SKY SPORTS FOOTBALL YEARBOOK 2006-2007

EDITORS: GLENDA ROLLIN AND JACK ROLLIN

headline

First published in 2006
by HEADLINE PUBLISHING GROUP

1

Front cover photographs: (left and background) Steven Gerrard (Liverpool) – *John Buckle/Empics*; (centre) Didier Drogba (Chelsea) – *Darren Walsh/Empics/ Chelsea FC*; (right) Rio Ferdinand (Manchester United) – *Getty Images/Alex Livesey*.

Spine photograph: Joe Cole (Chelsea and England) celebrates his goal against Sweden in the 2006 World Cup – *Action Images/Alex Morton Livepic*.

Back cover photographs: (top) Paul Telfer (Celtic) and Dado Prso (Rangers) – *Lynne Cameron/Empics/Rangers FC*; (bottom) Ledley King (Tottenham Hotspur) and Francesc Fabregas (Arsenal) – *Action Images/Andrew Couldridge Livepic.*

Cataloguing in Publication Data is available from the British Library

10-digit ISBN 0 7553 1525 1 (hardback)
13-digit ISBN 978 0 7553 1525 3 (hardback)
10-digit ISBN 0 7553 1526 X (trade paperback)
13-digit ISBN 978 0 7553 1526 0 (trade paperback)

Typeset by Wearset Ltd, Boldon, Tyne and Wear

Printed and bound in Great Britain by
Mackays of Chatham PLC,
Chatham, Kent

Headline's policy is to use papers that are natural, renewable and recyclable products and made from wood grown in sustainable forests. The logging and manufacturing processes are expected to conform to the environmental regulations of the country of origin.

HEADLINE PUBLISHING GROUP
A division of Hodder Headline
338 Euston Road
London NW1 3BH

www.headline.co.uk
www.hodderheadline.com

CONTENTS

INTERNATIONAL FOOTBALL

NON-LEAGUE FOOTBALL

INFORMATION AND RECORDS

FOREWORD

Football's been my life since I made my debut for Dundee United in 1973 and continues at Sky Sports where I'm fortunate enough to commentate on the game I love. Nothing compares to playing, but as we prepare for another new season, there's a similar sense of anticipation.

And after the World Cup Finals, we can welcome back players who've thrilled us on the biggest stage of all. Some are familiar, while some we've never seen in our domestic game before. Thierry Henry, John Terry and Steven Gerrard will be joined by the likes of Andriy Shevchenko, Michael Ballack and Tomas Rosicky. It's a credit to our game that these players are all set to illuminate the Premier League this season.

When I was a player, I was lucky enough to be the guy that put the ball in the back of the net but teamwork was as important then as it is now. Here at Sky Sports we broadcast around 400 live games a season. That requires some serious preparation and attention to detail and we leave nothing to chance. We need the best team behind us with the best resources at their disposal.

And as part of our pre-season training there's only ever been one source of reference, one that's been part of the fabric of football throughout my career on and off the pitch – *The* Yearbook.

Andy Gray, Sky Sports

Andy Gray in preparation for another match on Sky Sports.

INTRODUCTION

The 37th edition of the Yearbook, our fourth with new sponsors Sky Sports, has maintained its recent expansion to 1,056 pages. Once again, there is an A to Z index of names with a cross reference to the Players Directory, enabling readers to check on the whereabouts of any specific player during the 2005–06 season. The who's who style directory again provides a season-by-season account of individual player's appearances and goals. The fullest possible available details have been provided for players in this section, including all players who appeared in first-class matches.

Throughout the book players sent off are designated thus ■, substitutes in the club pages are 12, 13 and 14 with 15 for the substitute goalkeeper. Squad numbers are not used.

There are comprehensive details of the World Cup finals in Germany with a round-up of the qualifying matches in Europe and South America before the tournament's finale and other results of the competition from around the world.

With the continual increase in interest in non-League football, all Conference clubs have again been given the same style of recognition as the FA Premier League and Football League teams. In addition, the second echelon in the Conference North and South have featured as part of the non-league coverage.

As far as the club pages are concerned, a more uniform approach has been retained in respect of individual entries, without losing any of the essential information, including records over the previous ten seasons, latest sequences and runs of scoring and non-scoring.

Once more, every match played in the Champions League, including the qualifying competition, has full teams and line-ups. Also, with the expansion of the UEFA Cup with its group stage, there are full line-ups from that point onwards.

The usual detailed and varied coverage involves Scottish, Welsh and Irish football, amateur, schools, university, reserve team, extensive non-League information, awards, records and an international directory. Women's football, referees and the work of chaplains are also featured.

Transfer fees quoted in the Daily Round-up are invariably those initially mentioned when a deal is imminent. They may not reflect the figures which appear elsewhere in the edition. Moves during the summer months, together with any specific changes affecting the book appear in the Stop Press section.

The Editors would like to express their appreciation of the response from FA Premier League and Football League clubs when requesting information. Thanks are also due to Alan Elliott for the Scottish section, Tony Brown for sequences and instances of match results in the records section, Richard Beal for research into international anomalies and Ian Nannestad for the obituaries and additional information on foreign players. Thanks are also due to John English, who provided invaluable and conscientious reading of the proofs.

ACKNOWLEDGEMENTS

The Editors would like to express appreciation of the following individuals and organisations for their co-operation: David Barber, Dawn Keleher and Stuart Yeates (Football Association), David C. Thomson (Scottish League), Heather Elliott, Dr Malcolm Brodie, Wally Goss (AFA), Rev. Nigel Sands, Ken Goldman, Grahame Lloyd, Marshall Gillespie, Valery Karpoushkin, Andrew Howe, Mike Kelleher, Alan Platt and Wendy McCance (Headline Publishing Group). The highest praise is due to the indefatigable, ebullient and loquacious Lorraine Jerram, Headline's Managing Editor for her generosity, expertise, constant support, resilience, patience, sincerity, perspicacity and appreciation, not to mention her unfailing humour, stoicism, quick-wittedness, courtesy, consideration and understated authority.

Finally sincere thanks to John Anderson, Simon Dunnington, Geoff Turner, Brian Tait and the staff at Wearset for their efforts in the production of this book, which was much appreciated throughout the year.

EDITORIAL

Long, long ago when the Old Testament was merely the Testament and the Dead Sea was probably still feeling quite chipper, there were rumours of another wise man foretelling the future about someone destined one day to rule the sporting world.

A hot-blooded individual from a cold country, who despite many temptations and with a single-minded objective would achieve outstanding success for his adopted land.

Thus the words of this kind of fourth official adept at separating warring chiefs, controlling time itself and steeped in manipulating mystic numbers became part of mythology. But he foretold, too, that just as Moses had been encouraged to keep taking the tablets, there was a warning for the conqueror-in-waiting to ignore the wailings of the tabloids.

Success would not come easily, with many disappointments along the way, yet his ultimate goal achievable unless as occured when the AGM of the clairvoyants society had to be postponed for unforseen circumstances. Alas, fate cruelly conspired against him with a treble whammy – the loss of a key player, not allegedly from a first class stamp, but something of a secondary delivery, the obvious penalty clause and "Big Phil" – again, not we understand the first or any other choice.

So much for the predictions of an earlier poor man's Nostradamus. It all ended with Sven-Goran Eriksson packing his expensive kit and heading for the Job Centre, dropping off his Three Lions blazer to Oxfam, looking perhaps for something different – an opening with a ladies team, but with an assistant who could make notes (bank ones?).

Eriksson was never adventurous – at least on the field of play and while there were serious reservations about his ability to guide England to success in Germany, these were put aside by the understandable and formidable media campaign behind our brave lads. It was said there were individual doubts about certain players chosen or more importantly those ignored in the selection, yet the squad representing the country was generally agreed to be the best since 1990. No doubting the end of 40 years of despair was nigh.

Of course, at least one other forward should have been included, perhaps two in view of Michael Owen not back to full match fitness, Wayne Rooney yet to play at all since injury, Theo Walcott only just clear of nappy rash, destined to be dressed, not called upon.

Then the outcome: Owen injured and out of it. The defence did well enough apart from problems against Sweden, though Paul Robinson in goal appeared none to confident at times. Midfield was a disappointment though Owen Hargreaves was the big plus, given his first real chance to shine. Then he does play in Germany! And he was the sole successful penalty taker and the only one who looked likely to score.

Once Rooney was dismissed against Portugal, we simply retreated. It would have been better to move Joe Cole up front to support Peter Crouch rather than leave a lone striker. Instead Cole was taken off. Also nearing the end of extra time, Aaron Lennon himself a substitute was replaced by Jamie Carragher, presumably to boost the penalty shoot-out.

Alas, early in the season Carragher had scored his first Liverpool goal in six years and only the third in 363 outings. True, he did find the net with his shot – but it was a premature execution and he failed to repeat the feat. Frank Lampard, who we were constantly reminded *ad nauseum* had had more shots at goal than any other player in the finals, but had not found the net, was given the first penalty when clearly his scoring boots were still at Stamford Bridge.

Unfortunately, hardly anyone played to their Premier League standard. Or is it that the domestic competition does not make for a successful international team. Perhaps we do not do flair.

Lack of pace, invention and overmuch reliance on the long ball, did nothing to visually enhance any of England's matches. Worse, it did not work.

The obvious criticism after World Cup failure concerned foreign players in the Premier League. Far too many of them. Of all the competing countries who had players in the World Cup finals, Arsenal had 15, Chelsea 14 as first and second in the list, Manchester United were fifth with 12. Naturally they all also included some England players!

Alf Ramsey made wingers redundant in 1966. The word was erased from the football dictionary. Nowadays anyone straying near the touchline is known as a wide player. It is arguable that In the long run this did nothing to improve English football. Eriksson did precious little to champion the cause of the strikers.

Like Eriksson, Ramsey was not too clever when it came to substitutes. They were not introduced into the World Cup until 1970 so presumably he had little time to fathom out what was required. There was criticism when he made changes with England two up against the Germans in Mexico only to lose 3-2, but his *piece de resistance* came in the infamous 1973 qualifying match against Poland at Wembley when he brought Kevin Hector on for the last couple of minutes trying to salvage everything.

Had it not been for Bobby Moore (not playing) helping him off with his tracksuit – one doubts whether he would have made it before the final whistle! But Ramsey had won the World Cup in 1966.

Still he was not the only coach with problems over tactics. It took his Swedish colleague Lars Lagertop – sorry Lagerback, 54 minutes to realise that his right-side midfield player Mattias Jonson, once of Norwich City, was not getting to grips with either Joe or Ashley Cole, hence the acres of space they were enjoying. Once he brought on Christian Wilhelmsson, it ended the free reign of the Coles.

Another mistake – with Henrik Larsson about to take a penalty against Germany, the coach decided to make the same substitution. The Swedish striker kept waiting, lost concentration and missed.

Argentina were also poorly served by the bench when Jose Pekerman – another of the blazer brigade – thought he had wrapped up the game with Germany and made ill judged replacements including taking off the influential Juan Riquelme. Never underestimate the Germans. Spain's Aragones panicked too early with substitutions, too.

Referees were instructed to cut out the lunging tackles and simulation – that's diving to us. It became a charter for the cheats collapsed whenever touched. Again there was a wide interpretation of how to interpret the instructions. Valentin Ivanov the Russian in charge of Holland v Portugal proved Ivan had an off day – four times over. In addition to his quartet of red cards, he flashed 16 of the yellow variety.

With the four officials all wired up it was good to realise the old values of refereeing still essential. Graham Poll, again disgracefully known in some parts of the media as The Thing from Tring, succeeded in showing three yellow cards to one Croatian, when pencil and paper might have saved him an early trip home.

Now Sepp Blatter wants two referees for the 2010 finals! I recall Ken Aston, the referee who introduced red cards in the 1970 World Cup telling me that two referees could mean double the mistakes.

Not a good year for the Football Association, aside from the Wembley fiasco. They did not need to be constantly reminded of the money they poured down the Sven drain. Problems scratching around for an Eriksson replacement. So that trip to Portugal was in reality a jolly boys outing to the Algarve, nothing to do with interviewing Luiz Felipe Scolari for the manager's job. Why the fuss? Steve McClaren was always first choice.

Mind you, not sure how Big Phil's ranting and raving would have gone down with the FA. Contrast with the animation of Jurgen Klinsmann, the all-action German coach, like a man's best friend, eager to please. Then let us not forget the WAG's!

Television came in for its share of stick, too. Who was it that referred to the direction of expert opinion on the two terrestial channels as being reminiscent of Enid Blyton: Big Ears on one side, Totty on the other. Outrageous comment! The England players were unhappy, too, about the way their performances were being analysed, again unkindly as failed managers and half-forgotten old players. Not at all a kind comment. Anyway does panel beating carry a custodial sentence?

The actual commentaries did not escape either. The most used set control appeared to be the stadium sound only button where the atmosphere is broadcast, the description of play left to the viewer or via the radio.

In the last forty years, we know football has become enormous business. At its head is FIFA a money-making organisation concerned with promoting competitive international football but only a peripheral interest in anything else in the game. Most domestic club stuff does not matter much though just where they imagine the players come from is apparently either a mystery to them or of little matter. It is

Steven Gerrad (right) equalises for Liverpool in the FA Cup Final against West Ham United.
(Alastair Grant/AP/Empics)

Newcastle United's Alan Shearer is challenged by Chelsea's John Terry (left) and Asier Del Horno (right).
(Reuters/Kieran Doherty/Actionimages)

successful at corporate sponsorship and argue that without the huge financial imput from such sources it would not be able to provide large screens in city centres to allow the peasants, who cannot afford ticket prices or are unable to access them if they could, to watch World Cup final matches.

Some of those given freebies to attend – the junket junkies – have as much interest in the game as they would if seats and sustinance were on offer at the Fifth Test, world conker championship, or the donkey derby.

Little appreciation for the soul of the game for FIFA? Is this true? How else can you explain allowing penalty shoot-outs to decide any game at all let alone a World Cup final. The concept of a penalty kick is a punishment, not a door to success and as such at odds with the game's spirit. Extra time invariably becomes a mixture of either a comfort zone or fear-ridden until the spot kicks take over. If this is the game's only spectacle – why not dispense with the 90 minutes altogether and get down to the penalties. They are a sideshow. Once old goalkeepers would try to save them a penny a time on Blackpool beach. Now the stakes are higher in the carousel of the absurd.

Too many meaningless World Cup final group matches involving teams who are already qualified for the knock-out stages or those with their departure bags already packed. Not easy to provide a solution unless you have two seeded teams who do not meet each other in their group. But since FIFA doubled the number of finalists from 16 they have little scope for anything that revolutionary. Reducing the qualifiers to 28 would give some scope for such a system, but it would be fewer overall games and inevitably less income, so that is a non-runner for FIFA.

Yet if FIFA are serious about the effect on players' health, streamlining the finals with seven groups of four teams, two of whom are seeded, two unseeded, the four thus kept apart. Four games per group, 28 in total. The top two in each section, plus the two best third placed teams go straight into a knock-out competition. No extra time – play to a finish. Total matches 44 compared with 64.

Blatter also wants the Premier League reduced to 18 clubs. He considers the saving of four matches will allow leading players to have more rest and be available for even more international fixtures! Something of a contradiction in terms. There are hints, too, about a World Cup every two years.

In the first five years of the European Cup of the Champions as it was then titled, Real Madrid's handful of trophies was achieved playing a total of 37 matches including replays. When Liverpool won the Champions League two years back they completed 15.

UEFA and FIFA between them are responsible for the calendar congestion. Two days after the World Cup final in Germany, the Champions League started, four days and 35 UEFA Cup games were scheduled. Oh! yes, and the Intertoto even began in the middle of the finals!

While the Premier League has actually shrunk from its opening 22 clubs in 1992–93, the commitment of leading clubs outside domestic football has escalated. Judge for yourself who is causing the problem.

SKY SPORTS FOOTBALL YEARBOOK HONOURS

Chelsea's second FA Premier League title in successive seasons produced one more player for them than in the Sky Sports Football Yearbook Honours for 2004–05. The two changes were in midfield, where Arjen Robben was replaced by his colleague Joe Cole and at left-back where William Gallas made a comeback, having featured in the 2002–03 season as a central defender, received more votes from the Football Writers' Association in this different position.

Perhaps the one surprise for Chelsea was the edging out as Manager by Arsène Wenger of Arsenal, who just won the vote in front of Jose Mourinho. There had been other claims for this role with Alan Pardew, the West Ham United Manager and Paul Jewell, who did much to raise the status of newly promoted Wigan Athletic receiving strong support.

Seven of the successful team for 2004–05 retained their places in the final selection: Petr Cech, John Terry, Steven Gerrard, Frank Lampard, Claude Makelele, Wayne Rooney and Thierry Henry. There was fierce competition for one of the two central defensive positions before Jamie Carragher, who was in last year's line-up, just failed to push out Kolo Toure in a bid to keep his place.

At right-back Gary Neville regained the slot he had in 2003–04 and which he lost to Steve Finnan last year. On the opposite flank, Gabriel Heinze, the Argentine international of Manchester United, who spent most of the season on the injured list, understandably did not figure in the voting.

In attack, Thierry Henry has been an ever-present feature for five years and he was the Football Writers' Association choice as Player of the Year. In fact, it was a record third award for the Arsenal striker, having been featured in 2003 and 2004.

In the FWA voting, John Terry had finished second, Rooney third with Gerrard in fourth place.

It is also interesting to record that the favoured formation among journalists continues to be 4-4-2, but there were claims for both 4-3-3 and 3-5-2 as well as 5-3-2.

Sky Sports Football Yearbook Team of the Season 2005–06

Petr Cech
(Chelsea)

Gary Neville *(Manchester U)* | John Terry *(Chelsea)* | Kolo Toure *(Arsenal)* | William Gallas *(Chelsea)*

Steven Gerrard *(Liverpool)* | Frank Lampard *(Chelsea)* | Claude Makelele *(Chelsea)* | Joe Cole *(Chelsea)*

Wayne Rooney *(Manchester U)* | Thierry Henry *(Arsenal)*

Manager:
Arsène Wenger *(Arsenal)*

Substitutes:
Pascal Chimbonda (Wigan Ath)
Jamie Carragher (Liverpool)
Aaron Lennon (Tottenham H)

FOOTBALL AWARDS 2006

FOOTBALLER OF THE YEAR

The Football Writers' Association Sir Stanley Mathews Trophy for the Footballer of the Year went to Thierry Henry of Arsenal and France.

Past Winners
1947–48 Stanley Matthews (Blackpool), 1948–49 Johnny Carey (Manchester U), 1949–50 Joe Mercer (Arsenal), 1950–51 Harry Johnston (Blackpool), 1951–52 Billy Wright (Wolverhampton W), 1952–53 Nat Lofthouse (Bolton W), 1953–54 Tom Finney (Preston NE), 1954–55 Don Revie (Manchester C), 1955–56 Bert Trautmann (Manchester C), 1956–57 Tom Finney (Preston NE), 1957–58 Danny Blanchflower (Tottenham H), 1958–59 Syd Owen (Luton T), 1959–60 Bill Slater (Wolverhampton W), 1960–61 Danny Blanchflower (Tottenham H), 1961–62 Jimmy Adamson (Burnley), 1962–63 Stanley Matthews (Stoke C), 1963–64 Bobby Moore (West Ham U), 1964–65 Bobby Collins (Leeds U), 1965–66 Bobby Charlton (Manchester U), 1966–67 Jackie Charlton (Leeds U), 1967–68 George Best (Manchester U), 1968–69 Dave Mackay (Derby Co) shared with Tony Book (Manchester C), 1969–70 Billy Bremner (Leeds U), 1970–71 Frank McLintock (Arsenal), 1971–72 Gordon Banks (Stoke C), 1972–73 Pat Jennings (Tottenham H), 1973–74 Ian Callaghan (Liverpool), 1974–75 Alan Mullery (Fulham), 1975–76 Kevin Keegan (Liverpool), 1976–77 Emlyn Hughes (Liverpool), 1977–78 Kenny Burns (Nottingham F), 1978–79 Kenny Dalglish (Liverpool), 1979–80 Terry McDermott (Liverpool), 1980–81 Frans Thijssen (Ipswich T), 1981–82 Steve Perryman (Tottenham H), 1982–83 Kenny Dalglish (Liverpool), 1983–84 Ian Rush (Liverpool), 1984–85 Neville Southall (Everton), 1985–86 Gary Lineker (Everton), 1986–87 Clive Allen (Tottenham H), 1987–88 John Barnes (Liverpool), 1988–89 Steve Nicol (Liverpool), 1989–90 John Barnes (Liverpool), 1990–91 Gordon Strachan (Leeds U), 1991–92 Gary Lineker (Tottenham H), 1992–93 Chris Waddle (Sheffield W), 1993–94 Alan Shearer (Blackburn R), 1994–95 Jurgen Klinsmann (Tottenham H), 1995–96 Eric Cantona (Manchester U), 1996–97 Gianfranco Zola (Chelsea), 1997–98 Dennis Bergkamp (Arsenal), 1998–99 David Ginola (Tottenham H), 1999–2000 Roy Keane (Manchester U), 2000–01 Teddy Sheringham (Manchester U), 2001–02 Robert Pires (Arsenal), 2002–03 Thierry Henry (Arsenal), 2003–04 Thierry Henry (Arsenal), 2004–05 Frank Lampard (Chelsea).

THE PFA AWARDS 2006

Player of the Year: Steven Gerrard, Liverpool and England.
Young Player of the Year: Wayne Rooney, Manchester U and England.
Merit Award: The late George Best.

SCOTTISH FOOTBALL WRITERS' ASSOCIATION 2006

Player of the Year: Craig Gordon (Hearts).
Young Player of the Year: Steven Naismith (Kilmarnock).
Manager of the Year: Gordon Strachan (Celtic).

SCOTTISH PFA 'PLAYER OF THE YEAR' AWARDS 2006

Player of the Year: Shaun Maloney (Celtic).
First Division: John Rankin (Ross County).
Second Division: James Grady (Gretna).
Third Division: Markus Paatelainen (Cowdenbeath).
Young Player of the Year: Shaun Maloney (Celtic).

EUROPEAN FOOTBALLER OF THE YEAR 2005

Ronaldinho, Barcelona and Brazil.

WORLD PLAYER OF THE YEAR 2005

Ronaldinho, Barcelona and Brazil.

WOMEN'S PLAYER OF THE YEAR 2005

Birgit Prinz, FFC Frankfurt and Germany.

THE FOOTBALL RECORDS

LANDMARKS

Thierry Henry beat Ian Wright's 185 League and Cup goals for Arsenal as well as Cliff Bastin's 150 League goals for the club.
Arsenal establish Champions League record in their 8th game without conceding a goal.
Manchester United the first Premier League club to score 1000 goals in the competition.
Manchester United set a new Premier League attendance record at 73,006 v Charlton Ath 7 May 2006.
Andriy Shevchenko becomes the leading goalscorer in the European Cup with 52 goals all in the Champions League.
Alan Shearer breaks Jackie Milburn's 200 League and Cup goals for Newcastle United and finishes his career with 409 goals overall.
Reading become the first English club to achieve 106 points in a season.
Youngest Players: Theo Walcott 17 years 75 days for England v Hungary 30 May 2006; Lewin Nyatanga for Wales at 17 years 195 days v Paraguay 1 March 2006 and subsequently overtaken by Gareth Bale at 16 years 315 days v Trinidad & Tobago 27 May 2006.
Kevin Doyle achieves championship medals with two clubs in one year – Cork City and Reading.
Frank Lampard creates Premier League record with his 164th consecutive match.
John McDermott Grimsby Town extends his club record of appearances to 624.
Bolton Wanderers sign their 20th different national with Hidetoshi Nakata of Japan.
Celtic establish Scottish Premier League record with an 8-1 win at Dunfermline Ath.
Chelsea start season without conceding a goal in their first six matches.

CHAMPIONS LEAGUE AND EUROPEAN CUP RECORDS

ALL-TIME EUROPEAN CUP AND CHAMPIONS LEAGUE TOP SCORERS

Season	Player	Goals
1955–56	Milos Milutinovic (Partizan Belgrade)	8
1956–57	Dennis Viollet (Manchester United)	9
1957–58	Alfredo Di Stefano (Real Madrid)	10
1958–59	Just Fontaine (Reims)	10
1959–60	Ferenc Puskas (Real Madrid)	12
1960–61	Jose Aguas (Benfica)	11
1961–62	Alfredo Di Stefano (Real Madrid)	
	Ferenc Puskas (Real Madrid)	
	Justo Tejada (Real Madrid)	7
1962–63	Jose Altafini (AC Milan)	14
1963–64	Vladimir Kovacevic (Partizan Belgrade)	
	Ferenc Puskas (Real Madrid)	
	Alessandro Mazzola (Internazionale)	7
1964–65	Jose Torres (Benfica)	9
1965–66	Eusebio (Benfica)	
	Florian Albert (Ferencvaros)	7
1966–67	Paul Van Himst (Anderlecht)	
	Jurgen Piepenberg (Vorwaerts)	6
1967–68	Eusebio (Benfica)	6
1968–69	Denis Law (Manchester United)	9
1969–70	Mick Jones (Leeds United)	8
1970–71	Antonis Antoniadis (Panathinaikos)	10
1971–72	Sylvester Takac (Standard Liege)	
	Johan Cruyff (Ajax)	
	Lou Macari (Celtic)	5
1972–73	Gerd Muller (Bayern Munich)	11
1973–74	Gerd Muller (Bayern Munich)	9
1974–75	Gerd Muller (Bayern Munich)	6
1975–76	Josef Heynckes (Moenchengladbach)	
	Carlos Santillana (Real Madrid)	6
1976–77	Gerd Muller (Bayern Munich)	
	Franco Cucinotta (Zurich)	5
1977–78	Allan Simonsen (Moenchengladbach)	5
1978–79	Claudio Sulser (Grasshoppers)	11
1979–80	Soren Lerby (Ajax)	10
1980–81	Karl-Heinz Rummenigge (Bayern Munich)	
	Terry McDermott (Liverpool)	
	Graeme Souness (Liverpool)	6
1981–82	Dieter Hoeness (Bayern Munich)	7
1982–83	Paolo Rossi (Juventus)	6
1983–84	Viktor Sokol (Dynamo Minsk)	6
1984–85	Michel Platini (Juventus)	
	Torbjorn Nilsson (IFK Gothenburg)	7
1985–86	Torbjorn Nilsson (IFK Gothenburg)	7
1986–87	Borislav Cvetkovic (Red Star Belgrade)	7
1987–88	Rabah Madjer (Porto)	
	Jean-Marc Ferreri (Bordeaux)	
	Michel (Real Madrid)	
	Rui Aguas (Benfica)	
	Ally McCoist (Rangers)	
	Gheorghe Hagi (Steaua)	4
1988–89	Marco Van Basten (AC Milan)	10
1989–90	Romario (PSV Eindhoven)	
	Jean-Pierre Papin (Marseille)	6
1990–91	Peter Pacult (Tirol)	
	Jean-Pierre Papin (Marseille)	6
1991–92	Jean-Pierre Papin (Marseille)	7
1992–93	Romario (PSV Eindhoven)	7
1993–94	Ronald Koeman (Barcelona)	
	Wynton Rufer (Werder Bremen)	8
1994–95	George Weah (Paris St Germain)	7
1995–96	Jari Litmanen (Ajax)	9
1996–97	Ally McCoist (Rangers)	6
1997–98	Alessandro Del Piero (Juventus)	10
1998–99	Andrei Shevchenko (Dynamo Kiev)	10
1999–2000	Mario Jardel (Porto)	
	Rivaldo (Barcelona)	
	Raul (Real Madrid)	10
2000–01	Andrei Shevchenko (AC Milan)	
	Mario Jardel (Galatasaray)	9
2001–02	Ruud Van Nistelrooy (Manchester United)	10
2002–03	Ruud Van Nistelrooy (Manchester United)	14
2003–04	Fernando Morientes (Monaco)	9
2004–05	Adriano (Internazionale)	10
2005–06	Andriy Shevchenko (AC Milan)	9

EUROPEAN CUP AND CHAMPIONS LEAGUE RECORDS

CHAMPIONS LEAGUE ATTENDANCES AND GOALS FROM GROUP STAGES ONWARDS

Season	*Attendances*	*Average*	*Goals*	*Games*
1992–93	873,251	34,930	56	25
1993–94	1,202,289	44,529	71	27
1994–95	2,328,515	38,172	140	61
1995–96	1,874,316	30,726	159	61
1996–97	2,093,228	34,315	161	61
1997–98	2,868,271	33,744	239	85
1998–99	3,608,331	42,451	238	85
1999–2000	5,490,709	34,973	442	157
2000–01	5,773,486	36,774	449	157
2001–02	5,417,716	34,508	393	157
2002–03	6,461,112	41,154	431	157
2003–04	4,611,214	36,890	309	125
2004–05	4,946,820	39,575	331	125
2005–06	5,291,187	42,330	285	125

HIGHEST AVERAGE ATTENDANCE IN ONE EUROPEAN CUP SEASON
1959–60 50,545 from a total attendance of 2,780,000.

HIGHEST SCORE IN A EUROPEAN CUP MATCH
Feyenoord (Holland)12, KR Reykjavik (Iceland) 0
(First Round First Leg 1969–70)

HIGHEST AGGREGATE
Benfica (Portugal) 18, Dudelange (Luxembourg) 0
(Preliminary Round 1965–66)

MOST GOALS OVERALL
52 Andriy Shevchenko (Dynamo Kiev and AC Milan) *(1994–2006)*
49 Alfredo Di Stefano (Real Madrid) *(1955–64)*
46 Eusebio (Benfica) *(1959–74)*
43 Raul (Real Madrid) *(1995–2003)*
36 Gerd Muller (Bayern Munich) *(1969–77)*

CHAMPIONS LEAGUE BIGGEST WINS
Juventus 7, Olympiakos 0 10.12.2003
Marseille 6, CKSA Moscow 0 17.3.93
Leeds U 6, Besiktas 0 26.9.2000
Real Madrid 6, Genk 0 25.9.2002

FIRST TEAM TO SCORE SEVEN GOALS
Paris St Germain 7, Rosenborg 2 24.10.2000

HIGHEST AGGREGATE OF GOALS
Monaco 8, La Coruna 3 05.11.2003

HIGHEST SCORING DRAW
Hamburg 4, Juventus 4 13.9.2000

GREATEST COMEBACKS
Werder Bremen beat Anderlecht 5-3 after being three goals down in 33 minutes on 8.12.1993. They scored five goals in 23 second-half minutes.
La Coruna beat Paris St Germain 4-3 after being three goals down in 55 minutes on 7.3.2001. They scored four goals in 27 second-half minutes.
Liverpool after being three goals down in the first half on 25.5.2005 in the Champions League Final. They scored three goals in five second-half minutes and won the penalty shoot-out after extra time 3-2.
Liverpool 3 goals down to Basle in 29 minutes on 12.11.2002. They scored three second half goals in 24 minutes to draw 3-3.

MOST GOALS IN CHAMPIONS LEAGUE MATCH
4, Marco Van Basten AC Milan v IFK Gothenburg (33, 53 (pen), 61, 62 mins) 4-0 25.11.1992.
4, Simone Inzaghi Lazio v Marseille (17, 37, 38, 71 mins) 5-1 14.3.2000.
4, Ruud Van Nistelrooy Manchester U v Sparta Prague (14, 25 (pen), 60, 90 mins) 4-1 3.11.2004.
4, Dado Prso, Monaco v La Coruna (26, 30, 45, 49, 23 mins) 8-3 5.11.2003.
4, Andriy Shevchenko, AC Milan at Fenerbahce (16, 52, 70, 76,60 mins) 4-0 23.11.2005.

WINS WITH TWO DIFFERENT CLUBS
Miodrag Belodedici (Steaua) 1986; (Red Star Belgrade) 1991.
Ronald Koeman (PSV Eindhoven) 1988; (Barcelona) 1992.
Dejan Savicevic (Red Star Belgrade) 1991; (AC Milan) 1994.
Marcel Desailly (Marseille) 1993; (AC Milan) 1994.
Frank Rijkaard (AC Milan) 1989, 1990; (Ajax) 1995.
Vladimir Jugovic (Red Star Belgrade) 1991; (Juventus) 1996.
Didier Deschamps (Marseille) 1993; (Juventus) 1996.
Paulo Sousa (Juventus) 1996; (Borussia Dortmund) 1997.
Christian Panucci (AC Milan) 1994; (Real Madrid) 1998.
Jimmy Rimmer (Mancheser U) 1968, (Aston Villa) 1982 but as a non-playing substitute.

MOST WINS WITH DIFFERENT CLUBS
Clarence Seedorf (Ajax) 1995; (Real Madrid) 1998; (AC Milan) 2003.

MOST WINNERS MEDALS
6 Francisco Gento (Real Madrid) 1956, 1957, 1958, 1959, 1960, 1966.
5 Alfredo Di Stefano (Real Madrid) 1956, 1957, 1958, 1959, 1960.
5 Jose Maria Zarraga (Real Madrid) 1956, 1957, 1958, 1959, 1960.
4 Jose-Hector Rial (Real Madrid) 1956, 1957, 1958, 1959.
4 Marquitos (Real Madrid) 1956, 1957, 1959, 1960.
4 Phil Neal (Liverpool) 1977, 1978, 1981, 1984.

MOST GOALS SCORED IN FINALS
7 Alfredo Di Stefano (Real Madrid), 1956 (1), 1957 (1 pen), 1958 (1), 1959 (1), 1960 (3).
7 Ferenc Puskas (Real Madrid), 1960 (4), 1962 (3).

MOST FINAL APPEARANCES PER COUNTRY
Italy 24 (10 wins, 14 defeats).
Spain 20 (11 wins, 9 defeats).
England 13 (10 wins, 3 defeats).
Germany 13 (6 wins, 7 defeats).

MOST CLUB FINAL WINNERS
Real Madrid (Spain) 9 1956, 1957, 1958, 1959, 1960, 1966, 1998, 2000, 2002.
AC Milan (Italy) 6 1963, 1969, 1989, 1990, 1994, 2003.

MOST APPEARANCES IN FINAL
Real Madrid 12; AC Milan 10.

MOST EUROPEAN CUP APPEARANCES
Paolo Maldini (AC Milan)

Season	*European Cup*	*UEFA Cup*	*Super Cup*	*WCC*
1985–86	0	6	0	0
1987–88	0	2	0	0
1988–89	7	0	0	0
1989–90	8	0	2	1
1990–91	4	0	1	1
1992–93	10	0	0	0
1993–94	10	0	2	1
1994–95	11	0	1	1
1995–96	0	8	0	0
1996–97	6	0	0	0
1999–2000	6	0	0	0
2000–01	14	0	0	0
2001–02	0	4	0	0
2002–03	19	0	0	0
2003–04	9	0	1	1
2004–05	13	0	0	0
2005–06	9	0	0	0
Total	126	20	7	5

MOST SUCCESSFUL MANAGER
Bob Paisley (Liverpool) 1977, 1978, 1981.

FASTEST GOALS SCORED IN CHAMPIONS LEAGUE
20.07 sec Gilberto Silva for Arsenal at PSV Eindhoven 25 September 2002.
20.12 sec Alessandro Del Piero for Juventus at Manchester United 1 October 1997.

FASTEST HAT-TRICK SCORED IN CHAMPIONS LEAGUE
Mike Newell, 9 mins for Blackburn R v Rosenborg (4-1) 6.12.95.

MOST SUCCESSIVE CHAMPIONS LEAGUE APPEARANCES
Rosenborg (Norway) 11 1995–96 – 2005–06.

MOST SUCCESSIVE WINS IN THE CHAMPIONS LEAGUE
Barcelona (Spain) 11 2002–03.

OTHER BRITISH FOOTBALL RECORDS

ALL-TIME PREMIER LEAGUE CHAMPIONSHIP SEASONS ON POINTS AVERAGE

	Team	Season	P	W	D	L	F	A	Pts	Pts Av
1	Chelsea	2004–05	38	29	8	1	72	15	95	2.50
2	Manchester U	1999–2000	38	28	7	3	97	45	91	2.39
3	Chelsea	2005–06	38	29	4	5	72	22	91	2.39
4	Arsenal	2003–04	38	26	12	0	73	26	90	2.36
5	Arsenal	2001–02	38	26	9	3	79	36	87	2.28
6	Manchester U	1993–94	42	27	11	4	80	38	92	2.19
7	Manchester U	2002–03	38	25	8	5	74	34	83	2.18
8	Manchester U	1995–96	38	25	7	6	73	35	82	2.15
9	Blackburn R	1994–95	42	27	8	7	80	39	89	2.11
10	Manchester U	2000–01	38	24	8	6	79	31	80	2.10
11	Manchester U	1998–99	38	22	13	3	80	37	79	2.07
12	Arsenal	1997–98	38	23	9	6	68	33	78	2.05
13	Manchester U	1992–93	42	24	12	6	67	31	84	2.00
14	Manchester U	1996–97	38	21	12	5	76	44	75	1.97

TOP TEN WORLD TRANSFERS

	Player	Clubs	Fee (£m)	Year
1	Zinedine Zidane	Juventus to Real Madrid	46.5	2001
2	Luis Figo	Barcelona to Real Madrid	37.4	2000
3	Hernan Crespo	Parma to Lazio	35.7	2000
4	Gianluigi Buffon	Parma to Juventus	34	2001
5	Christian Vieri	Lazio to Internationale	31	1999
6	Andriy Shevchenko	AC Milan to Chelsea	29.5	2006
7	Giazka Mendieta	Valencia to Lazio	29	2001
8	Ronaldo	Internazionale to Real Madrid	28.9	2002
9	Rio Ferdinand	Leeds U to Manchester U	28.25	2002
10	Juan Sebastian Veron	Lazio to Manchester U	28.1	2001

Source: National Press.

TOP TEN BRITISH TRANSFERS (incoming only)

	Player	Clubs	Fee (£m)	Year
1	Andriy Shevchenko	AC Milan to Chelsea	29.5	2006
2	Rio Ferdinand	Leeds U to Manchester U	28.25	2002
3	Juan Sebastian Veron	Lazio to Manchester U	28.1	2001
4	Wayne Rooney	Everton to Manchester U	27	2004
5	Didier Drogba	Marseille to Chelsea	24	2004
6	Ruud Van Nistelrooy	PSV Eindhoven to Manchester U	19	2001
7	Rio Ferdinand	West Ham U to Leeds U	18	2000
8	José Antonio Reyes	Sevilla to Arsenal	17.6	2004
9	Damien Duff	Blackburn R to Chelsea	17	2003
20	Hernan Crespo	Inernazionale to Chelsea	16.8	2003

Source: National Press.

TOP TEN GOALSCORERS IN WORLD CUP FINAL TOURNAMENTS

1	Ronaldo (Brazil)	1998, 2002, 2006	15
2	Gerd Muller (West Germany)	1970, 74	14
3	Just Fontaine (France)	1958	13
4	Pele (Brazil)	1958, 70	12
5	Sandor Kocsis (Hungary)	1954	11
6	Jurgen Klinsmann (Germany)	1990, 98	11
7	Helmut Rahn (West Germany)	1954, 58	10
	Teofilo Cubillas (Peru)	1970, 78	10
	Grzegorz Lato (Poland)	1974, 82	10
	Gary Lineker (England)	1986, 90	10
	Gabriel Batistuta (Argentina)	1994, 2002	10
	Miroslav Klose (Germany)	2002, 2006	10

TOP TEN PREMIER LEAGUE AVERAGE ATTENDANCES 2005–06

1	Manchester U	68,765
2	Newcastle U	52,032
3	Liverpool	44,236
4	Manchester C	42,856
5	Chelsea	41,902
6	Arsenal	38,186
7	Everton	36,860
8	Tottenham H	36,074
9	Aston Villa	34,059
10	Sunderland	33,904

TOP TEN FOOTBALL LEAGUE AVERAGE ATTENDANCES 2005–06

1	Norwich C	24,952
2	Sheffield W	24,853
3	Ipswich T	24,253
4	Derby Co	24,166
5	Sheffield U	23,650
6	Wolverhampton W	23,624
7	Southampton	23,614
8	Leeds U	22,355
9	Leicester C	22,234
10	Coventry C	21,302

TOP TEN AVERAGE ATTENDANCES

1	Manchester United	2005–06	68,765
2	Manchester United	2004–05	67,871
3	Manchester United	2003–04	67,641
4	Manchester United	2002–03	67,630
5	Manchester United	2001–02	67,586
6	Manchester United	2000–01	67,544
7	Manchester United	1999–2000	58,017
8	Manchester United	1967–68	57,552
9	Newcastle United	1947–48	56,283
10	Tottenham Hotspur	1950–51	55,509

TOP TEN AVERAGE WORLD CUP FINAL CROWDS

1	In USA	1994	68,604
2	In Brazil	1950	60,772
3	In Germany	2006	52,416
4	In Mexico	1970	52,311
5	In England	1966	50,458
6	In Italy	1990	48,368
7	In Mexico	1986	46,956
8	In West Germany	1974	46,684
9	In France	1998	43,366
10	In Argentina	1978	42,374

TOP TEN ALL-TIME ENGLAND GOALSCORERS

1	Bobby Charlton	49
2	Gary Lineker	48
3	Jimmy Greaves	44
4	Michael Owen	36
5	Tom Finney	30
6	Nat Lofthouse	30
7	Alan Shearer	30
8	Vivian Woodward	29
9	Steve Bloomer	28
10	David Platt	27

TOP TEN ALL-TIME ENGLAND CAPS

1	Peter Shilton	125
2	Bobby Moore	108
3	Bobby Charlton	106
4	Billy Wright	105
5	David Beckham	94
6	Bryan Robson	90
7	Kenny Sansom	86
8	Ray Wilkins	84
9	Gary Neville	81
10	Gary Lineker and Michael Owen	80

MOST GOALS FOR IN A SEASON

FA PREMIER LEAGUE		*Goals*	*Games*
1999–2000	Manchester U	97	38
FOOTBALL LEAGUE			
Championship			
2005–06	Reading	99	46
Championship League One			
2004–05	Luton T	87	46
Championship League Two			
2004–05	Yeovil T	90	46
Division 1			
1930–31	Aston V	128	42
Division 2			
1926–27	Middlesbrough	122	42
Division 3(S)			
1927–28	Millwall	127	42
Division 3(N)			
1928–29	Bradford C	128	42
Division 3			
1961–62	QPR	111	46
Division 4			
1960–61	Peterborough U	134	46
SCOTTISH PREMIER LEAGUE			
2003–04	Celtic	105	38
SCOTTISH LEAGUE			
Premier Division			
1991–92	Rangers	101	44
1982–83	Dundee U	90	36
1982–83	Celtic	90	36
1986–87	Celtic	90	44
Division 1			
1957–58	Hearts	132	34
Division 2			
1937–38	Raith R	142	34
New Division 1			
1993–94	Dunfermline Ath	93	44
1981–82	Motherwell	92	39
New Division 2			
1987–88	Ayr U	95	39
New Division 3			
2004–05	Gretna	130	36

FEWEST GOALS AGAINST IN A SEASON

FA PREMIER LEAGUE		*Goals*	*Games*
2004–05	Chelsea	15	38
FOOTBALL LEAGUE (minimum 42 games)			
Championship			
2005–06	Preston NE	30	46
Championship League One			
2005–06	Colchester U	40	46
Championship League Two			
2005–06	Northampton T	37	46
Division 1			
1978–79	Liverpool	16	42
Division 2			
1924–25	Manchester U	23	42
2002–03	Wigan Ath	25	46
Division 3(S)			
1921–22	Southampton	21	42
Division 3(N)			
1953–54	Port Vale	21	46
Division 3			
1995–96	Gillingham	20	46
Division 4			
1980–81	Lincoln C	25	46
SCOTTISH PREMIER LEAGUE			
2001–02	Celtic	18	38
SCOTTISH LEAGUE (minimum 30 games)			
Premier Division			
1989–90	Rangers	19	36
1986–87	Rangers	23	44
1987–88	Celtic	23	44
Division 1			
1913–14	Celtic	14	38
Division 3			
1966–67	Morton	20	38
New Division 1			
1996–97	St Johnstone	23	36
1980–81	Hibernian	24	39
1993–94	Falkirk	32	44
New Division 2			
1987–88	St Johnstone	24	39
1990–91	Stirling Alb	24	39
New Division 3			
1995–96	Brechin C	21	36

FEWEST GOALS FOR IN A SEASON

FA PREMIER LEAGUE		*Goals*	*Games*
2002–03	Sunderland	21	38
FOOTBALL LEAGUE (minimum 42 games)			
Championship			
2004–05	Rotherham U	35	46
2005–06	Millwall	35	46
Championship League One			
2005–06	Hartlepool U	44	46
Championship League Two			
2004–05	Kidderminster H	39	46
2004–05	Cambridge U	39	46
Division 1			
1984–85	Stoke C	24	42
Division 2			
1971–72	Watford	24	42
1994–95	Leyton Orient	30	46
Division 3(S)			
1950–51	Crystal Palace	33	46
Division 3(N)			
1923–24	Crewe Alex	32	42
Division 3			
1969–70	Stockport Co	27	46
Division 4			
1981–82	Crewe Alex	29	46
SCOTTISH PREMIER LEAGUE			
2001–02	St Johnstone	24	38
SCOTTISH LEAGUE (minimum 30 games)			
Premier Division			
1988–89	Hamilton A	19	36
1991–92	Dunfermline Ath	22	44
Division 1			
1993–94	Brechin C	30	44
1966–67	Ayr U	20	34
Division 2			
1923–24	Lochgelly U	20	38
New Division 1			
1980–81	Stirling Alb	18	39
1995–96	Dumbarton	23	36
New Division 2			
1994–95	Brechin C	22	36
New Division 3			
1995–96	Alloa	26	36

MOST GOALS AGAINST IN A SEASON

FA PREMIER LEAGUE		*Goals*	*Games*
1993–94	Swindon T	100	42
FOOTBALL LEAGUE			
Championship			
2004–05	Crewe Alex	86	46
2005–06	Crewe Alex	86	46
Championship League One			
2004–05	Stockport Co	98	46
Championship League Two			
2004–05	Kidderminster H	85	46
Division 1			
1930–31	Blackpool	125	42
Division 2			
1898–99	Darwen	141	34
Division 3(S)			
1929–30	Merthyr T	135	42
Division 3(N)			
1927–28	Nelson	136	42
Division 3			
1959–60	Accrington S	123	46
Division 4			
1959–60	Hartlepools U	109	46
SCOTTISH PREMIER LEAGUE			
1999–2000	Aberdeen	83	36
SCOTTISH LEAGUE			
Premier Division			
1984–85	Morton	100	36
1987–88	Morton	100	44
Division 1			
1931–32	Leith Ath	137	38
Division 2			
1931–32	Edinburgh C	146	38
New Division 1			
1988–89	Queen of the S	99	39
1992–93	Cowdenbeath	109	44
New Division 2			
1977–78	Meadowbank T	89	39
New Division 3			
2003–04	East Stirling	118	36

GOALS PER GAME (from 1992–93)

Goals per game	Premier Games	Premier Goals	Championship/Div 1 Games	Championship/Div 1 Goals	League One/Div 2 Games	League One/Div 2 Goals	League Two/Div 3 Games	League Two/Div 3 Goals
0	490	0	663	0	638	0	632	0
1	1053	1053	1435	1435	1428	1428	1442	1442
2	1378	2756	1969	3938	1974	3948	1895	3790
3	1126	3378	1631	4893	1682	5046	1617	4851
4	778	3112	1065	4260	1074	4296	996	3984
5	401	2005	575	2875	556	2780	506	2530
6	204	1224	262	1572	227	1362	234	1404
7	92	644	89	623	106	742	92	644
8	36	288	29	232	28	224	32	256
9	8	72	5	45	12	108	9	81
10	0	0	3	30	3	30	2	20
11	0	0	2	22			1	11
	5566	**14532**	**7728**	**19925**	**7728**	**19964**	**7458**	**19013**

GOALS PER GAME (Football League to 1991–92)

Goals per game	Division 1 Games	Division 1 Goals	Division 2 Games	Division 2 Goals	Division 3 Games	Division 3 Goals	Division 4 Games	Division 4 Goals	Division 3(S) Games	Division 3(S) Goals	Division 3(N) Games	Division 3(N) Goals
0	2465	0	2665	0	1446	0	1438	0	997	0	803	0
1	5606	5606	5836	5836	3225	3225	3106	3106	2073	2073	1914	1914
2	8275	16550	8609	17218	4569	9138	4441	8882	3314	6628	2939	5878
3	7731	23193	7842	23526	3784	11352	4041	12123	2996	8988	2922	8766
4	6229	24920	5897	23588	2837	11348	2784	11136	2445	9780	2410	9640
5	3752	18755	3634	18170	1566	7830	1506	7530	1554	7770	1599	7995
6	2137	12822	2007	12042	769	4614	786	4716	870	5220	930	5580
7	1092	7644	1001	7007	357	2499	336	2352	451	3157	461	3227
8	542	4336	376	3008	135	1080	143	1144	209	1672	221	1768
9	197	1773	164	1476	64	576	35	315	76	684	102	918
10	83	830	68	680	13	130	8	80	33	330	45	450
11	37	407	19	209	2	22	7	77	15	165	15	165
12	12	144	17	204	1	12	0	0	7	84	8	96
13	4	52	4	52	0	0	0	0	2	26	4	52
14	2	28	1	14	0	0	0	0	0	0	0	0
17	0	0	0	0	0	0	0	0	0	0	1	17
	38164	**117061**	**38140**	**113030**	**18768**	**51826**	**18631**	**51461**	**15042**	**46577**	**14374**	**46466**

New Overall Totals (since 1992)		Totals (up to1991–92)		Complete Overall Totals (since 1888–89)	
Games	28480	Games	143119	Games	171599
Goals	73434	Goals	426421	Goals	499855

Extensive research by statisticians has unearthed six results from early years of the Football League which differ from the original scores. These are 26 January 1889 Wolverhampton W 5 Everton 0 (not 4-0), 16 March 1889 Notts Co 3 Derby Co 5 (not 2-5), 4 January 1896 Arsenal 5 Loughborough 0 (not 6-0), 28 November 1896 Leicester Fosse 4 Walsall 2 (not 4-1), 25 December 1902 Glossop NE 3 Stockport Co 0 (not 3-1), 26 April 1913 Hull C 2 Leicester C 0 (not 2-1).

MOST CUP GOALS IN A CAREER

FA CUP (Pre-Second World war)
Henry Cursham 48 (Notts Co)

FA CUP (post-war)
Ian Rush 43 (Chester, Liverpool)

LEAGUE CUP
Geoff Hurst 49 (West Ham U, Stoke C)
Ian Rush 49 (Chester, Liverpool, Newcastle U)

SCORED IN EVERY PREMIERSHIP GAME

Arsenal 2001–02 38 matches

MOST FA CUP FINAL GOALS

Ian Rush (Liverpool) 5: 1986(2), 1989(2), 1992(1)

MOST LEAGUE GOALS IN A SEASON

FA PREMIER LEAGUE		Goals	Games
1993–94	Andy Cole (Newcastle U)	34	40
1994–95	Alan Shearer (Blackburn R)	34	42
FOOTBALL LEAGUE			
Division 1			
1927–28	Dixie Dean (Everton)	60	39
Division 2			
1926–27	George Camsell (Middlesbrough)	59	37
Division 3(S)			
1936–37	Joe Payne (Luton T)	55	39
Division 3(N)			
1936–37	Ted Harston (Mansfield T)	55	41
Division 3			
1959–60	Derek Reeves (Southampton)	39	46
Division 4			
1960–61	Terry Bly (Peterborough U)	52	46
FA CUP			
1887–88	Jimmy Ross (Preston NE)	20	8
LEAGUE CUP			
1986–87	Clive Allen (Tottenham H)	12	9
SCOTTISH PREMIER LEAGUE			
2000–01	Henrik Larsson (Celtic)	35	37
SCOTTISH LEAGUE			
Division 1			
1931–32	William McFadyen (Motherwell)	52	34
Division 2			
1927–28	Jim Smith (Ayr U)	66	38

MOST LEAGUE GOALS IN A CAREER

FOOTBALL LEAGUE			
Arthur Rowley	*Goals*	*Games*	*Season*
WBA	4	24	1946–48
Fulham	27	56	1948–50
Leicester C	251	303	1950–58
Shrewsbury T	152	236	1958–65
	434	619	
SCOTTISH LEAGUE			
Jimmy McGrory			
Celtic	1	3	1922–23
Clydebank	13	30	1923–24
Celtic	396	375	1924–38
	410	408	

MOST HAT-TRICKS

Career
34 Dixie Dean (Tranmere R, Everton, Notts Co, England)

Division 1 (one season post-war)
6 Jimmy Greaves (Chelsea), 1960–61

Three for one team one match
West, Spouncer, Hooper, Nottingham F v Leicester Fosse, Division 1, 21 April 1909
Barnes, Ambler, Davies, Wrexham v Hartlepools U, Division 4, 3 March 1962
Adcock, Stewart, White, Manchester C v Huddersfield T, Division 2, 7 Nov 1987
Loasby, Smith, Wells, Northampton T v Walsall, Division 3S, 5 Nov 1927
Bowater, Hoyland, Readman, Mansfield T v Rotherham U, Division 3N, 27 Dec 1932

MOST GOALS IN A GAME

FA PREMIER LEAGUE	
19 Sept 1999	Alan Shearer (Newcastle U) 5 goals v Sheffield W
4 Mar 1995	Andy Cole (Manchester U) 5 goals v Ipswich T
FOOTBALL LEAGUE	
Division 1	
14 Dec 1935	Ted Drake (Arsenal) 7 goals v Aston V
Division 2	
5 Feb 1955	Tommy Briggs (Blackburn R) 7 goals v Bristol R
23 Feb 1957	Neville Coleman (Stoke C) 7 goals v Lincoln C
Division 3(S)	
13 April 1936	Joe Payne (Luton T) 10 goals v Bristol R
Division 3(N)	
26 Dec 1935	Bunny Bell (Tranmere R) 9 goals v Oldham Ath
Division 3	
16 Sept 1969	Steve Earle (Fulham) 5 goals v Halifax T
24 April 1965	Barrie Thomas (Scunthorpe U) 5 goals v Luton T
20 Nov 1965	Keith East (Swindon T) 5 goals v Mansfield T
2 Oct 1971	Alf Wood (Shrewsbury T) 5 goals v Blackburn R
10 Sept 1983	Tony Caldwell (Bolton W) 5 goals v Walsall
4 May 1987	Andy Jones (Port Vale) 5 goals v Newport Co
3 April 1990	Steve Wilkinson (Mansfield T) 5 goals v Birmingham C
5 Sept 1998	Giuliano Grazioli (Peterborough U) 5 goals v Barnet
6 April 2002	Lee Jones (Wrexham) 5 goals v Cambridge U
Division 4	
26 Dec 1962	Bert Lister (Oldham Ath) 6 goals v Southport
FA CUP	
20 Nov 1971	Ted MacDougall (Bournemouth) 9 goals v Margate (*1st Round*)
LEAGUE CUP	
25 Oct 1989	Frankie Bunn (Oldham Ath) 6 goals v Scarborough
SCOTTISH LEAGUE	
Premier Division	
17 Nov 1984	Paul Sturrock (Dundee U) 5 goals v Morton
Premier League	
23 Aug 1996	Marco Negri (Rangers) 5 goals v Dundee U
Division 1	
14 Sept 1928	Jimmy McGrory (Celtic) 8 goals v Dunfermline Ath
Division 2	
1 Oct 1927	Owen McNally (Arthurlie) 8 goals v Armadale
2 Jan 1930	Jim Dyet (King's Park) 8 goals v Forfar Ath
18 April 1936	John Calder (Morton) 8 goals v Raith R
20 Aug 1937	Norman Hayward (Raith R) 8 goals v Brechin C
SCOTTISH CUP	
12 Sept 1885	John Petrie (Arbroath) 13 goals v Bon Accord (*1st Round*)

HIGHEST WINS

Highest win in a First-Class Match
(Scottish Cup 1st Round)

Arbroath	36	Bon Accord	0	12 Sept 1885

Highest win in an International Match

England	13	Ireland	0	18 Feb 1882

Highest win in a FA Cup Match

Preston NE	26	Hyde U	0	15 Oct 1887

(1st Round)

Highest win in a League Cup Match

West Ham U	10	Bury	0	25 Oct 1983
(2nd Round, 2nd Leg)				
Liverpool	10	Fulham	0	23 Sept 1986
(2nd Round, 1st Leg)				

Highest win in an FA Premier League Match

Manchester U	9	Ipswich T	0	4 Mar 1995
Nottingham F	1	Manchester U	8	6 Feb 1999

Highest win in a Football League Match

Division 1 – highest home win				
WBA	12	Darwen	0	4 April 1892
Nottingham F	12	Leicester Fosse	0	21 April 1909
Division 1 – highest away win				
Newcastle U	1	Sunderland	9	5 Dec 1908
Cardiff C	1	Wolverhampton W	9	3 Sept 1955
Division 2 – highest home win				
Newcastle U	13	Newport Co	0	5 Oct 1946
Division 2 – highest away win				
Burslem PV	0	Sheffield U	10	10 Dec 1892
Division 3 – highest home win				
Gillingham	10	Chesterfield	0	5 Sept 1987
Division 3 – highest away win				
Barnet	1	Peterborough U	9	5 Sept 1998
Division 3(S) – highest home win				
Luton T	12	Bristol R	0	13 April 1936
Division 3(S – highest away win				
Northampton T	0	Walsall	8	2 Feb 1947
Division 3(N – highest home win				
Stockport Co	13	Halifax T	0	6 Jan 1934
Division 3(N) – highest away win				
Accrington S	0	Barnsley	9	3 Feb 1934
Division 4 – highest home win				
Oldham Ath	11	Southport	0	26 Dec 1962
Division 4 – highest away win				
Crewe Alex	1	Rotherham U	8	8 Sept 1973

Highest wins in a Scottish League Match

Scottish Premier League – highest home win				
Rangers	7	St Johnstone	0	8 Nov 1998
Celtic	7	Aberdeen	0	16 Oct 1999
Celtic	7	Aberdeen	0	2 Nov 2002
Hibernian	7	Livingston	0	8 Feb 2006
Scottish Premier Division – highest home win				
Aberdeen	8	Motherwell	0	26 Mar 1979
Scottish Premier League – highest away win				
Dunfermline Ath	1	Celtic	8	19 Feb 2006
Scottish Premier Division – highest away win				
Hamilton A	0	Celtic	8	5 Nov 1988
Scottish Division 1 – highest home win				
Celtic	11	Dundee	0	26 Oct 1895
Scottish Division 1 – highest away win				
Airdrieonians	1	Hibernian	11	24 Oct 1950
Scottish Division 2 – highest home win				
Airdrieonians	15	Dundee Wanderers	1	1 Dec 1894
Scottish Division 2 – highest away win				
Alloa Ath	0	Dundee	10	8 Mar 1947

MOST HOME WINS IN A SEASON

Brentford won all 21 games in Division 3(S), 1929–30

RECORD AWAY WINS IN A SEASON

Doncaster R won 18 of 21 games in Division 3(N), 1946–47

CONSECUTIVE AWAY WINS

FA PREMIER LEAGUE
Chelsea 9 games 2004–05

FEWEST WINS IN A SEASON

		Wins	*Games*
FA PREMIER LEAGUE			
2005–06	Sunderland	3	38
FOOTBALL LEAGUE			
Championship			
2004–05	Rotherham U	5	46
Championship League One			
2004–05	Stockport Co	6	46
Championship League Two			
2004–05	Cambridge U	8	46
Division 1			
1889–90	Stoke C	3	22
1912–13	Woolwich Arsenal	3	38
1984–85	Stoke C	3	42
Division 2			
1899–1900	Loughborough T	1	34
1983–84	Cambridge U	4	42
Division 3(S)			
1929–30	Merthyr T	6	42
1925–26	QPR	6	42
Division 3(N)			
1931–32	Rochdale	4	40
Division 3			
1973–74	Rochdale	2	46
Division 4			
1976–77	Southport	3	46
SCOTTISH PREMIER LEAGUE			
1998–99	Dunfermline Ath	4	36
SCOTTISH LEAGUE			
Premier Division			
1975–76	St Johnstone	3	36
1982–83	Kilmarnock	3	36
1987–88	Morton	3	44
Division 1			
1891–92	Vale of Leven	0	22
Division 2			
1905–06	East Stirlingshire	1	22
1974–75	Forfar Ath	1	38
New Division 1			
1988–89	Queen of the S	2	39
1992–93	Cowdenbeath	3	44
New Division 2			
1975–76	Forfar Ath	4	26
1987–88	Stranraer	4	39
New Division 3			
2002–03	East Stirling	2	36
2003–04	East Stirling	2	36

UNDEFEATED AT HOME OVERALL

Liverpool 85 games (63 League, 9 League Cup, 7 European, 6 FA Cup), Jan 1978–Jan 1981

UNDEFEATED IN A SEASON

FA PREMIER LEAGUE		
2003–04	Arsenal	38 games
FOOTBALL LEAGUE		
1889–90	Preston NE	22 games
Division 2		
1893–94	Liverpool	22 games

UNDEFEATED AWAY

Arsenal 19 games FA Premier League 2001–02 and 2003–04 (only Preston NE with 11 in 1888–89 had previously remained unbeaten away) in the top flight

HIGHEST AGGREGATE SCORES

Highest Aggregate Score England

Division 3(N)				
Tranmere R	13	Oldham Ath	4	26 Dec 1935

Highest Aggregate Score Scotland

Division 2				
Airdrieonians	15	Dundee Wanderers	1	1 Dec 1894

MOST WINS IN A SEASON

FA PREMIER LEAGUE		Wins	Games
2004–05	Chelsea	29	38
FOOTBALL LEAGUE			
Championship			
2005–06	Reading	31	46
Championship League One			
2004–05	Luton T	29	46
Championship League Two			
2004–05	Yeovil T	25	46
Division 1			
1960–61	Tottenham H	31	42
2001–02	Manchester C	31	46
Division 2			
1919–20	Tottenham H	32	42
Division 3(S)			
1927–28	Millwall	30	42
1929–30	Plymouth Arg	30	42
1946–47	Cardiff C	30	42
1950–51	Nottingham F	30	46
1954–55	Bristol C	30	46
Division 3(N)			
1946–47	Doncaster R	33	42
Division 3			
1971–72	Aston V	32	46
Division 4			
1975–76	Lincoln C	32	46
1985–86	Swindon T	32	46
SCOTTISH PREMIER LEAGUE			
2000–01	Celtic	31	38
2002–03	Rangers	31	38
	Celtic	31	38
2003–04	Celtic	31	38
SCOTTISH LEAGUE			
Premier Division			
1995–96	Rangers	27	36
1984–85	Aberdeen	27	36
1991–92	Rangers	33	44
1992–93	Rangers	33	44
Division 1			
1920–21	Rangers	35	42
Division 2			
1966–67	Morton	33	38
New Division 1			
1998–99	Hibernian	28	36
New Division 2			
1983–84	Forfar Ath	27	39
1987–88	Ayr U	27	39
New Division 3			
2004–05	Gretna	32	36

MOST POINTS IN A SEASON
(under old system of two points for a win)

FOOTBALL LEAGUE		Points	Games
Division 1			
1978–79	Liverpool	68	42
Division 2			
1919–20	Tottenham H	70	42
Division 3			
1971–72	Aston V	70	46
Division 3(S)			
1950–51	Nottingham F	70	46
1954–55	Bristol C	70	46
Division 3(N)			
1946–47	Doncaster R	72	42
Division 4			
1975–76	Lincoln C	74	46
SCOTTISH LEAGUE			
Premier Division			
1984–85	Aberdeen	59	36
1992–93	Rangers	73	44
Division 1			
1920–21	Rangers	76	42
Division 2			
1966–67	Morton	69	38
New Division 1			
1976–77	St Mirren	62	39
1993–94	Falkirk	66	44
New Division 2			
1983–84	Forfar Ath	63	39

MOST POINTS IN A SEASON
(three points for a win)

FA PREMIER LEAGUE		Points	Games
2004–05	Chelsea	95	38
FOOTBALL LEAGUE			
Championship			
2005–06	Reading	106	46
Championship League One			
2004–05	Luton T	98	46
Championship League Two			
2005–06	Carlisle U	86	46
Division 1			
1998–99	Sunderland	105	46
1984–85	Everton	90	42
1987–88	Liverpool	90	40
Division 2			
1998–99	Fulham	101	46
Division 3			
2001–02	Plymouth Arg	102	46
Division 4			
1985–86	Swindon T	102	46
SCOTTISH PREMIER LEAGUE			
2001–02	Celtic	103	38
SCOTTISH LEAGUE			
Premier League			
1995–96	Rangers	87	36
New Division 1			
1998–99	Hibernian	89	36
New Division 2			
1995–96	Stirling Alb	81	36
New Division 3			
2004–05	Gretna	98	36

FEWEST POINTS IN A SEASON

FA PREMIER LEAGUE		Points	Games
2005–06	Sunderland	15	38
FOOTBALL LEAGUE (minimum 34 games)			
Championship			
2004–05	Rotherham U	29	46
Championship League One			
2004–05	Stockport Co	26	46
Championship League Two			
2004–05	Kidderminster H	38	46
2004–05	Cambridge U*	30	46
**Deducted 10 points for entering administration.*			
Division 1			
1984–85	Stoke C	17	42
Division 2			
1904–05	Doncaster R	8	34
1899–1900	Loughborough T	8	34
Division 3			
1997–98	Doncaster R	20	46
Division 3(S)			
1924–25 & 1929–30	Merthyr T	21	42
1925–26	QPR	21	42
Division 3(N)			
1931–32	Rochdale	11	40
Division 4			
1976–77	Workington	19	46
SCOTTISH PREMIER LEAGUE			
2001–02	St Johnstone	21	38
SCOTTISH LEAGUE (minimum 30 games)			
Premier Division			
1975–76	St Johnstone	11	36
1987–88	Morton	16	44
Division 1			
1954–55	Stirling Alb	6	30
Division 2			
1936–37	Edinburgh C	7	34
New Division 1			
1988–89	Queen of the S	10	39
1992–93	Cowdenbeath	13	44
New Division 2			
1987–88	Berwick R	16	39
1987–88	Stranraer	16	39
New Division 3			
2003–04	East Stirling	8	36

FEWEST NUMBER OF DEFEATS IN A SEASON *(Minimum 20 games)*

FA PREMIER LEAGUE		*Defeats*	*Games*
2004–05	Chelsea	1	38
FOOTBALL LEAGUE			
Championship			
2005–06	Reading	2	46
Championship League One			
2004–05	Luton T	6	46
Championship League Two			
2005–06	Northampton T	7	46
Division 1			
1990–91	Arsenal	1	38
1987–88	Liverpool	2	40
1968–69	Leeds U	2	42
Division 2			
1897–98	Burnley	2	30
1905–06	Bristol C	2	38
1963–64	Leeds U	3	42
2002–03	Wigan Ath	4	46
Division 3			
1966–67	QPR	5	46
1989–90	Bristol R	5	46
1997–98	Notts Co	5	46
Division 3(S)			
1921–22	Southampton	4	42
1929–30	Plymouth Arg	4	42
Division 3(N)			
1953–54	Port Vale	3	46
1946–47	Doncaster R	3	42
1923–24	Wolverhampton W	3	42
Division 4			
1975–76	Lincoln C	4	46
1981–82	Sheffield U	4	46
1981–82	Bournemouth	4	46
SCOTTISH PREMIER LEAGUE			
2001–02	Celtic	1	38
SCOTTISH LEAGUE			
Premier Division			
1995–96	Rangers	3	36
1987–88	Celtic	3	44
Division 1			
1920–21	Rangers	1	42
Division 2			
1956–57	Clyde	1	36
1962–63	Morton	1	36
1967–68	St Mirren	1	36
New Division 1			
1975–76	Partick T	2	26
1976–77	St Mirren	2	39
1992–93	Raith R	4	44
1993–94	Falkirk	4	44
New Division 2			
1975–76	Raith R	1	26
1975–76	Clydebank	3	26
1983–84	Forfar Ath	3	39
1986–87	Raith R	3	39
1998–99	Livingston	3	36
New Division 3			
2004–05	Gretna	2	36

NO DEFEATS IN A SEASON

FA PREMIER LEAGUE		
2003–04	Arsenal	won 26, drew 12
FOOTBALL LEAGUE		
Division 1		
1888–89	Preston NE	won 18, drew 4
Division 2		
1893–94	Liverpool	won 22, drew 6
SCOTTISH LEAGUE DIVISION 1		
1898–99	Rangers	won 18

MOST LEAGUE MEDALS

Phil Neal (Liverpool) 8: 1976, 1977, 1979, 1980, 1982, 1983, 1984, 1986; Alan Hansen (Liverpool) 8: 1979, 1980, 1982, 1983, 1984, 1986, 1988, 1990; Ryan Giggs (Manchester U) 8: 1993, 1994, 1996, 1997, 1999, 2000, 2001, 2003

MOST DEFEATS IN A SEASON

FA PREMIER LEAGUE		*Defeats*	*Games*
1994–95	Ipswich T	29	42
FOOTBALL LEAGUE			
Championship			
2005–06	Crewe Alex	22	46
2005–06	Millwall	22	46
2005–06	Brighton & HA	22	46
Championship League One			
2004–05	Stockport Co	32	46
Championship League Two			
2004–05	Kidderminster H	28	46
Division 1			
1984–85	Stoke C	31	42
2003–04	Wimbledon	33	46
Division 2			
1938–39	Tranmere R	31	42
1992–93	Chester C	33	46
2000–01	Oxford U	33	46
Division 3			
1997–98	Doncaster R	34	46
Division 3(S)			
1924–25	Merthyr T	29	42
1952–53	Walsall	29	46
1953–54	Walsall	29	46
Division 3(N)			
1931–32	Rochdale	33	40
Division 4			
1987–88	Newport Co	33	46
SCOTTISH PREMIER LEAGUE			
2001–02	St Johnstone	27	38
SCOTTISH LEAGUE			
Premier Division			
1984–85	Morton	29	36
Division 1			
1920–21	St Mirren	31	42
Division 2			
1962–63	Brechin C	30	36
1923–24	Lochgelly	30	38
New Division 1			
1988–89	Queen of the S	29	39
1995–96	Dumbarton	31	36
1992–93	Cowdenbeath	34	44
New Division 2			
1987–88	Berwick R	29	39
New Division 3			
2003–04	East Stirling	32	36

MOST DRAWN GAMES IN A SEASON

FA PREMIER LEAGUE		*Draws*	*Games*
1993–94	Manchester C	18	42
1993–94	Sheffield U	18	42
1994–95	Southampton	18	42
FOOTBALL LEAGUE			
Championship			
2004–05	Wolverhampton W	21	46
2004–05	Leicester C	21	46
Championship League One			
2004–05	Barnsley	19	46
2005–06	Bradford	19	46
Championship League Two			
2004–05	Bristol R	21	46
2005–06	Lincoln C	21	46
Division 1			
1978–79	Norwich C	23	42
Division 3			
1997–98	Cardiff C	23	46
1997–98	Hartlepool U	23	46
Division 4			
1986–87	Exeter C	23	46
SCOTTISH LEAGUE			
Premier Division			
1993–94	Aberdeen	21	44
New Division 1			
1986–87	East Fife	21	44

LONGEST WINNING SEQUENCE

FA PREMIER LEAGUE	Team	Games
2001–02 and 2002–03	Arsenal	14
FOOTBALL LEAGUE		
Division 1		
1959–60 (2) and 1960–61 (11)	Tottenham H	13
1891–92	Preston NE	13
1891–92	Sunderland	13
Division 2		
1904–05	Manchester U	14
1905–06	Bristol C	14
1950–51	Preston NE	14
Division 3		
1985–86	Reading	13
FROM SEASON'S START		
Division 1		
1960–61	Tottenham H	11
1992–93	Newcastle U	11
2000–01	Fulham	11
Division 3		
1985–86	Reading	13
SCOTTISH LEAGUE		
Premier League		
2003–04	Celtic	25

LONGEST SEQUENCE OF CONSECUTIVE SCORING (Individual)

FA PREMIER LEAGUE
Ruud Van Nistelroy (Manchester U) 15 in 10 games 2003–04

FOOTBALL LEAGUE RECORD
Tom Phillipson (Wolverhampton W) 23 in 13 games 1926–27

LONGEST UNBEATEN SEQUENCE

FA PREMIER LEAGUE	Team	Games
May 2003–October 2004	Arsenal	49
FOOTBALL LEAGUE		
Division 1		
Nov 1977–Dec 1978	Nottingham F	42

LONGEST UNBEATEN CUP SEQUENCE

Liverpool 25 rounds League/Milk Cup 1980–84

LONGEST UNBEATEN SEQUENCE IN A SEASON

FA PREMIER LEAGUE	Team	Games
2003–04	Arsenal	38
FOOTBALL LEAGUE		
Division 1		
1920–21	Burnley	30

LONGEST UNBEATEN START TO A SEASON

FA PREMIER LEAGUE	Team	Games
2003–04	Arsenal	38
FOOTBALL LEAGUE		
Division 1		
1973–74	Leeds U	29
1987–88	Liverpool	29

LONGEST SEQUENCE WITHOUT A WIN IN A SEASON

FOOTBALL LEAGUE	Team	Games
Division 2		
1983–84	Cambridge U	31

LEAGUE CHAMPIONSHIP HAT-TRICKS

Huddersfield T	1923–24 to 1925–26
Arsenal	1932–33 to 1934–35
Liverpool	1981–82 to 1983–84
Manchester U	1998–99 to 2000–01

LONGEST SEQUENCE WITHOUT A WIN FROM SEASON'S START

FOOTBALL LEAGUE	Team	Games
Championship		
2004–05	Rotherham U	20
Division 4		
1970–71	Newport Co	25

LONGEST SEQUENCE OF CONSECUTIVE DEFEATS

FOOTBALL LEAGUE	Team	Games
Division 2		
1898–99	Darwen	18

East Stiling 24 in 2003–04.

A CENTURY OF LEAGUE AND CUP GOALS IN CONSECUTIVE SEASONS

George Camsell	League	Cup	Season
Middlesbrough	59	5	1926–27
(101 goals)	33	4	1927–28

(Camsell's cup goals were all scored in the FA Cup.)

Steve Bull			
Wolverhampton W	34	18	1987–88
(102 goals)	37	13	1988–89

(Bull had 12 in the Sherpa Van Trophy, 3 Littlewoods Cup, 3 FA Cup in 1987–88; 11 Sherpa Van Trophy, 2 Littlewoods Cup in 1988–89.)

PENALTIES

Most in a Season (individual)
Division 1 — Goals — Season
Francis Lee (Manchester C) 13 1971–72

Most awarded in one game
Five Crystal Palace (4 – 1 scored, 3 missed) v Brighton & HA (1 scored), Div 2 1988–89

Most saved in a Season
Division 1
Paul Cooper (Ipswich T) 8 (of 10) 1979–80

GOALKEEPING RECORDS

(without conceding a goal)

BRITISH RECORD (all competitive games)
Chris Woods, Rangers, in 1196 minutes from 26 November 1986 to 31 January 1987.

FOOTBALL LEAGUE
Steve Death, Reading, 1103 minutes from 24 March to 18 August 1979.

MOST SUCCESSFUL MANAGERS

Sir Alex Ferguson CBE
Manchester U
17 major trophies in 15 seasons:
8 Premier League, 5 FA Cup, 2 League Cup, 1 European Cup, 1 Cup-Winners' Cup.

Aberdeen
1976–86 – 9 trophies:
3 League, 4 Scottish Cup, 1 League Cup, 1 Cup-Winners' Cup.

Bob Paisley
Liverpool
1974–83 – 13 trophies:
6 League, 3 European Cup, 3 League Cup, 1 UEFA Cup.

MOST LEAGUE APPEARANCES (750+ matches)

1005 Peter Shilton (286 Leicester City, 110 Stoke City, 202 Nottingham Forest, 188 Southampton, 175 Derby County, 34 Plymouth Argyle, 1 Bolton Wanderers, 9 Leyton Orient) 1966–97

931 Tony Ford (355 Grimsby T, 9 Sunderland (loan), 112 Stoke C, 114 WBA, 68 Grimsby T, 5 Bradford C (loan), 76 Scunthorpe U, 103 Mansfield T, 89 Rochdale) 1975–2002

909 Graeme Armstrong (204 Stirling A, 83 Berwick R, 353 Meadowbank T, 268 Stenhousemuir, 1 Alloa) 1975–2001

863 Tommy Hutchison (165 Blackpool, 314 Coventry City, 46 Manchester City, 92 Burnley, 178 Swansea City, 68 Alloa) 1965–91

824 Terry Paine (713 Southampton, 111 Hereford United) 1957–77

790 Neil Redfearn (35 Bolton W, 10 Lincoln C (loan), 90 Lincoln C, 46 Doncaster R, 57 Crystal Palace, 24 Watford, 62 Oldham Ath, 292 Barnsley, 30 Charlton Ath, 17 Bradford C, 22 Wigan Ath, 42 Halifax T, 54 Boston U, 9 Rochdale) 1982–2004

782 Robbie James (484 Swansea C, 48 Stoke C, 87 QPR, 23 Leicester C, 89 Bradford C, 51 Cardiff C) 1973–94

777 Alan Oakes (565 Manchester C, 211 Chester C, 1 Port Vale) 1959–84

771 John Burridge (27 Workington, 134 Blackpool, 65 Aston Villa, 6 Southend U (loan), 88 Crystal Palace, 39 QPR, 74 Wolverhampton W, 6 Derby Co (loan), 109 Sheffield U, 62 Southampton, 67 Newcastle U, 65 Hibernian, 3 Scarborough, 4 Lincoln C, 3 Aberdeen, 3 Dumbarton, 3 Falkirk, 4 Manchester C, 3 Darlington, 6 Queen of the South) 1968–96

770 John Trollope (all for Swindon Town) 1960–80†

764 Jimmy Dickinson (all for Portsmouth) 1946–65

761 Roy Sproson (all for Port Vale) 1950–72

760 Mick Tait (64 Oxford U, 106 Carlisle U, 33 Hull C, 240 Portsmouth, 99 Reading, 79 Darlington, 139 Hartlepool U) 1975–97

758 Ray Clemence (48 Scunthorpe United, 470 Liverpool, 240 Tottenham Hotspur) 1966–87

758 Billy Bonds (95 Charlton Ath, 663 West Ham U) 1964–88

757 Pat Jennings (48 Watford, 472 Tottenham Hotspur, 237 Arsenal) 1963–86

757 Frank Worthington (171 Huddersfield T, 210 Leicester C, 84 Bolton W, 75 Birmingham C, 32 Leeds U, 19 Sunderland, 34 Southampton, 31 Brighton & HA, 59 Tranmere R, 23 Preston NE, 19 Stockport Co) 1966–88

† record for one club

CONSECUTIVE
401 Harold Bell (401 Tranmere R; 459 in all games) 1946–55

FA CUP
88 Ian Callaghan (79 Liverpool, 7 Swansea C, 2 Crewe Alex)

MOST SENIOR MATCHES
1390 Peter Shilton (1005 League, 86 FA Cup, 102 League Cup, 125 Internationals, 13 Under-23, 4 Football League XI, 20 European Cup, 7 Texaco Cup, 5 Simod Cup, 4 European Super Cup, 4 UEFA Cup, 3 Screen Sport Super Cup, 3 Zenith Data Systems Cup, 2 Autoglass Trophy, 2 Charity Shield, 2 Full Members Cup, 1 Anglo-Italian Cup, 1 Football League play-offs, 1 World Club Championship)

YOUNGEST PLAYERS

FA Premier League appearance
Aaron Lennon, 16 years 129 days, Leeds U v Tottenham H, 23.8.2003.

FA Premier League scorer
James Vaughan, 16 years 271 days, Everton v Crystal Palace 10.4.2005

Football League appearance
Albert Geldard, 15 years 158 days, Bradford Park Avenue v Millwall, Division 2, 16.9.29; and Ken Roberts, 15 years 158 days, Wrexham v Bradford Park Avenue, Division 3N, 1.9.51
If leap years are included, Ken Roberts was 157 days

Football League scorer
Ronnie Dix, 15 years 180 days, Bristol Rovers v Norwich City, Division 3S, 3.3.28.

Division 1 appearance
Derek Forster, 15 years 185 days, Sunderland v Leicester City, 22.8.64.

Division 1 scorer
Jason Dozzell, 16 years 57 days as substitute Ipswich Town v Coventry City, 4.2.84

Division 1 hat-tricks
Alan Shearer, 17 years 240 days, Southampton v Arsenal, 9.4.88
Jimmy Greaves, 17 years 10 months, Chelsea v Portsmouth, 25.12.57

FA Cup appearance (any round)
Andy Awford, 15 years 88 days as substitute Worcester City v Boreham Wood, 3rd Qual. rd, 10.10.87

FA Cup proper appearance
Lee Holmes, 15 years 277 days, Derby Co v Brentford 4.1.2003

FA Cup Final appearance
Curtis Weston, 17 years 119 days, Millwall v Manchester U, 2004

FA Cup Final scorer
Norman Whiteside, 18 years 18 days, Manchester United v Brighton & Hove Albion, 1983

FA Cup Final captain
David Nish, 21 years 212 days, Leicester City v Manchester City, 1969

League Cup appearance
Chris Coward, 16 years 30 days, Stockport Co v Sheffield W, 2005

League Cup Final scorer
Norman Whiteside, 17 years 324 days, Manchester United v Liverpool, 1983

League Cup Final captain
Barry Venison, 20 years 7 months 8 days, Sunderland v Norwich City, 1985

OLDEST PLAYERS

FA Premier League appearance
John Burridge 43 years 5 months, Manchester C v QPR 14.5.1995

Football League appearance
Neil McBain, 52 years 4 months, New Brighton v Hartlepools United, Div 3N, 15.3.47 (McBain was New Brighton's manager and had to play in an emergency)

Division 1 appearance
Stanley Matthews, 50 years 5 days, Stoke City v Fulham, 6.2.65

RECORD ATTENDANCES

FA PREMIER LEAGUE
73,006 Manchester U v Charlton Ath, Old Trafford 7.5.2006

FOOTBALL LEAGUE
83,260 Manchester U v Arsenal, Maine Road 17.1.1948

SCOTTISH LEAGUE
118,567 Rangers v Celtic, Ibrox Stadium 2.1.1939

FA CUP FINAL
126,047* Bolton W v West Ham U, Wembley 28.4.1923

EUROPEAN CUP
135,826 Celtic v Leeds U, semi-final at Hampden Park 15.4.1970

SCOTTISH CUP
146,433 Celtic v Aberdeen, Hampden Park 24.4.37

WORLD CUP
199,854† Brazil v Uruguay, Maracana, Rio 16.7.50

* It has been estimated that as many as 70,000 more broke in without paying.
† 173,830 paid.

SENDINGS-OFF

SEASON
451 (League alone) 2003–04
(Before rescinded cards taken into account)

DAY
19 (League) 13 Dec 2003

FA CUP FINAL
Kevin Moran, Manchester U v Everton 1985
Jose Antonio Reyes, Arsenal v Manchester U 2005

QUICKEST
Walter Boyd, Swansea C v Darlington Div 3 as substitute in zero seconds 23 Nov 1999

MOST IN ONE GAME
Five: Chesterfield (2) v Plymouth Arg (3) 22 Feb 1997
Five: Wigan Ath (1) v Bristol R (4) 2 Dec 1997
Five: Exeter C (3) v Cambridge U (2) 23 Nov 2002

MOST IN ONE TEAM
Wigan Ath (1) v Bristol R (4) 2 Dec 1997
Hereford U (4) v Northampton T (0) 11 Nov 1992

RED CARD ANOMALIES 2005–06

The following players were successful in appealing against their red cards:

Taggart (Stoke C), Welsh (Sunderland), Konchesky (West Ham U), Barker (Rotherham U), Sito (Ipswich T), Onuoha (Manchester C), Dichio (Preston NE), Khizanishvili (Blackburn R), Flitney (Barnet), O'Connor J (Burnley), Robinson (Millwall), Newman (Brentford), Gillet (Chester C), Johnson M (Derby Co), Beresford (Luton T), Herd (Shrewsbury T), Pouton (Gillingham), McAteer (Tranmere R), Carr (Newcastle U), Jones G (Grimsby T).

In addition, Jenas (Newcastle U) his red card was downgraded to a caution.

Pedersen (Nottingham F) his red card was rescinded at the request of the referee.

Khizanishvili (Blackburn R), Welsh (Sunderland), Konchesky (West Ham U) – rescinded on appeal, but the dismissal would remain on their records.

Diouf (Bolton W) received two yellow cards, but not generally picked up by the media.

Carr (Newcastle U) this was a case of mistaken identity. Scott Parker (Newcastle U) was booked when it should have been Carr.

Hutchinson (Darlington) and Jones RW (Grimsby T) both players dismissed after the final whistle.

PREMIER LEAGUE EVER-PRESENT CLUBS

	P	*W*	*D*	*L*	*F*	*A*	*Pts*
Manchester U	544	339	126	79	1057	489	1143
Arsenal	544	289	146	109	911	482	1013
Liverpool	544	265	136	143	868	552	931
Chelsea	544	261	147	136	848	556	930
Aston Villa	544	203	158	183	668	632	767
Tottenham H	544	195	143	206	716	732	728
Everton	544	177	146	221	651	739	677

TOP TEN PREMIERSHIP APPEARANCES

1	Gary Speed	483	**6**	Teddy Sheringham	401
2	Alan Shearer	441	**7**	Sol Campbell	390
3	David James	438	**8**	Andy Cole	389
4	Ryan Giggs	434	**9**	Ray Parlour	379
5	Gareth Southgate	426	**10**	Nigel Martyn	372

TOP TEN PREMIERSHIP GOALSCORERS

1	Alan Shearer	260	**6**	Teddy Sheringham	144
2	Andy Cole	184	**7**	Jimmy Floyd Hasselbaink	126
3	Thierry Henry	164	**8**	Michael Owen	125
4	Robbie Fowler	160	**9**	Dwight Yorke	122
5	Les Ferdinand	149	**10**	Ian Wright	113

INTERNATIONAL RECORDS

MOST GOALS IN AN INTERNATIONAL

Record/World Cup	Archie Thompson (Australia) 13 goals v American Samoa	11.4.2001
England	Malcolm Macdonald (Newcastle U) 5 goals v Cyprus, at Wembley	16.4.1975
	Willie Hall (Tottenham H) 5 goals v Ireland, at Old Trafford	16.11.1938
	Steve Bloomer (Derby Co) 5 goals v Wales, at Cardiff	16.3.1896
	Howard Vaughton (Aston Villa) 5 goals v Ireland, at Belfast	18.2.1882
Northern Ireland	Joe Bambrick (Linfield) 6 goals v Wales, at Belfast	1.2.1930
Wales	John Price (Wrexham) 4 goals v Ireland, at Wrexham	25.2.1882
	Mel Charles (Cardiff C) 4 goals v Ireland, at Cardiff	11.4.1962
	Ian Edwards (Chester) 4 goals v Malta, at Wrexham	25.10.1978

MOST GOALS IN AN INTERNATIONAL CAREER

		Goals	*Games*
England	Bobby Charlton (Manchester U)	49	106
Scotland	Denis Law (Huddersfield T, Manchester C, Torino, Manchester U)	30	55
	Kenny Dalglish (Celtic, Liverpool)	30	102
Northern Ireland	David Healy (Manchester U, Preston NE)	19	49
Wales	Ian Rush (Liverpool, Juventus)	28	73
Republic of Ireland	Robbie Keane (Wolverhampton W, Coventry C, Internazionale, Leeds U, Tottenham H)	26	66

HIGHEST SCORES

Record/World Cup Match	Australia	31	American Samoa	0	2001
European Championship	Spain	12	Malta	1	1983
Olympic Games	Denmark	17	France	1	1908
	Germany	16	USSR	0	1912
Other International Match	Libya	21	Oman	0	1966
European Cup	Feyenoord	12	K R Reykjavik	2	1969
European Cup-Winners' Cup	Sporting Lisbon	16	Apoel Nicosia	1	1963
Fairs & UEFA Cups	Ajax	14	Red Boys	0	1984

GOALSCORING RECORDS

World Cup Final	Geoff Hurst (England) 3 goals v West Germany	1966
World Cup Final tournament	Just Fontaine (France) 13 goals	1958
Career	Artur Friedenreich (Brazil) 1329 goals	1910–30
	Pele (Brazil) 1281 goals	*1956–78
	Franz 'Bimbo' Binder (Austria, Germany) 1006 goals	1930–50
World Cup Finals fastest	Hakan Sukur (Turkey) 10.8 secs v South Korea	2002

**Pele subsequently scored two goals in Testimonial matches making his total 1283.*

MOST CAPPED INTERNATIONALS IN THE BRITISH ISLES

England	Peter Shilton	125 appearances	1970–90
Northern Ireland	Pat Jennings	119 appearances	1964–86
Scotland	Kenny Dalglish	102 appearances	1971–86
Wales	Neville Southall	92 appearances	1982–97
Republic of Ireland	Steve Staunton	102 appearances	1988–2002

LONDON INTERNATIONAL VENUES

Eleven different venues in the London area have staged full England international games: Kennington Oval, Richmond Athletic Ground, Queen's Club, Crystal Palace, Craven Cottage, The Den, Stamford Bridge, Highbury, Wembley, Selhurst Park and White Hart Lane.

DAILY ROUND-UP 2005–06

JULY 2005

Gerrard decision at Anfield ... Vieira off to Italy ... Wigan season ticket boost ... Agents fees escalate ... Celtic humbled ... Football League want Euro recognition ... England U-19's beaten in final.

1 Joel Glazer, prospective Man Utd chairman speaks on MUTV about long term plans. Howard Kendall to get Everton testimonial.
2 Ace transfer fixer Pini Zahavi to sort out Chelsea's summer moves.
3 Liverpool and Gerrard are poles apart, but Zenden signs for them. Man Utd say Rooney is not for sale.
4 Could Gerrard be Chelsea bound for £32m? Everton confident of Bellamy capture. Kewell–Lineker settled out of court. Norwich sell Helveg to Moenchengladbach. Sir Clive role at Saints confirmed.
5 Gerrard walks out on Liverpool. As AC Milan sign Vieri, Crespo may return from loan to Chelsea.
6 London's Olympic 2012 award might revive GB soccer team. Jeff Burnige resigns as Millwall chairman.
7 Bellamy for Blackburn. Wigan face High Court summons over policing costs issue. Tony Adams to become trainee coach at Feyenoord.
8 Gerrard signs for Liverpool! Frank Arnesen will start work at Stamford Bridge in September. Stockport taken over by Supporters Trust.
9 As Essien demands Chelsea move, the Blues might pay £60m for Barca's Ronaldinho!
10 German FA target 14 lower division players and four referees amongst group suspected of fixing ten games.
11 Liverpool to unveil Jose Reina £6m goalkeeper from Villarreal against Welsh team in Ch Lge. Doncaster pay club record £175,000 for Sunderland's Thornton.
12 Newcastle's Bramble breaks elbow in training. Pompey hope to sign Collins Mbesuma, Kaizer Chiefs 35 goal Zambian striker.
13 Ch Lge treble for Gerrard as TNS the Welsh village (pop 1000) lose 49 days after Liverpool's trophy triumph. Sir Alex warns Ferdinand over contract. Chelsea defiant over Jose remarks about Arsenal's Dein.
14 Departing Vieira accumulated 10 red and 100 yellow cards in nine Arsenal years as Juventus pay £6.9m for him. Chelsea fined £9000 for Barcelona official melee.
15 Liverpool not interested in Owen return. Chelsea loan Smertin to Charlton.
16 Shaun Wright-Phillips leaves for Chelsea in expected £21m transfer from Man City, but Ashley Cole to stay at Arsenal after all. Sir Alex agrees with Jose – Arsenal have it too easy.
17 Dubnica beaten 3-1 by Newcastle in Intertoto Slovakian stroll. West Ham hoping to add Yossi Benayoun, Israeli international from Santander at £2.5m.
18 Sir Alex warned over conduct towards referees. Chelsea given Essien deadline. Wigan break club record with 7000 season ticket sales. Arsenal and Spurs chasing Julio Baptista.
19 Ch Lge: two more for Gerrard wraps up TNS tie as Liverpool pay £7m for Saints Crouch. Becks hamstring injury in Los Angeles. Fulham lose legal battle with Tigana. Ardilles sacked as Tokyo Verdy boss. Ferdinand jeered at Peterborough.
20 Shevchenko rubbishes Chelsea connection. Brighton's Virgo for Celtic at £1.5m. Spurs defend right to play in Peace Cup in Asia – sponsored by the Moonies! Newcastle's Muslim Emre denounces terrorist attacks.
21 Robinho joins Real to further undermine Owen's chances. FL spent £7.8m on agents' fees – £1.9m for Leeds players alone.
22 Man City's Barton sent home from Thailand for fighting. No joy for Newcastle after trying for Boa Morte and Anelka.
23 Newcastle beat Dubnica 2-0 to reach Intertoto semi. Dong Fangzhou, Man Utd's Chinese loanee at Antwerp, stars in 2-0 win in Hong Kong and club make £1.6m. AFC Wimbledon beat the other protesters FC United 1-0 in front of 3,301.
24 Inter agree to tour after all after terrorist re-think.
25 Arsenal confident of Julio Baptista from Sevilla at £16.5m. After life with the Lions, Sir Clive arrives at St Mary's. Sir Alex dismisses row over Keane. Inter beat Leicester 2-1 in off-on friendly in half filled Walkers Stadium.
26 Ch Lge joy for Carragher: first Liverpool goal in six years, third in 363 outings as Kaunas beaten 3-1.
27 Ch Lge crushing 5-0 disaster for Celtic and Strachan against Artmedia. FL claim Championship following with 9.8 million attendances, fourth best Euro League after Premiership 12.88, Bundesliga 11.57 and La Liga 10.92 and better than Serie A crowds and want Intertoto spot. Steve Claridge sacked after 36 non-playing days at Millwall! Intertoto defeat for Newcastle 2-1 in La Coruna. Man City's battling Barton fined £120,000. Neale Barry to head new FA refs dept.
28 UEFA Cup joy for Carmarthen, Cork, Linfield and Rhyl. Lyon insisting on £32m for Essien. Crespo handed No.9 shirt at Chelsea. Free man Davids heads for Spurs.
29 Ch Lge draw sees Everton get short straw against Villarreal; Liverpool likely to play CSKA Sofia, Man Utd, Debrecen or Hajduk. Lincoln's Hobbs, 16, likely £750,000 move to Anfield. Euro U-19 final: England lose lead and game 3-1 to France, finish with ten men. New boy Hleb lays on Lupoli goal as Arsenal edge Ajax 1-0.
30 Awesome Rooney strike as Man Utd beat Urawa 2-0 in Saitama. Sir Alex keen on Ballack. Celtic only concede four goals and get a point at Motherwell! New boys Falkirk go down to Caley. Bell's Cup: Gretna extra time defeat at Morton.
31 More Chelsea injuries in New Jersey draw with AC Milan. Glazer nod in Owen direction. Two goal Ljungberg gives Arsenal Amsterdam tourney 2-1 over Porto. Rangers already two points ahead of Celtic after 3-0 over Livi! Bell's defeat for East Stirling at Dundee. Even chairman Lowe takes Saints pay cut.

AUGUST 2005

Ferdinand gets the bird, then signs ... Swansea new ground interest ... Community success for Chelsea ... Lord Burns verdict on FA ... FIFA unhappy with FA over card attitude ... Sven boys bashed by Danes ... Essien saga ends ... Newcastle land Owen.

1 Man Utd ruling out Owen move. Real Madrid unveil £13.8m striker Julio Baptista from Sevilla to go with fellow Brazilian Robinho said to have cost £17m from Santos. Chelsea close in on Essien.
2 Ch Lge exit for Celtic despite valiant 4-0 comeback; Liverpool 2-0 sets club record of five Euro score games in a row. Le Tallec out on loan again – this time Sunderland. Johnson gets five year deal at Palace. Newcastle interest in Owen.
3 Intertoto dream ends for Newcastle after 2-1 home defeat. Man Utd will play Debrecen, 5-0 winners in Split, Liverpool face CSKA Sofia who beat Dinamo Tirana 2-0. Edgar Davids signs for Spurs. Ferdinand jeered by Man Utd fans during 6-1 win over Antwerp. Makelele and Zidane to make French national team return.

4 Phil Neville for Everton at £3.5m.

5 Eve of season sees universal determination to punish abusive players.

6 Low key FL opening; only 75 goals in 35 games, 14 of them drawn. Sheff Utd 4-1 over Leicester highest. Johnson for Palace but Luton top it and miss penalty. Walcott is youngest Saint in goalless with Wolves while also relegated Norwich held by Coventry. Some Hull fans disgrace game v QPR by London bomb jibes. Swansea baptise new home with best gate for 23 years. Oldham win with nine new signings. "Returnees" Barnet held by old boy Agogo for Bristol R, Carlisle draw at Wycombe. SPL: Nakamura lights up Celtic.

7 Community joy for Blues in Drogba duo as Chelsea edge Arsenal 2-1. Healy brace for Leeds against Millwall but gate 10,000 down on last season's start, though overall opening programme yields 404,028.

8 Ferdinand signs four-year Man Utd deal at £100,000 a week. Lyon snub Chelsea over Essien. Hull react quickly in bomb furore. Charlton solve goalie crisis by signing Myhre. Shock, horror, probe! Cambridge University claim to be oldest club, founded in 1856, one year before Sheffield. FA to investigate. Dream sequence convinced Zidane to return to French national team! Derby make a point with Idiakez penalty.

9 Ch Lge: Everton fail to classy Villarreal, Man Utd take a 3-0 lead over Debrecen but only 51,701 attend while Rangers win 2-1 against Anorthosis, FL: Palace, Soton lose and Norwich can only draw again. Just six teams remain with 100% records. Connolly treble for Leicester against ten-man Stoke. Yeovil's first goalless draw after 53 games. Wolves equal 80 year old unbeaten run.

10 Ch Lge: Liverpool in cruise control in Sofia, game marred by racial abuse; Artmedia find Partizan tougher than Celtic! Brentford make it seven FL teams with full points. CIS Cup: Gretna 2-1 winners at Albion. Anelka not for Mags but Sunderland get Sheff Utd's Gray at £1.1m. Peace-seeking Savage left out of Wales squad.

11 UEFA Cup: Irish jigging for Cork and Linfield with Swedish draws, similar Scottish reel for Dundee Utd in Finland, but more sober dance for Rhyl beaten by Viking and Carmarthen in Denmark. Wigan lose Ellington to WBA at £3m. Sven assures Owen of place.

12 Eve of season blast by Sir Alex over Peter Kenyon's remarks that title will be from a "select group of one." Lord Burns recommends more open disciplinary hearings, restructuring of the FA with a slimmer hierachy. Graeme Souness confident of Owen.

13 Premier return sees goal down Hammers dump Blackburn. Van and Roo show for Man Utd at Everton. Away day joy for Spurs and Charlton. Villa and Bolton share four goals but three games goalless. Other red cards: Ehiogu, Dickov. Only Orient remain with full points in FL with best start since 1912 – but everyone has a point. Saints win at Sheff Wed, Norwich and Palace draw with each other. Boardroom gun stick up at QPR! Gretna edge top place in Scots Div 2. Conf: four-play lifts Hereford and Stevenage.

14 Arsenal leave it late against Jenas banished Newcastle, Chelsea even later with far from peerless performance against unlucky Premier debutants Wigan. Ten-man Rangers lose at Aberdeen leaving Hearts as leaders following their 3-0 win over Dundee Utd.

15 Essien move to Chelsea on at last for £26m. England will bid for 2018 World Cup. Barwick expects Sven to stay to 2008. Wales, Northern Ireland hit by injuries. Scots may baptise Derek Riordan (Hibs). Brentford boss Martin Allen unhappy over ref Webster in Vale defeat player injury.

16 FIFA unhappy with FA's red card downgrading. U-21s: Ambrose late winner for England over ten-man Danes; Scots win in Austria, Wales at home to Malta while the Irish share all with each other. Conf: two rounds and only three with maximum points, Exeter, Accrington and Morecambe.

17 Half-baked England suffer Sven's rasher substitutions and crash 4-1 to Danish in worst defeat for 25 years; Scots even throw away a 2-0 lead to draw in Austria; Wales hold Slovenia; Northern Ireland draw ten-a-side game in Malta with Gillespie dismissed; Republic lose to Vieri inspired Italy. Ricardo Carvalho lambasts Jose. Kanoute bound for Sevilla. Blackburn fined £10,000 for poor disciplinary record of five red and 74 yellows. Fulham to let Marlet go free to Wolfsburg. Bellion loaned to Hammers. Emanuel Pogatetz to play for Boro after suspension for breaking an opponent's leg reduced. Coventry to play at Ricoh Arena at last.

18 Sven could upset clubs by fitness check on stars. "If" game links Baros with Lyon, Owen to Liverpool. Bolton to sign 20th different national with Hidetoshi Nakata (Japan). Iranian backed takeover for West Ham planned. After Socrates, Romario now Garforth get third ageing Brazilian connection – Careca.

19 Jose introduces Essien at £24.4m and the Ricardo revolution ends. Moneybags Real spend £78,000 on expenses connected with benefit game for Ferenc Puskas in Budapest. Real 3 Puskas all-stars 1. Blackburn want Bellamy to miss Wales.

20 Spurs 2-0 winners over Boro lead PL. Ten-man Hammers draw at Newcastle. Wigan, Portsmouth and Sunderland still searching for a point. Goals still scarce – 14 in eight games. Coventry baptise new ground with win over ten-man QPR. Victory for Palace, defeat for Wolves, Saints beat Norwich. Millwall have goalie sent off and crash 5-0 at Reading. Brentford and Oldham lead Lge 1, Barnet only team in double figure points head Lge 2. Rangers beat Celtic 3-1 but Hearts still top SPL. Conf: Exeter only 100% team.

21 Dour struggle ends with Chelsea's Drogba shinning one in to beat Arsenal on Arsene's 500th. London has four of top five PL teams.

22 Calf muscle injury to keep Gerrard out of England games. Pompey sign Brian Priske from Genk. Jarosik loaned to Brummies. Anderton goes to Wolves.

23 Ch Lge: Liverpool stumble to CSKA but hold on for 3-2 aggregate win. Viduka double helps Boro at Brum, Sunderland lose again, Villa draw at Pompey. C Cup: Barnet stun Bristol C, Yeovil win at Ipswich, Norwich need extra time to beat MK Dons, QPR slump to Northampton and Brentford ship five at Cheltenham. CIS Cup: Biggies all through but Dundee lose at Stranraer. FA uphold red card protests for Welsh (Sunderland), Konchesky (West Ham), but add further match ban for Eastwood (Southend) for frivolous appeal! Owen offered blighty lifeline by Everton. Villa get Baros for £6.5m. Woodgate gets four minute debut for Real.

24 Ch Lge: Collina disallows Fergie goal for Everton and Forlan seals it for Villarreal; Man Utd and Rangers ease into group stage. Chelsea go top with foursome over Baggies, Arsenal also four timers against Fulham; Magpies still scratching for a goal – and need Owen, another Blackburn red in goalless draw with Spurs. C Cup: Grimsby surprise Derby. Bolton unhappy over Liverpool approach for Giannakopoulos. Hammers get Aliadiere on loan, not Celtic after all. Ex-Strasbourg Christian Bassila's on-off transfer to Sunderland is on.

25 UEFA Cup: Cork away with it at home, but Carmarthen, Rhyl, Linfield and Dundee Utd hit the skids. Ch Lge draw pits Chelsea and Liverpool together; Man Utd to face Forlan, Arsenal have Ajax as chief threat.

26 The late late show gives Super Cup to Liverpool after the other CSKA (Moscow) prove less of a problem – and Anfield could be welcoming Owen back after all. Giannakopoulos to stay at Bolton. Blackburn Todd charged with violent conduct over Spurs' Reid. Solano gets three match ban for elbow. Newcastle pay £9.6m for La Coruna's Alberto Luque.

27 Spurs suffer Mido "touch" and Chelsea revel against the ten to go top; even Wigan pile agony on Sunderland; Baros makes scoring Villa bow; Man City shoot to second. Johnson at the double for Palace; no luck for Norwich again; debutant Unsworth's last gasp penalty puts Sheff Utd top against Coventry's ten, whose boss Micky Adams

is unhappy with ref. Still tough at the top in Lge 1 – five on ten points; Swansea win 5-2 at Walsall. Sodje gets Darlo treble but they still only draw 4-4 at Chester; Hurst brace lifts Notts; Barnet, Carlisle both lose at home. Conf: unbeaten Exeter opening gap already. SPL: Ivan Sproule super sub hat-trick for Hibs shakes Ibrox faithful; jolly Jambos of Hearts make it five out of five.

28 Charlton stun Boro at the Riverside; Mags latest hit by Roo and Van show for Man Utd. Eriksson furious over alleged witch-hunt against him. Owen left out of Real squad.

29 Shearer in the lead in trying to convince Owen. Sheff Utd consolidate with 3-1 at Crewe; Preston foursome at Ipswich; Norwich lose at Stoke. Huddersfield 2-1 at Donny have one point lead; Yeovil six without a win now. Another double for Hurst as Notts clip Stags 3-2; Kamudimba Kalala(!) is Grimsby penalty scorer. Conf: Forest Green draw at Exeter (4696); sad Shots lose again. Mourinho said to have recommended Nuno Valente to Everton before £1.5m move. Bug-eyed Collina hangs up whistle over car sponsorship deal.

30 Owen succumbs to Newcastle in £17m switch. Terry knee problem gives Carragher England chance. Villa sign Wilfred Bouma £3.5m from PSV. Bolton worry over playing Loko whose president was shot dead last week. Todd three game ban. Pompey sign Zvonimir Vukic, Saints to get Marcelo Tejera from Penarol. Cort treble for Wolves over Rangers.

31 Window shopping ends with Solano returning to Newcastle for £1.5m, Jenas moving to Spurs for £7m, Everton make third signing of the week with Andy van der Meyde £1.8m from Inter to join Nuno Valente and Matteo Ferrari, Fernandes – Saints to Trotters, Dario Silva from Sevilla and Frank Songo'o Barca both to Pompey who have Diao on loan from Liverpool, Jeffers on loan to Rangers, Connolly to Wigan from Leicester £2m. In addition Boro get Fabio Rochemback from Sporting and Xavier ex-Roma, let Reiziger go to PSV and Job on loan to Al Ittihad while Arsenal and Sunderland swap loans – Poom and Hoyte. Last completed deal Rasiak to Spurs for £2.25m. Lawrie Sanchez sends home Mulryne and Whitley for curfew breaking. 15,000 turn up for Owen viewing. FA Cup preliminary round replay on Wednesday Tunbridge Wells beat Littlehampton Town 16-15 on penalties from 40 kicks – four short of world record. Crowd variously said to be 109 or 122.

SEPTEMBER 2005

Ukraine first for World Cup ... Northern Ireland v England! ... Hearts early Scottish surprise ... Wycombe unbeaten run ... A crowds and goals famine in Premier League ... Maldini record.

1 Sven thinking of 4-5-1 against Wales. FA likely to incur FIFA wrath over yellow and red downgrading. Sproule is called up by Northern Ireland, Celtic's Beattie by Scots.

2 Wales fearful of England backlash as are Northern Ireland ahead of their meeting on Wednesday. Ashley Cole to take his "tapgate" case to court. Portuguese football racked by alleged match-fixing. U-21: England win 4-0 in Wrexham against Wales denied a goal by slow-moving officials; Scots held by Italy at Fir Park. Sunny Scunny leap to top of Lge 1 with 4-1 win at Huddersfield, Notts stay three points clear in Lge 2. Conf: new boys Grays are top.

3 WC: Joe Cole rescues unimpressive England in Cardiff; Scots hold wasteful Italians; first win for Northern Ireland against Azers; Ukraine first Euros to qualify, USA also make it. Yeovil victory but not off bottom, Brentford still on winning ways. Torquay foot of Lge 2.

4 WC: Brazil take five off Chile and join Argentina, South Korea, Japan, Iran and Saudi Arabia already in finals.

5 Sven to start Owen; Hartson suspension may give Earnshaw start; Scots must throw caution to the winds. Increase profit for Arsenal but new ground will eat into it. TV Shots first win.

6 Becks still has Sven support; Sanchez convincing his men; Scots need a win; Republic home record impresses French returnees. U-21: England with 4-5-1 of course draw 1-1 in Germany, Wales edged out 3-2 in Poland, France beat Republic and Scots win in Norway only to discover they fielded a suspended player against Italy and will lose the game 3-0! FIFA go bonkers in ordering WC replay after Uzbekistan beat Bahrain 1-0 but have a penalty kick nullified for encroachment! But KK is the Grimsby penalty king. Bobby Williamson leaves Plymouth post.

7 WC: Hero Healy jigs while Sven's sad 4-5-1 England reel to the Irish tune; 1-0 defeats, too, for Wales who pay the Polish penalty and the Republic where French king Henry rules in Dublin; but Miller grinds out two priceless goals for buoyant Scots in Norway. No clear-cut qualifiers from any other matches. Spurs appoint Damien Comolli as sporting director.

8 Crisis talks at FA but Sven sure to carry on. Chelsea to defend charge of misconduct over their own Mutu drug-testing. Fulham sign Philippe Christanval, French defender from Marseille. Noel Cantwell Man Utd and Irish international dies at 73.

9 Alam loses her case against the FA; alleged "third man Davies" cleared. Sam Allardyce would be keen on England job. Chelsea offer to play Brazil for £1m rejected.

10 Chelsea still in third gear go high five in 2-0 against Sunderland; Henry-less Gunners lose 2-1 at Boro; Owen not on score sheet and ten-man Toon held by Fulham; Barton grabs draw as Mancunian derby finishes all-square; Alan Curbishley celebrates 600th in charge as Charlton win at Brum; Wigan win away; Spurs held by Liverpool; Fergie own goal downs Everton. Sheff Utd four point lead in Championship. Bristol City suffer seven-goal Swans uppping and Brian Tinnion resigns as manager. Bees and Scunny lead the Lge l pack. Grimsby climb second on goal difference to leaders Notts. Scots: Rangers held at Falkirk are fifth level with the chasing pack behind Hearts. Gretna clear top of Div 2 already after 2-0 at Morton (3763). Conf: Exeter edge two points ahead in four play over Cambridge. FA Cup: Clacton have the Brook House brought down on them – 9-1.

11 Goalless Bolton and Rovers fail to divert viewers from Ashes. Hearts foursome keeps their 100% record. Asia suspend Japanese ref over Uzbekistan penalty fiasco.

12 Hat-trick Harewood hammers Villa. Henry sidelined by groin trouble.

13 Ch Lge: two early strikes see Liverpool 2-1 at Betis; Lampard in minimum Chelsea win over Anderlecht; Rangers edge it late 3-2 over Porto; Lyon maul Real 3-0 and miss penalty; Rosenborg surprise Olympiakos 3-1. Sheff Utd four clear in Champs after 1-0 at Brighton, first wins for Wednesday against Leeds, even Millwall at Wolves! Floodlight failure at Ipswich delays Saints leveller through Wise. Dundee out of the Bell's. Swansea reach Lge 1 top. Little Thun nine years after averaging 100 fans await trip to Highbury in Ch Lge.

14 Ch Lge: clap hands off goes Rooney but Man Utd hold Villarreal; Van Persie also sees red (60th under Wenger) as Arsenal need vet Bergkamp last gasp to turn part-timers Thun; Vieira another carded for Juve in 2-1 at Brugge. Hammers in good financial nick despite £5m loss, bank debts near £30m. Les Ferdinand, 36, joins Watford.

15 UEFA Cup: Borgetti belated boost for Bolton; Boro take 2-0 lead over Xanthi yet only 14,191 turn up, but Everton crash 5-1 to Dinamo Bucharest. Palace's Johnson faces knee injury lay off, Villa's Laursen out for season. FA charge Macclesfield over financial irregularities.

16 FA rejects 2018 World Cup bid as Australia could get it for Asia! Heinze to miss rest of season with cruciate ligament damage.

17 Six in a row Chelsea and best no goals start by a PL side see off nearest rivals Charlton; on fire Harewood dumps Fulham for Hammers; Sunderland end 20 PL match defeats but only draw with WBA – one of three such stale-

Bolton Wanderers' Jared Borgetti (left) scores the winning goal past Lokomotiv Plovdiv's Robert Petrov during the UEFA Cup first round match at the Reebok Stadium. (Martin Rickett/PA/Empics)

mates including Butt off for Brummies at Pompey. Watford discard two goal lead and lose to topping Sheff Utd while Wednesday hit bottom; Leeds ten minus Healy win at QPR; ten man Huddersfield turn Brentford over in injury time; Wycombe only unbeaten FL team; Grimsby march on after 3-0 v Torquay; Carlton Palmer resigns as Mansfield boss after crowd abuse. SPL: Six in a row, too, for jumping Jambos, Skacel makes it seven goals in seven games.

18 Owen on Mags mark in 3-0 at Rovers; Speed spot on for Bolton after Man City hit woodwork five times; no goals for boring Liverpool and Man Utd, Keane faces injury lay off, Wigan and Boro also 1-1. Saints leave it late to draw at Derby; Norwich win derby at Ipswich. Real rage at ref giving Espanyol late goal seconds after whistling for infringement.

19 Double header Campbell returns in Arsenal win over Everton; Crowd and goal slump hits PL. Doug Ellis to quit as Villa chairman. Sheff Wed sack Proudlock for breaches of discipline. Ronaldinho wins FIFPro World Player of the Year, Rooney Young Player by the 38,000 professional footballers in 40 countries, but only Terry, Lampard and Makelele – all Chelsea get in team. Graham Barrow axed at Bury, Chris Casper is caretaker boss. Maldini equals Zoff Serie A record 570 appearances – all games 939.

20 C Cup: Wycombe's 3-1 half-time lead ends with Villa winning 8-3!; Spurs go out to Grimsby's KK as McDermott makes 700th game; Pompey lose in extra time at Gillingham. CIS Cup: Rangers forced to extra time by Clyde.

21 C Cup: debutant sub keeper Budtz saves two Man City penalties as Doncaster knock them out with Onuoha wrongly red carded for breaking Warrington's leg; Fulham "reserves" just edge Lincoln 5-4 in extra time. CIS Cup: Celtic taken to extra time by Falkirk; Hearts trumped at last by Livi. Man Utd not to appeal Rooney's two match Ch Lge ban.

22 PL alarm over falling crowds and blame falls on TV – source of the bulk of the income! Harry Redknapp on Sir Clive alert. Fresh injury concerns for Solskjaer and Fowler. Bristol Rovers sack Ian Atkins. Woodgate competitive debut for Real ends with one own goal and two yellow cards!

23 Poll (Graham) to test hi-tech ear piece for Man C v Newcastle. Onuoha red rescinded. Gary Johnson leaves Yeovil for Bristol C; Tony Pulis lands Plymouth job. Howard rescues Luton against lowly Owls.

24 Chelsea shock: concede goal to Villa and need Lamps penalty to win; more upsets: Wigan win at Everton, Rovers at Old Trafford for first time in 43 years; Owen again a Mags scorer; Nolan overhead effort dumps Pompey for Bolton; Liverpool share four goals at ten-man Birmingham; Charlton still winning; Arsenal goalless at Hammers. Sheff Utd keep up momentum, four points ahead of Reading winners at Norwich and nine in front of Luton, Crewe first goalless game in 61. Palace just hold Preston nine. Swansea, Southend and Huddersfield level in Lge 1, MK Dons still seek first win. Barnsley nine lose to Donny. KK penalty king again for top Lge 2 Grimsby. SL; Hearts make it eight in a row beating Rangers 11 points below them. Conf: unbeaten Grays and Accrington now setting the pace. Getafe are surprise La Liga leaders in Spain.

25 Black Cats purr at Boro after first win. Real ease pressure by beating Alaves 3-0.

26 Defoe puts Spurs back on track against Fulham. Alain Perrin receives chairman's blessing! Andy King loses Swindon job, Iffy Onuora takes charge. Gazza might buy Kettering Town. Poll rates hi-tech a huge success.

27 Ch Lge: Pires penalty helps Arsenal 2-1 at Ajax after Ljungberg scores Gunners 100th Ch Lge goal in 70 ties; late Van arrival gives Man Utd Old Trafford win over Benfica; Ronaldinho treble for Barca against Udinese. Hungry Wolves hit four at Crewe; Luton take three off Preston, Burnley and Cardiff other Championship treble shooters. MK Dons break duck, Southend give Yeovil goal start and win 4-1. Four play for Grimsby and Wycombe in Lge 2 as goals trickle in again. Conf: Grays win at Dagenham and lead by three points. Bell's Cup: Hamilton win at St Johnstone, St Mirren and Morton draw in two quarter-finals. Lua Lua has malaria.

28 Ch Lge: Liverpool claim three penalties but have to settle for sharing no goals with Chelsea; Inter miss penalty but edge Rangers 1-0 in empty San Siro; Real leave it late against Olympiakos; PSV ship three at Fenerbahce; Artmedia stun Porto. Reading held by shot shy Saints. Hulse hat-trick for Leeds. UEFA quota system for foreigners likely to face EU sanction.
29 UEFA Cup: Bolton late win in Plovdiv, pride if nothing else restored for Everton in 1-0 v Dinamo; Boro draw enough for moving on, but Hibs crash 5-1 in Dnepr and Cork pop out. Bulgars celebrate three survivors – CSKA, Levski, Litets. Keane to leave Man Utd at season's end. Peace of a kind restored at Soton. TV battle hotting up for 13 Oct – unlucky for some?
30 FA's centre of excellence not quite going for a Burton (on Trent). WC opening ceremony now on 7 June. Microchip ball had some problems in FIFA U-17 tourney. Burnley stun Wolves at Molineux.

OCTOBER 2005

Wigan still raising eyebrows ... Real now world's richest ... England through to World Cup Finals ... Gretna keep up goal glut ... Another Henry record at Arsenal ... Death of Johnny Haynes ... Republic's Kerr axed ... Hearts axe Burley ... Chelsea still on the march.

1 Two 3-2 away wins for Man Utd at Fulham and Spurs at Charlton; Mags Given holds Pompey up; Kugi double for Rovers; Sunderland settle for a point. Reading snip Sheff Utd lead by cutting Blades down 2-1 while Wed actually win; seventh successive draw for Saints; Luton keep up the pressure, too. Swansea, Southend – with club equalling seventh win in a row – pacesetters but Huddersfield held; MK Dons win again. Yeovil two behind at Scunny win 4-3; Three wins in a week Orient close in on held Grimsby; SPL: Five alive for both Celtic and Rangers – and ten different scorers. SL: Partick hit six at Alloa. Conf: Grays still unbeaten, but York within two points.
2 Chelsea four play destroys Liverpool; Maik Taylor heroics and penalty save in vain as ten man Brum go down to own goal at Highbury; Boro enter the 3-2 vogue at Villa; Everton slump at Man City; Lancs joy for Wigan over Bolton. SPL: ten-man Hearts salvage late point at Falkirk. Becks shines in Real 4-0 win over Mallorca.
3 Real overtake Man Utd as world's richest at £183.8m. Roy Keane tipped as next Republic boss. Reich stars as Palace win at QPR.
4 UEFA Cup pot luck puts Boro in easier looking group than Bolton with Sevilla and Besiktas. Ashley Cole out of England game with foot injury. Ex-pro Mark Ward jailed for eight years for drug trafficking. Cardiff players hurt in car crash. Arsenal to sell off Highbury memorabilia.
5 Spurs announce profit of £4.9m. NTL plan to bid for TV rights.
6 Rio axed by Sven. Chelsea snubbed by Nacho, 12, Spanish wonder kid. Ref rage as assailant gets just 31 week Norfolk FA ban.
7 U-21s: England hit by double Janko against Austria; Belarus shake Scots, Republic draw in Cyprus and Wales crash in Germany. Irish eyeing third place, Kerr under Irish pressure, Scots faith in new tactics. Wycombe clip high riding Grimsby; Boston nine hold on for Notts win.
8 WC: Lamps spot on to lift limping England who definitely qualify as best runner-up thanks to Dutch treat, but lose Becks to controversial yellows; Wales upset Irish; Republic hanging in there courtesy of Elliott goal and Given penalty save, but Scots disaster hand Belarus only second ever away win. New qualifiers are Holland, Portugal, Italy and Poland. Republic's group still wide open with three teams still unbeaten! Ecuador held by Uruguay still book WC passage as do Paraguay winners in Venezuela. Tunisia draw with Morocco enough for finals – Togo, Ghana, Ivory Coast and Angola complete Africa's nap hand. Yeovil topple Swansea.
9 Southend club record eight wins on the spin spiral them top of Lge 1. Conf: Shots back on the bottom.
10 WC seeds likely after Wednesday; return of the Roo awaited. Zajec resigns as Pompey director of football. Yeovil confirm Steve Thompson as manager. Bolton appoint Ricky Sbragia ex-Man Utd reserve coach as No.2. Swindon face winding-up order.
11 U21s: England pull Poles apart at Hillsborough; Welsh rare bit of a 3-0 win over Azers; Scots slump at bottom; Republic hit by Swiss. Sven upbeat ahead of Poland and finals. Kerr job on line for Republic.
12 WC: England take Pole position in better display; Republic fail to make it; Another Welsh win; Scots blossom too late; Healy off target, Johnson sent off in Irish loss; Swedes grab last automatic place; Czechs win in Finland robs Romania; Turkey in play-offs as Danes miss out; Slovakia draw enough to foil Russians; unbeaten Israel out. Euro situ: Holland, Ukraine, Portugal, France, Italy, England, Poland, Serbia & Montenegro, Croatia and Sweden qualify: Czechs, Turkey, Slovakia, Switzerland, Norway and Spain for play-offs. Fans injured watching Brazil train. Caborn to plea for more WC final tickets for England fans. Gordon Taylor castigates Blatter over remarks about players.
13 WC: nervous Uruguay edge Argentina 1-0 to face Aussies in play-off; Trinidad & Tobago to meet Bahrain conquerers of unlucky Uzbeks as USA 2-0 winners over Panama, join Mexico and Costa Rica in finals. Premier League flexing muscles over TV battle with EU. Real reveal regular payments for Puskas over five years. Man Utd abandon casino idea.
14 WC: play-offs: Spain v Slovakia; Switzerland v Turkey; Norway v Czech Republic. Germany to ban English fans from boozing; FA arrange friendly with Argentina in Geneva on day Swiss play Turkey. England in top pot for Euro 2008. Grimsby also top again after 3-0 at Cheltenham in Lge 2.
15 Bolton lead Chelsea hit woodwork then suffer 5-1 crushing; Spurs hit struggling Everton to go second; Arsenal with no Brits lose to Baggies; Shearer "goal" ignored and ten man Wigan hold on to beat Mags; Hughes unhappy with ref Halsey for red card on Khiz and Cisse wonder strike gives Liverpool the points; Yakubu scores against old mates as Boro draw with Pompey; sub Rossi, 18, adds to Man Utd win at Sunderland. With Reading idle, Sheff Utd take six point lead with minimum win over Wolves with one of five gates over 20,000, but Luton slump at Crewe and Saints get their usual draw – a club record. Huddersfield take advantage of Southend defeat to top Lge 1, Rochdale sneak into second place after 3-1 over Notts. Conf: surprises Grays hammer Scarborough 5-0. SPL: Hearts hold Celtic at Parkhead. SL; Gretna and Berwick head the two lower divisions unbeaten.
16 Phillips strike earns Villa Midland derby win over Brummies, one of four PL teams without a home win; Cole brace for Man City shoots down Hammers. Reading beat Ipswich 2-0 to stay three points behind Sheff Utd. SPL: Rangers held at Dundee Utd are nine points adrift of Hearts.
17 Drug test failure Xavier banned. Charlton scrape draw with Fulham. Hearts could be boosted by signing free man Fredi Bobic, German international striker. Internet shoot-out ends with one dead, two critical in Brazil. Essien may get ban for Bolton challenge.
18 Ch Lge: supersub Henry back for Arsenal stuningly equals Wright's record then beats it in Prague; Scholes red carded, Giggs injured as Lille hold Man Utd. Shambles of dismissal system shown as Khiz is reprieved and FIFA prevent Essien ban. Impressive Sheff Utd get four at Millwall, Brighton stun Palace at Selhurst, where Johnson injury mars comeback. Reading draw at Hull, Luton beat Norwich 4-2. LDV Vans: goals galore – 96 in 27 ties – and shocks too with Halifax whacking ten-man Bury 6-1. Other Conf winners Cambridge, Morecambe, Kidderminster, Hereford and Woking 3-2 conquerors of Forest. Johnny Haynes, 71, Fulham and England inside-

forward dies after car crash; the first £100 a week footballer. Brian Kerr axed as Republic boss. PL confident of settling TV dispute with EU.

19 Ch Lge: Chelsea's four play too much for Betis; Cisse strike enough for Liverpool; squandering Rangers held by Artmedia; Woodgate scores at the right end for rampant Real; Porto surprise Inter. O'Leary defended by chairman Ellis in abuse allegations against Poll. Swindon avoid winding-up order.

20 UEFA Cup: Jimmy Floyd's first of the season puts Boro in credit at Grasshoppers; Mexican ace Borgetti secures draw for Bolton in Istanbul; unfancied Norwegians Viking beat Monaco; holders CSKA Moscow lose at home to Marseille. Spurs snubbed in bid to move to new London Olympic stadium. Liverpool Cisse cautioned by police over youth assault.

21 Yorkshire derby ends all square with Leeds and Sheff Utd. Ex-Darlo supremo George Reynolds jailed for tax evasion. TV deadline is Monday.

22 Pires converts one penalty then fluffs attempt to copy a Cruyff-Olsen gimmick for a second as Arsenal edge Man City 1-0; Charlton climb second as Spurs draw at Man Utd; Wigan go fourth 2-0 at Villa and similar wins for Rovers and Fulham against Brum and Liverpool respectively. Reading victory keeps them three points behind Sheff Utd, Cardiff take six goals off Crewe and Saints win at last. Southend stumble to a Barnsley draw but go top as Huddersfield fight back 3-0 down still finishes 4-3 and Swansea draw at Rotherham in Lge 1. In Lge 2 Orient win at Grimsby helps undefeated Wycombe 2-1 winners at Lincoln to go top. FA Cup: Conf giant-killing casualties are Cambridge, Crawley, Gravesend and Scarborough; no run for Exeter, beaten by Stevenage. SPL sensation: Hearts sack manager George Burley then beat Dunfermline. Gretna and Berwick keep winning ways in SL.

23 Shock, horror! Chelsea drop two points at Everton! Jose unhappy with Drogba goal ruled out. Boro fury, too, at West Ham goal which did not cross line in their 2-1 defeat; Mags win excellent Tyne-Wear derby 3-2; Bolton another for the 2-0 slot over WBA. Becks gets sixth red of his career – this one for clapping – as Real lose at home to Valencia. Juve equal their own record start with eighth successive win.

24 Late show gives Brighton point at Sheff Wed. Worcester win cup replay against Accrington and sackings in the wake elsewhere for Francis Vines (Crawley) and Nicky Henry (Scarborough). Hearts may look to Sir Bobby Robson. Mistaken identity at Newcastle might reprieve Parker at Carr expense. Keith Hackett, PL head of refs is now in favour of technology!

25 C Cup: Palace ko Liverpool, Reading end Sheff Utd run, Fulham "old boy" Inamoto scores winner there for WBA. FA Cup: Conf Canvey lose replay at Burnham; Hereford need penalties to beat Alfreton. Prince William to watch Charlton train. Scots to play USA. Hackett unhappy with Parker decision – "undermining refs"... Becks card clapped out.

26 C Cup: crisis club Chelsea! Now they lose shoot-out to Charlton; goalie Flitney controversially sees red as Barnet crash to Man Utd reserves; another crucial Borgetti strike for Bolton; Shearer scores but gets a Whittle elbow at Grimsby. SPL: Hearts, Celtic win but Rangers drop two points 11 behind the Jambos. Juve make it a record nine. Saints chairman Rupert Lowe wins High Court libel £250,000 against *The Times* for "shabby" remarks re-Dave Jones axing.

27 Gazza is new Kettering manager. England Ladies whack Hungary 13-0 in Tapolea for their biggest win. George Swindon pre-war Arsenal goalkeeper dies at 90.

28 Newcastle announce profit of £4.5m before deductions. Brighton get Prezza approval for new ground at Falmer. Flitney card rescinded.

29 Wigan second! Chimbonda goal enough against Fulham; Man Utd reach 1000 PL goals but crash 4-1 at Boro; Chelsea back winning in second half over Rovers and Lamps scores 100th career goal; Arsenal "ex-penalty king" Pires salvages a draw at Spurs on 32nd birthday; Everton off the foot at Brum; Bolton surprise Charlton; Liverpool knock the Hammers; Pompey four on target at sad Sunderland, but Robert goes on strike. Sheff Utd and Reading (club record 18 no loss) held up by their draws with Cardiff and Leeds while Watford close in on Luton beaten at Coventry; Walcott again for Saints. Eastwood hat-trick on 22nd birthday for Southend, Swansea celebrate new Liberty Stadium naming with Trundle treble, but Huddersfield held by cellar dwellers Swindon. Lge 2 have new leaders in Orient as Wycombe draw with Posh; Carlisle take six off Stockport. SPL: Hearts trumped at last by Hibs, Rangers only draw again. SL: Dundee slipping badly, but Gretna and Berwick unbeaten. Conf: soaring Grays set record with 15th undefeated. Gazza delight at Poppies blooming win before 2060. AC Milan end Juve run with 3-1 win.

30 Second half lift for Toon with Owen brace, one for Shearer dumps Albion. SPL; ominously for Hearts, Celtic win at Dundee Utd and resume top spot on goal difference.

31 Hearts in turmoil as chairman George Foulkes and chief executive Phil Anderson axed by Vladimir Romanov, who instals son Roman. Old boy Vassell sinks Villa for Man City.

NOVEMBER 2005

Reading in full Championship flow ... Milestones for Lampard and Henry ... Shevchenko record in Europe ... Death of George Best.

1 Ch Lge: Sensation: Chelsea crash to Betis; Liverpool ease past Anderlecht; Rangers scrape a point to Artmedia; Becks 100th for winners Real. Championship: Sheff Utd and Reading (club record 18 without loss) both winners striding ahead of opponents, Plymouth swamped by rain. Millwall have two sent off, Burnley one at fiery Turf Moor. Wenger to take action over JM taunting. Whistler Poll banned for pre-season incident holidays in Jamaica, refs a game! Peter Shirtliff gets Mansfield job after caretaking.

2 Ch Lge: Arsenal make it four out of four in Sparta victory; Man Utd lose in Lille before record 66,470 crowd in Paris while 64,321 see Eto'o treble chance spinning Barca into last 16. Saints called off because of waterlogging and reveal board was wrong to oppose Lowe over Hoddle return. Sunderland report loss of £8.8m. Alan Pardew gets five year contract at Hammers. Merson bid to get Seaman on board at Walsall fails.

3 JM threatens to have peace talks with Wenger. Sven may give James another chance in goal. UEFA Cup: Nolan strike enough for Bolton against Zenit; Viduka double sees Boro through against Dnepr as both English teams head their groups. Kevin Wilson leaves Kettering after Gazza appointment. Dyer mystery illness at Newcastle.

4 FA Cup: Walsall edge home at Merthyr with 3046 present. No peace in my time for Wenger with Mourinho.

5 Six in a row for peerless Wigan clear in second place after victory at Portsmouth; vintage Sherri downs WBA; Brummie plummeting; Henry brace as Sunderland lose again; Villa, too, adding to Midlands woe; Rovers whack four past Charlton; Malbranque double lifts Fulham. Away day successes for Sheff Utd and Reading make it hard for Championship chasing pack, but Millwall still short of a home win. FA Cup: Romance lives on as Unibond Burscough account for Gillingham and Conf Tamworth win at Bournemouth, while Eastbourne home to Oxford, Weymouth and Harrogate at Forest and Torquay respectively earn replays. But Leamington crash 9-1 at Colchester who equal their record score. Gazza men fail but 4548 have cup fever, though crowds, some hit by

adverse weather generally poor with only Forest getting five figures. SPL: Hearts pop back on top awaiting Celtic's Sunday response. SL: Gretna win, Berwick held.

6 Crisis hits Chelsea in Man Utd defeat, while even Everton win a home game, thanks to born-again Beattie. FA Cup: Oldham held by Midland Alliance Chasetown relying on Eyres, 41, to level. Celtic resume leadership. Woodgate injured again for Real. Now AC Milan go eight wins in a row.

7 Nolan again for Trotters as Spurs lose. Stoke suspend DoF John Rudge and assistant Jan De Koning for a week. Lennie Lawrence is DoF at Bristol Rovers, Trollope first team coach. Scarborough hope to sell ground. Graham Rix receives hostile reception after landing Hearts post.

8 Wembley date in doubt. Bournemouth on the brink. CIS Cup: Dunfermline, Livingston and Motherwell book semi-final spots.

9 Jerome double ensures Cardiff's highest placing for decades at Sheff Wed. CIS Cup: Celtic heap more problems on Rangers.

10 Ferdinand expected to keep Campbell out of England team. Mystery at Blackpool over manager Colin Hendry as Simon Grayson takes over first team. Scots and Welsh not interested in GB team for Olympics. After Roberto Carlos, Ronaldo becomes Spanish citizen but both to play for Brazil.

11 U21 play-offs: England scrape late draw with French; German look good, Italy draw in Hungary. Grimsby go top of Lge 2 again. High winds call off two SL games. Even crowd trouble in Paris for Tunisia v DR Congo! Fears over Wembley delay.

12 Owen sinks a late double to dampen Argentine; Scots held by the Yanks. Czechs, Spanish and Swiss look good for WC play-offs, but Uruguay take slender lead over Aussies and Bahrain hold Trinidad. Top of the table win for Swans at Southend attract 11,049; draw enough for Orient to recapture lead in Lge 2. SL: three in five minutes help Jags draw with Gretna, Berwick crash at Arbroath. Conf: Grays suffer first defeat to Stanley and Exeter stay ahead.

13 Man Utd to investigate bugging at Old Trafford.

14 Long serving Morecambe boss Jim Harvey suffers heart attack. Forest dampen Weymouth FA Cup hopes, Worcester through against Chippenham. Republic job interests Venables. Yank interest in Liverpool. Maldini to retire after one more season.

15 U21s: late penalty controversy ends England hopes; Germans and Italians through. Northern Ireland hold Portuguese in full international, Wales draw U21 game in Cyprus. Torquay, Rushden need penalties to oust Conf opposition. Neale Cooper resigns at Gillingham, Ronnie Jepson takes over. Rumours of trouble at Soton as Sir Clive assistant Simon Clifford gives up. England win semi-pro game in Belgium 2-0. Man Utd give training facilities to Chasetown.

16 Uruguay pay WC penalties as boss Guus Hiddink becomes the wizard of Aus, joined by Czechs, Spaniards, plus Swiss on away goals in fiery Turkey and Trinidad winners in Bahrain. Wales lose friendly in Cyprus. FA Cup: Conf Burton oust Posh, Chasetown go down four times. Sky TV monopoly likely to go. England will bid for 2018 World Cup.

17 TV free for all will involve several parties; decision next year for 2007-10. German ref Robert Hoyzer gets two years five months for match-fixing. Blatter vows to crack down on Turkish night fracas. England ladies win in Holland. WC injury will keep Forlan out of Villarreal for over a month. Bahrain to appeal over disallowed WC goal. Sky Sports Victory Shield: Wales beat Irish 1-0.

18 Roy Keane parts company with Man Utd, Celtic interested. FIFA to decide on 2018 WC in 2007. Hungry Wolves take three at Derby, Swansea clear top in Lge 1, Accrington sneak ahead in Conf. Pele unimpressed with latest Brazil.

19 Wigan press Arsenal all the way but lose 3-2; three goals and points for Chelsea back to winning as with Man Utd, Liverpool and Villa, but Baggies go one better clattering Everton 4-0 for their best PL win. No goals for Man City and Blackburn however. Saints chuck three goal lead and let Leeds win. Ten-man Sheff Utd scrape a point against Millwall, Reading dump Hull 3-1. Huddersfield held, Southend beaten in Lge 1 where bizarrely Rotherham finish with eight men and Barnsley only equalise in last minute! Wycombe stride on clipping rivals Grimsby. Shrewsbury v Mansfield called off when Stags goalkeeping coach Peter Wilson dies in warm-up. Conf: last gasping Grays win at Exeter to regain top spot. SPL: Celtic put more pressure on Alex McLeish as they take three goals off Rangers. Adverse weather hits Scottish League and Cup games, but Gretna win 6-2 at Preston Athletic.

20 Middlesbrough get the three goal habit, too, over Fulham while Ferdinand denies Spurs at the death for Hammers. Palace win local "derby" at Brighton. Rix starts with a Hearts draw leaving them two points behind Celtic. Barca win the 151st derby at Real thanks to vintage Ronaldinho performance, 3-0 of course.

21 England likely to be in WC pot 1 when draw made on December 9 with Brazil, Germany, Argentina, Italy, Spain, France and Holland. Pompey eye new manager. October 2004 Carling Cup disciplinary hearing involving Chelsea and West Ham still not settled! Brummies v Trotters fog off!

22 Ch Lge: Pires from the spot enough for Arsenal in Berne, but Man Utd stifled by Villarreal now on the brink; Lille and Benfica provide sixth Group D draw in ten games; 67,273 watch Barca beat Werder 3-1 while only 9623 turn up for Juve's 1-0 v FC Brugge. Championship: point for Sheff Utd at Wolves not enough as Reading 3-0 winners at Ipswich go top; Lions claw Canaries at The New Den to put pressure on at the bottom as Millwall appoint Peter De Savary as chairman. LDV Trophy: Conf joy for Cambridge and Hereford but Wycombe need penalties at Gillingham; Halifax frozen off, Woking fogged. Blatter wants to silence national anthems.

23 Ch Lge: Liverpool held by Betis and Chelsea winners at Anderlecht through; 67,302 see Real held by Lyon, but both qualify; nobody watches Inter make it 4-0 over Artmedia as Rangers hang in there with Porto draw; Shevchenko four at Fenerbahce for AC Milan makes him leading overall competition goalscorer. Xavier gets worldwide 18 month ban for drug abuse. John Hollins is the new Crawley manager. Hammers now keen on Keane.

24 UEFA Cup: away draws for Bolton and Boro, who reach last 32. Alain Perrin axed at Pompey. Ashley Cole out with injury until New Year.

25 George Best, 59, dies after long fight against illness. Neil Warnock linked with Portsmouth vacancy. Sky Sports Victory Shield: Scotland 1 England 2 (England share title with Wales).

26 Lampard completes 160th consecutive PL game and converts penalty in Chelsea's 2-0 win at managerless Pompey; Henry hits 100th PL goal at Highbury as Arsenal beat Blackburn 3-0; Wigan lose again to the other north Londoners Spurs; Riise lifts Liverpool at Man City; Charlton lose again this time at Villa; more depression for Sunderland as Brummies win at Stadium of Light. Reading undefeated in 20 open four point gap in Championship with 2-0 win at Plymouth as Sheff Utd slump at Leicester; some Leeds fans abuse Best tribute at Millwall. Swansea keep Lge 1 goal difference lead despite draw at Tranmere and Huddersfield win over nine man Forest; Southend go down again; Colchester take five off Gillingham. No stopping Wycombe 19 without defeat. Conf: Grays and next three Accrington, Exeter and Morecambe all win. SPL: Celtic below "Pars" as Dunfermline

stun Parkhead faithful; Hearts need late penalty to equalise at Motherwell. SL; Brechin only British team without a win. S Cup: Div 3 leaders Berwick put to sword by Spartans.

27 Souness fury at McFadden handball denies poor Toon a penalty in 1-0 reverse at Everton; Rooney rules in regal style as Man Utd edge Hammers; McBride double sees Fulham home against Bolton but Boro and Baggies share it. SPL: now Rangers lose at Hibs and Alex McLeish faces the axe. Ronaldinho shines as Barca return to Spanish leadership; the Brazilian expected to become European Player of the Year.

28 Ronaldinho 225 votes, Lampard 148, Gerrard 142 as 1.2.3 with Terry 10th and Carragher 20th. Chelsea to appeal over £30,000 fine for West Ham incident. Cardiff edge ten-man Ipswich. LDV Vans: Cheltenham swamp Woking in extra time. S Cup: Alloa give Selkirk one-over-the-eight feeling. Sudden death of David Di Tommaso, Utrecht player aged 26.

29 Mixed C Cup results: Reading lose to Arsenal reserves; Brum need penalties at Millwall and Donny easily account for sad Villa. Xavier appeals 18 month drug ban. Nationwide to end FA sponsorship after WC. Owen injury worries Souness. Pompey want McLeish!

30 UEFA Cup: AZ close gap to goal difference behind Boro. C Cup: Boro just better Palace as Bolton do for Leicester; Saha inspires Man Utd against WBA on Old Trafford night of Best remembrance; Wigan pen writes off Toon; Rovers return win at Charlton. More gloom at Stadium of Light as Liverpool ease in. West Ham keen on Keane, too.

DECEMBER 2005

Manchester United out of Europe ... Gazza in and out ... Blatter in restrictive mood ... Redknapp back at Pompey! ... Holders CSKA Moscow out of UEFA Cup ... Wycombe defeated at last.

1 UEFA Cup: Basle comeback to beat Tromso 4-3 after being 3-1 down; Eastern European leaders in Group F Levski and Bolton's Group H Zenit, but holders CSKA Moscow struggling to stay in. Harry Redknapp sensation: may return to Pompey! Graeme Souness under fire and Sam Allardyce tipped for Toon. Michael Ballack offered to Chelsea. Cahill banned for misconduct. Tear Gas needed on fans at Fiorentina–Juventus.

2 FA Cup: early dismissal too much for Grays at Mansfield; Vale level late against Bristol Rovers. Redknapp quits and future uncertain as south coast pantomime season starts. Man Utd appoint Neville captain in place of Keane.

3 Crouch ends his goal famine with Wigan on the slide; Trotters trip up Arsenal; managerless Pompey ship three at Man Utd; Spurs leave it late against Sunderland; Terry's the man for Chelsea; Shearer (198th United goal) edges nearer record but Villa still draw after Barry penalty gaffe; Everton ease their pressure at Blackburn who lose Todd to a card; no goals for Baggies or ten-man Fulham. Championship: with Redknapp quitting Saints draw No. 13; 30,558 for Sheffield derby as Utd edge it; Reading storm on at the head. QPR goalkeeper Royce attacked by spectator at Stoke. FA Cup: Tamworth Lambs lead Hartlepool to the slaughter; Stevenage hold Northampton, but goalie coach Lionel Perez caught poking two fingers in Cobblers coach Dave Watson's eye; Chester put ten-man Forest and boss Gary Megson under fire. Swindon off the foot of Lge 1. SPL: Rangers nine games without a win fritter two-goal lead to Falkirk leaving McLeish in crisis. Conf: Accrington take advantage of Grays cup involvement and Exeter defeat by Canvey to go top. Becks third red of season (one rescinded) as Real beat Getafe 1-0.

4 Charlton defence goes on holiday as Man City hit five. FA Cup: Huddersfield ten surface at Worcester; Donny do it at Boston. SPL: Celtic point ahead of Hearts after 3-1 at Aberdeen. Real sack coach Vanderlei Luxemburgo, their fifth coach in less than three years. German concern over crowd violence.

5 Gazza sacked by Kettering, but wants to buy the club. Lawrie Sanchez favourite for Pompey job. Goal-line technology not yet perfected. Hammers put more pressure on Birmingham.

6 Ch Lge: Chelsea and Livepool goalless, Essien tackle on Hamann goes unpunished; Rangers through, too! Real lose in Greece but qualify with AC Milan, PSV, Lyon and Inter. England seeded in WC finals. Scots beat Poles 2-0 in B match. FA Cup; Burton secure plumb tie at Man Utd after beating Burscough 4-1. Swansea clear in Lge 1 as Huddersfield lose two goal lead and two players at close in MK Dons draw. Eleventh draw for unbeaten Wycombe, Grimsby beat Rochdale 4-1 in Lge 2. Conf: Altrincham strike late for Grays point. Gazza arrested for being drunk and bailed.

7 Ch Lge: Man Utd bottom out of Europe; Villarreal and Benfica make it; Henry fluffs penalty – his 7th failure in 17 attempts to deprive them of being the fifth to be 100% Ch Lge group qualifiers as Ajax hold Arsenal but both go through; Juventus, Bayern, Barcelona and Werder complete the numbers. UEFA Cup will get their additional eight: FC Brugge, Thun, Udinese, Lille, Schalke, Rosenborg, Betis and Artmedia. Harry R – the return to Pompey! FA and PFA to come to aid of Gazza. Palace chairman Simon Jordan handed £10,000 suspended misconduct fine.

8 UEFA to act over Essien tackle. Sven fears no one in WC. Rangers give McLeish their backing. Kidderminster part with manager Stuart Watkiss.

9 WC draw has England paired with Paraguay, Trinidad & Tobago and Sweden. Most of the media have put us in the semis already! Germans get Costa Rica, Poland and Ecuador; Brazil with Croatia, Australia and Japan. Essien apologies to Hamann.

10 Liverpool equal club record ten League and Cup clean sheets and start thinking about the title after Morientes double over Boro; Chelsea, just the one (Terry) against Wigan; Birmingham no longer worst at home in Britain after first win. Newcastle surprise Arsenal who lose Silva (red); Charlton end slump against Sunderland; Baggies beat ten-man Man City; Rovers edge Hammers; Bolton all square with Villa. Reading take five off Brighton, Sheff Utd cling on four points behind – the rest trailing. Only ten no loss Barnsley of top eight in Lge 1 win 5-2 over Scunthorpe for whom Beagrie hits his 100th goal; Bristol City end nine defeats with 2-0 over Huddersfield; Rotherham 17th without a win axe manager Mick Harford. Wycombe 21 no loss extend lead to four points in Lge 2. SPL: Celtic edge Hibs 3-2 and with Hearts being held now lead by three points. SL: Dundee revival with 4-0 hammering of leaders St Mirren. S Cup: Gretna second half blitz to win 6-1 against Cove; Spartans on the march with high five at Lossiemouth. Conf: Grays crash at Morecambe, Accrington clear leaders.

11 Man Utd held by Everton. Rangers win League game after ten without one. Adriano seals Milan derby for Inter 3-2 in injury time. Barca equal club record 11th consecutive League and Cup win; Real new coach Juan Ramon Lopez Caro has winning start. Lifetime Achievement award for Pele at BBC Sports Personality Show and he tips England in WC.

12 Harry R rages over Spurs penalty for alleged hands given by referee Rennie as Pompey go down late at WHL. Real fancy Keane. Ijah Anderson, Swansea player tested positive for cocaine. Football League to have own awards in conjunction with *FourFourTwo* mag. Jose M and Sir Alex due for FA slap wrists. Sheff Utd to buy Chinese – Chengdu Five Bull a Div 2 team. Di Canio in bother over fascist salute for Lazio at Livorno.

13 Sir Alex gives 74 second press conference. FA Cup: Barnsley 5-3 replay win at Bradford; Northwich dump Woking to secure Sunderland date. Bothroyd suffers second blackout in six years.

14 Double helping of Roo helps Sir Alex smile after 4-0 against slipping Wigan. Hammers edge Everton at Goodison. UEFA Cup: Bolton just make it to ko stage after draw with Sevilla; non-playing holders CSKA Moscow out. FA Cup: Nuneaton win at Histon gives them home tie with Boro. Reduced Sunderland ticket pricing upsets Northwich. Keane to go green with Celtic. Essien awaiting punishment.

15 Keane unveiled at Parkhead. UEFA Cup: Maccarone duo for already qualified Boro keeps them top of Group D. FIFA WCC: Liverpool extend clean sheets to club record 11 after 3-0 win over Saprissa in Yokohama to reach final! Essien gets two match ban. UEFA give 2007 U-21 championship finals to Holland, not England.

16 Ch Lge draw pits Benfica v Liverpool; Real v Arsenal and Chelsea v Barcelona while Rangers get Villarreal. UEFA Cup: Bolton v Marseille and Stuttgart v Boro. Precious points for Brighton against Hull, Sheff Utd held at Preston. Forest go down at Scunny. Gazza may get FA job. Big Dunc Fergie might have to retire with injury.

17 Man Utd keep the pressure on Chelsea after 2-0 at Villa; Harry R Pompey joy; Treble-shooter Owen the difference for four Mags at West Ham, Shearer on 199 goals. Bolton hit four at Everton, Man City 4-1, against Birmingham; Fulham edge Rovers; Wigan winning again as Charlton lose. Championship: Reading now six points clear; Wolves hit 6,999th League goal; Saints lose lead at Norwich in 3-1 defeat. Lge 1: Brentford make ground as ten man Swans lose at Donny, Huddersfield and Southend draw; Colchester continue winning. Lge 2: Wycombe lose record in 22nd game – Bury score two in last four mins; Rotherham first win in 18 League and Cup attempts at Bradford; SPL: Hearts slump continues as Rangers beat them. Brechin ship six at Airdrie; Gretna only score once! Trophy: Conf giant-killing casualties: Burton, Cambridge and York; Hereford hit Bognor for six.

18 Wenger unhappy with disallowed goal then Chelsea 2-0 winners at Highbury, though Essien in bother again. Boro and Spurs share six goals. Celtic held by Caley but still have four point lead. CWC Final: Liverpool run ends as their finishing lets them down against Sao Paulo. Barca set club record 12 League and Cup wins in a row. Boca Juniors win Copa Sudamericana on penalties of course against UNAM (Mexico).

19 Blatter wants to restrict teams to five foreigners. Ronaldinho gets another award: FIFA World Player of the Year, Lamps second Eto'o third. Ijah Anderson six months ban. Macclesfield rocked by £62,000 fine and £195,000 repayment for ground funding, wrongly paid to their previous regime. Rangers hit by late Coventry penalty.

20 C Cup: Saha at the double as Man Utd add to Brummie worries; Roberts duo for Wigan cuts out Trotters. LDV Vans: Hereford, Kidderminster account for League opposition, Wycombe go down again. Trophy: holders Grays edge Shots in extra time replay. Graham Rix under pressure because of his past. Blatter renews fight against racism.

21 C Cup: late Silva strike hits unlucky Donny as Arsenal have something in reserve but still need penalties; Dickov at the death for Rovers ends Boro run. FA play down threat of Wembley delay. Millwall make Colin Lee DoF and assistant David Tuttle gets manager role. Soton may go Dutch with Mark Wotte and Cees Lok.

22 Double Dutch? Saints appoint George Burley as head coach, Sir Clive DoF! Di Canio Nazi salute investigation. Vote mix-up by Greek gave London 2012 Olympics!

23 Yeovil and Bournemouth share pre-Xmas penalties. Lajos Baroti, Hungarian coach in four WCs dies at 91.

24 Shock first defeat for Gretna 2-1 at home to Forfar. Real legend Alfredo di Stefano, 79, suffers heart attack. Liverpool do not rule out a return for Owen.

25 Christmas, but one Wise man falls out with the Saints. Eriksson admits he feared England might not qualify after Danish disaster.

26 Fulham make Chelsea go all the way in 3-2 thriller; Man Utd trio over Baggies; Liverpool beat Newcastle 2-0 as Bowyer sees red; Reyes for Gunners at Charlton; Everton savaged four times at Villa; Wigan edge seven-goal bonanza with Man City; Kuqi duo enough for Rovers at Boro; Izzet off as Brummies lose at Spurs; point only for Sunderland at home to Bolton and Pompey entertaining Hammers. Championship: Reading nine points clear as Sheff Utd lose at home to Norwich; no instant impact by Burley as Saints slump 3-0 at Watford. Lge 1: Brentford beat Swans 2-1 to take pole position; Huddersfield, Barnsley, Southend held and Colchester lose for first time in 12. Lge 2: Winners Grimsby and Orient move within two points of Wycombe; Macclesfield hit record League win 6-0 over ten-man Stockport. SPL: Celtic edge Livi 2-1, Hearts whack Falkirk 5-0 but Rangers can only draw at Dunfermline and are 17 points behind the leaders. SL; Brechin break their duck for the season 3-1 over Clyde; Stranraer just win nine-goal thriller with Accies. Conf: Accrington snatch draw, Exeter go second after easy 4-0 over Shots.

27 Gerrard faces ban after role in Bowyer fracas. More managerial calls for technological aids. Chris Turner leaves Stockport by mutual consent. Di Stefano to have by-pass surgery. Conf: Canvey spring surprise at Grays.

28 Big freeze accounts for three PL and 14 FL games. Chelsea extend lead to 11 points after Joe Cole goal at Man City while Man Utd held at Brum; Merseyside derby for Liverpool 3-1 against nine finishing Everton players; Wigan revival continues at Hammers; Arsenal take four goals off Pompey; Kanu double for Baggies ends Spurs hopes; Fulham and Villa share six goals. Championship: Reading, Sheff Utd win, Wolves hit record 7000th goal. Lge 1: Southend recapture winning ways at Hartlepool. Lge 2: Grimsby regain top spot after 3-0 over Lincoln. Death of Ted Ditchburn, 84, former Spurs and England goalkeeper. Di Stefano has his op.

29 Usual idiotic calls for winter breaks, but more sensible ones regarding local derbies at holiday times. Wycombe back on top after 4-2 against Orient.

30 MBEs for Rachel Yankey, Lawrie McMenemy and Clyde Best. Clubs awaiting end of window shopping and start of the sales. Conf: now waterlogged pitches hit two games while ten-man Hereford shake Exeter.

31 Owen breaks metatarsal bone in right foot as Mags go down at Spurs; Chelsea win hoists 101 points in the year, but Jose M threatens Cole J with non-starter role if any more horse play; Crouch 7th in eight games and another Liverpool clean sheet; double Ron for Man Utd in 4-1 over Bolton; Wigan hit by classic Pedersen and Reid strikes for Rovers; Cahill at the death relieves Everton at Black Cats expense; O'Neil goal cheers Harry R; Schwarzer thwarts Man City; Charlton derby winners against Hammers; Arsenal goalless draw at Villa. Long just lengthens Reading run in Derby draw; Sheff Utd close gap on them; Sheff Wed end goal fame after 634 mins with win at Burnley and Millwall braced by Brighton sea air. Lge 1: Trundle goal famine hits Swans again; Southend leapfrog second with win over ten-man Bournemouth; Brentford hit by Colchester. Lge 2: Away day wins for Wycombe and Grimsby as top five get maximum points. Panto season at Wrexham with ref Deadman carding Grimsby's Bolland then allowing him to stay as he had confused the player with Williams the opposing No.8 – who still gets sent off at the end! SPL: Rangers end recent Dundee Utd hoodoo. Conf: Grays drop two more points.

JANUARY 2006

Shearer hits no. 200 ... Managers life gets shorter ... News of bungs ... Henry goal record ... Arsenal sign wonder boy ... Hearts slipping up.

1 Undersoil heating failures at Bolton and Blackburn to be investigated. Sheff Wed sign Rotherham's Burton for £110,000 and Tudgay on loan from Derby. SPL: Jambos suicide as they lose two-goal lead, a player and game to Celtic – now seven points ahead.

2 Chelsea take advantage of Man Utd inactivity to go 14 points ahead after 3-1 at West Ham; Liverpool have to settle for draw at Bolton, but Gerrard in stamping row; Cahill again the twin spark in Everton revival; fourth holiday win for Blackburn; Villa win derby with Baggies; Brummies succeed at Wigan expense; Sunderland loss at Fulham leaves them ten points adrift; Mags and Boro share four goals; talk of a Pompey takeover. Championship: Reading storm on with 5-1 win over Cardiff; Millwall, Sheff Wed continue recent improvement; Preston 16th game without defeat, but Nowland suffers double fracture; Blackstock brace boosts Burley. Lge 1: Southend recapture top spot as Swansea, Brentford, Huddersfield all draw. Lge 2: Wycombe lose nine-goal thriller to Macclesfield, but Grimsby also beaten at home. Orient gain ground on both. Keith Alexander sent on home leave at Lincoln. Conf: Accrington draw, but go three points ahead as Exeter lose to the Shots and Canvey complete double over Grays.

3 Stalemate at Highbury and Arsenal and Man Utd may have to settle for places behind Chelsea. Gerrard OK as ref saw the incidents and took no action. Sheff Utd 3-1 at Hull are seven points behind Reading. Owen has his op.

4 Spurs have thoughts of Europe again after 2-0 at Man City. Liverpool into the January sales with two: Jan Kromkamp (Villarreal) and Paul Anderson (Hull) while Josemi moves to Spain in the exchange. Chelsea sign Maniche on loan from Dynamo Moscow. Man Utd pay £7m for Spartak Moscow's Nemanja Vidic; Birmingham get Chris Sutton from Celtic free. Ex-Leeds chairman Peter Ridsdale cleared of malpractice at Elland Road.

5 England fix friendlies with Uruguay, Hungary and Jamaica. Sommeil tackle on Spurs Lee under review.

6 Russian Alexandre Gaydamak becomes Pompey co-owner. Henry to stay a Gunner. Fulham sign NZ's Simon Elliott from USA. FA Cup: Vale loan star Togwell puts Donny in a state.

7 FA Cup: Romance lives on as Nuneaton hold Boro and Tamworth draw at Stoke, but broken hearts, too, as Luton chuck 3-1 lead over Liverpool and lose 5-3, Huddersfield pipped at Chelsea; Scunny sunk by Fowler hat-trick after leading at Man City; MK Dons just edged 4-3 at Saints. Eyebrows raised as Colchester shake Sheff Utd, Millwall hold Everton, Torquay similarly with Birmingham and Mags need Shearer's 200th to oust Mansfield. Lge 1 sees Southend extend lead with Oldham draw. Conf: Accrington three point lead and two games in hand of Exeter. S Cup: Premier casualties as Dunfermline lose 4-3 to Airdrie, Motherwell crash 3-0 at St Mirren. Alloa hold Livi and Ayr draw at Caley, but Hibs hit six against Arbroath and Rangers five over Peterhead. Ross nap hand, too, against Forfar. Non-league Spartans knock out Queens Park.

8 FA Cup: Man Utd held on sandy shores of Burton; Orient win 2-1 at Fulham and Spurs throw away 2-0 lead at Leicester and lose as upsets continue. S Cup: Keane nightmare debut as Celtic lose at Clyde.

9 Van Persie out with broken toe. FA seek sole sponsors for England and FA Cup. Fulham's Warner to play for Trinidad. 553 managers changed since 1992, average length of tenure now 21 months.

10 C Cup: new boy Paul Scharner, £1.5m from Brann gives Wigan first leg lead over Arsenal. Patrice Evra joins Man Utd from Monaco for £5.5m. Fears over WC ground safety refuted by Beckenbauer. Sommeil three-match ban. Knight makes Swans day with debut hat-trick after Brighton move. Alan Knill gets Rotherham job to season's end. Conf: Accrington win at Tamworth moves them further ahead. Dundee Utd sack manager Gordon Chisholm.

11 Luton manager Mike Newell says bung culture is ill-fitting football. Liverpool's Rick Parry unhappy with Liverpool missing out in New Year's honours. Jay-Jay may join Al-Ittihad. Pandiani to return to Spain with Espanyol.

12 Newell challenges FA. Sir Alex happy with Glazer connection. Arsenal to grab Abou Diaby, 19, from Auxerre and want Saints teenage wonder Walcott. Sadlier, ex-Millwall, may comeback with Sunderland after surgery in USA. Ehiogu back to Baggies. Steve Staunton lands Republic job. Waltham Forest, Youth Cup giant-killers finally beaten 2-1 by Brentford.

13 FL say agents fees are down! Jansen, Rovers to Bolton. Caley settle for compensation as Craig Brewster becomes Dundee Utd boss. Ince seals Wolves 2-1 win against Luton.

14 Seven-up Arsenal liquidate ten-man Boro as Henry equals Cliff Bastin's 150 League goals; City win Mancunian derby as Sir Alex and Roo rage over ref Bennett, Ron gets a controversial red and Evra has a nightmare debut; Kewell stunner as Liverpool down Spurs; woe for Pompey at home to Everton, Birmingham at Charlton; Hammers edge it at Villa; Rovers and ten Trotters goalless; more Toon concern as Fulham beat them. Championship: 28 unbeaten Reading may need only six wins to clinch promotion! Sheff Utd held at Ipswich; Derby hit five against Crewe; Preston 17th without defeat. Lge 1: Southend crack on – Brentford latest victims 4-1; Chesterfield draw at Donny, 12th without reverse. Lge 2: Wycombe sadden by death of Mike Philo in car crash as they and Grimsby make ground at the top. Trophy: Conf teams shown door by lower echelons: Gravesend, Canvey, Morecambe; Accrington, Woking held. SPL: Celtic still seven ahead of Hearts. SL: St Mirren walking away with Div 1 title it seems; Gretna held at Morton. Sven in trouble over fake interview.

15 Robben sent off for celebrating as Chelsea fight back to win at Sunderland; ten-man Albion shake Wigan. Rangers win at Motherwell. Becks hits bar for Real, Zidane treble; Barca go 12 without defeat. Del Piero scores 186th goal for Juve.

16 Sven to face FA. UEFA team of the year includes Cech, Terry, Gerrard and Luis Garcia; Mourinho top coach, but Henry misses out for first time since 2001. Steve Staunton confirmed Republic boss. Roy Hodgson to be Finnish coach. Marcus Bent to join Charlton for £2.5m. Six million WC tickets applied for by 677,900 Germans. Wigan boss Paul Jewell wants FA Cup replays scrapped.

17 FA Cup: sheepish Stoke need pens to dispose of Tamworth Lambs; Boro in another seven goal game, but get five of them against Nuneaton; Reading give WBA two goals start and beat them with Lita hat-trick; Wigan need penalties, too to oust Leeds. S Cup: Hamilton leave it late against QoS. Players to stand behind Sven. Chelsea also in for Walcott. Jim Gannon appointed Stockport boss to end of season.

18 FA Cup: Burton get the wonga, Man Utd high five; Millwall old boy Cahill sticks it in for the Toffees. Newell gives evidence to FA. New badge for Spurs. Carlisle hit five at Boston. Greg Dyke is new Brentford chairman.

19 Stuart Pearce rubbishes talk of England job. QPR manager Ian Holloway reveals bung tale. Xavier to appeal drug ban. Bridge not too far – goes to Fulham on loan from Chelsea. Wise sent to Coventry. Wigan pick up Rovers Thompson and Mellor on loan from Liverpool. Hibs Irish midfield player Shiels to have eye removed.

20 Arsenal grab expensive teenager Walcott from Soton in £5m deal, which could rise to £12m. Redknapp return to Pompey to be investigated. Mido on target in Egypt win. Important draw for Reading at Palace.

21 Fabregas is 62nd Arsenal red card under Wenger as Everton spike Gunners; two Wigan debutants score to edge Boro; WBA misery as Baggies own goal lets Black Cats out with the points; Rovers Pedersen "punch ball" downs Toon; even Birmingham hit Pompey for five; Bolton two better than Man City; Spurs held by ten Villans. Championship: Sheff Utd make up some ground on Reading; Coventry hit Derby for six – as a year ago; Preston 18 no loss, Crewe 12 no win. Hull's Myhill saves two Stoke penalties. Lge 1: late Colchester strike puts them top; Chesterfield 13 no loss, MK Dons 10 no win. Lge 2: with top three held, Orient gain ground. SPL: McLeish 47th birthday celebrations for Rangers; another defeat for Hearts leaves way open for Celtic again. more Sven revelations.

22 Chelsea drop first two points at home as Bent M makes scoring debut for Charlton; late Ferdi goal for Man Utd ends three month Liverpool run. SPL: Celtic go ten points clear of Hearts. Togo coach banishes new Arsenal man Adebayor from African Nations Cup.

23 Eriksson agrees to £2.5m pay-off. PL announce bung inquiry. Hammers edge Fulham 2-1.

24 C Cup: Wigan extra time surprise for indolent Arsenal after Pollitt saves Reyes penalty to reach first major final. Scholes out for season with eye problem, O'Shea with injury. Leicester defeat at Plymouth is sixth in a row. Lge 2: Grimsby lose at reviving Stockport. LDV Vans: Carlisle and Macclesfield win to reach Northern final, Colchester and Swansea via penalties in the South. Conf: Scarborough shake Morecambe with 3-0 win. WBA get Jan Kozak, Slovakian on loan from Artmedia. Drogba goal sends Ivory coasting to last African eight.

25 C Cup: Burns night eclipse for Blackburn at Man Utd, but Ferdi and Savage in tunnel scuffle. Johnson wastes chances for Palace at Soton in scoreless affair. Managerial axing: Craig Levein (Leicester), Leroy Rosenior (Torquay), while Peterborough's Mark Wright is on suspension. Rob Kelly caretaker at Leicester. Wolves sign £1.4m Polish striker Tomasz Frankowski from Elche. CIS Cup: Dunfermline boom final place in 1-0 v Livi. Eto'o helps quarter-final place for Cameroon in Africa. Missile at linesman ends Spanish tie between Valencia and La Coruna. Giant-killing German style: Div 3 St Pauli oust Werder Bremen.

26 Hiddink probably favourite foreigner for England job. Gary Neville charged with improper conduct for inappropriate celebrations in Liverpool game. Tamworth goalkeeper Bevan has kidney removed after injury in match with Forest Green. Karren Brady to have brain surgery. Sheff Utd sign twin strikers: Akinbiyi (Burnley) £1.75m, Dyer (Stoke) free. Tunisia, Guinea into last African eight respectively following 2-0 win over South Africa, 2-1 v Zambia.

27 Chelsea announce loss of £140m! – Abramovich investment £440m. England easy draw for Euro 2008, with Croatia, Russia, Israel, Estonia, Macedonia and Andorra! Scots have toughie with France, Italy etc, while Republic and Wales face Germany, Northern Ireland have Spain, Sweden and the Danes. Fowler rejoins Liverpool. Sir Alex unhappy over Neville charge. Lge 1: Southend consolidate, Barnsley move up after 2-0 at ten-man Forest.

28 FA Cup: DJ Campbell puts it on a platter for Brentford and Sunderland go spinning out; Lamps lights up Chelsea in scramble for a draw at Everton; Colchester's Danns double dumps Derby; Addicks sub Bothroyd hits unlucky Orient at the death; Arsenal lose another cup-tie at Bolton; Rovers 27 second strike but ends in 4-2 defeat at Hammers; Coventry hold Boro; Brum rally to level at Reading; Late, late Jones as Saints win at Leicester; Stoke edge Walsall 2-1; Cole fires Man City over Wigan; fifth FA Cup success for Villa against Vale; Cheltenham not at the Toon races; Preston and Palace all square. Lge 1: Bristol City indulge in Swans upping; Huddersfield give Oldham two goals start and beat them. Lge 2: Hartlepool suspended manager Martin Scott after Blackpool defeat. Cellar dwellers Stockport almost win at Wycombe; Rushden hit three against Oxford. SPL: Celtic allow Dundee Utd to take a point and Hibs win Edinburgh derby 4-1. Conf: Sad Shots crash 5-1 at Altrincham. Egypt win but Mido injured.

29 FA Cup: No bite in Wolves for Man Utd; Liverpool edge it at Portsmouth. Lge 2: Carlisle well beaten at Macc. DR Congo reach last eight despite losing to Cameroon. Woodgate gets on as Real sub in 2-1 win over Celta. Fascist flags in Roma game.

30 Man Utd to boycott TV interviews for a week over Neville "replays" – get Liverpool in the FA Cup and complain about Chelsea over Mikel affair. Wembley may not be ready for May final. Fowler goes back to Anfield. Derby sack manager Phil Brown. Pompey get another Spur – Routledge. Barton asks for Man City move. Veteran Dublin joins Celtic. Conf: Accrington win at Exeter might be eventual clincher for FL return after 44 years.

31 DJ Campbell in a year moves from £280 a week warehouseman to Premier League player with Birmingham after £500,000 transfer. Spurs nab Hossam Ghaly, Egyptian from Feyenoord and Charlton's Murphy, transfer Brown to Fulham. Bentley permanent at Blackburn now. Pompey's ninth is Andres Alessandro, Argie cap on loan. Delap free to Sunderland. Earnshaw to Norwich for £2.75m. Close of window. PL: Fulham at the death deny Spurs; Wigan and Everton scrap for a point; WBA hold Addicks; Boro heap more misery on Sunderland. Championship: Reading take four off Norwich; Palace go down at Preston this time; Leicester revive at QPR. Terry Westley is Derby caretaker-boss. Lge 1: Swans sink again. Lge 2: Orient, Wycombe settle for away point each. Senegal lose but still make last eight. Peterborough sack Mark Wright. Roma ban fans from next home game.

FEBRUARY 2006

Souness out at Newcastle ... Germans to sponsor FA Cup ... More records for Shearer and Henry ... Reading on a roll ... Sven successor sought ... Celtic record score.

1 Mancunian misery for Utd as Blackburn revenge with Bentley hat-trick and Ferdinand sees late red, joy for City as they hit sorry Toons for three; Arsenal lose again – at home to Hammers; Chelsea have to settle for point at Villa; Liverpool held by ten Brummies. Bolton draw at Portsmouth. Sheff Utd keeping up in the wake of Reading. CIS semi: Celtic leave it late at Motherwell.

2 Axe falls on Graeme Souness at Newcastle. Sol Campbell goes AWOL after being subbed. Beckenbauer reckons England are No.1 for WC after No.10 visit. FA seek life after Sven. Mark Wright to sue Peterborough. Kevin Wilson loses Kettering job again.

3 Lge 1: Swans win, Huddersfield lose at Tranmere. Davids with broken leg wants to play! Egypt in semis after 4-1 over DR Congo, Senegal edge Guinea to join them. German firm E.ON to sponsor FA Cup!

4 Record breaking for Shearer with 201st goal in 2-0 win over Pompey; Henry's 200th for Arsenal in same score at Birmingham; Man Utd beat Fulham but Chris Coleman riled over offside goal; rare win for Albion against Blackburn; Ashton goal as Hammers beat Sunderland; Boro in bother as Villa win 4-0 down by the Riverside; Bolton and Wigan settle for draw, Everton 1-0 naturally against Man City. Championship: Reading win odd goal in seven game at Crewe, 31st unbeaten record for "second tier" and are first to top 70 goals; Lge 1: leading pack all win and Brentford crash five past Walsall. Lge 2: Carlisle go top with high five against Chester. S Cup: now Hibs pile it on Rangers 3-0; Spartans earn replay against St Mirren; Ross hold Falkirk and Partick share it with Caley. Trophy: more Conf casualties – Crawley, Forest Green plus Stanley held by Worksop. Africa: Ivory Coast into semis after 12-11 shoot-out win over Cameroon and Nigeria make it 7-6 on spot kicks against Tunisia! Barca lose 3-1 to Atletico Madrid and fail to equal Real's 45 year old record of 14 successive League wins.

5 Chelsea better Liverpool but Rafael Benitez fury over Reina dismissal for friendly tap on Robben; Defoe brace in Spurs win over Addicks.

6 Watford shake Sheff Utd with 4-1 win at Bramall Lane. Sol Campbell returns. Steve McClaren issues wake up call to Boro players. Hartson retires from international football. Bolton give Sam Allardyce permission to talk to FA. Doubts over Paul Merson at Walsall and Ian Holloway suspended by QPR.

7 FA Cup: Reading lose at Birmingham in tie of not too-many-seniors, but Preston take it seriously at Palace. Colchester go top of Lge 1 after minimum against Scunny. SPL: Hearts scrape a draw at Dundee Utd. S Cup: Hamilton easily at Alloa. African: Egypt, Ivory Coast to dispute final after respective wins over Senegal and

Nigeria. Turkey must play all home Euro 2008 ties in neutral country. Graham Rix cannot select Hearts team – majority shareholder Vladimir Romanov will! Walsall sack Paul Merson. Ian Holloway on gardening leave at QPR told to dig for a new club.

8 FA Cup: Chelsea sweep Everton aside, Boro edge home against Coventry. PL: Gerrard absent and Liverpool lose at Charlton. SPL: Rangers lose to Dons, Hibs slaughter Livi 7-0 and Keane scores for Celtic. U-21: Northern Ireland win in Israel. Martin O'Neill latest name in England frame. Wembley finishing date still in doubt. FA Cup runners-up may lose UEFA Cup spot. Martin Scott axed by Hartlepool, Paul Stephenson as caretaker. Real hit for six by Zaragoza in cup clash first leg semi.

9 Death of ex-England manager Ron Greenwood at 84. Nigeria take third place in African win over Senegal. Match officials to get wired up in several UEFA Cup games. Rotherham on financial brink. Saints have spent £100m in wages in over four years. Alex McLeish to leave Rangers in summer.

10 Reading make it 32 without defeat in 2-0 over Saints. Southend stroll on against Rotherham. Conf: Exeter slip up at Burton. Egypt beat Ivory Coast in Nations Cup after Drogba misses not only easy chance, but one in the penalty shoot-out. Alex McLeish says he decided to quit Rangers last August. Big Dunc Ferguson banned until April! Karren Brady out of hospital after op.

11 Wheels come off for Chelsea at Boro – Steve McClaren for England?; Man Utd put skids under Pompey; Arsenal scrape a draw with Bolton; Fulham hit Baggies for six; managerless Toon smiling after win at Villa; Liverpool singly at Wigan; Beattie again for minimal Everton over Blackburn. Championship: Unbeaten in 24 Preston pan Luton with five, Watford hit Coventry for four. Lge 1: Colchester lose at Huddersfield, Swans win at Forest. Lge 2: draw specialists Wycombe held by Stags and with Orient drawing with Carlisle, Grimsby go top beating Boston; bottom two Stockport and Rushden both win. SPL: more Hearts fluttering after dumping by the Dons; Paul Lambert quits as Livi go down again. Barca lose to Valencia; Schalke 7 Leverkusen 4 in Bundesliga; Ajax fans banned after attacking Den Haag clubhouse!. SL: Hunter foursome has Stranraer reeling against Clyde. Conf: Accrington maintain 11 point lead; five goals each for Forest Green and Woking in impressive wins.

12 Late goal gives Sunderland a point with Spurs; The Bent boys fail to stop Man City win over Charlton. SPL: Celtic win at Rangers leaves them 21 points ahead, 13 more than Hearts.

14 Luis Garcia late strike spikes Gunners for Liverpool. Championship: Kenny penalty save from Kitson stops Reading win at Sheff Utd; Watford nine men edged out at Leeds. Lge 1: Southend beaten at Brentford; Colchester held by Walsall, Swansea by Bradford. Lge 2: Stockport revival carries on. S Cup: Spartans finally bow knee to St Mirren; Gretna's Grady threesome clips Clyde, Bairns make amends against Ross. Real cup fight-back at 4-0 still not good enough to oust Zaragoza. Ex-police chief to head PL illegal payments inquiry. FA split over desired nationality of Sven replacement.

15 UEFA Cup: Bolton rage as penalty claims dismissed and Marseille hold them; Lens leek three goals at Udinese. PL: Bellamy brace for Rovers hits Sunderland. Championship: Preston draw at Soton, Sheff Wed lose at Coventry. Lge 1: Forest ship three at Oldham. S Cup: Partick upset Caley on penalties. Non-League England beat Italy 3-1. Real now officially the world's richest – income £186.2m.

16 UEFA Cup: recalled Jimmy Floyd helps Boro win in Stuttgart. Gary Megson axed at Forest.

17 JM acknowledges the Chelsea pitch is not good, but good enough to play on. Anfield expects the Liverpool–Man Utd clash to be a fierce one. Reading's run comes to an end at last after 33 unbeaten, despite an 18 second lead, Luton came back to win 3-2. Northampton take three precious points. PL bung inquiry will cost £600,000. Conf: Accrington march on at Gravesend.

18 FA Cup: Liverpool end 108 years of failure to beat Man Utd at home with their first such cup win over them since 1921, but match marred by horrendous fractured leg and dislocated ankle accident to Utd's Smith; Newcastle rely on born-again Dyer to tip unlucky Soton out; Brentford Bees fail to sting Charlton; Hammers survive Bolton onslaught to get a replay. Championship: Utd win the Sheffield derby at Wednesday, 33,439 present. Lge 1: Southend recover at ten-man Chesterfield to win 4-3, Eastwood gets a treble; Scunny injury time leveller against Swans, but Huddersfield hit the Dons for five. Lge 2: and another nap hand for Carlisle, Wycombe's 17th draw. Conf: Halifax leave it late against Grays. SPL: Rangers end goal drought after 342 mins to beat Hibs SL: Cowdenbeath six packs off Queens Park.

19 FA Cup: Colchester shake Chelsea but supersub Cole J puts out their fire. Villa coasting until Richards levels for Man City; Preston shown the door by visiting Boro; Forssell maintains cup goal record for Birmingham to defeat Stoke. SPL: Celtic create competition highest scoring win 8-1 at Dunfermline making their goal difference 46; previous best victory 7-0.

20 UEFA warn Chelsea and Barca ahead of the Ch Lge clash. Three Man City players: Richards, Wright-Phillips and Musampa warned over their pitch cup celebrations. Chris Turner becomes DoF at Hartlepool, Paul Stephenson stays in charge of first team. Conf: Accrington take another step towards League return 2-0 over Morecambe.

21 Ch Lge: Arsenal triumph as King Henry the first to lead an England team to victory at Real; Liverpool narrowly down late to Benfica; ten-man Lyon happy in Eindhoven; Milan draw with Bayern in Munich. Wembley will not be ready by May. FL U-21 team beat Italy Serie B 1-0 at Hull – with four of Peter Taylor's City players! LDV Vans: Carlisle take narrow lead over Macclesfield in north final. Terry Westley confirmed as Derby manager, Mark Wright back at Chester. Conf: Hereford, Halifax and Stevenage of chasing pack all win.

22 Ch Lge: Del Horno's Argy bargy on Messi leaves Chelsea beached in Barca defeat; Rangers pegged level by Villarreal; Inter recover two goals to draw with Ajax; injury time strike gives Werder 3-2 edge over Juve. Liverpool's Sissoko in eyesight threat. No goals for Mags or Addicks, caretaker-manager Glenn Roeder fearful of more Dyer injury misery.

23 UEFA Cup: own misery for Bolton, Boro scrape through on away goals; surprise exits for Lens, Monaco. Russia causing problems over England's Euro 2008 fixtures. Paul Merson to play for Tamworth. Youth Cup Mancunian version: City 1 Utd 0 Kelvin Etuhu scorer, crowd 6492.

24 Chelsea to act on death threat fans over ref Terje Hauge. Arsenal have finance available despite move to new ground. Swansea squander two goal lead and draw again with Huddersfield.

25 JM's 600 days i/c Chelsea produces the points again as Pompey slip nearer the drop which seems certain for Sunderland beaten by fellow strugglers Birmingham; Blackburn climb to heady heights of fifth as Arsenal forgot Madrid form; caretaker Glenn Roeder sees another Toon tonic and Solano brace hits Everton; Charlton and Villa go goalless. Championship: Reading edge out Preston, but Sheff Utd Blades blunted by visiting Rangers; Watford, Leeds (Kelly's 500th), Palace impressively 4-1 over Norwich all win. Saints alive, too, 3-0 over Sheff Wed. Lge 1: Shrimpers find Saddlers stoic and defeats for Colchester, Brentford at home to Port Vale; managerless Forest fire seven against Swindon. Lge 2: top five all win; Rushden have a rare victory. Conf: Accrington stay on winning ways, York hit Forest Green for five. S Cup: high five for the Hibees at Falkirk; Gretna edge St Mirren, Dundee hold Accies and ten-man Hearts survive late fight back by Partick. Trophy: Exeter 3653 for win over Salisbury. Racist abuse hits Barca's Eto'o in Zaragoza,

Manchester United's Wayne Rooney celebrates his second goal in the 4-0 Carling Cup Final win over Wigan Athletic at the Millennium Stadium, Cardiff. (John Walton/Empics)

26 C Cup final: Wigan surrender to their peers as Roo sparks Man Utd four-play. PL: Bolton edge Fulham, Jimmy Floyd duo flattens WBA for Boro and Liverpool make it a hard fought 1-0 win over Man City who have Barton dismissed. Real lose again. Record 11 consecutive wins for Roma.

27 FA to have short list for Sven job. Ashley Cole reserve come back lasts seven minutes (twisted ankle). Pop star Robbie Williams buys into Port Vale. Del Horno ban cut to one game.

28 Becks outlines his wishes for next England boss! U-21s: Rovers Bentley twice on target in 3-1 over Norway; Scots take four off Iceland; Republic clip Swedes 1-0; Northern Ireland similarly take care of Wales. Vale beaten by Scunny. SL: Gretna five at Stirling. Lines drawn in TV battle ahead. Profit: Man City £16.8m; loss: Millwall: £2.4m.

MARCH 2006

Nyatanga youngest for Wales ... Mourinho best coach ... Scolari interviewed by FA ... Wembley in trouble ... TV Deal to change ... Keane century.

1 Late night Joe Cole delivery rescues fringe England in 2-1 win over Uruguay; Wales with Lewin Nyatanga their youngest ever at 17 years 195 days hold Paraguay but only 12,324 turn up; Republic give boss Staunton fine 3-0 start over Sweden; two minute Sproule sparks Northern Ireland against Estonia, but Scots clocked by Swiss at Hampden. Friendly shocks for France first defeat in 18 against Slovakia, Germany 4-1 in Italy worst there since 1939 and Argentina 3-2 in Croatia. Lamps hamstring blow to Chelsea. Liverpool condemn fans behaviour against Man Utd. Sudden death of Peter Osgood, Chelsea and England centre-forward at 59.

2 Real's new President warns underachieving players; Spain told to get tough on racism.

3 England's first 2008 opponents – Andorra the toughies! Now Crewe hold Sheff Utd. Sherry to stay another year at Hammers. Villa warn Hendrie after common assault charge. Michael Wilde buys more Saints shares in bid to oust Rupert Lowe.

4 JM and Robbo in touchline bust-up as Chelsea pull down the Baggies 2-1; awesome four-play Arsenal in cruise control at Fulham; Roeder rides on as Mags beat Bolton; Liverpool in blank blunted draw with Charlton; Villa hand Pompey another reverse; Boro similarly singular against Birmingham; Hammers and Toffees share four goals. Frost and snow hit 31 English and Scottish fixtures. Lita broken leg agony for Reading in win at Burnley; Palace fail in Leeds defeat; Late goal lifts Lions over Luton; injury-time salvage job for Watford in Derby draw. Lge 1: Southend impressively see off Colchester; Swans and Huddersfield held in stalemates; Lge 2: ten-man Wycombe go down at Cheltenham; Orient share six goals at Shrewsbury. Conf: high fives for Exeter, Grays. SPL: Celtic, Rangers both leave it late. SL: only three games survive weather. Hamburg complete double over Bundesliga leaders Bayern.

5 Mark Hughes fury over Keane alleged handled goal as Rovers edged out 3-2 by Spurs; Breen sent off for diving hands near Man City goal and Sunderland lose again.

6 Chelsea, Liverpool and Arsenal all confident prior to Ch Lge countdown. Wigan own goal gift to Man Utd. Mick McCarthy bites the dust at Sunderland.

7 Ch Lge: Lamps late penalty leveller not enough for Chelsea survival at Barca; Rangers restore pride in away goal outing at Villarreal; Wiese goalie error gives Juve similar decision over Werder. Preston and Wolves are separate point-takers in blank endings. Lge 1: Brentford edge Yeovil 2-1. Lge 2: more revival points for Stockport. LDV Vans: away goal success for Carlisle in north area final at Macclesfield, Swansea take slender lead over Colchester in south. Conf: Accrington gifted four goals at Shots move nearer return to League. Solskjaer in hospital after reserve game injury.

8 Ch Lge: chess masterpiece of a goalless draw sees Arsenal through against Real; Liverpool sink to Benfica brace; Lyon lash ten man PSV; AC Milan dump Bayern.

9 UEFA Cup: Yakubu penalty gives Boro first leg lead over Roma; Marseille shaken by Zenit. Hammers boss Alan Pardew hits out at the influx of too many foreign players. Chelsea may get Ballack in the summer. S Cup: Dundee extra time win over Hamilton. England ladies beat Iceland 1-0 (9616 at Norwich). Merson quits as a player! Bradford investment may save them.

10 Arsene Wenger replies to Alan Pardew's attack on foreign first policy. Southend power on, but Huddersfield lose at Hartlepool.

11 Injury-time rocket from Gallas and Spurs hoodoo with Chelsea continues; rare Pompey win, even rarer three goals for Everton; Black Cats 23rd defeat, lose to Wigan; Hammers, resting key players are stamped on by the Trotters; Blackburn ride high in fifth place; Baggies get a Brummie draw. Championship: Lita-less Reading held by Watford; Sheff Utd let in two at Coventry, Leeds have to share four goals with Norwich but Wolves move into sixth. Lge 1: Brentford take care of Barnsley, but Colchester's ten go down at Oldham. Lge 2: Wycombe, Grimsby and Orient all three-pointers, Mansfield hit Boston for five. SPL: Rangers celebrate 12th boss in 133 years Paul Le Guen starting in the summer by beating Killie 4-0. SL: shock for Gretna beaten at home by Morton; once mighty Dundee crash 7-0 at Airdrie. Conf: Accrington's ten have to settle for late Hereford equaliser. Ronaldo misses late penalty and Real are goalless at Valencia.

12 Swansea draw yet again, Celtic restore 15 point lead. Barca finish with nine and lose at Osasuna. Juve and AC in goalless game. California based German coach Klinsmann criticised for parlous state of national team.

13 International Federation of Football History and Statistics name Mourinho as world's best club coach – again. Palace 3-1 win at Stoke improves play-off position. Wembley stadium deal could boost cash-strapped Corinthians. Deaths of Jimmy Johnstone, 61, Celtic and Scotland and Roy Clarke, 80, Man City and Wales.

14 Ch Lge: Inter reached last eight after 1-0 over Ajax. FA Cup: Man City edge out Villa in replay. Nugent double for Preston then season-missing injury. LDV Vans: Swansea wrap up win at Colchester to meet Carlisle in final. Weather hits four Scottish games. FA hit out at FIFA over WC tickets. Lord Ashcroft takes Watford control! Fulham board support boss Chris Coleman. Brian Talbot sacked by Oxford, youth boss Darren Patterson installed.

15 UEFA Cup: Boro lose to Roma, but away goal enough. FA Cup: West Ham revenge: Trotters under the hammer now. Fulham suffer 5-1 PL defeat at Liverpool. Oxford beat Bristol Rovers! Scotland lose B game 3-2 to Turkey. Another betting scandal in Germany. FIFA farce: USA ranked fifth! Israel want 2008 UEFA Cup final. Sven will ban agents at WC.

16 UEFA Cup: Eastern Europeans do well: Levski, Steaua, Zenit. FIFA want clubs of racist offending fans relegated. Another Bosman-type cash looms: Moroccan international Abdelmajid Oulmers at Charleroi injured playing for his country.

17 Luis Felipe Scolari – "Big Phil" – apparently interviewed by FA for Sven job. Now Blatter to throw out WC countries with racist fans. Boro draw Basle in UEFA Cup last eight. Crucial win for Swans over Brentford.

18 Arsenal stroll on; tinkerman Alan Pardew and Pompey win at West Ham for first time in 75 years; first club red for Savage but Rovers still get a return over Boro; Bolton pile on Black Cats agony; Spurs take more points off Birmingham; now it's four play for Everton as Villa go down; Wigan win is woe for Man City; Saha double keeps Man Utd on track at The Hawthorns. Championship: Reading held by the Wolves, but Sheff Utd in the toils again at Norwich; Preston panned at Sheff Wed; Leeds need late penalty for parity at Coventry. Lge 1: Dons haul in the Shrimpers again; Colchester end six losing streak; Bristol City hit Gills ten for six; Booth treble boosts Huddersfield. Lge 2: high five for Carlisle again at Darlo; Torquay shake Wycombe. Conf: Stanley scrape draw with Stevenage, Hereford cut lead to 11 points. Trophy semis: advantage Woking at Boreham Wood, Exeter edge Grays. Barca have two injured in 2-0 win over Sociedad.

19 Creaking Chelsea caught out at Craven Cottage and Gallas sees red; Boumsong banished as Liverpool sing a different tune to Toon. CIS final: Celtic three goals better than Dunfermline. SPL: Hearts held by Rangers.

20 FA Cup: Hammers at full strength oust Man City. Saints boss George Burley may take court action against Hearts over his dismissal on day when Soton lose to Watford. Chelsea face FA wrath over Cottage pitch invasion. Roof collapse at Wembley.

21 FA Cup: Liverpool on cloud seven as Brummies humiliated. Palace lifted by win at Leeds. Brentford stung by the Gills. Conf: Accrington lose at lowly Southport, Scarborough beaten again. Stenhousemuir do a Liverpool at East Stirling. Chelsea and Leeds in dispute over two young players.

22 FA Cup: Terry shows rest of poor-finishing Chelsea the way against Newcastle. Now Hearts get rid of Graham Rix! Jim Smith the Bald Eagle returns to Oxford management. Celtic win could mean title in two weeks! Weakened USA (rated 6th by FIFA!) lose 4-1 to Germany (19th). Brummie co-owner David Sullivan hits at uncaring City players on and off the field. Bank of Scotland to end SPL sponsorship in 2007. No single TV broadcaster to have monopoly from 2007.

23 FA Cup: Boro satisfied with goalless draw at Charlton. FA Youth Cup: Man City aggregate win over Newcastle gives them final spot. Rooney gets his hands on the World Cup trophy. Chelsea in bother again after WBA and now Fulham match.

24 Sir Clive to go back to rugby? Fears for Owen fitness. Chelsea get Liverpool in the FA Cup draw. Hiddink to leave PSV in summer.

25 Drogba "hands" it to Chelsea, Man City's Distin refuses to hand ball to ref Styles and goes for second yellow; Liverpool win spicy Merseyside derby with Gerrard and Everton sub Van der Meyde dismissed; Rovers hold fifth place after downing Black Cats whose chairman Bob Murray is under fire; Wigan caught at the death by Hammers; Villa and Fulham goalless; Arsenal game at Pompey waterlogged off. Championship: Reading held at Leicester but are promoted; Millwall and Sheff Wed win crucial away games at wobbling Watford and Wolves; late penalty at Derby sinks Palace. Lge 1: Shrimpers haul in another three points, but Brentford beaten at home by Donny and Swans grabbed by the Gills. Lge 2: Free-scoring Carlisle again, but Lincoln high five trawls in Grimsby; Orient edge Wycombe. Conf: Stanley recover at York; Scarborough lifeline at Shots. Trophy: Grays and Woking 2-0 wins enough for final date. SL: Gretna seal Div 1 place.

26 Record PL gate as Man Utd (69,070) add to Brummie woes and Neville's 500th puts him 8th in the order; Boro late strike in odd goal in seven win over Bolton; Charlton confirm Mags slump.

27 Robbie Keane 99th and 100th career League goals hit unlucky Albion. Owen may return in a month. G14 clubs again threatened by Blatter.

28 Ch Lge: Ab fab Arsenal take command over nine-finishing Juve; Barca hold Benfica. Preston and Brentford back on track, Carlisle restricted to one goal, too. England U-17s held by Italy.

29 Ch Lge: Inter recover to snatch 2-1 lead over Villarreal, AC Milan hold Lyon in France. Van the man back for Man Utd nudges Hammers. Asamoah treble revives Chester. Chelsea plan expansion in USA, then China.

30 UEFA Cup: Boro concede twice in Basle; Sevilla 4-1 over Zenit's nine men; Schalke stun Levski; all square in Romania with Rapid and Steaua. England U-17s now held by the Bulgars. Leicester caretaker Rob Kelly is manager of the month. Shevchenko turns down Chelsea. Wembley out until 2007. FA's hope of retrospective diving ban doomed?

31 Henry to wait for WC before signing decision. Injury-hit Solskjaer to sign two-year deal. Palace late show beats Watford. Pogatetz out for season with facial injury sustained against Bolton. Graham Poll to be WC ref.

APRIL 2006

Milestones for Van Nistelrooy and Shearer ... Gretna are great ... Arsenal European record ... Henry in FWA choice again ... Reading points high ... Rooney injury blow.

1 Even Birmingham manage a draw with Chelsea; Arsenal in cruise control hit Villa for five; Pompey revival continues at Fulham; Spurs downed at Newcastle and Shearer strikes 300th Mags PL effort; Van Nistelrooy's 150th goal lifts him 8th in Man Utd history; Liverpool cause Baggies grief; Black Cats claw draw at Everton to boost caretaker Kevin Ball. Championship: Reading grab title in five star style over Derby; Sheff Utd manage a draw, Leeds lose, Preston win at Coventry. Crewe and Brighton win away at Rangers and Millwall respectively. Lge 1: Southend held at Bournemouth, Colchester and Brentford share one, too. Windass hat-trick for Bradford on 37th birthday. Lge 2: Wycombe caught at home by Bristol Rovers. Rushden leapfrog Torquay at the foot. Conf: Accrington clipped by Grays. S Cup: History-making Gretna dump Dundee to reach final. Real's ten get a draw at Barca, but title looks unlikely. Juve held by cellar dwellers Treviso.

2 40th birthday boy Sheringham second half outing but Hammers and Charlton in goalless affair; Boro hit poor Man City. FL trophy (ex-LDV) final sees Swansea beat Carlisle, but Trundle and Tate in hot water over obscene jibe at Cardiff. S Cup: Hearts hit Hibs four times to win semi. Dark Blue pain as Cambridge win 122nd University match, series dead-heated at 47 wins each, 28 draws.

3 Rovers and Wigan in a 1-1 draw, but Latics boss Paul Jewell unhappy over ref Dowd. Berti Vogts may be next Hearts manager.

4 Ch Lge: Good news for AC Milan as Shevchenko hits record 52nd competition goal against Lyon, but bad for Inter ousted on away goal by Villarreal. PL: revived Brummies beat Bolton. FA short list for Sven job believed to be Martin O'Neill, Alan Curbishley, Sam Allardyce and Steve McClaren. PL chairman David Richards may face quiz over alleged illegal payments when at Sheff Wed. FA get nowhere with FIFA over back-dated diving. Shock Welsh style: TNS beaten for first time 2-1 at Carmarthen.

5 Ch Lge: Arsenal's 8th consecutive clean sheet is a competition record, too, as Nedved red ends Juve hopes in stalemate. Ronaldinho misses a penalty but hits another goal as Barca beat Benfica 2-0. SPL: Celtic clinch 40th title beating nearest rivals Hearts with Hartson (31) birthday goal.

6 UEFA Cup: Amazing recovery by Boro against Basle turns 23rd minute 3-0 aggregate deficit into 4-1 win on the day to boost McClaren's England chances; Zenit out after ten-a-side draw with Sevilla; Rapid exit in Bucharest derby draw with Steaua; Levski 1-1 with Schalke not enough.

7 Palace hopes hit at Leicester, Accrington lift up stalled in draw at Forest Green. Ashley Cole agent facing FA charge. McClaren can go for England job if he wants to say Boro. Sir Clive has trouble with some board members and shareholders, too. Sunderland fans hope Niall Quinn fronted takeover will succeed

8 One win, three draws, another abandoned because of snow – Spurs points up against Man City, Pompey share with Rovers; Wigan with Birmingham and Charlton (sixth goalless of last nine) with Everton. Sunderland relegation delayed after Fulham lead cut short by saturated pitch. Championship: another five for Reading at Cardiff; Sheff Utd edge Hull 3-2 while Crewe beat Wednesday; Brighton, Millwall defeated; Stoke ruin boss Joe Royle's 57th birthday at Ipswich 4-1; fourth no goal tally for Leeds in a draw with Plymouth. Lge 1: Southend give Blackpool start and beat them; while rivals struggle, Brentford, Barnsley a point each, Huddersfield, Swansea, Colchester all lose; Dons win at Oldham. Lge 2: Carlisle win top of table clash with Grimsby; Rushden win away leaving Torquay bottom after Darlo win there. Conf: Hereford draw leaves Stanley a point away from elevation. SPL: Hearts, Rangers still fighting out second place. SL: Brechin beaten by St Johnstone are relegated from Div 1. work permit hit Gonzalez forced on loan to Sociedad from Liverpool equalises at Real.

9 Chelsea are back: goal behind, down to ten men recover to slam Hammers 4-1; Man Utd account opened by Rooney (said to have lost £7k in betting this term) show 2-0 profit over Arsenal with 70,908 present; Toon edge Boro at Riverside; Fowler strike enough for Liverpool over Bolton; Villa and Baggies share. Championship: Watford fall further behind in derby draw with Luton. SPL: Celtic ease in 4-1 at Killie. Conf: York held by Kiddy. Vase: Hillingdon edge Bury Town, Nantwich hit Cammell Laird for four, clinching final places.

10 Man Utd to raise ticket prices. Conf: Grays 3-0 winners end Exeter play-off reality.

11 Colchester, Swansea back to winning Lge 1 ways. SL: relegated Brechin win a Dundee; six for Gretna.

12 FA Cup: shot-shy Charlton score twice but Boro get four. Arsenal with Campbell breaking nose held at Pompey. Tribunal rules Sven misled FA over Alam affair. U-21: Northern Ireland win 4-1 in Liechtenstein. U-16: England beat China 2-0. FC United 25th win in 33 Lge games gives them promotion. Blackburn lose insurance claim over injured Dahlin. Mike Dean to ref FA Cup final.

13 Owen back in training. Liverpool take 3-0 FA Youth Cup lead over Man City (12,744). U-16: France beat England 1-0.

14 Freaky Friday: Sunderland relegated but get a point at Man Utd (another PL record 72,519). Sheff Utd step nearer 1-0 at Cardiff; Wolves 19th draw with ten-man Watford. Southend's 11,195 see Gills win; Conf: York two degrees under at Cambridge. Rob Kelly gets Leicester post; Ian Atkins in at Torquay. Guus Hiddink to lead Aussies in WC, then take on Russia with Abramovich input. AC win Milan derby.

15 *Deja-vu* Chelsea edge nearer title against ten Trotters; sub Bergkamp helps Gunners to beat Baggies on Bergkamp day at Highbury; Keane puts Everton on the spot in Spurs win; braces apiece for Shearer, Boa Morte as Newcastle and Fulham hit Charlton and Wigan respectively; Pompey revival continues at Boro expense; Hammers push Man City down further. Championship: Reading late equaliser at Leeds, who join Preston winners at Leicester and Palace held by Crewe in play-offs; Brighton get the points at Ipswich. Lge 1: Barnsley win at Oldham, but Brentford, Huddersfield in drawn games and Swans in deep water at Blackpool; life in the Dons in Swindon win. Lge 2: Carlisle held at Bristol Rovers but Northampton and Orient have away wins; looking ominous for Torquay at the bottom, Barnet lose and Rushden held. SPL: Hearts nearing permanent second place after 2-0 v Killie while Rangers are held by Aberdeen.

16 Villa's midland derby win puts Brummies at risk again; Fowler again the Liverpool marksman at Blackburn. SPL: Celtic only scrape a draw with Hibs. Now England U-16s lose to Tunisia. Becks only sub for Real.

17 Chelsea step nearer after downing ten-man Everton, but Man Utd hanging in after surviving Spurs pressure to win themselves; Sunderland shake Newcastle until late Toon revival and Shearer's 409th career goal might be last after knee ligament injury; Albion squander chances in Bolton draw and Pompey after six unbeaten caught late at Charlton; Boro see off Hammers. Championship: Reading top points century; Sheff Wed win sends Brighton,

Crewe and Millwall down! Lge 1: Southend concede two own goals then draw at Barnsley; Colchester win, but Brentford held and Swansea lose at home to Rotherham. Dons win again, but Walsall now bottom. Lge 2: Northampton 5th win in six move into second place as Orient and Grimsby share spoils. Torquay win puts more pressure on fellow strugglers. Conf: Hereford confirm play-off after 1-0 over Tamworth. England U-18s beat Slovenia 2-1. Death at 66 of former West Ham manager John Lyall.

18 Ch Lge semi: crucial lead for Barca in Milan. Wigan back to winning ways at Villa expense. Sheff Utd and Leeds draw but Blades boss Neil Warnock banished to the stands. Lge 1: Huddersfield held by Chesterfield. Lge 2: Rushden slump 4-1 at Shrewsbury. SL: already promoted Gretna take lead to 21 points.

19 Ch Lge semi: Toure turns tie in Arsenal's slender favour against Villarreal. Forssell strike sends Blues out of zone against Rovers. Chelsea nearing Ballack signing. Conf: confident Grays punish Scarborough Seadogs 7-2 on their own patch.

20 UEFA Cup: Boro go down 1-0 to Steaua on day Steve McClaren faces England job snub; scoreless Schalke and Sevilla. England ladies beat Austria 4-0. David Tuttle resigns at Millwall. Altrincham face 18 point deduction in Conf for ineligible player.

21 O'Neill, McClaren, Scolari in FA short list? Real resting Becks. Grimsby move into automatic frame again after 1-0 v Cheltenham.

22 FA Cup semi: JM picks the wrong starters and Chelsea run out of time as Liverpool beat them 2-1. PL: Davids sent off but Spurs make their point at Arsenal; Pompey recover late to beat Sunderland; Baggies beaten at Newcastle; Brummies get a point at Everton; Bolton hit Charlton 4-1. Championship: Reading draw at Sheff Wed means win needed for points record; Vine penalty miss costs Luton win over Sheff Utd. Lge 1: Shrimpers caught in Donny net, while Colchester, Brentford and Huddersfield – who relegated Walsall, all win. Lge 2: Carlisle get promotion point at Mansfield, Northampton secure second place with win at Oxford, but looking bleak for Rushden, while Torquay, Stockport both record victories. Steve Bleasdale resigns before Posh game. SPL: Hearts losing Edinburgh derby to Hibs gives Rangers hopes of second spot. FC United record home gate: 6023!

23 FA Cup semi: Harewood nails it for the Hammers at Boro expense. Gerrard is PFA Player choice, Rooney receives young award again. Rangers draw at Celtic and four points behind Hearts.

24 Malcolm Glazer, 78, suffers stroke. Campbell recall for Arsenal after Senderos injury. Scolari cools on England. Ref change for FA Cup final: Alan Wiley (Staffs) replaces Mike Dean (Cheshire) for geographical reasons. Fulham beat Wigan to hit Lancs Euro hopes. Kevan Broadhurst sacked at Walsall.

25 Ch Lge: Lehmann ignores Henry tip, dives left to save Riquelme penalty sending Arsenal to final. Vassell punishes old Villa mates for Man City. Lge 2: Torquay hit Stockport for four, Barnet snatch Rochdale draw. FA to delay England appointment. FIFA to ban WC betting. Death of Brian Labone, Everton and England defender at 66.

26 Ch Lge: Barca held by Milan but reach final watched by 95,661. Liverpool win at Hammers in cup rehearsal, but Garcia and Mullins red-carded. Scolari offered job.

27 UEFA Cup: Boro's finest: give Steaua two goal lead – three on aggregate – and whack them 4-2; Sevilla need extra time to oust Schalke. Scolari Oh! Oh! – Big Phil wants big bucks and Alan Ball hits out at FA wanting to go foreign again. Henry his third FWA award. Chelsea fined £10,000 for players surrounding ref at WBA game.

28 Scolari Oh! No! Big Phil turns England down. BSkyB get three of six TV packages. Bullard to leave Wigan for Fulham in £2.5m move.

Thierry Henry of Arsenal is presented with the Football Writers' Association Footballer of the Year award by Paul Hetherington of the *Daily Star on Sunday* and FAW chairman. (Paul Harding/Actionimages))

29 Focused Chelsea wrap up the title at lunchtime as Man Utd lose Rooney to fourth right metatarsal break in 3-0 defeat; Harry "Houdini" Redknapp sees Pompey escape in 2-1 win at Wigan to demote Baggies and Brummies; Alan Curbishley calls it a day at Charlton after Blackburn's 2-0 victory; ten-in-a-row Liverpool hit Villa 3-1; Boro on the downbeat with Everton the winners; Fulham steal it at the death over Man City. Lge 1: draw enough for Southend's promotion at Swansea; Swindon go down despite draw at Bristol City; Brentford caught by Hartlepool equaliser; Huddersfield lose at home but secure pl-off berth, Colchester win and either they or Brentford will get automatic lift; veteran Claridge hits Walsall winner at Gills. Lge 2: Northampton promoted, Rushden relegated, Orient overtake Grimsby. Cheltenham and Wycombe in pl-offs. Conf: Morecambe join Hereford, Halifax, Grays in play-offs after 2-1 at the latter's ground. SPL: Rangers within a point of Hearts after 3-1 over Killie.

30 Spurs close in on Ch Lge place after Lennon goal v Bolton. Championship: Reading hit 106th point record; Rooney (Adam) hat-trick man as Stoke hit Brighton for five but boss Johan Boskamp to leave; PNE's Nugent returns 47 days after Rooney (Wayne)-type injury; Evans scores in his 432nd and last Plymouth game. Hearts 3-0 win over Celtic could secure second spot.

MAY 2006

McClaren is FA choice ... Roeder for Toon ... Brave Arsenal beaten ... Walcott England's youngest ... Gareth Bale Wales even younger! ... Shevchenko to Chelsea £29.5m.

1 Arsene Wenger had refused to be considered for England, but angry over Diaby injury in win at Sunderland, while Arsenal Ladies beat Leeds 5-0 in Women's Cup final; Ashton injured in Hammers win at West Brom; Man Utd held by Boro, Pride Park record 33,475 for Ted McMinn benefit: Derby legends v Rangers 9-in-a-row legends.

2 Rovers return to Europe after edging Chelsea champs. Mixed medical thoughts on Rooney comeback date; Sir Clive blames FA and PL for England's long season. Another Carlisle win. SPL: Rangers still hoping to catch Hearts after 2-1 v Hibs. Doubts remain over Steve Bruce remaining at Birmingham.

3 McClaren celebrates 45th birthday expecting to be crowned for England as Boro hold Bolton to a draw. SPL: Hearts qualify for Ch Lge as first non-old firm team after 1-0 v Dons. SL pl-offs: Partick dump nine-man Stranraer, Peterhead goalless at Morton; Alloa draw at Arbroath, Berwick win at Stenhousemuir. Richard Money is new Walsall manager. Millwall get new chairman Stewart Till, though Peter de Savary continues as such at their plc.

4 McClaren to take over as England head coach 1 August. Arsenal win at Man City keeps them in for Spurs Ch Lge place; Sunderland first home win prevents unwanted record. Sir Alex warns on rushing Rooney back.

5 BSkyB to get 92 games from four packages; Setanta 46 from two; deals worth £7 billion (Sky £1.3b, Setanta £392m) 2007–10; Play-off: Preston draw at Leeds. Managerial casualties: Brian Little (Tranmere), Barry Hunter (Rushden). Spain name seven PL players in WC squad. Claridge on 999 games axed by Walsall!

6 Ups and downs: Colchester's point is automatically enough, Brentford's insufficient; Rotherham draw with MK Dons saves them, not the losers and Hartlepool also hit by point failure. Orient last gasp 3-2 win at Oxford promotes them, relegates United who 44 years ago had replaced now born-again Accrington! Play-off: Watford stun Palace 3-0 at Selhurst. SL play-offs: Jags through after Stranraer fright; Peterhead, Alloa and Berwick move on, too. Conf play-off: Grays claw back two goals at Halifax after three down. Vase final: Nantwich ease in against Hillingdon.

7 Spurs with ten suffering food poisoning lose at West Ham and fourth place to Arsenal (with Henry 3) 4-2 winners over Wigan; Intertoto spot failure for Bolton despite win over Brum, but Newcastle secure it beating eased up Chelsea; Big Dunc's last game for Everton and he rescues a draw with Baggies; Villa edge Black Cats; Liverpool second half flourish at Pompey, but lose Alonso with injury in 11th consecutive win; Boro rest stars in Fulham defeat; Rovers ten still good enough against Man City, while Sir Alex drops the Ruud one but relishes four play against Charlton. England may include untried Walcott. SPL: Quiet ending as Celtic held at Aberdeen, Rangers beat Hearts in Alex McLeish finale.

8 Rookie Walcott and injured Rooney in WC squad. Play-off: Leeds win at Preston. Jose Mourinho is Barclays manager of the season. Harry Redknapp gets three year deal.

9 Spurs want a replay. Play-off: Watford and Palace draw but Hornets manager Aidy Boothroyd stirs up a brawl. Charlton clear out management staff. Testimonial record crowd of 69,591 for Roy Kearne benefit at Old Trafford v Celtic.

10 UEFA Cup final: In Big Mac's 250th Boro buried 4-0 by Sevilla. PL reject Spurs. Conf play-off: Halifax draw ends Grays dream. SL play-offs: Peterhead surprise Partick, Alloa take four off Berwick. U-21s: Wales win 2-0 in Tallinn, Northern Ireland beat Liechtenstein 4-0. Milton Keynes sack Danny Wilson. Man Utd to sign identical Brazilian twins Fabio and Rafael Pereira, 15, from Fluminense.

11 Spurs may have suffered from a virus problem. Play-offs: Brentford have goalie sent off but hold Swansea; Huddersfield take lead at Barnsley. Joe Royle leaves Ipswich post. Conf: Hereford need extra time to finish Morecambe. Scotland beat Bulgaria 5-1 in Japan. England ladies defeat Hungary 2-0. U-21s: Republic 2-1 winners in Azerbaijan. Shearer penalty wins his benefit game with Celtic 3-2. Sir Clive suggest penalty shoot-out competition.

12 Shevchenko may be Chelsea target again. Leeds players alleged to have trashed PNE dressing-room. Match-fixing Italian style investigation on Juve, AC Milan, Fiorentina and Lazio. Watford boss Adrian Boothroyd cleared of misconduct. Rotherham will start with 10 point CVA deduction in 2006–07!

13 FA Cup final: excellent spectacle of two Liverpool defensive errors, a couple of Gerrard blockbusters, Reina atones with last gasp save and the three-all draw ruined by a penalty shoot-out to give Liverpool victory over West Ham. Play-offs: Grimsby narrow lead at Lincoln, Cheltenham similarly at Wycombe. Scotland win the Kirin Cup by drawing with Japan. S Cup final: Gallant Gretna thwarted by penalty shoot-out defeat against Hearts.

14 Michael Ballack likely to sign for Chelsea on a free from Bayern – but get £2m signing-on fee! Play-off: Knight double for Swans ends Brentford daydream. Trophy final: Grays retain it with 2-0 win over Woking. Scottish play-offs: Partick recover to beat Peterhead on penalties, Berwick win fails to stop Alloa.

15 Spurs get £34m shirt deal from online gamblers Mansion. Rupert Lowe facing Saints revolt. Play-off: Goalkeeping error lets in Barnsley at Huddersfield. Conf managers: Mark Stimson quits at Grays, Jim Harvey axed at Morecambe and Graham Westley to leave Stevenage.

16 Ole Hermann Borgan axed as Ch Lge final line-man for wearing Barca shirt! Fellow Norwegian Arild Sundet is in. Play-off: Grimsby edge Lincoln, but Gary Jones red will be challenged. Tests clear Spurs hotel of poisoning. Peter Taylor in for Charlton? Shearer to be Toon talent scout as Glenn Roeder handed manager's job. U-21s: Northern Ireland beat Scots 1-0, as do Wales over Cyprus.

17 Ch Lge: Bravery not enough for ten-man Arsenal after Lehmann red-carded and a Campbell headed lead as off-side-looking Eto'o levels and Belletti hits the winner for Barca with Norwegian ref Terje Hauge under fire. Spurs

£10.9m Leverkusen Bulgarian striker Dimitar Berbatov. Maurice Malpas, new Motherwell boss. Steve Thompson to stand down at Yeovil. Solano escapes Peru car crash. Terry Venables in Boro frame.

18 Hauge says he was wrong about the red card. Play-off: Cheltenham hold Wycombe to reach final. Taylor to stay at Hull. Peter Jackson gets extension to Huddersfield role. Fraud probe in Holland, Italian police search Juve offices. Pele tips England for WC final. U-21: Republic beat Azers 3-0.

19 Henry to reign at Arsenal until 2010. JM feels sorry for the Gunners. Italy coach Marcello Lippi questioned in corruption scandal. Managers: Steve Bruce likely to stay at Birmingham, Dennis Wise may go to Swindon and Billy Davies in Charlton frame.

20 Conf play-off: Hereford need extra time to beat Halifax and return to FL after nine years.

21 Play-off: Watford take giant step back to PL with 3-0 demolition of Leeds. Wales beat the Basque Country, Northern Ireland lose to a wonder strike by Uruguay's Estoyoff.

22 Iain Dowie quits at Palace but chairman Simon Jordan unhappy over possible Charlton destination. Dennis Wise is new Swindon boss with Gus Poyet as No.2. Former Man Utd secretary Les Olive dies at 78.

23 England players get looksee at unfinished Wembley. Terry Venables could return for England role in August. Arsenal sign Tomas Rosicky £7m from Borussia Dortmund. PL want No.10 to abandon salary capping and fewer foreigners ideas. Nigel Spackman is new Millwall boss. Sir Bobby Robson returns to consultant role for Republic. Gary Jones freed from suspension for Grimsby. Peter Coates is new Stoke chairman. Rushden appoint Paul Hart as manager. Ossie Ardiles to coach Beitar Jerusalem. Altrincham lose appeal Conf status.

24 Republic beaten by Chile in Dublin. Keith Alexander leaves Lincoln after four unsuccessful play-off appearances. Scandals in Italy show no sign of lessening. Man Utd sack doctor Mike Stone in wake of Rooney injury saga.

25 England B lose to ten-man Belarus but goalie Green injured, though baby Walcott gets a sub outing and Lennon delights. Swedes fail to down the Finns and are booed. Even more TV cash coming with £84m from late-night viewing. PL clubs want seven on the bench. Morientes to Valencia, Pires to Villarreal. Palace fined £77,000, Watford £35,000 for play-off brawl. Bury will start with one point deducted for playing Marrison time-expired loan.

26 Latest on Roo factor is encouraging. John Gorman resigns as Wycombe manager in wake of wife's death.

27 Northern Ireland lose to Romania in Chicago, Wales beat T & T in Graz! Gareth Bale at 16 years 315 days youngest. Play-off: Barnsley need penalties to beat Swansea for Championship berth.

28 Terry Venables declines Boro offer. Play-off: Cheltenham have penalty saved but still beat Grimsby for promotion.

29 Rooney looking unlikely for WC. Boro hoping to land Martin O'Neill.

30 With Gerrard fronting with Owen England beat Hungary 3-1 and sub Walcott breaks Rooney's record as youngest at 17 years 75 days. Germans held by the Japs. Iain Dowie unveiled as Charlton manager but Palace to claim damages. They also sell Johnson to Everton for club record £8.6m. Colin Calderwood leaves Northampton to take over Forest and Keith Alexander moves in at Peterborough. Chelsea sign Salomon Kalou from Feyenoord for £3.5m.

Chelsea's new signing Andriy Shevchenko with Chelsea manager Jose Mourinho.
(Darren Walsh/Empics/Chelsea FC.)

31 Andriy Shevchenko signs for Chelsea at £29.5m. Russell Slade loses Grimsby post. Longest-running disciplinary case – since October 2004 – ends with Chelsea and West Ham receiving reduced fines.

JUNE 2006

All-clear for Rooney ... Blatter wants 18 club Premier League ... World Cup starts with six goals ... Tentative England's opening ... Awesome Argentina ... Owen out with ligament injury.

1 Arsenal face allegations of illegal loan to Beveren. England players train, Prince William watches. Chelsea add goalkeeper Hilario to their signings. Gray moves from Sunderland to loan club Burnley. Ronnie Moore and Oldham part company, John Sheridan appointed.

2 Arsenal vice-chairman David Dein voted off FA board. Tug-of-war between Man Utd and Chelsea over John Obi Mikel resolved: Utd to get £12m, Lyn £4m Rafael Benitez gets Liverpool deal to 2010. Billy Davies is Derby manager.

3 England finish preparations with 6-0 demolition of Jamaica, Crouch scoring three and blasting a penalty over.

4 Brazil beat New Zealand 4-0 in their last warm-up. Scarborough are relegated after all because of an undisclosed breach of financial rules and Altrincham re-instated to Conf! Scarborough will also start with 10-point deduction.

5 Rooney hopes on a rise. Managerial appointments: Jim Magilton (Ipswich), John Gorman (Northampton), Graham Rodger (Grimsby).

6 FIFA to have final Rooney say-so. Boro to announce Gareth Southgate as manager though he lacks the right credentials.

7 All-clear sounds for Rooney. Djibril Cisse breaks leg playing for France against China. Brighton ground move hits yet another snag. Yeovil appoint Russell Slade as manager.

8 Sir Alex remains unhappy over Rooney decision, Sven reckons he is in charge now. Gerrard injury scare. France replace Djibril Cisse (broken leg) with Sidney Govou. Blatter tells PL to cut back to 18 clubs for 2007–08.

9 WC opens with unprecedented six-goals, Germany beating Costa Rica 4-2 with two memorable German strikes, two individual efforts by Wanchope and some wretched defending; Ecuador the high altitude team bring Poland down to earth 2-0, though the Poles have an goal disallowed for offside and late on hit the woodwork twice. Ronnie Moore is the new Tranmere boss.

10 Third-minute own goal joy from Becks free kick against Paraguay, then mounting misery as England hang on to win; Sweden unable to break down stoic T&T who have Avery John sent off 47 minutes and even hit the bar through Stern John; Argentina exuding class let a good Ivory Coast back in during 2-1 win.

11 Robben helps Dutch master Serbs; Portugal 1-0 but find old Angola colonials tougher than expected; Bravo brace boosts Mexico way over Iran.

12 Super-sub Cahill lifts land of Aus in late show against Japan; new Arsenal capture Rosicky stars as USA are bounced by the Czechs; Pirlo fizzes one as Italy survive two penalty appeals by Ghana. Roy Keane to retire. Peter Taylor expected to be new Palace manager. Steve Thompson appointed at Notts Co.

13 Lack-lustre Brazil thankful for cracker from Kaka; Uninspired France a shadow of bygone days in Swiss draw; Togo lead, lose a man and game to South Korea; Rooney may or may not return. Gudjohnsen likely for Barca at £8m. Taylor is sixth in seven years at Selhurst. Tony Pulis returns to Stoke job.

14 Sven pronounces Roo fit. Spanish masters paint four star panorama against ten-man Ukraine; Germany leave it late to finally achieve the Pole-axe; Jaidi header saves Tunisia in end-to-end four goal shared encounter with the Saudis. Phil Parkinson surprise resignation at Colchester. Sunderland chairman Bob Murray retires. Leroy Rosenior is new Brentford manager, Danny Wilson in at Hartlepool.

15 Unimpressive England fumble to 2-0 win over spirited T&T as Roo makes his sub comeback; altitude men from Ecuador bring Costa Rica down to earth; Ljungberg settles Swedes as Paraguay bow out. West Ham snap up Spector from Man Utd. Iain Dowie served with Palace writ. John Schofield is Lincoln head coach with John Deehan as D of F.

16 Awesome Argentine annihilate the Serbs 6-0 peaking with finest-ever WC movement: 9 players, 24 passes, one goal, 57 seconds; Orange van men give Dutch a lift but Ivorians make them sweat a little; Angola earn a goalless draw with Mexico. Paul Simpson leaves Carlisle for Preston post. Coventry pay £1m for West Ham's Ward.

17 Fluid Ghana blank the Czechs who also have Ujfalusi sent off; Italy in a battle with USA as De Rossi sent off for dreadful elbow on McBride and the Yanks finish with nine but still draw; Deco special delivery stops stoic Iran.

18 With Ronaldo out of sorts Brazil find disciplined, determined Aussies a tough outfit and sub Kewell misses an easy equaliser; France start brightly then fade into a South Korean draw; Japan hold Croatia who have a Srna penalty saved.

19 Spain caught early by spirited Tunisia have to struggle to assert themselves; Togo's bonus problems coupled with elimination as Swiss win 2-0; Ukraine put Saudis to the sword. Colchester sell Danns to Birmingham for £850,000.

20 Owen twisted knee, Joe Cole special, Gerrard saves us at both ends bit Swedes twice level against dire defence; Germans getting into gear against weakened Ecuador; Paraguay extinguish last T&T hopes; Costa Rica lead but lose to Poles in match of no importance. Kewell escapes ban as Merk had failed to red card him after whistle. FIFA to take over Togo pay dispute. Simon Grayson confirmed as Blackpool manager.

21 Owen out with ruptured anterior cruciate ligament in right knee; Newcastle seek compensation. Argentine and Holland in defence-dominated stalemate; Ivory Coast give Serbs two goals start and beat them in ten-a-side finish; Portugal – with Big Phil's tenth consecutive WC win, Brazil et al – edge the Mexican ten; Angola and Iran settle for draw. Coach departures: Henri Michel (Ivory Coast), Branko Ivankovic (Iran) was already leaving in July. Martin Allen is Milton Keynes manager.

22 Aussies rule OK? Kewell leveller against Croatia puts them through, but ref Poll is axed by FIFA after handing three yellow cards to one player and missing at least one obvious penalty; Ronaldo lives! Two goals overtake Pele's WC 12 and equals Gerd Muller's 14 in 4-1 over Zico's Brazil; Ghana beat USA to reach knock-out stage but Essien booking is costly; Italy ignore home problems – Juventus and AC Milan facing relegation in corruption trial – and beat faltering Czechs 2-0. Bellamy to Liverpool for £6m.

23 French old guard of birthday boy Vieira and Henry see them through against Togo and Senderos powers the Swiss past South Korea to join them in last 16; Ukraine scrape in against ten-man Tunisia and Spain reduced to one goal by goalkeeping of Saudis' Zaid. England prepare for 4-1-4-1 formation with Rooney to roam alone. Arsenal to escape sanction over Beveren dealings. Juve may be relegated, AC Milan, Fiorentina and Lazio sanctioned along with other officials over match-fixing allegations. Colchester go to court to keep manager Phil Parkinson.

24 Two-up Germans lack pedal power against ten-man Swedes and Larsson misses penalty; Argentina find fluid Mexicans a handful, push them to extra time, are fortunate Heinze was yellow not redded and grateful for Maxi wonder strike.

25 Sick Becks saves England with a free-kick against Ecuador; Red mist descends as Portugal beat Holland in nine-a-side affair; Figo fortunate to have survived, ref Ivanov loses the plot.

26 Dubious last minute penalty sees ten-man Italy through against unlucky Aussies; Swiss and Ukraine in stalemate, the former content to rely on spot kicks which the latter delivered! Albion sign Hartson from Celtic. Swansea pair Tate and Trundle get one-match bans for Trophy misdemeanour.

27 Ronaldo breaks Gerd Muller's WC record of 14 goals as Brazil are flattered by 3-0 over Ghana; underachievers Spain through lead to France old guard of Vieira and Zidane after panic substitutions by Aragones.

28 England camp getting more optimistic. Pompey appoint Tony Adams as assistant manager; Plymouth give Ian Holloway No.1 post. Birmingham sign Stephen Kelly from Spurs.

29 Poll axed from WC by FIFA. Polish coach Pawel Janas resigns. Blatter blasts wealthy English clubs. Italy's corruption trial postponed. Arsenal cleared over Beveren affair. Hull appoint Phil Parkinson as boss, pay Colchester £400,000 compensation.

30 Lehmann is Germany's spot kick hero with two saves after Argentina take second half lead, Germany equalise late and extra time brings fear of losing all round, Jose Pekerman having made over-hasty replacements; Toni twosome takes Italy on against Ukraine. Spurs pay £8.2m for Didier Zokora from St Etienne. Under-fire Rupert Lowe quits Soton. Paul Lambert is new Wycombe manager. Valdas Ivanauskas confirmed as Hearts head coach.

JULY

Exit England on penalties of course ... Italy beat Germany in best game to date ... One England player in FIFA 23 ... Germans finish third ... Zidane disgrace as Italy win Final.

1 England out – beaten on penalties of course after Rooney dismissed stamping on Ricardo Carvalho and Big Phil Scolari, not we were told the FA's first choice as Sven successor again has the last laugh with Ricardo saving three spot kicks. Man Utd's Ronaldo gets blame for goading Rooney; Improving France showing resolution and tenacity beat lethargic, uninspired Brazil.

2 Becks surrenders captain's armband. Eriksson having originally blamed Rooney, begs press not to castigate the striker. Glenn Hoddle quits Wolves. Sunderland hoping to get Martin O'Neill.

3 Greece suspended by FIFA because of government interference with FA. Frings ban to hit Germans. Wembley stadium – more delays forecast. Niall Quinn consortium agree £10m Sunderland takeover. Lawrie McMenemy to join Soton board, Sir Clive pledges future there. Roberto Carlos retires from international football. Roberts, Wigan to Blackburn £1m. Motty to break Wolstenholme WC record of five finals.

4 Free-flowing, attack-minded yet defensively peerless Italy hit Germany with two late extra time strikes after the woodwork twice and Lehmann heroics had held them up – on a day when judges ruled Italian domestic football in crisis with likelihood of relegation for four clubs involved in match-fixing. FA back Rooney over red card. Blatter wants two refs in 2010. Japan's Zico is now Fenerbahce boss. Ince hint for Wolves post.

5 Peerless Zidane penalty enough for France who surrender territory to Portugal but win the battle, despite occasional eccentricities from Barthez. Chilean winger Gonzalez gets a playing permit at Liverpool after a year.

6 FIFA pick Rooney ref Elizondo (Argentina) for WC final. Owen out for eight months. Heskey to Wigan for club record £5.5m.

7 Terry one England player in FIFA 23 selected from knock-out stages only. Premier League gets six including Ricardo Carvalho victim in Rooney incident and only one Brazilian Ze Roberto. Becks to get new deal at Real from new boss Fabio Capello.

8 Schweinsteiger hits two and forces an own goal, too, as Germany overcome Portugal to secure third place. Rooney gets a two-match ban. Arsenal's Campbell may go abroad.

9 Dramatic WC final: Zidane sent off for head butt on Italy's Materazzi and the French lose the penalty shoot-out after 1-1.

Zinedine Zidane fools Italian goalkeeper Gianluigi Buffon with his delicately chipped penalty off the underside of the crossbar to put France ahead in the World Cup Final, before his fall from grace. (Actionimages)

ENGLISH LEAGUE TABLES 2005–06

FA BARCLAYCARD PREMIERSHIP

			Home					*Away*					*Total*						
		P	*W*	*D*	*L*	*F*	*A*	*W*	*D*	*L*	*F*	*A*	*W*	*D*	*L*	*F*	*A*	*GD*	*Pts*
1	Chelsea	38	18	1	0	47	9	11	3	5	25	13	29	4	5	72	22	50	91
2	Manchester U	38	13	5	1	37	8	12	3	4	35	26	25	8	5	72	34	38	83
3	Liverpool	38	15	3	1	32	8	10	4	5	25	17	25	7	6	57	25	32	82
4	Arsenal	38	14	3	2	48	13	6	4	9	20	18	20	7	11	68	31	37	67
5	Tottenham H	38	12	5	2	31	16	6	6	7	22	22	18	11	9	53	38	15	65
6	Blackburn R	38	13	3	3	31	17	6	3	10	20	25	19	6	13	51	42	9	63
7	Newcastle U	38	11	5	3	28	15	6	2	11	19	27	17	7	14	47	42	5	58
8	Bolton W	38	11	5	3	29	13	4	6	9	20	28	15	11	12	49	41	8	56
9	West Ham U	38	9	3	7	30	25	7	4	8	22	30	16	7	15	52	55	–3	55
10	Wigan Ath	38	7	3	9	24	26	8	3	8	21	26	15	6	17	45	52	–7	51
11	Everton	38	8	4	7	22	22	6	4	9	12	27	14	8	16	34	49	–15	50
12	Fulham	38	13	2	4	31	21	1	4	14	17	37	14	6	18	48	58	–10	48
13	Charlton Ath	38	8	4	7	22	21	5	4	10	19	34	13	8	17	41	55	–14	47
14	Middlesbrough	38	7	5	7	28	30	5	4	10	20	28	12	9	17	48	58	–10	45
15	Manchester C	38	9	2	8	26	20	4	2	13	17	28	13	4	21	43	48	–5	43
16	Aston Villa	38	6	6	7	20	20	4	6	9	22	35	10	12	16	42	55	–13	42
17	Portsmouth	38	5	7	7	17	24	5	1	13	20	38	10	8	20	37	62	–25	38
18	Birmingham C	38	6	5	8	19	20	2	5	12	9	30	8	10	20	28	50	–22	34
19	WBA	38	6	2	11	21	24	1	7	11	10	34	7	9	22	31	58	–27	30
20	Sunderland	38	1	4	14	12	37	2	2	15	14	32	3	6	29	26	69	–43	15

COCA–COLA FOOTBALL LEAGUE CHAMPIONSHIP

			Home					*Away*					*Total*						
		P	*W*	*D*	*L*	*F*	*A*	*W*	*D*	*L*	*F*	*A*	*W*	*D*	*L*	*F*	*A*	*GD*	*Pts*
1	Reading	46	19	3	1	58	14	12	10	1	41	18	31	13	2	99	32	67	106
2	Sheffield U	46	15	5	3	43	22	11	7	5	33	24	26	12	8	76	46	30	90
3	Watford	46	11	7	5	39	24	11	8	4	38	29	22	15	9	77	53	24	81
4	Preston NE	46	11	10	2	31	12	9	10	4	28	18	20	20	6	59	30	29	80
5	Leeds U	46	13	7	3	35	18	8	8	7	22	20	21	15	10	57	38	19	78
6	Crystal Palace	46	13	6	4	39	20	8	6	9	28	28	21	12	13	67	48	19	75
7	Wolverhampton W	46	9	10	4	24	18	7	9	7	26	24	16	19	11	50	42	8	67
8	Coventry C	46	12	7	4	39	22	4	8	11	23	43	16	15	15	62	65	–3	63
9	Norwich C	46	12	4	7	34	25	6	4	13	22	40	18	8	20	56	65	–9	62
10	Luton T	46	11	6	6	45	31	6	4	13	21	36	17	10	19	66	67	–1	61
11	Cardiff C	46	10	7	6	32	24	6	5	12	26	35	16	12	18	58	59	–1	60
12	Southampton	46	9	10	4	26	17	4	9	10	23	33	13	19	14	49	50	–1	58
13	Stoke C	46	7	5	11	24	32	10	2	11	30	31	17	7	22	54	63	–9	58
14	Plymouth Arg	46	10	7	6	26	22	3	10	10	13	24	13	17	16	39	46	–7	56
15	Ipswich T	46	8	8	7	28	32	6	6	11	25	34	14	14	18	53	66	–13	56
16	Leicester C	46	8	9	6	30	25	5	6	12	21	34	13	15	18	51	59	–8	54
17	Burnley	46	11	6	6	34	22	3	6	14	12	32	14	12	20	46	54	–8	54
18	Hull C	46	8	8	7	24	21	4	8	11	25	34	12	16	18	49	55	–6	52
19	Sheffield W	46	7	8	8	22	24	6	5	12	17	28	13	13	20	39	52	–13	52
20	Derby Co	46	8	10	5	33	27	2	10	11	20	40	10	20	16	53	67	–14	50
21	QPR	46	7	7	9	24	26	5	7	11	26	39	12	14	20	50	65	–15	50
22	Crewe Alex	46	7	7	9	38	40	2	8	13	19	46	9	15	22	57	86	–29	42
23	Millwall	46	4	8	11	13	27	4	8	11	22	35	8	17	21	35	61	–27	40
24	Brighton & HA	46	4	8	11	21	34	3	9	11	18	37	7	17	22	39	71	–32	38

COCA–COLA FOOTBALL LEAGUE DIVISION 1

			Home					Away					Total						
		P	W	D	L	F	A	W	D	L	F	A	W	D	L	F	A	GD	Pts
1	Southend U	46	13	6	4	37	16	10	7	6	35	27	23	13	10	72	43	29	82
2	Colchester U	46	15	4	4	39	21	7	9	7	19	19	22	13	11	58	40	18	79
3	Brentford	46	10	8	5	35	23	10	8	5	37	29	20	16	10	72	52	20	76
4	Huddersfield T	46	13	6	4	40	25	6	10	7	32	34	19	16	11	72	59	13	73
5	Barnsley	46	11	11	1	37	19	7	7	9	25	25	18	18	10	62	44	18	72
6	Swansea C	46	11	9	3	42	23	7	8	8	36	32	18	17	11	78	55	23	71
7	Nottingham F	46	14	5	4	40	15	5	7	11	27	37	19	12	15	67	52	15	69
8	Doncaster R	46	11	6	6	30	19	9	3	11	25	32	20	9	17	55	51	4	69
9	Bristol C	46	11	7	5	38	22	7	4	12	28	40	18	11	17	66	62	4	65
10	Oldham Ath	46	12	4	7	32	24	6	7	10	26	36	18	11	17	58	60	–2	65
11	Bradford C	46	8	9	6	28	25	6	10	7	23	24	14	19	13	51	49	2	61
12	Scunthorpe U	46	8	8	7	36	33	7	7	9	32	40	15	15	16	68	73	–5	60
13	Port Vale	46	10	5	8	30	26	6	7	10	19	28	16	12	18	49	54	–5	60
14	Gillingham	46	13	4	6	31	21	3	8	12	19	43	16	12	18	50	64	–14	60
15	Yeovil T	46	8	8	7	27	24	7	3	13	27	38	15	11	20	54	62	–8	56
16	Chesterfield	46	6	7	10	31	37	8	7	8	32	36	14	14	18	63	73	–10	56
17	Bournemouth	46	7	11	5	25	20	5	8	10	24	33	12	19	15	49	53	–4	55
18	Tranmere R	46	7	8	8	32	30	6	7	10	18	22	13	15	18	50	52	–2	54
19	Blackpool	46	9	8	6	33	27	3	9	11	23	37	12	17	17	56	64	–8	53
20	Rotherham U	46	7	9	7	31	26	5	7	11	21	36	12	16	18	52	62	–10	52
21	Hartlepool U	46	6	10	7	28	30	5	7	11	16	29	11	17	18	44	59	–15	50
22	Milton Keynes D	46	8	8	7	28	25	4	6	13	17	41	12	14	20	45	66	–21	50
23	Swindon T	46	9	5	9	31	31	2	10	11	15	34	11	15	20	46	65	–19	48
24	Walsall	46	7	7	9	27	34	4	7	12	20	36	11	14	21	47	70	–23	47

COCA–COLA FOOTBALL LEAGUE DIVISION 2

			Home					Away					Total						
		P	W	D	L	F	A	W	D	L	F	A	W	D	L	F	A	GD	Pts
1	Carlisle U	46	14	3	6	47	23	11	8	4	37	19	25	11	10	84	42	42	86
2	Northampton T	46	11	8	4	30	15	11	9	3	33	22	22	17	7	63	37	26	83
3	Leyton Orient	46	11	6	6	29	21	11	9	3	38	30	22	15	9	67	51	16	81
4	Grimsby T	46	13	3	7	37	18	9	9	5	27	26	22	12	12	64	44	20	78
5	Cheltenham T	46	10	7	6	39	31	9	8	6	26	22	19	15	12	65	53	12	72
6	Wycombe W	46	9	9	5	41	29	9	8	6	31	27	18	17	11	72	56	16	71
7	Lincoln C	46	9	11	3	37	21	6	10	7	28	32	15	21	10	65	53	12	66
8	Darlington	46	10	7	6	32	26	6	8	9	26	26	16	15	15	58	52	6	63
9	Peterborough U	46	9	7	7	28	21	8	4	11	29	28	17	11	18	57	49	8	62
10	Shrewsbury T	46	10	9	4	33	20	6	4	13	22	35	16	13	17	55	55	0	61
11	Boston U	46	11	7	5	34	28	4	9	10	16	32	15	16	15	50	60	–10	61
12	Bristol R	46	8	6	9	30	29	9	3	11	29	38	17	9	20	59	67	–8	60
13	Wrexham	46	12	6	5	36	19	3	8	12	25	35	15	14	17	61	54	7	59
14	Rochdale	46	8	7	8	34	30	6	7	10	32	39	14	14	18	66	69	–3	56
15	Chester C	46	7	6	10	30	29	7	6	10	23	30	14	12	20	53	59	–6	54
16	Mansfield T	46	9	7	7	37	29	4	8	11	22	37	13	15	18	59	66	–7	54
17	Macclesfield T	46	10	9	4	35	27	2	9	12	25	44	12	18	16	60	71	–11	54
18	Barnet	46	9	8	6	24	22	3	10	10	20	35	12	18	16	44	57	–13	54
19	Bury	46	6	9	8	22	25	6	8	9	23	32	12	17	17	45	57	–12	53
20	Torquay U	46	7	9	7	33	31	6	4	13	20	35	13	13	20	53	66	–13	52
21	Notts Co	46	7	11	5	30	26	5	5	13	18	37	12	16	18	48	63	–15	52
22	Stockport Co	46	7	11	5	34	29	4	8	11	23	49	11	19	16	57	78	–21	52
23	Oxford U	46	7	7	9	25	30	4	9	10	18	27	11	16	19	43	57	–14	49
24	Rushden & D	46	8	5	10	25	31	3	7	13	19	45	11	12	23	44	76	–32	45

FOOTBALL LEAGUE PLAY-OFFS 2005–06

CHAMPIONSHIP FIRST LEG

Friday, 5 May 2006

Leeds U (0) 1 *(Lewis 74)*

Preston NE (0) 1 *(Nugent 48)* 35,239

Leeds U: Sullivan; Kelly, Crainey, Derry (Cresswell), Kilgallon, Gregan, Bakke (Stone), Miller, Hulse, Healy (Blake), Lewis.
Preston NE: Nash; Alexander, Mears, O'Neil (Whaley), Davis, Mawene, Jarrett, McKenna, Ormerod (Sedgwick), Dichio, Nugent (Agyemang).

Saturday, 6 May 2006

Crystal Palace (0) 0

Watford (0) 3 *(King 46, Young 67, Spring 85)* 22,880

Crystal Palace: Kiraly; Boyce, Ward (Butterfield), Popovic, Hall, Watson, McAnuff, Hughes, Johnson, Morrison, Soares (Freedman).
Watford: Foster; Doyley, Stewart, Spring, Mackay, DeMerit, Chambers (Eagles), Mahon, Henderson (Bangura), King, Young.

CHAMPIONSHIP SECOND LEG

Monday, 8 May 2006

Preston NE (0) 0

Leeds U (0) 2 *(Hulse 56, Richardson 61)* 20,383

Preston NE: Nash; Alexander, Mears, O'Neil, Davis, Mawene, Ormerod (Whaley), McKenna, Dichio, Nugent, Stewart (Agyemang).
Leeds U: Sullivan; Kelly, Crainey■, Derry, Kilgallon, Gregan, Douglas, Richardson, Hulse (Cresswell■), Miller, Lewis (Stone).

Tuesday, 9 May 2006

Watford (0) 0

Crystal Palace (0) 0 19,041

Watford: Foster; Doyley, Stewart, Bangura, Mackay, DeMerit, Spring, Mahon, Young, King, Chambers (Henderson).
Crystal Palace: Kiraly; Boyce, Borrowdale, Popovic (Reich), Hall, Leigertwood, McAnuff, Hughes (Watson), Johnson, Freedman (Macken), Soares.

CHAMPIONSHIP FINAL (at Millennium Stadium)

Sunday, 21 May 2006

Leeds U (0) 0

Watford (1) 3 *(DeMerit 25, Sullivan 57 (og), Henderson 84 (pen))* 64,736

Leeds U: Sullivan; Kelly, Kilgallon, Derry, Butler, Gregan (Bakke), Douglas, Richardson (Blake), Hulse, Miller (Healy), Lewis.
Watford: Foster; Doyley, Stewart, Spring, Mackay, DeMerit, Chambers (Bangoura), Mahon, Henderson, King, Young.
Referee: M. Dean (Wirral).

LEAGUE 1 FIRST LEG

Thursday, 11 May 2006

Barnsley (0) 0

Huddersfield T (0) 1 *(Taylor-Fletcher 85)* 16,127

Barnsley: Colgan; Hassell, Heckingbottom, Howard, Reid, Kay, Devaney, Shuker, Nardiello (Hayes), Richards (Wright), McPhail.
Huddersfield T: Rachubka; Holdsworth, Adams, Hudson, McIntosh, Clarke N, Worthington, Taylor-Fletcher, Graham (Abbott), Booth, Schofield.

Swansea C (0) 1 *(Ricketts 87)*

Brentford (1) 1 *(Tabb 29)* 19,060

Swansea C: Gueret; Ricketts, Austin, Tudur-Jones, Monk, Tate, Britton, MacDonald (Forbes), Knight (Trundle), Fallon (Akinfenwa), Robinson.
Brentford: Nelson■; O'Connor, Tillen, Newman, Frampton, Turner, Pratley, Smith, Gayle, Rankin (Bankole), Tabb (Brooker).

LEAGUE 1 SECOND LEG

Sunday, 14 May 2006

Brentford (0) 0

Swansea C (2) 2 *(Knight 8, 15)* 10,652

Brentford: Nelson; O'Connor, Frampton (Tillen), Newman (Willock), Sodje, Turner, Pratley, Smith (Brooker), Rhodes, Rankin, Tabb.
Swansea C: Gueret; Ricketts, Austin, Tudur-Jones, Monk, Tate, Britton, O'Leary, Knight (Forbes), Fallon (Trundle), Robinson (Williams).

Cheltenham Town players celebrate after winning the Coca-Cola League Two Play-off final against Grimsby Town at the Millennium Stadium, Cardiff. (Paul Harding/Actionimages)

Nick Colgan saves Alan Tate's shoot-out penalty in Barnsley's Coca-Cola League One Play-off win against Swansea City at the Millennium Stadium, Cardiff. (John Walton/EMPICS)

Monday, 15 May 2006
Huddersfield T (0) 1 *(Worthington 65)*
Barnsley (0) 3 *(Hayes 58 (pen), Reid 71, Nardiello 78)* 19,223
Huddersfield T: Rachubka; Holdsworth, Adams, Hudson (Brandon), McIntosh, Clarke N, Worthington, Taylor-Fletcher, Graham (Abbott), Booth, Schofield.
Barnsley: Colgan; Hassell, Heckingbottom, Howard, Reid, Kay, Devaney, Nardiello (Shuker), Hayes, Richards (Wright), McPhail.

LEAGUE 1 FINAL (at Millennium Stadium)

Saturday, 27 May 2006
Swansea C (2) 2 *(Fallon 28, Robinson 40)*
Barnsley (1) 2 *(Hayes 19, Nardiello 62)* 55,419
Swansea C: Gueret; Ricketts, Austin, O'Leary, Monk, Tate, Britton, Tudur-Jones, Knight (Trundle), Fallon (Akinfenwa), Robinson (McLeod).
Barnsley: Colgan; Hassell, Heckingbottom, Howard (Tonge), Reid, Kay, Devaney, Nardiello (Shuker), Hayes, Richards (Wright), McPhail.
aet; Barnsley won 4-3 on penalties.
Referee: L. Mason (Lancashire).

LEAGUE 2 FIRST LEG

Saturday, 13 May 2006
Lincoln C (0) 0
Grimsby T (1) 1 *(Jones G 22)* 8037
Lincoln C: Marriott; Beevers (Frecklington), Hughes, McAuley, Morgan, McCombe, Kerr, Robinson M (Birch), Green (Yeo), Forrester, Brown.
Grimsby T: Mildenhall; McDermott (Croft), Newey, Woodhouse, Whittle, Futcher, Cohen (Reddy), Bolland, Parkinson, Jones G, Mendes (Toner).

Wycombe W (0) 1 *(Mooney 90)*
Cheltenham T (1) 2 *(Finnigan 43, Guinan 75)* 5936
Wycombe W: Williams; Senda, Easton, Bloomfield (Oakes), Johnson, Antwi, Betsy, Martin, Mooney, Stonebridge (Easter), Lee (Burnell).
Cheltenham T: Higgs; Gill, Armstrong, McCann, Caines, Duff, Wilson (Bell), Finnigan, Odejayi (Spencer), Guinan (Gillespie), Vincent.

LEAGUE 2 SECOND LEG

Tuesday, 16 May 2006
Grimsby T (0) 2 *(Futcher 60, Jones G 82)*
Lincoln C (1) 1 *(Robinson M 27)* 8062
Grimsby T: Mildenhall; Croft, Newey, Woodhouse, Whittle, Jones R (Futcher), Cohen (Reddy), Bolland, Parkinson, Jones G■, Mendes (Toner).
Lincoln C: Marriott; Beevers (Green), Hughes, McAuley, Morgan, McCombe (Mayo), Kerr (Frecklington), Forrester, Robinson M, Yeo, Brown.

Thursday, 18 May 2006
Cheltenham T (0) 0
Wycombe W (0) 0 6813
Cheltenham T: Higgs; Gill, Armstrong, McCann, Caines, Duff, Vincent (Bird), Finnigan, Odejayi (Spencer), Guinan, Wilson.
Wycombe W: Williams; Senda, Easton (Williamson), Bloomfield (Oakes), Johnson, Antwi, Betsy, Martin, Mooney (Griffin), Easter, Lee.

LEAGUE 2 FINAL (at Millennium Stadium)

Sunday, 28 May 2006
Grimsby T (0) 0
Cheltenham T (0) 1 *(Guinan 63)* 29,196
Grimsby T: Mildenhall; Croft (Futcher), Newey, Woodhouse, Whittle, Jones R, Mendes (Goodfellow), Bolland, Parkinson, Jones G, Reddy (Cohen).
Cheltenham T: Higgs; Gill, Armstrong (Bell), McCann, Caines, Duff, Vincent (Spencer), Finnigan, Gillespie (Odejayi), Guinan, Wilson.
Referee: P. Taylor (Hertfordshire).

LEADING GOALSCORERS 2005–06

	League	Carling Cup	FA Cup	Other	Total
FA BARCLAYCARD PREMIERSHIP					
Players in this competition scoring ten or more League goals are listed. Other leading scorers classified by total number of goals in all competitions.					
Thierry Henry *(Arsenal)*	27	1	0	5	33
Ruud Van Nistelrooy *(Manchester U)*	21	1	0	2	24
Darren Bent *(Charlton Ath)*	18	2	2	0	22
Frank Lampard *(Chelsea)*	16	0	2	2	20
Wayne Rooney *(Manchester U)*	16	2	0	1	19
Robbie Keane *(Tottenham H)*	16	0	0	0	16
Marlon Harewood *(West Ham U)*	14	0	2	0	16
Ayegbeni Yakubu *(Middlesbrough)*	13	0	4	2	19
Craig Bellamy *(Blackburn R)*	13	2	2	0	17
Didier Drogba *(Chelsea)*	12	0	1	3	16
Henri Camara *(Wigan Ath)*	12	0	0	0	12
Collins John *(Fulham)*	11	0	1	0	12
Mido *(Tottenham H)*	11	0	0	0	11
Steven Gerrard *(Liverpool)*	10	1	4	8	23
Hernan Crespo *(Chelsea)*	10	0	1	2	13
Alan Shearer *(Newcastle U)*	10	1	1	0	12
James Beattie *(Everton)*	10	0	0	1	11
In order of total goals:					
Djibril Cisse *(Liverpool)*	9	0	2	8	19
Mark Viduka *(Middlesbrough)*	7	1	2	6	16
COCA-COLA CHAMPIONSHIP					
Players in this competition scoring 12 or more League goals are listed.					
Marlon King *(Watford)*	21	0	0	1	22
Dave Kitson *(Reading)*	18	4	0	0	22
Cameron Jerome *(Cardiff C) (now Birmingham C)*	18	1	1	0	20
Kevin Doyle *(Reading)*	18	0	1	0	19
Ade Akinbiyi *(Sheffield U)*	15	2	0	0	17
(Includes 12 League and 2 Carling Cup goals for Burnley).					
Andy Johnson *(Crystal Palace)*	15	0	2	0	17
Gary McSheffrey *(Coventry C)*	15	1	1	0	17
Steve Howard *(Luton T)*	14	0	1	0	15
Darius Henderson *(Watford)*	14	0	0	1	15
Ashley Young *(Watford)*	13	1	0	1	15
Clint Morrison *(Crystal Palace)*	13	0	0	0	13
David Healy *(Leeds U)*	12	0	2	0	14
Rob Hulse *(Leeds U)*	12	0	1	1	14
Jason Koumas *(Cardiff C)*	12	1	0	0	13
Dele Adebola *(Coventry C)*	12	0	0	0	12
COCA-COLA LEAGUE 1					
Freddy Eastwood *(Southend U)*	23	0	2	0	25
Billy Sharp *(Scunthorpe U)*	23	0	0	1	24
Lee Trundle *(Swansea C)*	20	0	0	1	21
James Hayter *(Bournemouth)*	20	0	0	0	20
Luke Beckett *(Oldham Ath)*	18	0	0	0	18
Chris Iwelumo *(Colchester U)*	17	0	2	0	19
Izale McLeod *(Milton Keynes D)*	17	0	1	0	18
Dean Windass *(Bradford C)*	16	3	1	0	20
Rory Fallon *(Swansea C)*	16	0	1	2	19
(Includes 12 League, 1 FA Cup and 1 other goal for Swindon T).					
Chris Greenacre *(Tranmere R)*	16	0	1	1	18
Steve Brooker *(Bristol C)*	16	0	0	0	16
Phil Jevons *(Yeovil T)*	15	0	1	0	16
Paul Hall *(Chesterfield)*	15	0	0	0	15
Andy Booth *(Huddersfield T)*	13	0	2	0	15
Darren Byfield *(Gillingham)*	13	1	0	0	14
Andy Robinson *(Swansea C)*	12	0	0	6	18
Lloyd Owusu *(Brentford)*	12	0	2	0	14
Pawel Abbott *(Huddersfield T)*	12	2	0	0	14
Deon Burton *(Rotherham U)*	12	1	1	0	14
Marc Richards *(Barnsley)*	12	0	0	0	12
COCA-COLA LEAGUE 2					
Karl Hawley *(Carlisle U)*	22	0	0	4	26
Rickie Lambert *(Rochdale)*	22	0	0	0	22
Richard Walker *(Bristol R)*	20	0	0	1	21
Richie Barker *(Mansfield T)*	18	1	4	0	23
Scott McGleish *(Northampton T)*	17	1	4	2	24
Tommy Mooney *(Wycombe W)*	17	1	0	1	19
Junior Agogo *(Bristol R)*	16	0	2	0	18
Danny Crow *(Peterborough U)*	15	0	0	2	17
Michael Bridges *(Carlisle U)*	15	1	0	0	16
(Includes 1 Carling Cup goal for Bristol City).					
Julian Joachim *(Boston U)*	14	0	2	0	16
Gary Alexander *(Leyton Orient)*	14	0	0	1	15
Gary Jones *(Grimsby T)*	13	1	1	2	17
Mark Jones *(Wrexham)*	13	0	0	2	15
Michael Reddy *(Grimsby T)*	13	0	0	0	13

Other matches consist of European, Super Cup and Club World Championship games, Football League Trophy, Community Shield and Football League play-offs. Players listed in order of League goals total.

REVIEW OF THE SEASON

A second Premier League success 50 years after the first, then along comes another immediately afterwards. In 2005–06 Chelsea's record was only just short of the points total achieved the year before. In fact had it not been for ringing the changes to give some more squad players a first team outing, there might well have been a similar points total rather than the four adrift of 2004–05.

The Blues were smartly away despite having to wait until the death to win at Wigan Athletic but recorded a Premier League record of six consecutive clean sheets. After 11 games only two points dropped in a draw at Everton and the pattern was largely set from then on.

First defeat away to Manchester United on 6 November, ending an impressive run of 40 unbeaten League matches, was followed crucially with ten straight wins – yet another club record. In the last third of the season, not such a straightforward performance, but any remote possibility of a drastic slip was erased when revenge was achieved in the return with Manchester United on 29 April. Bearing in mind there had been disappointments all round in various cup competitions, this was a significant moment. Chelsea rose to the occasion with a 3-0 victory which confirmed them as retaining champions. Jose Mourinho, despite not being given any of the monthly honours, was declared Manager of the season.

Twenty-five different players were called upon during the Premiership season, the days when a small squad would be capable of clearing the title unaided long gone. No ever-present members of the squad, but John Terry only missed the last two through injury. Frank Lampard just three after recording a Premier League record of 164 consecutive appearances. He was also top scorer with 16 goals, a more than creditable achievement for a midfield player.

If there was a problem area at Stamford Bridge it was trying to field both Didier Drogba and Hernan Crespo in the same team. International strikers in their own right, it was not the same trying to dovetail the pair together in Chelsea colours. Even so Drogba managed 12 goals from 29 overall outings, Crespo ten from 30.

Thus Manchester United had to be content with second place. Ruud Van Nistelrooy hit 21 goals, but was probably not as potent a force as in earlier times despite achieving his 150th goal in all games for the club, lifting him to eighth overall in the club's history. Old Trafford's ground improvements also meant a late season topping up to over 70,000 and another record for the competition. Talking of pieces of eight, Gary Neville with his 500th game, pushed himself to eighth in the list of United appearances. Their consolation prize was the not inconsiderable lifting of the Carling Cup.

Liverpool's third place seemed a likely destiny in the last half of the season after a ponderous start which at one time had them in the lower half of the table. But they finished strongly enough with nine successive wins. They played their part in the above average FA Cup, emerging as winners in the shoot-out with West Ham United. On the downside there was European failure as they were unable to retain the trophy won in the previous season.

Fourth place was pretty low by Arsenal standards in recent years, third in 1996–97 being the poorest. However, they did have Thierry Henry as top scorer in the League with 27 goals and in the process establishing himself as the highest overall goalscorer in the club's history plus the leading one in the League alone.

Didier Drogba gets the better of Rio Ferdinand as Chelsea see off Manchester United in the crucial Premier League meeting. (PA/Empics)

They also came within a whisker of success in the Champions League final, but the early handicap of losing their goalkeeper to a dismissal proved too much, but they stretched Barcelona all the way until the last quarter of an hour, the defence again showing its remarkable resilience. So it was the end of an era with the club moving house to a new headquarters and leaving Highbury after 92 years.

Tottenham Hotspur had fancied fourth place themselves, until the mystery of pre-match illness hit them before the last match of the season when they had seemed stuck on that number since December. In contrast, Blackburn Rovers slow away had a much improved second half of the season to finish fifth. Newcastle United's final position of seventh had seemed most unlikely, but stability was restored when a change of management occurred.

Bolton Wanderers had threatened to do even better but five successive defeats late in the season robbed them, though they acquitted themselves well in their first UEFA Cup experience as European newcomers.

West Ham United contributed to a much better final than in recent memory before losing on penalties to Liverpool who rarely fail from such a situation. Five straight wins in early January was Hammers best in the Premiership. Though Wigan finished tenth, they were enormously encouraged by the events of their initial season in the top echelon. Second place was their highest at one time and there was the Carling Cup runners-up to come in the second half.

After winning only one of the opening eight, Everton did well enough to steady the ship and the high spot for Fulham came in the deserved victory over neighbours Chelsea which halted four straight defeats.

Charlton Athletic won their first four and never again managed two in succession. Long serving manager Alan Curbishley decided at the end of the season that it was time to move to pastures new, while Middlesbrough's zenith was achieved when they gave Chelsea their biggest defeat of the season 3-0 at the Riverside in mid-February. Boro also played their best football in the UEFA Cup and reached the final after some stirring comebacks in earlier ties. In the League alone they used 37 different players and with the departure of manager Steve McClaren to assume the mantle of Sven-Goran Eriksson as England's No. 1, the club appointed player Gareth Southgate to take the reins.

Manchester City won only one of their last ten, Aston Villa managed just two consecutive wins in November, their other victories being isolated ones but Portsmouth made the great escape again having at one time appeared firm favourites for the drop. In the end it was the Midland pairing of Birmingham City and West Bromwich Albion who failed to hold on to their status. City's real problems were early season with one win in the first 12 and Albion scraped only four points from their last 13 outings. For their part Sunderland appeared doomed from the onset, only three wins overall, the first at home near the end.

In stark contrast Reading stormed the Championship in scintillating form. After losing 2-1 at home to Plymouth Argyle in the opening game, they did not lower their colours again until the 3-2 defeat at Luton Town on 17 February in what was their 35th League game. Moreover their 106 points total was a Football League record.

Sheffield United were the other automatic promotion team, never frightened to change a successful side – witness the 32 different players they used during the campaign. Watford joined them from the play-offs having finished third in the season. Six wins early in the New Year seemed to confirm their serious intentions.

Reading's Leroy Lita, Bobby Convey, Steven Sidwell and Stephen Hunt celebrate their promotion to the Premier League with a fan in a Scream mask and Kingsley Royal the Reading mascot. (Alex Morton/Actionimages)

Robbie Keane (left) puts Tottenham 1-0 ahead against Blackburn Rovers with a brilliant solo effort. (Reuters/Toby Melville/Actionimages)

Only one win in their last ten – and six goals in the process – when automatic promotion was not even out of the question seemed to be a heavy burden carried over into the play-offs where Leeds United lost in the final to Watford, having beaten Preston in the semi-final. North End for their part had stalled throughout by drawing as many as 20 League games. Crystal Palace the other team in the bracket had revealed some inconsistency in the last third of the season. It was a pity having changed up a gear from an indifferent start.

Wolverhampton Wanderers were again just short of what was required to secure a play-off place. They, too, drew as many as 19 matches. Coventry City's eighth place was the highest they reached all season which reflected credit on their determination to improve.

Norwich City might have expected to do better after relegation, but it was a transitional season for them and Luton were never able to match the first third of the season in terms of winning matches.

Cardiff City disappointingly did not win any of their last seven and Southampton, calling on 40 players, were another team obsessed with drawn games, sharing points in 19 of them. Stoke City had their most wretched run from Boxing Day with just one win in 13, Plymouth from the first win at Reading had to settle for safety rather than anything more ambitious.

Ipswich Town with one win in the last ten lost any hope of reaching the play-offs, Leicester City hauled themselves out of a sticky situation brought upon themselves by ten games without a win and Burnley's one win in 13 after the Christmas Holiday period was a clear indication of their final resting place.

Hull City were briefly ninth in late August but this was the high point, Sheffield Wednesday desperately needed those five wins in the last eight to avoid relegation and Derby County were never really completely free of worries either. Queens Park Rangers finished just above the drop zone, which by the end of the season had been confined to three clubs: Brighton & Hove Albion, Millwall and Crewe Alexandra.

Brighton had runs of nine and eleven without a win, Millwall capable of fine performances, hence late season success at Watford, were hugely inconsistent and Crewe enduring 16 games without a win seemed to have lost their way completely.

The chase for the top of League One chiefly concerned Southend United, the most consistent of the teams at the top. They survived their mid-December wobble and dropped fewer points at other times than their rivals to finish as champions. Neighbours Colchester United joined them, their biggest problem being a cup stutter after they had been drawn to play Chelsea. But four wins and two draws in the last six was enough for automatic promotion.

Through the play-offs it was fifth placed Barnsley who emerged. They might have done better had they not earlier drawn 11 times at home. But they accounted for Huddersfield Town the hard way, losing at home, winning away and then beat Swansea City who had looked in control until the turn of the year. City's consolation was winning the Football League Trophy.

Huddersfield also hit a bad patch when faced with Chelsea in the cup and needed longer winning runs to establish more confidence. Brentford were the other disappointed play-off team considering they did not lose any of their last eight and even drew at Swansea in the semi-final.

Nottingham Forest recovered from an erratic opening few matches to finish just outside the play-offs and Doncaster Rovers finished strongly with four wins. Bristol City looking flat and out of it before Christmas, pulled themselves together admirably but Oldham Athletic failing to win any of their last seven spoiled much of what had happened earlier.

Easy to see that 19 drawn games said much of the problem with Bradford City, Scunthorpe United never again measured up to second place early in September while Port Vale were unable to achieve more than two wins in a row.

Gillingham's six wins in a row from mid-March dispelled any further fears, Yeovil Town ninth in mid-October was their highest and Chesterfield's 15 unbeaten games in mid-season included 11 draws with eight successively! Bournemouth similarly lost only one of the last ten but seven of these ending in stalemate.

Almost any of the last ten finishing clubs were at one stage or another menaced by relegation. Tranmere Rovers 21 games without scoring, several successive groups of matches among them emphasised their trouble, Blackpool were concerned with their lowly position at the turn of the year as indeed were Rotherham United. In fact the final points total covering these involved clubs was just nine.

The unlucky quartet were Hartlepool United, Milton Keynes Dons, Swindon Town and Walsall. Hartlepool had scoring problems and won only one of the last eleven, the Dons did not win any of their first ten and Swindon were only once out of the bottom four after December with eight consecutive defeats to October, but Walsall fell dramatically recording only two wins from January onwards and used 46 different players.

League Two champions Carlisle United made it a rewarding two years having won their Football League place back the previous season. They lost only one game from February and judged their season exactly right. Northampton Town and Leyton Orient joined them automatically, the last games of the season settling it all in an exciting finale. Northampton also came through at the end with seven wins and two draws in the last nine. Orient lost only one of the last 16.

Cheltenham Town were the successful club from the play-offs, beating off the challenges of Wycombe Wanderers and finally Grimsby Town. Their most uncomfortable period had been around October with four defeats in five games. In contrast Wycombe had been off to a flier 21 games unbeaten, though with too many drawn affairs but crucially seven defeats in eight in the run up, six of them in a row.

Grimsby having beaten Lincoln in the semi-final were even top in early February, their opponents needing a second half of the term to improve prospects of their own.

Darlington missed out: just five wins from the last 16 proving decisive. Peterborough United had only two victories in the last ten and Shrewsbury Town had been as low as 21st before the turn of the year.

Ninth in late October with ten unbeaten games, Boston United needed this to launch a challenge but it was not to be, Bristol Rovers had to be content with second half of the season improvement and Wrexham could only reflect on sixth position on Boxing Day and what might have happened subsequently.

Rochdale second in mid-October gradually slipped away, Chester City still sixth in December did not score in 14 of their last 24 and Mansfield Town one win the first 12 immediately put themselves under pressure.

A 6-0 win over Stockport County in December was a tonic for Macclesfield Town and hoisted their highest League win, Barnet were never out of danger until unbeaten in the last five while Bury, utilising 40 players, had one defeat in the last ten to survive. Torquay United reacted smartly when it was necessary, winning four and drawing one of the last five, Notts County had enough points not to over worry about one win in the last 16 and Stockport, two victories in the first 24 had continual concerns.

However it was Oxford United and Rushden & Diamonds who were relegated to the Conference. Oddly enough Oxford had replaced Accrington Stanley in 1961 but found the Lancashire team repaying the compliment. Rushden newer to the League since 2001–02 scored only 14 goals in the last 16, whereas Oxford's damage was done when they were unable to win any of ten from the start of the New Year. Hereford United at the third attempt won back their old Football League place.

Watford's Jay DeMerit (centre) scores the opening goal against Leeds United in the Coca-Cola Championship Play-off final at the Millennium Stadium, Cardiff. (Barry Coombs/Empics)

THE FA CHARITY SHIELD WINNERS 1908–2005

1908	Manchester U v QPR	4-0 after 1-1 draw
1909	Newcastle U v Northampton T	2-0
1910	Brighton v Aston Villa	1-0
1911	Manchester U v Swindon T	8-4
1912	Blackburn R v QPR	2-1
1913	Professionals v Amateurs	7-2
1920	WBA v Tottenham H	2-0
1921	Tottenham H v Burnley	2-0
1922	Huddersfield T v Liverpool	1-0
1923	Professionals v Amateurs	2-0
1924	Professionals v Amateurs	3-1
1925	Amateurs v Professionals	6-1
1926	Amateurs v Professionals	6-3
1927	Cardiff C v Corinthians	2-1
1928	Everton v Blackburn R	2-1
1929	Professionals v Amateurs	3-0
1930	Arsenal v Sheffield W	2-1
1931	Arsenal v WBA	1-0
1932	Everton v Newcastle U	5-3
1933	Arsenal v Everton	3-0
1934	Arsenal v Manchester C	4-0
1935	Sheffield W v Arsenal	1-0
1936	Sunderland v Arsenal	2-1
1937	Manchester C v Sunderland	2-0
1938	Arsenal v Preston NE	2-1
1948	Arsenal v Manchester U	4-3
1949	Portsmouth v Wolverhampton W	1-1*
1950	World Cup Team v Canadian Touring Team	4-2
1951	Tottenham H v Newcastle U	2-1
1952	Manchester U v Newcastle U	4-2
1953	Arsenal v Blackpool	3-1
1954	Wolverhampton W v WBA	4-4*
1955	Chelsea v Newcastle U	3-0
1956	Manchester U v Manchester C	1-0
1957	Manchester U v Aston Villa	4-0
1958	Bolton W v Wolverhampton W	4-1
1959	Wolverhampton W v Nottingham F	3-1
1960	Burnley v Wolverhampton W	2-2*
1961	Tottenham H v FA XI	3-2
1962	Tottenham H v Ipswich T	5-1
1963	Everton v Manchester U	4-0
1964	Liverpool v West Ham U	2-2*
1965	Manchester U v Liverpool	2-2*
1966	Liverpool v Everton	1-0
1967	Manchester U v Tottenham H	3-3*
1968	Manchester C v WBA	6-1
1969	Leeds U v Manchester C	2-1
1970	Everton v Chelsea	2-1
1971	Leicester C v Liverpool	1-0
1972	Manchester C v Aston Villa	1-0
1973	Burnley v Manchester C	1-0
1974	Liverpool† v Leeds U	1-1
1975	Derby Co v West Ham U	2-0
1976	Liverpool v Southampton	1-0
1977	Liverpool v Manchester U	0-0*
1978	Nottingham F v Ipswich T	5-0
1979	Liverpool v Arsenal	3-1
1980	Liverpool v West Ham U	1-0
1981	Aston Villa v Tottenham H	2-2*
1982	Liverpool v Tottenham H	1-0
1983	Manchester U v Liverpool	2-0
1984	Everton v Liverpool	1-0
1985	Everton v Manchester U	2-0
1986	Everton v Liverpool	1-1*
1987	Everton v Coventry C	1-0
1988	Liverpool v Wimbledon	2-1
1989	Liverpool v Arsenal	1-0
1990	Liverpool v Manchester U	1-1*
1991	Arsenal v Tottenham H	0-0*
1992	Leeds U v Liverpool	4-3
1993	Manchester U† v Arsenal	1-1
1994	Manchester U v Blackburn R	2-0
1995	Everton v Blackburn R	1-0
1996	Manchester U v Newcastle U	4-0
1997	Manchester U† v Chelsea	1-1
1998	Arsenal v Manchester U	3-0
1999	Arsenal v Manchester U	2-1
2000	Chelsea v Manchester U	2-0
2001	Liverpool v Manchester U	2-1
2002	Arsenal v Liverpool	1-0
2003	Manchester U† v Arsenal	1-1
2004	Arsenal v Manchester U	3-1
2005	Chelsea v Arsenal	2-1

* *Each club retained shield for six months.* † *Won on penalties.*

THE FA COMMUNITY SHIELD 2005

Chelsea (1) 2, Arsenal (0) 1

At Millennium Stadium, 7 August 2005, attendance 58,014

Chelsea: Cech; Paulo Ferreira, Del Horno, Makelele, Terry, Gallas, Duff (Cole J), Lampard (Geremi), Drogba (Crespo), Gudjohnsen (Tiago), Robben (Wright-Phillips).

Scorers: Drogba 8, 57.

Arsenal: Lehmann; Lauren (Hoyte), Cole, Flamini (Hleb), Toure, Senderos (Cygan), Ljungberg (Reyes), Fabregas, Henry, Bergkamp (Van Persie), Pires (Silva).

Scorer: Fabregas 65.

Referee: H. Webb (Yorkshire).

ACCRINGTON STANLEY FL Championship 2

FOUNDATION

Accrington Football Club founder members of the Football League in 1888, were not connected with Accrington Stanley. In fact both clubs ran concurrently between 1891 when Stanley were formed and 1895 when Accington FC folded. Actually Stanley Villa was the original name, those responsible for forming the club living in Stanley Street and using the Stanley Arms as their meeting place. They became Accrington Stanley in 1893. In 1894–95 they joined the Accrington & District League, playing at Moorhead Park. Subsequently in the North-East Lancashire Combination and the Lancashire Combination before becoming founder members of the Third Division (North) in 1921, two years after moving to Peel Park. In 1962 they resigned from the Football League, were wound-up, reformed 1963, disbanded in 1966 only to restart as Accrington Stanley (1968), returning to the Lancashire Combination in 1970.

The Fraser Eagle Stadium, Livingstone Road, Accrington, Lancashire BB5, 5BX.

Telephone: (01254) 356 950.

Ticket Office: (01254) 356 904.

Fax: (01254) 356 951.

Website: www.accringtonstanley.co.uk.

Email: information@accringtonstanley.co.uk.

Ground Capacity: 5057 (1200 seats).

Record Attendance: 4368 v Colchester U, FA Cup 1st rd, 3 January 2004.

Pitch Measurements: 111yds × 72yds

Chairman: Eric Whalley.

Vice-Chairman: Frank Martindale.

Chief Executive: Robert Heys.

Secretary: Hannah Bailey.

Manager: John Coleman

Assistant Manager: Jimmy Bell.

Physio: Ian Liversedge.

Club Nickname: 'Reds'.

Colours: Red shirts, white shorts, red stockings.

Change Colours: All royal blue.

Year Formed: 1891, re-formed 1968.

Turned Professional: 1919.

HONOURS

Football League: Division 3 (N) – Runners-up 1954–55, 1957–58.

Conference: Champions 2005–06.

Northern Premier League: Champions 2002–03.

Northern League: Divison 1 – Champions 1999–2000.

North West Counties: Runners-up 1986–87.

Cheshire County League: Division 2 – Champions 1980–81; Runners-up 1979–80.

Lancashire Combination: Champions 1973–74, 1977–78; Runners-up 1971–72, 1975–76.

Lancashire Combination Cup: Winners 1971–72, 1972–73, 1973–74, 1976–77.

SKY SPORTS FACT FILE

In the two-legged FA Cup series of 1945–46, Accrington Stanley achieved the feat of holding Manchester United to a 2–2 draw at Peel Park, with Maurice Conroy and Walter Keeley their marksmen, watched by a crowd of 9968. United won the second leg 5–1.

Previous Grounds: 1891, Moorhead Park; 1897, Bell's Ground; 1919, Peel Park; 1970, Crown Inn.

First Football League Game: 27 August 1921, Division 3 (N), v Rochdale (a) L 3-6 – Tattersall; Newton, Baines, Crawshaw, Popplewell, Burkinshaw, Oxley, Makin, Green (1), Hosker (2), Hartles.

Record League Victory: 8-0 v New Brighton, Division 3 (N), 17 March 1934 – Maidment; Armstrong (pen), Price, Dodds, Crawshaw, McCulloch, Wyper, Lennox (2), Cheetham (4), Leedham (1), Watson.

Record Cup Victory: 7-0 v Spennymoor U, FA Cup 2nd rd, 8 December 1938 – Tootill; Armstrong, Whittaker, Latham, Curran, Lee, Parry (2), Chadwick, Jepson (3), McLoughlin (2), Barclay.

Record Defeat: 9-1 v Lincoln C, Division 3 (N), 3 March 1951.

Most League Points (2 for a win): 61, Division 3 (N), 1954–55.

Most League Goals: 96, Division 3 (N) 1954–55.

Highest League Scorer in Season: George Stewart, 35, 1955–56 Division 3 (N); George Hudson, 35, 1960–61, Division 4.

Most Leage Goals in Total Aggregate: George Stewart, 136, 1954–58.

Most League Goals in One Match: 5, Billy Harker v Gateshead, Division 3 (N), 16 November 1935; George Stewart v Gateshead, Division 3 (N), 27 November 1954.

Most Capped Player: none.

Most League Appearances: Jim Armstrong, 260, 1927–34.

Record Transfer Fee Received: £60,000 from Doncaster R for Gary Williams, January 2000.

Record Transfer Fee Paid: £25,000 to Doncaster R for Gary Williams, September 2000.

Football League Record: Original members of Division 3 (N) 1921–58; Division 3 1958–60; Divison 4 1960–62; FL 2 2006–.

MANAGERS

William Cronshaw c.1894
John Haworth 1897–1910
Johnson Haworth c.1916
Sam Pilkingson 1919–24
(Tommy Booth p-m 1923–24)
Ernie Blackburn 1924–32
Amos Wade 1932–35
John Hacking 1935–49
Jimmy Porter 1949–51
Walter Crook 1951–53
Walter Galbraith 1953–58
George Eastham snr 1958–59
Harold Bodle 1959–60
James Harrower 1960–61
Harold Mather 1962–63
Jimmy Hinksman 1963–64
Terry Neville 1964–65
Ian Bryson 1965
Danny Parker 1965–66

LATEST SEQUENCES

Longest Sequence of League Wins: 7, 27.12.1954 – 5.2.1955.

Longest Sequence of League Defeats: 9, 8.3.1030 – 21.4.1930.

Longest Sequence of League Draws: 4, 10.9.1927 – 27.9.1927.

Longest Sequence of Unbeaten League Matches: 11, 27.11.1954 – 5.2.1955.

TEN YEAR LEAGUE RECORD

		P	W	D	L	F	A	Pts	Pos
1996-97	U Pr	44	18	12	14	77	70	66	11
1997-98	U Pr	42	8	14	20	49	68	38	20
1998-99	U Pr	42	9	9	24	47	77	36	22
1999-2000	U D I	42	25	9	8	96	43	84	1
2000-01	U Pr	44	18	10	16	72	67	64	9
2001-02	U Pr	44	21	9	14	89	64	72	6
2002-03	U Pr	44	30	10	4	97	44	100	1
2003-04	Conf	42	15	13	14	68	61	58	10
2004-05	Conf	42	18	11	13	72	58	65	10
2005-06	Conf	42	28	7	7	76	45	91	1

DID YOU KNOW ?

Re-formed Accrington Stanley managed a notable FA Cup scalp on 14 November 1992 when they defeated former League opponents Gateshead in a first round tie, with Paul Beck scoring all three goals in the 3–2 success in front of an attendance of 2270.

ARSENAL FA Premiership

FOUNDATION

Formed by workers at the Royal Arsenal, Woolwich in 1886, they began as Dial Square (name of one of the workshops), and included two former Nottingham Forest players, Fred Beardsley and Morris Bates. Beardsley wrote to his old club seeking help and they provided the new club with a full set of red jerseys and a ball. The club became known as the 'Woolwich Reds' although their official title soon after formation was Woolwich Arsenal.

Emirates Stadium, Drayton Park, London N5.

Telephone: (020) 7704 4000.

Fax: (020) 7704 4001.

Ticket Office: (020) 7704 4040.

Website: www.arsenal.com

Email: info@arsenal.co.uk

Ground Capacity: 60,000.

Record Attendance: 73,295 v Sunderland, Div 1, 9 March 1935.

At Wembley: 73,707 v RC Lens, UEFA Champions League, 25 November 1998.

Pitch Measurements: 113m × 76m.

Chairman: Peter Hill-Wood.

Vice-chairman: David Dein.

Managing Director: Keith Edelman.

Secretary: David Miles.

Manager: Arsène Wenger.

Assistant Manager: Pat Rice.

Physio: Gary Lewin.

Colours: Red shirts with white sleeves, white shorts, white stockings.

Change Colours: Yellow shirts, black shorts, black stockings.

Year Formed: 1886.

Turned Professional: 1891.

Ltd Co: 1893.

Previous Names: 1886, Dial Square; 1886, Royal Arsenal; 1891, Woolwich Arsenal; 1914 Arsenal.

Club Nickname: 'Gunners'.

Previous Grounds: 1886, Plumstead Common; 1887, Sportsman Ground; 1888, Manor Ground; 1890, Invicta Ground; 1893, Manor Ground; 1913, Highbury.

HONOURS

FA Premier League: Champions 1997–98, 2001–02, 2003–04. Runners-up 1998–99, 1999–2000, 2000–01, 2002–03, 2004–05.

Football League: Division 1 – Champions 1930–31, 1932–33, 1933–34, 1934–35, 1937–38, 1947–48, 1952–53, 1970–71, 1988–89, 1990–91; Runners-up 1925–26, 1931–32, 1972–73; Division 2 – Runners-up 1903–04.

FA Cup: Winners 1930, 1936, 1950, 1971, 1979, 1993, 1998, 2002, 2003, 2005; Runners-up 1927, 1932, 1952, 1972, 1978, 1980, 2001.

Double performed: 1970–71, 1997–98, 2001–02.

Football League Cup: Winners 1987, 1993; Runners-up 1968, 1969, 1988.

European Competitions: *Fairs Cup:* 1963–64, 1969–70 (winners), 1970–71. *European Cup:* 1971–72, 1991–92. *UEFA Champions League:* 1998–99, 1999–2000, 2000–01, 2001–02, 2002–03, 2003–04, 2004–05, 2005–06 (runners-up). *UEFA Cup:* 1978–79, 1981–82, 1982–83, 1996–97, 1997–98, 1999–2000 (runners-up). *European Cup-Winners' Cup:* 1979–80 (runners-up), 1993–94 (winners), 1994–95 (runners-up).

SKY SPORTS FACT FILE

On 18 October 2005 in a Champions League match against Sparta Prague, Thierry Henry equalled then overtook Ian Wright's 185 League and Cup goals for Arsenal. On 1 February 2006 he beat Cliff Bastin's 150 League goals against West Ham United. It was the club's 2000th match at Highbury.

First Football League Game: 2 September 1893, Division 2, v Newcastle U (h) D 2–2 – Williams; Powell, Jeffrey; Devine, Buist, Howat; Gemmell, Henderson, Shaw (1), Elliott (1), Booth.

Record League Victory: 12–0 v Loughborough T, Division 2, 12 March 1900 – Orr; McNichol, Jackson; Moir, Dick (2), Anderson (1); Hunt, Cottrell (2), Main (2), Gaudie (3), Tennant (2).

Record Cup Victory: 11–1 v Darwen, FA Cup 3rd rd, 9 January 1932 – Moss; Parker, Hapgood; Jones, Roberts, John; Hulme (2), Jack (3), Lambert (2), James, Bastin (4).

Record Defeat: 0–8 v Loughborough T, Division 2, 12 December 1896.

Most League Points (2 for a win): 66, Division 1, 1930–31.

Most League Points (3 for a win): 90, Premier League 2003–04.

Most League Goals: 127, Division 1, 1930–31.

Highest League Scorer in Season: Ted Drake, 42, 1934–35.

Most League Goals in Total Aggregate: Thierry Henry, 164, 1999–.

Most League Goals in One Match: 7, Ted Drake v Aston Villa, Division 1, 14 December 1935.

Most Capped Player: Patrick Vieira, 79 (94), France.

Most League Appearances: David O'Leary, 558, 1975–93.

Youngest League Player: Gerry Ward, 16 years 321 days v Huddersfield T, 22 August 1953 (Jermaine Pennant, 16 years 319 days v Middlesbrough, League Cup, 30 November 1999).

Record Transfer Fee Received: A reported £22,900,000 from Real Madrid for Nicolas Anelka, August 1999.

Record Transfer Fee Paid: A reported £11,000,000 to Bordeaux for Sylvain Wiltord, August 2000.

Football League Record: 1893 Elected to Division 2; 1904–13 Division 1; 1913–19 Division 2; 1919–92 Division 1; 1992– FA Premier League.

MANAGERS

Sam Hollis 1894–97
Tom Mitchell 1897–98
George Elcoat 1898–99
Harry Bradshaw 1899–1904
Phil Kelso 1904–08
George Morrell 1908–15
Leslie Knighton 1919–25
Herbert Chapman 1925–34
George Allison 1934–47
Tom Whittaker 1947–56
Jack Crayston 1956–58
George Swindin 1958–62
Billy Wright 1962–66
Bertie Mee 1966–76
Terry Neill 1976–83
Don Howe 1984–86
George Graham 1986–95
Bruce Rioch 1995–96
Arsène Wenger September 1996–

LATEST SEQUENCES

Longest Sequence of League Wins: 14, 10.2.2002 – 18.8.2002.

Longest Sequence of League Defeats: 7, 12.2.1977 – 12.3.1977.

Longest Sequence of League Draws: 6, 4.3.1961 – 1.4.1961.

Longest Sequence of Unbeaten League Matches: 49, 7.5.2003 – 24.10.2004.

Longest Sequence Without a League Win: 23, 28.9.1912 – 1.3.1913.

Successive Scoring Runs: 55 from 19.5.2001.

Successive Non-scoring Runs: 6 from 25.2.1987.

TEN YEAR LEAGUE RECORD

		P	W	D	L	F	A	Pts	Pos
1996-97	PR Lge	38	19	11	8	62	32	68	3
1997-98	PR Lge	38	23	9	6	68	33	78	1
1998-99	PR Lge	38	22	12	4	59	17	78	2
1999-2000	PR Lge	38	22	7	9	73	43	73	2
2000-01	PR Lge	38	20	10	8	63	38	70	2
2001-02	PR Lge	38	26	9	3	79	36	87	1
2002-03	PR Lge	38	23	9	6	85	42	78	2
2003-04	PR Lge	38	26	12	0	73	26	90	1
2004-05	PR Lge	38	25	8	5	87	36	83	2
2005-06	PR Lge	38	20	7	11	68	31	67	4

DID YOU KNOW ?

On 22 October 2005 Arsenal manager Arsène Wenger was able to celebrate his 56th birthday with a 1–0 win over Manchester City, the goal being the 500th achieved by the club at Highbury in the FA Premier League since 1992–93.

ARSENAL 2005–06 LEAGUE RECORD

Match No.	*Date*	*Venue*	*Opponents*	*Result*		*H/T Score*	*Lg. Pos.*	*Goalscorers*	*Attendance*
1	Aug 14	H	Newcastle U	W	2-0	0-0	—	Henry (pen) [81], Van Persie [87]	38,072
2	21	A	Chelsea	L	0-1	0-0	9		42,136
3	24	H	Fulham	W	4-1	1-1	—	Cygan 2 [32, 90], Henry 2 [53, 82]	37,867
4	Sept 10	A	Middlesbrough	L	1-2	0-1	8	Reyes [90]	28,075
5	19	H	Everton	W	2-0	2-0	—	Campbell 2 [11, 30]	38,121
6	24	A	West Ham U	D	0-0	0-0	7		34,742
7	Oct 2	H	Birmingham C	W	1-0	0-0	7	Clemence (og) [81]	37,891
8	15	A	WBA	L	1-2	1-1	8	Senderos [17]	26,604
9	22	H	Manchester C	W	1-0	0-0	8	Pires (pen) [61]	38,189
10	29	A	Tottenham H	D	1-1	0-1	7	Pires [77]	36,154
11	Nov 5	H	Sunderland	W	3-1	2-0	4	Van Persie [12], Henry 2 [36, 82]	38,210
12	19	A	Wigan Ath	W	3-2	3-2	4	Van Persie [11], Henry 2 [21, 41]	25,004
13	26	H	Blackburn R	W	3-0	2-0	3	Fabregas [4], Henry [45], Van Persie [90]	38,192
14	Dec 3	A	Bolton W	L	0-2	0-2	5		26,792
15	10	A	Newcastle U	L	0-1	0-0	6		52,297
16	18	H	Chelsea	L	0-2	0-1	8		38,347
17	26	A	Charlton Ath	W	1-0	0-0	7	Reyes [58]	27,111
18	28	H	Portsmouth	W	4-0	4-0	6	Bergkamp [7], Reyes [13], Henry 2 (1 pen) [37, 43 (p)]	38,223
19	31	A	Aston Villa	D	0-0	0-0	6		37,114
20	Jan 3	H	Manchester U	D	0-0	0-0	—		38,313
21	14	H	Middlesbrough	W	7-0	4-0	5	Henry 3 [20, 30, 68], Senderos [22], Pires [45], Silva [59], Hleb [84]	38,186
22	21	A	Everton	L	0-1	0-1	5		36,920
23	Feb 1	H	West Ham U	L	2-3	1-2	—	Henry [45], Pires [89]	38,216
24	4	A	Birmingham C	W	2-0	1-0	5	Adebayor [21], Henry [63]	27,075
25	11	H	Bolton W	D	1-1	0-1	5	Silva [90]	38,193
26	14	A	Liverpool	L	0-1	0-0	—		44,065
27	25	A	Blackburn R	L	0-1	0-1	7		22,504
28	Mar 4	A	Fulham	W	4-0	2-0	5	Henry 2 [31, 77], Adebayor [35], Fabregas [86]	22,397
29	12	H	Liverpool	W	2-1	1-0	5	Henry 2 [21, 83]	38,221
30	18	H	Charlton Ath	W	3-0	2-0	5	Pires [13], Adebayor [32], Hleb [49]	38,223
31	Apr 1	H	Aston Villa	W	5-0	2-0	5	Adebayor [19], Henry 2 [25, 46], Van Persie [71], Diaby [80]	38,183
32	9	A	Manchester U	L	0-2	0-0	6		70,908
33	12	A	Portsmouth	D	1-1	1-0	—	Henry [36]	20,230
34	15	H	WBA	W	3-1	1-0	5	Hleb [44], Pires [76], Bergkamp [89]	38,167
35	22	H	Tottenham H	D	1-1	0-0	5	Henry [84]	38,326
36	May 1	A	Sunderland	W	3-0	3-0	—	Collins D (og) [29], Fabregas [40], Henry [43]	44,003
37	4	A	Manchester C	W	3-1	1-1	—	Ljungberg [30], Reyes 2 [78, 84]	41,875
38	7	H	Wigan Ath	W	4-2	2-2	4	Pires [8], Henry 3 (1 pen) [35, 56, 76 (p)]	38,389

Final League Position: 4

GOALSCORERS

League (68): Henry 27 (3 pens), Pires 7 (1 pen), Reyes 5, Van Persie 5, Adebayor 4, Fabregas 3, Hleb 3, Bergkamp 2, Campbell 2, Cygan 2, Senderos 2, Silva 2, Diaby 1, Ljungberg 1, own goals 2.
Carling Cup (10): Van Persie 4 (1 pen), Eboue 1, Henry 1, Lupoli 1, Owusu-Abeyie 1, Reyes 1, Silva 1.
FA Cup (2): Pires 2.
Champions League (15): Henry 5, Pires 2 (2 pens), Van Persie 2, Bergkamp 1, Campbell 1, Fabregas 1, Ljungberg 1, Silva 1, Toure 1.
Community Shield (1): Fabregas 1.

Lehmann J 38	Lauren E 22	Cole A 9+2	Silva G 33	Toure K 33	Senderos P 19+1	Ljungberg F 21+4	Fabregas F 30+5	Henry T 30+2	Bergkamp D 8+16	Pires R 23+10	Hleb A 17+8	Van Persie R 13+11	Flamini M 19+12	Cygan P 11+1	Clichy G 5+2	Reyes J 22+4	Campbell S 20	Song Billong A 3+2	Owusu-Abeyie Q —+4	Eboue E 11+7	Djourou J 6+1	Gilbert K 2	Diaby V 9+3	Larsson S 2+1	Adebayor E 12+1	Lupoli A —+1	*Match No.*
1	2	3	4	5	6	7	8^{1}	9	10^{2}	11^{3}	12	13	14														1
1	2	3	4	5	6	7^{1}	8^{2}	9		11	10	12	13														2
1	2	3	4	5			8	9	10		7^{2}		12	6	13	11^{1}											3
1	2	3	4	5			12		10	11^{2}	7	13	8^{1}	6		9											4
1	2	3	4	5		7	8		12	11^{2}	13	10^{1}				9^{3}	6	14									5
1	2	3	4^{1}	5		7	8				11	10^{2}	12		13	9^{3}	6		14								6
1	2	3	4	5		10^{2}	8		12	11^{3}	7^{1}	14	13			9	6										7
1	2			5	6	7^{2}	8		10	11			4^{1}		3	9			12	13							8
1	2		4	5			8	9	10	11			7	6	3												9
1	2		4	5		7^{2}	8		10	12		13	11^{1}	14	3	9^{3}	6										10
1	2		4	5			8	9	12	11		10^{1}			3	7^{2}	6			13							11
1	2		4	5	12	7^{1}	8	9	13	11^{3}		10^{2}	14	3			6										12
1	2		4	5		12	8	9	10^{2}	11^{3}		13	14	3		7^{1}	6										13
1	2^{3}		4	5		7	8^{2}	9	12	11		10^{1}		3		13	6			14							14
1	2		4▮	3	6	7	8^{1}	9		12	11^{2}	10^{3}	13				5		14								15
1	3			2	6	7^{1}	8	9	12	13	11^{2}	10^{3}	4				5		14								16
1	2		4	5		7	8	10		12	11^{1}		13	3		9^{2}	6										17
1	2		4^{1}	5			12	9	10	11			8	3		7^{2}	6			13							18
1	2			5		7^{2}	8	10	12	13	11^{3}	9^{1}	4	3		14	6										19
1	2		4	5			8^{2}	10	12	11	7^{1}		13	3		9^{3}	6			14							20
1	2	12	4^{2}		6	7	8	10		11^{3}	13		14	3^{1}		9					5						21
1	3		4		6	7	8▮	10		11^{2}	12					9	5					2^{1}	13				22
1			4		3	7		10	12	11		9	13				6^{3}				5	2^{2}	8^{1}	14			23
1			4		6		7	10			12		2			11^{1}					5		8	3	9		24
1			4		6	12	8	10	13	14			2			11^{3}					5		7^{1}	3^{2}	9		25
1			4	5	6	7	8	10		11^{1}	12		3							2					9		26
1			4^{3}	5	6		7	10		13	12		3			11^{2}				2			8^{1}		9	14	27
1			4	5	6	7	12	10^{3}	13		11^{1}		3			14				2			8		9^{2}		28
1			4	5	6	7^{2}	8	10	12	13	11		3							2					9^{1}		29
1			4	5	6		8^{3}	10	12	11	7^{2}	13	3					14		2					9^{1}		30
1			4	5	6		8^{3}	10^{1}		11		12	3			7				2^{2}	13		14		9		31
1			4	5	6	12	8^{3}	13		11	7^{1}	10^{2}	3							2			14		9		32
1				5		11		10			12	13	3			7^{1}	6^{3}	4		14	2		8		9^{2}		33
1			4	5	6			10^{3}	12	13	11^{2}	9^{1}	3			7				2			8		14		34
1			4	5	6^{3}		12	13		11		10^{2}	3			7				14	2		8^{1}		9		35
1		13		5			8	10^{1}	12	11^{2}		14			3		6	4		2			7		9^{3}		36
1		3	4	5		7	12	10		13	11^{2}	9^{3}				14	6	8^{1}		2							37
1		3	4	5		12	8	10	13	11^{1}	7^{2}	14				9^{3}	6			2							38

FA Cup

Third Round	Cardiff C	(h)	2-1
Fourth Round	Bolton W	(a)	0-1

Carling Cup

Third Round	Sunderland	(a)	3-0
Fourth Round	Reading	(h)	3-0
Quarter-Final	Doncaster R	(a)	2-2
Semi-Final	Wigan Ath	(a)	0-1
		(h)	2-1

Champions League

Group B	Thun	(h)	2-1
	Ajax	(a)	2-1
	Sparta Prague	(a)	2-0
		(h)	3-0
	Thun	(a)	1-0
	Ajax	(h)	0-0
First Round	Real Madrid	(a)	1-0
		(h)	0-0
Quarter-Final	Juventus	(h)	2-0
		(a)	0-0
Semi-Final	Villarreal	(h)	1-0
		(a)	0-0
Final *(in Paris)*	Barcelona		1-2

ASTON VILLA FA Premiership

FOUNDATION

Cricketing enthusiasts of Villa Cross Wesleyan Chapel, Aston, Birmingham decided to form a football club during the winter of 1874–75. Football clubs were few and far between in the Birmingham area and in their first game against Aston Brook St Mary's Rugby team they played one half rugby and the other soccer. In 1876 they were joined by a Scottish soccer enthusiast George Ramsay who was immediately appointed captain and went on to lead Aston Villa from obscurity to one of the country's top clubs in a period of less than 10 years.

Villa Park, Birmingham B6 6HE.

Telephone: (0871) 423 8100

Fax: (0871) 423 8102

Ticket Office/Consumer Sales: (0871) 423 8101

Website: www.avfc.co.uk

Email: postmaster@avfc.co.uk

Ground Capacity: 42,551.

Record Attendance: 76,588 v Derby Co, FA Cup 6th rd, 2 March 1946.

Pitch Measurements: 105m × 68m.

Chairman: H. D. Ellis OBE.

Club Secretary/Operations Director: Steven M. Stride.

Manager: TBC.

Assistant Manager: Roy Aitken.

Physio: Alan Smith.

Sports Science Manager: Dr Stephen McGregor.

Colours: Claret shirt with blue sleeves, side panel of blue chevrons, yellow piping to side. White shorts with claret side panel and blue chevrons. Blue stockings with claret top.

Change Colours: White shirts with claret trim, sky blue shorts with claret trim, white stockings with sky blue turnover.

Year Formed: 1874.

Turned Professional: 1885.

Ltd Co.: 1896.

Public Ltd Company: 1969.

Club Nickname: 'The Villans'.

Previous Grounds: 1874 Wilson Road and Aston Park (also used Aston Lower Grounds for some matches); 1876 Wellington Road, Perry Barr; 1897 Villa Park.

HONOURS

FA Premier League: Runners-up 1992–93.

Football League: Division 1 – Champions 1893–94, 1895–96, 1896–97, 1898–99, 1899–1900, 1909–10, 1980–81; Runners-up 1888–89, 1902–03, 1907–08, 1910–11, 1912–13, 1913–14, 1930–31, 1932–33, 1989–90; Division 2 – Champions 1937–38, 1959–60; Runners-up 1974–75, 1987–88; Division 3 – Champions 1971–72.

FA Cup: Winners 1887, 1895, 1897, 1905, 1913, 1920, 1957; Runners-up 1892, 1924, 2000.

Double Performed: 1896–97.

Football League Cup: Winners 1961, 1975, 1977, 1994, 1996; Runners-up 1963, 1971.

European Competitions: *European Cup:* 1981–82 (winners), 1982–83. *UEFA Cup:* 1975–76, 1977–78, 1983–84, 1990–91, 1993–94, 1994–95, 1996–97, 1997–98, 1998–99, 2001–02. *World Club Championship:* 1982. *European Super Cup:* 1982–83 (winners). *Intertoto Cup:* 2000, 2001 (winners), 2002.

SKY SPORTS FACT FILE

On 20 September 2005 in a Carling Cup second round tie at Wycombe Wanderers, Aston Villa found themselves trailing 3–1 at the interval. But they eventually won 8–3 which included scoring six times in the last 26 minutes.

First Football League Game: 8 September 1888, Football League, v Wolverhampton W (a) D 1–1 – Warner; Cox, Coulton; Yates, H. Devey, Dawson; A. Brown, Green (1), Allen, Garvey, Hodgetts.

Record League Victory: 12–2 v Accrington S, Division 1, 12 March 1892 – Warner; Evans, Cox; Harry Devey, Jimmy Cowan, Baird; Athersmith (1), Dickson (2), John Devey (4), L. Campbell (4), Hodgetts (1).

Record Cup Victory: 13–0 v Wednesbury Old Ath, FA Cup 1st rd, 30 October 1886 – Warner; Coulton, Simmonds; Yates, Robertson, Burton (2); R. Davis (1), A. Brown (3), Hunter (3), Loach (2), Hodgetts (2).

Record Defeat: 1–8 v Blackburn R, FA Cup 3rd rd, 16 February 1889.

Most League Points (2 for a win): 70, Division 3, 1971–72.

Most League Points (3 for a win): 78, Division 2, 1987–88.

Most League Goals: 128, Division 1, 1930–31.

Highest League Scorer in Season: 'Pongo' Waring, 49, Division 1, 1930–31.

Most League Goals in Total Aggregate: Harry Hampton, 215, 1904–15.

Most League Goals in One Match: 5, Harry Hampton v Sheffield W, Division 1, 5 October 1912; 5, Harold Halse v Derby Co, Division 1, 19 October 1912; 5, Len Capewell v Burnley, Division 1, 29 August 1925; 5, George Brown v Leicester C, Division 1, 2 January 1932; 5, Gerry Hitchens v Charlton Ath, Division 2, 18 November 1959.

Most Capped Player: Steve Staunton 64 (102), Republic of Ireland.

Most League Appearances: Charlie Aitken, 561, 1961–76.

Youngest League Player: Jimmy Brown, 15 years 349 days v Bolton W, 17 September 1969.

Record Transfer Fee Received: £12,600,000 from Manchester U for Dwight Yorke, August 1998.

Record Transfer Fee Paid: £9,500,000 to River Plate for Juan Pablo Angel, January 2001.

Football League Record: 1888 Founder Member of the League; 1936–38 Division 2; 1938–59 Division 1; 1959–60 Division 2; 1960–67 Division 1; 1967–70 Division 2; 1970–72 Division 3; 1972–75 Division 2; 1975–87 Division 1; 1987–88 Division 2; 1988–92 Division 1; 1992– FA Premier League.

MANAGERS

George Ramsay 1884–1926
(Secretary-Manager)
W. J. Smith 1926–34
(Secretary-Manager)
Jimmy McMullan 1934–35
Jimmy Hogan 1936–44
Alex Massie 1945–50
George Martin 1950–53
Eric Houghton 1953–58
Joe Mercer 1958–64
Dick Taylor 1964–67
Tommy Cummings 1967–68
Tommy Docherty 1968–70
Vic Crowe 1970–74
Ron Saunders 1974–82
Tony Barton 1982–84
Graham Turner 1984–86
Billy McNeill 1986–87
Graham Taylor 1987–90
Dr Jozef Venglos 1990–91
Ron Atkinson 1991–94
Brian Little 1994–98
John Gregory 1998–2002
Graham Taylor OBE 2002–03
David O'Leary 2003–2006

LATEST SEQUENCES

Longest Sequence of League Wins: 9, 15.10.1910 – 10.12.1910.

Longest Sequence of League Defeats: 11, 23.3.1963 – 4.5.1963.

Longest Sequence of League Draws: 6, 12.9.1981 – 10.10.1981.

Longest Sequence of Unbeaten League Matches: 15, 12.3.1949 – 27.8.1949.

Longest Sequence Without a League Win: 12, 27.12.1986 – 25.3.1987.

Successive Scoring Runs: 35 from 10.11.1895.

Successive Non-scoring Runs: 5 from 29.2.1992.

TEN YEAR LEAGUE RECORD

		P	*W*	*D*	*L*	*F*	*A*	*Pts*	*Pos*
1996-97	PR Lge	38	17	10	11	47	34	61	5
1997-98	PR Lge	38	17	6	15	49	48	57	7
1998-99	PR Lge	38	15	10	13	51	46	55	6
1999-2000	PR Lge	38	15	13	10	46	35	58	6
2000-01	PR Lge	38	13	15	10	46	43	54	8
2001-02	PR Lge	38	12	14	12	46	47	50	8
2002-03	PR Lge	38	12	9	17	42	47	45	16
2003-04	PR Lge	38	15	11	12	48	44	56	6
2004-05	PR Lge	38	12	11	15	45	52	47	10
2005-06	PR Lge	38	10	12	16	42	55	42	16

DID YOU KNOW ?

In 1949–50 Aston Villa did not strictly keep up with the Joneses but did better with those named Smith. Norman and Edward were directors, Billy secretary, plus two professionals Leslie and Herbert, as well as two amateurs Anthony and Jeffrey.

ASTON VILLA 2005–06 LEAGUE RECORD

Match No.	Date	Venue	Opponents	Result	H/T Score	Lg. Pos.	Goalscorers	Attendance
1	Aug 13	H	Bolton W	D 2-2	2-2	—	Phillips 4, Davis 9	32,263
2	20	A	Manchester U	L 0-1	0-0	12		67,934
3	23	A	Portsmouth	D 1-1	1-1	—	Hughes (og) 11	19,778
4	27	H	Blackburn R	W 1-0	1-0	8	Baros 11	31,010
5	Sept 12	A	West Ham U	L 0-4	0-2	—		29,582
6	17	H	Tottenham H	D 1-1	1-0	12	Milner 4	33,686
7	24	A	Chelsea	L 1-2	1-1	15	Moore 44	42,146
8	Oct 2	H	Middlesbrough	L 2-3	0-1	16	Moore 50, Davis 90	29,719
9	16	A	Birmingham C	W 1-0	1-0	14	Phillips 19	29,312
10	22	H	Wigan Ath	L 0-2	0-1	15		32,294
11	31	A	Manchester C	L 1-3	0-2	—	Ridgewell 65	42,069
12	Nov 5	H	Liverpool	L 0-2	0-0	17		42,551
13	19	A	Sunderland	W 3-1	0-0	15	Phillips 55, Barry 82, Baros 83	39,707
14	26	H	Charlton Ath	W 1-0	0-0	15	Davis 69	30,023
15	Dec 3	A	Newcastle U	D 1-1	0-1	15	McCann 75	52,267
16	10	A	Bolton W	D 1-1	0-0	14	Angel 88	23,646
17	17	H	Manchester U	L 0-2	0-1	15		37,128
18	26	H	Everton	W 4-0	1-0	14	Baros 2 35, 84, Delaney 48, Angel 82	32,432
19	28	A	Fulham	D 3-3	1-2	13	Moore 29, Ridgewell 2 60, 76	20,446
20	31	H	Arsenal	D 0-0	0-0	13		37,114
21	Jan 2	A	WBA	W 2-1	0-0	12	Davis 47, Baros (pen) 80	27,073
22	14	H	West Ham U	L 1-2	1-0	15	Hendrie 27	36,700
23	21	A	Tottenham H	D 0-0	0-0	15		36,243
24	Feb 1	H	Chelsea	D 1-1	0-1	—	Moore 77	38,562
25	4	A	Middlesbrough	W 4-0	2-0	12	Moore 3 18, 62, 64, Phillips 24	27,299
26	11	H	Newcastle U	L 1-2	1-2	15	Moore 16	37,140
27	25	A	Charlton Ath	D 0-0	0-0	15		26,594
28	Mar 4	H	Portsmouth	W 1-0	1-0	14	Baros 36	30,194
29	11	A	Blackburn R	L 0-2	0-0	14		21,932
30	18	A	Everton	L 1-4	0-3	15	Agbonlahor 64	36,507
31	25	H	Fulham	D 0-0	0-0	16		32,605
32	Apr 1	A	Arsenal	L 0-5	0-2	16		38,183
33	9	H	WBA	D 0-0	0-0	15		33,303
34	16	H	Birmingham C	W 3-1	1-1	15	Baros 2 10, 78, Cahill 56	40,158
35	18	A	Wigan Ath	L 2-3	0-1	—	Angel 53, Ridgewell 67	17,330
36	25	H	Manchester C	L 0-1	0-0	—		26,422
37	29	A	Liverpool	L 1-3	0-1	16	Barry 58	44,479
38	May 7	H	Sunderland	W 2-1	1-0	16	Barry 43, Ridgewell 78	33,820

Final League Position: 16

GOALSCORERS

League (42): Baros 8 (1 pen), Moore 8, Ridgewell 5, Davis 4, Phillips 4, Angel 3, Barry 3, Agbonlahor 1, Cahill 1, Delaney 1, Hendrie 1, McCann 1, Milner 1, own goal 1.
Carling Cup (9): Barry 2 (1 pen), Davis 2, Milner 2, Baros 1, Phillips 1, own goal 1.
FA Cup (6): Baros 3, Davis 2, Barry 1.

Sorensen T 36	Hughes A 35	Samuel J 14 + 5	Davis S 34 + 1	Mellberg O 27	Laursen M 1	Solano N 2 + 1	McCann G 32	Angel J 12 + 19	Phillips K 20 + 3	Barry G 36	Djemba-Djemba E — + 4	Ridgewell L 30 + 2	De la Cruz U 4 + 3	Whittingham P 4	Moore L 16 + 11	Berger P 3 + 5	Baros M 24 + 1	Bouma W 20	Milner J 27	Hendrie L 7 + 9	Bakke E 8 + 6	Taylor S 2	Delaney M 12	Gardner C 3 + 5	Agbonlahor G 3 + 6	Cahill G 6 + 1	*Match No.*
1	2	3	4	5	6	7	8	9	10	11																	1
1	2	3^3	4	5		12	8	9		11	14	6	7^1	10^2	13												2
1	2		4	5		7■	8	9^1	10^2	3		6	13	11	12												3
1	2	3	4	5			8		10	11		6		7^1		12	9										4
1	2		4	5			8^3	12	10^1	11^2		6				13	9	3	7	14							5
1	2	12	4	5				9		11		6				8	10	3^1	7								6
1	2	12	4	5				9		11^3	13	6			10	8^1		3^2	7	14							7
1		12	4	5				9		11		6	2^1		10	8		3^2	7		13						8
1	2		4	5				12	10^1	11^2	14	6			9	13		3	7		8^3						9
1	2	3	4	5				12	10	11		6			9^1	13			7		8^2						10
		3^1	4	5			8		10	11	13	6			9^3	12^2			7		14	1	2				11
1			4	5			8	12	10^1	3		6					9		7	13	11^2		2				12
1	2		4^3	5			8		10^1	11		6			12		9^2	3	7	13	14						13
1	2		4	5			8		10	11		6			12		9^1	3	7								14
1	2		4^2	5			8	10^1		11		6			12		9	3		7	13						15
1	2		12	5			8	13		11		6			14		9^3	3	10^1	7^2	4						16
1	5		4				8	12		11		6					9	3	7^1		10		2				17
1	5		4^3				8	12		11		6			10^1		9	3	7^2		13		2	14			18
1	2		4				8	12		11		6			10^1		9	3^2	7		13		5				19
1	2		4				8	12		3		6			10^1		9		7		11		5				20
	2		4	5			8	12		3					10^2		9		7		11^1	1	6	13			21
1	2	3	4	5			8	12							10^1		9		7	13	11^2		6				22
1	2	13	4	5			8	9		3■					12^2		10^1		7	11			6				23
1	2	3	4	5			8	12	10^2	11					13		9^1		7				6				24
1	2	3^3	4	5^2			8	12	10	11		13			9^1				7	14			6				25
1	2	3		5				12	10^1	11		13		4	9		14			8^3			6	7^2			26
1	2^2	3	4	5			8	9^1	12	11		6			13		10		7								27
1	5	2^1	4				8		10	11		6	12		13		9^2	3	7								28
1	2		4	5			8	12	10^1	11		6			7		9^2	3		13							29
1	2^1	12	4	5			8			11		6			9			3		13				7^2	10		30
1	5		4				8	12	10	11		6	2		9^1			3		7^2					13		31
1	5		4				8	12	10^1	11^2		6	2^3		9			3		7					13	14	32
1	2		4				8		10^1			6			12		9	3		7^2				13	11	5	33
1	2	3	4^2				8	12	10^1	11		6					9		7^3					13	14	5	34
1	2^1	3					8	9		11		6	12				10		7					4^2	13	5	35
1	2	3		5			8	9	12	11		6^1					10^2		7						13	4	36
1	2		4^3	5			8	12	13	11^2							10^1	3	7					14	9	6	37
1	2		4				8	9	10^2	11		6						3	7^1	12					13	5	38

FA Cup

Third Round	Hull C	(a)	1-0
Fourth Round	Port Vale	(h)	3-1
Fifth Round	Manchester C	(h)	1-1
		(a)	1-2

Carling Cup

Second Round	Wycombe W	(a)	8-3
Third Round	Burnley	(h)	1-0
Fourth Round	Doncaster R	(a)	0-3

BARNET FL Championship 2

FOUNDATION

Barnet Football Club was formed in 1888 as an amateur organisation and they played at a ground in Queen's Road until they disbanded in 1901. A club known as Alston Works FC was then formed and they played at Totteridge Lane until changing to Barnet Alston FC in 1906. They moved to their present ground a year later, combining with The Avenue to form Barnet and Alston in 1912. The club progressed to senior amateur football by way of the Athenian and Isthmian Leagues, turning professional in 1965. It was as a Southern League and Conference club that they made their name.

Underhill Stadium, Barnet Lane, Barnet, Herts EN5 2BE.

Telephone: 0870 1700 400.

Fax: 0870 1700 429.

Ticket Office: 0870 1700 444.

Website: www.barnetfc.com

Email: info@barnetfc.com

Ground Capacity: 4,800.

Record Attendance: 11,026 v Wycombe Wanderers, FA Amateur Cup 4th Round 1951–52.

Record Receipts: £31,202 v Portsmouth, FA Cup 3rd Round, 5 January 1991.

Pitch Measurements: 113yd × 72yd.

Chairman: A. A. Kleanthous.

Secretary: Andrew Adie.

Manager: Paul Fairclough.

Physio: Ato Chandler.

Colours: Amber with black trim.

Change Colours: White with red trim.

Year Formed: 1888.

Turned Professional: 1965.

Previous Names: 1906, Barnet Alston FC; 1919 Barnet.

Club Nickname: The Bees.

Previous Grounds: 1888, Queens Road; 1901, Totteridge Lane; 1907 Barnet Lane.

HONOURS

Football League: Division 2 best season: 24th, 1993–94.

FA Amateur Cup: Winners 1946.

FA Trophy: Finalists 1972.

GM Vauxhall Conference: Winners 1990–91. *Conference:* Winners 2004–05

FA Cup: never past 3rd rd.

League Cup: best season: 3rd rd, 2006.

SKY SPORTS FACT FILE

Legendary Barnet centre-forward Ron Phipps played his last game against Kingstonian in the London Senior Cup in 1957–58, scoring the equaliser a few minutes before the end of the game at 4–4 when injuries had reduced his team to only eight players!

First Football League Game: 17 August 1991, Division 4, v Crewe Alex (h) L 4–7 – Phillips; Blackford, Cooper (Murphy), Horton, Bodley (Stein), Johnson, Showler, Carter (2), Bull (2), Lowe, Evans.

Record League Victory: 7–0 v Blackpool, Division 3, 11 November 2000 – Naisbitt; Stockley, Sawyers, Niven (Brown), Heald, Arber (1), Currie (3), Doolan, Richards (2) (McGleish), Cottee (1) (Riza), Toms.

Record Cup Victory: 6–1 v Newport Co, FA Cup 1st rd, 21 November 1970 – McClelland; Lye, Jenkins, Ward, Embery, King, Powell (1), Ferry, Adams (1), Gray, George (3), (1 og).

Record Defeat: 1–9 v Peterborough U, Division 3, 5 September 1998.

Most League Points (3 for a win): 79, Division 3, 1992–93.

Most League Goals: 81, Division 4, 1991–92.

Highest League Scorer in Season: Dougie Freedman, 24, Division 3, 1994–95.

Most League Goals in Total Aggregate: Sean Devine, 47, 1995–99.

Most League Goals in One Match: 4, Dougie Freedman v Rochdale, Division 3, 13 September 1994; 4, Lee Hodges v Rochdale, Division 3, 8 April 1996.

Most Capped Player: Ken Charlery, 4, St. Lucia.

Most League Appearances: Paul Wilson, 263, 1991–2000.

Youngest League Player: Kieran Adams, 17 years 71 days v Mansfield T, 31 December 1994.

Record Transfer Fee Received: £800,000 from Crystal Palace for Dougie Freedman, September 1995.

Record Transfer Fee Paid: £130,000 to Peterborough U for Greg Heald, August 1997.

Football League Record: Promoted to Division 4 from GMVC 1991; 1991–92 Division 4; 1992–93 Division 3; 1993–94 Division 2; 1994–2001 Division 3; 2001–05 Conference; 2005– FL2.

MANAGERS

Lester Finch
George Wheeler
Dexter Adams
Tommy Coleman
Gerry Ward
Gordon Ferry
Brian Kelly
Bill Meadows
Barry Fry
Roger Thompson
Don McAllister
Barry Fry
Edwin Stein
Gary Phillips *(Player-Manager)* 1993–94
Ray Clemence 1994–96
Alan Mullery *(Director of Football)* 1996–97
Terry Bullivant 1997
John Still 1997–2000
Tony Cottee 2000–01
John Still 2001–02
Peter Shreeves 2002–04
Paul Fairclough March 2004–

LATEST SEQUENCES

Longest Sequence of League Wins: 6, 28.8.1993 – 25.9.1999.

Longest Sequence of League Defeats: 11, 8.5.1993 – 2.10.1993.

Longest Sequence of League Draws: 4, 22.1.1994 – 12.2.1994.

Longest Sequence of Unbeaten League Matches: 12, 5.12.1992 – 2.3.1993.

Longest Sequence Without a League Win: 14, 24.4.1993 – 10.10.1993.

TEN YEAR LEAGUE RECORD

		P	*W*	*D*	*L*	*F*	*A*	*Pts*	*Pos*
1996-97	Div 3	46	14	16	16	46	51	58	15
1997-98	Div 3	46	19	13	14	61	51	70	7
1998-99	Div 3	46	14	13	19	54	71	55	16
1999-2000	Div 3	46	21	12	13	59	53	75	6
2000–01	Div 3	46	12	9	25	67	81	45	24
2001–02	Conf	42	19	10	13	64	48	67	5
2002–03	Conf	42	13	14	15	65	68	53	11
2003–04	Conf	42	19	14	9	60	48	71	4
2004–05	Conf	42	26	8	8	90	44	86	1
2005-06	FL 2	46	12	18	16	44	57	54	18

DID YOU KNOW ?

Barnet celebrated their first FA Cup tie as a Football League club by beating Tiverton Town 5–0 in a first round encounter on 16 November 1991. They followed this up with a 4–1 success at neighbours Enfield and a Mark Carter hat-trick in round two.

BARNET 2005–06 LEAGUE RECORD

Match No.	Date	Venue	Opponents	Result	H/T Score	Lg. Pos.	Goalscorers	Attendance
1	Aug 6	H	Bristol R	D 1-1	0-0	—	Graham [77]	3237
2	9	A	Northampton T	W 2-1	0-1	—	Sinclair [56], Bailey [88]	5817
3	13	A	Carlisle U	W 3-1	0-1	2	Grazioli [51], Bailey [60], Sinclair [90]	6650
4	20	H	Macclesfield T	W 1-0	1-0	1	Bailey [26]	2005
5	27	H	Grimsby T	L 0-1	0-0	3		2447
6	29	A	Wrexham	L 1-3	1-2	7	Hendon (pen) [45]	3768
7	Sept 2	A	Cheltenham T	D 1-1	0-1	—	Lee [56]	3343
8	10	H	Leyton Orient	L 2-3	1-1	13	Grazioli 2 [1, 90]	3722
9	17	A	Wycombe W	L 0-1	0-1	15		4994
10	24	H	Rochdale	D 1-1	0-1	15	Grazioli [87]	2338
11	27	A	Shrewsbury T	D 2-2	2-1	—	Bailey (pen) [14], Soares [30]	3628
12	Oct 1	H	Oxford U	D 0-0	0-0	16		3272
13	7	A	Torquay U	D 0-0	0-0	—		2965
14	15	H	Chester C	L 1-3	0-2	19	Grazioli [78]	2206
15	22	A	Mansfield T	L 0-4	0-1	21		2809
16	29	H	Rushden & D	W 2-1	1-0	18	Lee [45], Strevens [74]	2564
17	Nov 13	A	Stockport Co	D 1-1	1-1	18	Norville [18]	6056
18	19	H	Torquay U	W 1-0	1-0	16	Bailey [13]	2368
19	26	A	Bristol R	L 1-2	0-2	16	Strevens [68]	5096
20	Dec 3	H	Bury	D 1-1	0-0	—	Strevens [84]	1796
21	10	H	Northampton T	L 0-1	0-0	19		2544
22	17	A	Macclesfield T	D 1-1	0-1	19	Bailey [90]	1663
23	26	H	Peterborough U	W 2-1	1-1	18	Yakubu [36], Lee [62]	2715
24	28	A	Darlington	L 1-2	0-1	18	Strevens [90]	2905
25	31	H	Boston U	W 1-0	0-0	15	Lee [47]	2287
26	Jan 2	A	Notts Co	L 0-1	0-1	18		5249
27	10	H	Cheltenham T	D 1-1	0-1	—	Grazioli [81]	1366
28	14	A	Lincoln C	L 1-4	1-1	19	Grazioli [13]	4033
29	21	H	Wycombe W	D 0-0	0-0	20		3602
30	Feb 4	H	Shrewsbury T	W 1-0	1-0	18	Kandol [29]	1789
31	14	H	Lincoln C	L 2-3	1-0	—	Strevens [21], Kandol [53]	1695
32	18	A	Bury	D 0-0	0-0	20		2083
33	25	H	Carlisle U	L 1-2	0-0	20	Holmes (og) [53]	2870
34	28	A	Leyton Orient	D 0-0	0-0	—		4910
35	Mar 4	H	Wrexham	D 2-2	2-1	18	Norville [30], Kandol [37]	2127
36	11	A	Grimsby T	L 0-3	0-3	20		5147
37	18	A	Peterborough U	D 2-2	1-0	20	Hessenthaler [10], Fuller [70]	3983
38	25	H	Darlington	W 1-0	0-0	21	Kandol [80]	2845
39	Apr 1	A	Boston U	L 1-2	0-2	22	Roache [73]	2066
40	8	H	Notts Co	W 2-1	0-0	21	Hendon 2 (2 pens) [64, 72]	2841
41	15	A	Oxford U	L 0-2	0-2	22		6948
42	17	H	Mansfield T	W 1-0	1-0	21	Hatch [11]	2784
43	22	A	Chester C	D 0-0	0-0	21		2367
44	25	A	Rochdale	D 1-1	1-1	—	Hendon (pen) [28]	1769
45	29	H	Stockport Co	D 0-0	0-0	20		3873
46	May 6	A	Rushden & D	W 2-1	0-0	18	Hatch [51], Bailey [55]	4174

Final League Position: 18

GOALSCORERS

League (44): Bailey 7 (1 pen), Grazioli 7, Strevens 5, Hendon 4 (4 pens), Kandol 4, Lee 4, Hatch 2, Norville 2, Sinclair 2, Fuller 1, Graham 1, Hessenthaler 1, Roache 1, Soares 1, Yakubu 1, own goal 1.
Carling Cup (7): Lee 2, Bailey 1, Grazioli 1, King 1, Roache 1, Sinclair 1.
FA Cup (0).
Football League Trophy (3): Bailey 1, Norville 1, Sinclair 1.

Tynan S 7	Hendon I 34 + 1	King S 31 + 1	Lee D 24 + 3	Yakubu I 26	Charles A 39 + 1	Bailey N 45	Sinclair D 39 + 5	Grazioli G 27 + 2	Strevens B 31 + 4	Graham R 13 + 2	Norville J 7 + 15	Hatch L 21 + 14	Gross A 18 + 2	Batt D 12 + 10	Roache L 2 + 6	Soares L 14 + 6	Flitney R 35	Bowditch B 3 + 3	Vernazza P 11 + 6	Clist S 12 + 2	Fuller B 15	Hessenthaler A 16	Varney A — + 1	Kandol T 13	Reed M 4	Warhurst P 7 + 2	*Match No.*
1	2	3	4	5	6	7	8	9^{1}	10^{2}	11	12	13															1
1	2	3	4	5^{2}	6	7	8	9^{1}	10	11^{3}	14	12	13														2
1	2	3	4		6	7	8	9^{1}	10	11	12		5														3
1	2	3	4		6	7	8	9^{1}	10	11	12		5														4
1	2^{3}	3	4		6	7	8	9	10^{1}	11		12	5^{2}	14	13												5
1	2	3	4		6	7	8	9	10^{2}	11^{1}			5		12	13											6
	2	3	4	5^{1}	6	7	8	9		11				12		10	1										7
	2	3	4		6	7	8	9		11				5	12	10^{1}	1										8
	2	3	4		6	7	8	9		11				5	12		1	10^{1}									9
	2	3	4		6	7	8	9	10^{1}	12		13		5		11^{2}	1										10
		3	4	2■	6	7	8	9^{1}	10^{2}			12		5		11	1	13									11
	2	3	4		6	7	8	9	10^{1}	12		13	14	5^{3}		11^{2}	1										12
	2		4		6	7	8		10	11		9	5	3			1										13
	2	12	13		6■	7	8	9	10^{3}	11^{2}	14	3	5^{1}	4			1										14
1	2	3^{1}	4	5	6	7^{3}	8	9		11^{2}	14	13		12		10											15
	2		4	5	6	7	8		10		12	11	3		9^{1}		1										16
	2	3		5	12	7	8	13	10		9^{2}	11	6^{1}			4	1										17
	2	3		5		7	8	9^{1}	10		12	11		6		4	1										18
	2	3		5	6	7	8	9	10		12	11				4^{1}	1										19
	2	3	12	5	6	7	13	9^{3}	10		14	11				8^{2}	1		4^{1}								20
		3	4	5	6	7	8	9	10^{1}			11		2			1			12							21
	2	3	4	5	6	7	8^{2}	9	10^{1}		12	11^{3}				13	1		14								22
	2	3	4	5	6^{3}	7		9^{2}	12		10	13				11^{1}	1		8	14							23
	2^{2}	3	4	5		7	12		10		9^{1}	11		13			1		8	6							24
			4	5	3	7	8		10^{1}		12	9		2			1		11	6							25
				5	3	7	8		10^{1}		12	11		2		13	1	9^{2}	4	6							26
	2				6		8	12	10			11	5	3	9^{1}	4^{2}	1	7	13								27
	2				6	7	8	9	10^{1}			11	3	12			1	13	4^{2}		5						28
		3		5^{1}		7	8	9^{2}		11			6	12		4	1				2	10	13				29
	12	3^{1}			6	7	8	9^{2}	13				5			4	1	14			2	10^{3}		11			30
			4	5	6	7	8^{1}	9	10				3			12	1				2			11			31
			4	5	6	7	8^{2}	9^{1}	10		12		3				1		13		2			11			32
				5	6	7	8	9^{1}	10		11	12	3								2	4			1		33
	2			5	6	7			10		9^{1}	12								4	3	8		11	1		34
	2		12	5	6	7^{2}	13		10^{3}		9	14								4	3	8^{1}		11	1		35
		3		5	6	7	8	9^{3}	10		11^{1}	12		13		14				2^{2}		4			1		36
		3	4	5	6	7	8					9					1		12	11	2	10^{1}					37
		3^{2}	4^{1}	5	6	7	8					12					1		13	11	2	10^{3}		9		14	38
	2^{3}			5	6	7	8		12			9^{1}			13		1		4	11	3	10^{2}				14	39
	2				6	7	12		10								1		4	5	8	11^{1}		9		3	40
	2^{3}				6	7	12		10^{2}			13		14			1		4	3	11	8^{1}		9		5	41
	2	3			6	7	8^{2}					10		12			1		13		11	4^{1}		9		5	42
	2	3				7	8		12			10^{1}					1			6	11	4		9		5	43
	2	3			6^{1}	7	8					10	4			12	1					11		9		5	44
	2	3				7	8					10^{1}	6	13	12		1		4			11^{2}		9		5	45
	2	3				7	8				12	10^{1}	6				1		4			11		9		5	46

FA Cup

First Round	Southend U	(h)	0-1

Carling Cup

First Round	Bristol C	(a)	4-2
Second Round	Plymouth Arg	(h)	2-1
Third Round	Manchester U	(a)	1-4

Football League Trophy

First Round	Bristol C	(h)	3-2
Second Round	Milton Keynes D	(h)	0-3

BARNSLEY FL Championship

FOUNDATION

Many clubs owe their inception to the church and Barnsley are among them, for they were formed in 1887 by the Rev. T. T. Preedy, curate of Barnsley St Peter's and went under that name until it was dropped in 1897 a year before being admitted to the Second Division of the Football League.

Oakwell Stadium, Grove Street, Barnsley, South Yorkshire S71 1ET.

Telephone: (01226) 211 211.

Fax: (01226) 211 444.

Ticket Office: (01226) 211 200.

Website: www.barnsleyfc.co.uk

Email: thereds@barnsleyfc.co.uk

Ground Capacity: 23,186.

Record Attendance: 40,255 v Stoke C, FA Cup 5th rd, 15 February 1936.

Pitch Measurements: 110yd × 73yd.

Chairman: J. G. Shepherd.

General Manager: A. D. Rowing.

Manager: Andy Ritchie.

Assistant Manager/Physio: Rick Holden.

Colours: Red shirts, white shorts, red stockings.

Change Colours: Yellow with black trim shirts, black with yellow trim shorts, black with yellow trim stockings.

Year Formed: 1887.

Turned Professional: 1888.

Ltd Co.: 1899.

Previous Name: 1887, Barnsley St Peter's; 1897, Barnsley.

Club Nickname: 'The Tykes', 'Reds' or 'Colliers'.

First Football League Game: 1 September 1898, Division 2, v Lincoln C (a) L 0–1 – Fawcett; McArtney, Nixon; King, Burleigh, Porteous; Davis, Lees, Murray, McCullough, McGee.

Record League Victory: 9–0 v Loughborough T, Division 2, 28 January 1899 – Greaves; McArtney, Nixon; Porteous, Burleigh, Howard; Davis (4), Hepworth (1), Lees (1), McCullough (1), Jones (2). 9–0 v Accrington S, Division 3 (N), 3 February 1934 – Ellis; Cookson, Shotton; Harper, Henderson, Whitworth; Spence (2), Smith (1), Blight (4), Andrews (1), Ashton (1).

Record Cup Victory: 6–0 v Blackpool, FA Cup 1st rd replay, 20 January 1910 – Mearns; Downs, Ness; Glendinning, Boyle (1), Utley; Bartrop, Gadsby (1), Lillycrop (2), Tufnell (2), Forman. 6–0 v Peterborough U, League Cup 1st rd 2nd leg, 15 September 1981 – Horn; Joyce, Chambers, Glavin (2), Banks, McCarthy, Evans, Parker (2), Aylott (1), McHale, Barrowclough (1).

HONOURS

Football League: Division 1 – Runners-up 1996–97; Promoted from Championship 1 (play-offs) 2005–06; Division 3 (N) – Champions 1933–34, 1938–39, 1954–55; Runners-up 1953–54; Division 3 – Runners-up 1980–81; Division 4 – Runners-up 1967–68; Promoted 1978–79.

FA Cup: Winners 1912; Runners-up 1910.

Football League Cup: best season: 5th rd, 1982.

SKY SPORTS FACT FILE

Abe Blight was snapped up by Barnsley from his home town team Blackhill in 1933–34. He set a scoring record of 31 League goals but injury forced him out early the following season, though he did play non-league football later with Annfield Plain.

Record Defeat: 0–9 v Notts Co, Division 2, 19 November 1927.

Most League Points (2 for a win): 67, Division 3 (N), 1938–39.

Most League Points (3 for a win): 82, Division 1, 1999–2000.

Most League Goals: 118, Division 3 (N), 1933–34.

Highest League Scorer in Season: Cecil McCormack, 33, Division 2, 1950–51.

Most League Goals in Total Aggregate: Ernest Hine, 123, 1921–26 and 1934–38.

Most League Goals in One Match: 5, Frank Eaton v South Shields, Division 3N, 9 April 1927; 5, Peter Cunningham v Darlington, Division 3N, 4 February 1933; 5, Beau Asquith v Darlington, Division 3N, 12 November 1938; 5, Cecil McCormack v Luton T, Division 2, 9 September 1950.

Most Capped Player: Gerry Taggart, 35 (50), Northern Ireland.

Most League Appearances: Barry Murphy, 514, 1962–78.

Youngest League Player: Alan Ogley, 16 years 226 days v Bristol R, 18 September 1962.

Record Transfer Fee Received: £4,500,000 from Blackburn R for Ashley Ward, December 1998.

Record Transfer Fee Paid: £1,500,000 to Partizan Belgrade for Georgi Hristov, July 1997.

Football League Record: 1898 Elected to Division 2; 1932–34 Division 3 (N); 1934–38 Division 2; 1938–39 Division 3 (N); 1946–53 Division 2; 1953–55 Division 3 (N); 1955–59 Division 2; 1959–65 Division 3; 1965–68 Division 4; 1968–72 Division 3; 1972–79 Division 4; 1979–81 Division 3; 1981–92 Division 2; 1992–97 Division 1; 1997–98 FA Premier League; 1998–2002 Division 1; 2002–04 Division 2; 2004–06 FL1; 2006– FLC.

MANAGERS

Arthur Fairclough 1898–1901 *(Secretary-Manager)*
John McCartney 1901–04 *(Secretary-Manager)*
Arthur Fairclough 1904–12
John Hastie 1912–14
Percy Lewis 1914–19
Peter Sant 1919–26
John Commins 1926–29
Arthur Fairclough 1929–30
Brough Fletcher 1930–37
Angus Seed 1937–53
Tim Ward 1953–60
Johnny Steele 1960–71 *(continued as General Manager)*
John McSeveney 1971–72
Johnny Steele *(General Manager)* 1972–73
Jim Iley 1973–78
Allan Clarke 1978–80
Norman Hunter 1980–84
Bobby Collins 1984–85
Allan Clarke 1985–89
Mel Machin 1989–93
Viv Anderson 1993–94
Danny Wilson 1994–98
John Hendrie 1998–99
Dave Bassett 1999–2000
Nigel Spackman 2001
Steve Parkin 2001–02
Glyn Hodges 2002–03
Gudjon Thordarson 2003–04
Paul Hart 2004–05
Andy Ritchie March 2005–

LATEST SEQUENCES

Longest Sequence of League Wins: 10, 5.3.1955 – 23.4.1955.

Longest Sequence of League Defeats: 9, 14.3.1953 – 25.4.1953.

Longest Sequence of League Draws: 7, 28.3.1911 – 22.4.1911.

Longest Sequence of Unbeaten League Matches: 21, 1.1.1934 – 5.5.1934.

Longest Sequence Without a League Win: 26, 13.12.1952 – 26.8.1953.

Successive Scoring Runs: 44 from 2.10.1926.

Successive Non-scoring Runs: 6 from 7.10.1899.

TEN YEAR LEAGUE RECORD

		P	W	D	L	F	A	Pts	Pos
1996-97	Div 1	46	22	14	10	76	55	80	2
1997-98	PR Lge	38	10	5	23	37	82	35	19
1998-99	Div 1	46	14	17	15	59	56	59	13
1999-2000	Div 1	46	24	10	12	88	67	82	4
2000-01	Div 1	46	15	9	22	49	62	54	16
2001-02	Div 1	46	11	15	20	59	86	48	23
2002-03	Div 2	46	13	13	20	51	64	52	19
2003-04	Div 2	46	15	17	14	54	58	62	12
2004-05	FL 1	46	14	19	13	69	64	61	13
2005-06	FL 1	46	18	18	10	62	44	72	5

DID YOU KNOW ?

Wing-half Lewis Clayton formed his own team L. Clayton's XI at 17 in 1941 but one day was persuaded to play for Monkton Athletic. Spotted by Barnsley he had the first of two spells there sandwiching a season at Carlisle United in 1946–47.

BARNSLEY 2005–06 LEAGUE RECORD

Match No.	Date	Venue	Opponents	Result		H/T Score	Lg. Pos.	Goalscorers	Attendance
1	Aug 6	H	Swindon T	W	2-0	1-0	—	Hayes [11], Shuker [47]	9358
2	9	A	Scunthorpe U	L	1-2	1-1	—	Hayes [16]	7152
3	13	A	Colchester U	L	0-1	0-0	15		2721
4	20	H	Yeovil T	W	1-0	0-0	9	Williams (pen) [79]	8153
5	27	H	Brentford	D	1-1	1-1	13	Turner (og) [24]	7462
6	29	A	Swansea C	L	1-3	1-1	15	Burns [35]	12,554
7	Sept 10	H	Nottingham F	W	2-0	2-0	11	Conlon [41], Shuker [45]	10,080
8	13	A	Gillingham	W	3-0	2-0	—	Shuker [40], Hayes [43], Nardiello [85]	5283
9	17	A	Milton Keynes D	D	0-0	0-0	6		4620
10	24	H	Doncaster R	L	0-2	0-1	11		12,002
11	27	A	Bristol C	L	0-3	0-3	—		10,771
12	Oct 1	H	Oldham Ath	W	4-0	3-0	8	Nardiello [8], Devaney [12], Shuker 2 [14, 54]	8077
13	15	H	Blackpool	D	2-2	0-1	12	Richards [81], Howard [84]	7945
14	22	A	Southend U	D	1-1	0-0	14	Richards [61]	6986
15	25	A	Rotherham U	W	1-0	0-0	—	Devaney [73]	5401
16	29	H	Walsall	W	2-1	1-0	5	Hayes [13], Howard [66]	8145
17	Nov 12	A	Bradford C	D	0-0	0-0	6		9486
18	19	H	Rotherham U	D	1-1	0-1	6	Watt [90]	9894
19	26	A	Swindon T	W	3-0	1-0	6	Devaney [8], Shuker 2 [51, 69]	5422
20	Dec 6	H	Tranmere R	W	2-1	0-0	—	Devaney [58], Richards (pen) [77]	6996
21	10	H	Scunthorpe U	W	5-2	3-0	4	Devaney [2], Hassell [7], Richards [33], Shuker [71], Hayes [89]	8197
22	17	A	Yeovil T	L	1-2	1-0	5	Williams [15]	5620
23	26	H	Hartlepool U	D	1-1	1-0	4	Richards (pen) [28]	9715
24	31	H	Huddersfield T	D	2-2	0-0	6	Burns [40], Nardiello [81]	13,263
25	Jan 2	A	Chesterfield	D	0-0	0-0	6		6046
26	10	H	Gillingham	W	1-0	1-0	—	Shuker [25]	7090
27	14	A	Port Vale	L	2-3	0-2	7	Burns [56], Carbon [67]	4468
28	21	H	Milton Keynes D	W	2-0	0-0	5	Richards [77], Hassell [79]	7588
29	27	A	Nottingham F	W	2-0	2-0	—	Richards 2 [15, 31]	16,237
30	Feb 4	H	Bristol C	W	2-0	1-0	4	Richards 2 (1 pen) [27, 81 (p)]	8092
31	11	A	Doncaster R	L	0-2	0-1	6		8144
32	14	H	Port Vale	D	1-1	0-0	—	Hayes [56]	7709
33	18	A	Tranmere R	W	1-0	1-0	6	Heckingbottom [16]	6802
34	25	H	Colchester U	W	1-0	0-0	5	Howard [72]	9411
35	28	A	Bournemouth	D	1-1	1-0	—	McPhail [21]	5191
36	Mar 4	H	Swansea C	D	2-2	0-0	3	Nardiello [56], Richards (pen) [61]	9743
37	11	A	Brentford	L	1-3	0-2	5	Wright [68]	7352
38	18	A	Hartlepool U	D	1-1	1-1	6	Kay [36]	5122
39	25	H	Bournemouth	D	0-0	0-0	6		9180
40	Apr 1	A	Huddersfield T	L	0-1	0-0	7		19,052
41	8	H	Chesterfield	D	1-1	1-0	6	Howard [31]	8303
42	15	A	Oldham Ath	W	3-0	0-0	6	Shuker [49], McPhail [62], Devaney [79]	7772
43	17	H	Southend U	D	2-2	2-0	5	Hunt (og) [18], Maher (og) [45]	10,663
44	22	A	Blackpool	D	1-1	0-1	5	Howard [53]	6912
45	29	H	Bradford C	D	0-0	0-0	5		11,178
46	May 6	A	Walsall	W	2-1	1-0	5	Richards [31], Nardiello (pen) [83]	7195

Final League Position: 5

GOALSCORERS

League (62): Richards 12 (4 pens), Shuker 10, Devaney 6, Hayes 6, Howard 5, Nardiello 5 (1 pen), Burns 3, Hassell 2, McPhail 2, Williams 2 (1 pen), Carbon 1, Conlon 1, Heckingbottom 1, Kay 1, Watt 1, Wright 1, own goals 3.
Carling Cup (2): Burns 2.
FA Cup (8): Hayes 5, Devaney 2, Reid 1.
Football League Trophy (2): Nardiello 1, own goal 1.
Play-Offs (5): Hayes 2 (1 pen), Nardiello 2, Reid 1.

Colgan N 43	Tonge D 14 + 10	Austin N 38	Williams R 13 + 9	Carbon M 21 + 3	Kay A 33 + 3	Burns J 32 + 1	Shuker C 45 + 1	Hayes P 38 + 7	Nardiello D 11 + 23	McPhail S 30 + 4	Wroe N 6 + 6	Conlon B 8 + 3	Jarman N — + 9	Vaughan T — + 1	Reid P 31 + 2	Devaney M 34 + 4	Richards M 29 + 9	Hassell B 25 + 3	Howard B 25 + 6	Watt S 3	Flinders S 3	Kell R — + 2	Wright T 7 + 10	Heckingbottom P 17 + 1	Laight R — + 1	McParland A — + 8	*Match No.*
1	2	3	4■	5	6	7	8	9[1]	10[2]	11	12	13															1
1	2[1]	3		5[2]	6	7	8	9	10	11	4[3]	14	12	13													2
1	2[1]	3	4[2]	5	6	7	12	9	10	11		13			8												3
1	2	3	4	5	12	7	8	9[2]		11[1]		10	13		6												4
1	12	2	3[1]	5	13	6	8	9	—	11		10[2]	14		4■	7[3]											5
1	2[2]	3	12	5	6	4	8	9	14	13	11	10[3]				7[1]											6
1		2	3	5	6	7[2]	8	9[1]	12		13	10[3]			4	11	14										7
1	2	3	12		6	4	8	9[2]	13		7	10[3]			5	11[1]	14										8
1	12	3	2		6	4	8[3]	9[2]	13		7	10			5	11[1]	14										9
1		3■		5	6■	7	8	9[1]	12			10			4	11[2]	13	2									10
1	2		4			6	8	9[1]	12		7	10[2]			5	11[3]	13	3	14								11
1	12		3	5[1]		6	8	9[3]	10		13				4	11	14	2	7[2]								12
1			3	5		7[1]	8[2]	9[3]	10	12			13		6	11	14	2	4								13
1	2	3			6	7	8[2]	9	12	11						13	10[1]	5	4								14
1	2	3			6	7	8[2]	9[3]	12	11			14			13	10[1]	5	4								15
1	2	3			6	7	8[2]	9[1]	12	11			14			13	10[3]		4	5							16
1	13	3		14	6		8	9	12[2]	11						7	10[1]	2	4■	5[3]							17
1	12	3[2]				4[1]	8	9		11			13		6	7	10	2		5							18
1	12	3		5	13	4[1]	8[3]	9		11	14				6	7[2]	10	2									19
	12	3	13	5[1]	6	7[3]	8	9			14					11[2]	10	2	4		1						20
	12	3[2]	13		6	7	8	9					14		5	11	10[3]	2[1]	4		1						21
		3	11[2]	12	6	7	8[3]	9		13	14				5		10	2	4[1]		1						22
1	12	3		13	6[2]	7[1]	8	9					14		5	11[3]	10	2	4								23
1	12	3	13	5		7	8	9[3]	14						6	11[2]	10	2[1]	4								24
1	2	6	3			4	8[3]	12	10[1]		7				5	11[2]			13			14	9				25
1	2	6	3[3]			4	8	9	12	11					5	7[2]	13					14	10[1]				26
1		6		5		4[3]	8	12	13	11						7	9[1]	2	14				10[2]	3			27
1		3		5		4	8[2]	9[1]	12	11					6	7	10[3]	2	13				14				28
1		3		5		4	8[3]	9[1]	12	11[2]					6	7	10	2	13					14			29
1			11		6	7	8[1]	9							5[2]		10	2	4				12	3	13		30
1				5	6	7	8[1]	9[2]	13	12					4		10	2[3]	11				14	3			31
1				5	6	4	8	9[1]	12	11						7[2]	10[3]	2	13				14	3			32
1		5	12		6	4	8	13	14	11						7[1]	10[3]	2					9[2]	3			33
1		5			6	12	8[3]	9		11[2]					13	7		2	4[1]				10	3		14	34
1		5			6		8	9[1]	12	11					13	7	10[3]	2[2]	4				14	3			35
1		2		5	6		8[2]	12	9	11					4	7[1]	10							3		13	36
1		3		5	2		8[1]	12	9	11					6	7[3]	10[2]		4				13			14	37
1		2		5	6		8[2]	12		11					7		10		4				9[1]	3		13	38
1		2			6		8[2]	9[1]	12	11					5	7	10		4					3		13	39
1		2[2]	13		6		8	9	12■	11					5	7[1]	10		4					3[3]		14	40
1		2			6		8[2]	9		11					5	7	10		4				12	3[1]		13	41
1		2[3]	12		6		8[2]	9	13	11					5	7	10[1]	14	4					3			42
1		2[3]			6		8	12	9	11					5	7[1]	13	14	4				10[2]	3			43
1		2[2]			6		8[1]	9	7	11					5■	12	10[3]	13	4				14	3			44
1	2				6		8[1]	9	12	11						7	10[2]	5	4				13	3			45
1	2		12		6		8[3]		9	11						7	10[2]	5	4[1]				13	3		14	46

FA Cup

First Round	Darlington	(h)	1-0
Second Round	Bradford C	(h)	1-1
		(a)	5-3
Third Round	Walsall	(h)	1-1
		(a)	0-2

Football League Trophy

First Round	Doncaster R	(h)	2-5

Carling Cup

First Round	Preston NE	(a)	2-2
Second Round	Burnley	(a)	0-3

Play-Offs

Semi-Final	Huddersfield T	(h)	0-1
		(a)	3-1
Final	Swansea C		2-2
(at Millennium Stadium)			

BIRMINGHAM CITY FL Championship

FOUNDATION

In 1875, cricketing enthusiasts who were largely members of Trinity Church, Bordesley, determined to continue their sporting relationships throughout the year by forming a football club which they called Small Heath Alliance. For their earliest games played on waste land in Arthur Street, the team included three Edden brothers and two James brothers.

St Andrews Stadium, Birmingham B9 4NH.

Telephone: 0871 226 1875.

Fax: 0871 226 1975.

Ticket Office: (0871) 226 1875 (extension 2).

Website: www.bcfc.com

Email: reception@bcfc.com

Ground Capacity: 30,007 (all seated).

Record Attendance: 66,844 v Everton, FA Cup 5th rd, 11 February 1939.

Pitch Measurements: 100m × 68m.

Chairman: David Sullivan (Plc), David Gold (FC).

Vice-chairman: Jack Wiseman.

Managing Director: Karren Brady.

Secretary: Julia Shelton.

Manager: Steve Bruce.

Assistant Manager: Eric Black.

Physio: Neil McDiamid.

Colours: Royal blue shirts with white trim, white shorts with royal blue trim, white stockings with royal blue trim.

Change Colours: All black with yellow trim.

Year Formed: 1875.

Turned Professional: 1885.

Ltd Co.: 1888.

Previous Names: 1875, Small Heath Alliance; 1888, dropped 'Alliance'; 1905, Birmingham; 1945, Birmingham City.

Club Nickname: 'Blues'.

Previous Grounds: 1875, waste ground near Arthur St; 1877, Muntz St, Small Heath; 1906, St Andrews.

First Football League game: 3 September 1892, Division 2, v Burslem Port Vale (h) W 5–1 – Charsley; Bayley, Speller; Ollis, Jenkyns, Devey; Hallam (1), Edwards (1), Short (1), Wheldon (2), Hands.

Record League Victory: 12–0 v Walsall T Swifts, Division 2, 17 December 1892 – Charsley; Bayley, Jones; Ollis, Jenkyns, Devey; Hallam (2), Walton (3), Mobley (3), Wheldon (2), Hands (2). 12–0 v Doncaster R, Division 2, 11 April 1903 – Dorrington; Goldie, Wassell; Beer, Dougherty (1), Howard; Athersmith (1), Leonard (3), McRoberts (1), Wilcox (4), Field (1). Aston, (1 og).

HONOURS

Football League: Promoted from Division 1 (play-offs) 2001–02; Division 2 – Champions 1892–93, 1920–21, 1947–48, 1954–55, 1994–95; Runners-up 1893–94, 1900–01, 1902–03, 1971–72, 1984–85; Division 3 Runners-up 1991–92.

FA Cup: Runners-up 1931, 1956.

Football League Cup: Winners 1963; Runners-up 2001.

Leyland Daf Cup: Winners 1991.

Auto Windscreens Shield: Winners 1995.

European Competitions: *European Fairs Cup:* 1955–58, 1958–60 (runners-up), 1960–61 (runners-up), 1961–62.

SKY SPORTS FACT FILE

Northern Ireland international inside-forward Bobby Brennan had previously won three schoolboy caps. Transferred from Distillery to Luton Town in 1947 for £2000 his value increased tenfold in two years when Birmingham City paid £20,000 for him.

Record Cup Victory: 9–2 v Burton W, FA Cup 1st rd, 31 October 1885 – Hedges; Jones, Evetts (1); F. James, Felton, A. James (1); Davenport (2), Stanley (4), Simms, Figures, Morris (1).

Record Defeat: 1–9 v Sheffield W, Division 1, 13 December 1930. 1–9 v Blackburn R, Division 1, 5 January 1895.

Most League Points (2 for a win): 59, Division 2, 1947–48.

Most League Points (3 for a win): 89, Division 2, 1994–95.

Most League Goals: 103, Division 2, 1893–94 (only 28 games).

Highest League Scorer in Season: Joe Bradford, 29, Division 1, 1927–28.

Most League Goals in Total Aggregate: Joe Bradford, 249, 1920–35.

Most League Goals in One Match: 5, Walter Abbott v Darwen, Division 2, 26 November, 1898; 5, John McMillan v Blackpool, Division 2, 2 March 1901; 5, James Windridge v Glossop, Division 2, 23 January 1915.

Most Capped Player: Kenny Cunningham, 32 (72), Republic of Ireland.

Most League Appearances: Frank Womack, 491, 1908–28.

Youngest League Player: Trevor Francis, 16 years 7 months v Cardiff C, 5 September 1970.

Record Transfer Fee Received: £5,500,000 from Wigan Ath for Emile Heskey, July 2006.

Record Transfer Fee Paid: £5,875,000 to Liverpool for Emile Heskey, July 2004.

Football League Record: 1892 elected to Division 2; 1894–96 Division 1; 1896–1901 Division 2; 1901–02 Division 1; 1902–03 Division 2; 1903–08 Division 1; 1908–21 Division 2; 1921–39 Division 1; 1946–48 Division 2; 1948–50 Division 1; 1950–55 Division 2; 1955–65 Division 1; 1965–72 Division 2; 1972–79 Division 1; 1979–80 Division 2; 1980–84 Division 1; 1984–85 Division 2; 1985–86 Division 1; 1986–89 Division 2; 1989–92 Division 3; 1992–94 Division 1; 1994–95 Division 2; 1995–2002 Division 1; 2002–06 FA Premier League; 2006– FLC.

MANAGERS

Alfred Jones 1892–1908
(Secretary-Manager)
Alec Watson 1908–10
Bob McRoberts 1910–15
Frank Richards 1915–23
Billy Beer 1923–27
Leslie Knighton 1928–33
George Liddell 1933–39
Harry Storer 1945–48
Bob Brocklebank 1949–54
Arthur Turner 1954–58
Pat Beasley 1959–60
Gil Merrick 1960–64
Joe Mallett 1965
Stan Cullis 1965–70
Fred Goodwin 1970–75
Willie Bell 1975–77
Jim Smith 1978–82
Ron Saunders 1982–86
John Bond 1986–87
Garry Pendrey 1987–89
Dave Mackay 1989–91
Lou Macari 1991
Terry Cooper 1991–93
Barry Fry 1993–96
Trevor Francis 1996–2001
Steve Bruce December 2001–

LATEST SEQUENCES

Longest Sequence of League Wins: 13, 17.12.1892 – 16.9.1893.

Longest Sequence of League Defeats: 8, 28.9.1985 – 23.11.1985.

Longest Sequence of League Draws: 8, 18.9.1990 – 23.10.1990.

Longest Sequence of Unbeaten League Matches: 20, 3.9.1994 – 2.1.1995.

Longest Sequence Without a League Win: 17, 28.9.1985 – 18.1.1986.

Successive Scoring Runs: 24 from 24.9.1892.

Successive Non-scoring Runs: 6 from 1.10.1949.

TEN YEAR LEAGUE RECORD

		P	W	D	L	F	A	Pts	Pos
1996-97	Div 1	46	17	15	14	52	48	66	10
1997-98	Div 1	46	19	17	10	60	35	74	7
1998-99	Div 1	46	23	12	11	66	37	81	4
1999-2000	Div 1	46	22	11	13	65	44	77	5
2000-01	Div 1	46	23	9	14	59	48	78	5
2001-02	Div 1	46	21	13	12	70	49	76	5
2002-03	PR Lge	38	13	9	16	41	49	48	13
2003-04	PR Lge	38	12	14	12	43	48	50	10
2004-05	PR Lge	38	11	12	15	40	46	45	12
2005-06	PR Lge	38	8	10	20	28	50	34	18

DID YOU KNOW ?

Though his previous club was listed as Erdington, centre-half Graham Sissons was actually spotted by Birmingham City assistant manager Walter Taylor while playing for The Country Girl, the name of a Saltley public house which ran a team in July 1954.

BIRMINGHAM CITY 2005–06 LEAGUE RECORD

Match No.	Date	Venue	Opponents	Result		H/T Score	Lg. Pos.	Goalscorers	Atten-dance
1	Aug 13	A	Fulham	D	0-0	0-0	—		16,550
2	20	H	Manchester C	L	1-2	1-1	14	Butt 7	26,366
3	23	H	Middlesbrough	L	0-3	0-2	—		27,998
4	27	A	WBA	W	3-2	3-1	13	Heskey 2 10, 33, Jarosik 26	23,993
5	Sept 10	H	Charlton Ath	L	0-1	0-1	16		26,846
6	17	A	Portsmouth	D	1-1	1-1	15	Jarosik 6	19,319
7	24	H	Liverpool	D	2-2	0-0	14	Warnock (og) 72, Pandiani 75	27,733
8	Oct 2	A	Arsenal	L	0-1	0-0	15		37,891
9	16	H	Aston Villa	L	0-1	0-1	17		29,312
10	22	A	Blackburn R	L	0-2	0-0	18		18,341
11	29	H	Everton	L	0-1	0-1	19		26,554
12	Nov 5	A	Newcastle U	L	0-1	0-0	19		52,191
13	26	A	Sunderland	W	1-0	0-0	19	Gray 68	32,442
14	Dec 5	H	West Ham U	L	1-2	1-2	—	Heskey 11	24,010
15	10	H	Fulham	W	1-0	0-0	18	Butt 84	27,597
16	17	A	Manchester C	L	1-4	0-3	19	Jarosik 76	41,343
17	26	A	Tottenham H	L	0-2	0-0	19		36,045
18	28	H	Manchester U	D	2-2	1-1	19	Clapham 18, Pandiani 78	28,459
19	31	A	Chelsea	L	0-2	0-2	19		40,652
20	Jan 2	H	Wigan Ath	W	2-0	2-0	19	Pennant 20, Melchiot 33	29,189
21	14	A	Charlton Ath	L	0-2	0-1	19		26,312
22	21	H	Portsmouth	W	5-0	2-0	18	Jarosik 5, Pennant 37, Upson 55, Forssell (pen) 89, Dunn 90	29,138
23	Feb 1	A	Liverpool	D	1-1	0-0	—	Xabi Alonso (og) 88	43,851
24	4	H	Arsenal	L	0-2	0-1	18		27,075
25	13	A	West Ham U	L	0-3	0-1	—		31,294
26	25	H	Sunderland	W	1-0	1-0	18	Heskey 39	29,257
27	Mar 4	A	Middlesbrough	L	0-1	0-1	18		28,141
28	11	H	WBA	D	1-1	0-0	18	Forssell (pen) 49	28,041
29	18	H	Tottenham H	L	0-2	0-0	18		26,398
30	26	A	Manchester U	L	0-3	0-2	18		69,070
31	Apr 1	H	Chelsea	D	0-0	0-0	19		26,364
32	4	H	Bolton W	W	1-0	1-0	—	Jarosik 37	26,493
33	8	A	Wigan Ath	D	1-1	0-0	17	Dunn 77	18,669
34	16	A	Aston Villa	L	1-3	1-1	18	Sutton 25	40,158
35	19	H	Blackburn R	W	2-1	0-0	—	Butt 62, Forssell 87	25,287
36	22	A	Everton	D	0-0	0-0	18		35,420
37	29	H	Newcastle U	D	0-0	0-0	18		28,331
38	May 7	A	Bolton W	L	0-1	0-0	18		26,275

Final League Position: 18

GOALSCORERS

League (28): Jarosik 5, Heskey 4, Butt 3, Forssell 3 (2 pens), Dunn 2, Pandiani 2, Pennant 2, Clapham 1, Gray 1, Melchiot 1, Sutton 1, Upson 1, own goals 2.
Carling Cup (7): Forssell 2 (1 pen), Jarosik 2, Gray 1, Heskey 1, Pennant 1.
FA Cup (6): Forssell 3, Dunn 1, Gray 1, Jarosik 1.

Taylor Maik 34	Melchiot M 22 + 1	Clapham J 13 + 3	Clemence S 13 + 2	Upson M 24	Cunningham K 31	Pennant J 35 + 3	Butt N 22 + 2	Pandiani W 7 + 10	Heskey E 34	Gray J 18 + 3	Forssell M 10 + 17	Morrison C — + 1	Lazaridis S 11 + 6	Izzet M 10 + 6	Tebily O 12 + 4	Jarosik J 19 + 5	Johnson D 31	Kilkenny N 6 + 12	Dunn D 8 + 7	Taylor Martin 20 + 1	Vaesen N 4	Painter M 2 + 2	Birley M — + 1	Sutton C 10	Latka M 6	Bruce A 3 + 3	Campbell D 4 + 7	Sadler M 8	Nafti M 1	Match No.
1	2	3	4	5	6	7	8	9^1	10^2	11	12	13																		1
1	2	3^1	4	5	6	7	8^2	9		11	10		12	13																2
1	2		4^3	5	6	7	8	9^1		12	13		3	14	11^2	10														3
1	2	3	12	5	6	7	4	13	10^2		9^3			14		11	8^1													4
1	2^1	3		5	6	7	4	13	10^2	12	9			14		11^3	8													5
1		12		5	6	7^2	4■	13	10	3	9^1			14	2	11^3	8													6
1	2	3		5	6	7		12	10^2	11	9^1				13		4	8■												7
1		3^1	4	5	6■	7		9^2	10	11	12		13		2		8													8
1		3^3	4^2	5		7		9^1	10	11	12				2	13	8		14	6										9
1		3		5	6	7	4		10		9		11^1		2^2	12	8	13												10
1		3		5	2^1	7	4^2	12	10		9					11	8	13		6										11
1		3		5	2	7		12	10		13		11^1	8^2		9		4		6										12
	2			5	3	12		13	9	14				8		10^2	7	4^1	11^3	6	1									13
	2^2			5	3	7	12		9	11			13	4^1			8	14	10	6^3	1									14
		12	4	5	6	13	8		9				11^2		2^3	14	7		10^1		1	3								15
		11	4	5	6	12	8	9^3			13				2^2	14	7		10^1		1■	3								16
1				5	2	7^1		12	9	11			3^2	8■		10		4	13	6										17
1		3^3	4^2	5	2	7^1	8	12	9							10	11	13		6		14								18
1			4^2	5^1	2	7	8	9	10^3	3					12		11	13		6			14							19
1	2^2			5	6	7		12	9	11			3	4^3		10^1	8	14		13										20
1	2			5	6^1	7			10		12		3	4		11^2	8		13					9						21
1	2			5	6^2	7			10^1		12		3	4		11^3	8	13	14					9						22
1	2			5		7			10	3			12^2		14		8■	4^3	11^1					9	6	13				23
1	2			5^2		7	4		10■	3	12			8^3		11^1								9	6	13	14			24
1	2	12	4		6	7				3	10^3					11^2						13		9	5^1	8	14			25
1	2					7	12		10	3				4^2		11	8^1		13	6				9^3	5		14			26
1	2					7	8		9	3	12					13	11^1	4^2	10^3	6						5	14			27
1	2					7^1	4		10		9^3		3	12			8	13	11^2	6					5		14			28
1	2	3			6	7	4		9^1		12		11^2				8	13		5							10			29
1	2^1		4		6	7			9^2				3^3		12	11	8	13							5	14	10			30
1			4		6	7	8^2		9		12				2		11	13		5							10^1	3		31
1			11^1		6	7	4^3		9		14		12^2		2	10	8		13	5								3		32
1					6	7			10		12			4^2	2	11	8		13	5				9^1				3		33
1					6^1	7	4		10		13		12		2		8		11^2	5				9				3		34
1	12				6	7^1	4		10^2	11	13				2		8			5				9				3		35
1	2				6	7^1	4		10^2	11	13						8			5				9			12	3		36
1	2		12		6^1	7			10	11^2	9					8	4			5							13	3		37
1	2					7	4		9								8	12		5						6	10	3	11^1	38

FA Cup

Third Round	Torquay U	(a)	0-0
		(h)	2-0
Fourth Round	Reading	(a)	1-1
		(h)	2-1
Fifth Round	Stoke C	(a)	1-0
Sixth Round	Liverpool	(h)	0-7

Carling Cup

Second Round	Scunthorpe U	(a)	2-0
Third Round	Norwich C	(h)	2-1
Fourth Round	Millwall	(a)	2-2
Quarter-Final	Manchester U	(h)	1-3

BLACKBURN ROVERS FA Premiership

FOUNDATION

It was in 1875 that some Public School old boys called a meeting at which the Blackburn Rovers club was formed and the colours blue and white adopted. The leading light was John Lewis, later to become a founder of the Lancashire FA, a famous referee who was in charge of two FA Cup Finals, and a vice-president of both the FA and the Football League.

Ewood Park, Blackburn BB2 4JF.

Telephone: 0870 111 3232.

Fax: (01254) 671 042.

Ticket Office: 0870 112 3456.

Website: www.rovers.co.uk

Email: enquiries@rovers.co.uk

Ground Capacity: 31,154.

Record Attendance: 62,522 v Bolton W, FA Cup 6th rd, 2 March 1929.

Pitch Measurements: 105m × 65m.

Chairman: John Williams.

Vice-chairman: David Brown.

Managing Director: Tom Finn.

Secretary: Andrew Pincher.

Manager: Mark Hughes.

Assistant Manager: Mark Bowen.

Physio: Dave Fevre.

Colours: Blue and white halved shirts.

Change Colours: All red.

Year Formed: 1875.

Turned Professional: 1880.

Ltd Co.: 1897.

Club Nickname: Rovers.

Previous Grounds: 1875, all matches played away; 1876, Oozehead Ground; 1877, Pleasington Cricket Ground; 1878, Alexandra Meadows; 1881, Leamington Road; 1890, Ewood Park.

First Football League Game: 15 September 1888, Football League, v Accrington (h) D 5–5 – Arthur; Beverley, James Southworth; Douglas, Almond, Forrest; Beresford (1), Walton, John Southworth (1), Fecitt (1), Townley (2).

Record League Victory: 9–0 v Middlesbrough, Division 2, 6 November 1954 – Elvy; Suart, Eckersley; Clayton, Kelly, Bell; Mooney (3), Crossan (2), Briggs, Quigley (3), Langton (1).

HONOURS

FA Premier League: Champions 1994–95; Runners-up 1993–94.

Football League: Division 1 – Champions 1911–12, 1913–14; 1991–92 (play-offs); Runners-up 2000–01; Division 2 – Champions 1938–39; Runners-up 1957–58; Division 3 – Champions 1974–75; Runners-up 1979–80.

FA Cup: Winners 1884, 1885, 1886, 1890, 1891, 1928; Runners-up 1882, 1960.

Football League Cup: Winners 2002.

Full Members' Cup: Winners 1987.

European Competitions: *European Cup:* 1995–96. *UEFA Cup:* 1994–95, 1998–99, 2002–03, 2003–04.

SKY SPORTS FACT FILE

Left-back Bill Eckersley was signed by Blackburn Rovers from High Park in March 1948 and made his debut against Manchester City on 1 May. He had to wait ten years before his next First Division match but meanwhile had collected 17 England caps.

Record Cup Victory: 11–0 v Rossendale, FA Cup 1st rd, 13 October 1884 – Arthur; Hopwood, McIntyre; Forrest, Blenkhorn, Lofthouse; Sowerbutts (2), J. Brown (1), Fecitt (4), Barton (3), Birtwistle (1).

Record Defeat: 0–8 v Arsenal, Division 1, 25 February 1933.

Most League Points (2 for a win): 60, Division 3, 1974–75.

Most League Points (3 for a win): 91, Division 1, 2000–01.

Most League Goals: 114, Division 2, 1954–55.

Highest League Scorer in Season: Ted Harper, 43, Division 1, 1925–26.

Most League Goals in Total Aggregate: Simon Garner, 168, 1978–92.

Most League Goals in One Match: 7, Tommy Briggs v Bristol R, Division 2, 5 February 1955.

Most Capped Player: Henning Berg, 58 (100), Norway.

Most League Appearances: Derek Fazackerley, 596, 1970–86.

Youngest League Player: Harry Dennison, 16 years 155 days v Bristol C, 8 April 1911.

Record Transfer Fee Received: £16,000,000 from Chelsea for Damian Duff, July 2003.

Record Transfer Fee Paid: £7,500,000 to Manchester U for Andy Cole, December 2001.

Football League Record: 1888 Founder Member of the League; 1936–39 Division 2; 1946–48 Division 1; 1948–58 Division 2; 1958–66 Division 1; 1966–71 Division 2; 1971–75 Division 3; 1975–79 Division 2; 1979–80 Division 3; 1980–92 Division 2; 1992–99 FA Premier League; 1999–2001 Division 1; 2001– FA Premier League.

MANAGERS

Thomas Mitchell 1884–96
(Secretary-Manager)
J. Walmsley 1896–1903
(Secretary-Manager)
R. B. Middleton 1903–25
Jack Carr 1922–26
(Team Manager under Middleton to 1925)
Bob Crompton 1926–30
(Hon. Team Manager)
Arthur Barritt 1931–36
(had been Secretary from 1927)
Reg Taylor 1936–38
Bob Crompton 1938–41
Eddie Hapgood 1944–47
Will Scott 1947
Jack Bruton 1947–49
Jackie Bestall 1949–53
Johnny Carey 1953–58
Dally Duncan 1958–60
Jack Marshall 1960–67
Eddie Quigley 1967–70
Johnny Carey 1970–71
Ken Furphy 1971–73
Gordon Lee 1974–75
Jim Smith 1975–78
Jim Iley 1978
John Pickering 1978–79
Howard Kendall 1979–81
Bobby Saxton 1981–86
Don Mackay 1987–91
Kenny Dalglish 1991–95
Ray Harford 1995–97
Roy Hodgson 1997–98
Brian Kidd 1998–99
Tony Parkes 1999–2000
Graeme Souness 2000–04
Mark Hughes September 2004–

LATEST SEQUENCES

Longest Sequence of League Wins: 8, 1.3.1980 – 7.4.1980.

Longest Sequence of League Defeats: 7, 12.3.1966 – 16.4.1966.

Longest Sequence of League Draws: 5, 11.10.1975 – 1.11.1975.

Longest Sequence of Unbeaten League Matches: 23, 30.9.1987 – 27.3.1988.

Longest Sequence Without a League Win: 16, 11.11.1978 – 24.3.1979.

Successive Scoring Runs: 32 from 24.4.1954.

Successive Non-scoring Runs: 4 from 12.12.1908.

TEN YEAR LEAGUE RECORD

		P	*W*	*D*	*L*	*F*	*A*	*Pts*	*Pos*
1996-97	PR Lge	38	9	15	14	42	43	42	13
1997-98	PR Lge	38	16	10	12	57	52	58	6
1998-99	PR Lge	38	7	14	17	38	52	35	19
1999-2000	Div 1	46	15	17	14	55	51	62	11
2000-01	Div 1	46	26	13	7	76	39	91	2
2001-02	PR Lge	38	12	10	16	55	51	46	10
2002-03	PR Lge	38	16	12	10	52	43	60	6
2003-04	PR Lge	38	12	8	18	51	59	44	15
2004-05	PR Lge	38	9	15	14	32	43	42	15
2005-06	PR Lge	38	19	6	13	51	42	63	6

DID YOU KNOW ?

When Blackburn Rovers won 2–1 at Old Trafford against Manchester United on 24 September 2005, it was their first League win there since 13 October 1962 when goals from Mick McGrath, Mike Harrison and Ian Lawther had produced a 3–0 victory.

BLACKBURN ROVERS 2005–06 LEAGUE RECORD

Match No.	*Date*	*Venue*	*Opponents*	*Result*		*H/T Score*	*Lg. Pos.*	*Goalscorers*	*Attendance*
1	Aug 13	A	West Ham U	L	1-3	1-0	—	Todd [18]	33,305
2	20	H	Fulham	W	2-1	1-0	10	Pedersen [15], Tugay [71]	16,953
3	24	H	Tottenham H	D	0-0	0-0	—		22,375
4	27	A	Aston Villa	L	0-1	0-1	11		31,010
5	Sept 11	A	Bolton W	D	0-0	0-0	12		24,405
6	18	H	Newcastle U	L	0-3	0-0	18		20,725
7	24	A	Manchester U	W	2-1	1-0	12	Pedersen 2 [33, 81]	67,765
8	Oct 1	H	WBA	W	2-0	0-0	11	Kuqi 2 [80, 88]	20,721
9	15	A	Liverpool	L	0-1	0-0	11		44,697
10	22	H	Birmingham C	W	2-0	0-0	10	Dickov (pen) [49], Bellamy [81]	18,341
11	29	A	Chelsea	L	2-4	2-2	12	Bellamy 2 (1 pen) [18 (p), 44]	41,553
12	Nov 5	H	Charlton Ath	W	4-1	2-1	11	Emerton [2], Dickov [18], Pedersen [59], Bellamy [90]	17,691
13	19	A	Manchester C	D	0-0	0-0	12		44,032
14	26	A	Arsenal	L	0-3	0-2	13		38,192
15	Dec 3	H	Everton	L	0-2	0-2	13		22,064
16	10	H	West Ham U	W	3-2	0-1	12	Dickov 2 (1 pen) [56 (p), 57], Kuqi [76]	20,370
17	17	A	Fulham	L	1-2	0-1	12	Knight (og) [90]	20,138
18	26	A	Middlesbrough	W	2-0	1-0	11	Kuqi 2 [38, 79]	29,881
19	31	A	Wigan Ath	W	3-0	1-0	9	Pedersen [15], Reid [53], Bellamy [85]	20,639
20	Jan 2	H	Portsmouth	W	2-1	2-1	8	Pedersen [9], Dickov [39]	19,521
21	14	H	Bolton W	D	0-0	0-0	9		18,180
22	21	A	Newcastle U	W	1-0	0-0	8	Pedersen [75]	51,323
23	Feb 1	H	Manchester U	W	4-3	3-1	—	Bentley 3 [35, 41, 56], Neill (pen) [45]	25,484
24	4	A	WBA	L	0-2	0-2	9		23,993
25	11	A	Everton	L	0-1	0-1	10		35,615
26	15	H	Sunderland	W	2-0	1-0	—	Bellamy 2 [38, 63]	18,220
27	25	H	Arsenal	W	1-0	1-0	5	Pedersen [18]	22,504
28	Mar 5	A	Tottenham H	L	2-3	1-2	6	Sinama-Pongolle [44], Bellamy [67]	36,080
29	11	H	Aston Villa	W	2-0	0-0	6	Todd [49], Bellamy [71]	21,932
30	18	H	Middlesbrough	W	3-2	2-1	6	Bellamy 2 [11, 68], Pedersen [28]	18,681
31	25	A	Sunderland	W	1-0	1-0	5	Reid [15]	29,593
32	Apr 3	H	Wigan Ath	D	1-1	0-0	—	Kuqi [84]	20,410
33	8	A	Portsmouth	D	2-2	1-1	5	Bellamy 2 [32, 62]	20,048
34	16	H	Liverpool	L	0-1	0-1	6		29,142
35	19	A	Birmingham C	L	1-2	0-0	—	Savage [78]	25,287
36	29	A	Charlton Ath	W	2-0	1-0	6	Reid [43], Powell (og) [65]	26,254
37	May 2	H	Chelsea	W	1-0	1-0	—	Reid [43]	20,243
38	7	H	Manchester C	W	2-0	1-0	6	Khizanishvili [35], Kuqi [52]	25,731

Final League Position: 6

GOALSCORERS

League (51): Bellamy 13 (1 pen), Pedersen 9, Kuqi 7, Dickov 5 (2 pens), Reid 4, Bentley 3, Todd 2, Emerton 1, Khizanishvili 1, Neill 1 (pen), Savage 1, Sinama-Pongolle 1, Tugay 1, own goals 2.
Carling Cup (12): Bellamy 2, Dickov 2, Bentley 1, Emerton 1, Khizanishvili 1, Kuqi 1, Neill 1, Pedersen 1, Reid 1, Thompson 1.
FA Cup (5): Bellamy 2, Bentley 1, Neill 1, Todd 1.

Friedel B 38	Neill L 35	Matteo D 6	Savage R 34	Todd A 20 + 2	Mokoena A 4 + 18	Emerton B 17 + 13	Reid S 31 + 3	Bellamy C 22 + 5	Kuqi S 15 + 18	Pedersen M 34	Dickov P 17 + 4	Gresko V 1 + 2	Tugay K 23 + 4	Nelsen R 31	Flitcroft G 1 + 1	Johnson J — + 3	Jansen M 1 + 3	Khizanishvili Z 24 + 2	Bentley D 23 + 6	Gray M 30	Thompson D 2 + 4	Peter S 1 + 7	Sinama-Pongolle F 8 + 2	Gallagher P — + 1	Match No.
1	2	3	4	5	6[1]	7	8	9	10[2]	11	12■	13													1
1	2	3	8	5		7[1]	11		10	9			4	6	12										2
1	2■	3	8	5[1]	12	7	11		10[2]	9			4	6		13									3
1		3[1]	4	2		7[3]	11		10	9		12	6	5	8[2]	14	13								4
1	2	3	8		6	7	11		12	9[2]				5			10[1]	4	13						5
1	2		8		6[2]		7	10	12	9		3[3]	13	5			14	4	11[1]						6
1	2		8		12	13	14	10		11	9[3]		4[1]	5				6	7[2]	3					7
1	2				12	13	8	10[3]	14	11	9		4[1]	5				6	7[2]	3					8
1	2		8	14	12	13			10	11[2]	9[3]		4[1]	5				6■	7	3					9
1	2		8	12		13		14	10	11	9[3]		4	5[1]				6	7[2]	3					10
1	2		8[3]	5	14	7	12	9	10[2]	11	13		4[1]					6		3					11
1	2			5[3]	12	7	8	10	13	11	9[2]		4					6	14	3[1]					12
1			8	5	12		7[3]	10	13	11	9[2]		4[1]	2				6		3	14				13
1	2		4	5		7[2]	8	9	10[1]	11	12			6						3	13				14
1	2			5■		13	8	9	12	11			4[1]	6				14	10[2]	3	7[3]				15
1	2		4		12	7[2]	8		13	11	9		6[1]				14	5	10[3]	3					16
1	2		8	5		7[1]			12	11[2]	9		4					6	10	3	13				17
1			8	5[1]	12	7	13	14	10				4	6				2	9[3]	3	11[2]				18
1	2		4			12	8	13	10	11[1]	9[2]			6				5	7[3]	3	14				19
1	2	3	4			12	8	13	10[3]	11	9[2]		14	6				5	7[1]						20
1	2		4	5		7[1]	8	13	12	11	9[2]			6					10	3					21
1	2		8		12	13	7		10	11[1]	9[3]		4[2]	6				5		3		14			22
1	2		8[1]	5	12	13	7		10	11			4[2]	6		14			9[3]	3					23
1	2		8	5		12	7		10[3]	11[2]			4[1]	6					9	3		13	14		24
1	2		4[1]	5		7[3]	8	9	13				12	6					10[2]	3		14	11		25
1	2		8	5			7	9	12	11[3]			4[2]	6				13		3		14	10[1]		26
1	2		8	5	12		7	9		11[3]			4[2]	6					13	3		14	10[1]		27
1	2		4	5		7[1]	8	9	12					6					11	3			10		28
1	2		4	5	12	13	8	9		11	14			6					7[2]	3[1]			10[3]		29
1	2		4■		12	7[1]	8	9		11				6				5	13	3			10[2]		30
1	2				12	7[3]	8	9[2]	13	11	10		4[1]	6				5	14	3					31
1	2		4				8	9	12	11	10[1]		13	6				5	7[2]	3					32
1	2		4		12	13	8	9		11[2]	10			6				5	7	3[1]					33
1	2		4				8	9	12	11	10[1]			6				5	7	3					34
1	2		4	5[2]	13	7[1]	8	9	12	11[3]				6				3	10			14			35
1	2		8				7	9	12	11			4	6[2]				5	13	3			10[1]		36
1	2		6		14		8[3]	9	12	11			4[2]					5	7	3		13	10[1]		37
1	2		8		6[1]	12			10		9[2]		4■					5	7	3		11[3]	13	14	38

FA Cup

Third Round	QPR	(h)	3-0
Fourth Round	West Ham U	(a)	2-4

Carling Cup

Second Round	Huddersfield T	(h)	3-1
Third Round	Leeds U	(h)	3-0
Fourth Round	Charlton Ath	(a)	3-2
Quarter-Final	Middlesbrough	(a)	1-0
Semi-Final	Manchester U	(h)	1-1
		(a)	1-2

BLACKPOOL FL Championship 1

FOUNDATION

Old boys of St John's School who had formed themselves into a football club decided to establish a club bearing the name of their town and Blackpool FC came into being at a meeting at the Stanley Arms Hotel in the summer of 1887. In their first season playing at Raikes Hall Gardens, the club won both the Lancashire Junior Cup and the Fylde Cup.

Bloomfield Road, Seasiders Way, Blackpool FY1 6JJ.

Telephone: 0870 443 1953.

Fax: (01253) 405 011.

Ticket Office: 0870 443 1953.

Website: www.blackpoolfc.co.uk

Email: info@blackpoolfc.co.uk

Ground Capacity: 9,612.

Record Attendance: 38,098 v Wolverhampton W, Division 1, 17 September 1955.

Pitch Measurements: 110yd × 74yd.

Chairman: Karl Oyston.

President: Valery Belokon.

Secretary: Matt Williams.

Manager: Simon Grayson.

Assistant Manager: Tony Parkes.

Physio: Phil Horner.

Colours: Tangerine shirts, white shorts, tangerine stockings.

Change Colours: White shirts, tangerine shorts, white stockings.

Year Formed: 1887.

Turned Professional: 1887.

Ltd Co.: 1896.

Previous Name: 'South Shore' combined with Blackpool in 1899, twelve years after the latter had been formed on the breaking up of the old 'Blackpool St John's' club.

Club Nickname: 'The Seasiders'.

Previous Grounds: 1887, Raikes Hall Gardens; 1897, Athletic Grounds; 1899, Raikes Hall Gardens; 1899, Bloomfield Road.

First Football League game: 5 September 1896, Division 2, v Lincoln C (a) L 1–3 – Douglas; Parr, Bowman; Stuart, Stirzaker, Norris; Clarkin, Donnelly, R. Parkinson, Mount (1), J. Parkinson.

Record League Victory: 7–0 v Reading, Division 2, 10 November 1928 – Mercer; Gibson, Hamilton, Watson, Wilson, Grant, Ritchie, Oxberry (2), Hampson (5), Tufnell, Neal. 7–0 v Preston NE (away), Division 1, 1 May 1948 – Robinson; Shimwell, Crosland; Buchan, Hayward, Kelly; Hobson, Munro (1), McIntosh (5), McCall, Rickett (1). 7–0 v Sunderland, Division 1, 5 October 1957 – Farm; Armfield, Garrett, Kelly (J), Gratrix, Kelly (H), Matthews, Taylor (2), Charnley (2), Durie (2), Perry (1).

HONOURS

Football League: Division 1 – Runners-up 1955–56; Division 2 – Champions 1929–30; Runners-up 1936–37, 1969–70; Promoted from Division 3 – 2000–01 (play-offs); Division 4 – Runners-up 1984–85.

FA Cup: Winners 1953; Runners-up 1948, 1951.

Football League Cup: Semi-final 1962.

Anglo-Italian Cup: Winners 1971; Runners-up 1972.

LDV Vans Trophy: Winners 2002, 2004.

SKY SPORTS FACT FILE

Inside-right Brian Petersen of Natal Province played in an exhibition match against a team including Blackpool maestro Stanley Matthews. He recommended Petersen and he made his Blackpool debut on 9 March 1957 in a 4–3 win at Cardiff City.

Record Cup Victory: 7–1 v Charlton Ath, League Cup 2nd rd, 25 September 1963 – Harvey; Armfield, Martin; Crawford, Gratrix, Cranston; Lea, Ball (1), Charnley (4), Durie (1), Oates (1).

Record Defeat: 1–10 v Small Heath, Division 2, 2 March 1901 and v Huddersfield T, Division 1, 13 December 1930.

Most League Points (2 for a win): 58, Division 2, 1929–30 and Division 2, 1967–68.

Most League Points (3 for a win): 86, Division 4, 1984–85.

Most League Goals: 98, Division 2, 1929–30.

Highest League Scorer in Season: Jimmy Hampson, 45, Division 2, 1929–30.

Most League Goals in Total Aggregate: Jimmy Hampson, 246, 1927–38.

Most League Goals in One Match: 5, Jimmy Hampson v Reading, Division 2, 10 November 1928; 5, Jimmy McIntosh v Preston NE, Division 1, 1 May 1948.

Most Capped Player: Jimmy Armfield, 43, England.

Most League Appearances: Jimmy Armfield, 568, 1952–71.

Youngest League Player: Matty Kay, 16 years 32 days v Scunthorpe U, 13 November 2005.

Record Transfer Fee Received: £1,750,000 from Southampton for Brett Ormerod, December 2001.

Record Transfer Fee Paid: £275,000 to Millwall for Chris Malkin, October 1996.

Football League Record: 1896 Elected to Division 2; 1899 Failed re-election; 1900 Re-elected; 1900–30 Division 2; 1930–33 Division 1; 1933–37 Division 2; 1937–67 Division 1; 1967–70 Division 2; 1970–71 Division 1; 1971–78 Division 2; 1978–81 Division 3; 1981–85 Division 4; 1985–90 Division 3; 1990–92 Division 4; 1992–2000 Division 2; 2000–01 Division 3; 2001–04 Division 2; 2004– FL1.

MANAGERS

Tom Barcroft 1903–33
(Secretary-Manager)
John Cox 1909–11
Bill Norman 1919–23
Maj. Frank Buckley 1923–27
Sid Beaumont 1927–28
Harry Evans 1928–33
(Hon. Team Manager)
Alex 'Sandy' Macfarlane 1933–35
Joe Smith 1935–58
Ronnie Suart 1958–67
Stan Mortensen 1967–69
Les Shannon 1969–70
Bob Stokoe 1970–72
Harry Potts 1972–76
Allan Brown 1976–78
Bob Stokoe 1978–79
Stan Ternent 1979–80
Alan Ball 1980–81
Allan Brown 1981–82
Sam Ellis 1982–89
Jimmy Mullen 1989–90
Graham Carr 1990
Bill Ayre 1990–94
Sam Allardyce 1994–96
Gary Megson 1996–97
Nigel Worthington 1997–99
Steve McMahon 2000–04
Colin Hendry 2004–06
Simon Grayson June 2006–

LATEST SEQUENCES

Longest Sequence of League Wins: 9, 21.11.1936 – 1.1.1937.

Longest Sequence of League Defeats: 8, 26.11.1898 – 7.1.1899.

Longest Sequence of League Draws: 5, 4.12.1976 – 1.1.1977.

Longest Sequence of Unbeaten League Matches: 17, 6.4.1968 – 21.9.1968.

Longest Sequence Without a League Win: 19, 19.12.1970 – 24.4.1971.

Successive Scoring Runs: 33 from 23.2.1929.

Successive Non-scoring Runs: 5 from 12.4.1975.

TEN YEAR LEAGUE RECORD

		P	W	D	L	F	A	Pts	Pos
1996-97	Div 2	46	18	15	13	60	47	69	7
1997-98	Div 2	46	17	11	18	59	67	62	12
1998-99	Div 2	46	14	14	18	44	54	56	14
1999-2000	Div 2	46	8	17	21	49	77	41	22
2000-01	Div 2	46	22	6	18	74	58	72	7
2001-02	Div 2	46	14	14	18	66	69	56	16
2002-03	Div 2	46	15	13	18	56	64	58	13
2003-04	Div 2	46	16	11	19	58	65	59	14
2004-05	FL 1	46	15	12	19	54	59	57	16
2005-06	FL 1	46	12	17	17	56	64	53	19

DID YOU KNOW ?

In 1962 Bill Perry the Blackpool left-winger set a record for the longest service achieved by an overseas player. Signed at 19 on the ship from South Africa on 28 October 1949, he won 3 England caps and completed over 400 League and Cup appearances.

BLACKPOOL 2005–06 LEAGUE RECORD

Match No.	Date	Venue	Opponents	Result	H/T Score	Lg. Pos.	Goalscorers	Attendance
1	Aug 6	H	Chesterfield	L 1-3	1-2	—	Parker [5]	6469
2	9	A	Tranmere R	D 2-2	1-2	—	Vernon [44], Murphy [69]	7509
3	13	A	Yeovil T	D 1-1	1-1	21	Murphy [15]	5698
4	20	H	Swindon T	D 0-0	0-0	21		4661
5	27	A	Rotherham U	L 0-4	0-1	23		4384
6	29	H	Bradford C	W 1-0	0-0	19	Wiles [84]	6468
7	Sept 2	A	Doncaster R	W 1-0	0-0	—	Donnelly [67]	5484
8	10	H	Hartlepool U	L 1-2	0-0	18	Wright [70]	5494
9	17	A	Bristol C	D 1-1	0-0	17	Blinkhorn [90]	9576
10	24	H	Milton Keynes D	W 3-2	1-2	17	Clarke (pen) [17], Mills (og) [50], Burns [68]	4723
11	27	A	Nottingham F	D 1-1	1-0	—	Parker [24]	17,071
12	Oct 1	A	Swansea C	L 2-3	1-2	19	Parker [36], Donnelly [70]	13,911
13	9	H	Colchester U	L 1-2	0-1	—	Wright [89]	4793
14	15	A	Barnsley	D 2-2	1-0	19	Wiles [29], Wright [68]	7945
15	22	H	Brentford	D 0-0	0-0	20		5041
16	29	A	Gillingham	L 1-2	1-0	21	Parker [23]	6300
17	Nov 13	H	Scunthorpe U	W 5-2	3-2	18	Murphy 2 [18, 84], Morris 2 [42, 90], Wright [45]	6016
18	19	A	Colchester U	L 2-3	0-1	22	Murphy [67], Wright [90]	3031
19	26	A	Chesterfield	D 1-1	0-1	20	Harkins [58]	4585
20	Dec 6	H	Bournemouth	L 1-3	1-2	—	Wright [5]	4326
21	10	H	Tranmere R	D 1-1	0-0	21	Clarke [90]	5069
22	17	A	Swindon T	D 0-0	0-0	21		5766
23	26	A	Port Vale	W 2-1	0-0	19	Wiles [52], Parker [54]	5666
24	31	A	Walsall	L 0-2	0-0	22		5046
25	Jan 2	H	Southend U	L 1-2	0-1	22	Parker [75]	5271
26	10	H	Oldham Ath	W 1-0	0-0	—	Gobern [48]	5977
27	14	A	Huddersfield T	L 0-2	0-1	21		11,977
28	21	H	Bristol C	D 1-1	1-1	21	Murphy [5]	4842
29	24	H	Doncaster R	W 4-2	3-1	—	Butler [16], Morris [42], Parker [44], Clarke [54]	4836
30	28	A	Hartlepool U	W 3-0	1-0	16	Clarke 2 (2 pens) [28, 74], Parker [82]	4421
31	Feb 4	H	Nottingham F	D 2-2	1-1	18	Bean [16], Fox [47]	8399
32	11	A	Milton Keynes D	L 0-3	0-1	19		5691
33	14	H	Huddersfield T	L 0-1	0-1	—		6004
34	18	A	Bournemouth	D 1-1	0-1	21	Murphy [61]	5349
35	25	H	Yeovil T	W 2-0	0-0	17	Lindegaard (og) [53], Murphy [54]	5747
36	Mar 11	H	Rotherham U	D 0-0	0-0	19		5934
37	18	H	Port Vale	W 1-0	0-0	17	Williams [66]	5494
38	21	A	Bradford C	L 0-1	0-0	—		7192
39	25	A	Oldham Ath	L 1-3	1-1	19	Southern [42]	6480
40	Apr 1	H	Walsall	W 2-0	0-0	18	Williams [49], Southern [57]	6129
41	8	A	Southend U	L 1-2	1-0	19	Williams [32]	8180
42	15	H	Swansea C	W 1-0	0-0	18	Parker [59]	6709
43	17	A	Brentford	D 1-1	0-0	18	Clarke [89]	7339
44	22	H	Barnsley	D 1-1	1-0	17	Parker [21]	6912
45	29	A	Scunthorpe U	L 0-1	0-0	19		5917
46	May 6	H	Gillingham	D 3-3	1-1	19	Blinkhorn [13], Parker 2 [56, 69]	8541

Final League Position: 19

GOALSCORERS

League (56): Parker 12, Murphy 8, Clarke 6 (3 pens), Wright 6, Morris 3, Wiles 3, Williams 3, Blinkhorn 2, Donnelly 2, Southern 2, Bean 1, Burns 1, Butler 1, Fox 1, Gobern 1, Harkins 1, Vernon 1, own goals 2.
Carling Cup (3): Clarke 1 (pen), Grayson 1, Parker 1.
FA Cup (1): Clarke 1 (pen).
Football League Trophy (5): Blinkhorn 1, Harkins 1, McGregor 1, Southern 1, Vernon 1.

Jones L 31	McGregor M 16+5	Coid D 13	Doolan J 15+4	Edwards R 28+4	Clarke P 46	Parker K 36+4	Southern K 36+6	Murphy J 28+6	Vernon S 10+7	Prendergast R 19+5	Blinkhorn M 4+12	Grayson S 8+4	Wiles S 14+13	Donnelly C 17+7	Edge L —+1	Pogliacomi L 15	Butler T 19+5	Burns J 4+2	Wright T 10+3	Morris I 21+9	Armstrong C 5	Warrender D 13+2	Kay M —+1	Harkins G 4	Gobern L 4+4	Wilcox J 26	Joseph M 15+1	Gordon D 1	Wood N 7	Fox D 4+3	Bean M 17	Kuqi N 1+3	Taylor S 3+1	Lasley K 4+4	Taylor A 3	Stockley S 3+4	Williams G 6+3	*Match No.*
1	2[1]	3	4[2]	5	6	7	8	9	10[3]	11	12	13	14																									1
1	2	3	4[1]	5	6	7	8	9	10[2]	11		12		13																								2
1[6]	2	3	4[1]	5	6	7	8	9	10[2]	11		12		13	15																							3
	2	3	4[1]	5	6	7	8	9	10[2]	11		12	13			1																						4
	2	3	8	5	6	10	12	9[2]	13	11[3]		4[1]	14	7		1																						5
	12	3	8[2]	5■	6	10	13	14	9[3]			4	11[1]	7		1	2																					6
	12	3[1]	4		6	10	8	13	9[2]			2	11[3]	7		1	5	14																				7
	12		4[1]	3	6	10[3]	8	13	9[2]			2	7	11		1	5		14																			8
	2			3	6	10[2]	8			12	13	4	7[1]	11		1	5		9																			9
		2		3	6	12	8		13		9[1]	4	7[3]	14		1	5	11	10[2]																			10
	2	3	12	5	6	10	8		13				7[1]	11		1		4[3]	9[2]	14																		11
	2			3[3]	6	10	8		12			4	13	11		1	5	14	9[1]	7[2]																		12
	2		12	3[3]	6		8		10[2]		13	4[1]	11			1	5	7	9	14																		13
	2	5	4		6	10	8				12		11			1		7[1]	9		3																	14
	5		4	12	6		8	13		11[1]	10[2]		7			1			9■		3	2																15
	2		4[2]	5	6	10■	8	9			12		7			1				13	3	11[1]																16
			4[3]	5	6		8	9	13	12			7[1]			1			10[2]	11	3	2	14															17
			12	5	6		8	9		13			7[2]			1	14		10	11	3[3]	2		4[1]														18
1	12	3		5	6	13		9						7■						8		2[1]		4	10[2]	11												19
1	12	2		5	6	13	3	9					14						10[3]	7[1]				4	8[2]	11												20
1		3[1]		5	6	10	8	9[3]					13				12		14	7		2		4		11[2]												21
1	5		4		6	10	8	9									3			7		2				11												22
1	3		4[1]		6	10	8	9[2]					7[3]	12			5		13			2			14	11												23
1	3		4		6	10	8	12	9[1]				13	7[3]			5					2			14	11[2]												24
1	3[2]				6	10	8	12	9[1]				7[3]	4			5			13		2			14	11												25
1			12		6	10	8	9					13	4			5			7[2]		2[3]			11[1]	3	14											26
1					6	10	8	9	12					13			5[3]			7[2]		14			11[1]	3	2	4										27
1					6	10[1]	8	9	12				13	7[2]			5			11						3	2		4[3]	14								28
1					6	10[3]		9		11							5			7[2]		12			13	3	2[1]		4		8	14						29
1					6[1]	10[3]	12	9		11							5			7						3[2]	2		4■		8	14	13					30
1				12	6	10	13	9		11							5			7							2[1]			4[2]	8		3					31
1				12	6			9		7	13						5■			2[1]						11				3[3]	4	8[2]	10	14				32
1				5	6		8	9		11[1]	10									7		2[2]				3■					4	12		13				33
1				5[2]	6	12	8	9					14				13			10									11[1]		7		2[3]	4	3			34
1				5	6	10	12	9					13							7						11			4[1]		8			2[2]	3			35
1					6	10[2]	8	9		12	13		14				5			7[1]		2				11			4[3]						3			36
1					6	10	12	9		11[1]				8[3]			13			7						3	5[2]				4					2	14	37
1					6	10	8[1]	9						13			12			7[3]						3	5			11[2]	4					2	14	38
1				12	6	10	8	9[3]		13										7[2]						3[1]	5			11	4					2	14	39
1				5	6	10	8[3]	9[2]		11[1]				12						13						3	2			14	4						7	40
1				5	6	10	8			11[2]	12									13[3]						3	2			14	4			7			9[1]	41
1				5	6	10	8			11[2]	12			7[3]						13						3	2				4					14	9[1]	42
1				5[3]	6	10	8			11	12			7[2]						13						3	2				4					14	9[1]	43
1				5	6	10	8			11	12			7[2]												3	2				4			13			9[1]	44
1				5	6	10	8			11[3]	12			7[2]												3	2				4			13		14	9[1]	45
1				5[2]	6	10				11[3]	9		12							13						3	2		8		4			7[1]		14		46

FA Cup

First Round	Doncaster R	(a)	1-4

Carling Cup

First Round	Hull C	(h)	2-1
Second Round	Leicester C	(a)	1-2

Football League Trophy

First Round	Wrexham	(h)	4-3
Second Round	Carlisle U	(a)	1-2

BOLTON WANDERERS FA Premiership

FOUNDATION

In 1874 boys of Christ Church Sunday School, Blackburn Street, led by their master Thomas Ogden, established a football club which went under the name of the school and whose president was Vicar of Christ Church. Membership was 6d (two and a half pence). When their president began to lay down too many rules about the use of church premises, the club broke away and formed Bolton Wanderers in 1877, holding their earliest meetings at the Gladstone Hotel.

Reebok Stadium, Burnden Way, Bolton BL6 6JW.

Telephone: (01204) 673 673.

Fax: (01204) 673 773.

Ticket Office: 0871 871 2932.

Website: www.bwfc.co.uk

Email: reception@bwfc.co.uk

Ground Capacity: 28,101.

Record Attendance: 69,912 v Manchester C, FA Cup 5th rd, 18 February 1933.

Pitch Measurements: 101m × 66m.

Chairman: Phil A. Gartside.

Vice-chairman: Brett Warburton.

Secretary: Simon Marland.

Manager: Sam Allardyce.

Assistant Manager: Sammy Lee.

Physio: Mark Taylor.

Colours: White shirts, white shorts, white stockings.

Change Colours: Maroon shirts, maroon shorts, maroon stockings.

Year Formed: 1874.

Turned Professional: 1880.

Ltd Co.: 1895.

Previous Name: 1874, Christ Church FC; 1877, Bolton Wanderers.

Club Nickname: 'The Trotters'.

Previous Grounds: Park Recreation Ground and Cockle's Field before moving to Pike's Lane ground 1881; 1895, Burnden Park; 1997, Reebok Stadium.

First Football League Game: 8 September 1888, Football League, v Derby Co (h) L 3–6 – Harrison; Robinson, Mitchell; Roberts, Weir, Bullough, Davenport (2), Milne, Coupar, Barbour, Brogan (1).

Record League Victory: 8–0 v Barnsley, Division 2, 6 October 1934 – Jones; Smith, Finney; Goslin, Atkinson, George Taylor; George T. Taylor (2), Eastham, Milsom (1), Westwood (4), Cook, (1 og).

HONOURS

Football League: Division 1 – Champions 1996–97; Promoted from Division 1 (play-offs) 2000–01. Division 2 – Champions 1908–09, 1977–78; Runners-up 1899–1900, 1904–05, 1910–11, 1934–35, 1992–93; Division 3 – Champions 1972–73; Promoted from Division 4 (3rd) 1987–88.

FA Cup: Winners 1923, 1926, 1929, 1958; Runners-up 1894, 1904, 1953.

Football League Cup: Runners-up 1995, 2004.

Freight Rover Trophy: Runners-up 1986.

Sherpa Van Trophy: Winners 1989.

European Competitions: *UEFA Cup:* 2005–06.

SKY SPORTS FACT FILE

On 8 May 1932, the last day of the season, Bolton Wanderers beat Liverpool 8–1 at Burnden Park but only 9209 spectators were present – the Trotters average attendance that season was 15,843. Jack Milsom scored four of their goals.

Record Cup Victory: 13–0 v Sheffield U, FA Cup 2nd rd, 1 February 1890 – Parkinson; Robinson (1), Jones; Bullough, Davenport, Roberts; Rushton, Brogan (3), Cassidy (5), McNee, Weir (4).

Record Defeat: 1–9 v Preston NE, FA Cup 2nd rd, 10 December 1887.

Most League Points (2 for a win): 61, Division 3, 1972–73.

Most League Points (3 for a win): 98, Division 1, 1996–97.

Most League Goals: 100, Division 1, 1996–97.

Highest League Scorer in Season: Joe Smith, 38, Division 1, 1920–21.

Most League Goals in Total Aggregate: Nat Lofthouse, 255, 1946–61.

Most League Goals in One Match: 5, Tony Caldwell v Walsall, Division 3, 10 September 1983.

Most Capped Player: Mark Fish, 34 (62), South Africa.

Most League Appearances: Eddie Hopkinson, 519, 1956–70.

Youngest League Player: Ray Parry, 15 years 267 days v Wolverhampton W, 13 October 1951.

Record Transfer Fee Received: £4,500,000 from Liverpool for Jason McAteer, September 1995.

Record Transfer Fee Paid: £3,500,000 for Dean Holdsworth from Wimbledon, October 1997.

Football League Record: 1888 Founder Member of the League; 1899–1900 Division 2; 1900–03 Division 1; 1903–05 Division 2; 1905–08 Division 1; 1908–09 Division 2; 1909–10 Division 1; 1910–11 Division 2; 1911–33 Division 1; 1933–35 Division 2; 1935–64 Division 1; 1964–71 Division 2; 1971–73 Division 3; 1973–78 Division 2; 1978–80 Division 1; 1980–83 Division 2; 1983–87 Division 3; 1987–88 Division 4; 1988–92 Division 3; 1992–93 Division 2; 1993–95 Division 1; 1995–96 FA Premier League; 1996–97 Division 1; 1997–98 FA Premier League; 1998–2001 Division 1; 2001– FA Premier League.

MANAGERS

Tom Rawthorne 1874–85 *(Secretary)*
J. J. Bentley 1885–86 *(Secretary)*
W. G. Struthers 1886–87 *(Secretary)*
Fitzroy Norris 1887 *(Secretary)*
J. J. Bentley 1887–95 *(Secretary)*
Harry Downs 1895–96 *(Secretary)*
Frank Brettell 1896–98 *(Secretary)*
John Somerville 1898–1910
Will Settle 1910–15
Tom Mather 1915–19
Charles Foweraker 1919–44
Walter Rowley 1944–50
Bill Ridding 1951–68
Nat Lofthouse 1968–70
Jimmy McIlroy 1970
Jimmy Meadows 1971
Nat Lofthouse 1971 *(then Admin. Manager to 1972)*
Jimmy Armfield 1971–74
Ian Greaves 1974–80
Stan Anderson 1980–81
George Mulhall 1981–82
John McGovern 1982–85
Charlie Wright 1985
Phil Neal 1985–92
Bruce Rioch 1992–95
Roy McFarland 1995–96
Colin Todd 1996–99
Sam Allardyce October 1999–

LATEST SEQUENCES

Longest Sequence of League Wins: 11, 5.11.1904 – 2.1.1905.

Longest Sequence of League Defeats: 11, 7.4.1902 – 18.10.1902.

Longest Sequence of League Draws: 6, 25.1.1913 – 8.3.1913.

Longest Sequence of Unbeaten League Matches: 23, 13.10.1990 – 9.3.1991.

Longest Sequence Without a League Win: 26, 7.4.1902 – 10.1.1903.

Successive Scoring Runs: 24 from 22.11.1996.

Successive Non-scoring Runs: 5 from 3.1.1898.

TEN YEAR LEAGUE RECORD

		P	*W*	*D*	*L*	*F*	*A*	*Pts*	*Pos*
1996-97	Div 1	46	28	14	4	100	53	98	1
1997-98	PR Lge	38	9	13	16	41	61	40	18
1998-99	Div 1	46	20	16	10	78	59	76	6
1999-2000	Div 1	46	21	13	12	69	50	76	6
2000-01	Div 1	46	24	15	7	76	45	87	3
2001-02	PR Lge	38	9	13	16	44	62	40	16
2002-03	PR Lge	38	10	14	14	41	51	44	17
2003-04	PR Lge	38	14	11	13	48	56	53	8
2004-05	PR Lge	38	16	10	12	49	44	58	6
2005-06	PR Lge	38	15	11	12	49	41	56	8

DID YOU KNOW ?

Shortly after signing as a Bolton Wanderers professional, Eric Bell scored three goals for the reserves on Christmas Eve 1949 at Preston North End, but had the misfortune to break his leg there on Easter Saturday missing the FA's tour to the West Indies.

BOLTON WANDERERS 2005–06 LEAGUE RECORD

Match No.	Date	Venue	Opponents	Result		H/T Score	Lg. Pos.	Goalscorers	Attendance
1	Aug 13	A	Aston Villa	D	2-2	2-2	—	Davies [6], Campo [8]	32,263
2	21	H	Everton	L	0-1	0-0	13		25,608
3	24	H	Newcastle U	W	2-0	1-0	—	Diouf [37], Giannakopoulos [50]	25,904
4	27	A	West Ham U	W	2-1	0-0	5	Nolan [59], Campo [85]	31,629
5	Sept 11	H	Blackburn R	D	0-0	0-0	5		24,405
6	18	A	Manchester C	W	1-0	0-0	4	Speed (pen) [90]	43,137
7	24	H	Portsmouth	W	1-0	1-0	3	Nolan [25]	23,134
8	Oct 2	A	Wigan Ath	L	1-2	0-0	5	Jaidi [68]	20,553
9	15	A	Chelsea	L	1-5	1-0	7	Giannakopoulos [4]	41,775
10	23	H	WBA	W	2-0	0-0	7	Nakata [81], Nolan [90]	24,151
11	29	A	Charlton Ath	W	1-0	0-0	4	Nolan [72]	26,175
12	Nov 7	H	Tottenham H	W	1-0	1-0	—	Nolan [32]	26,634
13	27	A	Fulham	L	1-2	0-2	6	Legwinski (og) [90]	19,768
14	Dec 3	H	Arsenal	W	2-0	2-0	6	Diagne-Faye [20], Giannakopoulos [32]	26,792
15	10	H	Aston Villa	D	1-1	0-0	5	Diouf [82]	23,646
16	17	A	Everton	W	4-0	1-0	5	Davies [32], Giannakopoulos 2 [75, 80], Speed (pen) [79]	34,500
17	26	A	Sunderland	D	0-0	0-0	5		32,232
18	31	A	Manchester U	L	1-4	1-2	7	Speed [33]	67,858
19	Jan 2	H	Liverpool	D	2-2	1-0	7	Jaidi [10], Diouf [71]	27,604
20	14	A	Blackburn R	D	0-0	0-0	7		18,180
21	21	H	Manchester C	W	2-0	2-0	7	Borgetti [37], Nolan [41]	26,466
22	Feb 1	A	Portsmouth	D	1-1	0-0	—	Fadiga [69]	19,128
23	4	H	Wigan Ath	D	1-1	0-0	7	Giannakopoulos [63]	25,854
24	11	A	Arsenal	D	1-1	1-0	6	Nolan [12]	38,193
25	26	H	Fulham	W	2-1	1-1	6	Helguson (og) [45], Nolan [68]	23,104
26	Mar 4	A	Newcastle U	L	1-3	0-2	7	Davies [72]	52,012
27	11	H	West Ham U	W	4-1	3-0	7	Giannakopoulos 2 [12, 33], Speed [45], Pedersen [81]	24,461
28	18	H	Sunderland	W	2-0	0-0	7	Davies [47], Nolan [85]	23,568
29	26	A	Middlesbrough	L	3-4	1-2	7	Giannakopoulos [3], Okocha [58], Jaidi [81]	25,971
30	Apr 1	H	Manchester U	L	1-2	1-1	7	Davies [26]	27,718
31	4	A	Birmingham C	L	0-1	0-1	—		26,493
32	9	A	Liverpool	L	0-1	0-1	7		44,194
33	15	H	Chelsea	L	0-2	0-1	8		27,266
34	17	A	WBA	D	0-0	0-0	8		23,181
35	22	H	Charlton Ath	W	4-1	3-0	8	Vaz Te [14], Davies 2 [21, 89], Borgetti [31]	24,713
36	30	A	Tottenham H	L	0-1	0-0	8		36,179
37	May 3	H	Middlesbrough	D	1-1	0-0	—	Vaz Te [51]	22,733
38	7	H	Birmingham C	W	1-0	0-0	8	Vaz Te [65]	26,275

Final League Position: 8

GOALSCORERS

League (49): Giannakopoulos 9, Nolan 9, Davies 7, Speed 4 (2 pens), Diouf 3, Jaidi 3, Vaz Te 3, Borgetti 2, Campo 2, Diagne-Faye 1, Fadiga 1, Nakata 1, Okocha 1, Pedersen 1, own goals 2.
Carling Cup (3): Borgetti 2, Vaz Te 1.
FA Cup (5): Giannakopoulos 2, Borgetti 1, Davies 1, Vaz Te 1.
UEFA Cup (9): Borgetti 2, Nolan 2, Diouf 1, Giannakopoulos 1, N'Gotty 1, Vaz Te 1, own goal 1.

Jaaskelainen J 38	Hunt N 12 + 8	Gardner R 27 + 3	Campo I 8 + 7	Ben Haim T 32 + 3	Jaidi R 15 + 1	Nolan K 35 + 1	Speed G 29 + 2	Pedersen H 15 + 6	Davies K 37	Diouf E 17 + 3	Okocha J 18 + 9	Vaz Te R 6 + 16	Giannakopoulos S 29 + 5	Diagne-Faye A 23 + 4	Borgetti J 5 + 14	N'Gotty B 27 + 2	Nakata H 14 + 7	O'Brien J 22 + 1	Fernandes F — + 1	Fadiga K 5 + 3	Djetou M 1 + 2	Jansen M 3 + 3	Fojut J — + 1	Match No.
1	2	3	4^{1}	5	6	7	8	9	10	11	12													1
1	2^{1}	3	12	5^{2}	6	7	4	9^{3}	10	8	11	13	14											2
1	2		12	5	6^{2}	8	4	3	10^{1}	9^{3}	7		11	13	14									3
1	2		12	5		8	4	3	10^{2}	9^{1}	7^{3}		11	13	14	6								4
1	12	13	2	5		8	4	3	10^{3}	9	7^{1}		11^{2}		14	6								5
1		12	13	2	6	7	8	3	10	9^{3}			11^{1}	4^{2}		5	14							6
1	2^{2}	11		5		9	4^{3}	3	10	13	7^{1}		12			6	8	14						7
1		11^{1}		2	6	9	4	3	10	12	7^{2}		13		14	5	8^{3}							8
1		12■		5	3	7	4^{2}	9^{1}	10^{3}	8			11	2		6	13		14					9
1				5		7		3	10	9^{1}			11	4		6	8	2		12				10
1		3		12	6	7	11		10^{3}	9^{2}	13			4	14	5	8^{1}	2						11
1		3		5	6	7	8		10^{2}	9^{1}			11^{3}	4	13	12	14	2						12
1		3		5	6^{1}	7	11		10	9■	13			4^{3}		12	8^{2}	2			14			13
1		3		5	12	7	8		10	9		13	11^{2}	4^{1}		6		2						14
1		3		5		7	8		10^{1}	9	12	13	11^{2}	4		6		2						15
1	12				6	8	3		10	9^{2}	7^{1}	13	11	4^{3}		5		2			14			16
1	2	3	12	5			8			9^{3}	13	10	11		14	6				7^{2}	4^{1}			17
1		3		5^{1}		8	10		9		7	12	11^{2}	4		6		2		13				18
1		3		12	6	7	8^{2}		10	9^{1}			11	4		5		2		13				19
1		3	12	5		7			10			13	11^{2}		9^{1}	6	8■	2		4^{3}		14		20
1	13	3	4	5		7			10			12^{2}	11		9^{3}	6		2		8^{1}		14		21
1	2^{1}	3		5		7			10			12	11			6		8		4^{2}		9	13	22
1	12	3		5		7			10^{3}			13	11		14	6	8	2		4^{1}		9^{2}		23
1	12	3		5		7			10		13	14	11^{2}	4^{1}		6	8	2				9^{3}		24
1		3		12	6	9	13		10		7^{1}	14	11	4^{2}		5	8^{3}	2						25
1		3			6	9	8	12	10		7^{2}	14	11	4		5^{1}	13^{3}	2						26
1	12	3		5	6	9	4	13	10		7^{3}	8	11^{2}				14	2^{1}						27
1		3^{1}		5		9	4	12	10		7^{2}	8^{3}	11	13	14	6		2						28
1		3		5	6	8^{2}	4^{1}	9^{3}	10		7		11	12	14		13	2						29
1	12			5		9	8^{2}	3	10^{3}	13	7		11	4	14	6		2^{1}						30
1	12			5		8^{2}		3	10	9^{3}	7	13	11	4	14	6		2^{1}						31
1	2	3	12	5		9	8	13	10		7^{3}		11^{2}	4^{1}		6						14		32
1		3	4	2■		7	8^{3}	12	10			11^{2}	13	5	9^{1}	6	14							33
1	2	3				9	4		10		7	12	11^{1}	5		6	8							34
1	2	3	4	5		12	7^{2}		10		13	11^{1}		6	9		8							35
1	2	3	4	5			7^{1}	12	10		13	14	11	6	9^{3}		8^{2}							36
1	2		4^{3}	5		9^{2}	12	3	10		7	11	13	6	14		8^{1}							37
1			4^{2}	5		9	7	3	10		12	13	11^{3}	6	14		8^{1}	2						38

FA Cup

Third Round	Watford	(a)	3-0
Fourth Round	Arsenal	(h)	1-0
Fifth Round	West Ham U	(h)	0-0
		(a)	1-2

Carling Cup

Third Round	West Ham U	(h)	1-0
Fourth Round	Leicester C	(h)	2-1
Quarter-Final	Wigan Ath	(a)	0-2

UEFA Cup

First Round	Lokomotiv Plovdiv	(h)	2-1
		(a)	2-1
Group H	Besiktas	(a)	1-1
	Zenit	(h)	1-0
	Guimaraes	(a)	1-1
	Sevilla	(h)	1-1
Third Round	Marseille	(h)	0-0
		(a)	1-2

BOSTON UNITED FL Championship 2

FOUNDATION

Although it was 1934 before the name Boston United first appeared, football had been played in the town since the late 1800s and indeed, always on the same site as the present York Street stadium. In fact Boston Football Club was established in March 1870 playing their first match against Louth the following month. Before the First World War, there were two clubs, Boston Town, whose headquarters were The Coach and Horses, and Boston Swifts, who used The Indian Queen. In fact, as both public houses were situated on Main Ridge and the pitch was virtually just opposite, it was not surprising that for the first forty years or so, that was what the ground was called. Swifts never reappeared after the First World War and it was left to the club called simply Boston to achieve the first giant-killing in the FA Cup by beating Bradford Park Avenue 1-0 on 12 December 1925. The club was now competing in the Midland League and subsequently reformed under the new title of Boston United.

Staffsmart Stadium, York Street, Boston, Lincolnshire, PE21 6HJ.

Telephone: (01205) 364 406. (01205) 365 525.

Fax: (01205) 354 063.

Ticket Office: (01205) 364 406.

Website: www.bostonunited.co.uk

Email: admin@bufc.co.uk

Ground Capacity: 6,613.

Record Attendance: 10,086 v Corby Town, Friendly, 1955.

Pitch Measurements: 110yd × 70yd.

Chairman: Jon Sotnick.

Chief Executive: James Rodwell.

Secretary: John Blackwell.

Manager: Steve Evans.

Assistant Manager: Paul Raynor.

Physio: Julie Frost.

HONOURS

FA Cup: best season: 3rd rd, 1926, 1956, 1972, 1974.
Football League Cup: never past 1st rd.
Conference: Champions 2001–02.
Dr. Martens: Champions 1999–2000. Runners-up: 1998–99.
Unibond League: Runners-up 1995–96, 1997–98.
Unibond Challenge Cup: Runners-up 1996–97.
FA Trophy: Runners-up 1984–85.
Northern Premier League: Champions 1972–73, 1973–74, 1976–77, 1977–78.
Northern Premier League Cup: Winners 1974, 1976.
Northern Premier League Challenge Shield: Winners 1974, 1975, 1977, 1978.
Lincolnshire Senior Cup: Winners 1935, 1937, 1938, 1946, 1950, 1955, 1956, 1960, 1977, 1979, 1986, 1988, 1989.
Non-League Champions of Champions Cup: Winners 1973, 1977.
East Anglian Cup: Winners 1961.
Central Alliance League: Champions 1961–62.
United Counties League: Champions 1965–66.
West Midlands League: Champions 1966–67, 1967–68.
Eastern Professional Floodlit Cup: Winners 1972.

SKY SPORTS FACT FILE

In 1967–68 Boston United won the West Midlands League title and the League Cup. They also reached the FA Cup first round proper and only lost to Leyton Orient in a replay in injury time. Boston had a season's squad of 12 part-timers and two amateurs.

Colours: Amber and black striped shirts, black shorts, black stockings.

Change Colours: All red.

Year formed: 1934.

Club Nickname: 'The Pilgrims'.

First Football League Game: 10 August 2002, Division 3, v Bournemouth (h), D 2–2 – Bastock; Hocking, Chapman, Morley (Rodwell), Warburton, Ellender, Gould (1), Bennett, Clare, Elding (Cook), Weatherstone S. (1 og).

MANAGERS

George Kerr/Dave Cusack
Dave Cusack
Peter Morris
Mel Sterland
Greg Fee
Steve Evans 1998–2002
Neil Thompson 2002–04
Steve Evans March 2004–

Record League Victory: 6–0 v Shrewsbury T, Division 3, 21 December 2002 – Bastock; Costello, Chapman, Redfearn (1), Balmer, Hocking (McCarthy), Weatherstone S, Higgins, Douglas (1), Logan (2) (Thompson L), Angel (Gould (1)). (1 og).

Most League Points (3 for a win): 61, League 2, 2005–06.

Most League Goals: 62, FL Championship 2, 2004–05.

Highest League Scorer in Season: Andy Kirk, 19, 2004–05.

Most Capped Player: Andy Kirk, 1, Northern Ireland.

Most League Appearances: Paul Ellender, 132, 2002–.

Youngest League Player: Rob Norris, 17 years 18 days v Bristol R, 30 October 2004.

Record Transfer Fee Received: £125,000 from Northampton T for Andy Kirk, March 2005.

Record Transfer Fee Paid: £30,000 to Scarborough for Paul Ellender, August 2001.

Football League Record: 2002 Promoted to Division 3; 2004– FL2.

LATEST SEQUENCES

Longest Sequence of League Wins: 4, 19.4.2003 – 3.5.2003.

Longest Sequence of League Defeats: 6, 29.10.2002 – 14.12.2002.

Longest Sequence of League Draws: 4, 6.12.2005 – 26.12.2005.

Longest Sequence of Unbeaten League Matches: 10, 4.9.2005 – 29.10.2005 .

Longest Sequence Without a League Win: 9, 30.4.2005 – 4.9.2005.

Successive Scoring Runs: 8 from 26.3.2005.

Successive Non-scoring Runs: 5 from 29.10.2002.

TEN YEAR LEAGUE RECORD

		P	*W*	*D*	*L*	*F*	*A*	*Pts*	*Pos*
1996-97	NP pr	44	22	13	9	74	47	79	6
1997-98	NP pr	42	22	12	8	55	40	78	2
1998-99	SL pr	42	17	16	9	69	51	67	2
1999-2000	SL pr	42	27	11	4	102	39	92	1
2000-01	Conf.	42	13	17	12	74	63	56	12
2001-02	Conf.	42	25	9	8	84	42	84	1
2002-03	Div 3	46	15	13	18	55	56	54*	15
2003-04	Div 3	46	16	11	19	50	54	59	11
2004-05	FL 2	46	14	16	16	62	58	58	16
2005-06	FL 2	46	15	16	15	50	60	61	11

**4 pts deducted at start of season.*

DID YOU KNOW ?

On 17 March 1951 Boston United, suffering a heavy injury list, were forced to field trainer Freddie Tunstall, 52, the one-time Sheffield United and England international at outside-left against Peterborough United.

BOSTON UNITED 2005–06 LEAGUE RECORD

Match No.	Date	Venue	Opponents	Result		H/T Score	Lg. Pos.	Goalscorers	Attendance
1	Aug 6	A	Wrexham	L	0-2	0-1	—		4503
2	10	H	Shrewsbury T	D	1-1	0-0	—	Lee [84]	2409
3	13	H	Stockport Co	D	2-2	0-0	20	Joachim 2 [50, 90]	2432
4	20	A	Cheltenham T	L	0-3	0-3	22		2680
5	27	H	Mansfield T	D	2-2	2-1	22	Thomas [9], White [34]	2848
6	29	A	Northampton T	L	2-3	1-2	23	White [40], Ross [86]	5012
7	Sept 4	A	Macclesfield T	D	2-2	0-2	22	Maylett [48], Whelan [75]	2130
8	10	H	Rochdale	W	3-2	1-1	20	Whelan 2 (1 pen) [8, 58 (p)], White [76]	2274
9	17	A	Bury	D	1-1	0-1	20	Dudfield [82]	1985
10	24	H	Grimsby T	D	1-1	0-1	20	Joachim [90]	4077
11	27	A	Darlington	D	0-0	0-0	—		3115
12	Oct 1	H	Peterborough U	W	1-0	0-0	18	Ross (pen) [63]	4126
13	7	A	Notts Co	W	2-1	2-0	—	Joachim [1], Pipe (og) [11]	6632
14	15	H	Bristol R	W	3-1	1-1	11	Dudfield [10], Ross [52], Joachim [80]	2469
15	22	A	Oxford U	D	0-0	0-0	11		5084
16	29	H	Torquay U	W	2-0	1-0	9	Ross [21], Joachim [61]	2220
17	Nov 11	A	Rushden & D	L	0-1	0-0	—		3205
18	19	H	Notts Co	L	1-2	0-1	12	Lee [49]	2921
19	26	H	Wrexham	W	2-1	1-0	10	Joachim 2 [14, 66]	1938
20	Dec 6	A	Wycombe W	D	1-1	1-0	—	Green [21]	4372
21	10	A	Shrewsbury T	D	1-1	0-1	—	Whelan [89]	3376
22	17	H	Cheltenham T	D	0-0	0-0	12		1906
23	26	A	Lincoln C	D	0-0	0-0	11		7077
24	31	A	Barnet	L	0-1	0-0	13		2287
25	Jan 2	H	Leyton Orient	L	1-2	0-1	17	Talbot [49]	2689
26	7	H	Macclesfield T	W	3-1	2-0	14	Talbot [15], Canoville [32], Ellender [81]	1975
27	14	A	Chester C	W	1-0	0-0	11	Rusk [82]	2956
28	18	H	Carlisle U	L	0-5	0-1	—		1924
29	21	H	Bury	W	3-1	2-1	10	Joachim 2 (1 pen) [26, 31 (p)], Till [60]	2018
30	28	A	Rochdale	D	1-1	1-1	11	Keene [8]	2384
31	Feb 4	H	Darlington	D	0-0	0-0	13		2268
32	11	A	Grimsby T	L	0-1	0-0	13		5028
33	18	H	Wycombe W	D	1-1	0-0	14	Joachim [56]	2283
34	25	A	Stockport Co	W	1-0	0-0	12	Joachim [67]	5133
35	Mar 11	A	Mansfield T	L	0-5	0-1	15		3121
36	18	H	Lincoln C	W	2-1	1-0	14	Joachim [26], Dudfield [90]	4476
37	22	H	Northampton T	L	0-1	0-0	—		2174
38	25	A	Carlisle U	L	2-4	0-2	14	Billy (og) [63], Rusk [84]	7596
39	29	H	Chester C	L	1-3	0-1	—	Rusk [87]	1651
40	Apr 1	H	Barnet	W	2-1	2-0	14	Dudfield [16], Greaves [35]	2066
41	8	A	Leyton Orient	L	0-2	0-0	14		4391
42	15	A	Peterborough U	W	1-0	0-0	13	Clarke J [69]	5092
43	17	H	Oxford U	W	1-0	1-0	12	White [6]	2313
44	22	A	Bristol R	L	1-3	0-1	13	Joachim [60]	4836
45	29	H	Rushden & D	W	2-0	0-0	11	Dudfield [89], Thomas [90]	2489
46	May 6	A	Torquay U	D	0-0	0-0	11		5697

Final League Position: 11

GOALSCORERS

League (50): Joachim 14 (1 pen), Dudfield 5, Ross 4 (1 pen), Whelan 4 (1 pen), White 4, Rusk 3, Lee 2, Talbot 2, Thomas 2, Canoville 1, Clarke J 1, Ellender 1, Greaves 1, Green 1, Keene 1, Maylett 1, Till 1, own goals 2.
Carling Cup (0).
FA Cup (7): Joachim 2, Futcher 1, Lee 1, Maylett 1, Rusk 1, Talbot 1.
Football League Trophy (2): Maylett 1, White 1.

Abbey N 17	Canoville L 42 + 1	McCann A 31 + 4	Holland C 29 + 5	Greaves M 31 + 3	Futcher B 13 + 1	Maylett B 23 + 15	Talbot S 28 + 2	Joachim J 41 + 2	Whelan N 8 + 7	Johnson G 3 + 1	Thomas D 15 + 20	Norris R — + 1	Rusk S 24 + 10	Lee J 11 + 6	Noble D 10 + 1	White A 37	Ross I 13 + 1	Ellender P 25	Clare D — + 1	Dudfield L 21 + 15	Wright C 1	Edkins A — + 1	Kuipers M 15	Galbraith D 6 + 6	Green F 5 + 1	Logan C 13	Hall A 5 + 7	Till P 10 + 6	Keene J 6	Silk G 11 + 3	Clarke J 12 + 3	McSporran J — + 2	Melton S — + 3	*Match No.*
1	2	3^{1}	4	5	6	7	8	9	10^{2}	11^{3}	12	13	14																					1
1	2	3^{1}	4	5	6	7	8^{3}		13	14	10		11^{2}	9	12																			2
1	2		4	5	6	7^{1}	8^{2}	9	12		11		13	10	3																			3
1	2	3	4^{1}		6■	12	8^{2}	9		11^{3}	14		13	10	7	5																		4
1	2	3		12		7	8^{3}	9^{1}	13		11			10^{2}	4	5	14	6																5
1	2			12	13		8^{1}		10^{3}	3^{2}	11			9	4	5	7	6	14															6
1	2^{1}			4^{2}	5	12		13	14		11			10	8	3	7	6		9^{3}														7
1		3		12	5^{1}	7		9^{3}	10^{2}		13			11	8	2	4	6		14														8
1	12	3^{2}		5		7^{1}		11	10^{3}		13			9	8	2	4	6		14														9
1		3■			5	7		11	10^{2}		12		13	9^{1}	8^{3}	2	4	6		14														10
1	2			5		7	12	9^{1}	10^{3}		13		11		8	3	4^{2}	6		14														11
1	2			5		7^{1}	12	9	10^{3}		13		11		8^{2}	3	4	6		14														12
1■	2		12	5^{2}		7	8^{1}	9^{3}	10■		13		11			3	4	6		14														13
	2		12	5	6	7	8	9^{3}					11^{1}	13		3	4			10^{2}	1	14												14
1	2	12	4	5	6	7^{3}	8	9					14	13		3	11^{1}			10^{2}														15
1	2	12	4^{3}	5^{1}	6	7	8	9					14	13		3	11			10^{2}														16
1	2			5	6	7^{1}	8	9			12		11	13		3	4			10^{2}														17
1		3^{2}	4^{1}	5	6	7	8	9			12		11	10		2				13														18
	2			5	6	7^{2}	8	9^{1}					11	10		3	4^{3}			12			1	13	14									19
	2	3	4			12	8■		13		11^{3}		7			5		6		9^{1}			1	14	10^{2}									20
	2	3^{2}	8	4^{1}		12		9	13		11^{3}		7■			5		6					1	14	10									21
	2^{1}	12	4	5		7^{2}	8	9			11					3		6		13			1		10									22
	2	3	4				8	9			11		7			5		6		10						1								23
	2	3	4			12		9	13		11^{1}		7	14		5^{3}		6		10^{2}					8	1								24
	2	12		4		7	8	9					11	13		5^{1}		6		14				3^{2}	10^{3}	1								25
	2	3	4^{3}			12	8	9^{1}			13		7			5		6		10				11^{2}		1	14							26
	2	3	12				8	9					7			5		6						11^{1}		1	4^{2}	13	10^{3}	14				27
	2	3	12				8	9					7^{1}			5		6		13				11^{3}		1	14	4	10^{2}					28
	2	3	4	5		12	8^{2}	9					13													1	14	11	10^{1}	6	7^{3}			29
	2	3	4	5		12	8	9					13							14						1	11^{2}	6^{1}	10^{3}	7				30
	2	3	4	5		12	8	9					13							14						1		6^{1}	10^{3}	7	11^{2}			31
	2	3^{1}	4	5^{3}			8^{2}	9			12		13													1	14	6	10	7	11			32
	2	3	4^{2}	5		12	8^{3}	9			13									10			1				14	6^{1}		7	11			33
	2^{3}		4	5			8^{1}	9^{2}			12		11			3				10			1				7			6	13	14		34
	2			5			8^{1}	9					11			3				10^{2}			1	12			7	6		4^{3}		13	14	35
	2	3	4^{1}				8	9			12					5				10^{2}			1				13	6		7	11			36
	2	3	4			12		9			13		7			5				10^{2}			1					8^{3}		6^{1}	11		14	37
	2	3	4^{2}			12		9			13		7			5				10			1				8^{1}	14		6^{3}	11			38
	2	3	4^{1}	5		7^{2}		9			12		8							10			1					13		6	11			39
	2	3	4	8		7^{2}		9^{3}			12		11			5		6		10^{1}			1				13				14			40
	2	3	4^{1}	8		7^{2}		9			12		11			5		6		10			1					13						41
	2	3	4^{2}	8		12		9^{1}			11		7^{3}			5		6		10			1	13							14			42
	2^{3}	3	12	4		7		13			11					5		6		10			1	9^{2}						14	8^{1}			43
	2	3	7	4^{1}		12		9^{2}			11					5		6		10^{3}				13		1		14			8			44
	2	3	4			12		9			11					5		6		13				10^{3}		1		8^{2}			7^{1}		14	45
	2^{2}	3	4	8		7^{3}		9			11^{1}					5		6		12						1		14		13	10			46

FA Cup

First Round	Swindon T	(a)	2-2
		(h)	4-1
Second Round	Doncaster R	(h)	1-2

Carling Cup

First Round	Sheffield U	(a)	0-1

Football League Trophy

First Round	Huddersfield T	(h)	2-1
Second Round	Kidderminster H	(h)	0-3

AFC BOURNEMOUTH FL Championship 1

FOUNDATION

There was a Bournemouth FC as early as 1875, but the present club arose out of the remnants of the Boscombe St John's club (formed 1890). The meeting at which Boscombe FC came into being was held at a house in Gladstone Road in 1899. They began by playing in the Boscombe and District Junior League.

The Fitness First Stadium at Dean Court, Bournemouth, Dorset BH7 7AF.

Telephone: (01202) 726 300.

Fax: (01202) 726 301.

Ticket Office: (01202) 726 334.
Booking line: 08700 340380.

Website: www.afcb.co.uk

Email: admin@afcb.co.uk

Ground Capacity: 10,375.

Record Attendance: 28,799 v Manchester U, FA Cup 6th rd, 2 March 1957.

Pitch Measurements: 115yd × 74yd.

Chairman: P. I. Phillips.

Vice-chairman: A. Jaffer.

Chief Executive: L. C. Jones.

Secretary: K. R. J. MacAlister.

Manager: Sean O'Driscoll.

Assistant Manager: Richard O'Kelly.

Physio: Steve Poole.

HONOURS

Football League: Division 3 – Champions 1986–87; Promoted from Division 3, 2002–03 (play-offs); Division 3 (S) – Runners-up 1947–48; Division 4 – Runners-up 1970–71; Promotion from Division 4 1981–82 (4th).

FA Cup: best season: 6th rd, 1957.

Football League Cup: best season: 4th rd, 1962, 1964.

Associate Members' Cup: Winners 1984.

Auto Windscreens Shield: Runners-up 1998.

Colours: Red shirts with three black stripes front and back, black shorts, black stockings.

Change Colours: Navy and sky blue shirts, navy shorts, navy stockings.

Year Formed: 1899.

Turned Professional: 1912.

Ltd Co.: 1914.

Previous Names: 1890, Boscombe St Johns; 1899, Boscombe FC; 1923, Bournemouth & Boscombe Ath FC; 1971, AFC Bournemouth.

Club Nickname: 'Cherries'.

Previous Grounds: 1899, Castlemain Road, Pokesdown; 1910, Dean Court.

First Football League Game: 25 August 1923, Division 3 (S), v Swindon T (a) L 1–3 – Heron; Wingham, Lamb; Butt, C. Smith, Voisey; Miller, Lister (1), Davey, Simpson, Robinson.

Record League Victory: 7–0 v Swindon T, Division 3 (S), 22 September 1956 – Godwin; Cunningham, Keetley; Clayton, Crosland, Rushworth; Siddall (1), Norris (2), Arnott (1), Newsham (2), Cutler (1). 10–0 win v Northampton T at start of 1939–40 expunged from the records on outbreak of war.

SKY SPORTS FACT FILE

In the immediate years before the Second World War no fewer than 25 different players joined Bournemouth from Wolverhampton Wanderers. They included Jack Rowley signed from Wolves nursery club Cradley Heath in February 1937.

Record Cup Victory: 11–0 v Margate, FA Cup 1st rd, 20 November 1971 – Davies; Machin (1), Kitchener, Benson, Jones, Powell, Cave (1), Boyer, MacDougall (9 incl. 1p), Miller, Scott (De Garis).

Record Defeat: 0–9 v Lincoln C, Division 3, 18 December 1982.

Most League Points (2 for a win): 62, Division 3, 1971–72.

Most League Points (3 for a win): 97, Division 3, 1986–87.

Most League Goals: 88, Division 3 (S), 1956–57.

Highest League Scorer in Season: Ted MacDougall, 42, 1970–71.

Most League Goals in Total Aggregate: Ron Eyre, 202, 1924–33.

Most League Goals in One Match: 4, Jack Russell v Clapton Orient, Division 3S, 7 January 1933; 4, Jack Russell v Bristol C, Division 3S, 28 January 1933; 4, Harry Mardon v Southend U, Division 3S, 1 January 1938; 4, Jack McDonald v Torquay U, Division 3S, 8 November 1947; 4, Ted MacDougall v Colchester U, 18 September 1970; 4, Brian Clark v Rotherham U, 10 October 1972, 4, Luther Blissett v Hull C, 29 November 1988; 4, James Hayter v Bury, Division 2, 21 October 2000.

Most Capped Player: Gerry Peyton, 7 (33), Republic of Ireland.

Most League Appearances: Steve Fletcher, 425, 1992–.

Youngest League Player: Jimmy White, 15 years 321 days v Brentford, 30 April 1958.

Record Transfer Fee Received: £800,000 from Everton for Joe Parkinson, March 1994.

Record Transfer Fee Paid: £210,000 to Gillingham for Gavin Peacock, August 1989.

Football League Record: 1923 Elected to Division 3 (S) and remained a Third Division club for record number of years until 1970; 1970–71 Division 4; 1971–75 Division 3; 1975–82 Division 4; 1982–87 Division 3; 1987–90 Division 2; 1990–92 Division 3; 1992–2002 Division 2; 2002–03 Division 3; 2003–04 Division 2; 2004– FL1.

MANAGERS

Vincent Kitcher 1914–23
(Secretary-Manager)
Harry Kinghorn 1923–25
Leslie Knighton 1925–28
Frank Richards 1928–30
Billy Birrell 1930–35
Bob Crompton 1935–36
Charlie Bell 1936–39
Harry Kinghorn 1939–47
Harry Lowe 1947–50
Jack Bruton 1950–56
Fred Cox 1956–58
Don Welsh 1958–61
Bill McGarry 1961–63
Reg Flewin 1963–65
Fred Cox 1965–70
John Bond 1970–73
Trevor Hartley 1974–75
John Benson 1975–78
Alec Stock 1979–80
David Webb 1980–82
Don Megson 1983
Harry Redknapp 1983–92
Tony Pulis 1992–94
Mel Machin 1994–2000
Sean O'Driscoll August 2000–

LATEST SEQUENCES

Longest Sequence of League Wins: 7, 22.8.1970 – 23.9.1970.

Longest Sequence of League Defeats: 7, 13.8.1994 – 13.9.1994.

Longest Sequence of League Draws: 5, 25.4.2000 – 12.8.2000.

Longest Sequence of Unbeaten League Matches: 18, 6.3.1982 – 28.8.1982.

Longest Sequence Without a League Win: 14, 6.3.1974 – 27.4.1974.

Successive Scoring Runs: 31 from 28.10.2000.

Successive Non-scoring Runs: 6 from 1.2.1975.

TEN YEAR LEAGUE RECORD

		P	*W*	*D*	*L*	*F*	*A*	*Pts*	*Pos*
1996-97	Div 2	46	15	15	16	43	45	60	16
1997-98	Div 2	46	18	12	16	57	52	66	9
1998-99	Div 2	46	21	13	12	63	41	76	7
1999-2000	Div 2	46	16	9	21	59	62	57	16
2000-01	Div 2	46	20	13	13	79	55	73	7
2001-02	Div 2	46	10	14	22	56	71	44	21
2002-03	Div 3	46	20	14	12	60	48	74	4
2003-04	Div 2	46	17	15	14	56	51	66	9
2004-05	FL 1	46	20	10	16	77	64	70	8
2005-06	FL 1	46	12	19	15	49	53	55	17

DID YOU KNOW ?

On 31 December 1949 goalkeeper Ken Bird had his benefit match arranged for the home fixture against Notts County. A crowd of 22,651 turned up at Dean Court and saw Bournemouth win 3–0 on what was Bird's 200th first team appearance.

AFC BOURNEMOUTH 2005–06 LEAGUE RECORD

Match No.	*Date*	*Venue*	*Opponents*	*Result*		*H/T Score*	*Lg. Pos.*	*Goalscorers*	*Attendance*
1	Aug 6	A	Milton Keynes D	D	2-2	0-1	—	Hayter ^{76}, Surman ^{90}	5163
2	9	H	Hartlepool U	D	1-1	0-0	—	Rodrigues ^{64}	5406
3	13	H	Bristol C	W	2-0	1-0	7	Stock ^{20}, Hayter (pen) ^{50}	6544
4	20	A	Gillingham	L	0-1	0-1	12		6568
5	27	A	Bradford C	W	2-1	0-1	8	Bower (og) ^{55}, Surman ^{64}	7621
6	29	H	Walsall	D	0-0	0-0	9		5953
7	Sept 2	H	Tranmere R	D	0-0	0-0	—		5695
8	10	A	Chesterfield	L	0-3	0-1	12		3540
9	17	H	Swindon T	W	2-1	1-1	9	Hayter 2 (1 pen) $^{24 (p), 68}$	7276
10	24	A	Oldham Ath	L	0-1	0-0	16		5058
11	27	H	Swansea C	L	0-1	0-1	—		5750
12	Oct 1	A	Huddersfield T	D	2-2	0-2	17	Hayter 2 (1 pen) $^{66 (p), 70}$	13,522
13	7	H	Doncaster R	W	2-1	0-1	—	Surman ^{82}, Stock ^{90}	6578
14	15	A	Colchester U	W	1-0	0-0	9	Keene ^{90}	3120
15	22	H	Port Vale	L	1-2	1-0	12	Surman ^{23}	6320
16	29	A	Brentford	W	2-0	2-0	11	Keene ^{26}, Hayter ^{41}	6625
17	Nov 12	H	Nottingham F	D	1-1	0-1	10	Stock ^{64}	9222
18	19	A	Doncaster R	L	2-4	0-1	13	Surman ^{64}, Rodrigues ^{79}	4803
19	26	H	Milton Keynes D	W	2-0	1-0	11	Foley-Sheridan ^{36}, Cooke ^{82}	5485
20	Dec 6	A	Blackpool	W	3-1	2-1	—	Hayter 3 (1 pen) $^{26, 27, 68 (p)}$	4326
21	10	A	Hartlepool U	L	1-2	0-2	10	Foley-Sheridan ^{68}	3755
22	17	H	Gillingham	W	2-1	0-0	9	Hayter ^{66}, Surman ^{90}	6177
23	23	A	Yeovil T	D	1-1	1-0	—	Hayter (pen) ^{19}	8178
24	31	A	Southend U	L	1-2	0-1	10	Foley-Sheridan ^{70}	6357
25	Jan 2	H	Scunthorpe U	D	1-1	0-1	10	Hayter ^{85}	6259
26	7	A	Tranmere R	D	0-0	0-0	9		6717
27	14	H	Rotherham U	W	2-0	2-0	9	Foley-Sheridan ^{2}, Hayter ^{11}	5700
28	21	A	Swindon T	L	2-4	0-1	10	Rodrigues ^{59}, Hayter (pen) ^{68}	6092
29	28	H	Chesterfield	L	1-2	0-1	11	Hayter (pen) ^{66}	5837
30	Feb 3	A	Swansea C	L	0-1	0-1	—		12,079
31	11	H	Oldham Ath	D	0-0	0-0	13		5453
32	14	A	Rotherham U	L	0-2	0-0	—		4498
33	18	H	Blackpool	D	1-1	1-0	14	Pitman ^{4}	5349
34	25	A	Bristol C	L	1-3	1-1	15	Hayter ^{44}	11,058
35	28	H	Barnsley	D	1-1	0-1	—	Griffiths ^{70}	5191
36	Mar 11	H	Bradford C	L	0-1	0-1	16		5749
37	18	H	Yeovil T	W	1-0	1-0	16	Fletcher ^{33}	7959
38	25	A	Barnsley	D	0-0	0-0	17		9180
39	Apr 1	H	Southend U	D	1-1	0-1	17	Hayter ^{82}	7638
40	8	A	Scunthorpe U	D	2-2	1-1	18	Hayter ^{33}, O'Connor ^{63}	4136
41	11	A	Walsall	W	1-0	1-0	—	Hayter ^{17}	4613
42	15	H	Huddersfield T	D	1-1	1-0	16	Fletcher ^{34}	7406
43	17	A	Port Vale	D	0-0	0-0	15		4006
44	22	H	Colchester U	L	1-2	1-1	16	Cooke ^{8}	6231
45	29	A	Nottingham F	D	1-1	0-0	18	Fletcher ^{48}	26,847
46	May 6	H	Brentford	D	2-2	1-1	17	Foley-Sheridan ^{45}, Fletcher ^{90}	9359

Final League Position: 17

GOALSCORERS

League (49): Hayter 20 (7 pens), Surman 6, Foley-Sheridan 5, Fletcher 4, Rodrigues 3, Stock 3, Cooke 2, Keene 2, Griffiths 1, O'Connor 1, Pitman 1, own goal 1.
Carling Cup (0).
FA Cup (1): Stock 1.
Football League Trophy (4): Keene 2, Cooke 1 (pen), Pitman 1 (pen).

Moss N 4	Young N 42	O'Connor J 37+2	Browning M 41+1	Howe E 16+4	Maher S 4+2	Spicer J 4	Stock B 26	Hayter J 46	Fletcher S 21+6	Surman A 24	Cooke S 18+13	Rodrigues D 13+16	Gowling J 11+2	Coutts J —+11	Stewart G 42	Cooper S 33+2	Pitman B 4+15	Hart C 32+7	Foley-Sheridan S 33+2	Keene J 6+5	Hudson K —+1	Purches S 22+4	Tindall J 5+6	Rix B 7+4	Rowe J —+2	Fordyce D 3	Broadhurst K 3+4	Brown A 3+1	Griffiths A 6+1	*Match No.*
1	2	3	4[1]	5	6	7	8	9	10[2]	11[3]	12	13	14																	1
1	2	3	4	5	6	7	8	9		11	12	10[1]																		2
1	2	3	4	5	6	7[1]	8	9[3]	10	11[2]	12	13		14																3
1	2	3	4	5	6[1]	7	8	9	10[3]	11[2]	13	14	12																	4
	2	3	4				8	9		11	7[1]	10[2]	6	12	1	5	13													5
	2	3	4				8[2]	9		11	7[3]	10[1]	6	12	1	5	13	14												6
	2	3	4				8	9	12	11	7[3]	10[1]	6		1	5[2]		13	14											7
	5	3	4				8[1]	9	12	11	7	10	6		1			2[2]	13											8
	5	2					6	9		11	7[1]	12	3■		1	4[2]		13	8	10[3]	14									9
	2	3	4				7	9		11[2]	13	12	5		1		14	6[1]	8	10[3]										10
	5	3	4				8	9		11			6		1			2	7	10										11
	2	3	4				8	9		11[2]		12	6		1	13		5	7	10[1]										12
	5	3	4[1]		13		8	9		11[2]	12				1	6	14	2	7	10[3]										13
	·5	7	4		12		8	9[3]		11[2]	13		6		1	3		2	10[1]	14										14
	5	3	4[1]				8	9		11	13	12	6	14	1			2	7[3]	10[2]										15
	5	3	4				8	9		11[1]	12	14	6[2]		1	10		2	7	13[3]										16
	5	3	4[1]				8	9	12	11	10[2]				1	6		2	7	13										17
	5	3	4[2]				8	9	12	11	10[1]	13			1	6		2	7[3]			14								18
	5	3	4				8[1]	9[2]	10	11	12				1	6		2	7	13										19
	5	3	4				8	9[1]	10	11		12			1	6		2[2]	7			13								20
	5[3]	3	4[2]				8	9	10[1]	11	13	12			1	6		2	7	14										21
	5	3	4	12			8	9	10	11		13			1	6[1]		2[3]	7[2]			14								22
	5	3	4				8	9	10	11		12			1	6		2	7[1]											23
	5■	3	4[1]	12			8	9	10[2]	11[3]		13			1	6		2	7			14								24
		3	4[2]	5[3]			8	9	10			11[1]		12	1	6	13	2				7	14							25
	5	3	4	12			8	9				10[1]			1	6		2	11[2]			7	13							26
	5	3	4					9	10[1]			11[3]		12[2]	1	6	14	2	8			7	13							27
	5	3	4	12				9				10[2]			1	6	13	2	11			7	8[1]							28
	5		4	6				9				10		12[2]	1	3	13	2	11[1]			7	8							29
	3		4	5				9				10[1]		13	1	6	12[2]	2				7	8	11[3]	14					30
	5			6				9						12	1	3	10[1]	2				7	8	11		4[2]	13			31
	5		4					9			12				1	3[2]	10	2				7	8[1]	11	14	6[3]	13			32
	5		4					9	12		7[3]			13	1		10[1]	2				3	14	11		8[2]		6		33
	5		4					9	10		8				1			2	7			3		11[1]				6	12	34
	5		4	6				9			8[1]				1		12	2	11			7						10	3	35
		12	4	5				9			8[3]	10[1]			1	13	14	3	7			2		11[2]					6	36
	3	12	4	5				9	10						1	8		2[1]	11[2]			7						13	6	37
	5	11		6				9	10		8[1]	12			1	4			7			2					13		3[2]	38
	5	3	4	6				9	10		12				1	11	13	2[2]	7[1]			8								39
	5	2	4	6				9	10		11[2]				1	3		12	7			8[1]		13						40
	5	3	4	6				9	10		8[2]				1	11		12	7			2[1]					13			41
	5	3	4	6				9	10		8[2]	12			1	11	13		7[1]			2								42
	5	3	12					9	13		8	10[1]			1	6	4[2]	2	11[3]			7		14						43
	2	3	4[3]					9	10		8				1	6	12	13	11[2]			7[1]		14			5			44
		3[1]	4					9	10		8[2]				1	6		12	11[3]			7	14	13			5		2	45
		3[1]						9	10					12	1	5	13	2	11			7	14	8[2]			4[3]		6■	46

FA Cup
First Round Tamworth (h) 1-2

Carling Cup
First Round Torquay U (a) 0-0
Second Round Wigan Ath (a) 0-1

Football League Trophy
First Round Aldershot T (h) 4-1
Second Round Walsall (a) 0-1

BRADFORD CITY FL Championship 1

FOUNDATION

Bradford was a rugby stronghold around the turn of the century but after Manningham RFC held an archery contest to help them out of financial difficulties in 1903, they were persuaded to give up the handling code and turn to soccer. So they formed Bradford City and continued at Valley Parade. Recognising this as an opportunity of spreading the dribbling code in this part of Yorkshire, the Football League immediately accepted the new club's first application for membership of the Second Division.

Bradford and Bingley Stadium, Valley Parade, Bradford, West Yorkshire BD8 7DY.

Telephone: 0870 822 0000.

Fax: (01274) 773 356.

Ticket Office: 0870 822 1911.

Website: www.bradfordcityfc.co.uk

Email: bradfordcityfc@compuserve.com

Ground Capacity: 25,136.

Record Attendance: 39,146 v Burnley, FA Cup 4th rd, 11 March 1911.

Pitch Measurements: 113yd × 70yd.

Chairman/Chief Executive: Julian Rhodes.

Vice-chairman: Jim Brown.

Secretary: Jon Pollard.

Manager: Colin Todd.

Assistant Manager: Bobby Davison.

Physio: Steve Redmond.

Colours: Claret and amber.

Change Colours: Blue.

Year Formed: 1903.

Turned Professional: 1903.

Ltd Co.: 1908.

Club Nickname: 'The Bantams'.

First Football League Game: 1 September 1903, Division 2, v Grimsby T (a) L 0–2 – Seymour; Wilson, Halliday; Robinson, Millar, Farnall; Guy, Beckram, Forrest, McMillan, Graham.

Record League Victory: 11–1 v Rotherham U, Division 3 (N), 25 August 1928 – Sherlaw; Russell, Watson; Burkinshaw (1), Summers, Bauld; Harvey (2), Edmunds (3), White (3), Cairns, Scriven (2).

Record Cup Victory: 11–3 v Walker Celtic, FA Cup 1st rd (replay), 1 December 1937 – Parker; Rookes, McDermott; Murphy, Mackie, Moore; Bagley (1), Whittingham (1), Deakin (4 incl. 1p), Cooke (1), Bartholomew (4).

HONOURS

Football League: Division 1 – Runners-up 1998–99; Division 2 – Champions 1907–08; Promoted from Division 2 1995–96 (play-offs); Division 3 – Champions 1984–85; Division 3 (N) – Champions 1928–29; Division 4 – Runners-up 1981–82.

FA Cup: Winners 1911.

Football League Cup: best season: 5th rd, 1965, 1989.

European Competitions: *Intertoto Cup:* 2000.

SKY SPORTS FACT FILE

Bradford born inside-forward Bobby Ham three spells with Bradford City, two with Park Avenue, played for Gainsborough Trinity, Grimsby Town, Preston North End and Rotherham United in a career of over 450 League appearances between 1961 and 1975.

Record Defeat: 1–9 v Colchester U, Division 4, 30 December 1961.

Most League Points (2 for a win): 63, Division 3 (N), 1928–29.

Most League Points (3 for a win): 94, Division 3, 1984–85.

Most League Goals: 128, Division 3 (N), 1928–29.

Highest League Scorer in Season: David Layne, 34, Division 4, 1961–62.

Most League Goals in Total Aggregate: Bobby Campbell, 121, 1981–84, 1984–86.

Most League Goals in One Match: 7, Albert Whitehurst v Tranmere R, Division 3N, 6 March 1929.

Most Capped Player: Jamie Lawrence, Jamaica.

Most League Appearances: Cec Podd, 502, 1970–84.

Youngest League Player: Robert Cullingford, 16 years 141 days v Mansfield T, 22 April 1970.

Record Transfer Fee Received: £2,000,000 from Newcastle U for Des Hamilton, March 1997 and £2,000,000 from Newcastle U for Andrew O'Brien, March 2001.

Record Transfer Fee Paid: £2,500,000 to Leeds U for David Hopkins, July 2000.

Football League Record: 1903 Elected to Division 2; 1908–22 Division 1; 1922–27 Division 2; 1927–29 Division 3 (N); 1929–37 Division 2; 1937–61 Division 3; 1961–69 Division 4; 1969–72 Division 3; 1972–77 Division 4; 1977–78 Division 3; 1978–82 Division 4; 1982–85 Division 3; 1985–90 Division 2; 1990–92 Division 3; 1992–96 Division 2; 1996–99 Division 1; 1999–2001 FA Premier League; 2001–04 Division 1; 2004– FL1.

MANAGERS

Robert Campbell 1903–05
Peter O'Rourke 1905–21
David Menzies 1921–26
Colin Veitch 1926–28
Peter O'Rourke 1928–30
Jack Peart 1930–35
Dick Ray 1935–37
Fred Westgarth 1938–43
Bob Sharp 1943–46
Jack Barker 1946–47
John Milburn 1947–48
David Steele 1948–52
Albert Harris 1952
Ivor Powell 1952–55
Peter Jackson 1955–61
Bob Brocklebank 1961–64
Bill Harris 1965–66
Willie Watson 1966–69
Grenville Hair 1967–68
Jimmy Wheeler 1968–71
Bryan Edwards 1971–75
Bobby Kennedy 1975–78
John Napier 1978
George Mulhall 1978–81
Roy McFarland 1981–82
Trevor Cherry 1982–87
Terry Dolan 1987–89
Terry Yorath 1989–90
John Docherty 1990–91
Frank Stapleton 1991–94
Lennie Lawrence 1994–95
Chris Kamara 1995–98
Paul Jewell 1998–2000
Chris Hutchings 2000
Jim Jefferies 2000–01
Nicky Law 2002–03
Bryan Robson 2003–04
Colin Todd June 2004–

LATEST SEQUENCES

Longest Sequence of League Wins: 10, 26.11.1983 – 3.2.1984.

Longest Sequence of League Defeats: 8, 21.1.1933 – 11.3.1933.

Longest Sequence of League Draws: 6, 30.1.1976 – 13.3.1976.

Longest Sequence of Unbeaten League Matches: 21, 11.1.1969 – 2.5.1969.

Longest Sequence Without a League Win: 16, 28.8.1948 – 20.11.1948.

Successive Scoring Runs: 30 from 26.12.1961.

Successive Non-scoring Runs: 7 from 18.4.1925.

TEN YEAR LEAGUE RECORD

		P	*W*	*D*	*L*	*F*	*A*	*Pts*	*Pos*
1996-97	Div 1	46	12	12	22	47	72	48	21
1997-98	Div 1	46	14	15	17	46	59	57	13
1998-99	Div 1	46	26	9	11	82	47	87	2
1999-2000	PR Lge	38	9	9	20	38	68	36	17
2000-01	PR Lge	38	5	11	22	30	70	26	20
2001-02	Div 1	46	15	10	21	69	76	55	15
2002-03	Div 1	46	14	10	22	51	73	52	19
2003-04	Div 1	46	10	6	30	38	69	36	23
2004-05	FL 1	46	17	14	15	64	62	65	11
2005-06	FL 1	46	14	19	13	51	49	61	11

DID YOU KNOW?

In 1934–35 centre-forward Harry Adamson had a unique record as he finished top scorer for Bradford City not only in the Second Division but also the Midland League, Yorkshire League and its mid-week section! He scored 10 in 12 League games.

BRADFORD CITY 2005–06 LEAGUE RECORD

Match No.	*Date*	*Venue*	*Opponents*	*Result*	*H/T Score*	*Lg. Pos.*	*Goalscorers*	*Attendance*
1	Aug 6	A	Hartlepool U	W 2-0	1-0	—	Windass [8], Petta [55]	6271
2	9	H	Southend U	L 0-2	0-1	—		8250
3	13	H	Milton Keynes D	W 2-0	1-0	4	Windass 2 (1 pen) [27 (p), 52]	7315
4	20	A	Rotherham U	D 1-1	0-0	6	Windass [84]	5222
5	27	H	Bournemouth	L 1-2	1-0	12	Cadamarteri [45]	7621
6	29	A	Blackpool	L 0-1	0-0	13		6468
7	Sept 2	H	Chesterfield	W 2-0	0-0	—	Windass [75], Bridge-Wilkinson [81]	7351
8	9	A	Tranmere R	D 2-2	2-1	—	Edghill [21], Wetherall [38]	8225
9	17	H	Yeovil T	D 1-1	0-1	12	Muirhead [64]	7826
10	24	A	Swindon T	W 3-2	1-1	7	Windass [34], Claridge 2 [64, 72]	4590
11	27	H	Colchester U	D 1-1	0-0	—	Petta [84]	6891
12	Oct 1	A	Doncaster R	D 2-2	1-0	7	Kearney [44], Claridge [47]	6800
13	10	H	Huddersfield T	L 1-2	1-1	—	Petta [35]	12,285
14	15	A	Port Vale	W 1-0	0-0	7	Claridge [64]	4892
15	22	H	Gillingham	W 1-0	0-0	6	Cooke [89]	7729
16	29	A	Nottingham F	L 0-1	0-1	9		17,983
17	Nov 12	H	Barnsley	D 0-0	0-0	8		9486
18	19	A	Huddersfield T	D 0-0	0-0	9		17,331
19	26	H	Hartlepool U	L 0-1	0-1	14		7499
20	Dec 6	A	Bristol C	W 1-0	0-0	—	Carey (og) [79]	9103
21	10	A	Southend U	D 1-1	1-1	11	Schumacher [33]	7307
22	17	H	Rotherham U	L 1-2	0-1	13	Windass (pen) [77]	7476
23	26	A	Oldham Ath	L 1-2	1-2	14	Windass (pen) [45]	6982
24	28	H	Walsall	W 2-0	2-0	12	Bridge-Wilkinson [29], Petta [35]	6745
25	31	A	Scunthorpe U	D 0-0	0-0	12		5269
26	Jan 2	H	Brentford	D 3-3	1-2	11	Bridge-Wilkinson 2 (1 pen) [44, 89 (p)], Wetherall [78]	7588
27	7	A	Chesterfield	L 0-1	0-0	12		4449
28	14	H	Swansea C	D 1-1	0-1	13	Windass [80]	7521
29	21	A	Yeovil T	W 1-0	0-0	11	Windass [87]	6168
30	28	H	Tranmere R	D 0-0	0-0	10		7697
31	Feb 4	A	Colchester U	L 1-3	1-1	11	Windass [37]	4503
32	11	H	Swindon T	D 1-1	0-0	12	Windass [79]	7283
33	14	A	Swansea C	D 1-1	0-1	—	Wetherall [72]	11,028
34	18	H	Bristol C	D 1-1	0-1	12	Wetherall [52]	7917
35	25	A	Milton Keynes D	L 1-2	0-0	12	Claridge [64]	8426
36	Mar 11	A	Bournemouth	W 1-0	1-0	14	Stewart [42]	5749
37	18	H	Oldham Ath	L 1-4	0-3	15	Wilbraham [50]	7959
38	21	H	Blackpool	W 1-0	0-0	—	Brown [90]	7192
39	25	A	Walsall	D 2-2	1-2	12	Bower [45], Wetherall [49]	4678
40	Apr 1	H	Scunthorpe U	W 4-2	1-2	10	Windass 3 [7, 54, 60], Bridge-Wilkinson [56]	8409
41	8	A	Brentford	D 1-1	1-1	12	Symes [36]	6533
42	15	H	Doncaster R	W 2-1	2-0	11	Emanuel 2 [20, 27]	9297
43	17	A	Gillingham	L 1-2	0-1	12	Cadamarteri [75]	7281
44	22	H	Port Vale	W 1-0	1-0	11	Bower [44]	7139
45	29	A	Barnsley	D 0-0	0-0	11		11,178
46	May 6	H	Nottingham F	D 1-1	1-0	11	Windass [20]	15,608

Final League Position: 11

GOALSCORERS

League (51): Windass 16 (3 pens), Bridge-Wilkinson 5 (1 pen), Claridge 5, Wetherall 5, Petta 4, Bower 2, Cadamarteri 2, Emanuel 2, Brown 1, Cooke 1, Edghill 1, Kearney 1, Muirhead 1, Schumacher 1, Stewart 1, Symes 1, Wilbraham 1, own goal 1.
Carling Cup (6): Windass 3, Bridge-Wilkinson 1, Cadamarteri 1, Schumacher 1.
FA Cup (6): Bower 1, Cooke 1, Crooks 1, Edghill 1, Wetherall 1, Windass 1 (pen).
Football League Trophy (2): Brown 2.

Ricketts D 36	Holloway D 21 + 3	Taylor A 24	Schumacher S 24 + 6	Wetherall D 46	Bower M 45	Bridge-Wilkinson M 36	Kearney T 11 + 4	Windass D 40	Cooke A 10 + 7	Petta B 23 + 4	Cadamarteri D 25 + 14	Muirhead B 26 + 6	Stewart D 20 + 3	Edghill R 19	Emanuel L 23 + 14	Howarth R 10 + 1	Crooks L 14 + 1	Morrison O 7 + 3	Swift J 4 + 1	Claridge S 14 + 12	Brown J 2 + 11	Colbeck J 5 + 6	Penford T 9 + 1	Wright J — + 1	Wilbraham A 5	Symes M 1 + 2	Bentham C 6 + 1	Match No.
1	2	3	4	5	6	7	8	9	10^{1}	11^{2}	12	13																1
1	2■	3	4	5	6	7	8^{1}	9	10^{2}	11	12		13															2
1		3	4	5	6	7		9^{2}	10	11^{1}	12	8		2	13													3
1^{6}		3		5	6	7	4	9	10^{1}	11^{2}	12	8		2		15	13											4
		3		5	6	8^{2}	13	9	12	11^{3}	10^{1}	7		2		1	4	14										5
	12	3	4^{2}	5	6			9		11^{1}	10^{3}	7		2	13	1	8			14								6
		3		5	6	8		9	10^{3}			7		2^{2}	11^{1}	1	4	12	13	14								7
		3		5	6	8	4^{2}	9	10^{3}	11	12	7^{1}		2	13	1				14								8
		3	4	5	6			9	10^{2}	11^{1}	12	7		2		1	8			13								9
	12	3	4	5	6			9		11^{2}	10^{3}	7^{1}		2	13	1	8			14								10
		3	4	5	6			9	12	11	13	7^{3}		2^{2}	14	1	8			10^{1}								11
		3	12	5	6		4^{1}	9		11		7		2		1	8			10								12
		3	12	5	6		4^{1}		10^{2}	11	13	7^{3}		2	14	1	8			9								13
1	12	3	4	5	6			9		11^{2}		7		2^{1}	13		8			10								14
1	2	3	4	5	6			9	12	11^{3}	13	7^{2}			14		8			10^{1}								15
1	2■	3	4	5	6		12	9	13		14	11^{3}			7		8^{1}			10^{2}								16
1		3	4	5	6			9			12	7■	2^{2}		13		8	11		10^{1}								17
1			4	5	6	7		9		12	10		2		3		8	11^{1}										18
1	2^{1}	3	4^{2}	5	6	7		9		12	10				11		8	13										19
1		3	4	5	6	8	12	9	13		10	7^{1}		2				11^{2}										20
1■		3	4	5	6	8	12	9	13		10^{2}	7^{1}		2	14			11^{3}										21
		3	4	5	6	7		9	10^{2}		8	11^{1}		2	12	1				13								22
1			4	5	6	8		9^{2}	12	11^{1}	10	7		2	3					13								23
1		3		5	6	8	4	9^{2}		11^{1}	10	12		2	7					13								24
1		3	12	5	6	8	4	9^{2}		11	10^{3}			2^{1}	7					13	14							25
1	2^{2}	3	4^{1}	5	6	8	7	9^{3}			10	12			11					13	14							26
1	2			5		7	4^{1}	9		11	8		6		3					10^{2}	12	13						27
1	2			5	6	8		4		11^{2}		7^{1}	12		3					10	9		13					28
1	2^{2}			5	6	7^{1}		8		12	9		3		11					10	13		4					29
1	2			5	6	7		9			8		3		11					10^{1}	12		4					30
1	2		4^{3}	5	6	8		9	10^{1}		12		3	7^{2}						14			11	13				31
1	2		4	5	6	7		9		11^{2}	10		12		3^{1}					13			8					32
1	2		4	5	6	7		9		11^{1}	10		3		12								8					33
1	2			5	6	7		9		11^{1}	10		3		4							12	8					34
1	2		4	5	6	7					10		3					11^{2}		9^{1}	12	13	8					35
1	2		4	5	6	8						7^{1}	3		12			11		10					9			36
1	2		4	5	6	8					12	7	3		13			11^{2}		10^{1}					9			37
1	2			5	6	8					10^{2}	7^{1}	3		11						12	13	4		9^{3}	14		38
1	2			5	6	8						12	3		11						10	7	4^{1}		9			39
1	2			5	6	8	4^{3}	10^{2}				12	3		11							7^{1}			9	13	14	40
1	2^{3}			5	6	8		9		12	13	7^{1}	3		11						14					10^{2}	4	41
1				5	6	8		9			10^{1}	7^{2}	3		11				2		12	13					4	42
1			12	5	6	8		9			10	7^{2}	3		11				2^{1}			13					4	43
1				5	6	8		9			10		3		11				2			7					4	44
1			12	5	6	8		9		11^{3}	10	13	3		2						14	7^{2}					4^{1}	45
1			12	5	6	8^{1}		9			10		3		11^{2}				2		13	7					4	46

FA Cup

First Round	Tranmere R	(h)	2-1
Second Round	Barnsley	(a)	1-1
		(h)	3-5

Carling Cup

First Round	Rochdale	(a)	5-0
Second Round	WBA	(a)	1-4

Football League Trophy

Second Round	Morecambe	(a)	1-0
Quarter-Final	Kidderminster H	(a)	1-2

BRENTFORD — FL Championship 1

FOUNDATION

Formed as a small amateur concern in 1889 they were very successful in local circles. They won the championship of the West London Alliance in 1893 and a year later the West Middlesex Junior Cup before carrying off the Senior Cup in 1895. After winning both the London Senior Amateur Cup and the Middlesex Senior Cup in 1898 they were admitted to the Second Division of the Southern League.

Griffin Park, Braemar Road, Brentford, Middlesex, TW8 0NT.

Telephone: 0845 3456 442.

Fax: (0208) 568 9940

Ticket Office: 0845 3456 442.

Website: www.brentfordfc.co.uk

E-mail: enquiries@brentfordfc.co.uk

Ground Capacity: 12,763.

Record Attendance: 38,678 v Leicester C, FA Cup 6th rd, 26 February 1949.

Pitch Measurements: 110yd × 73yd.

Chairman: Greg Dyke.

Secretary: Lisa Hall.

Manager: Leroy Rosenior.

First Team Coach: Adrian Whitbread.

Physio: Damien Doyle.

Colours: Red, white and black.

Change Colours: Black. ***Alternative change colours:*** White.

Year Formed: 1889.

Turned Professional: 1899.

Ltd Co.: 1901.

Club Nickname: 'The Bees'.

Previous Grounds: 1889, Clifden Road; 1891, Benns Fields, Little Ealing; 1895, Shotters Field; 1898, Cross Road, S. Ealing; 1900, Boston Park; 1904, Griffin Park.

First Football League Game: 28 August 1920, Division 3, v Exeter C (a) L 0–3 – Young; Hodson, Rosier, Elliott J, Levitt, Amos, Smith, Thompson, Spreadbury, Morley, Henery.

Record League Victory: 9–0 v Wrexham, Division 3, 15 October 1963 – Cakebread; Coote, Jones; Slater, Scott, Higginson; Summers (1), Brooks (2), McAdams (2), Ward (2), Hales (1), (1 og).

Record Cup Victory: 7–0 v Windsor & Eton (away), FA Cup 1st rd, 20 November 1982 – Roche; Rowe, Harris (Booker), McNichol (1), Whitehead, Hurlock (2), Kamara, Joseph (1), Mahoney (3), Bowles, Roberts. *N.B.* 8–0 v Uxbridge, FA Cup, 3rd Qual rd, 31 October 1903.

HONOURS

Football League: Division 1 best season: 5th, 1935–36; Division 2 – Champions 1934–35; Division 3 – Champions 1991–92, 1998–99; Division 3 (S) – Champions 1932–33, Runners-up 1929–30, 1957–58; Division 4 – Champions 1962–63.

FA Cup: best season: 6th rd, 1938, 1946, 1949, 1989.

Football League Cup: best season: 4th rd, 1983.

Freight Rover Trophy: Runners-up 1985.

LDV Vans Trophy: Runners-up 2001.

SKY SPORTS FACT FILE

Gary Roberts hit the fastest hat-trick for Brentford in a Freight Rover Trophy match against Newport County on 17 May 1985. His first came on the stroke of half-time, the second and third goals in the 47th and 48th minutes.

Record Defeat: 0–7 v Swansea T, Division 3 (S), 8 November 1924 and v Walsall, Division 3 (S), 19 January 1957.

Most League Points (2 for a win): 62, Division 3 (S), 1932–33 and Division 4, 1962–63.

Most League Points (3 for a win): 85, Division 2, 1994–95 and Division 3, 1998–99.

Most League Goals: 98, Division 4, 1962–63.

Highest League Scorer in Season: Jack Holliday, 38, Division 3 (S), 1932–33.

Most League Goals in Total Aggregate: Jim Towers, 153, 1954–61.

Most League Goals in One Match: 5, Jack Holliday v Luton T, Division 3S, 28 January 1933; Billy Scott v Barnsley, Division 2, 15 December 1934; Peter McKennan v Bury, Division 2, 18 February 1949.

Most Capped Player: John Buttigieg, 22 (98), Malta.

Most League Appearances: Ken Coote, 514, 1949–64.

Youngest League Player: Danis Salman, 15 years 243 days v Watford, 15 November 1975.

Record Transfer Fee Received: £2,500,000 from Wimbledon for Hermann Hreidarsson, October 1999.

Record Transfer Fee Paid: £750,000 to Crystal Palace for Hermann Hreidarsson, September 1998.

Football League Record: 1920 Original Member of Division 3; 1921–33 Division 3 (S); 1933–35 Division 2; 1935–47 Division 1; 1947–54 Division 2; 1954–62 Division 3 (S); 1962–63 Division 4; 1963–66 Division 3; 1966–72 Division 4; 1972–73 Division 3; 1973–78 Division 4; 1978–92 Division 3; 1992–93 Division 1; 1993–98 Division 2; 1998–99 Division 3; 1999–04 Division 2; 2004– FL1.

MANAGERS

Will Lewis 1900–03
(Secretary-Manager)
Dick Molyneux 1902–06
W. G. Brown 1906–08
Fred Halliday 1908–12, 1915–21, 1924–26
(only Secretary to 1922)
Ephraim Rhodes 1912–15
Archie Mitchell 1921–24
Harry Curtis 1926–49
Jackie Gibbons 1949–52
Jimmy Bain 1952–53
Tommy Lawton 1953
Bill Dodgin Snr 1953–57
Malcolm Macdonald 1957–65
Tommy Cavanagh 1965–66
Billy Gray 1966–67
Jimmy Sirrel 1967–69
Frank Blunstone 1969–73
Mike Everitt 1973–75
John Docherty 1975–76
Bill Dodgin Jnr 1976–80
Fred Callaghan 1980–84
Frank McLintock 1984–87
Steve Perryman 1987–90
Phil Holder 1990–93
David Webb 1993–97
Eddie May 1997
Micky Adams 1997–98
Ron Noades 1998–2000
Ray Lewington 2001
Steve Coppell 2001–02
Wally Downes 2002–04
Martin Allen 2004–2006
Leroy Rosenior June 2006–

LATEST SEQUENCES

Longest Sequence of League Wins: 9, 30.4.1932 – 24.9.1932.

Longest Sequence of League Defeats: 9, 20.10.1928 – 25.12.1928.

Longest Sequence of League Draws: 5, 16.3.1957 – 6.4.1957.

Longest Sequence of Unbeaten League Matches: 26, 20.2.1999 – 16.10.1999.

Longest Sequence Without a League Win: 16, 19.2.1994 – 7.5.1994.

Successive Scoring Runs: 26 from 4.3.1963.

Successive Non-scoring Runs: 7 from 7.3.2000.

TEN YEAR LEAGUE RECORD

		P	*W*	*D*	*L*	*F*	*A*	*Pts*	*Pos*
1996-97	Div 2	46	20	14	12	56	43	74	4
1997-98	Div 2	46	11	17	18	50	71	50	21
1998-99	Div 3	46	26	7	13	79	56	85	1
1999-2000	Div 2	46	13	13	20	47	61	52	17
2000-01	Div 2	46	14	17	15	56	70	59	14
2001-02	Div 2	46	24	11	11	77	43	83	3
2002-03	Div 2	46	14	12	20	47	56	54	16
2003-04	Div 2	46	14	11	21	52	69	53	17
2004-05	FL 1	46	22	9	15	57	60	75	4
2005-06	FL 1	46	20	16	10	72	52	76	3

DID YOU KNOW ?

Centre-forward Frank Dudley completed a unique treble of scoring for different clubs in different divisions when he joined Brentford (Div 2) in 1953–54. His previous two goals that season had been for Cardiff City (Div 1) and Southampton (Div 3S).

BRENTFORD 2005–06 LEAGUE RECORD

Match No.	Date	Venue	Opponents	Result	H/T Score	Lg. Pos.	Goalscorers	Attendance
1	Aug 6	H	Scunthorpe U	W 2-0	0-0	—	Tabb [71], Campbell (pen) [81]	5952
2	10	A	Chesterfield	W 3-1	1-1	—	Sodje [14], Rankin 2 [52, 56]	4121
3	15	A	Port Vale	L 0-1	0-0	—		4275
4	20	H	Tranmere R	W 2-0	1-0	1	Tabb [23], Hutchinson [50]	5438
5	27	A	Barnsley	D 1-1	1-1	1	Owusu [25]	7462
6	29	H	Gillingham	D 1-1	0-1	3	Peters [75]	6969
7	Sept 3	A	Nottingham F	W 2-1	0-0	1	Frampton [23], Pratley [78]	17,234
8	10	H	Milton Keynes D	W 1-0	0-0	1	O'Connor (pen) [62]	5862
9	17	A	Huddersfield T	L 2-3	1-1	4	Rankin [23], Campbell [46]	11,622
10	24	H	Bristol C	L 2-3	0-2	4	Brooker [66], Sodje [80]	6413
11	27	A	Walsall	D 0-0	0-0	—		4873
12	Oct 1	H	Rotherham U	W 2-1	2-1	4	O'Connor (pen) [11], Rankin [37]	5901
13	9	A	Oldham Ath	W 1-0	0-0	—	Fitzgerald [66]	5089
14	15	H	Swindon T	D 0-0	0-0	4		6969
15	22	A	Blackpool	D 0-0	0-0	4		5041
16	29	H	Bournemouth	L 0-2	0-2	4		6625
17	Nov 12	A	Hartlepool U	W 2-1	1-0	4	Campbell [22], Owusu [78]	4811
18	19	H	Oldham Ath	D 3-3	2-3	5	Pratley [17], Campbell [28], Owusu [89]	5450
19	26	A	Scunthorpe U	W 3-1	2-1	4	Pratley 2 [11, 24], Brooker [52]	4322
20	Dec 6	H	Yeovil T	W 3-2	2-1	—	Jones (og) [6], Tabb [13], Turner [88]	5131
21	10	H	Chesterfield	D 1-1	0-1	3	O'Connor [82]	5828
22	17	A	Tranmere R	W 4-1	3-1	2	Newman [12], Tabb [14], O'Connor (pen) [32], Owusu [53]	6210
23	26	H	Swansea C	W 2-1	2-0	1	O'Connor [26], Hutchinson [35]	9903
24	31	H	Colchester U	L 0-2	0-1	3		6397
25	Jan 2	A	Bradford C	D 3-3	2-1	3	Campbell 2 (1 pen) [4, 28 (p)], Sodje [58]	7588
26	14	A	Southend U	L 1-4	0-2	5	Campbell [65]	10,046
27	17	H	Nottingham F	D 1-1	1-1	—	Campbell [34]	7859
28	21	H	Huddersfield T	W 2-0	1-0	4	Owusu [25], Campbell [77]	7636
29	Feb 4	H	Walsall	W 5-0	2-0	5	Rankin [7], Newman [11], Brooker [65], Sodje [77], O'Connor (pen) [86]	5645
30	11	A	Bristol C	W 1-0	0-0	4	Owusu [78]	10,854
31	14	H	Southend U	W 2-0	2-0	—	Jupp (og) [23], Gayle [34]	7022
32	25	H	Port Vale	L 0-1	0-1	6		7542
33	28	A	Doncaster R	D 0-0	0-0	—		5250
34	Mar 7	A	Yeovil T	W 2-1	1-1	—	Rankin [12], Rhodes [58]	5137
35	11	H	Barnsley	W 3-1	2-0	2	Newman [12], Owusu 2 (1 pen) [22, 85 (p)]	7352
36	17	A	Swansea C	L 1-2	1-1	—	Frampton [30]	13,508
37	21	A	Gillingham	L 2-3	1-2	—	Turner [15], Tabb [79]	5745
38	25	H	Doncaster R	L 0-1	0-0	3		7323
39	28	A	Milton Keynes D	W 1-0	1-0	—	Owusu [8]	5592
40	Apr 1	A	Colchester U	D 1-1	1-1	2	Tabb [6]	5635
41	8	H	Bradford C	D 1-1	1-1	2	Owusu [43]	6533
42	15	A	Rotherham U	D 2-2	0-1	2	Owusu [68], Rankin [81]	5242
43	17	H	Blackpool	D 1-1	0-0	3	Owusu (pen) [54]	7339
44	22	A	Swindon T	W 3-1	2-0	3	Brooker [27], Gayle [39], Willock [75]	6845
45	29	H	Hartlepool U	D 1-1	0-0	3	O'Connor [84]	8725
46	May 6	A	Bournemouth	D 2-2	1-1	3	Sodje [22], Frampton [65]	9359

Final League Position: 3

GOALSCORERS

League (72): Owusu 12 (2 pens), Campbell 9 (2 pens), O'Connor 7 (4 pens), Rankin 7, Tabb 6, Sodje 5, Brooker 4, Pratley 4, Frampton 3, Newman 3, Gayle 2, Hutchinson 2, Turner 2, Fitzgerald 1, Peters 1, Rhodes 1, Willock 1, own goals 2.
Carling Cup (0).
FA Cup (9): Campbell 3, Owusu 2, Rankin 2, O'Connor 1 (pen), Sodje 1.
Football League Trophy (1): Fitzgerald 1.
Play-Offs (1): Tabb 1.

Nelson S 44 + 1	O'Connor K 30	Frampton A 36	Skulason O 2	Sodje S 43	Turner M 46	Brooker P 32 + 4	Hutchinson E 17 + 10	Owusu L 39 + 3	Rankin I 31 + 6	Tabb J 42	Dobson M 3 + 3	Fitzgerald S 3 + 8	Campbell D 13 + 10	Tillen S 20 + 13	Keenan J — + 3	Lewis J 11 + 3	Peters R 1 + 9	Pratley D 25 + 7	Gayle M 16 + 8	Osborne K 1	Rhodes A 5 + 12	Newman R 29 + 1	Charles D — + 2	Mousinho J 3 + 4	Bankole A 2	Willock C 5 + 8	Smith Jamie 7	Match No.
1	2^{1}	3	4	5	6	7	8	9^{2}	10^{3}	11	12	13	14															1
1	2	3	4^{1}	5	6	7^{2}	8	9	10^{3}	11			14	12	13													2
1	4	3		5	6	11^{2}	8	9	10		2^{3}	12	7^{1}	13	14													3
1	4	3		5	6	7^{3}	8	9	10^{1}	11^{2}	2	13	12		14													4
1	2	3		5	6	7^{2}	8	9^{1}	10	11	4		12			13												5
1	2	3		5	6		4	9	10^{2}	11	12		13			8^{1}	7											6
1	2	3		5	6		4		10	11		8^{1}					12	7	9									7
1	2	3		5	6		4		8^{2}	11		10^{1}	12				13	7	9									8
1		3■		5	6			12	10	11^{1}		4^{2}	13^{3}	2		8	14	7	9									9
1				5	6	12		9^{1}	8^{2}	11			13	3		4		7^{3}	10	2	14							10
1		3		5	6	8		9^{2}	10	11^{3}			12	2^{1}		4		7	13		14							11
1	2	3		5	6	8^{1}		9	10	11						4		7			12							12
1	2	3		5	6	8^{1}		9	10^{3}			14	12■	13		4		7			11^{2}							13
1	2	3		5	6	8^{2}		9^{1}	10	11		13				4		7	12									14
1	2	3			6	8^{3}	12	9^{2}	10	11		14		5		4^{1}		7	13									15
1	2	3		5	6	12	8^{3}	9	7	11^{2}			10	13		4^{1}						14						16
1	2	3		5	6	8^{2}	12	9		11	13		10^{1}					7				4						17
1	2	3^{1}		5	6	8^{2}		9		11		14	10^{3}	12			13	7				4						18
1	2	3^{3}		5	6	8	12	9	13	11			10^{2}	14				7^{1}				4						19
1	2	3^{3}		5	6	8^{2}	12	9	13	11			10^{1}	14				7				4						20
1	2			5	6	8^{1}	12	9	11^{2}				10				13	7	3^{3}			4	14					21
1	2			5^{3}	6	7	8	9^{2}		11^{1}				3		12	13		10			4		14				22
1	2			5	6	7^{2}	8	9	12				11^{1}	3		4			10					13				23
1	2^{1}			5	6	7^{2}	8	9		11			10	3		14	13^{3}		12			4						24
1				5	6		8	9	7	11^{1}			10	3								4	12	2				25
1	2	5			6	7^{1}	8■	9	12	11			10^{3}	3					13			4^{2}		14				26
	2	3^{3}		5	6	12		9	7^{1}	11		14	10	13					8^{2}			4			1			27
15	2	3^{2}		5	6	12	13	9^{1}	8	11			10	7								4■			1^{G}			28
1	2			5^{2}	6	8	12	9	10	11				3				7^{1}				4^{3}		13		14		29
1	7			5	6			9		11				3			12	8	13			4		2^{2}		10^{1}		30
1	2	3		5	6			12	10	11				8				7	9^{1}			4						31
1		3^{3}		5	6	8		12	10	11				13				7^{2}	9		14	4		2^{1}				32
1		2		5	6		8	9		11				3				7			12	4				10^{1}		33
1				5	6	2^{1}	8^{2}	9	7	11				3				12	10		13	4						34
1		3		5	6	2		9^{2}	10^{1}	11				7				13	12		8^{3}	4				14		35
1		3		5	6	8^{1}		9	10	11				2				7			12	4^{2}				13		36
1		3		5^{1}	6	8		9	10^{3}	11				12				13			7^{2}	4				14	2	37
1		5			6	7^{2}	8^{3}	9		11				3			13	12	10			4^{1}				14	2	38
1		3		5	6	8	12	9		11								7^{1}			13	4				10^{2}	2	39
1		3		5	6	7	12	9	13	11^{3}								14	10^{1}			4				8^{2}	2	40
1		3		5	6	7^{3}		9	10	11				12				13			8^{1}	4^{2}				14	2	41
1		3		5	6	8^{3}		9	10	11				12				7	13		14	4^{1}					2^{2}	42
1		3		5	6			9	10	11				2		8		12			7^{1}	4^{2}				13		43
1	2			5	6	8^{1}		9^{2}		11				3				7	10		12	4				13		44
1	2	3		5	6	8^{2}	13		12	11								7	9		14	4^{3}				10^{1}		45
1	2^{1}	3		5■	6				10^{2}	11				12				7	9		13	4					8	46

FA Cup

First Round	Rochdale	(a)	1-0
Second Round	Oldham Ath	(a)	1-1
		(h)	1-0
Third Round	Stockport Co	(a)	3-2
Fourth Round	Sunderland	(h)	2-1
Fifth Round	Charlton Ath	(a)	1-3

Carling Cup

First Round	Cheltenham T	(a)	0-5

Football League Trophy

First Round	Oxford U	(h)	1-1

Play-Offs

Semi-Final	Swansea C	(a)	1-1
		(h)	0-2

BRIGHTON & HOVE ALBION FL Championship 1

FOUNDATION

A professional club Brighton United was formed in November 1897 at the Imperial Hotel, Queen's Road, but folded in March 1900 after less than two seasons in the Southern League at the County Ground. An amateur team, Brighton & Hove Rangers was then formed by some prominent United supporters and after one season at Withdean, decided to turn semi-professional and play at the County Ground. Rangers were accepted into the Southern League but then also folded June 1901. John Jackson the former United manager organised a meeting at the Seven Stars public house, Ship Street on 24 June 1901 at which a new third club Brighton & Hove United was formed. They took over Rangers' place in the Southern League and pitch at County Ground. The name was changed to Brighton & Hove Albion before a match was played because of objections by Hove FC.

Withdean Stadium, Tongdean Lane, Brighton, East Sussex BN1 5JD.

Telephone: (01273) 695 400 (admin office 44 North Road, Brighton).

Fax: (01273) 648 179 (admin office 44 North Road, Brighton).

Ticket Office: (01273) 776 992.

Website: www.seagulls.co.uk

Email: seagulls@bhafc.co.uk

Ground Capacity: 8,850.

Record Attendance: 36,747 v Fulham, Division 2, 27 December 1958 (at Goldstone Ground).

Pitch Measurements: 110yd × 70yd.

Chairman: Dick Knight.

Chief Executive: Martin Perry.

Secretary: Derek J. Allan.

Manager: Mark McGhee.

Assistant Manager: Bob Booker.

Physio: Malcolm Stuart.

Colours: Blue and white vertical striped shirts, white shorts, white stockings.

Change Colours: White shirts, blue shorts, blue stockings.

Year Formed: 1901.

Turned Professional: 1901.

Ltd Co.: 1904.

Previous Grounds: 1901, County Ground; 1902, Goldstone Ground.

Club Nickname: 'The Seagulls'.

First Football League Game: 28 August 1920, Division 3, v Southend U (a) L 0–2 – Hayes; Woodhouse, Little; Hall, Comber, Bentley; Longstaff, Ritchie, Doran, Rodgerson, March.

HONOURS

Football League: Division 1 best season: 13th, 1981–82; Division 2 – Champions 2001–02; Runners-up 1978–79; Promoted from Division 2 2003–04 (play-offs); Division 3 (S) – Champions 1957–58; Runners-up 1953–54, 1955–56; Division 3 – Champions 2000–01; Runners-up 1971–72, 1976–77, 1987–88; Division 4 – Champions 1964–65.

FA Cup: Runners-up 1983.

Football League Cup: best season: 5th rd, 1979.

SKY SPORTS FACT FILE

Success for the Brighton & Hove Albion in winning the Charity Shield in 1910 by beating Aston Villa 1–0 at Stamford Bridge was rewarded with a £10 bonus for each player. But Charlie Webb the only amateur in the team merely received a gold tie pin!

Record League Victory: 9–1 v Newport Co, Division 3 (S), 18 April 1951 – Ball; Tennant (1p), Mansell (1p); Willard, McCoy, Wilson; Reed, McNichol (4), Garbutt, Bennett (2), Keene (1). 9–1 v Southend U, Division 3, 27 November 1965 – Powney; Magill, Baxter; Leck, Gall, Turner; Gould (1), Collins (1), Livesey (2), Smith (3), Goodchild (2).

Record Cup Victory: 10–1 v Wisbech, FA Cup 1st rd, 13 November 1965 – Powney; Magill, Baxter; Collins (1), Gall, Turner; Gould, Smith (2), Livesey (3), Cassidy (2), Goodchild (1), (1 og).

Record Defeat: 0–9 v Middlesbrough, Division 2, 23 August 1958.

Most League Points (2 for a win): 65, Division 3 (S), 1955–56 and Division 3, 1971–72.

Most League Points (3 for a win): 92, Division 3, 2000–01.

Most League Goals: 112, Division 3 (S), 1955–56.

Highest League Scorer in Season: Peter Ward, 32, Division 3, 1976–77.

Most League Goals in Total Aggregate: Tommy Cook, 114, 1922–29.

Most League Goals in One Match: 5, Jack Doran v Northampton T, Division 3S, 5 November 1921; 5, Adrian Thorne v Watford, Division 3S, 30 April 1958.

Most Capped Player: Steve Penney, 17, Northern Ireland.

Most League Appearances: 'Tug' Wilson, 509, 1922–36.

Youngest League Player: Ian Chapman, 16 years 259 days v Birmingham C, 14 February 1987.

Record Transfer Fee Received: £1,500,000 from Tottenham H for Bobby Zamora, July 2003.

Record Transfer Fee Paid: £500,000 to Manchester U for Andy Ritchie, October 1980.

Football League Record: 1920 Original Member of Division 3; 1921–58 Division 3 (S); 1958–62 Division 2; 1962–63 Division 3; 1963–65 Division 4; 1965–72 Division 3; 1972–73 Division 2; 1973–77 Division 3; 1977–79 Division 2; 1979–83 Division 1; 1983–87 Division 2; 1987–88 Division 3; 1988–96 Division 2; 1996–2001 Division 3; 2001–02 Division 2; 2002–03 Division 1; 2003–04 Division 2; 2004–06 FLC; 2006– FL1.

MANAGERS

John Jackson 1901–05
Frank Scott-Walford 1905–08
John Robson 1908–14
Charles Webb 1919–47
Tommy Cook 1947
Don Welsh 1947–51
Billy Lane 1951–61
George Curtis 1961–63
Archie Macaulay 1963–68
Fred Goodwin 1968–70
Pat Saward 1970–73
Brian Clough 1973–74
Peter Taylor 1974–76
Alan Mullery 1976–81
Mike Bailey 1981–82
Jimmy Melia 1982–83
Chris Cattlin 1983–86
Alan Mullery 1986–87
Barry Lloyd 1987–93
Liam Brady 1993–95
Jimmy Case 1995–96
Steve Gritt 1996–98
Brian Horton 1998–99
Jeff Wood 1999
Micky Adams 1999–2001
Peter Taylor 2001–02
Martin Hinshelwood 2002
Steve Coppell 2002–03
Mark McGhee October 2003–

LATEST SEQUENCES

Longest Sequence of League Wins: 9, 2.10.1926 – 20.11.1926.

Longest Sequence of League Defeats: 12, 17.8.2002 – 26.10.2002.

Longest Sequence of League Draws: 6, 16.2.1980 – 15.3.1980.

Longest Sequence of Unbeaten League Matches: 16, 8.10.1930 – 28.1.1931.

Longest Sequence Without a League Win: 15, 21.10.1972 – 27.1.1973

Successive Scoring Runs: 31 from 4.2.1956.

Successive Non-scoring Runs: 6 from 8.11.1924.

TEN YEAR LEAGUE RECORD

		P	W	D	L	F	A	Pts	Pos
1996-97	Div 3	46	13	10	23	53	70	47	23
1997-98	Div 3	46	6	17	23	38	66	35	23
1998-99	Div 3	46	16	7	23	49	66	55	17
1999-2000	Div 3	46	17	16	13	64	46	67	11
2000-01	Div 3	46	28	8	10	73	35	92	1
2001-02	Div 2	46	25	15	6	66	42	90	1
2002-03	Div 1	46	11	12	23	49	67	45	23
2003-04	Div 2	46	22	11	13	64	43	77	4
2004-05	FL C	46	13	12	21	40	65	51	20
2005-06	FL C	46	7	17	22	39	71	38	24

DID YOU KNOW ?

In 1953–54 Brighton & Hove Albion manager Billy Lane organised his defence to such a disciplined degree that in 48 League and Cup matches during the season they did not concede one penalty kick. They were runners-up in the Third Division (South).

BRIGHTON & HOVE ALBION 2005–06 LEAGUE RECORD

Match No.	Date	Venue	Opponents	Result		H/T Score	Lg. Pos.	Goalscorers	Attendance
1	Aug 6	A	Derby Co	D	1-1	1-1	—	Hammond 7	25,292
2	9	H	Reading	L	0-2	0-1	—		6676
3	13	H	Crewe Alex	D	2-2	1-0	21	Knight 42, Hammond 88	6132
4	20	A	Hull C	L	0-2	0-1	23		18,648
5	27	A	Preston NE	D	0-0	0-0	23		12,461
6	29	H	Plymouth Arg	W	2-0	1-0	16	Robinson 11, Carpenter 46	6238
7	Sept 10	A	Leeds U	D	3-3	1-0	16	Knight 28, Carole 51, Gregan (og) 83	21,212
8	13	H	Sheffield U	L	0-1	0-1	—		6553
9	17	H	Coventry C	D	2-2	0-1	19	Knight 50, Kazim-Richards 56	6529
10	24	A	Burnley	D	1-1	1-1	17	McShane 25	11,112
11	27	A	Leicester C	D	0-0	0-0	—		20,296
12	Oct 1	H	Norwich C	L	1-3	0-2	21	Frutos 67	6624
13	15	H	Cardiff C	L	1-2	0-1	24	McShane 61	6485
14	18	A	Crystal Palace	W	1-0	0-0	—	Boyce (og) 74	22,400
15	24	A	Sheffield W	D	1-1	0-0	—	Kazim-Richards 90	21,787
16	29	H	Ipswich T	D	1-1	1-1	22	Hammond 15	6867
17	Nov 1	H	Wolverhampton W	D	1-1	1-0	—	Frutos 40	6642
18	5	A	Stoke C	L	0-3	0-1	22		15,274
19	20	H	Crystal Palace	L	2-3	1-1	23	Knight 2 (1 pen) 22, 53 (p)	7273
20	22	A	Cardiff C	D	1-1	0-0	—	Kazim-Richards 76	9595
21	26	H	Derby Co	D	0-0	0-0	23		6855
22	Dec 3	A	Watford	D	1-1	0-1	22	Butters 52	14,455
23	10	A	Reading	L	1-5	0-1	22	Kazim-Richards 84	18,546
24	16	H	Hull C	W	2-1	2-1	—	Carole 16, Oatway 45	6929
25	26	H	QPR	W	1-0	1-0	21	Butters 7	7341
26	28	A	Luton T	L	0-3	0-2	21		9429
27	31	H	Millwall	L	1-2	1-0	21	Hammond 3	6847
28	Jan 2	A	Southampton	L	1-2	1-1	22	Mayo 21	24,630
29	14	H	Leeds U	W	2-1	1-1	21	Reid 10, Hart 80	7415
30	21	A	Sheffield U	L	1-3	0-0	21	Kazim-Richards 83	27,514
31	31	H	Burnley	D	0-0	0-0	—		6267
32	Feb 4	A	Coventry C	L	0-2	0-1	22		20,541
33	11	H	Leicester C	L	1-2	0-2	22	Frutos 56	7187
34	14	A	Norwich C	L	0-3	0-1	—		24,038
35	18	H	Watford	L	0-1	0-1	23		6658
36	25	A	Crewe Alex	L	1-2	1-0	23	Kazim-Richards 11	5925
37	Mar 4	A	Plymouth Arg	L	0-1	0-1	23		13,650
38	11	H	Preston NE	D	0-0	0-0	23		6361
39	18	A	QPR	D	1-1	0-1	23	Bignot (og) 80	13,907
40	25	H	Luton T	D	1-1	1-0	23	Noel-Williams 18	7139
41	Apr 1	A	Millwall	W	2-0	2-0	23	Reid 6, McShane 11	13,209
42	8	H	Southampton	L	0-2	0-1	24		7999
43	15	A	Ipswich T	W	2-1	1-0	22	Noel-Williams 45, Lynch 73	23,964
44	17	H	Sheffield W	L	0-2	0-1	23		7573
45	22	A	Wolverhampton W	L	0-1	0-1	24		22,555
46	30	H	Stoke C	L	1-5	0-3	24	Loft 84	5859

Final League Position: 24

GOALSCORERS

League (39): Kazim-Richards 6, Knight 5 (1 pen), Hammond 4, Frutos 3, McShane 3, Butters 2, Carole 2, Noel-Williams 2, Reid 2, Carpenter 1, Hart 1, Loft 1, Lynch 1, Mayo 1, Oatway 1, Robinson 1, own goals 3.
Carling Cup (2): McCammon 1, Robinson 1.
FA Cup (0).

Henderson W 32	Dodd J 6+1	Mayo K 14+4	McShane P 38	Butters G 43+2	Carpenter R 31+1	Reid P 36+2	Oatway C 17+1	Knight L 22+3	Kazim-Richards C 25+17	Hammond D 40+1	Turienzo F 1+3	Robinson J 15+12	Carole S 34+6	Nicolas A 4+7	McCammon M 3+4	Jarrett A 9+2	Hart G 31+4	Cox D —+1	Elphick G 1+1	Frutos A 27+9	Blayney A 8	El-Abd A 23+6	McPhee C 2+5	Elphick T —+1	Kuipers M 5	Chaigneau F 1	Lynch J 16	Gatting J 5+7	Hinshelwood A 10+1	Loft D —+3	Noel-Williams G 7	*Match No.*
1	2	3	4	5	6	7	8	9	10	11																						1
1	2[1]	3	4	5	6	7	8	9	10[2]	11	12	13																				2
1	3		4	5	6	2	8[2]	9	10[1]	11	12	13	7[3]	14																		3
1	2		4	5	6	3	8	9	10[1]	11		7[2]		12	13																	4
1	2[2]		4	5	6	3		9		8		10	7		13	11[1]	12															5
1			4	5	6	2		9	12	11		10[2]	7			8[1]	3	13														6
1			4	5	6	3	12	9	13	11		10[1]	7			8[2]	2															7
1			4	5	6	2		9	12	11		10[1]	7[3]			8	3[2]		13	14												8
			4	5	6	2		9	12	11		10[1]	7[2]			8	3			13	1											9
1		3	4	5	6[1]	2	8	9	12			10[3]	7	14		11[2]				13												10
1		3	4	5		2	8	9	10	6			7			11[1]				12												11
1		3[1]	4	5		2	8[2]	9	10	6		12	7			11[3]	13			14												12
1			4	5	6	3		9	12	11		10[1]	7			8[2]	2			13												13
1			4	5	6[2]	3	8	9[3]	12	11		10[1]	7				2			13		14										14
1			4	5		3	8	9	12	6		10[1]	7			13	2			11[2]												15
1			4[1]	5		3	8[2]	9	10	6		12	7	13			2			11[3]		14										16
1			4	5		3		9[1]	10	6		12	7	8			2			11[2]		13										17
			4	5		3			10[1]	6	12	9[2]	7	8			2			11	1		13									18
				5		4	8	9	12	6		10[1]	7				2■			11	1	3										19
	2[3]		4[2]	5		3	8	9	12	6			7	13						11	1	14	10[1]									20
				5		3	8[3]	9[2]	12	6		13	7	14			2			11[1]	1	4	10									21
				5		4	8	12	10[3]	6		9[1]	7[2]	13			2			11	1	3	14									22
				5		4[2]	8	9[3]	12	6		13	7[1]				2		10■	11	1	3		14								23
		3		5		2	8		10	6		13	7		12[2]		9			11[1]	1	4										24
		14	4	5	12	2	8[1]	9[2]	10	6					13		7			11[3]		3			1							25
		3[1]	4	5	6			12	13	11	10[2]		7		9[3]		8			14		2			1							26
			4	5	6	2		12	10[1]	8			7		9					11		3			1							27
		8	4	5	6							10[1]	7[2]		9	12				11		2				1	3	13				28
			4	5	6	10[1]				8		12	7				9			11		2			1		3					29
		12	4	5	6	10[2]			13	8			7				9			11[1]		2			1		3[3]	14				30
1			4	5	6	10			12	8			7[1]				9			11		2					3					31
1			4	5	6				12	8		10[2]	7				9			11[1]		2	13				3					32
1			4	5	6	3				8■		12	7[1]				9			11		2						10				33
1		3	4	5	6	12			13			14					9[2]			11		2					7[1]	10[3]	8■			34
1		3	4	5		12			10	6		13	7[1]				9			11		2						8[2]				35
1		3		5	6				10	12			13				7[2]			11[1]		2	14				4	9[3]	8			36
1		12		5	6				10	8			7							11[1]		2	13				3	9[2]	4			37
1			4	5	6				10	8			7				12			11[2]		2					3[1]		9	13		38
1	12		4	5	6				10	8			7[2]				9			11[3]		3[1]						13	2	14		39
1			4	5	6				10[3]	8			12				7[1]			11[2]		13					3	14	2		9	40
1		13	4	14	6	5			10	8							7[1]					2					3	12[2]	11		9[3]	41
1			4	12	6	7			10	8			13				11					2[2]					3	14	5[1]		9[3]	42
1		11	4	5	6	7[2]			10[1]	8			12				2					13					3	14			9[3]	43
1		11[2]	4	5[3]	6	7[1]			10	8■			12				2			13							3		14		9	44
1		3	4			7			10[2]				12	8			13			11[1]		2					5		6		9	45
1				5	6	2			10				7	8						11[1]							3		4	12	9	46

FA Cup				**Carling Cup**			
Third Round	Coventry C	(h)	0-1	First Round	Shrewsbury T	(a)	2-2

BRISTOL CITY — FL Championship 1

FOUNDATION

The name Bristol City came into being in 1897 when the Bristol South End club, formed three years earlier, decided to adopt professionalism and apply for admission to the Southern League after competing in the Western League. The historic meeting was held at The Albert Hall, Bedminster. Bristol City employed Sam Hollis from Woolwich Arsenal as manager and gave him £40 to buy players. In 1900 they merged with Bedminster, another leading Bristol club.

Ashton Gate Stadium, Bristol, North Somerset, BS3 2EJ.

Telephone: (0117) 9630 630.

Fax: (0117) 9630 700.

Ticket Office: 0870 112 1897.

Website: www.bcfc.co.uk

E-mail: commercial@bcfc.co.uk

Ground Capacity: 21,497.

Record Attendance: 43,335 v Preston NE, FA Cup 5th rd, 16 February 1935.

Pitch Measurements: 115yd × 75yd.

Chairman: Stephen Lansdown.

Vice-chairman: Keith Dawe.

Chief Executive: Colin Sexstone.

Secretary: Michelle McDonald.

Player Manager: Gary Johnson.

Assistant Manager: Keith Millen.

Physio: Anna Eason.

Colours: Red shirts, white shorts, white stockings.

Change Colours: White shirts, dark grey shorts, dark grey stockings.

Year Formed: 1894.

Turned Professional: 1897.

Ltd Co.: 1897. Bristol City Football Club Ltd.

Previous Name: 1894, Bristol South End; 1897, Bristol City.

Club Nickname: 'Robins'.

Previous Grounds: 1894, St John's Lane; 1904, Ashton Gate.

First Football League Game: 7 September 1901, Division 2, v Blackpool (a) W 2–0 – Moles; Tuft, Davies; Jones, McLean, Chambers; Bradbury, Connor, Boucher, O'Brien (2), Flynn.

Record League Victory: 9–0 v Aldershot, Division 3 (S), 28 December 1946 – Eddols; Morgan, Fox; Peacock, Roberts, Jones (1); Chilcott, Thomas, Clark (4 incl. 1p), Cyril Williams (1), Hargreaves (3).

HONOURS

Football League: Division 1 – Runners-up 1906–07; Division 2 – Champions 1905–06; Runners-up 1975–76, 1997–98; Division 3 (S) – Champions 1922–23, 1926–27, 1954–55; Runners-up 1937–38; Division 3 – Runners-up 1964–65, 1989–90.

FA Cup: Runners-up 1909.

Football League Cup: Semi-final 1971, 1989.

Welsh Cup: Winners 1934.

Anglo-Scottish Cup: Winners 1978.

Freight Rover Trophy: Winners 1986; Runners-up 1987.

Auto Windscreens Shield: Runners-up 2000.

LDV Vans Trophy: Winners 2003.

SKY SPORTS FACT FILE

On 3 September 1949 German forward Alec Eisentrager playing for Bristol City against Newport County scored four goals. Attached to the Hamburg club as a youngster this former POW who had joined the Luftwaffe at 16 had been captured three months later.

Record Cup Victory: 11–0 v Chichester C, FA Cup 1st rd, 5 November 1960 – Cook; Collinson, Thresher; Connor, Alan Williams, Etheridge; Tait (1), Bobby Williams (1), Atyeo (5), Adrian Williams (3), Derrick, (1 og).

Record Defeat: 0–9 v Coventry C, Division 3 (S), 28 April 1934.

Most League Points (2 for a win): 70, Division 3 (S), 1954–55.

Most League Points (3 for a win): 91, Division 3, 1989–90.

Most League Goals: 104, Division 3 (S), 1926–27.

Highest League Scorer in Season: Don Clark, 36, Division 3 (S), 1946–47.

Most League Goals in Total Aggregate: John Atyeo, 314, 1951–66.

Most League Goals in One Match: 6, Tommy 'Tot' Walsh v Gillingham, Division 3S, 15 January 1927.

Most Capped Player: Billy Wedlock, 26, England.

Most League Appearances: John Atyeo, 597, 1951–66.

Youngest League Player: Marvin Brown, 16 years 105 days v Bristol R, 17 October 1999.

Record Transfer Fee Received: £3,000,000 from Wolverhampton W for Ade Akinbiyi, September 1999.

Record Transfer Fee Paid: £1,200,000 to Gillingham for Ade Akinbiyi, May 1998.

Football League Record: 1901 Elected to Division 2; 1906–11 Division 1; 1911–22 Division 2; 1922–23 Division 3 (S); 1923–24 Division 2; 1924–27 Division 3 (S); 1927–32 Division 2; 1932–55 Division 3 (S); 1955–60 Division 2; 1960–65 Division 3; 1965–76 Division 2; 1976–80 Division 1; 1980–81 Division 2; 1981–82 Division 3; 1982–84 Division 4; 1984–90 Division 3; 1990–92 Division 2; 1992–95 Division 1; 1995–98 Division 2; 1998–99 Division 1; 1999–04 Division 2; 2004– FL1.

MANAGERS

Sam Hollis 1897–99
Bob Campbell 1899–1901
Sam Hollis 1901–05
Harry Thickett 1905–10
Sam Hollis 1911–13
George Hedley 1913–17
Jack Hamilton 1917–19
Joe Palmer 1919–21
Alex Raisbeck 1921–29
Joe Bradshaw 1929–32
Bob Hewison 1932–49
(under suspension 1938–39)
Bob Wright 1949–50
Pat Beasley 1950–58
Peter Doherty 1958–60
Fred Ford 1960–67
Alan Dicks 1967–80
Bobby Houghton 1980–82
Roy Hodgson 1982
Terry Cooper 1982–88
(Director from 1983)
Joe Jordan 1988–90
Jimmy Lumsden 1990–92
Denis Smith 1992–93
Russell Osman 1993–94
Joe Jordan 1994–97
John Ward 1997–98
Benny Lennartsson 1998–99
Tony Pulis 1999
Tony Fawthrop 2000
Danny Wilson 2000–04
Brian Tinnion 2004–05
Gary Johnson September 2005–

LATEST SEQUENCES

Longest Sequence of League Wins: 14, 9.9.1905 – 2.12.1905.

Longest Sequence of League Defeats: 7, 3.10.1970 – 7.11.1970.

Longest Sequence of League Draws: 4, 6.11.1999 – 27.11.1999.

Longest Sequence of Unbeaten League Matches: 24, 9.9.1905 – 10.2.1906.

Longest Sequence Without a League Win: 15, 29.4.1933 – 4.11.1933.

Successive Scoring Runs: 25 from 26.12.1905.

Successive Non-scoring Runs: 6 from 10.9.1910.

TEN YEAR LEAGUE RECORD

		P	*W*	*D*	*L*	*F*	*A*	*Pts*	*Pos*
1996-97	Div 2	46	21	10	15	69	51	73	5
1997-98	Div 2	46	25	10	11	69	39	85	2
1998-99	Div 1	46	9	15	22	57	80	42	24
1999-2000	Div 2	46	15	19	12	59	57	64	9
2000-01	Div 2	46	18	14	14	70	56	68	9
2001-02	Div 2	46	21	10	15	68	53	73	7
2002-03	Div 2	46	24	11	11	79	48	83	3
2003-04	Div 2	46	23	13	10	58	37	82	3
2004-05	FL 1	46	18	16	12	74	57	70	7
2005-06	FL 1	46	18	11	17	66	62	65	9

DID YOU KNOW ?

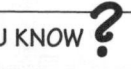

On 27 August 1958 Bristol City ran out 7–4 winners at Barnsley. However, the outcome had been in doubt until the 82nd minute when Bert Tindill made it 6–4 after a see-sawing game. Four days earlier they had beaten Rotherham United 6–1.

BRISTOL CITY 2005–06 LEAGUE RECORD

Match No.	Date	Venue	Opponents	Result		H/T Score	Lg. Pos.	Goalscorers	Attendance
1	Aug 6	H	Doncaster R	D	0-0	0-0	—		15,481
2	9	A	Huddersfield T	L	0-1	0-0	—		11,138
3	13	A	Bournemouth	L	0-2	0-1	24		6544
4	20	H	Port Vale	W	4-2	4-2	17	Brooker 2 [4, 28], Stewart [7], Murray [14]	11,120
5	27	H	Milton Keynes D	D	2-2	0-2	17	Brooker [53], Heywood [60]	10,011
6	Sept 3	H	Colchester U	D	0-0	0-0	18		10,180
7	10	A	Swansea C	L	1-7	0-1	22	Cotterill [81]	13,662
8	17	H	Blackpool	D	1-1	0-0	23	Cotterill [85]	9576
9	20	A	Nottingham F	L	1-3	1-2	—	Gillespie [15]	16,666
10	24	A	Brentford	W	3-2	2-0	22	Stewart [12], Wilkshire [40], Brooker [74]	6413
11	27	H	Barnsley	W	3-0	3-0	—	Brooker [24], Stewart 2 (1 pen) [39 (p), 45]	10,771
12	Oct 1	H	Hartlepool U	L	0-1	0-0	21		11,365
13	15	H	Tranmere R	W	1-0	0-0	18	Wilkshire [65]	10,495
14	22	A	Oldham Ath	L	3-4	0-2	19	Brown [48], Quinn [79], Murray [90]	5456
15	26	A	Chesterfield	L	0-3	0-0	—		5027
16	29	H	Southend U	L	0-3	0-1	22		10,625
17	Nov 11	A	Swindon T	L	1-2	1-2	—	Murray (pen) [4]	7572
18	19	H	Chesterfield	L	2-4	1-3	23	Wilkshire [6], Cotterill [85]	9752
19	26	A	Doncaster R	L	0-2	0-1	23		7876
20	Dec 6	H	Bradford C	L	0-1	0-0	—		9103
21	10	H	Huddersfield T	W	2-0	1-0	23	Murray [5], Cotterill [80]	9949
22	17	A	Port Vale	W	1-0	1-0	23	Brooker [45]	4214
23	26	A	Gillingham	D	1-1	1-0	23	Murray [10]	7786
24	28	H	Rotherham U	W	3-1	1-1	20	Brooker 2 [11, 77], Murray [48]	12,510
25	31	A	Yeovil T	D	1-1	0-1	20	Heywood [50]	9178
26	Jan 2	H	Walsall	W	3-0	2-0	20	Murray 2 [10, 30], Wilkshire [88]	12,652
27	14	H	Scunthorpe U	D	1-1	0-1	20	Savage [62]	11,692
28	17	A	Colchester U	L	2-3	1-2	—	Murray [2], Stewart [90]	4022
29	21	A	Blackpool	D	1-1	1-1	20	Brooker [26]	4842
30	28	H	Swansea C	W	1-0	1-0	19	Carey [45]	12,859
31	Feb 4	A	Barnsley	L	0-2	0-1	20		8092
32	11	H	Brentford	L	0-1	0-0	22		10,854
33	14	A	Scunthorpe U	W	2-0	1-0	—	Cotterill [32], Murray [79]	3786
34	18	A	Bradford C	D	1-1	1-0	16	Brooker [16]	7917
35	25	H	Bournemouth	W	3-1	1-1	13	McCammon [7], Brooker 2 [57, 64]	11,058
36	Mar 4	H	Nottingham F	D	1-1	0-0	13	Russell [78]	14,397
37	10	A	Milton Keynes D	W	1-0	1-0	—	Brooker [4]	6855
38	18	H	Gillingham	W	6-0	3-0	12	Brooker [11], Carey 2 [18, 50], Skuse (pen) [45], Wilkshire [67], McCammon [90]	10,932
39	25	A	Rotherham U	L	1-3	0-2	13	Skuse [80]	6682
40	Apr 1	H	Yeovil T	W	2-1	2-0	11	Orr [13], McCammon [21]	15,889
41	8	A	Walsall	W	3-0	1-0	10	Cotterill [44], Russell (pen) [51], Keogh [90]	5402
42	15	A	Hartlepool U	W	2-1	2-0	9	Noble [13], Russell [38]	5039
43	17	H	Oldham Ath	W	2-1	0-1	9	Russell (pen) [57], Brooker [76]	12,779
44	22	A	Tranmere R	W	3-0	2-0	8	Brooker [17], McCammon [34], Woodman (pen) [90]	6288
45	29	H	Swindon T	D	1-1	0-0	9	Cotterill [68]	15,632
46	May 6	A	Southend U	L	0-1	0-0	9		11,387

Final League Position: 9

GOALSCORERS

League (66): Brooker 16, Murray 10 (1 pen), Cotterill 7, Stewart 5 (1 pen), Wilkshire 5, McCammon 4, Russell 4 (2 pens), Carey 3, Heywood 2, Skuse 2 (1 pen), Brown 1, Gillespie 1, Keogh 1, Noble 1, Orr 1, Quinn 1, Savage 1, Woodman 1 (pen).
Carling Cup (2): Bridges 1, Golbourne 1.
FA Cup (0).
Football League Trophy (2): Madjo 1, Murray 1.

Phillips S 17 + 2	Carey L 38	Woodman C 36 + 1	Heywood M 22 + 2	Fortune C 4 + 2	Skuse C 29 + 9	Cotterill D 37 + 8	Wilkshire L 20 + 16	Bridges M 4 + 7	Stewart M 16 + 11	Smith G 4 + 7	Murray S 31 + 6	Brooker S 34 + 3	Brown S 23 + 6	Smith J 4 + 2	Partridge D 11	Golbourne S 4 + 1	Keogh R 4 + 5	Orr B 35 + 3	Gillespie S 3 + 1	Madjo G 1 + 4	Sankofa O 8	Youga K 4	Quinn J 2 + 1	Basso A 29	Russell A 21 + 6	Joseph M 3	Savage B 15 + 8	Noble D 23 + 1	Fontaine L 14 + 1	Andrew C 1 + 2	Green A 1 + 1	McCammon M 8 + 3	Abbey N — + 1	Myrie-Williams J — + 1	Match No.
1	2	3	4	5	6	7[1]	8	9[2]	10	11	12	13																							1
1	2	3	4	5	6	7[2]	8■	14	10	11[1]		9[3]	12	13																					2
1	2	3[2]	4		6	7		9	10[1]		12	11	8		5	13																			3
1	2		4[1]	12	6	13	8		10	14	7[2]	9	11[3]		5	3																			4
1	5		4		6	12	11[2]	13	10[1]		7	9	8	2		3																			5
1	2		4		6			9		12	7	10[2]	8			3[1]	5	11	13																6
1	6[1]			5		7	13	9	14		12		10	2		3	4	8[2]	11[3]																7
1	2	3	4[1]		6	13	14		10	11	7[2]		8		5			12	9[3]																8
1		11			6	12	13	14	10	3[2]	7[1]		8	2	4		5		9[3]																9
1		3	4		6	7[1]	8		10[2]		12	13	11		5		14	2		9[3]															10
1		3			6	7	8	12	10[3]		13	9[1]	11[2]		5			2		14	4														11
1		3[1]			6	7[2]	8	12	10[3]		13	9	11		5			2		14	4														12
1	2	3		12	6	11[3]	8	13	10[2]	14	7	9									4	5[1]													13
1	2[1]	3[2]			6	9	8	13	10[3]		7		11		5			12			4		14												14
1				5	6	9	8[1]			12	7		11[3]		3		13	2[2]		14	4		10												15
1	3	12			6	9	8		13		7		11[2]		5			2[1]		14	4		10[3]												16
			12			9			14	13	7[2]	10	11		5[1]			2[3]			6■	3		1	8	4									17
			4		6	12	8		10	13	7[3]	9[1]	11					2				3[2]		1	14	5									18
	2		12		6	9[3]	8				7	10						13			5	3[2]		1		4[1]	14	11							19
	5	3	4			7	11[2]		10[3]	12		9		13				2						1	6[1]		14	8							20
	5	3	4			11			10		7	9						2						1	6			8							21
	5	3	4			11					7	9						2						1	6		10	8							22
15	5	3	4		12	11	13				7	9						2						1[6]	6[2]		10	8[1]							23
	5	3	4		12	11[1]	13		14		7[2]	9						2						1	6		10[3]	8							24
15	5	3	4		12	11			13		7	9						2						1[6]	6		10[2]	8[1]							25
	5	3	4		12	11[2]	13				7	9						2						1	6[1]		10	8							26
	5	3	4		12	11[3]	14		13		7	9						2						1	6[1]		10[2]	8							27
	5	3	4		6[3]	11[2]			12		7	9	13					2						1	14		10[1]	8							28
	5	3	4		12	11[3]	14		13		7	9						2						1	6[1]		10[2]	8							29
	5	3	4		12	11					7	9						2						1	6		10[2]	8[1]	13						30
1	5■	3	4		6	11[1]			12		7		13	2[2]											8		10			9					31
			4			12	11[1]		13		7[3]	9						2						1	6		10[2]	8	5	14	3				32
	5	3			6	12	13		10[1]		7	9[3]	11[2]					2						1				8	4		14				33
	5	3			6[2]	10	12				7[3]	9	11[1]					2						1	13			8	4			14			34
	5	3			6[1]	11					7	9	13					2						1	12		14	8[2]	4			10[3]			35
	5	3			6	11	12		13		7	9						2[1]						1	8		10[2]		4						36
	5	3			6	11[1]	12				7[2]	9					13	2						1	8		10[3]	14	4						37
	5	3			6	11[2]	12				7[1]	9						2						1	8		10[3]		4	13		14			38
	5	3			6	11[2]	12				7[1]	9	13					2						1	8		10[3]		4			14			39
	5	3			6	12	11					9[1]	7[2]					2						1	14		13	8[3]	4			10			40
	5	3			6[1]	9	11						7[2]				14	2						1	12		13	8	4[3]			10			41
	5	3				9	7						11[2]				13	2						1	6		12	8	4			10[1]			42
	5	3				9	7[1]					12	11					2						1	6		13	8	4			10[2]			43
	5	3			12	7	13					9[1]	11[2]					2						1	6			8	4			10			44
	5	3			12	11	13					9	7[2]					2[1]						1	6		14	8	4			10[3]			45
	5	3			6	11	7[1]					9	12				4	2						1[6]				8				10[2]	15	13	46

FA Cup
First Round Notts Co (h) 0-2

Carling Cup
First Round Barnet (h) 2-4

Football League Trophy
First Round Barnet (a) 2-3

BRISTOL ROVERS FL Championship 2

FOUNDATION

Bristol Rovers were formed at a meeting in Stapleton Road, Eastville, in 1883. However, they first went under the name of the Black Arabs (wearing black shirts). Changing their name to Eastville Rovers in their second season, they won the Gloucestershire Senior Cup in 1888–89. Original members of the Bristol & District League in 1892, this eventually became the Western League and Eastville Rovers adopted professionalism in 1897.

The Memorial Stadium, Filton Avenue, Horfield, Bristol BS7 0BF.

Telephone: (0117) 952 4008.

Fax: (0117) 907 4312.

Ticket Office: (0117) 909 6648.

Website: www.bristolrovers.co.uk

Email: rodwesson@bristolrovers.co.uk

Ground Capacity: 11,900.

Record Attendance: 11,433 v Sunderland, Worthington Cup 3rd rd, 31 October 2000 (Memorial Stadium). 9464 v Liverpool, FA Cup 4th rd, 8 February 1992 (Twerton Park). 38,472 v Preston NE, FA Cup 4th rd, 30 January 1960 (Eastville).

Pitch Measurements: 110yd × 73yd.

Chairman: Geoff Dunford.

Vice-chairman: Ron Craig.

Secretary: Rod Wesson.

Director of Football: Lennie Lawrence.

First Team Coach: Paul Trollope.

Physio: Phil Kite.

Colours: Blue and white quartered shirts, blue shorts, white stockings.

Change Colours: Dark blue with yellow trim.

Year Formed: 1883. ***Turned Professional:*** 1897. ***Ltd Co.:*** 1896.

Previous Names: 1883, Black Arabs; 1884, Eastville Rovers; 1897, Bristol Eastville Rovers; 1898, Bristol Rovers. ***Club Nickname:*** 'Pirates'.

Previous Grounds: 1883, Purdown; Three Acres, Ashley Hill; Rudgeway, Fishponds; 1897, Eastville; 1986, Twerton Park; 1996, The Memorial Stadium.

First Football League Game: 28 August 1920, Division 3, v Millwall (a) L 0–2 – Stansfield; Bethune, Panes; Boxley, Kenny, Steele; Chance, Bird, Sims, Bell, Palmer.

Record League Victory: 7–0 v Brighton & HA, Division 3 (S), 29 November 1952 – Hoyle; Bamford, Fox; Pitt, Warren, Sampson; McIlvenny, Roost (2), Lambden (1), Bradford (1), Petherbridge (2), (1 og). 7–0 v Swansea T, Division 2, 2 October 1954 – Radford; Bamford, Watkins; Pitt, Muir, Anderson; Petherbridge, Bradford (2), Meyer, Roost (1), Hooper (2), (2 og). 7–0 v Shrewsbury T, Division 3, 21 March 1964 – Hall; Hillard, Gwyn Jones; Oldfield, Stone (1), Mabbutt; Jarman (2), Brown (1), Biggs (1p), Hamilton, Bobby Jones (2).

HONOURS

Football League: Division 2 best season: 4th, 1994–95; Division 3 (S) – Champions 1952–53; Division 3 – Champions 1989–90; Runners-up 1973–74.

FA Cup: best season: 6th rd, 1951, 1958.

Football League Cup: best season: 5th rd, 1971, 1972.

SKY SPORTS FACT FILE

Bristol Rovers' Geoff Bradford recovered from a serious leg injury which threatened his career and was capped for England against Denmark on 2 October 1955, making it a scoring debut. The club even chartered a Dakota and flew a party of 34 to Copenhagen.

Record Cup Victory: 6–0 v Merthyr Tydfil, FA Cup 1st rd, 14 November 1987 – Martyn; Alexander (Dryden), Tanner, Hibbitt, Twentyman, Jones, Holloway, Meacham (1), White (2), Penrice (3) (Reece), Purnell.

Most League Points (2 for a win): 64, Division 3 (S), 1952–53.

Most League Points (3 for a win): 93, Division 3, 1989–90.

Most League Goals: 92, Division 3 (S), 1952–53.

Highest League Scorer in Season: Geoff Bradford, 33, Division 3 (S), 1952–53.

Most League Goals in Total Aggregate: Geoff Bradford, 242, 1949–64.

Most League Goals in One Match: 4, Sidney Leigh v Exeter C, Division 3S, 2 May 1921; 4, Jonah Wilcox v Bournemouth, Division 3S, 12 December 1925; 4, Bill Culley v QPR, Division 3S, 5 March 1927; Frank Curran v Swindon T, Division 3S, 25 March 1939; Vic Lambden v Aldershot, Division 3S, 29 March 1947; George Petherbridge v Torquay U, Division 3S, 1 December 1951; Vic Lambden v Colchester U, Division 3S, 14 May 1952; Geoff Bradford v Rotherham U, Division 2, 14 March 1959; Robin Stubbs v Gillingham, Division 2, 10 October 1970; Alan Warboys v Brighton & HA, Division 3, 1 December 1973; Jamie Cureton v Reading, Division 2, 16 January 1999.

Most Capped Player: Vitalijs Astafjevs, 31 (125), Latvia.

Most League Appearances: Stuart Taylor, 546, 1966–80.

Youngest League Player: Ronnie Dix, 15 years 173 days v Charlton Ath, 25 February 1928.

Record Transfer Fee Received: £2,100,000 from Fulham for Barry Hayles, November 1998 and £2,100,000 from WBA for Jason Roberts, July 2000.

Record Transfer Fee Paid: £375,000 to QPR for Andy Tillson, November 1992.

Football League Record: 1920 Original Member of Division 3; 1921–53 Division 3 (S); 1953–62 Division 2; 1962–74 Division 3; 1974–81 Division 2; 1981–90 Division 3; 1990–92 Division 2. 1992–93 Division 1; 1993–2001 Division 2; 2001–04 Division 3; 2004– FL2.

MANAGERS

Alfred Homer 1899–1920
(continued as Secretary to 1928)
Ben Hall 1920–21
Andy Wilson 1921–26
Joe Palmer 1926–29
Dave McLean 1929–30
Albert Prince-Cox 1930–36
Percy Smith 1936–37
Brough Fletcher 1938–49
Bert Tann 1950–68 *(continued as General Manager to 1972)*
Fred Ford 1968–69
Bill Dodgin Snr 1969–72
Don Megson 1972–77
Bobby Campbell 1978–79
Harold Jarman 1979–80
Terry Cooper 1980–81
Bobby Gould 1981–83
David Williams 1983–85
Bobby Gould 1985–87
Gerry Francis 1987–91
Martin Dobson 1991
Dennis Rofe 1992
Malcolm Allison 1992–93
John Ward 1993–96
Ian Holloway 1996–2001
Garry Thompson 2001
Gerry Francis 2001
Garry Thompson 2001–02
Ray Graydon 2002–04
Ian Atkins 2004–05
Lennie Lawrence November 2005–

LATEST SEQUENCES

Longest Sequence of League Wins: 12, 18.10.1952 – 17.1.1953.

Longest Sequence of League Defeats: 8, 26.10.2002 – 21.12.2002.

Longest Sequence of League Draws: 5, 1.11.1975 – 22.11.1975.

Longest Sequence of Unbeaten League Matches: 32, 7.4.1973 – 27.1.1974.

Longest Sequence Without a League Win: 20, 5.4.1980 – 1.11.1980.

Successive Scoring Runs: 26 from 26.3.1927.

Successive Non-scoring Runs: 6 from 14.10.1922.

TEN YEAR LEAGUE RECORD

		P	W	D	L	F	A	Pts	Pos
1996-97	Div 2	46	15	11	20	47	50	56	17
1997-98	Div 2	46	20	10	16	70	64	70	5
1998-99	Div 2	46	13	17	16	65	56	56	13
1999-2000	Div 2	46	23	11	12	69	45	80	7
2000-01	Div 2	46	12	15	19	53	57	51	21
2001-02	Div 3	46	11	12	23	40	60	45	23
2002-03	Div 3	46	12	15	19	50	57	51	20
2003-04	Div 3	46	14	13	19	50	61	55	15
2004-05	FL 2	46	13	21	12	60	57	60	12
2005-06	FL 2	46	17	9	20	59	67	60	12

DID YOU KNOW ?

In 1963 Bristol Rovers signed goalkeeper Bernard Hall, 21, as a full-time professional. After some previous outings while serving his apprenticeship as a bricklayer he had been fixed up by the club with a firm of stonemasons. He became the regular choice.

BRISTOL ROVERS 2005–06 LEAGUE RECORD

Match No.	Date	Venue	Opponents	Result	H/T Score	Lg. Pos.	Goalscorers	Attendance
1	Aug 6	A	Barnet	D 1-1	0-0	—	Agogo ^{87}	3237
2	9	H	Grimsby T	L 1-2	0-0	—	Agogo ^{54}	6300
3	13	H	Peterborough U	L 2-3	1-2	22	Walker ^{45}, Elliott ^{59}	5169
4	20	A	Torquay U	W 3-2	0-1	17	Agogo 2 $^{74, 87}$, Walker ^{90}	3964
5	27	A	Notts Co	L 0-2	0-1	19		4405
6	Sept 3	A	Leyton Orient	W 3-2	1-0	17	Disley ^{15}, Agogo 2 (1 pen) $^{54 (p), 82}$	3481
7	10	H	Lincoln C	D 0-0	0-0	17		5057
8	13	H	Oxford U	D 1-1	0-1	—	Walker ^{64}	5098
9	17	A	Chester C	L 0-4	0-3	19		2874
10	24	H	Darlington	W 1-0	1-0	16	Walker ^{45}	5652
11	27	A	Bury	L 0-1	0-1	—		1673
12	Oct 1	A	Carlisle U	W 3-1	0-1	15	Gray (og) ^{57}, Aranalde (og) ^{82}, Agogo ^{90}	5317
13	7	H	Northampton T	D 0-0	0-0	—		6912
14	15	A	Boston U	L 1-3	1-1	18	Walker ^{12}	2469
15	22	H	Wrexham	W 2-1	0-0	14	Walker 2 $^{88, 90}$	5730
16	29	A	Macclesfield T	L 1-2	0-0	17	Disley ^{55}	1908
17	Nov 12	H	Rochdale	L 1-2	1-1	19	Agogo ^{38}	6042
18	19	A	Northampton T	L 0-4	0-2	19		5716
19	26	H	Barnet	W 2-1	2-0	17	Walker 2 $^{5, 20}$	5096
20	Dec 6	A	Stockport Co	W 1-0	1-0	—	Walker (pen) ^{35}	3460
21	10	A	Grimsby T	W 1-0	0-0	12	Carruthers ^{80}	4739
22	17	H	Torquay U	L 0-1	0-0	14		6061
23	26	H	Shrewsbury T	W 2-1	2-0	10	Disley ^{37}, Agogo (pen) ^{45}	7551
24	28	A	Mansfield T	D 3-3	2-2	10	Hunt ^{28}, Walker 2 (1 pen) $^{41 (p), 90}$	2357
25	31	H	Wycombe W	L 1-2	0-1	11	Walker ^{61}	6828
26	Jan 2	A	Rushden & D	W 3-2	1-1	8	Campbell ^{41}, Elliott ^{49}, Forrester ^{90}	2720
27	14	A	Cheltenham T	W 3-2	1-0	9	Forrester ^{18}, Disley ^{89}, Anderson ^{90}	6005
28	21	H	Chester C	W 2-1	2-0	8	Edwards ^{10}, Disley ^{42}	6310
29	28	A	Lincoln C	L 0-1	0-0	9		4258
30	31	H	Leyton Orient	D 3-3	1-0	—	Agogo ^{14}, Disley ^{58}, Walker (pen) ^{74}	5966
31	Feb 4	H	Bury	W 1-0	1-0	8	Agogo ^{28}	6027
32	11	A	Darlington	D 1-1	0-0	9	Agogo ^{68}	4579
33	14	H	Cheltenham T	L 0-1	0-0	—		6885
34	18	H	Stockport Co	D 2-2	1-0	9	Walker 2 (1 pen) $^{36, 50 (p)}$	5990
35	25	A	Peterborough U	W 2-1	1-0	9	Agogo ^{36}, Walker ^{54}	4292
36	Mar 11	H	Notts Co	L 1-2	0-1	9	Haldane ^{53}	6280
37	15	A	Oxford U	L 0-1	0-0	—		6424
38	18	A	Shrewsbury T	L 0-1	0-0	10		3641
39	25	H	Mansfield T	W 2-0	2-0	10	Igoe ^{14}, Walker ^{17}	5253
40	Apr 1	A	Wycombe W	W 3-1	1-0	9	Agogo 2 $^{31, 74}$, Walker (pen) ^{54}	6355
41	8	H	Rushden & D	L 0-1	0-0	10		6432
42	15	H	Carlisle U	D 1-1	0-0	10	Disley ^{55}	6181
43	17	A	Wrexham	L 0-1	0-1	11		3749
44	22	H	Boston U	W 3-1	1-0	9	Disley ^{27}, Walker (pen) ^{73}, Agogo ^{77}	4836
45	29	A	Rochdale	L 0-2	0-1	10		2649
46	May 6	H	Macclesfield T	L 2-3	1-2	12	Haldane 2 $^{12, 57}$	6100

Final League Position: 12

GOALSCORERS

League (59): Walker 20 (6 pens), Agogo 16 (2 pens), Disley 8, Haldane 3, Elliott 2, Forrester 2, Anderson 1, Campbell 1, Carruthers 1, Edwards 1, Hunt 1, Igoe 1, own goals 2.
Carling Cup (0).
FA Cup (3): Agogo 2, Gibb 1.
Football League Trophy (1): Walker 1.

Shearer S 45	Anderson J 10 + 2	Ryan R 14	Campbell S 31 + 7	Edwards C 12 + 3	Elliott S 45	Bass J 7 + 2	Disley C 37 + 5	Walker R 44 + 2	Agogo J 41 + 1	Lescott A 35 + 2	Hinton C 34 + 2	Williams R 2 + 5	Louis J 2 + 6	Carruthers C 39 + 1	Sommer M 1	Gibb A 21 + 12	Hunt J 40	Forrester J 3 + 14	Leary M 12 + 1	Haldane L 19 + 11	Mullings D — + 4	Igoe S 10 + 1	Lines C 1 + 3	Book S 1	*Match No.*
1	2^1	3	4	5	6	7^2	8	9^3	10	11	12	13	14												1
1	2		4	5	6			9^1	10	11^2		7	12	8	3	13									2
1	2^2	3^3	4	5	6			9	10^1		13	11	12			7	8	14							3
1	2	3	4^1		6		12	13	10	11	5	14	9^2			7^3	8								4
1	2^1	3	4^2		6	12		9^3	10	11■	5	13	14			7	8								5
1	5	3	12		6	13	8^1	9^2	10^3		2		14			11	4		7						6
1	5	3			6		4^1	13	10		2		9^2	12		11	8		7						7
1	5				6		4	9^1	10		2		12	3		11	8		7						8
1	5^3		4^1	14	6		12	9	10	13	2			3		11	8		7^2						9
1		3			6			9	10	4	5			2		11	8		7						10
1		3			6		12	9^2	10	4	5			2^1		11^3	8	13	7	14					11
1					6		4	9	10	3	5			2		11	8		7						12
1	5	3	12		6		11	9	10	2				4^1			8		7						13
1		3			6		12	9^2	10^3	2	5			4^1		11	8	13	7	14					14
1		3	12		6		11	9	10^3	2	5			4^2		7^1	8	13		14					15
1		3			6		4	9	10	2	5					11^1	8	12	7^2	13					16
1		3	4		6		8	9^2	10	2	5			11^1				12	7	13					17
1		3	4		6		12	9^3	10	2	5			11^2		13	8		7^1	14					18
1			4		6		11^1	9	10^2	2	5			3		7	8		12	13					19
1			4		6		11	9	10	2	5			3		7	8								20
1			4		6		11	9	10	2	5			3		7	8								21
1			4		6		11^2	9	10^3	2	5	12		3		7^1	8	13		14					22
1			4		6		11	9	10^1	2	5			3		7	8	12							23
1			4		6		11^1	9	10^3	2	5	12		3		7^2	8	13		14					24
1			4		6		11^3	9	10^2	2	5			3		7^1	8	12		13	14				25
1			4		6		11	9		2	5			3		12	8■	7		10^1					26
1	12		4	6			11	9	13	2	5^1			3		7^3		8		10^2		14			27
1			4	5	6		11	9	10	2				3						8^2	12	7^1	13		28
1			4	5	6		11^1	9	10	2				3		12				8		7			29
1	12		4	5	6		11	9	10	2^1				3			8					7			30
1			4^1	5	6	2	11	9	10					3			8	12		7^2	13				31
1			4	5	6	2	11	9	10					3			8			7					32
1			4	5	6	2	11	9	10					3			8	12		7^1					33
1			4	5	6	2	11	9	10					3			8	7^1		12					34
1			4		6	2	11	9	10■		5			3			8			7					35
			4		6	2^1	11^2	9		12	5			3		13	8			10^3	14	7		1	36
1			4^1		6		11	9		2	5			3		13	8	12		10^2		7			37
1			4^1		6		11	9		2	5			3		12	8	13		10^2		7			38
1					6		11	9	10^1	2	5			3		12	8			4		7			39
1			12	13	6		11	9	10	2	5			3^2		14	4			8^3		7^1			40
1			12		6		11^1	9	10	2	5			3		13	4			8^2		7			41
1			12		6		11	9	10	2	5			3			4			8^1		7			42
1			4^2		6		11	9	10	2	5			3		12	8			7^1			13		43
1			4		6		11	9	10	2	5			3			8			7					44
1			4^1	12	6		11	9	10	2	5■			3^3		13	8			7^2			14		45
1			12	5	6		11	9	10	2				3			4			7			8^1		46

FA Cup

First Round	Grimsby T	(a)	2-1
Second Round	Port Vale	(a)	1-1
		(h)	0-1

Carling Cup

First Round	Millwall	(a)	0-2

Football League Trophy

First Round	Peterborough U	(a)	1-2

BURNLEY — FL Championship

FOUNDATION

The majority of those responsible for the formation of the Burnley club in 1881 were from the defunct rugby club Burnley Rovers. Indeed, they continued to play rugby for a year before changing to soccer and dropping 'Rovers' from their name. The changes were decided at a meeting held in May 1882 at the Bull Hotel.

Turf Moor, Harry Potts Way, Burnley, Lancashire BB10 4BX.

Telephone: 0870 443 1882.

Fax: (01282) 700 014.

Ticket Office: 0870 443 1914.

Website: www.burnleyfc.com

Email: info@burnleyfootballclub.net

Ground Capacity: 22,610.

Record Attendance: 54,775 v Huddersfield T, FA Cup 3rd rd, 23 February 1924.

Pitch Measurements: 112yd × 70yd.

Chairman: Barry Kilby.

Vice-chairman: Ray Ingleby.

Chief Executive: Dave Edmundson.

Secretary: Cathy Pickup.

Manager: Steve Cotterill.

Assistant Manager: Dave Kevan.

Physio: Andy Mitchell.

Colours: Claret and blue shirts with white trim, claret shorts, claret stockings.

Change Colours: Yellow shirts with claret trim, yellow shorts with claret trim, yellow stockings.

Year Formed: 1882.

Turned Professional: 1883. ***Ltd Co.:*** 1897.

Previous Name: 1881, Burnley Rovers; 1882, Burnley.

Club Nickname: 'The Clarets'.

Previous Grounds: 1881, Calder Vale; 1882, Turf Moor.

First Football League Game: 8 September 1888, Football League, v Preston NE (a) L 2–5 – Smith; Lang, Bury, Abrams, Friel, Keenan, Brady, Tait, Poland (1), Gallocher (1), Yates.

Record League Victory: 9–0 v Darwen, Division 1, 9 January 1892 – Hillman; Walker, McFettridge, Lang, Matthews, Keenan, Nicol (3), Bowes, Espie (1), McLardie (3), Hill (2).

Record Cup Victory: 9–0 v Crystal Palace, FA Cup 2nd rd (replay), 10 February 1909 – Dawson; Barron, McLean; Cretney (2), Leake, Moffat; Morley, Ogden, Smith (3), Abbott (2), Smethams (1). 9–0 v New Brighton, FA Cup 4th rd, 26 January 1957 – Blacklaw; Angus, Winton; Seith, Adamson, Miller; Newlands (1), McIlroy (3), Lawson (3), Cheesebrough (1), Pilkington (1). 9–0 v Penrith, FA Cup 1st rd, 17 November 1984 – Hansbury; Miller, Hampton, Phelan, Overson (Kennedy), Hird (3 incl. 1p), Grewcock (1), Powell (2), Taylor (3), Biggins, Hutchison.

HONOURS

Football League: Division 1 – Champions 1920–21, 1959–60; Runners-up 1919–20, 1961–62; Division 2 – Champions 1897–98, 1972–73; Runners-up 1912–13, 1946–47, 1999–2000; Promoted from Division 2, 1993–94 (play-offs); Division 3 – Champions 1981–82; Division 4 – Champions 1991–92. Record 30 consecutive Division 1 games without defeat 1920–21.

FA Cup: Winners 1914; Runners-up 1947, 1962.

Football League Cup: Semi-final 1961, 1969, 1983.

Anglo-Scottish Cup: Winners 1979.

Sherpa Van Trophy: Runners-up 1988.

European Competitions: *European Cup:* 1960–61. *European Fairs Cup:* 1966–67.

SKY SPORTS FACT FILE

Few players have made such a dramatic start to their first class careers as Ian Lawson, 17, in February 1957 for Burnley. He scored four times on his debut in the FA Cup against Chesterfield and added a hat-trick in the next round against New Brighton.

Record Defeat: 0–10 v Aston Villa, Division 1, 29 August 1925 and v Sheffield U, Division 1, 19 January 1929.

Most League Points (2 for a win): 62, Division 2, 1972–73.

Most League Points (3 for a win): 88, Division 2, 1999–2000.

Most League Goals: 102, Division 1, 1960–61.

Highest League Scorer in Season: George Beel, 35, Division 1, 1927–28.

Most League Goals in Total Aggregate: George Beel, 178, 1923–32.

Most League Goals in One Match: 6, Louis Page v Birmingham C, Division 1, 10 April 1926.

Most Capped Player: Jimmy McIlroy, 51 (55), Northern Ireland.

Most League Appearances: Jerry Dawson, 522, 1907–28.

Youngest League Player: Tommy Lawton, 16 years 174 days v Doncaster R, 28 March 1936.

Record Transfer Fee Received: £1,750,000 from Sheffield United for Ade Akinbiyi, January 2006.

Record Transfer Fee Paid: £1,000,000 to Stockport C for Ian Moore, November 2000 and £1,000,000 to Bradford C for Robbie Blake, January 2002.

Football League Record: 1888 Original Member of the Football League; 1897–98 Division 2; 1898–1900 Division 1; 1900–13 Division 2; 1913–30 Division 1; 1930–47 Division 2; 1947–71 Division 1; 1971–73 Division 2; 1973–76 Division 1; 1976–80 Division 2; 1980–82 Division 3; 1982–83 Division 2; 1983–85 Division 3; 1985–92 Division 4; 1992–94 Division 2; 1994–95 Division 1; 1995–2000 Division 2; 2000–04 Division 1; 2004– FLC.

MANAGERS

Arthur F. Sutcliffe 1893–96
(Secretary-Manager)
Harry Bradshaw 1896–99
(Secretary-Manager)
Ernest Magnall 1899–1903
(Secretary-Manager)
Spen Whittaker 1903–10
R. H. Wadge 1910–11
(Secretary-Manager)
John Haworth 1911–25
Albert Pickles 1925–32
Tom Bromilow 1932–35
Alf Boland 1935–39
(Secretary-Manager)
Cliff Britton 1945–48
Frank Hill 1948–54
Alan Brown 1954–57
Billy Dougall 1957–58
Harry Potts 1958–70
(General Manager to 1972)
Jimmy Adamson 1970–76
Joe Brown 1976–77
Harry Potts 1977–79
Brian Miller 1979–83
John Bond 1983–84
John Benson 1984–85
Martin Buchan 1985
Tommy Cavanagh 1985–86
Brian Miller 1986–89
Frank Casper 1989–91
Jimmy Mullen 1991–96
Adrian Heath 1996–97
Chris Waddle 1997–98
Stan Ternent 1998–2004
Steve Cotterill June 2004–

LATEST SEQUENCES

Longest Sequence of League Wins: 10, 16.11.1912 – 18.1.1913.

Longest Sequence of League Defeats: 8, 2.1.1995 – 25.2.1995.

Longest Sequence of League Draws: 6, 21.2.1931 – 28.3.1931.

Longest Sequence of Unbeaten League Matches: 30, 6.9.1920 – 25.3.1921.

Longest Sequence Without a League Win: 24, 16.4.1979 – 17.11.1979.

Successive Scoring Runs: 27 from 13.2.1926.

Successive Non-scoring Runs: 6 from 9.8.1997.

TEN YEAR LEAGUE RECORD

		P	W	D	L	F	A	Pts	Pos
1996-97	Div 2	46	19	11	16	71	55	68	9
1997-98	Div 2	46	13	13	20	55	65	52	20
1998-99	Div 2	46	13	16	17	54	73	55	15
1999-2000	Div 2	46	25	13	8	69	47	88	2
2000-01	Div 2	46	21	9	16	50	54	72	7
2001-02	Div 1	46	21	12	13	70	62	75	7
2002-03	Div 1	46	15	10	21	65	89	55	16
2003-04	Div 1	46	13	14	19	60	77	53	19
2004-05	FL C	46	15	15	16	38	39	60	13
2005-06	FL C	46	14	12	20	46	54	54	17

Little did Gainsborough Trinity goalkeeper Ronnie Sewell plus full-backs Sam Gunton and Cliff Jones know they would be signed by Burnley after a 4–1 FA Cup defeat on 1 February 1913. All three played in the League and Sewell later won an England cap.

BURNLEY 2005–06 LEAGUE RECORD

Match No.	*Date*	*Venue*	*Opponents*	*Result*		*H/T Score*	*Lg. Pos.*	*Goalscorers*	*Attendance*
1	Aug 6	A	Crewe Alex	L	1-2	0-1	—	Noel-Williams 67	8006
2	9	H	Sheffield U	L	1-2	0-2	—	Akinbiyi 72	11,802
3	13	H	Coventry C	W	4-0	2-0	16	O'Connor G 28, Thomas 37, Akinbiyi 2 87, 90	11,683
4	20	A	Watford	L	1-3	1-2	19	O'Connor G (pen) 16	16,802
5	27	H	Derby Co	D	2-2	0-1	18	Akinbiyi 46, Noel-Williams 53	12,243
6	29	A	Reading	L	1-2	1-1	19	Akinbiyi 42	14,027
7	Sept 10	H	Cardiff C	D	3-3	2-2	20	Elliott 2 1, 23, O'Connor J 89	10,431
8	13	A	Preston NE	D	0-0	0-0	—		17,139
9	17	A	Plymouth Arg	L	0-1	0-0	23		11,829
10	24	H	Brighton & HA	D	1-1	1-1	23	O'Connor G (pen) 34	11,112
11	27	H	Ipswich T	W	3-0	1-0	—	O'Connor J 33, O'Connor G 72, McCann 87	10,496
12	30	A	Wolverhampton W	W	1-0	1-0	—	O'Connor G 23	21,747
13	Oct 15	H	Leeds U	L	1-2	0-0	18	O'Connor G (pen) 60	16,174
14	18	A	Leicester C	W	1-0	0-0	—	Akinbiyi 64	23,326
15	22	A	Crystal Palace	L	0-2	0-1	17		20,127
16	28	H	Hull C	W	1-0	1-0	—	Akinbiyi 29	11,701
17	Nov 1	H	Millwall	W	2-1	0-1	—	Dyer 76, Elliott 80	10,698
18	5	A	Luton T	W	3-2	2-1	8	Akinbiyi 3 (1 pen) 15, 31, 54 (p)	8518
19	19	H	Leicester C	W	1-0	1-0	6	Spicer 40	12,592
20	22	A	Leeds U	L	0-2	0-0	—		21,318
21	26	H	Crewe Alex	W	3-0	1-0	6	Spicer 2 27, 68, Dyer 72	11,151
22	Dec 3	A	Southampton	D	1-1	0-1	7	Akinbiyi 66	21,592
23	10	A	Sheffield U	L	0-3	0-2	11		23,118
24	17	H	Watford	W	4-1	2-0	8	Branch 32, Harley 2 (1 pen) 42, 77 (p), O'Connor J 79	13,815
25	26	H	Stoke C	W	1-0	0-0	5	Akinbiyi 56	17,912
26	28	A	Norwich C	L	1-2	0-2	7	Safri (og) 73	25,204
27	31	H	Sheffield W	L	1-2	0-1	9	O'Connor G (pen) 84	14,607
28	Jan 2	A	QPR	D	1-1	1-1	8	McCann 10	12,565
29	14	A	Cardiff C	L	0-3	0-0	9		10,872
30	21	H	Preston NE	L	0-2	0-1	10		17,220
31	31	A	Brighton & HA	D	0-0	0-0	—		6267
32	Feb 4	H	Plymouth Arg	W	1-0	1-0	10	Ricketts 24	11,292
33	11	A	Ipswich T	L	1-2	1-0	11	Ricketts 45	24,482
34	14	H	Wolverhampton W	L	0-1	0-1	—		11,056
35	25	A	Coventry C	L	0-1	0-0	14		19,641
36	Mar 4	H	Reading	L	0-3	0-1	15		12,888
37	11	A	Derby Co	L	0-3	0-3	17		23,292
38	18	A	Stoke C	L	0-1	0-0	18		12,082
39	24	H	Norwich C	W	2-0	1-0	—	Gray 18, Branch 51	11,938
40	28	H	Southampton	D	1-1	1-1	—	Gray 9	10,636
41	Apr 1	A	Sheffield W	D	0-0	0-0	17		24,485
42	8	H	QPR	W	1-0	0-0	15	Gray 79	11,247
43	15	A	Hull C	D	0-0	0-0	16		19,926
44	17	H	Crystal Palace	D	0-0	0-0	14		11,449
45	22	A	Millwall	L	0-1	0-1	16		7780
46	30	H	Luton T	D	1-1	0-1	17	Lafferty 78	12,473

Final League Position: 17

GOALSCORERS

League (46): Akinbiyi 12 (1 pen), O'Connor G 7 (4 pens), Elliott 3, Gray 3, O'Connor J 3, Spicer 3, Branch 2, Dyer 2, Harley 2 (1 pen), McCann 2, Noel-Williams 2, Ricketts 2, Lafferty 1, Thomas 1, own goal 1.
Carling Cup (5): Akinbiyi 2, Duff 1, Lowe 1, Spicer 1.
FA Cup (1): O'Connor G 1.

Coyne D 7 + 1	Sinclair F 36 + 1	Branch G 29 + 8	Hyde M 39 + 2	Thomas W 12 + 4	McGreal J 33 + 2	Elliott W 23 + 13	O'Connor J 46	Akinbiyi A 29	Noel-Williams G 17 + 12	O'Connor G 26 + 3	Lafferty K 3 + 8	Jensen B 38 + 1	Duff M 39 + 2	McCann C 15 + 8	Bermingham K 1 + 3	Harley J 41	Lowe K 10 + 6	Spicer J 22 + 12	Courtney D 1 + 6	Dyer N 4 + 1	Grant L 1	Karbassiyon D — + 5	Ricketts M 12 + 1	Bardsley P 6	Gray A 9	Mahon A 7 + 1	*Match No.*
1	2	3	4	5	6	7	8	9	10	11^{1}	12																1
	2^{1}	3	4	5	6	7	8	9	10	11	12	1															2
		3	4	5	6	7^{1}	8	9	10	11	13	1	2	12^{2}													3
15	5^{1}	3	4				8	9	10	11	12	1^{G}	2	7	6												4
1		11	4	5■	6		8	9	10^{1}	7			2			3	12										5
1		11	4^{2}	2^{1}	6		7	9	10	8■			5			3	12	13									6
1	5^{2}	11^{1}	4		6	7^{3}	8	9	10				2		14	3	13	12									7
1		12	4		6	7^{1}	8	9	10				2			3	5	11									8
1		12	4		6	7^{1}	8	9	10				2			3	5	11									9
1^{G}	12	11^{2}	4		6^{1}		8	9	10	7		15	2			3	5	13									10
	6	10	4				8	9^{2}		11		1	2	12	13	3	5	7^{1}									11
	6	10	4		5		8	9^{2}		11		1	2	12	13	3		7^{1}									12
	6	10^{2}	4		5	12	8	9	14	11		1	2	13^{3}		3		7^{1}									13
	6		4		5	7^{2}	8	9	12	10^{1}		1	2			3	13	11^{3}	14								14
	6		4		5	7^{2}	8	9	12	10		1	2			3		11^{1}	13								15
	6		4			7^{3}	8	9	12	10^{2}		1	2	13		3	5	11^{1}	14								16
	6		4			7^{2}	8■	9	12	10		1	2^{3}			3	5	11^{1}	13	14							17
	6		4		5	7^{2}	8	9	12	10^{1}		1■				3	13	11	2								18
			4		6	7^{2}	8	9		10^{1}			2	12		3	5	11	13		1						19
	4		8		6	12	7	9				1	2^{1}			3	5	11^{2}		10		13					20
	5		4		6^{2}	12	8	9		10^{3}		1	2			3	13	11		7^{1}		14					21
	5	10	4			7	8	9	12	6		1				3	2	11^{1}									22
	5	12	4		6	13	7	9	14	8^{1}		1	2^{2}				3	11^{3}		10							23
	5	10^{1}	4	12	6	13	8	9	14			1	2			3		11^{3}		7^{2}							24
	5	11^{1}	4	12	6	7	8	9	10			1	2			3											25
	5	12	4	11^{1}	6	13	8	9	10^{3}	14		1	2			3		7^{2}									26
	5	11^{2}	4	12	6^{1}	7	8	9	10	13		1	2			3^{3}						14					27
	5	12	4	13	6	7^{2}	8	9		11^{1}		1	2	10		3											28
	5	13	4	2	6	7^{3}	8	9	12	11^{1}		1		10^{2}		3		14									29
	5	9	4^{1}	2^{2}	6	7	8		10	11^{3}		1	13			3		12				14					30
	5	10	4		6	7^{2}	8			11^{1}		1	2	13		3		12					9				31
	5	11	4		6	12	8		10	7^{1}		1	2			3							9				32
		11^{3}	4	5■	6	12	8		10^{2}			1	2	14		3		7^{1}	13				9				33
		12	4		6	2	8		10			1	5	11^{1}		3		7					9				34
	5	10^{2}	4			2^{3}	8^{1}		12		14	1	6	11		3		7				13	9				35
	5		4	2	6	12	8				9	1	11	10		3		7^{1}									36
	5^{2}	12	4^{1}	2	6	7	8^{3}			11		1	13	10		3		14					9				37
		6^{3}		5		12	8		13	11^{1}		1	4	7^{2}		3		14					9	2	10		38
	5	11^{2}				7^{1}	8				13	1	6	4		3		12					9^{3}	2	10	14	39
	5	11	12				7^{1}				13	1	6	4		3							9^{2}	2	10	8	40
	5	11					7					1	6	4		3		12					9^{1}	2	10	8	41
	5	11^{2}	13		12	14	7					1	6	4^{1}		3							9^{3}	2	10	8	42
	5	11			12		7				9^{2}	1	6	4		3		13						2^{1}	10	8	43
	2	9	4		6		7				12	1	5	11^{1}		3									10	8	44
	2	11	4		6^{2}	12	7					1	5			3		13					9^{1}		10	8	45
	5	11^{2}				12	7			13	9^{3}	1	6	4		3		2					14		10	8^{1}	46

FA Cup

Third Round	Derby Co	(a)	1-2

Carling Cup

First Round	Carlisle U	(h)	2-1
Second Round	Barnsley	(h)	3-0
Third Round	Aston Villa	(a)	0-1

BURY FL Championship 2

FOUNDATION

A meeting at the Waggon & Horses Hotel, attended largely by members of Bury Wesleyans and Bury Unitarians football clubs, decided to form a new Bury club. This was officially formed at a subsequent gathering at the Old White Horse Hotel, Fleet Street, Bury on 24 April 1885.

Gigg Lane, Bury BL9 9HR.

Telephone: (0161) 764 4881.

Fax: (0161) 764 5521.

Ticket Office: (0161) 764 4881.

Website: www.buryfc.co.uk

Email: admin@buryfc.co.uk

Ground Capacity: 11,669.

Record Attendance: 35,000 v Bolton W, FA Cup 3rd rd, 9 January 1960.

Pitch Measurements: 112yd × 72yd.

Secretary: Mrs Jill Neville.

Manager: Chris Casper.

Assistant Manager: Martin Scott.

Physio: Nicky Reid.

Colours: White shirts, royal blue shorts, royal blue stockings.

Change Colours: Sky blue.

Year Formed: 1885.

Turned Professional: 1885.

Ltd Co.: 1897.

Club Nickname: 'Shakers'.

First Football League Game: 1 September 1894, Division 2, v Manchester C (h) W 4–2 – Lowe; Gillespie, Davies; White, Clegg, Ross; Wylie, Barbour (2), Millar (1), Ostler (1), Plant.

Record League Victory: 8–0 v Tranmere R, Division 3, 10 January 1970 – Forrest; Tinney, Saile; Anderson, Turner, McDermott; Hince (1), Arrowsmith (1), Jones (4), Kerr (1), Grundy, (1 og).

Record Cup Victory: 12–1 v Stockton, FA Cup 1st rd (replay), 2 February 1897 – Montgomery; Darroch, Barbour; Hendry (1), Clegg, Ross (1); Wylie (3), Pangbourn, Millar (4), Henderson (2), Plant, (1 og).

Record Defeat: 0–10 v Blackburn R, FA Cup pr rd, 1 October 1887. 0–10 v West Ham U, Milk Cup 2nd rd 2nd leg, 25 October 1983.

HONOURS

Football League: Division 1 best season: 4th, 1925–26; Division 2 – Champions 1894–95, 1996–97; Runners-up 1923–24; Division 3 – Champions 1960–61; Runners-up 1967–68; Promoted from Division 3 (3rd) 1995–96.

FA Cup: Winners 1900, 1903.

Football League Cup: Semi-final 1963.

SKY SPORTS FACT FILE

When Brian Barry-Murphy scored the first equalising goal for Bury in the 13th minute of the 2–2 draw with Wrexham on 27 August 2005 the club became the first to register 1000 goals in each of four divisions of the Football League.

Most League Points (2 for a win): 68, Division 3, 1960–61.

Most League Points (3 for a win): 84, Division 4, 1984–85 and Division 2, 1996–97.

Most League Goals: 108, Division 3, 1960–61.

Highest League Scorer in Season: Craig Madden, 35, Division 4, 1981–82.

Most League Goals in Total Aggregate: Craig Madden, 129, 1978–86.

Most League Goals in One Match: 5, Eddie Quigley v Millwall, Division 2, 15 February 1947; 5, Ray Pointer v Rotherham U, Division 2, 2 October 1965.

Most Capped Player: Bill Gorman, 11 (13), Republic of Ireland and (4), Northern Ireland.

Most League Appearances: Norman Bullock, 506, 1920–35.

Youngest League Player: Brian Williams, 16 years 133 days v Stockport Co, 18 March 1972.

Record Transfer Fee Received: £1,100,000 from Ipswich T for David Johnson, November 1997.

Record Transfer Fee Paid: £200,000 to Ipswich T for Chris Swailes, November 1997 and £200,000 to Swindon T for Darren Bullock, February 1999.

Football League Record: 1894 Elected to Division 2; 1895–1912 Division 1; 1912–24 Division 2; 1924–29 Division 1; 1929–57 Division 2; 1957–61 Division 3; 1961–67 Division 2; 1967–68 Division 3; 1968–69 Division 2; 1969–71 Division 3; 1971–74 Division 4; 1974–80 Division 3; 1980–85 Division 4; 1985–96 Division 3; 1996–97 Division 2; 1997–99 Division 1; 1999–2002 Division 2; 2002–04 Division 3; 2004– FL2.

MANAGERS

T. Hargreaves 1887
(Secretary-Manager)
H. S. Hamer 1887–1907
(Secretary-Manager)
Archie Montgomery 1907–15
William Cameron 1919–23
James Hunter Thompson 1923–27
Percy Smith 1927–30
Arthur Paine 1930–34
Norman Bullock 1934–38
Jim Porter 1944–45
Norman Bullock 1945–49
John McNeil 1950–53
Dave Russell 1953–61
Bob Stokoe 1961–65
Bert Head 1965–66
Les Shannon 1966–69
Jack Marshall 1969
Les Hart 1970
Tommy McAnearney 1970–72
Alan Brown 1972–73
Bobby Smith 1973–77
Bob Stokoe 1977–78
David Hatton 1978–79
Dave Connor 1979–80
Jim Iley 1980–84
Martin Dobson 1984–89
Sam Ellis 1989–90
Mike Walsh 1990–95
Stan Ternent 1995–98
Neil Warnock 1998–99
Andy Preece 2000–04
Graham Barrow 2004–05
Chris Casper October 2005–

LATEST SEQUENCES

Longest Sequence of League Wins: 9, 26.9.1960 – 19.11.1960.

Longest Sequence of League Defeats: 8, 18.8.2001 – 25.9.2001.

Longest Sequence of League Draws: 6, 6.3.1999 – 3.4.1999.

Longest Sequence of Unbeaten League Matches: 18, 4.2.1961 – 29.4.1961.

Longest Sequence Without a League Win: 19, 1.4.1911 – 2.12.1911.

Successive Scoring Runs: 24 from 1.9.1894.

Successive Non-scoring Runs: 6 from 11.1.1969.

TEN YEAR LEAGUE RECORD

		P	W	D	L	F	A	Pts	Pos
1996-97	Div 2	46	24	12	10	62	38	84	1
1997-98	Div 1	46	11	19	16	42	58	52	17
1998-99	Div 1	46	10	17	19	35	60	47	22
1999-2000	Div 2	46	13	18	15	61	64	57	15
2000-01	Div 2	46	16	10	20	45	59	58	16
2001-02	Div 2	46	11	11	24	43	75	44	22
2002-03	Div 3	46	18	16	12	57	56	70	7
2003-04	Div 3	46	15	11	20	54	64	56	12
2004-05	FL 2	46	14	16	16	54	54	58	17
2005-06	FL 2	46	12	17	17	45	57	53	19

DID YOU KNOW?

On 15 October 2005 midfield player Nicky Adams celebrated his debut on the eve of his 19th birthday with the only goal of the match against Darlington. He had been switched to a striking role because of injury problems.

BURY 2005–06 LEAGUE RECORD

Match No.	Date	Venue	Opponents	Result		H/T Score	Lg. Pos.	Goalscorers	Attendance
1	Aug 6	A	Cheltenham T	L	1-2	1-1	—	Mattis [19]	2967
2	9	H	Leyton Orient	L	1-2	0-1	—	Smart [78]	2053
3	13	H	Shrewsbury T	W	2-0	0-0	15	Newby [70], Barry-Murphy [90]	2261
4	20	A	Wycombe W	L	0-4	0-1	20		4421
5	27	H	Wrexham	D	2-2	1-2	20	Barry-Murphy [13], Tipton [52]	2468
6	29	A	Macclesfield T	L	0-1	0-1	22		1965
7	Sept 2	H	Carlisle U	L	0-1	0-0	—		3190
8	10	A	Northampton T	D	1-1	1-0	23	Whaley [26]	5147
9	17	H	Boston U	D	1-1	1-0	23	Mattis [38]	1985
10	24	A	Oxford U	L	1-2	0-2	24	Kennedy [83]	4198
11	27	H	Bristol R	W	1-0	1-0	—	Scott [42]	1673
12	Oct 1	H	Lincoln C	D	1-1	0-1	23	Whaley [90]	4118
13	7	A	Rushden & D	W	2-0	0-0	—	Mattis [59], Whaley [69]	2639
14	15	H	Darlington	W	1-0	1-0	17	Adams [35]	2630
15	22	A	Chester C	D	1-1	1-0	17	Mattis [10]	3471
16	29	H	Notts Co	L	2-3	0-2	19	Kennedy (pen) [59], Whaley [81]	2671
17	Nov 11	A	Mansfield T	W	3-0	2-0	—	Reet 2 [6, 75], Whaley [9]	4147
18	26	H	Cheltenham T	L	0-1	0-1	19		2251
19	Dec 3	A	Barnet	D	1-1	0-0	—	Reet [70]	1796
20	10	A	Leyton Orient	W	1-0	0-0	18	Whaley [54]	4095
21	17	H	Wycombe W	W	2-1	0-1	15	Scott [87], Whaley [90]	2384
22	26	H	Grimsby T	L	1-2	1-1	17	Reet [13]	3249
23	Jan 2	A	Peterborough U	L	1-4	0-2	20	Challinor [72]	3687
24	7	A	Carlisle U	L	0-4	0-2	21		6398
25	14	H	Torquay U	W	3-2	2-1	20	Hewlett (og) [40], Speight 2 [42, 49]	2102
26	21	A	Boston U	L	1-3	1-2	21	Canoville (og) [38]	2018
27	28	H	Northampton T	L	0-2	0-2	21		2456
28	Feb 4	A	Bristol R	L	0-1	0-1	22		6027
29	7	H	Rushden & D	D	1-1	0-0	—	Tipton [87]	1777
30	14	A	Torquay U	D	0-0	0-0	—		2129
31	18	H	Barnet	D	0-0	0-0	22		2083
32	25	A	Shrewsbury T	W	1-0	1-0	21	Hope (og) [2]	3586
33	28	A	Rochdale	D	1-1	0-0	—	Youngs [61]	3876
34	Mar 7	H	Stockport Co	L	0-1	0-0	—		3116
35	11	A	Wrexham	D	0-0	0-0	19		4134
36	18	A	Grimsby T	L	1-2	0-2	22	Daly [60]	5196
37	21	H	Oxford U	D	1-1	0-0	—	Kennedy (pen) [68]	1882
38	25	H	Rochdale	W	2-1	1-0	20	Youngs [33], Gobern [48]	4276
39	Apr 1	A	Stockport Co	W	1-0	1-0	18	Daly [32]	6014
40	4	H	Macclesfield T	D	0-0	0-0	—		2273
41	8	H	Peterborough U	L	1-3	0-1	19	Kennedy (pen) [66]	2233
42	15	A	Lincoln C	D	1-1	1-0	20	Pugh [37]	4439
43	17	H	Chester C	D	0-0	0-0	20		3421
44	22	A	Darlington	W	3-2	1-1	17	Flitcroft [22], Barry-Murphy [85], Tipton [90]	3739
45	29	H	Mansfield T	D	0-0	0-0	17		3105
46	May 6	A	Notts Co	D	2-2	1-0	19	Mattis [41], Youngs [81]	9817

Final League Position: 19

GOALSCORERS

League (45): Whaley 7, Mattis 5, Kennedy 4 (3 pens), Reet 4, Barry-Murphy 3, Tipton 3, Youngs 3, Daly 2, Scott 2, Speight 2, Adams 1, Challinor 1, Flitcroft 1, Gobern 1, Newby 1, Pugh 1, Smart 1, own goals 3.
Carling Cup (0).
FA Cup (2): Kennedy 1 (pen), Scott 1.
Football League Trophy (1): Sedgemore 1.

Edwards N 24	Scott P 40 + 1	Kennedy T 28 + 5	Fitzgerald J 22 + 5	Challinor D 46	Hardiker J 11	Flitcroft D 43	Mattis D 32 + 4	Smart A 11 + 2 / Pugh M 3 + 3	Whaley S 23	Barry-Murphy B 35 + 5	Sedgemore J 3 + 6	Youngs T 16 + 14	Barlow S 2 + 11	Newby J 4 + 6	Tipton M 15 + 9	Unsworth L — + 3 / Burns J 1	Dootson C 4 + 1	Parrish A 6 + 2	Buchanan D 22 + 1	Woodthorpe C 31 + 2	Adams N 9 + 6	Burke S — + 1	Quigley D — + 1	Reet D 6	Speight J 7 + 10	Saunders B 1	Williams T 3	Marrison C 8 + 8	Brass C 6 + 1	Jarman N 1 + 1	Hannah D 1 + 1	Anyinsah J 3	Grundy A — + 1	Schmeichel K 15	Daly J 11	Gobern L 7	Ross I 6 + 1	*Match No.*
1	2	3	4	5	6^{1}	7	8	9^{2}	10	11^{3}	12	13	14																									1
1	2	3^{2}	4	5	6	7^{1}	8	9	11	12	13	14	10^{3}																									2
1	2	3	4^{2}	5	6	7	8	9^{1}	10	11	12			13																								3
1	2	3^{1}	4	5	6	7	8	9	10	11				12																								4
1	2	3		5	6	7^{1}	8		4	11^{2}	12		14	10^{3}	9	13																						5
1	4	3^{3}		5	6^{1}	7^{2}	8		2	11	13		12	10	9	14																						6
1	4^{1}	3	12	5	6	7	8		2	11^{2}			13	10	9																							7
1^{G}	4	3		5	6	7	8	9■	2	11	10						15																					8
1	4	3		5	6	7	8		2	10^{1}	11	13	12		9^{2}																							9
1	2	12		5		7	8		9	11^{1}	3^{2}	13	10					4	6																			10
1	2	3		5	6	7	8	9^{1}	10				12						11	4																		11
1	2	3		5	6^{1}	7^{2}	8	9^{3}	10	13				12				14	11	4																		12
1	2	3		5		7	8	9^{2}	11	12				10^{1}	13				6	4																		13
1	4	3	12	5		7	8^{3}		2		14		13		9^{2}				11	6	10^{1}																	14
1	4	3		5		7	8		2			9^{2}	12						11	6	10^{1}	13																15
1■	2^{3}	3	14	5		7	8		4			12	13		9^{1}				11	6	10^{2}																	16
1	2	3		5		7^{1}	8		4^{3}			12			13				11	6	10		14	9^{2}														17
1		3	4^{2}	5			8		2	12		7^{1}			13				11	6	10			9^{3}	14													18
1	2	3		5					4	8		7^{2}			12			13	11	6	10^{3}			9^{1}	14													19
1	2	3		5		7			4	8		12							11	6	13			9^{1}	10^{2}													20
1	3		12	5		7			4	8		14	13					2	11	6^{1}				9^{2}	10^{3}													21
1	2			5		7	12	13	4			10^{2}	14					3	11	6	8^{1}			9^{3}														22
1	2			5		7	12		4	8		10^{2}						3	11^{1}	6	13				14	9^{3}												23
1	2	3^{3}		5		7	8	12		11		10				13			14	6^{2}	4^{1}				9													24
	2			5		7		9^{1}		8				12				3	11	6					10		1	4										25
	2			5		7	12	9		8^{1}				13	14				11	6					10^{2}		1	4^{3}	3									26
	2		4	5		7^{1}	8	9^{2}		12					10			3	11								1	13		6■								27
	2		4	5		7	8			11		12			9^{1}		1			6	10^{2}							3			13							28
	2		4	5		7	8			11^{1}		12			9		1			6	13							10			3^{2}							29
	2	3	4	5^{1}		7	8			11					9		1			12	13				14			10^{3}				6^{2}						30
	2	3^{1}	4	5		7	8			11^{2}					9		1^{G}			12					10					13		6	15					31
	2		4	5		7	8			11		12			9^{1}					3	13				10^{3}			14				6^{2}		1				32
	2		4	5		7	8			11		10^{1}			9^{2}				6	3					12			13						1				33
	2		4	5		7	8			11		9^{2}			12				6^{1}	3					13			10						1				34
	2		4	5		7^{1}	8			11		9^{2}							6	3	12				13			10						1				35
	2	12	4	5		7	8^{2}			11		9							6^{1}	3					13			14						1	10^{3}			36
	2	3	4	5		7		13		11		9		12	13				6^{1}									10						1	8^{2}			37
	2	3	4	5		7				11		9^{1}																12						1	10	8^{2}	6	38
	2	3		5		7				11		9^{1}								6								12	13					1	10	4	8^{2}	39
	2	3	12	5^{1}		7		13		11		9								6								13						1	10	4	8^{2}	40
	2	3		5		7		8^{3}		11		9^{1}				8^{2}				6					12									1	10	4		41
		3^{1}	4	5		7	12	9^{1}		11		9^{2}								6								13	2					1	10		14	42
		12	4	5		7^{2}	8	9^{2}		11					13					3					14				2					1	10^{3}		6	43
		12	4	5		7	8^{1}	13		11		13			14					3									2					1	10^{3}	6		44
			4	5		7				11		12			9^{1}					3									2					1	10^{2}	6	8	45
	12	13	4	5			8^{1}			11		14			9					3									2					1	10^{3}	6	7^{2}	46

FA Cup
First Round — Scunthorpe U — (h) 2-2; (a) 0-1

Carling Cup
First Round — Leicester C — (h) 0-3

Football League Trophy
First Round — Halifax T — (a) 1-6

CARDIFF CITY FL Championship

FOUNDATION

Credit for the establishment of a first class professional football club in such a rugby stronghold as Cardiff, is due to members of the Riverside club formed in 1899 out of a cricket club of that name. Cardiff became a city in 1905 and in 1908 the South Wales and Monmouthshire FA granted Riverside permission to call themselves Cardiff City. The club turned professional under that name in 1910.

Ninian Park, Sloper Road, Cardiff CF11 8SX.

Telephone: (029) 2022 1001.

Fax: (029) 2034 1148.

Ticket Office: 0845 345 1400.

Website: www.cardiffcityfc.co.uk

Email: club@cardiffcityfc.co.uk

Ground Capacity: 21,432.

Record Attendance: 62,634, Wales v England, 17 October 1959.

Club Record Attendance: 57,893 v Arsenal, Division 1, 22 April 1953.

Pitch Measurements: 110yd × 75yd.

Owner: Sam Hammam.

Executive Deputy Chairman: Peter Ridsdale.

Club Secretary: Jason Turner.

Manager: Dave Jones.

Assistant Manager: Terry Burton.

Physio: Sean Connelly.

Colours: Royal blue shirts, royal blue shorts, royal blue stockings.

Change Colours: All red.

Year Formed: 1899.

Turned Professional: 1910.

Ltd Co.: 1910.

Previous Names: 1899, Riverside; 1902, Riverside Albion; 1908, Cardiff City.

Club Nickname: 'Bluebirds'.

Previous Grounds: Riverside, Sophia Gardens, Old Park and Fir Gardens. Moved to Ninian Park, 1910.

First Football League Game: 28 August 1920, Division 2, v Stockport Co (a) W 5–2 – Kneeshaw; Brittan, Leyton; Keenor (1), Smith, Hardy; Grimshaw (1), Gill (2), Cashmore, West, Evans (1).

Record League Victory: 9–2 v Thames, Division 3 (S), 6 February 1932 – Farquharson; E. L. Morris, Roberts; Galbraith, Harris, Ronan; Emmerson (1), Keating (1), Jones (1), McCambridge (1), Robbins (5).

HONOURS

Football League: Division 1 – Runners-up 1923–24; Division 2 – Runners-up 1920–21, 1951–52, 1959–60; Division 2 – 2002–03 (play-offs); Division 3 (S) – Champions 1946–47; Division 3 – Champions 1992–93. Runners-up 1975–76, 1982–83, 2000–01; Division 4 – Runners-up 1987–88.

FA Cup: Winners 1927 (only occasion the Cup has been won by a club outside England); Runners-up 1925.

Football League Cup: Semi-final 1966.

Welsh Cup: Winners 22 times (joint record).

Charity Shield: Winners 1927.

European Competitions: *European Cup-Winners' Cup:* 1964–65, 1965–66, 1967–68 (semi-finalists), 1968–69, 1969–70, 1970–71, 1971–72, 1973–74, 1974–75, 1976–77, 1977–78, 1988–89, 1992–93, 1993–94.

SKY SPORTS FACT FILE

George Edwards, the Cardiff City and Welsh international outside-left, had a second string to his bow in 1952–53 as he had become one of the leading authorities on the coalfields of Pembrokeshire, achieving a Master of Arts for his thesis on the subject.

Record Cup Victory: 8–0 v Enfield, FA Cup 1st rd, 28 November 1931 – Farquharson; Smith, Roberts; Harris (1), Galbraith, Ronan; Emmerson (2), Keating (3); O'Neill (2), Robbins, McCambridge.

Record Defeat: 2–11 v Sheffield U, Division 1, 1 January 1926.

Most League Points (2 for a win): 66, Division 3 (S), 1946–47.

Most League Points (3 for a win): 86, Division 3, 1982–83.

Most League Goals: 95, Division 3, 2000–01.

Highest League Scorer in Season: Robert Earnshaw, 31, Division 2, 2002–03.

Most League Goals in Total Aggregate: Len Davies, 128, 1920–31.

Most League Goals in One Match: 5, Hugh Ferguson v Burnley, Division 1, 1 September 1928; 5, Walter Robbins v Thames, Division 3S, 6 February 1932; 5, William Henderson v Northampton T, Division 3S, 22 April 1933.

Most Capped Player: Alf Sherwood, 39 (41), Wales.

Most League Appearances: Phil Dwyer, 471, 1972–85.

Youngest League Player: John Toshack, 16 years 236 days v Leyton Orient, 13 November 1965.

Record Transfer Fee Received: Undisclosed from Birmingham C for Cameron Jerome, May 2006.

Record Transfer Fee Paid: £1,700,000 to Stoke C for Peter Thorne, September 2001.

Football League Record: 1920 Elected to Division 2; 1921–29 Division 1; 1929–31 Division 2; 1931–47 Division 3 (S); 1947–52 Division 2; 1952–57 Division 1; 1957–60 Division 2; 1960–62 Division 1; 1962–75 Division 2; 1975–76 Division 3; 1976–82 Division 2; 1982–83 Division 3; 1983–85 Division 2; 1985–86 Division 3; 1986–88 Division 4; 1988–90 Division 3; 1990–92 Division 4; 1992–93 Division 3; 1993–95 Division 2; 1995–99 Division 3; 1999–2000 Division 2; 2000–01 Division 3; 2001–03 Division 2; 2003–04 Division 1; 2004– FLC.

MANAGERS

Davy McDougall 1910–11
Fred Stewart 1911–33
Bartley Wilson 1933–34
B. Watts-Jones 1934–37
Bill Jennings 1937–39
Cyril Spiers 1939–46
Billy McCandless 1946–48
Cyril Spiers 1948–54
Trevor Morris 1954–58
Bill Jones 1958–62
George Swindin 1962–64
Jimmy Scoular 1964–73
Frank O'Farrell 1973–74
Jimmy Andrews 1974–78
Richie Morgan 1978–82
Len Ashurst 1982–84
Jimmy Goodfellow 1984
Alan Durban 1984–86
Frank Burrows 1986–89
Len Ashurst 1989–91
Eddie May 1991–94
Terry Yorath 1994–95
Eddie May 1995
Kenny Hibbitt *(Chief Coach)* 1995
Phil Neal 1996
Russell Osman 1996–97
Kenny Hibbitt 1996–98
Frank Burrows 1998–99
Billy Ayre 1999–2000
Bobby Gould 2000
Alan Cork 2000–02
Lennie Lawrence 2002–05
Dave Jones May 2005–

LATEST SEQUENCES

Longest Sequence of League Wins: 9, 26.10.1946 – 28.12.1946.

Longest Sequence of League Defeats: 7, 4.11.1933 – 25.12.1933.

Longest Sequence of League Draws: 6, 29.11.1980 – 17.1.1981.

Longest Sequence of Unbeaten League Matches: 21, 21.9.1946 – 1.3.1947.

Longest Sequence Without a League Win: 15, 21.11.1936 – 6.3.1937.

Successive Scoring Runs: 23 from 24.10.1992.

Successive Non-scoring Runs: 8 from 20.12.1952.

TEN YEAR LEAGUE RECORD

		P	W	D	L	F	A	Pts	Pos
1996-97	Div 3	46	20	9	17	56	54	69	7
1997-98	Div 3	46	9	23	14	48	52	50	21
1998-99	Div 3	46	22	14	10	60	39	80	3
1999-2000	Div 2	46	9	17	20	45	67	44	21
2000-01	Div 3	46	23	13	10	95	58	82	2
2001-02	Div 2	46	23	14	9	75	50	83	4
2002-03	Div 2	46	23	12	11	68	43	81	6
2003-04	Div 1	46	17	14	15	68	58	65	13
2004-05	FL C	46	13	15	18	48	51	54	16
2005-06	FL C	46	16	12	18	58	59	60	11

DID YOU KNOW?

In 1968 former Welsh international winger Jack Evans, who played for Cardiff City in the 1925 FA Cup Final, returned to his former school at Bala and presented them with one of his caps and the jersey he wore in 1913.

CARDIFF CITY 2005–06 LEAGUE RECORD

Match No.	Date	Venue	Opponents	Result		H/T Score	Lg. Pos.	Goalscorers	Atten-dance
1	Aug 6	A	Ipswich T	L	0-1	0-0	—		24,292
2	9	H	Leeds U	W	2-1	0-1	—	Koumas [60], Purse (pen) [67]	15,231
3	12	H	Watford	L	1-3	0-1	—	Jerome [80]	9256
4	20	A	Derby Co	L	1-2	0-2	21	Jerome [83]	23,153
5	27	H	Wolverhampton W	D	2-2	1-0	19	Jerome 2 [3, 49]	11,502
6	Sept 10	A	Burnley	D	3-3	2-2	21	Jerome [8], Loovens [45], Purse (pen) [72]	10,431
7	13	H	Leicester C	W	1-0	1-0	—	Ricketts [8]	9196
8	17	H	Crystal Palace	W	1-0	1-0	12	Ricketts [26]	11,647
9	24	A	Millwall	D	0-0	0-0	14		9254
10	27	A	Stoke C	W	3-0	3-0	—	Jerome 2 [10, 43], Purse [12]	12,240
11	Oct 1	H	Luton T	L	1-2	1-1	11	Ricketts [9]	14,657
12	15	A	Brighton & HA	W	2-1	1-0	9	Koumas [12], Lee [74]	6485
13	18	H	Preston NE	D	2-2	1-0	—	Ledley [31], Koumas [80]	9574
14	22	H	Crewe Alex	W	6-1	1-1	7	Ricketts [18], Ledley [48], Cooper [60], Purse (pen) [67], Jerome [68], Koumas [74]	10,815
15	29	A	Sheffield U	D	0-0	0-0	9		25,311
16	Nov 1	A	Norwich C	L	0-1	0-0	—		23,838
17	6	H	Coventry C	D	0-0	0-0	11		11,424
18	9	A	Sheffield W	W	3-1	3-0	—	Koumas [9], Jerome 2 [30, 38]	20,324
19	19	A	Preston NE	L	1-2	0-2	10	Loovens [68]	13,904
20	22	H	Brighton & HA	D	1-1	0-0	—	Lee [57]	9595
21	28	H	Ipswich T	W	2-1	1-0	—	Ricketts [30], Koumas [90]	8724
22	Dec 3	A	Hull C	L	0-2	0-0	10		18,364
23	10	A	Leeds U	W	1-0	1-0	5	Koumas [31]	20,597
24	17	H	Derby Co	D	0-0	0-0	7		12,500
25	26	H	Plymouth Arg	L	0-2	0-0	10		16,403
26	28	A	QPR	L	0-1	0-0	11		12,329
27	31	H	Southampton	W	2-1	2-1	8	Ledley [6], Jerome [9]	13,377
28	Jan 2	A	Reading	L	1-5	0-2	10	Jerome [62]	22,061
29	14	H	Burnley	W	3-0	0-0	8	Thompson 2 [58, 60], Koumas [63]	10,872
30	21	A	Leicester C	W	2-1	1-1	7	Jerome [13], Koumas [56]	20,140
31	31	H	Millwall	D	1-1	1-0	—	Jerome [28]	12,378
32	Feb 4	A	Crystal Palace	L	0-1	0-0	7		17,962
33	11	H	Stoke C	W	3-0	2-0	7	Cooper [18], Cox 2 [30, 68]	10,780
34	14	A	Luton T	D	3-3	0-2	—	Koumas 2 [55, 86], Scimeca [71]	7826
35	18	H	Hull C	W	1-0	1-0	7	Jerome [22]	11,047
36	25	A	Watford	L	1-2	0-0	8	Whitley [77]	17,419
37	Mar 4	H	Sheffield W	W	1-0	1-0	7	Jerome [19]	11,851
38	11	A	Wolverhampton W	L	0-2	0-1	8		23,996
39	18	A	Plymouth Arg	W	1-0	1-0	8	Thompson [34]	13,494
40	25	H	QPR	D	0-0	0-0	8		14,271
41	Apr 1	A	Southampton	L	2-3	0-0	8	Jerome [54], Purse [90]	22,388
42	8	H	Reading	L	2-5	0-2	8	Jerome [67], Parry [80]	11,866
43	14	H	Sheffield U	L	0-1	0-0	—		11,006
44	17	A	Crewe Alex	D	1-1	0-0	8	Koumas [76]	5865
45	22	H	Norwich C	L	0-1	0-1	9		11,590
46	30	A	Coventry C	L	1-3	1-1	11	Thompson [21]	22,536

Final League Position: 11

GOALSCORERS

League (58): Jerome 18, Koumas 12, Purse 5 (3 pens), Ricketts 5, Thompson 4, Ledley 3, Cooper 2, Cox 2, Lee 2, Loovens 2, Parry 1, Scimeca 1, Whitley 1.
Carling Cup (4): Jerome 1, Koumas 1, Ledley 1, Purse 1 (pen).
FA Cup (1): Jerome 1.

Alexander N 46	Darlington J 7 + 2	Barker C 41	Boland W 11 + 4	Purse D 39	Cox N 21 + 6	Ardley N 22 + 8	Whitley J 32 + 2	Jerome C 44	Parry P 11 + 16	Cooper K 31 + 5	Mulryne P 1 + 3	Lee A 6 + 19	Koumas J 42 + 2	Loovens G 32 + 1	Weston R 26 + 4	Ferretti A — + 4	Ledley J 42	Ricketts M 17	Thompson S 14	N'Dumbu Nsungu G 4 + 7	Scimeca R 17 + 1	Blake D — + 1	Jacobson J — + 1	McDonald C — + 1	*Match No.*
1	2	3	4^1	5	6	7	8	9	10^2	11	12	13													1
1	2	3	4^1	5	6	7	8	9	10^3	11^2	13	14	12												2
1	2	3		5	6^3	7	8	9	10^2	11	4^1	13	12	14											3
1	2	3	12	5	6	7	8	9	10^2	11^1		13	4												4
1			4	5		12	8	9		3^1		10^2	7	6	2	13	11								5
1		3		5			2	9	12	11^1		13	7	4	6		8	10^2							6
1		3		5		12	8	9	13	11^2		14	7^1	6	2		4	10^3							7
1		3		5			8	9	12	11^1			7	6	2		4	10							8
1		3		5			8	9		11		12	7	6	2		4	10^1							9
1		3		5			8	9	12	11^1		13	7	6	2		4	10^2							10
1		3		5		7		9	12	11^1	13	14	8^2	6	2^3		4	10							11
1		3		5			8	9	12	11^1		13	7	6	2		4	10^2							12
1		3		5			8	9^1	13	11^2		12	7	6	2		4	10							13
1		3		5	12		8	9	13	11^2		14	7	6^1	2		4	10^3							14
1		3		5			8	9		11		12	7	6	2		4	10^1							15
1		3		5		12	8	9	13	11^2		14	7	6	2^1		4	10^3							16
1		3		5			8	9	12	11^2		10^1	7	6	2	13	4								17
1		3		5		12	8	9	13	11^2		10^1	7	6	2		4								18
1		3	12	5		7	8		13			10	11	6	2^2		4	9^1							19
1		3		5	12	13	8	9	11			10	7	6^1	2^2		4								20
1		3			5		8	9	11			12	7	6	2		4	10^1							21
1		3^2		5■	12		8	9	11^1			13	7	6	2		4	10							22
1		3	7		5	12	8	9		11^1			10	6	2		4								23
1		3		5			8	9		11			7	6	2		4	10							24
1		3^3		5■	14		8	9^2	12	11^1		13	7	6	2		4	10							25
1		3	4		5	2	8^1	9	12	11^2		13	7	6			10								26
1		3			5	2	8	9	11			12	7	6			4	10^1							27
1	12	3		5		13	8	9		11^2		10	7	6	2^1		4								28
1		3	8	5^1	6	7		9		12			11^2		2		4		10^3	13	14				29
1		3	12	5	6	7		9^3		13			11		2^1		4		10^2	14	8				30
1		3		5	6	7		9		12			11		2^1		4		10^2	13	8				31
1	12	3^1	4^2	5	6	7		9		11			8				10			13	2				32
1		3	4	5	6	2		9		11							8			10	7				33
1		3		5	6	2	13	9		11^2			8			12	4			10^1	7				34
1		3		5	6	2	8	9^1					11		12		4		10		7				35
1		3		5	6	2	8^1	9					11		12		4		10		7				36
1		3		5	6	2	8	9					11				4		10^1	12	7				37
1		3		5	6	2^1	8^2	9		13			11		12		4		10^3	14	7				38
1		3		5		2		9^1		11			8	6			4		10	12	7				39
1		3		5		2		9		11^1			8	6	12		4		10		7				40
1		3	12	5	13	2		9		11^1			8	6^2		14	4			10^3	7				41
1			8	5		2		9	12	11^1			7	6			4		10		3				42
1			8^3	5^1	12		14	9	13	11^2			7	6	2		4		10		3				43
1	2				5		8^1	9	11				7	6			4		10		3	12			44
1	2	3^2			5			9^1	11	12			8	6			4		10		7		13		45
1	2^1		8		5	12			11				7	6			4		10	9^2	3			13	46

FA Cup

Third Round	Arsenal	(a)	1-2

Carling Cup

First Round	Colchester U	(a)	2-0
Second Round	Macclesfield T	(h)	2-1
Third Round	Leicester C	(h)	0-1

CARLISLE UNITED FL Championship 1

FOUNDATION

Carlisle United came into being in 1903 through the amalgamation of Shaddongate United and Carlisle Red Rose. The new club was admitted to the Second Division of the Lancashire Combination in 1905–06, winning promotion the following season. Devonshire Park was officially opened on 2 September 1905, when St Helens Town were the visitors. Despite defeat in a disappointing 3-2 start, a respectable mid-table position was achieved.

Brunton Park, Warwick Road, Carlisle CA1 1LL.

Telephone: (01228) 526 237.

Fax: (01228) 554 148.

Ticket Office: (01228) 526 237.

Website: www.carlisleunited.co.uk

Email: enquiries@carlisleunited.co.uk

Ground Capacity: 16,065.

Record Attendance: 27,500 v Birmingham C, FA Cup 3rd rd, 5 January 1957 and v Middlesbrough, FA Cup 5th rd, 7 February 1970.

Pitch Measurements: 114yd × 74yd.

Chairman: Andrew Jenkins.

Managing Director: John Nixon.

Secretary: Sarah McKnight.

Manager: Neil McDonald.

Assistant Manager: Denis Booth.

Physio: Mr Neil Dalton.

Colours: Blue shirts, white shorts, blue stockings.

Change Colours: White shirts, blue shorts, white stockings.

Year Formed: 1903.

Ltd Co.: 1921.

Previous Name: 1903, Shaddongate United; 1904, Carlisle United.

Club Nicknames: 'Cumbrians' or 'The Blues'.

Previous Grounds: 1903, Milholme Bank; 1905, Devonshire Park; 1909, Brunton Park.

First Football League Game: 25 August 1928, Division 3 (N), v Accrington S (a) W 3–2 – Prout; Coulthard, Cook; Harrison, Ross, Pigg; Agar (1), Hutchison, McConnell (1), Ward (1), Watson.

Record League Victory: 8–0 v Hartlepool U, Division 3 (N), 1 September 1928 – Prout; Smiles, Cook; Robinson (1) Ross, Pigg; Agar (1), Hutchison (1), McConnell (4), Ward (1), Watson. 8–0 v Scunthorpe U, Division 3 (N), 25 December 1952 – MacLaren; Hill, Scott; Stokoe, Twentyman, Waters; Harrison (1), Whitehouse (5), Ashman (2), Duffett, Bond.

Record Cup Victory: 6–0 v Shepshed Dynamo, FA Cup 1st rd, 16 November 1996 – Caig; Hopper, Archdeacon (pen), Walling, Robinson, Pounewatchy, Peacock (1), Conway (1) (Jansen), Smart (McAlindon (1)), Hayward, Aspinall (Thorpe), (2 og).

HONOURS

Football League: Division 1 best season: 22nd, 1974–75; Promoted from Division 2 (3rd) 1973–74; Division 3 – Champions 1964–65, 1994–95; Runners-up 1981–82; Promoted from Division 3 1996–97; Division 4 – Runners-up 1963–64; Championship 2 – Champions 2005–06. Promoted from Conference (play-offs) 2004–05.

FA Cup: best season: 6th rd 1975.

Football League Cup: Semi-final 1970.

Auto Windscreens Shield: Winners 1997; Runners-up 1995.

LDV Vans Trophy: Runners-up 2003, 2006.

SKY SPORTS FACT FILE

Carlisle United can claim to have had one of the outstanding Scots in football on their staff on two different occasions. As a right-half Bill Shankly joined them in 1932 and returned after the war to take over as manager in March 1949.

Record Defeat: 1–11 v Hull C, Division 3 (N), 14 January 1939.

Most League Points (2 for a win): 62, Division 3 (N), 1950–51.

Most League Points (3 for a win): 91, Division 3, 1994–95.

Most League Goals: 113, Division 4, 1963–64.

Highest League Scorer in Season: Jimmy McConnell, 42, Division 3 (N), 1928–29.

Most League Goals in Total Aggregate: Jimmy McConnell, 126, 1928–32.

Most League Goals in One Match: 5, Hugh Mills v Halifax T, Division 3N, 11 September 1937; 5, Jim Whitehouse v Scunthorpe U, Division 3N, 25 December 1952.

Most Capped Player: Eric Welsh, 4, Northern Ireland.

Most League Appearances: Allan Ross, 466, 1963–79.

Youngest League Player: John Slaven, 16 years 162 days v Scunthorpe U, 16 March 2002.

Record Transfer Fee Received: £1,500,000 from Crystal Palace for Matt Jansen, February 1998.

Record Transfer Fee Paid: £121,000 to Notts Co for David Reeves, December 1993.

Football League Record: 1928 Elected to Division 3 (N); 1958–62 Division 4; 1962–63 Division 3; 1963–64 Division 4; 1964–65 Division 3; 1965–74 Division 2; 1974–75 Division 1; 1975–77 Division 2; 1977–82 Division 3; 1982–86 Division 2; 1986–87 Division 3; 1987–92 Division 4; 1992–95 Division 3; 1995–96 Division 2; 1996–97 Division 3; 1997–98 Division 2; 1998–04 Division 3; 2004–05 Conference; 2005–06 FL2; 2006– FL1.

LATEST SEQUENCES

Longest Sequence of League Wins: 7, 18.2.06 – 8.4.06.

Longest Sequence of League Defeats: 12, 27.9.2003 – 13.12.2003.

Longest Sequence of League Draws: 6, 11.2.1978 – 11.3.1978.

Longest Sequence of Unbeaten League Matches: 19, 1.10.1994 – 11.2.1995.

Longest Sequence Without a League Win: 14, 19.1.1935 – 19.4.1935.

Successive Scoring Runs: 26 from 23.8.1947.

Successive Non-scoring Runs: 5 from 24.8.1968.

MANAGERS

Harry Kirkbride 1904–05 *(Secretary-Manager)*
McCumiskey 1905–06 *(Secretary-Manager)*
Jack Houston 1906–08 *(Secretary-Manager)*
Bert Stansfield 1908–10
Jack Houston 1910–12
Davie Graham 1912–13
George Bristow 1913–30
Billy Hampson 1930–33
Bill Clarke 1933–35
Robert Kelly 1935–36
Fred Westgarth 1936–38
David Taylor 1938–40
Howard Harkness 1940–45
Bill Clark 1945–46 *(Secretary-Manager)*
Ivor Broadis 1946–49
Bill Shankly 1949–51
Fred Emery 1951–58
Andy Beattie 1958–60
Ivor Powell 1960–63
Alan Ashman 1963–67
Tim Ward 1967–68
Bob Stokoe 1968–70
Ian MacFarlane 1970–72
Alan Ashman 1972–75
Dick Young 1975–76
Bobby Moncur 1976–80
Martin Harvey 1980
Bob Stokoe 1980–85
Bryan 'Pop' Robson 1985
Bob Stokoe 1985–86
Harry Gregg 1986–87
Cliff Middlemass 1987–91
Aidan McCaffery 1991–92
David McCreery 1992–93
Mick Wadsworth *(Director of Coaching)* 1993–96
Mervyn Day 1996–97
David Wilkes and John Halpin (*Directors of Coaching*), and Michael Knighton 1997–99
Martin Wilkinson 1999–2000
Ian Atkins 2000–01
Roddy Collins 2001–02; 2002–03
Paul Simpson 2003–06
Neil McDonald June 2006–

TEN YEAR LEAGUE RECORD

		P	*W*	*D*	*L*	*F*	*A*	*Pts*	*Pos*
1996-97	Div 3	46	24	12	10	67	44	84	3
1997-98	Div 2	46	12	8	26	57	73	44	23
1998-99	Div 3	46	11	16	19	43	53	49	23
1999-2000	Div 3	46	9	12	25	42	75	39	23
2000-01	Div 3	46	11	15	20	42	65	48	22
2001-02	Div 3	46	12	16	18	49	56	52	17
2002-03	Div 3	46	13	10	23	52	78	49	22
2003-04	Div 3	46	12	9	25	46	69	45	23
2004-05	Conf	42	20	13	9	74	37	73	3
2005-06	FL 2	46	25	11	10	84	42	86	1

DID YOU KNOW

At the age of 15 Geoff Twentyman was playing half-back for Swifts Rovers and about to leave school. His teacher recommended professional football! He was spotted by Carlisle United player-manager Ivor Broadis and turned professional in February 1947.

CARLISLE UNITED 2005–06 LEAGUE RECORD

Match No.	*Date*	*Venue*	*Opponents*	*Result*	*H/T Score*	*Lg. Pos.*	*Goalscorers*	*Attendance*
1	Aug 6	A	Wycombe W	D 1-1	1-1	—	Holmes [17]	5270
2	9	H	Peterborough U	W 1-0	1-0	—	Hawley [17]	6511
3	13	H	Barnet	L 1-3	1-0	14	Livesey [24]	6650
4	20	A	Wrexham	W 1-0	0-0	8	McGill [63]	4239
5	27	H	Northampton T	L 0-1	0-1	10		5730
6	29	A	Lincoln C	D 0-0	0-0	13		4303
7	Sept 2	A	Bury	W 1-0	0-0	—	Nade [57]	3190
8	10	H	Macclesfield T	W 2-0	0-0	3	Hawley [77], Murray G [82]	5190
9	17	A	Cheltenham T	W 3-2	1-1	2	Hawley 2 [22, 52], Aranalde [79]	3282
10	24	H	Leyton Orient	L 2-3	1-3	6	McGill [4], Murphy [90]	6584
11	27	A	Chester C	L 0-2	0-2	—		3394
12	Oct 1	H	Bristol R	L 1-3	1-0	11	O'Brien [7]	5317
13	7	A	Oxford U	L 0-1	0-1	—		5392
14	15	H	Mansfield T	W 1-0	0-0	9	Hawley [80]	5293
15	22	A	Notts Co	D 0-0	0-0	9		5347
16	29	H	Stockport Co	W 6-0	4-0	6	Hawley 3 [12, 77, 82], Holmes 2 [36, 41], Ikeme (og) [38]	5664
17	Nov 12	A	Torquay U	W 4-3	2-2	5	Hawley 3 [3, 15, 64], Gray [83]	2352
18	19	H	Oxford U	W 2-1	1-0	5	Nade [17], Hawley [57]	6097
19	26	H	Wycombe W	L 0-1	0-0	6		7033
20	Dec 6	A	Rushden & D	W 4-0	2-0	—	Holmes [19], Hawley [32], Lumsdon [65], Bridges [90]	2216
21	10	A	Peterborough U	D 1-1	0-0	3	Bridges [80]	3689
22	17	H	Wrexham	W 2-1	0-0	3	Gray [71], Lumsdon (pen) [81]	6213
23	26	H	Darlington	D 1-1	1-1	5	Lumsdon (pen) [29]	11,182
24	31	H	Rochdale	W 2-1	0-1	4	Livesey [60], Bridges [80]	6897
25	Jan 2	A	Grimsby T	W 2-1	1-1	4	Aranalde 2 [14, 76]	5882
26	7	H	Bury	W 4-0	2-0	2	Grand [10], Aranalde [28], Hawley [46], McGill [84]	6398
27	14	A	Shrewsbury T	L 1-2	1-1	3	Lumsdon (pen) [18]	4493
28	18	A	Boston U	W 5-0	1-0	—	Hawley 2 [5, 90], Bridges 3 [56, 63, 80]	1924
29	21	H	Cheltenham T	D 1-1	1-0	2	Bridges [40]	6759
30	29	A	Macclesfield T	L 0-3	0-3	2		4140
31	Feb 4	H	Chester C	W 5-0	2-0	1	Murray A [14], Bridges [45], Lumsdon (pen) [58], Hawley [64], Murray G [82]	6581
32	11	A	Leyton Orient	D 0-0	0-0	2		5833
33	14	H	Shrewsbury T	D 2-2	1-1	—	Lumsdon [2], Holmes [88]	5568
34	18	H	Rushden & D	W 5-0	2-0	1	Holmes [2], Hawley 2 [33, 49], Hackney 2 [60, 61]	6922
35	25	A	Barnet	W 2-1	0-0	1	Bridges [54], Hackney [75]	2870
36	Mar 10	A	Northampton T	W 3-0	1-0	—	Hawley [21], Bridges [74], Livesey [84]	7045
37	18	A	Darlington	W 5-0	1-0	1	Gray [45], Holmes [60], Bridges [62], Murray G [88], Grand [90]	8640
38	25	H	Boston U	W 4-2	2-0	1	Lumsdon [2], Hawley [20], Hackney 2 [75, 90]	7596
39	28	H	Lincoln C	W 1-0	0-0	—	Bridges [75]	6723
40	Apr 8	H	Grimsby T	W 1-0	0-0	1	Bridges [49]	10,909
41	15	A	Bristol R	D 1-1	0-0	1	Hackney [75]	6181
42	17	H	Notts Co	W 2-1	1-1	1	Bridges 2 [45, 89]	10,735
43	22	A	Mansfield T	D 1-1	0-0	1	Hawley [90]	4488
44	29	H	Torquay U	L 1-2	0-2	1	Aranalde [48]	13,467
45	May 2	A	Rochdale	W 2-0	2-0	—	Livesey [36], Murphy [44]	4439
46	6	A	Stockport Co	D 0-0	0-0	1		10,006

Final League Position: 1

GOALSCORERS

League (84): Hawley 22, Bridges 15, Holmes 7, Lumsdon 7 (4 pens), Hackney 6, Aranalde 5, Livesey 4, Gray 3, McGill 3, Murray G 3, Grand 2, Murphy 2, Nade 2, Murray A 1, O'Brien 1, own goal 1.
Carling Cup (1): Murray A 1.
FA Cup (0).
Football League Trophy (9): Hawley 4, Grand 1, Holmes 1, Murphy 1, Murray A 1, Murray G 1.

Williams T 11	Arnison P 39+2	Aranalde Z 38+1	Billy C 45	Gray K 44	Livesey D 34+2	McGill B 18+8	Murray A 29+8	Holmes D 30+10	Hawley K 46	Murphy P 38+6	Simpson P 4+5	Nade R 10+12	Murray G 3+23	Hackney S 9+21	Andrews L 1	Lumsdon C 37+1	McClen J —+2	Westwood K 35	Beharall D 6	O'Brien A 2+3	Grand S 2+6	Bridges M 23+2	Rivers M 2+2	Match No.
1	2	3	4	5	6	7	8[1]	9[2]	10	11	12	13												1
1	2	3	4	5	6	7[3]	8	9[1]	10	11[2]	13	12	14											2
1	2	3	4[1]	5	6	7	8	9[3]	10	11[2]	13	12	14											3
1	2[2]	3	4	5	6	7	8	9[1]	10	13	11	12												4
1	2	3	4[1]	5	6	7	8	9[2]	10	12	11[3]		13	14										5
1	12	3	4	5	6	7[1]	8	13	10[2]	11	9[3]	14			2									6
1	2	3	4	5	6	7	8	9[3]	10[2]	12	11[1]	14	13											7
1	2[1]	3	4	5	6	7	8		10[2]	13		12	14	9[3]		11								8
1	2	3	4	5	6	7	8		10	12		9[1]				11								9
1	2	3	4[3]	5	6	7	8[2]		10	12		9[1]	13			11	14							10
1	2	3	4	5	6	7	8		10	9			12			11[1]								11
		3	4[3]	5	6		8	9[2]	10[1]	11		12	13			14		1	2	7				12
		3	4	5			8	12	10	6		9[1]		13		11		1	2	7[2]				13
	12	3	4[2]	5			8	13	10	6		9		7[3]		11		1	2[1]	14				14
		3	4	5				8[1]	10	6		9[2]	12	7[3]		11	13	1	2	14				15
	2		4	5	12			8[2]	10	3		9	13	7[3]		11		1		14	6[1]			16
	2		4	5	6	12		8[2]	10	3		9		7[1]		11		1			13			17
	2		4	5	6	12	13	8[3]	10	3		9[1]		7[2]		11		1				14		18
			4	5	6	12	13	8[1]	10	3		9[2]		7[3]		11		1	2			14		19
	2	12	4	5	6	7	13	9[1]	10	3						11[2]		1				8		20
	2		4[2]	5	6	7[1]	13	9[3]	10	3		12		14		11		1				8		21
	2	3[1]	4	5	6	7		12	10	11						8		1				9		22
	2	11[2]	4	5	6	7		12	10	3				13		8		1				9[1]		23
	2		4	5	6	12	13	14	10	3		9[2]		7[3]		11		1				8[1]		24
	2	11	4	5■	6	7[3]	12	9[2]	10[1]	3			13			8		1			14			25
	2	11[3]			6	7	4	12	10[2]	3		13		14		8		1			5	9[1]		26
	2	11■	4	5	6	7[2]	13	12	10	3[1]						8		1				9		27
	2		4	5	6		8	9[2]	10	3			12	13		11		1				7[1]		28
	2	3	4	5	6		8	9[2]	10				12	13		11		1				7[1]		29
		11	4[1]	5	6			12	10	3				13		8		1	2			9	7[2]	30
	2	3	4	5		12	8	9[2]	10	6			13	14		11[1]		1				7[2]		31
	2	3	4	5			8	9[1]	10	6			12[2]	13		11		1				7[3]	14	32
	2[1]	3	4	5			8	9	10[2]	6				12		11		1				7	13	33
	2	3	4[3]	5[1]	12	13	8	9	10	6				14		11		1					7[2]	34
	2	3	4		5		8	9[1]	10[2]	6			12	13		11		1				7		35
	2	3	4	5	6		8	9[2]	10[1]				12	13		11		1				7		36
	2	3	4	5	6			9[2]	10[3]	11			12	13		8		1			14	7[1]		37
	2	3	4	5	6	12		9[3]	10	11[1]			13	14		8		1				7[2]		38
	2	3	4	5	6			9[1]	10	11			12			8		1				7		39
	2	3	4	5	6[1]		12	9[3]	10	11			13	14		8		1				7[2]		40
	2	3	4	5			8	9[1]	10	6				12		11		1			13	7[2]		41
	2[1]	3	4	5			8	12	10	6			11[2]	13		7		1				9		42
	2	3	4	5[1]			8[3]	9[2]	10	6			12	13		11		1			14	7		43
	2	3	4	5[1]			8	9[2]	10	6	14		12	13		11[3]		1				7		44
	2	3	4	5	6	12	8		10	11		13	9[2]			7[1]		1						45
	2	3	4	5	6		8[3]		10	11	12	13	9[2]	7[1]				1			14			46

FA Cup

First Round	Cheltenham T	(a)	0-1

Carling Cup

First Round	Burnley	(a)	1-2

Football League Trophy

First Round	Oldham Ath	(a)	1-1
Second Round	Blackpool	(h)	2-1
Quarter-Final	Tranmere R	(a)	0-0
Semi-Final	Kidderminster H	(h)	1-0
Northern Final	Macclesfield T	(h)	2-1
		(a)	2-3
Final	Swansea C		1-2

(at Millennium Stadium).

CHARLTON ATHLETIC FA Premiership

FOUNDATION

The club was formed on 9 June 1905, by a group of 14- and 15-year-old youths living in streets by the Thames in the area which now borders the Thames Barrier. The club's progress through local leagues was so rapid that after the First World War they joined the Kent League where they spent a season before turning professional and joining the Southern League in 1920. A year later they were elected to the Football League's Division 3 (South).

The Valley, Floyd Road, Charlton, London SE7 8BL.

Telephone: (020) 8333 4000.

Fax: (020) 8333 4001.

Ticket Office: (0871) 226 1905.

Website: www.cafc.co.uk

Email: info@cafc.co.uk

Ground Capacity: 27,113.

Record Attendance: 75,031 v Aston Villa, FA Cup 5th rd, 12 February 1938 (at The Valley).

Pitch Measurements: 101.5m × 65.8m.

Chairman: Martin Simons.

Vice Chairman: Richard Murray.

Chief Executive: Peter Varney.

Secretary: Chris Parkes.

Head Coach: Iain Dowie.

Assistant Head Coach: Les Reed.

Physio: George Cooper.

Colours: Red shirts, white shorts, red and white stockings.

Change Colours: Black, gold and white shirts, white shorts and stockings.

Year Formed: 1905.

Turned Professional: 1920.

Ltd Co.: 1919.

Club Nickname: 'Addicks'.

Previous Grounds: 1906, Siemen's Meadow; 1907, Woolwich Common; 1909, Pound Park; 1913, Horn Lane; 1920, The Valley; 1923, Catford (The Mount); 1924, The Valley; 1985, Selhurst Park; 1991, Upton Park; 1992, The Valley.

First Football League Game: 27 August 1921, Division 3 (S), v Exeter C (h) W 1–0 – Hughes; Mitchell, Goodman; Dowling (1), Hampson, Dunn; Castle, Bailey, Halse, Green, Wilson.

HONOURS

Football League: Division 1 – Champions 1999–2000; Runners-up 1936–37; Promoted from Division 1, 1997–98 (play-offs); Division 2 – Runners-up 1935–36, 1985–86; Division 3 (S) – Champions 1928–29, 1934–35; Promoted from Division 3 (3rd) 1974–75, 1980–81.

FA Cup: Winners 1947; Runners-up 1946.

Football League Cup: best season: 4th rd, 1963, 1966, 1979.

Full Members' Cup: Runners-up 1987.

SKY SPORTS FACT FILE

Charlton Athletic celebrated their 2000th League match entertaining Southampton at The Valley on 31 October 1975. The crowd included old Addicks favourites Peter Croker and Benny Fenton. Charlton marked the occasion with a 4–1 win.

Record League Victory: 8–1 v Middlesbrough, Division 1, 12 September 1953 – Bartram; Campbell, Ellis; Fenton, Ufton, Hammond; Hurst (2), O'Linn (2), Leary (1), Firmani (3), Kiernan.

Record Cup Victory: 7–0 v Burton A, FA Cup 3rd rd, 7 January 1956 – Bartram; Campbell, Townsend; Hewie, Ufton, Hammond; Hurst (1), Gauld (1), Leary (3), White, Kiernan (2).

Record Defeat: 1–11 v Aston Villa, Division 2, 14 November 1959.

Most League Points (2 for a win): 61, Division 3 (S), 1934–35.

Most League Points (3 for a win): 91, Division 1, 1999–2000.

Most League Goals: 107, Division 2, 1957–58.

Highest League Scorer in Season: Ralph Allen, 32, Division 3 (S), 1934–35.

Most League Goals in Total Aggregate: Stuart Leary, 153, 1953–62.

Most League Goals in One Match: 5, Wilson Lennox v Exeter C, Division 3S, 2 February 1929; 5, Eddie Firmani v Aston Villa, Division 1, 5 February 1955; 5, John Summers v Huddersfield T, Division 2, 21 December 1957; 5, John Summers v Portsmouth, Division 2, 1 October 1960.

MANAGERS

Walter Rayner 1920–25
Alex Macfarlane 1925–27
Albert Lindon 1928
Alex Macfarlane 1928–32
Albert Lindon 1932–33
Jimmy Seed 1933–56
Jimmy Trotter 1956–61
Frank Hill 1961–65
Bob Stokoe 1965–67
Eddie Firmani 1967–70
Theo Foley 1970–74
Andy Nelson 1974–79
Mike Bailey 1979–81
Alan Mullery 1981–82
Ken Craggs 1982
Lennie Lawrence 1982–91
Steve Gritt/Alan Curbishley 1991–95
Alan Curbishley 1995–2006
Iain Dowie May 2006–

Most Capped Player: Jonatan Johansson, 41 (70), Finland.

Most League Appearances: Sam Bartram, 583, 1934–56.

Youngest League Player: Paul Konchesky, 16 years 93 days v Oxford U, 16 August 1997.

Record Transfer Fee Received: £10,000,000 from Chelsea for Scott Parker, January 2004.

Record Transfer Fee Paid: £4,750,000 to Wimbledon for Jason Euell, July 2001.

Football League Record: 1921 Elected to Division 3 (S); 1929–33 Division 2; 1933–35 Division 3 (S); 1935–36 Division 2; 1936–57 Division 1; 1957–72 Division 2; 1972–75 Division 3; 1975–80 Division 2; 1980–81 Division 3; 1981–86 Division 2; 1986–90 Division 1; 1990–92 Division 2; 1992–98 Division 1; 1998–99 FA Premier League; 1999–2000 Division 1; 2000– FA Premier League.

LATEST SEQUENCES

Longest Sequence of League Wins: 12, 26.12.1999 – 7.3.2000.

Longest Sequence of League Defeats: 10, 11.4.1990 – 15.9.1990.

Longest Sequence of League Draws: 6, 13.12.1992 – 16.1.1993.

Longest Sequence of Unbeaten League Matches: 15, 4.10.1980 – 20.12.1980.

Longest Sequence Without a League Win: 16, 26.2.1955 – 22.8.1955.

Successive Scoring Runs: 25 from 26.12.1935.

Successive Non-scoring Runs: 5 from 6.9.1922.

TEN YEAR LEAGUE RECORD

		P	*W*	*D*	*L*	*F*	*A*	*Pts*	*Pos*
1996-97	Div 1	46	16	11	19	52	66	59	15
1997-98	Div 1	46	26	10	10	80	49	88	4
1998-99	PR Lge	38	8	12	18	41	56	36	18
1999-2000	Div 1	46	27	10	9	79	45	91	1
2000-01	PR Lge	38	14	10	14	50	57	52	9
2001-02	PR Lge	38	10	14	14	38	49	44	14
2002-03	PR Lge	38	14	7	17	45	56	49	12
2003-04	PR Lge	38	14	11	13	51	51	53	7
2004-05	PR Lge	38	12	10	16	42	58	46	11
2005-06	PR Lge	38	13	8	17	41	55	47	13

DID YOU KNOW ?

Jim Ryan scored an incredible 72 goals in the 75 matches he played for various Charlton Athletic teams in 1963–64. Manager Frank Hill suggested a set of gold cuff-links to commemorate the feat. Ryan asked for a gold watch and received one!

CHARLTON ATHLETIC 2005–06 LEAGUE RECORD

Match No.	*Date*	*Venue*	*Opponents*	*Result*	*H/T Score*	*Lg. Pos.*	*Goalscorers*	*Attendance*
1	Aug 13	A	Sunderland	W 3-1	1-1	—	Bent D 2 [11, 90], Murphy [64]	34,446
2	20	H	Wigan Ath	W 1-0	1-0	2	Bent D [42]	23,453
3	28	A	Middlesbrough	W 3-0	1-0	3	Rommedahl [38], Perry [81], Bent D [90]	26,206
4	Sept 10	A	Birmingham C	W 1-0	1-0	2	Bent D [15]	26,846
5	17	H	Chelsea	L 0-2	0-0	2		27,111
6	24	A	WBA	W 2-1	2-0	2	Murphy 2 (1 pen) [9 (p), 31]	23,909
7	Oct 1	H	Tottenham H	L 2-3	1-0	2	Bent D 2 [25, 48]	27,111
8	17	H	Fulham	D 1-1	0-1	—	Murphy [47]	26,310
9	22	A	Portsmouth	W 2-1	0-1	2	Ambrose [61], Rommedahl [77]	19,030
10	29	H	Bolton W	L 0-1	0-0	5		26,175
11	Nov 5	A	Blackburn R	L 1-4	1-2	8	Hughes [36]	17,691
12	19	H	Manchester U	L 1-3	0-1	10	Ambrose [65]	26,730
13	26	A	Aston Villa	L 0-1	0-0	11		30,023
14	Dec 4	H	Manchester C	L 2-5	1-2	12	Bent D [36], Bothroyd [73]	25,289
15	10	H	Sunderland	W 2-0	1-0	11	Bent D [42], Ambrose [49]	26,065
16	17	A	Wigan Ath	L 0-3	0-1	11		17,074
17	26	H	Arsenal	L 0-1	0-0	12		27,111
18	31	H	West Ham U	W 2-0	1-0	12	Bartlett [21], Bent D [63]	25,952
19	Jan 2	A	Everton	L 1-3	1-2	13	Holland [18]	34,333
20	14	H	Birmingham C	W 2-0	1-0	11	Hughes [29], Bent D [90]	26,312
21	22	A	Chelsea	D 1-1	0-1	11	Bent M [59]	41,355
22	31	H	WBA	D 0-0	0-0	—		25,921
23	Feb 5	A	Tottenham H	L 1-3	0-2	13	Thomas [70]	36,034
24	8	H	Liverpool	W 2-0	2-0	—	Bent D (pen) [42], Young [45]	27,111
25	12	A	Manchester C	L 2-3	0-1	12	Bent D [51], Bent M [66]	41,347
26	22	A	Newcastle U	D 0-0	0-0	—		50,451
27	25	H	Aston Villa	D 0-0	0-0	13		26,594
28	Mar 4	A	Liverpool	D 0-0	0-0	13		43,892
29	12	H	Middlesbrough	W 2-1	0-0	13	Bent D 2 [73, 86]	24,830
30	18	A	Arsenal	L 0-3	0-2	13		38,223
31	26	H	Newcastle U	W 3-1	2-1	11	Bent D (pen) [24], Bowyer (og) [37], Bothroyd [89]	27,019
32	Apr 2	A	West Ham U	D 0-0	0-0	11		34,753
33	8	H	Everton	D 0-0	0-0	12		26,954
34	15	A	Fulham	L 1-2	1-2	12	Euell [26]	19,146
35	17	H	Portsmouth	W 2-1	0-1	11	Hughes [76], Bent D [83]	25,419
36	22	A	Bolton W	L 1-4	0-3	11	Bent D (pen) [76]	24,713
37	29	H	Blackburn R	L 0-2	0-1	12		26,254
38	May 7	A	Manchester U	L 0-4	0-3	13		73,006

Final League Position: 13

GOALSCORERS

League (41): Bent D 18 (3 pens), Murphy 4 (1 pen), Ambrose 3, Hughes 3, Bent M 2, Bothroyd 2, Rommedahl 2, Bartlett 1, Euell 1, Holland 1, Perry 1, Thomas 1, Young 1, own goal 1.
Carling Cup (6): Bent D 2, Ambrose 1, Bothroyd 1, Johansson 1 (pen), Murphy 1.
FA Cup (11): Bothroyd 3, Bent D 2, Hughes 2, Rommedahl 2, Fortune 1, Holland 1.

Andersen S 15	Young L 32	Powell C 25 + 2	Smertin A 18	Perry C 27 + 1	Hreidarsson H 34	Kishishev R 34 + 3	Murphy D 17 + 1	Bent D 36	Ambrose D 19 + 9	Rommedahl D 19 + 2	Hughes B 22 + 11	Thomas J 16 + 9	Bartlett S 6 + 10	Johansson J 1 + 3	Fortune J 7 + 4	Spector J 13 + 7	Holland M 20 + 3	Bothroyd J 3 + 15	El Karkouri T 4 + 6	Lisbie K — + 6	Kiely D 3	Myhre T 20	Sorondo G 7	Bent M 12 + 1	Euell J 5 + 5	Sankofa O 3 + 1	Sam L — + 2	Match No.
1	2	3	4^{1}	5	6	7	8	9	10■	11^{2}	12	13																1
1	2	3	4	5	6	7	8^{1}	9		11^{3}	12	10^{2}	13	14														2
1	2	3	4^{1}	5	6	7	8	9		11	12	10^{2}	13															3
1	2	3	4^{3}	5	6	7	8	9		11^{1}	13	10^{2}	12		14													4
1	2	3^{2}		5	6	7^{3}	8	9	12	11	4	10^{1}				13	14											5
1	2	3^{2}	4	5	6	7	8^{1}	9		11^{3}	12	10				13		14										6
1	2	3	4	5		7^{3}	8	9^{2}		11	12	10^{1}	13			14			6									7
1	2	3	4^{1}	5	6	7^{2}	8	9		11	12	10^{3}						14	13									8
1	2		4	5	6	7	8^{2}	9	10	11^{1}				12		3			13									9
1	2		4^{1}	5	6	7^{2}	8		10	11^{3}	12			14		3	13	9										10
1	2			5	6	7	8^{2}	9	10^{1}	11^{3}	4	12				3		13	14									11
1	2	3	4		6	7^{2}	8	9	10	11^{1}		12						13	5									12
1	2	3^{1}	4	12	6	7^{2}	13	9	10^{3}			11					8		5	14								13
	2		4	5	6		8	9	10^{2}		13	12		11^{3}		3	7^{1}	14			1							14
	2	3	4^{1}	5	6	7	8	9^{2}	10		12	11^{3}	13						14		1							15
	2	3	4	5	6	7^{1}	8	9	10^{3}		12	11^{2}	13			14					1							16
	2				3	7^{1}	8■	9	12		11		10^{3}		5	13	4			14		1	6^{2}					17
	2	3			6	7		9		8	11		10^{1}		5		4			12		1						18
	2	3			6	12	8^{1}	9	13	11^{3}	7^{2}		10		5		4			14		1						19
	2	3			6	7^{2}		9	12	8^{1}	11		10		5		4			13		1						20
	2	3			6	7		9	10^{1}	8^{2}	11		12		5		4					1		13				21
	2	3	4		6	12		9	11^{2}		8	13			5		7^{1}	14				1		10^{3}				22
	2	3^{2}	4		6	7^{1}		9	8^{3}		11	12			5	13		14				1		10				23
	2		4^{2}	5	6	7		9	12		8	11^{1}				3			13			1		10				24
	2		4^{3}		6	7		9	12		8^{2}	11^{1}				3		13	5			1		10	14			25
	2			5	6	7		9	8		11^{1}					3	4					1		10	12			26
	2			5	6	7		9	8		11^{3}					3	4^{1}	13	12			1		10^{2}	14			27
	2	12		5	6	7^{3}		9	8^{1}		11					3	4	13				1		10^{2}	14			28
	2	3		5	6	7		9	8^{1}		11^{2}	13	12				4	10^{3}				1			14			29
	2^{1}	12		5	6	7		9		11	4^{2}	10^{3}	13			3	14					1			8			30
	2	3		5	6	7		9		12	8	11^{1}					4	13				1		10^{2}				31
	2^{2}	3		5	6	7		9		11^{1}	8	12				13	4	14				1		10^{3}				32
				5	3	7^{2}			12	13		11^{1}	14			2	4	9^{3}				1	6	10	8			33
				5	3	7^{1}		9	11			12				2	4^{2}	13				1	6	10	8			34
		3			6	7		9	12		8	11^{1}				2^{3}	4	13				1	5	10^{2}		14		35
		3		5		12		9	10^{2}	7^{3}	11				14		4	13				1	6		8	2^{1}		36
1		3		5		7^{3}		9	8		11		10^{2}		12		4			13			6^{1}			2	14	37
1		3		5		7		9^{3}	12		11		10		13		4						6		8^{1}	2^{2}	14	38

FA Cup

Third Round	Sheffield W	(a)	4-2
Fourth Round	Leyton Orient	(h)	2-1
Fifth Round	Brentford	(h)	3-1
Sixth Round	Middlesbrough	(h)	0-0
		(a)	2-4

Carling Cup

Second Round	Hartlepool U	(h)	3-1
Third Round	Chelsea	(a)	1-1
Fourth Round	Blackburn R	(h)	2-3

CHELSEA FA Premiership

FOUNDATION

Chelsea may never have existed but for the fact that Fulham rejected an offer to rent the Stamford Bridge ground from Mr H. A. Mears who had owned it since 1904. Fortunately he was determined to develop it as a football stadium rather than sell it to the Great Western Railway and got together with Frederick Parker, who persuaded Mears of the financial advantages of developing a major sporting venue. Chelsea FC was formed in 1905, and when admission to the Southern League was denied, they immediately gained admission to the Second Division of the Football League.

Stamford Bridge, Fulham Road, London SW6 1HS.

Telephone: 0870 300 1212.

Fax: (020) 7381 4831.

Ticket Office: 0870 300 2322.

Website: www.chelseafc.com

Email: media@chelseafc.com

Ground Capacity: 42,294.

Record Attendance: 82,905 v Arsenal, Division 1, 12 October 1935.

Pitch Measurements: 103m × 67.66m.

Chairman: Bruce Buck.

Director: Eugene Tenenbaum.

Chief Executive: Peter Kenyon.

Club Secretary: David Barnard.

Manager: José Mourinho.

Assistant Managers: Steve Clarke and Baltemar Brito.

Physio: Dean Kenneally.

Colours: Blue shirts and shorts, white stockings.

Change Colours: Sterling shirts, black shorts, sterling stockings.

Year Formed: 1905.

Turned Professional: 1905.

Ltd Co.: 1905.

Club Nickname: 'The Blues'.

First Football League Game: 2 September 1905, Division 2, v Stockport Co (a) L 0–1 – Foulke; Mackie, McEwan; Key, Harris, Miller; Moran, J. T. Robertson, Copeland, Windridge, Kirwan.

Record League Victory: 9–2 v Glossop N E, Division 2, 1 September 1906 – Byrne; Walton, Miller; Key (1), McRoberts, Henderson; Moran, McDermott (1), Hilsdon (5), Copeland (1), Kirwan (1).

HONOURS

FA Premier League: Champions 2004–05, 2005–06. Runners-up 2003–04.

Football League: Division 1 – Champions 1954–55; Division 2 – Champions 1983–84, 1988–89; Runners-up 1906–07, 1911–12, 1929–30, 1962–63, 1976–77.

FA Cup: Winners 1970, 1997, 2000; Runners-up 1915, 1967, 1994, 2002.

Football League Cup: Winners 1965, 1998, 2005; Runners-up 1972.

Full Members' Cup: Winners 1986.

Zenith Data Systems Cup: Winners 1990.

European Competitions: *Champions League:* 1999–2000, 2003–04 (semi-finals), 2004–05 (semi-finals). *European Fairs Cup:* 1958–60, 1965–66, 1968–69. *European Cup-Winners' Cup:* 1970–71 (winners), 1971–72, 1994–95, 1997–98 (winners), 1998–99 (semi-finals). *UEFA Cup:* 2000–01, 2001–02, 2002–03. *Super Cup:* 1998–99 (winners).

SKY SPORTS FACT FILE

In 1946–47 Scottish international inside-forward Tommy Walker set a 48-game League record likely to stand for all time. He made 39 League appearances for Chelsea having previously played nine times for Hearts before his transfer that season.

Record Cup Victory: 13–0 v Jeunesse Hautcharage, ECWC, 1st rd 2nd leg, 29 September 1971 – Bonetti; Boyle, Harris (1), Hollins (1p), Webb (1), Hinton, Cooke, Baldwin (3), Osgood (5), Hudson (1), Houseman (1).

Record Defeat: 1–8 v Wolverhampton W, Division 1, 26 September 1953.

Most League Points (2 for a win): 57, Division 2, 1906–07.

Most League Points (3 for a win): 99, Division 2, 1988–89.

Most League Goals: 98, Division 1, 1960–61.

Highest League Scorer in Season: Jimmy Greaves, 41, 1960–61.

Most League Goals in Total Aggregate: Bobby Tambling, 164, 1958–70.

Most League Goals in One Match: 5, George Hilsdon v Glossop, Division 2, 1 September 1906; 5, Jimmy Greaves v Wolverhampton W, Division 1, 30 August 1958; 5, Jimmy Greaves v Preston NE, Division 1, 19 December 1959; 5, Jimmy Greaves v WBA, Division 1, 3 December 1960; 5, Bobby Tambling v Aston Villa, Division 1, 17 September 1966; 5, Gordon Durie v Walsall, Division 2, 4 February 1989.

Most Capped Player: Marcel Desailly, 67 (116), France.

Most League Appearances: Ron Harris, 655, 1962–80.

Youngest League Player: Ian Hamilton, 16 years 138 days v Tottenham H, 18 March 1967.

Record Transfer Fee Received: £12,000,000 from Rangers for Tore Andre Flo, November 2000.

Record Transfer Fee Paid: £29,500,000 to AC Milan for Andriy Shevchenko, June 2006.

Football League Record: 1905 Elected to Division 2; 1907–10 Division 1; 1910–12 Division 2; 1912–24 Division 1; 1924–30 Division 2; 1930–62 Division 1; 1962–63 Division 2; 1963–75 Division 1; 1975–77 Division 2; 1977–79 Division 1; 1979–84 Division 2; 1984–88 Division 1; 1988–89 Division 2; 1989–92 Division 1; 1992– FA Premier League.

MANAGERS

John Tait Robertson 1905–07
David Calderhead 1907–33
Leslie Knighton 1933–39
Billy Birrell 1939–52
Ted Drake 1952–61
Tommy Docherty 1962–67
Dave Sexton 1967–74
Ron Suart 1974–75
Eddie McCreadie 1975–77
Ken Shellito 1977–78
Danny Blanchflower 1978–79
Geoff Hurst 1979–81
John Neal 1981–85 *(Director to 1986)*
John Hollins 1985–88
Bobby Campbell 1988–91
Ian Porterfield 1991–93
David Webb 1993
Glenn Hoddle 1993–96
Ruud Gullit 1996–98
Gianluca Vialli 1998–2000
Claudio Ranieri 2000–04
Jose Mourinho June 2004–

LATEST SEQUENCES

Longest Sequence of League Wins: 10, 19.11.2005 – 15.1.2006.

Longest Sequence of League Defeats: 7, 1.11.1952 – 20.12.1952.

Longest Sequence of League Draws: 6, 20.8.1969 – 13.9.1969.

Longest Sequence of Unbeaten League Matches: 40, 23.10.2004 – 29.10.2005.

Longest Sequence Without a League Win: 21, 3.11.1987 – 2.4.1988.

Successive Scoring Runs: 27 from 29.10.1988.

Successive Non-scoring Runs: 9 from 14.3.1981.

TEN YEAR LEAGUE RECORD

		P	W	D	L	F	A	Pts	Pos
1996-97	PR Lge	38	16	11	11	58	55	59	6
1997-98	PR Lge	38	20	3	15	71	43	63	4
1998-99	PR Lge	38	20	15	3	57	30	75	3
1999-2000	PR Lge	38	18	11	9	53	34	65	5
2000-01	PR Lge	38	17	10	11	68	45	61	6
2001-02	PR Lge	38	17	13	8	66	38	64	6
2002-03	PR Lge	38	19	10	9	68	38	67	4
2003-04	PR Lge	38	24	7	7	67	30	79	2
2004-05	PR Lge	38	29	8	1	72	15	95	1
2005-06	PR Lge	38	29	4	5	72	22	91	1

DID YOU KNOW ?

Frank Lampard established a new Premier League record for consecutive appearances in 2005–06. After 164 successive games he felt unwell during the pre-match warm-up at Manchester City on 28 December and was withdrawn from the line-up.

CHELSEA 2005–06 LEAGUE RECORD

Match No.	*Date*	*Venue*	*Opponents*	*Result*		*H/T Score*	*Lg. Pos.*	*Goalscorers*	*Attendance*
1	Aug 14	A	Wigan Ath	W	1-0	0-0	—	Crespo [90]	23,575
2	21	H	Arsenal	W	1-0	0-0	4	Drogba [73]	42,136
3	24	H	WBA	W	4-0	2-0	—	Lampard 2 [23, 80], Cole J [43], Drogba [68]	41,201
4	27	A	Tottenham H	W	2-0	1-0	1	Del Horno [39], Duff [71]	36,077
5	Sept 10	H	Sunderland	W	2-0	0-0	1	Geremi [54], Drogba [82]	41,969
6	17	A	Charlton Ath	W	2-0	0-0	1	Crespo [55], Robben [60]	27,111
7	24	H	Aston Villa	W	2-1	1-1	1	Lampard 2 (1 pen) [45, 75 (p)]	42,146
8	Oct 2	A	Liverpool	W	4-1	2-1	1	Lampard (pen) [27], Duff [43], Cole J [63], Geremi [82]	44,235
9	15	H	Bolton W	W	5-1	0-1	1	Drogba 2 [52, 61], Lampard 2 [55, 59], Gudjohnsen [74]	41,775
10	23	A	Everton	D	1-1	0-1	1	Lampard [50]	36,042
11	29	H	Blackburn R	W	4-2	2-2	1	Drogba [10], Lampard 2 (1 pen) [14 (p), 62], Khizanishvili (og) [74]	41,553
12	Nov 6	A	Manchester U	L	0-1	0-1	1		67,864
13	19	H	Newcastle U	W	3-0	0-0	1	Cole J [47], Crespo [51], Duff [90]	42,268
14	26	A	Portsmouth	W	2-0	1-0	1	Crespo [27], Lampard (pen) [67]	20,182
15	Dec 3	H	Middlesbrough	W	1-0	0-0	1	Terry [62]	41,666
16	10	H	Wigan Ath	W	1-0	0-0	1	Terry [67]	42,060
17	18	A	Arsenal	W	2-0	1-0	1	Robben [39], Cole J [73]	38,347
18	26	H	Fulham	W	3-2	2-1	1	Gallas [3], Lampard [24], Crespo [74]	42,313
19	28	A	Manchester C	W	1-0	0-0	1	Cole J [79]	46,587
20	31	H	Birmingham C	W	2-0	2-0	1	Crespo [25], Robben [43]	40,652
21	Jan 2	A	West Ham U	W	3-1	1-0	1	Lampard [25], Crespo [61], Drogba [80]	34,758
22	15	A	Sunderland	W	2-1	1-1	1	Crespo [28], Robben [69]	32,420
23	22	H	Charlton Ath	D	1-1	1-0	1	Gudjohnsen [19]	41,355
24	Feb 1	A	Aston Villa	D	1-1	1-0	—	Robben [14]	38,562
25	5	H	Liverpool	W	2-0	1-0	1	Gallas [35], Crespo [68]	42,316
26	11	A	Middlesbrough	L	0-3	0-2	1		31,037
27	25	H	Portsmouth	W	2-0	0-0	1	Lampard [65], Robben [78]	42,254
28	Mar 4	A	WBA	W	2-1	0-0	1	Drogba [51], Cole J [74]	26,581
29	11	H	Tottenham H	W	2-1	1-1	1	Essien [14], Gallas [90]	42,243
30	19	A	Fulham	L	0-1	0-1	1		22,486
31	25	H	Manchester C	W	2-0	2-0	1	Drogba 2 [30, 33]	42,321
32	Apr 1	A	Birmingham C	D	0-0	0-0	1		26,364
33	9	H	West Ham U	W	4-1	2-1	1	Drogba [28], Crespo [31], Terry [54], Gallas [69]	41,919
34	15	A	Bolton W	W	2-0	1-0	1	Terry [44], Lampard [59]	27,266
35	17	H	Everton	W	3-0	1-0	1	Lampard [28], Drogba [62], Essien [74]	41,765
36	29	H	Manchester U	W	3-0	1-0	1	Gallas [5], Cole J [61], Ricardo Carvalho [73]	42,219
37	May 2	A	Blackburn R	L	0-1	0-1	—		20,243
38	7	A	Newcastle U	L	0-1	0-0	1		52,309

Final League Position: 1

GOALSCORERS

League (72): Lampard 16 (4 pens), Drogba 12, Crespo 10, Cole J 7, Robben 6, Gallas 5, Terry 4, Duff 3, Essien 2, Geremi 2, Gudjohnsen 2, Del Horno 1, Ricardo Carvalho 1, own goal 1.
Carling Cup (1): Terry 1.
FA Cup (12): Cole J 2, Lampard 2 (1 pen), Terry 2, Cole C 1, Crespo 1, Drogba 1, Gudjohnsen 1, Paulo Ferreira 1, Robben 1.
Champions League (9): Crespo 2, Lampard 2 (1 pen), Ricardo Carvalho 2, Cole J 1, Drogba 1, own goal 1.
Community Shield (2): Drogba 2.

Cech P 34	Paulo Ferreira 18 + 3	Del Horno A 25	Makelele C 29 + 2	Terry J 36	Gallas W 33 + 1	Duff D 18 + 10	Lampard F 35	Drogba D 20 + 9	Gudjohnsen E 16 + 10	Robben A 21 + 7	Crespo H 20 + 10	Wright-Phillips S 10 + 17	Cole J 26 + 8	Essien M 27 + 4	Cudicini C 3 + 1	Johnson G 4	Huth R 7 + 6	Geremi 8 + 7	Ricardo Carvalho 22 + 2	Cole C — + 9	Maniche 3 + 5	Diarra L 2 + 1	Pidgeley L 1	Smith J — + 1	Match No.
1	2	3	4	5	6	7[1]	8	9	10[2]	11[3]	12	13	14												1
1	2	3	4	5	6	11	8	12	10[3]	7[2]	9[1]	13		14											2
		3	4	5	6	12	8	9[2]		14	13	7[1]	11[3]	10	1	2									3
1	2	3	4	5	6	7[3]	8	9[1]			12	13	11[2]	10			14								4
1		3		5	6	12	8	13	10[1]	11	9[2]	7[3]	14	4				2							5
1	2		4	5	3	7[3]	8	12		11[2]	9[1]	14	13	10					6						6
1	2		4	5	3	7	8	12	13	11[2]	9[1]	14		10					6[3]						7
1		3[2]	4	5	6	7[3]	8	9		12			11[1]	10			13	14	2						8
1	12	3[2]	4	5	2		8	9	13			7[3]	11[1]	10					6	14					9
1		3	4	5	2		8	9[1]	13	14	12	7[2]	11[3]	10			6								10
1		3	4	5	2		8	9[1]	13	14	12	7[3]	11[2]	10					6						11
1	2	3[3]	4	5	6	7	8	9	12			13	11[2]	10[1]						14					12
1		3	4[2]	5	12	7	8		10		9[3]	14	11	13		2[1]			6						13
1	2			5	3	7[2]	8		10		9[3]	12	11[1]	4				13	6	14					14
1		2		5	3	7	8	9[3]	10[2]	11[1]		12		4				13	6	14					15
		3		5	2	7[1]	8	12	13	11[2]	9[3]		10	4	1			14	6						16
1	2		4	5	3		8	9[1]		11[2]			7	10			12	13	6						17
1	2		4	5	3		8	12	13	11	9[3]	7[2]	10				6[1]	14							18
1	12	3	4	5	6	11[3]		9[2]	10[1]	14	13		7	8				2							19
1	2		12	5	3		8	13	10	11[3]	9[2]	14	7	4[1]					6						20
1		3	4	5		7[1]	8	9	14	11	12[2]	13		10[3]				2	6						21
1		3	4	5	2	12	8		10[2]	11■	9[3]		7[1]				13		6	14					22
1		3[2]	4[1]	5	2	11[3]	8		10		9	12	7						6■	13	14				23
1			4	5	3	12	8		10[2]	11	9[3]		7[1]			2	13		6		14				24
1		3	4[3]	5	2	12[2]	8		13	11	9		7[1]	10					6			14			25
1				5	3[3]		8		10	11	9	12	7[1]	4				2[2]	6	13	14				26
1	2	3[3]	12	5		14	8	9	13	11		7[1]	10[2]	4			6								27
1	2		4	5	3	7[1]		9[2]	10[3]	11■		13	12	8			6	14							28
1	2		4	5	3	12	8	13			9	7[2]	11[1]	10[3]			6				14				29
1	2		4	5	3■	12	8	13			9	7[1]	11[2]	10			6[3]		14						30
1	2	3	4	5		11[2]	8	9	10[1]		12	14	7[3]	13					6						31
1	2	3[1]	4	5		7[2]	8	9	10[3]	11	12		13	14					6						32
1		3	4	5	6		8	9[1]		13	10[2]		12	11[3]				2	14		7■				33
1	12	3	4	5	6		8	9[3]		13	10[2]		11[1]	7			14	2							34
1[G]		3	4	5	6		8	9		11[1]	10[2]	13	12	7	15			2							35
1	2		4	5	3	12	8	9[3]		11[1]	13		10[2]	7					6		14				36
		3[1]			5	12	8		10		9	7[2]	13		1			2[3]	6	14	11	4			37
	2				3	11[1]				8		12	9			7	5[2]		6[3]	13	10	4	1	14	38

FA Cup

Third Round	Huddersfield T	(h)	2-1
Fourth Round	Everton	(a)	1-1
		(h)	4-1
Fifth Round	Colchester U	(h)	3-1
Sixth Round	Newcastle U	(h)	1-0
Semi-Final	Liverpool		1-2
(at Old Trafford)			

Carling Cup

Third Round	Charlton Ath	(h)	1-1

Champions League

Group G	Anderlecht	(h)	1-0
	Liverpool	(a)	0-0
	Betis	(h)	4-0
		(a)	0-1
	Anderlecht	(a)	2-0
	Liverpool	(h)	0-0
First Round	Barcelona	(h)	1-2
		(a)	1-1

CHELTENHAM TOWN FL Championship 1

FOUNDATION

Although a scratch team representing Cheltenham played a match against Gloucester in 1884, the earliest recorded match for Cheltenham Town FC was a friendly against Dean Close School on 12 March 1892. The School won 4–3 and the match was played at Prestbury (half a mile from Whaddon Road). Cheltenham Town played Wednesday afternoon friendlies at a local cricket ground until entering the Mid Gloucester League. In those days the club played in deep red coloured shirts and were nicknamed 'the Rubies'. The club moved to Whaddon Lane for season 1901–02 and changed to red and white colours two years later.

Whaddon Road, Cheltenham, Gloucester GL52 5NA.

Telephone: (01242) 573 558.

Fax: (01242) 224 675.

Website: www.ctfc.com

Email: info@ctfc.com

Ground Capacity: 7,013.

Record Attendance: at Whaddon Road: 8,326 v Reading, FA Cup 1st rd, 17 November 1956; at Cheltenham Athletic Ground: 10,389 v Blackpool, FA Cup 3rd rd, 13 January 1934.

Pitch Measurements: 111yd × 72yd.

Chairman: Paul Baker.

Vice-chairman: Colin Farmer.

Secretary: Paul Godfrey.

Manager: John Ward.

Assistant Manager: Keith Downing.

Physio: Ian Weston.

Colours: Red and white striped shirts, white shorts, red stockings.

Change Colours: All yellow with blue trim.

Year Formed: 1892.

Turned Professional: 1932.

Ltd Co.: 1937.

Club Nickname: 'The Robins'.

Previous Grounds: Grafton Cricket Ground, Whaddon Lane, Carter's Field (pre 1932).

HONOURS

Football League: Promoted from Division 3 (play-offs) 2001–02; Promoted from Championship 2 (play-offs) 2005–06.

FA Cup: best season: 5th rd 2002.

Football League Cup: never past 2nd rd.

Football Conference: Champions 1998–99, runners-up 1997–98.

Trophy: Winners 1997–98.

Southern League: Champions 1984–85; *Southern League Cup:* Winners 1957–58, runners-up 1968–69, 1984–85; *Southern League Merit Cup:* Winners 1984–85; *Southern League Championship Shield:* Winners 1985.

Gloucestershire Senior Cup: Winners 1998–99; *Gloucestershire Northern Senior Professional Cup:* Winners 30 times; *Midland Floodlit Cup:* Winners 1985–86, 1986–87, 1987–88; *Mid Gloucester League:* Champions 1896–97; *Gloucester and District League:* Champions 1902–03, 1905–06; *Cheltenham League:* Champions 1910–11, 1913–14; *North Gloucestershire League:* Champions 1913–14; *Gloucestershire Northern Senior League:* Champions 1928–29, 1932–33; *Gloucestershire Northern Senior Amateur Cup:* Winners 1929–30, 1930–31, 1932–33, 1933–34, 1934–35; *Leamington Hospital Cup:* Winners 1934–35.

SKY SPORTS FACT FILE

Left-half George Blackburn was a clerk in Hampstead's electricity company. He became a professional with Aston Villa, Cardiff City and Mansfield Town, picking up an England cap on the way to becoming Cheltenham Town player-manager in 1932.

Record League Victory: 11–0 v Bourneville Ath, Birmingham Combination, 29 April 1933 – Davis; Jones, Williams; Lang (1), Blackburn, Draper; Evans, Hazard (4), Haycox (4), Goodger (1), Hill (1).

Record Cup Victory: 12–0 v Chippenham R, FA Cup 3rd qual. rd, 2 November 1935 – Bowles; Whitehouse, Williams; Lang, Devonport (1), Partridge (2); Perkins, Hackett, Jones (4), Black (4), Griffiths (1).

Record Defeat: 0–7 v Crystal Palace, League Cup 2nd rd, 2 October 2002.
N.B. 1–10 v Merthyr T, Southern League, 8 March 1952.

Most League Points (2 for a win): 60, Southern League Division 1, 1963–64.

Most League Points (3 for a win): 78, Division 3, 2001–02.

Most League Goals: 66, Division 3, 2001–02.

Highest League Scorer in Season: Julian Alsop, 20, Division 3, 2001–02.

Most League Goals in Total Aggregate: Martin Devaney, 38, 1999–2005.

Most Capped Player: Grant McCann, 6 (11), Northern Ireland.

Most League Appearances: Jamie Victory, 248, 1999–.

Record Transfer Fee Received: £60,000 from Southampton for Christer Warren, March 1995.

Record Transfer Fee Paid: £50,000 to West Ham U for Grant McCann, January 2003 and £50,000 to Stoke C for Brian Wilson, March 2004.

Football League Record: 1999 Promoted to Division 3; 2002 Division 2; 2003–04 Division 3; 2004–06 FL2; 2006– FL1.

MANAGERS

George Blackburn 1932–34
George Carr 1934–37
Jimmy Brain 1937–48
Cyril Dean 1948–50
George Summerbee 1950–52
William Raeside 1952–53
Arch Anderson 1953–58
Ron Lewin 1958–60
Peter Donnelly 1960–61
Tommy Cavanagh 1961
Arch Anderson 1961–65
Harold Fletcher 1965–66
Bob Etheridge 1966–73
Willie Penman 1973–74
Dennis Allen 1974–79
Terry Paine 1979
Alan Grundy 1979–82
Alan Wood 1982–83
John Murphy 1983–88
Jim Barron 1988–90
John Murphy 1990
Dave Lewis 1990–91
Ally Robertson 1991–92
Lindsay Parsons 1992–95
Chris Robinson 1995–97
Steve Cotterill 1997–2002
Graham Allner 2002–03
Bobby Gould 2003
John Ward November 2003–

LATEST SEQUENCES

Longest Sequence of League Wins: not more than 3.

Longest Sequence of League Defeats: 5, 13.1.2001 – 13.2.2001.

Longest Sequence of League Draws: 5, 5.4.2003 – 21.4.2003.

Longest Sequence of Unbeaten League Matches: 16, 1.12.2001 – 12.3.2002.

Longest Sequence Without a League Win: 10, 16.4.2002 – 14.9.2002.

Successive Scoring Runs: 15 from 15.2.2003.

Successive Non-scoring Runs: 4 from 12.9.1999.

TEN YEAR LEAGUE RECORD

		P	*W*	*D*	*L*	*F*	*A*	*Pts*	*Pos*
1996–97	Sth L	42	21	11	10	76	44	74	2
1997–98	Conf.	42	23	9	10	63	43	78	2
1998-99	Conf.	42	22	14	6	71	36	80	1
1999-2000	Div 3	46	20	10	16	50	42	70	8
2000-01	Div 3	46	18	14	14	59	52	68	9
2001-02	Div 3	46	21	15	10	66	49	78	4
2002-03	Div 2	46	10	18	18	53	68	48	21
2003-04	Div 3	46	14	14	18	57	71	56	14
2004-05	FL 2	46	16	12	18	51	54	60	14
2005-06	FL 2	46	19	15	12	65	53	72	5

DID YOU KNOW ?

Cheltenham Town signed three forwards in March 1962 to improve their poor goalscoring: Colin Moir and Paddy Roche from Nottingham Forest plus Ted Calland, a much travelled marksman from Lincoln City. Instant result: 5–1 v Folkestone Town.

CHELTENHAM TOWN 2005–06 LEAGUE RECORD

Match No.	Date	Venue	Opponents	Result		H/T Score	Lg. Pos.	Goalscorers	Attendance
1	Aug 6	H	Bury	W	2-1	1-1	—	Odejayi [9], Armstrong [74]	2967
2	9	A	Macclesfield T	D	2-2	1-0	—	Melligan [18], Odejayi [82]	1601
3	13	A	Rochdale	D	1-1	1-0	4	Spencer [37]	2344
4	20	H	Boston U	W	3-0	3-0	4	Spencer [19], Victory [43], Futcher (og) [45]	2680
5	27	H	Leyton Orient	D	1-1	0-1	6	Finnigan [90]	3274
6	29	A	Wycombe W	D	0-0	0-0	5		5244
7	Sept 2	H	Barnet	D	1-1	1-0	—	Finnigan [44]	3343
8	10	A	Wrexham	L	0-2	0-1	10		3671
9	17	H	Carlisle U	L	2-3	1-1	13	Melligan [19], McCann (pen) [87]	3282
10	24	A	Northampton T	W	2-1	2-1	10	Odejayi 2 [20, 45]	5407
11	27	H	Peterborough U	W	2-1	1-0	—	McCann [37], Armstrong [90]	2531
12	Oct 1	H	Torquay U	L	0-1	0-0	10		3578
13	7	A	Lincoln C	W	1-0	0-0	—	Odejayi [76]	4776
14	14	H	Grimsby T	L	0-3	0-1	—		3500
15	22	A	Darlington	L	1-3	1-0	12	Connolly [30]	3315
16	29	H	Mansfield T	L	0-2	0-1	15		3033
17	Nov 12	A	Notts Co	W	3-2	1-1	11	Wilson [35], Victory [78], McCann [84]	4903
18	18	H	Lincoln C	W	4-1	1-0	—	Guinan [31], Wilson 2 [64, 66], Gillespie [90]	3078
19	26	A	Bury	W	1-0	1-0	7	Melligan [43]	2251
20	Dec 6	H	Oxford U	L	1-2	1-2	—	Guinan [11]	2852
21	10	H	Macclesfield T	D	2-2	0-0	9	Odejayi [85], Caines [90]	2804
22	17	A	Boston U	D	0-0	0-0	9		1906
23	26	H	Chester C	W	1-0	0-0	7	Wilson [49]	3819
24	28	A	Rushden & D	W	1-0	0-0	6	McCann [48]	2244
25	31	H	Shrewsbury T	W	1-0	0-0	5	Gillespie [72]	3474
26	Jan 2	A	Stockport Co	D	2-2	0-1	5	Wilson [69], Finnigan [90]	3777
27	10	A	Barnet	D	1-1	1-0	—	Melligan [8]	1366
28	14	H	Bristol R	L	2-3	0-1	6	Gillespie [70], Odejayi [88]	6005
29	21	A	Carlisle U	D	1-1	0-1	6	Gray (og) [90]	6759
30	Feb 4	A	Peterborough U	L	0-1	0-0	9		3901
31	11	H	Northampton T	W	3-1	2-0	8	Guinan [38], Odejayi [45], Melligan (pen) [71]	3876
32	14	A	Bristol R	W	1-0	0-0	—	Wilson [73]	6885
33	18	A	Oxford U	D	1-1	0-0	7	Guinan [53]	5232
34	25	H	Rochdale	D	1-1	1-0	8	Guinan [43]	3184
35	Mar 4	H	Wycombe W	W	2-1	0-1	7	Caines [72], Gillespie [90]	4069
36	11	A	Leyton Orient	L	0-1	0-1	7		4879
37	18	A	Chester C	W	1-0	1-0	6	Wilson [2]	2281
38	21	H	Wrexham	D	2-2	1-1	—	McCann [35], Guinan [56]	2737
39	25	H	Rushden & D	W	3-1	3-0	6	Melligan [7], Wilson [13], Finnigan [33]	3447
40	Apr 1	A	Shrewsbury T	L	0-2	0-1	6		3724
41	8	H	Stockport Co	D	3-3	1-1	6	Odejayi [12], Wilson [66], McCann (pen) [88]	3525
42	15	A	Torquay U	W	2-1	0-1	6	Spencer [60], Odejayi [70]	3336
43	17	H	Darlington	D	1-1	0-0	5	McCann (pen) [59]	3851
44	21	A	Grimsby T	L	0-1	0-0	—		5863
45	29	H	Notts Co	W	2-0	1-0	5	Guinan [3], Vincent [82]	4518
46	May 6	A	Mansfield T	W	5-0	2-0	5	Gillespie [34], Vincent [45], McCann [50], Bird (pen) [81], Odejayi [85]	3728

Final League Position: 5

GOALSCORERS

League (65): Odejayi 11, Wilson 9, McCann 8 (3 pens), Guinan 7, Melligan 6 (1 pen), Gillespie 5, Finnigan 4, Spencer 3, Armstrong 2, Caines 2, Victory 2, Vincent 2, Bird 1 (pen), Connolly 1, own goals 2.
Carling Cup (5): McCann 2, Caines 1, Melligan 1, Victory 1.
FA Cup (7): Odejayi 2, Finnigan 1 (pen), Guinan 1, McCann 1, Melligan 1 (pen), Wilson 1.
Football League Trophy (9): Gillespie 2, Wilson 2, Armstrong 1, Connolly 1, Duff 1, Spicer 1, Victory 1.
Play-Offs (3): Guinan 2, Finnigan 1.

Higgs S 45	Gill J 41 + 1	Victory J 19 + 3	McCann G 38 + 1	Townsend M 30 + 1	Taylor M 9 + 1	Melligan J 40 + 2	Finnigan J 38 + 1	Odejayi K 38 + 3	Guinan S 27 + 3	Armstrong C 28 + 6	Spencer D 17 + 29	Vincent A 1 + 12	Wilson B 41 + 2	Caines G 35 + 4	Rose M 3	Bird D 18 + 18	Yao S — + 3	Brown A 3	Duff S 18 + 2	Connolly A 4 + 1	Bradshaw G — + 3	Gillespie S 4 + 10	Brown S 1	Wylde M — + 1	Bell M 7 + 2	Gallinagh A 1	*Match No.*
1	2	3	4	5	6	7	8	9	10[1]	11	12																1
1	2	3	4	5	6	7	8	9	12	11	10[1]																2
1	2	3	4	5	6	7[2]	8	9	12	11	10[1]	13															3
1	2	3	4	5	6	7[2]	8	9[3]		11	10[1]	12	13	14													4
1	2	3	4	5	6	7	8	9			10[2]	13	12		11[1]												5
1	2	3	4	5	6	7	8	9[1]			12	13	11[3]		10[2]	14											6
1	2[1]	3	4	5	6	7	8	9			12	13	11		10[2]												7
1	2	3	4	5[2]	6	7	8[3]	9			10[1]	12	11	13		14											8
1	2[1]	3	4	5	6[2]	7	8	9[3]			10	12	11	13			14										9
1	2	3	4	5			8	9[1]			12		11	6		7	13	10[2]									10
1	2	3	4	5			7[1]	9		13	12		11	6		8		10[2]									11
1	2	3	4	5		12	7[2]	9		13	14		11	6		8[3]		10[1]									12
1			4			7		9		10	11		6	5		8			2	3							13
1		12	4			7		9		3	10		2	5		8			6	11[1]							14
1		12	4			7[2]		9		3	10		2	5		8[1]	13		6	11							15
1	12	13	4[2]	5		7		9		3	10[3]		2			8			6	11[1]	14■						16
1	2	3	4			7[2]		9[1]	10[3]	11	12		8	5		13			6			14					17
1	2	3	4			7		9[3]	10[1]	11	12		8	5		13			6[2]			14					18
1	2	3	4			7	12	9[2]	10[3]	11	13		8[1]	5					6			14					19
1	2[1]		4			7	8[2]	9	10[3]	3	12		11	5		13			6			14					20
1	2		4			7[1]	8	9	10[2]	3	12		11	5					6			13					21
1	2		4			7	8[2]	9[1]	10	3	12		11	5		13			6								22
1	2		4			7[2]	8	9	10[1]	3	12		11	5		13			6								23
1	2	3[3]	4			7	8	9[2]	10[1]		12		11	5		14			6			13					24
1	2	3		12		7	8	9[2]	10[3]		13		11	5		4			6[1]			14					25
1	2	3		6		7[1]	8	12	10[2]		9	13	11	5		4											26
	2	3[1]		6		7	8[2]		10	12	9	13	11	5		4							1				27
1	2				12	7	8	9		3	13		11	5		4			6[1]			10[2]					28
1	2[3]			6		7[2]	8	9	10[1]		12		11	5		4						13		14	3		29
1	2[2]			6		7	8	9	10[1]	3	12		11	5		4						13■					30
1	2		12	6		7	8	9[2]	10[3]		13		11[1]	5		4					14				3		31
1	2		4[1]	6		7[2]	8			12	9		10	5		11					13				3		32
1	2		4	6		7[1]	8		10[2]	13	9		11	5		12									3		33
1	2		4	6		7[1]	8		10[3]	13	9		11	5		12						14			3[2]		34
1	2		4	6		12	8		10[2]	11	13		7	5								9			3[1]		35
1	2		4	6			7	12	10[1]	3	13		11[2]	5		8						9					36
1	2		4[2]	6		7	8	9[1]	10	3	12		11[3]	5		13									14		37
1	2		4	6		7[2]	8	9[1]	10	3	12		11	5		13											38
1	2		4[2]	6		7	8	9[1]	10	3	12		11[3]	5		13									14		39
1	2			6		7[2]	8	9[3]	10	3	12	14	11[1]	5		4			13								40
1	2		4	6		7[2]	8	9	10[1]	3	12		11	5		13											41
1	2		4	6		7	8	9[1]	12	3	10[2]		11	5[3]		13			14								42
1	2		4	6■		7[1]	8	9		3	10		11[2]	13		12			5								43
1	2		4			7[2]	8	9	10[1]	3	12	14	11[3]	5		13			6								44
1	2		4			7[3]	8	9[2]	10[1]	3	12	13	11	5		14			6								45
1			4[3]					12	10[1]		13	11	7	5		8			6	14		9[2]			3	2	46

FA Cup

First Round	Carlisle U	(h)	1-0
Second Round	Oxford U	(h)	1-1
		(a)	2-1
Third Round	Chester C	(h)	2-2
		(a)	1-0
Fourth Round	Newcastle U	(h)	0-2

Carling Cup

First Round	Brentford	(h)	5-0
Second Round	Sunderland	(a)	0-1

Football League Trophy

First Round	Shrewsbury T	(a)	2-0
Second Round	Woking	(a)	5-1
Quarter-Final	Oxford U	(h)	2-1
Semi-Final	Colchester U	(h)	0-1

Play-Offs

Semi-Final	Wycombe W	(a)	2-1
		(h)	0-0
Final	Grimsby T		1-0
(at Millennium Stadium)			

CHESTER CITY FL Championship 2

FOUNDATION

All students of soccer history have read about the medieval games of football in Chester, but the present club was not formed until 1884 through the amalgamation of King's School Old Boys with Chester Rovers. For many years Chester were overshadowed in Cheshire by Northwich Victoria and Crewe Alexandra who had both won the Senior Cup several times before Chester's first success in 1894–95. The final against Macclesfield saw Chester face the team that had not only beaten them in the previous year's final, but also knocked them out of the FA Cup two seasons in succession. The final was held at the Drill Field, Northwich and Chester had the support of more than 1000 fans. Chester won 2-1.

Saunders Honda Stadium, Bumpers Lane, Chester CH1 4LT.

Telephone: (01244) 371 376.

Fax: (01244) 390 265.

Ticket Offfice: (01244) 371 376.

Website: www.chestercityfc.net

Email: info@chestercityfc.net

Ground Capacity: 6,012.

Record Attendance: 20,500 v Chelsea, FA Cup 3rd rd (replay), 16 January 1952 (at Sealand Road).

Pitch Measurements: 115yd × 75yd.

Chairman: Stephen Vaughan.

Secretary: Tony Allan.

Manager: Mark Wright.

Physio: Joe Hinnigan.

Colours: Blue and white striped shirts, blue shorts, blue stockings.

Change Colours: Yellow shirts, yellow shorts, yellow stockings.

Year Formed: 1885.

Turned Professional: 1902.

Ltd Co.: 1909.

Previous Name: Chester until 1983.

Club Nickname: 'Blues' and 'City'.

Previous Grounds: 1885, Faulkner Street; 1898, The Old Showground; 1901, Whipcord Lane; 1906, Sealand Road; 1990, Moss Rose Ground, Macclesfield; 1992, Deva Stadium, Bumpers Lane.

First Football League Game: 2 September 1931, Division 3 (N), v Wrexham (a) D 1–1 – Johnson; Herod, Jones; Keeley, Skitt, Reilly; Thompson, Ranson, Jennings (1), Cresswell, Hedley.

HONOURS

Football League: Division 3 – Runners-up 1993–94; Division 3 (N) – Runners-up 1935–36; Division 4 – Runners-up 1985–86.

Conference: Champions 2003–04.

FA Cup: best season: 5th rd, 1977, 1980.

Football League Cup: Semi-final 1975.

Welsh Cup: Winners 1908, 1933, 1947.

Debenhams Cup: Winners 1977.

SKY SPORTS FACT FILE

Gary Talbot scored a hat-trick in three minutes for Chester against Crewe Alexandra in a first round FA Cup tie on 14 November 1964. Chester won 5–0 with Mike Metcalf scoring the other two including one from the penalty spot.

Record League Victory: 12–0 v York C, Division 3 (N), 1 February 1936 – Middleton; Common, Hall; Wharton, Wilson, Howarth; Horsman (2), Hughes, Wrightson (4), Cresswell (2), Sargeant (4).

Record Cup Victory: 6–1 v Darlington, FA Cup 1st rd, 25 November 1933 – Burke; Bennett, Little; Pitcairn, Skitt, Duckworth; Armes (3), Whittam, Mantle (2), Cresswell (1), McLachlan.

Record Defeat: 2–11 v Oldham Ath, Division 3 (N), 19 January 1952.

Most League Points (2 for a win): 56, Division 3 (N), 1946–47 and Division 4, 1964–65.

Most League Points (3 for a win): 84, Division 4, 1985–86.

Most League Goals: 119, Division 4, 1964–65.

Highest League Scorer in Season: Dick Yates, 36, Division 3 (N), 1946–47.

Most League Goals in Total Aggregate: Stuart Rimmer, 135, 1985–88, 1991–98.

Most League Goals in One Match: 5, Tom Jennings v Walsall, Division 3N, 30 January 1932; 5, Barry Jepson v York C, Division 4, 8 February 1958.

Most Capped Player: Angus Eve, 35 (117), Trinidad & Tobago.

Most League Appearances: Ray Gill, 406, 1951–62.

Youngest League Player: Aidan Newhouse, 15 years 350 days v Bury, 7 May 1988.

Record Transfer Fee Received: £300,000 from Liverpool for Ian Rush, May 1980.

Record Transfer Fee Paid: £100,000 to Doncaster R for Gregg Blundell, August 2005.

Football League Record: 1931 Elected Division 3 (N); 1958–75 Division 4; 1975–82 Division 3; 1982–86 Division 4; 1986–92 Division 3; 1992–93 Division 2; 1993–94 Division 3; 1994–95 Division 2; 1995–2000 Division 3; 2000–04 Conference; 2004– FL2.

MANAGERS

Charlie Hewitt 1930–36
Alex Raisbeck 1936–38
Frank Brown 1938–53
Louis Page 1953–56
John Harris 1956–59
Stan Pearson 1959–61
Bill Lambton 1962–63
Peter Hauser 1963–68
Ken Roberts 1968–76
Alan Oakes 1976–82
Cliff Sear 1982
John Sainty 1982–83
John McGrath 1984
Mick Speight 1985
Harry McNally 1985–92
Graham Barrow 1992–94
Mike Pejic 1994–95
Derek Mann 1995
Kevin Ratcliffe 1995–99
Terry Smith 1999
Ian Atkins 2000
Graham Barrow 2000–01
Gordon Hill 2001
Steve Mungall 2001
Mark Wright 2002–04
Ian Rush 2004–05
Keith Curle 2005–06.
Mark Wright March 2006–

LATEST SEQUENCES

Longest Sequence of League Wins: 8, 12.4.1978 – 26.8.1978.

Longest Sequence of League Defeats: 9, 30.4.1994 – 13.9.1994.

Longest Sequence of League Draws: 6, 11.10.1986 – 1.11.1986.

Longest Sequence of Unbeaten League Matches: 18, 27.10.1934 – 16.2.1935.

Longest Sequence Without a League Win: 25, 19.9.1961 – 3.3.1962.

TEN YEAR LEAGUE RECORD

		P	W	D	L	F	A	Pts	Pos
1996-97	Div 3	46	18	16	12	55	43	70	6
1997-98	Div 3	46	17	10	19	60	61	61	14
1998-99	Div 3	46	13	18	15	57	66	57	14
1999-2000	Div 3	46	10	9	27	44	79	39	24
2000-01	Conf.	42	16	14	12	49	43	62	8
2001-02	Conf.	42	15	9	18	54	51	54	14
2002-03	Conf.	42	21	12	9	59	31	75	4
2003-04	Conf.	42	27	11	4	85	34	92	1
2004-05	FL 2	46	12	16	18	43	69	52	20
2005-06	FL 2	46	14	12	20	53	59	54	15

DID YOU KNOW ?

Chester City players must have had that feeling of *déjà vu* when playing at Port Vale in 1992–93. What used to the main stand at Sealand Road, their home for 84 years had been bought by Vale chairman Bill Bell for a knockdown £350,000.

CHESTER CITY 2005–06 LEAGUE RECORD

Match No.	*Date*	*Venue*	*Opponents*	*Result*	*H/T Score*	*Lg. Pos.*	*Goalscorers*	*Attendance*
1	Aug 6	A	Peterborough U	W 1-0	0-0	—	Drummond [70]	4980
2	9	H	Lincoln C	D 2-2	0-2	—	Davies [50], Branch (pen) [90]	2637
3	20	A	Rushden & D	D 1-1	0-0	10	Lowe [56]	2682
4	27	H	Darlington	D 4-4	0-2	11	Richardson 2 [47, 90], Blundell 2 [55, 89]	2469
5	29	A	Torquay U	W 1-0	0-0	9	Lowe [90]	2245
6	Sept 2	H	Mansfield T	W 3-1	1-0	—	Blundell 2 [2, 60], Lowe [80]	3079
7	6	H	Grimsby T	L 1-2	0-0	—	Lowe [53]	3095
8	10	A	Notts Co	D 1-1	0-0	5	Davies [70]	5404
9	17	H	Bristol R	W 4-0	3-0	4	Lowe [34], Artell [35], Richardson [45], Blundell [87]	2874
10	24	A	Stockport Co	D 0-0	0-0	4		4873
11	27	H	Carlisle U	W 2-0	2-0	—	Artell [11], Blundell [40]	3394
12	Oct 1	A	Wycombe W	D 3-3	2-2	4	Drummond [10], Branch 2 [36, 60]	5145
13	7	H	Rochdale	L 2-3	0-1	—	Drummond [54], Davies [57]	4327
14	15	A	Barnet	W 3-1	2-0	5	Branch [14], Lowe [44], Curtis [69]	2206
15	22	H	Bury	D 1-1	0-1	5	Lowe (pen) [78]	3471
16	29	A	Shrewsbury T	L 1-3	1-2	5	Lowe [35]	5430
17	Nov 12	H	Northampton T	D 0-0	0-0	6		3295
18	19	A	Rochdale	D 2-2	1-0	6	Bolland [20], Davies [64]	3618
19	26	H	Peterborough U	W 3-1	1-0	5	Branch (pen) [35], Drummond [53], Lowe [66]	2701
20	Dec 6	A	Leyton Orient	W 1-0	1-0	—	Drummond [45]	3463
21	10	A	Lincoln C	L 1-3	0-0	5	Richardson [49]	3563
22	17	H	Rushden & D	L 1-2	1-1	6	Davies (pen) [33]	2265
23	26	A	Cheltenham T	L 0-1	0-0	8		3819
24	31	A	Macclesfield T	L 0-1	0-0	8		2910
25	Jan 2	H	Oxford U	L 0-1	0-0	12		2624
26	14	H	Boston U	L 0-1	0-0	17		2956
27	21	A	Bristol R	L 1-2	0-2	17	Davies [89]	6310
28	24	A	Mansfield T	W 2-1	0-0	—	McNiven [54], Asamoah [69]	3219
29	28	H	Notts Co	L 0-2	0-0	15		2599
30	Feb 4	A	Carlisle U	L 0-5	0-2	17		6581
31	11	H	Stockport Co	L 1-2	0-0	17	Lowe [81]	3446
32	18	H	Leyton Orient	L 0-2	0-1	19		2210
33	25	A	Grimsby T	L 0-1	0-1	19		4058
34	Mar 7	H	Torquay U	D 1-1	0-1	—	Blundell [58]	1806
35	11	A	Darlington	L 0-1	0-0	21		3593
36	18	H	Cheltenham T	L 0-1	0-1	24		2281
37	26	A	Wrexham	L 1-2	0-2	24	Edwards [89]	7240
38	29	A	Boston U	W 3-1	1-0	—	Asamoah 3 [43, 50, 61]	1651
39	Apr 1	H	Macclesfield T	W 2-1	0-0	20	Asamoah 2 [50, 90]	2939
40	8	A	Oxford U	W 1-0	1-0	18	Asamoah [19]	5754
41	12	H	Wrexham	W 2-1	0-0	—	Davies (pen) [56], Asamoah [75]	4801
42	15	H	Wycombe W	W 1-0	0-0	15	Drummond [64]	2797
43	17	A	Bury	D 0-0	0-0	14		3421
44	22	H	Barnet	D 0-0	0-0	14		2367
45	29	A	Northampton T	L 0-1	0-1	16		7114
46	May 6	H	Shrewsbury T	L 0-1	0-1	15		3744

Final League Position: 15

GOALSCORERS

League (53): Lowe 10 (1 pen), Asamoah 8, Blundell 7, Davies 7 (2 pens), Drummond 6, Branch 5 (2 pens), Richardson 4, Artell 2, Bolland 1, Curtis 1, Edwards 1, McNiven 1.
Carling Cup (1): Davies 1.
FA Cup (7): Lowe 3 (1 pen), Richardson 2, Branch 1 (pen), Drummond 1.
Football League Trophy (0).

MacKenzie C 30	McNiven S 41	Regan C 39 + 2	Curtis T 34 + 6	Bolland P 12 + 4	Dimech L 27 + 3	Drummond S 41 + 1	Davies B 42 + 3	Richardson M 22 + 12	Branch M 23 + 4	Lowe R 28 + 4	Walker J 13 + 8	El Kholti A 7 + 15	Artell D 34 + 3	Vaughan S 7 + 10	Hessey S 17 + 2	Blundell G 23 + 7	Bertos L 2 + 3	Dove C 2 + 3	Curle T — + 2	Rutherford P 1 + 5	Brookfield R — + 1	Ruddy J 4	Gillet S 8	Asamoah D 14 + 3	Corden W 2	Roberts M 1	Robertson C — + 1	Horwood E 1	Tait P 3 + 6	Albrighton M 9	Ellender P 5	Harrison P 4	Edwards J 10	*Match No.*
1	2	3	4	5	6	7	8	9	10	11^{3}	12																							1
1	2^{2}	3	4^{1}	5	6	7	8	9^{3}	10	11	12	13	14																					2
1	2	3	12	5		7	8	9^{2}	10	11■	6^{1}		4	13																				3
1	2	3^{1}	13	5	6	7^{2}	8	14	10		4				12	9	11^{3}																	4
1	2	3	4	5		12	8	9^{3}	10	14			6	7^{1}		13	11^{2}																	5
1	2	3	4		6	7	8^{1}	13	10^{3}	11	12		5			9^{2}	14																	6
1	2^{1}	3	4	5	6	7	8^{2}	14	10	11			12			9^{3}	13																	7
1	2		4^{2}	5^{1}	12	7	13	9^{3}	10	11	8		6		3	14																		8
1	2		4^{1}		6	7	8^{2}	9^{3}		11	12		5	13	3	10		14																9
1	2	3	4		6	7^{2}	8	9^{1}	12	11			5	13		10																		10
1	2	3	12		6	7	8	13	10^{2}	11^{3}	4^{1}	14	5			9																		11
1	2	3	4		6	7	8	9^{1}	10	11^{2}	12		5			13																		12
1	2	3	4	12	6	7	8	10^{3}	11	13			5^{1}			9^{2}	14																	13
1	2	3^{2}	4		6	7■	8	9^{1}	10^{3}	11	12		5		13				14															14
1	2		4	12	6		8^{1}	9^{3}	10	11	7^{2}	14	5	13	3																			15
1	2		4		6		8	12	10	11	13		5	7^{2}	3			9^{1}																16
1	2	3	4		6	7	8	9^{1}	10	11		12	5																					17
1	2	3	4	6		7	8	9	10^{1}	11			5	12																				18
1	2	3			6	7	8	9^{1}	10^{2}	11	4	12	5							13														19
1	2	3	4	6	12	7	8	9^{1}		11^{3}	10^{2}	13	5					14																20
1^{6}	2	3	4	6		7	8	9		11	10^{1}	12	5								15													21
			2	5	6	7	8	9				3		11				4^{1}	12	10		1												22
	2	3	12	4		7	8	9		10		11^{2}	5	6^{1}						13		1												23
	2^{3}	3	4	12	6	7	8	9^{2}		11■	14	13	5			10^{1}						1												24
	2^{1}	3^{2}	4	12	6	7	8	9			11^{3}	13	5			10		14				1												25
	2	3	4^{2}			7	12	9^{3}	13		8^{1}	6	5			14							1	10	11									26
	2	3	4^{2}		6	7	12	13	10	11			5	14									1■	9^{3}	8^{1}									27
	2	3	4		6	7	8	12	13	11^{2}			5	14		10^{1}							1	9^{3}										28
	2	3	4		6^{1}	7	8	10^{2}		11			5■	12		13							1	9										29
	2	5				7	8	12	10^{2}	11				4		13							1	9^{1}		6^{3}	14	3						30
	2	3				7	8		12	13	4		5		6	10^{2}							1	11^{1}					9					31
	2	3^{1}	4		6	7	8	12	10		11^{2}		5			13							1	14					9^{3}					32
	2	3	4			7		12	10^{1}	11			13		8	9							1							5	6^{2}			33
	2	3^{3}	13			7	8	12		11^{2}					5	10								14					9^{1}	4	6	1		34
	2	3^{2}	10			7	8			11		12			5^{1}	9													13	4	6	1		35
	2	3^{2}	4^{3}			7	8	12	10	11		14		13		9^{1}														5	6	1		36
	2	3^{1}				7	8		9	12		11^{2}	5							13										4	6	1	10	37
1	2	3^{1}			12	7	8					11	5		6					13				10^{2}					14	4			9^{3}	38
1	2	3				7	8						5		6	9^{1}				12				10						4			11	39
1	2	3	12			7	8						5		6	9^{1}								11					13	4			10^{2}	40
1	2	12	3			7	8					13	5		6^{2}	9^{1}								11					14	4			10^{3}	41
1	2^{1}	12	3		4	7	8					13	5		6	9								11									10^{2}	42
1		3	4^{1}		6	7	8					12	5		2	9								11					13				10^{2}	43
1		3	4		6	7^{1}	8					12	5^{2}	13	2	9								11									10	44
1		3	4		5		8				7^{1}	11		2	6	9								12					13				10^{2}	45
1		3	2		5		8					11		4	6	9								7									10	46

FA Cup

First Round	Folkestone I	(h)	2-1
Second Round	Nottingham F	(h)	3-0
Third Round	Cheltenham T	(a)	2-2
		(h)	0-1

Carling Cup

First Round	Wolverhampton W	(a)	1-5

Football League Trophy

First Round	Cambridge U	(a)	0-3

CHESTERFIELD FL Championship 1

FOUNDATION

Chesterfield are fourth only to Stoke, Notts County and Nottingham Forest in age for they can trace their existence as far back as 1866, although it is fair to say that they were somewhat casual in the first few years of their history playing only a few friendlies a year. However, their rules of 1871 are still in existence showing an annual membership of 2s (10p), but it was not until 1891 that they won a trophy (the Barnes Cup) and followed this a year later by winning the Sheffield Cup, Barnes Cup and the Derbyshire Junior Cup.

The Recreation Ground, Saltergate, Chesterfield, Derbyshire S40 4SX.

Telephone: (01246) 209 765.

Fax: (01246) 556 799.

Ticket Office: (01246) 209 765.

Website: www.chesterfield-fc.co.uk

Email: reception@chesterfield-fc.co.uk

Ground Capacity: 8,502.

Record Attendance: 30,968 v Newcastle U, Division 2, 7 April 1939.

Pitch Measurements: 111yd × 71yd.

Chairman: Barrie Hubbard.

Vice-chairman: Jason Elliott.

Chief Executive/Managing Director: Mike Warner.

Secretary: Alan Walters.

Manager: Roy McFarland.

Assistant Manager: Lee Richardson.

Physio: Jamie Hewitt.

Colours: Blue shirts, white shorts, blue stockings.

Change Colours: Maroon shirts, white shorts, maroon stockings.

Year Formed: 1866.

Turned Professional: 1891.

Ltd Co: 1871.

Previous Name: Chesterfield Town.

Club Nicknames: 'Blues' or 'Spireites'.

First Football League Game: 2 September 1899, Division 2, v Sheffield W (a) L 1–5 – Hancock; Pilgrim, Fletcher; Ballantyne, Bell, Downie; Morley, Thacker, Gooing, Munday (1), Geary.

Record League Victory: 10–0 v Glossop NE, Division 2, 17 January 1903 – Clutterbuck; Thorpe, Lerper; Haig, Banner, Thacker; Tomlinson (2), Newton (1), Milward (3), Munday (2), Steel (2).

Record Cup Victory: 5–0 v Wath Ath (a), FA Cup 1st rd, 28 November 1925 – Birch; Saxby, Dennis; Wass, Abbott, Thompson; Fisher (1), Roseboom (1), Cookson (2), Whitfield (1), Hopkinson.

HONOURS

Football League: Division 2 best season: 4th, 1946–47; Division 3 (N) – Champions 1930–31, 1935–36; Runners-up 1933–34; Promoted to Division 2 (3rd) – 2000–01; Division 4 – Champions 1969–70, 1984–85.

FA Cup: Semi-final 1997.

Football League Cup: best season: 4th rd, 1965.

Anglo-Scottish Cup: Winners 1981.

SKY SPORTS FACT FILE

On 23 August 1952 the former England international centre-forward Dennis Westcott made his debut for Chesterfield against Mansfield Town and scored all four goals in the 4–1 win. It was the first foursome by a Chesterfield player on an opening day.

Record Defeat: 0–10 v Gillingham, Division 3, 5 September 1987.

Most League Points (2 for a win): 64, Division 4, 1969–70.

Most League Points (3 for a win): 91, Division 4, 1984–85.

Most League Goals: 102, Division 3 (N), 1930–31.

Highest League Scorer in Season: Jimmy Cookson, 44, Division 3 (N), 1925–26.

Most League Goals in Total Aggregate: Ernie Moss, 161, 1969–76, 1979–81 and 1984–86.

Most League Goals in One Match: 4, Jimmy Cookson v Accrington S, Division 3N, 16 January 1926; 4, Jimmy Cookson v Ashington, Division 3N, 1 May 1926; 4, Jimmy Cookson v Wigan Borough, Division 3N, 4 September 1926; 4, Tommy Lyon v Southampton, Division 2, 3 December 1938.

Most Capped Player: Walter McMillen, 4 (7), Northern Ireland; Mark Williams, 4 (30), Northern Ireland.

Most League Appearances: Dave Blakey, 613, 1948–67.

Youngest League Player: Dennis Thompson, 16 years 160 days v Notts Co, 26 December 1950.

Record Transfer Fee Received: £750,000 from Southampton for Kevin Davies, May 1997.

Record Transfer Fee Paid: £250,000 to Watford for Jason Lee, August 1998.

Football League Record: 1899 Elected to Division 2; 1909 failed re-election; 1921–31 Division 3 (N); 1931–33 Division 2; 1933–36 Division 3 (N); 1936–51 Division 2; 1951–58 Division 3 (N); 1958–61 Division 3; 1961–70 Division 4; 1970–83 Division 3; 1983–85 Division 4; 1985–89 Division 3; 1989–92 Division 4; 1992–95 Division 3; 1995–2000 Division 2; 2000–01 Division 3; 2001–04 Division 2; 2004– FL1.

MANAGERS

E. Russell Timmeus 1891–95
(Secretary-Manager)
Gilbert Gillies 1895–1901
E. F. Hind 1901–02
Jack Hoskin 1902–06
W. Furness 1906–07
George Swift 1907–10
G. H. Jones 1911–13
R. L. Weston 1913–17
T. Callaghan 1919
J. J. Caffrey 1920–22
Harry Hadley 1922
Harry Parkes 1922–27
Alec Campbell 1927
Ted Davison 1927–32
Bill Harvey 1932–38
Norman Bullock 1938–45
Bob Brocklebank 1945–48
Bobby Marshall 1948–52
Ted Davison 1952–58
Duggie Livingstone 1958–62
Tony McShane 1962–67
Jimmy McGuigan 1967–73
Joe Shaw 1973–76
Arthur Cox 1976–80
Frank Barlow 1980–83
John Duncan 1983–87
Kevin Randall 1987–88
Paul Hart 1988–91
Chris McMenemy 1991–93
John Duncan 1993–2000
Nicky Law 2000–02
Dave Rushbury 2002–03
Roy McFarland May 2003–

LATEST SEQUENCES

Longest Sequence of League Wins: 10, 6.9.1933 – 4.11.1933.

Longest Sequence of League Defeats: 9, 22.10.1960 – 27.12.1960.

Longest Sequence of League Draws: 8, 26.11.2005 – 2.1.2006.

Longest Sequence of Unbeaten League Matches: 21, 26.12.1994 – 29.4.1995.

Longest Sequence Without a League Win: 18, 11.9.1999 – 3.1.2000.

Successive Scoring Runs: 46 from 25.12.1929.

Successive Non-scoring Runs: 7 from 23.9.1977.

TEN YEAR LEAGUE RECORD

		P	W	D	L	F	A	Pts	Pos
1996-97	Div 2	46	18	14	14	42	39	68	10
1997-98	Div 2	46	16	17	13	46	44	65	10
1998-99	Div 2	46	17	13	16	46	44	64	9
1999-2000	Div 2	46	7	15	24	34	63	36	24
2000-01	Div 3	46	25	14	7	79	42	80*	3
2001-02	Div 2	46	13	13	20	53	65	52	18
2002-03	Div 2	46	14	8	24	43	73	50	20
2003-04	Div 2	46	12	15	19	49	71	51	20
2004-05	FL 1	46	14	15	17	55	62	57	17
2005-06	FL 1	46	14	14	18	63	73	56	16

**9 pts deducted.*

DID YOU KNOW ?

Right back Stan Milburn, a former miner, joined Chesterfield from Ashington in January 1947 and was understudying elder brother George. He made his League debut on 25 October 1947 v Barnsley, partnered his brother for five games then replaced him.

CHESTERFIELD 2005–06 LEAGUE RECORD

Match No.	Date	Venue	Opponents	Result		H/T Score	Lg. Pos.	Goalscorers	Attendance
1	Aug 6	A	Blackpool	W	3-1	2-1	—	Allison [23], De Bolla [39], Blatherwick [67]	6469
2	10	H	Brentford	L	1-3	1-1	—	Hall [27]	4121
3	13	H	Rotherham U	L	0-1	0-0	17		5189
4	20	A	Oldham Ath	L	1-4	0-2	23	Niven [51]	5347
5	27	H	Tranmere R	L	0-2	0-0	22		3445
6	29	A	Yeovil T	W	3-1	1-1	18	Hall [44], Smith 2 [53, 75]	6079
7	Sept 2	A	Bradford C	L	0-2	0-0	—		7351
8	10	H	Bournemouth	W	3-0	1-0	16	Larkin [27], Allison [53], Nicholson [79]	3540
9	17	A	Walsall	W	3-2	0-2	14	Allott 2 [55, 68], Allison [77]	5177
10	24	H	Hartlepool U	W	3-1	0-1	8	Larkin [54], Niven [67], Hall [79]	4078
11	27	A	Gillingham	L	0-1	0-0	—		7472
12	Oct 1	A	Colchester U	W	2-1	1-0	6	Larkin [25], Hall [49]	3414
13	15	A	Milton Keynes D	D	0-0	0-0	10		5642
14	22	H	Huddersfield T	W	4-3	3-0	8	Allison [11], Hall [30], Larkin [45], Nicholson (pen) [85]	6206
15	26	H	Bristol C	W	3-0	0-0	—	Allison [57], Nicholson 2 (1 pen) [66, 88 (p)]	5027
16	29	A	Swansea C	L	1-5	1-4	7	Blatherwick [21]	13,264
17	Nov 12	H	Port Vale	W	2-0	1-0	5	Allison 2 [31, 67]	4714
18	19	A	Bristol C	W	4-2	3-1	4	Hall 3 (1 pen) [18, 30 (p), 61], Hurst [25]	9752
19	26	H	Blackpool	D	1-1	1-0	5	Clingan [8]	4585
20	Dec 6	A	Southend U	D	0-0	0-0	—		5767
21	10	A	Brentford	D	1-1	1-0	7	Hall [19]	5828
22	17	H	Oldham Ath	D	1-1	0-0	7	Allison [69]	4304
23	26	A	Scunthorpe U	D	2-2	1-0	7	Hall [4], Nicholson (pen) [58]	5866
24	28	H	Swindon T	D	1-1	1-0	7	Hall [19]	4265
25	31	A	Nottingham F	D	0-0	0-0	7		21,909
26	Jan 2	H	Barnsley	D	0-0	0-0	7		6046
27	7	H	Bradford C	W	1-0	0-0	6	Smith [89]	4449
28	14	A	Doncaster R	D	1-1	0-1	6	Allison [63]	6528
29	21	H	Walsall	D	2-2	1-1	7	Allison [36], Hurst [80]	4666
30	28	A	Bournemouth	W	2-1	1-0	7	Allison [25], O'Hara [74]	5837
31	Feb 4	H	Gillingham	D	1-1	0-0	7	Hall [89]	4652
32	10	A	Hartlepool U	L	0-1	0-0	—		4596
33	15	H	Doncaster R	L	0-1	0-1	—		5719
34	18	H	Southend U	L	3-4	1-0	8	Larkin [27], Niven [63], Hurst [66]	4527
35	25	A	Rotherham U	W	4-0	1-0	8	Hurst [45], Niven [49], Allott [54], O'Hara [87]	6919
36	Mar 4	H	Yeovil T	L	0-3	0-1	8		4843
37	11	A	Tranmere R	L	1-4	1-3	8	O'Hara [30]	6435
38	18	H	Scunthorpe U	L	1-2	1-0	9	Larkin [15]	4406
39	25	A	Swindon T	L	0-2	0-0	10		5661
40	Apr 1	H	Nottingham F	L	1-3	1-2	13	Picken [33]	7073
41	8	A	Barnsley	D	1-1	0-1	14	Niven [76]	8303
42	15	H	Colchester U	D	2-2	2-1	15	O'Hara [3], Hall (pen) [18]	3649
43	18	A	Huddersfield T	W	2-1	0-1	—	Hall 2 [54, 68]	13,368
44	22	H	Milton Keynes D	L	1-2	0-1	13	Larkin [50]	3965
45	29	A	Port Vale	L	1-3	1-2	15	O'Hara [3]	4478
46	May 6	H	Swansea C	L	0-4	0-2	16		6294

Final League Position: 16

GOALSCORERS

League (63): Hall 15 (2 pens), Allison 11, Larkin 7, Nicholson 5 (3 pens), Niven 5, O'Hara 5, Hurst 4, Allott 3, Smith 3, Blatherwick 2, Clingan 1, De Bolla 1, Picken 1.
Carling Cup (2): Hurst 1, Niven 1.
FA Cup (1): Hurst 1.
Football League Trophy (0).

Roche B 41	Bailey A 17 + 1	Nicholson S 24 + 1	Downes A 20 + 2	Blatherwick S 29 + 1	Davies G 13 + 7	Hall P 44 + 1	Allott M 43	De Bolla M 2 + 2	Allison W 26 + 6	Smith A 10 + 16	Folan C 8 + 19	Hazell R 30 + 3	Niven D 42	O'Hare A 15 + 7	N'Toya T 1 + 3	Kovacs J 9	Larkin C 31 + 10	Picken P 32	Hurst K 30 + 7	Lancaster S — + 1	Clingan S 14 + 7	O'Hara J 19	Muggleton C 3	Heath C 1 + 3	Beckwith R 2	Foyle A — + 1	Jackson J — + 2	*Match No.*
1	2	3	4	5	6	7	8	9¹	10	11²	12	13																1
1		3	4¹	5		7	8	9³	10²	11	14	2	6	12	13													2
1		3		5		7	8		13	11¹	9	2	6		10²	4	12											3
1		3				7	8		10¹		12	13	6³	5		4²	9	2	11	14								4
1		3		5		7	8		10¹	13	12		6			4	9	2	11²									5
1		3		5	11	7³	8		12	13	9¹	4	6	14				2	10²									6
1		3		5	11³	7¹	8			12	9²	4	6				13	2	10		14							7
1		3		5	2	7³	8		10²	12	13	4	6				9¹		11		14							8
1		3		5	2	7	8		12	13	9¹	4	6				14		10²		11³							9
1		3			2	7	8	12	10			4	6	5			9¹		11²		13							10
1				5	2	7²	8	12			9¹	4	6	3			10		13		11							11
1		3		5	2	7	8		10			4	6				9		11¹		12							12
1	12	3		5	2¹	7	8		10	13		4	6				9²		11³		14							13
1	2	3		5		7²	8		10	12		4	6				9		11¹		13							14
1	2	3		5		7¹	8		10			4	6				9		11		12							15
1	2	3		5	13	7	8		10²	12		4					9		11¹		6							16
1	2¹	3		5	12	7	8		10			4	6				9		11									17
1	2			5	12	7	8					4	6				9	3	10¹		11							18
1	2	3■		5	12	7	8				13	4	6				9¹		10²		11							19
1	2¹			5	12	7	8		10²		13	4	6				14	3	9³		11							20
1				5		7	8		10¹		12	4	6	3				2	9		11							21
1			12	5	6¹	7			10³	13	14	4		2			9	3	8²		11							22
1		3		5		7	8		10	12		4	6					2	9¹		11							23
1		3		5		7³	8			10²	14	4	6		12		9¹	2	13		11							24
1		3		5		7	8			10²	12	4	6				9¹	2	13		11							25
1		3		5		7	8			10¹	13	4	6		12		9²	2			11							26
1		3		5²		7			10	8	12	4	6	13			9¹	2			11							27
1		3	4			7			10	9¹			6	5			12	2			11	8						28
1		3¹	12			7	8		10			4	6	5			9²	2	13			11						29
1			5		3	7¹	8		10			4	6				12	2	9			11						30
1			5		2	7	8		10			4	6¹				12	3	9			11						31
1			5		2²	7	8		12		9	4¹	6	13			14	3	10			11³						32
1			5			7	8		10²	12	13			2		4	9	3	11¹			6						33
1			5	12		7	8				13		6	2		4■	9²	3	10¹			11						34
	2		4	5		7	8				12		6				9¹	3	10			11	1					35
	2		4	5		7	8			12	13		6³				9²	3	10¹			11	1	14				36
	2		4	5		7	8			12	13		6²				9³	3	10¹			11	1	14				37
	2		4	5²			8		10¹		12		6	13			9	3	11			7			1			38
	2		5			7¹	8			10²	9		6	4³			12	3	13			11			1	14		39
1	2		5			7¹	8		10²				6	4			9	3	12			11		13				40
1	2³		5		12	7	8				10		6	13		4	9²	3	14			11¹						41
1	2³		5		14	7¹	8		12	13			6	3		4	9²	11				10						42
1	2²		5			7¹	8		10				6	13		4	12	3	9			11						43
1			5			12	8			13		14	6²	2		4³	9	3	10			11		7¹				44
1		12	5			7	8		13	10		4¹	6²	3			9³	2				11					14	45
1			5			7²	8		10	12		4	6¹	3			9	2				11					13	46

FA Cup

First Round	Leyton Orient	(a)	0-0
		(h)	1-2

Carling Cup

First Round	Huddersfield T	(h)	2-4

Football League Trophy

First Round	Macclesfield T	(a)	0-2

COLCHESTER UNITED FL Championship

FOUNDATION

Colchester United was formed in 1937 when a number of enthusiasts of the much older Colchester Town club decided to establish a professional concern as a limited liability company. The new club continued at Layer Road which had been the amateur club's home since 1909.

Layer Road, Colchester, Essex CO2 7JJ.

Telephone: 0871 226 2161.

Fax: (01206) 715 327.

Ticket Office: 0871 226 2161.

Website: www.cu-fc.com

Email: caroline@colchesterunited.net

Ground Capacity: 6,189.

Record Attendance: 19,072 v Reading, FA Cup 1st rd, 27 November 1948.

Pitch Measurements: 111yd × 71yd.

Chairman: Peter Heard.

Chief Executive: Mrs Marie Partner.

Secretary: Miss Caroline Pugh.

Manager: TBC.

Assistant Manager: Geraint Williams.

Physio: Stuart Ayles.

Colours: Blue and white striped shirts, white shorts, white stockings.

Change Colours: Red with black trim shirts, red with black trim shorts, red stockings.

Year Formed: 1937.

Turned Professional: 1937.

Ltd Co.: 1937.

Club Nickname: 'The U's'.

First Football League Game: 19 August 1950, Division 3 (S), v Gillingham (a) D 0–0 – Wright; Kettle, Allen; Bearryman, Stewart, Elder; Jones, Curry, Turner, McKim, Church.

Record League Victory: 9–1 v Bradford C, Division 4, 30 December 1961 – Ames; Millar, Fowler; Harris, Abrey, Ron Hunt; Foster, Bobby Hunt (4), King (4), Hill (1), Wright.

Record Cup Victory: 9-1 v Leamington, FA Cup 1st rd, 5 November 2005 – Davison; Stockley (Garcia), Duguid, Brown (1), Chilvers, Watson (1), Halford (1), Izzet (Danns) (2), Iwelumo (1) (Williams), Cureton (2), Yeates (1).

Record Defeat: 0–8 v Leyton Orient, Division 4, 15 October 1989.

HONOURS

Football League: Promoted from Division 3 – 1997–98 (play-offs); Division 4 – Runners-up 1961–62; Championship 1 – Runners-up 2005–06.

FA Cup: best season: 6th rd, 1971.

Football League Cup: best season: 5th rd, 1975.

Auto Windscreens Shield: Runners-up 1997.

GM Vauxhall Conference: Winners 1991–92.

FA Trophy: Winners 1992.

SKY SPORTS FACT FILE

Ted Phillips scored goals in all four divisions of the Football League in 18 months from April 1964, for Ipswich Town (Div 1), Orient (Div 2), Luton Town (Div 3) and then a hat-trick for Colchester United (Div 4) v Barnsley on 11 September 1965.

Most League Points (2 for a win): 60, Division 4, 1973–74.

Most League Points (3 for a win): 81, Division 4, 1982–83.

Most League Goals: 104, Division 4, 1961–62.

Highest League Scorer in Season: Bobby Hunt, 38, Division 4, 1961–62.

Most League Goals in Total Aggregate: Martyn King, 130, 1956–64.

Most League Goals in One Match: 4, Bobby Hunt v Bradford C, Division 4, 30 December 1961; 4, Martyn King v Bradford C, Division 4, 30 December 1961; 4, Bobby Hunt v Doncaster R, Division 4, 30 April 1962.

Most Capped Player: None.

Most League Appearances: Micky Cook, 613, 1969–84.

Youngest League Player: Lindsay Smith, 16 years 218 days v Grimsby T, 24 April 1971.

Record Transfer Fee Received: £2,250,000 from Newcastle U for Lomano Lua-Lua, September 2000.

Record Transfer Fee Paid: £50,000 to Ipswich T for Neil Gregory, March 1998 and £50,000 to Norwich C for Adrian Coote, December 2001.

Football League Record: 1950 Elected to Division 3 (S); 1958–61 Division 3; 1961–62 Division 4; 1962–65 Division 3; 1965–66 Division 4; 1966–68 Division 3; 1968–74 Division 4; 1974–76 Division 3, 1976–77 Division 4; 1977–81 Division 3; 1981–90 Division 4; 1990–92 GM Vauxhall Conference; 1992–98 Division 3; 1998–04 Division 2; 2004–06 FL1; 2006– FLC.

MANAGERS

Ted Fenton 1946–48
Jimmy Allen 1948–53
Jack Butler 1953–55
Benny Fenton 1955–63
Neil Franklin 1963–68
Dick Graham 1968–72
Jim Smith 1972–75
Bobby Roberts 1975–82
Allan Hunter 1982–83
Cyril Lea 1983–86
Mike Walker 1986–87
Roger Brown 1987–88
Jock Wallace 1989
Mick Mills 1990
Ian Atkins 1990–91
Roy McDonough 1991–94
George Burley 1994
Steve Wignall 1995–99
Mick Wadsworth 1999
Steve Whitton 1999–2003
Phil Parkinson 2003–06

LATEST SEQUENCES

Longest Sequence of League Wins: 7, 29.11.1968 – 1.2.1969.

Longest Sequence of League Defeats: 8, 9.10.1954 – 4.12.1954.

Longest Sequence of League Draws: 6, 21.3.1977 – 11.4.1977.

Longest Sequence of Unbeaten League Matches: 20, 22.12.1956 – 19.4.1957.

Longest Sequence Without a League Win: 20, 2.3.1968 – 31.8.1968.

Successive Scoring Runs: 24 from 15.9.1962.

Successive Non-scoring Runs: 5 from 7.4.1981.

TEN YEAR LEAGUE RECORD

		P	*W*	*D*	*L*	*F*	*A*	*Pts*	*Pos*
1996-97	Div 3	46	17	17	12	62	51	68	8
1997-98	Div 3	46	21	11	14	72	60	74	4
1998-99	Div 2	46	12	16	18	52	70	52	18
1999-2000	Div 2	46	14	10	22	59	82	52	18
2000-01	Div 2	46	15	12	19	55	59	57	17
2001-02	Div 2	46	15	12	19	65	76	57	15
2002-03	Div 2	46	14	16	16	52	56	58	12
2003-04	Div 2	46	17	13	16	52	56	64	11
2004-05	FL 1	46	14	17	15	60	50	59	15
2005-06	FL 1	46	22	13	11	58	40	79	2

DID YOU KNOW?

Colchester-born winger Barrie Aitchison graduated at Tottenham Hotspur and signed professional forms in January 1955. But he had to move back home to Colchester United in August 1964 before he managed to make his first Football League appearance.

COLCHESTER UNITED 2005–06 LEAGUE RECORD

Match No.	*Date*		*Venue*	*Opponents*	*Result*		*H/T Score*	*Lg. Pos.*	*Goalscorers*	*Attendance*
1	Aug	6	A	Gillingham	L	1-2	0-0	—	Danns[50]	7293
2		9	H	Swansea C	L	1-2	0-1	—	Halford[67]	2950
3		13	H	Barnsley	W	1-0	0-0	18	Iwelumo[48]	2721
4		20	A	Milton Keynes D	D	1-1	0-1	18	Chilvers[79]	4423
5		27	H	Oldham Ath	D	0-0	0-0	18		2742
6		29	A	Southend U	L	1-3	1-2	22	Stockley[19]	7344
7	Sept	3	A	Bristol C	D	0-0	0-0	20		10,180
8		10	H	Doncaster R	W	3-2	3-1	15	Iwelumo[1], McDaid (og)[23], Foster (og)[27]	2721
9		17	A	Port Vale	W	1-0	1-0	13	Iwelumo[34]	5166
10		24	H	Huddersfield T	D	1-1	0-0	15	Elokobi[49]	3415
11		27	A	Bradford C	D	1-1	0-0	—	Halford[62]	6891
12	Oct	1	H	Chesterfield	L	1-2	0-1	16	Iwelumo[90]	3414
13		9	A	Blackpool	W	2-1	1-0	—	Halford 2[16, 90]	4793
14		15	H	Bournemouth	L	0-1	0-0	15		3120
15		22	A	Tranmere R	D	0-0	0-0	16		6612
16		29	H	Yeovil T	W	3-2	1-1	13	Iwelumo 2[43, 90], Cureton[68]	3409
17	Nov	12	A	Rotherham U	W	2-1	0-1	11	Barker (og)[55], Iwelumo[85]	3715
18		19	H	Blackpool	W	3-2	1-0	8	Iwelumo 2 (1 pen)[34, 54 (p)], Halford[81]	3031
19		26	H	Gillingham	W	5-0	1-0	7	Halford 2[32, 52], Cureton 2[54, 66], Brown[70]	3801
20	Dec	6	A	Hartlepool U	W	1-0	0-0	—	Cureton[59]	3375
21		10	A	Swansea C	D	1-1	1-1	6	Iwelumo[13]	13,230
22		17	H	Milton Keynes D	W	2-0	1-0	4	Danns[13], Iwelumo (pen)[90]	3400
23		26	A	Swindon T	L	0-1	0-0	6		5531
24		31	A	Brentford	W	2-0	1-0	5	Yeates 2[30, 86]	6397
25	Jan	2	H	Nottingham F	W	3-1	0-0	4	Danns[71], Yeates[89], Garcia[90]	5767
26		14	A	Walsall	W	2-0	0-0	4	Danns[76], Iwelumo[88]	5464
27		17	H	Bristol C	W	3-2	2-1	—	Williams[27], Danns 2[45, 61]	4022
28		21	H	Port Vale	W	2-1	0-0	1	Garcia 2[74, 87]	4316
29	Feb	4	H	Bradford C	W	3-1	1-1	2	Garcia 2[41, 56], Iwelumo[63]	4503
30		7	H	Scunthorpe U	W	1-0	1-0	—	Iwelumo[45]	4416
31		11	A	Huddersfield T	L	0-2	0-1	2		13,515
32		14	H	Walsall	D	0-0	0-0	—		3810
33		25	A	Barnsley	L	0-1	0-0	3		9411
34	Mar	4	H	Southend U	L	0-3	0-3	5		5920
35		11	A	Oldham Ath	L	0-1	0-0	6		5822
36		18	H	Swindon T	W	1-0	1-0	5	Iwelumo (pen)[14]	3767
37		21	A	Doncaster R	D	0-0	0-0	—		4262
38		25	A	Scunthorpe U	D	0-0	0-0	4		4608
39	Apr	1	H	Brentford	D	1-1	1-1	4	Iwelumo[31]	5635
40		8	A	Nottingham F	L	0-1	0-0	4		22,680
41		11	H	Hartlepool U	W	2-0	0-0	—	Danns 2[83, 90]	3916
42		15	A	Chesterfield	D	2-2	1-2	3	Yeates[45], Iwelumo[73]	3649
43		17	H	Tranmere R	W	1-0	0-0	2	Brown[63]	4757
44		22	A	Bournemouth	W	2-1	1-1	2	Chilvers[5], Vernon[51]	6231
45		29	H	Rotherham U	W	2-0	1-0	2	Barker (og)[29], Yeates[53]	5741
46	May	6	A	Yeovil T	D	0-0	0-0	2		8785

Final League Position: 2

GOALSCORERS

League (58): Iwelumo 17 (3 pens), Danns 8, Halford 7, Garcia 5, Yeates 5, Cureton 4, Brown 2, Chilvers 2, Elokobi 1, Stockley 1, Vernon 1, Williams 1, own goals 4.
Carling Cup (0).
FA Cup (17): Danns 5, Cureton 3, Iwelumo 2, Brown 1, Garcia 1, Halford 1, Watson 1, Williams 1, Yeates 1, own goal 1.
Football League Trophy (7): Danns 3, Garcia 2, Duguid 1, Elokobi 1.

Davison A 41	Stockley S 21 + 6	Duguid K 26 + 9	Brown W 38	Chilvers L 33 + 1	Baldwin P 20 + 5	Izzet K 19 + 14	Danns N 38 + 3	Iwelumo C 46	Halford G 45	Watson K 43 + 1	Yeates M 42 + 2	Williams G 6 + 12	Howell D 1 + 3	Guy J — + 2	Gerken D 5 + 2	Elokobi G 10 + 2	White J 32 + 3	Richards G 12 + 3	King R — + 3	Hunt S — + 2	Garcia R 9 + 13	Cureton J 7 + 1	Thorpe T 5 + 9	Vernon S 4 + 3	Clarke B 2 + 4	Campbell-Ryce J 1 + 3	Match No.
1	2	3	4	5	6^{1}	7^{2}	8	9	10	11	12	13															1
1	2	3^{2}	4	5		7^{3}	8	9	6	11^{1}	10	12	13	14													2
1	2	3	4	5	6	7	8	9	10		11^{1}	12															3
1■	2	3	4	5	6	7	8	9	10		11^{G}				15												4
	2		4	5		7	8^{2}	9	10	6	11^{1}	12	13		1	3^{3}	14										5
	2		4	5		7		9	10^{2}	6	11	12	8^{1}	13	1	3^{3}	14										6
1			4■		6^{2}	7		9	8	11	10^{1}		12			3	5	2	13								7
1	12				6	7		9	8	4	11^{3}	10				3^{2}	2^{1}	5	13	14							8
1	2			5	12	7		9	8	11		10^{2}				3	4	6^{1}		13							9
1	12			5	13	7		9	8	6	11^{3}	10				3	2^{1}	4^{2}			14						10
1	2			5		7	12	9	10	6	11^{1}					3	8	4									11
1	12			5		7	13	9	8	6^{2}	11	10^{1}				3	2^{3}	4			14						12
1	2		4^{2}	5		7	8^{1}	9	10	6	11						3	13			12						13
1	2		4	5		7	8	9	10	6	11^{1}	12					3										14
1	2	12	4	5		7	8^{2}	9	10	6	11^{1}						3					13					15
1	2^{3}	12	4	5		7^{2}	13	9	8	6	11						3^{1}				14	10					16
1	2	12	4	5		7	8	9	10	6	11^{2}						3^{1}				13						17
1	2	12	4	5		13	8^{2}	9	7	6	11^{1}						3				14	10^{3}					18
1	2	12	4	5		13	8^{2}	9	7^{3}	6	11						3				14	10^{1}					19
1	2	12	4	5		13	8^{2}	9	7	6	11^{1}						3				14	10^{3}					20
1	2	12	4	5			8	9	7	6	11^{1}						3				13	10^{2}					21
1	2	12	4	5			8	9	7	6	11^{1}						3				13	10^{2}					22
1	2		4	5		12	8^{1}	9	7	6	11						3				10						23
1		12	4	5		13	8^{2}	9	7	6	11^{1}					2	3				14	10^{3}					24
1	2	11	4	5		12	8^{1}	9		6	10						3				7						25
1		2	4		5^{3}	12	8^{1}	9	7	6	11	13					3	14			10^{2}						26
1		2	4		5	12	8^{1}	9	7^{3}	6	11	10^{2}					3				13		14				27
1^{G}		2	4		5		8	9	7	6	11	10^{1}			15		3^{2}				12		13				28
1		2			5		8^{2}	9	7	6	11	12					3	4	13		10^{1}						29
1	12	2			5		8	9	7	6	11^{1}	13					3	4			10^{2}						30
1		2	5		12		8	9	7	6	11^{1}	13				14	3^{3}	4■			10^{2}						31
1	12	2	4		5		8	9	7	6	11	13					3^{1}				10^{2}						32
1	12	2	4		5		8	9	7	6^{2}	11	13				3^{1}					10						33
1		2	4	5		6^{2}	8	9	7	12	11						3^{1}				10		13				34
1	2	3	4	5		6■	8^{2}	9	7	11	10^{1}					12							13				35
1		3	4	5	2	12	8	9	7	6	11^{2}						13						10^{1}				36
1		11	4	5	2	12	8^{1}	9^{3}	7	6	13						3						10^{2}	14			37
1		3	4		2	12	8^{1}	9	7	6	11							5					10^{2}		13		38
1		3	4		2		8	9	7	6	11							5					10^{1}		12		39
1		3	4	12	2		8	9	7	6	11^{3}							5^{1}						10^{2}	13	14	40
1		3	4	5	2^{2}		8	9^{1}	7	6	11							12					13		10		41
1		3	4	5	2^{3}		8	9^{1}	7	6	11												10^{2}	12	13	14	42
1		2	4	5			8	9^{1}	7	6	11						3^{3}						13	12	10^{2}	14	43
		2	4	5	12	13	8^{2}	9	7	6	11				1		3^{1}						14	10^{3}			44
		2	4	5	12	13	8^{2}	9	7	6	11^{1}				1		3						14	10^{3}			45
		2		5	4	12	8	9	7	6					1		3						13	10^{2}		11^{1}	46

FA Cup

First Round	Leamington	(h)	9-1
Second Round	Shrewsbury T	(a)	2-1
Third Round	Sheffield U	(a)	2-1
Fourth Round	Derby Co	(h)	3-1
Fifth Round	Chelsea	(a)	1-3

Carling Cup

First Round	Cardiff C	(h)	0-2

Football League Trophy

Second Round	Northampton T	(h)	3-2
Quarter-Final	Milton Keynes D	(a)	2-1
Semi-Final	Cheltenham T	(a)	1-0
Southern Final	Swansea C	(a)	0-1
		(h)	1-2

COVENTRY CITY FL Championship

FOUNDATION

Workers at Singers' cycle factory formed a club in 1883. The first success of Singers' FC was to win the Birmingham Junior Cup in 1891 and this led in 1894 to their election to the Birmingham and District League. Four years later they changed their name to Coventry City and joined the Southern League in 1908 at which time they were playing in blue and white quarters.

Ricoh Arena, Phoenix Way, Foleshill, Coventry CV6 6GE.

Telephone: 0870 421 1987.

Fax: 0870 421 1988.

Ticket Office: 0870 421 1 987 (option 1).

Website: www.ccfc.co.uk

Email: info@ccfc.co.uk

Ground Capacity: 32,000.

Record Attendance: 51,455 v Wolverhampton W, Division 2, 29 April 1967.

Pitch Measurements: 110yd × 75yd (at Highfield Road).

Chairman: Geoffrey Robinson MP (acting chairman).

Chief Executive: Paul Fletcher

Secretary: Roger Brinsford.

Manager: Micky Adams.

Assistant Manager: Adrian Heath.

Physio: Michael McBride.

Colours: All sky blue.

Change Colours: Red and black.

Year Formed: 1883.

Turned Professional: 1893.

Ltd Co.: 1907.

Previous Names: 1883, Singers FC; 1898, Coventry City FC.

Club Nickname: 'Sky Blues'.

Previous Grounds: 1883, Binley Road; 1887, Stoke Road; 1899, Highfield Road.

First Football League Game: 30 August 1919, Division 2, v Tottenham H (h) L 0–5 – Lindon; Roberts, Chaplin, Allan, Hawley, Clarke, Sheldon, Mercer, Sambrooke, Lowes, Gibson.

Record League Victory: 9–0 v Bristol C, Division 3 (S), 28 April 1934 – Pearson; Brown, Bisby; Perry, Davidson, Frith; White (2), Lauderdale, Bourton (5), Jones (2), Lake.

Record Cup Victory: 8–0 v Rushden & D, League Cup 2nd rd, 2 October 2002 – Debec; Caldwell, Quinn, Betts (1p), Konjic (Shaw), Davenport, Pipe, Safri (Stanford), Mills (2) (Bothroyd (2)), McSheffery (3), Partridge.

HONOURS

Football League: Division 1 best season: 6th, 1969–70; Division 2 – Champions 1966–67; Division 3 – Champions 1963–64; Division 3 (S) – Champions 1935–36; Runners-up 1933–34; Division 4 – Runners-up 1958–59.

FA Cup: Winners 1987.

Football League Cup: Semi-final 1981, 1990.

European Competitions: *European Fairs Cup:* 1970–71.

SKY SPORTS FACT FILE

Billy Frith was a pre-war and wartime half-back with Coventry City. Injury having apparently ended his career, he became Port Vale manager in August 1945. He resigned in October 1946 to return to play for City, later becoming their manager and a JP!

Record Defeat: 2–10 v Norwich C, Division 3 (S), 15 March 1930.

Most League Points (2 for a win): 60, Division 4, 1958–59 and Division 3, 1963–64.

Most League Points (3 for a win): 66, Division 1, 2001–02.

Most League Goals: 108, Division 3 (S), 1931–32.

Highest League Scorer in Season: Clarrie Bourton, 49, Division 3 (S), 1931–32.

Most League Goals in Total Aggregate: Clarrie Bourton, 171, 1931–37.

Most League Goals in One Match: 5, Clarrie Bourton v Bournemouth, Division 3S, 17 October 1931; 5, Arthur Bacon v Gillingham, Division 3S, 30 December 1933.

Most Capped Player: Magnus Hedman 44 (56), Sweden.

Most League Appearances: Steve Ogrizovic, 507, 1984–2000.

Youngest League Player: Ben Mackey, 16 years 167 days v Ipswich T, 12 April 2003.

Record Transfer Fee Received: £12,500,000 from Internazionale for Robbie Keane, July 2000.

Record Transfer Fee Paid: £6,000,000 to Wolverhampton W for Robbie Keane, August 1999.

Football League Record: 1919 Elected to Division 2; 1925–26 Division 3 (N); 1926–36 Division 3 (S); 1936–52 Division 2; 1952–58 Division 3 (S); 1958–59 Division 4; 1959–64 Division 3; 1964–67 Division 2; 1967–92 Division 1; 1992–2001 FA Premier League; 2001–04 Division 1; 2004– FLC.

LATEST SEQUENCES

Longest Sequence of League Wins: 6, 25.4.1964 – 5.9.1964.

Longest Sequence of League Defeats: 9, 30.8.1919 – 11.10.1919.

Longest Sequence of League Draws: 6, 1.11.2003 – 29.11.2003.

Longest Sequence of Unbeaten League Matches: 25, 26.11.1966 – 13.5.1967.

Longest Sequence Without a League Win: 19, 30.8.1919 – 20.12.1919.

Successive Scoring Runs: 25 from 10.9.1966.

Successive Non-scoring Runs: 11 from 11.10.1919.

MANAGERS

H. R. Buckle 1909–10
Robert Wallace 1910–13
(Secretary-Manager)
Frank Scott-Walford 1913–15
William Clayton 1917–19
H. Pollitt 1919–20
Albert Evans 1920–24
Jimmy Kerr 1924–28
James McIntyre 1928–31
Harry Storer 1931–45
Dick Bayliss 1945–47
Billy Frith 1947–48
Harry Storer 1948–53
Jack Fairbrother 1953–54
Charlie Elliott 1954–55
Jesse Carver 1955–56
Harry Warren 1956–57
Billy Frith 1957–61
Jimmy Hill 1961–67
Noel Cantwell 1967–72
Bob Dennison 1972
Joe Mercer 1972–75
Gordon Milne 1972–81
Dave Sexton 1981–83
Bobby Gould 1983–84
Don Mackay 1985–86
George Curtis 1986–87
(became Managing Director)
John Sillett 1987–90
Terry Butcher 1990–92
Don Howe 1992
Bobby Gould 1992–93
Phil Neal 1993–95
Ron Atkinson 1995–96
(became Director of Football)
Gordon Strachan 1996–2001
Roland Nilsson 2001–02
Gary McAllister 2002–04
Eric Black 2004
Peter Reid 2004–05
Micky Adams January 2005–

TEN YEAR LEAGUE RECORD

		P	W	D	L	F	A	Pts	Pos
1996-97	PR Lge	38	9	14	15	38	54	41	17
1997-98	PR Lge	38	12	16	10	46	44	52	11
1998-99	PR Lge	38	11	9	18	39	51	42	15
1999-2000	PR Lge	38	12	8	18	47	54	44	14
2000-01	PR Lge	38	8	10	20	36	63	34	19
2001-02	Div 1	46	20	6	20	59	53	66	11
2002-03	Div 1	46	12	14	20	46	62	50	20
2003-04	Div 1	46	17	14	15	67	54	65	12
2004-05	FL C	46	13	13	20	61	73	52	19
2005-06	FL C	46	16	15	15	62	65	63	8

DID YOU KNOW

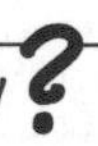

On 11 April 1931 Coventry City set off for a fixture at Exeter City but missed their connection at Gloucester. The players changed on the train, arrived four minutes late yet after a 15 minute delayed start managed to recover to win 3–2.

COVENTRY CITY 2005–06 LEAGUE RECORD

Match No.	*Date*	*Venue*	*Opponents*	*Result*		*H/T Score*	*Lg. Pos.*	*Goalscorers*	*Attendance*
1	Aug 6	A	Norwich C	D	1-1	0-1	—	Adebola [65]	25,355
2	9	A	Millwall	D	0-0	0-0	—		8344
3	13	A	Burnley	L	0-4	0-2	22		11,683
4	20	H	QPR	W	3-0	3-0	15	Jorgensen [11], Adebola 2 [24, 44]	23,000
5	27	A	Sheffield U	L	1-2	1-1	15	Scowcroft [24]	17,739
6	29	H	Southampton	D	1-1	1-1	15	Scowcroft [6]	23,000
7	Sept 10	H	Reading	D	1-1	0-0	17	Page [87]	22,074
8	14	A	Derby Co	D	1-1	0-1	—	Adebola [57]	21,840
9	17	A	Brighton & HA	D	2-2	1-0	16	McShane (og) [39], Jorgensen [50]	6529
10	24	H	Hull C	L	0-2	0-1	19		21,161
11	28	H	Watford	W	3-1	2-0	—	Adebola [2], Flood [20], McSheffrey [86]	16,978
12	Oct 1	A	Sheffield W	L	2-3	1-2	18	McSheffrey (pen) [33], Morrell [74]	22,732
13	15	H	Crystal Palace	L	1-4	1-2	20	Heath [45]	24,438
14	18	A	Ipswich T	D	2-2	1-2	—	McSheffrey [45], Nalis [56]	22,656
15	23	A	Leicester C	L	1-2	1-1	21	McSheffrey [24]	22,991
16	29	H	Luton T	W	1-0	0-0	19	Adebola [47]	22,228
17	Nov 2	H	Stoke C	L	1-2	1-1	—	Nalis [12]	16,617
18	6	A	Cardiff C	D	0-0	0-0	21		11,424
19	19	H	Ipswich T	D	1-1	0-0	21	McSheffrey [56]	18,316
20	22	A	Crystal Palace	L	0-2	0-2	—		17,343
21	26	H	Norwich C	D	2-2	2-1	21	McSheffrey [3], Adebola [10]	20,433
22	Dec 3	H	Plymouth Arg	W	3-1	2-1	19	Morrell [36], Hutchison [45], McSheffrey [49]	18,796
23	10	H	Millwall	W	1-0	1-0	18	Jorgensen [33]	16,156
24	19	A	QPR	W	1-0	0-0	—	McSheffrey (pen) [87]	13,556
25	26	A	Leeds U	L	1-3	0-1	17	Hutchison [58]	24,291
26	28	H	Crewe Alex	D	1-1	1-0	16	Hutchison [32]	19,045
27	31	A	Preston NE	L	1-3	0-3	18	John [59]	12,936
28	Jan 2	H	Wolverhampton W	W	2-0	2-0	16	Scowcroft [8], Lescott (og) [35]	26,851
29	14	A	Reading	L	0-2	0-0	17		22,813
30	21	H	Derby Co	W	6-1	1-1	15	John 2 [5, 47], Wise [59], Adebola [62], McSheffrey 2 (1 pen) [83 (p), 90]	20,267
31	31	A	Hull C	W	2-1	0-1	—	Wise [61], John [72]	18,381
32	Feb 4	H	Brighton & HA	W	2-0	1-0	11	Wise 2 [43, 68]	20,541
33	11	A	Watford	L	0-4	0-1	13		19,842
34	15	H	Sheffield W	W	2-1	1-0	—	John [45], McSheffrey [76]	20,021
35	18	A	Plymouth Arg	L	1-3	0-2	12	Wise [84]	12,958
36	25	H	Burnley	W	1-0	0-0	11	Adebola [54]	19,641
37	Mar 4	A	Southampton	D	1-1	0-0	12	Hutchison (pen) [88]	21,980
38	11	H	Sheffield U	W	2-0	2-0	9	McSheffrey [5], Adebola [32]	23,506
39	18	H	Leeds U	D	1-1	1-0	10	McSheffrey [26]	26,643
40	25	A	Crewe Alex	L	1-4	1-3	12	John [23]	6444
41	Apr 1	H	Preston NE	L	0-1	0-1	12		21,023
42	8	A	Wolverhampton W	D	2-2	1-2	12	John [25], McSheffrey [60]	23,702
43	15	A	Luton T	W	2-1	2-0	10	John [29], McSheffrey [30]	8752
44	17	H	Leicester C	D	1-1	1-1	11	John [11]	26,672
45	22	A	Stoke C	W	1-0	0-0	11	Adebola [85]	13,385
46	30	H	Cardiff C	W	3-1	1-1	8	John [8], Adebola [65], Wise [90]	22,536

Final League Position: 8

GOALSCORERS

League (62): McSheffrey 15 (3 pens), Adebola 12, John 10, Wise 6, Hutchison 4 (1 pen), Jorgensen 3, Scowcroft 3, Morrell 2, Nalis 2, Flood 1, Heath 1, Page 1, own goals 2.
Carling Cup (3): Heath 1, McSheffrey 1, Morrell 1.
FA Cup (2): John 1, McSheffrey 1.

Bywater S 14	Duffy R 30 + 2	Hall M 38 + 1	Hughes S 18 + 1	Page R 32	Heath M 23 + 2	McSheffrey G 43	Doyle M 44	Adebola D 39 + 5	John S 21 + 4	Scowcroft J 37 + 4	Jorgensen C 15 + 12	Morrell A 10 + 24	Wood N — + 4	Williams A 12 + 2	Flood W 7 + 1	Osbourne I 7 + 3	Whing A 24 + 8	Shaw R 24 + 1	Watson P 1 + 2	Impey A 4 + 12	Davis L — + 2	Sofiane Y — + 1	Nalis L 5 + 1	Ince C 1	Fulop M 31	Thornton K 4 + 12	Hutchison D 10 + 14	Wise D 11 + 2	Giddings S 1 + 1	Turner B — + 1	*Match No.*
1	2	3	4	5	6	7^1	8	9	10	11	12																				1
1	2	3	4	5	6	7	8	9^1	10^2	11		12	13																		2
1	2	3	4■	5	6	7^3	8	9^1	10^2	11	13	12		14																	3
1	2	3		5	6	7^2	4	9^3		11	8	12	13		10^1	14															4
1	2^1	3		5	6■	7^3	8	9	12	10		13			11^2	4	14														5
1	2	3		5		8	4	9^3	14	10	11^2	12			7^1	13		6													6
1	2^3	3		5		8	4	9		10	11^2	12	13		7^1		14	6													7
1	2	3			6^2	8	4	9		10	11	12	13		7^1		14	5^3													8
1	2^3	3	4^2	5		7^1	8	9		10	11	12				13	6		14												9
1	3		4	5		7^3	8^1	9		10	11^2	12			13				6	2	14										10
1	2	3	4	5		11^3	8	9^1		10	13	12			7^2		6			14											11
1	2	3	4^2		5	11	8			10	12	9			7^1		6		13												12
1	2	3	4^2		6	11	8	9^1		10^3	14■	12						5				13	7								13
1	2	3	4		6	11^1	8	9		10		12						5					7								14
	2^2	3	4		6	11	8	9		10		12					13	5					7^1	1							15
	2	3	4	5	6	7^2	8	9		10	11^1	12											13		1						16
	2	3	4	5	6		8	9		10										7^2	12		11^1		1	13					17
	2	3	4	5	6	9^1		12		10	13							7					11		1	8^2					18
		3	4	5	6	7	8^2	9^1		10	11	12					2								1	13					19
	2	3		5	6	7	8	9^1		10	11^2	12						4^3		14					1	13					20
	2	3		5	6	8	4	9		10	11^1	7^2													1	12	13				21
		3^2		5	6^1	8	4	9		10^3	11	7					2	12		13					1		14				22
	3^1			5		10	8	9			11^2	7				4	2	6		12					1	13					23
	3			5		11^2	8	9^1		12	13	7^3				4	2	6		14					1		10				24
	3			5		11	8	9^3		12	13	7^2				4^3	2	6		14					1		10				25
	3			5		7^2	8■	9^1	13	12	11					4	2	6		14					1		10^3				26
		12			6	9			13	10	11	14				4	2	5^1		3					1	8^3	7^2				27
	2	3				11^3	8^1	9	10^2	7	12	13		5		4	14	6							1						28
	4^2	3				7	8	12	9	10	11^1			5			2^3	6		13					1		14				29
	2^1	3				11	4	9^3	10	7				5			12	6							1	13	14	8^2			30
	2^1	3		6	12	11^2	4	9	10^3	7		13		5											1		14	8			31
		3		6		11^1	4	9^3	10	7		12		5			2			13					1		14	8^2			32
		3		5		7	8	9			12	13		4			2	6^1							1	14	11^2	10^3			33
				5	3	7	4	9	10^2		12	11^1		6			2								1		13	8			34
					6	11	4^3	9^2	10	7^1	12	13		5			2			3					1		8	14			35
		3		5			4	9	10^2	7		11^1					2	6		12					1		13	8			36
		3		5			4	9	10^3	7		11^2					2	6		12					1	13	14	8^1			37
		3		5		11^2	4	9	10^1	7		12					2	6							1	14	13	8^3			38
		3		5		11^1	4^2	9	10	7							2	6		12					1	13	8				39
	12	3	13	5		11	4	9	10	7^2				14			2^1	6^3							1		8				40
	12	3		5	13	11	4	9^3	10	7				6			2^1								1		14	8^2			41
	2^2	3	4	6		9^3	8	12	10	7^1				5			13								1		14	11			42
		3	4		6	11^1	8	13	10^2	12		9^3		5			2								1	14	7				43
	2^1	3				11^3	4	9^2	10	7				5			12	6							1	14	13	8			44
		3	4		6	11^2	8	12	10^3			13					2								1	7	9^1		5	14	45
		3	4^1		6	11	8	9	10^2								2	5^3							1	7	13	12	14		46

FA Cup

Third Round	Brighton & HA	(a)	1-0
Fourth Round	Middlesbrough	(h)	1-1
		(a)	0-1

Carling Cup

First Round	Rushden & D	(a)	3-0
Second Round	Crystal Palace	(a)	0-1

CREWE ALEXANDRA FL Championship 1

FOUNDATION

The first match played at Crewe was on 1 December 1877 against Basford, the leading North Staffordshire team of that time. During the club's history they have also played in a number of other leagues including the Football Alliance, Football Combination, Lancashire League, Manchester League, Central League and Lancashire Combination. Two former players, Aaron Scragg in 1899 and Jackie Pearson in 1911, had the distinction of refereeing FA Cup finals. Pearson was also capped for England against Ireland in 1892.

Alexandra Stadium, Gresty Road, Crewe, Cheshire CW2 6EB.

Telephone: (01270) 213 014.

Fax: (01270) 216 320.

Ticket Office: (01270) 252 610.

Website: www.crewealex.net

Email: info@crewealex.net

Ground Capacity: 10,046.

Record Attendance: 20,000 v Tottenham H, FA Cup 4th rd, 30 January 1960.

Pitch Measurements: 112yd × 74yd.

Chairman: John Bowler.

Vice-chairman: Norman Hassall.

Business Operations Manager: Alison Bowler.

Secretary: Andrew Blakemore.

Manager: Dario Gradi MBE.

Assistant Manager: Neil Baker.

Physio: Matt Radcliffe.

Colours: All red.

Change Colours: All blue.

Year Formed: 1877.

Turned Professional: 1893.

Ltd Co.: 1892.

Club Nickname: 'Railwaymen'.

First Football League Game: 3 September 1892, Division 2, v Burton Swifts (a) L 1–7 – Hickton; Moore, Cope; Linnell, Johnson, Osborne; Bennett, Pearson (1), Bailey, Barnett, Roberts.

Record League Victory: 8–0 v Rotherham U, Division 3 (N), 1 October 1932 – Foster; Pringle, Dawson; Ward, Keenor (1), Turner (1); Gillespie, Swindells (1), McConnell (2), Deacon (2), Weale (1).

HONOURS

Football League: Divison 2 – Runners-up 2002–03; Promoted from Division 2 1996–97 (play-offs).

FA Cup: Semi-final 1888.

Football League Cup: best season: 3rd rd, 1975, 1976, 1979, 1993, 1999, 2000, 2002.

Welsh Cup: Winners 1936, 1937.

SKY SPORTS FACT FILE

On 30 April 2006 Crewe Alexandra finished with a 4–2 win over Millwall. Half-time substitute Nicky Maynard, 19, took just 45 seconds to score on his debut with his first touch; Steve Jones, a 73rd minute replacement, scored in his last game for the club.

Record Cup Victory: 8–0 v Hartlepool U, Auto Windscreens Shield 1st rd, 17 October 1995 – Gayle; Collins (1), Booty, Westwood (Unsworth), Macauley (1), Whalley (1), Garvey (1), Murphy (1), Savage (1) (Rivers (1p)), Lennon, Edwards, (1 og). 8–0 v Doncaster R, LDV Vans Trophy 3rd rd, 10 November 2002 – Bankole; Wright, Walker, Foster, Tierney; Lunt (1), Brammer, Sorvel, Vaughan (1) (Bell); Ashton (3) (Miles), Jack (2) (Jones (1)).

Record Defeat: 2–13 v Tottenham H, FA Cup 4th rd replay, 3 February 1960.

Most League Points (2 for a win): 59, Division 4, 1962–63.

Most League Points (3 for a win): 86, Division 2, 2002–03.

Most League Goals: 95, Division 3 (N), 1931–32.

Highest League Scorer in Season: Terry Harkin, 35, Division 4, 1964–65.

Most League Goals in Total Aggregate: Bert Swindells, 126, 1928–37.

Most League Goals in One Match: 5, Tony Naylor v Colchester U, Division 3, 24 April 1993.

Most Capped Player: Clayton Ince, 38 (63), Trinidad & Tobago.

Most League Appearances: Tommy Lowry, 436, 1966–78.

Youngest League Player: Steve Walters, 16 years 119 days v Peterborough U, 6 May 1988.

Record Transfer Fee Received: £3,400,000 from Norwich C for Dean Ashton, January 2005.

Record Transfer Fee Paid: £650,000 to Torquay U for Rodney Jack, June 1998.

Football League Record: 1892 Original Member of Division 2; 1896 Failed re-election; 1921 Re-entered Division (N); 1958–63 Division 4; 1963–64 Division 3; 1964–68 Division 4; 1968–69 Division 3; 1969–89 Division 4; 1989–91 Division 3; 1991–92 Division 4; 1992–94 Division 3; 1994–97 Division 2; 1997–2002 Division 1; 2002–03 Division 2; 2003–04 Division 1; 2004–06 FLC; 2006– FL1.

MANAGERS

W. C. McNeill 1892–94 *(Secretary-Manager)*
J. G. Hall 1895–96 *(Secretary-Manager)*
R. Roberts *(1st team Secretary-Manager)* 1897
J. B. Blomerley 1898–1911 *(Secretary-Manager, continued as Hon. Secretary to 1925)*
Tom Bailey *(Secretary only)* 1925–38
George Lillycrop *(Trainer)* 1938–44
Frank Hill 1944–48
Arthur Turner 1948–51
Harry Catterick 1951–53
Ralph Ward 1953–55
Maurice Lindley 1956–57
Willie Cook 1957–58
Harry Ware 1958–60
Jimmy McGuigan 1960–64
Ernie Tagg 1964–71 *(continued as Secretary to 1972)*
Dennis Viollet 1971
Jimmy Melia 1972–74
Ernie Tagg 1974
Harry Gregg 1975–78
Warwick Rimmer 1978–79
Tony Waddington 1979–81
Arfon Griffiths 1981–82
Peter Morris 1982–83
Dario Gradi June 1983–

LATEST SEQUENCES

Longest Sequence of League Wins: 7, 30.4.1994 – 3.9.1994.

Longest Sequence of League Defeats: 10, 16.4.1979 – 22.8.1979.

Longest Sequence of League Draws: 5, 31.8.1987 – 18.9.1987.

Longest Sequence of Unbeaten League Matches: 17, 25.3.1995 – 16.9.1995.

Longest Sequence Without a League Win: 30, 22.9.1956 – 6.4.1957.

Successive Scoring Runs: 26 from 7.4.1934.

Successive Non-scoring Runs: 9 from 6.11.1974.

TEN YEAR LEAGUE RECORD

		P	*W*	*D*	*L*	*F*	*A*	*Pts*	*Pos*
1996-97	Div 2	46	22	7	17	56	47	73	6
1997-98	Div 1	46	18	5	23	58	65	59	11
1998-99	Div 1	46	12	12	22	54	78	48	18
1999-2000	Div 1	46	14	9	23	46	67	51	19
2000-01	Div 1	46	15	10	21	47	62	55	14
2001-02	Div 1	46	12	13	21	47	76	49	22
2002-03	Div 2	46	25	11	10	76	40	86	2
2003-04	Div 1	46	14	11	21	57	66	53	18
2004-05	FL C	46	12	14	20	66	86	50	21
2005-06	FL C	46	9	15	22	57	86	42	22

DID YOU KNOW

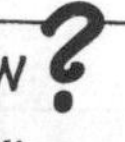

Goalkeeper Peter Ellison was a railway police officer in the local sidings when Crewe Alexandra needed an emergency replacement. Given two hours leave he made his debut on 30 April 1949, turned professional and made over 200 appearances.

CREWE ALEXANDRA 2005–06 LEAGUE RECORD

Match No.	Date	Venue	Opponents	Result	H/T Score	Lg. Pos.	Goalscorers	Attendance
1	Aug 6	H	Burnley	W 2-1	1-0	—	Jones B [44], Vaughan [89]	8006
2	9	A	Norwich C	D 1-1	1-0	—	Varney [19]	25,116
3	13	A	Brighton & HA	D 2-2	0-1	7	Rivers [77], Higdon [83]	6132
4	20	H	Leicester C	D 2-2	2-1	12	Varney [1], Rivers [17]	7053
5	27	A	Southampton	L 0-2	0-1	14		20,792
6	29	H	Sheffield U	L 1-3	1-1	17	Foster [17]	7501
7	Sept 11	H	Derby Co	D 1-1	1-0	18	Rivers [30]	5958
8	13	A	Plymouth Arg	D 1-1	1-1	—	Johnson [8]	10,460
9	17	A	Reading	L 0-1	0-0	20		17,668
10	24	H	Watford	D 0-0	0-0	20		6258
11	27	H	Wolverhampton W	L 0-4	0-4	—		7471
12	Oct 1	A	Ipswich T	L 1-2	1-0	24	Vaughan [26]	23,145
13	15	H	Luton T	W 3-1	1-1	21	Jones B [37], Lunt [88], Varney [90]	6604
14	18	A	Stoke C	L 0-2	0-1	—		14,080
15	22	A	Cardiff C	L 1-6	1-1	23	Foster [31]	10,815
16	29	H	Crystal Palace	D 2-2	1-0	23	Jones S [7], Higdon [90]	6766
17	Nov 1	H	Leeds U	W 1-0	1-0	—	Butler (og) [8]	7220
18	5	A	Millwall	W 3-1	1-1	18	Jones S 2 [15, 70], Roberts [63]	8120
19	19	H	Stoke C	L 1-2	0-1	19	Johnson [90]	8942
20	22	A	Luton T	L 1-4	0-0	—	Walker [83]	7474
21	26	A	Burnley	L 0-3	0-1	22		11,151
22	Dec 3	H	Preston NE	L 0-2	0-2	23		6364
23	10	H	Norwich C	L 1-2	1-0	23	Jones B [16]	6132
24	17	A	Leicester C	D 1-1	1-0	23	Higdon [40]	24,873
25	26	H	Hull C	D 2-2	2-1	23	Johnson [19], Roberts [41]	7942
26	28	A	Coventry C	D 1-1	0-1	22	Rodgers [90]	19,045
27	31	H	QPR	L 3-4	3-2	24	Johnson [15], Varney [39], Jones B [45]	5687
28	Jan 2	A	Sheffield W	L 0-3	0-1	24		25,656
29	14	A	Derby Co	L 1-5	0-2	24	Vaughan [79]	22,649
30	21	H	Plymouth Arg	L 1-2	0-2	24	Rodgers [68]	5984
31	28	A	Watford	L 1-4	0-2	—	Rodgers [81]	11,722
32	Feb 4	H	Reading	L 3-4	1-3	24	Bell [14], Taylor [51], Lunt (pen) [68]	6484
33	11	A	Wolverhampton W	D 1-1	1-1	24	Jones B [6]	21,683
34	14	H	Ipswich T	L 1-2	1-1	—	Jones S [15]	5686
35	25	H	Brighton & HA	W 2-1	0-1	24	Bell [59], Foster [65]	5925
36	Mar 3	A	Sheffield U	D 0-0	0-0	—		22,691
37	11	H	Southampton	D 1-1	0-0	24	Rodgers [78]	6588
38	18	A	Hull C	L 0-1	0-1	24		21,163
39	25	H	Coventry C	W 4-1	3-1	24	Jones B [4], Bougherra [17], Rodgers [24], Taylor [61]	6444
40	28	A	Preston NE	L 0-1	0-1	—		13,170
41	Apr 1	A	QPR	W 2-1	1-0	24	Lunt [39], Vaughan [73]	12,877
42	8	H	Sheffield W	W 2-0	2-0	22	Taylor 2 [31, 45]	8007
43	15	A	Crystal Palace	D 2-2	0-2	23	Rodgers [68], Lunt (pen) [79]	18,358
44	17	H	Cardiff C	D 1-1	0-0	22	Vaughan [58]	5865
45	22	A	Leeds U	L 0-1	0-0	23		21,046
46	30	H	Millwall	W 4-2	1-1	22	Johnson [43], Maynard [46], Varney [59], Jones S [84]	5945

Final League Position: 22

GOALSCORERS

League (57): Jones B 6, Rodgers 6, Johnson 5, Jones S 5, Varney 5, Vaughan 5, Lunt 4 (2 pens), Taylor 4, Foster 3, Higdon 3, Rivers 3, Bell 2, Roberts 2, Bougherra 1, Maynard 1, Walker 1, own goal 1.
Carling Cup (1): Walker 1.
FA Cup (1): Jones B 1.

Williams B 16 + 1	Moss D 30 + 1	Tonkin A 27	Jones B 43 + 1	Walker R 17 + 1	Moses A 12 + 3	Vaughan D 28 + 6	Lunt K 43	Johnson E 16 + 6	Jones S 36 + 5	Varney L 15 + 12	Higdon M 15 + 11	Rivers M 9 + 8	Roberts G 27 + 6	Cochrane J 2 + 2	Ugarte J — + 2	Turnbull R 29	Foster S 36 + 3	Suhaj P 1 + 5	McCready C 19 + 6	Bignot P 4 + 1	Rodgers L 13 + 13	Bell L 14 + 3	Rix B 1 + 1	Otsemobor J 16	Taylor G 15	Tomlinson S 1 + 1	Grant T 10	Bougherra M 11	O'Connor M — + 2	Maynard N — + 1	Match No.
1	2	3	4	5	6	7	8	9¹	10²	11	12	13																			1
1	2	3	4¹	5	6	7		9³	10²	11	14	13	8	12																	2
1	2	3	4¹	5	6	7	8	9³	10²	11	14	13	12																		3
1	2	3	12	5	6	7	4			11	9²	10	8¹		13																4
	2	3	4	5	6	7	8	12	13	11¹	9³	10²				1	14														5
	2	3	4	12	6¹	7²	8	13	10	11	9³					1	5	14													6
	2	3	4			7	8	9¹	12	11		10²	13			1	5		6												7
	2	3	4			7	8	9¹		11	12	10²	13			1	5		6												8
	2	3	4			7¹	8		10²		9³	12	11		13	1	5	14	6												9
15	2	3	4			7	8	9¹	10²		13	12	11			1⁶	5		6												10
1	2		4			7	8	9¹	10²				11				5	12	6	3	13										11
1	2		4			7¹	8	9²	10			12	11				5		6	3	13										12
1	2	3	4				8	9¹	10²	12		7³	11	13			5		6		14										13
1	2	3	4			7¹	8		12	9			13	11²			5	14	6		10³										14
1	2	3	4¹			12	8			9	13	10	11				5²	7	6³	14											15
1		3	4			7²	8		10		9	12	11	6¹			5			2	13										16
1	2	3	4	5		7	8		10¹		9		11				6				12										17
1	2	3	4	5	12	7¹	8		10		9		11				6														18
1	2	3	4	5		7¹	8	13	10		9	12	11²				6														19
1	2	3²	4	5	13		8		10³	12	9	7¹	11				6▪				14										20
1	2		4	5	3		8	12	10		9¹	7	11						6												21
1	2		4	5	3¹		8	7		10	9²		11				12		6		13										22
	2²	3	4	5		7	8		10	12	9¹		11			1			6			13									23
		3	4		2	7	8		10²	12	9¹		11			1	5		6		13										24
	2	3	4²		13	7	8	9¹	10	12			11			1	5		6												25
	2	3²	4			7¹	8	9	10	12			11			1	5		6		13										26
	2	3²	4			7	8	9¹	10	12			11			1	5		6		13										27
	2		4		3		8		10²	9			11³			1	5	12	6		13	14	7¹								28
	2		4¹	5	3	7		9	12			10	11²			1			6			8	13								29
	2		4	5	6¹	7²	8		10				11			1	12				13			3	9						30
	2		4	5		7	8		10	12			11²			1⁶	6				13			3	9¹	15					31
	12	3¹	4				8▪		10				11			1	5		13		7	6²		2	9						32
		3	4	5					10	12	9¹		11			1	6		13		8	7²		2							33
		3	4¹	5			7		10	12			11²			1	6				8	13		2	9						34
		3					8		10	9¹	12					1	6					7		2	11²		4	5	13		35
			3				8		10		12					1	6				11	7		2	9¹		4	5			36
			3			12	8		10							1	5				11	7		2	9		4¹	6			37
			3			12	8		10		13					1	6		14		11¹	7		2	9²		4³	5			38
			3			12	8		10							1	6¹				11	7		2	9		4	5			39
			3			12	8	13	10		14					1	6				11	7¹		2	9²		4³	5			40
			3			12	8		10	13						1	6				11¹	7		2	9²		4	5			41
			3				8		10	12						1	6				11¹	7		2	9		4	5			42
			3				8		10							1	6		12		11	7		2	9		4	5¹			43
			3			7	8	12	10				13			1	6		14		11¹			2	9		4²	5³			44
	2					7	8	9		10	12		13			1	6		14			4²		3	11¹			5³			45
			3			7	8	9¹	12	11	10³						6		5	2		4²				1			14	13	46

FA Cup
Third Round Preston NE (a) 1-2

Carling Cup
First Round Lincoln C (a) 1-5

CRYSTAL PALACE FL Championship

FOUNDATION

There was a Crystal Palace club as early as 1861 but the present organisation was born in 1905 after the formation of a club by the company that controlled the Crystal Palace (building), had been rejected by the FA who did not like the idea of the Cup Final hosts running their own club. A separate company had to be formed and they had their home on the old Cup Final ground until 1915.

Selhurst Park Stadium, Whitehorse Lane, London SE25 6PU.

Telephone: (020) 8768 6000.

Fax: (020) 8771 5311.

Ticket Office: 0871 200 0071

Website: www.cpfc.co.uk

Email: info@cpfc.co.uk

Ground Capacity: 26,225.

Record Attendance: 51,482 v Burnley, Division 2, 11 May 1979.

Pitch Measurements: 110yd × 74yd.

Chairman: Simon Jordan.

Vice-chairman: Dominic Jordan.

Chief Executive: Phil Alexander.

Secretary: Christine Dowdeswell.

Manager: Peter Taylor.

Assistant Manager: Neil McDonald.

Physio: Paul Caton.

Colours: Red and blue shirts, red shorts, red stockings.

Change Colours: White and grey shirts, grey and white shorts, grey and white stockings.

Year Formed: 1905.

Turned Professional: 1905.

Ltd Co.: 1905.

Club Nickname: 'The Eagles'.

Previous Grounds: 1905, Crystal Palace; 1915, Herne Hill; 1918, The Nest; 1924, Selhurst Park.

First Football League Game: 28 August 1920, Division 3, v Merthyr T (a) L 1–2 – Alderson; Little, Rhodes; McCracken, Jones, Feebury; Bateman, Conner, Smith, Milligan (1), Whibley.

Record League Victory: 9–0 v Barrow, Division 4, 10 October 1959 – Rouse; Long, Noakes; Truett, Evans, McNichol; Gavin (1), Summersby (4 incl. 1p), Sexton, Byrne (2), Colfar (2).

Record Cup Victory: 8–0 v Southend U, Rumbelows League Cup 2nd rd (1st leg), 25 September 1989 – Martyn; Humphrey (Thompson (1)), Shaw, Pardew, Young, Thorn, McGoldrick, Thomas, Bright (3), Wright (3), Barber (Hodges (1)).

HONOURS

Football League: Division 1 – Champions 1993–94; Promoted from Division 1, 1996–97 (play-offs), 2003–04 (play-offs); Division 2 – Champions 1978–79; Runners-up 1968–69; Division 3 – Runners-up 1963–64; Division 3 (S) – Champions 1920–21; Runners-up 1928–29, 1930–31, 1938–39; Division 4 – Runners-up 1960–61.

FA Cup: Runners-up 1990.

Football League Cup: Semi-final 1993, 1995, 2001.

Zenith Data Systems Cup: Winners 1991.

European Competition: *Intertoto Cup:* 1998.

SKY SPORTS FACT FILE

In 1961 Crystal Palace and former England international centre-forward Ronnie Allen regained his PFA Golf Championship title he lost to the then Leeds United player Don Revie. Allen went on to top 250 career League goals while at Selhurst Park.

Record Defeat: 0–9 v Burnley, FA Cup 2nd rd replay, 10 February 1909. 0–9 v Liverpool, Division 1, 12 September 1990.

Most League Points (2 for a win): 64, Division 4, 1960–61.

Most League Points (3 for a win): 90, Division 1, 1993–94.

Most League Goals: 110, Division 4, 1960–61.

Highest League Scorer in Season: Peter Simpson, 46, Division 3 (S), 1930–31.

Most League Goals in Total Aggregate: Peter Simpson, 153, 1930–36.

Most League Goals in One Match: 6, Peter Simpson v Exeter C, Division 3S, 4 October 1930.

Most Capped Player: Aleksandrs Kolinko 23 (66), Latvia.

Most League Appearances: Jim Cannon, 571, 1973–88.

Youngest League Player: Phil Hoadley, 16 years 112 days v Bolton W, 27 April 1968.

Record Transfer Fee Received: £8,500,000 from Everton for Andy Johnson, May 2006.

Record Transfer Fee Paid: £2,750,000 to RC Strasbourg for Valerien Ismael, January 1998.

Football League Record: 1920 Original Members of Division 3; 1921–25 Division 2; 1925–58 Division 3 (S); 1958–61 Division 4; 1961–64 Division 3; 1964–69 Division 2; 1969–73 Division 1; 1973–74 Division 2; 1974–77 Division 3; 1977–79 Division 2; 1979–81 Division 1; 1981–89 Division 2; 1989–92 Division 1; 1992–93 FA Premier League; 1993–94 Division 1; 1994–95 FA Premier League; 1995–97 Division 1; 1997–98 FA Premier League; 1998–2004 Division 1; 2004–05 FA Premier League; 2005– FLC.

LATEST SEQUENCES

Longest Sequence of League Wins: 8, 9.2.1921 – 26.3.1921.

Longest Sequence of League Defeats: 8, 10.1.1998 – 14.3.1998.

Longest Sequence of League Draws: 5, 21.9.2002 – 19.10.2002.

Longest Sequence of Unbeaten League Matches: 18, 22.2.1969 – 13.8.1969.

Longest Sequence Without a League Win: 20, 3.3.1962 – 8.9.1962.

Successive Scoring Runs: 24 from 27.4.1929.

Successive Non-scoring Runs: 9 from 19.11.1994.

MANAGERS

John T. Robson 1905–07
Edmund Goodman 1907–25 *(had been Secretary since 1905 and afterwards continued in this position to 1933)*
Alec Maley 1925–27
Fred Mavin 1927–30
Jack Tresadern 1930–35
Tom Bromilow 1935–36
R. S. Moyes 1936
Tom Bromilow 1936–39
George Irwin 1939–47
Jack Butler 1947–49
Ronnie Rooke 1949–50
Charlie Slade and Fred Dawes *(Joint Managers)* 1950–51
Laurie Scott 1951–54
Cyril Spiers 1954–58
George Smith 1958–60
Arthur Rowe 1960–62
Dick Graham 1962–66
Bert Head 1966–72 *(continued as General Manager to 1973)*
Malcolm Allison 1973–76
Terry Venables 1976–80
Ernie Walley 1980
Malcolm Allison 1980–81
Dario Gradi 1981
Steve Kember 1981–82
Alan Mullery 1982–84
Steve Coppell 1984–93
Alan Smith 1993–95
Steve Coppell *(Technical Director)* 1995–96
Dave Bassett 1996–97
Steve Coppell 1997–98
Attilio Lombardo 1998
Terry Venables *(Head Coach)* 1998–99
Steve Coppell 1999–2000
Alan Smith 2000–01
Steve Bruce 2001
Trevor Francis 2001–03
Steve Kember 2003
Iain Dowie 2003–06
Peter Taylor June 2006–

TEN YEAR LEAGUE RECORD

		P	W	D	L	F	A	Pts	Pos
1996-97	Div 1	46	19	14	13	78	48	71	6
1997-98	PR Lge	38	8	9	21	37	71	33	20
1998-99	Div 1	46	14	16	16	58	71	58	14
1999-2000	Div 1	46	13	15	18	57	67	54	15
2000-01	Div 1	46	12	13	21	57	70	49	21
2001-02	Div 1	46	20	6	20	70	62	66	10
2002-03	Div 1	46	14	17	15	59	52	59	14
2003-04	Div 1	46	21	10	15	72	61	73	6
2004-05	PR Lge	38	7	12	19	41	62	33	18
2005-06	FL C	46	21	12	13	67	48	75	6

DID YOU KNOW

In 1964 Crystal Palace undertook a successful tour to Bermuda and Canada, winning all six matches scoring 29 goals in the process and conceding just two. Top scorer was the much travelled Brian Whitehouse with nine of the total.

CRYSTAL PALACE 2005–06 LEAGUE RECORD

Match No.	Date	Venue	Opponents	Result	H/T Score	Lg. Pos.	Goalscorers	Attendance
1	Aug 6	H	Luton T	L 1-2	0-1	—	Johnson 52	21,166
2	9	A	Wolverhampton W	L 1-2	1-1	—	McAnuff 42	24,745
3	13	A	Norwich C	D 1-1	1-1	23	Johnson 42	25,102
4	20	H	Plymouth Arg	W 1-0	0-0	16	Ward 63	18,781
5	27	H	Stoke C	W 2-0	1-0	12	Johnson 2 44, 85	17,637
6	Sept 10	H	Hull C	W 2-0	1-0	9	Morrison 27, Johnson 89	18,630
7	13	A	Reading	L 2-3	1-1	—	Johnson 29, Morrison 47	17,562
8	17	A	Cardiff C	L 0-1	0-1	14		11,647
9	24	H	Preston NE	D 1-1	0-1	15	Morrison 90	17,291
10	27	H	Sheffield W	W 2-0	1-0	—	Morrison 17, Boyce 57	17,413
11	Oct 3	A	QPR	W 3-1	2-1	—	Reich 2 14, 17, Soares 89	13,433
12	15	A	Coventry C	W 4-1	2-1	5	Ward 14, Morrison 45, Watson 58, Macken 90	24,438
13	18	H	Brighton & HA	L 0-1	0-0	—		22,400
14	22	H	Burnley	W 2-0	1-0	5	Morrison 38, Freedman 78	20,127
15	29	A	Crewe Alex	D 2-2	0-1	6	Freedman 52, Morrison 65	6766
16	Nov 5	H	Sheffield U	L 2-3	1-2	10	Hughes 45, Freedman (pen) 85	20,344
17	20	A	Brighton & HA	W 3-2	1-1	9	Freedman 2 28, 60, McAnuff 90	7273
18	22	H	Coventry C	W 2-0	2-0	—	Andrews 1, Boyce 34	17,343
19	26	A	Luton T	L 0-2	0-2	8		10,248
20	Dec 3	H	Millwall	D 1-1	0-1	8	Watson 90	19,571
21	10	H	Wolverhampton W	D 1-1	1-1	9	Johnson 44	19,385
22	17	A	Plymouth Arg	L 0-2	0-1	11		14,582
23	26	A	Ipswich T	W 2-0	1-0	7	Macken 14, Hughes 61	27,392
24	28	H	Derby Co	W 2-0	2-0	5	Morrison 30, Ward 41	18,978
25	31	A	Watford	W 2-1	1-0	5	Ward 18, Johnson (pen) 72	15,856
26	Jan 2	H	Leicester C	W 2-0	0-0	5	McAnuff 78, Johnson 90	20,089
27	14	A	Hull C	W 2-1	2-1	4	Ward 9, Cort (og) 24	18,886
28	20	H	Reading	D 1-1	0-0	—	Johnson (pen) 79	19,888
29	25	A	Southampton	D 0-0	0-0	—		24,651
30	31	A	Preston NE	L 0-2	0-1	—		13,867
31	Feb 4	H	Cardiff C	W 1-0	0-0	5	Riihilahti 70	17,962
32	11	A	Sheffield W	D 0-0	0-0	6		24,784
33	14	H	QPR	W 2-1	2-0	—	Morrison 3, McAnuff 32	17,550
34	18	A	Millwall	D 1-1	0-0	5	Watson 67	12,296
35	25	H	Norwich C	W 4-1	2-0	5	Johnson 7, Watson 34, Morrison 54, Hall 62	19,066
36	Mar 4	H	Leeds U	L 1-2	0-1	5	McAnuff 90	23,843
37	13	A	Stoke C	W 3-1	1-0	—	Sidibe (og) 30, McAnuff 48, Johnson 58	10,121
38	18	H	Ipswich T	D 2-2	1-1	5	Riihilahti 10, Morrison 53	22,076
39	21	A	Leeds U	W 1-0	1-0	—	McAnuff 43	24,507
40	25	A	Derby Co	L 1-2	1-1	5	Morrison 18	24,857
41	31	H	Watford	W 3-1	0-1	—	Freedman 55, Stewart (og) 59, DeMerit (og) 86	18,619
42	Apr 7	A	Leicester C	L 0-2	0-1	—		23,211
43	15	H	Crewe Alex	D 2-2	2-0	6	Johnson 2 28, 45	18,358
44	17	A	Burnley	D 0-0	0-0	6		11,449
45	22	H	Southampton	W 2-1	0-0	6	Johnson 63, Morrison 81	20,995
46	30	A	Sheffield U	L 0-1	0-0	6		27,120

Final League Position: 6

GOALSCORERS

League (67): Johnson 15 (2 pens), Morrison 13, McAnuff 7, Freedman 6 (1 pen), Ward 5, Watson 4, Boyce 2, Hughes 2, Macken 2, Reich 2, Riihilahti 2, Andrews 1, Hall 1, Soares 1, own goals 4.
Carling Cup (7): Reich 2, Freedman 1, Granville 1, Hughes 1, Popovic 1 (pen), own goal 1.
FA Cup (6): Johnson 2 (1 pen), Freedman 1 (pen), Hughes 1, McAnuff 1, Ward 1.
Play-Offs (0).

Kiraly G 43	Boyce E 42	Borrowdale G 26 + 4	Hudson M 8 + 7	Hall F 39	Watson B 40 + 2	McAnuff J 35 + 6	Hughes M 30 + 10	Johnson A 30 + 3	Macken J 13 + 11	Soares T 38 + 6	Ward D 42 + 1	Andrews W 5 + 19	Kolkka J 1 + 2	Leigertwood M 18 + 9	Butterfield D 9 + 4	Riihilahti A 9 + 6	Freedman D 19 + 15	Morrison C 32 + 8	Reich M 14 + 7	Speroni J 3 + 1	Black T — + 1	Popovic T 10	*Match No.*
1	2	3	4^1	5	6	7	8	9	10^2	11^3	12	13	14										1
1	2	3^1	12	5	6	7		9	10	11^3	4	13	14	8^2									2
1	2	3		5	6			9	10^2	11	4	13	7^1	8	12								3
1	2	3		5	6^1	7		9		11^2	4	10^3		8	13	12	14						4
1	2	3		5	6^1	7^2	12	9	10^3	11	4			8		13		14					5
1	2	3		5	6		8	9	10^2	7^3	4	13			12	14		11^1					6
1	2	3		5	6		8	9^1	12	7	4	13				11^2		10					7
1		3^1	12	5	6	13	8		9^3	7	4	14			2	11^2		10					8
1	2	3	12		6^1	7	8			11^3	4				5	10^2	13	9	14				9
1	2	12		5	6^2	7	13			11	4	14			3		8^3	9	10^1				10
1	2	12		5	6^2	7^1	13			11	4	14			3		8^3	9	10				11
1	2			5	6^1	7	12	13	14	11	4				3		8^3	9^2	10				12
1	2			5	13	7^3	6		12	11	4	14			3		8^1	9	10^2				13
1	2			5	6	7^2	12		8^3	11	4	13			3		14	9	10^1				14
1^6	2	12		5	6	13	8			11	4				3^1		10	9	7^2	15			15
1	2	3^2		5	6^1	12	8			11	4	13					10	9	7				16
1	2	3^1	12	5	6^2	14	8			11	4	13					10	9	7^3				17
1	2	3		5	6	7^3			12	11	4	8^2		13			10^1	9			14		18
1	2	3^3		5	6^1	7^2	8	12	13	11	4	14					10	9					19
	2	3		5^1	6	7^2	12	9		13		8^3		11			10	14		1		4	20
	2				6	12	8	9	13	3	4			7			10^2	11^1		1		5	21
	2			5	6	12	8	9	13	3^3				7			10	11^1	14	1		4^2	22
1			12	2	6■	7	8^1	9^2	10■	11	4			3				13				5	23
1	2			5		7	12	9		11	3	13		4			8^1	10^2				6	24
1	2		12	3		7	8^1	9^2		11	4	14		6			13	10^3				5	25
1	2			3	6^1	7	12	9		11^3	4	14		8			13	10^2				5	26
1	2	3	4		6	7	8^2	9	10^3		5	11^1				13	12	14					27
1	2		4	5	6	7	8	9	10	11	3												28
1	3		4	2	6^1	7^2	8	9	10^3	11	5	12					14	13					29
1	3^2		4	5		7^3	8	9	12	11	2			6			13	10^1	14				30
1	3	12		5■	13	7^1	8	9^3			2			4		6	10	14	11^2				31
1	3		4			7	8	9^3	12	13	2			5		6^2	10	14	11^1				32
1	5	3			6	7	12		10^2	11	2	8^1		4			13	9					33
1	2	3		5	6^1	7	8			11	4	13		12			10^2	9					34
1	2	3		5	6	7^1	8	9^2		11^3	4	12		14			13	10					35
1	2	3		5	6^1	7	8	9		11^2	4			13		12		10					36
1	2	3		5	6^2	7^1	8	9		12	4			13		11		10					37
1	2	3^1		5	6	7^3		9		11^2	4			12		8	13	10	14				38
1	2			5	6	7^2	8	9		12	4			3		11		10^1	13				39
1	2			5	6	7^1	8	9		12	4			3		11^3	13	10^2	14				40
1	2			5	6^3	7	8^2	9^1		11	3			13		14	12	10				4	41
1	2	3		5	6	7	8	9	12	11^3	4^1						13	10^2	14				42
1	2	3	4		6		8	9		11	5			12			10		7^1				43
1	2	3	4		6		12	13	10^3	11	5			8^1			14	9^2	7				44
1		3		5	6^1	7	8	9		12				13	2		10^3	14	11^2			4	45
1		3	12	5^3	6	7			13	11	2^1				14		10^2	9	8			4	46

FA Cup

Third Round	Northampton T	(h)	4-1
Fourth Round	Preston NE	(a)	1-1
		(h)	1-2

Carling Cup

First Round	Walsall	(h)	3-0
Second Round	Coventry C	(h)	1-0
Third Round	Liverpool	(h)	2-1
Fourth Round	Middlesbrough	(a)	1-2

Play-Offs

Semi-Final	Watford	(h)	0-3
		(a)	0-0

DARLINGTON FL Championship 2

FOUNDATION

A football club was formed in Darlington as early as 1861 but the present club began in 1883 and reached the final of the Durham Senior Cup in their first season, losing to Sunderland in a replay after complaining that they had suffered from intimidation in the first. On 5 April 1884, Sunderland had defeated Darlington 4-3. Darlington's objection was upheld by the referee and the replay took place on 3 May. The new referee for the match was Major Marindin, appointed by the Football Association to ensure fair play. Sunderland won 2-0. The following season Darlington won this trophy and for many years were one of the leading amateur clubs in their area.

96.6 TFM Darlington Arena, Neasham Road, Darlington DL2 1GR.

Telephone: (01325) 387 000.

Fax: (01325) 387 050.

Ticket Office: 0870 0272 949.

Website: www.darlington-fc.net

Email: enquiries@darlington-fc.net

Ground Capacity: 25,000.

Record Attendance: 21,023 v Bolton W, League Cup 3rd rd, 14 November 1960.

Pitch Measurements: 105m × 68m.

Chairman: George Houghton.

Directors: George Luke and David Jones.

Football Secretary: Lisa Charlton.

Manager: David Hodgson.

Assistant Manager: Mark Proctor.

Physio: Paul Gough.

Colours: Black and white hoops.

Change Colours: All red.

Year Formed: 1883. ***Turned Professional:*** 1908. ***Ltd Co.:*** 1891.

Previous Grounds: Feethams Ground; 2003, Reynolds Arena, Hurworth Moor.

Club Nickname: 'The Quakers'.

First Football League Game: 27 August 1921, Division 3 (N), v Halifax T (h) W 2–0 – Ward; Greaves, Barbour; Dickson (1), Sutcliffe, Malcolm; Dolphin, Hooper (1), Edmunds, Wolstenholme, Winship.

Record League Victory: 9–2 v Lincoln C, Division 3 (N), 7 January 1928 – Archibald; Brooks, Mellen; Kelly, Waugh, McKinnell; Cochrane (1), Gregg (1), Ruddy (3), Lees (3), McGiffen (1).

Record Cup Victory: 7–2 v Evenwood T, FA Cup 1st rd, 17 November 1956 – Ward; Devlin, Henderson; Bell (1p), Greener, Furphy; Forster (1), Morton (3), Tulip (2), Davis, Moran.

HONOURS

Football League: Division 2 best season: 15th, 1925–26; Division 3 (N) – Champions 1924–25; Runners-up 1921–22; Division 4 – Champions 1990–91; Runners-up 1965–66.

FA Cup: best season: 5th rd, 1958.

Football League Cup: best season: 5th rd, 1968.

GM Vauxhall Conference: Champions 1989–90.

SKY SPORTS FACT FILE

Bob Thyne was a Darlington half-back who moved to Kilmarnock in October 1946. He played for Scotland in a wartime international against England while on convalescent leave and in the 1960s he became a member of the Scotland selection board.

Record Defeat: 0–10 v Doncaster R, Division 4, 25 January 1964.

Most League Points (2 for a win): 59, Division 4, 1965–66.

Most League Points (3 for a win): 85, Division 4, 1984–85.

Most League Goals: 108, Division 3 (N), 1929–30.

Highest League Scorer in Season: David Brown, 39, Division 3 (N), 1924–25.

Most League Goals in Total Aggregate: Alan Walsh, 90, 1978–84.

Most League Goals in One Match: 5, Tom Ruddy v South Shields, Division 2, 23 April 1927; 5, Maurice Wellock v Rotherham U, Division 3N, 15 February 1930.

Most Capped Player: Jason Devos, 3 (46), Canada; Adrian Webster, 3, New Zealand.

Most League Appearances: Ron Greener, 442, 1955–68.

Youngest League Player: Dale Anderson, 16 years 254 days v Chesterfield, 4 May 1987.

Record Transfer Fee Received: £400,000 from Dundee U for Jason Devos, October 1998.

Record Transfer Fee Paid: £95,000 to Motherwell for Nick Cusack, January 1992.

Football League Record: 1921 Original Member Division 3 (N); 1925–27 Division 2; 1927–58 Division 3 (N); 1958–66 Division 4; 1966–67 Division 3; 1967–85 Division 4; 1985–87 Division 3; 1987–89 Division 4; 1989–90 GM Vauxhall Conference; 1990–91 Division 4; 1991–2004 Division 3; 2004– FL2.

LATEST SEQUENCES

Longest Sequence of League Wins: 6, 6.2.2000 – 7.3.2000.

Longest Sequence of League Defeats: 8, 31.8.1985 – 19.10.1985.

Longest Sequence of League Draws: 5, 31.12.1988 – 28.1.1989.

Longest Sequence of Unbeaten League Matches: 17, 27.4.1968 – 19.10.1968.

Longest Sequence Without a League Win: 19, 27.4.1988 – 8.11.1988.

Successive Scoring Runs: 22 from 3.12.1932.

Successive Non-scoring Runs: 7 from 5.9.1975.

MANAGERS

Tom McIntosh 1902–11
W. L. Lane 1911–12
(Secretary-Manager)
Dick Jackson 1912–19
Jack English 1919–28
Jack Fairless 1928–33
George Collins 1933–36
George Brown 1936–38
Jackie Carr 1938–42
Jack Surtees 1942
Jack English 1945–46
Bill Forrest 1946–50
George Irwin 1950–52
Bob Gurney 1952–57
Dick Duckworth 1957–60
Eddie Carr 1960–64
Lol Morgan 1964–66
Jimmy Greenhalgh 1966–68
Ray Yeoman 1968–70
Len Richley 1970–71
Frank Brennan 1971
Ken Hale 1971–72
Allan Jones 1972
Ralph Brand 1972–73
Dick Conner 1973–74
Billy Horner 1974–76
Peter Madden 1976–78
Len Walker 1978–79
Billy Elliott 1979–83
Cyril Knowles 1983–87
Dave Booth 1987–89
Brian Little 1989–91
Frank Gray 1991–92
Ray Hankin 1992
Billy McEwan 1992–93
Alan Murray 1993–95
Paul Futcher 1995
David Hodgson/Jim Platt
(Director of Coaching) 1995
Jim Platt 1995–96
David Hodgson 1996–2000
Gary Bennett 2000–01
Tommy Taylor 2001–02
Mick Tait 2003
David Hodgson November 2003–

TEN YEAR LEAGUE RECORD

		P	W	D	L	F	A	Pts	Pos
1996-97	Div 3	46	14	10	22	64	78	52	18
1997-98	Div 3	46	14	12	20	56	72	54	19
1998-99	Div 3	46	18	11	17	69	58	65	11
1999-2000	Div 3	46	21	16	9	66	36	79	4
2000-01	Div 3	46	12	13	21	44	56	49	20
2001-02	Div 3	46	15	11	20	60	71	56	15
2002-03	Div 3	46	12	18	16	58	59	54	14
2003-04	Div 3	46	14	11	21	53	61	53	18
2004-05	FL 2	46	20	12	14	57	49	72	8
2005-06	FL 2	46	16	15	15	58	52	63	8

DID YOU KNOW?

In July 1965 goalkeeper Tony Moor was preparing to return to his former club Scarborough. He had been released by York City but Darlington stepped in, signed him and with the Quakers he went on to complete well over 200 League appearances.

DARLINGTON 2005–06 LEAGUE RECORD

Match No.	Date	Venue	Opponents	Result		H/T Score	Lg. Pos.	Goalscorers	Attendance
1	Aug 6	A	Rushden & D	D	1-1	0-0	—	Wijnhard (pen) [58]	2832
2	9	H	Stockport Co	W	2-0	1-0	—	Logan [28], Sodje [89]	4371
3	13	H	Leyton Orient	L	0-1	0-1	9		4021
4	20	A	Grimsby T	W	1-0	0-0	7	N'Dumbu Nsungu (pen) [81]	3904
5	27	A	Chester C	D	4-4	2-0	7	Johnson S (pen) [6], Sodje 3 [34, 49, 81]	2469
6	29	H	Rochdale	W	2-1	1-0	2	Johnson S [36], Logan [69]	4318
7	Sept 2	H	Notts Co	D	1-1	0-0	—	N'Dumbu Nsungu [80]	5273
8	10	A	Mansfield T	D	2-2	1-1	6	Clarke [39], N'Dumbu Nsungu [74]	2803
9	17	H	Oxford U	L	1-2	0-0	10	Webster [79]	4127
10	24	A	Bristol R	L	0-1	0-1	14		5652
11	27	H	Boston U	D	0-0	0-0	—		3115
12	Oct 1	A	Northampton T	D	0-0	0-0	14		5182
13	7	H	Macclesfield T	W	1-0	1-0	—	Johnson S (pen) [28]	3831
14	15	A	Bury	L	0-1	0-1	12		2630
15	22	H	Cheltenham T	W	3-1	0-1	8	Wainwright [75], Dickman [79], N'Dumbu Nsungu [90]	3315
16	29	A	Wrexham	L	0-1	0-0	13		4881
17	Nov 12	H	Wycombe W	D	1-1	1-0	12	Keogh (og) [36]	3928
18	19	A	Macclesfield T	L	0-1	0-1	13		1769
19	26	H	Rushden & D	D	1-1	0-1	13	N'Dumbu Nsungu (pen) [90]	3209
20	Dec 6	A	Shrewsbury T	L	1-3	1-1	—	Stamp [45]	2469
21	10	A	Stockport Co	W	3-0	1-0	14	Logan [37], N'Dumbu Nsungu [84], Sodje [86]	3502
22	26	A	Carlisle U	D	1-1	1-1	16	Johnson S [38]	11,182
23	28	H	Barnet	W	2-1	1-0	11	N'Dumbu Nsungu [44], Johnson S [53]	2905
24	31	A	Lincoln C	D	2-2	0-2	12	Kandol [64], N'Dumbu Nsungu [69]	4008
25	Jan 2	H	Torquay U	W	3-2	1-1	10	Kandol [14], N'Dumbu Nsungu 2 (1 pen) [76, 90 (p)]	3785
26	7	A	Notts Co	L	2-3	1-0	11	Lafferty [45], Logan [88]	4244
27	14	H	Peterborough U	W	2-1	0-1	10	Hopkins [77], Lafferty [88]	3822
28	17	H	Grimsby T	D	0-0	0-0	—		3924
29	21	A	Oxford U	W	2-0	0-0	7	Dickman [47], Johnson S [90]	4204
30	28	H	Mansfield T	W	4-0	1-0	6	Lafferty [6], Martis [53], Clarke [58], Sodje [64]	4282
31	Feb 4	A	Boston U	D	0-0	0-0	7		2268
32	11	H	Bristol R	D	1-1	0-0	6	Johnson S (pen) [75]	4579
33	14	A	Peterborough U	L	1-2	1-1	—	Cooke [26]	3960
34	18	H	Shrewsbury T	L	0-1	0-0	10		3898
35	25	A	Leyton Orient	L	0-1	0-1	10		4767
36	Mar 11	H	Chester C	W	1-0	0-0	10	Martis [75]	3593
37	18	H	Carlisle U	L	0-5	0-1	11		8640
38	25	A	Barnet	L	0-1	0-0	11		2845
39	Apr 1	H	Lincoln C	W	4-2	0-0	11	Bates [48], Clarke [57], Johnson J 2 [61, 71]	4028
40	4	A	Rochdale	W	2-0	1-0	—	Cooke [34], Johnson J [53]	1963
41	8	A	Torquay U	W	2-1	0-1	8	Sodje [66], Wainwright [89]	2715
42	15	H	Northampton T	L	0-1	0-0	9		5220
43	17	A	Cheltenham T	D	1-1	0-0	9	Wainwright [50]	3851
44	22	H	Bury	L	2-3	1-1	10	Brass (og) [8], Sodje [80]	3739
45	29	A	Wycombe W	W	1-0	0-0	9	Duke [50]	5840
46	May 6	H	Wrexham	D	1-1	0-1	8	Cooke [90]	4648

Final League Position: 8

GOALSCORERS

League (58): N'Dumbu Nsungu 10 (3 pens), Sodje 8, Johnson S 7 (3 pens), Logan 4, Clarke 3, Cooke 3, Johnson J 3, Lafferty 3, Wainwright 3, Dickman 2, Kandol 2, Martis 2, Bates 1, Duke 1, Hopkins 1, Stamp 1, Webster 1, Wijnhard 1 (pen), own goals 2.
Carling Cup (1): Logan 1.
FA Cup (0).
Football League Trophy (1): N'Dumbu-Nsungu 1 (pen).

Russell S 30	Valentine R 43	Logan C 27 + 6	Martis S 39 + 1	Clarke M 42 + 1	Hutchinson J 19	Dickman J 35 + 3	Appleby M 18 + 8	Johnson S 35 + 7	Wijnhard C 5 + 3	Webster A 6 + 7	N'Dumbu Nsungu G 11 + 10	Sodje A 17 + 19	Thomas S — + 6	Duke D 17 + 3	Wainwright N 23 + 16	Peacock A 17 + 10	Bossu B 9	Jameson N 1 + 4	Kendrick J 21	Close B 4 + 2	Keltie C 23 + 1	Kandol T 6 + 1	Stamp P 5 + 3	Knight D 3	Hopkins P 3 + 2	Lafferty K 9	Schmeichel K 4	McGurk D 2 + 1	Bates G 6 + 3	McDermott N 1 + 2	Cooke A 11 + 3	Stockdale R 3	Johnson J 9	McLeod M 2 + 2	Atieno T — + 3	Beaumont J — + 1	Maddison N — + 1	Match No.
1	2	3	4	5	6	7	8	9^{1}	10^{2}	11^{3}	12	13	14																									1
1	2	3^{1}	4^{2}	5	6	7^{3}	8	9	10			12		13	11	14																						2
1	2	3	4	5^{2}	6	7^{3}	8	9	10^{1}	13	14	12			11																							3
1	2	3	4	5	6	7		9^{2}	10^{1}		13	12		14	11^{3}	8																						4
	3	11	2^{2}	5	6	4		9		12		10		13	7^{3}	8^{1}	1	14																				5
	3	11		5■	6	4	12	9^{3}	13	14		10^{2}		2	7	8^{1}	1																					6
	2	11	4		5	6^{1}	12	9^{2}		14	13	10		3	7	8^{3}	1																					7
	2	11	3	5	6	4^{2}		9			12	10			7^{1}	8	1	13																				8
1	2	11^{1}	3	5	6		4	9	12	13	14	10^{3}			7	8^{2}																						9
1	3	11	2	5	6^{1}	12		9^{3}		13	8	10^{2}		7	14	4																						10
1	2	11	4	5	6			9^{1}	12		10			3	7	8																						11
1	2	11^{3}		5	6	12	8	9	10^{2}	7^{1}	13			3	14	4																						12
1	2		4	5	6		8^{1}	9^{3}		11	10		12	3	13	7^{2}		14																				13
1	2		4	5	6		8^{3}	9		11	10^{2}	13	12	3^{1}	7			14																				14
1	2		4	5	6	7		9		3^{1}	12	10	13		14	8^{2}		11^{3}																				15
1	2		4	5	6■	8		9			12	10	13	3^{2}	7	11^{1}																						16
1	2	12	4	5			8^{3}	9				10			7^{1}	6			3^{2}	13	14■	11																17
1	2	12	4	5		13	8^{2}	9^{3}			10			3	14	6				7^{1}		11																18
	2	11	4	5		7		9^{1}			10	13		3^{3}	12	6	1			14		8^{2}																19
	2	11^{3}	4^{1}	12	5	7		9			10	13			14		1		3		6		8^{2}															20
	2	11^{3}		5	6	7^{1}		9		12	10	13			14		1		3		4		8^{2}															21
		11	12	5	6^{1}	4	2^{2}	9^{3}			10	13					1		3	7	8	14																22
		12	4	5		6		9^{1}			10^{2}				7	13	1		3	2	8	11																23
		12	4	5		6	13	9^{3}			14	10■			7				3^{1}	2^{2}	8	11		1														24
	2	12	4	5		6^{2}		9^{1}			10	14			7	13			3		8	11^{3}		1														25
	2	11	4	5		6^{2}	12						13		7				3		8		15	1^{6}	10	9^{1}												26
	2	11		5		6^{1}	12	7^{2}								13			3^{3}		8		14		9	10	1	4										27
	2	12	4	5^{3}		6	7^{1}	13											3		8		11		9^{2}	10	1	14										28
	2	11^{3}	4	5		6	12	9				13							3		8		7^{2}		14	10^{1}	1											29
	2	11	4	5		6^{1}		7				9				12			3		8^{2}		13		14	10^{3}	1											30
1	2	11	4	5				7^{1}				9			12				3		6		8			10^{2}			13									31
1	2	11	4	5		6^{1}	12	13				9^{3}			7^{2}				3		8					10			14									32
1	2	11^{3}	4	5		6		12^{2}				14			7^{1}				3		8					10				13	9							33
1	2	11	4	5		6^{3}	12	7^{2}				13							3^{1}		8					10				14	9							34
1	2	11^{3}	4			6	5■					14			12	13					8								9^{2}	3^{1}	10	7						35
1	3		4	5		6		12		11^{1}		13			14	7^{3}					8■										10^{2}	2	9					36
1	2		4	5		6^{2}		11				12			7				3												10	8^{1}	9	13				37
1	2		4	5		11	6^{1}	8				13			7^{3}	12			3												10^{2}		9		14			38
1	2		4	5		6^{1}	8								13	12			3										11^{3}		10		9	7^{2}	14			39
1	2		4	5			6							7^{1}	12				3										9		10^{2}		11	8^{3}	13	14		40
1	2		4	5			6^{2}	12				14		7	13				3		8								9^{3}		10^{1}		11					41
1	2			5		6	4	11^{2}				13		3	7	12					8^{1}										10		9					42
1	2			5		6	4■	12				10		3	7	11^{2}					8										13		9^{1}					43
1	2		4	5		6^{2}		12				10		3^{1}	7	13					8								14		9^{3}		11					44
1	2	11^{3}	4	5■		6		7				10^{2}		3	12						8								9^{1}		13						14	45
1	2	11^{3}	4			6^{2}		7				10		3	12						8							5	9^{1}		13			14				46

FA Cup
First Round Barnsley (a) 0-1

Carling Cup
First Round Hartlepool U (a) 1-3

Football League Trophy
First Round Kidderminster H (a) 1-2

DERBY COUNTY FL Championship

FOUNDATION

Derby County was formed by members of the Derbyshire County Cricket Club in 1884, when football was booming in the area and the cricketers thought that a football club would help boost finances for the summer game. To begin with, they sported the cricket club's colours of amber, chocolate and pale blue, and went into the game at the top immediately entering the FA Cup.

Pride Park Stadium, Pride Park, Derby DE24 8XL.

Telephone: 0870 444 1884.

Fax: (01332) 667 522.

Ticket Office: 0870 444 1884.

Website: www.dcfc.co.uk

Email: derby-county@dcfc.co.uk

Ground Capacity: 33,597.

Record Attendance: Baseball ground: 41,826 v Tottenham H, Division 1, 20 September 1969. Pride Park: 33,475 Derby Co Legends v Rangers 9 in a row Legends, 1 May 2006 (Ted McMinn Benefit).

Pitch Measurements: 110yd × 74yd.

Chairman: Peter Gadsby.

Vice-chairman: Mike Horton.

Managing Director: Mike Horton.

Secretary: Marian McMinn.

Manager: Billy Davies.

Assistant Manager: TBC.

Physio: Dave Galley.

Colours: White and black.

Change Colours: Blue and yellow.

Year Formed: 1884.

Turned Professional: 1884.

Ltd Co.: 1896.

Club Nickname: 'The Rams'.

Previous Grounds: 1884, Racecourse Ground; 1895, Baseball Ground; 1997, Pride Park.

First Football League Game: 8 September 1888, Football League, v Bolton W (a) W 6–3 – Marshall; Latham, Ferguson, Williamson; Monks, W. Roulstone; Bakewell (2), Cooper (2), Higgins, H. Plackett, L. Plackett (2).

Record League Victory: 9–0 v Wolverhampton W, Division 1, 10 January 1891 – Bunyan; Archie Goodall, Roberts; Walker, Chalmers, Roulstone (1); Bakewell, McLachlan, Johnny Goodall (1), Holmes (2), McMillan (5). 9–0 v Sheffield W, Division 1, 21 January 1899 – Fryer; Methven, Staley; Cox, Archie Goodall, May; Oakden (1), Bloomer (6), Boag, McDonald (1), Allen, (1 og).

HONOURS

Football League: Division 1 – Champions 1971–72, 1974–75; Runners-up 1895–96, 1929–30, 1935–36, 1995–96; Division 2 – Champions 1911–12, 1914–15, 1968–69, 1986–87; Runners-up 1925–26; Division 3 (N) Champions 1956–57; Runners-up 1955–56.

FA Cup: Winners 1946; Runners-up 1898, 1899, 1903.

Football League Cup: Semi-final 1968.

Texaco Cup: Winners 1972.

European Competitions: *European Cup:* 1972–73, 1975–76. *UEFA Cup:* 1974–75, 1976–77. *Anglo-Italian Cup:* Runners-up 1993.

SKY SPORTS FACT FILE

Freddie Wheatcroft must have had an open-ended season ticket between Derby County and Swindon Town in the 1900s. He made the trip three times there and back, once returning from Fulham and another via Reading – and he scored goals at both clubs.

Record Cup Victory: 12–0 v Finn Harps, UEFA Cup 1st rd 1st leg, 15 September 1976 – Moseley; Thomas, Nish, Rioch (1), McFarland, Todd (King), Macken, Gemmill, Hector (5), George (3), James (3).

Record Defeat: 2–11 v Everton, FA Cup 1st rd, 1889–90.

Most League Points (2 for a win): 63, Division 2, 1968–69 and Division 3 (N), 1955–56 and 1956–57.

Most League Points (3 for a win): 84, Division 3, 1985–86 and Division 3, 1986–87.

Most League Goals: 111, Division 3 (N), 1956–57.

Highest League Scorer in Season: Jack Bowers, 37, Division 1, 1930–31; Ray Straw, 37 Division 3 (N), 1956–57.

Most League Goals in Total Aggregate: Steve Bloomer, 292, 1892–1906 and 1910–14.

Most League Goals in One Match: 6, Steve Bloomer v Sheffield W, Division 1, 2 January 1899.

Most Capped Players: Deon Burton, 41 (98), Jamaica and Mart Poom, 41 (101), Estonia.

Most League Appearances: Kevin Hector, 486, 1966–78 and 1980–82.

Youngest League Player: Lee Holmes, 15 years 268 days v Grimsby T, 26 December 2002.

Record Transfer Fee Received: £7,000,000 rising to £9,000,000 for Seth Johnson from Leeds U, October 2001.

Record Transfer Fee Paid: £3,000,000 for Horacio Carbonari from Club Rosario Central, May 1998.

Football League Record: 1888 Founder Member of the Football League; 1907–12 Division 2; 1912–14 Division 1; 1914–15 Division 2; 1915–21 Division 1; 1921–26 Division 2; 1926–53 Division 1; 1953–55 Division 2; 1955–57 Division 3 (N); 1957–69 Division 2; 1969–80 Division 1; 1980–84 Division 2; 1984–86 Division 3; 1986–87 Division 2; 1987–91 Division 1; 1991–92 Division 2; 1992–96 Division 1; 1996–2002 FA Premier League; 2002–04 Division 1; 2004– FLC.

MANAGERS

W. D. Clark 1896–1900
Harry Newbould 1900–06
Jimmy Methven 1906–22
Cecil Potter 1922–25
George Jobey 1925–41
Ted Magner 1944–46
Stuart McMillan 1946–53
Jack Barker 1953–55
Harry Storer 1955–62
Tim Ward 1962–67
Brian Clough 1967–73
Dave Mackay 1973–76
Colin Murphy 1977
Tommy Docherty 1977–79
Colin Addison 1979–82
Johnny Newman 1982
Peter Taylor 1982–84
Roy McFarland 1984
Arthur Cox 1984–93
Roy McFarland 1993–95
Jim Smith 1995–2001
Colin Todd 2001–02
John Gregory 2002–03
George Burley 2003–05
Phil Brown 2005–06
Billy Davies June 2006–

LATEST SEQUENCES

Longest Sequence of League Wins: 9, 15.3.1969 – 19.4.1969.

Longest Sequence of League Defeats: 8, 12.12.1987 – 10.2.1988.

Longest Sequence of League Draws: 6, 26.3.1927 – 18.4.1927.

Longest Sequence of Unbeaten League Matches: 22, 8.3.1969 – 20.9.1969.

Longest Sequence Without a League Win: 20, 15.12.1990 – 23.4.1991.

Successive Scoring Runs: 29 from 3.12.1960.

Successive Non-scoring Runs: 8 from 30.10.1920.

TEN YEAR LEAGUE RECORD

		P	W	D	L	F	A	Pts	Pos
1996-97	PR Lge	38	11	13	14	45	58	46	12
1997-98	PR Lge	38	16	7	15	52	49	55	9
1998-99	PR Lge	38	13	13	12	40	45	52	8
1999-2000	PR Lge	38	9	11	18	44	57	38	16
2000-01	PR Lge	38	10	12	16	37	59	42	17
2001-02	PR Lge	38	8	6	24	33	63	30	19
2002-03	Div 1	46	15	7	24	55	74	52	18
2003-04	Div 1	46	13	13	20	53	67	52	20
2004-05	FL C	46	22	10	14	71	60	76	4
2005-06	FL C	46	10	20	16	53	67	50	20

DID YOU KNOW ?

England international half-back Frank Forman had a long association with Nottingham Forest, but actually made his League debut for Derby County against Forest on 8 September 1894 in a 4–2 win while still an amateur with Beeston Town.

DERBY COUNTY 2005–06 LEAGUE RECORD

Match No.	Date	Venue	Opponents	Result		H/T Score	Lg. Pos.	Goalscorers	Attendance
1	Aug 6	H	Brighton & HA	D	1-1	1-1	—	Peschisolido [12]	25,292
2	8	A	Preston NE	D	1-1	1-1	—	Idiakez (pen) [43]	13,127
3	13	A	Plymouth Arg	W	2-0	2-0	6	Rasiak [20], Bisgaard [39]	14,279
4	20	H	Cardiff C	W	2-1	2-0	3	Bisgaard [21], Idiakez (pen) [45]	23,153
5	27	A	Burnley	D	2-2	1-0	7	Idiakez [30], Rasiak [90]	12,243
6	29	H	Watford	L	1-2	1-0	9	Bolder [4]	23,664
7	Sept 11	A	Crewe Alex	D	1-1	0-1	10	Bisgaard [49]	5958
8	14	H	Coventry C	D	1-1	1-0	—	Bisgaard [14]	21,840
9	18	H	Southampton	D	2-2	0-0	9	Idiakez (pen) [80], Davies [85]	22,348
10	24	A	Sheffield U	L	1-2	0-2	12	Peschisolido [53]	22,192
11	28	A	Leeds U	L	1-3	0-3	—	Gregan (og) [74]	18,353
12	Oct 1	H	Leicester C	D	1-1	0-0	16	El Hamdaoui [89]	25,044
13	15	H	Stoke C	W	2-1	1-0	12	Idiakez [45], Peschisolido [86]	22,229
14	18	A	Wolverhampton W	D	1-1	0-1	—	El Hamdaoui [46]	22,914
15	22	A	Hull C	L	1-2	0-1	15	Idiakez (pen) [56]	20,661
16	29	H	QPR	L	1-2	0-1	17	Blackstock [84]	24,447
17	Nov 2	H	Ipswich T	D	3-3	2-2	—	Blackstock 2 [35, 56], Tudgay [38]	21,598
18	5	A	Sheffield W	L	1-2	1-0	19	Tudgay [42]	26,334
19	18	H	Wolverhampton W	L	0-3	0-0	—		22,869
20	22	A	Stoke C	W	2-1	0-1	—	Smith [64], Nyatanga [69]	13,205
21	26	A	Brighton & HA	D	0-0	0-0	17		6855
22	Dec 3	H	Norwich C	W	2-0	1-0	14	Davies 2 [28, 52]	23,346
23	10	H	Preston NE	D	1-1	0-0	14	Smith (pen) [81]	22,740
24	17	A	Cardiff C	D	0-0	0-0	16		12,500
25	26	H	Luton T	D	1-1	0-0	16	Idiakez [72]	26,807
26	28	A	Crystal Palace	L	0-2	0-2	18		18,978
27	31	H	Reading	D	2-2	1-1	17	Johnson S 2 [32, 62]	21,434
28	Jan 2	A	Millwall	L	1-2	0-0	18	Johnson S [60]	9523
29	14	H	Crewe Alex	W	5-1	2-0	16	Peschisolido [11], Johnson M [21], Smith 2 [53, 63], Idiakez [71]	22,649
30	21	A	Coventry C	L	1-6	1-1	18	Peschisolido [2]	20,267
31	Feb 1	H	Sheffield U	L	0-1	0-1	—		26,275
32	4	A	Southampton	D	0-0	0-0	19		21,829
33	11	H	Leeds U	D	0-0	0-0	20		27,000
34	14	A	Leicester C	D	2-2	1-1	—	El Hamdaoui [24], Stearman (og) [58]	23,246
35	18	A	Norwich C	L	0-2	0-1	20		24,921
36	25	H	Plymouth Arg	W	1-0	1-0	19	Bolder [2]	25,170
37	Mar 4	A	Watford	D	2-2	1-1	19	Lisbie [19], Barnes [86]	16,769
38	11	H	Burnley	W	3-0	3-0	19	Smith [19], Idiakez [29], Moore [34]	23,292
39	18	A	Luton T	L	0-1	0-0	20		9163
40	25	H	Crystal Palace	W	2-1	1-1	18	Idiakez 2 [28, 90]	24,857
41	Apr 1	A	Reading	L	0-5	0-0	20		22,981
42	8	H	Millwall	W	1-0	1-0	20	Smith [31]	24,415
43	15	A	QPR	D	1-1	0-0	20	Smith [67]	12,606
44	17	H	Hull C	D	1-1	0-1	19	Smith (pen) [89]	24,961
45	22	A	Ipswich T	L	0-2	0-0	19		24,067
46	30	H	Sheffield W	L	0-2	0-1	20		30,391

Final League Position: 20

GOALSCORERS

League (53): Idiakez 11 (4 pens), Smith 8 (2 pens), Peschisolido 5, Bisgaard 4, Blackstock 3, Davies 3, El Hamdaoui 3, Johnson S 3, Bolder 2, Rasiak 2, Tudgay 2, Barnes 1, Johnson M 1, Lisbie 1, Moore 1, Nyatanga 1, own goals 2.
Carling Cup (0).
FA Cup (3): Peschisolido 2, Smith 1 (pen).

Camp L 40	Edworthy M 30	Jackson R 20 + 6	Thirlwell P 15 + 6	Davies A 22 + 1	Johnson M 30 + 1	Bisgaard M 25 + 8	Idiakez I 41 + 1	Rasiak G 6	Peschisolido P 14 + 20	Smith T 43	Holmes L 9 + 9	Tudgay M 11 + 10	Bolder A 25 + 10	Mills P — + 1	Johnson S 26 + 4	Kenna J 15 + 1	Barnes G 15 + 4	Fadiga K 2 + 2	Holdsworth D — + 3	El Hamdaoui M 5 + 4	John S 6 + 1	Whittingham P 11	Poole K 6	Nyatanga L 23 + 1	Jackson J 3 + 3	Emerson 3 + 1	Blackstock D 8 + 1	Doyle N — + 4	Graham D 11 + 3	Hajto T 5	Moore D 14	Wright A 7	Lisbie K 7	Ainsworth L — + 2	McIndoe M 6 + 2	Addison M 2	*Match No.*
1	2	3	4	5	6	7	8^1	9	10^2	11	12	13																									1
1	2	3		5	6	7^1	8	9	10^2	11		12	4	13																							2
1	2	3	4	5	6	7	8	9		10^1		12	11																								3
1	2	3	4	5	6	7^1	8	9		10^2		12	11		13																						4
1	2^3	3	4	5	6^1	7	8	9	13	10		12	11^2		14																						5
1		3■	4	5	6	7	8	9^3	12	10^2		14	11^1		13	2																					6
1			4	5■	6	7^1	8		12	10		9^2	11		3	2	13																				7
1	2^1		4^2		6	7	8		12	10		9^3	11		3	5		13	14																		8
1	2^2			5	6	7	8		12	10					3	13		4^3		14	9^1	11															9
1				5	6	7^3	8		12	10			4^2		3	2		14		13	9^1	11															10
1				5	6	7			8	10^2			12		3	2		4^1	14	13	9^3	11															11
				5^1	6	7	11		8^2	10			12		4	2			14	13	9^3	3	1														12
				5	6	7	8		9^2	10^3		12			11	2				4^1		3	1	13	14												13
					6	7^1	8		9^3	10		12			5	2				11^2	13	3	1	4	14												14
	4			5■		7	8		10^1	11^2		12			6	2					9	3	1		13												15
			12		6	7	8		10^2			13			4	2^1					9^3	3	1		11	5	14										16
	2				6	7	8					9			4		12					3	1		11^1	5	10										17
1			12		6	7^2	8		13			9			4	2						3			11^1	5	10										18
1		2		5	6^2	7	8		12	11		9^1			4							3				13	10										19
1	2	3	4	5			8^1			11		9^2	12		7									6			10	13									20
1	2	3	4^2	5		12	8			11		9^1	13		7									6			10^3		14								21
1	2	3	4	5			8			11		9	7											6			10										22
1	2	3	4^2	5		12	8			11		9^1	7		13									6			10^3		14								23
1		2	4	5	6	12	8			11		9^1			7									3			10^2		13								24
1		2	4	5	6	12	8		13	11		9^1	14		7^3									3					10^2								25
1		2	4^1	5	6	7^3	8		12	10	14		13		11									3					9^2								26
1	2	3	12	5■	13		8		14	10^2	11^1		4		7									6					9^3								27
1	2	3			5		8		12	10^2	11		4^1		7		13							6					9								28
1	3	12	13		5^1	14	8		11	10	4				7^2	2								6					9^3								29
1	2			12	3	13	8		10	11	4		14		7^3	5^1								6					9^2								30
1	3	12			6■		8		13	10	11^1		7^2				4^3											14	9	2	5						31
1	2	12			6^1	13	8			10	11^2		7				4^3											14	9	3	5						32
1	2	3^3				7^1			13	10	12		8				4			11								14	9^2	5	6						33
1	2		12			7^2			13	10			8			3	4			11^1									9	5	6						34
1	2						8		12	10	11^1		7			3	4												9	5	6						35
1	2						8		10^1	11	12		7				4							6							5	3	9^2	13			36
1	2						8		12	10	11		7				4							6							5	3	9^1				37
1	2		12				8		13	10	14		7				4^1							6							5	3	9^2		11^3		38
1	2						8^1		12	10	13		7				4							6							5	3	9		11^2		39
1		2					8			10			7				4							6							5	3	9		11		40
1		2				12	8		9^2	10			7^1				4							6							5	3		13	11		41
1	2	13					8			10			12		7^1		4			11^3				6							5	3^2	9		14		42
1		2			3		12		13	10	14		8^1		7		4^2							6							5■		9		11^3		43
1	2	12	4^3		5^1	7	8		9	10	11^2		13				14							6												3	44
1	2	12			5	7^1	8			10	13		14		9^3		4							6											11^2	3	45
1	2				3	7^2			9^1	10	12		8		11		4							6							5				13		46

FA Cup

Third Round	Burnley	(h)	2-1
Fourth Round	Colchester U	(a)	1-3

Carling Cup

First Round	Grimsby T	(h)	0-1

DONCASTER ROVERS FL Championship 1

FOUNDATION

In 1879, Mr Albert Jenkins assembled a team to play a match against the Yorkshire Institution for the Deaf. The players remained together as Doncaster Rovers, joining the Midland Alliance in 1889 and the Midland Counties League in 1891.

The Earth Stadium, Belle Vue, Bawtry Road, Doncaster, South Yorkshire DN4 5HT.

Telephone: (01302) 539 441.

Fax: (01302) 539 679.

Ticket Office: (01302) 539 441.

Website: www.doncasterroversfc.co.uk

Email: info@doncasterroversfc.co.uk

Ground Capacity: 10,593.

Record Attendance: 3,7149 v Hull C, Division 3 (N), 2 October 1948.

Pitch Measurements: 110yd × 76yd.

Chairman: John Ryan.

Vice-chairman: Jim Beresford

Managing Director: Stuart Highfield JP.

Chief Executive/Secretary: David Morris.

Manager: Dave Penney.

Assistant Manager: Mickey Walker.

Physio: Barrie Windle.

Colours: Red and white hoops.

Change Colours: All black.

Year Formed: 1879.

Turned Professional: 1885.

Ltd Co.: 1905 & 1920.

Club Nickname: 'Rovers'.

Previous Grounds: 1880–1916, Intake Ground; 1920, Benetthorpe Ground; 1922, Low Pasture, Belle Vue.

Record League Victory: 10–0 v Darlington, Division 4, 25 January 1964: Potter; Raine, Meadows, Windross (1), White, Ripley (2), Robinson, Book (2), Hale (4), Jeffrey, Broadbent (1).

Record Cup Victory: 7–0 v Blyth Spartans, FA Cup 1st rd, 27 November 1937: Imrie; Shaw, Rodgers, McFarlane, Bycroft, Cyril Smith, Burton (1), Killourhy (4), Morgan (2), Malam, Dutton.

HONOURS

Football League: Division 2 best season: 7th, 1901–02; Division 3 Champions 2003–04; Division 3 (N) Champions – 1934–35, 1946–47, 1949–50; Runners-up: 1937–38, 1938–39; Division 4 Champions 1965–66, 1968–69; Runners-up: 1983–84. Promoted 1980–81 (3rd).

FA Cup: best season 5th rd, 1952, 1954, 1955, 1956.

Football League Cup: best season: 5th rd, 1976.

Football Conference: Champions 2002–03

Sheffield County Cup: Winners 1891, 1912, 1936, 1938, 1956, 1968, 1976, 1986.

Midland Counties League: Champions 1897, 1899.

Conference Trophy: Winners 1999, 2000.

Sheffield & Hallamshire Senior Cup: Winners 2001, 2002.

SKY SPORTS FACT FILE

On 21 September 2005 Jan Budtz was called upon to replace injured goalkeeper Andy Warrington for his debut in the 105th minute of the Carling Cup game against Manchester City. In the penalty shoot-out he saved two shots and Rovers won 3–0.

Record Defeat: 0–12 v Small Heath, Division 2, 11 April 1903.

Most League Points (2 for a win): 72, Division 3 (N), 1946–47.

Most League Points (3 for a win): 92, Division 3, 2003–04.

Most League Goals: 123, Division 3 (N), 1946–47.

Highest League Scorer in Season: Clarrie Jordan, 42, Division 3 (N), 1946–47.

Most League Goals in Total Aggregate: Tom Keetley, 180, 1923–29.

Most Capped Player: Len Graham, 14, Northern Ireland.

Most League Appearances: Fred Emery, 417, 1925–36.

Record Transfer Fee Received: £275,000 from QPR for Rufus Brevett, February 1991.

Record Transfer Fee Paid: £175,000 to Sunderland for Sean Thornton, July 2005.

Football League Record: 1901 Elected to Division 2; 1903 Failed re-election; 1904 Re-elected; 1905 Failed re-election; 1923 Re-elected to Divison 3 (N); 1935–37 Division 2; 1937–47 Division 3 (N); 1947–48 Division 2; 1948–50 Division 3 (N); 1950–58 Division 2; 1958–59 Division 3; 1959–66 Division 4; 1966–67 Division 3; 1967–69 Division 4; 1969–71 Division 3; 1971–81 Division 4; 1981–83 Division 3; 1983–84 Division 4; 1984–88 Division 3; 1988–92 Division 4; 1992–98 Division 3; 1998–2003 Conference; 2003–04 Division 3; 2004– FL1.

LATEST SEQUENCES

Longest Sequence of League Wins: 10, 22.1.1947 – 4.4.1947.

Longest Sequence of League Defeats: 9, 14.1.1905 – 1.4.1905.

Longest Sequence of League Draws: 4, 29.10.1932 – 19.11.1932.

Longest Sequence of Unbeaten League Matches: 20, 26.12.1968 – 12.4.1969.

Longest Sequence Without a League Win: 20, 9.8.1997 – 29.11.1997.

Successive Scoring Runs: 27 from 10.11.1934.

Successive Non-scoring Runs: 7 from 27.9.1947.

MANAGERS

Arthur Porter 1920–21
Harry Tufnell 1921–22
Arthur Porter 1922–23
Dick Ray 1923–27
David Menzies 1928–36
Fred Emery 1936–40
Bill Marsden 1944–46
Jackie Bestall 1946–49
Peter Doherty 1949–58
Jack Hodgson & Sid Bycroft (*Joint Managers*) 1958
Jack Crayston 1958–59 (*continued as Secretary-Manager to 1961*)
Jackie Bestall (TM) 1959–60
Norman Curtis 1960–61
Danny Malloy 1961–62
Oscar Hold 1962–64
Bill Leivers 1964–66
Keith Kettleborough 1966–67
George Raynor 1967–68
Lawrie McMenemy 1968–71
Morris Setters 1971–74
Stan Anderson 1975–78
Billy Bremner 1978–85
Dave Cusack 1985–87
Dave Mackay 1987–89
Billy Bremner 1989–91
Steve Beaglehole 1991–93
Ian Atkins 1994
Sammy Chung 1994–96
Kerry Dixon (*Player–Manager*) 1996–97
Dave Cowling 1997
Mark Weaver 1997–98
Ian Snodin 1998–99
Steve Wignall 1999–2001
Dave Penney March 2002–

TEN YEAR LEAGUE RECORD

		P	W	D	L	F	A	Pts	Pos
1996-97	Div 3	46	14	10	22	52	65	52	19
1997-98	Div 3	46	4	8	34	30	113	20	24
1998-99	Conf.	42	12	12	18	51	55	48	16
1999-2000	Conf.	42	15	9	18	46	48	54	12
2000-01	Conf.	42	15	13	14	47	43	58	9
2001-02	Conf.	42	18	13	11	68	46	67	4
2002-03	Conf.	42	22	12	8	73	47	78	3
2003-04	Div 3	46	27	11	8	79	37	92	1
2004-05	FL 1	46	16	18	12	65	60	66	10
2005-06	FL 1	46	20	9	17	55	51	69	8

DID YOU KNOW?

On 14 March 1936 one Doncaster Rovers player earned more than the rest of his team despite not playing. Twelfth man at Bradford City he was pressed into service to act as linesman when the official failed to arrive and earned a fee of £1.11s.6d (£1.58).

DONCASTER ROVERS 2005–06 LEAGUE RECORD

Match No.	Date	Venue	Opponents	Result	H/T Score	Lg. Pos.	Goalscorers	Attendance
1	Aug 6	A	Bristol C	D 0-0	0-0	—		15,481
2	9	H	Milton Keynes D	D 1-1	0-0	—	Heffernan 66	5232
3	13	H	Hartlepool U	L 0-1	0-1	20		5061
4	20	A	Swansea C	W 2-1	0-1	13	Mulligan 74, Guy 85	12,744
5	27	A	Port Vale	L 0-2	0-1	20		4993
6	29	H	Huddersfield T	L 1-2	0-2	23	McIndoe (pen) 64	7222
7	Sept 2	H	Blackpool	L 0-1	0-0	—		5484
8	10	A	Colchester U	L 2-3	1-3	24	Forte 5, McIndoe (pen) 54	2721
9	17	H	Scunthorpe U	W 3-1	2-0	21	Fortune-West 15, McIndoe 25, Forte 60	6699
10	24	A	Barnsley	W 2-0	1-0	19	Green 13, Mulligan 83	12,002
11	27	H	Swindon T	W 1-0	1-0	—	Forte 36	5282
12	Oct 1	H	Bradford C	D 2-2	0-1	14	Ravenhill 55, Fenton 69	6800
13	7	A	Bournemouth	L 1-2	1-0	—	Heffernan 7	6578
14	15	H	Southend U	W 2-0	0-0	13	Ravenhill 77, Forte 88	5899
15	22	A	Walsall	L 0-1	0-0	15		5385
16	29	H	Tranmere R	L 0-2	0-0	18		5542
17	Nov 13	A	Oldham Ath	W 1-0	0-0	16	McIndoe (pen) 78	5800
18	19	H	Bournemouth	W 4-2	1-0	12	Heffernan 41, McIndoe (pen) 61, Ravenhill 63, Green 85	4803
19	26	H	Bristol C	W 2-0	1-0	9	Heffernan 5, Coppinger 68	7876
20	Dec 6	A	Gillingham	L 0-1	0-1	—		4861
21	10	A	Milton Keynes D	W 3-2	2-0	9	Fenton 13, Roberts S 23, Heffernan 86	5351
22	17	H	Swansea C	W 2-1	1-1	8	McIndoe (pen) 16, Heffernan 84	7159
23	26	A	Nottingham F	L 0-4	0-1	10		23,009
24	31	A	Rotherham U	L 0-1	0-0	13		6761
25	Jan 2	H	Yeovil T	L 0-1	0-1	13		5680
26	14	H	Chesterfield	D 1-1	1-0	15	Heffernan 45	6528
27	21	A	Scunthorpe U	W 2-1	0-0	12	McIndoe 63, Lee 89	6978
28	24	A	Blackpool	L 2-4	1-3	—	McIndoe (pen) 26, McCormack 90	4836
29	Feb 4	A	Swindon T	L 1-2	0-1	15	Heffernan 64	5100
30	11	H	Barnsley	W 2-0	1-0	14	Jason Price 2 36, 59	8144
31	15	A	Chesterfield	W 1-0	1-0	—	Jason Price 14	5719
32	18	H	Gillingham	W 2-0	2-0	9	Wheater 27, McCormack (pen) 45	5738
33	25	A	Hartlepool U	D 1-1	0-1	10	McCormack 90	5459
34	28	H	Brentford	D 0-0	0-0	—		5250
35	Mar 4	A	Huddersfield T	D 2-2	1-2	9	Jason Price 15, Green 57	14,490
36	11	H	Port Vale	D 1-1	0-0	9	Fortune-West 58	5511
37	18	H	Nottingham F	L 1-2	0-1	10	Coppinger (pen) 86	8299
38	21	H	Colchester U	D 0-0	0-0	—		4262
39	25	A	Brentford	W 1-0	0-0	9	Thornton 59	7323
40	Apr 1	H	Rotherham U	W 3-1	3-1	9	Roberts N 6, Thornton 10, Guy 21	7542
41	8	A	Yeovil T	L 0-3	0-1	9		5456
42	15	A	Bradford C	L 1-2	0-2	10	McCormack 68	9297
43	17	H	Walsall	W 1-0	1-0	10	Coppinger 43	5086
44	22	A	Southend U	W 1-0	0-0	10	Coppinger 46	10,397
45	29	H	Oldham Ath	W 1-0	0-0	8	Coppinger 66	6104
46	May 6	A	Tranmere R	W 2-0	2-0	8	Guy 12, Roberts N 43	8343

Final League Position: 8

GOALSCORERS

League (55): Heffernan 8, McIndoe 8 (6 pens), Coppinger 5 (1 pen), Forte 4, McCormack 4 (1 pen), Jason Price 4, Green 3, Guy 3, Ravenhill 3, Fenton 2, Fortune-West 2, Mulligan 2, Roberts N 2, Thornton 2, Lee 1, Roberts S 1, Wheater 1.
Carling Cup (9): Heffernan 3, McIndoe 3 (2 pens), Green 1, Hughes 1, Thornton 1.
FA Cup (7): Heffernan 3, McIndoe 2 (2 pens), Mulligan 2.
Football League Trophy (7): Fortune-West 2, Guy 2, Offiong 1, own goals 2.

Warrington A 9	McGuire P 11	Ryan T 7	Foster S 17	Fenton N 21 + 4	Green P 23 + 11	Mulligan D 22 + 10	Thornton S 23 + 6	Roberts N 17 + 13	Heffernan P 22 + 4	McIndoe M 29 + 4	Roberts S 23 + 4	Fortune-West L 16 + 11	Guy L 18 + 13	Coppinger J 32 + 4	Ravenhill R 23 + 4	Hughes A 4 + 2	Predic U 3 + 3	Offiong R 2 + 3	Forte J 9 + 4	McDaid S 35	Albrighton M 16	Budtz J 20	Marples S 12 + 3	Seremet D 1	Oji S 1 + 3	Blayney A 16	Lee G 20	McCormack R 12 + 7	Price Jason 11	Griffiths A 4	Wheater D 7	Horlock K 13	Armstrong A 1 + 5	Timlin M 3	McSporran J 2	Nelthorpe C 1	*Match No.*
1	2	3	4	5	6	7	8[1]	9[2]	10[3]	11	12	13	14																								1
1	2[1]	3	4	5	6		8	9[3]	10	11	12	14	13	7[2]																							2
1	2	3	4	5			8	9[2]	10	11		13	12	7[1]	6																						3
1	2	3	4	5		7	8[2]	9[3]	10[1]	11			12	13	6	14																					4
1	2[2]	3[3]	4	5		7	12	9	10	11			13	14	6[1]	8																					5
1		3	4	5		2	8[2]	9[1]	13	11		12	10■	7[3]		6	14																				6
1		3	4	5		2	8	9[1]	10			12			13	7[2]	6[3]	14	11																		7
1	2		4		6[1]	7[2]		12		11		9			8		13		10	3	5																8
1	3				6	12				11	5	9		7[1]	13		8[2]		10	2	4																9
	2				6[2]	13		9	12	11	5			7	8				10[1]	3	4	1															10
	2			12		13			14	11	5[1]	9		7[2]	6		8[3]		10■	3	4	1															11
	2			5	6[1]	12		9[3]	10	11			13	7[2]	8■		14			3	4	1															12
	2			5	6	8			10[3]	11		9[1]		7[2]		13			12	3	4	1	14														13
					6	12		9	10[2]	11	5			7	8				13	3[1]	4	1	2														14
					6[1]		12	9[3]		11	5	13	14	7[2]	8				10	3	4	1	2														15
					6[1]		12	9[3]	10	11	5	13	14	7[2]	8					3	4	1	2														16
			4	5	6	2[2]			10[1]	11	13	12	9		8			7[3]		3		1	14														17
			4	12	13	2	8[1]		10	11	5		7		6				9[2]	3		1															18
			4	2	12		8	13	10	11	5		9[2]	7	6					3[1]				1													19
			4	2	12	3[1]	8[2]		10		5		9	7	6[3]				13	11		1			14												20
			4	2	12		8	13	10	11	5[3]			7[1]	6				9[2]	3		1			14												21
			4	2			8[2]	12	10	11	5		9		6			7[1]	13	3		1															22
			4	2	6		12		10[2]	11	5[3]		13	7	8[1]				9	3		1			14												23
			4		12	13	8[1]		10■	11	5[2]	14	9	7[3]	6							1	2		3												24
			5	2		7[3]	12	13		11		10[2]	9		6	8[1]		14		3	4	1															25
				2	6	12	8[2]		10	11[1]			9	7				13		3	4					1	5										26
				2	6	7[2]	8		10	11			12	13■						3	4					1	5	9[1]									27
				2	6	12	13		10[3]	11		14	7[1]		8					3[2]	4					1	5	9									28
				2	12	13			10	11		14			6[1]					3	4[2]					1	5	9[3]	7	8							29
					6	2		12		11		10								3	4					1		9[1]	7		5	8					30
					6[2]	2		12		11[3]		10		14	13					3						1	5	9[1]	7		4	8					31
				12	6	2		13		14		10		11[3]						3						1	5	9[2]	7[1]		4	8					32
				12	6	2		13		14		10[2]		11						3[1]		1					5	9	7[3]		4	8					33
				4[3]	6	3		12		13		10		11[2]	14							1	2				5	9[1]	7			8					34
					6	3			12	13		10[1]		11[2]								1	2				5	9	7		4	8					35
					6	3		12			13	10[1]	14	11								1	2				5	9[3]	7		4[2]	8					36
					6	12		13			2	10[2]	14	11						3		1					5	9[3]	7[1]		4	8					37
						2	4	9[2]			6		10[1]	11						3						1	5	12	7			8	13				38
						2	4	9[2]			6		10[1]	11						3						1	5	12	7			8	13				39
					12	2	4[1]	9[2]			6		10	7						3						1	5	13				8		11			40
					12		4	9[2]			6		10[3]	7						3			2			1	5	13				8	14	11[1]			41
					12		4				5[3]		13	7[2]	10[1]					3	2		14			1	6	9				8	11				42
					12		8				4	9	10	7	6[1]					3			2			1	5	13						11[2]			43
					12		8				4	9[3]	10[2]	7						3			2			1	5	13		6[1]			14		11		44
							8	12			4	9[2]	10	7						3			2			1	5			6			13		11[1]		45
							8	9			4		10[1]	7						3			2			1	5	12		6						11	46

FA Cup

First Round	Blackpool	(h)	4-1
Second Round	Boston U	(a)	2-1
Third Round	Port Vale	(a)	1-2

Football League Trophy

First Round	Barnsley	(a)	5-2
Second Round	Cambridge U	(a)	2-3

Carling Cup

First Round	Wrexham	(a)	1-0
Second Round	Manchester C	(h)	1-1
Third Round	Gillingham	(h)	2-0
Fourth Round	Aston Villa	(h)	3-0
Quarter-Final	Arsenal	(h)	2-2

EVERTON FA Premiership

FOUNDATION

St Domingo Church Sunday School formed a football club in 1878 which played at Stanley Park. Enthusiasm was so great that in November 1879 they decided to expand membership and changed the name to Everton playing in black shirts with a scarlet sash and nicknamed the 'Black Watch'. After wearing several other colours, royal blue was adopted in 1901.

Goodison Park, Goodison Road, Liverpool L4 4EL.

Telephone: (0870) 442 1878.

Fax: (0151) 286 9114.

Ticket Office: 0870 442 1878.

Website: www.evertonfc.com

Email: everton@evertonfc.com

Ground Capacity: 40,394.

Record Attendance: 78,299 v Liverpool, Division 1, 18 September 1948.

Pitch Measurements: 100.58m × 68m.

Chairman: Bill Kenwright CBE.

Vice chairman: Jon Woods.

Chief Executive: Keith Wyness.

Secretary: David Harrison.

Manager: David Moyes.

Assistant Manager: Alan Irvine.

Head of Physiotherapy: Mick Rathbone Bsc (Hons), MCSP.

Colours: Blue shirts, white shorts, white stockings.

Change Colours: White shirts, navy shorts, navy stockings.

Year Formed: 1878.

Turned Professional: 1885.

Ltd Co.: 1892.

Previous Name: 1878, St Domingo FC; 1879, Everton.

Club Nickname: 'The Toffees'.

Previous Grounds: 1878, Stanley Park; 1882, Priory Road; 1884, Anfield Road; 1892, Goodison Park.

First Football League Game: 8 September 1888, Football League, v Accrington (h) W 2–1 – Smalley; Dick, Ross; Holt, Jones, Dobson; Fleming (2), Waugh, Lewis, E. Chadwick, Farmer.

HONOURS

Football League: Division 1 – Champions 1890–91, 1914–15, 1927–28, 1931–32, 1938–39, 1962–63, 1969–70, 1984–85, 1986–87; Runners-up 1889–90, 1894–95, 1901–02, 1904–05, 1908–09, 1911–12, 1985–86; Division 2 – Champions 1930–31; Runners-up 1953–54.

FA Cup: Winners 1906, 1933, 1966, 1984, 1995; Runners-up 1893, 1897, 1907, 1968, 1985, 1986, 1989.

Football League Cup: Runners-up 1977, 1984.

League Super Cup: Runners-up 1986.

Simod Cup: Runners-up 1989.

Zenith Data Systems Cup: Runners-up 1991.

European Competitions: *European Cup:* 1963–64, 1970–71. *European Cup-Winners' Cup:* 1966–67, 1984–85 (winners), 1995–96. *European Fairs Cup:* 1962–63, 1964–65, 1965–66. *Champions League:* 2005–06. *UEFA Cup:* 1975–76, 1978–79, 1979–80, 2005–06.

SKY SPORTS FACT FILE

On 31 August 1956 Everton paid Huddersfield Town £4000 for forward Jimmy Glazzard and gave him his 300th League appearance the following day against Wolverhampton Wanderers. On 7 April 1953 he had headed four goals against Everton.

Record League Victory: 9–1 v Manchester C, Division 1, 3 September 1906 – Scott; Balmer, Crelley; Booth, Taylor (1), Abbott (1); Sharp, Bolton (1), Young (4), Settle (2), George Wilson. 9–1 v Plymouth Arg, Division 2, 27 December 1930 – Coggins; Williams, Cresswell; McPherson, Griffiths, Thomson; Critchley, Dunn, Dean (4), Johnson (1), Stein (4).

Record Cup Victory: 11–2 v Derby Co, FA Cup 1st rd, 18 January 1890 – Smalley; Hannah, Doyle (1); Kirkwood, Holt (1), Parry; Latta, Brady (3), Geary (3), Chadwick, Millward (3).

Record Defeat: 4–10 v Tottenham H, Division 1, 11 October 1958.

Most League Points (2 for a win): 66, Division 1, 1969–70.

Most League Points (3 for a win): 90, Division 1, 1984–85.

Most League Goals: 121, Division 2, 1930–31.

Highest League Scorer in Season: William Ralph 'Dixie' Dean, 60, Division 1, 1927–28 (All-time League record).

Most League Goals in Total Aggregate: William Ralph 'Dixie' Dean, 349, 1925–37.

Most League Goals in One Match: 6, Jack Southworth v WBA, Division 1, 30 December 1893.

Most Capped Player: Neville Southall, 92, Wales.

Most League Appearances: Neville Southall, 578, 1981–98.

Youngest League Player: James Vaughan, 16 years 271 days v Crystal Palace, 10 April 2005.

Record Transfer Fee Received: £27,000,000 from Manchester U for Wayne Rooney, August 2004.

Record Transfer Fee Paid: £8,500,000 to Crystal Palace for Andy Johnson, June 2006.

Football League Record: 1888 Founder Member of the Football League; 1930–31 Division 2; 1931–51 Division 1; 1951–54 Division 2; 1954–92 Division 1; 1992– FA Premier League.

MANAGERS

W. E. Barclay 1888–89
(Secretary-Manager)
Dick Molyneux 1889–1901
(Secretary-Manager)
William C. Cuff 1901–18
(Secretary-Manager)
W. J. Sawyer 1918–19
(Secretary-Manager)
Thomas H. McIntosh 1919–35
(Secretary-Manager)
Theo Kelly 1936–48
Cliff Britton 1948–56
Ian Buchan 1956–58
Johnny Carey 1958–61
Harry Catterick 1961–73
Billy Bingham 1973–77
Gordon Lee 1977–81
Howard Kendall 1981–87
Colin Harvey 1987–90
Howard Kendall 1990–93
Mike Walker 1994
Joe Royle 1994–97
Howard Kendall 1997–98
Walter Smith 1998–2002
David Moyes March 2002–

LATEST SEQUENCES

Longest Sequence of League Wins: 12, 24.3.1894 – 13.10.1894.

Longest Sequence of League Defeats: 6, 26.12.1996 – 29.1.1997.

Longest Sequence of League Draws: 5, 4.5.1977 – 16.5.1977.

Longest Sequence of Unbeaten League Matches: 20, 29.4.1978 – 16.12.1978.

Longest Sequence Without a League Win: 14, 6.3.1937 – 4.9.1937.

Successive Scoring Runs: 40 from 15.3.1930.

Successive Non-scoring Runs: 6 from 3.3.1951.

TEN YEAR LEAGUE RECORD

		P	*W*	*D*	*L*	*F*	*A*	*Pts*	*Pos*
1996-97	PR Lge	38	10	12	16	44	57	42	15
1997-98	PR Lge	38	9	13	16	41	56	40	17
1998-99	PR Lge	38	11	10	17	42	47	43	14
1999-2000	PR Lge	38	12	14	12	59	49	50	13
2000-01	PR Lge	38	11	9	18	45	59	42	16
2001-02	PR Lge	38	11	10	17	45	57	43	15
2002-03	PR Lge	38	17	8	13	48	49	59	7
2003-04	PR Lge	38	9	12	17	45	57	39	17
2004-05	PR Lge	38	18	7	13	45	46	61	4
2005-06	PR Lge	38	14	8	16	34	49	50	11

DID YOU KNOW ?

In the last five matches of the 1955–56 season Albert Harris was in goal, Jimmy Harris at centre-forward. In three of the matches Brian Harris was on the right-wing. The relationship between the trio was that they were simply playing colleagues.

EVERTON 2005–06 LEAGUE RECORD

Match No.	Date	Venue	Opponents	Result	H/T Score	Lg. Pos.	Goalscorers	Attendance
1	Aug 13	H	Manchester U	L 0-2	0-1	—		38,610
2	21	A	Bolton W	W 1-0	0-0	11	Bent [52]	25,608
3	27	A	Fulham	L 0-1	0-0	17		17,169
4	Sept 10	H	Portsmouth	L 0-1	0-0	18		36,831
5	19	A	Arsenal	L 0-2	0-2	—		38,121
6	24	H	Wigan Ath	L 0-1	0-0	20		37,189
7	Oct 2	A	Manchester C	L 0-2	0-0	20		42,681
8	15	A	Tottenham H	L 0-2	0-0	20		36,247
9	23	H	Chelsea	D 1-1	1-0	20	Beattie (pen) [37]	36,042
10	29	A	Birmingham C	W 1-0	1-0	18	Davies [43]	26,554
11	Nov 6	H	Middlesbrough	W 1-0	1-0	16	Beattie [16]	34,349
12	19	A	WBA	L 0-4	0-1	18		24,784
13	27	H	Newcastle U	W 1-0	0-0	16	Yobo [46]	36,207
14	Dec 3	A	Blackburn R	W 2-0	2-0	16	McFadden [28], Arteta [45]	22,064
15	11	A	Manchester U	D 1-1	1-1	15	McFadden [7]	67,831
16	14	H	West Ham U	L 1-2	1-1	—	Beattie [9]	35,704
17	17	H	Bolton W	L 0-4	0-1	16		34,500
18	26	A	Aston Villa	L 0-4	0-1	16		32,432
19	28	H	Liverpool	L 1-3	1-2	17	Beattie [42]	40,158
20	31	A	Sunderland	W 1-0	0-0	16	Cahill [90]	30,576
21	Jan 2	H	Charlton Ath	W 3-1	2-1	15	Beattie [9], Cahill 2 [41, 59]	34,333
22	14	A	Portsmouth	W 1-0	1-0	14	O'Brien (og) [31]	20,094
23	21	H	Arsenal	W 1-0	1-0	12	Beattie [13]	36,920
24	31	A	Wigan Ath	D 1-1	1-1	—	Thompson (og) [9]	21,731
25	Feb 4	H	Manchester C	W 1-0	1-0	11	Weir [8]	37,827
26	11	H	Blackburn R	W 1-0	1-0	11	Beattie [33]	35,615
27	25	A	Newcastle U	L 0-2	0-0	12		51,916
28	Mar 4	A	West Ham U	D 2-2	1-2	12	Osman [18], Beattie [71]	34,866
29	11	H	Fulham	W 3-1	2-0	11	Beattie 2 (1 pen) [14 (p), 36], McFadden [55]	36,515
30	18	H	Aston Villa	W 4-1	3-0	9	McFadden [16], Cahill 2 [22, 90], Osman [45]	36,507
31	25	A	Liverpool	L 1-3	0-1	10	Cahill [61]	44,923
32	Apr 1	H	Sunderland	D 2-2	2-1	10	Osman [5], McFadden [26]	38,093
33	8	A	Charlton Ath	D 0-0	0-0	11		26,954
34	15	H	Tottenham H	L 0-1	0-1	11		39,856
35	17	A	Chelsea	L 0-3	0-1	12		41,765
36	22	H	Birmingham C	D 0-0	0-0	12		35,420
37	29	A	Middlesbrough	W 1-0	0-0	11	McFadden [89]	29,224
38	May 7	H	WBA	D 2-2	0-1	11	Anichebe [84], Ferguson [90]	39,671

Final League Position: 11

GOALSCORERS

League (34): Beattie 10 (2 pens), Cahill 6, McFadden 6, Osman 3, Anichebe 1, Arteta 1, Bent 1, Davies 1, Ferguson 1, Weir 1, Yobo 1, own goals 2.
Carling Cup (0).
FA Cup (4): Arteta 1 (pen), Cahill 1, McFadden 1, Osman 1.
UEFA Cup (2): Cahill 1, Yobo 1.
Champions League (2): Arteta 1, Beattie 1.

Martyn N 20	Hibbert T 29	Pistone A 2	Yobo J 29	Weir D 32 + 1	Arteta M 27 + 2	Osman L 28 + 7	Neville P 34	Beattie J 29 + 3	Cahill T 32	Davies S 22 + 8	Ferguson D 7 + 20	Bent M 7 + 11	Kilbane K 21 + 13	McFadden J 24 + 8	Vaughan J — + 1	Nuno Valente 20	Ferrari M 6 + 2	Van der Meyde A 7 + 3	Wright R 14 + 1	Kroldrup P 1	Stubbs A 13 + 1	Turner I 2 + 1	Carsley L 3 + 2	Ruddy J — + 1	Westerveld S 2	Naysmith G 7	Anichebe V — + 2	Match No.
1	2	3	4	5	6	7^{1}	8	9^{2}	10	11^{3}	12	13	14															1
1	2	3^{1}	4	5	6	12	8		7		10	9^{2}	11	13														2
1	2		4	5	6	7	3■		10	8^{3}	12	9^{2}	11^{1}	13	14													3
1	2		4	5	6	12		13	8	7^{3}	10	9^{2}	11^{1}	14		3												4
1	2		4	5	6^{1}	7	8		11^{2}	12	13	9^{3}	14	10			3											5
1			4	5	6	7	8		10	11^{2}	13	12	3^{1}	9		2												6
1			4	5		7^{1}	6	13	8	12	14	9^{2}	11	10^{3}		3	2											7
1			4	5		14	6	12	8^{1}	7	13	9	11	10^{3}		3	2^{2}											8
1	2		4	5	6		7	9	8^{1}	12	10^{2}	13	11			3^{3}	14											9
1	2		4	5	6	12	3	9^{1}	8	7	10		13					11^{2}										10
1	2		4	5	6		3	9	8	7^{1}	10^{2}	13	12	14				11^{3}										11
1	2		4	5	6^{1}	12	3	9^{2}		8	13	10	11	14				7^{3}										12
1	2		4	5	6^{1}	12	3	9^{3}	8	7		14	13	10				11^{2}										13
1^{G}	2		4	5	6^{2}	7	3	9		8	12		13	10				11^{1}	15									14
	2		4	5		7	6	9^{2}		8	13	12	11	10^{1}		3			1									15
	2^{1}		4	5	12	7	6	9		8	13	14	11^{2}	10^{3}		3			1									16
	2^{1}		4	5	6	12	8	9	7	11				10		3			1									17
1	2		4		6	11^{2}	3	9	8^{1}	7	12	13		10						5								18
1	2		4	5	6■		8■	9	10	7^{1}			11	12		3												19
1	2		4	5		7		9	6	8^{1}	12	13	11	10^{2}		3												20
1	2		4		6	7		9	8		10^{1}	12	11			3	5											21
1	2		4	12	6^{2}	7	8	9^{1}	10			13	11			3	5											22
1	2			5	6^{1}	7	8	9	10		12		11			3	4^{2}				13							23
	2			5	6^{1}	7	8		10		12■		11	9		3			1		4							24
	2			5	6	7^{2}	8	9^{1}	10	13			11	12		3			1		4							25
	2			5	6	7^{1}	8	9^{2}	10				12	11^{G}		3					4	1■	13	15				26
			2	5	6	7		9	10^{2}	8			11^{1}	12		3					4		13		1			27
	2			5	6^{2}	7	8	9	10	12			13	11^{1}		3					4				1			28
	2			5	6	7	8	9	10^{3}	12			13	11^{2}		3^{1}		14	1		4							29
	2			5	6^{1}	7	8	9	10				12	11					1		4					3		30
	2			5		7	6	9	10		12		11^{2}	8^{1}				13■	1		4					3		31
	2		5		12	7	6	9	10	8^{1}	13			11					1		4					3^{2}		32
	2		4		6	7^{1}	3	9^{2}	10	12	13			11					1		5		8					33
			4			7	2	9	10	8^{2}	13		12	11			14		1		5^{3}		6			3^{1}		34
			4	5		7	2	9^{1}	10	12	13		11^{2}	8					1				6■			3		35
			4	5		7	2	9	10^{1}	8	13		12	11^{3}				6^{2}	1							3	14	36
			4	5		7	2	9		8			12	10				11^{1}	1^{G}		6	15				3		37
				5	6	7	2			8^{2}	10		11^{1}	9		3		12			4	1					13	38

FA Cup

Third Round	Millwall	(a)	1-1
		(h)	1-0
Fourth Round	Chelsea	(h)	1-1
		(a)	1-4

Carling Cup

Third Round	Middlesbrough	(h)	0-1

Champions League

Third Qualifying Round	Villarreal	(h)	1-2
		(a)	1-2

UEFA Cup

First Round	Dinamo Bucharest	(a)	1-5
		(h)	1-0

FULHAM

FA Premiership

FOUNDATION

Churchgoers were responsible for the foundation of Fulham, which first saw the light of day as Fulham St Andrew's Church Sunday School FC in 1879. They won the West London Amateur Cup in 1887 and the championship of the West London League in its initial season of 1892–93. The name Fulham had been adopted in 1888.

Craven Cottage, Stevenage Road, London SW6 6HH
Telephone: 0870 442 1222.
Fax: 0870 442 0236.
Ticket Office: 0870 442 1234
Website: www.fulhamfc.co.uk
Email: enquiries@fulhamfc.com
Ground Capacity: 22,602.
Record Attendance: 49,335 v Millwall, Division 2, 8 October 1938.
Pitch Measurements: 100m × 68m.
Chairman: Mohamed Al Fayed.
Managing Director: David McNally.
Secretary: Zoe Ward.
Manager: Chris Coleman.
Assistant Manager: Steve Kean.
Physio: Jason Palmer.
Colours: White shirts, black shorts, white stockings.
Change Colours: Black shirts, white shorts, black stockings.
Year Formed: 1879.
Turned Professional: 1898.
Ltd Co.: 1903.
Reformed: 1987.
Previous Name: 1879, Fulham St Andrew's; 1888, Fulham.
Club Nickname: 'Cottagers'.

Previous Grounds: 1879, Star Road, Fulham; c.1883, Eel Brook Common, 1884, Lillie Road; 1885, Putney Lower Common; 1886, Ranelagh House, Fulham; 1888, Barn Elms, Castelnau; 1889, Purser's Cross (Roskell's Field), Parsons Green Lane; 1891, Eel Brook Common; 1891, Half Moon, Putney; 1895, Captain James Field, West Brompton; 1896, Craven Cottage.

First Football League Game: 3 September 1907, Division 2, v Hull C (h) L 0–1 – Skene; Ross, Lindsay; Collins, Morrison, Goldie; Dalrymple, Freeman, Bevan, Hubbard, Threlfall.

Record League Victory: 10–1 v Ipswich T, Division 1, 26 December 1963 – Macedo; Cohen, Langley; Mullery (1), Keetch, Robson (1); Key, Cook (1), Leggat (4), Haynes, Howfield (3).

Record Cup Victory: 7–0 v Swansea C, FA Cup 1st rd, 11 November 1995 – Lange; Jupp (1), Herrera, Barkus (Brooker (1)), Moore, Angus, Thomas (1), Morgan, Brazil (Hamill), Conroy (3) (Bolt), Cusack (1).

HONOURS

Football League: Division 1 – Champions 2000–01; Division 2 – Champions 1948–49, 1998–99; Runners-up 1958–59; Division 3 (S) – Champions 1931–32; Division 3 – Runners-up 1970–71, 1996–97.

FA Cup: Runners-up 1975.

Football League Cup: best season: 5th rd, 1968, 1971, 2000.

European Competitions: *UEFA Cup:* 2002–03. *Intertoto Cup:* 2002 (winners)

SKY SPORTS FACT FILE

On 23 March 1963 Rodney Marsh made his debut for Fulham against Aston Villa at Craven Cottage. The 18-year old who had scored 40 goals for the club's juniors had the distinction of scoring the only goal of the game.

Record Defeat: 0–10 v Liverpool, League Cup 2nd rd 1st leg, 23 September 1986.

Most League Points (2 for a win): 60, Division 2, 1958–59 and Division 3, 1970–71.

Most League Points (3 for a win): 101, Division 2, 1998–99.

Most League Goals: 111, Division 3 (S), 1931–32.

Highest League Scorer in Season: Frank Newton, 43, Division 3 (S), 1931–32.

Most League Goals in Total Aggregate: Gordon Davies, 159, 1978–84, 1986–91.

Most League Goals in One Match: 5, Fred Harrison v Stockport Co, Division 2, 5 September 1908; 5, Bedford Jezzard v Hull C, Division 2, 8 October 1955; 5, Jimmy Hill v Doncaster R, Division 2, 15 March 1958; 5, Steve Earle v Halifax T, Division 3, 16 September 1969.

Most Capped Player: Johnny Haynes, 56, England.

Most League Appearances: Johnny Haynes, 594, 1952–70.

Youngest League Player: Tony Mahoney, 17 years 38 days v Cardiff C, 6 November 1976.

Record Transfer Fee Received: £11,500,000 from Manchester U for Louis Saha, January 2004.

Record Transfer Fee Paid: £11,500,000 to Lyon for Steve Marlet, August 2001.

Football League Record: 1907 Elected to Division 2; 1928–32 Division 3 (S); 1932–49 Division 2; 1949–52 Division 1; 1952–59 Division 2; 1959–68 Division 1; 1968–69 Division 2; 1969–71 Division 3; 1971–80 Division 2; 1980–82 Division 3; 1982–86 Division 2; 1986–92 Division 3; 1992–94 Division 2; 1994–97 Division 3; 1997–99 Division 2; 1999–2001 Division 1; 2001– FA Premier League.

MANAGERS

Harry Bradshaw 1904–09
Phil Kelso 1909–24
Andy Ducat 1924–26
Joe Bradshaw 1926–29
Ned Liddell 1929–31
Jim MacIntyre 1931–34
Jimmy Hogan 1934–35
Jack Peart 1935–48
Frank Osborne 1948–64
(was Secretary-Manager or General Manager for most of this period)
Bill Dodgin Snr 1949–53
Duggie Livingstone 1956–58
Bedford Jezzard 1958–64
(General Manager for last two months)
Vic Buckingham 1965–68
Bobby Robson 1968
Bill Dodgin Jnr 1969–72
Alec Stock 1972–76
Bobby Campbell 1976–80
Malcolm Macdonald 1980–84
Ray Harford 1984–96
Ray Lewington 1986–90
Alan Dicks 1990–91
Don Mackay 1991–94
Ian Branfoot 1994–96
(continued as General Manager)
Micky Adams 1996–97
Ray Wilkins 1997–98
Kevin Keegan 1998–99
(Chief Operating Officer)
Paul Bracewell 1999–2000
Jean Tigana 2000–03
Chris Coleman April 2003–

LATEST SEQUENCES

Longest Sequence of League Wins: 12, 7.5.2000 – 18.10.2000.

Longest Sequence of League Defeats: 11, 2.12.1961 – 24.2.1962.

Longest Sequence of League Draws: 6, 14.10.1995 – 18.11.1995.

Longest Sequence of Unbeaten League Matches: 15, 26.1.1999 – 13.4.1999.

Longest Sequence Without a League Win: 15, 25.2.1950 – 23.8.1950.

Successive Scoring Runs: 26 from 28.3.1931.

Successive Non-scoring Runs: 6 from 21.8.1971.

TEN YEAR LEAGUE RECORD

		P	*W*	*D*	*L*	*F*	*A*	*Pts*	*Pos*
1996-97	Div 3	46	25	12	9	72	38	87	2
1997-98	Div 2	46	20	10	16	60	43	70	6
1998-99	Div 2	46	31	8	7	79	32	101	1
1999-2000	Div 1	46	17	16	13	49	41	67	9
2000-01	Div 1	46	30	11	5	90	32	101	1
2001-02	PR Lge	38	10	14	14	36	44	44	13
2002-03	PR Lge	38	13	9	16	41	50	48	14
2003-04	PR Lge	38	14	10	14	52	46	52	9
2004-05	PR Lge	38	12	8	18	52	60	44	13
2005-06	PR Lge	38	14	6	18	48	58	48	12

DID YOU KNOW ?

In 1904–05 Fulham reached the third round of the FA Cup starting in the sixth qualifying stage. Their victories included three-match marathons with both Manchester United and Reading and then ousting First Division Nottingham Forest.

FULHAM 2005–06 LEAGUE RECORD

Match No.	*Date*	*Venue*	*Opponents*	*Result*		*H/T Score*	*Lg. Pos.*	*Goalscorers*	*Attendance*
1	Aug 13	H	Birmingham C	D	0-0	0-0	—		16,550
2	20	A	Blackburn R	L	1-2	0-1	15	McBride [49]	16,953
3	24	A	Arsenal	L	1-4	1-1	—	Jensen C [22]	37,867
4	27	H	Everton	W	1-0	0-0	14	McBride [57]	17,169
5	Sept 10	A	Newcastle U	D	1-1	1-0	13	McBride [13]	52,208
6	17	H	West Ham U	L	1-2	0-0	16	Boa Morte [66]	21,907
7	26	A	Tottenham H	L	0-1	0-1	—		35,427
8	Oct 1	H	Manchester U	L	2-3	2-3	18	John [2], Jensen C [28]	21,862
9	17	A	Charlton Ath	D	1-1	1-0	—	John [28]	26,310
10	22	H	Liverpool	W	2-0	1-0	14	John [30], Boa Morte [90]	22,480
11	29	A	Wigan Ath	L	0-1	0-0	15		17,266
12	Nov 5	H	Manchester C	W	2-1	2-1	14	Malbranque 2 [6, 45]	22,241
13	20	A	Middlesbrough	L	2-3	1-0	14	John [9], Diop [70]	27,599
14	27	H	Bolton W	W	2-1	2-0	14	McBride 2 [4, 18]	19,768
15	Dec 3	A	WBA	D	0-0	0-0	14		23,144
16	10	A	Birmingham C	L	0-1	0-0	16		27,597
17	17	H	Blackburn R	W	2-1	1-0	14	Diop [45], Boa Morte [52]	20,138
18	26	A	Chelsea	L	2-3	1-2	15	McBride [29], Helguson (pen) [56]	42,313
19	28	H	Aston Villa	D	3-3	2-1	14	McBride 2 [13, 61], Helguson (pen) [32]	20,446
20	31	A	Portsmouth	L	0-1	0-1	15		19,101
21	Jan 2	H	Sunderland	W	2-1	1-1	14	John 2 [43, 61]	19,372
22	14	H	Newcastle U	W	1-0	0-0	12	Malbranque [75]	21,974
23	23	A	West Ham U	L	1-2	0-2	—	Helguson [52]	29,812
24	31	H	Tottenham H	W	1-0	0-0	—	Bocanegra [90]	21,081
25	Feb 4	A	Manchester U	L	2-4	2-3	14	McBride [22], Helguson [37]	67,844
26	11	H	WBA	W	6-1	2-0	13	Helguson 2 [4, 40], Radzinski [48], Davies (og) [58], John 2 [83, 90]	21,508
27	26	A	Bolton W	L	1-2	1-1	14	Helguson [22]	23,104
28	Mar 4	H	Arsenal	L	0-4	0-2	16		22,397
29	11	A	Everton	L	1-3	0-2	16	John (pen) [86]	36,515
30	15	A	Liverpool	L	1-5	1-2	—	John [25]	42,293
31	19	H	Chelsea	W	1-0	1-0	14	Boa Morte [17]	22,486
32	25	A	Aston Villa	D	0-0	0-0	15		32,605
33	Apr 1	H	Portsmouth	L	1-3	1-2	15	Malbranque [10]	22,322
34	15	H	Charlton Ath	W	2-1	2-1	16	Boa Morte 2 [15, 30]	19,146
35	24	H	Wigan Ath	W	1-0	1-0	—	Malbranque [45]	17,149
36	29	A	Manchester C	W	2-1	0-0	13	John [84], Malbranque [90]	41,128
37	May 4	A	Sunderland	L	1-2	0-1	—	Radzinski [76]	28,226
38	7	H	Middlesbrough	W	1-0	0-0	12	Helguson (pen) [84]	22,434

Final League Position: 12

GOALSCORERS

League (48): John 11 (1 pen), McBride 9, Helguson 8 (3 pens), Boa Morte 6, Malbranque 6, Diop 2, Jensen C 2, Radzinski 2, Bocanegra 1, own goal 1.
Carling Cup (7): Helguson 2, Boa Morte 1, McBride 1, Radzinski 1, Rehman 1, Rosenior 1.
FA Cup (1): John 1.

Warner T 16 + 2	Volz M 23	Jensen N 14 + 2	Malbranque S 32 + 2	Knight Z 29 + 1	Rehman Z 3	Legwinski S 10 + 3	Jensen C 11	McBride B 34 + 4	Radzinski T 23 + 10	Boa Morte L 35	Elrich A 2 + 4	John C 16 + 19	Diop P 21 + 1	Helguson H 15 + 12	Bocanegra C 20 + 1	Christanval P 7 + 8	Crossley M 13	Goma A 13	Rosenior L 22 + 2	Leacock D 5	Pearce I 10	Niemi A 9	Elliott S 12	Bridge W 12	Brown M 6 + 1	Pembridge M 5	Match No.
1	2	3	4	5	6	7[1]	8	9	10[2]	11	12	13															1
1	2	3	7	5	6		8	9[2]	10[1]	11		12	4	13													2
1	2	3	7	5	6		8	9[1]	10	11		12	4														3
1	2	3	7	5			8	9	10	11			4		6												4
1	2	3	7	5			8	9[2]	10[1]	11		12	4	13	6												5
1	2	3	7	5[2]			8	9	10[1]	11		12	4		6	13											6
1	2	3	7	5			8	9[1]	10	11		12	4		6												7
	2	3	7				8	9[2]	12	11		10[1]	4	13	6		1	5									8
	2	3	7				8	12	13	10		9[1]	4		6	11[2]	1	5									9
15	2	3[2]	7				8	12		11	10[1]	9	4		6		1[G]	5	13								10
1	2	3	7				8[2]	12	10	11	13	9[1]	4		6[3]			5	14								11
1	2	3	7					9[1]	8	10		11	4	12	6			5									12
1	2	3	11	5		8		9	10			7[1]	4	12				6									13
	2		7			12		9	8	10[1]		11[2]	4	13	6		1	5	3								14
	2[3]		7	14		12		9[2]	8	10[■]		11[1]	4	13	6		1	5	3								15
			7	5		8		9	10			11			3	4	1	6	2								16
				5		12		9	8	10[2]	13	11[3]	4[1]	14		7	1	6	3	2							17
15				5		7		9	8	11		12		10[1]		4	1[G]	6	3	2							18
		12		5		7[3]		9	8	11	14	13		10[2]	6	4	1		3	2[1]							19
1				5		7		9	8	11	4[2]	12		10[1]	13			6	3	2							20
1		12	13	5		7		9	8	11		10[2]	4[3]	14					3[1]	2	6						21
		3	12	5		7[2]		9	8[1]	11		13		10					2		6	1	4				22
			8[1]	5		7		9[2]	12	11		13		10	6				2			1	4	3			23
			8	5		7[1]		9[2]	12	11		13		10	6				2			1	4	3			24
			7	5				9	12	11		13		10[2]	6				2			1	4	3	8[1]		25
	2		7	5				9	8	11		12		10[1]	6							1	4	3			26
1	2		7	5				9[1]	8[2]	11		12	13	10	6								4	3			27
1	2		7	5				9	8	11		12		10[1]				6	3				4				28
1	2		7	5				9		11		12		10[1]	6	13			3				4[2]			8	29
1			7	5[2]				12	8[1]	10		9				13			2		6			3	4	11	30
	2		7[2]	5				9		11		10[1]		12		13	1		3		6				4	8	31
	2		7	5				9	12	11		10[1]					1		3		6				4	8	32
	2		7	5				9	12	11		10[2]		13		14	1				6[3]			3	4[■]	8[1]	33
			7	5				9		11			8	10		12			2		6	1	4[1]	3			34
			7	5				9	12	11			4	10[1]		13			2		6	1	8[2]	3			35
			7	5[2]				9		11		12	4	10[1]		13			2		6	1	8	3			36
			7					9[2]	12	11[1]		13	4	10		5	1		2		6[3]		8	3	14		37
	2		7					9[1]	12			10[2]	4	13	6	5			3			1		11	8		38

FA Cup

Third Round	Leyton Orient	(h)	1-2

Carling Cup

Second Round	Lincoln C	(h)	5-4
Third Round	WBA	(h)	2-3

GILLINGHAM FL Championship 1

FOUNDATION

The success of the pioneering Royal Engineers of Chatham excited the interest of the residents of the Medway Towns and led to the formation of many clubs including Excelsior. After winning the Kent Junior Cup and the Chatham District League in 1893, Excelsior decided to go for bigger things and it was at a meeting in the Napier Arms, Brompton, in 1893 that New Brompton FC came into being, buying and developing the ground which is now Priestfield Stadium. Changed name to Gillingham in 1913, when they also changed their strip from black and white stripes to predominantly blue.

Priestfield Stadium, Redfern Avenue, Gillingham, Kent ME7 4DD.

Telephone: (01634) 300 000.

Fax: (01634) 850 986.

Ticket Office: (01634) 300 000.

Website: www.gillinghamfootballclub.com

Email: info@gillinghamfootballclub.com

Ground Capacity: 11,400.

Record Attendance: 23,002 v QPR, FA Cup 3rd rd, 10 January 1948.

Pitch Measurements: 112yd × 70yd.

Chairman/Chief Executive: Paul D. P. Scally.

Vice-chairman: Peter A. Spokes.

Chief Executive: Paul D. P. Scally.

Secretary: Gwen E. Poynter.

Manager: Ronnie Jepson.

Assistant Manager: Mick Docherty.

Physio: Simon Webster.

Colours: Blue with white side/sleeve panel.

Change Colours: White with blue side/sleeve panel.

Year Formed: 1893.

Turned Professional: 1894.

Ltd Co.: 1893.

Previous Name: 1893, New Brompton; 1913, Gillingham.

Club Nickname: 'The Gills'.

First Football League Game: 28 August 1920, Division 3, v Southampton (h) D 1–1 – Branfield; Robertson, Sissons; Battiste, Baxter, Wigmore; Holt, Hall, Gilbey (1), Roe, Gore.

Record League Victory: 10–0 v Chesterfield, Division 3, 5 September 1987 – Kite; Haylock, Pearce, Shipley (2) (Lillis), West, Greenall (1), Pritchard (2), Shearer (2), Lovell, Elsey (2), David Smith (1).

HONOURS

Football League: Promoted from Division 2 1999–2000 (play-offs); Division 3 – Runners-up 1995-96; Division 4 – Champions 1963–64; Runners-up 1973–74.

FA Cup: best season: 6th rd, 2000.

Football League Cup: best season: 4th rd, 1964, 1997.

SKY SPORTS FACT FILE

In 1951–52 Gillingham re-signed goalkeeper Johnny Burke and enabled the veteran to complete 20 years professional service in England. Signed originally from Shelbourne by Chester in 1931 he later joined Millwall and Gillingham in 1948.

Record Cup Victory: 10–1 v Gorleston, FA Cup 1st rd, 16 November 1957 – Brodie; Parry, Hannaway; Riggs, Boswell, Laing; Payne, Fletcher (2), Saunders (5), Morgan (1), Clark (2).

Record Defeat: 2–9 v Nottingham F, Division 3 (S), 18 November 1950.

Most League Points (2 for a win): 62, Division 4, 1973–74.

Most League Points (3 for a win): 85, Division 2, 1999–2000.

Most League Goals: 90, Division 4, 1973–74.

Highest League Scorer in Season: Ernie Morgan, 31, Division 3 (S), 1954–55; Brian Yeo, 31, Division 4, 1973–74.

Most League Goals in Total Aggregate: Brian Yeo, 135, 1963–75.

Most League Goals in One Match: 6, Fred Cheesmur v Merthyr T, Division 3S, 26 April 1930.

Most Capped Player: Mamady Sidibe, 7, Mali.

Most League Appearances: John Simpson, 571, 1957–72.

Youngest League Player: Billy Hughes, 15 years 275 days v Southend U, 13 April 1976.

Record Transfer Fee Received: £1,500,000 from Manchester C for Robert Taylor, November 1999.

Record Transfer Fee Paid: £600,000 to Reading for Carl Asaba, August 1998.

Football League Record: 1920 Original Member of Division 3; 1921 Division 3 (S); 1938 Failed re-election; Southern League 1938–44; Kent League 1944–46; Southern League 1946–50; 1950 Re-elected to Division 3 (S); 1958–64 Division 4; 1964–71 Division 3; 1971–74 Division 4; 1974–89 Division 3; 1989–92 Division 4; 1992–96; Division 3; 1996–2000 Division 2; 2000–04 Division 1; 2004–05 FLC; 2005– FL1.

MANAGERS

W. Ironside Groombridge
1896–1906 *(Secretary-Manager)*
(previously Financial Secretary)
Steve Smith 1906–08
W. I. Groombridge 1908–19
(Secretary-Manager)
George Collins 1919–20
John McMillan 1920–23
Harry Curtis 1923–26
Albert Hoskins 1926–29
Dick Hendrie 1929–31
Fred Mavin 1932–37
Alan Ure 1937–38
Bill Harvey 1938–39
Archie Clark 1939–58
Harry Barratt 1958–62
Freddie Cox 1962–65
Basil Hayward 1966–71
Andy Nelson 1971–74
Len Ashurst 1974–75
Gerry Summers 1975–81
Keith Peacock 1981–87
Paul Taylor 1988
Keith Burkinshaw 1988–89
Damien Richardson 1989–93
Mike Flanagan 1993–95
Neil Smillie 1995
Tony Pulis 1995–99
Peter Taylor 1999–2000
Andy Hessenthaler 2000–04
Stan Ternent 2004–05
Neale Cooper 2005
Ronnie Jepson November 2005–

LATEST SEQUENCES

Longest Sequence of League Wins: 7, 18.12.1954 – 29.1.1955.

Longest Sequence of League Defeats: 10, 20.9.1988 – 5.11.1988.

Longest Sequence of League Draws: 5, 28.8.1993 – 18.9.1993.

Longest Sequence of Unbeaten League Matches: 20, 13.10.1973 – 10.2.1974.

Longest Sequence Without a League Win: 15, 1.4.1972 – 2.9.1972.

Successive Scoring Runs: 20 from 31.10.1959.

Successive Non-scoring Runs: 6 from 11.2.1961.

TEN YEAR LEAGUE RECORD

		P	*W*	*D*	*L*	*F*	*A*	*Pts*	*Pos*
1996-97	Div 2	46	19	10	17	60	59	67	11
1997-98	Div 2	46	19	13	14	52	47	70	8
1998-99	Div 2	46	22	14	10	75	44	80	4
1999-2000	Div 2	46	25	10	11	79	48	85	3
2000-01	Div 1	46	13	16	17	61	66	55	13
2001-02	Div 1	46	18	10	18	64	67	64	12
2002-03	Div 1	46	16	14	16	56	65	62	11
2003-04	Div 1	46	14	9	23	48	67	51	21
2004-05	FL C	46	12	14	20	45	66	50	22
2005-06	FL 1	46	16	12	18	50	64	60	14

DID YOU KNOW ?

Centre-forward Bill Brown had been discarded by both Southampton and Charlton Athletic, had toured the Southern League with Romford, Chelmsford City and Bedford Town before settling successfully for a stint with Gillingham in February 1966.

GILLINGHAM 2005–06 LEAGUE RECORD

Match No.	Date	Venue	Opponents	Result		H/T Score	Lg. Pos.	Goalscorers	Attendance
1	Aug 6	H	Colchester U	W	2-1	0-0	—	Crofts [75], Byfield [89]	7293
2	9	A	Port Vale	D	0-0	0-0	—		4931
3	13	A	Scunthorpe U	D	1-1	0-0	8	Hessenthaler [61]	5007
4	20	H	Bournemouth	W	1-0	1-0	4	Browning (og) [39]	6568
5	27	H	Nottingham F	L	1-3	0-2	9	Byfield [78]	7228
6	29	A	Brentford	D	1-1	1-0	10	Harris [45]	6969
7	Sept 10	A	Rotherham U	L	0-3	0-0	17		4253
8	13	H	Barnsley	L	0-3	0-2	—		5283
9	17	H	Oldham Ath	L	0-1	0-1	20		6259
10	24	A	Tranmere R	D	2-2	1-1	21	Byfield 2 (1 pen) [16, 63 (p)]	7003
11	27	H	Chesterfield	W	1-0	0-0	—	Sancho [86]	7472
12	Oct 1	H	Southend U	L	1-2	0-0	22	Pouton [86]	8128
13	15	H	Yeovil T	D	0-0	0-0	22		6848
14	22	A	Bradford C	L	0-1	0-0	23		7729
15	29	H	Blackpool	W	2-1	0-1	20	Hope [49], Harris [65]	6300
16	Nov 1	A	Hartlepool U	L	1-3	0-1	—	Collin [90]	4522
17	12	A	Walsall	L	0-2	0-1	22		4785
18	19	H	Hartlepool U	W	1-0	1-0	20	Shields [10]	6092
19	26	A	Colchester U	L	0-5	0-1	21		3801
20	Dec 6	H	Doncaster R	W	1-0	1-0	—	Flynn [18]	4861
21	10	H	Port Vale	W	3-0	1-0	16	Harris [41], Jarvis 2 [66, 82]	6210
22	17	A	Bournemouth	L	1-2	0-0	18	Harris [62]	6177
23	26	H	Bristol C	D	1-1	0-1	18	Flynn [69]	7786
24	31	H	Milton Keynes D	W	3-0	2-0	17	Johnson [27], Clohessy [41], Pouton [89]	6162
25	Jan 2	A	Huddersfield T	D	0-0	0-0	19		11,483
26	10	A	Barnsley	L	0-1	0-1	—		7090
27	14	H	Swindon T	W	3-0	1-0	17	Byfield [20], Flynn [73], Harris [89]	7300
28	21	A	Oldham Ath	L	0-2	0-0	17		5783
29	28	H	Rotherham U	D	1-1	0-0	18	Grant [63]	6107
30	31	A	Swansea C	W	2-1	1-0	—	Byfield [18], Harris [71]	14,357
31	Feb 4	A	Chesterfield	D	1-1	0-0	14	Black [48]	4652
32	11	H	Tranmere R	D	1-1	0-0	15	Byfield [73]	6803
33	14	A	Swindon T	L	0-1	0-1	—		5530
34	18	A	Doncaster R	L	0-2	0-2	15		5738
35	25	H	Scunthorpe U	L	1-3	1-1	18	Cochrane [39]	6029
36	Mar 11	A	Nottingham F	D	1-1	1-1	20	Bennett (og) [8]	19,446
37	18	A	Bristol C	L	0-6	0-3	21		10,932
38	21	H	Brentford	W	3-2	2-1	—	Sancho [9], Byfield 2 (1 pen) [45 (p), 76]	5745
39	25	H	Swansea C	W	1-0	0-0	16	Byfield (pen) [54]	6909
40	Apr 1	A	Milton Keynes D	W	2-1	0-1	15	Byfield [59], Black [61]	6432
41	8	H	Huddersfield T	W	2-0	1-0	13	Mulligan [4], Jarvis [90]	7014
42	14	A	Southend U	W	1-0	0-0	—	Black [46]	11,195
43	17	H	Bradford C	W	2-1	1-0	11	Black [9], Flynn [54]	7281
44	22	A	Yeovil T	L	3-4	1-2	12	Black [12], Flynn [77], Crofts [88]	6040
45	29	H	Walsall	L	0-1	0-0	14		7757
46	May 6	A	Blackpool	D	3-3	1-1	14	Byfield 2 [28, 52], Flynn [86]	8541

Final League Position: 14

GOALSCORERS

League (50): Byfield 13 (3 pens), Flynn 6, Harris 6, Black 5, Jarvis 3, Crofts 2, Pouton 2, Sancho 2, Clohessy 1, Cochrane 1, Collin 1, Grant 1, Hessenthaler 1, Hope 1, Johnson 1, Mulligan 1, Shields 1, own goals 2.
Carling Cup (4): Byfield 1, Crofts 1, Jarvis 1, own goal 1.
FA Cup (2): Jarvis 1, Saunders 1.
Football League Trophy (4): Jarvis 2, Collin 1, Jackman 1.

Brown J 39	Rose R 13 + 1	Jackman D 35 + 7	Flynn M 30 + 6	Cox I 36	Hope C 20 + 4	Crofts A 45	Hessenthaler A 14 + 2	Spiller D 21 + 11	Byfield D 27 + 2	Pouton A 19 + 4	Shields P 6 + 11	Corneille M — + 2	Jarvis M 30 + 5	Claridge S 1	Ashikodi M — + 4	Sancho B 16 + 3	Hislop S 2 + 6	Harris N 28 + 8	Williams T 13	Johnson L 25 + 3	Crichton P 1	Saunders M 3 + 1	Bullock T 6	Wallis J 16 + 1	Collin F 1 + 5	Smith P 3	Stone C — + 3	Clohessy S 18 + 2	Fobi-Edusei A 5 + 1	Grant G 1 + 9	Black T 17	Mulligan G 10 + 3	Cochrane J 5	*Match No.*
1	2	3	4	5	6	7	8^1	9^2	10	11^3	12	13	14																					1
1	2	3	4	5	6	7	8^2	9^3	10	11^1	14	12	13																					2
1	2	3	4	5	6	7	8^2	9^1	10▮	11	13		12																					3
1	2	3	4	5	6	7	8^1	12		11^3			10	9^2	13	14																		4
1	2	3	4^1	5	6	7	8		10		12		11		13		9^2																	5
1	2	3	12	5	6	7			10^2	11	13		8			4^1		9																6
1	2	3^1	4	5	6^2	7	12		10	11^3	13		8				14	9																7
1	2	3	12	5	6	7^2	8		10	4^1			11				13	9																8
1	3	12	4	5	6	7	8^2		10		13		11			2^3	14	9^1																9
1	2	12	4			7	8^1		10		9^2		11			6		13	3	5														10
1	2	12	4			7	8^1		10^2				11			6	13	9	3	5														11
1	2	12	4			7	8^3			13			11		14	6^2	10	9^1	3	5														12
	2	11^2	4^1		6	7	8^3	12					10		14▮			9	3	5	1	13												13
			12	5	6	7	8	11^3					10				13	9^2	3			4^1	1	2	14									14
			4	5	6	7	8						11					9	3				1	2		10								15
			4	5	6	7^2	8^3						10					9	3^1	12		11	1	2	13		14							16
		11^1			6	7^3		8			9^2		10					12	3	5		4	1	2	13		14							17
		12		5	6^3	7		8	13		10^2		11					9^1	3	2			1		14	4								18
		12	4	5		7		9^2	10				11					13	3	6			1			8^1		2						19
1		11	4	6		7		12	13				8					9^2	3	5				2					10^1					20
1		3	4	6		7^1	12	13					8					9	11^2	5				2					10^3	14				21
1		3	4	5				7			12		8			6		9	11					2					10^1					22
1		3	4	6^1		7		8			10^3		11			12		9		5				2^2				13	14					23
1		3	4			7		8^1		12	10		11^2			6		9^3		5					13			2		14				24
1		3	4			7		8			10^1					6	12	9		5								2	11^2	13				25
1		3	4			7		8	10^3	12	13					6		9		5				11^1				2^2		14				26
1		3	4	6	12	7		8	10^3	11^2								9^1		5				13				2		14				27
1		3	4	6	12	7		8^1		11								9		5								2	10^2	13				28
1		3	12	6		7		8	10	4^1								9^2		5								2		13	11			29
1		3	4▮	6		7		8	10	12								9^1		5								2		13	11^2			30
1		3		6^1	12	7		8	10	4								9		5								2			11^2	13		31
1		3			6	7		8^1	10									9		5								2			11	12	4	32
1		3	4	6		7		12	10▮											5								2			11	9	8^1	33
1		3	4	6	10	7					12									5								2		13	11	9^1	8^2	34
1	12	3		6		7		8^2			13							9		5								2^1		10	11		4	35
1		3^2	4^1	5	6	7		8		11			12							13								2			9		10	36
1		12		5	6^3	7		8		4			13			14		9^1		3▮								2			11^2	10		37
1		3		5		7		12	10	4▮			8			6		13										2▮			11^1	9^2		38
1		3		5		7		12	10	4			8			6		13						2							11^1	9^2		39
1		3		5		7		12	10^2	4			8			6		13						2							11^1	9		40
1		3	12	5		7^1		13	10	4			8			6								2							11^2	9		41
1		3		5		7		12	10	4			8			6								2							11^1	9		42
1		3	12	5		7		13	10^3	4^1			8			6		14						2							11^2	9		43
1		3^3	4	5		7			10				8			6▮		13		12				2				14			11^1	9^2		44
1			4	6^1	12	7			10				8					9		5				2				3			11^2	13		45
1		3	4		6	7			10				8					9		5					11^1		12	2						46

FA Cup
First Round Burscough (a) 2-3

Football League Trophy
First Round Crawley T (h) 2-0
Second Round Wycombe W (h) 2-2

Carling Cup
First Round Oxford U (h) 1-0
Second Round Portsmouth (h) 3-2
Third Round Doncaster R (a) 0-2

GRIMSBY TOWN — FL Championship 2

FOUNDATION

Grimsby Pelham FC, as they were first known, came into being at a meeting held at the Wellington Arms in September 1878. Pelham is the family name of big landowners in the area, the Earls of Yarborough. The receipts for their first game amounted to 6s. 9d. (approx. 39p). After a year, the club name was changed to Grimsby Town.

Blundell Park, Cleethorpes, North East Lincolnshire DN35 7PY.

Telephone: (01472) 605 050.

Fax: (01472) 317 958.

Ticket Office: (01472) 608 026.

Website: www.gtfc.co.uk.

Email: enquiries@gtfc.co.uk.

Ground Capacity: 9106.

Record Attendance: 31,657 v Wolverhampton W, FA Cup 5th rd, 20 February 1937.

Pitch Measurements: 111yd × 75yd.

Chairman: John Fenty.

Chief Executive: Ian Fleming.

Manager: Graham Rodger.

Assistant Manager: TBC.

Physio: David Moore.

Colours: Black and white striped shirts, black shorts, white stockings with black trim.

Change Colours: Redcurrant shirts, white shorts, redcurrant stockings.

Year Formed. 1878.

Turned Professional: 1890. ***Ltd Co.:*** 1890.

Previous Name: 1878, Grimsby Pelham; 1879, Grimsby Town.

Club Nickname: 'The Mariners'.

Previous Grounds: 1880, Clee Park; 1889, Abbey Park; 1899, Blundell Park.

First Football League Game: 3 September 1892, Division 2, v Northwich Victoria (h) W 2–1 – Whitehouse; Lundie, T. Frith; C. Frith, Walker, Murrell; Higgins, Henderson, Brayshaw, Riddoch (2), Ackroyd.

Record League Victory: 9–2 v Darwen, Division 2, 15 April 1899 – Bagshaw; Lockie, Nidd; Griffiths, Bell (1), Nelmes; Jenkinson (3), Richards (1), Cockshutt (3), Robinson, Chadburn (1).

Record Cup Victory: 8–0 v Darlington, FA Cup 2nd rd, 21 November 1885 – G. Atkinson; J. H. Taylor, H. Taylor; Hall, Kimpson, Hopewell; H. Atkinson (1), Garnham, Seal (3), Sharman, Monument (4).

HONOURS

Football League: Division 1 best season: 5th, 1934–35; Division 2 – Champions 1900–01, 1933–34; Runners-up 1928–29; Promoted from Division 2 1997–98 (play-offs); Division 3 (N) – Champions 1925–26, 1955–56; Runners-up 1951–52; Division 3 – Champions 1979–80; Runners-up 1961–62; Division 4 – Champions 1971–72; Runners-up 1978–79; 1989–90.

FA Cup: Semi-finals, 1936, 1939.

Football League Cup: best season: 5th rd, 1980, 1985.

League Group Cup: Winners 1982.

Auto Windscreen Shield: Winners 1998.

SKY SPORTS FACT FILE

When Ralph Hunt signed for Grimsby Town in August 1959 he embarked on a remarkable scoring spree, registering a goal in each of their first ten matches. Despite missing seven matches in the season he finished as top scorer with 33 League goals.

Record Defeat: 1–9 v Arsenal, Division 1, 28 January 1931.

Most League Points (2 for a win): 68, Division 3 (N), 1955–56.

Most League Points (3 for a win): 83, Division 3, 1990–91.

Most League Goals: 103, Division 2, 1933–34.

Highest League Scorer in Season: Pat Glover, 42, Division 2, 1933–34.

Most League Goals in Total Aggregate: Pat Glover, 180, 1930–39.

Most League Goals in One Match: 6, Tommy McCairns v Leicester Fosse, Division 2, 11 April 1896.

Most Capped Player: Pat Glover, 7, Wales.

Most League Appearances: John McDermott, 624, 1987– .

Youngest League Player: Tony Ford, 16 years 143 days v Walsall, 4 October 1975.

Record Transfer Fee Received: £1,500,000 from Everton for John Oster, July 1997.

Record Transfer Fee Paid: £500,000 to Preston NE for Lee Ashcroft, August 1998.

Football League Record: 1892 Original Member Division 2; 1901–03 Division 1; 1903 Division 2; 1910 Failed re-election; 1911 re-elected Division 2; 1920–21 Division 3; 1921–26 Division 3 (N); 1926–29 Division 2; 1929–32 Division 1; 1932–34 Division 2; 1934–48 Division 1; 1948–51 Division 2; 1951–56 Division 3 (N); 1956–59 Division 2; 1959–62 Division 3; 1962–64 Division 2; 1964–68 Division 3; 1968–72 Division 4; 1972–77 Division 3; 1977–79 Division 4; 1979–80 Division 3; 1980–87 Division 2; 1987–88 Division 3; 1988–90 Division 4; 1990–91 Division 3; 1991–92 Division 2; 1992–97 Division 1; 1997–98 Division 2; 1998–2003 Division 1; 2003–04 Division 2; 2004– FL2.

MANAGERS

H. N. Hickson 1902–20
(Secretary-Manager)
Haydn Price 1920
George Fraser 1921–24
Wilf Gillow 1924–32
Frank Womack 1932–36
Charles Spencer 1937–51
Bill Shankly 1951–53
Billy Walsh 1954–55
Allenby Chilton 1955–59
Tim Ward 1960–62
Tom Johnston 1962–64
Jimmy McGuigan 1964–67
Don McEvoy 1967–68
Bill Harvey 1968–69
Bobby Kennedy 1969–71
Lawrie McMenemy 1971–73
Ron Ashman 1973–75
Tom Casey 1975–76
Johnny Newman 1976–79
George Kerr 1979–82
David Booth 1982–85
Mike Lyons 1985–87
Bobby Roberts 1987–88
Alan Buckley 1988–94
Brian Laws 1994–96
Kenny Swain 1997
Alan Buckley 1997–2000
Lennie Lawrence 2000–01
Paul Groves 2001–04
Nicky Law 2004
Russell Slade 2004–06
Graham Rodger June 2006–

LATEST SEQUENCES

Longest Sequence of League Wins: 11, 19.1.1952 – 29.3.1952.

Longest Sequence of League Defeats: 9, 30.11.1907 – 18.1.1908.

Longest Sequence of League Draws: 5, 6.2.1965 – 6.3.1965.

Longest Sequence of Unbeaten League Matches: 19, 16.2.1980 – 30.8.1980.

Longest Sequence Without a League Win: 18, 10.10.1981 – 16.3.1982.

Successive Scoring Runs: 33 from 6.10.1928.

Successive Non-scoring Runs: 6 from 11.3.2000.

TEN YEAR LEAGUE RECORD

		P	W	D	L	F	A	Pts	Pos
1996-97	Div 1	46	11	13	22	60	81	46	22
1997-98	Div 2	46	19	15	12	55	37	72	3
1998-99	Div 1	46	17	10	19	40	52	61	11
1999-2000	Div 1	46	13	12	21	41	67	51	20
2000-01	Div 1	46	14	10	22	43	62	52	18
2001-02	Div 1	46	12	14	20	50	72	50	19
2002-03	Div 1	46	9	12	25	48	85	39	24
2003-04	Div 2	46	13	11	22	55	81	50	21
2004-05	FL 2	46	14	16	16	51	52	58	18
2005-06	FL 2	46	22	12	12	64	44	78	4

DID YOU KNOW ?

Long-serving right-back John McDermott made his 500th League appearance for Grimsby Town in the 1–0 win at Peterborough United on 10 September 2005 and his 700th League and Cup game on 17 September in the 3–0 win against Torquay United.

GRIMSBY TOWN 2005–06 LEAGUE RECORD

Match No.	*Date*	*Venue*	*Opponents*	*Result*	*H/T Score*	*Lg. Pos.*	*Goalscorers*	*Attendance*
1	Aug 6	H	Oxford U	D 1-1	0-0	—	Crane [62]	4706
2	9	A	Bristol R	W 2-1	0-0	—	Gritton [75], Jones R [88]	6300
3	20	H	Darlington	L 0-1	0-0	15		3904
4	27	A	Barnet	W 1-0	0-0	9	Andrew [46]	2447
5	29	H	Rushden & D	W 2-0	1-0	6	McDermott [8], Kamudimba Kalala (pen) [51]	3774
6	Sept 2	H	Stockport Co	L 1-3	1-0	—	Jones G [33]	5381
7	6	A	Chester C	W 2-1	0-0	—	Kamudimba Kalala (pen) [50], Reddy [80]	3095
8	10	A	Peterborough U	W 1-0	0-0	2	Jones G [48]	4263
9	17	H	Torquay U	W 3-0	1-0	1	Jones R [43], Reddy 2 [66, 77]	4026
10	24	A	Boston U	D 1-1	1-0	1	Kamudimba Kalala (pen) [12]	4077
11	27	H	Notts Co	W 4-0	2-0	—	Jones R [28], Gritton [45], Kamudimba Kalala [46], Cohen [81]	5577
12	Oct 1	A	Shrewsbury T	D 0-0	0-0	1		4607
13	7	H	Wycombe W	L 0-1	0-1	—		7206
14	14	A	Cheltenham T	W 3-0	1-0	—	Bolland [15], Reddy [65], Cohen [90]	3500
15	22	H	Leyton Orient	L 0-1	0-1	3		4963
16	29	A	Northampton T	D 0-0	0-0	3		6067
17	Nov 11	H	Macclesfield T	W 3-1	1-1	—	Jones G [41], Newey [61], Cohen [80]	3658
18	19	A	Wycombe W	L 1-3	1-2	3	Reddy [37]	6125
19	26	A	Oxford U	W 3-2	1-0	2	Parkinson [3], Bolland [61], Cohen [89]	4323
20	Dec 6	H	Rochdale	W 4-1	0-1	—	Jones G [67], Cohen [70], Jones R [74], Reddy [90]	3896
21	10	H	Bristol R	L 0-1	0-0	2		4739
22	26	A	Bury	W 2-1	1-1	2	Jones G [29], Cohen [75]	3249
23	28	H	Lincoln C	W 3-0	3-0	1	Toner [9], Reddy [25], Parkinson [44]	6056
24	31	A	Wrexham	W 2-1	0-1	2	Reddy [52], Downey [84]	4527
25	Jan 2	H	Carlisle U	L 1-2	1-1	2	Toner [8]	5882
26	14	H	Mansfield T	W 2-1	1-0	2	Reddy [9], Parkinson [86]	4506
27	17	A	Darlington	D 0-0	0-0	—		3924
28	21	A	Torquay U	D 2-2	1-1	3	Parkinson [6], Futcher [81]	2559
29	24	A	Stockport Co	L 1-2	0-0	—	Reddy [48]	3860
30	28	H	Peterborough U	L 1-2	1-1	3	Reddy [29]	4462
31	Feb 4	A	Notts Co	W 1-0	1-0	3	Reddy [40]	6456
32	11	H	Boston U	W 1-0	0-0	1	Mildenhall [72]	5028
33	14	A	Mansfield T	L 1-2	0-2	—	Woodhouse [79]	3053
34	25	H	Chester C	W 1-0	1-0	4	Jones G [42]	4058
35	Mar 4	A	Rushden & D	D 1-1	0-0	3	Futcher [61]	3366
36	11	H	Barnet	W 3-0	3-0	3	Jones G 2 [39, 41], Bolland [45]	5147
37	18	H	Bury	W 2-1	2-0	2	Jones G 2 [14, 20]	5196
38	21	A	Rochdale	D 2-2	1-0	—	Toner (pen) [24], Bolland [82]	1865
39	25	A	Lincoln C	L 0-5	0-4	2		7182
40	Apr 1	H	Wrexham	W 2-0	1-0	2	Jones G [25], Reddy [88]	6058
41	8	A	Carlisle U	L 0-1	0-0	2		10,909
42	15	H	Shrewsbury T	D 1-1	0-1	4	Goodfellow (pen) [66]	5935
43	17	A	Leyton Orient	D 0-0	0-0	4		6582
44	21	H	Cheltenham T	W 1-0	0-0	—	Jones G [69]	5863
45	29	A	Macclesfield T	D 1-1	1-1	4	Jones G [40]	3849
46	May 6	H	Northampton T	D 1-1	0-0	4	Kamudimba Kalala (pen) [75]	8458

Final League Position: 4

GOALSCORERS

League (64): Jones G 13, Reddy 13, Cohen 6, Kamudimba Kalala 5 (4 pens), Bolland 4, Jones R 4, Parkinson 4, Toner 3 (1 pen), Futcher 2, Gritton 2, Andrew 1, Crane 1, Downey 1, Goodfellow 1 (pen), McDermott 1, Mildenhall 1, Newey 1, Woodhouse 1.
Carling Cup (2): Jones G 1, Kamudimba Kalala 1.
FA Cup (1): Jones G 1.
Football League Trophy (1): Ashton 1.
Play-Offs (3): Jones G 2, Futcher 1.

Mildenhall S 46	McDermott J 32	Newey T 35 + 3	Ramsden S 8 + 4	Crane T 3 + 2	Jones R 38 + 2	Croft G 26 + 7	Bolland P 44	Parkinson A 32 + 8	Gritton M 7 + 19	Reddy M 42 + 2	Jones G 34 + 6	Cohen G 32 + 8	Andrew C 3 + 5	Toner C 24 + 7	Whittle J 32	Kamudimba Kalala J 14 + 7	Barwick T 2 + 6	Francis S 5	Hegarty N — + 2	Downey G — + 1	Bloomer M 3	Futcher B 12 + 3	North D — + 1	Mendes J 8 + 7	Woodhouse C 16	Goodfellow M 8 + 2	Match No.
1	2	3	4	5	6	7	8	9	10^{1}	11	12																1
1	2	3	4	5	6	7	8	9^{2}	10^{1}	11^{3}	12	13	14														2
1	2	3■	4	5■	6	7	8^{3}	9^{2}	10	11^{1}		13	12	14													3
1	2	3^{3}	4^{2}		6	13	8■	9	12	11^{1}	10		14		5	7											4
1	2	3		12	6^{1}	7		9	13	11	8^{2}		10		5	4											5
1	2^{1}		12		6	3^{2}	8	9	13	11	7		10		5	4											6
1	2			14	6	7	8	9	13	11^{3}	10^{2}	3^{1}			5	4	12										7
1	2	12			6	7	8	9^{2}	13	11	10^{1}	3^{3}			5	4	14										8
1	2	12			6	7^{1}	8		13	11	10^{2}	3		14	5	4	9^{3}										9
1	2	11			6	7^{1}	8	12	9	10		3			5	4											10
1	2	12			6	7	8^{3}	9^{1}	10	11^{2}		13		14	5	4		3									11
1	2	3			6		8		9^{1}	10	12	11^{2}		4	5		13	7									12
1	2^{1}	3	12		6		8	9	13	11	10^{2}	14		4	5			7^{3}									13
1	2	3	12		6		8	9^{3}	13	11	10^{2}	14			5	4		7^{1}									14
1	2	3			6		8	9^{1}	12	11	10^{2}	13			5	4		7									15
1	2	3			6		8		10^{2}	12	13	11^{3}	9^{1}	7	5	4	14										16
1	2	3	4				8	9^{1}		11	10	7	12	6	5												17
1	2	3^{2}	4			13	8	9	12	11	10^{1}	7^{3}	14	6	5												18
1	2		4			7	8	9^{1}		11	10	3		6	5	12											19
1	2^{1}	3			6	12	8	9		11	10	13		7	5	4^{2}											20
1		3			6	2	8	9	12	11	10^{1}	7		4	5												21
1		3			6	2	8	9	12	11^{1}	10	7		4	5												22
1		3	12		6	2^{1}	8	9		11^{2}	10	7		4	5				13								23
1		3	5^{3}		6^{1}	2^{2}	8■	9	12	11	10	7		4		13				14							24
1		3			6		8	9	12	11^{3}	10^{1}	7^{2}		4	5		13		14		2						25
1		3			6	12	8	9	13	11^{3}	10^{2}	7		4							2^{1}	5	14				26
1		3			6	2	8	9	12	11	10^{1}	7^{2}		4								5		13			27
1		3			6	2	8	9	12	11^{2}	10^{1}	13		4								5		7			28
1	3				6	2	8	9	12	11		7		4								5		10^{1}			29
1	2^{2}	3			6	13	8	9^{1}	12	11		7									5			10	4		30
1		3				7	8^{2}	12		11		2		6			13					5		10	4	9^{1}	31
1		5			6	3		9		11	12	2		7^{1}		13	8^{2}							10	4		32
1		3			6	2^{3}	8	9^{1}		11	12	7		13		14						5		10^{2}	4		33
1	2	3			6		8	9			10	11		7								5			4		34
1	2^{2}	3			6■	13	8	12		9	10	7^{1}		11^{3}								5			4	14	35
1	2	3					8^{1}			9^{2}	10	7		11	6	12						5		13	4		36
1	2	3					8	12		9	10	7		11^{1}	6							5			4		37
1	2	3			12		8			9^{1}	10	7^{2}		11	6	4						5		13			38
1		3			12	2^{3}	8			9	10	7		11^{2}	6^{1}	13						5			4	14	39
1	2	3			6		8	12		9	10	7^{1}			5										4	11	40
1	2^{2}	3			6		8	9^{3}		11	10			12	5							13		14	4	7^{1}	41
1	2	3^{1}			6	12	8	9^{3}		11	10				5^{2}							13		14	4	7	42
1	2^{2}				6	3	8	12			10	7			5	4^{1}								13	11	9	43
1					6	3	8	12		9^{1}	10	2		13	5									7	4	11^{2}	44
1					6^{2}	3	8	9		11^{3}	10	2		12	5							13		14	4	7^{1}	45
1	2				6	3^{3}	8	12		13	10	7			5	14								9^{2}	4	11^{1}	46

FA Cup
First Round Bristol R (h) 1-2

Carling Cup
First Round Derby Co (a) 1-0
Second Round Tottenham H (h) 1-0
Third Round Newcastle U (h) 0-1

Football League Trophy
First Round Morecambe (h) 1-1

Play-Offs
Semi-Final Lincoln C (a) 1-0
(h) 2-1
Final Cheltenham T 0-1
(at Millennium Stadium)

HARTLEPOOL UNITED FL Championship 2

FOUNDATION

The inspiration for the launching of Hartlepool United was the West Hartlepool club which won the FA Amateur Cup in 1904–05. They had been in existence since 1881 and their Cup success led in 1908 to the formation of the new professional concern which first joined the North-Eastern League. In those days they were Hartlepools United and won the Durham Senior Cup in their first two seasons.

Victoria Park, Clarence Road, Hartlepool TS24 8BZ.

Telephone: (01429) 272 584.

Fax: (01429) 863 007.

Ticket Office: (01429) 272 584 ext 2.

Website: www.hartlepoolunited.co.uk

Email: enquires@hartlepoolunited.co.uk

Ground Capacity: 7,691.

Record Attendance: 17,426 v Manchester U, FA Cup 3rd rd, 5 January 1957.

Pitch Measurements: 100m × 66m.

Chairman: Ken Hodcroft.

Chief Executive: Russ Green.

Secretary: Maureen Smith.

Manager: Danny Wilson.

Assistant Manager: TBC.

Physio: James Haycock.

Colours: Blue and white.

Change Colours: Black.

Year Formed: 1908.

Turned Professional: 1908.

Ltd Co.: 1908.

Previous Names: 1908, Hartlepools United; 1968, Hartlepool; 1977, Hartlepool United.

Club Nickname: 'The Pool'.

First Football League Game: 27 August 1921, Division 3 (N), v Wrexham (a) W 2–0 – Gill; Thomas, Crilly; Dougherty, Hopkins, Short; Kessler, Mulholland (1), Lister (1), Robertson, Donald.

Record League Victory: 10–1 v Barrow, Division 4, 4 April 1959 – Oakley; Cameron, Waugh; Johnson, Moore, Anderson; Scott (1), Langland (1), Smith (3), Clark (2), Luke (2), (1 og).

Record Cup Victory: 6–0 v North Shields, FA Cup 1st rd, 30 November 1946 – Heywood; Brown, Gregory; Spelman, Lambert, Jones; Price, Scott (2), Sloan (4), Moses, McMahon.

HONOURS

Football League: Division 3 – Runners-up 2002–03; Division 3 (N) – Runners-up 1956–57.

FA Cup: best season: 4th rd, 1955, 1978, 1989, 1993.

Football League Cup, best season: 4th rd, 1975.

SKY SPORTS FACT FILE

Ex-Bishop Auckland amateur centre-forward Fred Richardson had two goalscoring spells with Hartlepools United the first from October 1947. He had made his League debut the previous season for Chelsea understudying the always supportive Tommy Lawton.

Record Defeat: 1–10 v Wrexham, Division 4, 3 March 1962.

Most League Points (2 for a win): 60, Division 4, 1967–68.

Most League Points (3 for a win): 85, Division 3, 2002–03.

Most League Goals: 90, Division 3 (N), 1956–57.

Highest League Scorer in Season: William Robinson, 28, Division 3 (N), 1927–28; Joe Allon, 28, Division 4, 1990–91.

Most League Goals in Total Aggregate: Ken Johnson, 98, 1949–64.

Most League Goals in One Match: 5, Harry Simmons v Wigan Borough, Division 3N, 1 January 1931; 5, Bobby Folland v Oldham Ath, Division 3N, 15 April 1961.

Most Capped Player: Ambrose Fogarty, 1 (11), Republic of Ireland.

Most League Appearances: Wattie Moore, 447, 1948–64.

Youngest League Player: David Foley, 16 years 105 days v Port Vale, 25 August 2003.

Record Transfer Fee Received: £750,000 from Ipswich T for Tommy Miller, July 2001.

Record Transfer Fee Paid: £75,000 to Northampton for Chris Freestone, March 1993; £75,000 to Notts Co for Gary Jones, March 1999; £75,000 to Mansfield T for Darrell Clarke, July 2001.

Football League Record: 1921 Original Member of Division 3 (N); 1958–68 Division 4; 1968–69 Division 3; 1969–91 Division 4; 1991–92 Division 3; 1992–94 Division 2; 1994–2003 Division 3; 2003–04 Division 2; 2004–06 FL1; 2006– FL2.

LATEST SEQUENCES

Longest Sequence of League Wins: 7, 30.3.2002 – 13.8.2002.

Longest Sequence of League Defeats: 8, 27.1.1993 – 27.2.1993.

Longest Sequence of League Draws: 5, 24.2.2001 – 17.3.2001.

Longest Sequence of Unbeaten League Matches: 21, 2.12.2000 – 31.3.2001.

Longest Sequence Without a League Win: 18, 9.1.1993 – 3.4.1993.

Successive Scoring Runs: 17 from 28.2.1964.

Successive Non-scoring Runs: 11 from 9.1.1993.

MANAGERS

Alfred Priest 1908–12
Percy Humphreys 1912–13
Jack Manners 1913–20
Cecil Potter 1920–22
David Gordon 1922–24
Jack Manners 1924–27
Bill Norman 1927–31
Jack Carr 1932–35
(had been Player-Coach since 1931)
Jimmy Hamilton 1935–43
Fred Westgarth 1943–57
Ray Middleton 1957–59
Bill Robinson 1959–62
Allenby Chilton 1962–63
Bob Gurney 1963–64
Alvan Williams 1964–65
Geoff Twentyman 1965
Brian Clough 1965–67
Angus McLean 1967–70
John Simpson 1970–71
Len Ashurst 1971–74
Ken Hale 1974–76
Billy Horner 1976–83
Johnny Duncan 1983
Mike Docherty 1983
Billy Horner 1984–86
John Bird 1986–88
Bobby Moncur 1988–89
Cyril Knowles 1989–91
Alan Murray 1991–93
Viv Busby 1993
John MacPhail 1993–94
David McCreery 1994–95
Keith Houchen 1995–96
Mick Tait 1996–99
Chris Turner 1999–2002
Mike Newell 2002–03
Neale Cooper 2003–05
Martin Scott 2005–06
Danny Wilson June 2006–

TEN YEAR LEAGUE RECORD

		P	W	D	L	F	A	Pts	Pos
1996-97	Div 3	46	14	9	23	53	66	51	20
1997-98	Div 3	46	12	23	11	61	53	59	17
1998-99	Div 3	46	13	12	21	52	65	51	22
1999-2000	Div 3	46	21	9	16	60	49	72	7
2000-01	Div 3	46	21	14	11	71	54	77	4
2001-02	Div 3	46	20	11	15	74	48	71	7
2002-03	Div 3	46	24	13	9	71	51	85	2
2003-04	Div 2	46	20	13	13	76	61	73	6
2004-05	FL 1	46	21	8	17	76	66	71	6
2005-06	FL 1	46	11	17	18	44	59	50	21

DID YOU KNOW ?

In three successive seasons from 1933–34, Hartlepools United found themselves drawn against Halifax Town in the FA Cup. United avenged themselves in another replay in 1934–35 while in 1935–36 it took three attempts before winning 4–1 at St James' Park.

HARTLEPOOL UNITED 2005–06 LEAGUE RECORD

Match No.	Date	Venue	Opponents	Result		H/T Score	Lg. Pos.	Goalscorers	Attendance
1	Aug 6	H	Bradford C	L	0-2	0-1	—		6271
2	9	A	Bournemouth	D	1-1	0-0	—	Bullock 51	5406
3	13	A	Doncaster R	W	1-0	1-0	14	Daly 45	5061
4	20	H	Walsall	D	1-1	0-1	15	Sweeney 63	5060
5	27	A	Huddersfield T	L	1-2	0-2	19	Boyd 51	11,241
6	29	H	Scunthorpe U	D	3-3	1-1	17	Proctor 6, Williams E 71, Boyd (pen) 90	5044
7	Sept 3	H	Yeovil T	L	0-1	0-0	19		4572
8	10	A	Blackpool	W	2-1	0-0	14	Sweeney 86, Istead 90	5494
9	17	H	Swansea C	D	2-2	1-0	16	Humphreys 25, Sweeney 76	4743
10	24	A	Chesterfield	L	1-3	1-0	20	Proctor 11	4078
11	27	H	Rotherham U	D	0-0	0-0	—		4309
12	Oct 1	A	Bristol C	W	1-0	0-0	18	Proctor 54	11,365
13	15	A	Nottingham F	L	0-2	0-1	21		17,586
14	22	H	Milton Keynes D	W	2-1	0-1	18	Lewington (og) 50, Bullock 84	4337
15	29	A	Port Vale	W	2-1	1-1	16	Williams E 12, Butler 64	4550
16	Nov 1	H	Gillingham	W	3-1	1-0	—	Daly 15, Sweeney 50, Bullock 86	4522
17	12	H	Brentford	L	1-2	0-1	14	Sweeney 72	4811
18	19	A	Gillingham	L	0-1	0-1	15		6092
19	26	A	Bradford C	W	1-0	1-0	13	Tinkler 34	7499
20	Dec 6	H	Colchester U	L	0-1	0-0	—		3375
21	10	H	Bournemouth	W	2-1	2-0	12	Istead 28, McDonald 39	3755
22	17	A	Walsall	L	0-1	0-0	14		4293
23	26	A	Barnsley	D	1-1	0-1	13	Williams E 50	9715
24	28	H	Southend U	L	1-2	1-1	15	Williams E 20	3929
25	31	A	Oldham Ath	L	1-2	0-1	16	Williams E 75	5047
26	Jan 2	H	Swindon T	D	1-1	1-0	18	Strachan 36	4169
27	7	A	Yeovil T	L	0-2	0-1	18		5480
28	14	H	Tranmere R	D	0-0	0-0	19		4181
29	21	A	Swansea C	D	1-1	0-1	19	Williams E 90	13,960
30	28	H	Blackpool	L	0-3	0-1	21		4421
31	Feb 4	A	Rotherham U	D	0-0	0-0	22		5960
32	10	H	Chesterfield	W	1-0	0-0	—	Robson 65	4596
33	14	A	Tranmere R	D	0-0	0-0	—		6301
34	25	H	Doncaster R	D	1-1	1-0	19	Boyd 20	5459
35	Mar 10	H	Huddersfield T	W	3-1	1-1	—	Boyd 10, Maidens 53, Porter 82	5468
36	14	A	Scunthorpe U	L	0-2	0-1	—		4550
37	18	H	Barnsley	D	1-1	1-1	18	Porter 9	5122
38	25	A	Southend U	L	0-3	0-1	21		8496
39	31	H	Oldham Ath	D	1-1	1-1	—	Bullock 9	5259
40	Apr 8	A	Swindon T	D	1-1	1-0	21	Humphreys 31	5225
41	11	A	Colchester U	L	0-2	0-0	—		3916
42	15	H	Bristol C	L	1-2	0-2	21	Williams E 83	5039
43	17	A	Milton Keynes D	L	1-2	0-1	23	Proctor 50	6472
44	22	H	Nottingham F	W	3-2	1-1	22	Porter 32, Nelson 59, Proctor 60	5336
45	29	A	Brentford	D	1-1	0-0	21	Nelson 90	8725
46	May 6	H	Port Vale	D	1-1	0-0	21	Brown 86	6895

Final League Position: 21

GOALSCORERS

League (44): Williams E 7, Proctor 5, Sweeney 5, Boyd 4 (1 pen), Bullock 4, Porter 3, Daly 2, Humphreys 2, Istead 2, Nelson 2, Brown 1, Butler 1, Maidens 1, McDonald 1, Robson 1, Strachan 1, Tinkler 1, own goal 1.
Carling Cup (4): Daly 2, Proctor 2.
FA Cup (3): Butler 1, Llewellyn 1 (pen), Nelson 1.
Football League Trophy (0).

Konstantopoulos D 46	Clark B 28 + 4	Humphreys R 46	Williams D 33 + 6	Nelson M 43	Bullock L 22 + 9	Llewellyn C 24 + 5	Sweeney A 34 + 1	Proctor M 22 + 4	Boyd A 12 + 9	Butler T 26 + 2	Strachan G 6 + 3	Daly J 18 + 12	Williams E 24 + 12	Collins N 22	Robson M 13 + 6	Jones C 1	Tinkler M 11 + 4	Turnbull S 16 + 5	Maidens M 11 + 9	Istead S 4 + 6	Foley D 1 + 10	Craddock D 4	McDonald D 4 + 1	Brackstone J 2	Barron M 13 + 2	Robertson H 2	Clarke D 6 + 6	Walker J 1 + 3	Nash G 3	Pittman J 2 + 1	Porter J 6 + 2	Brown J — + 4	*Match No.*
1	2	3	4	5	6^{1}	7^{2}	8	9	10	11^{3}	12	13	14																				1
1	2	3	4	5	6	12	8	9^{2}	13	11^{1}		10	7																				2
1		3	4	5	6		8	9^{1}	12	11		10	7	2																			3
1		3	2	5	6^{1}	13	8	9^{2}	14	11	12	10	7^{3}	4																			4
1		11^{3}	2	5	12	14	8	9	13	7	6^{1}	10^{2}		4	3																		5
1	12	11^{2}	2	5	6^{1}	7^{3}	8	9	10			13	14	4	3																		6
1	4	11	2	5	12		8	9	10^{2}	7^{1}		14	13^{3}		3	6																	7
1		3	2	5			8	9^{3}		11		10		4			6^{1}	12	7^{2}	13	14												8
1		3	2	5			8	9^{3}		11		10		4			6^{1}	12	7^{2}	13	14												9
1		3	2	5	10	12	8	9^{3}		11				4			6^{2}	13	7^{1}		14												10
1		3	2	5	10^{3}	7^{2}	8	9		11				4			6^{1}	12	13		14												11
1		3	2	5	11	7	8^{2}	9^{1}				10^{3}	12	6			13	4	14														12
1		3	2	5■	11	7^{1}	8	9^{2}		12		10	13	6			14	4^{3}															13
1		3	4		12	7^{3}	8			11		10^{1}	9	5			13■	6^{2}	14			2											14
1		3	4		6	7^{2}	8	12		11^{1}		10	9	5					13			2											15
1		3	2	5	6^{2}	7^{3}	8	12		11		10	9^{1}	4				13	14														16
1		3	2	5			8	9^{1}		11		10	7	4			6		12														17
1	12	3	2	5			8			11■		10	9^{3}	4			6^{1}		7^{2}	13			14										18
1		11^{1}	2	5		7	8					12	9	4			6			13			10^{2}	3									19
1	12	3		5		9	8	13		11^{2}		14	7	4			6^{1}						10		2^{3}								20
1	6^{1}	11	12	5		9	8					13		4						7^{3}			10^{2}		2	3	14						21
1	4	3	12	5		9	8			11		13		6						7^{3}			10^{2}		2^{1}		14						22
1	4	3		5		10	8			11		12	9^{1}	6						7^{2}		2					13						23
1	4	3		5		10^{1}	8			11^{2}		12	9^{3}	6					13	14		2					7						24
1	4^{1}	11	12	5		10	8				13	14	9	6										3^{3}	2^{2}		7						25
1	12	3	4	5	13	10	8^{2}				6^{1}		9						7						2		11^{3}	14					26
1	8	11	4	5	12	10					6^{1}	13	9		3^{2}				7^{3}						2			14					27
1	4^{1}	3		5	12	11■	8				7	10													2			9^{2}	6	13			28
1	4^{3}	3		5	12		8			11^{2}	7^{1}	10	13												2			14	6	9			29
1	4^{2}	3		5	12		8		13		11^{1}	10	7								14				2■				6	9^{3}			30
1	5	3	2		12		8					10	9^{2}		4		6	11^{1}	7^{3}		13						14						31
1	4	3	2	5		10	8^{3}		9			12			13		6^{2}	7			11^{1}						14						32
1	4	3	2	5	6	7^{1}			9^{2}			10			11			8	12		13												33
1	4	3	2	5	6	7^{1}	12		10^{2}				9		14		13	8									11^{3}						34
1	4	3	2	5	6	11			10^{1}				9^{3}		13			8	7^{2}		12										14		35
1	4	3	2	5	6	11^{1}			10				9^{3}		13			8	7^{2}		12										14		36
1	4	3	2	5	6	11			10^{1}				12		13			8	7^{2}		14										9^{3}		37
1	4	3	2	5	6			9	12	11			13		7^{1}			8													10^{2}		38
1	4	3	2	5	6			9^{1}	13	11^{3}			12		7			8	14												10^{2}		39
1	2	3	4	5	6			9	10^{1}	11			12		7			8^{2}							13								40
1	2	3	4■	5	6			9^{1}	10^{2}	11^{3}			12					8	7						13							14	41
1	2	3		5	6^{2}			12	10^{3}	11			9		13			8							4	7^{1}						14	42
1	4	3	12	5		13		9					11		2		6^{2}	8^{3}		10					7^{1}		14						43
1	4	3	12	5			8^{1}	9					11^{3}		2					13					7		6				10^{2}	14	44
1	4	11	12	5			8	9	13	14			7^{2}		3										2^{1}		6^{3}				10		45
1	4	3	2	5	6^{1}		8^{3}	9^{2}	12	11			13		7																10	14	46

FA Cup

First Round	Dagenham & R	(h)	2-1
Second Round	Tamworth	(h)	1-2

Carling Cup

First Round	Darlington	(h)	3-1
Second Round	Charlton Ath	(a)	1-3

Football League Trophy

First Round	Scunthorpe U	(a)	0-1

HEREFORD UNITED FL Championship 2

FOUNDATION

Two local teams RAOC and St Martins amalgamated in 1924 under the chairmanship of Dr. E.W. Maples to form Hereford United and joined the Birmingham Combination. The first game at Edgar Street was against Atherstone Town on 24 August 1924, the visitors winning 3-2. The players used the Wellington Hotel as a changing room. They graduated to the Birmingham League four years later and the Southern League in 1939.

Edgar Street, Hereford HR4 9JU.

Telephone: (01432) 276666.

Fax: (01432) 341359.

Ticket Office: (01432) 276666.

Website: www.herefordunited.co.uk.

Email: hufc1939@hotmail.com.

Ground capacity: 7873

Record Attendance: 18,114 v Sheffield W, FA Cup 3rd rd, 4 January 1958.

Pitch measurements: 100m × 72m.

Chairman: Graham Turner.

Secretary: Mrs Joan Fennessey

Manager: Graham Turner.

Physio: Wayne Jones.

Colours: White shirts, black shorts, black stockings.

Change colours: Yellow shirts, blue shorts, blue stockings.

Year Formed: 1924.

Turned Professional: 1924.

Ltd Co.: 1939.

Club Nickname: 'United'.

First Football League game: 12 August 1972, Division 4, v Colchester U (a) L 0-1 – Potter; Mallender, Naylor; Jones, McLaughlin, Tucker; Slattery, Hollett, Owen, Radford, Wallace.

Record League Victory: 6–0 v Burnley (away), Division 4, 24 January 1987 – Rose; Rodgerson, Devine, Halliday, Pejic, Dalziel, Harvey (1p), Wells, Phillips (3), Kearns (2), Spooner.

HONOURS

Football League: Division 2 best season: 22nd, 1976–77; Division 3 – Champions 1975–76; Division 4 – Runners-up 1972–73.

FA Cup: best season: 4th rd, 1972, 1974, 1977, 1982, 1990, 1992.

Football League Cup: best season: 3rd rd, 1975.

Welsh Cup: Winners 1990.

Conference (runners-up): 2003–04, 2004–05. Promoted from Conference 2005–06 (Play-offs).

SKY SPORTS FACT FILE

When Hereford United won the Southern League First Division title in 1964–65, they dropped only 12 points and finished 11 points ahead of Wimbledon. Their 124 goals gave them The Merit Cup, too, while the defence conceded only 39 goals in 42 games.

Record Cup Victory: 6–1 v QPR, FA Cup 2nd rd, 7 December 1957 – Sewell; Tomkins, Wade; Masters, Niblett, Horton (2p); Reg Bowen (1), Clayton (1), Fidler, Williams (1), Cyril Beech (1).

Record Defeat: 0–7 v Middlesbrough, Coca-Cola Cup 2nd rd, 1st leg, 18 September 1996.

Most League Points (2 for a win): 63, Division 3, 1975–76.

Most League Points (3 for a win): 77, Division 4, 1984–85.

Most League Goals: 86, Division 3, 1975–76.

Highest League Scorer in Season: Dixie McNeil, 35, 1975–76.

Most League Goals in Total Aggregate: Stewart Phillips, 93, 1980–88, 1990–91.

Most Capped Player: Brian Evans, 1 (7), Wales.

Most League Appearances: Mel Pejic, 412, 1980–92.

Record Transfer Fee Received: £440,000 from QPR for Darren Peacock, December 1990.

Record Transfer Fee Paid: £80,000 to Walsall for Dean Smith, June 1994.

Football League Record: 1972 Elected to Division 4; 1973–76 Division 3; 1976–77 Division 2; 1977–78 Division 3; 1978–92 Division 4; 1992–97 Division 3; 1997–2006 Vauxhall Conference; 2006– FL2.

MANAGERS

Eric Keen 1939
George Tranter 1948–49
Alex Massie 1952
George Tranter 1953–55
Joe Wade 1956–62
Ray Daniels 1962–63
Bob Dennison 1963–67
John Charles 1967–71
Colin Addison 1971–74
John Sillett 1974–78
Mike Bailey 1978–79
Frank Lord 1979–82
Tommy Hughes 1982–83
Johnny Newman 1983–87
Ian Bowyer 1987–90
Colin Addison 1990–91
John Sillett 1991–92
Greg Downs 1992–94
John Layton 1994–95
Graham Turner 1995–

LATEST SEQUENCES

Longest Sequence of League Wins: 6, 2.4.1996 – 20.4.1996.

Longest Sequence of League Defeats: 8, 7.2.1987 – 18.3.1987.

Longest Sequence of League Draws: 6, 12.4.1975 – 23.8.1975.

Longest Sequence of Unbeaten League Matches: 14, 21.10.1972 – 17.1.1973.

Longest Sequence Without a League Win: 13, 19.11.1977 – 25.2.1978.

Successive Scoring Runs: 23 from 20.9.1975.

Successive Non-scoring Runs: 5 from 8.4.1978.

TEN YEAR LEAGUE RECORD

		P	W	D	L	F	A	Pts	Pos
1996–9	Div 3	46	11	14	21	50	65	47	24
1997–98	Conf	42	18	13	11	56	49	67	6
1998–99	Conf	42	15	10	17	49	46	55	13
1999–2000	Conf	42	15	14	13	61	52	59	8
2000–01	Conf	42	14	15	13	60	46	57	11
2001–02	Conf	42	14	10	18	50	53	52	17
2002–03	Conf	42	19	7	16	64	51	64	6
2003–04	Conf	42	28	7	7	103	44	91	2
2004–05	Conf	42	21	11	10	68	41	74	2
2005–06	Conf	42	22	14	6	59	33	80	2

DID YOU KNOW ?

Charlie Thompson not only scored more than 200 goals for Hereford United in the immediate post-war period, but achieved the feat of scoring a club record eight goals in an 11–0 preliminary round FA Cup win over Thynnes Athletic on 20 September 1947.

HUDDERSFIELD TOWN FL Championship 1

FOUNDATION

A meeting, attended largely by members of the Huddersfield & District FA, was held at the Imperial Hotel in 1906 to discuss the feasibility of establishing a football club in this rugby stronghold. However, it was not until a man with both the enthusiasm and the money to back the scheme came on the scene, that real progress was made. This benefactor was Mr Hilton Crowther and it was at a meeting at the Albert Hotel in 1908, that the club formally came into existence with a capital of £2,000 and joined the North-Eastern League.

The Galpharm Stadium, Stadium Way, Leeds Road, Huddersfield HD1 6PX.

Telephone: 0870 4444 677.

Fax: (01484) 484 101.

Ticket Office: 0870 4444 552.

Website: www.htafc.com

Email: info@htafc.com

Ground Capacity: 24,590.

Record Attendance: 67,037 v Arsenal, FA Cup 6th rd, 27 February 1932 (at Leeds Road); 23,678 v Liverpool, FA Cup 3rd rd, 12 December 1999 (at Alfred McAlpine Stadium).

Pitch Measurements: 115yd × 82yd.

Chairman: Ken Davy.

Chief Executive: Andrew Watson.

Secretary: Ann Hough.

Manager: Peter Jackson.

Physio: Lee Martin.

Colours: Blue and white striped shirts, white shorts, white stockings.

Change Colours: Red shirt, red shorts, red stockings.

Year Formed: 1908. ***Turned Professional:*** 1908. ***Ltd Co.:*** 1908.

Club Nickname: 'The Terriers'.

Previous Grounds: 1908, Leeds Road; 1994, The Alfred McAlpine Stadium.

First Football League Game: 3 September 1910, Division 2, v Bradford PA (a) W 1–0 – Mutch; Taylor, Morris; Beaton, Hall, Bartlett; Blackburn, Wood, Hamilton (1), McCubbin, Jee.

Record League Victory: 10–1 v Blackpool, Division 1, 13 December 1930 – Turner; Goodall, Spencer; Redfern, Wilson, Campbell; Bob Kelly (1), McLean (4), Robson (3), Davies (1), Smailes (1).

Record Cup Victory: 7–0 v Lincoln U, FA Cup 1st rd, 16 November 1991 – Clarke; Trevitt, Charlton, Donovan (2), Mitchell, Doherty, O'Regan (1), Stapleton (1) (Wright), Roberts (2), Onuora (1), Barnett (Ireland). *N.B.* 11-0 v Heckmondwike (a), FA Cup pr rd, 18 September 1909 – Doggart; Roberts, Ewing; Hooton, Stevenson, Randall; Kenworthy (2), McCreadie (1), Foster (4), Stacey (4), Jee.

HONOURS

Football League: Division 1 – Champions 1923–24, 1924–25, 1925–26; Runners-up 1926–27, 1927–28, 1933–34; Division 2 – Champions 1969–70; Runners-up 1919–20, 1952–53; Promoted from Division 2 1994–95 (play-offs); Promoted from Division 3 2003–04 (play-offs); Division 4 – Champions 1979–80.

FA Cup: Winners 1922; Runners-up 1920, 1928, 1930, 1938.

Football League Cup: Semi-final 1968.

Autoglass Trophy: Runners-up 1994.

SKY SPORTS FACT FILE

Long-serving Huddersfield Town goalkeeper Bob Hesford signed in 1933 had to choose between England's tour to South Africa in 1939 or taking his final scholastic examinations. He stayed and achieved a BA at Leeds University and also became a teacher.

Record Defeat: 1–10 v Manchester C, Division 2, 7 November 1987.

Most League Points (2 for a win): 66, Division 4, 1979–80.

Most League Points (3 for a win): 82, Division 3, 1982–83.

Most League Goals: 101, Division 4, 1979–80.

Highest League Scorer in Season: Sam Taylor, 35, Division 2, 1919–20; George Brown, 35, Division 1, 1925–26.

Most League Goals in Total Aggregate: George Brown, 142, 1921–29; Jimmy Glazzard, 142, 1946–56.

Most League Goals in One Match: 5, Dave Mangnall v Derby Co, Division 1, 21 November 1931; 5, Alf Lythgoe v Blackburn R, Division 1, 13 April 1935.

Most Capped Player: Jimmy Nicholson, 31 (41), Northern Ireland.

Most League Appearances: Billy Smith, 520, 1914–34.

Youngest League Player: Denis Law, 16 years 303 days v Notts Co, 24 December 1956.

Record Transfer Fee Received: £2,750,000 from Ipswich T for Marcus Stewart, February 2000.

Record Transfer Fee Paid: £1,200,000 to Bristol R for Marcus Stewart, July 1996.

Football League Record: 1910 Elected to Division 2; 1920–52 Division 1; 1952–53 Division 2; 1953–56 Division 1; 1956–70 Division 2; 1970–72 Division 1; 1972–73 Division 2; 1973–75 Division 3; 1975–80 Division 4; 1980–83 Division 3; 1983–88 Division 2; 1988–92 Division 3; 1992–95 Division 2; 1995–2001 Division 1; 2001–03 Division 2; 2003–04 Division 3; 2004– FL1.

MANAGERS

Fred Walker 1908–10
Richard Pudan 1910–12
Arthur Fairclough 1912–19
Ambrose Langley 1919–21
Herbert Chapman 1921–25
Cecil Potter 1925–26
Jack Chaplin 1926–29
Clem Stephenson 1929–42
David Steele 1943–47
George Stephenson 1947–52
Andy Beattie 1952–56
Bill Shankly 1956–59
Eddie Boot 1960–64
Tom Johnston 1964–68
Ian Greaves 1968–74
Bobby Collins 1974
Tom Johnston 1975–78
(had been General Manager since 1975)
Mike Buxton 1978–86
Steve Smith 1986–87
Malcolm Macdonald 1987–88
Eoin Hand 1988–92
Ian Ross 1992–93
Neil Warnock 1993–95
Brian Horton 1995–97
Peter Jackson 1997–99
Steve Bruce 1999–2000
Lou Macari 2000–02
Mick Wadsworth 2002–03
Peter Jackson June 2003–

LATEST SEQUENCES

Longest Sequence of League Wins: 11, 5.4.1920 – 4.9.1920.

Longest Sequence of League Defeats: 7, 8.10.1955 – 19.11.1955.

Longest Sequence of League Draws: 6, 3.3.1987 – 3.4.1987.

Longest Sequence of Unbeaten League Matches: 27, 24.1.1925 – 17.10.1925.

Longest Sequence Without a League Win: 22, 4.12.1971 – 29.4.1972.

Successive Scoring Runs: 27 from 12.3.2005.

Successive Non-scoring Runs: 7 from 22.1.1972.

TEN YEAR LEAGUE RECORD

		P	*W*	*D*	*L*	*F*	*A*	*Pts*	*Pos*
1996-97	Div 1	46	13	15	18	48	61	54	20
1997-98	Div 1	46	14	11	21	50	72	53	16
1998-99	Div 1	46	15	16	15	62	71	61	10
1999-2000	Div 1	46	21	11	14	62	49	74	8
2000-01	Div 1	46	11	15	20	48	57	48	22
2001-02	Div 2	46	21	15	10	65	47	78	6
2002-03	Div 2	46	11	12	23	39	61	45	22
2003-04	Div 3	46	23	12	11	68	52	81	4
2004-05	FL 1	46	20	10	16	74	65	70	9
2005-06	FL 1	46	19	16	11	72	59	73	4

DID YOU KNOW ?

Huddersfield Town were already gearing themselves up for their then record three championships in a row when in March and April 1923 they showed the type of consistency that was to come when they recorded five successive 2–0 victories to finish third.

HUDDERSFIELD TOWN 2005–06 LEAGUE RECORD

Match No.	*Date*	*Venue*	*Opponents*	*Result*		*H/T Score*	*Lg. Pos.*	*Goalscorers*	*Attendance*
1	Aug 6	A	Nottingham F	L	1-2	0-1	—	Abbott (pen) [64]	24,042
2	9	H	Bristol C	W	1-0	0-0	—	Abbott [89]	11,138
3	13	H	Swansea C	W	3-1	2-1	3	Booth [27], Abbott [41], Schofield [76]	10,304
4	20	A	Southend U	D	1-1	1-1	5	Abbott [45]	5567
5	27	H	Hartlepool U	W	2-1	2-0	2	Abbott [13], Schofield [18]	11,241
6	29	A	Doncaster R	W	2-1	2-0	1	Brandon [2], Worthington [40]	7222
7	Sept 2	H	Scunthorpe U	L	1-4	0-2	—	Abbott (pen) [64]	14,112
8	10	A	Oldham Ath	W	3-0	2-0	3	Schofield [27], Taylor-Fletcher 2 [37, 72]	6803
9	17	H	Brentford	W	3-2	1-1	2	Abbott [34], Schofield [89], Booth [90]	11,622
10	24	A	Colchester U	D	1-1	0-0	3	Taylor-Fletcher [65]	3415
11	27	H	Tranmere R	W	1-0	0-0	—	Schofield [87]	10,640
12	Oct 1	H	Bournemouth	D	2-2	2-0	3	Schofield [14], Taylor-Fletcher [21]	13,522
13	10	A	Bradford C	W	2-1	1-1	—	Hudson [21], Booth [79]	12,285
14	15	H	Walsall	W	3-1	2-1	1	Booth [15], Abbott 2 [34, 78]	11,642
15	22	A	Chesterfield	L	3-4	0-3	2	Hudson [80], Worthington [87], Holdsworth [90]	6206
16	29	H	Swindon T	D	1-1	0-1	3	Brandon [54]	11,352
17	Nov 12	A	Yeovil T	W	2-1	2-0	2	Booth [11], Hudson [39]	6742
18	19	H	Bradford C	D	0-0	0-0	2		17,331
19	26	H	Nottingham F	W	2-1	2-0	2	Schofield [21], Booth [26]	17,370
20	Dec 6	A	Milton Keynes D	D	2-2	1-0	—	Abbott [7], Booth [64]	4832
21	10	A	Bristol C	L	0-2	0-1	2		9949
22	17	H	Southend U	D	0-0	0-0	3		11,223
23	26	A	Rotherham U	D	1-1	0-1	3	Taylor-Fletcher [90]	7380
24	28	H	Port Vale	L	0-3	0-0	3		10,824
25	31	A	Barnsley	D	2-2	0-0	4	Booth [76], Taylor-Fletcher [90]	13,263
26	Jan 2	H	Gillingham	D	0-0	0-0	5		11,483
27	10	A	Scunthorpe U	D	2-2	1-1	—	Schofield [44], McIntosh [90]	4450
28	14	H	Blackpool	W	2-0	1-0	3	Clarke T [9], Schofield [73]	11,977
29	21	A	Brentford	L	0-2	0-1	5		7636
30	28	H	Oldham Ath	W	3-2	1-2	3	Branston (og) [45], Abbott [48], Graham [59]	12,973
31	Feb 3	A	Tranmere R	L	1-2	0-1	—	Graham [48]	8300
32	11	H	Colchester U	W	2-0	1-0	5	Worthington [14], Graham [68]	13,515
33	14	A	Blackpool	W	1-0	1-0	—	Brandon (pen) [43]	6004
34	18	H	Milton Keynes D	W	5-0	3-0	3	McIntosh [19], Taylor-Fletcher [24], Worthington [36], Mirfin [77], Collins [90]	11,423
35	24	A	Swansea C	D	2-2	0-2	—	McIntosh [70], Graham [82]	13,110
36	Mar 4	H	Doncaster R	D	2-2	2-1	2	McIntosh [8], Graham [40]	14,490
37	10	A	Hartlepool U	L	1-3	1-1	—	Graham [22]	5468
38	18	H	Rotherham U	W	4-1	2-1	3	Booth 3 [32, 39, 82], Taylor-Fletcher [84]	15,264
39	25	A	Port Vale	D	1-1	0-0	2	Booth [81]	5664
40	Apr 1	H	Barnsley	W	1-0	0-0	3	Taylor-Fletcher [55]	19,052
41	8	A	Gillingham	L	0-2	0-1	3		7014
42	15	A	Bournemouth	D	1-1	0-1	4	Taylor-Fletcher [71]	7406
43	18	H	Chesterfield	L	1-2	1-0	—	Graham [13]	13,368
44	22	A	Walsall	W	3-1	1-0	4	Graham [25], Abbott [83], Booth [90]	5554
45	29	H	Yeovil T	L	1-2	1-0	4	Graham [8]	14,473
46	May 6	A	Swindon T	D	0-0	0-0	4		6353

Final League Position: 4

GOALSCORERS

League (72): Booth 13, Abbott 12 (2 pens), Taylor-Fletcher 10, Graham 9, Schofield 9, McIntosh 4, Worthington 4, Brandon 3 (1 pen), Hudson 3, Clarke T 1, Collins 1, Holdsworth 1, Mirfin 1, own goal 1.
Carling Cup (5): Taylor-Fletcher 3, Abbott 2.
FA Cup (6): Booth 2, Brandon 1, Holdsworth 1, Schofield 1 (pen), Taylor-Fletcher 1.
Football League Trophy (1): Mirfin 1.
Play-Offs (2): Taylor-Fletcher 1, Worthington 1.

Rachubka P 34	Holdsworth A 37 + 5	Adams D 40	Hudson M 25 + 4	Mirfin D 27 + 4	Clarke N 46	Worthington J 41	Brandon C 36 + 4	Abbott P 27 + 9	Booth A 32 + 4	McIntosh M 20 + 2	Schofield D 37 + 4	Taylor-Fletcher G 30 + 13	Carss T 10 + 7	Collins M 9 + 8	Mendes J — + 5	Clarke T 16 + 1	Young M — + 2	Ahmed A 4 + 9	McAliskey J — + 9	Senior P 12 + 1	Smith D 7 + 1	Graham D 15 + 1	McCombe J 1	Match No.
1	2^{1}	3	4	5	6	7	8	9^{2}	10	11	12	13												1
1	12	3	4^{2}	5^{1}	6	7	8	9	10	11	2^{3}	14	13											2
1	2	3	4^{1}		6	7^{2}	8	9	10^{3}	5	11	14	12	13										3
1	2	3	4		6	7	8^{1}	9		5	11	10			12									4
1	2	3			6	7	8	9			11	10	12	4^{1}		5								5
1	2	3			6	7	8^{1}	9			11	10	12	4		5								6
1	2	3			6	7	8	9			11	10		4		5								7
1	2	3			6	7	8	9			4	10^{2}	11^{1}	12	13	5								8
1	2	3			6	7	8^{2}	9	12		4	10^{1}	11		13	5■								9
1	2	3			6	7	8	9^{1}	10		4	12	11			5								10
1	2	3	12		6	7	8^{2}	9^{3}	10		4	13	11^{1}		14	5								11
1	2	3	12		6	7^{1}	8	9^{3}	13		4^{2}	10	11		14	5								12
1	2	3	4	5	6	7	8^{2}	12	10			9^{1}	11	13										13
1	2	3	4^{2}	5	6	7		9	10^{1}		8^{3}	12	11	13			14							14
1	2	3	4	5	6	7	12	9	10		8^{2}	13	11^{1}											15
1	2	3	4	5	6		8^{2}	9	10		7	12	11^{1}	13										16
1	2	3	4■	5	6	7		9^{1}	10		11	8	12											17
1	2	3		5	6	7	12	9^{1}	10		4	8	11											18
1	2	3	4	5	6	7	8^{1}		10		11	9	12											19
1	2	3	4	5■	6	7	8■	9	10			11												20
1	2	3^{3}	4		6	7		9^{2}	10		11	8^{1}	12			5		14	13					21
1	2		4^{2}	3	6	7	8	9	10	12	11					5^{1}		13						22
1	2	3	4^{2}	5	6	7	8	9^{1}	10		11	12						13						23
1	2	3		5■	6	7	8	12	10	13	11	9^{1}						4^{2}						24
1	2	3			6	7	8^{1}	12	10	5	11	9						4						25
	2	3			6	7^{1}		9^{2}	10	5	11	8		12				4	13	1				26
1	2	3^{1}	4^{2}	12	6		8^{3}	9		5	11	10		14		7			13					27
1	2	3		12	6	7	8	9	10^{2}	5^{1}	11^{3}	13				4					14			28
1■	2	3	4	5	6	7	8^{1}				10	9		12^{6}		11^{2}			13	15				29
	2	3	12^{2}	13	6	7		9		5	11	14				4^{1}				1	8	10^{3}		30
	2	3^{2}			6	7	8	9^{1}	12	5		13		4						1	11	10		31
				2	6	7	8		10	5		11		4						1	3	9		32
	12			2	6	7	8	13	10	5		11		4						1	3^{1}	9^{2}		33
	12			2	6	7^{1}	8	13	10^{2}	5	14	11^{3}		4						1	3	9		34
	12			2	6	7^{3}	8		10	5	13	11^{2}		4^{1}					14	1	3	9		35
	2^{1}		12	4	6	7	8^{3}	13	10	5	14	11^{2}								1	3	9		36
	12	3	4^{2}	2^{1}	6	7	8		10	5	11								13	1		9		37
	2	3	4		6	7^{3}	8		10^{2}	5	11	12						14	13	1		9^{1}		38
	2	3	4	12	6	7	8		10	5^{1}	11	9								1				39
	2	3	4	5	6	7	8^{1}		10		11	9^{2}						12		1		13		40
1	2	3^{2}	4^{3}	5	6	7		12	10^{1}		11	8						14	13			9		41
1	2	3	4	5	6	7	12				11	10				8^{1}						9		42
1	2^{2}	3	4	5	6	7	8^{1}		12		11	10				13^{3}		14				9		43
1		3	4	2	6		8	12	10	5	11^{2}	7						13				9^{1}		44
1		3	4	2	6		8^{2}	12	10	5	11	7^{1}						13				9		45
1		3		2	6^{1}		12	10			11^{3}			8		4■	14	7	13			9^{2}	5	46

FA Cup

First Round	Welling U	(h)	4-1
Second Round	Worcester C	(a)	1-0
Third Round	Chelsea	(a)	1-2

Carling Cup

First Round	Chesterfield	(a)	4-2
Second Round	Blackburn R	(a)	1-3

Football League Trophy

First Round	Boston U	(a)	1-2

Play-Offs

Semi-Final	Barnsley	(a)	1-0
		(h)	1-3

HULL CITY FL Championship

FOUNDATION

The enthusiasts who formed Hull City in 1904 were brave men indeed. More than that they were audacious for they immediately put the club on the map in this Rugby League fortress by obtaining a three-year agreement with the Hull Rugby League club to rent their ground! They had obtained quite a number of conversions to the dribbling code, before the Rugby League forbade the use of any of their club grounds by Association Football clubs. By that time, Hull City were well away having entered the FA Cup in their initial season and the Football League, Second Division after only a year.

Kingston Communications Stadium, The Circle, Walton Street, Anlaby Road, Hull HU3 6HU.

Telephone: 0870 837 0003.

Fax: (01482) 304 882.

Ticket Office: 0870 837 0004.

Website: www.hullcityafc.net

Email: info@hulltigers.com

Ground Capacity: 25,404.

Record Attendance: KC Stadium: 23,495 v Huddersfield T, Division 3, 24 April 2004. Boothferry Park: 55,019 v Manchester U, FA Cup 6th rd, 26 February 1949.

Pitch Measurements: 105m × 68m.

Chairman/Chief Executive: Adam Pearson.

Secretary: Phil Hough.

Manager: Phil Parkinson.

Assistant Manager: Colin Murphy.

Physio: Simon Maltby.

HONOURS

Football League: Championship 1 runners-up 2004–05; Division 2 best season: 3rd, 1909–10; Division 3 (N) – Champions 1932–33, 1948–49; Division 3 – Champions 1965–66; Runners-up 1958–59, 2003–04; Division 4 – Runners-up 1982–83.

FA Cup: Semi-final 1930.

Football League Cup: best season: 4th, 1974, 1976, 1978.

Associate Members' Cup: Runners-up 1984.

Colours: Black and amber striped shirts, black shorts with amber trim, black stockings with amber turnover.

Change Colours: Black shirts with white side panel and amber trim, white shorts with black back yoke.

Year Formed: 1904. ***Turned Professional:*** 1905.

Ltd Co.: 1905.

Club Nickname: 'The Tigers'.

Previous Grounds: 1904, Boulevard Ground (Hull RFC); 1905, Anlaby Road (Hull CC); 1944, Boulevard Ground; 1946, Boothferry Park; 2002, Kingston Communications Stadium.

First Football League Game: 2 September 1905, Division 2, v Barnsley (h) W 4–1 – Spendiff; Langley, Jones; Martin, Robinson, Gordon (2); Rushton, Spence (1), Wilson (1), Howe, Raisbeck.

Record League Victory: 11–1 v Carlisle U, Division 3 (N), 14 January 1939 – Ellis; Woodhead, Dowen; Robinson (1), Blyth, Hardy; Hubbard (2), Richardson (2), Dickinson (2), Davies (2), Cunliffe (2).

SKY SPORTS FACT FILE

In 1948–49 Hull City won their first nine matches in the Third Division (North), at the time a season's start record for the Football League. In the process they scored 28 goals and it provided a fine springboard for promotion.

Record Cup Victory: 8–2 v Stalybridge Celtic (a), FA Cup 1st rd, 26 November 1932 – Maddison; Goldsmith, Woodhead; Gardner, Hill (1), Denby; Forward (1), Duncan, McNaughton (1), Wainscoat (4), Sargeant (1).

Record Defeat: 0–8 v Wolverhampton W, Division 2, 4 November 1911.

Most League Points (2 for a win): 69, Division 3, 1965–66.

Most League Points (3 for a win): 90, Division 4, 1982–83.

Most League Goals: 109, Division 3, 1965–66.

Highest League Scorer in Season: Bill McNaughton, 39, Division 3 (N), 1932–33.

Most League Goals in Total Aggregate: Chris Chilton, 195, 1960–71.

Most League Goals in One Match: 5, Ken McDonald v Bristol C, Division 2, 17 November 1928; 5, Simon 'Slim' Raleigh v Halifax T, Division 3N, 26 December 1930.

Most Capped Player: Theo Whitmore, Jamaica.

Most League Appearances: Andy Davidson, 520, 1952–67.

Youngest League Player: Matthew Edeson, 16 years 63 days v Fulham, 10 October 1992.

Record Transfer Fee Received: £750,000 from Middlesbrough for Andy Payton, November 1991.

Record Transfer Fee Paid: £250,000 to Falkirk for Darryl Duffy, January 2006.

Football League Record: 1905 Elected to Division 2; 1930–33 Division 3 (N); 1933–36 Division 2; 1936–49 Division 3 (N); 1949–56 Division 2; 1956–58 Division 3 (N); 1958–59 Division 3; 1959–60 Division 2; 1960–66 Division 3; 1966–78 Division 2; 1978–81 Division 3; 1981–83 Division 4; 1983–85 Division 3; 1985–91 Division 2; 1991–92 Division 3; 1992–96 Division 2; 1996–2004 Division 3; 2004–05 FL1; 2005– FLC.

MANAGERS

James Ramster 1904–05
(Secretary-Manager)
Ambrose Langley 1905–13
Harry Chapman 1913–14
Fred Stringer 1914–16
David Menzies 1916–21
Percy Lewis 1921–23
Bill McCracken 1923–31
Haydn Green 1931–34
John Hill 1934–36
David Menzies 1936
Ernest Blackburn 1936–46
Major Frank Buckley 1946–48
Raich Carter 1948–51
Bob Jackson 1952–55
Bob Brocklebank 1955–61
Cliff Britton 1961–70
(continued as General Manager to 1971)
Terry Neill 1970–74
John Kaye 1974–77
Bobby Collins 1977–78
Ken Houghton 1978–79
Mike Smith 1979–82
Bobby Brown 1982
Colin Appleton 1982–84
Brian Horton 1984–88
Eddie Gray 1988–89
Colin Appleton 1989
Stan Ternent 1989–91
Terry Dolan 1991–97
Mark Hateley 1997–98
Warren Joyce 1998–2000
Brian Little 2000–02
Jan Molby 2002
Peter Taylor 2002–06
Phil Parkinson June 2006–

LATEST SEQUENCES

Longest Sequence of League Wins: 10, 23.2.1966 – 20.4.1966.

Longest Sequence of League Defeats: 8, 7.4.1934 – 8.9.1934.

Longest Sequence of League Draws: 5, 30.3.1929 – 15.4.1929.

Longest Sequence of Unbeaten League Matches: 19, 13.3.2001 – 22.9.2001.

Longest Sequence Without a League Win: 27, 27.3.1989 – 4.11.1989.

Successive Scoring Runs: 26 from 10.4.1990.

Successive Non-scoring Runs: 6 from 13.11.1920.

TEN YEAR LEAGUE RECORD

		P	*W*	*D*	*L*	*F*	*A*	*Pts*	*Pos*
1996-97	Div 3	46	13	18	15	44	50	57	17
1997-98	Div 3	46	11	8	27	56	83	41	22
1998-99	Div 3	46	14	11	21	44	62	53	21
1999-2000	Div 3	46	15	14	17	43	43	59	14
2000-01	Div 3	46	19	17	10	47	39	74	6
2001-02	Div 3	46	16	13	17	57	51	61	11
2002-03	Div 3	46	14	17	15	58	53	59	13
2003-04	Div 3	46	25	13	8	82	44	88	2
2004-05	FL 1	46	26	8	12	80	53	86	2
2005-06	FL C	46	12	16	18	49	55	52	18

DID YOU KNOW ?

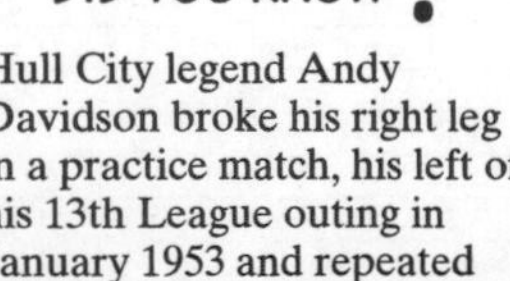

Hull City legend Andy Davidson broke his right leg in a practice match, his left on his 13th League outing in January 1953 and repeated the injury nine months later in the A team. A defender, he actually made his first team debut at centre-forward!

HULL CITY 2005–06 LEAGUE RECORD

Match No.	*Date*	*Venue*	*Opponents*	*Result*		*H/T Score*	*Lg. Pos.*	*Goalscorers*	*Atten-dance*
1	Aug 6	H	QPR	D	0-0	0-0	—		
2	9	A	Sheffield W	D	1-1	1-1	—	Barmby [23]	29,910
3	13	A	Wolverhampton W	L	0-1	0-1	19		24,333
4	20	H	Brighton & HA	W	2-0	1-0	13	France [40], Burgess [87]	18,648
5	27	A	Plymouth Arg	W	1-0	0-0	9	Elliott [58]	12,329
6	29	H	Leicester C	D	1-1	0-0	10	Fagan [51]	20,192
7	Sept 10	A	Crystal Palace	L	0-2	0-1	13		18,630
8	13	H	Stoke C	L	0-1	0-0	—		18,692
9	17	H	Luton T	L	0-1	0-0	18		19,184
10	24	A	Coventry C	W	2-0	1-0	13	Welsh 2 [17, 74]	21,161
11	27	A	Norwich C	L	1-2	1-2	—	Cort [2]	27,470
12	30	H	Millwall	D	1-1	0-0	—	Burgess [81]	18,761
13	Oct 15	A	Southampton	D	1-1	0-1	17	Ellison [79]	23,810
14	18	H	Reading	D	1-1	0-0	—	Brown [56]	17,698
15	22	H	Derby Co	W	2-1	1-0	12	Elliott [11], Green (pen) [84]	20,661
16	28	A	Burnley	L	0-1	0-1	—		11,701
17	Nov 1	A	Preston NE	L	0-3	0-0	—		13,536
18	5	H	Watford	L	1-2	1-2	20	Barmby [6]	18,444
19	19	A	Reading	L	1-3	0-1	22	Barmby [55]	17,864
20	22	H	Southampton	D	1-1	1-1	—	Barmby [45]	18,061
21	26	A	QPR	D	2-2	1-0	18	France [40], Paynter [50]	13,185
22	Dec 3	H	Cardiff C	W	2-0	0-0	17	Paynter [70], Fagan [88]	18,364
23	10	H	Sheffield W	W	1-0	0-0	15	Price [87]	21,329
24	16	A	Brighton & HA	L	1-2	1-2	—	Elliott [4]	6929
25	26	A	Crewe Alex	D	2-2	1-2	18	Fagan [33], Paynter [80]	7942
26	28	H	Ipswich T	W	2-0	0-0	15	Barmby [56], Fagan [70]	20,124
27	31	A	Leeds U	L	0-2	0-1	16		26,387
28	Jan 3	H	Sheffield U	L	1-3	1-2	—	Price [23]	21,929
29	14	H	Crystal Palace	L	1-2	1-2	18	Parkin [25]	18,886
30	21	A	Stoke C	W	3-0	1-0	17	Russell (og) [7], Parkin [55], Duffy [81]	13,444
31	31	H	Coventry C	L	1-2	1-0	—	Elliott [31]	18,381
32	Feb 4	A	Luton T	W	3-2	3-1	18	Elliott [14], Duffy [35], Parkin [38]	8835
33	11	H	Norwich C	D	1-1	1-0	17	Cort [26]	20,527
34	14	A	Millwall	D	1-1	0-0	—	Parkin [78]	7108
35	18	A	Cardiff C	L	0-1	0-1	17		11,047
36	25	H	Wolverhampton W	L	2-3	0-1	18	Cort [51], Edwards (og) [82]	19,841
37	Mar 4	A	Leicester C	L	2-3	1-1	20	Elliott [35], Green [73]	22,835
38	11	H	Plymouth Arg	W	1-0	0-0	20	Fagan [55]	20,137
39	18	H	Crewe Alex	W	1-0	1-0	17	Green [16]	21,163
40	25	A	Ipswich T	D	1-1	0-1	19	Cort [57]	23,968
41	Apr 1	H	Leeds U	W	1-0	0-0	16	Parkin [76]	23,486
42	8	A	Sheffield U	L	2-3	0-1	19	Elliott [65], Duffy [70]	26324
43	15	H	Burnley	D	0-0	0-0	19		19,926
44	17	A	Derby Co	D	1-1	1-0	18	Green [33]	24,961
45	22	H	Preston NE	D	1-1	1-1	18	Mawene (og) [43]	19,716
46	30	A	Watford	D	0-0	0-0	18		17,128

Final League Position: 18

GOALSCORERS

League (49): Elliott 7, Barmby 5, Fagan 5, Parkin 5, Cort 4, Green 4 (1 pen), Duffy 3, Paynter 3, Burgess 2, France 2, Price 2, Welsh 2, Brown 1, Ellison 1, own goals 3.
Carling Cup (1): Price 1.
FA Cup (0).

Myhill B 45	Lynch M 15 + 1	Dawson A 17 + 1	Ashbee I 6	Cort L 42	Coles D 9	France R 30 + 5	Green S 20 + 18	McPhee S 2 + 2	Barmby N 21 + 5	Elliott S 26 + 14	Delaney D 45 + 1	Price J 10 + 5	Fagan C 29 + 12	Andrews K 24 + 2	Edge R 8	Burgess B 3 + 11	Wiseman S 8 + 3	Ellison K 15 + 8	Woodhouse C 14 + 4	Joseph M 2 + 3	Welsh J 29 + 3	Brown C 13	Collins S 17	Fry R — + 1	Paynter B 11 + 11	Duke M 1 + 1	Duffy D 5 + 10	Parkin J 18	Thelwell A 7 + 2	Rogers A 9	Noble M 4 + 1	Rui Marques M 1	*Match No.*
1	2^1	3	4	5	6	7^2	8	9	10^3	11	12	13	14																				1
1			4	5	6		12	13	10^2	11	3	7^1	9^3	8	2	14																	2
1			4		6	14	13	7^1	10^3	12	5		9	8^2	3		2	11															3
1		3	4		6	7	8^2		10^1	11	5		9			12	2		13														4
1		3	4		6	12		13	10^1	11	5	7^3	9^2						8	2■	14												5
1		3	4		6	2	12		10^2	11	5	7	9^3			13			14		8^1												6
1				5	2	7^3	12		10^1	11	6	14			3			13	4^2		8	9											7
1				5	2	7^2	12		10	11	6	13			3	14			4^3		8	9^1											8
1		3		5	2^2	7	8		10^1	11	6		12			14				13	4	9^3											9
1	2■			5		7			10^1	12	6		9		3				4	13	8	11^2											10
1				5		7	12			11	6	13	9		3^2		2	14	4^3		8	10^1											11
1	2^1	3		5		12	7		10	11^3	6		13			14			4		8	9^2											12
1	2	3		5		7	12		10^3		6		9			14		13	4^1		8	11^2											13
1	2			5		7	3^1			12	6		9^2			13		11	4		8	10											14
1	2^1			5		7	12			11	6		13		3^3	9^2			4	14	8	10											15
1	2			5		7	12		13	11	6		9		3^2	14			4^1		8	10^3											16
1	2^2			5		7	12		13	11^3	3		9			14			4^1	6	8	10											17
1	2^1			5		12	7		10		3		13			14		11^2	4		8	9^3	6										18
1	2			5			6		10^1	11^2	3		9			7^3		12			8		4	13	14								19
1				5		2	7		12	13	3		14			11^1			4		8	9^3	6		10^2								20
1■	2			5		7			10^1	12	3		9						4		8		6		11^G	15							21
	2	3		5		7			10^1	12	6		9	13							8		4		11^2	1							22
1	2^3	3		5		7	12		10^1	13	6	14	9								8		4		11^2								23
1		3		5		7	12		10^3	11	6	2^2	9	13							8^1		4		14								24
1		3		5		7	8		12	13	6	2^1	9^2	10^3				11					4		14								25
1	12	3		5		2			10^2	13	6	7^1	9	8					14				4		11^3								26
1	2^3	3		5			12		13	10	6	7^2	9^1	8			14						4		11								27
1		3		5		2	12		10	11^1	6	7^2		8^3				13	14				4		9								28
1	3^1			5		2	12		10^2	13	6	7^3	9	8									4				14	11					29
1				5		2				11^1	6	7^3	9^2	4			13	12			8		3				14	10					30
1				5		2	12			11	6			7				3^2			8^1		4		13		9	10					31
1				5		2^2				7	3		12	6			13	11^3			8		4		14		9^1	10					32
1				5		2				7	3		12	4				11			8		6				9^1	10					33
1				5		2	12			11	3		9	4				7^2			8^1		6^3		13			10	14				34
1				5			12			13	6		9^1	4				7^2							11^3		14	10	2	3	8		35
1				5		7	8			10^1	6		12	4													13	9	2^2	3	11		36
1				5		7	8			10	6			4^2							12				13		14	9	2^3	3	11^1		37
1				5			8			11	6		12	4			2				7^2						9^1	10		3	13		38
1				5			8			11^1	6		9^3	4			2	12							13		14	10		3	7^2		39
1		3		5			8^1				6^2		12	4			2	11			13				9			10				7	40
1				5			8^2			12	6		9	4				11^1			7				13			10	2	3			41
1		3		5			8			12	6		9^2	4				11							7^1		13	10	2				42
1		3		5		7^3	8			12	6		13	4				11^1							14		9^2	10	2				43
1				5			8				6		9^2	4			2	12			7				11^1		13	10		3			44
1				5			8				6		9^3	4			2^2	11^1			7				12		14	10	13	3			45
1		12		5		13	8				6		9^3	4				11^2			7						14	10	2	3^1			46

FA Cup

Third Round Aston Villa (h) 0-1

Carling Cup

First Round Blackpool (a) 1-2

IPSWICH TOWN FL Championship

FOUNDATION

Considering that Ipswich Town only reached the Football League in 1938, many people outside of East Anglia may be surprised to learn that this club was formed at a meeting held in the Town Hall as far back as 1878 when Mr T. C. Cobbold, MP, was voted president. Originally it was the Ipswich Association FC to distinguish it from the older Ipswich Football Club which played rugby. These two amalgamated in 1888 and the handling game was dropped in 1893.

Portman Road, Ipswich, Suffolk IP1 2DA.

Telephone: (01473) 400 500.

Fax: (01473) 400 040.

Ticket Office: 0870 1110 555.

Website: www.itfc.co.uk

Email: enquiries@itfc.co.uk

Ground Capacity: 30,311.

Record Attendance: 38,010 v Leeds U, FA Cup 6th rd, 8 March 1975.

Pitch Measurements: 101m × 65m.

Chairman: David Sheepshanks.

Chief Executive: Derek Bowden.

Secretary: Sally Webb.

Manager: Jim Magilton.

Assistant Manager: Willie Donachie.

Physio: David Williams.

Colours: Blue and white.

Change Colours: White and navy.

Year Formed: 1878.

Turned Professional: 1936.

Ltd Co.: 1936.

Club Nicknames: 'Blues' or 'Town' or 'Tractor Boys'.

First Football League Game: 27 August 1938, Division 3 (S), v Southend U (h) W 4–2 – Burns; Dale, Parry; Perrett, Fillingham, McLuckie; Williams, Davies (1), Jones (2), Alsop (1), Little.

Record League Victory: 7–0 v Portsmouth, Division 2, 7 November 1964 – Thorburn; Smith, McNeil; Baxter, Bolton, Thompson; Broadfoot (1), Hegan (2), Baker (1), Leadbetter, Brogan (3). 7–0 v Southampton, Division 1, 2 February 1974 – Sivell; Burley, Mills (1), Morris, Hunter, Beattie (1), Hamilton (2), Viljoen, Johnson, Whymark (2), Lambert (1) (Woods). 7–0 v WBA, Division 1, 6 November 1976 – Sivell; Burley, Mills, Talbot, Hunter, Beattie (1), Osborne, Wark (1), Mariner (1) (Bertschin), Whymark (4), Woods.

HONOURS

Football League: Division 1 – Champions 1961–62; Runners-up 1980–81, 1981–82; Promoted from Division 1 1999–2000 (play-offs); Division 2 – Champions 1960–61, 1967–68, 1991–92; Division 3 (S) – Champions 1953–54, 1956–57.

FA Cup: Winners 1978.

Football League Cup: Semi-final 1982, 1985.

Texaco Cup: Winners 1973.

European Competitions: *European Cup:* 1962–63. *European Cup-Winners' Cup:* 1978–79. *UEFA Cup:* 1973–74, 1974–75, 1975–76, 1977–78, 1979–80, 1980–81 (winners), 1981–82, 1982–83, 2001–02, 2002–03.

SKY SPORTS FACT FILE

Ipswich Town signed Mick Hill, a forward from Sheffield United in October 1969. He had had a chequered career from Cardiff City groundstaff boy to Bethesda Athletic and working in a garage. But at Portman Road he was capped twice for Wales in 1971.

Record Cup Victory: 10–0 v Floriana, European Cup prel. rd, 25 September 1962 – Bailey; Malcolm, Compton; Baxter, Laurel, Elsworthy (1); Stephenson, Moran (2), Crawford (5), Phillips (2), Blackwood.

Record Defeat: 1–10 v Fulham, Division 1, 26 December 1963.

Most League Points (2 for a win): 64, Division 3 (S), 1953–54 and 1955–56.

Most League Points (3 for a win): 87, Division 1, 1999–2000.

Most League Goals: 106, Division 3 (S), 1955–56.

Highest League Scorer in Season: Ted Phillips, 41, Division 3 (S), 1956–57.

Most League Goals in Total Aggregate: Ray Crawford, 203, 1958–63 and 1966–69.

MANAGERS

Mick O'Brien 1936–37
Scott Duncan 1937–55
(continued as Secretary)
Alf Ramsey 1955–63
Jackie Milburn 1963–64
Bill McGarry 1964–68
Bobby Robson 1969–82
Bobby Ferguson 1982–87
Johnny Duncan 1987–90
John Lyall 1990–94
George Burley 1994–2002
Joe Royle 2002–06
Jim Magilton June 2006–

Most League Goals in One Match: 5, Alan Brazil v Southampton, Division 1, 16 February 1981.

Most Capped Player: Allan Hunter, 47 (53), Northern Ireland.

Most League Appearances: Mick Mills, 591, 1966–82.

Youngest League Player: Jason Dozzell, 16 years 56 days v Coventry C, 4 February 1984.

Record Transfer Fee Received: £6,000,000 from Newcastle U for Kieron Dyer, July 1999 and £6,000,000 from Arsenal for Richard Wright, July 2001.

Record Transfer Fee Paid: £4,750,000 to Sampdoria for Matteo Sereni, July 2001.

Football League Record: 1938 Elected to Division 3 (S); 1954–55 Division 2; 1955–57 Division 3 (S); 1957–61 Division 2; 1961–64 Division 1; 1964–68 Division 2; 1968–86 Division 1; 1986–92 Division 2; 1992–95 FA Premier League; 1995–2000 Division 1; 2000–02 FA Premier League; 2002–04 Division 1; 2004– FLC.

LATEST SEQUENCES

Longest Sequence of League Wins: 8, 23.9.1953 – 31.10.1953.

Longest Sequence of League Defeats: 10, 4.9.1954 – 16.10.1954.

Longest Sequence of League Draws: 7, 10.11.1990 – 21.12.1990.

Longest Sequence of Unbeaten League Matches: 23, 8.12.1979 – 26.4.1980.

Longest Sequence Without a League Win: 21, 28.8.1963 – 14.12.1963.

Successive Scoring Runs: 31 from 7.3.2004.

Successive Non-scoring Runs: 7 from 28.2.1995.

TEN YEAR LEAGUE RECORD

		P	W	D	L	F	A	Pts	Pos
1996-97	Div 1	46	20	14	12	68	50	74	4
1997-98	Div 1	46	23	14	9	77	43	83	5
1998-99	Div 1	46	26	8	12	69	32	86	3
1999-2000	Div 1	46	25	12	9	71	42	87	3
2000-01	PR Lge	38	20	6	12	57	42	66	5
2001-02	PR Lge	38	9	9	20	41	64	36	18
2002-03	Div 1	46	19	13	14	80	64	70	7
2003-04	Div 1	46	21	10	15	84	72	73	5
2004-05	FL C	46	24	13	9	85	56	85	3
2005-06	FL C	46	14	14	18	53	66	56	15

DID YOU KNOW ?

In 1961–62 Ipswich Town needed three attempts before managing to eliminate Luton Town from the FA Cup in a third round tie. Held 1–1 at Portman Road and again in the replay, it was at Highbury for the decider that Ipswich emphatically won 5–1.

IPSWICH TOWN 2005–06 LEAGUE RECORD

Match No.	Date	Venue	Opponents	Result		H/T Score	Lg. Pos.	Goalscorers	Attendance
1	Aug 6	H	Cardiff C	W	1-0	0-0	—	Forster 64	24,292
2	9	A	QPR	L	1-2	0-2	—	Parkin 54	14,632
3	13	A	Leicester C	D	0-0	0-0	11		21,879
4	20	H	Sheffield W	W	2-1	1-0	7	Naylor 7, Westlake 71	24,238
5	27	A	Millwall	W	2-1	1-0	6	Currie 13, Parkin 80	8277
6	29	H	Preston NE	L	0-4	0-3	8		22,551
7	Sept 10	A	Sheffield U	L	0-2	0-1	12		21,059
8	13	H	Southampton	D	2-2	1-0	—	Naylor 36, Garvan 61	22,997
9	18	H	Norwich C	L	0-1	0-0	13		29,184
10	24	A	Leeds U	W	2-0	1-0	10	Parkin 2 29, 70	21,676
11	27	A	Burnley	L	0-3	0-1	—		10,496
12	Oct 1	H	Crewe Alex	W	2-1	0-1	8	Currie 54, Forster 68	23,145
13	16	A	Reading	L	0-2	0-1	11		17,581
14	18	H	Coventry C	D	2-2	2-1	—	Currie 28, Juan 39	22,656
15	22	H	Watford	L	0-1	0-0	14		24,069
16	29	A	Brighton & HA	D	1-1	1-1	13	Parkin 39	6867
17	Nov 2	A	Derby Co	D	3-3	2-2	—	Naylor 10, Magilton 42, Richards 83	21,598
18	5	H	Plymouth Arg	W	3-1	2-0	13	McEveley 23, Juan 31, Richards (pen) 56	23,083
19	19	A	Coventry C	D	1-1	0-0	14	Williams 50	18,316
20	22	H	Reading	L	0-3	0-1	—		22,621
21	28	A	Cardiff C	L	1-2	0-1	—	Juan 86	8724
22	Dec 3	H	Wolverhampton W	D	1-1	0-0	15	Richards (pen) 60	23,563
23	10	H	QPR	D	2-2	1-2	17	De Vos 34, Haynes 90	24,628
24	17	A	Sheffield W	W	1-0	0-0	15	Forster 87	21,716
25	26	H	Crystal Palace	L	0-2	0-1	15		27,392
26	28	A	Hull C	L	0-2	0-0	17		20,124
27	31	H	Luton T	W	1-0	0-0	14	Westlake 69	23,957
28	Jan 2	A	Stoke C	D	2-2	2-1	15	De Vos 7, Wilnis 18	14,493
29	14	H	Sheffield U	D	1-1	0-0	15	Juan 54	23,794
30	21	A	Southampton	W	2-0	1-0	14	Lee 2 4, 89	22,250
31	31	H	Leeds U	D	1-1	0-0	—	Haynes 48	25,845
32	Feb 5	A	Norwich C	W	2-1	1-1	12	Juan 38, Doherty (og) 88	25,402
33	11	H	Burnley	W	2-1	0-1	10	Lee 62, Richards (pen) 83	24,482
34	14	A	Crewe Alex	W	2-1	1-1	—	Lee 19, McDonald 52	5686
35	18	A	Wolverhampton W	L	0-1	0-0	10		23,561
36	25	H	Leicester C	W	2-0	0-0	9	Garvan 52, Fuller 86	24,861
37	Mar 11	H	Millwall	D	1-1	1-0	10	Garvan 6	24,864
38	14	A	Preston NE	L	1-3	1-0	—	De Vos 38	14,507
39	18	A	Crystal Palace	D	2-2	1-1	11	Soares (og) 30, Fuller 67	22,076
40	25	H	Hull C	D	1-1	1-0	10	Currie 23	23,968
41	Apr 1	A	Luton T	L	0-1	0-0	11		9820
42	8	H	Stoke C	L	1-4	0-0	13	Haynes 67	23,592
43	15	H	Brighton & HA	L	1-2	0-1	14	Forster 90	23,964
44	17	A	Watford	L	1-2	0-1	16	Forster 57	16,721
45	22	H	Derby Co	W	2-0	0-0	12	Forster 46, Currie 65	24,067
46	30	A	Plymouth Arg	L	1-2	1-1	15	Forster 12	15,921

Final League Position: 15

GOALSCORERS

League (53): Forster 7, Currie 5, Juan 5, Parkin 5, Lee 4, Richards 4 (3 pens), De Vos 3, Garvan 3, Haynes 3, Naylor 3, Fuller 2, Westlake 2, Magilton 1, McDonald 1, McEveley 1, Williams 1, Wilnis 1, own goals 2.
Carling Cup (0).
FA Cup (0).

Price L 25	Wilnis F 33 + 2	Richards M 31 + 7	Garvan O 29 + 3	De Vos J 41	Naylor R 42	Currie D 39 + 7	Magilton J 25 + 9	Parkin S 17 + 3	Forster N 17 + 3	Westlake I 19 + 7	Juan J 24 + 10	Peters J 4 + 9	Sito 31 + 7	Fish M 1	Horlock K 13 + 4	Bowditch D 14 + 7	Supple S 21 + 1	McDonald D 4 + 10	Collins A 2 + 1	McEveley J 17 + 2	Haynes D 6 + 13	Proudlock A 3 + 6	Williams G 12	Clarke B 1 + 1	Barron S 14 + 1	Lee A 14	Fuller R 3	Brekke-Skard V 2 + 1	Casement C 2 + 3	Trotter L — + 1	*Match No.*
1	2	3	4	5	6	7	8^1	9	10^2	11	12	13																			1
1	2	12	4^2		6	7	8	9	10	11^3		14	3	5^1	13																2
1^G	2	3			6	12	8	9	10^2	11		4^1	5		7	13	15														3
	2	3	4^1		6	7^2	8^3			11	12	13	5		14	9	1	10													4
1	2	3	4^3		6■	7^1	8^2	9		11	12		5		10			13	14												5
1	2	3	4^3			7	8^2	9		11	13	14	5		10^1			12	6												6
1				5	6	7	8	9				4	2■		11	10^1		12		3											7
1	2^1	12	4^3	5	6	7		9			13	8^2			11	10		14		3											8
1		12	4^1	5	6	7	8	9				13	2■		11	10^2				3											9
1			4	5	6	7^1	8	9			12		2		11	10^2				3	13										10
1			4	5	6	7	8^1	9				12	2		11	10^2				3	13										11
1	12		4	5	6	7	8^3	9^1	13		14		2		11	10^2				3											12
1	2		12	5^3	6	7^2	8	9	10^1				4		11	13				3		14									13
1		11	4^2	5	6	7		12	10^3		13		2		8^1	14				3		9									14
		11		5	6	7	8^1	12	10		4		2			13	1			3		9^2									15
1	3	11^1		5	6	7^2	12	9			4		2			10		14		13		8^3									16
1	3^3	11		5	6	12	8	9			4		2			10^2		7^1		14		13									17
1		11^1		5	6	7		9	10^2	12	4		2		8	13				3											18
1		13		5	6	12	8^1	9	10^3	11^2	4		2			14				3			7								19
1	12	11		5	6	10		9^2	13	14	4^3		2		8^1					3			7								20
1	6■	11		5	9	14	8^2		10		4		2		12					3^1			7	13^3							21
1		3		5	6	7^3	8^1		10		4		2		12	9^2						13	11		14						22
1	3	11		5	6	7	12		10	13	4^3		2								14		8^1	9^2							23
1	3	12		5	6	13	8^3		10	14	4		2			9^1					11^2		7								24
1	3^2		4	5	6	9			10	11	8		2					12			13		7^1								25
	3	12	13	5	6	7	8^2		10^3	11^1	4		2				1				14		9								26
	3	11	4^1	5	6	7	12			13	8		2^2			9^3	1	14			10										27
	2	3^1	12	5		9	8^2			11	13						1	10^3	4			14	7		6						28
	3		4^1	5	6	9	12			11^3	8		13				1				14		7		2^2	10					29
	2	12	4	5	6	9	8^2			13	7						1						11^1		3	10					30
	2	3	4	5	6	12	8^1			11							1				9^2	13			7	10					31
1	2	3	4	5	6	9					8		13								12^2		7^1		11	10					32
	2	11	4	5	6	9				7^1	8		12				1								3	10					33
	6^1	11		5	9	7	12			8	4		2				1	13							3	10^2					34
	6	11	4	5	10	7	14			8		13^3	2				1	9^2				12			3^1						35
	2	11	4	5	6	7				8							1	12			10^1				3		9				36
	2	11^3	4	5	6	9	12			7	8		13				1				14				3^2	10^1					37
	2	11	4	5	6■	7^2				12	8^1		13				1				14				3	10	9^3				38
	2	6	4	5		7	8^1						3				1								11^2	10	9■	12	13		39
	6	11	4	5		9	8^1			7^2			2				1	13			12				3^3	10			14		40
	4	11^1	8	5	6	9					7		2^2			12	1			3	13					10					41
	3	11	4^1	5	6	7	12				8		13			9^3	1				14					10			2^2		42
	2	11	4	5	6^2	7			12		8^1						1				9				3	10			13		43
1		4		5	6	12			9		8	14	2			7^1				3	13					10^3		11^2			44
	2^1	11	4	5	6	7	8^3		10		13	14	12				1			3	9^2										45
			4^1	5	6	9	12	13	10	11^3		7					1			3								8^2	2	14	46

FA Cup
Third Round Portsmouth (h) 0-1

Carling Cup
First Round Yeovil T (h) 0-2

LEEDS UNITED FL Championship

FOUNDATION

Immediately the Leeds City club (founded in 1904) was wound up by the FA in October 1919, following allegations of illegal payments to players, a meeting was called by a Leeds solicitor, Mr Alf Masser, at which Leeds United was formed. They joined the Midland League playing their first game in that competition in November 1919. It was in this same month that the new club had discussions with the directors of a virtually bankrupt Huddersfield Town who wanted to move to Leeds in an amalgamation. But Huddersfield survived even that crisis.

Elland Road, Leeds, West Yorkshire LS11 0ES.

Telephone: (0113) 367 6000.

Fax: (0113) 367 6050.

Ticket Office: 0845 121 1992.

Website: www.leedsunited.com

Email: tickets@leedsunited.com

Ground Capacity: 39,460.

Record Attendance: 57,892 v Sunderland, FA Cup 5th rd (replay), 15 March 1967.

Pitch Measurements: 105m × 68m.

Chairman: Ken Bates.

Vice-chairman: Jayne McGuinness.

Chief Executive: Shaun Harvey.

Secretary: Alison Royston.

Manager: Kevin Blackwell.

Physio: Dave Hancock.

Colours: White shirts and shorts with navy blue trim.

Change Colours: Yellow with royal trim.

Year Formed: 1919, as Leeds United after disbandment (by FA order) of Leeds City (formed in 1904).

Turned Professional: 1920.

Ltd Co.: 1920.

Club Nickname: 'The Whites'.

First Football League Game: 28 August 1920, Division 2, v Port Vale (a) L 0–2 – Down; Duffield, Tillotson; Musgrove, Baker, Walton; Mason, Goldthorpe, Thompson, Lyon, Best.

HONOURS

Football League: Division 1 – Champions 1968–69, 1973–74, 1991–92; Runners-up 1964–65, 1965–66, 1969–70, 1970–71, 1971–72; Division 2 – Champions 1923–24, 1963–64, 1989–90; Runners-up 1927–28, 1931–32, 1955–56.

FA Cup: Winners 1972; Runners-up 1965, 1970, 1973.

Football League Cup: Winners 1968; Runners-up 1996.

European Competitions: *European Cup:* 1969–70, 1974–75 (runners-up). *Champions League:* 1992–93, 2000–01 (semi-finalists). *European Cup-Winners' Cup:* 1972–73 (runners-up). *European Fairs Cup:* 1965–66, 1966–67 (runners-up), 1967–68 (winners), 1968–69, 1970–71 (winners). *UEFA Cup:* 1971–72, 1973–74, 1979–80, 1995–96, 1998–99, 1999–2000 (semi-finalists), 2001–02, 2002–03.

SKY SPORTS FACT FILE

On 8 September 1962 with John Charles injured, Leeds United fielded Rod Johnson, 17, at centre-forward for his debut against Swansea Town at Vetch Field. He opened the scoring in the first half of the 2–0 win but was later stretchered off injured.

Record League Victory: 8–0 v Leicester C, Division 1, 7 April 1934 – Moore; George Milburn, Jack Milburn; Edwards, Hart, Copping; Mahon (2), Firth (2), Duggan (2), Furness (2), Cochrane.

Record Cup Victory: 10–0 v Lyn (Oslo), European Cup 1st rd 1st leg, 17 September 1969 – Sprake; Reaney, Cooper, Bremner (2), Charlton, Hunter, Madeley, Clarke (2), Jones (3), Giles (2) (Bates), O'Grady (1).

Record Defeat: 1–8 v Stoke C, Division 1, 27 August 1934.

Most League Points (2 for a win): 67, Division 1, 1968–69.

Most League Points (3 for a win): 85, Division 2, 1989–90.

Most League Goals: 98, Division 2, 1927–28.

Highest League Scorer in Season: John Charles, 42, Division 2, 1953–54.

Most League Goals in Total Aggregate: Peter Lorimer, 168, 1965–79 and 1983–86.

Most League Goals in One Match: 5, Gordon Hodgson v Leicester C, Division 1, 1 October 1938.

Most Capped Player: Lucas Radebe, 58 (70), South Africa.

Most League Appearances: Jack Charlton, 629, 1953–73.

Youngest League Player: Peter Lorimer, 15 years 289 days v Southampton, 29 September 1962.

Record Transfer Fee Received: £28,250,000 from Manchester U for Rio Ferdinand, July 2002 (see Manchester United page 249).

Record Transfer Fee Paid: £18,000,000 to West Ham United for Rio Ferdinand, November 2000.

Football League Record: 1920 Elected to Division 2; 1924–27 Division 1; 1927–28 Division 2; 1928–31 Division 1; 1931–32 Division 2; 1932–47 Division 1; 1947–56 Division 2; 1956–60 Division 1; 1960–64 Division 2; 1964–82 Division 1; 1982–90 Division 2; 1990–92 Division 1; 1992–2004 FA Premier League; 2004– FLC.

MANAGERS

Dick Ray 1919–20
Arthur Fairclough 1920–27
Dick Ray 1927–35
Bill Hampson 1935–47
Willis Edwards 1947–48
Major Frank Buckley 1948–53
Raich Carter 1953–58
Bill Lambton 1958–59
Jack Taylor 1959–61
Don Revie OBE 1961–74
Brian Clough 1974
Jimmy Armfield 1974–78
Jock Stein CBE 1978
Jimmy Adamson 1978–80
Allan Clarke 1980–82
Eddie Gray MBE 1982–85
Billy Bremner 1985–88
Howard Wilkinson 1988–96
George Graham 1996–98
David O'Leary 1998–2002
Terry Venables 2002–03
Peter Reid 2003
Eddie Gray *(Caretaker)* 2003–04
Kevin Blackwell May 2004–

LATEST SEQUENCES

Longest Sequence of League Wins: 9, 26.9.1931 – 21.11.1931.

Longest Sequence of League Defeats: 6, 28.12.2003 – 7.2.2004.

Longest Sequence of League Draws: 5, 19.4.1997 – 9.8.1997.

Longest Sequence of Unbeaten League Matches: 34, 26.10.1968 – 26.8.1969.

Longest Sequence Without a League Win: 17, 1.2.1947 – 26.5.1947.

Successive Scoring Runs: 30 from 27.8.1927.

Successive Non-scoring Runs: 6 from 30.1.1982.

TEN YEAR LEAGUE RECORD

		P	*W*	*D*	*L*	*F*	*A*	*Pts*	*Pos*
1996-97	PR Lge	38	11	13	14	28	38	46	11
1997-98	PR Lge	38	17	8	13	57	46	59	5
1998-99	PR Lge	38	18	13	7	62	34	67	4
1999-2000	PR Lge	38	21	6	11	58	43	69	3
2000-01	PR Lge	38	20	8	10	64	43	68	4
2001-02	PR Lge	38	18	12	8	53	37	66	5
2002-03	PR Lge	38	14	5	19	58	57	47	15
2003-04	PR Lge	38	8	9	21	40	79	33	19
2004-05	FL C	46	14	18	14	49	52	60	14
2005-06	FL C	46	21	15	10	57	38	78	5

DID YOU KNOW ?

Leeds United outside-left Jack Overfield scored in under a minute of the opening match of the season against Everton on 18 August 1956. They won 5–1, but it was his only goal despite playing in all 42 League games.

LEEDS UNITED 2005–06 LEAGUE RECORD

Match No.	Date	Venue	Opponents	Result		H/T Score	Lg. Pos.	Goalscorers	Attendance
1	Aug 7	H	Millwall	W	2-1	1-0	—	Healy 2 (1 pen) 28, 73 (p)	20,440
2	9	A	Cardiff C	L	1-2	1-0	—	Blake 22	15,231
3	13	A	Luton T	D	0-0	0-0	9		10,102
4	20	H	Wolverhampton W	W	2-0	1-0	5	Lewis 8, Hulse 60	21,229
5	27	A	Norwich C	W	1-0	0-0	4	Hulse 67	25,015
6	Sept 10	H	Brighton & HA	D	3-3	0-1	7	Healy 2 65, 70, Douglas 90	21,212
7	13	A	Sheffield W	L	0-1	0-1	—		29,986
8	17	A	QPR	W	1-0	1-0	7	Hulse 41	15,523
9	24	H	Ipswich T	L	0-2	0-1	9		21,676
10	28	H	Derby Co	W	3-1	3-0	—	Hulse 3 32, 37, 44	18,353
11	Oct 1	A	Watford	D	0-0	0-0	6		16,050
12	15	A	Burnley	W	2-1	0-0	4	Lewis 71, Hulse 75	16,174
13	18	H	Southampton	W	2-1	2-1	—	Hulse 11, Blake 19	18,881
14	21	H	Sheffield U	D	1-1	0-0	—	Richardson 53	23,600
15	29	A	Reading	D	1-1	0-0	5	Healy 75	22,012
16	Nov 1	A	Crewe Alex	L	0-1	0-1	—		7220
17	5	H	Preston NE	D	0-0	0-0	5		22,289
18	19	A	Southampton	W	4-3	0-3	4	Butler 71, Blake 77, Healy (pen) 84, Miller 86	30,173
19	22	H	Burnley	W	2-0	0-0	—	Healy (pen) 55, Blake 70	21,318
20	26	A	Millwall	W	1-0	0-0	4	May (og) 90	8134
21	Dec 3	H	Leicester C	W	2-1	1-0	3	Healy 41, Kilgallon 73	21,402
22	10	H	Cardiff C	L	0-1	0-1	4		20,597
23	17	A	Wolverhampton W	L	0-1	0-1	4		26,821
24	26	H	Coventry C	W	3-1	1-0	4	Douglas 34, Blake 61, Cresswell 80	24,291
25	28	A	Stoke C	W	1-0	0-0	3	Lewis 69	20,408
26	31	H	Hull C	W	2-0	1-0	3	Douglas 2 45, 57	26,387
27	Jan 2	A	Plymouth Arg	W	3-0	0-0	3	Cresswell 53, Blake 60, Hulse (pen) 86	17,726
28	14	A	Brighton & HA	L	1-2	1-1	3	Blake (pen) 38	7415
29	21	H	Sheffield W	W	3-0	0-0	3	Butler 70, Cresswell 2 82, 90	27,843
30	31	A	Ipswich T	D	1-1	0-0	—	Healy (pen) 88	25,845
31	Feb 4	H	QPR	W	2-0	1-0	3	Cresswell 39, Butler 84	21,807
32	11	A	Derby Co	D	0-0	0-0	4		27,000
33	14	H	Watford	W	2-1	0-1	—	Blake 2 (1 pen) 60 (p), 81	22,007
34	18	A	Leicester C	D	1-1	1-1	4	Blake (pen) 12	25,497
35	25	H	Luton T	W	2-1	0-0	4	Douglas 49, Lewis 53	23,644
36	Mar 4	A	Crystal Palace	W	2-1	1-0	3	Blake 33, Hulse 53	23,843
37	11	H	Norwich C	D	2-2	1-0	3	Hulse 20, Lewis 90	24,993
38	18	A	Coventry C	D	1-1	0-1	3	Healy (pen) 88	26,643
39	21	H	Crystal Palace	L	0-1	0-1	—		24,507
40	25	H	Stoke C	D	0-0	0-0	4		21,452
41	Apr 1	A	Hull C	L	0-1	0-0	4		23,486
42	8	H	Plymouth Arg	D	0-0	0-0	4		20,650
43	15	H	Reading	D	1-1	0-0	4	Hulse 47	24,535
44	18	A	Sheffield U	D	1-1	1-1	—	Healy 42	29,329
45	22	H	Crewe Alex	W	1-0	0-0	4	Healy 74	21,046
46	30	A	Preston NE	L	0-2	0-1	5		19,350

Final League Position: 5

GOALSCORERS

League (57): Healy 12 (5 pens), Hulse 12 (1 pen), Blake 11 (3 pens), Cresswell 5, Douglas 5, Lewis 5, Butler 3, Kilgallon 1, Miller 1, Richardson 1, own goal 1.
Carling Cup (4): Cresswell 2, Richardson 1, Ricketts 1.
FA Cup (4): Healy 2 (1 pen), Hulse 1, Kelly 1.
Play-Offs (3): Hulse 1, Lewis 1, Richardson 1.

Sullivan N 42	Kelly G 44	Harding D 20	Bakke E 7 + 3	Butler P 44	Gregan S 28	Wright J 3	Derry S 41	Blake R 31 + 10	Healy D 24 + 18	Lewis E 42 + 1	Richardson F 13 + 10	Ricketts M 1 + 3	Kilgallon M 22 + 3	Bennett I 4	Einarsson G 6 + 4	Hulse R 32 + 7	Douglas J 32 + 8	Cresswell R 12 + 4	Crainey S 24	Moore I 2 + 18	Pugh D 1 + 11	Miller L 26 + 2	Walton S 3 + 1	Beckford J — + 5	Griffiths J — + 2	Graham D 1 + 2	Stone S 1 + 1	*Match No.*
1	2	3	4	5	6	7^1	8	9^2	10	11	12	13																1
1	2	3	4	5^3	6	7^1	8	9	10^2	11	12	13	14															2
	2	3	4	5	6	7^1	8	9^2	13	11	12	10^3		1	14													3
	2	3		5	6		4	9^3	12	11	7^1	13		1	8	10^2	14											4
	2	3		5	6		4		10^2	11	7			1	8	9^1	12	13										5
	2	3		5	6		4	12	10	11^1	7^3			1	8	9^2	14	13										6
1	2			5	6		4	12	10^1	11	13				8^2	14	7	9^3	3									7
1	2			5	6		4		10■	11					8	9^1	7	12	3									8
1	2^2			5	6		4	13		11	12				8^1	9^3	7	10	3	14								9
1	2			5	6		4	12		11	8		13			9^3	7	10^1	3^2	14								10
1	2			5	6		4	10^1	12	11^3	8		3			9^2	7			13	14							11
1	2	3		5	6		4	10^3	12	11	8^1				14	9^2	7			13								12
1	2	3		5	6^1		4	10^2	13	11	8^3		12		14	9	7											13
1	2	3		5			4	10^1	12	11	8^3		6		14	9	7^2			13								14
1	2	3		5			4	10^1	12	11^3	8^2		6			9	7			13	14							15
1	2	3^3		5			4	12	10^1	11	13		6			9	7			8^2	14							16
1	2	3		5			4	12	10^1	11	8^3		6			9	14			13		7^2						17
1	2	3		5			4	10	12	11	7^1		6			9						8						18
1	2^2	3		5			4	7^3	10^1	11	12		6			9	13				14	8						19
1	2	3			6		4^2	7^1	10	11			5			9	13			12		8						20
1	2	3		5				7^3	10^2	11	12		6			9				13	14	8	4^1					21
1	2	3^3		5	6^1			7^2	10	11			4			9	12			13	14	8						22
1		3^1		5			4	7	10	11			6				12	9^2		13		8	2■					23
1	2	3		5			4	8^1	10^2	11	13		6			12	7	9										24
1	2	3		5			4	8^1	10^2	11			6			12	7	9				13						25
1	2			5			4	10^1	12	11			6			13	7	9^2	3^3		14	8						26
1	2			5			4	10^1		11			6			12	7	9	3			8						27
1	2			5			4	10^1	12	11^3			6			13	7	9	3		14	8^2						28
1	2			5	6		4	10^1	12	11							7	9	3			8^2	13					29
1	2			5	6		4		12	11						9	7	10	3			8^1						30
1	2			5	6		4	12	10^1	11						13	7	9^2	3			8						31
1	2			5	6		4	10^2		11^1						9	7		3	12	13	8						32
1	2			5	6		4	10	12	11						9^2	7^1	13	3			8						33
1	2		4^1	5	6			10^2	12	11						9	7		3	13		8						34
1	2		12	5	6			8^2	10^1	11						9	7		3	13		4						35
1	2			5	6		4	10^1	12	11^2						9	7		3		13	8						36
1	2		12	5	6		4	10^2	13	11						9	7		3			8^1						37
1	2			5			4	10^1	12	11			6			9	7^2		3	13		8						38
1	2		12	5			4	13	10^2	11			6			9	7^1		3^3			8		14				39
1	2			5	6		4	12	10^2	11^3						9	7^1		3			8		13	14			40
1	2			5	6		4	10^2	12	11^1	13					9	7		3			8^3				14		41
1	2^3			5	6		4	8	10^1	12	11					9	7^2		3			13		14				42
1	2		11^1	5			4		10^2				6			9^3	7		3	12		8		13		14		43
1	2		11^2	5			4		10^1				6			9	7		3	12	13	8						44
1	2		7	5			4	12	10	11^1			6						3	13		8^3				9^2	14	45
1					6			8^1	10		2		5				11			9^2	3		4	13	12		7	46

FA Cup
Third Round Wigan Ath (a) 1-1
(h) 3-3

Carling Cup
First Round Oldham Ath (h) 2-0
Second Round Rotherham U (a) 2-0
Third Round Blackburn R (a) 0-3

Play-Offs
Semi-Final Preston NE (h) 1-1
(a) 2-0
Final Watford 0-3
(at Millennium Stadium)

LEICESTER CITY FL Championship

FOUNDATION

In 1884 a number of young footballers who were mostly old boys of Wyggeston School, held a meeting at a house on the Roman Fosse Way and formed Leicester Fosse FC. They collected 9d (less than 4p) towards the cost of a ball, plus the same amount for membership. Their first professional, Harry Webb from Stafford Rangers, was signed in 1888 for 2s 6d (12p) per week, plus travelling expenses.

The Walkers Stadium, Filbert Way, Leicester LE2 7FL.

Telephone: 0870 040 6000.

Ticket Office: 0870 499 1884.

Website: www.lcfc.co.uk

Ground Capacity: 32,312.

Record Attendance: 47,298 v Tottenham H, FA Cup 5th rd, 18 February 1928.

Pitch Measurements: 110yd × 74yd.

Chairman: Andrew Taylor.

Vice-chairman: Jim McCahill.

Chief Executive: Tim Davies.

Secretary: Andrew Neville.

Manager: Robert Kelly.

Assistant Manager: TBC.

Physio: David Rennie.

Colours: Blue and white.

Change Colours: All yellow.

Year Formed: 1884.

Turned Professional: 1888.

Ltd Co: 1897.

Previous Name: 1884, Leicester Fosse; 1919, Leicester City.

Club Nickname: 'Foxes'.

Previous Grounds: 1884, Victoria Park; 1887, Belgrave Road; 1888, Victoria Park; 1891, Filbert Street; 2002, Walkers Stadium.

First Football League Game: 1 September 1894, Division 2, v Grimsby T (a) L 3–4 – Thraves; Smith, Bailey; Seymour, Brown, Henrys; Hill, Hughes, McArthur (1), Skea (2), Priestman.

Record League Victory: 10–0 v Portsmouth, Division 1, 20 October 1928 – McLaren; Black, Brown; Findlay, Carr, Watson; Adcock, Hine (3), Chandler (6), Lochhead, Barry (1).

Record Cup Victory: 8–1 v Coventry C (a), League Cup 5th rd, 1 December 1964 – Banks; Sjoberg, Norman (2); Roberts, King, McDerment; Hodgson (2), Cross, Goodfellow, Gibson (1), Stringfellow (2), (1 og).

HONOURS

Football League: Division 1 – Runners-up 1928–29; Promoted from Division 1 1993–94 (play-offs) and 1995–96 (play-offs); Division 2 – Champions 1924–25, 1936–37, 1953–54, 1956–57, 1970–71, 1979–80; Runners-up 1907–08.

FA Cup: Runners-up 1949, 1961, 1963, 1969.

Football League Cup: Winners 1964, 1997, 2000; Runners-up 1965, 1999.

European Competitions: *European Cup-Winners' Cup:* 1961–62. *UEFA Cup:* 1997–98, 2000–01.

SKY SPORTS FACT FILE

When ex-Newcastle United and Mansfield Town left-winger John Mitten signed for Leicester City in September 1961 he completed a football and cricket hat-trick having also been with Leicestershire CCC after spells with Notts and Lancs.

Record Defeat: 0–12 (as Leicester Fosse) v Nottingham F, Division 1, 21 April 1909.

Most League Points (2 for a win): 61, Division 2, 1956–57.

Most League Points (3 for a win): 92, Division 1, 2002–03.

Most League Goals: 109, Division 2, 1956–57.

Highest League Scorer in Season: Arthur Rowley, 44, Division 2, 1956–57.

Most League Goals in Total Aggregate: Arthur Chandler, 259, 1923–35.

Most League Goals in One Match: 6, John Duncan v Port Vale, Division 2, 25 December 1924; 6, Arthur Chandler v Portsmouth, Division 1, 20 October 1928.

Most Capped Player: John O'Neill, 39, Northern Ireland.

Most League Appearances: Adam Black, 528, 1920–35.

Youngest League Player: Dave Buchanan, 16 years 192 days v Oldham Ath, 1 January 1979.

Record Transfer Fee Received: £11,500,000 from Liverpool for Emile Heskey, February 2000.

Record Transfer Fee Paid: £5,500,000 to Wolverhampton W for Ade Akinbiyi, July 2000.

Football League Record: 1894 Elected to Division 2; 1908–09 Division 1; 1909–25 Division 2; 1925–35 Division 1; 1935–37 Division 2; 1937–39 Division 1; 1946–54 Division 2; 1954–55 Division 1; 1955–57 Division 2; 1957–69 Division 1; 1969–71 Division 2; 1971–78 Division 1; 1978–80 Division 2; 1980–81 Division 1; 1981–83 Division 2; 1983–87 Division 1; 1987–92 Division 2; 1992–94 Division 1; 1994–95 FA Premier League; 1995–96 Division 1; 1996–2002 FA Premier League; 2002–03 Division 1; 2003–04 FA Premier League; 2004– FLC.

MANAGERS

Frank Gardner 1884–92
Ernest Marson 1892–94
J. Lee 1894–95
Henry Jackson 1895–97
William Clark 1897–98
George Johnson 1898–1912
Jack Bartlett 1912–14
Louis Ford 1914–15
Harry Linney 1915–19
Peter Hodge 1919–26
Willie Orr 1926–32
Peter Hodge 1932–34
Arthur Lochhead 1934–36
Frank Womack 1936–39
Tom Bromilow 1939–45
Tom Mather 1945–46
John Duncan 1946–49
Norman Bullock 1949–55
David Halliday 1955–58
Matt Gillies 1958–68
Frank O'Farrell 1968–71
Jimmy Bloomfield 1971–77
Frank McLintock 1977–78
Jock Wallace 1978–82
Gordon Milne 1982–86
Bryan Hamilton 1986–87
David Pleat 1987–91
Gordon Lee 1991
Brian Little 1991–94
Mark McGhee 1994–95
Martin O'Neill 1995–2000
Peter Taylor 2000–01
Dave Bassett 2001–02
Micky Adams 2002–04
Craig Levein 2004–06
Robert Kelly April 2006–

LATEST SEQUENCES

Longest Sequence of League Wins: 7, 28.2.1993 – 27.3.1993.

Longest Sequence of League Defeats: 8, 17.3.2001 – 28.4.2001.

Longest Sequence of League Draws: 6, 21.8.1976 – 18.9.1976.

Longest Sequence of Unbeaten League Matches: 19, 6.2.1971 – 18.8.1971.

Longest Sequence Without a League Win: 18, 12.4.1975 – 1.11.1975.

Successive Scoring Runs: 31 from 12.11.1932.

Successive Non-scoring Runs: 7 from 21.11.1987.

TEN YEAR LEAGUE RECORD

		P	W	D	L	F	A	Pts	Pos
1996-97	PR Lge	38	12	11	15	46	54	47	9
1997-98	PR Lge	38	13	14	11	51	41	53	10
1998-99	PR Lge	38	12	13	13	40	46	49	10
1999-2000	PR Lge	38	16	7	15	55	55	55	8
2000-01	PR Lge	38	14	6	18	39	51	48	13
2001-02	PR Lge	38	5	13	20	30	64	28	20
2002-03	Div 1	46	26	14	6	73	40	92	2
2003-04	PR Lge	38	6	15	17	48	65	33	18
2004-05	FL C	46	12	21	13	49	46	57	15
2005-06	FL C	46	13	15	18	51	59	54	16

DID YOU KNOW 

An extra period injury time goal by Jack Lee forced a fifth round FA Cup replay for Leicester City against Luton Town on 12 February 1949 at 4–4. A week later he scored two more in another game of eight goals as Leicester ran out 5–3 winners.

LEICESTER CITY 2005–06 LEAGUE RECORD

Match No.	Date	Venue	Opponents	Result	H/T Score	Lg. Pos.	Goalscorers	Attendance
1	Aug 6	A	Sheffield U	L 1-4	0-1	—	Connolly 50	18,224
2	9	H	Stoke C	W 4-2	1-0	—	De Vries 14, Connolly 3 66, 82, 90	20,519
3	13	H	Ipswich T	D 0-0	0-0	12		21,879
4	20	A	Crewe Alex	D 2-2	1-2	14	Tiatto 45, Gudjonsson (pen) 50	7053
5	27	H	Luton T	L 0-2	0-1	16		22,048
6	29	A	Hull C	D 1-1	0-0	18	McCarthy 65	20,192
7	Sept 10	H	Sheffield W	W 2-0	2-0	14	De Vries 2 10, 12	22,618
8	13	A	Cardiff C	L 0-1	0-1	—		9196
9	17	A	Wolverhampton W	D 0-0	0-0	15		24,726
10	24	H	QPR	L 1-2	0-1	16	Hammond 73	20,148
11	27	H	Brighton & HA	D 0-0	0-0	—		20,296
12	Oct 1	A	Derby Co	D 1-1	0-0	19	Hume 85	25,044
13	15	A	Watford	W 2-1	1-0	15	De Vries 29, Kisnorbo 51	16,224
14	18	H	Burnley	L 0-1	0-0	—		23,326
15	23	H	Coventry C	W 2-1	1-1	13	De Vries 2 45, 46	22,991
16	29	A	Preston NE	D 0-0	0-0	12		13,904
17	Nov 5	H	Southampton	D 0-0	0-0	15		21,318
18	19	A	Burnley	L 0-1	0-1	16		12,592
19	22	H	Watford	D 2-2	2-1	—	Gudjonsson 2 (1 pen) 38, 45 (p)	18,856
20	26	H	Sheffield U	W 4-2	2-0	14	Hume 2 12, 89, Smith R 15, Hammond 74	22,382
21	Dec 3	A	Leeds U	L 1-2	0-1	16	Gudjonsson (pen) 69	21,402
22	9	A	Stoke C	L 2-3	1-1	—	Gudjonsson 21, Hammond 48	11,125
23	17	H	Crewe Alex	D 1-1	0-1	18	Hume 65	24,873
24	26	H	Millwall	D 1-1	0-1	20	Gudjonsson (pen) 64	22,520
25	28	A	Reading	L 0-2	0-0	20		22,061
26	31	H	Norwich C	L 0-1	0-0	20		21,072
27	Jan 2	A	Crystal Palace	L 0-2	0-0	21		20,089
28	14	A	Sheffield W	L 1-2	1-2	22	Stearman 7	25,398
29	21	H	Cardiff C	L 1-2	1-1	22	Fryatt 41	20,140
30	24	A	Plymouth Arg	L 0-1	0-0	—		12,591
31	31	A	QPR	W 3-2	1-1	—	Fryatt 10, Stearman 79, Hughes 88	11,785
32	Feb 4	H	Wolverhampton W	W 1-0	0-0	21	Fryatt 70	21,358
33	11	A	Brighton & HA	W 2-1	2-0	19	McCarthy 4, Hume 5	7187
34	14	H	Derby Co	D 2-2	1-1	—	Hume 27, Maybury 55	23,246
35	18	H	Leeds U	D 1-1	1-1	19	Hume 5	25,497
36	25	A	Ipswich T	L 0-2	0-0	20		24,861
37	Mar 4	H	Hull C	W 3-2	1-1	18	Hume 30, Gudjonsson 2 64, 84	22,835
38	11	A	Luton T	W 2-1	1-0	16	Fryatt 16, O'Grady 88	9783
39	18	A	Millwall	W 1-0	1-0	16	Hughes 31	10,523
40	25	H	Reading	D 1-1	1-0	16	Hume 38	25,578
41	Apr 1	A	Norwich C	L 1-2	0-1	18	Williams 63	24,718
42	7	H	Crystal Palace	W 2-0	1-0	—	Welsh 42, Hughes 87	23,211
43	15	H	Preston NE	L 1-2	1-1	17	Fryatt 1	21,865
44	17	A	Coventry C	D 1-1	1-1	17	Stearman 9	26,672
45	22	H	Plymouth Arg	W 1-0	0-0	15	Fryatt 55	22,796
46	30	A	Southampton	L 0-2	0-2	16		26,801

Final League Position: 16

GOALSCORERS

League (51): Hume 9, Gudjonsson 8 (4 pens), De Vries 6, Fryatt 6, Connolly 4, Hammond 3, Hughes 3, Stearman 3, McCarthy 2, Kisnorbo 1, Maybury 1, O'Grady 1, Smith R 1, Tiatto 1, Welsh 1, Williams 1.
Carling Cup (7): De Vries 2, Gudjonsson 1 (pen), Hamill 1, Johansson 1, Stearman 1, Williams 1.
FA Cup (3): De Vries 1, Hammond 1, Hughes 1.

Douglas R 32	Stearman R 31 + 3	Maybury A 40	Williams G 26 + 5	McCarthy P 37 + 1	Johansson N 39	Sylla M 24 + 4	Gudjonsson J 40 + 2	De Vries M 20 + 9	Connolly D 5	Wilcox J 3 + 3	Gilbert P 4 + 1	Hammond E 15 + 18	Tiatto D 11 + 7	Dublin D 15 + 6	Hamill J 7 + 5	Sheehan A 2	Hume I 28 + 9	Hughes S 28 + 6	Kisnorbo P 36 + 1	Henderson P 14 + 1	Gerrbrand P 14 + 3	Smith R 10 + 7	O'Grady C — + 13	Fryatt M 18 + 1	Wesolowski J 3 + 2	Brevett R — + 1	Welsh A 4 + 6	Match No.
1	2[1]	3	4	5	6	7	8	9	10	11[2]	12	13																1
1		2	4	5	6	7[1]	8	9	10	11	3	12																2
1		2	4	5	6	7[1]	8	9[2]	10		3	12	11	13														3
1	12	2	4	5	6	7[2]	8	14		13	3[1]	10	11	9[3]														4
1	2[3]	3	4	5	6	7[1]	8	14	10	13		12	11[2]	9														5
1	2	3	4	5	6	7	8	9[3]	10[2]	11[1]		12		14	13													6
1		2	4		6	7[1]	8	9		12		10[3]		5		3	14	11[2]	13									7
1		2	4[2]	12	6		8	9			3[1]	10[3]		5	13		14	11	7									8
1		2		6	3	7	8	9[2]				12		5	10		13	4[1]	11									9
1	12	2■		6	3	7	8	9				13	14	5			10[2]	4[3]	11[1]									10
	2		4	5	6	12	8	9[2]				14	11[1]	13			10	7[3]	3	1								11
	2[3]		4		6		8	12				9[1]	11	5			10	7[2]	3	1	13	14						12
1	2			4	6	7	12	9				10[2]		5	8		13	11[1]	3									13
1	2			6	3[2]	7	12	9				10[3]	13	5	8[1]		14	4	11									14
1	2			6	3	7	8	9				12	13	5	4[2]		10[1]		11									15
1		2		5	3	7	4	9[2]				12		13	8[3]		10[1]		11		6	14						16
1		2	4[2]	5	3	7[3]						10[1]	13	9	14		12		11		6	8						17
1		2		5	3[2]	7[1]	8	10				14	13	9[3]				12	11		6	4						18
1	2	3		5		7[1]	8	9[2]				10	14	13				12	11		6	4[3]						19
1		2		5	3	7	8	12				10[1]			13		9		11		6	4[2]						20
1	2	3		5■		7	8	12				10[2]		13			9		11[1]		6	4						21
1	2[1]	3	12			7	8[2]	13				10		5			9		11		6	4						22
1	5[1]	2	12			7[3]	8	13				10[2]				3■	9	14	11		6	4						23
1		2	12	5	3[1]		8	13				10[2]	11■				9	14	7		6	4[3]						24
1	12	2	4	5		7	8	9				13			11[3]			10[2]	3		6[1]	14						25
1	2	3	4	6		7[1]	8[2]	9				12		5	14		10	13				11[3]						26
1	2	3		6			8	12				10	11[2]	5			9[1]	4	7[3]			13	14					27
1	2[2]	3	4	5	6			9				10[1]			8[3]		12	7	11		13			14				28
1	2	3[2]	4	5	6			9				12					13	8	11[3]			7[1]		10	14			29
1	2	3[3]		5	6		8	9[2]				12					13	7	11			14		10[1]	4			30
1	2	3	4[2]	5	6		8										9[1]	7	11				12	10	13			31
1	2	3		5	6		8										9[1]	7	11				12	10	4			32
1	2			5	3	7	8										9[1]	6	11		12	13[3]	14	10	4[2]			33
1[6]	2	3		5	6	7[1]	8										9	4	11	15		12		10				34
	2	3	12	5■	6		8						11[1]				9	4	7	1			13	10[2]				35
	2	3	13		5		8					12	11[2]				9[3]	4[1]	7	1	6		14	10				36
	2	3	4		6		8										9	7[2]	11	1	5			10[1]		12	13	37
	2	3	4	5	6		8										9[2]	7[1]	11	1			13	10			12	38
	2	3	4	5	6		8										9[2]	7	11	1			12	10[1]			13	39
	2	3	4	5	6		8										9[2]	7	11	1			12	10[1]			13	40
	2	3	4	5	6[1]		8[2]										9	7	11	1			12	10			13	41
		2	4	5	6	12	8										9	11	3	1				10			7[1]	42
		2[2]	4		6	12	8										9	7[1]	3	1	5		13	10			11	43
	2	3	4		6		8					12	11[3]				9[1]	13	7■	1	5			10[2]			14	44
	2	3	4	5	6		8						12				9	7		1			13	10[2]			11[1]	45
	2	3	4[1]	5	6	12						13	11[2]				9	8		1			14	10			7[3]	46

FA Cup

Third Round	Tottenham H	(h)	3-2
Fourth Round	Southampton	(h)	0-1

Carling Cup

First Round	Bury	(a)	3-0
Second Round	Blackpool	(h)	2-1
Third Round	Cardiff C	(a)	1-0
Fourth Round	Bolton W	(a)	1-2

LEYTON ORIENT — FL Championship 1

FOUNDATION

There is some doubt about the foundation of Leyton Orient, and, indeed, some confusion with clubs like Leyton and Clapton over their early history. As regards the foundation, the most favoured version is that Leyton Orient was formed originally by members of Homerton Theological College who established Glyn Cricket Club in 1881 and then carried on through the following winter playing football. Eventually many employees of the Orient Shipping Line became involved and so the name Orient was chosen in 1888.

Matchroom Stadium, Brisbane Road, Leyton, London E10 5NE.

Telephone: 0871 310 1881.

Fax: 0871 310 1882.

Ticket Office: 0871 310 1883.

Website: www.leytonorient.com

Email: info@leytonorient.net

Ground Capacity: 7,872 (rising to approx 9,000 by 2007).

Record Attendance: 34,345 v West Ham U, FA Cup 4th rd, 25 January 1964.

Pitch Measurements: 110yd × 76yd.

Chairman: Barry Hearn.

Vice-chairman: Nick Levene.

Chief Executive: Matthew Porter.

Secretary: Lindsey Freeman.

Manager: Martin Ling.

Assistant Manager: Dean Smith.

Physio: Dave Appanah.

Colours: All red with white trim. ***Change Colours:*** White with red trim.

Year Formed: 1881. ***Turned Professional:*** 1903.

Ltd Co.: 1906.

Previous Names: 1881, Glyn Cricket and Football Club; 1886, Eagle Football Club; 1888, Orient Football Club; 1898, Clapton Orient; 1946, Leyton Orient; 1966, Orient; 1987, Leyton Orient.

Club Nickname: 'The O's'.

Previous Grounds: 1884, Glyn Road; 1896, Whittles Athletic Ground; 1900, Millfields Road; 1930, Lea Bridge Road; 1937, Brisbane Road.

First Football League Game: 2 September 1905, Division 2, v Leicester Fosse (a) L 1–2 – Butler; Holmes, Codling; Lamberton, Boden, Boyle; Kingaby (1), Wootten, Leigh, Evenson, Bourne.

Record League Victory: 8–0 v Crystal Palace, Division 3 (S), 12 November 1955 – Welton; Lee, Earl; Blizzard, Aldous, McKnight; White (1), Facey (3), Burgess (2), Heckman, Hartburn (2). 8–0 v Rochdale, Division 4, 20 October 1987 – Wells; Howard, Dickenson (1), Smalley (1), Day, Hull, Hales (2), Castle (Sussex), Shinners (2), Godfrey (Harvey), Comfort (2). 8–0 v Colchester U,

HONOURS

Football League: Division 1 best season: 22nd, 1962–63; Division 2 – Runners-up 1961–62; Division 3 – Champions 1969–70; Division 3 (S) – Champions 1955–56; Runners-up 1954–55; Promoted from Division 4 1988–89 (play-offs); Promoted from Championship 2 (3rd) 2005–06.

FA Cup: Semi-final 1978.

Football League Cup: best season: 5th rd, 1963.

SKY SPORTS FACT FILE

Left-half and captain Tommy Brown who joined Leyton Orient in 1950 had been given an early baptism in his native Scotland with Hearts, making five appearances at 17 in the abortive 1939–40 season and then making a wartime debut for Scotland in 1940.

Division 4, 15 October 1988 – Wells; Howard, Dickenson, Hales (1p), Day (1), Sitton (1), Baker (1), Ward, Hull (3), Juryeff, Comfort (1). 8–0 v Doncaster R, Division 3, 28 December 1997 – Hyde; Channing, Naylor, Smith (1p), Hicks, Clark, Ling, Joseph R, Griffiths (3) (Harris), Richards (2) (Baker (1)), Inglethorpe (1) (Simpson).

Record Cup Victory: 9–2 v Chester, League Cup 3rd rd, 15 October 1962 – Robertson; Charlton, Taylor; Gibbs, Bishop, Lea; Deeley (1), Waites (3), Dunmore (2), Graham (3), Wedge.

Record Defeat: 0–8 v Aston Villa, FA Cup 4th rd, 30 January 1929.

Most League Points (2 for a win): 66, Division 3 (S), 1955–56.

Most League Points (3 for a win): 75, Division 4, 1988–89.

Most League Goals: 106, Division 3 (S), 1955–56.

Highest League Scorer in Season: Tom Johnston, 35, Division 2, 1957–58.

Most League Goals in Total Aggregate: Tom Johnston, 121, 1956–58, 1959–61.

Most League Goals in One Match: 4, Wally Leigh v Bradford C, Division 2, 13 April 1906; 4, Albert Pape v Oldham Ath, Division 2, 1 September 1924; 4, Peter Kitchen v Millwall, Division 3, 21 April 1984.

Most Capped Players: Tunji Banjo, 7 (7), Nigeria; John Chiedozie, 7 (9), Nigeria; Tony Grealish, 7 (45), Eire.

Most League Appearances: Peter Allen, 432, 1965–78.

Youngest League Player: Paul Went, 15 years 327 days v Preston NE, 4 September 1965.

Record Transfer Fee Received: £600,000 from Notts Co for John Chiedozie, August 1981.

Record Transfer Fee Paid: £175,000 to Wigan Ath for Paul Beesley, October 1989.

Football League Record: 1905 Elected to Division 2; 1929–56 Division 3 (S); 1956–62 Division 2; 1962–63 Division 1; 1963–66 Division 2; 1966–70 Division 3; 1970–82 Division 2; 1982–85 Division 3; 1985–89 Division 4; 1989–92 Division 3; 1992–95 Division 2; 1995–2004 Division 3; 2004–06 FL2; 2006– FL1.

MANAGERS

Sam Omerod 1905–06
Ike Ivenson 1906
Billy Holmes 1907–22
Peter Proudfoot 1922–29
Arthur Grimsdell 1929–30
Peter Proudfoot 1930–31
Jimmy Seed 1931–33
David Pratt 1933–34
Peter Proudfoot 1935–39
Tom Halsey 1939
Bill Wright 1939–45
Willie Hall 1945
Bill Wright 1945–46
Charlie Hewitt 1946–48
Neil McBain 1948–49
Alec Stock 1949–59
Les Gore 1959–61
Johnny Carey 1961–63
Benny Fenton 1963–64
Dave Sexton 1965
Dick Graham 1966–68
Jimmy Bloomfield 1968–71
George Petchey 1971–77
Jimmy Bloomfield 1977–81
Paul Went 1981
Ken Knighton 1981
Frank Clark 1982–91 *(Managing Director)*
Peter Eustace 1991–94
Chris Turner/John Sitton 1994–95
Pat Holland 1995–96
Tommy Taylor 1996–2001
Paul Brush 2001–03
Martin Ling January 2004–

LATEST SEQUENCES

Longest Sequence of League Wins: 10, 21.1.1956 – 30.3.1956.

Longest Sequence of League Defeats: 9, 1.4.1995 – 6.5.1995.

Longest Sequence of League Draws: 6, 30.11.1974 – 28.12.1974.

Longest Sequence of Unbeaten League Matches: 13, 30.10.1954 – 19.2.1955.

Longest Sequence Without a League Win: 23, 6.10.1962 – 13.4.1963.

Successive Scoring Runs: 24 from 3.5.2003.

Successive Non-scoring Runs: 8 from 19.11.1994.

TEN YEAR LEAGUE RECORD

		P	*W*	*D*	*L*	*F*	*A*	*Pts*	*Pos*
1996-97	Div 3	46	15	12	19	50	58	57	16
1997-98	Div 3	46	19	12	15	62	47	66	11
1998-99	Div 3	46	19	15	12	68	59	72	6
1999-2000	Div 3	46	13	13	20	47	52	52	19
2000-01	Div 3	46	20	15	11	59	51	75	5
2001-02	Div 3	46	13	13	20	55	71	52	18
2002-03	Div 3	46	14	11	21	51	61	53	18
2003-04	Div 3	46	13	14	19	48	65	53	19
2004-05	FL 2	46	16	15	15	65	67	63	11
2005-06	FL 2	46	22	15	9	67	51	81	3

DID YOU KNOW ?

From 3 September 2005 Gary Alexander scored in nine successive League and Cup games for Leyton Orient. In 1957–58 Tom Johnston had registered in nine consecutive Football League games totalling 18 goals in the process.

LEYTON ORIENT 2005–06 LEAGUE RECORD

Match No.	*Date*	*Venue*	*Opponents*	*Result*		*H/T Score*	*Lg. Pos.*	*Goalscorers*	*Attendance*
1	Aug 6	H	Macclesfield T	W	2-1	1-0	—	Keith [2], Echanomi [90]	3600
2	9	A	Bury	W	2-1	1-0	—	Tudor [21], Zakuani [73]	2053
3	13	A	Darlington	W	1-0	1-0	1	Lockwood (pen) [41]	4021
4	20	H	Rochdale	L	1-4	0-2	2	Echanomi [76]	4223
5	27	A	Cheltenham T	D	1-1	1-0	4	Mackie [20]	3274
6	29	H	Shrewsbury T	L	0-1	0-1	8		3742
7	Sept 3	H	Bristol R	L	2-3	0-1	12	Alexander [75], McMahon [89]	3481
8	10	A	Barnet	W	3-2	1-1	7	Ibehre [40], Alexander 2 [75, 89]	3722
9	17	H	Wrexham	D	1-1	0-0	9	Alexander [80]	3733
10	24	A	Carlisle U	W	3-2	3-1	7	Alexander [10], Lockwood (pen) [33], Ibehre [36]	6584
11	27	H	Torquay U	W	2-1	1-0	—	Ibehre [25], Alexander [50]	4091
12	Oct 1	H	Mansfield T	W	3-1	1-0	2	Keith [16], Alexander [59], Echanomi [76]	4164
13	8	A	Stockport Co	D	1-1	0-1	—	Alexander [71]	3901
14	15	H	Lincoln C	D	1-1	1-0	4	Alexander [18]	4837
15	22	A	Grimsby T	W	1-0	1-0	2	Easton [44]	4963
16	29	H	Oxford U	W	1-0	1-0	1	Easton [45]	5268
17	Nov 12	A	Peterborough U	D	1-1	0-1	1	Miller [74]	5341
18	19	H	Stockport Co	D	2-2	1-0	2	Raynes (og) [24], Mackie [63]	4997
19	26	A	Macclesfield T	D	0-0	0-0	3		1649
20	Dec 6	H	Chester C	L	0-1	0-1	—		3463
21	10	H	Bury	L	0-1	0-0	4		4095
22	17	A	Rochdale	W	4-2	2-1	4	Alexander 2 [10, 47], Tudor [35], Mackie [76]	2666
23	26	H	Rushden & D	W	5-1	3-1	3	Mackie [27], Steele 2 [29, 36], Ibehre [74], Easton [87]	4558
24	29	A	Wycombe W	L	2-4	1-2	—	Steele [21], Tudor [68]	6240
25	31	H	Notts Co	W	1-0	1-0	3	Ibehre [45]	3715
26	Jan 2	A	Boston U	W	2-1	1-0	3	Ibehre [44], Alexander [58]	2689
27	14	H	Northampton T	L	1-2	0-1	4	McMahon [86]	5445
28	21	A	Wrexham	W	2-1	2-0	4	Alexander [4], Lockwood (pen) [43]	5031
29	31	A	Bristol R	D	3-3	0-1	—	Ibehre 2 [48, 57], Simpson [62]	5966
30	Feb 4	A	Torquay U	L	0-2	0-0	5		2687
31	11	H	Carlisle U	D	0-0	0-0	5		5833
32	14	A	Northampton T	D	1-1	0-1	—	Mackie [65]	5552
33	18	A	Chester C	W	2-0	1-0	5	Lockwood (pen) [35], Connor [72]	2210
34	25	H	Darlington	W	1-0	1-0	5	Tudor [13]	4767
35	28	H	Barnet	D	0-0	0-0	—		4910
36	Mar 4	A	Shrewsbury T	D	3-3	2-3	5	Lockwood [19], Connor [26], Tann [47]	3471
37	11	H	Cheltenham T	W	1-0	1-0	4	Connor [23]	4879
38	18	A	Rushden & D	L	0-1	0-1	4		3679
39	25	H	Wycombe W	W	1-0	1-0	4	Connor [6]	6720
40	Apr 1	A	Notts Co	D	1-1	0-0	4	Corden [48]	5007
41	8	H	Boston U	W	2-0	0-0	4	Lockwood (pen) [51], Connor [89]	4391
42	15	A	Mansfield T	W	1-0	0-0	3	Lockwood (pen) [75]	4763
43	17	H	Grimsby T	D	0-0	0-0	3		6582
44	22	A	Lincoln C	D	1-1	1-1	4	Mackie [2]	5660
45	29	H	Peterborough U	W	2-1	1-0	3	Lockwood (pen) [15], Corden [70]	6591
46	May 6	A	Oxford U	W	3-2	1-1	3	Easton [17], Alexander [64], Steele [90]	12,243

Final League Position: 3

GOALSCORERS

League (67): Alexander 14, Ibehre 8, Lockwood 8 (7 pens), Mackie 6, Connor 5, Easton 4, Steele 4, Tudor 4, Echanomi 3, Corden 2, Keith 2, McMahon 2, Miller 1, Simpson 1, Tann 1, Zakuani 1, own goal 1.
Carling Cup (1): McMahon 1.
FA Cup (6): Steele 2, Easton 1, Keith 1, Mackie 1, Tudor 1.
Football League Trophy (2): Alexander 1, Hanson 1.

Garner G 43	Barnard D 14 + 12	Lockwood M 42	McMahon D 17 + 16	Mackie J 40	Zakuani G 43	Tudor S 29 + 4	Simpson M 45	Alexander G 42 + 4	Steele L 14 + 13	Keith J 41 + 1	Carlisle W 3 + 9	Easton C 36 + 5	Echanomi E — + 16	Miller J 34 + 2	Palmer A 3	Dolan J 1	Ibehre J 22 + 11	Hanson C — + 2	Saah B 2 + 1	Morris G 3 + 1	Tann A 8 + 2	Connor P 15 + 1	Demetriou J 1 + 2	Corden W 8	Duncan D — + 1	*Match No.*
1	2	3^{1}	4	5	6	7^{2}	8	9	10^{3}	11	12	13	14													1
1	2	3	4	5	6	7^{1}	8	9	10^{2}	11		12	13													2
1	2	3	4	5	6	7^{1}	8	9	10^{2}	11		12	13													3
1	2^{3}	3	4^{1}	5	6	7	8	9	10	11^{2}		12	13	14												4
1	2		4	5	6		8	9	10^{1}			11	12	7	3											5
1	12		13	5^{1}	6	7	8	9^{3}	10	11		4	14	2	3^{2}											6
1	2^{1}		4	5		12	8^{2}	9	10^{3}	11	13	7	14	3		6										7
1		3	4	5	6		8	9			7	11	12	2			10^{1}									8
1		3	4	5	6	12	8	9			7^{1}	11	13	2			10^{2}									9
1		3		5	6	7^{1}	8	9		11	12	4		2			10									10
1	12	3		5	6	7^{1}	8	9		11		4	13	2			10^{2}									11
1		3		5	6	7	8	9		11		4	12	2			10^{1}									12
1	2^{1}	3	13	5		7	8	9		11^{2}	12	6	14	4			10^{3}									13
1	2^{2}	3	12		6	7	8	9		11^{1}	13	4	14	5			10^{3}									14
1		3		5	6	7^{2}	8	9		11		4	12	2			10^{1}	13								15
1		3	12	5	6	7	8	9		11^{1}		4		2			10									16
1		3	12	5	6	7	8	9		11^{1}		4	13	2			10^{2}									17
1		3	12	5	6^{3}	7	8	9		11^{1}		4	13	2			10^{2}	14								18
1	12	3		5■	6	7^{1}	8	9		11		4		2			10									19
1	2^{3}	3	12		6	7	8	9	13	11^{1}	14	4					10^{2}		5							20
1	2	3	12		6	7^{3}	8	9^{2}	13	11^{1}	14	4					10		5							21
1	12	3		5	6	7■	8	9	10	11^{1}		4		2												22
1		3	12	5	6		8	9^{3}	10	11^{2}	7^{1}	4		2			14								13	23
1		3	12	5	6	7	8	9	10^{3}	11^{1}	13	4		2^{2}			14									24
1		3		5	6	7	8	9		11		4		2			10									25
1		3	4	5	6	7		9		11		8		2			10									26
1^{6}		3	4	5	6	7	8	9	12	11^{1}	13			2^{2}			10			15						27
1		3	4	5	6^{2}	7	8	9	12	11				2			10^{1}		13							28
1	12	3	4	5	6	7^{1}	8	9	10^{2}	11				2^{3}			13				14					29
1			4	5	6	7	8	9^{3}	12	11^{2}		13			3		10^{1}				2	14				30
1		3	12	5	6	7^{1}	8	9^{2}	13	11		4		2			14					10^{3}				31
1		3		5	6		8	12	10^{1}	11		4		2			7					9				32
1	12	3	4^{3}	5	6		8	9	13	11^{1}		7		2								10^{2}	14			33
1	12	3	4	5	6	7	8	9^{2}		11^{1}				2			13					10				34
	12	3	4^{1}	5	6	7	8	9^{3}	13	11				2			14			1		10^{2}				35
1		3	4		6		8	9^{2}	12	11^{1}		7		2			13				5	10				36
1	12	3	13		6		8^{2}	14		11		4		2			9^{3}				5	10	7^{1}			37
	7	3	12		6		8^{1}	13	14	11^{3}		4		2			9^{2}			1	5	10				38
	12	3		5	6		8	9		11		4		2						1		10		7^{1}		39
1		3		5	6	12	8	9^{2}		11		4		2			13					10		7^{1}		40
1	12	3		5	6	7^{2}	8	9		13		4		2^{1}								10		11		41
1	2	3		5	6^{3}		8	9^{1}	12	11^{2}		4									14	10	13	7		42
1	2^{2}	3		5			8	9^{1}	12	11		4		13			14				6	10^{3}		7		43
1	2^{1}	3	12	5	6		8	9^{2}	13			4					14				11	10^{3}		7		44
1	12	3	13	5	6		8	14	10^{3}	11		4									2^{1}	9■		7^{2}		45
1		3	12	5	6	13	8^{1}	9	10	11^{2}		4					14				2			7^{3}		46

FA Cup			
First Round	Chesterfield	(h)	0-0
		(a)	2-1
Second Round	Rushden & D	(a)	1-0
Third Round	Fulham	(a)	2-1
Fourth Round	Charlton Ath	(a)	1-2

Carling Cup			
First Round	Luton T	(h)	1-3
Football League Trophy			
First Round	Yeovil T	(h)	2-0
Second Round	Oxford U	(a)	0-1

LINCOLN CITY FL Championship 2

FOUNDATION

The original Lincoln Football Club was established in the early 1860's and was one of the first provisional clubs to affiliate to the Football Association. In their early years, they regularly played matches against the famous Sheffield Club and later became known as Lincoln Lindum. The present organisation was formed at a public meeting held in the Monson Arms Hotel in June 1884 and won the Lincolnshire Cup in only their third season. They were founder members of the Midland League in 1889 and that competition's first champions.

Sincil Bank Stadium, Sincil Bank, Lincoln LN5 8LD.
Telephone: 0870 899 2005.
Fax: (01522) 880011
Ticket Office: 0870 899 1976.
Website: www.redimps.com
Email: lcfc@redimps.com
Ground Capacity: 10,127.
Record Attendance: 23,196 v Derby Co, League Cup 4th rd, 15 November 1967.
Pitch Measurements: 110yd × 70yd.
Chairman: Steff Wright.
Chief Executive: Dave Roberts.
Secretary: Fran Martin.
Head Coach: John Schofield.
Director of Football: John Deehan.
Physio: Michael Wait.
Colours: Red and white striped shirts, black shorts, red stockings.
Change Colours: Black shirts with red trim, red shorts, black stockings.
Year Formed: 1884.
Turned Professional: 1892.
Ltd Co.: 1895.
Club Nickname: 'The Red Imps'.
Previous Grounds: 1883, John O'Gaunt's; 1894, Sincil Bank.
First Football League Game: 3 September 1892, Division 2, v Sheffield U (a) L 2–4 – W. Gresham; Coulton, Neill; Shaw, Mettam, Moore; Smallman, Irving (1), Cameron (1), Kelly, J. Gresham.
Record League Victory: 11–1 v Crewe Alex, Division 3 (N), 29 September 1951 – Jones; Green (1p), Varney; Wright, Emery, Grummett (1); Troops (1), Garvey, Graver (6), Whittle (1), Johnson (1).
Record Cup Victory: 8–1 v Bromley, FA Cup 2nd rd, 10 December 1938 – McPhail; Hartshorne, Corbett; Bean, Leach, Whyte (1); Hancock, Wilson (1), Ponting (3), Deacon (1), Clare (2).

HONOURS

Football League: Division 2 best season: 5th, 1901–02; Promotion from Division 3, 1997–98; Division 3 (N) – Champions 1931–32, 1947–48, 1951–52; Runners-up 1927–28, 1930–31, 1936–37; Division 4 – Champions 1975–76; Runners-up 1980–81.

FA Cup: best season: 1st rd of Second Series (5th rd equivalent), 1887, 2nd rd (5th rd equivalent), 1890, 1902.

Football League Cup: best season: 4th rd, 1968.

GM Vauxhall Conference: Champions 1987–88.

SKY SPORTS FACT FILE

Versatile forward Jimmy McCormick was recruited by Lincoln City in August 1947 and helped them win promotion from the Third Division (North). It was not his first such success having helped Tottenham Hotspur into the First Division in 1932–33.

Record Defeat: 3–11 v Manchester C, Division 2, 23 March 1895.

Most League Points (2 for a win): 74, Division 4, 1975–76.

Most League Points (3 for a win): 77, Division 3, 1981–82.

Most League Goals: 121, Division 3 (N), 1951–52.

Highest League Scorer in Season: Allan Hall, 41, Division 3 (N), 1931–32.

Most League Goals in Total Aggregate: Andy Graver, 143, 1950–55 and 1958–61.

Most League Goals in One Match: 6, Frank Keetley v Halifax T, Division 3N, 16 January 1932; 6, Andy Graver v Crewe Alex, Division 3N, 29 September 1951.

Most Capped Player: Gareth McAuley, 5, Northern Ireland.

Most League Appearances: Grant Brown, 407, 1989–2002.

Youngest League Player: Shane Nicholson, 16 years 172 days v Burnley, 22 November 1986.

Record Transfer Fee Received: £500,000 from Port Vale for Gareth Ainsworth, September 1997.

Record Transfer Fee Paid: £75,000 to Carlisle U for Dean Walling, September 1997 and £75,000 to Bury for Tony Battersby, August 1998.

Football League Record: 1892 Founder member of Division 2. Remained in Division 2 until 1920 when they failed re-election but also missed seasons 1908–09 and 1911–12 when not re-elected. 1921–32 Division 3 (N); 1932–34 Division 2; 1934–48 Division 3 (N); 1948–49 Division 2; 1949–52 Division 3 (N); 1952–61 Division 2; 1961–62 Division 3; 1962–76 Division 4; 1976–79 Division 3; 1979–81 Division 4; 1981–86 Division 3; 1986–87 Division 4; 1987–88 GM Vauxhall Conference; 1988–92 Division 4; 1992–98 Division 3; 1998–99 Division 2; 1999–2004 Division 3; 2004– FL2.

MANAGERS

David Calderhead 1900–07
John Henry Strawson 1907–14
(had been Secretary)
George Fraser 1919–21
David Calderhead Jnr. 1921–24
Horace Henshall 1924–27
Harry Parkes 1927–36
Joe McClelland 1936–46
Bill Anderson 1946–65
(General Manager to 1966)
Roy Chapman 1965–66
Ron Gray 1966–70
Bert Loxley 1970–71
David Herd 1971–72
Graham Taylor 1972–77
George Kerr 1977–78
Willie Bell 1977–78
Colin Murphy 1978–85
John Pickering 1985
George Kerr 1985–87
Peter Daniel 1987
Colin Murphy 1987–90
Allan Clarke 1990
Steve Thompson 1990–93
Keith Alexander 1993–94
Sam Ellis 1994–95
Steve Wicks *(Head Coach)* 1995
John Beck 1995–98
Shane Westley 1998
John Reames 1998–99
Phil Stant 2000–01
Alan Buckley 2001–02
Keith Alexander 2002–06
John Schofield June 2006–

LATEST SEQUENCES

Longest Sequence of League Wins: 10, 1.9.1930 – 18.10.1930.

Longest Sequence of League Defeats: 12, 21.9.1896 – 9.1.1897.

Longest Sequence of League Draws: 5, 21.2.1981 – 7.3.1981.

Longest Sequence of Unbeaten League Matches: 18, 11.3.1980 – 13.9.1980.

Longest Sequence Without a League Win: 19, 22.8.1978 – 23.12.1978.

Successive Scoring Runs: 37 from 1.3.1930.

Successive Non-scoring Runs: 5 from 15.11.1913.

TEN YEAR LEAGUE RECORD

		P	*W*	*D*	*L*	*F*	*A*	*Pts*	*Pos*
1996-97	Div 3	46	18	12	16	70	69	66	9
1997-98	Div 3	46	20	15	11	60	51	72	3
1998-99	Div 2	46	13	7	26	42	74	46	23
1999-2000	Div 3	46	15	14	17	67	69	59	15
2000-01	Div 3	46	12	15	19	58	66	51	18
2001-02	Div 3	46	10	16	20	44	62	46	22
2002-03	Div 3	46	18	16	12	46	37	70	6
2003-04	Div 3	46	19	17	10	68	47	74	7
2004-05	FL 2	46	20	12	14	64	47	72	6
2005-06	FL 2	46	15	21	10	65	53	66	7

DID YOU KNOW ?

The first FA Cup tie in which Lincoln City participated was on 1 November 1884 when they defeated the long-since defunct Hull Town 5–1. One of the goals was recorded as "scrimmage", the result of observers being unable to name the player responsible!

LINCOLN CITY 2005–06 LEAGUE RECORD

Match No.	Date	Venue	Opponents	Result	H/T Score	Lg. Pos.	Goalscorers	Attendance
1	Aug 6	H	Northampton T	D 1-1	0-0	—	Birch 64	5397
2	9	A	Chester C	D 2-2	2-0	—	Brown 38, Birch 43	2637
3	13	A	Notts Co	L 1-2	1-1	17	Brown 20	6153
4	20	H	Oxford U	W 2-1	0-1	12	Birch 62, Asamoah 74	3724
5	27	A	Rushden & D	D 1-1	1-0	13	Keates 19	2860
6	29	H	Carlisle U	D 0-0	0-0	14		4303
7	Sept 10	A	Bristol R	D 0-0	0-0	16		5057
8	13	H	Wrexham	W 2-0	0-0	—	Brown 64, Keates 90	2956
9	17	H	Peterborough U	L 1-2	0-0	14	Keates 85	5526
10	24	A	Torquay U	L 1-2	1-0	17	McAuley 10	2281
11	27	H	Stockport Co	W 2-0	0-0	—	Birch 2 53, 78	3508
12	Oct 1	A	Bury	D 1-1	1-0	13	Keates 44	4118
13	7	H	Cheltenham T	L 0-1	0-0	—		4776
14	15	A	Leyton Orient	D 1-1	0-1	16	Butcher 70	4837
15	22	H	Wycombe W	L 1-2	0-0	18	Robinson M 52	4347
16	29	A	Rochdale	W 2-1	2-0	16	Robinson M 15, Brown 36	3420
17	Nov 12	H	Shrewsbury T	D 1-1	0-1	16	Brown 51	3748
18	18	A	Cheltenham T	L 1-4	0-1	—	Mayo 60	3078
19	26	A	Northampton T	D 1-1	1-0	18	Birch 14	5174
20	Dec 3	H	Macclesfield T	D 2-2	0-1	—	McAuley 72, Brown 79	3171
21	10	H	Chester C	W 3-1	0-0	17	Logan 68, Mayo (pen) 70, Asamoah 90	3563
22	16	A	Oxford U	W 1-0	0-0	—	Logan 80	3795
23	26	H	Boston U	D 0-0	0-0	14		7077
24	28	A	Grimsby T	L 0-3	0-3	15		6056
25	31	H	Darlington	D 2-2	2-0	14	McAuley 17, Robinson M 19	4008
26	Jan 2	A	Mansfield T	D 0-0	0-0	15		4946
27	7	A	Wrexham	D 1-1	0-0	16	Yeo 63	3809
28	14	H	Barnet	W 4-1	1-1	13	Yeo 38, McCombe 63, Robinson M 81, Kerr 82	4033
29	21	A	Peterborough U	D 1-1	0-1	13	Yeo 85	6227
30	28	H	Bristol R	W 1-0	0-0	12	Birch 73	4258
31	Feb 4	A	Stockport Co	W 3-2	0-0	11	Gritton 62, Yeo 69, Frecklington 79	4506
32	11	H	Torquay U	W 2-0	1-0	10	Kerr 12, Hughes 89	4454
33	14	A	Barnet	W 3-2	0-1	—	McCombe 54, Birch 65, Brown 87	1695
34	18	A	Macclesfield T	D 1-1	0-1	8	Hughes 76	2268
35	25	H	Notts Co	W 2-1	1-0	7	Green 45, McCombe 79	5262
36	Mar 11	H	Rushden & D	D 2-2	1-0	8	Yeo 22, McCombe 90	4383
37	18	A	Boston U	L 1-2	0-1	8	Robinson M 66	4476
38	25	H	Grimsby T	W 5-0	4-0	7	Foster 12, Forrester 16, Mayo (pen) 38, Robinson M 44, Beevers 83	7182
39	28	A	Carlisle U	L 0-1	0-0	—		6723
40	Apr 1	A	Darlington	L 2-4	0-0	8	Robinson M 53, Forrester 76	4028
41	8	H	Mansfield T	D 1-1	0-0	9	Green 53	6062
42	15	H	Bury	D 1-1	0-1	8	Frecklington 86	4439
43	17	A	Wycombe W	W 3-0	0-0	7	Forrester 2 61, 81, Green 73	5750
44	22	H	Leyton Orient	D 1-1	1-1	7	Forrester 36	5660
45	29	A	Shrewsbury T	W 1-0	0-0	7	McAuley 62	5170
46	May 6	H	Rochdale	D 1-1	0-0	7	McAuley 72	7165

Final League Position: 7

GOALSCORERS

League (65): Birch 8, Brown 7, Robinson M 7, Forrester 5, McAuley 5, Yeo 5, Keates 4, McCombe 4, Green 3, Mayo 3 (2 pens), Asamoah 2, Frecklington 2, Hughes 2, Kerr 2, Logan 2, Beevers 1, Butcher 1, Foster 1, Gritton 1.
Carling Cup (9): Birch 2, Robinson M 2, Beevers 1, Green 1, Kerr 1, Molango 1, own goal 1.
FA Cup (2): Mayo 1 (pen), Robinson M 1.
Football League Trophy (1): Brown 1.
Play-Offs (1): Robinson M 1.

Marriott A 43	Beevers L 28 + 5	Mayo P 25 + 3	McAuley G 33 + 2	Morgan P 19 + 1	McCombe J 38	Cryan C 37	Birch G 23 + 14	Green F 23 + 5	Molango M 5 + 5	Brown N 37 + 2	Asamoah D 19 + 6	Ryan O 4 + 6	Foster L 14 + 2	Bloomer M 7 + 5	Keates D 19 + 2	Bacon D — + 1	Kerr S 41	Robinson S 11 + 1	Hughes J 18 + 4	Rayner S 3	Robinson M 20 + 12	Butcher R 4	Logan R 8	Mettam L — + 1	Yeo S 11 + 1	Frecklington L 3 + 15	Stirling J — + 6	Gritton M 4 + 6	Forrester J 9	Wilkinson T — + 1	*Match No.*
1	2	3	4	5	6	7	8	9[1]	10[2]	11	12	13																			1
1	2	3	4	5■	6	7	8	9[1]	10[2]	11	13			12																	2
1	2	3			6	7	8	9[2]		11	10		5[1]	4	12	13															3
1	2	3■			6	4	8	12	10[3]	11	9[2]			5	13		7[1]				14										4
1	2	12		13	6	4	8		10[3]	3	9[1]			5	11[2]		7				14										5
1		3		5	6	4	8		12	2	9				11		7				10[1]										6
1	2[3]	3	12	5	6	4	8[2]			10	9[1]				11		7		14		13										7
1	2	11	12	5	6	3	8[1]	13		10	9[2]				4		7														8
1	2[2]	11		5	6	3	8	12	13	10[3]	9[1]				4		7				14										9
1■	2■	3	4	5■		6	12	9[2]	10		13	14			11[3]		7				8[1]										10
		3	4			2	8		12		9[2]	13	14	5	11		7	6[3]		1	10[1]										11
	12	3	4			2	8		13		9[1]		6	5	11		7			1	10[2]										12
	2					3	8	12			9[1]	10[2]	6	5	11		7		13	1		4									13
1	2		4			6	8			10[1]	12	9[2]	5	3	11						13	7									14
1	2		4	5		3			12	11	9			13	6		7[2]				10[1]	8									15
1	2		4	5		3				11	9[1]				6		7		12		10	8									16
1	2	3	4	5		6	8	12		11	9						7				10[1]										17
1	2[1]	3	4	5	6		8			11[2]	12		10				7		14		13		9[3]								18
1		3	4	5[1]	6		8[2]			11	10		13	12	2		7						9								19
1		3	4	5	6		8			11	10				2		7						9								20
1		3	4	5	6		8[1]			11	10				2■		7				12		9								21
1	2	3	4		6	5	8[1]			11	10						7				12		9								22
1	2	3	4		6	5	8[1]			11	10		7								12		9								23
1	2[1]	3	4		6	5				11	10[2]		8	12			7				13		9								24
1		3	4		6	5	12			13	14		8		2		7[2]		11[3]		10[1]		9								25
1		3	4		6	5							8		2		7		9[1]		10			12	11						26
1		3[3]	4		6	5	12	10[1]		14		13	8		2		7		9						11[2]						27
1			4		6	5	12	9				13			2[3]		7	8	3		10[1]				11[2]	14					28
1			4		5	2[3]		8		11		12					7[2]	6	3		9[1]				10■	13	14				29
1			4		6	5	12	8		2[1]		10[3]					7	11	3		9[2]					13	14				30
1			4		6	5		8[2]		2							7	11	3[3]		12				10	13	14	9[1]			31
1	12		4		6	5	13			2		8[3]					7		3						10	11[1]	14	9[2]			32
1			4		6	5	12	8		2							7	11[2]	3						10	13		9[1]			33
1	12		4		6	5	13	8		2							7	11[3]	3						10[1]	14		9[2]			34
1	12		4		6	5	8[2]	9					7				2[1]		3						10	11		13			35
1	12	3	4[1]		6	5	8[3]	9[2]		2							7	11							10	13		14			36
1	2	3			6	5	8[3]	9		11							7	4[2]			12				10[1]	13		14			37
1	2	3			6	5	12	9		11			4				7[2]				10[1]					13		14	8[3]		38
1	2				6	5	12	9[3]		3			4[2]				7				10					11[1]	13		8	14	39
1	2				6	5	12	9[1]		3			4[2]				7	13	11[3]		10					14			8		40
1	2				6	5	12	9		11							7	4[2]	3		10[1]						13		8		41
1	2		4[1]	5	6			9		10				12			7[2]	11[3]	3							13		14	8		42
1	2	12	4	5	6			9[1]		11							7		3		10[3]					13		14	8[2]		43
1	2		4	5	6		12	9		11							7[2]		3		10[1]					13			8		44
1	2	12	4	5	6			9		11							7[2]		3		10					13			8[1]		45
1	2		4	5	6		12	9[2]		11							7		3		10[1]				14	13			8[3]		46

FA Cup
First Round — Milton Keynes D — (h) 1-1; (a) 1-2

Carling Cup
First Round — Crewe Alex — (h) 5-1
Second Round — Fulham — (a) 4-5

Football League Trophy
First Round — Tranmere R — (a) 1-2

Play-Offs
Semi-Final — Grimsby T — (h) 0-1; (a) 1-2

LIVERPOOL — FA Premiership

FOUNDATION

But for a dispute between Everton FC and their landlord at Anfield in 1892, there may never have been a Liverpool club. This dispute persuaded the majority of Evertonians to quit Anfield for Goodison Park, leaving the landlord, Mr John Houlding, to form a new club. He originally tried to retain the name 'Everton' but when this failed, he founded Liverpool Association FC on 15 March 1892.

Anfield, Anfield Road, Liverpool L4 0TH.

Telephone: (0151) 263 2361.

Fax: (0151) 260 8813.

Ticket Office: 0870 220 2345.

Website: www.liverpoolfc.tv

Email: customercontact@liverpoolfc.tv

Ground Capacity: 45,362.

Record Attendance: 61,905 v Wolverhampton W, FA Cup 4th rd, 2 February 1952.

Pitch Measurements: 101m × 68m.

Chairman: David Moores.

Chief Executive: Rick Parry BSC, FCA.

Secretary: William Bryce Morrison.

Manager: Rafael Benitez.

Assistant Manager: Pako Ayestaran.

Colours: Red shirts, red shorts, red stockings.

Change Colours: Yellow shirts, yellow shorts, yellow stockings and White with green trim shirts, white with green trim shorts, white stockings.

Year Formed: 1892.

Turned Professional: 1892.

Ltd Co.: 1892.

Club Nicknames: 'Reds' or 'Pool'.

First Football League Game: 2 September 1893, Division 2, v Middlesbrough Ironopolis (a) W 2–0 – McOwen; Hannah, McLean; Henderson, McQue (1), McBride; Gordon, McVean (1), M. McQueen, Stott, H. McQueen.

Record League Victory: 10–1 v Rotherham T, Division 2, 18 February 1896 – Storer; Goldie, Wilkie; McCartney, McQue, Holmes; McVean (3), Ross (2), Allan (4), Becton (1), Bradshaw.

HONOURS

Football League: Division 1 – Champions 1900–01, 1905–06, 1921–22, 1922–23, 1946–47, 1963–64, 1965–66, 1972–73, 1975–76, 1976–77, 1978–79, 1979–80, 1981–82, 1982–83, 1983–84, 1985–86, 1987–88, 1989–90 (Liverpool have a record number of 18 League Championship wins); Runners-up 1898–99, 1909–10, 1968–69, 1973–74, 1974–75, 1977–78, 1984–85, 1986–87, 1988–89, 1990–91, 2001–02; Division 2 – Champions 1893–94, 1895–96, 1904–05, 1961–62.

FA Cup: Winners 1965, 1974, 1986, 1989, 1992, 2001, 2006; Runners-up 1914, 1950, 1971, 1977, 1988, 1996.

Football League Cup: Winners 1981, 1982, 1983, 1984, 1995, 2001, 2003; Runners-up 1978, 1987, 2005.

League Super Cup: Winners 1986.

European Competitions: *European Cup:* 1964–65, 1966–67, 1973–74, 1976–77 (winners), 1977–78 (winners), 1978–79, 1979–80, 1980–81 (winners), 1981–82, 1982–83, 1983–84 (winners), 1984–85 (runners-up). *Champions League:* 2001–02, 2002–03, 2004–05 (winners), 2005–06. *European Cup-Winners' Cup:* 1965–66 (runners-up), 1971–72, 1974–75, 1992–93, 1996–97 (s-f.). *European Fairs Cup:* 1967–68, 1968–69, 1969–70, 1970–71. *UEFA Cup:* 1972–73 (winners), 1975–76 (winners), 1991–92, 1995–96, 1997–98, 1998–99, 2000–01 (winners), 2002–03, 2003–04. *Super Cup:* 1977 (winners), 1978, 1984, 2001 (winners), 2005 (winners). *World Club Championship:* 1981 (runners-up), 1984 (runners-up). *FIFA Club World Championship:* 2005 (runners-up).

SKY SPORTS FACT FILE

In August 1939 Liverpool had under manager George Kay, Albert Shelley ex-Southampton as trainer, assisted by former full-back Ephraim Longworth with Jimmy Seddon once of Bolton Wanderers as coach, a trio with combined League appearances of over 1000.

Record Cup Victory: 11–0 v Stromsgodset Drammen, ECWC 1st rd 1st leg, 17 September 1974 – Clemence; Smith (1), Lindsay (1p), Thompson (2), Cormack (1), Hughes (1), Boersma (2), Hall, Heighway (1), Kennedy (1), Callaghan (1).

Record Defeat: 1–9 v Birmingham C, Division 2, 11 December 1954.

Most League Points (2 for a win): 68, Division 1, 1978–79.

Most League Points (3 for a win): 90, Division 1, 1987–88.

Most League Goals: 106, Division 2, 1895–96.

Highest League Scorer in Season: Roger Hunt, 41, Division 2, 1961–62.

Most League Goals in Total Aggregate: Roger Hunt, 245, 1959–69.

Most League Goals in One Match: 5, Andy McGuigan v Stoke C, Division 1, 4 January 1902; 5, John Evans v Bristol R, Division 2, 15 September 1954; 5, Ian Rush v Luton T, Division 1, 29 October 1983.

Most Capped Player: Ian Rush, 67 (73), Wales.

Most League Appearances: Ian Callaghan, 640, 1960–78.

Youngest League Player: Max Thompson, 17 years 128 days v Tottenham H, 8 May 1974.

Record Transfer Fee Received: £12,500,000 from Leeds U for Robbie Fowler, November 2001.

Record Transfer Fee Paid: £14,000,000 (reported figure) to Auxerre for Djibril Cisse, July 2004.

Football League Record: 1893 Elected to Division 2; 1894–95 Division 1; 1895–96 Division 2; 1896–1904 Division 1; 1904–05 Division 2; 1905–54 Division 1; 1954–62 Division 2; 1962–92 Division 1; 1992– FA Premier League.

MANAGERS

W. E. Barclay 1892–96
Tom Watson 1896–1915
David Ashworth 1920–23
Matt McQueen 1923–28
George Patterson 1928–36
(continued as Secretary)
George Kay 1936–51
Don Welsh 1951–56
Phil Taylor 1956–59
Bill Shankly 1959–74
Bob Paisley 1974–83
Joe Fagan 1983–85
Kenny Dalglish 1985–91
Graeme Souness 1991–94
Roy Evans 1994–98
(then Joint Manager)
Gerard Houllier 1998–2004
Rafael Benitez June 2004–

LATEST SEQUENCES

Longest Sequence of League Wins: 12, 21.4.1990 – 6.10.1990.

Longest Sequence of League Defeats: 9, 29.4.1899 – 14.10.1899.

Longest Sequence of League Draws: 6, 19.2.1975 – 19.3.1975.

Longest Sequence of Unbeaten League Matches: 31, 4.5.1987 – 16.3.1988.

Longest Sequence Without a League Win: 14, 12.12.1953 – 20.3.1954.

Successive Scoring Runs: 29 from 27.4.1957.

Successive Non-scoring Runs: 5 from 22.12.1906.

TEN YEAR LEAGUE RECORD

		P	W	D	L	F	A	Pts	Pos
1996-97	PR Lge	38	19	11	8	62	37	68	4
1997-98	PR Lge	38	18	11	9	68	42	65	3
1998-99	PR Lge	38	15	9	14	68	49	54	7
1999-2000	PR Lge	38	19	10	9	51	30	67	4
2000-01	PR Lge	38	20	9	9	71	39	69	3
2001-02	PR Lge	38	24	8	6	67	30	80	2
2002-03	PR Lge	38	18	10	10	61	41	64	5
2003-04	PR Lge	38	16	12	10	55	37	60	4
2004-05	PR Lge	38	17	7	14	52	41	58	5
2005-06	PR Lge	38	25	7	6	57	25	82	3

DID YOU KNOW

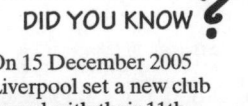

On 15 December 2005 Liverpool set a new club record with their 11th successive League and Cup clean sheet thanks to goals from Peter Crouch (2) and Steven Gerrard in a 3–0 win over Deportivo Saprissa in the Club World Championship semi-final at Yokohama.

LIVERPOOL 2005–06 LEAGUE RECORD

Match No.	Date	Venue	Opponents	Result		H/T Score	Lg. Pos.	Goalscorers	Attendance
1	Aug 13	A	Middlesbrough	D	0-0	0-0	—		31,908
2	20	H	Sunderland	W	1-0	1-0	8	Xabi Alonso 24	44,913
3	Sept 10	A	Tottenham H	D	0-0	0-0	10		36,148
4	18	H	Manchester U	D	0-0	0-0	11		44,917
5	24	A	Birmingham C	D	2-2	0-0	13	Luis Garcia 68, Cisse (pen) 85	27,733
6	Oct 2	H	Chelsea	L	1-4	1-2	13	Gerrard 36	44,235
7	15	H	Blackburn R	W	1-0	0-0	12	Cisse 75	44,697
8	22	A	Fulham	L	0-2	0-1	13		22,480
9	29	H	West Ham U	W	2-0	1-0	13	Xabi Alonso 18, Zenden 82	44,537
10	Nov 5	A	Aston Villa	W	2-0	0-0	12	Gerrard (pen) 85, Xabi Alonso 89	42,551
11	19	H	Portsmouth	W	3-0	2-0	9	Zenden 23, Cisse 39, Morientes 80	44,394
12	26	A	Manchester C	W	1-0	0-0	7	Riise 61	47,105
13	30	A	Sunderland	W	2-0	2-0	—	Luis Garcia 30, Gerrard 45	32,697
14	Dec 3	H	Wigan Ath	W	3-0	2-0	3	Crouch 2 19, 42, Luis Garcia 70	44,098
15	10	H	Middlesbrough	W	2-0	0-0	2	Morientes 2 72, 77	43,510
16	26	H	Newcastle U	W	2-0	2-0	3	Gerrard 14, Crouch 43	44,197
17	28	A	Everton	W	3-1	2-1	3	Crouch 11, Gerrard 18, Cisse 47	40,158
18	31	H	WBA	W	1-0	0-0	3	Crouch 52	44,192
19	Jan 2	A	Bolton W	D	2-2	0-1	3	Gerrard (pen) 67, Luis Garcia 82	27,604
20	14	H	Tottenham H	W	1-0	0-0	3	Kewell 59	44,983
21	22	A	Manchester U	L	0-1	0-0	3		67,874
22	Feb 1	H	Birmingham C	D	1-1	0-0	—	Gerrard 62	43,851
23	5	A	Chelsea	L	0-2	0-1	3		42,316
24	8	A	Charlton Ath	L	0-2	0-2	—		27,111
25	11	A	Wigan Ath	W	1-0	1-0	3	Hyypia 30	25,023
26	14	H	Arsenal	W	1-0	0-0	—	Luis Garcia 87	44,065
27	26	H	Manchester C	W	1-0	1-0	3	Kewell 40	44,121
28	Mar 4	H	Charlton Ath	D	0-0	0-0	2		43,892
29	12	A	Arsenal	L	1-2	0-1	3	Luis Garcia 76	38,221
30	15	H	Fulham	W	5-1	2-1	—	Fowler 16, Brown (og) 34, Morientes 71, Crouch 89, Warnock 90	42,293
31	19	A	Newcastle U	W	3-1	2-1	3	Crouch 10, Gerrard 35, Cisse (pen) 52	52,302
32	25	H	Everton	W	3-1	1-0	3	Neville (og) 45, Luis Garcia 47, Kewell 84	44,923
33	Apr 1	A	WBA	W	2-0	2-0	3	Fowler 7, Cisse 38	27,576
34	9	H	Bolton W	W	1-0	1-0	3	Fowler 45	44,194
35	16	A	Blackburn R	W	1-0	1-0	3	Fowler 29	29,142
36	26	A	West Ham U	W	2-1	1-0	—	Cisse 2 19, 54	34,852
37	29	H	Aston Villa	W	3-1	1-0	3	Morientes 4, Gerrard 2 61, 66	44,479
38	May 7	A	Portsmouth	W	3-1	0-0	3	Fowler 52, Crouch 84, Cisse 89	20,240

Final League Position: 3

GOALSCORERS

League (57): Gerrard 10 (2 pens), Cisse 9 (2 pens), Crouch 8, Luis Garcia 7, Fowler 5, Morientes 5, Xabi Alonso 3, Kewell 3, Zenden 2, Hyypia 1, Riise 1, Warnock 1, own goals 2.
Carling Cup (1): Gerrard 1.
FA Cup (20): Gerrard 4 (1 pen), Crouch 3, Riise 3, Cisse 2, Sinama-Pongolle 2, Xabi Alonso 2, Hyypia 1, Luis Garcia 1, Morientes 1, own goal 1.
Champions League (20): Gerrard 7 (1 pen), Cisse 6, Morientes 3, Luis Garcia 2, Carragher 1, Sinama-Pongolle 1.
Super Cup (3): Cisse 2, Luis Garcia 1.
Club World Championship (3): Crouch 2, Gerrard 1.

Reina J 33	Finnan S 33	Warnock S 15 + 5	Xabi Alonso 29 + 6	Carragher J 36	Hyypia S 35 + 1	Sissoko M 21 + 5	Gerrard S 32	Luis Garcia 15 + 16	Morientes F 20 + 8	Zenden B 5 + 2	Cisse D 19 + 14	Baros M — + 2	Riise J 24 + 8	Hamann D 13 + 4	Crouch P 27 + 5	Traore D 9 + 6	Sinama-Pongolle F 3 + 4	Josemi 3 + 3	Kewell H 22 + 5	Kromkamp J 6 + 7	Agger D 4	Fowler R 9 + 5	Dudek J 5 + 1	*Match No.*
1	2	3	4	5	6	7	8	9[2]	10[1]	11	13	12												1
1	2	3	4	5	6	7	8[1]	12	10	11[3]	9[2]	13	14											2
1	2	3[1]	12	5	6	13	8	7			10		11	4[2]	9[3]	14								3
1	2	3[2]	4	5	6	12	8	7			14		11		9[3]	13	10[1]							4
1		3	7	5	6		8	12		11[3]	14		13	4[2]	9		10[1]	2						5
1	2		7	5	6[1]	14	8	10			13		11	4[3]	9	3[2]	12							6
1	7	3[3]	4	5		8		12	13	11	10		14		9[2]	6		2[1]						7
1			4	5	6	7		12	10		9		11		13	3[1]		2	8[2]					8
1	2		4	5	6	7	8	11	10[2]	12	9[1]		3		13									9
1	2		4	5	6	7	8	11[1]	10[2]	12	9[3]		3		13				14					10
1	2	3	12	5	6		8[3]	7[2]	13	11	10[1]			4	9			14						11
1	2	3		5	6	7	8	12	13		10[3]		11[1]	4	9[2]				14					12
1	2	12	4	5	6	7■	8	11	10[3]				3[1]		9[2]	13			14					13
1	2	3	4[1]	5	6		8	7	10		13		14	12	9[2]				11[3]					14
1	2		4	5	6	7	8	12	10[3]		13		3		9[1]			14	11[2]					15
1	2[3]		4	5	6		8	7	10		12		3		9[1]		13	14	11[2]					16
1	2	3	4	5	6	7	8[1]	12	13		10		14		9[2]				11[3]					17
1	2		4	5	6	12	8	7			10[2]		3		9[1]	13	14		11[3]					18
1	2		12	5	6	7[3]	8	13			14			4[1]	9	3	10[2]		11					19
1	2	12	4	5	6	7[3]	8		10[1]		13		3		9[2]				11	14				20
1	2		4	5	6	7[3]	8		12		10[2]		3		9[1]		13		11	14				21
1	2		12		6		8[1]	7	10				3	4	9[2]				11		5	13		22
1■	2	3	4	5	6	7[1]	8	13[6]			12		11[2]		9				10				15	23
	2		4	5	6[1]	7			10		8[2]		12		9[3]	3			11	13		14	1	24
	2		4	5	6		8		10[1]		12		3	7					11	13		9[2]	1	25
	2		4[3]	5	6	7[1]	8	12	10		13		3	14					11			9[2]	1	26
1	2		4[2]		6		8	12	10				3	13	9[1]	14			11[3]	7	5			27
1			12	5	6[3]		8		13		7		14	4[1]	9[2]	3			11	2		10		28
1	2	3	4■	5	6		8	10						7[2]	9				12	11[1]		13		29
1	2	12		5			8	7	10[2]		14			4	13	3			11[1]		6	9[3]		30
1		3	12	5	6[3]		8[1]	13			10			4	9[2]				11	7	2	14		31
1	2	12	4	5	6	7	8■	10	13				3		9[2]				11[1]					32
1	2		4	5	6	7		12	13		8[3]		3		9[2]				11	14		10[1]		33
1	2		4	5	6		8	12			7[1]		3	13	9	14			11[3]			10[2]		34
1	2	3[2]	4	5	6	7		12	10[3]		8		11						13	14		9[1]		35
	2[1]	11		5	12	7		13■	10[3]		8		14	4		3				6		9[2]	1	36
1		12	4	5	6	13	8		10		7[2]		11[1]		9[3]	3				2		14		37
	2		4[3]	5	6	7	8		10[1]		13		3		12				11	14		9[2]	1	38

FA Cup

Third Round	Luton T	(a)	5-3
Fourth Round	Portsmouth	(a)	2-1
Fifth Round	Manchester U	(h)	1-0
Sixth Round	Birmingham C	(a)	7-0
Semi-Final *(at Old Trafford)*	Chelsea		2-1
Final *(at Millennium Stadium)*	West Ham U		3-3

Carling Cup

Third Round	Crystal Palace	(a)	1-2

Super Cup

	CSKA Moscow	(n)	3-1

Club World Championship

Semi-Final	Saprissa	(a)	3-0
Final	Sao Paulo	(a)	0-1

Champions League

First Qualifying Round	TNS	(h)	3-0
		(a)	3-0
Second Qualifying Round	Kaunas	(a)	3-1
		(h)	2-0
Third Qualifying Round	CSKA Sofia	(a)	3-1
		(h)	0-1
Group G	Betis	(a)	2-1
	Chelsea	(h)	0-0
	Anderlecht	(a)	1-0
		(h)	3-0
	Betis	(h)	0-0
	Chelsea	(a)	0-0
First Round	Benfica	(a)	0-1
		(h)	0-2

LUTON TOWN FL Championship

FOUNDATION

Formed by an amalgamation of two leading local clubs, Wanderers and Excelsior a works team, at a meeting in Luton Town Hall in April 1885. The Wanderers had three months earlier changed their name to Luton Town Wanderers and did not take too kindly to the formation of another Town club but were talked around at this meeting. Wanderers had already appeared in the FA Cup and the new club entered in its inaugural season.

Kenilworth Stadium, 1 Maple Road, Luton, Beds LU4 8AW.

Telephone: (01582) 411 622.

Fax: (01582) 405 070.

Ticket Office: 0870 017 0656.

Website: www.lutontown.co.uk

Email: clubsec@lutontown.co.uk

Ground Capacity: 10,260.

Record Attendance: 30,069 v Blackpool, FA Cup 6th rd replay, 4 March 1959.

Pitch Measurements: 110yd × 72yd.

Chairman: Bill Tomlins.

Secretary: Cherry Newbery.

Manager: Mike Newell.

First Team Coach: Brian Stein.

Physio: Jon Bowden.

Colours: White shirts, black shorts, white stockings.

Change Colours: Orange shirts, black shorts, black stockings.

Year Formed: 1885.

Turned Professional: 1890.

Ltd Co.: 1897.

Club Nickname: 'The Hatters'.

Previous Grounds: 1885, Excelsior, Dallow Lane; 1897, Dunstable Road; 1905, Kenilworth Road.

First Football League Game: 4 September 1897, Division 2, v Leicester Fosse (a) D 1–1 – Williams; McCartney, McEwen; Davies, Stewart, Docherty; Gallacher, Coupar, Birch, McInnes, Ekins (1).

Record League Victory: 12–0 v Bristol R, Division 3 (S), 13 April 1936 – Dolman; Mackey, Smith; Finlayson, Nelson, Godfrey; Rich, Martin (1), Payne (10), Roberts (1), Stephenson.

HONOURS

Football League: Championship 1 – Winners 2004–05; Division 1 best season: 7th, 1986–87; Division 2 – Champions 1981–82; Runners-up 1954–55, 1973–74; Division 3 – Runners-up 1969–70, 2001–02; Division 4 – Champions 1967–68; Division 3 (S) – Champions 1936–37; Runners-up 1935–36.

FA Cup: Runners-up 1959.

Football League Cup: Winners 1988; Runners-up 1989.

Simod Cup: Runners-up 1988.

SKY SPORTS FACT FILE

In October 1946 there was no shortage of leadership at Luton Town. Scottish international winger Dally Duncan (37) was player-manager under George Martin, wartime international Frank Soo (32) player-coach while captain and centre-half was Horace Gager (29).

Record Cup Victory: 9–0 v Clapton, FA Cup 1st rd (replay after abandoned game), 30 November 1927 – Abbott; Kingham, Graham; Black, Rennie, Fraser; Pointon, Yardley (4), Reid (2), Woods (1), Dennis (2).

Record Defeat: 0–9 v Small Heath, Division 2, 12 November 1898.

Most League Points (2 for a win): 66, Division 4, 1967–68.

Most League Points (3 for a win): 98, Championship 1 2004–05.

Most League Goals: 103, Division 3 (S), 1936–37.

Highest League Scorer in Season: Joe Payne, 55, Division 3 (S), 1936–37.

Most League Goals in Total Aggregate: Gordon Turner, 243, 1949–64.

Most League Goals in One Match: 10, Joe Payne v Bristol R, Division 3S, 13 April 1936.

Most Capped Player: Mal Donaghy, 58 (91), Northern Ireland.

Most League Appearances: Bob Morton, 495, 1948–64.

Youngest League Player: Mike O'Hara, 16 years 32 days v Stoke C, 1 October 1960.

Record Transfer Fee Received: £3,000,000 from WBA for Curtis Davies, August 2005.

Record Transfer Fee Paid: £850,000 to Odense for Lars Elstrup, August 1989.

Football League Record: 1897 Elected to Division 2; 1900 Failed re-election; 1920 Division 3; 1921–37 Division 3 (S); 1937–55 Division 2; 1955–60 Division 1; 1960–63 Division 2; 1963–65 Division 3; 1965–68 Division 4; 1968–70 Division 3; 1970–74 Division 2; 1974–75 Division 1; 1975–82 Division 2; 1982–96 Division 1; 1996–2001 Division 2; 2001–02 Division 3; 2002–04 Division 2; 2004–05 FL1; 2005– FLC.

MANAGERS

Charlie Green 1901–28
(Secretary-Manager)
George Thomson 1925
John McCartney 1927–29
George Kay 1929–31
Harold Wightman 1931–35
Ted Liddell 1936–38
Neil McBain 1938–39
George Martin 1939–47
Dally Duncan 1947–58
Syd Owen 1959–60
Sam Bartram 1960–62
Bill Harvey 1962–64
George Martin 1965–66
Allan Brown 1966–68
Alec Stock 1968–72
Harry Haslam 1972–78
David Pleat 1978–86
John Moore 1986–87
Ray Harford 1987–89
Jim Ryan 1900–91
David Pleat 1991–95
Terry Westley 1995
Lennie Lawrence 1995–2000
Ricky Hill 2000
Lil Fuccillo 2000
Joe Kinnear 2001–03
Mike Newell June 2003–

LATEST SEQUENCES

Longest Sequence of League Wins: 12, 19.2.2002 – 6.4.2002.

Longest Sequence of League Defeats: 8, 11.11.1899 – 6.1.1900.

Longest Sequence of League Draws: 5, 28.8.1971 – 18.9.1971.

Longest Sequence of Unbeaten League Matches: 19, 8.4.1969 – 7.10.1969.

Longest Sequence Without a League Win: 16, 9.9.1964 – 6.11.1964.

Successive Scoring Runs: 25 from 24.10.1931.

Successive Non-scoring Runs: 5 from 10.4.1973.

TEN YEAR LEAGUE RECORD

		P	*W*	*D*	*L*	*F*	*A*	*Pts*	*Pos*
1996-97	Div 2	46	21	15	10	71	45	78	3
1997-98	Div 2	46	14	15	17	60	64	57	17
1998-99	Div 2	46	16	10	20	51	60	58	12
1999-2000	Div 2	46	17	10	19	61	65	61	13
2000-01	Div 2	46	9	13	24	52	80	40	22
2001-02	Div 3	46	30	7	9	96	48	97	2
2002-03	Div 2	46	17	14	15	67	62	65	9
2003-04	Div 2	46	17	15	14	69	66	66	10
2004-05	FL 1	46	29	11	6	87	48	98	1
2005-06	FL C	46	17	10	19	66	67	61	10

DID YOU KNOW ?

In 1938–39 Hugh Billington had the unusual experience of scoring 42 goals in as many League games. However 28 were scored in the Football League from 27 matches, the remaining 14 having been registered in 15 London Combination fixtures!

LUTON TOWN 2005–06 LEAGUE RECORD

Match No.	*Date*	*Venue*	*Opponents*	*Result*		*H/T Score*	*Lg. Pos.*	*Goalscorers*	*Attendance*
1	Aug 6	A	Crystal Palace	W	2-1	1-0	—	Howard [44], Brkovic [79]	21,166
2	9	H	Southampton	W	3-2	1-2	—	Nicholls [41], Brkovic [52], Morgan [90]	9447
3	13	H	Leeds U	D	0-0	0-0	1		10,102
4	20	A	Stoke C	L	1-2	1-0	6	Morgan [9]	18,653
5	27	A	Leicester C	W	2-0	1-0	3	Brkovic [42], Nicholls (pen) [90]	22,048
6	29	H	Millwall	W	2-1	1-0	3	Feeney [12], Davies [78]	8220
7	Sept 10	H	Wolverhampton W	D	1-1	0-1	4	Nicholls [79]	10,248
8	13	A	QPR	L	0-1	0-0	—		13,492
9	17	A	Hull C	W	1-0	0-0	4	Howard [85]	19,184
10	23	H	Sheffield W	D	2-2	1-1	—	Howard 2 [2, 66]	8267
11	27	H	Preston NE	W	3-0	3-0	—	Feeney [4], Brkovic [11], Howard [38]	7815
12	Oct 1	A	Cardiff C	W	2-1	1-1	3	Morgan [30], Holmes [57]	14,657
13	15	A	Crewe Alex	L	1-3	1-1	3	Morgan [29]	6604
14	18	H	Norwich C	W	4-2	4-0	—	Feeney [16], Edwards [27], Holmes [34], Howard [41]	10,248
15	22	H	Plymouth Arg	D	1-1	0-0	3	Feeney [64]	8714
16	29	A	Coventry C	L	0-1	0-0	3		22,228
17	Nov 1	A	Sheffield U	L	0-4	0-1	—		22,554
18	5	H	Burnley	L	2-3	1-2	4	Howard [43], Feeney [60]	8518
19	19	A	Norwich C	L	0-2	0-2	7		25,383
20	22	H	Crewe Alex	W	4-1	0-0	—	Vine 2 (1 pen) [69, 72 (p)], Morgan [82], Showunmi [89]	7474
21	26	H	Crystal Palace	W	2-0	2-0	5	Heikkinen [11], Vine [21]	10,248
22	Dec 3	A	Reading	L	0-3	0-1	5		19,478
23	11	A	Southampton	L	0-1	0-1	6		19,086
24	17	H	Stoke C	L	2-3	1-1	10	Brkovic [21], Nicholls (pen) [88]	8296
25	26	A	Derby Co	D	1-1	0-0	11	Brkovic [80]	26,807
26	28	H	Brighton & HA	W	3-0	2-0	8	Howard [17], Feeney [44], Robinson [62]	9429
27	31	A	Ipswich T	L	0-1	0-0	10		23,957
28	Jan 2	H	Watford	L	1-2	0-2	9	Edwards [49]	10,248
29	13	A	Wolverhampton W	L	1-2	0-0	—	Howard [80]	21,823
30	21	H	QPR	W	2-0	1-0	9	Heikkinen [1], Howard [85]	9797
31	31	A	Sheffield W	W	2-0	0-0	—	Nicholls (pen) [52], Vine [56]	23,965
32	Feb 4	H	Hull C	L	2-3	1-3	8	Keane [9], Coyne [86]	8835
33	11	A	Preston NE	L	1-5	0-1	9	Mears (og) [82]	15,237
34	14	H	Cardiff C	D	3-3	2-0	—	Vine 2 [25, 26], Barker (og) [60]	7826
35	17	H	Reading	W	3-2	2-1	—	Vine 2 [20, 26], Morgan [51]	8705
36	25	A	Leeds U	L	1-2	0-0	10	Howard [83]	23,644
37	Mar 4	A	Millwall	L	1-2	0-1	11	Coyne [47]	9871
38	11	H	Leicester C	L	1-2	0-1	12	Howard [53]	9783
39	18	H	Derby Co	W	1-0	0-0	12	Howard [72]	9163
40	25	A	Brighton & HA	D	1-1	0-1	11	Robinson [61]	7139
41	Apr 1	H	Ipswich T	W	1-0	0-0	10	Howard [81]	9820
42	9	A	Watford	D	1-1	0-1	9	Brkovic [73]	15,922
43	15	H	Coventry C	L	1-2	0-2	9	Williams (og) [85]	8752
44	17	A	Plymouth Arg	W	2-1	0-0	9	Vine [79], Andrew [88]	13,486
45	22	H	Sheffield U	D	1-1	0-0	10	Brkovic [72]	10,248
46	30	A	Burnley	D	1-1	1-0	10	Vine [42]	12,473

Final League Position: 10

GOALSCORERS

League (66): Howard 14, Vine 10 (1 pen), Brkovic 8, Feeney 6, Morgan 6, Nicholls 5 (3 pens), Coyne 2, Edwards 2, Heikkinen 2, Holmes 2, Robinson 2, Andrew 1, Davies 1, Keane 1, Showunmi 1, own goals 3.
Carling Cup (3): Coyne 1, Feeney 1, own goal 1.
FA Cup (3): Howard 1, Nicholls 1 (pen), Robinson 1.

Brill D 5	Foley K 35 + 3	Underwood P 28 + 1	Robinson S 26	Davies C 6	Heikkinen M 38 + 1	Brkovic A 39 + 3	Nicholls K 31 + 1	Howard S 40 + 3	Feeney W 29 + 13	Morgan D 25 + 11	Showunmi E 15 + 26	Holmes P 16 + 7	Edwards C 38 + 4	Beresford M 41	Davis S 17 + 4	Coyne C 28 + 2	Perrett R 9 + 2	Barnett L 12 + 8	Keane K 5 + 5	Vine R 21 + 10	Bell D 2 + 7	Andrew C — + 1	Stevens D — + 1	Match No.
1	2	3	4	5	6	7^{1}	8	9	10	11^{2}	12	13												1
1	2	3	4	5	6	7	8	9	10^{1}	11	12													2
1	2	3	4	5	6	7	8	9	10^{1}	11^{2}	12		13											3
	2	3	4	5	6	7^{2}	8	9■	10^{1}	11^{3}	12		13	1	14									4
	2	3	4^{1}	5	6	7^{3}	8		10	11^{2}	9		14	1	13	12								5
	2	3	4	5	6	7	8		10^{2}	11^{1}	9^{3}		13	1	12	14								6
		7	4		6^{2}	11	8	9	10^{1}		12		2	1	3	5	13							7
		11^{3}	4^{2}			7	8	9	10^{1}	13	12	14	2	1	3	5	6							8
			4			7	8	9	10	11			2	1	3	5	6^{1}	12						9
			4		12	7	8	9	10	11^{2}	13		2	1	3^{1}	5	6							10
			4^{2}		6	7^{3}	8	9	10	11^{1}	12	13	2	1	3	5			14					11
		12			6	7^{1}	8	9	10^{2}	11^{3}	13	4	2	1	3	5			14					12
	12				6	7	8	9	10^{2}	11^{1}	13	4	2	1	3	5								13
	12		4^{1}		6	7		9	10^{2}	11^{3}	13	8	2	1	3	5				14				14
	12				6	7^{2}	8	9	10	11^{1}	13	4	2	1	3	5								15
	2				6	7	8	9	10	11^{2}	12	4^{1}	3	1		5^{3}		14	13					16
	2	11^{2}			6	7^{1}		9	10^{3}		12	4	3	1		5		8	13	14				17
	2	11			6			9	10^{2}	7^{1}	12	4	3	1			5	8		13				18
	2	3	4		6	7	8■	9	10^{1}	11^{2}	12			1			5■			13				19
	2	3	4		6	12			10^{2}	13	9	8	7	1				5		11^{1}				20
	2	3	4		6			12	13	11^{1}	9	8	7	1		5^{3}	14			10^{2}				21
	2	3	4		6^{3}			12	13	11^{2}	9	8	7	1			5	14		10^{1}				22
1	2	3	4		6	7	8	9			10^{2}	12	11^{1}			5				13				23
1	2	3	4^{2}		6	7	8	9	12		13		11			5				10^{1}				24
	2	3	4		6	7		9		12		8^{1}	11	1		5				10				25
	2	3	4		6	7^{1}	8	9^{3}	10^{2}	12	13		11	1		5				14				26
	2	3	4		6	7	8	12	10^{1}		13		11	1		5^{3}		14		9^{2}				27
	2	3	4		6	7^{2}	8	9	12		13		11	1				5		10^{1}				28
	2	3			6	7	4	9	12		8		11	1		5				10^{1}				29
	2	3			6	7^{2}	4	9	12	13	8^{3}		11	1		5		14		10^{1}				30
	2	3^{2}			6	7	4	9	12	13	8^{3}		11	1		5		14		10^{1}				31
	2				6	7^{2}	4	9	12	13	8^{3}		11	1		5			3	10^{1}	14			32
	2				6	7	8	9		12			11	1■	13	5^{3}		14	4^{2}	10	3^{1}			33
	2				6	8	4	9		11^{1}		12	7	1	5			3		10				34
	2				6	8	4	9	12	11^{2}	13	14	7	1	5^{3}			3		10^{1}				35
	2	3				7^{1}		9	12	11^{2}	13		8	1	6■	5		4		10				36
	2	3			6	7^{3}	8	9	12	13	14	4^{2}	11	1		5				10^{1}				37
	2	3^{2}					8^{3}	9	12		13	7	11	1	4	5		6		10^{1}	14			38
	2	11	4			8^{2}		9	10^{1}				7	1	3	5	6			12	13			39
	2	3	8		6	7^{2}		9	10^{1}		12		11^{3}	1	4	5				13	14			40
	2		8		6^{3}	12		9	13	11^{1}	14		7	1	3	5	4			10^{2}				41
	2^{1}		4		6	7		9	10^{2}	12	8		11	1	5^{3}		3	14		13				42
	2				6	7		9	10	12	8	4^{3}	3^{2}	1				5	13	11^{1}	14			43
					6^{3}	12		9	10^{2}	11	8	4	2	1				5	3	13	7^{1}	14		44
						7	12	6	10	11^{1}	8	4^{2}	2	1				5	3	9	13			45
	2					7^{2}	4^{1}	9	10	3^{3}	8	12		1				5	6	11	13		14	46

FA Cup

Third Round	Liverpool	(h)	3-5

Carling Cup

First Round	Leyton Orient	(a)	3-1
Second Round	Reading	(a)	0-1

MACCLESFIELD TOWN FL Championship 2

FOUNDATION

From the mid-19th Century until 1874, Macclesfield Town FC played under rugby rules. In 1891 they moved to the Moss Rose and finished champions of the Manchester & District League in 1906 and 1908. By 1911, they had carried off the Cheshire Senior Cup five times. Macclesfield were founder members of the Cheshire County League in 1919.

Moss Rose Ground, London Road, Macclesfield, Cheshire SK11 0DQ.

Telephone: (01625) 264 686.

Fax: (01625) 264 692.

Ticket Office: (01625) 264 686.

Website: www.mtfc.co.uk

Email: admin@mtfc.co.uk

Ground Capacity: 6,141.

Record Attendance: 9008 v Winsford U, Cheshire Senior Cup 2nd rd, 4 February 1948.

Pitch Measurements: 110yds × 72yds

Chairman: Robert Bickerton.

Chief Executive: Patrick Nelson.

Secretary: Dianne Hehir.

Manager: Brian Horton.

Physio: Paul Lake.

Colours: All blue.

Change Colours: All black.

Year formed: 1874.

Club Nickname: 'The Silkmen'.

Previous Ground: 1874, Rostron Field; 1891, Moss Rose.

First Football League Game: 9 August 1997, Division 3, v Torquay U (h) W 2–1 – Price; Tinson, Rose, Payne (Edey), Howarth, Sodje (1), Askey, Wood, Landon (1) (Power), Mason, Sorvel.

Record League Victory: 6–0 v Stockport Co, FL1, 26 December 2005 – Fettis; Harsley, Sandwith, Morley, Swailes (Teague), Navarro, Whitaker (Miles (1)), Bullock (1), Parkin (2), Wijnhard (2) (Townson), McIntyre.

HONOURS

Football League: Division 3 – Runners-up 1997–98.

FA Cup: best season: 3rd rd, 1968, 1988, 2002, 2003, 2004.

Football League Cup: never past 2nd rd.

Vauxhall Conference: Champions 1994–95, 1996–97.

FA Trophy: Winners 1969–70, 1995–96; Runners-up 1988–89.

Bob Lord Trophy: Winners 1993–94; Runners-up 1995–96, 1996–97.

Vauxhall Conference Championship Shield: Winners 1996, 1997, 1998.

Northern Premier League: Winners 1968–69, 1969–70, 1986–87; Runners-up 1984–85.

Northern Premier League Challenge Cup: Winners 1986–87; Runners-up 1969–70, 1970–71, 1982–83.

Northern Premier League Presidents Cup: Winners 1986–87; Runners-up 1984–85.

Cheshire Senior Cup: Winners 20 times; Runners-up 11.

SKY SPORTS FACT FILE

No other player at this level of football has made such an impact on his first team debut as Johnnie Mullington. Brought in from Macclesfield Town reserves because of injury, he scored all eight goals in the demolition of Witton Albion in May 1963.

Record Win: 15–0 v Chester St Marys, Cheshire Senior Cup, 2nd rd, 16 February 1886.

Record Defeat: 1–13 v Tranmere R reserves, 3 May 1929.

Most League Points (3 for a win): 82, Division 3, 1997–98.

Most League Goals: 66, Division 3, 1999–2000.

Highest League Scorer in Season: Jon Parkin, 22, League 2, 2004–05.

Most League Goals in Total Aggregate: Matt Tipton, 41, 2002–05.

Most Capped Player: George Abbey, 10, Nigeria.

Most League Appearances: Darren Tinson, 263, 1997–2003.

Youngest League Player: Peter Griffiths, 18 years 44 days v Reading, 26 September 1998.

Record Transfer Fee Received: £250,000 from Stockport Co for Rickie Lambert, April 2002.

Record Transfer Fee Paid: £40,000 to Bury for Danny Swailes, January 2005.

Football League Record: 1997 Promoted to Division 3; 1998–99 Division 2; 1999–2004 Division 3; 2004– FL2.

MANAGERS

Since 1967
Keith Goalen 1967–68
Frank Beaumont 1968–72
Billy Haydock 1972–74
Eddie Brown 1974
John Collins 1974
Willie Stevenson 1974
John Collins 1975–76
Tony Coleman 1976
John Barnes 1976
Brian Taylor 1976
Dave Connor 1976–78
Derek Partridge 1978
Phil Staley 1978–80
Jimmy Williams 1980–81
Brian Booth 1981–85
Neil Griffiths 1985–86
Roy Campbell 1986
Peter Wragg 1986–93
Sammy McIlroy 1993–2000
Peter Davenport 2000
Gil Prescott 2001
David Moss 2001–03
John Askey 2003–04
Brian Horton April 2004–

LATEST SEQUENCES

Longest Sequence of League Wins: 6, 25.1.2005 – 26.2.2005.

Longest Sequence of League Defeats: 6, 26.12.1998 –6.2.1999.

Longest Sequence of League Draws: 4, 26.11.2005 – 17.12.2005.

Longest Sequence of Unbeaten League Matches: 8, 16.10.1999 – 27.11.1999.

Longest Sequence Without a League Win: 10, 21.11.1998 – 6.2.1999.

Successive Scoring Runs: 14 from 11.10.2003.

Successive Non-scoring Runs: 5 from 18.12.1998.

TEN YEAR LEAGUE RECORD

		P	W	D	L	F	A	Pts	Pos
1996-97	Conf.	42	27	9	6	80	30	90	1
1997-98	Div 3	46	23	13	10	63	44	82	2
1998-99	Div 2	46	11	10	25	43	63	43	24
1999-2000	Div 3	46	18	11	17	66	61	65	13
2000-01	Div 3	46	14	14	18	51	62	56	14
2001-02	Div 3	46	15	13	18	41	52	58	13
2002-03	Div 3	46	14	12	20	57	63	54	16
2003-04	Div 3	46	13	13	20	54	69	52	20
2004-05	FL 2	46	22	9	15	60	49	75	5
2005-06	FL 2	46	12	18	16	60	71	54	17

DID YOU KNOW ?

Long before their record Football League victory during 2005–06 against Stockport County, the same team provided non-league Macclesfield Town with their first League scalp in the FA Cup when they beat County 2–1 in a replay on 13 December 1967.

MACCLESFIELD TOWN 2005–06 LEAGUE RECORD

Match No.	*Date*	*Venue*	*Opponents*	*Result*		*H/T Score*	*Lg. Pos.*	*Goalscorers*	*Attendance*
1	Aug 6	A	Leyton Orient	L	1-2	0-1	—	Harsley ^{57}	3600
2	9	H	Cheltenham T	D	2-2	0-1	—	MacKenzie ^{83}, Bullock ^{85}	1601
3	20	A	Barnet	L	0-1	0-1	23		2005
4	27	A	Rochdale	L	1-3	1-2	24	Townson ^{24}	2606
5	29	H	Bury	W	1-0	1-0	21	Bullock ^{18}	1965
6	Sept 4	H	Boston U	D	2-2	2-0	21	McIntyre ^{21}, Futcher (og) ^{32}	2130
7	10	A	Carlisle U	L	0-2	0-0	22		5190
8	13	H	Rushden & D	W	3-1	1-0	—	Bullock 2 ^{40,86}, Harsley (pen) ^{56}	2874
9	17	H	Northampton T	L	1-4	0-1	21	Bullock ^{62}	2014
10	24	A	Wrexham	D	1-1	0-0	21	Russell ^{72}	3830
11	27	H	Mansfield T	D	1-1	1-0	—	Russell ^{36}	1576
12	Oct 1	H	Notts Co	D	0-0	0-0	19		1892
13	7	A	Darlington	L	0-1	0-1	—		3831
14	15	H	Peterborough U	L	0-4	0-0	23		1810
15	22	A	Torquay U	D	1-1	0-0	24	Harsley ^{49}	2355
16	29	H	Bristol R	W	2-1	0-0	23	Wijnhard ^{52}, Harsley ^{65}	1908
17	Nov 11	A	Grimsby T	L	1-3	1-1	—	Parkin ^{43}	3658
18	19	H	Darlington	W	1-0	1-0	21	McIntyre ^{38}	1769
19	26	H	Leyton Orient	D	0-0	0-0	22		1649
20	Dec 3	A	Lincoln C	D	2-2	1-0	—	Wijnhard ^{45}, Teague ^{81}	3171
21	10	A	Cheltenham T	D	2-2	0-0	21	Sandwith ^{58}, Parkin ^{71}	2804
22	17	H	Barnet	D	1-1	1-0	22	Sandwith ^{18}	1663
23	26	H	Stockport Co	W	6-0	2-0	20	Wijnhard 2 ^{41,64}, Parkin 2 ^{43,63}, Bullock ^{59}, Miles ^{86}	4553
24	31	H	Chester C	W	1-0	0-0	18	McIntyre ^{60}	2910
25	Jan 2	A	Wycombe W	W	5-4	3-1	16	Wijnhard 2 ^{3,13}, Whitaker ^{10}, Parkin 2 ^{77,81}	5364
26	7	A	Boston U	L	1-3	0-2	18	Parkin ^{47}	1975
27	14	H	Oxford U	D	1-1	1-0	18	McIntyre ^{39}	1972
28	21	A	Northampton T	L	0-5	0-2	19		5428
29	29	H	Carlisle U	W	3-0	3-0	17	Swailes ^{6}, McIntyre ^{10}, Whitaker ^{42}	4140
30	31	A	Shrewsbury T	D	1-1	1-0	—	Wijnhard ^{26}	2642
31	Feb 4	A	Mansfield T	D	1-1	0-0	16	Swailes ^{79}	2901
32	15	A	Oxford U	D	1-1	1-1	—	Sandwith ^{16}	4331
33	18	H	Lincoln C	D	1-1	1-0	16	Wijnhard (pen) ^{32}	2268
34	25	A	Rushden & D	L	0-1	0-0	17		2479
35	Mar 11	H	Rochdale	L	1-3	0-1	18	Miles ^{56}	2211
36	14	H	Wrexham	W	3-2	1-2	—	Holt (og) ^{43}, Whitaker ^{74}, Briscoe ^{82}	1616
37	18	A	Stockport Co	L	0-2	0-1	18		6003
38	25	H	Shrewsbury T	W	2-0	1-0	17	McNeil ^{33}, Bullock ^{61}	2274
39	Apr 1	A	Chester C	L	1-2	0-0	17	Townson ^{75}	2939
40	4	A	Bury	D	0-0	0-0	—		2273
41	8	H	Wycombe W	W	2-1	1-0	15	Harsley (pen) ^{39}, Whitaker ^{53}	1869
42	15	A	Notts Co	D	1-1	0-1	16	Harsley (pen) ^{89}	4393
43	17	H	Torquay U	L	0-2	0-0	17		1808
44	22	A	Peterborough U	L	2-3	0-0	19	Miles 2 ^{62,89}	3002
45	29	H	Grimsby T	D	1-1	1-1	18	Richardson ^{43}	3849
46	May 6	A	Bristol R	W	3-2	2-1	17	Morley ^{7}, Richardson 2 ^{29,89}	6100

Final League Position: 17

GOALSCORERS

League (60): Wijnhard 8 (1 pen), Bullock 7, Parkin 7, Harsley 6 (3 pens), McIntyre 5, Miles 4, Whitaker 4, Richardson 3, Sandwith 3, Russell 2, Swailes 2, Townson 2, Briscoe 1, MacKenzie 1, McNeil 1, Morley 1, Teague 1, own goals 2.
Carling Cup (4): Bullock 1, MacKenzie 1, Townson 1, Whitaker 1.
FA Cup (1): Wijnhard 1.
Football League Trophy (14): Wijnhard 3, Parkin 2, Sandwith 2, Beresford 1, Harsley 1, McNeil 1, Smart 1, Teague 1, Townson 1, Whitaker 1.

Fettis A 33	Bailey M 5	Sandwith K 34 + 1	Morley D 45	Swailes D 39	Miles J 8 + 17	Harsley P 45	Bullock M 38 + 2	Townson K 3 + 15	Beresford D 9 + 7	McIntyre K 44	MacKenzie N 4 + 2	Barras T 7	Russell A 12 + 1	Whitaker D 41 + 1	Smart A 7 + 2	Briscoe M 11 + 2	Navarro A 27	Wijnhard C 19 + 1	Parkin J 9 + 2	Brightwell I 10 + 1	Teague A 23 + 2	Deasy T 2 + 1	Lee T 11	McNeil M 12	Richardson M 8	Match No.
1	2	3	4	5	6	7	8		10	11[1]	12		9													1
1	2[1]	3	4	5	13	7	8	12	10		11	6	9[2]													2
1		3	4	2	12	7	8	13	10[1]	11	6[2]	5	9													3
1		3[2]	4	5		11	12	9	13		6[1]	2	10	7	8											4
1			4	5	6	3	8			11			9	7	10	2										5
1			2	5	10	3[2]	6	12	13	11			9[1]	7	8	4										6
1		3	4	5	12	6[2]	8	9[1]	13	11			10	7		2										7
1		3	4	5	12	8	10			11		6	9[1]	7		2										8
1		3	4	5	9	8	10	12		11[1]		6		7		2										9
1		3[2]	2	5		8	10	9		11		6[1]	12	7	13	4										10
1			4	5	12	8	10		7[1]	11			9	2	3	6										11
1			4	5		6	10	12	9	11			8	7[1]	3	2										12
1			4	5	12	6	8	13	9[3]	11	14		10	7[1]	3	2[2]										13
1		3[2]	4	5	12	7	10			11	8[3]	2[1]	9	13			6	14								14
1	2		4	5		3	8		9	11				7			6	10								15
1	2		4	5		3	8		9	11				7			6[1]	10	12							16
1	2[1]		4		13	11	8[2]		9	3				7		5	6	10	12							17
1		3	2	5		8				11				7			6	10	9	4						18
1		3	4	5		8			12	11				7			6[1]	10	9	2						19
1		3	2			8				11				7			6	10	9	4	5					20
1		3	4			2	8			11				7			6	10	9		5					21
1		3	4	5		8				11				7			6	10	9		2					22
1		3	4	5[3]	12	2	8	13		11				7[1]			6	10[2]	9		14					23
1[6]		3	4			2	8			11				7			6	10	9		5	15				24
		3	4			2	8[1]			11				7		12	6	10	9		5	1				25
1		3	4			2	8			11				7			6	10	9		5					26
1		3	4	5		8	9	12		11				7			6[1]	10			2					27
1		3	4	5	12	8	9	13		11[2]				7			6[1]	10			2					28
1		3	4	5		8	9			11				7			6	10			2					29
1		3[2]	4	5	12	8	9[1]		13	11				7			6	10			2					30
1		3	4	5	12	8	9			11				7			6[1]	10			2					31
		3	4	5		8	9			11				7			6	10			2		1			32
		3	4	5	12	8	9			11				7			6[1]	10			2		1			33
		3	4	5	6	8[1]	9[2]	12	13	11				7	10						2		1			34
1		3[2]	4	5	6[1]	8	10	12		11				7	13						2			9		35
			4	5	13	8[1]	9			11				7		12	6			2[2]	3		1	10		36
		12	4[2]	5	13		9		14	11[1]				7		8[1]	6			2	3		1	10		37
		3		5		4	8			11				7			6				2		1	10	9	38
		3	4[1]	5		9		12		11				7			6			8	2		1	10		39
		3	4	5		8	6			11				7							2		1	10	9	40
		3	4	5		8	6			11				7							2		1	10	9	41
		3	4	5		8	6	12		11				7						13	2[2]		1	10	9[1]	42
		3[1]	4	5	12	8	6	13		11				7						2			1	10	9[2]	43
		3	4		12	8	7[1]	13		11							6			2	5	1		10	9[2]	44
1			2	5	8[1]	3	12			11				7			6			4				10	9	45
1			4	5	11	8				3[1]				7			6			2	12			10	9	46

FA Cup

First Round	Yeovil T	(h)	1-1
		(a)	0-4

Carling Cup

First Round	Nottingham F	(a)	3-2
Second Round	Cardiff C	(a)	1-2

Football League Trophy

First Round	Chesterfield	(h)	2-0
Second Round	Rotherham U	(a)	2-1
Quarter-Final	Cambridge U	(h)	4-2
Semi-Final	Hereford U	(h)	2-0
Northern Final	Carlisle U	(a)	1-2
		(h)	3-2

MANCHESTER CITY FA Premiership

FOUNDATION

Manchester City was formed as a Limited Company in 1894 after their predecessors Ardwick had been forced into bankruptcy. However, many historians like to trace the club's lineage as far back as 1880 when St Mark's Church, West Gorton added a football section to their cricket club. They amalgamated with Gorton Athletic in 1884 as Gorton FC. Because of a change of ground they became Ardwick in 1887.

The City of Manchester Stadium, SportCity, Manchester M11 3FF.

Telephone: 0870 062 1894.

Fax: (0161) 438 7999.

Ticket Office: 0870 062 1894.

Website: www.mcfc.co.uk

Email: mcfc@mcfc.co.uk

Ground Capacity: 47,500.

Record Attendance: 85,569 v Stoke C, FA Cup 6th rd, 3 March 1934 (British record for any game outside London or Glasgow).

Pitch Measurements: 105m × 68m.

Chairman: John Wardle.

Deputy chairman: Bryan Bodek.

Chief Executive: Alistair Mackintosh.

Secretary: J. B. Halford.

Manager: Stuart Pearce.

First Team Coach: Derek Fazackerley.

Physio: Jim Webb.

Colours: Sky blue shirts, white shorts, sky blue stockings.

Change Colours: Navy blue, navy blue shorts, navy blue stockings.

Year Formed: 1887 as Ardwick FC; 1894 as Manchester City.

Turned Professional: 1887 as Ardwick FC.

Ltd Co.: 1894.

Previous Names: 1887, Ardwick FC (formed through the amalgamation of West Gorton and Gorton Athletic, the latter having been formed in 1880); 1894, Manchester City.

Club Nicknames: 'Blues' or 'The Citizens'.

Previous Grounds: 1880, Clowes Street; 1881, Kirkmanshulme Cricket Ground; 1882, Queens Road; 1884, Pink Bank Lane; 1887, Hyde Road (1894–1923 as City); 1923, Maine Road; 2003, City of Manchester Stadium.

First Football League Game: 3 September 1892, Division 2, v Bootle (h) W 7–0 – Douglas; McVickers, Robson; Middleton, Russell, Hopkins; Davies (3), Morris (2), Angus (1), Weir (1), Milarvie.

Record League Victory: 10–1 v Huddersfield T, Division 2, 7 November 1987 – Nixon; Gidman, Hinchcliffe, Clements, Lake, Redmond, White (3), Stewart (3), Adcock (3), McNab (1), Simpson.

HONOURS

Football League: Division 1 – Champions 1936–37, 1967–68, 2001–02; Runners-up 1903–04, 1920–21, 1976–77, 1999–2000; Division 2 – Champions 1898–99, 1902–03, 1909–10, 1927–28, 1946–47, 1965–66; Runners-up 1895–96, 1950–51, 1987–88; Promoted from Division 2 (play-offs) 1998–99.

FA Cup: Winners 1904, 1934, 1956, 1969; Runners-up 1926, 1933, 1955, 1981.

Football League Cup: Winners 1970, 1976; Runners-up 1974.

European Competitions: *European Cup:* 1968–69. *European Cup-Winners' Cup:* 1969–70 (winners), 1970–71. *UEFA Cup:* 1972–73, 1976–77, 1977–78, 1978–79, 2003–04.

SKY SPORTS FACT FILE

Injury to goalkeeper Bert Trautmann gave a chance for David Williams, 17, against Blackpool at Maine Road on 9 February 1952. Still on amateur forms, he also had to get permission to miss a schools game on the same day and kept a clean sheet.

Record Cup Victory: 10–1 v Swindon T, FA Cup 4th rd, 29 January 1930 – Barber; Felton, McCloy; Barrass, Cowan, Heinemann; Toseland, Marshall (5), Tait (3), Johnson (1), Brook (1).

Record Defeat: 1–9 v Everton, Division 1, 3 September 1906.

Most League Points (2 for a win): 62, Division 2, 1946–47.

Most League Points (3 for a win): 99, Division 1, 2001–02.

Most League Goals: 108, Division 2, 1926–27, 108, Division 1, 2001–02.

Highest League Scorer in Season: Tommy Johnson, 38, Division 1, 1928–29.

Most League Goals in Total Aggregate: Tommy Johnson, 158, 1919–30.

Most League Goals in One Match: 5, Fred Williams v Darwen, Division 2, 18 February 1899; 5, Tom Browell v Burnley, Division 2, 24 October 1925; 5, Tom Johnson v Everton, Division 1, 15 September 1928; 5, George Smith v Newport Co, Division 2, 14 June 1947.

Most Capped Player: Colin Bell, 48, England.

Most League Appearances: Alan Oakes, 565, 1959–76.

Youngest League Player: Glyn Pardoe, 15 years 314 days v Birmingham C, 11 April 1962.

Record Transfer Fee Received: £7,000,000 from Fenerbahce for Nicolas Anelka, January 2005.

Record Transfer Fee Paid: £10,000,000 to Paris St Germain for Nicolas Anelka, June 2002.

Football League Record: 1892 Ardwick elected founder member of Division 2; 1894 Newly-formed Manchester C elected to Division 2; Division 1 1899–1902, 1903–09, 1910–26, 1928–38, 1947–50, 1951–63, 1966–83, 1985–87, 1989–92; Division 2 1902–03, 1909–10, 1926–28, 1938–47, 1950–51, 1963–66, 1983–85, 1987–89; 1992–96 FA Premier League; 1996–98 Division 1; 1998–99 Division 2; 1999–2000 Division 1; 2000–01 FA Premier League; 2001–02 Division 1; 2002– FA Premier League.

MANAGERS

Joshua Parlby 1893–95
(Secretary-Manager)
Sam Omerod 1895–1902
Tom Maley 1902–06
Harry Newbould 1906–12
Ernest Magnall 1912–24
David Ashworth 1924–25
Peter Hodge 1926–32
Wilf Wild 1932–46
(continued as Secretary to 1950)
Sam Cowan 1946–47
John 'Jock' Thomson 1947–50
Leslie McDowall 1950–63
George Poyser 1963–65
Joe Mercer 1965–71
(continued as General Manager to 1972)
Malcolm Allison 1972–73
Johnny Hart 1973
Ron Saunders 1973–74
Tony Book 1974–79
Malcolm Allison 1979–80
John Bond 1980–83
John Benson 1983
Billy McNeill 1983–86
Jimmy Frizzell 1986–87
(continued as General Manager)
Mel Machin 1987–89
Howard Kendall 1990
Peter Reid 1990–93
Brian Horton 1993–95
Alan Ball 1995–96
Steve Coppell 1996
Frank Clark 1996–98
Joe Royle 1998–2001
Kevin Keegan 2001–05
Stuart Pearce March 2005–

LATEST SEQUENCES

Longest Sequence of League Wins: 9, 8.4.1912 – 28.9.1912.

Longest Sequence of League Defeats: 8, 23.8.1995 – 14.10.1995.

Longest Sequence of League Draws: 6, 5.4.1913 – 6.9.1913.

Longest Sequence of Unbeaten League Matches: 22, 16.11.1946 – 19.4.1947.

Longest Sequence Without a League Win: 17, 26.12.1979 – 7.4.1980.

Successive Scoring Runs: 44 from 3.10.1936.

Successive Non-scoring Runs: 6 from 30.1.1971.

TEN YEAR LEAGUE RECORD

		P	W	D	L	F	A	Pts	Pos
1996-97	Div 1	46	17	10	19	59	60	61	14
1997-98	Div 1	46	12	12	22	56	57	48	22
1998-99	Div 2	46	22	16	8	69	33	82	3
1999-2000	Div 1	46	26	11	9	78	40	89	2
2000-01	PR Lge	38	8	10	20	41	65	34	18
2001-02	Div 1	46	31	6	9	108	52	99	1
2002-03	PR Lge	38	15	6	17	47	54	51	9
2003-04	PR Lge	38	9	14	15	55	54	41	16
2004-05	PR Lge	38	13	13	12	47	39	52	8
2005-06	PR Lge	38	13	4	21	43	48	43	15

DID YOU KNOW ?

The first Manchester City match televised at Maine Road was on 15 December 1956 against Wolverhampton Wanderers. It was notable for the reappearance of goalkeeper Bert Trautmann after breaking his neck in the FA Cup Final against Birmingham City that year.

MANCHESTER CITY 2005–06 LEAGUE RECORD

Match No.	Date	Venue	Opponents	Result		H/T Score	Lg. Pos.	Goalscorers	Attendance
1	Aug 13	H	WBA	D	0-0	0-0	—		42,983
2	20	A	Birmingham C	W	2-1	1-1	6	Barton[20], Cole[47]	26,366
3	23	A	Sunderland	W	2-1	2-1	—	Vassell[10], Sinclair[35]	33,357
4	27	H	Portsmouth	W	2-1	0-0	2	Reyna[66], Cole[69]	41,022
5	Sept 10	A	Manchester U	D	1-1	0-1	3	Barton[76]	67,839
6	18	H	Bolton W	L	0-1	0-0	5		43,137
7	24	A	Newcastle U	L	0-1	0-1	6		52,280
8	Oct 2	H	Everton	W	2-0	0-0	6	Mills D[72], Vassell[90]	42,681
9	16	H	West Ham U	W	2-1	1-0	4	Cole 2[18, 56]	43,647
10	22	A	Arsenal	L	0-1	0-0	6		38,189
11	31	H	Aston Villa	W	3-1	2-0	—	Vassell 2[4, 26], Cole[83]	42,069
12	Nov 5	A	Fulham	L	1-2	1-2	6	Croft[20]	22,241
13	19	H	Blackburn R	D	0-0	0-0	7		44,032
14	26	H	Liverpool	L	0-1	0-0	8		47,105
15	Dec 4	A	Charlton Ath	W	5-2	2-1	8	Cole 2[25, 84], Sinclair[37], Barton[69], Vassell[79]	25,289
16	10	A	WBA	L	0-2	0-1	8		25,472
17	17	H	Birmingham C	W	4-1	3-0	7	Sommeil[1], Barton (pen)[15], Sibierski[40], Wright-Phillips[70]	41,343
18	26	A	Wigan Ath	L	3-4	1-3	8	Sibierski[3], Barton[77], Cole[88]	25,017
19	28	H	Chelsea	L	0-1	0-0	8		46,587
20	31	A	Middlesbrough	D	0-0	0-0	8		28,022
21	Jan 4	H	Tottenham H	L	0-2	0-1	—		40,808
22	14	H	Manchester U	W	3-1	2-0	8	Sinclair[32], Vassell[39], Fowler[90]	47,192
23	21	A	Bolton W	L	0-2	0-2	9		26,466
24	Feb 1	H	Newcastle U	W	3-0	2-0	—	Riera[14], Cole[38], Vassell[62]	42,413
25	4	A	Everton	L	0-1	0-1	10		37,827
26	12	H	Charlton Ath	W	3-2	1-0	9	Dunne[22], Samaras[54], Barton[62]	41,347
27	26	A	Liverpool	L	0-1	0-1	10		44,121
28	Mar 5	H	Sunderland	W	2-1	2-1	9	Samaras 2[9, 10]	42,200
29	11	A	Portsmouth	L	1-2	0-0	10	Dunne[83]	19,556
30	18	H	Wigan Ath	L	0-1	0-0	11		42,444
31	25	A	Chelsea	L	0-2	0-2	12		42,321
32	Apr 2	H	Middlesbrough	L	0-1	0-1	13		40,256
33	8	A	Tottenham H	L	1-2	0-1	13	Samaras[52]	36,167
34	15	A	West Ham U	L	0-1	0-1	13		34,305
35	25	A	Aston Villa	W	1-0	0-0	—	Vassell[71]	26,422
36	29	H	Fulham	L	1-2	0-0	14	Dunne[69]	41,128
37	May 4	H	Arsenal	L	1-3	1-1	—	Sommeil[38]	41,875
38	7	A	Blackburn R	L	0-2	0-1	15		25,731

Final League Position: 15

GOALSCORERS

League (43): Cole 9, Vassell 8, Barton 6 (1 pen), Samaras 4, Dunne 3, Sinclair 3, Sibierski 2, Sommeil 2, Croft 1, Fowler 1, Mills D 1, Reyna 1, Riera 1, Wright-Phillips 1.
Carling Cup (1): Vassell 1 (pen).
FA Cup (8): Fowler 3 (1 pen), Cole 1, Musampa 1, Richards 1, Samaras 1, Vassell 1.

James D 38	Mills D 18	Thatcher B 18	Sommeil D 14 + 2	Jordan S 18	Barton J 31	Sinclair T 29 + 2	Reyna C 22	Cole A 20 + 2	Vassell D 36	Musampa K 24 + 3	Croft L 4 + 17	Wright-Phillips B 1 + 17	Sibierski A 12 + 12	Dunne R 31 + 1	Jihai S 16 + 13	Onuoha N 8 + 2	Distin S 31	Fowler R — + 4	Ireland S 13 + 11	Richards M 11 + 2	Riera A 12 + 3	Samaras G 10 + 4	Miller I — + 1	Mills M — + 1	Flood W 1 + 4	*Match No.*
1	2	3	4	5	6	7^{1}	8	9	10^{2}	11^{3}	12	13	14													1
1	2	3		5	6	7	8^{3}	9^{1}	10^{2}	11		13	12	4	14											2
1	2	3		5^{2}	6	7	8	9	10	11^{1}				4	12	13										3
1	2^{1}	3			6	7	8	9	10	11				4	12	5										4
1	2^{1}	3			6	7	8	9	10^{3}	11^{2}			13	4	12		5	14								5
1	2	3			6^{2}	7^{1}	8		10	11			9	4	12		5		13							6
1		3			6		8		10	11^{2}	12		9^{1}	4	7	2	5		13							7
1	2			3	6			9^{1}	10	11^{2}	13		7	4	12		5		8							8
1	2			3	6		8	9	10	11^{2}	12				13	4	5		7^{1}							9
1	2^{3}		4	3	6		8^{2}		10	9^{1}	13		11		12		5		7	14						10
1	2		4^{2}	3	6			9^{3}	10	11	7^{1}	14	12		13		5		8							11
1	2^{2}			3^{3}	6			9	10	11^{1}	7	14	12	4	13		5		8							12
1	2			3		12		9^{2}	10	11^{1}	7	13		4	6		5		8							13
1	2^{3}			3^{2}	6	12		9	10	11^{1}	7	14		4	13		5		8							14
1		3	2		6	7^{1}	8^{3}	9^{2}	10		12	13		4	11		5		14							15
1		3^{2}	2^{3}		6	7	8^{1}	9■	10		12	13		4	11		5		14							16
1		3	2		6	7	8^{2}		10^{1}			12	9^{3}		11	4	5	13	14							17
1		3	4^{2}		6	7	8^{1}	12	10				9	13	11	2	5									18
1		3^{3}			6	7^{2}		9	10		13	12	8^{1}	4	11	2	5		14							19
1				3	6	7		9	10^{1}			12	8^{2}	4	11	2	5		13							20
1		3	12		6	7		9	10^{3}		13	14		4	11	2^{1}	5		8^{2}							21
1				3	6	7		9^{1}	10	13				4^{3}	2	14	5	12	8		11^{2}					22
1				3	6	7		9^{3}	10^{2}		13		12	4	2		5	14	8		11^{1}					23
1				3	6^{2}	7		9^{3}	10^{1}	8			12	4	2		5			13	11	14				24
1				3■	6	7		12	10^{3}	8		14	13	4	2		5				11^{1}	9^{2}				25
1			3		6	7^{3}		9^{2}	10^{1}	8			12	4			5		13	2	11	14				26
1	2			3	6■	7^{3}				8	12	13	10^{2}	4			5		14		11^{1}	9				27
1				3		7	6^{3}		10^{2}	8		13		4	12		5		14	2	11^{1}	9				28
1				3^{3}	6	7^{1}	8^{2}		10	11	12	13		4	2				14	5		9				29
1	2	3	4			7	8^{1}				12	10	9^{2}		11		5		6			13^{3}	14			30
1	2^{3}	3	6^{2}						10	9	12			4			5■		8^{1}	11	13			14	7	31
1	2	3				7^{2}			10	12	13		8^{3}	4					6^{1}	5	11	9			14	32
1	2^{2}	3				7	8^{1}		10	11			12	4			5			6	13	9				33
1		3^{2}	13			7	6^{3}		10	8			12	4			5			2	11	9^{1}			14	34
1			2		6	7	8		10^{3}	12			13	4	14		5			3	11^{1}	9^{2}				35
1			2		6	7	8		10^{1}				9^{2}	4			5			3	11	12			13	36
1			2		6	7^{1}	8		10		12			4	3					5	11^{2}	9			13	37
1			2		6	7^{1}	8		10	11^{2}	12	14		4			5^{3}			3	13	9				38

FA Cup

Third Round	Scunthorpe U	(h)	3-1
Fourth Round	Wigan Ath	(h)	1-0
Fifth Round	Aston Villa	(a)	1-1
		(h)	2-1
Sixth Round	West Ham U	(h)	1-2

Carling Cup

Second Round	Doncaster R	(a)	1-1

MANCHESTER UNITED FA Premiership

FOUNDATION

Manchester United was formed as comparatively recently as 1902 after their predecessors, Newton Heath, went bankrupt. However, it is usual to give the date of the club's foundation as 1878 when the dining room committee of the carriage and waggon works of the Lancashire and Yorkshire Railway Company formed Newton Heath L and YR Cricket and Football Club. They won the Manchester Cup in 1886 and as Newton Heath FC were admitted to the Second Division in 1892.

Old Trafford, Sir Matt Busby Way, Manchester M16 0RA.

Telephone: (0161) 868 8000.

Fax: (0161) 868 8804.

Ticket Office: 0870 442 1968.

Website: www.manutd.com

Email: enquiries@manutd.co.uk

Ground Capacity: 76,212.

Record Attendance: 76,962 Wolverhampton W v Grimsby T, FA Cup semi-final, 25 March 1939.
Club Record Attendance: 73,006 v Charlton Ath, Premier League, 7 May 2006.

Pitch Measurements: 105m × 68m.

Chief Executive: David Gill.

Secretary: Kenneth R. Merrett.

Manager: Sir Alex Ferguson CBE.

Assistant Manager: Carlos Queiroz.

Physio: Robert Swire.

Colours: Red shirts, white shorts, black stockings.

Change Colours: Blue shirts, blue shorts, blue stockings.

Year Formed: 1878 as Newton Heath LYR; 1902, Manchester United.

Turned Professional: 1885. ***Ltd Co.:*** 1907.

Previous Name: 1880, Newton Heath; 1902, Manchester United.

Club Nickname: 'Red Devils'.

Previous Grounds: 1880, North Road, Monsall Road; 1893, Bank Street; 1910, Old Trafford (played at Maine Road 1941–49).

First Football League Game: 3 September 1892, Division 1, v Blackburn R (a) L 3–4 – Warner; Clements, Brown; Perrins, Stewart, Erentz; Farman (1), Coupar (1), Donaldson (1), Carson, Mathieson.

HONOURS

FA Premier League – Champions 1992–93, 1993–94, 1995–96, 1996–97, 1998–99, 1999–2000, 2000–01, 2002–03; Runners-up 1994–95, 1997–98, 2005–06.

Football League: Division 1 – Champions 1907–08, 1910–11, 1951–52, 1955–56, 1956–57, 1964–65, 1966–67; Runners-up 1946–47, 1947–48, 1948–49, 1950–51, 1958–59, 1963–64, 1967–68, 1979–80, 1987–88, 1991–92. Division 2 – Champions 1935–36, 1974–75; Runners-up 1896–97, 1905–06, 1924–25, 1937–38.

FA Cup: Winners 1909, 1948, 1963, 1977, 1983, 1985, 1990, 1994, 1996, 1999, 2004; Runners-up 1957, 1958, 1976, 1979, 1995, 2005.

Football League Cup: Winners 1992, 2006; Runners-up 1983, 1991, 1994, 2003.

European Competitions: *European Cup:* 1956–57 (s-f), 1957–58 (s-f), 1965–66 (s-f), 1967–68 (winners), 1968–69 (s-f). *Champions League:* 1993–94, 1994–95, 1996–97 (s-f), 1997–98, 1998–99 (winners), 1999–2000, 2000–01, 2001–02 (s-f), 2002–03, 2003–04, 2004–05, 2005–06. *European Cup-Winners' Cup:* 1963–64, 1977–78, 1983–84, 1990–91 (winners). 1991–92. *Inter Cities Fairs Cup:* 1964–65. *UEFA Cup:* 1976–77, 1980–81, 1982–83, 1984–85, 1992–93, 1995–96. *Super Cup:* 1991 (winners), 1999 (runners-up). *Inter-Continental Cup:* 1999 (winners), 1968 (runners-up).

SKY SPORTS FACT FILE

In the Vol 12 No 1 edition of the weekly *Soccer Star* it referred to Manchester United fielding a 17-year-old debutant on the right-wing in George Best against West Bromwich Albion on 14 September 1963. United won 1–0 with a David Sadler goal.

Record League Victory (as Newton Heath): 10–1 v Wolverhampton W, Division 1, 15 October 1892 – Warner; Mitchell, Clements; Perrins, Stewart (3), Erentz; Farman (1), Hood (1), Donaldson (3), Carson (1), Hendry (1).

Record League Victory (as Manchester U): 9–0 v Ipswich T, FA Premier League, 4 March 1995 – Schmeichel; Keane (1) (Sharpe), Irwin, Bruce (Butt), Kanchelskis, Pallister, Cole (5), Ince (1), McClair, Hughes (2), Giggs.

Record Cup Victory: 10–0 v RSC Anderlecht, European Cup prel. rd 2nd leg, 26 September 1956 – Wood; Foulkes, Byrne; Colman, Jones, Edwards; Berry (1), Whelan (2), Taylor (3), Viollet (4), Pegg.

Record Defeat: 0–7 v Blackburn R, Division 1, 10 April 1926. 0–7 v Aston Villa, Division 1, 27 December 1930. 0–7 v Wolverhampton W, Division 2, 26 December 1931.

Most League Points (2 for a win): 64, Division 1, 1956–57.

Most League Points (3 for a win): 92, FA Premier League, 1993–94.

Most League Goals: 103, Division 1, 1956–57 and 1958–59.

Highest League Scorer in Season: Dennis Viollet, 32, 1959–60.

Most League Goals in Total Aggregate: Bobby Charlton, 199, 1956–73.

Most Capped Player: Bobby Charlton, 106, England.

Most League Appearances: Bobby Charlton, 606, 1956–73.

Youngest League Player: Jeff Whitefoot, 16 years 105 days v Portsmouth, 15 April 1950.

Record Transfer Fee Received: £25,000,000 from Real Madrid for David Beckham, July 2003.

Record Transfer Fee Paid: £30,000,000 to Leeds U for Rio Ferdinand, July 2002 (see also Leeds United page 217).

Football League Record: 1892 Newton Heath elected to Division 1; 1894–1906 Division 2; 1906–22 Division 1; 1922–25 Division 2; 1925–31 Division 1; 1931–36 Division 2; 1936–37 Division 1; 1937–38 Division 2; 1938–74 Division 1; 1974–75 Division 2; 1975–92 Division 1; 1992– FA Premier League.

MANAGERS

J. Ernest Mangnall 1903–12
John Bentley 1912–14
John Robson 1914–21
(Secretary-Manager from 1916)
John Chapman 1921–26
Clarence Hilditch 1926–27
Herbert Bamlett 1927–31
Walter Crickmer 1931–32
Scott Duncan 1932–37
Walter Crickmer 1937–45
(Secretary-Manager)
Matt Busby 1945–69
(continued as General Manager then Director)
Wilf McGuinness 1969–70
Sir Matt Busby 1970–71
Frank O'Farrell 1971–72
Tommy Docherty 1972–77
Dave Sexton 1977–81
Ron Atkinson 1981–86
Sir Alex Ferguson November 1986–

LATEST SEQUENCES

Longest Sequence of League Wins: 14, 15.10.1904 – 3.1.1905.

Longest Sequence of League Defeats: 14, 26.4.1930 – 25.10.1930.

Longest Sequence of League Draws: 6, 30.10.1988 – 27.11.1988.

Longest Sequence of Unbeaten League Matches: 29, 26.12.1998 – 25.9.1999.

Longest Sequence Without a League Win: 16, 19.4.1930 – 25.10.1930.

Successive Scoring Runs: 27 from 11.10.1958.

Successive Non-scoring Runs: 5 from 22.2.1902.

TEN YEAR LEAGUE RECORD

		P	W	D	L	F	A	Pts	Pos
1996-97	PR Lge	38	21	12	5	76	44	75	1
1997-98	PR Lge	38	23	8	7	73	26	77	2
1998-99	PR Lge	38	22	13	3	80	37	79	1
1999-2000	PR Lge	38	28	7	3	97	45	91	1
2000-01	PR Lge	38	24	8	6	79	31	80	1
2001-02	PR Lge	38	24	5	9	87	45	77	3
2002-03	PR Lge	38	25	8	5	74	34	83	1
2003-04	PR Lge	38	23	6	9	64	35	75	3
2004-05	PR Lge	38	22	11	5	58	26	77	3
2005-06	PR Lge	38	25	8	5	72	34	83	2

DID YOU KNOW ?

On 1 April 2006 Ruud Van Nistelrooy scored his 150th goal to place him 8th in the Manchester United goalscoring list. On 26 March Gary Neville had played his 500th match for the club, leaving him 8th in this order of appearances.

MANCHESTER UNITED 2005–06 LEAGUE RECORD

Match No.	*Date*	*Venue*	*Opponents*	*Result*	*H/T Score*	*Lg. Pos.*	*Goalscorers*	*Attendance*
1	Aug 13	A	Everton	W 2-0	1-0	—	Van Nistelrooy [43], Rooney [46]	38,610
2	20	H	Aston Villa	W 1-0	0-0	3	Van Nistelrooy [66]	67,934
3	28	A	Newcastle U	W 2-0	0-0	4	Rooney [66], Van Nistelrooy [90]	52,327
4	Sept 10	H	Manchester C	D 1-1	1-0	4	Van Nistelrooy [45]	67,839
5	18	A	Liverpool	D 0-0	0-0	3		44,917
6	24	H	Blackburn R	L 1-2	0-1	5	Van Nistelrooy [67]	67,765
7	Oct 1	A	Fulham	W 3-2	3-2	4	Van Nistelrooy 2 (1 pen) [17 (p), 45], Rooney [18]	21,862
8	15	A	Sunderland	W 3-1	1-0	3	Rooney [40], Van Nistelrooy [76], Rossi [87]	39,085
9	22	H	Tottenham H	D 1-1	1-0	5	Silvestre [7]	67,856
10	29	A	Middlesbrough	L 1-4	0-3	6	Ronaldo [90]	30,579
11	Nov 6	H	Chelsea	W 1-0	1-0	3	Fletcher [31]	67,864
12	19	A	Charlton Ath	W 3-1	1-0	3	Smith [37], Van Nistelrooy 2 [70, 85]	26,730
13	27	A	West Ham U	W 2-1	0-1	2	Rooney [47], O'Shea [56]	34,755
14	Dec 3	H	Portsmouth	W 3-0	1-0	2	Scholes [20], Rooney [80], Van Nistelrooy [84]	67,684
15	11	H	Everton	D 1-1	1-1	3	Giggs [15]	67,831
16	14	H	Wigan Ath	W 4-0	2-0	—	Ferdinand [30], Rooney 2 [35, 55], Van Nistelrooy (pen) [70]	67,793
17	17	A	Aston Villa	W 2-0	1-0	2	Van Nistelrooy [10], Rooney [51]	37,128
18	26	H	WBA	W 3-0	2-0	2	Scholes [35], Ferdinand [45], Van Nistelrooy [63]	67,972
19	28	A	Birmingham C	D 2-2	1-1	2	Van Nistelrooy [5], Rooney [54]	28,459
20	31	H	Bolton W	W 4-1	2-1	2	N'Gotty (og) [8], Saha [44], Ronaldo 2 [68, 90]	67,858
21	Jan 3	A	Arsenal	D 0-0	0-0	—		38,313
22	14	A	Manchester C	L 1-3	0-2	2	Van Nistelrooy [76]	47,192
23	22	H	Liverpool	W 1-0	0-0	2	Ferdinand [90]	67,874
24	Feb 1	A	Blackburn R	L 3-4	1-3	—	Saha [37], Van Nistelrooy 2 [63, 68]	25,484
25	4	H	Fulham	W 4-2	3-2	2	Bocanegra (og) [6], Ronaldo 2 [14, 86], Saha [23]	67,844
26	11	A	Portsmouth	W 3-1	3-0	2	Van Nistelrooy [18], Ronaldo 2 [38, 45]	20,206
27	Mar 6	A	Wigan Ath	W 2-1	0-0	—	Ronaldo [74], Chimbonda (og) [90]	23,574
28	12	H	Newcastle U	W 2-0	2-0	2	Rooney 2 [8, 12]	67,858
29	18	A	WBA	W 2-1	1-0	2	Saha 2 [16, 64]	27,623
30	26	H	Birmingham C	W 3-0	2-0	2	Giggs 2 [3, 15], Rooney [83]	69,070
31	29	H	West Ham U	W 1-0	1-0	—	Van Nistelrooy [45]	69,522
32	Apr 1	A	Bolton W	W 2-1	1-1	2	Saha [33], Van Nistelrooy [79]	27,718
33	9	H	Arsenal	W 2-0	0-0	2	Rooney [54], Park [78]	70,908
34	14	H	Sunderland	D 0-0	0-0	—		72,519
35	17	A	Tottenham H	W 2-1	2-0	2	Rooney 2 [8, 36]	36,141
36	29	A	Chelsea	L 0-3	0-1	2		42,219
37	May 1	H	Middlesbrough	D 0-0	0-0	—		69,531
38	7	H	Charlton Ath	W 4-0	3-0	2	Saha [19], Ronaldo [23], Euell (og) [35], Richardson [58]	73,006

Final League Position: 2

GOALSCORERS

League (72): Van Nistelrooy 21 (2 pens), Rooney 16, Ronaldo 9, Saha 7, Ferdinand 3, Giggs 3, Scholes 2, Fletcher 1, O'Shea 1, Park 1, Richardson 1, Rossi 1, Silvestre 1, Smith 1, own goals 4.
Carling Cup (17): Saha 6, Ronaldo 2 (1 pen), Rooney 2, Ebanks-Blake 1, Miller 1, O'Shea 1, Park 1, Richardson 1, Rossi 1, Van Nistelrooy 1.
FA Cup (8): Richardson 3, Rossi 2, Saha 2, Giggs 1.
Champions League (9): Heinze 2, Van Nistelrooy 2, Giggs 1, Richardson 1, Ronaldo 1, Rooney 1, Scholes 1.

Van der Sar E 38	Neville G 24 + 1	O'Shea J 34	Keane R 4 + 1	Ferdinand R 37	Silvestre M 30 + 3	Fletcher D 23 + 4	Scholes P 18 + 2	Van Nistelrooy R 28 + 7	Rooney W 34 + 2	Park J 23 + 10	Heinze G 2 + 2	Smith A 15 + 6	Richardson K 12 + 10	Ronaldo C 24 + 9	Giggs R 22 + 5	Bardsley P 3 + 5	Pique G 1 + 2	Rossi G 1 + 4	Miller L — + 1	Brown W 17 + 2	Saha L 12 + 7	Solskjaer O — + 3	Evra P 7 + 4	Vidic N 9 + 2	Howard T — + 1	*Match No.*
1	2	3	4	5	6	7^1	8^2	9	10	11^3	12	13	14													1
1	2	3^1	4	5	6	7	8	9	10^2	11^3	12	13		14												2
1		2	4	5	6	7^2	8	9	10	12	3	13		11^1												3
1		2	12	5	6	7^1	8	9	10	11^3	3	4^2	13		14											4
1		2	4^3	5	6	12	8	9	10^1	13		7	3	11^2	14											5
1		2^3		5	6	7^1	8	9	12	10^2		4	3	11	13	14										6
1		2		5	6	7	12	9^1	10	11		4	3^3	13	8^2	14										7
1		3^1		5	6		8	9^2	10	7		4		11^3		2	12	13	14							8
1		3		5	6	7^1	8	9	10	11		4		12		2^2		13								9
1		3		5^3	6	7	8	9	10	11^1		4	13	12		2^2				14						10
1		2		5	3	7	8	9^1	10	12		4		11						6						11
1		2		5	3	7^3	8	9^2	10	12		4	13	11^1		14				6						12
1	12	3		5	6^1	7	8	9^2	10	11		4	13							2						13
1		3^2		5	6		8	9	10	7^3		4	13	12	11^1					2	14					14
1	2			5	6	12	8		10	7^2		4^1	3^3	13	11			14			9					15
1	2	3		5^3		7	8^1	9	10	12		4		13	11^2	14				6						16
1	2	3		5		7	8	9	10	4				12	11^1					6						17
1	2	3		5		7	8^1	9^3	10	4		12	13		11					6^2	14					18
1	2	6		5		7	8	9	10	12		4^1	3^2	11^3	13							14				19
1	2	4		5	6	8^3		12	10^2	13			3	7	11		14				9^1					20
1	2	6		5	3	8		9	10	12				7	11^1					4						21
1	2	4^2		5	6	8^3		9	10			12	13	7■	11						14		3^1			22
1	2	6^1		5		8		9	10				11		7					4	12		3			23
1	2			4■	12	8		13	10				11^2	7						5^1	9		3	6		24
1	2^3				6			9	12	8^1		4	11	7		13				5	10		3^2	14		25
1^G				5	3	8		9	10^2	4		12		7	11^1					2	13			6	15	26
1	2	6		5	3^2			12	10	8^1				7	11					4	9		13			27
1	2	6		5	3^2			12	10	8				7^1	11					4	9		13			28
1	2	4		5	3	12			10				8^1	7	11						9			6		29
1	2	4		5	3	12		13	10	14			8^3	7	11^1						9^2			6		30
1		2		5	12	8^2		9	10	11				7^3	13		4				14		3^1	6		31
1	2	4		5	3	8^1		12	10	13				7^2	11						9			6		32
1	2	4		5	3			9^1	10	8^2				7	11						12		13	6		33
1	2	6^2		5	12			9	10	8				7	11					4		13	3^1			34
1	2	4		5	3			9	10	8				7^1	11					12				6		35
1	2	4		5	3			12	10^3	8			13	7^1	11^2						9		14	6		36
1	2	6		5	3			9		8^1			13	12	7			14		4	10^3		11^2			37
1	2^2	6^1		5	3		12						8	7	11			9		4	10^3	14		13		38

FA Cup

Third Round	Burton Alb	(a)	0-0
		(h)	5-0
Fourth Round	Wolverhampton W	(a)	3-0
Fifth Round	Liverpool	(a)	0-1

Carling Cup

Third Round	Barnet	(h)	4-1
Fourth Round	WBA	(h)	3-1
Quarter-Final	Birmingham C	(a)	3-1
Semi-Final	Blackburn R	(a)	1-1
		(h)	2-1
Final	Wigan Ath		4-0
(at Millennium Stadium)			

Champions League

Third Qualifying Round			
	Debrecen	(h)	3-0
		(a)	3-0
Group D	Villarreal	(a)	0-0
	Benfica	(h)	2-1
	Lille	(h)	0-0
		(a)	0-1
	Villarreal	(h)	0-0
	Benfica	(a)	1-2

MANSFIELD TOWN FL Championship 2

FOUNDATION

The club was formed as Mansfield Wesleyans in 1897, and changed their name to Mansfield Wesley in 1906 and Mansfield Town in 1910. This was after the Mansfield Wesleyan Chapel trustees had requested that the club change its name as 'it has no longer had any connection with either the chapel or school'. The new club participated in the Notts and Derby District League, but in the following season 1911–12 joined the Central Alliance.

Field Mill Ground, Quarry Lane, Mansfield, Notts NG18 5DA.

Telephone: 0870 756 3160.

Fax: (01623) 482 495.

Ticket Office: 0870 756 3160.

Website: www.mansfieldtown.net

Email: mtfc@stags.plus.com

Ground Capacity: 9,365.

Record Attendance: 24,467 v Nottingham F, FA Cup 3rd rd, 10 January 1953.

Pitch Measurements: 114yd × 70yd.

Chairman: Peter Lee.

Chief Executive: Keith Haslam.

Secretary: Sharon Roberts.

Manager: Peter Shirtliff.

Assistant Manager: TBC.

Physio: Paul Madin IIST, Sports Therapy Dip.

Colours: Amber shirts with royal blue trim, royal blue shorts with amber side stripe, amber stockings.

Change Colours: Navy blue shirts with gold piping, white shorts with navy blue side stripe, white stockings or navy blue stockings.

Year Formed: 1897.

Turned Professional: 1906.

Ltd Co.: 1922.

Previous Name: 1897, Mansfield Wesleyans; 1906, Mansfield Wesley; 1910, Mansfield Town.

Previous Grounds: 1897–99, Westfield Lane; 1899–1901, Ratcliffe Gate; 1901–12, Newgate Lane; 1912–16, Ratcliffe Gate; Field Mill.

Club Nickname: 'The Stags'.

First Football League Game: 29 August 1931, Division 3 (S), v Swindon T (h) W 3–2 – Wilson; Clifford, England; Wake, Davis, Blackburn; Gilhespy, Readman (1), Johnson, Broom (2), Baxter.

Record League Victory: 9–2 v Rotherham U, Division 3 (N), 27 December 1932 – Wilson; Anthony, England; Davies, S. Robinson, Slack; Prior, Broom, Readman (3), Hoyland (3), Bowater (3).

HONOURS

Football League: Division 2 best season: 21st, 1977–78; Division 3 – Champions 1976–77; Promoted to Division 2 (3rd) 2001–02; Division 4 – Champions 1974–75; Division 3 (N) – Runners-up 1950–51.

FA Cup: best season: 6th rd, 1969.

Football League Cup: best season: 5th rd, 1976.

Freight Rover Trophy: Winners 1987.

SKY SPORTS FACT FILE

In 1961–62 former Derby County and Coventry City centre-forward Ray Straw joined Mansfield Town and was able to claim to have scored goals in six different divisions of the Football League including the North and South sections of Division Three.

Record Cup Victory: 8–0 v Scarborough (a), FA Cup 1st rd, 22 November 1952 – Bramley; Chessell, Bradley; Field, Plummer, Lewis; Scott, Fox (3), Marron (2), Sid Watson (1), Adam (2).

Record Defeat: 1–8 v Walsall, Division 3 (N), 19 January 1933.

Most League Points (2 for a win): 68, Division 4, 1974–75.

Most League Points (3 for a win): 81, Division 4, 1985–86.

Most League Goals: 108, Division 4, 1962–63.

Highest League Scorer in Season: Ted Harston, 55, Division 3 (N), 1936–37.

Most League Goals in Total Aggregate: Harry Johnson, 104, 1931–36.

Most League Goals in One Match: 7, Ted Harston v Hartlepools U, Division 3N, 23 January 1937.

Most Capped Player: John McClelland, 6 (53), Northern Ireland.

Most League Appearances: Rod Arnold, 440, 1970–83.

Youngest League Player: Cyril Poole, 15 years 351 days v New Brighton, 27 February 1937.

Record Transfer Fee Received: £655,000 from Tottenham H for Colin Calderwood, July 1993.

Record Transfer Fee Paid: £150,000 to Carlisle U for Lee Peacock, October 1997; £150,000 to Wolverhampton W for Colin Larkin, July 2002.

Football League Record: 1931 Elected to Division 3 (S); 1932–37 Division 3 (N); 1937–47 Division 3 (S); 1947–58 Division 3 (N); 1958–60 Division 3; 1960–63 Division 4; 1963–72 Division 3; 1972–75 Division 4; 1975–77 Division 3; 1977–78 Division 2; 1978–80 Division 3; 1980–86 Division 4; 1986–91 Division 3; 1991–92 Division 4; 1992–93 Division 2; 1993–2002 Division 3; 2002–03 Division 2; 2003–04 Division 3; 2004– FL2.

MANAGERS

John Baynes 1922–25
Ted Davison 1926–28
Jack Hickling 1928–33
Henry Martin 1933–35
Charlie Bell 1935
Harold Wightman 1936
Harold Parkes 1936–38
Jack Poole 1938–44
Lloyd Barke 1944–45
Roy Goodall 1945–49
Freddie Steele 1949–51
George Jobey 1952–53
Stan Mercer 1953–55
Charlie Mitten 1956–58
Sam Weaver 1958–60
Raich Carter 1960–63
Tommy Cummings 1963–67
Tommy Eggleston 1967–70
Jock Basford 1970–71
Danny Williams 1971–74
Dave Smith 1974–76
Peter Morris 1976–78
Billy Bingham 1978–79
Mick Jones 1979–81
Stuart Boam 1981–83
Ian Greaves 1983–89
George Foster 1989–93
Andy King 1993–96
Steve Parkin 1996–99
Bill Dearden 1999–2002
Stuart Watkiss 2002
Keith Curle 2002–05
Carlton Palmer 2005
Peter Shirtliff November 2005–

LATEST SEQUENCES

Longest Sequence of League Wins: 7, 13.9.1991 – 26.10.1991.

Longest Sequence of League Defeats: 7, 18.1.1947 – 15.3.1947.

Longest Sequence of League Draws: 5, 18.10.1986 – 22.11.1986.

Longest Sequence of Unbeaten League Matches: 20, 14.2.1976 – 21.8.1976.

Longest Sequence Without a League Win: 14, 25.3.2000 – 2.9.2000.

Successive Scoring Runs: 27 from 1.10.1962.

Successive Non-scoring Runs: 8 from 25.3.2000.

TEN YEAR LEAGUE RECORD

		P	*W*	*D*	*L*	*F*	*A*	*Pts*	*Pos*
1996-97	Div 3	46	16	16	14	47	45	64	11
1997-98	Div 3	46	16	17	13	64	55	65	12
1998-99	Div 3	46	19	10	17	60	58	67	8
1999-2000	Div 3	46	16	8	22	50	65	56	17
2000-01	Div 3	46	15	13	18	64	72	68	13
2001-02	Div 3	46	24	7	15	72	60	79	3
2002-03	Div 2	46	12	8	26	66	97	44	23
2003-04	Div 3	46	22	9	15	76	62	75	5
2004-05	FL 2	46	15	15	16	56	56	60	13
2005-06	FL 2	46	13	15	18	59	66	54	16

DID YOU KNOW ?

Chris Staniforth had five different spells with Mansfield Town inside and outside the Football League, scored 152 League and Cup goals in only 160 matches and with service for Oldham Athletic and Notts County appeared in all four divisions to 1931–32.

MANSFIELD TOWN 2005–06 LEAGUE RECORD

Match No.	*Date*	*Venue*	*Opponents*	*Result*		*H/T Score*	*Lg. Pos.*	*Goalscorers*	*Attendance*
1	Aug 6	A	Stockport Co	D	2-2	2-0	—	Dawson [22], Birchall [31]	4970
2	9	H	Rushden & D	L	0-1	0-1	—		3402
3	13	H	Torquay U	W	3-0	2-0	7	Rundle [15], Peers [43], Brown [82]	2632
4	20	A	Peterborough U	L	0-2	0-0	14		4056
5	27	A	Boston U	D	2-2	1-2	16	Barker (pen) [26], Brown [69]	2848
6	29	H	Notts Co	L	2-3	1-1	18	Barker [15], Jelleyman [60]	6444
7	Sept 2	A	Chester C	L	1-3	0-1	—	John-Baptiste [67]	3079
8	10	H	Darlington	D	2-2	1-1	21	Brown 2 [9, 64]	2803
9	17	A	Rochdale	L	0-2	0-1	22		2965
10	24	H	Wycombe W	L	2-3	0-3	23	Barker (pen) [66], Brown [75]	3237
11	27	A	Macclesfield T	D	1-1	0-1	—	Birchall [49]	1576
12	Oct 1	A	Leyton Orient	L	1-3	0-1	24	Coke [66]	4164
13	7	H	Shrewsbury T	W	4-0	1-0	—	Coke [6], Rundle [65], Barker [69], Uhlenbeek [71]	3334
14	15	A	Carlisle U	L	0-1	0-0	24		5293
15	22	H	Barnet	W	4-0	1-0	22	Barker 2 (1 pen) [11 (p), 83], Brown [65], Rundle [69]	2809
16	29	A	Cheltenham T	W	2-0	1-0	20	Barker [29], Brown [68]	3033
17	Nov 11	H	Bury	L	0-3	0-2	—		4147
18	26	H	Stockport Co	W	2-1	2-0	20	Peers [26], Barker [31]	2994
19	Dec 6	A	Wrexham	L	1-4	1-0	—	Barker (pen) [41]	3421
20	10	A	Rushden & D	W	2-1	1-0	20	Brown [19], Coke [50]	2477
21	17	H	Peterborough U	D	0-0	0-0	20		3891
22	26	A	Northampton T	L	0-1	0-0	21		6112
23	28	H	Bristol R	D	3-3	2-2	21	Arnold [14], Rundle [25], Russell [74]	2357
24	31	A	Oxford U	W	2-1	0-1	20	Day 2 [61, 79]	4005
25	Jan 2	H	Lincoln C	D	0-0	0-0	19		4946
26	14	A	Grimsby T	L	1-2	0-1	21	Barker (pen) [79]	4506
27	17	A	Shrewsbury T	D	0-0	0-0	—		3747
28	21	H	Rochdale	W	1-0	1-0	18	Reet [40]	3018
29	24	H	Chester C	L	1-2	0-0	—	Reet [51]	3219
30	28	A	Darlington	L	0-4	0-1	19		4282
31	Feb 4	H	Macclesfield T	D	1-1	0-0	20	Rundle [56]	2901
32	11	A	Wycombe W	D	2-2	2-0	20	Hjelde [27], Barker [33]	5041
33	14	H	Grimsby T	W	2-1	2-0	—	Barker [19], Coke [40]	3053
34	18	H	Wrexham	D	2-2	0-0	17	Barker 2 (1 pen) [64 (p), 67]	3139
35	25	A	Torquay U	W	2-0	1-0	15	Reet [11], Brown [83]	2494
36	Mar 4	A	Notts Co	D	2-2	0-1	15	Wilson [61], Barker [64]	9779
37	11	H	Boston U	W	5-0	1-0	13	Barker [43], Greaves (og) [47], Reet [51], Uhlenbeek [62], Brown (pen) [83]	3121
38	18	H	Northampton T	W	1-0	0-0	12	Barker [65]	3985
39	25	A	Bristol R	L	0-2	0-2	12		5253
40	Apr 1	H	Oxford U	W	1-0	0-0	12	Reet [84]	3480
41	8	A	Lincoln C	D	1-1	0-0	13	Russell [90]	6062
42	15	H	Leyton Orient	L	0-1	0-0	14		4763
43	17	A	Barnet	L	0-1	0-1	15		2784
44	22	H	Carlisle U	D	1-1	0-0	15	Barker [63]	4488
45	29	A	Bury	D	0-0	0-0	15		3105
46	May 6	H	Cheltenham T	L	0-5	0-2	16		3728

Final League Position: 16

GOALSCORERS

League (59): Barker 18 (6 pens), Brown 10 (1 pen), Reet 5, Rundle 5, Coke 4, Birchall 2, Day 2, Peers 2, Russell 2, Uhlenbeek 2, Arnold 1, Dawson 1, Hjelde 1, Jelleyman 1, John-Baptiste 1, Wilson 1, own goal 1.
Carling Cup (4): Barker 1, Brown 1, Coke 1, Jelleyman 1.
FA Cup (7): Barker 4 (1 pen), Birchall 1, Brown 1, Coke 1.
Football League Trophy (0).

Pressman K 41	Peers G 12 + 1	Jelleyman G 33 + 1	Palmer C 1	Day R 21	Hjelde J 30 + 1	Dawson S 31 + 9	McLachlan F 7 + 1	Barker R 41 + 2	Birchall A 15 + 16	Tipton M 4	Coke G 33 + 7	Rundle A 27 + 8	Uhlenbeek G 28 + 12	Buxton J 36 + 3	Beardsley C 2 + 1	Brown S 15 + 14	White J 5	John-Baptiste A 40 + 1	Talbot J 6	Lloyd C 3 + 9	Littlejohn A — + 7	D'Laryea J 29	Russell A 7 + 11	Arnold N 5 + 3	Reet D 16 + 2	Jacobs K 4 + 1	Wilson L 14 + 1	Match No.
1	2	3	4[1]	5	6	7	8	9	10[2]	11	12	13																1
1	2	3		5	6[1]	7	8	9	10	11[3]		14	4[2]	12		13												2
1	2	3		5		7	8	9[2]	10	11[1]		6[3]	12	4	13	14												3
	2	3		5		7	8	9	4	10[2]		11[1]	12	6[3]		13	1	14										4
1	2[1]	11[2]		5		14		9	13		8		7	4	10[3]	12		6	3									5
1		12			5	7[2]	8	9	4[1]		13		3	14	10[3]	11		6	2									6
1	2	11		5	12	13		9			8[2]	14	7	4[1]		10		6	3[3]									7
1	2	3		5		7[2]		9	12		8	11[1]	4			10		6		13								8
1		11		2	5■		7[1]	9	12		8	13[3]	3			10		6	4[2]		14							9
1	2	3[2]		5		12	7[3]	9	11		8	13	14			10		6	4[1]									10
1	2	11		5		7		9	10		4			3		8[1]		6			12							11
1	2[2]	3			6	7		9	10[3]		8	12	13	5[1]		11		4			14							12
1		3			5	7[1]	12	9			8	11	4[2]	2		10[3]		6		13	14							13
1		3			5	7[3]		9	12		8	11[2]	4	2		10[1]		6		14	13							14
1		3			6	12		9			8	11	2[1]	5		10[2]		4			13	7						15
1		3■			5			9			4	11	7	2		10		6				8						16
1	12				5			9	7		4	11		2		10[2]		6	3[1]		13	8						17
1	2				5	7		9	10[1]		4	11		3				6				8	12					18
1	2[3]	3		5		7[2]		9	10[1]		4		11	13		12		6				8	14					19
1		3		5		12		9			4	11	7[1]	2		10[2]		6				8	13					20
1		3		5		12		9	13		4	11	7[2]	2				6				8	10[1]					21
1		3		5		7			10[3]		4	11[1]	12	2				6		13		8[2]	9	14				22
1		3		5					12		4	11	7	2				6				8	10	9[1]				23
1		3		5		4		12	13		14	11	7[2]	2				6				8	10[1]	9[3]				24
1				5	6	7[3]		12	13		4	11	14	2				3				8	10[1]	9[2]				25
1		3			5	7		9	12		13	11[1]	2	4				6				8[2]	10[3]		14			26
1		3			5	7[2]		9	11[1]		4	12		2				6				8	13		10			27
1		3			5	8		9			4	11	7	2				6					12		10[1]			28
1		3			5	8		9■	12		4	11[2]	7[1]	2		13		6					14		10[3]			29
		3			5	7[1]			8		4	11[3]	12			9[2]	1	6		14				13	10	2		30
1		3						9	12		4	11	7	5				6				8			10[1]	2		31
1		3			6	12		9	13		4	11[3]	7[1]	2								8			10[2]	5	14	32
1		3■			5	7		9			4			2				6		12		8			10[1]		11	33
1					5	7		9			4[3]	11[1]	12	2		13		6		14		8			10[2]		3	34
1					5	7		9				11	3	2		12		6				8			10[1]		4	35
1		3			5	7[1]		9			4		12	2		13		6		14		8			10[2]		11[3]	36
1		3			5	4[2]		9	12		13		7	2		14		6				8			10[3]		11[1]	37
1		3			5	4[1]		9			12		7	2		13		6				8			10[2]		11	38
1		3		6	5	4		9	12		13		7[2]	2		14						8			10[3]		11[1]	39
1					5			9	12		4	11[1]	7	2				6				8			10		3	40
1					5	12		9			4	11[1]	7[2]	2		14		6				8	13		10[3]		3	41
1					5	12		9			4	11[2]	7[1]	2		14		6				8	13		10[3]		3	42
1					5	7[1]		9			4■	11[3]	12	2				6		14		8	10[2]		13■		3	43
				4	5[3]	7		9					2			10[2]	1	6[1]		11		8	12	13		14	3	44
				5		7		9	12		4[2]		13	2			1	6		11[3]		8	14	10[1]			3	45
				5		7[1]		9	10[2]			12	13				1	6		4		8	14	11[3]		3	2	46

FA Cup

First Round	Rotherham U	(a)	4-3
Second Round	Grays Ath	(h)	3-0
Third Round	Newcastle U	(a)	0-1

Carling Cup

First Round	Stoke C	(h)	1-1
Second Round	Southampton	(h)	1-0
Third Round	Millwall	(h)	2-3

Football League Trophy

First Round	Hereford U	(h)	0-1

MIDDLESBROUGH FA Premiership

FOUNDATION

A previous belief that Middlesbrough Football Club was founded at a tripe supper at the Corporation Hotel has proved to be erroneous. In fact, members of Middlesbrough Cricket Club were responsible for forming it at a meeting in the gymnasium of the Albert Park Hotel in 1875.

Riverside Stadium, Middlesbrough TS3 6RS.

Telephone: 0870 421 1986.

Fax: (01642) 757 690.

Ticket Office: 0870 421 1986. ***Hotline:*** 0845 070 1575.

Website: www.mfc.co.uk

Email: enquiries@mfc.co.uk

Ground Capacity: 35,041.

Record Attendance: Ayresome Park: 53,536 v Newcastle U, Division 1, 27 December 1949. Riverside Stadium: 34,814 v Newcastle U, FA Premier League, 5 March 2003.

Pitch Measurements: 105m × 68m.

Chairman: Steve Gibson.

Chief Executive: Keith Lamb.

Secretary: Karen Nelson.

Manager: Gareth Southgate.

Assistant Manager: Malcolm Crosby.

Physios: Grant Downie and Chris Moseley

Colours: Red with white chest band and gold trim.

Change Colours: White with blue chest band.

Year Formed: 1876; re-formed 1986.

Turned Professional: 1889; became amateur 1892, and professional again, 1899.

Ltd Co: 1892.

Club Nickname: 'Boro'.

Previous Grounds: 1877, Old Archery Ground, Albert Park; 1879, Breckon Hill; 1882, Linthorpe Road Ground; 1903, Ayresome Park; 1995, Cellnet Riverside Stadium.

First Football League Game: 2 September 1899, Division 2, v Lincoln C (a) L 0–3 – Smith; Shaw, Ramsey; Allport, McNally, McCracken; Wanless, Longstaffe, Gettins, Page, Pugh.

Record League Victory: 9–0 v Brighton & HA, Division 2, 23 August 1958 – Taylor; Bilcliff, Robinson; Harris (2p), Phillips, Walley; Day, McLean, Clough (5), Peacock (2), Holliday.

Record Cup Victory: 7–0 v Hereford U, Coca-Cola Cup 2nd rd, 1st leg, 18 September 1996 – Miller; Fleming (1), Branco (1), Whyte, Vickers, Whelan, Emerson (1), Mustoe, Stamp, Juninho, Ravanelli (4).

HONOURS

Football League: Division 1 – Champions 1994–95; Runners-up 1997–98; Division 2 – Champions 1926–27, 1928–29, 1973–74; Runners-up 1901–02, 1991–92; Division 3 – Runners-up 1966–67, 1986–87.

FA Cup: Runners-up 1997.

Football League Cup: Winners 2004; Runners-up 1997, 1998.

Amateur Cup: Winners 1895, 1898.

Anglo-Scottish Cup: Winners 1976.

Zenith Data Systems Cup: Runners-up 1990.

European Competitions: *UEFA Cup:* 2004–05, 2005–06 (runners-up).

SKY SPORTS FACT FILE

On 18 April 1931 Middlesbrough beat Blackburn Rovers 5–4 at Ewood Park after trailing 3–2 at the interval. Free-scoring centre-forward George Camsell scored twice to hoist his 200th career League goal having rattled in his first 20 for Durham City.

Record Defeat: 0–9 v Blackburn R, Division 2, 6 November 1954.

Most League Points (2 for a win): 65, Division 2, 1973–74.

Most League Points (3 for a win): 94, Division 3, 1986–87.

Most League Goals: 122, Division 2, 1926–27.

Highest League Scorer in Season: George Camsell, 59, Division 2, 1926–27 (Second Division record).

Most League Goals in Total Aggregate: George Camsell, 325, 1925–39.

Most League Goals in One Match: 5, Andy Wilson v Nottingham F, Division 1, 6 October 1923; 5, George Camsell v Manchester C, Division 2, 25 December 1926; 5, George Camsell v Aston Villa, Division 1, 9 September 1935; 5, Brian Clough v Brighton & HA, Division 2, 22 August 1958.

Most Capped Player: Wilf Mannion, 26, England.

Most League Appearances: Tim Williamson, 563, 1902–23.

Youngest League Player: Stephen Bell, 16 years 323 days v Southampton, 30 January 1982; Sam Lawrie, 16 years 323 days v Arsenal, 3 November 1951.

Record Transfer Fee Received: £12,000,000 from Atletico Madrid for Juninho, July 1997.

Record Transfer Fee Paid: £8,150,000 to Empoli for Massimo Maccarone, August 2002.

Football League Record: 1899 Elected to Division 2; 1902–24 Division 1; 1924–27 Division 2; 1927–28 Division 1; 1928–29 Division 2; 1929–54 Division 1; 1954–66 Division 2; 1966–67 Division 3; 1967–74 Division 2; 1974–82 Division 1; 1982–86 Division 2; 1986–87 Division 3; 1987–88 Division 2; 1988–89 Division 1; 1989–92 Division 2; 1992–93 FA Premier League; 1993–95 Division 1; 1995–97 FA Premier League; 1997–98 Division 1; 1998– FA Premier League.

MANAGERS

John Robson 1899–1905
Alex Mackie 1905–06
Andy Aitken 1906–09
J. Gunter 1908–10
(Secretary-Manager)
Andy Walker 1910–11
Tom McIntosh 1911–19
Jimmy Howie 1920–23
Herbert Bamlett 1923–26
Peter McWilliam 1927–34
Wilf Gillow 1934–44
David Jack 1944–52
Walter Rowley 1952–54
Bob Dennison 1954–63
Raich Carter 1963–66
Stan Anderson 1966–73
Jack Charlton 1973–77
John Neal 1977–81
Bobby Murdoch 1981–82
Malcolm Allison 1982–84
Willie Maddren 1984–86
Bruce Rioch 1986–90
Colin Todd 1990–91
Lennie Lawrence 1991–94
Bryan Robson 1994–2001
Steve McClaren 2001–06
Gareth Southgate June 2006–

LATEST SEQUENCES

Longest Sequence of League Wins: 9, 16.2.1974 – 6.4.1974.

Longest Sequence of League Defeats: 8, 26.12.1995 – 17.2.1996.

Longest Sequence of League Draws: 8, 3.4.1971 – 1.5.1971.

Longest Sequence of Unbeaten League Matches: 24, 8.9.1973 – 19.1.1974.

Longest Sequence Without a League Win: 19, 3.10.1981 – 6.3.1982.

Successive Scoring Runs: 26 from 21.9.1946.

Successive Non-scoring Runs: 4 from 24.11.1923.

TEN YEAR LEAGUE RECORD

		P	*W*	*D*	*L*	*F*	*A*	*Pts*	*Pos*
1996-97	PR Lge	38	10	12	16	51	60	39	19
1997-98	Div 1	46	27	10	9	77	41	91	2
1998-99	PR Lge	38	12	15	11	48	54	51	9
1999-2000	PR Lge	38	14	10	14	46	52	52	12
2000-01	PR Lge	38	9	15	14	44	44	42	14
2001-02	PR Lge	38	12	9	17	35	47	45	12
2002-03	PR Lge	38	13	10	15	48	44	49	11
2003-04	PR Lge	38	13	9	16	44	52	48	11
2004-05	PR Lge	38	14	13	11	53	46	55	7
2005-06	PR Lge	38	12	9	17	48	58	45	14

DID YOU KNOW ?

In May 1948 Middlesbrough signed goalkeeper Rolando Ugolini from Celtic, who stipulated that he should not be transferred subsequently to another Scottish club. In fact he later played for Wrexham in Wales before joining Dundee United!

MIDDLESBROUGH 2005–06 LEAGUE RECORD

Match No.	Date	Venue	Opponents	Result		H/T Score	Lg. Pos.	Goalscorers	Attendance
1	Aug 13	H	Liverpool	D	0-0	0-0	—		31,908
2	20	A	Tottenham H	L	0-2	0-0	16		35,844
3	23	A	Birmingham C	W	3-0	2-0	—	Viduka 2 [14, 45], Queudrue [71]	27,998
4	28	H	Charlton Ath	L	0-3	0-1	12		26,206
5	Sept 10	H	Arsenal	W	2-1	1-0	7	Yakubu [40], Maccarone [59]	28,075
6	18	A	Wigan Ath	D	1-1	1-0	8	Yakubu [14]	16,641
7	25	H	Sunderland	L	0-2	0-1	11		29,583
8	Oct 2	A	Aston Villa	W	3-2	1-0	10	Yakubu 2 (1 pen) [33, 88 (p)], Boateng [64]	29,719
9	15	H	Portsmouth	D	1-1	0-0	10	Yakubu [54]	26,551
10	23	A	West Ham U	L	1-2	0-0	12	Queudrue [87]	34,612
11	29	H	Manchester U	W	4-1	3-0	11	Mendieta 2 [2, 78], Hasselbaink [25], Yakubu (pen) [45]	30,579
12	Nov 6	A	Everton	L	0-1	0-1	13		34,349
13	20	H	Fulham	W	3-2	0-1	11	Morrison [64], Yakubu [76], Hasselbaink [84]	27,599
14	27	H	WBA	D	2-2	1-1	10	Viduka [12], Yakubu (pen) [66]	27,041
15	Dec 3	A	Chelsea	L	0-1	0-0	10		41,666
16	10	A	Liverpool	L	0-2	0-0	13		43,510
17	18	H	Tottenham H	D	3-3	2-1	13	Yakubu 2 [30, 43], Queudrue [69]	27,614
18	26	H	Blackburn R	L	0-2	0-1	13		29,881
19	31	H	Manchester C	D	0-0	0-0	14		28,022
20	Jan 2	A	Newcastle U	D	2-2	0-1	16	Yakubu [54], Hasselbaink [87]	52,302
21	14	A	Arsenal	L	0-7	0-4	17		38,186
22	21	H	Wigan Ath	L	2-3	0-2	17	Hasselbaink [56], Yakubu [66]	27,208
23	31	A	Sunderland	W	3-0	2-0	—	Pogatetz [19], Parnaby [31], Hasselbaink [71]	31,675
24	Feb 4	H	Aston Villa	L	0-4	0-2	17		27,299
25	11	H	Chelsea	W	3-0	2-0	16	Rochemback [2], Downing [45], Yakubu [68]	31,037
26	26	A	WBA	W	2-0	2-0	16	Hasselbaink [17], Wallwark (og) [44]	24,061
27	Mar 4	H	Birmingham C	W	1-0	1-0	15	Viduka [45]	28,141
28	12	A	Charlton Ath	L	1-2	0-0	15	Viduka [81]	24,830
29	18	A	Blackburn R	L	2-3	1-2	16	Viduka [16], Rochemback [62]	18,681
30	26	H	Bolton W	W	4-3	2-1	14	Hasselbaink 2 (1 pen) [8 (p), 47], Viduka [30], Parnaby [90]	25,971
31	Apr 2	A	Manchester C	W	1-0	1-0	14	Cattermole [42]	40,256
32	9	H	Newcastle U	L	1-2	0-2	14	Boateng [79]	31,202
33	15	A	Portsmouth	L	0-1	0-0	14		20,204
34	17	H	West Ham U	W	2-0	1-0	13	Hasselbaink [41], Maccarone (pen) [57]	27,658
35	29	H	Everton	L	0-1	0-0	15		29,224
36	May 1	A	Manchester U	D	0-0	0-0	—		69,531
37	3	A	Bolton W	D	1-1	0-0	—	Johnson [47]	22,733
38	7	A	Fulham	L	0-1	0-0	14		22,434

Final League Position: 14

GOALSCORERS

League (48): Yakubu 13 (3 pens), Hasselbaink 9 (1 pen), Viduka 7, Queudrue 3, Boateng 2, Maccarone 2 (1 pen), Mendieta 2, Parnaby 2, Rochemback 2, Cattermole 1, Downing 1, Johnson 1, Morrison 1, Pogatetz 1, own goal 1.
Carling Cup (3): Hasselbaink 1, Nemeth 1, Viduka 1.
FA Cup (14): Yakubu 4 (1 pen), Hasselbaink 3, Viduka 2, Mendieta 1, Morrison 1, Parnaby 1, Riggott 1, Rochemback 1.
UEFA Cup (20): Viduka 6, Maccarone 5, Hasselbaink 4, Yakubu 2 (1 pen), Boateng 1, Parnaby 1, Riggott 1.

Schwarzer M 27	Reiziger M 4	Queudrue F 26 + 3	Boateng G 25 + 1	Ehiogu U 16 + 2	Southgate G 24	Mendieta G 15 + 2	Parlour R 11 + 2	Hasselbaink J 12 + 10	Yakubu A 29 + 5	Downing S 11 + 1	Viduka M 19 + 8	Nemeth S 1 + 4	Bates M 12 + 4	Doriva 19 + 8	Morrison J 21 + 3	Maccarone M 6 + 11	Job J — + 1	Pogatetz E 21 + 3	Xavier A 4	Graham D 1 + 2	Johnson A 8 + 5	Rochemback F 22	Jones B 9	Riggott C 22	Parnaby S 19 + 1	Kennedy J 1 + 2	Cattermole L 10 + 4	Taylor A 7 + 6	Wheater D 4 + 2	Davies A 4 + 8	McMahon T 3	Christie M 3 + 3	Turnbull R 2	Cooper C — + 1	Craddock T — + 1	Walker J — + 1	*Match No.*
1	2	3	4	5■	6	7[1]	8	9[2]	10[3]	11	12	13	14																								1
1	2	3	4		6	7[2]	8	9	10[3]	11	14		5[1]	12	13																						2
1	2	3	4	5	6		8	9[2]		11	10[3]		12		7[1]	13	14																				3
1	2	3[3]	4	5	6	12[2]	8		9	11	10				7[1]	13		14																			4
1		3	4	5	6		8		10[3]					12		7[1]		13	2	14	9[2]	11															5
1		3	4	5	6				9		10[1]			13	7[2]	12		11	2			8															6
		11	4	5[3]	6		12	13	9[2]		10				7[1]	14		3	2			8	1														7
		12	8		6	7[1]			9			10[2]		4				3	2			11	1	5	13												8
1		11[3]	8		6	14		12	9		13			4		7[2]		3				10[1]		5	2												9
1		12	8		6[1]	7		13	9		14		2	4[3]		10[2]		3				11		5													10
1		11	4			7[3]		9[1]	10			12	6	13	14			3				8[2]		5	2												11
1		3	6	5[2]		7		9	10[1]		12			13	14			11				8[3]		4	2												12
		3	4		6			9[2]	10			12		13	7			11[1]				8	1	5	2												13
1		3[1]	4		6			13	9		10[2]	12		14	7[3]			11				8		5	2												14
1		12	8		6			9[2]	10		13		2	4	7[1]			3				11		5													15
1		3	8	12	6			13	9[1]		10		2	4	7[2]							11		5■													16
1		3	8	5	6				9		10		2	4	7[1]	12						11															17
1		3			6	7[1]		12	9		10			4[3]				11			13	8[2]		5	2	14											18
1		3			6	7		12	9[1]		10		13	4	8	14		11[3]						5	2[2]												19
1					6	7[2]		12	9[1]		10		13	4	8			3						5	2		11										20
						11			9		10[2]		5	6■	7						12	8[1]	1	4	2		13	3[3]	14								21
				12	6		8	13	9	11	10[2]		2[3]					3			14		1	5[1]	4		7										22
1					6	8		9[1]	12	11[2]	10[3]			4				5			13				2		7	3		14							23
1					6	7[3]		9[2]	12	11	10[1]			4		13		5							2		8	3		14							24
1			12		6	8[3]		13	9[2]	11				4	7[1]			3				10		5	2					14							25
1		3	4		6	7[3]		9[2]	10[1]		12					13		11						5	2		8			14							26
1		3	4		6	7[1]			9		10[2]			12		13		11						5	2[3]		8			14							27
1		3		5			8[3]		12		10			4		7[1]		6			9						14	2		13	11[2]						28
1		3	4	5			8[1]		12		10				7			13			9[3]	11		6[2]				14		2							29
1		3	8	5				9[1]	12	13	10				7[3]			6				11[2]			2		14			4							30
		3[2]	4	5					9	11					7[1]							10	1	6	2		8	13		12							31
1		3[3]	8	5					9		12			4	7	13					10[1]	11		6				14		2[2]							32
			8	5					9	11			6[2]	4[3]	7[1]						12	10	1		2			3	13			14					33
1		3					8	9[1]			10[3]		2	6		7					11[2]			5		12		13	4			14					34
				5			8		9					6[2]	7					12	11		1				13	3	4		2	10[1]					35
		3[2]	4				12			11			6		7[3]	9[1]						10	1	5	2		8	13				14					36
		3		5			7		10					6		12					11[2]						8	13	4	14	2[3]	9[1]	1				37
													5		7					10[2]	11					6[1]	8	3	4	2		9[3]	1	12	13	14	38

FA Cup

Third Round	Nuneaton B	(a)	1-1
		(h)	5-2
Fourth Round	Coventry C	(a)	1-1
		(h)	1-0
Fifth Round	Preston NE	(a)	2-0
Sixth Round	Charlton Ath	(a)	0-0
		(h)	4-2
Semi-Final *(at Villa Park)*	West Ham U		0-1

Carling Cup

Third Round	Everton	(a)	1-0
Fourth Round	Crystal Palace	(h)	2-1
Quarter-Final	Blackburn R	(h)	0-1

UEFA Cup

First Round	Xanthi	(h)	2-0
		(a)	0-0
Group D	Grasshoppers	(a)	1-0
	Dnepr	(h)	3-0
	AZ	(a)	0-0
	Litets	(h)	2-0
Third Round	Stuttgart	(a)	2-1
		(h)	0-1
Fourth Round	Roma	(h)	1-0
		(a)	1-2
Quarter-Final	Basle	(a)	0-2
		(h)	4-1
Semi-Final	Steaua	(a)	0-1
		(h)	4-2
Final *(in Eindhoven)*	Sevilla		0-4

MILLWALL FL Championship 1

FOUNDATION

Formed in 1885 as Millwall Rovers by employees of Morton & Co, a jam and marmalade factory in West Ferry Road. The founders were predominantly Scotsmen. Their first headquarters was The Islanders pub in Tooke Street, Millwall. Their first trophy was the East End Cup in 1887.

The Den, Zampa Road, London SE16 3LN.

Telephone: (020) 7232 1222.

Fax: (020) 7231 3663.

Ticket Office: (020) 7231 9999.

Website: www.millwallfc.co.uk

Email: questions@millwallplc.com

Ground Capacity: 20,146.

Record Attendance: 20,093 v Arsenal, FA Cup 3rd rd, 10 January 1994.

Pitch Measurements: 105m × 68m.

Company Chairman: Peter de Savary.

Football Club Chairman: Stewart Till.

Executive Deputy Chairman: Heather Rabbatts.

Chief Executive: Ken Brown

Secretary: Yvonne Haines.

Manager: Nigel Spackman.

Assistant Manager: Willie Donachie.

Physio: Colin Clifford.

Colours: Blue and white shirts, white and blue shorts, blue stockings.

Change Colours: Black shirts with plum, black shorts with plum, black stockings.

Year Formed: 1885. ***Turned Professional:*** 1893. ***Ltd Co.:*** 1894.

Previous Names: 1885, Millwall Rovers; 1889, Millwall Athletic; 1899, Millwall; 1985, Millwall Football & Athletic Company.

Club Nickname: 'The Lions'.

Previous Grounds: 1885, Glengall Road, Millwall; 1886, Back of 'Lord Nelson'; 1890, East Ferry Road; 1901, North Greenwich; 1910, The Den, Cold Blow Lane; 1993, The Den, Bermondsey.

First Football League Game: 28 August 1920, Division 3, v Bristol R (h) W 2–0 – Lansdale; Fort, Hodge; Voisey (1), Riddell, McAlpine; Waterall, Travers, Broad (1), Sutherland, Dempsey.

Record League Victory: 9–1 v Torquay U, Division 3 (S), 29 August 1927 – Lansdale, Tilling, Hill, Amos, Bryant (3), Graham, Chance, Hawkins (3), Landells (1), Phillips (2), Black. 9–1 v Coventry C, Division 3 (S), 19 November 1927 – Lansdale, Fort, Hill, Amos, Collins (1), Graham, Chance, Landells (4), Cock (2), Phillips (2), Black.

HONOURS

Football League: Division 1 best season: 3rd, 1993–94; Division 2 – Champions 1987–88, 2000–01; Division 3 (S) – Champions 1927–28, 1937–38; Runners-up 1952–53; Division 3 – Runners-up 1965–66, 1984–85; Division 4 – Champions 1961–62; Runners-up 1964–65.

FA Cup: Runners-up 2004; Semi-final 1900, 1903, 1937 (first Division 3 side to reach semi-final).

Football League Cup: best season: 5th rd, 1974, 1977, 1995.

Football League Trophy: Winners 1983.

Auto Windscreens Shield: Runners-up 1999.

European Competitions: *UEFA Cup:* 2004–05.

SKY SPORTS FACT FILE

The term Young Lions was certainly an appropriate one for the Millwall half-back line fielded in April 1959 when the trio of Ray White, Dave Harper and Len Vaessen totalled just 55 years between them.

Record Cup Victory: 7–0 v Gateshead, FA Cup 2nd rd, 12 December 1936 – Yuill; Ted Smith, Inns; Brolly, Hancock, Forsyth; Thomas (1), Mangnall (1), Ken Burditt (2), McCartney (2), Thorogood (1).

Record Defeat: 1–9 v Aston Villa, FA Cup 4th rd, 28 January 1946.

Most League Points (2 for a win): 65, Division 3 (S), 1927–28 and Division 3, 1965–66.

Most League Points (3 for a win): 93, Division 2, 2000–01.

Most League Goals: 127, Division 3 (S), 1927–28.

Highest League Scorer in Season: Richard Parker, 37, Division 3 (S), 1926–27.

Most League Goals in Total Aggregate: Teddy Sheringham, 93, 1984–91 and Neil Harris, 93, 1995–2004.

Most League Goals in One Match: 5, Richard Parker v Norwich C, Division 3S, 28 August 1926.

Most Capped Player: Eamonn Dunphy, 22 (23), Republic of Ireland.

Most League Appearances: Barry Kitchener, 523, 1967–82.

Youngest League Player: Moses Ashikodi, 15 years 240 days v Brighton & HA, 22 February 2003.

Record Transfer Fee Received: £2,300,000 from Liverpool for Mark Kennedy, March 1995.

Record Transfer Fee Paid: £800,000 to Derby Co for Paul Goddard, December 1989.

Football League Record: 1920 Original Members of Division 3; 1921 Division 3 (S); 1928–34 Division 2; 1934–38 Division 3 (S); 1938–48 Division 2; 1948–58 Division 3 (S); 1958–62 Division 4; 1962–64 Division 3; 1964–65 Division 4; 1965–66 Division 3; 1966–75 Division 2; 1975–76 Division 3; 1976–79 Division 2; 1979–85 Division 3; 1985–88 Division 2; 1988–90 Division 1; 1990–92 Division 2; 1992–96 Division 1; 1996–2001 Division 2; 2001–04 Division 1; 2004–06 FLC; 2006– FL1.

MANAGERS

F. B. Kidd 1894–99
(Hon. Treasurer/Manager)
E. R. Stopher 1899–1900
(Hon. Treasurer/Manager)
George Saunders 1900–11
(Hon. Treasurer/Manager)
Herbert Lipsham 1911–19
Robert Hunter 1919–33
Bill McCracken 1933–36
Charlie Hewitt 1936–40
Bill Voisey 1940–44
Jack Cock 1944–48
Charlie Hewitt 1948–56
Ron Gray 1956–57
Jimmy Seed 1958–59
Reg Smith 1959–61
Ron Gray 1961–63
Billy Gray 1963–66
Benny Fenton 1966–74
Gordon Jago 1974–77
George Petchey 1978–80
Peter Anderson 1980–82
George Graham 1982–86
John Docherty 1986–90
Bob Pearson 1990
Bruce Rioch 1990–92
Mick McCarthy 1992–96
Jimmy Nicholl 1996–97
John Docherty 1997
Billy Bonds 1997–98
Keith Stevens May 1998–2000
(then Joint Manager)
(*plus* Alan McLeary 1999–2000)
Mark McGhee 2000–03
Dennis Wise 2003–05
Steve Claridge 2005
Colin Lee 2005–06
Nigel Spackman May 2006–

LATEST SEQUENCES

Longest Sequence of League Wins: 10, 10.3.1928 – 25.4.1928.

Longest Sequence of League Defeats: 11, 10.4.1929 – 16.9.1929.

Longest Sequence of League Draws: 5, 22.12.1973 – 12.1.1974.

Longest Sequence of Unbeaten League Matches: 19, 22.8.1959 – 31.10.1959.

Longest Sequence Without a League Win: 20, 26.12.1989 – 5.5.1990.

Successive Scoring Runs: 22 from 8.12.1923.

Successive Non-scoring Runs: 6 from 20.12.1947.

TEN YEAR LEAGUE RECORD

		P	*W*	*D*	*L*	*F*	*A*	*Pts*	*Pos*
1996-97	Div 2	46	16	13	17	50	55	61	14
1997-98	Div 2	46	14	13	19	43	54	55	18
1998-99	Div 2	46	17	11	18	52	59	62	10
1999-2000	Div 2	46	23	13	10	76	50	82	5
2000-01	Div 2	46	28	9	9	89	38	93	1
2001-02	Div 1	46	22	11	13	69	48	77	4
2002-03	Div 1	46	19	9	18	59	69	66	9
2003-04	Div 1	46	18	15	13	55	48	69	10
2004-05	FL C	46	18	12	16	51	45	66	10
2005-06	FL C	46	8	17	21	35	61	40	23

DID YOU KNOW ?

Former Newcastle United left-winger Ken Prior joined Millwall in May 1954. Father George was an ex-Watford and Sheffield Wednesday full-back, uncle Jack an ex-Sunderland winger while Bobby Cowell of Newcastle was his brother-in-law.

MILLWALL 2005–06 LEAGUE RECORD

Match No.	Date	Venue	Opponents	Result		H/T Score	Lg. Pos.	Goalscorers	Attendance
1	Aug 7	A	Leeds U	L	1-2	0-1	—	Hutchison [61]	20,440
2	9	H	Coventry C	D	0-0	0-0	—		8344
3	13	H	Stoke C	L	0-1	0-1	24		8668
4	20	A	Reading	L	0-5	0-4	24		14,225
5	27	H	Ipswich T	L	1-2	0-1	24	May [68]	8277
6	29	A	Luton T	L	1-2	0-1	24	May [46]	8220
7	Sept 10	H	Preston NE	L	1-2	0-1	24	Hutchison [51]	7674
8	13	A	Wolverhampton W	W	2-1	1-1	—	Wright [27], Hayles [90]	21,897
9	17	A	Sheffield W	W	2-1	0-0	22	Hayles [50], Asaba [74]	22,446
10	24	H	Cardiff C	D	0-0	0-0	22		9254
11	27	H	QPR	D	1-1	1-1	—	Hayles [45]	10,322
12	30	A	Hull C	D	1-1	0-0	—	Asaba [61]	18,761
13	Oct 15	A	Norwich C	D	1-1	1-0	23	Williams A [23]	25,095
14	18	H	Sheffield U	L	0-4	0-2	—		9148
15	22	H	Southampton	L	0-2	0-2	24		10,759
16	30	A	Plymouth Arg	D	0-0	0-0	24		11,764
17	Nov 1	A	Burnley	L	1-2	1-0	—	Wright [1]	10,698
18	5	H	Crewe Alex	L	1-3	1-1	24	Hayles (pen) [38]	8120
19	19	A	Sheffield U	D	2-2	1-1	24	Dyer B 2 [34, 55]	22,292
20	22	H	Norwich C	W	1-0	0-0	—	Elliott [70]	7814
21	26	H	Leeds U	L	0-1	0-0	24		8134
22	Dec 3	A	Crystal Palace	D	1-1	1-0	24	May [41]	19,571
23	10	A	Coventry C	L	0-1	0-1	24		16,156
24	17	H	Reading	L	0-2	0-1	24		12,920
25	26	A	Leicester C	D	1-1	1-0	24	McCarthy (og) [28]	22,520
26	28	H	Watford	D	0-0	0-0	24		8450
27	31	A	Brighton & HA	W	2-1	0-1	23	May [46], Simpson [50]	6847
28	Jan 2	H	Derby Co	W	2-1	0-0	23	Elliott [73], Williams M [78]	9523
29	14	A	Preston NE	L	0-2	0-1	23		14,105
30	21	H	Wolverhampton W	D	0-0	0-0	23		9905
31	31	A	Cardiff C	D	1-1	0-1	—	Powel [60]	12,378
32	Feb 4	H	Sheffield W	L	0-1	0-0	23		11,896
33	11	A	QPR	L	0-1	0-0	23		12,355
34	14	H	Hull C	D	1-1	0-0	—	Livermore [80]	7108
35	18	H	Crystal Palace	D	1-1	0-0	22	May [89]	12,296
36	25	A	Stoke C	L	1-2	1-1	22	May [8]	11,340
37	Mar 4	H	Luton T	W	2-1	1-0	22	May [33], Williams M [90]	9871
38	11	A	Ipswich T	D	1-1	0-1	22	Livermore [85]	24,864
39	18	H	Leicester C	L	0-1	0-1	22		10,523
40	25	A	Watford	W	2-0	0-0	22	Asaba [66], May [90]	16,654
41	Apr 1	H	Brighton & HA	L	0-2	0-2	22		13,209
42	8	A	Derby Co	L	0-1	0-1	23		24,415
43	15	H	Plymouth Arg	D	1-1	1-1	24	Williams M [31]	9183
44	17	A	Southampton	L	0-2	0-1	24		22,043
45	22	H	Burnley	W	1-0	1-0	22	Williams M [45]	7780
46	30	A	Crewe Alex	L	2-4	1-1	23	May 2 [15, 58]	5945

Final League Position: 23

GOALSCORERS

League (35): May 10, Hayles 4 (1 pen), Williams M 4, Asaba 3, Dyer B 2, Elliott 2, Hutchison 2, Livermore 2, Wright 2, Powel 1, Simpson 1, Williams A 1, own goal 1.
Carling Cup (9): Dunne 2, Asaba 1, Elliott 1, Fangueiro 1, Hayles 1, Livermore 1, May 1, Robinson 1.
FA Cup (1): Williams M.

Marshall A 29	Dunne A 40	Vincent J 18 + 1	Elliott M 33 + 6	Lawrence M 30 + 1	Phillips M 19 + 3	Serioux A 2 + 3	Morris J 24	Hayles B 21 + 2	Hutchison D 7 + 4	Simpson J 8 + 5	Igoe S 3 + 2	Braniff K 9 + 6	May B 24 + 15	Peeters B — + 2	Fangueiro C 1 + 8	Livermore D 41	Robinson P 29 + 3	Asaba C 17 + 4	Craig T 26 + 2	Wright J 15	Williams A 12	Ifil P 16	Jones P 3	Cogan B 6 + 8	Dyer B 9 + 1	Doyle C 14	Whitbread Z 25	Williams M 8 + 14	Hendry W 2 + 1	Healy J — + 1	Dyer L 2 + 4	Powel B 8 + 4	Cameron C 5	Pooley D — + 1	Robinson T — + 1	Match No.
1	2	3	4^{1}	5	6	7^{2}	8	9	10	11^{3}	12	13	14																							1
1	2	3	4	5	6	7■	8	9^{2}	10	11^{1}				13	12																					2
1	2	3	4^{1}	5	6		8	9	10^{2}	11^{3}	13			12	14	7																				3
1■	2	3	12	5^{3}	6	13	8	9^{1}		11^{2}	7		10			4	14																			4
1	2	3	12		6		8^{1}	9	13	11			14		7^{3}	4	5	10^{2}																		5
1	2	3	4^{3}		6^{1}	14	8	13		12	7^{2}		9			11	5		10																	6
1	2	3	4^{1}		6			10	11	12	7^{2}		9		13	8	5																			7
1	2	3			6	12	8	10^{1}					9			4				11	5	7														8
1	2	3			6		8^{1}	10^{2}	12				9^{3}			4		14	13	11	5	7														9
1	2	3		12	6^{1}		8■	10								4		9		11	5	7														10
1	2	3		6				10	11^{1}				12			4		9		8	5	7														11
1	2	3		6	12			10^{1}	8				13			4		9^{2}		11	5	7														12
1	2^{2}	3	12				8^{1}	10■	13				14			4	6	9^{3}		11	5	7														13
1	2	3	12	4			8^{1}		14	11^{2}			9		13^{3}	6				10	5	7														14
1	2	3^{1}		4			8^{2}	10					9			6	12	13		11	5	7■														15
1	2^{1}		12	4			8	10					13			6	3	9^{2}	14	11	5^{3}	7														16
1■			12	5			8	10	11^{1}				13■			4	6	9^{2}	3	7		2														17
	2		4	5^{1}				10								8	6		3	11		7	1	12	9											18
	2		4					10^{1}				13			12	11	5	14	3	8	6	7^{3}	1		9^{2}											19
	2		4					10		12		9	13			6	5	7^{1}	3	8			1		11^{2}											20
	2		4					10					12				5	8	3		6	7			9^{1}	1	11									21
	2		4				8					12	9			11			3	7	5				10^{1}	1	6									22
	2		4	5■			8					9^{1}				11	6	12		7^{2}					10	1	3	13								23
	2		7		6					11		12	9			8	5		3■						10^{1}	1	4									24
	2		4		6		8			11^{1}		10^{2}	9^{3}			7	3■							13	14	1	5	12								25
	2		4^{1}		12		8					9^{3}	13			11	6		3					7	10^{2}	1	5	14								26
	7			6			8			12		9^{1}	10			4	2		3					13	11^{3}	1	5^{2}	14								27
	2		4	5			8^{1}			12		9^{2}	10			7	6		3					11		1		13								28
			4^{2}	5	6							9^{1}	10		12	11			3					7		1	2	8^{3}	13	14						29
1	2		7	5			8						9			11	4		3								6	10								30
1	2		7	5									9^{2}			8	4^{1}		3			11					6	10			12	13				31
1	2^{1}		7	5			8^{3}					13	12			11	4		3								6	10^{2}			14	9				32
1	2■		7	5								10^{2}	12			11	4		3					8^{3}			6	13			14	9^{1}				33
1			7	5			8^{2}						9			11	4■		3			2^{1}		12			6	13				10				34
1			7	5	4								9			8			3			2^{2}		12			6	13			11^{1}	10				35
1	2		7	5									9^{2}			8	4	10^{1}	3								6	12			11	13				36
1	2^{2}		7	5									9			11	4^{3}	10	3					12			6	13			14		8^{1}			37
1	2		7	5	12											11	4^{1}	9	3■								6	13				10^{2}	8			38
1	2	3^{1}	7	5				12					9			11	4	10^{2}									6	13					8			39
1	2	3	7	5				10^{2}					12			11	4	9^{1}									6	13					8			40
1	2	3^{1}	7	5				10				13	12^{2}			11	4	9^{3}									6	14					8			41
	2	12^{2}	7	5	4		8^{1}						10			11		9^{3}	3					13		1	6					14				42
	2^{1}		7	5	4								10			11		9^{2}	3					12		1	6	8				13				43
	2^{2}		7	5	4^{1}							9	13			11	12		3							1	6	8				10				44
			7		4								9		12		5		3					2		1	6^{2}	8^{3}	11			10^{1}		13	14	45
			7		4								9		12		5		3					2		1	6	8	11			10^{1}				46

FA Cup

Third Round	Everton	(h)	1-1
		(a)	0-1

Carling Cup

First Round	Bristol R	(h)	2-0
Second Round	Yeovil T	(a)	2-1
Third Round	Mansfield T	(a)	3-2
Fourth Round	Birmingham C	(h)	2-2

MILTON KEYNES DONS FL Championship 2

FOUNDATION

Old boys from Central School formed this club as Wimbledon Old Centrals in 1889. Their earliest successes were in the Clapham League before switching to the Southern Suburban League in 1902.

The National Hockey Stadium, Silbury Boulevard, Milton Keynes, Buckinghamshire MK9 1FA.

Telephone: (01908) 607 090.

Fax: (01908) 209 449.

Ticket Office: (01908) 609 000.

Website: www.mkdons.com

Email: info@mkdons.com

Ground Capacity: 8,836.

Record Attendance: 30,115 v Manchester U, FA Premier League, 9 May 1993 (at Selhurst Park).

Pitch Measurements: 110yd × 74yd.

Chairman: Pete Winkelman.

Vice-Chairman: Berni Winkelman.

Executive Director: Sue Dawson.

Acting Chief Executive: John Cove.

Head of Football Operations: Kirstine Nicholson.

Manager: Martin Allen.

Assistant Manager: Adrian Whitbread.

Sports Therapist: Damien Doyle.

Colours: All white.

Change Colours: All black.

Year Formed: 1889.

Turned Professional: 1964.

Ltd Co.: 1964.

Previous Names: Wimbledon Old Centrals, 1899–1905; Wimbledon 1905–2004.

Previous Grounds: 1899, Plough Lane; 1991, Selhurst Park.

HONOURS

FA Premier League: best season: 6th, 1993–94.

Football League: Division 3 – Runners-up 1983–84; Division 4 – Champions 1982–83.

FA Cup: Winners 1988.

Football League Cup: Semi-final 1996–97, 1998–99.

League Group Cup: Runners-up 1982.

Amateur Cup: Winners 1963; Runners-up 1935, 1947.

European Competitions: *Intertoto Cup:* 1995.

SKY SPORTS FACT FILE

Wimbledon had an excellent reputation as an amateur club and could claim to have won every major competition they had entered. Their outstanding season was 1930–31 when they won the Isthmian League and five other trophies.

Club Nicknames: 'The Dons', 'The Crazy Gang'.

First Football League Game: 20 August 1977, Division 4, v Halifax T (h) D 3–3 – Guy; Bryant (1), Galvin, Donaldson, Aitken, Davies, Galliers, Smith, Connell (1), Holmes, Leslie (1).

Record League Victory: 6–0 v Newport Co, Division 3, 3 September 1983 – Beasant; Peters, Winterburn, Galliers, Morris, Hatter, Evans (2), Ketteridge (1), Cork (3 incl. 1p), Downes, Hodges (Driver).

Record Cup Victory: 7–2 v Windsor & Eton, FA Cup 1st rd, 22 November 1980 – Beasant; Jones, Armstrong, Galliers, Mick Smith (2), Cunningham (1), Ketteridge, Hodges, Leslie, Cork (1), Hubbick (3).

Record Defeat: 0–8 v Everton, League Cup 2nd rd, 29 August 1978.

Most League Points (2 for a win): 61, Division 4, 1978–79.

Most League Points (3 for a win): 98, Division 4, 1982–83.

Most League Goals: 97, Division 3, 1983–84.

Highest League Scorer in Season: Alan Cork, 29, 1983–84.

Most League Goals in Total Aggregate: Alan Cork, 145, 1977–92.

Most League Goals in One Match: 4, Alan Cork v Torquay U, Division 4, 28 February 1979.

Most Capped Player: Kenny Cunningham, 40 (72), Republic of Ireland.

Most League Appearances: Alan Cork, 430, 1977–92.

Youngest League Player: Kevin Gage, 17 years 15 days v Bury, 2 May 1981.

Record Transfer Fee Received: £7,000,000 from Newcastle U for Carl Cort, July 2000.

Record Transfer Fee Paid: £7,500,000 to West Ham U for John Hartson, January 1999.

Football League Record: 1977 Elected to Division 4; 1979–80 Division 3; 1980–81 Division 4; 1981–82 Division 3; 1982–83 Division 4; 1983–84 Division 3; 1984–86 Division 2; 1986–92 Division 1; 1992–2000 FA Premier League; 2000–04 Division 1; 2004–06 FL1; 2006– FL2.

MANAGERS

Les Henley 1955–71
Mike Everitt 1971–73
Dick Graham 1973–74
Allen Batsford 1974–78
Dario Gradi 1978–81
Dave Bassett 1981–87
Bobby Gould 1987–90
Ray Harford 1990–91
Peter Withe 1991
Joe Kinnear 1992–99
Egil Olsen 1999–2000
Terry Burton 2000–02
Stuart Murdock 2002–04
Danny Wilson 2004–06
Martin Allen June 2006–

LATEST SEQUENCES

Longest Sequence of League Wins: 7, 4.9.1996 – 19.10.1996.

Longest Sequence of League Defeats: 14, 19.3.2000 – 28.8.2000.

Longest Sequence of League Draws: 4, 24.4.2001 – 6.5.2001.

Longest Sequence of Unbeaten League Matches: 22, 15.1.1983 – 14.5.1983.

Longest Sequence Without a League Win: 14, 19.3.2000 – 28.8.2000.

Successive Scoring Runs: 23 from 18.2.1984.

TEN YEAR LEAGUE RECORD

		P	*W*	*D*	*L*	*F*	*A*	*Pts*	*Pos*
1996-97	PR Lge	38	15	11	12	49	46	56	8
1997-98	PR Lge	38	10	14	14	34	46	44	15
1998-99	PR Lge	38	10	12	16	40	63	42	16
1999-2000	PR Lge	38	7	12	19	46	74	33	18
2000-01	Div 1	46	17	18	11	71	50	69	8
2001-02	Div 1	46	18	13	15	63	57	67	9
2002-03	Div 1	46	18	11	17	76	73	65	10
2003-04	Div 1	46	8	5	33	41	89	29	24
2004-05	FL 1	46	12	15	19	54	68	51	20
2005-06	FL 1	46	12	14	20	45	66	50	22

DID YOU KNOW ?

In 2005–06 Milton Keynes Dons had their share of players with overseas connections. Three Aussies: Trent McClenahan (loaned from West Ham), Gareth Edds and Nicky Rizzo, Aaron Wilbraham who had played in Norway plus Julien Hornuss from Auxerre in France.

MILTON KEYNES DONS FC 2005–06 LEAGUE RECORD

Match No.	Date	Venue	Opponents	Result	H/T Score	Lg. Pos.	Goalscorers	Attendance
1	Aug 6	H	Bournemouth	D 2-2	1-0	—	McLeod 2 [41, 46]	5163
2	9	A	Doncaster R	D 1-1	0-0	—	McLeod [76]	5232
3	13	A	Bradford C	L 0-2	0-1	22		7315
4	20	H	Colchester U	D 1-1	1-0	22	Wilbraham [23]	4423
5	27	A	Bristol C	D 2-2	2-0	21	Platt 2 [7, 17]	10,011
6	29	H	Port Vale	D 0-0	0-0	21		4592
7	Sept 10	A	Brentford	L 0-1	0-0	23		5862
8	13	H	Swansea C	L 1-3	1-1	—	Mills [35]	4798
9	17	H	Barnsley	D 0-0	0-0	24		4620
10	24	A	Blackpool	L 2-3	2-1	24	Rizzo (pen) [19], Small [34]	4723
11	27	H	Scunthorpe U	W 1-0	1-0	—	Platt [43]	4682
12	Oct 1	H	Swindon T	W 3-1	0-1	23	Kamara [49], Edds [77], McLeod [81]	5536
13	8	A	Walsall	D 1-1	0-0	—	Edds [72]	5041
14	15	H	Chesterfield	D 0-0	0-0	20		5642
15	22	A	Hartlepool U	L 1-2	1-0	22	McLeod [24]	4337
16	29	H	Rotherham U	D 1-1	0-1	23	Kamara [80]	5096
17	Nov 12	A	Tranmere R	W 2-1	0-1	20	McLeod 2 (1 pen) [57 (p), 58]	6611
18	19	H	Walsall	W 2-1	1-1	18	McLeod [6], Wilbraham [84]	5506
19	26	A	Bournemouth	L 0-2	0-1	19		5485
20	Dec 6	H	Huddersfield T	D 2-2	0-1	—	Rizzo [81], McLeod [83]	4832
21	10	H	Doncaster R	L 2-3	0-2	20	Smith [73], Wilbraham [87]	5351
22	17	A	Colchester U	L 0-2	0-1	22		3400
23	26	A	Southend U	D 0-0	0-0	22		7452
24	31	A	Gillingham	L 0-3	0-2	24		6162
25	Jan 2	H	Oldham Ath	L 0-1	0-1	24		5082
26	10	A	Swansea C	L 1-3	0-3	—	McLeod (pen) [80]	11,922
27	14	H	Yeovil T	D 1-1	0-1	24	McLeod [74]	5548
28	21	A	Barnsley	L 0-2	0-0	24		7588
29	31	H	Nottingham F	W 1-0	1-0	—	McLeod [22]	7670
30	Feb 4	A	Scunthorpe U	L 0-2	0-2	24		4631
31	11	H	Blackpool	W 3-0	1-0	24	McLeod 2 [26, 87], Taylor [51]	5691
32	14	A	Yeovil T	D 1-1	0-0	—	Harding [90]	5048
33	18	A	Huddersfield T	L 0-5	0-3	24		11,423
34	25	H	Bradford C	W 2-1	0-0	24	Harding [58], Lewington [89]	8426
35	Mar 10	H	Bristol C	L 0-1	0-1	—		6855
36	18	H	Southend U	W 2-1	1-1	24	Smith [16], Taylor [78]	7071
37	25	A	Nottingham F	L 0-3	0-2	24		18,214
38	28	H	Brentford	L 0-1	0-1	—		5592
39	Apr 1	H	Gillingham	L 1-2	1-0	24	Smith (pen) [40]	6432
40	4	A	Port Vale	L 1-3	1-3	—	Platt [28]	3452
41	8	A	Oldham Ath	W 2-1	2-1	24	McLeod 2 [40, 41]	5919
42	15	A	Swindon T	W 1-0	0-0	24	Platt [65]	7273
43	17	H	Hartlepool U	W 2-1	1-0	22	Wilbraham [25], Taylor [90]	6472
44	22	A	Chesterfield	W 2-1	1-0	21	Platt [13], Edds [86]	3965
45	29	H	Tranmere R	L 1-2	0-0	22	McLeod [89]	7777
46	May 6	A	Rotherham U	D 0-0	0-0	22		7625

Final League Position: 22

GOALSCORERS

League (45): McLeod 17 (2 pens), Platt 6, Wilbraham 4, Edds 3, Smith 3 (1 pen), Taylor 3, Harding 2, Kamara 2, Rizzo 2 (1 pen), Lewington 1, Mills 1, Small 1.
Carling Cup (0).
FA Cup (8): Edds 2, Platt 2, McLeod 1 (pen), Rizzo 1, Smith 1, own goal 1.
Football League Trophy (7): Smith 3 (1 pen), Wilbraham 2, Mills 1, Small 1.

Baker M 37	Crooks L 22 + 1	Lewington D 44	Mitchell P 39	Morgan C 38 + 2	Chorley B 25 + 1	Edds G 32 + 9	Small W 24 + 4	Wilbraham A 16 + 15	McLeod I 33 + 6	Smith G 18 + 7	Kamara M 6 + 17	Oyedele S 2 + 1	McKoy N 5 + 11	Palmer S 1 + 1	Harding B 8 + 2	McClenahan T 24 + 5	Puncheon J 1	Carrilho M 1 + 2	Platt C 34 + 6	Rizzo N 15 + 14	Mills P 16	Quinn S 13 + 2	Ricketts M 4 + 1	Batista R 9	Partridge D 18	Taylor S 10 + 7	Morais F 11 + 2	Match No.
1	2	3	4	5	6	7	8^1	9	10	11	12																	1
1	2	3		5	6	7	8	9	10	11^1		4	12															2
1	2	3		5^2	6▮	7	8	9^3	10	11^1		4	12	13	14													3
1		3		5		7	8^2	9	10	14	13	12	6^3	4		2	11^1											4
1	2	3	4^2	5		7	8	9^1			12		11			6		13	10									5
1	7	3^2	4	5		2^3	8	9		14	12		11^1			6		13	10									6
1	7		4	5			8^1	9			12		11			2		3^2	10	13	6							7
1	7	3^3	4^1	5				13	10^2	12	8		11			2			9	14	6							8
1		3	4^3	5		12		13	10	8	11^1		14			2			9	7^2	6							9
1		3	4	5		12	8^1	13	10				14			2			9^2	11^3	6	7						10
1		3	4	5		2		12	10		7^1		13						9	11^2	6	8						11
1	12	3	4	5		2		13	10		7^1		14						9^2	11^3	6	8						12
1	7	3	4	5		2			10	12			13						9	11^1	6	8^2						13
1	7	3	4▮	5		2		12	10	13			14						9^1	11^3	6	8^2						14
1	7	3	4	5		2^1		12▮	10		13								9	11^2	6	8						15
1	7^2	3	4^1	5		2			10	12	8		14			13			9	11^3	6							16
1		3	4	5		12	8		10							2^1			9		6	11	7					17
1		3	7	5		2	8^1	12	10^2		13					4			9	14	6	11^3						18
1		3	7	5		2^1	8	13	10^2	12						4^3			9	14	6	11						19
1		3	4^3	5	6		7^2	12	10	8	13					2			9^1	14		11						20
1		3	4	5	6	7^1		9	10	8	12					2				13		11^2						21
1		3	7	5	4▮	12	10	9		8^1						2				13	6	11^2						22
1	7	3	8	5		2^1	11	9					12			4			10		6							23
1	7^3	3	11	5		2^2	8^1		10		13					4			9	12	6	14						24
1		3	4	5	6	12	8^3	13	10^2		14					2			9	7		11^1						25
1	4^2	3	11	5	6	2	8^1	12	10										9	13		14	7^3					26
1		3	5^3		6	2	8^1	9^2	13		12		14			4			10	11			7					27
		3	4	12	6	2	8	13			14								9^2	11^3			7	1	5^1	10		28
		3	7^3	5		2		12	10						11	4			9^1				13	1	6	8^2	14	29
		3	7^3	5	12	2			10						8	4^1			9	13				1	6	11^2	14	30
		3	4		6	2			10		12				8^3	14			13	11^1				1	5	9^2	7	31
1		3	4^2		6	2	8		10		7^3				11	14			12	13					5	9^1		32
1		3	7^2	5^3	6	2	8		10^1						11	14			12	13					4	9		33
1^G		3		5		2	8^2	15	10						11	4			12	13					6	9^1	7	34
		3		5	6	2	8^3		10		12				11^1	4			13	14				1		9^2	7	35
		3	7	12	6	2	13		14	8						4			9^3	11^2				1	5^1	10		36
		3▮	7		6	2	12		13	8					11^1	4			9					1	5	10^2		37
	3		4		6		8^1		10	7	12					2^2			9	11				1	5	13		38
		3	4		6	2^2			10	8	12								9	11^1				1	5	13	7	39
1	8	3		5	6^3	2^2			10	11					12	13			9						4	14	7^1	40
1	2	3	8	5	6	12		9^2	10	11									13						4		7^1	41
1	2	3	7	5	6	12		10		8									9						4		11^1	42
1	2	3	11^1	5	6	13		10^3	12	8									9						4	14	7^2	43
1	2	3	11^1	5	6	12		10^2	13	8									9						4	14	7^3	44
1	2	3	11^3	5	6		12	10^1	13	8									9						4	14	7^2	45
1	7	3		5	6	2	12		10	8^2									9						4	13	11^1	46

FA Cup

First Round	Lincoln C	(a)	1-1
		(h)	2-1
Second Round	Southend U	(a)	2-1
Third Round	Southampton	(a)	3-4

Carling Cup

First Round	Norwich C	(h)	0-1

Football League Trophy

First Round	Exeter C	(h)	3-2
Second Round	Barnet	(a)	3-0
Quarter-Final	Colchester U	(h)	1-2

NEWCASTLE UNITED FA Premiership

FOUNDATION

It stemmed from a newly formed club called Stanley in 1881. In October 1882 they changed their name to Newcastle East End to avoid confusion with two other local clubs, Stanley Nops and Stanley Albion. Shortly afterwards another club Rosewood merged with them. Newcastle West End had been formed in August 1882 and they played on a pitch which was part of the Town Moor. Moved to Brandling Park 1885 and St James' Park 1886 (home of Newcastle Rangers). West End went out of existence after a bad run and the remaining committee men invited East End to move to St James' Park. They accepted and, at a meeting in Bath Lane Hall in 1892, changed their name to Newcastle United.

St James' Park, Newcastle-upon-Tyne NE1 4ST.

Telephone: (0191) 201 8400.

Fax: (0191) 201 8600.

Ticket Office: (0191) 261 1571.

Website: www.nufc.co.uk

Email: admin@nufc.co.uk

Ground Capacity: 52,387.

Record Attendance: 68,386 v Chelsea, Division 1, 3 September 1930.

Pitch Measurements: 105m × 68m.

Chairman: Freddy Shepherd.

Vice-chairman: Douglas Hall.

Chief Operating Officer: Russell Cushing.

Manager: Glenn Roeder.

Assistant Manager: Kevin Bond.

Physio: Derek Wright.

Colours: Black and white striped shirts, black shorts, black stockings.

Change Colours: Cardinal and navy shirts, navy shorts, navy stockings.

Year Formed: 1881.

Turned Professional: 1889.

Ltd Co.: 1890.

Previous Names: 1881, Stanley; 1882, Newcastle East End; 1892, Newcastle United.

Club Nickname: 'The Magpies'.

Previous Grounds: 1881, South Byker; 1886, Chillingham Road, Heaton, 1892, St James' Park.

First Football League Game: 2 September 1893, Division 2, v Royal Arsenal (a) D 2–2 – Ramsay; Jeffery, Miller; Crielly, Graham, McKane; Bowman, Crate (1), Thompson, Sorley (1), Wallace. Graham and not Crate scored according to some reports.

HONOURS

FA Premier League: Runners-up 1995–96, 1996–97; *Football League:* Division 1 – Champions 1904–05, 1906–07, 1908–09, 1926–27, 1992–93; Division 2 – Champions 1964–65; Runners-up 1897–98, 1947–48.

FA Cup: Winners 1910, 1924, 1932, 1951, 1952, 1955; Runners-up 1905, 1906, 1908, 1911, 1974, 1998, 1999.

Football League Cup: Runners-up 1976.

Texaco Cup: Winners 1974, 1975.

European Competitions: *Champions League:* 1997–98, 2002–03, 2003–04. *European Fairs Cup:* 1968–69 (winners), 1969–70, 1970–71. *UEFA Cup:* 1977–78, 1994–95, 1996–97, 1999–2000, 2003–04 (semi-final), 2004–05. *European Cup Winners' Cup:* 1998–99. *Anglo-Italian Cup:* Winners 1972–73. *Intertoto Cup:* 2001 (runners-up), 2005.

SKY SPORTS FACT FILE

On 7 January 2006 Alan Shearer scored his 200th goal for Newcastle United, hit his 201st on 4 February and finished his farewell playing season on 206 goals from 404 matches for the club.

Record League Victory: 13–0 v Newport Co, Division 2, 5 October 1946 – Garbutt; Cowell, Graham; Harvey, Brennan, Wright; Milburn (2), Bentley (1), Wayman (4), Shackleton (6), Pearson.

Record Cup Victory: 9–0 v Southport (at Hillsborough), FA Cup 4th rd, 1 February 1932 – McInroy; Nelson, Fairhurst; McKenzie, Davidson, Weaver (1); Boyd (1), Jimmy Richardson (3), Cape (2), McMenemy (1), Lang (1).

Record Defeat: 0–9 v Burton Wanderers, Division 2, 15 April 1895.

Most League Points (2 for a win): 57, Division 2, 1964–65.

Most League Points (3 for a win): 96, Division 1, 1992–93.

Most League Goals: 98, Division 1, 1951–52.

Highest League Scorer in Season: Hughie Gallacher, 36, Division 1, 1926–27.

Most League Goals in Total Aggregate: Jackie Milburn, 177, 1946–57.

Most League Goals in One Match: 6, Len Shackleton v Newport Co, Division 2, 5 October 1946.

Most Capped Player: Shay Given, 67 (76), Republic of Ireland.

Most League Appearances: Jim Lawrence, 432, 1904–22.

Youngest League Player: Steve Watson, 16 years 223 days v Wolverhampton W, 10 November 1990.

Record Transfer Fee Received: £13,650,000 from Real Madrid for Jonathan Woodgate, August 2004.

Record Transfer Fee Paid: £16,000,000 to Real Madrid for Michael Owen, September 2005.

Football League Record: 1893 Elected to Division 2; 1898–1934 Division 1; 1934–48 Division 2; 1948–61 Division 1; 1961–65 Division 2; 1965–78 Division 1; 1978–84 Division 2; 1984–89 Division 1; 1989–92 Division 2; 1992–93 Division 1; 1993– FA Premier League.

MANAGERS

Frank Watt 1895–32
(Secretary-Manager)
Andy Cunningham 1930–35
Tom Mather 1935–39
Stan Seymour 1939–47
(Hon. Manager)
George Martin 1947–50
Stan Seymour 1950–54
(Hon. Manager)
Duggie Livingstone 1954–56
Stan Seymour 1956–58
(Hon. Manager)
Charlie Mitten 1958–61
Norman Smith 1961–62
Joe Harvey 1962–75
Gordon Lee 1975–77
Richard Dinnis 1977
Bill McGarry 1977–80
Arthur Cox 1980–84
Jack Charlton 1984
Willie McFaul 1985–88
Jim Smith 1988–91
Ossie Ardiles 1991–92
Kevin Keegan 1992–97
Kenny Dalglish 1997–98
Ruud Gullit 1998–99
Sir Bobby Robson 1999–2004
Graeme Souness 2004–06
Glenn Roeder May 2006–

LATEST SEQUENCES

Longest Sequence of League Wins: 13, 25.4.1992 – 18.10.1992.

Longest Sequence of League Defeats: 10, 23.8.1977 – 15.10.1977.

Longest Sequence of League Draws: 4, 20.1.1990 – 24.2.1990.

Longest Sequence of Unbeaten League Matches: 14, 22.4.1950 – 30.9.1950.

Longest Sequence Without a League Win: 21, 14.1.1978 – 23.8.1978.

Successive Scoring Runs: 25 from 15.4.1939.

Successive Non-scoring Runs: 6 from 31.12.1938.

TEN YEAR LEAGUE RECORD

		P	*W*	*D*	*L*	*F*	*A*	*Pts*	*Pos*
1996-97	PR Lge	38	19	11	8	73	40	68	2
1997-98	PR Lge	38	11	11	16	35	44	44	13
1998-99	PR Lge	38	11	13	14	48	54	46	13
1999-2000	PR Lge	38	14	10	14	63	54	52	11
2000-01	PR Lge	38	14	9	15	44	50	51	11
2001-02	PR Lge	38	21	8	9	74	52	71	4
2002-03	PR Lge	38	21	6	11	63	48	69	3
2003-04	PR Lge	38	13	17	8	52	40	56	5
2004-05	PR Lge	38	10	14	14	47	57	44	14
2005-06	PR Lge	38	17	7	14	47	42	58	7

DID YOU KNOW ?

What could have been the betting odds on Newcastle United between 1904 and 1910 finishing in successive League seasons in the following positions: 4 1 4 1 4 1 4? In 1910–11 the sequence ended when their final place was eighth in the First Division.

NEWCASTLE UNITED 2005–06 LEAGUE RECORD

Match No.	*Date*	*Venue*	*Opponents*	*Result*	*H/T Score*	*Lg. Pos.*	*Goalscorers*	*Atten-dance*
1	Aug 14	A	Arsenal	L 0-2	0-0	—		38,072
2	20	H	West Ham U	D 0-0	0-0	17		51,620
3	24	A	Bolton W	L 0-2	0-1	—		25,904
4	28	H	Manchester U	L 0-2	0-0	19		52,327
5	Sept 10	H	Fulham	D 1-1	0-1	19	N'Zogbia [78]	52,208
6	18	A	Blackburn R	W 3-0	0-0	14	Shearer [62], Owen [66], N'Zogbia [85]	20,725
7	24	H	Manchester C	W 1-0	1-0	10	Owen [18]	52,280
8	Oct 1	A	Portsmouth	D 0-0	0-0	12		20,220
9	15	A	Wigan Ath	L 0-1	0-1	13		22,374
10	23	H	Sunderland	W 3-2	2-2	11	Ameobi 2 [34, 37], Emre [63]	52,302
11	30	A	WBA	W 3-0	0-0	10	Owen 2 [46, 78], Shearer [80]	26,216
12	Nov 5	H	Birmingham C	W 1-0	0-0	10	Emre [78]	52,191
13	19	A	Chelsea	L 0-3	0-0	13		42,268
14	27	A	Everton	L 0-1	0-0	12		36,207
15	Dec 3	H	Aston Villa	D 1-1	1-0	11	Shearer (pen) [32]	52,267
16	10	H	Arsenal	W 1-0	0-0	10	Solano [82]	52,297
17	17	A	West Ham U	W 4-2	2-1	10	Owen 3 [5, 43, 90], Shearer [66]	34,836
18	26	A	Liverpool	L 0-2	0-2	10		44,197
19	31	A	Tottenham H	L 0-2	0-1	11		36,246
20	Jan 2	H	Middlesbrough	D 2-2	1-0	11	Solano [27], Clark [90]	52,302
21	14	A	Fulham	L 0-1	0-0	13		21,974
22	21	H	Blackburn R	L 0-1	0-0	14		51,323
23	Feb 1	A	Manchester C	L 0-3	0-2	—		42,413
24	4	H	Portsmouth	W 2-0	1-0	15	N'Zogbia [41], Shearer [64]	51,627
25	11	A	Aston Villa	W 2-1	2-1	14	Ameobi [2], N'Zogbia [29]	37,140
26	22	H	Charlton Ath	D 0-0	0-0	—		50,451
27	25	H	Everton	W 2-0	0-0	11	Solano 2 [64, 76]	51,916
28	Mar 4	H	Bolton W	W 3-1	2-0	11	Solano [34], Shearer [45], Ameobi [70]	52,012
29	12	A	Manchester U	L 0-2	0-2	12		67,858
30	19	H	Liverpool	L 1-3	1-2	12	Ameobi [41]	52,302
31	26	A	Charlton Ath	L 1-3	1-2	13	Parker [35]	27,019
32	Apr 1	H	Tottenham H	W 3-1	3-1	12	Bowyer [2], Ameobi [25], Shearer (pen) [30]	52,301
33	9	A	Middlesbrough	W 2-1	2-0	10	Boateng (og) [29], Ameobi [44]	31,202
34	15	H	Wigan Ath	W 3-1	2-1	9	Shearer 2 (1 pen) [28 (p), 66], Bramble [36]	52,302
35	17	A	Sunderland	W 4-1	0-1	7	Chopra [60], Shearer (pen) [61], N'Zogbia [66], Luque [87]	40,032
36	22	H	WBA	W 3-0	2-0	7	Solano [30], Ameobi 2 (1 pen) [40 (p), 90]	52,272
37	29	A	Birmingham C	D 0-0	0-0	7		28,331
38	May 7	H	Chelsea	W 1-0	0-0	7	Bramble [73]	52,309

Final League Position: 7

GOALSCORERS

League (47): Shearer 10 (4 pens), Ameobi 9 (1 pen), Owen 7, Solano 6, N'Zogbia 5, Bramble 2, Emre 2, Bowyer 1, Chopra 1, Clark 1, Luque 1, Parker 1, own goal 1.
Carling Cup (1): Shearer 1.
FA Cup (4): Chopra 1, Dyer 1, Parker 1, Shearer 1.

Given S 38	Carr S 19	Babayaro C 26 + 2	Parker S 26	Taylor S 12	Boumsong J 30 + 3	Dyer K 4 + 7	Jenas J 3 + 1	Shearer A 31 + 1	Bowyer L 18 + 10	Emre B 19 + 1	Faye A 14 + 8	N'Zogbia C 27 + 5	Milner J 1 + 2	Clark L 8 + 14	Ameobi F 25 + 5	Luque A 6 + 8	Bramble T 21 + 3	Owen M 10 + 1	Elliott R 14 + 3	Ramage P 23	Solano N 27 + 2	Chopra M 6 + 7	O'Brien A — + 3	Pattison M 2 + 1	Moore C 8	Match No.
1	2	3	4^{1}	5	6	7^{2}	8■	9^{3}	10	11	12	13	14													1
1	2	3	4	5	6		8	9	10			11^{1}	7	12												2
1	2	3	8	5	6		7	9	11^{1}		4^{2}		12	13	10											3
1	2	3	4	5	6	7^{2}	12	9	8^{3}	11^{1}	13				14	10										4
1	7	3	8■	2^{1}	6			9	12		4^{2}	14		13		11^{3}	5	10								5
1	2	3		5■	6			9^{1}	7		4	11		8			12	10								6
1	2	3	4		6			9^{1}	7^{2}		13	11		8	12		5	10								7
1	2	3^{2}	4	5	6			9	7		12	11		8^{1}	10				13							8
1	2		8	5	6			9	7^{2}	12	4^{1}	11		14	13			10	3^{3}							9
1	2■		4	5	6			9		8^{1}	12	11		13	10^{3}					3	7^{2}	14				10
1		3	4	5	6^{3}	13		12		8		11^{2}			9^{1}		14	10		2	7					11
1		3	4	5				9		8		11^{1}		13	12		6	10		2	7^{2}					12
1		3	4		6				9	8		11			10		5			2	7^{1}	12				13
1		3^{2}	4		6			9	12	8		11			10	13	5			2	7^{1}					14
1			8		6			9	12		4				10	13	5		3	2	7^{1}	11^{2}				15
1			8^{1}		6			9	12		4				11		5	10^{2}	3	2	7	13				16
1			8		6			9	12		4				11		5	10	3	2	7^{1}					17
1		3		5^{2}	6			9	8■		4	7^{3}			12	11^{1}	13	10		2	14					18
1		12	8		6			9			4	13			11	14	5	10^{1}	3	2^{3}	7^{2}					19
1		12			6			9			4	13		8	11^{2}	10	5		3^{1}	2	7					20
1	2^{1}	3			6			9	8			11^{3}		4		10^{2}			12	5	7	14	13			21
1		3			6			9	8					4		11^{1}	5			2	7	10	12			22
1		3	8		6			9		7^{3}		11^{1}		4		13	5			2	12	10^{2}	14			23
1		3	4^{1}		6	13		9	14	8^{3}		11		12	10		5			2	7^{2}					24
1		3■	4		6	12		9	13	8		11^{2}			10^{1}		5		14	2	7^{3}					25
1			4		6				10	8		11			9	12	5^{1}		3	2	7					26
1		3	4		6				10	8^{1}		11^{2}		12	9				5	2	7			13		27
1		3	4		6			9	12	8^{1}		11			10^{2}	13			5	2	7					28
1		3	4		6	12		9	13	8		11^{3}			10^{2}	14			5	2	7^{1}					29
1		3	4		6■	12		9	13	8^{3}		11^{2}		14	10^{1}				5	2	7					30
1	2		4		6	12		9	11	8		13			10^{2}					3	7^{1}				5	31
1	2							9	8	4^{2}	12	11^{3}		13	10				3	5	7^{1}	14			6	32
1	2					12		9	8	4^{2}	13	11			10		5		3		7^{1}				6	33
1	2					8^{2}		9	4^{1}		12	11		13	10^{3}		5		3		7	14			6	34
1	2	3			12	10		9^{2}			4	11^{1}		8^{3}		13	5				7	14			6	35
1	2	3									4	11		12	10		5				7	9		8^{1}	6	36
1	2	3			12						4^{1}	11		13	10		5	14			7	9^{3}		8^{2}	6	37
1	2■	3			12					8	4	11		13	10		5				7^{1}	9^{2}			6	38

FA Cup

Third Round	Mansfield T	(h)	1-0
Fourth Round	Cheltenham T	(a)	2-0
Fifth Round	Southampton	(h)	1-0
Sixth Round	Chelsea	(a)	0-1

Carling Cup

Third Round	Grimsby T	(a)	1-0
Fourth Round	Wigan Ath	(a)	0-1

NORTHAMPTON TOWN FL Championship 1

FOUNDATION

Formed in 1897 by school teachers connected with the Northampton and District Elementary Schools' Association, they survived a financial crisis at the end of their first year when they were £675 in the red and became members of the Midland League – a fast move indeed for a new club. They achieved Southern League membership in 1901.

Sixfields Stadium, Upton Way, Northampton NN5 5QA.

Telephone: 0870 822 1997.

Fax: (01604) 751 613.

Ticket Office: 0870 822 1966.

Website: www.ntfc.co.uk

Email: secretary@ntfc.co.uk

Ground Capacity: 7,653.

Record Attendance: (at County Ground): 24,523 v Fulham, Division 1, 23 April 1966; (at Sixfields Stadium): 7,557 v Manchester C, Division 2, 26 September 1998.

Pitch Measurements: 116yd × 72yd.

Chairman: D. Cardoza.

Secretary: N. Howells.

Manager: John Gorman.

Director of Football: John Deehan.

Physio: D. Casey.

Colours: Claret shirts, white shorts, claret stockings.

Change Colours: Blue shirts, blue shorts, blue stockings.

Year Formed: 1897.

Turned Professional: 1901.

Ltd Co.: 1901.

Previous Ground: 1897, County Ground; 1994, Sixfields Stadium.

Club Nickname: 'The Cobblers'.

First Football League Game: 28 August 1920, Division 3, v Grimsby T (a) L 0–2 – Thorpe; Sproston, Hewison; Jobey, Tomkins, Pease; Whitworth, Lockett, Thomas, Freeman, MacKechnie.

Record League Victory: 10–0 v Walsall, Division 3 (S), 5 November 1927 – Hammond; Watson, Jeffs; Allen, Brett, Odell; Daley, Smith (3), Loasby (3), Hoten (1), Wells (3).

Record Cup Victory: 10–0 v Sutton T, FA Cup prel rd, 7 December 1907 – Cooch; Drennan, Lloyd Davies, Tirrell (1), McCartney, Hickleton, Badenock (3), Platt (3), Lowe (1), Chapman (2), McDiarmid.

HONOURS

Football League: Division 1 best season: 21st, 1965–66; Division 2 – Runners-up 1964–65; Division 3 – Champions 1962–63; Promoted from Division 3 1996–97 (play-offs); Division 3 (S) – Runners-up 1927–28, 1949–50; Division 4 – Champions 1986–87; Runners-up 1975–76; Championship 2 – Runners-up 2005–06.

FA Cup: best season: 5th rd, 1934, 1950, 1970.

Football League Cup: best season: 5th rd, 1965, 1967.

SKY SPORTS FACT FILE

On 7 February 1923 Northampton Town had to include local amateur Ian Sorenson, a schoolmaster, to lead their attack because of injury to Bill Lockett. A crowd of 7663 saw the Cobblers win 3–1. It was Sorenson's only League appearance.

Record Defeat: 0–11 v Southampton, Southern League, 28 December 1901.

Most League Points (2 for a win): 68, Division 4, 1975–76.

Most League Points (3 for a win): 99, Division 4, 1986–87.

Most League Goals: 109, Division 3, 1962–63 and Division 3 (S), 1952–53.

Highest League Scorer in Season: Cliff Holton, 36, Division 3, 1961–62.

Most League Goals in Total Aggregate: Jack English, 135, 1947–60.

Most League Goals in One Match: 5, Ralph Hoten v Crystal Palace, Division 3S, 27 October 1928.

Most Capped Player: Edwin Lloyd Davies, 12 (16), Wales.

Most League Appearances: Tommy Fowler, 521, 1946–61.

Youngest League Player: Adrian Mann, 16 years 297 days v Bury, 5 May 1984.

Record Transfer Fee Received: £265,000 from Watford for Richard Hill, July 1987.

Record Transfer Fee Paid: £165,000 to Oldham Ath for Josh Low, July 2003.

Football League Record: 1920 Original Member of Division 3; 1921 Division 3 (S); 1958–61 Division 4; 1961–63 Division 3; 1963–65 Division 2; 1965–66 Division 1; 1966–67 Division 2; 1967–69 Division 3; 1969–76 Division 4; 1976–77 Division 3; 1977–87 Division 4; 1987–90 Division 3; 1990–92 Division 4; 1992–97 Division 3; 1997–99 Division 2; 1999–2000 Division 3; 2000–03 Division 2; 2003–04 Division 3; 2004–06 FL2; 2006– FLC.

LATEST SEQUENCES

Longest Sequence of League Wins: 8, 27.8.1960 – 19.9.1960.

Longest Sequence of League Defeats: 8, 26.10.1935 – 21.12.1935.

Longest Sequence of League Draws: 6, 18.9.1983 – 15.10.1983.

Longest Sequence of Unbeaten League Matches: 21, 27.9.1986 – 6.2.1987.

Longest Sequence Without a League Win: 18, 26.3.1969 – 20.9.1969.

Successive Scoring Runs: 27 from 23.8.1986.

Successive Non-scoring Runs: 7 from 7.4.1939.

MANAGERS

Arthur Jones 1897–1907
(Secretary-Manager)
Herbert Chapman 1907–12
Walter Bull 1912–13
Fred Lessons 1913–19
Bob Hewison 1920–25
Jack Tresadern 1925–30
Jack English 1931–35
Syd Puddefoot 1935–37
Warney Cresswell 1937–39
Tom Smith 1939–49
Bob Dennison 1949–54
Dave Smith 1954–59
David Bowen 1959–67
Tony Marchi 1967–68
Ron Flowers 1968–69
Dave Bowen 1969–72
(continued as General Manager and Secretary to 1985 when joined the board)
Billy Baxter 1972–73
Bill Dodgin Jnr 1973–76
Pat Crerand 1976–77
Bill Dodgin Jnr 1977
John Petts 1977–78
Mike Keen 1978–79
Clive Walker 1979–80
Bill Dodgin Jnr 1980–82
Clive Walker 1982–84
Tony Barton 1984–85
Graham Carr 1985–90
Theo Foley 1990–92
Phil Chard 1992–93
John Barnwell 1993–95
Ian Atkins 1995–99
Kevin Wilson 1999–2001
Kevan Broadhurst 2001–03
Terry Fenwick 2003
Martin Wilkinson 2003
Colin Calderwood 2003–06
John Gorman June 2006–

TEN YEAR LEAGUE RECORD

		P	W	D	L	F	A	Pts	Pos
1996-97	Div 3	46	20	12	14	67	44	72	4
1997-98	Div 2	46	18	17	11	52	37	71	4
1998-99	Div 2	46	10	18	18	43	57	48	22
1999-2000	Div 3	46	25	7	14	63	45	82	3
2000-01	Div 2	46	15	12	19	46	59	57	18
2001-02	Div 2	46	14	7	25	54	79	49	20
2002-03	Div 2	46	10	9	27	40	79	39	24
2003-04	Div 3	46	22	9	15	58	51	75	6
2004-05	FL 2	46	20	12	14	62	51	72	7
2005-06	FL 2	46	22	17	7	63	37	83	2

DID YOU KNOW ?

Between 1960–61 and 1965–66 Mike Everitt and Barry Lines scored goals for Northampton Town in all four divisions of the Football League. Both players made more than 200 League appearances during their time with the club.

NORTHAMPTON TOWN 2005–06 LEAGUE RECORD

Match No.	Date	Venue	Opponents	Result		H/T Score	Lg. Pos.	Goalscorers	Attendance
1	Aug 6	A	Lincoln C	D	1-1	0-0	—	Bojic [53]	5397
2	9	H	Barnet	L	1-2	1-0	—	Dudfield [32]	5817
3	13	H	Wrexham	D	0-0	0-0	18		5075
4	20	A	Shrewsbury T	D	1-1	0-1	18	Kirk (pen) [80]	3562
5	27	A	Carlisle U	W	1-0	1-0	15	Bojic [37]	5730
6	29	H	Boston U	W	3-2	2-1	18	Kirk [22], Taylor [45], Crowe [83]	5012
7	Sept 2	A	Wycombe W	D	1-1	1-0	—	Hunt [31]	5650
8	10	H	Bury	D	1-1	0-1	12	Gilligan [83]	5147
9	17	A	Macclesfield T	W	4-1	1-0	7	McGleish 2 (1 pen) [44 (p), 79], Taylor [51], Low [90]	2014
10	24	H	Cheltenham T	L	1-2	1-2	9	Taylor [30]	5407
11	27	A	Rushden & D	W	3-1	1-0	—	Gilligan [9], Gier (og) [80], McGleish [84]	5211
12	Oct 1	H	Darlington	D	0-0	0-0	6		5182
13	7	A	Bristol R	D	0-0	0-0	—		6912
14	14	H	Oxford U	W	1-0	0-0	—	Taylor [74]	6802
15	22	A	Stockport Co	L	2-4	2-1	6	Mendes [18], McGleish [31]	4150
16	29	H	Grimsby T	D	0-0	0-0	8		6067
17	Nov 12	A	Chester C	D	0-0	0-0	8		3295
18	19	H	Bristol R	W	4-0	2-0	7	Kirk 2 (1 pen) [34 (p), 43], Smith [48], Bojic [89]	5716
19	26	H	Lincoln C	D	1-1	0-1	8	Low [90]	5174
20	Dec 6	A	Torquay U	D	3-3	1-0	—	McGleish 2 [21, 67], Mendes [77]	2010
21	10	A	Barnet	W	1-0	0-0	7	McGleish (pen) [48]	2544
22	17	H	Shrewsbury T	W	1-0	0-0	5	McGleish [50]	5380
23	26	H	Mansfield T	W	1-0	0-0	4	Hunt [66]	6112
24	31	H	Peterborough U	L	0-1	0-1	6		7023
25	Jan 2	A	Rochdale	D	1-1	0-0	6	Bojic [49]	3030
26	14	A	Leyton Orient	W	2-1	1-0	5	McGleish [35], Doig [54]	5445
27	21	H	Macclesfield T	W	5-0	2-0	5	Taylor 2 [35, 89], Kirk 2 [38, 90], McGleish [61]	5428
28	24	A	Notts Co	D	2-2	0-1	—	Crowe [69], Jess [77]	4884
29	28	A	Bury	W	2-0	2-0	4	Parrish (og) [29], Kirk [40]	2456
30	31	H	Wycombe W	D	0-0	0-0	—		6438
31	Feb 4	H	Rushden & D	W	2-0	1-0	4	Hunt [11], McGleish [86]	7036
32	11	A	Cheltenham T	L	1-3	0-2	4	McGleish [90]	3876
33	14	H	Leyton Orient	D	1-1	1-0	—	Kirk [8]	5552
34	17	H	Torquay U	W	1-0	0-0	—	Taylor [81]	5636
35	25	A	Wrexham	W	1-0	0-0	3	Gilligan [68]	5012
36	Mar 10	H	Carlisle U	L	0-3	0-1	—		7045
37	18	A	Mansfield T	L	0-1	0-0	5		3985
38	22	A	Boston U	W	1-0	0-0	—	Johnson G [79]	2174
39	25	H	Notts Co	W	2-0	1-0	3	Lee [39], Low [90]	6077
40	Apr 1	A	Peterborough U	W	1-0	1-0	3	McGleish [21]	8637
41	8	H	Rochdale	D	2-2	2-0	3	Low [6], McGleish [35]	5732
42	15	A	Darlington	W	1-0	0-0	2	McGleish [70]	5220
43	17	H	Stockport Co	W	2-0	0-0	2	McGleish [54], Smith [73]	6544
44	22	A	Oxford U	W	3-1	1-0	2	Doig [16], Smith [69], Low [71]	8264
45	29	H	Chester C	W	1-0	1-0	2	McGleish [26]	7114
46	May 6	A	Grimsby T	D	1-1	0-0	2	Gilligan [90]	8458

Final League Position: 2

GOALSCORERS

League (63): McGleish 17 (2 pens), Kirk 8 (2 pens), Taylor 7, Low 5, Bojic 4, Gilligan 4, Hunt 3, Smith 3, Crowe 2, Doig 2, Mendes 2, Dudfield 1, Jess 1, Johnson G 1, Lee 1, own goals 2.
Carling Cup (3): Kirk 1, McGleish 1, Sabin 1 (pen).
FA Cup (8): McGleish 4 (1 pen), Bojic 1, Doig 1, Low 1, Smith 1.
Football League Trophy (7): Cross 2, McGleish 2, Bojic 1, Kirk 1, Mendes 1.

Harper L 46	Bojic P 18 + 18	Johnson Brett 2 + 4	Chambers L 42 + 1	Dyche S 34 + 1	Hunt D 35 + 5	Low J 29 + 6	Taylor I 33	Sabin E 4 + 2	Jess E 35 + 3	Galbraith D 1 + 3	Dudfield L 2 + 4	Crowe J 41	Gilligan R 4 + 19	Kirk A 20 + 9	McGleish S 39 + 3	Rowson D 13 + 16	Johnson Brad 1 + 2	Johnson G 22 + 2	Mikolanda P 2	Doig C 36 + 2	Smith M 22 + 4	Mendes J 9 + 3	Cross S — + 4	Lee J 8 + 3	Hand J 8 + 3	Westwood A — + 3	Match No.
1	2	3	4	5	6	7	8	9	10	11^{1}	12																1
1	2	12	4	5	6	7^{1}	8	9	10^{2}	13	11	3															2
1	2^{1}	12	4	5	6	7^{2}	8	9^{3}	10		11	3	13	14													3
1	12	3^{1}	4	5	6	7^{3}	8	13	11		14	2		10	9^{2}												4
1	2		4	5	6		8	10^{3}	11^{1}		13	3	7^{2}		9	14	12										5
1	2		4	5	6^{1}		8	13	11		14	3	7^{3}	10^{2}	9	12											6
1	2■	14	4	5	6^{2}	12	8		11^{3}	13		3			9	7^{1}		10									7
1			4	5	6^{2}	7	8		10	12		2	13		9		11^{1}	3									8
1			4	5	6	12	8		11^{3}			2	13		9^{2}	7		3	10^{1}	14							9
1			4	5	6^{1}	7^{2}	8		11			2	13		9	12		3^{3}	10	14							10
1	12	13	4		6	14	8		10^{1}			2	11^{2}		9	7^{3}		3		5							11
1	12		4^{1}	5	11	13	8		10			2	3^{3}		9	7^{2}				6	14						12
1	12		4^{1}		6	7^{2}	8		10			2	13		9	11^{3}		3		5	14						13
1	12			5	6	7^{1}	8		10^{3}			2			9	13		3		4	11^{2}	14					14
1				5	2■	12	8		11^{1}			4			9	13		3^{3}		6	7^{2}	10	14				15
1	2			5^{1}		7^{3}	8		11			3		13	9	14	12^{2}			6	4	10					16
1	2		4		12	7	6		11^{1}			3		13	9					5	8	10^{2}					17
1	2		4		12	7	8		11			3		10^{2}	13	14				5	6^{1}	9^{3}					18
1	2		4		12	7	6		11^{2}			3		10	9^{1}					5	8	13					19
1	2		4	12	6^{1}	7						3	13		9	11				5	8	10^{2}					20
1	12		4	5	6^{1}	2						3	13		9	11				8	7	10^{2}					21
1	12		4	5	7^{1}	2	8		11^{3}					13	9	14				6	3^{2}	10					22
1	2		12	5	6	7	8		11			3		13	9					4^{1}		10^{2}					23
1	12		4	5	7	2	8		11^{2}			3^{1}		9	13					6		10^{3}	14				24
1	2		4	5	8	7	3		11					10^{1}	9					6		12					25
1	12		4	5	11	2^{1}	8		13			3		10^{2}	9					6				7			26
1	2		4		6^{2}	3	8		13			7		11	9^{1}	14				5	12			10^{3}			27
1	12		4	5		7	8		11			2		13	9^{1}	14				6	3^{2}			10^{3}			28
1	12		4	5	7^{3}	11^{2}	8					2		10	9	14		13		6	3^{1}						29
1	7		4	5			8		11^{1}			2	13	10^{2}	9	12				6	3						30
1	7		2	5^{2}	8		4		11^{1}			3	12		9	14		13		6	10^{3}						31
1	7^{1}		4		6^{2}		8		11			2	12	10	9			3		5			13				32
1	12		4	5	8^{1}		11					2	13	10	9^{3}			3		6			14		7^{2}		33
1	12		4	5	7^{2}		8		11^{1}			2	13	10	9^{3}			3		6					14		34
1	12		4	5	8^{1}				11^{3}			2	13	10^{2}	9			3		6					7	14	35
1			4	5	8^{3}		7^{2}		11			2	13	10	9^{1}			3		6	12			14			36
1	12		4	5	13	7^{3}			11			2		10	14					6	8^{1}			9	3^{2}		37
1	12		4	5	8^{2}							2	14	10^{3}	9	13		11^{1}		6	7				3		38
1	12		4	5■		13			11^{2}			2			9^{3}	14		3		6	8			10^{1}	7		39
1	2		4									5	12		9^{1}	7		3		6	11			10	8		40
1			4			7^{1}			11^{2}			2	12	14	9^{3}	13		3		6	8			10	5		41
1			4		12	7			10^{3}			2^{1}		14	9	11		3^{2}		6	8				5	13	42
1			4	5	8	2							13	10	9^{2}	7		3		6^{1}	11^{3}				14	12	43
1	12		4	5	8	2^{1}								13	9^{2}	7		3		6	11^{3}			10	14		44
1			4		8	7			12			2		10^{1}	9^{2}	11		3		6	5			13			45
1			4	5	11	7			10^{1}			2	13	9^{2}		8		3		6				12			46

FA Cup

First Round	Wycombe W	(a)	3-1
Second Round	Stevenage B	(a)	2-2
		(h)	2-0
Third Round	Crystal Palace	(a)	1-4

Carling Cup

First Round	QPR	(h)	3-0
Second Round	Norwich C	(a)	0-2

Football League Trophy

First Round	Notts Co	(h)	5-2
Second Round	Colchester U	(a)	2-3

NORWICH CITY FL Championship

FOUNDATION

Formed in 1902, largely through the initiative of two local schoolmasters who called a meeting at the Criterion Cafe, they were shocked by an FA Commission which in 1904 declared the club professional and ejected them from the FA Amateur Cup. However, this only served to strengthen their determination. New officials were appointed and a professional club established at a meeting in the Agricultural Hall in March 1905.

Carrow Road, Norwich NR1 1JE.

Telephone: (01603) 760 760.

Fax: (01603) 613 886.

Ticket Office: 0870 444 1902.

Website: www.canaries.co.uk

Email: reception@ncfc-canaries.co.uk

Ground Capacity: 26,034.

Record Attendance: 43,984 v Leicester C, FA Cup 6th rd, 30 March 1963.

Pitch Measurements: 105m × 67m.

Chairman: Roger Munby.

Vice-chairman: Barry Skipper.

Chief Executive: Neil Doncaster.

Secretary: Kevan Platt.

Manager: Nigel Worthington.

Assistant Manager: Doug Livermore.

Physio: Neil Reynolds MCSP, SRP.

Colours: Yellow shirts, green shorts, yellow stockings.

Change Colours: White shirts, white shorts, white stockings.

Year Formed: 1902.

Turned Professional: 1905.

Ltd Co.: 1905.

Club Nickname: 'The Canaries'.

Previous Grounds: 1902, Newmarket Road; 1908, The Nest, Rosary Road; 1935, Carrow Road.

First Football League Game: 28 August 1920, Division 3, v Plymouth Arg (a) D 1–1 – Skermer; Gray, Gadsden; Wilkinson, Addy, Martin; Laxton, Kidger, Parker, Whitham (1), Dobson.

Record League Victory: 10–2 v Coventry C, Division 3 (S), 15 March 1930 – Jarvie; Hannah, Graham; Brown, O'Brien, Lochhead (1); Porter (1), Anderson, Hunt (5), Scott (2), Slicer (1).

HONOURS

FA Premier League: best season: 3rd 1992–93.

Football League: Division 1 – Champions 2003–04; Division 2 – Champions 1971–72, 1985–86; Division 3 (S) – Champions 1933–34; Division 3 – Runners-up 1959–60.

FA Cup: Semi-finals 1959, 1989, 1992.

Football League Cup: Winners 1962, 1985; Runners-up 1973, 1975.

European Competitions: *UEFA Cup:* 1993–94.

SKY SPORTS FACT FILE

Few players have become first-class referees, even fewer referees have become football managers. However, Jimmy Jewell, the BBC's pre-war commentator, had refereed the 1938 Cup Final and in January 1939 was appointed manager of Norwich City.

Record Cup Victory: 8–0 v Sutton U, FA Cup 4th rd, 28 January 1989 – Gunn; Culverhouse, Bowen, Butterworth, Linighan, Townsend (Crook), Gordon, Fleck (3), Allen (4), Phelan, Putney (1).

Record Defeat: 2–10 v Swindon T, Southern League, 5 September 1908.

Most League Points (2 for a win): 64, Division 3 (S), 1950–51.

Most League Points (3 for a win): 94, Division 1, 2003–04.

Most League Goals: 99, Division 3 (S), 1952–53.

Highest League Scorer in Season: Ralph Hunt, 31, Division 3 (S), 1955–56.

Most League Goals in Total Aggregate: Johnny Gavin, 122, 1945–54, 1955–58.

Most League Goals in One Match: 5, Tommy Hunt v Coventry C, Division 3S, 15 March 1930; 5, Roy Hollis v Walsall, Division 3S, 29 December 1951.

Most Capped Player: Mark Bowen, 35 (41), Wales.

Most League Appearances: Ron Ashman, 592, 1947–64.

Youngest League Player: Ryan Jarvis, 16 years 282 days v Walsall, 19 April 2003.

Record Transfer Fee Received: £7,250,000 from West Ham U for Dean Ashton, January 2006.

Record Transfer Fee Paid: £3,250,000 to WBA for Robert Earnshaw, January 2006.

Football League Record: 1920 Original Member of Division 3; 1921 Division 3 (S): 1934–39 Division 2; 1946–58 Division 3 (S); 1958–60 Division 3; 1960–72 Division 2; 1972–74 Division 1; 1974–75 Division 2; 1975–81 Division 1; 1981–82 Division 2; 1982–85 Division 1; 1985–86 Division 2; 1986–92 Division 1; 1992–95 FA Premier League; 1995–2004 Division 1; 2004–05 FA Premier League; 2005– FLC.

MANAGERS

John Bowman 1905–07
James McEwen 1907–08
Arthur Turner 1909–10
Bert Stansfield 1910–15
Major Frank Buckley 1919–20
Charles O'Hagan 1920–21
Albert Gosnell 1921–26
Bert Stansfield 1926
Cecil Potter 1926–29
James Kerr 1929–33
Tom Parker 1933–37
Bob Young 1937–39
Jimmy Jewell 1939
Bob Young 1939–45
Cyril Spiers 1946–47
Duggie Lochhead 1947–50
Norman Low 1950–55
Tom Parker 1955–57
Archie Macaulay 1957–61
Willie Reid 1961–62
George Swindin 1962
Ron Ashman 1962–66
Lol Morgan 1966–69
Ron Saunders 1969–73
John Bond 1973–80
Ken Brown 1980–87
Dave Stringer 1987–92
Mike Walker 1992–94
John Deehan 1994–95
Martin O'Neill 1995
Gary Megson 1995–96
Mike Walker 1996–98
Bruce Rioch 1998–2000
Bryan Hamilton 2000
Nigel Worthington January 2001–

LATEST SEQUENCES

Longest Sequence of League Wins: 10, 23.11.1985 – 25.1.1986.

Longest Sequence of League Defeats: 7, 1.4.1995 – 6.5.1995.

Longest Sequence of League Draws: 7, 15.1.1994 – 26.2.1994.

Longest Sequence of Unbeaten League Matches: 20, 31.8.1950 – 30.12.1950.

Longest Sequence Without a League Win: 25, 22.9.1956 – 23.2.1957.

Successive Scoring Runs: 25 from 31.8.1963.

Successive Non-scoring Runs: 5 from 21.2.1925.

TEN YEAR LEAGUE RECORD

		P	W	D	L	F	A	Pts	Pos
1996-97	Div 1	46	17	12	17	63	68	63	13
1997-98	Div 1	46	14	13	19	52	69	55	15
1998-99	Div 1	46	15	17	14	62	61	62	9
1999-2000	Div 1	46	14	15	17	45	50	57	12
2000-01	Div 1	46	14	12	20	46	58	54	15
2001-02	Div 1	46	22	9	15	60	51	75	6
2002-03	Div 1	46	19	12	15	60	49	69	8
2003-04	Div 1	46	28	10	8	79	39	94	1
2004-05	PR Lge	38	7	12	19	42	77	33	19
2005-06	FL C	46	18	8	20	56	65	62	9

DID YOU KNOW

George Ansell was not only the first University Blue – triple at Oxford – to turn professional, but the first to play for two Football League clubs. After playing inside-forward for Brighton & Hove Albion, he joined Norwich City in February 1936.

NORWICH CITY 2005–06 LEAGUE RECORD

Match No.	*Date*	*Venue*	*Opponents*	*Result*		*H/T Score*	*Lg. Pos.*	*Goalscorers*	*Attendance*
1	Aug 6	H	Coventry C	D	1-1	1-0	—	Ashton [21]	25,355
2	9	H	Crewe Alex	D	1-1	0-1	—	McKenzie [50]	25,116
3	13	H	Crystal Palace	D	1-1	1-1	17	Ashton [6]	25,102
4	20	A	Southampton	L	0-1	0-1	20		23,498
5	27	H	Leeds U	L	0-1	0-0	21		25,015
6	29	A	Stoke C	L	1-3	1-2	23	Ashton [38]	14,249
7	Sept 10	H	Plymouth Arg	W	2-0	2-0	19	Doumbe (og) [20], Ashton [37]	23,981
8	13	A	Watford	L	1-2	0-2	—	Lisbie [62]	13,502
9	18	A	Ipswich T	W	1-0	0-0	17	Huckerby [51]	29,184
10	24	H	Reading	L	0-1	0-0	18		24,850
11	27	H	Hull C	W	2-1	2-1	—	Safri [15], Doherty [39]	27,470
12	Oct 1	A	Brighton & HA	W	3-1	2-0	12	Huckerby [22], McVeigh [41], Henderson [85]	6624
13	15	H	Millwall	D	1-1	0-1	13	Ashton [52]	25,095
14	18	A	Luton T	L	2-4	0-4	—	Ashton [56], Ryan Jarvis [85]	10,248
15	22	A	QPR	L	0-3	0-3	18		15,976
16	29	H	Sheffield W	L	0-1	0-0	20		25,383
17	Nov 1	H	Cardiff C	W	1-0	0-0	—	Alexander (og) [77]	23,838
18	5	A	Wolverhampton W	L	0-2	0-2	17		23,808
19	19	H	Luton T	W	2-0	2-0	15	Hughes [3], Huckerby [25]	25,383
20	22	A	Millwall	L	0-1	0-0	—		7814
21	26	A	Coventry C	D	2-2	1-2	16	Davenport [40], Fleming [84]	20,433
22	Dec 3	A	Derby Co	L	0-2	0-1	18		23,346
23	10	A	Crewe Alex	W	2-1	0-1	16	McVeigh 2 [64, 85]	6132
24	17	H	Southampton	W	3-1	1-1	15	Ashton 3 [30, 51, 66]	24,836
25	26	A	Sheffield U	W	3-1	1-1	12	McVeigh [33], Ashton [62], Morgan (og) [71]	26,505
26	28	H	Burnley	W	2-1	2-0	12	Charlton [16], Huckerby [39]	25,204
27	31	A	Leicester C	W	1-0	0-0	11	McVeigh [71]	21,072
28	Jan 2	H	Preston NE	L	0-3	0-1	11		25,032
29	14	A	Plymouth Arg	D	1-1	0-1	10	Huckerby [48]	13,906
30	21	H	Watford	L	2-3	1-0	11	McVeigh (pen) [44], Thorne [62]	25,384
31	31	A	Reading	L	0-4	0-2	—		21,442
32	Feb 5	H	Ipswich T	L	1-2	1-1	14	Johansson [33]	25,402
33	11	A	Hull C	D	1-1	0-1	14	Elliott (og) [87]	20,527
34	14	H	Brighton & HA	W	3-0	1-0	—	Huckerby [28], Earnshaw 2 [87, 90]	24,038
35	18	H	Derby Co	W	2-0	1-0	11	Johansson [26], Huckerby [83]	24,921
36	25	A	Crystal Palace	L	1-4	0-2	12	Ward (og) [88]	19,066
37	Mar 4	H	Stoke C	W	2-1	0-0	10	McKenzie [52], Johansson [89]	24,223
38	11	A	Leeds U	D	2-2	0-1	11	Hughes [57], McVeigh [75]	24,993
39	18	H	Sheffield U	W	2-1	2-1	9	McKenzie [33], Earnshaw [45]	25,346
40	24	A	Burnley	L	0-2	0-1	—		11,938
41	Apr 1	H	Leicester C	W	2-1	1-0	9	Earnshaw [28], McKenzie (pen) [77]	24,718
42	8	A	Preston NE	L	0-2	0-2	10		15,714
43	15	A	Sheffield W	L	0-1	0-1	11		30,755
44	17	H	QPR	W	3-2	0-1	10	Huckerby [78], Earnshaw 2 [85, 90]	24,126
45	22	A	Cardiff C	W	1-0	1-0	8	Earnshaw [16]	11,590
46	30	H	Wolverhampton W	L	1-2	0-1	9	Earnshaw [73]	24,081

Final League Position: 9

GOALSCORERS

League (56): Ashton 10, Earnshaw 8, Huckerby 8, McVeigh 7 (1 pen), McKenzie 4 (1 pen), Johansson 3, Hughes 2, Charlton 1, Davenport 1, Doherty 1, Fleming 1, Henderson 1, Ryan Jarvis 1, Lisbie 1, Safri 1, Thorne 1, own goals 5.
Carling Cup (4): Ashton 1, Huckerby 1 (pen), McKenzie 1, own goal 1.
FA Cup (1): McVeigh 1 (pen).

Green R 42	Louis-Jean M 2	Drury A 39	Fleming C 31 + 5	Doherty G 39 + 3	Charlton S 17 + 4	Marney D 12 + 1	Hughes A 35 + 1	McKenzie L 11 + 9	Ashton D 28	Huckerby D 39 + 4	Jarrett J 6 + 5	Thorne P 11 + 10	Shackell J 16 + 1	Safri Y 25 + 5	Colin J 24 + 1	Brennan J 12 + 6	McVeigh P 22 + 14	Henderson I 8 + 16	Lisbie K 4 + 2	Davenport C 14 + 1	Jarvis Ryan 1 + 3	Wright D 5	Etuhu D 15 + 4	Robinson C 18 + 4	Johansson J 6 + 6	Rehman Z 5	Earnshaw R 13 + 2	Jarvis Rossi — + 3	Gallacher P 4	Spillane M 2	*Match No.*
1	2	3	4	5	6^{1}	7^{2}	8	9	10	11	12	13																			1
1	2	3	4			7^{1}	8	9	10	11	6^{2}	12	5	13																	2
1		3^{1}	4		12	7	8	9^{3}	10	11	13	14	5	6^{2}	2																3
1			4		3^{1}	7	8^{2}	12	10	9	13	14	5	6	2^{3}	11															4
1			4	12	3^{2}	7		9	10	11			5	6	2^{1}	8	13														5
1			4	13	3	7		9^{1}	10^{2}	11■			5	6	2	8	12														6
1		3	4			7^{1}	8		10				5	6	2	11	9^{2}	12	13												7
1		3	4	12		7	8		10				5^{3}	6	2^{1}	11^{2}	13		9	14											8
1		3		5		7^{1}	8		10	12				6	2	13	11^{3}	14	9^{2}	4											9
1		3	12	5			8		10	13				6	2^{1}	11^{3}	7^{2}	14	9	4											10
1		3		5		7^{1}	8		10^{2}	11				6	2	12	9		13	4											11
1		3		5	12	7^{2}	8			10^{1}				6^{3}	2	13	11	14	9	4											12
1		3		5	6				10	9	8^{1}				2	7	11	12		4											13
1				5	6		8^{1}		10	11	12				2	3	9^{2}	7		4■	13										14
1			4	5	6	12	8		10	11					2	3	9^{2}	7^{1}			13										15
1		3	2^{3}	5		7^{1}	8		10	9		13		6	14	11^{2}		12		4											16
1		3	12	5			8^{3}		10	11	7			6^{2}	2^{1}	13	14	9		4											17
1		3		5					10	11	6	12			2	8^{2}	7^{1}	9		4								13			18
1		3	12	5			8		10^{2}	9		11		6				13		4		2^{1}	7								19
1		3		5			8		10	11		9		6^{2}			12			4		2^{1}	7					13			20
1		3	12	5			8^{3}		10	11^{2}		9				13	14	7		4		2^{1}		6							21
1		3^{2}		5					10			9^{1}		12	2	11	13	7		4			8	6							22
1		3	12	5			8^{2}		10	13		9^{3}		6			14			4		2^{1}	11	7							23
1		3	4	5	12		8^{3}	13	10	11^{1}				6			9^{2}					2	14	7							24
1		3	4	5	11			12	10^{2}	9^{3}		13		6	2		7^{1}	14						8							25
1		3	4	5	11			12^{2}	10^{1}	9		13		6	2		7						14	8^{3}							26
1		3	4	5	11				10	9				6	2^{1}		7						8					12			27
1		3^{3}	4	5	6				10	9		12			2^{1}	13	11	14					7	8^{2}							28
1		3	4	5	6		12		10^{2}	9	8^{1}	13			2			7					11								29
1			4	5	3		8			9	6	10			2		11^{1}	12					7								30
1		3^{3}	4	5	6		8			9	14	10^{2}			2		11^{1}	12					7		13						31
1		3	2^{2}	5			8^{1}			12			13	6			11						7^{3}	14	10	4	9				32
1		3	2	5			8	12		11		7^{1}		6^{3}			13							14	10^{2}	4	9				33
1		3	2	5			8	12		11		10^{1}		6^{3}			13							14	7^{2}	4	9				34
1		3	2	5			8^{3}	12		11		10^{1}		6			13							14	7^{2}	4	9				35
1		3	2	5				12		11		10^{1}		6^{3}			13						14	8	7^{2}	4	9				36
1			2	5	3		8^{1}	10^{2}		11			4				7						12	6	13		9				37
1		3	2	5	11^{1}		8	10^{2}		9^{3}			4	12			7							6	13		14				38
1		3	2	5	12		8	9^{3}		11^{1}			4	13			7^{2}							6	14		10				39
1		3^{3}	2	5	11^{1}		8	10		9			4	12				13						6	7^{2}		14				40
1		3	2	5			8	9		11			4	6										7			10				41
1		3	2	5			8	9^{2}		11			4					12					7	6^{1}	13		10				42
		3		5			8^{2}			11			4				12	10			13		7	6			9		1	2^{1}	43
		3		5			8^{2}			11			4				12	13			10^{3}		7	6	14		9		1	2^{1}	44
		3	2	5			8			11			4				10^{1}	12					7	6			9		1		45
		3	4	5			8^{1}	12		11					2^{2}		10	13					7	6			9		1		46

FA Cup

Third Round	West Ham U	(h)	1-2

Carling Cup

First Round	Milton Keynes D	(a)	1-0
Second Round	Northampton T	(h)	2-0
Third Round	Birmingham C	(a)	1-2

NOTTINGHAM FOREST FL Championship 1

FOUNDATION

One of the oldest football clubs in the world, Nottingham Forest was formed at a meeting in the Clinton Arms in 1865. Known originally as the Forest Football Club, the game which first drew the founders together was 'shinney', a form of hockey. When they determined to change to football in 1865, one of their first moves was to buy a set of red caps to wear on the field.

The City Ground, Nottingham NG2 5FJ.

Telephone: (0115) 982 4444.

Fax: (0115) 982 4455.

Ticket Office: 0871 226 1980.

Website: www.nottinghamforest.co.uk

Email: info@nottinghamforest.co.uk

Ground Capacity: 30,602.

Record Attendance: 49,946 v Manchester U, Division 1, 28 October 1967.

Pitch Measurements: 112yd × 74yd.

Chairman: Nigel Doughty.

Chief Executive: Mark Arthur.

Football Administrator: Jane Carnelly.

Manager: Colin Calderwood.

Physios: Gary Fleming and Steve Devine.

Colours: Red shirts, white shorts, red stockings.

Change Colours: Blue shirts, blue shorts, blue stockings.

Year Formed: 1865.

Turned Professional: 1889.

Ltd Co.: 1982.

Club Nickname: 'Reds'.

Previous Grounds: 1865, Forest Racecourse; 1879, The Meadows; 1880, Trent Bridge Cricket Ground; 1882, Parkside, Lenton; 1885, Gregory, Lenton; 1890, Town Ground; 1898, City Ground.

First Football League Game: 3 September 1892, Division 1, v Everton (a) D 2–2 – Brown; Earp, Scott; Hamilton, A. Smith, McCracken; McCallum, W. Smith, Higgins (2), Pike, McInnes.

Record League Victory: 12–0 v Leicester Fosse, Division 1, 12 April 1909 – Iremonger; Dudley, Maltby; Hughes (1), Needham, Armstrong; Hooper (3), Marrison, West (3), Morris (2), Spouncer (3 incl. 1p).

Record Cup Victory: 14–0 v Clapton (away), FA Cup 1st rd, 17 January 1891 – Brown; Earp, Scott; A. Smith, Russell, Jeacock; McCallum (2), 'Tich' Smith (1), Higgins (5), Lindley (4), Shaw (2).

Record Defeat: 1–9 v Blackburn R, Division 2, 10 April 1937.

HONOURS

Football League: Division 1 – Champions 1977–78, 1997–98; Runners-up 1966–67, 1978–79; Division 2 – Champions 1906–07, 1921–22; Runners-up 1956–57; Division 3 (S) – Champions 1950–51.

FA Cup: Winners 1898, 1959; Runners-up 1991.

Football League Cup: Winners 1978, 1979, 1989, 1990; Runners-up 1980, 1992.

Anglo-Scottish Cup: Winners 1977;

Simod Cup: Winners 1989.

Zenith Data Systems Cup: Winners: 1992.

European Competitions: *European Cup:* 1978–79 (winners), 1979–80 (winners), 1980–81. *European Fairs Cup:* 1961–62, 1967–68. *UEFA Cup:* 1983–84, 1984–85, 1995–96. *Super Cup:* 1979–80 (winners), 1980–81 (runners-up).*World Club Championship:* 1980.

SKY SPORTS FACT FILE

The first Nottingham Forest player to score as many as four goals in an FA Cup tie for the club was Sam Widdowson, also famous on a wider scale as the man who invented shinguards. His foursome came on 2 December 1882 in a 7–2 win over Sheffield Heeley.

Most League Points (2 for a win): 70, Division 3 (S), 1950–51.

Most League Points (3 for a win): 94, Division 1, 1997–98.

Most League Goals: 110, Division 3 (S), 1950–51.

Highest League Scorer in Season: Wally Ardron, 36, Division 3 (S), 1950–51.

Most League Goals in Total Aggregate: Grenville Morris, 199, 1898–1913.

Most League Goals in One Match: 4, Enoch West v Sunderland, Division 1, 9 November 1907; 4, Tommy Gibson v Burnley, Division 2, 25 January 1913; 4, Tom Peacock v Port Vale, Division 2, 23 December 1933; 4, Tom Peacock v Barnsley, Division 2, 9 November 1935; 4, Tom Peacock v Port Vale, Division 2, 23 November 1935; 4, Tom Peacock v Doncaster R, Division 2, 26 December 1935; 4, Tommy Capel v Gillingham, Division 3S, 18 November 1950; 4, Wally Ardron v Hull C, Division 2, 26 December 1952; 4, Tommy Wilson v Barnsley, Division 2, 9 February 1957; 4, Peter Withe v Ipswich T, Division 1, 4 October 1977.

Most Capped Player: Stuart Pearce, 76 (78), England.

Most League Appearances: Bob McKinlay, 614, 1951–70.

Youngest League Player: Craig Westcarr, 16 years 257 days v Burnley, 13 October 2001.

Record Transfer Fee Received: £8,500,000 from Liverpool for Stan Collymore, June 1995.

Record Transfer Fee Paid: £3,500,000 to Celtic for Pierre van Hooijdonk, March 1997.

Football League Record: 1892 Elected to Division 1; 1906–07 Division 2; 1907–11 Division 1; 1911–22 Division 2; 1922–25 Division 1; 1925–49 Division 2; 1949–51 Division 3 (S); 1951–57 Division 2; 1957–72 Division 1; 1972–77 Division 2; 1977–92 Division 1; 1992–93 FA Premier League; 1993–94 Division 1; 1994–97 FA Premier League; 1997–98 Division 1; 1998–99 FA Premier League; 1999–2004 Division 1; 2004–05 FLC; 2005– FL1.

MANAGERS

Harry Radford 1889–97 *(Secretary-Manager)*
Harry Haslam 1897–1909 *(Secretary-Manager)*
Fred Earp 1909–12
Bob Masters 1912–25
John Baynes 1925–29
Stan Hardy 1930–31
Noel Watson 1931–36
Harold Wightman 1936–39
Billy Walker 1939–60
Andy Beattie 1960–63
Johnny Carey 1963–68
Matt Gillies 1969–72
Dave Mackay 1972
Allan Brown 1973–75
Brian Clough 1975–93
Frank Clark 1993–96
Stuart Pearce 1996–97
Dave Bassett 1997–98 *(previously General Manager from February)*
Ron Atkinson 1998–99
David Platt 1999–2001
Paul Hart 2001–04
Joe Kinnear 2004
Gary Megson 2005
Colin Calderwood May 2006–

LATEST SEQUENCES

Longest Sequence of League Wins: 7, 9.5.1979 – 1.9.1979.

Longest Sequence of League Defeats: 14, 21.3.1913 – 27.9.1913.

Longest Sequence of League Draws: 7, 29.4.1978 – 2.9.1978.

Longest Sequence of Unbeaten League Matches: 42, 26.11.1977 – 25.11.1978.

Longest Sequence Without a League Win: 19, 8.9.1998 – 16.1.1999.

Successive Scoring Runs: 22 from 28.3.1931.

Successive Non-scoring Runs: 7 from 13.12.2003.

TEN YEAR LEAGUE RECORD

		P	*W*	*D*	*L*	*F*	*A*	*Pts*	*Pos*
1996-97	PR Lge	38	6	16	16	31	59	34	20
1997-98	Div 1	46	28	10	8	82	42	94	1
1998-99	PR Lge	38	7	9	22	35	69	30	20
1999-2000	Div 1	46	14	14	18	53	55	56	14
2000-01	Div 1	46	20	8	18	55	53	68	11
2001-02	Div 1	46	12	18	16	50	51	54	16
2002-03	Div 1	46	20	14	12	82	50	74	6
2003-04	Div 1	46	15	15	16	61	58	60	14
2004-05	FL C	46	9	17	20	42	66	44	23
2005-06	FL 1	46	19	12	15	67	52	69	7

DID YOU KNOW

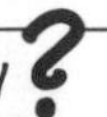

One historical event in the 1905 tour of Argentina by Nottingham Forest which produced seven wins and a 51–2 goal ratio, concerned a young spectator attending his first match. He was Juan Domingo Peron, later to become President of Argentina!

NOTTINGHAM FOREST 2005–06 LEAGUE RECORD

Match No.	Date	Venue	Opponents	Result		H/T Score	Lg. Pos.	Goalscorers	Attendance
1	Aug 6	H	Huddersfield T	W	2-1	1-0	—	Dobie 45, Johnson 87	24,042
2	9	A	Walsall	L	2-3	1-0	—	Commons 36, Friio 85	8703
3	13	A	Swindon T	L	1-2	1-1	16	Commons 39	8108
4	20	H	Scunthorpe U	L	0-1	0-0	20		19,091
5	27	A	Gillingham	W	3-1	2-0	15	Johnson 8, Dobie 44, Weir-Daley 79	7228
6	Sept 3	H	Brentford	L	1-2	0-0	17	Thompson 48	17,234
7	10	A	Barnsley	L	0-2	0-2	21		10,080
8	17	H	Rotherham U	W	2-0	0-0	18	Lester (pen) 76, Commons 88	20,123
9	20	H	Bristol C	W	3-1	2-1	—	Lester (pen) 25, Perch 27, Commons 55	16,666
10	24	A	Swansea C	D	1-1	0-0	14	Lester 54	18,212
11	27	H	Blackpool	D	1-1	0-1	—	Breckin 79	17,071
12	Oct 1	H	Tranmere R	W	1-0	0-0	9	Taylor 70	22,022
13	9	A	Southend U	L	0-1	0-0	—		10,104
14	15	H	Hartlepool U	W	2-0	1-0	8	Taylor 34, Bopp (pen) 90	17,586
15	22	A	Yeovil T	L	0-3	0-2	11		9072
16	29	H	Bradford C	W	1-0	1-0	10	Johnson 24	17,983
17	Nov 12	A	Bournemouth	D	1-1	1-0	9	Southall 19	9222
18	19	H	Southend U	W	2-0	0-0	7	Wilson (og) 51, Southall 70	19,576
19	26	A	Huddersfield T	L	1-2	0-2	10	Lester 46	17,370
20	Dec 6	H	Port Vale	W	1-0	1-0	—	Tyson 31	17,696
21	10	H	Walsall	D	1-1	1-1	8	Breckin 35	20,912
22	16	A	Scunthorpe U	L	1-3	0-1	—	Taylor (pen) 65	5857
23	26	H	Doncaster R	W	4-0	1-0	8	Breckin 45, Thompson 50, Southall 53, Taylor 67	23,009
24	31	H	Chesterfield	D	0-0	0-0	9		21,909
25	Jan 2	A	Colchester U	L	1-3	0-0	9	Tyson 88	5767
26	14	H	Oldham Ath	W	3-0	1-0	10	Grant Holt 25, Tyson 63, Southall 67	17,807
27	17	A	Brentford	D	1-1	1-1	—	Commons 5	7859
28	21	A	Rotherham U	D	1-1	1-0	9	Tyson 34	7222
29	27	H	Barnsley	L	0-2	0-2	—		16,237
30	31	A	Milton Keynes D	L	0-1	0-1	—		7670
31	Feb 4	A	Blackpool	D	2-2	1-1	9	Breckin 45, Bennett 90	8399
32	11	H	Swansea C	L	1-2	1-1	10	Tyson 21	19,132
33	15	A	Oldham Ath	L	0-3	0-0	—		5584
34	18	A	Port Vale	W	2-0	1-0	10	Commons 40, Tyson 90	6793
35	25	H	Swindon T	W	7-1	3-0	9	Southall 3 3, 51, 55, Morgan 2 17, 57, Breckin 29, Lester 90	22,444
36	Mar 4	A	Bristol C	D	1-1	0-0	10	Perch 66	14,397
37	11	H	Gillingham	D	1-1	1-1	10	Tyson 45	19,446
38	18	A	Doncaster R	W	2-1	1-0	8	Commons 25, Grant Holt 47	8299
39	25	H	Milton Keynes D	W	3-0	2-0	8	McClenahan (og) 20, Grant Holt 34, Breckin 90	18,214
40	Apr 1	A	Chesterfield	W	3-1	2-1	8	Breckin 19, Tyson 29, Thompson 87	7073
41	8	H	Colchester U	W	1-0	0-0	8	Perch 72	22,680
42	15	A	Tranmere R	W	1-0	1-0	7	Grant Holt 17	9152
43	17	H	Yeovil T	W	2-1	1-1	6	Breckin 40, Southall 68	28,193
44	22	A	Hartlepool U	L	2-3	1-1	7	Tyson 15, Commons 67	5336
45	29	H	Bournemouth	D	1-1	0-0	7	Tyson 56	26,847
46	May 6	A	Bradford C	D	1-1	0-1	7	Bennett 88	15,608

Final League Position: 7

GOALSCORERS

League (67): Tyson 10, Breckin 8, Commons 8, Southall 8, Lester 5 (2 pens), Grant Holt 4, Taylor 4 (1 pen), Johnson 3, Perch 3, Thompson 3, Bennett 2, Dobie 2, Morgan 2, Bopp 1 (pen), Friio 1, Weir-Daley 1, own goals 2.
Carling Cup (2): Breckin 2.
FA Cup (3): Taylor 2, Gary Holt 1.
Football League Trophy (2): Bopp 1, Weir-Daly 1.

Pedersen R 17 + 1	Eaden N 26 + 2	Curtis J 27	Cullip D 10 + 1	Breckin I 46	Holt Gary 23 + 3	Southall N 37 + 3	Gardner R 6 + 6	Dobie S 6 + 2	Taylor G 17 + 3	Commons K 36 + 1	Johnson D 12 + 5	Friio D 11 + 6	Morgan W 41 + 2	Gerrard P 21 + 1	Perch J 34 + 4	Harris N — + 1	Padula G 3	Thompson J 28 + 7	Weir-Daley S — + 6	Dadi E — + 5	Lester J 15 + 23	Bopp E 2 + 10	Hoult R 8	Fernandez V — + 1	Bastians F 2 + 9	Tyson N 28	Bennett J 18	Holt Grant 18 + 1	Clingan S 14 + 1	Vickerton M — + 1	Match No.
1	2	3	4	5	6	7[1]	8[2]	9	10[3]	11	12	13	14																		1
1■	2[1]	3	4	5	6	7	8[G]	9	10[2]	11	13	12		15																	2
1	2[2]	3	4[3]	5	6	7	8	9	10[1]	11	12	13	14																		3
1	12			5	6[3]	7[2]	13		10	11	9	4	2		8[1]	14	3														4
	2			5	6	7	12	9	10	11[1]	8[3]		4	1			3[2]	13	14												5
	2			5	6	7[1]		9[3]	10[2]	11	8		3	1	12			4	13	14											6
1	2		4	5		7[1]	6	9	10[2]	11	8[3]	13			12		3			14											7
	2			5		7				11	9	4	6		8			3			10[1]	12	1								8
	2			5		7	12			11[3]	9	4	6		8			3[1]		13	10[2]	14	1								9
	2			5		7	12			11[2]	9	4	6		8			3			10[1]		1	13							10
	2			5		7			12	11	9[1]	4[2]	6		8			3	14		10[3]	13	1								11
	2			5		7			12	11[2]	9[1]	4	6		8			3	14		10[3]	13	1								12
	2			5		7			12	11	9[1]	4[2]	6		8			3	14		10[3]	13	1								13
	2			5		7[2]			9	11	12	4	6		8			3			10[1]	13	1								14
	2[1]		12	5		7[2]			9■	11[3]	13	4	6		8			3			10	14	1								15
	2			5	6	7					9[2]		4	1	8			3		12	10	11[1]			13						16
	2		4	5	11	7					9		6	1	8			3	12		10[1]										17
	2	3	4	5		7			9				6	1	8			11			12					10[1]					18
	2[1]	11	4	5■	12	7			9				3[2]	1	8[3]			6			13■				14	10					19
	2	4		5		7			9				6	1	8			3			12				11[1]	10					20
	2	4		5		7[1]			9				6	1	8			3		13	12				11[2]	10					21
	2	3		5	6[1]	7	11		9				4	1	8[1]						12					10					22
	2	3		5		7			9[1]	11[3]		12	6	1	8			4			13	14				10[2]					23
	2	3		5		7			9	11[2]		12	6[1]	1	8			4			13					10					24
	2			5	6	7	12		9[2]	11[3]			4	1	8[1]			3			13	14				10					25
		2[2]		5	13	7				11[3]			6	1	8			4			12				14	10	3	9[1]			26
				5		7	12			11[1]		4	6	1	8			2			13					10	3■	9[2]			27
	12			5	6	7[2]				11[3]		4[1]	3	1	8			2			13				14	10		9			28
	2[1]			5	12	7[2]				11[3]			6	1	8			3			13				14	10■		9	4		29
	2[2]		4	5			7[1]	13					6	1	8			3			10	12						9[3]	11	14	30
		2	4	5		7		12					6■	1							9	8[1]				10	3		11		31
		2	4	5		7				11				1				6[1]			9				12	10	3		8		32
15		2		5		7				12			4	1[G]	13			6			11[1]					10	3	9	8[2]		33
1		2		5		7				11[3]			4		8[1]			12			13				14	10	3	9[2]	6		34
1		2[1]		5	6	7				11[2]			4		8			12			13				14	10[3]	3	9			35
1		2		5	6	7[2]				11[3]			4		8			12							14	10	3	9[1]	13		36
1		2		5	6					11			4		8						12					10	3	9[1]	7		37
1		2		5	6					11			4		8			12			13					10	3	9[2]	7[1]		38
1		2		5	6					11			4		8						12					10	3	9[1]	7		39
1		2		5	6					11			4		8			12			13					10	3	9[2]	7[1]		40
1		2		5	6					11			4		8			12			13					10	3	9[2]	7[1]		41
1		2		5	6	12				11			4					8			13					10	3	9[2]	7[1]		42
1		2		5	6	12				11			4					8			13					10[2]	3	9	7[1]		43
1		2		5	6	12				11			4		13			8[2]			14					10	3	9[3]	7[1]		44
1		2		5	6	7				11			4		8						9[1]					10	3	12			45
		2[1]		5	6	7				11			4	1	8						12					10	3	9			46

FA Cup

First Round	Weymouth	(h)	1-1
		(a)	2-0
Second Round	Chester C	(a)	0-3

Carling Cup

First Round	Macclesfield T	(h)	2-3

Football League Trophy

First Round	Woking	(a)	2-3

NOTTS COUNTY — FL Championship 2

FOUNDATION

According to the official history of Notts County 'the true date of Notts' foundation has to be the meeting at the George Hotel on 7 December 1864'. However, in the same opening chapter is the following: *The Nottingham Guardian* on 28 November 1862 carried the following report: 'The opening of the Nottingham Football Club commenced on Tuesday last at Cremorne Gardens. A side was chosen by W. Arkwright and Chas Deakin. A very spirited game resulted in the latter scoring two goals and two rouges against one and one.'

Meadow Lane Stadium, Meadow Lane, Nottingham NG2 3HJ.

Telephone: (0115) 952 9000.

Fax: (0115) 955 3994.

Ticket Office: (0115) 955 7204 (weekdays), (0115) 955 7210 (match days).

Website: www.nottscountyfc.co.uk

Email: info@nottscountyfc.co.uk

Ground Capacity: 20,300.

Record Attendance: 47,310 v York C, FA Cup 6th rd, 12 March 1955.

Pitch Measurements: 113yd × 72yd.

Chairman: Jeff Moore.

Chief Executive: Geoff Davey.

Secretary: Tony Cuthbert.

Manager: Steve Thompson.

First Team Coach: John Gannon.

Physio: John Haselden.

Colours: Black and white striped shirts, black shorts, black stockings.

Change Colours: All yellow.

Year Formed: 1862* (*see Foundation*).

Turned Professional: 1885. ***Ltd Co.:*** 1888.

Club Nickname: 'Magpies'.

Previous Grounds: 1862, The Park; 1864, The Meadows; 1877, Beeston Cricket Ground; 1880, Castle Ground; 1883, Trent Bridge; 1910, Meadow Lane.

First Football League Game: 15 September 1888, Football League, v Everton (a) L 1–2 – Holland; Guttridge, McLean; Brown, Warburton, Shelton; Hodder, Harker, Jardine, Moore (1), Wardle.

Record League Victory: 11–1 v Newport Co, Division 3 (S), 15 January 1949 – Smith; Southwell, Purvis; Gannon, Baxter, Adamson; Houghton (1), Sewell (4), Lawton (4), Pimbley, Johnston (2).

Record Cup Victory: 15–0 v Rotherham T (at Trent Bridge), FA Cup 1st rd, 24 October 1885 – Sherwin; Snook, H. T. Moore; Dobson (1), Emmett (1), Chapman; Gunn (1), Albert Moore (2), Jackson (3), Daft (2), Cursham (4), (1 og).

HONOURS

Football League: Division 1 best season: 3rd, 1890–91, 1900–01; Division 2 – Champions 1896–97, 1913–14, 1922–23; Runners-up 1894–95, 1980–81; Promoted from Division 2 1990–91 (play-offs); Division 3 (S) – Champions 1930–31, 1949–50; Runners-up 1936–37; Division 3 – Champions 1997–98; Runners-up 1972–73; Promoted from Division 3 1989–90 (play-offs); Division 4 – Champions 1970–71; Runners-up 1959–60.

FA Cup: Winners 1894; Runners-up 1891.

Football League Cup: best season: 5th rd, 1964, 1973, 1976.

Anglo-Italian Cup: Winners 1995; Runners-up 1994.

SKY SPORTS FACT FILE

Notts County can claim to have had on their books at the same time the two most prolific pre-war goalscorers in English football during 1937–38, Hughie Gallacher and Dixie Dean though the former preceded the latter in the team.

Record Defeat: 1–9 v Blackburn R, Division 1, 16 November 1889. 1–9 v Aston Villa, Division 1, 29 September 1888. 1–9 v Portsmouth, Division 2, 9 April 1927.

Most League Points (2 for a win): 69, Division 4, 1970–71.

Most League Points (3 for a win): 99, Division 3, 1997–98.

Most League Goals: 107, Division 4, 1959–60.

Highest League Scorer in Season: Tom Keetley, 39, Division 3 (S), 1930–31.

Most League Goals in Total Aggregate: Les Bradd, 124, 1967–78.

Most League Goals in One Match: 5, Robert Jardine v Burnley, Division 1, 27 October 1888; 5, Daniel Bruce v Port Vale, Division 2, 26 February 1895; 5, Bertie Mills v Barnsley, Division 2, 19 November 1927.

Most Capped Player: Kevin Wilson, 15 (42), Northern Ireland.

Most League Appearances: Albert Iremonger, 564, 1904–26.

Youngest League Player: Tony Bircumshaw, 16 years 54 days v Brentford, 3 April 1961.

Record Transfer Fee Received: £2,500,000 from Derby Co for Craig Short, September 1992.

Record Transfer Fee Paid: £685,000 to Sheffield U for Tony Agana, November 1991.

Football League Record: 1888 Founder Member of the Football League; 1893–97 Division 2; 1897–1913 Division 1; 1913–14 Division 2; 1914–20 Division 1; 1920–23 Division 2; 1923–26 Division 1; 1926–30 Division 2; 1930–31 Division 3 (S); 1931–35 Division 2; 1935–50 Division 3 (S); 1950–58 Division 2; 1958–59 Division 3; 1959–60 Division 4; 1960–64 Division 3; 1964–71 Division 4; 1971–73 Division 3; 1973–81 Division 2; 1981–84 Division 1; 1984–85 Division 2; 1985–90 Division 3; 1990–91 Division 2; 1991–95 Division 1; 1995–97 Division 2; 1997–98 Division 3; 1998–2004 Division 2; 2004– FL2.

LATEST SEQUENCES

Longest Sequence of League Wins: 10, 3.12.1997 – 31.1.1998.

Longest Sequence of League Defeats: 7, 3.9.1983 – 16.10.1983.

Longest Sequence of League Draws: 5, 2.12.1978 – 26.12.1978.

Longest Sequence of Unbeaten League Matches: 19, 26.4.1930 – 6.12.1930.

Longest Sequence Without a League Win: 20, 3.12.1996 – 31.3.1997.

Successive Scoring Runs: 35 from 26.4.1930.

Successive Non-scoring Runs: 5 from 30.11.1912.

MANAGERS

Edwin Browne 1883–93 *(Secretary-Manager)*
Tom Featherstone 1893 *(Secretary-Manager)*
Tom Harris 1893–1913 *(Secretary-Manager)*
Albert Fisher 1913–27
Horace Henshall 1927–34
Charlie Jones 1934–35
David Pratt 1935
Percy Smith 1935–36
Jimmy McMullan 1936–37
Harry Parkes 1938–39
Tony Towers 1939–42
Frank Womack 1942–43
Major Frank Buckley 1944–46
Arthur Stollery 1946–49
Eric Houghton 1949–53
George Poyser 1953–57
Tommy Lawton 1957–58
Frank Hill 1958–61
Tim Coleman 1961–63
Eddie Lowe 1963–65
Tim Coleman 1965–66
Jack Burkitt 1966–67
Andy Beattie *(General Manager)* 1967
Billy Gray 1967–68
Jimmy Sirrel 1969–75
Ron Fenton 1975–77
Jimmy Sirrel 1978–82 *(continued as General Manager to 1984)*
Howard Wilkinson 1982–83
Larry Lloyd 1983–84
Richie Barker 1984–85
Jimmy Sirrel 1985–87
John Barnwell 1987–88
Neil Warnock 1989–93
Mick Walker 1993–94
Russell Slade 1994–95
Howard Kendall 1995
Colin Murphy 1995 *(continued as General Manager to 1996)*
Steve Thompson 1996
Sam Allardyce 1997–99
Gary Brazil 1999–2000
Jocky Scott 2000–01
Gary Brazil 2001
Billy Dearden 2002–04
Gary Mills 2004
Ian Richardson 2004–05
Gudjon Thordarson 2005–06
Steve Thompson June 2006–

TEN YEAR LEAGUE RECORD

		P	W	D	L	F	A	Pts	Pos
1996-97	Div 2	46	7	14	25	33	59	35	24
1997-98	Div 3	46	29	12	5	82	43	99	1
1998-99	Div 2	46	14	12	20	52	61	54	16
1999-2000	Div 2	46	18	11	17	61	55	65	8
2000-01	Div 2	46	19	12	15	62	66	69	8
2001-02	Div 2	46	13	11	22	59	71	50	19
2002-03	Div 2	46	13	16	17	62	70	55	15
2003-04	Div 2	46	10	12	24	50	78	42	23
2004-05	FL 2	46	13	13	20	46	62	52	19
2005-06	FL 2	46	12	16	18	48	63	52	21

DID YOU KNOW 

Legendary Notts County goalkeeper Albert Iremonger was introduced to the Prince of Wales before the match at Lea Bridge Road against Clapton Orient on 7 February 1914. Afterwards he received an autographed souvenir from HRH.

NOTTS COUNTY 2005–06 LEAGUE RECORD

Match No.	*Date*	*Venue*	*Opponents*	*Result*		*H/T Score*	*Lg. Pos.*	*Goalscorers*	*Attendance*
1	Aug 6	A	Torquay U	D	0-0	0-0	—		3754
2	9	H	Wrexham	W	1-0	0-0	—	Long [90]	4382
3	13	H	Lincoln C	W	2-1	1-1	3	Scoffham [40], Baudet [56]	6153
4	20	A	Stockport Co	D	1-1	1-1	5	Williams (og) [14]	3922
5	27	H	Bristol R	W	2-0	1-0	1	Hurst 2 [1, 79]	4405
6	29	A	Mansfield T	W	3-2	1-1	1	Hurst 2 [18, 87], Edwards [82]	6444
7	Sept 2	A	Darlington	D	1-1	0-0	—	White [85]	5273
8	10	H	Chester C	D	1-1	0-0	1	Hurst [56]	5404
9	17	A	Shrewsbury T	L	0-2	0-2	5		4011
10	24	H	Rushden & D	D	0-0	0-0	5		5142
11	27	A	Grimsby T	L	0-4	0-2	—		5577
12	Oct 1	A	Macclesfield T	D	0-0	0-0	8		1892
13	7	H	Boston U	L	1-2	0-2	—	Edwards [90]	6632
14	15	A	Rochdale	L	0-3	0-3	14		3348
15	22	H	Carlisle U	D	0-0	0-0	15		5347
16	29	A	Bury	W	3-2	2-0	12	Hurst 3 [35, 45, 57]	2671
17	Nov 12	H	Cheltenham T	L	2-3	1-1	15	Baudet (pen) [45], Edwards [57]	4903
18	19	A	Boston U	W	2-1	1-0	10	Hurst [7], White [82]	2921
19	26	H	Torquay U	D	2-2	1-0	11	Edwards [8], De Bolla [79]	4442
20	Dec 6	A	Peterborough U	L	0-2	0-1	—		2833
21	10	A	Wrexham	D	1-1	0-0	13	Sheridan [84]	4726
22	17	H	Stockport Co	W	2-0	1-0	10	Baudet [40], Friars [73]	4261
23	26	A	Oxford U	L	0-3	0-0	12		5626
24	31	A	Leyton Orient	L	0-1	0-1	16		3715
25	Jan 2	H	Barnet	W	1-0	1-0	13	Martin [10]	5249
26	7	H	Darlington	W	3-2	0-1	8	Scoffham [55], Martin [82], Baudet (pen) [87]	4244
27	14	A	Wycombe W	L	0-2	0-0	12		5185
28	21	H	Shrewsbury T	W	2-1	2-0	11	Pipe [20], Wilson [37]	5438
29	24	H	Northampton T	D	2-2	1-0	—	Pipe [24], Crooks [75]	4884
30	28	A	Chester C	W	2-0	0-0	8	Baudet (pen) [66], Dadi (pen) [85]	2599
31	Feb 4	H	Grimsby T	L	0-1	0-1	10		6456
32	11	A	Rushden & D	L	0-1	0-1	11		3113
33	14	H	Wycombe W	L	1-2	0-1	—	O'Callaghan [55]	3710
34	18	H	Peterborough U	L	1-2	0-1	13	Dadi (pen) [77]	6012
35	25	A	Lincoln C	L	1-2	0-1	14	Edwards [71]	5262
36	Mar 4	H	Mansfield T	D	2-2	1-0	14	Palmer [43], Chillingworth [76]	9779
37	11	A	Bristol R	W	2-1	1-0	12	Chillingworth [5], Scoffham [74]	6280
38	18	H	Oxford U	D	0-0	0-0	15		5265
39	25	A	Northampton T	L	0-2	0-1	15		6077
40	Apr 1	H	Leyton Orient	D	1-1	0-0	15	Edwards [74]	5007
41	8	A	Barnet	L	1-2	0-0	16	Scoffham [46]	2841
42	15	H	Macclesfield T	D	1-1	1-0	17	Edwards [45]	4393
43	17	A	Carlisle U	L	1-2	1-1	18	Scoffham [25]	10,735
44	22	H	Rochdale	D	1-1	0-0	18	Martin [72]	4413
45	29	A	Cheltenham T	L	0-2	0-1	21		4518
46	May 6	H	Bury	D	2-2	0-1	21	Martin [86], Baudet (pen) [89]	9817

Final League Position: 21

GOALSCORERS

League (48): Hurst 9, Edwards 7, Baudet 6 (4 pens), Scoffham 5, Martin 4, Chillingworth 2, Dadi 2 (2 pens), Pipe 2, White 2, Crooks 1, De Bolla 1, Friars 1, Long 1, O'Callaghan 1, Palmer 1, Sheridan 1, Wilson 1, own goal 1.
Carling Cup (1): Palmer 1.
FA Cup (3): Baudet 1, McMahon 1, Tann 1.
Football League Trophy (2): Long 1, McMahon 1 (pen).

Pilkington K 45	O'Callaghan B 30 + 3	Martin D 16 + 6	Edwards M 45 + 1	Wilson K 33 + 1	Baudet J 42	Pipe D 43	McMahon L 23 + 6	Scoffham S 22 + 8	Hurst G 15 + 3	Palmer C 25 + 4	Sheridan J 13 + 14	Ullathorne R 31 + 2	White A 10 + 16	Long S 7 + 12	Gill M 7 + 7	Gordon G 4 + 2	McGoldrick D 4 + 2	Berry T 4 + 1	Zadkovich R — + 1	Friars E 5	Tann A 4 + 1	Williams M — + 1	De Bolla M 8 + 6	Needham L 21 + 1	Crooks L 18	Dadi E 9 + 2	Sissoko N 1 + 2	Chillingworth D 8 + 5	Doyle N 12	Marshall S 1	Frost S — + 4	*Match No.*
1	2[1]	3[2]	4	5	6	7	8	9	10[3]	11	12	13	14																			1
1	2		4	5	6	7	8	9[1]	12	11[3]		3	10[2]	14	13																	2
1	2		4	5	6	7	8	9		11[1]		3	10[2]	12		13																3
1	2	12	4	5	6	7	8	9				3[1]	13	11[3]	14	10[2]																4
1	2		4	5	6	7[1]	13	9[3]	10	11[2]		3	14	12	8																	5
1	2	12	4	5	6		8	9[3]	10	7[1]	13	3	14	11[2]																		6
1	2		4	5	6	7	8[3]	9[2]	10[1]		12	3	14		11	13																7
1	2		4	5	6	7		9▮	10[1]	11[2]	12	3	13		8																	8
1	2	8[2]	4	5	6▮	7			10[3]	12	13	3[1]	14		11	9																9
1	2		4	5		7	8		10[3]		11	3		12	6[1]	9[2]	13	14														10
1	2	12	4	5		7[2]	8▮				6	3[1]		13	11		10	9														11
1	2		4	5		7		12	13		6	3		14	11[3]	9[1]	10[2]	8														12
1	2[1]		4	5	6	7		9[2]	13		8[3]	3	14		12		10	11														13
1	2	3[3]	4	5	6	7[2]		12	10		13			11			9[1]	8	14													14
1			4	5	6		8	9[2]	10		7[1]	3		11	12		13			2												15
1	12		4	5	6	2	8[2]	9[3]	10			11	14	7	13					3[1]												16
1			2	5	6	7	8[2]		10			3	9	11[1]	12						4	13										17
1	2		4	5	6	7	8		10			3	9								11											18
1	2		4	5	6	7	8[1]		10			11	9[2]	12							3▮		13									19
1	2[3]		4	5	6	7	8		10[2]		13		9	12							3[1]		14	11								20
1			4	5	6	7	8		10[1]		12	3	13							2			9[2]	11								21
1			8	5	6	2					10	3	12	11[2]	13					4			9[1]	7								22
1	2[3]		4	5	6		8	12		13	10[1]	3	14							7[2]			9	11								23
1	2	3	4		6	7	12			8	13	5[1]	10										9[2]	11								24
1	2	3	4		6	7	8	12		5	10[1]		9											11								25
1	2	3	4	13	6	7	8	12		5	10[1]		9[2]											11								26
1	2[1]		4	5	6	7	8[2]			10	9										12		13	11	3							27
1		3	4	5	6	7				8	12	13											9[1]	11[2]	2	10						28
1		3	4	5	6	7				8	12												9[1]	11	2	10						29
1	12	3	4	5	6	7		13		8													9[2]	11[1]	2	10						30
1		3[2]	4	5	6	7		12		8				13									9	11[1]	2	10						31
1	2	3[3]	4	5	6	7	12	9[2]			11												14	13	8[1]	10						32
1	2		4[2]	5	6	7	8																12	11	3	9	13	10[1]				33
1	2		12	5	6	7	8			13													14	11[3]	3[1]	9	4[2]	10				34
1	2	12	4	5		7	8[3]	9[2]		6		3[1]														13	14	10	11			35
1			4	5	6	7	12			11	9	3[1]													8	10[2]		13	2			36
1	2	12	4		6	7[2]		14		11	13	3	9[3]												5[1]			10	8			37
1	2		4		6	7		9		11[2]	12	3[3]	14	13											5			10	8[1]			38
1	2		5		6	7		9[2]		11	12	3[3]	13												4[1]	14		10	8			39
1		12	5		6	7		9[1]		13	8[2]	3	14											11	2			10[3]	4			40
1			5		6	7		9		11		3	12	13										8[2]	4			10[1]	2			41
	2	3[1]	5		6	7	12	9[2]		8														11	4			13	10	1		42
1	12	3[1]	5		6	2[3]		9		8		7[2]		13										11	10				4		14	43
1		3	5		6	10	4[2]	9[1]		7														11	8			12	2		13	44
1		4	5		6	10		9[2]		7		3												11	8[1]			12	2		13	45
1		4	5		6	7	12	9[3]		8		3												11[1]		10[2]		13	2		14	46

FA Cup

First Round	Bristol C	(a)	2-0
Second Round	Torquay U	(a)	1-2

Carling Cup

First Round	Watford	(a)	1-3

Football League Trophy

First Round	Northampton T	(a)	2-5

OLDHAM ATHLETIC FL Championship 1

FOUNDATION

It was in 1895 that John Garland, the landlord of the Featherstall and Junction Hotel, decided to form a football club. As Pine Villa they played in the Oldham Junior League. In 1899 the local professional club, Oldham County, went out of existence and one of the liquidators persuaded Pine Villa to take over their ground at Sheepfoot Lane and change their name to Oldham Athletic.

Boundary Park, Furtherwood Road, Oldham OL1 2PA.

Telephone: 0871 226 2235.

Fax: 0871 226 1715.

Ticket Office: 0871 226 1653.

Website: www.oldhamathletic.co.uk

Email: enquiries@oldhamathletic.co.uk

Ground Capacity: 13,624.

Record Attendance: 46,471 v Sheffield W, FA Cup 4th rd, 25 January 1930.

Pitch Measurements: 110yd × 72yd.

Chairman: Barry Chaytow.

Chief Executive/Secretary: Alan Hardy.

Manager: John Sheridan.

Assistant Manager: John Breckin.

Physio: Lee Nobes.

Colours: Royal blue shirts with white trim, royal blue shorts with white trim, white stockings.

Change Colours: Navy shirts, navy shorts, navy stockings.

Year Formed: 1895.

Turned Professional: 1899.

Ltd Co.: 1906.

Previous Name: 1895, Pine Villa; 1899, Oldham Athletic.

Club Nickname: 'The Latics'.

Previous Grounds: 1895, Sheepfoot Lane; 1900, Hudson Field; 1906, Sheepfoot Lane; 1907, Boundary Park.

First Football League Game: 9 September 1907, Division 2, v Stoke (a) W 3–1 – Hewitson; Hodson, Hamilton; Fay, Walders, Wilson; Ward, W. Dodds (1), Newton (1), Hancock, Swarbrick (1).

Record League Victory: 11–0 v Southport, Division 4, 26 December 1962 – Bollands; Branagan, Marshall; McCall, Williams, Scott; Ledger (1), Johnstone, Lister (6), Colquhoun (1), Whitaker (3).

HONOURS

Football League: Division 1 – Runners-up 1914–15; Division 2 – Champions 1990–91; Runners-up 1909–10; Division 3 (N) – Champions 1952–53; Division 3 – Champions 1973–74; Division 4 – Runners-up 1962–63.

FA Cup: Semi-final 1913, 1990, 1994.

Football League Cup: Runners-up 1990.

SKY SPORTS FACT FILE

When centre-half Jack Martin joined Oldham Athletic from the defunct Wigan Borough in 1931 he completed League appearances for seven Lancashire clubs: Accrington Stanley, Blackpool, Southport and Nelson. He had also been on Burnley's books!

Record Cup Victory: 10–1 v Lytham, FA Cup 1st rd, 28 November 1925 – Gray; Wynne, Grundy; Adlam, Heaton, Naylor (1), Douglas, Pynegar (2), Ormston (2), Barnes (3), Watson (2).

Record Defeat: 4–13 v Tranmere R, Division 3 (N), 26 December 1935.

Most League Points (2 for a win): 62, Division 3, 1973–74.

Most League Points (3 for a win): 88, Division 2, 1990–91.

Most League Goals: 95, Division 4, 1962–63.

Highest League Scorer in Season: Tom Davis, 33, Division 3 (N), 1936–37.

Most League Goals in Total Aggregate: Roger Palmer, 141, 1980–94.

Most League Goals in One Match: 7, Eric Gemmell v Chester, Division 3N, 19 January 1952.

Most Capped Player: Gunnar Halle, 24 (64), Norway.

Most League Appearances: Ian Wood, 525, 1966–80.

Youngest League Player: Wayne Harrison, 15 years 11 months v Notts Co, 27 October 1984.

Record Transfer Fee Received: £1,700,000 from Aston Villa for Earl Barrett, February 1992.

Record Transfer Fee Paid: £750,000 to Aston Villa for Ian Olney, June 1992.

Football League Record: 1907 Elected to Division 2; 1910–23 Division 1; 1923–35 Division 2; 1935–53 Division 3 (N); 1953–54 Division 2; 1954–58 Division 3 (N); 1958–63 Division 4; 1963–69 Division 3; 1969–71 Division 4; 1971–74 Division 3; 1974–91 Division 2; 1991–92 Division 1; 1992–94 FA Premier League; 1994–97 Division 1; 1997–2004 Division 2; 2004– FL1.

MANAGERS

David Ashworth 1906–14
Herbert Bamlett 1914–21
Charlie Roberts 1921–22
David Ashworth 1923–24
Bob Mellor 1924–27
Andy Wilson 1927–32
Jimmy McMullan 1933–34
Bob Mellor 1934–45
(continued as Secretary to 1953)
Frank Womack 1945–47
Billy Wootton 1947–50
George Hardwick 1950–56
Ted Goodier 1956–58
Norman Dodgin 1958–60
Jack Rowley 1960–63
Les McDowall 1963–65
Gordon Hurst 1965–66
Jimmy McIlroy 1966–68
Jack Rowley 1968–69
Jimmy Frizzell 1970–82
Joe Royle 1982–94
Graeme Sharp 1994–97
Neil Warnock 1997–98
Andy Ritchie 1998–2001
Mick Wadsworth 2001–02
Iain Dowie 2002–03
Brian Talbot 2004–05
Ronnie Moore 2005–06
John Sheridan June 2006–

LATEST SEQUENCES

Longest Sequence of League Wins: 10, 12.1.1974 – 12.3.1974.

Longest Sequence of League Defeats: 8, 15.12.1934 – 2.2.1935.

Longest Sequence of League Draws: 5, 26.12.1982 – 15.1.1983.

Longest Sequence of Unbeaten League Matches: 20, 1.5.1990 – 10.11.1990.

Longest Sequence Without a League Win: 17, 4.9.1920 – 18.12.1920.

Successive Scoring Runs: 25 from 15.1.1927.

Successive Non-scoring Runs: 6 from 4.2.1922.

TEN YEAR LEAGUE RECORD

		P	W	D	L	F	A	Pts	Pos
1996-97	Div 1	46	10	13	23	51	66	43	23
1997-98	Div 2	46	15	16	15	62	54	61	13
1998-99	Div 2	46	14	9	23	48	66	51	20
1999-2000	Div 2	46	16	12	18	50	55	60	14
2000-01	Div 2	46	15	13	18	53	65	58	15
2001-02	Div 2	46	18	16	12	77	65	70	9
2002-03	Div 2	46	22	16	8	68	38	82	5
2003-04	Div 2	46	12	21	13	66	60	57	15
2004-05	FL 1	46	14	10	22	60	73	52	19
2005-06	FL 1	46	18	11	17	58	60	65	10

DID YOU KNOW ?

On Easter Monday morning 1934 Fred Swift, goalkeeping brother of Frank, played for Oldham Athletic against Preston North End at Deepdale. In the afternoon he turned out in the club's reserves Central League fixture at Boundary Park.

OLDHAM ATHLETIC 2005–06 LEAGUE RECORD

Match No.	Date	Venue	Opponents	Result	H/T Score	Lg. Pos.	Goalscorers	Attendance
1	Aug 6	H	Yeovil T	W 2-0	2-0	—	Porter [24], Warne [26]	6979
2	9	A	Swindon T	W 3-2	2-0	—	Scott [13], Liddell 2 (1 pen) [38, 51 (p)]	5294
3	12	A	Tranmere R	L 0-4	0-1	—		8466
4	20	H	Chesterfield	W 4-1	2-0	2	Branston [2], Liddell [4], Warne 2 [57, 86]	5347
5	27	A	Colchester U	D 0-0	0-0	3		2742
6	29	H	Rotherham U	L 0-1	0-0	8		6950
7	Sept 4	A	Southend U	L 1-2	0-2	12	Bonner [69]	5261
8	10	H	Huddersfield T	L 0-3	0-2	13		6803
9	17	A	Gillingham	W 1-0	1-0	10	Killen [6]	6259
10	24	H	Bournemouth	W 1-0	0-0	6	Liddell (pen) [62]	5058
11	28	A	Port Vale	D 2-2	1-0	—	Beckett [15], Killen [81]	3796
12	Oct 1	A	Barnsley	L 0-4	0-3	11		8077
13	9	H	Brentford	L 0-1	0-0	—		5089
14	15	A	Swansea C	D 0-0	0-0	14		14,029
15	22	H	Bristol C	W 4-3	2-0	10	Hughes [4], Wellens [25], Porter [56], Liddell [87]	5456
16	29	A	Scunthorpe U	L 2-4	2-2	14	Liddell 2 [17, 33]	5055
17	Nov 13	H	Doncaster R	L 0-1	0-0	17		5800
18	19	A	Brentford	D 3-3	3-2	17	Porter 3 [11, 21, 23]	5450
19	26	A	Yeovil T	W 2-0	1-0	16	Warne 2 [39, 82]	5852
20	Dec 6	H	Walsall	W 2-1	0-0	—	Porter [34], Warne [72]	3878
21	10	H	Swindon T	D 2-2	0-1	13	Wellens [56], Liddell [71]	5354
22	17	A	Chesterfield	D 1-1	0-0	12	Warne [47]	4304
23	26	H	Bradford C	W 2-1	2-1	11	Butcher [8], Beckett [13]	6982
24	31	H	Hartlepool U	W 2-1	1-0	8	Beckett [37], Liddell [61]	5047
25	Jan 2	A	Milton Keynes D	W 1-0	1-0	8	Beckett [43]	5082
26	7	H	Southend U	D 0-0	0-0	7		5662
27	10	A	Blackpool	L 0-1	0-0	—		5977
28	14	A	Nottingham F	L 0-3	0-1	8		17,807
29	21	H	Gillingham	W 2-0	0-0	8	Beckett 2 [84, 87]	5783
30	28	A	Huddersfield T	L 2-3	2-1	8	Porter [13], Beckett [33]	12,973
31	Feb 4	H	Port Vale	L 0-1	0-1	8		5555
32	11	A	Bournemouth	D 0-0	0-0	8		5453
33	15	H	Nottingham F	W 3-0	0-0	—	Wellens [53], Butcher [73], Beckett [82]	5584
34	18	A	Walsall	W 2-0	0-0	7	Beckett [72], Warne [74]	5816
35	25	H	Tranmere R	W 1-0	1-0	7	Wellens [35]	5281
36	Mar 11	H	Colchester U	W 1-0	0-0	7	Butcher [90]	5822
37	14	A	Rotherham U	L 0-2	0-1	—		5823
38	18	A	Bradford C	W 4-1	3-0	7	Warne [16], Beckett 2 [17, 82], Butcher [34]	7959
39	25	H	Blackpool	W 3-1	1-1	7	Beckett 3 (1 pen) [45, 55, 86 (p)]	6480
40	31	A	Hartlepool U	D 1-1	1-1	—	Beckett (pen) [45]	5259
41	Apr 8	H	Milton Keynes D	L 1-2	1-2	7	Beckett (pen) [28]	5919
42	15	H	Barnsley	L 0-3	0-0	8		7772
43	17	A	Bristol C	L 1-2	1-0	8	Beckett [45]	12,779
44	22	H	Swansea C	D 1-1	0-0	9	Beckett (pen) [60]	5179
45	29	A	Doncaster R	L 0-1	0-0	10		6104
46	May 6	H	Scunthorpe U	D 1-1	1-0	10	Eyres [45]	5544

Final League Position: 10

GOALSCORERS

League (58): Beckett 18 (4 pens), Liddell 9 (2 pens), Warne 9, Porter 7, Butcher 4, Wellens 4, Killen 2, Bonner 1, Branston 1, Eyres 1, Hughes 1, Scott 1.
Carling Cup (0).
FA Cup (6): Porter 2, Eyres 1, Hall C 1, Liddell 1 (pen), Warne 1.
Football League Trophy (1): Liddell 1 (pen).

Day C 30	Forbes T 33+6	Tierney M 13+6	Scott R 19+2	Branston G 38	Owen G 17	Wellens R 45	Butcher R 32+4	Porter C 18+13	Warne P 38+2	Liddell A 29	Facey D —+3	Bonner M 5+2	Eyres D 15+6	Edwards P 29+5	Stam S 9+4	Killen C 10+2	Beckett L 27+7	Hughes M 30+3	Hall D 9+1	Hall C 3+14	Haining W 13+2	Swailes C 14+1	Grant A 2	Wolfenden M —+1	Grant L 16	Taylor C 11+3	Eardley I 1	Match No.
1	2	3	4	5	6	7	8	9	10	11																		1
1	2	3	4	5	6	7	8	9[1]	10	11	12																	2
1	2	3	4	5	6[1]	7	8[2]	9[3]	10	11	14	13	12															3
1	2	3	4	5	6	7	8	9[1]	10	11[2]	12			13														4
1	2	3	4	5	6	7[1]	8	9	10[2]	11		12		13														5
1	2	3	4	5[3]	6	7	8	12	10[2]	11				13	14	9[1]												6
1	2	3	4		6	7	12	13	10[2]	11		5[1]	14	8[3]		9												7
1	2	3	4		5	7	8[1]	12	10■	11		6				9[2]	13											8
1	2	12	4		5	7		9[2]		11		6	8		3[1]	10	13											9
1	2	3	4	5		7		12		11		6	8			9[1]	10											10
1	2	3	4	5		7	12	13		11		6[1]	8			9	10[2]											11
1	2	12	4	5	6[1]	7	8		13	11			3			9	10[2]											12
1	2		4[2]	5		7		12	13	11			8			9[1]	10	3	6									13
1	2		4	5		7		12	9	11			8				10[1]	3	6									14
1	12	3	2	5		7[1]		9	10	11			8[2]	13				6	4									15
1	12	3	2	5		7		9[2]	10	11			8				13	6	4[1]									16
1	2	3			6	7		9[1]	10	11			8[2]	13			12	4	5									17
1	2				6	7	8	9[1]	10	11				3				4	5	12								18
1	2			5		7	8	9	10	11				3■				4			6							19
1	2		6	5		7	8	9	10	11				3				4										20
1	2		3	5		7	8	9[1]	10	11				6			12	4										21
1	2		3			7[2]		12	10	11				8	6		9[1]	4	5	13								22
1				5	6	7	8	12	10	11				3	13		9[1]	2	4[2]									23
1				5	6	7	8		10	11				3	4		9	2										24
1	2	13	12[2]	5	6[1]		8	9		11				7	4		10[3]	3		14								25
1	2			5		7	8[1]		10	11			13	6[3]	4	12	9[2]	3				14						26
1	2			5		7	8[1]	12	10[3]	11			14		4	13	9[2]	3				6						27
1	2[1]		13	5		7			10	11				8		9[3]	14	12			3[2]	4	6					28
1	2			5		7			10[1]	11			13	8		9[3]	12	3		14		6	4[2]					29
1	2			5		7	6	9	10[2]				11[1]	3	12		8			13		4						30
	2			5		7	8[1]		10[2]				11[3]	3	13		9	12		6		4		14	1			31
	2			5		7	8							11	6		10	3		9		4			1			32
				5		7	8	9[1]						2	6		10	3		12	13	4			1	11[2]		33
				5		7	8		10					2	6[2]		9	3[1]		12	13	4			1	11		34
				5		7	8		10[1]					2			9	3		12	6	4			1	11		35
	12			5		7	8	9[2]	10					3				2[1]		13	6	4			1	11		36
		12		5		7	8[1]	13	10[3]					11			9[2]	3		14	2	4			1	6		37
	12			5		7[1]	8		10[2]					11			9	6		13	2	4			1	3		38
	2			5		7[1]	8		10					6			9	3	12		4				1	11		39
	2			5		7	8		10					11			9	6		12	4				1	3[1]		40
	12				6	7	8[3]	13	10					3			9	2		14	5	4[1]			1	11[2]		41
	12				6	7	8	13	10				14	3			9	2[2]			5	4[1]			1	11[3]		42
	2			5		7	12	9	10[2]				11[1]	3			8	4			6				1	13		43
	2			5		7[1]	12		10				8	3			9	4		13	6				1	11[2]		44
	2	12		5		7	8		10				11[1]	3			9	4[2]	6						1	13		45
		12		5		7	8[2]		10				11[1]	3			9	13		2[3]	6				1	14	4	46

FA Cup

First Round	Chasetown	(a)	1-1
		(h)	4-0
Second Round	Brentford	(h)	1-1
		(a)	0-1

Carling Cup

First Round	Leeds U	(a)	0-2

Football League Trophy

First Round	Carlisle U	(h)	1-1

OXFORD UNITED Conference

FOUNDATION

There had been an Oxford United club around the time of World War I but only in the Oxfordshire Thursday League and there is no connection with the modern club which began as Headington in 1893, adding 'United' a year later. Playing first on Quarry Fields and subsequently Wootten's Fields, they owe much to a Dr Hitchings for their early development.

The Kassam Stadium, Grenoble Road, Oxford OX4 4XP.

Telephone: (01865) 337 500.

Fax: (01865) 337 555.

Ticket Office: (01865) 337 533.

Website: www.oufc.co.uk

Email: admin@oufc.co.uk

Ground Capacity: 12,500.

Record Attendance: 22,730 v Preston NE, FA Cup 6th rd, 29 February 1964.

Pitch Measurements: 115yd × 71yd.

Chairman: Nick Merry.

Secretary: Mick Brown.

Manager: Jim Smith.

Colours: Yellow shirts with navy trim, navy shorts with yellow trim, navy stockings with yellow trim.

Change Colours: White shirts, white shorts, white stockings.

Year Formed: 1893.

Turned Professional: 1949.

Ltd Co.: 1949.

Club Nickname: 'The U's'.

Previous Names: 1893, Headington; 1894, Headington United; 1960, Oxford United.

Previous Grounds: 1893, Headington Quarry; 1894, Wootten's Field; 1898, Sandy Lane Ground; 1902, Britannia Field; 1909, Sandy Lane; 1910, Quarry Recreation Ground; 1914, Sandy Lane; 1922, The Paddock Manor Road; 1925, Manor Ground; 2001, The Kassam Stadium.

First Football League Game: 18 August 1962, Division 4, v Barrow (a) L 2–3 – Medlock; Beavon, Quartermain; R. Atkinson, Kyle, Jones; Knight, G. Atkinson (1), Houghton (1), Cornwell, Colfar.

Record League Victory: 7–0 v Barrow, Division 4, 19 December 1964 – Fearnley; Beavon, Quartermain; R. Atkinson (1), Kyle, Jones; Morris, Booth (3), Willey (1), G. Atkinson (1), Harrington (1).

HONOURS

Football League: Division 1 best season: 12th, 1997–98; Division 2 – Champions 1984–85; Runners-up 1995–96; Division 3 – Champions 1967–68, 1983–84; Division 4 – Promoted 1964–65 (4th).

FA Cup: best season: 6th rd, 1964 (shared record for 4th Division club).

Football League Cup: Winners 1986.

SKY SPORTS FACT FILE

The first player signed by Oxford United after entry to the Football League in 1962 was left-winger Ray Colfar who had impressed the previous season while playing for Cambridge United. He was formerly with Sutton United and Crystal Palace.

Record Cup Victory: 9–1 v Dorchester T, FA Cup 1st rd, 11 November 1995 – Whitehead; Wood (2), Ford M (1), Smith, Elliott, Gilchrist, Rush (1), Massey (Murphy), Moody (3), Ford R (1), Angel (Beauchamp (1)).

Record Defeat: 0–7 v Sunderland, Division 1, 19 September 1998.

Most League Points (2 for a win): 61, Division 4, 1964–65.

Most League Points (3 for a win): 95, Division 3, 1983–84.

Most League Goals: 91, Division 3, 1983–84.

Highest League Scorer in Season: John Aldridge, 30, Division 2, 1984–85.

Most League Goals in Total Aggregate: Graham Atkinson, 77, 1962–73.

Most League Goals in One Match: 4, Tony Jones v Newport Co, Division 4, 22 September 1962; 4, Arthur Longbottom v Darlington, Division 4, 26 October 1963; 4, Richard Hill v Walsall, Division 2, 26 December 1988; 4, John Durnin v Luton T, 14 November 1992.

Most Capped Player: Jim Magilton, 18 (52), Northern Ireland.

Most League Appearances: John Shuker, 478, 1962–77.

Youngest League Player: Jason Seacole, 16 years 149 days v Mansfield T, 7 September 1976.

Record Transfer Fee Received: £1,600,000 from Leicester C for Matt Elliott, January 1997.

Record Transfer Fee Paid: £475,000 to Aberdeen for Dean Windass, August 1998.

Football League Record: 1962 Elected to Division 4; 1965–68 Division 3; 1968–76 Division 2; 1976–84 Division 3; 1984–85 Division 2; 1985–88 Division 1; 1988–92 Division 2; 1992–94 Division 1; 1994–96 Division 2; 1996–99 Division 1; 1999–2001 Division 2; 2001–04 Division 3; 2004–06 FL2; 2006– Conference.

MANAGERS

Harry Thompson 1949–58
(Player-Manager) 1949-51
Arthur Turner 1959–69
(continued as General Manager to 1972)
Ron Saunders 1969
Gerry Summers 1969–75
Mick Brown 1975–79
Bill Asprey 1979–80
Ian Greaves 1980–82
Jim Smith 1982–85
Maurice Evans 1985–88
Mark Lawrenson 1988
Brian Horton 1988–93
Denis Smith 1993–97
Malcolm Crosby 1997
Malcolm Shotton 1998–99
Denis Smith 2000
David Kemp 2000–01
Mark Wright 2001
Ian Atkins 2001–04
Graham Rix 2004
Ramon Diaz 2004–05
Brian Talbot 2005–2006
Darren Patterson 2006
Jim Smith March 2006–

LATEST SEQUENCES

Longest Sequence of League Wins: 6, 6.4.1985 – 24.4.1985.

Longest Sequence of League Defeats: 7, 4.5.1991 – 7.9.1991.

Longest Sequence of League Draws: 5, 7.10.1978 – 28.10.1978.

Longest Sequence of Unbeaten League Matches: 20, 17.3.1984 – 29.9.1984.

Longest Sequence Without a League Win: 27, 14.11.1987 – 27.8.1988.

Successive Scoring Runs: 17 from 10.9.1983.

Successive Non-scoring Runs: 6 from 26.3.1988.

TEN YEAR LEAGUE RECORD

		P	W	D	L	F	A	Pts	Pos
1996-97	Div 1	46	16	9	21	64	68	57	17
1997-98	Div 1	46	16	10	20	60	64	58	12
1998-99	Div 1	46	10	14	22	48	71	44	23
1999-2000	Div 2	46	12	9	25	43	73	45	20
2000-01	Div 2	46	7	6	33	53	100	27	24
2001-02	Div 3	46	11	14	21	53	62	47	21
2002-03	Div 3	46	19	12	15	57	47	69	8
2003-04	Div 3	46	18	17	11	55	44	71	9
2004-05	FL 2	46	16	11	19	50	63	59	15
2005-06	FL 2	46	11	16	19	43	57	49	23

DID YOU KNOW ?

Still as Headington United in 1955–56 the leading scorer for Oxford United was Jimmy Smillie, an outside-right signed from Third Lanark. Unusually for a wing forward he broke the club's then individual scoring record with 25 League and Cup goals.

OXFORD UNITED 2005–06 LEAGUE RECORD

Match No.	Date	Venue	Opponents	Result	H/T Score	Lg. Pos.	Goalscorers	Attendance
1	Aug 6	A	Grimsby T	D 1-1	0-0	—	Hargreaves 86	4706
2	10	H	Torquay U	W 1-0	0-0	—	Bradbury 55	4820
3	13	H	Wycombe W	D 2-2	1-0	6	Hackett 17, Morgan 88	6364
4	20	A	Lincoln C	L 1-2	1-0	13	Davies 2	3724
5	27	H	Stockport Co	D 1-1	1-1	14	Roget 21	4329
6	Sept 2	A	Shrewsbury T	L 0-2	0-2	—		4073
7	10	H	Rushden & D	D 2-2	2-0	18	Sabin 24, Roget 25	4189
8	13	A	Bristol R	D 1-1	1-0	—	Hackett 45	5098
9	17	A	Darlington	W 2-1	0-0	16	Sabin 67, Davies 76	4127
10	24	H	Bury	W 2-1	2-0	12	Mansell 33, Bradbury (pen) 36	4198
11	27	A	Rochdale	W 1-0	0-0	—	Quinn 60	2347
12	Oct 1	A	Barnet	D 0-0	0-0	7		3272
13	7	H	Carlisle U	W 1-0	1-0	—	Basham 22	5392
14	14	A	Northampton T	L 0-1	0-0	—		6802
15	22	H	Boston U	D 0-0	0-0	7		5084
16	29	A	Leyton Orient	L 0-1	0-1	11		5268
17	Nov 12	H	Wrexham	L 0-3	0-1	14		4491
18	19	A	Carlisle U	L 1-2	0-1	15	Bradbury 90	6097
19	26	H	Grimsby T	L 2-3	0-1	15	Fitzgerald 51, Basham (pen) 90	4323
20	Dec 6	A	Cheltenham T	W 2-1	2-1	—	Basham 9, Sabin 41	2852
21	10	A	Torquay U	D 3-3	3-2	16	Sabin 2 5, 19, Bradbury (pen) 17	2678
22	16	H	Lincoln C	L 0-1	0-0	—		3795
23	26	H	Notts Co	W 3-0	0-0	15	Basham 63, Sabin 68, Quinn 77	5626
24	31	H	Mansfield T	L 1-2	1-0	17	Bradbury 38	4005
25	Jan 2	A	Chester C	W 1-0	0-0	14	Basham 75	2624
26	7	H	Shrewsbury T	L 0-3	0-0	17		3702
27	10	A	Peterborough U	D 0-0	0-0	—		2926
28	14	A	Macclesfield T	D 1-1	0-1	16	Basham 47	1972
29	21	H	Darlington	L 0-2	0-0	16		4204
30	28	A	Rushden & D	L 0-3	0-3	18		3823
31	Feb 4	H	Rochdale	D 1-1	1-1	19	Ashton 17	3978
32	15	H	Macclesfield T	D 1-1	1-1	—	E'Beyer 26	4331
33	18	H	Cheltenham T	D 1-1	0-0	18	Basham (pen) 76	5232
34	25	A	Wycombe W	L 1-2	0-1	18	Odubade 72	7016
35	Mar 11	A	Stockport Co	L 1-2	0-1	22	Sills 61	4424
36	15	H	Bristol R	W 1-0	0-0	—	Basham (pen) 65	6424
37	18	A	Notts Co	D 0-0	0-0	19		5265
38	21	A	Bury	D 1-1	0-0	—	Burgess 71	1882
39	25	H	Peterborough U	W 1-0	0-0	18	N'Toya 67	7486
40	Apr 1	A	Mansfield T	L 0-1	0-0	19		3480
41	8	H	Chester C	L 0-1	0-1	20		5754
42	15	H	Barnet	W 2-0	2-0	18	N'Toya 2 1, 25	6948
43	17	A	Boston U	L 0-1	0-1	19		2313
44	22	H	Northampton T	L 1-3	0-1	22	Willmott 75	8264
45	29	A	Wrexham	D 1-1	0-1	23	N'Toya (pen) 54	4575
46	May 6	H	Leyton Orient	L 2-3	1-1	23	Sabin 14, Willmott 66	12,243

Final League Position: 23

GOALSCORERS

League (43): Basham 8 (3 pens), Sabin 7, Bradbury 5 (2 pens), N'Toya 4 (1 pen), Davies 2, Hackett 2, Quinn 2, Roget 2, Willmott 2, Ashton 1, Burgess 1, E'Beyer 1, Fitzgerald 1, Hargreaves 1, Mansell 1, Morgan 1, Odubade 1, Sills 1.
Carling Cup (0).
FA Cup (6): Basham 5 (1 pen), Sabin 1.
Football League Trophy (3): Mansell 1, Roget 1, Sabin 1.

Turley B 32 + 1	Mansell L 44	Robinson M 44	Quinn B 44	Willmott C 38 + 3	Ashton J 32 + 1	Hackett C 19 + 2	Hargreaves C 34 + 1	Basham S 30 + 10	Bradbury L 18 + 4	Gray S 10	Davies C 10 + 10	Hughes R — + 3	Morgan D 1 + 2	Stirling J 6 + 4	Roget L 32 + 1	Sabin E 28 + 1	Campbell A 3 + 2	Griffin A 8 + 1	E'Beyer M 3 + 3	Roach N 1 + 6	Fitzgerald S 2 + 1	Tardif C 10 + 1	Burgess A 12 + 4	Dempster J 6	Odubade Y 4 + 4	Brooks J 4 + 5	Weedon B 1 + 1	Sills T 9 + 4	Goodhind W 4 + 2	Guatelli A 4	Smith J 5 + 1	N'Toya T 7 + 1	Horsted L 1 + 3	Gemmill S — + 1	Beechers B — + 1	Match No.
1	2	3	4	5	6	7	8	9^1	10	11^2	12	13																								1
1	2	3	4	5	6	7	8	9^1	10	11	12																									2
1	2	3	4	5	6	7	8	12	10^2	11	9^1		13																							3
1	2	3	4	5	6^3	7	8■		10^1	11^2	9	14	12	13																						4
1	2	3	4		6	7	8	12^2		11	10		9^1	13	5																					5
1	2	3	4■		6	7	8	9^3	10^2	11^1		12			5	13	14																			6
1	2	3			6	7	8		12	11	13			4^1	5	9	10^2																			7
1	2	3	4	6		7	8		12	11^1	13				5	9	10^2																			8
1	2	11	4	3	6	7			8		12				5	9	10^1																			9
1	2	11	4	3	6	7^2		12	8		10^1			13	5	9																				10
1	2	3	11	4	6			7	8		10				5	9																				11
1	2	3	11	4	6			7	8		10				5	9																				12
1	2	3	4	11	6	7		10	8						5	9																				13
1	2	3	4	5	8^1	7		11			10				6	9	12																			14
1	2	3	4	6	11	7		10^1	8		12				5	9																				15
1	2	3	4	8	6^3	7^1	12	13	10		11^2			14	5	9																				16
1	2	3	4^3	7	6	12	8	10	11^1		13				5	9^2		14																		17
1	2	3	4	5		7	8	9	12		10^1			6				11^2	13																	18
1	2	3	4	6		7■	8	12							5	9^2		11		13	10^1															19
1	2	3	4	6	12		8	9^1	7		13				5^2	10		11																		20
1		3	4	6	2		8	9^1	7		12				5	10		11																		21
1	2	3	4	7^1	6	12	8				11				5	10					9															22
	2	3	4	5	6	7		9^2	12					8		10			11^1	13		1														23
	2	3	4	5	6	7^2		9^3	11					8^1	12	10				13	14	1														24
	2	3	4	5	6			9	8					7		10		11				1														25
		3	4		6	7^1		9	8		12			2^2	5	10		11^3	13	14		1														26
	2	3	4	6	7		8	9							5	10		11				1														27
	2	3	4	6	7		8	9^1							5	10		11^2		12		1	13													28
	2	3	4^1	6	7		8	9^2							5	10			12	13		1	11													29
	2		4	6	7		8	12												9		1	3	5■	10^1	11^2	13									30
	2	3	4		6		8	9							5							1	11				7	10								31
1	2	3	4	12	6		8	9							5				7				11^1					10								32
15	2	3	4	12	6^1		8	9		11					5				7^2			1^6			13			10								33
1	2	3	4^3	12	6^1		8	9		11					5								7^2		13			10	14							34
1	4	3		5	6		8	7															11		9			10	2							35
1	7	3	4	6			8	11^2							5								13		9^1	12		10	2							36
1	7	3	4	6			8	11							5										9^1	12		10	2							37
1	7	3	4	6			8								5								11		12	9^1		10	2							38
	2	3	4	6			8	12							5								11^2			13		10^1		1	7	9^3	14			39
	2		4	5			8	9^1																3		7^2		12	13	1	6	10	11^3	14		40
	2	3	4	5			8	9^3								10^1							11	6				12		1	7^2	14	13			41
1	2	3	4	6			8	9^1							5	11^3							12			13		14			7^2	10				42
1	2	3^1	4	5	6^2		8	12							9	10							13			7^3						11	14			43
1	2	3	4	6			8	12							5	10^1							11	7	13							9^2				44
	2	3	4	5			8^1	7^2								9						15	11	6				13		1^8	12	10				45
1	2^2	3	4	5■			8	12								9^1							11	6		13					7^3	10			14	46

FA Cup

First Round	Eastbourne B	(a)	1-1
		(h)	3-0
Second Round	Cheltenham T	(a)	1-1
		(h)	1-2

Carling Cup

First Round	Gillingham	(a)	0-1

Football League Trophy

First Round	Brentford	(a)	1-1
Second Round	Leyton Orient	(h)	1-0
Quarter-Final	Cheltenham T	(a)	1-2

PETERBOROUGH UNITED FL Championship 2

FOUNDATION

The old Peterborough & Fletton club, founded in 1923, was suspended by the FA during season 1932–33 and disbanded. Local enthusiasts determined to carry on and in 1934 a new professional club, Peterborough United, was formed and entered the Midland League the following year. Peterborough's first success came in 1939–40, but from 1955–56 to 1959–60 they won five successive titles. During the 1958–59 season they were undefeated in the Midland League. They reached the third round of the FA Cup, won the Northamptonshire Senior Cup, the Maunsell Cup and were runners-up in the East Anglian Cup.

London Road Stadium, Peterborough PE2 8AL.

Telephone: (01733) 563 947.

Fax: (01733) 344 140.

Ticket Office: (01733) 865 674.

Website: www.theposh.com

Email: info@theposh.com

Ground Capacity: 15,460.

Record Attendance: 30,096 v Swansea T, FA Cup 5th rd, 20 February 1965.

Pitch Measurements: 112yd × 71yd.

Chairman: Steve Holt.

Director of Football: Barry Fry.

Executive Director: Bob Symns.

Secretary: Mary Faxon.

Manager: Keith Alexander.

First Team Coach: Gary Simpson.

Physio: Keith Oakes.

Colours: All blue.

Change Colours: All red.

Year Formed: 1934.

Turned Professional: 1934.

Ltd Co.: 1934.

Club Nickname: 'The Posh'.

First Football League Game: 20 August 1960, Division 4, v Wrexham (h) W 3–0 – Walls; Stafford, Walker; Rayner, Rigby, Norris; Hails, Emery (1), Bly (1), Smith, McNamee (1).

Record League Victory: 9–1 v Barnet (a) Division 3, 5 September 1998 – Griemink; Hooper (1), Drury (Farell), Gill, Bodley, Edwards, Davies, Payne, Grazioli (5), Quinn (2) (Rowe), Houghton (Etherington) (1).

HONOURS

Football League: Division 1 best season: 10th, 1992–93; Division 2 1991–92 (play-offs). Promoted from Division 3 1999–2000 (play-offs); Division 4 – Champions 1960–61, 1973–74.

FA Cup: best season: 6th rd, 1965.

Football League Cup: Semi-final 1966.

SKY SPORTS FACT FILE

In May 1966 John Mason, a schoolmaster and England amateur international forward with Alvechurch, had to decide whether to turn professional with Peterborough United and give up teaching. He did and scored 18 goals in 37 League appearances.

Record Cup Victory: 7–0 v Harlow T, FA Cup 1st rd, 16 November 1991 – Barber; Luke, Johnson, Halsall (1), Robinson D, Welsh, Sterling (1) (Butterworth), Cooper G (2 incl. 1p), Riley (1) (Culpin (1)), Charlery (1), Kimble.

Record Defeat: 1–8 v Northampton T, FA Cup 2nd rd (2nd replay), 18 December 1946.

Most League Points (2 for a win): 66, Division 4, 1960–61.

Most League Points (3 for a win): 82, Division 4, 1981–82.

Most League Goals: 134, Division 4, 1960–61.

Highest League Scorer in Season: Terry Bly, 52, Division 4, 1960–61.

Most League Goals in Total Aggregate: Jim Hall, 122, 1967–75.

Most League Goals in One Match: 5, Guiliano Grazioli v Barnet, Division 3, 5 September 1998.

Most Capped Player: James Quinn, 9 (46), Northern Ireland.

Most League Appearances: Tommy Robson, 482, 1968–81.

Youngest League Player: Matthew Etherington, 15 years 262 days v Brentford, 3 May 1997.

Record Transfer Fee Received: £700,000 from Tottenham H for Simon Davies, December 1999.

Record Transfer Fee Paid: £350,000 to Walsall for Martin O'Connor, July 1996.

Football League Record: 1960 Elected to Division 4; 1961–68 Division 3, when they were demoted for financial irregularities; 1968–74 Division 4; 1974–79 Division 3; 1979–91 Division 4; 1991–92 Division 3; 1992–94 Division 1; 1994–97 Division 2; 1997–2000 Division 3; 2000–04 Division 2; 2004–05 FL1; 2005– FL2.

MANAGERS

Jock Porter 1934–36
Fred Taylor 1936–37
Vic Poulter 1937–38
Sam Madden 1938–48
Jack Blood 1948–50
Bob Gurney 1950–52
Jack Fairbrother 1952–54
George Swindin 1954–58
Jimmy Hagan 1958–62
Jack Fairbrother 1962–64
Gordon Clark 1964–67
Norman Rigby 1967–69
Jim Iley 1969–72
Noel Cantwell 1972–77
John Barnwell 1977–78
Billy Hails 1978–79
Peter Morris 1979–82
Martin Wilkinson 1982–83
John Wile 1983–86
Noel Cantwell 1986–88 *(continued as General Manager)*
Mick Jones 1988–89
Mark Lawrenson 1989–90
Chris Turner 1991–92
Lil Fuccillo 1992–93
John Still 1994–95
Mick Halsall 1995–96
Barry Fry 1996–2005
Mark Wright 2005–06
Keith Alexander May 2006–

LATEST SEQUENCES

Longest Sequence of League Wins: 9, 1.2.1992 – 14.3.1992.

Longest Sequence of League Defeats: 5, 8.10.1996 – 26.10.1996.

Longest Sequence of League Draws: 8, 18.12.1971 – 12.2.1972.

Longest Sequence of Unbeaten League Matches: 17, 17.12.1960 – 8.4.1961.

Longest Sequence Without a League Win: 17, 23.9.1978 – 30.12.1978.

Successive Scoring Runs: 33 from 20.9.1960.

Successive Non-scoring Runs: 6 from 13.8.2002.

TEN YEAR LEAGUE RECORD

		P	*W*	*D*	*L*	*F*	*A*	*Pts*	*Pos*
1996-97	Div 2	46	11	14	21	55	73	47	21
1997-98	Div 3	46	18	13	15	63	51	67	10
1998-99	Div 3	46	18	12	16	72	56	66	9
1999-2000	Div 3	46	22	12	12	63	54	78	5
2000-01	Div 2	46	15	14	17	61	66	59	12
2001-02	Div 2	46	15	10	21	64	59	55	17
2002-03	Div 2	46	14	16	16	51	54	58	11
2003-04	Div 2	46	12	16	18	58	58	52	18
2004-05	FL 1	46	9	12	25	49	73	39	23
2005-06	FL 2	46	17	11	18	57	49	62	9

DID YOU KNOW ?

No other English League club has managed to achieve the feat performed by Peterborough United in their first four seasons in the Football League to average 100 goals. From 1960–61 they scored 136, 107, 93 and hit number 64 on 28 March 1964.

PETERBOROUGH UNITED 2005–06 LEAGUE RECORD

Match No.	*Date*	*Venue*	*Opponents*	*Result*	*H/T Score*	*Lg. Pos.*	*Goalscorers*	*Attendance*
1	Aug 6	H	Chester C	L 0-1	0-0	—		4980
2	9	A	Carlisle U	L 0-1	0-1	—		6511
3	13	A	Bristol R	W 3-2	2-1	16	Newton [5], Farrell [23], Logan [73]	5169
4	20	H	Mansfield T	W 2-0	0-0	9	Farrell [50], St Ledger-Hall [60]	4056
5	27	H	Torquay U	D 0-0	0-0	8		3502
6	29	A	Stockport Co	D 1-1	1-0	12	Quinn [2]	3774
7	Sept 2	A	Rushden & D	W 2-0	1-0	—	Logan [22], Gain [77]	4403
8	10	H	Grimsby T	L 0-1	0-0	11		4263
9	17	A	Lincoln C	W 2-1	0-0	8	Quinn [61], Newton [69]	5526
10	24	H	Shrewsbury T	L 0-2	0-0	11		4274
11	27	A	Cheltenham T	L 1-2	0-1	—	Quinn [75]	2531
12	Oct 1	A	Boston U	L 0-1	0-0	17		4126
13	15	A	Macclesfield T	W 4-0	0-0	15	Crow [47], Farrell 2 [67, 70], Willock [71]	1810
14	22	H	Rochdale	W 3-1	0-1	10	Crow 2 [54, 73], Burton (pen) [68]	4314
15	25	H	Wrexham	D 1-1	1-0	—	Farrell [30]	4014
16	29	A	Wycombe W	D 2-2	2-0	10	Crow [33], Benjamin [38]	5214
17	Nov 12	H	Leyton Orient	D 1-1	1-0	9	Willock [45]	5341
18	19	A	Wrexham	D 1-1	0-0	11	Crow [59]	4480
19	26	A	Chester C	L 1-3	0-1	12	Semple [75]	2701
20	Dec 6	H	Notts Co	W 2-0	1-0	—	Semple [41], Willock [57]	2833
21	10	H	Carlisle U	D 1-1	0-0	10	Crow [56]	3689
22	17	A	Mansfield T	D 0-0	0-0	11		3891
23	26	A	Barnet	L 1-2	1-1	13	Crow [13]	2715
24	31	A	Northampton T	W 1-0	1-0	10	Plummer [9]	7023
25	Jan 2	H	Bury	W 4-1	2-0	7	Quinn [6], Woodthorpe (og) [40], Burton [47], Day [64]	3687
26	7	H	Rushden & D	W 2-0	1-0	7	Holden [17], Quinn (pen) [76]	4613
27	10	H	Oxford U	D 0-0	0-0	—		2926
28	14	A	Darlington	L 1-2	1-0	7	Quinn [26]	3822
29	21	H	Lincoln C	D 1-1	1-0	9	Gain [30]	6227
30	28	A	Grimsby T	W 2-1	1-1	10	Gain [30], Crow [71]	4462
31	Feb 4	H	Cheltenham T	W 1-0	0-0	6	Logan [55]	3901
32	11	A	Shrewsbury T	L 1-2	1-0	7	Crow (pen) [39]	3295
33	14	H	Darlington	W 2-1	1-1	—	Arber 2 [43, 74]	3960
34	18	A	Notts Co	W 2-1	1-0	6	Crow [40], Quinn [58]	6012
35	25	H	Bristol R	L 1-2	0-1	6	Holden [90]	4292
36	Mar 4	H	Stockport Co	W 2-0	0-0	6	Holden [70], Semple [88]	3406
37	11	A	Torquay U	L 0-1	0-0	6		2438
38	18	H	Barnet	D 2-2	0-1	7	Crow [53], Logan [75]	3983
39	25	A	Oxford U	L 0-1	0-0	8		7486
40	Apr 1	H	Northampton T	L 0-1	0-1	7		8637
41	8	A	Bury	W 3-1	1-0	7	Crow 2 [49, 90], Newton [62]	2233
42	15	H	Boston U	L 0-1	0-0	7		5092
43	17	A	Rochdale	L 0-1	0-0	8		2318
44	22	H	Macclesfield T	W 3-2	0-0	8	Crow 2 [71, 90], Farrell [83]	3002
45	29	A	Leyton Orient	L 1-2	0-1	8	Opara [85]	6591
46	May 6	H	Wycombe W	L 0-2	0-1	9		5376

Final League Position: 9

GOALSCORERS

League (57): Crow 15 (1 pen), Quinn 7 (1 pen), Farrell 6, Logan 4, Gain 3, Holden 3, Newton 3, Semple 3, Willock 3, Arber 2, Burton 2 (1 pen), Benjamin 1, Day 1, Opara 1, Plummer 1, St Ledger-Hall 1, own goal 1.
Carling Cup (1): Plummer 1.
FA Cup (0).
Football League Trophy (5): Crow 2, Benjamin 1 (pen), Hand 1, Logan 1.

Tyler M 40	Holden D 34 + 1	Kennedy P 10 + 4	Arber M 46	St Ledger-Hall S 43	Burton S 17 + 2	Boucaud A 2 + 1	Carden P 42	Benjamin T 5 + 15	Crow D 34 + 4	Gain P 37	Day J 19 + 6	Plummer C 16 + 6	Semple R 11 + 17	Logan R 13 + 15	Farrell D 19 + 10	Newton A 36 + 4	Quinn J 21 + 3	Hand J 9	Miller A 2	Harrison L 6	Thorpe L 6	Willock C 9 + 6	Huke S 3	Bolland P 17	Kuqi N 1	Opara L 2 + 6	Ryan T 6 + 1	*Match No.*
1	2	3^{1}	4	5	6^{2}	7^{3}	8	9	10	11	12	13	14															1
1	2	3■	4	5			8	9^{2}	10^{3}	11	13	12	6^{1}	14	7													2
1	2■		4	5^{2}	6		8	12		11		3		13	7	9	10^{1}											3
1			4	5	6		8	12		11	3	2	13	14	7^{3}	10^{2}	9^{1}											4
1			4	2	5		6	12		11	7^{1}	3	14	13	9	8^{2}	10^{3}											5
1	14	3	4	2	5		6	12	13	11				9^{1}	7^{3}	8	10^{2}											6
1	3	7	4	2	5^{1}		6	10	13	11		12	14	9^{3}		8^{2}												7
1	3		4	2	5		6	12	13	11			14	9^{2}	7^{3}	8	10^{1}											8
1	3		4	2	5		6■	12	9^{2}	11		14		13	7^{3}	8	10^{1}											9
1	3		4	2	5				9^{2}	11			12	13	14	8	10	6^{1}	7^{3}									10
1	3	12	4	2	5^{1}		6					7			9	8	10	11										11
	3		4	2			6		12			5	13		11^{2}	8	10^{1}		7	1	9							12
1	3		4	2			6		10^{3}	11		5	12		7^{1}	8	13				9^{2}	14						13
1	3		4	2	5		6	12	9^{2}	11				13	7	8					10^{1}							14
1	3	12	4	2	5		6		9^{2}						11^{1}	8		7			10	13						15
1	3		4	2	5^{2}		6	10^{3}	9^{1}				13	12	11	8		7				14						16
1	3		4	2	5		6	12	9^{2}	11	13					8					10^{1}	7						17
1	3		4		6		2		9^{1}	11		5				8		7			10	12						18
1	3		4	2			6	10	9^{1}	11		5	13			8		7^{2}				12						19
1	2	3	4	5			6		9		11		8					7				10						20
1	2	3^{1}	4	5	12		6	13	9		11		8^{3}			14		7				10^{2}						21
1	2		4	3	5	12		13	9^{3}		11		7				14	8				10^{2}	6^{1}					22
1	2		4	3				12	9^{1}	11	7	5	8^{2}			13						10	6					23
1	2		4	3			6	12	9^{1}	11	13	5	7			8	10^{2}											24
1			4	2	6		8	12		11	3	5	7	13			10^{1}					9^{2}						25
1	2		4	3^{1}	12		6			11	7^{2}	5	8^{3}		13	14	10					9						26
1	2	3	4	5			8	12		11		6		13		7	10^{2}					9^{1}						27
1	2	3^{2}	4	5			8	12		11		6		14	13	7	10^{1}					9^{3}						28
1	2		4				8		9^{2}	11	3	6		12		7	10^{1}					13		5				29
1^{6}	2		4	6			8		9	11	3	15		10		7								5				30
	2		4	3		8	6		9		11		12	10		7^{1}				1				5				31
	2		4	3					9^{1}	11	7		13	10	12	8^{2}				1			6	5				32
	2		4	3			6		9	11	7			10^{1}	12	13	8^{2}			1				5				33
	2		4	3			6		9	11	7				12	8	10^{1}			1				5				34
	2	12	4				6		9^{3}	11^{2}	7	3^{1}	13	14		8	10			1				5				35
1	2		4	3			6		9^{1}	11			12		7	8	10							5				36
1	2		4	3			6		9	11	7		12		13	8^{1}	10^{2}							5				37
1		3	4	2			6		9	11	7^{1}		8	13	12									5	10^{2}			38
1		3	4	2			6		9	11	7^{2}			10^{1}		8	12							5		13		39
1	2^{2}		4	3			6		9^{1}	11			12		7	8								5		10	13	40
1			4	2			6		9	11			7^{2}	12	13	8								5		10^{1}	3	41
1			4	3			6		9	11				10^{1}	7	8								5		12	2	42
1			4	2			6		9	11	12			10^{2}	7^{1}	8								5		13	3	43
1			4	2			6		9	11	7^{1}			10	12	8								5^{2}		13	3	44
1		12	4	2			6		9	11^{2}			13	10	7^{1}	8								5^{3}		14	3	45
1			4	5			6		9		12	13	7^{3}	8	11^{1}	2	10^{2}									14	3	46

FA Cup

First Round	Burton Alb	(h)	0-0
		(a)	0-1

Carling Cup

First Round	Plymouth Arg	(a)	1-2

Football League Trophy

First Round	Bristol R	(h)	2-1
Second Round	Swindon T	(h)	2-1
Quarter-Final	Swansea C	(a)	1-3

PLYMOUTH ARGYLE FL Championship

FOUNDATION

The club was formed in September 1886 as the Argyle Football Club by former public and private school pupils who wanted to continue playing the game. The meeting was held in a room above the Borough Arms (a Coffee House), Bedford Street, Plymouth. It was common then to choose a local street/terrace as a club name and Argyle or Argyll was a fashionable name throughout the land due to Queen Victoria's great interest in Scotland.

Home Park, Plymouth, Devon PL2 3DQ.

Telephone: (01752) 562 561.

Fax: (01752) 606 167.

Ticket Office: 0871 222 1288.

Website: www.pafc.co.uk

Email: argyle@pafc.co.uk

Ground Capacity: 20,922.

Record Attendance: 43,596 v Aston Villa, Division 2, 10 October 1936.

Pitch Measurements: 110yd × 72yd.

Chairman: Paul Stapleton.

Vice-chairman: Robert Dennerly.

Chief Executive: Michael Dunford.

Secretary: Carole Rowntree.

Manager: Ian Holloway.

Assistant Managers: Gerry McCabe and Jocky Scott.

Physio: Paul Maxwell.

Colours: Green shirts, white shorts, green stockings.

Change Colours: White shirts, green shorts, white stockings.

Year Formed: 1886.

Turned Professional: 1903.

Ltd Co.: 1903.

Previous Name: 1886, Argyle Athletic Club; 1903, Plymouth Argyle.

Club Nickname: 'The Pilgrims'.

First Football League Game: 28 August 1920, Division 3, v Norwich C (h) D 1–1 – Craig; Russell, Atterbury; Logan, Dickinson, Forbes; Kirkpatrick, Jack, Bowler, Heeps (1), Dixon.

Record League Victory: 8–1 v Millwall, Division 2, 16 January 1932 – Harper; Roberts, Titmuss; Mackay, Pullan, Reed; Grozier, Bowden (2), Vidler (3), Leslie (1), Black (1), (1 og). 8–1 v Hartlepool U (a), Division 2, 7 May 1994 – Nicholls; Patterson (Naylor), Hill, Burrows, Comyn, McCall (1), Barlow, Castle (1), Landon (3), Marshall (1), Dalton (2).

HONOURS

Football League: Division 2 – Champions 2003–04; Division 3 (S) – Champions 1929–30, 1951–52; Runners-up 1921–22, 1922–23, 1923–24, 1924–25, 1925–26, 1926–27 (record of six consecutive years); Division 3 – Champions 1958–59, 2001–02; Runners-up 1974–75, 1985–86, Promoted 1995–96 (play-offs).

FA Cup: Semi-final 1984.

Football League Cup: Semi-final 1965, 1974.

SKY SPORTS FACT FILE

Jackie Wharton, 18, scored in the first minute of his debut for Plymouth Argyle against West Bromwich Albion on 3 September 1938. His son Terry making his bow for Wolverhampton Wanderers was also a marksman against Ipswich Town 23 years later.

Record Cup Victory: 6–0 v Corby T, FA Cup 3rd rd, 22 January 1966 – Leiper; Book, Baird; Williams, Nelson, Newman; Jones (1), Jackson (1), Bickle (3), Piper (1), Jennings.

Record Defeat: 0–9 v Stoke C, Division 2, 17 December 1960.

Most League Points (2 for a win): 68, Division 3 (S), 1929–30.

Most League Points (3 for a win): 102, Division 3, 2001–02.

Most League Goals: 107, Division 3 (S), 1925–26 and 1951–52.

Highest League Scorer in Season: Jack Cock, 32, Division 3 (S), 1926–27.

Most League Goals in Total Aggregate: Sammy Black, 180, 1924–38.

Most League Goals in One Match: 5, Wilf Carter v Charlton Ath, Division 2, 27 December 1960.

Most Capped Player: Moses Russell, 20 (23), Wales.

Most League Appearances: Kevin Hodges, 530, 1978–92.

Youngest League Player: Lee Phillips, 16 years 43 days v Gillingham, 29 October 1996.

Record Transfer Fee Received: £750,000 from Southampton for Mickey Evans, March 1997.

Record Transfer Fee Paid: £250,000 to Hartlepool U for Paul Dalton, June 1992.

Football League Record: 1920 Original Member of Division 3; 1921–30 Division 3 (S); 1930–50 Division 2; 1950–52 Division 3 (S); 1952–56 Division 2; 1956–58 Division 3 (S); 1958–59 Division 3; 1959–68 Division 2; 1968–75 Division 3; 1975–77 Division 2; 1977–86 Division 3; 1986–95 Division 2; 1995–96 Division 3; 1996–98 Division 2; 1998–2002 Division 3; 2002–04 Division 2; 2004– FLC.

MANAGERS

Frank Brettell 1903–05
Bob Jack 1905–06
Bill Fullerton 1906–07
Bob Jack 1910–38
Jack Tresadern 1938–47
Jimmy Rae 1948–55
Jack Rowley 1955–60
Neil Dougall 1961
Ellis Stuttard 1961–63
Andy Beattie 1963–64
Malcolm Allison 1964–65
Derek Ufton 1965–68
Billy Bingham 1968–70
Ellis Stuttard 1970–72
Tony Waiters 1972–77
Mike Kelly 1977–78
Malcolm Allison 1978–79
Bobby Saxton 1979–81
Bobby Moncur 1981–83
Johnny Hore 1983–84
Dave Smith 1984–88
Ken Brown 1988–90
David Kemp 1990–92
Peter Shilton 1992–95
Steve McCall 1995
Neil Warnock 1995–97
Mick Jones 1997–98
Kevin Hodges 1998–2000
Paul Sturrock 2000–04
Bobby Williamson 2004–05
Tony Pulis 2005–06
Ian Holloway June 2006–

LATEST SEQUENCES

Longest Sequence of League Wins: 9, 8.3.1986 – 12.4.1986.

Longest Sequence of League Defeats: 9, 12.10.1963 – 7.12.1963.

Longest Sequence of League Draws: 5, 26.2.2000 – 14.3.2000.

Longest Sequence of Unbeaten League Matches: 22, 20.4.1929 – 21.12.1929.

Longest Sequence Without a League Win: 13, 27.4.1963 – 2.10.1963.

Successive Scoring Runs: 39 from 15.4.1939.

Successive Non-scoring Runs: 5 from 20.9.1947.

TEN YEAR LEAGUE RECORD

		P	W	D	L	F	A	Pts	Pos
1996-97	Div 2	46	12	18	16	47	58	54	19
1997-98	Div 2	46	12	13	21	55	70	49	22
1998-99	Div 3	46	17	10	19	58	54	61	13
1999-2000	Div 3	46	16	18	12	55	51	66	12
2000-01	Div 3	46	15	13	18	54	61	58	12
2001-02	Div 3	46	31	9	6	71	28	102	1
2002-03	Div 2	46	17	14	15	63	52	65	8
2003-04	Div 2	46	26	12	8	85	41	90	1
2004-05	FL C	46	14	11	21	52	64	53	17
2005-06	FL C	46	13	17	16	39	46	56	14

DID YOU KNOW?

In blitz recovering Home Park, Plymouth Argyle struggled in 1945–46 and had to wait until January for their first win. Their top scorer Irishman Ron (Paddy) Brown out of the Navy scored a hat-trick in a 3–2 win over Wolverhampton Wanderers.

PLYMOUTH ARGYLE 2005–06 LEAGUE RECORD

Match No.	*Date*	*Venue*	*Opponents*	*Result*		*H/T Score*	*Lg. Pos.*	*Goalscorers*	*Attendance*
1	Aug 6	A	Reading	W	2-1	1-0	—	Evans [21], Chadwick [90]	16,836
2	9	H	Watford	D	3-3	3-1	—	Evans [4], Capaldi [12], Wotton [43]	13,813
3	13	H	Derby Co	L	0-2	0-2	13		14,279
4	20	A	Crystal Palace	L	0-1	0-0	17		18,781
5	27	H	Hull C	L	0-1	0-0	20		12,329
6	29	A	Brighton & HA	L	0-2	0-1	21		6238
7	Sept 10	A	Norwich C	L	0-2	0-2	22		23,981
8	13	H	Crewe Alex	D	1-1	1-1	—	Taylor [12]	10,460
9	17	H	Burnley	W	1-0	0-0	21	Evans [46]	11,829
10	24	A	Southampton	D	0-0	0-0	21		26,331
11	27	A	Sheffield U	L	0-2	0-2	—		20,111
12	Oct 1	H	Stoke C	W	2-1	0-0	20	Russell (og) [50], Buzsaky [77]	12,604
13	15	H	Sheffield W	D	1-1	0-1	19	Wotton (pen) [79]	16,534
14	18	A	QPR	D	1-1	1-0	—	Buzsaky [39]	11,741
15	22	A	Luton T	D	1-1	0-0	19	Djordjic [90]	8714
16	30	H	Millwall	D	0-0	0-0	21		11,764
17	Nov 5	A	Ipswich T	L	1-3	0-2	23	Buzsaky [51]	23,083
18	19	H	QPR	W	3-1	2-0	17	Wotton (pen) [7], Doumbe [37], Chadwick [51]	13,213
19	22	A	Sheffield W	D	0-0	0-0	—		20,244
20	26	H	Reading	L	0-2	0-1	19		14,020
21	Dec 3	A	Coventry C	L	1-3	1-2	20	Norris [25]	18,796
22	10	A	Watford	D	1-1	0-0	20	Chadwick [48]	12,884
23	17	H	Crystal Palace	W	2-0	1-0	20	Chadwick [1], Capaldi [90]	14,582
24	26	A	Cardiff C	W	2-0	0-0	19	Wotton (pen) [72], Norris [80]	16,403
25	31	A	Wolverhampton W	D	1-1	1-1	19	Ward [22]	22,790
26	Jan 2	H	Leeds U	L	0-3	0-0	19		17,726
27	14	H	Norwich C	D	1-1	1-0	20	Charlton (og) [24]	13,906
28	21	A	Crewe Alex	W	2-1	2-0	19	Wotton 2 (1 pen) [3 (p), 45]	5984
29	24	H	Leicester C	W	1-0	0-0	—	Wotton [47]	12,591
30	31	H	Southampton	W	2-1	1-0	—	Chadwick [45], Wotton (pen) [84]	15,936
31	Feb 4	A	Burnley	L	0-1	0-1	16		11,292
32	11	H	Sheffield U	D	0-0	0-0	15		15,017
33	14	A	Stoke C	D	0-0	0-0	—		10,242
34	18	H	Coventry C	W	3-1	2-0	14	Pericard 3 [13, 41, 74]	12,958
35	25	A	Derby Co	L	0-1	0-1	15		25,170
36	Mar 4	H	Brighton & HA	W	1-0	1-0	13	Nalis [37]	13,650
37	7	H	Preston NE	D	0-0	0-0	—		10,874
38	11	A	Hull C	L	0-1	0-0	13		20,137
39	18	H	Cardiff C	L	0-1	0-1	14		13,494
40	25	A	Preston NE	D	0-0	0-0	14		13,925
41	Apr 1	H	Wolverhampton W	W	2-0	1-0	14	Aljofree [9], Ince (og) [80]	15,871
42	8	A	Leeds U	D	0-0	0-0	14		20,650
43	15	A	Millwall	D	1-1	1-1	13	Pericard [10]	9183
44	17	H	Luton T	L	1-2	0-0	15	Buzsaky [70]	13,486
45	22	A	Leicester C	L	0-1	0-0	17		22,796
46	30	H	Ipswich T	W	2-1	1-1	14	Capaldi [28], Evans [57]	15,921

Final League Position: 14

GOALSCORERS

League (39): Wotton 8 (5 pens), Chadwick 5, Buzsaky 4, Evans 4, Pericard 4, Capaldi 3, Norris 2, Aljofree 1, Djordjic 1, Doumbe 1, Nalis 1, Taylor 1, Ward 1, own goals 3.
Carling Cup (3): Buzsaky 1, Taylor 1, Wotton 1 (pen).
FA Cup (0).

Larrieu R 45	Barness A 33 + 3	Brevett R 12 + 1	Wotton P 45	Doumbe S 43	Aljofree H 36 + 1	Norris D 44 + 1	Gudjonsson B 6 + 4	Evans M 36 + 9	Buzsaky A 16 + 18	Capaldi T 38 + 3	Chadwick N 26 + 11	Djordjic B 9 + 13	Taylor S 8 + 10	Connolly P 27 + 4	Mendes N 2	West T 4	Zebroski C — + 4	Derbyshire M 2 + 10	Lasley K — + 5	Ward E 15 + 1	Jarrett J 7	Nalis L 20	Hodges L 12 + 1	Pericard V 14 + 1	Clarke L 5	Pulis A — + 5	McCormick L 1	Reid R — + 1	Match No.
1	2	3	4	5	6	7	8	9¹	10²	11	12	13																	1
1	2	3	4	5	6	7		9	8	11¹	10²	12	13																2
1	2	3¹	4	5	6	13	8	9	7			11²	10	12															3
1	2	3	4	5	6¹	7	12	9	10	13		11²	14		8³														4
1	2	3²	4	5		7	8³	9¹	12			11	10	13		6	14												5
1	2	3	4	5		7	12	9	8³			11¹	13		10²	6	14												6
1	2	3²	8	5	6	7		9	12	13	10³	11¹				4		14											7
1	2¹	3	4	5	6	7		13	12		9²	11	10					8											8
1	12	3¹	4	2	6	7		9		13	14	11²	10			5		8³											9
1	2		4	5	6	7	8³	9	12	3	10¹	11²	13					14											10
1	2	3²	4	5	6	7	8¹	9	12	11	10³	13	14																11
1	2	3	4	5	6	7	8¹	9	12	11	10²		13																12
1		3²	4	5	6	7	12	9	8¹	11	10³	13	14	2															13
1		12	4	5	6	7	13	9	8¹	3	14	11³	10²	2															14
1	3		4	5	6	7		9³	8¹	11	13	12	10²	2				14											15
1	3²		4	5	6	7		9¹	8	11	12	13	10³	2				14											16
1	3		4	5	6	7		9	8	11	10			2															17
1	3		4	5	6	7		9²	8³	11	10¹		12	2				13	14										18
1	3		4	5	6	7		9	8²	11	10¹	12		2³					13	14									19
1	2			5	3	7		9²	8¹	11	10	12						13		6	4								20
1	2²		4	5	3³	7		9		11	10¹		12	13				14		6	8								21
1	3		4	5	12	7		9²		11	10¹			2				13		6	8								22
1	3		4	5		7		9¹	12	11	10			2						6	8								23
1	2		4	5	3	7		9¹		11	10								12	6	8								24
1	3		4	5		7		9		11	10¹			2²				12	13	6	8								25
1	3		4	5				9	7³	11		12	10²	2¹				13	14	6	8								26
1	3		4	5		7		9		11	10¹		12	2						6		8							27
1	2		4	5	3	7		9		11	10¹									6		8	12						28
1	2		4	5	3	7		9		11	10									6		8							29
1	2		4	5	3²	7		9	11¹		10	12		13						6		8							30
1	2¹		4	5		7		9²	12	11	10			3			13			6		8							31
1	3		4	5		7		9¹		11	10			2						6		8		12					32
1	3		4	5		7		12		11	10¹			2						6		8		9					33
1			4	5	3²	7¹		9³	12	11	14	13		2						6		8		10					34
1	3		4		5	7		12	13	11	10¹			2								8	6²	9					35
1	2		4	5	3	7		12		11	10¹											8	6	9					36
1	12		4	5²	6	7		9³	13	11	14			2								8	3¹	10					37
1	3³		4		5	7		9²	12	11	13	14		2								8	6¹	10					38
1			4	5	6	7		9³	12	11		13		2¹			14					8	3²	10					39
1	12		4	5	6	7		13		11	14			2¹								8	3	10²	9³				40
1			4	5	6	7		12	13	11²	9¹			2								8	3	10³		14			41
1			4	5	6	7		12	13	11				2								8	3³	10²	9¹	14			42
1			4	5	6	7		12	13	11²				2								8	3	10³	9¹	14			43
			4	5	6	7		12	13	11				2								8	3²	10	9¹		1		44
1			4	5	6	7			12	11	13			2³								8	3¹	10	9²	14			45
1			4		5	7		9¹	6²	11	12			2								8	3	10³		13		14	46

FA Cup
Third Round Wolverhampton W (a) 0-1

Carling Cup
First Round Peterborough U (h) 2-1
Second Round Barnet (a) 1-2

PORTSMOUTH FA Premiership

FOUNDATION

At a meeting held in his High Street, Portsmouth offices in 1898, solicitor Alderman J. E. Pink and five other business and professional men agreed to buy some ground close to Goldsmith Avenue for £4,950 which they developed into Fratton Park in record breaking time. A team of professionals was signed up by manager Frank Brettell and entry to the Southern League obtained for the new club's September 1899 kick-off.

Fratton Park, Frogmore Road, Portsmouth, Hampshire PO4 8RA.

Telephone: (02392) 731 204.

Fax: (02392) 734 129.

Ticket Office: 0871 230 1898.

Website: www.pompeyfc.co.uk

Email: info@pompeyfc.co.uk

Ground Capacity: 20,328.

Record Attendance: 51,385 v Derby Co, FA Cup 6th rd, 26 February 1949.

Pitch Measurements: 100m × 65m.

Owner: Alexander Gaydamak.

Chief Executive: Peter Storrie.

Secretary: Paul Weld.

Manager: Harry Redknapp.

Assistant Manager: Tony Adams.

Physio: Gary Sadler.

Colours: Blue shirts, white shorts, red stockings.

Change Colours: TBC.

Year Formed: 1898.

Turned Professional: 1898.

Ltd Co.: 1898.

Club Nickname: 'Pompey'.

First Football League Game: 28 August 1920, Division 3, v Swansea T (h) W 3–0 – Robson; Probert, Potts; Abbott, Harwood, Turner; Thompson, Stringfellow (1), Reid (1), James (1), Beedie.

Record League Victory: 9–1 v Notts Co, Division 2, 9 April 1927 – McPhail; Clifford, Ted Smith; Reg Davies (1), Foxall, Moffat; Forward (1), Mackie (2), Haines (3), Watson, Cook (2).

Record Cup Victory: 7–0 v Stockport Co, FA Cup 3rd rd, 8 January 1949 – Butler; Rookes, Ferrier; Scoular, Flewin, Dickinson; Harris (3), Barlow, Clarke (2), Phillips (2), Froggatt.

HONOURS

Football League: Division 1 – Champions 1948–49, 1949–50, 2002–03; Division 2 – Runners-up 1926–27, 1986–87; Division 3 (S) – Champions 1923–24; Division 3 – Champions 1961–62, 1982–83.

FA Cup: Winners 1939; Runners-up 1929, 1934.

Football League Cup: best season: 5th rd, 1961, 1986.

SKY SPORTS FACT FILE

On 21 February 1959 England international wing-half Jimmy Dickinson made his 500th appearance for Portsmouth at Tottenham Hotspur, his 600th v Barnsley on 9 September 1961 while No. 700 arrived on 16 November 1963 against Charlton Athletic.

Record Defeat: 0–10 v Leicester C, Division 1, 20 October 1928.

Most League Points (2 for a win): 65, Division 3, 1961–62.

Most League Points (3 for a win): 98, Division 1, 2002–03.

Most League Goals: 97, Division 1, 2002–03.

Highest League Scorer in Season: Guy Whittingham, 42, Division 1, 1992–93.

Most League Goals in Total Aggregate: Peter Harris, 194, 1946–60.

Most League Goals in One Match: 5, Alf Strange v Gillingham, Division 3, 27 January 1923; 5, Peter Harris v Aston Villa, Division 1, 3 September 1958.

Most Capped Player: Jimmy Dickinson, 48, England.

Most League Appearances: Jimmy Dickinson, 764, 1946–65.

Youngest League Player: Clive Green, 16 years 259 days v Wrexham, 21 August 1976.

Record Transfer Fee Received: £7,300,000 from Middlesbrough for Ayegbeni Yakubu, July 2005.

Record Transfer Fee Paid: £4,100,000 to Auxerre for Benjani Mwaruwari, January 2006.

Football League Record: 1920 Original Member of Division 3; 1921 Division 3 (S); 1924–27 Division 2; 1927–59 Division 1; 1959–61 Division 2; 1961–62 Division 3; 1962–76 Division 2; 1976–78 Division 3; 1978–80 Division 4; 1980–83 Division 3; 1983–87 Division 2; 1987–88 Division 1; 1988–92 Division 2; 1992–2003 Division 1; 2003– FA Premier League.

MANAGERS

Frank Brettell 1898–1901
Bob Blyth 1901–04
Richard Bonney 1905–08
Bob Brown 1911–20
John McCartney 1920–27
Jack Tinn 1927–47
Bob Jackson 1947–52
Eddie Lever 1952–58
Freddie Cox 1958–61
George Smith 1961–70
Ron Tindall 1970–73
(General Manager to 1974)
John Mortimore 1973–74
Ian St John 1974–77
Jimmy Dickinson 1977–79
Frank Burrows 1979–82
Bobby Campbell 1982–84
Alan Ball 1984–89
John Gregory 1989–90
Frank Burrows 1990–91
Jim Smith 1991–95
Terry Fenwick 1995–98
Alan Ball 1998–99
Tony Pulis 2000
Steve Claridge 2000–01
Graham Rix 2001–02
Harry Redknapp 2002–04
Velimir Zajec 2004–05
Alain Perrin 2005
Harry Redknapp December 2005–

LATEST SEQUENCES

Longest Sequence of League Wins: 7, 17.8.2002 – 17.9.2002.

Longest Sequence of League Defeats: 9, 21.10.1975 – 6.12.1975.

Longest Sequence of League Draws: 5, 16.12.2000 – 13.1.2001.

Longest Sequence of Unbeaten League Matches: 15, 18.4.1924 – 18.10.1924.

Longest Sequence Without a League Win: 25, 29.11.1958 – 22.8.1959.

Successive Scoring Runs: 23 from 30.8.1930.

Successive Non-scoring Runs: 6 from 14.1.1939.

TEN YEAR LEAGUE RECORD

		P	W	D	L	F	A	Pts	Pos
1996-97	Div 1	46	20	8	18	59	53	68	7
1997-98	Div 1	46	13	10	23	51	63	49	20
1998-99	Div 1	46	11	14	21	57	73	47	19
1999-2000	Div 1	46	13	12	21	55	66	51	18
2000-01	Div 1	46	10	19	17	47	59	49	20
2001-02	Div 1	46	13	14	19	60	72	53	17
2002-03	Div 1	46	29	11	6	97	45	98	1
2003-04	PR Lge	38	12	9	17	47	54	45	13
2004-05	PR Lge	38	10	9	19	43	59	39	16
2005-06	PR Lge	38	10	8	20	37	62	38	17

DID YOU KNOW?

When Jimmy Scoular made his Portsmouth debut on 15 December 1945 he was under close arrest and escorted to the ground! Petty Officer Scoular had gone AWOL to watch a midweek game but manager Jack Tinn persuaded the Royal Navy to allow him to play.

PORTSMOUTH 2005–06 LEAGUE RECORD

Match No.	*Date*	*Venue*	*Opponents*	*Result*	*H/T Score*	*Lg. Pos.*	*Goalscorers*	*Attendance*
1	Aug 13	H	Tottenham H	L 0-2	0-1	—		20,215
2	20	A	WBA	L 1-2	0-1	19	Robert [63]	24,404
3	23	H	Aston Villa	D 1-1	1-1	—	Lua-Lua [42]	19,778
4	27	A	Manchester C	L 1-2	0-0	18	Viafara [52]	41,022
5	Sept 10	A	Everton	W 1-0	0-0	15	Ferguson (og) [60]	36,831
6	17	H	Birmingham C	D 1-1	1-1	13	Lua-Lua [4]	19,319
7	24	A	Bolton W	L 0-1	0-1	17		23,134
8	Oct 1	H	Newcastle U	D 0-0	0-0	14		20,220
9	15	A	Middlesbrough	D 1-1	0-0	16	O'Neil [46]	26,551
10	22	H	Charlton Ath	L 1-2	1-0	17	Dario Silva [14]	19,030
11	29	A	Sunderland	W 4-1	0-1	14	Vukic [48], Taylor 2 [59, 67], Dario Silva [74]	34,926
12	Nov 5	H	Wigan Ath	L 0-2	0-0	15		19,102
13	19	A	Liverpool	L 0-3	0-2	17		44,394
14	26	H	Chelsea	L 0-2	0-1	18		20,182
15	Dec 3	A	Manchester U	L 0-3	0-1	18		67,684
16	12	A	Tottenham H	L 1-3	1-0	—	Lua-Lua [24]	36,141
17	17	H	WBA	W 1-0	0-0	18	Todorov [56]	20,052
18	26	H	West Ham U	D 1-1	1-0	18	O'Neil [17]	20,168
19	28	A	Arsenal	L 0-4	0-4	18		38,223
20	31	H	Fulham	W 1-0	1-0	18	O'Neil [43]	19,101
21	Jan 2	A	Blackburn R	L 1-2	1-2	18	Taylor [3]	19,521
22	14	H	Everton	L 0-1	0-1	18		20,094
23	21	A	Birmingham C	L 0-5	0-2	19		29,138
24	Feb 1	H	Bolton W	D 1-1	0-0	—	Karadas [85]	19,128
25	4	A	Newcastle U	L 0-2	0-1	19		51,627
26	11	H	Manchester U	L 1-3	0-3	19	Taylor [87]	20,206
27	25	A	Chelsea	L 0-2	0-0	19		42,254
28	Mar 4	A	Aston Villa	L 0-1	0-1	19		30,194
29	11	H	Manchester C	W 2-1	0-0	19	Pedro Mendes 2 [60, 90]	19,556
30	18	A	West Ham U	W 4-2	3-0	19	Lua-Lua [19], Davis [25], Pedro Mendes [42], Todorov [77]	34,837
31	Apr 1	A	Fulham	W 3-1	2-1	18	O'Neil 2 [1, 62], Lua-Lua [24]	22,322
32	8	H	Blackburn R	D 2-2	1-1	19	Lua-Lua [41], Todorov [78]	20,048
33	12	H	Arsenal	D 1-1	0-1	—	Lua-Lua [66]	20,230
34	15	H	Middlesbrough	W 1-0	0-0	17	O'Neil [54]	20,204
35	17	A	Charlton Ath	L 1-2	1-0	17	D'Alessandro [40]	25,419
36	22	H	Sunderland	W 2-1	0-0	17	Todorov [73], Taylor (pen) [88]	20,078
37	29	A	Wigan Ath	W 2-1	0-1	17	Mwaruwari [63], Taylor (pen) [71]	21,126
38	May 7	H	Liverpool	L 1-3	0-0	17	Koroman [85]	20,240

Final League Position: 17

GOALSCORERS

League (37): Lua-Lua 7, O'Neil 6, Taylor 6 (2 pens), Todorov 4, Pedro Mendes 3, Dario Silva 2, D'Alessandro 1, Davis 1, Karadas 1, Koroman 1, Mwaruwari 1, Robert 1, Viafara 1, Vukic 1, own goal 1.
Carling Cup (2): O'Neil 1, Taylor 1 (pen).
FA Cup (2): Dario Silva 1, Davis 1.

Westerveld S 6	Griffin A 20 + 2	Vignal G 13 + 1	Hughes R 21 + 5	O'Brien A 29	Stefanovic D 27 + 1	Mornar I 1 + 1	Viafara J 10 + 4	Karadas A 4 + 13	Lua-Lua L 24 + 1	Robert L 13 + 4	Pericard V 3 + 3	Taylor M 32 + 2	Mbesuma C — + 4	Skopelitis G — + 5	O'Neil G 36	Todorov S 6 + 18	Priske B 26 + 4	Ashdown J 17	Diao S 7 + 4	Dario Silva D 13	Vukic Z 6 + 3	Songo'o F — + 2	Primus L 20	Cisse A 2 + 1	Davis S 16 + 1	Pamarot N 4 + 4	Pedro Mendes 14	Mwaruwari B 16	Olisadebe E — + 2	Kiely D 15	Routledge W 3 + 10	D'Alessandro A 13	Koroman O 1 + 2	*Match No.*
1	2	3	4	5	6	7^{1}	8^{2}	9^{3}	10	11	12	13	14																					1
1	2^{2}	3	4	5	6		8	9^{3}	10	11	14			13	7^{1}	12																		2
1		3	4	5	6		8	9^{2}	10	11	13				7^{1}	12	2																	3
1	2^{2}	3	4	5	6		8^{3}	12	10	11		14		13	9^{1}		7																	4
		3	4	5	6		12	13	10^{2}	11^{3}					7		2	1	8	9^{1}	14													5
		3	4^{2}	5	6			12	10^{1}	11					7		2	1	8	9	13													6
		3	4	5	6			12		11		7^{1}			8^{3}	13	2	1	10	9^{2}		14												7
	4^{2}	3	12	5	6							11			7		2	1	8^{1}	9	10	13												8
	3^{2}	12		5	6		8			11^{1}		7		13	4	14	2	1		9^{3}	10													9
		3	12	5	6		8			11^{2}		7^{1}	14		4	13	2	1		9	10^{3}													10
	7	3	4		6		12					11^{2}	14		8	13	2	1		9^{3}	10^{1}		5											11
	3^{3}	11^{1}	4		6				13	12		7			8		2	1	14	9	10^{2}		5											12
	2	3	4^{2}	5			8		10^{1}	11^{3}		7	12	13	9		6	1			14													13
	3		4^{1}	5	6		12		10			11			7	13	2	1	8	9^{2}														14
	3			5	6		8		10	12		11^{1}			7	13	2	1	4	9^{2}														15
	3		4	5	6		8		10	12	9	11^{1}			7			1					2											16
	3		4	5	6				10	7	9^{1}	11			8	12^{2}	13	1					2											17
	3		4	5	6		12		10	11[illegible]		7			8		13	1		9^{1}			2^{2}											18
	2	3	4^{3}	5		12	8		10^{1}			11		14		13	6	1			9^{2}			7										19
1	3		4	5	6			12	10	11^{2}		7			8		2			9^{1}				13										20
1	3			5	6			12	10	13		11^{1}			7	14	2		4	9^{3}				8^{2}										21
	2		4^{3}	5				12	10			3			7			1	13						11^{1}	6	8^{2}	9	14					22
	3			5	6^{2}			12			10^{3}	11			7		13	1							4	2^{1}	8	9	14					23
	12			5	6^{1}			13				3			11^{3}	14							2		4		8	9^{2}		1	7	10		24
	2^{3}			5								3			11	12			13				6		4^{2}	14	8	9		1	7^{1}	10		25
	12			5					10			3			7								6		4^{1}	2	8	9		1	13	11^{2}		26
			4^{2}	5				6	10			3			7								2		13		8	9		1	12		11^{1}	27
	2^{2}			5				12	10			3			11	9^{1}	13						6		4^{3}		8			1	7		14	28
				5					10			3			7	12	2						6		4^{2}		8	9^{1}		1	13	11		29
				5					10			3			7	12	2						6		4		8	9^{1}		1		11		30
				5	12			13	10^{2}			3			7	14	2						6		4		8	9^{3}		1		11^{1}		31
					6				10			3			7	12	2						5		4^{2}		8	9^{1}		1	13	11		32
			12		6				10^{1}			3			7	13	2						5		4^{3}		8	9^{2}		1	14	11		33
			12		6			13				3			7	10^{1}	2						5		4^{3}		8	9^{2}		1	14	11		34
			8^{2}					12				3			7	10^{1}	2						5		4	6		9		1	13	11		35
			8^{3}		6							3			7	10^{2}	2		12				5		4	13		9		1	14	11^{1}		36
			12		6							3			7	10^{3}	2						5		4^{2}	13	8^{1}	9		1	14	11		37
			4^{3}		6							3			7	10	2						5^{1}		8	12		9		1	13	11^{2}	14	38

FA Cup

Third Round	Ipswich T	(a)	1-0
Fourth Round	Liverpool	(h)	1-2

Carling Cup

Second Round	Gillingham	(a)	2-3

PORT VALE — FL Championship 1

FOUNDATION

Formed in 1876 as Port Vale, adopting the prefix 'Burslem' in 1884 upon moving to that part of the city. It was dropped in 1909.

Vale Park, Hamil Road, Burslem, Stoke-on-Trent ST6 1AW.

Telephone: (01782) 655 800.

Fax: (01782) 834 981.

Ticket Office: (01782) 655 832.

Website: www.port-vale.co.uk

Email: lodey@port-vale.co.uk

Ground Capacity: 18,982.

Record Attendance: 49,768 v Aston Villa, FA Cup 5th rd, 20 February 1960.

Pitch Measurements: 114yd × 75yd.

Chairman/Chief Executive: William A. Bratt.

Vice-chairmen: David Smith, Peter L. Jackson.

Secretary: Bill Lodey.

Manager: Martin Foyle.

Assistant Manager: Dean Glover.

Physios: Ian Baddiley, John Bowers.

Colours: White shirts with gold and black trim, black shorts with white and gold trim, black stockings.

Change Colours: Sky blue shirts with navy trim, navy blue shorts, sky and navy blue stockings.

Year Formed: 1876.

Turned Professional: 1885.

Ltd Co.: 1911.

Previous Names: 1876, Port Vale; 1884, Burslem Port Vale; 1909, Port Vale.

Club Nickname: 'Valiants'.

Previous Grounds: 1876, Limekin Lane, Longport; 1881, Westport; 1884, Moorland Road, Burslem; 1886, Athletic Ground, Cobridge; 1913, Recreation Ground, Hanley; 1950, Vale Park.

First Football League Game: 3 September 1892, Division 2, v Small Heath (a) L 1–5 – Frail; Clutton, Elson; Farrington, McCrindle, Delves; Walker, Scarratt, Bliss (1), Jones. (Only 10 men).

Record League Victory: 9–1 v Chesterfield, Division 2, 24 September 1932 – Leckie; Shenton, Poyser; Sherlock, Round, Jones; McGrath, Mills, Littlewood (6), Kirkham (2), Morton (1).

Record Cup Victory: 7–1 v Irthlingborough, FA Cup 1st rd, 12 January 1907 – Matthews; Dunn, Hamilton; Eardley, Baddeley, Holyhead; Carter, Dodds (2), Beats, Mountford (2), Coxon (3).

Record Defeat: 0–10 v Sheffield U, Division 2, 10 December 1892. 0–10 v Notts Co, Division 2, 26 February 1895.

HONOURS

Football League: Division 2 – Runners-up 1993–94; Division 3 (N) – Champions 1929–30, 1953–54; Runners-up 1952–53; Division 4 – Champions 1958–59; Promoted 1969–70 (4th).

FA Cup: Semi-final 1954, when in Division 3.

Football League Cup: best season: 3rd rd 1992, 1997.

Autoglass Trophy: Winners 1993.

Anglo-Italian Cup: Runners-up 1996.

LDV Vans Trophy: Winners 2001.

SKY SPORTS FACT FILE

Chris Birchall, the Port Vale midfield player, was the first white to be capped by Trinidad & Tobago for 60 years when he made his debut against Panama on 4 June 2005. His grandparents had emigrated to Trinidad and his mother was born there.

Most League Points (2 for a win): 69, Division 3 (N), 1953–54.

Most League Points (3 for a win): 89, Division 2, 1992–93.

Most League Goals: 110, Division 4, 1958–59.

Highest League Scorer in Season: Wilf Kirkham 38, Division 2, 1926–27.

Most League Goals in Total Aggregate: Wilf Kirkham, 154, 1923–29, 1931–33.

Most League Goals in One Match: 6, Stewart Littlewood v Chesterfield, Division 2, 24 September 1922.

Most Capped Player: Chris Birchall, 22, Trinidad & Tobago.

Most League Appearances: Roy Sproson, 761, 1950–72.

Youngest League Player: Malcolm McKenzie, 15 years 347 days v Newport Co, 12 April 1966.

Record Transfer Fee Received: £2,000,000 from Wimbledon for Gareth Ainsworth, October 1998.

Record Transfer Fee Paid: £500,000 to York C for Jon McCarthy, August 1995 and £500,000 to Lincoln C for Gareth Ainsworth, September 1997.

Football League Record: 1892 Original Member of Division 2. Failed re-election in 1896; Re-elected 1898; Resigned 1907; Returned in Oct, 1919, when they took over the fixtures of Leeds City; 1929–30 Division 3 (N); 1930–36 Division 2; 1936–38 Division 3 (N); 1938–52 Division 3 (S); 1952–54 Division 3 (N); 1954–57 Division 2; 1957–58 Division 3 (S); 1958–59 Division 4; 1959–65 Division 3; 1965–70 Division 4; 1970–78 Division 3; 1978–83 Division 4; 1983–84 Division 3; 1984–86 Division 4; 1986–89 Division 3; 1989–94 Division 2; 1994–2000 Division 1; 2000–04 Division 2; 2004– FL1.

MANAGERS

Sam Gleaves 1896–1905
(Secretary-Manager)
Tom Clare 1905–11
A. S. Walker 1911–12
H. Myatt 1912–14
Tom Holford 1919–24
(continued as Trainer)
Joe Schofield 1924–30
Tom Morgan 1930–32
Tom Holford 1932–35
Warney Cresswell 1936–37
Tom Morgan 1937–38
Billy Frith 1945–46
Gordon Hodgson 1946–51
Ivor Powell 1951
Freddie Steele 1951–57
Norman Low 1957–62
Freddie Steele 1962–65
Jackie Mudie 1965–67
Sir Stanley Matthews
(General Manager) 1965–68
Gordon Lee 1968–74
Roy Sproson 1974–77
Colin Harper 1977
Bobby Smith 1977–78
Dennis Butler 1978–79
Alan Bloor 1979
John McGrath 1980–83
John Rudge 1984–99
Brian Horton 1999–2004
Martin Foyle February 2004–

LATEST SEQUENCES

Longest Sequence of League Wins: 8, 8.4.1893 – 30.9.1893.

Longest Sequence of League Defeats: 9, 9.3.1957 – 20.4.1957.

Longest Sequence of League Draws: 6, 26.4.1981 – 12.9.1981.

Longest Sequence of Unbeaten League Matches: 19, 5.5.1969 – 8.11.1969.

Longest Sequence Without a League Win: 17, 7.12.1991 – 21.3.1992.

Successive Scoring Runs: 22 from 12.9.1992.

Successive Non-scoring Runs: 4 from 10.2.1896.

TEN YEAR LEAGUE RECORD

		P	*W*	*D*	*L*	*F*	*A*	*Pts*	*Pos*
1996-97	Div 1	46	17	16	13	58	55	67	8
1997-98	Div 1	46	13	10	23	56	66	49	19
1998-99	Div 1	46	13	8	25	45	75	47	21
1999-2000	Div 1	46	7	15	24	48	69	36	23
2000-01	Div 2	46	16	14	16	55	49	62	11
2001-02	Div 2	46	16	10	20	51	62	58	14
2002-03	Div 2	46	14	11	21	54	70	53	17
2003-04	Div 2	46	21	10	15	73	63	73	7
2004-05	FL 1	46	17	5	24	49	59	56	18
2005-06	FL 1	46	16	12	18	49	54	60	13

DID YOU KNOW ?

Praying for victory is understandable whether religion enters the equation or not. But from May 1946 Port Vale had as a part-time professional Methodist minister Rev. Norman Hallam at wing-half before he moved to Halifax Town in 1953.

PORT VALE 2005–06 LEAGUE RECORD

Match No.	Date	Venue	Opponents	Result	H/T Score	Lg. Pos.	Goalscorers	Attendance
1	Aug 6	A	Southend U	W 2-1	2-0	—	Lowndes 2 [12, 28]	6543
2	9	H	Gillingham	D 0-0	0-0	—		4931
3	15	H	Brentford	W 1-0	0-0	—	Cummins [53]	4275
4	20	A	Bristol C	L 2-4	2-4	7	Lowndes [35], Bell [40]	11,120
5	27	H	Doncaster R	W 2-0	1-0	4	Lowndes [30], Dinning [48]	4993
6	29	A	Milton Keynes D	D 0-0	0-0	5		4592
7	Sept 3	H	Rotherham U	W 2-0	1-0	3	Lowndes [45], Paynter [90]	4528
8	10	A	Scunthorpe U	L 0-2	0-2	7		5694
9	17	H	Colchester U	L 0-1	0-1	8		5166
10	24	A	Yeovil T	L 0-1	0-0	12		5901
11	28	H	Oldham Ath	D 2-2	0-1	—	Cornes [71], Scott (og) [90]	3796
12	Oct 1	H	Walsall	W 3-2	1-2	5	Birchall [8], Mulligan [55], Cornes [72]	5314
13	8	A	Swindon T	W 2-1	1-1	—	Bell [44], Cornes [53]	4531
14	15	H	Bradford C	L 0-1	0-0	6		4892
15	22	A	Bournemouth	W 2-1	0-1	5	Cummins [75], Paynter [86]	6320
16	29	H	Hartlepool U	L 1-2	1-1	8	Cummins [43]	4550
17	Nov 12	A	Chesterfield	L 0-2	0-1	12		4714
18	19	H	Swindon T	D 1-1	0-0	11	Husbands [87]	4108
19	26	H	Southend U	W 2-1	1-0	8	Constantine [18], Husbands [55]	3961
20	Dec 6	A	Nottingham F	L 0-1	0-1	—		17,696
21	10	A	Gillingham	L 0-3	0-1	14		6210
22	17	H	Bristol C	L 0-1	0-1	16		4214
23	26	H	Blackpool	L 1-2	0-0	17	Fortune [58]	5666
24	28	A	Huddersfield T	W 3-0	0-0	14	Constantine 2 [48, 65], Dinning (pen) [80]	10,824
25	31	H	Tranmere R	L 0-2	0-1	14		4289
26	Jan 2	A	Swansea C	D 0-0	0-0	16		14,747
27	10	A	Rotherham U	D 1-1	1-1	—	Husbands [7]	3883
28	14	H	Barnsley	W 3-2	2-0	12	Sonner [24], Constantine [27], Togwell [73]	4468
29	21	A	Colchester U	L 1-2	0-0	14	Husbands (pen) [79]	4316
30	Feb 4	A	Oldham Ath	W 1-0	1-0	13	Constantine [44]	5555
31	11	H	Yeovil T	W 1-0	0-0	9	Constantine [52]	4732
32	14	A	Barnsley	D 1-1	0-0	—	Cummins [84]	7709
33	18	H	Nottingham F	L 0-2	0-1	11		6793
34	25	A	Brentford	W 1-0	1-0	11	Smith [36]	7542
35	28	H	Scunthorpe U	L 1-2	1-1	—	Cummins [18]	3984
36	Mar 11	A	Doncaster R	D 1-1	0-0	12	Constantine [86]	5511
37	18	A	Blackpool	L 0-1	0-0	14		5494
38	25	H	Huddersfield T	D 1-1	0-0	15	Cummins [59]	5664
39	31	A	Tranmere R	L 0-3	0-1	—		6926
40	Apr 4	H	Milton Keynes D	W 3-1	3-1	—	Constantine 2 (1 pen) [13, 35 (p)], Cummins [45]	3452
41	8	H	Swansea C	W 3-2	1-0	11	Togwell [43], Cummins [58], Constantine [63]	4850
42	15	A	Walsall	D 1-1	0-0	14	Fortune [86]	4876
43	17	H	Bournemouth	D 0-0	0-0	13		4006
44	22	A	Bradford C	L 0-1	0-1	15		7139
45	29	H	Chesterfield	W 3-1	2-1	13	Pilkington 2 [5, 15], Cummins [81]	4478
46	May 6	A	Hartlepool U	D 1-1	0-0	13	Cummins [77]	6895

Final League Position: 13

GOALSCORERS

League (49): Constantine 10 (1 pen), Cummins 10, Lowndes 5, Husbands 4 (1 pen), Cornes 3, Bell 2, Dinning 2 (1 pen), Fortune 2, Paynter 2, Pilkington 2, Togwell 2, Birchall 1, Mulligan 1, Smith 1, Sonner 1, own goal 1.
Carling Cup (1): Cummins 1.
FA Cup (7): Constantine 2, Togwell 2, Birchall 1, Husbands 1, Lowndes 1.
Football League Trophy (1): Smith 1.

Goodlad M 46	Abbey G 19 + 1	Bell M 14 + 1	Dinning T 33 + 2	Pilkington G 46	Collins S 15	Cummins M 36 + 3	Sonner D 25 + 4	Lowndes N 30 + 5	Paynter B 16	Innes M 17 + 6	James C 30 + 5	Birchall C 23 + 8	Sam H — + 4	Smith J 18 + 9	Rowland S 13 + 5	Matthews L — + 3	Cornes C 7 + 3	Porter A 2	Cardle J 1 + 5	Mulligan G 8 + 2	Clarke D — + 1	Husbands M 6 + 18	Hulbert R — + 1	Togwell S 26 + 1	Fortune C 20 + 5	Constantine L 30	Briscoe L — + 4	Doherty S 3 + 3	McGregor M 14	Talbot J 4 + 1	Walsh M 4	*Match No.*
1	2	3[1]	4	5	6	7	8[2]	9[3]	10	11	12	13	14																			1
1	2	3	4	5	6	7	8[1]	9	10[2]	11[3]		12	13	14																		2
1	2	3	4	5	6	7	8	9[2]	10	11[1]				12	13																	3
1	2[1]	3	4	5	6	7	8	9	10	11[2]		12		13																		4
1		3[2]	4	5	6	7	8	9[3]	10		13	12		11[1]	2■	14																5
1			4	5		7	8	9[1]	10		2	12		11			3	6														6
1			4	5	6	7	8	9	10		3			12	2		11[1]															7
1			4	5	6	7	8[2]	9	10		3	12			2		11[1]		13													8
1		12	4	5	6	7	8	9	10		3[1]	11			2[2]		13															9
1	2		4[2]	5	6	7	8	9[3]	10	13		11			3[1]		12			14												10
1	2	3[1]	4	5	6	7	8[2]		10	12		11					13			9												11
1	2[1]	3[2]		5	6	7	8		10	13		4			12		11[3]			9	14											12
1		3	4	5	6	7	8		10	11[1]	12						2			9												13
1		3[2]	4	5	6	7	8	12	9			11					2[1]			10		13										14
1		3	4	5	6	2	8[1]	9	7			11			12					10[2]		13										15
1		3	4	5	6[3]	7		9[2]	10		12	11			2					8[1]		13	14									16
1		3	4	5				9[2]		11	7[1]			12					13	10				2	6	8						17
1		3[1]	4	5				9		11	8			12	13		7[3]					14		2[2]	6	10						18
1			4	5			8	12		13	3			11[2]	2					9		7[1]			6	10						19
1			4	5			8[1]	9		12	3			11	2					13		7[2]			6	10						20
1			4■	5			8	9		12	3			11[1]	2							7[2]		13	6	10						21
1		11[2]		5			8	9			3	7			6			4[1]	12			13		2		10[3]	14					22
1	2[1]		4	5				9[2]		11	3	8							12			13		7	6	10						23
1			4[2]	5		12	13	9[3]		11[1]	3	8			2							14		7	6	10						24
1			4[1]	5		12		9		11[2]	3	8[3]			2	13						14		7	6	10						25
1	2[1]		4	5		8		9[2]		11	3				12							13		7	6	10						26
1	12		4	5		8				11	3				2[1]							9		7	6	10						27
1	2			5		8	4	12		11[2]	3											9[1]		7	6	10		13				28
1	2			5		8		12		11[2]	3	4[1]										9		7	6	10		13				29
1	2		4	5		12		9[2]		11	3	8[1]										13		7[3]		10		14	6			30
1	2		4[1]	5		8	12	9		11[2]	3			13								14				10		7[3]	6			31
1	2			5		8		9[3]		11	3			12								13		7		10[2]		4[1]	6	14		32
1	2			5		8		9			3[3]	11[2]		12								13		7	14	10		4[1]	6			33
1	2		12	5		8		9[2]				4[1]		11								13		7	6	10				3		34
1	2		4[2]	5		8		9			12			11[1]								13		7	6	10				3■		35
1	2		4[1]	5		8	12	9[2]			3	13		11[3]								14		7	6	10						36
1			4	5		8					3	9		11[1]								12		7	6	10			2			37
1			4	5		8		12			3	9		11										7[1]	6	10			2			38
1				5		8	12	9			3	11		2								13		7	6	10[2]			4[1]			39
1				5		8	4	9[1]			3	12		11										7	6	10			2			40
1				5		8	4				3	9		11		12								7	13	10[1]			2		6[2]	41
1				5		8	4				3	9	12	11[2]										7	13	10[1]			2		6	42
1				5		8	4				3	9		11										7	6	10[1]	12		2			43
1			12	5		8	4[1]				3	9[2]	13	11										7	14	10[3]			2		6	44
1			4	5		8						9[1]		11					12					7	13	10[3]	14		2	3[2]	6	45
1	2		4	5		8								11					9[1]					7		10	12		6	3		46

FA Cup

First Round	Wrexham	(h)	2-1
Second Round	Bristol R	(h)	1-1
		(a)	1-0
Third Round	Doncaster R	(h)	2-1
Fourth Round	Aston Villa	(a)	1-3

Carling Cup

First Round	Rotherham U	(a)	1-3

Football League Trophy

Second Round	Hereford U	(a)	1-2

PRESTON NORTH END FL Championship

FOUNDATION

North End Cricket and Rugby Club which was formed in 1863, indulged in most sports before taking up soccer in about 1879. In 1881 they decided to stick to football to the exclusion of other sports and even a 16–0 drubbing by Blackburn Rovers in an invitation game at Deepdale, a few weeks after taking this decision, did not deter them for they immediately became affiliated to the Lancashire FA.

Sir Tom Finney Way, Deepdale, Preston PR1 6RU.

Telephone: 0870 442 1964.

Fax: (01772) 693 366.

Ticket Office: 0870 442 1966.

Website: www.pne.com, www.mypne.com

Email: enquiries@pne.com

Ground Capacity: 20,600.

Record Attendance: 42,684 v Arsenal, Division 1, 23 April 1938.

Pitch Measurements: 110yd × 77yd.

Chairman: Derek Shaw.

Vice-chairman: David Taylor.

Chief Executive: Steve Jackson.

Secretary: Janet Parr.

Manager: Paul Simpson.

Assistant Manager: David Kelly.

Physio: Andrew Balderston.

Colours: White shirts, blue shorts, white stockings.

Change Colours: Yellow shirts, royal blue shorts, yellow stockings.

Year Formed: 1881.

Turned Professional: 1885. ***Ltd Co.:*** 1893.

Club Nicknames: 'The Lilywhites' or 'North End'.

First Football League Game: 8 September 1888, Football League, v Burnley (h) W 5–2 – Trainer; Howarth, Holmes; Robertson, W. Graham, J. Graham; Gordon (1), Ross (2), Goodall, Dewhurst (2), Drummond.

Record League Victory: 10–0 v Stoke, Division 1, 14 September 1889 – Trainer; Howarth, Holmes; Kelso, Russell (1), Graham; Gordon, Jimmy Ross (2), Nick Ross (3), Thomson (2), Drummond (2).

Record Cup Victory: 26–0 v Hyde, FA Cup 1st rd, 15 October 1887 – Addision; Howarth, Nick Ross; Russell (1), Thomson (5), Graham (1); Gordon (5), Jimmy Ross (8), John Goodall (1), Dewhurst (3), Drummond (2).

Record Defeat: 0–7 v Blackpool, Division 1, 1 May 1948.

Most League Points (2 for a win): 61, Division 3, 1970–71.

Most League Points (3 for a win): 95, Division 2, 1999–2000.

HONOURS

Football League: Division 1 – Champions 1888–89 (first champions) 1889–90; Runners-up 1890–91, 1891–92, 1892–93, 1905–06, 1952–53, 1957–58; Division 2 – Champions 1903–04, 1912–13, 1950–51, 1999–2000; Runners-up 1914–15, 1933–34; Division 3 – Champions 1970–71, 1995–96; Division 4 – Runners-up 1986–87.

FA Cup: Winners 1889, 1938; Runners-up 1888, 1922, 1937, 1954, 1964.

Football League Cup: best season: 4th rd, 2003.

Double Performed: 1888–89.

Football League Cup: best season: 4th rd, 1963, 1966, 1972, 1981.

SKY SPORTS FACT FILE

In a remarkable sequence from 1934–35 to 1948–49 inclusive, the team which knocked Preston North End out of the FA Cup always reached the final. The exception of course was in 1937–38 when Preston were the winners themselves.

Most League Goals: 100, Division 2, 1927–28 and Division 1, 1957–58.

Highest League Scorer in Season: Ted Harper, 37, Division 2, 1932–33.

Most League Goals in Total Aggregate: Tom Finney, 187, 1946–60.

Most League Goals in One Match: 4, Jimmy Ross v Stoke, Division 1, 6 October 1888; 4, Nick Ross v Derby Co, Division 1, 11 January 1890; 4, George Drummond v Notts Co, Division 1, 12 December 1891; 4, Frank Becton v Notts Co, Division 1, 31 March 1893; 4, George Harrison v Grimsby T, Division 2, 3 November 1928; 4, Alex Reid v Port Vale, Division 2, 23 February 1929; 4, James McClelland v Reading, Division 2, 6 September 1930; 4, Dick Rowley v Notts Co, Division 2, 16 April 1932; 4, Ted Harper v Burnley, Division 2, 29 August 1932; 4, Ted Harper v Lincoln C, Division 2, 11 March 1933; 4, Charlie Wayman v QPR, Division 2, 25 December 1950; 4, Alex Bruce v Colchester U, Division 3, 28 February 1978.

Most Capped Player: Tom Finney, 76, England.

Most League Appearances: Alan Kelly, 447, 1961–75.

Youngest League Player: Steve Doyle, 16 years 166 days v Tranmere R, 15 November 1974.

Record Transfer Fee Received: £5,000,000 from Manchester C for Jon Macken, March 2002.

Record Transfer Fee Paid: £1,500,000 to Manchester U for David Healy, December 2000.

Football League Record: 1888 Founder Member of League; 1901–04 Division 2; 1904–12 Division 1; 1912–13 Division 2; 1913–14 Division 1; 1914–15 Division 2; 1919–25 Division 1; 1925–34 Division 2; 1934–49 Division 1; 1949–51 Division 2; 1951–61 Division 1; 1961–70 Division 2; 1970–71 Division 3; 1971–74 Division 2; 1974–78 Division 3; 1978–81 Division 2; 1981–85 Division 3; 1985–87 Division 4; 1987–92 Division 3; 1992–93 Division 2; 1993–96 Division 3; 1996–2000 Division 2; 2000–04 Division 1; 2004– FLC.

MANAGERS

Charlie Parker 1906–15
Vincent Hayes 1919–23
Jim Lawrence 1923–25
Frank Richards 1925–27
Alex Gibson 1927–31
Lincoln Hayes 1931–32
Run by committee 1932–36
Tommy Muirhead 1936–37
Run by committee 1937–49
Will Scott 1949–53
Scot Symon 1953–54
Frank Hill 1954–56
Cliff Britton 1956–61
Jimmy Milne 1961–68
Bobby Seith 1968–70
Alan Ball Sr 1970–73
Bobby Charlton 1973–75
Harry Catterick 1975–77
Nobby Stiles 1977–81
Tommy Docherty 1981
Gordon Lee 1981–83
Alan Kelly 1983–85
Tommy Booth 1985–86
Brian Kidd 1986
John McGrath 1986–90
Les Chapman 1990–92
Sam Allardyce 1992 (*Caretaker*)
John Beck 1992–94
Gary Peters 1994–98
David Moyes 1998–2002
Kelham O'Hanlon 2002 (*Caretaker*)
Craig Brown 2002–04
Billy Davies 2004–06
Paul Simpson June 2006–

LATEST SEQUENCES

Longest Sequence of League Wins: 14, 25.12.1950 – 27.3.1951.

Longest Sequence of League Defeats: 8, 22.9.1984 – 27.10.1984.

Longest Sequence of League Draws: 6, 24.2.1979 – 20.3.1979.

Longest Sequence of Unbeaten League Matches: 23, 8.9.1888 – 14.9.1889.

Longest Sequence Without a League Win: 15, 14.4.1923 – 20.10.1923.

Successive Scoring Runs: 30 from 15.11.1952.

Successive Non-scoring Runs: 6 from 8.4.1897.

TEN YEAR LEAGUE RECORD

		P	*W*	*D*	*L*	*F*	*A*	*Pts*	*Pos*
1996-97	Div 2	46	18	7	21	49	55	61	15
1997-98	Div 2	46	15	14	17	56	56	59	15
1998-99	Div 2	46	22	13	11	78	50	79	5
1999-2000	Div 2	46	28	11	7	74	37	95	1
2000-01	Div 1	46	23	9	14	64	52	78	4
2001-02	Div 1	46	20	12	14	71	59	72	8
2002-03	Div 1	46	16	13	17	68	70	61	12
2003-04	Div 1	46	15	14	17	69	71	59	15
2004-05	FL C	46	21	12	13	67	58	75	5
2005-06	FL C	46	20	20	6	59	30	80	4

DID YOU KNOW ?

That 1938 Preston North End cup final victory proved size does not always matter. Their five-man forward line on the occasion boasted the tallest of the bunch as Bud Maxwell, something of a giant standing at 5ft 8in!

PRESTON NORTH END 2005–06 LEAGUE RECORD

Match No.	*Date*	*Venue*	*Opponents*	*Result*		*H/T Score*	*Lg. Pos.*	*Goalscorers*	*Attendance*
1	Aug 6	A	Watford	W	2-1	2-1	—	Nugent [22], Etuhu [37]	12,597
2	8	H	Derby Co	D	1-1	1-1	—	Nugent [15]	13,127
3	13	H	Reading	L	0-3	0-1	15		13,154
4	20	A	Sheffield U	L	1-2	1-1	18	McKenna [35]	20,519
5	27	H	Brighton & HA	D	0-0	0-0	17		12,461
6	29	A	Ipswich T	W	4-0	3-0	11	Nugent 2 [31, 34], Jones [45], Agyemang [85]	22,551
7	Sept 10	A	Millwall	W	2-1	1-0	8	Jones [19], Agyemang [77]	7674
8	13	H	Burnley	D	0-0	0-0	—		17,139
9	16	H	Stoke C	L	0-1	0-0	—		12,453
10	24	A	Crystal Palace	D	1-1	1-0	11	Lucketti [43]	17,291
11	27	A	Luton T	L	0-3	0-3	—		7815
12	Oct 1	H	Southampton	D	1-1	0-1	14	Agyemang [65]	15,263
13	15	H	QPR	D	1-1	0-0	16	Mawene [90]	13,660
14	18	A	Cardiff C	D	2-2	0-1	—	Mears [62], Sedgwick [90]	9574
15	22	A	Wolverhampton W	D	1-1	1-0	16	Etuhu [45]	22,802
16	29	H	Leicester C	D	0-0	0-0	16		13,904
17	Nov 1	H	Hull C	W	3-0	0-0	—	Johnson [59], Jones [73], McKenna [76]	13,536
18	5	A	Leeds U	D	0-0	0-0	14		22,289
19	19	H	Cardiff C	W	2-1	2-0	12	Sedgwick [22], Agyemang [42]	13,904
20	22	A	QPR	W	2-0	0-0	—	Nugent [60], Davidson [85]	10,901
21	26	H	Watford	D	1-1	1-1	10	Davidson [14]	14,638
22	Dec 3	A	Crewe Alex	W	2-0	2-0	6	Davidson [24], Nowland [37]	6364
23	10	A	Derby Co	D	1-1	0-0	8	Davis [54]	22,740
24	16	H	Sheffield U	D	0-0	0-0	—		14,378
25	26	H	Sheffield W	D	0-0	0-0	9		18,867
26	31	H	Coventry C	W	3-1	3-0	7	Nowland [26], Alexander (pen) [41], Sedgwick [45]	12,936
27	Jan 2	A	Norwich C	W	3-0	1-0	6	Nowland [45], Alexander (pen) [69], Nugent [74]	25,032
28	14	H	Millwall	W	2-0	1-0	6	Agyemang [43], Davis [51]	14,105
29	21	A	Burnley	W	2-0	1-0	6	Nugent [13], Alexander (pen) [86]	17,220
30	31	H	Crystal Palace	W	2-0	1-0	—	Ormerod [13], O'Neil [49]	13,867
31	Feb 4	A	Stoke C	D	0-0	0-0	6		13,218
32	11	H	Luton T	W	5-1	1-0	5	Neal L [20], Nugent [53], Mears [84], Sedgwick (pen) [89], Davis [90]	15,237
33	15	A	Southampton	D	0-0	0-0	—		19,534
34	25	A	Reading	L	1-2	1-2	6	Davidson [8]	23,011
35	Mar 7	A	Plymouth Arg	D	0-0	0-0	—		10,874
36	11	A	Brighton & HA	D	0-0	0-0	7		6361
37	14	H	Ipswich T	W	3-1	0-1	—	Nugent 2 [53, 62], Agyemang [71]	14,507
38	18	A	Sheffield W	L	0-2	0-1	6		23,429
39	25	H	Plymouth Arg	D	0-0	0-0	6		13,925
40	28	H	Crewe Alex	W	1-0	1-0	—	Ormerod [37]	13,170
41	Apr 1	A	Coventry C	W	1-0	1-0	6	Whaley [30]	21,023
42	8	H	Norwich C	W	2-0	2-0	5	Shackell (og) [20], Doherty (og) [38]	15,714
43	15	A	Leicester C	W	2-1	1-1	5	Whaley [45], Jarrett [49]	21,865
44	17	H	Wolverhampton W	W	2-0	1-0	4	Neal L [42], Ormerod [71]	16,885
45	22	A	Hull C	D	1-1	1-1	5	Whaley [33]	19,716
46	30	H	Leeds U	W	2-0	1-0	4	Stock [38], Ormerod [77]	19,350

Final League Position: 4

GOALSCORERS

League (59): Nugent 10, Agyemang 6, Davidson 4, Ormerod 4, Sedgwick 4 (1 pen), Alexander 3 (3 pens), Davis 3, Jones 3, Nowland 3, Whaley 3, Etuhu 2, McKenna 2, Mears 2, Neal L 2, Jarrett 1, Johnson 1, Lucketti 1, Mawene 1, O'Neil 1, Stock 1, own goals 2.
Carling Cup (2): Alexander 1 (pen), Dichio 1.
FA Cup (5): Dichio 2, Alexander 1, O'Neil 1, Sedgwick 1.
Play-Offs (1): Nugent 1.

Nash C 46	Alexander G 39 + 1	Davidson C 26 + 1	O'Neil B 22 + 3	Lucketti C 23 + 5	Mawene Y 26 + 4	Sedgwick C 39 + 7	McKenna P 40 + 1	Cresswell R 3	Nugent D 27 + 5	Etuhu D 6 + 7	Davis C 37 + 3	Jones D 21 + 3	Agyemang P 19 + 23	Dichio D 18 + 15	Neal L 13 + 11	Mears T 27 + 5	Anyinsah J — + 3	Hill M 24 + 2	Nowland A 9 + 4	Hibbert D — + 10	Johnson J 2 + 1	Stock B 4 + 2	Whaley S 7 + 9	Ormerod B 13 + 2	Jarrett J 8 + 2	Stewart M 4	Wilson K 3 + 3	*Match No.*
1	2	3^{1}	4^{2}	5	6	7	8	9	10^{3}	11	12	13	14															1
1	2	3	4^{1}	5	6	7^{2}	8	9	10^{3}	11			14	13	12													2
1	2	3	4	5	6	7^{1}	8^{2}	9^{3}	10	11		12		13	14													3
1	2		4	5		7^{3}	8		10^{1}		6	11	13	9^{2}	12	3	14											4
1	2		4^{1}		6	7^{2}	8		10	11^{3}	5	12	14	9	13			3										5
1	2		4	5		13	8		10^{2}	12	6	7^{1}	14	9^{3}		11		3										6
1	12		4^{2}	5		11^{1}	8		10	13	6	7	14	9^{3}		2		3										7
1	2	3		5		7^{2}	8^{1}		10	11	6	4	12	9		13												8
1	2	3	4^{3}	5		11^{2}	8		10		6	7	9^{1}	12			13		14									9
1	2	3		5		7^{1}	8			12	6■	11	13	10■	4^{3}			14	9^{2}									10
1	2	3		5		7	8^{1}			4		11	12	10^{3}	9^{2}	13		6		14								11
1	2	3		5		7^{2}	8^{1}			12		4	9^{3}	10	11	6	13			14								12
1		3		5	6	7^{1}	8					4	9	10^{2}	11	2			12	13								13
1	2	3		5		12	8		13		6	4	9	14	11^{3}	7^{1}			10^{2}									14
1	2			5^{1}	12	13	8			14	6	4	9		11^{2}	7		3	10^{3}									15
1	2^{1}	11		5		12	8^{2}			13	6	4	9			7		3		14	10^{3}							16
1	2	11		5	12	7	8		13		6^{1}	4	9^{2}					3		14	10^{3}							17
1	2^{1}	11	10^{2}	5	12	7	8		14	13	6	4^{3}	9					3										18
1	2	11	12	5		7^{2}	8		10^{3}		6	4^{1}	9	13				3			14							19
1	2	11	4^{1}	5	12	7	8		13		6		9^{3}	14				3	10^{2}									20
1	2	11	4^{2}	5		7			10		6	8	9^{1}	12	14			3^{3}	13									21
1	2	11^{3}	12	5		7	8		10^{2}		6	4		13	14			3	9^{1}									22
1	2		12		6	7	8		10^{2}		5	4		13	11^{3}	14		3	9^{1}									23
1	2				6	7^{2}			10^{1}		5	4	12	9	13	3		11	8									24
1	2		4^{2}		6	7^{3}			10		5	8	12	9^{1}	11	14		3	13									25
1	2	12		13	6^{2}	7			10^{3}		5	4	9		11			3	8^{1}	14								26
1	2	11		12	6	7			10^{1}		5		13	9		4		3	8^{2}									27
1	2	11			6	7	8^{2}		10		5		9^{1}	12	13	3						4^{3}	14					28
1	2	11		12	6	7	8		10^{2}		5		13	9		3						4^{1}						29
1	2	11	4^{3}	12	6	7^{1}	8		10		5		13			3							14	9^{2}				30
1	2^{3}	11	4^{1}	12	6	7^{2}	8		10		5		13		14	3								9				31
1			4	5	6	7	8^{2}		10^{1}		13		12		11^{3}	2		3					14	9				32
1		11	4	5	6	7^{2}	8		10^{1}		13		12	14		2		3						9^{3}				33
1		11	4		6	7^{3}	8		10^{1}		5		12	13		2		3					14	9^{2}				34
1	2		4			7	8		10^{3}		5		12	9^{1}	13	3							11^{2}	14	6			35
1	2	11			6	7^{2}	8		10^{3}		5		12	9^{1}		3							13	14	4			36
1		11			6	7	8		10^{2}		5		12	13		2		3					14	9^{1}	4^{3}			37
1	2		4^{3}		6	7	8				5		9^{1}	10^{2}		3				12			13	11	14			38
1	2		4		6	7	8				5		12		11^{3}	13		3^{2}					14	9		10^{1}		39
1	2		4^{3}			7	8^{2}				5		9			3				12			13	11	14	10^{1}	6	40
1	2				6	7^{2}	8				5		9^{3}			3				12		13	4		11	10^{1}	14	41
1	2		4^{1}		6	12	8				5		9			3				13			7^{3}	11		10^{2}	14	42
1	2				6	7^{3}	8				5		9^{2}	12	13	3						14	11	10^{1}	4			43
1	2					12	8				5		9^{2}	13	7^{1}	3		14					11	10^{3}	4		6	44
1					6	7	12						13	10	9^{2}	2		3				4	11		8^{1}		5	45
1	2				6	12	8^{1}		13		5^{3}			10				3				4^{2}	11	9	7		14	46

FA Cup

Third Round	Crewe Alex	(h)	2-1
Fourth Round	Crystal Palace	(h)	1-1
		(a)	2-1
Fifth Round	Middlesbrough	(h)	0-2

Carling Cup

First Round	Barnsley	(h)	2-2

Play-Offs

Semi-Final	Leeds U	(a)	1-1
		(h)	0-2

QUEENS PARK RANGERS FL Championship

FOUNDATION

There is an element of doubt about the date of the foundation of this club, but it is believed that in either 1885 or 1886 it was formed through the amalgamation of Christchurch Rangers and St Jude's Institute FC. The leading light was George Wodehouse, whose family maintained a connection with the club until comparatively recent times. Most of the players came from the Queen's Park district so this name was adopted after a year as St Jude's Institute.

Loftus Road Stadium, South Africa Road, Shepherds Bush, London W12 7PA.

Telephone: (020) 8743 0262.

Fax: (020) 8749 0994.

Ticket Office: 0870 112 1967.

Website: www.qpr.co.uk

Email: feedback@qpr.co.uk

Ground Capacity: 18,769.

Record Attendance: 35,353 v Leeds U, Division 1, 27 April 1974.

Pitch Measurements: 110yd × 73yd.

Chairman: Gianni Paladini.

Secretary: Sheila Marson.

Manager: Gary Waddock (caretaker).

Assistant Manager: Alan McDonald (caretaker).

Physio: Prav Mathema.

Colours: Blue and white hooped shirts, white shorts, white stockings.

Change Colours: All black.

Year Formed: 1885* (*see Foundation*).

Turned Professional: 1898. ***Ltd Co.:*** 1899.

Previous Names: 1885, St Jude's; 1887, Queens Park Rangers. ***Club Nicknames:*** 'Rangers' or 'Rs'.

Previous Grounds: 1885* (*see Foundation*), Welford's Fields; 1888–99; London Scottish Ground, Brondesbury, Home Farm, Kensal Rise Green, Gun Club Wormwood Scrubs, Kilburn Cricket Ground; 1899, Kensal Rise Athletic Ground; 1901, Latimer Road, Notting Hill; 1904, Agricultural Society, Park Royal; 1907, Park Royal Ground; 1917, Loftus Road; 1931, White City; 1933, Loftus Road; 1962, White City; 1963, Loftus Road.

First Football League Game: 28 August 1920, Division 3, v Watford (h) L 1–2 – Price; Blackman, Wingrove; McGovern, Grant, O'Brien; Faulkner, Birch (1), Smith, Gregory, Middlemiss.

Record League Victory: 9–2 v Tranmere R, Division 3, 3 December 1960 – Drinkwater; Woods, Ingham; Keen, Rutter, Angell; Lazarus (2), Bedford (2), Evans (2), Andrews (1), Clark (2).

Record Cup Victory: 8–1 v Bristol R (away), FA Cup 1st rd, 27 November 1937 – Gilfillan; Smith, Jefferson; Lowe, James, March; Cape, Mallett, Cheetham (3), Fitzgerald (3) Bott (2). 8–1 v Crewe Alex, Milk Cup 1st rd, 3 October 1983 – Hucker; Neill, Dawes, Waddock (1), McDonald (1), Fenwick, Micklewhite (1), Stewart (1), Allen (1), Stainrod (3), Gregory.

HONOURS

Football League: Division 1 – Runners-up 1975–76; Division 2 – Champions 1982–83; Runners-up 1967–68, 1972–73, 2003–04; Division 3 (S) – Champions 1947–48; Runners-up 1946–47; Division 3 – Champions 1966–67.

FA Cup: Runners-up 1982.

Football League Cup: Winners 1967; Runners-up 1986. (In 1966–67 won Division 3 and Football League Cup).

European Competitions: *UEFA Cup:* 1976–77, 1984–85.

SKY SPORTS FACT FILE

Queens Park Rangers, who came back from being four down at half-time to Newcastle United on 22 September 1984 to draw 5–5, also found themselves similarly placed at Port Vale on 19 January 1997. With five minutes left they were losing 4–1 but drew 4–4.

Record Defeat: 1–8 v Mansfield T, Division 3, 15 March 1965. 1–8 v Manchester U, Division 1, 19 March 1969.

Most League Points (2 for a win): 67, Division 3, 1966–67.

Most League Points (3 for a win): 85, Division 2, 1982–83.

Most League Goals: 111, Division 3, 1961–62.

Highest League Scorer in Season: George Goddard, 37, Division 3 (S), 1929–30.

Most League Goals in Total Aggregate: George Goddard, 172, 1926–34.

Most League Goals in One Match: 4, George Goddard v Merthyr T, Division 3S, 9 March 1929; 4, George Goddard v Swindon T, Division 3S, 12 April 1930; 4, George Goddard v Exeter C, Division 3S, 20 December 1930; 4, George Goddard v Watford, Division 3S, 19 September 1931; 4, Tom Cheetham v Aldershot, Division 3S, 14 September 1935; 4, Tom Cheetham v Aldershot, Division 3S, 12 November 1938.

Most Capped Player: Alan McDonald, 52, Northern Ireland.

Most League Appearances: Tony Ingham, 519, 1950–63.

Youngest League Player: Frank Sibley, 16 years 97 days v Bristol C, 10 March 1964.

Record Transfer Fee Received: £6,000,000 from Newcastle U for Les Ferdinand, June 1995.

Record Transfer Fee Paid: £2,750,000 to Stoke C for Mike Sheron, July 1997.

Football League Record: 1920 Original Members of Division 3; 1921–48 Division 3 (S); 1948–52 Division 2; 1952–58 Division 3 (S); 1958–67 Division 3; 1967–68 Division 2; 1968–69 Division 1; 1969–73 Division 2; 1973–79 Division 1; 1979–83 Division 2; 1983–92 Division 1; 1992–96 FA Premier League; 1996–2001 Division 1; 2001–04 Division 2; 2004– FLC.

MANAGERS

James Cowan 1906–13
Jimmy Howie 1913–20
Ted Liddell 1920–24
Will Wood 1924–25
(had been Secretary since 1903)
Bob Hewison 1925–30
John Bowman 1930–31
Archie Mitchell 1931–33
Mick O'Brien 1933–35
Billy Birrell 1935–39
Ted Vizard 1939–44
Dave Mangnall 1944–52
Jack Taylor 1952–59
Alec Stock 1959–65
(General Manager to 1968)
Bill Dodgin Jnr 1968
Tommy Docherty 1968
Les Allen 1968–71
Gordon Jago 1971–74
Dave Sexton 1974–77
Frank Sibley 1977–78
Steve Burtenshaw 1978–79
Tommy Docherty 1979–80
Terry Venables 1980–84
Gordon Jago 1984
Alan Mullery 1984
Frank Sibley 1984–85
Jim Smith 1985–88
Trevor Francis 1988–90
Don Howe 1990–91
Gerry Francis 1991–94
Ray Wilkins 1994–96
Stewart Houston 1996–97
Ray Harford 1997–98
Gerry Francis 1998–2001
Ian Holloway 2001–06

LATEST SEQUENCES

Longest Sequence of League Wins: 8, 7.11.1931 – 28.12.1931.

Longest Sequence of League Defeats: 9, 25.2.1969 – 5.4.1969.

Longest Sequence of League Draws: 6, 29.1.2000 – 5.3.2000.

Longest Sequence of Unbeaten League Matches: 20, 11.3.1972 – 23.9.1972.

Longest Sequence Without a League Win: 20, 7.12.1968 – 7.4.1969.

Successive Scoring Runs: 33 from 9.12.1961.

Successive Non-scoring Runs: 6 from 18.3.1939.

TEN YEAR LEAGUE RECORD

		P	W	D	L	F	A	Pts	Pos
1996-97	Div 1	46	18	12	16	64	60	66	9
1997-98	Div 1	46	10	19	17	51	63	49	21
1998-99	Div 1	46	12	11	23	52	61	47	20
1999-2000	Div 1	46	16	18	12	62	53	66	10
2000-01	Div 1	46	7	19	20	45	75	40	23
2001-02	Div 2	46	19	14	13	60	49	71	8
2002-03	Div 2	46	24	11	11	69	45	83	4
2003-04	Div 2	46	22	17	7	80	45	83	2
2004-05	FL C	46	17	11	18	54	58	62	11
2005-06	FL C	46	12	14	20	50	65	50	21

DID YOU KNOW

In 1963–64 Queens Park Rangers had identical twins Ian and Roger Morgan playing on opposite wings in their reserve team. Left-winger Roger was the elder by ten minutes, but Ian made his League debut at 17 a week earlier on 25 September 1964.

QUEENS PARK RANGERS 2005–06 LEAGUE RECORD

Match No.	Date	Venue	Opponents	Result	H/T Score	Lg. Pos.	Goalscorers	Attendance
1	Aug 6	A	Hull C	D 0-0	0-0	—		
2	9	H	Ipswich T	W 2-1	2-0	—	Gallen 37, Rowlands 45	14,632
3	13	H	Sheffield U	W 2-1	0-0	2	Bircham 56, Moore 89	13,497
4	20	A	Coventry C	L 0-3	0-3	11		23,000
5	26	H	Sheffield W	D 0-0	0-0	—		12,131
6	30	A	Wolverhampton W	L 1-3	1-2	—	Gallen 12	22,426
7	Sept 10	A	Southampton	D 1-1	1-1	15	Shittu 32	25,744
8	13	H	Luton T	W 1-0	0-0	—	Cook 58	13,492
9	17	H	Leeds U	L 0-1	0-1	11		15,523
10	24	A	Leicester C	W 2-1	1-0	8	Nygaard 12, Furlong 86	20,148
11	27	A	Millwall	D 1-1	1-1	—	Nygaard 25	10,322
12	Oct 3	H	Crystal Palace	L 1-3	1-2	—	Ainsworth 19	13,433
13	15	A	Preston NE	D 1-1	0-0	10	Shittu 62	13,660
14	18	H	Plymouth Arg	D 1-1	0-1	—	Gallen (pen) 69	11,741
15	22	H	Norwich C	W 3-0	3-0	10	Nygaard 11, Furlong 18, Santos 42	15,976
16	29	A	Derby Co	W 2-1	1-0	8	Ainsworth 30, Gallen 80	24,447
17	Nov 1	A	Watford	L 1-3	0-1	—	Shittu 90	16,476
18	5	H	Reading	L 1-2	0-1	12	Cook 47	15,347
19	19	A	Plymouth Arg	L 1-3	0-2	13	Baidoo 61	13,213
20	22	H	Preston NE	L 0-2	0-0	—		10,901
21	26	H	Hull C	D 2-2	0-1	13	Ainsworth 2 56, 66	13,185
22	Dec 3	A	Stoke C	W 2-1	1-1	13	Furlong 2, Langley (pen) 52	15,367
23	10	A	Ipswich T	D 2-2	2-1	13	Moore 26, Furlong 42	24,628
24	19	H	Coventry C	L 0-1	0-0	—		13,556
25	26	A	Brighton & HA	L 0-1	0-1	14		7341
26	28	H	Cardiff C	W 1-0	0-0	13	Nygaard 47	12,329
27	31	A	Crewe Alex	W 4-3	2-3	13	Cook 35, Baidoo 37, Rowlands 57, Langley 81	5687
28	Jan 2	H	Burnley	D 1-1	1-1	13	Ainsworth 45	12,565
29	14	H	Southampton	W 1-0	0-0	11	Langley (pen) 21	15,494
30	21	A	Luton T	L 0-2	0-1	12		9797
31	31	H	Leicester C	L 2-3	1-1	—	Ainsworth 6, Shittu 83	11,785
32	Feb 4	A	Leeds U	L 0-2	0-1	15		21,807
33	11	H	Millwall	W 1-0	0-0	12	Nygaard 56	12,355
34	14	A	Crystal Palace	L 1-2	0-2	—	Furlong 56	17,550
35	25	A	Sheffield U	W 3-2	1-2	13	Nygaard 6, Morgan (og) 56, Furlong 74	25,360
36	Mar 4	H	Wolverhampton W	D 0-0	0-0	14		14,731
37	11	A	Sheffield W	D 1-1	1-1	14	Bircham 43	22,788
38	18	H	Brighton & HA	D 1-1	1-0	13	Ainsworth 13	13,907
39	25	A	Cardiff C	D 0-0	0-0	13		14,271
40	29	H	Stoke C	L 1-2	1-0	—	Nygaard 7	10,918
41	Apr 1	H	Crewe Alex	L 1-2	0-1	15	Ainsworth 90	12,877
42	8	A	Burnley	L 0-1	0-0	18		11,247
43	15	H	Derby Co	D 1-1	0-0	18	Nygaard 59	12,606
44	17	A	Norwich C	L 2-3	1-0	20	Ainsworth 45, Cook 61	24,126
45	22	H	Watford	L 1-2	1-1	20	Nygaard (pen) 39	16,152
46	30	A	Reading	L 1-2	0-1	21	Furlong 72	23,156

Final League Position: 21

GOALSCORERS

League (50): Ainsworth 9, Nygaard 9 (1 pen), Furlong 7, Cook 4, Gallen 4 (1 pen), Shittu 4, Langley 3 (2 pens), Baidoo 2, Bircham 2, Moore 2, Rowlands 2, Santos 1, own goal 1.
Carling Cup (0).
FA Cup (0).

Royce S 30	Bignot M 44	Rose M 15	Doherty T 14 + 1	Shittu D 45	Santos G 25 + 6	Rowlands M 12 + 2	Bircham M 24 + 2	Furlong P 31 + 6	Gallen K 18	Cook L 34 + 6	Ainsworth G 33 + 10	Sturridge D 6 + 3	Moore S 11 + 14	Nygaard M 20 + 7	Bean M 4 + 5	Brown A 1 + 1	Ukah U — + 1	Milanese M 22 + 4	Shimmin D 1 + 1	Miller A 1	Evatt I 21 + 6	Lomas S 18 + 3	Langley R 22 + 11	Hislop M 1	Dyer L 15	Baidoo S 6 + 9	Cole J 1 + 2	Donnelly S 3 + 5	Taylor A 1 + 2	Barnes P 1	Lowe K 1	Kus M 3	Youssouf S 2 + 4	Clarke L 1	Jones P 14	Bailey S 5	Jones R — + 2	*Match No.*
1	2	3	4^1	5	6	7^2	8	9	10	11	12	13^3	14																									1
1	2	3	4	5	6	11	8	9^2	10		7^1		12	13																								2
1	2	3	4^2	5	6	11^3	8	9	10		7^1		13		14	12																						3
1	2^2	3		5■			8^1	9	10		7		11		12	4^3	13	14	6																			4
1	2	6	4	5			8	9	10		7		12					3		11^1																		5
1	2		4^1	5	6		8^2	9	10		12		11		13			7			3																	6
1	2		4^2	5	6		8	9^3		11		10^1	7	12				3				13	14															7
1	2		4■	5	6		8	9^1		11	7^3		10^2	12				3				13	14															8
1	2			5	6	12	8	9		11	7^1	10^2	13					3^3			14	4																9
1	2			5	6		8	9■		11^2	12			10					14		13	4	7^1	3^3														10
1	2			5	6		8			11	12	9^2	13	10								4	7^1		3													11
1	2^2		4^1	5	6		8	9		11	7		10^3								13		12		3	14												12
1	2		12	5	6			9	10	11^2	13			8							4	7^1			3													13
1	2		4^2	5	12		8	9^3	7	11^1	13	14		10							6				3													14
1	2		4	5	12		8^1	9	7	11^2	13	14		10^3							6				3													15
1	2		4^2	5	6			9■	11		7^3	10^1	12					14			8		13		3													16
1	2		3	5	6^3				11	12	7^1	10	9^2	14							4		13		8													17
1	2		8	5	6				10	11	12	9^1									4		7		3													18
1	2		4^1	5	9^3	12			10	11	7				14						6		8^2		3	13												19
1	2			5	12	4			10	11^2	7^3		13		14						6		8		3	9^1												20
1	2				5^1	4		9	10^2	12	7		13					3			6		8		11													21
1	2			5		4		9		12	11^1		10^3		7			6			13		8		3^2	14												22
1	2			5	12	7^2		9		13	11		10		4			6			14		8^3		3^1													23
1■	2			5	9^2	4	13			12	7^G		10		11^1						6		8		3		15											24
	2			5		4	12	9		13	7^1		10^3	14	11^2						6		8		3		1											25
1	2	3		5	6	7	8^2	9		11^1	12			10^3				13					4			14												26
1	2	3		5	6^3	7	8^2	12		11	13			10^1				14					4			9												27
1	2	6^1		5	12	4		13		11	7			10^2				3					8^3			9		14										28
1	2	3		5	6^3			9		11	7^2		12									4	8			10^1		13	14									29
1	2^3	3		5	6			9		11	7^1		12	13								4	8			10^2			14									30
1	2	3		5	6			9^1		11	7^2		12	10^3								4	8			14		13										31
	2			5						11^1	7^3		10	12								4	13						8	1	3	6^2	14	9				32
	2			5			8^1	9		11	7			10^2				3			6	4	12			13									1			33
	2^1	3		5				12		11				10				9			6	4	8			13		7^2							1			34
	2	3		5	12		7	9		11				10^2							6	4^1	8										13		1			35
	2	6		5				9	10^1	11	7							3					8										12		1	4		36
	2	6^1		5			8	9^3	10	11^2	7							3			12	4	13			14									1			37
	2			5			8		10■	11^1	7			9^2				3			6	4				12							13		1			38
	2			5			8	12		11	7			9^2				3			6	4	13										10^1		1			39
	2			5			8^2	12		11	7^1		14	9				3			6	4	13										10^3		1			40
	2^2			5			8	9^1		11	7		12	10				3			6	4	13												1			41
				5			4^2			11	7			9				3			6	12	8			10		13				2^1			1			42
				5				12		11	7			9				3			6		8					4^1				2			1	10		43
	2			5	6			9		11	7			10				3				4													1	8		44
	2^1			5	6			9		11	7			10■				3				4^2						12							1	8	13	45
	2			5	6			9		11	7							3					8				15	10							1^G	4^1	12	46

FA Cup
Third Round Blackburn R (a) 0-3

Carling Cup
First Round Northampton T (a) 0-3

READING FA Premiership

FOUNDATION

Reading was formed as far back as 1871 at a public meeting held at the Bridge Street Rooms. They first entered the FA Cup as early as 1877 when they amalgamated with the Reading Hornets. The club was further strengthened in 1889 when Earley FC joined them. They were the first winners of the Berks and Bucks Cup in 1878–79.

Madejski Stadium, Junction 11, M4, Reading, Berkshire RG2 0FL.

Telephone: (0118) 968 1100.

Fax: (0118) 968 1101.

Ticket Office: 0870 999 1871.

Website: www.readingfc.co.uk

Email: comments@readingfc.co.uk

Ground Capacity: 24,225.

Record Attendance: 33,042 v Brentford, FA Cup 5th rd, 19 February 1927.

Pitch Measurements: 111yd × 74yd.

Chairman: John Madejski OBE, DL.

Director of Football: Nick Hammond.

Chief Executive: Nigel Howe.

Secretary: Sue Hewett.

Manager: Steve Coppell.

First Team Coaches: Kevin Dillon, Wally Downes.

Physio: Jon Fearn MMACP, MCSP.

Colours: Blue and white hooped shirts, blue shorts, blue stockings.

Change Colours: Navy shirts with silver trim, silver shorts, navy stockings.

Year Formed: 1871.

Turned Professional: 1895.

Ltd Co.: 1895.

Club Nickname: 'The Royals'.

Previous Grounds: 1871, Reading Recreation; Reading Cricket Ground; 1882, Coley Park; 1889, Caversham Cricket Ground; 1896, Elm Park; 1998, Madejski Stadium.

First Football League Game: 28 August 1920, Division 3, v Newport Co (a) W 1–0 – Crawford; Smith, Horler; Christie, Mavin, Getgood; Spence, Weston, Yarnell, Bailey (1), Andrews.

Record League Victory: 10–2 v Crystal Palace, Division 3 (S), 4 September 1946 – Groves; Glidden, Gulliver; McKenna, Ratcliffe, Young; Chitty, Maurice Edelston (3), McPhee (4), Barney (1), Deverell (2).

HONOURS

Football League: Championship – Champions 2005–06; Division 1 – Runners-up 1994–95; Division 2 – Champions 1993–94; Runners-up 2001–02; Division 3 – Champions 1985–86; Division 3 (S) – Champions 1925–26; Runners-up 1931–32, 1934–35, 1948–49, 1951–52; Division 4 – Champions 1978–79.

FA Cup: Semi-final 1927.

Football League Cup: best season: 5th rd, 1996.

Simod Cup: Winners 1988.

SKY SPORTS FACT FILE

Prior to their club unbeaten record sequence in 2005–06, Reading had gone 19 League matches without defeat starting on 21 April 1973 and finishing on 27 October. However, they finished only seventh at the end of the first season, sixth in 1973–74.

Record Cup Victory: 6–0 v Leyton, FA Cup 2nd rd, 12 December 1925 – Duckworth; Eggo, McConnell; Wilson, Messer, Evans; Smith (2), Braithwaite (1), Davey (1), Tinsley, Robson (2).

Record Defeat: 0–18 v Preston NE, FA Cup 1st rd, 1893–94.

Most League Points (2 for a win): 65, Division 4, 1978–79.

Most League Points (3 for a win): 106, Championship, 2005–06.

Most League Goals: 112, Division 3 (S), 1951–52.

Highest League Scorer in Season: Ronnie Blackman, 39, Division 3 (S), 1951–52.

Most League Goals in Total Aggregate: Ronnie Blackman, 158, 1947–54.

Most League Goals in One Match: 6, Arthur Bacon v Stoke C, Division 2, 3 April 1931.

Most Capped Player: Jimmy Quinn, 17 (46), Northern Ireland.

Most League Appearances: Martin Hicks, 500, 1978–91.

Youngest League Player: Peter Castle, 16 years 49 days v Watford, 30 April 2003.

Record Transfer Fee Received: £1,575,000 from Newcastle U for Shaka Hislop, August 1995.

Record Transfer Fee Paid: £1,000,000 to Bristol C for Leroy Lita, July 2005.

Football League Record: 1920 Original Member of Division 3; 1921–26 Division 3 (S); 1926–31 Division 2; 1931–58 Division 3 (S); 1958–71 Division 3; 1971–76 Division 4; 1976–77 Division 3; 1977–79 Division 4; 1979–83 Division 3; 1983–84 Division 4; 1984–86 Division 3; 1986–88 Division 2; 1988–92 Division 3; 1992–94 Division 2; 1994–98 Division 1; 1998–2002 Division 2; 2002–04 Division 1; 2004–06 FLC; 2006– FA Premier League.

MANAGERS

Thomas Sefton 1897–1901
(Secretary-Manager)
James Sharp 1901–02
Harry Matthews 1902–20
Harry Marshall 1920–22
Arthur Chadwick 1923–25
H. S. Bray 1925–26
(Secretary only since 1922 and 1926–35)
Andrew Wylie 1926–31
Joe Smith 1931–35
Billy Butler 1935–39
John Cochrane 1939
Joe Edelston 1939–47
Ted Drake 1947–52
Jack Smith 1952–55
Harry Johnston 1955–63
Roy Bentley 1963–69
Jack Mansell 1969–71
Charlie Hurley 1972–77
Maurice Evans 1977–84
Ian Branfoot 1984–89
Ian Porterfield 1989–91
Mark McGhee 1991–94
Jimmy Quinn/Mick Gooding 1994–97
Terry Bullivant 1997–98
Tommy Burns 1998–99
Alan Pardew 1999–2003
Steve Coppell October 2003–

LATEST SEQUENCES

Longest Sequence of League Wins: 13, 17.8.1985 – 19.10.1985.

Longest Sequence of League Defeats: 7, 10.4.1998 – 15.8.1998.

Longest Sequence of League Draws: 6, 23.3.2002 – 20.4.2002.

Longest Sequence of Unbeaten League Matches: 33, 9.8.2005 – 14.2.2006.

Longest Sequence Without a League Win: 14, 30.4.1927 – 29.10.1927.

Successive Scoring Runs: 32 from 1.10.1932.

Successive Non-scoring Runs: 6 from 13.4.1925.

TEN YEAR LEAGUE RECORD

		P	*W*	*D*	*L*	*F*	*A*	*Pts*	*Pos*
1996-97	Div 1	46	15	12	19	58	67	57	18
1997-98	Div 1	46	11	9	26	39	78	42	24
1998-99	Div 2	46	16	13	17	54	63	61	11
1999-2000	Div 2	46	16	14	16	57	63	62	10
2000-01	Div 2	46	25	11	10	86	52	86	3
2001-02	Div 2	46	23	15	8	70	43	84	2
2002-03	Div 1	46	25	4	17	61	46	79	4
2003-04	Div 1	46	20	10	16	55	57	70	9
2004-05	FL C	46	19	13	14	51	44	70	7
2005-06	FL C	46	31	13	2	99	32	106	1

DID YOU KNOW ?

The much travelled Tommy Tait scored in seven of the FA Cup ties in which Reading scored in 1934–35 and 1935–36 seasons. His total of ten included two in an 8–3 victory over Corinthians on 30 November 1935 in which Jimmy Liddle hit a hat-trick himself.

READING 2005–06 LEAGUE RECORD

Match No.	*Date*	*Venue*	*Opponents*	*Result*		*H/T Score*	*Lg. Pos.*	*Goalscorers*	*Attendance*
1	Aug 6	H	Plymouth Arg	L	1-2	0-1	—	Lita [54]	16,836
2	9	A	Brighton & HA	W	2-0	1-0	—	Little [15], Kitson [63]	6676
3	13	A	Preston NE	W	3-0	1-0	4	Lita 2 [34, 46], Little [57]	13,154
4	20	H	Millwall	W	5-0	4-0	1	Convey 2 [6, 25], Harper [38], Kitson (pen) [43], Sidwell [79]	14,225
5	27	A	Watford	D	0-0	0-0	2		11,358
6	29	H	Burnley	W	2-1	1-1	2	Lita [7], Doyle [70]	14,027
7	Sept 10	A	Coventry C	D	1-1	0-0	2	Doyle [68]	22,074
8	13	H	Crystal Palace	W	3-2	1-1	—	Doyle [26], Lita [68], Sonko [87]	17,562
9	17	H	Crewe Alex	W	1-0	0-0	2	Ingimarsson [81]	17,668
10	24	A	Norwich C	W	1-0	0-0	2	Harper [61]	24,850
11	28	A	Southampton	D	0-0	0-0	—		24,946
12	Oct 1	H	Sheffield U	W	2-1	1-1	2	Gunnarsson 2 [3, 89]	22,068
13	16	H	Ipswich T	W	2-0	1-0	2	Naylor (og) [18], Doyle [47]	17,581
14	18	A	Hull C	D	1-1	0-0	—	Little [74]	17,698
15	22	A	Stoke C	W	1-0	0-0	2	Kitson (pen) [77]	13,484
16	29	H	Leeds U	D	1-1	0-0	2	Gunnarsson [63]	22,012
17	Nov 1	H	Sheffield W	W	2-0	1-0	—	Whelan (og) [38], Kitson [64]	16,188
18	5	A	QPR	W	2-1	1-0	2	Harper [10], Ingimarsson [66]	15,347
19	19	H	Hull C	W	3-1	1-0	2	Convey [7], Doyle [69], Little [70]	17,864
20	22	A	Ipswich T	W	3-0	1-0	—	Sidwell [29], Lita [53], Doyle [77]	22,621
21	26	A	Plymouth Arg	W	2-0	1-0	1	Little [20], Doyle [57]	14,020
22	Dec 3	H	Luton T	W	3-0	1-0	1	Sidwell [44], Kitson [76], Doyle [88]	19,478
23	10	H	Brighton & HA	W	5-1	1-0	1	Oatway (og) [27], Kitson 3 (1 pen) [51 (p), 71, 90], Hunt [76]	18,546
24	17	A	Millwall	W	2-0	1-0	1	Sidwell [40], Doyle [68]	12,920
25	26	A	Wolverhampton W	W	2-0	1-0	1	Convey [64], Kitson [79]	27,980
26	28	H	Leicester C	W	2-0	0-0	1	Doyle [60], Gunnarsson [87]	22,061
27	31	A	Derby Co	D	2-2	1-1	1	Doyle [34], Long [88]	21,434
28	Jan 2	H	Cardiff C	W	5-1	2-0	1	Sidwell 2 [11, 71], Sonko [32], Kitson 2 (1 pen) [51, 76 (p)]	22,061
29	14	H	Coventry C	W	2-0	0-0	1	Kitson 2 [46, 78]	22,813
30	20	A	Crystal Palace	D	1-1	0-0	—	Harper [81]	19,888
31	31	H	Norwich C	W	4-0	2-0	—	Shorey [6], Sidwell [17], Lita [55], Convey [69]	21,442
32	Feb 4	A	Crewe Alex	W	4-3	3-1	1	Shorey [24], Sidwell [26], Lita 2 [43, 53]	6484
33	10	H	Southampton	W	2-0	2-0	—	Lita [16], Doyle [38]	23,845
34	14	A	Sheffield U	D	1-1	1-1	—	Kitson [12]	25,011
35	17	A	Luton T	L	2-3	1-2	—	Doyle 2 [1, 90]	8705
36	25	H	Preston NE	W	2-1	2-1	1	Sidwell [6], Lita [45]	23,011
37	Mar 4	A	Burnley	W	3-0	1-0	1	Convey [10], Sonko [55], Kitson [90]	12,888
38	11	H	Watford	D	0-0	0-0	1		23,724
39	18	H	Wolverhampton W	D	1-1	1-0	1	Convey [23]	23,502
40	25	A	Leicester C	D	1-1	0-1	1	Doyle [85]	25,578
41	Apr 1	H	Derby Co	W	5-0	0-0	1	Harper [59], Doyle [65], Oster [70], Long 2 [74, 83]	22,981
42	8	A	Cardiff C	W	5-2	2-0	1	Harper 2 [10, 90], Kitson [39], Loovens (og) [52], Doyle [87]	11,866
43	15	A	Leeds U	D	1-1	0-0	1	Hunt [85]	24,535
44	17	H	Stoke C	W	3-1	1-0	1	Sidwell [25], Doyle (pen) [56], Halls [62]	22,119
45	22	A	Sheffield W	D	1-1	1-0	1	Kitson [34]	27,307
46	30	H	QPR	W	2-1	1-0	1	Kitson [40], Murty (pen) [84]	23,156

Final League Position: 1

GOALSCORERS

League (99): Doyle 18 (1 pen), Kitson 18 (4 pens), Lita 11, Sidwell 10, Convey 7, Harper 7, Little 5, Gunnarsson 4, Long 3, Sonko 3, Hunt 2, Ingimarsson 2, Shorey 2, Halls 1, Murty 1 (pen), Oster 1, own goals 4.
Carling Cup (6): Kitson 4, Lita 1, Oster 1.
FA Cup (6): Lita 3, Doyle 1 (pen), Hunt 1, Long 1.

Hahnemann M 45	Murty G 40	Shorey N 40	Ingimarsson I 46	Sonko I 46	Harper J 44 + 1	Little G 34 + 1	Sidwell S 29 + 4	Lita L 22 + 4	Doyle K 41 + 4	Convey B 45	Kitson D 27 + 7	Hunt S 3 + 35	Oster J 11 + 22	Makin C 11 + 1	Gunnarsson B 19 + 10	Obinna E — + 6	Baradji S — + 1	Cox S — + 2	Long S 1 + 10	Stack G 1	Golbourne S — + 1	Halls J 1	Dobson M — + 1	*Match No.*
1	2	3	4	5	6	7^{1}	8	9	10	11^{2}	12	13												1
1	2	3	4	5	6	7^{1}	8	9^{2}	13	11^{3}	10	14	12											2
1	2	3	4	5	6	7^{1}	8	9		11^{2}	10	13	12											3
1	2	3	4	5	6	7^{3}	8	9	12	11^{2}	10^{1}	13	14											4
1	2	3	4	5	6	7	8	9^{1}	12	11	10													5
1	2	3^{2}	4	5	6	7	8	9	12	11	10^{1}			13										6
1	2		4	5	6	7^{1}		9^{2}	10	11			12	3	8	13								7
1	2		4	5	6	7		9	10	11^{1}		12		3	8									8
1	2		4	5	6	7^{1}		9^{3}	10	11^{2}		13	12	3	8	14								9
1	2		4	5	6	7		9^{1}	10	11				3	8	12								10
1	2^{1}		4	5	6	7		9^{2}	10	11		12		3	8	13								11
1			4	5	6	7^{1}		9^{2}	10	11^{3}		2	12	3	8	13	14							12
1		3	4	5	6	7^{2}		9	10^{1}	11^{3}	12	14	13	2	8									13
1		3	4	5	6	7		9^{2}	10	11^{1}	13		12	2	8									14
1		3	4	5	6	7^{2}	12		10	11^{3}	9	14	13	2^{1}	8									15
1	2	3	4	5	6	7	12		10	11^{2}	9	13			8^{1}									16
1	2	3	4	5	6	7^{1}	8		10	11^{2}	9	13	12											17
1	2	3	4	5	6	7^{1}	8		10	11^{2}	9	13	12											18
1	2	3	4	5	6	7^{2}	8	9	10^{3}	11^{1}		12	13			14								19
1	2	3	4	5	6	7^{2}	8	9	10	11^{1}		12	13											20
1	2	3	4	5	6	7^{2}	8	9	10^{3}	11^{1}		12	13					14						21
1	2	3	4	5	6	7^{3}	8	9^{2}	10	11^{1}	13	12	14											22
1	2	3	4	5	6^{3}	7^{2}	8		10^{1}	11	9	12	13		14									23
1	2	3	4	5	6	7^{2}	8^{3}		10^{1}	11	9	12	13		14									24
1	2	3	4	5	6	7^{2}			10	11^{1}	9	12	13		8									25
1	2	3	4	5	6		8		10	11^{1}	9^{3}	12	7^{2}		13				14					26
1	2^{1}	3	4	5	12	7	8		10	11^{3}		9^{2}	13		6				14					27
1	2	3	4	5	6	7^{2}	8		10	11^{1}	9^{3}	12	13						14					28
1	2	3	4	5	6	7		12	10^{1}	11^{2}	9	13			8									29
1	2	3	4	5	6	7	8	12	10	11	9^{1}													30
1	2	3	4	5	6	7^{1}	8^{2}	9	10^{3}	11			12		13				14					31
1	2	3	4	5	6	7^{3}	8	9^{1}	10	11^{2}	12	13			14									32
1	2	3	4	5	6	7	8	9^{1}	10	11^{2}	12	13												33
1	2	3	4	5	6	7	8		10	11	9													34
1	2	3	4	5	6			12	10	11^{2}	9	13	7^{1}		8									35
1	2	3	4	5	6		8^{3}	12	10	11	9^{1}	13	7^{2}		14									36
1	2	3	4	5	6	12^{2}		9^{3}	10	11	14	13	7^{1}		8									37
1	2	3	4	5	6				10	11	9	12	7^{1}		8									38
1	2	3	4	5	6		12		10	11	9	13	7^{2}		8^{1}									39
1	2	3	4	5	6		12		10	11^{2}	9	13	7^{3}		8^{1}				14					40
1	2	3	4	5	6	7^{2}	8		10^{3}	11^{1}	9	12	13						14					41
1	2	3	4	5	6		8		10	11^{1}	9^{3}	12	7^{2}		13				14					42
1	2^{2}	3	4	5	6		8		10^{3}	11	9	12	7^{1}		13				14					43
		3^{2}	4	5			8^{3}		10^{1}			11		6	7			12	9	1	13	2	14	44
1		3	4	5	6		8^{2}		10	11^{1}	9^{3}	12	7	2	13				14					45
1	2	3	4	5	6		8		10^{3}	11^{2}	9	12	7^{1}		13				14					46

FA Cup

Third Round	WBA	(a)	1-1
		(h)	3-2
Fourth Round	Birmingham C	(h)	1-1
		(a)	1-2

Carling Cup

First Round	Swansea C	(h)	3-1
Second Round	Luton T	(h)	1-0
Third Round	Sheffield U	(h)	2-0
Fourth Round	Arsenal	(a)	0-3

ROCHDALE FL Championship 2

FOUNDATION

Considering the love of rugby in their area, it is not surprising that Rochdale had difficulty in establishing an Association Football club. The earlier Rochdale Town club formed in 1900 went out of existence in 1907 when the present club was immediately established and joined the Manchester League, before graduating to the Lancashire Combination in 1908.

Spotland Stadium, Sandy Lane, Rochdale OL11 5DS.

Telephone: (0870) 822 1907.

Fax: (01706) 648 466.

Ticket Office: (0870) 822 1907.

Website: www.rochdaleafc.co.uk

Email: office@rochdaleafc.co.uk

Ground Capacity: 10,208.

Record Attendance: 24,231 v Notts Co, FA Cup 2nd rd, 10 December 1949.

Pitch Measurements: 114yd × 76yd.

Chairman: Chris Dunphy.

General Manager/Secretary: Colin Garlick.

Manager: Steve Parkin.

Assistant Manager: Tony Ford

Physio: Andy Thorpe.

Colours: All blue.

Change Colours: All white.

Year Formed: 1907.

Turned Professional: 1907.

Ltd Co.: 1910.

Club Nickname: 'The Dale'.

First Football League Game: 27 August 1921, Division 3 (N), v Accrington Stanley (h) W 6–3 – Crabtree; Nuttall, Sheehan; Hill, Farrer, Yarwood; Hoad, Sandiford, Dennison (2), Owens (3), Carney (1).

Record League Victory: 8–1 v Chesterfield, Division 3 (N), 18 December 1926 – Hill; Brown, Ward; Hillhouse, Parkes, Braidwood; Hughes, Bertram, Whitehurst (5), Schofield (2), Martin (1).

Record Cup Victory: 8–2 v Crook T, FA Cup 1st rd, 26 November 1927 – Moody; Hopkins, Ward; Braidwood, Parkes, Barker; Tompkinson, Clennell (3) Whitehurst (4), Hall, Martin (1).

HONOURS

Football League: Division 3 best season: 9th, 1969–70; Division 3 (N) – Runners-up 1923–24, 1926–27.

FA Cup: best season: 5th rd, 1990, 2003.

Football League Cup: Runners-up 1962 (record for 4th Division club).

SKY SPORTS FACT FILE

Rochdale won the Lancashire Senior Cup in 1948–49. In the semi-final goals from John Livesey and Jack Connor accounted for Manchester City then one from goalkeeper Noel Bywater secured the final against Blackpool!

Record Defeat: 1–9 v Tranmere R, Division 3 (N), 25 December 1931.

Most League Points (2 for a win): 62, Division 3 (N), 1923–24.

Most League Points (3 for a win): 78, Division 3, 2001–02.

Most League Goals: 105, Division 3 (N), 1926–27.

Highest League Scorer in Season: Albert Whitehurst, 44, Division 3 (N), 1926–27.

Most League Goals in Total Aggregate: Reg Jenkins, 119, 1964–73.

Most League Goals in One Match: 6, Tommy Tippett v Hartlepools U, Division 3N, 21 April 1930.

Most Capped Player: Leo Bertos, 6 (7), New Zealand.

Most League Appearances: Graham Smith, 317, 1966–74.

Youngest League Player: Zac Hughes, 16 years 105 days v Exeter C, 19 September 1987.

Record Transfer Fee Received: £400,000 from West Ham U for Stephen Bywater, August 1998.

Record Transfer Fee Paid: £150,000 to Stoke C for Paul Connor, March 2001.

Football League Record: 1921 Elected to Division 3 (N); 1958–59 Division 3; 1959–69 Division 4; 1969–74 Division 3; 1974–92 Division 4; 1992–2004 Division 3; 2004– FL2.

MANAGERS

Billy Bradshaw 1920
Run by committee 1920–22
Tom Wilson 1922–23
Jack Peart 1923–30
Will Cameron 1930–31
Herbert Hopkinson 1932–34
Billy Smith 1934–35
Ernest Nixon 1935–37
Sam Jennings 1937–38
Ted Goodier 1938–52
Jack Warner 1952–53
Harry Catterick 1953–58
Jack Marshall 1958–60
Tony Collins 1960–68
Bob Stokoe 1967–68
Len Richley 1968–70
Dick Conner 1970–73
Walter Joyce 1973–76
Brian Green 1976–77
Mike Ferguson 1977–78
Doug Collins 1979
Bob Stokoe 1979–80
Peter Madden 1980–83
Jimmy Greenhoff 1983–84
Vic Halom 1984–86
Eddie Gray 1986–88
Danny Bergara 1988–89
Terry Dolan 1989–91
Dave Sutton 1991–94
Mick Docherty 1995–96
Graham Barrow 1996–99
Steve Parkin 1999–2001
John Hollins 2001–02
Paul Simpson 2002–03
Alan Buckley 2003–04
Steve Parkin January 2004–

LATEST SEQUENCES

Longest Sequence of League Wins: 8, 29.9.1969 – 3.11.1969.

Longest Sequence of League Defeats: 17, 14.11.1931 – 12.3.1932.

Longest Sequence of League Draws: 6, 17.8.1968 – 14.9.1968.

Longest Sequence of Unbeaten League Matches: 20, 15.9.1923 – 19.1.1924.

Longest Sequence Without a League Win: 28, 14.11.1931 – 29.8.1932.

Successive Scoring Runs: 29 from 8.1.1927.

Successive Non-scoring Runs: 9 from 14.3.1980.

TEN YEAR LEAGUE RECORD

		P	*W*	*D*	*L*	*F*	*A*	*Pts*	*Pos*
1996-97	Div 3	46	14	16	16	58	58	58	14
1997-98	Div 3	46	17	7	22	56	55	58	18
1998-99	Div 3	46	13	15	18	42	55	54	19
1999-2000	Div 3	46	18	14	14	57	54	68	10
2000-01	Div 3	46	18	17	11	59	48	71	8
2001-02	Div 3	46	21	15	10	65	52	78	5
2002-03	Div 3	46	12	16	18	63	70	52	19
2003-04	Div 3	46	12	14	20	49	58	50	21
2004-05	FL 2	46	16	18	12	54	48	66	9
2005-06	FL 2	46	14	14	18	66	69	56	14

DID YOU KNOW ?

Reaching the final of the League Cup was an outstanding achievement for Rochdale. However, strangely enough they had received a bye in the fourth round! The only ever present in 60 League and Cup games was top scorer Ron Cairns with 22.

ROCHDALE 2005–06 LEAGUE RECORD

Match No.	Date	Venue	Opponents	Result	H/T Score	Lg. Pos.	Goalscorers	Attendance
1	Aug 6	A	Shrewsbury T	W 1-0	1-0	—	Holt [15]	4927
2	9	H	Wycombe W	L 1-2	0-2	—	Jones (pen) [79]	2755
3	13	H	Cheltenham T	D 1-1	0-1	13	Lambert [53]	2344
4	20	A	Leyton Orient	W 4-1	2-0	6	Holt [24], Lambert 2 [29, 68], Goodall [74]	4223
5	27	H	Macclesfield T	W 3-1	2-1	2	Holt 2 [31, 76], Goodall [33]	2606
6	29	A	Darlington	L 1-2	0-1	4	Holt (pen) [61]	4318
7	Sept 3	H	Torquay U	W 4-1	2-1	2	Lambert 2 [14, 67], Warner [22], Holt (pen) [54]	2388
8	10	A	Boston U	L 2-3	1-1	4	Holt [16], Griffiths [53]	2274
9	17	H	Mansfield T	W 2-0	1-0	3	Sturrock [25], Holt [83]	2965
10	24	A	Barnet	D 1-1	1-0	3	Holt [36]	2338
11	27	H	Oxford U	L 0-1	0-0	—		2347
12	Oct 1	H	Rushden & D	W 2-1	1-0	5	Sturrock [45], Boardman [90]	2606
13	7	A	Chester C	W 3-2	1-0	—	Jones [40], Holt [69], Lambert [85]	4327
14	15	H	Notts Co	W 3-0	3-0	2	Lambert 2 [4, 12], Cartwright [20]	3348
15	22	A	Peterborough U	L 1-3	1-0	4	Holt (pen) [28]	4314
16	29	H	Lincoln C	L 1-2	0-2	4	Cooksey [54]	3420
17	Nov 12	A	Bristol R	W 2-1	1-1	4	Holt (pen) [31], Sturrock [66]	6042
18	19	H	Chester C	D 2-2	0-1	4	Sturrock [69], Lambert [82]	3618
19	26	H	Shrewsbury T	W 4-3	1-3	4	Holt 2 (1 pen) [6 (p), 78], Lambert 2 [47, 81]	2843
20	Dec 6	A	Grimsby T	L 1-4	1-0	—	Lambert [27]	3896
21	10	A	Wycombe W	L 0-3	0-1	6		4928
22	17	H	Leyton Orient	L 2-4	1-2	7	Goodall [24], Sturrock [65]	2666
23	26	A	Wrexham	L 1-2	1-1	9	Tait [21]	5127
24	31	A	Carlisle U	L 1-2	1-0	9	Sturrock [2]	6897
25	Jan 2	H	Northampton T	D 1-1	0-0	11	Low (og) [71]	3030
26	14	H	Stockport Co	L 0-1	0-1	15		3520
27	21	A	Mansfield T	L 0-1	0-1	15		3018
28	24	A	Torquay U	W 3-1	1-0	—	Dagnall [29], Jones [48], Lambert [68]	2043
29	28	H	Boston U	D 1-1	1-1	14	Griffiths [30]	2384
30	Feb 4	A	Oxford U	D 1-1	1-1	14	Cooksey [45]	3978
31	14	A	Stockport Co	L 0-3	0-2	—		4312
32	25	A	Cheltenham T	D 1-1	0-1	16	Lambert [82]	3184
33	28	H	Bury	D 1-1	0-0	—	Lambert (pen) [70]	3876
34	Mar 11	A	Macclesfield T	W 3-1	1-0	16	McArdle [27], Christie [49], Lambert [83]	2211
35	18	H	Wrexham	L 0-1	0-1	16		2856
36	21	H	Grimsby T	D 2-2	0-1	—	Ramsden [52], Lambert [90]	1865
37	25	A	Bury	L 1-2	0-1	16	Jones [71]	4276
38	Apr 4	H	Darlington	L 0-2	0-1	—		1963
39	8	A	Northampton T	D 2-2	0-2	17	Lambert 2 (1 pen) [51, 90 (p)]	5732
40	15	A	Rushden & D	D 1-1	0-0	19	Dagnall [90]	3135
41	17	H	Peterborough U	W 1-0	0-0	16	Christie [72]	2318
42	22	A	Notts Co	D 1-1	0-0	16	Lambert (pen) [81]	4413
43	25	H	Barnet	D 1-1	1-1	—	Dagnall [23]	1769
44	29	H	Bristol R	W 2-0	1-0	14	Lambert (pen) [45], Cooksey [90]	2649
45	May 2	H	Carlisle U	L 0-2	0-2	—		4439
46	6	A	Lincoln C	D 1-1	0-0	14	Lambert [88]	7165

Final League Position: 14

GOALSCORERS

League (66): Lambert 22 (4 pens), Holt 14 (5 pens), Sturrock 6, Jones 4 (1 pen), Cooksey 3, Dagnall 3, Goodall 3, Christie 2, Griffiths 2, Boardman 1, Cartwright 1, McArdle 1, Ramsden 1, Tait 1, Warner 1, own goal 1.
Carling Cup (0).
FA Cup (0).
Football League Trophy (5): Tait 2, Holt 1 (pen), own goals 2.

Gilks M 46	Clarke J 21 + 1	Gallimore T 32 + 2	Brisco N 14 + 2	Griffiths G 29	Boardman J 17 + 4	Cartwright L 21 + 6	Jones G 42	Lambert R 43 + 3	Holt G 21	Jaszczun T 12 + 5	Sturrock B 15 + 16	Warner S 16 + 8	Goodall A 37 + 3	Tait P 4 + 7	Cooksey E 27 + 7	Kitchen B 3 + 5	Moyo-Modise C 1 + 8	Brown G 6 + 10	McArdle R 16 + 3	Goodhind W 10	Dagnall C 15 + 6	Doolan J 16 + 2	Ramsden S 15	Jackson M 12	Christie I 10 + 4	Bayliss D 4	Coleman T 1	Thompson J — + 1	*Match No.*
1	2	3	4	5	6	7	8	9^{1}	10	11	12																		1
1	2	3	4^{2}	5	6	7	8	9^{1}	10	11^{3}	12	13	14																2
1	2	5	4■		6	7	8	9^{1}	10	11^{3}	12		3^{2}	13	14														3
1	2	3			6	7	8	9	10^{1}	11	12		5		4														4
1	2	5			6	7^{1}		9	10	12	11^{2}	8	3		4	13													5
1	2	5	12		6			9	10	11	8^{2}	7^{1}	3		4		13												6
1	2	5	4^{1}		6			9	10^{3}	13	8^{2}	7	3		11		14	12											7
1	2	3	4	5	6		8	12	10		13	7^{1}	9^{2}		11														8
1	2	6	4	5^{3}			8	9^{1}	10	12	11^{2}	7	3				13		14										9
1	2	6	4^{2}	5			8	9^{1}	10	3	11	7		12				13											10
1	2	3		5			8	9^{1}	10	4	11	7	13	12					6^{2}										11
1	4	3		5^{1}	12		8	9		10	11^{2}	7	6	13				14		2^{3}									12
1	4	6		5		7	8	9	10	11^{1}		12	3					13		2^{2}									13
1	4	3		5	6	7	8	9^{1}	10^{2}		13		11		12			14		2^{3}									14
1	4	3^{3}		5	6	7^{2}	8	9^{1}	10		12		11		13			14		2									15
1	2^{3}	3		5■		7^{1}	4	9^{2}	10		13	12	11		8			14	6										16
1	2	5				7	4	12	10^{2}	3	9	13	11^{1}		8				6										17
1	4	5				7^{1}	8	12	10	11	9		3					2	6										18
1	4	5	7				8	9	10		11^{1}		3	12				2■	6										19
1	7	5	4^{1}			12	8	9	10^{3}	13	11^{2}		3	14					6	2									20
1	12	6	4^{2}	5		7	8	9^{3}	10■	3^{1}	13		11	14						2■									21
1	2	3^{2}	4^{1}	5	6	7	8	9			12		11	10	13														22
1		6	4	5^{1}			8	9			11		3	10	7				12	2									23
1		5	4^{2}			12	8	9		13	11^{3}		3	10^{1}	7		14		6	2									24
1		5	12		6		4	9	10		11^{2}	7^{1}	3		8		13			2									25
1		5			6	12	4	9			13	8^{2}	3	10^{3}	7		11			2^{1}	14								26
1		12		5		7	8	9			11^{1}		3				13	2	6		10^{2}	4							27
1				5		7	8	9			12	13	3		11			2^{2}	6		10^{1}	4							28
1				5	12	7^{2}	8	9				2^{1}	3		11	13	14		6		10^{3}	4							29
1		12	4	5				9					3		7^{1}				13		11	8	2	6^{2}	10				30
1		3			6		8	9					12		7^{1}				5		11	4	2		10				31
1						7^{1}	8	9					3		11				5		12	4	2		10	6			32
1					6	7^{1}	8	9					3^{2}		11			12			13	4	2		10	5			33
1		3					8	9							11				6		7	4	2		10	5			34
1		3					8^{2}	9				12			11^{1}	13		14	6		7	4^{3}	2		10	5■			35
1		3		5	12	13	8	9							11				6		14	4^{3}	2^{2}	7^{1}	10				36
1		3		5^{1}		12	8	9							11^{3}	14			6		13	4	2^{2}	7	10				37
1				5			8	9				7^{2}	3		12	14		13			10	4^{1}	2	6	11^{3}				38
1				5			8	9				12	3		11	10^{1}		7^{2}			13	4^{3}	2	6	14				39
1				5		12	4	9				8^{2}	3		11^{1}	7^{3}					10	13	2	6	14				40
1				5		7	4	9					3		8^{1}	11^{2}					10	12	2	6	13				41
1		3^{3}		5			8	9			12	13	11		14						10^{1}	4	2	6	7^{2}				42
1				5		7^{1}	4	9			12	8	3		11						10		2	6					43
1				5	12	7	4	9			13	8	3		11						10^{2}		2^{1}	6					44
1				5	6^{1}		8	9			12	11	3		13						10^{3}	4^{2}		2			7	14	45
1				5	6		8	9					3^{1}		11		12	7			10^{2}	4		2	13				46

FA Cup

First Round	Brentford	(h)	0-1

Carling Cup

First Round	Bradford C	(h)	0-5

Football League Trophy

First Round	Stockport Co	(h)	3-1
Second Round	Tranmere R	(a)	2-3

ROTHERHAM UNITED FL Championship 1

FOUNDATION

Rotherham were formed in 1870 before becoming Town in the late 1880s. Thornhill United were founded in 1877 and changed their name to Rotherham County in 1905. The Town amalgamated with Rotherham County to form Rotherham United in 1925.

Millmoor, Rotherham S60 1HR.
Telephone: (01709) 512 434.
Fax: (01709) 512 762.
Ticket Office: 0870 443 1884.
Website: www.themillers.co.uk
Email: office@rotherhamunited.net
Ground Capacity: 8,200.
Record Attendance: 25,170 v Sheffield U, Division 2, 13 December 1952.
Pitch Measurements. 115yd × 70yd.
Chairman: Denis Coleman.
Vice-chairman: Dino Maccio.
Chief Executive: Paul Douglas.
Manager: Alan Knill.
Media Manager: Gerry Somerton.
Physio: Denis Circuit.
Colours: Red shirts with white sleeves, white shorts, red stockings.

HONOURS

Football League: Division 2 – runners-up 2000–01; Division 3 – Champions 1980–81; Runners-up 1999–2000; Division 3 (N) – Champions 1950–51; Runners-up 1946–47, 1947–48, 1948–49; Division 4 – Champions 1988–89; Runners-up 1991–92.

FA Cup: best season: 5th rd, 1953, 1968.

Football League Cup: Runners-up 1961.

Auto Windscreens Shield: Winners 1996.

Change Colours: Black shirts with white stripes, black shorts, black stockings.
Year Formed: 1870.
Turned Professional: 1905.
Ltd Co.: 1920.
Club Nickname: 'The Merry Millers'.
Previous Names: 1877, Thornhill United; 1905, Rotherham County; 1925, amalgamated with Rotherham Town under Rotherham United.
Previous Ground: 1870, Red House Ground; 1907, Millmoor.
First Football League Game: 2 September 1893, Division 2, Rotherham T v Lincoln C (a) D 1–1 – McKay; Thickett, Watson; Barr, Brown, Broadhead; Longden, Cutts, Leatherbarrow, McCormick, Pickering, (1 og). 30 August 1919, Division 2, Rotherham Co v Nottingham F (h) W 2–0 – Branston; Alton, Baines; Bailey, Coe, Stanton; Lee (1), Cawley (1), Glennon, Lees, Lamb.
Record League Victory: 8–0 v Oldham Ath, Division 3 (N), 26 May 1947 – Warnes; Selkirk, Ibbotson; Edwards, Horace Williams, Danny Williams; Wilson (2), Shaw (1), Ardron (3), Guest (1), Hainsworth (1).
Record Cup Victory: 6–0 v Spennymoor U, FA Cup 2nd rd, 17 December 1977 – McAlister; Forrest, Breckin, Womble, Stancliffe, Green, Finney, Phillips (3), Gwyther (2) (Smith), Goodfellow, Crawford (1). 6–0 v Wolverhampton W, FA Cup 1st rd, 16 November 1985 – O'Hanlon; Forrest, Dungworth, Gooding (1), Smith (1), Pickering, Birch (2), Emerson, Tynan (1), Simmons (1), Pugh. 6–0 v Kings Lynn, FA Cup 2nd rd, 6 December 1997 – Mimms; Clark, Hurst (Goodwin), Garner (1) (Hudson) (1), Warner (Bass), Richardson (1), Berry (1), Thompson, Druce (1), Glover (1), Roscoe.

SKY SPORTS FACT FILE

In 1951–52 Rotherham United claimed to be the only team in the top two divisions of the Football League whose regular side were all Englishmen. Indeed with the exception of Colin Rawson who had been born at Shirebrook, Derbyshire they were all Yorkshiremen.

Record Defeat: 1–11 v Bradford C, Division 3 (N), 25 August 1928.

Most League Points (2 for a win): 71, Division 3 (N), 1950–51.

Most League Points (3 for a win): 91, Division 2, 2000–01.

Most League Goals: 114, Division 3 (N), 1946–47.

Highest League Scorer in Season: Wally Ardron, 38, Division 3 (N), 1946–47.

Most League Goals in Total Aggregate: Gladstone Guest, 130, 1946–56.

Most League Goals in One Match: 4, Roland Bastow v York C, Division 3N, 9 November 1935; 4, Roland Bastow v Rochdale, Division 3N, 7 March 1936; 4, Wally Ardron v Crewe Alex, Division 3N, 5 October 1946; 4, Wally Ardron v Carlisle U, Division 3N, 13 September 1947; 4, Wally Ardron v Hartlepools U, Division 3N, 13 October 1948; 4, Ian Wilson v Liverpool, Division 2, 2 May 1955; 4, Carl Gilbert v Swansea C, Division 3, 28 September 1971; 4, Carl Airey v Chester, Division 3, 31 August 1987; 4, Shaun Goater v Hartlepool U, Division 3, 9 April 1994; 4, Lee Glover v Hull C, Division 3, 28 December 1997; 4, Darren Byfield v Millwall, Division 1, 10 August 2002.

Most Capped Player: Shaun Goater 14 (19), Bermuda.

Most League Appearances: Danny Williams, 459, 1946–62.

Youngest League Player: Kevin Eley, 16 years 72 days v Scunthorpe U, 15 May 1984.

Record Transfer Fee Received: £900,000 from Cardiff C for Alan Lee, August 2003.

Record Transfer Fee Paid: £150,000 to Millwall for Tony Towner, August 1980; £150,000 to Port Vale for Lee Glover, August 1996; £150,000 to Burnley for Alan Lee, September 2000; £150,000 to Reading for Martin Butler, September 2003.

Football League Record: 1893 Rotherham Town elected to Division 2; 1896 Failed re-election; 1919 Rotherham County elected to Division 2; 1923–51 Division 3 (N); 1951–68 Division 2; 1968–73 Division 3; 1973–75 Division 4; 1975–81 Division 3; 1981–83 Division 2; 1983–88 Division 3; 1988–89 Division 4; 1989–91 Division 3; 1991–92 Division 4; 1992–97 Division 2; 1997–2000 Division 3; 2000–01 Division 2; 2001–04 Division 1; 2004–05 FLC; 2005– FL1.

MANAGERS

Billy Heald 1925–29 *(Secretary only for long spell)*
Stanley Davies 1929–30
Billy Heald 1930–33
Reg Freeman 1934–52
Andy Smailes 1952–58
Tom Johnston 1958–62
Danny Williams 1962–65
Jack Mansell 1965–67
Tommy Docherty 1967–68
Jimmy McAnearney 1968–73
Jimmy McGuigan 1973–79
Ian Porterfield 1979–81
Emlyn Hughes 1981–83
George Kerr 1983–85
Norman Hunter 1985–87
Dave Cusack 1987–88
Billy McEwan 1988–91
Phil Henson 1991–94
Archie Gemmill/John McGovern 1994–96
Danny Bergara 1996–97
Ronnie Moore 1997–2005
Mick Harford 2005
Alan Knill December 2005–

LATEST SEQUENCES

Longest Sequence of League Wins: 9, 2.2.1982 – 6.3.1982.

Longest Sequence of League Defeats: 8, 7.4.1956 – 18.8.1956.

Longest Sequence of League Draws: 6, 13.10.1969 – 22.11.1969.

Longest Sequence of Unbeaten League Matches: 18, 13.10.1969 – 7.2.1970.

Longest Sequence Without a League Win: 21, 9.5.2004 – 20.11.2004.

Successive Scoring Runs: 30 from 3.4.1954.

Successive Non-scoring Runs: 6 from 21.8.2004.

TEN YEAR LEAGUE RECORD

		P	*W*	*D*	*L*	*F*	*A*	*Pts*	*Pos*
1996-97	Div 2	46	7	14	25	39	70	35	23
1997-98	Div 3	46	16	19	11	67	61	67	9
1998-99	Div 3	46	20	13	13	79	61	73	5
1999-2000	Div 3	46	24	12	10	72	36	84	2
2000-01	Div 2	46	27	10	9	79	55	91	2
2001-02	Div 1	46	10	19	17	52	66	49	21
2002-03	Div 1	46	15	14	17	62	62	59	15
2003-04	Div 1	46	13	15	18	53	61	54	17
2004-05	FL C	46	5	14	27	35	69	29	24
2005-06	FL 1	46	12	16	18	52	62	52	20

DID YOU KNOW ?

Rotherham United can claim a left-back in Irvine Rhodes who made a scoring debut with a long-range free-kick on 6 March 1937, and Tom Hall, an inside-right who provided an explosive bow on 5 November 1927 with four debut goals against Wigan Borough.

ROTHERHAM UNITED 2005–06 LEAGUE RECORD

Match No.	Date	Venue	Opponents	Result		H/T Score	Lg. Pos.	Goalscorers	Attendance
1	Aug 6	H	Walsall	L	1-2	1-1	—	Butler 42	5386
2	9	A	Yeovil T	D	0-0	0-0	—		5856
3	13	A	Chesterfield	W	1-0	0-0	12	Butler 59	5189
4	20	H	Bradford C	D	1-1	0-0	14	Burton 81	5222
5	27	H	Blackpool	W	4-0	1-0	7	Mullin 40, Burton 3 (1 pen) 58 (p), 59, 86	4384
6	29	A	Oldham Ath	W	1-0	0-0	4	Burton 80	6950
7	Sept 3	A	Port Vale	L	0-2	0-1	9		4528
8	10	H	Gillingham	W	3-0	0-0	5	McLaren 46, Burton 81, Butler 90	4253
9	17	A	Nottingham F	L	0-2	0-0	7		20,123
10	24	H	Southend U	L	2-4	2-2	10	Murdock 34, Burton (pen) 45	4259
11	27	A	Hartlepool U	D	0-0	0-0	—		4309
12	Oct 1	A	Brentford	L	1-2	1-2	13	Burton 8	5901
13	15	A	Scunthorpe U	D	2-2	2-1	17	Butler (og) 3, McLaren 29	6649
14	22	H	Swansea C	D	2-2	1-1	17	Leadbitter 41, Conlon 90	4056
15	25	H	Barnsley	L	0-1	0-0	—		5401
16	29	A	Milton Keynes D	D	1-1	1-0	17	Monkhouse 24	5096
17	Nov 12	H	Colchester U	L	1-2	1-0	19	Burton (pen) 23	3715
18	19	A	Barnsley	D	1-1	1-0	21	Barker 31	9894
19	26	A	Walsall	L	1-3	0-2	22	Hoskins 78	4563
20	Dec 3	H	Swindon T	L	0-1	0-1	—		3537
21	10	H	Yeovil T	L	1-2	1-2	22	Burton 18	3929
22	17	A	Bradford C	W	2-1	1-0	19	Williamson 21, Burton 60	7476
23	26	H	Huddersfield T	D	1-1	1-0	20	Burton 8	7380
24	28	A	Bristol C	L	1-3	1-1	22	Murdock 26	12,510
25	31	H	Doncaster R	W	1-0	0-0	22	Williamson 90	6761
26	Jan 2	A	Tranmere R	L	2-3	1-1	21	Barker 14, Hoskins 77	7361
27	10	H	Port Vale	D	1-1	1-1	—	Hoskins 26	3883
28	14	A	Bournemouth	L	0-2	0-2	22		5700
29	21	H	Nottingham F	D	1-1	0-1	22	Shaw 86	7222
30	28	A	Gillingham	D	1-1	0-0	22	Williamson 54	6107
31	Feb 4	H	Hartlepool U	D	0-0	0-0	23		5960
32	10	A	Southend U	L	0-2	0-2	—		7879
33	14	H	Bournemouth	W	2-0	0-0	—	Butler 58, Williamson 60	4498
34	18	A	Swindon T	W	3-2	2-2	23	Butler 2 22, 49, Barker 31	7518
35	25	H	Chesterfield	L	0-4	0-1	23		6919
36	Mar 11	A	Blackpool	D	0-0	0-0	23		5934
37	14	H	Oldham Ath	W	2-0	1-0	—	Swailes (og) 21, McLaren 85	5823
38	18	A	Huddersfield T	L	1-4	1-2	22	Forte 13	15,264
39	25	H	Bristol C	W	3-1	2-0	20	Forte 2 27, 47, Shaw 39	6682
40	Apr 1	A	Doncaster R	L	1-3	1-3	21	Forte 15	7542
41	8	H	Tranmere R	W	2-0	0-0	20	Butler 73, Shaw 78	4129
42	15	H	Brentford	D	2-2	1-0	20	Mullin 43, Shaw 69	5242
43	17	A	Swansea C	W	2-0	2-0	19	Monk (og) 16, Robertson 30	14,118
44	22	H	Scunthorpe U	D	1-1	0-1	20	Hoskins 83	5778
45	29	A	Colchester U	L	0-2	0-1	20		5741
46	May 6	H	Milton Keynes D	D	0-0	0-0	20		7625

Final League Position: 20

GOALSCORERS

League (52): Burton 12 (3 pens), Butler 7, Forte 4, Hoskins 4, Shaw 4, Williamson 4, Barker 3, McLaren 3, Mullin 2, Murdock 2, Conlon 1, Leadbitter 1, Monkhouse 1, Robertson 1, own goals 3.
Carling Cup (3): Burton 1, Otsemobor 1, own goal 1.
FA Cup (3): McLaren 2, Burton 1.
Football League Trophy (4): Butler 1, Evans 1, Hoskins 1, Newsham 1.

Montgomery G 24	Worrell D 40 + 1	Minto S 5 + 1	McLaren P 35 + 4	Murdock C 39	Barker S 42 + 1	Campbell-Ryce J 4 + 3	Williamson L 37	Butler M 33 + 6	Burton D 24	Robertson G 30 + 5	Cutler N 22	Mullin J 40 + 3	Keane M 26 + 2	Otsemobor J 4 + 6	Gilchrist P 9 + 2	Hurst P 28 + 3	Hoskins W 7 + 16	Leadbitter G 3 + 2	Conlon B 3	Monkhouse A 7 + 5	Newsham M — + 3	Brogan S — + 3	Evans P 4	Taylor R — + 1	Duncum S 1	Forte J 8 + 3	Shaw P 15 + 2	Quinn S 16	*Match No.*
1	2	3	4	5	6	7	8	9	10	11																			1
	2	3	4	5	6	7	8	9^{2}	10	11^{1}	1	13	12																2
	2	3	4	5	6	7^{1}	8	9	10		1	12	11																3
	2	3	4	5	6	7^{1}	8	9	10		1	12	11																4
	2		4	5	6	12	8^{2}	9	10	3	1	7^{1}	11	13															5
	2		4		6	12	8	9	10	3	1	7	11^{1}		5														6
	2		4		6■	12	8^{2}	9	10		1	7	11^{1}	13	5	3													7
	2		4		6		8	9	10^{1}	3	1	7	11	12	5														8
	2^{2}		4		6		8^{1}	9	10	3	1	7	11	12	5		13												9
	2^{2}		4	5	6		8^{1}	9	10	3	1	7	11	12			13												10
1	2		4	5	6			9	10	3		8	11	7															11
1	2^{2}		4	5	6			9	10	3		8	11^{1}	7			12	13											12
1	2		4■	5^{1}	6			13	10	3		7	11		12			8	9^{2}										13
1	2			5	6			12	10	11			7			3^{1}		4	9	8									14
1	2			5	6			9	10	3		7	11^{2}				12	4^{1}		8	13								15
1	2		4		6			12	10			7	11^{2}		5	3		13	9^{1}	8^{3}		14							16
	2		4		6		11	9	10^{1}		1	7			5	3^{2}	12			8	13								17
	2		4	5■	6		8■	9	10■		1	7^{1}			12	3							11						18
	2	5^{1}	4		6		8^{2}	9	10	12	1	7^{3}				3	14			13			11						19
	2	12	4	5^{1}	6		8	9	10	3^{2}	1	7										13	11^{3}	14					20
	2^{1}		4^{2}	5	6		8	9	10	3	1	7^{3}	14				12			13			11						21
	2		4	5			8^{2}	9	10	3	1	7	11^{1}	12	6	13													22
	2		4	5			8	9	10^{2}	3	1	7	11^{1}		6	12	13												23
1	2		4	5	12		8	9	10	3^{3}		7	11^{2}		6^{1}	13	14												24
1	2		4	5	6		8	9		11		7				3	10												25
1			4	5	6■		8	9		11				2		3	10					12			7^{1}				26
1	2			5						3		7	11■	4		6	10			8						9			27
1	2		4	5	6		8	9				7				3	10^{1}				12					11			28
1	2		4^{1}	5	6		8			12		7				3	10										9	11	29
1	2		4	5	6		8					7				3	9^{1}									12	10	11	30
1	2		4^{2}	5	6		8	12				7				3	9^{3}			13						14	10^{1}	11	31
1	2			5	6		8					7	4^{1}			3	12									9	10	11	32
1	2		12	5	6		8^{1}	9		13		7	4			3											10^{2}	11	33
1	2		12	5	6		8	9		13		7				3				4^{2}							10^{1}	11	34
1	2		4	5	6			9				7				3	12			8^{1}							10	11	35
1			4	5	6			9■		2		7	8			3	13									12^{2}	10^{1}	11	36
1			4	5	6		8			2		7	10			3	12									9^{1}		11	37
1			4^{1}	5	6		8			2		7	10			3	12									9^{2}	13	11	38
1			4^{1}	5	6		8			2		7	10			3										9	12	11	39
1	12			5	6		8	13		2^{1}		7	4^{2}			3										9	10	11	40
	2			5	6		8	12		13	1	7^{1}	4■			3										9^{2}	10	11	41
	2		12	5	6		8	9		4	1	7				3											10^{1}	11	42
	2		12	5	6		8^{1}	9		4	1	7				3											10	11	43
	2			5	6		8	9		4^{1}	1	7				3	12			13							10	11^{2}	44
	2		4^{2}	5	6		8	9		11^{1}	1	7				3	12			13							10		45
	2		4	5	6		8	9		11	1	7				3											10		46

FA Cup

First Round	Mansfield T	(h)	3-4

Carling Cup

First Round	Port Vale	(h)	3-1
Second Round	Leeds U	(h)	0-2

Football League Trophy

First Round	Accrington S	(h)	3-3
Second Round	Macclesfield T	(h)	1-2

RUSHDEN & DIAMONDS Conference

FOUNDATION

Rushden & Diamonds were formed in 1992 from an amalgamation of Rushden Town and Irthlingborough Diamonds. At the end of 1990–91, Rushden Town had been relegated to the Southern League Midland Division as their ground was unfit for Premier Division football. Irthlingborough Diamonds were competing in the United Counties League at the time. The idea for this merger came from Max Griggs (owner of Dr Martens), a local multi-millionaire businessman. He invested several million pounds and they were able to achieve Football League status in nine years.

Nene Park, Irthlingborough, Northants NN9 5QF.

Telephone: (01933) 652 000.

Fax: (01933) 652 606.

Ticket Office: (01933) 652 936.

Website: www.thediamondsfc.com

Email: secretary@rd-fc.co.uk

Ground Capacity: 6,441.

Record Attendance: 6,431 v Leeds U, FA Cup 3rd rd, 2 January 1999.

Pitch Measurements: 111yd × 74yd.

Chairman: Richard Palmer.

Chief Executive: Helen Thompson.

Secretary: Helen Thompson.

Manager: Paul Hart.

Assistant Manager: Ian Bowyer.

Physio: Simon Parsell.

Colours: Red shirts, red shorts, red stockings.

Change Colours: Blue shirts, blue shorts, blue stockings or white shirts, white shorts, white stockings.

Year formed: 1992.

Turned Professional: 1992.

Ltd Co.: 1992.

Club Nickname: 'The Diamonds'.

HONOURS

Football League: Division 3 – Champions 2002–03

FA Cup: best season 3rd rd 1999.

Football League Cup: never past 2nd rd.

Conference: Champions 2000–01.

Conference Championship Shield: Winners 2001.

Southern League Midland Division: Champions 1993–94.

Premier Division: Champions 1995–96.

FA Trophy: Semi-finalists 1994.

Northants FA Hillier Senior Cup: Winners 1993–94, 1998–99.

Maunsell Premier Cup: Winners 1994–95, 1998–99; Finalists 2001–02.

SKY SPORTS FACT FILE

In 2000–01 Rushden & Diamonds were the best-supported team in the Nationwide Conference with an average of 3876. Brian Talbot was the competition's manager of the year, while top scorer Duane Darby with 24 took the individual player's honour.

MANAGERS

Roger Ashby 1992–97
Brian Talbot 1997–2004
Ernie Tippett 2004–05
Barry Hunter 2005–06
Paul Hart June 2006–

First Football League Match: 11 August 2001, Division 3, v York C (a) W 1–0 – Turley; Mustafa, Underwood, Talbot (Setchell), Peters, Rodwell, Butterworth, Brady, Patmore (1) (Darby), Jackson, Mills (Carey).

Record League Victory: 7–0 v Redditch U, Southern League, Midland Division, 7 May 1994 – Fox; Wooding (1), Johnson, Flower (1), Beech, Page, Coe, Mann (2), Nuttell (1), Watkins (1), Keast (1).

Record Cup Victory: 8–0 v Desborough T, Northants FA Hillier Senior Cup, 1st rd, 27 September 1994 – Fox; Wooding, Johnson, Flower, Keast, Page, Collins, Butterworth, Nuttell (2), Watkins (2), Mann (2). Subs:– Capone (2), Mason.

Record Defeat: 0–8 v Coventry C, League Cup 2nd rd, 2 October 2002.

Most League Points (3 for a win): 87, Division 3, 2002–03.

Most League Goals: 73, Division 3, 2002–03.

Highest League Scorer in Season: Onandi Lowe, 19, Division 3, 2001–02.

Most League Goals in Total Aggregate: Onandi Lowe, 49, 2001–05.

Most Capped Player: Onandi Lowe, 9, Jamaica.

Most League Appearances: Andy Burgess, 147, 2001–06.

Youngest League Player: Lee Tomlin, 16 years 276 days v Wycombe W, 15 October 2005.

Record Transfer Fee Received: Undisclosed for Justin Jackson from Doncaster R, May 2003.

Record Transfer Fee Paid: Undisclosed to Morecambe for Justin Jackson, June 2000.

Football League Record: 2001 Promoted to Division 3; 2003–04 Division 2; 2004–06 FL2; 2006– Conference.

LATEST SEQUENCES

Longest Sequence of League Wins: 6, 29.10.2002 – 14.12.2002.

Longest Sequence of League Defeats: 4, 27.8.2001 – 15.9.2001.

Longest Sequence of League Draws: not more than 2.

Longest Sequence of Unbeaten League Matches: 12, 18.9.2001 – 20.11.2001.

Longest Sequence Without a League Win: 12, 6.11.2004 – 22.1.2005.

Successive Scoring Runs: 16 from 26.1.2002.

Successive Non-scoring Runs: 7 from 12.4.2004.

TEN YEAR LEAGUE RECORD

		P	W	D	L	F	A	Pts	Pos
1996-97	Conf.	42	14	11	17	61	63	53	12
1997-98	Conf.	42	23	5	14	79	57	74	4
1998-99	Conf.	42	20	12	10	71	42	72	4
1999-2000	Conf.	42	21	13	8	71	42	76	2
2000-01	Conf.	42	25	11	6	78	36	86	1
2001-02	Div 3	46	20	13	13	69	53	73	6
2002-03	Div 3	46	24	15	7	73	47	87	1
2003-04	Div 2	46	13	9	24	60	74	48	22
2004-05	FL 2	46	10	14	22	42	63	44	22
2005-06	FL 2	46	11	12	23	44	76	45	24

DID YOU KNOW?

Rushden & Diamonds' elevation to the Football League did not come easily in 2000–01. Half-way they were seven points adrift of Yeovil Town and had played two games more than the leaders. But in fine finishing style they won with six points to spare.

RUSHDEN & DIAMONDS 2005–06 LEAGUE RECORD

Match No.	Date	Venue	Opponents	Result		H/T Score	Lg. Pos.	Goalscorers	Attendance
1	Aug 6	H	Darlington	D	1-1	0-0	—	Bell 60	2832
2	9	A	Mansfield T	W	1-0	1-0	—	Allen 45	3402
3	20	H	Chester C	D	1-1	0-0	11	O'Grady 61	2682
4	27	H	Lincoln C	D	1-1	0-1	12	Pearson 64	2860
5	29	A	Grimsby T	L	0-2	0-1	16		3774
6	Sept 2	H	Peterborough U	L	0-2	0-1	—		4403
7	10	A	Oxford U	D	2-2	0-2	19	Taylor 54, Grainger 58	4189
8	13	A	Macclesfield T	L	1-3	0-1	—	Broughton 84	2874
9	17	H	Stockport Co	W	3-2	0-1	17	Gulliver 53, O'Grady 71, Dempster 90	2710
10	24	A	Notts Co	D	0-0	0-0	18		5142
11	27	H	Northampton T	L	1-3	0-1	—	Savage 63	5211
12	Oct 1	A	Rochdale	L	1-2	0-1	20	Okuonghae 50	2606
13	7	H	Bury	L	0-2	0-0	—		2639
14	15	A	Wycombe W	D	0-0	0-0	21		5231
15	22	H	Shrewsbury T	W	3-0	0-0	20	Savage 49, Bell 66, O'Grady 85	2954
16	29	A	Barnet	L	1-2	0-1	21	Dempster 65	2564
17	Nov 11	H	Boston U	W	1-0	0-0	—	Gulliver 90	3205
18	26	A	Darlington	D	1-1	1-0	21	Bell 9	3209
19	Dec 6	H	Carlisle U	L	0-4	0-2	—		2216
20	10	H	Mansfield T	L	1-2	0-1	22	Dempster 57	2477
21	17	A	Chester C	W	2-1	1-1	21	Broughton (pen) 11, Bolland (og) 55	2265
22	26	A	Leyton Orient	L	1-5	1-3	22	Broughton 25	4558
23	28	H	Cheltenham T	L	0-1	0-0	22		2244
24	31	A	Torquay U	L	1-2	0-2	23	O'Grady 65	2668
25	Jan 2	H	Bristol R	L	2-3	1-1	23	Broughton 2 44, 84	2720
26	7	A	Peterborough U	L	0-2	0-1	23		4613
27	14	H	Wrexham	L	0-2	0-1	23		2617
28	21	A	Stockport Co	D	2-2	0-0	23	Gulliver 49, Jackson 68	4574
29	28	H	Oxford U	W	3-0	3-0	23	Kelly 2 15, 22, Gulliver 20	3823
30	Feb 4	A	Northampton T	L	0-2	0-1	24		7036
31	7	A	Bury	D	1-1	0-0	—	Hatswell 82	1777
32	11	H	Notts Co	W	1-0	1-0	23	Mikolanda 33	3113
33	14	A	Wrexham	L	0-2	0-2	—		3195
34	18	A	Carlisle U	L	0-5	0-2	24		6922
35	25	H	Macclesfield T	W	1-0	0-0	23	Broughton 81	2479
36	Mar 4	H	Grimsby T	D	1-1	0-0	23	Jackson 72	3366
37	11	A	Lincoln C	D	2-2	0-1	24	Turner 82, Jackson 84	4383
38	18	H	Leyton Orient	W	1-0	1-0	23	Broughton 8	3679
39	25	A	Cheltenham T	L	1-3	0-3	23	Jackson 53	3447
40	Apr 1	H	Torquay U	W	1-0	1-0	23	Broughton 43	3795
41	8	A	Bristol R	W	1-0	0-0	23	Broughton 79	6432
42	15	H	Rochdale	D	1-1	0-0	23	Broughton 55	3135
43	18	A	Shrewsbury T	L	1-4	0-2	—	Caskey 47	4239
44	22	H	Wycombe W	L	1-3	1-0	24	Kelly 24	3396
45	29	A	Boston U	L	0-2	0-0	24		2489
46	May 6	H	Barnet	L	1-2	0-0	24	Jackson 86	4174

Final League Position: 24

GOALSCORERS

League (44): Broughton 10 (1 pen), Jackson 5, Gulliver 4, O'Grady 4, Bell 3, Dempster 3, Kelly 3, Savage 2, Allen 1, Caskey 1, Grainger 1, Hatswell 1, Mikolanda 1, Okuonghae 1, Pearson 1, Taylor 1, Turner 1, own goal 1.
Carling Cup (0).
FA Cup (1): Armstrong 1.
Football League Trophy (1): Pearson 1.

Young J 19 + 1	Gier R 34 + 1	Hawkins P 20 + 1	McCafferty N 19 + 4	Allen G 5	Gulliver P 40	Bell D 13 + 1	Savage D 30 + 2	Pearson G 16 + 6	Chillingworth D 3 + 3	Kelly M 39 + 2	Grainger D 2 + 12	Taylor J 4 + 8	Nicholls A 26 + 4	Okuonghae M 15 + 6	O'Grady C 20 + 2	Dempster J 13 + 1	Broughton D 32 + 5	Woodman A 3	Tomlin L 4 + 17	Armstrong A 6 + 3	Burgess A 7 + 2	Ruddy J 3	Mills G 7 + 4	Crane D 8	Stokes T 18 + 1	Turner J 4 + 7	Joseph R 1	Castle P 1	Berry T 13 + 7	Bull R 19	Hatswell W 17	Jackson S 8 + 6	Tynan S 13 + 1	Mikolanda P 7 + 2	Caskey D 17 + 1	Hunter B — + 5	Shaw T — + 1	Match No.
1	2	3	4	5	6	7	8^1	9	10^2	11	12	13																										1
1	2	3	4	5	6	7		9^1	10^2	11		12	8	13																								2
1	2	3	4	5	6	7	8^2	9	10^1	11		12			13																							3
1		3	4		6	7	8^1	9^2		11	12	13	2	5	10																							4
1		3	4		6	7		8	12	11		9^1	2	5	10																							5
1		3▪	4		6			7^1		11	12	9^2	2	5	10	8	13▪																					6
1			4^2		6		8	7	12	3	13	9^1	11	5	10	2																						7
1		3			6		8	7^2	12	11	13	9^3	4	5	10^1	2	14																					8
1		3			6		8	7^2		11	13	12	2	5	10	4	9^1																					9
1	2	3	12		6		8^1	13		11	4^2	14	7	5	10		9^3																					10
1	2	3	12		6		8	13		11	4^3	14	7^1	5	10		9^2																					11
1	2	3	4		6		8	12		11	13		7^2	5	10		9^1																					12
1	2	3	4		6		8	7^2		11	13	14		5^1	10	12	9^3																					13
	2	3	4		6		8	7^1		11	12				10	5	9^2	1	13																			14
	2	3	4		6	12	8	7^1		11^2					10	5	9	1	13																			15
15	2	3			6	7	8	11^2					4^1		10	5	9▪	1^6		13	12																	16
	2		4		6	7	8			11					10	5				9	3	1																17
	2^1	12	4		6	7	8^3			11					10	5	13			9^2	3	1	14															18
		2	4^1		6	7	8								10	5	12		13	9^2	3	1	11															19
1	2		4		6	7	8			12					10^2	5	13		14	9^3	3		11^1															20
1	2^3	3	12		6	7^2	8	13		11					10	5	9^1				14		4															21
1	2	3	12		6	7^3	8^1			11					10	5▪	9^2		14	13			4															22
1	2	3			6	7	8	12		11					13		9^1		14	10^2	5		4^3															23
1	2	3	4^1		6		8	7^2							10		9		13	12	5		11															24
1	5		4^1		6		8	7^2			12		2				9		13	10▪	3		11															25
	2		4^1	5	6		8	9^3			12		3	13					11^2					1	7	14	10											26
			4^1	5^2	6		8			12			3^3	13			9		10					1	7			2	14	11								27
	2				6		8			11							9		10^2				12	1	7^1				4	3	5	13						28
	2				6		8^1			11			12				9^2								7				4	3	5	13	1	10^3	14			29
	2				6					11							9								7	12			4	3^1	5	13	1	10^2	8			30
	2				6					11			12				9		13				14		7^1				4^3	3	5		1	10^2	8			31
	2				6					11			12				9		13				14		7				4^1	3	5		1	10^2	8^3			32
	2				6		12			11							9		13						7^1				4	3	5		1	10^2	8			33
	2				6		7			11^2			13	12			9		14					1					4	3	5^1			10^3	8			34
	2									11			7	6			9^2		12					1	10^1				4^3	3	5			13	8	14		35
	2				6					11			7				9							1	10^1				4^2	3	5	12			8	13		36
					6		7			11			2	12			9^1								10^2	14			4^3	3	5	13	1		8			37
	2				6^2					11			7				9		12							14			4^3	3	5	10^1	1		8	13		38
	2									11			4^2	6^1			9^3		12						13	7			14	3	5	10	1		8			39
	2									11			4	5			9^2							1^6	7	8^1			12	3		10	15		6	13		40
	5						4			11^3			2	6			9^2								7	13			12	3		10^1	1		8	14		41
					6^1		13			11			2	12			9^3								7	14			4^2	3	5	10	1		8			42
	12						8			11			2	6^1			9^3								7	14			13	3	5	10^2	1		4			43
	6▪							12		11			2				9		13						7	8^1			14	3^3	5	10^2	1		4			44
					6					11			2				9^2		12						7	8^3			14	3^1	5	10	1	13	4			45
	3				6					11	12		2						10					1	7^3				8^1		5	13		9^2	4		14	46

FA Cup

First Round	Halifax T	(a)	1-1
		(h)	0-0
Second Round	Leyton Orient	(h)	0-1

Carling Cup

First Round	Coventry C	(h)	0-3

Football League Trophy

First Round	Southend U	(h)	1-0
Second Round	Swansea C	(a)	0-4

SCUNTHORPE UNITED FL Championship 1

FOUNDATION

The year of foundation for Scunthorpe United has often been quoted as 1910, but the club can trace its history back to 1899 when Brumby Hall FC, who played on the Old Showground, consolidated their position by amalgamating with some other clubs and changing their name to Scunthorpe United. The year 1910 was when that club amalgamated with North Lindsey United as Scunthorpe and Lindsey United. The link is Mr W. T. Lockwood whose chairmanship covers both years.

Glanford Park, Doncaster Road, Scunthorpe DN15 8TD.

Telephone: 01724 747 671.

Fax: 01604 871 448.

Website: www.scunthorpe-united.co.uk

Email: admin@scunthorpe-united.co.uk

Ground Capacity: 9,182.

Record Attendance: Old Showground: 23,935 v Portsmouth, FA Cup 4th rd, 30 January 1954. Glanford Park: 8,775 v Rotherham U, Division 4, 1 May 1989.

Pitch Measurements: 110yd × 71yd.

Chairman: J. S. Wharton.

Vice-chairman: R. Garton.

General Manager: J. Hammond.

Manager: Brian Laws.

Assistant Manager: Russ Wilcox.

Physio: Nigel Adkins.

Colours: Claret and blue.

Change Colours: Black with blue trim.

Year Formed: 1899.

Turned Professional: 1912.

Ltd Co.: 1912.

Club Nickname: 'The Iron'.

Previous Names: Amalgamated first with Brumby Hall then North Lindsey United to become Scunthorpe & Lindsey United, 1910; dropped '& Lindsey' in 1958.

Previous Ground: 1899, Old Showground; 1988, Glanford Park.

First Football League Game: 19 August 1950, Division 3 (N), v Shrewsbury T (h) D 0–0 – Thompson; Barker, Brownsword; Allen, Taylor, McCormick; Mosby, Payne, Gorin, Rees, Boyes.

HONOURS

Football League: Division 2 best season: 4th, 1961–62; Championship 2 – Runners-up 2004–05; Division 3 (N) – Champions 1957–58. Promoted from Division 3 1998–99 (play-offs).

FA Cup: best season: 5th rd, 1958, 1970.

Football League Cup: never past 3rd rd.

SKY SPORTS FACT FILE

A losing sequence forced Scunthorpe United to switch full-back Jack Hubbard to inside-right against Hartlepools United on 26 March 1955. He responded by scoring four times including a hat-trick in the last 12 minutes. He later resumed in defence.

Record League Victory: 8–1 v Luton T, Division 3, 24 April 1965 – Sidebottom; Horstead, Hemstead; Smith, Neale, Lindsey; Bramley (1), Scott, Thomas (5), Mahy (1), Wilson (1). 8–1 v Torquay U (a), Division 3, 28 October 1995 – Samways; Housham, Wilson, Ford (1), Knill (1), Hope (Nicholson), Thornber, Bullimore (Walsh), McFarlane (4) (Young), Eyre (2), Paterson.

Record Cup Victory: 9–0 v Boston U, FA Cup 1st rd, 21 November 1953 – Malan; Hubbard, Brownsword; Sharpe, White, Bushby; Mosby (1), Haigh (3), Whitfield (2), Gregory (1), Mervyn Jones (2).

Record Defeat: 0–8 v Carlisle U, Division 3 (N), 25 December 1952.

Most League Points (2 for a win): 66, Division 3 (N), 1956–57, 1957–58.

Most League Points (3 for a win): 83, Division 4, 1982–83.

Most League Goals: 88, Division 3 (N), 1957–58.

Highest League Scorer in Season: Barrie Thomas, 31, Division 2, 1961–62.

Most League Goals in Total Aggregate: Steve Cammack, 110, 1979–81, 1981–86.

Most League Goals in One Match: 5, Barrie Thomas v Luton T, Division 3, 24 April 1965.

Most Capped Player: None.

Most League Appearances: Jack Brownsword, 595, 1950–65.

Youngest League Player: Mike Farrell, 16 years 240 days v Workington, 8 November 1975.

Record Transfer Fee Received: £350,000 from Aston Villa for Neil Cox, February 1991.

Record Transfer Fee Paid: £175,000 to Bristol C for Steve Torpey, February 2000.

Football League Record: 1950 Elected to Division 3 (N); 1958–64 Division 2; 1964–68 Division 3; 1968–72 Division 4; 1972–73 Division 3; 1973–83 Division 4; 1983–84 Division 3; 1984–92 Division 4; 1992–99 Division 3; 1999–2000 Division 2; 2000–04 Division 3; 2004–05 FL2; 2005– FL1.

MANAGERS

Harry Allcock 1915–53
(Secretary-Manager)
Tom Crilly 1936–37
Bernard Harper 1946–48
Leslie Jones 1950–51
Bill Corkhill 1952–56
Ron Suart 1956–58
Tony McShane 1959
Bill Lambton 1959
Frank Soo 1959–60
Dick Duckworth 1960–64
Fred Goodwin 1964–66
Ron Ashman 1967–73
Ron Bradley 1973–74
Dick Rooks 1974–76
Ron Ashman 1976–81
John Duncan 1981–83
Allan Clarke 1983–84
Frank Barlow 1984–87
Mick Buxton 1987–91
Bill Green 1991–93
Richard Money 1993–94
David Moore 1994–96
Mick Buxton 1996–97
Brian Laws February 1997–

LATEST SEQUENCES

Longest Sequence of League Wins: 6, 18.10.1969 – 25.11.1969.

Longest Sequence of League Defeats: 8, 29.11.1997 – 20.1.1998.

Longest Sequence of League Draws: 6, 2.1.1984 – 25.2.1984.

Longest Sequence of Unbeaten League Matches: 15, 13.11.1971 – 26.2.1972.

Longest Sequence Without a League Win: 14, 22.3.1975 – 6.9.1975.

Successive Scoring Runs: 23 from 18.8.1951.

Successive Non-scoring Runs: 7 from 19.4.1975.

TEN YEAR LEAGUE RECORD

		P	W	D	L	F	A	Pts	Pos
1996-97	Div 3	46	18	9	19	59	62	63	13
1997-98	Div 3	46	19	12	15	56	52	69	8
1998-99	Div 3	46	22	8	16	69	58	74	4
1999-2000	Div 2	46	9	12	25	40	74	39	23
2000-01	Div 3	46	18	11	17	62	52	65	10
2001-02	Div 3	46	19	14	13	74	56	71	8
2002-03	Div 3	46	19	15	12	68	49	72	5
2003-04	Div 3	46	11	16	19	69	72	49	22
2004-05	FL 2	46	22	14	10	69	42	80	2
2005-06	FL 1	46	15	15	16	68	73	60	12

DID YOU KNOW ?

Scunthorpe United can claim to have had three England captains who at one time played for them. Kevin Keegan and Ray Clemence went on to skipper their country in the 1980s, the third Ian Botham achieved his honour as a Test cricketer.

SCUNTHORPE UNITED 2005–06 LEAGUE RECORD

Match No.	Date	Venue	Opponents	Result		H/T Score	Lg. Pos.	Goalscorers	Attendance
1	Aug 6	A	Brentford	L	0-2	0-0	—		5952
2	9	H	Barnsley	W	2-1	1-1	—	Crosby (pen) [28], Taylor [71]	7152
3	13	H	Gillingham	D	1-1	0-0	13	Hinds [90]	5007
4	20	A	Nottingham F	W	1-0	0-0	8	Sharp [71]	19,091
5	26	H	Southend U	W	1-0	1-0	—	Baraclough [36]	5569
6	29	A	Hartlepool U	D	3-3	1-1	6	Sharp 2 [9, 50], Keogh [65]	5044
7	Sept 2	A	Huddersfield T	W	4-1	2-0	—	Beagrie (pen) [8], Keogh 2 [45, 83], Sparrow [74]	14,112
8	10	H	Port Vale	W	2-0	2-0	2	Hinds [32], Keogh [37]	5694
9	17	A	Doncaster R	L	1-3	0-2	5	Sharp [51]	6699
10	24	H	Walsall	L	1-3	0-1	5	Sharp [55]	4973
11	27	A	Milton Keynes D	L	0-1	0-1	—		4682
12	Oct 1	H	Yeovil T	L	3-4	2-2	10	Keogh [13], Sharp 2 [20, 77]	4311
13	7	A	Tranmere R	W	2-0	2-0	—	Keogh [1], Sharp [39]	7522
14	15	H	Rotherham U	D	2-2	1-2	5	Sharp 2 [20, 60]	6649
15	22	A	Swindon T	D	1-1	1-0	7	Sparrow [35]	4972
16	29	H	Oldham Ath	W	4-2	2-2	6	Butler [28], Sharp 2 [31, 56], Crosby [52]	5055
17	Nov 13	A	Blackpool	L	2-5	2-3	7	Sharp 2 (1 pen) [3, 35 (p)]	6016
18	19	H	Tranmere R	L	1-2	0-0	10	Sharp (pen) [68]	4602
19	26	H	Brentford	L	1-3	1-2	15	Goodwin [8]	4322
20	Dec 6	A	Swansea C	L	0-2	0-0	—		13,207
21	10	A	Barnsley	L	2-5	0-3	17	Beagrie (pen) [88], MacKenzie [90]	8197
22	16	H	Nottingham F	W	3-1	1-0	—	Ridley [29], Taylor [72], Byrne [83]	5857
23	26	H	Chesterfield	D	2-2	0-1	15	Baraclough [65], Johnson [90]	5866
24	31	H	Bradford C	D	0-0	0-0	15		5269
25	Jan 2	A	Bournemouth	D	1-1	1-0	17	Sharp [6]	6259
26	10	H	Huddersfield T	D	2-2	1-1	—	Beagrie [17], Keogh [70]	4450
27	14	A	Bristol C	D	1-1	1-0	18	Keogh [5]	11,692
28	21	H	Doncaster R	L	1-2	0-0	18	Goodwin [48]	6978
29	Feb 4	H	Milton Keynes D	W	2-0	2-0	17	Sharp 2 (1 pen) [3, 10 (p)]	4631
30	7	A	Colchester U	L	0-1	0-1	—		4416
31	11	A	Walsall	D	2-2	2-1	16	Keogh [19], MacKenzie [45]	4911
32	14	H	Bristol C	L	0-2	0-1	—		3786
33	18	H	Swansea C	D	2-2	1-2	17	Sharp [6], Torpey [90]	4352
34	25	A	Gillingham	W	3-1	1-1	16	Sparrow [42], Hinds [59], Keogh [64]	6029
35	28	A	Port Vale	W	2-1	1-1	—	Sparrow [11], Taylor [59]	3984
36	Mar 10	A	Southend U	L	0-3	0-1	—		8717
37	14	H	Hartlepool U	W	2-0	1-0	—	Baraclough [44], Sparrow [70]	4550
38	18	A	Chesterfield	W	2-1	0-1	11	Hinds [47], Crosby [63]	4406
39	25	H	Colchester U	D	0-0	0-0	11		4608
40	Apr 1	A	Bradford C	L	2-4	2-1	14	Beagrie (pen) [13], Hinds [29]	8409
41	8	H	Bournemouth	D	2-2	1-1	15	Beagrie (pen) [12], Hinds [84]	4136
42	14	A	Yeovil T	W	1-0	0-0	—	Sharp [57]	6759
43	17	H	Swindon T	L	1-2	1-2	14	Sharp [9]	5207
44	22	A	Rotherham U	D	1-1	1-0	14	Keogh [41]	5778
45	29	H	Blackpool	W	1-0	0-0	12	Sharp [90]	5917
46	May 6	A	Oldham Ath	D	1-1	0-1	12	Sharp [88]	5544

Final League Position: 12

GOALSCORERS

League (68): Sharp 23 (3 pens), Keogh 11, Hinds 6, Beagrie 5 (4 pens), Sparrow 5, Baraclough 3, Crosby 3 (1 pen), Taylor 3, Goodwin 2, MacKenzie 2, Butler 1, Byrne 1, Johnson 1, Ridley 1, Torpey 1.
Carling Cup (2): Hinds 1, Ryan 1.
FA Cup (5): Keogh 3, Baraclough 1, Johnson 1.
Football League Trophy (4): Crosby 1 (pen), Johnson 1, Keogh 1, Sharp 1.

Musselwhite P 28	Byrne C 25 + 7	Williams M 28 + 1	Crosby A 38 + 4	Butler A 15 + 1	Baraclough I 37 + 1	Taylor C 31 + 14	Hinds R 42	Parton A 3 + 3	Torpey S 16 + 10	Sparrow M 30 + 9	Keogh A 40 + 5	Corden W 5 + 4	Beagrie P 21 + 9	Stanton N 21 + 1	Sharp B 35 + 2	Ryan R 7 + 6	Johnson T 3 + 11	Ridley L 2 + 1	Till P 6 + 2	MacKenzie N 12 + 2	Goodwin J 10 + 3	Allanson A — + 1	Evans T 18	Rose M 15	Foster S 18	Ehui I — + 3	Timlin M — + 1	*Match No.*
1	2	3	4	5	6	7	8	9	10¹	11	12																	1
1	2	3	4	5	6	13	8¹	9³	10	7	14	11²	12															2
1	2	3	4	5	6	12	8	9²	10	7³	13	11¹	14															3
1		3	4	5	6³	7	8	12	10²	11	13		14	2	9¹													4
1		3	4		6	12	5			7	9		11	2	10²	8¹	13											5
1	12	3	4			7	5			8	9²		11	2	10	6¹	13											6
1	12	3	4		6	7	5			13	9³		11	2¹	10	8²	14											7
1		3	4		6	7¹	5			12	9		11	2	10	8												8
1		3	4		6	7	5			12	9³	13	11²	2	10	8¹	14											9
1		3	4	12	6²	13	5	14		7	9³	11¹		2	10	8■												10
1		3	4	5	6	12	8¹	13		7	9	11²		2	10													11
1	12	6	4¹	5		7²				8	9	13	11	2	10			3										12
1	2	3		5	6		4			7	9		11		10				8									13
1	2	3	12	5¹	6	13	4			7	9	14	11³		10				8²									14
1	2	3	4		6	12	5			7	9		11²		10	13			8¹									15
1	2	3	4	5	6	12	8				9		11		10²		13		7¹									16
1	2	3	4■	5	6	12	8			7	9	11¹			10													17
1	2¹	3	12	5	6	7³	8■			11²	9			4	10		13		14									18
1	2	3	4	5		12					9³			6	10	8¹			13	11²	7■	14						19
	2	3	4	5		12					9	13	11		10				8²	7	6¹		1					20
	2	3	4¹	5	12	13	6				9		11		10³		14		8²	7			1					21
	2		4		6	7	5		12		9¹		11		10²		13	3		8			1					22
	2		4		6	7	5		12	13	9³		11²		10		14			8	3¹		1					23
	2		4		6	7³	5		12	13	9¹		11		10		14			8	3²		1					24
	2		4		6	12	5		11	7	9				10¹					8			1	3				25
	2		4		6¹	7	5		13	12	9		11		10²					8³	14		1	3				26
	12		4	5¹		7	2		14	13	9		11³		10					8	6²		1	3				27
			4		6	7¹	2		13■	12	9		11		10²					8³	14		1	3	5			28
	2				6	7¹	4			11	9				10		12				8		1	3	5			29
	2					7	5			11	9				10		8¹			12	4		1	3	6			30
	2		12			7	5			11	9				10					8	4		1	3	6¹			31
	2²	12				7	5		14	11				13	10		9			8	4³		1	3¹	6			32
1		3	12		6	7	4		13	11	14			2	10²		9³				8¹				5			33
1		3	4		6	7¹	8		10	11	9			2											5	12		34
1			4		6	7	8		10	11	9¹			2										3	5	12		35
1			4		6	7	8		10¹	11²	9			2										3	5	12	13	36
1			4¹		6	7	8		10	11	9		12	2										3	5			37
1	12		4		6	7²	8		10	11	9		13	2¹										3	5			38
1			4		6	7	8		10	11¹	9		12	2										3	5			39
1			4		6³	12	8		10²	7¹	9		11	2	13					14				3	5			40
1	12		4		6	7²	8		10		9		11³	2¹	13	14								3	5			41
	2	3	4		6²	7	8		11		9¹		12		10³	14					13		1		5			42
	2	3¹	4		6	7	8		11²	12	9		13		10	14							1		5³			43
	12	3¹	2		6	7	4		8	11	9				10								1		5			44
	2	3	4		6³	7¹	8²		12	11	9		13		10	14							1		5			45
	2	3²	4		6¹	7			12	8	9		11³	5	10	14		13					1					46

FA Cup

First Round	Bury	(a)	2-2
		(h)	1-0
Second Round	Aldershot T	(a)	1-0
Third Round	Manchester C	(a)	1-3

Carling Cup

First Round	Tranmere R	(h)	2-1
Second Round	Birmingham C	(h)	0-2

Football League Trophy

First Round	Hartlepool U	(h)	1-0
Second Round	Halifax T	(a)	3-1
Quarter-Final	Hereford U	(a)	0-2

SHEFFIELD UNITED FA Premiership

FOUNDATION

In March 1889, Yorkshire County Cricket Club formed Sheffield United six days after an FA Cup semi-final between Preston North End and West Bromwich Albion had finally convinced Charles Stokes, a member of the cricket club, that the formation of a professional football club would prove successful at Bramall Lane. The United's first secretary, Mr J. B. Wostinholm was also secretary of the cricket club.

Bramall Lane Ground, Cherry Street, Bramall Lane, Sheffield S2 4SU.

Telephone: 0870 787 1960.

Fax: 0870 787 3345.

Ticket Office: 0870 787 1799.

Website: www.sufc.co.uk

Email: info@sufc.co.uk

Ground Capacity: 30,864.

Record Attendance: 68,287 v Leeds U, FA Cup 5th rd, 15 February 1936.

Pitch Measurements: 110yd × 74yd.

Chairman: Terry Robinson.

Vice-chairman: Chris Steer.

Secretary: Donna Fletcher.

Manager: Neil Warnock.

Assistant Manager: Stuart McCall.

Physio: Dennis Pettitt.

Colours: Red and white striped shirts, black shorts, black stockings.

Change Colours: Black and white striped shirts, white shorts, white stockings.

Year Formed: 1889.

Turned Professional: 1889.

Ltd Co.: 1899.

Club Nickname: 'The Blades'.

First Football League Game: 3 September 1892, Division 2, v Lincoln C (h) W 4–2 – Lilley; Witham, Cain; Howell, Hendry, Needham (1); Wallace, Dobson, Hammond (3), Davies, Drummond.

Record League Victory: 10–0 v Burslem Port Vale (a), Division 2, 10 December 1892 – Howlett; Witham, Lilley; Howell, Hendry, Needham; Drummond (1), Wallace (1), Hammond (4), Davies (2), Watson (2).

HONOURS

Football League: Championship – Runners-up 2005–06; Division 1 – Champions 1897–98; Runners-up 1896–97, 1899–1900; Division 2 – Champions 1952–53; Runners-up 1892–93, 1938–39, 1960–61, 1970–71, 1989–90; Division 4 – Champions 1981–82.

FA Cup: Winners 1899, 1902, 1915, 1925; Runners-up 1901, 1936.

Football League Cup: semi-final 2003.

SKY SPORTS FACT FILE

In the first issue of the Sheffield United programme at the beginning of the 1897–98 season one of the aims stated was "to gain the Championship". The ambition was achieved in the penultimate game 1–0 at Bolton Wanderers on 8 April.

Record Cup Victory: 6–1 v Lincoln C, League Cup, 22 August 2000 – Tracey; Uhlenbeek, Weber, Woodhouse (Ford), Murphy, Sandford, Devlin (pen), Ribeiro (Santos), Bent (3), Kelly (1) (Thompson), Jagielka, og (1). 6–1 v Loughborough, FA Cup 4th qualifying rd, 6 December 1890; 6–1 v Scarborough (a), FA Cup 1st qualifying rd, 5 October 1889.

Record Defeat: 0–13 v Bolton W, FA Cup 2nd rd, 1 February 1890.

Most League Points (2 for a win): 60, Division 2, 1952–53.

Most League Points (3 for a win): 96, Division 4, 1981–82.

Most League Goals: 102, Division 1, 1925–26.

Highest League Scorer in Season: Jimmy Dunne, 41, Division 1, 1930–31.

Most League Goals in Total Aggregate: Harry Johnson, 205, 1919–30.

Most League Goals in One Match: 5, Harry Hammond v Bootle, Division 2, 26 November 1892; 5, Harry Johnson v West Ham U, Division 1, 26 December 1927.

Most Capped Player: Billy Gillespie, 25, Northern Ireland.

Most League Appearances: Joe Shaw, 629, 1948–66.

Youngest League Player: Steve Hawes, 17 years 47 days v WBA, 2 September 1995.

Record Transfer Fee Received: £3,000,000 (dependant on appearances) from Derby Co for Lee Morris, October 1999.

MANAGERS

J. B. Wostinholm 1889–99
(Secretary-Manager)
John Nicholson 1899–1932
Ted Davison 1932–52
Reg Freeman 1952–55
Joe Mercer 1955–58
Johnny Harris 1959–68
(continued as General Manager to 1970)
Arthur Rowley 1968–69
Johnny Harris *(General Manager resumed Team Manager duties)* 1969–73
Ken Furphy 1973–75
Jimmy Sirrel 1975–77
Harry Haslam 1978–81
Martin Peters 1981
Ian Porterfield 1981–86
Billy McEwan 1986–88
Dave Bassett 1988–95
Howard Kendall 1995–97
Nigel Spackman 1997–98
Steve Bruce 1998–99
Adrian Heath 1999
Neil Warnock December 1999–

Record Transfer Fee Paid: £3,000,000 to Preston NE for Claude Davis, July 2006.

Football League Record: 1892 Elected to Division 2; 1893–1934 Division 1; 1934–39 Division 2; 1946–49 Division 1; 1949–53 Division 2; 1953–56 Division 1; 1956–61 Division 2; 1961–68 Division 1; 1968–71 Division 2; 1971–76 Division 1; 1976–79 Division 2; 1979–81 Division 3; 1981–82 Division 4; 1982–84 Division 3; 1984–88 Division 2; 1988–89 Division 3; 1989–90 Division 2; 1990–92 Division 1; 1992–94 FA Premier League; 1994–2004 Division 1; 2004–06 FLC; 2006– FA Premier League.

LATEST SEQUENCES

Longest Sequence of League Wins: 8, 14.9.1960 – 22.10.1960.

Longest Sequence of League Defeats: 7, 19.8.1975 – 20.9.1975.

Longest Sequence of League Draws: 6, 6.5.2001 – 8.9.2001.

Longest Sequence of Unbeaten League Matches: 22, 2.9.1899 – 13.1.1900.

Longest Sequence Without a League Win: 19, 27.9.1975 – 7.2.1976.

Successive Scoring Runs: 34 from 30.3.1956.

Successive Non-scoring Runs: 6 from 4.12.1993.

TEN YEAR LEAGUE RECORD

		P	W	D	L	F	A	Pts	Pos
1996-97	Div 1	46	20	13	13	75	52	73	5
1997-98	Div 1	46	19	17	10	69	54	74	6
1998-99	Div 1	46	18	13	15	71	66	67	8
1999-2000	Div 1	46	13	15	18	59	71	54	16
2000-01	Div 1	46	19	11	16	52	49	68	10
2001-02	Div 1	46	15	15	16	53	54	60	13
2002-03	Div 1	46	23	11	12	72	52	80	3
2003-04	Div 1	46	20	11	15	65	56	71	8
2004-05	FL C	46	18	13	15	57	56	67	8
2005-06	FL C	46	26	12	8	76	46	90	2

DID YOU KNOW?

In August 1953 Sheffield United manager Teddy Davison signed 5ft 7in goalkeeper Alan Hodgkinson who went on to play for England, the smallest goalkeeper for his country since 5ft 7in Davison himself had been capped v Wales on 13 March 1922.

SHEFFIELD UNITED 2005–06 LEAGUE RECORD

Match No.	Date	Venue	Opponents	Result		H/T Score	Lg. Pos.	Goalscorers	Attendance
1	Aug 6	H	Leicester C	W	4-1	1-0	—	Gray (pen) 34, Kabba (pen) 61, Ifill 84, Bromby 90	18,224
2	9	A	Burnley	W	2-1	2-0	—	Shipperley 5, Webber 40	11,802
3	13	A	QPR	L	1-2	0-0	5	Kabba 90	13,497
4	20	H	Preston NE	W	2-1	1-1	2	Shipperley 45, Webber 90	20,519
5	27	H	Coventry C	W	2-1	1-1	1	Kabba 27, Unsworth (pen) 90	17,739
6	29	A	Crewe Alex	W	3-1	1-1	1	Shipperley 15, Quinn 50, Kabba 56	7501
7	Sept 10	H	Ipswich T	W	2-0	1-0	1	Kabba 2 5, 90	21,059
8	13	A	Brighton & HA	W	1-0	1-0	—	Jagielka 25	6553
9	17	A	Watford	W	3-2	0-1	1	Jagielka 56, Ifill 66, Carlisle (og) 81	15,399
10	24	H	Derby Co	W	2-1	2-0	1	Unsworth 7, Ifill 37	22,192
11	27	H	Plymouth Arg	W	2-0	2-0	—	Shipperley 10, Quinn 31	20,111
12	Oct 1	A	Reading	L	1-2	1-1	1	Kabba 15	22,068
13	15	H	Wolverhampton W	W	1-0	1-0	1	Shipperley 16	25,533
14	18	A	Millwall	W	4-0	2-0	—	Webber 2 33, 73, Pericard 36, Quinn 68	9148
15	21	A	Leeds U	D	1-1	0-0	—	Kabba 69	23,600
16	29	H	Cardiff C	D	0-0	0-0	1		25,311
17	Nov 1	H	Luton T	W	4-0	1-0	—	Jagielka 2 34, 88, Morgan 50, Pericard 71	22,554
18	5	A	Crystal Palace	W	3-2	2-1	1	Jagielka 15, Ifill 45, Shipperley 56	20,344
19	19	H	Millwall	D	2-2	1-1	1	Unsworth 5, Webber 84	22,292
20	22	A	Wolverhampton W	D	0-0	0-0	—		24,240
21	26	A	Leicester C	L	2-4	0-2	2	Kabba 52, Short 90	22,382
22	Dec 3	H	Sheffield W	W	1-0	1-0	2	Quinn 24	30,558
23	10	H	Burnley	W	3-0	2-0	2	Shipperley 2 29, 81, Webber 34	23,118
24	16	A	Preston NE	D	0-0	0-0	—		14,378
25	26	H	Norwich C	L	1-3	1-1	2	Jagielka 22	26,505
26	28	A	Southampton	W	1-0	0-0	2	Shipperley 55	27,443
27	31	H	Stoke C	W	2-1	1-0	2	Montgomery 28, Morgan 90	21,279
28	Jan 3	A	Hull C	W	3-1	2-1	—	Ifill 31, Webber 45, Armstrong 52	21,929
29	14	A	Ipswich T	D	1-1	0-0	2	Webber 77	23,794
30	21	H	Brighton & HA	W	3-1	0-0	2	Jagielka 53, Ifill 64, Tonge 75	27,514
31	Feb 1	A	Derby Co	W	1-0	1-0	—	Akinbiyi 12	26,275
32	6	H	Watford	L	1-4	0-1	—	Ifill 58	20,791
33	11	A	Plymouth Arg	D	0-0	0-0	2		15,017
34	14	H	Reading	D	1-1	1-1	—	Dyer 9	25,011
35	18	A	Sheffield W	W	2-1	2-0	2	Tonge 38, Akinbiyi 45	33,439
36	25	H	QPR	L	2-3	2-1	2	Akinbiyi 21, Bircham (og) 29	25,360
37	Mar 3	H	Crewe Alex	D	0-0	0-0	—		22,691
38	11	A	Coventry C	L	0-2	0-2	2		23,506
39	18	A	Norwich C	L	1-2	1-2	2	Armstrong 17	25,346
40	25	H	Southampton	W	3-0	2-0	2	Jagielka 43, Ifill 45, Shipperley 77	22,824
41	Apr 1	A	Stoke C	D	1-1	0-1	2	Webber 83	17,544
42	8	H	Hull C	W	3-2	1-0	2	Shipperley 36, Ifill 52, Unsworth 90	26324
43	14	A	Cardiff C	W	1-0	0-0	—	Webber 76	11,006
44	18	H	Leeds U	D	1-1	1-1	—	Bakke (og) 10	29,329
45	22	A	Luton T	D	1-1	0-0	2	Tonge 90	10,248
46	30	H	Crystal Palace	W	1-0	0-0	2	Morgan 81	27,120

Final League Position: 2

GOALSCORERS

League (76): Shipperley 11, Webber 10, Ifill 9, Kabba 9 (1 pen), Jagielka 8, Quinn 4, Unsworth 4 (1 pen), Akinbiyi 3, Morgan 3, Tonge 3, Armstrong 2, Pericard 2, Bromby 1, Dyer 1, Gray 1 (pen), Montgomery 1, Short 1, own goals 3.
Carling Cup (1): Ross 1.
FA Cup (1): Kabba 1.

Kenny P 46	Bromby L 35	Harley J 4	Montgomery N 34 + 5	Morgan C 37 + 2	Jagielka P 46	Ifill P 28 + 11	Nalis L 3 + 1	Webber D 24 + 11	Gray A 1	Tonge M 23 + 7	Gillespie K 8 + 22	Kabba S 21 + 13	Shipperley N 34 + 5	Kozluk R 21 + 6	Short C 20 + 3	Shaw P — + 1	Quinn A 23 + 4	Unsworth D 33 + 1	Armstrong C 21 + 3	Pericard V 3 + 8	Geary D 17 + 3	Wright A 3 + 3	Flitcroft G 3 + 3	Deane B — + 2	Akinbiyi A 10 + 5	Dyer B 3 + 2	Collins N 2	Horsfield G 1 + 2	Luckett C 2 + 1	Forte J — + 1	Francis S — + 1	*Match No.*
1	2	3	4	5	6	7	8	9[1]	10[2]	11[3]	12	13	14																			1
1	2	3	4	5	6	7[1]	8	9[2]		11[3]	12	13	10	14																		2
1	2	3[1]	4	5	6	7	8[3]	9			12	13	10[2]	11	14																	3
1	2	3	4	5	8	7[1]		9		11[3]	12		10[2]		6	13	14															4
1	2		4	5[2]	8	7				12	13	9[1]	10	14	6		11[3]	3														5
1	2		4	5	8	13					7	9[2]	10		6		11[1]	3	12													6
1	2		4	5	8	7[2]				12	13	9	10[1]		6		11	3														7
1	6		4	5	8	12				13	7	9[2]	10[1]	2			11[3]	3	14													8
1	6		4	5	8	7	12	13			14	9[1]	10[2]	2			11[3]	3														9
1	6		4	5	8	7[2]		12			13	9[1]	10[3]	2			11	3		14												10
1	5		4	6	8	7[2]		12			13	9[1]	10[3]	2			11	3		14												11
1	5		4	6	8	7[2]		12			13	9	10[3]	2			11[1]	3		14												12
1	5		4	6	8	7[2]		12			13	9[1]	10[3]	2			11	3		14												13
1	5		4	6	8	7[1]		9		11	12			2[3]			13	3[2]		10	14											14
1	5		4	6	8	7[1]		13			12	9[3]	10[2]				11			14	2	3										15
1	5		4	6	8	12		13			7[1]	9	10[2]	2[3]			11	3			14											16
1	5		4	6	8	7		12				9[1]	10[2]				11	3		13	2[3]	14										17
1	5		4	6	8	7[2]		12			13	9[1]	10				11[3]	3			2	14										18
1	5		4[2]	6■	8	7		12			13	9[1]					11	3[3]		10	2	14										19
1	5		4		6	12		9[1]		8	7		10[2]				11			13	2	3										20
1	5		4		6			9		8[3]	7[1]	12	13		14		11			10[2]	2	3										21
1	5		4		6	12		7[1]		13		9[2]	10[3]	2	8		11	3		14												22
1	5		4	12	8	13		9[2]		14			10	2	6		7[1]	3	11[3]													23
1	5		4		8			9					10	2	6		7	3	11													24
1	5		4[3]	6	8	12		9		11[1]	14	13	10[2]	2			7	3														25
1	5		4	6	7			9[1]		12		8	10	13				3	11		2[2]											26
1	5		4[1]	6	7	13		9		12		8[2]	10	14			11	3[3]			2											27
1	5		12	6	4	7[2]		9		8[1]	13		10					3	11		2											28
1	5		12	6	4	7[2]		9[1]		8		13	10				14	3	11[3]		2											29
1	5				4	7				8		9[2]	10[3]		6		12	3[1]	11		2		13	14								30
1	5				4	7[2]				8	13	12	10[1]		6			3	11		2				9							31
1	5			12	4	7[3]				8	14	10[2]	13		6			3■	11		2[1]				9							32
1	2		12	5	4	7					13	10[3]	14		6		11[2]		3				8[1]		9							33
1	2[2]		4	5	8	7				11		12		13	6[3]				3				14		9	10[1]						34
1			4	5	8	7[1]				11				2					3		12		13		9[2]	10[3]	6	14				35
1			4[3]	5	8	7		12		11			13	2				14	3						9[2]		6	10[1]				36
1	5[1]		12	6	4	13		10			8[3]	14					11[2]		3		2		7		9							37
1			4	6	2			8				12	10[3]	13	5				11		3		7[2]		9[1]			14				38
1			4[1]	6	7			9[3]		8	12		10[2]	2	5			3	11						13	14						39
1			12	6	4	7[2]		9[3]		8	13		10	2	5			3[1]	11						14							40
1				6	4	7[1]		9		8		12	10[2]	2	5			3	11						13							41
1				6	4	7[1]		9		8		12	10	2	5			3	11													42
1			4	6	7	12		9[1]		8		13	10[3]	2	5			3	11[2]						14							43
1			4[2]		7	12		10[1]		11		8[3]			5			3	13		2				9	14			6			44
1				5	4					8	7				12			3[2]	11		2[1]				9	10[3]			6	13	14	45
1				6	4			9		8	7		10[1]	2	5[3]			3[2]	11					13	12				14			46

FA Cup

Third Round	Colchester U	(a)	1-2

Carling Cup

First Round	Boston U	(h)	1-0
Second Round	Shrewsbury T	(a)	0-0
Third Round	Reading	(a)	0-2

SHEFFIELD WEDNESDAY FL Championship

FOUNDATION

Sheffield being one of the principal centres of early Association Football, this club was formed as long ago as 1867 by the Sheffield Wednesday Cricket Club (formed 1825) and their colours from the start were blue and white. The inaugural meeting was held at the Adelphi Hotel and the original committee included Charles Stokes who was subsequently a founder member of Sheffield United.

Hillsborough, Sheffield S6 1SW.

Telephone: 0870 999 1867.

Fax: (0114) 221 2122.

Ticket Office: 0870 999 1867.

Website: www.swfc.co.uk

Email: enquiries@swfc.co.uk

Ground Capacity: 39,812.

Record Attendance: 72,841 v Manchester C, FA Cup 5th rd, 17 February 1934.

Pitch Measurements: 115yd × 74yd.

Chairman: Dave E. D. Allen.

Chief Executive/Secretary: Kaven Walker.

Manager: Paul Sturrock.

Assistant Manager: Kevin Summerfield.

Physio: John Dickens.

Colours: Blue and white striped shirts, black shorts, blue stockings.

Change Colours: All yellow.

Year Formed: 1867 (fifth oldest League club).

Turned Professional: 1887.

Ltd Co.: 1899.

Former Names: The Wednesday until 1929.

Club Nickname: 'The Owls'.

Previous Grounds: 1867, Highfield; 1869, Myrtle Road; 1877, Sheaf House; 1887, Olive Grove; 1899, Owlerton (since 1912 known as Hillsborough). Some games were played at Endcliffe in the 1880s. Until 1895 Bramall Lane was used for some games.

First Football League Game: 3 September 1892, Division 1, v Notts Co (a) W 1–0 – Allan; Tom Brandon (1), Mumford; Hall, Betts, Harry Brandon; Spiksley, Brady, Davis, R. N. Brown, Dunlop.

Record League Victory: 9–1 v Birmingham, Division 1, 13 December 1930 – Brown; Walker, Blenkinsop; Strange, Leach, Wilson; Hooper (3), Seed (2), Ball (2), Burgess (1), Rimmer (1).

HONOURS

Football League: Division 1 – Champions 1902–03, 1903–04, 1928–29, 1929–30; Runners-up 1960–61; Promotion from Championship 1 2004–05 (play-offs); Division 2 – Champions 1899–1900, 1925–26, 1951–52, 1955–56, 1958–59; Runners-up 1949–50, 1983–84.

FA Cup: Winners 1896, 1907, 1935; Runners-up 1890, 1966, 1993.

Football League Cup: Winners 1991; Runners-up 1993.

European Competitions: *European Fairs Cup:* 1961–62, 1963–64. *UEFA Cup:* 1992–93. *Intertoto Cup:* 1995.

SKY SPORTS FACT FILE

Billy Betts the Sheffield Wednesday and England centre-half began with the Owls in 1882. His grandson Dennis Woodhead became their left-winger in 1955, thus establishing the longest existing family connection with a club in the Football League at the time.

Record Cup Victory: 12–0 v Halliwell, FA Cup 1st rd, 17 January 1891 – Smith; Thompson, Brayshaw; Harry Brandon (1), Betts, Cawley (2); Winterbottom, Mumford (2), Bob Brandon (1), Woolhouse (5), Ingram (1).

Record Defeat: 0–10 v Aston Villa, Division 1, 5 October 1912.

Most League Points (2 for a win): 62, Division 2, 1958–59.

Most League Points (3 for a win): 88, Division 2, 1983–84.

Most League Goals: 106, Division 2, 1958–59.

Highest League Scorer in Season: Derek Dooley, 46, Division 2, 1951–52.

Most League Goals in Total Aggregate: Andrew Wilson, 199, 1900–20.

Most League Goals in One Match: 6, Doug Hunt v Norwich C, Division 2, 19 November 1938.

Most Capped Player: Nigel Worthington, 50 (66), Northern Ireland.

Most League Appearances: Andrew Wilson, 501, 1900–20.

Youngest League Player: Peter Fox, 15 years 269 days v Orient, 31 March 1973.

Record Transfer Fee Received: £2,750,000 from Blackburn R for Paul Warhurst, September 1993.

Record Transfer Fee Paid: £4,500,000 to Celtic for Paolo Di Canio, August 1997.

Football League Record: 1892 Elected to Division 1; 1899–1900 Division 2; 1900–20 Division 1; 1920–26 Division 2; 1926–37 Division 1; 1937–50 Division 2; 1950–51 Division 1; 1951–52 Division 2; 1952–55 Division 1; 1955–56 Division 2; 1956–58 Division 1; 1958–59 Division 2; 1959–70 Division 1; 1970–75 Division 2; 1975–80 Division 3; 1980–84 Division 2; 1984–90 Division 1; 1990–91 Division 2; 1991–92 Division 1; 1992–2000 FA Premier League; 2000–03 Division 1; 2003–04 Division 2; 2004–05 FL1; 2005– FLC.

MANAGERS

Arthur Dickinson 1891–1920
(Secretary-Manager)
Robert Brown 1920–33
Billy Walker 1933–37
Jimmy McMullan 1937–42
Eric Taylor 1942–58
(continued as General Manager to 1974)
Harry Catterick 1958–61
Vic Buckingham 1961–64
Alan Brown 1964–68
Jack Marshall 1968–69
Danny Williams 1969–71
Derek Dooley 1971–73
Steve Burtenshaw 1974–75
Len Ashurst 1975–77
Jackie Charlton 1977–83
Howard Wilkinson 1983–88
Peter Eustace 1988–89
Ron Atkinson 1989–91
Trevor Francis 1991–95
David Pleat 1995–97
Ron Atkinson 1997–98
Danny Wilson 1998–2000
Peter Shreeves (Acting) 2000
Paul Jewell 2000–01
Peter Shreeves 2001
Terry Yorath 2001–02
Chris Turner 2002–04
Paul Sturrock September 2004–

LATEST SEQUENCES

Longest Sequence of League Wins: 9, 23.4.1904 – 15.10.1904.

Longest Sequence of League Defeats: 8, 9.9.2000 – 17.10.2000.

Longest Sequence of League Draws: 5, 24.10.1992 – 28.11.1992.

Longest Sequence of Unbeaten League Matches: 19, 10.12.1960 – 8.4.1961.

Longest Sequence Without a League Win: 20, 11.1.1975 – 30.8.1975.

Successive Scoring Runs: 40 from 14.11.1959.

Successive Non-scoring Runs: 8 from 8.3.1975.

TEN YEAR LEAGUE RECORD

		P	*W*	*D*	*L*	*F*	*A*	*Pts*	*Pos*
1996-97	PR Lge	38	14	15	9	50	51	57	7
1997-98	PR Lge	38	12	8	18	52	67	44	16
1998-99	PR Lge	38	13	7	18	41	42	46	12
1999-2000	PR Lge	38	8	7	23	38	70	31	19
2000-01	Div 1	46	15	8	23	52	71	53	17
2001-02	Div 1	46	12	14	20	49	71	50	20
2002-03	Div 1	46	10	16	20	56	73	46	22
2003-04	Div 2	46	13	14	19	48	64	53	16
2004-05	FL 1	46	19	15	12	77	59	72	5
2005-06	FL C	46	13	13	20	39	52	52	19

DID YOU KNOW ?

Harry Woolhouse, scorer of five Sheffield Wednesday goals in their biggest FA Cup win, established an individual scoring record for the club in the competition. Signed in 1888 he made the transition from the Football Alliance to Football League.

SHEFFIELD WEDNESDAY 2005–06 LEAGUE RECORD

Match No.	Date	Venue	Opponents	Result		H/T Score	Lg. Pos.	Goalscorers	Attendance
1	Aug 6	A	Stoke C	D	0-0	0-0	—		18,744
2	9	H	Hull C	D	1-1	1-1	—	Best [8]	29,910
3	13	H	Southampton	L	0-1	0-1	20		26,688
4	20	A	Ipswich T	L	1-2	0-1	22	Peacock [81]	24,238
5	26	A	QPR	D	0-0	0-0	—		12,131
6	Sept 10	A	Leicester C	L	0-2	0-2	23		22,618
7	13	H	Leeds U	W	1-0	1-0	—	Eagles [9]	29,986
8	17	H	Millwall	L	1-2	0-0	24	Coughlan [66]	22,446
9	23	A	Luton T	D	2-2	1-1	—	Lee [14], Graham [64]	8267
10	27	A	Crystal Palace	L	0-2	0-1	—		17,413
11	Oct 1	H	Coventry C	W	3-2	2-1	22	Coughlan [17], Brunt 2 (1 pen) [43, 79 (p)]	22,732
12	15	A	Plymouth Arg	D	1-1	1-0	22	Buzsaki (og) [24]	16,534
13	18	H	Watford	D	1-1	0-0	—	Brunt [64]	21,187
14	24	H	Brighton & HA	D	1-1	0-0	—	Peacock [55]	21,787
15	29	A	Norwich C	W	1-0	0-0	18	Brunt [79]	25,383
16	Nov 1	A	Reading	L	0-2	0-1	—		16,188
17	5	H	Derby Co	W	2-1	0-1	16	Brunt [69], Graham [74]	26,334
18	9	H	Cardiff C	L	1-3	0-3	—	Eagles [65]	20,324
19	19	A	Watford	L	1-2	0-2	18	Whelan [90]	16,988
20	22	H	Plymouth Arg	D	0-0	0-0	—		20,244
21	26	H	Stoke C	L	0-2	0-1	20		21,970
22	Dec 3	A	Sheffield U	L	0-1	0-1	21		30,558
23	10	A	Hull C	L	0-1	0-0	21		21,329
24	17	H	Ipswich T	L	0-1	0-0	22		21,716
25	26	A	Preston NE	D	0-0	0-0	22		18,867
26	28	H	Wolverhampton W	L	0-2	0-1	23		24,295
27	31	A	Burnley	W	2-1	1-0	22	Eagles [5], Coughlan [56]	14,607
28	Jan 2	H	Crewe Alex	W	3-0	1-0	20	Wood [7], Tudgay [62], McCready (og) [81]	25,656
29	14	H	Leicester C	W	2-1	2-1	19	Brunt [31], Coughlan [40]	25,398
30	21	A	Leeds U	L	0-3	0-0	20		27,843
31	31	H	Luton T	L	0-2	0-0	—		23,965
32	Feb 4	A	Millwall	W	1-0	0-0	20	Simek [63]	11,896
33	11	H	Crystal Palace	D	0-0	0-0	21		24,784
34	15	A	Coventry C	L	1-2	0-1	—	Brunt [79]	20,021
35	18	H	Sheffield U	L	1-2	0-2	21	MacLean (pen) [80]	33,439
36	25	A	Southampton	L	0-3	0-0	21		26,236
37	Mar 4	A	Cardiff C	L	0-1	0-1	21		11,851
38	11	H	QPR	D	1-1	1-1	21	Burton [13]	22,788
39	18	H	Preston NE	W	2-0	1-0	21	Burton [38], O'Brien [51]	23,429
40	25	A	Wolverhampton W	W	3-1	1-0	21	Tudgay 2 [45, 86], Burton [67]	25,161
41	Apr 1	H	Burnley	D	0-0	0-0	21		24,485
42	8	A	Crewe Alex	L	0-2	0-2	21		8007
43	15	H	Norwich C	W	1-0	1-0	21	Tudgay [45]	30,755
44	17	A	Brighton & HA	W	2-0	1-0	21	Hart 8 (og) [09], O'Brien [69]	7573
45	22	H	Reading	D	1-1	0-1	21	MacLean (pen) [59]	27,307
46	30	A	Derby Co	W	2-0	1-0	19	Tudgay [5], Best [85]	30,391

Final League Position: 19

GOALSCORERS

League (39): Brunt 7 (1 pen), Tudgay 5, Coughlan 4, Burton 3, Eagles 3, Best 2, Graham 2, MacLean 2 (2 pens), O'Brien 2, Peacock 2, Lee 1, Simek 1, Whelan 1, Wood 1, own goals 3.
Carling Cup (6): Proudlock 2, Coughlan 1, Graham 1, Partridge 1, Peacock 1.
FA Cup (2): Heckingbottom 2.

Lucas D 18	Simek F 42 + 1	Hills J 26 + 1	Whelan G 40 + 3	Lee G 14 + 1	Wood R 27 + 3	Eagles C 21 + 4	Rocastle C 14 + 3	Best L 5 + 8	Peacock L 19 + 3	Brunt C 35 + 9	Proudlock A — + 6	Partridge R 6 + 12	Graham D 19 + 5	O'Brien B 34 + 10	Coughlan G 33	Adams S 8	Diallo D 8 + 3	Ross M 1	Corr B 7 + 9	Bullen L 12 + 16	McGovern J 3 + 4	Agbonlahor G 4 + 4	Weaver N 14	Heckingbottom P 4	Murphy D 4	Gilbert P 17	Tudgay M 14 + 4	Burton D 15 + 2	Folly Y 14	Adamson C 5	MacLean S 4 + 2	Collins P 3	McAllister S 1 + 1	Carson S 9	Bischoff M 4	Spurr T 2	*Match No.*
1	2	3	4	5	6	7[2]	8	9[1]	10	11	12	13																									1
1	2	3	4	5	6	7[1]	8	9[2]	10	11	13	12																									2
1	2	3	4	5	6	7[1]	8[3]		10	11	13	12	9[2]	14																							3
1	2	3	4		6	7[1]			12	11	13		9[2]	10	5	8[3]	14																				4
1	2	3[3]	4[2]		12		8		10[3]	13	14	7	9	11	5		6[1]																				5
1	2		4		6	7	8[1]		10	12			9[3]	11	5			3[2]	13	14																	6
1	2	3	4		6	7	12		10	11[1]			9[2]	8	5					13																	7
1	2	3	4		6	7[2]	12		10	11[1]	14		9[3]	8	5					13																	8
1	2	3	4	5	6	7[3]	12		10[2]	11			9	8[1]						13	14																9
1	2[2]	3	4	5	6	7			10	11[1]		12	9[3]	8					14	13																	10
1	2	3	4	5		7[1]	8		10	11			9[2]	12	6					13																	11
1	2	3	4[3]	5	12	7	8		10	11[1]			9[2]	14	6					13																	12
1	2	3	4	5	12	7	8[2]		10	11		13	9[3]	14	6[1]																						13
1	2[2]	3	4	5		7	8		10	11			9[1]	12	6					13																	14
1	2	3	4	5	6	7[2]	8		10	11[3]		13	12	14								9[1]															15
1	2	3[2]	4	5	6	12	8		10[3]	11		7[1]	13	14								9															16
	2	3	4	5	6	7	8[3]		10[2]	11			12	14						13		9[1]	1														17
	2		4	5	6	7[1]				11		12	9[3]	8					10[2]	13		14	1	3													18
			4	12	6	7			10	11			9[2]	8			5			2[1]		13	1	3													19
	2		4	10[3]	6	7[2]				11		13	12	8			5		14			9[1]	1	3													20
	2		4				8			11		7[1]	9[2]	14	6		5				13	12	1	3[3]	10												21
	2		4		6	12	8[2]			11		7[1]	9	13	5								1		10	3											22
	2		4[2]		6	12			10[1]	13			9[3]	8	5	11						14	1		7	3											23
	2		4		6	12			10[3]	13			9[2]	7	5	11[1]			14				1		8	3											24
	2		4		6	7			12	9[2]			13	8	5	11			10[1]				1			3											25
	2		4		6	7			12	13		14	9[3]	8	5	11[2]			10[1]				1			3											26
	2	4	12		6	7[3]				11				8	5	9[1]	13		10[2]	14			1			3											27
	2	11[3]	4		6					12		8[1]		7	5				14	13			1			3	9	10[2]									28
	2	11	4[1]		6					7				8	5				13	12			1			3	9[2]	10									29
	2	11	4[1]		6					7		12		8	5				13				1			3	9[2]	10									30
1	2	11[2]			6			13		7				8	5				12							3[1]	9	10	4								31
1[G]	2		4		6					11				8			15		9[1]	5						3	12	10	7								32
					6			12		11				8	5[2]		4		9[3]	2						3	13	10[1]	7	1	14						33
	2		4					12		13		14		8	5		6[2]		10[1]	11						3			7[3]	1	9						34
	2		4					10[2]		11		12		8	5					6						3	13		7[1]	1	9						35
	2		4							7		11[2]		8[1]	5				12	3							10	13		1	9[3]	6	14				36
	2		4					12		11[1]				8	5					3							9	10	7	1		6					37
	13		4					12		11[1]				8	5					2						3	9[3]	10	7		14			1	6[2]		38
	2		4							11				8	5											3	9	10	7					1	6		39
	2	12	4							11[2]				8	5					13						3[1]	9	10	7					1	6		40
	2	3	4					12		11[1]				8	5					13	14						9	10[3]	7					1	6[2]		41
	2	3	4[1]					13		12				8[2]	5					14	11[3]						9	10	7			6		1			42
	2	3	12							11[2]				8	5	4[1]				6	13						9	10	7					1			43
	2	3	4					7[1]		12				8	5	11				6							9	10						1			44
	2	3[1]	12					10[3]						8			5			6	11[2]						13	14	7		9			1		4	45
								12						8	5		6			2	4[1]						9	10	7				11	1		3	46

FA Cup

Third Round	Charlton Ath	(h)	2-4

Carling Cup

First Round	Stockport Co	(a)	4-2
Second Round	West Ham U	(h)	2-4

SHREWSBURY TOWN FL Championship 2

FOUNDATION

Shrewsbury School having provided a number of the early England and Wales international players it is not surprising that there was a Town club as early as 1876 which won the Birmingham Senior Cup in 1879. However, the present Shrewsbury Town club was formed in 1886 and won the Welsh FA Cup as early as 1891.

Gay Meadow, Abbey Foregate, Shrewsbury, Shropshire SY2 6AB.

Telephone: (01743) 360 111.

Fax: (01743) 236 384.

Ticket Office: (01743) 360 111.

Website: www.shrewsburytown.com

Email: info@shrewsburytown.co.uk

Ground Capacity: 8,000.

Record Attendance: 18,917 v Walsall, Division 3, 26 April 1961.

Pitch Measurements: 114yd × 73yd.

Chairman: Roland E. Wycherley.

Vice-chairman: Keith J. Sayfritz.

Secretary: John W. Howarth.

Manager: Gary Peters.

First Team Coach: TBC.

Physio: Rachel Greenley MCSP.

Colours: Blue and amber.

Change Colours: Red and black.

Year Formed: 1886.

Turned Professional: 1896.

Ltd Co.: 1936.

HONOURS

Football League: Division 2 best season: 8th, 1983–84, 1984–85; Division 3 – Champions 1978–79, 1993–94; Division 4 – Runners-up 1974–75.

Conference: Promotion 2003–04 (play-offs)

FA Cup: best season: 6th rd, 1979, 1982.

Football League Cup: Semi-final 1961.

Welsh Cup: Winners 1891, 1938, 1977, 1979, 1984, 1985; Runners-up 1931, 1948, 1980.

Auto Windscreens Shield: Runners-up 1996

Club Nickname: 'Town', 'Blues' or 'Salop'. The name 'Salop' is a colloquialism for the county of Shropshire. Since Shrewsbury is the only club in Shropshire, cries of 'Come on Salop' are frequently used!

Previous Ground: 1886, Old Shrewsbury Racecourse; 1910, Gay Meadow.

First Football League Game: 19 August 1950, Division 3 (N), v Scunthorpe U (a) D 0–0 – Egglestone; Fisher, Lewis; Wheatley, Depear, Robinson; Griffin, Hope, Jackson, Brown, Barker.

Record League Victory: 7–0 v Swindon T, Division 3 (S), 6 May 1955 – McBride; Bannister, Skeech; Wallace, Maloney, Candlin; Price, O'Donnell (1), Weigh (4), Russell, McCue (2).

SKY SPORTS FACT FILE

On 17 February 1951 former England right-winger Sammy Crooks took over as player-manager of Shrewsbury Town at 42. Made his debut in a 3–1 friendly win over Western Command and later sold Frank Griffin to West Bromwich Albion for £10,000.

Record Cup Victory: 11–2 v Marine, FA Cup 1st rd, 11 November 1995 – Edwards, Seabury (Dempsey (1)), Withe (1), Evans (1), Whiston (2), Scott (1), Woods, Stevens (1), Spink (3) (Anthrobus), Walton, Berkley, (1 og).

Record Defeat: 1–8 v Norwich C, Division 3 (S), 13 September 1952. 1–8 v Coventry C, Division 3, 22 October 1963.

Most League Points (2 for a win): 62, Division 4, 1974–75.

Most League Points (3 for a win): 79, Division 3, 1993–94.

Most League Goals: 101, Division 4, 1958–59.

Highest League Scorer in Season: Arthur Rowley, 38, Division 4, 1958–59.

Most League Goals in Total Aggregate: Arthur Rowley, 152, 1958–65 (thus completing his League record of 434 goals).

Most League Goals in One Match: 5, Alf Wood v Blackburn R, Division 3, 2 October 1971.

Most Capped Player: Jimmy McLaughlin, 5 (12), Northern Ireland; Bernard McNally, 5, Northern Ireland.

Most League Appearances: Mickey Brown, 418, 1986–91; 1992–94; 1996–2001.

Youngest League Player: Graham French, 16 years 177 days v Reading, 30 September 1961.

Record Transfer Fee Received: £500,000 from Crewe Alex for Dave Walton, December 1997.

Record Transfer Fee Paid: £100,000 to Aldershot for John Dungworth, November 1979 and £100,000 to Southampton for Mark Blake, August 1990.

Football League Record: 1950 Elected to Division 3 (N); 1951–58 Division 3 (S); 1958–59 Division 4; 1959–74 Division 3; 1974–75 Division 4; 1975–79 Division 3; 1979–89 Division 2; 1989–94 Division 3; 1994–97 Division 2; 1997–2003 Division 3; 2003–04 Conference; 2004– FL2.

MANAGERS

W. Adams 1905–12
(Secretary-Manager)
A. Weston 1912–34
(Secretary-Manager)
Jack Roscamp 1934–35
Sam Ramsey 1935–36
Ted Bousted 1936–40
Leslie Knighton 1945–49
Harry Chapman 1949–50
Sammy Crooks 1950–54
Walter Rowley 1955–57
Harry Potts 1957–58
Johnny Spuhler 1958
Arthur Rowley 1958–68
Harry Gregg 1968–72
Maurice Evans 1972–73
Alan Durban 1974–78
Richie Barker 1978
Graham Turner 1978–84
Chic Bates 1984–87
Ian McNeill 1987–90
Asa Hartford 1990–91
John Bond 1991–93
Fred Davies 1994–97
(previously Caretaker-Manager 1993–94)
Jake King 1997–99
Kevin Ratcliffe 1999–2003
Jimmy Quinn 2003–04
Gary Peters November 2004–

LATEST SEQUENCES

Longest Sequence of League Wins: 7, 28.10.1995 – 16.12.1995.

Longest Sequence of League Defeats: 11, 9.4.2003 – 14.8.2004.

Longest Sequence of League Draws: 6, 30.10.1963 – 14.12.1963.

Longest Sequence of Unbeaten League Matches: 16, 30.10.1993 – 26.2.1994.

Longest Sequence Without a League Win: 18, 8.3.2003 – 14.8.2004.

Successive Scoring Runs: 28 from 7.9.1960.

Successive Non-scoring Runs: 6 from 1.1.1991.

TEN YEAR LEAGUE RECORD

		P	*W*	*D*	*L*	*F*	*A*	*Pts*	*Pos*
1996-97	Div 2	46	11	13	22	49	74	46	22
1997-98	Div 3	46	16	13	17	61	62	61	13
1998-99	Div 3	46	14	14	18	52	63	56	15
1999-2000	Div 3	46	9	13	24	40	67	40	22
2000-01	Div 3	46	15	10	21	49	65	55	15
2001-02	Div 3	46	20	10	16	64	53	70	9
2002-03	Div 3	46	9	14	23	62	92	41	24
2003-04	Conf.	42	20	14	8	67	42	74	3
2004-05	FL 2	46	11	16	19	48	53	49	21
2005-06	FL 2	46	16	13	17	55	55	61	10

DID YOU KNOW ?

In 1960–61 Shrewsbury Town created a then record for the number of competitive domestic matches played by a Football League club in one season. In addition to their 46 League fixtures, they appeared in five FA Cup and eight League Cup games. Total: 59.

SHREWSBURY TOWN 2005–06 LEAGUE RECORD

Match No.	Date	Venue	Opponents	Result		H/T Score	Lg. Pos.	Goalscorers	Attendance
1	Aug 6	H	Rochdale	L	0-1	0-1	—		4927
2	10	A	Boston U	D	1-1	0-0	—	Smith [69]	2409
3	13	A	Bury	L	0-2	0-0	23		2261
4	20	H	Northampton T	D	1-1	1-0	21	Edwards [6]	3562
5	27	H	Wycombe W	D	1-1	0-1	21	McMenamin [85]	3533
6	29	A	Leyton Orient	W	1-0	1-0	17	McMenamin (pen) [3]	3742
7	Sept 2	H	Oxford U	W	2-0	2-0	—	McMenamin (pen) [8], Tolley [19]	4073
8	10	A	Torquay U	L	1-2	1-2	15	Langmead [28]	2287
9	17	H	Notts Co	W	2-0	2-0	12	McMenamin [21], Walton [45]	4011
10	24	A	Peterborough U	W	2-0	0-0	8	Sorvel [55], Darby [83]	4274
11	27	H	Barnet	D	2-2	1-2	—	McMenamin (pen) [12], Herd [90]	3628
12	Oct 1	H	Grimsby T	D	0-0	0-0	9		4607
13	7	A	Mansfield T	L	0-4	0-1	—		3334
14	15	H	Stockport Co	D	2-2	1-1	13	Walton [45], Langmead [90]	4316
15	22	A	Rushden & D	L	0-3	0-0	16		2954
16	29	H	Chester C	W	3-1	2-1	14	McMenamin [1], Stallard [8], Langmead [58]	5430
17	Nov 12	A	Lincoln C	D	1-1	1-0	13	Tolley [18]	3748
18	26	A	Rochdale	L	3-4	3-1	14	McMenamin [3], Cowan [9], Stallard [42]	2843
19	Dec 6	H	Darlington	W	3-1	1-1	—	Stallard [8], Sorvel [51], Ashton [68]	2469
20	10	H	Boston U	D	1-1	1-0	—	Hope [2]	3376
21	17	A	Northampton T	L	0-1	0-0	17		5380
22	26	A	Bristol R	L	1-2	0-2	19	Darby [50]	7551
23	31	A	Cheltenham T	L	0-1	0-0	21		3474
24	Jan 3	H	Wrexham	W	1-0	0-0	—	Hurst [72]	6249
25	7	A	Oxford U	W	3-0	0-0	15	Langmead [65], Herd [83], Tolley [90]	3702
26	14	H	Carlisle U	W	2-1	1-1	14	McMenamin (pen) [32], Sharp (pen) [75]	4493
27	17	H	Mansfield T	D	0-0	0-0	—		3747
28	21	A	Notts Co	L	1-2	0-2	14	Langmead [88]	5438
29	28	H	Torquay U	L	0-1	0-0	16		3741
30	31	H	Macclesfield T	D	1-1	0-1	—	Burton (pen) [50]	2642
31	Feb 4	A	Barnet	L	0-1	0-1	15		1789
32	11	H	Peterborough U	W	2-1	0-1	14	Sorvel [60], Langmead [87]	3295
33	14	A	Carlisle U	D	2-2	1-1	—	Sorvel [12], Hope [72]	5568
34	18	A	Darlington	W	1-0	0-0	12	McMenamin [55]	3898
35	25	H	Bury	L	0-1	0-1	13		3586
36	Mar 4	H	Leyton Orient	D	3-3	3-2	12	Stallard [39], Edwards [41], Burton [45]	3471
37	11	A	Wycombe W	L	0-2	0-1	14		5035
38	18	H	Bristol R	W	1-0	0-0	13	Hurst [73]	3641
39	25	A	Macclesfield T	L	0-2	0-1	13		2274
40	Apr 1	H	Cheltenham T	W	2-0	1-0	13	Langmead 2 [32, 75]	3724
41	9	A	Wrexham	W	2-1	2-0	12	Lawrence (og) [3], McMenamin (pen) [15]	6310
42	15	A	Grimsby T	D	1-1	1-0	11	Burton [27]	5935
43	18	H	Rushden & D	W	4-1	2-0	—	Stallard 2 [7, 55], Tolley [36], Burton [81]	4239
44	22	A	Stockport Co	L	1-3	0-1	11	Hurst [64]	5831
45	29	H	Lincoln C	L	0-1	0-0	13		5170
46	May 6	A	Chester C	W	1-0	1-0	10	Langmead [9]	3744

Final League Position: 10

GOALSCORERS

League (55): McMenamin 10 (5 pens), Langmead 9, Stallard 6, Burton 4 (1 pen), Sorvel 4, Tolley 4, Hurst 3, Darby 2, Edwards 2, Herd 2, Hope 2, Walton 2, Ashton 1, Cowan 1, Sharp 1 (pen), Smith 1, own goal 1.
Carling Cup (3): Denny 2, Stallard 1.
FA Cup (5): Edwards 2, Hope 1, McMenamin 1 (pen), Tolley 1.
Football League Trophy (0).

Hart J 46	Herd B 45 + 1	Sharp K 27 + 3	Ashton N 39 + 5	Walton D 15 + 1	Cowan G 9 + 6	Denny J 7 + 7	Sorvel N 44 + 1	Stallard M 25 + 12	McMenamin C 40 + 3	Smith B 9 + 3	Hogg S 7 + 5	Langmead K 29 + 13	Tolley J 30 + 6	Whitehead S 20 + 3	Edwards D 27 + 3	Hope R 42	Darby D 7 + 4	Jackson M 2 + 3	Lyng C — + 1	Hurst G 15 + 1	Evans R 2 + 4	Burton S 15 + 1	Cadwallader G — + 2	Adaggio M — + 5	McClen J 4	Leslie S — + 1	*Match No.*
1	2	3	4^{1}	5	6	7^{2}	8	9	10^{3}	11	12	13	14														1
1	2	3	4^{2}	5	6^{1}	7	8	9	13	11^{3}			10	12	14												2
1	2	3	13	5		7	8	9^{1}	10	11^{2}		12	4^{3}	6	14												3
1	2	3	12^{2}	5		13	8	9^{3}	10	11		14	4	6	7^{1}												4
1	2	3	12	5		13	8	9^{3}	10	11^{1}	7^{2}	14	4			6											5
1	14	12	4^{2}	5		7	8		10		13	9^{3}	6	2	11^{1}	3											6
1	2	3	12	5		13	7	14	10	11^{2}		9^{3}	8		4^{1}	6											7
1	2	3	4^{1}	5		12	7	9^{2}	10	13	14	11	8^{3}			6											8
1	2	3	12	5		13	8	9^{1}	10	7^{2}		11■	4			6											9
1	2	3	4	5		12	8	9^{2}	10				7^{1}	11		6	13										10
1	2	3	4	5		7^{1}	8	13	10				11■	12		6	9^{2}										11
1	2	3	4	5		7^{1}	8	13	10	14		11^{2}		12		6	9^{3}										12
1	2^{2}	3	4	5		7	8	12	10			13		11		6	9^{1}										13
1	2	3	4	5			8		10	7		11				6	9^{1}	12									14
1	2	3		5			8	12	10	13		11^{1}	4			6	9^{2}	7									15
1	2		3				8^{2}	9^{1}	10	11	14	12	4	5	13	6		7^{3}									16
1	2		4		6				10			11	8	3	7	5	9										17
1	2		4		6		8	9	10				7	3	11	5											18
1	2^{1}		3	12			8	9^{2}	10			11	7	5	4	6	13										19
1	2	3					8	9^{1}	10			11	7	5	4	6	12										20
1	2		3				8	9^{2}	10^{1}			11	7	5	4	6		12	13								21
1	2	3	4		12	13	8^{2}		10^{3}			11		5	7	6^{1}	9	14									22
1	2	3^{1}	4^{2}		12		8	9^{3}	10			14	7	5	11	6	13										23
1	2	3	4				8		10			12	7	5	11	6				9^{1}							24
1	2	3	4				8		10^{1}			12	7	5	11	6				9							25
1	2	3	4				8	12	10^{2}			13	7	5	11	6				9^{1}							26
1	2	3^{1}	4		12		8	13	10			14	7	5	11^{3}	6				9^{2}							27
1	2	3^{2}	4				8	9^{1}	10			12	7	5^{3}	11	6					13	14					28
1	2	3	4^{1}		12		8		10^{2}			11			7	6				9	13	5					29
1	2		3				8		12			11	7		4	6				9	10^{1}	5					30
1	2	3^{1}	4				8	12	13			10^{2}	7		11	6				9		5					31
1	2		4		12		8	13	10			14	7^{1}		3	6				9^{2}	11^{3}	5					32
1	2■	3	4		6		8	9^{1}	10		7	11				5							12				33
1	2	3	4		6		8	9	10			11	12			7						5^{1}					34
1	2	3	7		6^{1}		8^{2}	9	10			11	12			4						5		13			35
1	2		3		6^{1}		8	9^{2}	10			11	12		7	4						5		13			36
1	2^{1}		3		12		8	9^{2}	10			11			4	6						5		13	7		37
1	2	12	3		6^{2}		13		10		8^{3}	9		5	7	4				14					11^{1}		38
1	2		3				8	12	10		13	11^{1}		5	7	6				9					4^{2}		39
1	2	12	3				8	13	10			11			7	6				9^{2}		5			4^{1}		40
1	2		3				8	12	10■		4^{2}	11	13		7	6				9^{1}		5					41
1	2		3				8	9			4	11	12		7^{1}	6				10^{2}		5	13				42
1	2		3^{2}				8	9^{1}			4	11	7			6				10		5		12		13	43
1	2		3				8	9			4^{1}	11	7			6				10	12	5					44
1	2		3				8	9	7^{1}			11	4			6				10^{2}	12	5		13			45
1	2		3				8	9	10			11	7		4	6						5					46

FA Cup

First Round	Braintree T	(h)	4-1
Second Round	Colchester U	(h)	1-2

Carling Cup

First Round	Brighton & HA	(h)	3-2
Second Round	Sheffield U	(h)	0-0

Football League Trophy

First Round	Cheltenham T	(h)	0-2

SOUTHAMPTON FL Championship

FOUNDATION

Formed largely by players from the Deanery FC, which had been established by school teachers in 1880. Most of the founders were connected with the young men's association of St Mary's Church. At the inaugural meeting held in November 1885 the club was named Southampton St Mary's and the church's curate was elected president.

St Mary's Stadium, Britannia Road, Southampton SO14 5FP.

Telephone: 0870 220 0000.

Fax: (02380) 727 727.

Ticket Office: 0870 220 0150.

Website: www.saintsfc.co.uk

Email: sfc@saintsfc.co.uk

Ground Capacity: 32,689.

Record Attendance: 32,104 v Liverpool, FA Premier League, 18 January 2003.

Pitch Measurements: 112yd × 72yd.

Chairman of SFC Ltd: Michael Wilde.

Chairman: Ken Dulieu.

Chief Executive: Jim Hone.

Secretary: Liz Coley.

Manager: George Burley.

Assistant Manager: Malcolm Webster.

Physio: TBC.

Colours: Red and white striped shirts, black shorts, white stockings.

Change Colours: Black shirts, red shorts, black and red stockings.

Year Formed: 1885.

Turned Professional: 1894.

Ltd Co.: 1897.

Previous Name: 1885, Southampton St Mary's; 1897, Southampton.

Club Nickname: 'The Saints'.

Previous Grounds: 1885, Antelope Ground; 1897, County Cricket Ground; 1898, The Dell; 2001, St Mary's.

First Football League Game: 28 August 1920, Division 3, v Gillingham (a) D 1–1 – Allen; Parker, Titmuss; Shelley, Campbell, Turner; Barratt, Dominy (1), Rawlings, Moore, Foxall.

Record League Victory: 9–3 v Wolverhampton W, Division 2, 18 September 1965 – Godfrey; Jones, Williams; Walker, Knapp, Huxford; Paine (2), O'Brien (1), Melia, Chivers (4), Sydenham (2).

HONOURS

Football League: Division 1 – Runners-up 1983–84; Division 2 – Runners-up 1965–66, 1977–78; Division 3 (S) – Champions 1921–22; Runners-up 1920–21; Division 3 – Champions 1959–60.

FA Cup: Winners 1976; Runners-up 1900, 1902, 2003.

Football League Cup: Runners-up 1979.

Zenith Data Systems Cup: Runners-up 1992.

European Competitions: *European Fairs Cup:* 1969–70. *UEFA Cup:* 1971–72, 1981–82, 1982–83, 1984–85, 2003–04. *European Cup-Winners' Cup:* 1976–77.

SKY SPORTS FACT FILE

Theo Walcott was not only the youngest player to appear for Southampton first team but also their youngest goalscorer on 18 October 2005 at Leeds United as well as having been previously the youngest reserves debutant at the age of 15 years 175 days.

Record Cup Victory: 7–1 v Ipswich T, FA Cup 3rd rd, 7 January 1961 – Reynolds; Davies, Traynor; Conner, Page, Huxford; Paine (1), O'Brien (3 incl. 1p), Reeves, Mulgrew (2), Penk (1).

Record Defeat: 0–8 v Tottenham H, Division 2, 28 March 1936. 0–8 v Everton, Division 1, 20 November 1971.

Most League Points (2 for a win): 61, Division 3 (S), 1921–22 and Division 3, 1959–60.

Most League Points (3 for a win): 77, Division 1, 1983–84.

Most League Goals: 112, Division 3 (S), 1957–58.

Highest League Scorer in Season: Derek Reeves, 39, Division 3, 1959–60.

Most League Goals in Total Aggregate: Mike Channon, 185, 1966–77, 1979–82.

Most League Goals in One Match: 5, Charlie Wayman v Leicester C, Division 2, 23 October 1948.

Most Capped Player: Peter Shilton, 49 (125), England.

Most League Appearances: Terry Paine, 713, 1956–74.

Youngest League Player: Theo Walcott, 16 years 143 days v Wolverhampton W, 6 August 2005.

Record Transfer Fee Received: £8,000,000 from Tottenham H for Dean Richards, October 2001.

Record Transfer Fee Paid: £4,000,000 to Derby Co for Rory Delap, July 2001.

Football League Record: 1920 Original Member of Division 3; 1921–22 Division 3 (S); 1922–53 Division 2; 1953–58 Division 3 (S); 1958–60 Division 3; 1960–66 Division 2; 1966–74 Division 1; 1974–78 Division 2; 1978–92 Division 1; 1992–2005 FA Premier League; 2005– FLC.

MANAGERS

Cecil Knight 1894–95
(Secretary-Manager)
Charles Robson 1895–97
E. Arnfield 1897–1911
(Secretary-Manager)
(continued as Secretary)
George Swift 1911–12
Ernest Arnfield 1912–19
Jimmy McIntyre 1919–24
Arthur Chadwick 1925–31
George Kay 1931–36
George Gross 1936–37
Tom Parker 1937–43
J. R. Sarjantson stepped down from the board to act as Secretary-Manager 1943–47 with the next two listed being team Managers during this period
Arthur Dominy 1943–46
Bill Dodgin Snr 1946–49
Sid Cann 1949–51
George Roughton 1952–55
Ted Bates 1955–73
Lawrie McMenemy 1973–85
Chris Nicholl 1985–91
Ian Branfoot 1991–94
Alan Ball 1994–95
Dave Merrington 1995–96
Graeme Souness 1996–97
Dave Jones 1997–2000
Glenn Hoddle 2000–01
Stuart Gray 2001
Gordon Strachan 2001–04
Paul Sturrock 2004
Steve Wigley 2004
Harry Redknapp 2004–05
George Burley December 2005–

LATEST SEQUENCES

Longest Sequence of League Wins: 6, 3.3.1992 – 4.4.1992.

Longest Sequence of League Defeats: 5, 16.8.1998 – 12.9.1998.

Longest Sequence of League Draws: 8, 29.8.2005 – 15.10.2005.

Longest Sequence of Unbeaten League Matches: 19, 5.9.1921 – 31.12.1921.

Longest Sequence Without a League Win: 20, 30.8.1969 – 27.12.1969.

Successive Scoring Runs: 24 from 5.9.1966.

Successive Non-scoring Runs: 5 from 1.9.1937.

TEN YEAR LEAGUE RECORD

		P	W	D	L	F	A	Pts	Pos
1996-97	PR Lge	38	10	11	17	50	56	41	16
1997-98	PR Lge	38	14	6	18	50	55	48	12
1998-99	PR Lge	38	11	8	19	37	64	41	17
1999-2000	PR Lge	38	12	8	18	45	62	44	15
2000-01	PR Lge	38	14	10	14	40	48	52	10
2001-02	PR Lge	38	12	9	17	46	54	45	11
2002-03	PR Lge	38	13	13	12	43	46	52	8
2003-04	PR Lge	38	12	11	15	44	45	47	12
2004-05	PR Lge	38	6	14	18	45	66	32	20
2005-06	FL C	46	13	19	14	49	50	58	12

DID YOU KNOW ?

George Reader made his one appearance for Exeter City in 1919–20 and scored against Southampton for whom he subsequently played. A former schoolmaster, he became a referee officiating at the 1950 World Cup Final, then Saints director and chairman.

SOUTHAMPTON 2005–06 LEAGUE RECORD

Match No.	Date	Venue	Opponents	Result		H/T Score	Lg. Pos.	Goalscorers	Attendance
1	Aug 6	H	Wolverhampton W	D	0-0	0-0	—		24,061
2	9	A	Luton T	L	2-3	2-1	—	Oakley [18], Jones [45]	9447
3	13	A	Sheffield W	W	1-0	1-0	10	Jones [22]	26,688
4	20	H	Norwich C	W	1-0	1-0	8	Quashie (pen) [15]	23,498
5	27	H	Crewe Alex	W	2-0	1-0	5	Belmadi [11], Quashie [66]	20,792
6	29	A	Coventry C	D	1-1	1-1	5	Fuller [12]	23,000
7	Sept 10	H	QPR	D	1-1	1-1	5	Higginbotham [37]	25,744
8	13	A	Ipswich T	D	2-2	0-1	—	Powell [50], Wise [69]	22,997
9	18	A	Derby Co	D	2-2	0-0	6	Ormerod [58], Fuller [90]	22,348
10	24	H	Plymouth Arg	D	0-0	0-0	7		26,331
11	28	H	Reading	D	0-0	0-0	—		24,946
12	Oct 1	A	Preston NE	D	1-1	1-0	7	Davidson (og) [27]	15,263
13	15	H	Hull C	D	1-1	1-0	8	Oakley [44]	23,810
14	18	A	Leeds U	L	1-2	1-2	—	Walcott [25]	18,881
15	22	A	Millwall	W	2-0	2-0	9	Walcott [18], Fuller [25]	10,759
16	29	H	Stoke C	W	2-0	1-0	7	Walcott [16], Belmadi [90]	24,095
17	Nov 5	A	Leicester C	D	0-0	0-0	6		21,318
18	19	H	Leeds U	L	3-4	3-0	11	Pahars [27], Quashie 2 (1 pen) [35, 45 (p)]	30,173
19	22	A	Hull C	D	1-1	1-1	—	Kosowski [6]	18,061
20	26	A	Wolverhampton W	D	0-0	0-0	12		24,628
21	Dec 3	H	Burnley	D	1-1	1-0	12	Higginbotham (pen) [34]	21,592
22	11	H	Luton T	W	1-0	1-0	12	Walcott [23]	19,086
23	17	A	Norwich C	L	1-3	1-1	12	Belmadi [9]	24,836
24	26	A	Watford	L	0-3	0-2	13		16,972
25	28	H	Sheffield U	L	0-1	0-0	14		27,443
26	31	A	Cardiff C	L	1-2	1-2	15	Blackstock [25]	13,377
27	Jan 2	H	Brighton & HA	W	2-1	1-1	14	Blackstock 2 [10, 86]	24,630
28	14	A	QPR	L	0-1	0-0	14		15,494
29	21	H	Ipswich T	L	0-2	0-1	16		22,250
30	25	H	Crystal Palace	D	0-0	0-0	—		24,651
31	31	A	Plymouth Arg	L	1-2	0-1	—	Surman [70]	15,936
32	Feb 4	H	Derby Co	D	0-0	0-0	17		21,829
33	10	A	Reading	L	0-2	0-2	—		23,845
34	15	H	Preston NE	D	0-0	0-0	—		19,534
35	25	H	Sheffield W	W	3-0	0-0	17	Higginbotham [34], Rasiak [49], Jones [55]	26,236
36	Mar 4	H	Coventry C	D	1-1	0-0	17	Rasiak [81]	21,980
37	11	A	Crewe Alex	D	1-1	0-0	18	Madsen [61]	6588
38	20	H	Watford	L	1-3	0-1	—	Madsen [85]	19,202
39	25	A	Sheffield U	L	0-3	0-2	20		22,824
40	28	A	Burnley	D	1-1	1-1	—	Bardsley (og) [1]	10,636
41	Apr 1	H	Cardiff C	W	3-2	0-0	19	Lundekvam [47], Fuller 2 [70, 75]	22,388
42	8	A	Brighton & HA	W	2-0	1-0	17	Fuller [37], Chaplow [63]	7999
43	15	A	Stoke C	W	2-1	2-0	15	Rasiak 2 (1 pen) [24 (p), 31]	16,501
44	17	H	Millwall	W	2-0	1-0	12	Jones (pen) [13], Fuller [90]	22,043
45	22	A	Crystal Palace	L	1-2	0-0	13	Fuller [69]	20,995
46	30	H	Leicester C	W	2-0	2-0	12	Fuller [22], Surman [25]	26,801

Final League Position: 12

GOALSCORERS

League (49): Fuller 9, Jones 4 (1 pen), Quashie 4 (2 pens), Rasiak 4 (1 pen), Walcott 4, Belmadi 3, Blackstock 3, Higginbotham 3 (1 pen), Madsen 2, Oakley 2, Surman 2, Chaplow 1, Kosowski 1, Lundekvam 1, Ormerod 1, Pahars 1, Powell 1, Wise 1, own goals 2.
Carling Cup (3): Blackstock 1, Dyer 1, Ormerod 1.
FA Cup (5): Jones 1, Kenton 1, Prutton 1, Quashie 1, Walcott.

Niemi A 25	Hajto T 15 + 5	Higginbotham D 37	Oakley M 29	Lundekvam C 34	Powell D 24 + 1	Prutton D 14 + 3	Quashie N 24	Jones K 17 + 17	Fuller R 21 + 9	Belmadi D 21 + 1	Walcott T 13 + 8	Delap R 12 + 4 / Bale G 2	Wise D 8 + 3	Blackstock D 7 + 12	Cranie M 7 + 4	Ormerod B 13 + 6 / McGoldrick D 1	Dyer N 10 + 7	Kosowski K 12 + 6	McCann N 7 + 4	Pahars M 5 + 3	Svensson M 7	Kenton D 12 + 1	Folly Y 2	Baird C 16 + 1	Best L 1 + 2	Smith P 9	Mills J 3 + 1	Bialkowski B 5	Surman A 11 + 1	Brennan J 13 + 1	Potter D 8 + 2	Ostlund A 10 + 2	Madsen P 8 + 1	Chaplow R 11	Rasiak G 12 + 1	Wright J 13	Miller K 7	*Match No.*
1	2	3	4	5■	6	7	8	9^1	10^2	11^3	12	13	14																									1
1	2	3	4		6	7^1	8	9^2	10		12	5	11	13																								2
1	2	3	4	5	6	7	8	9^2		11	12	13		10^1																								3
1	2	3	4	5^3	6	7	8	9^1	10^2	11	12			13	14																							4
1	2	3	4	5	6	7	8	9^2	10^1	11						13	12																					5
1	2	3	4	5	6	7	8		10	11				12		9^1																						6
1	2	3	4^1	5	6	7^3	8	9^2	10	11			12			13		14																				7
1	2	3	4	5	6		8		10^2		12		11	13		9		7^1																				8
1	2■	3	4	5	6		8	12	10^2			13	11			9^1		7^3	14																			9
1	2^1	3	4^3	5	6		8	12	10		13		11		14	9^2		7																				10
1	2	3	4	5	6		8	9^1	10				11			12		7^2		13																		11
1	2	3	4		6		8	12	10				11			9^1		7^2		13	5																	12
1	2	3	4	5			8		10^2	11	12			13		9		7^1			6																	13
1	6^2	3	4	5			8	12	10^1	7^3	9	13			2			14	11																			14
1		3	4^2	5			8	12	10^1	7	9^3		13		2			14	11		6																	15
1		3		5			8	12	10^1	7	9	2	4						11		6																	16
1		3	4	5			8		10^1	7	9	2						12	11^2	13	6																	17
1	12	3	4	5^1			8		13		10	2	11^2			9			14	7^3	6																	18
1	12	3	4		5		8■		13	11	10	2				9^2		7^1			6																	19
1		3	4		5			12	13	11^2	10^1	2				9		7^3	14			6	8															20
1		3	4		5	8		12	13	11^3	10^1	2				9^2		7	14			6																21
1		3	4		5	8		9^1			10^2	2■			12			7^3	11			6		14	13													22
1		3	4		5	8		9^1	12	7^2	10^3				2	13			11			6			14													23
	12		4^1			11	8		13		10	5			3	9^2	7							2		1	6											24
	12				5^1		8	10		11^3	13	4		14	3	9^2	7							2		1	6											25
1						7		10^1			9	4		8	3	12			11			5		2			6											26
1	5					12	8			11				10	3^1	13	7					6^3	4	2	9^2		14											27
		3	4	5	6	7	8	12	13	11	9			10^1			2^2									1												28
	12	3	7	5	6^1	13	8	14		11^2		2^3		9						10		4				1												29
		3	4	5		7		10^1						12		9^2	13			8		6		2				1	11									30
		6	4	5				12						10			7			9^1		13		2				1	11	3^2	8							31
		6	4	5				9^1	12					13			14	7^3										1	11	3	8	2	10^2					32
		3		5	6			12									7^2											1	13		8	2	10^1	4	9	11		33
		6		5^1	12									13			14											1	11	3	8^3	2	10^2	4	9	7		34
		6	4^2	5				10						12			13									1			11	3		2		8	9^1	7		35
		6		5				10^1						12			7									1			11	3	13	2^2		4	9	8		36
		6		5										8^1				12						2		1			11	3			10	4	9	7		37
		6						12										13				5		7		1			11	3		2	10	4^1	9	8^2		38
		6		5				9						12			13	8^1						7		1			11	3		2	10^2	4				39
		4		5				12														6		7						3	13	2^2	10^1	8	9	11	1	40
		3		5				12	10^1	13												6		2						11			7^2	4	9	8	1	41
				5	6				10	11														7						3		2^1	12	4	9	8	1	42
				5	6				10	11^1							12							7						3	2	13		4^2	9	8	1	43
				5	6^2			10	12			3				9^1	7			11^3				2						13	4				14	8	1	44
				5				12	10								7					6^2		2					11	3	4	13			9^1	8	1	45
				5^2		12		14	10^3			3			13		7							6					11		4^1	2			9	8	1	46

FA Cup

Third Round	Milton Keynes D	(h)	4-3
Fourth Round	Leicester C	(a)	1-0
Fifth Round	Newcastle U	(a)	0-1

Carling Cup

First Round	Southend U	(a)	3-0
Second Round	Mansfield T	(a)	0-1

SOUTHEND UNITED FL Championship

FOUNDATION

The leading club in Southend around the turn of the century was Southend Athletic, but they were an amateur concern. Southend United was a more ambitious professional club when they were founded in 1906, employing Bob Jack as secretary-manager and immediately joining the Second Division of the Southern League.

Roots Hall, Victoria Avenue, Southend-on-Sea, Essex SS2 6NQ.

Telephone: (01702) 304 050.

Fax: (01702) 304 124.

Ticket Office: (08444) 770077.

Website: www.southendunited.co.uk

Email: info@southend-united.co.uk

Ground Capacity: 12,268.

Record Attendance: 31,090 v Liverpool, FA Cup 3rd rd, 10 January 1979.

Pitch Measurements: 110yd × 74yd.

Chairman: Ron Martin.

Chief Executive: Geoffrey King.

Secretary: Mrs Helen Norbury.

Manager: Steve Tilson.

Assistant Manager: Paul Brush.

Physio: John Stannard.

Club Nickname: 'The Blues' or 'The Shrimpers'.

Colours: Navy blue with white panel on sleeve.

Change Colours: White shirts with black sleeves, white shorts, white stockings

Year Formed: 1906.

Turned Professional: 1906. ***Ltd Co.:*** 1919.

Previous Grounds: 1906, Roots Hall, Prittlewell; 1920, Kursaal; 1934, Southend Stadium; 1955, Roots Hall Football Ground.

First Football League Game: 28 August 1920, Division 3, v Brighton & HA (a) W 2–0 – Capper; Reid, Newton; Wileman, Henderson, Martin; Nicholls, Nuttall, Fairclough (2), Myers, Dorsett.

Record League Victory: 9–2 v Newport Co, Division 3 (S), 5 September 1936 – McKenzie; Nelson, Everest (1); Deacon, Turner, Carr; Bolan, Lane (1), Goddard (4), Dickinson (2), Oswald (1).

Record Cup Victory: 10–1 v Golders Green, FA Cup 1st rd, 24 November 1934 – Moore; Morfitt, Kelly; Mackay, Joe Wilson, Carr (1); Lane (1), Johnson (5), Cheesmuir (2), Deacon (1), Oswald. 10–1 v Brentwood, FA Cup 2nd rd, 7 December 1968 – Roberts; Bentley, Birks; McMillan (1) Beesley, Kurila; Clayton, Chisnall, Moore (4), Best (5), Hamilton. 10–1 v Aldershot, Leyland Daf Cup Prel rd, 6 November 1990 – Sansome; Austin, Powell, Cornwell, Prior (1), Tilson (3), Cawley, Butler, Ansah (1), Benjamin (1), Angell (4).

HONOURS

Football League: Championship 1 – Champions 2005–06; Division 1 best season: 13th, 1994–95; Promoted from Championship 2 2004–05 (play-offs); Division 3 – Runners-up 1990–91; Division 4 – Champions 1980–81; Runners-up 1971–72, 1977–78.

FA Cup: best season: old 3rd rd, 1921; 5th rd, 1926, 1952, 1976, 1993.

Football League Cup: never past 3rd rd.

LDV Vans Trophy: Runners-up 2004, 2005.

SKY SPORTS FACT FILE

On 29 October 2005 Freddy Eastwood celebrated his 22nd birthday with all three Southend United goals at Bristol City. He had hit a hat-trick on his debut for the club on 16 October a year earlier against Swansea City.

Record Defeat: 1–9 v Brighton & HA, Division 3, 27 November 1965.

Most League Points (2 for a win): 67, Division 4, 1980–81.

Most League Points (3 for a win): 85, Division 3, 1990–91.

Most League Goals: 92, Division 3 (S), 1950–51.

Highest League Scorer in Season: Jim Shankly, 31, 1928–29; Sammy McCrory, 1957–58, both in Division 3 (S).

Most League Goals in Total Aggregate: Roy Hollis, 122, 1953–60.

Most League Goals in One Match: 5, Jim Shankly v Merthyr T, Division 3S, 1 March 1930.

Most Capped Player: George Mackenzie, 9, Eire.

Most League Appearances: Sandy Anderson, 452, 1950–63.

Youngest League Player: Phil O'Connor, 16 years 76 days v Lincoln C, 26 December 1969.

Record Transfer Fee Received: £3,570,000 from Nottingham F for Stan Collymore, June 1993.

Record Transfer Fee Paid: £750,000 to Crystal Palace for Stan Collymore, November 1992.

Football League Record: 1920 Original Member of Division 3; 1921–58 Division 3 (S); 1958–66 Division 3; 1966–72 Division 4; 1972–76 Division 3; 1976–78 Division 4; 1978–80 Division 3; 1980–81 Division 4; 1981–84 Division 3; 1984–87 Division 4; 1987–89 Division 3; 1989–90 Division 4; 1990–91 Division 3; 1991–92 Division 2; 1992–97 Division 1; 1997–98 Division 2; 1998–2004 Division 3; 2004–05 FL2; 2005–06 FL1; 2006– FLC.

MANAGERS

Bob Jack 1906–10
George Molyneux 1910–11
O. M. Howard 1911–12
Joe Bradshaw 1912–19
Ned Liddell 1919–20
Tom Mather 1920–21
Ted Birnie 1921–34
David Jack 1934–40
Harry Warren 1946–56
Eddie Perry 1956–60
Frank Broome 1960
Ted Fenton 1961–65
Alvan Williams 1965–67
Ernie Shepherd 1967–69
Geoff Hudson 1969–70
Arthur Rowley 1970–76
Dave Smith 1976–83
Peter Morris 1983–84
Bobby Moore 1984–86
Dave Webb 1986–87
Dick Bate 1987
Paul Clark 1987–88
Dave Webb *(General Manager)* 1988–92
Colin Murphy 1992–93
Barry Fry 1993
Peter Taylor 1993–95
Steve Thompson 1995
Ronnie Whelan 1995–97
Alvin Martin 1997–99
Alan Little 1999–2000
David Webb 2000–01
Rob Newman 2001–03
Steve Wignall 2003–04
Steve Tilson May 2004–

LATEST SEQUENCES

Longest Sequence of League Wins: 8, 29.8.2005 – 9.10.2005.

Longest Sequence of League Defeats: 6, 29.8.1987 – 19.9.1987.

Longest Sequence of League Draws: 6, 30.1.1982 – 19.2.1982.

Longest Sequence of Unbeaten League Matches: 16, 20.2.1932 – 29.8.1932.

Longest Sequence Without a League Win: 17, 31.12.1983 – 14.4.1984.

Successive Scoring Runs: 24 from 23.3.1929.

Successive Non-scoring Runs: 6 from 28.10.1933.

TEN YEAR LEAGUE RECORD

		P	*W*	*D*	*L*	*F*	*A*	*Pts*	*Pos*
1996-97	Div 1	46	8	15	23	42	86	39	24
1997-98	Div 2	46	11	10	25	47	79	43	24
1998-99	Div 3	46	14	12	20	52	58	54	18
1999-2000	Div 3	46	15	11	20	53	61	56	16
2000-01	Div 3	46	15	18	13	55	53	63	11
2001-02	Div 3	46	15	13	18	51	54	58	12
2002-03	Div 3	46	17	3	26	47	59	54	17
2003-04	Div 3	46	14	12	20	51	63	54	17
2004-05	FL 2	46	22	12	12	65	46	78	4
2005-06	FL 1	46	23	13	10	72	43	82	1

DID YOU KNOW ?

Southend United set a new club record in 2005–06 with eight successive wins in League games. Their previous equal best had occurred from 27 April 1990 when they had started a seven consecutive sequence with a 2–0 success over Halifax Town.

SOUTHEND UNITED 2005–06 LEAGUE RECORD

Match No.	Date	Venue	Opponents	Result		H/T Score	Lg. Pos.	Goalscorers	Attendance
1	Aug 6	H	Port Vale	L	1-2	0-2	—	Gray [72]	6543
2	9	A	Bradford C	W	2-0	1-0	—	Wetherall (og) [15], Guttridge [62]	8250
3	13	A	Walsall	D	2-2	0-0	10	Gray [49], Goater [89]	5569
4	20	H	Huddersfield T	D	1-1	1-1	11	Eastwood [14]	5567
5	26	A	Scunthorpe U	L	0-1	0-1	—		5569
6	29	H	Colchester U	W	3-1	2-1	12	Goater 2 [3, 78], Cole [30]	7344
7	Sept 4	H	Oldham Ath	W	2-1	2-0	8	Lawson [11], Gower [45]	5261
8	10	A	Swindon T	W	2-1	1-0	6	Barrett [2], Gray [88]	4785
9	17	H	Tranmere R	W	3-1	2-0	3	Lawson [16], Goater 2 (1 pen) [33 (p), 82]	6691
10	24	A	Rotherham U	W	4-2	2-2	2	Bentley [18], Barrett [26], Gray 2 (1 pen) [84, 88 (p)]	4259
11	27	H	Yeovil T	W	4-1	0-1	—	Guttridge [60], Gray [69], Eastwood 2 [89, 90]	6654
12	Oct 1	A	Gillingham	W	2-1	0-0	2	Bentley 2 [56, 70]	8128
13	9	H	Nottingham F	W	1-0	0-0	—	Eastwood [81]	10,104
14	15	A	Doncaster R	L	0-2	0-0	2		5899
15	22	H	Barnsley	D	1-1	0-0	1	Goater (pen) [59]	6986
16	29	A	Bristol C	W	3-0	1-0	1	Eastwood 3 [25, 48, 76]	10,625
17	Nov 12	H	Swansea C	L	1-2	0-1	3	Eastwood [81]	11,049
18	19	A	Nottingham F	L	0-2	0-0	3		19,576
19	26	A	Port Vale	L	1-2	0-1	3	Smith [90]	3961
20	Dec 6	H	Chesterfield	D	0-0	0-0	—		5767
21	10	H	Bradford C	D	1-1	1-1	5	Gower [45]	7307
22	17	A	Huddersfield T	D	0-0	0-0	6		11,223
23	26	H	Milton Keynes D	D	0-0	0-0	5		7452
24	28	A	Hartlepool U	W	2-1	1-1	4	Eastwood [32], Gray (pen) [85]	3929
25	31	H	Bournemouth	W	2-1	1-0	2	Gray (pen) [22], Guttridge [78]	6357
26	Jan 2	A	Blackpool	W	2-1	1-0	1	Bentley [39], Eastwood [89]	5271
27	7	A	Oldham Ath	D	0-0	0-0	1		5662
28	14	H	Brentford	W	4-1	2-0	1	Sodje [19], Gower [31], Barrett [63], Wilson [78]	10,046
29	21	A	Tranmere R	D	0-0	0-0	2		7058
30	27	H	Swindon T	W	2-0	2-0	—	Guttridge [31], Gower [32]	7945
31	Feb 4	A	Yeovil T	W	2-0	1-0	1	Bentley [36], Goater [75]	6289
32	10	H	Rotherham U	W	2-0	2-0	—	Goater [12], Eastwood [36]	7879
33	14	A	Brentford	L	0-2	0-2	—		7022
34	18	A	Chesterfield	W	4-3	0-1	1	Eastwood 3 (1 pen) [52 (p), 56, 83], Goater [74]	4527
35	25	H	Walsall	D	0-0	0-0	1		7906
36	Mar 4	A	Colchester U	W	3-0	3-0	1	Eastwood [11], Maher [21], Wilson [32]	5920
37	10	H	Scunthorpe U	W	3-0	1-0	—	Eastwood [7], Bradbury [54], Goater [75]	8717
38	18	A	Milton Keynes D	L	1-2	1-1	1	Goater [13]	7071
39	25	H	Hartlepool U	W	3-0	1-0	1	Gower [1], Eastwood 2 [51, 71]	8496
40	Apr 1	A	Bournemouth	D	1-1	1-0	1	Eastwood [20]	7638
41	8	H	Blackpool	W	2-1	0-1	1	Eastwood [60], Guttridge [86]	8180
42	14	H	Gillingham	L	0-1	0-0	—		11,195
43	17	A	Barnsley	D	2-2	0-2	1	Gower [53], Eastwood [62]	10,663
44	22	H	Doncaster R	L	0-1	0-0	1		10,397
45	29	A	Swansea C	D	2-2	1-2	1	Eastwood 2 [28, 63]	19,176
46	May 6	H	Bristol C	W	1-0	0-0	1	Gray [87]	11,387

Final League Position: 1

GOALSCORERS

League (72): Eastwood 23 (1 pen), Goater 11 (2 pens), Gray 9 (3 pens), Gower 6, Bentley 5, Guttridge 5, Barrett 3, Lawson 2, Wilson 2, Bradbury 1, Cole 1, Maher 1, Smith 1, Sodje 1, own goal 1.
Carling Cup (0).
FA Cup (2): Eastwood 2.
Football League Trophy (0).

Flahavan D 43	Jupp D 29	Wilson C 41 + 3	Maher K 44	Barrett A 45	Prior S 15 + 2	Guttridge L 41	Bentley M 20 + 13	Gray W 23 + 16	Eastwood F 34 + 6	Cole M 19 + 10	Hunt L 23 + 7	Gower M 34 + 6	Lawson J 7 + 16	Edwards A 19 + 1	Pettefer C 5 + 6	Goater S 28 + 6	Smith J 3 + 10	Campbell-Ryce J 7 + 6	Griemink B 3	Sodje E 12 + 1	Ademeno C — + 1	Bradbury L 11 + 4	Moussa F — + 1	*Match No.*
1	2	3	4	5	6^{1}	7^{2}	8	9	10	11^{3}	12	13	14											1
1	2	3	4	5		7^{1}	8^{2}	9	10	11^{3}	13	14		6	12									2
1	2	3	4	5		8^{2}		9	10			11		6	7^{1}	12	13							3
1	2^{2}	3	4	5		8^{1}	12	9	10■		13	11^{3}		6	7	14								4
1		3	4	5		8		9		12	2	11		6	7^{1}	10								5
1		3	4	5		8^{2}	12	9^{3}		11^{1}	2	7	14	6		10	13							6
1		3	4	5	12	8	13			11^{3}	2	7	9^{2}	6		10^{1}	14							7
1		3	4	5	12	8^{3}	14	13		11	2	7	9^{2}	6		10^{1}								8
1		3	4	5		8		12	13	11^{2}	2	7^{1}	9	6		10								9
1		3	4	5		7^{3}	8^{1}	12	13	11	2		9^{2}	6		10	14							10
1		3	4	5		7^{2}	8	9	12	11^{3}	2			6		10^{1}	13	14						11
1		3	4	5		7^{1}	8	9	10	11^{2}	2		13	6			12							12
1		3	4	5		7	8	9^{1}	12	11^{2}	2			6		10		13						13
1		3	4	5		7	8	9^{1}	12	11^{3}	2		13	6		10^{2}		14						14
1		3	4	5		8^{3}		12	9		2	13	7^{2}	6		10	14	11^{1}						15
		3	4	5		8		12	9	11^{2}	2	14	13	6		10^{1}		7^{3}	1					16
		3	4	5		8^{1}	12	13	9	11^{3}	2		14	6		10^{2}		7	1					17
		3	4	5			8^{3}	9	10^{1}	11^{2}	2	13	12	6			14	7	1					18
1		3	4	5			8^{2}	9	10		2	11^{1}	12	6		13	14	7^{3}						19
1		3	4	5	6		12	13	9		2	11^{3}	14			10^{2}	8^{1}	7						20
1		3	4	5	6		12	9	10	13	2	11^{2}	14				8^{1}	7^{3}						21
1	2	3		5	6	7^{1}	8	9		12		11	10^{3}		13		4^{2}	14						22
1	2	3	4	5	6	8^{2}		9^{1}	10	11^{3}		7	12		13			14						23
1	2	3	4	5	6	8^{2}	12	9	10	11^{1}		7						13						24
1	2	3	4	5	6	8	12	9	10^{2}	11^{1}		7^{3}	13		14									25
1	2	3	4	5		7	8	9	12			13	10^{1}	6	11^{2}									26
1	2		4	5	3	7	8	9	10			11		12						6^{1}				27
1	2	12	4	3	6^{1}	7	8	9^{3}	10^{2}			11				13				5	14			28
1	2	12	4	3	6^{1}		8	9^{3}	10^{2}			11	13		7	14				5				29
1	2	3	4	5		7^{1}	8	9^{2}	10	12		11				13				6				30
1	2	12	4	3■	6	7	8		9^{2}		13	11				10^{3}				5^{1}		14		31
1	2	3	4		6	7^{2}	8		9	12		11^{1}			13	10^{3}				5		14		32
1	2		4	3	6	7	8^{1}		9	12		11				10^{2}				5		13		33
1	2	3	4^{2}	5	6	8			9	11^{1}		7	12		13	10^{3}						14		34
1	2	3	4	5	6^{2}	8				11^{1}		7	12			10				13		9		35
1	2	3	4	5		8^{2}			9			11	12			10^{1}				6		7	13	36
1	2	3	4	5		8^{3}		12	9^{1}		13	11				10	14			6^{2}		7		37
1	2	3		5		8	4	12	9			11				10^{1}				6		7		38
1	2	3	4^{1}	5		8^{2}	12	14	9		13	11^{3}				10				6		7		39
1	2	3	4	5		7	8	12	9		13	11				10^{1}				6^{2}				40
1	2	3	4	5		8		12	9	13	6	11^{2}				10^{1}						7		41
1	2	3	4	5		8		9	10	12	6	11^{1}										7		42
1	2	3	4	5		8		12	9		6	11				10^{1}						7		43
1	2	3	4	5		8^{1}	12	13	9	14	6	11^{3}				10^{2}						7		44
1	2	3	4	5		8	12	13	9		6	11				10^{2}						7^{1}		45
1	2	3	4	5		8^{1}	12	13	9	14	6	11^{3}				10^{2}						7		46

FA Cup

First Round	Barnet	(a)	1-0
Second Round	Milton Keynes D	(h)	1-2

Carling Cup

First Round	Southampton	(h)	0-3

Football League Trophy

First Round	Rushden & D	(a)	0-1

STOCKPORT COUNTY FL Championship 2

FOUNDATION

Formed at a meeting held at Wellington Road South by members of Wycliffe Congregational Chapel in 1883, they called themselves Heaton Norris Rovers until changing to Stockport County in 1890, a year before joining the Football Combination.

Edgeley Park, Hardcastle Road, Edgeley, Stockport, Cheshire SK3 9DD.

Telephone: (0161) 286 8888.

Fax: (0161) 286 8900.

Ticket Office: 08712 220 120.

Website: www.stockportcounty.com

Email: fans@stockportcounty.com

Ground Capacity: 10,641.

Record Attendance: 27,833 v Liverpool, FA Cup 5th rd, 11 February 1950.

Pitch Measurements: 104m × 66m.

Chairman (acting): Norman Beverley.

Chief Executive/Secretary: Kevan Taylor.

Manager: Jim Gannon.

Assistant Manager: Peter Ward.

Physio: Rodger Wylde.

Colours: Blue shirts with white chestband, blue shorts, white stockings.

Change Colours: Black and yellow shirts, yellow shorts, yellow stockings.

Year Formed: 1883.

Turned Professional: 1891.

Ltd Co.: 1908.

Previous Names: 1883, Heaton Norris Rovers; 1888, Heaton Norris; 1890, Stockport County.

Club Nicknames: 'County' or 'Hatters'.

Previous Grounds: 1883 Heaton Norris Recreation Ground; 1884 Heaton Norris Wanderers Cricket Ground; 1885 Chorlton's Farm, Chorlton's Lane; 1886 Heaton Norris Cricket Ground; 1887 Wilkes' Field, Belmont Street; 1889 Nursery Inn, Green Lane; 1902 Edgeley Park.

First Football League Game: 1 September 1900, Division 2, v Leicester Fosse (a) D 2–2 – Moores; Earp, Wainwright; Pickford, Limond, Harvey; Stansfield, Smith (1), Patterson, Foster, Betteley (1).

Record League Victory: 13–0 v Halifax T, Division 3 (N), 6 January 1934 – McGann; Vincent (1p), Jenkinson; Robinson, Stevens, Len Jones; Foulkes (1), Hill (3), Lythgoe (2), Stevenson (2), Downes (4).

Record Cup Victory: 5–0 v Lincoln C, FA Cup 1st rd, 11 November 1995 – Edwards; Connelly, Todd, Bennett, Flynn, Gannon (Dinning), Beaumont, Oliver, Ware, Eckhardt (3), Armstrong (1) (Mike), Chalk, (1 og).

HONOURS

Football League: Division 1 best season: 8th, 1997–98; Division 2 – Runners-up 1996–97; Division 3 (N) – Champions 1921–22, 1936–37; Runners-up 1928–29, 1929-30, 1996–97; Division 4 – Champions 1966–67; Runners-up 1990–91.

FA Cup: best season: 5th rd, 1935, 1950, 2001.

Football League Cup: Semi-final 1997.

Autoglass Trophy: Runners-up 1992, 1993.

SKY SPORTS FACT FILE

In November 1968 Scottish international inside-forward Alex Young quit his player-manager post with Glentoran to join Stockport County and the former Hearts and Everton player completed a career 250 Football League appearances.

Record Defeat: 1–8 v Chesterfield, Division 2, 19 April 1902.

Most League Points (2 for a win): 64, Division 4, 1966–67.

Most League Points (3 for a win): 85, Division 2, 1993–94.

Most League Goals: 115, Division 3 (N), 1933–34.

Highest League Scorer in Season: Alf Lythgoe, 46, Division 3 (N), 1933–34.

Most League Goals in Total Aggregate: Jack Connor, 132, 1951–56.

Most League Goals in One Match: 5, Joe Smith v Southport, Division 3N, 7 January 1928; 5, Joe Smith v Lincoln C, Division 3N, 15 September 1928; 5, Frank Newton v Nelson, Division 3N, 21 September 1929; 5, Alf Lythgoe v Southport, Division 3N, 25 August 1934; 5, Billy McNaughton v Mansfield T, Division 3N, 14 December 1935; 5, Jack Connor v Workington, Division 3N, 8 November 1952; 5, Jack Connor v Carlisle U, Division 3N, 7 April 1956.

Most Capped Player: Jarkko Wiss, 9 (36), Finland.

Most League Appearances: Andy Thorpe, 489, 1978–86, 1988–92.

Youngest League Player: Paul Turnbull, 16 years 97 days v Wrexham, 30 April 2005.

Record Transfer Fee Received: £1,600,000 from Middlesbrough for Alun Armstrong, February 1998.

Record Transfer Fee Paid: £800,000 to Nottingham F for Ian Moore, July 1998.

Football League Record: 1900 Elected to Division 2; 1904 Failed re-election; 1905–21 Division 2; 1921–22 Division 3 (N); 1922–26 Division 2; 1926–37 Division 3 (N); 1937–38 Division 2; 1938–58 Division 3 (N); 1958–59 Division 3; 1959–67 Division 4; 1967–70 Division 3; 1970–91 Division 4; 1991–92 Division 3; 1992–97 Division 2; 1997–2002 Division 1; 2002–04 Division 2; 2004–05 FL1; 2005– FL2.

LATEST SEQUENCES

Longest Sequence of League Wins: 8, 26.12.1927 – 28.1.1928.

Longest Sequence of League Defeats: 10, 24.11.2001 – 13.01.2002

Longest Sequence of League Draws: 7, 17.3.1989 – 14.4.1989.

Longest Sequence of Unbeaten League Matches: 18, 28.1.1933 – 28.8.1933.

Longest Sequence Without a League Win: 19, 28.12.1999 – 22.4.2000.

Successive Scoring Runs: 24 from 8.9.1928.

Successive Non-scoring Runs: 7 from 10.3.1923.

MANAGERS

Fred Stewart 1894–1911
Harry Lewis 1911–14
David Ashworth 1914–19
Albert Williams 1919–24
Fred Scotchbrook 1924–26
Lincoln Hyde 1926–31
Andrew Wilson 1932–33
Fred Westgarth 1934–36
Bob Kelly 1936–38
George Hunt 1938–39
Bob Marshall 1939–49
Andy Beattie 1949–52
Dick Duckworth 1952–56
Billy Moir 1956–60
Reg Flewin 1960–63
Trevor Porteous 1963–65
Bert Trautmann *(General Manager)* 1965–66
Eddie Quigley *(Team Manager)* 1965–66
Jimmy Meadows 1966–69
Wally Galbraith 1969–70
Matt Woods 1970–71
Brian Doyle 1972–74
Jimmy Meadows 1974–75
Roy Chapman 1975–76
Eddie Quigley 1976–77
Alan Thompson 1977–78
Mike Summerbee 1978–79
Jimmy McGuigan 1979–82
Eric Webster 1982–85
Colin Murphy 1985
Les Chapman 1985–86
Jimmy Melia 1986
Colin Murphy 1986–87
Asa Hartford 1987–89
Danny Bergara 1989–95
Dave Jones 1995–97
Gary Megson 1997–99
Andy Kilner 1999–2001
Carlton Palmer 2001–03
Sammy McIlroy 2003–04
Chris Turner 2004–05
Jim Gannon January 2006–

TEN YEAR LEAGUE RECORD

		P	W	D	L	F	A	Pts	Pos
1996-97	Div 2	46	23	13	10	59	41	82	2
1997-98	Div 1	46	19	8	19	71	69	65	8
1998-99	Div 1	46	12	17	17	49	60	53	16
1999-2000	Div 1	46	13	15	18	55	67	54	17
2000-01	Div 1	46	11	18	17	58	65	51	19
2001-02	Div 1	46	6	8	32	42	102	26	24
2002-03	Div 2	46	15	10	21	65	70	55	14
2003-04	Div 2	46	11	19	16	62	70	52	19
2004-05	FL 1	46	6	8	32	49	98	26	24
2005-06	FL 2	46	11	19	16	57	78	52	22

DID YOU KNOW

After Bill Holden scored a hat-trick for Stockport County on 2 November 1957 against Chesterfield, it was 18 September 1965 before another treble when Len White obliged at Bradford City.

STOCKPORT COUNTY 2005–06 LEAGUE RECORD

Match No.	Date	Venue	Opponents	Result		H/T Score	Lg. Pos.	Goalscorers	Attendance
1	Aug 6	H	Mansfield T	D	2-2	0-2	—	Easter 2 [48, 66]	4970
2	9	A	Darlington	L	0-2	0-1	—		4371
3	13	A	Boston U	D	2-2	0-0	19	Bramble [64], Hamshaw [67]	2432
4	20	H	Notts Co	D	1-1	1-1	19	Easter [35]	3922
5	27	A	Oxford U	D	1-1	1-1	18	Clare [35]	4329
6	29	H	Peterborough U	D	1-1	0-1	19	St Ledger-Hall (og) [28]	3774
7	Sept 2	A	Grimsby T	W	3-1	0-1	—	Whittle (og) [56], Hamshaw [75], Wolski [79]	5381
8	10	H	Wycombe W	D	3-3	2-2	14	Easter 2 (1 pen) [15, 80 (p)], Malcolm [45]	3507
9	17	A	Rushden & D	L	2-3	1-0	18	Gulliver (og) [19], Malcolm [61]	2710
10	24	H	Chester C	D	0-0	0-0	19		4873
11	27	A	Lincoln C	L	0-2	0-0	—		3508
12	Oct 1	A	Wrexham	L	0-3	0-1	22		4153
13	8	H	Leyton Orient	D	1-1	1-0	—	Vaughan [22]	3901
14	15	A	Shrewsbury T	D	2-2	1-1	20	Bramble [32], Malcolm [53]	4316
15	22	H	Northampton T	W	4-2	1-2	19	Bramble 2 [8, 62], Singh [54], Briggs [84]	4150
16	29	A	Carlisle U	L	0-6	0-4	22		5664
17	Nov 13	H	Barnet	D	1-1	1-1	22	Hamshaw [15]	6056
18	19	A	Leyton Orient	D	2-2	0-1	22	Clare [56], Easter [64]	4997
19	26	A	Mansfield T	L	1-2	0-2	23	Easter [80]	2994
20	Dec 6	H	Bristol R	L	0-1	0-1	—		3460
21	10	H	Darlington	L	0-3	0-1	23		3502
22	17	A	Notts Co	L	0-2	0-1	24		4261
23	26	A	Macclesfield T	L	0-6	0-2	24		4553
24	Jan 2	H	Cheltenham T	D	2-2	1-0	24	Hamshaw [35], Dickinson [76]	3777
25	14	A	Rochdale	W	1-0	1-0	24	Easter [8]	3520
26	21	H	Rushden & D	D	2-2	0-0	24	Griffin A [47], Dickinson [90]	4574
27	24	H	Grimsby T	W	2-1	0-0	—	Le Fondre 2 [72, 79]	3860
28	28	A	Wycombe W	D	1-1	1-0	24	Hamshaw [38]	5512
29	31	H	Torquay U	D	1-1	0-1	—	Le Fondre [64]	4455
30	Feb 4	H	Lincoln C	L	2-3	0-0	23	Briggs [64], Dickinson [83]	4506
31	11	A	Chester C	W	2-1	0-0	24	Dickinson 2 [76, 89]	3446
32	14	H	Rochdale	W	3-0	2-0	—	Boshell [27], Griffin A [33], Briggs [88]	4312
33	18	A	Bristol R	D	2-2	0-1	21	Le Fondre [68], Hughes [88]	5990
34	25	H	Boston U	L	0-1	0-0	22		5133
35	Mar 4	A	Peterborough U	L	0-2	0-0	22		3406
36	7	A	Bury	W	1-0	0-0	—	Dickinson [85]	3116
37	11	H	Oxford U	W	2-1	1-0	17	Bramble [21], Le Fondre (pen) [87]	4424
38	18	H	Macclesfield T	W	2-0	1-0	17	Briscoe (og) [12], Le Fondre [90]	6003
39	Apr 1	H	Bury	L	0-1	0-1	21		6014
40	8	A	Cheltenham T	D	3-3	1-1	22	Robinson (pen) [34], Briggs [56], Dickinson [90]	3525
41	15	H	Wrexham	W	2-1	2-1	21	Williams A [6], Raynes [42]	4750
42	17	A	Northampton T	L	0-2	0-0	22		6544
43	22	H	Shrewsbury T	W	3-1	1-0	20	Ward [36], O'Connor [54], Robinson (pen) [84]	5831
44	25	A	Torquay U	L	0-4	0-3	—		3565
45	29	A	Barnet	D	0-0	0-0	22		3873
46	May 6	H	Carlisle U	D	0-0	0-0	22		10,006

Final League Position: 22

GOALSCORERS

League (57): Easter 8 (1 pen), Dickinson 7, Le Fondre 6 (1 pen), Bramble 5, Hamshaw 5, Briggs 4, Malcolm 3, Clare 2, Griffin A 2, Robinson 2 (2 pens), Boshell 1, Hughes 1, O'Connor 1, Raynes 1, Singh 1, Vaughan 1, Ward 1, Williams A 1, Wolski 1, own goals 4.
Carling Cup (2): Boshell 1, Le Fondre 1.
FA Cup (6): Easter 3, Briggs 2, Wolski 1.
Football League Trophy (1): own goal 1.

Spencer J 34	Clare R 31 + 3	Robinson M 46	Wolski M 14 + 6	Raynes M 23 + 2	Williams A 33 + 3	Briggs K 39 + 2	Boshell D 28 + 5	Easter J 18 + 1	Ellis D — + 3	Bramble T 33 + 4	Singh H 19 + 5	Greenwood R 17 + 5	Malcolm M 10 + 13	Hamshaw M 35 + 4	Le Fondre A 4 + 18	Allen D 13 + 9	Duke M 3	Vaughan T 10	Crowe D 1 + 5	Dje L 5 + 2	Ikeme C 9	Williams C 1 + 2	Griffin D 4	Strachan G 4	Dolan J 2	Tunnicliffe J — + 1	Crowther R — + 1	Dickinson L 12 + 9	Symes M — + 1	Foster L — + 1	Griffin A 20 + 1	Beharall D 10 + 2	Hughes M 3	Smylie D 1 + 2	Ward J 7 + 2	Collins A 2 + 1	Taylor J 9	O'Connor K 6 + 1	*Match No.*
1	2	3	4	5^1	6	7^2	8	9		10	11^3	12	13	14																									1
1	2	3	4^2	5^1	6	7	8	9^3		10	11	12		13	14																								2
1	2	3	4		6	13	8^2	9^3		10	11^1	5	12	7	14																								3
1	2	3	4^1		6	12	8	9			11^2	5	13	7^3	10	14																							4
	5	3	4			2	8	9^3			11		12	7^2	10^1	13	1	6	14																				5
	5	3	4			2	8^1	9			11^3		13	7	10^2	12	1	6	14																				6
	5	3^1	4			2	8^2	9			11	12	13	7^3		14	1	6		10																			7
	5	3	4^2			2	8	9		12		14	11	7^3		13		6		10^1	1																		8
	5	3				4^2	8			9^3	11^1	2	10	7	12	13		6		14	1																		9
	5	3				2	8^1			9		7	10	11		4		6			1	12																	10
	6	3			5	7				9^2		2	10^1	11	12			4		13	1	8																	11
	6^2	3		5	4	7^3				12		2	10^1	11				8	14	9■	1	13																	12
		11		5	12		8^1			9^2	13	3	10	7				4			1		2	6															13
		11		5	12		8^2			9	13	3	10■	7				4			1		2^1	6															14
		11		5		8		12		9	13	3	10^2	7							1		2^1	6	4														15
	12	3			6^1		13	9			11	2	14	7						10^3	1		5^2	8	4														16
1	6	3^3	12	5		4^1	8	9		13	11	2	14	7						10^2																			17
1	6	3		5	12	4	8	9		10	11	2^1		7																									18
1	6	3	12	5		4^1	8^3	9		10^2	11	2	13	7		14																							19
1	5	3	4^2		6		8^1	9		10	11	2	12	7		13																							20
1	5	3			6	4	8			10	11^1	2	9	7					12																				21
1	5	3			6■	4	8	9		10	11^1	2		7												12													22
1	6	3^1		5		4	8	9		10■	11	2		7					12																				23
1	2	3		5	6	4		9			11			7^1		8			10^2								12	13											24
1	2	3	12	5	6	10	8	9^3			11^1			7^2	13	4												14											25
1	2	3		5	6	7^3	8^1	9		12	11^2			10		4												14			13								26
1	2	3	4^3	5	6	7	14			10^1				11	12	8												13			9^2								27
1	2	3	12	5	6	7	8			10^3				11^2	13	4												14			9^1								28
1	2	3	12	5^1	6	7^2	8			10^3				9	13	4													14		11								29
1	5	3	4^3		6	2	12						13	7	10	8^1												9		14	11^2								30
1	2	3	12		6	8				9	13		14	7^3		4^1												10			11^2	5							31
1		3	4		6	7	8			9^2				12	13													10^1			11	2	5						32
1		3^1	4		6	7^3	8			9	12			10^2	13																11	2	5	14					33
1		3	4^3		6		8			9^1				7	12	13												10			11	2	5^2	14					34
1	5	3		12	6	4^2	8					13		7^3	14													10			11	2		9^1					35
1	5	3			6	8				9^1				7^2	12	4												10			11	2			13				36
1	5^1	3			6	8	12			9				7^3	13	4												10^2			11	2			14				37
1		3			6	2				9					12	4												10^1			11				7	5	8		38
1		3^3		12	6	7				9				13	14	4^1												10			11	2^2				5	8		39
1	4^2	3		5^3	6	7				9																		12			11	2^1			8	13	10	14	40
1		3		5^3	6	2	12			9^2			10^1															13			11	14			4		7	8	41
1		3		5	6	2	8			9^3			12	7^2														14			11^1	13					4	10	42
1		3		5	6	2			12	9																		10			11^1				4		7	8	43
1		3		5	6	2			13	9					12													10			11				4^1		8^2	7	44
1	12	3		5	6	2			14	9																		13			11	10^1			4^3		8	7^2	45
1	12	3		5	6	2				9^2					13													10			11				4^1		7	8	46

FA Cup

First Round	Swansea C	(h)	2-0
Second Round	Hereford U	(a)	2-0
Third Round	Brentford	(h)	2-3

Carling Cup

First Round	Sheffield W	(h)	2-4

Football League Trophy

First Round	Rochdale	(a)	1-3

STOKE CITY FL Championship

FOUNDATION

The date of the formation of this club has long been in doubt. The year 1863 was claimed, but more recent research by Wade Martin has uncovered nothing earlier than 1868, when a couple of Old Carthusians, who were apprentices at the local works of the old North Staffordshire Railway Company, met with some others from that works, to form Stoke Ramblers. It should also be noted that the old Stoke club went bankrupt in 1908 when a new club was formed.

Britannia Stadium, Stanley Matthews Way, Stoke-on-Trent, Staffs ST4 4EG.

Telephone: (01782) 592 222.

Fax: (01782) 592 221.

Ticket Office: (01782) 592204.

Website: www.stokecityfc.com

Email: info@stokecityfc.com

Ground Capacity: 28,218.

Record Attendance: 51,380 v Arsenal, Division 1, 29 March 1937.

Pitch Measurements: 116yd × 74yd.

Chairman: Peter Coates.

Chief Executive: Tony Scholes.

Secretary: Diane Richardson.

Manager: Tony Pulis.

Physio: Dave Watson.

HONOURS

Football League: Division 1 best season: 4th, 1935–36, 1946–47; Division 2 – Champions 1932–33, 1962–63, 1992–93; Runners-up 1921–22; Promoted 1978–79 (3rd), Promoted from Division 2 (play-offs) 2001–02; Division 3 (N) – Champions 1926–27.

FA Cup: Semi-finals 1899, 1971, 1972.

Football League Cup: Winners 1972.

Autoglass Trophy: Winners: 1992.

Auto Windscreens Shield: Winners: 2000.

European Competitions: *UEFA Cup:* 1972–73, 1974–75.

Colours: Red and white striped shirts, white shorts with red trim, white stockings with red trim.

Change Colours: White shirts with navy and sky blue trim, navy shorts, navy stockings.

Year Formed: 1863 *(*see Foundation*). ***Turned Professional:*** 1885. ***Ltd Co.:*** 1908.

Previous Names: 1868, Stoke Ramblers; 1870, Stoke; 1925, Stoke City.

Club Nickname: 'The Potters'.

Previous Grounds: 1875, Sweeting's Field; 1878, Victoria Ground (previously known as the Athletic Club Ground); 1997, Britannia Stadium.

First Football League Game: 8 September 1888, Football League, v WBA (h) L 0–2 – Rowley; Clare, Underwood; Ramsey, Shutt, Smith; Sayer, McSkimming, Staton, Edge, Tunnicliffe.

Record League Victory: 10–3 v WBA, Division 1, 4 February 1937 – Doug Westland; Brigham, Harbot; Tutin, Turner (1p), Kirton; Matthews, Antonio (2), Freddie Steele (5), Jimmy Westland, Johnson (2).

SKY SPORTS FACT FILE

At the start of the 1968–69 season Stoke City had four experienced forwards who had career aggregates of over 650 League goals between them: David Herd (216), Peter Dobing (184), Roy Vernon (170) and Harry Burrows (97).

Record Cup Victory: 7–1 v Burnley, FA Cup 2nd rd (replay), 20 February 1896 – Clawley; Clare, Eccles; Turner, Grewe, Robertson; Willie Maxwell, Dickson, A. Maxwell (3), Hyslop (4), Schofield.

Record Defeat: 0–10 v Preston NE, Division 1, 14 September 1889.

Most League Points (2 for a win): 63, Division 3 (N), 1926–27.

Most League Points (3 for a win): 93, Division 2, 1992–93.

Most League Goals: 92, Division 3 (N), 1926–27.

Highest League Scorer in Season: Freddie Steele, 33, Division 1, 1936–37.

Most League Goals in Total Aggregate: Freddie Steele, 142, 1934–49.

Most League Goals in One Match: 7, Neville Coleman v Lincoln C, Division 2, 23 February 1957.

Most Capped Player: Gordon Banks, 36 (73), England.

Most League Appearances: Eric Skeels, 506, 1958–76.

Youngest League Player: Peter Bullock, 16 years 163 days v Swansea C, 19 April 1958.

Record Transfer Fee Received: £2,750,000 from QPR for Mike Sheron, July 1997.

Record Transfer Fee Paid: £950,000 to Standard Liege for Sambegou Bangoura, August 2005.

Football League Record: 1888 Founder Member of Football League; 1890 Not re-elected; 1891 Re-elected; relegated in 1907, and after one year in Division 2, resigned for financial reasons; 1919 re-elected to Division 2; 1922–23 Division 1; 1923–26 Division 2; 1926–27 Division 3 (N); 1927–33 Division 2; 1933–53 Division 1; 1953–63 Division 2; 1963–77 Division 1; 1977–79 Division 2; 1979–85 Division 1; 1985–90 Division 2; 1990–92 Division 3; 1992–93 Division 2; 1993–98 Division 1; 1998–2002 Division 2; 2002–04 Division 1; 2004– FLC.

MANAGERS

Tom Slaney 1874–83
(Secretary-Manager)
Walter Cox 1883–84
(Secretary-Manager)
Harry Lockett 1884–90
Joseph Bradshaw 1890–92
Arthur Reeves 1892–95
William Rowley 1895–97
H. D. Austerberry 1897–1908
A. J. Barker 1908–14
Peter Hodge 1914–15
Joe Schofield 1915–19
Arthur Shallcross 1919–23
John 'Jock' Rutherford 1923
Tom Mather 1923–35
Bob McGrory 1935–52
Frank Taylor 1952–60
Tony Waddington 1960–77
George Eastham 1977–78
Alan A'Court 1978
Alan Durban 1978–81
Richie Barker 1981–83
Bill Asprey 1984–85
Mick Mills 1985–89
Alan Ball 1989–91
Lou Macari 1991–93
Joe Jordan 1993–94
Lou Macari 1994–97
Chic Bates 1997–98
Chris Kamara 1998
Brian Little 1998–99
Gary Megson 1999
Gudjon Thordarson 1999–2002
Steve Cotterill 2002
Tony Pulis 2002–05
Johan Boskamp 2005–06
Tony Pulis June 2006–

LATEST SEQUENCES

Longest Sequence of League Wins: 8, 30.3.1895 – 21.9.1895.

Longest Sequence of League Defeats: 11, 6.4.1985 – 17.8.1985.

Longest Sequence of League Draws: 5, 21.3.1987 – 11.4.1987.

Longest Sequence of Unbeaten League Matches: 25, 5.9.1992 – 20.2.1993.

Longest Sequence Without a League Win: 17, 22.4.1989 – 14.10.1989.

Successive Scoring Runs: 21 from 24.12.1921.

Successive Non-scoring Runs: 8 from 29.12.1984.

TEN YEAR LEAGUE RECORD

		P	W	D	L	F	A	Pts	Pos
1996-97	Div 1	46	18	10	18	51	57	64	12
1997-98	Div 1	46	11	13	22	44	74	46	23
1998-99	Div 2	46	21	6	19	59	63	69	8
1999-2000	Div 2	46	23	13	10	68	42	82	6
2000-01	Div 2	46	21	14	11	74	49	77	5
2001-02	Div 2	46	23	11	12	67	40	80	5
2002-03	Div 1	46	12	14	20	45	69	50	21
2003-04	Div 1	46	18	12	16	58	55	66	11
2004-05	FL C	46	17	10	19	36	38	61	12
2005-06	FL C	46	17	7	22	54	63	58	13

DID YOU KNOW

Scottish international inside-left Tommy Hyslop scored only four FA Cup goals for Stoke during two spells, but all in one tie – their record win in the competition. Previously he had been the first Stoke player to score a debut hat-trick, against Derby County.

STOKE CITY 2005–06 LEAGUE RECORD

Match No.	Date	Venue	Opponents	Result	H/T Score	Lg. Pos.	Goalscorers	Atten-dance
1	Aug 6	H	Sheffield W	D 0-0	0-0	—		18,744
2	9	A	Leicester C	L 2-4	0-1	—	Broomes [64], Halls [89]	20,519
3	13	A	Millwall	W 1-0	1-0	14	Halls [38]	8668
4	20	H	Luton T	W 2-1	0-1	9	Broomes [63], Brammer [90]	18,653
5	27	A	Crystal Palace	L 0-2	0-1	13		17,637
6	29	H	Norwich C	W 3-1	2-1	7	Kolar [9], Harper [45], Sidibe [69]	14,249
7	Sept 10	H	Watford	L 0-3	0-1	11		14,565
8	13	A	Hull C	W 1-0	0-0	—	Gallagher [74]	18,692
9	16	A	Preston NE	W 1-0	0-0	—	Gallagher [76]	12,453
10	24	H	Wolverhampton W	L 1-3	0-1	6	Buxton [90]	18,183
11	27	H	Cardiff C	L 0-3	0-3	—		12,240
12	Oct 1	A	Plymouth Arg	L 1-2	0-0	10	Chadwick [47]	12,604
13	15	A	Derby Co	L 1-2	0-1	14	Hoefkens [59]	22,229
14	18	H	Crewe Alex	W 2-0	1-0	—	Bangoura [41], Duberry [64]	14,080
15	22	H	Reading	L 0-1	0-0	11		13,484
16	29	A	Southampton	L 0-2	0-1	14		24,095
17	Nov 2	A	Coventry C	W 2-1	1-1	—	Taggart [37], Gallagher [55]	16,617
18	5	H	Brighton & HA	W 3-0	1-0	9	Bangoura 2 [35, 75], Russell [68]	15,274
19	19	A	Crewe Alex	W 2-1	1-0	8	Bangoura [16], Gallagher [89]	8942
20	22	H	Derby Co	L 1-2	1-0	—	Bangoura [33]	13,205
21	26	A	Sheffield W	W 2-0	1-0	7	Bangoura [17], Sidibe [86]	21,970
22	Dec 3	H	QPR	L 1-2	1-1	11	Bangoura [26]	15,367
23	9	H	Leicester C	W 3-2	1-1	—	Gallagher (pen) [36], Sidibe [75], Bangoura [78]	11,125
24	17	A	Luton T	W 3-2	1-1	5	Gallagher 2 [45, 83], Coyne (og) [90]	8296
25	26	A	Burnley	L 0-1	0-0	6		17,912
26	28	H	Leeds U	L 0-1	0-0	9		20,408
27	31	A	Sheffield U	L 1-2	0-1	12	Sidibe [57]	21,279
28	Jan 2	H	Ipswich T	D 2-2	1-2	12	Russell [27], Sidibe [73]	14,493
29	14	A	Watford	L 0-1	0-0	13		12,247
30	21	H	Hull C	L 0-3	0-1	13		13,444
31	Feb 4	H	Preston NE	D 0-0	0-0	13		13,218
32	11	A	Cardiff C	L 0-3	0-2	16		10,780
33	14	H	Plymouth Arg	D 0-0	0-0	—		10,242
34	25	H	Millwall	W 2-1	1-1	16	Hoefkens (pen) [15], Gallagher [57]	11,340
35	Mar 4	A	Norwich C	L 1-2	0-0	16	Gallagher [58]	24,223
36	7	A	Wolverhampton W	D 0-0	0-0	—		22,439
37	13	H	Crystal Palace	L 1-3	0-1	—	Skoko [47]	10,121
38	18	H	Burnley	W 1-0	0-0	15	Gallagher [52]	12,082
39	25	A	Leeds U	D 0-0	0-0	15		21,452
40	29	A	QPR	W 2-1	0-1	—	Hoefkens (pen) [73], Sigurdsson [79]	10,918
41	Apr 1	H	Sheffield U	D 1-1	1-0	13	Skoko [16]	17,544
42	8	A	Ipswich T	W 4-1	0-0	11	Wilnis (og) [51], Bangoura [82], Chadwick [89], Russell [90]	23,592
43	15	H	Southampton	L 1-2	0-2	12	Gallagher [83]	16,501
44	17	A	Reading	L 1-3	0-1	13	Rooney [59]	22,119
45	22	H	Coventry C	L 0-1	0-0	14		13,385
46	30	A	Brighton & HA	W 5-1	3-0	13	Rooney 3 [6, 22, 63], Sidibe [40], Sweeney [82]	5859

Final League Position: 13

GOALSCORERS

League (54): Gallagher 11 (1 pen), Bangoura 9, Sidibe 6, Rooney 4, Hoefkens 3 (2 pens), Russell 3, Broomes 2, Chadwick 2, Halls 2, Skoko 2, Brammer 1, Buxton 1, Duberry 1, Harper 1, Kolar 1, Sigurdsson 1, Sweeney 1, Taggart 1, own goals 2.
Carling Cup (1): Brammer 1 (pen).
FA Cup (3): Chadwick 1, Gallagher 1, Sidibe 1.

Simonsen S 45	Halls J 13	Broomes M 36 + 1	Hoefkens C 44	Taggart G 3	Junior 16 + 6	Chadwick L 33 + 3	Brammer D 38 + 2	Sidibe M 37 + 5	Russell D 35 + 2	Kolar M 12 + 2	Henry K 11 + 13	Buxton L 25 + 7	Harper K 5 + 9	Dyer B 2 + 9	Duberry M 41	Wilkinson A 4 + 2	Gallagher P 32 + 5	Sigurdsson H 10 + 13	De Goey E 1 + 1	Bangoura S 23 + 1	Sweeney P 8 + 9	Paterson M 2 + 1	Kopteff P 3 + 3	Rooney A 2 + 3	Hill C 12 + 1	Skoko J 9	Dickinson C 4 + 1	Garret R — + 2	Hazley M — + 1	*Match No.*
1	2	3	4	5■	6^{1}	7	8	9	10^{2}	11^{3}	12	13	14																	1
1	2	3	4		6■	7	8	9	10^{1}	11				12	5															2
1	2	3	4			7	8	9		11	6		12	10^{1}	5															3
1	2	3	4			7	8	9		11^{1}	6		12	10	5															4
1		3	4		10^{2}	7^{3}	8	9		11^{1}	6	2	12	13	5	14														5
1		3	4		6^{1}	7	8	9^{3}		11	12	2	10^{2}	14	5		13													6
1■		3	4		10	7^{1}	8	9		11^{6}		2	6^{2}	12	5		13		15											7
		3	4		14		8	9	12	11^{3}	6^{1}	2	7^{2}	13	5		10		1											8
1		3	4			7^{1}	8	9^{2}	6	11		2	12	13	5		10													9
1		3	4		13	7^{1}	8^{2}	9	6	11^{3}		2	12	14	5		10													10
1		3	4		6	7^{1}		9	8	12		2	11		5		10													11
1		3	4		8	7^{1}		9^{2}	6	11^{3}	12	2		13	5		10	14												12
1		3	4			7^{1}	8	9	6	12		2			5		10	11^{2}		13										13
1		3	4			7^{1}	8	12	6		13	2			5■		10^{2}	11^{3}		9	14									14
1		3	4	5^{2}		7^{1}	8	12	6	11^{3}		2				13	10			9	14									15
1	2	3■	4		6		8	9	7							5	10^{2}	11^{1}			12	13								16
1	3		4	5			8	9	6		12	2					10^{1}	11		7										17
1	3		4		12	13	8	9	6		14	2			5		10^{3}	11^{2}		7^{1}										18
1	3		4			7^{2}	8	9	6		12	2			5		11^{1}	13		10										19
1	3		4			7		9	8		6	2			5		11^{1}	12		10										20
1	2	3	4			7^{2}	8	12	6		13	14			5		11	9^{1}		10^{3}										21
1	2■	3	4			11	8	9			6				5			12		10	7^{1}									22
1		3	4				8	9	6		12	2			5		7^{1}	13		10	11^{2}									23
1			4			7^{1}	8	9	6		3	2	12		5		10	11^{2}			13									24
1	2	3	4			7	8	9	6						5		11			10										25
1	2^{1}	3^{2}	4			7	8	9	6			12			5		11	13		10										26
1		3	4			7^{1}	8	9	6		12	2			5		11^{2}	13		10										27
1		3^{1}	4			7^{2}	8	9	6		12	2	13		5		11^{3}			10			14							28
1		3	4		6	7	8	9			2		11^{1}	12	5		10													29
1		3	4			7^{1}		9	6		8	2	12^{2}		5		10				11			13						30
1		3	4		12	7		9	6■		8	2			5		10^{2}	13			11^{1}									31
1		3^{3}	4		12		8^{1}	9			6	2			5			11			7^{2}		13		14	10				32
1		3	4			7	8	9^{1}							5			12		10	13		6^{2}		2	11				33
1		3	4			7	8	9	12						5		13	10			11^{2}				2	6^{1}				34
1		3			6	7			8			2			5		11^{1}			10	12				4	9				35
1		3	4		12	7^{2}	8	13	10						5		11			9					2	6^{1}				36
1		3	4^{1}				8	9	6			12			5		11^{2}	13		10					2	7				37
1		3^{1}	4			13	8	9	6^{2}			12			5		11	14		10^{3}					2	7				38
1			4		6^{1}		12	9	8			2			5		11^{3}	13		10^{2}	14	7			3					39
1		3	4			7^{3}	8	12	6			14			5	2	13	9		10^{1}	11^{2}									40
1		3	4		6^{1}	7	12	9	8			13					10^{3}	14							5^{2}	11	2			41
1		12	4^{1}		6	13	8^{3}		7						5	2	9			10			11^{2}		3			14		42
1		3	4		6	7^{1}	8		11^{2}						5	2^{3}	9			10	12			13			14			43
1			4		6		8		9		12				5		13			10^{1}	11^{2}		7^{3}	14	3		2			44
1			4				8^{1}	9	6		12				5		11					7^{2}		10	3		2		13	45
1					6		8^{3}	9	7			2			5						12		13	10^{1}	3	11^{2}	4	14		46

FA Cup

Third Round	Tamworth	(h)	0-0
		(a)	1-1
Fourth Round	Walsall	(h)	2-1
Fifth Round	Birmingham C	(h)	0-1

Carling Cup

First Round	Mansfield T	(a)	1-1

SUNDERLAND FL Championship

FOUNDATION

A Scottish schoolmaster named James Allan, working at Hendon Board School, took the initiative in the foundation of Sunderland in 1879 when they were formed as The Sunderland and District Teachers' Association FC at a meeting in the Adults School, Norfolk Street. Due to financial difficulties, they quickly allowed members from outside the teaching profession and so became Sunderland AFC in October 1880.

Stadium of Light, Sunderland, Tyne and Wear SR5 1SU.

Telephone: (0191) 551 5000.

Fax: (0191) 551 5123.

Ticket Office: 0845 671 1973.

Website: www.safc.com

Ground Capacity: 49,000.

Record Attendance: Stadium of Light: 48,353 v Liverpool, FA Premier League, 13 April 2002. FA Premier League figure (46,062). Roker Park: 75,118 v Derby Co, FA Cup 6th rd replay, 8 March 1933.

Pitch Measurements: 105m × 68m.

Chairman: TBC.

Vice-chairman: TBC.

Chief Executive: TBC.

Secretary: TBC.

Manager: TBC.

Assistant Manager: TBC.

Head of Sports Therapy: Pete Friar.

Colours: Red and white striped shirts, black shorts, black and red stockings.

Change Colours: Sky blue shirts, dark blue shorts, dark blue stockings.

Year Formed: 1879.

Turned Professional: 1886.

Ltd Co.: 1906.

Previous Name: 1879, Sunderland and District Teacher's AFC; 1880, Sunderland.

Previous Grounds: 1879, Blue House Field, Hendon; 1882, Groves Field, Ashbrooke; 1883, Horatio Street; 1884, Abbs Field, Fulwell; 1886, Newcastle Road; 1898, Roker Park; 1997, Stadium of Light.

First Football League Game: 13 September 1890, Football League, v Burnley (h) L 2–3 – Kirtley; Porteous, Oliver; Wilson, Auld, Gibson; Spence (1), Miller, Campbell (1), Scott, D. Hannah.

Record League Victory: 9–1 v Newcastle U (a), Division 1, 5 December 1908 – Roose; Forster, Melton; Daykin, Thomson, Low; Mordue (1), Hogg (3), Brown, Holley (3), Bridgett (2).

HONOURS

Football League: Championship – Winners 2004–05; Division 1 – Champions 1891–92, 1892–93, 1894–95, 1901–02, 1912–13, 1935–36, 1995–96, 1998–99; Runners-up 1893–94, 1897–98, 1900–01, 1922–23, 1934–35; Division 2 – Champions 1975–76; Runners-up 1963–64, 1979–80; 1989–90 (play-offs). Division 3 – Champions 1987–88.

FA Cup: Winners 1937, 1973; Runners-up 1913, 1992.

Football League Cup: Runners-up 1985.

European Competitions: *European Cup-Winners' Cup:* 1973–74.

SKY SPORTS FACT FILE

In November 1951 George Aitken was a Third Lanark half-back. One night a policeman called with an urgent message from his manager! The next day Aitken was transferred to Sunderland where he made over 250 League and Cup appearances and won Scottish caps.

Record Cup Victory: 11–1 v Fairfield, FA Cup 1st rd, 2 February 1895 – Doig; McNeill, Johnston; Dunlop, McCreadie (1), Wilson; Gillespie (1), Millar (5), Campbell, Hannah (3), Scott (1).

Record Defeat: 0–8 v Sheff Wed, Division 1, 26 December 1911. 0–8 v West Ham U, Division 1, 19 October 1968. 0–8 v Watford, Division 1, 25 September 1982.

Most League Points (2 for a win): 61, Division 2, 1963–64.

Most League Points (3 for a win): 105, Division 1, 1998–99 (Football League Record).

Most League Goals: 109, Division 1, 1935–36.

Highest League Scorer in Season: Dave Halliday, 43, Division 1, 1928–29.

Most League Goals in Total Aggregate: Charlie Buchan, 209, 1911–25.

Most League Goals in One Match: 5, Charlie Buchan v Liverpool, Division 1, 7 December 1919; 5, Bobby Gurney v Bolton W, Division 1, 7 December 1935; 5, Dominic Sharkey v Norwich C, Division 2, 20 February 1962.

Most Capped Player: Charlie Hurley, 38 (40), Republic of Ireland.

Most League Appearances: Jim Montgomery, 537, 1962–77.

Youngest League Player: Derek Forster, 15 years 184 days v Leicester C, 22 August 1964.

Record Transfer Fee Received: £5,500,000 from Leeds U for Michael Bridges, July 1999.

Record Transfer Fee Paid: £8,000,000 to Rangers for Tore Andre Flo, August 2002.

Football League Record: 1890 Elected to Division 1; 1958–64 Division 2; 1964–70 Division 1; 1970–76 Division 2; 1976–77 Division 1; 1977–80 Division 2; 1980–85 Division 1; 1985–87 Division 2; 1987–88 Division 3; 1988–90 Division 2; 1990–91 Division 1; 1991–92 Division 2; 1992–96 Division 1; 1996–97 FA Premier League; 1997–99 Division 1; 1999–2003 FA Premier League; 2003–04 Division 1; 2004–05 FLC; 2005–06 FA Premier League; 2006– FLC.

MANAGERS

Tom Watson 1888–96
Bob Campbell 1896–99
Alex Mackie 1899–1905
Bob Kyle 1905–28
Johnny Cochrane 1928–39
Bill Murray 1939–57
Alan Brown 1957–64
George Hardwick 1964–65
Ian McColl 1965–68
Alan Brown 1968–72
Bob Stokoe 1972–76
Jimmy Adamson 1976–78
Ken Knighton 1979–81
Alan Durban 1981–84
Len Ashurst 1984–85
Lawrie McMenemy 1985–87
Denis Smith 1987–91
Malcolm Crosby 1992–93
Terry Butcher 1993
Mick Buxton 1993–95
Peter Reid 1995–2002
Howard Wilkinson 2002–03
Mick McCarthy 2003–06

LATEST SEQUENCES

Longest Sequence of League Wins: 13, 14.11.1891 – 2.4.1892.

Longest Sequence of League Defeats: 17, 18.1.2003 – 16.8.2003.

Longest Sequence of League Draws: 6, 26.3.1949 – 19.4.1949.

Longest Sequence of Unbeaten League Matches: 19, 3.5.1998 – 14.11.1998.

Longest Sequence Without a League Win: 22, 21.12.2002 – 16.8.2003.

Successive Scoring Runs: 29 from 8.11.1997

Successive Non-scoring Runs: 10 from 27.11.1976.

TEN YEAR LEAGUE RECORD

		P	*W*	*D*	*L*	*F*	*A*	*Pts*	*Pos*
1996-97	PR Lge	38	10	10	18	35	53	40	18
1997-98	Div 1	46	26	12	8	86	50	90	3
1998-99	Div 1	46	31	12	3	91	28	105	1
1999-2000	PR Lge	38	16	10	12	57	56	58	7
2000-01	PR Lge	38	15	12	11	46	41	57	7
2001-02	PR Lge	38	10	10	18	29	51	40	17
2002-03	PR Lge	38	4	7	27	21	65	19	20
2003-04	Div 1	46	22	13	11	62	45	79	3
2004-05	FL C	46	29	7	10	76	41	94	1
2005-06	PR Lge	38	3	6	29	26	69	15	20

DID YOU KNOW ?

When Alan Brown was appointed manager of Sunderland in August 1957 he was the first Englishman to hold the position there since Tom Watson in 1888. The previous incumbents had all been Scots with the exception of Irishman Bob Kyle.

SUNDERLAND 2005–06 LEAGUE RECORD

Match No.	Date	Venue	Opponents	Result		H/T Score	Lg. Pos.	Goalscorers	Attendance
1	Aug 13	H	Charlton Ath	L	1-3	1-1	—	Gray 32	34,446
2	20	A	Liverpool	L	0-1	0-1	20		44,913
3	23	H	Manchester C	L	1-2	1-2	—	Le Tallec 41	33,357
4	27	A	Wigan Ath	L	0-1	0-1	20		17,223
5	Sept 10	A	Chelsea	L	0-2	0-0	20		41,969
6	17	H	WBA	D	1-1	1-0	20	Breen 7	31,657
7	25	A	Middlesbrough	W	2-0	1-0	19	Miller 2, Arca 60	29,583
8	Oct 1	H	West Ham U	D	1-1	1-0	17	Miller 45	31,212
9	15	H	Manchester U	L	1-3	0-1	19	Elliott 82	39,085
10	23	A	Newcastle U	L	2-3	2-2	19	Lawrence 35, Elliott 41	52,302
11	29	H	Portsmouth	L	1-4	1-0	20	Whitehead (pen) 4	34,926
12	Nov 5	A	Arsenal	L	1-3	0-2	20	Stubbs 75	38,210
13	19	H	Aston Villa	L	1-3	0-0	20	Whitehead (pen) 90	39,707
14	26	H	Birmingham C	L	0-1	0-0	20		32,442
15	30	H	Liverpool	L	0-2	0-2	—		32,697
16	Dec 3	A	Tottenham H	L	2-3	1-1	20	Whitehead 16, Le Tallec 60	36,244
17	10	A	Charlton Ath	L	0-2	0-1	20		26,065
18	26	H	Bolton W	D	0-0	0-0	20		32,232
19	31	H	Everton	L	0-1	0-0	20		30,576
20	Jan 2	A	Fulham	L	1-2	1-1	20	Lawrence 7	19,372
21	15	H	Chelsea	L	1-2	1-1	20	Lawrence 12	32,420
22	21	A	WBA	W	1-0	0-0	20	Watson (og) 72	26,464
23	31	H	Middlesbrough	L	0-3	0-2	—		31,675
24	Feb 4	A	West Ham U	L	0-2	0-0	20		34,745
25	12	H	Tottenham H	D	1-1	0-1	20	Murphy 89	34,700
26	15	A	Blackburn R	L	0-2	0-1	—		18,220
27	25	A	Birmingham C	L	0-1	0-1	20		29,257
28	Mar 5	A	Manchester C	L	1-2	1-2	20	Kyle 25	42,200
29	11	H	Wigan Ath	L	0-1	0-1	20		31,194
30	18	A	Bolton W	L	0-2	0-0	20		23,568
31	25	H	Blackburn R	L	0-1	0-1	20		29,593
32	Apr 1	A	Everton	D	2-2	1-2	20	Stead 16, Delap 80	38,093
33	14	A	Manchester U	D	0-0	0-0	—		72,519
34	17	H	Newcastle U	L	1-4	1-0	20	Hoyte 32	40,032
35	22	A	Portsmouth	L	1-2	0-0	20	Miller 70	20,078
36	May 1	H	Arsenal	L	0-3	0-3	—		44,003
37	4	H	Fulham	W	2-1	1-0	—	Le Tallec 32, Brown 57	28,226
38	7	A	Aston Villa	L	1-2	0-1	20	Collins D 88	33,820

Final League Position: 20

GOALSCORERS

League (26): Lawrence 3, Le Tallec 3, Miller 3, Whitehead 3 (2 pens), Elliott 2, Arca 1, Breen 1, Brown 1, Collins D 1, Delap 1, Gray 1, Hoyte 1, Kyle 1, Murphy 1, Stead 1, Stubbs 1, own goal 1.
Carling Cup (1): Le Tallec 1.
FA Cup (4): Arca 1, Collins N 1, Le Tallec 1, Whitehead 1.

Davis K 33	Wright S 2	Arca J 22 + 2	Robinson C 3 + 2	Breen G 33 + 2	Caldwell S 23 + 1	Whitehead D 37	Miller T 27 + 2	Stead J 21 + 9	Gray A 13 + 8	Welsh A 12 + 2	Nosworthy N 24 + 6	Lawrence L 19 + 10	Elliott S 11 + 4	Woods M 1 + 6	Stubbs A 8 + 2	Brown C 10 + 3	Le Tallec A 12 + 15	Hoyte J 27	Bassila C 12 + 1	Murphy D 5 + 13	Alnwick B 5	Collins D 22 + 1	Leadbitter G 8 + 4	Kyle K 9 + 4	McCartney G 13	Delap R 5 + 1	Smith D 1 + 2	*Match No.*
1	2[1]	3	4[2]	5	6	7	8	9	10	11[3]	12	13	14															1
1		3	4[2]	5		7	8		10[3]	9■	2	11[1]	12	13	6	14												2
1		3		5		7	8	12	10[1]	11	2	13	9		4		6[2]											3
1		3		5		7	8	9[1]	12	11[2]	2		10	13	4		6											4
1		11		5		7	8[2]	9[3]	14	12	2		10		6[1]		13	3	4									5
1		11[1]		5		7	8[2]	12	10		2	13	9[3]		6		14	3	4									6
1		11		5	6	7[1]	8		10		2	12	9[2]				13	3	4									7
1				5	6	7	8		10	11[2]	2	12	9					3	4[1]	13								8
1			12	5	6	7	8	13	10[2]	11[1]	2	4[3]	9				14	3										9
1		12		5[2]	6	7	8		10[3]	11[1]	2	4	9		13		14	3										10
1			12		6	7	8[1]	13	10	11	2	4[2]	9		5			3										11
			4	5	6	7	12	9[3]	10[2]		2[1]		13		3		14			8	1	11						12
				5		7	8	9		11[1]	2[2]			13	6		10	3	4	12	1							13
				5		7	8	9	12	11[2]	2	13				14	10[3]	3	4[1]		1	6						14
				5	6	7	8[3]	9	12	14	13	11[1]				10		2[2]	4		1	3						15
				5	6	7		9[3]	12		2	13		8[2]		10[1]	14	11	4		1	3						16
1		11		5	6	7		12	10		2[2]	8					9[1]	3	4				13					17
1		11		5	6	7		9[2]	10[3]			8			12		13	2	4[1]	14		3						18
1		11		5	6	7	8	9[2]	10[1]			4					12	2		13		3						19
1		3		5	6■	7	8	9[1]	12		13	4					11[2]	2[3]		14		10						20
1		11		5	6	7	8	9[2]	12			4					10[1]	2		13		3						21
1		11		5	6	7	8	9[1]	12		13	4[2]					10[3]	2	14			3						22
1		11		5	6	7	8	9[1]				4					10	2		12		3[2]		13				23
1	2■	11[3]		5	6	7		12			13	4[1]		14			10[2]		8					9	3			24
1		11		5			8	9[1]			2	7[3]					12	3	4[2]	14		6	13	10				25
1		11		5		7	8[3]	12			2	4[1]		14						13		6	10[2]	9	3			26
1		11		5[2]		7					2	4[3]	12	13				3		10[1]		6	8	9		14		27
1		11		5■		7		12			2	13	10[3]				14					6	8	9[1]	3	4[2]		28
1		11[2]			5	7		12			2	13	10[1]				14					6	8	9	3	4[3]		29
1				12	5	7	8				2					13				14		6	11[1]	9[2]	3	4	10[3]	30
1		11		12	5[1]	7		9[3]				13				10		2				6	8	14	3	4[2]		31
1				5		7		9[2]				11[1]				10[3]	12	2		14		6	8		3	4	13	32
1				5[1]	12	7	13	9[3]				4				10	14	2		11		6	8[2]		3			33
1		12			6	7	8	9[2]				4				10		2		11[1]		5		13	3			34
1		11		5		7	4	9[1]			12					10		2				6		8	3			35
1				5		4	8[3]	7[1]			2					10	12			11[2]		6	14	9	3		13	36
1				5	6	4	8			11	2					10	9[1]	7[2]		12				13	3			37
1				5	6[2]	4	8[3]			11	2					10	9	7		13		12	14		3[1]			38

FA Cup

Third Round	Northwich Vic	(h)	3-0
Fourth Round	Brentford	(a)	1-2

Carling Cup

Second Round	Cheltenham T	(h)	1-0
Third Round	Arsenal	(h)	0-3

SWANSEA CITY FL Championship 1

FOUNDATION

The earliest Association Football in Wales was played in the Northern part of the country and no international took place in the South until 1894, when a local paper still thought it necessary to publish an outline of the rules and an illustration of the pitch markings. There had been an earlier Swansea club, but this has no connection with Swansea Town (now City) formed at a public meeting in June 1912.

Liberty Stadium, Landore, Swansea SA1 2FA.

Telephone: (01792) 616 600.

Fax: (01792) 616 606.

Ticket Office: (0870) 040 0004.

Website: www.swanseacity.net

Email: jackie@swanseacity

Ground Capacity: 20,520.

Record Attendance: 32,796 v Arsenal, FA Cup 4th rd, 17 February 1968 (at Vetch Field).

Pitch Measurements: 115yd × 74yd.

Chairman: Huw Jenkins.

Vice-chairman: Leigh Dineen.

Secretary: Jackie Rockey.

Manager: Kenny Jackett.

Assistant Manager: Kevin Nugent.

Physio: Richard Evans.

Colours: All white.

Change Colours: All black.

Year Formed: 1912.

Turned Professional: 1912.

Ltd Co.: 1912.

Previous Name: 1912, Swansea Town; 1970, Swansea City.

Club Nicknames: 'The Swans', 'The Jacks'.

Previous Ground: 1912, Vetch field; 2005, Liberty Stadium.

First Football League Game: 28 August 1920, Division 3, v Portsmouth (a) L 0–3 – Crumley; Robson, Evans; Smith, Holdsworth, Williams; Hole, I. Jones, Edmundson, Rigsby, Spottiswood.

Record League Victory: 8–0 v Hartlepool U, Division 4, 1 April 1978 – Barber; Evans, Bartley, Lally (1) (Morris), May, Bruton, Kevin Moore, Robbie James (3 incl. 1p), Curtis (3), Toshack (1), Chappell.

Record Cup Victory: 12–0 v Sliema W (Malta), ECWC 1st rd 1st leg, 15 September 1982 – Davies; Marustik, Hadziabdic (1), Irwin (1), Kennedy, Rajkovic (1), Loveridge (2) (Leighton James), Robbie James, Charles (2), Stevenson (1), Latchford (1) (Walsh (3)).

HONOURS

Football League: Championship 2 – promoted 2004–05 (3rd); Division 1 best season: 6th, 1981–82; Division 2 – Promoted 1980–81 (3rd); Division 3 (S) – Champions 1924–25, 1948–49; Division 3 – Champions 1999–2000; Promoted 1978–79 (3rd); Division 4 – Promoted 1969–70 (3rd), 1977–78 (3rd), 1987–88 (play-offs).

FA Cup: Semi-finals 1926, 1964.

Football League Cup: best season: 4th rd, 1965, 1977.

Welsh Cup: Winners 11 times; Runners-up 8 times.

Autoglass Trophy: Winners 1994, 2006.

Football League Trophy: Winners 2006.

European Competitions: *European Cup-Winners' Cup:* 1961–62, 1966–67, 1981–82, 1982–83, 1983–84, 1989–90, 1991–92.

SKY SPORTS FACT FILE

On the opening day of the 2005–06 season on 6 August, Swansea City played their first competitive match at their new headquarters. An attendance of 16,733 witnessed the 1–0 win over Tranmere Rovers.

Record Defeat: 0–8 v Liverpool, FA Cup 3rd rd, 9 January 1990. 0–8 v Monaco, ECWC, 1st rd 2nd leg, 1 October 1991.

Most League Points (2 for a win): 62, Division 3 (S), 1948–49.

Most League Points (3 for a win): 85, Division 3, 1999–2000.

Most League Goals: 90, Division 2, 1956–57.

Highest League Scorer in Season: Cyril Pearce, 35, Division 2, 1931–32.

Most League Goals in Total Aggregate: Ivor Allchurch, 166, 1949–58, 1965–68.

Most League Goals in One Match: 5, Jack Fowler v Charlton Ath, Division 3S, 27 December 1924.

Most Capped Player: Ivor Allchurch, 42 (68), Wales.

Most League Appearances: Wilfred Milne, 585, 1919–37.

Youngest League Player: Nigel Dalling, 15 years 289 days v Southport, 6 December 1974.

Record Transfer Fee Received: £400,000 from Bristol C for Steve Torpey, August 1997.

Record Transfer Fee Paid: £340,000 to Liverpool for Colin Irwin, August 1981.

Football League Record: 1920 Original Member of Division 3; 1921–25 Division 3 (S); 1925–47 Division 2; 1947–49 Division 3 (S); 1949–65 Division 2; 1965–67 Division 3; 1967–70 Division 4; 1970–73 Division 3; 1973–78 Division 4; 1978–79 Division 3; 1979–81 Division 2; 1981–83 Division 1; 1983–84 Division 2; 1984–86 Division 3; 1986–88 Division 4; 1988–92 Division 3; 1992–96 Division 2; 1996–2000 Division 3; 2000–01 Division 2; 2001–04 Division 3; 2004–05 FL2; 2005– FL1.

MANAGERS

Walter Whittaker 1912–14
William Bartlett 1914–15
Joe Bradshaw 1919–26
Jimmy Thomson 1927–31
Neil Harris 1934–39
Haydn Green 1939–47
Bill McCandless 1947–55
Ron Burgess 1955–58
Trevor Morris 1958–65
Glyn Davies 1965–66
Billy Lucas 1967–69
Roy Bentley 1969–72
Harry Gregg 1972–75
Harry Griffiths 1975–77
John Toshack 1978–83
(resigned October re-appointed in December) 1983–84
Colin Appleton 1984
John Bond 1984–85
Tommy Hutchison 1985–86
Terry Yorath 1986–89
Ian Evans 1989–90
Terry Yorath 1990–91
Frank Burrows 1991–95
Bobby Smith 1995
Kevin Cullis 1996
Jan Molby 1996–97
Micky Adams 1997
Alan Cork 1997–98
John Hollins 1998–2001
Colin Addison 2001–02
Nick Cusack 2002
Brian Flynn 2002–04
Kenny Jackett April 2004–

LATEST SEQUENCES

Longest Sequence of League Wins: 9, 27.11.1999 – 22.01.2000.

Longest Sequence of League Defeats: 9, 26.1.1991 – 19.3.1991.

Longest Sequence of League Draws: 5, 5.1.1993 – 5.2.1993.

Longest Sequence of Unbeaten League Matches: 19, 19.10.1970 – 9.3.1971.

Longest Sequence Without a League Win: 15, 25.3.1989 – 2.9.1989.

Successive Scoring Runs: 27 from 28.8.1947.

Successive Non-scoring Runs: 6 from 6.2.1996.

TEN YEAR LEAGUE RECORD

		P	W	D	L	F	A	Pts	Pos
1996-97	Div 3	46	21	8	17	62	58	71	5
1997-98	Div 3	46	13	11	22	49	62	50	20
1998-99	Div 3	46	19	14	13	56	48	71	7
1999-2000	Div 3	46	24	13	9	51	30	85	1
2000-01	Div 2	46	8	13	25	47	73	37	23
2001-02	Div 3	46	13	12	21	53	77	51	20
2002-03	Div 3	46	12	13	21	48	65	49	21
2003-04	Div 3	46	15	14	17	58	61	59	10
2004-05	FL 2	46	24	8	14	62	43	80	3
2005-06	FL 1	46	18	17	11	78	55	71	6

DID YOU KNOW ?

On 29 October 2005 Swansea City celebrated the renaming of their new ground as the Liberty Stadium by beating Chesterfield 5–1. Lee Trundle, who had signed an image-rights deal the previous week, scored a hat-trick.

SWANSEA CITY 2005–06 LEAGUE RECORD

Match No.	*Date*	*Venue*	*Opponents*	*Result*		*H/T Score*	*Lg. Pos.*	*Goalscorers*	*Attendance*
1	Aug 6	H	Tranmere R	W	1-0	1-0	—	Akinfenwa [30]	16,733
2	9	A	Colchester U	W	2-1	1-0	—	Forbes [35], Trundle [68]	2950
3	13	A	Huddersfield T	L	1-3	1-2	5	Trundle (pen) [32]	10,304
4	20	H	Doncaster R	L	1-2	1-0	10	McLeod [44]	12,744
5	27	A	Walsall	W	5-2	1-1	6	Martinez [15], Akinfenwa [47], Tudur Jones [63], McLeod [65], Connor [71]	5745
6	29	H	Barnsley	W	3-1	1-1	2	McLeod 2 [14, 90], Trundle [58]	12,554
7	Sept 10	H	Bristol C	W	7-1	1-0	4	McLeod 3 [45, 69, 87], Akinfenwa [50], Trundle 2 (1 pen) [58 (p), 71], Britton [75]	13,662
8	13	A	Milton Keynes D	W	3-1	1-1	—	Trundle [16], Robinson 2 [72, 77]	4798
9	17	A	Hartlepool U	D	2-2	0-1	1	Trundle 2 [56, 61]	4743
10	24	H	Nottingham F	D	1-1	0-0	1	Martinez [84]	18,212
11	27	A	Bournemouth	W	1-0	1-0	—	Trundle [30]	5750
12	Oct 1	H	Blackpool	W	3-2	2-1	1	Trundle [22], Akinfenwa [44], Britton [81]	13,911
13	8	A	Yeovil T	L	0-1	0-1	—		7578
14	15	H	Oldham Ath	D	0-0	0-0	3		14,029
15	22	A	Rotherham U	D	2-2	1-1	3	Trundle [42], Bean [59]	4056
16	29	H	Chesterfield	W	5-1	4-1	2	Akinfenwa [7], Trundle 3 [11, 28, 72], Tudur-Jones [45]	13,264
17	Nov 12	A	Southend U	W	2-1	1-0	1	Trundle [40], Akinfenwa [47]	11,049
18	18	H	Yeovil T	W	2-0	1-0	—	Trundle 2 (1 pen) [25 (p), 67]	19,288
19	26	A	Tranmere R	D	2-2	1-2	1	Tudur-Jones [45], Robinson [88]	7518
20	Dec 6	H	Scunthorpe U	W	2-0	0-0	—	Robinson [53], Forbes [87]	13,207
21	10	H	Colchester U	D	1-1	1-1	1	Robinson [30]	13,230
22	17	A	Doncaster R	L	1-2	1-1	1	Ricketts [24]	7159
23	26	A	Brentford	L	1-2	0-2	2	Robinson [90]	9903
24	31	A	Swindon T	D	0-0	0-0	1		8985
25	Jan 2	H	Port Vale	D	0-0	0-0	2		14,747
26	10	H	Milton Keynes D	W	3-1	3-0	—	Knight 3 [5, 12, 27]	11,922
27	14	A	Bradford C	D	1-1	1-0	2	Monk [44]	7521
28	21	H	Hartlepool U	D	1-1	1-0	3	Britton [20]	13,960
29	28	A	Bristol C	L	0-1	0-1	4		12,859
30	31	H	Gillingham	L	1-2	0-1	—	Robinson (pen) [84]	14,357
31	Feb 3	H	Bournemouth	W	1-0	1-0	—	Robinson [45]	12,079
32	11	A	Nottingham F	W	2-1	1-1	3	Forbes [27], Trundle [67]	19,132
33	14	H	Bradford C	D	1-1	1-0	—	Knight [45]	11,028
34	18	A	Scunthorpe U	D	2-2	2-1	4	Robinson (pen) [24], Knight [28]	4352
35	24	H	Huddersfield T	D	2-2	2-0	—	Trundle [19], Britton [45]	13,110
36	Mar 4	A	Barnsley	D	2-2	0-0	4	Robinson [48], Trundle [64]	9743
37	12	H	Walsall	D	1-1	0-1	4	Akinfenwa [88]	13,262
38	17	H	Brentford	W	2-1	1-1	—	Akinfenwa [20], Robinson [80]	13,508
39	25	A	Gillingham	L	0-1	0-0	5		6909
40	Apr 8	A	Port Vale	L	2-3	0-1	5	Akinfenwa [47], Fallon [88]	4850
41	11	H	Swindon T	W	2-1	0-0	—	Robinson [72], Forbes [79]	12,465
42	15	A	Blackpool	L	0-1	0-0	5		6709
43	17	H	Rotherham U	L	0-2	0-2	7		14,118
44	22	A	Oldham Ath	D	1-1	0-0	6	O'Leary [68]	5179
45	29	H	Southend U	D	2-2	2-1	6	Fallon 2 [19, 34]	19,176
46	May 6	A	Chesterfield	W	4-0	2-0	6	Knight 3 [5, 79, 89], Fallon [33]	6294

Final League Position: 6

GOALSCORERS

League (78): Trundle 20 (3 pens), Robinson 12 (2 pens), Akinfenwa 9, Knight 8, McLeod 7, Britton 4, Fallon 4, Forbes 4, Tudur-Jones 3, Martinez 2, Bean 1, Connor 1, Monk 1, O'Leary 1, Ricketts 1.
Carling Cup (1): Akinfenwa 1.
FA Cup (0).
Football League Trophy (17): Akinfenwa 5, Robinson 5, Knight 2, Britton 1, Connor 1, Forbes 1, Monk 1, Trundle 1.
Play-Offs (5): Knight 2, Fallon 1, Ricketts 1, Robinson 1.

Gueret W 46	Ricketts S 43 + 1	Austin K 23 + 3	O'Leary K 12 + 3	Monk G 33	Iriekpen E 28	Forbes A 12 + 17	Martinez R 34 + 5	Akinfenwa A 29 + 5	Trundle L 34 + 2	Goodfellow M 5 + 6	Tate A 42 + 1	Tudur-Jones O 17 + 4	McLeod K 23 + 6	Britton L 36 + 2	Anderson I — + 5	Edwards C 1 + 1	Thorpe L — + 3	Connor P 5 + 8	Macdonald S 2 + 5	Robinson A 29 + 10	Bean M 9	Nugent K — + 1	Knight L 10 + 7	Williams T 13 + 4	Watt S 2	Way D 2 + 3	Fallon R 12 + 5	Lowe K 4	*Match No.*
1	2	3	4	5^{1}	6	7	8	9	10^{2}	11	12	13																	1
1	2	3	4		6	7	8	9	10	11^{1}	5		12																2
1	2	3	4■		6■	7^{3}	8^{1}	9	10	11^{2}	5	12		14	13														3
1	2	3					8	9^{2}		11^{3}	5	10	7^{1}	4	12	6	13	14											4
1	2	3^{1}			6		8	9^{2}			5	7	11^{3}	4		12		10	13	14									5
1	2	3	12		6		8^{3}	9	10^{2}		5	7	11	4^{1}				13		14									6
1	2^{3}	3■			6		8	9^{2}	10		5		11	4^{1}	14			13		12	7								7
1	2			5	6		8		10^{2}		3		11^{1}		12		13	9		7	4								8
1	2	13		5	6		8		10		3		11				12^{2}	9^{1}		7	4								9
1	2			5	6		8	9	10	12	3		11^{1}	4						13	7^{2}								10
1	2	3			6		8	9^{1}	10		5		11	4						12	7								11
1	2	3	12		6		8	9	10		5		11	4^{1}						13	7^{2}								12
1		3		5	6	9^{1}	8		10	12	2			4	14					11^{2}	7	13^{3}							13
1	2	3			6	12	8^{2}	9	10	11^{1}	5			4						13	7								14
1	3	5	12		6	13	8^{1}	9	10^{3}		2	14	11	4^{2}							7								15
1	2	3			6		8	9^{1}	10		5	7	11	4				12											16
1	2		4	5	6			9	10		3	7	11^{1}	8						12									17
1	2	12	4	5	6			9	10^{2}		3^{1}	8	11	7				13											18
1	2		4^{1}	5	6	13	12	9	10		3	8	11^{3}	7^{2}						14									19
1	2			5	6	12	8	9^{2}	10		3	4		7				13		11^{1}									20
1	2			5	6	12	8	9^{2}	10	14	3	4		7^{3}				13		11^{1}									21
1	2	3■		5		12	8		10		6^{2}	4	13	7				9^{1}		11									22
1	2			5	6	7^{1}		9	10	12	3■	8		4						11									23
1	2			5	6	12	8	9	10^{1}	13		4^{2}	3	7						11									24
1	2	12		5	6^{1}	10^{3}	8	13		14	3		7^{2}	4				9		11									25
1	2	3		5			8	9^{1}			6		13	4				12		7			10	11^{2}					26
1	2	3		5		12	8	9			6		13	4^{1}						7			10	11^{2}					27
1	2			5	6	12	8	9^{1}	13		3		11	4						7			10^{2}						28
1		3		5	6	7^{2}	8^{3}		10					12						11			13	4■	2^{1}	14	9		29
1	2			5	6	12	8						3	4^{2}					13	11			9			7^{1}	10		30
1	2			5	6	12	8	13			3		11^{1}						14	7^{3}			9	4			10^{2}		31
1	2				6^{2}	12	8		10^{3}		4			7					13	11			14	3	5^{1}		9		32
1	2	6		5		12	8	13			4		14	7^{1}						11^{3}			9	3			10^{2}		33
1	2	6		5		7^{1}		10			4		12	8						11			9^{2}	3			13		34
1	2	6		5					10		4		8	7						11				3			9		35
1	2		4■	5		12	13		10^{3}		6		8^{1}	7^{2}						11				3		14	9		36
1	12			5		2^{1}	8	13	10		6			7^{3}						11			14	3		4	9^{2}		37
1	2		4	5		12	8^{1}	9^{2}	10^{3}		3			7						11						14	13	6	38
1	2^{2}		4	5		8	12	9	10^{3}		3			7^{1}						11			14	13				6	39
1	2		4^{1}	5			12	9	10		3	8		7^{3}						13			11^{2}				14	6	40
1	2			5		12	8	9^{3}	10		3	4		7^{1}						11				13			14	6^{2}	41
1	2			5		7	8^{1}		10		6	4								11			12	3			9		42
1	2			5		7^{3}	8^{1}	9^{2}	10		6	4							14	11			12	3			13		43
1	2	5	4			12			13		6	14	8	7^{1}						11^{3}			9^{2}	3			10		44
1	2	3	4	5					10^{1}		6		7^{2}						8	11			12	13			9		45
1	2	3		5			12	13			6	4		7					8^{3}	11			9^{1}	14			10^{2}		46

FA Cup
First Round | Stockport Co | (a) | 0-2

Carling Cup
First Round | Reading | (a) | 1-3

Play-Offs
Semi-Final | Brentford | (h) | 1-1
 | | (a) | 2-0
Final | Barnsley | | 2-2
(at Millennium Stadium)

Football League Trophy
First Round | Torquay U | (a) | 3-1
Second Round | Rushden & D | (h) | 4-0
Quarter-Final | Peterborough U | (h) | 3-1
Semi-Final | Walsall | (h) | 2-2
Southern Final | Colchester U | (h) | 1-0
 | | (a) | 2-1
Final | Carlisle U | | 2-1
(at Millennium Stadium)

SWINDON TOWN FL Championship 2

FOUNDATION

It is generally accepted that Swindon Town came into being in 1881, although there is no firm evidence that the club's founder, Rev. William Pitt, captain of the Spartans (an offshoot of a cricket club) changed his club's name to Swindon Town before 1883, when the Spartans amalgamated with St Mark's Young Men's Friendly Society.

County Ground, County Road, Swindon SN1 2ED.

Telephone: 0870 443 1969.

Fax: (01793) 333 703.

Ticket Office: 0870 443 1894.

Website: www.swindontownfc.co.uk

Email: enquiries@swindontownfc.co.uk

Ground Capacity: 14,255.

Record Attendance: 32,000 v Arsenal, FA Cup 3rd rd, 15 January 1972.

Pitch Measurements: 110yd × 70yd.

Chairman: Willie Carson.

Deputy Chairman: Mark Devlin.

Chief Executive: Sandy Gray.

Secretary: Linda Birrell.

Manager: Dennis Wise.

Assistant Manager: Gus Poyet.

Physio: Dick Mackey.

Colours: Red shirts with white and green, red shorts with white stripe, red stockings with white turnover.

Change Colours: Navy shirts with pale blue stripe, navy shorts, navy stockings with white turnover.

Year Formed: 1881* (*see Foundation*).

Turned Professional: 1894.

Ltd Co.: 1894.

Club Nickname: 'Robins'.

Previous Ground: 1881, The Croft; 1896, County Ground.

First Football League Game: 28 August 1920, Division 3, v Luton T (h) W 9–1 – Nash; Kay, Macconachie; Langford, Hawley, Wareing; Jefferson (1), Fleming (4), Rogers, Batty (2), Davies (1), (1 og).

Record League Victory: 9–1 v Luton T, Division 3 (S), 28 August 1920 – Nash; Kay, Macconachie; Langford, Hawley, Wareing; Jefferson (1), Fleming (4), Rogers, Batty (2), Davies (1), (1 og).

HONOURS

FA Premier League: best season: 22nd 1993–94; Division 1 – 1992–93 (play-offs).

Football League: Division 2 – Champions 1995–96; Division 3 – Runners-up 1962–63, 1968–69; Division 4 – Champions 1985–86 (with record 102 points).

FA Cup: Semi-finals 1910, 1912.

Football League Cup: Winners 1969.

Anglo-Italian Cup: Winners 1970.

SKY SPORTS FACT FILE

In August 1952 Swindon Town manager Louis Page signed wing-half Ralph Prouton from Arsenal, the transfer forms being completed when the player was acting as twelfth man for Hampshire against Sussex in a County Cricket Championship match.

Record Cup Victory: 10–1 v Farnham U Breweries (away), FA Cup 1st rd (replay), 28 November 1925 – Nash; Dickenson, Weston, Archer, Bew, Adey; Denyer (2), Wall (1), Richardson (4), Johnson (3), Davies.

Record Defeat: 1–10 v Manchester C, FA Cup 4th rd (replay), 25 January 1930.

Most League Points (2 for a win): 64, Division 3, 1968–69.

Most League Points (3 for a win): 102, Division 4, 1985–86.

Most League Goals: 100, Division 3 (S), 1926–27.

Highest League Scorer in Season: Harry Morris, 47, Division 3 (S), 1926–27.

Most League Goals in Total Aggregate: Harry Morris, 216, 1926–33.

Most League Goals in One Match: 5, Harry Morris v QPR, Division 3S, 18 December 1926; 5, Harry Morris v Norwich C, Division 3S, 26 April 1930; 5, Keith East v Mansfield T, Division 3, 20 November 1965.

Most Capped Player: Rod Thomas, 30 (50), Wales.

Most League Appearances: John Trollope, 770, 1960–80.

Youngest League Player: Paul Rideout, 16 years 107 days v Hull C, 29 November 1980.

Record Transfer Fee Received: £1,500,000 from Manchester C for Kevin Horlock, January 1997.

Record Transfer Fee Paid: £800,000 to West Ham U for Joey Beauchamp, August 1994.

Football League Record: 1920 Original Member of Division 3; 1921–58 Division 3 (S); 1958–63 Division 3; 1963–65 Division 2; 1965–69 Division 3; 1969–74 Division 2; 1974–82 Division 3; 1982–86 Division 4; 1986–87 Division 3; 1987–92 Division 2; 1992–93 Division 1; 1993–94 FA Premier League; 1994–95 Division 1; 1995–96 Division 2; 1996–2000 Division 1; 2000–04 Division 2; 2004–06 FL1; 2006– FL2.

MANAGERS

Sam Allen 1902–33
Ted Vizard 1933–39
Neil Harris 1939–41
Louis Page 1945–53
Maurice Lindley 1953–55
Bert Head 1956–65
Danny Williams 1965–69
Fred Ford 1969–71
Dave Mackay 1971–72
Les Allen 1972–74
Danny Williams 1974–78
Bobby Smith 1978–80
John Trollope 1980–83
Ken Beamish 1983–84
Lou Macari 1984–89
Ossie Ardiles 1989–91
Glenn Hoddle 1991–93
John Gorman 1993–94
Steve McMahon 1994–99
Jimmy Quinn 1999–2000
Colin Todd 2000
Andy King 2000–01
Roy Evans 2001
Andy King 2002–06
Iffy Onuora 2006
Dennis Wise May 2006–

LATEST SEQUENCES

Longest Sequence of League Wins: 8, 12.1.1986 – 15.3.1986.

Longest Sequence of League Defeats: 8, 29.8.2005 – 8.10.2005.

Longest Sequence of League Draws: 6, 22.11.1991 – 28.12.1991.

Longest Sequence of Unbeaten League Matches: 22, 12.1.1986 – 23.8.86.

Longest Sequence Without a League Win: 19, 30.10.1999 – 4.3.2000.

Successive Scoring Runs: 31 from 17.4.1926.

Successive Non-scoring Runs: 5 from 16.11.1963.

TEN YEAR LEAGUE RECORD

		P	W	D	L	F	A	Pts	Pos
1996-97	Div 1	46	15	9	22	52	71	54	19
1997-98	Div 1	46	14	10	22	42	73	52	18
1998-99	Div 1	46	13	11	22	59	81	50	17
1999-2000	Div 1	46	8	12	26	38	77	36	24
2000-01	Div 2	46	13	13	20	47	65	52	20
2001-02	Div 2	46	15	14	17	46	56	59	13
2002-03	Div 2	46	16	12	18	59	63	60	10
2003-04	Div 2	46	20	13	13	76	58	73	5
2004-05	FL 1	46	17	12	17	66	68	63	12
2005-06	FL 1	46	11	15	20	46	65	48	23

DID YOU KNOW ?

George Morrall was a 1931 FA Cup finalist with Birmingham for whom he made 250 League and Cup appearances at centre-half. He joined Swindon Town in August 1936 and was outstanding in their 2–1 FA Cup replay win over Grimsby Town on 12 January 1938.

SWINDON TOWN 2005–06 LEAGUE RECORD

Match No.	Date	Venue	Opponents	Result	H/T Score	Lg. Pos.	Goalscorers	Attendance
1	Aug 6	A	Barnsley	L 0-2	0-1	—		9358
2	9	H	Oldham Ath	L 2-3	0-2	—	Roberts 79, Thorpe 85	5294
3	13	H	Nottingham F	W 2-1	1-1	19	Fallon 31, O'Hanlon 73	8108
4	20	A	Blackpool	D 0-0	0-0	19		4661
5	27	H	Yeovil T	W 4-2	1-1	14	Skiverton (og) 24, Fallon 50, Heath 66, Roberts 90	6973
6	29	A	Tranmere R	L 0-1	0-0	14		7557
7	Sept 3	A	Walsall	L 0-1	0-0	16		5392
8	10	H	Southend U	L 1-2	0-1	20	Fallon 90	4785
9	17	A	Bournemouth	L 1-2	1-1	22	Jenkins 44	7276
10	24	H	Bradford C	L 2-3	1-1	23	Fallon 2 19, 76	4590
11	27	A	Doncaster R	L 0-1	0-1	—		5282
12	Oct 1	A	Milton Keynes D	L 1-3	1-0	24	Fallon 7	5536
13	8	H	Port Vale	L 1-2	1-1	—	Fallon 24	4531
14	15	A	Brentford	D 0-0	0-0	24		6969
15	22	H	Scunthorpe U	D 1-1	0-1	24	Roberts (pen) 78	4972
16	29	A	Huddersfield T	D 1-1	1-0	24	Gurney (pen) 40	11,352
17	Nov 11	H	Bristol C	W 2-1	2-1	—	McDermott 12, Fallon 31	7572
18	19	A	Port Vale	D 1-1	0-0	24	Bouazza 66	4108
19	26	H	Barnsley	L 0-3	0-1	24		5422
20	Dec 3	A	Rotherham U	W 1-0	1-0	—	Fallon 45	3537
21	10	A	Oldham Ath	D 2-2	1-0	24	O'Hanlon 12, McDermott 48	5354
22	17	H	Blackpool	D 0-0	0-0	24		5766
23	26	H	Colchester U	W 1-0	0-0	24	Fallon 90	5531
24	28	A	Chesterfield	D 1-1	0-1	24	Bouazza (pen) 63	4265
25	31	H	Swansea C	D 0-0	0-0	23		8985
26	Jan 2	A	Hartlepool U	D 1-1	0-1	23	Fallon 78	4169
27	14	A	Gillingham	L 0-3	0-1	23		7300
28	21	H	Bournemouth	W 4-2	1-0	23	Cureton 37, Miglioranzi 52, Fallon 79, Peacock 90	6092
29	27	A	Southend U	L 0-2	0-2	—		7945
30	31	H	Walsall	W 1-0	1-0	—	Cureton 43	4597
31	Feb 4	H	Doncaster R	W 2-1	1-0	21	Shakes 29, Comyn-Platt 57	5100
32	11	A	Bradford C	D 1-1	0-0	21	O'Hanlon 90	7283
33	14	H	Gillingham	W 1-0	1-0	—	Cureton 27	5530
34	18	H	Rotherham U	L 2-3	2-2	19	Cureton 20, O'Hanlon 25	7518
35	25	A	Nottingham F	L 1-7	0-3	22	Benjamin 76	22,444
36	Mar 7	H	Tranmere R	L 1-2	0-2	—	Cureton 69	4139
37	11	A	Yeovil T	D 0-0	0-0	22		7451
38	18	A	Colchester U	L 0-1	0-1	23		3767
39	25	H	Chesterfield	W 2-0	0-0	23	Cureton 2 53, 90	5661
40	Apr 8	H	Hartlepool U	D 1-1	0-1	22	Peacock 54	5225
41	11	A	Swansea C	L 1-2	0-0	—	Shakes 62	12,465
42	15	H	Milton Keynes D	L 0-1	0-0	23		7273
43	17	A	Scunthorpe U	W 2-1	2-1	21	Benjamin (pen) 26, Shakes 39	5207
44	22	H	Brentford	L 1-3	0-2	23	Brown 71	6845
45	29	A	Bristol C	D 1-1	0-0	23	Brown 49	15,632
46	May 6	H	Huddersfield T	D 0-0	0-0	23		6353

Final League Position: 23

GOALSCORERS

League (46): Fallon 12, Cureton 7, O'Hanlon 4, Roberts 3 (1 pen), Shakes 3, Benjamin 2 (1 pen), Bouazza 2 (1 pen), Brown 2, McDermott 2, Peacock 2, Comyn-Platt 1, Gurney 1 (pen), Heath 1, Jenkins 1, Miglioranzi 1, Thorpe 1, own goal 1.
Carling Cup (1): Pook 1.
FA Cup (3): Comyn-Platt 1, Fallon 1 (pen), Gurney 1.
Football League Trophy (3): Bouazza 1, Fallon 1, Roberts 1.

Evans R 32	Smith J 38	Jenkins S 17+7	Ifil J 34+2	O'Hanlon S 40	Collins P 13	Shakes R 26+11	Whalley G 23+1	Thorpe T 6+1	Cureton J 22+8	Pook M 26+4	Wells B —+4	Roberts C 4+17	Nicholas A 31+2	Reeves A —+1	Nicolau N 3+2	Summerbee N 1	Fallon R 25	Heath C 8+3	Heaton T 14	Miglioranzi S 22+5	Gurney A 24+4	McDermott N 9+4	Bouazza H 11+2	Comyn-Platt C 13+9	Stroud D 1+1	Brown A 23+4	Mikolanda P 1+4	Holgate A 2+4	Smith P 5+4	Peacock L 11+4	Jarrett A 2+4	Benjamin T 5+3	Diagouraga T 5+3	McPhee C 6+2	Jutkiewicz L 3+2	*Match No.*
1	2	3^{1}	4	5	6	7	8	9	10	11^{2}	12	13																							1
1	2		4	5^{1}	6	14	8	9	10	11^{2}		7	3^{3}	12	13																				2
1	2		4	5	6	12	8		10^{2}	11		13			3	7^{1}	9																		3
1	2	12	4	5	6	13	8^{1}		10^{3}	11		14			3		9	7^{2}																	4
	2		4	5^{3}	6	7	8		10^{1}	11		12					9	3^{2}	1	13	14														5
	3		4		5	6^{1}	8^{3}		12	11	14	13					9	10^{2}	1	7	2														6
	3	13	4		5	6^{1}	8		12	11		14					9	10^{3}	1	7^{2}	2														7
	2		4		6	12	8^{3}	14	10^{1}	11		13			3^{2}		9		1	7	5														8
	11	3^{3}	4		5		8^{2}	10^{1}		6		12					9	13	1	7	2■	14													9
	11		4	5	6		8^{2}	10^{1}		2		12	3				9	13	1	7^{3}		14													10
	3		4■	5	6^{1}	7		10	12	2		13					9	11^{2}	1			8													11
	3			5	6	7^{2}		10^{1}	12	4			2		13		9	11	1			8													12
	2	3	4	5		12	8^{3}			11	14		13				9	6^{1}	1			7	10^{2}												13
	3^{3}	2^{1}	4■	5			8			11		13	12				9	7^{2}	1		6	14	10												14
		2		5		12	8^{1}			7		11	3				9■		1		4	6^{2}	10	13											15
		2	4	5		6^{3}				11^{1}			3					12	1	7	9^{2}	13	10	14	8										16
	2^{1}	12	4	5						11^{2}		13	3				9		1	7	8	6^{3}	10	14											17
1		2	4	5		12	8					11^{1}	3				9			7			10	6											18
		2	4	5								11	3				9		1	7^{2}	8^{1}		10	6		13	12								19
1	2^{1}				6		13			11		12	3				9^{3}			7		4	10^{2}	5		8	14								20
1	2		12	5		6				11			3				9^{3}			7		8^{2}	10	4^{1}		13	14								21
1	2		4	5		12				11			3				9			7		6^{1}	10^{3}			13	8^{2}	14							22
1	2		4	5		6				12			3				9			7		8^{1}	13			11		10^{2}							23
1	2	12	4	5		6				7^{2}			3				9				8		10^{1}			11		13							24
1	2^{1}	12	4	5		6							3				9			7^{3}	8		13	14		11		10^{2}							25
1		2	4	5		6			10^{3}	12			3				9			7^{1}				8	13	11^{2}	14								26
1		2	4	5^{1}		6			10				3^{2}				9			7				8		11		13	12						27
1		2	4			6			10^{3}				3				9			7^{1}	8			5		11^{2}			12	14	13					28
1		2	4	5		6			12				3							7^{3}	9			13		11^{1}			14	10	8^{2}					29
1	2		4	5		6			8				3							7^{1}	9^{2}			12		11			13	10^{3}		14				30
1	2		4	5		6			10				3								12			8^{1}		11		13	7	9^{2}						31
1	2		4	5		6			10^{1}			12	3								8^{2}					11			7	9	13					32
1	2		4	5		6^{2}			10			13	3							12	8					11			7^{1}	9						33
1	2		4	5		6^{2}			10	12		13	3							7^{1}	8^{3}					11				9	14					34
1	2	12	4■	5		6^{2}			10				3							7^{1}	13					11				9	8^{3}	14				35
1	2^{1}			5		12			10	11			3							7^{2}	4					6				9	13	8				36
1	2	3^{1}		5		13	8		10	7^{2}			11							12	4					6				9						37
1	2	3		5			8^{1}		10	7		12	11^{2}								4			13		6				9^{3}		14				38
1	2	3	12	5			8		10	7^{2}											4^{1}			6		11						9^{3}	13	14		39
1	2	3	4^{1}	5		12	8^{3}		10															6		11				13		9^{2}	7	14		40
1	2			5		6	8^{1}		12				3							13				4		7				9^{3}			11^{2}	10	14	41
1	2			5		6	8^{1}		10				3							12	4			13^{3}		7^{2}				14			11	9		42
1	2	12		5		6							3								4			13					7^{1}	14		8	11	9^{2}	10^{3}	43
1	2			5		6	8^{1}		10				3								4					12			7^{2}			11^{3}	13	9	14	44
1	2	3^{2}	4	5			8^{1}		12	14											13			6		11							7^{3}	9	10	45
1	2		4	5^{2}		7	8^{3}		12	11	13													6^{1}		3							14	9	10	46

FA Cup

First Round	Boston U	(h)	2-2
		(a)	1-4

Carling Cup

First Round	Wycombe W	(h)	1-3

Football League Trophy

First Round	Stevenage B	(h)	2-0
Second Round	Peterborough U	(a)	1-2

TORQUAY UNITED FL Championship 2

FOUNDATION

The idea of establishing a Torquay club was agreed by old boys of Torquay College and Torbay College, while sitting in Princess Gardens listening to the band. A proper meeting was subsequently held at Tor Abbey Hotel at which officers were elected. This was on 1 May 1899 and the club's first competition was the Eastern League (later known as the East Devon League). As an amateur club it played at Teignmouth Road, Torquay Recreation Ground and Cricket Field Road before settling down for four years at Torquay Cricket Ground where the rugby club now plays. They became Torquay United in 1921 after merging with Babbacombe FC.

Plainmoor Ground, Torquay, Devon TQ1 3PS.

Telephone: (01803) 328 666.

Fax: (01803) 323 976.

Ticket Office: (01803) 328 666.

Website: www.torquayunited.com

Email: gullsfc@aol.com

Ground Capacity: 6,285.

Record Attendance: 21,908 v Huddersfield T, FA Cup 4th rd, 29 January 1955.

Pitch Measurements: 110yd × 74yd.

Chairman: Michael Bateson.

Vice-chairman: Mervyn Benney.

Secretary: Deborah Hancox.

Manager: Ian Atkins.

Physio: Darren James.

Colours: Yellow shirt with royal blue sleeves, yellow shorts, yellow stockings.

Change Colours: All blue.

Year Formed: 1899.

Turned Professional: 1921.

Ltd Co.: 1921.

Previous Name: 1910, Torquay Town; 1921, Torquay United.

Club Nickname: 'The Gulls'.

Previous Grounds: 1899, Teignmouth Road; 1900, Torquay Recreation Ground; 1904, Cricket Field Road; 1906, Torquay Cricket Ground; 1910, Plainmoor Ground.

First Football League Game: 27 August 1927, Division 3 (S), v Exeter C (h) D 1–1 – Millsom; Cook,

HONOURS

Football League: Division 3 – Promoted 2003–04 (3rd); Division 3 (S) – Runners-up 1956–57; Division 4 – Promoted 1959–60 (3rd), 1965–66 (3rd), 1990–91 (play-offs).

FA Cup: best season: 4th rd, 1949, 1955, 1971, 1983, 1990.

Football League Cup: never past 3rd rd.

Sherpa Van Trophy: Runners-up 1989.

SKY SPORTS FACT FILE

On 19 October 1963 when Robin Stubbs scored his club record five goals, Torquay United were leading Newport County 2–1 with less than 20 minutes remaining in the match. The final score was 8–3 in favour of Torquay who also had a goal disallowed.

Smith; Wellock, Wragg, Connor, Mackey, Turner (1), Jones, McGovern, Thomson.

Record League Victory: 9–0 v Swindon T, Division 3 (S), 8 March 1952 – George Webber; Topping, Ralph Calland; Brown, Eric Webber, Towers; Shaw (1), Marchant (1), Northcott (2), Collins (3), Edds (2).

Record Cup Victory: 7–1 v Northampton T, FA Cup 1st rd, 14 November 1959 – Gill; Penford, Downs; Bettany, George Northcott, Rawson; Baxter, Cox, Tommy Northcott (1), Bond (3), Pym (3).

Record Defeat: 2–10 v Fulham, Division 3 (S), 7 September 1931. 2–10 v Luton T, Division 3 (S), 2 September 1933.

Most League Points (2 for a win): 60, Division 4, 1959–60.

Most League Points (3 for a win): 81, Division 3, 2003–04.

Most League Goals: 89, Division 3 (S), 1956–57.

Highest League Scorer in Season: Sammy Collins, 40, Division 3 (S), 1955–56.

Most League Goals in Total Aggregate: Sammy Collins, 204, 1948–58.

Most League Goals in One Match: 5, Robin Stubbs v Newport Co, Division 4, 19 October 1963.

Most Capped Player: Rodney Jack, St Vincent.

Most League Appearances: Dennis Lewis, 443, 1947–59.

Youngest League Player: David Byng, 16 years 36 days v Walsall, 14 August 1993.

Record Transfer Fee Received: £400,000 from Crystal Palace for Matthew Greg, October 1998.

Record Transfer Fee Paid: £500,000 to Crewe Alex for Rodney Jack, August 1998.

Football League Record: 1927 Elected to Division 3 (S); 1958–60 Division 4; 1960–62 Division 3; 1962–66 Division 4; 1966–72 Division 3; 1972–91 Division 4; 1991–2004 Division 3; 2004–05 FL1; 2005– FL2.

MANAGERS

Percy Mackrill 1927–29
A. H. Hoskins 1929 *(Secretary-Manager)*
Frank Womack 1929–32
Frank Brown 1932–38
Alf Steward 1938–40
Billy Butler 1945–46
Jack Butler 1946–47
John McNeil 1947–50
Bob John 1950
Alex Massie 1950–51
Eric Webber 1951–65
Frank O'Farrell 1965–68
Alan Brown 1969–71
Jack Edwards 1971–73
Malcolm Musgrove 1973–76
Mike Green 1977–81
Frank O'Farrell 1981–82 *(continued as General Manager to 1983)*
Bruce Rioch 1982–84
Dave Webb 1984–85
John Sims 1985
Stuart Morgan 1985–87
Cyril Knowles 1987–89
Dave Smith 1989–91
John Impey 1991–92
Ivan Golac 1992
Paul Compton 1992–93
Don O'Riordan 1993–95
Eddie May 1995–96
Kevin Hodges *(Head Coach)* 1996–98
Wes Saunders 1998–2001
Roy McFarland 2001–02
Leroy Rosenior 2002–06
Ian Atkins April 2006–

LATEST SEQUENCES

Longest Sequence of League Wins: 8, 24.1.1998 – 3.3.1998.

Longest Sequence of League Defeats: 8, 30.9.1995 – 18.11.1995.

Longest Sequence of League Draws: 8, 25.10.1969 – 13.12.1969.

Longest Sequence of Unbeaten League Matches: 15, 5.5.1990 – 3.11.1990.

Longest Sequence Without a League Win: 17, 5.3.1938 – 10.9.1938.

Successive Scoring Runs: 19 from 3.10.1953.

TEN YEAR LEAGUE RECORD

		P	W	D	L	F	A	Pts	Pos
1996-97	Div 3	46	13	11	22	46	62	50	21
1997-98	Div 3	46	21	11	14	68	59	74	5
1998-99	Div 3	46	12	17	17	47	58	53	20
1999-2000	Div 3	46	19	12	15	62	52	69	9
2000-01	Div 3	46	12	13	21	52	77	49	21
2001-02	Div 3	46	12	15	19	46	63	51	19
2002-03	Div 3	46	16	18	12	71	71	66	9
2003-04	Div 3	46	23	12	11	68	44	81	3
2004-05	FL 1	46	12	15	19	55	79	51	21
2005-06	FL 2	46	13	13	20	53	66	52	20

DID YOU KNOW?

From Celtic's "A" team, Scottish junior football, Stirling Albion, Clyde, Millwall and Weymouth, goalkeeper Andy Donnelly had to wait ten years until his debut for Torquay United on 28 October 1968 and at long last a regular senior slot.

TORQUAY UNITED 2005–06 LEAGUE RECORD

Match No.	Date	Venue	Opponents	Result		H/T Score	Lg. Pos.	Goalscorers	Attendance
1	Aug 6	H	Notts Co	D	0-0	0-0	—		3754
2	10	A	Oxford U	L	0-1	0-0	—		4820
3	13	A	Mansfield T	L	0-3	0-2	24		2632
4	20	H	Bristol R	L	2-3	1-0	24	Constantine[21], Hewlett[58]	3964
5	27	A	Peterborough U	D	0-0	0-0	23		3502
6	29	H	Chester C	L	0-1	0-0	24		2245
7	Sept 3	A	Rochdale	L	1-4	1-2	24	Connell[16]	2388
8	10	H	Shrewsbury T	W	2-1	2-1	24	Connell[2], Garner[45]	2287
9	17	A	Grimsby T	L	0-3	0-1	24		4026
10	24	H	Lincoln C	W	2-1	0-1	22	Garner[51], Connell[66]	2281
11	27	A	Leyton Orient	L	1-2	0-1	—	Osei-Kuffour[67]	4091
12	Oct 1	A	Cheltenham T	W	1-0	0-0	21	Connell[67]	3578
13	7	H	Barnet	D	0-0	0-0	—		2965
14	15	A	Wrexham	L	2-4	0-2	22	Connell[66], Bedeau[90]	4301
15	22	H	Macclesfield T	D	1-1	0-0	23	Connell[68]	2355
16	29	A	Boston U	L	0-2	0-1	24		2220
17	Nov 12	H	Carlisle U	L	3-4	2-2	24	Robinson 2 (1 pen)[13, 78 (p)], Hill[45]	2352
18	19	A	Barnet	L	0-1	0-1	24		2368
19	26	A	Notts Co	D	2-2	0-1	24	Lockwood[71], Osei-Kuffour[90]	4442
20	Dec 6	H	Northampton T	D	3-3	0-1	—	Bedeau (pen)[56], Osei-Kuffour[82], Hill[90]	2010
21	10	H	Oxford U	D	3-3	2-3	24	Lockwood[7], Hill 2[27, 73]	2678
22	17	A	Bristol R	W	1-0	0-0	23	Sako[88]	6061
23	26	H	Wycombe W	D	2-2	2-0	23	Sako[13], Bedeau[31]	3733
24	31	H	Rushden & D	W	2-1	2-0	22	Osei-Kuffour[2], Hill[33]	2668
25	Jan 2	A	Darlington	L	2-3	1-1	22	Phillips[45], Connell[89]	3785
26	14	A	Bury	L	2-3	1-2	22	Lockwood[10], Hill[90]	2102
27	21	H	Grimsby T	D	2-2	1-1	22	Bedeau 2[34, 89]	2559
28	24	H	Rochdale	L	1-3	0-1	—	Sako[55]	2043
29	28	A	Shrewsbury T	W	1-0	0-0	22	Robinson[64]	3741
30	31	A	Stockport Co	D	1-1	1-0	—	Bedeau[7]	4455
31	Feb 4	H	Leyton Orient	W	2-0	0-0	21	Phillips[47], Bedeau[62]	2687
32	11	A	Lincoln C	L	0-2	0-1	22		4454
33	14	H	Bury	D	0-0	0-0	—		2129
34	17	A	Northampton T	L	0-1	0-0	—		5636
35	25	H	Mansfield T	L	0-2	0-1	24		2494
36	Mar 7	A	Chester C	D	1-1	1-0	—	Hill[22]	1806
37	11	H	Peterborough U	W	1-0	0-0	23	Bedeau[65]	2438
38	18	A	Wycombe W	W	1-0	0-0	21	Bedeau[57]	7134
39	Apr 1	A	Rushden & D	L	0-1	0-1	24		3795
40	8	H	Darlington	L	1-2	1-0	24	Hill[37]	2715
41	15	H	Cheltenham T	L	1-2	1-0	24	Thorpe[26]	3336
42	17	A	Macclesfield T	W	2-0	0-0	24	Osei-Kuffour 2[54, 90]	1808
43	22	H	Wrexham	W	1-0	1-0	23	Phillips[9]	2623
44	25	H	Stockport Co	W	4-0	3-0	—	Thorpe 2[4, 18], Osei-Kuffour[23], Hollands[48]	3565
45	29	A	Carlisle U	W	2-1	2-0	19	Hill[8], Osei-Kuffour[41]	13,467
46	May 6	H	Boston U	D	0-0	0-0	20		5697

Final League Position: 20

GOALSCORERS

League (53): Bedeau 9 (1 pen), Hill 9, Osei-Kuffour 8, Connell 7, Lockwood 3, Phillips 3, Robinson 3 (1 pen), Sako 3, Thorpe 3, Garner 2, Constantine 1, Hewlett 1, Hollands 1.
Carling Cup (0).
FA Cup (3): Bedeau 2, Stonebridge 1.
Football League Trophy (1): Osei Kuffour 1.

Marriott A 46	Hockley M 25 + 11	McGlinchey B 4 + 1	Hewlett M 18 + 6	Taylor C 27 + 4	Woods S 35 + 3	Hill K 41 + 1	Garner D 40 + 3	Connell A 12 + 10	Osei-Kuffour J 34 + 9	Lawless A 11 + 3	Sow M 9 + 2	Constantine L 10 + 5	Bedeau A 26 + 5	Villis M 11 + 1	Coleman L 7 + 7	Sako M 10 + 15	Priso C 1 + 2	Sharp J 30 + 2	Hancox R — + 1	Flynn P 1	McAliskey J 3	Phillips M 23 + 3	Lloyd A 19 + 1	Woodman C 2	Robinson P 12 + 9	Stonebridge I 3	Lockwood A 9	Afful L — + 5	Thorpe L 10	Reed S 11	Hollands D 10	Andrews L 6 + 1	Match No.
1	2	3	4	5	6	7¹	8	9	10²	11³	12	13	14■																				1
1	2	3	4³	5	6	7	8²	12	10	13	11	9¹		14																			2
1	2	3		5	6	7	8²	12	10	4	11³				13	14	9¹																3
1	2	3	4	5	6	7	12		13			10		11	8¹	9²																	4
1	2		4	5	13	11			14		12²	9	7¹	6	8	10³		3															5
1	2	12	4³	5	6	7¹	14		10			8	13		11²	9		3															6
1	2			5■	6		8	9	10²			11	7³	4¹	13	12		3	14														7
1	4				6	3	8	9	10	2	7²	11¹			13	12		5															8
1	4		12	13	6	3	8	9	10²		7³	11					14	5		2¹													9
1	2		4	5	12	3	8	9	10		7¹	11						6															10
1	2		4²	5		3	8	9	10		7¹	11			12		13	6															11
1	2		4	5		3	8	9	10		7	12						6			11¹												12
1	2²		4	5		3		9	10		7¹	11	8		13	12		6															13
1			4	5	2	3	8	9²	10		7¹	12	11		13			6															14
1	2		4²	5		3	8	9	10¹			12	7³		13			6			11	14											15
1	2		4	5	6	11	8³	12				13			10¹	14		3			9²	7											16
1				5²	6	11	4		12						8¹			13				7	2	3	9	10							17
1			14	5	6²	11¹	4						12		7							13	2	3	9³	10	8						18
1	12		4¹		6		8		11				7					5				13	2		9²	10	3						19
1	4²			12	6¹	11	8		10				9		7³	13		3					2		14		5						20
1	4¹			5		11	8		10				9			12		3				7	2				6						21
1	4²			5	14	11	8	12	10	2³			9			13						7¹	3				6						22
1	12			5		11	4	13	10	2			9			8¹						7²	6				3						23
1	12			5		11	4		10	2²			9³			8¹		13				7	3		14		6						24
1	12				4	11		13	10	2²						8■		6				7	3		9¹		5						25
1			4²		8	11	12	14	10	2			9¹			13		6				7³	3				5						26
1			4		6¹	11	8		10	2			9					5				7	3		12								27
1	12		4²		6	11	8		10	2¹			9			13		5				7	3³		14								28
1	2¹				6		4		10	12			9			8		5				7²	3		11			13					29
1	2²		12		6		4		10³	13			9¹			8		5				7	3		11			14					30
1	2					11	4		10				9	6				5				7	3		8								31
1			12		6	11	8	13	10	2				4¹		7		5					3		9²								32
1	2		12		6	11	4		8³				9²			7¹		5					3		13			14	10				33
1	2¹		4		6	11	8	12	7				9²					5					3		13				10				34
1			4¹		6	12	8	9²	10				7	5				3					2		11			13					35
1	2				6	11¹	8		12				9²	4				5				7³	14		13				10■	3			36
1	12				2	11	4		13				9²	6				5				7³			10¹			14		3	8		37
1	12			14	6	11	4						9²			13		5				7³			10¹					3	8	2	38
1			12	13	6²	11	4¹		14				9					5				7			10³					3	8	2	39
1				5	6	11	4²		12				9			13						7¹			14				10³	3	8	2	40
1				5	6	11	4¹	9	12				13	2		14						7²							10	3	8³		41
1	12			5	6	11	4		13				9²	2³								7¹							10	3	8	14	42
1	12			5	6	11	4		9¹													7							10	3	8	2	43
1	12			5	6	11	4	13	9²							14						7¹							10³	3	8	2	44
1	12			5	6	11	4		9³					2		13						7¹			14				10	3	8²		45
1	7			5	6	11	4		9¹				12																10	3	8	2	46

FA Cup

First Round	Harrogate T	(h)	1-1
		(a)	0-0
Second Round	Notts Co	(h)	2-1
Third Round	Birmingham C	(h)	0-0
		(a)	0-2

Carling Cup

First Round	Bournemouth	(h)	0-0

Football League Trophy

First Round	Swansea C	(h)	1-3

TOTTENHAM HOTSPUR FA Premiership

FOUNDATION

The Hotspur Football Club was formed from an older cricket club in 1882. Most of the founders were old boys of St John's Presbyterian School and Tottenham Grammar School. The Casey brothers were well to the fore as the family provided the club's first goalposts (painted blue and white) and their first ball. They soon adopted the local YMCA as their meeting place, but after a couple of moves settled at the Red House, which is still their headquarters, although now known simply as 748 High Road.

White Hart Lane, Bill Nicholson Way, 748 High Road, Tottenham, London N17 0AP.

Telephone: 0870 420 5000.

Fax: (020) 8365 5175.

Ticket Office: 0870 420 5000.

Website: www.tottenhamhotspur.co.uk

Email: email@tottenhamhotspur.co.uk

Ground Capacity: 36,237.

Record Attendance: 75,038 v Sunderland, FA Cup 6th rd. 5 March 1938.

Pitch Measurements: 100m × 67m.

Chairman: Daniel Levy.

Vice-chairman: Paul Kemsley.

Secretary: John Alexander.

Head Coach: Martin Jol.

First Assistant to Head Coach: Chris Hughton.

Head of Medical Services: Dr Charlotte Cowie.

Colours: White shirts, navy shorts, white stockings.

Change Colours: Blue atoll and navy shirts, navy and blue atoll shorts, blue atoll and navy stockings.

Year Formed: 1882.

Turned Professional: 1895.

Ltd Co.: 1898.

Previous Names: 1882, Hotspur Football Club; 1884, Tottenham Hotspur.

Club Nickname: 'Spurs'.

Previous Grounds: 1882, Tottenham Marshes; 1888, Northumberland Park; 1899, White Hart Lane.

First Football League Game: 1 September 1908, Division 2, v Wolverhampton W (h) W 3–0 – Hewitson; Coquet, Burton; Morris (1), D. Steel, Darnell; Walton, Woodward (2), Macfarlane, R. Steel, Middlemiss.

Record League Victory: 9–0 v Bristol R, Division 2, 22 October 1977 – Daines; Naylor, Holmes, Hoddle (1), McAllister, Perryman, Pratt, McNab, Moores (3), Lee (4), Taylor (1).

HONOURS

Football League: Division 1 – Champions 1950–51, 1960–61; Runners-up 1921–22, 1951–52, 1956–57, 1962–63; Division 2 – Champions 1919–20, 1949–50; Runners-up 1908–09, 1932–33; Promoted 1977–78 (3rd).

FA Cup: Winners 1901 (as non-League club), 1921, 1961, 1962, 1967, 1981, 1982, 1991; Runners-up 1987.

Football League Cup: Winners 1971, 1973, 1999; Runners-up 1982, 2002.

European Competitions: *European Cup:* 1961–62. *European Cup-Winners' Cup:* 1962–63 (winners), 1963–64, 1967–68, 1981–82, 1982–83, 1991–92. *UEFA Cup:* 1971–72 (winners), 1972–73, 1973–74 (runners-up), 1983–84 (winners), 1984–85, 1999–2000. *Intertoto Cup:* 1995.

SKY SPORTS FACT FILE

When Tottenham Hotspur signed former Barking and Northampton Town amateur winger Les Miller from Sochaux in September 1936 he became the first player to be signed by an English club having played professionally in France.

Record Cup Victory: 13–2 v Crewe Alex, FA Cup 4th rd (replay), 3 February 1960 – Brown; Hills, Henry; Blanchflower, Norman, Mackay; White, Harmer (1), Smith (4), Allen (5), Jones (3 incl. 1p).

Record Defeat: 0–8 v Cologne, UEFA Intertoto Cup, 22 July 1995.

Most League Points (2 for a win): 70, Division 2, 1919–20.

Most League Points (3 for a win): 77, Division 1, 1984–85.

Most League Goals: 115, Division 1, 1960–61.

Highest League Scorer in Season: Jimmy Greaves, 37, Division 1, 1962–63.

Most League Goals in Total Aggregate: Jimmy Greaves, 220, 1961–70.

Most League Goals in One Match: 5, Ted Harper v Reading, Division 2, 30 August 1930; 5, Alf Stokes v Birmingham C, Division 1, 18 September 1957; 5, Bobby Smith v Aston Villa, Division 1, 29 March 1958.

Most Capped Player: Pat Jennings, 74 (119), Northern Ireland.

Most League Appearances: Steve Perryman, 655, 1969–86.

Youngest League Player: Ally Dick, 16 years 301 days v Manchester C, 20 February 1982.

Record Transfer Fee Received: £5,500,000 from Lazio for Paul Gascoigne, May 1992.

Record Transfer Fee Paid: £11,000,000 to Dynamo Kiev for Sergei Rebrov, May 2000.

Football League Record: 1908 Elected to Division 2; 1909–15 Division 1; 1919–20 Division 2; 1920–28 Division 1; 1928–33 Division 2; 1933–35 Division 1; 1935–50 Division 2; 1950–77 Division 1; 1977–78 Division 2; 1978–92 Division 1; 1992– FA Premier League.

MANAGERS

Frank Brettell 1898–99
John Cameron 1899–1906
Fred Kirkham 1907–08
Peter McWilliam 1912–27
Billy Minter 1927–29
Percy Smith 1930–35
Jack Tresadern 1935–38
Peter McWilliam 1938–42
Arthur Turner 1942–46
Joe Hulme 1946–49
Arthur Rowe 1949–55
Jimmy Anderson 1955–58
Bill Nicholson 1958–74
Terry Neill 1974–76
Keith Burkinshaw 1976–84
Peter Shreeves 1984–86
David Pleat 1986–87
Terry Venables 1987–91
Peter Shreeves 1991–92
Ossie Ardiles 1993–94
Gerry Francis 1994–97
Christian Gross *(Head Coach)* 1997–98
George Graham 1998–2001
Glenn Hoddle 2001–03
David Pleat (*Caretaker*) 2003–04
Jacques Santini 2004
Martin Jol November 2004–

LATEST SEQUENCES

Longest Sequence of League Wins: 13, 23.4.1960 – 1.10.1960.

Longest Sequence of League Defeats: 7, 1.1.1994 – 27.2.1994.

Longest Sequence of League Draws: 6, 9.1.1999 – 27.2.1999.

Longest Sequence of Unbeaten League Matches: 22, 31.8.1949 – 31.12.1949.

Longest Sequence Without a League Win: 16, 29.12.1934 – 13.4.1935.

Successive Scoring Runs: 32 from 24.2.1962.

Successive Non-scoring Runs: 6 from 28.12.1985.

TEN YEAR LEAGUE RECORD

		P	*W*	*D*	*L*	*F*	*A*	*Pts*	*Pos*
1996-97	PR Lge	38	13	7	18	44	51	46	10
1997-98	PR Lge	38	11	11	16	44	56	44	14
1998-99	PR Lge	38	11	14	13	47	50	47	11
1999-2000	PR Lge	38	15	8	15	57	49	53	10
2000-01	PR Lge	38	13	10	15	47	54	49	12
2001-02	PR Lge	38	14	8	16	49	53	50	9
2002-03	PR Lge	38	14	8	16	51	62	50	10
2003-04	PR Lge	38	13	6	19	47	57	45	14
2004-05	PR Lge	38	14	10	14	47	41	52	9
2005-06	PR Lge	38	18	11	9	53	38	65	5

DID YOU KNOW

The railway engine named "Tottenham Hotspur" was scrapped at Doncaster in December 1958 and the plates displayed at White Hart Lane. In May 1937 it had been named at Hoe Street station, Walthamstow by Spurs chairman Charles Roberts.

TOTTENHAM HOTSPUR 2005–06 LEAGUE RECORD

Match No.	Date	Venue	Opponents	Result		H/T Score	Lg. Pos.	Goalscorers	Attendance
1	Aug 13	A	Portsmouth	W	2-0	1-0	—	Griffin (og) [45], Defoe [64]	20,215
2	20	H	Middlesbrough	W	2-0	0-0	1	Defoe [49], Mido [75]	35,844
3	24	A	Blackburn R	D	0-0	0-0	—		22,375
4	27	H	Chelsea	L	0-2	0-1	6		36,077
5	Sept 10	H	Liverpool	D	0-0	0-0	6		36,148
6	17	A	Aston Villa	D	1-1	0-1	7	Keane [78]	33,686
7	26	H	Fulham	W	1-0	1-0	—	Defoe [8]	35,427
8	Oct 1	A	Charlton Ath	W	3-2	0-1	3	King [51], Mido [64], Keane [80]	27,111
9	15	H	Everton	W	2-0	0-0	2	Mido [58], Jenas [63]	36,247
10	22	A	Manchester U	D	1-1	0-1	3	Jenas [72]	67,856
11	29	H	Arsenal	D	1-1	1-0	3	King [17]	36,154
12	Nov 7	A	Bolton W	L	0-1	0-1	—		26,634
13	20	H	West Ham U	D	1-1	1-0	6	Mido [16]	36,154
14	26	A	Wigan Ath	W	2-1	1-0	5	Keane [8], Davids [77]	22,611
15	Dec 3	H	Sunderland	W	3-2	1-1	4	Mido [37], Keane [51], Carrick [77]	36,244
16	12	H	Portsmouth	W	3-1	0-1	—	King [57], Mido (pen) [85], Defoe [90]	36,141
17	18	A	Middlesbrough	D	3-3	1-2	4	Keane [25], Jenas [63], Mido [83]	27,614
18	26	H	Birmingham C	W	2-0	0-0	4	Keane (pen) [58], Defoe [90]	36,045
19	28	A	WBA	L	0-2	0-1	4		27,510
20	31	H	Newcastle U	W	2-0	1-0	4	Tainio [43], Mido [66]	36,246
21	Jan 4	A	Manchester C	W	2-0	1-0	—	Mido [31], Keane [83]	40,808
22	14	A	Liverpool	L	0-1	0-0	4		44,983
23	21	H	Aston Villa	D	0-0	0-0	4		36,243
24	31	A	Fulham	L	0-1	0-0	—		21,081
25	Feb 5	H	Charlton Ath	W	3-1	2-0	4	Defoe 2 [14, 46], Jenas [41]	36,034
26	12	A	Sunderland	D	1-1	1-0	4	Keane [38]	34,700
27	19	H	Wigan Ath	D	2-2	1-1	—	Mido [23], Defoe [68]	35,676
28	Mar 5	H	Blackburn R	W	3-2	2-1	4	Keane 2 [9, 42], Mido [70]	36,080
29	11	A	Chelsea	L	1-2	1-1	4	Jenas [45]	42,243
30	18	A	Birmingham C	W	2-0	0-0	4	Lennon [65], Keane [77]	26,398
31	27	H	WBA	W	2-1	0-1	—	Keane 2 (1 pen) [68, 89 (p)]	36,152
32	Apr 1	A	Newcastle U	L	1-3	1-3	4	Keane [19]	52,301
33	8	H	Manchester C	W	2-1	1-0	4	Stalteri [44], Carrick [49]	36,167
34	15	A	Everton	W	1-0	1-0	4	Keane (pen) [33]	39,856
35	17	H	Manchester U	L	1-2	0-2	4	Jenas [53]	36,141
36	22	A	Arsenal	D	1-1	0-0	4	Keane [66]	38,326
37	30	H	Bolton W	W	1-0	0-0	4	Lennon [60]	36,179
38	May 7	A	West Ham U	L	1-2	1-1	5	Defoe [35]	34,970

Final League Position: 5

GOALSCORERS

League (53): Keane 16 (3 pens), Mido 11 (1 pen), Defoe 9, Jenas 6, King 3, Carrick 2, Lennon 2, Davids 1, Stalteri 1, Tainio 1, own goal 1.
Carling Cup (0).
FA Cup (2): Jenas 1, Stalteri 1.

Robinson P 38	Stalteri P 33	Edman E 3	Gardner A 16 + 1	Dawson M 31 + 1	Tainio T 22 + 2	Routledge W 2 + 1	Carrick M 35	Mido 24 + 3	Defoe J 23 + 13	Reid A 7 + 6	Pedro Mendes3 + 3	Kanoute F — + 1	Davids E 28 + 3	Keane R 25 + 11	Brown M 2 + 7	Kelly S 9	Lennon A 21 + 6	Lee Y 31	King L 26	Rasiak G 4 + 4	Jenas J 30	Naybet N 2 + 1	Pamarot N — + 2	Huddlestone T — + 4	Jackson J — + 1	Murphy D 2 + 8	Davenport C 1 + 3	Barnard L — + 3	Match No.
1	2	3	4	5	6	7¹	8	9²	10	11	12	13																	1
1	2	3	4	5	6		8	9	10¹	11			7	12															2
1	2	3	4	5	6			9²	12	11	7¹		13	10	8														3
1	2		4	5	6¹		8	9■	10	11			7			3	12												4
1	2		4				8		10				11	12	13		6²	3	5	9¹	7								5
1	2		4²		6		8		10	11¹				12				3	5	9	7	13							6
1	2							9³	10²	12	7		11	13			4¹	3	6	14	8	5							7
1	2			14	12			9³	10		7¹		11	13		3	4		6		8²	5							8
1	2			5			8	9	10²	12			11	13			4¹	3	6		7								9
1	2			5			8	9	10²		13		11	12			4¹	3	6		7								10
1	2			5	11³		8	9	10²	12	14			13			4¹	3	6		7								11
1	2			5	6		8	9	10				11	12	13			3¹	4		7²								12
1	2			5	6²		8	9	12				11	10¹			13	3	4		7								13
1	2			5	6		8	9					11	10				3	4		7								14
1	2			5	6		8	9	12				11	10¹			13	3	4		7²								15
1	2			5	6¹	12²	8	9	14	13			11	10³				3	4		7								16
1	2			5			8	9	12²	11¹			6	10	13			3	4	14	7³								17
1	2			5			8	9	12				11	10²	13		4¹	3	6³		7		14						18
1	2		4	5		7²	8	12	10				6	13	14			3		9¹	11³								19
1	2		4	5	6²		8	9	12				11	10¹	13			3			7								20
1	2		4	5			8	9²	12					10	11		6¹	3³		13	7		14						21
1	2■			5	6¹		8	9	12				11²	10			13	3	4		7								22
1				5	6		8		10³				11²	9	13	2	12	3	4	14	7¹								23
1	3		12	5■			8		13	11³				10		2	4¹		6	9²	7			14					24
1	2		4		6¹		8		10					9		3	11²		5		7			12	13				25
1	2			5			8	12	10				11³	9¹			4²	3	6		7			13		14			26
1	2			5			8	9	10				11²	12			4	3	6					13		7¹			27
1	2			5	6²		8	9					11¹	10			12	3	4		7					13			28
1	2			5	6		8	9	12				11	10¹				3	4		7								29
1				5			8		10				11	9¹		2	4	3	6		7					12			30
1				5	13		8	12	10				11³	9		2¹	4²	3	6		7					14			31
1			4	5■			8	10	12				11²	9		2	6¹	3			7					13			32
1	2		4		11²		8	10	12				13	9			6¹	3	5		7								33
1	2		4		11²		8		10				12	9			6³	3	5¹		7					13	14		34
1	2			5			8		10				11¹	9			6²	3			7					12	4	13	35
1	2		4	5	7		8		10				11■	9			6¹	3								12			36
1	2		4	5	11		8		10¹	12				9³			6	3								7²	13	14	37
1			4	5	7²		8¹		10	12			11	9		2	6	3³									13	14	38

FA Cup
Third Round Leicester C (a) 2-3

Carling Cup
Second Round Grimsby T (a) 0-1

TRANMERE ROVERS FL Championship 1

FOUNDATION

Formed in 1884 as Belmont they adopted their present title the following year and eventually joined their first league, the West Lancashire League in 1889–90, the same year as their first success in the Wirral Challenge Cup. The club almost folded in 1899–1900 when all the players left en bloc to join a rival club, but they survived the crisis and went from strength to strength winning the 'Combination' title in 1907–08 and the Lancashire Combination in 1913–14. They joined the Football League in 1921 from the Central League.

Prenton Park, Prenton Road West, Birkenhead, Merseyside CH42 9PY.

Telephone: 0870 460 3333.

Fax: (0151) 609 0606.

Ticket Office: 0870 460 3332.

Website: www.tranmererovers.co.uk

Email: Main: info@tranmererovers.co.uk; Ticket office: tickets@tranmererovers.co.uk; Club shop: shop@tranmererovers.co.uk

Ground Capacity: 16,567.

Record Attendance: 24,424 v Stoke C, FA Cup 4th rd, 5 February 1972.

Pitch Measurements: 110yd × 70yd.

Chairperson: Lorraine Rogers.

Chief Executive/Secretary: Mick Horton.

Manager: Ronnie Moore.

Assistant Manager: John McMahon.

Physio: Les Parry.

Colours: White shirts with reflex blue trim, white shorts with reflex blue trim, white stockings with reflex blue trim.

Change Colours: Black shirts, black shorts, black stockings.

Year Formed: 1884.

Turned Professional: 1912.

Ltd Co.: 1920.

Previous Name: 1884, Belmont AFC; 1885, Tranmere Rovers.

Club Nickname: 'The Rovers'.

Previous Grounds: 1884, Steeles Field; 1887, Ravenshaws Field/Old Prenton Park; 1912, Prenton Park.

First Football League Game: 27 August 1921, Division 3 (N), v Crewe Alex (h) W 4–1 – Bradshaw; Grainger, Stuart (1); Campbell, Milnes (1), Heslop; Moreton, Groves (1), Hyam, Ford (1), Hughes.

HONOURS

Football League Division 1 best season: 4th, 1992–93; Promoted from Division 3 1990–91 (play-offs); Division 3 (N) – Champions 1937–38; Promotion to 3rd Division: 1966–67, 1975–76; Division 4 – Runners-up 1988–89.

FA Cup: best season: 6th rd, 2000, 2001, 2004.

Football League Cup: Runners-up, 2000.

Welsh Cup: Winners 1935; Runners-up 1934.

Leyland Daf Cup: Winners 1990; Runners-up 1991.

SKY SPORTS FACT FILE

Albert Payne, a wing-half at Tranmere Rovers during and after the Second World War, recommended his cousin George Payne, a goalkeeper with the RAF in South Africa. He was signed in April 1947 and went on to make over 450 League and Cup appearances.

Record League Victory: 13–4 v Oldham Ath, Division 3 (N), 26 December 1935 – Gray; Platt, Fairhurst; McLaren, Newton, Spencer; Eden, MacDonald (1), Bell (9), Woodward (2), Urmson (1).

Record Cup Victory: 13–0 v Oswestry U, FA Cup 2nd prel rd, 10 October 1914 – Ashcroft; Stevenson, Bullough, Hancock, Taylor, Holden (1), Moreton (1), Cunningham (2), Smith (5), Leck (3), Gould (1).

Record Defeat: 1–9 v Tottenham H, FA Cup 3rd rd (replay), 14 January 1953.

Most League Points (2 for a win): 60, Division 4, 1964–65.

Most League Points (3 for a win): 80, Division 4, 1988–89; Division 3, 1989–90; Division 2, 2002–03.

Most League Goals: 111, Division 3 (N), 1930–31.

Highest League Scorer in Season: Bunny Bell, 35, Division 3 (N), 1933–34.

Most League Goals in Total Aggregate: Ian Muir, 142, 1985–95.

Most League Goals in One Match: 9, Bunny Bell v Oldham Ath, Division 3N, 26 December 1935.

Most Capped Player: John Aldridge, 30 (69), Republic of Ireland.

Most League Appearances: Harold Bell, 595, 1946–64 (incl. League record 401 consecutive appearances).

Youngest League Player: Iain Hume, 16 years 167 days v Swindon T, 15 April 2000.

Record Transfer Fee Received: £3,300,000 from Everton for Steve Simonsen, September 1998.

Record Transfer Fee Paid: £450,000 to Aston Villa for Shaun Teale, August 1995.

Football League Record: 1921 Original Member of Division 3 (N): 1938–39 Division 2; 1946–58 Division 3 (N); 1958–61 Division 3; 1961–67 Division 4; 1967–75 Division 3; 1975–76 Division 4; 1976–79 Division 3; 1979–89 Division 4; 1989–91 Division 3; 1991–92 Division 2; 1992–2001 Division 1; 2001–04 Division 2; 2004– FL1.

MANAGERS

Bert Cooke 1912–35
Jackie Carr 1935–36
Jim Knowles 1936–39
Bill Ridding 1939–45
Ernie Blackburn 1946–55
Noel Kelly 1955–57
Peter Farrell 1957–60
Walter Galbraith 1961
Dave Russell 1961–69
Jackie Wright 1969–72
Ron Yeats 1972–75
John King 1975–80
Bryan Hamilton 1980–85
Frank Worthington 1985–87
Ronnie Moore 1987
John King 1987–96
John Aldridge 1996–2001
Dave Watson 2001–02
Ray Mathias 2002–03
Brian Little 2003–06
Ronnie Moore June 2006–

LATEST SEQUENCES

Longest Sequence of League Wins: 9, 9.2.1990 – 19.3.1990.

Longest Sequence of League Defeats: 8, 29.10.1938 – 17.12.1938.

Longest Sequence of League Draws: 5, 26.12.1997 – 31.1.1998.

Longest Sequence of Unbeaten League Matches: 18, 16.3.1970 – 4.9.1970.

Longest Sequence Without a League Win: 16, 8.11.1969 – 14.3.1970.

Successive Scoring Runs: 32 from 24.2.1934.

Successive Non-scoring Runs: 7 from 20.12.1997.

TEN YEAR LEAGUE RECORD

		P	*W*	*D*	*L*	*F*	*A*	*Pts*	*Pos*
1996-97	Div 1	46	17	14	15	63	56	65	11
1997-98	Div 1	46	14	14	18	54	57	56	14
1998-99	Div 1	46	12	20	14	63	61	56	15
1999-2000	Div 1	46	15	12	19	57	68	57	13
2000-01	Div 1	46	9	11	26	46	77	38	24
2001-02	Div 2	46	16	15	15	63	60	63	12
2002-03	Div 2	46	23	11	12	66	57	80	7
2003-04	Div 2	46	17	16	13	59	56	67	8
2004-05	FL 1	46	22	13	11	73	55	79	3
2005-06	FL 1	46	13	15	18	50	52	54	18

DID YOU KNOW ?

Tranmere Rovers met Blyth Spartans in the 1951–52 FA Cup, the tie lasting 405 minutes! Held 1–1 at Prenton Park and in Blyth where bad light stopped play after 105 minutes, the teams drew 2–2 at Carlisle before Tranmere finally won 5–1 at nearby Everton.

TRANMERE ROVERS 2005–06 LEAGUE RECORD

Match No.	*Date*	*Venue*	*Opponents*	*Result*	*H/T Score*	*Lg. Pos.*	*Goalscorers*	*Attendance*
1	Aug 6	A	Swansea C	L 0-1	0-1	—		16,733
2	9	H	Blackpool	D 2-2	2-1	—	Hume 38, Greenacre 45	7509
3	12	H	Oldham Ath	W 4-0	1-0	—	Greenacre 2 (1 pen) 45, 90 (p), Sharps 54, Roberts 77	8466
4	20	A	Brentford	L 0-2	0-1	16		5438
5	27	A	Chesterfield	W 2-0	0-0	11	Jackson 76, Roberts 90	3445
6	29	H	Swindon T	W 1-0	0-0	7	Greenacre 58	7557
7	Sept 2	A	Bournemouth	D 0-0	0-0	—		5695
8	9	H	Bradford C	D 2-2	1-2	—	Facey 24, Greenacre 72	8225
9	17	A	Southend U	L 1-3	0-2	11	Facey 46	6691
10	24	H	Gillingham	D 2-2	1-1	13	Jackson 10, Greenacre 46	7003
11	27	A	Huddersfield T	L 0-1	0-0	—		10,640
12	Oct 1	A	Nottingham F	L 0-1	0-0	20		22,022
13	7	H	Scunthorpe U	L 0-2	0-2	—		7522
14	15	A	Bristol C	L 0-1	0-0	23		10,495
15	22	H	Colchester U	D 0-0	0-0	21		6612
16	29	A	Doncaster R	W 2-0	0-0	19	Davies 62, Jennings 90	5542
17	Nov 12	H	Milton Keynes D	L 1-2	1-0	21	Jackson 38	6611
18	19	A	Scunthorpe U	W 2-1	0-0	19	Greenacre (pen) 58, Facey 76	4602
19	26	H	Swansea C	D 2-2	2-1	18	Francis 18, Facey 45	7518
20	Dec 6	A	Barnsley	L 1-2	0-0	—	Facey 90	6996
21	10	A	Blackpool	D 1-1	0-0	19	Facey 81	5069
22	17	H	Brentford	L 1-4	1-3	20	Zola 23	6210
23	26	A	Walsall	D 0-0	0-0	21		6476
24	28	H	Yeovil T	W 4-1	0-1	19	Greenacre 3 50, 74, 86, Zola 72	6327
25	31	A	Port Vale	W 2-0	1-0	19	Harrison 8, Greenacre 90	4289
26	Jan 2	H	Rotherham U	W 3-2	1-1	15	Greenacre 45, Zola 54, Harrison 62	7361
27	7	H	Bournemouth	D 0-0	0-0	14		6717
28	14	A	Hartlepool U	D 0-0	0-0	14		4181
29	21	H	Southend U	D 0-0	0-0	15		7058
30	28	A	Bradford C	D 0-0	0-0	14		7697
31	Feb 3	H	Huddersfield T	W 2-1	1-0	—	Tremarco 4, Facey 84	8300
32	11	A	Gillingham	D 1-1	0-0	11	O'Leary 48	6803
33	14	H	Hartlepool U	D 0-0	0-0	—		6301
34	18	H	Barnsley	L 0-1	0-1	13		6802
35	25	A	Oldham Ath	L 0-1	0-1	14		5281
36	Mar 7	A	Swindon T	W 2-1	2-0	—	Greenacre 21, Aiston 33	4139
37	11	H	Chesterfield	W 4-1	3-1	11	Aiston 2 36, 39, Greenacre 45, O'Leary 65	6435
38	17	H	Walsall	L 1-2	0-1	—	Greenacre 64	6615
39	25	A	Yeovil T	D 2-2	1-1	14	Goodison 39, Greenacre 77	5409
40	31	H	Port Vale	W 3-0	1-0	—	Zola 28, O'Leary 58, Davies 78	6926
41	Apr 8	A	Rotherham U	L 0-2	0-0	16		4129
42	15	H	Nottingham F	L 0-1	0-1	17		9152
43	17	A	Colchester U	L 0-1	0-0	17		4757
44	22	H	Bristol C	L 0-3	0-2	19		6288
45	29	A	Milton Keynes D	W 2-1	0-0	17	Partridge (og) 88, Facey 90	7777
46	May 6	H	Doncaster R	L 0-2	0-2	18		8343

Final League Position: 18

GOALSCORERS

League (50): Greenacre 16 (2 pens), Facey 8, Zola 4, Aiston 3, Jackson 3, O'Leary 3, Davies 2, Harrison 2, Roberts 2, Francis 1, Goodison 1, Hume 1, Jennings 1, Sharps 1, Tremarco 1, own goal 1.
Carling Cup (1): Sharps 1.
FA Cup (1): Greenacre 1.
Football League Trophy (5): Facey 1, Greenacre 1 (pen), Harrison 1, Jennings 1, Rankine 1.

Achterberg J 19	Goodison I 32 + 6	Roberts G 44	Linwood P 12 + 2	Jackson M 41	Sharps I 39	McAteer J 23 + 6	Rankine M 20 + 4	Zola C 15 + 7	Greenacre C 45	Aiston S 23 + 13	Harrison D 26 + 9	Jennings S 24 + 14	Hume I 5 + 1	Whitmore T — + 4	Davies S 6 + 16	Bruce A 10 + 1	Dagnall C — + 6	Tremarco C 14 + 4	Facey D 30 + 7	Summerbee N 4 + 2	O'Leary S 19 + 2	Francis S 16 + 1	Wilson S 12	Seremet D 13	Raven D 11	Murray M 2	James O — + 1	Jones M 1	Match No.
1	2^{1}	3	4	5	6	7	8^{2}	9	10	11^{3}	12	13	14																1
1	2	3	4	5	6	7	8^{1}		10	11^{2}	12		9	13															2
1	2	3	4	5	6	7^{1}	8^{2}		10	11	13	12	9^{3}		14														3
1	2	3	4^{3}	5^{1}	6	7	8		10	11		12	9^{2}		13	14													4
1	4	3		5	6				10	11^{2}	7	8	9^{1}		12	2	13												5
1	4	3^{1}		5	6				10^{3}	11	7	8	9^{2}	12	13	2	14												6
1	4			5		6			10	11	7	8^{1}		12		2	13	3	9^{2}										7
1	4	3		5		7	8^{2}		10	11	13	12				2		6^{1}	9										8
1	6	3		5		4^{1}	12		10	11	8	13				2^{2}	14		9	7^{3}									9
1	6	3		5		12	8		10	11	4^{1}	13				2			9	7^{2}									10
1	6	3		5		4	8^{1}		10	11		12				2			9	7									11
1	6	3		5		4			10	12^{2}		11				2	13	8	9	7^{1}									12
1	3^{2}			5	6	4^{1}	8		10	12		7				2		11	9	13									13
1	4^{3}	3		5	6		8^{1}	11^{2}	10	12		7		13		2			9	14									14
1	2	3	4	5	6		8^{3}	12	10^{2}	11^{1}		7			13				9		14								15
1	12	3	2	5	6		8		10			7			11^{1}				9		4								16
1	12	3	2	5	6			13	10	14	11^{3}	7			8^{1}				9^{2}		4								17
1	2	3	4^{3}	5	6			12	10^{2}		11	7					13		9^{1}		8	14							18
1	2	3		5	6		8	12	10^{2}	11^{3}	7	14			13				9^{1}			4							19
	4	3		5^{2}	6		8		10	12	11^{1}	7						13	9			2	1						20
	4	3			6		8	13	10^{1}		11	5			12^{2}			7	9			2	1						21
	2	3		5	6^{2}		8	10^{1}		12	11	7			13				9			4	1						22
	2^{2}	3	12	5	6		8		10		11	7			13				9^{1}			4	1						23
		3	4^{2}	5	6	8^{3}		13	10	12	7	11^{1}			9			14				2	1						24
	12	3		5	6	13	8^{2}	9	10	11^{1}	4	14			7^{3}							2	1						25
	12	3		5	6	8		9^{2}	10	11^{1}	7	13			14▮			4^{3}				2		1					26
	2	3		5	6	8^{1}	12	9^{2}	10	11	7^{3}								13		14	4		1					27
	2	3		5	6		12	9^{3}	10	13	7^{2}	11							14		8^{1}	4		1					28
		3	12	5	6	4^{2}		11^{1}	10	13	7								9		8	2		1					29
	2	3		5	6		8		10		7								9		11	4		1					30
		3		5	6	12		9▮	10	11^{1}	7	13						8^{3}	14		4^{2}	2		1					31
	8	3		5	6	7^{1}	13		10	12	11								9^{2}		4	2		1					32
		3		5	6				10	11	7				12			8	9^{1}		4	2		1					33
	6	3		5			8^{1}		10	11^{2}		12			13				9		4	2		1	7				34
	4	3	5		6	12	8^{1}	13	10		11								9		7^{2}			1	2				35
	12	3		5	6	7		9^{2}	10	11^{3}	14							8^{1}	13		4			1	2				36
		3		5	6	7^{2}		9^{1}	10	11	14	13						8^{3}	12		4			1	2				37
		3		5	6	7		9	10	11^{1}		13						8^{2}	12		4			1	2				38
	2	3		5	6	7^{2}		9^{1}	10		13	8							12		4				11	1			39
	12	3		5	6^{1}	7		9^{3}	10	13		8			14				11^{2}		4		1		2				40
	4^{1}	3		5▮	6			9^{2}	10	12	13	8			14				11		7^{3}		1		2				41
	5	3			6	7			10	12		8			9^{2}			13	11		4^{1}		1		2				42
	5	3			6	12			10	11^{2}	13	7			14			8^{1}	9		4▮		1		2^{3}				43
	5	3			6	4▮			10		8	7			9^{1}			12	11						2	1			44
		3	4	5	6	7			10		2	8						11	9				1						45
		3	2^{3}	5	6	12			10		7	11			13			8^{1}	9^{2}				1				14	4	46

FA Cup

First Round	Bradford C	(a)	1-2

Carling Cup

First Round	Scunthorpe U	(a)	1-2

Football League Trophy

First Round	Lincoln C	(h)	2-1
Second Round	Rochdale	(h)	3-2
Quarter-Final	Carlisle U	(h)	0-0

WALSALL FL Championship 2

FOUNDATION

Two of the leading clubs around Walsall in the 1880s were Walsall Swifts (formed 1877) and Walsall Town (formed 1879). The Swifts were winners of the Birmingham Senior Cup in 1881, while the Town reached the 4th round (5th round modern equivalent) of the FA Cup in 1883. These clubs amalgamated as Walsall Town Swifts in 1888, becoming simply Walsall in 1895.

Bescot Stadium, Bescot Crescent, Walsall WS1 4SA.

Telephone: 0870 442 0442.

Fax: (01922) 613 202.

Ticket Office: 0870 442 0111.

Website: www.saddlers@walsallfc.co.uk

Email: info@walsallfc.co.uk

Ground Capacity: 11,126.

Record Attendance: 11,037 v Wolverhampton W, Division 1, 11 January 2003.

Pitch Measurements: 110yd × 73yd.

Chairman: Jeff Bonser.

Chief Executive/Secretary: K. R. Whalley.

Manager: Richard Money.

Physio: John Whitney.

Colours: Red shirts, white shorts, red stockings.

Change Colours: White shirts, red shorts, white stockings.

Year Formed: 1888.

Turned Professional: 1888.

Ltd Co.: 1921.

Previous Names: Walsall Swifts (founded 1877) and Walsall Town (founded 1879) amalgamated in 1888 and were known as Walsall Town Swifts until 1895.

Club Nickname: 'The Saddlers'.

Previous Ground: 1888, Fellows Park; 1990, Bescot Stadium.

First Football League Game: 3 September 1892, Division 2, v Darwen (h) L 1–2 – Hawkins; Withington, Pinches; Robinson, Whitrick, Forsyth; Marshall, Holmes, Turner, Gray (1), Pangbourn.

Record League Victory: 10–0 v Darwen, Division 2, 4 March 1899 – Tennent; E. Peers (1), Davies; Hickinbotham, Jenkyns, Taggart; Dean (3), Vail (2), Aston (4), Martin, Griffin.

Record Cup Victory: 7–0 v Macclesfield T (a), FA Cup 2nd rd, 6 December 1997 – Walker; Evans, Marsh, Viveash (1), Ryder, Peron, Boli (2 incl. 1p) (Ricketts), Porter (2), Keates, Watson (Platt), Hodge (2 incl. 1p).

Record Defeat: 0–12 v Small Heath, 17 December 1892. 0–12 v Darwen, 26 December 1896, both Division 2.

HONOURS

Football League: Division 2: Runners-up, 1998–99, Promoted to Division 1 – 2000–01 (play-offs); Division 3 – Runners-up 1960–61, 1994–95; Division 4 – Champions 1959–60; Runners-up 1979–80.

FA Cup: best season: 5th rd, 1939, 1975, 1978, 1987, 2002, 2003 and last 16 1889.

Football League Cup: Semi-final 1984.

SKY SPORTS FACT FILE

The youngest Walsall first team player in any competition was midfield player David McDermott. He was 16 years 191 days on his debut as a substitute 12 minutes from the end of the first round League Cup tie at Sheffield Wednesday on 25 August 2004.

Most League Points (2 for a win): 65, Division 4, 1959–60.

Most League Points (3 for a win): 87, Division 2, 1998–99.

Most League Goals: 102, Division 4, 1959–60.

Highest League Scorer in Season: Gilbert Alsop, 40, Division 3 (N), 1933–34 and 1934–35.

Most League Goals in Total Aggregate: Tony Richards, 184, 1954–63; Colin Taylor, 184, 1958–63, 1964–68, 1969–73.

Most League Goals in One Match: 5, Gilbert Alsop v Carlisle U, Division 3N, 2 February 1935; 5, Bill Evans v Mansfield T, Division 3N, 5 October 1935; 5, Johnny Devlin v Torquay U, Division 3S, 1 September 1949.

Most Capped Player: Mick Kearns, 15 (18), Republic of Ireland.

Most League Appearances: Colin Harrison, 467, 1964–82.

Youngest League Player: Geoff Morris, 16 years 218 days v Scunthorpe U, 14 September 1965.

Record Transfer Fee Received: £600,000 from West Ham U for David Kelly, July 1988.

Record Transfer Fee Paid: £175,000 to Birmingham C for Alan Buckley, June 1979.

Football League Record: 1892 Elected to Division 2; 1895 Failed re-election; 1896–1901 Division 2; 1901 Failed re-election; 1921 Original Member of Division 3 (N); 1927–31 Division 3 (S); 1931–36 Division 3 (N); 1936–58 Division 3 (S); 1958–60 Division 4; 1960–61 Division 3; 1961–63 Division 2; 1963–79 Division 3; 1979–80 Division 4; 1980–88 Division 3; 1988–89 Division 2; 1989–90 Division 3; 1990–92 Division 4; 1992–95 Division 3; 1995–99 Division 2; 1999–2000 Division 1; 2000–01 Division 2; 2001–04 Division 1; 2004–06 FL1; 2006– FL2.

LATEST SEQUENCES

Longest Sequence of League Wins: 7, 10.10.1959 – 21.11.1959.

Longest Sequence of League Defeats: 15, 29.10.1988 – 4.2.1989.

Longest Sequence of League Draws: 5, 7.5.1988 – 17.9.1988.

Longest Sequence of Unbeaten League Matches: 21, 6.11.1979 – 22.3.1980.

Longest Sequence Without a League Win: 18, 15.10.1988 – 4.2.1989.

Successive Scoring Runs: 27 from 9.2.1928.

Successive Non-scoring Runs: 5 from 8.10.1927.

MANAGERS

H. Smallwood 1888–91 *(Secretary-Manager)*
A. G. Burton 1891–93
J. H. Robinson 1893–95
C. H. Ailso 1895–96 *(Secretary-Manager)*
A. E. Parsloe 1896–97 *(Secretary-Manager)*
L. Ford 1897–98 *(Secretary-Manager)*
G. Hughes 1898–99 *(Secretary-Manager)*
L. Ford 1899–1901 *(Secretary-Manager)*
J. E. Shutt 1908–13 *(Secretary-Manager)*
Haydn Price 1914–20
Joe Burchell 1920–26
David Ashworth 1926–27
Jack Torrance 1927–28
James Kerr 1928–29
Sid Scholey 1929–30
Peter O'Rourke 1930–32
Bill Slade 1932–34
Andy Wilson 1934–37
Tommy Lowes 1937–44
Harry Hibbs 1944–51
Tony McPhee 1951
Brough Fletcher 1952–53
Major Frank Buckley 1953–55
John Love 1955–57
Billy Moore 1957–64
Alf Wood 1964
Reg Shaw 1964–68
Dick Graham 1968
Ron Lewin 1968–69
Billy Moore 1969–72
John Smith 1972–73
Doug Fraser 1973–77
Dave Mackay 1977–78
Alan Ashman 1978
Frank Sibley 1979
Alan Buckley 1979–86
Neil Martin *(Joint Manager with Buckley)* 1981–82
Tommy Coakley 1986–88
John Barnwell 1989–90
Kenny Hibbitt 1990–94
Chris Nicholl 1994–97
Jan Sorensen 1997–98
Ray Graydon 1998–2002
Colin Lee 2002–04
Paul Merson 2004–06
Richard Money May 2006–

TEN YEAR LEAGUE RECORD

		P	W	D	L	F	A	Pts	Pos
1996-97	Div 2	46	19	10	17	54	53	67	12
1997-98	Div 2	46	14	12	20	43	52	54	19
1998-99	Div 2	46	26	9	11	63	47	87	2
1999-2000	Div 1	46	11	13	22	52	77	46	22
2000-01	Div 2	46	23	12	11	79	50	81	4
2001-02	Div 1	46	13	12	21	51	71	51	18
2002-03	Div 1	46	15	9	22	57	69	54	17
2003-04	Div 1	46	13	12	21	45	65	51	22
2004-05	FL 1	46	16	12	18	65	69	60	14
2005-06	FL 1	46	11	14	21	47	70	47	24

DID YOU KNOW

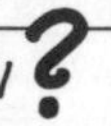

Ex-Chelsea and Northern Ireland international centre-forward Joe Bambrick was an instant scoring success for Walsall in 1938. In addition to 15 goals in 35 League goals he also scored a hat-trick in his first FA Cup tie, a 4–1 win over Carlisle United.

WALSALL 2005–06 LEAGUE RECORD

Match No.	*Date*	*Venue*	*Opponents*	*Result*		*H/T Score*	*Lg. Pos.*	*Goalscorers*	*Attendance*
1	Aug 6	A	Rotherham U	W	2-1	1-1	—	Taylor K [2], Leitao [90]	5386
2	9	H	Nottingham F	W	3-2	0-1	—	Wright [50], Westwood [52], Fryatt (pen) [61]	8703
3	13	H	Southend U	D	2-2	0-0	1	Fryatt [65], Leitao [68]	5569
4	20	A	Hartlepool U	D	1-1	1-0	3	Westwood [7]	5060
5	27	H	Swansea C	L	2-5	1-1	10	Fryatt (pen) [24], Gueret (og) [51]	5745
6	29	A	Bournemouth	D	0-0	0-0	11		5953
7	Sept 3	H	Swindon T	W	1-0	0-0	6	Fryatt [57]	5392
8	10	A	Yeovil T	L	1-2	1-0	9	Fryatt (pen) [34]	9579
9	17	H	Chesterfield	L	2-3	2-0	15	Leitao [14], Wright [35]	5177
10	24	A	Scunthorpe U	W	3-1	1-0	9	Fryatt (pen) [15], Osborn 2 [66, 75]	4973
11	27	H	Brentford	D	0-0	0-0	—		4873
12	Oct 1	A	Port Vale	L	2-3	2-1	12	Collins (og) [24], De Montagnac [36]	5314
13	8	H	Milton Keynes D	D	1-1	0-0	—	Bennett [90]	5041
14	15	A	Huddersfield T	L	1-3	1-2	16	Smith P [31]	11,642
15	22	H	Doncaster R	W	1-0	0-0	13	Leitao [72]	5385
16	29	A	Barnsley	L	1-2	0-1	15	Fryatt [63]	8145
17	Nov 12	H	Gillingham	W	2-0	1-0	13	De Montagnac [15], Skora [57]	4785
18	19	A	Milton Keynes D	L	1-2	1-1	14	Skora [13]	5506
19	26	H	Rotherham U	W	3-1	2-0	12	Fryatt 2 [42, 45], Leitao [69]	4563
20	Dec 6	A	Oldham Ath	L	1-2	0-0	—	Taylor K [73]	3878
21	10	A	Nottingham F	D	1-1	1-1	15	Fryatt [6]	20,912
22	17	H	Hartlepool U	W	1-0	0-0	11	Fryatt [85]	4293
23	26	H	Tranmere R	D	0-0	0-0	12		6476
24	28	A	Bradford C	L	0-2	0-2	13		6745
25	31	H	Blackpool	W	2-0	0-0	11	Constable 2 [46, 52]	5046
26	Jan 2	A	Bristol C	L	0-3	0-2	12		12,652
27	14	H	Colchester U	L	0-2	0-0	16		5464
28	21	A	Chesterfield	D	2-2	1-1	16	Timm [33], Smith G [50]	4666
29	31	A	Swindon T	L	0-1	0-1	—		4597
30	Feb 4	A	Brentford	L	0-5	0-2	19		5645
31	11	H	Scunthorpe U	D	2-2	1-2	20	Keates [30], Barrowman [77]	4911
32	14	A	Colchester U	D	0-0	0-0	—		3810
33	18	H	Oldham Ath	L	0-2	0-0	22		5816
34	25	A	Southend U	D	0-0	0-0	20		7906
35	Mar 12	A	Swansea C	D	1-1	1-0	21	Devlin [17]	13,262
36	17	A	Tranmere R	W	2-1	1-0	—	Smith G 2 [41, 72]	6615
37	21	H	Yeovil T	L	0-2	0-2	—		4464
38	25	H	Bradford C	D	2-2	2-1	22	James [17], Westwood [37]	4678
39	Apr 1	A	Blackpool	L	0-2	0-0	22		6129
40	8	H	Bristol C	L	0-3	0-1	23		5402
41	11	H	Bournemouth	L	0-1	0-1	—		4613
42	15	H	Port Vale	D	1-1	0-0	22	Constable [50]	4876
43	17	A	Doncaster R	L	0-1	0-1	24		5086
44	22	H	Huddersfield T	L	1-3	0-1	24	Leary [90]	5554
45	29	A	Gillingham	W	1-0	0-0	24	Claridge [56]	7757
46	May 6	H	Barnsley	L	1-2	0-1	24	Keates (pen) [59]	7195

Final League Position: 24

GOALSCORERS

League (47): Fryatt 11 (4 pens), Leitao 5, Constable 3, Smith G 3, Westwood 3, Demontagnac 2, Keates 2 (1 pen), Osborn 2, Skora 2, Taylor K 2, Wright 2, Barrowman 1, Bennett 1, Claridge 1, Devlin 1, James 1, Leary 1, Smith P 1, Timm 1, own goals 2.
Carling Cup (0).
FA Cup (8): James 3, Fryatt 2 (1 pen), Kinsella 1, Leary 1, Leitao 1.
Football League Trophy (6): Constable 2, Bennett 1, Fryatt 1, Leitao 1, Nicholls 1.

Oakes A 25	Pead C 38+1	Fox D 33	Osborn S 27+5	Gerrard A 32+2	Bennett J 17+2	Wright M 23+7	Standing M 10+10	Fryatt M 23 / Timm M 6+3	Wrack D 7	Taylor K 15+7	Leitao J 20+3	Westwood C 26+3	Kinsella M 6+3	Larrosa R 2+5 / Devlin P 8	Staunton S 5+2	Smith P 8 / Tilt L —+1	Roper I 24+1	Merson P 6+1 / Barrowman A 10+3	Husbands M 1+3	Gilmartin R 2	Ruddy J 5	Demontagnac I 14+10	Gillett S 2	Broad J 2 / Keates D 14	McDermott D —+1	Murphy J 14 / Mills P 14	Sztybel J 1	Skora E 4 / Fitzgerald S 1+4	Taylor D 4+7	Constable J 7+10	Bradley M —+3	Nicholls A 4+4 / Claridge S	Harkness J 1	James K 12+3	Leary M 12+3	Smith G 13	Atieno T 1+1	*Match No.*
1	2	3	4	5	6	7^1	8	9	10	11	12																											1
1	2	3	4^1		6	13	8^2	9	7	11	10^3	5	12	14																								2
1	2	3	12		6^2	7		9	8	11	10	5			13	4^1																						3
1	2	3	4				12	9	11	7^1	10	5			6	8																						4
1	2		12		3	7	13	9	11^1	8	10	5			6	4^2																						5
1	2		4	6^1	3■	14	7^2	9		11	10^3	5	13				12	8																				6
1	2		4	6		12	7^1	9	3	11	10	5	13					8^2																				7
1	2	3	4^1	6		12	13	9	11^3	7	10	5	8^2						14																			8
	2	3	4	6		11^1	7^2	9^3		12	10	5				8		13	14	1																		9
	2	3	4	6		12		9		11^2	10^1	5				7		8	13		1																	10
	2	3	4	6	12	13		9			10	5				11		8^2	7^1		1																	11
		3^1	4	6	12	2	7			14	10	5		13		8					1	9^2	11^3															12
	2^1	3	4		6	7	12	9				5		13							1	10	11^2	8														13
	2	3			6			9^2		12	10	5	4^3	13		11					1	8		7^1	14													14
	2	3	4^2	14	6	7^3	13	9		11	12			8^1			5					10				1												15
	2■	3		12	6		8^1	9		11	13		4^2				5					10				1	7											16
		3			6			9			8	2	4	11	12		5					10^1				1		7										17
		2		4	7^1			9			8^2	6		12	3		5					10				1		11	13									18
	2	3	8^2		6			9		13	10^3				4		5					7^1				1		11	12	14								19
	2	3	4^1	6	7			9		12	10						5					13				1		8^2	11^3	14								20
	2	3	4^1	6	7			9		12							5	8				10■				1			11^2		13							21
	2	11^1	4	6	3			9		12							5	8								1			7^2	13		10						22
	2		4	6	3		8^1	9		7	10						5									1			13	11^2		12						23
	2		8	6			7^1				10	3	4				5					9				1			11^2	12		13						24
	2		4^3	6		7		9^1		11	10				3		5					8^2				1				12	14	13						25
	2		12	6	3		13			7^2	10^3	5	4^1													1			14	9		8	11					26
	2	3		6		7	12	10^1									5									1				9^2				11	8	4	13	27
	2			6		7	12	10				5		9^1								8				1								11	4	3		28
1	2	3		6		7^2	12	9				5																		13		11^1		10	4	8		29
1^6	2	3	12	6		13						5^2				15		9						11										10	4^1	8	7	30
1	2		4^3			3		10^1						7■			5	9				14		8		6						13		12^2		11		31
1	2			6		3											5	9				12		8		4					13	7^1		10^2		11		32
1	2			6		3											5	9^2				12		8		4		13						10	7	11^1		33
1	2		4	6		7^2											5	9^1						11		8		10^3		12				14	13	3		34
1	2		4^2	5		7^1						12		11				9^3				13				3		14						10	6	8		35
1		3^2	4	6		2^1						12		7			5	9^3				13				8								10	14	11		36
1		3		6		2^2		13				12		7			5	9				8■												10	4	11^1		37
	12	3		6^2		7		9^3				2		11			5			1				8				14		13				10^1	4			38
1		3	4^3	6		7^2		13				2		9			5	12						11		8		14				10^1						39
1		3	12	6		2								7			5					13		11		8^2				9^1		10			4			40
1	3	11	4^2					13				2					5					12		8		6				9		10^1			7			41
1	2	3	4^2				12					5						13						8		6				9		10			7^1	11		42
1	2	3					7^1					5						9^3				13		8		6			12	14		10			4	11^2		43
1	2	3	7^1	4				11^2				5■												8		6				9		10		13	12			44
1	2	3		6		7											5	13				8^1		11		4			12			10^2		9				45
1	2	3		6		7^2				11^1							5■	9^3				13		8		4			12	14				10				46

FA Cup

First Round	Merthyr T	(a)	2-1
Second Round	Yeovil T	(h)	2-0
Third Round	Barnsley	(a)	1-1
		(h)	2-0
Fourth Round	Stoke C	(a)	1-2

Carling Cup

First Round	Crystal Palace	(a)	0-3

Football League Trophy

Second Round	Bournemouth	(h)	1-0
Quarter-Final	Wycombe W	(h)	3-2
Semi-Final	Swansea C	(a)	2-2

WATFORD FA Premiership

FOUNDATION

The club was formed as Watford Rovers in 1881. The name was changed to West Herts in 1893 and then the name Watford was adopted after rival club Watford St Mary's was absorbed in 1898.

Vicarage Road Stadium, Vicarage Road, Watford, Herts WD18 0ER.

Telephone: 0870 111 1881.

Fax: (01923) 496 001.

Ticket Office: 0870 111 1881.

Website: www.watfordfc.com

Email: yourvoice@watfordfc.com

Ground Capacity: 19,920.

Record Attendance: 34,099 v Manchester U, FA Cup 4th rd (replay), 3 February 1969.

Pitch Measurements: 103m × 65m.

Chairman: Graham Simpson.

Vice-chairman: Jimmy Russo.

Chief Executive: Mark Ashton.

Secretary: Michelle Ives.

Manager: Adrian Boothroyd.

Assistant Manager: Keith Burkinshaw.

Physio: Andy Rolls.

Colours: Yellow shirts, red shorts, red stockings.

Change Colours: Navy shirts, navy shorts, navy stockings.

Year Formed: 1881.

Turned Professional: 1897.

Ltd Co.: 1909.

Club Nickname: 'The Hornets'.

Previous Names: 1881, Watford Rovers; 1893, West Herts; 1898, Watford.

Previous Grounds: 1883, Vicarage Meadow, Rose and Crown Meadow; 1889, Colney Butts; 1890, Cassio Road; 1922, Vicarage Road.

First Football League Game: 28 August 1920, Division 3, v QPR (a) W 2–1 – Williams; Horseman, F. Gregory; Bacon, Toone, Wilkinson; Bassett, Ronald (1), Hoddinott, White (1), Waterall.

Record League Victory: 8–0 v Sunderland, Division 1, 25 September 1982 – Sherwood; Rice, Rostron, Taylor, Terry, Bolton, Callaghan (2), Blissett (4), Jenkins (2), Jackett, Barnes.

Record Cup Victory: 10–1 v Lowestoft T, FA Cup 1st rd, 27 November 1926 – Yates; Prior, Fletcher (1); F. Smith, 'Bert' Smith, Strain; Stephenson, Warner (3), Edmonds (3), Swan (1), Daniels (1), (1 og).

HONOURS

Football League: Division 1 – Runners-up 1982–83, promoted from Division 1 1998–99 (play-offs); promoted from Championship (play-offs) 2005–06; Division 2 – Champions 1997–98; Runners-up 1981–82; Division 3 – Champions 1968–69; Runners-up 1978–79; Division 4 – Champions 1977–78; Promoted 1959–60 (4th).

FA Cup: Runners-up 1984, semi-finals 1970, 1984, 1987, 2003.

Football League Cup: Semi-final 1979.

European Competitions: *UEFA Cup:* 1983–84.

SKY SPORTS FACT FILE

Frank "Leftie" McPherson scored twice on his debut for Watford against Fulham on 29 September 1928. He then averaged a goal a game until the end of the season, registering 33 in his 33 League appearances in what was his first of two spells at the club.

Record Defeat: 0–10 v Wolverhampton W, FA Cup 1st rd (replay), 24 January 1912.

Most League Points (2 for a win): 71, Division 4, 1977–78.

Most League Points (3 for a win): 88, Division 2, 1997–98.

Most League Goals: 92, Division 4, 1959–60.

Highest League Scorer in Season: Cliff Holton, 42, Division 4, 1959–60.

Most League Goals in Total Aggregate: Luther Blissett, 148, 1976–83, 1984–88, 1991–92.

Most League Goals in One Match: 5, Eddie Mummery v Newport Co, Division 3S, 5 January 1924.

Most Capped Player: John Barnes, 31 (79), England and Kenny Jackett, 31, Wales.

Most League Appearances: Luther Blissett, 415, 1976–83, 1984–88, 1991–92.

Youngest League Player: Keith Mercer, 16 years 125 days v Tranmere R, 16 February 1973.

Record Transfer Fee Received: £2,300,000 from Chelsea for Paul Furlong, May 1994.

Record Transfer Fee Paid: £2,250,000 to Tottenham H for Allan Nielsen, August 2000.

Football League Record: 1920 Original Member of Division 3; 1921–58 Division 3 (S); 1958–60 Division 4; 1960–69 Division 3; 1969–72 Division 2; 1972–75 Division 3; 1975–78 Division 4; 1978–79 Division 3; 1979–82 Division 2; 1982–88 Division 1; 1988–92 Division 2; 1992–96 Division 1; 1996–98 Division 2; 1998–99 Division 1; 1999–2000 FA Premier League; 2000–04 Division 1; 2004–06 FLC; 2006– FA Premier League.

MANAGERS

John Goodall 1903–10
Harry Kent 1910–26
Fred Pagnam 1926–29
Neil McBain 1929–37
Bill Findlay 1938–47
Jack Bray 1947–48
Eddie Hapgood 1948–50
Ron Gray 1950–51
Haydn Green 1951–52
Len Goulden 1952–55
(General Manager to 1956)
Johnny Paton 1955–56
Neil McBain 1956–59
Ron Burgess 1959–63
Bill McGarry 1963–64
Ken Furphy 1964–71
George Kirby 1971–73
Mike Keen 1973–77
Graham Taylor 1977–87
Dave Bassett 1987–88
Steve Harrison 1988–90
Colin Lee 1990
Steve Perryman 1990–93
Glenn Roeder 1993–96
Kenny Jackett 1996–97
Graham Taylor 1997–2001
Gianluca Vialli 2001–02
Ray Lewington 2002–05
Adrian Boothroyd March 2005–

LATEST SEQUENCES

Longest Sequence of League Wins: 7, 28.8.2000 – 14.10.2000.

Longest Sequence of League Defeats: 9, 26.12.1972 – 27.2.1973.

Longest Sequence of League Draws: 7, 30.11.1996 – 27.1.1997.

Longest Sequence of Unbeaten League Matches: 22, 1.10.1996 – 1.3.1997.

Longest Sequence Without a League Win: 19, 27.11.1971 – 8.4.1972.

Successive Scoring Runs: 22 from 20.8.1985.

Successive Non-scoring Runs: 7 from 18.12.1971.

TEN YEAR LEAGUE RECORD

		P	*W*	*D*	*L*	*F*	*A*	*Pts*	*Pos*
1996-97	Div 2	46	16	19	11	45	38	67	13
1997-98	Div 2	46	24	16	6	67	41	88	1
1998-99	Div 1	46	21	14	11	65	56	77	5
1999-2000	PR Lge	38	6	6	26	35	77	24	20
2000-01	Div 1	46	20	9	17	76	67	69	9
2001-02	Div 1	46	16	11	19	62	56	59	14
2002-03	Div 1	46	17	9	20	54	70	60	13
2003-04	Div 1	46	15	12	19	54	68	57	16
2004-05	FL C	46	12	16	18	52	59	52	18
2005-06	FL C	46	22	15	9	77	53	81	3

DID YOU KNOW ?

Two goals on his League debut and a hat-trick two games later made attacking midfield player Tony Currie an instant hit with Watford in 1967–68. He was transferred to Sheffield United for £27,000 and went on to win England international honours.

WATFORD 2005–06 LEAGUE RECORD

Match No.	*Date*	*Venue*	*Opponents*	*Result*	*H/T Score*	*Lg. Pos.*	*Goalscorers*	*Attendance*
1	Aug 6	H	Preston NE	L 1-2	1-2	—	Henderson [9]	12,597
2	9	A	Plymouth Arg	D 3-3	1-3	—	King [35], Young 2 [52, 61]	13,813
3	12	A	Cardiff C	W 3-1	1-0	—	King 2 [7, 67], Henderson [52]	9256
4	20	H	Burnley	W 3-1	2-1	4	King [11], Mahon [30], Spring [83]	16,802
5	27	H	Reading	D 0-0	0-0	8		11,358
6	29	A	Derby Co	W 2-1	0-1	4	Spring [67], Carlisle [89]	23,664
7	Sept 10	A	Stoke C	W 3-0	1-0	3	Devlin [24], Young [67], King (pen) [72]	14,565
8	13	H	Norwich C	W 2-1	2-0	—	King [13], Young [25]	13,502
9	17	H	Sheffield U	L 2-3	1-0	3	Henderson 2 [39, 53]	15,399
10	24	A	Crewe Alex	D 0-0	0-0	3		6258
11	28	A	Coventry C	L 1-3	0-2	—	Young [51]	16,978
12	Oct 1	H	Leeds U	D 0-0	0-0	5		16,050
13	15	H	Leicester C	L 1-2	0-1	7	Young [49]	16,224
14	18	A	Sheffield W	D 1-1	0-0	—	Young [86]	21,187
15	22	A	Ipswich T	W 1-0	0-0	6	Young [55]	24,069
16	29	H	Wolverhampton W	W 3-1	0-0	4	DeMerit [69], King [77], Devlin [80]	14,561
17	Nov 1	H	QPR	W 3-1	1-0	—	Spring [39], McNamee [70], Young [76]	16,476
18	5	A	Hull C	W 2-1	2-1	3	Mahon [8], Spring [44]	18,444
19	19	H	Sheffield W	W 2-1	2-0	3	Carlisle [17], King [24]	16,988
20	22	A	Leicester C	D 2-2	1-2	—	King [11], MacKay [85]	18,856
21	26	A	Preston NE	D 1-1	1-1	3	Spring [11]	14,638
22	Dec 3	H	Brighton & HA	D 1-1	1-0	4	King [45]	14,455
23	10	H	Plymouth Arg	D 1-1	0-0	3	King [90]	12,884
24	17	A	Burnley	L 1-4	0-2	3	King [62]	13,815
25	26	H	Southampton	W 3-0	2-0	3	Henderson [28], Carlisle [40], Hajto (og) [47]	16,972
26	28	A	Millwall	D 0-0	0-0	4		8450
27	31	H	Crystal Palace	L 1-2	0-1	4	Henderson [59]	15,856
28	Jan 2	A	Luton T	W 2-1	2-0	4	Henderson [9], MacKay [30]	10,248
29	14	H	Stoke C	W 1-0	0-0	4	Eagles [54]	12,247
30	21	A	Norwich C	W 3-2	0-1	4	Henderson 2 [47, 65], Spring [90]	25,384
31	28	H	Crewe Alex	W 4-1	2-0	—	Spring 2 [18, 26], King [58], Young [62]	11,722
32	Feb 6	A	Sheffield U	W 4-1	1-0	—	Eagles [6], King 2 [47, 69], Bouazza [88]	20,791
33	11	H	Coventry C	W 4-0	1-0	3	Young [32], King [59], Henderson [78], DeMerit [82]	19,842
34	14	A	Leeds U	L 1-2	1-0	—	Young [40]	22,007
35	18	A	Brighton & HA	W 1-0	1-0	3	Eagles [45]	6658
36	25	H	Cardiff C	W 2-1	0-0	3	MacKay [69], King [88]	17,419
37	Mar 4	H	Derby Co	D 2-2	1-1	4	King [35], Bangura [90]	16,769
38	11	A	Reading	D 0-0	0-0	4		23,724
39	20	A	Southampton	W 3-1	1-0	—	Mahon [3], Henderson 2 [67, 72]	19,202
40	25	H	Millwall	L 0-2	0-0	3		16,654
41	31	A	Crystal Palace	L 1-3	1-0	—	King [28]	18,619
42	Apr 9	H	Luton T	D 1-1	1-0	3	King [36]	15,922
43	14	A	Wolverhampton W	D 1-1	0-1	—	King [65]	22,584
44	17	H	Ipswich T	W 2-1	1-0	3	Henderson 2 [33, 77]	16,721
45	22	A	QPR	W 2-1	1-1	3	Young [42], Santos (og) [78]	16,152
46	30	H	Hull C	D 0-0	0-0	3		17,128

Final League Position: 3

GOALSCORERS

League (77): King 21 (1 pen), Henderson 14, Young 13, Spring 8, Carlisle 3, Eagles 3, MacKay 3, Mahon 3, DeMerit 2, Devlin 2, Bangura 1, Bouazza 1, McNamee 1, own goals 2.
Carling Cup (5): Carlisle 2, Blizzard 1, Bouazza 1 (pen), Young 1.
FA Cup (0).
Play-Offs (6): DeMerit 1, Henderson 1 (pen), King 1, Spring 1, Young 1, own goal 1.

Foster B 44	Doyley L 40 + 4	Stewart J 29 + 6	Bangura A 11 + 24	DeMerit J 27 + 5	Carlisle C 30 + 2	Young A 38 + 1	Blizzard D 9 + 1	Henderson D 27 + 3	King M 40 + 1	McNamee A 26 + 12	Bouazza H 3 + 11	Chambers J 26 + 12	Mahon G 35 + 3	Devlin P 21 + 2	MacKay M 35 + 3	Spring M 36 + 3	Fletcher C 3	Osborne J 1	Grant J 2 + 5	Benjamin T 2	Agbonlahor G 1 + 1	Francis F — + 1	Diagouraga T 1	Eagles C 16 + 1	Chamberlain A 2 + 1	Mariappa A 1 + 2	Robinson T — + 1	Match No.
1	2	3^1	4	5	6	7	8	9	10	11^2	12	13																1
1	2^1	12	4^2	5	6	7	8	9	10	11^3		3	13	14														2
1		3	12	5	6	7^2	8	9	10	13		2	4	11^1														3
1	12	3^1			6	7^2	8	9	10			2	4	11	5	13												4
1	2				6	7	8	9^1	10	11	12	3			5	4												5
1	2	13	9		6	7	8^2		10	11	12	3^1			5	4												6
1	12	3^2	14		6	9	8^3		10	11	13	2		7^1	5	4												7
1	12	3	13		6	9	8^2		10	11^3	14	2		7^1	5	4												8
1	2	3			6	9	12	13	10^2	11^3		14		7^1	5■	4	8											9
1	6	12			5	9				11		3	13	7^3		4^2	8	2^1	14	10								10
1	5	3			6	9	8^1			11^2		2	12	13			4		7	10^3	14							11
1	6	3				9				11^1		2	8	7	5	4			12		10^2	13						12
1	12	3^1			6	9			10	11		2	8	7^2	5	4			13									13
1	2		12	13	6	11		9^3	10	14		3	8	7^2	5	4^1												14
1	2		12	5	6	11		9^2	10			3	8	7	13	4^1												15
1	2		12	5	6	11		9^2	10	13		3	8	7^1		4												16
1	2		12	5	6	9			10	11		3	8	7		4^1												17
1	2		12	5^2	6	9		14	10	11^1		3	8	7^3	13	4												18
1	2	12		5^3	6	9^1		13	10^2	11		3	8	7	14	4												19
1	2		12	13	6■	9			10	11^1		3	8	7^2	5	4												20
1	2	3	11	6		9			10	12			8	7^1	5	4												21
1		3	4	12	6				10	11		2	8	7	5				9^1									22
1	2	3^2	12	4	6				10	11		13	8	9	5	7^1												23
1	2	11		14	6				10	12		3^1	8	7^2	5	4			13				9^3					24
1	2		12		6			9^1	10	11		3	8	7^2	5	4			13									25
1	2		12		6			9	10	11^1		3	8	7	5	4												26
1	2		7		6	12		9	10	11		3	8		5	4^1												27
1	2	12	4^2	14	6	7■		9	10	11^1		3^3	8		5	13												28
1	2	3	12	6				9^2	10	11^1	13		8		5	4								7				29
1	2	3	12	6^2	13			9	10	11^3	14		8		5	4								7^1				30
	2	3	12	6		11		9^3	10^1		14	13	8		5	4								7^2	1			31
1	2	3	12	6		11^2		9	10		13	14	8		5	4^1								7^3				32
1	2	3		6		7		9^3	10	11^1	12	13	8^2		5	4								14				33
1■	2	3	4^2	6		11		9■	10^1		12	8			5									7^G	15	13		34
	2	3^2	12	6	13	9			10		11^1	14	8		5	4								7^3	1			35
1	2	3		6		9			10	12	11^1	13	8		5	4								7^2				36
1	2	3	12		6	9			10	13	11^1		8		5	4								7^2				37
1	2	3	12	6		10^1		9	13	11^2			8		5	4								7				38
1	2	3	12	6		11		9^2	10			13	8		5	4								7^1				39
1	2	3^1	12	6		11		9	10	13			8		5^2	4								7				40
1	2	3^1	12	6		11		9	10	13			8		5	4								7^2				41
1	2	3^2	12	6		11		9	10			13	8		5	4								7^1				42
1	2		12	3	6	11		9^2	10■	13		14	8		5	4^1								7^3				43
1	2	12	4	3	6	10		9		11^1		13	8		5									7^2				44
1	2	11	4	3	6^1	10		9^3		12		7			5	8^2										13	14	45
1	2	3	4	5		11^1		9^2	10	12			8			13								7		6		46

FA Cup

Third Round	Bolton W	(h)	0-3

Carling Cup

First Round	Notts Co	(h)	3-1
Second Round	Wolverhampton W	(h)	2-1
Third Round	Wigan Ath	(a)	0-3

Play-Offs

Semi-Final	Crystal Palace	(a)	3-0
		(h)	0-0
Final	Leeds U		3-0
(at Millennium Stadium)			

WEST BROMWICH ALBION FL Championship

FOUNDATION

There is a well known story that when employees of Salter's Spring Works in West Bromwich decided to form a football club, they had to send someone to the nearby Association Football stronghold of Wednesbury to purchase a football. A weekly subscription of 2d (less than 1p) was imposed and the name of the new club was West Bromwich Strollers.

The Hawthorns, West Bromwich, West Midlands B71 4LF.

Telephone: 0870 066 8888.

Fax: 0870 066 2861.

Ticket Office: 0870 066 2800.

Website: www.wbafc.co.uk

Email: enquiries@wbafc.co.uk

Ground Capacity: 28,000.

Record Attendance: 64,815 v Arsenal, FA Cup 6th rd, 6 March 1937.

Pitch Measurements: 115yd × 74yd.

Chairman: Jeremy Peace.

Secretary: John Evans.

Manager: Bryan Robson.

Assistant Manager: Nigel Pearson.

Physio: Nick Worth.

Colours: Navy blue and white striped shirts, white shorts, navy blue stockings.

Change Colours: Navy blue shirts with red and white diagonal strip, white shorts, white stockings.

Year Formed: 1878.

Turned Professional: 1885.

Ltd Co.: 1892.

Plc: 1996.

Previous Name: 1878, West Bromwich Strollers; 1881, West Bromwich Albion.

Club Nicknames: 'Throstles', 'Baggies', 'Albion'.

Previous Grounds: 1878, Coopers Hill; 1879, Dartmouth Park; 1881, Bunns Field, Walsall Street; 1882, Four Acres (Dartmouth Cricket Club); 1885, Stoney Lane; 1900, The Hawthorns.

First Football League Game: 8 September 1888, Football League, v Stoke (a) W 2–0 – Roberts; J. Horton, Green; E. Horton, Perry, Bayliss; Bassett, Woodhall (1), Hendry, Pearson, Wilson (1).

Record League Victory: 12–0 v Darwen, Division 1, 4 April 1892 – Reader; J. Horton, McCulloch; Reynolds (2), Perry, Groves; Bassett (3), McLeod, Nicholls (1), Pearson (4), Geddes (1), (1 og).

HONOURS

Football League: Division 1 – Champions 1919–20; Runners-up 1924–25, 1953–54, 2001–02, 2003–04; Division 2 – Champions 1901–02, 1910–11; Runners-up 1930–31, 1948–49; Promoted to Division 1 1975–76 (3rd); 1992–93 (play-offs); Promoted to FA Premier League 2001–02.

FA Cup: Winners 1888, 1892, 1931, 1954, 1968; Runners-up 1886, 1887, 1895, 1912, 1935.

Football League Cup: Winners 1966; Runners-up 1967, 1970.

European Competitions: *European Cup-Winners' Cup:* 1968–69. *European Fairs Cup:* 1966–67. *UEFA Cup:* 1978–79, 1979–80, 1981–82.

SKY SPORTS FACT FILE

On 15 October 2005 West Bromwich Albion beat Arsenal 2–1. It was their first League victory over their opponents at The Hawthorns since 28 February 1973 when a goal from Tony Brown ensured the points for the Baggies.

Record Cup Victory: 10–1 v Chatham (away), FA Cup 3rd rd, 2 March 1889 – Roberts; J. Horton, Green; Timmins (1), Charles Perry, E. Horton; Bassett (2), Perry (1), Bayliss (2), Pearson, Wilson (3), (1 og).

Record Defeat: 3–10 v Stoke C, Division 1, 4 February 1937.

Most League Points (2 for a win): 60, Division 1, 1919–20.

Most League Points (3 for a win): 89, Division 1, 2001–02.

Most League Goals: 105, Division 2, 1929–30.

Highest League Scorer in Season: William 'Ginger' Richardson, 39, Division 1, 1935–36.

Most League Goals in Total Aggregate: Tony Brown, 218, 1963–79.

Most League Goals in One Match: 6, Jimmy Cookson v Blackpool, Division 2, 17 September 1927.

Most Capped Player: Stuart Williams, 33 (43), Wales.

Most League Appearances: Tony Brown, 574, 1963–80.

Youngest League Player: Charlie Wilson, 16 years 73 days v Oldham Ath, 1 October 1921.

Record Transfer Fee Received: £5,000,001 from Coventry C for Lee Hughes, July 2001.

Record Transfer Fee Paid: £3,500,000 to Cardiff C for Robert Earnshaw, August 2004.

Football League Record: 1888 Founder Member of Football League; 1901–02 Division 2; 1902–04 Division 1; 1904–11 Division 2; 1911–27 Division 1; 1927–31 Division 2; 1931–38 Division 1; 1938–49 Division 2; 1949–73 Division 1; 1973–76 Division 2; 1976–86 Division 1; 1986–91 Division 2; 1991–92 Division 3; 1992–93 Division 2; 1993–2002 Division 1; 2002–03 FA Premier League; 2003–04 Division 1; 2004–06 FA Premier League; 2006– FLC.

MANAGERS

Louis Ford 1890–92
(Secretary-Manager)
Henry Jackson 1892–94
(Secretary-Manager)
Edward Stephenson 1894–95
(Secretary-Manager)
Clement Keys 1895–96
(Secretary-Manager)
Frank Heaven 1896–1902
(Secretary-Manager)
Fred Everiss 1902–48
Jack Smith 1948–52
Jesse Carver 1952
Vic Buckingham 1953–59
Gordon Clark 1959–61
Archie Macaulay 1961–63
Jimmy Hagan 1963–67
Alan Ashman 1967–71
Don Howe 1971–75
Johnny Giles 1975–77
Ronnie Allen 1977
Ron Atkinson 1978–81
Ronnie Allen 1981–82
Ron Wylie 1982–84
Johnny Giles 1984–85
Ron Saunders 1986–87
Ron Atkinson 1987–88
Brian Talbot 1988–91
Bobby Gould 1991–92
Ossie Ardiles 1992–93
Keith Burkinshaw 1993–94
Alan Buckley 1994–97
Ray Harford 1997
Denis Smith 1997–2000
Brian Little 2000
Gary Megson 2000–04
Bryan Robson November 2004–

LATEST SEQUENCES

Longest Sequence of League Wins: 11, 5.4.1930 – 8.9.1930.

Longest Sequence of League Defeats: 11, 28.10.1995 – 26.12.1995.

Longest Sequence of League Draws: 5, 30.8.1999 – 3.10.1999.

Longest Sequence of Unbeaten League Matches: 17, 7.9.1957 – 7.12.1957.

Longest Sequence Without a League Win: 15, 16.10.2004 – 25.9.2004.

Successive Scoring Runs: 36 from 26.4.1958.

Successive Non-scoring Runs: 4 from 15.2.1913.

TEN YEAR LEAGUE RECORD

		P	W	D	L	F	A	Pts	Pos
1996-97	Div 1	46	14	15	17	68	72	57	16
1997-98	Div 1	46	16	13	17	50	56	61	10
1998-99	Div 1	46	16	11	19	69	76	59	12
1999-2000	Div 1	46	10	19	17	43	60	49	21
2000-01	Div 1	46	21	11	14	60	52	74	6
2001-02	Div 1	46	27	8	11	61	29	89	2
2002-03	PR Lge	38	6	8	24	29	65	26	19
2003-04	Div 1	46	25	11	10	64	42	86	2
2004-05	PR Lge	38	6	16	16	36	61	34	17
2005-06	PR Lge	38	7	9	22	31	58	30	19

DID YOU KNOW

Left-back Len Millard made his 350th League appearance for West Bromwich Albion on 23 December 1950 against Stoke City, but suffered influenza and missed the Christmas matches, two of only 13 he was absent from in the first ten post-war seasons.

WEST BROMWICH ALBION 2005–06 LEAGUE RECORD

Match No.	Date	Venue	Opponents	Result		H/T Score	Lg. Pos.	Goalscorers	Attendance
1	Aug 13	A	Manchester C	D	0-0	0-0	—		42,983
2	20	H	Portsmouth	W	2-1	1-0	7	Horsfield 2 [2, 59]	24,404
3	24	A	Chelsea	L	0-4	0-2	—		41,201
4	27	H	Birmingham C	L	2-3	1-3	15	Horsfield 2 [12, 64]	23,993
5	Sept 10	H	Wigan Ath	L	1-2	1-1	17	Greening [26]	25,617
6	17	A	Sunderland	D	1-1	0-1	17	Gera [90]	31,657
7	24	H	Charlton Ath	L	1-2	0-2	18	Davies [51]	23,909
8	Oct 1	A	Blackburn R	L	0-2	0-0	19		20,721
9	15	H	Arsenal	W	2-1	1-1	15	Kanu [38], Carter [76]	26,604
10	23	A	Bolton W	L	0-2	0-0	16		24,151
11	30	H	Newcastle U	L	0-3	0-0	17		26,216
12	Nov 5	A	West Ham U	L	0-1	0-0	18		34,325
13	19	H	Everton	W	4-0	1-0	16	Ellington 2 (1 pen) [45 (p), 69], Clement [51], Earnshaw [90]	24,784
14	27	A	Middlesbrough	D	2-2	1-1	17	Ellington [18], Kanu [57]	27,041
15	Dec 3	H	Fulham	D	0-0	0-0	17		23,144
16	10	H	Manchester C	W	2-0	1-0	17	Kamara [5], Campbell [61]	25,472
17	17	A	Portsmouth	L	0-1	0-0	17		20,052
18	26	A	Manchester U	L	0-3	0-2	17		67,972
19	28	H	Tottenham H	W	2-0	1-0	16	Kanu 2 [23, 52]	27,510
20	31	A	Liverpool	L	0-1	0-0	17		44,192
21	Jan 2	H	Aston Villa	L	1-2	0-0	17	Watson [76]	27,073
22	15	A	Wigan Ath	W	1-0	0-0	16	Albrechtsen [56]	17,421
23	21	H	Sunderland	L	0-1	0-0	16		26,464
24	31	A	Charlton Ath	D	0-0	0-0	—		25,921
25	Feb 4	H	Blackburn R	W	2-0	2-0	16	Campbell [6], Greening [32]	23,993
26	11	A	Fulham	L	1-6	0-2	17	Campbell [85]	21,508
27	26	H	Middlesbrough	L	0-2	0-2	17		24,061
28	Mar 4	H	Chelsea	L	1-2	0-0	17	Kanu [88]	26,581
29	11	A	Birmingham C	D	1-1	0-0	17	Ellington [70]	28,041
30	18	H	Manchester U	L	1-2	0-1	17	Ellington [78]	27,623
31	27	A	Tottenham H	L	1-2	1-0	—	Davies [21]	36,152
32	Apr 1	H	Liverpool	L	0-2	0-2	17		27,576
33	9	A	Aston Villa	D	0-0	0-0	18		33,303
34	15	A	Arsenal	L	1-3	0-1	19	Quashie [72]	38,167
35	17	H	Bolton W	D	0-0	0-0	19		23,181
36	22	A	Newcastle U	L	0-3	0-2	19		52,272
37	May 1	H	West Ham U	L	0-1	0-1	—		24,462
38	7	A	Everton	D	2-2	1-0	19	Gera [14], Martinez [47]	39,671

Final League Position: 19

GOALSCORERS

League (31): Ellington 5 (1 pen), Kanu 5, Horsfield 4, Campbell 3, Davies 2, Gera 2, Greening 2, Albrechtsen 1, Carter 1, Clement 1, Earnshaw 1, Kamara 1, Martinez 1, Quashie 1, Watson 1.
Carling Cup (8): Ellington 3, Earnshaw 2, Inamoto 1, Kamara 1, Kanu 1.
FA Cup (3): Chaplow 2, Gera 1 (pen).

Kirkland C 10	Albrechtsen M 26 + 5	Robinson P 33	Wallwork R 31	Gaardsoe T 7	Clement N 29 + 2	Gera Z 12 + 3	Inamoto J 16 + 6	Campbell K 19 + 10	Kanu N 17 + 8	Greening J 37 + 1	Chaplow R 4 + 3	Kamara D 21 + 5	Watson S 28 + 2	Earnshaw R 4 + 8	Johnson A 8	Horsfield G 10 + 8	Scimeca R 2	Ellington N 15 + 16	Carter D 11 + 9	Davies C 33	Moore D 3 + 2	Kuszczak T 28	Nicholson S — + 4	Quashie N 9	Kozak J 4 + 2	Hoult R — + 1	Martinez W 1 + 1	Hodgkiss J — + 1	*Match No.*
1	2	3	4[1]	5	6	7	8	9	10[2]	11[3]	12	13	14																1
1	12	3	4	5	6	7[1]		9		11			2[2]	13	8	10													2
1	2	3		5	6		12		10	11[2]	7	9			8[1]		4	13											3
1	12	3	4	5	6	7		9[3]		11			2[1]	13		10		14	8[2]										4
1	2	3	4[1]	5	6			12		11	13		7	14		10		9[3]	8[2]										5
1		3	4		6	7		9		11[2]		13	2	10[1]	8			12		5									6
1		3	4		6	7		9[1]		11		13	2	10[3]	8[2]	12		14		5									7
1	2	3	4		6	7		9[2]		11	8	10[1]				12		13		5									8
1	2	3	4[2]		6				9[3]	11		8	7			10[1]		12	13	5	14								9
1	2	3			6[1]				13	11		9	7	12		10[2]			8	5	4								10
					3		4		9[2]	11[1]			7	10		12	2	13	8	5	6	1							11
	3		4		6		8	12	9[1]	11		7	2	10[2]		13				5		1							12
	3		4		6		8		12	11		7[3]	2	13		10[1]		9[2]	14	5		1							13
	12	3	4		6		8		10	11		7[2]	2[1]					9	13	5		1							14
		3	4		6		8		10[1]	11[2]		7[3]	2	13		12		9	14	5		1							15
	12	3	4		6		8	13	10	11		7[3]	2[1]					9[2]	14	5		1							16
	2	3	4		6		8	12	10	11[1]		7[2]		13				9		5		1							17
	2	3[2]	4	6[1]		12		14		11	10	13	7					9[3]	8	5		1							18
	3		4		6			12	10[1]	11		7[3]	2			13		9[2]	8	5	14	1							19
	2	3	4[3]		6			9[2]		12	8[1]	14	7			10		13	11	5		1							20
	2	3			6[2]			12	10	11		4	7			13		9[1]	8	5		1							21
	12	3	4				8	9[2]		11			2	13				10[1]	7	5	6■	1							22
	2	3	4[2]				8[1]	9		7	13		6			12		10[3]	11	5		1	14						23
	2	3			6		4	9[1]		7					8	10		12	11	5		1							24
	2	3	4		6		8	9[1]		11						10[3]		12	13	5		1		7[2]	14				25
	2		4	6[2]	3		8	9		11						10[1]		12		5		1[6]		7		15	13		26
	2[1]	3	4		6		12	9[3]	10[2]	11		7						13		5		1		8■	14				27
	2[3]	3	4		6		8[2]	9[1]	12	11		10	14					13		5		1			7				28
	6	3[1]	4		12		8[2]	9[3]	13	11		10	2					14		5		1			7				29
	2	3	4				8	9[1]	12	11		10[2]	6					13	14	5		1			7[3]				30
	2	3	4			12	13	14	10[3]	11			6		8			9[1]		5		1			7[2]				31
	2	3	4		12	13		14	10[3]	11		7[2]	6[1]		8			9		5		1							32
		3	4[2]		6	7	13	9[1]	12	11		10[3]	5							2		1	14	8					33
	2	3	4[3]		6	7[1]	12	13	10[2]	11		9							14	5		1		8					34
		3			6	7		9[1]	12	11		10[2]	2		4					5		1	13	8					35
	2	3			6	7	12	9[2]	13	11		10[3]	4[1]					14		5		1		8					36
	2	3	4			7			10	11			6					9		5		1		8					37
		3	4			7[1]			10	11			2[3]					9[2]	12	5		1	13	8			6	14	38

FA Cup

Third Round	Reading	(h)	1-1
		(a)	2-3

Carling Cup

Second Round	Bradford C	(h)	4-1
Third Round	Fulham	(a)	3-2
Fourth Round	Manchester U	(a)	1-3

WEST HAM UNITED FA Premiership

FOUNDATION

Thames Iron Works FC was formed by employees of this famous shipbuilding company in 1895 and entered the FA Cup in their initial season at Chatham and the London League in their second. The committee wanted to introduce professional players, so Thames Iron Works was wound up in June 1900 and relaunched a month later as West Ham United.

The Boleyn Ground, Green Street, Upton Park, London E13 9AZ.

Telephone: (020) 8548 2748.

Fax: (020) 8548 2758.

Ticket Office: 0870 112 2700.

Website: www.whufc.co.uk

Ground Capacity: 35,303.

Record Attendance: 42,322 v Tottenham H, Division 1, 17 October 1970.

Pitch Measurements: 112yd × 72yd.

Chairman: Terence Brown FCIS, AII, FCCA.

Vice-chairman: Martin Cearns ACIB.

Chief Executive: Paul Aldridge.

Secretary: Peter Barnes.

Manager: Alan Pardew.

Assistant Manager: Peter Grant.

Physio: Steve Allen.

Colours: Claret shirts with sky blue sleeves, white shorts, sky blue stockings.

Change Colours: Navy blue shirts, shorts and stockings.

Year Formed: 1895.

Turned Professional: 1900.

Ltd Co.: 1900.

Previous Names: 1895, Thames Iron Works FC; 1900, West Ham United.

Club Nicknames: 'The Hammers', 'The Irons'.

Previous Grounds: 1895, Memorial Recreation Ground, Canning Town; 1904, Boleyn Ground.

First Football League Game: 30 August 1919, Division 2, v Lincoln C (h) D 1–1 – Hufton; Cope, Lee; Lane, Fenwick, McCrae; D. Smith, Moyes (1), Puddefoot, Morris, Bradshaw.

HONOURS

Football League: Promotion from Championship 2004–05 (play-offs); Division 2 – Champions 1957–58, 1980–81; Runners-up 1922–23, 1990–91.

FA Cup: Winners 1964, 1975, 1980; Runners-up 1923, 2006.

Football League Cup: Runners-up 1966, 1981.

European Competitions: *European Cup-Winners' Cup:* 1964–65 (winners), 1965–66, 1975–76 (runners-up), 1980–81. *UEFA Cup:* 1999–2000. *Intertoto Cup:* 1999 (winners).

SKY SPORTS FACT FILE

West Ham United had a memorable fourth round FA Cup tie with Tottenham Hotspur during 1938–39. The teams shared six goals at Upton Park, drew 1–1 at White Hart Lane before goals from Stan Foxall and Archie Macaulay edged Hammers home 2–1 at Highbury.

MANAGERS

Syd King 1902–32
Charlie Paynter 1932–50
Ted Fenton 1950–61
Ron Greenwood 1961–74
(continued as General Manager to 1977)
John Lyall 1974–89
Lou Macari 1989–90
Billy Bonds 1990–94
Harry Redknapp 1994–2001
Glenn Roeder 2001–03
Alan Pardew October 2003–

Record League Victory: 8–0 v Rotherham U, Division 2, 8 March 1958 – Gregory; Bond, Wright; Malcolm, Brown, Lansdowne; Grice, Smith (2), Keeble (2), Dick (4), Musgrove. 8–0 v Sunderland, Division 1, 19 October 1968 – Ferguson; Bonds, Charles; Peters, Stephenson, Moore (1); Redknapp, Boyce, Brooking (1), Hurst (6), Sissons.

Record Cup Victory: 10–0 v Bury, League Cup 2nd rd (2nd leg), 25 October 1983 – Parkes; Stewart (1), Walford, Bonds (Orr), Martin (1), Devonshire (2), Allen, Cottee (4), Swindlehurst, Brooking (2), Pike.

Record Defeat: 2–8 v Blackburn R, Division 1, 26 December 1963.

Most League Points (2 for a win): 66, Division 2, 1980–81.

Most League Points (3 for a win): 88, Division 1, 1992–93.

Most League Goals: 101, Division 2, 1957–58.

Highest League Scorer in Season: Vic Watson, 42, Division 1, 1929–30.

Most League Goals in Total Aggregate: Vic Watson, 298, 1920–35.

Most League Goals in One Match: 6, Vic Watson v Leeds U, Division 1, 9 February 1929; 6, Geoff Hurst v Sunderland, Division 1, 19 October 1968.

Most Capped Player: Bobby Moore, 108, England.

Most League Appearances: Billy Bonds, 663, 1967–88.

Youngest League Player: Neil Finn, 17 years 3 days v Manchester C, 1 January 1996.

Record Transfer Fee Received: £18,000,000 from Leeds U for Rio Ferdinand, November 2000.

Record Transfer Fee Paid: £7,250,000 to Norwich C for Dean Ashton, January 2006.

Football League Record: 1919 Elected to Division 2; 1923–32 Division 1; 1932–58 Division 2; 1958–78 Division 1; 1978–81 Division 2; 1981–89 Division 1; 1989–91 Division 2; 1991–93 Division 1; 1993–2003 FA Premier League; 2003–04 Division 1; 2004–05 FLC; 2005– FA Premier League.

LATEST SEQUENCES

Longest Sequence of League Wins: 9, 19.10.1985 – 14.12.1985.

Longest Sequence of League Defeats: 9, 28.3.1932 – 29.8.1932.

Longest Sequence of League Draws: 5, 15.10.2003 – 1.11.2003.

Longest Sequence of Unbeaten League Matches: 27, 27.12.80 – 10.10.81.

Longest Sequence Without a League Win: 17, 31.1.1976 – 21.8.1976.

Successive Scoring Runs: 27 from 5.10.1957.

Successive Non-scoring Runs: 5 from 1.5.1971.

TEN YEAR LEAGUE RECORD

		P	W	D	L	F	A	Pts	Pos
1996-97	PR Lge	38	10	12	16	39	48	42	14
1997-98	PR Lge	38	16	8	14	56	57	56	8
1998-99	PR Lge	38	16	9	13	46	53	57	5
1999-2000	PR Lge	38	15	10	13	52	53	55	9
2000-01	PR Lge	38	10	12	16	45	50	42	15
2001-02	PR Lge	38	15	8	15	48	57	53	7
2002-03	PR Lge	38	10	12	16	42	59	42	18
2003-04	Div 1	46	19	17	10	67	45	74	4
2004-05	FL C	46	21	10	15	66	56	73	6
2005-06	PR Lge	38	16	7	15	52	55	55	9

In November 1957 West Ham United entertained Polish League leaders and Cup holders LKS Lodz, said to be their 100th against foreign opposition. Actually it was their 108th and the Hammers won 4–1 against a team with six full and 2 B internationals.

WEST HAM UNITED 2005–06 LEAGUE RECORD

Match No.	*Date*	*Venue*	*Opponents*	*Result*		*H/T Score*	*Lg. Pos.*	*Goalscorers*	*Attendance*
1	Aug 13	H	Blackburn R	W	3-1	0-1	—	Sheringham [46], Reo-Coker [62], Etherington [80]	33,305
2	20	A	Newcastle U	D	0-0	0-0	5		51,620
3	27	H	Bolton W	L	1-2	0-0	9	Sheringham (pen) [90]	31,629
4	Sept 12	H	Aston Villa	W	4-0	2-0	—	Harewood 3 [25, 29, 50], Benayoun [89]	29,582
5	17	A	Fulham	W	2-1	0-0	6	Harewood [46], Warner (og) [52]	21,907
6	24	H	Arsenal	D	0-0	0-0	4		34,742
7	Oct 1	A	Sunderland	D	1-1	0-1	9	Benayoun [72]	31,212
8	16	A	Manchester C	L	1-2	0-1	9	Zamora [90]	43,647
9	23	H	Middlesbrough	W	2-1	0-0	9	Sheringham [66], Riggott (og) [74]	34,612
10	29	A	Liverpool	L	0-2	0-1	9		44,537
11	Nov 5	H	WBA	W	1-0	0-0	9	Sheringham [57]	34,325
12	20	A	Tottenham H	D	1-1	0-1	8	Ferdinand [90]	36,154
13	27	H	Manchester U	L	1-2	1-0	9	Harewood [2]	34,755
14	Dec 5	A	Birmingham C	W	2-1	2-1	—	Zamora [36], Harewood [45]	24,010
15	10	A	Blackburn R	L	2-3	1-0	9	Zamora [45], Harewood [63]	20,370
16	14	A	Everton	W	2-1	1-1	—	Weir (og) [19], Zamora [67]	35,704
17	17	H	Newcastle U	L	2-4	1-2	9	Solano (og) [20], Harewood (pen) [73]	34,836
18	26	A	Portsmouth	D	1-1	0-1	9	Collins [56]	20,168
19	28	H	Wigan Ath	L	0-2	0-2	9		34,131
20	31	A	Charlton Ath	L	0-2	0-1	10		25,952
21	Jan 2	H	Chelsea	L	1-3	0-1	10	Harewood [46]	34,758
22	14	A	Aston Villa	W	2-1	0-1	10	Zamora [51], Harewood (pen) [60]	36,700
23	23	H	Fulham	W	2-1	2-0	—	Ferdinand [17], Benayoun [28]	29,812
24	Feb 1	A	Arsenal	W	3-2	2-1	—	Reo-Coker [25], Zamora [32], Etherington [80]	38,216
25	4	H	Sunderland	W	2-0	0-0	8	Ashton [81], Konchesky [87]	34,745
26	13	H	Birmingham C	W	3-0	1-0	—	Harewood 2 [11, 63], Ashton [65]	31,294
27	Mar 4	H	Everton	D	2-2	2-1	8	Harewood [10], Ashton [23]	34,866
28	11	A	Bolton W	L	1-4	0-3	9	Sheringham [79]	24,461
29	18	H	Portsmouth	L	2-4	0-3	10	Sheringham [69], Benayoun [90]	34,837
30	25	A	Wigan Ath	W	2-1	0-1	9	Harewood [52], Reo-Coker [90]	18,736
31	29	A	Manchester U	L	0-1	0-1	—		69,522
32	Apr 2	H	Charlton Ath	D	0-0	0-0	8		34,753
33	9	A	Chelsea	L	1-4	1-2	9	Collins [10]	41,919
34	15	H	Manchester C	W	1-0	1-0	7	Newton [15]	34,305
35	17	A	Middlesbrough	L	0-2	0-1	9		27,658
36	26	H	Liverpool	L	1-2	0-1	—	Reo-Coker [46]	34,852
37	May 1	A	WBA	W	1-0	1-0	—	Reo-Coker [42]	24,462
38	7	H	Tottenham H	W	2-1	1-1	9	Fletcher [10], Benayoun [80]	34,970

Final League Position: 9

GOALSCORERS

League (52): Harewood 14 (2 pens), Sheringham 6 (1 pen), Zamora 6, Benayoun 5, Reo-Coker 5, Ashton 3, Collins 2, Etherington 2, Ferdinand 2, Fletcher 1, Konchesky 1, Newton 1, own goals 4.
Carling Cup (4): Zamora 2, Bellion 1, Daily 1.
FA Cup (14): Ashton 3, Harewood 2, Zamora 2, Etherington 1, Konchesky 1, Mullins 1, Sheringham 1 (pen), own goal 3.

Carroll R 19	Dailly C 6 + 16	Konchesky P 36 + 1	Gabbidon D 31 + 1	Ferdinand A 32 + 1	Mullins H 35	Benayoun Y 30 + 4	Reo-Coker N 31	Harewood M 31 + 6	Sheringham T 15 + 11	Etherington M 33	Noble M 4 + 1	Newton S 8 + 18	Repka T 19	Zamora B 17 + 17	Ward E 3 + 1	Aliadiere J 1 + 6	Hislop S 16	Collins J 13 + 1	Bellion D 2 + 6	Bywater S — + 1	Fletcher C 6 + 6	Katan Y 2 + 4	Clarke C 2	Ashton D 9 + 2	Scaloni L 13	Walker J 3	Reid K 1 + 1	*Match No.*
1	2	3	4	5	6^{1}	7	8	9	10^{2}	11	12	13																1
1	12	3■	4	5	6	7^{1}	8	9^{3}	10^{2}	11		13	2	14														2
1		3	4^{2}	5	6	7	8	9^{1}	10	11^{3}			2	12	13	14												3
1	12	3	4	5	6^{1}	7	8	9^{2}	10	11^{3}		14	2	13														4
1		3	4	5	6	7^{1}	8	9^{3}	12	11		13	2	10^{2}		14												5
1		3	4	5	6	7	8	9	10^{1}	11^{2}		13	2	12														6
1	12	3	4	5	6	7	8	9	10^{2}	11^{3}		14	2^{1}	13														7
1	12	3	4	5	6	7	8	9	10^{2}	11^{3}		14	2^{1}	13														8
	12	3	4	5	6	7^{1}	8	9	13	11^{3}		14	2	10^{2}			1											9
		3	4	5	6	7	8	9	12	11^{1}			2^{3}			13	1	14	10^{2}									10
	12	3	4	5	6	7^{2}	8^{1}	9	10	11		13	2				1^{G}			15								11
		3	4	5	6	7		9^{1}	10	11^{2}	8	14	2^{3}	12			1		13									12
1	12	3	4	5	6^{2}	7		9	10^{1}	11^{3}	8	14	2	13														13
1	12	3	4	5	6	7^{2}		9		11	8^{1}	13	2	10^{3}					14									14
1	12	3	4^{1}	5	6	7		9		11	8^{2}		2	10^{3}		14			13									15
1	12	3		5	6	7		9		11^{1}		13	2	10^{2}				4			8							16
1		3		5	6	7^{2}		9		11			2^{1}	10		12		4	13		8							17
1	13	3	12^{2}	5	6^{3}		8	9		11		7	2^{1}	10				4			14							18
1	2	3		5	6		8	9^{3}		11		12		13		14		4	7^{1}		10^{2}							19
1	2^{1}	3		5	6	12	8	9		11		7				10^{2}		4	13									20
1	2	3		5	6^{1}	7	8	9		11^{2}				12				4	13		10							21
1	12	3	4	5	6	13	8	9		11^{1}		7^{2}	2	10^{3}								14						22
1	12	3	4	5	6	7^{3}	8	9		11^{2}		13	2	10^{1}								14						23
		3	4	5	6	7^{1}	8	9		11		12		10^{3}			1				13		2^{2}	14				24
	12	3	4	5	6^{2}	7	8	13	14	11				10^{2}			1							9^{1}	2			25
	12	3	4	5	6^{1}	7	8	9		11^{3}				13			1					14		10^{2}	2			26
		3	4	5	6	7^{2}	8	9	12	11^{3}		14		13			1							10^{1}	2			27
	12	3	4	5	8	13			10	11		7^{2}		9	6^{1}		1								2			28
	6	3	4	5^{3}		12	8	13	10					9							14	7^{2}	11^{1}		2	1		29
		3	4		6	7^{2}	8	9	12	11^{3}		13		14			1	5						10^{1}	2			30
		3	4	12	6	7	8	9	13	11^{3}				14			1	5						10^{2}	2^{1}			31
		3	4	2	6	7	8^{2}	9^{3}	12	11				13			1	5				14		10^{1}				32
		3	4		6	7^{1}	8	9	12	11				13			1	5						10^{2}	2			33
		3	4		6	7	8	12	13			11^{3}		9^{1}				5			14			10^{2}	2	1		34
		3	4		6		8	9^{3}	10			7		12			1	5			13	11^{1}		14	2^{2}			35
				5	6■	7^{1}	8	12	10	11				9	3			4^{2}			13				2	1		36
	3^{1}	12	4				8	13	14			7		9^{2}	5		1				6			10^{3}	2		11	37
		3	4	5		11^{2}	8	12	10^{1}			7		9			1				6				2		13	38

FA Cup

Third Round	Norwich C	(a)	2-1
Fourth Round	Blackburn R	(h)	4-2
Fifth Round	Bolton W	(a)	0-0
		(h)	2-1
Sixth Round	Manchester C	(a)	2-1
Semi-Final *(at Villa Park)*	Middlesbrough		1-0
Final *(at Millennium Stadium)*	Liverpool		3-3

Carling Cup

Second Round	Sheffield W	(a)	4-2
Third Round	Bolton W	(a)	0-1

WIGAN ATHLETIC FA Premiership

FOUNDATION

Following the demise of Wigan Borough and their resignation from the Football League in 1931, a public meeting was called in Wigan at the Queen's Hall in May 1932 at which a new club, Wigan Athletic, was founded in the hope of carrying on in the Football League. With this in mind, they bought Springfield Park for £2,250, but failed to gain admission to the Football League until 46 years later.

JJB Stadium, Robin Park, Newtown, Wigan WN5 0UZ.

Telephone: (01942) 774 000.

Fax: (01942) 770 477.

Ticket Office: 0870 112 2552.

Website: www.wiganathletic.tv

Email: latics@jjbstadium.co.uk

Ground Capacity: 25,138.

Record Attendance: 27,526 v Hereford U, 12 December 1953 (at Springfield Park).

Pitch Measurements: 114yd × 74yd.

Chairman: David Whelan.

Vice-chairman: Phillip Williams.

Chief Executive: Brenda Spencer.

Secretary: Stuart Hayton.

Manager: Paul Jewell.

Assistant Manager: Chris Hutchings.

Physio: Alex Cribley.

Colours: Blue shirts, blue shorts, white stockings.

Change Colours: Black shirts, black shorts, black stockings.

Year Formed: 1932.

Previous Grounds: 1932, Springfield Park; 1999, JJB Stadium.

Club Nickname: 'The Latics'.

First Football League Game: 19 August 1978, Division 4, v Hereford U (a) D 0–0 – Brown; Hinnigan, Gore, Gillibrand, Ward, Davids, Corrigan, Purdie, Houghton, Wilkie, Wright.

Record League Victory: 7–1 v Scarborough, Division 3, 11 March 1997 – Butler L, Butler J, Sharp (Morgan), Greenall, McGibbon (Biggins (1)), Martinez (1), Diaz (2), Jones (Lancashire (1)), Lowe (2), Rogers, Kilford.

Record Cup Victory: 6–0 v Carlisle U (away), FA Cup 1st rd, 24 November 1934 – Caunce; Robinson, Talbot; Paterson, Watson, Tufnell; Armes (2), Robson (1), Roberts (2), Felton, Scott (1).

HONOURS

Football League: Championship – Runners-up 2004–05; Division 2 Champions, 2002–03; Division 3 Champions, 1996–97; Division 4 – Promoted (3rd) 1981–82.

FA Cup: best season: 6th rd, 1987.

Football League Cup: Runners up: 2006.

Freight Rover Trophy: Winners 1985.

Auto Windscreens Shield: Winners 1999.

SKY SPORTS FACT FILE

On 22 October 2005 midfield player Jimmy Bullard set a club record for Wigan Athletic by making his 118th consecutive appearance for the club in the 2–0 win at Aston Villa. He was signed in January 2003 from Peterborough United.

Record Defeat: 1–6 v Bristol R, Division 3, 3 March 1990.

Most League Points (2 for a win): 55, Division 4, 1978–79 and 1979–80.

Most League Points (3 for a win): 100, Division 2, 2002–03.

Most League Goals: 84, Division 3, 1996–97.

Highest League Scorer in Season: Graeme Jones, 31, Division 3, 1996–97.

Most League Goals in Total Aggregate: Andy Liddell, 70, 1998–2004.

Most League Goals in One Match: Not more than three goals by one player.

Most Capped Player: Roy Carroll, 9 (17), Northern Ireland.

Most League Appearances: Kevin Langley, 317, 1981–86, 1990–94.

Youngest League Player: Steve Nugent, 16 years 132 days v Leyton Orient, 16 September 1989.

Record Transfer Fee Received: £3,000,001 from WBA for Nathan Ellington, August 2005.

Record Transfer Fee Paid: £3,100,000 to Wolverhampton W for Henri Camara, August 2005.

Football League Record: 1978 Elected to Division 4; 1982–92 Division 3; 1992–93 Division 2; 1993–97 Division 3; 1997–2003 Division 2; 2003–04 Division 1; 2004–05 FLC; 2005– FA Premier League.

MANAGERS

Charlie Spencer 1932–37
Jimmy Milne 1946–47
Bob Pryde 1949–52
Ted Goodier 1952–54
Walter Crook 1954–55
Ron Suart 1955–56
Billy Cooke 1956
Sam Barkas 1957
Trevor Hitchen 1957–58
Malcolm Barrass 1958–59
Jimmy Shirley 1959
Pat Murphy 1959–60
Allenby Chilton 1960
Johnny Ball 1961–63
Allan Brown 1963–66
Alf Craig 1966–67
Harry Leyland 1967–68
Alan Saunders 1968
Ian McNeill 1968–70
Gordon Milne 1970–72
Les Rigby 1972–74
Brian Tiler 1974–76
Ian McNeill 1976–81
Larry Lloyd 1981–83
Harry McNally 1983–85
Bryan Hamilton 1985–86
Ray Mathias 1986–89
Bryan Hamilton 1989–93
Dave Philpotts 1993
Kenny Swain 1993–94
Graham Barrow 1994–95
John Deehan 1995–98
Ray Mathias 1998–99
John Benson 1999–2000
Bruce Rioch 2000–01
Steve Bruce 2001
Paul Jewell June 2001–

LATEST SEQUENCES

Longest Sequence of League Wins: 11, 2.11.2002 – 18.1.2003.

Longest Sequence of League Defeats: 7, 6.4.1993 – 4.5.1993.

Longest Sequence of League Draws: 6, 11.12.2001 – 5.1.2002.

Longest Sequence of Unbeaten League Matches: 25, 8.5.1999 – 3.1.2000.

Longest Sequence Without a League Win: 14, 9.5.1989 – 17.10.1989.

Successive Scoring Runs: 24 from 27.4.1996.

Successive Non-scoring Runs: 4 from 15.4.1995.

TEN YEAR LEAGUE RECORD

		P	W	D	L	F	A	Pts	Pos
1996-97	Div 3	46	26	9	11	84	51	87	1
1997-98	Div 2	46	17	11	18	64	66	62	11
1998-99	Div 2	46	22	10	14	75	48	76	6
1999-2000	Div 2	46	22	17	7	72	38	83	4
2000-01	Div 2	46	19	18	9	53	42	75	6
2001-02	Div 2	46	16	16	14	66	51	64	10
2002-03	Div 2	46	29	13	4	68	25	100	1
2003-04	Div 1	46	18	17	11	60	45	71	7
2004-05	FL C	46	25	12	9	79	35	87	2
2005-06	PR Lge	38	15	6	17	45	52	51	10

DID YOU KNOW ?

In 1951–52 Wigan Athletic had uncle and nephew in the same team. Sammy Lyon, signed from Prescot Cables, was the uncle of Jackie. Between them they made 54 League appearances for the club in the Lancashire Combination.

WIGAN ATHLETIC 2005–06 LEAGUE RECORD

Match No.	*Date*	*Venue*	*Opponents*	*Result*	*H/T Score*	*Lg. Pos.*	*Goalscorers*	*Attendance*
1	Aug 14	H	Chelsea	L 0-1	0-0	—		23,575
2	20	A	Charlton Ath	L 0-1	0-1	18		23,453
3	27	H	Sunderland	W 1-0	1-0	16	Roberts (pen) [2]	17,223
4	Sept 10	A	WBA	W 2-1	1-1	9	Connolly [40], Bullard [90]	25,617
5	18	H	Middlesbrough	D 1-1	0-1	9	Camara [68]	16,641
6	24	A	Everton	W 1-0	0-0	8	Francis [47]	37,189
7	Oct 2	H	Bolton W	W 2-1	0-0	8	Camara [48], McCulloch [63]	20,553
8	15	H	Newcastle U	W 1-0	1-0	5	Roberts [40]	22,374
9	22	A	Aston Villa	W 2-0	1-0	4	Hughes (og) [32], Mahon [82]	32,294
10	29	H	Fulham	W 1-0	0-0	2	Chimbonda [90]	17,266
11	Nov 5	A	Portsmouth	W 2-0	0-0	2	Chimbonda [48], Roberts [79]	19,102
12	19	H	Arsenal	L 2-3	2-3	2	Camara [28], Bullard [45]	25,004
13	26	H	Tottenham H	L 1-2	0-1	4	McCulloch [88]	22,611
14	Dec 3	A	Liverpool	L 0-3	0-2	7		44,098
15	10	A	Chelsea	L 0-1	0-0	7		42,060
16	14	A	Manchester U	L 0-4	0-2	—		67,793
17	17	H	Charlton Ath	W 3-0	1-0	6	Camara 3 [9, 51, 63]	17,074
18	26	H	Manchester C	W 4-3	3-1	6	Roberts 2 [11, 45], McCulloch [23], Camara [71]	25,017
19	28	A	West Ham U	W 2-0	2-0	5	Roberts [43], Camara [45]	34,131
20	31	H	Blackburn R	L 0-3	0-1	5		20,639
21	Jan 2	A	Birmingham C	L 0-2	0-2	5		29,189
22	15	H	WBA	L 0-1	0-0	6		17,421
23	21	A	Middlesbrough	W 3-2	2-0	6	Roberts [2], Thompson [29], Mellor [90]	27,208
24	31	H	Everton	D 1-1	1-1	—	Scharner [45]	21,731
25	Feb 4	A	Bolton W	D 1-1	0-0	6	Johansson [77]	25,854
26	11	H	Liverpool	L 0-1	0-1	7		25,023
27	19	A	Tottenham H	D 2-2	1-1	—	Johansson 2 [10, 67]	35,676
28	Mar 6	H	Manchester U	L 1-2	0-0	—	Scharner [60]	23,574
29	11	A	Sunderland	W 1-0	1-0	8	Camara [8]	31,194
30	18	A	Manchester C	W 1-0	0-0	8	McCulloch [55]	42,444
31	25	H	West Ham U	L 1-2	1-0	8	McCulloch [45]	18,736
32	Apr 3	A	Blackburn R	D 1-1	0-0	—	Roberts [53]	20,410
33	8	H	Birmingham C	D 1-1	0-0	8	Johansson [49]	18,669
34	15	A	Newcastle U	L 1-3	1-2	10	Bullard [5]	52,302
35	18	H	Aston Villa	W 3-2	1-0	—	Bullard [25], Camara 2 [56, 60]	17,330
36	24	A	Fulham	L 0-1	0-1	—		17,149
37	29	H	Portsmouth	L 1-2	1-0	9	Camara [34]	21,126
38	May 7	A	Arsenal	L 2-4	2-2	10	Scharner [10], Thompson [33]	38,389

Final League Position: 10

GOALSCORERS

League (45): Camara 12, Roberts 8 (1 pen), McCulloch 5, Bullard 4, Johansson 4, Scharner 3, Chimbonda 2, Thompson 2, Connolly 1, Francis 1, Mahon 1, Mellor 1, own goal 1.
Carling Cup (9): Roberts 4, Johansson 2, Connolly 1 (pen), Scharner 1, Taylor 1 (pen).
FA Cup (4): Roberts 2, Connolly 1, Johansson 1.

Pollitt M 23 + 1	Chimbonda P 37	Baines L 35 + 2	Francis D 16 + 4	Henchoz S 26	De Zeeuw A 31	Teale G 20 + 4	Bullard J 35 + 1	Camara H 25 + 4	Roberts J 34	Mahon A 5 + 1	Johansson A 6 + 10	Taylor R 3 + 8	McMillan S — + 2	Kavanagh G 32 + 3	Jackson M 11 + 5	McCulloch L 27 + 3	Skoko J 3 + 2	Connolly D 4 + 13	Filan J 15	Wright D 1 + 1	Scharner P 14 + 2	Thompson D 7 + 3	Mellor N 3	Ziegler R 5 + 5	*Match No.*
1	2	3	4	5	6	7	8	9[1]	10	11	12														1
1	2	3	4	5	6	7[1]	8		9	11[2]	10	12	13												2
1	2	3	4	5[1]	6		8		9	13		11		7[2]	12	10									3
1	2	3	7[2]	5	6		8		9			12		4[1]		11	13	10							4
1	2	3	7	5	6		8	12	9					4		11		10[1]							5
	2	3	7	5	6		8	9[1]	10					4		11		12	1						6
	2[1]	3	7	5	6		8	9[2]	10			12		4		11		13	1						7
	2	3	7	5	6		8[1]	9[2]	10			12		4		11■		13	1						8
	2	3	7	5	6	12	8	9	10[1]	11				4					1						9
	2	3[2]	7	5	6	12	8[1]	9		11[3]	14	10	13	4					1						10
	2	3	7	5	6		8	9[1]	10[2]			12		4	13	11			1						11
	2	3	7[1]	5	6		8	9	10			12		4		11[2]		13	1						12
1	2	3	7[1]	5	6		8	9	10					4		11		12							13
1	2	3	7[2]	5	6[1]		8	9	10					4[3]	13	11	14	12							14
1	2	3		5		12	13	14	10[3]			7[1]		4[2]	6	11	8	9							15
1	2	3		5			8	9	10	11[2]				12	6	13	4[1]	7							16
1	2	3			6	7[2]	8	9[1]	10		12	13		4	5	11									17
1	2	3	12		6	7[2]	8	9[3]	10			13		4[1]	5	11		14							18
1	2	3	12		6	7[1]	8	9[2]	10					4	5	11		13							19
1	2	3[1]	13		6	7[3]	8	9	10					4[2]	5	11		14		12					20
1	2		7	5	6	12	8[2]	9	10					13		11[3]	4[1]	14		3					21
1	2	3[1]		5	6	11	8		10		12			4		9					7				22
1	2	3		5		11	8		10		12			4							6	7[1]	9		23
1	2	3		5	6	7	8		10■												4	11[1]	9	12	24
1	2	3[2]		5	6	7	8				12			4							10	13	9[1]	11	25
1		12		5	6	7	8				9[1]			4	2						10	11		3	26
1	2	3		5[2]	6		8	9[1]			10			4	13	12					7	11			27
	2	3			6	7	8	9	10					4		11[1]			1		5			12	28
	2	3			6	7[3]	8	9[1]	10		12			4[2]		11			1		5	14		13	29
	2	3			6	7	8	9[1]	10		12			4		11			1		5				30
15	2	3			6	7[1]	8	9	10					4[2]		11			1[G]		5	12		13	31
	2	3			6	7	8		10		9			4	12	11			1		5[1]				32
	2	3[2]			6	7	8	12	10		9[1]			4		11			1		5			13	33
	2	12			6[3]		8	13	10		9			4	5[1]	11[2]			1		14	7		3	34
	2	3	4[1]	5		7	8	9	10					12		13			1		6			11[2]	35
1	2	3		5		7[1]	8	9	10					4	6	11		12							36
1	2	3		5		7■		9[2]	10		12			4[1]	6	11		13			14	8[3]			37
1	2	3	13					9[3]	10		12■			4	6	8		14			5	7[1]		11[2]	38

FA Cup

Third Round	Leeds U	(h)	1-1
		(a)	3-3
Fourth Round	Manchester C	(a)	0-1

Carling Cup

Second Round	Bournemouth	(h)	1-0
Third Round	Watford	(h)	3-0
Fourth Round	Newcastle U	(h)	1-0
Quarter-Final	Bolton W	(h)	2-0
Semi-Final	Arsenal	(h)	1-0
		(a)	1-2
Final *(at Millennium Stadium)*	Manchester U		0-4

WOLVERHAMPTON WANDERERS FL Championship

FOUNDATION

Enthusiasts of the game at St Luke's School, Blakenhall formed a club in 1877. In the same neighbourhood a cricket club called Blakenhall Wanderers had a football section. Several St Luke's footballers played cricket for them and shortly before the start of the 1879–80 season the two amalgamated and Wolverhampton Wanderers FC was brought into being.

Molineux, Waterloo Road, Wolverhampton WV1 4QR.

Telephone: 0870 442 0123.

Fax: (01902) 687 006.

Ticket Office: 0870 442 0123.

Website: wolves.co.uk

Email: info@wolves.co.uk

Ground Capacity: 29,277.

Record Attendance: 61,315 v Liverpool, FA Cup 5th rd, 11 February 1939.

Pitch Measurements: 110yd × 75yd.

Chairman: Rick Hayward.

Vice-chairman: Derek Harrington CBE.

Chief Executive: Jez Moxey.

Secretary: Richard Skirrow.

Manager: Mick McCarthy.

Coach: Stuart Gray.

Physio: Barry Holmes.

Colours: Gold and black.

Change Colours: Black with gold trim.

Year Formed: 1877* (*see Foundation*).

Turned Professional: 1888.

Ltd Co.: 1923 (but current club is WWFC (1986) Ltd).

Previous Names: 1879, St Luke's combined with Wanderers Cricket Club to become Wolverhampton Wanderers (1923) Ltd. New limited companies followed in 1982 and 1986 (current).

Club Nickname: 'Wolves'.

Previous Grounds: 1877, Windmill Field; 1879, John Harper's Field; 1881, Dudley Road; 1889, Molineux.

First Football League Game: 8 September 1888, Football League, v Aston Villa (h) D 1–1 – Baynton; Baugh, Mason; Fletcher, Allen, Lowder; Hunter, Cooper, Anderson, White, Cannon, (1 og).

Record League Victory: 10–1 v Leicester C, Division 1, 15 April 1938 – Sidlow; Morris, Dowen; Galley, Cullis, Gardiner; Maguire (1), Horace Wright, Westcott (4), Jones (1), Dorsett (4).

HONOURS

Football League: Division 1 – Champions 1953–54, 1957–58, 1958–59; Runners-up 1937–38, 1938–39, 1949–50, 1954–55, 1959–60; 2002–03 (play-offs). Division 2 – Champions 1931–32, 1976–77; Runners-up 1966–67, 1982–83; Division 3 (N) – Champions 1923–24; Division 3 – Champions 1988–89; Division 4 – Champions 1987–88.

FA Cup: Winners 1893, 1908, 1949, 1960; Runners-up 1889, 1896, 1921, 1939.

Football League Cup: Winners 1974, 1980.

Texaco Cup: Winners 1971.

Sherpa Van Trophy: Winners 1988.

European Competitions: *European Cup:* 1958–59, 1959–60. *European Cup-Winners' Cup:* 1960–61. *UEFA Cup:* 1971–72 (runners-up), 1973–74, 1974–75, 1980–81.

SKY SPORTS FACT FILE

In 1952 Mark Crook, a pre-war Wolverhampton Wanderers half-back, started a nursery team called Wath Wanderers for his former club at Brampton, Wombwell in South Yorkshire, some 100 miles from Molineux. In 1968 the name was changed to the parent club.

Record Cup Victory: 14–0 v Crosswell's Brewery, FA Cup 2nd rd, 13 November 1886 – I. Griffiths; Baugh, Mason; Pearson, Allen (1), Lowder; Hunter (4), Knight (2), Brodie (4), B. Griffiths (2), Wood. Plus one goal 'scrambled through'.

Record Defeat: 1–10 v Newton Heath, Division 1, 15 October 1892.

Most League Points (2 for a win): 64, Division 1, 1957–58.

Most League Points (3 for a win): 92, Division 3, 1988–89.

Most League Goals: 115, Division 2, 1931–32.

Highest League Scorer in Season: Dennis Westcott, 38, Division 1, 1946–47.

Most League Goals in Total Aggregate: Steve Bull, 250, 1986–99.

Most League Goals in One Match: 5, Joe Butcher v Accrington, Division 1, 19 November 1892; 5, Tom Phillipson v Barnsley, Division 2, 26 April 1926; 5, Tom Phillipson v Bradford C, Division 2, 25 December 1926; 5, Billy Hartill v Notts Co, Division 2, 12 October 1929; 5, Billy Hartill v Aston Villa, Division 1, 3 September 1934.

Most Capped Player: Billy Wright, 105, England (70 consecutive).

Most League Appearances: Derek Parkin, 501, 1967–82.

Youngest League Player: Jimmy Mullen, 16 years 43 days v Leeds U, 18 February 1939.

Record Transfer Fee Received: £6,000,000 from Coventry C for Robbie Keane, August 1999.

Record Transfer Fee Paid: £3,500,000 to Bristol C for Ade Akinbiyi, September 1999.

Football League Record: 1888 Founder Member of Football League: 1906–23 Division 2; 1923–24 Division 3 (N); 1924–32 Division 2; 1932–65 Division 1; 1965–67 Division 2; 1967–76 Division 1; 1976–77 Division 2; 1977–82 Division 1; 1982–83 Division 2; 1983–84 Division 1; 1984–85 Division 2; 1985–86 Division 3; 1986–88 Division 4; 1988–89 Division 3; 1989–92 Division 2; 1992–2003 Division 1; 2003–04 FA Premier League; 2004– FLC.

MANAGERS

George Worrall 1877–85
(Secretary-Manager)
John Addenbrooke 1885–1922
George Jobey 1922–24
Albert Hoskins 1924–26
(had been Secretary since 1922)
Fred Scotchbrook 1926–27
Major Frank Buckley 1927–44
Ted Vizard 1944–48
Stan Cullis 1948–64
Andy Beattie 1964–65
Ronnie Allen 1966–68
Bill McGarry 1968–76
Sammy Chung 1976–78
John Barnwell 1978–81
Ian Greaves 1982
Graham Hawkins 1982–84
Tommy Docherty 1984–85
Bill McGarry 1985
Sammy Chapman 1985–86
Brian Little 1986
Graham Turner 1986–94
Graham Taylor 1994–95
Mark McGhee 1995–98
Colin Lee 1998–2000
Dave Jones 2001–04
Glenn Hoddle 2004–2006
Mick McCarthy July 2006–

LATEST SEQUENCES

Longest Sequence of League Wins: 8, 15.10.1988 – 26.11.1988.

Longest Sequence of League Defeats: 8, 5.12.1981 – 13.2.1982.

Longest Sequence of League Draws: 6, 22.4.1995 – 20.8.1995.

Longest Sequence of Unbeaten League Matches: 21, 15.1.2005 – 13.8.2005.

Longest Sequence Without a League Win: 19, 1.12.1984 – 6.4.1985.

Successive Scoring Runs: 41 from 20.12.1958.

Successive Non-scoring Runs: 7 from 2.2.1985.

TEN YEAR LEAGUE RECORD

		P	W	D	L	F	A	Pts	Pos
1996-97	Div 1	46	22	10	14	68	51	76	3
1997-98	Div 1	46	18	11	17	57	53	65	9
1998-99	Div 1	46	19	16	11	64	43	73	7
1999-2000	Div 1	46	21	11	14	64	48	74	7
2000-01	Div 1	46	14	13	19	45	48	55	12
2001-02	Div 1	46	25	11	10	76	43	86	3
2002-03	Div 1	46	20	16	10	81	44	76	5
2003-04	PR Lge	38	7	12	19	38	77	33	20
2004-05	FL C	46	15	21	10	72	59	66	9
2005-06	FL C	46	16	19	11	50	42	67	7

DID YOU KNOW ?

On 28 December 2005 Wolverhampton Wanderers became the first English club to score 7000 League goals when Darren Anderton registered in the 34th minute at Sheffield Wednesday. Wolves had been the first club to score via an own goal in the League!

WOLVERHAMPTON WANDERERS 2005–06 LEAGUE RECORD

Match No.	Date	Venue	Opponents	Result	H/T Score	Lg. Pos.	Goalscorers	Attendance
1	Aug 6	A	Southampton	D 0-0	0-0	—		24,061
2	9	H	Crystal Palace	W 2-1	1-1	—	Seol 4, Cort 84	24,745
3	13	H	Hull C	W 1-0	1-0	3	Delaney (og) 19	24,333
4	20	A	Leeds U	L 0-2	0-1	10		21,229
5	27	A	Cardiff C	D 2-2	0-1	10	Clarke 73, Lescott 90	11,502
6	30	H	QPR	W 3-1	2-1	—	Cort 3 8, 24, 90	22,426
7	Sept 10	A	Luton T	D 1-1	1-0	6	Cort 25	10,248
8	13	H	Millwall	L 1-2	1-1	—	Cort 19	21,897
9	17	H	Leicester C	D 0-0	0-0	8		24,726
10	24	A	Stoke C	W 3-1	1-0	5	Cort 42, Miller 48, Naylor 73	18,183
11	27	A	Crewe Alex	W 4-0	4-0	—	Cort 2 13, 36, Miller 2 27, 34	7471
12	30	H	Burnley	L 0-1	0-1	—		21,747
13	Oct 15	A	Sheffield U	L 0-1	0-1	6		25,533
14	18	H	Derby Co	D 1-1	1-0	—	Miller 6	22,914
15	22	H	Preston NE	D 1-1	0-1	8	Ganea 59	22,802
16	29	A	Watford	L 1-3	0-0	10	Seol 90	14,561
17	Nov 1	A	Brighton & HA	D 1-1	0-1	—	Cameron 82	6642
18	5	H	Norwich C	W 2-0	2-0	7	Seol 2, Ganea 37	23,808
19	18	A	Derby Co	W 3-0	0-0	—	Ndah 67, Huddlestone 80, Ganea 86	22,869
20	22	H	Sheffield U	D 0-0	0-0	—		24,240
21	26	H	Southampton	D 0-0	0-0	9		24,628
22	Dec 3	A	Ipswich T	D 1-1	0-0	9	Cameron 51	23,563
23	10	A	Crystal Palace	D 1-1	1-1	10	Seol 19	19,385
24	17	H	Leeds U	W 1-0	1-0	6	Ganea 38	26,821
25	26	H	Reading	L 0-2	0-1	8		27,980
26	28	A	Sheffield W	W 2-0	1-0	6	Anderton 34, Miller 63	24,295
27	31	H	Plymouth Arg	D 1-1	1-1	6	Cameron 31	22,790
28	Jan 2	A	Coventry C	L 0-2	0-2	7		26,851
29	13	H	Luton T	W 2-1	0-0	—	Davies 57, Ince 88	21,823
30	21	A	Millwall	D 0-0	0-0	8		9905
31	Feb 4	A	Leicester C	L 0-1	0-0	9		21,358
32	11	H	Crewe Alex	D 1-1	1-1	8	Kennedy 45	21,683
33	14	A	Burnley	W 1-0	1-0	—	Ince 15	11,056
34	18	H	Ipswich T	W 1-0	0-0	8	Miller (pen) 74	23,561
35	25	A	Hull C	W 3-2	1-0	7	Aliadiere 28, Miller 59, Cort 89	19,841
36	Mar 4	A	QPR	D 0-0	0-0	8		14,731
37	7	H	Stoke C	D 0-0	0-0	—		22,439
38	11	H	Cardiff C	W 2-0	1-0	6	Rosa 16, Miller (pen) 54	23,996
39	18	A	Reading	D 1-1	0-1	7	Miller 64	23,502
40	25	H	Sheffield W	L 1-3	0-1	7	Cort 50	25,161
41	Apr 1	A	Plymouth Arg	L 0-2	0-1	7		15,871
42	8	H	Coventry C	D 2-2	2-1	7	Ince 2, Cameron 22	23,702
43	14	H	Watford	D 1-1	1-0	—	Aliadiere 17	22,584
44	17	A	Preston NE	L 0-2	0-1	7		16,885
45	22	H	Brighton & HA	W 1-0	1-0	7	Miller (pen) 31	22,555
46	30	A	Norwich C	W 2-1	1-0	7	Rosa 45, Kennedy 71	24,081

Final League Position: 7

GOALSCORERS

League (50): Cort 11, Miller 10 (3 pens), Cameron 4, Ganea 4, Seol 4, Ince 3, Aliadiere 2, Kennedy 2, Rosa 2, Anderton 1, Clarke 1, Davies 1, Huddlestone 1, Lescott 1, Naylor 1, Ndah 1, own goal 1.
Carling Cup (6): Cameron 2, Miller 2, Anderton 1, Ganea 1.
FA Cup (1): Clarke 1.

Oakes M 16 + 1	Edwards R 39 + 3	Naylor L 38 + 2	Ince P 15 + 3	McNamara J 9 + 1	Lescott J 46	Ricketts R 17 + 8	Seol K 22 + 10	Cort C 24 + 7	Miller K 33 + 2	Kennedy M 37 + 3	Olofinjana S 6 + 7	Clarke L 10 + 14	Craddock J 17 + 1	Ndah G 6 + 8	Cameron C 20 + 7	Davies M 12 + 8	Anderton D 20 + 4	Gyepes G 19 + 1	Ganea V 11 + 7	Ross M 13 + 5	Huddlestone T 12 + 1	Postma S 29	Gobern L — + 1	Rosa D 6 + 3	Frankowski T 12 + 4	Aliadiere J 12 + 2	Jones D 1	Lowe K 3	Murray M 1	*Match No.*
1	2	3	4	5	6	7	8^{1}	9	10^{2}	11	12	13																		1
1	12	3		5	6	7	8^{2}	9	10^{3}	11	4	13	2^{1}	14																2
1	2	3	4	5	6	7^{2}	8	9	10^{1}	11		12			13															3
1	2	3		5	6	7^{2}	8^{3}	9	10		4	12		14	11^{1}	13														4
1	2	12		5	6	13		9	10^{3}	3	4	14		8^{1}	7^{2}		11													5
1	2	3		5	6	7		9	10	11	13	8^{2}		12			4^{1}													6
1	2	3			6	7	8^{3}	9	10^{1}	11	13	12			14		4^{2}	5												7
1		3		2	6	7^{1}	8	9		11	13	10^{3}		14	12		4^{2}	5												8
1	2	3		5	6		12	9		11	4	10^{3}		8^{1}	7^{2}	13			14											9
1	2	3			6	7	8	9	10^{1}	11				12	4			5												10
1	2	3			6	7	8	9^{2}	10	11		13			4^{1}	12		5												11
1	2	3			6	7^{2}	8	9	10	11		13			4^{1}	12		5												12
1	2	3			6		8	9	10^{1}	11	4^{2}		5	12	7^{3}	14	13													13
1	2	3			6		8^{2}	9	10	11		12				7	4^{1}	5	13											14
1	2	3			6		8^{3}		10	11	12	14			13	7^{2}	4^{1}	5	9■											15
1	2	3			6		12		10^{2}	11	13	9	5				7^{1}	4^{3}		14	8									16
	2	3			6		12			11	4^{1}	10	5		13		8^{2}		9		7	1								17
	2	3			6		8			11		10^{1}	5		7				9		4	1	12							18
	2	3			6		8			11		10^{1}	5	12	7				9		4	1								19
	2^{3}	3			6		8			11		12	5	10^{1}	7^{2}		13	14	9		4	1								20
	2	3			6		12			11	13	14		10	7^{2}		8^{1}	5	9^{3}		4	1								21
	2	3			6		8			11		12		10^{2}	7		13	5	9		4^{1}	1								22
	2	3			6		8		10	11		12					7	5	9^{1}		4	1								23
	2	3			6	7	8		10						12		11^{1}	5	9		4	1								24
	2	3			6	7^{1}	8		10	11			14	13	12		4^{2}	5^{3}	9			1								25
	2	3^{3}	12		6		8		13	11			5	10^{2}	7		4^{1}		9		14	1								26
			12		6		13		10	11		9^{3}	2		7		8^{1}	5	14	3^{2}	4	1								27
	2				3		12		10	11		9	6^{1}		7^{2}		8^{3}	5	13		4	1		14						28
	2		4		6			9		11		10^{1}	5			7			12	3	8	1								29
	2	12	4		6		13	9	10	11			5			7^{2}	8^{3}			3^{1}		1		14						30
	2	3	4		6	7		9^{2}	10^{1}	11								5	12			1		13	8					31
	2^{3}	3	4		6		8^{1}	9	12	11			5						13	14		1		7	10^{2}					32
		3	4		6			11	10				5			7	12			2		1		8^{1}	9^{2}	13				33
	12	3			6	13		11	10				5^{1}			7	8			2		1		4^{2}	9^{3}	14				34
	2	3	4		6	12		9	10^{3}	13						7	8^{2}			5		1			14	11^{1}				35
	5	3	4		6	12		11	10^{3}	13						7^{1}	8^{2}			2		1			14	9				36
	5	3	12		6	13		8^{3}	10	11							7^{1}			2		1		4^{2}	14	9				37
	2	3	4		6	7			10							12		5				1		8^{1}	11	9				38
	2^{2}	3	4		6	7		12	10^{1}							11		5		13		1			8	9				39
	2^{3}	3^{2}	4		6	7		12	10^{1}	13						11		5		14		1			8	9				40
	12		4		6	13		9	10^{3}	11			5			7				2^{2}		1			14	8	3^{1}			41
		3	4		6	13	8^{3}	12		11			5		7	14				2		1			10^{1}	9^{2}				42
	2	3	4^{1}		6	12	13	14		11					8					7^{2}		1			10^{3}	9		5		43
	5				6	7^{2}	12	13	10^{1}	3					11^{3}	14				2		1			8	9		4		44
15	5			12	6			13	10	3					7	11				2		1^{6}			8^{2}	9		4^{1}		45
	5	3		2	6		12	13	10^{1}	11					7■					14				4	8^{2}	9^{3}			1	46

FA Cup

Third Round	Plymouth Arg	(h)	1-0
Fourth Round	Manchester U	(h)	0-3

Carling Cup

First Round	Chester C	(h)	5-1
Second Round	Watford	(a)	1-2

WREXHAM FL Championship 2

FOUNDATION

The club was formed on 28 September 1872 by members of Wrexham Cricket Club, so they could continue playing a sport during the winter months. This meeting was held at the Turf Hotel, which although rebuilt since, still stands at one corner of the present ground. Their first game was a few weeks later and matches often included 17 players on either side! By 1875 team formations were reduced to 11 men and a year later the club was among the founder members of the Cambrian Football Association, which quickly changed its title to the Football Association of Wales.

Racecourse Ground, Mold Road, Wrexham LL11 2AH.

Telephone: (01978) 262 129.

Fax: (01978) 357 821.

Website: www.wrexhamafc.co.uk

Email: info@wrexhamafc.co.uk

Ground Capacity: 15,500.

Record Attendance: 34,445 v Manchester U, FA Cup 4th rd, 26 January 1957.

Pitch Measurements: 111yd × 75yd.

Secretary: Geraint Parry.

Manager: Denis Smith.

Assistant Manager: Kevin Russell.

Physio: Mel Pejic BSc (Hons).

Colours: Red shirts, white shorts, red stockings.

Change Colours: Black shirts with red trim, black shorts, black stockings.

Year Formed: 1872 (oldest club in Wales).

Turned Professional: 1912.

Ltd Co.: 1912.

Club Nickname: 'Red Dragons'.

Previous Grounds: 1872, Racecourse Ground; 1883, Rhosddu Recreation Ground; 1887, Racecourse Ground.

First Football League Game: 27 August 1921, Division 3 (N), v Hartlepools U (h) L 0–2 – Godding; Ellis, Simpson; Matthias, Foster, Griffiths; Burton, Goode, Cotton, Edwards, Lloyd.

Record League Victory: 10–1 v Hartlepool U, Division 4, 3 March 1962 – Keelan; Peter Jones, McGavan; Tecwyn Jones, Fox, Ken Barnes; Ron Barnes (3), Bennion (1), Davies (3), Ambler (3), Ron Roberts.

HONOURS

Football League: Division 3 – Champions 1977–78; Runners-up 1992–93; Promoted (3rd) 2002–03; Division 3 (N) – Runners-up 1932–33; Division 4 – Runners-up 1969–70.

FA Cup: best season: 6th rd, 1974, 1978, 1997.

Football League Cup: best season: 5th rd, 1961, 1978.

Welsh Cup: Winners 22 times (joint record); Runners-up 22 times (record).

FAW Premier Cup: Winners 1998, 2000, 2001, 2003.

LDV Vans Trophy: Winners 2005

European Competition: *European Cup-Winners' Cup:* 1972–73, 1975–76, 1978–79, 1979–80, 1984–85, 1986–87, 1990–91, 1995–96.

SKY SPORTS FACT FILE

In 1932–33 Wrexham had seven players on their staff by the name of Jones. Four of them – full-back Alf, winger Arthur, centre-forwards Charlie Wilson and Ossie – made League appearances that season. Moreover the chairman was Dr. Edward Jones.

Record Cup Victory: 11–1 v New Brighton, Football League Northern Section Cup 1st rd, 3 January 1934 – Foster; Alfred Jones, Hamilton, Bulling, McMahon, Lawrence, Bryant (3), Findlay (1), Bamford (5), Snow, Waller (1), (o.g. 1).

Record Defeat: 0–9 v Brentford, Division 3, 15 October 1963.

Most League Points (2 for a win): 61, Division 4, 1969–70 and Division 3, 1977–78.

Most League Points (3 for a win): 84, Division 3, 2002–03.

Most League Goals: 106, Division 3 (N), 1932–33.

Highest League Scorer in Season: Tom Bamford, 44, Division 3 (N), 1933–34.

Most League Goals in Total Aggregate: Tom Bamford, 175, 1928–34.

Most League Goals in One Match: 5, Tom Bamford v Carlisle U, Division 3N, 17 March 1934; 5, Lee Jones v Cambridge U, Division 2, 6 April 2002; 5 Juan Ugarte v Hartlepool U, League Championship 1, 5 March 2005.

Most Capped Player: Joey Jones, 29 (72), Wales.

Most League Appearances: Arfon Griffiths, 592, 1959–61, 1962–79.

Youngest League Player: Ken Roberts, 15 years 158 days v Bradford PA, 1 September 1951.

Record Transfer Fee Received: £800,000 from Birmingham C for Bryan Hughes, March 1997.

Record Transfer Fee Paid: £210,000 to Liverpool for Joey Jones, October 1978.

Football League Record: 1921 Original Member of Division 3 (N); 1958–60 Division 3; 1960–62 Division 4; 1962–64 Division 3; 1964–70 Division 4; 1970–78 Division 3; 1978–82 Division 2; 1982–83 Division 3; 1983–92 Division 4; 1992–93 Division 3; 1993–2002 Division 2; 2002–03 Division 3; 2003–04 Division 2; 2004–05 FL1; 2005– FL2.

MANAGERS

Selection Committee 1872–1924
Charlie Hewitt 1924–25
Selection Committee 1925–29
Jack Baynes 1929–31
Ernest Blackburn 1932–37
James Logan 1937–38
Arthur Cowell 1938
Tom Morgan 1938–42
Tom Williams 1942–49
Les McDowell 1949–50
Peter Jackson 1950–55
Cliff Lloyd 1955–57
John Love 1957–59
Cliff Lloyd 1959–60
Billy Morris 1960–61
Ken Barnes 1961–65
Billy Morris 1965
Jack Rowley 1966–67
Alvan Williams 1967–68
John Neal 1968–77
Arfon Griffiths 1977–81
Mel Sutton 1981–82
Bobby Roberts 1982–85
Dixie McNeil 1985–89
Brian Flynn 1989–2001
Denis Smith October 2001–

LATEST SEQUENCES

Longest Sequence of League Wins: 8, 5.4.2003 – 3.5.2003.

Longest Sequence of League Defeats: 9, 2.10.1963 – 30.10.1963.

Longest Sequence of League Draws: 6, 12.11.1999 – 26.12.1999.

Longest Sequence of Unbeaten League Matches: 18, 8.3.2003 – 25.8.2003.

Longest Sequence Without a League Win: 16, 25.9.1999 – 3.1.2000.

Successive Scoring Runs: 25 from 5.5.1928.

Successive Non-scoring Runs: 6 from 12.9.1973.

TEN YEAR LEAGUE RECORD

		P	W	D	L	F	A	Pts	Pos
1996-97	Div 2	46	17	18	11	54	50	69	8
1997-98	Div 2	46	18	16	12	55	51	70	7
1998-99	Div 2	46	13	14	19	43	62	53	17
1999-2000	Div 2	46	17	11	18	52	61	62	11
2000-01	Div 2	46	17	12	17	65	71	63	10
2001-02	Div 2	46	11	10	25	56	89	43	23
2002-03	Div 3	46	23	15	8	84	50	84	3
2003-04	Div 2	46	17	9	20	50	60	60	13
2004-05	FL 1	46	13	14	19	62	80	43*	22
2005-06	FL 2	46	15	14	17	61	54	59	13

**10 points deducted for entering administration.*

DID YOU KNOW?

Seventeen-year-old centre-forward Bernard Evans made a dramatic start to his professional career with Wrexham against Bradford City on 15 September 1954, scoring after 25 seconds. It enabled his team to secure a point from the 2–2 draw.

WREXHAM 2005–06 LEAGUE RECORD

Match No.	Date	Venue	Opponents	Result	H/T Score	Lg. Pos.	Goalscorers	Attendance
1	Aug 6	H	Boston U	W 2-0	1-0	—	MarkJones 23, Roche 83	4503
2	9	A	Notts Co	L 0-1	0-0	—		4382
3	13	A	Northampton T	D 0-0	0-0	12		5075
4	20	H	Carlisle U	L 0-1	0-0	16		4239
5	27	A	Bury	D 2-2	2-1	17	McEvilly 11, Foy 24	2468
6	29	H	Barnet	W 3-1	2-1	11	MarkJones 1, Warhurst 32, Foy 59	3768
7	Sept 10	H	Cheltenham T	W 2-0	1-0	9	Holt 8, Walters 69	3671
8	13	A	Lincoln C	L 0-2	0-0	—		2956
9	17	A	Leyton Orient	D 1-1	0-0	11	Ferguson 53	3733
10	24	H	Macclesfield T	D 1-1	0-0	13	Williams D 65	3830
11	27	A	Wycombe W	L 1-4	0-2	—	Mark Jones 54	4166
12	Oct 1	H	Stockport Co	W 3-0	1-0	12	Walters 21, Mark Jones 2 51, 57	4153
13	15	H	Torquay U	W 4-2	2-0	10	Walters 2 17, 76, Bennett 44, Spender 49	4301
14	22	A	Bristol R	L 1-2	0-0	13	Lawrence 57	5730
15	25	A	Peterborough U	D 1-1	0-1	—	Holt 88	4014
16	29	H	Darlington	W 1-0	0-0	7	McEvilly (pen) 89	4881
17	Nov 12	A	Oxford U	W 3-0	1-0	7	McEvilly 2 39, 58, Mark Jones 75	4491
18	19	H	Peterborough U	D 1-1	0-0	8	Burton (og) 69	4480
19	26	A	Boston U	L 1-2	0-1	9	McEvilly 60	1938
20	Dec 6	H	Mansfield T	W 4-1	0-1	—	Williams D 49, McEvilly 53, Walters 61, Mark Jones 87	3421
21	10	H	Notts Co	D 1-1	0-0	8	Foy 90	4726
22	17	A	Carlisle U	L 1-2	0-0	8	Crowell (pen) 50	6213
23	26	H	Rochdale	W 2-1	1-1	6	Crowell (pen) 41, Ferguson 65	5127
24	31	H	Grimsby T	L 1-2	1-0	7	Mark Jones 42	4527
25	Jan 3	A	Shrewsbury T	L 0-1	0-0	—		6249
26	7	H	Lincoln C	D 1-1	0-0	9	Mark Jones 90	3809
27	14	A	Rushden & D	W 2-0	1-0	8	Mark Jones 2 36, 67	2617
28	21	H	Leyton Orient	L 1-2	0-2	12	Bennett 89	5031
29	Feb 4	H	Wycombe W	W 2-0	2-0	12	Lawrence 12, Williams S 15	4311
30	14	H	Rushden & D	W 2-0	2-0	—	Derbyshire 2 24, 36	3195
31	18	A	Mansfield T	D 2-2	0-0	11	Derbyshire 2 51, 62	3139
32	25	H	Northampton T	L 0-1	0-0	11		5012
33	Mar 4	A	Barnet	D 2-2	1-2	10	Mark Jones 44, Derbyshire 51	2127
34	11	H	Bury	D 0-0	0-0	11		4134
35	14	A	Macclesfield T	L 2-3	2-1	—	Williams S 9, Holt 33	1616
36	18	A	Rochdale	W 1-0	1-0	9	Derbyshire 20	2856
37	21	A	Cheltenham T	D 2-2	1-1	—	Derbyshire 2 1, 64	2737
38	26	H	Chester C	W 2-1	2-0	9	Williams D 11, Mark Jones 36	7240
39	Apr 1	A	Grimsby T	L 0-2	0-1	10		6058
40	9	H	Shrewsbury T	L 1-2	0-2	11	Derbyshire 78	6310
41	12	A	Chester C	L 1-2	0-0	—	McEvilly 69	4801
42	15	A	Stockport Co	L 1-2	1-2	12	Spender 38	4750
43	17	H	Bristol R	W 1-0	1-0	10	Derbyshire 5	3749
44	22	A	Torquay U	L 0-1	0-1	12		2623
45	29	H	Oxford U	D 1-1	1-0	12	Crowell 28	4575
46	May 6	A	Darlington	D 1-1	1-0	13	Williams D 31	4648

Final League Position: 13

GOALSCORERS

League (61): Mark Jones 13, Derbyshire 10, McEvilly 7 (1 pen), Walters 5, Williams D 4, Crowell 3 (2 pens), Foy 3, Holt 3, Bennett 2, Ferguson 2, Lawrence 2, Spender 2, Williams S 2, Roche 1, Warhurst 1, own goal 1.
Carling Cup (0).
FA Cup (1): McEvilly 1.
Football League Trophy (3): Mark Jones 2, Ferguson 1.

Ingham M 40	Roche L 17	Holt A 35 + 1	Bayliss D 21 + 1	Lawrence D 38 + 1	Pejic S 26	Jones Mark 42	Ferguson D 36 + 3	Walters J 33 + 5	McEvilly L 15 + 8	Williams D 45	Bennett D 20 + 13	Mackin L 3 + 14	Spender S 15 + 4	Warhurst P 6 + 5	Linwood P 8 + 1	Foy R 7 + 10	Smith A 15 + 5	Jones Michael 6 + 1	Williams Mike 7 + 5	Reed J — + 3	Ugarte J 2	Crowell M 26 + 3	Williams Marc 2 + 2	Whitley J 10	Williams S 14 + 1	Derbyshire M 16	Done M 1 + 5	*Match No.*
1	2	3	4	5	6	7	8	9	10^{1}	11	12																	1
1	2	3	4	5^{2}	6	7	8	9	10^{1}	11	12	13																2
1	2	3	4	5	6	7	8	9	10^{1}	11	12																	3
1	2^{3}	3	4	5	6	7	8	9	10^{1}	11^{2}	12	13	14■															4
1		3	4■	5		7	8^{1}	9	10^{2}	11		12		6	2	13												5
1		3		5		7^{1}	8	9		11		12		6	2	10	4											6
1		3				7^{2}	8	9	12	11	6	13	14	5	4^{3}	10^{1}	2											7
1		3^{2}		5		7	8	9	12	11	4			6	13	10^{1}	2											8
			4	5		7^{1}	8	9	12	11^{3}	6	13		14	2	10^{2}	3	1										9
1^{6}				5		7	8	9		11	4		12	6	2	10^{1}	3	15										10
			4	5		7	8	9^{2}		11	2				6^{1}	10	3	1	12	13								11
			4	5		7	8^{2}	9^{1}	12	11	10^{3}	13	6		2	14	3	1										12
1		3^{2}	4			7	8	9	12	11	10^{1}	14	6	13^{3}	5		2											13
1		3	4	5		7	8	9^{1}	12	11			6			13	2				10^{2}							14
1		3	4	5		7	8	9	10	11^{2}		13		6		12	2^{1}											15
1	2	3	4	5			8	9	10	11		6^{1}				12	7^{2}					13						16
1	2		4			7	8	9	10	11	6								5			3						17
1	2		4			7	8	9	10	11	3^{1}					12			5			6						18
1	2		4	5		7	8	9	10	11	3^{1}						12			13		6^{2}						19
1	2		4	5		7^{2}	8	9	10^{1}	11	12			13			3					6						20
1	2		4	5^{3}		7	8	9	10	11	12					13	3^{1}		14			6^{2}						21
1	2	12	4	5		7	8	9	10^{2}	11			13			14	3^{1}					6^{3}						22
1	2	3	4	5		7	8	9		11	12					10^{1}						6						23
1	2	3	4	5		7	8	9		11■	10^{1}			12								6						24
1	2	3	4^{2}	5	6	7	8	9			10			13		12						11^{1}						25
1	2	3	12	5^{1}	6	7	8	9		11	10^{2}					13				14		4^{3}						26
1		3			6	7	8	9		11	12		2						5				10^{1}	4				27
1		3			6	7	8	9		11	12		2^{1}				13		5^{2}				10	4				28
1		3		5	6	7^{1}				11		12	2								10^{2}	4	13	8	9			29
1		3		5	6	7				11		12	2									4^{1}		8	9	10		30
1		3		5	6	7				11			2									4		8	9	10		31
1		3		5	6	7				11^{1}		12	2									4^{2}		8	9	10	13	32
1		3		5	6	7	12			11	13		2^{2}									4		8^{1}	9	10		33
1		3		5	6	7				11	4	12										2^{2}		8^{1}	9	10	13	34
1		3		5	6	7		12		11	4	2^{2}										13		8^{1}	9^{3}	10	14	35
1		3		5	6	7				11^{2}	2	12							13			4		8^{1}	9	10		36
1		3		5^{3}	6	7	12	13		11	2	8^{1}							14			4			9^{2}	10		37
1		3		5	6	7	8			11	2											4			9	10		38
1		3		5	6	7	8	10		11			2				12					4			9^{1}			39
1		3		5	6	7	8	12	13	11	2■											4^{2}			9^{1}	10		40
1		3		5	6	7	8	12	10	11			2^{1}									4^{2}			13	9		41
1		3		5	6		8	10	12	11			2				13		4^{2}			14			7^{3}	9^{1}		42
		3^{2}		5	6		8^{3}	12	10^{1}	11	14		2				13	1				4			7	9		43
				5	6	7^{1}	8	10		11	12		2				3^{2}	1	13			4^{3}				9	14	44
	2	3		12	6	7^{2}	8^{3}	10^{1}		11	13							1	5			4				9	14	45
1	2	3			6		12	10^{2}		11	7								5			4	13			9	8^{1}	46

FA Cup
First Round Port Vale (a) 1-2

Carling Cup
First Round Doncaster R (h) 0-1

Football League Trophy
First Round Blackpool (a) 3-4

WYCOMBE WANDERERS FL Championship 2

FOUNDATION

In 1887 a group of young furniture trade workers called a meeting at the Steam Engine public house with the aim of forming a football club and entering junior football. It is thought that they were named after the famous FA Cup winners, The Wanderers who had visited the town in 1877 for a tie with the original High Wycombe club. It is also possible that they played informally before their formation, although there is no proof of this.

Adams Park, Hillbottom Road, Sands, High Wycombe HP12 4HJ.

Telephone: (01494) 472 100.

Fax: (01494) 527 633.

Ticket Office: (01494) 441 118.

Website: www.wwfc.org

Email: wwfc@wycombewanderers.co.uk

Ground Capacity: 10,000.

Record Attendance: 9,650 v Wimbledon, FA Cup 5th rd, 17 February 2001.

Pitch Measurements: 115yd × 75yd.

Chairman: Ivor L. Beeks.

Vice-chairman: Brian Kane.

Managing Director: Steve Hayes.

Secretary: Keith J. Allen.

Manager: Paul Lambert.

Assistant Manager: TBC.

Physio: Shay Connolly.

Colours: Light blue and dark blue quarters.

Change Colours: All white.

Year Formed: 1887.

Turned Professional: 1974.

Club Nicknames: 'Chairboys' (after High Wycombe's tradition of furniture making), 'The Blues'.

Previous Grounds: 1887, The Rye; 1893, Spring Meadow; 1895, Loakes Park; 1899, Daws Hill Park; 1901, Loakes Park; 1990, Adams Park.

First Football League Game: 14 August 1993, Division 3 v Carlisle U (a) D 2–2: Hyde; Cousins, Horton (Langford), Kerr, Crossley, Ryan, Carroll, Stapleton, Thompson, Scott, Guppy (1) (Hutchinson), (1 og).

Record League Victory: 5–0 v Burnley, Division 2, 15 April 1997 – Parkin; Cousins, Bell, Kavanagh, McCarthy, Forsyth, Carroll (2p) (Simpson), Scott (Farrell), Stallard (1), McGavin (1) (Read (1)), Brown.

HONOURS

Football League: Division 2 best season: 6th, 1994–95. Division 3 1993–94 (play-offs).

FA Amateur Cup: Winners 1931.

FA Trophy: Winners 1991, 1993.

GM Vauxhall Conference: Winners 1992–93.

FA Cup: semi-final 2001.

Football League Cup: never beyond 2nd rd.

SKY SPORTS FACT FILE

The first League hat-trick by a Wycombe Wanderers player was achieved in the Southern League on 19 February 1898 at Maidenhead when Bill Buchanan scored three times in the 5–1 win there. He was one of four brothers who played for the club.

Record Cup Victory: 5–0 v Hitchin T (a), FA Cup 2nd rd, 3 December 1994 – Hyde; Cousins, Brown, Crossley, Evans, Ryan (1), Carroll, Bell (1), Thompson, Garner (3) (Hemmings), Stapleton (Langford).

Record Defeat: 0–5 v Walsall, Auto Windscreens Shield 1st rd, 7 November 1995.

Most League Points (3 for a win): 78, Division 2, 1994–95.

Most League Goals: 72, Championship 2, 2005–06.

Highest League Goalscorer in Season: Sean Devine, 23, 1999–2000.

Most League Goals in Total Aggregate: Nathan Tyson, 42, 2004–06.

Most League Goals in One Match: 3, Miquel Desouza v Bradford C, Division 2, 2 September 1995; 3, John Williams v Stockport Co, Division 2, 24 February 1996; 3, Mark Stallard v Walsall, Division 2, 21 October 1997; 3, Sean Devine v Reading, Division 2, 2 October 1999; 3, Sean Divine v Bury, Division 2, 26 February 2000; 3, Nathan Tyson v Lincoln C, FL 2, 5 March 2005; 3 Nathan Tyson v Kidderminster H, FL 2, 2 April 2005; 3 Nathan Tyson v Stockport Co, FL 2, 10 September 2005.

Most Capped Player: Mark Rogers, 7, Canada.

Most League Appearances: Steve Brown, 371, 1994–2004.

Youngest League Player: Ikechi Anya, 16 years 279 days v Scunthorpe U, 8 October 2004.

Record Transfer Fee Received: £600,000 from Nottingham F for Nathan Tyson, January 2006.

Record Transfer Fee Paid: £200,000 to Barnet for Sean Devine, 15 April 1999 and £200,000 to Ipswich T for Darren Currie, December 2004.

Football League Record: Promoted to Division 3 from GM Vauxhall Conference in 1993; 1993–94 Division 3; 1994–2004 Division 2; 2004– FL2.

MANAGERS

First coach appointed 1951.
Prior to Brian Lee's appointment in 1969 the team was selected by a Match Committee which met every Monday evening.
James McCormack 1951–52
Sid Cann 1952–61
Graham Adams 1961–62
Don Welsh 1962–64
Barry Darvill 1964–68
Brian Lee 1969–76
Ted Powell 1976–77
John Reardon 1977–78
Andy Williams 1978–80
Mike Keen 1980–84
Paul Bence 1984–86
Alan Gane 1986–87
Peter Suddaby 1987–88
Jim Kelman 1988–90
Martin O'Neill 1990–95
Alan Smith 1995–96
John Gregory 1996–98
Neil Smillie 1998–99
Lawrie Sanchez 1999–2003
Tony Adams 2003–04
John Gorman 2004–06
Paul Lambert June 2006–

LATEST SEQUENCES

Longest Sequence of League Wins: 4, 26.2.1994 – 19.3.1994.

Longest Sequence of League Defeats: 6, 18.3.2006 – 17.4.2006.

Longest Sequence of League Draws: 5, 24.1.2004 – 21.2.2004

Longest Sequence of Unbeaten League Matches: 21, 6.8.2005 – 10.12.2005.

Longest Sequence Without a League Win: 13, 16.8.2003 – 18.10.2003 and 10.1.2004 – 20.3.2004.

Successive Scoring Runs: 15 from 28.12.2004.

Successive Non-scoring Runs: 5 from 15.10.1996

TEN YEAR LEAGUE RECORD

		P	W	D	L	F	A	Pts	Pos
1996-97	Div 2	46	15	10	21	51	56	55	18
1997-98	Div 2	46	14	18	14	51	53	60	14
1998-99	Div 2	46	13	12	21	52	58	51	19
1999-2000	Div 2	46	16	13	17	56	53	61	12
2000-01	Div 2	46	15	14	17	46	53	59	13
2001-02	Div 2	46	17	13	16	58	64	64	11
2002-03	Div 2	46	13	13	20	59	66	52	18
2003-04	Div 2	46	6	19	21	50	75	37	24
2004-05	FL 2	46	17	14	15	58	52	65	10
2005-06	FL 2	46	18	17	11	72	56	71	6

DID YOU KNOW

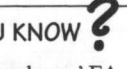

Wycombe Wanderers' FA Amateur Cup success in 1930–31 came from a seven match run in which they scored 23 goals. In the final at Highbury a strike by Alf Britnell defeated Hayes 1–0.

WYCOMBE WANDERERS 2005–06 LEAGUE RECORD

Match No.	*Date*	*Venue*	*Opponents*	*Result*	*H/T Score*	*Lg. Pos.*	*Goalscorers*	*Attendance*
1	Aug 6	H	Carlisle U	D 1-1	1-1	—	Mooney [37]	5270
2	9	A	Rochdale	W 2-1	2-0	—	Williamson [7], Bloomfield [23]	2755
3	13	A	Oxford U	D 2-2	0-1	5	Tyson 2 [70, 85]	6364
4	20	H	Bury	W 4-0	1-0	3	Johnson [37], Mooney [68], Tyson 2 [74, 80]	4421
5	27	A	Shrewsbury T	D 1-1	1-0	5	Tyson [32]	3533
6	29	H	Cheltenham T	D 0-0	0-0	3		5244
7	Sept 2	H	Northampton T	D 1-1	0-1	—	Williamson [58]	5650
8	10	A	Stockport Co	D 3-3	2-2	8	Tyson 3 (1 pen) [13, 21 (p), 53]	3507
9	17	H	Barnet	W 1-0	1-0	6	Tyson [21]	4994
10	24	A	Mansfield T	W 3-2	3-0	2	Betsy 3 [1, 15, 43]	3237
11	27	H	Wrexham	W 4-1	2-0	—	Tyson 2 [16, 81], Betsy [22], Mooney [58]	4166
12	Oct 1	H	Chester C	D 3-3	2-2	3	Mooney 2 [24, 50], Johnson [44]	5145
13	7	A	Grimsby T	W 1-0	1-0	—	Mooney [11]	7206
14	15	H	Rushden & D	D 0-0	0-0	3		5231
15	22	A	Lincoln C	W 2-1	0-0	1	Williamson 2 [69, 90]	4347
16	29	H	Peterborough U	D 2-2	0-2	2	Johnson [74], Easton [80]	5214
17	Nov 12	A	Darlington	D 1-1	0-1	3	Mooney [66]	3928
18	19	H	Grimsby T	W 3-1	2-1	1	Griffin [20], Bloomfield [36], Johnson [78]	6125
19	26	A	Carlisle U	W 1-0	0-0	1	Johnson [88]	7033
20	Dec 6	H	Boston U	D 1-1	0-1	—	Bloomfield [71]	4372
21	10	H	Rochdale	W 3-0	1-0	1	Mooney 2 [9, 53], Griffin [85]	4928
22	17	A	Bury	L 1-2	1-0	1	Betsy [21]	2384
23	26	A	Torquay U	D 2-2	0-2	1	Betsy [71], Lawless (og) [86]	3733
24	29	H	Leyton Orient	W 4-2	2-1	—	Griffin [2], Zakuani (og) [22], Bloomfield [50], Oakes [54]	6240
25	31	A	Bristol R	W 2-1	1-0	1	Mooney 2 (1 pen) [4 (p), 46]	6828
26	Jan 2	H	Macclesfield T	L 4-5	1-3	1	Mooney 2 (1 pen) [31 (p), 61], Martin [71], Morley (og) [76]	5364
27	14	H	Notts Co	W 2-0	0-0	1	Collins [58], Torres [72]	5185
28	21	A	Barnet	D 0-0	0-0	1		3602
29	28	H	Stockport Co	D 1-1	0-1	1	Stonebridge [89]	5512
30	31	A	Northampton T	D 0-0	0-0	—		6438
31	Feb 4	A	Wrexham	L 0-2	0-2	2		4311
32	11	H	Mansfield T	D 2-2	0-2	3	Mooney [53], Oakes [77]	5041
33	14	A	Notts Co	W 2-1	1-0	—	Bowditch [32], Stonebridge [76]	3710
34	18	A	Boston U	D 1-1	0-0	2	Betsy [71]	2283
35	25	H	Oxford U	W 2-1	1-0	2	Betsy [17], Mooney [60]	7016
36	Mar 4	A	Cheltenham T	L 1-2	1-0	2	Johnson [16]	4069
37	11	H	Shrewsbury T	W 2-0	1-0	2	Bloomfield [15], Martin [73]	5035
38	18	H	Torquay U	L 0-1	0-0	3		7134
39	25	A	Leyton Orient	L 0-1	0-1	5		6720
40	Apr 1	H	Bristol R	L 1-3	0-1	5	Easter [81]	6355
41	8	A	Macclesfield T	L 1-2	0-1	5	Martin [86]	1869
42	15	A	Chester C	L 0-1	0-0	5		2797
43	17	H	Lincoln C	L 0-3	0-0	6		5750
44	22	A	Rushden & D	W 3-1	0-1	5	Mooney 2 (1 pen) [62, 88 (p)], Johnson [65]	3396
45	29	H	Darlington	L 0-1	0-0	6		5840
46	May 6	A	Peterborough U	W 2-0	1-0	6	Easter [14], Williamson [85]	5376

Final League Position: 6

GOALSCORERS

League (72): Mooney 17 (3 pens), Tyson 11 (1 pen), Betsy 8, Johnson 7, Bloomfield 5, Williamson 5, Griffin 3, Martin 3, Easter 2, Oakes 2, Stonebridge 2, Bowditch 1, Collins 1, Easton 1, Torres 1, own goals 3.
Carling Cup (6): Tyson 2, Dixon 1, Johnson 1, Mooney 1, Stonebridge 1.
FA Cup (1): Burnell 1.
Football League Trophy (6): Griffin 4 (1 pen), Easton 2.
Play-Offs (1): Mooney 1.

Talia F 35	Senda D 44	Easton C 40 + 4	Oakes S 31 + 6	Johnson R 45	Williamson M 38 + 1	Betsy K 41 + 1	Burnell J 27 + 6	Mooney T 44 + 1	Tyson N 15	Lee R 28 + 3	Bloomfield M 35 + 4	Stonebridge I 8 + 19	Dixon J — + 17	Anya I — + 2	Torres S 13 + 11	Lonergan A 2	Martin R 11 + 12	Griffin C 13 + 9	Turner I 3	Keogh R 2 + 1	Duke M 5	Collins A 3 + 2	Bowditch D 9 + 2	Easter J 8 + 7	Antwi W 5	Williams S 1	Gregory S — + 1	*Match No.*
1	2	3	4¹	5	6	7	8²	9³	10	11	12	13	14															1
1	2	3	4	5	6	7	8¹	9	10²		11	12	13															2
1	2	3	12	5	6	7	8	9	10	4¹	11²	13																3
1	2	3	4	5	6	7	8¹	9³	10	13	11²	12	14															4
1	2	3	4	5	6	7		9¹	10	11		8	12															5
1	2	3	4³	5	6	7	12	9	10	11¹		8²		14	13													6
1	2	3	4	5	6	7	8¹	9	10			11²	12		13													7
1	2	3	4	5	6	7	8	9	10²	11¹	13		12															8
1	2	3	4	5	6	12	8¹	9	10	11³	14	13			7²													9
1	2	3	4	5	6	7		9	10²	11	8¹	12	13															10
1	2	3	4	5	6	7	12	9²	10³		11	14	13		8¹													11
1	2	3	4	5	6	7	12	9	10¹		11³	14	13		8²													12
	2	3	4	5	6	7	8	9			11		12		10¹	1												13
	2	3	4²	5	6	7	8¹	9	10	12	11³		13		14	1												14
1	2	3²	4	5	6		8	9	10	11¹	7³				12		13	14										15
1	2	3	4¹	5	6		8	9	10	11³	7²			13	12			14										16
	2	3	4¹	5		10	8	9			11				7			12	1	6								17
	2	3		5		7	8	9		11²	6		12				13	10¹	1	4								18
	2	3		5	6	7	8	9		11¹	4²				13		12	10	1									19
1	2	3¹		5	6	7	8	9		11³	4		13		14		12	10²										20
1	2	3		5	6	7	8¹	9		11³			13		4²		12	10		14								21
1	2	3		5	6	7		9		11	4		12		8²		13	10¹										22
1	2	3²	13	5	6	7	12	9		11¹	4						8	10										23
1		3	4²	5	6	7	8¹	9		12	11				13		2	10										24
1	2	12	4¹	5	6	7		9		11	8		13				3	10²										25
1	2	12	4	5	6	7		9		11¹	8²				13		3	10										26
	2	3	4		6	7	12	9			11				8			10¹			1	5						27
	2	3	4	5	6²	10	8	9				13	12		7¹						1	11						28
	2¹	3	4²	5		7	8	9			11	13			10³		12				1	6	14					29
	2	3	4¹	5	6	7	8	9			11				12						1		10²	13				30
		3³	4	5	6	7	8	9			11¹	12					2²				1	13	14	10				31
1	2	3	12	5	6	7	8¹	9			4	13			14								11³	10²				32
1	2³	3	4²	5	6	7		9		11		13			8¹		12					14	10					33
1	2			5	6	7		9		11¹		10			8		3						4	12				34
1	2	3		5	6	7		9		11	4¹	12			8								10²	13				35
1	2	3	12	5	6	7■		9		11	4							13					8²	10¹				36
1	2	3	4²	5	6			9		11	7	12					13	14					8¹	10³				37
1	2	3¹	4	5	6			9		11	7	12					13	14					8²	10³				38
1	2	12	4	5	6	7		9		11³	8	10²						13					3¹	14				39
1	2	12	4	5	6	7	8³	9		3¹	11²						13	10						14				40
1	2	3³	4	5		7	8	9			11¹	12					13	10²						14	6			41
1	2		12	5		7	8²	9³		11¹	4	14					3	13						10	6			42
1	2	3	4²	5	6	7	8³	12			13	14					11	9						10¹				43
1	2	3¹	12	5		7	13	9		11²	8	10					4³							14	6			44
1	2	3		5		7		9		11	8	10					4								6			45
	2	3		5	12	7	8				4³	9					11	13						10²	6¹	1	14	46

FA Cup

First Round	Northampton T	(h)	1-3

Carling Cup

First Round	Swindon T	(a)	3-1
Second Round	Aston Villa	(h)	3-8

Football League Trophy

First Round	Dagenham & R	(h)	2-1
Second Round	Gillingham	(a)	2-2
Quarter-Final	Walsall	(a)	2-3

Pla-Offs

Semi-Final	Cheltenham T	(h)	1-2
		(a)	0-0

YEOVIL TOWN — FL Championship 1

FOUNDATION

One of the prime movers of Yeovil football was Ernest J. Sercombe. His association with the club began in 1895 as a playing member of Yeovil Casuals, of which team he became vice-captain and in his last season 1899–1900, he was chosen to play for Somerset against Devon. Upon the reorganisation of the club, he became secretary of the old Yeovil Town FC and with the amalgamation with Petters United in 1914, he continued to serve until his resignation in 1930.

Huish Park, Lufton Way, Yeovil, Somerset BA22 8YF.

Telephone: (01935) 423 662.

Fax: (01935) 473 956.

Ticket Office: (01935) 847 888.

Website: www.ytfc.net

Email: jcotton@ytfc.co.uk

Ground Capacity: 9,665.

Record Attendance: 8,612 v Arsenal, F.A. Cup 3rd rd, 2 January 1993 (16,318 v Sunderland at Huish).

Pitch Measurements: 118yd × 75yd.

Chairman/Chief Executive: John R. Fry.

Secretary: Jean Cotton.

Manager: Russell Slade.

First Team Coach: Steve Thompson.

Physio: Glen Schmidt.

Colours: Green and white hooped shirts, white shorts, white stockings.

Change Colours: Black shirts with amber trim, black shorts with amber trim, black stockings with amber trim.

Year formed: 1895.

Turned Professional: 1921.

Ltd Co.: 1923.

HONOURS

FL Championship 2 winners 2004–05.

Conference: Champions 2002–03.

FA Cup: 5th rd 1949.

League Cup: 1st rd 2004.

Southern League: Champions 1954–55, 1963–64, 1970–71; Runners-up: 1923–24, 1931–32, 1934–35, 1969–70, 1972–73.

Southern League Cup: Winners 1948–49, 1954–55, 1960–61, 1965–66; Runners-up: 1946–47, 1955–56.

Isthmian League: Winners 1987–88; Runners-up: 1985–86, 1986–87, 1996–97.

AC Delco Cup: Winners 1987–88.

Bob Lord Trophy: Winners 1989–90.

FA Trophy: Winners 2002.

London Combination: Runners-up 1930–31, 1932–33.

SKY SPORTS FACT FILE

In 1950–51 Yeovil Town had the services of three outstanding Scots. Left-half George Paterson as player-manager and a former international, centre-half Willie Corbett and outside-right Jimmy Rae who completed a trio formerly with Celtic.

Club Nickname: "Glovers".

Previous names: 1895, Yeovil; 1907, Yeovil Town; 1914, Yeovil & Petters United; 1946, Yeovil Town.

Previous grounds: 1895–1921, Pen Mill Ground; 1921–1990, Huish; 1990, Huish Park.

First Football League Game: 9 August 2003, Division 3 v Rochdale (h) W 3-1: Weale; Williams (Lindegaard), Crittenden, Lockwood, O'Brien, Pluck (Rodrigues), Gosling (El Kholti), Way, Jackson, Gall (2), Johnson (1).

Record League Victory: 10–0 v Kidderminster H, Southern League, 27 December 1955. 10–0 v Bedford T, Southern League, 4 March 1961.

MANAGERS

(since 1990)
Clive Whitehead
Steve Rutter
Brian Hall
Graham Roberts
Colin Lippiatt
Steve Thompson
Dave Webb
Gary Johnson 2001–05
Steve Thompson 2005–06
Russell Slade June 2006–

Record Cup Victory: 12–1 v Westbury United, FA Cup 1st qual rd, 1923–24.

Record Defeat: 0–8 v Manchester United, FA Cup 5th rd, 12 February 1949.

Most League Goals: 90, FL Championship 2, 2004–05.

Highest League Goalscorer in Season: Phil Jevons, 27, 2004–05

Most League Goals in Total Aggregate: Phil Jevons, 42, 2004–06

Most Capped Player: Andrejs Stolcers, 1 (81) Latvia and Arron Davies, 1, Wales.

Most League Appearances: Lee Johnson, 115, 2003–06.

Record Transfer Fee Received: Undisclosed from West Ham U for Gavin Williams, December 2004.

Record Transfer Fee Paid: Undisclosed to Atletico Penarol de Rafaela (Argentina) for Pablo Bastianini, August 2005.

Football League Record: 2003 Promoted to Division 3 from Conference; 2003–04 Division 3; 2004–05 FL2; 2005– FL1.

LATEST SEQUENCES

Longest Sequence of League Wins: 7, 7.12.2004 – 15.1.2005.

Longest Sequence of League Defeats: 5, 29.10.05 – 6.12.05.

Longest Sequence of Unbeaten League Matches: 7, 7.12.2004 – 15.1.2005.

Longest Sequence Without a League Win: 6, 6.8.05 – 29.8.05.

Successive Scoring Runs: 22 from 30.10.2004.

Successive Non-scoring Runs: 3 from 21.1.2006.

TEN YEAR LEAGUE RECORD

		P	*W*	*D*	*L*	*F*	*A*	*Pts*	*Pos*
1996–97	Isth.	42	31	8	3	83	34	101	1
1997–98	Conf.	42	17	8	17	73	63	59	11
1998–99	Conf.	42	20	11	11	68	54	71	5
1999–2000	Conf.	42	18	10	14	60	63	64	7
2000–01	Conf.	42	24	8	10	73	50	80	2
2001–02	Conf.	42	19	13	10	66	53	70	3
2002–03	Conf.	42	28	11	3	100	37	95	1
2003-04	Div 3	46	23	5	18	70	57	74	8
2004-05	FL 2	46	25	8	13	90	65	83	1
2005-06	FL 1	46	15	11	20	54	62	56	15

DID YOU KNOW ?

On 13 April 1960 Yeovil Town appointed Basil Hayward as player-manager, but only to take charge after the end of the season, using the remainder of it to acclimatise himself with club and players, an unusual situation at the time.

YEOVIL TOWN 2005–06 LEAGUE RECORD

Match No.	*Date*	*Venue*	*Opponents*	*Result*		*H/T Score*	*Lg. Pos.*	*Goalscorers*	*Attendance*
1	Aug 6	A	Oldham Ath	L	0-2	0-2	—		6979
2	9	H	Rotherham U	D	0-0	0-0	—		5856
3	13	H	Blackpool	D	1-1	1-1	23	Amankwaah [45]	5698
4	20	A	Barnsley	L	0-1	0-0	24		8153
5	27	A	Swindon T	L	2-4	1-1	24	Bastianini [1], Skiverton [87]	6973
6	29	H	Chesterfield	L	1-3	1-1	24	Alvarez [36]	6079
7	Sept 3	A	Hartlepool U	W	1-0	0-0	24	Bastianini [68]	4572
8	10	H	Walsall	W	2-1	0-1	19	Jevons [65], Gall [70]	9579
9	17	A	Bradford C	D	1-1	1-0	19	Skiverton [6]	7826
10	24	H	Port Vale	W	1-0	0-0	18	Harrold [85]	5901
11	27	A	Southend U	L	1-4	1-0	—	Jevons [45]	6654
12	Oct 1	A	Scunthorpe U	W	4-3	2-2	15	Way [26], Jevons [37], Harrold 2 [59, 66]	4311
13	8	H	Swansea C	W	1-0	1-0	—	Skiverton [39]	7578
14	15	A	Gillingham	D	0-0	0-0	11		6848
15	22	H	Nottingham F	W	3-0	2-0	9	Jevons 2 [6, 26], Davies [82]	9072
16	29	A	Colchester U	L	2-3	1-1	12	Bastianini [32], Harrold [51]	3409
17	Nov 12	H	Huddersfield T	L	1-2	0-2	15	Johnson [47]	6742
18	18	A	Swansea C	L	0-2	0-1	—		19,288
19	26	H	Oldham Ath	L	0-2	0-1	17		5852
20	Dec 6	A	Brentford	L	2-3	1-2	—	Harrold [38], Johnson [68]	5131
21	10	A	Rotherham U	W	2-1	2-1	18	Murdock (og) [32], Harrold [36]	3929
22	17	H	Barnsley	W	2-1	0-1	17	Poole [46], Sodje [73]	5620
23	23	H	Bournemouth	D	1-1	0-1	—	Jevons (pen) [80]	8178
24	28	A	Tranmere R	L	1-4	1-0	17	Jevons (pen) [32]	6327
25	31	H	Bristol C	D	1-1	1-0	18	Poole [3]	9178
26	Jan 2	A	Doncaster R	W	1-0	1-0	14	Jevons [12]	5680
27	7	H	Hartlepool U	W	2-0	1-0	10	Jevons 2 [26, 60]	5480
28	14	A	Milton Keynes D	D	1-1	1-0	11	Skiverton [13]	5548
29	21	H	Bradford C	L	0-1	0-0	13		6168
30	Feb 4	H	Southend U	L	0-2	0-1	16		6289
31	11	A	Port Vale	L	0-1	0-0	18		4732
32	14	H	Milton Keynes D	D	1-1	0-0	—	Gall [71]	5048
33	25	A	Blackpool	L	0-2	0-0	21		5747
34	Mar 4	A	Chesterfield	W	3-0	1-0	17	Davies 3 [37, 89, 90]	4843
35	7	H	Brentford	L	1-2	1-1	—	Skiverton [26]	5137
36	11	H	Swindon T	D	0-0	0-0	18		7451
37	18	A	Bournemouth	L	0-1	0-1	20		7959
38	21	A	Walsall	W	2-0	2-0	—	Harrold [24], Davies [33]	4464
39	25	H	Tranmere R	D	2-2	1-1	18	Harrold 2 [5, 69]	5409
40	Apr 1	A	Bristol C	L	1-2	0-2	19	Davies [64]	15,889
41	8	H	Doncaster R	W	3-0	1-0	17	Skiverton [8], Jevons [57], Davies [86]	5456
42	14	H	Scunthorpe U	L	0-1	0-0	—		6759
43	17	A	Nottingham F	L	1-2	1-1	20	Jevons [9]	28,193
44	22	H	Gillingham	W	4-3	2-1	18	Jevons (pen) [18], Cohen [36], Terry [52], Davies [56]	6040
45	29	A	Huddersfield T	W	2-1	0-1	16	Jevons 2 (1 pen) [66 (p), 72]	14,473
46	May 6	H	Colchester U	D	0-0	0-0	15		8785

Final League Position: 15

GOALSCORERS

League (54): Jevons 15 (4 pens), Harrold 9, Davies 8, Skiverton 6, Bastianini 3, Gall 2, Johnson 2, Poole 2, Alvarez 1, Amankwaah 1, Cohen 1, Sodje 1, Terry 1, Way 1, own goal 1.
Carling Cup (3): Davies 1, Gall 1, Way 1.
FA Cup (5): Davies 1, Jevons 1, Johnson 1, Terry 1, Way 1.
Football League Trophy (0).

Collis S 21 + 2	Amankwaah K 38	Jones N 37 + 6	Way D 15	Skiverton T 36	Sodje E 17 + 2	Terry P 34 + 8	Johnson L 26	Jevons P 35 + 3	Davies A 27 + 12	Poole D 20 + 5	Miles C 18 + 12	Oliver L — + 3	Gall K 11 + 26	Weale C 25	Harrold M 28 + 14	Bastianini P 15 + 5	Alvarez L 4	Lockwood A 18 + 2	Lindegaard A 14 + 9	Fontaine L 10	Melono A 1	Guyett S 16 + 5	Rose M — + 1	Cohen C 29 + 1	Barry A 4	Webb D — + 4	Doherty T 1	Wilson M 1 + 1	Rocastle C 5 + 3	Williams D — + 1	*Match No.*
1	2	3	4	5	6	7^{1}	8	9	10^{2}	11^{3}	12	13	14																		1
	2	3	4	5^{1}	6	7^{2}	8	9	13		12	14	11	1	10^{3}																2
	2	3	4	5	6	7^{1}	8	9	12	13		14	11^{2}	1	10^{3}																3
	2	3	4	5	6	7^{2}	8	9^{1}	10				12	1	13	11															4
	2	3	4	5	6■	12	8^{2}		11^{1}		7		13	1	14	9	10^{3}														5
	2	11	4	5			8			12	6^{3}		13	1	14	9	10^{2}	3	7^{1}												6
	2	11	4	5		12	8				3		7	1	13	9^{2}	10^{1}			6											7
	2	11^{1}	4	5			8	12	13		3		7	1		9	10^{2}			6											8
	2	12	4	5	13		8	10	11		3^{1}		7	1	14	9^{3}				6^{2}											9
	2	11	4	5	6	12	8	10^{1}	7					1	13	9^{2}					3■										10
	2	11	4	5	6^{1}	13	8	10	7		12^{2}			1	14	9^{3}				3											11
	2	11^{2}	4	5	6	12	8	10	7					1	13	9^{1}				3											12
	2	12	4	5	6	7^{1}	8	10			13		14	1	11^{3}	9				3^{2}											13
	2		4	5	6	7	8	10	12		3		13	1	11^{1}	9^{2}															14
	2	3		5^{3}		7^{2}	8	10	4		6		12	1	11	9^{1}						14	13								15
	2	3		5		7	8	10	4^{2}		6^{3}		12	1	11	9^{1}		13				14									16
	2	3		5		7	8	10	12		13		14	1	11^{3}	9^{1}				6^{2}				4							17
	2	11^{3}	4	5	6	7	8■	10^{2}	9^{1}		3		12	1	13									14							18
	2	12		5	6	11		10	8		3^{1}		7^{2}	1	13	9								4							19
15	2	3		5	6	7	8	10^{6}					11	1■	9^{1}	12			13					4^{2}							20
1	2	11^{2}			6		8	10^{1}		13	12		7^{3}		9				14	3		5		4							21
1	2	11			6	12	8	9^{3}	13	7^{1}			14		10					3^{2}		5		4							22
1	2	11			6	12	8	9^{2}	14	7^{3}			13		10					3^{1}		5		4							23
1	2^{2}	12			6	7	8	9	14	11^{3}	3^{1}		13		10							5		4							24
1	2	3		5		7	8	9^{3}		11^{1}	6^{2}		12		10	14						13		4							25
1	2^{3}	3		5	12	7^{1}	8	9^{2}		11			13		10				14			6		4							26
1	2^{3}	3		5		7	8	9^{1}	13	11^{2}			12		10				14			6		4							27
1	2	3		5		7		9^{1}	8^{2}	11			12		10				13			6		4							28
1	2	3				7		9	8^{3}	11	6^{1}		13		10^{2}	14		12				5		4							29
1	2	3^{2}				7		9	8^{3}	11	6		12		10^{1}	14		5	13					4							30
	2	3				7^{2}		9	12	11^{3}			10^{1}	1	13			5	6					4	8	14					31
	2	3				7^{2}		9^{1}	13	11	12		10^{3}	1	14			5	6					4	8						32
	2	3				7^{2}		9	13	11^{1}	12		10^{3}	1		14		5	6					4	8						33
	2	3		5		12			9	11				1	10			6	13					4	8^{2}		7^{1}				34
1	2^{2}	3		5^{3}		7			9	11^{1}			12		10			6	4			13		8		14					35
1		3		5^{1}		7			9	11^{2}	13		12		10^{3}			2	4			6		8		14					36
1	2	3^{1}		5		7			9	11^{2}			12		10			4	13			6^{3}		8		14					37
1	2^{1}	12		5		7			9^{2}				13		10			4	3			6		8				11			38
1		3		5^{2}		7		12	9^{1}		13				10			4	2			6		8				14	11^{3}		39
1	2^{3}	3				7		12	9	13	6^{2}				10^{1}			4	14			5		8					11		40
		3		5		7^{3}		9	11		12		13	1	10^{2}			2	4^{1}			6		8					14		41
15		11^{2}		5		7		9	8	12				1^{6}	10			2	3			6^{1}		4					13		42
1		3^{1}		5		7		9	11		12		13		10^{3}			2	4			6^{2}		8					14		43
1		12		5		7		9	10	11^{2}	3^{1}		13					2	6			14		4					8^{3}		44
1				5		7		9	10^{1}	11	6				12			2	3					4					8		45
1				5		7		9	10^{2}	11^{1}	6				12			2	3					4					8	13	46

FA Cup

First Round	Macclesfield T	(a)	1-1
		(h)	4-0
Second Round	Walsall	(a)	0-2

Carling Cup

First Round	Ipswich T	(a)	2-0
Second Round	Millwall	(h)	1-2

Football League Trophy

First Round	Leyton Orient	(a)	0-2

ENGLISH LEAGUE PLAYERS DIRECTORY

Players listed represent those with their clubs during the 2005–06 season.

Players are listed alphabetically on pages 563–569.
The number alongside each player corresponds to the team number heading. (Abbey, George 62 = team 62 (Port Vale))

ARSENAL (1)

ADEBAYOR, Emmanuel (F) **135 37**
H: 6 4 W: 11 08 b.Lome 26-2-84
Source: Lome. *Honours:* Togo 32 full caps, 12 goals.
2001–02 Metz 10 2
2002–03 Metz 34 13 **44 15**
2003–04 Monaco 31 8
2004–05 Monaco 34 9
2005–06 Monaco 13 1 **78 18**
2005–06 Arsenal 13 4 **13 4**

ALIADIERE, Jeremie (F) **39 3**
H: 6 0 W: 11 00 b.Rambouillet 30-3-83
Source: Scholarship. *Honours:* France Under-21.
1999–2000 Arsenal 0 0
2000–01 Arsenal 0 0
2001–02 Arsenal 1 0
2002–03 Arsenal 3 1
2003–04 Arsenal 10 0
2004–05 Arsenal 4 0
2005–06 Arsenal 0 0 **18 1**
2005–06 *West Ham U* 7 0 **7 0**
2005–06 *Wolverhampton W* 14 2 **14 2**

ALMUNIA, Manuel (G) **143 0**
H: 6 3 W: 13 00 b.Pamplona 19-5-77
1997–98 Osasuna B 31 0
1998–99 Osasuna B 13 0 **44 0**
1999–2000 Cartagonova 3 0 **3 0**
2000–01 Sabadell 25 0 **25 0**
2001–02 Celta Vigo 0 0
2001–02 *Eibar* 35 0 **35 0**
2002–03 *Recreativo* 2 0 **2 0**
2003–04 Albacete 24 0 **24 0**
2004–05 Arsenal 10 0
2005–06 Arsenal 0 0 **10 0**

BENDTNER, Nicklas (F) **0 0**
H: 6 2 W: 13 00 b.Copenhagen 16-1-88
Source: Scholar. *Honours:* Denmark Youth, Under-21.
2005–06 Arsenal 0 0

BERGKAMP, Dennis (F) **552 201**
H: 6 0 W: 12 10 b.Amsterdam 18-5-69
Honours: Holland 79 full caps, 36 goals.
1986–87 Ajax 14 2
1987–88 Ajax 25 5
1988–89 Ajax 30 13
1989–90 Ajax 25 8
1990–91 Ajax 33 25
1991–92 Ajax 30 24
1992–93 Ajax 28 26 **185 103**
1993–94 Internazionale 31 8
1994–95 Internazionale 21 3 **52 11**
1995–96 Arsenal 33 11
1996–97 Arsenal 29 12
1997–98 Arsenal 28 16
1998–99 Arsenal 29 12
1999–2000 Arsenal 28 6
2000–01 Arsenal 25 3
2001–02 Arsenal 33 9
2002–03 Arsenal 29 4
2003–04 Arsenal 28 4
2004–05 Arsenal 29 8
2005–06 Arsenal 24 2 **315 87**

CAMPBELL, Sol (D) **390 18**
H: 6 2 W: 15 07 b.Newham 18-9-74
Source: Trainee. *Honours:* England Youth, Under-21, B, 69 full caps, 1 goal.
1992–93 Tottenham H 1 1
1993–94 Tottenham H 34 0
1994–95 Tottenham H 30 0
1995–96 Tottenham H 31 1
1996–97 Tottenham H 38 0
1997–98 Tottenham H 34 0
1998–99 Tottenham H 37 6
1999–2000 Tottenham H 29 0
2000–01 Tottenham H 21 2 **255 10**
2001–02 Arsenal 31 2
2002–03 Arsenal 33 2
2003–04 Arsenal 35 1
2004–05 Arsenal 16 1
2005–06 Arsenal 20 2 **135 8**

CLICHY, Gael (D) **34 0**
H: 5 9 W: 10 04 b.Toulouse 26-7-85
Source: Cannes. *Honours:* France Under-21.
2003–04 Arsenal 12 0
2004–05 Arsenal 15 0
2005–06 Arsenal 7 0 **34 0**

COLE, Ashley (D) **170 9**
H: 5 8 W: 10 05 b.Stepney 20-12-80
Source: Trainee. *Honours:* England Youth, Under-21, B, 51 full caps.
1998–99 Arsenal 0 0
1999–2000 Arsenal 1 0
1999–2000 *Crystal Palace* 14 1 **14 1**
2000–01 Arsenal 17 3
2001–02 Arsenal 29 2
2002–03 Arsenal 31 1
2003–04 Arsenal 32 0
2004–05 Arsenal 35 2
2005–06 Arsenal 11 0 **156 8**

CONNOLLY, Matthew (D) **0 0**
H: 6 1 W: 11 03 b.Barnet 24-9-87
Source: Scholar. *Honours:* England Youth.
2005–06 Arsenal 0 0

CREGG, Patrick (M) **0 0**
H: 5 9 W: 10 04 b.Dublin 21-2-86
Source: Trainee. *Honours:* Eire Youth, Under-21.
2002–03 Arsenal 0 0
2003–04 Arsenal 0 0
2004–05 Arsenal 0 0
2005–06 Arsenal 0 0
To Falkirk January 2006

CYGAN, Pascal (D) **242 12**
H: 6 4 W: 13 12 b.Lens 19-4-74
Source: Wasquehal.
1995–96 Lille 27 0
1996–97 Lille 14 0
1997–98 Lille 26 3
1998–99 Lille 21 1
1999–2000 Lille 33 2
2000–01 Lille 29 2
2001–02 Lille 29 1 **179 9**
2002–03 Arsenal 18 1
2003–04 Arsenal 18 0
2004–05 Arsenal 15 0
2005–06 Arsenal 12 2 **63 3**

DIABY, Vassiriki (M) **22 2**
H: 6 2 W: 12 04 b.Paris 11-5-86
Honours: France Youth.
2004–05 Auxerre 5 0
2005–06 Auxerre 5 1 **10 1**
2005–06 Arsenal 12 1 **12 1**

DJOUROU, Johan (D) **7 0**
H: 6 2 W: 12 05 b.Ivory Coast 18-1-87
Source: Scholar. *Honours:* Switzerland Youth, 5 full caps.
2004–05 Arsenal 0 0
2005–06 Arsenal 7 0 **7 0**

EBOUE, Emmanuel (D) **89 4**
H: 5 10 W: 11 08 b.Abidjan 4-6-83
Honours: Ivory Coast 14 full caps.
2002–03 Beveren 23 0
2003–04 Beveren 30 2
2004–05 Beveren 17 2 **70 4**
2004–05 Arsenal 1 0
2005–06 Arsenal 18 0 **19 0**

FABREGAS, Francesc (M) **68 5**
H: 5 11 W: 11 01 b.Vilessoc de Mar 4-5-87
Source: Barcelona. *Honours:* Spain Youth, Under-21, 8 full caps.
2003–04 Arsenal 0 0
2004–05 Arsenal 33 2
2005–06 Arsenal 35 3 **68 5**

FLAMINI, Mathieu (M) **66 1**
H: 5 11 W: 11 10 b.Marseille 7-3-84
Source: Marseille. *Honours:* France Under-21.
2003–04 Marseille 14 0 **14 0**
2004–05 Arsenal 21 1
2005–06 Arsenal 31 0 **52 1**

GARRY, Ryan (D) **1 0**
H: 6 0 W: 11 05 b.Hornchurch 29-9-83
Source: Scholar. *Honours:* England Youth, Under-20.
2001–02 Arsenal 0 0
2002–03 Arsenal 1 0
2003–04 Arsenal 0 0
2004–05 Arsenal 0 0
2005–06 Arsenal 0 0 **1 0**

GILBERT, Kerrea (D) **2 0**
H: 5 6 W: 11 03 b.Hammersmith 28-2-87
Source: Scholar. *Honours:* England Youth.
2005–06 Arsenal 2 0 **2 0**

HENRY, Thierry (F) **358 187**
H: 6 2 W: 13 05 b.Paris 17-8-77
Honours: France 85 full caps, 36 goals.
1994–95 Monaco 8 3
1995–96 Monaco 18 3
1996–97 Monaco 36 9
1997–98 Monaco 30 4
1998–99 Monaco 13 1 **105 20**
1998–99 Juventus 16 3 **16 3**
1999–2000 Arsenal 31 17
2000–01 Arsenal 35 17
2001–02 Arsenal 33 24
2002–03 Arsenal 37 24
2003–04 Arsenal 37 30
2004–05 Arsenal 32 25
2005–06 Arsenal 32 27 **237 164**

HLEB, Aleksandr (M) **204 24**
H: 5 10 W: 11 07 b.Minsk 1-5-81
Honours: Belarus 22 full caps, 3 goals.
1999 BATE 13 1
2000 BATE 12 3 **25 4**
2000–01 Stuttgart B 17 4 **17 4**
2000–01 Stuttgart 6 0
2001–02 Stuttgart 32 2
2002–03 Stuttgart 34 4
2003–04 Stuttgart 31 5
2004–05 Stuttgart 34 2 **137 13**
2005–06 Arsenal 25 3 **25 3**

HOWARD, Mark (G) **0 0**
H: 6 2 W: 12 00 b.Southwark 21 9 86
Source: Scholar. *Honours:* England Under-20.
2004–05 Arsenal 0 0
2005–06 Arsenal 0 0

HOYTE, Justin (D) **34 1**
H: 5 11 W: 11 00 b.Waltham Forest 20-11-84
Source: Scholar. *Honours:* England Youth, Under-20, Under-21.
2002–03 Arsenal 1 0
2003–04 Arsenal 1 0
2004–05 Arsenal 5 0
2005–06 Arsenal 0 0 **7 0**
2005–06 *Sunderland* 27 1 **27 1**

JORDAN, Michael (G) **0 0**
H: 6 2 W: 13 02 b.Enfield 7-4-86
Source: Scholar.

2003–04	Arsenal	0	0		
2004–05	Arsenal	0	0		
2005–06	Arsenal	0	0		
2005–06	*Yeovil T*	0	0		

LARSSON, Sebastian (M) **3 0**
H: 5 11 W: 11 02 b.Eskilstuna 6-6-85
Source: Trainee. *Honours:* Sweden Under-21.

2002–03	Arsenal	0	0		
2003–04	Arsenal	0	0		
2004–05	Arsenal	0	0		
2005–06	Arsenal	3	0	**3**	**0**

LAUREN, Etame-Mayer (D) **302 24**
H: 5 11 W: 11 07 b.Londi Kribi 19-1-77
Honours: Cameroon 25 full caps, 1 goal.

1995–96	Utrera	30	5	**30**	**5**
1996–97	Sevilla B	17	3	**17**	**3**
1997–98	Levante	34	6	**34**	**6**
1998–99	Mallorca	32	1		
1999–2000	Mallorca	30	3	**62**	**4**
2000–01	Arsenal	18	2		
2001–02	Arsenal	27	2		
2002–03	Arsenal	27	1		
2003–04	Arsenal	32	0		
2004–05	Arsenal	33	1		
2005–06	Arsenal	22	0	**159**	**6**

LEHMANN, Jens (G) **438 2**
H: 6 4 W: 13 05 b.Essen 10-11-69
Honours: Germany 38 full caps.

1991–92	Schalke	37	0		
1992–93	Schalke	8	0		
1993–94	Schalke	21	0		
1994–95	Schalke	34	1		
1995–96	Schalke	32	0		
1996–97	Schalke	34	0		
1997–98	Schalke	34	1	**200**	**2**
1998–99	AC Milan	5	0	**5**	**0**
1998–99	Borussia Dortmd	13	0		
1999–2000	Borussia Dortmd	31	0		
2000–01	Borussia Dortmd	31	0		
2001–02	Borussia Dortmd	30	0		
2002–03	Borussia Dortmd	24	0	**129**	**0**
2003–04	Arsenal	38	0		
2004–05	Arsenal	28	0		
2005–06	Arsenal	38	0	**104**	**0**

LJUNGBERG, Frederik (M) **277 56**
H: 5 9 W: 11 00 b.Vittsjo 16-4-77
Honours: Sweden 61 full caps, 13 goals.

1994	Halmstad	1	0		
1995	Halmstad	16	1		
1996	Halmstad	20	2		
1997	Halmstad	24	5		
1998	Halmstad	18	2	**79**	**10**
1998–99	Arsenal	16	1		
1999–2000	Arsenal	26	6		
2000–01	Arsenal	30	6		
2001–02	Arsenal	25	12		
2002–03	Arsenal	20	6		
2003–04	Arsenal	30	4		
2004–05	Arsenal	26	10		
2005–06	Arsenal	25	1	**198**	**46**

LUPOLI, Arturo (F) **1 0**
H: 5 7 W: 11 04 b.Brescia 24-6-87
Source: Parma. *Honours:* Italy Youth.

2004–05	Arsenal	0	0		
2005–06	Arsenal	1	0	**1**	**0**

MANNONE, Vito (G) **0 0**
H: 6 0 W: 11 08 b.Desio 2-3-88
Source: Atalanta.

2005–06	Arsenal	0	0		

MUAMBA, Fabrice (M) **0 0**
H: 6 1 W: 11 10 b.DR Congo 6-4-88
Source: Scholar. *Honours:* England Youth.

2005–06	Arsenal	0	0		

OWUSU-ABEYIE, Quincy (F) **5 0**
H: 5 11 W: 11 10 b.Amsterdam 15-4-86
Source: Scholar. *Honours:* Holland Youth.

2003–04	Arsenal	0	0		
2004–05	Arsenal	1	0		
2005–06	Arsenal	4	0	**5**	**0**

To Spartak Moscow January 2006

PIRES, Robert (M) **417 113**
H: 6 1 W: 12 09 b.Reims 29-10-73
Honours: France 79 full caps, 14 goals.

1992–93	Metz	2	0		
1993–94	Metz	24	1		
1994–95	Metz	35	9		
1995–96	Metz	38	11		
1996–97	Metz	32	11		
1997–98	Metz	31	11	**162**	**43**
1998–99	Marseille	34	6		
1999–2008	Marseille	32	2	**66**	**8**
2000–01	Arsenal	33	4		
2001–02	Arsenal	28	9		
2002–03	Arsenal	26	14		
2003–04	Arsenal	36	14		
2004–05	Arsenal	33	14		
2005–06	Arsenal	33	7	**189**	**62**

POOM, Mart (G) **249 1**
H: 6 4 W: 14 02 b.Tallinn 3-2-72
Honours: Estonia 101 full caps.

1992–93	Flora Tallinn	11	0		
1993–94	Flora Tallinn	11	0		
1994–95	Portsmouth	0	0		
1995–96	Portsmouth	4	0		
1995–96	Flora Tallinn	7	0		
1996–97	Portsmouth	0	0	**4**	**0**
1996–97	Flora Tallinn	12	0	**41**	**0**
1996–97	Derby Co	4	0		
1997–98	Derby Co	36	0		
1998–99	Derby Co	17	0		
1999–2000	Derby Co	28	0		
2000–01	Derby Co	33	0		
2001–02	Derby Co	15	0		
2002–03	Derby Co	13	0	**146**	**0**
2002–03	Sunderland	4	0		
2003–04	Sunderland	43	1		
2004–05	Sunderland	11	0		
2005–06	Sunderland	0	0	**58**	**1**
2005–06	Arsenal	0	0		

REYES, Jose Antonio (F) **186 39**
H: 5 9 W: 12 01 b.Utrera 1-9-83
Honours: Spain 20 full caps, 4 goals.

1999–2000	Sevilla B	32	1		
1999–2000	Sevilla	1	0		
2000–01	Sevilla B	0	0	**32**	**1**
2000–01	Sevilla	1	0		
2001–02	Sevilla	29	8		
2002–03	Sevilla	34	9		
2003–04	Sevilla	20	5	**85**	**22**
2003–04	Arsenal	13	2		
2004–05	Arsenal	30	9		
2005–06	Arsenal	26	5	**69**	**16**

SENDEROS, Philippe (D) **59 5**
H: 6 1 W: 13 10 b.Geneva 14-2-85
Honours: Switzerland Youth, Under-21, 15 full caps, 3 goals.

2001–02	Servette	3	0		
2002–03	Servette	23	3	**26**	**3**
2003–04	Arsenal	0	0		
2004–05	Arsenal	13	0		
2005–06	Arsenal	20	2	**33**	**2**

SILVA, Gilberto (M) **140 9**
H: 6 3 W: 12 04 b.Lagoa da Prata 7-10-76
Honours: Brazil 40 full caps, 3 goals.

2000	Atletico Mineiro	1	0		
2001	Atletico Mineiro	26	3	**27**	**3**
2002–03	Arsenal	35	0		
2003–04	Arsenal	32	4		
2004–05	Arsenal	13	0		
2005–06	Arsenal	33	2	**113**	**6**

SMITH, Ryan (M) **17 1**
H: 5 10 W: 11 00 b.Islington 10-11-86
Source: Scholar. *Honours:* England Youth, Under-20.

2004–05	Arsenal	0	0		
2005–06	Arsenal	0	0		
2005–06	*Leicester C*	17	1	**17**	**1**

SONG BILLONG, Alexandre (M) **5 0**
H: 5 11 W: 12 04 b.Douala 9-9-87
Source: Bastia. *Honours:* Cameroon full caps.

2005–06	Arsenal	5	0	**5**	**0**

STOKES, Anthony (F) **0 0**
H: 5 11 W: 11 06 b.Dublin 25-7-88
Source: Scholar. *Honours:* Eire Youth, Under-21.

2005–06	Arsenal	0	0		

TOURE, Kolo (D) **131 3**
H: 5 10 W: 13 08 b.Sokuora Bouake 19-3-81
Source: ASEC Mimosas. *Honours:* Ivory Coast 44 full caps, 1 goal.

2001–02	Arsenal	0	0		
2002–03	Arsenal	26	2		
2003–04	Arsenal	37	1		
2004–05	Arsenal	35	0		
2005–06	Arsenal	33	0	**131**	**3**

VAN PERSIE, Robin (F) **111 24**
H: 6 0 W: 11 00 b.Rotterdam 6-8-83
Honours: Holland Under-21, 14 full caps, 2 goals.

2001–02	Feyenoord	10	0		
2002–03	Feyenoord	23	8		
2003–04	Feyenoord	28	6	**61**	**14**
2004–05	Arsenal	26	5		
2005–06	Arsenal	24	5	**50**	**10**

WALCOTT, Theo (F) **21 4**
H: 5 9 W: 11 01 b.Compton 16-3-89
Source: Scholar. *Honours:* England Youth, B, 1 full cap.

2005–06	Southampton	21	4	**21**	**4**
2005–06	Arsenal	0	0		

Scholars
Butcher, Lee Anthony; Efrem, Giorgos; Elston, Marc Stephen; Parisio, Carl; Simpson, Jay-Alistaire Frederick; Stokes, Anthony; Tracy, Shane.

ASTON VILLA (2)

AGBONLAHOR, Gabriel (F) **19 1**
H: 5 11 W: 12 05 b.Birmingham 13-10-86
Source: Scholar. *Honours:* England Under-20.

2005–06	Aston Villa	9	1	**9**	**1**
2005–06	*Watford*	2	0	**2**	**0**
2005–06	*Sheffield W*	8	0	**8**	**0**

ANGEL, Juan Pablo (F) **243 85**
H: 6 0 W: 12 10 b.Medellin 24-10-75
Source: Nacional. *Honours:* Colombia 33 full caps, 8 goals.

1997–98	River Plate	12	2		
1998–99	River Plate	27	11		
1999–2000	River Plate	34	19		
2000–01	River Plate	18	13	**91**	**45**
2000–01	Aston Villa	9	1		
2001–02	Aston Villa	29	12		
2002–03	Aston Villa	15	1		
2003–04	Aston Villa	33	16		
2004–05	Aston Villa	35	7		
2005–06	Aston Villa	31	3	**152**	**40**

BAROS, Milan (F) **154 38**
H: 6 0 W: 12 00 b.Valasske Mezirici 28-10-81
Honours: Czech Republic Youth, Under-21, 50 full caps, 27 goals.

1998–99	Banik Ostrava	6	0		
1999–2000	Banik Ostrava	29	6		
2000–01	Banik Ostrava	26	5	**61**	**11**
2001–02	Liverpool	0	0		
2002–03	Liverpool	27	9		
2003–04	Liverpool	13	1		
2004–05	Liverpool	26	9		
2005–06	Liverpool	2	0	**68**	**19**
2005–06	Aston Villa	25	8	**25**	**8**

BARRY, Gareth (D) **255 19**
H: 5 11 W: 12 06 b.Hastings 23-2-81
Source: Trainee. *Honours:* England Youth, Under-21, 8 full caps.

1997–98	Aston Villa	2	0		
1998–99	Aston Villa	32	2		
1999–2000	Aston Villa	30	1		
2000–01	Aston Villa	30	0		
2001–02	Aston Villa	20	0		
2002–03	Aston Villa	35	3		
2003–04	Aston Villa	36	3		

2004–05	Aston Villa	34	7		
2005–06	Aston Villa	36	3	**255**	**19**

BERGER, Patrik (M) 322 64
H: 6 1 W: 12 06 b.Prague 10-11-73
Honours: Czechoslovakia 2 full caps.Czech Republic 44 full caps, 18 goals.

1991–92	Slavia Prague	20	3		
1992–93	Slavia Prague	29	10		
1993–94	Slavia Prague	12	4		
1994–95	Slavia Prague	28	7	**89**	**24**
1995–96	Borussia Dortmd	25	4	**25**	**4**
1996–97	Liverpool	23	6		
1997–98	Liverpool	22	3		
1998–99	Liverpool	32	7		
1999–2000	Liverpool	34	9		
2000–01	Liverpool	14	2		
2001–02	Liverpool	21	1		
2002–03	Liverpool	2	0	**148**	**28**
2003–04	Portsmouth	20	5		
2004–05	Portsmouth	32	3	**52**	**8**
2005–06	Aston Villa	8	0	**8**	**0**

BERSON, Mathieu (M) 133 7
H: 5 9 W: 11 06 b.Vannes 23-2-80
Honours: France Under-21.

1999–2000	Nantes	12	0		
2000–01	Nantes	28	0		
2001–02	Nantes	29	3		
2002–03	Nantes	29	2		
2003–04	Nantes	24	2	**122**	**7**
2004–05	Aston Villa	11	0		
2005–06	Aston Villa	0	0	**11**	**0**

To Auxerre (loan) August 2005

BOUMA, Wilfred (D) 271 37
H: 5 10 W: 13 01 b.Helmond 15-6-78
Honours: Holland 20 full caps, 1 goal.

1994–95	PSV Eindhoven	1	0		
1995–96	PSV Eindhoven	4	0		
1996–97	PSV Eindhoven	1	0		
1996–97	MVV	18	7		
1997–98	MVV	33	6	**51**	**13**
1998–99	Fortuna Sittard	33	5	**33**	**5**
1999–2000	PSV Eindhoven	27	9		
2000–01	PSV Eindhoven	20	0		
2001–02	PSV Eindhoven	27	3		
2002–03	PSV Eindhoven	27	1		
2003–04	PSV Eindhoven	32	5		
2004–05	PSV Eindhoven	28	1	**167**	**19**
2005–06	Aston Villa	20	0	**20**	**0**

BOYLE, Lee (G) 0 0
H: 5 11 W: 10 08 b.Donegal 22-1-88
Source: Scholar.

2005–06	Aston Villa	0	0		

BRIDGES, Scott (D) 0 0
H: 5 7 W: 13 08 b.Oxford 3-5-88
Source: Scholar.

2005–06	Aston Villa	0	0		

CAHILL, Gary (D) 34 2
H: 6 2 W: 12 06 b.Dronfield 19-12-85
Source: Trainee. *Honours:* England Youth, Under-20.

2003–04	Aston Villa	0	0		
2004–05	Aston Villa	0	0		
2004–05	*Burnley*	27	1	**27**	**1**
2005–06	Aston Villa	7	1	**7**	**1**

DAVIS, Steven (M) 63 5
H: 5 7 W: 9 07 b.Ballymena 1-1-85
Source: Scholar. *Honours:* Northern Ireland Schools, Youth, Under-21, Under-23, 13 full caps, 1 goal.

2001–02	Aston Villa	0	0		
2002–03	Aston Villa	0	0		
2003–04	Aston Villa	0	0		
2004–05	Aston Villa	28	1		
2005–06	Aston Villa	35	4	**63**	**5**

DE LA CRUZ, Ulises (D) 289 26
H: 5 8 W: 12 10 b.Piqulucho 8-2-74
Source: Cruzeiro. *Honours:* Ecuador 88 full caps, 5 goals.

1996	Aucas	32	3	**32**	**3**
1997	LDU Quito	38	4		
1998	LDU Quito	42	7		
1999	LDU Quito	22	4		
1999	Cruzeiro	4	0	**4**	**0**
2000	LDU Quito	30	5	**132**	**20**
2001–02	Hibernian	32	2	**32**	**2**
2002–03	Aston Villa	20	1		
2003–04	Aston Villa	28	0		
2004–05	Aston Villa	34	0		
2005–06	Aston Villa	7	0	**89**	**1**

DELANEY, Mark (D) 186 2
H: 6 1 W: 11 07 b.Haverfordwest 13-5-76
Source: Carmarthen T. *Honours:* Wales 34 full caps.

1998–99	Cardiff C	28	0	**28**	**0**
1998–99	Aston Villa	2	0		
1999–2000	Aston Villa	28	1		
2000–01	Aston Villa	19	0		
2001–02	Aston Villa	30	0		
2002–03	Aston Villa	12	0		
2003–04	Aston Villa	25	0		
2004–05	Aston Villa	30	0		
2005–06	Aston Villa	12	1	**158**	**2**

DJEMBA-DJEMBA, Eric (M) 72 1
H: 5 8 W: 12 07 b.Douala 4-5-81
Source: Kadji Sport, UCB Douala. *Honours:* Cameroon 26 full caps.

2001–02	Nantes	14	0		
2002–03	Nantes	28	1	**42**	**1**
2003–04	Manchester U	15	0		
2004–05	Manchester U	5	0	**20**	**0**
2004–05	Aston Villa	6	0		
2005–06	Aston Villa	4	0	**10**	**0**

GARDNER, Craig (M) 8 0
H: 5 10 W: 11 13 b.Solihull 25-11-86
Source: Scholar.

2004–05	Aston Villa	0	0		
2005–06	Aston Villa	8	0	**8**	**0**

GRANT, Lee (M) 0 0
H: 6 2 W: 12 02 b.York 31-12-85
Source: Trainee.

2003–04	Aston Villa	0	0		
2004–05	Aston Villa	0	0		
2005–06	Aston Villa	0	0		

GREEN, Paul (D) 0 0
H: 5 8 W: 10 04 b.Birmingham 15-4-87
Source: Scholar.

2005–06	Aston Villa	0	0		

HENDERSON, Stephen (G) 0 0
H: 6 3 W: 11 00 b.Dublin 2-5-88
Source: Scholar.

2005–06	Aston Villa	0	0		

HENDRIE, Lee (M) 250 27
H: 5 10 W: 11 00 b.Birmingham 18-5-77
Source: Trainee. *Honours:* England Youth, Under-21, B, 1 full cap.

1993–94	Aston Villa	0	0		
1994–95	Aston Villa	0	0		
1995–96	Aston Villa	3	0		
1996–97	Aston Villa	4	0		
1997–98	Aston Villa	17	3		
1998–99	Aston Villa	32	3		
1999–2000	Aston Villa	29	1		
2000–01	Aston Villa	32	6		
2001–02	Aston Villa	29	2		
2002–03	Aston Villa	27	4		
2003–04	Aston Villa	32	2		
2004–05	Aston Villa	29	5		
2005–06	Aston Villa	16	1	**250**	**27**

HUGHES, Aaron (D) 240 4
H: 6 0 W: 11 02 b.Cookstown 8-11-79
Source: Trainee. *Honours:* Northern Ireland Youth, B, 46 full caps.

1996–97	Newcastle U	0	0		
1997–98	Newcastle U	4	0		
1998–99	Newcastle U	14	0		
1999–2000	Newcastle U	27	2		
2000–01	Newcastle U	35	0		
2001–02	Newcastle U	34	0		
2002–03	Newcastle U	35	1		
2003–04	Newcastle U	34	0		
2004–05	Newcastle U	22	1	**205**	**4**
2005–06	Aston Villa	35	0	**35**	**0**

LAURSEN, Martin (D) 146 6
H: 6 2 W: 12 05 b.Farvoug 26-7-77
Honours: Denmark Youth, Under-21, 41 full caps.

1995–96	Silkeborg	1	0		
1996–97	Silkeborg	12	0		
1997–98	Silkeborg	22	1	**35**	**1**
1998–99	Verona	6	0		
1999–2000	Verona	19	2		
2000–01	Verona	31	0	**56**	**2**
2001–02	AC Milan	22	2		
2002–03	AC Milan	10	0		
2003–04	AC Milan	10	0	**42**	**2**
2004–05	Aston Villa	12	1		
2005–06	Aston Villa	1	0	**13**	**1**

McCANN, Gavin (M) 207 10
H: 5 11 W: 11 00 b.Blackpool 10-1-78
Source: Trainee. *Honours:* England 1 full cap.

1995–96	Everton	0	0		
1996–97	Everton	0	0		
1997–98	Everton	11	0		
1998–99	Everton	0	0	**11**	**0**
1998–99	Sunderland	11	0		
1999–2000	Sunderland	24	4		
2000–01	Sunderland	22	3		
2001–02	Sunderland	29	0		
2002–03	Sunderland	30	1	**116**	**8**
2003–04	Aston Villa	28	0		
2004–05	Aston Villa	20	1		
2005–06	Aston Villa	32	1	**80**	**2**

McGURK, Adam (F) 0 0
H: 5 9 W: 12 13 b.St Helier 24-1-89
Source: Scholar.

2005–06	Aston Villa	0	0		

MELLBERG, Olof (D) 322 5
H: 6 1 W: 12 10 b.Amncharad 3-9-77
Honours: Sweden 68 full caps, 2 goals.

1996	Degerfors	22	0		
1997	Degerfors	25	0	**47**	**0**
1998	AIK Stockholm	17	0	**17**	**0**
1998–99	Santander	25	0		
1999–2000	Santander	37	0		
2000–01	Santander	36	0	**98**	**0**
2001–02	Aston Villa	32	0		
2002–03	Aston Villa	38	1		
2003–04	Aston Villa	33	1		
2004–05	Aston Villa	30	3		
2005–06	Aston Villa	27	0	**160**	**5**

MIKAELSSON, Tobias (F) 0 0
H: 6 3 W: 11 04 b.Jorlanda 17-11-88
Source: Scholar.

2005–06	Aston Villa	0	0		

MOORE, Luke (F) 65 13
H: 5 11 W: 11 13 b.Birmingham 13-2-86
Source: Trainee. *Honours:* FA Schools, England Youth, Under-21.

2002–03	Aston Villa	0	0		
2003–04	Aston Villa	7	0		
2003–04	*Wycombe W*	6	4	**6**	**4**
2004–05	Aston Villa	25	1		
2005–06	Aston Villa	27	8	**59**	**9**

O'HALLORAN, Stephen (D) 0 0
H: 6 0 W: 11 07 b.Cork 29-11-87
Source: Scholar.

2005–06	Aston Villa	0	0		

OLEJNIK, Robert (G) 0 0
H: 6 0 W: 15 06 b.Vienna 26-11-86
Source: Scholar.

2004–05	Aston Villa	0	0		
2005–06	Aston Villa	0	0		

OSBOURNE, Isaiah (M) 0 0
H: 6 2 W: 12 07 b.Birmingham 5-11-87
Source: Scholar.

2005–06	Aston Villa	0	0		

PAUL, Shane (F) 0 0
H: 5 6 W: 10 07 b.Walsall 25-1-87
Source: Scholar. *Honours:* England Youth.

2004–05	Aston Villa	0	0		
2005–06	Aston Villa	0	0		

PHILLIPS, Kevin (F) 354 163
H: 5 7 W: 11 00 b.Hitchin 25-7-73
Source: Baldock T. *Honours:* England B, 8 full caps.

1994–95	Watford	16	9		
1995–96	Watford	27	11		
1996–97	Watford	16	4	**59**	**24**
1997–98	Sunderland	43	29		
1998–99	Sunderland	26	23		
1999–2000	Sunderland	36	30		
2000–01	Sunderland	34	14		

2001–02 Sunderland 37 11
2002–03 Sunderland 32 6 **208 113**
2003–04 Southampton 34 12
2004–05 Southampton 30 10 **64 22**
2005–06 Aston Villa 23 4 **23 4**

RIDGEWELL, Liam (D) 63 5
H: 5 10 W: 10 03 b.Bexley 21-7-84
Source: Scholar. *Honours:* England Youth, Under-20, Under-21.
2001–02 Aston Villa 0 0
2002–03 Aston Villa 0 0
2002–03 *Bournemouth* 5 0 **5 0**
2003–04 Aston Villa 11 0
2004–05 Aston Villa 15 0
2005–06 Aston Villa 32 5 **58 5**

SAMUEL, J Lloyd (D) 173 2
H: 5 11 W: 11 04 b.Trinidad 29-3-81
Source: Charlton Ath Trainee. *Honours:* England Youth, Under-20, Under-21.
1998–99 Aston Villa 0 0
1999–2000 Aston Villa 9 0
2000–01 Aston Villa 3 0
2001–02 *Gillingham* 8 0 **8 0**
2001–02 Aston Villa 23 0
2002–03 Aston Villa 38 0
2003–04 Aston Villa 38 2
2004–05 Aston Villa 35 0
2005–06 Aston Villa 19 0 **165 2**

SORENSEN, Thomas (G) 281 0
H: 6 4 W: 13 10 b.Fredericia 12-6-76
Source: Odense. *Honours:* Denmark Youth, Under-21, B, 54 full caps.
1998–99 Sunderland 45 0
1999–2000 Sunderland 37 0
2000–01 Sunderland 34 0
2001–02 Sunderland 34 0
2002–03 Sunderland 21 0 **171 0**
2003–04 Aston Villa 38 0
2004–05 Aston Villa 36 0
2005–06 Aston Villa 36 0 **110 0**

TAYLOR, Stuart (G) 50 0
H: 6 5 W: 13 07 b.Romford 28-11-80
Source: Trainee. *Honours:* FA Schools, England Youth, Under-21.
1998–99 Arsenal 0 0
1999–2000 Arsenal 0 0
1999–2000 *Bristol R* 4 0 **4 0**
2000–01 Arsenal 0 0
2000–01 *Crystal Palace* 10 0 **10 0**
2000–01 *Peterborough U* 6 0 **6 0**
2001–02 Arsenal 10 0
2002–03 Arsenal 8 0
2003–04 Arsenal 0 0
2004–05 Arsenal 0 0 **18 0**
2004–05 *Leicester C* 10 0 **10 0**
2005–06 Aston Villa 2 0 **2 0**

TSHIMANGA, Christian (M) 0 0
H: 5 9 W: 11 10 b.Kinshasa 16-6-87
Source: Scholar.
2004–05 Aston Villa 0 0
2005–06 Aston Villa 0 0

WARD, Jamie (M) 9 1
H: 5 5 W: 9 04 b.Birmingham 12-5-86
Source: Scholar. *Honours:* Northern Ireland Youth, Under-21.
2003–04 Aston Villa 0 0
2004–05 Aston Villa 0 0
2005–06 Aston Villa 0 0
2005–06 *Stockport Co* 9 1 **9 1**

WHITTINGHAM, Peter (D) 71 1
H: 5 10 W: 9 13 b.Nuneaton 8-9-84
Source: Trainee. *Honours:* England Youth, Under-20, Under-21.
2002–03 Aston Villa 4 0
2003–04 Aston Villa 32 0
2004–05 Aston Villa 13 1
2004–05 *Burnley* 7 0 **7 0**
2005–06 Aston Villa 4 0 **53 1**
2005–06 *Derby Co* 11 0 **11 0**

WILLIAMS, Sam (M) 15 2
H: 5 11 W: 10 08 b.London 9-6-87
Source: Scholar.
2004–05 Aston Villa 0 0
2005–06 Aston Villa 0 0
2005–06 *Wrexham* 15 2 **15 2**

Scholars
Bevan, David; Collins, Jordan; Earls, Daniel; Evans, Morgan Kaighn; Green, Phillip Richard; Herd, Christopher; Hogg, Jonathan; Lowry, Shane Thomas; Lund, Eric; Morgan, Oluwaseyi; Stieber, Zoltan.

BARNET (3)

BAILEY, Nicky (M) 45 7
H: 5 10 W: 12 06 b.Hammersmith 10-6-84
Source: Sutton U.
2005–06 Barnet 45 7 **45 7**

BATT, Damian (D) 22 0
H: 5 10 W: 11 06 b.Hoddesdon 16-9-84
Source: Norwich C Trainee.
2005–06 Barnet 22 0 **22 0**

BOWDITCH, Ben (M) 11 0
H: 5 11 W: 13 05 b.Bishops Stortford 19-2-84
Source: Scholar. *Honours:* England Youth, Under-20.
2000–01 Tottenham H 0 0
2001–02 Tottenham H 0 0
2002–03 Tottenham H 0 0
2003–04 Tottenham H 0 0
2004–05 Colchester U 5 0 **5 0**
2005–06 Barnet 6 0 **6 0**

CHARLES, Anthony (D) 40 0
H: 6 1 W: 12 07 b.Isleworth 11-3-81
Source: Brook House.
1999–2000 Crewe Alex 0 0
2000–01 Crewe Alex 0 0
From Farnborough T
2005–06 Barnet 40 0 **40 0**

CLIST, Simon (D) 96 8
H: 5 9 W: 11 09 b.Bournemouth 13-6-81
Source: Tottenham H Trainee.
1999–2000 Bristol C 9 0
2000–01 Bristol C 38 4
2001–02 Bristol C 20 1
2002–03 Bristol C 3 1
2002–03 *Torquay U* 11 2 **11 2**
2003–04 Bristol C 1 0
2004–05 Bristol C 0 0 **71 6**
2005–06 Barnet 14 0 **14 0**

DEVERA, Joe (D) 0 0
H: 6 2 W: 12 00 b.Southgate 6-2-87
2005–06 Barnet 0 0

FLITNEY, Ross (G) 38 0
H: 6 3 W: 12 07 b.Hitchin 1-6-84
Source: Scholar.
2003–04 Fulham 0 0
2003–04 *Brighton & HA* 3 0 **3 0**
2004–05 Fulham 0 0
2004–05 *Doncaster R* 0 0
2005–06 Barnet 35 0 **35 0**

GRAHAM, Richard (M) 17 1
H: 5 10 W: 11 10 b.Newry 5-8-79
Source: Trainee. *Honours:* Northern Ireland Youth, Under-21.
1996–97 QPR 0 0
1997–98 QPR 0 0
1998–99 QPR 2 0
1999–2000 QPR 0 0
2000–01 QPR 0 0 **2 0**
From Chesham, Billericay,
2005–06 Barnet 15 1 **15 1**

GRAZIOLI, Giuliano (F) 182 52
H: 5 10 W: 12 00 b.Marylebone 23-3-75
Source: Wembley.
1995–96 Peterborough U 3 1
1996–97 Peterborough U 4 0
1997–98 Peterborough U 0 0
1998–99 Peterborough U 34 15 **41 16**
1999–2000 Swindon T 19 8
2000–01 Swindon T 28 2
2001–02 Swindon T 31 8 **78 18**
2002–03 Bristol R 34 11 **34 11**
2003–04 Barnet 0 0
2004–05 Barnet 0 0
2005–06 Barnet 29 7 **29 7**

GROSS, Adam (D) 20 0
H: 5 10 W: 10 09 b.Greenwich 16-2-86
Source: Charlton Ath Scholar.
2005–06 Barnet 20 0 **20 0**

HATCH, Liam (F) 35 2
H: 6 4 W: 13 09 b.Hitchin 3-4-84
Source: Herne Bay, Gravesend & N.
2005–06 Barnet 35 2 **35 2**

HENDON, Ian (D) 388 21
H: 6 1 W: 13 02 b.Ilford 5-12-71
Source: Trainee. *Honours:* England Youth, Under-21.
1989–90 Tottenham H 0 0
1990–91 Tottenham H 2 0
1991–92 Tottenham H 2 0
1991–92 *Portsmouth* 4 0 **4 0**
1991–92 *Leyton Orient* 6 0
1992–93 Tottenham H 0 0 **4 0**
1992–93 *Barnsley* 6 0 **6 0**
1993–94 Leyton Orient 36 2
1994–95 Leyton Orient 29 0
1994–95 *Birmingham C* 4 0 **4 0**
1995–96 Leyton Orient 38 2
1996–97 Leyton Orient 28 1 **137 5**
1996–97 Notts Co 12 0
1997–98 Notts Co 38 0
1998–99 Notts Co 32 6 **82 6**
1998–99 Northampton T 7 0
1999–2000 Northampton T 44 2
2000–01 Northampton T 9 1 **60 3**
2000–01 Sheffield W 31 2
2001–02 Sheffield W 9 0
2002–03 Sheffield W 9 0 **49 2**
2002–03 Peterborough U 7 1 **7 1**
2004–05 Barnet 0 0
2005–06 Barnet 35 4 **35 4**

HESSENTHALER, Andy (M) 524 32
H: 5 7 W: 11 10 b.Gravesend 17-8-65
Source: Dartford, Redbridge Forest.
1991–92 Watford 35 1
1992–93 Watford 45 3
1993–94 Watford 42 5
1994–95 Watford 43 2
1995–96 Watford 30 0 **195 11**
1996–97 Gillingham 38 2
1997–98 Gillingham 42 0
1998–99 Gillingham 39 7
1999–2000 Gillingham 42 5
2000–01 Gillingham 23 2
2001–02 Gillingham 17 0
2002–03 Gillingham 33 1
2003–04 Gillingham 36 2
2004–05 Gillingham 17 0
2004–05 *Hull C* 10 0 **10 0**
2005–06 Gillingham 16 1 **303 20**
2005–06 Barnet 16 1 **16 1**

HICKIE, Luke (M) 0 0
H: 5 11 W: 11 07 b.Croydon 17-8-88
Source: Crystal Palace Scholar.
2005–06 Barnet 0 0

JONES, Ryan (G) 0 0
H: 6 2 W: 13 00
2005–06 Barnet 0 0

KANDOL, Tresor (F) 53 9
H: 6 0 W: 13 07 b.Banga 30-8-81
Source: Trainee.
1998–99 Luton T 4 0
1999–2000 Luton T 4 0
2000–01 Luton T 13 3 **21 3**
2001–02 Bournemouth 12 0 **12 0**
From Thurrock, Dagen
2005–06 Darlington7 **2**
From Dagenham & R.
2005–06 Barnet 13 4 **13 4**

KING, Simon (D) 36 0
H: 6 0 W: 13 00 b.Oxford 11-4-83
Source: Scholar.
2000–01 Oxford U 2 0
2001–02 Oxford U 2 0
2002–03 Oxford U 0 0
2003–04 Oxford U 0 0
2004–05 Oxford U 0 0 **4 0**
2005–06 Barnet 32 0 **32 0**

LEE, Dwane (M) **27 4**
H: 6 3 W: 13 09 b.Hillingdon 26-11-79
Source: Yeading, Exeter C.

2005–06	Barnet	27	4	**27**	**4**

NORVILLE, Jason (F) **36 3**
H: 6 0 W: 11 03 b.Trinidad 9-9-83
Source: Scholar.

2001–02	Watford	2	0		
2002–03	Watford	12	1		
2003–04	Watford	0	0		
2004–05	Watford	0	0	**14**	**1**
2005–06	Barnet	22	2	**22**	**2**

ROACHE, Lee (M) **8 1**
H: 5 9 W: 11 00 b.Leytonstone 30-4-84

2005–06	Barnet	8	1	**8**	**1**

SINCLAIR, Dean (M) **46 2**
H: 5 10 W: 11 03 b.St Albans 17-12-84
Source: Scholar.

2002–03	Norwich C	2	0		
2003–04	Norwich C	0	0	**2**	**0**
2004–05	Barnet	0	0		
2005–06	Barnet	44	2	**44**	**2**

SOARES, Louie (D) **21 1**
H: 5 11 W: 13 05 b.Reading 8-1-85
Source: Scholar.

2004–05	Reading	0	0		
2004–05	Bristol R	1	0	**1**	**0**
2005–06	Barnet	20	1	**20**	**1**

STREVENS, Ben (M) **69 9**
H: 6 1 W: 12 00 b.Edgware 24-5-80
Source: Wingate & Finchley.

1998–99	Barnet	0	0		
1999–2000	Barnet	6	0		
2000–01	Barnet	28	4		
2001–02	Barnet	0	0		
2002–03	Barnet	0	0		
2003–04	Barnet	0	0		
2004–05	Barnet	0	0		
2005–06	Barnet	35	5	**69**	**9**

WARHURST, Paul (D) **353 18**
H: 6 1 W: 13 00 b.Stockport 26-9-69
Source: Trainee. *Honours:* England Under-21.

1987–88	Manchester C	0	0		
1988–89	Oldham Ath	4	0		
1989–90	Oldham Ath	30	1		
1990–91	Oldham Ath	33	1	**67**	**2**
1991–92	Sheffield W	33	0		
1992–93	Sheffield W	29	6		
1993–94	Sheffield W	4	0	**66**	**6**
1993–94	Blackburn R	9	0		
1994–95	Blackburn R	27	2		
1995–96	Blackburn R	10	0		
1996–97	Blackburn R	11	2	**57**	**4**
1997–98	Crystal Palace	22	3		
1998–99	Crystal Palace	5	1	**27**	**4**
1998–99	Bolton W	20	0		
1999–2000	Bolton W	19	0		
2000–01	Bolton W	20	0		
2001–02	Bolton W	25	0		
2002–03	Bolton W	7	0	**91**	**0**
2002–03	*Stoke C*	5	1	**5**	**1**
2003–04	Chesterfield	4	0	**4**	**0**
2003–04	Barnsley	4	0	**4**	**0**
2003–04	Carlisle U	1	0	**1**	**0**
2003–04	Grimsby T	7	0		
2004–05	Grimsby T	0	0	**7**	**0**
2004–05	Blackpool	4	0	**4**	**0**
From Forest Green R.					
2005–06	Wrexham	11	1	**11**	**1**
2005–06	Barnet	9	0	**9**	**0**

YAKUBU, Ismail (D) **26 1**
H: 6 1 W: 13 09 b.Kano 8-4-85
Source: Trainee.

2005–06	Barnet	26	1	**26**	**1**

BARNSLEY (4)

ATKINSON, Rob (D) **2 0**
H: 6 1 W: 12 00 b.Beverley 29-4-87
Source: Scholar.

2003–04	Barnsley	1	0		
2004–05	Barnsley	1	0		
2005–06	Barnsley	0	0	**2**	**0**

AUSTIN, Neil (D) **124 0**
H: 5 10 W: 11 09 b.Barnsley 26-4-83
Source: Trainee. *Honours:* England Youth, Under-20.

1999–2000	Barnsley	0	0		
2000–01	Barnsley	0	0		
2001–02	Barnsley	0	0		
2002–03	Barnsley	34	0		
2003–04	Barnsley	37	0		
2004–05	Barnsley	15	0		
2005–06	Barnsley	38	0	**124**	**0**

BURNS, Jacob (M) **177 14**
H: 5 10 W: 11 08 b.Sydney 21-1-78
Honours: Australia Under-23, 2 full caps.

1996–97	Sydney U	5	0		
1997–98	Sydney U	25	2		
1998–99	Sydney U	27	3	**57**	**5**
1999–2000	Parramatta Power	25	3	**25**	**3**
2000–01	Leeds U	4	0		
2001–02	Leeds U	0	0		
2002–03	Leeds U	2	0		
2003–04	Leeds U	0	0	**6**	**0**
2003–04	Barnsley	22	1		
2004–05	Barnsley	34	2		
2005–06	Barnsley	33	3	**89**	**6**

To Wisla Krakow February 2006

CARBON, Matt (D) **308 18**
H: 6 2 W: 11 13 b.Nottingham 8-6-75
Source: Trainee. *Honours:* England Under-21.

1992–93	Lincoln C	1	0		
1993–94	Lincoln C	9	0		
1994–95	Lincoln C	33	7		
1995–96	Lincoln C	26	3		
1995–96	Derby Co	6	0		
1996–97	Derby Co	10	0		
1997–98	Derby Co	4	0	**20**	**0**
1997–98	WBA	16	1		
1998–99	WBA	39	2		
1999–2000	WBA	34	2		
2000–01	WBA	24	0	**113**	**5**
2001–02	Walsall	22	1		
2002–03	Walsall	25	1		
2003–04	Walsall	8	0	**55**	**2**
2003–04	*Lincoln C*	1	0	**70**	**10**
2004–05	Barnsley	26	0		
2005–06	Barnsley	24	1	**50**	**1**

COLGAN, Nick (G) **203 0**
H: 6 1 W: 12 00 b.Drogheda 19-9-73
Source: Drogheda. *Honours:* Eire Under-21, 8 full caps.

1992–93	Chelsea	0	0		
1993–94	Chelsea	0	0		
1993–94	*Crewe Alex*	0	0		
1994–95	Chelsea	0	0		
1994–95	*Grimsby T*	0	0		
1995–96	Chelsea	0	0		
1995–96	*Millwall*	0	0		
1996–97	Chelsea	1	0		
1997–98	Chelsea	0	0	**1**	**0**
1997–98	*Brentford*	5	0	**5**	**0**
1997–98	*Reading*	5	0	**5**	**0**
1998–99	Bournemouth	0	0		
1999–2000	Hibernian	24	0		
2000–01	Hibernian	37	0		
2001–02	Hibernian	30	0		
2002–03	Hibernian	30	0		
2003–04	Hibernian	0	0	**121**	**0**
2003–04	*Stockport Co*	15	0	**15**	**0**
2004–05	Barnsley	13	0		
2005–06	Barnsley	43	0	**56**	**0**

CONLON, Barry (M) **281 75**
H: 6 3 W: 14 00 b.Drogheda 1-10-78
Source: QPR Trainee. *Honours:* Eire Under-21.

1997–98	Manchester C	7	0		
1997–98	*Plymouth Arg*	13	2	**13**	**2**
1998–99	Manchester C	0	0	**7**	**0**
1998–99	Southend U	34	7	**34**	**7**
1999–2000	York C	40	11		
2000–01	York C	8	0	**48**	**11**
2000–01	*Colchester U*	26	8	**26**	**8**
2001–02	Darlington	35	10		
2002–03	Darlington	41	15		
2003–04	Darlington	39	14	**115**	**39**
2004–05	Barnsley	24	6		
2005–06	Barnsley	11	1	**35**	**7**
2005–06	*Rotherham U*	3	1	**3**	**1**

DEVANEY, Martin (M) **241 44**
H: 5 11 W: 12 00 b.Cheltenham 1-6-80
Source: Trainee.

1997–98	Coventry C	0	0		
1998–99	Coventry C	0	0		
1999–2000	Cheltenham T	26	6		
2000–01	Cheltenham T	34	10		
2001–02	Cheltenham T	25	1		
2002–03	Cheltenham T	40	6		
2003–04	Cheltenham T	40	5		
2004–05	Cheltenham T	38	10	**203**	**38**
2005–06	Watford	0	0		
2005–06	Barnsley	38	6	**38**	**6**

FLINDERS, Scott (G) **14 0**
H: 6 4 W: 13 00 b.Rotherham 12-6-86
Source: Scholar. *Honours:* England Youth, Under-20.

2004–05	Barnsley	11	0		
2005–06	Barnsley	3	0	**14**	**0**

HARBAN, Thomas (D) **0 0**
H: 6 0 W: 11 09 b.Barnsley 12-11-85
Source: Scholar.

2005–06	Barnsley	0	0		

HASSELL, Bobby (D) **227 5**
H: 5 10 W: 12 00 b.Derby 4-6-80
Source: Trainee.

1997–98	Mansfield T	9	0		
1998–99	Mansfield T	3	0		
1999–2000	Mansfield T	11	1		
2000–01	Mansfield T	40	1		
2001–02	Mansfield T	43	1		
2002–03	Mansfield T	20	0		
2003–04	Mansfield T	34	0	**160**	**3**
2004–05	Barnsley	39	0		
2005–06	Barnsley	28	2	**67**	**2**

HAYES, Paul (F) **144 34**
H: 6 0 W: 12 12 b.Dagenham 20-9-83
Source: Norwich C Scholar.

2002–03	Scunthorpe U	18	8		
2003–04	Scunthorpe U	35	2		
2004–05	Scunthorpe U	46	18	**99**	**28**
2005–06	Barnsley	45	6	**45**	**6**

HECKINGBOTTOM, Paul (D) **267 11**
H: 6 0 W: 13 01 b.Barnsley 17-7-77
Source: Manchester U Trainee.

1995–96	Sunderland	0	0		
1996–97	Sunderland	0	0		
1997–98	Sunderland	0	0		
1997–98	*Scarborough*	29	0	**29**	**0**
1998–99	Sunderland	0	0		
1998–99	*Hartlepool U*	5	1	**5**	**1**
1998–99	*Darlington*	10	0		
1999–2000	Darlington	45	1		
2000–01	Darlington	18	1		
2001–02	Darlington	42	3	**115**	**5**
2002–03	Norwich C	15	0	**15**	**0**
2003–04	Bradford C	43	0	**43**	**0**
2004–05	Sheffield W	38	4		
2005–06	Sheffield W	4	0	**42**	**4**
2005–06	Barnsley	18	1	**18**	**1**

HESLOP, Simon (M) **0 0**
H: 5 11 W: 11 00 b.York 1-5-87
Source: Scholar.

2005–06	Barnsley	0	0		

HOWARD, Brian (M) **101 14**
H: 5 8 W: 11 00 b.Winchester 23-1-83
Source: Trainee. *Honours:* England Schools, Youth, Under-20.

1999–2000	Southampton	0	0		
2000–01	Southampton	0	0		
2001–02	Southampton	0	0		
2002–03	Southampton	0	0		
2003–04	Swindon T	35	4		
2004–05	Swindon T	35	5	**70**	**9**
2005–06	Barnsley	31	5	**31**	**5**

JARMAN, Nathan (F) **17 0**
H: 5 11 W: 11 03 b.Scunthorpe 19-9-86
Source: Scholar.

2004–05	Barnsley	6	0		
2005–06	Barnsley	9	0	**15**	**0**
2005–06	*Bury*	2	0	**2**	**0**

JOYNES, Nathan (F) **1 0**

H: 6 1 W: 12 02 b.Hoyland 7-8-85

Source: Scholar.

2004–05	Barnsley	1	0		
2005–06	Barnsley	0	0	**1**	**0**

KAY, Antony (D) **142 10**

H: 5 11 W: 11 08 b.Barnsley 21-10-82

Source: Trainee. *Honours:* England Youth.

1999–2000	Barnsley	0	0		
2000–01	Barnsley	7	0		
2001–02	Barnsley	1	0		
2002–03	Barnsley	16	0		
2003–04	Barnsley	43	3		
2004–05	Barnsley	39	6		
2005–06	Barnsley	36	1	**142**	**10**

KELL, Richard (M) **100 11**

H: 6 1 W: 10 13 b.Bishop Auckland 15-9-79

Source: Trainee.

1998–99	Middlesbrough	0	0		
1999–2000	Middlesbrough	0	0		
2000–01	Middlesbrough	0	0		
2000–01	Torquay U	15	3		
2001–02	Torquay U	0	0	**15**	**3**
2001–02	Scunthorpe U	16	1		
2002–03	Scunthorpe U	0	0		
2003–04	Scunthorpe U	24	2		
2004–05	Scunthorpe U	43	5	**83**	**8**
2005–06	Barnsley	2	0	**2**	**0**

LAIGHT, Ryan (D) **1 0**

H: 6 2 W: 11 09 b.Barnsley 16-11-85

Source: Scholar.

2002–03	Barnsley	0	0		
2003–04	Barnsley	0	0		
2004–05	Barnsley	0	0		
2005–06	Barnsley	1	0	**1**	**0**

McPARLAND, Anthony (M) **8 0**

H: 5 7 W: 10 07 b.Rutherglen 20-9-82

Source: Celtic.

2005–06	Barnsley	8	0	**8**	**0**

McPHAIL, Stephen (M) **165 7**

H: 5 8 W: 11 04 b.Westminster 9-12-79

Source: Trainee. *Honours:* Eire Under-21, 10 full caps, 1 goal.

1996–97	Leeds U	0	0		
1997–98	Leeds U	4	0		
1998–99	Leeds U	17	0		
1999–2000	Leeds U	24	2		
2000–01	Leeds U	7	0		
2001–02	Leeds U	1	0		
2001–02	*Millwall*	3	0	**3**	**0**
2002–03	Leeds U	13	0		
2003–04	Leeds U	12	1	**78**	**3**
2003–04	*Nottingham F*	14	0	**14**	**0**
2004–05	Barnsley	36	2		
2005–06	Barnsley	34	2	**70**	**4**

NARDIELLO, Daniel (F) **82 19**

H: 5 11 W: 11 04 b.Coventry 22-10-82

Source: Trainee.

1999–2000	Manchester U	0	0		
2000–01	Manchester U	0	0		
2001–02	Manchester U	0	0		
2002–03	Manchester U	0	0		
2003–04	Manchester U	0	0		
2003–04	*Swansea C*	4	0	**4**	**0**
2003–04	*Barnsley*	16	7		
2004–05	Manchester U	0	0		
2004–05	*Barnsley*	28	7		
2005–06	Barnsley	34	5	**78**	**19**

REID, Paul (D) **146 6**

H: 6 2 W: 11 08 b.Carlisle 18-2-82

Source: Trainee. *Honours:* England Youth, Under-20.

1998–99	Carlisle U	0	0		
1999–2000	Carlisle U	19	0	**19**	**0**
2000–01	Rangers	0	0		
2001–02	Rangers	0	0		
2001–02	*Preston NE*	1	1	**1**	**1**
2002–03	Rangers	0	0		
2002–03	*Northampton T*	19	0		
2003–04	Northampton T	33	2	**52**	**2**
2004–05	Barnsley	41	3		
2005–06	Barnsley	33	0	**74**	**3**

RICHARDS, Marc (F) **127 31**

H: 6 2 W: 12 06 b.Wolverhampton 8-7-82

Source: Trainee. *Honours:* England Youth, Under-20.

1999–2000	Blackburn R	0	0		
2000–01	Blackburn R	0	0		
2001–02	Blackburn R	0	0		
2001–02	*Crewe Alex*	4	0	**4**	**0**
2001–02	*Oldham Ath*	5	0	**5**	**0**
2001–02	*Halifax T*	5	0	**5**	**0**
2002–03	Blackburn R	0	0		
2002–03	*Swansea C*	17	7	**17**	**7**
2003–04	Northampton T	41	8		
2004–05	Northampton T	12	2		
2004–05	*Rochdale*	5	2	**5**	**2**
2005–06	Northampton T	0	0	**53**	**10**
2005–06	Barnsley	38	12	**38**	**12**

SCARSELLA, David (G) **32 0**

H: 6 2 W: 11 03 b.Australia 2-10-82

Honours: Australia Schools.

2002–03	Adelaide City	8	0	**8**	**0**
2003–04	Adelaide United	24	0	**24**	**0**
2004–05	Barnsley	0	0		
2005–06	Barnsley	0	0		

SHUKER, Chris (M) **147 20**

H: 5 5 W: 9 03 b.Liverpool 9-5-82

Source: Scholarship.

1999–2000	Manchester C	0	0		
2000–01	Manchester C	0	0		
2000–01	*Macclesfield T*	9	1	**9**	**1**
2001–02	Manchester C	2	0		
2002–03	Manchester C	3	0		
2002–03	*Walsall*	5	0	**5**	**0**
2003–04	Manchester C	0	0	**5**	**0**
2003–04	*Rochdale*	14	1	**14**	**1**
2003–04	*Hartlepool U*	14	1	**14**	**1**
2003–04	Barnsley	9	0		
2004–05	Barnsley	45	7		
2005–06	Barnsley	46	10	**100**	**17**

TONGE, Dale (D) **39 0**

H: 5 10 W: 10 06 b.Doncaster 7-5-85

Source: Scholar.

2003–04	Barnsley	1	0		
2004–05	Barnsley	14	0		
2005–06	Barnsley	24	0	**39**	**0**

VAUGHAN, Tony (D) **260 13**

H: 6 1 W: 11 02 b.Manchester 11-10-75

Source: Trainee. *Honours:* England Schools.

1994–95	Ipswich T	10	0		
1995–96	Ipswich T	25	1		
1996–97	Ipswich T	32	2	**67**	**3**
1997–98	Manchester C	19	1		
1998–99	Manchester C	38	1		
1999–2000	Manchester C	1	0	**58**	**2**
1999–2000	*Cardiff C*	14	0	**14**	**0**
1999–2000	Nottingham F	10	0		
2000–01	Nottingham F	25	1		
2001–02	Nottingham F	8	0		
2001–02	*Scunthorpe U*	5	0	**5**	**0**
2002–03	Nottingham F	0	0	**43**	**1**
2002–03	*Mansfield T*	4	0		
2003–04	Mansfield T	32	2	**36**	**2**
2004–05	Barnsley	26	4		
2005–06	Barnsley	1	0	**27**	**4**
2005–06	*Stockport Co*	10	1	**10**	**1**

WILLIAMS, Robbie (D) **51 4**

H: 5 10 W: 11 13 b.Pontefract 2-10-84

Source: Scholar.

2002–03	Barnsley	8	0		
2003–04	Barnsley	4	1		
2004–05	Barnsley	17	1		
2005–06	Barnsley	22	2	**51**	**4**

WRIGHT, Tommy (F) **76 12**

H: 6 0 W: 12 02 b.Leicester 28-9-84

Source: Scholar. *Honours:* England Youth, Under-20.

2001–02	Leicester C	1	0		
2002–03	Leicester C	13	2		
2003–04	Leicester C	0	0		
2003–04	*Brentford*	25	3	**25**	**3**
2004–05	Leicester C	7	0		
2005–06	Leicester C	0	0	**21**	**2**
2005–06	*Blackpool*	13	6	**13**	**6**
2005–06	Barnsley	17	1	**17**	**1**

WROE, Nicky (M) **46 1**

H: 5 11 W: 10 02 b.Sheffield 28-9-85

Source: Scholar.

2002–03	Barnsley	1	0		
2003–04	Barnsley	2	1		
2004–05	Barnsley	31	0		
2005–06	Barnsley	12	0	**46**	**1**

BIRMINGHAM C (5)

ALLEN, Oliver (F) **0 0**

H: 5 9 W: 10 05 b.Essex 7-9-86

Source: Scholar.

2005–06	Birmingham C	0	0		

ALSOP, Sam (D) **0 0**

H: 5 11 W: 11 07 b.Birmingham 7-3-85

Source: Scholar.

2004–05	Birmingham C	0	0		
2005–06	Birmingham C	0	0		
2005–06	*Yeovil T*	0	0		

ALUKO, Sone (F) **0 0**

H: 5 8 W: 9 11 b.Birmingham 19-2-89

Source: Scholar. *Honours:* England Schools, Youth.

2005–06	Birmingham C	0	0		

BIRLEY, Matt (M) **1 0**

H: 5 8 W: 11 01 b.Bromsgrove 26-7-86

Source: Scholar.

2005–06	Birmingham C	1	0	**1**	**0**

BRUCE, Alex (D) **35 0**

H: 6 0 W: 11 06 b.Norwich 28-9-84

Source: Trainee. *Honours:* Eire Under-21.

2002–03	Blackburn R	0	0		
2003–04	Blackburn R	0	0		
2004–05	Blackburn R	0	0		
2004–05	*Oldham Ath*	12	0	**12**	**0**
2004–05	Birmingham C	0	0		
2004–05	*Sheffield W*	6	0	**6**	**0**
2005–06	Birmingham C	6	0	**6**	**0**
2005–06	*Tranmere R*	11	0	**11**	**0**

BURGE, Ryan (M) **0 0**

H: 5 10 W: 10 03 b.Cheltenham 12-10-88

Source: Scholar.

2005–06	Birmingham C	0	0		

CAMPBELL, Dudley (F) **34 9**

H: 5 10 W: 11 00 b.London 12-11-81

Source: Aston Villa Trainee, QPR, Chesham U, Stevenage B, Yeading.

2005–06	Brentford	23	9	**23**	**9**
2005–06	Birmingham C	11	0	**11**	**0**

CLAPHAM, Jamie (M) **303 11**

H: 5 9 W: 11 09 b.Lincoln 7-12-75

Source: Trainee.

1994–95	Tottenham H	0	0		
1995–96	Tottenham H	0	0		
1996–97	Tottenham H	1	0		
1996–97	*Leyton Orient*	6	0	**6**	**0**
1996–97	*Bristol R*	5	0	**5**	**0**
1997–98	Tottenham H	0	0	**1**	**0**
1997–98	Ipswich T	22	0		
1998–99	Ipswich T	46	3		
1999–2000	Ipswich T	46	2		
2000–01	Ipswich T	35	2		
2001–02	Ipswich T	32	2		
2002–03	Ipswich T	26	1	**207**	**10**
2002–03	Birmingham C	16	0		
2003–04	Birmingham C	25	0		
2004–05	Birmingham C	27	0		
2005–06	Birmingham C	16	1	**84**	**1**

CLEMENCE, Stephen (M) **177 6**

H: 6 0 W: 12 09 b.Liverpool 31-3-78

Source: Trainee. *Honours:* England Schools, Youth, Under-21.

1994–95	Tottenham H	0	0		
1995–96	Tottenham H	0	0		
1996–97	Tottenham H	0	0		
1997–98	Tottenham H	17	0		
1998–99	Tottenham H	18	0		
1999–2000	Tottenham H	20	1		
2000–01	Tottenham H	29	1		
2001–02	Tottenham H	6	0		
2002–03	Tottenham H	0	0	**90**	**2**
2002–03	Birmingham C	15	2		

2003–04	Birmingham C	35	2		
2004–05	Birmingham C	22	0		
2005–06	Birmingham C	15	0	**87**	**4**

COTTRILL, Chris (M) **0** **0**
H: 5 10 W: 11 00 b.Birmingham 4-9-84
Source: Scholar.

2004–05	Birmingham C	0	0		
2005–06	Birmingham C	0	0		

CUNNINGHAM, Kenny (D) **520** **1**
H: 5 11 W: 12 07 b.Dublin 28-6-71
Source: Tolka R. *Honours:* Eire Youth, Under-21, B, 72 full caps.

1989–90	Millwall	5	0		
1990–91	Millwall	23	0		
1991–92	Millwall	17	0		
1992–93	Millwall	37	0		
1993–94	Millwall	39	1		
1994–95	Millwall	15	0	**136**	**1**
1994–95	Wimbledon	28	0		
1995–96	Wimbledon	33	0		
1996–97	Wimbledon	36	0		
1997–98	Wimbledon	32	0		
1998–99	Wimbledon	35	0		
1999–2000	Wimbledon	37	0		
2000–01	Wimbledon	15	0		
2001–02	Wimbledon	34	0	**250**	**0**
2002–03	Birmingham C	31	0		
2003–04	Birmingham C	36	0		
2004–05	Birmingham C	36	0		
2005–06	Birmingham C	31	0	**134**	**0**

DORMAND, James (G) **0** **0**
H: 6 1 W: 14 09 b.Birmingham 13-6-86
Source: Scholar.

2005–06	Birmingham C	0	0		

DOYLE, Colin (G) **17** **0**
H: 6 5 W: 14 05 b.Cork 12-8-85
Honours: Eire Youth, Under-21.

2004–05	Birmingham C	0	0		
2004–05	*Chester C*	0	0		
2004–05	*Nottingham F*	3	0	**3**	**0**
2005–06	Birmingham C	0	0		
2005–06	*Millwall*	14	0	**14**	**0**

DUNN, David (M) **183** **36**
H: 5 9 W: 12 03 b.Gt Harwood 27-12-79
Source: Trainee. *Honours:* England Youth, Under-21, 1 full cap.

1997–98	Blackburn R	0	0		
1998–99	Blackburn R	15	1		
1999–2000	Blackburn R	22	2		
2000–01	Blackburn R	42	12		
2001–02	Blackburn R	29	7		
2002–03	Blackburn R	28	8	**136**	**30**
2003–04	Birmingham C	21	2		
2004–05	Birmingham C	11	2		
2005–06	Birmingham C	15	2	**47**	**6**

FORSSELL, Mikael (F) **181** **49**
H: 5 10 W: 10 10 b.Steinfurt 15-3-81
Honours: Finland Youth, Under-21, 40 full caps, 16 goals.

1997	HJK Helsinki	1	0		
1998	HJK Helsinki	16	1	**17**	**1**
1998–99	Chelsea	10	1		
1999–2000	Chelsea	0	0		
1999–2000	*Crystal Palace*	13	3		
2000–01	Chelsea	0	0		
2000–01	*Crystal Palace*	39	13	**52**	**16**
2001–02	Chelsea	22	4		
2002–03	*M'gladbach*	16	7	**16**	**7**
2002–03	Chelsea	0	0		
2003–04	Chelsea	0	0		
2003–04	*Birmingham C*	32	17		
2004–05	Chelsea	1	0	**33**	**5**
2004–05	*Birmingham C*	4	0		
2005–06	Birmingham C	27	3	**63**	**20**

GRAY, Julian (M) **188** **13**
H: 6 1 W: 11 00 b.Lewisham 21-9-79
Source: Trainee.

1998–99	Arsenal	0	0		
1999–2000	Arsenal	1	0	**1**	**0**
2000–01	Crystal Palace	23	1		
2001–02	Crystal Palace	43	2		
2002–03	Crystal Palace	35	5		
2003–04	Crystal Palace	24	2	**125**	**10**
2003–04	*Cardiff C*	9	0	**9**	**0**
2004–05	Birmingham C	32	2		
2005–06	Birmingham C	21	1	**53**	**3**

HALL, Asa (M) **12** **0**
H: 6 2 W: 11 09 b.Sandwell 29-11-86
Source: Scholar. *Honours:* England Youth, Under-20.

2004–05	Birmingham C	0	0		
2005–06	Birmingham C	0	0		
2005–06	*Boston U*	12	0	**12**	**0**

HARTHILL, Oliver (M) **0** **0**
H: 5 11 W: 11 05 b.Birmingham 7-9-88
Source: Scholar.

2005–06	Birmingham C	0	0		

HESKEY, Emile (F) **372** **93**
H: 6 2 W: 13 12 b.Leicester 11-1-78
Source: Trainee. *Honours:* England Youth, Under-21, B, 43 full caps, 5 goals.

1994–95	Leicester C	1	0		
1995–96	Leicester C	30	7		
1996–97	Leicester C	35	10		
1997–98	Leicester C	35	10		
1998–99	Leicester C	30	6		
1999–2000	Leicester C	23	7	**154**	**40**
1999–2000	Liverpool	12	3		
2000–01	Liverpool	36	14		
2001–02	Liverpool	35	9		
2002–03	Liverpool	32	6		
2003–04	Liverpool	35	7	**150**	**39**
2004–05	Birmingham C	34	10		
2005–06	Birmingham C	34	4	**68**	**14**

HINKS, Brett (M) **0** **0**
b.Birmingham
Source: Scholar.

2005–06	Birmingham C	0	0		

HOJSTED, Ingi (M) **0** **0**
H: 5 9 W: 9 10 b.Torshavn 12-12-85
Source: Trainee.

2002–03	Arsenal	0	0		
2003–04	Arsenal	0	0		
2004–05	Arsenal	0	0		
2005–06	Birmingham C	0	0		

HOWLAND, David (M) **0** **0**
H: 5 11 W: 10 08 b.Ballynahinch 17-9-86
Source: Scholar.

2004–05	Birmingham C	0	0		
2005–06	Birmingham C	0	0		

IZZET, Muzzy (M) **295** **39**
H: 5 10 W: 10 03 b.Mile End 31-10-74
Source: Trainee. *Honours:* Turkey 9 full caps.

1993–94	Chelsea	0	0		
1994–95	Chelsea	0	0		
1995–96	Chelsea	0	0		
1995–96	*Leicester C*	9	1		
1996–97	Leicester C	35	3		
1997–98	Leicester C	36	4		
1998–99	Leicester C	31	5		
1999–2000	Leicester C	32	8		
2000–01	Leicester C	27	7		
2001–02	Leicester C	31	4		
2002–03	Leicester C	38	4		
2003–04	Leicester C	30	2	**269**	**38**
2004–05	Birmingham C	10	1		
2005–06	Birmingham C	16	0	**26**	**1**

JEROME, Cameron (F) **73** **24**
H: 6 1 W: 13 06 b.Huddersfield 14-8-86
Honours: England Under-21.

2004–05	Cardiff C	29	6		
2005–06	Cardiff C	44	18	**73**	**24**
2005–06	Birmingham C	0	0		

JOHNSON, Damien (M) **206** **6**
H: 5 9 W: 11 09 b.Lisburn 18-11-78
Source: Trainee. *Honours:* Northern Ireland Youth, Under-21, 42 full caps.

1995–96	Blackburn R	0	0		
1996–97	Blackburn R	0	0		
1997–98	Blackburn R	0	0		
1997–98	*Nottingham F*	6	0	**6**	**0**
1998–99	Blackburn R	21	1		
1999–2000	Blackburn R	16	1		
2000–01	Blackburn R	16	0		
2001–02	Blackburn R	7	1	**60**	**3**
2001–02	Birmingham C	8	1		
2002–03	Birmingham C	30	1		
2003–04	Birmingham C	35	1		
2004–05	Birmingham C	36	0		
2005–06	Birmingham C	31	0	**140**	**3**

KILKENNY, Neil (M) **45** **4**
H: 5 8 W: 10 08 b.Enfield 19-12-85
Source: Arsenal Trainee. *Honours:* England Youth, Under-20.

2003–04	Birmingham C	0	0		
2004–05	Birmingham C	0	0		
2004–05	*Oldham Ath*	27	4	**27**	**4**
2005–06	Birmingham C	18	0	**18**	**0**

KUQI, Njazi (F) **5** **0**
H: 6 3 W: 13 05 b.Vushtrri 25-3-83
Source: Lahti. *Honours:* Finland Under-21.

2004–05	Birmingham C	0	0		
2005–06	Birmingham C	0	0		
2005–06	*Blackpool*	4	0	**4**	**0**
2005–06	*Peterborough U*	1	0	**1**	**0**

LATKA, Martin (D) **71** **8**
H: 6 4 W: 13 07 b.Ceske Budojovice 28-9-84
Honours: Czech Republic Under-21.

2003–04	Slavia Prague	24	1		
2004–05	Slavia Prague	28	5		
2005–06	Slavia Prague	13	2	**65**	**8**
2005–06	Birmingham C	6	0	**6**	**0**

LAZARIDIS, Stan (M) **333** **16**
H: 5 9 W: 11 12 b.Perth 16-8-72
Honours: Australia Youth, Under-23, 59 full caps.

1992–93	Adelaide Sharks	28	2		
1993–94	Adelaide Sharks	23	3		
1994–95	Adelaide Sharks	22	0	**73**	**5**
1995–96	West Ham U	4	0		
1996–97	West Ham U	22	1		
1997–98	West Ham U	28	2		
1998–99	West Ham U	15	0	**69**	**3**
1999–2000	Birmingham C	31	2		
2000–01	Birmingham C	31	2		
2001–02	Birmingham C	32	0		
2002–03	*Portsmouth*	0	0		
2002–03	Birmingham C	30	2		
2003–04	Birmingham C	30	2		
2004–05	Birmingham C	20	0		
2005–06	Birmingham C	17	0	**191**	**8**

McPIKE, James (F) **0** **0**
H: 5 10 W: 11 02 b.Birmingham 4-10-88
Source: Scholar.

2005–06	Birmingham C	0	0		

MELCHIOT, Mario (D) **260** **7**
H: 6 2 W: 11 09 b.Amsterdam 4-11-76
Honours: Holland 13 full caps.

1996–97	Ajax	23	0		
1997–98	Ajax	26	0		
1998–99	Ajax	24	1	**73**	**1**
1999–2000	Chelsea	5	0		
2000–01	Chelsea	31	0		
2001–02	Chelsea	37	2		
2002–03	Chelsea	34	0		
2003–04	Chelsea	23	2	**130**	**4**
2004–05	Birmingham C	34	1		
2005–06	Birmingham C	23	1	**57**	**2**

MOTTERAM, Carl (M) **0** **0**
H: 5 8 W: 9 11 b.Birmingham 3-9-84
Source: Scholar.

2004–05	Birmingham C	0	0		
2005–06	Birmingham C	0	0		

NAFTI, Mehdi (M) **156** **4**
H: 5 10 W: 12 02 b.Toulouse 28-11-78
Honours: Tunisia 32 full caps, 1 goal.

1998–99	Toulouse	0	0		
1999–2000	Toulouse	13	1	**13**	**1**
2000–01	Santander B	21	0	**21**	**0**
2000–01	Santander	3	0		
2001–02	Santander	30	0		
2002–03	Santander	31	2		
2003–04	Santander	31	1		
2004–05	Santander	16	0	**111**	**3**
2004–05	Birmingham C	10	0		
2005–06	Birmingham C	1	0	**11**	**0**

OJI, Sam (D) **4** **0**
H: 6 0 W: 14 05 b.Westminster 9-10-85

2003–04	Birmingham C	0	0		
2004–05	Birmingham C	0	0		
2005–06	Birmingham C	0	0		
2005–06	*Doncaster R*	4	0	**4**	**0**

PAINTER, Marcos (D) **4 0**
H: 5 11 W: 12 04 b.Solihull 17-8-86
Source: Scholar. *Honours:* Eire Youth, Under-21.

2005–06	Birmingham C	4	0	**4**	**0**

PANDIANI, Walter (F) **221 75**
H: 6 0 W: 11 09 b.Montevideo 27-4-76
Honours: Uruguay 3 full caps.

1996	Progreso	0	0		
1997	Basanez	0	0		
1998	Penarol	21	3		
1999	Penarol	35	17		
2000	Penarol	15	9	**71**	**29**
2000–01	La Coruna	25	7		
2001–02	La Coruna	18	0		
2002–03	Mallorca	33	13	**33**	**13**
2003–04	La Coruna	28	14		
2004–05	La Coruna	15	6	**86**	**27**
2004–05	Birmingham C	14	4		
2005–06	Birmingham C	17	2	**31**	**6**

To Espanyol January 2006

PENNANT, Jermaine (M) **126 9**
H: 5 9 W: 10 06 b.Nottingham 15-1-83
Honours: England Schools, Youth, Under-21.

1998–99	Notts Co	0	0		
1998–99	Arsenal	0	0		
1999–2000	Arsenal	0	0		
2000–01	Arsenal	0	0		
2001–02	Arsenal	0	0		
2001–02	*Watford*	9	2		
2002–03	Arsenal	5	3		
2002–03	*Watford*	12	0	**21**	**2**
2003–04	Arsenal	7	0		
2003–04	*Leeds U*	36	2	**36**	**2**
2004–05	Arsenal	7	0	**19**	**3**
2004–05	Birmingham C	12	0		
2005–06	Birmingham C	38	2	**50**	**2**

SADLER, Matthew (D) **17 0**
H: 5 11 W: 11 08 b.Birmingham 26-2-85
Source: Scholar. *Honours:* England Youth.

2001–02	Birmingham C	0	0		
2002–03	Birmingham C	2	0		
2003–04	Birmingham C	0	0		
2003–04	*Northampton T*	7	0	**7**	**0**
2004–05	Birmingham C	0	0		
2005–06	Birmingham C	8	0	**10**	**0**

SUTTON, Chris (F) **400 147**
H: 6 3 W: 13 08 b.Nottingham 10-3-73
Source: Trainee. *Honours:* England Under-21, B, 1 full cap.

1990–91	Norwich C	2	0		
1991–92	Norwich C	21	2		
1992–93	Norwich C	38	8		
1993–94	Norwich C	41	25	**102**	**35**
1994–95	Blackburn R	40	15		
1995–96	Blackburn R	13	0		
1996–97	Blackburn R	25	11		
1997–98	Blackburn R	35	18		
1998–99	Blackburn R	17	3	**130**	**47**
1999–2000	Chelsea	28	1	**28**	**1**
2000–01	Celtic	24	11		
2001–02	Celtic	18	4		
2002–03	Celtic	28	15		
2003–04	Celtic	25	19		
2004–05	Celtic	27	12		
2005–06	Celtic	8	2	**130**	**63**
2005–06	Birmingham C	10	1	**10**	**1**

TAYLOR, Maik (G) **378 0**
H: 6 4 W: 14 02 b.Hildeshein 4-9-71
Source: Farnborough T. *Honours:* Northern Ireland Under-21, B, 52 full caps.

1995–96	Barnet	45	0		
1996–97	Barnet	25	0	**70**	**0**
1996–97	Southampton	18	0		
1997–98	Southampton	0	0	**18**	**0**
1997–98	Fulham	28	0		
1998–99	Fulham	46	0		
1999–2000	Fulham	46	0		
2000–01	Fulham	44	0		
2001–02	Fulham	1	0		
2002–03	Fulham	19	0		
2003–04	Fulham	0	0	**184**	**0**
2003–04	Birmingham C	34	0		
2004–05	Birmingham C	38	0		
2005–06	Birmingham C	34	0	**106**	**0**

TAYLOR, Martin (D) **139 6**
H: 6 4 W: 15 00 b.Ashington 9-11-79
Source: Trainee. *Honours:* England Youth, Under-21.

1997–98	Blackburn R	0	0		
1998–99	Blackburn R	3	0		
1999–2000	Blackburn R	6	0		
1999–2000	*Darlington*	4	0	**4**	**0**
1999–2000	*Stockport Co*	7	0	**7**	**0**
2000–01	Blackburn R	16	3		
2001–02	Blackburn R	19	0		
2002–03	Blackburn R	33	2		
2003–04	Blackburn R	11	0	**88**	**5**
2003–04	Birmingham C	12	1		
2004–05	Birmingham C	7	0		
2005–06	Birmingham C	21	0	**40**	**1**

TEBILY, Oliver (D) **134 1**
H: 6 0 W: 13 05 b.Abidjan 19-12-75
Source: Chateauroux. *Honours:* France Under-21. Ivory Coast full caps.

1997–98	Chateauroux	11	1	**11**	**1**
1998–99	Sheffield U	8	0	**8**	**0**
1999–2000	Celtic	23	0		
2000–01	Celtic	4	0		
2001–02	Celtic	11	0	**38**	**0**
2001–02	Birmingham C	7	0		
2002–03	Birmingham C	12	0		
2003–04	Birmingham C	27	0		
2004–05	Birmingham C	15	0		
2005–06	Birmingham C	16	0	**77**	**0**

TILL, Peter (M) **24 1**
H: 5 11 W: 11 04 b.Walsall 7-9-85
Source: Scholar.

2005–06	Birmingham C	0	0		
2005–06	*Scunthorpe U*	8	0	**8**	**0**
2005–06	*Boston U*	16	1	**16**	**1**

UPSON, Matthew (D) **161 3**
H: 6 1 W: 11 04 b.Stowmarket 18-4-79
Source: Trainee. *Honours:* England Youth, Under-21, 7 full caps.

1995–96	Luton T	0	0		
1996–97	Luton T	1	0	**1**	**0**
1996–97	Arsenal	0	0		
1997–98	Arsenal	5	0		
1998–99	Arsenal	5	0		
1999–2000	Arsenal	8	0		
2000–01	Arsenal	2	0		
2000–01	*Nottingham F*	1	0	**1**	**0**
2000–01	*Crystal Palace*	7	0	**7**	**0**
2001–02	Arsenal	14	0		
2002–03	Arsenal	0	0	**34**	**0**
2002–03	*Reading*	14	0	**14**	**0**
2002–03	Birmingham C	14	0		
2003–04	Birmingham C	30	0		
2004–05	Birmingham C	36	2		
2005–06	Birmingham C	24	1	**104**	**3**

VAESEN, Nico (G) **259 0**
H: 6 3 W: 12 13 b.Hasselt 28-9-69
Source: Tongeren.

1993–94	CS Brugge	13	0		
1994–95	CS Brugge	3	0	**16**	**0**
1995–96	Aalst	20	0		
1996–97	Aalst	0	0		
1997–98	Aalst	14	0	**34**	**0**
1998–99	Huddersfield T	43	0		
1999–2000	Huddersfield T	46	0		
2000–01	Huddersfield T	45	0	**134**	**0**
2001–02	Birmingham C	23	0		
2002–03	Birmingham C	27	0		
2003–04	Birmingham C	0	0		
2003–04	*Gillingham*	5	0	**5**	**0**
2003–04	*Bradford C*	6	0	**6**	**0**
2003–04	*Crystal Palace*	10	0	**10**	**0**
2004–05	Birmingham C	0	0		
2005–06	Birmingham C	4	0	**54**	**0**

Scholars
Aluko, Sone; Blake, James; Campion, Darren; De Las, Stefan Leonce Nicholas; Green, Lewis; Hall, Mark Stephen John; Howell, Michael Robert; Howell, Nathaniel Marlon; Johnson, James; Legzdins, Adam Richard; Meredith, Jake Leslie; Murdock, Chris; Ndiaye, Amadou Cardinar; Price, Jamie Michael; Wilson, Jared Andrew; Wright, Nicholas.

BLACKBURN R (6)

AHMED, Abdi (M) **0 0**
b.Cardiff 10-10-88
Source: Scholar.

2005–06	Blackburn R	0	0		

AMORUSO, Lorenzo (D) **216 17**
H: 6 2 W: 13 10 b.Bari 28-6-71

1988–89	Bari	3	0		
1989–90	Bari	3	0		
1990–91	Bari	5	1		
1991–92	Bari	0	0		
1991–92	Mantova	13	1	**13**	**1**
1992–93	Bari	0	0		
1992–93	Pescavo	19	1	**19**	**1**
1993–94	Bari	37	3		
1994–95	Bari	27	4	**75**	**8**
1995–96	Fiorentina	31	2		
1996–97	Fiorentina	23	1	**54**	**3**
1997–98	Rangers	4	0		
1998–99	Rangers	33	1		
1999–2000	Rangers	0	0		
2000–01	Rangers	0	0		
2001–02	Rangers	0	0	**37**	**1**
2003–04	Blackburn R	12	3		
2004–05	Blackburn R	6	0		
2005–06	Blackburn R	0	0	**18**	**3**

BARKER, Keith (F) **0 0**
H: 6 2 W: 12 12 b.Accrington 21-10-86
Source: Scholar. *Honours:* England Youth, Under-20.

2004–05	Blackburn R	0	0		
2005–06	Blackburn R	0	0		

To CS Brugge (loan) January 2006

BARR, Craig (D) **0 0**
b.Edinburgh 29-3-87
Source: Scholar.

2005–06	Blackburn R	0	0		

BELLAMY, Craig (F) **250 85**
H: 5 9 W: 10 12 b.Cardiff 13-7-79
Source: Trainee. *Honours:* Wales Schools, Youth, Under-21, 35 full caps, 9 goals.

1996–97	Norwich C	3	0		
1997–98	Norwich C	36	13		
1998–99	Norwich C	40	17		
1999–2000	Norwich C	4	2		
2000–01	Norwich C	1	0	**84**	**32**
2000–01	Coventry C	34	6	**34**	**6**
2001–02	Newcastle U	27	9		
2002–03	Newcastle U	29	7		
2003–04	Newcastle U	16	4		
2004–05	Newcastle U	21	7	**93**	**27**
2004–05	*Celtic*	12	7	**12**	**7**
2005–06	Blackburn R	27	13	**27**	**13**

BENTLEY, David (F) **56 5**
H: 5 10 W: 11 03 b.Peterborough 27-8-84
Source: Scholar. *Honours:* England Youth, Under-20, Under-21.

2001–02	Arsenal	0	0		
2002–03	Arsenal	0	0		
2003–04	Arsenal	1	0		
2004–05	Arsenal	0	0		
2004–05	*Norwich C*	26	2	**26**	**2**
2005–06	Arsenal	0	0	**1**	**0**
2005–06	Blackburn R	29	3	**29**	**3**

BYROM, Joel (M) **0 0**
H: 6 0 W: 12 04 b.Oswaldtwistle 14-9-86
Source: Scholar.

2004–05	Blackburn R	0	0		
2005–06	Blackburn R	0	0		

DE VITA, Raffaele (F) **0 0**
b.Rome 23-9-87
Source: Scholar.

2005–06	Blackburn R	0	0		

DERBYSHIRE, Matt (F) **29 10**
H: 5 10 W: 11 01 b.Gt Harwood 14-4-86
Source: Gt Harwood T.

2003–04	Blackburn R	0	0		
2004–05	Blackburn R	1	0		
2005–06	Blackburn R	0	0	**1**	**0**
2005–06	*Plymouth Arg*	12	0	**12**	**0**
2005–06	*Wrexham*	16	10	**16**	**10**

DICKOV, Paul (F) 339 88
H: 5 6 W: 10 06 b.Livingston 1-11-72
Source: Trainee. *Honours:* Scotland Schools, Youth, Under-21, 10 full caps, 1 goal.

1992–93	Arsenal	3	2		
1993–94	Arsenal	1	0		
1993–94	*Luton T*	15	1	**15**	**1**
1993–94	*Brighton & HA*	8	5	**8**	**5**
1994–95	Arsenal	9	0		
1995–96	Arsenal	7	1		
1996–97	Arsenal	1	0	**21**	**3**
1996–97	Manchester C	29	5		
1997–98	Manchester C	30	9		
1998–99	Manchester C	35	10		
1999–2000	Manchester C	34	5		
2000–01	Manchester C	21	4		
2001–02	Manchester C	7	0	**156**	**33**
2001–02	Leicester C	12	4		
2002–03	Leicester C	42	17		
2003–04	Leicester C	35	11	**89**	**32**
2004–05	Blackburn R	29	9		
2005–06	Blackburn R	21	5	**50**	**14**

DOUGLAS, Jonathan (M) 89 10
H: 5 11 W: 11 11 b.Monaghan 22-11-81
Source: Trainee. *Honours:* Eire 2 full caps, Under-21.

1999–2000	Blackburn R	0	0		
2000–01	Blackburn R	0	0		
2001–02	Blackburn R	0	0		
2002–03	Blackburn R	1	0		
2002–03	*Chesterfield*	7	1	**7**	**1**
2003–04	Blackpool	16	3	**16**	**3**
2003–04	Blackburn R	14	1		
2004–05	Blackburn R	1	0		
2004–05	*Gillingham*	10	0	**10**	**0**
2005–06	Blackburn R	0	0	**16**	**1**
2005–06	*Leeds U*	40	5	**40**	**5**

DRENCH, Steven (G) 0 0
H: 5 11 W: 12 08 b.Salford 11-9-85
Source: Trainee.

2002–03	Blackburn R	0	0		
2003–04	Blackburn R	0	0		
2004–05	Blackburn R	0	0		
2005–06	Blackburn R	0	0		

EMERTON, Brett (M) 290 34
H: 6 1 W: 13 05 b.Bankstown 22-2-79
Honours: Australia Youth, Under-20, Under-23, 51 full caps, 11 goals.

1996–97	Sydney Olympic	18	2		
1997–98	Sydney Olympic	24	3		
1998–99	Sydney Olympic	21	2		
1999–2000	Sydney Olympic	31	9	**94**	**16**
2000–01	Feyenoord	28	2		
2001–02	Feyenoord	31	6		
2002–03	Feyenoord	33	3	**92**	**11**
2003–04	Blackburn R	37	2		
2004–05	Blackburn R	37	4		
2005–06	Blackburn R	30	1	**104**	**7**

ENCKELMAN, Peter (G) 133 0
H: 6 2 W: 12 05 b.Turku 10-3-77
Source: TPS Turku. *Honours:* Finland Under-21, 7 full caps.

1995	TPS Turku	6	0		
1996	TPS Turku	24	0		
1997	TPS Turku	25	0		
1998	TPS Turku	24	0	**79**	**0**
1998–99	Aston Villa	0	0		
1999–2000	Aston Villa	10	0		
2000–01	Aston Villa	0	0		
2001–02	Aston Villa	9	0		
2002–03	Aston Villa	33	0		
2003–04	Aston Villa	0	0	**52**	**0**
2003–04	Blackburn R	2	0		
2004–05	Blackburn R	0	0		
2005–06	Blackburn R	0	0	**2**	**0**

FLITCROFT, Garry (M) 379 27
H: 6 0 W: 11 08 b.Bolton 6-11-72
Source: Trainee. *Honours:* England Schools, Under-21.

1991–92	Manchester C	0	0		
1991–92	*Bury*	12	0	**12**	**0**
1992–93	Manchester C	32	5		
1993–94	Manchester C	21	3		
1994–95	Manchester C	37	5		
1995–96	Manchester C	25	0	**115**	**13**
1995–96	Blackburn R	3	0		
1996–97	Blackburn R	28	3		
1997–98	Blackburn R	33	0		
1998–99	Blackburn R	8	2		
1999–2000	Blackburn R	19	0		
2000–01	Blackburn R	41	3		
2001–02	Blackburn R	29	1		
2002–03	Blackburn R	33	2		
2003–04	Blackburn R	31	3		
2004–05	Blackburn R	19	0		
2005–06	Blackburn R	2	0	**246**	**14**
2005–06	*Sheffield U*	6	0	**6**	**0**

FRIEDEL, Brad (G) 275 1
H: 6 3 W: 14 00 b.Lakewood 18-5-71
Honours: USA 82 full caps.

1996	Columbus Crew	9	0		
1997	Columbus Crew	29	0	**38**	**0**
1997–98	Liverpool	11	0		
1998–99	Liverpool	12	0		
1999–2000	Liverpool	2	0		
2000–01	Liverpool	0	0	**25**	**0**
2000–01	Blackburn R	27	0		
2001–02	Blackburn R	36	0		
2002–03	Blackburn R	37	0		
2003–04	Blackburn R	36	1		
2004–05	Blackburn R	38	0		
2005–06	Blackburn R	38	0	**212**	**1**

GALLAGHER, Paul (F) 81 16
H: 6 1 W: 11 00 b.Glasgow 9-8-84
Source: Trainee. *Honours:* Scotland Under-21, B, 1 full cap.

2002–03	Blackburn R	1	0		
2003–04	Blackburn R	26	3		
2004–05	Blackburn R	16	2		
2005–06	Blackburn R	1	0	**44**	**5**
2005–06	*Stoke C*	37	11	**37**	**11**

GARNER, Joseph (F) 0 0
b.Blackburn 12-4-88
Source: Scholar. *Honours:* England Schools, Youth.

2004–05	Blackburn R	0	0		
2005–06	Blackburn R	0	0		

GRAY, Michael (D) 426 16
H: 5 8 W: 10 07 b.Sunderland 3-8-74
Source: Trainee. *Honours:* England 3 full caps.

1992–93	Sunderland	27	2		
1993–94	Sunderland	22	1		
1994–95	Sunderland	16	0		
1995–96	Sunderland	46	4		
1996–97	Sunderland	34	3		
1997–98	Sunderland	44	2		
1998–99	Sunderland	37	2		
1999–2000	Sunderland	33	0		
2000–01	Sunderland	36	1		
2001–02	Sunderland	35	0		
2002–03	Sunderland	32	1		
2003–04	Sunderland	1	0	**363**	**16**
2003–04	Blackburn R	14	0		
2004–05	Blackburn R	9	0		
2004–05	*Leeds U*	10	0	**10**	**0**
2005–06	Blackburn R	30	0	**53**	**0**

GRESKO, Vratislav (D) 161 6
H: 6 0 W: 11 05 b.Bratislava 24-7-77
Honours: Slovakia 29 full caps, 2 goals.

1995–96	Dukla Banska	1	0		
1996–97	Dukla Banska	7	0	**8**	**0**
1997–98	Internazionale	22	0		
1998–99	Internazionale	29	5		
1999–2000	Leverkusen	9	0		
2000–01	Leverkusen	7	0	**16**	**0**
2000–01	Internazionale	18	0		
2001–02	Internazionale	23	0	**92**	**5**
2002–03	Parma	5	0	**5**	**0**
2002–03	Blackburn R	10	0		
2003–04	Blackburn R	24	1		
2004–05	Blackburn R	3	0		
2005–06	Blackburn R	3	0	**40**	**1**

GRIFFITHS, Rostyn (M) 0 0
b.Stoke 10-3-88
Source: Scholar.

2005–06	Blackburn R	0	0		

HARKINS, Gary (M) 12 1
H: 6 2 W: 12 10 b.Greenock 2-1-85
Source: Trainee.

2003–04	Blackburn R	0	0		
2003–04	*Huddersfield T*	3	0	**3**	**0**
2004–05	Blackburn R	0	0		
2004–05	*Bury*	5	0	**5**	**0**
2005–06	Blackburn R	0	0		
2005–06	*Blackpool*	4	1	**4**	**1**

HODGE, Bryan (M) 0 0
H: 5 10 W: 12 02 b.Hamilton 23-9-87
Source: Scholar.

2004–05	Blackburn R	0	0		
2005–06	Blackburn R	0	0		

JOHNSON, Jemal (F) 18 4
H: 5 8 W: 11 09 b.New Jersey 3-5-84
Source: Scholar.

2001–02	Blackburn R	0	0		
2002–03	Blackburn R	0	0		
2003–04	Blackburn R	0	0		
2004–05	Blackburn R	3	0		
2005–06	Blackburn R	3	0	**6**	**0**
2005–06	*Preston NE*	3	1	**3**	**1**
2005–06	*Darlington*	9	3	**9**	**3**

JONES, Luke (D) 0 0
b.Blackburn 10-4-87
Source: Scholar.

2005–06	Blackburn R	0	0		

JONES, Zak (G) 0 0
b.Darwen 24-11-88
Source: Scholar. *Honours:* England Youth.

2005–06	Blackburn R	0	0		

KANE, Tony (D) 0 0
H: 5 11 W: 11 00 b.Belfast 29-8-87
Source: Scholar.

2004–05	Blackburn R	0	0		
2005–06	Blackburn R	0	0		

KUQI, Shefki (F) 333 95
H: 6 2 W: 13 13 b.Albania 10-11-76
Source: Trepka, Miki. *Honours:* Albania 8 full caps, 1 goal, Finland 42 full caps, 5 goals.

1995	MP	24	3		
1996	MP	26	7	**50**	**10**
1997	HJK Helsinki	25	6		
1998	HJK Helsinki	22	1		
1999	HJK Helsinki	25	11	**72**	**18**
From Jokerit					
2000–01	Stockport Co	17	6		
2001–02	Stockport Co	18	5	**35**	**11**
2001–02	Sheffield W	17	6		
2002–03	Sheffield W	40	8		
2003–04	Sheffield W	7	5	**64**	**19**
2003–04	Ipswich T	36	11		
2004–05	Ipswich T	43	19	**79**	**30**
2005–06	Blackburn R	33	7	**33**	**7**

MATTEO, Dominic (D) 277 3
H: 6 1 W: 13 08 b.Dumfries 28-4-74
Source: Trainee. *Honours:* England Youth, Under-21, B, Scotland 6 full caps.

1992–93	Liverpool	0	0		
1993–94	Liverpool	11	0		
1994–95	Liverpool	7	0		
1994–95	*Sunderland*	1	0	**1**	**0**
1995–96	Liverpool	5	0		
1996–97	Liverpool	26	0		
1997–98	Liverpool	26	0		
1998–99	Liverpool	20	1		
1999–2000	Liverpool	32	0		
2000–01	Liverpool	0	0	**127**	**1**
2000–01	Leeds U	30	0		
2001–02	Leeds U	32	0		
2002–03	Leeds U	20	0		
2003–04	Leeds U	33	2	**115**	**2**
2004–05	Blackburn R	28	0		
2005–06	Blackburn R	6	0	**34**	**0**

McEVELEY, James (D) 47 2
H: 6 1 W: 13 03 b.Liverpool 11-2-85
Source: Trainee. *Honours:* England Under-20, Under-21.

2002–03	Blackburn R	9	0		
2003–04	Blackburn R	0	0		
2003–04	*Burnley*	4	0	**4**	**0**
2004–05	Blackburn R	5	0		
2004–05	*Gillingham*	10	1	**10**	**1**

2005–06 Blackburn R 0 0 **14 0**
2005–06 *Ipswich T* 19 1 **19 1**

MOKOENA, Aaron (D) 104 2
H: 6 2 W: 14 00 b.Johannesburg 25-11-80
Honours: South Africa 51 full caps.
2000–01 Ajax 0 0
2000–01 Antwerp 6 0
2001–02 Antwerp 13 1
2002–03 Antwerp 29 1 **48 2**
2003–04 Genk 18 0 **18 0**
2004–05 Blackburn R 16 0
2005–06 Blackburn R 22 0 **38 0**

NEILL, Lucas (D) 320 18
H: 6 0 W: 12 03 b.Sydney 9-3-78
Source: NSW Soccer Academy. *Honours:* Australia Under-20, Under-23, 29 full caps.
1995–96 Millwall 13 0
1996–97 Millwall 39 3
1997–98 Millwall 6 0
1998–99 Millwall 35 6
1999–2000 Millwall 31 1
2000–01 Millwall 24 2
2001–02 Millwall 4 1 **152 13**
2001–02 Blackburn R 31 1
2002–03 Blackburn R 34 0
2003–04 Blackburn R 32 2
2004–05 Blackburn R 36 1
2005–06 Blackburn R 35 1 **168 5**

NELSEN, Ryan (D) 127 7
H: 5 11 W: 14 02 b.Christchurch, NZ 18-10-77
Honours: New Zealand 29 full caps, 3 goals.
2001 DC United 19 0
2002 DC United 20 4
2003 DC United 25 1
2004 DC United 17 2 **81 7**
2004–05 Blackburn R 15 0
2005–06 Blackburn R 31 0 **46 0**

NOLAN, Eddie (D) 0 0
H: 6 0 W: 13 05 b.Waterford 5-8-88
Source: Scholar.
2005–06 Blackburn R 0 0

O'KEEFE, Josh (M) 0 0
b.Whalley 22-12-88
Source: Scholar.
2005–06 Blackburn R 0 0

OLSSON, Martin (D) 0 0
b.Sweden 17-5-88
Source: Hogaborg.
2005–06 Blackburn R 0 0

PEDERSEN, Morten (F) 216 58
H: 5 11 W: 11 00 b.Vadso 8-9-81
Honours: Norway Youth, Under-21, 23 full caps, 5 goals.
2004 Tromso 18 7
1997 Norlid 21 0
1998 Pola 20 4 **20 4**
1999 Norlid 19 0 **40 0**
2000 Tromso 10 3
2001 Tromso 26 5
2002 Tromso 23 18
2003 Tromso 26 8 **103 41**
2004–05 Blackburn R 19 4
2005–06 Blackburn R 34 9 **53 13**

PETER, Sergio (M) 8 0
H: 5 8 W: 11 00 b.Ludwigshafen 12-10-86
Source: Scholar. *Honours:* Germany Youth.
2004–05 Blackburn R 0 0
2005–06 Blackburn R 8 0 **8 0**

REID, Steven (M) 217 24
H: 6 0 W: 12 07 b.Kingston 10-3-81
Source: Trainee. *Honours:* England Youth. Eire 16 full caps, 2 goals.
1997–98 Millwall 1 0
1998–99 Millwall 25 0
1999–2000 Millwall 21 0
2000–01 Millwall 37 7
2001–02 Millwall 35 5
2002–03 Millwall 20 6 **139 18**
2003–04 Blackburn R 16 0
2004–05 Blackburn R 28 2
2005–06 Blackburn R 34 4 **78 6**

SAVAGE, Robbie (M) 374 30
H: 5 11 W: 11 00 b.Wrexham 18-10-74
Source: Trainee. *Honours:* Wales Schools, Youth, Under-21, 39 full caps, 2 goals.
1993–94 Manchester U 0 0
1994–95 Crewe Alex 6 2
1995–96 Crewe Alex 30 7
1996–97 Crewe Alex 41 1 **77 10**
1997–98 Leicester C 35 2
1998–99 Leicester C 34 1
1999–2000 Leicester C 35 1
2000–01 Leicester C 33 4
2001–02 Leicester C 35 0 **172 8**
2002–03 Birmingham C 33 4
2003–04 Birmingham C 31 3
2004–05 Birmingham C 18 4 **82 11**
2004–05 Blackburn R 9 0
2005–06 Blackburn R 34 1 **43 1**

TAYLOR, Andy (D) 6 0
H: 5 11 W: 11 07 b.Blackburn 14-3-86
Source: Scholar. *Honours:* England Youth, Under-20.
2004–05 Blackburn R 0 0
2005–06 Blackburn R 0 0
2005–06 *QPR* 3 0 **3 0**
2005–06 *Blackpool* 3 0 **3 0**

THOMAS, Adam (D) 0 0
b.Stockport 1-1-88
Source: Scholar.
2005–06 Blackburn R 0 0

THOMSON, Stephen (D) 0 0
b.Edinburgh 7-3-88
Source: Scholar.
2005–06 Blackburn R 0 0

TODD, Andy (D) 243 10
H: 5 11 W: 13 04 b.Derby 21-9-74
Source: Trainee.
1991–92 Middlesbrough 0 0
1992–93 Middlesbrough 0 0
1993–94 Middlesbrough 3 0
1994–95 Middlesbrough 5 0 **8 0**
1994–95 *Swindon T* 13 0 **13 0**
1995–96 Bolton W 12 2
1996–97 Bolton W 15 0
1997–98 Bolton W 25 0
1998–99 Bolton W 20 0
1999–2000 Bolton W 12 0 **84 2**
1999–2000 Charlton Ath 12 0
2000–01 Charlton Ath 23 1
2001–02 Charlton Ath 5 0 **40 1**
2001–02 *Grimsby T* 12 3 **12 3**
2002–03 Blackburn R 12 1
2003–04 Blackburn R 19 0
2003–04 *Burnley* 7 0 **7 0**
2004–05 Blackburn R 26 1
2005–06 Blackburn R 22 2 **79 4**

TREACY, Keith (M) 0 0
b.Dublin 13-9-88
Source: Scholar.
2005–06 Blackburn R 0 0

TUGAY, Kerimoglu (M) 471 44
H: 5 9 W: 11 07 b.Istanbul 24-8-70
Honours: Turkey 92 full caps, 2 goals.
1988–89 Galatasaray 16 0
1989–90 Galatasaray 23 0
1990–91 Galatasaray 12 0
1991–92 Galatasaray 26 3
1992–93 Galatasaray 25 6
1993–94 Galatasaray 25 12
1994–95 Galatasaray 23 1
1995–96 Galatasaray 30 3
1996–97 Galatasaray 33 4
1997–98 Galatasaray 30 2
1998–99 Galatasaray 22 2
1999–2000 Galatasaray 10 1 **275 34**
1999–2000 Rangers 16 1
2000–01 Rangers 26 3 **42 4**
2001–02 Blackburn R 33 3
2002–03 Blackburn R 37 1
2003–04 Blackburn R 36 1
2004–05 Blackburn R 21 0
2005–06 Blackburn R 27 1 **154 6**

WATT, Jerome (M) 0 0
b.Preston 20-10-84
Source: Scholar. *Honours:* England Youth.
2001–02 Blackburn R 0 0
2002–03 Blackburn R 0 0
2003–04 Blackburn R 0 0
2004–05 Blackburn R 0 0
2005–06 Blackburn R 0 0

WELCH, Ralph (M) 0 0
b.Liverpool 10-3-87
Source: Scholar.
2004–05 Blackburn R 0 0
2005–06 Blackburn R 0 0

WOODS, Ryan (M) 0 0
b.Preston 16-5-88
Source: Scholar. *Honours:* England Youth.
2005–06 Blackburn R 0 0

Scholars
Clarke, Jamie Andre; Dadson, Junior; Fielding, Francis David; Haworth, Andrew Alan David; Judge, Alan; King, Mark; Pezzoni, Kevin; Rowntree, Gari Richard; Somodi, Bence; Stopforth, Gary; Winnard, Dean.

BLACKPOOL (7)

ANDERSON, Stuart (M) 4 0
H: 6 0 W: 11 09 b.Banff 22-4-86
Source: Scholar. *Honours:* Scotland Youth.
2003–04 Southampton 0 0
2004–05 Southampton 0 0
2004–05 Blackpool 4 0
2005–06 Blackpool 0 0 **4 0**

BEAN, Marcus (M) 101 4
H: 5 11 W: 11 06 b.Hammersmith 2-11-84
Source: Scholar.
2002–03 QPR 7 0
2003–04 QPR 31 1
2004–05 QPR 20 1
2004–05 *Swansea C* 8 0
2005–06 QPR 9 0 **67 2**
2005–06 *Swansea C* 9 1 **17 1**
2005–06 Blackpool 17 1 **17 1**

BLINKHORN, Matthew (F) 44 5
H: 5 11 W: 10 10 b.Blackpool 2-3-85
Source: Scholar.
2001–02 Blackpool 3 0
2002–03 Blackpool 7 2
2003–04 Blackpool 12 1
2004–05 Blackpool 4 0
2004–05 *Luton T* 2 0 **2 0**
2005–06 Blackpool 16 2 **42 5**

BURNS, Jamie (F) 48 1
H: 5 9 W: 10 11 b.Blackpool 6-3-84
Source: Scholar.
2002–03 Blackpool 7 0
2003–04 Blackpool 11 0
2004–05 Blackpool 23 0
2005–06 Blackpool 6 1 **47 1**
2005–06 *Bury* 1 0 **1 0**

BUTLER, Tony (D) 466 11
H: 6 2 W: 12 00 b.Stockport 28-9-72
Source: Trainee.
1990–91 Gillingham 6 0
1991–92 Gillingham 5 0
1992–93 Gillingham 41 0
1993–94 Gillingham 27 1
1994–95 Gillingham 33 2
1995–96 Gillingham 36 2 **148 5**
1996–97 Blackpool 42 0
1997–98 Blackpool 37 0
1998–99 Blackpool 20 0
1998–99 Port Vale 4 0
1999–2000 Port Vale 15 0 **19 0**
1999–2000 WBA 7 0
2000–01 WBA 44 1
2001–02 WBA 19 0
2002–03 WBA 0 0 **70 1**
2002–03 Bristol C 38 1
2003–04 Bristol C 38 1
2004–05 Bristol C 22 2 **98 4**
2004–05 Blackpool 8 0
2005–06 Blackpool 24 1 **131 1**

CLANCY, Sean (M) **2** **0**
H: 5 8 W: 9 12 b.Liverpool 16-9-87
Source: School.

2003–04	Blackpool	2	0		
2004–05	Blackpool	0	0		
2005–06	Blackpool	0	0	**2**	**0**

CLARKE, Peter (D) **127** **15**
H: 6 0 W: 12 00 b.Southport 3-1-82
Source: Trainee. *Honours:* England Youth, Under-20, Under-21.

1998–99	Everton	0	0		
1999–2000	Everton	0	0		
2000–01	Everton	1	0		
2001–02	Everton	7	0		
2002–03	Everton	0	0		
2002–03	*Blackpool*	16	3		
2002–03	*Port Vale*	13	1	**13**	**1**
2003–04	Everton	1	0		
2003–04	*Coventry C*	5	0	**5**	**0**
2004–05	Everton	0	0	**9**	**0**
2004–05	Blackpool	38	5		
2005–06	Blackpool	46	6	**100**	**14**

COID, Danny (D) **214** **9**
H: 5 11 W: 11 07 b.Liverpool 3-10-81
Source: Trainee.

1998–99	Blackpool	1	0		
1999–2000	Blackpool	21	1		
2000–01	Blackpool	46	1		
2001–02	Blackpool	27	3		
2002–03	Blackpool	36	1		
2003–04	Blackpool	35	3		
2004–05	Blackpool	35	0		
2005–06	Blackpool	13	0	**214**	**9**

DONNELLY, Ciaran (M) **41** **2**
H: 5 10 W: 11 08 b.Blackpool 2-4-84
Source: Scholar. *Honours:* England Youth.

2001–02	Blackburn R	0	0		
2002–03	Blackburn R	0	0		
2003–04	*Blackpool*	9	0		
2004–05	Blackburn R	0	0		
2004–05	Blackpool	8	0		
2005–06	Blackpool	24	2	**41**	**2**

DOUGHTY, Phil (D) **0** **0**
H: 6 2 W: 13 02 b.Kirkham 6-9-86
Source: Scholar.

2003–04	Blackpool	0	0		
2004–05	Blackpool	0	0		
2005–06	Blackpool	0	0		

EDGE, Lewis (G) **2** **0**
H: 6 1 W: 12 10 b.Lancaster 12-1-87
Source: Scholar.

2003–04	Blackpool	1	0		
2004–05	Blackpool	0	0		
2005–06	Blackpool	1	0	**2**	**0**

EDWARDS, Rob (D) **491** **15**
H: 6 0 W: 12 02 b.Kendal 1-7-73
Source: Trainee. *Honours:* Wales Youth, Under-21, B, 4 full caps.

1989–90	Carlisle U	12	0		
1990–91	Carlisle U	36	5	**48**	**5**
1990–91	Bristol C	0	0		
1991–92	Bristol C	20	1		
1992–93	Bristol C	18	0		
1993–94	Bristol C	38	2		
1994–95	Bristol C	30	0		
1995–96	Bristol C	19	0		
1996–97	Bristol C	31	0		
1997–98	Bristol C	37	2		
1998–99	Bristol C	23	0	**216**	**5**
1999–2000	Preston NE	41	2		
2000–01	Preston NE	42	0		
2001–02	Preston NE	36	2		
2002–03	Preston NE	26	0		
2003–04	Preston NE	24	0	**169**	**4**
2004–05	Blackpool	26	1		
2005–06	Blackpool	32	0	**58**	**1**

FOX, David (M) **11** **2**
H: 5 9 W: 11 08 b.Leek 13-12-83
Source: Scholar. *Honours:* England Youth, Under-20.

2000–01	Manchester U	0	0		
2001–02	Manchester U	0	0		
2002–03	Manchester U	0	0		
2003–04	Manchester U	0	0		
2004–05	Manchester U	0	0		
2004–05	*Shrewsbury T*	4	1	**4**	**1**
2005–06	Manchester U	0	0		
2005–06	Blackpool	7	1	**7**	**1**

GORDON, Dean (D) **338** **29**
H: 5 11 W: 13 08 b.Croydon 10-2-73
Source: Trainee. *Honours:* England Under-21.

1991–92	Crystal Palace	4	0		
1992–93	Crystal Palace	10	0		
1993–94	Crystal Palace	45	5		
1994–95	Crystal Palace	41	2		
1995–96	Crystal Palace	34	8		
1996–97	Crystal Palace	30	3		
1997–98	Crystal Palace	37	2	**201**	**20**
1998–99	Middlesbrough	38	3		
1999–2000	Middlesbrough	4	0		
2000–01	Middlesbrough	20	1		
2001–02	Middlesbrough	1	0	**63**	**4**
2001–02	*Cardiff C*	7	2	**7**	**2**
2002–03	Coventry C	30	1		
2003–04	Coventry C	5	0		
2003–04	*Reading*	3	0	**3**	**0**
2004–05	Coventry C	0	0	**35**	**1**
2004–05	Grimsby T	20	2	**20**	**2**
2004–05	Apoel	8	0	**8**	**0**
From Crook T.					
2005–06	Blackpool	1	0	**1**	**0**

GRAYSON, Simon (M) **433** **11**
H: 6 0 W: 13 07 b.Ripon 16-12-69
Source: Trainee.

1987–88	Leeds U	2	0		
1988–89	Leeds U	0	0		
1989–90	Leeds U	0	0		
1990–91	Leeds U	0	0		
1991–92	Leeds U	0	0	**2**	**0**
1991–92	Leicester C	13	0		
1992–93	Leicester C	24	1		
1993–94	Leicester C	40	1		
1994–95	Leicester C	34	0		
1995–96	Leicester C	41	2		
1996–97	Leicester C	36	0	**188**	**4**
1997–98	Aston Villa	33	0		
1998–99	Aston Villa	15	0	**48**	**0**
1999–2000	Blackburn R	34	0		
2000–01	Blackburn R	0	0		
2000–01	*Sheffield W*	5	0	**5**	**0**
2000–01	*Stockport Co*	13	0	**13**	**0**
2001–02	Blackburn R	0	0	**34**	**0**
2001–02	*Notts Co*	10	1	**10**	**1**
2001–02	*Bradford C*	7	0	**7**	**0**
2002–03	Blackpool	45	3		
2003–04	Blackpool	33	1		
2004–05	Blackpool	36	2		
2005–06	Blackpool	12	0	**126**	**6**

JONES, Lee (G) **238** **0**
H: 6 3 W: 14 04 b.Pontypridd 9-8-70
Source: Porth.

1993–94	Swansea C	0	0		
1994–95	Swansea C	2	0		
1995–96	Swansea C	1	0		
1995–96	*Crewe Alex*	0	0		
1996–97	Swansea C	1	0		
1997–98	Swansea C	2	0	**6**	**0**
1997–98	Bristol R	8	0		
1998–99	Bristol R	32	0		
1999–2000	Bristol R	36	0	**76**	**0**
2000–01	Stockport Co	27	0		
2001–02	Stockport Co	24	0		
2002–03	Stockport Co	24	0		
2003–04	Stockport Co	0	0	**75**	**0**
2003–04	Blackpool	21	0		
2004–05	Blackpool	29	0		
2005–06	Blackpool	31	0	**81**	**0**

JOSEPH, Marc (D) **322** **3**
H: 6 0 W: 12 05 b.Leicester 10-11-76
Source: Trainee.

1995–96	Cambridge U	12	0		
1996–97	Cambridge U	8	0		
1997–98	Cambridge U	41	0		
1998–99	Cambridge U	29	0		
1999–2000	Cambridge U	33	0		
2000–01	Cambridge U	30	0	**153**	**0**
2001–02	Peterborough U	44	2		
2002–03	Peterborough U	17	0	**61**	**2**
2002–03	Hull C	23	0		
2003–04	Hull C	32	1		
2004–05	Hull C	29	0		
2005–06	Hull C	5	0	**89**	**1**
2005–06	*Bristol C*	3	0	**3**	**0**
2005–06	Blackpool	16	0	**16**	**0**

KAY, Matty (M) **1** **0**
H: 5 9 W: 11 00 b.Blackpool 12-10-89

2005–06	Blackpool	1	0	**1**	**0**

MURPHY, John (F) **355** **103**
H: 6 2 W: 14 00 b.Whiston 18-10-76
Source: Trainee.

1994–95	Chester C	5	0		
1995–96	Chester C	18	3		
1996–97	Chester C	11	1		
1997–98	Chester C	27	4		
1998–99	Chester C	42	12	**103**	**20**
1999–2000	Blackpool	39	10		
2000–01	Blackpool	46	18		
2001–02	Blackpool	37	13		
2002–03	Blackpool	35	16		
2003–04	Blackpool	30	9		
2004–05	Blackpool	31	9		
2005–06	Blackpool	34	8	**252**	**83**

PARKER, Keigan (F) **207** **42**
H: 5 7 W: 10 05 b.Livingston 8-6-82
Source: St Johnstone BC. *Honours:* Scotland Youth, Under-21.

1998–99	St Johnstone	2	0		
1999–2000	St Johnstone	10	2		
2000–01	St Johnstone	37	9		
2001–02	St Johnstone	21	1		
2002–03	St Johnstone	31	1		
2003–04	St Johnstone	31	8	**132**	**21**
2004–05	Blackpool	35	9		
2005–06	Blackpool	40	12	**75**	**21**

PATERSON, Sean (M) **2** **0**
H: 5 11 W: 11 05 b.Greenock 26-3-87
Source: Scholar.

2004–05	Blackpool	2	0		
2005–06	Blackpool	0	0	**2**	**0**

POGLIACOMI, Les (G) **240** **0**
H: 6 4 W: 13 02 b.Sydney 3-5-76
Honours: Australia Schools, Under-20.

1994–95	Marconi Stallions	11	0		
1995–96	Marconi Stallions	1	0		
1996–97	Marconi Stallions	10	0	**22**	**0**
1997–98	Adelaide City	0	0		
1998–99	Wollongong W	22	0		
1999–2000	Wollongong W	34	0	**56**	**0**
2000–01	Parramatta Power	8	0		
2001–02	Parramatta Power	19	0	**27**	**0**
2002–03	Oldham Ath	37	0		
2003–04	Oldham Ath	46	0		
2004–05	Oldham Ath	37	0		
2005–06	Oldham Ath	0	0	**120**	**0**
2005–06	Blackpool	15	0	**15**	**0**

PRENDERGAST, Rory (F) **27** **0**
H: 5 8 W: 12 00 b.Pontefract 6-4-78
Source: Rochdale.

1995–96	Barnsley	0	0		
1996–97	Barnsley	0	0		
1997–98	Barnsley	0	0		
1998–99	York C	3	0	**3**	**0**
1998–99	Oldham Ath	0	0		
From Accrington S					
2005–06	Blackpool	24	0	**24**	**0**

SHAW, Matt (F) **11** **0**
H: 6 1 W: 11 09 b.Blackpool 17-5-84
Source: Stockport Co Trainee.

2001–02	Sheffield W	0	0		
2002–03	Sheffield W	0	0		
2003–04	Sheffield W	0	0		
2004–05	Sheffield W	0	0		
2004–05	Wrexham	1	0	**1**	**0**
2004–05	Blackpool	10	0		
2005–06	Blackpool	0	0	**10**	**0**

SOUTHERN, Keith (M) **135** **11**
H: 5 10 W: 12 06 b.Gateshead 24-4-81
Source: Trainee.

1998–99	Everton	0	0		
1999–2000	Everton	0	0		
2000–01	Everton	0	0		
2001–02	Everton	0	0		
2002–03	Everton	0	0		

2002–03 Blackpool 38 1
2003–04 Blackpool 28 2
2004–05 Blackpool 27 6
2005–06 Blackpool 42 2 **135 11**

VERNON, Scott (F) 103 25
H: 6 1 W: 11 06 b.Manchester 13-12-83
Source: Scholar.
2002–03 Oldham Ath 8 1
2003–04 Oldham Ath 45 12
2004–05 Oldham Ath 22 7 **75 20**
2004–05 *Blackpool* 4 3
2005–06 Blackpool 17 1 **21 4**
2005–06 *Colchester U* 7 1 **7 1**

WARRENDER, Danny (D) 15 0
H: 5 9 W: 11 06 b.Manchester 28-4-86
2005–06 Manchester C 0 0
2005–06 Blackpool 15 0 **15 0**

WHITTAKER, Danny (M) 0 0
H: 6 0 W: 11 10 b.Blackpool 13-1-87
Source: Scholar.
2004–05 Blackpool 0 0
2005–06 Blackpool 0 0

WILCOX, Jason (M) 396 36
H: 5 11 W: 11 01 b.Bolton 15-7-71
Source: Trainee. *Honours:* England B, 3 full caps.
1989–90 Blackburn R 1 0
1990–91 Blackburn R 18 0
1991–92 Blackburn R 38 4
1992–93 Blackburn R 33 4
1993–94 Blackburn R 33 6
1994–95 Blackburn R 27 5
1995–96 Blackburn R 10 3
1996–97 Blackburn R 28 2
1997–98 Blackburn R 31 4
1998–99 Blackburn R 30 3
1999–2000 Blackburn R 20 0 **269 31**
1999–2000 Leeds U 20 3
2000–01 Leeds U 17 0
2001–02 Leeds U 13 0
2002–03 Leeds U 25 1
2003–04 Leeds U 6 0 **81 4**
2004–05 Leicester C 14 1
2005–06 Leicester C 6 0 **20 1**
2005–06 Blackpool 26 0 **26 0**

WILES, Simon (F) 31 3
H: 5 11 W: 11 04 b.Preston 22-4-85
Source: Scholar.
2003–04 Blackpool 4 0
2004–05 Blackpool 0 0
2005–06 Blackpool 27 3 **31 3**

WOOD, Neil (M) 37 2
H: 5 10 W: 13 02 b.Manchester 4-1-83
Source: Trainee. *Honours:* England Youth.
1999–2000 Manchester U 0 0
2000–01 Manchester U 0 0
2001–02 Manchester U 0 0
2002–03 Manchester U 0 0
2003–04 Manchester U 0 0
2003–04 *Peterborough U* 3 1 **3 1**
2003–04 *Burnley* 10 1 **10 1**
2004–05 Coventry C 13 0
2005–06 Coventry C 4 0 **17 0**
2005–06 Blackpool 7 0 **7 0**

BOLTON W (8)

AL-HABSI, Ali (G) 62 0
H: 6 4 W: 12 06 b.Oman 30-12-81
Source: Al-Nasser, Al-Mudhaibi.
2003 Lyn 13 0
2004 Lyn 24 0
2005 Lyn 25 0 **62 0**
2005–06 Bolton W 0 0

BEN HAIM, Tal (D) 142 3
H: 5 11 W: 11 09 b.Rishon Le Zion 31-3-82
Source: Maccabi Tel Aviv. *Honours:* Israel 26 full caps.
2000–01 Maccabi Tel Aviv 1 0
2001–02 Maccabi Tel Aviv 29 1
2002–03 Maccabi Tel Aviv 30 0
2003–04 Maccabi Tel Aviv 26 1 **86 2**
2004–05 Bolton W 21 1
2005–06 Bolton W 35 0 **56 1**

BORGETTI, Jared (F) 405 227
H: 6 0 W: 12 04 b.Culiacan 14-8-73
Honours: Mexico 77 full caps, 38 goals.
1993–94 Atlas 2 0
1994–95 Atlas 29 13
1995–96 Atlas 32 8 **63 21**
1996–97 Santos (Mex) 41 20
1997–98 Santos (Mex) 28 14
1998–99 Santos (Mex) 38 19
1999–2000 Santos (Mex) 39 22
2000–01 Santos (Mex) 43 41
2001–02 Santos (Mex) 31 23
2002–03 Santos (Mex) 39 27
2003–04 Santos (Mex) 35 22 **294 188**
2004 Dorados 14 8 **14 8**
2005 Pachuca 15 8 **15 8**
2005–06 Bolton W 19 2 **19 2**

BUVAL, Bedi (F) 0 0
H: 5 11 W: 11 01 b.Domont 16-6-86
Source: Scholar.
2004–05 Bolton W 0 0
2005–06 Bolton W 0 0

CAMPO, Ivan (M) 280 15
H: 6 1 W: 12 10 b.San Sebastian 21-2-74
Honours: Spain 4 full caps.
1993–94 Alaves 11 1
1994–95 Alaves 23 1
1995–96 Alaves 11 0 **45 2**
1995–96 Valladolid 24 2 **24 2**
1996–97 Valencia 7 1 **7 1**
1997–98 Mallorca 33 1 **33 1**
1998–99 Real Madrid 27 1
1999–2000 Real Madrid 20 0
2000–01 Real Madrid 10 0
2001–02 Real Madrid 3 0 **60 1**
2002–03 Bolton W 31 2
2003–04 Bolton W 38 4
2004–05 Bolton W 27 0
2005–06 Bolton W 15 2 **111 8**

DAVIES, Kevin (F) 378 69
H: 6 0 W: 12 10 b.Sheffield 26-3-77
Source: Trainee. *Honours:* England Youth, Under-21.
1993–94 Chesterfield 24 4
1994–95 Chesterfield 41 11
1995–96 Chesterfield 30 4
1996–97 Chesterfield 34 3 **129 22**
1996–97 Southampton 0 0
1997–98 Southampton 25 9
1998–99 Blackburn R 21 1
1999–2000 Blackburn R 2 0 **23 1**
1999–2000 Southampton 23 6
2000–01 Southampton 27 1
2001–02 Southampton 23 2
2002–03 Southampton 9 1 **107 19**
2002–03 *Millwall* 9 3 **9 3**
2003–04 Bolton W 38 9
2004–05 Bolton W 35 8
2005–06 Bolton W 37 7 **110 24**

DIAGNE-FAYE, Aboulaye (M) 121 5
H: 6 2 W: 13 10 b.Dakar 26-2-78
Source: Ndiambour Louga. *Honours:* Senegal 6 full caps, 1 goal.
2001–02 Jeanne D'Arc Dakar 32 4 **32 4**
2002–03 Lens 15 0
2003–04 Lens 19 0 **34 0**
2004–05 Istres 28 0 **28 0**
2005–06 Bolton W 27 1 **27 1**

DIOUF, El Hadji (F) 199 34
H: 5 11 W: 11 11 b.Dakar 15-1-81
Honours: Senegal 37 full caps, 19 goals.
1998–99 Sochaux 15 0 **15 0**
1999–2000 Rennes 28 1 **28 1**
2000–01 Lens 28 8
2001–02 Lens 26 10 **54 18**
2002–03 Liverpool 29 3
2003–04 Liverpool 26 0
2004–05 Liverpool 0 0 **55 3**
2004–05 *Bolton W* 27 9
2005–06 Bolton W 20 3 **47 12**

DJETOU, Martin (M) 281 8
H: 5 11 W: 12 06 b.Brogohlo 15-12-74
Honours: France 6 full caps.
1992–93 Strasbourg 28 0
1993–94 Strasbourg 4 0
1994–95 Strasbourg 21 0
1995–96 Strasbourg 30 1 **83 1**
1996–97 Monaco 26 0
1997–98 Monaco 24 3
1998–99 Monaco 15 0
1999–2000 Monaco 22 0
2000–01 Monaco 29 1 **116 4**
2001–02 Parma 23 2 **23 2**
2002–03 Fulham 25 1
2003–04 Fulham 26 0 **51 1**
2004–05 Nice 5 0 **5 0**
2005–06 Bolton W 3 0 **3 0**
To Istres January 2006

FADIGA, Khalilou (M) 219 26
H: 6 0 W: 12 02 b.Dakar 30-12-74
Honours: Senegal full caps.
1995–96 Lommel 20 0
1996–97 Lommel 28 2 **48 2**
1997–98 FC Brugge 31 3
1998–99 FC Brugge 21 4
1999–2000 FC Brugge 17 2
2000–01 FC Brugge 3 4 **72 13**
2000–01 Auxerre 21 1
2001–02 Auxerre 27 8
2002–03 Auxerre 34 1 **82 10**
2004–05 Bolton W 5 0
2005–06 Bolton W 8 1 **13 1**
2005–06 *Derby Co* 4 0 **4 0**

FERNANDES, Fabrice (M) 162 11
H: 5 9 W: 11 07 b.Aubervilliers 29-10-79
1998–99 Rennes 15 2
1999–2000 Rennes 17 1
2000–01 Fulham 29 2 **29 2**
2000–01 Rangers 4 1 **4 1**
2001–02 Marseille 4 0 **4 0**
2001–02 Southampton 11 1
2001–02 Rennes 1 0 **33 3**
2002–03 Southampton 37 3
2003–04 Southampton 27 1
2004–05 Southampton 16 0
2005–06 Southampton 0 0 **91 5**
2005–06 Bolton W 1 0 **1 0**

FOJUT, Jaroslaw (D) 1 0
H: 6 2 W: 13 00 b.Legionowo 17-10-87
Source: Scholar. *Honours:* Poland Youth.
2005–06 Bolton W 1 0 **1 0**

GARDNER, Ricardo (D) 239 15
H: 5 9 W: 11 00 b.St Andrews 25-9-78
Source: Harbour View. *Honours:* Jamaica 60 full caps, 5 goals.
1998–99 Bolton W 30 2
1999–2000 Bolton W 29 5
2000–01 Bolton W 32 3
2001–02 Bolton W 31 3
2002–03 Bolton W 32 2
2003–04 Bolton W 22 0
2004–05 Bolton W 33 0
2005–06 Bolton W 30 0 **239 15**

GIANNAKOPOULOS, Stelios (M) 405 114
H: 5 8 W: 11 00 b.Athens 12-7-74
Honours: Greece 61 full caps, 12 goals.
1992–93 Ethnikos 32 6 **32 6**
1993–94 Paniliakos 26 9
1994–95 Paniliakos 31 10
1995–96 Paniliakos 27 7 **84 26**
1996–97 Olympiakos 31 7
1997–98 Olympiakos 31 3
1998–99 Olympiakos 23 7
1999–2000 Olympiakos 29 10
2000–01 Olympiakos 26 11
2001–02 Olympiakos 21 11
2002–03 Olympiakos 29 15 **190 64**
2003–04 Bolton W 31 2
2004–05 Bolton W 34 7
2005–06 Bolton W 34 9 **99 18**

HOWARTH, Chris (G) 0 0
b.Bolton 23-5-86
Source: Scholar.
2005–06 Bolton W 0 0
2005–06 *Stockport Co* 0 0

HUNT, Nicky (D) 81 1
H: 6 1 W: 13 07 b.Westhoughton 3-9-83
Source: Scholar. *Honours:* England Under-21.
2000–01 Bolton W 1 0

2001–02 Bolton W 0 0
2002–03 Bolton W 0 0
2003–04 Bolton W 31 1
2004–05 Bolton W 29 0
2005–06 Bolton W 20 0 **81 1**

JAASKELAINEN, Jussi (G) 397 0
H: 6 3 W: 12 10 b.Vaasa 19-4-75
Honours: Finland Youth, Under-21, 27 full caps.
1992 MP 6 0
1993 MP 6 0
1994 MP 26 0
1995 MP 26 0 **64 0**
1996 VPS 27 0
1997 VPS 27 0 **54 0**
1997–98 Bolton W 0 0
1998–99 Bolton W 34 0
1999–2000 Bolton W 34 0
2000–01 Bolton W 27 0
2001–02 Bolton W 34 0
2002–03 Bolton W 38 0
2003–04 Bolton W 38 0
2004–05 Bolton W 36 0
2005–06 Bolton W 38 0 **279 0**

JAIDI, Radhi (D) 43 8
H: 6 2 W: 14 00 b.Tunis 30-8-75
Source: Esperance. *Honours:* Tunisia 92 full caps, six goals.
2004–05 Bolton W 27 5
2005–06 Bolton W 16 3 **43 8**

JANSEN, Matt (F) 236 65
H: 5 11 W: 10 12 b.Carlisle 20-10-77
Source: Trainee. *Honours:* England Under-21.
1995–96 Carlisle U 0 0
1996–97 Carlisle U 19 1
1997–98 Carlisle U 23 9 **42 10**
1997–98 Crystal Palace 8 3
1998–99 Crystal Palace 18 7 **26 10**
1998–99 Blackburn R 11 2
1999–2000 Blackburn R 30 4
2000–01 Blackburn R 40 23
2001–02 Blackburn R 35 10
2002–03 Blackburn R 7 0
2002–03 *Coventry C* 9 2 **9 2**
2003–04 Blackburn R 19 2
2004–05 Blackburn R 7 2
2005–06 Blackburn R 4 0 **153 43**
2005–06 Bolton W 6 0 **6 0**

N'GOTTY, Bruno (D) 515 24
H: 6 1 W: 13 07 b.Lyon 10-6-71
Honours: France 6 full caps.
1989–90 Lyon 27 0
1990–91 Lyon 37 2
1991–92 Lyon 36 1
1992–93 Lyon 36 3
1993–94 Lyon 36 3
1994–95 Lyon 35 3 **207 12**
1995–96 Paris St Germain 24 1
1996–97 Paris St Germain 30 4
1997–98 Paris St Germain 26 2 **80 7**
1998–99 AC Milan 25 1
1999–2000 AC Milan 9 0 **34 1**
1999–2000 Venezia 16 0 **16 0**
2000–01 Marseille 30 0 **30 0**
2001–02 Bolton W 26 1
2002–03 Bolton W 23 1
2003–04 Bolton W 33 2
2004–05 Bolton W 37 0
2005–06 Bolton W 29 0 **148 4**

NAKATA, Hidetoshi (M) 276 41
H: 5 9 W: 11 05 b.Yamanashi 22-1-77
Honours: Japan 77 full caps, 11 goals.
1995 Bellmare 26 8
1996 Bellmare 26 2
1997 Bellmare 11 3
1998 Bellmare 11 3 **74 16**
1998–99 Perugia 33 10
1999–2000 Perugia 15 2 **48 12**
1999–2000 Roma 15 3
2000–01 Roma 15 2 **30 5**
2001–02 Parma 24 1
2002–03 Parma 31 4
2003–04 Parma 12 0 **67 5**
2003–04 Bologna 17 2 **17 2**
2004–05 Fiorentina 19 0 **19 0**
2005–06 Bolton W 21 1 **21 1**

NOLAN, Kevin (M) 212 32
H: 6 0 W: 14 00 b.Liverpool 24-6-82
Source: Scholar. *Honours:* England Youth, Under-20, Under-21.
1999–2000 Bolton W 4 0
2000–01 Bolton W 31 1
2001–02 Bolton W 35 8
2002–03 Bolton W 33 1
2003–04 Bolton W 37 9
2004–05 Bolton W 36 4
2005–06 Bolton W 36 9 **212 32**

O'BRIEN, Joey (M) 39 2
H: 5 11 W: 10 13 b.Dublin 17-2-86
Source: Scholar. *Honours:* Eire Youth, Under-21, 1 full cap.
2004–05 Bolton W 1 0
2004–05 *Sheffield W* 15 2 **15 2**
2005–06 Bolton W 23 0 **24 0**

OKOCHA, Jay-Jay (M) 360 73
H: 5 8 W: 11 00 b.Enugu 14-8-73
Source: Enugu Rangers, Neunkirchen.
Honours: Nigeria 65 full caps, 12 goals.
1992–93 Eintracht Frankfurt 20 2
1993–94 Eintracht Frankfurt 19 2
1994–95 Eintracht Frankfurt 27 6
1995–96 Eintracht Frankfurt 24 7 **90 17**
1996–97 Fenerbahce 33 16
1997–98 Fenerbahce 30 14 **63 30**
1998–99 Paris St Germain 25 4
1999–2000 Paris St Germain 23 2
2000–01 Paris St Germain 15 2
2001–02 Paris St Germain 20 4 **83 12**
2002–03 Bolton W 31 7
2003–04 Bolton W 35 0
2004–05 Bolton W 31 6
2005–06 Bolton W 27 1 **124 14**

PEDERSEN, Henrik (F) 247 83
H: 6 1 W: 13 03 b.Copenhagen 10-6-75
Honours: Denmark 3 full caps.
1995–96 Silkeborg 12 4
1996–97 Silkeborg 2 0
1997–98 Silkeborg 15 9
1998–99 Silkeborg 33 16
1999–2000 Silkeborg 28 13
2000–01 Silkeborg 32 20 **122 62**
2001–02 Bolton W 11 0
2002–03 Bolton W 33 7
2003–04 Bolton W 33 7
2004–05 Bolton W 27 6
2005–06 Bolton W 21 1 **125 21**

PEREZ, Oscar (M) 0 0
H: 5 9 W: 11 03 b.Oviedo 27-8-81
Source: Eibar, Oviedo, Lealtad, Cordoba.
Honours:
2005–06 Bolton W 0 0

POWELL, Rhys (D) 0 0
H: 5 8 W: 11 08 b.Cardiff 25-2-87
Source: Scholar. *Honours:* Wales Under-21.
2004–05 Bolton W 0 0
2005–06 Bolton W 0 0

SINCLAIR, James (F) 0 0
H: 5 6 W: 10 05 b.Newcastle 22-10-87
Source: Scholar.
2005–06 Bolton W 0 0

SISSONS, Robert (M) 0 0
H: 5 8 W: 11 02 b.Stockport 29-9-88
Source: Scholar. *Honours:* England Youth.
2005–06 Bolton W 0 0

SMITH, Johann (M) 0 0
b.Hartford 25-4-87
Source: Scholar.
2005–06 Bolton W 0 0

SPEED, Gary (M) 588 89
H: 5 10 W: 12 10 b.Deeside 8-9-69
Source: Trainee. *Honours:* Wales Youth, Under-21, 85 full caps, 7 goals.
1988–89 Leeds U 1 0
1989–90 Leeds U 25 3
1990–91 Leeds U 38 7
1991–92 Leeds U 41 7
1992–93 Leeds U 39 7
1993–94 Leeds U 36 10
1994–95 Leeds U 39 3
1995–96 Leeds U 29 2 **248 39**
1996–97 Everton 37 9
1997–98 Everton 21 7 **58 16**
1997–98 Newcastle U 13 1
1998–99 Newcastle U 38 4
1999–2000 Newcastle U 36 9
2000–01 Newcastle U 35 5
2001–02 Newcastle U 29 5
2002–03 Newcastle U 24 2
2003–04 Newcastle U 38 3 **213 29**
2004–05 Bolton W 38 1
2005–06 Bolton W 31 4 **69 5**

VAZ TE, Ricardo (F) 30 3
H: 6 2 W: 12 07 b.Lisbon 1-10-86
Source: Trainee. *Honours:* Portugal Youth.
2003–04 Bolton W 1 0
2004–05 Bolton W 7 0
2005–06 Bolton W 22 3 **30 3**

WALKER, Ian (G) 401 0
H: 6 2 W: 13 01 b.Watford 31-10-71
Source: Trainee. *Honours:* England Youth, Under-21, B, 4 full caps.
1989–90 Tottenham H 0 0
1990–91 Tottenham H 1 0
1990–91 *Oxford U* 2 0 **2 0**
1990–91 *Ipswich T* 0 0
1991–92 Tottenham H 18 0
1992–93 Tottenham H 17 0
1993–94 Tottenham H 11 0
1994–95 Tottenham H 41 0
1995–96 Tottenham H 38 0
1996–97 Tottenham H 37 0
1997–98 Tottenham H 29 0
1998–99 Tottenham H 25 0
1999–2000 Tottenham H 38 0
2000–01 Tottenham H 4 0 **259 0**
2001–02 Leicester C 35 0
2002–03 Leicester C 46 0
2003–04 Leicester C 37 0
2004–05 Leicester C 22 0 **140 0**
2005–06 Bolton W 0 0

Scholars
Augustyn, Blazej Szozepan; Cassidy, Matthew Stephen; Charlesworth, Mark; Ellis, Mark Ian; Fojut, Jaroslaw; Jamieson, Scott; Kazimierczak, Prezemek; Mountford, Sean; Roddy, Michael John; Sinclair, James Alexander; Sissons, Robert; Smith, Johann Anwar Ryan; Stott, Daniel Adam; Thompson, Leslie; Woolfe, Nathan Bret.

BOSTON U (9)

CANOVILLE, Lee (D) 157 3
H: 6 1 W: 12 00 b.Ealing 14-3-81
Source: Trainee. *Honours:* FA Schools, England Youth.
1998–99 Arsenal 0 0
1999–2000 Arsenal 0 0
2000–01 Arsenal 0 0
2000–01 *Northampton T* 2 0 **2 0**
2001–02 Torquay U 12 1
2002–03 Torquay U 36 0
2003–04 Torquay U 33 1
2004–05 Torquay U 31 0 **112 2**
2005–06 Boston U 43 1 **43 1**

CLARE, Daryl (F) 131 17
H: 5 9 W: 11 00 b.Jersey 1-8-78
Source: Trainee. *Honours:* Eire Under-21.
1995–96 Grimsby T 1 0
1996–97 Grimsby T 0 0
1997–98 Grimsby T 22 3
1998–99 Grimsby T 22 3
1999–2000 Grimsby T 17 3
1999–2000 *Northampton T* 10 3
2000–01 Grimsby T 17 0 **79 9**
2000–01 *Northampton T* 4 0 **14 3**
2000–01 *Cheltenham T* 4 0 **4 0**
2002–03 Boston U 7 1
2003–04 Boston U 0 0
2004–05 Chester C 7 1 **7 1**
2004–05 Boston U 19 3
2005–06 Boston U 1 0 **27 4**

CLARKE, Jamie (D) **112** **3**
H: 6 2 W: 12 03 b.Sunderland 18-9-82
Source: Scholar.
2001–02 Mansfield T 1 0
2002–03 Mansfield T 21 1
2003–04 Mansfield T 12 0 **34** **1**
2004–05 Rochdale 41 1
2005–06 Rochdale 22 0 **63** **1**
2005–06 Boston U 15 1 **15** **1**

DUDFIELD, Lawrie (F) **198** **35**
H: 6 1 W: 13 05 b.Southwark 7-5-80
Source: Kettering T.
1997–98 Leicester C 0 0
1998–99 Leicester C 0 0
1999–2000 Leicester C 2 0
2000–01 Leicester C 0 0 **2** **0**
2000–01 *Lincoln C* 3 0 **3** **0**
2000–01 *Chesterfield* 14 3 **14** **3**
2001–02 Hull C 38 12
2002–03 Hull C 21 1 **59** **13**
2002–03 Northampton T 10 1
2003–04 Northampton T 19 3
2003–04 Southend U 13 5
2004–05 Southend U 36 4 **49** **9**
2005–06 Northampton T 6 1 **35** **5**
2005–06 Boston U 36 5 **36** **5**

EDKINS, Ashley (M) **1** **0**
H: 5 9 W: 12 02 b.Leicester 23-12-86
Source: Scholar.
2005–06 Boston U 1 0 **1** **0**

ELLENDER, Paul (D) **137** **7**
H: 6 1 W: 12 07 b.Scunthorpe 21-10-74
Source: Trainee.
1992–93 Scunthorpe U 0 0
1993–94 Scunthorpe U 0 0
From Altrincham, Scarborough
2002–03 Boston
2003–04 Boston U 42 4
2004–05 Boston U 39 2
2005–06 Boston U 25 1 **132** **7**
2005–06 *Chester C* 5 0 **5** **0**

FORBES, Luke (M) **0** **0**
H: 5 9 W: 10 11 b.Lincoln 13-2-88
Source: Scholar.
2005–06 Boston U 0 0

GALBRAITH, David (M) **41** **1**
H: 5 8 W: 11 03 b.Luton 20-12-83
Source: Trainee.
2003–04 Tottenham H 0 0
2003–04 Northampton T 0 0
2004–05 Northampton T 25 1
2005–06 Northampton T 4 0 **29** **1**
2005–06 Boston U 12 0 **12** **0**

GREAVES, Mark (D) **296** **12**
H: 6 1 W: 13 00 b.Hull 22-1-75
Source: Brigg Town.
1996–97 Hull C 30 2
1997–98 Hull C 25 2
1998–99 Hull C 25 0
1999–2000 Hull C 38 3
2000–01 Hull C 30 2
2001–02 Hull C 26 1
2002–03 Hull C 3 0 **177** **10**
2002–03 Boston U 26 1
2003–04 Boston U 37 0
2004–05 Boston U 22 0
2005–06 Boston U 34 1 **119** **2**

HOLLAND, Chris (M) **265** **2**
H: 5 9 W: 11 05 b.Clitheroe 11-9-75
Source: Trainee. *Honours:* England Youth, Under-21.
1993–94 Preston NE 1 0 **1** **0**
1993–94 Newcastle U 3 0
1994–95 Newcastle U 0 0
1995–96 Newcastle U 0 0
1996–97 Newcastle U 0 0 **3** **0**
1996–97 Birmingham C 32 0
1997–98 Birmingham C 10 0
1998–99 Birmingham C 14 0
1999–2000 Birmingham C 14 0 **70** **0**
1999–2000 Huddersfield T 17 1
2000–01 Huddersfield T 29 0
2001–02 Huddersfield T 37 1
2002–03 Huddersfield T 34 0
2003–04 Huddersfield T 3 0 **120** **2**
2003–04 Boston U 5 0
2004–05 Boston U 32 0
2005–06 Boston U 34 0 **71** **0**

HURST, Tom (M) **1** **0**
H: 6 1 W: 11 00 b.Leicester 23-9-87
Source: Scholar.
2004–05 Boston U 1 0
2005–06 Boston U 0 0 **1** **0**

JOACHIM, Julian (F) **374** **97**
H: 5 6 W: 12 02 b.Boston 20-9-74
Source: Trainee. *Honours:* England Youth, Under-21.
1992–93 Leicester C 26 10
1993–94 Leicester C 36 11
1994–95 Leicester C 15 3
1995–96 Leicester C 22 1 **99** **25**
1995–96 Aston Villa 11 1
1996–97 Aston Villa 15 3
1997–98 Aston Villa 26 8
1998–99 Aston Villa 36 14
1999–2000 Aston Villa 33 6
2000–01 Aston Villa 20 7 **141** **39**
2001–02 Coventry C 16 1
2002–03 Coventry C 11 2
2003–04 Coventry C 29 8 **56** **11**
2004–05 Leeds U 27 2 **27** **2**
2004–05 *Walsall* 8 6 **8** **6**
2005–06 Boston U 43 14 **43** **14**

MAYLETT, Brad (M) **147** **9**
H: 5 8 W: 10 04 b.Manchester 24-12-80
Source: Trainee.
1998–99 Burnley 17 0
1999–2000 Burnley 0 0
2000–01 Burnley 12 0
2001–02 Burnley 10 0
2002–03 Burnley 6 0 **45** **0**
2002–03 *Swansea C* 6 0
2003–04 Swansea C 33 5
2004–05 Swansea C 16 0 **55** **5**
2004–05 *Boston U* 9 3
2005–06 Boston U 38 1 **47** **4**

McCANN, Austin (D) **219** **9**
H: 5 9 W: 11 13 b.Alexandria 21-1-80
Source: Wolverhampton W Trainee.
1997–98 Airdrieonians 14 0
1998–99 Airdrieonians 31 4
1999–2000 Airdrieonians 29 2
2000–01 Airdrieonians 20 1 **94** **7**
2000–01 Hearts 10 0
2001–02 Hearts 6 0
2002–03 Hearts 17 1
2003–04 Hearts 6 0 **39** **1**
2003–04 Clyde 6 0 **6** **0**
2004–05 Boston U 45 1
2005–06 Boston U 35 0 **80** **1**

MELTON, Steve (M) **105** **5**
H: 5 11 W: 12 03 b.Lincoln 3-10-78
Source: Trainee.
1995–96 Nottingham F 0 0
1996–97 Nottingham F 0 0
1997–98 Nottingham F 0 0
1998–99 Nottingham F 1 0
1999–2000 Nottingham F 2 0 **3** **0**
1999–2000 Stoke C 5 0 **5** **0**
2000–01 Brighton & HA 28 1
2001–02 Brighton & HA 10 1
2002–03 Brighton & HA 8 1 **46** **3**
2002–03 Hull C 25 0
2003–04 Hull C 5 0 **30** **0**
2003–04 Boston U 9 1
2004–05 Boston U 9 1
2005–06 Boston U 3 0 **21** **2**

NORRIS, Rob (M) **3** **0**
H: 5 10 W: 10 00 b.Nottingham 12-10-87
Source: Scholar.
2004–05 Boston U 2 0
2005–06 Boston U 1 0 **3** **0**

RUSK, Simon (M) **102** **8**
H: 5 11 W: 12 08 b.Peterborough 17-12-81
Source: Peterborough U.
2002–03 Boston U 18 2
2003–04 Boston U 19 0
2004–05 Boston U 31 3
2005–06 Boston U 34 3 **102** **8**

TALBOT, Stewart (M) **338** **23**
H: 6 0 W: 13 07 b.Birmingham 14-6-73
Source: Doncaster R, Moor Green.
1994–95 Port Vale 2 0
1995–96 Port Vale 20 0
1996–97 Port Vale 34 4
1997–98 Port Vale 42 6
1998–99 Port Vale 33 0
1999–2000 Port Vale 6 0 **137** **10**
2000–01 Rotherham U 38 5
2001–02 Rotherham U 38 1
2002–03 Rotherham U 15 1
2002–03 *Shrewsbury T* 5 0 **5** **0**
2003–04 Rotherham U 23 1 **114** **8**
2003–04 Brentford 15 2
2004–05 Brentford 37 1 **52** **3**
2005–06 Boston U 30 2 **30** **2**

THOMAS, Danny (M) **144** **10**
H: 5 7 W: 10 10 b.Leamington Spa 1-5-81
Source: Trainee.
1997–98 Nottingham F 0 0
1997–98 Leicester C 0 0
1998–99 Leicester C 0 0
1999–2000 Leicester C 3 0
2000–01 Leicester C 0 0
2001–02 Leicester C 0 0 **3** **0**
2001–02 Bournemouth 12 0
2002–03 Bournemouth 37 2
2003–04 Bournemouth 10 0 **59** **2**
2003–04 Boston U 8 3
2004–05 Boston U 39 3
2005–06 Boston U 35 2 **82** **8**

WHELAN, Noel (F) **309** **59**
H: 6 2 W: 12 03 b.Leeds 30-12-74
Source: Trainee. *Honours:* England Under-21.
1992–93 Leeds U 1 0
1993–94 Leeds U 16 0
1994–95 Leeds U 23 7
1995–96 Leeds U 8 0 **48** **7**
1995–96 Coventry C 21 8
1996–97 Coventry C 35 6
1997–98 Coventry C 21 6
1998–99 Coventry C 31 10
1999–2000 Coventry C 26 1 **134** **31**
2000–01 Middlesbrough 27 1
2001–02 Middlesbrough 19 4
2002–03 Middlesbrough 15 1 **61** **6**
2002–03 *Crystal Palace* 8 3 **8** **3**
2003–04 Millwall 15 4 **15** **4**
2003–04 Derby Co 8 0 **8** **0**
2004–05 Aberdeen 20 4 **20** **4**
2005–06 Boston U 15 4 **15** **4**
To Livingston March 2006

WHITE, Alan (D) **297** **11**
H: 6 0 W: 13 04 b.Darlington 22-3-76
Source: Derby Co Schoolboy.
1994–95 Middlesbrough 0 0
1995–96 Middlesbrough 0 0
1996–97 Middlesbrough 0 0
1997–98 Middlesbrough 0 0
1997–98 Luton T 28 1
1998–99 Luton T 33 1
1999–2000 Luton T 19 1 **80** **3**
1999–2000 *Colchester U* 4 0
2000–01 Colchester U 32 0
2001–02 Colchester U 33 3
2002–03 Colchester U 41 0
2003–04 Colchester U 33 1 **143** **4**
2004–05 Leyton Orient 26 0 **26** **0**
2004–05 Boston U 11 0
2005–06 Boston U 37 4 **48** **4**

WRIGHT, Chris (G) **1** **0**
H: 6 0 W: 13 00 b.Clacton 27-9-86
Source: Arsenal Scholar.
2005–06 Boston U 1 0 **1** **0**

BOURNEMOUTH (10)

BROADHURST, Karl (D) **165** **3**
H: 6 1 W: 11 07 b.Portsmouth 18-3-80
Source: Trainee.
1998–99 Bournemouth 0 0
1999–2000 Bournemouth 16 0

2000–01 Bournemouth 30 0
2001–02 Bournemouth 23 0
2002–03 Bournemouth 21 1
2003–04 Bournemouth 39 1
2004–05 Bournemouth 29 1
2005–06 Bournemouth 7 0 **165 3**

BROWNING, Marcus (M) 459 22
H: 6 0 W: 12 10 b.Bristol 22-4-71
Source: Trainee. *Honours:* Wales 5 full caps.
1989–90 Bristol R 1 0
1990–91 Bristol R 0 0
1991–92 Bristol R 11 0
1992–93 Bristol R 19 1
1992–93 *Hereford U* 7 5 **7 5**
1993–94 Bristol R 31 4
1994–95 Bristol R 41 2
1995–96 Bristol R 45 4
1996–97 Bristol R 26 2 **174 13**
1996–97 Huddersfield T 13 0
1997–98 Huddersfield T 14 0
1998–99 Huddersfield T 6 0 **33 0**
1998–99 Gillingham 4 0
1999–2000 Gillingham 1 0
2000–01 Gillingham 31 0
2001–02 Gillingham 42 3 **78 3**
2002–03 Bournemouth 43 1
2003–04 Bournemouth 42 0
2004–05 Bournemouth 40 0
2005–06 Bournemouth 42 0 **167 1**

COOKE, Stephen (M) 50 2
H: 5 8 W: 9 02 b.Walsall 15-2-83
Source: Scholar. *Honours:* England Youth, Under-20.
1999–2000 Aston Villa 0 0
2000–01 Aston Villa 0 0
2001–02 Aston Villa 0 0
2001–02 *Bournemouth* 7 0
2002–03 Aston Villa 3 0
2003–04 Aston Villa 0 0
2003–04 *Bournemouth* 3 0
2004–05 Aston Villa 0 0 **3 0**
2004–05 *Wycombe W* 6 0 **6 0**
2005–06 Bournemouth 31 2 **41 2**

COOPER, Shaun (D) 61 0
H: 5 10 W: 10 05 b.Newport (IW) 5-10-83
Source: School.
2000–01 Portsmouth 0 0
2001–02 Portsmouth 7 0
2002–03 Portsmouth 0 0
2003–04 Portsmouth 0 0
2003–04 *Leyton Orient* 9 0 **9 0**
2004–05 Portsmouth 0 0
2004–05 *Kidderminster H* 10 0 **10 0**
2005–06 Portsmouth 0 0 **7 0**
2005–06 Bournemouth 35 0 **35 0**

COUTTS, James (M) 12 0
H: 5 6 W: 9 01 b.Weymouth 15-4-87
Source: Southampton Juniors.
2004–05 Bournemouth 1 0
2005–06 Bournemouth 11 0 **12 0**

CUMMINGS, Warren (D) 119 5
H: 5 9 W: 11 05 b.Aberdeen 15-10-80
Source: Trainee. *Honours:* Scotland Under-21, 1 full cap.
1999–2000 Chelsea 0 0
2000–01 Chelsea 0 0
2000–01 *Bournemouth* 10 1
2000–01 *WBA* 3 0
2001–02 Chelsea 0 0
2001–02 *WBA* 14 0 **17 0**
2002–03 Chelsea 0 0
2002–03 Bournemouth 20 0
2003–04 Bournemouth 42 2
2004–05 Bournemouth 30 2
2005–06 Bournemouth 0 0 **102 5**

FLETCHER, Steve (F) 484 91
H: 6 2 W: 14 09 b.Hartlepool 26-7-72
Source: Trainee.
1990–91 Hartlepool U 14 2
1991–92 Hartlepool U 18 2 **32 4**
1992–93 Bournemouth 31 4
1993–94 Bournemouth 36 6
1994–95 Bournemouth 40 6
1995–96 Bournemouth 7 1
1996–97 Bournemouth 35 7
1997–98 Bournemouth 42 12
1998–99 Bournemouth 39 8
1999–2000 Bournemouth 36 7
2000–01 Bournemouth 45 9
2001–02 Bournemouth 2 0
2002–03 Bournemouth 35 5
2003–04 Bournemouth 41 9
2004–05 Bournemouth 36 9
2005–06 Bournemouth 27 4 **452 87**

FOLEY-SHERIDAN, Steven (M) 35 5
H: 5 4 W: 9 00 b.Dublin 10-2-86
Source: Trainee. *Honours:* Eire Youth.
2002–03 Aston Villa 0 0
2003–04 Aston Villa 0 0
2004–05 Aston Villa 0 0
2005–06 Aston Villa 0 0
2005–06 Bournemouth 35 5 **35 5**

GOWLING, Josh (D) 26 0
H: 6 3 W: 12 08 b.Coventry 29-11-83
Source: WBA Scholar.
2004–05 Herfolge 13 0 **13 0**
2005–06 Bournemouth 13 0 **13 0**

GRIFFITHS, Adam (D) 34 1
H: 6 2 W: 12 13 b.Sydney 21-8-79
2004–05 Ostend 27 0 **27 0**
2005–06 Watford 0 0
2005–06 Bournemouth 7 1 **7 1**

HART, Callum (D) 39 0
H: 6 0 W: 11 00 b.Cardiff 21-12-85
Source: Bristol C Scholar.
2005–06 Bournemouth 39 0 **39 0**

HAYTER, James (F) 316 84
H: 5 9 W: 10 13 b.Newport (IW) 9-4-79
Source: Trainee.
1996–97 Bournemouth 2 0
1997–98 Bournemouth 5 0
1998–99 Bournemouth 20 2
1999–2000 Bournemouth 31 2
2000–01 Bournemouth 40 11
2001–02 Bournemouth 44 7
2002–03 Bournemouth 45 9
2003–04 Bournemouth 44 14
2004–05 Bournemouth 39 19
2005–06 Bournemouth 46 20 **316 84**

HOWE, Eddie (D) 257 11
H: 5 11 W: 11 10 b.Amersham 29-11-77
Source: Trainee.
1995–96 Bournemouth 5 0
1996–97 Bournemouth 13 0
1997–98 Bournemouth 40 1
1998–99 Bournemouth 45 2
1999–2000 Bournemouth 28 1
2000–01 Bournemouth 31 2
2001–02 Bournemouth 38 4
2001–02 Portsmouth 1 0
2002–03 Portsmouth 1 0
2003–04 Portsmouth 0 0
2003–04 *Swindon T* 0 0
2004–05 Portsmouth 0 0 **2 0**
2004–05 Bournemouth 35 1
2005–06 Bournemouth 20 0 **255 11**

HUDSON, Kirk (F) 1 0
H: 5 8 W: 10 00 b.Rochford 12-12-86
Source: Ipswich T Scholar, Celtic.
2005–06 Bournemouth 1 0 **1 0**

MAHER, Shaun (D) 176 7
H: 6 2 W: 13 06 b.Dublin 20-6-78
Source: Bohemians.
1996–97 Bohemians 2 0
1997–98 Fulham 0 0
1997–98 Bohemians 11 0
1998–99 Bohemians 25 1
1999–2000 Bohemians 28 1
2000–01 Bohemians 0 0 **66 2**
2001–02 Bournemouth 31 0
2002–03 Bournemouth 8 2
2003–04 Bournemouth 29 1
2004–05 Bournemouth 36 2
2005–06 Bournemouth 6 0 **110 5**

MOSS, Neil (G) 185 0
H: 6 0 W: 13 10 b.New Milton 10-5-75
Source: Trainee.
1992–93 Bournemouth 1 0
1993–94 Bournemouth 6 0
1994–95 Bournemouth 8 0
1995–96 Bournemouth 7 0
1995–96 Southampton 0 0
1996–97 Southampton 3 0
1997–98 Southampton 0 0
1997–98 *Gillingham* 10 0 **10 0**
1998–99 Southampton 7 0
1999–2000 Southampton 9 0
2000–01 Southampton 3 0
2001–02 Southampton 2 0
2002–03 Southampton 0 0 **24 0**
2002–03 Bournemouth 33 0
2003–04 Bournemouth 46 0
2004–05 Bournemouth 46 0
2005–06 Bournemouth 4 0 **151 0**

O'CONNOR, James (D) 58 1
H: 5 10 W: 12 05 b.Birmingham 20-11-84
Source: Scholar.
2003–04 Aston Villa 0 0
2004–05 Aston Villa 0 0
2004–05 *Port Vale* 13 0 **13 0**
2004–05 Bournemouth 6 0
2005–06 Bournemouth 39 1 **45 1**

PITMAN, Brett (M) 19 1
H: 6 0 W: 11 00 b.Jersey 31-1-88
2005–06 Bournemouth 19 1 **19 1**

PURCHES, Stephen (M) 201 9
H: 5 11 W: 11 13 b.Ilford 14-1-80
Source: Trainee.
1998–99 West Ham U 0 0
1999–2000 West Ham U 0 0
2000–01 Bournemouth 34 0
2001–02 Bournemouth 41 2
2002–03 Bournemouth 44 3
2003–04 Bournemouth 42 3
2004–05 Bournemouth 14 1
2005–06 Bournemouth 26 0 **201 9**

RODRIGUES, Dani (F) 86 11
H: 5 11 W: 11 08 b.Oporto 3-3-80
Source: Farense.
1998–99 Bournemouth 5 0
1998–99 Southampton 0 0
1999–2000 Southampton 2 0
2000–01 Southampton 0 0
2000–01 *Bristol C* 4 0
2001–02 Southampton 0 0 **2 0**
2001–02 *Bristol C* 4 0 **8 0**
2002–03 Walsall 1 0 **1 0**
2002–03 Ionikos 14 1 **14 1**
2003–04 Yeovil T 4 4 **4 4**
2004–05 Bournemouth 23 3
2005–06 Bournemouth 29 3 **57 6**

ROWE, James (M) 4 0
H: 5 8 W: 11 00 b.Frimley 10-3-87
Source: Scholar.
2004–05 Bournemouth 2 0
2005–06 Bournemouth 2 0 **4 0**

STEWART, Gareth (G) 126 0
H: 6 0 W: 12 08 b.Preston 3-2-80
Source: Trainee. *Honours:* England Schools, Youth.
1996–97 Blackburn R 0 0
1997–98 Blackburn R 0 0
1998–99 Blackburn R 0 0
1999–2000 Bournemouth 3 0
2000–01 Bournemouth 35 0
2001–02 Bournemouth 45 0
2002–03 Bournemouth 1 0
2003–04 Bournemouth 0 0
2004–05 Bournemouth 0 0
2005–06 Bournemouth 42 0 **126 0**

TINDALL, Jason (M) 171 6
H: 6 1 W: 11 09 b.Stepney 15-11-77
Source: Trainee.
1996–97 Charlton Ath 0 0
1997–98 Charlton Ath 0 0
1998–99 Bournemouth 17 1
1999–2000 Bournemouth 8 0
2000–01 Bournemouth 45 1
2001–02 Bournemouth 44 3
2002–03 Bournemouth 27 1
2003–04 Bournemouth 19 0
2004–05 Bournemouth 0 0
2005–06 Bournemouth 11 0 **171 6**

YOUNG, Neil (D) 374 4
H: 5 9 W: 12 04 b.Harlow 31-8-73
Source: Trainee.

1991–92	Tottenham H	0	0		
1992–93	Tottenham H	0	0		
1993–94	Tottenham H	0	0		
1994–95	Bournemouth	32	0		
1995–96	Bournemouth	41	0		
1996–97	Bournemouth	44	0		
1997–98	Bournemouth	44	2		
1998–99	Bournemouth	44	1		
1999–2000	Bournemouth	37	0		
2000–01	Bournemouth	7	0		
2001–02	Bournemouth	11	0		
2002–03	Bournemouth	32	1		
2003–04	Bournemouth	10	0		
2004–05	Bournemouth	30	0		
2005–06	Bournemouth	42	0	**374**	**4**

BRADFORD C (11)

AINGE, Simon (D) 0 0
H: 6 1 W: 12 02 b.Bradford 18-2-88
Source: Scholar.

2005–06	Bradford C	0	0		

BENTHAM, Craig (D) 9 0
H: 5 9 W: 11 06 b.Bingley 7-3-85
Source: Scholar.

2004–05	Bradford C	2	0		
2005–06	Bradford C	7	0	**9**	**0**

BOWER, Mark (D) 191 8
H: 5 10 W: 11 00 b.Bradford 23-1-80
Source: Trainee.

1997–98	Bradford C	3	0		
1998–99	Bradford C	0	0		
1999–2000	Bradford C	0	0		
1999–2000	*York C*	15	1		
2000–01	Bradford C	0	0		
2000–01	*York C*	21	1	**36**	**2**
2001–02	Bradford C	10	2		
2002–03	Bradford C	37	0		
2003–04	Bradford C	14	0		
2004–05	Bradford C	46	2		
2005–06	Bradford C	45	2	**155**	**6**

BRIDGE-WILKINSON, Marc (M) 202 41
H: 5 6 W: 11 00 b.Coventry 16-3-79
Source: Trainee.

1996–97	Derby Co	0	0		
1997–98	Derby Co	0	0		
1998–99	Derby Co	1	0		
1998–99	*Carlisle U*	7	0	**7**	**0**
1999–2000	Derby Co	0	0	**1**	**0**
2000–01	Port Vale	42	9		
2001–02	Port Vale	19	6		
2002–03	Port Vale	31	9		
2003–04	Port Vale	32	7	**124**	**31**
2004–05	Stockport Co	22	2	**22**	**2**
2004–05	*Bradford C*	12	3		
2005–06	Bradford C	36	5	**48**	**8**

BROWN, Joe (M) 13 1
H: 5 10 W: 11 04 b.Bradford 3-4-88
Source: Scholar.

2005–06	Bradford C	13	1	**13**	**1**

CADAMARTERI, Danny (F) 210 22
H: 5 7 W: 13 05 b.Bradford 12-10-79
Source: Trainee. *Honours:* England Youth, Under-21.

1996–97	Everton	1	0		
1997–98	Everton	26	4		
1998–99	Everton	30	4		
1999–2000	Everton	17	1		
1999–2000	*Fulham*	5	1	**5**	**1**
2000–01	Everton	16	4		
2001–02	Everton	3	0	**93**	**13**
2001–02	Bradford C	14	2		
2002–03	Bradford C	20	0		
2003–04	Bradford C	18	3		
2004–05	Leeds U	0	0		
2004–05	Sheffield U	21	1	**21**	**1**
2005–06	Bradford C	39	2	**91**	**7**

CLARIDGE, Steve (F) 640 194
H: 6 0 W: 12 10 b.Portsmouth 10-4-66
Source: Portsmouth, Fareham T.

1984–85	Bournemouth	6	1		
1985–86	Bournemouth	1	0	**7**	**1**
From Weymouth, Basingstoke T					
1988–89	Crystal				
1988–89	Aldershot	37	9		
1989–90	Aldershot	25	10	**62**	**19**
1989–90	Cambridge U	20	4		
1990–91	Cambridge U	30	12		
1991–92	Cambridge U	29	12		
1992–93	Luton T	16	2	**16**	**2**
1992–93	Cambridge U	29	7		
1993–94	Cambridge U	24	11	**132**	**46**
1993–94	Birmingham C	18	7		
1994–95	Birmingham C	42	20		
1995–96	Birmingham C	28	8	**88**	**35**
1995–96	Leicester C	14	5		
1996–97	Leicester C	32	11		
1997–98	Leicester C	17	0	**63**	**16**
1997–98	*Portsmouth*	10	2		
1997–98	Wolverhampton W	5	0	**5**	**0**
1998–99	Portsmouth	39	9		
1999–2000	Portsmouth	34	14		
2000–01	Portsmouth	31	11	**114**	**36**
2000–01	*Millwall*	6	3		
2001–02	Millwall	41	17		
2002–03	Millwall	44	9	**91**	**29**
From Weymouth					
2004–05	Brighton & HA	5	0	**5**	**0**
2004–05	Brentford	4	0	**4**	**0**
2004–05	*Wycombe W*	19	4	**19**	**4**
2005–06	Gillingham	1	0	**1**	**0**
2005–06	Bradford C	26	5	**26**	**5**
2005–06	*Walsall*	7	1	**7**	**1**

COLBECK, Joe (M) 11 0
H: 5 10 W: 10 12 b.Bradford 29-11-86
Source: Scholar.

2004–05	Bradford C	0	0		
2005–06	Bradford C	11	0	**11**	**0**

COOKE, Andy (F) 310 81
H: 6 0 W: 12 07 b.Shrewsbury 20-1-74
Source: Newtown.

1994–95	Burnley	0	0		
1995–96	Burnley	23	5		
1996–97	Burnley	31	13		
1997–98	Burnley	34	16		
1998–99	Burnley	36	9		
1999–2000	Burnley	36	7		
2000–01	Burnley	11	2	**171**	**52**
2000–01	Stoke C	22	6		
2001–02	Stoke C	35	9		
2002–03	Stoke C	31	6		
2003–04	Stoke C	0	0	**88**	**21**
From Pusan Icons.					
2004–05	Bradford C	20	4		
2005–06	Bradford C	17	1	**37**	**5**
2005–06	*Darlington*	14	3	**14**	**3**

CROOKS, Lee (M) 211 4
H: 6 2 W: 12 01 b.Wakefield 14-1-78
Source: Trainee. *Honours:* England Youth.

1994–95	Manchester C	0	0		
1995–96	Manchester C	0	0		
1996–97	Manchester C	15	0		
1997–98	Manchester C	5	0		
1998–99	Manchester C	34	1		
1999–2000	Manchester C	20	1		
2000–01	Manchester C	2	0	**76**	**2**
2000–01	*Northampton T*	3	0	**3**	**0**
2000–01	Barnsley	0	0		
2001–02	Barnsley	26	0		
2002–03	Barnsley	18	0		
2003–04	Barnsley	23	0	**67**	**0**
2004–05	Bradford C	32	1		
2005–06	Bradford C	15	0	**47**	**1**
2005–06	*Notts Co*	18	1	**18**	**1**

DENTON, Sam (D) 0 0
H: 6 2 W: 13 02 b.Leeds 31-7-86
Source: Scholar.

2004–05	Bradford C	0	0		
2005–06	Bradford C	0	0		

EDGHILL, Richard (D) 244 2
H: 5 9 W: 12 01 b.Oldham 23-9-74
Source: Trainee. *Honours:* England Under-21.

1992–93	Manchester C	0	0		
1993–94	Manchester C	22	0		
1994–95	Manchester C	14	0		
1995–96	Manchester C	13	0		
1996–97	Manchester C	0	0		
1997–98	Manchester C	36	0		
1998–99	Manchester C	38	0		
1999–2000	Manchester C	41	1		
2000–01	Manchester C	6	0		
2000–01	*Birmingham C*	3	0	**3**	**0**
2001–02	Manchester C	11	0	**181**	**1**
2002–03	Wigan Ath	0	0		
2002–03	Sheffield U	1	0	**1**	**0**
2003–04	QPR	20	0		
2004–05	QPR	20	0	**40**	**0**
2005–06	Bradford C	19	1	**19**	**1**

ELLIS, Danny (D) 0 0
H: 6 0 W: 12 00 b.Bradford 23-11-85
Source: Scholar.

2005–06	Bradford C	0	0		

EMANUEL, Lewis (D) 139 4
H: 5 8 W: 12 01 b.Bradford 14-10-83
Source: Scholar. *Honours:* England Schools, Youth.

2001–02	Bradford C	9	0		
2002–03	Bradford C	29	0		
2003–04	Bradford C	28	2		
2004–05	Bradford C	36	0		
2005–06	Bradford C	37	2	**139**	**4**

FORREST, Danny (F) 50 5
H: 5 10 W: 11 07 b.Keighley 23-10-84
Source: Trainee. *Honours:* England Youth.

2002–03	Bradford C	17	3		
2003–04	Bradford C	13	0		
2004–05	Bradford C	20	2		
2005–06	Bradford C	0	0	**50**	**5**

HOLLOWAY, Darren (D) 221 2
H: 6 0 W: 12 05 b.Crook 3-10-77
Source: Trainee. *Honours:* England Under-21.

1995–96	Sunderland	0	0		
1996–97	Sunderland	0	0		
1997–98	Sunderland	32	0		
1997–98	*Carlisle U*	5	0	**5**	**0**
1998–99	Sunderland	6	0		
1999–2000	Sunderland	15	0		
1999–2000	*Bolton W*	4	0	**4**	**0**
2000–01	Sunderland	5	0	**58**	**0**
2000–01	Wimbledon	31	0		
2001–02	Wimbledon	32	0		
2002–03	Wimbledon	16	0		
2003–04	Wimbledon	13	0	**92**	**0**
2003–04	*Scunthorpe U*	5	1	**5**	**1**
2004–05	Bradford C	33	1		
2005–06	Bradford C	24	0	**57**	**1**

HOWARTH, Russell (G) 31 0
H: 6 2 W: 14 05 b.York 27-3-82
Source: Scholar. *Honours:* England Youth, Under-20.

1999–2000	York C	6	0		
2000–01	York C	0	0		
2001–02	York C	2	0		
2002–03	York C	0	0	**8**	**0**
2002–03	Tranmere R	3	0		
2003–04	Tranmere R	1	0		
2004–05	Tranmere R	8	0	**12**	**0**
2005–06	Bradford C	11	0	**11**	**0**

KEARNEY, Tom (M) 54 2
H: 5 11 W: 10 08 b.Liverpool 7-10-81
Source: Trainee.

1999–2000	Everton	0	0		
2000–01	Everton	0	0		
2001–02	Everton	0	0		
2001–02	Bradford C	5	0		
2002–03	Bradford C	4	0		
2003–04	Bradford C	17	0		
2004–05	Bradford C	13	1		
2005–06	Bradford C	15	1	**54**	**2**

McGUIRE, Patrick (M) **0 0**
H: 5 10 W: 10 07 b.Bradford 29-7-87
Source: Scholar.

2005–06	Bradford C	0	0		

MORRISON, Owen (M) **121 11**
H: 5 8 W: 11 12 b.Derry 8-12-81
Source: Trainee. *Honours:* Northern Ireland Schools, Youth, Under-21.

1998–99	Sheffield W	1	0		
1999–2000	Sheffield W	0	0		
2000–01	Sheffield W	30	6		
2001–02	Sheffield W	24	2		
2002–03	Sheffield W	1	0	**56**	**8**
2002–03	*Hull C*	2	0	**2**	**0**
2002–03	Sheffield U	8	0	**8**	**0**
2003–04	Stockport Co	22	1		
2004–05	Stockport Co	1	0	**23**	**1**
2004–05	Bradford C	22	2		
2005–06	Bradford C	10	0	**32**	**2**

MUIRHEAD, Ben (M) **108 4**
H: 5 9 W: 11 02 b.Doncaster 5-1-83
Source: Trainee. *Honours:* England Youth.

1999–2000	Manchester U	0	0		
2000–01	Manchester U	0	0		
2001–02	Manchester U	0	0		
2002–03	Manchester U	0	0		
2002–03	Bradford C	8	0		
2003–04	Bradford C	28	2		
2004–05	Bradford C	40	1		
2005–06	Bradford C	32	1	**108**	**4**

PENFORD, Tom (M) **20 0**
H: 5 10 W: 11 03 b.Leeds 5-1-85
Source: Scholar.

2002–03	Bradford C	3	0		
2003–04	Bradford C	4	0		
2004–05	Bradford C	3	0		
2005–06	Bradford C	10	0	**20**	**0**

PETTA, Bobby (M) **170 14**
H: 5 7 W: 11 05 b.Rotterdam 6-8-74
Source: Feyenoord.

1996–97	Ipswich T	6	0		
1997–98	Ipswich T	32	7		
1998–99	Ipswich T	32	2	**70**	**9**
1999–2000	Celtic	12	0		
2000–01	Celtic	20	0		
2001–02	Celtic	18	0		
2002–03	Celtic	2	0		
2003–04	Celtic	0	0		
2003–04	*Fulham*	9	0	**9**	**0**
2004–05	Celtic	0	0	**52**	**0**
2004–05	Darlington	12	1	**12**	**1**
2005–06	Bradford C	27	4	**27**	**4**

RICHARDSON, Luke (D) **0 0**
H: 5 11 W: 11 04 b.Keighley 11-7-86
Source: Scholar.

2005–06	Bradford C	0	0		

RICKETTS, Donovan (G) **40 0**
H: 6 1 W: 11 05 b.Kingston 7-6-77
Source: Village U.

2003–04	Bolton W	0	0		
2004–05	Bolton W	0	0		
2004–05	Bradford C	4	0		
2005–06	Bradford C	36	0	**40**	**0**

SANASY, Kevin (F) **9 1**
H: 5 8 W: 10 05 b.Leeds 2-11-84
Source: Scholar.

2002–03	Bradford C	1	0		
2003–04	Bradford C	5	1		
2004–05	Bradford C	3	0		
2005–06	Bradford C	0	0	**9**	**1**

SCHUMACHER, Steven (M) **77 7**
H: 5 10 W: 11 00 b.Liverpool 30-4-84
Source: Scholar. *Honours:* England Youth.

2000–01	Everton	0	0		
2001–02	Everton	0	0		
2002–03	Everton	0	0		
2003–04	Everton	0	0		
2003–04	*Carlisle U*	4	0	**4**	**0**
2004–05	Bradford C	43	6		
2005–06	Bradford C	30	1	**73**	**7**

STEWART, Damion (D) **23 1**
H: 6 3 W: 13 10 b.Jamaica 18-8-80
Source: Harbour View. *Honours:* Jamaica full caps.

2005–06	Bradford C	23	1	**23**	**1**

SWIFT, John (D) **10 0**
H: 5 7 W: 10 06 b.Leeds 20-9-84
Source: Scholar.

2004–05	Bradford C	5	0		
2005–06	Bradford C	5	0	**10**	**0**

SYMES, Michael (F) **20 4**
H: 6 3 W: 12 04 b.Gt Yarmouth 31-10-83
Source: Scholar.

2001–02	Everton	0	0		
2002–03	Everton	0	0		
2003–04	Everton	0	0		
2003–04	*Crewe Alex*	4	1	**4**	**1**
2004–05	Bradford C	12	2		
2004–05	*Darlington*	0	0		
2005–06	Bradford C	3	1	**15**	**3**
2005–06	*Stockport Co*	1	0	**1**	**0**

WETHERALL, David (D) **419 27**
H: 6 3 W: 13 12 b.Sheffield 14-3-71
Source: School. *Honours:* England Schools.

1989–90	Sheffield W	0	0		
1990–91	Sheffield W	0	0		
1991–92	Leeds U	1	0		
1992–93	Leeds U	13	1		
1993–94	Leeds U	32	1		
1994–95	Leeds U	38	3		
1995–96	Leeds U	34	4		
1996–97	Leeds U	29	0		
1997–98	Leeds U	34	3		
1998–99	Leeds U	21	0	**202**	**12**
1999–2000	Bradford C	38	2		
2000–01	Bradford C	18	1		
2001–02	Bradford C	19	2		
2002–03	Bradford C	17	0		
2003–04	Bradford C	34	1		
2004–05	Bradford C	45	4		
2005–06	Bradford C	46	5	**217**	**15**

WINDASS, Dean (F) **532 167**
H: 5 10 W: 12 03 b.North Ferriby 1-4-69
Source: N Ferriby U.

1991–92	Hull C	32	6		
1992–93	Hull C	41	7		
1993–94	Hull C	43	23		
1994–95	Hull C	44	17		
1995–96	Hull C	16	4	**176**	**57**
1995–96	Aberdeen	20	6		
1996–97	Aberdeen	29	10		
1997–98	Aberdeen	24	5	**73**	**21**
1998–99	Oxford U	33	15	**33**	**15**
1998–99	Bradford C	12	3		
1999–2000	Bradford C	38	10		
2000–01	Bradford C	24	3		
2000–01	Middlesbrough	8	2		
2001–02	Middlesbrough	27	1		
2001–02	*Sheffield W*	2	0	**2**	**0**
2002–03	Middlesbrough	2	0	**37**	**3**
2002–03	Sheffield U	20	6	**20**	**6**
2003–04	Bradford C	36	6		
2004–05	Bradford C	41	27		
2005–06	Bradford C	40	16	**191**	**65**

WRIGHT, Jake (D) **1 0**
H: 5 10 W: 11 07 b.Keighley 11-3-86
Source: Scholar.

2005–06	Bradford C	1	0	**1**	**0**

BRENTFORD (12)

BANKOLE, Ademola (G) **64 0**
H: 6 3 W: 13 00 b.Lagos 9-9-69
Source: Leyton Orient.

1996–97	Crewe Alex	3	0		
1997–98	Crewe Alex	3	0		
1998–99	QPR	0	0		
1998–99	*Grimsby T*	0	0		
1999–2000	QPR	1	0	**1**	**0**
1999–2000	*Bradford C*	0	0		
2000–01	Crewe Alex	21	0		
2001–02	Crewe Alex	28	0		
2002–03	Crewe Alex	3	0		
2003–04	Crewe Alex	0	0	**58**	**0**
2004–05	Brentford	3	0		
2005–06	Brentford	2	0	**5**	**0**

BROOKER, Paul (M) **271 23**
H: 5 8 W: 10 00 b.Hammersmith 25-11-76
Source: Trainee.

1995–96	Fulham	20	2		
1996–97	Fulham	26	2		
1997–98	Fulham	9	0		
1998–99	Fulham	1	0		
1999–2000	Fulham	0	0	**56**	**4**
1999–2000	*Brighton & HA*	15	2		
2000–01	Brighton & HA	41	3		
2001–02	Brighton & HA	41	4		
2002–03	Brighton & HA	37	6	**134**	**15**
2003–04	Leicester C	3	0	**3**	**0**
2003–04	*Reading*	11	0		
2004–05	Reading	31	0	**42**	**0**
2005–06	Brentford	36	4	**36**	**4**

CHARLES, Darius (M) **3 0**
H: 6 1 W: 13 05 b.Ealing 10-12-87
Source: Scholar.

2004–05	Brentford	1	0		
2005–06	Brentford	2	0	**3**	**0**

DOBSON, Michael (D) **178 3**
H: 6 0 W: 12 04 b.Isleworth 9-4-81
Source: Trainee.

1999–2000	Brentford	0	0		
2000–01	Brentford	26	0		
2001–02	Brentford	39	0		
2002–03	Brentford	46	1		
2003–04	Brentford	42	1		
2004–05	Brentford	18	1		
2005–06	Brentford	6	0	**177**	**3**
2005–06	*Reading*	1	0	**1**	**0**

FITZGERALD, Scott (F) **90 17**
H: 5 11 W: 12 00 b.Hillingdon 18-11-79
Source: Northwood.

2002–03	Watford	4	1		
2003–04	Watford	44	10		
2004–05	Watford	7	0	**55**	**11**
2004–05	*Swansea C*	3	0	**3**	**0**
2004–05	*Leyton Orient*	1	0	**1**	**0**
2004–05	Brentford	12	4		
2005–06	Brentford	11	1	**23**	**5**
2005–06	*Oxford U*	3	1	**3**	**1**
2005–06	*Walsall*	5	0	**5**	**0**

FITZGERALD, Scott B (D) **338 2**
H: 6 1 W: 13 00 b.Westminster 13-8-69
Source: Trainee. *Honours:* Eire Under-21, B.

1988–89	Wimbledon	0	0		
1989–90	Wimbledon	1	0		
1990–91	Wimbledon	0	0		
1991–92	Wimbledon	36	1		
1992–93	Wimbledon	20	0		
1993–94	Wimbledon	28	0		
1994–95	Wimbledon	17	0		
1995–96	Wimbledon	4	0		
1995–96	*Sheffield U*	6	0	**6**	**0**
1996–97	Wimbledon	0	0	**106**	**1**
1996–97	*Millwall*	7	0		
1997–98	Millwall	18	0		
1998–99	Millwall	32	1		
1999–2000	Millwall	31	0		
2000–01	Millwall	1	0	**89**	**1**
2000–01	Colchester U	30	0		
2001–02	Colchester U	37	0		
2002–03	Colchester U	26	0		
2003–04	Colchester U	23	0	**116**	**0**
2003–04	*Brentford*	9	0		
2004–05	Brentford	12	0		
2005–06	Brentford	0	0	**21**	**0**

FRAMPTON, Andrew (D) **130 3**
H: 5 11 W: 10 10 b.Wimbledon 3-9-79
Source: Trainee.

1998–99	Crystal Palace	6	0		
1999–2000	Crystal Palace	9	0		
2000–01	Crystal Palace	10	0		
2001–02	Crystal Palace	2	0		
2002–03	Crystal Palace	1	0	**28**	**0**
2002–03	Brentford	15	0		
2003–04	Brentford	16	0		
2004–05	Brentford	35	0		
2005–06	Brentford	36	3	**102**	**3**

GAYLE, Marcus (D) 528 66
H: 6 2 W: 12 09 b.Hammersmith 27-9-70
Source: Trainee. *Honours:* England Youth. Jamaica 14 full caps, 3 goals.
1988–89 Brentford 3 0
1989–90 Brentford 9 0
1990–91 Brentford 33 6
1991–92 Brentford 38 6
1992–93 Brentford 38 4
1993–94 Brentford 35 6
1993–94 Wimbledon 10 0
1994–95 Wimbledon 23 2
1995–96 Wimbledon 34 5
1996–97 Wimbledon 36 8
1997–98 Wimbledon 30 2
1998–99 Wimbledon 35 10
1999–2000 Wimbledon 36 7
2000–01 Wimbledon 32 3 **236 37**
2000–01 Rangers 4 0 **4 0**
2001–02 Watford 36 4
2002–03 Watford 31 0
2003–04 Watford 32 1
2004–05 Watford 3 0 **102 5**
2004–05 Brentford 6 0
2005–06 Brentford 24 2 **186 24**

HUTCHINSON, Eddie (M) 117 8
H: 6 2 W: 13 00 b.Kingston 23-2-82
Source: Sutton U.
2000–01 Brentford 7 0
2001–02 Brentford 9 0
2002–03 Brentford 23 0
2003–04 Brentford 36 5
2004–05 Brentford 15 1
2005–06 Brentford 27 2 **117 8**

IDE, Charlie (M) 1 0
H: 5 9 W: 11 00 b.Sunbury 10-5-88
2004–05 Brentford 1 0
2005–06 Brentford 0 0 **1 0**

LEWIS, Junior (M) 189 15
H: 6 2 W: 13 00 b.Wembley 9-10-73
Source: Trainee.
1992–93 Fulham 6 0 **6 0**
From Dover, Hendon
1999–2000 Gillingham 42 6
2000–01 Gillingham 17 2 **59 8**
2000–01 Leicester C 15 0
2001–02 Leicester C 6 0
2001–02 *Brighton & HA* 15 3 **15 3**
2002–03 Leicester C 9 1
2002–03 *Swindon T* 9 0
2003–04 Leicester C 0 0 **30 1**
2003–04 *Swindon T* 4 0 **13 0**
2003–04 *Hull C* 13 1
2004–05 Hull C 39 2
2005–06 Hull C 0 0 **52 3**
2005–06 Brentford 14 0 **14 0**

MASTERS, Clark (G) 0 0
H: 6 3 W: 13 12 b.Hastings 31-5-87
Source: Scholar.
2005–06 Brentford 0 0

MOLESKI, George (M) 1 0
H: 5 7 W: 11 09 b.Hillingdon 24-7-87
Source: Scholar.
2004–05 Brentford 1 0
2005–06 Brentford 0 0 **1 0**

MOUSINHO, John (D) 7 0
H: 6 1 W: 12 07 b.Buckingham 30-4-86
Source: Univ of Notre Dame.
2005–06 Brentford 7 0 **7 0**

NELSON, Stuart (G) 97 0
H: 6 1 W: 12 12 b.Stroud 17-9-81
Source: Doncaster R, Hucknall T.
2003–04 Brentford 9 0
2004–05 Brentford 43 0
2005–06 Brentford 45 0 **97 0**

NEWMAN, Ricky (D) 359 13
H: 5 10 W: 12 06 b.Guildford 5-8-70
Source: Trainee.
1987–88 Crystal Palace 0 0
1988–89 Crystal Palace 0 0
1989–90 Crystal Palace 0 0
1990–91 Crystal Palace 0 0
1991–92 Crystal Palace 0 0
1991–92 *Maidstone U* 10 1 **10 1**
1992–93 Crystal Palace 2 0
1993–94 Crystal Palace 11 0
1994–95 Crystal Palace 35 3 **48 3**
1995–96 Millwall 36 1
1996–97 Millwall 41 3
1997–98 Millwall 35 1
1998–99 Millwall 24 0
1999–2000 Millwall 14 0 **150 5**
1999–2000 *Reading* 7 1
2000–01 Reading 39 0
2001–02 Reading 0 0
2002–03 Reading 28 0
2003–04 Reading 30 0
2004–05 Reading 17 0 **121 1**
2005–06 Brentford 30 3 **30 3**

O'CONNOR, Kevin (F) 197 16
H: 5 11 W: 12 00 b.Blackburn 24-2-82
Source: Trainee. *Honours:* Eire Under-21.
1999–2000 Brentford 6 0
2000–01 Brentford 11 1
2001–02 Brentford 25 0
2002–03 Brentford 45 5
2003–04 Brentford 43 1
2004–05 Brentford 37 2
2005–06 Brentford 30 7 **197 16**

OSBORNE, Karleigh (D) 2 0
H: 6 2 W: 12 04 b.Southall 19-3-88
Source: Scholar.
2004–05 Brentford 1 0
2005–06 Brentford 1 0 **2 0**

OWUSU, Lloyd (F) 299 95
H: 6 2 W: 14 00 b.Slough 12-12-76
Source: Slough T.
1998–99 Brentford 46 22
1999–2000 Brentford 41 12
2000–01 Brentford 33 10
2001–02 Brentford 44 20
2002–03 Sheffield W 32 4
2003–04 Sheffield W 20 5 **52 9**
2003–04 Reading 16 4
2004–05 Reading 25 6 **41 10**
2005–06 Brentford 42 12 **206 76**

PETERS, Ryan (F) 30 2
H: 5 8 W: 10 05 b.Wandsworth 21-8-87
Source: Scholar.
2000–01 Southampton 0 0
2001–02 Southampton 0 0
2001–02 Brentford 0 0
2002–03 Brentford 11 1
2003–04 Brentford 9 0
2004–05 Brentford 0 0
2005–06 Brentford 10 1 **30 2**

RANKIN, Isiah (F) 215 42
H: 5 10 W: 11 00 b.London 22-5-78
Source: Trainee.
1995–96 Arsenal 0 0
1996–97 Arsenal 0 0
1997–98 Arsenal 1 0 **1 0**
1997–98 *Colchester U* 11 5 **11 5**
1998–99 Bradford C 27 4
1999–2000 Bradford C 9 0
1999–2000 *Birmingham C* 13 4 **13 4**
2000–01 Bradford C 1 0 **37 4**
2000–01 *Bolton W* 16 2 **16 2**
2000–01 Barnsley 9 1
2001–02 Barnsley 9 1
2002–03 Barnsley 9 1
2003–04 Barnsley 20 5 **47 8**
2003–04 Grimsby T 12 4 **12 4**
2004–05 Brentford 41 8
2005–06 Brentford 37 7 **78 15**

RHODES, Alex (F) 42 5
H: 5 9 W: 10 04 b.Cambridge 23-1-82
Source: Newmarket T.
2003–04 Brentford 3 1
2004–05 Brentford 22 3
2005–06 Brentford 17 1 **42 5**

SKULASON, Olafur-Ingi (M) 2 0
H: 6 0 W: 11 10 b.Reykjavik 1-4-83
Source: Fylkir. *Honours:* Iceland Youth, Under-21, 2 full caps.
2001–02 Arsenal 0 0
2002–03 Arsenal 0 0
2003–04 Arsenal 0 0
2004–05 Arsenal 0 0
2005–06 Brentford 2 0 **2 0**

SODJE, Sam (D) 83 12
H: 6 0 W: 12 00 b.Greenwich 29-5-79
Source: Stevenage B, Margate. *Honours:* Nigeria full caps.
2004–05 Brentford 40 7
2005–06 Brentford 43 5 **83 12**

STEELE, Aaron (M) 0 0
H: 5 10 W: 12 04 b.Twickenham 1-2-87
Source: Scholar.
2005–06 Brentford 0 0

TABB, Jay (M) 128 20
H: 5 7 W: 10 00 b.Tooting 21-2-84
Source: Trainee. *Honours:* Eire Under-21.
2000–01 Brentford 2 0
2001–02 Brentford 3 0
2002–03 Brentford 5 0
2003–04 Brentford 36 9
2004–05 Brentford 40 5
2005–06 Brentford 42 6 **128 20**

TILLEN, Sam (D) 33 0
H: 5 10 W: 11 09 b.Reading 16-4-85
Source: Trainee. *Honours:* England Youth.
2002–03 Chelsea 0 0
2003–04 Chelsea 0 0
2004–05 Chelsea 0 0
2005–06 Brentford 33 0 **33 0**

TURNER, Michael (D) 98 4
H: 6 4 W: 13 05 b.Lewisham 9-11-83
Source: Scholar.
2001–02 Charlton Ath 0 0
2002–03 Charlton Ath 0 0
2002–03 *Leyton Orient* 7 1 **7 1**
2003–04 Charlton Ath 0 0
2004–05 Charlton Ath 0 0
2004–05 Brentford 45 1
2005–06 Brentford 46 2 **91 3**

WATTS, Ryan (M) 1 0
H: 5 10 W: 10 10 b.Greenford 18-5-88
Source: Scholar.
2004–05 Brentford 1 0
2005–06 Brentford 0 0 **1 0**

WEIGHT, Scott (M) 0 0
H: 5 11 W: 10 04 b.Hounslow 3-4-87
Source: Scholar.
2004–05 Brentford 0 0
2005–06 Brentford 0 0

WILLOCK, Calum (F) 105 24
H: 6 1 W: 12 08 b.Lambeth 29-10-81
Source: Scholar. *Honours:* England Schools. St Kitts & Nevis full caps.
2000–01 Fulham 1 0
2001–02 Fulham 2 0
2002–03 Fulham 2 0
2002–03 *QPR* 3 0 **3 0**
2003–04 Fulham 0 0 **5 0**
2003–04 *Bristol R* 5 0 **5 0**
2003–04 Peterborough U 29 8
2004–05 Peterborough U 35 12
2005–06 Peterborough U 15 3 **79 23**
2005–06 Brentford 13 1 **13 1**

BRIGHTON & HA (13)

BREACH, Chris (D) 0 0
H: 5 10 W: 12 04 b.Brighton 19-4-86
Source: Scholar.
2005–06 Brighton & HA 0 0

BUTTERS, Guy (D) 502 34
H: 6 3 W: 13 00 b.Hillingdon 30-10-69
Source: Trainee. *Honours:* England Under-21.
1988–89 Tottenham H 28 1
1989–90 Tottenham H 7 0 **35 1**
1989–90 *Southend U* 16 3 **16 3**
1990–91 Portsmouth 23 0
1991–92 Portsmouth 33 2
1992–93 Portsmouth 15 1
1993–94 Portsmouth 15 1
1994–95 Portsmouth 24 0
1994–95 *Oxford U* 3 1 **3 1**

1995–96 Portsmouth 37 2
1996–97 Portsmouth 7 0 **154 6**
1996–97 Gillingham 30 0
1997–98 Gillingham 31 7
1998–99 Gillingham 23 3
1999–2000 Gillingham 40 2
2000–01 Gillingham 12 3
2001–02 Gillingham 23 1 **159 16**
2002–03 Brighton & HA 6 0
2003–04 Brighton & HA 43 3
2004–05 Brighton & HA 41 2
2005–06 Brighton & HA 45 2 **135 7**

CAROLE, Sebastien (M) 52 3
H: 5 7 W: 11 05 b.Pontoise 8-9-82
Source: Monaco.
2003–04 West Ham U 1 0 **1 0**
2004–05 Chateauroux 11 1 **11 1**
2005–06 Brighton & HA 40 2 **40 2**

CARPENTER, Richard (M) 492 32
H: 6 0 W: 13 00 b.Sheerness 30-9-72
Source: Trainee.
1990–91 Gillingham 9 1
1991–92 Gillingham 3 0
1992–93 Gillingham 28 0
1993–94 Gillingham 40 3
1994–95 Gillingham 29 0
1995–96 Gillingham 12 0
1996–97 Gillingham 1 0 **122 4**
1996–97 Fulham 34 5
1997–98 Fulham 24 2 **58 7**
1998–99 Cardiff C 42 1
1999–2000 Cardiff C 33 1 **75 2**
2000–01 Brighton & HA 42 6
2001–02 Brighton & HA 45 3
2002–03 Brighton & HA 44 2
2003–04 Brighton & HA 42 4
2004–05 Brighton & HA 32 3
2005–06 Brighton & HA 32 1 **237 19**

CHAIGNEAU, Florent (G) 7 0
H: 6 6 W: 14 02 b.La Roche-sur-Yon 21-3-84
Honours: France Under-21.
2003–04 Rennes 6 0
2004–05 Rennes 0 0
2005–06 Rennes 0 0 **6 0**
2005–06 Brighton & HA 1 0 **1 0**

COX, Dean (M) 1 0
H: 5 4 W: 9 08 b.Cuckfield 12-8-87
Source: Scholar.
2005–06 Brighton & HA 1 0 **1 0**

DODD, Jason (D) 409 9
H: 5 11 W: 12 03 b.Bath 2-11-70
Source: Bath C. *Honours:* England Under-21.
1988–89 Southampton 0 0
1989–90 Southampton 22 0
1990–91 Southampton 19 0
1991–92 Southampton 28 0
1992–93 Southampton 30 1
1993–94 Southampton 10 0
1994–95 Southampton 26 2
1995–96 Southampton 37 2
1996–97 Southampton 23 1
1997–98 Southampton 36 1
1998–99 Southampton 28 1
1999–2000 Southampton 31 0
2000–01 Southampton 31 1
2001–02 Southampton 29 0
2002–03 Southampton 15 0
2003–04 Southampton 28 0
2004–05 Southampton 5 0 **398 9**
2004–05 *Plymouth Arg* 4 0 **4 0**
2005–06 Brighton & HA 7 0 **7 0**

EL-ABD, Adam (D) 56 0
H: 5 10 W: 13 05 b.Brighton 11-9-84
Source: Scholar.
2003–04 Brighton & HA 11 0
2004–05 Brighton & HA 16 0
2005–06 Brighton & HA 29 0 **56 0**

ELPHICK, Gary (D) 2 0
H: 6 1 W: 13 02 b.Brighton 17-10-85
Source: Scholar.
2005–06 Brighton & HA 2 0 **2 0**

ELPHICK, Tommy (M) 1 0
H: 5 11 W: 11 07 b.Brighton 7-9-87
Source: Scholar.
2005–06 Brighton & HA 1 0 **1 0**

FRUTOS, Alexandre (M) 36 3
H: 5 9 W: 10 03 b.Vitry-le-Francois 23-4-82
Source: Chateauroux, Metz. *Honours:* France Youth.
2005–06 Brighton & HA 36 3 **36 3**

GATTING, Joe (D) 12 0
H: 5 11 W: 12 04 b.Brighton 25-11-87
Source: Scholar.
2005–06 Brighton & HA 12 0 **12 0**

HAMMOND, Dean (M) 83 8
H: 6 0 W: 11 09 b.Hastings 7-3-83
Source: Scholar.
2002–03 Brighton & HA 4 0
2003–04 Brighton & HA 0 0
2003–04 *Leyton Orient* 8 0 **8 0**
2004–05 Brighton & HA 30 4
2005–06 Brighton & HA 41 4 **75 8**

HART, Gary (F) 310 42
H: 5 9 W: 12 03 b.Harlow 21-9-76
Source: Stansted.
1998–99 Brighton & HA 44 12
1999–2000 Brighton & HA 43 9
2000–01 Brighton & HA 45 7
2001–02 Brighton & HA 39 4
2002–03 Brighton & HA 36 4
2003–04 Brighton & HA 42 3
2004–05 Brighton & HA 26 2
2005–06 Brighton & HA 35 1 **310 42**

HENDERSON, Wayne (G) 46 0
H: 5 11 W: 12 02 b.Dublin 16-9-83
Source: Scholar. *Honours:* Eire Youth, Under-21, 2 full caps.
2000–01 Aston Villa 0 0
2001–02 Aston Villa 0 0
2002–03 Aston Villa 0 0
2003–04 Aston Villa 0 0
2003–04 *Wycombe W* 3 0 **3 0**
2004–05 Aston Villa 0 0
2004–05 *Notts Co* 11 0 **11 0**
2005–06 Aston Villa 0 0
2005–06 Brighton & HA 32 0 **32 0**

HINSHELWOOD, Adam (D) 73 1
H: 5 10 W: 12 10 b.Oxford 8-1-84
Source: Scholar.
2002–03 Brighton & HA 7 0
2003–04 Brighton & HA 17 0
2004–05 Brighton & HA 38 1
2005–06 Brighton & HA 11 0 **73 1**

JARRETT, Albert (M) 38 1
H: 6 1 W: 10 07 b.Sierra Leone 23-10-84
Source: Dulwich Hamlet.
2002–03 Wimbledon 0 0
2003–04 Wimbledon 9 0 **9 0**
2004–05 Brighton & HA 12 1
2005–06 Brighton & HA 11 0 **23 1**
2005–06 *Swindon T* 6 0 **6 0**

KAZIM-RICHARDS, Colin (F) 72 9
H: 6 1 W: 10 10 b.Leyton 26-8-86
Source: Scholar.
2004–05 Bury 30 3 **30 3**
2005–06 Brighton & HA 42 6 **42 6**

KUIPERS, Michels (G) 158 0
H: 6 2 W: 14 03 b.Amsterdam 26-6-74
Source: SDW Amsterdam.
1998–99 Bristol R 1 0
1999–2000 Bristol R 0 0 **1 0**
2000–01 Brighton & HA 34 0
2001–02 Brighton & HA 39 0
2002–03 Brighton & HA 21 0
2003–04 Brighton & HA 10 0
2003–04 *Hull C* 3 0 **3 0**
2004–05 Brighton & HA 30 0
2005–06 Brighton & HA 5 0 **139 0**
2005–06 *Boston U* 15 0 **15 0**

LOFT, Doug (M) 3 1
H: 6 0 W: 12 01 b.Maidstone 25-12-86
Source: Hastings U.
2005–06 Brighton & HA 3 1 **3 1**

LYNCH, Joel (G) 16 1
H: 6 1 W: 12 10 b.Eastbourne 3-10-87
Source: Scholar. *Honours:* England Youth.
2005–06 Brighton & HA 16 1 **16 1**

MARTIN, Richard (G) 0 0
H: 6 2 W: 12 13 b.Chelmsford 1-9-87
Source: Scholar.
2005–06 Brighton & HA 0 0

MAYO, Kerry (D) 321 12
H: 5 10 W: 12 08 b.Haywards Heath 21-9-77
Source: Trainee.
1996–97 Brighton & HA 24 0
1997–98 Brighton & HA 44 6
1998–99 Brighton & HA 25 1
1999–2000 Brighton & HA 31 1
2000–01 Brighton & HA 45 1
2001–02 Brighton & HA 33 0
2002–03 Brighton & HA 41 1
2003–04 Brighton & HA 33 0
2004–05 Brighton & HA 27 1
2005–06 Brighton & HA 18 1 **321 12**

McARTHUR, Duncan (M) 3 0
H: 5 9 W: 12 06 b.Brighton 6-5-81
Source: Trainee.
1998–99 Brighton & HA 3 0
1999–2000 Brighton & HA 0 0
2000–01 Brighton & HA 0 0
2001–02 Brighton & HA 0 0
2002–03 Brighton & HA 0 0
2003–04 Brighton & HA 0 0
2004–05 Brighton & HA 0 0
2005–06 Brighton & HA 0 0 **3 0**

McCAMMON, Mark (F) 145 19
H: 6 2 W: 14 05 b.Barnet 7-8-78
Source: Cambridge C.
1997–98 Cambridge U 2 0
1998–99 Cambridge U 2 0 **4 0**
1998–99 Charlton Ath 0 0
1999–2000 Charlton Ath 4 0 **4 0**
1999–2000 *Swindon T* 4 0 **4 0**
2000–01 Brentford 24 3
2001–02 Brentford 14 0
2002–03 Brentford 37 7 **75 10**
2002–03 Millwall 7 2
2003–04 Millwall 7 0
2004–05 Millwall 8 0 **22 2**
2004–05 Brighton & HA 18 3
2005–06 Brighton & HA 7 0 **25 3**
2005–06 *Bristol C* 11 4 **11 4**

McPHEE, Chris (F) 68 4
H: 5 11 W: 11 09 b.Eastbourne 20-3-83
Source: Scholarship.
1999–2000 Brighton & HA 4 0
2000–01 Brighton & HA 0 0
2001–02 Brighton & HA 2 0
2002–03 Brighton & HA 2 0
2003–04 Brighton & HA 29 4
2004–05 Brighton & HA 16 0
2005–06 Brighton & HA 7 0 **60 4**
2005–06 *Swindon T* 8 0 **8 0**

MOLANGO, Maheta (F) 15 1
H: 6 1 W: 12 06 b.St Imier 24-7-82
Source: SV Burghausen.
2004–05 Brighton & HA 5 1
2005–06 Brighton & HA 0 0 **5 1**
2005–06 *Lincoln C* 10 0 **10 0**
To UB Conquense (loan) January 2006

NICOLAS, Alexis (M) 46 0
H: 5 10 W: 9 12 b.Westminster 13-2-83
Source: Scholar. *Honours:* Cyprus Youth, Under-21.
2000–01 Aston Villa 0 0
2001–02 Aston Villa 0 0
2001–02 Chelsea 0 0
2002–03 Chelsea 0 0
2003–04 Chelsea 2 0
2004–05 Chelsea 0 0 **2 0**
2004–05 Brighton & HA 33 0
2005–06 Brighton & HA 11 0 **44 0**

OATWAY, Charlie (M) 383 10
H: 5 7 W: 10 10 b.Hammersmith 28-11-73
Source: Yeading.
1994–95 Cardiff C 30 0

1995–96 Cardiff C 2 0 **32 0**
1995–96 Torquay U 24 0
1996–97 Torquay U 41 1
1997–98 Torquay U 2 0 **67 1**
1997–98 Brentford 33 0
1998–99 Brentford 24 0 **57 0**
1998–99 *Lincoln C* 3 0 **3 0**
1999–2000 Brighton & HA 42 4
2000–01 Brighton & HA 38 0
2001–02 Brighton & HA 32 1
2002–03 Brighton & HA 29 1
2003–04 Brighton & HA 31 1
2004–05 Brighton & HA 34 1
2005–06 Brighton & HA 18 1 **224 9**

REID, Paul (M) 183 21
H: 5 10 W: 10 10 b.Sydney 6-7-79
Honours: Australia Under-20.
1998–99 Wollongong Wolves 22 2
1999–2000 Wollongong Wolves 31 3
2000–01 Wollongong Wolves 30 7
2001–02 Wollongong Wolves 15 3 **98 15**
2002–03 Bradford C 8 2
2003–04 Bradford C 0 0 **8 2**
2003–04 Brighton & HA 5 0
2004–05 Brighton & HA 34 2
2005–06 Brighton & HA 38 2 **77 4**

ROBINSON, Jake (F) 46 2
H: 5 7 W: 10 10 b.Brighton 23-10-86
Source: Scholar.
2003–04 Brighton & HA 9 0
2004–05 Brighton & HA 10 1
2005–06 Brighton & HA 27 1 **46 2**

SULLIVAN, John (M) 0 0
H: 5 10 W: 11 04 b.Brighton 8-3-88
Source: Scholar. *Honours:* England Youth.
2005–06 Brighton & HA 0 0

TURIENZO, Federico (F) 56 7
H: 6 2 W: 11 13 b.La Plata 6-2-83
2001–02 Gimnasia 12 3
2002–03 Gimnasia 25 4
2003–04 Gimnasia 6 0
2004–05 Gimnasia 9 0 **52 7**
2005–06 Brighton & HA 4 0 **4 0**

BRISTOL C (14)

ABBEY, Nathan (G) 168 0
H: 6 1 W: 11 13 b.Islington 11-7-78
Source: Trainee.
1995–96 Luton T 0 0
1996–97 Luton T 0 0
1997–98 Luton T 0 0
1998–99 Luton T 2 0
1999–2000 Luton T 33 0
2000–01 Luton T 20 0
2001–02 Chesterfield 46 0 **46 0**
2002–03 Northampton T 5 0 **5 0**
2003–04 Luton T 0 0 **55 0**
2003–04 Macclesfield T 0 0
2003–04 Ipswich T 0 0
2003–04 Burnley 0 0
2004–05 Boston U 44 0
2005–06 Boston U 17 0 **61 0**
2005–06 *Leyton Orient* 0 0
2005–06 Bristol C 1 0 **1 0**

ARTUS, Frankie (M) 0 0
b.Bristol
Source: Scholar.
2005–06 Bristol C 0 0

BASSO, Adriano (G) 29 0
H: 6 1 W: 11 07 b.Jundiai 18-4-75
Source: Woking.
2005–06 Bristol C 29 0 **29 0**

BENYON, Elliot (M) 0 0
b.Wycombe 29-8-87
Source: Scholar.
2005–06 Bristol C 0 0

BROOKER, Stephen (F) 202 67
H: 6 0 W: 14 00 b.Newport Pagnell 21-5-81
Source: Trainee.
1999–2000 Watford 1 0
2000–01 Watford 0 0 **1 0**
2000–01 Port Vale 23 8
2001–02 Port Vale 41 9
2002–03 Port Vale 26 5
2003–04 Port Vale 32 8
2004–05 Port Vale 9 5 **131 35**
2004–05 Bristol C 33 16
2005–06 Bristol C 37 16 **70 32**

BROWN, Scott (M) 48 1
H: 5 9 W: 10 03 b.Runcorn 8-5-85
Source: Scholar. *Honours:* England Youth.
2001–02 Everton 0 0
2002–03 Everton 0 0
2003–04 Everton 0 0
2004–05 Bristol C 19 0
2005–06 Bristol C 29 1 **48 1**

CAREY, Louis (D) 387 8
H: 5 10 W: 11 00 b.Bristol 20-1-77
Source: Trainee. *Honours:* Scotland Under-21.
1995–96 Bristol C 23 0
1996–97 Bristol C 42 0
1997–98 Bristol C 38 0
1998–99 Bristol C 41 0
1999–2000 Bristol C 22 0
2000–01 Bristol C 46 3
2001–02 Bristol C 35 0
2002–03 Bristol C 24 1
2003–04 Bristol C 41 1
2004–05 Coventry C 23 0 **23 0**
2004–05 Bristol C 14 0
2005–06 Bristol C 38 3 **364 8**

COTTERILL, David (F) 57 7
H: 5 9 W: 11 02 b.Cardiff 4-12-87
Source: Scholar. *Honours:* Wales Youth, Under-21, 3 full caps.
2004–05 Bristol C 12 0
2005–06 Bristol C 45 7 **57 7**

FORTUNE, Clayton (D) 78 2
H: 6 3 W: 13 10 b.Forest Gate 10-11-82
Source: Tottenham H Scholar.
2000–01 Bristol C 0 0
2001–02 Bristol C 1 0
2002–03 Bristol C 10 0
2003–04 Bristol C 6 0
2004–05 Bristol C 30 0
2005–06 Bristol C 6 0 **53 0**
2005–06 *Port Vale* 25 2 **25 2**

HARLEY, Ryan (D) 2 0
H: 5 11 W: 11 00 b.Bristol 22-1-85
Source: Scholar.
2004–05 Bristol C 2 0
2005–06 Bristol C 0 0 **2 0**

HEYWOOD, Matthew (D) 220 10
H: 6 3 W: 14 00 b.Chatham 26-8-79
Source: Trainee.
1998–99 Burnley 13 0
1999–2000 Burnley 0 0
2000–01 Burnley 0 0 **13 0**
2000–01 Swindon T 21 2
2001–02 Swindon T 44 3
2002–03 Swindon T 46 1
2003–04 Swindon T 40 1
2004–05 Swindon T 32 1 **183 8**
2005–06 Bristol C 24 2 **24 2**

KEOGH, Richard (M) 12 1
H: 6 0 W: 11 02 b.Harlow 11-8-86
Source: Scholar. *Honours:* Eire Under-21.
2004–05 Stoke C 0 0
2005–06 Bristol C 9 1 **9 1**
2005–06 *Wycombe W* 3 0 **3 0**

LAMB, Shaun (D) 0 0
b.Bristol 17-11-86
Source: Scholar.
2005–06 Bristol C 0 0

MADJO, Guy (F) 5 0
H: 6 0 W: 13 05 b.Cameroon 1-6-84
2005–06 Bristol C 5 0 **5 0**

MURRAY, Scott (M) 347 69
H: 5 9 W: 11 00 b.Aberdeen 26-5-74
Source: Fraserburgh. *Honours:* Scotland B.
1993–94 Aston Villa 0 0
1994–95 Aston Villa 0 0
1995–96 Aston Villa 3 0
1996–97 Aston Villa 1 0
1997–98 Aston Villa 0 0 **4 0**
1997–98 Bristol C 23 0
1998–99 Bristol C 32 3
1999–2000 Bristol C 41 6
2000–01 Bristol C 46 10
2001–02 Bristol C 37 8
2002–03 Bristol C 45 19
2003–04 Reading 34 5 **34 5**
2003–04 Bristol C 6 0
2004–05 Bristol C 42 8
2005–06 Bristol C 37 10 **309 64**

MYRIE-WILLIAMS, Jennison (F) 1 0
H: 5 11 W: 12 08 b.London 17-5-88
Source: Scholar.
2005–06 Bristol C 1 0 **1 0**

NOBLE, David (M) 99 7
H: 6 0 W: 12 04 b.Hitchin 2-2-82
Source: Scholar. *Honours:* England Youth, Under-20. Scotland Under-21.
2000–01 Arsenal 0 0
2001–02 Arsenal 0 0
2001–02 *Watford* 15 1 **15 1**
2002–03 Arsenal 0 0
2002–03 West Ham U 0 0
2003–04 West Ham U 3 0 **3 0**
2003–04 Boston U 14 2
2004–05 Boston U 32 3
2005–06 Boston U 11 0 **57 5**
2005–06 Bristol C 24 1 **24 1**

ORR, Bradley (M) 79 1
H: 6 0 W: 11 11 b.Liverpool 1-11-82
Source: Scholar.
2001–02 Newcastle U 0 0
2002–03 Newcastle U 0 0
2003–04 Newcastle U 0 0
2003–04 *Burnley* 4 0 **4 0**
2004–05 Bristol C 37 0
2005–06 Bristol C 38 1 **75 1**

PARTRIDGE, David (D) 174 2
H: 6 1 W: 13 06 b.Westminster 26-11-78
Source: Trainee. *Honours:* Wales Under-21, 7 full caps.
1997–98 West Ham U 0 0
1998–99 Dundee U 1 0
1999–2000 Dundee U 29 0
2000–01 Dundee U 19 0
2001–02 Dundee U 13 0 **62 0**
2001–02 *Leyton Orient* 7 0 **7 0**
2002–03 Motherwell 32 1
2003–04 Motherwell 15 0
2004–05 Motherwell 29 1 **76 2**
2005–06 Bristol C 11 0 **11 0**
2005–06 *Milton Keynes D* 18 0 **18 0**

PEARCE, Sam (G) 0 0
b.Newport 24-2-86
Source: Scholar. *Honours:* Wales Under-21.
2005–06 Bristol C 0 0

PHILLIPS, Steve (G) 257 0
H: 6 1 W: 11 10 b.Bath 6-5-78
Source: Paulton R.
1996–97 Bristol C 0 0
1997–98 Bristol C 0 0
1998–99 Bristol C 15 0
1999–2000 Bristol C 21 0
2000–01 Bristol C 42 0
2001–02 Bristol C 22 0
2002–03 Bristol C 46 0
2003–04 Bristol C 46 0
2004–05 Bristol C 46 0
2005–06 Bristol C 19 0 **257 0**

RUSSELL, Alex (M) 363 47
H: 5 10 W: 11 07 b.Crosby 17-3-73
Source: Burscough.
1994–95 Rochdale 7 1
1995–96 Rochdale 25 0
1996–97 Rochdale 39 9
1997–98 Rochdale 31 4 **102 14**
1998–99 Cambridge U 37 6
1999–2000 Cambridge U 15 0
2000–01 Cambridge U 29 2 **81 8**
2001–02 Torquay U 33 7
2002–03 Torquay U 39 9
2003–04 Torquay U 43 2
2004–05 Torquay U 38 3 **153 21**
2005–06 Bristol C 27 4 **27 4**

SAVAGE, Bas (F) 48 1
H: 6 3 W: 13 08 b.London 7-1-82
Source: Walton & Hersham.
2001–02 Reading 1 0
2002–03 Reading 0 0
2003–04 Reading 15 0
2004–05 Reading 0 0 **16 0**
2004–05 *Wycombe W* 4 0 **4 0**
2004–05 *Bury* 5 0 **5 0**
2005–06 Bristol C 23 1 **23 1**

SKUSE, Cole (M) 45 2
H: 6 1 W: 11 05 b.Bristol 29-3-86
Source: Scholar.
2004–05 Bristol C 7 0
2005–06 Bristol C 38 2 **45 2**

SMITH, Grant (M) 87 14
H: 6 1 W: 12 07 b.Irvine 5-5-80
1998–99 Reading 0 0
1999–2000 Reading 0 0
2000–01 Reading 0 0
2001–02 *Halifax T* 11 0 **11 0**
2001–02 Sheffield U 7 0
2002–03 Sheffield U 3 0 **10 0**
2002–03 *Plymouth Arg* 5 1 **5 1**
2003–04 Swindon T 7 0
2004–05 Swindon T 30 10 **37 10**
2005–06 Bristol C 11 0 **11 0**
2005–06 *Walsall* 13 3 **13 3**

SMITH, Jamie (M) 297 7
H: 5 6 W: 10 08 b.Birmingham 17-9-74
Source: Trainee.
1993–94 Wolverhampton W 0 0
1994–95 Wolverhampton W 25 0
1995–96 Wolverhampton W 13 0
1996–97 Wolverhampton W 38 0
1997–98 Wolverhampton W 11 0 **87 0**
1997–98 Crystal Palace 18 0
1998–99 Crystal Palace 26 0
1998–99 *Fulham* 9 1 **9 1**
1999–2000 Crystal Palace 27 0
2000–01 Crystal Palace 29 0
2001–02 Crystal Palace 32 4
2002–03 Crystal Palace 2 0
2003–04 Crystal Palace 15 0 **149 4**
2004–05 Bristol C 39 2
2005–06 Bristol C 6 0 **45 2**
2005–06 *Brentford* 7 0 **7 0**

STEWART, Marcus (F) 512 178
H: 5 10 W: 11 00 b.Bristol 7-11-72
Source: Trainee. *Honours:* England Schools, Football League.
1991–92 Bristol R 33 5
1992–93 Bristol R 38 11
1993–94 Bristol R 29 5
1994–95 Bristol R 27 15
1995–96 Bristol R 44 21 **171 57**
1996–97 Huddersfield T 20 7
1997–98 Huddersfield T 41 15
1998–99 Huddersfield T 43 22
1999–2000 Huddersfield T 29 14 **133 58**
1999–2000 Ipswich T 10 2
2000–01 Ipswich T 34 19
2001–02 Ipswich T 28 6
2002–03 Ipswich T 3 0 **75 27**
2002–03 Sunderland 19 1
2003–04 Sunderland 40 14
2004–05 Sunderland 43 16 **102 31**
2005–06 Bristol C 27 5 **27 5**
2005–06 *Preston NE* 4 0 **4 0**

WILKSHIRE, Luke (M) 131 17
H: 5 9 W: 11 05 b.Wollongong 2-10-81
Honours: Australia Under-20, Under-23, 10 full caps.
1998–99 Middlesbrough 0 0
1999–2000 Middlesbrough 0 0
2000–01 Middlesbrough 0 0
2001–02 Middlesbrough 7 0
2002–03 Middlesbrough 14 0 **21 0**
2003–04 Bristol C 37 2
2004–05 Bristol C 37 10
2005–06 Bristol C 36 5 **110 17**

WILSON, James (D) 0 0
b.Chepstow 26-2-89
Source: Scholar.
2005–06 Bristol C 0 0

WOODMAN, Craig (D) 111 3
H: 5 9 W: 10 11 b.Tiverton 22-12-82
Source: Trainee.
1999–2000 Bristol C 0 0
2000–01 Bristol C 2 0
2001–02 Bristol C 6 0
2002–03 Bristol C 10 0
2003–04 Bristol C 21 0
2004–05 Bristol C 3 0
2004–05 *Mansfield T* 8 1 **8 1**
2004–05 *Torquay U* 22 1
2005–06 Bristol C 37 1 **79 1**
2005–06 *Torquay U* 2 0 **24 1**

WRING, Danny (M) 1 0
H: 5 10 W: 10 03 b.Portishead 26-10-86
Source: Scholar.
2004–05 Bristol C 1 0
2005–06 Bristol C 0 0 **1 0**

BRISTOL R (15)

AGOGO, Junior (F) 146 48
H: 5 10 W: 11 07 b.Accra 1-8-79
Source: Willesden.
1996–97 Sheffield W 0 0
1997–98 Sheffield W 1 0
1998–99 Sheffield W 1 0
1999–2000 Sheffield W 0 0 **2 0**
1999–2000 *Oldham Ath* 2 0 **2 0**
1999–2000 *Chester C* 10 6 **10 6**
1999–2000 *Chesterfield* 4 0 **4 0**
1999–2000 *Lincoln C* 3 1 **3 1**
From Colorado R, San Jose E.
2001–02 QPR 2 0 **2 0**
2002–03 Barnet 0 0
2003–04 Bristol R 38 6
2004–05 Bristol R 43 19
2005–06 Bristol R 42 16 **123 41**

ANDERSON, John (D) 343 34
H: 6 2 W: 12 02 b.Greenock 2-10-72
Source: Gourock YAC.
1993–94 Morton 19 2
1994–95 Morton 30 3
1995–96 Morton 30 4
1996–97 Morton 31 4
1997–98 Morton 33 4
1998–99 Morton 33 6
1999–2000 Morton 29 5 **205 28**
2000–01 Livingston 30 3
2001–02 Livingston 11 0 **41 3**
2002–03 Hull C 43 1
2003–04 Hull C 0 0 **43 1**
2003–04 Bristol R 8 0
2004–05 Bristol R 34 1
2005–06 Bristol R 12 1 **54 2**

BASS, Jon (D) 114 1
H: 6 0 W: 13 05 b.Weston-Super-Mare 1-7-76
Source: Trainee. *Honours:* England Schools.
1994–95 Birmingham C 0 0
1995–96 Birmingham C 5 0
1996–97 Birmingham C 13 0
1996–97 *Carlisle U* 3 0 **3 0**
1997–98 Birmingham C 30 0
1998–99 Birmingham C 11 0
1999–2000 Birmingham C 8 0
1999–2000 *Gillingham* 7 0 **7 0**
2000–01 Birmingham C 1 0 **68 0**
2001–02 Hartlepool U 20 1
2002–03 Hartlepool U 4 0
2003–04 Hartlepool U 0 0 **24 1**
2004–05 Bristol R 3 0
2005–06 Bristol R 9 0 **12 0**

BOOK, Steve (G) 175 0
H: 5 11 W: 11 01 b.Bournemouth 7-7-69
1997–98 Brighton & HA 0 0
1998–99 Lincoln C 0 0
From Forest Green R.
1999–2000 Cheltenham T 46 0
2000–01 Cheltenham T 46 0
2001–02 Cheltenham T 39 0
2002–03 Cheltenham T 36 0
2003–04 Cheltenham T 5 0 **172 0**
2004–05 Swindon T 2 0
2005–06 Swindon T 0 0 **2 0**
From Cirencester T
2005–06 Bristol R 1 0 **1 0**

CAMPBELL, Stuart (M) 257 13
H: 5 10 W: 10 08 b.Corby 9-12-77
Source: Trainee. *Honours:* Scotland Under-21.
1996–97 Leicester C 10 0
1997–98 Leicester C 11 0
1998–99 Leicester C 12 0
1999–2000 Leicester C 4 0
1999–2000 *Birmingham C* 2 0 **2 0**
2000–01 Leicester C 0 0 **37 0**
2000–01 *Grimsby T* 38 2
2001–02 Grimsby T 33 3
2002–03 Grimsby T 45 6
2003–04 Grimsby T 39 1 **155 12**
2004–05 Bristol R 25 0
2005–06 Bristol R 38 1 **63 1**

CARRUTHERS, Chris (M) 119 2
H: 5 10 W: 12 00 b.Kettering 19-8-83
Source: Scholar. *Honours:* England Under-20.
2000–01 Northampton T 3 0
2001–02 Northampton T 13 1
2002–03 Northampton T 33 0
2003–04 Northampton T 24 0
2004–05 Northampton T 1 0 **74 1**
2004–05 *Bristol R* 5 0
2005–06 Bristol R 40 1 **45 1**

CLARKE, Ryan (G) 30 0
H: 6 3 W: 13 00 b.Bristol 30-4-82
Source: Scholar.
2001–02 Bristol R 1 0
2002–03 Bristol R 2 0
2003–04 Bristol R 2 0
2004–05 Bristol R 18 0
2004–05 *Southend U* 1 0 **1 0**
2004–05 *Kidderminster H* 6 0 **6 0**
2005–06 Bristol R 0 0 **23 0**

DISLEY, Craig (M) 211 28
H: 5 10 W: 10 13 b.Worksop 24-8-81
Source: Trainee.
1999–2000 Mansfield T 5 0
2000–01 Mansfield T 24 0
2001–02 Mansfield T 36 7
2002–03 Mansfield T 42 4
2003–04 Mansfield T 34 5 **141 16**
2004–05 Bristol R 28 4
2005–06 Bristol R 42 8 **70 12**

EDWARDS, Christian (D) 305 11
H: 6 2 W: 11 09 b.Caerphilly 23-11-75
Source: Trainee. *Honours:* Wales Under-21, B, 1 full cap.
1994–95 Swansea C 9 0
1995–96 Swansea C 38 2
1996–97 Swansea C 36 0
1997–98 Swansea C 32 2
1997–98 Nottingham F 0 0
1998–99 Nottingham F 12 0
1998–99 *Bristol C* 3 0 **3 0**
1999–2000 Nottingham F 0 0
1999–2000 *Oxford U* 5 1
2000–01 Nottingham F 36 3
2001–02 Nottingham F 6 0
2001–02 *Crystal Palace* 9 0 **9 0**
2002–03 Nottingham F 0 0 **54 3**
2002–03 *Tranmere R* 12 0 **12 0**
2002–03 *Oxford U* 6 0 **11 1**
2003–04 Bristol R 42 0
2004–05 Bristol R 42 2
2005–06 Bristol R 15 1 **99 3**
2005–06 Swansea C 2 0 **117 4**

ELLIOTT, Steve (D) 187 5
H: 6 1 W: 14 00 b.Derby 29-10-78
Source: Trainee.
1996–97 Derby Co 0 0
1997–98 Derby Co 3 0
1998–99 Derby Co 11 0
1999–2000 Derby Co 20 0
2000–01 Derby Co 6 0
2001–02 Derby Co 6 0
2002–03 Derby Co 23 1
2003–04 Derby Co 4 0 **73 1**
2003–04 Blackpool 28 0 **28 0**
2004–05 Bristol R 41 2

2005–06 Bristol R 45 2 **86 4**

FORRESTER, Jamie (F) 385 110
H: 5 7 W: 11 00 b.Bradford 1-11-74
Source: Auxerre. *Honours:* England Schools, Youth.

1992–93	Leeds U	6	0		
1993–94	Leeds U	3	0		
1994–95	Leeds U	0	0		
1994–95	*Southend U*	5	0	**5**	**0**
1994–95	*Grimsby T*	9	1		
1995–96	Leeds U	0	0	**9**	**0**
1995–96	Grimsby T	28	5		
1996–97	Grimsby T	13	1	**50**	**7**
1996–97	Scunthorpe U	10	6		
1997–98	Scunthorpe U	45	11		
1998–99	Scunthorpe U	46	20	**101**	**37**
1999–2000	Utrecht	1	0	**1**	**0**
1999–2000	Walsall	5	0	**5**	**0**
1999–2000	*Northampton T*	10	6		
2000–01	Northampton T	43	17		
2001–02	Northampton T	43	17		
2002–03	Northampton T	25	5	**121**	**45**
2002–03	Hull C	11	3		
2003–04	Hull C	21	4	**32**	**7**
2004–05	Bristol R	35	7		
2005–06	Bristol R	17	2	**52**	**9**
2005–06	*Lincoln C*	9	5	**9**	**5**

GIBB, Ali (M) 360 6
H: 5 9 W: 11 07 b.Salisbury 17-2-76
Source: Trainee.

1994–95	Norwich C	0	0		
1995–96	Norwich C	0	0		
1995–96	Northampton T	23	2		
1996–97	Northampton T	18	1		
1997–98	Northampton T	35	1		
1998–99	Northampton T	41	0		
1999–2000	Northampton T	14	0	**131**	**4**
1999–2000	Stockport Co	14	0		
2000–01	Stockport Co	39	0		
2001–02	Stockport Co	41	0		
2002–03	Stockport Co	45	1		
2003–04	Stockport Co	26	0	**165**	**1**
2003–04	Bristol R	8	1		
2004–05	Bristol R	23	0		
2005–06	Bristol R	33	0	**64**	**1**

HALDANE, Lewis (F) 70 8
H: 6 0 W: 11 03 b.Trowbridge 13-3-85
Source: Scholar.

2003–04	Bristol R	27	5		
2004–05	Bristol R	13	0		
2005–06	Bristol R	30	3	**70**	**8**

HINTON, Craig (D) 247 3
H: 6 0 W: 12 00 b.Wolverhampton 26-11-77
Source: Trainee.

1996–97	Birmingham C	0	0		
1997–98	Birmingham C	0	0		
2000–01	Kidderminster H	46	2		
2001–02	Kidderminster H	41	0		
2002–03	Kidderminster H	44	0		
2003–04	Kidderminster H	42	1	**173**	**3**
2004–05	Bristol R	38	0		
2005–06	Bristol R	36	0	**74**	**0**

HORSELL, Martin (G) 0 0
H: 6 0 W: 12 00 b.Torquay 10-12-86
Source: Scholar.

2005–06	Bristol R	0	0		

HUNT, James (M) 352 17
H: 5 8 W: 10 03 b.Derby 17-12-76
Source: Trainee.

1994–95	Notts Co	0	0		
1995–96	Notts Co	10	1		
1996–97	Notts Co	9	0	**19**	**1**
1997–98	Northampton T	21	0		
1998–99	Northampton T	35	2		
1999–2000	Northampton T	37	1		
2000–01	Northampton T	41	1		
2001–02	Northampton T	38	4	**172**	**8**
2002–03	Oxford U	39	1		
2003–04	Oxford U	41	2	**80**	**3**
2004–05	Bristol R	41	4		
2005–06	Bristol R	40	1	**81**	**5**

LESCOTT, Aaron (M) 185 1
H: 5 8 W: 10 09 b.Birmingham 2-12-78
Source: Trainee. *Honours:* England Schools.

1996–97	Aston Villa	0	0		
1997–98	Aston Villa	0	0		
1998–99	Aston Villa	0	0		
1999–2000	Aston Villa	0	0		
1999–2000	*Lincoln C*	5	0	**5**	**0**
2000–01	Aston Villa	0	0		
2000–01	Sheffield W	30	0		
2001–02	Sheffield W	7	0	**37**	**0**
2001–02	Stockport Co	17	0		
2002–03	Stockport Co	41	1		
2003–04	Stockport Co	14	0	**72**	**1**
2003–04	*Bristol R*	8	0		
2004–05	Bristol R	26	0		
2005–06	Bristol R	37	0	**71**	**0**

LINES, Chris (M) 4 0
H: 6 2 W: 12 00 b.Bristol 30-11-85

2005–06	Bristol R	4	0	**4**	**0**

LOUIS, Jefferson (F) 65 8
H: 6 2 W: 15 00 b.Harrow 22-2-79
Source: Thame U.

2001–02	Oxford U	1	0		
2002–03	Oxford U	34	6		
2003–04	Oxford U	20	2		
2004–05	Oxford U	1	0	**56**	**8**
From For GR, Woking					
2004–05	Bristol R	1	0		
2005–06	Bristol R	8	0	**9**	**0**

MULLINGS, Darren (M) 4 0
H: 6 1 W: 12 00 b.Bristol 3-3-87

2005–06	Bristol R	4	0	**4**	**0**

RYAN, Robbie (D) 295 2
H: 5 11 W: 11 05 b.Dublin 16-5-77
Source: Belvedere. *Honours:* Eire Youth, Under-21.

1994–95	Huddersfield T	0	0		
1995–96	Huddersfield T	0	0		
1996–97	Huddersfield T	5	0		
1997–98	Huddersfield T	10	0	**15**	**0**
1997–98	Millwall	16	0		
1998–99	Millwall	26	0		
1999–2000	Millwall	34	0		
2000–01	Millwall	42	0		
2001–02	Millwall	37	0		
2002–03	Millwall	41	2		
2003–04	Millwall	30	0	**226**	**2**
2004–05	Bristol R	40	0		
2005–06	Bristol R	14	0	**54**	**0**

SANDELL, Andy (M) 0 0
b.Swindon 8-9-83
Source: Bath C.

2005–06	Bristol R	0	0		

SHEARER, Scott (G) 145 0
H: 6 3 W: 12 00 b.Glasgow 15-2-81
Source: Tower Hearts. *Honours:* Scotland B.

2000–01	Albion R	3	0		
2001–02	Albion R	10	0		
2002–03	Albion R	36	0	**49**	**0**
2003–04	Coventry C	30	0		
2004–05	Coventry C	8	0	**38**	**0**
2004–05	*Rushden & D*	13	0	**13**	**0**
2005–06	Bristol R	45	0	**45**	**0**

SOMNER, Matt (D) 109 1
H: 6 0 W: 13 00 b.Isleworth 8-12-82
Source: Trainee. *Honours:* Wales Under-21.

2000–01	Brentford	3	0		
2001–02	Brentford	0	0		
2002–03	Brentford	40	1		
2003–04	Brentford	39	0		
2004–05	Brentford	2	0	**84**	**1**
2004–05	Cambridge U	24	0	**24**	**0**
2005–06	Bristol R	1	0	**1**	**0**

TROLLOPE, Paul (M) 383 37
H: 6 0 W: 12 06 b.Swindon 3-6-72
Source: Trainee. *Honours:* Wales B, 9 full caps.

1989–90	Swindon T	0	0		
1990–91	Swindon T	0	0		
1991–92	Swindon T	0	0		
1991–92	*Torquay U*	10	0		
1992–93	Torquay U	36	2		
1993–94	Torquay U	42	10		
1994–95	Torquay U	18	4	**106**	**16**
1994–95	Derby Co	24	4		
1995–96	Derby Co	17	0		
1996–97	Derby Co	14	1		
1996–97	*Grimsby T*	7	1	**7**	**1**
1996–97	*Crystal Palace*	9	0	**9**	**0**
1997–98	Derby Co	10	0	**65**	**5**
1997–98	Fulham	24	3		
1998–99	Fulham	20	2		
1999–2000	Fulham	22	0		
2000–01	Fulham	10	0		
2001–02	Fulham	0	0	**76**	**5**
2001–02	Coventry C	6	0	**6**	**0**
2002–03	Northampton T	41	2		
2003–04	Northampton T	43	6	**84**	**8**
2004–05	Bristol R	30	2		
2005–06	Bristol R	0	0	**30**	**2**

WALKER, Richard (F) 208 57
H: 6 0 W: 12 04 b.Sutton Coldfield 8-11-77
Source: Trainee.

1995–96	Aston Villa	0	0		
1996–97	Aston Villa	0	0		
1997–98	Aston Villa	1	0		
1998–99	Aston Villa	0	0		
1998–99	*Cambridge U*	21	3	**21**	**3**
1999–2000	Aston Villa	5	2		
2000–01	Aston Villa	0	0		
2000–01	*Blackpool*	18	3		
2001–02	Aston Villa	0	0	**6**	**2**
2001–02	*Wycombe W*	12	3	**12**	**3**
2001–02	Blackpool	21	8		
2002–03	Blackpool	32	4		
2003–04	Blackpool	9	0	**80**	**15**
2003–04	*Northampton T*	12	4	**12**	**4**
2003–04	Oxford U	4	0	**4**	**0**
2004–05	Bristol R	27	10		
2005–06	Bristol R	46	20	**73**	**30**

WILLIAMS, Ryan (M) 201 22
H: 5 5 W: 11 04 b.Sutton-in-Ashfield 31-8-78
Source: Trainee. *Honours:* England Youth.

1995–96	Mansfield T	10	3		
1996–97	Mansfield T	16	0	**26**	**3**
1997–98	Tranmere R	0	0		
1998–99	Tranmere R	5	0		
1999–2000	Tranmere R	0	0	**5**	**0**
1999–2000	Chesterfield	30	5		
2000–01	Chesterfield	45	8	**75**	**13**
2001–02	Hull C	29	2		
2002–03	Hull C	23	0		
2003–04	Hull C	0	0	**52**	**2**
2003–04	Bristol R	19	1		
2004–05	Bristol R	17	3		
2005–06	Bristol R	7	0	**43**	**4**

BURNLEY (16)

BRANCH, Graham (F) 382 31
H: 6 2 W: 12 02 b.Liverpool 12-2-72
Source: Heswall.

1991–92	Tranmere R	4	0		
1992–93	Tranmere R	3	0		
1992–93	*Bury*	4	1	**4**	**1**
1993–94	Tranmere R	13	0		
1994–95	Tranmere R	1	0		
1995–96	Tranmere R	21	2		
1996–97	Tranmere R	35	5		
1997–98	Tranmere R	25	3	**102**	**10**
1997–98	*Wigan Ath*	3	0	**3**	**0**
1998–99	Stockport Co	14	3	**14**	**3**
1998–99	Burnley	20	1		
1999–2000	Burnley	44	3		
2000–01	Burnley	35	5		
2001–02	Burnley	10	0		
2002–03	Burnley	32	0		
2003–04	Burnley	38	3		
2004–05	Burnley	43	3		
2005–06	Burnley	37	2	**259**	**17**

COURTNEY, Duane (D) 7 0
H: 5 11 W: 11 03 b.Birmingham 7-1-85
Source: AFC Telford U.

2005–06	Burnley	7	0	**7**	**0**

COYNE, Danny (G) **324 0**
H: 6 0 W: 13 00 b.Prestatyn 27-8-73
Source: Trainee. *Honours:* Wales Schools, Youth, Under-21, B, 11 full caps.

1991–92	Tranmere R	0	0		
1992–93	Tranmere R	1	0		
1993–94	Tranmere R	5	0		
1994–95	Tranmere R	5	0		
1995–96	Tranmere R	46	0		
1996–97	Tranmere R	21	0		
1997–98	Tranmere R	16	0		
1998–99	Tranmere R	17	0	**111**	**0**
1999–2000	Grimsby T	44	0		
2000–01	Grimsby T	46	0		
2001–02	Grimsby T	45	0		
2002–03	Grimsby T	46	0	**181**	**0**
2003–04	Leicester C	4	0	**4**	**0**
2004–05	Burnley	20	0		
2005–06	Burnley	8	0	**28**	**0**

CROSSLEY, Mark (G) **0 0**
H: 6 0 W: 12 02 b.Burnley 3-12-87
Source: Scholar.

2005–06	Burnley	0	0		

DUFF, Michael (D) **284 12**
H: 6 1 W: 11 08 b.Belfast 11-1-78
Source: Trainee. *Honours:* Northern Ireland 10 full caps.

1999–2000	Cheltenham T	31	2		
2000–01	Cheltenham T	39	5		
2001–02	Cheltenham T	45	3		
2002–03	Cheltenham T	44	2		
2003–04	Cheltenham T	42	0	**201**	**12**
2004–05	Burnley	42	0		
2005–06	Burnley	41	0	**83**	**0**

ELLIOTT, Wade (M) **256 34**
H: 5 10 W: 10 03 b.Southampton 14-12-78

1999–2000	Bournemouth	12	3		
2000–01	Bournemouth	36	9		
2001–02	Bournemouth	46	8		
2002–03	Bournemouth	44	4		
2003–04	Bournemouth	39	3		
2004–05	Bournemouth	43	4	**220**	**31**
2005–06	Burnley	36	3	**36**	**3**

GRAY, Andy (F) **266 51**
H: 6 1 W: 13 00 b.Harrogate 15-11-77
Source: Trainee. *Honours:* Scotland Youth, 2 full caps.

1995–96	Leeds U	15	0		
1996–97	Leeds U	7	0		
1997–98	Leeds U	0	0		
1997–98	*Bury*	6	1	**6**	**1**
1998–99	Leeds U	0	0	**22**	**0**
1998–99	Nottingham F	8	0		
1998–99	*Preston NE*	5	0	**5**	**0**
1998–99	*Oldham Ath*	4	0	**4**	**0**
1999–2000	Nottingham F	22	0		
2000–01	Nottingham F	18	0		
2001–02	Nottingham F	16	1	**64**	**1**
2002–03	Bradford C	44	15		
2003–04	Bradford C	33	5	**77**	**20**
2003–04	Sheffield U	14	9		
2004–05	Sheffield U	43	15		
2005–06	Sheffield U	1	1	**58**	**25**
2005–06	Sunderland	21	1	**21**	**1**
2005–06	Burnley	9	3	**9**	**3**

HARLEY, Jon (D) **179 11**
H: 5 8 W: 10 03 b.Maidstone 26-9-79
Source: Trainee. *Honours:* England Under-21.

1996–97	Chelsea	0	0		
1997–98	Chelsea	3	0		
1998–99	Chelsea	0	0		
1999–2000	Chelsea	17	2		
2000–01	Chelsea	10	0	**30**	**2**
2000–01	*Wimbledon*	6	2	**6**	**2**
2001–02	Fulham	10	0		
2002–03	Fulham	11	1		
2002–03	*Sheffield U*	9	1		
2003–04	Fulham	4	0	**25**	**1**
2003–04	*Sheffield U*	5	0		
2003–04	*West Ham U*	15	1	**15**	**1**
2004–05	Sheffield U	44	2		
2005–06	Sheffield U	4	0	**62**	**3**
2005–06	Burnley	41	2	**41**	**2**

HYDE, Micah (M) **439 38**
H: 5 10 W: 11 02 b.Newham 10-11-74
Source: Trainee. *Honours:* Jamaica 16 full caps.

1993–94	Cambridge U	18	2		
1994–95	Cambridge U	27	0		
1995–96	Cambridge U	24	4		
1996–97	Cambridge U	38	7	**107**	**13**
1997–98	Watford	40	4		
1998–99	Watford	44	2		
1999–2000	Watford	34	3		
2000–01	Watford	26	6		
2001–02	Watford	39	4		
2002–03	Watford	37	4		
2003–04	Watford	33	1	**253**	**24**
2004–05	Burnley	38	1		
2005–06	Burnley	41	0	**79**	**1**

JENSEN, Brian (G) **159 0**
H: 6 1 W: 12 04 b.Copenhagen 8-6-75
Source: Hvidovre, B93.

1997–98	AZ	0	0		
1998–99	AZ	1	0	**1**	**0**
1999–2000	WBA	12	0		
2000–01	WBA	33	0		
2001–02	WBA	1	0		
2002–03	WBA	0	0	**46**	**0**
2003–04	Burnley	46	0		
2004–05	Burnley	27	0		
2005–06	Burnley	39	0	**112**	**0**

KARBASSIYON, Daniel (D) **10 0**
H: 5 8 W: 11 07 b.Virginia 10-8-84
Source: Roanoke Star. *Honours:* USA Youth.

2003–04	Arsenal	0	0		
2004–05	Arsenal	0	0		
2004–05	*Ipswich T*	5	0	**5**	**0**
2005–06	Burnley	5	0	**5**	**0**

LAFFERTY, Kyle (F) **20 4**
H: 6 4 W: 11 02 b.Belfast 21-7-87
Source: Scholar. *Honours:* Northern Ireland Youth, Under-21, 2 full caps.

2005–06	Burnley	11	1	**11**	**1**
2005–06	*Darlington*	9	3	**9**	**3**

MAHON, Alan (M) **238 26**
H: 5 8 W: 12 03 b.Dublin 4-4-78
Source: Crumplin U. *Honours:* Eire Under-21, 2 full caps.

1994–95	Tranmere R	0	0		
1995–96	Tranmere R	2	0		
1996–97	Tranmere R	25	2		
1997–98	Tranmere R	18	1		
1998–99	Tranmere R	39	6		
1999–2000	Tranmere R	36	4	**120**	**13**
2000–01	Sporting Lisbon	1	0	**1**	**0**
2000–01	Blackburn R	18	0		
2001–02	Blackburn R	13	1		
2002–03	Blackburn R	2	0		
2002–03	*Cardiff C*	15	2	**15**	**2**
2003–04	Blackburn R	3	0	**36**	**1**
2003–04	*Ipswich T*	11	1	**11**	**1**
2003–04	Wigan Ath	14	1		
2004–05	Wigan Ath	27	7		
2005–06	Wigan Ath	6	1	**47**	**9**
2005–06	Burnley	8	0	**8**	**0**

McCANN, Chris (M) **23 2**
H: 6 1 W: 11 11 b.Dublin 21-7-87
Source: Scholar. *Honours:* Eire Youth.

2005–06	Burnley	23	2	**23**	**2**

McGREAL, John (D) **392 6**
H: 5 11 W: 12 08 b.Birkenhead 2-6-72
Source: Trainee.

1990–91	Tranmere R	3	0		
1991–92	Tranmere R	0	0		
1992–93	Tranmere R	0	0		
1993–94	Tranmere R	15	1		
1994–95	Tranmere R	43	0		
1995–96	Tranmere R	32	0		
1996–97	Tranmere R	24	0		
1997–98	Tranmere R	42	0		
1998–99	Tranmere R	36	0	**195**	**1**
1999–2000	Ipswich T	34	0		
2000–01	Ipswich T	28	1		
2001–02	Ipswich T	27	1		
2002–03	Ipswich T	16	1		
2003–04	Ipswich T	18	1	**123**	**4**
2004–05	Burnley	39	1		
2005–06	Burnley	35	0	**74**	**1**

NOEL-WILLIAMS, Gifton (F) **293 60**
H: 6 3 W: 13 06 b.Islington 21-1-80
Source: Trainee. *Honours:* England Youth.

1996–97	Watford	25	2		
1997–98	Watford	38	7		
1998–99	Watford	26	10		
1999–2000	Watford	3	0		
2000–01	Watford	32	8		
2001–02	Watford	29	6		
2002–03	Watford	16	0	**169**	**33**
2003–04	Stoke C	42	10		
2004–05	Stoke C	46	13	**88**	**23**
2005–06	Burnley	29	2	**29**	**2**
2005–06	*Brighton & HA*	7	2	**7**	**2**

O'CONNOR, Gareth (M) **227 35**
H: 5 10 W: 11 00 b.Dublin 10-11-78
Source: Bohemians.

1998–99	Shamrock R	8	0	**8**	**0**
1999–2000	Bohemians	22	4	**22**	**4**
2000–01	Bournemouth	22	1		
2001–02	Bournemouth	28	0		
2002–03	Bournemouth	41	8		
2003–04	Bournemouth	37	2		
2004–05	Bournemouth	40	13	**168**	**24**
2005–06	Burnley	29	7	**29**	**7**

O'CONNOR, James (M) **273 21**
H: 5 8 W: 11 00 b.Dublin 1-9-79
Source: Trainee. *Honours:* Eire Under-21.

1996–97	Stoke C	0	0		
1997–98	Stoke C	0	0		
1998–99	Stoke C	4	0		
1999–2000	Stoke C	42	6		
2000–01	Stoke C	44	8		
2001–02	Stoke C	43	2		
2002–03	Stoke C	43	0	**176**	**16**
2003–04	WBA	30	0		
2004–05	WBA	0	0	**30**	**0**
2004–05	Burnley	21	2		
2005–06	Burnley	46	3	**67**	**5**

REILLY, Martin (M) **0 0**
H: 5 11 W: 11 00 b.Cavan 3-5-87
Source: Scholar.

2005–06	Burnley	0	0		

SINCLAIR, Frank (D) **412 12**
H: 5 8 W: 12 09 b.Lambeth 3-12-71
Source: Trainee. *Honours:* Jamaica 24 full caps, 1 goal.

1989–90	Chelsea	0	0		
1990–91	Chelsea	4	0		
1991–92	Chelsea	8	1		
1991–92	*WBA*	6	1	**6**	**1**
1992–93	Chelsea	32	0		
1993–94	Chelsea	35	0		
1994–95	Chelsea	35	3		
1995–96	Chelsea	13	1		
1996–97	Chelsea	20	1		
1997–98	Chelsea	22	1	**169**	**7**
1998–99	Leicester C	31	1		
1999–2000	Leicester C	34	0		
2000–01	Leicester C	17	0		
2001–02	Leicester C	35	0		
2002–03	Leicester C	33	1		
2003–04	Leicester C	14	1	**164**	**3**
2004–05	Burnley	36	1		
2005–06	Burnley	37	0	**73**	**1**

SPICER, John (M) **77 9**
H: 5 11 W: 11 07 b.Romford 13-9-83
Source: Scholar. *Honours:* England Schools, Youth, Under-20.

2001–02	Arsenal	0	0		
2002–03	Arsenal	0	0		
2003–04	Arsenal	0	0		
2004–05	Arsenal	0	0		
2004–05	Bournemouth	39	6		
2005–06	Bournemouth	4	0	**43**	**6**
2005–06	Burnley	34	3	**34**	**3**

THOMAS, Wayne (D) **328 13**
H: 6 2 W: 14 12 b.Gloucester 17-5-79
Source: Trainee.

1995–96	Torquay U	6	0		
1996–97	Torquay U	12	0		
1997–98	Torquay U	21	1		
1998–99	Torquay U	44	1		

1999–2000 Torquay U 40 3 **123 5**
2000–01 Stoke C 34 0
2001–02 Stoke C 40 2
2002–03 Stoke C 41 0
2003–04 Stoke C 39 3
2004–05 Stoke C 35 2 **189 7**
2005–06 Burnley 16 1 **16 1**

BURY (17)

ADAMS, Nicky (F) 15 1
H: 5 10 W: 11 00 b.Bolton 16-10-86
Source: Scholar.
2005–06 Bury 15 1 **15 1**

BARLOW, Stuart (F) 415 111
H: 5 10 W: 11 05 b.Liverpool 16-7-68
Source: School.
1990–91 Everton 2 0
1991–92 Everton 7 0
1991–92 *Rotherham U* 0 0
1992–93 Everton 26 5
1993–94 Everton 22 3
1994–95 Everton 11 2
1995–96 Everton 3 0 **71 10**
1995–96 Oldham Ath 26 7
1996–97 Oldham Ath 35 12
1997–98 Oldham Ath 32 12 **93 31**
1997–98 Wigan Ath 9 3
1998–99 Wigan Ath 41 19
1999–2000 Wigan Ath 33 18 **83 40**
2000–01 Tranmere R 27 2
2001–02 Tranmere R 38 14
2002–03 Tranmere R 29 3 **94 19**
2003–04 Stockport Co 30 8
2004–05 Stockport Co 31 3 **61 11**
2005–06 Bury 13 0 **13 0**

BARROW, James (D) 0 0
H: 5 10 W: 12 01 b.Chorley 14-6-86
Source: Scholar.
2005–06 Bury 0 0

BARRY-MURPHY, Brian (M) 259 12
H: 5 10 W: 13 01 b.Cork 27-7-78
Honours: Eire Under-21.
1995–96 Cork City 13 0
1996–97 Cork City 25 0
1997–98 Cork City 15 1
1998–99 Cork City 27 1 **80 2**
1999–2000 Preston NE 1 0
2000–01 Preston NE 14 0
2001–02 Preston NE 4 0
2001–02 *Southend U* 8 1 **8 1**
2002–03 Preston NE 2 0 **21 0**
2002–03 *Hartlepool U* 7 0 **7 0**
2002–03 Sheffield W 17 0
2003–04 Sheffield W 41 0 **58 0**
2004–05 Bury 45 6
2005–06 Bury 40 3 **85 9**

BRASS, Chris (M) 284 6
H: 5 10 W: 11 13 b.Easington 24-7-75
Source: Trainee.
1993–94 Burnley 0 0
1994–95 Burnley 5 0
1994–95 *Torquay U* 7 0 **7 0**
1995–96 Burnley 9 0
1996–97 Burnley 39 0
1997–98 Burnley 40 1
1998–99 Burnley 34 0
1999–2000 Burnley 7 0
2000–01 Burnley 0 0 **134 1**
2000–01 *Halifax T* 6 0 **6 0**
2000–01 York C 10 1
2001–02 York C 41 2
2002–03 York C 40 1
2003–04 York C 39 1
2004–05 York C 0 0 **130 5**
2005–06 Bury 7 0 **7 0**

BUCHANAN, David (M) 26 0
H: 5 7 W: 11 03 b.Rochdale 6-5-86
Source: Scholar. *Honours:* Northern Ireland Youth, Under-21.
2004–05 Bury 3 0
2005–06 Bury 23 0 **26 0**

BURKE, Steve (F) 1 0
H: 6 0 W: 12 10 b.Bolton 13-1-88
2005–06 Bury 1 0 **1 0**

CHALLINOR, Dave (D) 325 9
H: 6 1 W: 12 06 b.Chester 2-10-75
Source: Brombrough Pool. *Honours:* England Schools.
1994–95 Tranmere R 0 0
1995–96 Tranmere R 0 0
1996–97 Tranmere R 5 0
1997–98 Tranmere R 32 1
1998–99 Tranmere R 34 2
1999–2000 Tranmere R 41 3
2000–01 Tranmere R 22 0
2001–02 Tranmere R 6 0 **140 6**
2001–02 Stockport Co 18 0
2002–03 Stockport Co 46 1
2003–04 Stockport Co 17 0 **81 1**
2003–04 *Bury* 15 0
2004–05 Bury 43 1
2005–06 Bury 46 1 **104 2**

DOOTSON, Craig (G) 5 0
H: 6 4 W: 14 00 b.Preston 23-5-79
Source: Bamber Bridge, Leigh RMI, Stalybridge C.
2005–06 Bury 5 0 **5 0**

EDWARDS, Neil (G) 427 0
H: 5 9 W: 12 11 b.Aberdare 5-12-70
Source: Trainee.
1988–89 Leeds U 0 0
1989–90 Leeds U 0 0
1990–91 Leeds U 0 0
1990–91 *Huddersfield T* 0 0
1991–92 Stockport Co 39 0
1992–93 Stockport Co 35 0
1993–94 Stockport Co 26 0
1994–95 Stockport Co 19 0
1995–96 Stockport Co 45 0
1996–97 Stockport Co 0 0
1997–98 Stockport Co 0 0 **164 0**
1997–98 Rochdale 27 0
1998–99 Rochdale 45 0
1999–2000 Rochdale 40 0
2000–01 Rochdale 44 0
2001–02 Rochdale 7 0
2002–03 Rochdale 26 0
2003–04 Rochdale 34 0
2004–05 Rochdale 16 0 **239 0**
2005–06 Bury 24 0 **24 0**

FITZGERALD, John (D) 41 0
H: 6 2 W: 12 13 b.Dublin 10-2-84
Source: Scholar. *Honours:* Eire Youth, Under-21.
2000–01 Blackburn R 0 0
2001–02 Blackburn R 0 0
2002–03 Blackburn R 0 0
2003–04 Blackburn R 0 0
2004–05 Blackburn R 0 0
2004–05 *Bury* 14 0
2005–06 Bury 27 0 **41 0**

FLITCROFT, David (M) 448 28
H: 5 11 W: 14 05 b.Bolton 14-1-74
Source: Trainee.
1991–92 Preston NE 0 0
1992–93 Preston NE 8 2
1993–94 Preston NE 0 0 **8 2**
1993–94 *Lincoln C* 2 0 **2 0**
1993–94 Chester C 8 1
1994–95 Chester C 32 0
1995–96 Chester C 9 1
1996–97 Chester C 32 6
1997–98 Chester C 44 4
1998–99 Chester C 42 6 **167 18**
1999–2000 Rochdale 43 2
2000–01 Rochdale 41 0
2001–02 Rochdale 35 0
2002–03 Rochdale 41 2 **160 4**
2003–04 Macclesfield T 15 0 **15 0**
2003–04 Bury 17 0
2004–05 Bury 36 3
2005–06 Bury 43 1 **96 4**

GRUNDY, Aaron (G) 1 0
H: 6 1 W: 12 07 b.Bolton 21-1-88
Source: Scholar.
2005–06 Bury 1 0 **1 0**

HANNAH, David (M) 123 7
H: 5 11 W: 11 01 b.Coatbridge 4-8-74
Source: Hamilton Th. *Honours:* Scotland Under-21.
1991–92 Dundee U 0 0
1992–93 Dundee U 5 0
1993–94 Dundee U 10 2
1994–95 Dundee U 32 2
1995–96 Dundee U 7 1
1996–97 Dundee U 12 1
1996–97 Celtic 18 0
1997–98 Celtic 15 0
1998–99 Celtic 9 0 **42 0**
1998–99 Dundee U 13 1
1999–2000 Dundee U 0 0
2000–01 Dundee U 0 0
2001–02 Dundee U 0 0 **79 7**
2005–06 Bury 2 0 **2 0**

HARDIKER, John (M) 114 3
H: 5 11 W: 11 01 b.Preston 17-7-82
Source: Morecambe.
2001–02 Stockport Co 12 3
2002–03 Stockport Co 23 0
2003–04 Stockport Co 39 0
2004–05 Stockport Co 29 0 **103 3**
2005–06 Bury 11 0 **11 0**

HITCHEN, Russell (D) 0 0
H: 6 0 W: 11 06 b.West Houghton 24-12-86
Source: Scholar.
2005–06 Bury 0 0

KENNEDY, Tom (D) 106 5
H: 5 10 W: 11 01 b.Bury 24-6-85
Source: Scholar.
2002–03 Bury 0 0
2003–04 Bury 27 0
2004–05 Bury 46 1
2005–06 Bury 33 4 **106 5**

MATTIS, Dwayne (M) 144 12
H: 6 1 W: 11 12 b.Huddersfield 31-7-81
Source: Trainee. *Honours:* Eire Under-21.
1998–99 Huddersfield T 2 0
1999–2000 Huddersfield T 0 0
2000–01 Huddersfield T 0 0
2001–02 Huddersfield T 29 1
2002–03 Huddersfield T 33 1
2003–04 Huddersfield T 5 0 **69 2**
2004–05 Bury 39 5
2005–06 Bury 36 5 **75 10**

NEWBY, Jon (F) 196 26
H: 5 11 W: 11 00 b.Warrington 28-11-78
Source: Trainee.
1998–99 Liverpool 0 0
1999–2000 Liverpool 1 0
1999–2000 *Crewe Alex* 6 0 **6 0**
2000–01 Liverpool 0 0 **1 0**
2000–01 *Sheffield U* 13 0 **13 0**
2000–01 Bury 17 5
2001–02 Bury 46 6
2002–03 Bury 46 10
2003–04 Huddersfield T 14 0 **14 0**
2003–04 *York C* 7 0 **7 0**
2004–05 Bury 36 4
2005–06 Bury 10 1 **155 26**

PARRISH, Andy (D) 8 0
H: 6 0 W: 11 00 b.Bolton 22-6-88
2005–06 Bury 8 0 **8 0**

PUGH, Marc (M) 6 1
H: 5 11 W: 11 04 b.Burnley 2-4-87
Source: Scholar.
2005–06 Burnley 0 0
2005–06 Bury 6 1 **6 1**

QUIGLEY, Damien (M) 1 0
H: 5 8 W: 11 06 b.Rochdale 20-9-87
Source: Scholar.
2005–06 Bury 1 0 **1 0**

SCOTT, Paul (D) 96 4
H: 5 11 W: 12 00 b.Wakefield 5-11-79
Source: Trainee.
1998–99 Huddersfield T 0 0
1999–2000 Huddersfield T 0 0
2000–01 Huddersfield T 0 0
2001–02 Huddersfield T 0 0
2002–03 Huddersfield T 13 0
2003–04 Huddersfield T 19 2

2004–05	Huddersfield T	0	0	**32**	**2**
2004–05	Bury	23	0		
2005–06	Bury	41	2	**64**	**2**

SEDGEMORE, Jake (D) **40 5**
H: 6 1 W: 12 10 b.Wolverhampton 10-10-78
Source: WBA, Hednesford T, Hereford U, Northwich Vic.

2004–05	Shrewsbury T	31	5	**31**	**5**
2005–06	Bury	9	0	**9**	**0**

SMART, Allan (F) **214 46**
H: 6 2 W: 12 07 b.Perth 8-7-74

1994–95	Caledonian Th	4	0	**4**	**0**
1994–95	Preston NE	19	6		
1995–96	Preston NE	2	0		
1995–96	*Carlisle U*	4	0		
1996–97	Preston NE	0	0	**21**	**6**
1996–97	*Northampton T*	1	0	**1**	**0**
1996–97	Carlisle U	28	10		
1997–98	Carlisle U	16	6	**48**	**16**
1998–99	Watford	35	7		
1999–2000	Watford	14	5		
2000–01	Watford	8	0		
2001–02	Watford	0	0	**57**	**12**
2001–02	*Hibernian*	5	1	**5**	**1**
2001–02	*Stoke C*	2	0	**2**	**0**
2001–02	Oldham Ath	21	6	**21**	**6**
2002–03	Dundee U	18	0	**18**	**0**
2003–04	Crewe Alex	6	0	**6**	**0**
2004–05	Milton Keynes D	18	4	**18**	**4**
2005–06	Bury	13	1	**13**	**1**

SPEIGHT, Jake (F) **17 2**
H: 5 7 W: 11 02 b.Sheffield 28-9-85
Source: Sheffield W Scholar.
From Scarborough.

2005–06	Bury	17	2	**17**	**2**

TIPTON, Matt (F) **271 59**
H: 5 10 W: 11 02 b.Bangor 29-6-80
Source: Trainee. *Honours:* Wales Youth, Under-21.

1997–98	Oldham Ath	3	0		
1998–99	Oldham Ath	28	2		
1999–2000	Oldham Ath	29	3		
2000–01	Oldham Ath	30	5		
2001–02	Oldham Ath	22	5	**112**	**15**
2001–02	Macclesfield T	13	3		
2002–03	Macclesfield T	36	10		
2003–04	Macclesfield T	38	16		
2004–05	Macclesfield T	44	12	**131**	**41**
2005–06	Mansfield T	4	0	**4**	**0**
2005–06	Bury	24	3	**24**	**3**

UNSWORTH, Lee (D) **277 6**
H: 5 11 W: 11 09 b.Eccles 25-2-73
Source: Ashton U.

1994–95	Crewe Alex	0	0		
1995–96	Crewe Alex	29	0		
1996–97	Crewe Alex	29	0		
1997–98	Crewe Alex	36	0		
1998–99	Crewe Alex	24	0		
1999–2000	Crewe Alex	8	0	**126**	**0**
2000–01	Bury	15	0		
2001–02	Bury	35	1		
2002–03	Bury	35	2		
2003–04	Bury	27	2		
2004–05	Bury	36	1		
2005–06	Bury	3	0	**151**	**6**

WOODTHORPE, Colin (D) **533 12**
H: 6 0 W: 11 08 b.Ellesmere Pt 13-1-69
Source: Apprentice.

1986–87	Chester C	30	2		
1987–88	Chester C	35	0		
1988–89	Chester C	44	3		
1989–90	Chester C	46	1	**155**	**6**
1990–91	Norwich C	1	0		
1991–92	Norwich C	15	1		
1992–93	Norwich C	7	0		
1993–94	Norwich C	20	0	**43**	**1**
1994–95	Aberdeen	14	0		
1995–96	Aberdeen	15	1		
1996–97	Aberdeen	19	0	**48**	**1**
1997–98	Stockport Co	32	1		
1998–99	Stockport Co	37	2		
1999–2000	Stockport Co	26	0		
2000–01	Stockport Co	24	1		
2001–02	Stockport Co	34	0		
2002–03	Stockport Co	0	0	**153**	**4**
2002–03	Bury	32	0		
2003–04	Bury	39	0		
2004–05	Bury	30	0		
2005–06	Bury	33	0	**134**	**0**

YOUNGS, Tom (F) **216 47**
H: 5 9 W: 11 13 b.Bury St Edmunds 31-8-79
Source: Trainee.

1997–98	Cambridge U	4	0		
1998–99	Cambridge U	10	0		
1999–2000	Cambridge U	21	8		
2000–01	Cambridge U	38	14		
2001–02	Cambridge U	42	11		
2002–03	Cambridge U	35	10	**150**	**43**
2002–03	Northampton T	5	0		
2003–04	Northampton T	12	0		
2004–05	Northampton T	9	0	**26**	**0**
2004–05	Leyton Orient	10	1	**10**	**1**
2005–06	Bury	30	3	**30**	**3**

CARDIFF C (18)

ALEXANDER, Neil (G) **282 0**
H: 6 1 W: 12 08 b.Edinburgh 10-3-78
Source: Edina Hibs. *Honours:* Scotland Under-21, B, 3 full caps.

1996–97	Stenhousemuir	12	0		
1997–98	Stenhousemuir	36	0	**48**	**0**
1998–99	Livingston	21	0		
1999–2000	Livingston	13	0		
2000–01	Livingston	26	0	**60**	**0**
2001–02	Cardiff C	46	0		
2002–03	Cardiff C	40	0		
2003–04	Cardiff C	25	0		
2004–05	Cardiff C	17	0		
2005–06	Cardiff C	46	0	**174**	**0**

ANTHONY, Byron (D) **0 0**
H: 6 1 W: 11 02 b.Newport 20-9-84
Source: Scholar. *Honours:* Wales Youth, Under-21.

2003–04	Cardiff C	0	0		
2004–05	Cardiff C	0	0		
2005–06	Cardiff C	0	0		

ARDLEY, Neal (M) **394 26**
H: 5 10 W: 12 12 b.Epsom 1-9-72
Source: Trainee. *Honours:* England Under-21.

1990–91	Wimbledon	1	0		
1991–92	Wimbledon	8	0		
1992–93	Wimbledon	26	4		
1993–94	Wimbledon	16	1		
1994–95	Wimbledon	14	1		
1995–96	Wimbledon	6	0		
1996–97	Wimbledon	34	2		
1997–98	Wimbledon	34	2		
1998–99	Wimbledon	23	0		
1999–2000	Wimbledon	17	2		
2000–01	Wimbledon	37	3		
2001–02	Wimbledon	29	3	**245**	**18**
2002–03	Watford	43	2		
2003–04	Watford	38	1		
2004–05	Watford	30	4	**111**	**7**
2004–05	Cardiff C	8	1		
2005–06	Cardiff C	30	0	**38**	**1**

BARKER, Chris (D) **276 3**
H: 6 2 W: 13 08 b.Sheffield 2-3-80
Source: Alfreton.

1998–99	Barnsley	0	0		
1999–2000	Barnsley	29	0		
2000–01	Barnsley	40	0		
2001–02	Barnsley	44	3	**113**	**3**
2002–03	Cardiff C	40	0		
2003–04	Cardiff C	39	0		
2004–05	*Stoke C*	4	0	**4**	**0**
2004–05	Cardiff C	39	0		
2005–06	Cardiff C	41	0	**159**	**0**

BLAKE, Darcy (M) **1 0**
H: 5 10 W: 12 05 b.Caerphilly 13-12-88
Source: Scholar. *Honours:* Wales Youth.

2005–06	Cardiff C	1	0	**1**	**0**

BOLAND, Willie (M) **272 3**
H: 5 9 W: 12 04 b.Ennis 6-8-75
Source: Trainee. *Honours:* Eire Youth, Under-21.

1992–93	Coventry C	1	0		
1993–94	Coventry C	27	0		
1994–95	Coventry C	12	0		
1995–96	Coventry C	3	0		
1996–97	Coventry C	1	0		
1997–98	Coventry C	19	0		
1998–99	Coventry C	0	0	**63**	**0**
1999–2000	Cardiff C	28	1		
2000–01	Cardiff C	25	1		
2001–02	Cardiff C	42	1		
2002–03	Cardiff C	41	0		
2003–04	Cardiff C	37	0		
2004–05	Cardiff C	21	0		
2005–06	Cardiff C	15	0	**209**	**3**

CAMPBELL, Andy (F) **154 19**
H: 5 11 W: 12 04 b.Middlesbrough 18-4-79
Source: Trainee. *Honours:* England Youth, Under-21.

1995–96	Middlesbrough	2	0		
1996–97	Middlesbrough	3	0		
1997–98	Middlesbrough	7	0		
1998–99	Middlesbrough	8	0		
1998–99	*Sheffield U*	11	3	**11**	**3**
1999–2000	Middlesbrough	25	4		
2000–01	Middlesbrough	7	0		
2000–01	*Bolton W*	6	0	**6**	**0**
2001–02	Middlesbrough	4	0	**56**	**4**
2001–02	Cardiff C	8	7		
2002–03	Cardiff C	28	3		
2003–04	Cardiff C	25	2		
2004–05	Cardiff C	12	0		
2004–05	*Doncaster R*	3	0	**3**	**0**
2005–06	Cardiff C	0	0	**73**	**12**
2005–06	*Oxford U*	5	0	**5**	**0**

COOMBES, Gregg (M) **0 0**
b.Porth 1-3-88
Source: Scholar.

2005–06	Cardiff C	0	0		

COOPER, Kevin (M) **330 45**
H: 5 8 W: 10 04 b.Derby 8-2-75
Source: Trainee.

1993–94	Derby Co	0	0		
1994–95	Derby Co	1	0		
1995–96	Derby Co	1	0		
1996–97	Derby Co	0	0	**2**	**0**
1996–97	*Stockport Co*	12	3		
1997–98	Stockport Co	38	8		
1998–99	Stockport Co	38	1		
1999–2000	Stockport Co	46	4		
2000–01	Stockport Co	34	5	**168**	**21**
2000–01	Wimbledon	11	3		
2001–02	Wimbledon	40	10	**51**	**13**
2001–02	Wolverhampton W	5	0		
2002–03	Wolverhampton W	26	3		
2003–04	Wolverhampton W	1	0		
2003–04	*Sunderland*	1	0	**1**	**0**
2003–04	*Norwich C*	10	0	**10**	**0**
2004–05	Wolverhampton W	30	6	**62**	**9**
2005–06	Cardiff C	36	2	**36**	**2**

COX, Neil (D) **491 36**
H: 5 11 W: 13 08 b.Scunthorpe 8-10-71
Source: Trainee. *Honours:* England Under-21.

1989–90	Scunthorpe U	0	0		
1990–91	Scunthorpe U	17	1	**17**	**1**
1990–91	Aston Villa	0	0		
1991–92	Aston Villa	7	0		
1992–93	Aston Villa	15	1		
1993–94	Aston Villa	20	2	**42**	**3**
1994–95	Middlesbrough	40	1		
1995–96	Middlesbrough	35	2		
1996–97	Middlesbrough	31	0	**106**	**3**
1997–98	Bolton W	21	1		
1998–99	Bolton W	44	4		
1999–2000	Bolton W	15	2	**80**	**7**
1999–2000	Watford	21	0		
2000–01	Watford	44	5		
2001–02	Watford	40	2		
2002–03	Watford	40	9		
2003–04	Watford	35	4		
2004–05	Watford	39	0	**219**	**20**
2005–06	Cardiff C	27	2	**27**	**2**

DARLINGTON, Jermaine (D) 211 5
H: 5 8 W: 11 05 b.Hackney 11-4-74
Source: Aylesbury U.

1998–99	QPR	4	0		
1999–2000	QPR	34	2		
2000–01	QPR	33	0	**71**	**2**
2001–02	Wimbledon	29	0		
2002–03	Wimbledon	35	2		
2003–04	Wimbledon	41	1	**105**	**3**
2004–05	Watford	26	0	**26**	**0**
2005–06	Cardiff C	9	0	**9**	**0**

FERRETTI, Andrea (F) 4 0
H: 5 10 W: 11 10 b.Parma 18-9-86
Source: Parma.

2005–06	Cardiff C	4	0	**4**	**0**

FISH, Nicky (M) 0 0
H: 5 10 W: 11 02 b.Cardiff 15-9-84
Source: Scholar. *Honours:* Wales Youth, Under-21.

2001–02	Cardiff C	0	0		
2002–03	Cardiff C	0	0		
2003–04	Cardiff C	0	0		
2004–05	Cardiff C	0	0		
2005–06	Cardiff C	0	0		

FLEETWOOD, Stuart (F) 8 0
H: 5 10 W: 12 07 b.Gloucester 23-4-86
Source: Scholar. *Honours:* Wales Youth, Under-21.

2003–04	Cardiff C	2	0		
2004–05	Cardiff C	6	0		
2005–06	Cardiff C	0	0	**8**	**0**

JACOBSON, Joe (D) 1 0
H: 5 11 W: 12 06 b.Cardiff 17-11-86
Source: Scholar. *Honours:* Wales Under-21.

2005–06	Cardiff C	1	0	**1**	**0**

KIFT, Jonathan (F) 0 0
b.Cardiff 16-2-86
Source: Scholar.

2005–06	Cardiff C	0	0		

LEDLEY, Joe (M) 70 6
H: 6 0 W: 11 07 b.Cardiff 23-1-87
Source: Scholar. *Honours:* Wales Youth, Under-21, 3 full caps.

2004–05	Cardiff C	28	3		
2005–06	Cardiff C	42	3	**70**	**6**

LOOVENS, Glenn (D) 95 4
H: 6 1 W: 12 11 b.Doetinchem 22-9-83
Honours: Holland Youth.

2001–02	Feyenoord	8	0		
2002–03	Feyenoord	12	0		
2003–04	Feyenoord	1	0		
2003–04	Excelsior	24	2	**24**	**2**
2004–05	Feyenoord	6	0	**27**	**0**
2004–05	De Graafschap	11	0	**11**	**0**
2005–06	Cardiff C	33	2	**33**	**2**

MARGETSON, Martyn (G) 166 0
H: 6 0 W: 14 00 b.West Neath 8-9-71
Source: Trainee. *Honours:* Wales Schools, Youth, Under-21, B, 1 full cap.

1990–91	Manchester C	2	0		
1991–92	Manchester C	3	0		
1992–93	Manchester C	1	0		
1993–94	Manchester C	0	0		
1993–94	*Bristol R*	3	0	**3**	**0**
1993–94	*Bolton W*	0	0		
1994–95	Manchester C	0	0		
1994–95	*Luton T*	0	0		
1995–96	Manchester C	0	0		
1996–97	Manchester C	17	0		
1997–98	Manchester C	28	0	**51**	**0**
1998–99	Southend U	32	0	**32**	**0**
1999–2000	Huddersfield T	0	0		
2000–01	Huddersfield T	2	0		
2001–02	Huddersfield T	46	0	**48**	**0**
2002–03	Cardiff C	6	0		
2003–04	Cardiff C	22	0		
2004–05	Cardiff C	4	0		
2005–06	Cardiff C	0	0	**32**	**0**

McDONALD, Curtis (M) 1 0
H: 5 10 W: 10 08 b.Cardiff 24-3-88
Source: Scholar. *Honours:* Wales Youth, Under-21.

2005–06	Cardiff C	1	0	**1**	**0**

MULRYNE, Phil (M) 166 18
H: 5 9 W: 11 03 b.Belfast 1-1-78
Source: Trainee. *Honours:* Northern Ireland Youth, Under-21, B, 27 full caps, 3 goals.

1994–95	Manchester U	0	0		
1995–96	Manchester U	0	0		
1996–97	Manchester U	0	0		
1997–98	Manchester U	1	0		
1998–99	Manchester U	0	0	**1**	**0**
1998–99	Norwich C	7	2		
1999–2000	Norwich C	9	0		
2000–01	Norwich C	28	1		
2001–02	Norwich C	40	6		
2002–03	Norwich C	33	6		
2003–04	Norwich C	34	3		
2004–05	Norwich C	10	0	**161**	**18**
2005–06	Cardiff C	4	0	**4**	**0**

N'DUMBU NSUNGU, Guylain (F) 81 21
H: 6 1 W: 12 08 b.Kinshasa 26-12-82
Source: Amiens.

2003–04	Sheffield W	24	9		
2004–05	Sheffield W	11	1	**35**	**10**
2004–05	*Preston NE*	6	0	**6**	**0**
2004–05	Colchester U	8	1	**8**	**1**
2005–06	Darlington	21	10	**21**	**10**
2005–06	Cardiff C	11	0	**11**	**0**

PARRY, Paul (M) 68 6
H: 5 11 W: 12 12 b.Chepstow 19-8-80
Source: Hereford U. *Honours:* Wales 6 full caps, 1 goal.

2003–04	Cardiff C	17	1		
2004–05	Cardiff C	24	4		
2005–06	Cardiff C	27	1	**68**	**6**

PARSLOW, Danny (D) 0 0
H: 5 11 W: 12 05 b.Rhymney Valley 11-9-85

2005–06	Cardiff C	0	0		

PURSE, Darren (D) 343 22
H: 6 2 W: 12 08 b.Stepney 14-2-77
Source: Trainee. *Honours:* England Under-21.

1993–94	Leyton Orient	5	0		
1994–95	Leyton Orient	38	3		
1995–96	Leyton Orient	12	0	**55**	**3**
1996–97	Oxford U	31	1		
1997–98	Oxford U	28	4	**59**	**5**
1997–98	Birmingham C	8	0		
1998–99	Birmingham C	20	0		
1999–2000	Birmingham C	38	2		
2000–01	Birmingham C	37	3		
2001–02	Birmingham C	36	3		
2002–03	Birmingham C	20	1		
2003–04	Birmingham C	9	0	**168**	**9**
2004–05	WBA	22	0	**22**	**0**
2005–06	Cardiff C	39	5	**39**	**5**

SCIMECA, Riccardo (D) 306 11
H: 6 1 W: 12 09 b.Leamington Spa 13-6-75
Source: Trainee. *Honours:* England Under-21, B.

1993–94	Aston Villa	0	0		
1994–95	Aston Villa	0	0		
1995–96	Aston Villa	17	0		
1996–97	Aston Villa	17	0		
1997–98	Aston Villa	21	0		
1998–99	Aston Villa	18	2	**73**	**2**
1999–2000	Nottingham F	38	0		
2000–01	Nottingham F	36	4		
2001–02	Nottingham F	37	0		
2002–03	Nottingham F	40	3	**151**	**7**
2003–04	Leicester C	29	1	**29**	**1**
2004–05	WBA	33	0		
2005–06	WBA	2	0	**35**	**0**
2005–06	Cardiff C	18	1	**18**	**1**

TAYLOR, Anthony (D) 0 0
b.Rhymney Valley 31-3-86
Source: Scholar.

2005–06	Cardiff C	0	0		

THOMPSON, Steven (F) 205 39
H: 6 2 W: 12 05 b.Paisley 14-10-78
Source: Dundee U BC. *Honours:* Scotland Under-21, 16 full caps, 3 goals.

1996–97	Dundee U	1	0		
1997–98	Dundee U	8	0		
1998–99	Dundee U	15	1		
1999–2000	Dundee U	27	1		
2000–01	Dundee U	31	4		
2001–02	Dundee U	32	6		
2002–03	Dundee U	20	6	**134**	**18**
2002–03	Rangers	8	2		
2003–04	Rangers	16	8		
2004–05	Rangers	19	5		
2005–06	Rangers	14	2	**57**	**17**
2005–06	Cardiff C	14	4	**14**	**4**

WESTON, Rhys (D) 183 2
H: 6 1 W: 12 12 b.Kingston 27-10-80
Source: Trainee. *Honours:* England Schools, Youth, Wales Under-21, 7 full caps.

1999–2000	Arsenal	1	0		
2000–01	Arsenal	0	0	**1**	**0**
2000–01	Cardiff C	28	0		
2001–02	Cardiff C	37	0		
2002–03	Cardiff C	38	2		
2003–04	Cardiff C	24	0		
2004–05	Cardiff C	25	0		
2005–06	Cardiff C	30	0	**182**	**2**

WHITLEY, Jeff (M) 252 13
H: 5 8 W: 11 06 b.Zambia 28-1-79
Source: Trainee. *Honours:* Northern Ireland Under-21, B, 20 full caps, 2 goals.

1995–96	Manchester C	0	0		
1996–97	Manchester C	23	1		
1997–98	Manchester C	17	1		
1998–99	Manchester C	8	1		
1998–99	*Wrexham*	9	2	**9**	**2**
1999–2000	Manchester C	42	4		
2000–01	Manchester C	31	1		
2001–02	Manchester C	2	0		
2001–02	*Notts Co*	6	0		
2002–03	Manchester C	0	0	**123**	**8**
2002–03	*Notts Co*	12	0	**18**	**0**
2003–04	Sunderland	33	2		
2004–05	Sunderland	35	0	**68**	**2**
2005–06	Cardiff C	34	1	**34**	**1**

CARLISLE U (19)

ANDREWS, Lee (D) 107 0
H: 6 0 W: 10 12 b.Carlisle 23-4-83
Source: Scholar.

2001–02	Carlisle U	39	0		
2002–03	Carlisle U	15	0		
2002–03	*Rochdale*	8	0	**8**	**0**
2003–04	Carlisle U	37	0		
2004–05	Carlisle U	0	0		
2005–06	Carlisle U	1	0	**92**	**0**
2005–06	*Torquay U*	7	0	**7**	**0**

ARANALDE, Zigor (D) 236 10
H: 6 1 W: 13 03 b.Ibarra 28-2-73
Source: Logrones.

2000–01	Walsall	45	0		
2001–02	Walsall	45	2		
2002–03	Walsall	39	3		
2003–04	Walsall	36	0		
2004–05	Walsall	30	0	**195**	**5**
2004–05	Sheffield W	2	0	**2**	**0**
2005–06	Carlisle U	39	5	**39**	**5**

ARNISON, Paul (D) 144 4
H: 5 10 W: 10 12 b.Hartlepool 18-9-77
Source: Trainee.

1995–96	Newcastle U	0	0		
1996–97	Newcastle U	0	0		
1997–98	Newcastle U	0	0		
1998–99	Newcastle U	0	0		
1999–2000	Newcastle U	0	0		
1999–2000	Hartlepool U	8	1		
2000–01	Hartlepool U	27	1		
2001–02	Hartlepool U	19	0		
2002–03	Hartlepool U	19	1		
2003–04	Hartlepool U	4	0	**77**	**3**
2003–04	Carlisle U	26	1		
2004–05	Carlisle U	0	0		
2005–06	Carlisle U	41	0	**67**	**1**

BILLY, Chris (M) 480 25
H: 5 11 W: 11 08 b.Huddersfield 2-1-73
Source: Trainee.

1991–92	Huddersfield T	10	2		
1992–93	Huddersfield T	13	0		
1993–94	Huddersfield T	34	0		

1994–95 Huddersfield T 37 2 **94 4**
1995–96 Plymouth Arg 32 4
1996–97 Plymouth Arg 45 3
1997–98 Plymouth Arg 41 2 **118 9**
1998–99 Notts Co 6 0 **6 0**
1998–99 Bury 37 0
1999–2000 Bury 36 4
2000–01 Bury 46 0
2001–02 Bury 21 3
2002–03 Bury 38 4 **178 11**
2003–04 Carlisle U 39 1
2004–05 Carlisle U 0 0
2005–06 Carlisle U 45 0 **84 1**

BRADLEY, Adam (G) 0 0
H: 6 0 W: 12 06 b.Carlisle 25-8-88
2005–06 Carlisle U 0 0

BRIDGES, Michael (F) 196 51
H: 6 1 W: 10 11 b.North Shields 5-8-78
Source: Trainee. *Honours:* England Schools, Youth, Under-21.
1995–96 Sunderland 15 4
1996–97 Sunderland 25 3
1997–98 Sunderland 9 1
1998–99 Sunderland 30 8
1999–2000 Leeds U 34 19
2000–01 Leeds U 7 0
2001–02 Leeds U 0 0
2002–03 Leeds U 5 0
2003–04 Leeds U 10 0 **56 19**
2003–04 *Newcastle U* 6 0 **6 0**
2004–05 Bolton W 0 0
2004–05 Sunderland 19 1 **98 17**
2005–06 Bristol C 11 0 **11 0**
2005–06 Carlisle U 25 15 **25 15**

DILLON, Dan (M) 1 0
H: 5 9 W: 10 07 b.Huntingdon 6-9-86
Source: Scholar.
2002–03 Carlisle U 1 0
2003–04 Carlisle U 0 0
2004–05 Carlisle U 0 0
2005–06 Carlisle U 0 0 **1 0**

GRAND, Simon (D) 48 4
H: 6 0 W: 10 03 b.Chorley 23-2-84
Source: Scholar.
2002–03 Rochdale 23 2
2003–04 Rochdale 17 0 **40 2**
2004–05 Carlisle U 0 0
2005–06 Carlisle U 8 2 **8 2**

GRAY, Kevin (D) 453 16
H: 6 0 W: 14 00 b.Sheffield 7-1-72
Source: Trainee.
1988–89 Mansfield T 1 0
1989–90 Mansfield T 16 0
1990–91 Mansfield T 31 1
1991–92 Mansfield T 18 0
1992–93 Mansfield T 33 0
1993–94 Mansfield T 42 2 **141 3**
1994–95 Huddersfield T 5 0
1995–96 Huddersfield T 38 0
1996–97 Huddersfield T 39 1
1997–98 Huddersfield T 35 1
1998–99 Huddersfield T 34 1
1999–2000 Huddersfield T 18 2
2000–01 *Stockport Co* 1 0 **1 0**
2000–01 Huddersfield T 17 0
2001–02 Huddersfield T 44 1 **230 6**
2002–03 Tranmere R 10 1
2003–04 Tranmere R 2 0 **12 1**
2003–04 Carlisle U 25 3
2004–05 Carlisle U 0 0
2005–06 Carlisle U 44 3 **69 6**

HACKNEY, Simon (M) 30 6
H: 5 8 W: 9 13 b.Manchester 5-2-84
Source: Woodley Sports.
2005–06 Carlisle U 30 6 **30 6**

HAWLEY, Karl (F) 75 31
H: 5 8 W: 12 02 b.Walsall 6-12-81
Source: Scholar.
2000–01 Walsall 0 0
2001–02 Walsall 1 0
2002–03 Walsall 0 0
2002–03 *Raith R* 17 7
2003–04 Walsall 0 0 **1 0**
2003–04 *Raith R* 11 2 **28 9**
2004–05 Carlisle U 0 0
2005–06 Carlisle U 46 22 **46 22**

HOLMES, Derek (F) 201 37
H: 6 2 W: 13 00 b.Lanark 18-10-78
Source: Royal Albert.
1995–96 Hearts 0 0
1996–97 Hearts 1 0
1997–98 Hearts 1 1
1997–98 Cowdenbeath 13 5 **13 5**
1998–99 Hearts 6 0 **8 1**
1999–2000 Ross Co 25 8
2000–01 Ross Co 0 0 **25 8**
2001–02 Bournemouth 37 9
2002–03 Bournemouth 29 3
2003–04 Bournemouth 26 2
2004–05 Bournemouth 23 2 **115 16**
2004–05 Carlisle U 0 0
2005–06 Carlisle U 40 7 **40 7**

JOYCE, Luke (M) 0 0
b.Bolton 9-7-87
Source: Scholar.
2005–06 Wigan Ath 0 0
2005–06 Carlisle U 0 0

KELLY, Darren (D) 42 2
H: 6 0 W: 13 00 b.Derry 30-6-79
Source: Derry C.
2002–03 Carlisle U 32 1
2003–04 Carlisle U 10 1
2004–05 Carlisle U 0 0
2005–06 Carlisle U 0 0 **42 2**

LIVESEY, Danny (D) 63 4
H: 6 3 W: 13 01 b.Salford 31-12-84
Source: Trainee.
2002–03 Bolton W 2 0
2003–04 Bolton W 0 0
2003–04 *Notts Co* 11 0 **11 0**
2003–04 *Rochdale* 13 0 **13 0**
2004–05 Bolton W 0 0 **2 0**
2004–05 *Blackpool* 1 0 **1 0**
2005–06 Carlisle U 36 4 **36 4**

LUMSDON, Chris (M) 147 21
H: 5 11 W: 10 06 b.Newcastle 15-12-79
Source: Trainee.
1997–98 Sunderland 1 0
1998–99 Sunderland 0 0
1999–2000 Sunderland 1 0
1999–2000 *Blackpool* 6 1 **6 1**
2000–01 Sunderland 0 0
2000–01 *Crewe Alex* 16 0 **16 0**
2001–02 Sunderland 0 0 **2 0**
2001–02 Barnsley 32 7
2002–03 Barnsley 25 3
2003–04 Barnsley 28 3
2004–05 Barnsley 0 0 **85 13**
2005–06 Carlisle U 38 7 **38 7**

McGILL, Brendan (M) 132 15
H: 5 8 W: 9 02 b.Dublin 22-3-81
Source: River Valley R.
1998–99 Sunderland 0 0
1999–2000 Sunderland 0 0
2000–01 Sunderland 0 0
2001–02 Sunderland 0 0
2001–02 *Carlisle U* 28 2
2002–03 Sunderland 0 0
2002–03 Carlisle U 34 3
2003–04 Carlisle U 44 7
2004–05 Carlisle U 0 0
2005–06 Carlisle U 26 3 **132 15**

MOLLOY, David (M) 7 0
H: 5 11 W: 11 01 b.Newcastle 29-8-86
Source: Scholar.
2003–04 Carlisle U 7 0
2004–05 Carlisle U 0 0
2005–06 Carlisle U 0 0 **7 0**

MURPHY, Peter (M) 180 6
H: 5 10 W: 12 10 b.Dublin 27-10-80
Source: Trainee. *Honours:* Eire Under-21.
1998–99 Blackburn R 0 0
1999–2000 Blackburn R 0 0
2000–01 Blackburn R 0 0
2000–01 *Halifax T* 21 1 **21 1**
2001–02 Blackburn R 0 0
2001–02 Carlisle U 40 0
2002–03 Carlisle U 40 2
2003–04 Carlisle U 35 1
2004–05 Carlisle U 0 0
2005–06 Carlisle U 44 2 **159 5**

MURRAY, Adam (M) 163 16
H: 5 8 W: 10 12 b.Birmingham 30-9-81
Source: Trainee. *Honours:* England Youth, Under-20.
1998–99 Derby Co 4 0
1999–2000 Derby Co 8 0
2000–01 Derby Co 14 0
2001–02 Derby Co 6 0
2001–02 *Mansfield T* 13 7
2002–03 Derby Co 24 0
2003–04 Derby Co 0 0 **56 0**
2003–04 Kidderminster H 22 3 **22 3**
From Burton Alb.
2003–04 Notts Co 3 0 **3 0**
2004–05 Mansfield T 32 5 **45 12**
2004–05 Carlisle U 0 0
2005–06 Carlisle U 37 1 **37 1**

MURRAY, Glenn (F) 26 3
H: 6 1 W: 12 12 b.Maryport 25-9-83
Source: Wilmington Hammerheads, Workington.
2005–06 Carlisle U 26 3 **26 3**

MURRAY, Paul (M) 294 25
H: 5 9 W: 10 08 b.Carlisle 31-8-76
Source: Trainee. *Honours:* England Youth, Under-21, B.
1993–94 Carlisle U 8 0
1994–95 Carlisle U 5 0
1995–96 Carlisle U 28 1
1995–96 QPR 1 0
1996–97 QPR 32 5
1997–98 QPR 32 1
1997–98 QPR 0 0
1998–99 QPR 39 1
1999–2000 QPR 30 0
2000–01 QPR 6 0 **140 7**
2001–02 Southampton 1 0 **1 0**
2001–02 Oldham Ath 24 5
2002–03 Oldham Ath 30 1
2003–04 Oldham Ath 41 9 **95 15**
2004–05 Beira Mar 17 2 **17 2**
2005–06 Carlisle U 0 0 **41 1**

NADE, Raphael (M) 22 2
H: 6 0 W: 12 08 b.Abidjan 18-10-80
Source: Le Havre, Troyes, Hampton & Richmond B, Welling U, Woking.
2005–06 Carlisle U 22 2 **22 2**

RIVERS, Mark (F) 332 63
H: 5 10 W: 11 04 b.Crewe 26-11-75
Source: Trainee.
1993–94 Crewe Alex 0 0
1994–95 Crewe Alex 0 0
1995–96 Crewe Alex 33 10
1996–97 Crewe Alex 27 6
1997–98 Crewe Alex 35 6
1998–99 Crewe Alex 43 7
1999–2000 Crewe Alex 32 7
2000–01 Crewe Alex 33 7
2001–02 Norwich C 32 2
2002–03 Norwich C 30 4
2003–04 Norwich C 12 4 **74 10**
2004–05 Crewe Alex 34 7
2005–06 Crewe Alex 17 3 **254 53**
2005–06 Carlisle U 4 0 **4 0**

SHELLEY, Brian (D) 66 1
H: 6 0 W: 13 00 b.Dublin 15-11-81
Source: Bohemians. *Honours:* Eire Under-21.
2002–03 Carlisle U 35 1
2003–04 Carlisle U 31 0
2004–05 Carlisle U 0 0
2005–06 Carlisle U 0 0 **66 1**

SIMPSON, Paul (M) 671 150
H: 5 8 W: 11 11 b.Carlisle 26-7-66
Source: Apprentice. *Honours:* England Youth, Under-21.
1982–83 Manchester C 3 0
1983–84 Manchester C 0 0
1984–85 Manchester C 10 6
1985–86 Manchester C 37 8
1986–87 Manchester C 32 3
1987–88 Manchester C 38 1
1988–89 Manchester C 1 0 **121 18**

1988–89	Oxford U	25	8		
1989–90	Oxford U	42	9		
1990–91	Oxford U	46	17		
1991–92	Oxford U	31	9	**144**	**43**
1991–92	Derby Co	16	7		
1992–93	Derby Co	35	12		
1993–94	Derby Co	34	9		
1994–95	Derby Co	42	8		
1995–96	Derby Co	39	10		
1996–97	Derby Co	19	2		
1996–97	*Sheffield U*	6	0	**6**	**0**
1997–98	Derby Co	1	0	**186**	**48**
1997–98	Wolverhampton W	28	4		
1998–99	Wolverhampton W	11	2		
1998–99	*Walsall*	10	1	**10**	**1**
1999–2000	Wolverhampton W	13	0		
2000–01	Wolverhampton W	0	0	**52**	**6**
2000–01	Blackpool	44	12		
2001–02	Blackpool	32	1	**76**	**13**
2001–02	Rochdale	7	5		
2002–03	Rochdale	35	10	**42**	**15**
2003–04	Carlisle U	25	6		
2004–05	Carlisle U	0	0		
2005–06	Carlisle U	9	0	**34**	**6**

WESTWOOD, Keiren (G) 35 0
H: 6 1 W: 13 10 b.Manchester 23-10-84

2001–02	Manchester C	0	0		
2002–03	Manchester C	0	0		
2003–04	Manchester C	0	0		
2003–04	*Oldham Ath*	0	0		
2004–05	Manchester C	0	0		
2005–06	Manchester C	0	0		
2005–06	Carlisle U	35	0	**35**	**0**

WILLIAMS, Tony (G) 232 0
H: 6 2 W: 13 09 b.Maesteg 20-9-77
Source: Trainee. *Honours:* Wales Youth, Under-21.

1996–97	Blackburn R	0	0		
1997–98	Blackburn R	0	0		
1997–98	*QPR*	0	0		
1998–99	Blackburn R	0	0		
1998–99	*Macclesfield T*	4	0		
1998–99	*Huddersfield T*	0	0		
1998–99	*Bristol R*	9	0	**9**	**0**
1999–2000	Blackburn R	0	0		
1999–2000	*Gillingham*	2	0	**2**	**0**
1999–2000	*Macclesfield T*	11	0	**15**	**0**
2000–01	Hartlepool U	41	0		
2001–02	Hartlepool U	43	0		
2002–03	Hartlepool U	46	0		
2003–04	Hartlepool U	1	0	**131**	**0**
2003–04	*Swansea C*	0	0		
2003–04	*Stockport Co*	15	0	**15**	**0**
2004–05	Grimsby T	46	0	**46**	**0**
2005–06	Carlisle U	11	0	**11**	**0**
2005–06	*Bury*	3	0	**3**	**0**

CHARLTON ATH (20)

AMBROSE, Darren (M) 95 16
H: 6 0 W: 11 00 b.Harlow 29-2-84
Source: Scholar. *Honours:* England Youth, Under-20, Under-21.

2001–02	Ipswich T	1	0		
2002–03	Ipswich T	29	8	**30**	**8**
2002–03	Newcastle U	1	0		
2003–04	Newcastle U	24	2		
2004–05	Newcastle U	12	3	**37**	**5**
2005–06	Charlton Ath	28	3	**28**	**3**

ANDERSEN, Stephan (G) 17 0
H: 6 2 W: 13 07 b.Copenhagen 26-11-81
Source: AB Copenhagen. *Honours:* Denmark Youth, Under-21, 2 full caps.

2004–05	Charlton Ath	2	0		
2005–06	Charlton Ath	15	0	**17**	**0**

ASHTON, Nathan (D) 0 0
H: 5 8 W: 9 07 b.Plaistow 30-1-87
Source: Scholar. *Honours:* England Youth, Under-20.

2004–05	Charlton Ath	0	0		
2005–06	Charlton Ath	0	0		

BARTLETT, Shaun (F) 257 66
H: 6 0 W: 12 06 b.Cape Town 31-10-72
Honours: Cape Town Spurs. South Africa 72 full caps, 28 goals.

1996	Colorado Rapids	26	8		
1996–97	Amazulu	0	0		
1997	NY/NJ Metros	13	2	**13**	**2**
1997	Colorado Rapids	10	1	**36**	**9**
1998	Cape Town Spurs	18	8	**18**	**8**
1998–99	Zurich	27	13		
1999–2000	Zurich	20	2		
2000–01	Zurich	20	8	**67**	**23**
2000–01	Charlton Ath	18	7		
2001–02	Charlton Ath	14	1		
2002–03	Charlton Ath	31	4		
2003–04	Charlton Ath	19	5		
2004–05	Charlton Ath	25	6		
2005–06	Charlton Ath	16	1	**123**	**24**

BENT, Darren (F) 158 67
H: 5 11 W: 12 07 b.Wandsworth 6-2-84
Source: Scholar. *Honours:* England Youth, Under-21, 1 full cap.

2001–02	Ipswich T	5	1		
2002–03	Ipswich T	35	12		
2003–04	Ipswich T	37	16		
2004–05	Ipswich T	45	20	**122**	**49**
2005–06	Charlton Ath	36	18	**36**	**18**

BENT, Marcus (F) 368 81
H: 6 2 W: 13 03 b.Hammersmith 19-5-78
Source: Trainee. *Honours:* England Under-21.

1995–96	Brentford	12	1		
1996–97	Brentford	34	3		
1997–98	Brentford	24	4	**70**	**8**
1997–98	Crystal Palace	16	5		
1998–99	Crystal Palace	12	0	**28**	**5**
1998–99	Port Vale	15	0		
1999–2000	Port Vale	8	1	**23**	**1**
1999–2000	Sheffield U	32	15		
2000–01	Sheffield U	16	5	**48**	**20**
2000–01	Blackburn R	28	8		
2001–02	Blackburn R	9	0	**37**	**8**
2001–02	Ipswich T	25	9		
2002–03	Ipswich T	32	11		
2003–04	Ipswich T	4	1	**61**	**21**
2003–04	*Leicester C*	33	9	**33**	**9**
2004–05	Everton	37	6		
2005–06	Everton	18	1	**55**	**7**
2005–06	Charlton Ath	13	2	**13**	**2**

BOTHROYD, Jay (F) 127 21
H: 6 3 W: 14 13 b.Islington 7-5-82
Source: Trainee. *Honours:* England Youth, Under-20, Under-21.

1999–2000	Arsenal	0	0		
2000–01	Coventry C	8	0		
2001–02	Coventry C	31	6		
2002–03	Coventry C	33	8	**72**	**14**
2003–04	*Perugia*	26	4	**26**	**4**
2004–05	Blackburn R	11	1	**11**	**1**
2005–06	Charlton Ath	18	2	**18**	**2**

BRANDAO, Goncarlo (D) 0 0
H: 5 11 W: 12 03 b.Lisbon 9-10-86
Source: Belenenses.

2005–06	Charlton Ath	0	0		

CARVILL, Michael (F) 0 0
b.Belfast 3-4-88
Source: Scholar.

2005–06	Charlton Ath	0	0		

EL KARKOURI, Talal (D) 125 5
H: 6 1 W: 12 03 b.Casablanca 8-7-76
Source: Casablanca School of Sportsmen. *Honours:* Morocco 31 full caps, 1 goal.

1999–2000	Paris St Germain	10	0		
2000–01	Paris St Germain	11	0		
2000–01	Aris Salonika	11	0	**11**	**0**
2001–02	Paris St Germain	16	0		
2002–03	Sunderland	8	0	**8**	**0**
2003–04	Paris St Germain	27	0	**64**	**0**
2004–05	Charlton Ath	32	5		
2005–06	Charlton Ath	10	0	**42**	**5**

ELLIOT, Rob (G) 4 0
H: 6 3 W: 14 10 b.Greenwich 30-4-86
Source: Scholar.

2004–05	Charlton Ath	0	0		
2004–05	*Notts Co*	4	0	**4**	**0**
2005–06	Charlton Ath	0	0		

EUELL, Jason (F) 280 75
H: 5 11 W: 11 13 b.Lambeth 6-2-77
Source: Trainee. *Honours:* England Youth, Under-21, Jamaica full caps.

1995–96	Wimbledon	9	2		
1996–97	Wimbledon	7	2		
1997–98	Wimbledon	19	4		
1998–99	Wimbledon	33	10		
1999–2000	Wimbledon	37	4		
2000–01	Wimbledon	36	19	**141**	**41**
2001–02	Charlton Ath	36	11		
2002–03	Charlton Ath	36	10		
2003–04	Charlton Ath	31	10		
2004–05	Charlton Ath	26	2		
2005–06	Charlton Ath	10	1	**139**	**34**

FISH, Mark (D) 351 14
H: 6 4 W: 12 07 b.Cape Town 14-3-74
Source: Arcadia Shepherds. *Honours:* South Africa 62 full caps, 2 goals.

1992	Jomo Cosmos	14	1		
1993	Jomo Cosmos	41	1	**55**	**2**
1994	Orlando Pirates	37	5		
1995	Orlando Pirates	38	1	**75**	**6**
1996–97	Lazio	15	1	**15**	**1**
1997–98	Bolton W	22	2		
1998–99	Bolton W	36	1		
1999–2000	Bolton W	31	0		
2000–01	Bolton W	14	0	**103**	**3**
2000–01	Charlton Ath	24	1		
2001–02	Charlton Ath	25	0		
2002–03	Charlton Ath	23	1		
2003–04	Charlton Ath	23	0		
2004–05	Charlton Ath	7	0		
2005–06	Charlton Ath	0	0	**102**	**2**
2005–06	*Ipswich T*	1	0	**1**	**0**

FORTUNE, Jon (D) 133 5
H: 6 2 W: 12 12 b.Islington 23-8-80
Source: Trainee.

1998–99	Charlton Ath	0	0		
1999–2000	Charlton Ath	0	0		
1999–2000	*Mansfield T*	4	0		
2000–01	Charlton Ath	0	0		
2000–01	*Mansfield T*	14	0	**18**	**0**
2001–02	Charlton Ath	19	0		
2002–03	Charlton Ath	26	1		
2003–04	Charlton Ath	28	2		
2004–05	Charlton Ath	31	2		
2005–06	Charlton Ath	11	0	**115**	**5**

FULLER, Barry (M) 15 1
H: 5 10 W: 11 10 b.Ashford 25-9-84
Source: Scholar.

2004–05	Charlton Ath	0	0		
2005–06	Charlton Ath	0	0		
2005–06	*Barnet*	15	1	**15**	**1**

GISLASON, Rurik (M) 0 0
H: 6 0 W: 11 04 b.Reykjavik 25-2-88
Source: Kopavogur, Anderlecht. *Honours:* Iceland 1 full cap.

2005–06	Charlton Ath	0	0		

HOLLAND, Matt (M) 456 66
H: 5 10 W: 12 03 b.Bury 11-4-74
Source: Trainee. *Honours:* Eire B, 49 full caps, 5 goals.

1992–93	West Ham U	0	0		
1993–94	West Ham U	0	0		
1994–95	West Ham U	0	0		
1994–95	Bournemouth	16	1		
1995–96	Bournemouth	43	10		
1996–97	Bournemouth	45	7	**104**	**18**
1997–98	Ipswich T	46	10		
1998–99	Ipswich T	46	5		
1999–2000	Ipswich T	46	10		
2000–01	Ipswich T	38	3		
2001–02	Ipswich T	38	3		
2002–03	Ipswich T	45	7	**259**	**38**
2003–04	Charlton Ath	38	6		
2004–05	Charlton Ath	32	3		
2005–06	Charlton Ath	23	1	**93**	**10**

HREIDARSSON, Hermann (D) 371 19
H: 6 3 W: 12 12 b.Reykjavik 11-7-74
Honours: Iceland Under-21, 64 full caps, 4 goals.

1993	IBV	2	0		
1994	IBV	18	2		

1995	IBV	18	1		
1996	IBV	17	2		
1997	IBV	11	0	**66**	**5**
1997–98	Crystal Palace	30	2		
1998–99	Crystal Palace	7	0	**37**	**2**
1998–99	Brentford	33	4		
1999–2000	Brentford	8	2	**41**	**6**
1999–2000	Wimbledon	24	1	**24**	**1**
2000–01	Ipswich T	36	1		
2001–02	Ipswich T	38	1		
2002–03	Ipswich T	28	0	**102**	**2**
2002–03	Charlton Ath	0	0		
2003–04	Charlton Ath	33	2		
2004–05	Charlton Ath	34	1		
2005–06	Charlton Ath	34	0	**101**	**3**

HUGHES, Bryan (M) 392 50
H: 5 10 W: 11 08 b.Liverpool 19-6-76
Source: Trainee.

1993–94	Wrexham	11	0		
1994–95	Wrexham	38	9		
1995–96	Wrexham	22	0		
1996–97	Wrexham	23	3	**94**	**12**
1996–97	Birmingham C	11	0		
1997–98	Birmingham C	40	5		
1998–99	Birmingham C	28	3		
1999–2000	Birmingham C	45	10		
2000–01	Birmingham C	45	4		
2001–02	Birmingham C	31	7		
2002–03	Birmingham C	22	2		
2003–04	Birmingham C	26	3	**248**	**34**
2004–05	Charlton Ath	17	1		
2005–06	Charlton Ath	33	3	**50**	**4**

JEFFERS, Francis (F) 117 25
H: 5 10 W: 11 02 b.Liverpool 25-1-81
Source: Trainee. *Honours:* England Schools, Youth, Under-21, 1 full cap, 1 goal.

1997–98	Everton	1	0		
1998–99	Everton	15	6		
1999–2000	Everton	21	6		
2000–01	Everton	12	6		
2001–02	Arsenal	6	2		
2002–03	Arsenal	16	2		
2003–04	Arsenal	0	0	**22**	**4**
2003–04	*Everton*	18	0	**67**	**18**
2004–05	Charlton Ath	20	3		
2005–06	Charlton Ath	0	0	**20**	**3**
2005–06	*Rangers*	8	0	**8**	**0**

JOHANSSON, Jonatan (F) 248 59
H: 6 2 W: 12 08 b.Stockholm 16-8-75
Source: Flora Tallinn. *Honours:* Finland Under-21, 70 full caps, 12 goals.

1995	TPS Turku	9	0		
1996	TPS Turku	23	6	**32**	**6**
1996–97	Flora Tallinn	9	9	**9**	**9**
1997–98	Rangers	6	0		
1998–99	Rangers	25	8		
1999–2000	Rangers	16	6	**47**	**14**
2000–01	Charlton Ath	31	11		
2001–02	Charlton Ath	30	5		
2002–03	Charlton Ath	31	3		
2003–04	Charlton Ath	26	4		
2004–05	Charlton Ath	26	4		
2005–06	Charlton Ath	4	0	**148**	**27**
2005–06	*Norwich C*	12	3	**12**	**3**

JOHN, Alistar (M) 0 0
b. 28-11-87
Source: Scholar.

2005–06	Charlton Ath	0	0		

KEMENES, Szabolcs (G) 0 0
H: 6 2 W: 12 12 b.Budapest 18-5-86
Source: ferencvaros.

2004–05	Charlton Ath	0	0		
2005–06	Charlton Ath	0	0		

KISHISHEV, Radostin (D) 358 19
H: 5 11 W: 12 03 b.Bourgas 30-7-74
Honours: Bulgaria 63 full caps.

1991–92	Chernomorets	6	1		
1992–93	Chernomorets	23	2		
1993–94	Chernomorets	23	1	**52**	**4**
1994–95	Neftochimik	14	0		
1995–96	Neftochimik	30	0		
1996–97	Neftochimik	30	6		
1997–98	Neftochimik	1	0	**75**	**6**
1997–98	Bursaspor	20	3	**20**	**3**
1997–98	Litets Lovech	5	0		
1998–99	Litets Lovech	26	2		
1999–2000	Litets Lovech	15	2	**46**	**4**
2000–01	Charlton Ath	27	0		
2001–02	Charlton Ath	3	0		
2002–03	Charlton Ath	34	2		
2003–04	Charlton Ath	33	0		
2004–05	Charlton Ath	31	0		
2005–06	Charlton Ath	37	0	**165**	**2**

LISBIE, Kevin (F) 171 22
H: 5 10 W: 11 06 b.Hackney 17-10-78
Source: Trainee. *Honours:* England Youth. Jamaica 6 full caps.

1996–97	Charlton Ath	25	1		
1997–98	Charlton Ath	17	1		
1998–99	Charlton Ath	1	0		
1998–99	*Gillingham*	7	4	**7**	**4**
1999–2000	Charlton Ath	0	0		
1999–2000	*Reading*	2	0	**2**	**0**
2000–01	Charlton Ath	18	0		
2000–01	*QPR*	2	0	**2**	**0**
2001–02	Charlton Ath	22	5		
2002–03	Charlton Ath	32	4		
2003–04	Charlton Ath	9	4		
2004–05	Charlton Ath	17	1		
2005–06	Charlton Ath	6	0	**147**	**16**
2005–06	*Norwich C*	6	1	**6**	**1**
2005–06	*Derby Co*	7	1	**7**	**1**

MYHRE, Thomas (G) 276 0
H: 6 4 W: 14 02 b.Sarpsborg 16-10-73
Honours: Norway Youth, Under-21, 50 full caps.

1993	Viking	22	0		
1994	Viking	22	0		
1995	Viking	24	0		
1996	Viking	0	0		
1997	Viking	26	0	**94**	**0**
1997–98	Everton	22	0		
1998–99	Everton	38	0		
1999–2000	Everton	4	0		
1999–2000	*Rangers*	3	0	**3**	**0**
1999–2000	*Birmingham C*	7	0	**7**	**0**
2000–01	Everton	6	0		
2000–01	*Tranmere R*	3	0	**3**	**0**
2000–01	FC Copenhagen	14	0	**14**	**0**
2001–02	Everton	0	0	**70**	**0**
2001–02	Besiktas	13	0	**13**	**0**
2002–03	Sunderland	2	0		
2003–04	Sunderland	4	0		
2003–04	*Crystal Palace*	15	0	**15**	**0**
2004–05	Sunderland	31	0	**37**	**0**
2005–06	Charlton Ath	20	0	**20**	**0**

PERRY, Chris (D) 363 8
H: 5 8 W: 11 03 b.Carshalton 26-4-73
Source: Trainee.

1991–92	Wimbledon	0	0		
1992–93	Wimbledon	0	0		
1993–94	Wimbledon	2	0		
1994–95	Wimbledon	22	0		
1995–96	Wimbledon	37	0		
1996–97	Wimbledon	37	1		
1997–98	Wimbledon	35	1		
1998–99	Wimbledon	34	0	**167**	**2**
1999–2000	Tottenham H	37	1		
2000–01	Tottenham H	32	1		
2001–02	Tottenham H	33	0		
2002–03	Tottenham H	18	1		
2003–04	Tottenham H	0	0	**120**	**3**
2003–04	Charlton Ath	29	1		
2004–05	Charlton Ath	19	1		
2005–06	Charlton Ath	28	1	**76**	**3**

POWELL, Chris (D) 616 5
H: 5 11 W: 11 12 b.Lambeth 8-9-69
Source: Trainee. *Honours:* England 5 full caps.

1987–88	Crystal Palace	0	0		
1988–89	Crystal Palace	3	0		
1989–90	Crystal Palace	0	0	**3**	**0**
1989–90	*Aldershot*	11	0	**11**	**0**
1990–91	Southend U	45	1		
1991–92	Southend U	44	0		
1992–93	Southend U	42	2		
1993–94	Southend U	46	0		
1994–95	Southend U	44	0		
1995–96	Southend U	27	0	**248**	**3**
1995–96	Derby Co	19	0		
1996–97	Derby Co	35	0		
1997–98	Derby Co	37	1	**91**	**1**
1998–99	Charlton Ath	38	0		
1999–2000	Charlton Ath	40	0		
2000–01	Charlton Ath	33	0		
2001–02	Charlton Ath	36	1		
2002–03	Charlton Ath	37	0		
2003–04	Charlton Ath	16	0		
2004–05	Charlton Ath	0	0		
2004–05	West Ham U	36	0	**36**	**0**
2005–06	Charlton Ath	27	0	**227**	**1**

RANDOLPH, Darren (G) 0 0
H: 6 2 W: 14 00 b.Dublin 12-5-87
Source: Ardmore R Scholar, Eire Under-21.

2004–05	Charlton Ath	0	0		
2005–06	Charlton Ath	0	0		

RICKETTS, Mark (D) 5 0
H: 6 0 W: 11 02 b.Sidcup 7-10-84
Source: Scholar.

2005–06	Charlton Ath	0	0		
2005–06	*Milton Keynes D*	5	0	**5**	**0**

ROMMEDAHL, Dennis (F) 251 38
H: 5 9 W: 11 08 b.Copenhagen 22-7-78
Honours: Denmark Youth, Under-21, 58 full caps, 11 goals.

1995–96	Lyngby	9	0	**9**	**0**
1996–97	PSV Eindhoven	2	0		
1997–98	RKC	34	5	**34**	**5**
1998–99	PSV Eindhoven	19	2		
1999–2000	PSV Eindhoven	23	0		
2000–01	PSV Eindhoven	31	5		
2001–02	PSV Eindhoven	34	12		
2002–03	PSV Eindhoven	33	6		
2003–04	PSV Eindhoven	19	4	**161**	**29**
2004–05	Charlton Ath	26	2		
2005–06	Charlton Ath	21	2	**47**	**4**

SAM, Lloyd (F) 13 0
H: 5 10 W: 11 00 b.Leeds 27-9-84
Honours: England Youth, Under-20.

2002–03	Charlton Ath	0	0		
2003–04	Charlton Ath	0	0		
2003–04	*Leyton Orient*	10	0	**10**	**0**
2004–05	Charlton Ath	1	0		
2005–06	Charlton Ath	2	0	**3**	**0**

SANKOFA, Osei (D) 13 0
H: 6 0 W: 12 04 b.London 19-3-85
Source: Scholar. *Honours:* England Youth, Under-20.

2002–03	Charlton Ath	1	0		
2003–04	Charlton Ath	0	0		
2004–05	Charlton Ath	0	0		
2005–06	Charlton Ath	4	0	**5**	**0**
2005–06	*Bristol C*	8	0	**8**	**0**

SORONDO, Gonzalo (D) 121 6
H: 5 11 W: 12 08 b.Montevideo 9-10-79
Honours: Uruguay 27 full caps, 1 goal.

1998	Defensor	4	0		
1999	Defensor	12	0		
2000	Defensor	27	4		
2001	Defensor	17	0	**60**	**4**
2001–02	Internazionale	11	0		
2002–03	Internazionale	0	0		
2003–04	Internazionale	0	0	**11**	**0**
2003–04	Standard Liege	23	2	**23**	**2**
2004–05	Crystal Palace	20	0	**20**	**0**
2005–06	Charlton Ath	7	0	**7**	**0**

TANSKA, Jani (D) 0 0
H: 6 4 W: 12 12 b.Anjalankoski 29-7-88
Source: Scholar.

2005–06	Charlton Ath	0	0		

THOMAS, Jerome (M) 60 7
H: 5 9 W: 11 09 b.Wembley 23-3-83
Source: Scholar. *Honours:* England Youth, Under-20, Under-21.

2001–02	Arsenal	0	0		
2001–02	*QPR*	4	1		
2002–03	Arsenal	0	0		
2002–03	*QPR*	6	2	**10**	**3**
2003–04	Arsenal	0	0		
2003–04	Charlton Ath	1	0		
2004–05	Charlton Ath	24	3		
2005–06	Charlton Ath	25	1	**50**	**4**

VARNEY, Alex (F) **1 0**
H: 5 11 W: 11 13 b.Bromley 27-12-84
Source: Trainee.
2003–04 Charlton Ath 0 0
2004–05 Charlton Ath 0 0
2005–06 Charlton Ath 0 0
2005–06 *Barnet* 1 0 **1 0**

WALKER, James (F) **4 0**
H: 5 10 W: 11 10 b.Hackney 25-11-87
Source: Scholar. *Honours:* England Youth.
2004–05 Charlton Ath 0 0
2005–06 Charlton Ath 0 0
2005–06 *Hartlepool U* 4 0 **4 0**

YOUGA, Kelly (D) **4 0**
H: 6 1 W: 12 00 b.Bangui 22-9-85
Source: Lyon.
2005–06 Charlton Ath 0 0
2005–06 *Bristol C* 4 0 **4 0**

YOUNG, Luke (D) **216 3**
H: 6 0 W: 12 04 b.Harlow 19-7-79
Source: Trainee. *Honours:* England Youth, Under-21, 7 full caps.
1997–98 Tottenham H 0 0
1998–99 Tottenham H 15 0
1999–2000 Tottenham H 20 0
2000–01 Tottenham H 23 0 **58 0**
2001–02 Charlton Ath 34 0
2002–03 Charlton Ath 32 0
2003–04 Charlton Ath 24 0
2004–05 Charlton Ath 36 2
2005–06 Charlton Ath 32 1 **158 3**

Scholars
Basey, Grant William; Baxter, Nicholas James; Kamara, Sheku; Murtagh, Keiran Zac; Nielsen, Mads Frederik Wagner; Saunders, Christopher Michael; Simmonds, Donovan; Springer, Dane; Thomas, Aswad; Weston, Myles Arthur.

CHELSEA (21)

BRIDGE, Wayne (D) **212 3**
H: 5 10 W: 12 13 b.Southampton 5-8-80
Source: Trainee. *Honours:* England Youth, Under-21, 23 full caps, 1 goal.
1997–98 Southampton 0 0
1998–99 Southampton 23 0
1999–2000 Southampton 19 1
2000–01 Southampton 38 0
2001–02 Southampton 38 0
2002–03 Southampton 34 1 **152 2**
2003–04 Chelsea 33 1
2004–05 Chelsea 15 0
2005–06 Chelsea 0 0 **48 1**
2005–06 *Fulham* 12 0 **12 0**

CECH, Petr (G) **197 0**
H: 6 5 W: 14 07 b.Plzen 20-5-82
Honours: Czech Republic 44 full caps.
1998–99 Viktoria Plzen 0 0
1999–2000 Chmel 1 0
2000–01 Chmel 26 0 **27 0**
2001–02 Sparta Prague 26 0 **26 0**
2002–03 Rennes 37 0
2003–04 Rennes 38 0 **75 0**
2004–05 Chelsea 35 0
2005–06 Chelsea 34 0 **69 0**

COLE, Carlton (F) **80 12**
H: 6 3 W: 14 02 b.Croydon 12-11-83
Source: Scholar. *Honours:* England Youth, Under-20, Under-21.
2000–01 Chelsea 0 0
2001–02 Chelsea 3 1
2002–03 Chelsea 13 3
2002–03 *Wolverhampton W* 7 1 **7 1**
2003–04 Chelsea 0 0
2003–04 *Charlton Ath* 21 4 **21 4**
2004–05 Chelsea 0 0
2004–05 *Aston Villa* 27 3 **27 3**
2005–06 Chelsea 9 0 **25 4**

COLE, Joe (M) **223 26**
H: 5 9 W: 11 09 b.Islington 8-11-81
Source: Trainee. *Honours:* England Schools, Youth, Under-21, B, 37 full caps, 6 goals.
1998–99 West Ham U 8 0
1999–2000 West Ham U 22 1
2000–01 West Ham U 30 5
2001–02 West Ham U 30 0
2002–03 West Ham U 36 4 **126 10**
2003–04 Chelsea 35 1
2004–05 Chelsea 28 8
2005–06 Chelsea 34 7 **97 16**

CRESPO, Hernan (F) **329 161**
H: 6 0 W: 12 11 b.Florida, Arg 5-7-75
Honours: Argentina 59 full caps, 32 goals.
1993–94 River Plate 25 13
1994–95 River Plate 18 5
1995–96 River Plate 21 5 **64 23**
1996–97 Parma 27 12
1997–98 Parma 25 12
1998–99 Parma 30 16
1999–2000 Parma 34 22 **116 62**
2000–01 Lazio 32 26
2001–02 Lazio 22 13 **54 39**
2002–03 Internazionale 18 7 **18 7**
2003–04 Chelsea 19 10
2004–05 *AC Milan* 28 10 **28 10**
2005–06 Chelsea 30 10 **49 20**

CUDICINI, Carlo (G) **205 0**
H: 6 1 W: 12 08 b.Milan 6-9-73
Honours: Italy Under-21.
1991–92 AC Milan 0 0
1992–93 AC Milan 0 0
1993–94 Como 6 0 **6 0**
1994–95 AC Milan 0 0
1995–96 AC Milan 0 0
1995–96 Prato 30 0 **30 0**
1996–97 Lazio 1 0 **1 0**
1997–98 Castel di Sangro 14 0
1998–99 Castel di Sangro 32 0 **46 0**
1999–2000 Chelsea 1 0
2000–01 Chelsea 24 0
2001–02 Chelsea 28 0
2002–03 Chelsea 36 0
2003–04 Chelsea 26 0
2004–05 Chelsea 3 0
2005–06 Chelsea 4 0 **122 0**

DEL HORNO, Asier (D) **159 14**
H: 5 11 W: 11 12 b.Portugalete 19-1-81
Honours: Spain 10 full caps, 2 goals.
1999–2000 Athletic Bilbao B 26 0 **26 0**
2000–01 Athletic Bilbao 14 0
2001–02 Athletic Bilbao 10 1
2002–03 Athletic Bilbao 24 4
2003–04 Athletic Bilbao 31 5
2004–05 Athletic Bilbao 29 3 **108 13**
2005–06 Chelsea 25 1 **25 1**

DIARRA, Lassana (M) **3 0**
H: 5 8 W: 11 02 b.Paris 10-3-85
Source: Le Havre. *Honours:* France Youth, Under-21.
2005–06 Chelsea 3 0 **3 0**

DROGBA, Didier (F) **199 71**
H: 6 2 W: 14 05 b.Abidjan 11-3-78
Honours: Ivory Coast 34 full caps, 24 goals.
1998–99 Le Mans 2 0
1999–2000 Le Mans 30 6
2000–01 Le Mans 11 0
2001–02 Le Mans 21 5 **64 11**
2001–02 Guingamp 11 3
2002–03 Guingamp 34 17 **45 20**
2003–04 Marseille 35 18 **35 18**
2004–05 Chelsea 26 10
2005–06 Chelsea 29 12 **55 22**

DUFF, Damien (F) **265 41**
H: 5 9 W: 12 06 b.Ballyboden 2-3-79
Source: Lourdes Celtic. *Honours:* Eire Schools, Youth, B, 59 full caps, 7 goals.
1995–96 Blackburn R 0 0
1996–97 Blackburn R 1 0
1997–98 Blackburn R 26 4
1998–99 Blackburn R 28 1
1999–2000 Blackburn R 39 5
2000–01 Blackburn R 32 1
2001–02 Blackburn R 32 7
2002–03 Blackburn R 26 9 **184 27**
2003–04 Chelsea 23 5
2004–05 Chelsea 30 6
2005–06 Chelsea 28 3 **81 14**

ELMER, Jonas (D) **0 0**
b.Zurich 28-2-88
Source: Grasshoppers, Chelsea Scholar.
2005–06 Chelsea 0 0

ESSIEN, Mickael (M) **168 20**
H: 5 10 W: 13 06 b.Accra 3-12-82
Honours: Ghana 20 full caps, 4 goals.
2000–01 Bastia 13 1
2001–02 Bastia 24 4
2002–03 Bastia 29 6 **66 11**
2003–04 Lyon 34 3
2004–05 Lyon 37 4 **71 7**
2005–06 Chelsea 31 2 **31 2**

GALLAS, William (D) **262 14**
H: 6 0 W: 12 12 b.Asnieres 17-8-77
Honours: France Under-21, 47 full caps, 1 goal.
1996–97 Caen 18 0 **18 0**
1997–98 Marseille 3 0
1998–99 Marseille 30 0
1999–2000 Marseille 22 0
2000–01 Marseille 30 2 **85 2**
2001–02 Chelsea 30 1
2002–03 Chelsea 38 4
2003–04 Chelsea 29 0
2004–05 Chelsea 28 2
2005–06 Chelsea 34 5 **159 12**

GEREMI (M) **194 19**
H: 5 9 W: 13 01 b.Bafoussam 20-12-78
Source: Racing Bafousam. *Honours:* Cameroon 72 full caps, 6 goals.
1997 Cerro Porteno 6 0 **6 0**
1997–98 Genclerbirligi 28 4
1998–99 Genclerbirligi 29 5 **57 9**
1999–2000 Real Madrid 20 0
2000–01 Real Madrid 16 0
2001–02 Real Madrid 9 0 **45 0**
2002–03 Middlesbrough 33 7 **33 7**
2003–04 Chelsea 25 1
2004–05 Chelsea 13 0
2005–06 Chelsea 15 2 **53 3**

GRANT, Anthony (M) **3 0**
H: 5 10 W: 11 01 b.Lambeth 4-6-87
Source: Scholar. *Honours:* England Youth.
2004–05 Chelsea 1 0
2005–06 Chelsea 0 0 **1 0**
2005–06 *Oldham Ath* 2 0 **2 0**

GUDJOHNSEN, Eidur (F) **277 82**
H: 6 1 W: 14 02 b.Reykjavik 15-9-78
Honours: Iceland Youth, Under-21, 39 full caps, 16 goals.
1994–95 Valur 17 7 **17 7**
1995–96 PSV Eindhoven 13 3
1996–97 PSV Eindhoven 0 0 **13 3**
1998 KR 6 0 **6 0**
1998–99 Bolton W 14 5
1999–2000 Bolton W 41 13 **55 18**
2000–01 Chelsea 30 10
2001–02 Chelsea 32 14
2002–03 Chelsea 35 10
2003–04 Chelsea 26 6
2004–05 Chelsea 37 12
2005–06 Chelsea 26 2 **186 54**

HOLLANDS, Danny (M) **10 1**
H: 6 0 W: 11 11 b.Ashford 6-11-85
Source: Trainee.
2003–04 Chelsea 0 0
2004–05 Chelsea 0 0
2005–06 Chelsea 0 0
2005–06 *Torquay U* 10 1 **10 1**

HURRELL, Sam (D) **0 0**
2005–06 Chelsea 0 0

HUTH, Robert (D) **42 0**
H: 6 3 W: 14 07 b.Berlin 18-8-84
Source: Scholar. *Honours:* Germany Youth, Under-21, 17 full caps, 2 goals.
2001–02 Chelsea 1 0
2002–03 Chelsea 2 0
2003–04 Chelsea 16 0

2004–05 Chelsea 10 0
2005–06 Chelsea 13 0 **42** **0**

JAROSIK, Jiri (M) 224 39
H: 6 4 W: 14 01 b.Usti Nad Lebem 27-10-77
Source: Teplice, Sparta Prague. *Honours:* Czech Republic 23 full caps.
1997–98 Slovan Liberec 18 0
1998–99 Slovan Liberec 21 2 **39** **2**
1999–2000 Sparta Prague 21 3
2000–01 Sparta Prague 28 8
2001–02 Sparta Prague 27 6
2002–03 Sparta Prague 15 3 **91** **20**
2003 CSKA Moscow 27 7
2004 CSKA Moscow 29 5 **56** **12**
2004–05 Chelsea 14 0
2005–06 Chelsea 0 0 **14** **0**
2005–06 *Birmingham C* 24 5 **24** **5**

JOHNSON, Glen (D) 63 3
H: 6 0 W: 13 04 b.Greenwich 23-8-84
Source: Scholar. *Honours:* England Youth, Under-20, Under-21, 5 full caps.
2001–02 West Ham U 0 0
2002–03 West Ham U 15 0 **15** **0**
2002–03 *Millwall* 8 0 **8** **0**
2003–04 Chelsea 19 3
2004–05 Chelsea 17 0
2005–06 Chelsea 4 0 **40** **3**

KEENAN, Joe (M) 5 0
H: 5 7 W: 10 00 b.Southampton 14-10-82
Source: Trainee. *Honours:* England Schools, Youth, Under-20.
1999–2000 Chelsea 0 0
2000–01 Chelsea 0 0
2001–02 Chelsea 1 0
2002–03 Chelsea 1 0
2003–04 Chelsea 0 0
2004–05 Chelsea 0 0
2005–06 Chelsea 0 0 **2** **0**
2005–06 *Brentford* 3 0 **3** **0**
To Willem II (loan) January 2006

LAMPARD, Frank (M) 343 74
H: 6 0 W: 14 02 b.Romford 20-6-78
Source: Trainee. *Honours:* England Youth, Under-21, B, 45 full caps, 11 goals.
1994–95 West Ham U 0 0
1995–96 West Ham U 2 0
1995–96 *Swansea C* 9 1 **9** **1**
1996–97 West Ham U 13 0
1997–98 West Ham U 31 4
1998–99 West Ham U 38 5
1999–2000 West Ham U 34 7
2000–01 West Ham U 30 7 **148** **23**
2001–02 Chelsea 37 5
2002–03 Chelsea 38 6
2003–04 Chelsea 38 10
2004–05 Chelsea 38 13
2005–06 Chelsea 35 16 **186** **50**

MA KALAMBAY, Yves (G) 0 0
H: 6 5 W: 14 10 b.Brussels 31-1-86
Source: PSV Eindhoven. *Honours:* Belgium Youth.
2003–04 Chelsea 0 0
2004–05 Chelsea 0 0
2005–06 Chelsea 0 0
2005–06 *Watford* 0 0

MAKELELE, Claude (M) 463 17
H: 5 7 W: 10 05 b.Kinshasa 18-2-73
Source: Brest. *Honours:* France Under-21, B, 50 full caps.
1992–93 Nantes 34 1
1993–94 Nantes 30 0
1994–95 Nantes 36 3
1995–96 Nantes 33 0
1996–97 Nantes 36 5 **169** **9**
1997–98 Marseille 33 4 **33** **4**
1998–99 Celta Vigo 36 2
1999–2000 Celta Vigo 34 1 **70** **3**
2000–01 Real Madrid 33 0
2001–02 Real Madrid 32 0
2002–03 Real Madrid 29 0 **94** **0**
2003–04 Chelsea 30 0
2004–05 Chelsea 36 1
2005–06 Chelsea 31 0 **97** **1**

MANCIENNE, Michael (D) 0 0
b.Isleworth 8-1-88
Source: Scholar. *Honours:* England Youth.
2005–06 Chelsea 0 0

McKINLAY, Kevin (F) 0 0
H: 5 11 W: 11 01 b.Stirling 28-2-86
Source: Trainee.
2003–04 Chelsea 0 0
2004–05 Chelsea 0 0
2005–06 Chelsea 0 0

MORAIS, Filipe (M) 13 0
H: 5 9 W: 11 10 b.Lisbon 21-11-85
Source: Trainee. *Honours:* Portugal Youth.
2003–04 Chelsea 0 0
2004–05 Chelsea 0 0
2005–06 Chelsea 0 0
2005–06 *Milton Keynes D* 13 0 **13** **0**

NUNO MORAIS (D) 2 0
H: 6 0 W: 12 04 b.Penafiel 29-1-84
Source: Penafiel. *Honours:* Portugal Under-21.
2004–05 Chelsea 2 0
2005–06 Chelsea 0 0 **2** **0**
To Maritimo (loan) August 2005

PAULO FERREIRA (D) 215 4
H: 6 0 W: 11 13 b.Cascais 18-1-79
Honours: Portugal 33 full caps.
1997–98 Estoril 1 0
1998–99 Estoril 16 0
1999–2000 Estoril 18 2 **35** **2**
2000–01 Vitoria Setubal 34 2
2001–02 Vitoria Setubal 34 0 **68** **2**
2002–03 Porto 30 0
2003–04 Porto 32 0 **62** **0**
2004–05 Chelsea 29 0
2005–06 Chelsea 21 0 **50** **0**

PETTIGREW, Adrian (D) 0 0
H: 6 0 W: 13 01 b.Hackney 12-11-86
Source: Scholar.
2004–05 Chelsea 0 0
2005–06 Chelsea 0 0

PIDGELEY, Lenny (G) 29 0
H: 6 4 W: 14 09 b.Isleworth 7-2-84
Source: Scholar. *Honours:* England Under-20.
2003–04 Chelsea 0 0
2003–04 *Watford* 27 0 **27** **0**
2004–05 Chelsea 1 0
2005–06 Chelsea 1 0 **2** **0**
2005–06 *Millwall* 0 0

RICARDO CARVALHO (D) 197 9
H: 6 0 W: 12 04 b.Amarante 18-5-78
Honours: Portugal 30 full caps, 1 goal.
1996–97 Leca 0 0
1997–98 Leca 22 1 **22** **1**
1998–99 Porto 1 0
1999–2000 Vitoria Setubal 25 2 **25** **2**
2000–01 Alverca 29 1 **29** **1**
2001–02 Porto 25 0
2002–03 Porto 17 1
2003–04 Porto 29 2 **72** **3**
2004–05 Chelsea 25 1
2005–06 Chelsea 24 1 **49** **2**

ROBBEN, Arjen (F) 153 38
H: 5 11 W: 12 08 b.Bedum 23-1-84
Honours: Holland 23 full caps, 7 goals.
2000–01 Groningen 18 2
2001–02 Groningen 28 6 **46** **8**
2002–03 PSV Eindhoven 33 12
2003–04 PSV Eindhoven 28 5 **61** **17**
2004–05 Chelsea 18 7
2005–06 Chelsea 28 6 **46** **13**

SARKI, Emmanuel (M) 0 0
b.Nigeria 26-12-87
2005–06 Chelsea 0 *0*
To Westerlo January 2006.

SIMMONDS, James (M) 0 0
b.Hammersmith 3-12-87
Source: Scholar.
2005–06 Chelsea 0 0

SINCLAIR, Scott (F) 2 0
H: 5 10 W: 10 00 b.Bath 26-3-89
Source: Bristol R Schoolboy, England Youth.
2004–05 Bristol R 2 0 **2** **0**
2005–06 Chelsea 0 0

SMERTIN, Alexei (M) 407 27
H: 5 9 W: 10 10 b.Barnaul 1-5-75
Honours: Russia 54 full caps.
1992 Dynamo Barnaul 18 2
1993 Dynamo Barnaul 24 0 **42** **2**
1994 Zarya 49 2
1995 Zarya 37 7
1996 Zarya 34 4
1997 Zarya 13 0 **133** **13**
1997 Uralan 23 0
1998 Uralan 26 3 **49** **3**
1999 Lokomotiv Moscow 29 6
2000 Lokomotiv Moscow 10 1 **39** **7**
2000–01 Bordeaux 23 0
2001–02 Bordeaux 28 0
2002–03 Bordeaux 33 2 **84** **2**
2003–04 Chelsea 0 0
2003–04 *Portsmouth* 26 0 **26** **0**
2004–05 Chelsea 16 0
2005–06 Chelsea 0 0 **16** **0**
2005–06 *Charlton Ath* 18 0 **18** **0**
To Dynamo Moscow March 2006

SMITH, Dean (D) 0 0
H: 5 10 W: 10 00 b.Islington 13-8-86
Source: Trainee. *Honours:* England Schools, Youth.
2003–04 Chelsea 0 0
2004–05 Chelsea 0 0
2005–06 Chelsea 0 0

SMITH, Jimmy (M) 1 0
H: 6 0 W: 10 03 b.Newham 7-1-87
Source: Scholar. *Honours:* England Youth.
2004–05 Chelsea 0 0
2005–06 Chelsea 1 0 **1** **0**

TERRY, John (D) 192 14
H: 6 1 W: 14 02 b.Barking 7-12-80
Source: Trainee. *Honours:* England Under-21, 29 full caps, 1 goal.
1997–98 Chelsea 0 0
1998–99 Chelsea 2 0
1999–2000 Chelsea 4 0
1999–2000 *Nottingham F* 6 0 **6** **0**
2000–01 Chelsea 22 1
2001–02 Chelsea 33 1
2002–03 Chelsea 20 3
2003–04 Chelsea 33 2
2004–05 Chelsea 36 3
2005–06 Chelsea 36 4 **186** **14**

TILLEN, Joe (M) 0 0
H: 5 10 W: 11 07 b.Reading 15-12-86
Source: Scholar. *Honours:* England Youth.
2004–05 Chelsea 0 0
2005–06 Chelsea 0 0

VERON, Juan Sebastian (M) 324 41
H: 5 11 W: 12 04 b.La Plata 9-3-75
Honours: Argentina 58 full caps, 9 goals.
1993–94 Estudiantes 7 0
1994–95 Estudiantes 38 5
1995–96 Estudiantes 15 2 **60** **7**
1995–96 Boca Juniors 17 4 **17** **4**
1996–97 Sampdoria 32 5
1997–98 Sampdoria 29 2 **61** **7**
1998–99 Parma 26 1 **26** **1**
1999–2000 Lazio 31 8
2000–01 Lazio 22 3 **53** **11**
2001–02 Manchester U 26 5
2002–03 Manchester U 25 2 **51** **7**
2003–04 Chelsea 7 1
2004–05 *Internazionale* 24 3
2005–06 *Internazionale* 25 0 **49** **3**
2005–06 Chelsea 0 0 **7** **1**

WORLEY, Harry (D) 0 0
H: 6 3 W: 13 00 b.Warrington 25-11-88
Source: Scholar.
2005–06 Chelsea 0 0

WRIGHT-PHILLIPS, Shaun (F) 180 26
H: 5 5 W: 10 01 b.Lewisham 25-10-81
Source: Scholar. *Honours:* England Under-21, 8 full caps, 1 goal.
1998–99 Manchester C 0 0
1999–2000 Manchester C 4 0
2000–01 Manchester C 15 0
2001–02 Manchester C 35 8
2002–03 Manchester C 31 1

2003–04 Manchester C 34 7
2004–05 Manchester C 34 10 **153 26**
2005–06 Chelsea 27 0 **27 0**

YOUNGHUSBAND, Phil (F) 0 0
H: 5 10 W: 10 08 b.Ashford 4-8-87
Source: Scholar.
2004–05 Chelsea 0 0
2005–06 Chelsea 0 0

Scholars
Bertrand, Ryan; Bridcutt, Liam Robert; Cork, Jack Frank Porteous; Cummings, Shaun; Fernandes, Ricardo; Ferreira, Fabio Miguel; Hamann, Nick; Hutchinson, Samuel Edward; Ismail, Hamze; Russell, James Peter; Saarelma, Tomi.

CHELTENHAM T (22)

ARMSTRONG, Craig (M) 275 9
H: 5 11 W: 12 09 b.South Shields 23-5-75
Source: Trainee.
1992–93 Nottingham F 0 0
1993–94 Nottingham F 0 0
1994–95 Nottingham F 0 0
1994–95 *Burnley* 4 0 **4 0**
1995–96 Nottingham F 0 0
1995–96 *Bristol R* 14 0 **14 0**
1996–97 Nottingham F 0 0
1996–97 *Gillingham* 10 0 **10 0**
1996–97 *Watford* 15 0 **15 0**
1997–98 Nottingham F 18 0
1998–99 Nottingham F 22 0 **40 0**
1998–99 Huddersfield T 13 1
1999–2000 Huddersfield T 39 0
2000–01 Huddersfield T 44 3
2001–02 Huddersfield T 11 1 **107 5**
2001–02 Sheffield W 8 0
2002–03 Sheffield W 17 1
2003–04 Sheffield W 10 0
2003–04 *Grimsby T* 9 1 **9 1**
2004–05 Sheffield W 0 0 **35 1**
2004–05 Bradford C 7 0 **7 0**
2005–06 Cheltenham T 34 2 **34 2**

BELL, Mickey (D) 587 52
H: 5 9 W: 12 02 b.Newcastle 15-11-71
Source: Trainee.
1989–90 Northampton T 6 0
1990–91 Northampton T 28 0
1991–92 Northampton T 30 4
1992–93 Northampton T 39 5
1993–94 Northampton T 38 0
1994–95 Northampton T 12 1 **153 10**
1994–95 Wycombe W 31 3
1995–96 Wycombe W 41 1
1996–97 Wycombe W 46 2 **118 6**
1997–98 Bristol C 44 10
1998–99 Bristol C 33 5
1999–2000 Bristol C 36 5
2000–01 Bristol C 41 4
2001–02 Bristol C 42 7
2002–03 Bristol C 38 2
2003–04 Bristol C 27 0
2004–05 Bristol C 31 1 **292 34**
2005–06 Port Vale 15 2 **15 2**
2005–06 Cheltenham T 9 0 **9 0**

BIRD, David (M) 108 1
H: 5 9 W: 12 00 b.Gloucester 26-12-84
Source: Cinderford T.
2001–02 Cheltenham T 0 0
2002–03 Cheltenham T 14 0
2003–04 Cheltenham T 24 0
2004–05 Cheltenham T 34 0
2005–06 Cheltenham T 36 1 **108 1**

BRADSHAW, Gary (M) 25 1
H: 5 6 W: 10 06 b.Hull 30-12-82
Source: Scholarship.
1999–2000 Hull C 12 0
2000–01 Hull C 2 0
2001–02 Hull C 3 1
2002–03 Hull C 5 0
2003–04 Hull C 0 0
2004–05 Hull C 0 0 **22 1**
From North Ferriby U
2005–06 Cheltenham T 3 0 **3 0**

BROWN, Scott (G) 1 0
H: 6 2 W: 13 01 b.Wolverhampton 26-4-85
Source: Wolverhampton W Trainee.
From Welshpool T
2003–04 Bristol C 0 0
2004–05 Cheltenham T 0 0
2005–06 Cheltenham T 1 0 **1 0**

CAINES, Gavin (D) 68 4
H: 6 1 W: 12 00 b.Birmingham 20-9-83
Source: Scholar.
2003–04 Walsall 0 0
2004–05 Cheltenham T 29 2
2005–06 Cheltenham T 39 2 **68 4**

CONNOLLY, Adam (M) 9 1
H: 5 9 W: 12 04 b.Manchester 10-4-86
Source: Scholar.
2004–05 Cheltenham T 4 0
2005–06 Cheltenham T 5 1 **9 1**

DUFF, Shane (D) 98 2
H: 6 1 W: 12 10 b.Wroughton 2-4-82
Source: Juniors. *Honours:* Northern Ireland Under-21.
2000–01 Cheltenham T 0 0
2001–02 Cheltenham T 0 0
2002–03 Cheltenham T 18 0
2003–04 Cheltenham T 15 1
2004–05 Cheltenham T 45 1
2005–06 Cheltenham T 20 0 **98 2**

FINNIGAN, John (M) 296 14
H: 5 8 W: 10 09 b.Wakefield 29-3-76
Source: Trainee.
1992–93 Nottingham F 0 0
1993–94 Nottingham F 0 0
1994–95 Nottingham F 0 0
1995–96 Nottingham F 0 0
1996–97 Nottingham F 0 0
1997–98 Nottingham F 0 0
1997–98 *Lincoln C* 6 0
1998–99 Lincoln C 37 1
1999–2000 Lincoln C 37 2
2000–01 Lincoln C 40 0
2001–02 Lincoln C 23 0 **143 3**
2001–02 Cheltenham T 12 2
2002–03 Cheltenham T 37 1
2003–04 Cheltenham T 33 1
2004–05 Cheltenham T 32 3
2005–06 Cheltenham T 39 4 **153 11**

FOLEY, Sam (M) 0 0
H: 6 0 W: 10 08 b.Upton-on-Severn 17-10-86
Source: Scholar.
2005–06 Cheltenham T 0 0

GALLINAGH, Andy (D) 1 0
H: 5 8 W: 11 08 b.Sutton Coldfield 16-3-85
Source: Stratford T.
2004–05 Cheltenham T 0 0
2005–06 Cheltenham T 1 0 **1 0**

GILL, Jeremy (D) 194 0
H: 5 11 W: 12 00 b.Clevedon 8-9-70
Source: Yeovil T.
1997–98 Birmingham C 3 0
1998–99 Birmingham C 3 0
1999–2000 Birmingham C 11 0
2000–01 Birmingham C 29 0
2001–02 Birmingham C 14 0
2002–03 Birmingham C 0 0 **60 0**
2002–03 Northampton T 41 0
2003–04 Northampton T 0 0 **41 0**
2003–04 Cheltenham T 7 0
2004–05 Cheltenham T 44 0
2005–06 Cheltenham T 42 0 **93 0**

GILLESPIE, Steven (F) 38 11
H: 5 9 W: 11 02 b.Liverpool 4-6-84
Source: Liverpool Scholar.
2004–05 Bristol C 8 0
2004–05 *Cheltenham T* 12 5
2005–06 Bristol C 4 1 **12 1**
2005–06 Cheltenham T 14 5 **26 10**

GUINAN, Stephen (F) 159 27
H: 6 1 W: 13 02 b.Birmingham 24-12-75
Source: Trainee.
1992–93 Nottingham F 0 0
1993–94 Nottingham F 0 0
1994–95 Nottingham F 0 0
1995–96 Nottingham F 2 0
1995–96 *Darlington* 3 1 **3 1**
1996–97 Nottingham F 2 0
1996–97 *Burnley* 6 0 **6 0**
1997–98 Nottingham F 2 0
1997–98 *Crewe Alex* 3 0 **3 0**
1998–99 Nottingham F 0 0
1998–99 *Halifax T* 12 2 **12 2**
1998–99 *Plymouth Arg* 11 7
1999–2000 Nottingham F 1 0 **7 0**
1999–2000 *Scunthorpe U* 3 1 **3 1**
1999–2000 Cambridge U 6 0 **6 0**
1999–2000 Plymouth Arg 8 2
2000–01 Plymouth Arg 22 1
2001–02 Plymouth Arg 0 0 **41 10**
2001–02 Shrewsbury T 5 0
2002–03 Shrewsbury T 0 0
2003–04 Shrewsbury T 0 0 **5 0**
2004–05 Cheltenham T 43 6
2005–06 Cheltenham T 30 7 **73 13**

HIGGS, Shane (G) 155 0
H: 6 3 W: 14 06 b.Oxford 13-5-77
Source: Trainee.
1994–95 Bristol R 0 0
1995–96 Bristol R 0 0
1996–97 Bristol R 2 0
1997–98 Bristol R 8 0 **10 0**
From Worcester C.
1999–2000 Cheltenham T 0 0
2000–01 Cheltenham T 1 0
2001–02 Cheltenham T 1 0
2002–03 Cheltenham T 10 0
2003–04 Cheltenham T 42 0
2004–05 Cheltenham T 46 0
2005–06 Cheltenham T 45 0 **145 0**

LEWIS, Greg (D) 0 0
b.Coleford
Source: Scholar.
2005–06 Cheltenham T 0 0

McCANN, Grant (M) 184 29
H: 5 10 W: 11 00 b.Belfast 14-4-80
Source: Trainee. *Honours:* Northern Ireland Youth, Under-21, 11 full caps.
1998–99 West Ham U 0 0
1999–2000 West Ham U 0 0
2000–01 West Ham U 1 0
2000–01 *Notts Co* 2 0 **2 0**
2000–01 *Cheltenham T* 30 3
2001–02 West Ham U 3 0
2002–03 West Ham U 0 0 **4 0**
2002–03 Cheltenham T 27 6
2003–04 Cheltenham T 43 8
2004–05 Cheltenham T 39 4
2005–06 Cheltenham T 39 8 **178 29**

MELLIGAN, John (M) 136 21
H: 5 9 W: 11 02 b.Dublin 11-2-82
Source: Trainee. *Honours:* Eire Under-21.
2000–01 Wolverhampton W 0 0
2001–02 Wolverhampton W 0 0
2001–02 *Bournemouth* 8 0 **8 0**
2002–03 Wolverhampton W 2 0
2002–03 *Kidderminster H* 29 10
2003–04 Wolverhampton W 0 0 **2 0**
2003–04 *Kidderminster H* 5 1 **34 11**
2003–04 *Doncaster R* 21 2 **21 2**
2004–05 Cheltenham T 29 2
2005–06 Cheltenham T 42 6 **71 8**

MUSGROVE, Scott (M) 0 0
b.Stamford 21-6-87
Source: Stoke C Scholar.
2005–06 Cheltenham T 0 0

ODEJAYI, Kayode (F) 109 17
H: 6 2 W: 12 02 b.Ibadon 21-2-82
Source: Scholarship.
1999–2000 Bristol C 3 0
2000–01 Bristol C 3 0
2001–02 Bristol C 0 0
2002–03 Bristol C 0 0 **6 0**
2003–04 Cheltenham T 30 5
2004–05 Cheltenham T 32 1
2005–06 Cheltenham T 41 11 **103 17**

PUDDY, Will (G) 0 0
H: 5 10 W: 11 07 b.Salisbury 4-10-87
Source: Scholar.
2005–06 Cheltenham T 0 0

SPENCER, Damien (F) **172 27**

H: 6 1 W: 14 00 b.Ascot 19-9-81

Source: Scholarship.

1999–2000	Bristol C	9	1		
2000–01	Bristol C	4	0		
2000–01	*Exeter C*	6	0	**6**	**0**
2001–02	Bristol C	0	0	**13**	**1**
2002–03	Cheltenham T	30	6		
2003–04	Cheltenham T	36	9		
2004–05	Cheltenham T	41	8		
2005–06	Cheltenham T	46	3	**153**	**26**

TAYLOR, Michael (D) **35 0**

H: 6 1 W: 13 08 b.Liverpool 21-11-82

Source: Scholarship.

1999–2000	Blackburn R	0	0		
2000–01	Blackburn R	0	0		
2001–02	Blackburn R	0	0		
2002–03	Blackburn R	0	0		
2002–03	*Carlisle U*	10	0	**10**	**0**
2002–03	*Rochdale*	2	0	**2**	**0**
2003–04	Blackburn R	0	0		
2004–05	Cheltenham T	13	0		
2005–06	Cheltenham T	10	0	**23**	**0**

TOWNSEND, Michael (D) **31 0**

H: 6 1 W: 13 12 b.Walsall 17-5-86

Source: Wolverhampton W scholar.

2004–05	Cheltenham T	0	0		
2005–06	Cheltenham T	31	0	**31**	**0**

VICTORY, Jamie (D) **264 22**

H: 5 10 W: 12 13 b.Hackney 14-11-75

Source: Trainee.

1994–95	West Ham U	0	0		
1995–96	Bournemouth	16	1		
1996–97	Bournemouth	0	0	**16**	**1**
1999–2000	Cheltenham T	46	4		
2000–01	Cheltenham T	3	1		
2001–02	Cheltenham T	46	7		
2002–03	Cheltenham T	45	2		
2003–04	Cheltenham T	44	2		
2004–05	Cheltenham T	42	3		
2005–06	Cheltenham T	22	2	**248**	**21**

VINCENT, Ashley (F) **39 3**

H: 5 10 W: 11 08 b.Oldbury 26-5-85

Source: Wolverhampton W Scholar.

2004–05	Cheltenham T	26	1		
2005–06	Cheltenham T	13	2	**39**	**3**

WHITTINGTON, Michael (F) **0 0**

H: 5 8 W: 11 00 b.Bristol 16-12-86

Source: Scholar.

2005–06	Cheltenham T	0	0		

WILSON, Brian (D) **106 12**

H: 5 10 W: 11 00 b.Manchester 9-5-83

Source: Scholar.

2001–02	Stoke C	1	0		
2002–03	Stoke C	3	0		
2003–04	Stoke C	2	0	**6**	**0**
2003–04	Cheltenham T	14	0		
2004–05	Cheltenham T	43	3		
2005–06	Cheltenham T	43	9	**100**	**12**

WYLDE, Michael (M) **1 0**

H: 6 2 W: 13 02 b.Birmingham 6-1-87

Source: Scholar.

2005–06	Cheltenham T	1	0	**1**	**0**

YAO, Sosthene (M) **3 0**

H: 5 4 W: 11 09 b.Ivory Coast 7-8-87

Source: West Ham U Scholar.

2005–06	Cheltenham T	3	0	**3**	**0**

CHESTER C (23)

ARTELL, Dave (D) **147 12**

H: 6 3 W: 14 01 b.Rotherham 22-11-80

Source: Trainee.

1999–2000	Rotherham U	1	0		
2000–01	Rotherham U	36	4		
2001–02	Rotherham U	0	0		
2002–03	Rotherham U	0	0	**37**	**4**
2002–03	*Shrewsbury T*	28	1	**28**	**1**
2003–04	Mansfield T	26	3		
2004–05	Mansfield T	19	2	**45**	**5**
2005–06	Chester C	37	2	**37**	**2**

BERTOS, Leo (M) **99 14**

H: 5 10 W: 12 04 b.Wellington, NZ 20-12-81

Honours: New Zealand Schools, Youth, Under-23, 7 full caps.

2000–01	Barnsley	2	0		
2001–02	Barnsley	4	0		
2002–03	Barnsley	6	1	**12**	**1**
2003–04	Rochdale	40	9		
2004–05	Rochdale	42	4		
2005–06	Rochdale	0	0	**82**	**13**
2005–06	Chester C	5	0	**5**	**0**

BLUNDELL, Greg (F) **115 34**

H: 5 10 W: 11 06 b.Liverpool 3-10-77

Source: Tranmere R Trainee, Vauxhall M, Northwich Vic.

2003–04	Doncaster R	44	18		
2004–05	Doncaster R	41	9	**85**	**27**
2005–06	Chester C	30	7	**30**	**7**

BRANCH, Michael (F) **219 38**

H: 5 9 W: 12 08 b.Liverpool 18-10-78

Source: Trainee. *Honours:* England Schools, Youth, Under-21.

1995–96	Everton	3	0		
1996–97	Everton	25	3		
1997–98	Everton	6	0		
1998–99	Everton	7	0		
1998–99	*Manchester C*	4	0	**4**	**0**
1999–2000	Everton	0	0	**41**	**3**
2000–01	Wolverhampton W	38	4		
1999–2000	Wolverhampton W	27	6		
2001–02	Wolverhampton W	7	0		
2001–02	*Reading*	2	0	**2**	**0**
2002–03	Wolverhampton W	0	0	**72**	**10**
2002–03	*Hull C*	7	3	**7**	**3**
2003–04	Bradford C	33	6	**33**	**6**
2004–05	Chester C	33	11		
2005–06	Chester C	27	5	**60**	**16**

BROOKFIELD, Ryan (G) **1 0**

H: 6 0 W: 12 06 b.Liverpool 10-5-87

2005–06	Chester C	1	0	**1**	**0**

BROWN, Wayne (G) **108 0**

H: 6 0 W: 13 11 b.Southampton 14-1-77

Source: Trainee.

1993–94	Bristol C	1	0		
1994–95	Bristol C	0	0		
1995–96	Bristol C	0	0	**1**	**0**
From Weston-S-Mare					
1996–97	Chester C	2	0		
1997–98	Chester C	13	0		
1998–99	Chester C	23	0		
1999–2000	Chester C	46	0		
2000–01	Chester C	0	0		
2001–02	Chester C	0	0		
2004–05	Chester C	23	0		
2005–06	Chester C	0	0	**107**	**0**

CURLE, Tom (M) **3 0**

H: 5 9 W: 10 13 b.Bristol 3-3-86

Source: Scholar.

2003–04	Mansfield T	1	0		
2004–05	Mansfield T	0	0	**1**	**0**
2005–06	Chester C	2	0	**2**	**0**

CURTIS, Tom (M) **398 13**

H: 5 8 W: 11 12 b.Exeter 1-3-73

Source: School.

1991–92	Derby Co	0	0		
1992–93	Derby Co	0	0		
1993–94	Chesterfield	36	3		
1994–95	Chesterfield	40	2		
1995–96	Chesterfield	46	0		
1996–97	Chesterfield	40	3		
1997–98	Chesterfield	36	1		
1998–99	Chesterfield	24	3		
1999–2000	Chesterfield	18	0	**240**	**12**
2000–01	Portsmouth	4	0		
2001–02	Portsmouth	9	0		
2001–02	*Walsall*	4	0	**4**	**0**
2002–03	Portsmouth	0	0	**13**	**0**
2002–03	*Tranmere R*	8	0	**8**	**0**
2002–03	Mansfield T	23	0		
2003–04	Mansfield T	38	0		
2004–05	Mansfield T	32	0	**93**	**0**
2005–06	Chester C	40	1	**40**	**1**

DAVIES, Ben (M) **101 9**

H: 5 7 W: 12 03 b.Birmingham 27-5-81

Source: Walsall trainee.

2000–01	Kidderminster H	3	0		
2001–02	Kidderminster H	9	0	**12**	**0**
2004–05	Chester C	44	2		
2005–06	Chester C	45	7	**89**	**9**

DIMECH, Luke (D) **75 1**

H: 5 11 W: 14 10 b.Malta 11-1-77

Source: Shamrock R. *Honours:* Malta 40 full caps, 1 goal.

2003–04	Mansfield T	20	1		
2004–05	Mansfield T	25	0	**45**	**1**
2005–06	Chester C	30	0	**30**	**0**

DOVE, Craig (M) **42 6**

H: 5 11 W: 11 01 b.Hartlepool 16-8-83

Source: Scholar. *Honours:* England Youth, Under-20.

2000–01	Middlesbrough	0	0		
2001–02	Middlesbrough	0	0		
2002–03	Middlesbrough	0	0		
2003–04	Middlesbrough	0	0		
2003–04	*York C*	1	0	**1**	**0**
2004–05	Rushden & D	36	6	**36**	**6**
2005–06	Chester C	5	0	**5**	**0**

DRUMMOND, Stuart (M) **87 12**

H: 6 2 W: 13 08 b.Preston 11-12-75

Source: Morecambe.

2004–05	Chester C	45	6		
2005–06	Chester C	42	6	**87**	**12**

EL KHOLTI, Abdelhalim (D) **60 1**

H: 5 9 W: 11 00 b.Annemasse 17-10-80

Source: Raja.

2003–04	Yeovil T	23	1	**23**	**1**
2004–05	Cambridge U	15	0	**15**	**0**
2005–06	Chester C	22	0	**22**	**0**

GILLET, Stephane (G) **8 0**

H: 6 2 W: 12 02 b.Luxembourg 20-8-77

Source: Union Luxembourg.

2005–06	Chester C	8	0	**8**	**0**

HARRISON, Paul (G) **4 0**

H: 5 9 W: 13 04 b.Liverpool 18-12-84

Source: Scholar.

2003–04	Liverpool	0	0		
2004–05	Liverpool	0	0		
2004–05	*Leeds U*	0	0		
2005–06	Liverpool	0	0		
2005–06	Wolverhampton W	0	0		
2005–06	Chester C	4	0	**4**	**0**

HESSEY, Sean (D) **114 2**

H: 5 11 W: 12 08 b.Whiston 19-9-78

Source: Liverpool Trainee.

1997–98	Wigan Ath	0	0		
1997–98	Leeds U	0	0		
1997–98	Huddersfield T	1	0		
1998–99	Huddersfield T	10	0	**11**	**0**
1999–2000	Kilmarnock	11	0		
2000–01	Kilmarnock	6	0		
2001–02	Kilmarnock	15	0		
2002–03	Kilmarnock	5	0		
2003–04	Kilmarnock	7	1	**44**	**1**
2003–04	Blackpool	6	0	**6**	**0**
2004–05	Chester C	34	1		
2005–06	Chester C	19	0	**53**	**1**

HOLROYD, Chris (M) **0 0**

b.Macclesfield 24-10-86

2005–06	Chester C	0	0		

MACKENZIE, Chris (G) **144 1**

H: 5 11 W: 14 02 b.Northampton 14-5-72

Source: Corby T.

1994–95	Hereford U	22	0		
1995–96	Hereford U	38	1		
1996–97	Hereford U	0	0	**60**	**1**
1997–98	Leyton Orient	4	0		
1998–99	Leyton Orient	26	0	**30**	**0**
From Telford U					
2004–05	Chester C	24	0		
2005–06	Chester C	30	0	**54**	**0**

McNIVEN, Scott (D) **373 5**

H: 5 10 W: 13 09 b.Leeds 27-5-78

Source: Trainee. *Honours:* Scotland Youth, Under-21.

1994–95	Oldham Ath	1	0		

1995–96	Oldham Ath	15	0		
1996–97	Oldham Ath	12	0		
1997–98	Oldham Ath	32	1		
1998–99	Oldham Ath	37	1		
1999–2000	Oldham Ath	45	1		
2000–01	Oldham Ath	45	0		
2001–02	Oldham Ath	35	0	**222**	**3**
2002–03	Oxford U	44	1		
2003–04	Oxford U	41	0	**85**	**1**
2004–05	Mansfield T	25	0	**25**	**0**
2005–06	Chester C	41	1	**41**	**1**

REGAN, Carl (D) 122 0
H: 5 11 W: 11 12 b.Liverpool 14-1-80
Source: Trainee. *Honours:* England Youth.

1997–98	Everton	0	0		
1998–99	Everton	0	0		
1999–2000	Everton	0	0		
2000–01	Barnsley	27	0		
2001–02	Barnsley	10	0		
2002–03	Barnsley	0	0	**37**	**0**
2002–03	Hull C	38	0		
2003–04	Hull C	0	0		
2004–05	Hull C	0	0	**38**	**0**
2004–05	Chester C	6	0		
2005–06	Chester C	41	0	**47**	**0**

RICHARDSON, Marcus (F) 182 36
H: 6 1 W: 14 10 b.Reading 31-8-77
Source: Harrow B.

2000–01	Cambridge U	10	2		
2001–02	Cambridge U	6	0	**16**	**2**
2001–02	Torquay U	30	6		
2002–03	Torquay U	9	2	**39**	**8**
2002–03	Hartlepool U	24	5		
2003–04	Hartlepool U	3	0	**27**	**5**
2003–04	Lincoln C	38	10		
2004–05	Lincoln C	14	4	**52**	**14**
2004–05	*Rochdale*	2	0	**2**	**0**
2004–05	Yeovil T	4	0	**4**	**0**
2005–06	Chester C	34	4	**34**	**4**
2005–06	*Macclesfield T*	8	3	**8**	**3**

RUTHERFORD, Paul (M) 6 0
H: 5 9 W: 11 07 b.Moreton 10-7-87

2005–06	Chester C	6	0	**6**	**0**

TAIT, Paul (F) 200 28
H: 6 2 W: 12 05 b.Newcastle 24-10-74
Source: Trainee.

1993–94	Everton	0	0		
1994–95	Wigan Ath	5	0		
1995–96	Wigan Ath	0	0	**5**	**0**
From Northwich Vic.					
1999–2000	Crewe Alex	33	6		
2000–01	Crewe Alex	18	0		
2001–02	*Hull C*	2	0	**2**	**0**
2001–02	Crewe Alex	12	0	**63**	**6**
2002–03	Bristol R	41	7		
2003–04	Bristol R	33	12	**74**	**19**
2004–05	Rochdale	36	2		
2005–06	Rochdale	11	1	**47**	**3**
2005–06	Chester C	9	0	**9**	**0**

VAUGHAN, James (D) 0 0
H: 5 10 W: 12 09 b.Liverpool 6-12-86

2005–06	Chester C	0	0		

VAUGHAN, Stephen (D) 38 0
H: 5 6 W: 11 11 b.Liverpool 22-1-85
Source: Scholar.

2001–02	Liverpool	0	0		
2002–03	Liverpool	0	0		
2003–04	Liverpool	0	0		
2004–05	Chester C	21	0		
2005–06	Chester C	17	0	**38**	**0**

WALKER, Justin (M) 336 13
H: 5 10 W: 13 05 b.Nottingham 6-9-75
Source: Trainee. *Honours:* England Schools, Youth.

1992–93	Nottingham F	0	0		
1993–94	Nottingham F	0	0		
1994–95	Nottingham F	0	0		
1995–96	Nottingham F	0	0		
1996–97	Nottingham F	0	0		
1996–97	Scunthorpe U	9	0		
1997–98	Scunthorpe U	40	1		
1998–99	Scunthorpe U	41	1		
1999–2000	Scunthorpe U	42	0	**132**	**2**
2000–01	Lincoln C	45	1		
2001–02	Lincoln C	31	3	**76**	**4**
2002–03	Exeter C	39	5	**39**	**5**
2003–04	Cambridge U	23	1		
2003–04	*York C*	9	0	**9**	**0**
2004–05	Cambridge U	36	1	**59**	**2**
2005–06	Chester C	21	0	**21**	**0**

CHESTERFIELD (24)

ALLISON, Wayne (F) 707 167
H: 6 0 W: 14 13 b.Huddersfield 16-10-68
Source: Trainee.

1986–87	Halifax T	8	4		
1987–88	Halifax T	35	4		
1988–89	Halifax T	41	15	**84**	**23**
1989–90	Watford	7	0	**7**	**0**
1990–91	Bristol C	37	6		
1991–92	Bristol C	43	10		
1992–93	Bristol C	39	4		
1993–94	Bristol C	39	15		
1994–95	Bristol C	37	13	**195**	**48**
1995–96	Swindon T	44	17		
1996–97	Swindon T	41	11		
1997–98	Swindon T	16	3	**101**	**31**
1997–98	Huddersfield T	27	6		
1998–99	Huddersfield T	44	9		
1999–2000	Huddersfield T	3	0	**74**	**15**
1999–2000	Tranmere R	40	16		
2000–01	Tranmere R	36	6		
2001–02	Tranmere R	27	4	**103**	**26**
2002–03	Sheffield U	34	6		
2003–04	Sheffield U	39	1	**73**	**7**
2004–05	Chesterfield	38	6		
2005–06	Chesterfield	32	11	**70**	**17**

ALLOTT, Mark (M) 336 42
H: 5 11 W: 11 07 b.Manchester 3-10-77
Source: Trainee.

1995–96	Oldham Ath	0	0		
1996–97	Oldham Ath	5	1		
1997–98	Oldham Ath	22	2		
1998–99	Oldham Ath	41	7		
1999–2000	Oldham Ath	32	10		
2000–01	Oldham Ath	39	7		
2001–02	Oldham Ath	15	4	**154**	**31**
2001–02	Chesterfield	21	4		
2002–03	Chesterfield	33	0		
2003–04	Chesterfield	40	2		
2004–05	Chesterfield	45	2		
2005–06	Chesterfield	43	3	**182**	**11**

BAILEY, Alex (D) 63 1
H: 5 9 W: 11 08 b.Newham 21-9-83
Source: Scholar. *Honours:* England Youth.

2001–02	Arsenal	0	0		
2002–03	Arsenal	0	0		
2003–04	Arsenal	0	0		
2004–05	Chesterfield	45	1		
2005–06	Chesterfield	18	0	**63**	**1**

BLATHERWICK, Steve (D) 278 11
H: 6 2 W: 14 06 b.Nottingham 20-9-73
Source: Notts Co.

1992–93	Nottingham F	0	0		
1993–94	Nottingham F	3	0		
1993–94	*Wycombe W*	2	0	**2**	**0**
1994–95	Nottingham F	0	0		
1995–96	Nottingham F	0	0		
1995–96	*Hereford U*	10	1	**10**	**1**
1996–97	Nottingham F	7	0	**10**	**0**
1996–97	*Reading*	7	0	**7**	**0**
1997–98	Burnley	21	0		
1998–99	Burnley	3	0	**24**	**0**
1998–99	Chesterfield	14	1		
1999–2000	Chesterfield	36	0		
2000–01	Chesterfield	38	1		
2001–02	Chesterfield	5	0		
2002–03	Chesterfield	31	0		
2003–04	Chesterfield	36	2		
2004–05	Chesterfield	35	4		
2005–06	Chesterfield	30	2	**225**	**10**

DAVIES, Gareth (M) 101 2
H: 6 1 W: 12 10 b.Chesterfield 4-2-83
Source: Trainee.

2001–02	Chesterfield	0	0		
2002–03	Chesterfield	34	1		
2003–04	Chesterfield	28	0		
2004–05	Chesterfield	19	1		
2005–06	Chesterfield	20	0	**101**	**2**

DE BOLLA, Mark (F) 54 6
H: 5 8 W: 11 07 b.Camberwell 1-1-83
Source: Trainee.

1999–2000	Aston Villa	0	0		
2000–01	Charlton Ath	0	0		
2001–02	Charlton Ath	0	0		
2002–03	Charlton Ath	0	0		
2003–04	Charlton Ath	0	0		
2003–04	Chesterfield	8	1		
2004–05	Chesterfield	28	3		
2005–06	Chesterfield	4	1	**40**	**5**
2005–06	*Notts Co*	14	1	**14**	**1**

DOWNES, Aaron (D) 31 2
H: 6 2 W: 13 02 b.Mudgee 15-5-85
Honours: Australia Under-20.

2004–05	Chesterfield	9	2		
2005–06	Chesterfield	22	0	**31**	**2**

FOLAN, Caleb (F) 86 7
H: 6 2 W: 14 07 b.Leeds 26-10-82
Source: Trainee.

1999–2000	Leeds U	0	0		
2000–01	Leeds U	0	0		
2001–02	Leeds U	0	0		
2001–02	*Rushden & D*	6	0	**6**	**0**
2001–02	*Hull C*	1	0	**1**	**0**
2002–03	Leeds U	0	0		
2002–03	Chesterfield	13	1		
2003–04	Chesterfield	7	0		
2004–05	Chesterfield	32	6		
2005–06	Chesterfield	27	0	**79**	**7**

FOX, Michael (M) 1 0
H: 5 11 W: 11 00 b.Mansfield 7-9-85
Source: Scholar.

2004–05	Chesterfield	1	0		
2005–06	Chesterfield	0	0	**1**	**0**

FOYLE, Ashley (D) 1 0
H: 5 11 W: 12 07 b.Sheffield 17-9-86
Source: Scholar.

2005–06	Chesterfield	1	0	**1**	**0**

HALL, Paul (M) 570 103
H: 5 8 W: 12 00 b.Manchester 3-7-72
Source: Trainee. *Honours:* Jamaica 41 full caps, 9 goals.

1989–90	Torquay U	10	0		
1990–91	Torquay U	17	0		
1991–92	Torquay U	38	1		
1992–93	Torquay U	28	0	**93**	**1**
1992–93	Portsmouth	0	0		
1993–94	Portsmouth	28	4		
1994–95	Portsmouth	43	5		
1995–96	Portsmouth	46	10		
1996–97	Portsmouth	42	13		
1997–98	Portsmouth	29	5	**188**	**37**
1998–99	Coventry C	9	0		
1998–99	*Bury*	7	0	**7**	**0**
1999–2000	Coventry C	1	0	**10**	**0**
1999–2000	*Sheffield U*	4	1	**4**	**1**
1999–2000	*WBA*	4	0	**4**	**0**
1999–2000	Walsall	10	4		
2000–01	Walsall	42	6		
2001–02	Walsall	0	0	**52**	**10**
2001–02	Rushden & D	34	8		
2002–03	Rushden & D	45	16		
2003–04	Rushden & D	33	2	**112**	**26**
2003–04	Tranmere R	9	2		
2004–05	Tranmere R	46	11	**55**	**13**
2005–06	Chesterfield	45	15	**45**	**15**

HAZELL, Reuben (D) 159 3
H: 5 11 W: 12 05 b.Birmingham 24-4-79
Source: Trainee.

1996–97	Aston Villa	0	0		
1997–98	Aston Villa	0	0		
1998–99	Aston Villa	0	0		
1999–2000	Tranmere R	23	1		
2000–01	Tranmere R	13	0		
2001–02	Tranmere R	6	0	**42**	**1**
2001–02	Torquay U	19	0		
2002–03	Torquay U	46	1		
2003–04	Torquay U	19	1		
2004–05	Torquay U	0	0	**84**	**2**
2005–06	Chesterfield	33	0	**33**	**0**

HEATH, Colin (F) **21 1**
H: 6 0 W: 11 13 b.Matlock 31-12-83
Source: Scholar.

2000–01	Manchester U	0	0		
2001–02	Manchester U	0	0		
2002–03	Manchester U	0	0		
2003–04	Manchester U	0	0		
2004–05	Manchester U	0	0		
2004–05	*Cambridge U*	6	0	**6**	**0**
2005–06	Manchester U	0	0		
2005–06	*Swindon T*	11	1	**11**	**1**
2005–06	Chesterfield	4	0	**4**	**0**

JACKSON, Jamie (F) **2 0**
H: 5 6 W: 10 04 b.Sheffield 1-11-86
Source: Scholar.

2005–06	Chesterfield	2	0	**2**	**0**

JUBB, Anthony (M) **0 0**
b.Sheffield 2-12-85
Source: Scholar.

2005–06	Chesterfield	0	0		

KOVACS, Janos (D) **9 0**
H: 6 4 W: 14 10 b.Budapest 11-9-85
Source: MTK.

2005–06	Chesterfield	9	0	**9**	**0**

LANCASTER, Sam (M) **1 0**
H: 6 0 W: 12 07 b.Leicester 17-2-86
Source: Scholar.

2005–06	Chesterfield	1	0	**1**	**0**

LARKIN, Colin (F) **169 38**
H: 5 9 W: 11 07 b.Dundalk 27-4-82
Source: Trainee.

1998–99	Wolverhampton W	0	0		
1999–2000	Wolverhampton W	1	0		
2000–01	Wolverhampton W	2	0		
2001–02	Wolverhampton W	0	0	**3**	**0**
2001–02	*Kidderminster H*	33	6	**33**	**6**
2002–03	Mansfield T	22	7		
2003–04	Mansfield T	37	7		
2004–05	Mansfield T	33	11	**92**	**25**
2005–06	Chesterfield	41	7	**41**	**7**

MUGGLETON, Carl (G) **394 0**
H: 6 2 W: 14 12 b.Leicester 13-9-68
Source: Apprentice. *Honours:* England Under-21.

1986–87	Leicester C	0	0		
1987–88	Leicester C	0	0		
1987–88	*Chesterfield*	17	0		
1987–88	*Blackpool*	2	0	**2**	**0**
1988–89	Leicester C	3	0		
1988–89	*Hartlepool U*	8	0	**8**	**0**
1989–90	Leicester C	0	0		
1989–90	*Stockport Co*	4	0	**4**	**0**
1990–91	Leicester C	22	0		
1990–91	*Liverpool*	0	0		
1991–92	Leicester C	4	0		
1992–93	Leicester C	17	0		
1993–94	Leicester C	0	0	**46**	**0**
1993–94	*Stoke C*	6	0		
1993–94	*Sheffield U*	0	0		
1993–94	Celtic	12	0	**12**	**0**
1994–95	Stoke C	24	0		
1995–96	Stoke C	6	0		
1995–96	*Rotherham U*	6	0	**6**	**0**
1995–96	*Sheffield U*	1	0	**1**	**0**
1996–97	Stoke C	33	0		
1997–98	Stoke C	34	0		
1998–99	Stoke C	40	0		
1999–2000	Stoke C	0	0		
1999–2000	*Mansfield T*	9	0	**9**	**0**
1999–2000	*Chesterfield*	5	0		
2000–01	Stoke C	12	0	**155**	**0**
2000–01	*Cardiff C*	6	0	**6**	**0**
2001–02	Cheltenham T	7	0	**7**	**0**
2001–02	*Bradford C*	4	0	**4**	**0**
2002–03	Chesterfield	26	0		
2003–04	Chesterfield	46	0		
2004–05	Chesterfield	37	0		
2005–06	Chesterfield	3	0	**134**	**0**

N'TOYA, Tcham (F) **56 12**
H: 5 11 W: 12 11 b.Kinshasa 3-11-83
Source: Troyes.

2003–04	Chesterfield	6	0		
2004–05	Chesterfield	38	8		
2005–06	Chesterfield	4	0	**48**	**8**
2005–06	*Oxford U*	8	4	**8**	**4**

NICHOLSON, Shane (D) **507 31**
H: 5 11 W: 12 06 b.Newark 3-6-70
Source: Trainee.

1986–87	Lincoln C	7	0		
1987–88	Lincoln C	0	0		
1988–89	Lincoln C	34	1		
1989–90	Lincoln C	23	0		
1990–91	Lincoln C	40	4		
1991–92	Lincoln C	29	1	**133**	**6**
1991–92	Derby Co	0	0		
1992–93	Derby Co	17	0		
1993–94	Derby Co	22	1		
1994–95	Derby Co	15	0		
1995–96	Derby Co	20	0	**74**	**1**
1995–96	WBA	18	0		
1996–97	WBA	18	0		
1997–98	WBA	16	0	**52**	**0**
1998–99	Chesterfield	24	0		
1999–2000	Stockport Co	42	1		
2000–01	Stockport Co	35	2	**77**	**3**
2001–02	Sheffield U	25	3	**25**	**3**
2002–03	Tranmere R	38	4		
2003–04	Tranmere R	16	2	**54**	**6**
2004–05	Chesterfield	43	7		
2005–06	Chesterfield	25	5	**92**	**12**

NIVEN, Derek (M) **103 7**
H: 5 11 W: 12 05 b.Falkirk 12-12-83
Source: Stenhousemuir.

2000–01	Raith R	1	0	**1**	**0**
2001–02	Bolton W	0	0		
2002–03	Bolton W	0	0		
2003–04	Bolton W	0	0		
2003–04	Chesterfield	22	1		
2004–05	Chesterfield	38	1		
2005–06	Chesterfield	42	5	**102**	**7**

O'HARE, Alan (D) **124 1**
H: 6 1 W: 12 09 b.Drogheda 31-7-82
Source: Scholar. *Honours:* Eire Youth.

2001–02	Bolton W	0	0		
2001–02	*Chesterfield*	19	0		
2002–03	Bolton W	0	0		
2002–03	Chesterfield	22	0		
2003–04	Chesterfield	40	1		
2004–05	Chesterfield	21	0		
2005–06	Chesterfield	22	0	**124**	**1**

ROCHE, Barry (G) **54 0**
H: 6 5 W: 14 08 b.Dublin 6-4-82
Source: Trainee.

1999–2000	Nottingham F	0	0		
2000–01	Nottingham F	2	0		
2001–02	Nottingham F	0	0		
2002–03	Nottingham F	1	0		
2003–04	Nottingham F	8	0		
2004–05	Nottingham F	2	0	**13**	**0**
2005–06	Chesterfield	41	0	**41**	**0**

SMITH, Adam (M) **45 3**
H: 5 11 W: 12 00 b.Huddersfield 20-2-85
Source: Scholar.

2003–04	Chesterfield	3	0		
2004–05	Chesterfield	16	0		
2005–06	Chesterfield	26	3	**45**	**3**

COLCHESTER U (25)

BALDWIN, Pat (D) **86 0**
H: 6 3 W: 12 07 b.City of London 12-11-82
Source: Chelsea Academy.

2002–03	Colchester U	19	0		
2003–04	Colchester U	4	0		
2004–05	Colchester U	38	0		
2005–06	Colchester U	25	0	**86**	**0**

BROWN, Wayne (D) **195 9**
H: 6 0 W: 12 06 b.Barking 20-8-77
Source: Trainee.

1995–96	Ipswich T	0	0		
1996–97	Ipswich T	0	0		
1997–98	Ipswich T	1	0		
1997–98	*Colchester U*	2	0		
1998–99	Ipswich T	1	0		
1999–2000	Ipswich T	25	0		
2000–01	Ipswich T	4	0		
2000–01	*QPR*	2	0	**2**	**0**
2001–02	Ipswich T	0	0		
2001–02	*Wimbledon*	17	1	**17**	**1**
2001–02	*Watford*	11	3		
2002–03	Ipswich T	9	0	**40**	**0**
2002–03	Watford	13	1		
2003–04	Watford	12	0	**36**	**4**
2003–04	*Gillingham*	4	1	**4**	**1**
2003–04	*Colchester U*	16	0		
2004–05	Colchester U	40	1		
2005–06	Colchester U	38	2	**96**	**3**

CHILVERS, Liam (D) **129 4**
H: 6 2 W: 12 03 b.Chelmsford 6-11-81
Source: Scholar.

2000–01	Arsenal	0	0		
2000–01	*Northampton T*	7	0	**7**	**0**
2001–02	Arsenal	0	0		
2001–02	*Notts Co*	9	1	**9**	**1**
2002–03	Arsenal	0	0		
2002–03	*Colchester U*	6	0		
2003–04	Arsenal	0	0		
2003–04	*Colchester U*	32	0		
2004–05	Colchester U	41	1		
2005–06	Colchester U	34	2	**113**	**3**

COUSINS, Mark (G) **0 0**
b.Chelmsford 9-1-87
Source: Scholar.

2005–06	Colchester U	0	0		

DANNS, Neil (M) **97 22**
H: 5 10 W: 10 12 b.Liverpool 23-11-82
Source: Scholar.

2000–01	Blackburn R	0	0		
2001–02	Blackburn R	0	0		
2002–03	Blackburn R	2	0		
2003–04	Blackpool	12	2	**12**	**2**
2003–04	Blackburn R	1	0		
2003–04	*Hartlepool U*	9	1	**9**	**1**
2004–05	Blackburn R	0	0	**3**	**0**
2004–05	Colchester U	32	11		
2005–06	Colchester U	41	8	**73**	**19**

DAVISON, Aidan (G) **327 0**
H: 6 2 W: 13 12 b.Sedgefield 11-5-68
Source: Billingham Synthonia. *Honours:* Northern Ireland B, 3 full caps.

1987–88	Notts Co	0	0		
1988–89	Notts Co	1	0		
1989–90	Notts Co	0	0	**1**	**0**
1989–90	*Leyton Orient*	0	0		
1989–90	Bury	0	0		
1989–90	*Chester C*	0	0		
1990–91	Bury	0	0		
1990–91	*Blackpool*	0	0		
1991–92	Millwall	33	0		
1992–93	Millwall	1	0	**34**	**0**
1993–94	Bolton W	31	0		
1994–95	Bolton W	4	0		
1995–96	Bolton W	2	0		
1996–97	Bolton W	0	0	**37**	**0**
1996–97	*Ipswich T*	0	0		
1996–97	*Hull C*	9	0	**9**	**0**
1996–97	Bradford C	10	0		
1997–98	Grimsby T	42	0		
1998–99	Grimsby T	35	0		
1999–2000	Grimsby T	0	0		
1999–2000	Sheffield U	2	0	**2**	**0**
1999–2000	Bradford C	6	0		
2000–01	Bradford C	2	0		
2001–02	Bradford C	9	0		
2002–03	Bradford C	34	0	**61**	**0**
2003–04	Grimsby T	32	0	**109**	**0**
2004–05	Colchester U	33	0		
2005–06	Colchester U	41	0	**74**	**0**

DUGUID, Karl (M) **305 37**
H: 5 11 W: 11 06 b.Hitchin 21-3-78
Source: Trainee.

1995–96	Colchester U	16	1		
1996–97	Colchester U	20	3		
1997–98	Colchester U	21	3		
1998–99	Colchester U	33	4		
1999–2000	Colchester U	41	12		
2000–01	Colchester U	41	5		
2001–02	Colchester U	41	4		
2002–03	Colchester U	27	3		
2003–04	Colchester U	30	2		
2004–05	Colchester U	0	0		
2005–06	Colchester U	35	0	**305**	**37**

ELOKOBI, George (D) 17 1
H: 5 10 W: 13 02 b.Cameroon 31-1-86
Source: Dulwich Hamlet.
2004–05 Colchester U 0 0
2004–05 *Chester C* 5 0 **5 0**
2005–06 Colchester U 12 1 **12 1**

GARCIA, Richard (F) 80 13
H: 5 11 W: 12 01 b.Perth 4-9-81
Source: Trainee. *Honours:* Australia Under-23.
1998–99 West Ham U 0 0
1999–2000 West Ham U 0 0
2000–01 West Ham U 0 0
2000–01 *Leyton Orient* 18 4 **18 4**
2001–02 West Ham U 8 0
2002–03 West Ham U 0 0
2003–04 West Ham U 7 0
2004–05 West Ham U 1 0 **16 0**
2004–05 Colchester U 24 4
2005–06 Colchester U 22 5 **46 9**

GERKEN, Dean (G) 21 0
H: 6 3 W: 12 08 b.Rochford 22-5-85
Source: Scholar.
2003–04 Colchester U 1 0
2004–05 Colchester U 13 0
2005–06 Colchester U 7 0 **21 0**

GUY, Jamie (M) 4 0
H: 6 1 W: 13 00 b.Barking 1-8-87
Source: Scholar.
2004–05 Colchester U 2 0
2005–06 Colchester U 2 0 **4 0**

HALFORD, Greg (D) 108 15
H: 6 4 W: 12 10 b.Chelmsford 8-12-84
Source: Scholar. *Honours:* England Youth, Under-20.
2002–03 Colchester U 1 0
2003–04 Colchester U 18 4
2004–05 Colchester U 44 4
2005–06 Colchester U 45 7 **108 15**

HOWELL, Dean (D) 9 0
H: 6 1 W: 12 05 b.Burton-on-Trent 29-11-80
Source: Trainee.
1999–2000 Notts Co 1 0 **1 0**
2000–01 Crewe Alex 1 0 **1 0**
2000–01 *Rochdale* 3 0 **3 0**
2005–06 Colchester U 4 0 **4 0**

HUGHES, Craig (F) 0 0
Source: Scholar.
2005–06 Colchester U 0 0

HUNT, Stephen (D) 22 1
H: 6 2 W: 13 00 b.Southampton 11-11-84
Source: Southampton Scholar.
2004–05 Colchester U 20 1
2005–06 Colchester U 2 0 **22 1**

IWELUMO, Chris (F) 218 44
H: 6 3 W: 15 03 b.Coatbridge 1-8-78
1996–97 St Mirren 14 0
1997–98 St Mirren 12 0 **26 0**
1998–99 Aarhus Fremad 27 4 **27 4**
1999–2000 Stoke C 3 0
2000–01 Stoke C 2 1
2000–01 *York C* 12 2 **12 2**
2000–01 *Cheltenham T* 4 1 **4 1**
2001–02 Stoke C 38 10
2002–03 Stoke C 32 5
2003–04 Stoke C 9 0 **84 16**
2003–04 Brighton & HA 10 4 **10 4**
2004–05 Aachen 9 0 **9 0**
2005–06 Colchester U 46 17 **46 17**

IZZET, Kem (M) 172 15
H: 5 7 W: 10 05 b.Mile End 29-9-80
Source: Trainee.
1998–99 Charlton Ath 0 0
1999–2000 Charlton Ath 0 0
2000–01 Charlton Ath 0 0
2000–01 Colchester U 6 1
2001–02 Colchester U 40 3
2002–03 Colchester U 45 8
2003–04 Colchester U 44 3
2004–05 Colchester U 4 0
2005–06 Colchester U 33 0 **172 15**

KEITH, Marino (F) 216 68
H: 5 10 W: 12 13 b.Peterhead 16-12-74
Source: Fraserburgh.
1995–96 Dundee U 4 0
1996–97 Dundee U 0 0 **4 0**
1997–98 Falkirk 32 10
1998–99 Falkirk 29 17 **61 27**
1999–2000 Livingston 9 4
2000–01 Livingston 13 3 **22 7**
2001–02 Plymouth Arg 23 9
2002–03 Plymouth Arg 37 11
2003–04 Plymouth Arg 40 9
2004–05 Plymouth Arg 17 1 **117 30**
2004–05 Colchester U 12 4
2005–06 Colchester U 0 0 **12 4**

KING, Robbie (M) 3 0
H: 5 11 W: 12 05 b.Chelmsford 1-10-86
Source: Scholar.
2005–06 Colchester U 3 0 **3 0**

PAINE, Matt (D) 0 0
H: 6 1 W: 12 12 b.Sidcup 22-12-87
Source: Scholar.
2005–06 Colchester U 0 0

POND, Russell (M) 0 0
H: 5 8 W: 11 10 b.Leytonstone 27-1-87
Source: Scholar.
2005–06 Colchester U 0 0

RICHARDS, Garry (D) 15 0
H: 6 3 W: 13 00 b.Romford 11-6-86
Source: Scholar.
2005–06 Colchester U 15 0 **15 0**

STOCKLEY, Sam (D) 371 5
H: 6 0 W: 12 08 b.Tiverton 5-9-77
Source: Trainee.
1996–97 Southampton 0 0
1996–97 Barnet 21 0
1997–98 Barnet 41 0
1998–99 Barnet 41 0
1999–2000 Barnet 34 1
2000–01 Barnet 45 1 **182 2**
2001–02 Oxford U 41 0
2002–03 Oxford U 0 0 **41 0**
2002–03 Colchester U 33 1
2003–04 Colchester U 44 0
2004–05 Colchester U 37 1
2005–06 Colchester U 27 1 **141 3**
2005–06 *Blackpool* 7 0 **7 0**

THORPE, Tony (F) 378 136
H: 5 9 W: 12 06 b.Leicester 10-4-74
Source: Leicester C.
1992–93 Luton T 0 0
1993–94 Luton T 14 1
1994–95 Luton T 4 0
1995–96 Luton T 33 7
1996–97 Luton T 41 28
1997–98 Luton T 28 14
1997–98 Fulham 13 3 **13 3**
1998–99 Bristol C 16 2
1998–99 *Reading* 6 1 **6 1**
1998–99 *Luton T* 8 4
1999–2000 Bristol C 31 13
1999–2000 *Luton T* 4 1
2000–01 Bristol C 39 19
2001–02 Bristol C 42 16 **128 50**
2002–03 Luton T 30 13
2003–04 Luton T 2 2 **164 70**
2003–04 QPR 31 10
2004–05 QPR 10 0 **41 10**
2004–05 *Rotherham U* 5 1 **5 1**
2005–06 Swindon T 7 1 **7 1**
2005–06 Colchester U 14 0 **14 0**

WATSON, Kevin (M) 349 12
H: 6 0 W: 12 06 b.Hackney 3-1-74
Source: Trainee.
1991–92 Tottenham H 0 0
1992–93 Tottenham H 5 0
1993–94 Tottenham H 0 0
1993–94 *Brentford* 3 0 **3 0**
1994–95 Tottenham H 0 0
1994–95 *Bristol C* 2 0 **2 0**
1994–95 *Barnet* 13 0 **13 0**
1995–96 Tottenham H 0 0 **5 0**
1996–97 Swindon T 27 1
1997–98 Swindon T 18 0
1998–99 Swindon T 18 0 **63 1**
1999–2000 Rotherham U 44 1
2000–01 Rotherham U 46 5
2001–02 Rotherham U 19 1 **109 7**
2001–02 Reading 12 1
2002–03 Reading 32 1
2003–04 Reading 22 0 **66 2**
2004–05 Colchester U 44 2
2005–06 Colchester U 44 0 **88 2**

WHITE, John (D) 55 0
H: 6 0 W: 12 01 b.Maldon 26-7-86
Source: Scholar.
2004–05 Colchester U 20 0
2005–06 Colchester U 35 0 **55 0**

WILLIAMS, Gareth (M) 81 16
H: 5 10 W: 11 13 b.Germiston 10-9-82
Source: Scholar. *Honours:* Wales Under-21.
2002–03 Crystal Palace 5 0
2002–03 *Colchester U* 8 6
2003–04 Crystal Palace 0 0
2003–04 *Cambridge U* 4 1 **4 1**
2003–04 *Bournemouth* 1 0 **1 0**
2003–04 *Colchester U* 7 2
2004–05 Crystal Palace 0 0 **5 0**
2004–05 Colchester U 29 3
2005–06 Colchester U 18 1 **62 12**
2005–06 *Blackpool* 9 3 **9 3**

COVENTRY C (26)

ADEBOLA, Dele (F) 412 98
H: 6 3 W: 12 08 b.Lagos 23-6-75
Source: Trainee.
1992–93 Crewe Alex 6 0
1993–94 Crewe Alex 0 0
1994–95 Crewe Alex 30 8
1995–96 Crewe Alex 29 8
1996–97 Crewe Alex 32 16
1997–98 Crewe Alex 27 7 **124 39**
1997–98 Birmingham C 17 7
1998–99 Birmingham C 39 13
1999–2000 Birmingham C 42 5
2000–01 Birmingham C 31 6
2001–02 Birmingham C 0 0 **129 31**
2001–02 *Oldham Ath* 5 0 **5 0**
2002–03 Crystal Palace 39 5 **39 5**
2003–04 Coventry C 28 2
2003–04 *Burnley* 3 1 **3 1**
2004–05 Coventry C 25 5
2004–05 *Bradford C* 15 3 **15 3**
2005–06 Coventry C 44 12 **97 19**

BARRETT, Graham (F) 117 12
H: 5 10 W: 11 07 b.Dublin 6-10-81
Source: Trainee. *Honours:* Eire Schools, Youth, Under-21, 6 full caps, 2 goals.
1998–99 Arsenal 0 0
1999–2000 Arsenal 2 0
2000–01 Arsenal 0 0
2000–01 *Bristol R* 1 0 **1 0**
2001–02 Arsenal 0 0
2001–02 *Crewe Alex* 3 0 **3 0**
2001–02 *Colchester U* 20 4 **20 4**
2002–03 Arsenal 0 0 **2 0**
2002–03 *Brighton & HA* 30 1 **30 1**
2003–04 Coventry C 31 2
2004–05 Coventry C 24 4
2004–05 *Sheffield W* 6 1 **6 1**
2005–06 Coventry C 0 0 **55 6**

DAVIS, Liam (M) 2 0
H: 5 9 W: 11 07 b.Wandsworth 23-11-86
Source: Scholar.
2005–06 Coventry C 2 0 **2 0**

DOYLE, Micky (M) 128 7
H: 5 10 W: 11 00 b.Dublin 8-7-81
Source: Celtic. *Honours:* Eire Under-21, 1 full cap.
2003–04 Coventry C 40 5
2004–05 Coventry C 44 2
2005–06 Coventry C 44 0 **128 7**

GIDDINGS, Stuart (M) 15 0
H: 6 0 W: 11 08 b.Coventry 27-3-86
Source: Scholar. *Honours:* England Youth.
2003–04 Coventry C 1 0
2004–05 Coventry C 12 0
2005–06 Coventry C 2 0 **15 0**

HALL, Marcus (D) **261 3**
H: 6 1 W: 12 02 b.Coventry 24-3-76
Source: Trainee. *Honours:* England Under-21, B.
1994–95 Coventry C 5 0
1995–96 Coventry C 25 0
1996–97 Coventry C 13 0
1997–98 Coventry C 25 1
1998–99 Coventry C 5 0
1999–2000 Coventry C 9 0
2000–01 Coventry C 21 0
2001–02 Coventry C 29 1
2002–03 Nottingham F 1 0 **1 0**
2002–03 Stoke C 24 0
2003–04 Stoke C 35 0
2004–05 Stoke C 20 1 **79 1**
2004–05 Coventry C 10 0
2005–06 Coventry C 39 0 **181 2**

HEATH, Matt (D) **84 7**
H: 6 4 W: 13 13 b.Leicester 1-11-81
Source: Scholar.
2000–01 Leicester C 0 0
2001–02 Leicester C 5 0
2002–03 Leicester C 11 3
2003–04 Leicester C 13 0
2003–04 *Stockport Co* 8 0 **8 0**
2004–05 Leicester C 22 3 **51 6**
2005–06 Coventry C 25 1 **25 1**

HUGHES, Stephen (M) **155 9**
H: 6 0 W: 12 12 b.Wokingham 18-9-76
Source: Trainee. *Honours:* England Schools, Youth, Under-21.
1994–95 Arsenal 1 0
1995–96 Arsenal 1 0
1996–97 Arsenal 14 1
1997–98 Arsenal 17 2
1998–99 Arsenal 14 1
1999–2000 Fulham 3 0 **3 0**
1999–2000 Arsenal 2 0 **49 4**
1999–2000 Everton 11 1
2000–01 Everton 18 0 **29 1**
2001–02 Watford 15 0
2002–03 Watford 0 0 **15 0**
2003–04 Charlton Ath 0 0
2004–05 Coventry C 40 4
2005–06 Coventry C 19 0 **59 4**

HUTCHISON, Don (M) **389 54**
H: 6 1 W: 11 08 b.Gateshead 9-5-71
Source: Trainee. *Honours:* Scotland B, 26 full caps, 6 goals.
1989–90 Hartlepool U 13 2
1990–91 Hartlepool U 11 0 **24 2**
1990–91 Liverpool 0 0
1991–92 Liverpool 3 0
1992–93 Liverpool 31 7
1993–94 Liverpool 11 0 **45 7**
1994–95 West Ham U 23 9
1995–96 West Ham U 12 2
1995–96 Sheffield U 19 2
1996–97 Sheffield U 41 3
1997–98 Sheffield U 18 0 **78 5**
1997–98 Everton 11 1
1998–99 Everton 33 3
1999–2000 Everton 31 6 **75 10**
2000–01 Sunderland 32 8
2001–02 Sunderland 2 0 **34 8**
2001–02 West Ham U 24 1
2002–03 West Ham U 10 0
2003–04 West Ham U 24 4
2004–05 West Ham U 5 0 **98 16**
2005–06 Millwall 11 2 **11 2**
2005–06 Coventry C 24 4 **24 4**

IMPEY, Andrew (M) **423 15**
H: 5 8 W: 11 02 b.Hammersmith 30-9-71
Source: Yeading. *Honours:* England Under-21.
1990–91 QPR 0 0
1991–92 QPR 13 0
1992–93 QPR 40 2
1993–94 QPR 33 3
1994–95 QPR 40 3
1995–96 QPR 29 3
1996–97 QPR 32 2 **187 13**
1997–98 West Ham U 19 0
1998–99 West Ham U 8 0 **27 0**
1998–99 Leicester C 18 0
1999–2000 Leicester C 29 1
2000–01 Leicester C 33 0
2001–02 Leicester C 27 0
2002–03 Leicester C 32 0
2003–04 Leicester C 13 0 **152 1**
2003–04 *Nottingham F* 16 1
2004–05 Nottingham F 20 0
2004–05 *Millwall* 5 0 **5 0**
2005–06 Nottingham F 0 0 **36 1**
2005–06 Coventry C 16 0 **16 0**

INCE, Clayton (G) **124 0**
H: 6 3 W: 13 03 b.Trinidad 13-7-72
Source: Defence Force. *Honours:* Trinidad & Tobago 63 full caps.
1999–2000 Crewe Alex 1 0
2000–01 Crewe Alex 1 0
2001–02 Crewe Alex 19 0
2002–03 Crewe Alex 43 0
2003–04 Crewe Alex 36 0
2004–05 Crewe Alex 23 0 **123 0**
2005–06 Coventry C 1 0 **1 0**

JOHN, Stern (F) **266 99**
H: 6 1 W: 12 13 b.Tunapuna 30-10-76
Honours: Trinidad & Tobago 98 full caps, 65 goals.
1998 Columbus Crew 27 26
1999 Columbus Crew 28 18 **55 44**
1999–2000 Nottingham F 17 3
2000–01 Nottingham F 29 2
2001–02 Nottingham F 26 13 **72 18**
2001–02 Birmingham C 15 7
2002–03 Birmingham C 30 5
2003–04 Birmingham C 29 4
2004–05 Birmingham C 3 0 **77 16**
2004–05 Coventry C 30 11
2005–06 Coventry C 25 10 **55 21**
2005–06 *Derby Co* 7 0 **7 0**

JORGENSEN, Claus (M) **206 32**
H: 5 10 W: 10 06 b.Holstebro 27-4-76
Source: Resen-Humlum, Struer BK, Holstebro, Aarhus, AC Horsens. *Honours:* Faroe Islands 5 full caps, 1 goal.
1999–2000 Bournemouth 44 6
2000–01 Bournemouth 43 8
2001–02 Bradford C 18 1
2002–03 Bradford C 32 11 **50 12**
2003–04 Coventry C 8 0
2003–04 *Bournemouth* 17 0 **104 14**
2004–05 Coventry C 17 3
2005–06 Coventry C 27 3 **52 6**

LYNCH, Ryan (M) **0 0**
H: 5 11 W: 11 09 b.Solihull 13-3-87
Source: Scholar.
2005–06 Coventry C 0 0

McCRINK, Paul (M) **0 0**
b.Newry 10-11-87
2004–05 Coventry C 0 0
2005–06 Coventry C 0 0

McSHEFFREY, Gary (F) **168 54**
H: 5 8 W: 10 06 b.Coventry 13-8-82
Source: Trainee. *Honours:* England Youth, Under-20.
1998–99 Coventry C 1 0
1999–2000 Coventry C 3 0
2000–01 Coventry C 0 0
2001–02 *Stockport Co* 5 1 **5 1**
2001–02 Coventry C 8 1
2002–03 Coventry C 29 4
2003–04 Coventry C 19 11
2003–04 *Luton T* 18 9
2004–05 Coventry C 37 12
2004–05 *Luton T* 5 1 **23 10**
2005–06 Coventry C 43 15 **140 43**

MORRELL, Andy (F) **208 57**
H: 5 11 W: 12 00 b.Doncaster 28-9-74
Source: Newcastle Blue Star.
1998–99 Wrexham 7 0
1999–2000 Wrexham 13 1
2000–01 Wrexham 20 3
2001–02 Wrexham 25 2
2002–03 Wrexham 45 34 **110 40**
2003–04 Coventry C 30 9
2004–05 Coventry C 34 6
2005–06 Coventry C 34 2 **98 17**

OSBOURNE, Isaac (M) **21 0**
H: 5 10 W: 11 11 b.Birmingham 22-6-86
Source: Scholar.
2002–03 Coventry C 2 0
2003–04 Coventry C 0 0
2004–05 Coventry C 9 0
2005–06 Coventry C 10 0 **21 0**

PAGE, Robert (D) **373 4**
H: 6 0 W: 12 05 b.Llwynpia 3-9-74
Source: Trainee. *Honours:* Wales Schools, Youth, Under-21, B, 41 full caps.
1992–93 Watford 0 0
1993–94 Watford 4 0
1994–95 Watford 5 0
1995–96 Watford 19 0
1996–97 Watford 36 0
1997–98 Watford 41 0
1998–99 Watford 39 0
1999–2000 Watford 36 1
2000–01 Watford 36 1
2001–02 Watford 0 0 **216 2**
2001–02 Sheffield U 43 0
2002–03 Sheffield U 34 0
2003–04 Sheffield U 30 1 **107 1**
2004–05 Cardiff C 9 0 **9 0**
2004–05 Coventry C 9 0
2005–06 Coventry C 32 1 **41 1**

REID, Craig (F) **0 0**
H: 5 10 W: 11 10 b.Coventry 17-12-85
Honours: Ipswich T Scholar.
2004–05 Coventry C 0 0
2005–06 Coventry C 0 0

SCOWCROFT, James (F) **385 74**
H: 6 1 W: 14 07 b.Bury St Edmunds 15-11-75
Source: Trainee. *Honours:* England Under-21.
1994–95 Ipswich T 0 0
1995–96 Ipswich T 23 2
1996–97 Ipswich T 41 9
1997–98 Ipswich T 31 6
1998–99 Ipswich T 32 13
1999–2000 Ipswich T 41 13
2000–01 Ipswich T 34 4
2001–02 Leicester C 24 5
2002–03 Leicester C 43 10
2003–04 Leicester C 35 5
2004–05 Leicester C 31 4 **133 24**
2004–05 *Ipswich T* 9 0 **211 47**
2005–06 Coventry C 41 3 **41 3**

SHAW, Richard (D) **528 4**
H: 5 9 W: 12 08 b.Brentford 11-9-68
Source: Apprentice.
1986–87 Crystal Palace 0 0
1987–88 Crystal Palace 3 0
1988–89 Crystal Palace 14 0
1989–90 Crystal Palace 21 0
1989–90 *Hull C* 4 0 **4 0**
1990–91 Crystal Palace 36 1
1991–92 Crystal Palace 10 0
1992–93 Crystal Palace 33 0
1993–94 Crystal Palace 34 2
1994–95 Crystal Palace 41 0
1995–96 Crystal Palace 15 0 **207 3**
1995–96 Coventry C 21 0
1996–97 Coventry C 35 0
1997–98 Coventry C 33 0
1998–99 Coventry C 37 0
1999–2000 Coventry C 29 0
2000–01 Coventry C 24 0
2001–02 Coventry C 32 0
2002–03 Coventry C 29 0
2003–04 Coventry C 19 1
2004–05 Coventry C 33 0
2005–06 Coventry C 25 0 **317 1**

SOFIANE, Youssef (F) **6 0**
H: 5 8 W: 11 01 b.Lyon 8-7-84
Honours: France Youth.
2001–02 Auxerre 0 0
2002–03 West Ham U 0 0
2003–04 West Ham U 1 0
2004–05 West Ham U 0 0
2004–05 *Notts Co* 4 0 **4 0**
2005–06 West Ham U 0 0 **1 0**
2005–06 Coventry C 1 0 **1 0**

THORNTON, Kevin (M) **16 0**
H: 5 7 W: 11 00 b.Drogheda 9-7-86
Source: Scholar. *Honours:* Eire Youth.

2003–04	Coventry C	0	0		
2004–05	Coventry C	0	0		
2005–06	Coventry C	16	0	**16**	**0**

TUFFEY, Jonathan (G) **0 0**
H: 6 0 W: 12 08 b.Newry 20-1-87
Source: Scholar.

2003–04	Coventry C	0	0		
2004–05	Coventry C	0	0		
2005–06	Coventry C	0	0		

TURNER, Ben (D) **1 0**
H: 6 4 W: 14 04 b.Birmingham 21-1-88
Source: Scholar.

2005–06	Coventry C	1	0	**1**	**0**

WATSON, Paul (D) **349 20**
H: 5 8 W: 10 10 b.Hastings 4-1-75
Source: Trainee.

1992–93	Gillingham	1	0		
1993–94	Gillingham	14	0		
1994–95	Gillingham	39	2		
1995–96	Gillingham	8	0	**62**	**2**
1996–97	Fulham	44	3		
1997–98	Fulham	6	1	**50**	**4**
1997–98	Brentford	25	0		
1998–99	Brentford	12	0	**37**	**0**
1999–2000	Brighton & HA	42	4		
2000–01	Brighton & HA	46	5		
2001–02	Brighton & HA	45	5		
2002–03	Brighton & HA	45	0		
2003–04	Brighton & HA	15	0		
2004–05	Brighton & HA	4	0		
2005–06	Brighton & HA	0	0	**197**	**14**
2005–06	Coventry C	3	0	**3**	**0**

WEBB, Luke (M) **0 0**
H: 6 0 W: 12 01 b.Nottingham 12-9-86

2005–06	Coventry C	0	0		

WHING, Andrew (D) **90 2**
H: 6 0 W: 12 00 b.Birmingham 20-9-84
Source: Scholar.

2002–03	Coventry C	14	0		
2003–04	Coventry C	28	1		
2004–05	Coventry C	16	1		
2005–06	Coventry C	32	0	**90**	**2**

WILLIAMS, Ady (D) **407 21**
H: 6 2 W: 13 02 b.Reading 16-8-71
Source: Trainee. *Honours:* Wales 13 full caps, 1 goal.

1988–89	Reading	8	0		
1989–90	Reading	16	2		
1990–91	Reading	7	0		
1991–92	Reading	40	4		
1992–93	Reading	31	4		
1993–94	Reading	41	0		
1994–95	Reading	22	1		
1995–96	Reading	31	3		
1996–97	Wolverhampton W	6	0		
1997–98	Wolverhampton W	20	0		
1998–99	Wolverhampton W	0	0		
1999–2000	Wolverhampton W	1	0	**27**	**0**
1999–2000	*Reading*	15	1		
2000–01	Reading	5	0		
2001–02	Reading	35	1		
2002–03	Reading	38	1		
2003–04	Reading	33	1		
2004–05	Reading	11	0	**333**	**18**
2004–05	Coventry C	21	2		
2005–06	Coventry C	14	0	**35**	**2**
2005–06	*Millwall*	12	1	**12**	**1**

WISE, Dennis (M) **593 95**
H: 5 6 W: 10 09 b.Kensington 16-12-66
Source: Southampton Apprentice. *Honours:* England Under-21, B, 21 full caps, 1 goal.

1984–85	Wimbledon	1	0		
1985–86	Wimbledon	4	0		
1986–87	Wimbledon	28	4		
1987–88	Wimbledon	30	10		
1988–89	Wimbledon	37	5		
1989–90	Wimbledon	35	8	**135**	**27**
1990–91	Chelsea	33	10		
1991–92	Chelsea	38	10		
1992–93	Chelsea	27	3		
1993–94	Chelsea	35	4		
1994–95	Chelsea	19	6		
1995–96	Chelsea	35	7		
1996–97	Chelsea	31	3		
1997–98	Chelsea	26	3		
1998–99	Chelsea	22	0		
1999–2000	Chelsea	30	4		
2000–01	Chelsea	36	3	**332**	**53**
2001–02	Leicester C	17	1		
2002–03	Leicester C	0	0	**17**	**1**
2002–03	Millwall	29	3		
2003–04	Millwall	31	1		
2004–05	Millwall	25	3	**85**	**7**
2005–06	Southampton	11	1	**11**	**1**
2005–06	Coventry C	13	6	**13**	**6**

CREWE ALEX (27)

BAILEY, Matt (F) **5 0**
H: 6 4 W: 11 06 b.Crewe 12-3-86
Source: Nantwich T.

2003–04	Stockport Co	0	0		
2004–05	Stockport Co	1	0	**1**	**0**
2004–05	*Scunthorpe U*	4	0	**4**	**0**
From Northwich Vic.					
2005–06	Crewe Alex	0	0		

BELL, Lee (M) **54 3**
H: 5 11 W: 12 04 b.Crewe 26-1-83
Source: Scholar.

2000–01	Crewe Alex	0	0		
2001–02	Crewe Alex	0	0		
2002–03	Crewe Alex	17	1		
2003–04	Crewe Alex	3	0		
2004–05	Crewe Alex	17	0		
2005–06	Crewe Alex	17	2	**54**	**3**

BIGNOT, Paul (D) **10 0**
H: 6 1 W: 12 03 b.Birmingham 14-2-86
Source: Scholar.

2004–05	Crewe Alex	5	0		
2005–06	Crewe Alex	5	0	**10**	**0**

BOND, Andrew (M) **0 0**
H: 5 10 W: 11 06 b.Wigan 16-3-86
Source: Scholar.

2005–06	Crewe Alex	0	0		

BOUGHERRA, Madjid (D) **60 2**
H: 6 2 W: 14 00 b.Dijon 7-10-82
Source: Longvic.

2002–03	Gueugnon	1	0		
2003–04	Gueugnon	8	1		
2004–05	Gueugnon	30	0		
2005–06	Gueugnon	10	0	**49**	**1**
2005–06	Crewe Alex	11	1	**11**	**1**

COCHRANE, Justin (M) **78 1**
H: 5 11 W: 11 07 b.Hackney 26-1-82
Source: Scholarship.

1999–2000	QPR	0	0		
2000–01	QPR	1	0		
2001–02	QPR	0	0		
2002–03	QPR	0	0	**1**	**0**
From Hayes.					
2003–04	Crewe Alex	39	0		
2004–05	Crewe Alex	29	0		
2005–06	Crewe Alex	4	0	**72**	**0**
2005–06	*Gillingham*	5	1	**5**	**1**

FOSTER, Stephen (D) **218 15**
H: 6 0 W: 11 05 b.Warrington 10-9-80
Source: Trainee. *Honours:* England Schools.

1998–99	Crewe Alex	1	0		
1999–2000	Crewe Alex	0	0		
2000–01	Crewe Alex	30	0		
2001–02	Crewe Alex	34	5		
2002–03	Crewe Alex	35	4		
2003–04	Crewe Alex	45	2		
2004–05	Crewe Alex	34	1		
2005–06	Crewe Alex	39	3	**218**	**15**

GRANT, Tony (M) **250 6**
H: 5 9 W: 11 00 b.Liverpool 14-11-74
Source: Trainee. *Honours:* England Under-21.

1993–94	Everton	0	0		
1994–95	Everton	5	0		
1995–96	Everton	13	1		
1995–96	*Swindon T*	3	1	**3**	**1**
1996–97	Everton	18	0		
1997–98	Everton	7	1		
1998–99	Everton	16	0		
1999–2000	Everton	2	0	**61**	**2**
1999–2000	*Tranmere R*	9	0	**9**	**0**
1999–2000	Manchester C	8	0		
2000–01	Manchester C	10	0		
2000–01	*WBA*	5	0	**5**	**0**
2001–02	Manchester C	3	0	**21**	**0**
2001–02	Burnley	28	0		
2002–03	Burnley	34	1		
2003–04	Burnley	37	0		
2004–05	Burnley	42	2	**141**	**3**
2005–06	Bristol C	0	0		
2005–06	Crewe Alex	10	0	**10**	**0**

HIGDON, Michael (F) **56 7**
H: 6 2 W: 11 05 b.Liverpool 2-9-83
Source: School.

2000–01	Crewe Alex	0	0		
2001–02	Crewe Alex	0	0		
2002–03	Crewe Alex	0	0		
2003–04	Crewe Alex	10	1		
2004–05	Crewe Alex	20	3		
2005–06	Crewe Alex	26	3	**56**	**7**

JONES, Billy (M) **91 7**
H: 5 11 W: 13 00 b.Shrewsbury 24-3-87
Source: Scholar. *Honours:* England Youth, Under-20.

2003–04	Crewe Alex	27	1		
2004–05	Crewe Alex	20	0		
2005–06	Crewe Alex	44	6	**91**	**7**

JONES, Steve (F) **168 40**
H: 5 10 W: 10 05 b.Derry 25-10-76
Source: Leigh RMI. *Honours:* Northern Ireland 24 full caps, 2 goals.

2001–02	*Rochdale*	9	1	**9**	**1**
2001–02	Crewe Alex	6	0		
2002–03	Crewe Alex	31	9		
2003–04	Crewe Alex	45	15		
2004–05	Crewe Alex	36	10		
2005–06	Crewe Alex	41	5	**159**	**39**

LLOYD, Rob (D) **0 0**
H: 6 0 W: 11 10 b.Chester 13-8-86
Source: Scholar.

2005–06	Crewe Alex	0	0		

LOWE, Ryan (F) **207 40**
H: 5 10 W: 12 08 b.Liverpool 18-9-78
Source: Burscough.

2000–01	Shrewsbury T	30	4		
2001–02	Shrewsbury T	38	7		
2002–03	Shrewsbury T	39	9		
2003–04	Shrewsbury T	30	3		
2004–05	Shrewsbury T	30	3	**167**	**26**
2004–05	Chester C	8	4		
2005–06	Chester C	32	10	**40**	**14**
2005–06	Crewe Alex	0	0		

LUNT, Kenny (M) **373 35**
H: 5 10 W: 10 05 b.Runcorn 20-11-79
Source: Trainee. *Honours:* England Schools, Youth.

1997–98	Crewe Alex	41	2		
1998–99	Crewe Alex	18	1		
1999–2000	Crewe Alex	43	3		
2000–01	Crewe Alex	46	1		
2001–02	Crewe Alex	45	5		
2002–03	Crewe Alex	46	7		
2003–04	Crewe Alex	45	7		
2004–05	Crewe Alex	46	5		
2005–06	Crewe Alex	43	4	**373**	**35**

MAYNARD, Nicky (F) **1 1**
H: 5 11 W: 11 00 b.Winsford 11-12-86
Source: Scholar.

2005–06	Crewe Alex	1	1	**1**	**1**

McCREADY, Chris (D) **76 0**
H: 6 1 W: 12 05 b.Ellesmere Port 5-9-81
Source: Scholar.

2000–01	Crewe Alex	0	0		
2001–02	Crewe Alex	1	0		
2002–03	Crewe Alex	8	0		
2003–04	Crewe Alex	22	0		
2004–05	Crewe Alex	20	0		
2005–06	Crewe Alex	25	0	**76**	**0**

MOSES, Adi (D) **277 4**
H: 5 11 W: 13 01 b.Doncaster 4-5-75
Source: School. *Honours:* England Under-21.
1993–94 Barnsley 0 0
1994–95 Barnsley 4 0
1995–96 Barnsley 24 1
1996–97 Barnsley 28 2
1997–98 Barnsley 35 0
1998–99 Barnsley 34 0
1999–2000 Barnsley 12 0
2000–01 Barnsley 14 0 **151 3**
2000–01 Huddersfield T 12 0
2001–02 Huddersfield T 17 0
2002–03 Huddersfield T 40 1 **69 1**
2003–04 Crewe Alex 21 0
2004–05 Crewe Alex 21 0
2005–06 Crewe Alex 15 0 **57 0**

MOSS, Darren (D) **202 16**
H: 5 10 W: 11 00 b.Wrexham 24-5-81
Source: Trainee. *Honours:* Wales Under-21.
1998–99 Chester C 7 0
1999–2000 Chester C 35 0
2000–01 Chester C 0 0 **42 0**
2001–02 Shrewsbury T 31 2
2002–03 Shrewsbury T 40 2
2003–04 Shrewsbury T 26 6
2004–05 Shrewsbury T 26 6 **123 16**
2004–05 Crewe Alex 6 0
2005–06 Crewe Alex 31 0 **37 0**

O'CONNOR, Michael (M) **2 0**
H: 6 1 W: 11 08 b.Belfast 6-10-87
Source: Scholar. *Honours:* Northern Ireland Youth.
2005–06 Crewe Alex 2 0 **2 0**

OTSEMOBOR, John (D) **54 4**
H: 5 10 W: 12 07 b.Liverpool 23-3-83
Source: Trainee. *Honours:* England Youth, Under-20.
1999–2000 Liverpool 0 0
2000–01 Liverpool 0 0
2001–02 Liverpool 0 0
2002–03 Liverpool 0 0
2002–03 *Hull C* 9 3 **9 3**
2003–04 Liverpool 4 0
2003–04 *Bolton W* 1 0 **1 0**
2004–05 Liverpool 0 0 **4 0**
2004–05 *Crewe Alex* 14 1
2005–06 Rotherham U 10 0 **10 0**
2005–06 Crewe Alex 16 0 **30 1**

POPE, Tom (M) **0 0**
b.Stoke 27-8-85
Source: Lancaster C.
2005–06 Crewe Alex 0 0

RIX, Ben (M) **83 2**
H: 5 9 W: 11 13 b.Wolverhampton 11-12-82
Source: Scholar.
2000–01 Crewe Alex 0 0
2001–02 Crewe Alex 21 0
2002–03 Crewe Alex 23 0
2003–04 Crewe Alex 26 2
2004–05 Crewe Alex 0 0
2005–06 Crewe Alex 2 0 **72 2**
2005–06 *Bournemouth* 11 0 **11 0**

ROBERTS, Gary (M) **37 2**
H: 5 8 W: 10 05 b.Chester 4-2-87
Source: Scholar. *Honours:* England Youth.
2003–04 Crewe Alex 2 0
2004–05 Crewe Alex 2 0
2005–06 Crewe Alex 33 2 **37 2**

ROBERTS, Mark (D) **9 0**
H: 6 1 W: 12 00 b.Northwich 16-10-83
Source: Scholar.
2002–03 Crewe Alex 0 0
2003–04 Crewe Alex 2 0
2004–05 Crewe Alex 6 0
2005–06 Crewe Alex 0 0 **8 0**
2005–06 *Chester C* 1 0 **1 0**

RODGERS, Luke (F) **168 58**
H: 5 8 W: 11 00 b.Birmingham 1-1-82
Source: Trainee.
1999–2000 Shrewsbury T 6 1
2000–01 Shrewsbury T 26 7
2001–02 Shrewsbury T 38 22
2002–03 Shrewsbury T 36 16
2003–04 Shrewsbury T 0 0
2004–05 Shrewsbury T 36 6 **142 52**
2005–06 Crewe Alex 26 6 **26 6**

SUHAJ, Pavol (F) **49 5**
H: 6 3 W: 12 00 b.Lipany 16-4-81
Source: Patraikos.
2003–04 Trencin 16 2
2004–05 Trencin 27 3 **43 5**
2005–06 Crewe Alex 6 0 **6 0**

SUTTON, Ritchie (D) **0 0**
H: 6 0 W: 11 05 b.Stoke 29-4-86
Source: Scholar.
2005–06 Crewe Alex 0 0

TOMLINSON, Stuart (G) **4 0**
H: 6 1 W: 11 02 b.Chester 10-5-85
Source: Scholar.
2002–03 Crewe Alex 1 0
2003–04 Crewe Alex 1 0
2004–05 Crewe Alex 0 0
2005–06 Crewe Alex 2 0 **4 0**

TONKIN, Anthony (D) **112 0**
H: 5 11 W: 12 02 b.Newlyn 17-1-80
Source: Yeovil T.
2002–03 Stockport Co 24 0
2003–04 Stockport Co 0 0 **24 0**
2003–04 Crewe Alex 26 0
2004–05 Crewe Alex 35 0
2005–06 Crewe Alex 27 0 **88 0**

UGARTE, Juan (F) **35 17**
H: 5 10 W: 10 08 b.San Sebastian 7-11-80
2001–02 Real Sociedad 1 0
2002–03 Real Sociedad 0 0
2003–04 Real Sociedad 0 0 **1 0**
From Dorchester T
2004–05 Wrexham 30 17
2005–06 Crewe Alex 2 0 **2 0**
2005–06 *Wrexham* 2 0 **32 17**

VARNEY, Luke (F) **61 10**
H: 5 11 W: 11 00 b.Leicester 28-9-82
Source: Quorn.
2002–03 Crewe Alex 0 0
2003–04 Crewe Alex 8 1
2004–05 Crewe Alex 26 4
2005–06 Crewe Alex 27 5 **61 10**

VAUGHAN, David (M) **155 14**
H: 5 7 W: 11 00 b.Rhuddlan 18-2-83
Source: Scholar. *Honours:* Wales Youth, Under-21, 7 full caps.
2000–01 Crewe Alex 1 0
2001–02 Crewe Alex 13 0
2002–03 Crewe Alex 32 3
2003–04 Crewe Alex 31 0
2004–05 Crewe Alex 44 6
2005–06 Crewe Alex 34 5 **155 14**

WALKER, Richard (D) **100 6**
H: 6 2 W: 12 08 b.Stafford 17-9-80
Source: Brook House.
1999–2000 Crewe Alex 0 0
2000–01 Crewe Alex 3 0
2001–02 Crewe Alex 1 0
2002–03 Crewe Alex 35 2
2003–04 Crewe Alex 20 1
2004–05 Crewe Alex 23 2
2005–06 Crewe Alex 18 1 **100 6**

WILLIAMS, Ben (G) **64 0**
H: 6 0 W: 13 01 b.Manchester 27-8-82
Source: Scholar. *Honours:* England Schools.
2001–02 Manchester U 0 0
2002–03 Manchester U 0 0
2002–03 *Coventry C* 0 0
2002–03 *Chesterfield* 14 0 **14 0**
2003–04 Manchester U 0 0
2003–04 *Crewe Alex* 10 0
2004–05 Crewe Alex 23 0
2005–06 Crewe Alex 17 0 **50 0**

WILLIAMS, Owain Fon (G) **0 0**
H: 6 1 W: 12 09 b.Gwynedd 17-3-87
Source: Scholar.
2005–06 Crewe Alex 0 0

WILSON, Kyle (F) **0 0**
H: 5 10 W: 11 05 b.Wirrall 14-11-85
Source: Scholar. *Honours:* England Youth.
2003–04 Crewe Alex 0 0
2004–05 Crewe Alex 0 0
2005–06 Crewe Alex 0 0

CRYSTAL PALACE (28)

ANDREWS, Wayne (F) **156 35**
H: 5 10 W: 11 06 b.Paddington 25-11-77
Source: Trainee.
1995–96 Watford 1 0
1996–97 Watford 25 4
1997–98 Watford 2 0
1998–99 Watford 0 0 **28 4**
1998–99 *Cambridge U* 2 0 **2 0**
1998–99 *Peterborough U* 10 5 **10 5**
From Aldershot T, Chesham U
2001–02 Oldham
2002–03 Oldham Ath 37 11 **37 11**
2003–04 Colchester U 41 12
2004–05 Colchester U 5 2 **46 14**
2004–05 Crystal Palace 9 0
2005–06 Crystal Palace 24 1 **33 1**

BLACK, Tommy (M) **158 17**
H: 5 7 W: 11 10 b.Chigwell 26-11-79
Source: Trainee.
1998–99 Arsenal 0 0
1999–2000 Arsenal 1 0 **1 0**
1999–2000 *Carlisle U* 5 1 **5 1**
1999–2000 *Bristol C* 4 0 **4 0**
2000–01 Crystal Palace 40 4
2001–02 Crystal Palace 25 0
2002–03 Crystal Palace 36 6
2003–04 Crystal Palace 25 0
2004–05 Crystal Palace 0 0
2004–05 *Sheffield U* 4 1 **4 1**
2005–06 Crystal Palace 1 0 **127 10**
2005–06 *Gillingham* 17 5 **17 5**

BORROWDALE, Gary (D) **73 0**
H: 6 0 W: 12 01 b.Sutton 16-7-85
Source: Scholar. *Honours:* England Youth, Under-20.
2002–03 Crystal Palace 13 0
2003–04 Crystal Palace 23 0
2004–05 Crystal Palace 7 0
2005–06 Crystal Palace 30 0 **73 0**

BOYCE, Emmerson (D) **255 10**
H: 6 0 W: 12 03 b.Aylesbury 24-9-79
Source: Trainee.
1997–98 Luton T 0 0
1998–99 Luton T 1 0
1999–2000 Luton T 30 1
2000–01 Luton T 42 3
2001–02 Luton T 37 0
2002–03 Luton T 34 0
2003–04 Luton T 42 4 **186 8**
2004–05 Crystal Palace 27 0
2005–06 Crystal Palace 42 2 **69 2**

BUTTERFIELD, Danny (D) **235 8**
H: 5 10 W: 11 06 b.Boston 21-11-79
Source: Trainee. *Honours:* England Youth.
1997–98 Grimsby T 7 0
1998–99 Grimsby T 12 0
1999–2000 Grimsby T 29 0
2000–01 Grimsby T 30 1
2001–02 Grimsby T 46 2 **124 3**
2002–03 Crystal Palace 46 1
2003–04 Crystal Palace 45 4
2004–05 Crystal Palace 7 0
2005–06 Crystal Palace 13 0 **111 5**

DANZE, Anthony (M) **13 0**
H: 6 0 W: 12 00 b.Perth 15-3-84
Honours: Australia Youth, Under-20, Under-23.
2002–03 Perth Glory 7 0
2003–04 Perth Glory 4 0 **11 0**
2004–05 Crystal Palace 0 0
2004–05 *Milton Keynes D* 2 0 **2 0**
2005–06 Crystal Palace 0 0

FRAY, Arron (D) 0 0
H: 5 11 W: 11 02 b.Bromley 1-5-87
Source: Scholar.
2005–06 Crystal Palace 0 0

FREEDMAN, Dougie (F) 420 145
H: 5 9 W: 12 05 b.Glasgow 21-1-74
Source: Trainee. *Honours:* Scotland Schools, Under-21, B, 2 full caps, 1 goal.
1991–92 QPR 0 0
1992–93 QPR 0 0
1993–94 QPR 0 0
1994–95 Barnet 42 24
1995–96 Barnet 5 3 **47 27**
1995–96 Crystal Palace 39 20
1996–97 Crystal Palace 44 11
1997–98 Crystal Palace 7 0
1997–98 Wolverhampton W 29 10 **29 10**
1998–99 Nottingham F 31 9
1999–2000 Nottingham F 34 9
2000–01 Nottingham F 5 0 **70 18**
2000–01 Crystal Palace 26 11
2001–02 Crystal Palace 40 20
2002–03 Crystal Palace 29 9
2003–04 Crystal Palace 35 13
2004–05 Crystal Palace 20 1
2005–06 Crystal Palace 34 5 **274 90**

GRABBAN, Lewis (F) 0 0
H: 6 0 W: 11 03 b.Croydon 12-1-88
Source: Scholar.
2005–06 Crystal Palace 0 0

GRANVILLE, Danny (D) 309 19
H: 6 0 W: 12 00 b.Islington 19-1-75
Source: Trainee. *Honours:* England Under-21.
1993–94 Cambridge U 11 5
1994–95 Cambridge U 16 2
1995–96 Cambridge U 35 0
1996–97 Cambridge U 37 0 **99 7**
1996–97 Chelsea 5 0
1997–98 Chelsea 13 0 **18 0**
1998–99 Leeds U 9 0
1999–2000 Leeds U 0 0 **9 0**
1999–2000 Manchester C 35 2
2000–01 Manchester C 19 0
2000–01 *Norwich C* 6 0 **6 0**
2001–02 Manchester C 16 1 **70 3**
2001–02 Crystal Palace 16 0
2002–03 Crystal Palace 35 3
2003–04 Crystal Palace 21 3
2004–05 Crystal Palace 35 3
2005–06 Crystal Palace 0 0 **107 9**

HALL, Fitz (D) 130 8
H: 6 3 W: 13 00 b.Leytonstone 20-12-80
Source: Barnet Trainee, Chesham U.
2001–02 Oldham Ath 4 1
2002–03 Oldham Ath 40 4 **44 5**
2003–04 Southampton 11 0 **11 0**
2004–05 Crystal Palace 36 2
2005–06 Crystal Palace 39 1 **75 3**

HALL, Ryan (M) 0 0
H: 5 10 W: 10 04 b.Dulwich 4-1-88
Source: Scholar.
2005–06 Crystal Palace 0 0

HUDSON, Mark (D) 51 1
H: 6 1 W: 12 01 b.Guildford 30-3-82
Source: Trainee.
1998–99 Fulham 0 0
1999–2000 Fulham 0 0
2000–01 Fulham 0 0
2001–02 Fulham 0 0
2002–03 Fulham 0 0
2003–04 Fulham 0 0
2003–04 *Oldham Ath* 15 0 **15 0**
2003–04 *Crystal Palace* 14 0
2004–05 Crystal Palace 7 1
2005–06 Crystal Palace 15 0 **36 1**

HUGHES, Michael (M) 420 35
H: 5 6 W: 10 08 b.Larne 2-8-71
Source: Carrick R. *Honours:* Northern Ireland Schools, Youth, Under-21, Under-23, 71 full caps, 5 goals.
1988–89 Manchester C 1 0
1989–90 Manchester C 0 0
1990–91 Manchester C 1 0
1991–92 Manchester C 24 1 **26 1**
1992–93 Strasbourg 36 2
1993–94 Strasbourg 34 7
1994–95 Strasbourg 13 0 **83 9**
1994–95 *West Ham U* 17 2
1995–96 *West Ham U* 28 0
1996–97 West Ham U 33 3
1997–98 West Ham U 5 0 **83 5**
1997–98 Wimbledon 29 4
1998–99 Wimbledon 30 2
1999–2000 Wimbledon 20 2
2000–01 Wimbledon 10 1
2001–02 Wimbledon 26 4
2001–02 *Birmingham C* 3 0 **3 0**
2002–03 Wimbledon 0 0 **115 13**
2003–04 Crystal Palace 34 3
2004–05 Crystal Palace 36 2
2005–06 Crystal Palace 40 2 **110 7**

JOHNSON, Andy (F) 223 82
H: 5 7 W: 10 09 b.Bedford 10-2-81
Source: Trainee. *Honours:* England Youth, Under-20, 2 full caps.
1997–98 Birmingham C 0 0
1998–99 Birmingham C 4 0
1999–2000 Birmingham C 22 1
2000–01 Birmingham C 34 4
2001–02 Birmingham C 23 3 **83 8**
2002–03 Crystal Palace 28 11
2003–04 Crystal Palace 42 27
2004–05 Crystal Palace 37 21
2005–06 Crystal Palace 33 15 **140 74**

KIRALY, Gabor (G) 340 0
H: 6 3 W: 13 06 b.Szombathely 1-4-76
Honours: Hungary 65 full caps.
1993–94 Haladas 15 0
1994–95 Haladas 0 0
1995–96 Haladas 19 0
1996–97 Haladas 33 0 **67 0**
1997–98 Hertha Berlin 27 0
1998–99 Hertha Berlin 34 0
1999–2000 Hertha Berlin 27 0
2000–01 Hertha Berlin 34 0
2001–02 Hertha Berlin 25 0
2002–03 Hertha Berlin 33 0
2003–04 Hertha Berlin 18 0 **198 0**
2004–05 Crystal Palace 32 0
2005–06 Crystal Palace 43 0 **75 0**

KOLKKA, Joonas (M) 275 48
H: 5 9 W: 11 08 b.Lahti 28-9-74
Source: Reipas Lahti. *Honours:* Finland 68 full caps, 11 goals.
1994 MyPa 21 11
1995 MyPa 22 6 **43 17**
1995–96 Willem II 7 0
1996–97 Willem II 19 4
1997–98 Willem II 29 9 **55 13**
1998–99 PSV Eindhoven 19 1
1999–2000 PSV Eindhoven 32 5
2000–01 PSV Eindhoven 27 4 **78 10**
2001–02 Panathinaikos 23 2
2002–03 Panathinaikos 22 1 **45 3**
2003–04 M'gladbach 28 2 **28 2**
2004–05 Crystal Palace 23 3
2005–06 Crystal Palace 3 0 **26 3**

LEIGERTWOOD, Mikele (D) 123 3
H: 6 1 W: 11 04 b.Enfield 12-11-82
Source: Scholar.
2001–02 Wimbledon 1 0
2001–02 *Leyton Orient* 8 0 **8 0**
2002–03 Wimbledon 28 0
2003–04 Wimbledon 27 2 **56 2**
2003–04 Crystal Palace 12 0
2004–05 Crystal Palace 20 1
2005–06 Crystal Palace 27 0 **59 1**

MACKEN, Jon (F) 259 72
H: 5 11 W: 12 04 b.Manchester 7-9-77
Source: Trainee. *Honours:* England Youth. Eire 1 full cap.
1996–97 Manchester U 0 0
1997–98 Preston NE 29 6
1998–99 Preston NE 42 8
1999–2000 Preston NE 44 22
2000–01 Preston NE 38 19
2001–02 Preston NE 31 8 **184 63**
2001–02 Manchester C 8 5
2002–03 Manchester C 5 0
2003–04 Manchester C 15 1
2004–05 Manchester C 23 1 **51 7**
2005–06 Crystal Palace 24 2 **24 2**

McANUFF, Jobi (M) 193 24
H: 5 11 W: 11 05 b.Edmonton 9-11-81
Source: Scholar. *Honours:* Jamaica 1 full cap.
2000–01 Wimbledon 0 0
2001–02 Wimbledon 38 4
2002–03 Wimbledon 31 4
2003–04 Wimbledon 27 5 **96 13**
2003–04 West Ham U 12 1
2004–05 West Ham U 1 0 **13 1**
2004–05 Cardiff C 43 2 **43 2**
2005–06 Crystal Palace 41 8 **41 8**

MORRISON, Clinton (F) 284 89
H: 6 0 W: 12 00 b.Tooting 14-5-79
Source: Trainee. *Honours:* Eire Under-21, 34 full caps, 9 goals.
1996–97 Crystal Palace 0 0
1997–98 Crystal Palace 1 1
1998–99 Crystal Palace 37 12
1999–2000 Crystal Palace 29 13
2000–01 Crystal Palace 45 14
2001–02 Crystal Palace 45 22
2002–03 Birmingham C 28 6
2003–04 Birmingham C 32 4
2004–05 Birmingham C 26 4
2005–06 Birmingham C 1 0 **87 14**
2005–06 Crystal Palace 40 13 **197 75**

PELTONEN, Eero (F) 0 0
H: 5 9 W: 11 07 b.Finland 22-12-86
Source: PK39.
2005–06 Crystal Palace 0 0

POPOVIC, Tony (D) 372 34
H: 6 5 W: 13 01 b.Sydney 4-7-73
Honours: Australia Youth, Under-20, Under-23, 57 full caps, 7 goals.
1989–90 Sydney U 13 0
1990–91 Sydney U 17 1
1991–92 Sydney U 20 1
1992–93 Sydney U 24 2
1993–94 Sydney U 27 2
1994–95 Sydney U 25 3
1995–96 Sydney U 29 4
1995–96 Wolverhampton W 0 0
1996–97 Wolverhampton W 0 0
1996–97 Sydney U 7 2 **162 15**
1997 Sanfrecce 11 0
1998 Sanfrecce 25 4
1999 Sanfrecce 23 6
2000 Sanfrecce 21 3
2001 Sanfrecce 7 0 **87 13**
2001–02 Crystal Palace 20 2
2002–03 Crystal Palace 36 3
2003–04 Crystal Palace 34 1
2004–05 Crystal Palace 23 0
2005–06 Crystal Palace 10 0 **123 6**

REICH, Marco (M) 214 17
H: 6 0 W: 12 00 b.Meisenheim 30-12-77
Honours: Germany 1 full cap.
1996–97 Kaiserslautern 0 0
1997–98 Kaiserslautern 31 1
1998–99 Kaiserslautern 27 3
1999–2000 Kaiserslautern 28 2
2000–01 Kaiserslautern 18 2 **104 8**
2001–02 Cologne 24 0 **24 0**
2002–03 Werder Bremen 15 0 **15 0**
2003–04 Derby Co 13 1
2004–05 Derby Co 37 6 **50 7**
2005–06 Crystal Palace 21 2 **21 2**

RIIHILAHTI, Aki (M) 182 18
H: 5 11 W: 12 06 b.Helsinki 9-9-76
Honours: Finland Youth, Under-21, 63 full caps, 11 goals.
1999 Valerenga 25 5 **25 5**
2000–01 Crystal Palace 9 1
2001–02 Crystal Palace 45 5
2002–03 Crystal Palace 25 1
2003–04 Crystal Palace 31 0
2004–05 Crystal Palace 32 4
2005–06 Crystal Palace 15 2 **157 13**

SOARES, Tom (M) **69 1**
H: 6 0 W: 11 04 b.Reading 10-7-86
Source: Scholar. *Honours:* England Youth, Under-20, Under-21.

2003–04	Crystal Palace	3	0		
2004–05	Crystal Palace	22	0		
2005–06	Crystal Palace	44	1	**69**	**1**

SPERONI, Julian (G) **104 0**
H: 6 0 W: 11 00 b.Buenos Aires 18-5-79

1999–2000	Platense	2	0		
2000–01	Platense	0	0	**2**	**0**
2001–02	Dundee	17	0		
2002–03	Dundee	38	0		
2003–04	Dundee	37	0	**92**	**0**
2004–05	Crystal Palace	6	0		
2005–06	Crystal Palace	4	0	**10**	**0**

SYMONS, Kit (D) **436 27**
H: 6 1 W: 13 00 b.Basingstoke 8-3-71
Source: Trainee. *Honours:* Wales Youth, Under-21, B, 37 full caps, 2 goals.

1988–89	Portsmouth	2	0		
1989–90	Portsmouth	1	0		
1990–91	Portsmouth	1	0		
1991–92	Portsmouth	46	1		
1992–93	Portsmouth	41	2		
1993–94	Portsmouth	29	3		
1994–95	Portsmouth	40	4		
1995–96	Portsmouth	1	0	**161**	**10**
1995–96	Manchester C	38	2		
1996–97	Manchester C	44	0		
1997–98	Manchester C	42	2	**124**	**4**
1998–99	Fulham	45	11		
1999–2000	Fulham	29	2		
2000–01	Fulham	24	0		
2001–02	Fulham	4	0	**102**	**13**
2001–02	Crystal Palace	9	0		
2002–03	Crystal Palace	25	0		
2003–04	Crystal Palace	15	0		
2004–05	Crystal Palace	0	0		
2005–06	Crystal Palace	0	0	**49**	**0**

TOGWELL, Sam (D) **40 2**
H: 5 11 W: 12 04 b.Beaconsfield 14-10-84
Source: Scholar.

2002–03	Crystal Palace	1	0		
2003–04	Crystal Palace	0	0		
2004–05	Crystal Palace	0	0		
2004–05	*Oxford U*	4	0	**4**	**0**
2004–05	*Northampton T*	8	0	**8**	**0**
2005–06	Crystal Palace	0	0	**1**	**0**
2005–06	*Port Vale*	27	2	**27**	**2**

TORGHELLE, Sandor (F) **112 24**
H: 6 1 W: 13 06 b.Budapest 5-5-82
Honours: Hungary 13 full caps, 4 goals.

1999–2000	Kispest Honved	7	0		
2000–01	Kispest Honved	25	1		
2001–02	Kispest Honved	19	4		
2002–03	Kispest Honved	27	10	**78**	**15**
2003–04	MTK	22	9	**22**	**9**
2004–05	Crystal Palace	12	0		
2005–06	Crystal Palace	0	0	**12**	**0**

To Panathinaikos (loan) August 2005

WARD, Darren (D) **258 11**
H: 6 3 W: 11 04 b.Kenton 13-9-78
Source: Trainee.

1995–96	Watford	1	0		
1996–97	Watford	7	0		
1997–98	Watford	0	0		
1998–99	Watford	1	0		
1999–2000	Watford	9	1		
1999–2000	*QPR*	14	0	**14**	**0**
2000–01	Watford	40	1		
2001–02	Watford	1	0	**59**	**2**
2001–02	Millwall	14	0		
2002–03	Millwall	39	1		
2003–04	Millwall	46	3		
2004–05	Millwall	43	0	**142**	**4**
2005–06	Crystal Palace	43	5	**43**	**5**

WATSON, Ben (M) **84 5**
H: 5 10 W: 10 11 b.Camberwell 9-7-85
Source: Scholar. *Honours:* England Under-21.

2002–03	Crystal Palace	5	0		
2003–04	Crystal Palace	16	1		
2004–05	Crystal Palace	21	0		
2005–06	Crystal Palace	42	4	**84**	**5**

WILSON, Glenn (D) **0 0**
H: 6 1 W: 12 08 b.Lewisham 16-3-86
Source: Scholar.

2005–06	Crystal Palace	0	0

DARLINGTON (29)

APPLEBY, Matty (M) **347 17**
H: 5 10 W: 11 05 b.Middlesbrough 16-4-72
Source: Trainee.

1989–90	Newcastle U	0	0		
1990–91	Newcastle U	1	0		
1991–92	Newcastle U	18	0		
1992–93	Newcastle U	0	0		
1993–94	Newcastle U	1	0	**20**	**0**
1993–94	*Darlington*	10	1		
1994–95	Darlington	36	1		
1995–96	Darlington	43	6		
1996–97	Barnsley	35	0		
1997–98	Barnsley	15	0		
1998–99	Barnsley	34	0		
1999–2000	Barnsley	36	5		
2000–01	Barnsley	19	2		
2001–02	Barnsley	0	0	**139**	**7**
2001–02	Oldham Ath	17	2		
2002–03	Oldham Ath	12	0		
2003–04	Oldham Ath	17	0		
2004–05	Oldham Ath	17	0	**63**	**2**
2004–05	Darlington	10	0		
2005–06	Darlington	26	0	**125**	**8**

BATES, Guy (F) **9 1**
H: 6 0 W: 13 05 b.Newcastle 31-10-85
Source: Newcastle Jets.

2005–06	Darlington	9	1	**9**	**1**

BOSSU, Bertrand (G) **17 0**
H: 6 7 W: 14 00 b.Calais 14-10-80

1999–2000	Barnet	0	0		
2000–01	Barnet	0	0		
2001–02	Barnet	0	0		
2002–03	Barnet	0	0		

From Hayes.

2003–04	Gillingham	4	0		
2004–05	Gillingham	2	0	**6**	**0**
2004–05	*Torquay U*	2	0	**2**	**0**
2004–05	*Oldham Ath*	0	0		
2005–06	Darlington	9	0	**9**	**0**

CLARKE, Matthew (D) **238 15**
H: 6 3 W: 13 00 b.Leeds 18-12-80
Source: Wolverhampton W Trainee.

1999–2000	Halifax T	19	0		
2000–01	Halifax T	19	1		
2001–02	Halifax T	31	1	**69**	**2**
2002–03	Darlington	38	3		
2003–04	Darlington	45	4		
2004–05	Darlington	43	3		
2005–06	Darlington	43	3	**169**	**13**

CLOSE, Brian (M) **64 1**
H: 5 10 W: 12 03 b.Belfast 27-1-82
Honours: Northern Ireland Under-21.

1999–2000	Middlesbrough	0	0		
2000–01	Middlesbrough	0	0		
2001–02	Middlesbrough	0	0		
2002–03	Middlesbrough	0	0		
2002–03	*Chesterfield*	8	1	**8**	**1**
2003–04	Middlesbrough	0	0		
2003–04	Darlington	12	0		
2004–05	Darlington	38	0		
2005–06	Darlington	6	0	**56**	**0**

DICKMAN, Jonjo (M) **49 3**
H: 5 9 W: 9 08 b.Hexham 22-9-81

1998–99	Sunderland	0	0		
1999–2000	Sunderland	0	0		
2000–01	Sunderland	0	0		
2001–02	Sunderland	0	0		
2002–03	Sunderland	1	0		
2003–04	Sunderland	0	0		
2003–04	*York C*	2	0	**2**	**0**
2004–05	Sunderland	0	0	**1**	**0**
2004–05	Darlington	8	1		
2005–06	Darlington	38	2	**46**	**3**

DUKE, David (D) **224 8**
H: 5 10 W: 11 00 b.Inverness 7-11-78
Source: Redby CA.

1997–98	Sunderland	0	0		
1998–99	Sunderland	0	0		
1999–2000	Sunderland	0	0		
2000–01	Swindon T	32	1		
2001–02	Swindon T	42	2		
2002–03	Swindon T	44	2		
2003–04	Swindon T	42	1		
2004–05	Swindon T	44	1	**204**	**7**
2005–06	Darlington	20	1	**20**	**1**

HUTCHINSON, Joey (D) **70 0**
H: 5 11 W: 11 11 b.Middlesbrough 2-4-82
Source: Scholar.

2000–01	Birmingham C	0	0		
2001–02	Birmingham C	3	0		
2002–03	Birmingham C	1	0	**4**	**0**
2003–04	Darlington	39	0		
2004–05	Darlington	8	0		
2005–06	Darlington	19	0	**66**	**0**

JAMESON, Nathan (M) **5 0**
H: 5 11 W: 12 03 b.Middlesbrough 20-3-85
Source: Scholar.

2004–05	Walsall	0	0		
2005–06	Walsall	0	0		
2005–06	Darlington	5	0	**5**	**0**

JANES, Alex (D) **0 0**
b.York
Source: Scholar.

2005–06	Darlington	0	0

JOHNSON, Simon (F) **96 15**
H: 5 9 W: 11 09 b.West Bromwich 9-3-83
Source: Scholar. *Honours:* England Youth, Under-20.

2000–01	Leeds U	0	0		
2001–02	Leeds U	0	0		
2002–03	Leeds U	4	0		
2002–03	*Hull C*	12	2	**12**	**2**
2003–04	Leeds U	5	0		
2003–04	*Blackpool*	4	1	**4**	**1**
2004–05	Leeds U	2	0	**11**	**0**
2004–05	*Sunderland*	5	0	**5**	**0**
2004–05	*Doncaster R*	11	3	**11**	**3**
2004–05	*Barnsley*	11	2	**11**	**2**
2005–06	Darlington	42	7	**42**	**7**

KELTIE, Clark (M) **107 4**
H: 5 11 W: 11 08 b.Newcastle 31-8-83
Source: Shildon.

2001–02	Darlington	1	0		
2002–03	Darlington	30	3		
2003–04	Darlington	31	1		
2004–05	Darlington	21	0		
2005–06	Darlington	24	0	**107**	**4**

KENDRICK, Joe (D) **52 1**
H: 5 11 W: 11 03 b.Dublin 26-6-83
Source: Scholar. *Honours:* Eire Youth, Under-21.

2000–01	Newcastle U	0	0		
2001–02	Newcastle U	0	0		
2002–03	Newcastle U	0	0		
2003–04	Munich 1860	0	0		
2004–05	Darlington	31	1		
2005–06	Darlington	21	0	**52**	**1**

LOGAN, Carlos (M) **42 5**
H: 5 10 W: 12 06 b.Wythenshawe 7-11-85
Source: Scholar.

2004–05	Manchester C	0	0		
2004–05	*Chesterfield*	9	1	**9**	**1**
2005–06	Darlington	33	4	**33**	**4**

LOGAN, Richard (M) **1 0**
H: 6 0 W: 11 12 b.Washington 18-2-88
Source: Scholar.

2004–05	Darlington	1	0		
2005–06	Darlington	0	0	**1**	**0**

MADDISON, Neil (M) **350 28**
H: 5 10 W: 12 00 b.Darlington 2-10-69
Source: Trainee.

1987–88	Southampton	0	0
1988–89	Southampton	5	2
1989–90	Southampton	2	0
1990–91	Southampton	4	0
1991–92	Southampton	6	0
1992–93	Southampton	37	4

1993–94 Southampton 41 7
1994–95 Southampton 35 3
1995–96 Southampton 15 1
1996–97 Southampton 18 1
1997–98 Southampton 6 1 **169 19**
1997–98 Middlesbrough 22 4
1998–99 Middlesbrough 21 0
1999–2000 Middlesbrough 13 0
2000–01 Middlesbrough 0 0 **56 4**
2000–01 *Barnsley* 3 0 **3 0**
2000–01 *Bristol C* 7 1 **7 1**
2001–02 Darlington 30 1
2002–03 Darlington 28 1
2003–04 Darlington 32 1
2004–05 Darlington 24 1
2005–06 Darlington 1 0 **115 4**

MARTIS, Shelton (D) 62 2
H: 6 0 W: 11 11 b.Willemstad 29-11-82
2002–03 Excelsior 12 0
2003–04 Excelsior 10 0 **22 0**
2005–06 Darlington 40 2 **40 2**

McGURK, David (D) 56 6
H: 5 9 W: 12 03 b.Middlesbrough 30-9-82
Source: Scholar.
2001–02 Darlington 12 0
2002–03 Darlington 4 0
2003–04 Darlington 27 4
2004–05 Darlington 10 2
2005–06 Darlington 3 0 **56 6**

McLEOD, Mark (M) 4 0
H: 6 0 W: 12 00 b.Sunderland 15-12-86
Source: Scholar.
2005–06 Darlington 4 0 **4 0**

NORTON, Jack (G) 0 0
H: 6 0 b. 27-3-87
Source: Scholar.
2005–06 Darlington 0 0

PARKIN, Gavin (F) 0 0
H: 6 0 W: 12 00 b.Stockton 19-11-86
Source: Scholar.
2005–06 Darlington 0 0

PEACOCK, Anthony (M) 27 0
H: 5 5 W: 11 11 b.Middlesbrough 6-9-85
Source: Trainee.
2003–04 Middlesbrough 0 0
2004–05 Middlesbrough 0 0
2005–06 Darlington 27 0 **27 0**

REAY, Sean (F) 0 0
Source: Scholar.
2005–06 Darlington 0 0

RUSSELL, Sam (G) 87 0
H: 6 0 W: 10 13 b.Middlesbrough 4-10-82
Source: Scholar.
2000–01 Middlesbrough 0 0
2001–02 Middlesbrough 0 0
2002–03 Middlesbrough 0 0
2002–03 *Darlington* 1 0
2003–04 Middlesbrough 0 0
2003–04 *Scunthorpe U* 10 0 **10 0**
2004–05 Darlington 46 0
2005–06 Darlington 30 0 **77 0**

SODJE, Akpo (F) 50 9
H: 6 2 W: 12 08 b.Greenwich 31-1-81
Source: QPR, Stevenage B, Margate, Gravesend & N, Erith & Belvedere.
2004–05 Huddersfield T 7 0 **7 0**
2004–05 *Darlington* 7 1
2005–06 Darlington 36 8 **43 9**

STAMP, Phil (M) 125 7
H: 5 11 W: 13 05 b.Middlesbrough 12-12-75
Source: Trainee. *Honours:* England Youth.
1992–93 Middlesbrough 0 0
1993–94 Middlesbrough 10 0
1994–95 Middlesbrough 3 0
1995–96 Middlesbrough 12 2
1996–97 Middlesbrough 24 1
1997–98 Middlesbrough 10 0
1998–99 Middlesbrough 16 2
1999–2000 Middlesbrough 16 0
2000–01 Middlesbrough 19 1
2001–02 Middlesbrough 6 0
2001–02 *Millwall* 1 0 **1 0**
2002–03 Middlesbrough 0 0
2003–04 Middlesbrough 0 0
2004–05 Middlesbrough 0 0 **116 6**
2005–06 Darlington 8 1 **8 1**

THOMAS, Steve (M) 133 7
H: 5 10 W: 11 12 b.Hartlepool 23-6-79
Source: Trainee. *Honours:* Wales Youth, Under-21.
1997–98 Wrexham 0 0
1998–99 Wrexham 4 0
1999–2000 Wrexham 2 0
2000–01 Wrexham 6 0
2001–02 Wrexham 38 3
2002–03 Wrexham 25 2
2003–04 Wrexham 40 2 **115 7**
2004–05 Darlington 12 0
2005–06 Darlington 6 0 **18 0**

VALENTINE, Ryan (D) 162 4
H: 5 10 W: 11 05 b.Wrexham 19-8-82
Source: Trainee. *Honours:* Wales Under-21.
1999–2000 Everton 0 0
2000–01 Everton 0 0
2001–02 Everton 0 0
2002–03 Darlington 43 1
2003–04 Darlington 40 2
2004–05 Darlington 36 1
2005–06 Darlington 43 0 **162 4**

WAINWRIGHT, Neil (M) 223 26
H: 6 0 W: 12 00 b.Warrington 4-11-77
Source: Trainee.
1996–97 Wrexham 0 0
1997–98 Wrexham 11 3 **11 3**
1998–99 Sunderland 2 0
1999–2000 Sunderland 0 0
1999–2000 *Darlington* 17 4
2000–01 Sunderland 0 0
2000–01 *Halifax T* 13 0 **13 0**
2001–02 Sunderland 0 0 **2 0**
2001–02 Darlington 35 4
2002–03 Darlington 33 1
2003–04 Darlington 35 7
2004–05 Darlington 38 4
2005–06 Darlington 39 3 **197 23**

WEBSTER, Adrian (M) 35 1
H: 5 8 W: 10 09 b.Hawkes Bay 11-10-80
Source: Charlton Ath. *Honours:* New Zealand 3 full caps.
1999–2000 Colchester U 0 0
2000–01 Colchester U 0 0
2001–02 Colchester U 0 0
From Mgate, Mstn
2004–05 Darlington 22 0
2005–06 Darlington 13 1 **35 1**

WRIGHT, Nathan (G) 0 0
b. 8-11-89
Source: Scholar.
2005–06 Darlington 0 0

DERBY CO (30)

ADDISON, Miles (D) 2 0
H: 6 2 W: 13 03 b.London 7-1-89
Source: Scholar.
2005–06 Derby Co 2 0 **2 0**

AINSWORTH, Lionel (F) 2 0
H: 5 9 W: 9 10 b.Nottingham 1-10-87
Source: Scholar. *Honours:* England Youth.
2005–06 Derby Co 2 0 **2 0**

BARNES, Giles (M) 19 1
H: 6 0 W: 12 10 b.Barking 5-8-88
Source: Scholar. *Honours:* England Youth.
2005–06 Derby Co 19 1 **19 1**

BISGAARD, Morten (M) 300 54
H: 6 1 W: 12 04 b.Randers 25-6-74
Honours: Denmark Youth, Under-21, 8 full caps, 1 goal.
1993–94 Odense 7 1
1994–95 Odense 27 4
1995–96 Odense 25 6
1996–97 Odense 33 16
1997–98 Odense 29 8 **121 35**
1998–99 Udinese 3 0
1999–2000 Udinese 20 1
2000–01 Udinese 13 0 **36 1**
2001–02 FC Copenhagen 27 6
2002–03 FC Copenhagen 27 1
2003–04 FC Copenhagen 20 3 **74 10**
2004–05 Derby Co 36 4
2005–06 Derby Co 33 4 **69 8**

BOERTIEN, Paul (D) 127 3
H: 5 10 W: 11 02 b.Haltwhistle 21-1-79
Source: Trainee.
1996–97 Carlisle U 0 0
1997–98 Carlisle U 9 0
1998–99 Carlisle U 8 1 **17 1**
1998–99 Derby Co 1 0
1999–2000 Derby Co 2 0
1999–2000 *Crewe Alex* 2 0 **2 0**
2000–01 Derby Co 8 1
2001–02 Derby Co 32 0
2002–03 Derby Co 42 1
2003–04 Derby Co 18 0
2003–04 *Notts Co* 5 0 **5 0**
2004–05 Derby Co 0 0
2005–06 Derby Co 0 0 **103 2**

BOLDER, Adam (M) 173 11
H: 5 9 W: 10 08 b.Hull 25-10-80
Source: Trainee.
1998–99 Hull C 1 0
1999–2000 Hull C 19 0 **20 0**
1999–2000 Derby Co 0 0
2000–01 Derby Co 2 0
2001–02 Derby Co 11 0
2002–03 Derby Co 45 6
2003–04 Derby Co 24 1
2004–05 Derby Co 36 2
2005–06 Derby Co 35 2 **153 11**

CAMP, Lee (G) 98 0
H: 5 11 W: 11 11 b.Derby 22-8-84
Source: Scholar. *Honours:* England Youth, Under-20, Under-21.
2002–03 Derby Co 1 0
2003–04 Derby Co 0 0
2003–04 *QPR* 12 0 **12 0**
2004–05 Derby Co 45 0
2005–06 Derby Co 40 0 **86 0**

DOYLE, Nathan (M) 21 0
H: 5 11 W: 12 06 b.Derby 12-1-87
Source: Scholar. *Honours:* England Youth, Under-20.
2003–04 Derby Co 2 0
2004–05 Derby Co 3 0
2005–06 Derby Co 4 0 **9 0**
2005–06 *Notts Co* 12 0 **12 0**

EDWORTHY, Marc (D) 394 2
H: 5 10 W: 11 11 b.Barnstaple 24-12-72
Source: Trainee.
1990–91 Plymouth Arg 0 0
1991–92 Plymouth Arg 15 0
1992–93 Plymouth Arg 15 0
1993–94 Plymouth Arg 12 0
1994–95 Plymouth Arg 27 1 **69 1**
1995–96 Crystal Palace 44 0
1996–97 Crystal Palace 45 0
1997–98 Crystal Palace 34 0
1998–99 Crystal Palace 3 0 **126 0**
1998–99 Coventry C 22 0
1999–2000 Coventry C 10 0
2000–01 Coventry C 24 1
2001–02 Coventry C 20 0 **76 1**
2002–03 Wolverhampton W 22 0 **22 0**
2003–04 Norwich C 43 0
2004–05 Norwich C 28 0 **71 0**
2005–06 Derby Co 30 0 **30 0**

GRANT, Lee (G) 84 0
H: 6 3 W: 13 01 b.Hemel Hempstead 27-1-83
Source: Scholar. *Honours:* England Youth, Under-21.
2000–01 Derby Co 0 0
2001–02 Derby Co 0 0
2002–03 Derby Co 29 0
2003–04 Derby Co 36 0
2004–05 Derby Co 2 0
2005–06 Derby Co 0 0 **67 0**
2005–06 *Burnley* 1 0 **1 0**
2005–06 *Oldham Ath* 16 0 **16 0**

HAJTO, Tomasz (D) **367 24**
H: 6 3 W: 14 05 b.Makow Podh 16-10-72
Honours: Poland 62 full caps, 6 goals.

1990–91	Hutnik	1	0		
1991–92	Hutnik	4	0		
1992–93	Hutnik	28	2	**33**	**2**
1993–94	Gornik Zabrze	21	2		
1994–95	Gornik Zabrze	30	1		
1995–96	Gornik Zabrze	25	1		
1996–97	Gornik Zabrze	29	4	**105**	**8**
1997–98	Duisburg	25	3		
1998–99	Duisburg	29	4		
1999–2000	Duisburg	26	1	**80**	**8**
2000–01	Schalke	32	0		
2001–02	Schalke	24	2		
2002–03	Schalke	32	3		
2003–04	Schalke	19	1	**107**	**6**
2004–05	Nuremberg	17	0	**17**	**0**
2005–06	Southampton	20	0	**20**	**0**
2005–06	Derby Co	5	0	**5**	**0**

HOLDSWORTH, Dean (F) **530 163**
H: 5 11 W: 11 13 b.Walthamstow 8-11-68
Source: Trainee.

1986–87	Watford	2	0		
1987–88	*Carlisle U*	4	1	**4**	**1**
1987–88	*Port Vale*	6	2	**6**	**2**
1988–89	Watford	10	2		
1988–89	*Swansea C*	5	1	**5**	**1**
1988–89	*Brentford*	7	1		
1989–90	Watford	4	1	**16**	**3**
1989–90	Brentford	39	24		
1990–91	Brentford	30	5		
1991–92	Brentford	41	24	**117**	**54**
1992–93	Wimbledon	36	19		
1993–94	Wimbledon	42	17		
1994–95	Wimbledon	28	7		
1995–96	Wimbledon	33	10		
1996–97	Wimbledon	25	5		
1997–98	Wimbledon	5	0		
1997–98	Bolton W	20	3		
1998–99	Bolton W	32	12		
1999–2000	Bolton W	35	11		
2000–01	Bolton W	31	11		
2001–02	Bolton W	31	2		
2002–03	Bolton W	9	0	**158**	**39**
2002–03	Coventry C	17	0	**17**	**0**
2002–03	Rushden & D	7	2	**7**	**2**
2003–04	Wimbledon	28	3	**197**	**61**
2004–05	Milton Keynes D	0	0		
From Havant & W.					
2005–06	Derby Co	3	0	**3**	**0**

HOLMES, Lee (M) **61 3**
H: 5 8 W: 10 06 b.Mansfield 2-4-87
Source: Scholar. *Honours:* FA Schools, England Youth.

2002–03	Derby Co	2	0		
2003–04	Derby Co	23	2		
2004–05	Derby Co	3	0		
2004–05	*Swindon T*	15	1	**15**	**1**
2005–06	Derby Co	18	0	**46**	**2**

IDIAKEZ, Inigo (M) **402 75**
H: 6 0 W: 12 02 b.San Sebastian 8-11-73

1992–93	Real Sociedad	1	0		
1993–94	Real Sociedad B	25	13		
1993–94	Real Sociedad	2	0		
1994–95	Real Sociedad	26	4		
1995–96	Real Sociedad	33	4		
1996–97	Real Sociedad	31	4		
1997–98	Real Sociedad	16	1		
1998–99	Real Sociedad	29	7		
1999–2000	Real Sociedad	27	4		
2000–01	Real Sociedad	33	7		
2001–02	Real Sociedad	34	2	**232**	**33**
2002–03	Oviedo	33	4	**33**	**4**
2003–04	Rayo Vallecano	29	5	**29**	**5**
2004–05	Derby Co	41	9		
2005–06	Derby Co	42	11	**83**	**20**

JACKSON, Richard (D) **135 0**
H: 5 8 W: 12 10 b.Whitby 18-4-80
Source: Trainee.

1997–98	Scarborough	2	0		
1998–99	Scarborough	20	0	**22**	**0**
1998–99	Derby Co	0	0		
1999–2000	Derby Co	2	0		
2000–01	Derby Co	2	0		
2001–02	Derby Co	7	0		
2002–03	Derby Co	21	0		
2003–04	Derby Co	36	0		
2004–05	Derby Co	19	0		
2005–06	Derby Co	26	0	**113**	**0**

JOHNSON, Michael (D) **475 16**
H: 5 11 W: 11 12 b.Nottingham 4-7-73
Source: Trainee. *Honours:* Jamaica 14 full caps.

1991–92	Notts Co	5	0		
1992–93	Notts Co	37	0		
1993–94	Notts Co	34	0		
1994–95	Notts Co	31	0		
1995–96	Notts Co	0	0	**107**	**0**
1995–96	Birmingham C	33	0		
1996–97	Birmingham C	35	0		
1997–98	Birmingham C	38	3		
1998–99	Birmingham C	45	5		
1999–2000	Birmingham C	34	2		
2000–01	Birmingham C	39	2		
2001–02	Birmingham C	32	1		
2002–03	Birmingham C	6	0		
2003–04	Birmingham C	0	0	**262**	**13**
2003–04	Derby Co	39	1		
2004–05	Derby Co	36	1		
2005–06	Derby Co	31	1	**106**	**3**

JOHNSON, Seth (M) **250 15**
H: 5 10 W: 12 13 b.Birmingham 12-3-79
Source: Trainee. *Honours:* England, Youth, Under-21, 1 full cap.

1996–97	Crewe Alex	11	1		
1997–98	Crewe Alex	40	1		
1998–99	Crewe Alex	42	4	**93**	**6**
1999–2000	Derby Co	36	1		
2000–01	Derby Co	30	1		
2001–02	Derby Co	7	0		
2001–02	Leeds U	14	0		
2002–03	Leeds U	9	1		
2003–04	Leeds U	25	2		
2004–05	Leeds U	6	1	**54**	**4**
2005–06	Derby Co	30	3	**103**	**5**

KENNA, Jeff (D) **426 9**
H: 5 11 W: 12 12 b.Dublin 27-8-70
Source: Trainee. *Honours:* Eire Youth, Under-21, B, 27 full caps.

1988–89	Southampton	0	0		
1989–90	Southampton	0	0		
1990–91	Southampton	2	0		
1991–92	Southampton	14	0		
1992–93	Southampton	29	2		
1993–94	Southampton	41	2		
1994–95	Southampton	28	0	**114**	**4**
1994–95	Blackburn R	9	1		
1995–96	Blackburn R	32	0		
1996–97	Blackburn R	37	0		
1997–98	Blackburn R	37	0		
1998–99	Blackburn R	23	0		
1999–2000	Blackburn R	11	0		
2000–01	Blackburn R	6	0		
2000–01	*Tranmere R*	11	0	**11**	**0**
2001–02	Blackburn R	0	0	**155**	**1**
2001–02	*Wigan Ath*	6	1	**6**	**1**
2001–02	Birmingham C	21	0		
2002–03	Birmingham C	37	1		
2003–04	Birmingham C	17	2	**75**	**3**
2003–04	Derby Co	9	0		
2004–05	Derby Co	40	0		
2005–06	Derby Co	16	0	**65**	**0**

KONJIC, Muhamed (D) **316 16**
H: 6 3 W: 13 00 b.Doboj 14-5-70
Honours: Bosnia 38 full caps, 3 goals.

1990–91	Tuzla	3	0		
1991–92	Tuzla	5	0	**8**	**0**
1992–93	Belisce	18	0	**18**	**0**
1993–94	Zagreb	29	3		
1994–95	Zagreb	19	1		
1995–96	Zagreb	15	1	**63**	**5**
1996–97	Zurich	29	2		
1997–98	Zurich	7	3	**36**	**5**
1997–98	Monaco	19	0		
1998–99	Monaco	18	2	**37**	**2**
1998–99	Coventry C	4	0		
1999–2000	Coventry C	4	0		
2000–01	Coventry C	8	0		
2001–02	Coventry C	38	2		
2002–03	Coventry C	42	0		
2003–04	Coventry C	42	2	**138**	**4**
2003–04	Derby Co	0	0		
2004–05	Derby Co	16	0		
2005–06	Derby Co	0	0	**16**	**0**

MILLS, Pablo (D) **88 1**
H: 5 9 W: 11 04 b.Birmingham 27-5-84
Source: Trainee. *Honours:* England Youth.

2002–03	Derby Co	16	0		
2003–04	Derby Co	19	0		
2004–05	Derby Co	22	0		
2005–06	Derby Co	1	0	**58**	**0**
2005–06	*Milton Keynes D*	16	1	**16**	**1**
2005–06	*Walsall*	14	0	**14**	**0**

MOORE, Darren (D) **418 27**
H: 6 2 W: 15 07 b.Birmingham 22-4-74
Source: Trainee. *Honours:* Jamaica 3 full caps.

1991–92	Torquay U	5	1		
1992–93	Torquay U	31	2		
1993–94	Torquay U	37	2		
1994–95	Torquay U	30	3	**103**	**8**
1995–96	Doncaster R	35	2		
1996–97	Doncaster R	41	5	**76**	**7**
1997–98	Bradford C	18	0		
1998–99	Bradford C	44	3		
1999–2000	Bradford C	0	0	**62**	**3**
1999–2000	Portsmouth	25	1		
2000–01	Portsmouth	32	1		
2001–02	Portsmouth	2	0	**59**	**2**
2001–02	WBA	32	2		
2002–03	WBA	29	2		
2003–04	WBA	22	2		
2004–05	WBA	16	0		
2005–06	WBA	5	0	**104**	**6**
2005–06	Derby Co	14	1	**14**	**1**

NYATANGA, Lewin (D) **24 1**
H: 6 2 W: 12 08 b.Burton 18-8-88
Source: Scholar. *Honours:* Wales Under-21, 2 full caps.

2005–06	Derby Co	24	1	**24**	**1**

PESCHISOLIDO, Paul (F) **429 115**
H: 5 7 W: 10 12 b.Scarborough, Can 25-5-71
Source: Toronto Blizzard. *Honours:* Canada Youth, Under-21, 53 full caps, 10 goals.

1992–93	Birmingham C	19	7		
1993–94	Birmingham C	24	9		
1994–95	Stoke C	40	13		
1995–96	Stoke C	26	6	**66**	**19**
1995–96	Birmingham C	9	1	**52**	**17**
1996–97	WBA	37	15		
1997–98	WBA	8	3	**45**	**18**
1997–98	Fulham	32	13		
1998–99	Fulham	33	7		
1999–2000	Fulham	30	4		
2000–01	Fulham	0	0	**95**	**24**
2000–01	*QPR*	5	1	**5**	**1**
2000–01	*Sheffield U*	5	2		
2000–01	*Norwich C*	5	0	**5**	**0**
2001–02	Sheffield U	29	6		
2002–03	Sheffield U	23	3		
2003–04	Sheffield U	27	8	**84**	**19**
2003–04	Derby Co	11	4		
2004–05	Derby Co	32	8		
2005–06	Derby Co	34	5	**77**	**17**

POOLE, Kevin (G) **307 0**
H: 5 10 W: 12 11 b.Bromsgrove 21-7-63
Source: Apprentice.

1981–82	Aston Villa	0	0		
1982–83	Aston Villa	0	0		
1983–84	Aston Villa	0	0		
1984–85	Aston Villa	7	0		
1984–85	*Northampton T*	3	0	**3**	**0**
1985–86	Aston Villa	11	0		
1986–87	Aston Villa	10	0	**28**	**0**
1987–88	Middlesbrough	1	0		
1988–89	Middlesbrough	12	0		
1989–90	Middlesbrough	21	0		
1990–91	Middlesbrough	0	0	**34**	**0**
1990–91	*Hartlepool U*	12	0	**12**	**0**
1991–92	Leicester C	42	0		
1992–93	Leicester C	19	0		
1993–94	Leicester C	14	0		
1994–95	Leicester C	36	0		
1995–96	Leicester C	45	0		
1996–97	Leicester C	7	0	**163**	**0**

1997–98 Birmingham C 1 0
1998–99 Birmingham C 36 0
1999–2000 Birmingham C 18 0
2000–01 Birmingham C 1 0
2001–02 Birmingham C 0 0 **56 0**
2001–02 Bolton W 3 0
2002–03 Bolton W 0 0
2003–04 Bolton W 0 0
2004–05 Bolton W 2 0 **5 0**
2005–06 Derby Co 6 0 **6 0**

SMITH, Tommy (F) 269 56
H: 5 8 W: 11 04 b.Hemel Hempstead 22-5-80
Source: Trainee. *Honours:* England Youth, Under-21.
1997–98 Watford 1 0
1998–99 Watford 8 2
1999–2000 Watford 22 2
2000–01 Watford 43 11
2001–02 Watford 40 11
2002–03 Watford 35 7
2003–04 Watford 0 0 **149 33**
2003–04 Sunderland 35 4 **35 4**
2004–05 Derby Co 42 11
2005–06 Derby Co 43 8 **85 19**

THIRLWELL, Paul (M) 140 1
H: 5 11 W: 12 08 b.Springwell 13-2-79
Source: Trainee. *Honours:* England Under-21.
1996–97 Sunderland 0 0
1997–98 Sunderland 0 0
1998–99 Sunderland 2 0
1999–2000 Sunderland 8 0
1999–2000 *Swindon T* 12 0 **12 0**
2000–01 Sunderland 5 0
2001–02 Sunderland 14 0
2002–03 Sunderland 19 0
2003–04 Sunderland 29 0 **77 0**
2004–05 Sheffield U 30 1 **30 1**
2005–06 Derby Co 21 0 **21 0**

TURNER, Chris (D) 0 0
H: 5 9 W: 11 09 b.Ballymoney 3-1-87
Source: Scholar.
2004–05 Derby Co 0 0
2005–06 Derby Co 0 0

DONCASTER R (31)

ALBRIGHTON, Mark (D) 70 4
H: 6 1 W: 12 07 b.Nuneaton 6-3-76
Source: Atherstone U, Nuneaton B, Telford U.
2003–04 Doncaster R 28 3
2004–05 Doncaster R 17 1
2005–06 Doncaster R 16 0 **61 4**
2005–06 *Chester C* 9 0 **9 0**

ARMSTRONG, Alun (F) 326 81
H: 6 0 W: 12 00 b.Gateshead 22-2-75
Source: School.
1993–94 Newcastle U 0 0
1994–95 Stockport Co 45 14
1995–96 Stockport Co 46 13
1996–97 Stockport Co 39 9
1997–98 Stockport Co 29 12 **159 48**
1997–98 Middlesbrough 11 7
1998–99 Middlesbrough 6 1
1999–2000 Middlesbrough 12 1
1999–2000 *Huddersfield T* 6 0 **6 0**
2000–01 Middlesbrough 0 0 **29 9**
2000–01 Ipswich T 21 7
2001–02 Ipswich T 32 4
2002–03 Ipswich T 19 1
2003–04 Ipswich T 7 2
2003–04 *Bradford C* 6 1 **6 1**
2004–05 Ipswich T 0 0 **79 14**
2004–05 Darlington 32 9
2005–06 Darlington 0 0 **32 9**
2005–06 Rushden & D 9 0 **9 0**
2005–06 Doncaster R 6 0 **6 0**

BLAYNEY, Alan (G) 42 0
H: 6 2 W: 13 12 b.Belfast 9-10-81
Source: Scholar. *Honours:* Northern Ireland Under-21, Under-23, 1 full cap.
2001–02 Southampton 0 0
2002–03 Southampton 0 0
2002–03 *Stockport Co* 2 0 **2 0**
2002–03 *Bournemouth* 2 0 **2 0**
2003–04 Southampton 2 0
2004–05 Southampton 1 0
2004–05 *Rushden & D* 4 0 **4 0**
2004–05 *Brighton & HA* 7 0
2005–06 Southampton 0 0 **3 0**
2005–06 *Brighton & HA* 8 0 **15 0**
2005–06 Doncaster R 16 0 **16 0**

BROWN, Adam (M) 3 1
H: 5 10 W: 10 07 b.Sunderland 17-12-87
Source: Scholar.
2004–05 Doncaster R 3 1
2005–06 Doncaster R 0 0 **3 1**

BUDTZ, Jan (G) 20 0
H: 6 0 W: 13 05 b.Denmark 20-4-79
Source: B1909 Odense.
2004–05 Nordsjaelland 0 0
2005–06 Doncaster R 20 0 **20 0**

COCKERHAM, Lee (G) 0 0
H: 6 3 W: 13 00 b.Pontefract 12-8-87
Source: Scholar.
2005–06 Doncaster R 0 0

COPPINGER, James (F) 135 15
H: 5 7 W: 10 03 b.Middlesbrough 10-1-81
Source: Darlington Trainee. *Honours:* England Youth.
1997–98 Newcastle U 0 0
1998–99 Newcastle U 0 0
1999–2000 Newcastle U 0 0
1999–2000 *Hartlepool U* 10 3
2000–01 Newcastle U 1 0
2001–02 Newcastle U 0 0 **1 0**
2001–02 *Hartlepool U* 14 2 **24 5**
2002–03 Exeter C 43 5
2003–04 Exeter C 0 0 **43 5**
2004–05 Doncaster R 31 0
2005–06 Doncaster R 36 5 **67 5**

FENTON, Nick (D) 259 13
H: 6 0 W: 10 02 b.Preston 23-11-79
Source: Trainee. *Honours:* England Youth.
1996–97 Manchester C 0 0
1997–98 Manchester C 0 0
1998–99 Manchester C 15 0
1999–2000 Manchester C 0 0
1999–2000 *Notts Co* 13 1
1999–2000 *Bournemouth* 8 0
2000–01 Manchester C 0 0 **15 0**
2000–01 *Bournemouth* 5 0 **13 0**
2000–01 Notts Co 30 2
2001–02 Notts Co 42 3
2002–03 Notts Co 40 3
2003–04 Notts Co 43 1 **168 10**
2004–05 Doncaster R 38 1
2005–06 Doncaster R 25 2 **63 3**

FORTUNE-WEST, Leo (F) 338 91
H: 6 4 W: 13 10 b.Stratford 9-4-71
Source: Tiptree, Dagenham, Dartford, Bishops Stortford, Stevenage Bor.
1995–96 Gillingham 40 12
1996–97 Gillingham 7 2
1996–97 *Leyton Orient* 5 0 **5 0**
1997–98 Gillingham 20 4 **67 18**
1998–99 Lincoln C 9 1 **9 1**
1998–99 Brentford 11 0 **11 0**
1998–99 Rotherham U 20 12
1999–2000 Rotherham U 39 17
2000–01 Rotherham U 5 1 **64 30**
2000–01 Cardiff C 37 12
2001–02 Cardiff C 36 9
2002–03 Cardiff C 19 2 **92 23**
2003–04 Doncaster R 39 11
2004–05 Doncaster R 24 6
2005–06 Doncaster R 27 2 **90 19**

GREEN, Paul (M) 119 18
H: 5 9 W: 12 02 b.Pontefract 10-4-83
Source: Trainee.
2003–04 Doncaster R 43 8
2004–05 Doncaster R 42 7
2005–06 Doncaster R 34 3 **119 18**

GRIFFITH, Anthony (M) 4 0
b.Huddersfield 28-10-86
2005–06 Doncaster R 4 0 **4 0**
2005–06 *Oxford U* 0 0

GUY, Lewis (F) 40 6
H: 5 10 W: 10 07 b.Penrith 27-8-85
Source: Trainee. *Honours:* England Youth, Under-20.
2002–03 Newcastle U 0 0
2003–04 Newcastle U 0 0
2004–05 Newcastle U 0 0
2004–05 Doncaster R 9 3
2005–06 Doncaster R 31 3 **40 6**

HEFFERNAN, Paul (F) 153 49
H: 5 10 W: 11 00 b.Dublin 29-12-81
Source: Newton.
1999–2000 Notts Co 2 0
2000–01 Notts Co 1 0
2001–02 Notts Co 23 6
2002–03 Notts Co 36 10
2003–04 Notts Co 38 20 **100 36**
2004–05 Bristol C 27 5 **27 5**
2005–06 Doncaster R 26 8 **26 8**

HUGHES, Adam (M) 6 0
b.Australia 14-7-82
2005–06 Doncaster R 6 0 **6 0**

LEE, Graeme (D) 306 25
H: 6 2 W: 13 07 b.Middlesbrough 31-5-78
Source: Trainee.
1995–96 Hartlepool U 6 0
1996–97 Hartlepool U 24 0
1997–98 Hartlepool U 37 3
1998–99 Hartlepool U 24 3
1999–2000 Hartlepool U 38 7
2000–01 Hartlepool U 6 0
2001–02 Hartlepool U 39 4
2002–03 Hartlepool U 45 2 **219 19**
2003–04 Sheffield W 30 3
2004–05 Sheffield W 22 1
2005–06 Sheffield W 15 1 **67 5**
2005–06 Doncaster R 20 1 **20 1**

MARPLES, Simon (D) 43 0
H: 5 10 W: 11 00 b.Sheffield 30-7-75
Source: Stocksbridge Park Steels.
2003–04 Doncaster R 16 0
2004–05 Doncaster R 12 0
2005–06 Doncaster R 15 0 **43 0**

McCORMACK, Ross (F) 30 6
H: 5 9 W: 11 00 b.Glasgow 18-8-86
Honours: Scotland Youth, Under-21.
2003–04 Rangers 2 1
2004–05 Rangers 1 0
2005–06 Rangers 8 1 **11 2**
2005–06 Doncaster R 19 4 **19 4**

McDAID, Sean (D) 35 0
H: 5 6 W: 9 08 b.Harrogate 6-3-86
Source: Trainee.
2002–03 Leeds U 0 0
2003–04 Leeds U 0 0
2004–05 Leeds U 0 0
2005–06 Doncaster R 35 0 **35 0**

McGUIRE, Phil (D) 164 10
H: 5 11 W: 10 06 b.Glasgow 4-3-80
Source: Dyce J.
1999–2000 Aberdeen 3 0
2000–01 Aberdeen 29 0
2001–02 Aberdeen 38 3
2002–03 Aberdeen 36 5
2003–04 Aberdeen 17 2
2004–05 Aberdeen 30 0 **153 10**
2005–06 Doncaster R 11 0 **11 0**

McINDOE, Michael (M) 169 28
H: 5 8 W: 11 00 b.Edinburgh 2-12-79
Source: Trainee. *Honours:* Scotland B.
1997–98 Luton T 0 0
1998–99 Luton T 22 0
1999–2000 Luton T 17 0 **39 0**
Fr Hereford, Yeovil
2003–04 Doncaster R 45 10
2004–05 Doncaster R 44 10
2005–06 Doncaster R 33 8 **122 28**
2005–06 *Derby Co* 8 0 **8 0**

McSPORRAN, Jermaine (M) 194 31
H: 5 10 W: 10 12 b.Manchester 1-1-77
Source: Oxford C.
1998–99 Wycombe W 26 4
1999–2000 Wycombe W 38 9
2000–01 Wycombe W 20 2

2001–02 Wycombe W 32 7
2002–03 Wycombe W 9 1
2003–04 Wycombe W 33 7 **158 30**
2003–04 Walsall 6 0 **6 0**
2004–05 Doncaster R 26 1
2005–06 Doncaster R 2 0 **28 1**
2005–06 *Boston U* 2 0 **2 0**

MULLIGAN, Dave (D) 142 5
H: 5 8 W: 9 13 b.Bootle 24-3-82
Source: Scholar. *Honours:* New Zealand Youth, Under-23, 6 full caps.
2000–01 Barnsley 0 0
2001–02 Barnsley 28 0
2002–03 Barnsley 33 1
2003–04 Barnsley 4 0 **65 1**
2003–04 Doncaster R 14 1
2004–05 Doncaster R 31 1
2005–06 Doncaster R 32 2 **77 4**

NELTHORPE, Craig (M) 2 0
H: 5 10 W: 11 00 b.Doncaster 10-6-87
Source: Scholar.
2004–05 Doncaster R 1 0
2005–06 Doncaster R 1 0 **2 0**

NIELSEN, Tonny (M) 0 0
H: 6 9 W: 13 08 b.Denmark 10-2-84
Source: Fremad.
2005–06 Doncaster R 0 0

OFFIONG, Richard (F) 25 2
H: 5 11 W: 12 02 b.South Shields 17-12-83
Source: Scholar. *Honours:* England Youth, Under-20.
2001–02 Newcastle U 0 0
2002–03 Newcastle U 0 0
2002–03 *Darlington* 7 2 **7 2**
2002–03 *Motherwell* 9 0 **9 0**
2003–04 Newcastle U 0 0
2003–04 *York C* 4 0 **4 0**
2004–05 Newcastle U 0 0
2005–06 Doncaster R 5 0 **5 0**

PACEY, Rob (D) 0 0
H: 6 4 W: 12 07 b.Leeds 18-6-87
Source: Scholar.
2005–06 Doncaster R 0 0

PREDIC, Uros (M) 6 0
H: 5 10 W: 11 00 b.Novi Sad 11-8-73
Source: Hajduk Kula.
2005–06 Doncaster R 6 0 **6 0**

PRICE, Jason (M) 294 46
H: 6 2 W: 11 05 b.Pontypridd 12-4-77
Source: Aberaman Ath. *Honours:* Wales Under-21.
1995–96 Swansea C 0 0
1996–97 Swansea C 2 0
1997–98 Swansea C 34 3
1998–99 Swansea C 28 4
1999–2000 Swansea C 39 6
2000–01 Swansea C 41 4 **144 17**
2001–02 Brentford 15 1 **15 1**
2001–02 Tranmere R 24 7
2002–03 Tranmere R 25 4 **49 11**
2003–04 Hull C 33 9
2004–05 Hull C 27 2
2005–06 Hull C 15 2 **75 13**
2005–06 Doncaster R 11 4 **11 4**

RAVENHILL, Ricky (M) 98 9
H: 5 10 W: 11 02 b.Doncaster 16-1-81
Source: Barnsley Trainee.
2003–04 Doncaster R 36 3
2004–05 Doncaster R 35 3
2005–06 Doncaster R 27 3 **98 9**

RIGOGLIOSO, Adriano (M) 29 0
H: 6 1 W: 12 07 b.Liverpool 28-5-79
Source: Morecambe.
2003–04 Doncaster R 17 0
2004–05 Doncaster R 12 0
2005–06 Doncaster R 0 0 **29 0**

ROBERTS, Neil (F) 270 45
H: 5 10 W: 11 00 b.Wrexham 7-4-78
Source: Trainee. *Honours:* Wales Youth, Under-21, B, 3 full caps.
1996–97 Wrexham 0 0
1997–98 Wrexham 34 8
1998–99 Wrexham 22 3
1999–2000 Wrexham 19 6 **75 17**
1999–2000 Wigan Ath 9 1
2000–01 Wigan Ath 34 6
2001–02 *Hull C* 6 0 **6 0**
2001–02 Wigan Ath 17 4
2002–03 Wigan Ath 37 6
2003–04 Wigan Ath 28 2
2004–05 Wigan Ath 0 0 **125 19**
2004–05 *Bradford C* 3 1 **3 1**
2004–05 Doncaster R 31 6
2005–06 Doncaster R 30 2 **61 8**

ROBERTS, Steve (D) 177 7
H: 6 1 W: 11 02 b.Wrexham 24-2-80
Source: Trainee. *Honours:* Wales Youth, Under-21, 1 full cap.
1997–98 Wrexham 0 0
1998–99 Wrexham 0 0
1999–2000 Wrexham 19 0
2000–01 Wrexham 7 0
2001–02 Wrexham 24 1
2002–03 Wrexham 39 2
2003–04 Wrexham 27 0
2004–05 Wrexham 34 3 **150 6**
2005–06 Doncaster R 27 1 **27 1**

SAUNDERS, Ben (F) 1 0
H: 6 1 W: 13 07 b.Southwell 12-10-84
Source: Southwell C.
2005–06 Doncaster R 0 0
2005–06 *Bury* 1 0 **1 0**

THORNTON, Sean (M) 92 12
H: 5 10 W: 11 00 b.Drogheda 18-5-83
Source: Scholar. *Honours:* Eire Under-21.
2001–02 Tranmere R 11 1 **11 1**
2002–03 Sunderland 11 1
2002–03 *Blackpool* 3 0 **3 0**
2003–04 Sunderland 22 4
2004–05 Sunderland 16 4 **49 9**
2005–06 Doncaster R 29 2 **29 2**

WARRINGTON, Andy (G) 150 0
H: 6 3 W: 12 13 b.Sheffield 10-6-76
Source: Trainee.
1994–95 York C 0 0
1995–96 York C 6 0
1996–97 York C 27 0
1997–98 York C 17 0
1998–99 York C 11 0 **61 0**
2003–04 Doncaster R 46 0
2004–05 Doncaster R 34 0
2005–06 Doncaster R 9 0 **89 0**

EVERTON (32)

ANICHEBE, Victor (F) 2 1
H: 6 1 W: 13 00 b.Nigeria 23-4-88
Source: Scholar.
2005–06 Everton 2 1 **2 1**

ARTETA, Mikel (M) 136 17
H: 5 9 W: 10 08 b.San Sebastian 26-3-82
2000–01 Barcelona B 0 0
2000–01 Paris St Germain 6 1
2001–02 Paris St Germain 25 1 **31 2**
2002–03 Rangers 27 4
2003–04 Rangers 23 8 **50 12**
2004–05 Real Sociedad 14 1 **14 1**
2004–05 Everton 12 1
2005–06 Everton 29 1 **41 2**

BEATTIE, James (F) 251 79
H: 6 1 W: 13 06 b.Lancaster 27-2-78
Source: Trainee. *Honours:* England Under-21, 5 full caps.
1994–95 Blackburn R 0 0
1995–96 Blackburn R 0 0
1996–97 Blackburn R 1 0
1997–98 Blackburn R 3 0 **4 0**
1998–99 Southampton 35 5
1999–2000 Southampton 18 0
2000–01 Southampton 37 11
2001–02 Southampton 28 12
2002–03 Southampton 38 23
2003–04 Southampton 37 14
2004–05 Southampton 11 3 **204 68**
2004–05 Everton 11 1
2005–06 Everton 32 10 **43 11**

BOYLE, Patrick (D) 0 0
H: 6 0 W: 12 09 b.Glasgow 20-3-87
Source: Scholar.
2005–06 Everton 0 0

CAHILL, Tim (M) 282 69
H: 5 10 W: 10 12 b.Sydney 6-12-79
Source: Sydney U. *Honours:* Western Samoa Youth, Australia Under-23, 20 full caps, 11 goals.
1997–98 Millwall 1 0
1998–99 Millwall 36 6
1999–2000 Millwall 45 12
2000–01 Millwall 41 9
2001–02 Millwall 43 13
2002–03 Millwall 11 3
2003–04 Millwall 40 9 **217 52**
2004–05 Everton 33 11
2005–06 Everton 32 6 **65 17**

CARSLEY, Lee (M) 325 29
H: 5 10 W: 12 04 b.Birmingham 28-2-74
Source: Trainee. *Honours:* Eire 29 full caps.
1992–93 Derby Co 0 0
1993–94 Derby Co 0 0
1994–95 Derby Co 23 2
1995–96 Derby Co 35 1
1996–97 Derby Co 24 0
1997–98 Derby Co 34 1
1998–99 Derby Co 22 1 **138 5**
1998–99 Blackburn R 8 0
1999–2000 Blackburn R 30 10
2000–01 Blackburn R 8 0 **46 10**
2000–01 Coventry C 21 2
2001–02 Coventry C 26 2 **47 4**
2001–02 Everton 8 1
2002–03 Everton 24 3
2003–04 Everton 21 2
2004–05 Everton 36 4
2005–06 Everton 5 0 **94 10**

DAVIES, Simon (M) 216 20
H: 5 10 W: 11 07 b.Haverfordwest 23-10-79
Source: Trainee. *Honours:* Wales Youth, Under-21, B, 30 full caps, 5 goals.
1997–98 Peterborough U 6 0
1998–99 Peterborough U 43 4
1999–2000 Peterborough U 16 2 **65 6**
1999–2000 Tottenham H 3 0
2000–01 Tottenham H 13 2
2001–02 Tottenham H 31 4
2002–03 Tottenham H 36 5
2003–04 Tottenham H 17 2
2004–05 Tottenham H 21 0 **121 13**
2005–06 Everton 30 1 **30 1**

DENNEHY, Darren (D) 0 0
H: 6 3 W: 11 11 b.Republic of Ireland 21-9-88
Source: Scholar.
2005–06 Everton 0 0

DOWNES, Aiden (F) 0 0
H: 5 8 W: 11 07 b.Republic of Ireland 24-7-88
Source: Scholar.
2005–06 Everton 0 0

FERGUSON, Duncan (F) 360 98
H: 6 4 W: 13 07 b.Stirling 27-12-71
Source: Carse T. *Honours:* Scotland Schools, Youth, Under-21, B, 7 full caps.
1990–91 Dundee U 9 1
1991–92 Dundee U 38 15
1992–93 Dundee U 30 12 **77 28**
1993–94 Rangers 10 1
1994–95 Rangers 4 1 **14 2**
1994–95 Everton 23 7
1995–96 Everton 18 5
1996–97 Everton 33 10
1997–98 Everton 29 11
1998–99 Everton 13 4
1998–99 Newcastle U 7 2
1999–2000 Newcastle U 23 6 **30 8**
2000–01 Everton 12 6
2001–02 Everton 22 6
2002–03 Everton 7 0
2003–04 Everton 20 5
2004–05 Everton 35 5
2005–06 Everton 27 1 **239 60**

FERRARI, Matteo (D) 185 3
H: 6 0 W: 12 06 b.Aflou 5-12-79
Honours: Italy Youth, Under-21, 11 full caps.

1995–96	Spal	0	0		
1996–97	Internazionale	0	0		
1997–98	Genoa	3	0	**3**	**0**
1998–99	Lecce	13	0	**13**	**0**
1999–2000	Bari	26	0	**26**	**0**
2000–01	Internazionale	19	0	**19**	**0**
2001–02	Parma	16	0		
2002–03	Parma	32	2		
2003–04	Parma	33	1	**81**	**3**
2004–05	Roma	35	0	**35**	**0**
2005–06	Everton	8	0	**8**	**0**

HARPUR, Ryan (M) 0 0
H: 5 9 W: 11 11 b.Craigavon 1-12-88
Source: Scholar.

2005–06	Everton	0	0		

HARRIS, James (M) 0 0
H: 5 7 W: 11 06 b.Liverpool 15-4-87
Source: Scholar.

2005–06	Everton	0	0		

HIBBERT, Tony (D) 127 0
H: 5 9 W: 11 05 b.Liverpool 20-2-81
Source: Trainee.

1998–99	Everton	0	0		
1999–2000	Everton	0	0		
2000–01	Everton	3	0		
2001–02	Everton	10	0		
2002–03	Everton	24	0		
2003–04	Everton	25	0		
2004–05	Everton	36	0		
2005–06	Everton	29	0	**127**	**0**

HOPKINS, Paul (F) 5 1
H: 5 8 W: 11 13 b.Liverpool 29-11-86
Source: Scholar. *Honours:* England Under-20.

2004–05	Everton	0	0		
2005–06	Everton	0	0		
2005–06	*Darlington*	5	1	**5**	**1**

HUGHES, Mark (D) 3 1
H: 6 1 W: 13 03 b.Liverpool 9-12-86
Source: Scholar.

2004–05	Everton	0	0		
2005–06	Everton	0	0		
2005–06	*Stockport Co*	3	1	**3**	**1**

INGASON, Thordur (M) 0 0
b.Iceland

2005–06	Everton	0	0		

IRVING, John (M) 0 0
H: 5 10 W: 11 00 b.Liverpool 17-9-88
Source: Scholar.

2005–06	Everton	0	0		

KEARNEY, Alan (M) 0 0
H: 6 1 W: 12 06 b.Cork 22-9-87
Source: Scholar.

2005–06	Everton	0	0		

KILBANE, Kevin (M) 368 30
H: 6 1 W: 13 05 b.Preston 1-2-77
Source: Trainee. *Honours:* Eire Under-21, 70 full caps, 5 goals.

1993–94	Preston NE	0	0		
1994–95	Preston NE	0	0		
1995–96	Preston NE	11	1		
1996–97	Preston NE	36	2	**47**	**3**
1997–98	WBA	43	4		
1998–99	WBA	44	6		
1999–2000	WBA	19	5	**106**	**15**
1999–2000	Sunderland	20	1		
2000–01	Sunderland	30	4		
2001–02	Sunderland	28	2		
2002–03	Sunderland	30	1		
2003–04	Sunderland	5	0	**113**	**8**
2003–04	Everton	30	3		
2004–05	Everton	38	1		
2005–06	Everton	34	0	**102**	**4**

KROLDRUP, Per (D) 92 3
H: 6 3 W: 13 09 b.Viborg 31-7-79
Source: B93 Copenhagen. *Honours:* Denmark 15 full caps.

2001–02	Udinese	10	1		
2002–03	Udinese	26	0		
2003–04	Udinese	30	2		
2004–05	Udinese	25	0	**91**	**3**
2005–06	Everton	1	0	**1**	**0**

To Fiorentina January 2006

LI TIE (M) 34 0
H: 6 0 W: 11 10 b.Liaoning 18-9-77
Source: Liaoning Bodao. *Honours:* China 79 full caps, 5 goals.

2002–03	Everton	29	0		
2003–04	Everton	5	0		
2004–05	Everton	0	0		
2005–06	Everton	0	0	**34**	**0**

MARTYN, Nigel (G) 666 0
H: 6 1 W: 15 11 b.St Austell 11-8-66
Source: St Blazey. *Honours:* England Under-21, B, 23 full caps.

1987–88	Bristol R	39	0		
1988–89	Bristol R	46	0		
1989–90	Bristol R	16	0	**101**	**0**
1989–90	Crystal Palace	25	0		
1990–91	Crystal Palace	38	0		
1991–92	Crystal Palace	38	0		
1992–93	Crystal Palace	42	0		
1993–94	Crystal Palace	46	0		
1994–95	Crystal Palace	37	0		
1995–96	Crystal Palace	46	0	**272**	**0**
1996–97	Leeds U	37	0		
1997–98	Leeds U	37	0		
1998–99	Leeds U	34	0		
1999–2000	Leeds U	38	0		
2000–01	Leeds U	23	0		
2001–02	Leeds U	38	0		
2002–03	Leeds U	0	0		
2003–04	Leeds U	0	0	**207**	**0**
2003–04	Everton	34	0		
2004–05	Everton	32	0		
2005–06	Everton	20	0	**86**	**0**

McFADDEN, James (M) 141 33
H: 6 0 W: 12 11 b.Glasgow 14-4-83
Honours: Scotland Under-21, B, 27 full caps, 4 goals.

2000–01	Motherwell	6	0		
2001–02	Motherwell	24	10		
2002–03	Motherwell	30	13		
2003–04	Motherwell	3	3	**63**	**26**
2003–04	Everton	23	0		
2004–05	Everton	23	1		
2005–06	Everton	32	6	**78**	**7**

MOLYNEUX, Lee (D) 0 0
H: 5 10 W: 11 07 b.Liverpool 24-2-89
Source: Scholar. *Honours:* England Schools, Youth.

2005–06	Everton	0	0		

MORRISON, Steven (M) 0 0
H: 6 0 W: 10 13 b.Southport 10-9-88
Source: Scholar.

2005–06	Everton	0	0		

NAYSMITH, Gary (D) 216 8
H: 5 9 W: 12 01 b.Edinburgh 16-11-78
Source: Whitehill Welfare Colts. *Honours:* Scotland Schools, Under-21, B, 30 full caps, 1 goal.

1995–96	Hearts	1	0		
1996–97	Hearts	10	0		
1997–98	Hearts	16	2		
1998–99	Hearts	26	0		
1999–2000	Hearts	35	1		
2000–01	Hearts	9	0	**97**	**3**
2000–01	Everton	20	2		
2001–02	Everton	24	0		
2002–03	Everton	28	1		
2003–04	Everton	29	2		
2004–05	Everton	11	0		
2005–06	Everton	7	0	**119**	**5**

NEVILLE, Phil (M) 297 5
H: 5 11 W: 12 00 b.Bury 21-1-77
Source: Trainee. *Honours:* England Schools, Youth, Under-21, 52 full caps.

1994–95	Manchester U	2	0		
1995–96	Manchester U	24	0		
1996–97	Manchester U	18	0		
1997–98	Manchester U	30	1		
1998–99	Manchester U	28	0		
1999–2000	Manchester U	29	0		
2000–01	Manchester U	29	1		
2001–02	Manchester U	28	2		
2002–03	Manchester U	25	1		
2003–04	Manchester U	31	0		
2004–05	Manchester U	19	0	**263**	**5**
2005–06	Everton	34	0	**34**	**0**

NUNO VALENTE (D) 255 4
H: 6 0 W: 12 03 b.Lisbon 12-9-74
Honours: Portugal 29 full caps, 1 goal.

1993–94	Portimonense	26	1	**26**	**1**
1994–95	Sporting Lisbon	9	0		
1995–96	Sporting Lisbon	9	0		
1996–97	Maritimo	30	0	**30**	**0**
1997–98	Sporting Lisbon	6	0		
1998–99	Sporting Lisbon	12	1	**36**	**1**
1999–2000	Uniao Leiria	28	0		
2000–01	Uniao Leiria	31	2		
2001–02	Uniao Leiria	28	0	**87**	**2**
2002–03	Porto	21	0		
2003–04	Porto	27	0		
2004–05	Porto	8	0	**56**	**0**
2005–06	Everton	20	0	**20**	**0**

OSMAN, Leon (F) 99 14
H: 5 8 W: 10 09 b.Billinge 17-5-81
Source: Trainee. *Honours:* England Schools, Youth.

1998–99	Everton	0	0		
1999–2000	Everton	0	0		
2000–01	Everton	0	0		
2001–02	Everton	0	0		
2002–03	Everton	2	0		
2002–03	*Carlisle U*	12	1	**12**	**1**
2003–04	Everton	4	1		
2003–04	*Derby Co*	17	3	**17**	**3**
2004–05	Everton	29	6		
2005–06	Everton	35	3	**70**	**10**

PHELAN, Scott (M) 0 0
H: 5 7 W: 10 07 b.Liverpool 13-3-88
Source: Scholar. *Honours:* England Youth.

2005–06	Everton	0	0		

PISTONE, Alessandro (D) 249 8
H: 5 11 W: 11 08 b.Milan 27-7-75

1992–93	Vicenza	0	0		
1993–94	Solbiatese	20	1	**20**	**1**
1994–95	Crevalcore	29	4	**29**	**4**
1995–96	Vicenza	6	0	**6**	**0**
1995–96	Internazionale	19	1		
1996–97	Internazionale	26	0	**45**	**1**
1997–98	Newcastle U	28	0		
1998–99	Newcastle U	3	0		
1999–2000	Newcastle U	15	1	**46**	**1**
2000–01	Everton	7	0		
2001–02	Everton	25	1		
2002–03	Everton	15	0		
2003–04	Everton	21	0		
2004–05	Everton	33	0		
2005–06	Everton	2	0	**103**	**1**

RUDDY, John (G) 52 0
H: 6 3 W: 12 07 b.St Ives 24-10-86
Source: Scholar. *Honours:* England Youth.

2003–04	Cambridge U	1	0		
2004–05	Cambridge U	38	0	**39**	**0**
2005–06	Everton	1	0	**1**	**0**
2005–06	*Walsall*	5	0	**5**	**0**
2005–06	*Rushden & D*	3	0	**3**	**0**
2005–06	*Chester C*	4	0	**4**	**0**

SEARGEANT, Christian (M) 0 0
H: 5 10 W: 11 07 b.Liverpool 13-9-86
Source: Scholar.

2005–06	Everton	0	0		

STUBBS, Alan (D) 456 16
H: 6 2 W: 14 02 b.Kirkby 6-10-71
Source: Trainee.

1990–91	Bolton W	23	0		
1991–92	Bolton W	32	1		
1992–93	Bolton W	42	2		
1993–94	Bolton W	41	1		
1994–95	Bolton W	39	1		
1995–96	Bolton W	25	4	**202**	**9**
1996–97	Celtic	20	0		
1997–98	Celtic	29	1		
1998–99	Celtic	23	1		
1999–2000	Celtic	23	0		
2000–01	Celtic	11	1	**106**	**3**
2001–02	Everton	31	2		
2002–03	Everton	35	0		
2003–04	Everton	27	0		
2004–05	Everton	31	1		

2005–06	Sunderland	10	1	**10**	**1**
2005–06	Everton	14	0	**138**	**3**

TURNER, Iain (G) **28** **0**
H: 6 3 W: 12 10 b.Stirling 26-1-84
Source: Riverside BC. *Honours:* Scotland Under-21, B.

2002–03	Stirling A	14	0	**14**	**0**
2002–03	Everton	0	0		
2003–04	Everton	0	0		
2004–05	Everton	0	0		
2004–05	*Doncaster R*	8	0	**8**	**0**
2005–06	Everton	3	0	**3**	**0**
2005–06	*Wycombe W*	3	0	**3**	**0**

VAN DER MEYDE, Andy (M) **165** **22**
H: 5 10 W: 12 04 b.Arnhem 30-9-79
Honours: Holland 18 full caps, 1 goal.

1997–98	Ajax	4	0		
1998–99	Ajax	1	0		
1999–2000	Twente	32	2	**32**	**2**
2000–01	Ajax	27	3		
2001–02	Ajax	30	5		
2002–03	Ajax	29	11	**91**	**19**
2003–04	Internazionale	14	1		
2004–05	Internazionale	18	0	**32**	**1**
2005–06	Everton	10	0	**10**	**0**

VAUGHAN, James (F) **3** **1**
H: 5 11 W: 13 00 b.Birmingham 14-7-88
Source: Scholar. *Honours:* England Youth.

2004–05	Everton	2	1		
2005–06	Everton	1	0	**3**	**1**

VIDARSSON, Bjarni (M) **0** **0**
H: 6 1 W: 11 08 b.Iceland 5-3-88
Source: Scholar. *Honours:* Iceland Youth, Under-21

2005–06	Everton	0	0

WEIR, David (D) **455** **25**
H: 6 5 W: 14 03 b.Falkirk 10-5-70
Source: Celtic BC. *Honours:* Scotland 48 full caps, 1 goal.

1992–93	Falkirk	30	1		
1993–94	Falkirk	37	3		
1994–95	Falkirk	32	1		
1995–96	Falkirk	34	3	**133**	**8**
1996–97	Hearts	34	6		
1997–98	Hearts	35	1		
1998–99	Hearts	23	1	**92**	**8**
1998–99	Everton	14	0		
1999–2000	Everton	35	2		
2000–01	Everton	37	1		
2001–02	Everton	36	4		
2002–03	Everton	31	0		
2003–04	Everton	10	0		
2004–05	Everton	34	1		
2005–06	Everton	33	1	**230**	**9**

WILSON, Laurence (M) **15** **1**
H: 5 10 W: 10 09 b.Huyton 10-10-86
Source: Scholar. *Honours:* England Youth.

2004–05	Everton	0	0		
2005–06	Everton	0	0		
2005–06	*Mansfield T*	15	1	**15**	**1**

WRIGHT, Richard (G) **311** **0**
H: 6 2 W: 14 04 b.Ipswich 5-11-77
Source: Trainee. *Honours:* England Schools, Youth, Under-21, 2 full caps.

1994–95	Ipswich T	3	0		
1995–96	Ipswich T	23	0		
1996–97	Ipswich T	40	0		
1997–98	Ipswich T	46	0		
1998–99	Ipswich T	46	0		
1999–2000	Ipswich T	46	0		
2000–01	Ipswich T	36	0	**240**	**0**
2001–02	Arsenal	12	0	**12**	**0**
2002–03	Everton	33	0		
2003–04	Everton	4	0		
2004–05	Everton	7	0		
2005–06	Everton	15	0	**59**	**0**

WRIGHT, Sean (D) **0** **0**
H: 5 10 W: 12 03 b.Liverpool 5-7-87
Source: Scholar.

2005–06	Everton	0	0

WYNNE, Stephen (D) **0** **0**
H: 5 9 W: 11 10 b.Liverpool 8-12-86
Source: Scholar.

2005–06	Everton	0	0

YOBO, Joseph (D) **179** **5**
H: 6 1 W: 13 00 b.Kano 6-9-80
Source: Mechelen. *Honours:* Nigeria 23 full caps, 1 goal.

1998–99	Standard Liege	0	0		
1999–2000	Standard Liege	18	0		
2000–01	Standard Liege	30	2	**48**	**2**
2001–02	Marseille	23	0	**23**	**0**
2002–03	Everton	24	0		
2003–04	Everton	28	2		
2004–05	Everton	27	0		
2005–06	Everton	29	1	**108**	**3**

Scholars
Connor, Stephen Jeffrey; Densmore, Shaun Peter; Elder, Matthew; Hall, Walter Alonte James; Hoogerwerf; Dax; Jones, Jamie.

FULHAM (33)

BATISTA, Ricardo (G) **9** **0**
H: 6 2 W: 12 06 b.Portugal 19-11-86
Source: Vitoria Setubal. *Honours:* Portugal Under-21.

2004–05	Fulham	0	0		
2005–06	Fulham	0	0		
2005–06	*Milton Keynes D*	9	0	**9**	**0**

BOA MORTE, Luis (F) **229** **45**
H: 5 9 W: 12 06 b.Lisbon 4-8-77
Source: Sporting Lisbon, Lourihanense (loan). *Honours:* Portugal Youth, Under-21, 25 full caps, 1 goal.

1997–98	Arsenal	15	0		
1998–99	Arsenal	8	0		
1999–2000	Arsenal	2	0	**25**	**0**
1999–2000	Southampton	14	1		
2000–01	Southampton	0	0	**14**	**1**
2000–01	*Fulham*	39	18		
2001–02	Fulham	23	1		
2002–03	Fulham	29	2		
2003–04	Fulham	33	9		
2004–05	Fulham	31	8		
2005–06	Fulham	35	6	**190**	**44**

BOCANEGRA, Carlos (D) **151** **7**
H: 5 11 W: 12 07 b.Alta Loma 25-5-79
Honours: USA 42 full caps, 6 goals.

2000	Chicago Fire	27	1		
2001	Chicago Fire	15	1		
2002	Chicago Fire	26	2		
2003	Chicago Fire	19	1	**87**	**5**
2003–04	Fulham	15	0		
2004–05	Fulham	28	1		
2005–06	Fulham	21	1	**64**	**2**

BROWN, Michael (M) **307** **32**
H: 5 9 W: 12 04 b.Hartlepool 25-1-77
Source: Trainee. *Honours:* England Under-21.

1994–95	Manchester C	0	0		
1995–96	Manchester C	21	0		
1996–97	Manchester C	11	0		
1996–97	*Hartlepool U*	6	1	**6**	**1**
1997–98	Manchester C	26	0		
1998–99	Manchester C	31	2		
1999–2000	Manchester C	0	0	**89**	**2**
1999–2000	*Portsmouth*	4	0	**4**	**0**
1999–2000	Sheffield U	24	3		
2000–01	Sheffield U	36	1		
2001–02	Sheffield U	36	5		
2002–03	Sheffield U	40	16		
2003–04	Sheffield U	15	2	**151**	**27**
2003–04	Tottenham H	17	1		
2004–05	Tottenham H	24	1		
2005–06	Tottenham H	9	0	**50**	**2**
2005–06	Fulham	7	0	**7**	**0**

BULLARD, Jimmy (M) **211** **21**
H: 5 10 W: 11 05 b.Newham 23-10-78
Source: Corinthian, Dartford, Gravesend & N.

1998–99	West Ham U	0	0		
1999–2000	West Ham U	0	0		
2000–01	West Ham U	0	0		
2001–02	Peterborough U	40	8		
2002–03	Peterborough U	26	3	**66**	**11**
2002–03	Wigan Ath	17	1		
2003–04	Wigan Ath	46	2		
2004–05	Wigan Ath	46	3		
2005–06	Wigan Ath	36	4	**145**	**10**
2005–06	Fulham	0	0		

CHRISTANVAL, Philippe (D) **140** **1**
H: 6 2 W: 12 10 b.Paris 31-8-78
Honours: France Under-21.

1997–98	Monaco	10	0		
1998–99	Monaco	23	1		
1999–2000	Monaco	25	0		
2000–01	Monaco	23	0	**81**	**1**
2001–02	Barcelona	26	0		
2002–03	Barcelona	5	0	**31**	**0**
2003–04	Marseille	13	0		
2004–05	Marseille	0	0	**13**	**0**
2005–06	Fulham	15	0	**15**	**0**

COLLINS, Matthew (M) **0** **0**
b.Merthyr 31-3-86
Source: Trainee.

2002–03	Fulham	0	0
2003–04	Fulham	0	0
2004–05	Fulham	0	0
2005–06	Fulham	0	0

CROSSLEY, Mark (G) **371** **0**
H: 6 3 W: 15 09 b.Barnsley 16-6-69
Source: Trainee. *Honours:* England Under-21, Wales B, 8 full caps.

1987–88	Nottingham F	0	0		
1988–89	Nottingham F	2	0		
1989–90	Nottingham F	8	0		
1989–90	*Manchester U*	0	0		
1990–91	Nottingham F	38	0		
1991–92	Nottingham F	36	0		
1992–93	Nottingham F	37	0		
1993–94	Nottingham F	37	0		
1994–95	Nottingham F	42	0		
1995–96	Nottingham F	38	0		
1996–97	Nottingham F	33	0		
1997–98	Nottingham F	0	0		
1997–98	*Millwall*	13	0	**13**	**0**
1998–99	Nottingham F	12	0		
1999–2000	Nottingham F	20	0	**303**	**0**
2000–01	Middlesbrough	5	0		
2001–02	Middlesbrough	18	0		
2002–03	Middlesbrough	0	0	**23**	**0**
2002–03	*Stoke C*	12	0	**12**	**0**
2003–04	Fulham	1	0		
2004–05	Fulham	6	0		
2005–06	Fulham	13	0	**20**	**0**

DE VILLIERS, Richard (G) **0** **0**
b.Johannesburg 15-12-87
Source: Balfour Park.

2005–06	Fulham	0	0

DIOP, Papa Bouba (M) **145** **23**
H: 6 4 W: 14 12 b.Dakar 28-1-78
Source: Espoir, Jaraaf, Vevey Sports. *Honours:* Senegal 25 full caps, 9 goals.

1999–2000	Neuchatel Xamax	0	0		
2000–01	Neuchatel Xamax	18	4	**18**	**4**
2000–01	Grasshoppers	11	1		
2001–02	Grasshoppers	18	4	**29**	**5**
2001–02	Lens	5	0		
2002–03	Lens	16	3		
2003–04	Lens	26	3	**47**	**6**
2004–05	Fulham	29	6		
2005–06	Fulham	22	2	**51**	**8**

DROBNY, Jaroslav (G) **0** **0**
H: 6 4 W: 14 00 b.Pocatky 19-10-79
Source: Panionios.

2005–06	Fulham	0	0

EHUI, Ismael (F) **3** **0**
H: 5 5 W: 10 02 b.Lille 10-12-86
Source: Scholar.

2004–05	Fulham	0	0		
2005–06	Fulham	0	0		
2005–06	*Scunthorpe U*	3	0	**3**	**0**

ELLIOTT, Simon (M) **193** **11**
H: 6 0 W: 13 02 b.Wellington 10-6-74
Source: Waterside Karori, Wellington Coll, Wellington U, Wellington Olympic AFC, Miramar R, Western Suburbs, Stanford Univ, Boston Bulldogs. *Honours:* New Zealand full caps.

1999	Los Angeles G	23	2
2000	Los Angeles G	27	5

2001 Los Angeles G 23 1
2002 Los Angeles G 25 1
2003 Los Angeles G 24 1 **122 10**
2004 Columbus Crew 27 0
2005 Columbus Crew 32 1 **59 1**
2005–06 Fulham 12 0 **12 0**

ELRICH, Ahmed (M) 136 20
H: 5 11 W: 12 00 b.Sydney 30-5-81
Honours: Australia Under-20, Under-23, 16 full caps, 5 goals.
1999–2000 Parramatta Power 21 1
2000–01 Parramatta Power 24 2
2001–02 Parramatta Power 22 2
2002–03 Parramatta Power 32 10
2003–04 Parramatta Power 21 4 **120 19**
2003–04 Busan Icons 10 1
2004–05 Busan Icons 0 0 **10 1**
2005–06 Fulham 6 0 **6 0**

FONTAINE, Liam (D) 41 0
H: 5 11 W: 11 09 b.Beckenham 7-1-86
Source: Trainee. *Honours:* England Under-20.
2003–04 Fulham 0 0
2004–05 Fulham 1 0
2004–05 *Yeovil T* 15 0
2005–06 Fulham 0 0 **1 0**
2005–06 *Yeovil T* 10 0 **25 0**
2005–06 *Bristol C* 15 0 **15 0**

GOMA, Alain (D) 346 5
H: 6 0 W: 13 01 b.Sault 5-10-72
Honours: France 2 full caps.
1990–91 Auxerre 1 0
1991–92 Auxerre 1 0
1992–93 Auxerre 15 1
1993–94 Auxerre 33 0
1994–95 Auxerre 28 0
1995–96 Auxerre 32 0
1996–97 Auxerre 34 2
1997–98 Auxerre 22 1 **166 4**
1998–99 Paris St Germain 30 0 **30 0**
1999–2000 Newcastle U 14 0
2000–01 Newcastle U 19 1 **33 1**
2000–01 Fulham 3 0
2001–02 Fulham 33 0
2002–03 Fulham 29 0
2003–04 Fulham 23 0
2004–05 Fulham 16 0
2005–06 Fulham 13 0 **117 0**

GREEN, Adam (D) 16 0
H: 5 8 W: 10 11 b.Hillingdon 12-1-84
Source: Scholar.
2003–04 Fulham 4 0
2004–05 Fulham 4 0
2004–05 *Sheffield W* 3 0 **3 0**
2004–05 *Bournemouth* 3 0 **3 0**
2005–06 Fulham 0 0 **8 0**
2005–06 *Bristol C* 2 0 **2 0**

HELGUSON, Heidar (F) 245 81
H: 5 10 W: 12 09 b.Akureyri 22-8-77
Source: Throttur. *Honours:* Iceland Youth, Under-21, 38 full caps, 6 goals.
1998 Lillestrom 19 2
1999 Lillestrom 25 16 **44 18**
1999–2000 Watford 16 6
2000–01 Watford 33 8
2001–02 Watford 34 6
2002–03 Watford 30 11
2003–04 Watford 22 8
2004–05 Watford 39 16 **174 55**
2005–06 Fulham 27 8 **27 8**

JAMES, Chris (M) 0 0
H: 5 8 W: 10 12 b.New Zealand 4-7-87
Source: Scholar. *Honours:* England Youth.
2005–06 Fulham 0 0

JENSEN, Claus (M) 297 40
H: 6 0 W: 13 01 b.Nykobing 29-4-77
Source: Stubbekobing, Nykobing. *Honours:* Denmark Under-21, 41 full caps, 8 goals.
1995–96 Naestved 4 0 **4 0**
1996–97 Lyngby 31 3
1997–98 Lyngby 31 11 **62 14**
1998–99 Bolton W 44 2
1999–2000 Bolton W 42 6 **86 8**
2000–01 Charlton Ath 38 5
2001–02 Charlton Ath 18 1
2002–03 Charlton Ath 35 6
2003–04 Charlton Ath 31 4 **122 16**
2004–05 Fulham 12 0
2005–06 Fulham 11 2 **23 2**

JENSEN, Niclas (D) 328 18
H: 5 9 W: 13 00 b.Copenhagen 17-8-74
Honours: Denmark Youth, Under-21, 49 full caps.
1992–93 Lyngby 12 2
1993–94 Lyngby 21 0
1994–95 Lyngby 20 1
1995–96 Lyngby 32 3
1996–97 Lyngby 7 1 **92 7**
1996–97 PSV Eindhoven 2 0
1997–98 PSV Eindhoven 2 0 **4 0**
1997–98 FC Copenhagen 10 0
1998–99 FC Copenhagen 33 4
1999–2000 FC Copenhagen 29 1
2000–01 FC Copenhagen 32 1
2001–02 FC Copenhagen 18 1 **122 7**
2001–02 Manchester C 18 1
2002–03 Manchester C 33 1 **51 2**
2003–04 Bor Dortmund 27 1
2004–05 Bor Dortmund 16 1 **43 2**
2005–06 Fulham 16 0 **16 0**

JOHN, Collins (F) 105 30
H: 5 11 W: 12 13 b.Zwandru 17-10-85
Honours: Holland Youth, Under-21, 2 full caps.
2002–03 Twente 17 2
2003–04 Twente 18 9 **35 11**
2003–04 Fulham 8 4
2004–05 Fulham 27 4
2005–06 Fulham 35 11 **70 19**

KNIGHT, Zat (D) 131 1
H: 6 6 W: 15 02 b.Solihull 2-5-80
Source: Rushall Olympic. *Honours:* England Under-21, 2 full caps.
1998–99 Fulham 0 0
1999–2000 Fulham 0 0
1999–2000 *Peterborough U* 8 0 **8 0**
2000–01 Fulham 0 0
2001–02 Fulham 10 0
2002–03 Fulham 17 0
2003–04 Fulham 31 0
2004–05 Fulham 35 1
2005–06 Fulham 30 0 **123 1**

LEACOCK, Dean (D) 22 0
H: 6 2 W: 12 04 b.Croydon 10-6-84
Source: Trainee. *Honours:* England Youth, Under-20.
2002–03 Fulham 0 0
2003–04 Fulham 4 0
2004–05 Fulham 0 0
2004–05 *Coventry C* 13 0 **13 0**
2005–06 Fulham 5 0 **9 0**

LEGWINSKI, Sylvain (M) 302 23
H: 6 1 W: 11 07 b.Clermont-Ferrand 6-10-73
Honours: France Under-21.
1992–93 Monaco 2 0
1993–94 Monaco 0 0
1994–95 Monaco 21 1
1995–96 Monaco 29 2
1996–97 Monaco 37 9
1997–98 Monaco 22 0
1998–99 Monaco 14 1 **125 13**
1999–2000 Bordeaux 13 1
2000–01 Bordeaux 32 1
2001–02 Bordeaux 4 0 **49 2**
2001–02 Fulham 33 3
2002–03 Fulham 35 4
2003–04 Fulham 32 0
2004–05 Fulham 15 1
2005–06 Fulham 13 0 **128 8**

MALBRANQUE, Steed (M) 249 37
H: 5 7 W: 11 07 b.Mouscron 6-1-80
Honours: France Under-21.
1997–98 Lyon 2 0
1998–99 Lyon 21 0
1999–2000 Lyon 28 3
2000–01 Lyon 26 2 **77 5**
2001–02 Fulham 37 8
2002–03 Fulham 37 6
2003–04 Fulham 38 6
2004–05 Fulham 26 6
2005–06 Fulham 34 6 **172 32**

McBRIDE, Brian (F) 275 87
H: 6 0 W: 12 08 b.Chicago 19-6-72
Source: St Louis Univ. *Honours:* USA 95 full caps, 30 goals.
1994–95 Wolfsburg 12 1 **12 1**
1996 Columbus Crew 28 17
1997 Columbus Crew 13 6
1998 Columbus Crew 24 10
1999 Columbus Crew 25 5
2000 Columbus Crew 18 6
2000–01 Preston NE 9 1 **9 1**
2001 Columbus Crew 15 1
2002 Columbus Crew 14 5
2002–03 Everton 8 4 **8 4**
2003 Columbus Crew 24 12 **161 62**
2003–04 Fulham 16 4
2004–05 Fulham 31 6
2005–06 Fulham 38 9 **85 19**

McDERMOTT, Neale (M) 16 2
H: 5 9 W: 10 11 b.Newcastle 8-3-85
Source: Scholar. *Honours:* England Youth.
2001–02 Newcastle U 0 0
2002–03 Newcastle U 0 0
2002–03 Fulham 0 0
2003–04 Fulham 0 0
2004–05 Fulham 0 0
2005–06 Fulham 0 0
2005–06 *Swindon T* 13 2 **13 2**
2005–06 *Darlington* 3 0 **3 0**

MILSOM, Robert (D) 0 0
b.Redhill 2-1-87
Source: Scholar.
2005–06 Fulham 0 0

MONCUR, Tom (D) 0 0
b.Hackney 23-9-87
Source: Scholar.
2005–06 Fulham 0 0

NIEMI, Antti (G) 366 0
H: 6 1 W: 12 04 b.Oulu 31-5-72
Honours: Finland Youth, Under-21, 66 full caps.
1991 HJK Helsinki 2 0
1992 HJK Helsinki 28 0
1993 HJK Helsinki 24 0
1994 HJK Helsinki 24 0
1995 HJK Helsinki 24 0 **102 0**
1995–96 FC Copenhagen 17 0
1996–97 FC Copenhagen 30 0 **47 0**
1997–98 Rangers 5 0
1998–99 Rangers 7 0
1999–2000 Rangers 1 0 **13 0**
1999–2000 Hearts 17 0
2000–01 Hearts 37 0
2001–02 Hearts 32 0
2002–03 Hearts 3 0 **89 0**
2002–03 Southampton 25 0
2003–04 Southampton 28 0
2004–05 Southampton 28 0
2005–06 Southampton 25 0 **106 0**
2005–06 Fulham 9 0 **9 0**

OMOZUSI, Elliot (D) 0 0
b.Hackney 15-12-88
Source: Scholar. *Honours:* England Youth.
2005–06 Fulham 0 0

PEARCE, Ian (D) 242 11
H: 6 3 W: 15 06 b.Bury St Edmunds 7-5-74
Source: School. *Honours:* England Youth, Under-21.
1990–91 Chelsea 1 0
1991–92 Chelsea 2 0
1992–93 Chelsea 1 0
1993–94 Chelsea 0 0 **4 0**
1993–94 Blackburn R 5 1
1994–95 Blackburn R 28 0
1995–96 Blackburn R 12 1
1996–97 Blackburn R 12 0
1997–98 Blackburn R 5 0 **62 2**
1997–98 West Ham U 30 1
1998–99 West Ham U 33 2
1999–2000 West Ham U 1 0
2000–01 West Ham U 15 1
2001–02 West Ham U 9 2
2002–03 West Ham U 30 2

2003–04	West Ham U	24	1	142	9
2003–04	Fulham	13	0		
2004–05	Fulham	11	0		
2005–06	Fulham	10	0	34	0

PEMBRIDGE, Mark (M) **418 51**
H: 5 7 W: 11 13 b.Merthyr 29-11-70
Source: Trainee. *Honours:* Wales Schools, Under-21, B, 54 full caps, 6 goals.

1989–90	Luton T	0	0		
1990–91	Luton T	18	1		
1991–92	Luton T	42	5	60	6
1992–93	Derby Co	42	8		
1993–94	Derby Co	41	11		
1994–95	Derby Co	27	9	110	28
1995–96	Sheffield W	25	1		
1996–97	Sheffield W	34	6		
1997–98	Sheffield W	34	4	93	11
1998–99	Benfica	19	1	19	1
1999–2000	Everton	31	2		
2000–01	Everton	21	0		
2001–02	Everton	14	1		
2002–03	Everton	21	1		
2003–04	Everton	4	0	91	4
2003–04	Fulham	12	1		
2004–05	Fulham	28	0		
2005–06	Fulham	5	0	45	1

PRATLEY, Darren (M) **47 5**
H: 6 1 W: 10 12 b.Barking 22-4-85
Source: Scholar.

2001–02	Fulham	0	0		
2002–03	Fulham	0	0		
2003–04	Fulham	1	0		
2004–05	Fulham	0	0		
2004–05	*Brentford*	14	1		
2005–06	Fulham	0	0	1	0
2005–06	*Brentford*	32	4	46	5

RADZINSKI, Tomasz (F) **341 127**
H: 5 8 W: 11 11 b.Poznan 14-12-73
Source: Toronto Rockets, St Catherines Roma. *Honours:* Canada Under-23, 29 full caps, 7 goals.

1994–95	Ekeren	28	6		
1995–96	Ekeren	22	9		
1996–97	Ekeren	23	8		
1997–98	Ekeren	31	19	104	42
1998–99	Anderlecht	22	15		
1999–2000	Anderlecht	25	14		
2000–01	Anderlecht	31	23	78	52
2001–02	Everton	27	6		
2002–03	Everton	30	11		
2003–04	Everton	34	8	91	25
2004–05	Fulham	35	6		
2005–06	Fulham	33	2	68	8

REHMAN, Zesh (D) **37 2**
H: 6 2 W: 12 08 b.Birmingham 14-10-83
Source: Scholar. *Honours:* England Youth, Pakistan full caps.

2001–02	Fulham	0	0		
2002–03	Fulham	0	0		
2003–04	Fulham	1	0		
2003–04	*Brighton & HA*	11	2	11	2
2004–05	Fulham	17	0		
2005–06	Fulham	3	0	21	0
2005–06	*Norwich C*	5	0	5	0

ROSENIOR, Liam (D) **73 2**
H: 5 10 W: 11 05 b.Wandsworth 9-7-84
Source: Scholar. *Honours:* England Youth, Under-20, Under-21.

2001–02	Bristol C	1	0		
2002–03	Bristol C	21	2		
2003–04	Bristol C	0	0	22	2
2003–04	Fulham	0	0		
2003–04	*Torquay U*	10	0	10	0
2004–05	Fulham	17	0		
2005–06	Fulham	24	0	41	0

SAVA, Facundo (F) **299 82**
H: 6 0 W: 13 01 b.Ituzaingo 3-7-74

1993–94	Ferro Carril	27	3		
1994–95	Ferro Carril	18	0		
1995–96	Ferro Carril	34	4		
1996–97	Ferro Carril	1	0	80	7
1996–97	Boca Juniors	7	0	7	0
1997–98	Gimnasia	32	8		
1998–99	Gimnasia	28	10		
1999–2000	Gimnasia	35	12		
2000–01	Gimnasia	34	13		
2001–02	Gimnasia	34	23	163	66
2002–03	Fulham	20	5		
2003–04	Fulham	6	1		
2004–05	*Celta Vigo*	23	3	23	3
2005–06	Fulham	0	0	26	6

TIMLIN, Michael (M) **4 0**
H: 5 8 W: 11 08 b.Lambeth 19-3-85
Source: Trainee. *Honours:* Eire Youth, Under-21.

2002–03	Fulham	0	0		
2003–04	Fulham	0	0		
2004–05	Fulham	0	0		
2005–06	Fulham	0	0		
2005–06	*Scunthorpe U*	1	0	1	0
2005–06	*Doncaster R*	3	0	3	0

VOLZ, Moritz (D) **97 1**
H: 5 10 W: 11 07 b.Siegen 21-1-83
Source: Schalke. *Honours:* Germany Youth, Under-21.

1999–2000	Arsenal	0	0		
2000–01	Arsenal	0	0		
2001–02	Arsenal	0	0		
2002–03	Arsenal	0	0		
2002–03	*Wimbledon*	10	1	10	1
2003–04	Arsenal	0	0		
2003–04	Fulham	33	0		
2004–05	Fulham	31	0		
2005–06	Fulham	23	0	87	0

WARNER, Tony (G) **255 0**
H: 6 4 W: 15 06 b.Liverpool 11-5-74
Source: School.

1993–94	Liverpool	0	0		
1994–95	Liverpool	0	0		
1995–96	Liverpool	0	0		
1996–97	Liverpool	0	0		
1997–98	Liverpool	0	0		
1997–98	*Swindon T*	2	0	2	0
1998–99	Liverpool	0	0		
1998–99	*Celtic*	3	0	3	0
1998–99	*Aberdeen*	6	0	6	0
1999–2000	Millwall	45	0		
2000–01	Millwall	35	0		
2001–02	Millwall	46	0		
2002–03	Millwall	46	0		
2003–04	Millwall	28	0	200	0
2004–05	Cardiff C	26	0		
2005–06	Cardiff C	0	0	26	0
2005–06	Fulham	18	0	18	0

WATKINS, Robert (D) **0 0**
b.Carshalton 14-10-85
Source: Trainee.

2003–04	Fulham	0	0		
2004–05	Fulham	0	0		
2005–06	Fulham	0	0		

Scholars
Bent, Eliot; Brooks-Meade, Corrin; Brown, Wayne Johnathon; Casal, Yinka; Goncalves, Lino; Gowland, Jefferson; Hudson-Odoi, Bradley; Mabbutt, Gary David; Orelaja, Kazeem Kareem; Watts, Adam; Wilson, Jack.

GILLINGHAM (34)

BROWN, Jason (G) **126 0**
H: 6 0 W: 15 07 b.Southwark 18-5-82
Source: Charlton Ath Scholar. *Honours:* Wales Youth, Under-21, 1 full cap.

2000–01	Gillingham	0	0		
2001–02	Gillingham	10	0		
2002–03	Gillingham	39	0		
2003–04	Gillingham	22	0		
2004–05	Gillingham	16	0		
2005–06	Gillingham	39	0	126	0

BULLOCK, Tony (G) **177 0**
H: 6 1 W: 15 03 b.Warrington 18-2-72
Source: Northwich V, Leek T.

1996–97	Barnsley	0	0		
1997–98	Barnsley	0	0		
1998–99	Barnsley	32	0		
1999–2000	Barnsley	6	0	38	0
2000–01	Macclesfield T	24	0	24	0
2000–01	Lincoln C	2	0	2	0
2001–02	Ross Co	33	0		
2002–03	Ross Co	36	0	69	0
2003–04	Dundee U	5	0		
2004–05	Dundee U	26	0		
2005–06	Dundee U	7	0	38	0
2005–06	Gillingham	6	0	6	0

To St Mirren January 2006

BYFIELD, Darren (F) **254 61**
H: 5 11 W: 12 07 b.Sutton Coldfield 29-9-76
Source: Trainee. *Honours:* Jamaica 7 full caps.

1993–94	Aston Villa	0	0		
1994–95	Aston Villa	0	0		
1995–96	Aston Villa	0	0		
1996–97	Aston Villa	0	0		
1997–98	Aston Villa	7	0		
1998–99	Aston Villa	0	0		
1998–99	*Preston NE*	5	1	5	1
1999–2000	Aston Villa	0	0	7	0
1999–2000	*Northampton T*	6	1	6	1
1999–2000	*Cambridge U*	4	0	4	0
1999–2000	*Blackpool*	3	0	3	0
2000–01	Walsall	40	9		
2001–02	Walsall	37	4	77	13
2001–02	Rotherham U	3	2		
2002–03	Rotherham U	37	13		
2003–04	Rotherham U	28	7	68	22
2003–04	Sunderland	17	5	17	5
2004–05	Gillingham	38	6		
2005–06	Gillingham	29	13	67	19

CLOHESSY, Sean (D) **20 1**
H: 5 11 W: 12 07 b.Croydon 12-12-86
Source: Arsenal Scholar.

2005–06	Gillingham	20	1	20	1

COLLIN, Frannie (F) **6 1**
H: 5 10 W: 11 07 b.Chatham 20-4-87

2005–06	Gillingham	6	1	6	1

CORNEILLE, Mark (D) **2 0**
H: 5 7 W: 10 05 b.London 31-5-86

2005–06	Gillingham	2	0	2	0

COX, Ian (D) **402 23**
H: 6 1 W: 12 08 b.Croydon 25-3-71
Source: Carshalton Ath. *Honours:* Trinidad & Tobago 16 full caps.

1993–94	Crystal Palace	0	0		
1994–95	Crystal Palace	11	0		
1995–96	Crystal Palace	4	0	15	0
1995–96	Bournemouth	8	0		
1996–97	Bournemouth	44	8		
1997–98	Bournemouth	46	3		
1998–99	Bournemouth	46	5		
1999–2000	Bournemouth	28	0	172	16
1999–2000	Burnley	17	1		
2000–01	Burnley	38	1		
2001–02	Burnley	34	2		
2002–03	Burnley	26	1	115	5
2003–04	Gillingham	33	0		
2004–05	Gillingham	31	2		
2005–06	Gillingham	36	0	100	2

CRICHTON, Paul (G) **419 0**
H: 6 1 W: 14 04 b.Pontefract 3-10-68
Source: Apprentice.

1986–87	Nottingham F	0	0		
1986–87	*Notts Co*	5	0	5	0
1986–87	*Darlington*	5	0		
1986–87	*Peterborough U*	4	0		
1987–88	Nottingham F	0	0		
1987–88	*Darlington*	3	0	8	0
1987–88	*Swindon T*	4	0	4	0
1987–88	*Rotherham U*	6	0	6	0
1988–89	Nottingham F	0	0		
1988–89	*Torquay U*	13	0	13	0
1988–89	Peterborough U	31	0		
1989–90	Peterborough U	16	0	51	0
1990–91	Doncaster R	20	0		
1991–92	Doncaster R	16	0		
1992–93	Doncaster R	41	0	77	0
1993–94	Grimsby T	46	0		
1994–95	Grimsby T	43	0		
1995–96	Grimsby T	44	0		
1996–97	Grimsby T	0	0	133	0
1996–97	WBA	30	0		
1997–98	WBA	2	0		
1997–98	*Aston Villa*	0	0		
1998–99	WBA	0	0	32	0
1998–99	Burnley	29	0		

1999–2000 Burnley 46 0
2000–01 Burnley 8 0 **83 0**
2001–02 Norwich C 6 0
2002–03 Norwich C 0 0
2003–04 Norwich C 0 0
2004–05 Norwich C 0 0 **6 0**
From Accrington S.
2005–06 Gillingham 1 0 **1 0**

CROFTS, Andrew (D) 81 4
H: 5 10 W: 12 09 b.Chatham 29-5-84
Source: Trainee. *Honours:* Wales Youth, Under-21, 3 full caps.
2000–01 Gillingham 1 0
2001–02 Gillingham 0 0
2002–03 Gillingham 0 0
2003–04 Gillingham 8 0
2004–05 Gillingham 27 2
2005–06 Gillingham 45 2 **81 4**

FLYNN, Michael (M) 96 11
H: 5 10 W: 13 04 b.Newport 17-10-80
Source: Barry T.
2002–03 Wigan Ath 17 1
2003–04 Wigan Ath 8 0
2004–05 Wigan Ath 13 1 **38 2**
2004–05 *Blackpool* 6 0 **6 0**
2004–05 Gillingham 16 3
2005–06 Gillingham 36 6 **52 9**

FOBI-EDUSEI, Akwasi (F) 8 0
H: 5 9 W: 11 00 b.London 12-10-86
Source: Scholar.
2002–03 Gillingham 2 0
2003–04 Gillingham 0 0
2004–05 Gillingham 0 0
2005–06 Gillingham 6 0 **8 0**

HISLOP, Steve (F) 138 44
H: 6 1 W: 12 10 b.Edinburgh 14-6-78
2000–01 East Stirling 36 16 **36 16**
2001–02 Ross Co 33 14
2002–03 Ross Co 14 3 **47 17**
2002–03 Inverness CT 14 2
2003–04 Inverness CT 26 9
2004–05 Inverness CT 7 0 **47 11**
2005–06 Gillingham 8 0 **8 0**
To Livingston January 2006

HOPE, Chris (D) 523 32
H: 6 1 W: 13 07 b.Sheffield 14-11-72
Source: Darlington.
1991–92 Nottingham F 0 0
1992–93 Nottingham F 0 0
1993–94 Scunthorpe U 41 0
1994–95 Scunthorpe U 24 0
1995–96 Scunthorpe U 40 3
1996–97 Scunthorpe U 46 3
1997–98 Scunthorpe U 46 5
1998–99 Scunthorpe U 46 5
1999–2000 Scunthorpe U 44 3 **287 19**
2000–01 Gillingham 46 2
2001–02 Gillingham 46 4
2002–03 Gillingham 46 1
2003–04 Gillingham 37 3
2004–05 Gillingham 37 2
2005–06 Gillingham 24 1 **236 13**

JACKMAN, Danny (D) 109 5
H: 5 4 W: 10 00 b.Worcester 3-1-83
Source: Scholar.
2000–01 Aston Villa 0 0
2001–02 Aston Villa 0 0
2001–02 *Cambridge U* 7 1 **7 1**
2002–03 Aston Villa 0 0
2003–04 Aston Villa 0 0
2003–04 Stockport Co 27 2
2004–05 Stockport Co 33 2 **60 4**
2005–06 Gillingham 42 0 **42 0**

JARVIS, Matthew (M) 75 6
H: 5 8 W: 11 10 b.Middlesbrough 22-5-86
Source: Scholar.
2003–04 Gillingham 10 0
2004–05 Gillingham 30 3
2005–06 Gillingham 35 3 **75 6**

JOHNSON, Leon (M) 122 4
H: 6 1 W: 13 05 b.Shoreditch 10-5-81
Source: Scholarship.
1999–2000 Southend U 0 0
2000–01 Southend U 20 1
2001–02 Southend U 28 2 **48 3**
2002–03 Gillingham 18 0
2003–04 Gillingham 20 0
2004–05 Gillingham 8 0
2005–06 Gillingham 28 1 **74 1**

KNOWLES, Danny (G) 0 0
H: 6 0 W: 13 02 b.Sidcup 7-1-86
Source: Scholar.
2005–06 Gillingham 0 0

POUTON, Alan (M) 270 21
H: 6 2 W: 13 09 b.Newcastle 1-2-77
Source: Newcastle U Trainee.
1995–96 Oxford U 0 0
1995–96 York C 0 0
1996–97 York C 22 1
1997–98 York C 41 5
1998–99 York C 27 1
1999–2000 York C 0 0 **90 7**
1999–2000 Grimsby T 35 1
2000–01 Grimsby T 21 1
2001–02 Grimsby T 35 5
2002–03 Grimsby T 25 5
2003–04 Grimsby T 5 0 **121 12**
2003–04 Gillingham 19 0
2004–05 Gillingham 12 0
2004–05 *Hartlepool U* 5 0 **5 0**
2005–06 Gillingham 23 2 **54 2**

ROBERTS, Iwan (F) 647 202
H: 6 4 W: 14 08 b.Bangor 26-6-68
Source: Trainee. *Honours:* Wales Schools, Youth, B, 15 full caps.
1985–86 Watford 4 0
1986–87 Watford 3 1
1987–88 Watford 25 2
1988–89 Watford 22 6
1989–90 Watford 9 0 **63 9**
1990–91 Huddersfield T 44 13
1991–92 Huddersfield T 46 24
1992–93 Huddersfield T 37 9
1993–94 Huddersfield T 15 4 **142 50**
1993–94 Leicester C 26 13
1994–95 Leicester C 37 9
1995–96 Leicester C 37 19 **100 41**
1996–97 Wolverhampton W 33 12 **33 12**
1997–98 Norwich C 31 5
1998–99 Norwich C 45 19
1999–2000 Norwich C 44 17
2000–01 Norwich C 44 15
2001–02 Norwich C 30 13
2002–03 Norwich C 43 7
2003–04 Norwich C 41 8 **278 84**
2004–05 Gillingham 20 3
2004–05 *Cambridge U* 11 3 **11 3**
2005–06 Gillingham 0 0 **20 3**

ROSE, Richard (D) 67 0
H: 6 0 W: 12 04 b.Pembury 8-9-82
Source: Trainee.
2000–01 Gillingham 4 0
2001–02 Gillingham 3 0
2002–03 Gillingham 2 0
2002–03 *Bristol R* 9 0 **9 0**
2003–04 Gillingham 17 0
2004–05 Gillingham 18 0
2005–06 Gillingham 14 0 **58 0**

SANCHO, Brent (D) 67 4
H: 6 1 W: 14 01 b.Belmont 13-3-77
Source: Portland T. *Honours:* Trinidad & Tobago 43 full caps.
2003–04 Dundee 21 0
2004–05 Dundee 27 2 **48 2**
2005–06 Gillingham 19 2 **19 2**

SAUNDERS, Mark (M) 248 26
H: 6 0 W: 13 01 b.Reading 23-7-71
Source: Tiverton.
1995–96 Plymouth Arg 10 1
1996–97 Plymouth Arg 25 3
1997–98 Plymouth Arg 37 7 **72 11**
1998–99 Gillingham 34 4
1999–2000 Gillingham 26 1
2000–01 Gillingham 35 5
2001–02 Gillingham 19 1
2002–03 Gillingham 34 3
2003–04 Gillingham 21 1
2004–05 Gillingham 3 0
2005–06 Gillingham 4 0 **176 15**

SHIELDS, Paul (F) 136 33
H: 6 0 W: 13 07 b.Dunfermline 15-8-81
Source: Milton Green.
1998–99 Raith R 14 0
1999–2000 Raith R 9 1 **23 1**
1999–2000 Celtic 1 0
2000–01 Celtic 0 0
2001–02 Celtic 0 0 **1 0**
2002–03 Queen of South 13 1 **13 1**
2002–03 Clyde 13 1 **13 1**
2003–04 Forfar Ath 33 9
2004–05 Forfar Ath 36 20 **69 29**
2005–06 Gillingham 17 1 **17 1**

SPILLER, Danny (M) 104 6
H: 5 8 W: 11 00 b.Maidstone 10-10-81
Source: Trainee.
2000–01 Gillingham 0 0
2001–02 Gillingham 1 0
2002–03 Gillingham 10 0
2003–04 Gillingham 39 6
2004–05 Gillingham 22 0
2005–06 Gillingham 32 0 **104 6**

STONE, Craig (M) 3 0
H: 6 0 W: 10 05 b.Rochester 29-12-88
Source: Scholar.
2005–06 Gillingham 3 0 **3 0**

WALLIS, John (M) 17 0
H: 5 7 W: 11 04 b.Gravesend 4-4-86
Source: Scholar.
2005–06 Gillingham 17 0 **17 0**

GRIMSBY T (35)

ASHTON, Paul (G) 0 0
H: 6 2 W: 12 08 b.Maesteg 25-10-86
Source: Scholar.
2004–05 Grimsby T 0 0
2005–06 Grimsby T 0 0

BARWICK, Terry (M) 54 1
H: 5 11 W: 10 12 b.Doncaster 11-1-83
Source: Scholarship.
1999–2000 Scunthorpe U 1 0
2000–01 Scunthorpe U 0 0
2001–02 Scunthorpe U 10 0
2002–03 Scunthorpe U 5 0
2003–04 Scunthorpe U 30 1
2004–05 Scunthorpe U 0 0 **46 1**
2005–06 Grimsby T 8 0 **8 0**

BOLLAND, Paul (M) 228 10
H: 5 10 W: 10 12 b.Bradford 23-12-79
Source: Trainee.
1997–98 Bradford C 10 0
1998–99 Bradford C 2 0 **12 0**
1998–99 Notts Co 13 0
1999–2000 Notts Co 25 1
2000–01 Notts Co 7 0
2001–02 Notts Co 19 0
2002–03 Notts Co 29 3
2003–04 Notts Co 39 1
2004–05 Notts Co 40 1 **172 6**
2005–06 Grimsby T 44 4 **44 4**

CHAMBERLAIN, Miles (D) 0 0
H: 6 0 W: 12 00 b.Boston 14-12-86
Source: Scholar.
2004–05 Grimsby T 0 0
2005–06 Grimsby T 0 0

COHEN, Gary (F) 66 6
H: 5 11 W: 11 02 b.Leyton 20-1-84
Source: Academy.
2002–03 Watford 0 0
From Scarborough
2003–04 Gretna 26 0
2004–05 Gretna 0 0 **26 0**
2005–06 Grimsby T 40 6 **40 6**

CRANE, Tony (D) 94 8
H: 6 5 W: 12 05 b.Liverpool 8-9-82
Source: Trainee. *Honours:* England Youth.
1999–2000 Sheffield W 0 0
2000–01 Sheffield W 15 2
2001–02 Sheffield W 15 0
2002–03 Sheffield W 19 2 **49 4**
2003–04 Grimsby T 37 3

2004–05 Grimsby T 3 0
2005–06 Grimsby T 5 1 **45 4**

CROFT, Gary (D) 335 8
H: 5 9 W: 11 08 b.Burton-on-Trent 17-2-74
Source: Trainee. *Honours:* England Under-21.
1990–91 Grimsby T 1 0
1991–92 Grimsby T 0 0
1992–93 Grimsby T 32 0
1993–94 Grimsby T 36 1
1994–95 Grimsby T 44 1
1995–96 Grimsby T 36 1
1995–96 Blackburn R 0 0
1996–97 Blackburn R 5 0
1997–98 Blackburn R 23 1
1998–99 Blackburn R 12 0
1999–2000 Blackburn R 0 0 **40 1**
1999–2000 Ipswich T 21 1
2000–01 Ipswich T 8 0
2001–02 Ipswich T 0 0 **29 1**
2001–02 *Wigan Ath* 7 0 **7 0**
2001–02 *Cardiff C* 6 1
2002–03 Cardiff C 43 1
2003–04 Cardiff C 27 1
2004–05 Cardiff C 1 0 **77 3**
2005–06 Grimsby T 33 0 **182 3**

DOWNEY, Glen (D) 2 1
H: 6 1 W: 13 00 b.Sunderland 20-9-78
1997–98 Hartlepool U 0 0
1998–99 Hartlepool U 0 0
1999–2000 Hartlepool U 0 0
2000–01 Hartlepool U 0 0
2001–02 Hartlepool U 0 0
From Scarborough.
2004–05 Grimsby T 1 0
2005–06 Grimsby T 1 1 **2 1**

FUTCHER, Ben (D) 160 15
H: 6 7 W: 12 05 b.Manchester 20-2-81
Source: Trainee.
1999–2000 Oldham Ath 5 0
2000–01 Oldham Ath 5 0
2001–02 Oldham Ath 0 0 **10 0**
From Stalybridge C, Doncaster R
2002–03 Lincoln
2003–04 Lincoln C 43 2
2004–05 Lincoln C 35 3 **121 13**
2005–06 Boston U 14 0 **14 0**
2005–06 Grimsby T 15 2 **15 2**

GOODFELLOW, Marc (M) 111 15
H: 5 10 W: 11 00 b.Swadlincote 20-9-81
1998–99 Stoke C 0 0
1999–2000 Stoke C 0 0
2000–01 Stoke C 7 0
2001–02 Stoke C 23 5
2002–03 Stoke C 20 1
2003–04 Stoke C 4 0 **54 6**
2003–04 Bristol C 15 4
2004–05 Bristol C 5 0 **20 4**
2004–05 *Port Vale* 5 0 **5 0**
2004–05 *Swansea C* 6 3
2004–05 *Colchester U* 5 1 **5 1**
2005–06 Swansea C 11 0 **17 3**
2005–06 Grimsby T 10 1 **10 1**

HEGARTY, Nick (M) 3 0
H: 5 10 W: 11 00 b.Hemsworth 25-6-86
Source: Scholar.
2004–05 Grimsby T 1 0
2005–06 Grimsby T 2 0 **3 0**

HIGGINS, Ben (M) 0 0
H: 5 11 W: 12 00 b.Grimsby 13-9-87
Source: Scholar.
2004–05 Grimsby T 0 0
2005–06 Grimsby T 0 0

JONES, Gary (M) 346 59
H: 6 3 W: 15 02 b.Chester 10-5-75
Source: Trainee.
1993–94 Tranmere R 6 2
1994–95 Tranmere R 19 3
1995–96 Tranmere R 23 1
1996–97 Tranmere R 30 6
1997–98 Tranmere R 43 8
1998–99 Tranmere R 26 5
1999–2000 Tranmere R 31 3
2000–01 Nottingham F 31 1
2001–02 Nottingham F 5 1
2002–03 Nottingham F 0 0 **36 2**
2002–03 Tranmere R 40 6
2003–04 Tranmere R 42 9
2004–05 Tranmere R 10 1 **270 44**
2005–06 Grimsby T 40 13 **40 13**

JONES, Rob (D) 77 7
H: 6 7 W: 12 02 b.Stockton 30-11-79
Source: Gateshead.
2002–03 Stockport Co 0 0
2003–04 Stockport Co 16 2 **16 2**
2003–04 *Macclesfield T* 1 0 **1 0**
2004–05 Grimsby T 20 1
2005–06 Grimsby T 40 4 **60 5**

KAMUDIMBA KALALA, Jean-Paul (M) 23 5
H: 5 10 W: 12 02 b.Lubumbashi 16-2-82
Honours: DR Congo full caps.
2003–04 Nice 2 0
2004–05 Nice 0 0 **2 0**
2005–06 Grimsby T 21 5 **21 5**

LAMB, Alan (M) 0 0
H: 5 10 W: 11 00 b.Grimsby 20-12-85
Source: Scholar.
2004–05 Grimsby T 0 0
2005–06 Grimsby T 0 0

LUKIC, John (G) 0 0
H: 6 2 W: 13 00 b.Enfield 25-4-86
Source: Scholar.
2002–03 Nottingham F 0 0
2003–04 Nottingham F 0 0
2004–05 Nottingham F 0 0
2005–06 Grimsby T 0 0

McDERMOTT, John (D) 624 11
H: 5 7 W: 10 00 b.Middlesbrough 3-2-69
Source: Trainee.
1986–87 Grimsby T 13 0
1987–88 Grimsby T 28 1
1988–89 Grimsby T 38 1
1989–90 Grimsby T 39 0
1990–91 Grimsby T 43 0
1991–92 Grimsby T 39 1
1992–93 Grimsby T 38 2
1993–94 Grimsby T 26 0
1994–95 Grimsby T 12 0
1995–96 Grimsby T 28 1
1996–97 Grimsby T 29 1
1997–98 Grimsby T 41 1
1998–99 Grimsby T 37 0
1999–2000 Grimsby T 26 0
2000–01 Grimsby T 36 0
2001–02 Grimsby T 24 0
2002–03 Grimsby T 35 0
2003–04 Grimsby T 21 0
2004–05 Grimsby T 39 2
2005–06 Grimsby T 32 1 **624 11**

MILDENHALL, Steve (G) 161 1
H: 6 4 W: 14 01 b.Swindon 13-5-78
Source: Trainee.
1996–97 Swindon T 1 0
1997–98 Swindon T 4 0
1998–99 Swindon T 0 0
1999–2000 Swindon T 5 0
2000–01 Swindon T 23 0 **33 0**
2001–02 Notts Co 26 0
2002–03 Notts Co 21 0
2003–04 Notts Co 28 0
2004–05 Notts Co 1 0 **76 0**
2004–05 Oldham Ath 6 0 **6 0**
2005–06 Grimsby T 46 1 **46 1**

MURRAY, Robert (M) 0 0
H: 5 8 W: 9 00 b.Leamington Spa 11-7-88
Source: Scholar.
2004–05 Grimsby T 0 0
2005–06 Grimsby T 0 0

NEWEY, Tom (D) 121 5
H: 5 10 W: 10 02 b.Sheffield 31-10-82
Source: Scholar.
2000–01 Leeds U 0 0
2001–02 Leeds U 0 0
2002–03 Leeds U 0 0
2002–03 *Cambridge U* 6 0
2002–03 *Darlington* 7 1 **7 1**
2003–04 Leyton Orient 34 2
2004–05 Leyton Orient 20 1 **54 3**
2004–05 *Cambridge U* 16 0 **22 0**
2005–06 Grimsby T 38 1 **38 1**

NORTH, Danny (F) 2 0
H: 5 9 W: 12 08 b.Grimsby 7-9-87
Source: Scholar.
2004–05 Grimsby T 1 0
2005–06 Grimsby T 1 0 **2 0**

PALMER, Jermaine (F) 4 0
H: 6 1 W: 11 03 b.Nottingham 28-8-86
Source: Scholar.
2003–04 Stoke C 3 0
2004–05 Stoke C 1 0 **4 0**
2005–06 Grimsby T 0 0

PARKINSON, Andy (F) 270 33
H: 5 8 W: 10 12 b.Liverpool 27-5-79
Source: Liverpool Trainee.
1996–97 Tranmere R 0 0
1997–98 Tranmere R 18 1
1998–99 Tranmere R 29 2
1999–2000 Tranmere R 37 7
2000–01 Tranmere R 39 6
2001–02 Tranmere R 31 2
2002–03 Tranmere R 10 0 **164 18**
2003–04 Sheffield U 7 0 **7 0**
2003–04 *Notts Co* 14 3 **14 3**
2004–05 Grimsby T 45 8
2005–06 Grimsby T 40 4 **85 12**

REDDY, Michael (F) 155 37
H: 6 1 W: 11 07 b.Kilkenny City 24-3-80
Source: Kilkenny C. *Honours:* Eire Under-21.
1999–2000 Sunderland 8 1
2000–01 Sunderland 2 0
2000–01 *Swindon T* 18 4 **18 4**
2001–02 Sunderland 0 0
2001–02 *Hull C* 5 4 **5 4**
2001–02 *Barnsley* 0 0
2002–03 Sunderland 0 0
2002–03 *York C* 11 2 **11 2**
2002–03 *Sheffield W* 15 3
2003–04 Sunderland 0 0 **10 1**
2003–04 *Sheffield W* 12 1 **27 4**
2004–05 Grimsby T 40 9
2005–06 Grimsby T 44 13 **84 22**

RICHARDSON, Oliver (G) 0 0
H: 5 10 W: 12 00 b.Grimsby 12-2-87
Source: Scholar.
2004–05 Grimsby T 0 0
2005–06 Grimsby T 0 0

ROCK, Stephen (M) 0 0
b.Grimsby 30-11-87
Source: Scholar.
2004–05 Grimsby T 0 0
2005–06 Grimsby T 0 0

TAYLOR, Andy (M) 0 0
H: 6 2 W: 13 00 b.Grimsby 30-10-88
Source: Scholar.
2005–06 Grimsby T 0 0

TAYLOR, Tom (G) 0 0
Source: Viking, BAT Sports.
2005–06 Grimsby T 0 0

TONER, Ciaran (M) 118 7
H: 6 1 W: 12 02 b.Craigavon 30-6-81
Source: Trainee. *Honours:* Northern Ireland Under-21, 2 full caps.
1999–2000 Tottenham H 0 0
2000–01 Tottenham H 0 0
2001–02 Tottenham H 0 0
2001–02 *Peterborough U* 6 0 **6 0**
2001–02 Bristol R 6 0 **6 0**
2001–02 Leyton Orient 0 0
2002–03 Leyton Orient 25 1
2003–04 Leyton Orient 27 1 **52 2**
2004–05 Lincoln C 15 2 **15 2**
2004–05 *Cambridge U* 8 0 **8 0**
2005–06 Grimsby T 31 3 **31 3**

WARD, Andrew (M) 0 0
H: 6 0 W: 10 12 b.Grimsby 10-9-86
Source: Scholar.
2004–05 Grimsby T 0 0
2005–06 Grimsby T 0 0

WHITTLE, Justin (D) **344 4**
H: 6 1 W: 12 12 b.Derby 18-3-71
Source: Celtic.

1994–95	Stoke C	0	0		
1995–96	Stoke C	8	0		
1996–97	Stoke C	37	0		
1997–98	Stoke C	20	0		
1998–99	Stoke C	14	1	**79**	**1**
1998–99	Hull C	24	1		
1999–2000	Hull C	38	0		
2000–01	Hull C	38	0		
2001–02	Hull C	36	0		
2002–03	Hull C	39	1		
2003–04	Hull C	18	0	**193**	**2**
2004–05	Grimsby T	40	1		
2005–06	Grimsby T	32	0	**72**	**1**

WOODHOUSE, Curtis (M) **258 20**
H: 5 8 W: 11 00 b.Driffield 17-4-80
Source: Trainee. *Honours:* England Youth, Under-21.

1997–98	Sheffield U	9	0		
1998–99	Sheffield U	33	3		
1999–2000	Sheffield U	37	3		
2000–01	Sheffield U	25	0	**104**	**6**
2000–01	Birmingham C	17	2		
2001–02	Birmingham C	28	0		
2002–03	Birmingham C	3	0		
2002–03	*Rotherham U*	11	0	**11**	**0**
2003–04	Birmingham C	0	0	**48**	**2**
2003–04	Peterborough U	27	7		
2004–05	Peterborough U	34	4	**61**	**11**
2005–06	Hull C	18	0	**18**	**0**
2005–06	Grimsby T	16	1	**16**	**1**

HARTLEPOOL U (36)

APPLEBY, Andy (F) **15 2**
H: 5 10 W: 11 00 b.Seaham 11-10-85
Source: Scholar.

2004–05	Hartlepool U	15	2		
2005–06	Hartlepool U	0	0	**15**	**2**

BARRON, Micky (D) **299 3**
H: 5 11 W: 11 10 b.Chester-le-Street 22-12-74
Source: Trainee.

1992–93	Middlesbrough	0	0		
1993–94	Middlesbrough	2	0		
1994–95	Middlesbrough	0	0		
1995–96	Middlesbrough	1	0		
1996–97	Middlesbrough	0	0	**3**	**0**
1996–97	*Hartlepool U*	16	0		
1997–98	Hartlepool U	33	0		
1998–99	Hartlepool U	38	1		
1999–2000	Hartlepool U	40	0		
2000–01	Hartlepool U	28	0		
2001–02	Hartlepool U	39	1		
2002–03	Hartlepool U	42	0		
2003–04	Hartlepool U	32	1		
2004–05	Hartlepool U	13	0		
2005–06	Hartlepool U	15	0	**296**	**3**

BOYD, Adam (F) **158 57**
H: 5 9 W: 10 12 b.Hartlepool 25-5-82
Source: Scholarship.

1999–2000	Hartlepool U	4	1		
2000–01	Hartlepool U	5	0		
2001–02	Hartlepool U	29	9		
2002–03	Hartlepool U	22	5		
2003–04	Hartlepool U	18	12		
2003–04	*Boston U*	14	4	**14**	**4**
2004–05	Hartlepool U	45	22		
2005–06	Hartlepool U	21	4	**144**	**53**

BRACKSTONE, John (D) **17 0**
H: 6 0 W: 11 06 b.Hartlepool 9-2-85
Source: Scholar.

2003–04	Hartlepool U	6	0		
2004–05	Hartlepool U	9	0		
2005–06	Hartlepool U	2	0	**17**	**0**

BROWN, James (F) **4 1**
H: 5 11 W: 11 00 b.Newcastle 3-1-87
Source: Cramlington Jun.

2004–05	Hartlepool U	0	0		
2005–06	Hartlepool U	4	1	**4**	**1**

BULLOCK, Lee (M) **234 34**
H: 6 0 W: 11 04 b.Stockton 22-5-81
Source: Trainee.

1999–2000	York C	24	0		
2000–01	York C	33	3		
2001–02	York C	40	8		
2002–03	York C	39	6		
2003–04	York C	35	7	**171**	**24**
2003–04	*Cardiff C*	11	3		
2004–05	Cardiff C	21	3	**32**	**6**
2005–06	Hartlepool U	31	4	**31**	**4**

BUTLER, Thomas (M) **88 2**
H: 5 7 W: 12 00 b.Dublin 25-4-81
Source: Trainee. *Honours:* Eire Under-21, 2 full caps.

1998–99	Sunderland	0	0		
1999–2000	Sunderland	1	0		
2000–01	Sunderland	4	0		
2000–01	*Darlington*	8	0	**8**	**0**
2001–02	Sunderland	7	0		
2002–03	Sunderland	7	0		
2003–04	Sunderland	12	0	**31**	**0**
2004–05	Dunfermline Ath	12	0	**12**	**0**
2004–05	Hartlepool U	9	1		
2005–06	Hartlepool U	28	1	**37**	**2**

CLARK, Ben (D) **65 0**
H: 6 1 W: 13 11 b.Shotley Bridge 24-1-83
Source: Manchester U Trainee. *Honours:* England Youth, Under-20.

2000–01	Sunderland	0	0		
2001–02	Sunderland	0	0		
2002–03	Sunderland	1	0		
2003–04	Sunderland	5	0		
2004–05	Sunderland	2	0	**8**	**0**
2004–05	Hartlepool U	25	0		
2005–06	Hartlepool U	32	0	**57**	**0**

CLARKE, Darrell (M) **286 43**
H: 5 10 W: 11 05 b.Mansfield 16-12-77
Source: Trainee.

1995–96	Mansfield T	3	0		
1996–97	Mansfield T	19	2		
1997–98	Mansfield T	35	4		
1998–99	Mansfield T	33	5		
1999–2000	Mansfield T	39	7		
2000–01	Mansfield T	32	6	**161**	**24**
2001–02	Hartlepool U	33	7		
2002–03	Hartlepool U	45	7		
2003–04	Hartlepool U	33	5		
2004–05	Hartlepool U	0	0		
2004–05	*Stockport Co*	1	0	**1**	**0**
2005–06	Hartlepool U	12	0	**123**	**19**
2005–06	*Port Vale*	1	0	**1**	**0**

CRADDOCK, Darren (D) **24 0**
H: 6 0 W: 12 02 b.Bishop Auckland 23-2-85
Source: Scholar.

2003–04	Hartlepool U	10	0		
2004–05	Hartlepool U	10	0		
2005–06	Hartlepool U	4	0	**24**	**0**

DALY, Jon (F) **154 21**
H: 6 3 W: 12 00 b.Dublin 8-1-83
Source: Trainee. *Honours:* Eire Under-21.

1999–2000	Stockport Co	4	0		
2000–01	Stockport Co	0	0		
2001–02	Stockport Co	13	1		
2002–03	Stockport Co	35	7		
2003–04	Stockport Co	25	3		
2003–04	Bury	7	1		
2004–05	Stockport Co	14	3	**91**	**14**
2004–05	*Grimsby T*	3	1	**3**	**1**
2004–05	Hartlepool U	12	1		
2005–06	Hartlepool U	30	2	**42**	**3**
2005–06	*Bury*	11	2	**18**	**3**

FOLEY, David (F) **14 0**
H: 5 4 W: 8 09 b.South Shields 12-5-87
Source: Scholar.

2003–04	Hartlepool U	1	0		
2004–05	Hartlepool U	2	0		
2005–06	Hartlepool U	11	0	**14**	**0**

HUMPHREYS, Richie (M) **319 35**
H: 5 11 W: 12 07 b.Sheffield 30-11-77
Source: Trainee. *Honours:* England Youth, Under-21.

1995–96	Sheffield W	5	0		
1996–97	Sheffield W	29	3		
1997–98	Sheffield W	7	0		
1998–99	Sheffield W	19	1		
1999–2000	Sheffield W	0	0		
1999–2000	*Scunthorpe U*	6	2	**6**	**2**
1999–2000	*Cardiff C*	9	2	**9**	**2**
2000–01	Sheffield W	7	0	**67**	**4**
2000–01	Cambridge U	7	3	**7**	**3**
2001–02	Hartlepool U	46	5		
2002–03	Hartlepool U	46	11		
2003–04	Hartlepool U	46	3		
2004–05	Hartlepool U	46	3		
2005–06	Hartlepool U	46	2	**230**	**24**

ISTEAD, Steven (M) **64 3**
H: 5 8 W: 11 04 b.South Shields 23-4-86
Source: Scholar.

2002–03	Hartlepool U	6	0		
2003–04	Hartlepool U	31	1		
2004–05	Hartlepool U	17	0		
2005–06	Hartlepool U	10	2	**64**	**3**

JONES, Carl (D) **1 0**
H: 6 1 W: 12 02 b.Sunderland 3-9-86
Source: Chester-Le-Street.

2005–06	Hartlepool U	1	0	**1**	**0**

KONSTANTOPOULOS, Dimitrios (G) **71 0**
H: 6 4 W: 14 02 b.Kalamata 29-11-78
Source: Farense.

2003–04	Hartlepool U	0	0		
2004–05	Hartlepool U	25	0		
2005–06	Hartlepool U	46	0	**71**	**0**

LLEWELLYN, Chris (F) **276 35**
H: 5 11 W: 11 06 b.Swansea 29-8-79
Source: Trainee. *Honours:* Wales Youth, Under-21, B, 4 full caps.

1996–97	Norwich C	0	0		
1997–98	Norwich C	15	4		
1998–99	Norwich C	31	2		
1999–2000	Norwich C	36	3		
2000–01	Norwich C	42	8		
2001–02	Norwich C	13	0		
2002–03	Norwich C	5	0	**142**	**17**
2002–03	*Bristol R*	14	3	**14**	**3**
2003–04	Wrexham	46	8		
2004–05	Wrexham	45	7	**91**	**15**
2005–06	Hartlepool U	29	0	**29**	**0**

MAIDENS, Michael (M) **21 1**
H: 5 11 W: 11 04 b.Middlesbrough 7-5-87
Source: Scholar.

2004–05	Hartlepool U	1	0		
2005–06	Hartlepool U	20	1	**21**	**1**

NELSON, Michael (D) **198 14**
H: 6 2 W: 13 03 b.Gateshead 15-3-82

2000–01	Bury	2	1		
2001–02	Bury	31	2		
2002–03	Bury	39	5	**72**	**8**
2003–04	Hartlepool U	40	3		
2004–05	Hartlepool U	43	1		
2005–06	Hartlepool U	43	2	**126**	**6**

PORTER, Joel (F) **182 55**
H: 5 9 W: 11 13 b.Adelaide 25-12-78
Honours: Australia 4 full caps, 5 goals.

1998–99	West Adelaide	20	3	**20**	**3**
2000–01	Melbrne Knights	30	12		
2001–02	Melbrne Knights	26	12	**56**	**24**
2002–03	Sydney Olympic	32	8	**32**	**8**
2003–04	Hartlepool U	27	3		
2004–05	Hartlepool U	39	14		
2005–06	Hartlepool U	8	3	**74**	**20**

PROCTOR, Michael (F) **178 39**
H: 5 11 W: 11 11 b.Sunderland 3-10-80
Source: Trainee.

1997–98	Sunderland	0	0		
1998–99	Sunderland	0	0		
1999–2000	Sunderland	0	0		
2000–01	Sunderland	0	0		
2000–01	*Halifax T*	12	4	**12**	**4**
2001–02	Sunderland	0	0		
2001–02	*York C*	41	14	**41**	**14**
2002–03	Sunderland	21	2		
2002–03	*Bradford C*	12	4	**12**	**4**
2003–04	Sunderland	17	1	**38**	**3**
2003–04	Rotherham U	17	6		
2004–05	Rotherham U	28	1	**45**	**7**

2004–05 *Swindon T* 4 2 **4 2**
2005–06 Hartlepool U 26 5 **26 5**

PROVETT, Jim (G) 66 0
H: 6 0 W: 13 04 b.Stockton 22-12-82
Source: Trainee.
1999–2000 Hartlepool U 0 0
2000–01 Hartlepool U 0 0
2001–02 Hartlepool U 0 0
2002–03 Hartlepool U 0 0
2003–04 Hartlepool U 45 0
2004–05 Hartlepool U 21 0
2005–06 Hartlepool U 0 0 **66 0**

ROBERTSON, Hugh (D) 218 24
H: 5 9 W: 13 11 b.Aberdeen 19-3-75
Source: Lewis U. *Honours:* Scotland Under-21.
1993–94 Aberdeen 8 0
1994–95 Aberdeen 3 2
1995–96 Aberdeen 11 0
1996–97 Aberdeen 0 0 **22 2**
1996–97 Dundee 15 1
1997–98 Dundee 0 0
1997–98 *Brechin C* 7 0 **7 0**
1998–99 Dundee 10 0
1998–99 Inverness CT 12 1 **12 1**
1999–2000 Dundee 0 0
2000–01 Dundee 0 0 **25 1**
2000–01 Ayr U 8 1 **8 1**
2000–01 Ross Co 16 1
2001–02 Ross Co 36 6
2002–03 Ross Co 32 4
2003–04 Ross Co 20 2 **104 13**
2003–04 Hartlepool U 18 4
2004–05 Hartlepool U 20 2
2005–06 Hartlepool U 2 0 **40 6**

ROBSON, Matty (D) 69 4
H: 5 10 W: 11 02 b.Durham 23-1-85
Source: Scholar.
2002–03 Hartlepool U 0 0
2003–04 Hartlepool U 23 1
2004–05 Hartlepool U 27 2
2005–06 Hartlepool U 19 1 **69 4**

STRACHAN, Gavin (M) 109 7
H: 5 10 W: 11 07 b.Aberdeen 23-12-78
Source: Trainee. *Honours:* Scotland Youth, Under-21.
1996–97 Coventry C 0 0
1997–98 Coventry C 9 0
1998–99 Coventry C 0 0
1998–99 *Dundee* 6 0 **6 0**
1999–2000 Coventry C 3 0
2000–01 Coventry C 2 0
2001–02 Coventry C 1 0
2002–03 Coventry C 1 0 **16 0**
2002–03 *Peterborough U* 2 0 **2 0**
2002–03 Southend U 7 0 **7 0**
2003–04 Hartlepool U 36 5
2004–05 Hartlepool U 29 1
2005–06 Hartlepool U 9 1 **74 7**
2005–06 *Stockport Co* 4 0 **4 0**

SWEENEY, Anthony (M) 96 19
H: 6 0 W: 11 07 b.Stockton 5-9-83
Source: Scholar.
2001–02 Hartlepool U 2 0
2002–03 Hartlepool U 4 0
2003–04 Hartlepool U 11 1
2004–05 Hartlepool U 44 13
2005–06 Hartlepool U 35 5 **96 19**

TINKLER, Mark (M) 376 43
H: 6 2 W: 12 00 b.Bishop Auckland 24-10-74
Source: Trainee. *Honours:* England Schools, Youth.
1991–92 Leeds U 0 0
1992–93 Leeds U 7 0
1993–94 Leeds U 3 0
1994–95 Leeds U 3 0
1995–96 Leeds U 9 0
1996–97 Leeds U 3 0 **25 0**
1996–97 York C 9 1
1997–98 York C 44 5
1998–99 York C 37 2
1999–2000 York C 0 0 **90 8**
1999–2000 Southend U 41 0
2000–01 Southend U 15 1 **56 1**
2000–01 Hartlepool U 28 3
2001–02 Hartlepool U 40 9
2002–03 Hartlepool U 45 13
2003–04 Hartlepool U 44 6
2004–05 Hartlepool U 33 2
2005–06 Hartlepool U 15 1 **205 34**

TURNBULL, Stephen (M) 23 0
H: 5 10 W: 11 00 b.South Shields 7-1-87
Source: Scholar.
2004–05 Hartlepool U 2 0
2005–06 Hartlepool U 21 0 **23 0**

WILKINSON, Jack (F) 7 2
H: 5 8 W: 10 08 b.Beverley 12-9-85
Source: Scholar.
2003–04 Hartlepool U 4 2
2004–05 Hartlepool U 3 0
2005–06 Hartlepool U 0 0 **7 2**

WILKINSON, Neil (D) 0 0
H: 6 0 W: 12 06 b.Middlesbrough 12-10-85
Source: Scholar.
2005–06 Hartlepool U 0 0

WILLIAMS, Darren (D) 278 4
H: 5 11 W: 11 00 b.Middlesbrough 28-4-77
Source: Trainee. *Honours:* England Under-21, B.
1994–95 York C 1 0
1995–96 York C 18 0
1996–97 York C 1 0 **20 0**
1996–97 Sunderland 11 2
1997–98 Sunderland 36 2
1998–99 Sunderland 25 0
1999–2000 Sunderland 25 0
2000–01 Sunderland 28 0
2001–02 Sunderland 28 0
2002–03 Sunderland 16 0
2003–04 Sunderland 29 0
2004–05 Sunderland 1 0 **199 4**
2004–05 Cardiff C 20 0 **20 0**
2005–06 Hartlepool U 39 0 **39 0**

WILLIAMS, Eifion (F) 279 68
H: 5 11 W: 11 02 b.Bangor 15-11-75
Source: Barry T. *Honours:* Wales B.
1998–99 Torquay U 7 5
1999–2000 Torquay U 42 9
2000–01 Torquay U 37 9
2001–02 Torquay U 25 1 **111 24**
2001–02 Hartlepool U 8 4
2002–03 Hartlepool U 45 15
2003–04 Hartlepool U 41 13
2004–05 Hartlepool U 38 5
2005–06 Hartlepool U 36 7 **168 44**

WINTER, James (G) 0 0
H: 6 0 W: 12 00 b.Durham 18-9-85
Source: Scholar.
2005–06 Hartlepool U 0 0

HUDDERSFIELD T (37)

ABBOTT, Pawel (F) 135 55
H: 6 2 W: 13 10 b.York 5-5-82
Source: LKS Lodz. *Honours:* Poland Under-21.
2000–01 Preston NE 0 0
2001–02 Preston NE 0 0
2002–03 Preston NE 16 4
2002–03 *Bury* 17 6 **17 6**
2003–04 Preston NE 9 2 **25 6**
2003–04 Huddersfield T 13 5
2004–05 Huddersfield T 44 26
2005–06 Huddersfield T 36 12 **93 43**

ADAMS, Danny (D) 232 2
H: 5 8 W: 13 08 b.Manchester 3-1-76
Source: Altrincham.
2000–01 Macclesfield T 37 0
2001–02 Macclesfield T 39 0
2002–03 Macclesfield T 45 1
2003–04 Macclesfield T 27 0 **148 1**
2003–04 Stockport Co 12 0
2004–05 Stockport Co 27 1 **39 1**
2004–05 Huddersfield T 5 0
2005–06 Huddersfield T 40 0 **45 0**

AHMED, Adnan (M) 32 1
H: 5 10 W: 11 02 b.Burnley 7-6-84
Source: Scholar.
2003–04 Huddersfield T 1 0
2004–05 Huddersfield T 18 1
2005–06 Huddersfield T 13 0 **32 1**

BOOTH, Andy (F) 439 138
H: 6 0 W: 12 06 b.Huddersfield 6-12-73
Source: Trainee. *Honours:* England Under-21.
1991–92 Huddersfield T 3 0
1992–93 Huddersfield T 5 2
1993–94 Huddersfield T 26 10
1994–95 Huddersfield T 46 26
1995–96 Huddersfield T 43 16
1996–97 Sheffield W 35 10
1997–98 Sheffield W 23 7
1998–99 Sheffield W 34 6
1999–2000 Sheffield W 23 2
2000–01 Sheffield W 18 3 **133 28**
2000–01 *Tottenham H* 4 0 **4 0**
2000–01 Huddersfield T 8 3
2001–02 Huddersfield T 36 11
2002–03 Huddersfield T 33 6
2003–04 Huddersfield T 37 13
2004–05 Huddersfield T 29 10
2005–06 Huddersfield T 36 13 **302 110**

BRANDON, Chris (M) 234 28
H: 5 8 W: 10 00 b.Bradford 7-4-76
Source: Bradford PA.
1999–2000 Torquay U 42 5
2000–01 Torquay U 2 0
2001–02 Torquay U 27 3 **71 8**
2002–03 Chesterfield 36 7
2003–04 Chesterfield 43 4 **79 11**
2004–05 Huddersfield T 44 6
2005–06 Huddersfield T 40 3 **84 9**

CARSS, Tony (M) 296 12
H: 5 11 W: 12 00 b.Alnwick 31-3-76
Source: Bradford C Trainee.
1994–95 Blackburn R 0 0
1995–96 Darlington 28 2
1996–97 Darlington 29 0 **57 2**
1997–98 Cardiff C 42 1 **42 1**
1998–99 Chesterfield 4 0
1999–2000 Chesterfield 31 1 **35 1**
2000–01 Carlisle U 7 0 **7 0**
2000–01 Oldham Ath 35 2
2001–02 Oldham Ath 14 1
2002–03 Oldham Ath 26 2 **75 5**
2003–04 Huddersfield T 36 2
2004–05 Huddersfield T 27 1
2005–06 Huddersfield T 17 0 **80 3**

CLARKE, Nathan (D) 148 2
H: 6 2 W: 12 00 b.Halifax 30-11-83
Source: Scholar.
2001–02 Huddersfield T 36 1
2002–03 Huddersfield T 3 0
2003–04 Huddersfield T 26 1
2004–05 Huddersfield T 37 0
2005–06 Huddersfield T 46 0 **148 2**

CLARKE, Tom (D) 29 1
H: 6 0 W: 11 02 b.Halifax 21-12-87
Source: Scholar. *Honours:* England Youth.
2004–05 Huddersfield T 12 0
2005–06 Huddersfield T 17 1 **29 1**

COLLINS, Michael (M) 25 1
H: 6 0 W: 11 00 b.Halifax 30-4-86
Source: Scholar. *Honours:* Eire Youth.
2004–05 Huddersfield T 8 0
2005–06 Huddersfield T 17 1 **25 1**

EASTWOOD, Simon (G) 0 0
H: 6 2 W: 13 00 b.Luton 26-6-89
Source: Scholar.
2005–06 Huddersfield T 0 0

FOWLER, Lee (M) 63 0
H: 5 7 W: 10 00 b.Cardiff 10-6-83
Source: Scholar. *Honours:* Wales Youth, Under-21.
2000–01 Coventry C 0 0
2001–02 Coventry C 13 0
2002–03 Coventry C 1 0
2003–04 Coventry C 0 0 **14 0**
2003–04 Huddersfield T 29 0

2004–05 Huddersfield T 20 0
2005–06 Huddersfield T 0 0 **49 0**

HAND, James (M) 0 0
H: 5 9 W: 11 00 b.Drogheda 22-10-86
Source: Scholar. *Honours:* Eire Youth, Under-21.
2005–06 Huddersfield T 0 0

HARDY, Aaron (M) 0 0
H: 5 8 W: 11 04 b.Pontefract 26-5-86
Source: Scholar.
2005–06 Huddersfield T 0 0

HOLDSWORTH, Andy (D) 118 1
H: 5 9 W: 11 02 b.Pontefract 29-1-84
Source: Scholar.
2003–04 Huddersfield T 36 0
2004–05 Huddersfield T 40 0
2005–06 Huddersfield T 42 1 **118 1**

HUDSON, Mark (M) 142 13
H: 5 10 W: 11 03 b.Bishop Auckland 24-10-80
Source: Trainee.
1999–2000 Middlesbrough 0 0
2000–01 Middlesbrough 3 0
2001–02 Middlesbrough 2 0
2002–03 Middlesbrough 0 0 **5 0**
2002–03 *Carlisle U* 15 1 **15 1**
2002–03 Chesterfield 24 3
2003–04 Chesterfield 35 2
2004–05 Chesterfield 34 4 **93 9**
2005–06 Huddersfield T 29 3 **29 3**

McALISKEY, John (F) 38 6
H: 6 4 W: 12 01 b.Huddersfield 2-9-84
Source: Scholar. *Honours:* Eire Under-21.
2003–04 Huddersfield T 8 4
2004–05 Huddersfield T 18 2
2005–06 Huddersfield T 9 0 **35 6**
2005–06 *Torquay U* 3 0 **3 0**

McCOMBE, John (D) 7 0
H: 6 2 W: 13 00 b.Pontefract 7-5-85
Source: Scholar.
2002–03 Huddersfield T 1 0
2003–04 Huddersfield T 0 0
2004–05 Huddersfield T 5 0
2005–06 Huddersfield T 1 0 **7 0**
2005–06 *Torquay U* 0 0

McINTOSH, Martin (D) 420 47
H: 6 3 W: 13 07 b.East Kilbride 19-3-71
Honours: Scotland B.
1988–89 St Mirren 2 0
1989–90 St Mirren 2 0
1990–91 St Mirren 0 0 **4 0**
1991–92 Clydebank 28 5
1992–93 Clydebank 33 4
1993–94 Clydebank 4 1 **65 10**
1993–94 Hamilton A 13 2
1994–95 Hamilton A 30 2
1995–96 Hamilton A 23 1
1996–97 Hamilton A 33 7 **99 12**
1997–98 Stockport Co 38 2
1998–99 Stockport Co 41 3
1999–2000 Stockport Co 20 0 **99 5**
1999–2000 Hibernian 9 0
2000–01 Hibernian 0 0
2001–02 Hibernian 0 0 **9 0**
2001–02 Rotherham U 39 4
2002–03 Rotherham U 42 5
2003–04 Rotherham U 18 2
2004–05 Rotherham U 23 5 **122 16**
2005–06 Huddersfield T 22 4 **22 4**

MENDES, Junior (F) 270 47
H: 5 10 W: 11 00 b.Balham 15-9-76
Source: Trainee. *Honours:* Montserrat full caps.
1995–96 Chelsea 0 0
1995–96 St Mirren 0 0
1996–97 St Mirren 36 3
1997–98 St Mirren 29 9
1998–99 St Mirren 22 4
1998–99 *Carlisle U* 6 1 **6 1**
1999–2000 St Mirren 33 5
2000–01 Dunfermline Ath 13 0 **13 0**
2001–02 Rushden & D 0 0
2002–03 St Mirren 17 6 **137 27**
2002–03 Mansfield T 18 1
2003–04 Mansfield T 39 11 **57 12**
2004–05 Huddersfield T 25 5
2005–06 Huddersfield T 5 0 **30 5**
2005–06 *Northampton T* 12 2 **12 2**
2005–06 *Grimsby T* 15 0 **15 0**

MIRFIN, David (M) 94 7
H: 6 3 W: 13 00 b.Sheffield 18-4-85
Source: Scholar.
2002–03 Huddersfield T 1 0
2003–04 Huddersfield T 21 2
2004–05 Huddersfield T 41 4
2005–06 Huddersfield T 31 1 **94 7**

RACHUBKA, Paul (G) 107 0
H: 6 1 W: 13 05 b.San Luis Opispo 21-5-81
Source: Trainee. *Honours:* England Youth.
1999–2000 Manchester U 0 0
2000–01 Manchester U 1 0
2001–02 Manchester U 0 0 **1 0**
2001–02 *Oldham Ath* 16 0 **16 0**
2001–02 Charlton Ath 0 0
2002–03 Charlton Ath 0 0
2003–04 Charlton Ath 0 0
2003–04 *Huddersfield T* 13 0
2004–05 Charlton Ath 0 0
2004–05 *Milton Keynes D* 4 0 **4 0**
2004–05 *Northampton T* 10 0 **10 0**
2004–05 Huddersfield T 29 0
2005–06 Huddersfield T 34 0 **76 0**

SCHOFIELD, Danny (F) 188 32
H: 5 10 W: 11 02 b.Doncaster 10-4-80
Source: Brodsworth.
1998–99 Huddersfield T 1 0
1999–2000 Huddersfield T 2 0
2000–01 Huddersfield T 1 0
2001–02 Huddersfield T 40 8
2002–03 Huddersfield T 30 2
2003–04 Huddersfield T 40 8
2004–05 Huddersfield T 33 5
2005–06 Huddersfield T 41 9 **188 32**

SENIOR, Philip (G) 53 0
H: 5 11 W: 11 00 b.Huddersfield 30-10-82
Source: Trainee.
1999–2000 Huddersfield T 0 0
2000–01 Huddersfield T 0 0
2001–02 Huddersfield T 0 0
2002–03 Huddersfield T 18 0
2003–04 Huddersfield T 16 0
2004–05 Huddersfield T 6 0
2005–06 Huddersfield T 13 0 **53 0**

TAYLOR-FLETCHER, Gary (F) 149 38
H: 6 0 W: 11 00 b.Liverpool 4-6-81
Source: Northwich Vic. *Honours:* England Schools.
2000–01 Hull C 5 0 **5 0**
2001–02 Leyton Orient 9 0
2002–03 Leyton Orient 12 1 **21 1**
2003–04 Lincoln C 42 16
2004–05 Lincoln C 38 11 **80 27**
2005–06 Huddersfield T 43 10 **43 10**

WALLS, David (D) 0 0
H: 6 0 W: 12 00 b.Leeds 22-11-86
Source: Scholar.
2005–06 Huddersfield T 0 0

WORTHINGTON, Jon (M) 141 10
H: 5 9 W: 11 05 b.Dewsbury 16-4-83
Source: Scholar.
2001–02 Huddersfield T 0 0
2002–03 Huddersfield T 22 0
2003–04 Huddersfield T 39 3
2004–05 Huddersfield T 39 3
2005–06 Huddersfield T 41 4 **141 10**

YOUNG, Matthew (M) 2 0
H: 5 8 W: 11 03 b.Woodlesford 25-10-85
Source: Scholar.
2005–06 Huddersfield T 2 0 **2 0**

HULL C (38)

ANDREWS, Keith (M) 121 3
H: 6 0 W: 12 04 b.Dublin 13-9-80
Source: Trainee. *Honours:* Eire Youth.
1997–98 Wolverhampton W 0 0
1998–99 Wolverhampton W 0 0
1999–2000 Wolverhampton W 2 0
2000–01 Wolverhampton W 22 0
2000–01 *Oxford U* 4 1 **4 1**
2001–02 Wolverhampton W 11 0
2002–03 Wolverhampton W 9 0
2003–04 Wolverhampton W 1 0
2003–04 *Stoke C* 16 0 **16 0**
2003–04 *Walsall* 10 2 **10 2**
2004–05 Wolverhampton W 20 0 **65 0**
2005–06 Hull C 26 0 **26 0**

ASHBEE, Ian (M) 320 15
H: 6 1 W: 13 07 b.Birmingham 6-9-76
Source: Trainee. *Honours:* England Youth.
1994–95 Derby Co 1 0
1995–96 Derby Co 0 0
1996–97 Derby Co 0 0 **1 0**
1996–97 Cambridge U 18 0
1997–98 Cambridge U 27 1
1998–99 Cambridge U 31 4
1999–2000 Cambridge U 45 1
2000–01 Cambridge U 44 3
2001–02 Cambridge U 38 2 **203 11**
2002–03 Hull C 31 1
2003–04 Hull C 39 2
2004–05 Hull C 40 1
2005–06 Hull C 6 0 **116 4**

ASPDEN, Curtis (G) 0 0
H: 6 1 W: 11 12 b.Blackburn 16-11-87
Source: Scholar.
2005–06 Hull C 0 0

BARMBY, Nick (F) 373 67
H: 5 7 W: 11 03 b.Hull 11-2-74
Source: Trainee. *Honours:* England Schools, Youth, Under-21, B, 23 full caps, 4 goals.
1991–92 Tottenham H 0 0
1992–93 Tottenham H 22 6
1993–94 Tottenham H 27 5
1994–95 Tottenham H 38 9 **87 20**
1995–96 Middlesbrough 32 7
1996–97 Middlesbrough 10 1 **42 8**
1996–97 Everton 25 4
1997–98 Everton 30 2
1998–99 Everton 24 3
1999–2000 Everton 37 9 **116 18**
2000–01 Liverpool 26 2
2001–02 Liverpool 6 0 **32 2**
2002–03 Leeds U 19 4
2003–04 *Nottingham F* 6 1 **6 1**
2003–04 Leeds U 6 0 **25 4**
2004–05 Hull C 39 9
2005–06 Hull C 26 5 **65 14**

BURGESS, Ben (F) 165 61
H: 6 3 W: 14 04 b.Buxton 9-11-81
Source: Trainee. *Honours:* Eire Under-21.
1998–99 Blackburn R 0 0
1999–2000 Blackburn R 2 0
2000–01 Blackburn R 0 0
2000–01 Northern Spirit 27 16 **27 16**
2001–02 Blackburn R 0 0 **2 0**
2001–02 *Brentford* 43 17 **43 17**
2002–03 Stockport Co 19 4 **19 4**
2002–03 *Oldham Ath* 7 0 **7 0**
2002–03 Hull C 7 4
2003–04 Hull C 44 18
2004–05 Hull C 2 0
2005–06 Hull C 14 2 **67 24**

COLES, Danny (D) 157 5
H: 6 1 W: 11 05 b.Bristol 31-10-81
Source: Scholarship.
1999–2000 Bristol C 1 0
2000–01 Bristol C 2 0
2001–02 Bristol C 23 0
2002–03 Bristol C 39 2
2003–04 Bristol C 45 2
2004–05 Bristol C 38 1 **148 5**
2005–06 Hull C 9 0 **9 0**

COLLINS, Sam (D) 271 13
H: 6 2 W: 14 03 b.Pontefract 5-6-77
Source: Trainee.
1994–95 Huddersfield T 0 0
1995–96 Huddersfield T 0 0
1996–97 Huddersfield T 4 0
1997–98 Huddersfield T 10 0
1998–99 Huddersfield T 23 0 **37 0**
1999–2000 Bury 19 0

2000–01 Bury 34 2
2001–02 Bury 29 0 **82** **2**
2002–03 Port Vale 44 5
2003–04 Port Vale 43 4
2004–05 Port Vale 33 2
2005–06 Port Vale 15 0 **135** **11**
2005–06 Hull C 17 0 **17** **0**

CORT, Leon (D) **223** **21**
H: 6 3 W: 13 01 b.Bermondsey 11-9-79
Source: Dulwich H.
1997–98 Millwall 0 0
1998–99 Millwall 0 0
1999–2000 Millwall 0 0
2000–01 Millwall 0 0
2001–02 Southend U 45 4
2002–03 Southend U 46 6
2003–04 Southend U 46 1 **137** **11**
2004–05 Hull C 44 6
2005–06 Hull C 42 4 **86** **10**

DAWSON, Andy (D) **280** **11**
H: 5 9 W: 11 02 b.Northallerton 20-10-78
Source: Trainee.
1995–96 Nottingham F 0 0
1996–97 Nottingham F 0 0
1997–98 Nottingham F 0 0
1998–99 Nottingham F 0 0
1998–99 Scunthorpe U 24 0
1999–2000 Scunthorpe U 43 2
2000–01 Scunthorpe U 41 4
2001–02 Scunthorpe U 44 0
2002–03 Scunthorpe U 43 2 **195** **8**
2003–04 Hull C 33 3
2004–05 Hull C 34 0
2005–06 Hull C 18 0 **85** **3**

DELANEY, Damien (D) **194** **5**
H: 6 3 W: 14 00 b.Cork 20-7-81
Source: Cork C.
2000–01 Leicester C 5 0
2001–02 Leicester C 3 0
2001–02 *Stockport Co* 12 1 **12** **1**
2001–02 *Huddersfield T* 2 0 **2** **0**
2002–03 Leicester C 0 0 **8** **0**
2002–03 *Mansfield T* 7 0 **7** **0**
2002–03 Hull C 30 1
2003–04 Hull C 46 2
2004–05 Hull C 43 1
2005–06 Hull C 46 0 **165** **4**

DUFFY, Darryl (F) **72** **29**
H: 5 11 W: 12 01 b.Glasgow 16-4-84
Honours: Scotland Under-21, B.
2003–04 Rangers 1 0 **1** **0**
2004–05 Falkirk 35 17
2005–06 Falkirk 21 9 **56** **26**
2005–06 Hull C 15 3 **15** **3**

DUKE, Matt (G) **12** **0**
H: 6 5 W: 13 04 b.Sheffield 16-7-77
Source: Alfreton T.
1999–2000 Sheffield U 0 0
2000–01 Sheffield U 0 0
2001–02 Sheffield U 0 0
2004–05 Hull C 2 0
2005–06 Hull C 2 0 **4** **0**
2005–06 *Stockport Co* 3 0 **3** **0**
2005–06 *Wycombe W* 5 0 **5** **0**

EDGE, Roland (D) **124** **1**
H: 5 9 W: 11 07 b.Gillingham 25-11-78
Source: Trainee.
1997–98 Gillingham 0 0
1998–99 Gillingham 8 0
1999–2000 Gillingham 26 1
2000–01 Gillingham 20 0
2001–02 Gillingham 14 0
2002–03 Gillingham 34 0
2003–04 Gillingham 0 0 **102** **1**
2004–05 Hull C 14 0
2005–06 Hull C 8 0 **22** **0**

ELLIOTT, Stuart (M) **320** **109**
H: 5 10 W: 11 09 b.Belfast 23-7-78
Honours: Northern Ireland Under-21, 34 full caps, 4 goals.
1994–95 Glentoran 0 0
1995–96 Glentoran 1 0
1996–97 Glentoran 8 1
1997–98 Glentoran 22 5
1998–99 Glentoran 31 7
1999–2000 Glentoran 34 16 **96** **29**
2000–01 Motherwell 33 10
2001–02 Motherwell 37 10 **70** **20**
2002–03 Hull C 36 12
2003–04 Hull C 42 14
2004–05 Hull C 36 27
2005–06 Hull C 40 7 **154** **60**

ELLISON, Kevin (M) **123** **13**
H: 6 0 W: 12 00 b.Liverpool 23-2-79
Source: Altrincham.
2000–01 Leicester C 1 0
2001–02 Leicester C 0 0 **1** **0**
2001–02 Stockport Co 11 0
2002–03 Stockport Co 23 1
2003–04 Stockport Co 14 1 **48** **2**
2003–04 *Lincoln C* 11 0 **11** **0**
2004–05 Chester C 24 9 **24** **9**
2004–05 Hull C 16 1
2005–06 Hull C 23 1 **39** **2**

FAGAN, Craig (F) **123** **27**
H: 5 11 W: 11 11 b.Birmingham 11-12-82
Source: Scholar.
2001–02 Birmingham C 0 0
2002–03 Birmingham C 1 0
2002–03 *Bristol C* 6 1 **6** **1**
2003–04 Birmingham C 0 0 **1** **0**
2003–04 Colchester U 37 9
2004–05 Colchester U 26 8 **63** **17**
2004–05 Hull C 12 4
2005–06 Hull C 41 5 **53** **9**

FRANCE, Ryan (M) **94** **6**
H: 5 11 W: 11 11 b.Sheffield 13-12-80
Source: Alfreton T.
2003–04 Hull C 28 2
2004–05 Hull C 31 2
2005–06 Hull C 35 2 **94** **6**

FRY, Russell (M) **2** **0**
H: 6 0 W: 12 01 b.Hull 4-12-85
Source: Scholar. *Honours:* England Under-20.
2002–03 Hull C 0 0
2003–04 Hull C 0 0
2004–05 Hull C 1 0
2005–06 Hull C 1 0 **2** **0**

GREEN, Stuart (M) **163** **29**
H: 5 10 W: 11 01 b.Whitehaven 15-6-81
Source: Trainee.
1999–2000 Newcastle U 0 0
2000–01 Newcastle U 0 0
2001–02 Newcastle U 0 0
2001–02 *Carlisle U* 16 3
2002–03 Newcastle U 0 0
2002–03 Hull C 28 6
2002–03 *Carlisle U* 10 2 **26** **5**
2003–04 Hull C 42 6
2004–05 Hull C 29 8
2005–06 Hull C 38 4 **137** **24**

LEITE, Sergio (G) **0** **0**
H: 5 11 W: 12 08 b.Oporto 16-8-79
Source: Boavista. *Honours:* Portugal Under-21.
2003–04 Charlton Ath 0 0
2004–05 Charlton Ath 0 0
2005–06 Hull C 0 0

LYNCH, Mark (D) **47** **0**
H: 5 11 W: 11 03 b.Manchester 2-9-81
Source: Trainee.
1999–2000 Manchester U 0 0
2000–01 Manchester U 0 0
2001–02 Manchester U 0 0
2001–02 *St Johnstone* 20 0 **20** **0**
2002–03 Manchester U 0 0
2003–04 Manchester U 0 0
2004–05 Sunderland 11 0 **11** **0**
2005–06 Hull C 16 0 **16** **0**

McPHEE, Stephen (F) **165** **44**
H: 5 7 W: 10 08 b.Glasgow 5-6-81
Honours: Scotland Under-21.
1998–99 Coventry C 0 0
1999–2000 Coventry C 0 0
2000–01 Coventry C 0 0
2001–02 Port Vale 44 11
2002–03 Port Vale 40 3
2003–04 Port Vale 46 25 **130** **39**
2004–05 Beira Mar 31 5 **31** **5**
2005–06 Hull C 4 0 **4** **0**

MYHILL, Boaz (G) **132** **0**
H: 6 3 W: 14 06 b.Modesto 9-11-82
Source: Scholar. *Honours:* England Youth, Under-20.
2000–01 Aston Villa 0 0
2001–02 Aston Villa 0 0
2001–02 *Stoke C* 0 0
2002–03 Aston Villa 0 0
2002–03 *Bristol C* 0 0
2002–03 *Bradford C* 2 0 **2** **0**
2003–04 Aston Villa 0 0
2003–04 *Macclesfield T* 15 0 **15** **0**
2003–04 *Stockport Co* 2 0 **2** **0**
2003–04 Hull C 23 0
2004–05 Hull C 45 0
2005–06 Hull C 45 0 **113** **0**

PARKIN, Jon (F) **168** **49**
H: 6 4 W: 13 07 b.Barnsley 30-12-81
Source: Scholarship.
1998–99 Barnsley 2 0
1999–2000 Barnsley 0 0
2000–01 Barnsley 4 0
2001–02 Barnsley 4 0 **10** **0**
2001–02 *Hartlepool U* 1 0 **1** **0**
2001–02 York C 18 2
2002–03 York C 41 10
2003–04 York C 15 2 **74** **14**
2003–04 Macclesfield T 12 1
2004–05 Macclesfield T 42 22
2005–06 Macclesfield T 11 7 **65** **30**
2005–06 Hull C 18 5 **18** **5**

PAYNTER, Billy (F) **166** **33**
H: 6 1 W: 14 01 b.Liverpool 13-7-84
Source: Schoolboy.
2000–01 Port Vale 1 0
2001–02 Port Vale 7 0
2002–03 Port Vale 31 5
2003–04 Port Vale 44 13
2004–05 Port Vale 45 10
2005–06 Port Vale 16 2 **144** **30**
2005–06 Hull C 22 3 **22** **3**

STOCKDALE, Robbie (D) **148** **3**
H: 6 0 W: 11 03 b.Middlesbrough 30-11-79
Source: Trainee. *Honours:* England Under-21, Scotland 5 full caps.
1997–98 Middlesbrough 1 0
1998–99 Middlesbrough 19 0
1999–2000 Middlesbrough 11 1
2000–01 Middlesbrough 0 0
2000–01 *Sheffield W* 6 0 **6** **0**
2001–02 Middlesbrough 28 1
2002–03 Middlesbrough 14 0
2003–04 Middlesbrough 2 0 **75** **2**
2003–04 *West Ham U* 7 0 **7** **0**
2003–04 *Rotherham U* 16 1
2004–05 Rotherham U 27 0 **43** **1**
2004–05 Hull C 14 0
2005–06 Hull C 0 0 **14** **0**
2005–06 *Darlington* 3 0 **3** **0**

THELWELL, Alton (D) **56** **1**
H: 6 0 W: 12 05 b.Islington 5-9-80
Source: Trainee.
1998–99 Tottenham H 0 0
1999–2000 Tottenham H 0 0
2000–01 Tottenham H 16 0
2001–02 Tottenham H 2 0
2002–03 Tottenham H 0 0 **18** **0**
2003–04 Hull C 26 1
2004–05 Hull C 3 0
2005–06 Hull C 9 0 **38** **1**

WELSH, John (M) **36** **2**
H: 5 7 W: 12 02 b.Liverpool 10-1-84
Source: Scholar. *Honours:* England Youth, Under-20, Under-21.
2000–01 Liverpool 0 0
2001–02 Liverpool 0 0
2002–03 Liverpool 0 0
2003–04 Liverpool 1 0
2004–05 Liverpool 3 0
2005–06 Liverpool 0 0 **4** **0**
2005–06 Hull C 32 2 **32** **2**

WILKINSON, Alistair (M) 0 0
b.Sheffield
Source: Derby Co Scholar.
2005–06 Hull C 0 0

WISEMAN, Scott (D) 18 0
H: 6 0 W: 11 06 b.Hull 9-10-85
Source: Scholar. *Honours:* England Youth, Under-20.
2003–04 Hull C 2 0
2004–05 Hull C 3 0
2004–05 *Boston U* 2 0 **2 0**
2005–06 Hull C 11 0 **16 0**

IPSWICH T (39)

BARRON, Scott (D) 15 0
H: 5 9 W: 9 08 b.Preston 2-9-85
Source: Scholar.
2003–04 Ipswich T 0 0
2004–05 Ipswich T 0 0
2005–06 Ipswich T 15 0 **15 0**

BOWDITCH, Dean (F) 84 9
H: 5 11 W: 11 05 b.Bishops Stortford 15-6-86
Source: Trainee. *Honours:* FA Schools, England Youth.
2002–03 Ipswich T 5 0
2003–04 Ipswich T 16 4
2004–05 Ipswich T 21 3
2004–05 *Burnley* 10 1 **10 1**
2005–06 Ipswich T 21 0 **63 7**
2005–06 *Wycombe W* 11 1 **11 1**

BREKKE-SKARD, Vemund (M) 3 0
H: 5 8 W: 13 03 b.Norway 11-9-81
Source: Brumunddal.
2005–06 Ipswich T 3 0 **3 0**

CASEMENT, Chris (M) 5 0
H: 6 0 W: 12 02 b.Belfast 12-1-88
Source: Scholar. *Honours:* Northern Ireland Youth.
2005–06 Ipswich T 5 0 **5 0**

CLARKE, Billy (F) 8 0
H: 5 7 W: 10 01 b.Cork 13-12-87
Source: Scholar. *Honours:* Republic of Ireland Youth.
2004–05 Ipswich T 0 0
2005–06 Ipswich T 2 0 **2 0**
2005–06 *Colchester U* 6 0 **6 0**

COLLINS, Aidan (D) 12 1
H: 6 2 W: 13 09 b.Harlow 18-10-86
Honours: England Youth.
2002–03 Ipswich T 1 0
2003–04 Ipswich T 0 0
2004–05 Ipswich T 0 0
2005–06 Ipswich T 3 0 **4 0**
2005–06 *Wycombe W* 5 1 **5 1**
2005–06 *Stockport Co* 3 0 **3 0**

CURRIE, Darren (M) 445 53
H: 5 11 W: 12 07 b.Hampstead 29-11-74
Source: Trainee.
1993–94 West Ham U 0 0
1994–95 West Ham U 0 0
1994–95 *Shrewsbury T* 17 2
1995–96 West Ham U 0 0
1995–96 *Leyton Orient* 10 0 **10 0**
1995–96 Shrewsbury T 13 2
1996–97 Shrewsbury T 37 2
1997–98 Shrewsbury T 16 4 **83 10**
1997–98 Plymouth Arg 7 0 **7 0**
1998–99 Barnet 38 4
1999–2000 Barnet 44 5
2000–01 Barnet 45 10 **127 19**
2001–02 Wycombe W 46 3
2002–03 Wycombe W 38 4
2003–04 Wycombe W 42 7 **126 14**
2004–05 Brighton & HA 22 2 **22 2**
2004–05 Ipswich T 24 3
2005–06 Ipswich T 46 5 **70 8**

DE VOS, Jason (D) 313 28
H: 6 4 W: 13 07 b.London, Can 2-1-74
Source: Montreal Impact. *Honours:* Canada Youth, Under-23, 49 full caps, 4 goals.
1996–97 Darlington 8 0
1997–98 Darlington 24 3
1998–99 Darlington 12 2 **44 5**
1998–99 Dundee U 25 0
1999–2000 Dundee U 35 2
2000–01 Dundee U 33 0 **93 2**
2001–02 Wigan Ath 20 5
2002–03 Wigan Ath 43 8
2003–04 Wigan Ath 27 2 **90 15**
2004–05 Ipswich T 45 3
2005–06 Ipswich T 41 3 **86 6**

FORSTER, Nicky (F) 451 141
H: 5 9 W: 11 05 b.Caterham 8-9-73
Source: Horley T. *Honours:* England Under-21.
1992–93 Gillingham 26 6
1993–94 Gillingham 41 18 **67 24**
1994–95 Brentford 46 24
1995–96 Brentford 38 5
1996–97 Brentford 25 10 **109 39**
1996–97 Birmingham C 7 3
1997–98 Birmingham C 28 3
1998–99 Birmingham C 33 5 **68 11**
1999–2000 Reading 36 10
2000–01 Reading 9 1
2001–02 Reading 42 19
2002–03 Reading 40 16
2003–04 Reading 30 7
2004–05 Reading 30 7 **187 60**
2005–06 Ipswich T 20 7 **20 7**

GARVAN, Owen (M) 32 3
H: 6 0 W: 10 07 b.Dublin 29-1-88
Source: Scholar. *Honours:* Eire Youth.
2005–06 Ipswich T 32 3 **32 3**

HAYNES, Danny (F) 19 3
H: 5 11 W: 12 04 b.London 19-1-88
Source: Scholar.
2005–06 Ipswich T 19 3 **19 3**

HORLOCK, Kevin (M) 465 60
H: 6 0 W: 12 00 b.Erith 1-11-72
Source: Trainee. *Honours:* Northern Ireland B, 32 full caps.
1991–92 West Ham U 0 0
1992–93 West Ham U 0 0
1992–93 Swindon T 14 1
1993–94 Swindon T 38 0
1994–95 Swindon T 38 1
1995–96 Swindon T 45 12
1996–97 Swindon T 28 8 **163 22**
1996–97 Manchester C 18 4
1997–98 Manchester C 25 5
1998–99 Manchester C 37 9
1999–2000 Manchester C 38 10
2000–01 Manchester C 14 2
2001–02 Manchester C 42 7
2002–03 Manchester C 30 0 **204 37**
2003–04 West Ham U 27 1 **27 1**
2004–05 Ipswich T 41 0
2005–06 Ipswich T 17 0 **58 0**
2005–06 *Doncaster R* 13 0 **13 0**

JUAN, Jimmy (M) 39 5
H: 6 2 W: 11 11 b.Valence 10-6-83
2003–04 Monaco 1 0
2004–05 Monaco 4 0 **5 0**
2004–05 Ipswich T 0 0
2005–06 Ipswich T 34 5 **34 5**

KNIGHTS, Darryl (F) 1 0
H: 5 7 W: 10 01 b.Ipswich 1-5-88
Source: Scholar. *Honours:* England Youth.
2004–05 Ipswich T 1 0
2005–06 Ipswich T 0 0 **1 0**

KRAUSE, James (D) 0 0
H: 5 11 W: 10 03 b.Bury St Edmunds 9-1-87
Source: Scholar.
2005–06 Ipswich T 0 0

LEE, Alan (F) 244 55
H: 6 2 W: 13 09 b.Galway 21-8-78
Source: Trainee. *Honours:* Eire Under-21, 8 full caps.
1995–96 Aston Villa 0 0
1996–97 Aston Villa 0 0
1997–98 Aston Villa 0 0
1998–99 Aston Villa 0 0
1998–99 *Torquay U* 7 2 **7 2**
1998–99 *Port Vale* 11 2 **11 2**
1999–2000 Burnley 15 0
2000–01 Burnley 0 0 **15 0**
2000–01 Rotherham U 31 13
2001–02 Rotherham U 38 9
2002–03 Rotherham U 41 15
2003–04 Rotherham U 1 0 **111 37**
2003–04 Cardiff C 23 3
2004–05 Cardiff C 38 5
2005–06 Cardiff C 25 2 **86 10**
2005–06 Ipswich T 14 4 **14 4**

MAGILTON, Jim (M) 580 64
H: 6 1 W: 14 00 b.Belfast 6-5-69
Source: Apprentice. *Honours:* Northern Ireland Schools, Youth, Under-21, Under-23, 52 full caps, 5 goals. Football League.
1986–87 Liverpool 0 0
1987–88 Liverpool 0 0
1988–89 Liverpool 0 0
1989–90 Liverpool 0 0
1990–91 Liverpool 0 0
1990–91 Oxford U 37 6
1991–92 Oxford U 44 12
1992–93 Oxford U 40 11
1993–94 Oxford U 29 5 **150 34**
1993–94 Southampton 15 0
1994–95 Southampton 42 6
1995–96 Southampton 31 3
1996–97 Southampton 37 4
1997–98 Southampton 5 0 **130 13**
1997–98 Sheffield W 21 1
1998–99 Sheffield W 6 0 **27 1**
1998–99 Ipswich T 19 3
1999–2000 Ipswich T 38 4
2000–01 Ipswich T 33 1
2001–02 Ipswich T 24 0
2002–03 Ipswich T 40 3
2003–04 Ipswich T 46 1
2004–05 Ipswich T 39 3
2005–06 Ipswich T 34 1 **273 16**

McDONALD, Dean (F) 19 2
H: 5 7 W: 11 00 b.Lambeth 19-2-86
2004–05 Ipswich T 0 0
2005–06 Ipswich T 14 1 **14 1**
2005–06 *Hartlepool U* 5 1 **5 1**

NASH, Gerard (D) 4 0
H: 6 1 W: 11 08 b.Dublin 11-7-86
Source: Scholar. *Honours:* Eire Youth.
2003–04 Ipswich T 1 0
2004–05 Ipswich T 0 0
2005–06 Ipswich T 0 0 **1 0**
2005–06 *Hartlepool U* 3 0 **3 0**
2005–06 *Southend U* 0 0

NAYLOR, Richard (D) 280 37
H: 6 1 W: 13 07 b.Leeds 28-2-77
Source: Trainee.
1995–96 Ipswich T 0 0
1996–97 Ipswich T 27 4
1997–98 Ipswich T 5 2
1998–99 Ipswich T 30 5
1999–2000 Ipswich T 36 8
2000–01 Ipswich T 13 1
2001–02 Ipswich T 14 1
2001–02 *Millwall* 3 0 **3 0**
2001–02 *Barnsley* 8 0 **8 0**
2002–03 Ipswich T 17 2
2003–04 Ipswich T 39 5
2004–05 Ipswich T 46 6
2005–06 Ipswich T 42 3 **269 37**

PARKIN, Sam (F) 206 84
H: 6 2 W: 13 00 b.Roehampton 14-3-81
Honours: England Schools.
1998–99 Chelsea 0 0
1999–2000 Chelsea 0 0
2000–01 Chelsea 0 0
2000–01 *Millwall* 7 4 **7 4**
2000–01 *Wycombe W* 8 1 **8 1**
2000–01 *Oldham Ath* 7 3 **7 3**
2001–02 Chelsea 0 0
2001–02 *Northampton T* 40 4 **40 4**
2002–03 Swindon T 43 25
2003–04 Swindon T 40 19
2004–05 Swindon T 41 23 **124 67**
2005–06 Ipswich T 20 5 **20 5**

PETERS, Jaime (M) **13 0**
H: 5 7 W: 10 12 b.Pickering 4-5-87
Source: Moor Green. *Honours:* Canada 12 full caps.

2005–06	Ipswich T	13	0	**13**	**0**

PRICE, Lewis (G) **40 0**
H: 6 3 W: 13 05 b.Bournemouth 19-7-84
Source: Southampton Academy. *Honours:* Wales Youth, Under-21, 2 full caps.

2002–03	Ipswich T	0	0		
2003–04	Ipswich T	1	0		
2004–05	Ipswich T	8	0		
2004–05	*Cambridge U*	6	0	**6**	**0**
2005–06	Ipswich T	25	0	**34**	**0**

PROUDLOCK, Adam (F) **147 28**
H: 6 0 W: 13 07 b.Wellington 9-5-81
Source: Trainee.

1999–2000	Wolverhampton W	0	0		
2000–01	*Clyde*	4	4	**4**	**4**
2000–01	Wolverhampton W	35	8		
2001–02	Wolverhampton W	19	3		
2001–02	*Nottingham F*	3	0	**3**	**0**
2002–03	Wolverhampton W	17	2		
2002–03	*Tranmere R*	5	0	**5**	**0**
2002–03	*Sheffield W*	5	2		
2003–04	Wolverhampton W	0	0	**71**	**13**
2003–04	Sheffield W	30	3		
2004–05	Sheffield W	14	6		
2005–06	Sheffield W	6	0	**55**	**11**
2005–06	Ipswich T	9	0	**9**	**0**

RHODES, Andy (G) **437 0**
H: 6 0 W: 13 06 b.Doncaster 23-8-64
Source: Apprentice.

1982–83	Barnsley	0	0		
1983–84	Barnsley	31	0		
1984–85	Barnsley	5	0		
1985–86	Barnsley	0	0	**36**	**0**
1985–86	Doncaster R	30	0		
1986–87	Doncaster R	41	0		
1987–88	Doncaster R	35	0	**106**	**0**
1987–88	Oldham Ath	11	0		
1988–89	Oldham Ath	27	0		
1989–90	Oldham Ath	31	0	**69**	**0**
1990–91	Dunfermline Ath	35	0		
1991–92	Dunfermline Ath	44	0	**79**	**0**
1992–93	St Johnstone	44	0		
1993–94	St Johnstone	44	0		
1994–95	St Johnstone	19	0	**107**	**0**
1994–95	*Bolton W*	0	0		
1995–96	Airdrieonians	16	0		
1996–97	Airdrieonians	9	0		
1997–98	Airdrieonians	4	0	**29**	**0**
1997–98	Scarborough	11	0		
1998–99	Scarborough	0	0		
1999–2000	Scarborough	0	0		
2000–01	Scarborough	0	0		
2001–02	Scarborough	0	0	**11**	**0**
From Emley.					
2005–06	Ipswich T	0	0		

RICHARDS, Matt (D) **119 6**
H: 5 8 W: 11 00 b.Harlow 26-12-84
Source: Scholar. *Honours:* England Under-21.

2001–02	Ipswich T	0	0		
2002–03	Ipswich T	13	0		
2003–04	Ipswich T	44	1		
2004–05	Ipswich T	24	1		
2005–06	Ipswich T	38	4	**119**	**6**

SITO (D) **99 0**
H: 5 8 W: 11 07 b.Coruna 21-5-80

2001–02	Lugo	10	0	**10**	**0**
2001–02	Calahorra	18	0	**18**	**0**
2002–03	Racing Ferrol	12	0		
2003–04	Racing Ferrol	21	0		
2004–05	Racing Ferrol	0	0	**33**	**0**
2005–06	Ipswich T	38	0	**38**	**0**

SUPPLE, Shane (G) **22 0**
H: 6 0 W: 11 13 b.Dublin 4-5-87
Source: Scholar. *Honours:* Eire Youth.

2004–05	Ipswich T	0	0		
2005–06	Ipswich T	22	0	**22**	**0**

TROTTER, Liam (M) **1 0**
H: 6 2 W: 12 02 b.Ipswich 24-8-88
Source: Scholar.

2005–06	Ipswich T	1	0	**1**	**0**

WESTLAKE, Ian (M) **114 15**
H: 5 10 W: 11 06 b.Clacton 10-7-83
Source: Scholar.

2002–03	Ipswich T	4	0		
2003–04	Ipswich T	39	6		
2004–05	Ipswich T	45	7		
2005–06	Ipswich T	26	2	**114**	**15**

WILLIAMS, Gavin (M) **77 13**
H: 5 10 W: 11 05 b.Pontypridd 20-6-80
Source: Hereford U. *Honours:* Wales 2 full caps.

2003–04	Yeovil T	42	9		
2004–05	Yeovil T	13	2	**55**	**11**
2004–05	West Ham U	10	1		
2005–06	West Ham U	0	0	**10**	**1**
2005–06	Ipswich T	12	1	**12**	**1**

WILNIS, Fabian (D) **489 10**
H: 5 8 W: 12 06 b.Paramaribo 23-8-70
Source: Het Noorden, NOC, De Zwervers, Sparta.

1990–91	NAC	7	3		
1991–92	NAC	30	0		
1992–93	NAC	32	0		
1993–94	NAC	34	0		
1994–95	NAC	31	0	**134**	**3**
1995–96	De Graafschap	32	0		
1996–97	De Graafschap	23	0		
1997–98	De Graafschap	33	1		
1998–99	De Graafschap	19	0	**107**	**1**
1998–99	Ipswich T	18	1		
1999–2000	Ipswich T	35	0		
2000–01	Ipswich T	29	2		
2001–02	Ipswich T	14	0		
2002–03	Ipswich T	35	2		
2003–04	Ipswich T	41	0		
2004–05	Ipswich T	41	0		
2005–06	Ipswich T	35	1	**248**	**6**

LEEDS U (40)

BAKKE, Eirik (M) **230 25**
H: 6 1 W: 12 08 b.Sogndal 13-9-77
Honours: Norway 25 full caps.

1994	Sogndal	5	0		
1995	Sogndal	0	0		
1996	Sogndal	19	8		
1997	Sogndal	25	4		
1998	Sogndal	19	2		
1999	Sogndal	8	3	**76**	**17**
1999–2000	Leeds U	29	2		
2000–01	Leeds U	29	2		
2001–02	Leeds U	27	2		
2002–03	Leeds U	34	1		
2003–04	Leeds U	10	1		
2004–05	Leeds U	1	0		
2005–06	Leeds U	10	0	**140**	**8**
2005–06	*Aston Villa*	14	0	**14**	**0**

BAYLY, Robert (M) **0 0**
b.Dublin 22-2-88
Source: Scholar.

2005–06	Leeds U	0	0		

BECKFORD, Jermaine (F) **5 0**
H: 6 2 W: 13 02 b.London 9-12-83
Source: Wealdstone.

2005–06	Leeds U	5	0	**5**	**0**

BENNETT, Ian (G) **374 0**
H: 6 0 W: 12 10 b.Worksop 10-10-71
Source: Newcastle U Trainee.

1991–92	Peterborough U	7	0		
1992–93	Peterborough U	46	0		
1993–94	Peterborough U	19	0	**72**	**0**
1993–94	Birmingham C	22	0		
1994–95	Birmingham C	46	0		
1995–96	Birmingham C	24	0		
1996–97	Birmingham C	40	0		
1997–98	Birmingham C	45	0		
1998–99	Birmingham C	10	0		
1999–2000	Birmingham C	21	0		
2000–01	Birmingham C	45	0		
2001–02	Birmingham C	18	0		
2002–03	Birmingham C	10	0		
2003–04	Birmingham C	6	0		
2004–05	Birmingham C	0	0	**287**	**0**
2004–05	*Sheffield U*	5	0	**5**	**0**
2004–05	*Coventry C*	6	0	**6**	**0**
2005–06	Leeds U	4	0	**4**	**0**

BLAKE, Robbie (F) **404 117**
H: 5 9 W: 12 00 b.Middlesbrough 4-3-76
Source: Trainee.

1994–95	Darlington	9	0		
1995–96	Darlington	29	11		
1996–97	Darlington	30	10	**68**	**21**
1996–97	Bradford C	5	0		
1997–98	Bradford C	34	8		
1998–99	Bradford C	39	16		
1999–2000	Bradford C	28	2		
2000–01	Bradford C	21	4		
2000–01	*Nottingham F*	11	1	**11**	**1**
2001–02	Bradford C	26	10	**153**	**40**
2001–02	Burnley	10	0		
2002–03	Burnley	41	13		
2003–04	Burnley	45	19		
2004–05	Burnley	24	10	**120**	**42**
2004–05	Birmingham C	11	2	**11**	**2**
2005–06	Leeds U	41	11	**41**	**11**

BUTLER, Paul (D) **528 23**
H: 6 2 W: 13 00 b.Manchester 2-11-72
Source: Trainee. *Honours:* Eire 1 full cap.

1990–91	Rochdale	2	0		
1991–92	Rochdale	25	0		
1992–93	Rochdale	16	2		
1993–94	Rochdale	38	2		
1994–95	Rochdale	39	3		
1995–96	Rochdale	38	3	**158**	**10**
1996–97	Bury	41	2		
1997–98	Bury	43	2	**84**	**4**
1998–99	Sunderland	44	2		
1999–2000	Sunderland	32	1		
2000–01	Sunderland	3	0	**79**	**3**
2000–01	Wolverhampton W	12	0		
2001–02	Wolverhampton W	43	1		
2002–03	Wolverhampton W	32	1		
2003–04	Wolverhampton W	37	1	**124**	**3**
2004–05	Leeds U	39	0		
2005–06	Leeds U	44	3	**83**	**3**

CAMFIELD, Bailey (D) **0 0**
b.Wakefield 22-1-88
Source: Scholar.

2005–06	Leeds U	0	0		

CRAINEY, Stephen (D) **79 0**
H: 5 9 W: 9 11 b.Glasgow 22-6-81
Honours: Scotland 6 full caps.

1999–2000	Celtic	9	0		
2000–01	Celtic	2	0		
2001–02	Celtic	15	0		
2002–03	Celtic	13	0		
2003–04	Celtic	2	0	**41**	**0**
2003–04	Southampton	5	0	**5**	**0**
2004–05	Leeds U	9	0		
2005–06	Leeds U	24	0	**33**	**0**

CRESSWELL, Richard (F) **342 78**
H: 6 0 W: 11 08 b.Bridlington 20-9-77
Source: Trainee. *Honours:* England Under-21.

1995–96	York C	16	1		
1996–97	York C	17	0		
1996–97	*Mansfield T*	5	1	**5**	**1**
1997–98	York C	26	4		
1998–99	York C	36	16	**95**	**21**
1998–99	Sheffield W	7	1		
1999–2000	Sheffield W	20	1		
2000–01	Sheffield W	4	0	**31**	**2**
2000–01	Leicester C	8	0	**8**	**0**
2000–01	*Preston NE*	11	2		
2001–02	Preston NE	40	13		
2002–03	Preston NE	42	16		
2003–04	Preston NE	45	2		
2004–05	Preston NE	46	16		
2005–06	Preston NE	3	0	**187**	**49**
2005–06	Leeds U	16	5	**16**	**5**

DERRY, Shaun (M) **338 10**
H: 5 10 W: 10 13 b.Nottingham 6-12-77
Source: Trainee.

1995–96	Notts Co	12	0		
1996–97	Notts Co	39	2		
1997–98	Notts Co	28	2	**79**	**4**
1997–98	Sheffield U	12	0		
1998–99	Sheffield U	26	0		
1999–2000	Sheffield U	34	0	**72**	**0**

1999–2000 Portsmouth 9 1
2000–01 Portsmouth 28 0
2001–02 Portsmouth 12 0 **49 1**
2002–03 Crystal Palace 39 1
2003–04 Crystal Palace 37 2
2004–05 Crystal Palace 7 0 **83 3**
2004–05 *Nottingham F* 7 0 **7 0**
2004–05 Leeds U 7 2
2005–06 Leeds U 41 0 **48 2**

EINARSSON, Gylfi (M) 121 27
H: 6 1 W: 11 11 b.Iceland 27-10-78
Honours: Iceland Youth, 23 full caps, 1 goal.
1996 Fylkir 2 0
1997 Fylkir 0 0
1998 Fylkir 0 0
1999 Fylkir 0 0
2000 Fylkir 18 10 **20 10**
2000–01 Lille 18 1
2001–02 Lille 22 1
2002–03 Lille 17 2
2003–04 Lille 26 12 **83 16**
2004–05 Leeds U 8 1
2005–06 Leeds U 10 0 **18 1**

GARDNER, Scott (M) 0 0
b.Luxembourg 1-4-88
Source: Scholar. *Honours:* England Youth.
2005–06 Leeds U 0 0

GREGAN, Sean (M) 490 18
H: 6 2 W: 14 00 b.Guisborough 29-3-74
Source: Trainee.
1991–92 Darlington 17 0
1992–93 Darlington 17 1
1993–94 Darlington 23 1
1994–95 Darlington 25 2
1995–96 Darlington 38 0
1996–97 Darlington 16 0 **136 4**
1996–97 Preston NE 21 1
1997–98 Preston NE 35 2
1998–99 Preston NE 41 3
1999–2000 Preston NE 33 3
2000–01 Preston NE 41 2
2001–02 Preston NE 41 1 **212 12**
2002–03 WBA 36 1
2003–04 WBA 43 1
2004–05 WBA 0 0 **79 2**
2004–05 Leeds U 35 0
2005–06 Leeds U 28 0 **63 0**

GRIFFITHS, Joel (M) 74 4
H: 6 0 W: 11 11 b.Australia 21-8-79
Honours: Australia 1 full cap.
2003–04 Neuchatel Xamax 29 2
2004–05 Neuchatel Xamax 30 1
2005–06 Neuchatel Xamax 13 1 **72 4**
2005–06 Leeds U 2 0 **2 0**

HARDING, Dan (D) 87 1
H: 6 0 W: 11 11 b.Gloucester 23-12-83
Source: Scholar. *Honours:* England Under-21.
2002–03 Brighton & HA 1 0
2003–04 Brighton & HA 23 0
2004–05 Brighton & HA 43 1 **67 1**
2005–06 Leeds U 20 0 **20 0**

HEALY, David (F) 239 68
H: 5 8 W: 10 09 b.Downpatrick 5-8-79
Source: Trainee. *Honours:* Northern Ireland Schools, Youth, Under-21, B, 49 full caps, 19 goals.
1997–98 Manchester U 0 0
1998–99 Manchester U 0 0
1999–2000 Manchester U 0 0
1999–2000 *Port Vale* 16 3 **16 3**
2000–01 Manchester U 1 0 **1 0**
2000–01 Preston NE 22 9
2001–02 Preston NE 44 10
2002–03 Preston NE 24 5
2002–03 *Norwich C* 13 2 **13 2**
2003–04 Preston NE 38 15
2004–05 Preston NE 11 5 **139 44**
2004–05 Leeds U 28 7
2005–06 Leeds U 42 12 **70 19**

HIRD, Samuel (D) 0 0
b.Doncaster 7-9-87
Source: Scholar.
2005–06 Leeds U 0 0

HULSE, Rob (F) 206 74
H: 6 1 W: 12 04 b.Crewe 25-10-79
Source: Trainee.
1998–99 Crewe Alex 0 0
1999–2000 Crewe Alex 4 1
2000–01 Crewe Alex 33 11
2001–02 Crewe Alex 41 12
2002–03 Crewe Alex 38 22 **116 46**
2003–04 WBA 33 10
2004–05 WBA 5 0 **38 10**
2004–05 *Leeds U* 13 6
2005–06 Leeds U 39 12 **52 18**

KELLY, Gary (D) 414 2
H: 5 8 W: 13 03 b.Drogheda 9-7-74
Source: Home Farm. *Honours:* Eire Youth, 52 full caps, 2 goals.
1991–92 Leeds U 2 0
1992–93 Leeds U 0 0
1993–94 Leeds U 42 0
1994–95 Leeds U 42 0
1995–96 Leeds U 34 0
1996–97 Leeds U 36 2
1997–98 Leeds U 34 0
1998–99 Leeds U 0 0
1999–2000 Leeds U 31 0
2000–01 Leeds U 24 0
2001–02 Leeds U 20 0
2002–03 Leeds U 25 0
2003–04 Leeds U 37 0
2004–05 Leeds U 43 0
2005–06 Leeds U 44 0 **414 2**

KILGALLON, Matthew (D) 64 3
H: 6 1 W: 12 10 b.York 8-1-84
Source: Scholar. *Honours:* England Youth, Under-20, Under-21.
2000–01 Leeds U 0 0
2001–02 Leeds U 0 0
2002–03 Leeds U 2 0
2003–04 Leeds U 8 2
2003–04 *West Ham U* 3 0 **3 0**
2004–05 Leeds U 26 0
2005–06 Leeds U 25 1 **61 3**

LEWIS, Eddie (M) 285 29
H: 5 10 W: 11 02 b.Cerritos 17-5-74
Honours: USA 71 full caps, 8 goals.
1996 San Jose Clash 25 0
1997 San Jose Clash 29 2
1998 San Jose Clash 32 3
1999 San Jose Clash 29 4 **115 9**
1999–2000 Fulham 8 0
2000–01 Fulham 7 0
2001–02 Fulham 1 0 **16 0**
2002–03 Preston NE 38 5
2003–04 Preston NE 33 6
2004–05 Preston NE 40 4 **111 15**
2005–06 Leeds U 43 5 **43 5**

MADDEN, Simon (D) 0 0
b.Dublin 1-5-88
Source: Shelbourne.
2005–06 Leeds U 0 0

McKEOWN, Steven (D) 0 0
H: 5 10 W: 10 08 b.Paisley 3-6-87
Source: Livingston.
2003–04 Leeds U 0 0
2004–05 Leeds U 0 0
2005–06 Leeds U 0 0

MOORE, Ian (F) 391 70
H: 5 11 W: 12 00 b.Birkenhead 26-8-76
Source: Trainee. *Honours:* England Youth, Under-21.
1994–95 Tranmere R 1 0
1995–96 Tranmere R 36 9
1996–97 Tranmere R 21 3 **58 12**
1996–97 *Bradford C* 6 0 **6 0**
1996–97 Nottingham F 5 0
1997–98 Nottingham F 10 1 **15 1**
1997–98 *West Ham U* 1 0 **1 0**
1998–99 Stockport Co 38 3
1999–2000 Stockport Co 38 10
2000–01 Stockport Co 17 7 **93 20**
2000–01 Burnley 27 5
2001–02 Burnley 46 11
2002–03 Burnley 44 8
2003–04 Burnley 40 9
2004–05 Burnley 35 4 **192 37**
2004–05 Leeds U 6 0
2005–06 Leeds U 20 0 **26 0**

MORRIS, Ian (D) 30 3
H: 6 0 W: 11 05 b.Dublin 27-2-87
Source: Scholar.
2003–04 Leeds U 0 0
2004–05 Leeds U 0 0
2005–06 Leeds U 0 0
2005–06 *Blackpool* 30 3 **30 3**

PARKER, Ben (D) 0 0
b.Pontefract 8-11-87
Source: Scholar. *Honours:* England Youth.
2004–05 Leeds U 0 0
2005–06 Leeds U 0 0

PUGH, Danny (M) 51 5
H: 6 0 W: 12 10 b.Manchester 19-10-82
Source: Scholar.
2000–01 Manchester U 0 0
2001–02 Manchester U 0 0
2002–03 Manchester U 1 0
2003–04 Manchester U 0 0 **1 0**
2004–05 Leeds U 38 5
2005–06 Leeds U 12 0 **50 5**

RICHARDSON, Frazer (D) 78 3
H: 5 11 W: 11 12 b.Rotherham 29-10-82
Source: Trainee. *Honours:* England Youth, Under-20.
1999–2000 Leeds U 0 0
2000–01 Leeds U 0 0
2001–02 Leeds U 0 0
2002–03 Leeds U 0 0
2002–03 *Stoke C* 7 0
2003–04 Leeds U 4 0
2003–04 *Stoke C* 6 1 **13 1**
2004–05 Leeds U 38 1
2005–06 Leeds U 23 1 **65 2**

RICKETTS, Michael (F) 272 61
H: 6 2 W: 11 12 b.Birmingham 4-12-78
Source: Trainee. *Honours:* England 1 full cap.
1995–96 Walsall 1 1
1996–97 Walsall 11 1
1997–98 Walsall 24 1
1998–99 Walsall 8 0
1999–2000 Walsall 32 11 **76 14**
2000–01 Bolton W 39 19
2001–02 Bolton W 37 12
2002–03 Bolton W 22 6 **98 37**
2002–03 Middlesbrough 9 1
2003–04 Middlesbrough 23 2 **32 3**
2004–05 Leeds U 21 0
2004–05 *Stoke C* 11 0 **11 0**
2005–06 Leeds U 4 0 **25 0**
2005–06 *Cardiff C* 17 5 **17 5**
2005–06 *Burnley* 13 2 **13 2**

ROTHERY, Gavin (F) 0 0
b.Morley 22-9-87
Source: Scholar. *Honours:* England Youth.
2005–06 Leeds U 0 0

RUI MARQUES, Manuel (D) 116 0
H: 5 11 W: 11 13 b.Luanda 3-9-77
Source: Benfica. *Honours:* Angola 3 full caps.
1998–99 Baden 27 0 **27 0**
1999–2000 SSV Ulm 32 0 **32 0**
2000–01 Hertha 1 0 **1 0**
2000–01 Stuttgart 12 0
2001–02 Stuttgart 23 0
2002–03 Stuttgart 12 0
2003–04 Stuttgart 0 0 **47 0**
2004–05 Maritimo 8 0 **8 0**
2005–06 Leeds U 0 0
2005–06 *Hull C* 1 0 **1 0**

STONE, Steve (F) 358 36
H: 5 9 W: 12 07 b.Gateshead 20-8-71
Source: Trainee. *Honours:* England 9 full caps, 2 goals.
1989–90 Nottingham F 0 0
1990–91 Nottingham F 0 0
1991–92 Nottingham F 1 0
1992–93 Nottingham F 12 1
1993–94 Nottingham F 45 5
1994–95 Nottingham F 41 5
1995–96 Nottingham F 34 7
1996–97 Nottingham F 5 0
1997–98 Nottingham F 29 2

1998–99 Nottingham F 26 3 193 23
1998–99 Aston Villa 10 0
1999–2000 Aston Villa 24 1
2000–01 Aston Villa 34 2
2001–02 Aston Villa 22 1
2002–03 Aston Villa 0 0 90 4
2002–03 Portsmouth 18 4
2003–04 Portsmouth 32 2
2004–05 Portsmouth 23 3 73 9
2005–06 Leeds U 2 0 2 0

SULLIVAN, Neil (G) 338 0
H: 6 2 W: 12 00 b.Sutton 24-2-70
Source: Trainee. *Honours:* Scotland 28 full caps.
1988–89 Wimbledon 0 0
1989–90 Wimbledon 0 0
1990–91 Wimbledon 1 0
1991–92 Wimbledon 1 0
1991–92 *Crystal Palace* 1 0 1 0
1992–93 Wimbledon 1 0
1993–94 Wimbledon 2 0
1994–95 Wimbledon 11 0
1995–96 Wimbledon 16 0
1996–97 Wimbledon 36 0
1997–98 Wimbledon 38 0
1998–99 Wimbledon 38 0
1999–2000 Wimbledon 37 0 181 0
2000–01 Tottenham H 35 0
2001–02 Tottenham H 29 0
2002–03 Tottenham H 0 0 64 0
2003–04 Chelsea 4 0 4 0
2004–05 Leeds U 46 0
2005–06 Leeds U 42 0 88 0

WALTON, Simon (D) 34 3
H: 6 1 W: 13 05 b.Sherburn-in-Elmet 13-9-87
Source: Scholar. *Honours:* England Youth.
2004–05 Leeds U 30 3
2005–06 Leeds U 4 0 34 3

WILBERFORCE, Mark (G) 0 0
H: 5 10 W: 11 07 b.Hull 30-1-87
Source: Scholar.
2003–04 Leeds U 0 0
2004–05 Leeds U 0 0
2005–06 Leeds U 0 0

WRIGHT, Jermaine (M) 332 20
H: 5 9 W: 11 09 b.Greenwich 21-10-75
Source: Trainee. *Honours:* England Youth.
1992–93 Millwall 0 0
1993–94 Millwall 0 0
1994–95 Millwall 0 0
1994–95 Wolverhampton W 6 0
1995–96 Wolverhampton W 7 0
1995–96 *Doncaster R* 13 0 13 0
1996–97 Wolverhampton W 3 0
1997–98 Wolverhampton W 4 0 20 0
1997–98 Crewe Alex 5 0
1998–99 Crewe Alex 44 5 49 5
1999–2000 Ipswich T 34 1
2000–01 Ipswich T 37 2
2001–02 Ipswich T 29 1
2002–03 Ipswich T 39 1
2003–04 Ipswich T 45 5 184 10
2004–05 Leeds U 35 3
2005–06 Leeds U 3 0 38 3
2005–06 *Millwall* 15 2 15 2
2005–06 *Southampton* 13 0 13 0

LEICESTER C (41)

CANERO, Peter (D) 130 10
H: 5 9 W: 12 06 b.Glasgow 18-1-81
Honours: Scotland 1 full cap.
1999–2000 Kilmarnock 11 0
2000–01 Kilmarnock 28 1
2001–02 Kilmarnock 32 1
2002–03 Kilmarnock 33 6
2003–04 Kilmarnock 13 2 117 10
2003–04 Leicester C 7 0
2004–05 Leicester C 6 0
2005–06 Leicester C 0 0 13 0
To Red Bull New York September 2005

CHAMBERS, Ashley (F) 0 0
H: 5 10 W: 11 06 b.Leicester 1-3-90
Honours: England Schools, Youth.
2005–06 Leicester C 0 0

DE VRIES, Mark (F) 183 47
H: 6 3 W: 13 05 b.Surinam 24-8-75
1995–96 Volendam 4 0
1996–97 Volendam 10 0
1997–98 Volendam 14 1 28 1
1998–99 Niort 0 0
1999–2000 Dordrecht 8 0
2000–01 Dordrecht 30 11
2001–02 Dordrecht 0 0 38 11
2002–03 Hearts 32 15
2003–04 Hearts 31 12
2004–05 Hearts 9 1 72 28
2004–05 Leicester C 16 1
2005–06 Leicester C 29 6 45 7
To Heerenveen (loan) January 2006

DODDS, Louis (F) 0 0
H: 5 10 W: 12 04 b.Leicester 8-10-86
Source: Scholar.
2005–06 Leicester C 0 0

DOUGLAS, Rab (G) 329 0
H: 6 3 W: 14 12 b.Lanark 24-4-72
Source: Forth Wanderers. *Honours:* Scotland B, 19 full caps.
1992–93 Meadowbank T 0 0
1993–94 Meadowbank T 4 0
1994–95 Meadowbank T 8 0 12 0
1995–96 Livingston 24 0
1996–97 Livingston 36 0 60 0
1997–98 Dundee 36 0
1998–99 Dundee 35 0
1999–2000 Dundee 35 0
2000–01 Dundee 11 0 117 0
2000–01 Celtic 22 0
2001–02 Celtic 35 0
2002–03 Celtic 21 0
2003–04 Celtic 16 0
2004–05 Celtic 14 0 108 0
2005–06 Leicester C 32 0 32 0

DUBLIN, Dion (F) 531 170
H: 6 2 W: 15 00 b.Leicester 22-4-69
Source: Oakham U. *Honours:* England 4 full caps.
1987–88 Norwich C 0 0
1988–89 Cambridge U 21 6
1989–90 Cambridge U 46 15
1990–91 Cambridge U 46 16
1991–92 Cambridge U 43 15 156 52
1992–93 Manchester U 7 1
1993–94 Manchester U 5 1 12 2
1994–95 Coventry C 31 13
1995–96 Coventry C 34 14
1996–97 Coventry C 34 13
1997–98 Coventry C 36 18
1998–99 Coventry C 10 3 145 61
1998–99 Aston Villa 24 11
1999–2000 Aston Villa 26 12
2000–01 Aston Villa 33 8
2001–02 Aston Villa 21 4
2001–02 *Millwall* 5 2 5 2
2002–03 Aston Villa 28 10
2003–04 Aston Villa 23 3 155 48
2004–05 Leicester C 37 5
2005–06 Leicester C 21 0 58 5
To Celtic January 2006

FRYATT, Matty (F) 99 34
H: 5 10 W: 11 00 b.Nuneaton 5-3-86
Source: Scholar. *Honours:* England Youth.
2002–03 Walsall 0 0
2003–04 Walsall 11 1
2003–04 *Carlisle U* 10 1 10 1
2004–05 Walsall 36 15
2005–06 Walsall 23 11 70 27
2005–06 Leicester C 19 6 19 6

GERRBRAND, Patrik (D) 82 2
H: 6 2 W: 12 06 b.Stockholm 27-4-81
Source: Alvsjo. *Honours:* Sweden Under-21.
2000 Hammarby 6 0
2001 Hammarby 5 0
2002 Hammarby 0 0
2003 Hammarby 16 1
2004 Hammarby 25 1
2005 Hammarby 13 0 65 2
2005–06 Leicester C 17 0 17 0

GRADEL, Max (M) 0 0
H: 5 8 W: 12 03 b.Ivory Coast 30-9-87
2005–06 Leicester C 0 0

GUDJONSSON, Joey (M) 165 21
H: 5 9 W: 12 04 b.Akranes 25-5-80
Honours: Iceland Youth, Under-21, 24 full caps, 1 goal.
1998–99 Genk 5 0 5 0
1999–2000 MVV 19 5 19 5
2000–01 RKC 31 4 31 4
2001–02 Betis 11 0 11 0
2002–03 Aston Villa 11 2 11 2
2003–04 Wolverhampton W 11 0 11 0
2004–05 Leicester C 35 2
2005–06 Leicester C 42 8 77 10

HAMILL, Joe (M) 69 4
H: 5 9 W: 10 10 b.Bellshill 25-2-84
2001–02 Hearts 3 0
2002–03 Hearts 4 0
2003–04 Hearts 18 2
2004–05 Hearts 32 2 57 4
2005–06 Leicester C 12 0 12 0

HAMMOND, Elvis (F) 69 5
H: 5 10 W: 11 02 b.Accra 6-10-80
Source: Trainee. *Honours:* Ghana 1 full cap.
1999–2000 Fulham 0 0
2000–01 Fulham 0 0
2001–02 Fulham 0 0
2001–02 *Bristol R* 7 0 7 0
2002–03 Fulham 10 0
2003–04 Fulham 0 0
2003–04 *Norwich C* 4 0 4 0
2004–05 Fulham 1 0
2004–05 RBC Roosendaal 14 2 14 2
2005–06 Fulham 0 0 11 0
2005–06 Leicester C 33 3 33 3

HENDERSON, Paul (G) 189 0
H: 6 1 W: 12 06 b.Sydney 22-4-76
1998–99 Northern Spirit 30 0
1999–2000 Northern Spirit 14 0
2000–01 Northern Spirit 21 0
2001–02 Northern Spirit 13 0
2002–03 Northern Spirit 33 0
2003–04 Northern Spirit 23 0 134 0
2004–05 Bradford C 40 0 40 0
2005–06 Leicester C 15 0 15 0

HUGHES, Stephen (M) 113 11
H: 5 11 W: 9 06 b.Motherwell 14-11-82
2000–01 Rangers 1 0
2001–02 Rangers 17 1
2002–03 Rangers 12 1
2003–04 Rangers 22 3
2004–05 Rangers 11 2 63 7
2004–05 Leicester C 16 1
2005–06 Leicester C 34 3 50 4

HUME, Iain (F) 187 41
H: 5 7 W: 11 02 b.Brampton 31-10-83
Source: Juniors. *Honours:* Canada Youth, 14 full caps, 1 goal.
1999–2000 Tranmere R 3 0
2000–01 Tranmere R 10 0
2001–02 Tranmere R 14 0
2002–03 Tranmere R 35 6
2003–04 Tranmere R 40 10
2004–05 Tranmere R 42 15
2005–06 Tranmere R 6 1 150 32
2005–06 Leicester C 37 9 37 9

JOHANSSON, Nils-Eric (D) 135 0
H: 6 1 W: 12 10 b.Stockholm 13-1-80
Source: Viksjo, Brommapojkana. *Honours:* Sweden 4 full caps.
1998 AIK Stockholm 0 0
1998–99 Bayern Munich 2 0
1999–2000 Bayern Munich 0 0
2000–01 Bayern Munich 0 0 2 0
2001–02 Nuremberg 8 0 8 0
2001–02 Blackburn R 20 0
2002–03 Blackburn R 30 0
2003–04 Blackburn R 14 0
2004–05 Blackburn R 22 0 86 0
2005–06 Leicester C 39 0 39 0

KISNORBO, Patrick (D) 152 5
H: 6 1 W: 11 11 b.Melbourne 24-3-81
Honours: Australia Schools, Under-20, Under-23, 7 full caps.
2000–01 South Melbourne 25 0
2001–02 South Melbourne 23 2
2002–03 South Melbourne 19 1 **67 3**
2003–04 Hearts 31 0
2004–05 Hearts 17 1 **48 1**
2005–06 Leicester C 37 1 **37 1**

LOGAN, Conrad (G) 13 0
H: 6 2 W: 14 00 b.Letterkenny 18-4-86
Source: Scholar. *Honours:* Eire Youth.
2003–04 Leicester C 0 0
2004–05 Leicester C 0 0
2005–06 Leicester C 0 0
2005–06 *Boston U* 13 0 **13 0**

MAYBURY, Alan (D) 195 7
H: 5 8 W: 11 08 b.Dublin 8-8-78
Source: Trainee. *Honours:* Eire Youth, Under-21, 10 full caps.
1995–96 Leeds U 1 0
1996–97 Leeds U 0 0
1997–98 Leeds U 12 0
1998–99 Leeds U 0 0
1998–99 *Reading* 8 0 **8 0**
1999–2000 Leeds U 0 0
2000–01 Leeds U 0 0
2000–01 *Crewe Alex* 6 0 **6 0**
2001–02 Leeds U 1 0 **14 0**
2001–02 Hearts 27 0
2002–03 Hearts 35 2
2003–04 Hearts 33 2
2004–05 Hearts 15 0 **110 4**
2004–05 Leicester C 17 2
2005–06 Leicester C 40 1 **57 3**

McCARTHY, Patrick (D) 68 2
H: 6 2 W: 13 07 b.Dublin 31-5-83
Source: Scholar. *Honours:* Eire Youth, Under-21.
2000–01 Manchester C 0 0
2001–02 Manchester C 0 0
2002–03 Manchester C 0 0
2002–03 *Boston U* 12 0 **12 0**
2002–03 *Notts Co* 6 0 **6 0**
2003–04 Manchester C 0 0
2004–05 Manchester C 0 0
2004–05 Leicester C 12 0
2005–06 Leicester C 38 2 **50 2**

MORRIS, Lee (F) 132 24
H: 5 10 W: 11 07 b.Blackpool 30-4-80
Source: Trainee. *Honours:* England Youth.
1997–98 Sheffield U 5 0
1998–99 Sheffield U 20 6
1999–2000 Sheffield U 1 0 **26 6**
1999–2000 Derby Co 3 0
2000–01 Derby Co 20 0
2000–01 *Huddersfield T* 5 1 **5 1**
2001–02 Derby Co 15 4
2002–03 Derby Co 30 8
2003–04 Derby Co 23 5 **91 17**
2003–04 Leicester C 0 0
2004–05 Leicester C 10 0
2005–06 Leicester C 0 0 **10 0**

O'GRADY, Chris (F) 45 5
H: 6 3 W: 12 04 b.Nottingham 25-1-86
Source: Trainee. *Honours:* England Youth.
2002–03 Leicester C 1 0
2003–04 Leicester C 0 0
2004–05 Leicester C 0 0
2004–05 *Notts Co* 9 0 **9 0**
2005–06 Leicester C 13 1 **14 1**
2005–06 *Rushden & D* 22 4 **22 4**

PORTER, Levi (F) 0 0
H: 5 4 W: 10 05 b.Leicester 6-4-87
Source: Scholar. *Honours:* England Youth.
2005–06 Leicester C 0 0

SHEEHAN, Alan (D) 3 0
H: 5 11 W: 11 02 b.Athlone 14-9-86
Source: Scholar. *Honours:* Eire Youth, Under-21.
2004–05 Leicester C 1 0
2005–06 Leicester C 2 0 **3 0**

SMEDLEY, Jay (D) 0 0
H: 6 0 W: 10 12 b.Nottingham 18-2-87
Source: Scholar.
2005–06 Leicester C 0 0

STEARMAN, Richard (D) 42 4
H: 6 2 W: 10 08 b.Wolverhampton 19-8-87
Source: Scholar. *Honours:* England Youth.
2004–05 Leicester C 8 1
2005–06 Leicester C 34 3 **42 4**

SYLLA, Momo (M) 149 10
H: 6 0 W: 11 09 b.Conakry 13-3-77
Honours: Guinea full caps.
1997–98 Ayr U 3 0 **3 0**
1998–99 Le Havre 10 0 **10 0**
1999–2000 Le Mans 27 1 **27 1**
2000–01 St Johnstone 34 6
2001–02 St Johnstone 1 0 **35 6**
2001–02 Celtic 8 1
2002–03 Celtic 18 2
2003–04 Celtic 14 0
2004–05 Celtic 6 0 **46 3**
2005–06 Leicester C 28 0 **28 0**

TIATTO, Danny (D) 257 10
H: 5 8 W: 11 08 b.Melbourne 22-5-73
Honours: Australia Under-23, 23 full caps, 1 goal.
1994–95 Melbourne Knights 25 3
1995–96 Melbourne Knights 18 0 **43 3**
1996–97 Salernitana 11 1 **11 1**
1997–98 Stoke C 15 1 **15 1**
From Baden
1998–99 Manchester C 17 0
1999–2000 Manchester C 35 0
2000–01 Manchester C 33 2
2001–02 Manchester C 37 1
2002–03 Manchester C 13 0
2003–04 Manchester C 5 0 **140 3**
2004–05 Leicester C 30 1
2005–06 Leicester C 18 1 **48 2**

WESOLOWSKI, James (D) 5 0
H: 5 8 W: 11 11 b.Sydney 25-8-87
Source: Scholar. *Honours:* Australia Youth, Under-20.
2004–05 Leicester C 0 0
2005–06 Leicester C 5 0 **5 0**

WILLIAMS, Gareth (M) 206 11
H: 6 1 W: 12 03 b.Glasgow 16-12-81
Source: Trainee. *Honours:* Scotland Youth, Under-21, 5 full caps.
1998–99 Nottingham F 0 0
1999–2000 Nottingham F 2 0
2000–01 Nottingham F 17 0
2001–02 Nottingham F 44 0
2002–03 Nottingham F 40 3
2003–04 Nottingham F 39 6 **142 9**
2004–05 Leicester C 33 1
2005–06 Leicester C 31 1 **64 2**

LEYTON ORIENT (42)

ALEXANDER, Gary (F) 277 86
H: 6 0 W: 13 04 b.Lambeth 15-8-79
Source: Trainee.
1998–99 West Ham U 0 0
1999–2000 West Ham U 0 0
1999–2000 *Exeter C* 37 16 **37 16**
2000–01 Swindon T 37 7 **37 7**
2001–02 Hull C 43 17
2002–03 Hull C 25 6 **68 23**
2002–03 Leyton Orient 17 2
2003–04 Leyton Orient 44 15
2004–05 Leyton Orient 28 9
2005–06 Leyton Orient 46 14 **135 40**

BARNARD, Donny (D) 121 1
H: 5 10 W: 12 01 b.Forest Gate 1-7-84
Source: Trainee.
2001–02 Leyton Orient 10 0
2002–03 Leyton Orient 29 0
2003–04 Leyton Orient 23 0
2004–05 Leyton Orient 33 1
2005–06 Leyton Orient 26 0 **121 1**

CARLISLE, Wayne (M) 168 22
H: 5 11 W: 11 06 b.Lisburn 9-9-79
Source: Trainee. *Honours:* Northern Ireland Schools, Youth, Under-21.
1996–97 Crystal Palace 0 0
1997–98 Crystal Palace 0 0
1998–99 Crystal Palace 6 0
1999–2000 Crystal Palace 26 3
2000–01 Crystal Palace 14 0
2001–02 Crystal Palace 0 0 **46 3**
2001–02 *Swindon T* 11 2 **11 2**
2001–02 Bristol R 5 0
2002–03 Bristol R 41 7
2003–04 Bristol R 25 7 **71 14**
2004–05 Leyton Orient 28 3
2005–06 Leyton Orient 12 0 **40 3**

CONNOR, Paul (F) 229 61
H: 6 2 W: 11 08 b.Bishop Auckland 12-1-79
Source: Trainee.
1996–97 Middlesbrough 0 0
1997–98 Middlesbrough 0 0
1997–98 *Hartlepool U* 5 0 **5 0**
1998–99 Middlesbrough 0 0
1998–99 *Stoke C* 3 2
1999–2000 Stoke C 26 5
2000–01 Stoke C 7 0 **36 7**
2000–01 *Cambridge U* 13 5 **13 5**
2000–01 Rochdale 14 10
2001–02 Rochdale 17 1
2002–03 Rochdale 39 12
2003–04 Rochdale 24 5 **94 28**
2003–04 Swansea C 12 5
2004–05 Swansea C 40 10
2005–06 Swansea C 13 1 **65 16**
2005–06 Leyton Orient 16 5 **16 5**

DEMETRIOU, Jason (M) 3 0
H: 5 11 W: 10 08 b.Newham 18-11-87
Source: Scholar.
2005–06 Leyton Orient 3 0 **3 0**

DOLAN, Joe (D) 66 4
H: 6 4 W: 14 12 b.Harrow 27-5-80
Source: Chelsea Trainee. *Honours:* Northern Ireland Youth, Under-21.
1998–99 Millwall 9 1
1999–2000 Millwall 17 1
2000–01 Millwall 20 1
2001–02 Millwall 0 0
2002–03 Millwall 2 0
2003–04 Millwall 1 0
2004–05 Millwall 0 0 **49 3**
2004–05 *Stockport Co* 11 1
2004–05 *Brighton & HA* 3 0 **3 0**
2005–06 Leyton Orient 1 0 **1 0**
2005–06 *Stockport Co* 2 0 **13 1**

DUNCAN, Derek (M) 17 0
H: 5 10 W: 10 11 b.Newham 23-4-87
Source: Scholar.
2003–04 Leyton Orient 1 0
2004–05 Leyton Orient 15 0
2005–06 Leyton Orient 1 0 **17 0**

EASTON, Craig (M) 102 6
H: 5 11 W: 11 03 b.Bellshill 26-2-79
Source: Dundee U BC. *Honours:* Scotland Under-21, Under-18.
1995–96 Dundee U 0 0
1996–97 Dundee U 2 0
1997–98 Dundee U 29 1
1998–99 Dundee U 30 1
1999–2000 Dundee U 0 0
2000–01 Dundee U 0 0
2001–02 Dundee U 0 0 **61 2**
2005–06 Leyton Orient 41 4 **41 4**

ECHANOMI, Efe (F) 34 8
H: 5 7 W: 11 13 b.Nigeria 27-9-86
2004–05 Leyton Orient 18 5
2005–06 Leyton Orient 16 3 **34 8**

GARNER, Glyn (G) 169 0
H: 6 2 W: 13 11 b.Pontypool 9-12-76
Source: Llanelli. *Honours:* Wales 1 full cap.
2000–01 Bury 0 0
2001–02 Bury 7 0
2002–03 Bury 46 0
2003–04 Bury 46 0

2004–05 Bury 27 0 **126 0**
2005–06 Leyton Orient 43 0 **43 0**

GOURGEL, Nuno (F) 0 0
b.Angola 28-10-87
Source: Scholar.
2004–05 Leyton Orient 0 0
2005–06 Leyton Orient 0 0

HANSON, Christian (D) 21 0
H: 6 1 W: 13 02 b.Middlesbrough 3-8-81
Source: Trainee. *Honours:* England Schools, Youth.
1998–99 Middlesbrough 0 0
1999–2000 Middlesbrough 0 0
2000–01 Middlesbrough 0 0
2000–01 *Cambridge U* 8 0 **8 0**
2001–02 Middlesbrough 0 0
2001–02 *Torquay U* 6 0 **6 0**
2002–03 Middlesbrough 0 0
2003–04 Middlesbrough 0 0
From Havant & W
2004–05 Port Vale 5 0 **5 0**
2005–06 Leyton Orient 2 0 **2 0**

IBEHRE, Jabo (F) 148 25
H: 6 2 W: 13 13 b.Islington 28-1-83
Source: Trainee.
1999–2000 Leyton Orient 3 0
2000–01 Leyton Orient 5 2
2001–02 Leyton Orient 28 4
2002–03 Leyton Orient 25 5
2003–04 Leyton Orient 35 4
2004–05 Leyton Orient 19 2
2005–06 Leyton Orient 33 8 **148 25**

KEITH, Joe (M) 253 25
H: 5 7 W: 11 02 b.Plaistow 1-10-78
Source: Trainee.
1997–98 West Ham U 0 0
1998–99 West Ham U 0 0
1999–2000 Colchester U 45 1
2000–01 Colchester U 27 3
2001–02 Colchester U 41 4
2002–03 Colchester U 36 9
2003–04 Colchester U 28 2
2004–05 Colchester U 31 4 **208 23**
2004–05 *Bristol C* 3 0 **3 0**
2005–06 Leyton Orient 42 2 **42 2**

LOCKWOOD, Matt (D) 350 40
H: 5 11 W: 11 10 b.Southend 17-10-76
Source: Trainee.
1994–95 QPR 0 0
1995–96 QPR 0 0
1996–97 Bristol R 39 1
1997–98 Bristol R 24 0 **63 1**
1998–99 Leyton Orient 37 3
1999–2000 Leyton Orient 41 6
2000–01 Leyton Orient 32 7
2001–02 Leyton Orient 24 2
2002–03 Leyton Orient 43 5
2003–04 Leyton Orient 25 2
2004–05 Leyton Orient 43 6
2005–06 Leyton Orient 42 8 **287 39**

MACKIE, John (D) 158 14
H: 6 1 W: 12 08 b.Enfield 5-7-76
Source: Sutton U.
1999–2000 Reading 0 0
2000–01 Reading 10 0
2001–02 Reading 27 2
2002–03 Reading 25 0
2003–04 Reading 9 1 **71 3**
2003–04 Leyton Orient 20 1
2004–05 Leyton Orient 27 4
2005–06 Leyton Orient 40 6 **87 11**

McMAHON, Daryl (M) 63 5
H: 6 0 W: 12 07 b.Dublin 10-10-83
Honours: Eire Youth.
2000–01 West Ham U 0 0
2001–02 West Ham U 0 0
2002–03 West Ham U 0 0
2003–04 West Ham U 0 0
2003–04 *Torquay U* 1 0 **1 0**
2004–05 Port Vale 5 0 **5 0**
2004–05 Leyton Orient 24 3
2005–06 Leyton Orient 33 2 **57 5**

MILLER, Justin (D) 132 3
H: 6 1 W: 12 12 b.Johannesburg 16-12-80
Source: Academy.
1999–2000 Ipswich T 0 0
2000–01 Ipswich T 0 0
2001–02 Ipswich T 0 0
2002–03 Ipswich T 0 0
2002–03 Leyton Orient 19 0
2003–04 Leyton Orient 34 2
2004–05 Leyton Orient 43 0
2005–06 Leyton Orient 36 1 **132 3**

MORRIS, Glenn (G) 68 0
H: 6 0 W: 12 03 b.Woolwich 20-12-83
Source: Scholar.
2001–02 Leyton Orient 2 0
2002–03 Leyton Orient 23 0
2003–04 Leyton Orient 27 0
2004–05 Leyton Orient 12 0
2005–06 Leyton Orient 4 0 **68 0**

PALMER, Aiden (D) 8 0
H: 5 8 W: 10 10 b.Enfield 2-1-87
Source: Scholar.
2004–05 Leyton Orient 5 0
2005–06 Leyton Orient 3 0 **8 0**

SAAH, Brian (M) 21 0
H: 6 3 W: 12 03 b.Rush Green 16-12-86
Source: Scholar.
2003–04 Leyton Orient 6 0
2004–05 Leyton Orient 12 0
2005–06 Leyton Orient 3 0 **21 0**

SIMPSON, Michael (M) 436 22
H: 5 8 W: 10 12 b.Nottingham 28-2-74
Source: Trainee.
1992–93 Notts Co 0 0
1993–94 Notts Co 6 1
1994–95 Notts Co 19 2
1995–96 Notts Co 23 0
1996–97 Notts Co 1 0 **49 3**
1996–97 *Plymouth Arg* 12 0 **12 0**
1996–97 Wycombe W 20 1
1997–98 Wycombe W 21 0
1998–99 Wycombe W 33 4
1999–2000 Wycombe W 43 0
2000–01 Wycombe W 45 3
2001–02 Wycombe W 43 1
2002–03 Wycombe W 42 5
2003–04 Wycombe W 38 2 **285 16**
2004–05 Leyton Orient 45 2
2005–06 Leyton Orient 45 1 **90 3**

SMITH, Dean (D) 566 54
H: 6 1 W: 13 10 b.West Bromwich 19-3-71
Source: Trainee.
1988–89 Walsall 15 0
1989–90 Walsall 7 0
1990–91 Walsall 33 0
1991–92 Walsall 9 0
1992–93 Walsall 42 1
1993–94 Walsall 36 1 **142 2**
1994–95 Hereford U 35 3
1995–96 Hereford U 40 8
1996–97 Hereford U 42 8 **117 19**
1997–98 Leyton Orient 43 9
1998–99 Leyton Orient 37 9
1999–2000 Leyton Orient 44 4
2000–01 Leyton Orient 43 5
2001–02 Leyton Orient 45 2
2002–03 Leyton Orient 27 3
2002–03 Sheffield W 14 0
2003–04 Sheffield W 41 1 **55 1**
2004–05 Port Vale 13 0 **13 0**
2004–05 Leyton Orient 0 0
2005–06 Leyton Orient 0 0 **239 32**

STEELE, Lee (F) 265 72
H: 5 8 W: 12 05 b.Liverpool 2-12-73
Source: Bootle, Northwich V.
1997–98 Shrewsbury T 38 13
1998–99 Shrewsbury T 38 13
1999–2000 Shrewsbury T 37 11 **113 37**
2000–01 Brighton & HA 23 2
2001–02 Brighton & HA 37 9 **60 11**
2002–03 Oxford U 10 3
2003–04 Oxford U 16 1 **26 4**
2004–05 Leyton Orient 39 16
2005–06 Leyton Orient 27 4 **66 20**

TANN, Adam (D) 136 5
H: 6 0 W: 11 05 b.Fakenham 12-5-82
Source: Scholar. *Honours:* England Youth.
1999–2000 Cambridge U 0 0
2000–01 Cambridge U 1 0
2001–02 Cambridge U 25 0
2002–03 Cambridge U 25 1
2003–04 Cambridge U 34 2
2004–05 Cambridge U 36 1 **121 4**
From Gravesend & N.
2005–06 Notts Co 5 0 **5 0**
2005–06 Leyton Orient 10 1 **10 1**

TUDOR, Shane (M) 155 25
H: 5 7 W: 11 12 b.Wolverhampton 10-2-82
Source: Trainee.
1999–2000 Wolverhampton W 0 0
2000–01 Wolverhampton W 1 0
2001–02 Wolverhampton W 0 0 **1 0**
2001–02 Cambridge U 32 3
2002–03 Cambridge U 27 9
2003–04 Cambridge U 36 3
2004–05 Cambridge U 26 6 **121 21**
2005–06 Leyton Orient 33 4 **33 4**

WALLIS, Scott (M) 3 0
H: 5 10 W: 10 10 b.Enfield 28-6-88
Source: Scholar.
2004–05 Leyton Orient 3 0
2005–06 Leyton Orient 0 0 **3 0**

ZAKUANI, Gaby (D) 87 3
H: 6 1 W: 12 13 b.DR Congo 31-5-86
Source: Scholar. *Honours:* DR Congo full caps.
2002–03 Leyton Orient 1 0
2003–04 Leyton Orient 10 2
2004–05 Leyton Orient 33 0
2005–06 Leyton Orient 43 1 **87 3**

LINCOLN C (43)

ASAMOAH, Derek (F) 195 25
H: 5 6 W: 10 04 b.Ghana 1-5-81
Source: Slough T.
2001–02 Northampton T 40 3
2002–03 Northampton T 42 4
2003–04 Northampton T 31 3 **113 10**
2004–05 Mansfield T 30 5 **30 5**
2004–05 Lincoln C 10 0
2005–06 Lincoln C 25 2 **35 2**
2005–06 *Chester C* 17 8 **17 8**

BACON, Danny (F) 45 4
H: 5 10 W: 10 12 b.Mansfield 20-9-80
Source: Trainee.
1999–2000 Mansfield T 8 2
2000–01 Mansfield T 22 1
2001–02 Mansfield T 8 1
2002–03 Mansfield T 6 0 **44 4**
From Hucknall T
2005–06 Lincoln C 1 0 **1 0**

BEEVERS, Lee (D) 113 4
H: 6 2 W: 11 07 b.Doncaster 4-12-83
Source: Scholar. *Honours:* Wales Youth, Under-21.
2000–01 Ipswich T 0 0
2001–02 Ipswich T 0 0
2002–03 Ipswich T 0 0
2002–03 *Boston U* 1 0
2003–04 Boston U 40 2
2004–05 Boston U 31 1 **72 3**
2004–05 Lincoln C 8 0
2005–06 Lincoln C 33 1 **41 1**

BIRCH, Gary (F) 151 23
H: 6 0 W: 12 03 b.Birmingham 8-10-81
Source: Trainee.
1998–99 Walsall 0 0
1999–2000 Walsall 0 0
2000–01 Walsall 0 0
2000–01 *Exeter C* 9 2
2001–02 *Exeter C* 15 0 **24 2**
2001–02 Walsall 1 0
2002–03 Walsall 19 1
2003–04 Walsall 35 4
2003–04 *Barnsley* 8 2 **8 2**
2004–05 Walsall 13 2 **68 7**

2004–05 Kidderminster H 14 4 **14 4**
2005–06 Lincoln C 37 8 **37 8**

BLOOMER, Matt (D) 112 3
H: 6 1 W: 13 00 b.Cleethorpes 3-11-78
Source: Trainee.
1997–98 Grimsby T 0 0
1998–99 Grimsby T 4 0
1999–2000 Grimsby T 2 0
2000–01 Grimsby T 6 0
2001–02 Grimsby T 0 0
2001–02 Hull C 3 0
2001–02 *Lincoln C* 5 0
2002–03 Hull C 0 0 **3 0**
2002–03 Lincoln C 13 1
2003–04 Lincoln C 27 0
2004–05 Lincoln C 37 2
2005–06 Lincoln C 12 0 **94 3**
2005–06 *Grimsby T* 3 0 **15 0**

BROWN, Nat (F) 115 7
H: 6 2 W: 12 05 b.Sheffield 15-6-81
Source: Trainee.
1999–2000 Huddersfield T 0 0
2000–01 Huddersfield T 0 0
2001–02 Huddersfield T 0 0
2002–03 Huddersfield T 38 0
2003–04 Huddersfield T 21 0
2004–05 Huddersfield T 17 0 **76 0**
2005–06 Lincoln C 39 7 **39 7**

COLEMAN, Omari (F) 0 0
H: 5 10 W: 12 05 b.Birmingham 23-11-81
Source: Dulwich Hamlet.
2004–05 Watford 0 0
2005–06 Lincoln C 0 0

CRYAN, Colin (D) 42 0
H: 5 9 W: 11 08 b.Dublin 23-3-81
Source: Scholar. *Honours:* Eire Under-21.
1999–2000 Sheffield U 0 0
2000–01 Sheffield U 1 0
2001–02 Sheffield U 1 0
2002–03 Sheffield U 2 0
2003–04 Sheffield U 1 0
2004–05 Sheffield U 0 0 **5 0**
2005–06 Lincoln C 37 0 **37 0**

FOSTER, Luke (D) 16 1
H: 6 2 W: 12 08 b.Mexborough 8-9-85
Source: Scholar.
2004–05 Sheffield W 0 0
2005–06 Lincoln C 16 1 **16 1**

FRECKLINGTON, Lee (M) 21 2
H: 5 8 W: 11 00 b.Lincoln 8-9-85
Source: Scholar.
2003–04 Lincoln C 0 0
2004–05 Lincoln C 3 0
2005–06 Lincoln C 18 2 **21 2**

GORDON, Chris (D) 0 0
H: 6 0 W: 13 10 b.Grimsby 18-10-85
Source: Scholar.
2005–06 Lincoln C 0 0

GREEN, Francis (F) 214 33
H: 5 9 W: 11 04 b.Nottingham 25-4-80
Source: Ilkeston T.
1997–98 Peterborough U 4 1
1998–99 Peterborough U 7 1
1999–2000 Peterborough U 20 1
2000–01 Peterborough U 32 6
2001–02 Peterborough U 23 3
2002–03 Peterborough U 19 2
2003–04 Peterborough U 3 0 **108 14**
2003–04 Lincoln C 35 7
2004–05 Lincoln C 37 8
2005–06 Lincoln C 28 3 **100 18**
2005–06 *Boston U* 6 1 **6 1**

GRITTON, Martin (F) 196 37
H: 6 1 W: 12 02 b.Glasgow 1-6-78
Source: Porthleven.
1998–99 Plymouth Arg 2 0
1999–2000 Plymouth Arg 30 6
2000–01 Plymouth Arg 10 1
2001–02 Plymouth Arg 2 0
2002–03 Plymouth Arg 0 0 **44 7**
2002–03 Torquay U 43 13
2003–04 Torquay U 31 4
2004–05 Torquay U 19 6 **93 23**
2004–05 Grimsby T 23 4
2005–06 Grimsby T 26 2 **49 6**
2005–06 Lincoln C 10 1 **10 1**

HUGHES, Jeff (D) 22 2
H: 6 1 W: 11 00 b.Larne 29-5-85
Source: Larne. *Honours:* Northern Ireland Under-21, 2 full caps.
2005–06 Lincoln C 22 2 **22 2**

KERR, Scott (M) 42 2
H: 5 9 W: 10 07 b.Leeds 11-12-81
Source: Scholar.
2000–01 Bradford C 1 0 **1 0**
2001–02 Hull C 0 0
2002–03 Hull C 0 0
2003–04 Hull C 0 0
2004–05 Hull C 0 0
From Scarborough.
2005–06 Lincoln C 41 2 **41 2**

MARRIOTT, Alan (G) 271 0
H: 5 11 W: 12 05 b.Bedford 3-9-78
Source: Trainee.
1997–98 Tottenham H 0 0
1998–99 Tottenham H 0 0
1999–2000 Lincoln C 18 0
2000–01 Lincoln C 30 0
2001–02 Lincoln C 43 0
2002–03 Lincoln C 46 0
2003–04 Lincoln C 46 0
2004–05 Lincoln C 45 0
2005–06 Lincoln C 43 0 **271 0**

MAYO, Paul (D) 159 9
H: 5 11 W: 11 09 b.Lincoln 13-10-81
Source: Scholarship.
1999–2000 Lincoln C 19 0
2000–01 Lincoln C 27 0
2001–02 Lincoln C 14 0
2002–03 Lincoln C 15 0
2003–04 Lincoln C 31 6
2003–04 Watford 12 0
2004–05 Watford 13 0 **25 0**
2005–06 Lincoln C 28 3 **134 9**

McAULEY, Gareth (D) 72 8
H: 6 3 W: 13 00 b.Larne 5-12-79
Source: Coleraine. *Honours:* Northern Ireland 5 full caps.
2004–05 Lincoln C 37 3
2005–06 Lincoln C 35 5 **72 8**

McCOMBE, Jamie (D) 150 8
H: 6 5 W: 12 05 b.Scunthorpe 1-1-83
Source: Scholar.
2001–02 Scunthorpe U 17 0
2002–03 Scunthorpe U 31 1
2003–04 Scunthorpe U 15 0 **63 1**
2003–04 Lincoln C 8 0
2004–05 Lincoln C 41 3
2005–06 Lincoln C 38 4 **87 7**

METTAM, Leon (F) 1 0
H: 5 9 W: 11 01 b.Lincoln 9-12-86
Source: Scholar.
2005–06 Lincoln C 1 0 **1 0**

MORGAN, Paul (D) 179 1
H: 6 0 W: 11 05 b.Belfast 23-10-78
Source: Trainee. *Honours:* Northern Ireland Under-21.
1997–98 Preston NE 0 0
1998–99 Preston NE 0 0
1999–2000 Preston NE 0 0
2000–01 Preston NE 0 0
2001–02 Lincoln C 34 1
2002–03 Lincoln C 45 0
2003–04 Lincoln C 41 0
2004–05 Lincoln C 39 0
2005–06 Lincoln C 20 0 **179 1**

RAYNER, Simon (G) 4 0
H: 6 4 W: 15 00 b.Vancouver 8-7-83
Source: Bournemouth, Barry T, Port Talbot. *Honours:* Canada Under-23.
2004–05 Lincoln C 1 0
2005–06 Lincoln C 3 0 **4 0**

ROBINSON, Marvin (F) 102 20
H: 5 11 W: 12 13 b.Crewe 11-4-80
Source: Trainee.
1998–99 Derby Co 1 0
1999–2000 Derby Co 8 0
2000–01 Derby Co 0 0
2000–01 *Stoke C* 3 1 **3 1**
2001–02 Derby Co 2 1
2002–03 Derby Co 1 0 **12 1**
2002–03 *Tranmere R* 6 1 **6 1**
2003–04 Chesterfield 32 6
2004–05 Chesterfield 0 0 **32 6**
2004–05 Notts Co 2 0 **2 0**
2004–05 Rushden & D 2 0 **2 0**
2004–05 Walsall 10 4 **10 4**
2004–05 Stockport Co 3 0 **3 0**
2005–06 Lincoln C 32 7 **32 7**

ROBINSON, Steve (M) 240 5
H: 5 9 W: 11 00 b.Nottingham 17-1-75
Source: Trainee.
1993–94 Birmingham C 0 0
1994–95 Birmingham C 6 0
1995–96 Birmingham C 0 0
1995–96 *Peterborough U* 5 0 **5 0**
1996–97 Birmingham C 9 0
1997–98 Birmingham C 25 0
1998–99 Birmingham C 31 0
1999–2000 Birmingham C 6 0
2000–01 Birmingham C 4 0 **81 0**
2000–01 Swindon T 18 2
2001–02 Swindon T 40 0
2002–03 Swindon T 44 2
2003–04 Swindon T 22 1
2004–05 Swindon T 18 0 **142 5**
2005–06 Lincoln C 12 0 **12 0**

RYAN, Oliver (M) 16 0
H: 5 9 W: 11 00 b.Boston 26-9-85
Source: Scholar.
2004–05 Lincoln C 6 0
2005–06 Lincoln C 10 0 **16 0**

SHERLOCK, Jamie (D) 0 0
H: 6 1 W: 13 00 b.Hull 25-4-83
Source: N.Ferriby U, Brigg T, Scarborough, Gainsborough T.
2005–06 Lincoln C 0 0

STIRLING, Jude (D) 26 0
H: 6 2 W: 11 12 b.Enfield 29-6-82
Source: Trainee.
1999–2000 Luton T 0 0
2000–01 Luton T 9 0
2001–02 Luton T 1 0 **10 0**
From Tamworth.
2005–06 Oxford U 10 0 **10 0**
From Stevenage B, Hornchurch,**6 0**

WILKINSON, Tom (D) 1 0
H: 5 7 W: 11 03 b.Lincoln 26-9-85
Source: Scholar.
2005–06 Lincoln C 1 0 **1 0**

YEO, Simon (F) 134 42
H: 5 10 W: 11 08 b.Stockport 20-10-73
Source: Hyde U.
2002–03 Lincoln C 37 5
2003–04 Lincoln C 41 11
2004–05 Lincoln C 44 21
From New Zealand Knights
2005–06 Lincoln C 12 5 **134 42**

LIVERPOOL (44)

AGGER, Daniel (D) 38 5
H: 6 2 W: 12 06 b.Hvidovre 12-12-84
Honours: Denmark Youth, Under-21, 4 full caps, 1 goal.
2004–05 Brondby 26 5
2005–06 Brondby 8 0 **34 5**
2005–06 Liverpool 4 0 **4 0**

ALONSO, Xabi (M) 188 14
H: 6 0 W: 12 02 b.Tolosa 25-11-81
Honours: Spain 29 full caps, 1 goal.
1999–2000 Real Sociedad 0 0
2000–01 Eibar 14 0 **14 0**
2000–01 Real Sociedad 18 0
2001–02 Real Sociedad 29 3
2002–03 Real Sociedad 33 3
2003–04 Real Sociedad 35 3 **115 9**
2004–05 Liverpool 24 2
2005–06 Liverpool 35 3 **59 5**

ANDERSON, Paul (M) 0 0
H: 5 9 W: 10 04 b.Leicester 23-7-88
Source: Scholar.

2005–06	Hull C	0	0		
2005–06	Liverpool	0	0		

ANTWI-BIRAGO, Godwin (D) 0 0
H: 6 1 W: 13 09 b.Tafu 7-6-88
Source: San Gregorio.

2005–06	Liverpool	0	0		

BARRAGAN, Juan Antonio (D) 0 0
H: 6 1 W: 11 09 b.Seville 12-6-87
Source: Sevilla. *Honours:* Spain Youth.

2005–06	Liverpool	0	0		

CALLISTE, Ramon (F) 0 0
H: 5 10 W: 11 06 b.Cardiff 16-12-85
Source: Trainee. *Honours:* Wales Under-21.

2003–04	Manchester U	0	0		
2004–05	Manchester U	0	0		
2005–06	Liverpool	0	0		

CARRAGHER, Jamie (D) 290 2
H: 5 9 W: 12 01 b.Liverpool 28-1-78
Source: Trainee. *Honours:* England Youth, Under-21, B, 29 full caps.

1995–96	Liverpool	0	0		
1996–97	Liverpool	2	1		
1997–98	Liverpool	20	0		
1998–99	Liverpool	34	1		
1999–2000	Liverpool	36	0		
2000–01	Liverpool	34	0		
2001–02	Liverpool	33	0		
2002–03	Liverpool	35	0		
2003–04	Liverpool	22	0		
2004–05	Liverpool	38	0		
2005–06	Liverpool	36	0	**290**	**2**

CARSON, Scott (G) 16 0
H: 6 3 W: 14 00 b.Whitehaven 3-9-85
Source: Scholar. *Honours:* England Youth, Under-21, B.

2002–03	Leeds U	0	0		
2003–04	Leeds U	3	0		
2004–05	Leeds U	0	0	**3**	**0**
2004–05	Liverpool	4	0		
2005–06	Liverpool	0	0	**4**	**0**
2005–06	*Sheffield W*	9	0	**9**	**0**

CHEYROU, Bruno (M) 171 32
H: 6 1 W: 13 03 b.Suresnes 10-5-78
Source: Lens, Racing. *Honours:* France 2 full caps.

1998–99	Lille	20	6		
1999–2000	Lille	21	5		
2000–01	Lille	27	6		
2001–02	Lille	27	11	**95**	**28**
2002–03	Liverpool	19	0		
2003–04	Liverpool	12	2		
2004–05	*Marseille*	19	1	**19**	**1**
2005–06	*Bordeaux*	26	1	**26**	**1**
2005–06	Liverpool	0	0	**31**	**2**

CISSE, Djibril (F) 177 83
H: 6 0 W: 13 00 b.Arles 12-8-81
Honours: France 30 full caps, 9 goals.

1998–99	Auxerre	1	0		
1999–2000	Auxerre	2	0		
2000–01	Auxerre	25	8		
2001–02	Auxerre	29	22		
2002–03	Auxerre	33	14		
2003–04	Auxerre	38	26	**128**	**70**
2004–05	Liverpool	16	4		
2005–06	Liverpool	33	9	**49**	**13**

CROUCH, Peter (F) 190 58
H: 6 7 W: 13 03 b.Macclesfield 30-1-81
Source: Trainee. *Honours:* England Youth, Under-20, Under-21, B, 11 full caps, 6 goals.

1998–99	Tottenham H	0	0		
1999–2000	Tottenham H	0	0		
2000–01	QPR	42	10	**42**	**10**
2001–02	Portsmouth	37	18	**37**	**18**
2001–02	Aston Villa	7	2		
2002–03	Aston Villa	14	0		
2003–04	Aston Villa	16	4	**37**	**6**
2003–04	*Norwich C*	15	4	**15**	**4**
2004–05	Southampton	27	12	**27**	**12**
2005–06	Liverpool	32	8	**32**	**8**

DIAO, Salif (M) 127 1
H: 6 1 W: 12 08 b.Kedougou 10-2-77
Honours: Senegal 29 full caps, 3 goals.

1996–97	Epinal	2	0	**2**	**0**
1996–97	Monaco	0	0		
1997–98	Monaco	12	0		
1998–99	Monaco	14	0		
1999–2000	Monaco	1	0	**27**	**0**
2000–01	Sedan	26	0		
2001–02	Sedan	22	0	**48**	**0**
2002–03	Liverpool	26	1		
2003–04	Liverpool	3	0		
2004–05	Liverpool	8	0		
2004–05	*Birmingham C*	2	0	**2**	**0**
2005–06	Liverpool	0	0	**37**	**1**
2005–06	*Portsmouth*	11	0	**11**	**0**

DIARRA, Alou (M) 94 6
H: 6 1 W: 12 03 b.Villepinte 15-7-81
Source: Louhans, Bayern Munich.

2002–03	Le Havre	25	0	**25**	**0**
2003–04	*Bastia*	35	4	**35**	**4**
2004–05	*Lens*	34	2	**34**	**2**
2005–06	Liverpool	0	0		

DUDEK, Jerzy (G) 276 0
H: 6 2 W: 12 08 b.Ribnek 23-3-73
Source: GKS Tychy. *Honours:* Poland 51 full caps.

1995–96	Sokol Tychy	15	0	**15**	**0**
1996–97	Feyenoord	0	0		
1997–98	Feyenoord	34	0		
1998–99	Feyenoord	34	0		
1999–2000	Feyenoord	34	0		
2000–01	Feyenoord	34	0	**136**	**0**
2001–02	Liverpool	35	0		
2002–03	Liverpool	30	0		
2003–04	Liverpool	30	0		
2004–05	Liverpool	24	0		
2005–06	Liverpool	6	0	**125**	**0**

FINNAN, Steve (D) 372 15
H: 6 0 W: 12 03 b.Limerick 24-4-76
Source: Welling U. *Honours:* Eire Under-21, B, 38 full caps, 1 goal.

1995–96	Birmingham C	12	1		
1995–96	*Notts Co*	17	2		
1996–97	Birmingham C	3	0	**15**	**1**
1996–97	Notts Co	23	0		
1997–98	Notts Co	44	5		
1998–99	Notts Co	13	0	**97**	**7**
1998–99	Fulham	22	2		
1999–2000	Fulham	35	2		
2000–01	Fulham	45	2		
2001–02	Fulham	38	0		
2002–03	Fulham	32	0	**172**	**6**
2003–04	Liverpool	22	0		
2004–05	Liverpool	33	1		
2005–06	Liverpool	33	0	**88**	**1**

FOWLER, Robbie (F) 360 160
H: 5 10 W: 12 05 b.Liverpool 9-4-75
Source: Trainee. *Honours:* England Youth, B, Under-21, 26 full caps, 7 goals.

1991–92	Liverpool	0	0		
1992–93	Liverpool	0	0		
1993–94	Liverpool	28	12		
1994–95	Liverpool	42	25		
1995–96	Liverpool	38	28		
1996–97	Liverpool	32	18		
1997–98	Liverpool	20	9		
1998–99	Liverpool	25	14		
1999–2000	Liverpool	14	3		
2000–01	Liverpool	27	8		
2001–02	Liverpool	10	3		
2001–02	Leeds U	22	12		
2002–03	Leeds U	8	2	**30**	**14**
2002–03	Manchester C	13	2		
2003–04	Manchester C	31	7		
2004–05	Manchester C	32	11		
2005–06	Manchester C	4	1	**80**	**21**
2005–06	Liverpool	14	5	**250**	**125**

FOY, Robbie (F) 30 3
H: 5 9 W: 10 07 b.Edinburgh 29-10-85
Source: Trainee. *Honours:* Scotland Under-21.

2002–03	Liverpool	0	0		
2003–04	Liverpool	0	0		
2004–05	Liverpool	0	0		
2004–05	*Chester C*	13	0	**13**	**0**
2005–06	Liverpool	0	0		
2005–06	*Wrexham*	17	3	**17**	**3**

GERRARD, Steven (M) 232 37
H: 6 0 W: 12 05 b.Whiston 30-5-80
Source: Trainee. *Honours:* England Youth, Under-21, 47 full caps, 9 goals.

1997–98	Liverpool	0	0		
1998–99	Liverpool	12	0		
1999–2000	Liverpool	29	1		
2000–01	Liverpool	33	7		
2001–02	Liverpool	28	3		
2002–03	Liverpool	34	5		
2003–04	Liverpool	34	4		
2004–05	Liverpool	30	7		
2005–06	Liverpool	32	10	**232**	**37**

GONZALEZ, Jose Miguel (D) 80 20
H: 5 9 W: 12 08 b.Malaga 15-11-79
Honours: Chile 14 caps, 3 goals.

2002	Univ Catolica	6	0		
2003	Univ Catolica	28	9		
2004	Univ Catolica	8	1	**42**	**10**
2004–05	Albacete	26	5	**26**	**5**
2005–06	Real Sociedad	12	5	**12**	**5**
2005–06	Liverpool	0	0		

To Real Sociedad (loan) January 2006

GUTHRIE, Danny (M) 0 0
H: 5 9 W: 11 06 b.Shrewsbury 18-4-87
Source: Scholar. *Honours:* England Schools, Youth.

2004–05	Liverpool	0	0		
2005–06	Liverpool	0	0		

HAMANN, Dietmar (M) 319 18
H: 6 2 W: 13 00 b.Waldasson 27-8-73
Source: Wacker Munich. *Honours:* Germany Youth, Under-21, 59 full caps, 5 goals.

1993–94	Bayern Munich	5	1		
1994–95	Bayern Munich	30	0		
1995–96	Bayern Munich	20	2		
1996–97	Bayern Munich	22	1		
1997–98	Bayern Munich	28	2	**105**	**6**
1998–99	Newcastle U	23	4	**23**	**4**
1999–2000	Liverpool	28	1		
2000–01	Liverpool	30	2		
2001–02	Liverpool	31	1		
2002–03	Liverpool	30	2		
2003–04	Liverpool	25	2		
2004–05	Liverpool	30	0		
2005–06	Liverpool	17	0	**191**	**8**

HAMMILL, Adam (M) 0 0
b.Liverpool 25-1-88
Source: Scholar.

2005–06	Liverpool	0	0		

HOBBS, Jack (D) 1 0
H: 6 3 W: 13 05 b.Portsmouth 18-8-88
Source: Scholar.

2004–05	Lincoln C	1	0	**1**	**0**
2005–06	Liverpool	0	0		

HYYPIA, Sami (D) 415 24
H: 6 3 W: 13 09 b.Porvoo 7-10-73
Source: KuMu. *Honours:* Finland Youth, Under-21, 75 full caps, 4 goals.

1993	MyPa 47	12	0		
1994	MyPa 47	25	0		
1995	MyPa 47	26	3	**63**	**3**
1995–96	Willem II	14	0		
1996–97	Willem II	30	1		
1997–98	Willem II	30	0		
1998–99	Willem II	26	2	**100**	**3**
1999–2000	Liverpool	38	2		
2000–01	Liverpool	35	3		
2001–02	Liverpool	37	3		
2002–03	Liverpool	36	3		
2003–04	Liverpool	38	4		
2004–05	Liverpool	32	2		
2005–06	Liverpool	36	1	**252**	**18**

IDRIZAJ, Bezian (F) 0 0
H: 6 2 W: 12 02 b.Austria 12-10-87
Source: LASK Linz.

2005–06	Liverpool	0	0		

JOSEMI (D) 114 0
H: 5 9 W: 12 08 b.Malaga 15-11-79

2000–01	Malaga	1	0		
2001–02	Malaga	23	0		

2002–03	Malaga	32	0		
2003–04	Malaga	37	0	**93**	**0**
2004–05	Liverpool	15	0		
2005–06	Liverpool	6	0	**21**	**0**

To Villarreal January 2006

KEWELL, Harry (M) 262 56
H: 5 9 W: 12 06 b.Sydney 22-9-78
Source: NSW Soccer Academy. *Honours:* Australia Youth, Under-20, 23 full caps, 7 goals.

1995–96	Leeds U	2	0		
1996–97	Leeds U	1	0		
1997–98	Leeds U	29	5		
1998–99	Leeds U	38	6		
1999–2000	Leeds U	36	10		
2000–01	Leeds U	17	2		
2001–02	Leeds U	27	8		
2002–03	Leeds U	31	14	**181**	**45**
2003–04	Liverpool	36	7		
2004–05	Liverpool	18	1		
2005–06	Liverpool	27	3	**81**	**11**

KIRKLAND, Christopher (G) 59 0
H: 6 5 W: 14 08 b.Leicester 2-5-81
Source: Trainee. *Honours:* England Youth, Under-21.

1997–98	Coventry C	0	0		
1998–99	Coventry C	0	0		
1999–2000	Coventry C	0	0		
2000–01	Coventry C	23	0		
2001–02	Coventry C	1	0	**24**	**0**
2001–02	Liverpool	1	0		
2002–03	Liverpool	8	0		
2003–04	Liverpool	6	0		
2004–05	Liverpool	10	0		
2005–06	Liverpool	0	0	**25**	**0**
2005–06	*WBA*	10	0	**10**	**0**

KROMKAMP, Jan (D) 213 11
H: 6 3 W: 13 06 b.Makkinga 17-8-80
Honours: Holland 11 full caps.

1998–99	Go Ahead	28	1		
1999–2000	Go Ahead	33	4	**61**	**5**
2000–01	AZ	25	2		
2001–02	AZ	22	1		
2002–03	AZ	25	2		
2003–04	AZ	34	0		
2004–05	AZ	27	1	**133**	**6**
2005–06	Villarreal	6	0	**6**	**0**
2005–06	Liverpool	13	0	**13**	**0**

LE TALLEC, Anthony (M) 105 11
H: 6 0 W: 12 00 b.Hennebont 3-10-84
Honours: France Under-21.

2001–02	Le Havre	24	5		
2002–03	Le Havre	30	2	**54**	**7**
2003–04	Liverpool	13	0		
2004–05	Liverpool	4	0		
2004–05	*St Etienne*	7	1	**7**	**1**
2005–06	Liverpool	0	0	**17**	**0**
2005–06	*Sunderland*	27	3	**27**	**3**

LUIS GARCIA (M) 275 79
H: 5 6 W: 10 05 b.Badalona 24-6-78
Honours: Spain 13 full caps, 3 goals.

1997–98	Barcelona B	36	15		
1998–99	Barcelona B	36	10	**72**	**25**
1999–2000	Valladolid	6	0		
1999–2000	Toledo	17	4	**17**	**4**
2000–01	Tenerife	40	16	**40**	**16**
2001–02	Valladolid	25	6	**31**	**6**
2002–03	Atletico Madrid	30	9	**30**	**9**
2003–04	Barcelona	25	4	**25**	**4**
2004–05	Liverpool	29	8		
2005–06	Liverpool	31	7	**60**	**15**

MANNIX, David (M) 0 0
H: 5 8 W: 11 06 b.Crewe 24-9-85
Source: Trainee. *Honours:* England Under-20.

2003–04	Liverpool	0	0		
2004–05	Liverpool	0	0		
2005–06	Liverpool	0	0		

MARTIN, David (G) 17 0
H: 6 1 W: 13 04 b.Romford 22-1-86
Source: Scholar. *Honours:* England Youth, Under-20.

2003–04	Wimbledon	2	0	**2**	**0**
2004–05	Milton Keynes D	15	0		
2005–06	Milton Keynes D	0	0	**15**	**0**
2005–06	Liverpool	0	0		

MEDJANI, Carl (D) 48 0
H: 6 0 W: 13 04 b.Lyon 15-5-85
Source: St Etienne.

2003–04	Liverpool	0	0		
2004–05	*Lorient*	25	0	**25**	**0**
2005–06	*Metz*	23	0	**23**	**0**
2005–06	Liverpool	0	0		

MELLOR, Neil (F) 31 5
H: 6 0 W: 13 05 b.Sheffield 4-11-82
Source: Scholar.

2001–02	Liverpool	0	0		
2002–03	Liverpool	3	0		
2003–04	Liverpool	0	0		
2003–04	*West Ham U*	16	2	**16**	**2**
2004–05	Liverpool	9	2		
2005–06	Liverpool	0	0	**12**	**2**
2005–06	*Wigan Ath*	3	1	**3**	**1**

MORIENTES, Fernando (F) 335 123
H: 6 0 W: 12 09 b.Caceres 5-4-76
Honours: Spain 43 full caps, 27 goals.

1993–94	Albacete	2	0		
1994–95	Albacete	20	5	**22**	**5**
1995–96	Zaragoza	29	13		
1996–97	Zaragoza	37	15	**66**	**28**
1997–98	Real Madrid	33	12		
1998–99	Real Madrid	33	19		
1999–2000	Real Madrid	26	12		
2000–01	Real Madrid	22	6		
2001–02	Real Madrid	33	18		
2002–03	Real Madrid	19	5		
2003–04	Monaco	28	10	**28**	**10**
2004–05	Real Madrid	12	0	**178**	**72**
2004–05	Liverpool	13	3		
2005–06	Liverpool	28	5	**41**	**8**

O'DONNELL, Daniel (D) 0 0
b.Livepool 10-3-86
Source: Scholar.

2004–05	Liverpool	0	0		
2005–06	Liverpool	0	0		

PELTIER, Lee (F) 0 0
H: 5 10 W: 12 00 b.Liverpool 11-12-86
Source: Scholar.

2004–05	Liverpool	0	0		
2005–06	Liverpool	0	0		

POTTER, Darren (M) 12 0
H: 6 0 W: 10 08 b.Liverpool 21-12-84
Source: Scholar. *Honours:* Eire Youth, Under-21.

2001–02	Liverpool	0	0		
2002–03	Liverpool	0	0		
2003–04	Liverpool	0	0		
2004–05	Liverpool	2	0		
2005–06	Liverpool	0	0	**2**	**0**
2005–06	*Southampton*	10	0	**10**	**0**

RAVEN, David (D) 12 0
H: 6 0 W: 11 04 b.Birkenhead 10-3-85
Source: Scholar. *Honours:* England Youth, Under-20.

2001–02	Liverpool	0	0		
2002–03	Liverpool	0	0		
2003–04	Liverpool	0	0		
2004–05	Liverpool	1	0		
2005–06	Liverpool	0	0	**1**	**0**
2005–06	*Tranmere R*	11	0	**11**	**0**

REINA, Jose (G) 164 0
H: 6 2 W: 14 06 b.Madrid 31-8-82
Honours: Spain 3 full caps.

1999–2000	Barcelona B	30	0	**30**	**0**
2000–01	Barcelona	19	0		
2001–02	Barcelona	11	0	**30**	**0**
2002–03	Villarreal	33	0		
2003–04	Villarreal	38	0		
2004–05	Villarreal	0	0	**71**	**0**
2005–06	Liverpool	33	0	**33**	**0**

RIISE, John Arne (M) 216 24
H: 6 1 W: 14 00 b.Molde 24-9-80
Honours: Norway Youth, Under-21, 54 full caps, 7 goals.

1998–99	Monaco	7	0		
1999–2000	Monaco	21	1		
2000–01	Monaco	16	3	**44**	**4**
2001–02	Liverpool	38	7		
2002–03	Liverpool	37	6		
2003–04	Liverpool	28	0		
2004–05	Liverpool	37	6		
2005–06	Liverpool	32	1	**172**	**20**

ROQUE, Miguel (D) 0 0
H: 6 2 W: 12 03 b.Lleida 8-7-88
Source: EU Lleida.

2005–06	Liverpool	0	0		

SINAMA-PONGOLLE, Florent (F) 59 7
H: 5 7 W: 11 05 b.Saint-Pierre 20-10-84
Honours: France Under-21.

2001–02	Le Havre	11	2		
2002–03	Le Havre	0	0	**11**	**2**
2003–04	Liverpool	15	2		
2004–05	Liverpool	16	2		
2005–06	Liverpool	7	0	**38**	**4**
2005–06	*Blackburn R*	10	1	**10**	**1**

SISSOKO, Mohamed (M) 71 0
H: 6 2 W: 12 08 b.Mont Saint Aigan 22-1-85
Source: Auxerre. *Honours:* Mali 11 full caps, 2 goals.

2003–04	Valencia	21	0		
2004–05	Valencia	24	0	**45**	**0**
2005–06	Liverpool	26	0	**26**	**0**

SMITH, James (M) 0 0
b.Liverpool 17-10-85

2004–05	Liverpool	0	0		
2005–06	Liverpool	0	0		

TRAORE, Djimi (D) 107 0
H: 6 2 W: 12 07 b.Saint-Ouen 1-3-80
Source: Laval. *Honours:* France Youth, Under-21, Mali full caps.

1998–99	Liverpool	0	0		
1999–2000	Liverpool	0	0		
2000–01	Liverpool	8	0		
2001–02	Liverpool	0	0		
2001–02	Lens	19	0	**19**	**0**
2002–03	Liverpool	32	0		
2003–04	Liverpool	7	0		
2004–05	Liverpool	26	0		
2005–06	Liverpool	15	0	**88**	**0**

WARNOCK, Stephen (D) 95 5
H: 5 7 W: 11 09 b.Ormskirk 12-12-81
Source: Trainee. *Honours:* England Schools, Youth.

1998–99	Liverpool	0	0		
1999–2000	Liverpool	0	0		
2000–01	Liverpool	0	0		
2001–02	Liverpool	0	0		
2002–03	Liverpool	0	0		
2002–03	*Bradford C*	12	1	**12**	**1**
2003–04	Liverpool	0	0		
2003–04	*Coventry C*	44	3	**44**	**3**
2004–05	Liverpool	19	0		
2005–06	Liverpool	20	1	**39**	**1**

WHITBREAD, Zak (D) 25 0
H: 6 2 W: 12 07 b.Houston 4-3-84
Honours: USA Under-23.

2002–03	Liverpool	0	0		
2003–04	Liverpool	0	0		
2004–05	Liverpool	0	0		
2005–06	Liverpool	0	0		
2005–06	*Millwall*	25	0	**25**	**0**

WILKIE, Ryan (M) 0 0
H: 5 9 W: 11 06 b.Glasgow 11-12-85
Source: Trainee.

2002–03	Liverpool	0	0		
2003–04	Liverpool	0	0		
2004–05	Liverpool	0	0		
2005–06	Liverpool	0	0		

WILLIS, Paul (G) 0 0
H: 5 10 W: 12 00 b.Belfast 5-3-86
Source: Trainee. *Honours:* Northern Ireland Under-21.

2003–04	Liverpool	0	0		
2004–05	Liverpool	0	0		
2005–06	Liverpool	0	0		
2005–06	*Stockport Co*	0	0		

ZENDEN, Boudewijn (M) 292 41
H: 5 8 W: 11 01 b.Maastricht 15-8-76
Honours: Holland 54 full caps, 7 goals.

1994–95	PSV Eindhoven	27	5		
1995–96	PSV Eindhoven	25	7		

1996–97	PSV Eindhoven	34	8		
1997–98	PSV Eindhoven	25	3	**111**	**23**
1998–99	Barcelona	25	0		
1999–2000	Barcelona	29	2		
2000–01	Barcelona	10	1	**64**	**3**
2001–02	Chelsea	22	3		
2002–03	Chelsea	21	1		
2003–04	Chelsea	0	0	**43**	**4**
2003–04	*Middlesbrough*	31	4		
2004–05	Middlesbrough	36	5	**67**	**9**
2005–06	Liverpool	7	2	**7**	**2**

Scholars
Barnett, Charlie; Barratt, Paul James; Behan, John; Burns, Michael; Darby, Stephen; Flynn, Ryan; Lindfield, Craig; Mimms, Josh; Nardiello, Michael Antonio; Pringle, Jonathon; Putterill, Raymond; Roberts, David; Ryan, James; Spearing, Jay Francis; Threlfall, Robert Richard; Wignall, Ryan; Woodward, Lee Thomas.

LUTON T (45)

ANDREW, Calvin (F) **20 2**
H: 6 0 W: 12 11 b.Luton 19-12-86
Source: Scholar.

2004–05	Luton T	8	0		
2005–06	Luton T	1	1	**9**	**1**
2005–06	*Grimsby T*	8	1	**8**	**1**
2005–06	*Bristol C*	3	0	**3**	**0**

BARNETT, Leon (D) **20 0**
H: 6 0 W: 12 04 b.Stevenage 30-11-85
Source: Scholar.

2003–04	Luton T	0	0		
2004–05	Luton T	0	0		
2005–06	Luton T	20	0	**20**	**0**

BECKWITH, Rob (G) **19 0**
H: 6 1 W: 13 12 b.Hackney 12-9-84
Source: Scholar.

2002–03	Luton T	4	0		
2003–04	Luton T	13	0		
2004–05	Luton T	0	0		
2005–06	Luton T	0	0	**17**	**0**
2005–06	*Chesterfield*	2	0	**2**	**0**

BELL, David (M) **130 10**
H: 5 10 W: 11 05 b.Kettering 21-1-84
Source: Trainee. *Honours:* Eire Under-21.

2001–02	Rushden & D	0	0		
2002–03	Rushden & D	30	3		
2003–04	Rushden & D	37	1		
2004–05	Rushden & D	40	3		
2005–06	Rushden & D	14	3	**121**	**10**
2005–06	Luton T	9	0	**9**	**0**

BERESFORD, Marlon (G) **448 0**
H: 6 1 W: 13 10 b.Lincoln 2-9-69
Source: Trainee.

1987–88	Sheffield W	0	0		
1988–89	Sheffield W	0	0		
1989–90	Sheffield W	0	0		
1989–90	*Bury*	1	0	**1**	**0**
1989–90	*Ipswich T*	0	0		
1990–91	Sheffield W	0	0		
1990–91	*Northampton T*	13	0		
1990–91	*Crewe Alex*	3	0	**3**	**0**
1991–92	Sheffield W	0	0		
1991–92	*Northampton T*	15	0	**28**	**0**
1992–93	Burnley	44	0		
1993–94	Burnley	46	0		
1994–95	Burnley	40	0		
1995–96	Burnley	36	0		
1996–97	Burnley	40	0		
1997–98	Burnley	34	0		
1997–98	Middlesbrough	3	0		
1998–99	Middlesbrough	4	0		
1999–2000	Middlesbrough	1	0		
2000–01	Middlesbrough	1	0		
2000–01	*Sheffield W*	4	0	**4**	**0**
2001–02	Middlesbrough	1	0	**10**	**0**
2001–02	*Wolverhampton W*	0	0		
2001–02	*Burnley*	13	0		
2002–03	York C	6	0	**6**	**0**
2002–03	Burnley	34	0		
2003–04	Burnley	0	0	**287**	**0**
2003–04	Bradford C	5	0	**5**	**0**
2003–04	Luton T	11	0		
2003–04	Barnsley	14	0	**14**	**0**
2004–05	Luton T	38	0		
2005–06	Luton T	41	0	**90**	**0**

BRILL, Dean (G) **10 0**
H: 6 2 W: 14 05 b.Luton 2-12-85
Source: Scholar.

2003–04	Luton T	5	0		
2004–05	Luton T	0	0		
2005–06	Luton T	5	0	**10**	**0**

BRKOVIC, Ahmet (M) **242 36**
H: 5 8 W: 11 11 b.Dubrovnik 23-9-74
Source: Dubrovnik.

1999–2000	Leyton Orient	29	5		
2000–01	Leyton Orient	40	3		
2001–02	Leyton Orient	0	0	**69**	**8**
2001–02	Luton T	21	1		
2002–03	Luton T	36	3		
2003–04	Luton T	32	1		
2004–05	Luton T	42	15		
2005–06	Luton T	42	8	**173**	**28**

COYNE, Chris (D) **214 13**
H: 6 2 W: 13 10 b.Brisbane 20-12-78
Source: Perth SC. *Honours:* Australia Youth, Under-23.

1995–96	West Ham U	0	0		
1996–97	West Ham U	0	0		
1997–98	West Ham U	0	0		
1998–99	West Ham U	1	0	**1**	**0**
1998–99	*Brentford*	7	0	**7**	**0**
1998–99	*Southend U*	1	0	**1**	**0**
1999–2000	Dundee	2	0		
2000–01	Dundee	18	0	**20**	**0**
2001–02	Luton T	31	3		
2002–03	Luton T	40	1		
2003–04	Luton T	44	2		
2004–05	Luton T	40	5		
2005–06	Luton T	30	2	**185**	**13**

DAVIS, Sol (D) **253 2**
H: 5 7 W: 12 04 b.Cheltenham 4-9-79
Source: Trainee.

1997–98	Swindon T	6	0		
1998–99	Swindon T	25	0		
1999–2000	Swindon T	29	0		
2000–01	Swindon T	36	0		
2001–02	Swindon T	21	0		
2002–03	Swindon T	0	0	**117**	**0**
2002–03	Luton T	34	0		
2003–04	Luton T	36	0		
2004–05	Luton T	45	2		
2005–06	Luton T	21	0	**136**	**2**

DEENEY, David (D) **0 0**
H: 5 9 W: 10 06 b.Bulawayo 12-1-87
Source: Scholar.

2003–04	Luton T	0	0		
2004–05	Luton T	0	0		
2005–06	Luton T	0	0		

EDWARDS, Carlos (M) **208 25**
H: 5 8 W: 11 02 b.Port of Spain 24-10-78
Source: Defence Force. *Honours:* Trinidad & Tobago 54 full caps, 1 goal.

2000–01	Wrexham	36	4		
2001–02	Wrexham	26	5		
2002–03	Wrexham	44	8		
2003–04	Wrexham	42	5		
2004–05	Wrexham	18	1	**166**	**23**
2005–06	Luton T	42	2	**42**	**2**

FEENEY, Warren (F) **187 57**
H: 5 8 W: 12 04 b.Belfast 17-1-81
Source: Trainee. *Honours:* Northern Ireland Schools, Youth, Under-21, 11 full caps, 2 goals.

1997–98	Leeds U	0	0		
1998–99	Leeds U	0	0		
1999–2000	Leeds U	0	0		
2000–01	Leeds U	0	0		
2000–01	*Bournemouth*	10	4		
2001–02	Bournemouth	37	13		
2002–03	Bournemouth	21	7		
2003–04	Bournemouth	40	12	**108**	**36**
2004–05	Stockport Co	31	15	**31**	**15**
2004–05	Luton T	6	0		
2005–06	Luton T	42	6	**48**	**6**

FOLEY, Kevin (D) **112 3**
H: 5 9 W: 11 11 b.Luton 1-11-84
Source: Scholar. *Honours:* Eire Under-21.

2002–03	Luton T	2	0		
2003–04	Luton T	33	1		
2004–05	Luton T	39	2		
2005–06	Luton T	38	0	**112**	**3**

HEIKKINEN, Markus (D) **259 6**
H: 6 1 W: 12 13 b.Katrineholm 13-10-78
Honours: Finland 22 full caps.

1996	TPS Turku	0	0		
1997	TPS Turku	22	0	**22**	**0**
1998	MyPa	14	0		
1999	MyPa	29	1	**43**	**1**
2000	HJK Helsinki	32	0		
2001	HJK Helsinki	33	1		
2002	HJK Helsinki	20	0	**85**	**1**
2002–03	Portsmouth	2	0	**2**	**0**
2003–04	Aberdeen	38	0		
2004–05	Aberdeen	30	2	**68**	**2**
2005–06	Luton T	39	2	**39**	**2**

HOLMES, Peter (M) **100 11**
H: 5 11 W: 11 13 b.Bishop Auckland 18-11-80
Source: Trainee. *Honours:* England Schools.

1997–98	Sheffield W	0	0		
1998–99	Sheffield W	0	0		
1999–2000	Sheffield W	0	0		
2000–01	Luton T	18	1		
2001–02	Luton T	7	1		
2002–03	Luton T	17	1		
2003–04	Luton T	16	3		
2004–05	Luton T	19	3		
2005–06	Luton T	23	2	**100**	**11**

HOWARD, Steve (F) **440 140**
H: 6 3 W: 15 00 b.Durham 10-5-76
Source: Tow Law T.

1995–96	Hartlepool U	39	7		
1996–97	Hartlepool U	32	8		
1997–98	Hartlepool U	43	7		
1998–99	Hartlepool U	28	5	**142**	**27**
1998–99	Northampton T	12	0		
1999–2000	Northampton T	41	10		
2000–01	Northampton T	33	8	**86**	**18**
2000–01	Luton T	12	3		
2001–02	Luton T	42	24		
2002–03	Luton T	41	22		
2003–04	Luton T	34	14		
2004–05	Luton T	40	18		
2005–06	Luton T	43	14	**212**	**95**

HUGHES, Paul (M) **111 9**
H: 6 0 W: 12 06 b.Hammersmith 19-4-76
Source: Trainee. *Honours:* England Schools.

1994–95	Chelsea	0	0		
1995–96	Chelsea	0	0		
1996–97	Chelsea	12	2		
1997–98	Chelsea	9	0		
1998–99	Chelsea	0	0		
1998–99	*Stockport Co*	7	0	**7**	**0**
1998–99	*Norwich C*	4	1	**4**	**1**
1999–2000	Chelsea	0	0	**21**	**2**
1999–2000	*Crewe Alex*	0	0		
1999–2000	Southampton	0	0		
2000–01	Southampton	0	0		
2001–02	Southampton	0	0		
2001–02	Luton T	22	2		
2002–03	Luton T	35	3		
2003–04	Luton T	22	1		
2004–05	Luton T	0	0		
2005–06	Luton T	0	0	**79**	**6**

KEANE, Keith (M) **42 2**
H: 5 9 W: 12 02 b.Luton 20-11-86
Source: Scholar. *Honours:* Eire Youth, Under-21.

2003–04	Luton T	15	1		
2004–05	Luton T	17	0		
2005–06	Luton T	10	1	**42**	**2**

LEARY, Michael (M) **50 3**
H: 6 0 W: 11 11 b.Ealing 17-4-83
Source: Scholar.

2001–02	Luton T	0	0		
2002–03	Luton T	0	0		
2003–04	Luton T	14	2		
2004–05	Luton T	8	0		
2005–06	Luton T	0	0	**22**	**2**

2005–06 *Bristol R* 13 0 **13 0**
2005–06 *Walsall* 15 1 **15 1**

MORGAN, Dean (M) 138 15
H: 5 11 W: 13 00 b.Enfield 3-10-83
Source: Scholar.
2000–01 Colchester U 4 0
2001–02 Colchester U 30 0
2002–03 Colchester U 37 6
2003–04 Colchester U 0 0 **71 6**
2003–04 Reading 13 1
2004–05 Reading 18 2 **31 3**
2005–06 Luton T 36 6 **36 6**

NICHOLLS, Kevin (M) 219 33
H: 5 10 W: 11 13 b.Newham 2-1-79
Source: Trainee. *Honours:* England Youth.
1995–96 Charlton Ath 0 0
1996–97 Charlton Ath 6 1
1997–98 Charlton Ath 6 0
1998–99 Charlton Ath 0 0 **12 1**
1998–99 *Brighton & HA* 4 1 **4 1**
1999–2000 Wigan Ath 8 0
2000–01 Wigan Ath 20 0 **28 0**
2001–02 Luton T 42 7
2002–03 Luton T 36 5
2003–04 Luton T 21 2
2004–05 Luton T 44 12
2005–06 Luton T 32 5 **175 31**

O'LEARY, Stephen (M) 43 5
H: 6 0 W: 11 09 b.Barnet 12-2-85
Source: Scholar. *Honours:* Eire Youth.
2003–04 Luton T 5 1
2004–05 Luton T 17 1
2005–06 Luton T 0 0 **22 2**
2005–06 *Tranmere R* 21 3 **21 3**

PERRETT, Russell (D) 190 11
H: 6 1 W: 12 08 b.Barton-on-Sea 18-6-73
Source: AFC Lymington.
1995–96 Portsmouth 9 0
1996–97 Portsmouth 32 1
1997–98 Portsmouth 16 1
1998–99 Portsmouth 15 0 **72 2**
1999–2000 Cardiff C 27 1
2000–01 Cardiff C 2 0 **29 1**
2001–02 Luton T 40 3
2002–03 Luton T 20 2
2003–04 Luton T 6 2
2004–05 Luton T 12 1
2005–06 Luton T 11 0 **89 8**

ROBINSON, Steve (M) 392 62
H: 5 7 W: 11 09 b.Lisburn 10-12-74
Source: Trainee. *Honours:* Northern Ireland Schools, Youth, Under-21, B, 6 full caps.
1992–93 Tottenham H 0 0
1993–94 Tottenham H 2 0
1994–95 Tottenham H 0 0 **2 0**
1994–95 *Leyton Orient* 0 0
1994–95 Bournemouth 32 5
1995–96 Bournemouth 41 7
1996–97 Bournemouth 40 7
1997–98 Bournemouth 45 10
1998–99 Bournemouth 42 13
1999–2000 Bournemouth 40 9 **240 51**
2000–01 Preston NE 22 1
2001–02 Preston NE 2 0 **24 1**
2001–02 *Bristol C* 6 1 **6 1**
2002–03 Luton T 29 1
2003–04 Luton T 34 2
2004–05 Luton T 31 4
2005–06 Luton T 26 2 **120 9**

SEREMET, Dino (G) 27 0
H: 6 4 W: 14 05 b.Slovenia 16-8-80
2002–03 Maribor 6 0 **6 0**
2004–05 Luton T 7 0
2005–06 Luton T 0 0 **7 0**
2005–06 *Doncaster R* 1 0 **1 0**
2005–06 *Tranmere R* 13 0 **13 0**

SHOWUNMI, Enoch (F) 102 14
H: 6 3 W: 14 11 b.Kilburn 21-4-82
Source: Willesden Constantine. *Honours:* Nigeria 1 full cap.
2003–04 Luton T 26 7
2004–05 Luton T 35 6
2005–06 Luton T 41 1 **102 14**

STEVENS, Danny (F) 1 0
H: 5 5 W: 9 09 b.Enfield 26-11-86
Source: Tottenham H Scholar.
2004–05 Luton T 0 0
2005–06 Luton T 1 0 **1 0**

UNDERWOOD, Paul (M) 177 6
H: 5 9 W: 12 13 b.Wimbledon 16-8-73
Source: Enfield.
2001–02 Rushden & D 40 0
2002–03 Rushden & D 40 1
2003–04 Rushden & D 30 0 **110 1**
2003–04 Luton T 1 0
2004–05 Luton T 37 5
2005–06 Luton T 29 0 **67 5**

VINE, Rowan (F) 166 35
H: 5 11 W: 12 10 b.Basingstoke 21-9-82
Source: Scholar.
2000–01 Portsmouth 2 0
2001–02 Portsmouth 11 0
2002–03 Portsmouth 0 0
2002–03 *Brentford* 42 10 **42 10**
2003–04 Portsmouth 0 0
2003–04 *Colchester U* 35 6 **35 6**
2004–05 Portsmouth 0 0 **13 0**
2004–05 *Luton T* 45 9
2005–06 Luton T 31 10 **76 19**

MACCLESFIELD T (46)

BAILEY, Mark (D) 191 4
H: 5 8 W: 10 07 b.Stoke 12-8-76
Source: Trainee.
1994–95 Stoke C 0 0
1995–96 Stoke C 0 0
1996–97 Stoke C 0 0
1996–97 Rochdale 15 0
1997–98 Rochdale 33 0
1998–99 Rochdale 19 1
1999–2000 Rochdale 0 0
2000–01 Rochdale 0 0 **67 1**
From Northwich Vic.
2001–02 Lincoln C 18 0
2002–03 Lincoln C 45 0
2003–04 Lincoln C 35 1 **98 1**
2004–05 Macclesfield T 21 2
2005–06 Macclesfield T 5 0 **26 2**

BARRAS, Tony (D) 473 30
H: 6 0 W: 13 00 b.Billingham 29-3-71
Source: Trainee.
1988–89 Hartlepool U 3 0
1989–90 Hartlepool U 9 0 **12 0**
1990–91 Stockport Co 40 0
1991–92 Stockport Co 42 5
1992–93 Stockport Co 14 0
1993–94 Stockport Co 3 0 **99 5**
1993–94 *Rotherham U* 5 1 **5 1**
1994–95 York C 31 1
1995–96 York C 32 3
1996–97 York C 46 1
1997–98 York C 38 6
1998–99 York C 24 0 **171 11**
1998–99 Reading 6 1 **6 1**
1999–2000 Walsall 24 4
2000–01 Walsall 36 1
2001–02 Walsall 26 4
2002–03 Walsall 19 0 **105 9**
2002–03 *Plymouth Arg* 4 0 **4 0**
2003–04 Notts Co 40 2 **40 2**
2004–05 Macclesfield T 24 1
2005–06 Macclesfield T 7 0 **31 1**

BERESFORD, David (M) 236 9
H: 5 8 W: 11 09 b.Middleton 11-11-76
Source: Trainee. *Honours:* England Schools, Youth.
1993–94 Oldham Ath 1 0
1994–95 Oldham Ath 2 0
1995–96 Oldham Ath 28 2
1995–96 *Swansea C* 6 0 **6 0**
1996–97 Oldham Ath 33 0 **64 2**
1996–97 Huddersfield T 6 1
1997–98 Huddersfield T 8 0
1998–99 Huddersfield T 19 2
1999–2000 Huddersfield T 0 0
1999–2000 *Preston NE* 4 0 **4 0**
2000–01 Huddersfield T 2 0 **35 3**
2000–01 *Port Vale* 4 0 **4 0**
2001–02 Hull C 41 1 **41 1**
2002–03 Plymouth Arg 16 0
2003–04 Plymouth Arg 1 0 **17 0**
2003–04 *Macclesfield T* 5 0
2003–04 Tranmere R 25 1
2004–05 Tranmere R 19 2 **44 3**
2005–06 Macclesfield T 16 0 **21 0**

BRIGHTWELL, Ian (D) 460 18
H: 5 10 W: 12 07 b.Lutterworth 9-4-68
Source: Congleton T. *Honours:* England Schools, Youth, Under-21.
1986–87 Manchester C 16 1
1987–88 Manchester C 33 5
1988–89 Manchester C 26 6
1989–90 Manchester C 28 2
1990–91 Manchester C 33 0
1991–92 Manchester C 40 1
1992–93 Manchester C 21 1
1993–94 Manchester C 7 0
1994–95 Manchester C 30 0
1995–96 Manchester C 29 0
1996–97 Manchester C 37 2
1997–98 Manchester C 21 0 **321 18**
1998–99 Coventry C 0 0
1999–2000 Coventry C 0 0
1999–2000 Walsall 10 0
2000–01 Walsall 44 0
2001–02 Walsall 27 0 **81 0**
2001–02 Stoke C 4 0 **4 0**
2002–03 Port Vale 35 0
2003–04 Port Vale 2 0 **37 0**
2004–05 Macclesfield T 6 0
2005–06 Macclesfield T 11 0 **17 0**

BRISCOE, Michael (D) 27 1
H: 5 11 W: 12 00 b.Northampton 4-7-83
Source: Harpole.
2002–03 Coventry C 0 0
2003–04 Coventry C 0 0
2004–05 Macclesfield T 14 0
2005–06 Macclesfield T 13 1 **27 1**

BULLOCK, Martin (M) 384 16
H: 5 5 W: 10 07 b.Derby 5-3-75
Source: Eastwood T. *Honours:* England Under-21.
1993–94 Barnsley 0 0
1994–95 Barnsley 29 0
1995–96 Barnsley 41 1
1996–97 Barnsley 28 0
1997–98 Barnsley 33 0
1998–99 Barnsley 32 2
1999–2000 Barnsley 4 0
1999–2000 *Port Vale* 6 1 **6 1**
2000–01 Barnsley 18 1
2001–02 Barnsley 0 0 **185 4**
2001–02 Blackpool 43 2
2002–03 Blackpool 38 1
2003–04 Blackpool 44 1
2004–05 Blackpool 28 0 **153 4**
2005–06 Macclesfield T 40 7 **40 7**

DEASY, Tim (G) 3 0
H: 6 0 W: 12 06 b.Salford 1-10-85
Source: Scholar.
2004–05 Macclesfield T 0 0
2005–06 Macclesfield T 3 0 **3 0**

FETTIS, Alan (G) 373 2
H: 6 1 W: 13 09 b.Belfast 1-2-71
Source: Ards. *Honours:* Northern Ireland Schools, Youth, B, 25 full caps.
1991–92 Hull C 43 0
1992–93 Hull C 20 0
1993–94 Hull C 37 0
1994–95 Hull C 28 2
1995–96 Hull C 7 0
1995–96 *WBA* 3 0 **3 0**
1996–97 Nottingham F 4 0
1997–98 Nottingham F 0 0 **4 0**
1997–98 Blackburn R 8 0
1998–99 Blackburn R 2 0
1999–2000 Blackburn R 1 0 **11 0**
1999–2000 *Leicester C* 0 0
1999–2000 York C 13 0
2000–01 York C 46 0
2001–02 York C 45 0

2002–03 York C 21 0 125 0
2002–03 Hull C 17 0
2003–04 Hull C 3 0 155 2
2003–04 *Sheffield U* 3 0 3 0
2003–04 *Grimsby T* 11 0 11 0
2004–05 Macclesfield T 28 0
2005–06 Macclesfield T 33 0 61 0

HARSLEY, Paul (M) 339 29
H: 5 8 W: 11 05 b.Scunthorpe 29-5-78
Source: Trainee.
1996–97 Grimsby T 0 0
1997–98 Scunthorpe U 15 1
1998–99 Scunthorpe U 34 0
1999–2000 Scunthorpe U 46 3
2000–01 Scunthorpe U 33 1 128 5
2001–02 Halifax T 45 11 45 11
2002–03 Northampton T 45 2
2003–04 Northampton T 14 0 59 2
2003–04 Macclesfield T 16 2
2004–05 Macclesfield T 46 3
2005–06 Macclesfield T 45 6 107 11

McDONALD, Marvin (F) 0 0
H: 5 7 W: 10 00 b.Wythenshawe 24-8-86
Source: Scholar.
2005–06 Macclesfield T 0 0

McINTYRE, Kevin (M) 79 5
H: 6 0 W: 11 10 b.Liverpool 23-12-77
Source: Trainee.
1996–97 Tranmere R 0 0
1997–98 Tranmere R 2 0
1998–99 Tranmere R 0 0
1999–2000 Tranmere R 0 0
2000–01 Tranmere R 0 0
2001–02 Tranmere R 0 0 2 0
2004–05 Chester C 10 0 10 0
2004–05 Macclesfield T 23 0
2005–06 Macclesfield T 44 5 67 5

McNEIL, Matthew (F) 12 1
H: 6 5 W: 14 03 b.Macclesfield 14-7-76
Source: Burnley, Curzon Ashton, Altrincham, Woodley Sp, Stalybridge C, Woking, Runcorn, Hyde U.
2005–06 Macclesfield T 12 1 12 1

MILES, John (F) 98 18
H: 5 10 W: 10 08 b.Fazackerley 28-9-81
Source: Trainee.
1998–99 Liverpool 0 0
1999–2000 Liverpool 0 0
2000–01 Liverpool 0 0
2001–02 Liverpool 0 0
2001–02 Stoke C 1 0 1 0
2002–03 Crewe Alex 5 1 5 1
2002–03 Macclesfield T 8 4
2003–04 Macclesfield T 29 6
2004–05 Macclesfield T 30 3
2005–06 Macclesfield T 25 4 92 17

MORGAN, Neil (M) 0 0
H: 5 11 W: 12 00 b.Coventry 6-2-85
Source: Nottingham F scholar.
2004–05 Macclesfield T 0 0
2005–06 Macclesfield T 0 0

MORLEY, Dave (D) 236 9
H: 6 1 W: 13 02 b.St Helens 25-9-77
Source: Trainee.
1995–96 Manchester C 0 0
1996–97 Manchester C 0 0
1997–98 Manchester C 3 1
1997–98 *Ayr U* 4 0 4 0
1998–99 Manchester C 0 0 3 1
1998–99 Southend U 27 0
1999–2000 Southend U 32 0
2000–01 Southend U 17 0 76 0
2000–01 Carlisle U 23 1
2001–02 Carlisle U 18 0 41 1
2001–02 Oxford U 18 3 18 3
2003–04 Doncaster R 21 1
2004–05 Doncaster R 9 0 30 1
2004–05 Macclesfield T 19 2
2005–06 Macclesfield T 45 1 64 3

NAVARRO, Alan (M) 101 3
H: 5 10 W: 11 07 b.Liverpool 31-5-81
Source: Trainee.
1998–99 Liverpool 0 0
1999–2000 Liverpool 0 0
2000–01 Liverpool 0 0
2000–01 *Crewe Alex* 8 1
2001–02 Liverpool 0 0
2001–02 *Crewe Alex* 7 0 15 1
2001–02 Tranmere R 21 1
2002–03 Tranmere R 5 0
2003–04 Tranmere R 19 0
2004–05 Tranmere R 0 0
2004–05 *Chester C* 3 0 3 0
2004–05 *Macclesfield T* 11 1
2005–06 Tranmere R 0 0 45 1
From Accrington S.
2005–06 Macclesfield T 27 0 38 1

RUSSELL, Allan (M) 147 26
H: 6 0 W: 12 01 b.Glasgow 13-12-80
Source: Hibernian.
1999–2000 Hamilton A 6 0
2000–01 Hamilton A 24 6
2001–02 Hamilton A 12 1
2002–03 Hamilton A 23 6 65 13
2003–04 St Mirren 26 4
2004–05 St Mirren 25 5 51 9
2005–06 Macclesfield T 13 2 13 2
2005–06 *Mansfield T* 18 2 18 2

SANDWITH, Kevin (D) 78 5
H: 5 11 W: 12 05 b.Workington 30-4-78
Source: Trainee.
1996–97 Carlisle U 0 0
1997–98 Carlisle U 3 0
1998–99 Carlisle U 0 0 3 0
From Halifax T
2003–04 Lincoln C 3 0
2004–05 Lincoln C 37 2 40 2
2005–06 Macclesfield T 35 3 35 3

SMART, Andrew (D) 9 0
H: 6 1 W: 14 00 b.Altrincham 17-3-86
Source: Scholar.
2004–05 Macclesfield T 0 0
2005–06 Macclesfield T 9 0 9 0

SWAILES, Danny (D) 220 15
H: 6 3 W: 12 06 b.Bolton 1-4-79
Source: Trainee.
1997–98 Bury 0 0
1998–99 Bury 0 0
1999–2000 Bury 24 3
2000–01 Bury 11 0
2001–02 Bury 28 1
2002–03 Bury 39 3
2003–04 Bury 42 5
2004–05 Bury 20 1 164 13
2004–05 Macclesfield T 17 0
2005–06 Macclesfield T 39 2 56 2

TEAGUE, Andrew (D) 30 1
H: 6 2 W: 12 00 b.Preston 5-2-86
Source: Scholar.
2004–05 Macclesfield T 5 0
2005–06 Macclesfield T 25 1 30 1

TOWNSON, Kevin (F) 126 27
H: 5 5 W: 10 02 b.Kirby 19-4-83
Honours: England Youth.
2000–01 Rochdale 3 0
2001–02 Rochdale 41 14
2002–03 Rochdale 24 1
2003–04 Rochdale 33 10
2004–05 Rochdale 1 0 102 25
2004–05 *Macclesfield T* 6 0
2005–06 Macclesfield T 18 2 24 2

WHITAKER, Danny (M) 171 23
H: 5 10 W: 11 00 b.Manchester 14-11-80
Source: Wilmslow Sports.
2000–01 Macclesfield T 0 0
2001–02 Macclesfield T 16 2
2002–03 Macclesfield T 41 10
2003–04 Macclesfield T 36 5
2004–05 Macclesfield T 36 2
2005–06 Macclesfield T 42 4 171 23

WIJNHARD, Clyde (F) 305 101
H: 5 11 W: 11 11 b.Paramaribo 1-11-73
1992–93 Ajax 4 2
1993–94 Groningen 23 3 23 3
1994–95 Ajax 0 0 4 2
1995–96 RKC 33 8
1996–97 RKC 17 10 50 18
1997–98 Willem II 29 14 29 14
1998–99 Leeds U 18 3 18 3
1999–2000 Huddersfield T 45 15
2000–01 Huddersfield T 4 0
2001–02 Huddersfield T 13 1 62 16
2001–02 Preston NE 6 3 6 3
2002–03 Oldham Ath 25 10 25 10
2003–04 Beira Mar 29 9 29 9
2004–05 Darlington 31 14
2005–06 Darlington 8 1 39 15
2005–06 Macclesfield T 20 8 20 8

MANCHESTER C (47)

BARTON, Joey (M) 97 9
H: 5 11 W: 12 05 b.Huyton 2-9-82
Source: Scholar. *Honours:* England Under-21.
2001–02 Manchester C 0 0
2002–03 Manchester C 7 1
2003–04 Manchester C 28 1
2004–05 Manchester C 31 1
2005–06 Manchester C 31 6 97 9

BENNETT, Ian (M) 0 0
b.Rochdale 24-2-86
Source: Trainee.
2003–04 Manchester C 0 0
2004–05 Manchester C 0 0
2005–06 Manchester C 0 0

BERMINGHAM, Karl (F) 6 0
H: 5 11 W: 12 07 b.Dublin 6-10-85
Source: Scholar. *Honours:* Eire Youth, Under-21.
2002–03 Manchester C 0 0
2003–04 Manchester C 0 0
2004–05 Manchester C 0 0
2004–05 *Lincoln C* 2 0 2 0
2005–06 Manchester C 0 0
2005–06 *Burnley* 4 0 4 0

BISCHOFF, Mikkel (D) 26 1
H: 6 3 W: 13 11 b.Copenhagen 3-2-82
Honours: Denmark Under-21.
2001–02 AB Copenhagen 10 0 10 0
2002–03 Manchester C 1 0
2003–04 Manchester C 0 0
2004–05 Manchester C 0 0
2004–05 *Wolverhampton W* 11 1 11 1
2005–06 Manchester C 0 0 1 0
2005–06 *Sheffield W* 4 0 4 0

COLE, Andy (F) 456 219
H: 5 11 W: 12 11 b.Nottingham 15-10-71
Source: Trainee. *Honours:* England Schools, Youth, Under-21, B, 15 full caps, 1 goal. Football League.
1989–90 Arsenal 0 0
1990–91 Arsenal 1 0
1991–92 Arsenal 0 0 1 0
1991–92 *Fulham* 13 3
1991–92 *Bristol C* 12 8
1992–93 Bristol C 29 12 41 20
1992–93 Newcastle U 12 12
1993–94 Newcastle U 40 34
1994–95 Newcastle U 18 9 70 55
1994–95 Manchester U 18 12
1995–96 Manchester U 34 11
1996–97 Manchester U 20 6
1997–98 Manchester U 33 15
1998–99 Manchester U 32 17
1999–2000 Manchester U 28 19
2000–01 Manchester U 19 9
2001–02 Manchester U 11 4 195 93
2001–02 Blackburn R 15 9
2002–03 Blackburn R 34 7
2003–04 Blackburn R 34 11 83 27
2004–05 Fulham 31 12 44 15
2005–06 Manchester C 22 9 22 9

COLLINS, Paul (D) 0 0
H: 5 10 W: 11 12 b.Droylsden
Source: Scholar.
2004–05 Manchester C 0 0
2005–06 Manchester C 0 0

CROFT, Lee (F) 40 1
H: 5 11 W: 13 00 b.Wigan 21-6-85
Source: Scholar. *Honours:* England Youth, Under-20, Under-21.
2002–03 Manchester C 0 0

2003–04 Manchester C 0 0
2004–05 Manchester C 7 0
2004–05 *Oldham Ath* 12 0 **12 0**
2005–06 Manchester C 21 1 **28 1**

D'LARYEA, Nathan (D) 0 0
b.Manchester 3-9-85
Source: Trainee.
2003–04 Manchester C 0 0
2004–05 Manchester C 0 0
2005–06 Manchester C 0 0

DE VLIEGER, Geert (G) 0 0
H: 6 1 W: 12 07 b.Dendermonde 16-10-71
2004–05 Manchester C 0 0
2005–06 Manchester C 0 0

DISTIN, Sylvain (D) 256 7
H: 6 3 W: 14 06 b.Bagnolet 16-12-77
1998–99 Tours 26 3 **26 3**
1999–2000 Gueugnon 33 1 **33 1**
2000–01 Paris St Germain 28 0 **28 0**
2001–02 Newcastle U 28 0 **28 0**
2002–03 Manchester C 34 0
2003–04 Manchester C 38 2
2004–05 Manchester C 38 1
2005–06 Manchester C 31 0 **141 3**

DUNNE, Richard (D) 249 6
H: 6 2 W: 15 10 b.Dublin 21-9-79
Source: Trainee. *Honours:* Eire Schools, Youth, Under-21, B, 29 full caps, 4 goals.
1996–97 Everton 7 0
1997–98 Everton 3 0
1998–99 Everton 16 0
1999–2000 Everton 31 0
2000–01 Everton 3 0 **60 0**
2000–01 Manchester C 25 0
2001–02 Manchester C 43 1
2002–03 Manchester C 25 0
2003–04 Manchester C 29 0
2004–05 Manchester C 35 2
2005–06 Manchester C 32 3 **189 6**

ETUHU, Calvin (F) 0 0
b.Nigeria 30-5-88
Source: Scholar.
2005–06 Manchester C 0 0

FLOOD, Willo (M) 28 2
H: 5 7 W: 10 05 b.Dublin 10-4-85
Source: Trainee. *Honours:* Eire Youth, Under-21.
2001–02 Manchester C 0 0
2002–03 Manchester C 0 0
2003–04 Manchester C 0 0
2003–04 *Rochdale* 6 0 **6 0**
2004–05 Manchester C 9 1
2005–06 Manchester C 5 0 **14 1**
2005–06 *Coventry C* 8 1 **8 1**

HAAPALA, Tuomas (M) 129 14
H: 5 11 W: 12 02 b.Lahti 20-4-79
Honours: Finland 3 full caps.
2000 Lahti 24 1
2001 Lahti 27 5
2002 Lahti 28 2
2003 Lahti 26 5 **105 13**
2004 MyPa 24 1 **24 1**
2005–06 Manchester C 0 0

HUSSAIN, Yassar (M) 0 0
H: 5 6 W: 9 10 b.Qatar 1-9-84
Source: Al Sadd. *Honours:* Qatar full caps.
2005–06 Manchester C 0 0

IRELAND, Stephen (F) 24 0
H: 5 8 W: 10 07 b.Cork 22-8-86
Source: Scholar. *Honours:* Eire Youth, 1 full cap.
2005–06 Manchester C 24 0 **24 0**

JAMES, David (G) 554 0
H: 6 5 W: 15 07 b.Welwyn 1-8-70
Source: Trainee. *Honours:* England Youth, Under-21, B, 34 full caps.
1988–89 Watford 0 0
1989–90 Watford 0 0
1990–91 Watford 46 0
1991–92 Watford 43 0 **89 0**
1992–93 Liverpool 29 0
1993–94 Liverpool 14 0
1994–95 Liverpool 42 0
1995–96 Liverpool 38 0
1996–97 Liverpool 38 0
1997–98 Liverpool 27 0
1998–99 Liverpool 26 0 **214 0**
1999–2000 Aston Villa 29 0
2000–01 Aston Villa 38 0 **67 0**
2001–02 West Ham U 26 0
2002–03 West Ham U 38 0
2003–04 West Ham U 27 0 **91 0**
2003–04 Manchester C 17 0
2004–05 Manchester C 38 0
2005–06 Manchester C 38 0 **93 0**

JIHAI, Sun (D) 126 3
H: 5 9 W: 12 02 b.Dalian 30-9-77
Source: Dalian Wanda. *Honours:* China 62 full caps, 8 goals.
1998–99 Crystal Palace 23 0 **23 0**
From Dalian Wanda.
2001–02 Manchester C 7 0
2002–03 Manchester C 28 2
2003–04 Manchester C 33 1
2004–05 Manchester C 6 0
2005–06 Manchester C 29 0 **103 3**

JOHNSON, Michael (M) 0 0
b.Urmston
Source: Scholar.
2005–06 Manchester C 0 0

JORDAN, Stephen (D) 51 0
H: 6 1 W: 13 00 b.Warrington 6-3-82
Source: Scholarship.
1998–99 Manchester C 0 0
1999–2000 Manchester C 0 0
2000–01 Manchester C 0 0
2001–02 Manchester C 0 0
2002–03 Manchester C 1 0
2002–03 *Cambridge U* 11 0 **11 0**
2003–04 Manchester C 2 0
2004–05 Manchester C 19 0
2005–06 Manchester C 18 0 **40 0**

LAIRD, Marc (M) 0 0
b.Edinburgh 23-1-86
Source: Trainee.
2003–04 Manchester C 0 0
2004–05 Manchester C 0 0
2005–06 Manchester C 0 0

MILLER, Ishmael (F) 1 0
H: 6 3 W: 14 00 b.Manchester 5-3-87
Source: Scholar.
2005–06 Manchester C 1 0 **1 0**

MILLS, Danny (D) 290 7
H: 5 11 W: 12 13 b.Norwich 18-5-77
Source: Trainee. *Honours:* England Youth, Under-21, 19 full caps.
1994–95 Norwich C 0 0
1995–96 Norwich C 14 0
1996–97 Norwich C 32 0
1997–98 Norwich C 20 0 **66 0**
1997–98 Charlton Ath 9 1
1998–99 Charlton Ath 36 2 **45 3**
1999–2000 Leeds U 17 1
2000–01 Leeds U 23 0
2001–02 Leeds U 28 1
2002–03 Leeds U 33 1
2003–04 Leeds U 0 0 **101 3**
2003–04 *Middlesbrough* 28 0 **28 0**
2004–05 Manchester C 32 0
2005–06 Manchester C 18 1 **50 1**

MILLS, Matthew (D) 21 3
H: 6 3 W: 12 12 b.Swindon 14-7-86
Source: Scholar. *Honours:* England Youth.
2004–05 Southampton 0 0
2004–05 *Coventry C* 4 0 **4 0**
2004–05 *Bournemouth* 12 3 **12 3**
2005–06 Southampton 4 0 **4 0**
2005–06 Manchester C 1 0 **1 0**

MUSAMPA, Kiki (M) 245 38
H: 5 8 W: 12 07 b.Kinshasa 20-7-77
Honours: Holland Under-21.
1994–95 Ajax 1 0
1995–96 Ajax 17 1
1996–97 Ajax 24 5 **42 6**
1997–98 Bordeaux 16 4
1998–99 Bordeaux 17 1 **33 5**
1999–2000 Malaga 13 2
2000–01 Malaga 11 3
2001–02 Malaga 37 9
2002–03 Malaga 35 8 **96 22**
2003–04 Atletico Madrid 26 2
2004–05 Atletico Madrid 7 0 **33 2**
2004–05 Manchester C 14 3
2005–06 Manchester C 27 0 **41 3**

ONUOHA, Nedum (D) 27 0
H: 6 2 W: 12 04 b.Warri 12-11-86
Source: Scholar. *Honours:* England Youth, Under-20, Under-21.
2004–05 Manchester C 17 0
2005–06 Manchester C 10 0 **27 0**

REYNA, Claudio (M) 206 21
H: 5 9 W: 11 08 b.New Jersey 20-7-73
Source: Union County SC, Univ Virginia. *Honours:* USA 112 full caps, 8 goals.
1996–97 Leverkusen 5 0 **5 0**
1997–98 Wolfsburg 28 4
1998–99 Wolfsburg 20 2 **48 6**
1998–99 Rangers 6 0
1999–2000 Rangers 29 5
2000–01 Rangers 18 2
2001–02 Rangers 10 1 **63 8**
2001–02 Sunderland 17 3
2002–03 Sunderland 11 0
2003–04 Sunderland 0 0 **28 3**
2003–04 Manchester C 23 1
2004–05 Manchester C 17 2
2005–06 Manchester C 22 1 **62 4**

RICHARDS, Micah (D) 13 0
H: 5 11 W: 13 00 b.Birmingham 24-6-88
Source: Scholar. *Honours:* England Youth.
2005–06 Manchester C 13 0 **13 0**

SAMARAS, Georgios (F) 100 29
H: 6 3 W: 13 07 b.Heraklion 21-2-85
Source: OFI Crete. *Honours:* Greece Under-21, 3 full caps, 2 goals.
2002–03 Heerenveen 15 4
2003–04 Heerenveen 27 4
2004–05 Heerenveen 31 11
2005–06 Heerenveen 13 6 **86 25**
2005–06 Manchester C 14 4 **14 4**

SCHMEICHEL, Kasper (G) 19 0
H: 6 1 W: 13 00 b.Denmark 5-11-86
Source: Scholar. *Honours:* Denmark Youth.
2003–04 Manchester C 0 0
2004–05 Manchester C 0 0
2005–06 Manchester C 0 0
2005–06 *Darlington* 4 0 **4 0**
2005–06 *Bury* 15 0 **15 0**

SIBIERSKI, Antoine (M) 352 72
H: 6 2 W: 12 04 b.Lille 5-8-74
Honours: France Youth.
1992–93 Lille 6 0
1993–94 Lille 22 1
1994–95 Lille 36 7
1995–96 Lille 33 9 **97 17**
1996–97 Auxerre 30 7
1997–98 Auxerre 12 1 **42 8**
1998–99 Nantes 4 0
1999–2000 Nantes 28 13 **32 13**
2000–01 Lens 27 5
2001–02 Lens 25 6
2002–03 Lens 37 12 **89 23**
2003–04 Manchester C 33 5
2004–05 Manchester C 35 4
2005–06 Manchester C 24 2 **92 11**

SINCLAIR, Trevor (M) 520 73
H: 5 9 W: 13 05 b.Dulwich 2-3-73
Source: Trainee. *Honours:* England Youth, Under-21, B, 12 full caps.
1989–90 Blackpool 9 0
1990–91 Blackpool 31 1
1991–92 Blackpool 27 3
1992–93 Blackpool 45 11 **112 15**
1993–94 QPR 32 4
1994–95 QPR 33 4
1995–96 QPR 37 2
1996–97 QPR 39 3
1997–98 QPR 26 3 **167 16**
1997–98 West Ham U 14 7
1998–99 West Ham U 36 7
1999–2000 West Ham U 36 7
2000–01 West Ham U 19 3
2001–02 West Ham U 34 5
2002–03 West Ham U 38 8 **177 37**

2003–04	Manchester C	29	1		
2004–05	Manchester C	4	1		
2005–06	Manchester C	31	3	**64**	**5**

SOMMEIL, David (D) **327 7**
H: 5 10 W: 12 12 b.Ponte-a-Pitre 10-8-74
Honours: France B.

1993–94	Caen	1	0		
1994–95	Caen	25	0		
1995–96	Caen	30	0		
1996–97	Caen	25	0		
1997–98	Caen	38	1	**119**	**1**
1998–99	Rennes	33	0		
1999–2000	Rennes	30	1	**63**	**1**
2000–01	Bordeaux	29	0		
2001–02	Bordeaux	31	0		
2002–03	Bordeaux	17	1	**77**	**1**
2002–03	Manchester C	14	1		
2003–04	Manchester C	18	1		
2003–04	*Marseille*	19	0	**19**	**0**
2004–05	Manchester C	1	0		
2005–06	Manchester C	16	2	**49**	**4**

THATCHER, Ben (D) **277 2**
H: 5 10 W: 12 07 b.Swindon 30-11-75
Source: Trainee. *Honours:* England Youth, Under-21, Wales 7 full caps.

1992–93	Millwall	0	0		
1993–94	Millwall	8	0		
1994–95	Millwall	40	1		
1995–96	Millwall	42	0	**90**	**1**
1996–97	Wimbledon	9	0		
1997–98	Wimbledon	26	0		
1998–99	Wimbledon	31	0		
1999–2000	Wimbledon	20	0	**86**	**0**
2000–01	Tottenham H	12	0		
2001–02	Tottenham H	12	0		
2002–03	Tottenham H	12	0	**36**	**0**
2003–04	Leicester C	29	1	**29**	**1**
2004–05	Manchester C	18	0		
2005–06	Manchester C	18	0	**36**	**0**

VASSELL, Darius (F) **198 43**
H: 5 9 W: 13 00 b.Birmingham 13-6-80
Source: Trainee. *Honours:* England Youth, Under-21, 22 full caps, 6 goals.

1998–99	Aston Villa	6	0		
1999–2000	Aston Villa	11	0		
2000–01	Aston Villa	23	4		
2001–02	Aston Villa	36	12		
2002–03	Aston Villa	33	8		
2003–04	Aston Villa	32	9		
2004–05	Aston Villa	21	2	**162**	**35**
2005–06	Manchester C	36	8	**36**	**8**

WEAVER, Nick (G) **162 0**
H: 6 4 W: 14 07 b.Sheffield 2-3-79
Source: Trainee. *Honours:* England Under-21.

1995–96	Mansfield T	1	0		
1996–97	Mansfield T	0	0	**1**	**0**
1996–97	Manchester C	0	0		
1997–98	Manchester C	0	0		
1998–99	Manchester C	45	0		
1999–2000	Manchester C	45	0		
2000–01	Manchester C	31	0		
2001–02	Manchester C	25	0		
2002–03	Manchester C	0	0		
2003–04	Manchester C	0	0		
2004–05	Manchester C	1	0		
2005–06	Manchester C	0	0	**147**	**0**
2005–06	*Sheffield W*	14	0	**14**	**0**

WRIGHT-PHILLIPS, Bradley (M) **32 2**
H: 5 10 W: 10 07 b.Lewisham 12-3-85
Source: Scholar. *Honours:* England Youth, Under-20.

2002–03	Manchester C	0	0		
2003–04	Manchester C	0	0		
2004–05	Manchester C	14	1		
2005–06	Manchester C	18	1	**32**	**2**

Scholars
Breen, Garry; Campbell, John Terrance; Clayton, Adam Stephen; Daly, Michael; Evans, Chedwyn Michael; Evans, Scott Christopher; Logan, Shaleum; Marshall, Paul Anthony; Matthewson, Lawrence; McDonald, Clayton; Moore, Karl; Mouritsen, Christian; Obeng, Curtis; Pollitt, Daniel; Vadon, David; Vidal, Javan; Williams, Ashley David; Williamson, Samuel James.

MANCHESTER U (48)

BARDSLEY, Phillip (D) **14 0**
H: 5 11 W: 11 13 b.Salford 28-6-85
Source: Trainee.

2003–04	Manchester U	0	0		
2004–05	Manchester U	0	0		
2005–06	Manchester U	8	0	**8**	**0**
2005–06	*Burnley*	6	0	**6**	**0**

BELLION, David (F) **52 4**
H: 6 0 W: 11 09 b.Sevres 27-11-82
Source: Cannes. *Honours:* France Under-21.

2001–02	Sunderland	9	0		
2002–03	Sunderland	11	1	**20**	**1**
2003–04	Manchester U	14	2		
2004–05	Manchester U	10	1		
2005–06	Manchester U	0	0	**24**	**3**
2005–06	*West Ham U*	8	0	**8**	**0**

To Nice (loan) January 2006

BROWN, Wes (D) **140 1**
H: 6 1 W: 13 08 b.Manchester 13-10-79
Source: Trainee. *Honours:* England Schools, Youth, Under-21, 9 full caps.

1996–97	Manchester U	0	0		
1997–98	Manchester U	2	0		
1998–99	Manchester U	14	0		
1999–2000	Manchester U	0	0		
2000–01	Manchester U	28	0		
2001–02	Manchester U	17	0		
2002–03	Manchester U	22	0		
2003–04	Manchester U	17	0		
2004–05	Manchester U	21	1		
2005–06	Manchester U	19	0	**140**	**1**

CAMPBELL, Frazier (F) **0 0**
b.Huddersfield 13-9-87
Source: Scholar. *Honours:* England Youth.

2005–06	Manchester U	0	0		

CATHCART, Craig (D) **0 0**
H: 6 2 W: 11 06 b.Belfast 6-2-89
Source: Scholar.

2005–06	Manchester U	0	0		

COOPER, Kenny (F) **7 3**
H: 6 6 W: 15 04 b.Baltimore 21-10-84

2003–04	Manchester U	0	0		
2004–05	Manchester U	0	0		
2004–05	*Oldham Ath*	7	3	**7**	**3**
2005–06	Manchester U	0	0		

EAGLES, Chris (M) **55 7**
H: 5 10 W: 11 07 b.Hemel Hempstead 19-11-85
Source: Trainee. *Honours:* England Youth.

2003–04	Manchester U	0	0		
2004–05	Manchester U	0	0		
2004–05	*Watford*	13	1		
2005–06	Manchester U	0	0		
2005–06	*Sheffield W*	25	3	**25**	**3**
2005–06	*Watford*	17	3	**30**	**4**

EBANKS-BLAKE, Sylvan (F) **0 0**
H: 5 10 W: 13 04 b.Cambridge 29-3-86
Source: Scholar.

2004–05	Manchester U	0	0		
2005–06	Manchester U	0	0		

ECKERSLEY, Adam (D) **0 0**
H: 5 9 W: 11 13 b.Manchester 7-9-85
Source: Scholar. *Honours:* England Youth.

2004–05	Manchester U	0	0		
2005–06	Manchester U	0	*0*		

To Antwerp January 2006

EVANS, Jonny (D) **0 0**
H: 6 2 W: 12 02 b.Belfast 3-1-88
Source: Scholar. *Honours:* Northern Ireland Schools, Youth, Under-21.

2004–05	Manchester U	0	0		
2005–06	Manchester U	0	0		

EVRA, Patrice (D) **197 5**
H: 5 8 W: 11 10 b.Dakar 15-5-81
Honours: France 5 full caps.

1998–99	Marsala	24	3	**24**	**3**
1999–2000	Monza	3	0	**3**	**0**
2000–01	Nice	5	0		
2001–02	Nice	34	1	**39**	**1**
2002–03	Monaco	36	1		
2003–04	Monaco	33	0		
2004–05	Monaco	36	0		
2005–06	Monaco	15	0	**120**	**1**
2005–06	Manchester U	11	0	**11**	**0**

FERDINAND, Rio (D) **307 7**
H: 6 2 W: 13 12 b.Peckham 7-11-78
Source: Trainee. *Honours:* England Youth, Under-21, B, 52 full caps, 1 goal.

1995–96	West Ham U	1	0		
1996–97	West Ham U	15	2		
1996–97	*Bournemouth*	10	0	**10**	**0**
1997–98	West Ham U	35	0		
1998–99	West Ham U	31	0		
1999–2000	West Ham U	33	0		
2000–01	West Ham U	12	0	**127**	**2**
2000–01	Leeds U	23	2		
2001–02	Leeds U	31	0	**54**	**2**
2002–03	Manchester U	28	0		
2003–04	Manchester U	20	0		
2004–05	Manchester U	31	0		
2005–06	Manchester U	37	3	**116**	**3**

FLETCHER, Darren (M) **67 4**
H: 6 0 W: 11 09 b.Edinburgh 1-2-84
Source: Scholar. *Honours:* Scotland Under-21, B, 23 full caps, 3 goals.

2000–01	Manchester U	0	0		
2001–02	Manchester U	0	0		
2002–03	Manchester U	0	0		
2003–04	Manchester U	22	0		
2004–05	Manchester U	18	3		
2005–06	Manchester U	27	1	**67**	**4**

FORTUNE, Quinton (F) **172 13**
H: 5 10 W: 12 09 b.Cape Town 21-5-77
Source: Kaizer Chiefs, Tottenham H schoolboy. *Honours:* South Africa Under-23, 47 full caps, 2 goals.

1995–96	Mallorca	8	1	**8**	**1**
1995–96	Atletico Madrid	3	0		
1996–97	Atletico Madrid B	30	2		
1996–97	Atletico Madrid	2	0		
1997–98	Atletico Madrid B	31	1		
1997–98	Atletico Madrid	0	0		
1998–99	Atletico Madrid	2	0		
1998–99	Atletico Madrid B	20	4	**7**	**0**
1999–2000	Manchester U	6	2		
2000–01	Manchester U	7	2		
2001–02	Manchester U	14	1		
2002–03	Manchester U	9	0		
2003–04	Manchester U	23	0		
2004–05	Manchester U	17	0		
2005–06	Manchester U	0	0	**76**	**5**

FOSTER, Ben (G) **63 0**
H: 6 2 W: 12 08 b.Leamington Spa 3-4-83
Source: Racing Club Warwick.

2000–01	Stoke C	0	0		
2001–02	Stoke C	0	0		
2002–03	Stoke C	0	0		
2003–04	Stoke C	0	0		
2004–05	Stoke C	0	0		
2004–05	*Kidderminster H*	2	0	**2**	**0**
2004–05	*Wrexham*	17	0	**17**	**0**
2005–06	Manchester U	0	0		
2005–06	*Watford*	44	0	**44**	**0**

GIBSON, Darron (M) **0 0**
H: 6 0 W: 12 04 b.Londonderry 25-10-87
Source: Scholar. *Honours:* Eire Youth.

2005–06	Manchester U	0	0		

GIGGS, Ryan (F) **474 94**
H: 5 11 W: 11 02 b.Cardiff 29-11-73
Source: School. *Honours:* England Schools, Wales Youth, Under-21, 56 full caps, 11 goals.

1990–91	Manchester U	2	1		
1991–92	Manchester U	38	4		
1992–93	Manchester U	41	9		
1993–94	Manchester U	38	13		
1994–95	Manchester U	29	1		
1995–96	Manchester U	33	11		
1996–97	Manchester U	26	3		
1997–98	Manchester U	29	8		
1998–99	Manchester U	24	3		
1999–2000	Manchester U	30	6		
2000–01	Manchester U	31	5		

2001–02 Manchester U 25 7
2002–03 Manchester U 36 8
2003–04 Manchester U 33 7
2004–05 Manchester U 32 5
2005–06 Manchester U 27 3 **474 94**

GRAY, David (F) 0 0
H: 5 11 W: 11 02 b.Edinburgh 4-5-88
Source: Scholar.
2005–06 Manchester U 0 0

HEATON, Tom (G) 14 0
H: 6 1 W: 13 12 b.Chester 15-4-86
Source: Trainee. *Honours:* England Youth.
2003–04 Manchester U 0 0
2004–05 Manchester U 0 0
2005–06 Manchester U 0 0
2005–06 *Swindon T* 14 0 **14 0**

HEINZE, Gabriel (D) 196 7
H: 5 10 W: 12 08 b.Crespo 19-4-78
Source: Union de Crespo. *Honours:* Argentina 33 full caps, 1 goal.
1997–98 Newell's Old Boys 8 0 **8 0**
1997–98 Valladolid 0 0
1998–99 Sporting Lisbon 5 1 **5 1**
1999–2000 Valladolid 18 0
2000–01 Valladolid 36 1 **54 1**
2001–02 Paris St Germain 31 0
2002–03 Paris St Germain 35 2
2003–04 Paris St Germain 33 2 **99 4**
2004–05 Manchester U 26 1
2005–06 Manchester U 4 0 **30 1**

HOWARD, Mark (D) 0 0
H: 6 1 W: 12 08 b.Manchester 29-1-86
Source: Scholar.
2005–06 Manchester U 0 0

HOWARD, Tim (G) 130 0
H: 6 3 W: 14 12 b.North Brunswick 6-3-79
Honours: USA 16 full caps.
1998 NY/NJ MetrStars 1 0
1999 NY/NJ MetrStars 9 0
2000 NY/NJ MetrStars 9 0
2001 NY/NJ MetrStars 26 0
2002 NY/NJ MetrStars 27 0
2003 NY/NJ MetrStars 13 0 **85 0**
2003–04 Manchester U 32 0
2004–05 Manchester U 12 0
2005–06 Manchester U 1 0 **45 0**

JOHNSON, Eddie (F) 48 10
H: 5 10 W: 13 05 b.Chester 20-9-84
Source: Scholar. *Honours:* England Youth, Under-20.
2001–02 Manchester U 0 0
2002–03 Manchester U 0 0
2003–04 Manchester U 0 0
2004–05 Manchester U 0 0
2004–05 *Coventry C* 26 5 **26 5**
2005–06 Manchester U 0 0
2005–06 *Crewe Alex* 22 5 **22 5**

JONES, David (M) 24 3
H: 5 11 W: 10 10 b.Southport 4-11-84
Source: Trainee. *Honours:* England Youth, Under-21.
2003–04 Manchester U 0 0
2004–05 Manchester U 0 0
2005–06 Manchester U 0 0
2005–06 *Preston NE* 24 3 **24 3**
To NEC Nijmegen (loan) January 2006

JONES, Richie (M) 0 0
H: 6 0 W: 11 00 b.Manchester 26-9-86
Source: Scholar. *Honours:* England Youth.
2004–05 Manchester U 0 0
2005–06 Manchester U 0 *0*
To Antwerp January 2006

KEANE, Roy (M) 440 55
H: 5 11 W: 11 10 b.Cork 10-8-71
Source: Cobh Ramb. *Honours:* Eire Schools, Youth, Under-21, 67 full caps, 9 goals.
1990–91 Nottingham F 35 8
1991–92 Nottingham F 39 8
1992–93 Nottingham F 40 6 **114 22**
1993–94 Manchester U 37 5
1994–95 Manchester U 25 2
1995–96 Manchester U 29 6
1996–97 Manchester U 21 2
1997–98 Manchester U 9 2
1998–99 Manchester U 35 2
1999–2000 Manchester U 29 5
2000–01 Manchester U 28 2
2001–02 Manchester U 28 3
2002–03 Manchester U 21 0
2003–04 Manchester U 28 3
2004–05 Manchester U 31 1
2005–06 Manchester U 5 0 **326 33**
To Celtic December 2005

LEE, Tommy (G) 11 0
H: 6 2 W: 12 00 b.Keighley 3-1-86
Source: Scholar.
2005–06 Manchester U 0 0
2005–06 *Macclesfield T* 11 0 **11 0**

MARTIN, Lee (M) 0 0
H: 5 10 W: 10 03 b.Taunton 9-2-87
Source: Scholar. *Honours:* England Youth.
2004–05 Manchester U 0 0
2005–06 Manchester U 0 *0*
To Antwerp January 2006

McSHANE, Paul (D) 42 4
H: 6 0 W: 11 05 b.Wicklow 6-1-86
Source: Trainee. *Honours:* Eire Youth, Under-21.
2002–03 Manchester U 0 0
2003–04 Manchester U 0 0
2004–05 Manchester U 0 0
2004–05 *Walsall* 4 1 **4 1**
2005–06 Manchester U 0 0
2005–06 *Brighton & HA* 38 3 **38 3**

MILLER, Liam (M) 81 9
H: 5 7 W: 10 05 b.Cork 13-2-81
Honours: Eire Under-21, 12 full caps, 1 goal.
1999–2000 Celtic 1 0
2000–01 Celtic 0 0
2001–02 Celtic 0 0
2001–02 Aarhus 18 6 **18 6**
2002–03 Celtic 0 0
2003–04 Celtic 25 2 **26 2**
2004–05 Manchester U 8 0
2005–06 Manchester U 1 0 **9 0**
2005–06 *Leeds U* 28 1 **28 1**

N'GALULA, Floribert (D) 0 0
H: 6 0 W: 12 06 b.Brussels 7-3-87
Source: Scholar.
2004–05 Manchester U 0 0
2005–06 Manchester U 0 0

NEUMAYR, Marcus (M) 0 0
H: 5 11 W: 11 05 b.Aschaffenburg 26-3-86
Source: Scholar.
2003–04 Manchester U 0 0
2004–05 Manchester U 0 0
2005–06 Manchester U 0 0

NEVILLE, Gary (D) 340 5
H: 5 11 W: 12 10 b.Bury 18-2-75
Source: Trainee. *Honours:* England Youth, 81 full caps.
1992–93 Manchester U 0 0
1993–94 Manchester U 1 0
1994–95 Manchester U 18 0
1995–96 Manchester U 31 0
1996–97 Manchester U 31 1
1997–98 Manchester U 34 0
1998–99 Manchester U 34 1
1999–2000 Manchester U 22 0
2000–01 Manchester U 32 1
2001–02 Manchester U 34 0
2002–03 Manchester U 26 0
2003–04 Manchester U 30 2
2004–05 Manchester U 22 0
2005–06 Manchester U 25 0 **340 5**

O'SHEA, John (D) 141 6
H: 6 3 W: 13 07 b.Waterford 30-4-81
Source: Waterford. *Honours:* Eire Youth, Under-21, 30 full caps, 1 goal.
1998–99 Manchester U 0 0
1999–2000 Manchester U 0 0
1999–2000 *Bournemouth* 10 1 **10 1**
2000–01 Manchester U 0 0
2001–02 Manchester U 9 0
2002–03 Manchester U 32 0
2003–04 Manchester U 33 2
2004–05 Manchester U 23 2
2005–06 Manchester U 34 1 **131 5**

PARK, Ji-Sung (M) 173 25
H: 5 9 W: 11 06 b.Seoul 25-2-81
Honours: South Korea 63 full caps, 6 goals.
2000 Kyoto Purple S 13 1
2001 Kyoto Purple S 38 3
2002 Kyoto Purple S 25 7 **76 11**
2002–03 PSV Eindhoven 8 0
2003–04 PSV Eindhoven 28 6
2004–05 PSV Eindhoven 28 7 **64 13**
2005–06 Manchester U 33 1 **33 1**

PICKEN, Phil (D) 32 1
H: 5 9 W: 10 07 b.Droylsden 12-11-85
Source: Scholar.
2004–05 Manchester U 0 0
2005–06 Manchester U 0 0
2005–06 *Chesterfield* 32 1 **32 1**

PIQUE, Gerard (D) 3 0
H: 6 3 W: 13 03 b.Barcelona 2-2-87
Source: Scholar. *Honours:* Spain Youth.
2004–05 Manchester U 0 0
2005–06 Manchester U 3 0 **3 0**

RICHARDSON, Kieran (M) 40 4
H: 5 9 W: 11 13 b.Greenwich 21-10-84
Source: Scholar. *Honours:* England Under-21, 4 full caps, 2 goals.
2002–03 Manchester U 2 0
2003–04 Manchester U 2 0
2004–05 Manchester U 2 0
2004–05 *WBA* 12 3 **12 3**
2005–06 Manchester U 22 1 **28 1**

RONALDO, Cristiano (M) 120 21
H: 6 1 W: 13 02 b.Funchal 5-2-85
Honours: Portugal Youth, Under-21, 38 full caps, 12 goals.
2002–03 Sporting Lisbon 25 3 **25 3**
2003–04 Manchester U 29 4
2004–05 Manchester U 33 5
2005–06 Manchester U 33 9 **95 18**

ROONEY, Wayne (F) 132 42
H: 5 10 W: 12 13 b.Liverpool 24-10-85
Source: Scholar. *Honours:* FA Schools, England Youth, 33 full caps, 11 goals.
2002–03 Everton 33 6
2003–04 Everton 34 9 **67 15**
2004–05 Manchester U 29 11
2005–06 Manchester U 36 16 **65 27**

ROSSI, Giuseppe (F) 5 1
H: 5 9 W: 11 06 b.New Jersey 1-2-87
Honours: Italy Youth.
2004–05 Manchester U 0 0
2005–06 Manchester U 5 1 **5 1**

SAHA, Louis (F) 220 74
H: 6 1 W: 12 08 b.Paris 8-8-78
Honours: France Youth, Under-21, 12 full caps, 2 goals.
1997–98 Metz 21 1
1998–99 Metz 3 0
1998–99 Newcastle U 11 1 **11 1**
1999–2000 Metz 23 4 **47 5**
2000–01 Fulham 43 27
2001–02 Fulham 36 8
2002–03 Fulham 17 5
2003–04 Fulham 21 13 **117 53**
2003–04 Manchester U 12 7
2004–05 Manchester U 14 1
2005–06 Manchester U 19 7 **45 15**

SCHOLES, Paul (M) 341 89
H: 5 7 W: 11 00 b.Salford 16-11-74
Source: Trainee. *Honours:* England Youth, 66 full caps, 14 goals.
1992–93 Manchester U 0 0
1993–94 Manchester U 0 0
1994–95 Manchester U 17 5
1995–96 Manchester U 26 10
1996–97 Manchester U 24 3
1997–98 Manchester U 31 8
1998–99 Manchester U 31 6
1999–2000 Manchester U 31 9
2000–01 Manchester U 32 6
2001–02 Manchester U 35 8
2002–03 Manchester U 33 14
2003–04 Manchester U 28 9
2004–05 Manchester U 33 9
2005–06 Manchester U 20 2 **341 89**

SILVESTRE, Mikael (D) **299 6**
H: 6 0 W: 13 12 b.Chambray les Tours 9-8-77
Honours: France Youth, Under-21, 40 full caps, 2 goals.

1995–96	Rennes	1	0		
1996–97	Rennes	16	0		
1997–98	Rennes	32	0	**49**	**0**
1998–99	Internazionale	18	1	**18**	**1**
1999–2000	Manchester U	31	0		
2000–01	Manchester U	30	1		
2001–02	Manchester U	35	0		
2002–03	Manchester U	34	1		
2003–04	Manchester U	34	0		
2004–05	Manchester U	35	2		
2005–06	Manchester U	33	1	**232**	**5**

SIMPSON, Danny (D) **0 0**
b.Salford 4-1-87
Source: Scholar.

2005–06	Manchester U	0	*0*		

To Antwerp January 2006

SMITH, Alan (F) **224 45**
H: 5 10 W: 12 04 b.Rothwell 28-10-80
Source: Trainee. *Honours:* England Youth, Under-21, 16 full caps, 1 goal.

1997–98	Leeds U	0	0		
1998–99	Leeds U	22	7		
1999–2000	Leeds U	26	4		
2000–01	Leeds U	33	11		
2001–02	Leeds U	23	4		
2002–03	Leeds U	33	3		
2003–04	Leeds U	35	9	**172**	**38**
2004–05	Manchester U	31	6		
2005–06	Manchester U	21	1	**52**	**7**

SOLSKJAER, Ole Gunnar (F) **258 115**
H: 5 10 W: 11 07 b.Kristiansund 26-2-73
Honours: Norway Under-21, 62 full caps, 21 goals.

1995	Molde	26	20		
1996	Molde	16	11	**42**	**31**
1996–97	Manchester U	33	18		
1997–98	Manchester U	22	6		
1998–99	Manchester U	19	12		
1999–2000	Manchester U	28	12		
2000–01	Manchester U	31	10		
2001–02	Manchester U	30	17		
2002–03	Manchester U	37	9		
2003–04	Manchester U	13	0		
2004–05	Manchester U	0	0		
2005–06	Manchester U	3	0	**216**	**84**

SPECTOR, Jonathan (D) **23 0**
H: 6 0 W: 12 08 b.Arlington Heights 1-3-86
Source: Chicago Sockers, USA Youth.

2003–04	Manchester U	0	0		
2004–05	Manchester U	3	0		
2005–06	Manchester U	0	0	**3**	**0**
2005–06	*Charlton Ath*	20	0	**20**	**0**

STEELE, Luke (G) **34 0**
H: 6 2 W: 12 00 b.Peterborough 24-9-84
Source: Scholar. *Honours:* England Youth, Under-20.

2001–02	Peterborough U	2	0	**2**	**0**
2001–02	Manchester U	0	0		
2002–03	Manchester U	0	0		
2003–04	Manchester U	0	0		
2004–05	Manchester U	0	0		
2004–05	*Coventry C*	32	0	**32**	**0**
2005–06	Manchester U	0	0		

TIMM, Mads (F) **9 1**
H: 5 9 W: 12 10 b.Odense 31-10-84
Source: Scholar.

2001–02	Manchester U	0	0		
2002–03	Manchester U	0	0		
2003–04	Manchester U	0	0		
2004–05	Manchester U	0	0		
2005–06	Manchester U	0	0		
2005–06	*Walsall*	9	1	**9**	**1**

VAN NISTELROOY, Ruud (F) **317 187**
H: 6 2 W: 13 03 b.Oss 1-7-76
Source: Nooit Gedacht, Margriet. *Honours:* Holland 54 full caps, 28 goals.

1993–94	Den Bosch	2	0		
1994–95	Den Bosch	15	3		
1995–96	Den Bosch	21	2		
1996–97	Den Bosch	31	12	**69**	**17**
1997–98	Heerenveen	31	13	**31**	**13**
1998–99	PSV Eindhoven	34	31		
1999–2000	PSV Eindhoven	23	29		
2000–01	PSV Eindhoven	10	2	**67**	**62**
2001–02	Manchester U	32	23		
2002–03	Manchester U	34	25		
2003–04	Manchester U	32	20		
2004–05	Manchester U	17	6		
2005–06	Manchester U	35	21	**150**	**95**

VAN DER SAR, Edwin (G) **457 1**
H: 6 5 W: 14 11 b.Voorhout 29-10-70
Honours: Holland 113 full caps.

1990–91	Ajax	9	0		
1991–92	Ajax	0	0		
1992–93	Ajax	19	0		
1993–94	Ajax	32	0		
1994–95	Ajax	33	0		
1995–96	Ajax	33	0		
1996–97	Ajax	33	0		
1997–98	Ajax	33	1	**192**	**1**
1998–99	Juventus	34	0		
1999–2000	Juventus	32	0		
2000–01	Juventus	34	0	**100**	**0**
2001–02	Fulham	37	0		
2002–03	Fulham	19	0		
2003–04	Fulham	37	0		
2004–05	Fulham	34	0	**127**	**0**
2005–06	Manchester U	38	0	**38**	**0**

VIDIC, Nemanja (D) **145 22**
H: 6 1 W: 13 02 b.Uzice 21-10-81
Honours: Serbia & Montenegro 20 full caps, 1 goal.

2000–01	Subotica	27	6	**27**	**6**
2001–02	Red Star Belgrade	22	2		
2002–03	Red Star Belgrade	26	5		
2003–04	Red Star Belgrade	20	5	**68**	**12**
2004	Spartak Moscow	12	2		
2005	Spartak Moscow	27	2	**39**	**4**
2005–06	Manchester U	11	0	**11**	**0**

Scholars
Brandy, Febian E; Burns, Aaron Tyrone Stewart; Chester, James Grant; Crockett, Lee Adam; Eckersley, Richard John; Evans, Sean William; Fagan, Christopher Joseph; Hewson, Sam; Lea, Michael Robert; Lee, Kieran Christopher; Marsh, Philip; Mullan, Jamie John; Rose, Daniel Stephen; Shawcross, Ryan James; Zieler, Ron-Robert.

MANSFIELD T (49)

ARNOLD, Nathan (F) **8 1**
H: 5 8 W: 10 07 b.Mansfield 26-7-87

2005–06	Mansfield T	8	1	**8**	**1**

BARKER, Richard (F) **335 75**
H: 6 0 W: 14 03 b.Sheffield 30-5-75
Source: Trainee. *Honours:* England Schools.

1993–94	Sheffield W	0	0		
1994–95	Sheffield W	0	0		
1995–96	Sheffield W	0	0		
1995–96	*Doncaster R*	6	0	**6**	**0**
1996–97	Sheffield W	0	0		
From Linfield					
1997–98	Brighton & HA	17	2		
1998–99	Brighton & HA	43	10	**60**	**12**
1999–2000	Macclesfield T	35	16		
2000–01	Macclesfield T	23	7	**58**	**23**
2000–01	Rotherham U	19	1		
2001–02	Rotherham U	35	3		
2002–03	Rotherham U	37	7		
2003–04	Rotherham U	32	1		
2004–05	Rotherham U	17	0	**140**	**12**
2004–05	Mansfield T	28	10		
2005–06	Mansfield T	43	18	**71**	**28**

BEARDSLEY, Chris (F) **52 6**
H: 6 0 W: 12 12 b.Derby 28-2-84
Source: Scholar.

2002–03	Mansfield T	5	0		
2003–04	Mansfield T	15	1		
2004–05	Doncaster R	4	0	**4**	**0**
2004–05	Kidderminster H	25	5	**25**	**5**
2005–06	Mansfield T	3	0	**23**	**1**

BIRCHALL, Adam (F) **43 6**
H: 5 7 W: 10 09 b.Maidstone 2-12-84
Source: Trainee. *Honours:* Wales Under-21.

2002–03	Arsenal	0	0		
2003–04	Arsenal	0	0		
2004–05	Arsenal	0	0		
2004–05	*Wycombe W*	12	4	**12**	**4**
2005–06	Mansfield T	31	2	**31**	**2**

BROWN, Simon (F) **71 14**
H: 5 10 W: 11 00 b.West Bromwich 18-9-83
Source: Scholar.

2003–04	WBA	0	0		
2003–04	*Kidderminster H*	8	2		
2004–05	WBA	0	0		
2004–05	*Kidderminster H*	13	0	**21**	**2**
2004–05	Mansfield T	21	2		
2005–06	Mansfield T	29	10	**50**	**12**

BUXTON, Jake (D) **81 2**
H: 6 1 W: 13 05 b.Sutton-in-Ashfield 4---85
Source: Scholar.

2002–03	Mansfield T	3	0		
2003–04	Mansfield T	9	1		
2004–05	Mansfield T	30	1		
2005–06	Mansfield T	39	0	**81**	**2**

COKE, Gilles (M) **49 4**
H: 6 0 W: 11 11 b.London 3-6-86
Source: Kingstonian.

2004–05	Mansfield T	9	0		
2005–06	Mansfield T	40	4	**49**	**4**

D'LARYEA, Jonathan (M) **29 0**
H: 5 10 W: 12 02 b.Manchester 3-9-85
Source: Trainee.

2003–04	Manchester C	0	0		
2004–05	Manchester C	0	0		
2005–06	Manchester C	0	0		
2005–06	Mansfield T	29	0	**29**	**0**

DAWSON, Stephen (M) **40 1**
H: 5 9 W: 11 09 b.Dublin 4-12-85
Source: Scholar. *Honours:* Eire Under-21.

2003–04	Leicester C	0	0		
2004–05	Leicester C	0	0		
2005–06	Mansfield T	40	1	**40**	**1**

DAY, Rhys (D) **112 12**
H: 6 1 W: 12 08 b.Bridgend 31-8-82
Source: Scholarship. *Honours:* Wales Under-21.

1999–2000	Manchester C	0	0		
2000–01	Manchester C	0	0		
2001–02	Manchester C	0	0		
2001–02	*Blackpool*	9	0	**9**	**0**
2002–03	Manchester C	0	0		
2002–03	Mansfield T	23	1		
2003–04	Mansfield T	41	6		
2004–05	Mansfield T	18	3		
2005–06	Mansfield T	21	2	**103**	**12**

HERON, Danny (M) **3 0**
H: 5 11 W: 10 09 b.Cambridge 9-10-86
Source: Scholar.

2004–05	Mansfield T	3	0		
2005–06	Mansfield T	0	0	**3**	**0**

HJELDE, Jon Olav (D) **229 6**
H: 6 2 W: 13 07 b.Levanger 30-7-72

1994	Rosenborg	1	0		
1995	Rosenborg	7	0		
1996	Rosenborg	16	1		
1997	Rosenborg	3	0	**27**	**1**
1997–98	Nottingham F	28	1		
1998–99	Nottingham F	17	1		
1999–2000	Nottingham F	33	0		
2000–01	Nottingham F	11	2		
2001–02	Nottingham F	42	0		
2002–03	Nottingham F	26	0		
2003–04	Nottingham F	0	0		
2004–05	Nottingham F	14	0	**171**	**4**
2005–06	Mansfield T	31	1	**31**	**1**

JACOBS, Kyle (M) **5 0**
H: 5 10 W: 13 03 b.Manchester 18-10-86

2005–06	Mansfield T	5	0	**5**	**0**

JELLEYMAN, Gareth (D) 152 1
H: 5 10 W: 10 02 b.Holywell 14-11-80
Source: Trainee. *Honours:* Wales Youth, Under-21.
1998–99 Peterborough U 0 0
1999–2000 Peterborough U 20 0
2000–01 Peterborough U 8 0
2001–02 Peterborough U 10 0
2002–03 Peterborough U 32 0
2003–04 Peterborough U 17 0
2004–05 Peterborough U 14 0 **101 0**
2004–05 *Boston U* 3 0 **3 0**
2004–05 Mansfield T 14 0
2005–06 Mansfield T 34 1 **48 1**

JOHN-BAPTISTE, Alex (D) 103 2
H: 6 0 W: 11 11 b.Sutton-in-Ashfield 31-1-86
Source: Scholar.
2002–03 Mansfield T 4 0
2003–04 Mansfield T 17 0
2004–05 Mansfield T 41 1
2005–06 Mansfield T 41 1 **103 2**

LANGFORD, Michael (G) 0 0
H: 5 11 W: 11 02 b.Wolverhampton 10-5-88
Source: Scholar.
2005–06 Mansfield T 0 0

LITTLEJOHN, Adrian (M) 425 71
H: 5 9 W: 10 07 b.Wolverhampton 26-9-70
Source: WBA Trainee.
1989–90 Walsall 11 0
1990–91 Walsall 33 1 **44 1**
1991–92 Sheffield U 7 0
1992–93 Sheffield U 27 8
1993–94 Sheffield U 19 3
1994–95 Sheffield U 16 1
1995–96 Plymouth Arg 42 17
1996–97 Plymouth Arg 37 6
1997–98 Plymouth Arg 31 6 **110 29**
1997–98 Oldham Ath 5 3
1998–99 Oldham Ath 16 2 **21 5**
1998–99 Bury 20 1
1999–2000 Bury 42 9
2000–01 Bury 37 4 **99 14**
2001–02 Sheffield U 3 0
2002–03 Sheffield U 0 0 **72 12**
2002–03 Port Vale 13 3
2003–04 Port Vale 36 7
2004–05 Port Vale 0 0 **49 10**
2004–05 Lincoln C 8 0 **8 0**
2004–05 Rushden & D 15 0
2005–06 Rushden & D 0 0 **15 0**
2005–06 Mansfield T 7 0 **7 0**

LLOYD, Callum (M) 22 4
H: 5 9 W: 11 07 b.Nottingham 1-1-86
Source: Scholar.
2004–05 Mansfield T 10 4
2005–06 Mansfield T 12 0 **22 4**

LONSDALE, Richard (M) 0 0
H: 5 9 W: 10 10 b.Burton 29-10-87
Source: Scholar.
2004–05 Mansfield T 0 0
2005–06 Mansfield T 0 0

McINTOSH, Austin (M) 1 0
H: 5 11 W: 10 09 b.Newham 5-11-87
Source: Scholar.
2004–05 Mansfield T 1 0
2005–06 Mansfield T 0 0 **1 0**

McLACHLAN, Fraser (M) 82 4
H: 5 11 W: 12 07 b.Manchester 9-11-82
Source: Scholar.
2001–02 Stockport Co 11 1
2002–03 Stockport Co 22 0
2003–04 Stockport Co 20 3
2004–05 Stockport Co 0 0 **53 4**
2004–05 Mansfield T 21 0
2005–06 Mansfield T 8 0 **29 0**

PALMER, Carlton (M) 590 32
H: 6 2 W: 12 04 b.West Bromwich 5-12-65
Source: Trainee. *Honours:* England Under-21, B, 18 full caps, 1 goal.
1984–85 WBA 0 0
1985–86 WBA 20 0
1986–87 WBA 37 1
1987–88 WBA 38 3
1988–89 WBA 26 0 **121 4**
1988–89 Sheffield W 13 1
1989–90 Sheffield W 34 0
1990–91 Sheffield W 45 2
1991–92 Sheffield W 42 5
1992–93 Sheffield W 34 1
1993–94 Sheffield W 37 5
1994–95 Leeds U 39 3
1995–96 Leeds U 35 2
1996–97 Leeds U 28 0
1997–98 Leeds U 0 0 **102 5**
1997–98 Southampton 26 3
1998–99 Southampton 19 0 **45 3**
1998–99 Nottingham F 13 0
1999–2000 Nottingham F 3 1 **16 1**
1999–2000 Coventry C 15 1
2000–01 Coventry C 15 0
2000–01 *Watford* 5 0 **5 0**
2000–01 *Sheffield W* 12 0
2001–02 Coventry C 0 0 **30 1**
2001–02 *Sheffield W* 10 0 **227 14**
2001–02 Stockport Co 21 3
2002–03 Stockport Co 22 1
2003–04 Stockport Co 0 0
2004–05 Stockport Co 0 0 **43 4**
2005–06 Mansfield T 1 0 **1 0**

PARKS, Ryan (M) 0 0
b.Mansfield 1-5-87
Source: Scholar.
2005–06 Mansfield T 0 0

PEERS, Gavin (D) 13 2
H: 5 11 W: 13 05 b.Dublin 10-11-85
Source: Trainee.
2002–03 Blackburn R 0 0
2003–04 Blackburn R 0 0
2004–05 Blackburn R 0 0
2005–06 Mansfield T 13 2 **13 2**

PRESSMAN, Kevin (G) 462 0
H: 6 1 W: 14 12 b.Fareham 6-11-67
Source: Apprentice. *Honours:* England Schools, Youth, Under-21, B.
1985–86 Sheffield W 0 0
1986–87 Sheffield W 0 0
1987–88 Sheffield W 11 0
1988–89 Sheffield W 9 0
1989–90 Sheffield W 15 0
1990–91 Sheffield W 23 0
1991–92 Sheffield W 1 0
1991–92 *Stoke C* 4 0 **4 0**
1992–93 Sheffield W 3 0
1993–94 Sheffield W 32 0
1994–95 Sheffield W 34 0
1995–96 Sheffield W 30 0
1996–97 Sheffield W 38 0
1997–98 Sheffield W 36 0
1998–99 Sheffield W 15 0
1999–2000 Sheffield W 19 0
2000–01 Sheffield W 39 0
2001–02 Sheffield W 40 0
2002–03 Sheffield W 38 0
2003–04 *WBA* 0 0
2003–04 Sheffield W 21 0 **404 0**
2004–05 Leicester C 13 0 **13 0**
2005–06 Mansfield T 41 0 **41 0**

REET, Danny (F) 24 9
H: 6 1 W: 14 02 b.Sheffield 31-1-87
2005–06 Sheffield W 0 0
2005–06 *Bury* 6 4 **6 4**
2005–06 Mansfield T 18 5 **18 5**

RUNDLE, Adam (F) 114 10
H: 5 8 W: 11 02 b.Durham 8-7-84
Source: Scholar.
2001–02 Darlington 12 0
2002–03 Darlington 5 0 **17 0**
2002–03 Carlisle U 21 1
2003–04 Carlisle U 23 0
2004–05 Carlisle U 0 0 **44 1**
2004–05 Mansfield T 18 4
2005–06 Mansfield T 35 5 **53 9**

SLEATH, Danny (M) 0 0
H: 5 8 W: 9 07 b.Derby 14-12-86
2005–06 Mansfield T 0 0

TALBOT, Jason (D) 15 0
H: 5 8 W: 10 01 b.Irlam 30-9-85
Source: Scholar.
2004–05 Bolton W 0 0
2004–05 *Derby Co* 2 0 **2 0**
2004–05 *Mansfield T* 2 0
2005–06 Mansfield T 6 0 **8 0**
2005–06 *Port Vale* 5 0 **5 0**

UHLENBEEK, Gus (D) 408 15
H: 5 9 W: 12 00 b.Paramaribo 20-8-70
1990–91 Ajax 2 0
1991–92 Ajax 0 0 **2 0**
1992–93 Cambuur 24 0
1993–94 Cambuur 15 0 **39 0**
1994–95 TOPS SV 22 3 **22 3**
1995–96 Ipswich T 40 4
1996–97 Ipswich T 38 0
1997–98 Ipswich T 11 0 **89 4**
1998–99 Fulham 23 1
1999–2000 Fulham 16 0 **39 1**
2000–01 Sheffield U 31 0
2001–02 Sheffield U 20 0 **51 0**
2001–02 *Walsall* 5 0 **5 0**
2002–03 Bradford C 42 1 **42 1**
2003–04 Chesterfield 37 0 **37 0**
2004–05 Wycombe W 42 4 **42 4**
2005–06 Mansfield T 40 2 **40 2**

WHITE, Jason (G) 10 0
H: 6 2 W: 12 01 b.Sutton-in-Ashfield 28-1-84
Source: Trainee.
2002–03 Mansfield T 1 0
2003–04 Mansfield T 0 0
2004–05 Mansfield T 4 0
2005–06 Mansfield T 5 0 **10 0**

WOOD, Chris (M) 1 0
H: 6 0 W: 10 11 b.Worksop 24-1-87
2004–05 Mansfield T 1 0
2005–06 Mansfield T 0 0 **1 0**

MIDDLESBROUGH (50)

BATES, Matthew (D) 24 0
H: 5 10 W: 12 03 b.Stockton 10-12-86
Source: Scholar. *Honours:* England Youth.
2003–04 Middlesbrough 2 0
2004–05 Middlesbrough 2 0
2004–05 *Darlington* 4 0 **4 0**
2005–06 Middlesbrough 16 0 **20 0**

BOATENG, George (M) 341 15
H: 5 9 W: 12 06 b.Nkawkaw 5-9-75
Honours: Holland 2 full caps.
1994–95 Excelsior 9 0 **9 0**
1995–96 Feyenoord 24 1
1996–97 Feyenoord 26 0
1997–98 Feyenoord 18 0 **68 1**
1997–98 Coventry C 14 1
1998–99 Coventry C 33 4 **47 5**
1999–2000 Aston Villa 33 2
2000–01 Aston Villa 33 1
2001–02 Aston Villa 37 1 **103 4**
2002–03 Middlesbrough 28 0
2003–04 Middlesbrough 35 0
2004–05 Middlesbrough 25 3
2005–06 Middlesbrough 26 2 **114 5**

CATTERMOLE, Lee (M) 14 1
H: 5 10 W: 11 13 b.Stockton 21-3-88
Source: Scholar. *Honours:* England Youth.
2005–06 Middlesbrough 14 1 **14 1**

CHRISTIE, Malcolm (F) 146 36
H: 6 0 W: 12 06 b.Peterborough 11-4-79
Source: Nuneaton B. *Honours:* England Under-21.
1998–99 Derby Co 2 0
1999–2000 Derby Co 21 5
2000–01 Derby Co 34 8
2001–02 Derby Co 35 9
2002–03 Derby Co 24 8 **116 30**
2002–03 Middlesbrough 12 4
2003–04 Middlesbrough 10 1
2004–05 Middlesbrough 2 1
2005–06 Middlesbrough 6 0 **30 6**

COOPER, Colin (D) 606 37
H: 5 11 W: 11 11 b.Sedgefield 28-2-67
Honours: England Under-21, 2 full caps.

1984–85	Middlesbrough	0	0		
1985–86	Middlesbrough	11	0		
1986–87	Middlesbrough	46	0		
1987–88	Middlesbrough	43	2		
1988–89	Middlesbrough	35	2		
1989–90	Middlesbrough	21	2		
1990–91	Middlesbrough	32	0		
1991–92	Millwall	36	2		
1992–93	Millwall	41	4	**77**	**6**
1993–94	Nottingham F	37	7		
1994–95	Nottingham F	35	1		
1995–96	Nottingham F	37	5		
1996–97	Nottingham F	36	2		
1997–98	Nottingham F	35	5		
1998–99	Nottingham F	0	0	**180**	**20**
1998–99	Middlesbrough	32	1		
1999–2000	Middlesbrough	26	0		
2000–01	Middlesbrough	27	2		
2001–02	Middlesbrough	18	2		
2002–03	Middlesbrough	20	0		
2003–04	Middlesbrough	19	0		
2003–04	*Sunderland*	3	0	**3**	**0**
2004–05	Middlesbrough	15	0		
2005–06	Middlesbrough	1	0	**346**	**11**

CRADDOCK, Tom (F) 1 0
H: 5 11 W: 11 10 b.Durham 14-10-86
Source: Scholar.

2005–06	Middlesbrough	1	0	**1**	**0**

DAVIES, Andrew (D) 58 3
H: 6 3 W: 14 08 b.Stockton 17-12-84
Source: Scholar. *Honours:* England Youth, Under-20, Under-21.

2002–03	Middlesbrough	1	0		
2003–04	Middlesbrough	10	0		
2004–05	Middlesbrough	3	0		
2004–05	*QPR*	9	0	**9**	**0**
2005–06	Middlesbrough	12	0	**26**	**0**
2005–06	*Derby Co*	23	3	**23**	**3**

DORIVA (M) 260 10
H: 5 7 W: 11 04 b.Landeara 28-5-72
Honours: Brazil 12 full caps.

1993	Sao Paulo	12	0		
1994	Sao Paulo	15	0	**27**	**0**
1995	Atletico Mineiro	11	1		
1996	Atletico Mineiro	24	0		
1997	Atletico Mineiro	24	0	**59**	**1**
1997–98	Porto	13	1		
1998–99	Porto	17	4	**30**	**5**
1999–2000	Sampdoria	31	3	**31**	**3**
2000–01	Celta Vigo	17	1		
2001–02	Celta Vigo	14	0		
2002–03	Celta Vigo	3	0	**34**	**1**
2002–03	Middlesbrough	5	0		
2003–04	Middlesbrough	21	0		
2004–05	Middlesbrough	26	0		
2005–06	Middlesbrough	27	0	**79**	**0**

DOWNING, Stewart (M) 79 9
H: 5 11 W: 10 04 b.Middlesbrough 22-7-84
Source: Scholar. *Honours:* England Youth, Under-21, B, 4 full caps.

2001–02	Middlesbrough	3	0		
2002–03	Middlesbrough	2	0		
2003–04	Middlesbrough	20	0		
2003–04	*Sunderland*	7	3	**7**	**3**
2004–05	Middlesbrough	35	5		
2005–06	Middlesbrough	12	1	**72**	**6**

EHIOGU, Ugo (D) 365 19
H: 6 2 W: 14 10 b.Hackney 3-11-72
Source: Trainee. *Honours:* England Under-21, B, 4 full caps, 1 goal.

1990–91	WBA	2	0	**2**	**0**
1991–92	Aston Villa	8	0		
1992–93	Aston Villa	4	0		
1993–94	Aston Villa	17	0		
1994–95	Aston Villa	39	3		
1995–96	Aston Villa	36	1		
1996–97	Aston Villa	38	3		
1997–98	Aston Villa	37	2		
1998–99	Aston Villa	25	2		
1999–2000	Aston Villa	31	1		
2000–01	Aston Villa	2	0	**237**	**12**
2000–01	Middlesbrough	21	3		
2001–02	Middlesbrough	29	1		
2002–03	Middlesbrough	32	3		
2003–04	Middlesbrough	16	0		
2004–05	Middlesbrough	10	0		
2005–06	Middlesbrough	18	0	**126**	**7**

GRAHAM, Danny (F) 40 3
H: 5 11 W: 12 05 b.Gateshead 12-8-85
Source: Trainee. *Honours:* England Youth, Under-20.

2003–04	Middlesbrough	0	0		
2003–04	*Darlington*	9	2	**9**	**2**
2004–05	Middlesbrough	11	1		
2005–06	Middlesbrough	3	0	**14**	**1**
2005–06	*Derby Co*	14	0	**14**	**0**
2005–06	*Leeds U*	3	0	**3**	**0**

HASSELBAINK, Jimmy Floyd (F) 357 181
H: 5 10 W: 13 10 b.Paramaribo 27-3-72
Honours: Holland 23 full caps, 9 goals.

1995–96	Campomairorense	31	12	**31**	**12**
1996–97	Boavista	29	20	**29**	**20**
1997–98	Leeds U	33	16		
1998–99	Leeds U	36	18	**69**	**34**
1999–2000	Atletico Madrid	34	24	**34**	**24**
2000–01	Chelsea	35	23		
2001–02	Chelsea	35	23		
2002–03	Chelsea	36	11		
2003–04	Chelsea	30	12	**136**	**69**
2004–05	Middlesbrough	36	13		
2005–06	Middlesbrough	22	9	**58**	**22**

HINES, Sebastian (M) 0 0
H: 6 2 W: 12 04 b.Wetherby 29-5-88
Source: Scholar. *Honours:* England Youth.

2005–06	Middlesbrough	0	0		

HUTCHINSON, Ben (F) 0 0
b.Nottingham
Source: Arnold T.

2005–06	Middlesbrough	0	0		

JOB, Joseph-Desire (F) 170 33
H: 5 11 W: 11 00 b.Venissieux 1-12-77
Honours: Cameroon 48 full caps, 7 goals.

1997–98	Lyon	22	5		
1998–99	Lyon	19	6	**41**	**11**
1999–2000	Lens	24	4	**24**	**4**
2000–01	Middlesbrough	12	3		
2001–02	Middlesbrough	4	0		
2001–02	Metz	13	2	13	2
2002–03	Middlesbrough	28	4		
2003–04	Middlesbrough	24	5		
2004–05	Middlesbrough	23	4		
2005–06	Middlesbrough	1	0	**92**	**16**

To Al Ittihad (loan) August 2005

JOHNSON, Adam (M) 13 1
H: 5 8 W: 10 00 b.Sunderland 14-7-87
Source: Scholar. *Honours:* England Youth.

2004–05	Middlesbrough	0	0		
2005–06	Middlesbrough	13	1	**13**	**1**

JONES, Brad (G) 35 0
H: 6 3 W: 12 01 b.Armadale 19-3-82
Source: Trainee. *Honours:* Australia Under-20, Under-23.

1998–99	Middlesbrough	0	0		
1999–2000	Middlesbrough	0	0		
2000–01	Middlesbrough	0	0		
2001–02	Middlesbrough	0	0		
2002	Shelbourne	2	0	**2**	**0**
2002–03	Middlesbrough	0	0		
2002–03	*Stockport Co*	1	0	**1**	**0**
2003–04	Middlesbrough	1	0		
2003–04	*Blackpool*	5	0		
2003–04	*Rotherham U*	0	0		
2004–05	Middlesbrough	5	0		
2004–05	*Blackpool*	12	0	**17**	**0**
2005–06	Middlesbrough	9	0	**15**	**0**

KENNEDY, Jason (M) 4 0
H: 6 1 W: 13 02 b.Stockton 11-9-86
Source: Scholar.

2004–05	Middlesbrough	1	0		
2005–06	Middlesbrough	3	0	**4**	**0**

KNIGHT, David (G) 3 0
H: 6 0 W: 11 07 b.Sunderland 15-1-87
Source: Scholar. *Honours:* England Youth.

2004–05	Middlesbrough	0	0		
2005–06	Middlesbrough	0	0		
2005–06	*Darlington*	3	0	**3**	**0**

LIDDLE, Gary (D) 0 0
H: 6 1 W: 12 06 b.Middlesbrough 15-6-86
Source: Trainee. *Honours:* England Youth.

2003–04	Middlesbrough	0	0		
2004–05	Middlesbrough	0	0		
2005–06	Middlesbrough	0	0		

MACCARONE, Massimo (F) 126 39
H: 5 10 W: 12 05 b.Galliate 6-9-79
Honours: Italy 2 full caps.

2000–01	Empoli	35	16		
2001–02	Empoli	0	0	**35**	**16**
2002–03	Middlesbrough	34	9		
2003–04	Middlesbrough	23	6		
2004–05	Middlesbrough	0	0		
2004–05	*Siena*	17	6	**17**	**6**
2005–06	Middlesbrough	17	2	**74**	**17**

McMAHON, Tony (D) 16 0
H: 5 10 W: 11 04 b.Bishop Auckland 24-3-86
Source: Scholar. *Honours:* England Youth.

2003–04	Middlesbrough	0	0		
2004–05	Middlesbrough	13	0		
2005–06	Middlesbrough	3	0	**16**	**0**

MENDIETA, Gaizka (M) 402 52
H: 5 9 W: 11 02 b.Bilbao 27-3-74
Honours: Spain 40 full caps, 8 goals.

1991–92	Castellon	16	0	**16**	**0**
1992–93	Valencia B	31	2		
1992–93	Valencia	2	0		
1993–94	Valencia B	17	0	**48**	**2**
1993–94	Valencia	20	0		
1994–95	Valencia	13	1		
1995–96	Valencia	34	0		
1996–97	Valencia	29	1		
1997–98	Valencia	30	10		
1998–99	Valencia	38	7		
1999–2000	Valencia	33	13		
2000–01	Valencia	31	10	**230**	**42**
2001–02	Lazio	20	0	**20**	**0**
2002–03	Barcelona	33	4	**33**	**4**
2003–04	Middlesbrough	31	2		
2004–05	Middlesbrough	7	0		
2005–06	Middlesbrough	17	2	**55**	**4**

MORRISON, James (M) 39 1
H: 5 10 W: 10 06 b.Darlington 25-5-86
Source: Trainee. *Honours:* England Youth, Under-20.

2003–04	Middlesbrough	1	0		
2004–05	Middlesbrough	14	0		
2005–06	Middlesbrough	24	1	**39**	**1**

NEMETH, Szilard (F) 273 107
H: 5 11 W: 11 04 b.Komarno 8-8-77
Honours: Slovakia 56 full caps, 22 goals.

1994–95	Slovan Bratislava	3	0		
1995–96	Slovan Bratislava	28	12		
1996–97	Slovan Bratislava	30	13	**61**	**25**
1997–98	Kosice	18	12		
1998–99	Kosice	19	8	**37**	**20**
1999–2000	Inter Bratislava	26	16		
2000–01	Inter Bratislava	32	23	**58**	**39**
2001–02	Middlesbrough	21	3		
2002–03	Middlesbrough	28	7		
2003–04	Middlesbrough	32	9		
2004–05	Middlesbrough	31	4		
2005–06	Middlesbrough	5	0	**117**	**23**

To Strasbourg January 2006

PARLOUR, Ray (M) 385 22
H: 5 10 W: 11 12 b.Romford 7-3-73
Source: Trainee. *Honours:* England Under-21, B, 10 full caps.

1990–91	Arsenal	0	0		
1991–92	Arsenal	6	1		
1992–93	Arsenal	21	1		
1993–94	Arsenal	27	2		
1994–95	Arsenal	30	0		
1995–96	Arsenal	22	0		
1996–97	Arsenal	30	2		
1997–98	Arsenal	34	5		
1998–99	Arsenal	35	6		
1999–2000	Arsenal	30	1		
2000–01	Arsenal	33	4		
2001–02	Arsenal	27	0		
2002–03	Arsenal	19	0		
2003–04	Arsenal	25	0	**339**	**22**
2004–05	Middlesbrough	33	0		
2005–06	Middlesbrough	13	0	**46**	**0**

PARNABY, Stuart (M) 79 2
H: 5 11 W: 11 00 b.Durham 19-7-82
Source: Trainee. *Honours:* England Youth, Under-20, Under-21.
1999–2000 Middlesbrough 0 0
2000–01 Middlesbrough 0 0
2000–01 *Halifax T* 6 0 **6 0**
2001–02 Middlesbrough 0 0
2002–03 Middlesbrough 21 0
2003–04 Middlesbrough 13 0
2004–05 Middlesbrough 19 0
2005–06 Middlesbrough 20 2 **73 2**

POGATETZ, Emanuel (D) 147 3
H: 6 2 W: 13 05 b.Steinbock 16-1-83
Honours: Austria 20 full caps, 1 goal.
1999–2000 Sturm Graz 0 0
2000–01 Karntern 33 0 **33 0**
2001–02 Leverkusen B 23 0
2001–02 Leverkusen 0 0
2002–03 Leverkusen B 3 0 **26 0**
2002–03 Leverkusen 0 0
2002–03 Aarau 11 0 **11 0**
2003–04 Graz 31 1
2004–05 Graz 22 1 **53 2**
2005–06 Middlesbrough 24 1 **24 1**

QUEUDRUE, Franck (D) 192 13
H: 6 1 W: 12 01 b.Paris 27-8-78
Source: Meaux.
1999–2000 Lens 16 1
2000–01 Lens 24 1
2001–02 Lens 2 0 **42 2**
2001–02 Middlesbrough 28 2
2002–03 Middlesbrough 31 1
2003–04 Middlesbrough 31 0
2004–05 Middlesbrough 31 5
2005–06 Middlesbrough 29 3 **150 11**

RIGGOTT, Chris (D) 156 9
H: 6 2 W: 13 09 b.Derby 1-9-80
Source: Trainee. *Honours:* England Youth, Under-21.
1998–99 Derby Co 0 0
1999–2000 Derby Co 1 0
2000–01 Derby Co 31 3
2001–02 Derby Co 37 0
2002–03 Derby Co 22 2 **91 5**
2002–03 Middlesbrough 5 2
2003–04 Middlesbrough 17 0
2004–05 Middlesbrough 21 2
2005–06 Middlesbrough 22 0 **65 4**

ROCHEMBACK, Fabio (M) 131 17
H: 6 0 W: 13 01 b.Soledade 10-12-81
Honours: Brazil 7 full caps.
2000 Internacional 20 4
2001 Internacional 0 0 **20 4**
2001–02 Barcelona 24 1
2002–03 Barcelona 21 1 **45 2**
2003–04 Sporting Lisbon 21 8
2004–05 Sporting Lisbon 23 1 **44 9**
2005–06 Middlesbrough 22 2 **22 2**

SCHWARZER, Mark (G) 374 0
H: 6 4 W: 14 07 b.Sydney 6-10-72
Honours: Australia Youth, Under-20, 40 full caps.
1990–91 Marconi Stallions 1 0
1991–92 Marconi Stallions 9 0
1992–93 Marconi Stallions 23 0
1993–94 Marconi Stallions 25 0 **58 0**
1994–95 Dynamo Dresden 2 0 **2 0**
1995–96 Kaiserslautern 4 0
1996–97 Kaiserslautern 0 0 **4 0**
1996–97 Bradford C 13 0 **13 0**
1996–97 Middlesbrough 7 0
1997–98 Middlesbrough 35 0
1998–99 Middlesbrough 34 0
1999–2000 Middlesbrough 37 0
2000–01 Middlesbrough 31 0
2001–02 Middlesbrough 21 0
2002–03 Middlesbrough 38 0
2003–04 Middlesbrough 36 0
2004–05 Middlesbrough 31 0
2005–06 Middlesbrough 27 0 **297 0**

SOUTHGATE, Gareth (D) 503 26
H: 6 0 W: 12 03 b.Watford 3-9-70
Source: Trainee. *Honours:* England 57 full caps, 2 goals.
1988–89 Crystal Palace 0 0
1989–90 Crystal Palace 0 0
1990–91 Crystal Palace 1 0
1991–92 Crystal Palace 30 0
1992–93 Crystal Palace 33 3
1993–94 Crystal Palace 46 9
1994–95 Crystal Palace 42 3 **152 15**
1995–96 Aston Villa 31 1
1996–97 Aston Villa 28 1
1997–98 Aston Villa 32 0
1998–99 Aston Villa 38 1
1999–2000 Aston Villa 31 2
2000–01 Aston Villa 31 2 **191 7**
2001–02 Middlesbrough 37 1
2002–03 Middlesbrough 36 2
2003–04 Middlesbrough 27 1
2004–05 Middlesbrough 36 0
2005–06 Middlesbrough 24 0 **160 4**

TAYLOR, Andrew (D) 37 0
H: 5 10 W: 11 04 b.Hartlepool 1-8-86
Source: Trainee. *Honours:* England Youth, Under-20, Under-21.
2003–04 Middlesbrough 0 0
2004–05 Middlesbrough 0 0
2005–06 Middlesbrough 13 0 **13 0**
2005–06 *Bradford C* 24 0 **24 0**

TURNBULL, Ross (G) 60 0
H: 6 4 W: 15 00 b.Bishop Auckland 4-1-85
Source: Trainee. *Honours:* England Youth, Under-20.
2002–03 Middlesbrough 0 0
2003–04 Middlesbrough 0 0
2003–04 *Darlington* 1 0 **1 0**
2003–04 *Barnsley* 3 0
2004–05 Middlesbrough 0 0
2004–05 *Bradford C* 2 0 **2 0**
2004–05 *Barnsley* 23 0 **26 0**
2005–06 Middlesbrough 2 0 **2 0**
2005–06 *Crewe Alex* 29 0 **29 0**

VIDUKA, Mark (F) 342 181
H: 6 2 W: 15 01 b.Melbourne 9-10-75
Honours: Australia Youth, Under-20, Under-23, 37 full caps, 6 goals.
1992–93 Melbourne Knights 4 2
1993–94 Melbourne Knights 20 17
1994–95 Melbourne Knights 24 21 **48 40**
1995–96 Croatia Zagreb 27 12
1996–97 Croatia Zagreb 25 18
1997–98 Croatia Zagreb 25 8
1998–99 Croatia Zagreb 7 2 **84 40**
1998–99 Celtic 9 5
1999–2000 Celtic 28 25 **37 30**
2000–01 Leeds U 34 17
2001–02 Leeds U 33 11
2002–03 Leeds U 33 20
2003–04 Leeds U 30 11 **130 59**
2004–05 Middlesbrough 16 5
2005–06 Middlesbrough 27 7 **43 12**

WALKER, Josh (M) 1 0
H: 5 11 W: 11 13 b.Newcastle 21-2-89
Source: Scholar. *Honours:* England Schools, Youth.
2005–06 Middlesbrough 1 0 **1 0**

WHEATER, David (D) 13 1
H: 6 5 W: 12 12 b.Redcar 14-2-87
Source: Scholar. *Honours:* England Youth.
2004–05 Middlesbrough 0 0
2005–06 Middlesbrough 6 0 **6 0**
2005–06 *Doncaster R* 7 1 **7 1**

XAVIER, Abel (D) 246 7
H: 6 3 W: 12 07 b.Mozambique 30-11-72
Honours: Portugal 19 full caps, 2 goals.
1990–91 Amadora 22 0
1991–92 Amadora 21 0
1992–93 Amadora 0 0 **43 0**
1993–94 Benfica 24 1
1994–95 Benfica 22 3 **46 4**
1995–96 Bari 8 0 **8 0**
1996–97 Oviedo 27 0
1997–98 Oviedo 31 0 **58 0**
1998–99 PSV Eindhoven 19 2 **19 2**
1999–2000 Everton 20 0
2000–01 Everton 11 0
2001–02 Everton 12 0 **43 0**
2001–02 Liverpool 10 1
2002–03 Liverpool 4 0
2002–03 Galatasaray 11 0 **11 0**
2003–04 Liverpool 0 0
2004–05 Liverpool 0 0 **14 1**
2005–06 Middlesbrough 4 0 **4 0**

YAKUBU, Ayegbeni (F) 174 70
H: 6 0 W: 14 07 b.Benin City 22-11-82
Source: Julius Berger. *Honours:* Nigeria 19 full caps, 5 goals.
1999–2000 Gil Vicente 0 0
1999–2000 Hapoel Kfar-Sava 23 6 **23 6**
2000–01 Maccabi Haifa 14 3
2001–02 Maccabi Haifa 22 13 **36 16**
2002–03 Portsmouth 14 7
2003–04 Portsmouth 37 16
2004–05 Portsmouth 30 12 **81 35**
2005–06 Middlesbrough 34 13 **34 13**

Scholars
Burgess, Kevin; Craddock, Thomas; Fisher, Nathan; Grounds, Jonathan Martin; Honeyman, Jason; Johnson, John James; Langthorne, Richard; Owens, Graeme Adams; Robson, Daryl Andrew; Thompson, Stephen; **Watling, Peter;** Williams, Rhys.

MILLWALL (51)

ASABA, Carl (F) 334 106
H: 6 2 W: 13 00 b.Westminster 28-1-73
Source: Dulwich Hamlet.
1994–95 Brentford 0 0
1994–95 *Colchester U* 12 2 **12 2**
1995–96 Brentford 10 2
1996–97 Brentford 44 23 **54 25**
1997–98 Reading 32 8
1998–99 Reading 1 0 **33 8**
1998–99 Gillingham 41 20
1999–2000 Gillingham 11 6
2000–01 Gillingham 25 10 **77 36**
2000–01 Sheffield U 10 5
2001–02 Sheffield U 29 7
2002–03 Sheffield U 28 11 **67 23**
2003–04 Stoke C 37 8
2004–05 Stoke C 33 1
2005–06 Stoke C 0 0 **70 9**
2005–06 Millwall 21 3 **21 3**

BOSTWICK, Michael (D) 0 0
2005–06 Millwall 0 0

BRANIFF, Kevin (F) 60 4
H: 5 11 W: 10 03 b.Belfast 4-3-83
Source: Scholarship. *Honours:* Northern Ireland Schools, Youth, Under-21, Under-23.
1999–2000 Millwall 0 0
2000–01 Millwall 5 0
2001–02 Millwall 1 0
2002–03 Millwall 10 0
2003–04 Millwall 16 1
2004–05 Millwall 1 0
2004–05 *Rushden & D* 12 3 **12 3**
2005–06 Millwall 15 0 **48 1**

BROOKS, Alan (G) 0 0
b.Ennis 26-2-87
Source: Scholar.
2005–06 Millwall 0 0

COGAN, Barry (F) 24 0
H: 5 9 W: 9 0 b.Sligo 4-11-84
Source: Scholar. *Honours:* Eire Under-21.
2001–02 Millwall 0 0
2002–03 Millwall 0 0
2003–04 Millwall 3 0
2004–05 Millwall 7 0
2005–06 Millwall 14 0 **24 0**

CRAIG, Tony (D) 63 1
H: 6 0 W: 10 03 b.Greenwich 20-4-85
Source: Scholar.
2002–03 Millwall 2 1
2003–04 Millwall 9 0
2004–05 Millwall 10 0
2004–05 *Wycombe W* 14 0 **14 0**
2005–06 Millwall 28 0 **49 1**

DUNNE, Alan (D) 72 3
H: 5 10 W: 10 13 b.Dublin 23-8-82
Source: Trainee.
1999–2000 Millwall 0 0
2000–01 Millwall 0 0
2001–02 Millwall 1 0
2002–03 Millwall 4 0
2003–04 Millwall 8 0
2004–05 Millwall 19 3
2005–06 Millwall 40 0 **72 3**

DYER, Lloyd (M) 55 3
H: 5 8 W: 10 03 b.Birmingham 13-9-82
Source: Aston Villa Juniors.
2001–02 WBA 0 0
2002–03 WBA 0 0
2003–04 WBA 17 2
2003–04 *Kidderminster H* 7 1 **7 1**
2004–05 WBA 4 0
2004–05 *Coventry C* 6 0 **6 0**
2005–06 WBA 0 0 **21 2**
2005–06 *QPR* 15 0 **15 0**
2005–06 Millwall 6 0 **6 0**

ELLIOTT, Marvin (M) 102 3
H: 6 0 W: 12 02 b.Wandsworth 15-9-84
Source: Scholar.
2001–02 Millwall 0 0
2002–03 Millwall 1 0
2003–04 Millwall 21 0
2004–05 Millwall 41 1
2005–06 Millwall 39 2 **102 3**

FANGUEIRO, Carlos (M) 283 50
H: 5 9 W: 11 05 b.Matosinhos 19-12-76
1995–96 Leixoes 29 8
1996–97 Leixoes 32 7 **61 15**
1997–98 Guimaraes 19 1
1998–99 Maia 30 3 **30 3**
1999–2000 Gil Vicente 31 7 **31 7**
2000–01 Guimaraes 30 4
2001–02 Guimaraes 30 10
2002–03 Guimaraes 27 7
2003–04 Guimaraes 17 2 **123 24**
2004–05 Uniao Leiria 29 1 **29 1**
2005–06 Millwall 9 0 **9 0**

GAYNOR, Ross (F) 0 0
b.Ardee
Source: Scholar.
2005–06 Millwall 0 0

GRANT, Gavin (F) 10 1
H: 5 11 W: 11 00 b.Middlesex 27-3-84
Source: Tooting & Mitcham U.
2005–06 Gillingham 10 1 **10 1**
2005–06 Millwall 0 0

HAYLES, Barry (F) 296 92
H: 5 10 W: 12 11 b.Lambeth 17-5-72
Source: Stevenage Bor. *Honours:* Jamaica 10 full caps.
1997–98 Bristol R 45 23
1998–99 Bristol R 17 9 **62 32**
1998–99 Fulham 30 8
1999–2000 Fulham 35 5
2000–01 Fulham 35 18
2001–02 Fulham 35 8
2002–03 Fulham 14 1
2003–04 Fulham 26 4 **175 44**
2004–05 Sheffield U 4 0 **4 0**
2004–05 Millwall 32 12
2005–06 Millwall 23 4 **55 16**

HEALY, Joe (F) 3 0
H: 6 0 W: 12 04 b.Sidcup 26-12-86
2003–04 Millwall 0 0
2004–05 Millwall 2 0
2005–06 Millwall 1 0 **3 0**

HENDRY, Will (M) 3 0
H: 5 11 W: 12 10 b.Slough 10-11-86
Source: Scholar.
2005–06 Millwall 3 0 **3 0**

IGOE, Sammy (M) 344 28
H: 5 6 W: 10 00 b.Staines 30-9-75
Source: Trainee.
1993–94 Portsmouth 0 0
1994–95 Portsmouth 1 0
1995–96 Portsmouth 22 0
1996–97 Portsmouth 40 2
1997–98 Portsmouth 31 3
1998–99 Portsmouth 40 5
1999–2000 Portsmouth 26 1 **160 11**
1999–2000 Reading 6 0
2000–01 Reading 31 6
2001–02 Reading 35 1
2002–03 Reading 15 0 **87 7**
2002–03 *Luton T* 2 0 **2 0**
2003–04 Swindon T 36 5
2004–05 Swindon T 43 4 **79 9**
2005–06 Millwall 5 0 **5 0**
2005–06 *Bristol R* 11 1 **11 1**

LAWRENCE, Matthew (D) 362 5
H: 6 1 W: 12 12 b.Northampton 19-6-74
Source: Grays Ath. *Honours:* England Schools.
1995–96 Wycombe W 3 0
1996–97 Wycombe W 13 1
1996–97 Fulham 15 0
1997–98 Fulham 43 0
1998–99 Fulham 1 0 **59 0**
1998–99 Wycombe W 34 2
1999–2000 Wycombe W 29 2 **79 5**
1999–2000 Millwall 9 0
2000–01 Millwall 45 0
2001–02 Millwall 26 0
2002–03 Millwall 33 0
2003–04 Millwall 36 0
2004–05 Millwall 44 0
2005–06 Millwall 31 0 **224 0**

LIVERMORE, David (M) 273 12
H: 5 11 W: 12 02 b.Edmonton 20-5-80
Source: Trainee.
1998–99 Arsenal 0 0
1999–2000 Millwall 32 2
2000–01 Millwall 39 3
2001–02 Millwall 43 0
2002–03 Millwall 41 2
2003–04 Millwall 36 1
2004–05 Millwall 41 2
2005–06 Millwall 41 2 **273 12**

MARSHALL, Andy (G) 331 0
H: 6 3 W: 14 08 b.Bury St Edmunds 14-4-75
Source: Trainee. *Honours:* England Under-21.
1993–94 Norwich C 0 0
1994–95 Norwich C 21 0
1995–96 Norwich C 3 0
1996–97 Norwich C 7 0
1996–97 *Bournemouth* 11 0 **11 0**
1996–97 *Gillingham* 5 0 **5 0**
1997–98 Norwich C 42 0
1998–99 Norwich C 37 0
1999–2000 Norwich C 44 0
2000–01 Norwich C 41 0 **195 0**
2001–02 Ipswich T 13 0
2002–03 Ipswich T 40 0
2003–04 Ipswich T 0 0 **53 0**
2003–04 Millwall 16 0
2004–05 Millwall 22 0
2005–06 Millwall 29 0 **67 0**

MAY, Ben (F) 128 21
H: 6 3 W: 12 12 b.Gravesend 10-3-84
Source: Juniors.
2000–01 Millwall 0 0
2001–02 Millwall 0 0
2002–03 Millwall 10 1
2002–03 *Colchester U* 6 0
2003–04 Millwall 0 0
2003–04 *Brentford* 41 7
2004–05 Millwall 8 1
2004–05 *Colchester U* 14 1 **20 1**
2004–05 Brentford 10 1 **51 8**
2005–06 Millwall 39 10 **57 12**

MORRIS, Jody (F) 207 11
H: 5 5 W: 10 03 b.Hammersmith 22-12-78
Source: Trainee. *Honours:* England Schools, Youth, Under-21.
1995–96 Chelsea 1 0
1996–97 Chelsea 12 0
1997–98 Chelsea 12 1
1998–99 Chelsea 18 1
1999–2000 Chelsea 30 3
2000–01 Chelsea 21 0
2001–02 Chelsea 5 0
2002–03 Chelsea 25 0 **124 5**
2003–04 Leeds U 12 0 **12 0**
2003–04 Rotherham U 10 1 **10 1**
2004–05 Millwall 37 5
2005–06 Millwall 24 0 **61 5**

PEETERS, Bob (F) 278 74
H: 6 5 W: 13 12 b.Lier 28-1-74
Source: Ternesse. *Honours:* Belgium 13 full caps, 4 goals.
1992–93 Lierse 12 0
1993–94 Lierse 17 0
1994–95 Lierse 26 8
1995–96 Lierse 29 7
1996–97 Lierse 34 7 **118 22**
1997–98 Roda 30 11
1998–99 Roda 33 13
1999–2000 Roda 30 15 **93 39**
2000–01 Vitesse 32 8
2001–02 Vitesse 10 2 **42 10**
2003–04 Millwall 20 3
2004–05 Millwall 3 0
2005–06 Millwall 2 0 **25 3**

PHILLIPS, Mark (D) 55 1
H: 6 2 W: 11 00 b.Lambeth 27-1-82
Source: Scholarship.
1999–2000 Millwall 0 0
2000–01 Millwall 0 0
2001–02 Millwall 1 0
2002–03 Millwall 7 0
2003–04 Millwall 0 0
2004–05 Millwall 25 1
2005–06 Millwall 22 0 **55 1**

POOLEY, Dean (D) 1 0
H: 6 1 W: 11 02 b.Sidcup 10-9-86
Source: Scholar.
2005–06 Millwall 1 0 **1 0**

POWEL, Berry (F) 91 31
H: 6 2 W: 13 00 b.Utrecht 2-5-80
2003–04 Den Bosch 26 9
2004–05 Den Bosch 29 2
2005–06 Den Bosch 24 19 **79 30**
2005–06 Millwall 12 1 **12 1**

ROBINSON, Paul (D) 67 0
H: 6 1 W: 11 09 b.Barnet 7-1-82
Source: Scholar.
2000–01 Millwall 0 0
2001–02 Millwall 0 0
2002–03 Millwall 14 0
2003–04 Millwall 9 0
2004–05 Millwall 0 0
2004–05 *Torquay U* 12 0 **12 0**
2005–06 Millwall 32 0 **55 0**

ROBINSON, Trevor (M) 11 1
H: 5 9 W: 12 11 b.Jamaica 20-9-84
Source: Scholar.
2003–04 Millwall 1 0
2004–05 Millwall 9 1
2005–06 Millwall 1 0 **11 1**

ROSE, Jason (D) 0 0
H: 6 1 W: 10 13 b.Sidcup 28-1-85
Source: Scholar.
2003–04 Millwall 0 0
2004–05 Millwall 0 0
2005–06 Millwall 0 0

SERIOUX, Adrian (D) 24 0
H: 6 0 W: 12 12 b.Scarborough, Can 12-5-79
Source: Toronto Lynx. *Honours:* Canada 9 full caps.
2004–05 Millwall 19 0
2005–06 Millwall 5 0 **24 0**

SIMPSON, Josh (M) 43 2
H: 5 10 W: 12 02 b.Vancouver 15-5-83
Source: Univ of Portland. *Honours:* Canada 13 full caps.
2004–05 Millwall 30 1
2005–06 Millwall 13 1 **43 2**

WESTON, Curtis (M) 4 0
H: 5 11 W: 11 09 b.Greenwich 24-1-87
Source: Scholar.
2003–04 Millwall 1 0
2004–05 Millwall 3 0
2005–06 Millwall 0 0 **4 0**

WILLIAMS, Marvin (M) 22 4
H: 5 11 W: 11 06 b.London 12-8-87
Source: Scholar.
2005–06 Millwall 22 4 **22 4**

MILTON KEYNES D (52)

BAKER, Matt (G) 72 0
H: 6 0 W: 14 00 b.Harrogate 18-12-79
Source: Trainee.
1998–99 Hull C 0 0
1999–2000 Hull C 2 0
2000–01 Hull C 0 0
2001–02 Hull C 0 0 **2 0**
From Hereford U.
2004–05 Wrexham 13 0 **13 0**
2004–05 Milton Keynes D 20 0
2005–06 Milton Keynes D 37 0 **57 0**

BALDOCK, Sam (F) 0 0
H: 5 7 W: 10 07 b.Bedford 15-3-89
Source: Scholar.
2005–06 Milton Keynes D 0 0

BEVAN, Scott (G) 52 0
H: 6 6 W: 15 10 b.Southampton 16-9-79
Source: Trainee.
1997–98 Southampton 0 0
1998–99 Southampton 0 0
1999–2000 Southampton 0 0
2000–01 Southampton 0 0
2001–02 Southampton 0 0
2001–02 *Stoke C* 0 0
2002–03 Southampton 0 0
2002–03 *Huddersfield T* 30 0 **30 0**
2003–04 Southampton 0 0
2003–04 *Wycombe W* 5 0 **5 0**
2003–04 Wimbledon 10 0 **10 0**
2004–05 Milton Keynes D 7 0
2005–06 Milton Keynes D 0 0 **7 0**

CARRILHO, Mirano (D) 3 0
H: 5 10 W: 12 11 b.Amsterdam 17-7-75
Source: RW Essen.
2005–06 Milton Keynes D 3 0 **3 0**
To Apeldoorn January 2006

CHORLEY, Ben (M) 114 4
H: 6 3 W: 13 02 b.Sidcup 30-9-82
Source: Scholar.
2001–02 Arsenal 0 0
2002–03 Arsenal 0 0
2002–03 *Brentford* 2 0 **2 0**
2002–03 Wimbledon 10 0
2003–04 Wimbledon 35 2 **45 2**
2004–05 Milton Keynes D 41 2
2005–06 Milton Keynes D 26 0 **67 2**

CROOKS, Leon (M) 40 0
H: 6 0 W: 11 12 b.Greenwich 21-11-85
Source: Scholar.
2004–05 Milton Keynes D 17 0
2005–06 Milton Keynes D 23 0 **40 0**

EDDS, Gareth (D) 133 9
H: 5 11 W: 11 01 b.Sydney 3-2-81
Source: Trainee. *Honours:* Australia Under-20, Under-23.
1997–98 Nottingham F 0 0
1998–99 Nottingham F 0 0
1999–2000 Nottingham F 2 0
2000–01 Nottingham F 13 1
2001–02 Nottingham F 1 0 **16 1**
2002–03 Swindon T 14 0 **14 0**
2003–04 Bradford C 23 0 **23 0**
2004–05 Milton Keynes D 39 5
2005–06 Milton Keynes D 41 3 **80 8**

HARDING, Ben (M) 51 6
H: 5 10 W: 11 02 b.Carshalton 6-9-84
Source: Scholar. *Honours:* England Youth.
2001–02 Wimbledon 0 0
2002–03 Wimbledon 0 0
2003–04 Wimbledon 15 0 **15 0**
2004–05 Milton Keynes D 26 4
2005–06 Milton Keynes D 10 2 **36 6**

HORNUSS, Julien (F) 3 0
H: 5 10 W: 11 00 b.Paris 12-6-86
Source: Sedan.
2004–05 Milton Keynes D 3 0
2005–06 Milton Keynes D 0 0 **3 0**

KAMARA, Malvin (M) 77 5
H: 5 11 W: 13 00 b.Southwark 17-11-83
Source: Scholar.
2002–03 Wimbledon 2 0
2003–04 Wimbledon 27 2 **29 2**
2004–05 Milton Keynes D 25 1
2005–06 Milton Keynes D 23 2 **48 3**

KOO-BOOTHE, Nathan (D) 1 0
H: 6 4 W: 13 12 b.Westminster 18-7-84
2002–03 Watford 0 0
2003–04 Watford 0 0
2004–05 Milton Keynes D 1 0
2005–06 Milton Keynes D 0 0 **1 0**

LEWINGTON, Dean (D) 116 4
H: 5 11 W: 11 07 b.Kingston 18-5-84
Source: Scholar.
2002–03 Wimbledon 1 0
2003–04 Wimbledon 28 1 **29 1**
2004–05 Milton Keynes D 43 2
2005–06 Milton Keynes D 44 1 **87 3**

MAKOFO, Serge (M) 1 0
H: 5 11 W: 12 06 b.Kinshasa 22-10-86
Source: Scholar.
2004–05 Milton Keynes D 1 0
2005–06 Milton Keynes D 0 0 **1 0**

McKOY, Nick (M) 19 0
H: 6 0 W: 12 06 b.Newham 3-9-86
Source: Scholar.
2003–04 Wimbledon 3 0 **3 0**
2004–05 Milton Keynes D 0 0
2005–06 Milton Keynes D 16 0 **16 0**

McLEOD, Izale (F) 128 37
H: 6 1 W: 11 02 b.Birmingham 15-10-84
Source: Scholar. *Honours:* England Under-21.
2002–03 Derby Co 29 3
2003–04 Derby Co 10 1 **39 4**
2003–04 *Sheffield U* 7 0 **7 0**
2004–05 Milton Keynes D 43 16
2005–06 Milton Keynes D 39 17 **82 33**

MITCHELL, Paul (M) 134 0
H: 5 9 W: 12 01 b.Manchester 26-8-81
Source: Trainee.
2000–01 Wigan Ath 1 0
2000–01 *Halifax T* 11 0 **11 0**
2001–02 Wigan Ath 23 0
2002–03 Wigan Ath 27 0
2003–04 Wigan Ath 12 0
2004–05 Wigan Ath 1 0 **64 0**
2004–05 *Swindon T* 7 0 **7 0**
2004–05 *Milton Keynes D* 13 0
2005–06 Milton Keynes D 39 0 **52 0**

MORGAN, Craig (D) 92 1
H: 6 0 W: 11 04 b.St Asaph 18-6-85
Source: Scholar. *Honours:* Wales Youth, Under-21.
2001–02 Wrexham 2 0
2002–03 Wrexham 6 1
2003–04 Wrexham 18 0
2004–05 Wrexham 26 0 **52 1**
2005–06 Milton Keynes D 40 0 **40 0**

OYEDELE, Shola (D) 37 0
H: 5 11 W: 12 07 b.Kano 14-9-84
Source: Scholar.
2003–04 Wimbledon 9 0 **9 0**
2004–05 Milton Keynes D 25 0
2005–06 Milton Keynes D 3 0 **28 0**

PALMER, Steve (D) 507 20
H: 6 1 W: 12 13 b.Brighton 31-3-68
Source: Cambridge Univ. *Honours:* England Schools.
1989–90 Ipswich T 5 0
1990–91 Ipswich T 23 1
1991–92 Ipswich T 23 0
1992–93 Ipswich T 7 0
1993–94 Ipswich T 36 1
1994–95 Ipswich T 12 0
1995–96 Ipswich T 5 0 **111 2**
1995–96 Watford 35 1
1996–97 Watford 41 2
1997–98 Watford 41 2
1998–99 Watford 41 2
1999–2000 Watford 38 0
2000–01 Watford 39 1 **235 8**
2001–02 QPR 46 4
2002–03 QPR 46 1
2003–04 QPR 35 4 **127 9**
2004–05 Milton Keynes D 32 1
2005–06 Milton Keynes D 2 0 **34 1**

PLATT, Clive (F) 317 52
H: 6 4 W: 12 07 b.Wolverhampton 27-10-77
Source: Trainee.
1995–96 Walsall 4 2
1996–97 Walsall 1 0
1997–98 Walsall 20 1
1998–99 Walsall 7 1
1999–2000 Walsall 0 0 **32 4**
1999–2000 Rochdale 41 9
2000–01 Rochdale 43 8
2001–02 Rochdale 43 7
2002–03 Rochdale 42 6 **169 30**
2003–04 Notts Co 19 3 **19 3**
2003–04 Peterborough U 18 2
2004–05 Peterborough U 19 4 **37 6**
2004–05 Milton Keynes D 20 3
2005–06 Milton Keynes D 40 6 **60 9**

PUNCHEON, Jason (M) 34 1
H: 5 9 W: 12 05 b.Croydon 26-6-86
Source: Scholar.
2003–04 Wimbledon 8 0 **8 0**
2004–05 Milton Keynes D 25 1
2005–06 Milton Keynes D 1 0 **26 1**

RIZZO, Nicky (M) 104 7
H: 5 10 W: 12 00 b.Sydney 9-6-79
Source: Sydney Olympic. *Honours:* Australia Youth, Under-20, Under-23, 1 full cap.
1996–97 Liverpool 0 0
1997–98 Liverpool 0 0
1998–99 Crystal Palace 19 1
1999–2000 Crystal Palace 17 0 **36 1**
2000–01 Ternana 0 0
2001–02 Ternana 1 0
2002–03 Ternana 0 0 **1 0**
2003–04 Prato 20 2 **20 2**
2004–05 Milton Keynes D 18 2
2005–06 Milton Keynes D 29 2 **47 4**

SMALL, Wade (M) 99 12
H: 5 8 W: 11 05 b.Croydon 23-2-84
Source: Scholar.
2003–04 Wimbledon 27 1 **27 1**
2004–05 Milton Keynes D 44 10
2005–06 Milton Keynes D 28 1 **72 11**

SMITH, Gary (M) 59 7
H: 5 8 W: 10 09 b.Middlesbrough 30-1-84
Source: Trainee.
2002–03 Middlesbrough 0 0
2003–04 Middlesbrough 0 0
2003–04 *Wimbledon* 11 3 **11 3**
2004–05 Milton Keynes D 23 1
2005–06 Milton Keynes D 25 3 **48 4**

TAPP, Alex (M) 50 4
H: 5 8 W: 10 13 b.Redhill 7-6-82
Source: Trainee.
1999–2000 Wimbledon 0 0
2000–01 Wimbledon 0 0
2001–02 Wimbledon 0 0
2002–03 Wimbledon 24 2
2003–04 Wimbledon 14 1 **38 3**
2004–05 Milton Keynes D 12 1
2005–06 Milton Keynes D 0 0 **12 1**

TAYLOR, Scott (F) 358 76
H: 5 10 W: 11 04 b.Chertsey 5-5-76
Source: Staines T.
1994–95 Millwall 6 0
1995–96 Millwall 22 0 **28 0**
1995–96 Bolton W 1 0
1996–97 Bolton W 11 1
1997–98 Bolton W 0 0
1997–98 *Rotherham U* 10 3 **10 3**
1997–98 *Blackpool* 5 1
1998–99 Bolton W 0 0 **12 1**
1998–99 Tranmere R 36 9
1999–2000 Tranmere R 35 3
2000–01 Tranmere R 37 5 **108 17**
2001–02 Stockport Co 28 4 **28 4**
2001–02 Blackpool 17 2
2002–03 Blackpool 44 13
2003–04 Blackpool 31 16
2004–05 Blackpool 24 12 **121 44**

2004–05 Plymouth Arg 16 3
2005–06 Plymouth Arg 18 1 **34 4**
2005–06 Milton Keynes D 17 3 **17 3**

WILBRAHAM, Aaron (F) 231 44
H: 6 3 W: 12 04 b.Knutsford 21-10-79
Source: Trainee.
1997–98 Stockport Co 7 1
1998–99 Stockport Co 26 0
1999–2000 Stockport Co 26 4
2000–01 Stockport Co 36 12
2001–02 Stockport Co 21 3
2002–03 Stockport Co 15 7
2003–04 Stockport Co 41 8 **172 35**
2004–05 Hull C 19 2 **19 2**
2004–05 *Oldham Ath* 4 2 **4 2**
2005–06 Milton Keynes D 31 4 **31 4**
2005–06 *Bradford C* 5 1 **5 1**

NEWCASTLE U (53)

AMEOBI, Foluwashola (F) 150 25
H: 6 3 W: 11 13 b.Zaria 12-10-81
Source: Trainee. *Honours:* England Under-21.
1998–99 Newcastle U 0 0
1999–2000 Newcastle U 0 0
2000–01 Newcastle U 20 2
2001–02 Newcastle U 15 0
2002–03 Newcastle U 28 5
2003–04 Newcastle U 26 7
2004–05 Newcastle U 31 2
2005–06 Newcastle U 30 9 **150 25**

ATKIN, Liam (M) 0 0
H: 6 2 W: 12 03 b.Ashington 12-12-86
Source: Scholar.
2005–06 Newcastle U 0 0

BABAYARO, Celestine (D) 242 13
H: 5 10 W: 11 11 b.Kaduna 29-8-78
Source: Plateau U. *Honours:* Nigeria 26 full caps.
1994–95 Anderlecht 22 0
1995–96 Anderlecht 28 5
1996–97 Anderlecht 25 3 **75 8**
1997–98 Chelsea 8 0
1998–99 Chelsea 28 3
1999–2000 Chelsea 25 0
2000–01 Chelsea 24 0
2001–02 Chelsea 18 0
2002–03 Chelsea 19 1
2003–04 Chelsea 6 1
2004–05 Chelsea 4 0 **132 5**
2004–05 Newcastle U 7 0
2005–06 Newcastle U 28 0 **35 0**

BOUMSONG, Jean-Alain (D) 238 6
H: 6 3 W: 13 03 b.Douala 14-12-79
Source: US Palaiseau. *Honours:* France 19 full caps, 1 goal.
1997–98 Le Havre 1 0
1998–99 Le Havre 18 1
1999–2000 Le Havre 23 0 **42 1**
2000–01 Auxerre 32 0
2001–02 Auxerre 34 1
2002–03 Auxerre 33 1
2003–04 Auxerre 32 1 **131 3**
2004–05 Rangers 18 2 **18 2**
2004–05 Newcastle U 14 0
2005–06 Newcastle U 33 0 **47 0**

BOWYER, Lee (M) 338 52
H: 5 9 W: 10 12 b.Canning Town 3-1-77
Source: Trainee. *Honours:* England Youth, Under-21, 1 full cap.
1993–94 Charlton Ath 0 0
1994–95 Charlton Ath 5 0
1995–96 Charlton Ath 41 8 **46 8**
1996–97 Leeds U 32 4
1997–98 Leeds U 25 3
1998–99 Leeds U 35 9
1999–2000 Leeds U 33 5
2000–01 Leeds U 38 9
2001–02 Leeds U 25 5
2002–03 Leeds U 15 3 **203 38**
2002–03 West Ham U 10 0 **10 0**
2003–04 Newcastle U 24 2
2004–05 Newcastle U 27 3
2005–06 Newcastle U 28 1 **79 6**

BRAMBLE, Titus (D) 138 4
H: 6 2 W: 13 10 b.Ipswich 21-7-81
Source: Trainee. *Honours:* England Under-21.
1998–99 Ipswich T 4 0
1999–2000 Ipswich T 0 0
1999–2000 *Colchester U* 2 0 **2 0**
2000–01 Ipswich T 26 1
2001–02 Ipswich T 18 0 **48 1**
2002–03 Newcastle U 16 0
2003–04 Newcastle U 29 0
2004–05 Newcastle U 19 1
2005–06 Newcastle U 24 2 **88 3**

BRITTAIN, Martin (M) 1 0
H: 5 8 W: 10 07 b.Newcastle 29-12-84
Source: Trainee.
2003–04 Newcastle U 1 0
2004–05 Newcastle U 0 0
2005–06 Newcastle U 0 0 **1 0**

BUTT, Nicky (M) 312 25
H: 5 10 W: 11 05 b.Manchester 21-1-75
Source: Trainee. *Honours:* England Schools, Youth, Under-21, 39 full caps.
1992–93 Manchester U 1 0
1993–94 Manchester U 1 0
1994–95 Manchester U 22 1
1995–96 Manchester U 32 2
1996–97 Manchester U 26 5
1997–98 Manchester U 33 3
1998–99 Manchester U 31 2
1999–2000 Manchester U 32 3
2000–01 Manchester U 28 3
2001–02 Manchester U 25 1
2002–03 Manchester U 18 0
2003–04 Manchester U 21 1 **270 21**
2004–05 Newcastle U 18 1 **18 1**
2005–06 *Birmingham C* 24 3 **24 3**

CARR, Stephen (D) 271 8
H: 5 9 W: 11 13 b.Dublin 29-8-76
Source: Trainee. *Honours:* Eire Schools, Youth, Under-21, 41 full caps.
1993–94 Tottenham H 1 0
1994–95 Tottenham H 0 0
1995–96 Tottenham H 0 0
1996–97 Tottenham H 26 0
1997–98 Tottenham H 38 0
1998–99 Tottenham H 37 0
1999–2000 Tottenham H 34 3
2000–01 Tottenham H 28 3
2001–02 Tottenham H 0 0
2002–03 Tottenham H 30 0
2003–04 Tottenham H 32 1 **226 7**
2004–05 Newcastle U 26 1
2005–06 Newcastle U 19 0 **45 1**

CHOPRA, Michael (F) 70 23
H: 5 9 W: 10 10 b.Newcastle 23-12-83
Source: Scholar. *Honours:* England Youth, Under-20, Under-21.
2000–01 Newcastle U 0 0
2001–02 Newcastle U 0 0
2002–03 Newcastle U 1 0
2002–03 *Watford* 5 5 **5 5**
2003–04 Newcastle U 6 0
2003–04 *Nottingham F* 5 0 **5 0**
2004–05 Newcastle U 1 0
2004–05 *Barnsley* 39 17 **39 17**
2005–06 Newcastle U 13 1 **21 1**

CLARK, Lee (M) 439 60
H: 5 8 W: 11 07 b.Wallsend 27-10-72
Source: Trainee. *Honours:* England Schools, Youth, Under-21.
1989–90 Newcastle U 0 0
1990–91 Newcastle U 19 2
1991–92 Newcastle U 29 5
1992–93 Newcastle U 46 9
1993–94 Newcastle U 29 2
1994–95 Newcastle U 19 1
1995–96 Newcastle U 28 2
1996–97 Newcastle U 25 2
1997–98 Sunderland 46 13
1998–99 Sunderland 27 3 **73 16**
1999–2000 Fulham 42 8
2000–01 Fulham 45 7
2001–02 Fulham 9 0
2002–03 Fulham 11 2
2003–04 Fulham 25 2
2004–05 Fulham 17 1 **149 20**
2005–06 Newcastle U 22 1 **217 24**

DYER, Kieron (M) 259 27
H: 5 8 W: 10 01 b.Ipswich 29-12-78
Source: Trainee. *Honours:* England Youth, Under-21, B, 28 full caps.
1996–97 Ipswich T 13 0
1997–98 Ipswich T 41 4
1998–99 Ipswich T 37 5 **91 9**
1999–2000 Newcastle U 30 3
2000–01 Newcastle U 26 5
2001–02 Newcastle U 18 3
2002–03 Newcastle U 35 2
2003–04 Newcastle U 25 1
2004–05 Newcastle U 23 4
2005–06 Newcastle U 11 0 **168 18**

EDGAR, David (D) 0 0
H: 6 2 W: 12 13 b.Ontario 19-5-87
Source: Scholar. *Honours:* Canada Under-20.
2005–06 Newcastle U 0 0

ELLIOTT, Robbie (D) 228 16
H: 5 10 W: 10 12 b.Gosforth 25-12-73
Source: Trainee. *Honours:* England Under-21.
1990–91 Newcastle U 6 0
1991–92 Newcastle U 9 0
1992–93 Newcastle U 0 0
1993–94 Newcastle U 15 0
1994–95 Newcastle U 14 2
1995–96 Newcastle U 6 0
1996–97 Newcastle U 29 7
1997–98 Bolton W 4 0
1998–99 Bolton W 22 0
1999–2000 Bolton W 27 3
2000–01 Bolton W 33 2 **86 5**
2001–02 Newcastle U 27 1
2002–03 Newcastle U 2 0
2003–04 Newcastle U 0 0
2004–05 Newcastle U 17 1
2005–06 Newcastle U 17 0 **142 11**

EMRE, Belezoglu (M) 181 18
H: 5 8 W: 10 10 b.Istanbul 7-9-80
Honours: Turkey 43 full caps, 3 goals.
1997–98 Galatasaray 24 2
1998–99 Galatasaray 27 2
1999–2000 Galatasaray 24 5
2000–01 Galatasaray 26 4 **101 13**
2001–02 Internazionale 14 0
2002–03 Internazionale 25 3
2003–04 Internazionale 21 0
2004–05 Internazionale 0 0 **60 3**
2005–06 Newcastle U 20 2 **20 2**

FAYE, Amdy (M) 158 2
H: 6 1 W: 12 06 b.Dakar 12-3-77
Source: Frejus. *Honours:* Senegal full caps.
1998–99 Auxerre 0 0
1999–2000 Auxerre 3 0
2000–01 Auxerre 23 0
2001–02 Auxerre 20 0
2002–03 Auxerre 34 2 **80 2**
2003–04 Portsmouth 27 0
2004–05 Portsmouth 20 0 **47 0**
2004–05 Newcastle U 9 0
2005–06 Newcastle U 22 0 **31 0**

GATE, Kris (D) 0 0
H: 5 7 W: 10 03 b.Newcastle 1-1-85
Source: Trainee.
2003–04 Newcastle U 0 0
2004–05 Newcastle U 0 0
2005–06 Newcastle U 0 0

GIVEN, Shay (G) 315 0
H: 6 0 W: 13 03 b.Lifford 20-4-76
Source: Celtic. *Honours:* Eire Youth, Under-21, 76 full caps.
1994–95 Blackburn R 0 0
1994–95 *Swindon T* 0 0
1995–96 Blackburn R 0 0
1995–96 *Swindon T* 5 0 **5 0**
1995–96 *Sunderland* 17 0 **17 0**
1996–97 Blackburn R 2 0 **2 0**
1997–98 Newcastle U 24 0
1998–99 Newcastle U 31 0
1999–2000 Newcastle U 14 0
2000–01 Newcastle U 34 0

2001–02 Newcastle U 38 0
2002–03 Newcastle U 38 0
2003–04 Newcastle U 38 0
2004–05 Newcastle U 36 0
2005–06 Newcastle U 38 0 **291 0**

HARPER, Steve (G) 73 0
H: 6 2 W: 13 10 b.Easington 14-3-75
Source: Seaham Red Star.
1993–94 Newcastle U 0 0
1994–95 Newcastle U 0 0
1995–96 Newcastle U 0 0
1995–96 *Bradford C* 1 0 **1 0**
1996–97 Newcastle U 0 0
1996–97 *Stockport Co* 0 0
1997–98 Newcastle U 0 0
1997–98 *Hartlepool U* 15 0 **15 0**
1997–98 *Huddersfield T* 24 0 **24 0**
1998–99 Newcastle U 8 0
1999–2000 Newcastle U 18 0
2000–01 Newcastle U 5 0
2001–02 Newcastle U 0 0
2002–03 Newcastle U 0 0
2003–04 Newcastle U 0 0
2004–05 Newcastle U 2 0
2005–06 Newcastle U 0 0 **33 0**

HUNTINGTON, Paul (D) 0 0
H: 6 3 W: 12 08 b.Carlisle 17-9-87
Source: Scholar. *Honours:* England Youth.
2005–06 Newcastle U 0 0

KRUL, Tim (G) 0 0
H: 6 2 W: 11 08 b.Den Haag 3-4-88
Source: Academy.
2005–06 Newcastle U 0 0

LUQUE, Alberto (F) 275 78
H: 6 0 W: 11 11 b.Barcelona 11-3-78
Honours: Spain 16 full caps, 2 goals.
1997–98 Mallorca B 31 10
1998–99 Mallorca B 31 15 **62 25**
1998–99 Mallorca 5 0
1999–2000 Malaga 23 3 **23 3**
2000–01 Mallorca 32 9
2001–02 Mallorca 36 14 **73 23**
2002–03 La Coruna 32 7
2003–04 La Coruna 34 8
2004–05 La Coruna 37 11 **103 26**
2005–06 Newcastle U 14 1 **14 1**

MILNER, James (M) 109 9
H: 5 9 W: 11 00 b.Leeds 4-1-86
Source: Trainee. *Honours:* FA Schools, Youth, England Under-20, Under-21.
2002–03 Leeds U 18 2
2003–04 Leeds U 30 3 **48 5**
2003–04 *Swindon T* 6 2 **6 2**
2004–05 Newcastle U 25 1
2005–06 Newcastle U 3 0 **28 1**
2005–06 *Aston Villa* 27 1 **27 1**

MOORE, Craig (D) 220 18
H: 6 1 W: 12 00 b.Canterbury, Australia 12-12-75
Source: Australian Institute of Sport.
Honours: Australia Schools, Youth, Under-20, Under-23, 37 full caps, 3 goals.
1993–94 Rangers 1 0
1994–95 Rangers 21 2
1995–96 Rangers 11 1
1996–97 Rangers 23 1
1997–98 Rangers 10 0
1998–99 Rangers 8 1
1998–99 Crystal Palace 23 3 **23 3**
1999–2000 Rangers 22 1
2000–01 Rangers 5 0
2001–02 Rangers 18 3
2002–03 Rangers 35 3
2003–04 Rangers 19 2
2004–05 Rangers 3 0 **176 14**
2004–05 M'gladbach 13 1 **13 1**
2005–06 Newcastle U 8 0 **8 0**

N'ZOGBIA, Charles (M) 46 5
H: 5 9 W: 11 00 b.Le Havre 28-5-86
Honours: France Youth.
2004–05 Newcastle U 14 0
2005–06 Newcastle U 32 5 **46 5**

O'BRIEN, Alan (M) 8 1
H: 5 10 W: 10 10 b.Dublin 20-2-85
Source: Scholar. *Honours:* Eire Youth, Under-21.
2001–02 Newcastle U 0 0
2002–03 Newcastle U 0 0
2003–04 Newcastle U 0 0
2004–05 Newcastle U 0 0
2005–06 Newcastle U 3 0 **3 0**
2005–06 *Carlisle U* 5 1 **5 1**

OWEN, Michael (F) 227 125
H: 5 8 W: 10 12 b.Chester 14-12-79
Source: Trainee. *Honours:* England Schools, Youth, Under-21, B, 80 full caps, 30 goals.
1996–97 Liverpool 2 1
1997–98 Liverpool 36 18
1998–99 Liverpool 30 18
1999–2000 Liverpool 27 11
2000–01 Liverpool 28 16
2001–02 Liverpool 29 19
2002–03 Liverpool 35 19
2003–04 Liverpool 29 16
2004–05 Liverpool 0 0 **216 118**
2005–06 Newcastle U 11 7 **11 7**

PARKER, Scott (M) 175 12
H: 5 9 W: 11 10 b.Lambeth 13-10-80
Source: Trainee. *Honours:* England Schools, Youth, Under-21, 2 full caps.
1997–98 Charlton Ath 3 0
1998–99 Charlton Ath 4 0
1999–2000 Charlton Ath 15 1
2000–01 Charlton Ath 20 1
2000–01 *Norwich C* 6 1 **6 1**
2001–02 Charlton Ath 38 1
2002–03 Charlton Ath 28 4
2003–04 Charlton Ath 20 2 **128 9**
2003–04 Chelsea 11 1
2004–05 Chelsea 4 0 **15 1**
2005–06 Newcastle U 26 1 **26 1**

PATTISON, Matt (M) 3 0
H: 5 9 W: 11 00 b.Johannesburg 27-10-86
Source: Scholar.
2005–06 Newcastle U 3 0 **3 0**

RAMAGE, Peter (D) 27 0
H: 6 3 W: 11 02 b.Whitley Bay 22-11-83
Source: Trainee.
2003–04 Newcastle U 0 0
2004–05 Newcastle U 4 0
2005–06 Newcastle U 23 0 **27 0**

ROBERT, Laurent (M) 331 65
H: 5 9 W: 11 02 b.Saint-Benoit 21-5-75
Honours: France 9 full caps, 1 goal.
1994–95 Montpellier 7 0
1995–96 Montpellier 21 5
1996–97 Nancy 38 1 **38 1**
1997–98 Montpellier 26 2
1998–99 Montpellier 32 11 **86 18**
1999–2000 Paris St Germain 28 9
2000–01 Paris St Germain 32 14
2001–02 Paris St Germain 1 0 **61 23**
2001–02 Newcastle U 36 8
2002–03 Newcastle U 27 5
2003–04 Newcastle U 35 6
2004–05 Newcastle U 31 3 **129 22**
2005–06 *Portsmouth* 17 1 **17 1**
To Benfica January 2006

SHANKS, Chris (D) 0 0
H: 6 0 W: 11 00 b.Ashington 16-10-86
Source: Scholar.
2004–05 Newcastle U 0 0
2005–06 Newcastle U 0 0

SHEARER, Alan (F) 559 283
H: 5 11 W: 12 06 b.Newcastle 13-8-70
Source: Trainee. *Honours:* England Youth, Under-21, B, 63 full caps, 30 goals.
1987–88 Southampton 5 3
1988–89 Southampton 10 0
1989–90 Southampton 26 3
1990–91 Southampton 36 4
1991–92 Southampton 41 13 **118 23**
1992–93 Blackburn R 21 16
1993–94 Blackburn R 40 31
1994–95 Blackburn R 42 34
1995–96 Blackburn R 35 31 **138 112**
1996–97 Newcastle U 31 25
1997–98 Newcastle U 17 2
1998–99 Newcastle U 30 14
1999–2000 Newcastle U 37 23
2000–01 Newcastle U 19 5
2001–02 Newcastle U 37 23
2002–03 Newcastle U 35 17
2003–04 Newcastle U 37 22
2004–05 Newcastle U 28 7
2005–06 Newcastle U 32 10 **303 148**

SMYLIE, Daryl (M) 3 0
b.Portadown 10-9-85
Honours: Northern Ireland Youth, Under-21.
2005–06 Newcastle U 0 0
2005–06 *Stockport Co* 3 0 **3 0**

SOLANO, Nolberto (M) 357 80
H: 5 8 W: 10 07 b.Callao 12-12-74
Honours: Peru 77 full caps, 20 goals.
1994–95 Sporting Cristal 38 12
1995–96 Sporting Cristal 26 13
1996–97 Sporting Cristal 11 7 **75 32**
1997–98 Boca Juniors 32 5 **32 5**
1998–99 Newcastle U 29 6
1999–2000 Newcastle U 30 3
2000–01 Newcastle U 33 6
2001–02 Newcastle U 37 7
2002–03 Newcastle U 31 7
2003–04 Newcastle U 12 0
2003–04 Aston Villa 10 0
2004–05 Aston Villa 36 8
2005–06 Aston Villa 3 0 **49 8**
2005–06 Newcastle U 29 6 **201 35**

TAYLOR, Steven (D) 32 0
H: 6 2 W: 13 01 b.Greenwich 23-1-86
Source: Trainee. *Honours:* FA Schools, Youth, England Under-20, Under-21.
2002–03 Newcastle U 0 0
2003–04 Newcastle U 1 0
2003–04 *Wycombe W* 6 0 **6 0**
2004–05 Newcastle U 13 0
2005–06 Newcastle U 12 0 **26 0**

VIANA, Hugo (M) 65 3
H: 5 9 W: 11 09 b.Barcelos 15-1-83
Honours: Portugal 23 full caps, 1 goal.
2001–02 Sporting Lisbon 26 1 **26 1**
2002–03 Newcastle U 23 2
2003–04 Newcastle U 16 0
2004–05 Newcastle U 0 0
2005–06 Newcastle U 0 0 **39 2**
To Valencia (loan) March 2006

Scholars
Carroll, Andrew Thomas; Cave, Philip Adam; Cavener, Robert; Cook, Mark Daniel; Cowan, Ross Alexander; Critchlow, Dean Carl; Finnigan, Carl John; Forster, Fraser Gerard; Little, Callum Thomas; Marr, Lewis William; Reay, Glenn Mark; Troisi, James.

NORTHAMPTON T (54)

BOJIC, Pedj (D) 88 5
H: 5 11 W: 11 12 b.Sydney 9-4-84
Honours: Australia Youth.
2001–02 Parramatta Power 3 0
2002–03 Parramatta Power 0 0 **3 0**
2003–04 Sydney Olympic 13 1 **13 1**
2004–05 Northampton T 36 0
2005–06 Northampton T 36 4 **72 4**

BONNER, Tom (D) 0 0
H: 6 0 W: 11 06 b.Camden 6-2-88
Source: Scholar.
2005–06 Northampton T 0 0

BUNN, Mark (G) 0 0
H: 6 0 W: 12 02 b.Camden 16-11-84
Source: Scholar.
2004–05 Northampton T 0 0
2005–06 Northampton T 0 0

CHAMBERS, Luke (D) 95 0
H: 6 1 W: 11 13 b.Kettering 29-8-85
Source: Scholar.
2002–03 Northampton T 1 0
2003–04 Northampton T 24 0
2004–05 Northampton T 27 0
2005–06 Northampton T 43 0 **95 0**

CROSS, Scott (M) **5 0**
H: 5 10 W: 11 00 b.Northampton 30-10-87
Source: Scholar.
2004–05 Northampton T 1 0
2005–06 Northampton T 4 0 **5 0**

CROWE, Jason (D) **213 11**
H: 5 9 W: 10 09 b.Sidcup 30-9-78
Source: Trainee. *Honours:* England Schools, Youth.
1995–96 Arsenal 0 0
1996–97 Arsenal 0 0
1997–98 Arsenal 0 0
1998–99 Arsenal 0 0
1998–99 *Crystal Palace* 8 0 **8 0**
1999–2000 Portsmouth 25 0
2000–01 Portsmouth 23 0
2000–01 *Brentford* 9 0 **9 0**
2001–02 Portsmouth 22 1
2002–03 Portsmouth 16 4 **86 5**
2003–04 Grimsby T 32 0
2004–05 Grimsby T 37 4 **69 4**
2005–06 Northampton T 41 2 **41 2**

DOCKER, Jon (M) **0 0**
b.London 12-2-86
Source: RKC Waalwijk.
2005–06 Northampton T 0 0

DOIG, Chris (D) **124 3**
H: 6 2 W: 12 06 b.Dumfries 13-2-81
Source: Trainee. *Honours:* Scotland Schools, Youth, Under-21.
1997–98 Nottingham F 0 0
1998–99 Nottingham F 2 0
1999–2000 Nottingham F 11 0
2000–01 Nottingham F 15 0
2001–02 Nottingham F 8 1
2002–03 Nottingham F 10 0
2003–04 Nottingham F 10 0
2003–04 *Northampton T* 9 0
2004–05 Nottingham F 21 0 **77 1**
2005–06 Northampton T 38 2 **47 2**

DOLMAN, Liam (D) **0 0**
b.Northampton 26-9-87
Source: Scholar.
2005–06 Northampton T 0 0

DYCHE, Sean (D) **438 12**
H: 6 0 W: 13 10 b.Kettering 28-6-71
Source: Trainee.
1988–89 Nottingham F 0 0
1989–90 Nottingham F 0 0
1989–90 Chesterfield 22 2
1990–91 Chesterfield 28 2
1991–92 Chesterfield 42 3
1992–93 Chesterfield 20 1
1993–94 Chesterfield 20 0
1994–95 Chesterfield 22 0
1995–96 Chesterfield 41 0
1996–97 Chesterfield 36 0 **231 8**
1997–98 Bristol C 11 0
1998–99 Bristol C 6 0 **17 0**
1998–99 *Luton T* 14 1 **14 1**
1999–2000 Millwall 1 0
2000–01 Millwall 33 0
2001–02 Millwall 35 3 **69 3**
2002–03 Watford 24 0
2003–04 Watford 25 0
2004–05 Watford 23 0 **72 0**
2005–06 Northampton T 35 0 **35 0**

GEARING, Matthew (F) **0 0**
H: 5 7 W: 11 07 b.Northampton 11-9-86
Source: Scholar.
2005–06 Northampton T 0 0

GILLIGAN, Ryan (M) **23 4**
H: 5 10 W: 11 07 b.Swindon 18-1-87
Source: Watford Scholar.
2005–06 Northampton T 23 4 **23 4**

GRAHAM, Luke (D) **0 0**
H: 6 2 W: 13 04 b.Kettering 27-4-86
Source: Scholar.
2004–05 Northampton T 0 0
2005–06 Northampton T 0 0

HARPER, Lee (G) **274 0**
H: 6 1 W: 15 06 b.Chelsea 30-10-71
Source: Sittingbourne.
1994–95 Arsenal 0 0
1995–96 Arsenal 0 0
1996–97 Arsenal 1 0 **1 0**
1997–98 QPR 36 0
1998–99 QPR 15 0
1999–2000 QPR 38 0
2000–01 QPR 29 0 **118 0**
2001–02 Walsall 3 0 **3 0**
2002–03 Northampton T 31 0
2003–04 Northampton T 39 0
2004–05 Northampton T 36 0
2005–06 Northampton T 46 0 **152 0**

HICKS, David (M) **3 0**
H: 5 10 W: 10 12 b.Enfield 13-11-85
Source: Tottenham H Scholar.
2003–04 Northampton T 0 0
2004–05 Northampton T 3 0
2005–06 Northampton T 0 0 **3 0**

HUNT, David (M) **111 4**
H: 5 11 W: 11 09 b.Dulwich 10-9-82
Source: Scholar.
2002–03 Crystal Palace 2 0 **2 0**
2003–04 Leyton Orient 38 1
2004–05 Leyton Orient 27 0 **65 1**
2004–05 Northampton T 4 0
2005–06 Northampton T 40 3 **44 3**

JESS, Eoin (M) **522 104**
H: 5 10 W: 11 06 b.Aberdeen 13-12-70
Source: Rangers 'S' Form. *Honours:* Scotland Under-21, B, 18 full caps, 2 goals.
1987–88 Aberdeen 0 0
1988–89 Aberdeen 2 0
1989–90 Aberdeen 11 3
1990–91 Aberdeen 27 13
1991–92 Aberdeen 39 12
1992–93 Aberdeen 31 12
1993–94 Aberdeen 41 6
1994–95 Aberdeen 25 1
1995–96 Aberdeen 25 3
1995–96 Coventry C 12 1
1996–97 Coventry C 27 0 **39 1**
1997–98 Aberdeen 34 9
1998–99 Aberdeen 36 14
1999–2000 Aberdeen 26 5
2000–01 Aberdeen 0 0 **297 78**
2000–01 Bradford C 17 3
2001–02 Bradford C 45 14 **62 17**
2002–03 Nottingham F 32 3
2003–04 Nottingham F 34 2
2004–05 Nottingham F 20 2 **86 7**
2005–06 Northampton T 38 1 **38 1**

JOHNSON, Brad (M) **4 0**
H: 6 0 W: 12 10 b.Hackney 28-4-87
Source: Cambridge U Juniors.
2004–05 Cambridge U 1 0 **1 0**
2005–06 Northampton T 3 0 **3 0**

JOHNSON, Brett (D) **6 0**
H: 6 1 W: 13 00 b.Hammersmith 15-8-85
Source: Ashford T, Aldershot T.
2005–06 Northampton T 6 0 **6 0**

JOHNSON, Gavin (M) **414 33**
H: 5 11 W: 11 12 b.Stowmarket 10-10-70
Source: Trainee.
1988–89 Ipswich T 4 0
1989–90 Ipswich T 6 0
1990–91 Ipswich T 7 0
1991–92 Ipswich T 42 5
1992–93 Ipswich T 40 5
1993–94 Ipswich T 16 1
1994–95 Ipswich T 17 0 **132 11**
1995–96 Luton T 5 0 **5 0**
1995–96 Wigan Ath 27 3
1996–97 Wigan Ath 37 3
1997–98 Wigan Ath 20 2 **84 8**
1998–99 Dunfermline Ath 18 0 **18 0**
1999–2000 Colchester U 27 0
2000–01 Colchester U 37 2
2001–02 Colchester U 20 1
2002–03 Colchester U 8 0
2003–04 Colchester U 18 1
2004–05 Colchester U 37 9 **147 13**
2005–06 Boston U 4 0 **4 0**
2005–06 Northampton T 24 1 **24 1**

KIRK, Andy (F) **226 84**
H: 5 11 W: 11 01 b.Belfast 29-5-79
Honours: Northern Ireland Under-21, 8 full caps.
1995–96 Glentoran 1 1
1996–97 Glentoran 25 8
1997–98 Glentoran 25 9 **51 18**
1998–99 Hearts 5 0
1999–2000 Hearts 4 0
2000–01 Hearts 31 13
2001–02 Hearts 20 1
2002–03 Hearts 29 10
2003–04 Hearts 24 8 **113 32**
2004–05 Boston U 25 19 **25 19**
2004–05 Northampton T 8 7
2005–06 Northampton T 29 8 **37 15**

LEE, Jason (F) **450 91**
H: 6 3 W: 13 08 b.Forest Gate 9-5-71
Source: Trainee.
1989–90 Charlton Ath 1 0
1990–91 Charlton Ath 0 0
1990–91 *Stockport Co* 2 0 **2 0**
1990–91 Lincoln C 17 3
1991–92 Lincoln C 35 6
1992–93 Lincoln C 41 12 **93 21**
1993–94 Southend U 24 3 **24 3**
1993–94 Nottingham F 13 2
1994–95 Nottingham F 22 3
1995–96 Nottingham F 28 8
1996–97 Nottingham F 13 1 **76 14**
1996–97 *Charlton Ath* 8 3 **9 3**
1996–97 *Grimsby T* 7 1 **7 1**
1997–98 Watford 36 10
1998–99 Watford 1 1 **37 11**
1998–99 Chesterfield 22 1
1999–2000 Chesterfield 6 0 **28 1**
1999–2000 Peterborough U 23 6
2000–01 Peterborough U 30 8
2001–02 Peterborough U 0 0
2002–03 Peterborough U 25 3 **78 17**
2003–04 Falkirk 29 8 **29 8**
2004–05 Boston U 39 9
2005–06 Boston U 17 2 **56 11**
2005–06 Northampton T 11 1 **11 1**

LOW, Josh (M) **225 25**
H: 6 2 W: 14 03 b.Bristol 15-2-79
Source: Trainee. *Honours:* Wales Youth, Under-21.
1995–96 Bristol R 1 0
1996–97 Bristol R 3 0
1997–98 Bristol R 10 0
1998–99 Bristol R 8 0 **22 0**
1999–2000 Leyton Orient 5 1 **5 1**
1999–2000 Cardiff C 17 2
2000–01 Cardiff C 36 4
2001–02 Cardiff C 22 0
2002–03 Cardiff C 0 0 **75 6**
2002–03 Oldham Ath 21 3 **21 3**
2003–04 Northampton T 33 3
2004–05 Northampton T 34 7
2005–06 Northampton T 35 5 **102 15**

McGLEISH, Scott (F) **450 125**
H: 5 9 W: 11 09 b.Barnet 10-2-74
Source: Edgware T.
1994–95 Charlton Ath 6 0 **6 0**
1994–95 *Leyton Orient* 6 1
1995–96 Peterborough U 12 0
1995–96 *Colchester U* 15 6
1996–97 Peterborough U 1 0 **13 0**
1996–97 *Cambridge U* 10 7 **10 7**
1996–97 Leyton Orient 28 7
1997–98 Leyton Orient 8 0 **42 8**
1997–98 Barnet 37 13
1998–99 Barnet 36 8
1999–2000 Barnet 42 10
2000–01 Barnet 19 5 **134 36**
2000–01 Colchester U 21 5
2001–02 Colchester U 46 15
2002–03 Colchester U 43 8
2003–04 Colchester U 34 10 **159 44**
2004–05 Northampton T 44 13
2005–06 Northampton T 42 17 **86 30**

MURRAY, Fred (D) 126 0
H: 5 10 W: 11 12 b.Clonmel 22-5-82
Source: Trainee.
1998–99 Blackburn R 0 0
1999–2000 Blackburn R 0 0
2000–01 Blackburn R 0 0
2001–02 Blackburn R 0 0
2001–02 Cambridge U 21 0
2002–03 Cambridge U 29 0
2003–04 Cambridge U 38 0 **88 0**
2004–05 Northampton T 38 0
2005–06 Northampton T 0 0 **38 0**

NGOYI, Greg (F) 0 0
b.Zaire 20-7-87
Source: Scholar.
2004–05 Northampton T 0 0
2005–06 Northampton T 0 0

ROWSON, David (M) 209 11
H: 5 10 W: 11 10 b.Aberdeen 14-9-76
Source: FC Stoneywood. *Honours:* Scotland Under-21.
1994–95 Aberdeen 0 0
1995–96 Aberdeen 9 0
1996–97 Aberdeen 34 2
1997–98 Aberdeen 30 5
1998–99 Aberdeen 22 0
1999–2000 Aberdeen 0 0
2000–01 Aberdeen 0 0 **95 7**
2001–02 Stoke C 13 0
2002–03 Stoke C 0 0 **13 0**
2003–04 Partick T 35 2 **35 2**
2004–05 Northampton T 37 2
2005–06 Northampton T 29 0 **66 2**

SMITH, Martin (F) 329 88
H: 5 11 W: 12 07 b.Sunderland 13-11-74
Source: Trainee. *Honours:* England Schools, Under-21.
1992–93 Sunderland 0 0
1993–94 Sunderland 29 8
1994–95 Sunderland 35 10
1995–96 Sunderland 20 2
1996–97 Sunderland 11 0
1997–98 Sunderland 16 2
1998–99 Sunderland 8 3 **119 25**
1999–2000 Sheffield U 26 10 **26 10**
1999–2000 Huddersfield T 12 4
2000–01 Huddersfield T 30 8
2001–02 Huddersfield T 0 0
2002–03 Huddersfield T 38 17 **80 29**
2003–04 Northampton T 44 11
2004–05 Northampton T 34 10
2005–06 Northampton T 26 3 **104 24**

TAYLOR, Ian (M) 444 78
H: 6 2 W: 11 06 b.Birmingham 4-6-68
Source: Moor Green.
1992–93 Port Vale 41 15
1993–94 Port Vale 42 13 **83 28**
1994–95 Sheffield W 14 1 **14 1**
1994–95 Aston Villa 22 1
1995–96 Aston Villa 25 3
1996–97 Aston Villa 34 2
1997–98 Aston Villa 32 6
1998–99 Aston Villa 33 4
1999–2000 Aston Villa 29 5
2000–01 Aston Villa 29 4
2001–02 Aston Villa 16 3
2002–03 Aston Villa 13 0 **233 28**
2003–04 Derby Co 42 11
2004–05 Derby Co 39 3 **81 14**
2005–06 Northampton T 33 7 **33 7**

WESTWOOD, Ashley (D) 235 18
H: 6 0 W: 12 09 b.Bridgnorth 31-8-76
Source: Trainee. *Honours:* England Youth.
1994–95 Manchester U 0 0
1995–96 Crewe Alex 33 4
1996–97 Crewe Alex 44 2
1997–98 Crewe Alex 21 3 **98 9**
1998–99 Bradford C 19 2
1999–2000 Bradford C 5 0
2000–01 Bradford C 0 0 **24 2**
2000–01 Sheffield W 33 2
2001–02 Sheffield W 26 1
2002–03 Sheffield W 23 2 **82 5**
2003–04 Northampton T 9 0
2004–05 Northampton T 19 2
2005–06 Northampton T 3 0 **31 2**

NORWICH C (55)

CAVE-BROWN, Andrew (D) 0 0
H: 5 10 W: 12 02 b.Gravesend 5-8-88
Source: Scholar. *Honours:* Scotland Youth.
2005–06 Norwich C 0 0

CHARLTON, Simon (D) 475 5
H: 5 9 W: 12 01 b.Huddersfield 25-10-71
Source: Trainee. *Honours:* FA Schools.
1989–90 Huddersfield T 3 0
1990–91 Huddersfield T 30 0
1991–92 Huddersfield T 45 0
1992–93 Huddersfield T 46 1 **124 1**
1993–94 Southampton 33 1
1994–95 Southampton 25 1
1995–96 Southampton 26 0
1996–97 Southampton 27 0
1997–98 Southampton 3 0 **114 2**
1998–99 Birmingham C 28 0
1997–98 Birmingham C 24 0
1999–2000 Birmingham C 20 0 **72 0**
2000–01 Bolton W 22 0
2001–02 Bolton W 36 0
2002–03 Bolton W 31 0
2003–04 Bolton W 31 0 **120 0**
2004–05 Norwich C 24 1
2005–06 Norwich C 21 1 **45 2**

COLIN, Jurgen (D) 90 1
H: 5 10 W: 11 10 b.Utrecht 20-1-81
Honours: Holland Youth.
2001–02 PSV Eindhoven 4 0
2001–02 Genk 7 0 **7 0**
2002–03 NAC Breda 34 0 **34 0**
2003–04 PSV Eindhoven 20 1
2004–05 PSV Eindhoven 0 0 **24 1**
2005–06 Norwich C 25 0 **25 0**

DOHERTY, Gary (D) 196 19
H: 6 3 W: 13 13 b.Carndonagh 31-1-80
Source: Trainee. *Honours:* Eire Youth, Under-21, 33 full caps, 4 goals.
1997–98 Luton T 10 0
1998–99 Luton T 20 6
1999–2000 Luton T 40 6 **70 12**
1999–2000 Tottenham H 2 0
2000–01 Tottenham H 22 3
2001–02 Tottenham H 7 0
2002–03 Tottenham H 15 1
2003–04 Tottenham H 17 0
2004–05 Tottenham H 1 0 **64 4**
2004–05 Norwich C 20 2
2005–06 Norwich C 42 1 **62 3**

DRURY, Adam (D) 348 5
H: 5 10 W: 11 09 b.Cambridge 29-8-78
Source: Trainee.
1995–96 Peterborough U 1 0
1996–97 Peterborough U 5 1
1997–98 Peterborough U 31 0
1998–99 Peterborough U 40 0
1999–2000 Peterborough U 42 1
2000–01 Peterborough U 29 0 **148 2**
2000–01 Norwich C 6 0
2001–02 Norwich C 35 0
2002–03 Norwich C 45 2
2003–04 Norwich C 42 0
2004–05 Norwich C 33 1
2005–06 Norwich C 39 0 **200 3**

EARNSHAW, Robert (F) 239 107
H: 5 6 W: 9 09 b.Mulfulira 6-4-81
Source: Trainee. *Honours:* Wales Youth, Under-21, 26 full caps, 11 goals.
1997–98 Cardiff C 5 0
1998–99 Cardiff C 5 1
1998–99 *Middlesbrough* 0 0
1999–2000 Cardiff C 6 1
1999–2000 *Morton* 3 2 **3 2**
2000–01 Cardiff C 36 19
2001–02 Cardiff C 30 11
2002–03 Cardiff C 46 31
2003–04 Cardiff C 46 21
2004–05 Cardiff C 4 1 **178 85**
2004–05 WBA 31 11
2005–06 WBA 12 1 **43 12**
2005–06 Norwich C 15 8 **15 8**

ETUHU, Dickson (M) 165 17
H: 6 2 W: 13 04 b.Kano 8-6-82
Source: Scholarship.
1999–2000 Manchester C 0 0
2000–01 Manchester C 0 0
2001–02 Manchester C 12 0 **12 0**
2001–02 Preston NE 16 3
2002–03 Preston NE 39 6
2003–04 Preston NE 31 3
2004–05 Preston NE 35 3
2005–06 Preston NE 13 2 **134 17**
2005–06 Norwich C 19 0 **19 0**

FLEMING, Craig (D) 554 13
H: 6 0 W: 12 11 b.Halifax 6-10-71
Source: Trainee.
1988–89 Halifax T 1 0
1989–90 Halifax T 10 0
1990–91 Halifax T 46 0 **57 0**
1991–92 Oldham Ath 32 1
1992–93 Oldham Ath 24 0
1993–94 Oldham Ath 37 0
1994–95 Oldham Ath 5 0
1995–96 Oldham Ath 22 0
1996–97 Oldham Ath 44 0 **164 1**
1997–98 Norwich C 22 1
1998–99 Norwich C 37 3
1999–2000 Norwich C 39 3
2000–01 Norwich C 39 0
2001–02 Norwich C 46 0
2002–03 Norwich C 30 0
2003–04 Norwich C 46 3
2004–05 Norwich C 38 1
2005–06 Norwich C 36 1 **333 12**

GALLACHER, Paul (G) 126 0
H: 6 1 W: 12 04 b.Glasgow 16-8-79
Honours: Scotland Under-21, 8 full caps.
1999–2000 Dundee U 1 0
2000–01 Dundee U 15 0
2001–02 Dundee U 38 0
2002–03 Dundee U 34 0
2003–04 Dundee U 23 0 **111 0**
2004–05 Norwich C 0 0
2004–05 *Gillingham* 3 0 **3 0**
2004–05 *Sheffield W* 8 0 **8 0**
2005–06 Norwich C 4 0 **4 0**

GREEN, Robert (G) 223 0
H: 6 3 W: 14 09 b.Chertsey 18-1-80
Source: Trainee. *Honours:* England Youth, B, 1 full cap.
1997–98 Norwich C 0 0
1998–99 Norwich C 2 0
1999–2000 Norwich C 3 0
2000–01 Norwich C 5 0
2001–02 Norwich C 41 0
2002–03 Norwich C 46 0
2003–04 Norwich C 46 0
2004–05 Norwich C 38 0
2005–06 Norwich C 42 0 **223 0**

HENDERSON, Ian (F) 66 6
H: 5 10 W: 11 06 b.Thetford 24-1-85
Source: Scholar. *Honours:* England Youth, Under-20.
2002–03 Norwich C 20 1
2003–04 Norwich C 19 4
2004–05 Norwich C 3 0
2005–06 Norwich C 24 1 **66 6**

HUCKERBY, Darren (F) 363 93
H: 5 10 W: 12 09 b.Nottingham 23-4-76
Source: Trainee. *Honours:* England Under-21, B.
1993–94 Lincoln C 6 1
1994–95 Lincoln C 6 2
1995–96 Lincoln C 16 2 **28 5**
1995–96 Newcastle U 1 0
1996–97 Newcastle U 0 0 **1 0**
1996–97 *Millwall* 6 3 **6 3**
1996–97 Coventry C 25 5
1997–98 Coventry C 34 14
1998–99 Coventry C 34 9
1999–2000 Coventry C 1 0 **94 28**
1999–2000 Leeds U 33 2
2000–01 Leeds U 7 0 **40 2**
2000–01 Manchester C 13 1
2001–02 Manchester C 40 20
2002–03 Manchester C 16 1

2002–03	*Nottingham F*	9	5	**9**	**5**
2003–04	Manchester C	0	0	**69**	**22**
2003–04	Norwich C	36	14		
2004–05	Norwich C	37	6		
2005–06	Norwich C	43	8	**116**	**28**

HUGHES, Andy (M) 345 38
H: 5 11 W: 12 01 b.Stockport 2-1-78
Source: Trainee.

1995–96	Oldham Ath	15	1		
1996–97	Oldham Ath	8	0		
1997–98	Oldham Ath	10	0	**33**	**1**
1997–98	Notts Co	15	2		
1998–99	Notts Co	30	3		
1999–2000	Notts Co	35	7		
2000–01	Notts Co	30	5	**110**	**17**
2001–02	Reading	39	6		
2002–03	Reading	43	9		
2003–04	Reading	43	3		
2004–05	Reading	41	0	**166**	**18**
2005–06	Norwich C	36	2	**36**	**2**

JARRETT, Jason (M) 190 6
H: 6 1 W: 13 10 b.Bury 14-9-79
Source: Trainee.

1998–99	Blackpool	2	0		
1999–2000	Blackpool	0	0	**2**	**0**
1999–2000	Wrexham	1	0	**1**	**0**
2000–01	Bury	25	2		
2001–02	Bury	37	2	**62**	**4**
2001–02	Wigan Ath	5	0		
2002–03	Wigan Ath	35	0		
2003–04	Wigan Ath	41	1		
2004–05	Wigan Ath	14	0	**95**	**1**
2004–05	*Stoke C*	2	0	**2**	**0**
2005–06	Norwich C	11	0	**11**	**0**
2005–06	*Plymouth Arg*	7	0	**7**	**0**
2005–06	*Preston NE*	10	1	**10**	**1**

JARVIS, Rossi (D) 3 0
H: 5 11 W: 11 12 b.Fakenham 11-3-88
Source: Scholar. *Honours:* England Youth.

2005–06	Norwich C	3	0	**3**	**0**

JARVIS, Ryan (F) 29 3
H: 6 1 W: 11 11 b.Fakenham 11-7-86
Source: Scholar. *Honours:* FA Schools, England Youth.

2002–03	Norwich C	3	0		
2003–04	Norwich C	12	1		
2004–05	Norwich C	4	1		
2004–05	*Colchester U*	6	0	**6**	**0**
2005–06	Norwich C	4	1	**23**	**3**

LEWIS, Joe (G) 0 0
H: 6 5 W: 12 10 b.Bury St Edmunds 6-10-87
Source: Scholar. *Honours:* England Youth.

2004–05	Norwich C	0	0		
2005–06	Norwich C	0	0		

LOUIS-JEAN, Mathieu (D) 278 3
H: 5 9 W: 11 07 b.Mont-St-Aignan 22-2-76

1993–94	Le Havre	7	0		
1994–95	Le Havre	9	0		
1995–96	Le Havre	15	0		
1996–97	Le Havre	31	0		
1997–98	Le Havre	16	0	**78**	**0**
1998–99	Nottingham F	16	0		
1999–2000	Nottingham F	27	0		
2000–01	Nottingham F	13	0		
2001–02	Nottingham F	38	1		
2002–03	Nottingham F	41	1		
2003–04	Nottingham F	38	1		
2004–05	Nottingham F	25	0	**198**	**3**
2005–06	Norwich C	2	0	**2**	**0**

McKENZIE, Leon (F) 267 80
H: 5 11 W: 12 11 b.Croydon 17-5-78
Source: Trainee.

1995–96	Crystal Palace	12	0		
1996–97	Crystal Palace	21	2		
1997–98	Crystal Palace	3	0		
1997–98	*Fulham*	3	0	**3**	**0**
1998–99	Crystal Palace	16	1		
1998–99	*Peterborough U*	14	8		
1999–2000	Crystal Palace	25	4		
2000–01	Crystal Palace	8	0	**85**	**7**
2000–01	Peterborough U	30	13		
2001–02	Peterborough U	30	18		
2002–03	Peterborough U	11	5		
2003–04	Peterborough U	19	9	**104**	**53**
2003–04	Norwich C	18	9		
2004–05	Norwich C	37	7		
2005–06	Norwich C	20	4	**75**	**20**

McVEIGH, Paul (F) 198 37
H: 5 7 W: 11 00 b.Belfast 6-12-77
Source: Trainee. *Honours:* Northern Ireland Schools, Youth, Under-21, 20 full caps.

1995–96	Tottenham H	0	0		
1996–97	Tottenham H	3	1		
1997–98	Tottenham H	0	0		
1998–99	Tottenham H	0	0		
1999–2000	Tottenham H	0	0	**3**	**1**
1999–2000	Norwich C	1	0		
2000–01	Norwich C	11	1		
2001–02	Norwich C	42	8		
2002–03	Norwich C	44	14		
2003–04	Norwich C	44	5		
2004–05	Norwich C	17	1		
2005–06	Norwich C	36	7	**195**	**36**

ROBINSON, Carl (M) 292 26
H: 5 11 W: 12 08 b.Llandrindod Wells 13-10-76
Source: Trainee. *Honours:* Wales Youth, Under-21, B, 29 full caps, 1 goal.

1995–96	Wolverhampton W	0	0		
1995–96	*Shrewsbury T*	4	0	**4**	**0**
1996–97	Wolverhampton W	2	0		
1997–98	Wolverhampton W	32	3		
1998–99	Wolverhampton W	34	8		
1999–2000	Wolverhampton W	33	3		
2000–01	Wolverhampton W	40	3		
2001–02	Wolverhampton W	23	2	**164**	**19**
2002–03	Portsmouth	15	0		
2002–03	*Sheffield W*	4	1	**4**	**1**
2002–03	*Walsall*	11	1	**11**	**1**
2003–04	Portsmouth	1	0	**16**	**0**
2003–04	*Rotherham U*	14	0	**14**	**0**
2003–04	*Sheffield U*	5	0	**5**	**0**
2003–04	*Sunderland*	7	1		
2004–05	Sunderland	40	4		
2005–06	Sunderland	5	0	**52**	**5**
2005–06	Norwich C	22	0	**22**	**0**

SAFRI, Youseff (M) 139 3
H: 5 9 W: 12 09 b.Casablanca 1-3-77
Source: Raja. *Honours:* Morocco full caps.

2001–02	Coventry C	33	1		
2002–03	Coventry C	27	0		
2003–04	Coventry C	31	0	**91**	**1**
2004–05	Norwich C	18	1		
2005–06	Norwich C	30	1	**48**	**2**

SHACKELL, Jason (D) 36 0
H: 6 4 W: 13 06 b.Stevenage 27-9-83
Source: Scholar.

2002–03	Norwich C	2	0		
2003–04	Norwich C	6	0		
2004–05	Norwich C	11	0		
2005–06	Norwich C	17	0	**36**	**0**

SPILLANE, Michael (M) 2 0
H: 5 9 W: 11 10 b.Cambridge 23-3-89
Source: Scholar. *Honours:* Eire Youth.

2005–06	Norwich C	2	0	**2**	**0**

THORNE, Peter (F) 393 139
H: 6 1 W: 13 13 b.Manchester 21-6-73
Source: Trainee.

1991–92	Blackburn R	0	0		
1992–93	Blackburn R	0	0		
1993–94	Blackburn R	0	0		
1993–94	*Wigan Ath*	11	0	**11**	**0**
1994–95	Blackburn R	0	0		
1994–95	Swindon T	20	9		
1995–96	Swindon T	26	10		
1996–97	Swindon T	31	8	**77**	**27**
1997–98	Stoke C	36	12		
1998–99	Stoke C	34	9		
1999–2000	Stoke C	45	24		
2000–01	Stoke C	38	16		
2001–02	Stoke C	5	4	**158**	**65**
2001–02	Cardiff C	26	8		
2002–03	Cardiff C	46	13		
2003–04	Cardiff C	23	13		
2004–05	Cardiff C	31	12	**126**	**46**
2005–06	Norwich C	21	1	**21**	**1**

WARD, Darren (G) 456 0
H: 6 0 W: 13 09 b.Worksop 11-5-74
Source: Trainee. *Honours:* Wales Under-21, B, 5 full caps.

1992–93	Mansfield T	13	0		
1993–94	Mansfield T	33	0		
1994–95	Mansfield T	35	0	**81**	**0**
1995–96	Notts Co	46	0		
1996–97	Notts Co	38	0		
1997–98	Notts Co	44	0		
1998–99	Notts Co	43	0		
1999–2000	Notts Co	45	0		
2000–01	Notts Co	35	0	**251**	**0**
2000–01	Nottingham F	0	0		
2001–02	Nottingham F	46	0		
2002–03	Nottingham F	45	0		
2003–04	Nottingham F	32	0		
2004–05	Nottingham F	0	0	**123**	**0**
2004–05	Norwich C	1	0		
2005–06	Norwich C	0	0	**1**	**0**

NOTTINGHAM F (56)

BASTIANS, Felix (M) 11 0
H: 6 2 W: 12 00 b.Bochum 9-5-88
Source: Scholar. *Honours:* Germany Youth.

2005–06	Nottingham F	11	0	**11**	**0**

BEAUMONT, James (M) 1 0
H: 5 7 W: 10 10 b.Stockton 11-11-84
Source: Scholar.

2001–02	Newcastle U	0	0		
2002–03	Newcastle U	0	0		
2003–04	Nottingham F	0	0		
2004–05	Nottingham F	0	0		
2005–06	Nottingham F	0	0		
2005–06	*Darlington*	1	0	**1**	**0**

BENNETT, Julian (D) 69 5
H: 6 1 W: 13 00 b.Nottingham 17-12-84
Source: Scholar.

2003–04	Walsall	1	0		
2004–05	Walsall	31	2		
2005–06	Walsall	19	1	**51**	**3**
2005–06	Nottingham F	18	2	**18**	**2**

BOPP, Eugene (M) 77 8
H: 5 11 W: 12 03 b.Kiev 5-9-83
Source: Bayern Munich.

2000–01	Nottingham F	0	0		
2001–02	Nottingham F	19	1		
2002–03	Nottingham F	13	2		
2003–04	Nottingham F	15	1		
2004–05	Nottingham F	18	3		
2005–06	Nottingham F	12	1	**77**	**8**

BRECKIN, Ian (D) 486 22
H: 6 2 W: 13 05 b.Rotherham 24-2-75
Source: Trainee.

1993–94	Rotherham U	10	0		
1994–95	Rotherham U	41	2		
1995–96	Rotherham U	39	1		
1996–97	Rotherham U	42	3	**132**	**6**
1997–98	Chesterfield	43	1		
1998–99	Chesterfield	44	2		
1999–2000	Chesterfield	38	1		
2000–01	Chesterfield	45	3		
2001–02	Chesterfield	42	1	**212**	**8**
2002–03	Wigan Ath	9	0		
2003–04	Wigan Ath	45	0		
2004–05	Wigan Ath	42	0	**96**	**0**
2005–06	Nottingham F	46	8	**46**	**8**

CLINGAN, Sammy (M) 51 3
H: 5 11 W: 11 06 b.Belfast 13-1-84
Source: Scholar. *Honours:* Northern Ireland Schools, Youth, Under-21, Under-23, 2 full caps.

2001–02	Wolverhampton W	0	0		
2002–03	Wolverhampton W	0	0		
2003–04	Wolverhampton W	0	0		
2004–05	Wolverhampton W	0	0		
2004–05	*Chesterfield*	15	2		
2005–06	Wolverhampton W	0	0		
2005–06	*Chesterfield*	21	1	**36**	**3**
2005–06	Nottingham F	15	0	**15**	**0**

COMMONS, Kris (M) **108 19**
H: 5 6 W: 9 08 b.Mansfield 30-8-83
Source: Scholar.
2000–01 Stoke C 0 0
2001–02 Stoke C 0 0
2002–03 Stoke C 8 1
2003–04 Stoke C 33 4 **41 5**
2004–05 Nottingham F 30 6
2005–06 Nottingham F 37 8 **67 14**

CULLINGWORTH, James (M) **0 0**
b.Nottingham 18-9-87
Source: Scholar.
2004–05 Nottingham F 0 0
2005–06 Nottingham F 0 0

CULLIP, Danny (D) **308 9**
H: 6 0 W: 12 12 b.Bracknell 17-9-76
Source: Trainee.
1995–96 Oxford U 0 0
1996–97 Fulham 29 1
1997–98 Fulham 21 1 **50 2**
1997–98 Brentford 13 0
1998–99 Brentford 2 0
1999–2000 Brentford 0 0 **15 0**
1999–2000 Brighton & HA 33 2
2000–01 Brighton & HA 38 2
2001–02 Brighton & HA 44 0
2002–03 Brighton & HA 44 2
2003–04 Brighton & HA 40 1
2004–05 Brighton & HA 18 0 **217 7**
2004–05 Sheffield U 11 0 **11 0**
2004–05 *Watford* 4 0 **4 0**
2005–06 Nottingham F 11 0 **11 0**

CURTIS, John (D) **186 2**
H: 5 10 W: 11 07 b.Nuneaton 3-9-78
Source: Trainee. *Honours:* England Schools, Youth, Under-21, B.
1995–96 Manchester U 0 0
1996–97 Manchester U 0 0
1997–98 Manchester U 8 0
1998–99 Manchester U 4 0
1999–2000 Manchester U 1 0 **13 0**
1999–2000 *Barnsley* 28 2 **28 2**
2000–01 Blackburn R 46 0
2001–02 Blackburn R 10 0
2002–03 Blackburn R 5 0 **61 0**
2002–03 *Sheffield U* 12 0 **12 0**
2003–04 Leicester C 15 0 **15 0**
2003–04 Portsmouth 6 0
2004–05 Portsmouth 1 0 **7 0**
2004–05 *Preston NE* 12 0 **12 0**
2004–05 Nottingham F 11 0
2005–06 Nottingham F 27 0 **38 0**

DADI, Eugene (F) **191 44**
H: 6 2 W: 13 04 b.Abidjan 20-8-73
1997–98 Linz 19 4
1998–99 Linz 20 3
1999–2000 Linz 13 3 **52 10**
2000–01 Toulouse 3 0 **3 0**
2001–02 Aberdeen 28 4 **28 4**
2002–03 Livingston 23 3 **23 3**
2003–04 Tranmere R 38 16
2004–05 Tranmere R 31 9
2005–06 Tranmere R 0 0 **69 25**
2005–06 Nottingham F 5 0 **5 0**
2005–06 *Notts Co* 11 2 **11 2**

DOBIE, Scott (F) **288 51**
H: 6 1 W: 12 05 b.Workington 10-10-78
Source: Trainee. *Honours:* Scotland 6 full caps, 1 goal.
1996–97 Carlisle U 2 1
1997–98 Carlisle U 23 0
1998–99 Carlisle U 33 6
1998–99 *Clydebank* 6 0 **6 0**
1999–2000 Carlisle U 34 7
2000–01 Carlisle U 44 10 **136 24**
2001–02 WBA 43 10
2002–03 WBA 31 5
2003–04 WBA 31 5
2004–05 WBA 5 1 **110 21**
2004–05 Millwall 16 3 **16 3**
2004–05 Nottingham F 12 1
2005–06 Nottingham F 8 2 **20 3**

EADEN, Nicky (D) **517 13**
H: 5 9 W: 12 02 b.Sheffield 12-12-72
Source: Trainee.
1991–92 Barnsley 0 0
1992–93 Barnsley 2 0
1993–94 Barnsley 37 2
1994–95 Barnsley 45 1
1995–96 Barnsley 46 2
1996–97 Barnsley 46 3
1997–98 Barnsley 35 0
1998–99 Barnsley 40 1
1999–2000 Barnsley 42 1 **293 10**
2000–01 Birmingham C 45 2
2001–02 Birmingham C 29 1
2002–03 Birmingham C 0 0 **74 3**
2002–03 Wigan Ath 37 0
2003–04 Wigan Ath 46 0
2004–05 Wigan Ath 39 0 **122 0**
2005–06 Nottingham F 28 0 **28 0**

EVANS, Paul (M) **431 67**
H: 5 8 W: 12 06 b.Oswestry 1-9-74
Source: Trainee. *Honours:* Wales Youth, Under-21, 1 full cap.
1991–92 Shrewsbury T 2 0
1992–93 Shrewsbury T 4 0
1993–94 Shrewsbury T 13 0
1994–95 Shrewsbury T 32 5
1995–96 Shrewsbury T 34 3
1996–97 Shrewsbury T 42 6
1997–98 Shrewsbury T 39 6
1998–99 Shrewsbury T 32 6 **198 26**
1998–99 Brentford 14 3
1999–2000 Brentford 33 7
2000–01 Brentford 43 7
2001–02 Brentford 40 14 **130 31**
2002–03 Bradford C 19 2
2002–03 *Blackpool* 10 1 **10 1**
2003–04 Bradford C 23 3 **42 5**
2003–04 Nottingham F 8 0
2004–05 Nottingham F 39 4
2005–06 Nottingham F 0 0 **47 4**
2005–06 *Rotherham U* 4 0 **4 0**

FERNANDEZ, Vincent (D) **1 0**
H: 6 3 W: 10 11 b.Lyon 19-9-86
Source: Scholar.
2004–05 Nottingham F 0 0
2005–06 Nottingham F 1 0 **1 0**

FRIIO, David (M) **189 40**
H: 6 0 W: 11 05 b.Thionville 17-2-73
Source: Epinal, Nimes, ASOA Valence.
2000–01 Plymouth Arg 26 5
2001–02 Plymouth Arg 41 8
2002–03 Plymouth Arg 36 6
2003–04 Plymouth Arg 36 14
2004–05 Plymouth Arg 28 6 **167 39**
2004–05 Nottingham F 5 0
2005–06 Nottingham F 17 1 **22 1**

GAMBLE, Paddy (G) **0 0**
b.Nottingham 1-9-88
Source: Scholar. *Honours:* England Youth.
2005–06 Nottingham F 0 0

GARDNER, Ross (M) **28 0**
H: 5 8 W: 10 06 b.South Shields 15-12-85
Source: Scholar. *Honours:* England Youth, Under-20.
2001–02 Newcastle U 0 0
2002–03 Newcastle U 0 0
2003–04 Nottingham F 2 0
2004–05 Nottingham F 14 0
2005–06 Nottingham F 12 0 **28 0**

GERRARD, Paul (G) **318 1**
H: 6 2 W: 13 11 b.Heywood 22-1-73
Source: Trainee. *Honours:* England Under-21.
1991–92 Oldham Ath 0 0
1992–93 Oldham Ath 25 0
1993–94 Oldham Ath 16 0
1994–95 Oldham Ath 42 0
1995–96 Oldham Ath 36 1 **119 1**
1996–97 Everton 5 0
1997–98 Everton 4 0
1998–99 Everton 0 0
1998–99 *Oxford U* 16 0 **16 0**
1999–2000 Everton 34 0
2000–01 Everton 32 0
2001–02 Everton 13 0
2002–03 Everton 2 0
2002–03 *Ipswich T* 5 0 **5 0**
2003–04 Everton 0 0 **90 0**
2003–04 *Sheffield U* 16 0 **16 0**
2003–04 *Nottingham F* 8 0
2004–05 Nottingham F 42 0
2005–06 Nottingham F 22 0 **72 0**

GLASS, Matt (F) **0 0**
b.Swindon 28-5-88
Source: Scholar.
2005–06 Nottingham F 0 0

HARRIS, Neil (F) **286 100**
H: 5 10 W: 12 08 b.Orsett 12-7-77
Source: Cambridge C.
1997–98 Millwall 3 0
1998–99 Millwall 39 15
1999–2000 Millwall 38 25
2000–01 Millwall 42 27
2001–02 Millwall 21 4
2002–03 Millwall 40 12
2003–04 Millwall 38 9
2004–05 Millwall 12 1 **233 93**
2004–05 *Cardiff C* 3 1 **3 1**
2004–05 Nottingham F 13 0
2005–06 Nottingham F 1 0 **14 0**
2005–06 *Gillingham* 36 6 **36 6**

HEATH, Joe (D) **0 0**
b.Birkenhead 4-10-88
2005–06 Nottingham F 0 0

HOLT, Gary (M) **346 12**
H: 6 0 W: 12 00 b.Irvine 9-3-73
Source: Celtic. *Honours:* Scotland 10 full caps, 1 goal.
1994–95 Stoke C 0 0
1995–96 Kilmarnock 26 0
1996–97 Kilmarnock 12 1
1997–98 Kilmarnock 27 2
1998–99 Kilmarnock 33 3
1999–2000 Kilmarnock 35 0
2000–01 Kilmarnock 19 3 **152 9**
2000–01 Norwich C 4 0
2001–02 Norwich C 46 2
2002–03 Norwich C 45 0
2003–04 Norwich C 46 1
2004–05 Norwich C 27 0 **168 3**
2005–06 Nottingham F 26 0 **26 0**

HOLT, Grant (F) **124 42**
H: 6 1 W: 14 02 b.Carlisle 12-4-81
Source: Workington.
1999–2000 Halifax T 4 0
2000–01 Halifax T 2 0 **6 0**
From Sengkang,Barrow
2002–03 Sheffield W 7 1
2003–04 Sheffield W 17 2 **24 3**
2003–04 Rochdale 14 4
2004–05 Rochdale 40 17
2005–06 Rochdale 21 14 **75 35**
2005–06 Nottingham F 19 4 **19 4**

JAMES, Kevin (M) **77 5**
H: 5 7 W: 11 12 b.Southwark 3-1-80
Source: Trainee.
1998–99 Charlton Ath 0 0
1999–2000 Charlton Ath 0 0
2000–01 Gillingham 7 0
2001–02 Gillingham 10 0
2002–03 Gillingham 15 3
2003–04 Gillingham 17 1 **49 4**
2004–05 Nottingham F 7 0
2004–05 *Boston U* 6 0 **6 0**
2005–06 Nottingham F 0 0 **7 0**
2005–06 *Walsall* 15 1 **15 1**

JOHNSON, David (F) **391 126**
H: 5 6 W: 12 00 b.Kingston, Jamaica 15-8-76
Source: Trainee. *Honours:* England Schools, B, Jamaica 4 full caps.
1994–95 Manchester U 0 0
1995–96 Bury 36 5
1996–97 Bury 44 8
1997–98 Bury 17 5 **97 18**
1997–98 Ipswich T 31 20
1998–99 Ipswich T 42 13
1999–2000 Ipswich T 44 22
2000–01 Ipswich T 14 0 **131 55**

2000–01	Nottingham F	19	2		
2001–02	Nottingham F	22	3		
2001–02	*Sheffield W*	7	2	**7**	**2**
2001–02	*Burnley*	8	5	**8**	**5**
2002–03	Nottingham F	42	25		
2003–04	Nottingham F	17	7		
2004–05	Nottingham F	31	6		
2004–05	*Sheffield U*	0	0		
2005–06	Nottingham F	17	3	**148**	**46**

LESTER, Jack (F) **328** **57**

H: 5 9 W: 12 08 b.Sheffield 8-10-75

Source: Trainee. *Honours:* England Schools.

1994–95	Grimsby T	7	0		
1995–96	Grimsby T	5	0		
1996–97	Grimsby T	22	5		
1996–97	*Doncaster R*	11	1	**11**	**1**
1997–98	Grimsby T	40	4		
1998–99	Grimsby T	33	4		
1999–2000	Grimsby T	26	4	**133**	**17**
1999–2000	Nottingham F	15	2		
2000–01	Nottingham F	19	7		
2001–02	Nottingham F	32	5		
2002–03	Nottingham F	33	7		
2003–04	Sheffield U	32	12		
2004–05	Sheffield U	12	0	**44**	**12**
2004–05	Nottingham F	3	1		
2005–06	Nottingham F	38	5	**140**	**27**

MOLONEY, Brendan (M) **0** **0**

b.Enfield 18-1-89

Source: Scholar.

2005–06	Nottingham F	0	0		

MORGAN, Wes (D) **123** **6**

H: 6 2 W: 14 00 b.Nottingham 21-1-84

Source: Scholar.

2002–03	Nottingham F	0	0		
2002–03	*Kidderminster H*	5	1	**5**	**1**
2003–04	Nottingham F	32	2		
2004–05	Nottingham F	43	1		
2005–06	Nottingham F	43	2	**118**	**5**

MULLARKEY, Sam (M) **0** **0**

b.Lincoln 24-9-87

Source: Scholar.

2004–05	Nottingham F	0	0		
2005–06	Nottingham F	0	0		

PADULA, Gino (D) **122** **4**

H: 5 9 W: 12 11 b.Buenos Aires 11-7-76

Source: Xerex.

1999–2000	Bristol R	0	0		
1999–2000	Walsall	25	0	**25**	**0**
2000–01	Wigan Ath	4	0		
2001–02	Wigan Ath	0	0	**4**	**0**
2002–03	QPR	21	1		
2003–04	QPR	36	3		
2004–05	QPR	33	0	**90**	**4**
2005–06	Nottingham F	3	0	**3**	**0**

PEDERSEN, Rune (G) **57** **0**

H: 6 3 W: 13 08 b.Rigshospitalet 9-10-79

Source: Hvidovre. *Honours:* Denmark Youth, Under-21.

1999–2000	FC Copenhagen	0	0		
2000–01	FC Copenhagen	16	0		
2001–02	FC Copenhagen	2	0		
2002–03	FC Copenhagen	14	0	**32**	**0**
2003–04	Aarhus	7	0	**7**	**0**
2005–06	Nottingham F	18	0	**18**	**0**

PERCH, James (D) **60** **3**

H: 5 11 W: 11 05 b.Mansfield 29-9-85

Source: Scholar.

2002–03	Nottingham F	0	0		
2003–04	Nottingham F	0	0		
2004–05	Nottingham F	22	0		
2005–06	Nottingham F	38	3	**60**	**3**

PITTMAN, Jon-Paul (F) **3** **0**

H: 5 9 W: 11 00 b.Oklahoma City 24-10-86

Source: Scholar.

2005–06	Nottingham F	0	0		
2005–06	*Hartlepool U*	3	0	**3**	**0**

POWER, Alan (M) **0** **0**

b.Dublin 23-1-88

Source: Scholar.

2005–06	Nottingham F	0	0		

RIGBY, Andrew (M) **0** **0**

b.Nottingham 19-1-87

2003–04	Nottingham F	0	0		
2004–05	Nottingham F	0	0		
2005–06	Nottingham F	0	0		

ROBERTS, Dale (M) **0** **0**

H: 6 3 W: 11 06 b.Horden 22-10-86

Source: Scholar.

2005–06	Nottingham F	0	0		

ROBERTS, Justyn (D) **0** **0**

b.Lewisham 12-2-86

Source: Scholar.

2002–03	Nottingham F	0	0		
2003–04	Nottingham F	0	0		
2004–05	Nottingham F	0	0		
2005–06	Nottingham F	0	0		

ROGERS, Alan (D) **315** **18**

H: 5 9 W: 12 10 b.Liverpool 3-1-77

Source: Trainee.

1995–96	Tranmere R	26	2		
1996–97	Tranmere R	31	0	**57**	**2**
1997–98	Nottingham F	46	1		
1998–99	Nottingham F	34	3		
1999–2000	Nottingham F	37	9		
2000–01	Nottingham F	17	3		
2001–02	Nottingham F	3	0		
2001–02	Leicester C	13	0		
2002–03	Leicester C	41	0		
2003–04	Leicester C	8	0	**62**	**0**
2003–04	*Wigan Ath*	5	0	**5**	**0**
2003–04	*Nottingham F*	12	0		
2004–05	Nottingham F	33	0		
2005–06	Nottingham F	0	0	**182**	**16**
2005–06	*Hull C*	9	0	**9**	**0**

SOUTHALL, Nicky (M) **523** **57**

H: 5 11 W: 12 04 b.Stockton 28-1-72

Source: Trainee.

1990–91	Hartlepool U	0	0		
1991–92	Hartlepool U	22	3		
1992–93	Hartlepool U	39	6		
1993–94	Hartlepool U	40	9		
1994–95	Hartlepool U	37	6	**138**	**24**
1995–96	Grimsby T	33	2		
1996–97	Grimsby T	34	3		
1997–98	Grimsby T	5	0	**72**	**5**
1997–98	Gillingham	23	2		
1998–99	Gillingham	42	4		
1999–2000	Gillingham	45	9		
2000–01	Gillingham	44	2		
2001–02	Bolton W	18	1		
2002–03	Bolton W	0	0	**18**	**1**
2002–03	*Norwich C*	9	0	**9**	**0**
2002–03	Gillingham	24	1		
2003–04	Gillingham	35	0		
2004–05	Gillingham	33	1	**246**	**19**
2005–06	Nottingham F	40	8	**40**	**8**

TAYLOR, Gareth (F) **404** **111**

H: 6 2 W: 13 07 b.Weston-Super-Mare 25-2-73

Source: Southampton Trainee. *Honours:* Wales Under-21, 15 full caps, 1 goal.

1991–92	Bristol R	1	0		
1992–93	Bristol R	0	0		
1993–94	Bristol R	0	0		
1994–95	Bristol R	39	12		
1995–96	Bristol R	7	4	**47**	**16**
1995–96	Crystal Palace	20	1	**20**	**1**
1995–96	Sheffield U	10	2		
1996–97	Sheffield U	34	12		
1997–98	Sheffield U	28	10		
1998–99	Sheffield U	12	1	**84**	**25**
1998–99	Manchester C	26	4		
1999–2000	Manchester C	17	5		
1999–2000	*Port Vale*	4	0	**4**	**0**
1999–2000	*QPR*	6	1	**6**	**1**
2000–01	Manchester C	0	0	**43**	**9**
2000–01	*Burnley*	15	4		
2001–02	Burnley	40	16		
2002–03	Burnley	40	16		
2003–04	Burnley	0	0	**95**	**36**
2003–04	Nottingham F	34	8		
2004–05	Nottingham F	36	7		
2005–06	Nottingham F	20	4	**90**	**19**
2005–06	*Crewe Alex*	15	4	**15**	**4**

THOMPSON, John (D) **115** **7**

H: 6 0 W: 12 01 b.Dublin 12-10-81

Source: Home Farm. *Honours:* Eire Under-21, 1 full cap.

1999–2000	Nottingham F	0	0		
2000–01	Nottingham F	0	0		
2001–02	Nottingham F	8	0		
2002–03	Nottingham F	20	3		
2003–04	Nottingham F	32	1		
2004–05	Nottingham F	20	0		
2005–06	Nottingham F	35	3	**115**	**7**

TYSON, Nathan (F) **158** **55**

H: 5 10 W: 10 02 b.Reading 4-5-82

Source: Trainee. *Honours:* England Under-20.

1999–2000	Reading	1	0		
2000–01	Reading	0	0		
2001–02	Reading	1	0		
2001–02	*Swansea C*	11	1	**11**	**1**
2001–02	*Cheltenham T*	8	1	**8**	**1**
2002–03	Reading	23	1		
2003–04	Reading	8	0	**33**	**1**
2003–04	Wycombe W	21	9		
2004–05	Wycombe W	42	22		
2005–06	Wycombe W	15	11	**78**	**42**
2005–06	Nottingham F	28	10	**28**	**10**

VICKERTON, Martin (D) **1** **0**

H: 5 10 W: 11 02 b.Nottingham 24-6-87

Source: Scholar.

2005–06	Nottingham F	1	0	**1**	**0**

WEIR-DALEY, Spencer (F) **6** **1**

H: 5 9 W: 10 11 b.Leicester 5-9-85

Source: Scholar.

2003–04	Nottingham F	0	0		
2004–05	Nottingham F	0	0		
2005–06	Nottingham F	6	1	**6**	**1**

NOTTS CO (57)

BAUDET, Julien (D) **136** **14**

H: 6 2 W: 13 07 b.Grenoble 13-1-79

Source: Toulouse.

2001–02	Oldham Ath	20	1		
2002–03	Oldham Ath	24	2	**44**	**3**
2003–04	Rotherham U	11	0	**11**	**0**
2004–05	Notts Co	39	5		
2005–06	Notts Co	42	6	**81**	**11**

CHILAKA, Ohlizov (M) **0** **0**

H: 5 9 W: 13 00 b.Nigeria 21-10-86

2005–06	Notts Co	0	0		

EDWARDS, Mike (D) **271** **14**

H: 6 0 W: 12 10 b.Hessle 25-4-80

Source: Trainee.

1997–98	Hull C	21	0		
1998–99	Hull C	30	0		
1999–2000	Hull C	40	1		
2000–01	Hull C	42	4		
2001–02	Hull C	39	1		
2002–03	Hull C	6	0	**178**	**6**
2002–03	Colchester U	5	0	**5**	**0**
2003–04	Grimsby T	33	1	**33**	**1**
2004–05	Notts Co	9	0		
2005–06	Notts Co	46	7	**55**	**7**

FRIARS, Emmet (D) **14** **1**

H: 6 2 W: 11 09 b.Derry 14-9-85

Honours: Northern Ireland Under-21.

2003–04	Notts Co	0	0		
2004–05	Notts Co	9	0		
2005–06	Notts Co	5	1	**14**	**1**

FROST, Stef (M) **4** **0**

H: 6 2 W: 11 05 b.Nottingham 3-7-89

Source: Scholar.

2005–06	Notts Co	4	0	**4**	**0**

GILL, Matthew (M) **208** **5**

H: 5 11 W: 11 10 b.Cambridge 8-11-80

Source: Trainee.

1997–98	Peterborough U	2	0		
1998–99	Peterborough U	26	0		
1999–2000	Peterborough U	20	1		
2000–01	Peterborough U	17	1		
2001–02	Peterborough U	12	2		
2002–03	Peterborough U	41	1		
2003–04	Peterborough U	33	0	**151**	**5**

2004–05 Notts Co 43 0
2005–06 Notts Co 14 0 **57** **0**

GORDON, Gavin (F) 226 48
H: 6 1 W: 12 00 b.Manchester 24-6-79
Source: Trainee.
1995–96 Hull C 13 3
1996–97 Hull C 20 4
1997–98 Hull C 5 2 **38** **9**
1997–98 Lincoln C 13 3
1998–99 Lincoln C 27 5
1999–2000 Lincoln C 41 11
2000–01 Lincoln C 18 9 **99** **28**
2000–01 Cardiff C 10 1
2001–02 Cardiff C 15 1
2002–03 Cardiff C 10 2
2002–03 *Oxford U* 6 1 **6** **1**
2003–04 Cardiff C 15 1 **50** **5**
2004–05 Notts Co 27 5
2005–06 Notts Co 6 0 **33** **5**

LONG, Stacy (M) 19 1
H: 5 8 W: 10 00 b.Farnborough 11-1-85
Source: Scholar. *Honours:* England Under-20, Youth.
2001–02 Charlton Ath 0 0
2002–03 Charlton Ath 0 0
2003–04 Charlton Ath 0 0
2004–05 Charlton Ath 0 0
2005–06 Notts Co 19 1 **19** **1**

MARSHALL, Shaun (G) 156 0
H: 6 1 W: 13 00 b.Fakenham 3-10-78
Source: Trainee.
1996–97 Cambridge U 1 0
1997–98 Cambridge U 2 0
1998–99 Cambridge U 19 0
1999–2000 Cambridge U 24 0
2000–01 Cambridge U 11 0
2001–02 Cambridge U 7 0
2002–03 Cambridge U 45 0
2003–04 Cambridge U 45 0
2004–05 Cambridge U 1 0 **155** **0**
2005–06 Notts Co 1 0 **1** **0**

MARTIN, Dan (D) 22 4
H: 6 1 W: 12 13 b.Derby 27-9-86
Source: Scholar. *Honours:* Wales Under-21.
2004–05 Derby Co 0 0
2005–06 Notts Co 22 4 **22** **4**

McMAHON, Lewis (M) 54 2
H: 5 9 W: 10 10 b.Doncaster 2-5-85
Source: Scholar.
2003–04 Sheffield W 10 0
2004–05 Sheffield W 15 2 **25** **2**
2005–06 Notts Co 29 0 **29** **0**

NEEDHAM, Liam (M) 22 0
H: 6 1 W: 12 02 b.Sheffield 19-10-85
Source: Scholar.
2004–05 Sheffield W 0 0
From Gainsborough T.
2005–06 Notts Co 22 0 **22** **0**

O'CALLAGHAN, Brian (D) 108 2
H: 6 1 W: 12 10 b.Limerick 24-2-81
Source: Pike Rovers.
1998–99 Barnsley 0 0
1999–2000 Barnsley 0 0
2000–01 Barnsley 26 0
2001–02 Barnsley 6 0
2002–03 Barnsley 14 1
2003–04 Barnsley 29 0 **75** **1**
2004–05 IBV 0 0
From Worksop T
2005–06 Notts Co 33 1 **33** **1**

PALMER, Chris (M) 54 5
H: 5 7 W: 11 00 b.Derby 16-10-83
Source: Scholar.
2003–04 Derby Co 0 0
2004–05 Notts Co 25 4
2005–06 Notts Co 29 1 **54** **5**

PILKINGTON, Kevin (G) 264 0
H: 6 1 W: 13 00 b.Hitchin 8-3-74
Source: Trainee. *Honours:* England Schools.
1992–93 Manchester U 0 0
1993–94 Manchester U 0 0
1994–95 Manchester U 1 0
1995–96 Manchester U 3 0
1995–96 *Rochdale* 6 0 **6** **0**
1996–97 Manchester U 0 0
1996–97 *Rotherham U* 17 0 **17** **0**
1997–98 Manchester U 2 0
1998–99 Manchester U 0 0 **6** **0**
1998–99 Port Vale 8 0
1999–2000 Port Vale 15 0 **23** **0**
2000–01 Macclesfield T 0 0
2000–01 Wigan Ath 0 0
2000–01 Mansfield T 2 0
2001–02 Mansfield T 45 0
2002–03 Mansfield T 32 0
2003–04 Mansfield T 46 0
2004–05 Mansfield T 42 0 **167** **0**
2005–06 Notts Co 45 0 **45** **0**

PIPE, David (M) 123 5
H: 5 9 W: 12 01 b.Caerphilly 5-11-83
Source: Scholar. *Honours:* Wales Under-21, 1 full cap.
2000–01 Coventry C 0 0
2001–02 Coventry C 0 0
2002–03 Coventry C 21 1
2003–04 Coventry C 0 0 **21** **1**
2003–04 Notts Co 18 0
2004–05 Notts Co 41 2
2005–06 Notts Co 43 2 **102** **4**

RHODES, Chris (M) 1 0
H: 5 9 W: 10 12 b.Mansfield 9-1-87
Source: Scholar.
2003–04 Notts Co 1 0
2004–05 Notts Co 0 0
2005–06 Notts Co 0 0 **1** **0**

SCOFFHAM, Steve (F) 52 7
H: 5 11 W: 11 04 b.Munster 12-7-83
Source: Gedling.
2003–04 Notts Co 15 2
2004–05 Notts Co 7 0
2005–06 Notts Co 30 5 **52** **7**

SCULLY, Tony (M) 166 9
H: 5 8 W: 11 02 b.Dublin 12-6-76
Source: Trainee. *Honours:* Eire Under-21.
1993–94 Crystal Palace 0 0
1994–95 Crystal Palace 0 0
1994–95 *Bournemouth* 10 0 **10** **0**
1995–96 Crystal Palace 2 0
1995–96 *Cardiff C* 14 0 **14** **0**
1996–97 Crystal Palace 1 0
1997–98 Crystal Palace 0 0 **3** **0**
1997–98 Manchester C 9 0 **9** **0**
1997–98 *Stoke C* 7 0 **7** **0**
1997–98 QPR 7 0
1998–99 QPR 23 2
1999–2000 QPR 8 0
2000–01 QPR 2 0 **40** **2**
2001–02 Cambridge U 25 2
2002–03 Cambridge U 6 0 **31** **2**
2002–03 *Southend U* 8 0 **8** **0**
2002–03 *Peterborough U* 3 0
2003–04 Peterborough U 0 0 **3** **0**
From Dagenham & R
2003–04 Notts Co 10 3
2004–05 Notts Co 31 2
2005–06 Notts Co 0 0 **41** **5**

SHERIDAN, Jake (M) 27 1
H: 5 9 W: 11 06 b.Nottingham 8-7-86
Source: Dunkirk.
2005–06 Notts Co 27 1 **27** **1**

SISSOKO, Noe (M) 3 0
H: 6 3 W: 14 00 b.Bamako 2-6-83
Source: Creteil.
2005–06 Notts Co 3 0 **3** **0**

ULLATHORNE, Robert (D) 265 9
H: 5 8 W: 10 10 b.Wakefield 11-10-71
Source: Trainee.
1989–90 Norwich C 0 0
1990–91 Norwich C 2 0
1991–92 Norwich C 20 3
1992–93 Norwich C 0 0
1993–94 Norwich C 16 2
1994–95 Norwich C 27 2
1995–96 Norwich C 29 0 **94** **7**
1996–97 Osasuna 18 0 **18** **0**
1996–97 Leicester C 0 0
1997–98 Leicester C 6 1
1998–99 Leicester C 25 0
1999–2000 Leicester C 0 0 **31** **1**
2000–01 Sheffield U 14 0
2001–02 Sheffield U 14 0
2002–03 Sheffield U 12 0 **40** **0**
2003–04 Northampton T 13 1 **13** **1**
2004–05 Notts Co 36 0
2005–06 Notts Co 33 0 **69** **0**

WHITE, Andy (F) 131 17
H: 6 4 W: 14 00 b.Derby 6-11-81
Source: Hucknall T.
2000–01 Mansfield T 4 0
2001–02 Mansfield T 22 4
2002–03 Mansfield T 28 6
2002–03 *Crewe Alex* 2 0
2003–04 Mansfield T 14 0 **68** **10**
2003–04 *Boston U* 6 0 **6** **0**
2003–04 *Kidderminster H* 7 1 **7** **1**
2004–05 Crewe Alex 22 4 **24** **4**
2005–06 Notts Co 26 2 **26** **2**

WHITLOW, Mike (D) 397 15
H: 6 0 W: 12 13 b.Northwich 13-1-68
Source: Witton Alb.
1988–89 Leeds U 20 1
1989–90 Leeds U 29 1
1990–91 Leeds U 18 1
1991–92 Leeds U 10 1 **77** **4**
1991–92 Leicester C 5 0
1992–93 Leicester C 24 1
1993–94 Leicester C 31 2
1994–95 Leicester C 28 2
1995–96 Leicester C 42 3
1996–97 Leicester C 17 0
1997–98 Leicester C 0 0 **147** **8**
1997–98 Bolton W 13 0
1998–99 Bolton W 28 0
1999–2000 Bolton W 37 1
2000–01 Bolton W 8 1
2001–02 Bolton W 29 0
2002–03 Bolton W 17 0 **132** **2**
2003–04 Sheffield U 17 1 **17** **1**
2004–05 Notts Co 24 0
2005–06 Notts Co 0 0 **24** **0**

WILLIAMS, Matthew (F) 26 1
H: 5 8 W: 9 11 b.Flint 5-11-82
Honours: Wales Under-21.
1999–2000 Manchester U 0 0
2000–01 Manchester U 0 0
2001–02 Manchester U 0 0
2002–03 Manchester U 0 0
2003–04 Manchester U 0 0
2003–04 Notts Co 7 0
2004–05 Notts Co 18 1
2005–06 Notts Co 1 0 **26** **1**

WILSON, Kelvin (D) 84 3
H: 6 2 W: 12 12 b.Nottingham 3-9-85
Source: Scholar.
2003–04 Notts Co 3 0
2004–05 Notts Co 41 2
2005–06 Notts Co 34 1 **78** **3**
2005–06 *Preston NE* 6 0 **6** **0**

ZADKOVICH, Ruben (M) 9 1
H: 5 11 W: 11 00 b.Australia 23-5-86
Source: Wollongong R, QPR. *Honours:* Australia Under-20.
2004–05 Notts Co 8 1
2005–06 Notts Co 1 0 **9** **1**

OLDHAM ATH (58)

BARLOW, Matty (F) 10 0
H: 5 11 W: 10 04 b.Oldham 25-6-87
Source: Scholar.
2003–04 Oldham Ath 1 0
2004–05 Oldham Ath 9 0
2005–06 Oldham Ath 0 0 **10** **0**

BONNER, Mark (M) 355 18
H: 5 10 W: 11 01 b.Ormskirk 7-6-74
Source: Trainee.
1991–92 Blackpool 3 0
1992–93 Blackpool 15 0
1993–94 Blackpool 40 7
1994–95 Blackpool 17 0
1995–96 Blackpool 42 3
1996–97 Blackpool 29 1
1997–98 Blackpool 32 3 **178** **14**

1998–99 Cardiff C 25 1
1998–99 *Hull C* 1 1 **1 1**
1999–2000 Cardiff C 31 0
2000–01 Cardiff C 24 1
2001–02 Cardiff C 29 0
2002–03 Cardiff C 14 0
2003–04 Cardiff C 20 0 **143 2**
2003–04 Oldham Ath 7 0
2004–05 Oldham Ath 19 0
2005–06 Oldham Ath 7 1 **33 1**

BRANSTON, Guy (D) 211 18
H: 6 1 W: 15 01 b.Leicester 9-1-79
Source: Trainee.
1997–98 Leicester C 0 0
1997–98 *Colchester U* 12 1
1998–99 Leicester C 0 0
1998–99 *Colchester U* 1 0 **13 1**
1998–99 *Plymouth Arg* 7 1 **7 1**
1999–2000 Leicester C 0 0
1999–2000 *Lincoln C* 4 0 **4 0**
1999–2000 Rotherham U 30 4
2000–01 Rotherham U 41 6
2001–02 Rotherham U 10 1
2002–03 Rotherham U 15 2
2003–04 Rotherham U 8 0 **104 13**
2003–04 *Wycombe W* 9 0 **9 0**
2003–04 *Peterborough U* 14 0
2004–05 Sheffield W 11 0 **11 0**
2004–05 *Peterborough U* 4 1 **18 1**
2004–05 Oldham Ath 7 1
2005–06 Oldham Ath 38 1 **45 2**

BUTCHER, Richard (M) 144 16
H: 6 0 W: 13 01 b.Peterborough 22-1-81
Source: Kettering T.
2002–03 Lincoln C 26 3
2003–04 Lincoln C 32 6
2004–05 Lincoln C 46 2
2005–06 Oldham Ath 36 4 **36 4**
2005–06 *Lincoln C* 4 1 **108 12**

DAINECHE, Nasser (D) 0 0
H: 6 3 W: 14 00 b.Martigues 17-6-84
2005–06 Oldham Ath 0 0

DAY, Chris (G) 172 0
H: 6 2 W: 13 07 b.Whipps Cross 28-7-75
Source: Trainee. *Honours:* England Under-21.
1992–93 Tottenham H 0 0
1993–94 Tottenham H 0 0
1994–95 Tottenham H 0 0
1995–96 Tottenham H 0 0
1996–97 Crystal Palace 24 0 **24 0**
1997–98 Watford 0 0
1998–99 Watford 0 0
1999–2000 Watford 11 0
2000–01 Watford 0 0 **11 0**
2000–01 *Lincoln C* 14 0 **14 0**
2001–02 QPR 16 0
2002–03 QPR 12 0
2003–04 QPR 29 0
2004–05 QPR 30 0 **87 0**
2004–05 *Preston NE* 6 0 **6 0**
2005–06 Oldham Ath 30 0 **30 0**

EARDLEY, Ian (M) 1 0
b.Llandudno 6-11-88
Source: Scholar. *Honours:* England Youth.
2005–06 Oldham Ath 1 0 **1 0**

EDWARDS, Paul (M) 161 7
H: 5 11 W: 10 12 b.Manchester 1-1-80
Source: Altrincham.
2001–02 Swindon T 20 0 **20 0**
2002–03 Wrexham 38 4
2003–04 Wrexham 41 0 **79 4**
2004–05 Blackpool 28 3 **28 3**
2005–06 Oldham Ath 34 0 **34 0**

EYRES, David (M) 648 127
H: 5 11 W: 11 06 b.Liverpool 26-2-64
Source: Rhyl.
1989–90 Blackpool 35 7
1990–91 Blackpool 36 6
1991–92 Blackpool 41 9
1992–93 Blackpool 46 16 **158 38**
1993–94 Burnley 45 19
1994–95 Burnley 39 8
1995–96 Burnley 42 6
1996–97 Burnley 36 3
1997–98 Burnley 13 1 **175 37**
1997–98 Preston NE 28 4
1998–99 Preston NE 34 8
1999–2000 Preston NE 41 7
2000–01 Preston NE 5 0 **108 19**
2000–01 Oldham Ath 30 3
2001–02 Oldham Ath 45 9
2002–03 Oldham Ath 40 13
2003–04 Oldham Ath 29 3
2004–05 Oldham Ath 42 4
2005–06 Oldham Ath 21 1 **207 33**

FORBES, Terrell (D) 189 0
H: 5 11 W: 12 07 b.Southwark 17-8-81
Source: Trainee.
1999–2000 West Ham U 0 0
1999–2000 *Bournemouth* 3 0 **3 0**
2000–01 West Ham U 0 0
2001–02 QPR 43 0
2002–03 QPR 38 0
2003–04 QPR 30 0
2004–05 QPR 3 0 **114 0**
2004–05 Grimsby T 33 0 **33 0**
2005–06 Oldham Ath 39 0 **39 0**

GRIFFIN, Adam (D) 92 5
H: 5 7 W: 10 04 b.Salford 26-8-84
Source: Scholar.
2001–02 Oldham Ath 1 0
2002–03 Oldham Ath 0 0
2003–04 Oldham Ath 26 1
2004–05 Oldham Ath 35 2
2005–06 Oldham Ath 0 0 **62 3**
2005–06 *Oxford U* 9 0 **9 0**
2005–06 *Stockport Co* 21 2 **21 2**

HAINING, Will (D) 111 9
H: 6 0 W: 11 02 b.Glasgow 2-10-82
Source: Scholar.
2001–02 Oldham Ath 4 0
2002–03 Oldham Ath 26 2
2003–04 Oldham Ath 31 2
2004–05 Oldham Ath 35 5
2005–06 Oldham Ath 15 0 **111 9**

HALL, Chris (F) 24 0
H: 6 2 W: 11 07 b.Manchester 27-11-86
Source: Scholar.
2003–04 Oldham Ath 1 0
2004–05 Oldham Ath 6 0
2005–06 Oldham Ath 17 0 **24 0**

HALL, Danny (D) 64 1
H: 6 0 W: 12 02 b.Ashton-under-Lyne 14-11-83
Source: Scholar.
2002–03 Oldham Ath 2 0
2003–04 Oldham Ath 31 1
2004–05 Oldham Ath 21 0
2005–06 Oldham Ath 10 0 **64 1**

HUGHES, Mark (M) 63 1
H: 5 10 W: 12 05 b.Dungannon 16-9-83
Source: Scholar. *Honours:* Northern Ireland Schools, Youth, Under-21, Under-23, 2 full caps.
2001–02 Tottenham H 0 0
2002–03 Tottenham H 0 0
2003–04 Tottenham H 0 0
2004–05 Tottenham H 0 0
2004–05 *Northampton T* 3 0 **3 0**
2004–05 *Oldham Ath* 27 0
2005–06 Oldham Ath 33 1 **60 1**

KILLEN, Chris (F) 102 26
H: 6 1 W: 11 07 b.Wellington 8-10-81
Source: Miramar R. *Honours:* New Zealand Under-20, Under-23, 16 full caps, 7 goals.
1998–99 Manchester C 0 0
1999–2000 Manchester C 0 0
2000–01 Manchester C 0 0
2000–01 *Wrexham* 12 3 **12 3**
2001–02 *Port Vale* 9 6 **9 6**
2001–02 Manchester C 3 0 **3 0**
2002–03 Oldham Ath 27 3
2003–04 Oldham Ath 13 2
2004–05 Oldham Ath 26 10
2005–06 Oldham Ath 12 2 **78 17**
To Hibernian January 2006

LIDDELL, Andy (F) 477 116
H: 5 7 W: 11 11 b.Leeds 28-6-73
Source: Trainee. *Honours:* Scotland Under-21.
1990–91 Barnsley 0 0
1991–92 Barnsley 1 0
1992–93 Barnsley 21 2
1993–94 Barnsley 22 1
1994–95 Barnsley 39 13
1995–96 Barnsley 43 9
1996–97 Barnsley 38 8
1997–98 Barnsley 26 1
1998–99 Barnsley 8 0 **198 34**
1998–99 Wigan Ath 28 10
1999–2000 Wigan Ath 41 8
2000–01 Wigan Ath 37 9
2001–02 Wigan Ath 34 18
2002–03 Wigan Ath 37 16
2003–04 Wigan Ath 40 9 **217 70**
2004–05 Sheffield U 33 3 **33 3**
2005–06 Oldham Ath 29 9 **29 9**

LOMAX, Kelvin (D) 10 0
H: 5 11 W: 12 03 b.Bury 12-11-86
Source: Scholar.
2003–04 Oldham Ath 1 0
2004–05 Oldham Ath 9 0
2005–06 Oldham Ath 0 0 **10 0**

OWEN, Gareth (D) 51 1
H: 6 1 W: 11 07 b.Stoke 21-9-82
Source: Scholar. *Honours:* Wales Youth.
2001–02 Stoke C 0 0
2002–03 Stoke C 0 0
2003–04 Stoke C 3 0
2003–04 *Oldham Ath* 15 1
2004–05 Stoke C 2 0 **5 0**
2004–05 *Torquay U* 5 0 **5 0**
2004–05 *Oldham Ath* 9 0
2005–06 Oldham Ath 17 0 **41 1**

PORTER, Chris (F) 102 25
H: 6 1 W: 12 09 b.Wigan 12-12-83
Source: School.
2002–03 Bury 2 0
2003–04 Bury 37 9
2004–05 Bury 32 9 **71 18**
2005–06 Oldham Ath 31 7 **31 7**

SCOTT, Rob (D) 305 34
H: 6 0 W: 12 09 b.Epsom 15-8-73
Source: Sutton U.
1993–94 Sheffield U 0 0
1994–95 Sheffield U 1 0
1994–95 *Scarborough* 8 3 **8 3**
1995–96 Sheffield U 5 1 **6 1**
1995–96 *Northampton T* 5 0 **5 0**
1995–96 Fulham 21 5
1996–97 Fulham 43 9
1997–98 Fulham 17 3
1998–99 Fulham 3 0 **84 17**
1998–99 *Carlisle U* 7 3 **7 3**
1998–99 Rotherham U 6 1
1999–2000 Rotherham U 34 1
2000–01 Rotherham U 39 2
2001–02 Rotherham U 38 3
2002–03 Rotherham U 23 0
2003–04 Rotherham U 10 0
2004–05 Rotherham U 24 2 **174 9**
2005–06 Oldham Ath 21 1 **21 1**

SMITH, Terry (G) 0 0
H: 6 0 W: 11 00 b.Chester 16-9-87
Source: Scholar.
2005–06 Oldham Ath 0 0

STAM, Stefan (D) 26 0
H: 6 2 W: 13 02 b.Amersfoort 14-9-79
Honours: Holland Under-21.
2004–05 Oldham Ath 13 0
2005–06 Oldham Ath 13 0 **26 0**

SWAILES, Chris (D) 390 25
H: 6 2 W: 13 09 b.Gateshead 19-10-70
Source: Ipswich T Trainee, Peterborough U, Boston U, Birmingham C, Bridlington T.
1993–94 Doncaster R 17 0
1994–95 Doncaster R 32 0 **49 0**
1995–96 Ipswich T 5 0
1996–97 Ipswich T 23 1
1997–98 Ipswich T 5 0 **33 1**

1997–98 Bury 13 1
1998–99 Bury 43 3
1999–2000 Bury 27 2
2000–01 Bury 43 4 **126 10**
2001–02 Rotherham U 44 6
2002–03 Rotherham U 43 3
2003–04 Rotherham U 43 3
2004–05 Rotherham U 37 2 **167 14**
2005–06 Oldham Ath 15 0 **15 0**

TAYLOR, Chris (M) 14 0
H: 5 11 W: 11 00 b.Oldham 20-12-86
Source: Scholar.
2005–06 Oldham Ath 14 0 **14 0**

TAYLOR, Jason (M) 9 0
H: 6 1 W: 11 03 b.Ashton-under-Lyne 28-1-87
Source: Scholar.
2005–06 Oldham Ath 0 0
2005–06 *Stockport Co* 9 0 **9 0**

TIERNEY, Marc (D) 32 0
H: 5 11 W: 11 04 b.Manchester 7-9-86
Source: Trainee.
2003–04 Oldham Ath 2 0
2004–05 Oldham Ath 11 0
2005–06 Oldham Ath 19 0 **32 0**

WARNE, Paul (M) 313 41
H: 5 10 W: 11 07 b.Norwich 8-5-73
Source: Wroxham.
1997–98 Wigan Ath 25 2
1998–99 Wigan Ath 11 1 **36 3**
1998–99 Rotherham U 19 8
1999–2000 Rotherham U 43 10
2000–01 Rotherham U 44 7
2001–02 Rotherham U 25 0
2002–03 Rotherham U 40 1
2003–04 Rotherham U 35 1
2004–05 Rotherham U 24 1 **230 28**
2004–05 *Mansfield T* 7 1 **7 1**
2005–06 Oldham Ath 40 9 **40 9**

WELLENS, Richard (M) 233 20
H: 5 9 W: 11 06 b.Manchester 26-3-80
Source: Trainee. *Honours:* England Youth.
1996–97 Manchester U 0 0
1997–98 Manchester U 0 0
1998–99 Manchester U 0 0
1999–2000 Manchester U 0 0
1999–2000 Blackpool 8 0
2000–01 Blackpool 36 8
2001–02 Blackpool 36 1
2002–03 Blackpool 39 1
2003–04 Blackpool 41 3
2004–05 Blackpool 28 3 **188 16**
2005–06 Oldham Ath 45 4 **45 4**

WOLFENDEN, Matthew (F) 3 0
H: 5 9 W: 11 02 b.Oldham 23-7-87
Source: Scholar.
2003–04 Oldham Ath 1 0
2004–05 Oldham Ath 1 0
2005–06 Oldham Ath 1 0 **3 0**

OXFORD U (59)

ASHTON, Jon (D) 108 1
H: 6 2 W: 13 12 b.Nuneaton 4-10-82
Source: Scholar.
2000–01 Leicester C 0 0
2001–02 Leicester C 7 0
2002–03 *Notts Co* 4 0 **4 0**
2003–04 Leicester C 0 0 **7 0**
2003–04 Oxford U 34 0
2004–05 Oxford U 30 0
2005–06 Oxford U 33 1 **97 1**

BASHAM, Steve (F) 240 55
H: 6 0 W: 12 04 b.Southampton 2-12-77
Source: Trainee.
1996–97 Southampton 6 0
1997–98 Southampton 9 0
1997–98 *Wrexham* 5 0 **5 0**
1998–99 Southampton 4 1 **19 1**
1998–99 *Preston NE* 17 10
1999–2000 Preston NE 24 2
2000–01 Preston NE 11 2
2001–02 Preston NE 16 1 **68 15**
2002–03 Oxford U 31 8
2003–04 Oxford U 38 14
2004–05 Oxford U 39 9
2005–06 Oxford U 40 8 **148 39**

BEECHERS, Billy (M) 4 0
H: 5 9 W: 11 10 b.Oxford 1-6-87
Source: Scholar.
2004–05 Oxford U 3 0
2005–06 Oxford U 1 0 **4 0**

BROOKS, Jamie (F) 50 13
H: 5 10 W: 11 12 b.Oxford 12-8-83
Source: Scholar.
2000–01 Oxford U 4 1
2001–02 Oxford U 25 10
2002–03 Oxford U 0 0
2003–04 Oxford U 0 0
2004–05 Oxford U 12 2
2005–06 Oxford U 9 0 **50 13**

BURGESS, Andy (M) 163 11
H: 6 2 W: 11 12 b.Bedford 10-8-81
Source: Juniors.
2001–02 Rushden & D 32 4
2002–03 Rushden & D 27 1
2003–04 Rushden & D 37 4
2004–05 Rushden & D 42 1
2005–06 Rushden & D 9 0 **147 10**
2005–06 Oxford U 16 1 **16 1**

BURTON, Paul (M) 1 0
H: 6 0 W: 11 12 b.London 30-11-85
Source: Scholar.
2004–05 Oxford U 1 0
2005–06 Oxford U 0 0 **1 0**

CLARKE, Bradie (G) 4 0
H: 6 2 W: 13 08 b.Cambridge 26-5-86
Source: Scholar.
2004–05 Oxford U 4 0
2005–06 Oxford U 0 0 **4 0**

DAVIES, Craig (F) 48 8
H: 6 2 W: 13 01 b.Burton-on-Trent 9-1-86
Source: Manchester C. *Honours:* Wales Youth, Under-21, 3 full caps.
2004–05 Oxford U 28 6
2005–06 Oxford U 20 2 **48 8**
To Verona January 2006

DEMPSTER, John (D) 72 4
H: 6 1 W: 11 07 b.Kettering 1-4-83
Source: Trainee. *Honours:* Scotland Youth, Under-21.
2001–02 Rushden & D 2 0
2002–03 Rushden & D 16 1
2003–04 Rushden & D 19 0
2004–05 Rushden & D 15 0
2005–06 Rushden & D 14 3 **66 4**
2005–06 Oxford U 6 0 **6 0**

E'BEYER, Mark (M) 16 3
H: 5 11 W: 12 03 b.Stevenage 21-9-84
Source: Milton Keynes Dons Scholar.
2004–05 Oxford U 10 2
2005–06 Oxford U 6 1 **16 3**

FRANKLIN, Tom (D) 0 0
H: 6 1 W: 12 00 b.Oxford 12-5-89
Source: Scholar.
2005–06 Oxford U 0 0

GEMMILL, Scot (M) 367 27
H: 5 10 W: 11 08 b.Paisley 2-1-71
Source: School. *Honours:* Scotland Under-21, B, 26 full caps, 1 goal.
1989–90 Nottingham F 0 0
1990–91 Nottingham F 4 0
1991–92 Nottingham F 39 8
1992–93 Nottingham F 33 1
1993–94 Nottingham F 31 8
1994–95 Nottingham F 19 1
1995–96 Nottingham F 31 1
1996–97 Nottingham F 24 0
1997–98 Nottingham F 44 2
1998–99 Nottingham F 20 0 **245 21**
1998–99 Everton 7 1
1999–2000 Everton 14 1
2000–01 Everton 28 2
2001–02 Everton 32 1
2002–03 Everton 16 0
2003–04 Everton 0 0 **97 5**
2003–04 *Preston NE* 7 1 **7 1**
2004–05 Leicester C 17 0
2005–06 Leicester C 0 0 **17 0**
2005–06 Oxford U 1 0 **1 0**

GRAY, Stuart (M) 213 16
H: 6 0 W: 13 05 b.Harrogate 18-12-73
Source: Giffnock N. *Honours:* Scotland Under-21.
1992–93 Celtic 1 0
1993–94 Celtic 0 0
1994–95 Celtic 11 0
1995–96 Celtic 5 1
1996–97 Celtic 11 0
1997–98 Celtic 0 0 **28 1**
1997–98 Reading 7 0
1998–99 Reading 27 2
1999–2000 Reading 15 0
2000–01 Reading 3 0 **52 2**
2001–02 Rushden & D 12 0
2002–03 Rushden & D 38 7
2003–04 Rushden & D 35 5
2004–05 Rushden & D 38 1 **123 13**
2005–06 Oxford U 10 0 **10 0**

HACKETT, Chris (M) 125 9
H: 6 0 W: 12 08 b.Oxford 1-3-83
Source: Scholarship.
1999–2000 Oxford U 2 0
2000–01 Oxford U 16 2
2001–02 Oxford U 15 0
2002–03 Oxford U 12 0
2003–04 Oxford U 22 1
2004–05 Oxford U 37 4
2005–06 Oxford U 21 2 **125 9**
To Hearts January 2006

HARGREAVES, Chris (M) 457 25
H: 6 0 W: 12 13 b.Cleethorpes 12-5-72
Source: Trainee.
1989–90 Grimsby T 19 2
1990–91 Grimsby T 18 3
1991–92 Grimsby T 10 0
1992–93 Grimsby T 4 0
1992–93 *Scarborough* 3 0 **3 0**
1993–94 Grimsby T 0 0 **51 5**
1993–94 Hull C 28 0
1994–95 Hull C 21 0 **49 0**
1995–96 WBA 1 0 **1 0**
1995–96 *Hereford U* 17 2
1996–97 Hereford U 44 4
1997–98 Hereford U 0 0 **61 6**
From Hereford U.
1998–99 Plymouth Arg 32 2
1999–2000 Plymouth Arg 44 3 **76 5**
2000–01 Northampton T 31 0
2001–02 Northampton T 39 3
2002–03 Northampton T 39 0
2003–04 Northampton T 42 3 **151 6**
2004–05 Brentford 30 2 **30 2**
2005–06 Oxford U 35 1 **35 1**

HUGHES, Rob (M) 3 0
H: 5 8 W: 11 10 b.Sutton 6-9-80
Source: Farnborough T.
2005–06 Oxford U 3 0 **3 0**

MANSELL, Lee (D) 91 9
H: 5 10 W: 11 10 b.Gloucester 28-10-82
Source: Scholar.
2000–01 Luton T 18 5
2001–02 Luton T 11 1
2002–03 Luton T 1 0
2003–04 Luton T 16 2
2004–05 Luton T 1 0 **47 8**
2005–06 Oxford U 44 1 **44 1**

McCOY, Kyle (F) 0 0
H: 5 7 W: 10 07 b.Oxford 13-9-87
Source: Scholar.
2005–06 Oxford U 0 0

MORGAN, Danny (F) 6 1
H: 6 0 W: 14 02 b.Stepney 4-11-84
Source: Milton Keynes D Scholar.
2004–05 Oxford U 3 0
2005–06 Oxford U 3 1 **6 1**

ODUBADE, Yemi (F) 12 1
H: 5 7 W: 11 07 b.Lagos 4-7-84
Source: Eastbourne B.
2004–05 Yeovil T 4 0 **4 0**
From Eastbourne B.
2005–06 Oxford U 8 1 **8 1**

OLDFIELD, David (F) 551 73
H: 6 1 W: 13 02 b.Perth (Aus) 30-5-68
Source: Apprentice. *Honours:* England Under-21.
1986–87 Luton T 0 0
1987–88 Luton T 8 3
1988–89 Luton T 21 1
1988–89 Manchester C 11 3
1989–90 Manchester C 15 3 **26 6**
1989–90 Leicester C 20 5
1990–91 Leicester C 42 7
1991–92 Leicester C 41 4
1992–93 Leicester C 44 5
1993–94 Leicester C 27 4
1994–95 Leicester C 14 1 **188 26**
1994–95 *Millwall* 17 6 **17 6**
1995–96 Luton T 34 2
1996–97 Luton T 38 6
1997–98 Luton T 45 10 **146 22**
1998–99 Stoke C 46 6
1999–2000 Stoke C 19 1 **65 7**
1999–2000 Peterborough U 9 0
2000–01 Peterborough U 39 3
2001–02 Peterborough U 30 1 **78 4**
2002–03 Oxford U 28 2
2003–04 Oxford U 3 0
2004–05 Oxford U 0 0
2005–06 Oxford U 0 0 **31 2**

QUINN, Barry (M) 173 2
H: 6 1 W: 13 01 b.Dublin 9-5-79
Source: Trainee. *Honours:* Eire Under-21, 4 full caps.
1996–97 Coventry C 0 0
1997–98 Coventry C 0 0
1998–99 Coventry C 7 0
1999–2000 Coventry C 11 0
2000–01 Coventry C 25 0
2001–02 Coventry C 22 0
2002–03 Coventry C 18 0
2003–04 Coventry C 0 0 **83 0**
2003–04 *Rushden & D* 4 0 **4 0**
2003–04 *Oxford U* 6 0
2004–05 Oxford U 36 0
2005–06 Oxford U 44 2 **86 2**

ROACH, Neville (F) 52 4
H: 5 11 W: 12 00 b.Reading 29-9-78
Source: Trainee.
1996–97 Reading 3 1
1997–98 Reading 8 0
1998–99 Reading 5 0 **16 1**
1998–99 Southend U 8 1
1999–2000 Southend U 8 1
2000–01 Southend U 0 0 **16 2**
2000–01 Oldham Ath 1 0 **1 0**
2001–02 Torquay U 12 1
2002–03 Torquay U 0 0
2003–04 Torquay U 0 0
2004–05 Torquay U 0 0 **12 1**
From Eastleigh.
2005–06 Oxford U 7 0 **7 0**

ROBINSON, Matt (D) 319 5
H: 5 11 W: 11 05 b.Exeter 23-12-74
Source: Trainee.
1993–94 Southampton 0 0
1994–95 Southampton 1 0
1995–96 Southampton 5 0
1996–97 Southampton 7 0
1997–98 Southampton 1 0 **14 0**
1997–98 Portsmouth 15 0
1998–99 Portsmouth 29 1
1999–2000 Portsmouth 25 0 **69 1**
1999–2000 Reading 19 0
2000–01 Reading 32 0
2001–02 Reading 14 0 **65 0**
2002–03 Oxford U 42 1
2003–04 Oxford U 40 1
2004–05 Oxford U 45 2
2005–06 Oxford U 44 0 **171 4**

ROGET, Leo (D) 266 12
H: 6 1 W: 13 06 b.Ilford 1-8-77
Source: Trainee.
1995–96 Southend U 8 1
1996–97 Southend U 25 0
1997–98 Southend U 11 0
1998–99 Southend U 14 0
1999–2000 Southend U 36 2
2000–01 Southend U 26 4 **120 7**
2000–01 Stockport Co 9 0
2001–02 Stockport Co 22 1 **31 1**
2001–02 *Reading* 1 0 **1 0**
2002–03 Brentford 14 0
2003–04 Brentford 15 0 **29 0**
2003–04 Rushden & D 17 0 **17 0**
2004–05 Oxford U 35 2
2005–06 Oxford U 33 2 **68 4**

SABIN, Eric (F) 199 33
H: 6 1 W: 12 05 b.Sarcelles 22-1-75
Source: Ajaccio, Nimes.
2000–01 Wasquehal 28 3 **28 3**
2001–02 Swindon T 34 5
2002–03 Swindon T 39 4 **73 9**
2003–04 QPR 10 1 **10 1**
2003–04 *Boston U* 2 0 **2 0**
2003–04 Northampton T 11 5
2004–05 Northampton T 40 8
2005–06 Northampton T 6 0 **57 13**
2005–06 Oxford U 29 7 **29 7**

SILLS, Tim (F) 13 1
H: 6 1 W: 14 00 b.Romsey 10-9-79
Source: Camberley T, Basingstoke T, Kingstonian, Aldershot T.
2005–06 Oxford U 13 1 **13 1**

TARDIF, Chris (G) 65 0
H: 6 2 W: 13 02 b.Guernsey 19-9-79
Source: Trainee.
1998–99 Portsmouth 0 0
1999–2000 Portsmouth 0 0
2000–01 Portsmouth 4 0
2001–02 Portsmouth 1 0
2002–03 Portsmouth 0 0
2002–03 *Bournemouth* 9 0 **9 0**
2003–04 Portsmouth 0 0 **5 0**
2004–05 Oxford U 40 0
2005–06 Oxford U 11 0 **51 0**

TURLEY, Billy (G) 209 0
H: 6 3 W: 15 04 b.Wolverhampton 15-7-73
Source: Evesham U.
1995–96 Northampton T 2 0
1996–97 Northampton T 1 0
1997–98 Northampton T 0 0
1997–98 *Leyton Orient* 14 0 **14 0**
1998–99 Northampton T 25 0 **28 0**
2001–02 Rushden & D 43 0
2002–03 Rushden & D 44 0
2003–04 Rushden & D 25 0
2004–05 Rushden & D 22 0 **134 0**
2005–06 Oxford U 33 0 **33 0**

WEEDON, Ben (D) 2 0
H: 5 9 W: 11 00 b.Oxford 30-3-89
Source: Scholar.
2005–06 Oxford U 2 0 **2 0**

WILLMOTT, Chris (D) 202 5
H: 6 2 W: 13 08 b.Bedford 30-9-77
Source: Trainee.
1995–96 Luton T 0 0
1996–97 Luton T 0 0
1997–98 Luton T 0 0
1998–99 Luton T 14 0
1999–2000 Wimbledon 7 0
2000–01 Wimbledon 14 1
2001–02 Wimbledon 27 1
2002–03 Wimbledon 5 0 **53 2**
2002–03 *Luton T* 13 0 **27 0**
2003–04 Northampton T 36 1
2004–05 Northampton T 45 0 **81 1**
2005–06 Oxford U 41 2 **41 2**

WINTERS, Tom (M) 5 0
H: 5 9 W: 11 05 b.Banbury 11-12-85
Source: Scholar.
2003–04 Oxford U 1 0
2004–05 Oxford U 4 0
2005–06 Oxford U 0 0 **5 0**

PETERBOROUGH U (60)

ARBER, Mark (D) 275 23
H: 6 1 W: 11 09 b.Johannesburg 9-10-77
Source: Trainee.
1995–96 Tottenham H 0 0
1996–97 Tottenham H 0 0
1997–98 Tottenham H 0 0
1998–99 Tottenham H 0 0
1998–99 Barnet 35 2
1999–2000 Barnet 45 6
2000–01 Barnet 45 7
2001–02 Barnet 0 0 **125 15**
2002–03 Peterborough U 25 2
2003–04 Peterborough U 44 3
2004–05 Oldham Ath 14 1 **14 1**
2004–05 Peterborough U 21 0
2005–06 Peterborough U 46 2 **136 7**

BENJAMIN, Trevor (F) 286 61
H: 6 2 W: 13 07 b.Kettering 8-2-79
Source: Trainee. *Honours:* England Under-21, Jamaica 2 full caps.
1995–96 Cambridge U 5 0
1996–97 Cambridge U 7 1
1997–98 Cambridge U 25 4
1998–99 Cambridge U 42 10
1999–2000 Cambridge U 44 20 **123 35**
2000–01 Leicester C 21 1
2001–02 Leicester C 11 0
2001–02 *Crystal Palace* 6 1 **6 1**
2001–02 *Norwich C* 6 0 **6 0**
2001–02 *WBA* 3 1 **3 1**
2002–03 Leicester C 35 8
2003–04 Leicester C 4 0
2003–04 *Gillingham* 4 1 **4 1**
2003–04 *Rushden & D* 6 1 **6 1**
2003–04 *Brighton & HA* 10 5 **10 5**
2004–05 Leicester C 10 2 **81 11**
2004–05 *Northampton T* 5 2 **5 2**
2004–05 Coventry C 12 1 **12 1**
2005–06 Peterborough U 20 1 **20 1**
2005–06 *Watford* 2 0 **2 0**
2005–06 *Swindon T* 8 2 **8 2**

BOLLAND, Phil (D) 95 3
H: 6 4 W: 13 03 b.Liverpool 26-8-76
Source: Altrincham, Knowsley U, Trafford, Salford C, Altrincham, Southport.
2001–02 Oxford U 20 1 **20 1**
2001–02 Chester C 0 0
2002–03 Chester C 0 0
2003–04 Chester C 0 0
2004–05 Chester C 42 1
2005–06 Chester C 16 1 **58 2**
2005–06 Peterborough U 17 0 **17 0**

BOUCAUD, Andre (M) 39 2
H: 5 10 W: 11 02 b.Enfield 9-10-84
Source: Scholar. *Honours:* Trinidad & Tobago 6 full caps.
2001–02 Reading 0 0
2002–03 Reading 0 0
2002–03 *Peterborough U* 6 0
2003–04 Reading 0 0
2003–04 *Peterborough U* 8 1
2004–05 Peterborough U 22 1
2005–06 Peterborough U 3 0 **39 2**

CARDEN, Paul (M) 139 0
H: 5 9 W: 11 10 b.Liverpool 29-3-79
Source: Trainee.
1996–97 Blackpool 1 0
1997–98 Blackpool 0 0 **1 0**
1997–98 Rochdale 7 0
1998–99 Rochdale 25 0
1999–2000 Rochdale 13 0 **45 0**
1999–2000 Chester C 11 0
From Doncaster R.
2004–05 Chester C 40 0 **51 0**
2005–06 Peterborough U 42 0 **42 0**

CROW, Danny (F) 51 17
H: 5 10 W: 11 00 b.Great Yarmouth 26-1-86
Source: Scholar.
2004–05 Norwich C 3 0 **3 0**
2004–05 *Northampton T* 10 2 **10 2**
2005–06 Peterborough U 38 15 **38 15**

DAY, Jamie (M) **26 1**

H: 5 9 W: 10 07 b.Wycombe 7-5-86

Source: Scholar.

2003–04	Peterborough U	0	0		
2004–05	Peterborough U	1	0		
2005–06	Peterborough U	25	1	**26**	**1**

FARRELL, Dave (M) **408 51**

H: 5 11 W: 11 08 b.Birmingham 11-11-71

Source: Redditch U.

1992–93	Aston Villa	2	0		
1992–93	*Scunthorpe U*	5	1	**5**	**1**
1993–94	Aston Villa	4	0		
1994–95	Aston Villa	0	0		
1995–96	Aston Villa	0	0	**6**	**0**
1995–96	Wycombe W	33	7		
1996–97	Wycombe W	27	1	**60**	**8**
1997–98	Peterborough U	42	6		
1998–99	Peterborough U	37	4		
1999–2000	Peterborough U	35	3		
2000–01	Peterborough U	44	7		
2001–02	Peterborough U	38	6		
2002–03	Peterborough U	37	3		
2003–04	Peterborough U	44	5		
2004–05	Peterborough U	31	2		
2005–06	Peterborough U	29	6	**337**	**42**

FRY, Adam (M) **3 0**

H: 5 8 W: 10 07 b.Bedford 9-2-85

Source: Scholar.

2002–03	Peterborough U	0	0		
2003–04	Peterborough U	0	0		
2004–05	Peterborough U	3	0		
2005–06	Peterborough U	0	0	**3**	**0**

GAIN, Peter (M) **264 24**

H: 5 9 W: 11 07 b.Hammersmith 11-11-76

Source: Trainee.

1995–96	Tottenham H	0	0		
1996–97	Tottenham H	0	0		
1997–98	Tottenham H	0	0		
1998–99	Tottenham H	0	0		
1998–99	Lincoln C	4	0		
1999–2000	Lincoln C	32	2		
2000–01	Lincoln C	24	5		
2001–02	Lincoln C	42	2		
2002–03	Lincoln C	43	5		
2003–04	Lincoln C	42	7		
2004–05	Lincoln C	40	0	**227**	**21**
2005–06	Peterborough U	37	3	**37**	**3**

HARRISON, Lee (G) **275 0**

H: 6 2 W: 11 13 b.Billericay 12-9-71

Source: Trainee.

1990–91	Charlton Ath	0	0		
1991–92	Charlton Ath	0	0		
1991–92	*Fulham*	0	0		
1991–92	*Gillingham*	2	0	**2**	**0**
1992–93	Charlton Ath	0	0		
1992–93	*Fulham*	0	0		
1993–94	Fulham	0	0		
1994–95	Fulham	7	0		
1995–96	Fulham	5	0	**12**	**0**
1996–97	Barnet	21	0		
1997–98	Barnet	46	0		
1998–99	Barnet	43	0		
1999–2000	Barnet	43	0		
2000–01	Barnet	30	0		
2001–02	Barnet	0	0	**183**	**0**
2002–03	Peterborough U	12	0		
2002–03	Leyton Orient	6	0		
2003–04	Leyton Orient	20	0		
2004–05	Leyton Orient	34	0	**60**	**0**
2005–06	Peterborough U	6	0	**18**	**0**

HOLDEN, Dean (D) **156 14**

H: 6 1 W: 12 04 b.Salford 15-9-79

Source: Trainee. *Honours:* England Youth.

1997–98	Bolton W	0	0		
1998–99	Bolton W	0	0		
1999–2000	Bolton W	12	0		
2000–01	Bolton W	1	1		
2001–02	Bolton W	0	0	**13**	**1**
2001–02	*Oldham Ath*	23	2		
2002–03	Oldham Ath	6	2		
2003–04	Oldham Ath	39	4		
2004–05	Oldham Ath	40	2	**108**	**10**
2005–06	Peterborough U	35	3	**35**	**3**

HUKE, Shane (M) **11 0**

H: 5 11 W: 12 07 b.Reading 2-10-85

Source: Scholar.

2003–04	Peterborough U	0	0		
2004–05	Peterborough U	8	0		
2005–06	Peterborough U	3	0	**11**	**0**

KENNEDY, Peter (D) **238 23**

H: 5 10 W: 11 11 b.Lurgan 10-9-73

Source: Portadown. *Honours:* Northern Ireland B, 20 full caps.

1996–97	Notts Co	22	0	**22**	**0**
1997–98	Watford	34	11		
1998–99	Watford	46	6		
1999–2000	Watford	18	1		
2000–01	Watford	17	0	**115**	**18**
2001–02	Wigan Ath	31	0		
2002–03	Wigan Ath	22	1		
2003–04	Wigan Ath	12	1	**65**	**2**
2003–04	*Derby Co*	5	1	**5**	**1**
2004–05	Peterborough U	17	2		
2005–06	Peterborough U	14	0	**31**	**2**

LOGAN, Richard (F) **155 33**

H: 6 1 W: 12 05 b.Bury St Edmunds 4-1-82

Source: Trainee. *Honours:* England Youth.

1998–99	Ipswich T	2	0		
1999–2000	Ipswich T	1	0		
2000–01	Ipswich T	0	0		
2000–01	*Cambridge U*	5	1	**5**	**1**
2001–02	Ipswich T	0	0		
2001–02	*Torquay U*	16	4	**16**	**4**
2002–03	Ipswich T	0	0	**3**	**0**
2002–03	Boston U	27	10		
2003–04	Boston U	8	0	**35**	**10**
2003–04	Peterborough U	29	7		
2004–05	Peterborough U	26	4		
2004–05	*Shrewsbury T*	5	1	**5**	**1**
2005–06	Peterborough U	28	4	**83**	**15**
2005–06	*Lincoln C*	8	2	**8**	**2**

McSHANE, Luke (G) **0 0**

H: 6 1 W: 10 09 b.Peterborough 6-11-85

Source: Scholar.

2003–04	Peterborough U	0	0		
2004–05	Peterborough U	0	0		
2005–06	Peterborough U	0	0		

NEWTON, Adam (M) **178 9**

H: 5 10 W: 11 00 b.Ascot 4-12-80

Source: West Ham U Trainee. *Honours:* England Under-21. St Kitts & Nevis full caps.

1999–2000	West Ham U	2	0		
1999–2000	*Portsmouth*	3	0	**3**	**0**
2000–01	West Ham U	0	0		
2000–01	*Notts Co*	20	1	**20**	**1**
2001–02	West Ham U	0	0	**2**	**0**
2001–02	*Leyton Orient*	10	1	**10**	**1**
2002–03	Peterborough U	36	2		
2003–04	Peterborough U	37	2		
2004–05	Peterborough U	30	0		
2005–06	Peterborough U	40	3	**143**	**7**

OPARA, Lloyd (F) **24 2**

H: 6 1 W: 12 08 b.Enfield 6-1-84

Source: Scholar.

2001–02	Colchester U	1	0		
2002–03	Colchester U	5	0	**6**	**0**
2002–03	Cambridge U	2	0		
2003–04	Cambridge U	8	1	**10**	**1**
From Grays Ath.					
2004–05	Swindon T	0	0		
From Cheshunt.					
2005–06	Peterborough U	8	1	**8**	**1**

PLUMMER, Chris (D) **107 3**

H: 6 2 W: 13 08 b.Isleworth 12-10-76

Source: Trainee. *Honours:* England Youth, Under-21.

1994–95	QPR	0	0		
1995–96	QPR	1	0		
1996–97	QPR	5	0		
1997–98	QPR	0	0		
1998–99	QPR	10	0		
1999–2000	QPR	18	0		
2000–01	QPR	25	2		
2001–02	QPR	1	0		
2002–03	QPR	2	0		
2002–03	*Bristol R*	2	0	**2**	**0**
2003–04	QPR	0	0		
2004–05	QPR	0	0	**62**	**2**
2004–05	Peterborough U	21	0		
2005–06	Peterborough U	22	1	**43**	**1**

QUINN, James (M) **324 60**

H: 6 1 W: 12 10 b.Coventry 15-12-74

Source: Trainee. *Honours:* Northern Ireland Youth, Under-21, B, 46 full caps, 4 goals.

1992–93	Birmingham C	4	0	**4**	**0**
1993–94	Blackpool	14	2		
1993–94	*Stockport Co*	1	0	**1**	**0**
1994–95	Blackpool	41	9		
1995–96	Blackpool	44	9		
1996–97	Blackpool	38	13		
1997–98	Blackpool	14	4	**151**	**37**
1997–98	WBA	13	2		
1998–99	WBA	43	6		
1999–2000	WBA	37	0		
2000–01	WBA	14	1		
2001–02	WBA	7	0		
2001–02	*Notts Co*	6	3	**6**	**3**
2001–02	*Bristol R*	6	1	**6**	**1**
2002–03	WBA	0	0		
2003–04	WBA	0	0	**114**	**9**
2004–05	Sheffield W	15	2	**15**	**2**
2005–06	Peterborough U	24	7	**24**	**7**
2005–06	*Bristol C*	3	1	**3**	**1**

RYAN, Tim (D) **125 6**

H: 5 10 W: 11 00 b.Stockport 10-12-74

Source: Trainee.

1992–93	Scunthorpe U	1	0		
1993–94	Scunthorpe U	1	0		
1994–95	Scunthorpe U	0	0	**2**	**0**
From Buxton.					
1996–97	Doncaster R	28	0		
From Southport					
2003–04	Doncaster R	42	2		
2004–05	Doncaster R	39	4		
2005–06	Doncaster R	7	0	**116**	**6**
2005–06	Peterborough U	7	0	**7**	**0**

SEMPLE, Ryan (M) **41 3**

H: 5 11 W: 10 11 b.Belfast 4-7-85

Source: Scholar.

2002–03	Peterborough U	3	0		
2003–04	Peterborough U	2	0		
2004–05	Peterborough U	8	0		
2005–06	Peterborough U	28	3	**41**	**3**

ST LEDGER-HALL, Sean (D) **79 1**

H: 6 0 W: 11 09 b.Solihull 28-12-84

Source: Scholar.

2002–03	Peterborough U	1	0		
2003–04	Peterborough U	2	0		
2004–05	Peterborough U	33	0		
2005–06	Peterborough U	43	1	**79**	**1**

STAVROULAKIS, Nick (M) **0 0**

H: 5 8 W: 11 03 b.Sydney 30-4-85

2005–06	Peterborough U	0	0		

TYLER, Mark (G) **355 0**

H: 6 0 W: 12 09 b.Norwich 2-4-77

Source: Trainee. *Honours:* England Youth.

1994–95	Peterborough U	5	0		
1995–96	Peterborough U	0	0		
1996–97	Peterborough U	3	0		
1997–98	Peterborough U	46	0		
1998–99	Peterborough U	27	0		
1999–2000	Peterborough U	32	0		
2000–01	Peterborough U	40	0		
2001–02	Peterborough U	44	0		
2002–03	Peterborough U	29	0		
2003–04	Peterborough U	43	0		
2004–05	Peterborough U	46	0		
2005–06	Peterborough U	40	0	**355**	**0**

PLYMOUTH ARG (61)

ALJOFREE, Hasney (D) **161 7**

H: 6 0 W: 12 00 b.Manchester 11-7-78

Source: Trainee.

1996–97	Bolton W	0	0		
1997–98	Bolton W	2	0		
1998–98	Bolton W	4	0		
1999–2000	Bolton W	8	0	**14**	**0**
2000–01	Dundee U	26	2		
2001–02	Dundee U	27	2	**53**	**4**
2002–03	Plymouth Arg	19	1		
2003–04	Plymouth Arg	24	0		

2004–05	Plymouth Arg	12	1		
2004–05	*Sheffield W*	2	0	**2**	**0**
2005–06	Plymouth Arg	37	1	**92**	**3**

BARNESS, Anthony (D) **271** **4**

H: 5 10 W: 13 01 b.Lewisham 25-3-73

Source: Trainee.

1990–91	Charlton Ath	0	0		
1991–92	Charlton Ath	22	1		
1992–93	Charlton Ath	5	0		
1992–93	Chelsea	2	0		
1993–94	Chelsea	0	0		
1993–94	*Middlesbrough*	0	0		
1994–95	Chelsea	12	0		
1995–96	Chelsea	0	0	**14**	**0**
1995–96	*Southend U*	5	0	**5**	**0**
1996–97	Charlton Ath	45	2		
1997–98	Charlton Ath	29	1		
1998–99	Charlton Ath	3	0		
1999–2000	Charlton Ath	19	0	**123**	**4**
2000–01	Bolton W	20	0		
2001–02	Bolton W	25	0		
2002–03	Bolton W	25	0		
2003–04	Bolton W	15	0		
2004–05	Bolton W	8	0	**93**	**0**
2005–06	Plymouth Arg	36	0	**36**	**0**

BOND, Clay (M) **0** **0**

H: 5 10 W: 10 10 b.Torquay 15-12-87

Source: Scholar.

2005–06	Plymouth Arg	0	0		
2005–06	*Torquay U*	0	0		

BREVETT, Rufus (D) **473** **6**

H: 5 8 W: 11 06 b.Derby 24-9-69

Source: Trainee.

1987–88	Doncaster R	17	0		
1988–89	Doncaster R	23	0		
1989–90	Doncaster R	42	0		
1990–91	Doncaster R	27	3	**109**	**3**
1990–91	QPR	10	0		
1991–92	QPR	7	0		
1992–93	QPR	15	0		
1993–94	QPR	7	0		
1994–95	QPR	19	0		
1995–96	QPR	27	1		
1996–97	QPR	44	0		
1997–98	QPR	23	0	**152**	**1**
1997–98	Fulham	11	0		
1998–99	Fulham	45	1		
1999–2000	Fulham	23	0		
2000–01	Fulham	39	0		
2001–02	Fulham	35	0		
2002–03	Fulham	20	0	**173**	**1**
2002–03	West Ham U	13	0		
2003–04	West Ham U	2	0		
2004–05	West Ham U	10	1	**25**	**1**
2005–06	Plymouth Arg	13	0	**13**	**0**
2005–06	*Leicester C*	1	0	**1**	**0**

BUZSAKY, Akos (M) **49** **5**

H: 5 11 W: 11 09 b.Hungary 7-5-82

Source: MTK, Porto. *Honours:* Hungary Under-21, 3 full caps.

2004–05	Plymouth Arg	15	1		
2005–06	Plymouth Arg	34	4	**49**	**5**

CAPALDI, Tony (M) **110** **12**

H: 6 0 W: 11 08 b.Porsgrunn 12-8-81

Source: Trainee. *Honours:* Northern Ireland Youth, Under-21, 18 full caps.

1999–2000	Birmingham C	0	0		
2000–01	Birmingham C	0	0		
2001–02	Birmingham C	0	0		
2002–03	Birmingham C	0	0		
2002–03	Plymouth Arg	1	0		
2003–04	Plymouth Arg	33	7		
2004–05	Plymouth Arg	35	2		
2005–06	Plymouth Arg	41	3	**110**	**12**

CHADWICK, Nick (F) **87** **13**

H: 6 0 W: 12 08 b.Market Drayton 26-10-82

Source: Scholar.

1999–2000	Everton	0	0		
2000–01	Everton	0	0		
2001–02	Everton	9	3		
2002–03	Everton	1	0		
2002–03	*Derby Co*	6	0	**6**	**0**
2003–04	Everton	3	0		
2003–04	*Millwall*	15	4	**15**	**4**
2004–05	Everton	1	0	**14**	**3**
2004–05	Plymouth Arg	15	1		
2005–06	Plymouth Arg	37	5	**52**	**6**

CONNOLLY, Paul (D) **82** **0**

H: 6 0 W: 11 09 b.Liverpool 29-9-83

Source: Scholar.

2000–01	Plymouth Arg	1	0		
2001–02	Plymouth Arg	0	0		
2002–03	Plymouth Arg	2	0		
2003–04	Plymouth Arg	29	0		
2004–05	Plymouth Arg	19	0		
2005–06	Plymouth Arg	31	0	**82**	**0**

DEBBAGE, James (G) **0** **0**

H: 6 3 W: 12 09 b.Cramlington

Source: Scholar.

2005–06	Plymouth Arg	0	0		

DICKSON, Ryan (M) **3** **0**

H: 5 10 W: 11 05 b.Saltash 14-12-86

Source: Scholar.

2004–05	Plymouth Arg	3	0		
2005–06	Plymouth Arg	0	0	**3**	**0**

DJORDJIC, Bojan (M) **51** **1**

H: 5 10 W: 11 01 b.Belgrade 6-2-82

1998–99	Manchester U	0	0		
1999–2000	Manchester U	0	0		
2000–01	Manchester U	1	0		
2001–02	Manchester U	0	0		
2001–02	*Sheffield W*	5	0	**5**	**0**
2002–03	Manchester U	0	0		
2003–04	*Red St Belgrade*	19	0	**19**	**0**
2004–05	Manchester U	0	0	**1**	**0**
2004–05	Rangers	4	0	**4**	**0**
2005–06	Plymouth Arg	22	1	**22**	**1**

DOUMBE, Stephen (D) **114** **5**

H: 6 1 W: 12 05 b.Paris 28-10-79

Source: Paris St Germain. *Honours:* France Youth.

2001–02	Hibernian	0	0		
2002–03	Hibernian	12	0		
2003–04	Hibernian	33	2	**45**	**2**
2004–05	Plymouth Arg	26	2		
2005–06	Plymouth Arg	43	1	**69**	**3**

EVANS, Micky (F) **490** **86**

H: 6 1 W: 13 04 b.Plymouth 1-1-73

Source: Trainee. *Honours:* Eire 1 full cap.

1990–91	Plymouth Arg	4	0		
1991–92	Plymouth Arg	13	0		
1992–93	Plymouth Arg	23	1		
1992–93	*Blackburn R*	0	0		
1993–94	Plymouth Arg	22	9		
1994–95	Plymouth Arg	23	4		
1995–96	Plymouth Arg	45	12		
1996–97	Plymouth Arg	33	12		
1996–97	Southampton	12	4		
1997–98	Southampton	10	0	**22**	**4**
1997–98	WBA	10	1		
1998–99	WBA	20	2		
1999–2000	WBA	33	3		
2000–01	WBA	0	0	**63**	**6**
2000–01	Bristol R	21	4	**21**	**4**
2000–01	Plymouth Arg	10	4		
2001–02	Plymouth Arg	38	7		
2002–03	Plymouth Arg	42	4		
2003–04	Plymouth Arg	44	11		
2004–05	Plymouth Arg	42	4		
2005–06	Plymouth Arg	45	4	**384**	**72**

GUDJONSSON, Bjarni (M) **224** **29**

H: 5 9 W: 11 09 b.Akranes 26-2-79

Honours: Iceland Youth, Under-21, 17 full caps, 1 goal.

1995	IA Akranes	2	0		
1996	IA Akranes	17	13		
1997	IA Akranes	6	2	**25**	**15**
1997–98	Newcastle U	0	0		
1998–99	Newcastle U	0	0		
1999–2000	Genk	14	0	**14**	**0**
1999–2000	Stoke C	8	1		
2000–01	Stoke C	42	6		
2001–02	Stoke C	46	3		
2002–03	Stoke C	36	1	**132**	**11**
2003–04	Coventry C	18	3		
2004–05	Coventry C	10	0	**28**	**3**
2004–05	Plymouth Arg	15	0		
2005–06	Plymouth Arg	10	0	**25**	**0**

HODGES, Lee (M) **352** **49**

H: 6 0 W: 12 01 b.Epping 4-9-73

Source: Trainee.

1991–92	Tottenham H	0	0		
1992–93	Tottenham H	4	0		
1992–93	*Plymouth Arg*	7	2		
1993–94	Tottenham H	0	0	**4**	**0**
1993–94	*Wycombe W*	4	0	**4**	**0**
1994–95	Barnet	34	4		
1995–96	Barnet	40	17		
1996–97	Barnet	31	5	**105**	**26**
1997–98	Reading	24	6		
1998–99	Reading	1	0		
1999–2000	Reading	25	2		
2000–01	Reading	29	2		
2001–02	Reading	0	0	**79**	**10**
2001–02	Plymouth Arg	45	6		
2002–03	Plymouth Arg	39	2		
2003–04	Plymouth Arg	37	3		
2004–05	Plymouth Arg	19	0		
2005–06	Plymouth Arg	13	0	**160**	**13**

LARRIEU, Romain (G) **177** **0**

H: 6 4 W: 13 01 b.Mont-de-Marsan 31-8-76

Source: Montpellier, ASOA Valence.

2000–01	Plymouth Arg	15	0		
2001–02	Plymouth Arg	45	0		
2002–03	Plymouth Arg	43	0		
2003–04	Plymouth Arg	6	0		
2004–05	Plymouth Arg	23	0		
2005–06	Plymouth Arg	45	0	**177**	**0**

LASLEY, Keith (M) **134** **9**

H: 5 8 W: 10 07 b.Glasgow 21-9-79

2000–01	Motherwell	12	1		
2001–02	Motherwell	28	2		
2002–03	Motherwell	24	3		
2003–04	Motherwell	33	3	**97**	**9**
2004–05	Plymouth Arg	24	0		
2005–06	Plymouth Arg	5	0	**29**	**0**
2005–06	*Blackpool*	8	0	**8**	**0**

McCORMICK, Luke (G) **70** **0**

H: 6 0 W: 13 12 b.Coventry 15-8-83

Source: Scholar.

2000–01	Plymouth Arg	1	0		
2001–02	Plymouth Arg	0	0		
2002–03	Plymouth Arg	3	0		
2003–04	Plymouth Arg	40	0		
2004–05	Plymouth Arg	23	0		
2004–05	*Boston U*	2	0	**2**	**0**
2005–06	Plymouth Arg	1	0	**68**	**0**

MENDES, Nuno (D) **2** **0**

H: 5 11 W: 12 13 b.Guimaraes 7-4-78

Source: Guimaraes, Felgueiras, Chaves, leiria, Braga, Moreirense, Strasbourg, Santa Clara. *Honours:*

2005–06	Plymouth Arg	2	0	**2**	**0**

NALIS, Lilian (M) **337** **28**

H: 6 1 W: 11 00 b.Nogent sur Marne 29-9-71

1992–93	Auxerre	0	0		
1993–94	Caen	16	0		
1994–95	Caen	4	0	**20**	**0**
1995–96	Laval	42	4		
1996–97	Laval	39	8	**81**	**12**
1997–98	Guingamp	30	0	**30**	**0**
1998–99	Le Havre	27	3	**27**	**3**
1999–2000	Bastia	28	1		
2000–01	Bastia	28	1		
2001–02	Bastia	26	2	**82**	**4**
2002–03	Chievo	8	0	**8**	**0**
2003–04	Leicester C	20	1		
2004–05	Leicester C	39	5	**59**	**6**
2005–06	Sheffield U	4	0	**4**	**0**
2005–06	*Coventry C*	6	2	**6**	**2**
2005–06	Plymouth Arg	20	1	**20**	**1**

NORRIS, David (M) **164** **17**

H: 5 7 W: 11 06 b.Stamford 22-2-81

Source: Boston U.

1999–2000	Bolton W	0	0		
2000–01	Bolton W	0	0		
2001–02	Bolton W	0	0		
2001–02	*Hull C*	6	1	**6**	**1**
2002–03	Bolton W	0	0		
2002–03	Plymouth Arg	33	6		
2003–04	Plymouth Arg	45	5		

2004–05 Plymouth Arg 35 3
2005–06 Plymouth Arg 45 2 158 16

REID, Reuben (F) 1 0
H: 6 0 W: 12 02 b.Bristol 26-7-88
2005–06 Plymouth Arg 1 0 1 0

SAWYER, Gary (D) 0 0
b.Bideford 5-7-85
Source: Scholar.
2004–05 Plymouth Arg 0 0
2005–06 Plymouth Arg 0 0

SUMMERFIELD, Luke (M) 1 0
H: 6 0 W: 11 00 b.Ivybridge 6-12-87
Source: Scholar.
2004–05 Plymouth Arg 1 0
2005–06 Plymouth Arg 0 0 1 0

WEST, Taribo (D) 170 4
H: 6 0 W: 12 08 b.Port Harcourt 26-3-74
Source: Sharks, Julius Berger. *Honours:* Nigeria 13 full caps.
1993–94 Auxerre 1 0
1994–95 Auxerre 23 0
1995–96 Auxerre 22 0
1996–97 Auxerre 27 1 73 1
1997–98 Internazionale 23 1
1998–99 Internazionale 21 0 44 1
1999–2000 AC Milan 4 1 4 1
2000–01 Derby Co 18 0 18 0
2001–02 Kaiserslautern 10 0 10 0
2002–03 Partizan Belgrade 12 1
2003–04 Partizan Belgrade 5 0 17 1
From Al Arabi.
2005–06 Plymouth Arg 4 0 4 0

WOTTON, Paul (D) 364 49
H: 5 11 W: 12 00 b.Plymouth 17-8-77
Source: Trainee.
1994–95 Plymouth Arg 7 0
1995–96 Plymouth Arg 1 0
1996–97 Plymouth Arg 9 1
1997–98 Plymouth Arg 34 1
1998–99 Plymouth Arg 36 1
1999–2000 Plymouth Arg 23 0
2000–01 Plymouth Arg 42 4
2001–02 Plymouth Arg 46 5
2002–03 Plymouth Arg 43 8
2003–04 Plymouth Arg 38 9
2004–05 Plymouth Arg 40 12
2005–06 Plymouth Arg 45 8 364 49

ZEBROSKI, Chris (F) 4 0
H: 6 1 W: 11 08 b.Swindon 29-10-86
Source: Cirencester T, Scholar.
2005–06 Plymouth Arg 4 0 4 0

PORT VALE (62)

ABBEY, George (D) 138 1
H: 5 10 W: 12 04 b.Port Harcourt 20-10-78
Source: Sharks. *Honours:* Nigeria 16 full caps.
1999–2000 Macclesfield T 18 0
2000–01 Macclesfield T 18 0
2001–02 Macclesfield T 17 0
2002–03 Macclesfield T 22 1
2003–04 Macclesfield T 25 0
2004–05 Macclesfield T 0 0 100 1
2004–05 Port Vale 18 0
2005–06 Port Vale 20 0 38 0

ANYON, Joe (G) 0 0
H: 6 1 W: 12 11 b.Blackpool 29-12-86
Source: Scholar.
2005–06 Port Vale 0 0

BIRCHALL, Chris (M) 78 7
H: 5 7 W: 13 05 b.Stafford 5-5-84
Source: Scholar. *Honours:* Trinidad & Tobago 22 full caps, 3 goals.
2001–02 Port Vale 1 0
2002–03 Port Vale 2 0
2003–04 Port Vale 10 0
2004–05 Port Vale 34 6
2005–06 Port Vale 31 1 78 7

BRAIN, Jonny (G) 59 0
H: 6 3 W: 13 05 b.Carlisle 11-2-83
Source: Newcastle U Trainee.
2003–04 Port Vale 32 0
2004–05 Port Vale 27 0
2005–06 Port Vale 0 0 59 0

BRISCOE, Louie (F) 4 0
H: 6 0 W: 12 00 b.Burton 2-4-88
Source: Scholar.
2005–06 Port Vale 4 0 4 0

CARDLE, Joe (M) 6 0
H: 5 8 W: 9 05 b.Blackpool 27-2-87
Source: Scholar.
2005–06 Port Vale 6 0 6 0

CONSTANTINE, Leon (F) 156 45
H: 6 2 W: 12 00 b.Hackney 24-2-78
Source: Edgware T.
2000–01 Millwall 1 0
2001–02 Millwall 0 0 1 0
2001–02 *Leyton Orient* 10 3 10 3
2001–02 *Partick T* 2 0 2 0
2002–03 Brentford 17 0 17 0
2003–04 Southend U 43 21 43 21
2004–05 Peterborough U 11 1 11 1
2004–05 Torquay U 27 9
2005–06 Torquay U 15 1 42 10
2005–06 Port Vale 30 10 30 10

CUMMINS, Michael (M) 255 31
H: 6 0 W: 13 06 b.Dublin 1-6-78
Source: Trainee. *Honours:* Eire Youth, Under-21.
1995–96 Middlesbrough 0 0
1996–97 Middlesbrough 0 0
1997–98 Middlesbrough 0 0
1998–99 Middlesbrough 1 0
1999–2000 Middlesbrough 1 0 2 0
1999–2000 Port Vale 12 1
2000–01 Port Vale 45 2
2001–02 Port Vale 46 8
2002–03 Port Vale 30 4
2003–04 Port Vale 42 4
2004–05 Port Vale 39 2
2005–06 Port Vale 39 10 253 31

DINNING, Tony (M) 398 51
H: 6 0 W: 13 05 b.Wallsend 12-4-75
Source: Trainee.
1993–94 Newcastle U 0 0
1994–95 Stockport Co 40 1
1995–96 Stockport Co 10 1
1996–97 Stockport Co 20 2
1997–98 Stockport Co 30 4
1998–99 Stockport Co 41 5
1999–2000 Stockport Co 44 12
2000–01 Stockport Co 6 0 191 25
2000–01 Wolverhampton W 31 6
2001–02 Wolverhampton W 4 0 35 6
2001–02 Wigan Ath 33 5
2001–02 *Stoke C* 5 0 5 0
2002–03 Wigan Ath 38 7
2003–04 Wigan Ath 13 0
2003–04 *Walsall* 5 0 5 0
2003–04 *Blackpool* 10 3 10 3
2004–05 Wigan Ath 0 0 84 12
2004–05 *Ipswich T* 7 0 7 0
2004–05 *Bristol C* 19 0 19 0
2004–05 *Port Vale* 7 3
2005–06 Port Vale 35 2 42 5

DOHERTY, Sean (M) 7 0
H: 5 8 W: 10 08 b.Basingstoke 10-5-85
Source: Scholar. *Honours:* England Youth, Under-20.
2001–02 Fulham 0 0
2002–03 Fulham 0 0
2003–04 Fulham 0 0
2003–04 *Blackpool* 1 0 1 0
2004–05 Fulham 0 0
2005–06 Port Vale 6 0 6 0
To Den Haag January 2006

GOODLAD, Mark (G) 190 0
H: 6 1 W: 14 05 b.Barnsley 9-9-79
Source: Trainee.
1996–97 Nottingham F 0 0
1997–98 Nottingham F 0 0
1998–99 Nottingham F 0 0
1998–99 *Scarborough* 3 0 3 0
1999–2000 Nottingham F 0 0
1999–2000 Port Vale 1 0
2000–01 Port Vale 40 0
2001–02 Port Vale 43 0
2002–03 Port Vale 37 0
2003–04 Port Vale 0 0
2004–05 Port Vale 20 0
2005–06 Port Vale 46 0 187 0

HOLMES, Daniel (M) 0 0
H: 6 0 W: 12 00 b.Burton 17-11-86
Source: Scholar.
2005–06 Port Vale 0 0

HULBERT, Robin (M) 100 0
H: 5 9 W: 12 02 b.Plymouth 14-3-80
Source: Trainee. *Honours:* England Youth.
1997–98 Swindon T 1 0
1997–98 *Newcastle U* 0 0
1998–99 Swindon T 16 0
1999–2000 Swindon T 12 0 29 0
1999–2000 Bristol C 2 0
2000–01 Bristol C 19 0
2001–02 Bristol C 11 0
2002–03 Bristol C 7 0
2002–03 *Shrewsbury T* 7 0 7 0
2003–04 Bristol C 0 0 39 0
2004–05 Port Vale 24 0
2005–06 Port Vale 1 0 25 0

HUSBANDS, Michael (F) 39 4
H: 5 8 W: 10 10 b.Birmingham 13-11-83
Source: Scholar.
2001–02 Aston Villa 0 0
2002–03 Aston Villa 0 0
2003–04 Southend U 9 0
2004–05 Southend U 2 0 11 0
2005–06 Bristol R 0 0
2005–06 Walsall 4 0 4 0
From Rushall Olympic.
2005–06 Port Vale 24 4 24 4

INNES, Mark (M) 177 3
H: 5 9 W: 12 10 b.Bellshill 27-9-78
Source: Trainee.
1995–96 Oldham Ath 0 0
1996–97 Oldham Ath 0 0
1997–98 Oldham Ath 4 0
1998–99 Oldham Ath 13 1
1999–2000 Oldham Ath 21 0
2000–01 Oldham Ath 30 0
2001–02 Oldham Ath 5 0 73 1
2001–02 Chesterfield 23 2
2002–03 Chesterfield 10 0
2003–04 Chesterfield 22 0
2004–05 Chesterfield 21 0 76 2
2004–05 Port Vale 5 0
2005–06 Port Vale 23 0 28 0

JAMES, Craig (D) 84 2
H: 6 0 W: 13 00 b.Middlesbrough 15-11-82
Source: Scholar.
2000–01 Sunderland 0 0
2001–02 Sunderland 0 0
2002–03 Sunderland 0 0
2003–04 Sunderland 1 0 1 0
2003–04 *Darlington* 10 1 10 1
2003–04 Port Vale 8 0
2004–05 Port Vale 30 1
2005–06 Port Vale 35 0 73 1

LOWNDES, Nathan (F) 194 33
H: 6 0 W: 11 10 b.Salford 2-6-77
Source: Trainee.
1994–95 Leeds U 0 0
1995–96 Leeds U 0 0
1995–96 Watford 0 0
1996–97 Watford 3 0
1997–98 Watford 4 0 7 0
1998–99 St Johnstone 29 2
1999–2000 St Johnstone 25 10
2000–01 St Johnstone 10 2 64 14
2001–02 Livingston 21 3 21 3
2001–02 *Rotherham U* 2 0 2 0
2002–03 Plymouth Arg 16 2
2003–04 Plymouth Arg 33 8
2004–05 Plymouth Arg 4 0 53 10
2004–05 Port Vale 12 1
2005–06 Port Vale 35 5 47 6

MATTHEWS, Lee (F) 109 20
H: 6 2 W: 14 02 b.Middlesbrough 16-1-79
Source: Trainee. *Honours:* England Youth.
1995–96 Leeds U 0 0
1996–97 Leeds U 0 0
1997–98 Leeds U 3 0
1998–99 Leeds U 0 0
1998–99 *Notts Co* 5 0 5 0

Season	Club	App	Gls	Tot App	Tot Gls
1999–2000	Leeds U	0	0		
1999–2000	*Gillingham*	5	0	**5**	**0**
2000–01	Leeds U	0	0	**3**	**0**
2000–01	Bristol C	6	3		
2001–02	Bristol C	22	3		
2002–03	Bristol C	7	1		
2003–04	Bristol C	8	2	**43**	**9**
2003–04	*Darlington*	6	1	**6**	**1**
2003–04	*Bristol R*	9	0	**9**	**0**
2003–04	*Yeovil T*	4	0	**4**	**0**
2004–05	Port Vale	31	10		
2005–06	Port Vale	3	0	**34**	**10**

McGREGOR, Mark (D) 371 13
H: 5 11 W: 11 05 b.Chester 16-2-77
Source: Trainee.

Season	Club	App	Gls	Tot App	Tot Gls
1994–95	Wrexham	1	0		
1995–96	Wrexham	32	1		
1996–97	Wrexham	38	1		
1997–98	Wrexham	42	2		
1998–99	Wrexham	43	1		
1999–2000	Wrexham	45	1		
2000–01	Wrexham	43	5		
2001–02	Wrexham	0	0	**244**	**11**
2001–02	Burnley	1	0		
2002–03	Burnley	30	1		
2003–04	Burnley	23	1	**54**	**2**
2004–05	Blackpool	38	0		
2005–06	Blackpool	21	0	**59**	**0**
2005–06	Port Vale	14	0	**14**	**0**

PILKINGTON, George (D) 140 3
H: 5 11 W: 12 05 b.Rugeley 7-11-81
Source: Trainee. *Honours:* England Youth.

Season	Club	App	Gls	Tot App	Tot Gls
1998–99	Everton	0	0		
1999–2000	Everton	0	0		
2000–01	Everton	0	0		
2001–02	Everton	0	0		
2002–03	Everton	0	0		
2002–03	*Exeter C*	7	0	**7**	**0**
2003–04	Port Vale	44	1		
2004–05	Port Vale	43	0		
2005–06	Port Vale	46	2	**133**	**3**

PORTER, Andy (F) 403 23
H: 5 9 W: 12 03 b.Holmes Chapel 17-9-68
Source: Trainee.

Season	Club	App	Gls	Tot App	Tot Gls
1986–87	Port Vale	1	0		
1987–88	Port Vale	6	0		
1988–89	Port Vale	14	1		
1989–90	Port Vale	36	1		
1990–91	Port Vale	40	0		
1991–92	Port Vale	32	1		
1992–93	Port Vale	17	1		
1993–94	Port Vale	37	0		
1994–95	Port Vale	44	3		
1995–96	Port Vale	45	10		
1996–97	Port Vale	44	4		
1997–98	Port Vale	41	1		
1998–99	Wigan Ath	16	1		
1999–2000	Wigan Ath	5	0	**21**	**1**
1999–2000	*Mansfield T*	5	0	**5**	**0**
1999–2000	*Chester C*	16	0	**16**	**0**
Fr Northwh,Kidsgrove					
2004–05	Port Vale	2	0		
2005–06	Port Vale	2	0	**361**	**22**

PROSSER, Luke (M) 0 0
H: 6 3 W: 10 05 b.Hertfordshire 28-5-88
Source: Scholar.

Season	Club	App	Gls	Tot App	Tot Gls
2005–06	Port Vale	0	0		

ROWLAND, Stephen (D) 121 1
H: 5 10 W: 12 06 b.Wrexham 2-11-81
Source: Scholar.

Season	Club	App	Gls	Tot App	Tot Gls
2001–02	Port Vale	25	1		
2002–03	Port Vale	25	0		
2003–04	Port Vale	29	0		
2004–05	Port Vale	24	0		
2005–06	Port Vale	18	0	**121**	**1**

SAM, Hector (F) 154 35
H: 5 10 W: 12 07 b.Mount Hope 25-2-78
Source: San Juan Jabloteh. *Honours:* Trinidad & Tobago 20 full caps, 2 goals.

Season	Club	App	Gls	Tot App	Tot Gls
2000–01	Wrexham	20	6		
2001–02	Wrexham	29	5		
2002–03	Wrexham	26	5		
2003–04	Wrexham	37	10		
2004–05	Wrexham	38	9	**150**	**35**
2005–06	Port Vale	4	0	**4**	**0**

SMITH, Jeff (M) 81 4
H: 5 11 W: 11 10 b.Middlesbrough 28-6-80
Source: Trainee.

Season	Club	App	Gls	Tot App	Tot Gls
1998–99	Hartlepool U	3	0		
1999–2000	Hartlepool U	0	0	**3**	**0**
From Bishop Auckland					
2000–01	Bolton W	1	0		
2001–02	*Macclesfield T*	8	2	**8**	**2**
2001–02	Bolton W	1	0		
2002–03	Bolton W	0	0		
2003–04	Bolton W	0	0	**2**	**0**
2003–04	*Scunthorpe U*	1	0	**1**	**0**
2003–04	*Rochdale*	1	0	**1**	**0**
2003–04	Preston NE	5	0	**5**	**0**
2004–05	Port Vale	34	1		
2005–06	Port Vale	27	1	**61**	**2**

SONNER, Danny (M) 270 16
H: 6 0 W: 12 03 b.Wigan 9-1-72
Source: Wigan Ath. *Honours:* Northern Ireland B, 13 full caps.

Season	Club	App	Gls	Tot App	Tot Gls
1990–91	Burnley	2	0		
1991–92	Burnley	3	0		
1992–93	Burnley	1	0	**6**	**0**
1992–93	*Bury*	5	3	**5**	**3**
From Erzgebirge Aue					
1996–97	Ipswich T	29	2		
1997–98	Ipswich T	23	1		
1998–99	Ipswich T	4	0	**56**	**3**
1998–99	Sheffield W	26	3		
1999–2000	Sheffield W	27	0	**53**	**3**
2000–01	Birmingham C	26	1		
2001–02	Birmingham C	15	1	**41**	**2**
2002–03	Walsall	24	4	**24**	**4**
2003–04	Nottingham F	28	0		
2004–05	Nottingham F	0	0	**28**	**0**
2004–05	Peterborough U	15	0	**15**	**0**
2004–05	*Port Vale*	13	0		
2005–06	Port Vale	29	1	**42**	**1**

WALSH, Michael (D) 258 5
H: 5 11 W: 13 11 b.Rotherham 5-8-77
Source: Trainee.

Season	Club	App	Gls	Tot App	Tot Gls
1994–95	Scunthorpe U	3	0		
1995–96	Scunthorpe U	25	0		
1996–97	Scunthorpe U	36	0		
1997–98	Scunthorpe U	39	1	**103**	**1**
1998–99	Port Vale	19	1		
1999–2000	Port Vale	12	1		
2000–01	Port Vale	39	1		
2001–02	Port Vale	28	0		
2002–03	Port Vale	17	1		
2003–04	Port Vale	13	0		
2004–05	Port Vale	23	0		
2005–06	Port Vale	4	0	**155**	**4**

PORTSMOUTH (63)

ASHDOWN, Jamie (G) 67 0
H: 6 1 W: 13 05 b.Reading 30-11-80
Source: Scholar.

Season	Club	App	Gls	Tot App	Tot Gls
1999–2000	Reading	0	0		
2000–01	Reading	1	0		
2001–02	Reading	1	0		
2001–02	*Arsenal*	0	0		
2002–03	Reading	1	0		
2002–03	*Bournemouth*	2	0	**2**	**0**
2003–04	Reading	10	0	**13**	**0**
2003–04	*Rushden & D*	19	0	**19**	**0**
2004–05	Portsmouth	16	0		
2005–06	Portsmouth	17	0	**33**	**0**

CHALKIAS, Kostas (G) 161 0
H: 6 6 W: 15 03 b.Larisa 30-5-74
Honours: Greece 5 full caps.

Season	Club	App	Gls	Tot App	Tot Gls
1995–96	Panathinaikos	0	0		
1996–97	Apollon	29	0		
1997–98	Apollon	30	0		
1998–99	Panathinaikos	0	0		
1998–99	Apollon	16	0	**75**	**0**
1999–2000	Panathinaikos	6	0		
2000–01	Panathinaikos	4	0		
2001–02	Iraklis	25	0		
2002–03	Iraklis	25	0	**50**	**0**
2003–04	Panathinaikos	11	0		
2004–05	Panathinaikos	10	0	**31**	**0**
2004–05	Portsmouth	5	0		
2005–06	Portsmouth	0	0	**5**	**0**

CISSE, Aliou (M) 125 2
H: 5 9 W: 12 02 b.Zinguichor 24-3-76
Honours: Senegal 23 full caps, 1 goal.

Season	Club	App	Gls	Tot App	Tot Gls
1994–95	Lille	6	0		
1995–96	Lille	0	0		
1996–97	Lille	0	0	**6**	**0**
From Sedan					
1998–99	Paris St Germain	8	0		
1999–2000	Paris St Germain	25	1		
2000–01	Paris St Germain	10	0	**43**	**1**
2001–02	Montpellier	17	1	**17**	**1**
2002–03	Birmingham C	21	0		
2003–04	Birmingham C	15	0	**36**	**0**
2004–05	Portsmouth	20	0		
2005–06	Portsmouth	3	0	**23**	**0**

D'ALESSANDRO, Andres (M) 144 28
H: 5 9 W: 10 08 b.Buenos Aires 15-4-81
Honours: Argentina Youth, Under-23.

Season	Club	App	Gls	Tot App	Tot Gls
1999–2000	River Plate	1	0		
2000–01	River Plate	4	0		
2001–02	River Plate	36	9		
2002–03	River Plate	29	10	**70**	**19**
2003–04	Wolfsburg	29	3		
2004–05	Wolfsburg	19	3		
2005–06	Wolfsburg	13	2	**61**	**8**
2005–06	Portsmouth	13	1	**13**	**1**

DARIO SILVA, Dobray (F) 339 108
H: 5 10 W: 11 07 b.Treinta y Tres 2-11-72
Honours: Uruguay 49 full caps, 14 goals.

Season	Club	App	Gls	Tot App	Tot Gls
1992	Defensor	18	4	**18**	**4**
1993	Penarol	20	9		
1994	Penarol	24	18		
1995	Penarol	12	8	**56**	**35**
1995–96	Cagliari	33	3		
1996–97	Cagliari	29	4		
1997–98	Cagliari	27	13		
1998–99	Cagliari	0	0	**89**	**20**
1998–99	Espanyol	15	3	**15**	**3**
1999–2000	Malaga	23	4		
2000–01	Malaga	26	12		
2001–02	Malaga	23	9		
2002–03	Malaga	28	10	**100**	**35**
2003–04	Sevilla	27	7		
2004–05	Sevilla	21	2	**48**	**9**
2005–06	Portsmouth	13	2	**13**	**2**

DAVIS, Sean (M) 187 15
H: 5 10 W: 12 00 b.Clapham 20-9-79
Source: Trainee. *Honours:* England Under-21.

Season	Club	App	Gls	Tot App	Tot Gls
1996–97	Fulham	1	0		
1997–98	Fulham	0	0		
1998–99	Fulham	6	0		
1999–2000	Fulham	26	0		
2000–01	Fulham	40	6		
2001–02	Fulham	30	0		
2002–03	Fulham	28	3		
2003–04	Fulham	24	5	**155**	**14**
2004–05	Tottenham H	15	0		
2005–06	Tottenham H	0	0	**15**	**0**
2005–06	Portsmouth	17	1	**17**	**1**

DUFFY, Richard (D) 72 2
H: 5 9 W: 10 03 b.Swansea 30-8-85
Source: Scholar. *Honours:* Wales Youth, Under-21, 6 full caps.

Season	Club	App	Gls	Tot App	Tot Gls
2002–03	Swansea C	0	0		
2003–04	Swansea C	18	1	**18**	**1**
2003–04	Portsmouth	1	0		
2004–05	Portsmouth	0	0		
2004–05	*Burnley*	7	1	**7**	**1**
2004–05	*Coventry C*	14	0		
2005–06	Portsmouth	0	0	**1**	**0**
2005–06	*Coventry C*	32	0	**46**	**0**

FORDYCE, Daryl (M) 3 0
H: 6 0 W: 11 08 b.Belfast 2-1-87
Source: Scholar. *Honours:* Northern Ireland Youth.

Season	Club	App	Gls	Tot App	Tot Gls
2005–06	Portsmouth	0	0		
2005–06	*Bournemouth*	3	0	**3**	**0**

GRIFFIN, Andy (D) 177 4
H: 5 9 W: 10 10 b.Billinge 7-3-79
Source: Trainee. *Honours:* England Youth, Under-21.

Season	Club	App	Gls	Tot App	Tot Gls
1996–97	Stoke C	34	1		
1997–98	Stoke C	23	1	**57**	**2**
1997–98	Newcastle U	4	0		

1998–99	Newcastle U	14	0		
1999–2000	Newcastle U	3	1		
2000–01	Newcastle U	19	0		
2001–02	Newcastle U	4	0		
2002–03	Newcastle U	27	1		
2003–04	Newcastle U	5	0	**76**	**2**
2004–05	Portsmouth	22	0		
2005–06	Portsmouth	22	0	**44**	**0**

GUATELLI, Andrea (G) **4** **0**
H: 6 0 W: 12 00 b.Parma 5-5-84
Source: Parma. *Honours:* Italy Youth.

2004–05	Portsmouth	0	0		
2005–06	Portsmouth	0	0		
2005–06	*Oxford U*	4	0	**4**	**0**

HARRIS, Scott (M) **0** **0**
b.Worthing 24-7-85
Source: Scholar.

2004–05	Portsmouth	0	0		
2005–06	Portsmouth	0	0		

HORSTED, Liam (M) **4** **0**
H: 6 1 W: 12 06 b.Portsmouth 28-10-85
Source: Scholar.

2004–05	Portsmouth	0	0		
2005–06	Portsmouth	0	0		
2005–06	*Oxford U*	4	0	**4**	**0**

HUGHES, Richard (M) **202** **15**
H: 6 0 W: 13 03 b.Glasgow 25-6-79
Source: Atalanta. *Honours:* Scotland Youth, Under-21, 5 full caps.

1997–98	Arsenal	0	0		
1998–99	Bournemouth	44	2		
1999–2000	Bournemouth	21	2		
2000–01	Bournemouth	44	8		
2001–02	Bournemouth	22	2	**131**	**14**
2002–03	Portsmouth	6	0		
2002–03	*Grimsby T*	12	1	**12**	**1**
2003–04	Portsmouth	11	0		
2004–05	Portsmouth	16	0		
2005–06	Portsmouth	26	0	**59**	**0**

KARADAS, Azar (F) **127** **26**
H: 6 2 W: 13 07 b.Nordfjordeid 9-8-81
Honours: Norway Under-21, 8 full caps, 1 goal.

1999	Brann	6	0		
2000	Brann	21	7		
2001	Brann	23	5	**50**	**12**
2002	Rosenborg	23	5		
2003	Rosenborg	22	5		
2004	Rosenborg	15	3	**60**	**13**
2004–05	Benfica	0	0		
2005–06	Portsmouth	17	1	**17**	**1**

KEENE, James (F) **24** **3**
H: 5 11 W: 11 08 b.Wells 26-12-85
Source: Portsmouth Scholar.

2004–05	*Kidderminster H*	5	0	**5**	**0**
2004–05	Portsmouth	2	0		
2005–06	Portsmouth	0	0	**2**	**0**
2005–06	*Bournemouth*	11	2	**11**	**2**
2005–06	*Boston U*	6	1	**6**	**1**

KIELY, Dean (G) **584** **0**
H: 6 1 W: 13 10 b.Salford 10-10-70
Source: WBA School. *Honours:* England Schools, FA Schools, Youth, Eire 8 full caps.

1987–88	Coventry C	0	0		
1988–89	Coventry C	0	0		
1989–90	Coventry C	0	0		
1989–90	*Ipswich T*	0	0		
1989–90	*York C*	0	0		
1990–91	York C	17	0		
1991–92	York C	21	0		
1992–93	York C	40	0		
1993–94	York C	46	0		
1994–95	York C	46	0		
1995–96	York C	40	0	**210**	**0**
1996–97	Bury	46	0		
1997–98	Bury	46	0		
1998–99	Bury	45	0	**137**	**0**
1999–2000	Charlton Ath	45	0		
2000–01	Charlton Ath	25	0		
2001–02	Charlton Ath	38	0		
2002–03	Charlton Ath	38	0		
2003–04	Charlton Ath	37	0		
2004–05	Charlton Ath	36	0		
2005–06	Charlton Ath	3	0	**222**	**0**
2005–06	Portsmouth	15	0	**15**	**0**

KOROMAN, Ognjen (D) **89** **12**
H: 5 9 W: 11 00 b.Sarajevo 19-9-78
Honours: Serbia & Montenegro 27 full caps, 1 goal.

2002	Dynamo Moscow	24	6	**24**	**6**
2003	Kryliya	6	1		
2004	Kryliya	24	2		
2005	Kryliya	26	1	**56**	**4**
2005	Terek Grozny	6	1	**6**	**1**
2005–06	Portsmouth	3	1	**3**	**1**

LUA-LUA, Lomano (F) **185** **37**
H: 5 8 W: 12 02 b.Kinshasa 28-12-80
Honours: DR Congo 6 full caps.

1998–99	Colchester U	13	1		
1999–2000	Colchester U	41	12		
2000–01	Colchester U	7	2	**61**	**15**
2000–01	Newcastle U	21	0		
2001–02	Newcastle U	20	3		
2002–03	Newcastle U	11	2		
2003–04	Newcastle U	7	0	**59**	**5**
2003–04	*Portsmouth*	15	4		
2004–05	Portsmouth	25	6		
2005–06	Portsmouth	25	7	**65**	**17**

MBESUMA, Collins (F) **4** **0**
H: 6 0 W: 12 04 b.Luanshya 3-2-84
Source: Kaizer Chiefs. *Honours:* Zambia full caps.

2005–06	Portsmouth	4	0	**4**	**0**

MORNAR, Ivica (F) **253** **67**
H: 6 0 W: 12 04 b.Split 12-1-74
Honours: Croatia 20 full caps, 1 goal.

1992–93	Hajduk Split	21	7		
1993–94	Hajduk Split	27	8		
1994–95	Hajduk Split	9	3		
1995–96	Hajduk Split	1	0	**58**	**18**
1995–96	Eintracht Frankfurt	19	1	**19**	**1**
1996–97	Sevilla	11	2	**11**	**2**
1997–98	Ourense	28	8	**28**	**8**
1998–99	Standard Liege	15	3		
1999–2000	Standard Liege	24	8		
2000–01	Standard Liege	30	12	**69**	**23**
2001–02	Anderlecht	23	8		
2002–03	Anderlecht	20	6	**43**	**14**
2003–04	Portsmouth	8	1		
2004–05	*Rennes*	15	0	**15**	**0**
2005–06	Portsmouth	2	0	**10**	**1**

MWARUWARI, Benjamin (F) **158** **41**
H: 6 2 W: 12 03 b.Harare 13-8-78
Honours: Zimbabwe 20 full caps, 7 goals.

1999–2000	Jomo Cosmos	15	7		
2000–01	Jomo Cosmos	30	13	**45**	**20**
2001–02	Grasshoppers	25	1	**25**	**1**
2002–03	Auxerre	27	7		
2003–04	Auxerre	3	0		
2004–05	Auxerre	31	11		
2005–06	Auxerre	11	1	**72**	**19**
2005–06	Portsmouth	16	1	**16**	**1**

O'BRIEN, Andy (D) **282** **9**
H: 6 2 W: 11 13 b.Harrogate 29-6-79
Source: Trainee. *Honours:* England Youth, Under-21, Eire Under-21, 23 full caps, 1 goal.

1996–97	Bradford C	22	2		
1997–98	Bradford C	26	0		
1998–99	Bradford C	31	0		
1999–2000	Bradford C	36	1		
2000–01	Bradford C	18	0	**133**	**3**
2000–01	Newcastle U	9	1		
2001–02	Newcastle U	34	2		
2002–03	Newcastle U	26	0		
2003–04	Newcastle U	28	1		
2004–05	Newcastle U	23	2	**120**	**6**
2005–06	Portsmouth	29	0	**29**	**0**

O'NEIL, Gary (M) **154** **16**
H: 5 10 W: 11 00 b.Bromley 18-5-83
Source: Scholar. *Honours:* England Youth, Under-20, Under-21.

1999–2000	Portsmouth	1	0		
2000–01	Portsmouth	10	1		
2001–02	Portsmouth	33	1		
2002–03	Portsmouth	31	3		
2003–04	Portsmouth	3	2		
2003–04	*Walsall*	7	0	**7**	**0**
2004–05	Portsmouth	24	2		
2004–05	*Cardiff C*	9	1	**9**	**1**
2005–06	Portsmouth	36	6	**138**	**15**

OLISADEBE, Emanuel (F) **141** **44**
H: 6 0 W: 11 09 b.Waria 22-12-78
Honours: Poland 25 full caps, 11 goals.

1997–98	Polonia	13	1		
1998–99	Polonia	16	4		
1999–2000	Polonia	24	12		
2000–01	Polonia	13	3	**66**	**20**
2000–01	Panathinaikos	8	4		
2001–02	Panathinaikos	19	9		
2002–03	Panathinaikos	19	8		
2003–04	Panathinaikos	9	3		
2004–05	Panathinaikos	13	0		
2005–06	Panathinaikos	5	0	**73**	**24**
2005–06	Portsmouth	2	0	**2**	**0**

PAMAROT, Noe (D) **182** **9**
H: 5 11 W: 13 07 b.Fontenay-sous-Bois 14-4-79
Source: Martigues, Nice.

1997–98	Martigues	25	2		
1998–99	Martigues	0	0	**25**	**2**
1999–2000	Nice	0	0		
1999–2000	Portsmouth	2	0		
2000–01	Nice	23	0		
2001–02	Nice	33	3		
2002–03	Nice	33	1		
2003–04	Nice	33	2	**122**	**6**
2004–05	Tottenham H	23	1		
2005–06	Tottenham H	2	0	**25**	**1**
2005–06	Portsmouth	8	0	**10**	**0**

PEDRO MENDES (M) **184** **13**
H: 5 9 W: 12 04 b.Guimaraes 26-2-79
Honours: Portugal 2 full caps.

1998–99	Felgueiras	31	2	**31**	**2**
1999–2000	Guimaraes	13	1		
2000–01	Guimaraes	12	0		
2001–02	Guimaraes	26	0		
2002–03	Guimaraes	32	6	**83**	**7**
2003–04	Porto	26	0	**26**	**0**
2004–05	Tottenham H	24	1		
2005–06	Tottenham H	6	0	**30**	**1**
2005–06	Portsmouth	14	3	**14**	**3**

PERICARD, Vincent de Paul (F) **70** **15**
H: 6 1 W: 13 08 b.Efok 3-10-82
Source: Juventus.

2002–03	Portsmouth	32	9		
2003–04	Portsmouth	6	0		
2004–05	Portsmouth	0	0		
2005–06	Portsmouth	6	0	**44**	**9**
2005–06	*Sheffield U*	11	2	**11**	**2**
2005–06	*Plymouth Arg*	15	4	**15**	**4**

PRIMUS, Linvoy (D) **387** **11**
H: 5 10 W: 12 04 b.Forest Gate 14-9-73
Source: Trainee.

1992–93	Charlton Ath	4	0		
1993–94	Charlton Ath	0	0	**4**	**0**
1994–95	Barnet	39	0		
1995–96	Barnet	42	4		
1996–97	Barnet	46	3	**127**	**7**
1997–98	Reading	36	1		
1998–99	Reading	31	0		
1999–2000	Reading	28	0	**95**	**1**
2000–01	Portsmouth	23	0		
2001–02	Portsmouth	22	2		
2002–03	Portsmouth	40	0		
2003–04	Portsmouth	21	0		
2004–05	Portsmouth	35	1		
2005–06	Portsmouth	20	0	**161**	**3**

PRISKE, Brian (D) **252** **6**
H: 6 3 W: 12 02 b.Horsens 14-5-77
Honours: Denmark Under-21, 21 full caps.

1997–98	Fremad	33	2		
1998–99	Fremad	17	3	**50**	**5**
1998–99	Aalborg	18	0		
1999–2000	Aalborg	27	1		
2000–01	Aalborg	33	0		
2001–02	Aalborg	32	0		
2002–03	Aalborg	29	0	**139**	**1**
2003–04	Genk	33	0		
2004–05	Genk	0	0	**33**	**0**
2005–06	Portsmouth	30	0	**30**	**0**

RODIC, Alexsander (F) **63** **17**
H: 6 2 W: 12 11 b.Serbia 26-12-79
Honours: Slovenia 4 full caps, 1 goal.

2002–03	Gorica	16	1		
2003–04	Gorica	29	8		

2004–05	Gorica	14	8	**59**	**17**
2004–05	Portsmouth	4	0		
2005–06	Portsmouth	0	0	**4**	**0**

SILK, Gary (M) 36 0
H: 5 9 W: 13 07 b.Newport (IW) 13-9-84
Source: Scholar.

2003–04	Portsmouth	0	0		
2004–05	Portsmouth	0	0		
2004–05	*Wycombe W*	22	0	**22**	**0**
2005–06	Portsmouth	0	0		
2005–06	*Boston U*	14	0	**14**	**0**

SKOPELITIS, Giannis (M) 197 6
H: 5 11 W: 11 11 b.Athens 2-3-78

1996–97	Apollon	0	0		
1996–97	Aigaleo	11	1		
1997–98	Aigaleo	8	1		
1998–99	Aigaleo	21	0		
1999–2000	Aigaleo	23	2		
2000–01	Aigaleo	28	0		
2001–02	Aigaleo	23	0		
2002–03	Aigaleo	25	0		
2003–04	Aigaleo	25	2		
2004–05	Aigaleo	15	0	**179**	**6**
2004–05	Portsmouth	13	0		
2005–06	Portsmouth	5	0	**18**	**0**

SONGO'O, Frank (M) 2 0
H: 6 2 W: 12 06 b.Yaounde 14-5-87
Source: Barcelona. *Honours:* France Youth.

2005–06	Portsmouth	2	0	**2**	**0**

STEFANOVIC, Dejan (D) 298 20
H: 6 2 W: 13 01 b.Belgrade 28-10-74
Honours: Serbia-Montenegro 23 full caps.

1992–93	Red Star Belgrade	14	0		
1993–94	Red Star Belgrade	2	0		
1994–95	Red Star Belgrade	30	9	**46**	**9**
1995–96	Sheffield W	6	0		
1996–97	Sheffield W	29	2		
1997–98	Sheffield W	20	2		
1998–99	Sheffield W	11	0	**66**	**4**
1999–2000	Perugia	0	0		
1999–2000	OFK Belgrade	0	0		
1999–2000	Vitesse	14	0		
2000–01	Vitesse	27	1		
2001–02	Vitesse	25	3		
2002–03	Vitesse	28	0	**94**	**4**
2003–04	Portsmouth	32	3		
2004–05	Portsmouth	32	0		
2005–06	Portsmouth	28	0	**92**	**3**

TAYLOR, Matthew (D) 260 30
H: 5 11 W: 12 03 b.Oxford 27-11-81
Source: Trainee. *Honours:* England Under-21.

1998–99	Luton T	0	0		
1999–2000	Luton T	41	4		
2000–01	Luton T	45	1		
2001–02	Luton T	43	11	**129**	**16**
2002–03	Portsmouth	35	7		
2003–04	Portsmouth	30	0		
2004–05	Portsmouth	32	1		
2005–06	Portsmouth	34	6	**131**	**14**

TODOROV, Svetoslav (F) 170 71
H: 5 8 W: 11 11 b.Dobrich 30-8-78
Honours: Bulgaria Youth, 37 full caps, 4 goals.

1996–97	Dobrudzha	12	2	**12**	**2**
1997–98	Litets Lovech	19	9		
1998–99	Litets Lovech	11	2		
1999–2000	Litets Lovech	26	19		
2000–01	Litets Lovech	15	7	**71**	**37**
2000–01	West Ham U	8	1		
2001–02	West Ham U	6	0	**14**	**1**
2001–02	Portsmouth	3	1		
2002–03	Portsmouth	45	26		
2003–04	Portsmouth	1	0		
2004–05	Portsmouth	0	0		
2005–06	Portsmouth	24	4	**73**	**31**

VIAFARA, John (M) 199 12
H: 6 0 W: 13 01 b.Robles 27-10-78
Honours: Colombia full caps.

1999	Pasto	44	2		
2000	America	27	0		
2001	America	10	0	**37**	**0**
2001	Pasto	18	0	**62**	**2**
2002	Once Caldas	37	2		
2003	Once Caldas	32	4		
2004	Once Caldas	17	3	**86**	**9**
2005–06	Portsmouth	14	1	**14**	**1**

To Real Sociedad (loan) January 2006

VIGNAL, Gregory (D) 75 3
H: 5 9 W: 11 06 b.Montpellier 19-7-81
Source: Montpellier Herault SC.

2000–01	Liverpool	6	0		
2001–02	Liverpool	4	0		
2002–03	Liverpool	1	0	**11**	**0**
2002–03	Bastia	15	0	**15**	**0**
2003–04	*Rennes*	5	0	**5**	**0**
2004–05	*Rangers*	30	3	**30**	**3**
2005–06	Portsmouth	14	0	**14**	**0**

VUKIC, Zvonimir (M) 244 68
H: 6 0 W: 11 07 b.Zernjanin 17-9-79
Honours: Serbia & Montenegro 26 full caps, 6 goals.

1994–95	Begej	4	0		
1995–96	Begej	24	6	**28**	**6**
1996–97	Proleter	6	0		
1997–98	Proleter	30	3	**36**	**3**
1998–99	Atletico Madrid B	31	4		
1999–2000	Atletico Madrid B	0	0	**31**	**4**
1999–2000	Partizan Belgrade	6	1		
2000–01	Partizan Belgrade	21	7		
2001–02	Partizan Belgrade	29	14		
2002–03	Partizan Belgrade	30	22	**86**	**44**
2003–04	Shakhtjor Donetsk	27	10		
2004–05	Shakhtjor Donetsk	27	0	**54**	**10**
2005–06	Portsmouth	9	1	**9**	**1**

To Partizan Belgrade (loan) Feb 2006

WESTERVELD, Sander (G) 274 0
H: 6 4 W: 13 08 b.Enschede 23-10-74
Source: Tubanters. *Honours:* Holland 6 full caps.

1994–95	Twente	3	0		
1995–96	Twente	11	0	**14**	**0**
1996–97	Vitesse	34	0		
1997–98	Vitesse	34	0		
1998–99	Vitesse	32	0	**100**	**0**
1999–2000	Liverpool	36	0		
2000–01	Liverpool	38	0		
2001–02	Liverpool	1	0	**75**	**0**
2001–02	Real Sociedad	20	0		
2002–03	Real Sociedad	37	0		
2003–04	Real Sociedad	20	0		
2004–05	Real Sociedad	0	0	**77**	**0**
2005–06	Portsmouth	6	0	**6**	**0**
2005–06	*Everton*	2	0	**2**	**0**

WILSON, Marc (M) 2 0
H: 6 2 W: 12 07 b.Belfast 17-8-87
Source: Scholar.

2005–06	Portsmouth	0	0		
2005–06	*Yeovil T*	2	0	**2**	**0**

Scholars
Bell, Louis Peter; Compton, Jack Louis Paul; Hartmann, Matthew James; McClory-Cuthbertson, Tj; Pearce, Jason Daniel; Plummer, Jack; Roberts, Thomas Michael; Rogers, Raymond; Torre, Giovanni.

PRESTON NE (64)

AGYEMANG, Patrick (F) 235 38
H: 6 1 W: 12 00 b.Walthamstow 29-9-80
Source: Trainee. *Honours:* Ghana 1 full cap.

1998–99	Wimbledon	0	0		
1999–2000	Wimbledon	0	0		
1999–2000	*Brentford*	12	0	**12**	**0**
2000–01	Wimbledon	29	4		
2001–02	Wimbledon	33	4		
2002–03	Wimbledon	33	5		
2003–04	Wimbledon	26	7	**121**	**20**
2003–04	Gillingham	20	6		
2004–05	Gillingham	13	2	**33**	**8**
2004–05	Preston NE	27	4		
2005–06	Preston NE	42	6	**69**	**10**

ALEXANDER, Graham (D) 616 79
H: 5 10 W: 12 07 b.Coventry 10-10-71
Source: Trainee. *Honours:* Scotland B, 23 full caps.

1989–90	Scunthorpe U	0	0		
1990–91	Scunthorpe U	1	0		
1991–92	Scunthorpe U	36	5		
1992–93	Scunthorpe U	41	5		
1993–94	Scunthorpe U	41	4		
1994–95	Scunthorpe U	40	4	**159**	**18**
1995–96	Luton T	37	1		
1996–97	Luton T	45	2		
1997–98	Luton T	39	8		
1998–99	Luton T	29	4	**150**	**15**
1998–99	Preston NE	10	0		
1999–2000	Preston NE	46	6		
2000–01	Preston NE	34	5		
2001–02	Preston NE	45	6		
2002–03	Preston NE	45	10		
2003–04	Preston NE	45	9		
2004–05	Preston NE	42	7		
2005–06	Preston NE	40	3	**307**	**46**

ANYINSAH, Joe (M) 13 0
H: 5 8 W: 11 00 b.Bristol 8-10-84
Source: Scholar.

2001–02	Bristol C	0	0		
2002–03	Bristol C	0	0		
2003–04	Bristol C	0	0		
2004–05	Bristol C	7	0	**7**	**0**
2005–06	Preston NE	3	0	**3**	**0**
2005–06	*Bury*	3	0	**3**	**0**

BEATTIE, Warren (M) 0 0
H: 5 8 W: 10 12 b.Preston 18-10-86
Source: Scholar.

2005–06	Preston NE	0	0		

BROWN, Michael (M) 18 0
H: 5 11 W: 11 05 b.Preston 27-2-85
Source: Scholar.

2004–05	Preston NE	0	0		
2004–05	*Chester C*	18	0	**18**	**0**
2005–06	Preston NE	0	0		

CUDWORTH, Stephen (M) 0 0
b.Heysham 5-11-87

2005–06	Preston NE	0	0		

DAVIDSON, Callum (D) 256 12
H: 5 10 W: 11 08 b.Stirling 25-6-76
Source: 'S' Form. *Honours:* Scotland Under-21, 17 full caps.

1994–95	St Johnstone	7	1		
1995–96	St Johnstone	2	0		
1996–97	St Johnstone	20	2		
1997–98	St Johnstone	15	1	**44**	**4**
1997–98	Blackburn R	1	0		
1998–99	Blackburn R	34	1		
1999–2000	Blackburn R	30	0	**65**	**1**
2000–01	Leicester C	28	1		
2001–02	Leicester C	30	0		
2002–03	Leicester C	30	1		
2003–04	Leicester C	13	0	**101**	**2**
2004–05	Preston NE	19	1		
2005–06	Preston NE	27	4	**46**	**5**

DAVIS, Claude (D) 94 4
H: 6 3 W: 14 04 b.Kingston, Jam 6-3-79
Source: Portmore U. *Honours:* Jamaica full caps.

2003–04	Preston NE	22	1		
2004–05	Preston NE	32	0		
2005–06	Preston NE	40	3	**94**	**4**

DICHIO, Danny (F) 315 66
H: 6 3 W: 12 03 b.Hammersmith 19-10-74
Source: Trainee. *Honours:* England Schools, Under-21.

1993–94	QPR	0	0		
1993–94	*Barnet*	9	2	**9**	**2**
1994–95	QPR	9	3		
1995–96	QPR	29	10		
1996–97	QPR	37	7	**75**	**20**
1997–98	Sampdoria	0	0		
1997–98	Lecce	4	1	**4**	**1**
1997–98	Sunderland	13	0		
1998–99	Sunderland	36	10		
1999–2000	Sunderland	12	0		
2000–01	Sunderland	15	1		
2001–02	Sunderland	0	0	**76**	**11**
2001–02	WBA	27	9		
2002–03	WBA	28	5		
2003–04	WBA	11	0	**66**	**14**
2003–04	*Derby Co*	6	1	**6**	**1**
2003–04	Millwall	15	7		
2004–05	Millwall	31	10	**46**	**17**
2005–06	Preston NE	33	0	**33**	**0**

ELEBERT, David (D)				**0**	**0**
b.Dublin 21-3-86					
Source: Scholar.					
2002–03	Preston NE	0	0		
2003–04	Preston NE	0	0		
2004–05	Preston NE	0	0		
2005–06	Preston NE	0	0		
To Hamilton A January 2006					

HIBBERT, Dave (F)				**19**	**2**
H: 6 2 W: 12 00 b.Eccleshall 28-1-86					
Source: Scholar.					
2004–05	Port Vale	9	2	**9**	**2**
2005–06	Preston NE	10	0	**10**	**0**

HILL, Matt (D)				**238**	**6**
H: 5 7 W: 12 06 b.Bristol 26-3-81					
Source: Trainee.					
1998–99	Bristol C	3	0		
1999–2000	Bristol C	14	0		
2000–01	Bristol C	34	0		
2001–02	Bristol C	40	1		
2002–03	Bristol C	42	3		
2003–04	Bristol C	42	2		
2004–05	Bristol C	23	0	**198**	**6**
2004–05	Preston NE	14	0		
2005–06	Preston NE	26	0	**40**	**0**

JACKSON, Mark (F)				**8**	**0**
H: 5 11 W: 11 09 b.Preston 3-2-86					
Source: Scholar.					
2003–04	Preston NE	1	0		
2004–05	Preston NE	2	0		
2005–06	Preston NE	0	0	**3**	**0**
2005–06	*Shrewsbury T*	5	0	**5**	**0**

LONERGAN, Andrew (G)				**36**	**1**
H: 6 4 W: 13 02 b.Preston 19-10-83					
Source: Scholar. *Honours:* England Youth, Under-20.					
2000–01	Preston NE	1	0		
2001–02	Preston NE	0	0		
2002–03	Preston NE	0	0		
2002–03	*Darlington*	2	0	**2**	**0**
2003–04	Preston NE	8	0		
2004–05	Preston NE	23	1		
2005–06	Preston NE	0	0	**32**	**1**
2005–06	*Wycombe W*	2	0	**2**	**0**

LUCKETTI, Chris (D)				**574**	**21**
H: 6 1 W: 13 06 b.Rochdale 28-9-71					
Source: Trainee.					
1988–89	Rochdale	1	0		
1989–90	Rochdale	0	0	**1**	**0**
1990–91	Stockport Co	0	0		
1991–92	Halifax T	36	0		
1992–93	Halifax T	42	2	**78**	**2**
1993–94	Bury	27	1		
1994–95	Bury	39	3		
1995–96	Bury	42	1		
1996–97	Bury	38	0		
1997–98	Bury	46	2		
1998–99	Bury	43	1	**235**	**8**
1999–2000	Huddersfield T	26	0		
2000–01	Huddersfield T	40	1		
2001–02	Huddersfield T	2	0	**68**	**1**
2001–02	Preston NE	40	2		
2002–03	Preston NE	43	2		
2003–04	Preston NE	37	1		
2004–05	Preston NE	41	4		
2005–06	Preston NE	28	1	**189**	**10**
2005–06	*Sheffield U*	3	0	**3**	**0**

MAWENE, Youl (D)				**137**	**4**
H: 6 2 W: 12 06 b.Caen 16-7-79					
1999–2000	Lens	6	0	**6**	**0**
2000–01	Derby Co	8	0		
2001–02	Derby Co	17	1		
2002–03	Derby Co	0	0		
2003–04	Derby Co	30	0	**55**	**1**
2004–05	Preston NE	46	2		
2005–06	Preston NE	30	1	**76**	**3**

McCORMACK, Alan (M)				**25**	**2**
H: 5 8 W: 11 00 b.Dublin 10-1-84					
2002–03	Preston NE	0	0		
2003–04	Preston NE	5	0		
2003–04	*Leyton Orient*	10	0	**10**	**0**
2004–05	Preston NE	3	0		
2004–05	*Southend U*	7	2	**7**	**2**
2005–06	Preston NE	0	0	**8**	**0**

McKENNA, Paul (M)				**312**	**26**
H: 5 7 W: 11 12 b.Eccleston 20-10-77					
Source: Trainee.					
1995–96	Preston NE	0	0		
1996–97	Preston NE	5	1		
1997–98	Preston NE	5	0		
1998–99	Preston NE	36	0		
1999–2000	Preston NE	24	2		
2000–01	Preston NE	44	5		
2001–02	Preston NE	38	4		
2002–03	Preston NE	41	3		
2003–04	Preston NE	39	6		
2004–05	Preston NE	39	3		
2005–06	Preston NE	41	2	**312**	**26**

MEARS, Tyrone (D)				**71**	**4**
H: 5 11 W: 11 10 b.Stockport 18-2-83					
Source: Manchester C Juniors.					
2000–01	Manchester C	0	0		
2001–02	Manchester C	1	0	**1**	**0**
2002–03	Preston NE	22	1		
2003–04	Preston NE	12	1		
2004–05	Preston NE	4	0		
2005–06	Preston NE	32	2	**70**	**4**

NASH, Carlo (G)				**204**	**0**
H: 6 5 W: 14 01 b.Bolton 13-9-73					
Source: Clitheroe.					
1996–97	Crystal Palace	21	0		
1997–98	Crystal Palace	0	0	**21**	**0**
1998–99	Stockport Co	43	0		
1999–2000	Stockport Co	38	0		
2000–01	Stockport Co	8	0	**89**	**0**
2000–01	Manchester C	6	0		
2001–02	Manchester C	23	0		
2002–03	Manchester C	9	0	**38**	**0**
2003–04	Middlesbrough	1	0		
2004–05	Middlesbrough	2	0	**3**	**0**
2004–05	Preston NE	7	0		
2005–06	Preston NE	46	0	**53**	**0**

NEAL, Chris (G)				**1**	**0**
H: 6 2 W: 12 04 b.St Albans 23-10-85					
Source: Scholar.					
2004–05	Preston NE	1	0		
2005–06	Preston NE	0	0	**1**	**0**

NEAL, Lewis (M)				**94**	**4**
H: 5 10 W: 11 02 b.Leicester 14-7-81					
Source: Juniors.					
1998–99	Stoke C	0	0		
1999–2000	Stoke C	0	0		
2000–01	Stoke C	1	0		
2001–02	Stoke C	11	0		
2002–03	Stoke C	16	0		
2003–04	Stoke C	19	1		
2004–05	Stoke C	23	1	**70**	**2**
2005–06	Preston NE	24	2	**24**	**2**

NOWLAND, Adam (M)				**161**	**15**
H: 5 11 W: 11 06 b.Preston 6-7-81					
Source: Trainee.					
1997–98	Blackpool	1	0		
1998–99	Blackpool	37	2		
1999–2000	Blackpool	21	3		
2000–01	Blackpool	10	0	**69**	**5**
2001–02	Wimbledon	7	0		
2002–03	Wimbledon	24	2		
2003–04	Wimbledon	25	3	**56**	**5**
2003–04	West Ham U	11	0		
2004–05	West Ham U	4	1	**15**	**1**
2004–05	*Gillingham*	3	1	**3**	**1**
2004–05	Nottingham F	5	0		
2005–06	Nottingham F	0	0	**5**	**0**
2005–06	Preston NE	13	3	**13**	**3**

NUGENT, Dave (F)				**138**	**36**
H: 5 11 W: 12 13 b.Liverpool 2-5-85					
Source: Scholar. *Honours:* England Youth, Under-20, Under-21.					
2001–02	Bury	5	0		
2002–03	Bury	31	4		
2003–04	Bury	26	3		
2004–05	Bury	26	11	**88**	**18**
2004–05	Preston NE	18	8		
2005–06	Preston NE	32	10	**50**	**18**

O'NEIL, Brian (M)				**333**	**17**
H: 6 1 W: 12 04 b.Paisley 6-9-72					
Source: X Form. *Honours:* Scotland Schools, Youth, Under-21, 7 full caps.					
1991–92	Celtic	28	1		
1992–93	Celtic	17	3		
1993–94	Celtic	28	2		
1994–95	Celtic	26	0		
1995–96	Celtic	5	0		
1996–97	Celtic	16	2	**120**	**8**
1996–97	*Nottingham F*	5	0	**5**	**0**
1997–98	Aberdeen	29	1	**29**	**1**
1998–99	Wolfsburg	26	2		
1999–2000	Wolfsburg	16	1		
2000–01	Wolfsburg	8	0	**50**	**3**
2000–01	Derby Co	4	0		
2001–02	Derby Co	10	0		
2002–03	Derby Co	3	0	**17**	**0**
2002–03	Preston NE	15	0		
2003–04	Preston NE	29	1		
2004–05	Preston NE	43	3		
2005–06	Preston NE	25	1	**112**	**5**

ORMEROD, Brett (F)				**254**	**63**
H: 5 11 W: 11 12 b.Blackburn 18-10-76					
Source: Blackburn R Trainee, Accrington S.					
1996–97	Blackpool	4	0		
1997–98	Blackpool	9	2		
1998–99	Blackpool	40	8		
1999–2000	Blackpool	13	5		
2000–01	Blackpool	41	17		
2001–02	Blackpool	21	13	**128**	**45**
2001–02	Southampton	18	1		
2002–03	Southampton	31	5		
2003–04	Southampton	22	5		
2004–05	Southampton	9	0		
2004–05	*Leeds U*	6	0	**6**	**0**
2004–05	*Wigan Ath*	6	2	**6**	**2**
2005–06	Southampton	19	1	**99**	**12**
2005–06	Preston NE	15	4	**15**	**4**

PARILLON, Ashley (M)				**0**	**0**
b.Blackburn					
Source: Scholar.					
2005–06	Preston NE	0	0		

SEDGWICK, Chris (M)				**313**	**24**
H: 5 11 W: 11 10 b.Sheffield 28-4-80					
Source: Trainee.					
1997–98	Rotherham U	4	0		
1998–99	Rotherham U	33	4		
1999–2000	Rotherham U	38	5		
2000–01	Rotherham U	21	2		
2001–02	Rotherham U	44	1		
2002–03	Rotherham U	43	1		
2003–04	Rotherham U	40	2		
2004–05	Rotherham U	20	2	**243**	**17**
2004–05	Preston NE	24	3		
2005–06	Preston NE	46	4	**70**	**7**

SKORA, Eric (M)				**72**	**4**
H: 6 1 W: 11 10 b.Metz 20-8-81					
Source: Nancy.					
2001–02	Preston NE	4	0		
2002–03	Preston NE	36	0		
2003–04	Preston NE	2	0		
2003–04	*Kilmarnock*	17	2	**17**	**2**
2004–05	Preston NE	9	0		
2005–06	Preston NE	0	0	**51**	**0**
2005–06	*Walsall*	4	2	**4**	**2**
To Kilmarnock (loan) January 2006					

SMITH, Andy (F)				**22**	**0**
H: 5 11 W: 12 02 b.Lisburn 25-9-80					
Honours: Northern Ireland B, 11 full caps.					
2004–05	Preston NE	14	0		
2004–05	*Stockport Co*	1	0	**1**	**0**
2005–06	*Motherwell*	7	0	**7**	**0**
2005–06	Preston NE	0	0	**14**	**0**

STOCK, Brian (M)				**151**	**17**
H: 5 11 W: 11 02 b.Winchester 24-12-81					
Source: Trainee. *Honours:* Wales Under-21.					
1999–2000	Bournemouth	5	0		
2000–01	Bournemouth	1	0		
2001–02	Bournemouth	26	2		
2002–03	Bournemouth	27	2		
2003–04	Bournemouth	19	3		
2004–05	Bournemouth	41	6		
2005–06	Bournemouth	26	3	**145**	**16**
2005–06	Preston NE	6	1	**6**	**1**

WARD, Gavin (G) **278 0**
H: 6 3 W: 14 12 b.Sutton Coldfield 30-6-70
Source: Aston Villa Trainee.

1988–89	Shrewsbury T	0	0		
1989–90	WBA	0	0		
1989–90	Cardiff C	2	0		
1990–91	Cardiff C	1	0		
1991–92	Cardiff C	24	0		
1992–93	Cardiff C	32	0	**59**	**0**
1993–94	Leicester C	32	0		
1994–95	Leicester C	6	0	**38**	**0**
1995–96	Bradford C	36	0	**36**	**0**
1995–96	Bolton W	5	0		
1996–97	Bolton W	11	0		
1997–98	Bolton W	6	0		
1998–99	Bolton W	0	0	**22**	**0**
1998–99	*Burnley*	17	0	**17**	**0**
1998–99	Stoke C	6	0		
1999–2000	Stoke C	46	0		
2000–01	Stoke C	17	0		
2001–02	Stoke C	10	0	**79**	**0**
2002–03	Walsall	7	0	**7**	**0**
2003–04	Coventry C	12	0	**12**	**0**
2003–04	*Barnsley*	1	0	**1**	**0**
2004–05	Preston NE	7	0		
2005–06	Preston NE	0	0	**7**	**0**

WHALEY, Simon (M) **89 14**
H: 5 10 W: 11 11 b.Bolton 7-6-85
Source: Scholar.

2002–03	Bury	2	0		
2003–04	Bury	10	1		
2004–05	Bury	38	3		
2005–06	Bury	23	7	**73**	**11**
2005–06	Preston NE	16	3	**16**	**3**

QPR (65)

AINSWORTH, Gareth (M) **378 85**
H: 5 10 W: 12 05 b.Blackburn 10-5-73
Source: Blackburn R Trainee.

1991–92	Preston NE	5	0		
1992–93	Cambridge U	4	1	**4**	**1**
1992–93	Preston NE	26	0		
1993–94	Preston NE	38	11		
1994–95	Preston NE	16	1		
1995–96	Preston NE	2	0		
1995–96	Lincoln C	31	12		
1996–97	Lincoln C	46	22		
1997–98	Lincoln C	6	3	**83**	**37**
1997–98	Port Vale	40	5		
1998–99	Port Vale	15	5	**55**	**10**
1998–99	Wimbledon	8	0		
1999–2000	Wimbledon	2	2		
2000–01	Wimbledon	12	2		
2001–02	Wimbledon	2	0		
2001–02	*Preston NE*	5	1	**92**	**13**
2002–03	Wimbledon	12	2	**36**	**6**
2002–03	*Walsall*	5	1	**5**	**1**
2002–03	Cardiff C	9	0	**9**	**0**
2003–04	QPR	29	6		
2004–05	QPR	22	2		
2005–06	QPR	43	9	**94**	**17**

BAIDOO, Shabazz (M) **19 2**
H: 5 8 W: 10 07 b.Hackney 13-4-88
Source: Scholar.

2004–05	QPR	4	0		
2005–06	QPR	15	2	**19**	**2**

BAILEY, Stefan (M) **7 0**
H: 5 11 W: 12 08 b.Brent 10-11-87
Source: Scholar.

2004–05	QPR	2	0		
2005–06	QPR	5	0	**7**	**0**

BIGNOT, Marcus (D) **336 4**
H: 5 7 W: 11 04 b.Birmingham 22-8-74
Source: Kidderminster H.

1997–98	Crewe Alex	42	0		
1998–99	Crewe Alex	26	0		
1999–2000	Crewe Alex	27	0	**95**	**0**
2000–01	Bristol R	26	1	**26**	**1**
2000–01	QPR	9	1		
2001–02	QPR	45	0		
2002–03	Rushden & D	33	0		
2003–04	Rushden & D	35	2	**68**	**2**
2003–04	QPR	6	0		
2004–05	QPR	43	0		
2005–06	QPR	44	0	**147**	**1**

BIRCHAM, Marc (M) **239 10**
H: 5 11 W: 11 06 b.Wembley 11-5-78
Source: Trainee. *Honours:* Canada 17 full caps, 1 goal.

1996–97	Millwall	6	0		
1997–98	Millwall	4	0		
1998–99	Millwall	28	0		
1999–2000	Millwall	22	1		
2000–01	Millwall	20	2		
2001–02	Millwall	24	0	**104**	**3**
2002–03	QPR	36	2		
2003–04	QPR	38	2		
2004–05	QPR	35	1		
2005–06	QPR	26	2	**135**	**7**

COLE, Jake (G) **3 0**
H: 6 2 W: 13 00 b.Hammersmith 11-9-85
Source: Scholar.

2005–06	QPR	3	0	**3**	**0**

COOK, Lee (M) **161 15**
H: 5 8 W: 11 10 b.Hammersmith 3-8-82
Source: Aylesbury U.

1999–2000	Watford	0	0		
2000–01	Watford	4	0		
2001–02	Watford	10	0		
2002–03	Watford	4	0		
2002–03	*York C*	7	1	**7**	**1**
2002–03	*QPR*	13	1		
2003–04	Watford	41	7	**59**	**7**
2004–05	QPR	42	2		
2005–06	QPR	40	4	**95**	**7**

DOHERTY, Tom (M) **204 7**
H: 5 8 W: 10 06 b.Bristol 17-3-79
Source: Trainee. *Honours:* Northern Ireland 9 full caps.

1997–98	Bristol C	30	2		
1998–99	Bristol C	23	1		
1999–2000	Bristol C	1	0		
2000–01	Bristol C	0	0		
2001–02	Bristol C	34	1		
2002–03	Bristol C	38	0		
2003–04	Bristol C	33	2		
2004–05	Bristol C	29	1	**188**	**7**
2005–06	QPR	15	0	**15**	**0**
2005–06	*Yeovil T*	1	0	**1**	**0**

DONNELLY, Scott (M) **10 0**
H: 5 8 W: 11 10 b.Hammersmith 25-12-87
Source: Scholar.

2004–05	QPR	2	0		
2005–06	QPR	8	0	**10**	**0**

EVATT, Ian (D) **156 9**
H: 6 3 W: 13 12 b.Coventry 19-11-81
Source: Trainee.

1998–99	Derby Co	0	0		
1999–2000	Derby Co	0	0		
2000–01	Derby Co	1	0		
2001–02	*Northampton T*	11	0	**11**	**0**
2001–02	Derby Co	3	0		
2002–03	Derby Co	30	0	**34**	**0**
2003–04	Chesterfield	43	5		
2004–05	Chesterfield	41	4	**84**	**9**
2005–06	QPR	27	0	**27**	**0**

FURLONG, Paul (F) **464 161**
H: 6 0 W: 13 11 b.Wood Green 1-10-68
Source: Enfield.

1991–92	Coventry C	37	4	**37**	**4**
1992–93	Watford	41	19		
1993–94	Watford	38	18	**79**	**37**
1994–95	Chelsea	36	10		
1995–96	Chelsea	28	3	**64**	**13**
1996–97	Birmingham C	43	10		
1997–98	Birmingham C	25	15		
1998–99	Birmingham C	29	13		
1999–2000	Birmingham C	19	11		
2000–01	Birmingham C	4	0		
2000–01	*QPR*	3	1		
2001–02	Birmingham C	11	1		
2001–02	*Sheffield U*	4	2	**4**	**2**
2002–03	Birmingham C	0	0	**131**	**50**
2002–03	QPR	33	13		
2003–04	QPR	36	16		
2004–05	QPR	40	18		
2005–06	QPR	37	7	**149**	**55**

GALLEN, Kevin (F) **394 99**
H: 5 11 W: 13 05 b.Hammersmith 21-9-75
Source: Trainee. *Honours:* England Schools, Youth, Under-21.

1992–93	QPR	0	0		
1993–94	QPR	0	0		
1994–95	QPR	37	10		
1995–96	QPR	30	8		
1996–97	QPR	2	3		
1997–98	QPR	27	3		
1998–99	QPR	44	8		
1999–2000	QPR	31	4		
2000–01	Huddersfield T	38	10	**38**	**10**
2001–02	Barnsley	9	2	**9**	**2**
2001–02	QPR	25	7		
2002–03	QPR	42	13		
2003–04	QPR	45	17		
2004–05	QPR	46	10		
2005–06	QPR	18	4	**347**	**87**

HISLOP, Matthew (D) **1 0**
H: 5 11 W: 12 00 b.Wolverhampton 31-1-87
Source: Arsenal Scholar.

2004–05	QPR	0	0		
2005–06	QPR	1	0	**1**	**0**

HOWELL, Andrew (D) **0 0**
b.Gt Yarmouth 18-3-89
Source: Scholar.

2005–06	QPR	0	0		

JOHNSON, Ryan (D) **0 0**
b.Dartford 15-1-87
Source: Scholar.

2005–06	QPR	0	0		

JONES, Paul (G) **326 0**
H: 6 3 W: 15 02 b.Chirk 18-4-67
Source: Bridgnorth, Kidderminster H. *Honours:* Wales 46 full caps.

1991–92	Wolverhampton W	0	0		
1992–93	Wolverhampton W	16	0		
1993–94	Wolverhampton W	0	0		
1994–95	Wolverhampton W	9	0		
1995–96	Wolverhampton W	8	0		
1996–97	Stockport Co	46	0	**46**	**0**
1997–98	Southampton	38	0		
1998–99	Southampton	31	0		
1999–2000	Southampton	31	0		
2000–01	Southampton	35	0		
2001–02	Southampton	36	0		
2002–03	Southampton	14	0		
2003–04	Southampton	8	0	**193**	**0**
2003–04	*Liverpool*	2	0	**2**	**0**
2003–04	Wolverhampton W	16	0		
2004–05	Wolverhampton W	10	0		
2004–05	*Watford*	9	0	**9**	**0**
2005–06	Wolverhampton W	0	0	**59**	**0**
2005–06	*Millwall*	3	0	**3**	**0**
2005–06	QPR	14	0	**14**	**0**

JONES, Ray (F) **2 0**
H: 6 4 W: 14 05 b.Newham 28-8-88
Source: Scholar.

2005–06	QPR	2	0	**2**	**0**

KANYUKA, Patrick (D) **1 0**
H: 6 0 W: 12 06 b.Kinshasa 19-7-87
Source: QPR Juniors.

2004–05	QPR	1	0		
2005–06	QPR	0	0	**1**	**0**

KUS, Marcin (D) **84 5**
H: 6 0 W: 11 07 b.Warsaw 2-9-81
Honours: Poland 5 full caps.

1999–2000	Polonia	1	0		
2000–01	Polonia	14	0		
2001–02	Polonia	20	1		
2002–03	Polonia	23	4		
2003–04	Polonia	0	0	**58**	**5**
2004–05	Lech	10	0		
2005–06	Lech	13	0	**23**	**0**
2005–06	*QPR*	3	0	**3**	**0**

LANGLEY, Richard (M) **235 29**
H: 6 0 W: 11 04 b.Harlesden 27-12-79
Source: Trainee. *Honours:* England Youth, Jamaica 17 full caps.

1996–97	QPR	0	0		
1997–98	QPR	0	0		
1998–99	QPR	8	1		

1999–2000 QPR 41 3
2000–01 QPR 26 1
2001–02 QPR 18 3
2002–03 QPR 39 9
2003–04 QPR 1 1
2003–04 Cardiff C 44 6
2004–05 Cardiff C 25 2
2005–06 Cardiff C 0 0 **69 8**
2005–06 QPR 33 3 **166 21**

LOMAS, Steve (M) 319 18
H: 6 0 W: 12 08 b.Hanover 18-1-74
Source: Trainee. *Honours:* Northern Ireland Schools, Youth, B, 45 full caps, 3 goals.
1991–92 Manchester C 0 0
1992–93 Manchester C 0 0
1993–94 Manchester C 23 0
1994–95 Manchester C 20 2
1995–96 Manchester C 33 3
1996–97 Manchester C 35 3 **111 8**
1996–97 West Ham U 7 0
1997–98 West Ham U 33 2
1998–99 West Ham U 30 1
1999–2000 West Ham U 25 1
2000–01 West Ham U 20 1
2001–02 West Ham U 15 4
2002–03 West Ham U 29 0
2003–04 West Ham U 5 0
2004–05 West Ham U 23 1
2005–06 West Ham U 0 0 **187 10**
2005–06 QPR 21 0 **21 0**

MILANESE, Mauro (D) 396 22
H: 6 1 W: 13 01 b.Trieste 17-9-71
1989–90 Triestina 0 0
1990–91 Monfalcone 33 5 **33 5**
1991–92 Massese 22 2 **22 2**
1992–93 Triestina 25 2
1993–94 Triestina 25 1 **50 3**
1994–95 Cremonese 27 3 **27 3**
1995–96 Torino 31 0 **31 0**
1996–97 Napoli 29 1 **29 1**
1997–98 Parma 6 0 **6 0**
1997–98 Internazionale 9 1
1998–99 Internazionale 7 0 **16 1**
1999–2000 Perugia 25 0
2000–01 Perugia 4 0
2001–02 Perugia 30 1
2002–03 Perugia 31 1
2003–04 Ancona 27 1 **27 1**
2004–05 Perugia 39 4 **129 6**
2005–06 QPR 26 0 **26 0**

MILLER, Adam (M) 17 0
H: 5 11 W: 11 06 b.Hemel Hempstead 19-2-82
Source: Aldershot T.
From Aldershot T
2004–05 QPR 14 0
2005–06 QPR 1 0 **15 0**
2005–06 *Peterborough U* 2 0 **2 0**

MOORE, Stefan (F) 62 4
H: 5 10 W: 10 12 b.Birmingham 28-9-83
Source: Scholar. *Honours:* England Youth.
2000–01 Aston Villa 0 0
2001–02 Aston Villa 0 0
2001–02 *Chesterfield* 2 0 **2 0**
2002–03 Aston Villa 13 1
2003–04 Aston Villa 8 1
2004–05 Aston Villa 1 0 **22 2**
2004–05 *Millwall* 6 0 **6 0**
2004–05 *Leicester C* 7 0 **7 0**
2005–06 QPR 25 2 **25 2**

MULHOLLAND, Scott (M) 1 0
H: 5 8 W: 10 05 b.Bexleyheath 7-9-86
Source: Scholar.
2004–05 QPR 1 0
2005–06 QPR 0 0 **1 0**

MUNDAY, Jonathan (D) 0 0
b. *Honours:* 13-4-88
Source: Scholar.
2005–06 QPR 0 0

NYGAARD, Marc (F) 202 35
H: 6 5 W: 14 05 b.Copenhagen 1-9-76
Source: FC Copenhagen. *Honours:* Denmark Youth, Under-21, 6 full caps.
1995–96 Heerenveen 6 1
1996–97 Heerenveen 20 5 **26 6**
1997–98 MVV 34 3 **34 3**
1998–99 Roda JC 30 10
1999–2000 Roda JC 2 0
2000–01 Roda JC 24 1
2001–02 Roda JC 21 1 **77 12**
2002–03 Lommel 4 1 **4 1**
2002–03 Excelsior 8 1 **8 1**
2003–04 Catania 12 3 **12 3**
2003–04 Vicenza 4 0 **4 0**
2004–05 Brescia 10 0 **10 0**
2005–06 QPR 27 9 **27 9**

ROSE, Matthew (D) 236 8
H: 5 11 W: 12 02 b.Dartford 24-9-75
Source: Trainee. *Honours:* England Under-21.
1994–95 Arsenal 0 0
1995–96 Arsenal 4 0
1996–97 Arsenal 1 0 **5 0**
1997–98 QPR 16 0
1998–99 QPR 29 0
1999–2000 QPR 29 1
2000–01 QPR 27 0
2001–02 QPR 39 3
2002–03 QPR 28 2
2003–04 QPR 20 0
2004–05 QPR 28 2
2005–06 QPR 15 0 **231 8**

ROWLANDS, Martin (M) 240 35
H: 5 9 W: 10 10 b.Hammersmith 8-2-79
Source: Farnborough T. *Honours:* Eire Under-21, 3 full caps.
1998–99 Brentford 36 4
1999–2000 Brentford 40 6
2000–01 Brentford 32 2
2001–02 Brentford 23 7
2002–03 Brentford 18 1 **149 20**
2003–04 QPR 42 10
2004–05 QPR 35 3
2005–06 QPR 14 2 **91 15**

ROYCE, Simon (G) 244 0
H: 6 2 W: 12 10 b.Forest Gate 9-9-71
Source: Heybridge Swifts.
1991–92 Southend U 1 0
1992–93 Southend U 3 0
1993–94 Southend U 6 0
1994–95 Southend U 13 0
1995–96 Southend U 46 0
1996–97 Southend U 43 0
1997–98 Southend U 37 0 **149 0**
1998–99 Charlton Ath 8 0
1999–2000 Charlton Ath 0 0
2000–01 Leicester C 19 0
2001–02 Leicester C 0 0
2001–02 *Brighton & HA* 6 0 **6 0**
2001–02 *Manchester C* 0 0
2002–03 Leicester C 0 0 **19 0**
2002–03 *QPR* 16 0
2003–04 Charlton Ath 1 0
2004–05 Charlton Ath 0 0 **9 0**
2004–05 *Luton T* 2 0 **2 0**
2004–05 *QPR* 13 0
2005–06 QPR 30 0 **59 0**

SANTOS, Georges (M) 250 16
H: 6 3 W: 14 00 b.Marseille 15-8-70
Source: Toulon.
1998–99 Tranmere R 37 1
1999–2000 Tranmere R 10 1 **47 2**
1999–2000 WBA 8 0 **8 0**
2000–01 Sheffield U 31 4
2001–02 Sheffield U 30 2 **61 6**
2002–03 Grimsby T 26 1 **26 1**
2003–04 Ipswich T 34 1 **34 1**
2004–05 QPR 43 5
2005–06 QPR 31 1 **74 6**

SHIMMIN, Dominic (D) 2 0
H: 6 0 W: 12 06 b.Bermondsey 13-10-87
Source: Arsenal Scholar.
2004–05 QPR 0 0
2005–06 QPR 2 0 **2 0**

SHITTU, Dan (D) 186 19
H: 6 2 W: 16 03 b.Lagos 2-9-80
Honours: Nigeria 1 full cap.
1999–2000 Charlton Ath 0 0
2000–01 Charlton Ath 0 0
2000–01 *Blackpool* 17 2 **17 2**
2001–02 Charlton Ath 0 0
2001–02 QPR 27 2
2002–03 QPR 43 7
2003–04 QPR 20 0
2004–05 QPR 34 4
2005–06 QPR 45 4 **169 17**

STURRIDGE, Dean (F) 319 95
H: 5 8 W: 12 02 b.Birmingham 27-7-73
Source: Trainee.
1991–92 Derby Co 1 0
1992–93 Derby Co 10 0
1993–94 Derby Co 0 0
1994–95 Derby Co 12 1
1994–95 *Torquay U* 10 5 **10 5**
1995–96 Derby Co 39 20
1996–97 Derby Co 30 11
1997–98 Derby Co 30 9
1998–99 Derby Co 29 5
1999–2000 Derby Co 25 6
2000–01 Derby Co 14 1 **190 53**
2000–01 Leicester C 13 3
2001–02 Leicester C 9 3 **22 6**
2001–02 Wolverhampton W 27 20
2002–03 Wolverhampton W 39 10
2003–04 Wolverhampton W 5 0
2003–04 *Sheffield U* 4 0 **4 0**
2004–05 Wolverhampton W 11 1 **82 31**
2004–05 QPR 2 0
2005–06 QPR 9 0 **11 0**

THOMAS, Sean (G) 0 0
H: 6 1 W: 12 03 b.Edgware 5-9-87
Source: Scholar.
2005–06 QPR 0 0

TOWNSEND, Luke (M) 2 0
H: 6 0 W: 11 10 b.Guildford 28-9-86
Source: Scholar.
2004–05 QPR 2 0
2005–06 QPR 0 0 **2 0**

UKAH, Ugo (D) 1 0
H: 6 0 W: 12 11 b.Nigeria 18-1-84
Source: Pro Vasto. *Honours:* Nigeria Under-21.
2005–06 QPR 1 0 **1 0**

YOUSSOUF, Sammy (F) 6 0
H: 6 0 W: 13 01 b.Copenhagen 7-9-76
Source: Hvidovre, St Johnstone, Maritimo.
2005–06 QPR 6 0 **6 0**

READING (66)

BROWN, Aaron (D) 4 0
H: 6 4 W: 14 07 b.Birmingham 23-6-83
Source: Tamworth.
2005–06 Reading 0 0
2005–06 *Bournemouth* 4 0 **4 0**

BROWN, Steve (D) 282 10
H: 6 1 W: 13 10 b.Brighton 13-5-72
Source: Trainee.
1990–91 Charlton Ath 0 0
1991–92 Charlton Ath 1 0
1992–93 Charlton Ath 0 0
1993–94 Charlton Ath 19 0
1994–95 Charlton Ath 42 3
1995–96 Charlton Ath 19 0
1996–97 Charlton Ath 27 0
1997–98 Charlton Ath 34 2
1998–99 Charlton Ath 18 0
1999–2000 Charlton Ath 40 2
2000–01 Charlton Ath 25 0
2001–02 Charlton Ath 14 2
2002–03 Charlton Ath 3 0 **242 9**
2002–03 Reading 21 1
2003–04 Reading 19 0
2004–05 Reading 0 0
2005–06 Reading 0 0 **40 1**

CAMPBELL, Darren (M) 1 0
H: 5 7 W: 10 08 b.Huntingdon 16-4-86
Source: Scholar. *Honours:* England Youth.
2002–03 Reading 1 0
2003–04 Reading 0 0
2004–05 Reading 0 0
2005–06 Reading 0 0 **1 0**

CATNEY, Ryan (M) **0 0**
b.Northern Ireland 17-2-87
Source: Scholar.
2005–06 Reading 0 0

CONVEY, Bobby (M) **63 7**
H: 5 8 W: 10 12 b.Philadelphia 27-5-83
Source: DC United. *Honours:* USA 42 full caps, 1 goal.
2004–05 Reading 18 0
2005–06 Reading 45 7 **63 7**

COX, Simon (M) **2 0**
H: 5 10 W: 10 12 b.Reading 28-4-87
Source: Scholar.
2005–06 Reading 2 0 **2 0**

DOYLE, Kevin (F) **88 38**
H: 5 11 W: 12 06 b.Adamstown 18-9-83
Source: Adamstown, Wexford, St Patrick's Ath. *Honours:* Eire Under-21, 2 full caps.
2004 Cork C 32 13
2005 Cork C 11 7 **43 20**
2005–06 Reading 45 18 **45 18**

FEDERICI, Adam (G) **0 0**
H: 6 2 W: 14 02 b.Nowra 31-1-85
Honours: Australia Youth.
2005–06 Reading 0 0

GOLBOURNE, Scott (M) **15 0**
H: 5 8 W: 11 08 b.Bristol 29-2-88
Source: Scholar. *Honours:* England Youth.
2004–05 Bristol C 9 0
2005–06 Bristol C 5 0 **14 0**
2005–06 Reading 1 0 **1 0**

GUNNARSSON, Brynjar (M) **267 26**
H: 6 1 W: 12 01 b.Reykjavik 16-10-75
Honours: Iceland Youth, Under-21, 54 full caps, 3 goals.
1995 KR 16 1
1996 KR 18 0
1997 KR 16 0 **50 1**
1998 Moss 5 2 **5 2**
1999–2000 Stoke C 22 1
2000–01 Stoke C 46 5
2001–02 Stoke C 23 5
2002–03 Stoke C 40 5
2003–04 Nottingham F 13 0 **13 0**
2003–04 *Stoke C* 3 0 **134 16**
2004–05 Watford 36 3 **36 3**
2005–06 Reading 29 4 **29 4**

HAHNEMANN, Marcus (G) **247 0**
H: 6 3 W: 13 03 b.Seattle 15-6-72
Honours: USA 6 full caps.
1997 Colorado Rapids 25 0
1998 Colorado Rapids 28 0
1999 Colorado Rapids 13 0 **66 0**
1999–2000 Fulham 0 0
2000–01 Fulham 2 0
2001–02 Fulham 0 0 **2 0**
2001–02 *Rochdale* 5 0 **5 0**
2001–02 *Reading* 6 0
2002–03 Reading 41 0
2003–04 Reading 36 0
2004–05 Reading 46 0
2005–06 Reading 45 0 **174 0**

HALLS, John (M) **76 3**
H: 6 0 W: 11 11 b.Islington 14-2-82
Source: Scholar. *Honours:* England Youth, Under-20.
2000–01 Arsenal 0 0
2001–02 Arsenal 0 0
2001–02 *Colchester U* 6 0 **6 0**
2002–03 Arsenal 0 0
2003–04 Arsenal 0 0
2003–04 Stoke C 34 0
2004–05 Stoke C 22 0
2005–06 Stoke C 13 2 **69 2**
2005–06 Reading 1 1 **1 1**

HARPER, James (M) **202 15**
H: 5 10 W: 11 02 b.Chelmsford 9-11-80
Source: Trainee.
1999–2000 Arsenal 0 0
2000–01 Arsenal 0 0
2000–01 *Cardiff C* 3 0 **3 0**
2000–01 Reading 12 1
2001–02 Reading 26 1
2002–03 Reading 36 2
2003–04 Reading 39 1
2004–05 Reading 41 3
2005–06 Reading 45 7 **199 15**

HAYES, Jonathan (M) **0 0**
H: 5 7 W: 11 00 b.Dublin 9-7-87
Source: Scholar. *Honours:* Eire Under-21.
2004–05 Reading 0 0
2005–06 Reading 0 0

HOWELL, Simieon (M) **0 0**
H: 5 11 W: 12 00 b.Reading 26-8-85
Source: Scholar.
2004–05 Reading 0 0
2005–06 Reading 0 0

HUNT, Steve (M) **177 27**
H: 5 9 W: 10 10 b.Port Laoise 1-8-80
Source: Trainee.
1999–2000 Crystal Palace 3 0
2000–01 Crystal Palace 0 0 **3 0**
2001–02 Brentford 35 4
2002–03 Brentford 42 7
2003–04 Brentford 40 11
2004–05 Brentford 19 3 **136 25**
2005–06 Reading 38 2 **38 2**

INGIMARSSON, Ivar (D) **341 29**
H: 6 0 W: 12 07 b.Reykjavik 20-8-77
Honours: Iceland Youth, Under-21, 16 full caps.
1995 Valur 12 0
1996 Valur 17 2
1997 Valur 16 3 **45 5**
1998 IBV 18 1
1999 IBV 18 4 **36 5**
1999–2000 Torquay U 4 1 **4 1**
1999–2000 Brentford 25 1
2000–01 Brentford 42 3
2001–02 Brentford 46 6 **113 10**
2002–03 Wolverhampton W 13 2
2002–03 *Brighton & HA* 15 0 **15 0**
2003–04 Wolverhampton W 0 0 **13 2**
2003–04 Reading 25 1
2004–05 Reading 44 3
2005–06 Reading 46 2 **115 6**

KITSON, Dave (F) **190 82**
H: 6 3 W: 12 07 b.Hitchin 21-1-80
Source: Arlesey.
2000–01 Cambridge U 8 1
2001–02 Cambridge U 33 9
2002–03 Cambridge U 44 20
2003–04 Cambridge U 17 10 **102 40**
2003–04 Reading 17 5
2004–05 Reading 37 19
2005–06 Reading 34 18 **88 42**

LITA, Leroy (F) **111 42**
H: 5 7 W: 11 12 b.DR Congo 28-12-84
Source: Scholar. *Honours:* England Under-21.
2002–03 Bristol C 15 2
2003–04 Bristol C 26 5
2004–05 Bristol C 44 24 **85 31**
2005–06 Reading 26 11 **26 11**

LITTLE, Glen (M) **332 40**
H: 6 3 W: 13 00 b.Wimbledon 15-10-75
Source: Trainee.
1994–95 Crystal Palace 0 0
1995–96 Crystal Palace 0 0
1996–97 Glentoran 6 2 **6 2**
1996–97 Burnley 9 0
1997–98 Burnley 24 4
1998–99 Burnley 34 5
1999–2000 Burnley 41 3
2000–01 Burnley 34 3
2001–02 Burnley 37 9
2002–03 Burnley 33 5
2002–03 *Reading* 6 1
2003–04 Burnley 34 3 **246 32**
2003–04 *Bolton W* 4 0 **4 0**
2004–05 Reading 35 0
2005–06 Reading 35 5 **76 6**

LONG, Shane (F) **11 3**
H: 5 10 W: 11 02 b.Gortnahoe 22-1-87
Source: Cork C. *Honours:* Eire Youth, Under-21.
2005–06 Reading 11 3 **11 3**

MAKIN, Chris (D) **382 7**
H: 5 11 W: 11 02 b.Manchester 8-5-73
Source: Trainee. *Honours:* England Schools, Under-21.
1991–92 Oldham Ath 0 0
1992–93 Oldham Ath 0 0
1992–93 *Wigan Ath* 15 2 **15 2**
1993–94 Oldham Ath 27 1
1994–95 Oldham Ath 28 1
1995–96 Oldham Ath 39 2 **94 4**
1996–97 Marseille 29 0 **29 0**
1997–98 Sunderland 25 0
1998–99 Sunderland 38 0
1999–2000 Sunderland 34 1
2000–01 Sunderland 23 0 **120 1**
2000–01 Ipswich T 10 0
2001–02 Ipswich T 30 0
2002–03 Ipswich T 33 0
2003–04 Ipswich T 5 0 **78 0**
2004–05 Leicester C 21 0 **21 0**
2004–05 *Derby Co* 13 0 **13 0**
2005–06 Reading 12 0 **12 0**

MULLINS, John (D) **21 2**
H: 5 11 W: 12 07 b.Hampstead 6-11-85
Source: Scholar.
2004–05 Reading 0 0
2004–05 *Kidderminster H* 21 2 **21 2**
2005–06 Reading 0 0

MURTY, Graeme (D) **372 9**
H: 5 10 W: 11 10 b.Saltburn 13-11-74
Source: Trainee. *Honours:* Scotland B, 3 full caps.
1992–93 York C 0 0
1993–94 York C 1 0
1994–95 York C 20 2
1995–96 York C 35 2
1996–97 York C 27 2
1997–98 York C 34 1 **117 7**
1998–99 Reading 9 0
1999–2000 Reading 17 0
2000–01 Reading 23 1
2001–02 Reading 43 0
2002–03 Reading 44 0
2003–04 Reading 38 0
2004–05 Reading 41 0
2005–06 Reading 40 1 **255 2**

OBINNA, Eric (F) **37 6**
H: 6 3 W: 13 03 b.Nigeria 10-6-81
Source: Vitoria Bahia.
1998–99 St Etienne 5 0
1999–2000 Red Star 93 0 0
2000–01 St Etienne 0 0 **5 0**
2000–01 Rouen 0 0
2001–02 Rouen 0 0
2002–03 Stuttgart Kickers 26 6
2003–04 Stuttgart Kickers 0 0 **26 6**
2003–04 Kaiserslautern 0 0
2005–06 Reading 6 0 **6 0**

OSANO, Curtis (M) **0 0**
H: 5 11 W: 11 04 b.Nakuru 8-3-87
Source: Scholar.
2005–06 Reading 0 0

OSTER, John (M) **207 18**
H: 5 9 W: 10 08 b.Boston 8-12-78
Source: Trainee. *Honours:* Wales Youth, Under-21, B, 13 full caps.
1996–97 Grimsby T 24 3
1997–98 Everton 31 1
1998–99 Everton 9 0 **40 1**
1999–2000 Sunderland 10 0
2000–01 Sunderland 8 0
2001–02 Sunderland 0 0
2001–02 *Barnsley* 2 0 **2 0**
2002–03 Sunderland 3 0
2002–03 *Grimsby T* 17 6 **41 9**
2003–04 Sunderland 38 5
2004–05 Sunderland 9 0 **68 5**
2004–05 *Leeds U* 8 1 **8 1**
2004–05 Burnley 15 1 **15 1**
2005–06 Reading 33 1 **33 1**

SHOREY, Nicky (D) **209 9**
H: 5 9 W: 10 08 b.Romford 19-2-81
Source: Trainee.
1999–2000 Leyton Orient 7 0
2000–01 Leyton Orient 8 0 **15 0**

2000–01	Reading	0	0		
2001–02	Reading	32	0		
2002–03	Reading	43	2		
2003–04	Reading	35	2		
2004–05	Reading	44	3		
2005–06	Reading	40	2	**194**	**9**

SIDWELL, Steve (M) **175** **34**
H: 5 10 W: 11 00 b.Wandsworth 14-12-82
Source: Scholar. *Honours:* England Under-20, Under-21.

2001–02	Arsenal	0	0		
2001–02	*Brentford*	30	4	**30**	**4**
2002–03	Arsenal	0	0		
2002–03	*Brighton & HA*	12	5	**12**	**5**
2002–03	Reading	13	2		
2003–04	Reading	43	8		
2004–05	Reading	44	5		
2005–06	Reading	33	10	**133**	**25**

SINNOTT, Conor (M) **0** **0**
H: 6 0 W: 11 05 b.Wexford 19-1-86
Source: Bray W.

2005–06	Reading	0	0		

SONKO, Ibrahima (D) **165** **12**
H: 6 3 W: 13 07 b.Bignola 22-1-81
Source: St Etienne, Grenoble.

2002–03	Brentford	37	5		
2003–04	Brentford	43	3	**80**	**8**
2004–05	Reading	39	1		
2005–06	Reading	46	3	**85**	**4**

STACK, Graham (G) **27** **0**
H: 6 2 W: 12 07 b.Hampstead 26-9-81
Honours: Eire Under-21.

2000–01	Arsenal	0	0		
2001–02	Arsenal	0	0		
2002–03	Arsenal	0	0		
2003–04	Arsenal	0	0		
2004–05	Arsenal	0	0		
2004–05	*Millwall*	26	0	**26**	**0**
2005–06	Arsenal	0	0		
2005–06	Reading	1	0	**1**	**0**

YOUNG, Jamie (G) **21** **0**
H: 5 11 W: 13 00 b.Brisbane 25-8-85
Source: Scholar. *Honours:* England Youth, Under-20.

2003–04	Reading	1	0		
2004–05	Reading	0	0		
2005–06	Reading	0	0	**1**	**0**
2005–06	*Rushden & D*	20	0	**20**	**0**

ROCHDALE (67)

BOARDMAN, Jon (D) **21** **1**
H: 6 2 W: 12 09 b.Reading 27-1-81
Source: Trainee.

1999–2000	Crystal Palace	0	0		
2000–01	Crystal Palace	0	0		
2001–02	Crystal Palace	0	0		
From Woking.					
2005–06	Rochdale	21	1	**21**	**1**

BRISCO, Neil (M) **145** **2**
H: 5 11 W: 13 07 b.Wigan 26-1-78
Source: Trainee.

1996–97	Manchester C	0	0		
1997–98	Manchester C	0	0		
1998–99	Port Vale	1	0		
1999–2000	Port Vale	12	0		
2000–01	Port Vale	17	1		
2001–02	Port Vale	37	0		
2002–03	Port Vale	24	1		
2003–04	Port Vale	27	0	**118**	**2**
2004–05	Rochdale	11	0		
2005–06	Rochdale	16	0	**27**	**0**

BROWN, Gary (D) **17** **0**
H: 5 6 W: 10 00 b.Darwen 29-10-85
Source: Scholar.

2004–05	Rochdale	1	0		
2005–06	Rochdale	16	0	**17**	**0**

CARTWRIGHT, Lee (M) **458** **24**
H: 5 9 W: 11 07 b.Rawtenstall 19-9-72
Source: Trainee.

1990–91	Preston NE	14	1		
1991–92	Preston NE	33	3		
1992–93	Preston NE	34	3		
1993–94	Preston NE	39	1		
1994–95	Preston NE	36	1		
1995–96	Preston NE	26	3		
1996–97	Preston NE	14	1		
1997–98	Preston NE	36	2		
1998–99	Preston NE	27	4		
1999–2000	Preston NE	30	1		
2000–01	Preston NE	38	0		
2001–02	Preston NE	36	1		
2002–03	Preston NE	22	1		
2003–04	Preston NE	12	0	**397**	**22**
2003–04	Stockport Co	15	0		
2004–05	Stockport Co	19	1	**34**	**1**
2005–06	Rochdale	27	1	**27**	**1**

CHRISTIE, Iyseden (F) **238** **58**
H: 5 10 W: 12 02 b.Coventry 14-11-76
Source: Trainee.

1994–95	Coventry C	0	0		
1995–96	Coventry C	1	0		
1996–97	Coventry C	0	0	**1**	**0**
1996–97	*Bournemouth*	4	0	**4**	**0**
1996–97	*Mansfield T*	8	0		
1997–98	Mansfield T	39	10		
1998–99	Mansfield T	42	8		
1999–2000	Leyton Orient	36	7		
2000–01	Leyton Orient	7	2		
2001–02	Leyton Orient	15	3	**58**	**12**
2002–03	Mansfield T	37	18		
2003–04	Mansfield T	27	8	**153**	**44**
2004–05	Kidderminster H	8	0		
2005–06	Kidderminster H	0	0	**8**	**0**
2005–06	Rochdale	14	2	**14**	**2**

COLEMAN, Theo (M) **1** **0**
H: 5 11 W: 10 07 b.Manchester 5-5-89

2005–06	Rochdale	1	0	**1**	**0**

COOKSEY, Ernie (M) **105** **12**
H: 5 6 W: 12 04 b.Bishop's Stortford 11-6-80
Source: Crawley T.

2003–04	Oldham Ath	36	4		
2004–05	Oldham Ath	1	0	**37**	**4**
2004–05	Rochdale	34	5		
2005–06	Rochdale	34	3	**68**	**8**

DAGNALL, Chris (F) **60** **10**
H: 5 8 W: 12 03 b.Liverpool 15-4-86
Source: Scholar.

2003–04	Tranmere R	10	1		
2004–05	Tranmere R	23	6		
2005–06	Tranmere R	6	0	**39**	**7**
2005–06	Rochdale	21	3	**21**	**3**

DOOLAN, John (M) **379** **19**
H: 6 1 W: 13 00 b.Liverpool 7-5-74
Source: Trainee.

1992–93	Everton	0	0		
1993–94	Everton	0	0		
1994–95	Mansfield T	24	1		
1995–96	Mansfield T	42	2		
1996–97	Mansfield T	41	6		
1997–98	Mansfield T	24	1	**131**	**10**
1997–98	Barnet	17	0		
1998–99	Barnet	42	2		
1999–2000	Barnet	44	2		
2000–01	Barnet	31	3		
2001–02	Barnet	0	0		
2002–03	Barnet	0	0	**134**	**7**
2003–04	Doncaster R	39	0		
2004–05	Doncaster R	38	2	**77**	**2**
2005–06	Blackpool	19	0	**19**	**0**
2005–06	Rochdale	18	0	**18**	**0**

GALLIMORE, Tony (D) **512** **13**
H: 5 11 W: 12 12 b.Nantwich 21-2-72
Source: Trainee.

1989–90	Stoke C	1	0		
1990–91	Stoke C	7	0		
1991–92	Stoke C	3	0		
1991–92	*Carlisle U*	16	0		
1992–93	Stoke C	0	0	**11**	**0**
1992–93	*Carlisle U*	8	1		
1993–94	Carlisle U	40	1		
1994–95	Carlisle U	40	5		
1995–96	Carlisle U	36	2	**140**	**9**
1995–96	Grimsby T	10	1		
1996–97	Grimsby T	42	1		
1997–98	Grimsby T	35	2		
1998–99	Grimsby T	43	0		
1999–2000	Grimsby T	39	0		
2000–01	Grimsby T	28	0		
2001–02	Grimsby T	38	0		
2002–03	Grimsby T	38	0	**273**	**4**
2003–04	Barnsley	20	0		
2004–05	Barnsley	0	0	**20**	**0**
2004–05	Rochdale	34	0		
2005–06	Rochdale	34	0	**68**	**0**

GIBBINS, Kevin (D) **0** **0**
H: 6 1 W: 11 07 b.Manchester 3-9-85
Source: Scholar.

2005–06	Rochdale	0	0		

GILKS, Matthew (G) **130** **0**
H: 6 3 W: 13 12 b.Rochdale 4-6-82
Source: Scholar.

2000–01	Rochdale	3	0		
2001–02	Rochdale	19	0		
2002–03	Rochdale	20	0		
2003–04	Rochdale	12	0		
2004–05	Rochdale	30	0		
2005–06	Rochdale	46	0	**130**	**0**

GOODALL, Alan (D) **74** **5**
H: 5 7 W: 11 08 b.Birkenhead 2-12-81
Source: Bangor C.

2004–05	Rochdale	34	2		
2005–06	Rochdale	40	3	**74**	**5**

GOODHIND, Warren (D) **212** **3**
H: 5 11 W: 11 02 b.Johannesburg 16-8-77
Source: Trainee.

1996–97	Barnet	3	0		
1997–98	Barnet	35	1		
1998–99	Barnet	15	1		
1999–2000	Barnet	9	0		
2000–01	Barnet	31	1		
2001–02	Barnet	0	0	**93**	**3**
2001–02	Cambridge U	14	0		
2002–03	Cambridge U	37	0		
2003–04	Cambridge U	26	0		
2004–05	Cambridge U	26	0	**103**	**0**
2005–06	Rochdale	10	0	**10**	**0**
2005–06	*Oxford U*	6	0	**6**	**0**

GRIFFITHS, Gareth (D) **337** **20**
H: 6 4 W: 13 13 b.Winsford 10-4-70
Source: Rhyl.

1992–93	Port Vale	0	0		
1993–94	Port Vale	4	2		
1994–95	Port Vale	20	0		
1995–96	Port Vale	41	2		
1996–97	Port Vale	26	0		
1997–98	Port Vale	3	0	**94**	**4**
1997–98	*Shrewsbury T*	6	0	**6**	**0**
1998–99	Wigan Ath	20	0		
1999–2000	Wigan Ath	16	1		
2000–01	Wigan Ath	17	1	**53**	**2**
2001–02	Rochdale	41	4		
2002–03	Rochdale	42	6		
2003–04	Rochdale	33	1		
2004–05	Rochdale	39	1		
2005–06	Rochdale	29	2	**184**	**14**

JACKSON, Mark (D) **186** **4**
H: 5 11 W: 12 00 b.Barnsley 30-9-77
Source: Trainee. *Honours:* England Youth.

1995–96	Leeds U	1	0		
1996–97	Leeds U	17	0		
1997–98	Leeds U	1	0		
1998–99	Leeds U	0	0		
1998–99	*Huddersfield T*	5	0	**5**	**0**
1999–2000	Leeds U	0	0	**19**	**0**
1999–2000	*Barnsley*	1	0	**1**	**0**
1999–2000	Scunthorpe U	6	0		
2000–01	Scunthorpe U	32	1		
2001–02	Scunthorpe U	45	3		
2002–03	Scunthorpe U	33	0		
2003–04	Scunthorpe U	17	0		
2004–05	Scunthorpe U	3	0	**136**	**4**
2004–05	Kidderminster H	13	0		
2005–06	Kidderminster H	0	0	**13**	**0**
2005–06	Rochdale	12	0	**12**	**0**

JASZCZUN, Tommy (M) **171** **0**
H: 5 11 W: 12 09 b.Kettering 16-9-77
Source: Trainee.

1996–97	Aston Villa	0	0		
1997–98	Aston Villa	0	0		
1998–99	Aston Villa	0	0		
1999–2000	Aston Villa	0	0		

1999–2000 Blackpool 19 0
2000–01 Blackpool 35 0
2001–02 Blackpool 40 0
2002–03 Blackpool 21 0
2003–04 Blackpool 7 0 **122 0**
2004–05 Northampton T 32 0 **32 0**
2005–06 Rochdale 17 0 **17 0**

JONES, Gary (M) 311 40
H: 5 11 W: 12 05 b.Birkenhead 3-6-77
Source: Caernarfon T.
1997–98 Swansea C 8 0 **8 0**
1997–98 Rochdale 17 2
1998–99 Rochdale 20 0
1999–2000 Rochdale 39 7
2000–01 Rochdale 44 8
2001–02 Rochdale 20 5
2001–02 Barnsley 25 1
2002–03 Barnsley 31 1
2003–04 Barnsley 0 0 **56 2**
2003–04 Rochdale 26 4
2004–05 Rochdale 39 8
2005–06 Rochdale 42 4 **247 38**

KITCHEN, Ben (M) 9 0
H: 5 9 W: 11 01 b.Bolton 19-8-86
Source: Scholar.
2004–05 Rochdale 1 0
2005–06 Rochdale 8 0 **9 0**

LAMBERT, Ricky (F) 206 54
H: 6 2 W: 14 08 b.Liverpool 16-2-82
Source: Trainee.
1999–2000 Blackpool 3 0
2000–01 Blackpool 0 0 **3 0**
2000–01 Macclesfield T 9 0
2001–02 Macclesfield T 35 8 **44 8**
2001–02 Stockport Co 0 0
2002–03 Stockport Co 29 2
2003–04 Stockport Co 40 12
2004–05 Stockport Co 29 4 **98 18**
2004–05 Rochdale 15 6
2005–06 Rochdale 46 22 **61 28**

MOYO-MODISE, Clive (F) 9 0
H: 5 10 W: 11 00 b.London 20-9-87
2005–06 Rochdale 9 0 **9 0**

RAMSDEN, Simon (D) 84 1
H: 6 0 W: 12 06 b.Bishop Auckland 17-12-81
Source: Scholar.
2000–01 Sunderland 0 0
2001–02 Sunderland 0 0
2002–03 Sunderland 0 0
2002–03 *Notts Co* 32 0 **32 0**
2003–04 Sunderland 0 0
2004–05 Grimsby T 25 0
2005–06 Grimsby T 12 0 **37 0**
2005–06 Rochdale 15 1 **15 1**

STURROCK, Blair (F) 143 19
H: 5 10 W: 12 09 b.Dundee 25-8-81
Source: Dundee U.
2000–01 Brechin C 27 6 **27 6**
2001–02 Plymouth Arg 19 1
2002–03 Plymouth Arg 20 1
2003–04 Plymouth Arg 24 0
2004–05 Plymouth Arg 0 0 **63 2**
2004–05 Kidderminster H 22 5 **22 5**
2005–06 Rochdale 31 6 **31 6**

THOMPSON, Joe (M) 1 0
H: 6 0 W: 9 07 b.Rochdale 5-3-89
Source: Scholar.
2005–06 Rochdale 1 0 **1 0**

WARNER, Scott (M) 73 2
H: 5 11 W: 12 06 b.Rochdale 3-12-83
Source: Scholar.
2002–03 Rochdale 7 0
2003–04 Rochdale 14 1
2004–05 Rochdale 28 0
2005–06 Rochdale 24 1 **73 2**

WILLIAMS, Matt (M) 1 0
H: 5 11 W: 12 00 b.Bury 21-6-88
Source: Scholar.
2004–05 Rochdale 1 0
2005–06 Rochdale 0 0 **1 0**

WOODHALL, Danny (G) 0 0
H: 6 1 W: 12 07 b.West Birch 10-12-87
Source: Scholar.
2005–06 Rochdale 0 0

ROTHERHAM U (68)

BARKER, Shaun (D) 123 7
H: 6 2 W: 12 08 b.Nottingham 19-9-82
Source: Scholar.
2002–03 Rotherham U 11 0
2003–04 Rotherham U 36 2
2004–05 Rotherham U 33 2
2005–06 Rotherham U 43 3 **123 7**

BOULDING, Mick (F) 185 49
H: 5 10 W: 11 05 b.Sheffield 8-2-76
Source: Hallam.
1999–2000 Mansfield T 33 6
2000–01 Mansfield T 33 6
2001–02 Mansfield T 0 0 **66 12**
2001–02 Grimsby T 35 11
2002–03 Aston Villa 0 0
2002–03 *Sheffield U* 6 0 **6 0**
2002–03 Grimsby T 12 4
2003–04 Grimsby T 27 12 **74 27**
2003–04 Barnsley 6 0
2004–05 Barnsley 29 10 **35 10**
2004–05 *Cardiff C* 4 0 **4 0**
2005–06 Rotherham U 0 0

BROGAN, Stephen (D) 3 0
H: 5 7 W: 10 04 b.Rotherham 12-4-88
Source: Scholar.
2005–06 Rotherham U 3 0 **3 0**

BUTLER, Martin (F) 377 109
H: 5 11 W: 11 09 b.Wordsley 15-9-74
Source: Trainee.
1993–94 Walsall 15 3
1994–95 Walsall 8 0
1995–96 Walsall 28 4
1996–97 Walsall 23 1 **74 8**
1997–98 Cambridge U 31 10
1998–99 Cambridge U 46 17
1999–2000 Cambridge U 26 14 **103 41**
1999–2000 Reading 17 4
2000–01 Reading 45 24
2001–02 Reading 17 2
2002–03 Reading 21 2
2003–04 Reading 3 0 **103 32**
2003–04 Rotherham U 37 15
2004–05 Rotherham U 21 6
2005–06 Rotherham U 39 7 **97 28**

CAMPBELL-RYCE, Jamal (M) 86 2
H: 5 7 W: 12 03 b.Lambeth 6-4-83
Source: Scholar. *Honours:* Jamaica 1 full cap.
2002–03 Charlton Ath 1 0
2002–03 *Leyton Orient* 17 2 **17 2**
2003–04 Charlton Ath 2 0
2003–04 *Wimbledon* 4 0 **4 0**
2004–05 Charlton Ath 0 0 **3 0**
2004–05 *Chesterfield* 14 0 **14 0**
2004–05 Rotherham U 24 0
2005–06 Rotherham U 7 0 **31 0**
2005–06 *Southend U* 13 0 **13 0**
2005–06 *Colchester U* 4 0 **4 0**

CUTLER, Neil (G) 167 0
H: 6 1 W: 12 00 b.Cannock 3-9-76
Source: Trainee. *Honours:* England Schools, Youth.
1993–94 WBA 0 0
1994–95 WBA 0 0
1995–96 WBA 0 0
1995–96 *Coventry C* 0 0
1995–96 *Chester C* 1 0
1996–97 Crewe Alex 0 0
1996–97 *Chester C* 5 0
1997–98 Crewe Alex 0 0
1998–99 Chester C 23 0
1999–2000 Chester C 0 0 **29 0**
1999–2000 Aston Villa 1 0
2000–01 Aston Villa 0 0
2000–01 *Oxford U* 11 0 **11 0**
2001–02 Aston Villa 0 0 **1 0**
2001–02 Stoke C 36 0
2002–03 Stoke C 20 0
2002–03 *Swansea C* 13 0 **13 0**
2003–04 Stoke C 13 0 **69 0**
2004–05 Stockport Co 22 0 **22 0**
2005–06 Rotherham U 22 0 **22 0**

DAWS, Nick (M) 458 18
H: 5 11 W: 13 12 b.Salford 15-3-70
Source: Altrincham.
1992–93 Bury 36 1
1993–94 Bury 37 1
1994–95 Bury 34 2
1995–96 Bury 37 1
1996–97 Bury 46 2
1997–98 Bury 46 2
1998–99 Bury 46 2
1999–2000 Bury 43 2
2000–01 Bury 44 3 **369 16**
2001–02 Rotherham U 35 1
2002–03 Rotherham U 33 1
2003–04 Rotherham U 4 0
2003–04 Grimsby T 17 0 **17 0**
2004–05 Rotherham U 0 0
2005–06 Rotherham U 0 0 **72 2**

DUNCUM, Sam (M) 3 0
H: 5 9 W: 11 02 b.Sheffield 18-2-87
Source: Scholar.
2004–05 Rotherham U 2 0
2005–06 Rotherham U 1 0 **3 0**

GILCHRIST, Phil (D) 433 12
H: 5 11 W: 13 12 b.Stockton 25-8-73
Source: Trainee.
1990–91 Nottingham F 0 0
1991–92 Middlesbrough 0 0
1992–93 Hartlepool U 24 0
1993–94 Hartlepool U 35 0
1994–95 Hartlepool U 23 0 **82 0**
1994–95 Oxford U 18 1
1995–96 Oxford U 42 3
1996–97 Oxford U 38 2
1997–98 Oxford U 39 2
1998–99 Oxford U 39 2
1999–2000 Oxford U 1 0 **177 10**
1999–2000 Leicester C 27 1
2000–01 Leicester C 12 0 **39 1**
2000–01 WBA 8 0
2001–02 WBA 43 0
2002–03 WBA 22 0
2003–04 WBA 17 0 **90 0**
2003–04 *Rotherham U* 10 0
2004–05 Rotherham U 24 1
2005–06 Rotherham U 11 0 **45 1**

HEDGE, Jonathan (G) 0 0
H: 6 2 W: 13 02 b.Rotherham 19-7-88
Source: Scholar.
2005–06 Rotherham U 0 0

HOSKINS, Will (F) 49 8
H: 5 11 W: 11 02 b.Nottingham 6-5-86
Source: Scholar. *Honours:* England Youth, Under-20.
2003–04 Rotherham U 4 2
2004–05 Rotherham U 22 2
2005–06 Rotherham U 23 4 **49 8**

HURST, Paul (D) 410 13
H: 5 4 W: 9 04 b.Sheffield 25-9-74
Source: Trainee.
1993–94 Rotherham U 4 0
1994–95 Rotherham U 13 0
1995–96 Rotherham U 40 1
1996–97 Rotherham U 30 3
1997–98 Rotherham U 30 0
1998–99 Rotherham U 32 2
1999–2000 Rotherham U 30 2
2000–01 Rotherham U 44 3
2001–02 Rotherham U 45 0
2002–03 Rotherham U 44 1
2003–04 Rotherham U 28 1
2004–05 Rotherham U 39 0
2005–06 Rotherham U 31 0 **410 13**

KEANE, Michael (M) 122 8
H: 5 7 W: 10 10 b.Dublin 29-12-82
Source: Scholar. *Honours:* Eire Under-21.
2000–01 Preston NE 2 0
2001–02 Preston NE 20 2
2002–03 Preston NE 5 0
2002–03 *Grimsby T* 7 2 **7 2**
2003–04 Preston NE 30 1 **57 3**

2004–05	Hull C	20	3	**20**	**3**
2004–05	Rotherham U	10	0		
2005–06	Rotherham U	28	0	**38**	**0**

KING, Liam (D) **0** **0**
H: 5 9 W: 10 02 b.Rotherham 3-12-87
Source: Scholar.

2005–06	Rotherham U	0	0		

McLAREN, Paul (M) **335** **16**
H: 6 0 W: 13 04 b.High Wycombe 17-11-76
Source: Trainee.

1993–94	Luton T	1	0		
1994–95	Luton T	0	0		
1995–96	Luton T	12	1		
1996–97	Luton T	24	0		
1997–98	Luton T	43	0		
1998–99	Luton T	23	0		
1999–2000	Luton T	29	1		
2000–01	Luton T	35	2	**167**	**4**
2001–02	Sheffield W	35	2		
2002–03	Sheffield W	36	4		
2003–04	Sheffield W	25	2	**96**	**8**
2004–05	Rotherham U	33	1		
2005–06	Rotherham U	39	3	**72**	**4**

MINTO, Scott (D) **368** **11**
H: 5 9 W: 12 07 b.Bromborough 6-8-71
Source: Trainee. *Honours:* England Youth, Under-21.

1988–89	Charlton Ath	3	0		
1989–90	Charlton Ath	23	2		
1990–91	Charlton Ath	43	1		
1991–92	Charlton Ath	33	1		
1992–93	Charlton Ath	36	1		
1993–94	Charlton Ath	42	2	**180**	**7**
1994–95	Chelsea	19	0		
1995–96	Chelsea	10	0		
1996–97	Chelsea	25	4	**54**	**4**
1997–98	Benfica	21	0		
1998–99	Benfica	10	0	**31**	**0**
1998–99	West Ham U	15	0		
1999–2000	West Ham U	18	0		
2000–01	West Ham U	1	0		
2001–02	West Ham U	5	0		
2002–03	West Ham U	12	0	**51**	**0**
2003–04	Rotherham U	32	0		
2004–05	Rotherham U	14	0		
2005–06	Rotherham U	6	0	**52**	**0**

MONKHOUSE, Andy (M) **128** **9**
H: 6 1 W: 11 06 b.Leeds 23-10-80
Source: Trainee.

1998–99	Rotherham U	5	1		
1999–2000	Rotherham U	0	0		
2000–01	Rotherham U	12	0		
2001–02	Rotherham U	38	2		
2002–03	Rotherham U	20	0		
2003–04	Rotherham U	27	3		
2004–05	Rotherham U	14	2		
2005–06	Rotherham U	12	1	**128**	**9**

MONTGOMERY, Gary (G) **39** **0**
H: 5 11 W: 13 08 b.Leamington Spa 8-10-82
Source: Scholar.

2000–01	Coventry C	0	0		
2001–02	Coventry C	0	0		
2001–02	*Crewe Alex*	0	0		
2001–02	*Kidderminster H*	2	0	**2**	**0**
2002–03	Coventry C	8	0	**8**	**0**
2003–04	Rotherham U	4	0		
2004–05	Rotherham U	1	0		
2005–06	Rotherham U	24	0	**29**	**0**

MULLIN, John (M) **323** **26**
H: 6 0 W: 11 10 b.Bury 11-8-75
Source: School.

1992–93	Burnley	0	0		
1993–94	Burnley	6	1		
1994–95	Burnley	12	1		
1995–96	Sunderland	10	1		
1996–97	Sunderland	10	1		
1997–98	Sunderland	6	0		
1997–98	*Preston NE*	7	0	**7**	**0**
1997–98	*Burnley*	6	0		
1998–99	Sunderland	9	2	**35**	**4**
1999–2000	Burnley	37	5		
2000–01	Burnley	36	3		
2001–02	Burnley	4	0	**101**	**10**
2001–02	Rotherham U	34	2		
2002–03	Rotherham U	34	3		
2003–04	Rotherham U	38	4		
2004–05	Rotherham U	31	1		
2005–06	Rotherham U	43	2	**180**	**12**

MURDOCK, Colin (D) **269** **11**
H: 6 2 W: 13 00 b.Ballymena 2-7-75
Source: Trainee. *Honours:* Northern Ireland Schools, Youth, B, 34 full caps, 1 goal.

1992–93	Manchester U	0	0		
1993–94	Manchester U	0	0		
1994–95	Manchester U	0	0		
1995–96	Manchester U	0	0		
1996–97	Manchester U	0	0		
1997–98	Preston NE	27	1		
1998–99	Preston NE	33	1		
1999–2000	Preston NE	33	2		
2000–01	Preston NE	37	0		
2001–02	Preston NE	23	2		
2002–03	Preston NE	24	0	**177**	**6**
2003–04	Hibernian	32	3		
2004–05	Hibernian	5	0	**37**	**3**
2004–05	Crewe Alex	16	0	**16**	**0**
2005–06	Rotherham U	39	2	**39**	**2**

NEWSHAM, Mark (F) **7** **0**
H: 5 10 W: 9 11 b.Hatfield 24-3-87
Source: Scholar.

2004–05	Rotherham U	4	0		
2005–06	Rotherham U	3	0	**7**	**0**

ROBERTSON, Gregor (D) **71** **1**
H: 6 0 W: 12 04 b.Edinburgh 19-1-84
Honours: Scotland Under-21.

2000–01	Nottingham F	0	0		
2001–02	Nottingham F	0	0		
2002–03	Nottingham F	0	0		
2003–04	Nottingham F	16	0		
2004–05	Nottingham F	20	0	**36**	**0**
2005–06	Rotherham U	35	1	**35**	**1**

SHAW, Paul (F) **344** **77**
H: 5 11 W: 12 04 b.Burnham 4-9-73
Source: Trainee.

1991–92	Arsenal	0	0		
1992–93	Arsenal	0	0		
1993–94	Arsenal	0	0		
1994–95	Arsenal	1	0		
1994–95	*Burnley*	9	4	**9**	**4**
1995–96	Arsenal	3	0		
1995–96	*Cardiff C*	6	0	**6**	**0**
1995–96	*Peterborough U*	12	5	**12**	**5**
1996–97	Arsenal	8	2		
1997–98	Arsenal	0	0	**12**	**2**
1997–98	Millwall	40	11		
1998–99	Millwall	34	10		
1999–2000	Millwall	35	5	**109**	**26**
2000–01	Gillingham	33	1		
2001–02	Gillingham	37	7		
2002–03	Gillingham	44	12		
2003–04	Gillingham	21	6	**135**	**26**
2003–04	Sheffield U	13	1		
2004–05	Sheffield U	21	7		
2004–05	*Rotherham U*	9	2		
2005–06	Sheffield U	1	0	**35**	**8**
2005–06	Rotherham U	17	4	**26**	**6**

TAYLOR, Ryan (F) **1** **0**
H: 6 2 W: 10 10 b.Rotherham 4-5-88
Source: Scholar.

2005–06	Rotherham U	1	0	**1**	**0**

VERNAZZA, Paulo (M) **154** **3**
H: 6 0 W: 12 02 b.Islington 1-11-79
Source: Trainee. *Honours:* England Youth, Under-21.

1997–98	Arsenal	1	0		
1998–99	Arsenal	0	0		
1998–99	*Ipswich T*	2	0	**2**	**0**
1999–2000	Arsenal	2	0		
1999–2000	*Portsmouth*	7	0	**7**	**0**
2000–01	Arsenal	2	1	**5**	**1**
2000–01	Watford	23	2		
2001–02	Watford	21	0		
2002–03	Watford	23	0		
2003–04	Watford	29	0	**96**	**2**
2004–05	Rotherham U	27	0		
2005–06	Rotherham U	0	0	**27**	**0**
2005–06	*Barnet*	17	0	**17**	**0**

WHITTINGTON, Lee (M) **0** **0**
H: 5 8 W: 9 13 b.Sheffield 10-5-87
Source: Scholar.

2005–06	Rotherham U	0	0		

WILLIAMSON, Lee (M) **218** **7**
H: 5 10 W: 10 04 b.Derby 7-6-82
Source: Trainee.

1999–2000	Mansfield T	4	0		
2000–01	Mansfield T	15	0		
2001–02	Mansfield T	46	3		
2002–03	Mansfield T	40	0		
2003–04	Mansfield T	35	0		
2004–05	Mansfield T	4	0	**144**	**3**
2004–05	Northampton T	37	0	**37**	**0**
2005–06	Rotherham U	37	4	**37**	**4**

WORRELL, David (D) **205** **0**
H: 5 11 W: 12 04 b.Dublin 12-1-78
Source: Trainee. *Honours:* Eire Youth, Under-21.

1994–95	Blackburn R	0	0		
1995–96	Blackburn R	0	0		
1996–97	Blackburn R	0	0		
1997–98	Blackburn R	0	0		
1998–99	Blackburn R	0	0		
1998–99	Dundee U	4	0		
1999–2000	Dundee U	13	0	**17**	**0**
2000–01	Plymouth Arg	14	0		
2001–02	Plymouth Arg	42	0		
2002–03	Plymouth Arg	43	0		
2003–04	Plymouth Arg	18	0		
2004–05	Plymouth Arg	30	0	**147**	**0**
2005–06	Rotherham U	41	0	**41**	**0**

RUSHDEN & D (69)

ALLEN, Graham (D) **237** **12**
H: 6 1 W: 12 00 b.Bolton 8-4-77
Source: Trainee. *Honours:* England Youth.

1994–95	Everton	0	0		
1995–96	Everton	0	0		
1996–97	Everton	1	0		
1997–98	Everton	5	0		
1998–99	Everton	0	0	**6**	**0**
1998–99	Tranmere R	41	5		
1999–2000	Tranmere R	24	0		
2000–01	Tranmere R	22	0		
2001–02	Tranmere R	31	1		
2002–03	Tranmere R	41	3		
2003–04	Tranmere R	41	1	**200**	**10**
2004–05	Rushden & D	26	1		
2005–06	Rushden & D	5	1	**31**	**2**

BERRY, Tyrone (F) **25** **0**
H: 5 8 W: 10 03 b.Brixton 11-3-87
Source: Scholar.

2004–05	Crystal Palace	0	0		
2005–06	Crystal Palace	0	0		
2005–06	*Notts Co*	5	0	**5**	**0**
2005–06	Rushden & D	20	0	**20**	**0**

BOLT, Alex (M) **0** **0**
H: 5 8 W: 10 00 b. 11-6-89
Source: Scholar.

2005–06	Rushden & D	0	0		

BROUGHTON, Drewe (F) **248** **46**
H: 6 3 W: 12 01 b.Hitchin 25-10-78
Source: Trainee.

1996–97	Norwich C	8	1		
1997–98	Norwich C	1	0		
1997–98	*Wigan Ath*	4	0	**4**	**0**
1998–99	Norwich C	0	0	**9**	**1**
1998–99	Brentford	1	0	**1**	**0**
1998–99	Peterborough U	25	7		
1999–2000	Peterborough U	10	1		
2000–01	Peterborough U	0	0	**35**	**8**
2000–01	Kidderminster H	19	7		
2001–02	Kidderminster H	38	8		
2002–03	Kidderminster H	37	4	**94**	**19**
2003–04	Southend U	35	2		
2004–05	Southend U	9	0	**44**	**2**
2004–05	Rushden & D	21	6		
2004–05	*Wycombe W*	3	0	**3**	**0**
2005–06	Rushden & D	37	10	**58**	**16**

BULL, Ronnie (D) 123 2

H: 5 7 W: 10 12 b.Hackney 26-12-80
Source: Trainee.

1998–99	Millwall	1	0		
1999–2000	Millwall	9	0		
2000–01	Millwall	2	0		
2001–02	Millwall	26	0		
2002–03	Millwall	12	0		
2003–04	Millwall	0	0	**50**	**0**
2003–04	*Yeovil T*	7	0	**7**	**0**
2003–04	Brentford	20	0	**20**	**0**
2004–05	Grimsby T	27	2		
2005–06	Grimsby T	0	0	**27**	**2**
From New Zealand Knights					
2005–06	Rushden & D	19	0	**19**	**0**

CASKEY, Darren (M) 376 51

H: 5 8 W: 12 04 b.Basildon 21-8-74
Source: Trainee. *Honours:* England Schools, Youth.

1991–92	Tottenham H	0	0		
1992–93	Tottenham H	0	0		
1993–94	Tottenham H	25	4		
1994–95	Tottenham H	4	0		
1995–96	Tottenham H	3	0	**32**	**4**
1995–96	*Watford*	6	1	**6**	**1**
1995–96	Reading	15	2		
1996–97	Reading	35	0		
1997–98	Reading	23	0		
1998–99	Reading	42	7		
1999–2000	Reading	44	17		
2000–01	Reading	43	9	**202**	**35**
2001–02	Notts Co	42	5		
2002–03	Notts Co	39	3		
2003–04	Notts Co	33	2	**114**	**10**
2003–04	Bristol C	0	0		
From Hornchurch					
2004–05	Peterborough U	4	0	**4**	**0**
From Virginia Beach M.					
2005–06	Rushden & D	18	1	**18**	**1**

CASTLE, Peter (D) 2 0

H: 6 0 W: 12 02 b.Southampton 12-3-87
Source: Scholar. *Honours:* FA Schools.

2002–03	Reading	1	0		
2003–04	Reading	0	0		
2004–05	Reading	0	0		
2005–06	Reading	0	0	**1**	**0**
2005–06	Rushden & D	1	0	**1**	**0**

CHILLINGWORTH, Daniel (F) 118 18

H: 6 0 W: 12 06 b.Cambridge 13-9-81
Source: Scholarship.

1999–2000	Cambridge U	3	0		
2000–01	Cambridge U	1	0		
2001–02	*Darlington*	4	1	**4**	**1**
2001–02	Cambridge U	12	2		
2002–03	Cambridge U	30	0		
2003–04	Cambridge U	13	7		
2004–05	Cambridge U	28	4	**87**	**13**
2004–05	*Leyton Orient*	8	2	**8**	**2**
2005–06	Rushden & D	6	0	**6**	**0**
2005–06	*Notts Co*	13	2	**13**	**2**

CRANE, Daniel (G) 8 0

H: 6 3 W: 14 11 b.Birmingham 27-5-84
Source: Scholar.

2003–04	WBA	0	0		
2004–05	WBA	0	0		
From Burton Alb.					
2005–06	Rushden & D	8	0	**8**	**0**

GIER, Rob (D) 138 2

H: 5 10 W: 11 07 b.Ascot 6-1-80
Source: Trainee.

1998–99	Wimbledon	0	0		
1999–2000	Wimbledon	0	0		
2000–01	Wimbledon	14	0		
2001–02	Wimbledon	3	0		
2002–03	Wimbledon	29	0		
2003–04	Wimbledon	25	0	**71**	**0**
2004–05	Rushden & D	32	2		
2005–06	Rushden & D	35	0	**67**	**2**

GRAINGER, Daniel (D) 14 1

H: 5 10 W: 10 10 b.Thrapston 15-10-86
Source: Scholar.

2005–06	Rushden & D	14	1	**14**	**1**

GULLIVER, Phil (D) 94 4

H: 6 2 W: 13 05 b.Bishop Auckland 12-9-82
Source: Scholar.

2000–01	Middlesbrough	0	0		
2001–02	Middlesbrough	0	0		
2002–03	Middlesbrough	0	0		
2002–03	*Blackpool*	3	0	**3**	**0**
2002–03	*Carlisle U*	1	0	**1**	**0**
2002–03	*Bournemouth*	6	0	**6**	**0**
2003–04	Middlesbrough	0	0		
2003–04	*Bury*	10	0	**10**	**0**
2003–04	*Scunthorpe U*	2	0	**2**	**0**
2004–05	Rushden & D	32	0		
2005–06	Rushden & D	40	4	**72**	**4**

HATSWELL, Wayne (D) 137 4

H: 6 0 W: 13 10 b.Swindon 8-2-75
Source: Forest Green R.

2000–01	Oxford U	27	0		
2001–02	Oxford U	21	0		
2002–03	Oxford U	0	0	**48**	**0**
From Chester C.					
2003–04	Kidderminster H	32	2		
2004–05	Kidderminster H	40	1	**72**	**3**
2005–06	Rushden & D	17	1	**17**	**1**

HAWKINS, Peter (D) 196 1

H: 6 0 W: 11 04 b.Maidstone 19-9-78
Source: Trainee.

1996–97	Wimbledon	0	0		
1997–98	Wimbledon	0	0		
1998–99	Wimbledon	0	0		
1999–2000	Wimbledon	0	0		
1999–2000	*York C*	14	0	**14**	**0**
2000–01	Wimbledon	30	0		
2001–02	Wimbledon	29	0		
2002–03	Wimbledon	43	0		
2003–04	Wimbledon	18	0	**120**	**0**
2004–05	Rushden & D	41	1		
2005–06	Rushden & D	21	0	**62**	**1**

HUNTER, Barry (D) 292 16

H: 6 4 W: 12 00 b.Coleraine 18-11-68
Source: Crusaders. *Honours:* Northern Ireland Youth, B, 15 full caps, 1 goal.

1993–94	Wrexham	23	1		
1994–95	Wrexham	37	0		
1995–96	Wrexham	31	3	**91**	**4**
1996–97	Reading	27	2		
1997–98	Reading	0	0		
1998–99	Reading	3	0		
1998–99	*Southend U*	5	2	**5**	**2**
1999–2000	Reading	31	1		
2000–01	Reading	23	1		
2001–02	Reading	0	0	**84**	**4**
2001–02	Rushden & D	23	1		
2002–03	Rushden & D	40	1		
2003–04	Rushden & D	43	4		
2004–05	Rushden & D	1	0		
2005–06	Rushden & D	5	0	**112**	**6**

IOANNOU, Nicky (M) 0 0

H: 5 11 W: 11 00 b.Camden 3-7-87
Source: Scholar.

2005–06	Rushden & D	0	0		

JACKSON, Simeon (M) 17 5

H: 5 10 W: 10 12 b.Kingston, Jamaica 28-3-87
Source: Scholar. *Honours:* Canada Youth.

2004–05	Rushden & D	3	0		
2005–06	Rushden & D	14	5	**17**	**5**

JONES, Ashley (G) 0 0

Source: Scholar.

2005–06	Rushden & D	0	0		

JOSEPH, Ricardo (M) 1 0

H: 5 11 W: 12 06 b.Jamaica 17-1-87
Source: Scholar.

2005–06	Rushden & D	1	0	**1**	**0**

KELLY, Marcus (M) 60 3

H: 5 7 W: 10 00 b.Kettering 16-3-86
Source: Juniors.

2003–04	Rushden & D	8	0		
2004–05	Rushden & D	11	0		
2005–06	Rushden & D	41	3	**60**	**3**

KENNEDY, Luke (M) 3 0

H: 6 1 W: 11 03 b.Peterborough 22-5-86
Source: Scholar.

2004–05	Rushden & D	3	0		
2005–06	Rushden & D	0	0	**3**	**0**

KITSON, Paul (F) 302 78

H: 6 0 W: 13 00 b.Murton 9-1-71
Source: Trainee. *Honours:* England Under-21.

1988–89	Leicester C	0	0		
1989–90	Leicester C	13	0		
1990–91	Leicester C	7	0		
1991–92	Leicester C	30	6	**50**	**6**
1991–92	Derby Co	12	4		
1992–93	Derby Co	44	17		
1993–94	Derby Co	41	13		
1994–95	Derby Co	8	2	**105**	**36**
1994–95	Newcastle U	26	8		
1995–96	Newcastle U	7	2		
1996–97	Newcastle U	3	0	**36**	**10**
1996–97	West Ham U	14	8		
1997–98	West Ham U	13	4		
1998–99	West Ham U	17	3		
1999–2000	West Ham U	10	0		
1999–2000	*Charlton Ath*	6	1	**6**	**1**
2000–01	West Ham U	2	0		
2000–01	*Crystal Palace*	4	0	**4**	**0**
2001–02	West Ham U	7	3		
2002–03	West Ham U	0	0	**63**	**18**
2002–03	Brighton & HA	10	2		
2003–04	Brighton & HA	0	0	**10**	**2**
2003–04	Rushden & D	28	5		
From Aldershot T					
2005–06	Rushden & D	0	0	**28**	**5**

LAMBLEY, Lawrence (M) 0 0

H: 5 10 W: 12 00 b. 20-6-89
Source: Scholar.

2005–06	Rushden & D	0	0		

LANGDON, Dominic (M) 0 0

H: 6 2 W: 11 00 b. *Honours:* 14-9-88

2005–06	Rushden & D	0	0		

McCAFFERTY, Neil (M) 45 0

H: 5 7 W: 10 00 b.Derry 19-7-84
Source: Scholar.

2001–02	Charlton Ath	0	0		
2002–03	Charlton Ath	0	0		
2003–04	Charlton Ath	0	0		
2003–04	*Cambridge U*	6	0	**6**	**0**
2004–05	Charlton Ath	0	0		
2004–05	*Rushden & D*	16	0		
2005–06	Rushden & D	23	0	**39**	**0**

MILLS, Gary (M) 87 2

H: 5 9 W: 11 06 b.Sheppey 20-5-81
Source: Juniors.

2001–02	Rushden & D	9	0		
2002–03	Rushden & D	30	0		
2003–04	Rushden & D	30	1		
2004–05	Rushden & D	7	1		
2005–06	Rushden & D	11	0	**87**	**2**

NICHOLLS, Ashley (M) 141 7

H: 5 11 W: 11 11 b.Ipswich 30-10-81
Source: Ipswich W. *Honours:* England Schools.

2000–01	Ipswich T	0	0		
2001–02	Ipswich T	0	0		
2002–03	Darlington	41	6		
2003–04	Darlington	26	0	**67**	**6**
2003–04	*Cambridge U*	16	1		
2004–05	Cambridge U	28	0		
2005–06	Cambridge U	0	0	**44**	**1**
2005–06	Rushden & D	30	0	**30**	**0**

O'KEEFE, Sean (M) 0 0

H: 5 11 W: 11 00
Source: Scholar.

2005–06	Rushden & D	0	0		

OKUONGHAE, Magnus (F) 22 1

H: 6 3 W: 13 04 b.Nigeria 16-2-86
Source: Scholar.

2003–04	Rushden & D	1	0		
2004–05	Rushden & D	0	0		
2005–06	Rushden & D	21	1	**22**	**1**

PEARSON, Greg (F) 25 1
H: 6 0 W: 12 00 b.Birmingham 3-4-85
Source: Trainee.
2003–04 West Ham U 0 0
2004–05 West Ham U 0 0
2004–05 *Lincoln C* 3 0 **3 0**
2005–06 Rushden & D 22 1 **22 1**

REYNOLDS, Ben (M) 0 0
H: 5 10 W: 10 00 b. 27-9-88
2005–06 Rushden & D 0 0

RIDGEWAY, Sean (M) 0 0
H: 5 11 W: 12 03 b.London 10-12-86
2005–06 Rushden & D 0 0

SAVAGE, David (M) 427 34
H: 6 2 W: 13 05 b.Dublin 30-7-73
Source: Longford T. *Honours:* Eire Under-21, 5 full caps.
1994–95 Millwall 37 2
1995–96 Millwall 27 0
1996–97 Millwall 35 3
1997–98 Millwall 31 1
1998–99 Millwall 2 0 **132 6**
1998–99 Northampton T 27 5
1999–2000 Northampton T 43 5
2000–01 Northampton T 43 8 **113 18**
2001–02 Oxford U 42 1
2002–03 Oxford U 43 4 **85 5**
2003–04 Bristol R 38 2
2004–05 Bristol R 27 1 **65 3**
2005–06 Rushden & D 32 2 **32 2**

SHAW, Tom (M) 1 0
H: 6 0 W: 12 00 b.Nottingham 1-12-86
Source: Scholar.
2005–06 Rushden & D 1 0 **1 0**

STEAD, Jon (M) 0 0
H: 5 11 W: 11 00 b.Peterborough 6-1-88
Source: Scholar.
2005–06 Rushden & D 0 0

TAYLOR, Jason (M) 32 3
H: 6 2 W: 12 00 b.Burgess Hill 12-10-85
2004–05 Rushden & D 20 2
2005–06 Rushden & D 12 1 **32 3**

TOMLIN, Lee (F) 21 0
H: 5 11 W: 11 00 b.Leicester 12-1-89
2005–06 Rushden & D 21 0 **21 0**

TURNER, John (F) 86 11
H: 5 10 W: 11 00 b.Harrow 12-2-86
Source: Scholar.
2002–03 Cambridge U 1 1
2003–04 Cambridge U 36 3
2004–05 Cambridge U 38 6
2005–06 Cambridge U 0 0 **75 10**
2005–06 Rushden & D 11 1 **11 1**

TYNAN, Scott (G) 21 0
H: 6 2 W: 13 03 b.Knowsley 27-11-83
Source: Wigan Ath Scholar.
2001–02 Nottingham F 0 0
2002–03 Nottingham F 0 0
2003–04 Nottingham F 0 0
2004–05 Nottingham F 0 0
2005–06 Barnet 7 0 **7 0**
2005–06 Rushden & D 14 0 **14 0**

UDOJI, Ugo (M) 0 0
b. 9-1-89
Source: Scholar.
2005–06 Rushden & D 0 0

WARK, Scott (M) 1 0
H: 6 3 W: 13 00 b.Glasgow 9-6-87
Source: Scholar.
2004–05 Rushden & D 1 0
2005–06 Rushden & D 0 0 **1 0**

WOODMAN, Andy (G) 405 0
H: 6 3 W: 15 08 b.Camberwell 11-8-71
Source: Apprentice.
1989–90 Crystal Palace 0 0
1990–91 Crystal Palace 0 0
1991–92 Crystal Palace 0 0
1992–93 Crystal Palace 0 0
1993–94 Crystal Palace 0 0
1994–95 Exeter C 6 0 **6 0**
1994–95 Northampton T 10 0
1995–96 Northampton T 44 0
1996–97 Northampton T 45 0
1997–98 Northampton T 46 0
1998–99 Northampton T 18 0 **163 0**
1998–99 Brentford 22 0
1999–2000 Brentford 39 0
1999–2000 *Peterborough U* 0 0
2000–01 Brentford 0 0 **61 0**
2000–01 *Southend U* 17 0 **17 0**
2000–01 Colchester U 28 0
2001–02 Colchester U 26 0 **54 0**
2001–02 Oxford U 15 0
2002–03 Oxford U 45 0
2003–04 Oxford U 41 0 **101 0**
From Stevenage B
2005–06 Barnsley 0 0
2005–06 Rushden & D 3 0 **3 0**

SCUNTHORPE U (70)

ALLANSON, Ashley (M) 1 0
H: 5 11 W: 12 00 b.Hull 13-11-86
Source: Hull C Scholar.
2005–06 Scunthorpe U 1 0 **1 0**

BARACLOUGH, Ian (M) 554 39
H: 6 1 W: 12 09 b.Leicester 4-12-70
Source: Trainee.
1988–89 Leicester C 0 0
1989–90 Leicester C 0 0
1989–90 *Wigan Ath* 9 2 **9 2**
1990–91 Leicester C 0 0
1990–91 *Grimsby T* 4 0
1991–92 Grimsby T 0 0
1992–93 Grimsby T 1 0 **5 0**
1992–93 Lincoln C 36 5
1993–94 Lincoln C 37 5 **73 10**
1994–95 Mansfield T 36 3
1995–96 Mansfield T 11 2 **47 5**
1995–96 Notts Co 35 2
1996–97 Notts Co 38 2
1997–98 Notts Co 38 6
1997–98 QPR 8 0
1998–99 QPR 43 1
1999–2000 QPR 45 0
2000–01 QPR 29 0 **125 1**
2001–02 Notts Co 33 3
2002–03 Notts Co 34 2
2003–04 Notts Co 34 0 **212 15**
2004–05 Scunthorpe U 45 3
2005–06 Scunthorpe U 38 3 **83 6**

BEAGRIE, Peter (M) 661 90
H: 5 8 W: 12 04 b.Middlesbrough 28-11-65
Source: Local. *Honours:* England Under-21, B.
1983–84 Middlesbrough 0 0
1984–85 Middlesbrough 7 1
1985–86 Middlesbrough 26 1 **33 2**
1986–87 Sheffield U 41 9
1987–88 Sheffield U 43 2 **84 11**
1988–89 Stoke C 41 7
1989–90 Stoke C 13 0 **54 7**
1989–90 Everton 19 0
1990–91 Everton 17 2
1991–92 Everton 27 3
1991–92 *Sunderland* 5 1 **5 1**
1992–93 Everton 22 3
1993–94 Everton 29 3
1993–94 Manchester C 9 1
1994–95 Manchester C 37 2
1995–96 Manchester C 5 0
1996–97 Manchester C 1 0 **52 3**
1997–98 Bradford C 34 0
1997–98 *Everton* 6 0 **120 11**
1998–99 Bradford C 43 12
1999–2000 Bradford C 35 7
2000–01 Bradford C 19 1 **131 20**
2000–01 Wigan Ath 10 1 **10 1**
2001–02 Scunthorpe U 40 11
2002–03 Scunthorpe U 34 5
2003–04 Scunthorpe U 32 11
2004–05 Scunthorpe U 36 2
2005–06 Scunthorpe U 30 5 **172 34**

BUTLER, Andy (D) 88 13
H: 6 0 W: 13 00 b.Doncaster 4-11-83
Source: Scholar.
2003–04 Scunthorpe U 35 2
2004–05 Scunthorpe U 37 10
2005–06 Scunthorpe U 16 1 **88 13**

BYRNE, Cliff (D) 113 3
H: 6 0 W: 12 11 b.Dublin 27-4-82
Honours: Eire Under-21.
1999–2000 Sunderland 0 0
2000–01 Sunderland 0 0
2001–02 Sunderland 0 0
2002–03 Sunderland 0 0
2002–03 *Scunthorpe U* 13 0
2003–04 Scunthorpe U 39 1
2004–05 Scunthorpe U 29 1
2005–06 Scunthorpe U 32 1 **113 3**

CORDEN, Wayne (M) 285 38
H: 5 10 W: 11 05 b.Leek 1-11-75
Source: Trainee.
1994–95 Port Vale 1 0
1995–96 Port Vale 2 0
1996–97 Port Vale 12 0
1997–98 Port Vale 33 1
1998–99 Port Vale 16 0
1999–2000 Port Vale 2 0 **66 1**
2000–01 Mansfield T 34 3
2001–02 Mansfield T 46 8
2002–03 Mansfield T 44 13
2003–04 Mansfield T 44 8
2004–05 Mansfield T 24 3 **192 35**
2004–05 Scunthorpe U 8 0
2005–06 Scunthorpe U 9 0 **17 0**
2005–06 *Chester C* 2 0 **2 0**
2005–06 *Leyton Orient* 8 2 **8 2**

CROSBY, Andy (D) 542 30
H: 6 2 W: 13 13 b.Rotherham 3-3-73
Source: Leeds U Trainee.
1991–92 Doncaster R 22 0
1992–93 Doncaster R 29 0
1993–94 Doncaster R 0 0 **51 0**
1993–94 Darlington 25 0
1994–95 Darlington 35 0
1995–96 Darlington 45 1
1996–97 Darlington 42 1
1997–98 Darlington 34 1 **181 3**
1998–99 Chester C 41 4 **41 4**
1999–2000 Brighton & HA 36 3
2000–01 Brighton & HA 34 2
2001–02 Brighton & HA 2 0 **72 5**
2001–02 Oxford U 23 1
2002–03 Oxford U 46 6
2003–04 Oxford U 42 5 **111 12**
2004–05 Scunthorpe U 44 3
2005–06 Scunthorpe U 42 3 **86 6**

EVANS, Tom (G) 245 0
H: 6 1 W: 13 11 b.Doncaster 31-12-76
Source: Trainee. *Honours:* Northern Ireland Youth.
1995–96 Sheffield U 0 0
1996–97 Crystal Palace 0 0
1996–97 *Coventry C* 0 0
1997–98 Scunthorpe U 5 0
1998–99 Scunthorpe U 24 0
1999–2000 Scunthorpe U 28 0
2000–01 Scunthorpe U 46 0
2001–02 Scunthorpe U 42 0
2002–03 Scunthorpe U 46 0
2003–04 Scunthorpe U 36 0
2004–05 Scunthorpe U 0 0
2005–06 Scunthorpe U 18 0 **245 0**

FOSTER, Steve (D) 315 9
H: 6 1 W: 13 00 b.Mansfield 3-12-74
Source: Trainee.
1993–94 Mansfield T 5 0 **5 0**
From Telford U, Woking
1997–98 Bristol R 34 0
1998–99 Bristol R 43 1
1999–2000 Bristol R 43 1
2000–01 Bristol R 44 4
2001–02 Bristol R 33 1 **197 7**
2002–03 Doncaster R 0 0
2003–04 Doncaster R 44 1
2004–05 Doncaster R 34 1
2005–06 Doncaster R 17 0 **95 2**
2005–06 Scunthorpe U 18 0 **18 0**

GOODWIN, Jim (M) 116 9
H: 5 9 W: 12 01 b.Waterford 20-11-81
Source: Tramore. *Honours:* Eire Under-21, 1 full cap.
2001–02 Celtic 0 0

2002–03 Stockport Co 33 3
2003–04 Stockport Co 34 4
2004–05 Stockport Co 36 0 **103 7**
2005–06 Scunthorpe U 13 2 **13 2**

HINDS, Richard (D) 149 7
H: 6 2 W: 12 02 b.Sheffield 22-8-80
Source: Schoolboy.
1998–99 Tranmere R 2 0
1999–2000 Tranmere R 6 0
2000–01 Tranmere R 29 0
2001–02 Tranmere R 10 0
2002–03 Tranmere R 8 0 **55 0**
2003–04 Hull C 39 1
2004–05 Hull C 6 0 **45 1**
2004–05 *Scunthorpe U* 7 0
2005–06 Scunthorpe U 42 6 **49 6**

JOHNSON, Tommy (F) 397 126
H: 5 10 W: 12 04 b.Newcastle 15-1-71
Source: Trainee. *Honours:* England Under-21.
1988–89 Notts Co 10 4
1989–90 Notts Co 40 18
1990–91 Notts Co 37 16
1991–92 Notts Co 31 9 **118 47**
1991–92 Derby Co 12 2
1992–93 Derby Co 35 8
1993–94 Derby Co 37 13
1994–95 Derby Co 14 7 **98 30**
1994–95 Aston Villa 14 4
1995–96 Aston Villa 23 5
1996–97 Aston Villa 20 4 **57 13**
1996–97 Celtic 4 1
1997–98 Celtic 2 0
1998–99 Celtic 3 3
1999–2000 Celtic 10 9
1999–2000 *Everton* 3 0 **3 0**
2000–01 Celtic 16 5 **35 18**
2001–02 Sheffield W 8 3 **8 3**
2001–02 Kilmarnock 10 7 **10 7**
2002–03 Gillingham 26 2
2003–04 Gillingham 15 3
2004–05 Gillingham 8 2 **49 7**
2004–05 Sheffield U 5 0 **5 0**
2005–06 Scunthorpe U 14 1 **14 1**

KEOGH, Andrew (F) 74 16
H: 6 0 W: 11 00 b.Dublin 16-5-86
Source: Scholar. *Honours:* Eire Youth, Under-21.
2003–04 Leeds U 0 0
2004–05 Leeds U 0 0
2004–05 *Bury* 4 2 **4 2**
2004–05 Scunthorpe U 25 3
2005–06 Scunthorpe U 45 11 **70 14**

MACKENZIE, Neil (M) 220 13
H: 6 2 W: 12 05 b.Birmingham 15-4-76
Source: WBA schoolboy.
1996–97 Stoke C 22 1
1997–98 Stoke C 12 0
1998–99 Stoke C 6 0
1998–99 *Cambridge U* 4 1
1999–2000 Stoke C 2 0 **42 1**
1999–2000 Cambridge U 22 0
2000–01 Cambridge U 6 0 **32 1**
2000–01 Kidderminster H 23 3 **23 3**
2001–02 Blackpool 14 1 **14 1**
2002–03 Mansfield T 24 1
2003–04 Mansfield T 32 2
2004–05 Mansfield T 15 1 **71 4**
2004–05 Macclesfield T 18 0
2005–06 Macclesfield T 6 1 **24 1**
2005–06 Scunthorpe U 14 2 **14 2**

MUSSELWHITE, Paul (G) 613 0
H: 6 2 W: 14 02 b.Portsmouth 22-12-68
Source: Apprentice.
1987–88 Portsmouth 0 0
1988–89 Scunthorpe U 41 0
1989–90 Scunthorpe U 29 0
1990–91 Scunthorpe U 38 0
1991–92 Scunthorpe U 24 0
1992–93 Port Vale 41 0
1993–94 Port Vale 46 0
1994–95 Port Vale 44 0
1995–96 Port Vale 39 0
1996–97 Port Vale 33 0
1997–98 Port Vale 41 0
1998–99 Port Vale 38 0
1999–2000 Port Vale 30 0 **312 0**
2000–01 Sheffield W 0 0
2000–01 Hull C 37 0
2001–02 Hull C 20 0
2002–03 Hull C 20 0
2003–04 Hull C 18 0 **95 0**
2004–05 Scunthorpe U 46 0
2005–06 Scunthorpe U 28 0 **206 0**

PARTON, Andy (F) 19 0
H: 5 10 W: 12 00 b.Doncaster 29-9-83
Source: Scholar.
2001–02 Scunthorpe U 1 0
2002–03 Scunthorpe U 8 0
2003–04 Scunthorpe U 3 0
2004–05 Scunthorpe U 1 0
2005–06 Scunthorpe U 6 0 **19 0**

RANKINE, Michael (F) 21 1
H: 6 1 W: 14 12 b.Doncaster 15-1-85
Source: Doncaster R, Barrow.
2004–05 Scunthorpe U 21 1
2005–06 Scunthorpe U 0 0 **21 1**

RIDLEY, Lee (D) 82 2
H: 5 9 W: 11 11 b.Scunthorpe 5-12-81
Source: Scholar.
2000–01 Scunthorpe U 2 0
2001–02 Scunthorpe U 4 0
2002–03 Scunthorpe U 11 0
2003–04 Scunthorpe U 18 1
2004–05 Scunthorpe U 44 0
2005–06 Scunthorpe U 3 1 **82 2**

RYAN, Richie (M) 15 0
H: 5 10 W: 10 07 b.Kilkenny 6-1-85
Source: Scholar.
2001–02 Sunderland 0 0
2002–03 Sunderland 2 0
2003–04 Sunderland 0 0
2004–05 Sunderland 0 0 **2 0**
2004–05 *Scunthorpe U* 0 0
2005–06 Scunthorpe U 13 0 **13 0**

SHARP, Billy (F) 55 32
H: 5 9 W: 11 00 b.Sheffield 5-2-86
Source: Scholar.
2004–05 Sheffield U 2 0
2004–05 *Rushden & D* 16 9 **16 9**
2005–06 Sheffield U 0 0 **2 0**
2005–06 Scunthorpe U 37 23 **37 23**

SMITH, Rob (M) 0 0
H: 6 0 W: 12 06 b.Newcastle 22-10-86
Source: Scholar.
2005–06 Scunthorpe U 0 0

SPARROW, Matt (M) 209 27
H: 5 11 W: 10 06 b.Wembley 3-10-81
Source: Scholarship.
1999–2000 Scunthorpe U 11 0
2000–01 Scunthorpe U 11 4
2001–02 Scunthorpe U 24 1
2002–03 Scunthorpe U 42 9
2003–04 Scunthorpe U 38 3
2004–05 Scunthorpe U 44 5
2005–06 Scunthorpe U 39 5 **209 27**

STANTON, Nathan (D) 237 0
H: 5 9 W: 12 06 b.Nottingham 6-5-81
Source: Trainee. *Honours:* England Youth.
1997–98 Scunthorpe U 1 0
1998–99 Scunthorpe U 4 0
1999–2000 Scunthorpe U 34 0
2000–01 Scunthorpe U 38 0
2001–02 Scunthorpe U 42 0
2002–03 Scunthorpe U 42 0
2003–04 Scunthorpe U 33 0
2004–05 Scunthorpe U 21 0
2005–06 Scunthorpe U 22 0 **237 0**

TAYLOR, Cleveland (M) 112 12
H: 5 8 W: 10 07 b.Leicester 9-9-83
Source: Scholar.
2001–02 Bolton W 0 0
2002–03 Bolton W 0 0
2002–03 *Exeter C* 3 0 **3 0**
2003–04 Bolton W 0 0
2003–04 Scunthorpe U 20 3
2004–05 Scunthorpe U 44 6
2005–06 Scunthorpe U 45 3 **109 12**

TORPEY, Steve (F) 566 138
H: 6 3 W: 13 06 b.Islington 8-12-70
Source: Trainee.
1988–89 Millwall 0 0
1989–90 Millwall 7 0
1990–91 Millwall 0 0 **7 0**
1990–91 Bradford C 29 7
1991–92 Bradford C 43 10
1992–93 Bradford C 24 5 **96 22**
1993–94 Swansea C 40 9
1994–95 Swansea C 41 11
1995–96 Swansea C 42 15
1996–97 Swansea C 39 9 **162 44**
1997–98 Bristol C 29 8
1998–99 Bristol C 21 4
1998–99 *Notts Co* 6 1 **6 1**
1999–2000 Bristol C 20 1 **70 13**
1999–2000 Scunthorpe U 15 1
2000–01 Scunthorpe U 40 10
2001–02 Scunthorpe U 39 13
2002–03 Scunthorpe U 28 10
2003–04 Scunthorpe U 43 11
2004–05 Scunthorpe U 34 12
2005–06 Scunthorpe U 26 1 **225 58**

TWIBEY, Dean (D) 0 0
H: 5 9 W: 10 05 b.Pontefract 6-9-86
Source: Scholar.
2005–06 Scunthorpe U 0 0

WILLIAMS, Marcus (D) 34 0
H: 5 8 W: 10 07 b.Doncaster 8-4-86
Source: Scholar.
2003–04 Scunthorpe U 1 0
2004–05 Scunthorpe U 4 0
2005–06 Scunthorpe U 29 0 **34 0**

SHEFFIELD U (71)

AKINBIYI, Ade (F) 406 126
H: 6 1 W: 13 08 b.Hackney 10-10-74
Source: Trainee. *Honours:* Nigeria full caps.
1992–93 Norwich C 0 0
1993–94 Norwich C 2 0
1993–94 *Hereford U* 4 2 **4 2**
1994–95 Norwich C 13 0
1994–95 *Brighton & HA* 7 4 **7 4**
1995–96 Norwich C 22 3
1996–97 Norwich C 12 0 **49 3**
1996–97 Gillingham 19 7
1997–98 Gillingham 44 21 **63 28**
1998–99 Bristol C 44 19
1999–2000 Bristol C 3 2 **47 21**
1999–2000 Wolverhampton W 37 16 **37 16**
2000–01 Leicester C 37 9
2001–02 Leicester C 21 2 **58 11**
2001–02 Crystal Palace 14 2
2002–03 Crystal Palace 10 1
2002–03 *Stoke C* 4 2
2003–04 Crystal Palace 0 0 **24 3**
2003–04 Stoke C 30 10
2004–05 Stoke C 29 7 **63 19**
2004–05 Burnley 10 4
2005–06 Burnley 29 12 **39 16**
2005–06 Sheffield U 15 3 **15 3**

ANNERSON, Jamie (G) 0 0
b.Sheffield 21-6-88
Source: Scholar.
2005–06 Sheffield U 0 0

ARMSTRONG, Chris (D) 139 5
H: 5 9 W: 11 00 b.Newcastle 5-8-82
Source: Scholar. *Honours:* England Under-20.
2000–01 Bury 22 1
2001–02 Bury 11 0 **33 1**
2001–02 Oldham Ath 32 0
2002–03 Oldham Ath 33 1 **65 1**
2003–04 Sheffield U 12 1
2004–05 Sheffield U 0 0
2005–06 Sheffield U 24 2 **36 3**
2005–06 *Blackpool* 5 0 **5 0**

ASHMORE, James (M) 0 0
H: 5 8 W: 11 00 b.Sheffield 2-3-86
Source: Scholar.
2004–05 Sheffield U 0 0
2005–06 Sheffield U 0 0

BARNES, Phil (G) 150 0
H: 6 1 W: 11 01 b.Sheffield 2-3-79
Source: Trainee.
1996–97 Rotherham U 2 0 **2 0**
1997–98 Blackpool 1 0
1998–99 Blackpool 1 0
1999–2000 Blackpool 12 0
2000–01 Blackpool 34 0
2001–02 Blackpool 30 0
2002–03 Blackpool 44 0
2003–04 Blackpool 19 0 **141 0**
2004–05 Sheffield U 1 0
2004–05 *Torquay U* 5 0 **5 0**
2005–06 Sheffield U 0 0 **1 0**
2005–06 *QPR* 1 0 **1 0**

BECKETT, Luke (F) 275 122
H: 5 11 W: 11 02 b.Sheffield 25-11-76
Source: Trainee.
1995–96 Barnsley 0 0
1996–97 Barnsley 0 0
1997–98 Barnsley 0 0
1998–99 Chester C 28 11
1999–2000 Chester C 46 14 **74 25**
2000–01 Chesterfield 41 16
2001–02 Chesterfield 21 6 **62 22**
2001–02 Stockport Co 19 7
2002–03 Stockport Co 42 27
2003–04 Stockport Co 8 4
2004–05 Stockport Co 15 7 **84 45**
2004–05 Sheffield U 5 0
2004–05 *Huddersfield T* 7 6 **7 6**
2004–05 *Oldham Ath* 9 6
2005–06 Sheffield U 0 0 **5 0**
2005–06 *Oldham Ath* 34 18 **43 24**

BINNION, Travis (M) 0 0
H: 5 10 W: 11 02 b.Derby 10-11-86
Source: Scholar.
2005–06 Sheffield U 0 0

BROMBY, Leigh (D) 196 9
H: 5 11 W: 11 06 b.Dewsbury 2-6-80
Honours: England Schools.
1998–99 Sheffield W 0 0
1999–2000 Sheffield W 0 0
1999–2000 *Mansfield T* 10 1 **10 1**
2000–01 Sheffield W 18 0
2001–02 Sheffield W 26 1
2002–03 Sheffield W 27 0
2002–03 *Norwich C* 5 0 **5 0**
2003–04 Sheffield W 29 1 **100 2**
2004–05 Sheffield U 46 5
2005–06 Sheffield U 35 1 **81 6**

DEANE, Brian (F) 652 194
H: 6 3 W: 14 04 b.Leeds 7-2-68
Source: Apprentice. *Honours:* England B, 3 full caps.
1985–86 Doncaster R 3 0
1986–87 Doncaster R 20 2
1987–88 Doncaster R 43 10 **66 12**
1988–89 Sheffield U 43 22
1989–90 Sheffield U 45 21
1990–91 Sheffield U 38 13
1991–92 Sheffield U 30 12
1992–93 Sheffield U 41 14
1993–94 Leeds U 41 11
1994–95 Leeds U 35 9
1995–96 Leeds U 34 7
1996–97 Leeds U 28 5
1997–98 Sheffield U 24 11
1997–98 Benfica 14 7
1998–99 Benfica 4 0 **18 7**
1998–99 Middlesbrough 26 6
1999–2000 Middlesbrough 29 9
2000–01 Middlesbrough 25 2
2001–02 Middlesbrough 7 1 **87 18**
2001–02 Leicester C 15 6
2002–03 Leicester C 32 13
2003–04 Leicester C 5 0 **52 19**
2003–04 West Ham U 26 6 **26 6**
2004–05 Leeds U 31 6 **169 38**
2004–05 Sunderland 4 0 **4 0**
2005 Perth Glory 7 1 **7 1**
2005–06 Sheffield U 2 0 **223 93**

DYER, Bruce (F) 442 117
H: 6 0 W: 11 03 b.Ilford 13-4-75
Source: Trainee. *Honours:* England Under-21.
1992–93 Watford 2 0
1993–94 Watford 29 6
1993–94 Crystal Palace 11 0
1994–95 Crystal Palace 16 1
1995–96 Crystal Palace 35 13
1996–97 Crystal Palace 43 17
1997–98 Crystal Palace 24 4
1998–99 Crystal Palace 6 2 **135 37**
1998–99 Barnsley 28 7
1999–2000 Barnsley 32 6
2000–01 Barnsley 38 15
2001–02 Barnsley 44 14
2002–03 Barnsley 40 17 **182 59**
2003–04 Watford 32 3
2004–05 Watford 36 9 **99 18**
2005–06 Stoke C 11 0 **11 0**
2005–06 *Millwall* 10 2 **10 2**
2005–06 Sheffield U 5 1 **5 1**

FORTE, Jonathan (M) 54 9
H: 6 0 W: 12 02 b.Sheffield 25-7-86
Source: Scholar. *Honours:* England Youth.
2003–04 Sheffield U 7 0
2004–05 Sheffield U 22 1
2005–06 Sheffield U 1 0 **30 1**
2005–06 *Doncaster R* 13 4 **13 4**
2005–06 *Rotherham U* 11 4 **11 4**

FRANCIS, Simon (D) 89 2
H: 6 0 W: 12 06 b.Nottingham 16-2-85
Source: Scholar. *Honours:* England Youth, Under-20.
2002–03 Bradford C 25 1
2003–04 Bradford C 30 0 **55 1**
2003–04 Sheffield U 5 0
2004–05 Sheffield U 6 0
2005–06 Sheffield U 1 0 **12 0**
2005–06 *Grimsby T* 5 0 **5 0**
2005–06 *Tranmere R* 17 1 **17 1**

GEARY, Derek (D) 156 1
H: 5 6 W: 10 00 b.Dublin 19-6-80
1997–98 Sheffield W 0 0
1998–99 Sheffield W 0 0
1999–2000 Sheffield W 0 0
2000–01 Sheffield W 5 0
2001–02 Sheffield W 32 0
2002–03 Sheffield W 26 0
2003–04 Sheffield W 41 0 **104 0**
2004–05 Stockport Co 13 0 **13 0**
2004–05 Sheffield U 19 1
2005–06 Sheffield U 20 0 **39 1**

GILLESPIE, Keith (M) 320 23
H: 5 10 W: 11 03 b.Larne 18-2-75
Source: Trainee. *Honours:* Northern Ireland Schools, Youth, Under-21, 68 full caps, 2 goals.
1992–93 Manchester U 0 0
1993–94 Manchester U 0 0
1993–94 *Wigan Ath* 8 4
1994–95 Manchester U 9 1 **9 1**
1994–95 Newcastle U 17 2
1995–96 Newcastle U 28 4
1996–97 Newcastle U 32 1
1997–98 Newcastle U 29 4
1998–99 Newcastle U 7 0 **113 11**
1998–99 Blackburn R 16 1
1999–2000 Blackburn R 22 2
2000–01 Blackburn R 18 0
2000–01 *Wigan Ath* 5 0 **13 4**
2001–02 Blackburn R 32 2
2002–03 Blackburn R 25 0 **113 5**
2003–04 Leicester C 12 0
2004–05 Leicester C 30 2 **42 2**
2005–06 Sheffield U 30 0 **30 0**

GYAKI, Ryan (G) 0 0
H: 5 10 W: 11 02 b.Toronto 6-12-85
Source: Scholar. *Honours:* Canada Under-20.
2005–06 Sheffield U 0 0

HAIDONG, Hao (F) 0 0
H: 5 11 W: 11 00 b.Qingdao 9-5-70
Source: Dalian Shide. *Honours:* China 115 full caps, 41 goals.
2004–05 Sheffield U 0 0
2005–06 Sheffield U 0 0

HARPER, Adrian (M) 0 0
H: 5 9 W: 10 07 b.Dublin 4-5-85
Source: Scholar.
2004–05 Sheffield U 0 0
2005–06 Sheffield U 0 0

HILL, Shane (M) 0 0
b.London 5-8-87
2005–06 Sheffield U 0 0

HORWOOD, Evan (D) 11 0
H: 6 0 W: 10 06 b.Billingham 10-3-86
Source: Scholar.
2004–05 Sheffield U 0 0
2004–05 *Stockport Co* 10 0 **10 0**
2005–06 Sheffield U 0 0
2005–06 *Scunthorpe U* 0 0
2005–06 *Chester C* 1 0 **1 0**

HURST, Kevan (M) 59 6
H: 5 10 W: 11 07 b.Chesterfield 27-8-85
Source: Sheffield U Scholar.
2003–04 *Boston U* 7 1 **7 1**
2004–05 Sheffield U 1 0
2004–05 *Stockport Co* 14 1 **14 1**
2005–06 Sheffield U 0 0 **1 0**
2005–06 *Chesterfield* 37 4 **37 4**

IFILL, Paul (M) 269 49
H: 6 0 W: 12 09 b.Brighton 20-10-79
Source: Trainee. *Honours:* England Youth, Barbados full caps.
1998–99 Millwall 15 1
1999–2000 Millwall 44 11
2000–01 Millwall 35 6
2001–02 Millwall 40 4
2002–03 Millwall 45 6
2003–04 Millwall 33 8
2004–05 Millwall 18 4 **230 40**
2005–06 Sheffield U 39 9 **39 9**

JAGIELKA, Phil (D) 216 14
H: 6 0 W: 13 01 b.Manchester 17-8-82
Source: Scholar. *Honours:* England Youth, Under-20, Under-21.
1999–2000 Sheffield U 1 0
2000–01 Sheffield U 15 0
2001–02 Sheffield U 23 3
2002–03 Sheffield U 42 0
2003–04 Sheffield U 43 3
2004–05 Sheffield U 46 0
2005–06 Sheffield U 46 8 **216 14**

KABBA, Steven (F) 97 25
H: 5 10 W: 11 03 b.Lambeth 7-3-81
Source: Trainee.
1999–2000 Crystal Palace 1 0
2000–01 Crystal Palace 1 0
2001–02 Crystal Palace 4 0
2001–02 *Luton T* 3 0 **3 0**
2002–03 Crystal Palace 4 1 **10 1**
2002–03 *Grimsby T* 13 6 **13 6**
2002–03 Sheffield U 25 7
2003–04 Sheffield U 1 0
2004–05 Sheffield U 11 2
2005–06 Sheffield U 34 9 **71 18**

KENNY, Paddy (G) 291 0
H: 6 1 W: 14 01 b.Halifax 17-5-78
Source: Bradford PA. *Honours:* Eire 5 full caps.
1998–99 Bury 0 0
1999–2000 Bury 46 0
2000–01 Bury 46 0
2001–02 Bury 41 0
2002–03 Bury 0 0 **133 0**
2002–03 Sheffield U 45 0
2003–04 Sheffield U 27 0
2004–05 Sheffield U 40 0
2005–06 Sheffield U 46 0 **158 0**

KOZLUK, Rob (D) 225 2
H: 5 8 W: 10 02 b.Mansfield 5-8-77
Source: Trainee. *Honours:* England Under-21.
1995–96 Derby Co 0 0
1996–97 Derby Co 0 0
1997–98 Derby Co 9 0
1998–99 Derby Co 7 0 **16 0**
1998–99 Sheffield U 10 0
1999–2000 Sheffield U 39 0
2000–01 Sheffield U 27 0

2000–01 *Huddersfield T* 14 0 **14 0**
2001–02 Sheffield U 8 0
2002–03 Sheffield U 32 1
2003–04 Sheffield U 42 1
2004–05 Sheffield U 9 0
2004–05 *Preston NE* 1 0 **1 0**
2005–06 Sheffield U 27 0 **194 2**

LAW, Nicky (M) 0 0
H: 5 10 W: 11 06 b.Nottingham 29-3-88
Source: Scholar. *Honours:* England Youth.
2005–06 Sheffield U 0 0

LEE, San (F) 0 0
H: 5 9 W: 11 02 b.Seoul 5-10-85
Source: Brentford.
2005–06 Sheffield U 0 0

MARRISON, Colin (F) 16 0
H: 6 1 W: 12 05 b.Sheffield 23-9-85
Source: Scholar.
2005–06 Sheffield U 0 0
2005–06 *Bury* 16 0 **16 0**

McCALL, Stuart (M) 763 67
H: 5 7 W: 10 01 b.Leeds 10-6-64
Source: Apprentice. *Honours:* Scotland Under-21, 40 full caps, 1 goal.
1982–83 Bradford C 28 4
1983–84 Bradford C 46 5
1984–85 Bradford C 46 8
1985–86 Bradford C 38 4
1986–87 Bradford C 36 7
1987–88 Bradford C 44 9
1988–89 Everton 33 0
1989–90 Everton 37 3
1990–91 Everton 33 3 **103 6**
1991–92 Rangers 36 1
1992–93 Rangers 36 5
1993–94 Rangers 34 3
1994–95 Rangers 30 2
1995–96 Rangers 21 3
1996–97 Rangers 7 0
1997–98 Rangers 30 0 **194 14**
1998–99 Bradford C 43 3
1999–2000 Bradford C 34 1
2000–01 Bradford C 37 1
2001–02 Bradford C 43 3 **395 45**
2002–03 Sheffield U 34 0
2003–04 Sheffield U 37 2
2004–05 Sheffield U 0 0
2005–06 Sheffield U 0 0 **71 2**

McFADZEAN, Kyle (D) 0 0
H: 6 1 W: 13 04 b.Sheffield 20-2-87
Source: Scholar.
2004–05 Sheffield U 0 0
2005–06 Sheffield U 0 0

MONTGOMERY, Nick (M) 181 7
H: 5 9 W: 11 08 b.Leeds 28-10-81
Source: Scholar. *Honours:* Scotland Under-21, B.
2000–01 Sheffield U 27 0
2001–02 Sheffield U 31 2
2002–03 Sheffield U 23 0
2003–04 Sheffield U 36 3
2004–05 Sheffield U 25 1
2005–06 Sheffield U 39 1 **181 7**

MORGAN, Chris (D) 297 13
H: 6 1 W: 12 03 b.Barnsley 9-11-77
Source: Trainee.
1996–97 Barnsley 0 0
1997–98 Barnsley 11 0
1998–99 Barnsley 19 0
1999–2000 Barnsley 37 0
2000–01 Barnsley 40 1
2001–02 Barnsley 42 4
2002–03 Barnsley 36 2 **185 7**
2003–04 Sheffield U 32 1
2004–05 Sheffield U 41 2
2005–06 Sheffield U 39 3 **112 6**

MULLIGAN, Gary (M) 37 5
H: 6 1 W: 12 03 b.Dublin 23-4-85
Source: Scholar.
2002–03 Wolverhampton W 0 0
2003–04 Wolverhampton W 0 0
2004–05 Wolverhampton W 1 0 **1 0**
2004–05 *Rushden & D* 13 3 **13 3**
2005–06 Sheffield U 0 0
2005–06 *Port Vale* 10 1 **10 1**
2005–06 *Gillingham* 13 1 **13 1**

NARAJI, Sharu (M) 0 0
H: 5 10 W: 11 11 b.Bolton 7-2-84
Source: Real Sociedad.
2005–06 Sheffield U 0 0

NIX, Kyle (F) 0 0
H: 5 6 W: 9 10 b.Sydney 21-1-86
Source: Manchester U Trainee. *Honours:* FA Schools, England Youth, Under-20.
2002–03 Aston Villa 0 0
2003–04 Aston Villa 0 0
2004–05 Aston Villa 0 0
2005–06 Sheffield U 0 0
2005–06 *Barnsley* 0 0

QUINN, Alan (M) 233 27
H: 5 9 W: 10 06 b.Dublin 13-6-79
Source: Cherry Orchard. *Honours:* Eire Youth, Under-21, 6 full caps.
1997–98 Sheffield W 1 0
1998–99 Sheffield W 1 0
1999–2000 Sheffield W 19 3
2000–01 Sheffield W 37 2
2001–02 Sheffield W 38 2
2002–03 Sheffield W 37 5
2003–04 Sheffield W 24 4 **157 16**
2003–04 *Sunderland* 6 0 **6 0**
2004–05 Sheffield U 43 7
2005–06 Sheffield U 27 4 **70 11**

QUINN, Stephen (M) 31 0
H: 5 6 W: 9 08 b.Dublin 4-4-86
Source: Trainee.
2005–06 Sheffield U 0 0
2005–06 *Milton Keynes D* 15 0 **15 0**
2005–06 *Rotherham U* 16 0 **16 0**

ROBERTSON, Chris (D) 1 0
H: 6 3 W: 11 08 b.Dundee 11-10-85
Source: Scholar.
2005–06 Sheffield U 0 0
2005–06 *Chester C* 1 0 **1 0**

ROMA, Dominic (D) 2 0
H: 5 9 W: 12 04 b.Sheffield 29-11-85
Source: Scholar. *Honours:* Endgland Youth.
2004–05 Sheffield U 0 0
2004–05 *Boston U* 2 0 **2 0**
2005–06 Sheffield U 0 0

ROSS, Ian (M) 21 4
H: 5 10 W: 11 00 b.Sheffield 23-1-86
Source: Scholar. *Honours:* England Under-20.
2004–05 Sheffield U 0 0
2005–06 Sheffield U 0 0
2005–06 *Boston U* 14 4 **14 4**
2005–06 *Bury* 7 0 **7 0**

SHIPPERLEY, Neil (F) 435 120
H: 6 1 W: 13 12 b.Chatham 30-10-74
Source: Trainee. *Honours:* England Under-21.
1992–93 Chelsea 3 1
1993–94 Chelsea 24 4
1994–95 Chelsea 10 2 **37 7**
1994–95 *Watford* 6 1 **6 1**
1994–95 Southampton 19 4
1995–96 Southampton 37 7
1996–97 Southampton 10 1 **66 12**
1996–97 Crystal Palace 32 12
1997–98 Crystal Palace 26 7
1998–99 Crystal Palace 3 1
1998–99 Nottingham F 20 1 **20 1**
1999–2000 Barnsley 39 13
2000–01 Barnsley 39 14 **78 27**
2001–02 Wimbledon 41 12
2002–03 Wimbledon 46 20 **87 32**
2003–04 Crystal Palace 40 9
2004–05 Crystal Palace 1 0 **102 29**
2005–06 Sheffield U 39 11 **39 11**

SHORT, Craig (D) 565 31
H: 6 1 W: 13 08 b.Bridlington 25-6-68
Source: Pickering T. *Honours:* England Schools.
1987–88 Scarborough 21 2
1988–89 Scarborough 42 5 **63 7**
1989–90 Notts Co 44 2
1990–91 Notts Co 0 0
1990–91 Notts Co 43 0
1991–92 Notts Co 38 3
1992–93 Notts Co 3 1 **128 6**
1992–93 Derby Co 38 3
1993–94 Derby Co 43 3
1994–95 Derby Co 37 3 **118 9**
1995–96 Everton 23 2
1996–97 Everton 23 2
1997–98 Everton 31 0
1998–99 Everton 22 0 **99 4**
1999–2000 Blackburn R 17 0
2000–01 Blackburn R 35 1
2001–02 Blackburn R 22 0
2002–03 Blackburn R 27 1
2003–04 Blackburn R 19 1
2004–05 Blackburn R 14 1 **134 4**
2005–06 Sheffield U 23 1 **23 1**

TONGE, Michael (M) 186 18
H: 6 0 W: 11 10 b.Manchester 7-4-83
Source: Scholar. *Honours:* England Under-20, Under-21.
2000–01 Sheffield U 2 0
2001–02 Sheffield U 30 3
2002–03 Sheffield U 44 6
2003–04 Sheffield U 46 4
2004–05 Sheffield U 34 2
2005–06 Sheffield U 30 3 **186 18**

TRAVIS, Nicky (M) 0 0
H: 6 0 W: 12 01 b.Sheffield 12-3-87
Source: Scholar.
2004–05 Sheffield U 0 0
2005–06 Sheffield U 0 0

UNSWORTH, Dave (D) 401 43
H: 6 1 W: 13 07 b.Chorley 16-10-73
Source: Trainee. *Honours:* England Youth, Under-21, 1 full cap.
1991–92 Everton 2 1
1992–93 Everton 3 0
1993–94 Everton 8 0
1994–95 Everton 38 3
1995–96 Everton 31 2
1996–97 Everton 34 5
1997–98 West Ham U 32 2 **32 2**
1998–99 Aston Villa 0 0
1998–99 Everton 34 1
1999–2000 Everton 33 6
2000–01 Everton 29 5
2001–02 Everton 33 3
2002–03 Everton 33 5
2003–04 Everton 26 3 **304 34**
2004–05 Portsmouth 15 2
2004–05 *Ipswich T* 16 1 **16 1**
2005–06 Portsmouth 0 0 **15 2**
2005–06 Sheffield U 34 4 **34 4**

WEBBER, Danny (F) 118 34
H: 5 10 W: 11 04 b.Manchester 28-12-81
Source: Trainee. *Honours:* England Youth, Under-20.
1998–99 Manchester U 0 0
1999–2000 Manchester U 0 0
2000–01 Manchester U 0 0
2001–02 Manchester U 0 0
2001–02 *Port Vale* 4 0 **4 0**
2001–02 *Watford* 5 2
2002–03 Manchester U 0 0
2002–03 *Watford* 12 2
2003–04 Watford 27 5
2004–05 Watford 28 12 **72 21**
2004–05 *Sheffield U* 7 3
2005–06 Sheffield U 35 10 **42 13**

WRIGHT, Alan (D) 482 7
H: 5 4 W: 9 09 b.Ashton-under-Lyme 28-9-71
Source: Trainee. *Honours:* England Schools, Youth, Under-21.
1987–88 Blackpool 1 0
1988–89 Blackpool 16 0
1989–90 Blackpool 24 0
1990–91 Blackpool 45 0
1991–92 Blackpool 12 0 **98 0**
1991–92 Blackburn R 33 1
1992–93 Blackburn R 24 0
1993–94 Blackburn R 12 0
1994–95 Blackburn R 5 0 **74 1**
1994–95 Aston Villa 8 0
1995–96 Aston Villa 38 2

1996–97 Aston Villa 38 1
1997–98 Aston Villa 37 0
1998–99 Aston Villa 38 0
1999–2000 Aston Villa 32 1
2000–01 Aston Villa 36 1
2001–02 Aston Villa 23 0
2002–03 Aston Villa 10 0 **260 5**
2003–04 Middlesbrough 2 0 **2 0**
2003–04 Sheffield U 21 1
2004–05 Sheffield U 14 0
2005–06 Sheffield U 6 0 **41 1**
2005–06 *Derby Co* 7 0 **7 0**

SHEFFIELD W (72)

ADAMS, Steve (M) 174 7
H: 6 0 W: 12 03 b.Plymouth 25-9-80
Source: Trainee.
1999–2000 Plymouth Arg 1 0
2000–01 Plymouth Arg 17 0
2001–02 Plymouth Arg 46 2
2002–03 Plymouth Arg 37 2
2003–04 Plymouth Arg 36 2
2004–05 Plymouth Arg 20 1 **157 7**
2004–05 Sheffield W 9 0
2005–06 Sheffield W 8 0 **17 0**

ADAMSON, Chris (G) 29 0
H: 6 2 W: 13 07 b.Ashington 4-11-78
Source: Trainee.
1997–98 WBA 3 0
1998–99 WBA 0 0
1998–99 *Mansfield T* 2 0 **2 0**
1999–2000 WBA 9 0
1999–2000 *Halifax T* 7 0 **7 0**
2000–01 WBA 0 0
2001–02 WBA 0 0 **12 0**
2001–02 *Plymouth Arg* 1 0 **1 0**
From St Patrick's At
2004–05 Sheffield W 2 0
2005–06 Sheffield W 5 0 **7 0**

BRUNT, Chris (M) 95 13
H: 6 1 W: 13 04 b.Belfast 14-12-84
Source: Trainee. *Honours:* Northern Ireland Under-21, Under-23, 7 full caps.
2002–03 Middlesbrough 0 0
2003–04 Middlesbrough 0 0
2003–04 Sheffield W 9 2
2004–05 Sheffield W 42 4
2005–06 Sheffield W 44 7 **95 13**

BULLEN, Lee (D) 327 86
H: 6 1 W: 12 07 b.Edinburgh 29-3-71
1990–91 Meadowbank T 3 0 **3 0**
1991–92 Stenhousemuir 35 22
1992–93 Stenhousemuir 35 24 **70 46**
From Stanmore, Golden, South
1998–99 Kalamata 27 7
1999–2000 Kalamata 5 0 **50 11**
1999–2000 Dunfermline Ath 13 7
2000–01 Dunfermline Ath 24 4
2001–02 Dunfermline Ath 31 4
2002–03 Dunfermline Ath 35 5
2003–04 Dunfermline Ath 27 2 **130 22**
2004–05 Sheffield W 46 7
2005–06 Sheffield W 28 0 **74 7**

BURTON, Deon (F) 311 69
H: 5 9 W: 11 09 b.Ashford 25-10-76
Source: Trainee. *Honours:* Jamaica 49 full caps, 8 goals.
1993–94 Portsmouth 2 0
1994–95 Portsmouth 7 2
1995–96 Portsmouth 32 7
1996–97 Portsmouth 21 1
1996–97 *Cardiff C* 5 2 **5 2**
1997–98 Derby Co 29 3
1998–99 Derby Co 21 9
1998–99 *Barnsley* 3 0 **3 0**
1999–2000 Derby Co 19 4
2000–01 Derby Co 32 5
2001–02 Derby Co 17 1
2001–02 *Stoke C* 12 2 **12 2**
2002–03 Derby Co 7 3 **125 25**
2002–03 Portsmouth 15 4
2003–04 Portsmouth 1 0 **78 14**
2003–04 *Walsall* 3 0 **3 0**
2003–04 *Swindon T* 4 1 **4 1**
2004–05 Brentford 40 10 **40 10**
2005–06 Rotherham U 24 12 **24 12**
2005–06 Sheffield W 17 3 **17 3**

COLLINS, Patrick (D) 44 1
H: 6 2 W: 12 08 b.Oman 4-2-85
Source: Scholar. *Honours:* England Youth, Under-20.
2001–02 Sunderland 0 0
2002–03 Sunderland 0 0
2003–04 Sunderland 0 0
2004–05 Sheffield W 28 1
2005–06 Sheffield W 3 0 **31 1**
2005–06 *Swindon T* 13 0 **13 0**

CORR, Barry (F) 16 0
H: 6 3 W: 12 07 b.Co. Wicklow 2-4-85
Honours: Eire Youth.
2001–02 Leeds U 0 0
2002–03 Leeds U 0 0
2003–04 Leeds U 0 0
2004–05 Leeds U 0 0
2005–06 Sheffield W 16 0 **16 0**

COUGHLAN, Graham (D) 269 31
H: 6 2 W: 13 07 b.Dublin 18-11-74
Source: Bray Wanderers.
1995–96 Blackburn R 0 0
1996–97 Blackburn R 0 0
1996–97 *Swindon T* 3 0 **3 0**
1997–98 Blackburn R 0 0
1998–99 Livingston 6 0
1999–2000 Livingston 29 0
2000–01 Livingston 21 2 **56 2**
2001–02 Plymouth Arg 46 11
2002–03 Plymouth Arg 42 5
2003–04 Plymouth Arg 46 7
2004–05 Plymouth Arg 43 2 **177 25**
2005–06 Sheffield W 33 4 **33 4**

DIALLO, Drissa (D) 70 1
H: 6 1 W: 11 13 b.Nouadhibou 4-1-73
Honours: Guinea full caps.
2002–03 Burnley 14 1 **14 1**
2003–04 Ipswich T 19 0
2004–05 Ipswich T 26 0 **45 0**
2005–06 Sheffield W 11 0 **11 0**

GILBERT, Peter (D) 100 1
H: 5 11 W: 12 00 b.Newcastle 31-7-83
Source: Scholar. *Honours:* Wales Under-21.
2001–02 Birmingham C 0 0
2002–03 Birmingham C 0 0
2003–04 Birmingham C 0 0
2003–04 Plymouth Arg 40 1
2004–05 Plymouth Arg 38 0 **78 1**
2005–06 Leicester C 5 0 **5 0**
2005–06 Sheffield W 17 0 **17 0**

GRAHAM, David (F) 233 63
H: 5 10 W: 11 02 b.Edinburgh 6-10-78
Source: Rangers SABC. *Honours:* Scotland Under-21.
1995–96 Rangers 0 0
1996–97 Rangers 0 0
1997–98 Rangers 0 0
1998–99 Rangers 3 0 **3 0**
1998–99 Dunfermline Ath 21 2
1999–2000 Dunfermline Ath 15 2
2000–01 Dunfermline Ath 4 0 **40 4**
2000–01 Torquay U 5 2
2001–02 Torquay U 36 8
2002–03 Torquay U 34 15
2003–04 Torquay U 45 22 **120 47**
2004–05 Wigan Ath 30 1
2005–06 Wigan Ath 0 0 **30 1**
2005–06 Sheffield W 24 2 **24 2**
2005–06 *Huddersfield T* 16 9 **16 9**

HILLS, John (D) 262 19
H: 5 9 W: 12 08 b.St Annes-on-Sea 21-4-78
Source: Trainee.
1995–96 Blackpool 0 0
1995–96 Everton 0 0
1996–97 Everton 3 0
1996–97 *Swansea C* 11 0
1997–98 Everton 0 0 **3 0**
1997–98 *Swansea C* 7 1 **18 1**
1997–98 Blackpool 19 1
1998–99 Blackpool 28 1
1999–2000 Blackpool 33 2
2000–01 Blackpool 18 2
2001–02 Blackpool 37 5
2002–03 Blackpool 27 5 **162 16**
2003–04 Gillingham 29 2
2004–05 Gillingham 23 0 **52 2**
2005–06 Sheffield W 27 0 **27 0**

KIRBY, Ben (G) 0 0
H: 6 1 W: 12 02 b.Reading 16-3-87
Source: Scholar.
2005–06 Sheffield W 0 0

LUCAS, David (G) 209 0
H: 6 1 W: 13 07 b.Preston 23-11-77
Source: Trainee. *Honours:* England Youth.
1995–96 Preston NE 1 0
1995–96 *Darlington* 6 0
1996–97 Preston NE 2 0
1996–97 *Darlington* 7 0 **13 0**
1996–97 *Scunthorpe U* 6 0 **6 0**
1997–98 Preston NE 6 0
1998–99 Preston NE 30 0
1999–2000 Preston NE 6 0
2000–01 Preston NE 29 0
2001–02 Preston NE 24 0
2002–03 Preston NE 21 0
2003–04 Preston NE 2 0 **121 0**
2003–04 *Sheffield W* 17 0
2004–05 Sheffield W 34 0
2005–06 Sheffield W 18 0 **69 0**

MACLEAN, Steve (F) 87 43
H: 5 11 W: 12 06 b.Edinburgh 23-8-82
Honours: Scotland Under-21.
2002–03 Rangers 3 0 **3 0**
2003–04 Scunthorpe U 42 23 **42 23**
2004–05 Sheffield W 36 18
2005–06 Sheffield W 6 2 **42 20**

McALLISTER, Sean (M) 2 0
H: 5 8 W: 10 07 b.Bolton 15-8-87
Source: Scholar.
2005–06 Sheffield W 2 0 **2 0**

McARDLE, Rory (D) 19 1
H: 6 1 W: 11 11 b.Doncaster 1-5-87
Source: Scholar. *Honours:* Northern Ireland Youth, Under-21.
2004–05 Sheffield W 0 0
2005–06 Sheffield W 0 0
2005–06 *Rochdale* 19 1 **19 1**

McGOVERN, John-Paul (M) 68 7
H: 5 10 W: 12 02 b.Glasgow 3-10-80
Source: Celtic BC.
2001–02 Celtic 0 0
2002–03 Celtic 0 0
2002–03 *Sheffield U* 15 1 **15 1**
2003–04 Celtic 0 0
2004–05 Sheffield W 46 6
2005–06 Sheffield W 7 0 **53 6**

O'BRIEN, Burton (M) 165 18
H: 5 10 W: 11 09 b.South Africa 10-6-81
Source: S Form. *Honours:* Scotland Youth, Under-21.
1998–99 St Mirren 22 1 **22 1**
1998–99 Blackburn R 0 0
1999–2000 Blackburn R 0 0
2000–01 Blackburn R 0 0
2001–02 Blackburn R 0 0
2002–03 Livingston 28 1
2003–04 Livingston 33 6
2004–05 Livingston 38 8 **99 15**
2005–06 Sheffield W 44 2 **44 2**

PARTRIDGE, Richie (M) 51 5
H: 5 8 W: 11 00 b.Dublin 12-9-80
Source: Trainee. *Honours:* Eire Under-21.
1998–99 Liverpool 0 0
1999–2000 Liverpool 0 0
2000–01 Liverpool 0 0
2000–01 *Bristol R* 6 1 **6 1**
2001–02 Liverpool 0 0
2002–03 Liverpool 0 0
2002–03 *Coventry C* 27 4 **27 4**
2003–04 Liverpool 0 0
2004–05 Liverpool 0 0
2005–06 Sheffield W 18 0 **18 0**

ROCASTLE, Craig (M) **43** **1**
H: 6 1 W: 13 09 b.Lewisham 17-8-81
Source: Kingstonian.
2003–04 Chelsea 0 0
2003–04 *Barnsley* 5 0 **5** **0**
2003–04 *Lincoln C* 2 0 **2** **0**
2004–05 Chelsea 0 0
2004–05 Sheffield W 11 1
2005–06 Sheffield W 17 0 **28** **1**
2005–06 *Yeovil T* 8 0 **8** **0**

SIMEK, Frankie (D) **56** **1**
H: 6 0 W: 11 06 b.St Louis 13-10-84
Source: Trainee.
2002–03 Arsenal 0 0
2003–04 Arsenal 0 0
2004–05 Arsenal 0 0
2004–05 *QPR* 5 0 **5** **0**
2004–05 *Bournemouth* 8 0 **8** **0**
2005–06 Sheffield W 43 1 **43** **1**

SPURR, Tommy (D) **2** **0**
H: 6 1 W: 11 05 b.Leeds 13-9-87
Source: Scholar.
2005–06 Sheffield W 2 0 **2** **0**

TALBOT, Drew (F) **21** **4**
H: 5 10 W: 11 00 b.Barnsley 19-7-86
Source: Trainee.
2003–04 Sheffield W 0 0
2004–05 Sheffield W 21 4
2005–06 Sheffield W 0 0 **21** **4**

THORPE, Matt (M) **0** **0**
H: 5 11 W: 11 07 b.Chesterfield 28-10-86
2005–06 Sheffield W 0 0

TUDGAY, Marcus (F) **110** **22**
H: 5 10 W: 12 04 b.Worthing 3-2-83
Source: Trainee.
2002–03 Derby Co 8 0
2003–04 Derby Co 29 6
2004–05 Derby Co 34 9
2005–06 Derby Co 21 2 **92** **17**
2005–06 Sheffield W 18 5 **18** **5**

WHELAN, Glenn (M) **92** **3**
H: 5 11 W: 12 07 b.Dublin 13-1-84
Source: Scholar. *Honours:* Eire Youth, Under-21.
2000–01 Manchester C 0 0
2001–02 Manchester C 0 0
2002–03 Manchester C 0 0
2003–04 Manchester C 0 0
2003–04 *Bury* 13 0 **13** **0**
2004–05 Sheffield W 36 2
2005–06 Sheffield W 43 1 **79** **3**

WOOD, Richard (D) **79** **3**
H: 6 3 W: 12 13 b.Wakefield 5-7-85
Source: Scholar.
2002–03 Sheffield W 3 1
2003–04 Sheffield W 12 0
2004–05 Sheffield W 34 1
2005–06 Sheffield W 30 1 **79** **3**

SHREWSBURY T (73)

ADAGGIO, Marco (F) **10** **0**
H: 5 8 W: 12 04 b.Malaga 6-10-87
Source: Shrewsbury T Juniors.
2004–05 Shrewsbury T 5 0
2005–06 Shrewsbury T 5 0 **10** **0**

ASHTON, Neil (M) **69** **1**
H: 5 8 W: 12 04 b.Liverpool 15-1-85
Source: Scholar.
2002–03 Tranmere R 0 0
2003–04 Tranmere R 1 0
2004–05 Tranmere R 0 0 **1** **0**
2004–05 *Shrewsbury T* 24 0
2005–06 Shrewsbury T 44 1 **68** **1**

BURTON, Sagi (D) **233** **11**
H: 6 2 W: 14 02 b.Birmingham 25-11-77
Source: Trainee. *Honours:* St Kitts & Nevis full caps.
1995–96 Crystal Palace 0 0
1996–97 Crystal Palace 0 0
1997–98 Crystal Palace 2 0
1998–99 Crystal Palace 23 1 **25** **1**
1999–2000 Colchester U 9 0 **9** **0**
1999–2000 Sheffield U 0 0
1999–2000 Port Vale 20 2
2000–01 Port Vale 29 0
2001–02 Port Vale 37 0 **86** **2**
2002–03 Crewe Alex 1 0 **1** **0**
2002–03 Peterborough U 31 0
2003–04 Peterborough U 30 1
2004–05 Peterborough U 16 1
2005–06 Peterborough U 19 2 **96** **4**
2005–06 Shrewsbury T 16 4 **16** **4**

CADWALLADER, Gav (D) **2** **0**
H: 6 2 W: 12 01 b.Shrewsbury 18-4-86
2005–06 Shrewsbury T 2 0 **2** **0**

COWAN, Gavin (D) **20** **1**
H: 6 4 W: 14 04 b.Hanover 24-5-81
Source: Braintree T, Canvey Island.
2004–05 Shrewsbury T 5 0
2005–06 Shrewsbury T 15 1 **20** **1**

CRONIN, Lance (G) **1** **0**
H: 6 1 W: 12 00 b.Brighton 11-9-85
Source: Scholar. *Honours:* England Youth.
2002–03 Crystal Palace 0 0
2003–04 Crystal Palace 0 0
2004–05 Crystal Palace 0 0
2004–05 *Wycombe W* 1 0 **1** **0**
2005–06 Crystal Palace 0 0
2005–06 Shrewsbury T 0 0

DARBY, Duane (F) **345** **88**
H: 5 11 W: 13 11 b.Birmingham 17-10-73
Source: Trainee.
1991–92 Torquay U 14 2
1992–93 Torquay U 34 12
1993–94 Torquay U 36 8
1994–95 Torquay U 24 4 **108** **26**
1995–96 Doncaster R 17 4 **17** **4**
1995–96 Hull C 8 1
1996–97 Hull C 41 13
1997–98 Hull C 29 13
1998–99 Notts Co 0 0
1998–99 *Hull C* 8 0 **86** **27**
1999–2000 Notts Co 28 5
2000–01 Notts Co 0 0 **28** **5**
2001–02 Rushden & D 30 7
2002–03 Rushden & D 37 14
2003–04 Rushden & D 12 2 **79** **23**
2004–05 Shrewsbury T 16 1
2005–06 Shrewsbury T 11 2 **27** **3**

DENNY, Jay (M) **14** **0**
H: 5 11 W: 12 00 b.Los Angeles 6-1-86
Source: Scholar.
2004–05 Stoke C 0 0
2005–06 Shrewsbury T 14 0 **14** **0**

EDWARDS, Dave (M) **58** **7**
H: 5 11 W: 11 04 b.Shrewsbury 3-2-86
Source: Scholar. *Honours:* Wales Youth, Under-21.
2002–03 Shrewsbury T 1 0
2003–04 Shrewsbury T 0 0
2004–05 Shrewsbury T 27 5
2005–06 Shrewsbury T 30 2 **58** **7**

EVANS, Richard (M) **16** **1**
H: 5 9 W: 11 08 b.Cardiff 19-6-83
Source: Scholar.
2002–03 Birmingham C 0 0
2002–03 Sheffield W 4 1
2003–04 Sheffield W 6 0
2004–05 Sheffield W 0 0
2005–06 Sheffield W 0 0 **10** **1**
2005–06 Shrewsbury T 6 0 **6** **0**

HART, Joe (G) **52** **0**
H: 6 3 W: 13 03 b.Shrewsbury 19-4-87
Source: Scholar, England Youth.
2004–05 Shrewsbury T 6 0
2005–06 Shrewsbury T 46 0 **52** **0**

HERD, Ben (D) **46** **2**
H: 5 9 W: 10 12 b.Welwyn 21-6-85
Source: Scholar.
2002–03 Watford 0 0
2003–04 Watford 0 0
2004–05 Watford 0 0
2005–06 Shrewsbury T 46 2 **46** **2**

HOGG, Steven (M) **12** **0**
H: 6 3 W: 11 11 b.Bury 1-10-85
Source: Manchester U Scholar.
2005–06 Shrewsbury T 12 0 **12** **0**

HOPE, Richard (D) **304** **12**
H: 6 2 W: 12 06 b.Stockton 22-6-78
Source: Trainee.
1995–96 Blackburn R 0 0
1996–97 Blackburn R 0 0
1996–97 Darlington 20 0
1997–98 Darlington 35 1
1998–99 Darlington 8 0 **63** **1**
1998–99 Northampton T 19 0
1999–2000 Northampton T 17 0
2000–01 Northampton T 33 0
2001–02 Northampton T 43 6
2002–03 Northampton T 23 1 **135** **7**
2003–04 York C 36 2 **36** **2**
2004–05 Chester C 28 0 **28** **0**
2005–06 Shrewsbury T 42 2 **42** **2**

HURST, Glynn (F) **260** **92**
H: 5 10 W: 11 06 b.Barnsley 17-1-76
Source: Tottenham H Trainee.
1994–95 Barnsley 2 0
1995–96 Barnsley 5 0
1995–96 *Swansea C* 2 1 **2** **1**
1996–97 Barnsley 1 0 **8** **0**
1996–97 *Mansfield T* 6 0 **6** **0**
1998–99 Ayr U 34 18
1999–2000 Ayr U 25 14 **59** **32**
2000–01 Stockport Co 11 0
2001–02 Stockport Co 15 4 **26** **4**
2001–02 Chesterfield 23 9
2002–03 Chesterfield 32 7
2003–04 Chesterfield 29 13 **84** **29**
2004–05 Notts Co 41 14
2005–06 Notts Co 18 9 **59** **23**
2005–06 Shrewsbury T 16 3 **16** **3**

LANGMEAD, Kelvin (F) **93** **14**
H: 6 1 W: 12 00 b.Coventry 23-3-85
Source: Scholar.
2003–04 Preston NE 1 0
2003–04 *Carlisle U* 11 1 **11** **1**
2004–05 Preston NE 1 0 **2** **0**
2004–05 *Kidderminster H* 10 1 **10** **1**
2004–05 Shrewsbury T 28 3
2005–06 Shrewsbury T 42 9 **70** **12**

LESLIE, Steven (M) **1** **0**
H: 5 10 W: 11 02 b.Shrewsbury 5-11-87
2005–06 Shrewsbury T 1 0 **1** **0**

LYNG, Ciaran (M) **5** **0**
H: 5 11 W: 12 08 b.Wexford 24-7-85
Source: Scholar. *Honours:* Eire Youth.
2003–04 Preston NE 0 0
2004–05 Preston NE 0 0
2004–05 Shrewsbury T 4 0
2005–06 Shrewsbury T 1 0 **5** **0**

McCLEN, Jamie (M) **20** **0**
H: 5 9 W: 11 03 b.Newcastle 13-5-79
Source: Trainee.
1997–98 Newcastle U 0 0
1998–99 Newcastle U 1 0
1999–2000 Newcastle U 9 0
2000–01 Newcastle U 0 0
2001–02 Newcastle U 3 0
2002–03 Newcastle U 1 0
2003–04 Newcastle U 0 0
2004–05 Newcastle U 0 0 **14** **0**
2005–06 Carlisle U 2 0 **2** **0**
2005–06 Shrewsbury T 4 0 **4** **0**

McMENAMIN, Colin (F) **94** **21**
H: 5 10 W: 10 12 b.Glasgow 12-2-81
2000–01 Newcastle U 0 0
2001–02 Newcastle U 0 0
2002–03 Livingston 14 2
2003–04 Livingston 15 7
2004–05 Livingston 22 2 **51** **11**
2005–06 Shrewsbury T 43 10 **43** **10**

SHARP, Kevin (D) **325** **13**
H: 5 9 W: 11 11 b.Ontario 19-9-74
Source: Auxerre. *Honours:* England Schools, Youth.
1992–93 Leeds U 4 0
1993–94 Leeds U 10 0

1994–95 Leeds U 2 0
1995–96 Leeds U 1 0 **17 0**
1995–96 Wigan Ath 20 6
1996–97 Wigan Ath 35 2
1997–98 Wigan Ath 38 0
1998–99 Wigan Ath 31 2
1999–2000 Wigan Ath 21 0
2000–01 Wigan Ath 31 0
2001–02 Wigan Ath 2 0 **178 10**
2001–02 Wrexham 15 0 **15 0**
2002–03 Huddersfield T 39 0 **39 0**
2003–04 Scunthorpe U 40 2
2004–05 Scunthorpe U 6 0 **46 2**
2005–06 Shrewsbury T 30 1 **30 1**

SMITH, Ben (M) 25 4
H: 5 9 W: 11 09 b.Chelmsford 23-11-78
Source: Yeovil T.
2001–02 Southend U 1 0 **1 0**
From Hereford U
2004–05 Shrewsbury T 12 3
2005–06 Shrewsbury T 12 1 **24 4**

SORVEL, Neil (M) 390 24
H: 5 10 W: 11 04 b.Whiston 2-3-73
Source: Trainee.
1991–92 Crewe Alex 9 0
1992–93 Crewe Alex 0 0
1997–98 Macclesfield T 45 3
1998–99 Macclesfield T 41 4 **86 7**
1999–2000 Crewe Alex 46 6
2000–01 Crewe Alex 46 1
2001–02 Crewe Alex 38 0
2002–03 Crewe Alex 43 3
2003–04 Crewe Alex 31 0
2004–05 Crewe Alex 46 3 **259 13**
2005–06 Shrewsbury T 45 4 **45 4**

STALLARD, Mark (F) 410 118
H: 6 0 W: 13 09 b.Derby 24-10-74
Source: Trainee.
1991–92 Derby Co 3 0
1992–93 Derby Co 5 0
1993–94 Derby Co 0 0
1994–95 Derby Co 16 2
1994–95 *Fulham* 4 3 **4 3**
1995–96 Derby Co 3 0 **27 2**
1995–96 Bradford C 21 9
1996–97 Bradford C 22 1 **43 10**
1996–97 *Preston NE* 4 1 **4 1**
1996–97 Wycombe W 12 4
1997–98 Wycombe W 43 17
1998–99 Wycombe W 15 2 **70 23**
1998–99 Notts Co 14 4
1999–2000 Notts Co 36 14
2000–01 Notts Co 42 17
2001–02 Notts Co 26 4
2002–03 Notts Co 45 24
2003–04 Notts Co 22 4
2003–04 Barnsley 10 1
2004–05 Barnsley 5 0 **15 1**
2004–05 *Chesterfield* 9 2 **9 2**
2004–05 *Notts Co* 16 3 **201 70**
2005–06 Shrewsbury T 37 6 **37 6**

THOMPSON, Glyn (G) 37 0
H: 6 2 W: 13 01 b.Telford 24-2-81
Source: Trainee.
1998–99 Shrewsbury T 1 0
1999–2000 Shrewsbury T 0 0
1999–2000 Fulham 0 0
1999–2000 *Mansfield T* 16 0 **16 0**
2000–01 Fulham 0 0
2000–01 *Shrewsbury T* 0 0
2001–02 Fulham 0 0
2002–03 Fulham 0 0
2002–03 Northampton T 11 0
2003–04 Northampton T 8 0 **19 0**
2004–05 Walsall 0 0
2004–05 Chesterfield 1 0 **1 0**
2005–06 Shrewsbury T 0 0 **1 0**

TOLLEY, Jamie (M) 160 14
H: 6 1 W: 11 03 b.Ludlow 12-5-83
Source: Scholarship. *Honours:* Wales Under-21.
1999–2000 Shrewsbury T 2 0
2000–01 Shrewsbury T 24 2
2001–02 Shrewsbury T 23 1
2002–03 Shrewsbury T 39 3
2003–04 Shrewsbury T 0 0
2004–05 Shrewsbury T 36 4
2005–06 Shrewsbury T 36 4 **160 14**

WALTON, David (D) 333 17
H: 6 2 W: 13 04 b.Bedlington 10-4-73
Source: Trainee.
1991–92 Sheffield U 0 0
1992–93 Sheffield U 0 0
1993–94 Sheffield U 0 0
1993–94 Shrewsbury T 27 5
1994–95 Shrewsbury T 36 3
1995–96 Shrewsbury T 35 0
1996–97 Shrewsbury T 24 1
1997–98 Shrewsbury T 6 1
1997–98 Crewe Alex 27 0
1998–99 Crewe Alex 38 1
1999–2000 Crewe Alex 11 0
2000–01 Crewe Alex 20 0
2001–02 Crewe Alex 31 1
2002–03 Crewe Alex 28 1 **155 3**
2003–04 Derby Co 5 0 **5 0**
2003–04 *Stockport Co* 7 0 **7 0**
2004–05 Shrewsbury T 22 2
2005–06 Shrewsbury T 16 2 **166 14**

WHITEHEAD, Stuart (D) 238 2
H: 6 0 W: 12 04 b.Bromsgrove 17-7-76
Source: Bromsgrove R.
1995–96 Bolton W 0 0
1996–97 Bolton W 0 0
1997–98 Bolton W 0 0
1998–99 Carlisle U 37 0
1999–2000 Carlisle U 29 0
2000–01 Carlisle U 45 1
2001–02 Carlisle U 32 1
2002–03 Carlisle U 9 0 **152 2**
2002–03 Darlington 23 0 **23 0**
From Telford U
2004–05 Shrewsbury T 40 0
2005–06 Shrewsbury T 23 0 **63 0**

SOUTHAMPTON (74)

ANACLET, Edward (F) 0 0
H: 5 9 W: 10 01 b.Tanzania 31-8-85
Source: Scholar.
2004–05 Southampton 0 0
2005–06 Southampton 0 0

BAIRD, Chris (D) 42 0
H: 5 10 W: 11 11 b.Ballymoney 25-2-82
Source: Scholar. *Honours:* Northern Ireland Youth, Under-21, 20 full caps.
2000–01 Southampton 0 0
2001–02 Southampton 0 0
2002–03 Southampton 3 0
2003–04 Southampton 4 0
2003–04 *Walsall* 10 0 **10 0**
2003–04 *Watford* 8 0 **8 0**
2004–05 Southampton 0 0
2005–06 Southampton 17 0 **24 0**

BALE, Gareth (D) 2 0
H: 6 0 W: 11 10 b.Cardiff 16-7-89
Source: Scholar. *Honours:* Wales Under-21, 1 full cap.
2005–06 Southampton 2 0 **2 0**

BELMADI, Djamel (M) 161 26
H: 5 7 W: 11 00 b.Champigny-sur-Marne 27-3-76
Honours: Algeria full caps.
1995–96 Paris St Germain 1 0 **1 0**
1996–97 Martigues 31 8 **31 8**
1997–98 Marseille 0 0
1998–99 Cannes 26 6 **26 6**
1999–2000 Marseille 9 1
1999–2000 Celta Vigo 10 0 **10 0**
2000–01 Marseille 29 8
2001–02 Marseille 10 0
2002–03 Marseille 15 0 **63 9**
2002–03 Manchester C 8 0
2003–04 Manchester C 0 0
2004–05 Manchester C 0 0 **8 0**
2005–06 Southampton 22 3 **22 3**

BEST, Leon (F) 24 2
H: 6 1 W: 13 03 b.Nottingham 19-9-86
Source: Scholar. *Honours:* Eire Youth.
2004–05 Southampton 3 0
2004–05 *QPR* 5 0 **5 0**
2005–06 Southampton 3 0 **6 0**
2005–06 *Sheffield W* 13 2 **13 2**

BIALKOWSKI, Bartosz (G) 12 0
H: 6 3 W: 12 10 b.Braniewo 6-7-87
Honours: Poland Under-21.
2004–05 Gornik Zabrze 7 0 **7 0**
2005–06 Southampton 5 0 **5 0**

BLACKSTOCK, Dexter (F) 51 11
H: 6 2 W: 13 00 b.Oxford 20-5-86
Source: Scholar. *Honours:* England Youth, Under-20.
2004–05 Southampton 9 1
2004–05 *Plymouth Arg* 14 4 **14 4**
2005–06 Southampton 19 3 **28 4**
2005–06 *Derby Co* 9 3 **9 3**

BRENNAN, Jim (M) 237 5
H: 5 11 W: 12 12 b.Toronto 8-5-77
Source: Sora Lazio. *Honours:* Canada Under-23, 43 full caps, 6 goals.
1994–95 Bristol C 0 0
1995–96 Bristol C 0 0
1996–97 Bristol C 8 0
1997–98 Bristol C 6 0
1998–99 Bristol C 29 1
1999–2000 Bristol C 12 2 **55 3**
1999–2000 Nottingham F 25 0
2000–01 Nottingham F 12 0
2000–01 *Huddersfield T* 2 0 **2 0**
2001–02 Nottingham F 41 0
2002–03 Nottingham F 45 1 **123 1**
2003–04 Norwich C 15 1
2004–05 Norwich C 10 0
2005–06 Norwich C 18 0 **43 1**
2005–06 Southampton 14 0 **14 0**

CONDESSO, Feliciano (M) 0 0
H: 6 0 W: 11 13 b.Congo 6-4-87
2005–06 Southampton 0 0

CRANIE, Martin (D) 18 0
H: 6 1 W: 12 09 b.Yeovil 23-9-86
Source: Scholar. *Honours:* England Youth, Under-20.
2003–04 Southampton 1 0
2004–05 Southampton 3 0
2004–05 *Bournemouth* 3 0 **3 0**
2005–06 Southampton 11 0 **15 0**

CRITCHELL, Kyle (D) 0 0
H: 6 0 W: 12 02 b.Dorchester 18-1-87
Source: Scholar. *Honours:* Wales Under-21.
2005–06 Southampton 0 0

DUTTON-BLACK, Josh (M) 0 0
b. 29-12-87
Source: Oxford U, Southampton Scholar.
2005–06 Southampton 0 0

DYER, Nathan (M) 22 2
H: 5 5 W: 9 00 b.Trowbridge 29-11-87
Source: Scholar. *Honours:* England Youth.
2005–06 Southampton 17 0 **17 0**
2005–06 *Burnley* 5 2 **5 2**

FOLLY, Yoann (M) 31 0
H: 5 9 W: 11 04 b.Togo 6-6-85
Source: St Etienne. *Honours:* France Youth.
2003–04 Southampton 9 0
2004–05 Southampton 3 0
2004–05 *Nottingham F* 1 0 **1 0**
2004–05 *Preston NE* 2 0 **2 0**
2005–06 Southampton 2 0 **14 0**
2005–06 *Sheffield W* 14 0 **14 0**

FULLER, Ricardo (F) 157 47
H: 6 3 W: 12 10 b.Kingston, Jamaica 31-10-79
Source: Tivoli Gardens. *Honours:* Jamaica full caps.
2000–01 Crystal Palace 8 0 **8 0**
2001–02 Hearts 27 8 **27 8**
From Tivoli Gardens.
2002–03 Preston NE 18 9
2003–04 Preston NE 38 17
2004–05 Preston NE 2 1 **58 27**

2004–05	Portsmouth	31	1	**31**	**1**
2005–06	Southampton	30	9	**30**	**9**
2005–06	*Ipswich T*	3	2	**3**	**2**

GILLETT, Simon (M) 2 0
H: 5 6 W: 11 07 b.London 6-11-85
Source: Trainee. *Honours:* Luxembourg full caps.

2003–04	Southampton	0	0		
2004–05	Southampton	0	0		
2005–06	Southampton	0	0		
2005–06	*Walsall*	2	0	**2**	**0**

GRIFFIT, Leandre (M) 10 2
H: 5 8 W: 11 04 b.Maubeuge 21-5-84
Source: Amiens.

2003–04	Southampton	5	2		
2003–04	Southampton	0	0		
2004–05	Southampton	2	0		
2004–05	*Leeds U*	1	0	**1**	**0**
2004–05	*Rotherham U*	2	0	**2**	**0**
2005–06	Southampton	0	0	**7**	**2**

To Elfsborg March 2006

HIGGINBOTHAM, Danny (D) 184 7
H: 6 2 W: 13 01 b.Manchester 29-12-78
Source: Trainee.

1997–98	Manchester U	1	0		
1998–99	Manchester U	0	0		
1999–2000	Manchester U	3	0	**4**	**0**
2000–01	Derby Co	26	0		
2001–02	Derby Co	37	1		
2002–03	Derby Co	23	2	**86**	**3**
2002–03	Southampton	9	0		
2003–04	Southampton	27	0		
2004–05	Southampton	21	1		
2005–06	Southampton	37	3	**94**	**4**

JAMES, Lloyd (M) 0 0
H: 5 11 W: 11 01 b.Bristol 16-2-88
Source: Scholar. *Honours:* Wales Under-21.

2005–06	Southampton	0	0		

JONES, Kenwyne (F) 56 14
H: 6 2 W: 13 06 b.Trinidad & Tobago 5-10-84
Source: W Connection. *Honours:* Trindad & Tobago 31 full caps, 2 goals.

2004–05	Southampton	2	0		
2004–05	*Sheffield W*	7	7	**7**	**7**
2004–05	*Stoke C*	13	3	**13**	**3**
2005–06	Southampton	34	4	**36**	**4**

KENTON, Darren (D) 197 9
H: 5 10 W: 12 06 b.Wandsworth 13-9-78
Source: Trainee.

1997–98	Norwich C	11	0		
1998–99	Norwich C	22	1		
1999–2000	Norwich C	26	1		
2000–01	Norwich C	29	2		
2001–02	Norwich C	33	4		
2002–03	Norwich C	37	1	**158**	**9**
2002–03	Southampton	0	0		
2003–04	Southampton	7	0		
2004–05	Southampton	9	0		
2004–05	*Leicester C*	10	0	**10**	**0**
2005–06	Southampton	13	0	**29**	**0**

KOSOWSKI, Kamil (M) 164 14
H: 6 2 W: 12 07 b.Ostrowiec 30-8-77
Source: Gornik Zabrze. *Honours:* Poland 46 full caps, 4 goals.

1999–2000	Wisla	19	1		
2000–01	Wisla	27	1		
2001–02	Wisla	27	3		
2002–03	Wisla	29	7	**102**	**12**
2003–04	Kaiserslautern	23	0		
2003–04	Kaiserslautern B	1	0		
2004–05	Kaiserslautern	20	1	**43**	**1**
2005–06	Southampton	18	1	**18**	**1**

LALLANA, Adam (M) 0 0
b.Southampton 10-5-88
Source: Scholar. *Honours:* England Youth.

2005–06	Southampton	0	0		

LUNDEKVAM, Claus (D) 377 3
H: 6 3 W: 13 05 b.Austevoll 22-2-73
Honours: Norway Under-21, 40 full caps, 2 goals.

1993	Brann	3	0		
1994	Brann	20	0		
1995	Brann	14	0		
1996	Brann	16	1	**53**	**1**
1996–97	Southampton	29	0		
1997–98	Southampton	31	0		
1998–99	Southampton	33	0		
1999–2000	Southampton	27	0		
2000–01	Southampton	38	0		
2001–02	Southampton	34	0		
2002–03	Southampton	33	0		
2003–04	Southampton	31	1		
2004–05	Southampton	34	0		
2005–06	Southampton	34	1	**324**	**2**

MADSEN, Peter (F) 182 58
H: 6 0 W: 11 13 b.Roskilde 26-4-78
Honours: Denmark Youth, Under-21, 13 full caps, 3 goals.

1996–97	Brondby	8	2		
1997–98	Brondby	5	0		
1998–99	Brondby	18	3		
1999–2000	Brondby	28	7		
2000–01	Brondby	5	0		
2001–02	Brondby	31	22		
2002–03	Brondby	15	4	**110**	**38**
2002–03	Arminia	0	0		
2002–03	Wolfsburg	4	0	**4**	**0**
2003–04	Bochum	32	13		
2004–05	Bochum	19	5	**51**	**18**
2005–06	Cologne	8	0	**8**	**0**
2005–06	Southampton	9	2	**9**	**2**

McCANN, Neil (M) 305 42
H: 5 10 W: 11 00 b.Greenock 11-8-74
Source: Port Glasgow BC. *Honours:* Scotland Under-21, B, 26 full caps, 3 goals.

1992–93	Dundee	3	0		
1993–94	Dundee	22	1		
1994–95	Dundee	32	2		
1995–96	Dundee	22	2	**79**	**5**
1996–97	Hearts	30	5		
1997–98	Hearts	35	10		
1998–99	Hearts	8	3	**73**	**18**
1998–99	Rangers	19	5		
1999–2000	Rangers	30	3		
2000–01	Rangers	21	3		
2001–02	Rangers	25	7		
2002–03	Rangers	18	1	**113**	**19**
2003–04	Southampton	18	0		
2004–05	Southampton	11	0		
2005–06	Southampton	11	0	**40**	**0**

To Hearts January 2006

McGOLDRICK, David (F) 11 0
H: 6 1 W: 11 10 b.Nottingham 29-11-87
Source: Schoolboy.

2003–04	Notts Co	4	0		
2004–05	Notts Co	0	0		
2005–06	Southampton	1	0	**1**	**0**
2005–06	*Notts Co*	6	0	**10**	**0**

McNEIL, Andrew (G) 0 0
H: 5 11 W: 13 03 b.Edinburgh 19-1-87
Source: Scholar.

2004–05	Southampton	0	0		
2005–06	Southampton	0	0		

MILLER, Kevin (G) 621 0
H: 6 1 W: 13 00 b.Falmouth 15-3-69
Source: Newquay.

1988–89	Exeter C	3	0		
1989–90	Exeter C	28	0		
1990–91	Exeter C	46	0		
1991–92	Exeter C	42	0		
1992–93	Exeter C	44	0		
1993–94	Birmingham C	24	0	**24**	**0**
1994–95	Watford	44	0		
1995–96	Watford	42	0		
1996–97	Watford	42	0	**128**	**0**
1997–98	Crystal Palace	38	0		
1998–99	Crystal Palace	28	0		
1999–2000	Crystal Palace	0	0	**66**	**0**
1999–2000	Barnsley	41	0		
2000–01	Barnsley	46	0		
2001–02	Barnsley	28	0	**115**	**0**
2002–03	Exeter C	46	0	**209**	**0**
2003–04	Bristol R	44	0		
2004–05	*Derby Co*	0	0		
2004–05	Bristol R	28	0	**72**	**0**
2005–06	Southampton	7	0	**7**	**0**

OAKLEY, Matthew (M) 261 14
H: 5 10 W: 12 06 b.Peterborough 17-8-77
Source: Trainee. *Honours:* England Under-21.

1994–95	Southampton	1	0		
1995–96	Southampton	10	0		
1996–97	Southampton	28	3		
1997–98	Southampton	33	1		
1998–99	Southampton	22	2		
1999–2000	Southampton	31	3		
2000–01	Southampton	35	1		
2001–02	Southampton	27	1		
2002–03	Southampton	31	0		
2003–04	Southampton	7	0		
2004–05	Southampton	7	1		
2005–06	Southampton	29	2	**261**	**14**

OSTLUND, Alexander (D) 225 9
H: 5 11 W: 11 13 b.Akersborg 2-11-78
Honours: Sweden 22 full caps.

1994	AIK Stockholm	3	1		
1995	AIK Stockholm	17	1		
1996	AIK Stockholm	2	0		
1997	Brommapojkarna	13	2	**13**	**2**
1998	AIK Stockholm	24	1	**46**	**3**
1998–99	Guimaraes	0	0		
1999	Norrkoping	11	1		
2000	Norrkoping	22	1		
2001	Norrkoping	21	1		
2002	Norrkoping	23	0	**77**	**3**
2003	Hammarby	20	0		
2004	Hammarby	25	0	**45**	**0**
2004–05	Feyenoord	16	0		
2005–06	Feyenoord	16	1	**32**	**1**
2005–06	Southampton	12	0	**12**	**0**

PAHARS, Marian (F) 255 94
H: 5 8 W: 10 08 b.Latvia 5-8-76
Honours: Latvia 63 full caps, 15 goals.

1994	Pardaugava Riga	17	3	**17**	**3**
1995	Skonto/Metals Riga	16	4	**16**	**4**
1995	Skonto Riga	9	8		
1996	Skonto Riga	28	12		
1997	Skonto Riga	22	5		
1998	Skonto Riga	26	19	**85**	**44**
1998–99	Southampton	6	3		
1999–2000	Southampton	33	13		
2000–01	Southampton	31	9		
2001–02	Southampton	36	14		
2002–03	Southampton	9	1		
2003–04	Southampton	14	2		
2004–05	Southampton	0	0		
2005–06	Southampton	8	1	**137**	**43**

POKE, Michael (G) 0 0
H: 6 1 W: 13 12 b.Spelthorne 21-11-85
Source: Trainee.

2003–04	Southampton	0	0		
2004–05	Southampton	0	0		
2005–06	Southampton	0	0		
2005–06	*Oldham Ath*	0	0		
2005–06	*Northampton T*	0	0		

POWELL, Darren (D) 213 10
H: 6 2 W: 13 07 b.Hammersmith 10-3-76
Source: Hampton.

1998–99	Brentford	33	2		
1999–2000	Brentford	36	2		
2000–01	Brentford	18	1		
2001–02	Brentford	41	1	**128**	**6**
2002–03	Crystal Palace	39	1		
2003–04	Crystal Palace	10	0		
2004–05	Crystal Palace	6	1	**55**	**2**
2004–05	*West Ham U*	5	1	**5**	**1**
2005–06	Southampton	25	1	**25**	**1**

PRUTTON, David (M) 222 9
H: 5 10 W: 13 00 b.Hull 12-9-81
Source: Trainee. *Honours:* England Youth, Under-21.

1998–99	Nottingham F	0	0		
1999–2000	Nottingham F	34	2		
2000–01	Nottingham F	42	1		
2001–02	Nottingham F	43	3		
2002–03	Nottingham F	24	1	**143**	**7**
2002–03	Southampton	12	0		
2003–04	Southampton	27	1		
2004–05	Southampton	23	1		
2005–06	Southampton	17	0	**79**	**2**

RASIAK, Grzegorz (F) **156 65**
H: 6 3 W: 13 03 b.Szczecin 12-1-79
Honours: Poland 31 full caps, 8 goals.

2000–01	Odra	28	9	**28**	**9**
2001–02	Groclin	26	14		
2002–03	Groclin	22	10		
2003–04	Groclin	18	10	**66**	**34**
2003–04	Siena	0	0		
2004–05	Derby Co	35	16		
2005–06	Derby Co	6	2	**41**	**18**
2005–06	Tottenham H	8	0	**8**	**0**
2005–06	Southampton	13	4	**13**	**4**

RICHARDS, Craig (D) **0 0**
b.Southampton 24-11-86
Source: Scholar.

2005–06	Southampton	0	0		

RUDD, Sean (D) **0 0**
H: 6 2 W: 11 03 b.Oxford 23-10-87
Source: Scholar. *Honours:* England Youth.

2005–06	Southampton	0	0		

SMITH, Paul (G) **102 0**
H: 6 3 W: 14 00 b.Epsom 17-12-79

1998–99	Charlton Ath	0	0		
1998–99	*Brentford*	0	0		
1999–2000	Charlton Ath	0	0		
From Carshalton Ath.					
2000–01	Brentford	2	0		
2001–02	Brentford	18	0		
2002–03	Brentford	43	0		
2003–04	Brentford	24	0	**87**	**0**
2003–04	Southampton	0	0		
2004–05	Southampton	6	0		
2005–06	Southampton	9	0	**15**	**0**

SPARV, Tim (M) **0 0**
H: 6 4 W: 12 05 b.Vasa 20-2-87
Source: Scholar.

2004–05	Southampton	0	0		
2005–06	Southampton	0	0		

ST JUSTE, Jason (M) **15 2**
H: 5 6 W: 10 05 b.Leeds 21-9-85

2004–05	Darlington	15	2	**15**	**2**
2005–06	Southampton	0	0		

SURMAN, Andrew (M) **50 10**
H: 5 10 W: 11 06 b.Johannesburg 20-8-86
Source: Trainee.

2003–04	Southampton	0	0		
2004–05	Southampton	0	0		
2004–05	*Walsall*	14	2	**14**	**2**
2005–06	Southampton	12	2	**12**	**2**
2005–06	*Bournemouth*	24	6	**24**	**6**

SVENSSON, Michael (D) **245 11**
H: 6 2 W: 12 02 b.Varnamo 25-11-75
Honours: Sweden 25 full caps.

1992	Skillingaryds	21	0	**21**	**0**
1993	Varnamo	20	0		
1994	Varnamo	20	0		
1995	Varnamo	17	1		
1996	Varnamo	0	0	**57**	**1**
1997	Halmstad	0	0		
1998	Halmstad	14	2		
1999	Halmstad	20	0		
2000	Halmstad	25	2		
2001	Halmstad	18	1	**77**	**5**
2001–02	Troyes	23	1	**23**	**1**
2002–03	Southampton	34	2		
2003–04	Southampton	26	2		
2004–05	Southampton	0	0		
2005–06	Southampton	7	0	**67**	**4**

TEJERA, Marcos (F) **0 0**
H: 6 2 W: 12 03 b.Montevideo 6-8-73
Source: Penarol.

2005–06	Southampton	0	0		

VAN DAMME, Jelle (D) **31 0**
H: 6 4 W: 13 01 b.Lokeren 10-10-83
Honours: Belgium 7 full caps.

2001–02	Beerschot	7	0	**7**	**0**
2001–02	Ajax	1	0		
2002–03	Ajax	11	0		
2003–04	Ajax	6	0	**18**	**0**
2004–05	Southampton	6	0		
2005–06	Southampton	0	0	**6**	**0**

To Werder Bremen (loan) August 2005

SOUTHEND U (75)

ADEMENO, Charles (F) **1 0**
H: 5 10 W: 11 13 b.Milton Keynes 12-12-88
Source: Scholar.

2005–06	Southend U	1	0	**1**	**0**

BARRETT, Adam (D) **267 23**
H: 5 10 W: 12 00 b.Dagenham 29-11-79
Source: Leyton Orient Trainee.

1998–99	Plymouth Arg	1	0		
1999–2000	Plymouth Arg	42	3		
2000–01	Plymouth Arg	9	0	**52**	**3**
2000–01	Mansfield T	8	1		
2001–02	Mansfield T	29	0	**37**	**1**
2002–03	Bristol R	45	1		
2003–04	Bristol R	45	4	**90**	**5**
2004–05	Southend U	43	11		
2005–06	Southend U	45	3	**88**	**14**

BENTLEY, Mark (M) **93 12**
H: 6 2 W: 13 04 b.Hertford 7-1-78
Source: Enfield, Aldershot T, Gravesend & N, Dagenham & R.

2003–04	Southend U	21	2		
2004–05	Southend U	39	5		
2005–06	Southend U	33	5	**93**	**12**

BRADBURY, Lee (F) **350 78**
H: 6 0 W: 12 07 b.Isle of Wight 3-7-75
Source: Cowes. *Honours:* England Under-21.

1995–96	Portsmouth	12	0		
1995–96	*Exeter C*	14	5	**14**	**5**
1996–97	Portsmouth	42	15		
1997–98	Manchester C	27	7		
1998–99	Manchester C	13	3	**40**	**10**
1998–99	Crystal Palace	22	4		
1998–99	*Birmingham C*	7	0	**7**	**0**
1999–2000	Crystal Palace	10	2	**32**	**6**
1999–2000	Portsmouth	35	10		
2000–01	Portsmouth	39	10		
2001–02	Portsmouth	22	7		
2002–03	Portsmouth	3	1		
2002–03	*Sheffield W*	11	3	**11**	**3**
2003–04	Portsmouth	0	0	**153**	**43**
2003–04	*Derby Co*	7	0	**7**	**0**
2003–04	Walsall	8	1	**8**	**1**
2004–05	Oxford U	41	4		
2005–06	Oxford U	22	5	**63**	**9**
2005–06	Southend U	15	1	**15**	**1**

BYRNE, Paul (M) **125 11**
H: 5 11 W: 13 00 b.Dublin 30-6-72
Source: Trainee. *Honours:* Eire Youth.

1989–90	Oxford U	3	0		
1990–91	Oxford U	2	0		
1991–92	Oxford U	1	0	**6**	**0**
From Bangor					
1993–94	Celtic	22	2		
1994–95	Celtic	6	2	**28**	**4**
1994–95	*Brighton & HA*	8	1	**8**	**1**
1995–96	Southend U	41	5		
1996–97	Southend U	32	1		
1997–98	Southend U	10	0		
1998–99	Southend U	0	0		
1999–2000	Southend U	0	0		
2000–01	Southend U	0	0		
2001–02	Southend U	0	0		
2002–03	Southend U	0	0		
2003–04	Southend U	0	0		
2004–05	Southend U	0	0		
2005–06	Southend U	0	0	**83**	**6**

COLE, Mitchell (M) **29 1**
H: 5 11 W: 11 05 b.London 6-10-85
Source: Trainee. *Honours:* England Youth.

2002–03	West Ham U	0	0		
2003–04	West Ham U	0	0		
2004–05	West Ham U	0	0		
From Grays Ath.					
2005–06	Southend U	29	1	**29**	**1**

EASTWOOD, Freddy (F) **73 42**
H: 5 11 W: 12 04 b.Epsom 29-10-83
Source: West Ham U Trainee, Grays Ath.

2004–05	Southend U	33	19		
2005–06	Southend U	40	23	**73**	**42**

EDWARDS, Andy (D) **526 21**
H: 6 3 W: 12 13 b.Epping 17-9-71
Source: Trainee.

1988–89	Southend U	1	0		
1989–90	Southend U	8	0		
1990–91	Southend U	2	1		
1991–92	Southend U	9	0		
1992–93	Southend U	41	0		
1993–94	Southend U	42	1		
1994–95	Southend U	44	3		
1995–96	Birmingham C	37	1		
1996–97	Birmingham C	3	0	**40**	**1**
1996–97	Peterborough U	25	0		
1997–98	Peterborough U	46	2		
1998–99	Peterborough U	41	2		
1999–2000	Peterborough U	44	2		
2000–01	Peterborough U	43	1		
2001–02	Peterborough U	44	2		
2002–03	Peterborough U	23	1	**266**	**10**
2002–03	Rushden & D	12	1		
2003–04	Rushden & D	29	3	**41**	**4**
2004–05	Southend U	12	1		
2005–06	Southend U	20	0	**179**	**6**

FLAHAVAN, Darryl (G) **219 0**
H: 5 11 W: 12 05 b.Southampton 28-11-78
Source: Trainee.

From Woking.					
2000–01	Southend U	29	0		
2001–02	Southend U	41	0		
2002–03	Southend U	41	0		
2003–04	Southend U	37	0		
2004–05	Southend U	28	0		
2005–06	Southend U	43	0	**219**	**0**

GOATER, Shaun (F) **552 217**
H: 6 1 W: 12 00 b.Hamilton, Bermuda 25-2-70
Honours: Bermuda 19 full caps.

1988–89	Manchester U	0	0		
1989–90	Manchester U	0	0		
1989–90	Rotherham U	12	2		
1990–91	Rotherham U	22	2		
1991–92	Rotherham U	24	9		
1992–93	Rotherham U	23	7		
1993–94	Rotherham U	39	13		
1993–94	*Notts Co*	1	0	**1**	**0**
1994–95	Rotherham U	45	19		
1995–96	Rotherham U	44	18	**209**	**70**
1996–97	Bristol C	42	23		
1997–98	Bristol C	33	17	**75**	**40**
1997–98	Manchester C	7	3		
1998–99	Manchester C	43	17		
1999–2000	Manchester C	40	23		
2000–01	Manchester C	26	6		
2001–02	Manchester C	42	28		
2002–03	Manchester C	26	7	**184**	**84**
2003–04	Reading	34	12		
2004–05	Reading	9	0	**43**	**12**
2004–05	*Coventry C*	6	0	**6**	**0**
2005–06	Southend U	34	11	**34**	**11**

GOWER, Mark (M) **141 20**
H: 5 11 W: 11 12 b.Edmonton 5-10-78
Source: Trainee. *Honours:* England Schools, Youth.

1996–97	Tottenham H	0	0		
1997–98	Tottenham H	0	0		
1998–99	Tottenham H	0	0		
1998–99	*Motherwell*	9	1	**9**	**1**
1999–2000	Tottenham H	0	0		
2000–01	Tottenham H	0	0		
2000–01	Barnet	14	1		
2001–02	Barnet	0	0		
2002–03	Barnet	0	0	**14**	**1**
2003–04	Southend U	40	6		
2004–05	Southend U	38	6		
2005–06	Southend U	40	6	**118**	**18**

GRAY, Wayne (F) **192 34**
H: 5 10 W: 11 05 b.Dulwich 7-11-80
Source: Trainee.

1998–99	Wimbledon	0	0		
1999–2000	Wimbledon	1	0		
1999–2000	*Swindon T*	12	2	**12**	**2**
2000–01	Wimbledon	11	0		
2000–01	*Port Vale*	3	0	**3**	**0**
2001–02	Wimbledon	0	0		
2001–02	*Leyton Orient*	15	5	**15**	**5**

2001–02 *Brighton & HA* 4 1 **4 1**
2002–03 Wimbledon 30 2
2003–04 Wimbledon 33 4 **75 6**
2004–05 Southend U 44 11
2005–06 Southend U 39 9 **83 20**

GRIEMINK, Bart (G) **224 0**
H: 6 3 W: 15 04 b.Oss 29-3-72
Source: WKE.
1995–96 Birmingham C 20 0
1996–97 Birmingham C 0 0 **20 0**
1996–97 *Barnsley* 0 0
1996–97 Peterborough U 27 0
1997–98 Peterborough U 0 0
1998–99 Peterborough U 17 0
1999–2000 Peterborough U 14 0 **58 0**
1999–2000 *Swindon T* 4 0
2000–01 Swindon T 25 0
2001–02 Swindon T 45 0
2002–03 Swindon T 44 0
2003–04 Swindon T 6 0 **124 0**
2004–05 Southend U 19 0
2005–06 Southend U 3 0 **22 0**

GUTTRIDGE, Luke (M) **183 22**
H: 5 6 W: 8 07 b.Barnstaple 27-3-82
Source: Trainee.
1999–2000 Torquay U 1 0
2000–01 Torquay U 0 0 **1 0**
2000–01 Cambridge U 1 1
2001–02 Cambridge U 29 2
2002–03 Cambridge U 43 3
2003–04 Cambridge U 46 11
2004–05 Cambridge U 17 0 **136 17**
2004–05 Southend U 5 0
2005–06 Southend U 41 5 **46 5**

HUNT, Lewis (D) **98 0**
H: 5 11 W: 12 09 b.Birmingham 25-8-82
Source: Scholar.
2000–01 Derby Co 0 0
2001–02 Derby Co 0 0
2002–03 Derby Co 10 0
2003–04 Derby Co 1 0 **11 0**
2003–04 *Southend U* 26 0
2004–05 Southend U 31 0
2005–06 Southend U 30 0 **87 0**

JUPP, Duncan (D) **248 2**
H: 6 0 W: 12 12 b.Guildford 25-1-75
Source: Trainee. *Honours:* Scotland Under-21.
1992–93 Fulham 3 0
1993–94 Fulham 30 0
1994–95 Fulham 36 2
1995–96 Fulham 36 0 **105 2**
1996–97 Wimbledon 6 0
1997–98 Wimbledon 3 0
1998–99 Wimbledon 6 0
1999–2000 Wimbledon 9 0
2000–01 Wimbledon 4 0
2001–02 Wimbledon 2 0
2002–03 Wimbledon 0 0 **30 0**
2002–03 *Notts Co* 8 0 **8 0**
2002–03 Luton T 5 0 **5 0**
2003–04 Southend U 40 0
2004–05 Southend U 31 0
2005–06 Southend U 29 0 **100 0**

LAWSON, James (M) **24 2**
H: 6 0 W: 11 07 b.Basildon 21-1-87
Source: Scholar.
2004–05 Southend U 1 0
2005–06 Southend U 23 2 **24 2**

MAHER, Kevin (M) **323 17**
H: 6 0 W: 12 13 b.Ilford 17-10-76
Source: Trainee.
1995–96 Tottenham H 0 0
1996–97 Tottenham H 0 0
1997–98 Tottenham H 0 0
1997–98 Southend U 18 1
1998–99 Southend U 34 4
1999–2000 Southend U 24 0
2000–01 Southend U 41 2
2001–02 Southend U 36 5
2002–03 Southend U 42 2
2003–04 Southend U 42 1
2004–05 Southend U 42 1
2005–06 Southend U 44 1 **323 17**

MOUSSA, Franck (M) **1 0**
H: 5 8 W: 10 08 b.Brussels 24-9-87
Source: Scholar.
2005–06 Southend U 1 0 **1 0**

PETTEFER, Carl (M) **102 1**
H: 5 7 W: 10 02 b.Burnham 22-3-81
Source: Trainee.
1998–99 Portsmouth 0 0
1999–2000 Portsmouth 0 0
2000–01 Portsmouth 1 0
2001–02 Portsmouth 2 0
2002–03 Portsmouth 0 0
2002–03 *Exeter C* 31 1 **31 1**
2003–04 Portsmouth 0 0 **3 0**
2003–04 *Southend U* 11 0
2004–05 Southend U 46 0
2005–06 Southend U 11 0 **68 0**

PRIOR, Spencer (D) **496 13**
H: 6 3 W: 13 04 b.Rochford 22-4-71
Source: Trainee.
1988–89 Southend U 14 1
1989–90 Southend U 15 1
1990–91 Southend U 19 0
1991–92 Southend U 42 1
1992–93 Southend U 45 0
1993–94 Norwich C 13 0
1994–95 Norwich C 17 0
1995–96 Norwich C 44 1 **74 1**
1996–97 Leicester C 34 0
1997–98 Leicester C 30 0 **64 0**
1998–99 Derby Co 34 1
1999–2000 Derby Co 20 0 **54 1**
1999–2000 Manchester C 9 3
2000–01 Manchester C 21 1 **30 4**
2001–02 Cardiff C 37 2
2002–03 Cardiff C 37 0
2003–04 Cardiff C 7 0 **81 2**
2004–05 Southend U 41 2
2005–06 Southend U 17 0 **193 5**

SMITH, Jay (M) **68 7**
H: 5 7 W: 12 00 b.Lambeth 24-9-81
Source: Scholar.
2000–01 Aston Villa 0 0
2001–02 Aston Villa 0 0
2002–03 Aston Villa 0 0
2002–03 Southend U 31 5
2003–04 Southend U 18 1
2004–05 Southend U 0 0
2005–06 Southend U 13 1 **62 7**
2005–06 *Oxford U* 6 0 **6 0**

SODJE, Efe (D) **298 18**
H: 6 1 W: 12 00 b.Greenwich 5-10-72
Source: Delta Steel Pioneer, Stevenage Bor. *Honours:* Nigeria 10 full caps, 1 goal.
1997–98 Macclesfield T 41 3
1998–99 Macclesfield T 42 3 **83 6**
1999–2000 Luton T 9 0 **9 0**
1999–2000 Colchester U 3 0 **3 0**
2000–01 Crewe Alex 32 0
2001–02 Crewe Alex 36 2
2002–03 Crewe Alex 30 1 **98 3**
2003–04 Huddersfield T 39 4
2004–05 Huddersfield T 28 1 **67 5**
2004–05 Yeovil T 6 2
2005–06 Yeovil T 19 1 **25 3**
2005–06 Southend U 13 1 **13 1**

WILSON, Che (D) **195 2**
H: 5 9 W: 11 04 b.Ely 17-1-79
Source: Trainee.
1997–98 Norwich C 0 0
1998–99 Norwich C 17 0
1999–2000 Norwich C 5 0 **22 0**
2000–01 Bristol R 37 0
2001–02 Bristol R 38 0
2002–03 Bristol R 0 0 **75 0**
From Cambridge C.
2003–04 Southend U 14 0
2004–05 Southend U 40 0
2005–06 Southend U 44 2 **98 2**

WRIGHT, Mark (M) **0 0**
b.London 20-1-87
Source: Scholar.
2005–06 Southend U 0 0

STOCKPORT CO (76)

ALLEN, Damien (M) **43 1**
H: 5 11 W: 11 04 b.Cheadle 1-8-86
Source: Trainee.
2004–05 Stockport Co 21 1
2005–06 Stockport Co 22 0 **43 1**

BEHARALL, David (D) **98 3**
H: 6 2 W: 11 07 b.Wallsend 8-3-79
Source: Trainee.
1997–98 Newcastle U 0 0
1998–99 Newcastle U 4 0
1999–2000 Newcastle U 2 0
2000–01 Newcastle U 0 0 **6 0**
2001–02 Grimsby T 14 0 **14 0**
2001–02 Oldham Ath 18 1
2002–03 Oldham Ath 32 0
2003–04 Oldham Ath 7 2
2004–05 Oldham Ath 3 0 **60 3**
2005–06 Carlisle U 6 0 **6 0**
2005–06 Stockport Co 12 0 **12 0**

BOSHELL, Danny (M) **109 3**
H: 5 11 W: 11 09 b.Bradford 30-5-81
Source: Trainee.
1998–99 Oldham Ath 0 0
1999–2000 Oldham Ath 8 0
2000–01 Oldham Ath 18 1
2001–02 Oldham Ath 4 0
2002–03 Oldham Ath 2 0
2003–04 Oldham Ath 22 0
2004–05 Oldham Ath 16 1 **70 2**
2004–05 *Bury* 6 0 **6 0**
2005–06 Stockport Co 33 1 **33 1**

BRAMBLE, Tes (F) **185 37**
H: 6 2 W: 13 05 b.Ipswich 20-7-80
Source: Cambridge C.
2000–01 Southend U 16 6
2001–02 Southend U 35 9
2002–03 Southend U 34 9
2003–04 Southend U 34 4
2004–05 Southend U 20 1 **139 29**
2004–05 *Cambridge U* 9 3 **9 3**
2005–06 Stockport Co 37 5 **37 5**

BRIGGS, Keith (D) **123 8**
H: 6 0 W: 11 00 b.Glossop 11-12-81
Source: Trainee.
1999–2000 Stockport Co 7 1
2000–01 Stockport Co 0 0
2001–02 Stockport Co 32 0
2002–03 Stockport Co 19 1
2002–03 Norwich C 2 0
2003–04 Norwich C 3 0
2004–05 Norwich C 0 0 **5 0**
2004–05 *Crewe Alex* 3 0 **3 0**
2004–05 Stockport Co 16 2
2005–06 Stockport Co 41 4 **115 8**

CLARE, Rob (D) **174 5**
H: 6 2 W: 13 00 b.Belper 28-2-83
Source: Trainee. *Honours:* England Under-20.
1999–2000 Stockport Co 0 0
2000–01 Stockport Co 22 0
2001–02 Stockport Co 23 0
2002–03 Stockport Co 36 0
2003–04 Stockport Co 36 3
2004–05 Blackpool 23 0 **23 0**
2005–06 Stockport Co 34 2 **151 5**

COWARD, Chris (F) **0 0**
H: 6 1 W: 11 07 b.Manchester 23-7-89
Source: Scholar.
2005–06 Stockport Co 0 0

CROWE, Dean (F) **162 32**
H: 5 6 W: 11 03 b.Stockport 6-6-79
Source: Trainee.
1996–97 Stoke C 0 0
1997–98 Stoke C 16 4
1998–99 Stoke C 38 8
1999–2000 Stoke C 6 0
1999–2000 *Northampton T* 5 0 **5 0**
1999–2000 *Bury* 4 1
2000–01 Stoke C 0 0
2000–01 *Bury* 7 1 **11 2**
2001–02 Stoke C 0 0 **60 12**
2001–02 *Plymouth Arg* 1 0 **1 0**

2001–02 Luton T 34 15
2002–03 Luton T 27 2
2003–04 Luton T 8 0 **69 17**
2003–04 *York C* 5 0 **5 0**
2003–04 Oldham Ath 5 1
2004–05 Oldham Ath 0 0
2005–06 Oldham Ath 0 0 **5 1**
2005–06 Stockport Co 6 0 **6 0**

CROWTHER, Ryan (M) 1 0
H: 5 11 W: 11 00 b.Stockport 17-9-88
Source: Scholar.
2005–06 Stockport Co 1 0 **1 0**

DICKINSON, Liam (F) 21 7
H: 6 4 W: 11 07 b.Salford 4-10-85
Source: Woodley Sports.
2005–06 Stockport Co 21 7 **21 7**

DJE, Ludovic (D) 10 0
H: 6 3 W: 14 02 b.Paris 22-7-77
Source: RFB.
2004–05 Stockport Co 3 0
2005–06 Stockport Co 7 0 **10 0**

DUNCAN, Craig (G) 0 0
H: 6 1 W: 11 07 b.Manchester 17-10-87
Source: Scholar.
2005–06 Stockport Co 0 0

ELLIS, Dan (M) 3 0
H: 5 10 W: 12 07 b.Stockport 18-11-88
Source: Scholar.
2005–06 Stockport Co 3 0 **3 0**

FOSTER, Liam (D) 1 0
H: 5 10 W: 11 02 b.Eccles 4-9-87
Source: Scholar.
2005–06 Stockport Co 1 0 **1 0**

GREENWOOD, Ross (M) 24 0
H: 5 11 W: 11 05 b.York 1-11-85
Source: Scholar.
2004–05 Sheffield W 2 0 **2 0**
2005–06 Stockport Co 22 0 **22 0**

GRIFFIN, Danny (D) 236 9
H: 5 11 W: 10 02 b.Belfast 10-8-77
Source: St Andrews, Belfast. *Honours:* Northern Ireland Under-21, 29 full caps, 1 goal.
1993–94 St Johnstone 0 0
1994–95 St Johnstone 3 0
1995–96 St Johnstone 31 1
1996–97 St Johnstone 29 1
1997–98 St Johnstone 13 0
1998–99 St Johnstone 19 1
1999–2000 St Johnstone 29 1 **124 4**
2000–01 Dundee U 18 1
2001–02 Dundee U 29 2
2002–03 Dundee U 17 1
2003–04 Dundee U 13 0 **77 4**
2003–04 Stockport Co 15 1
2004–05 Stockport Co 16 0
2005–06 Stockport Co 4 0 **35 1**
To Aberdeen March 2006

HAMSHAW, Matt (M) 113 7
H: 5 10 W: 11 08 b.Rotherham 1-1-82
Source: Trainee. *Honours:* England Youth, Under-20.
1998–99 Sheffield W 0 0
1999–2000 Sheffield W 0 0
2000–01 Sheffield W 18 0
2001–02 Sheffield W 21 0
2002–03 Sheffield W 15 1
2003–04 Sheffield W 0 0
2004–05 Sheffield W 20 1 **74 2**
2005–06 Stockport Co 39 5 **39 5**

KAY, Jamie (D) 0 0
H: 5 10 W: 11 07 b.Stockport 12-12-86
2005–06 Stockport Co 0 0

LE FONDRE, Adam (F) 42 10
H: 5 9 W: 11 04 b.Stockport 2-12-86
Source: Trainee.
2004–05 Stockport Co 20 4
2005–06 Stockport Co 22 6 **42 10**

MALCOLM, Michael (F) 23 3
H: 5 10 W: 11 07 b.Harrow 13-10-85
Source: Trainee. *Honours:* England Youth.
2002–03 Tottenham H 0 0
2003–04 Tottenham H 0 0
2004–05 Tottenham H 0 0
2005–06 Stockport Co 23 3 **23 3**

RAYNES, Michael (D) 44 1
H: 6 4 W: 12 00 b.Wythenshawe 15-10-87
Source: Scholar.
2004–05 Stockport Co 19 0
2005–06 Stockport Co 25 1 **44 1**

ROBINSON, Mark (D) 131 2
H: 5 9 W: 11 00 b.Guisborough 24-7-81
Source: Trainee.
1999–2000 Hartlepool U 0 0
2000–01 Hartlepool U 6 0
2001–02 Hartlepool U 37 0
2002–03 Hartlepool U 38 0
2003–04 Hartlepool U 4 0 **85 0**
From Hereford U
2005–06 Stockport Co 46 2 **46 2**

SINGH, Harpal (M) 76 5
H: 5 7 W: 10 02 b.Bradford 15-9-81
Source: Trainee.
1998–99 Leeds U 0 0
1999–2000 Leeds U 0 0
2000–01 Leeds U 0 0
2001–02 Leeds U 0 0
2001–02 *Bury* 12 2
2001–02 *Bristol C* 3 0 **3 0**
2002–03 Leeds U 0 0
2002–03 *Bradford C* 3 0 **3 0**
2003–04 Leeds U 0 0
2003–04 *Bury* 28 2 **40 4**
2004–05 Leeds U 0 0
2004–05 *Stockport Co* 6 0
2005–06 Stockport Co 24 1 **30 1**

SPENCER, James (G) 76 0
H: 6 3 W: 15 04 b.Stockport 11-4-85
Source: Trainee.
2001–02 Stockport Co 2 0
2002–03 Stockport Co 1 0
2003–04 Stockport Co 15 0
2004–05 Stockport Co 24 0
2005–06 Stockport Co 34 0 **76 0**

TOMLINSON, Ezekiel (M) 5 0
H: 5 9 W: 11 00 b.Birmingham 9-11-85
Source: Scholar.
2004–05 WBA 0 0
2004–05 Stockport Co 5 0
2005–06 Stockport Co 0 0 **5 0**

TUNNICLIFFE, James (D) 1 0
H: 6 4 W: 12 03 b.Denton 17-1-89
Source: Scholar.
2005–06 Stockport Co 1 0 **1 0**

TURNBULL, Paul (F) 1 0
H: 6 0 W: 12 07 b.Handforth 23-1-89
Source: Scholar.
2004–05 Stockport Co 1 0
2005–06 Stockport Co 0 0 **1 0**

WILLIAMS, Ashley (D) 90 2
H: 6 0 W: 11 02 b.Wolverhampton 23-8-84
Source: Hednesford T.
2003–04 Stockport Co 10 0
2004–05 Stockport Co 44 1
2005–06 Stockport Co 36 1 **90 2**

WILLIAMS, Chris (F) 37 3
H: 5 7 W: 9 0 b.Manchester 2-2-85
Source: Scholar.
2001–02 Stockport Co 5 0
2002–03 Stockport Co 1 0
2003–04 Stockport Co 16 3
2004–05 Stockport Co 9 0
2004–05 *Grimsby T* 3 0 **3 0**
2005–06 Stockport Co 3 0 **34 3**

WOLSKI, Makael (M) 20 1
H: 6 0 W: 13 07 b.Moulins 5-3-79
Source: Shamrock R.
2005–06 Stockport Co 20 1 **20 1**

STOKE C (77)

BANGOURA, Sammy (F) 158 70
H: 6 0 W: 12 02 b.Guinea 3-4-82
Source: Kindia, AS Kaloum. *Honours:* Guinea full caps.
2000–01 Lokeren 30 13
2001–02 Lokeren 25 12
2002–03 Lokeren 29 16 **84 41**
2003–04 Standard Liege 20 5
2004–05 Standard Liege 30 15 **50 20**
2005–06 Stoke C 24 9 **24 9**

BRAMMER, Dave (M) 380 21
H: 5 8 W: 12 00 b.Bromborough 28-2-75
Source: Trainee.
1992–93 Wrexham 2 0
1993–94 Wrexham 22 2
1994–95 Wrexham 14 1
1995–96 Wrexham 11 2
1996–97 Wrexham 21 1
1997–98 Wrexham 33 4
1998–99 Wrexham 34 2 **137 12**
1998–99 Port Vale 9 0
1999–2000 Port Vale 29 0
2000–01 Port Vale 35 3 **73 3**
2001–02 Crewe Alex 30 2
2002–03 Crewe Alex 41 1
2003–04 Crewe Alex 16 1 **87 4**
2004–05 Stoke C 43 1
2005–06 Stoke C 40 1 **83 2**

BROOMES, Marlon (D) 188 4
H: 6 0 W: 12 12 b.Birmingham 28-11-77
Source: Trainee. *Honours:* England Schools, Youth, Under-21.
1994–95 Blackburn R 0 0
1995–96 Blackburn R 0 0
1996–97 Blackburn R 0 0
1996–97 *Swindon T* 12 1 **12 1**
1997–98 Blackburn R 4 0
1998–99 Blackburn R 13 0
1999–2000 Blackburn R 13 1
2000–01 Blackburn R 1 0
2000–01 *QPR* 5 0 **5 0**
2001–02 Blackburn R 0 0 **31 1**
2001–02 *Grimsby T* 15 0 **15 0**
2001–02 Sheffield W 19 0 **19 0**
2002–03 Preston NE 28 0
2003–04 Preston NE 30 0
2004–05 Preston NE 11 0 **69 0**
2005–06 Stoke C 37 2 **37 2**

BUXTON, Lewis (D) 125 1
H: 6 1 W: 13 11 b.Newport (IW) 10-12-83
Source: School.
2000–01 Portsmouth 0 0
2001–02 Portsmouth 29 0
2002–03 Portsmouth 1 0
2002–03 *Exeter C* 4 0 **4 0**
2002–03 *Bournemouth* 17 0
2003–04 Portsmouth 0 0
2003–04 *Bournemouth* 26 0 **43 0**
2004–05 Portsmouth 0 0 **30 0**
2004–05 Stoke C 16 0
2005–06 Stoke C 32 1 **48 1**

CHADWICK, Luke (M) 144 11
H: 5 11 W: 11 08 b.Cambridge 18-11-80
Source: Trainee. *Honours:* England Youth, Under-21.
1998–99 Manchester U 0 0
1999–2000 Manchester U 0 0
2000–01 Manchester U 16 2
2001–02 Manchester U 8 0
2002–03 Manchester U 1 0
2002–03 *Reading* 15 1 **15 1**
2003–04 Manchester U 0 0 **25 2**
2003–04 *Burnley* 36 5 **36 5**
2004–05 West Ham U 32 1
2005–06 West Ham U 0 0 **32 1**
2005–06 Stoke C 36 2 **36 2**

DE GOEY, Ed (G) 525 0
H: 6 6 W: 12 00 b.Gouda 20-12-66
Honours: Holland 31 full caps.
1985–86 Sparta 12 0
1986–87 Sparta 34 0
1987–88 Sparta 34 0

1988–89	Sparta	31	0		
1989–90	Sparta	34	0	**145**	**0**
1990–91	Feyenoord	34	0		
1991–92	Feyenoord	34	0		
1992–93	Feyenoord	33	0		
1993–94	Feyenoord	34	0		
1994–95	Feyenoord	32	0		
1995–96	Feyenoord	34	0	**201**	**0**
1997–98	Chelsea	28	0		
1998–99	Chelsea	35	0		
1999–2000	Chelsea	37	0		
2000–01	Chelsea	15	0		
2001–02	Chelsea	6	0		
2002–03	Chelsea	2	0	**123**	**0**
2003–04	Stoke C	37	0		
2004–05	Stoke C	17	0		
2005–06	Stoke C	2	0	**56**	**0**

DICKINSON, Carl (D) **6** **0**
H: 6 1 W: 12 04 b.Swadlincote 31-3-87
Source: Scholar.

2004–05	Stoke C	1	0		
2005–06	Stoke C	5	0	**6**	**0**

DUBERRY, Michael (D) **217** **6**
H: 6 1 W: 13 10 b.Enfield 14-10-75
Source: Trainee. *Honours:* England Under-21.

1993–94	Chelsea	1	0		
1994–95	Chelsea	0	0		
1995–96	Chelsea	22	0		
1995–96	*Bournemouth*	7	0	**7**	**0**
1996–97	Chelsea	15	1		
1997–98	Chelsea	23	0		
1998–99	Chelsea	25	0	**86**	**1**
1999–2000	Leeds U	13	1		
2000–01	Leeds U	5	0		
2001–02	Leeds U	3	0		
2002–03	Leeds U	14	0		
2003–04	Leeds U	19	3		
2004–05	Leeds U	4	0	**58**	**4**
2004–05	Stoke C	25	0		
2005–06	Stoke C	41	1	**66**	**1**

DUGGAN, Robert (G) **0** **0**
H: 6 1 W: 12 07 b.Dublin 1-4-87
Source: Scholar.

2005–06	Stoke C	0	0		

EUSTACE, John (M) **131** **13**
H: 5 11 W: 11 12 b.Solihull 3-11-79
Source: Trainee.

1996–97	Coventry C	0	0		
1997–98	Coventry C	0	0		
1998–99	Coventry C	0	0		
1998–99	Dundee U	11	1	**11**	**1**
1999–2000	Coventry C	16	1		
2000–01	Coventry C	32	2		
2001–02	Coventry C	6	0		
2002–03	Coventry C	32	4	**86**	**7**
2002–03	*Middlesbrough*	1	0	**1**	**0**
2003–04	Stoke C	26	5		
2004–05	Stoke C	7	0		
2005–06	Stoke C	0	0	**33**	**5**

GARRET, Robert (M) **2** **0**
b.Belfast 5-5-88
Source: Scholar. *Honours:* Northern Ireland Youth.

2005–06	Stoke C	2	0	**2**	**0**

GUDJONSSON, Thordur (M) **263** **68**
H: 5 10 W: 11 06 b.Reykjavik 23-1-73
Honours: Iceland Youth, Under-21, 58 full caps, 13 goals.

1990	KA	16	2	**16**	**2**
1991	IA Akranes	0	0		
1992	IA Akranes	18	6		
1993	IA Akranes	18	19	**36**	**25**
1994–95	Bochum	16	3		
1995–96	Bochum	28	3		
1996–97	Bochum	13	1		
1997–98	Genk	33	9		
1998–99	Genk	28	9		
1999–2000	Genk	33	10	**94**	**28**
2000–01	Las Palmas	9	1		
2000–01	Derby Co	10	1	**10**	**1**
2001–02	Las Palmas	0	0	**9**	**1**
2001–02	Preston NE	7	0	**7**	**0**
2002–03	Bochum	29	3		
2003–04	Bochum	3	1	**89**	**11**
2004–05	Stoke C	2	0		
2005–06	Stoke C	0	0	**2**	**0**

HARPER, Kevin (M) **290** **27**
H: 5 6 W: 10 09 b.Oldham 15-1-76
Source: Hutcheson Vale BC. *Honours:* Scotland Schools, Under-21, B.

1993–94	Hibernian	2	0		
1994–95	Hibernian	23	5		
1995–96	Hibernian	16	3		
1996–97	Hibernian	26	5		
1997–98	Hibernian	27	1		
1998–99	Hibernian	2	1	**96**	**15**
1998–99	Derby Co	27	1		
1999–2000	Derby Co	5	0	**32**	**1**
1999–2000	*Walsall*	9	1	**9**	**1**
1999–2000	Portsmouth	12	2		
2000–01	Portsmouth	24	2		
2001–02	Portsmouth	39	1		
2002–03	Portsmouth	37	4		
2003–04	Portsmouth	7	0		
2003–04	*Norwich C*	9	0	**9**	**0**
2004–05	Portsmouth	0	0	**119**	**9**
2004–05	*Leicester C*	2	0	**2**	**0**
2004–05	Stoke C	9	0		
2005–06	Stoke C	14	1	**23**	**1**

HAZLEY, Matthew (M) **1** **0**
b.Banbridge 30-12-87
Source: Scholar. *Honours:* Northern Ireland Youth.

2005–06	Stoke C	1	0	**1**	**0**

HENRY, Karl (M) **129** **2**
H: 6 0 W: 12 00 b.Wolverhampton 26-11-82
Source: Trainee. *Honours:* England Youth, Under-20.

1999–2000	Stoke C	0	0		
2000–01	Stoke C	0	0		
2001–02	Stoke C	24	0		
2002–03	Stoke C	18	1		
2003–04	Stoke C	20	0		
2003–04	*Cheltenham T*	9	1	**9**	**1**
2004–05	Stoke C	34	0		
2005–06	Stoke C	24	0	**120**	**1**

HILL, Clint (D) **214** **18**
H: 6 0 W: 11 06 b.Liverpool 19-10-78
Source: Trainee.

1997–98	Tranmere R	14	0		
1998–99	Tranmere R	33	4		
1999–2000	Tranmere R	29	5		
2000–01	Tranmere R	34	5		
2001–02	Tranmere R	30	2	**140**	**16**
2002–03	Oldham Ath	17	1	**17**	**1**
2003–04	Stoke C	12	0		
2004–05	Stoke C	32	1		
2005–06	Stoke C	13	0	**57**	**1**

HOEFKENS, Carl (D) **270** **11**
H: 6 1 W: 12 13 b.Lier 6-10-78
Honours: Belgium 10 full caps.

1996–97	Lierse	17	0		
1997–98	Lierse	27	1		
1998–99	Lierse	30	0		
1999–2000	Lierse	31	0		
2000–01	Lierse	27	0	**132**	**1**
2001–02	Lommel	33	3		
2002–03	Lommel	22	0	**55**	**3**
2002–03	Westerlo	7	0	**7**	**0**
2003–04	Beerschot	32	4		
2004–05	Beerschot	0	0	**32**	**4**
2005–06	Stoke C	44	3	**44**	**3**

JUNIOR (M) **47** **1**
H: 6 0 W: 11 00 b.Kinshasa 1-6-82
Honours: Belgium Under-21.

2001–02	Anderlecht	12	0		
2002–03	Anderlecht	4	1		
2003–04	Anderlecht	3	0		
2004–05	Anderlecht	6	0	**25**	**1**
2005–06	Stoke C	22	0	**22**	**0**

KOLAR, Martin (M) **67** **4**
H: 5 10 W: 11 00 b.Nymburk 18-9-83
Honours: Czech Republic Under-21.

2001–02	Bohemians	11	1	**11**	**1**
2002–03	Anderlecht	24	1		
2003–04	Anderlecht	18	1		
2004–05	Anderlecht	0	0	**42**	**2**
2005–06	Stoke C	14	1	**14**	**1**

KOPTEFF, Peter (M) **173** **15**
H: 5 11 W: 11 11 b.Helsingfors 10-4-79
Honours: Finland 39 full caps, 1 goal.

1997	HJK Helsinki	4	1		
1998	HJK Helsinki	6	0		
1999	HJK Helsinki	10	0		
2000	HJK Helsinki	17	1		
2001	HJK Helsinki	29	2	**66**	**4**
2002	Viking	25	3		
2003	Viking	26	2		
2004	Viking	24	3		
2005	Viking	26	3	**101**	**11**
2005–06	Stoke C	6	0	**6**	**0**

PATERSON, Martin (F) **6** **0**
H: 5 9 W: 10 11 b.Tunstall 13-5-87
Source: Scholar.

2004–05	Stoke C	3	0		
2005–06	Stoke C	3	0	**6**	**0**

PULIS, Anthony (M) **8** **0**
H: 5 10 W: 10 10 b.Bristol 21-7-84
Source: Scholar. *Honours:* Wales Under-21.

2002–03	Portsmouth	0	0		
2003–04	Portsmouth	0	0		
2004–05	Portsmouth	0	0		
2004–05	Stoke C	0	0		
2004–05	*Torquay U*	3	0	**3**	**0**
2005–06	Stoke C	0	0		
2005–06	*Plymouth Arg*	5	0	**5**	**0**

ROONEY, Adam (F) **5** **4**
H: 5 10 W: 12 03 b.Dublin 21-4-87
Source: Scholar. *Honours:* Eire Youth.

2005–06	Stoke C	5	4	**5**	**4**

RUSSELL, Darel (M) **260** **16**
H: 5 10 W: 11 09 b.Mile End 22-10-80
Source: Trainee. *Honours:* England Youth.

1997–98	Norwich C	1	0		
1998–99	Norwich C	13	1		
1999–2000	Norwich C	33	4		
2000–01	Norwich C	41	2		
2001–02	Norwich C	23	0		
2002–03	Norwich C	21	0	**132**	**7**
2003–04	Stoke C	46	4		
2004–05	Stoke C	45	2		
2005–06	Stoke C	37	3	**128**	**9**

SANNA, Chris (G) **0** **0**
b.Birkenhead
Source: Scholar.

2005–06	Stoke C	0	0		
2005–06	*Watford*	0	0		

SIDIBE, Mamady (F) **179** **23**
H: 6 4 W: 12 02 b.Bamako 18-12-79
Source: CA Paris. *Honours:* Mali 7 full caps.

2001–02	Swansea C	31	7	**31**	**7**
2002–03	Gillingham	30	3		
2003–04	Gillingham	41	5		
2004–05	Gillingham	35	2	**106**	**10**
2005–06	Stoke C	42	6	**42**	**6**

SIGURDSSON, Hannes (F) **103** **17**
H: 6 2 W: 13 02 b.Reykjavik 10-4-83
Honours: Iceland Youth, Under-21, 4 full caps, 1 goal.

2001	FH	11	1	**11**	**1**
2002	Viking	12	4		
2003	Viking	23	5		
2004	Viking	20	3		
2005	Viking	14	3	**69**	**15**
2005–06	Stoke C	23	1	**23**	**1**

SIMONSEN, Steve (G) **141** **0**
H: 6 2 W: 12 08 b.South Shields 3-4-79
Source: Trainee. *Honours:* England Youth, Under-21.

1996–97	Tranmere R	0	0		
1997–98	Tranmere R	30	0		
1998–99	Tranmere R	5	0	**35**	**0**
1998–99	Everton	0	0		
1999–2000	Everton	1	0		
2000–01	Everton	1	0		
2001–02	Everton	25	0		
2002–03	Everton	2	0		
2003–04	Everton	1	0	**30**	**0**
2004–05	Stoke C	31	0		
2005–06	Stoke C	45	0	**76**	**0**

SWEENEY, Peter (M) **76 6**
H: 6 0 W: 12 11 b.Glasgow 25-9-84
Source: Scholar. *Honours:* Scotland Youth, Under-21, B.

2001–02	Millwall	1	0		
2002–03	Millwall	5	1		
2003–04	Millwall	29	2		
2004–05	Millwall	24	2	**59**	**5**
2005–06	Stoke C	17	1	**17**	**1**

TAGGART, Gerry (D) **465 35**
H: 6 1 W: 14 00 b.Belfast 18-10-70
Source: Trainee. *Honours:* Northern Ireland Schools, Youth, Under-23, 51 full caps, 7 goals.

1988–89	Manchester C	11	1		
1989–90	Manchester C	1	0	**12**	**1**
1989–90	Barnsley	21	2		
1990–91	Barnsley	30	2		
1991–92	Barnsley	38	3		
1992–93	Barnsley	44	4		
1993–94	Barnsley	38	2		
1994–95	Barnsley	41	3	**212**	**16**
1995–96	Bolton W	11	1		
1996–97	Bolton W	43	3		
1997–98	Bolton W	15	0	**69**	**4**
1998–99	Leicester C	15	0		
1999–2000	Leicester C	31	6		
2000–01	Leicester C	24	2		
2001–02	Leicester C	1	0		
2002–03	Leicester C	37	1		
2003–04	Leicester C	9	0	**117**	**9**
2003–04	Stoke C	21	2		
2004–05	Stoke C	31	2		
2005–06	Stoke C	3	1	**55**	**5**

WILKINSON, Andy (D) **19 0**
H: 5 11 W: 11 00 b.Stone 6-8-84
Source: Scholar.

2001–02	Stoke C	0	0		
2002–03	Stoke C	0	0		
2003–04	Stoke C	3	0		
2004–05	Stoke C	1	0		
2004–05	*Shrewsbury T*	9	0	**9**	**0**
2005–06	Stoke C	6	0	**10**	**0**

SUNDERLAND (78)

ALNWICK, Ben (G) **8 0**
H: 6 2 W: 13 12 b.Prudhoe 1-1-87
Source: Scholar. *Honours:* England Youth.

2003–04	Sunderland	0	0		
2004–05	Sunderland	3	0		
2005–06	Sunderland	5	0	**8**	**0**

ARCA, Julio (M) **193 18**
H: 5 9 W: 11 13 b.Quilmes 31-1-81

1999–2000	Argentinos Jun	19	0		
2000–01	Argentinos Jun	17	1	**36**	**1**
2000–01	Sunderland	27	2		
2001–02	Sunderland	22	1		
2002–03	Sunderland	13	0		
2003–04	Sunderland	31	4		
2004–05	Sunderland	40	9		
2005–06	Sunderland	24	1	**157**	**17**

BASSILA, Christian (M) **205 13**
H: 6 4 W: 13 01 b.Paris 5-10-77

1996–97	Lyon	1	0		
1997–98	Lyon	21	1		
1998–99	Lyon	22	1	**44**	**2**
1999–2000	Rennes	23	1		
2000–01	Rennes	1	0	**24**	**1**
2000–01	West Ham U	3	0	**3**	**0**
2001–02	Strasbourg	33	3		
2002–03	Strasbourg	31	3		
2003–04	Strasbourg	34	4		
2004–05	Strasbourg	23	0	**121**	**10**
2005–06	Sunderland	13	0	**13**	**0**

BREEN, Gary (D) **446 12**
H: 6 3 W: 13 03 b.Hendon 12-12-73
Source: Charlton Ath. *Honours:* Eire Under-21, 63 full caps, 6 goals.

1991–92	Maidstone U	19	0	**19**	**0**
1992–93	Gillingham	29	0		
1993–94	Gillingham	22	0	**51**	**0**
1994–95	Peterborough U	44	1		
1995–96	Peterborough U	25	0	**69**	**1**
1995–96	Birmingham C	18	1		
1996–97	Birmingham C	22	1	**40**	**2**
1996–97	Coventry C	9	0		
1997–98	Coventry C	30	1		
1998–99	Coventry C	25	0		
1999–2000	Coventry C	21	0		
2000–01	Coventry C	31	1		
2001–02	Coventry C	30	0	**146**	**2**
2002–03	West Ham U	14	0	**14**	**0**
2003–04	Sunderland	32	4		
2004–05	Sunderland	40	2		
2005–06	Sunderland	35	1	**107**	**7**

BROWN, Chris (F) **85 17**
H: 6 3 W: 13 01 b.Doncaster 11-12-84
Source: Trainee. *Honours:* England Youth.

2002–03	Sunderland	0	0		
2003–04	Sunderland	0	0		
2003–04	*Doncaster R*	22	10	**22**	**10**
2004–05	Sunderland	37	5		
2005–06	Sunderland	13	1	**50**	**6**
2005–06	*Hull C*	13	1	**13**	**1**

CALDWELL, Steven (D) **121 6**
H: 6 2 W: 13 12 b.Stirling 12-9-80
Source: Trainee. *Honours:* Scotland Youth, Under-21, B, 9 full caps.

1997–98	Newcastle U	0	0		
1998–99	Newcastle U	0	0		
1999–2000	Newcastle U	0	0		
2000–01	Newcastle U	9	0		
2001–02	Newcastle U	0	0		
2001–02	*Blackpool*	6	0	**6**	**0**
2001–02	*Bradford C*	9	0	**9**	**0**
2002–03	Newcastle U	14	1		
2003–04	Newcastle U	5	0	**28**	**1**
2003–04	*Leeds U*	13	1	**13**	**1**
2004–05	Sunderland	41	4		
2005–06	Sunderland	24	0	**65**	**4**

COLLINS, Danny (D) **49 2**
H: 6 2 W: 11 13 b.Buckley 6-8-80
Source: Buckley T. *Honours:* Wales 3 full caps.

2004–05	Chester C	12	1	**12**	**1**
2004–05	Sunderland	14	0		
2005–06	Sunderland	23	1	**37**	**1**

COLLINS, Neill (D) **131 4**
H: 6 3 W: 12 07 b.Irvine 2-9-83
Honours: Scoland Under-21.

2000–01	Queen's Park	4	0		
2001–02	Queen's Park	28	0	**32**	**0**
2002–03	Dumbarton	33	2		
2003–04	Dumbarton	30	2	**63**	**4**
2004–05	Sunderland	11	0		
2005–06	Sunderland	1	0	**12**	**0**
2005–06	*Hartlepool U*	22	0	**22**	**0**
2005–06	*Sheffield U*	2	0	**2**	**0**

DAVIS, Kelvin (G) **344 0**
H: 6 1 W: 11 05 b.Bedford 29-9-76
Source: Trainee. *Honours:* England Youth, Under-21.

1993–94	Luton T	1	0		
1994–95	Luton T	9	0		
1994–95	*Torquay U*	2	0	**2**	**0**
1995–96	Luton T	6	0		
1996–97	Luton T	0	0		
1997–98	Luton T	32	0		
1997–98	*Hartlepool U*	2	0	**2**	**0**
1998–99	Luton T	44	0	**92**	**0**
1999–2000	Wimbledon	0	0		
2000–01	Wimbledon	45	0		
2001–02	Wimbledon	40	0		
2002–03	Wimbledon	46	0	**131**	**0**
2003–04	Ipswich T	45	0		
2004–05	Ipswich T	39	0	**84**	**0**
2005–06	Sunderland	33	0	**33**	**0**

DELAP, Rory (M) **306 24**
H: 6 3 W: 13 00 b.Sutton Coldfield 6-7-76
Source: Trainee. *Honours:* Eire 11 full caps.

1992–93	Carlisle U	1	0		
1993–94	Carlisle U	1	0		
1994–95	Carlisle U	3	0		
1995–96	Carlisle U	19	3		
1996–97	Carlisle U	32	4		
1997–98	Carlisle U	9	0	**65**	**7**
1997–98	Derby Co	13	0		
1998–99	Derby Co	23	0		
1999–2000	Derby Co	34	8		
2000–01	Derby Co	33	3	**103**	**11**
2001–02	Southampton	28	2		
2002–03	Southampton	24	0		
2003–04	Southampton	27	1		
2004–05	Southampton	37	2		
2005–06	Southampton	16	0	**132**	**5**
2005–06	Sunderland	6	1	**6**	**1**

DENNEHY, Billy (F) **0 0**
b.Tralee 17-2-87

2004–05	Sunderland	0	0		
2005–06	Sunderland	0	0		

ELLIOTT, Stephen (F) **59 17**
H: 5 8 W: 11 07 b.Dublin 6-1-84
Source: School. *Honours:* Eire Youth, Under-21, 7 full caps, 1 goal.

2000–01	Manchester C	0	0		
2001–02	Manchester C	0	0		
2002–03	Manchester C	0	0		
2003–04	Manchester C	2	0	**2**	**0**
2004–05	Sunderland	42	15		
2005–06	Sunderland	15	2	**57**	**17**

KYLE, Kevin (F) **104 12**
H: 6 4 W: 14 07 b.Stranraer 7-6-81
Source: Ayr Boswell. *Honours:* Scotland Under-21, B, 9 full caps, 1 goal.

1998–99	Sunderland	0	0		
1999–2000	Sunderland	0	0		
2000–01	Sunderland	3	0		
2000–01	*Huddersfield T*	4	0	**4**	**0**
2000–01	*Darlington*	5	1	**5**	**1**
2000–01	*Rochdale*	6	0	**6**	**0**
2001–02	Sunderland	6	0		
2002–03	Sunderland	17	0		
2003–04	Sunderland	44	10		
2004–05	Sunderland	6	0		
2005–06	Sunderland	13	1	**89**	**11**

LAWRENCE, Liam (M) **197 44**
H: 5 11 W: 12 06 b.Retford 14-12-81
Source: Trainee.

1999–2000	Mansfield T	2	0		
2000–01	Mansfield T	18	4		
2001–02	Mansfield T	32	2		
2002–03	Mansfield T	43	10		
2003–04	Mansfield T	41	18	**136**	**34**
2004–05	Sunderland	32	7		
2005–06	Sunderland	29	3	**61**	**10**

LEADBITTER, Grant (M) **17 1**
H: 5 9 W: 11 06 b.Sunderland 7-1-86
Source: Trainee. *Honours:* FA Schools, England Youth, Under-20.

2002–03	Sunderland	0	0		
2003–04	Sunderland	0	0		
2004–05	Sunderland	0	0		
2005–06	Sunderland	12	0	**12**	**0**
2005–06	*Rotherham U*	5	1	**5**	**1**

McCARTNEY, George (D) **134 0**
H: 5 11 W: 11 02 b.Belfast 29-4-81
Source: Trainee. *Honours:* Northern Ireland Schools, Youth, Under-21, 19 full caps, 1 goal.

1998–99	Sunderland	0	0		
1999–2000	Sunderland	0	0		
2000–01	Sunderland	2	0		
2001–02	Sunderland	18	0		
2002–03	Sunderland	24	0		
2003–04	Sunderland	41	0		
2004–05	Sunderland	36	0		
2005–06	Sunderland	13	0	**134**	**0**

MILLER, Tommy (M) **283 68**
H: 6 0 W: 11 07 b.Easington 8-1-79
Source: Trainee.

1997–98	Hartlepool U	13	1		
1998–99	Hartlepool U	34	4		
1999–2000	Hartlepool U	44	14		
2000–01	Hartlepool U	46	16		
2001–02	Hartlepool U	0	0	**137**	**35**
2001–02	Ipswich T	8	0		
2002–03	Ipswich T	30	6		
2003–04	Ipswich T	34	11		
2004–05	Ipswich T	45	13	**117**	**30**
2005–06	Sunderland	29	3	**29**	**3**

MURPHY, Daryl (F) **22** **1**
H: 6 2 W: 13 12 b.Waterford 15-3-83
Honours: Eire Under-21.
2000–01 Luton T 0 0
2001–02 Luton T 0 0
2005–06 Sunderland 18 1 **18** **1**
2005–06 *Sheffield W* 4 0 **4** **0**

MURPHY, Joe (G) **107** **0**
H: 6 2 W: 13 06 b.Dublin 21-8-81
Source: Trainee. *Honours:* Eire Under-21, 1 full cap.
1999–2000 Tranmere R 21 0
2000–01 Tranmere R 20 0
2001–02 Tranmere R 22 0 **63** **0**
2002–03 WBA 2 0
2003–04 WBA 3 0
2004–05 WBA 0 0 **5** **0**
2004–05 *Walsall* 25 0
2005–06 Sunderland 0 0
2005–06 *Walsall* 14 0 **39** **0**

NOSWORTHY, Nayron (D) **204** **5**
H: 6 0 W: 12 08 b.Brixton 11-10-80
Source: Trainee.
1998–99 Gillingham 3 0
1999–2000 Gillingham 29 1
2000–01 Gillingham 10 0
2001–02 Gillingham 29 0
2002–03 Gillingham 39 2
2003–04 Gillingham 27 2
2004–05 Gillingham 37 0 **174** **5**
2005–06 Sunderland 30 0 **30** **0**

PIPER, Matt (M) **48** **2**
H: 6 1 W: 13 07 b.Leicester 29-9-81
Source: Trainee.
1999–2000 Leicester C 0 0
2000–01 Leicester C 0 0
2001–02 *Mansfield T* 8 1 **8** **1**
2001–02 Leicester C 16 1
2002–03 Leicester C 0 0 **16** **1**
2002–03 Sunderland 13 0
2003–04 Sunderland 9 0
2004–05 Sunderland 2 0
2005–06 Sunderland 0 0 **24** **0**

SMITH, Dan (D) **11** **0**
H: 5 10 W: 10 07 b.Sunderland 5-10-86
Source: Scholar.
2003–04 Sunderland 0 0
2004–05 Sunderland 0 0
2005–06 Sunderland 3 0 **3** **0**
2005–06 *Huddersfield T* 8 0 **8** **0**

SMITH, Kevin (F) **0** **0**
H: 5 11 W: 11 09 b.Edinburgh 20-3-87
Source: Scholar.
2003–04 Leeds U 0 0
2004–05 Leeds U 0 0
2005–06 Leeds U 0 0
2005–06 Sunderland 0 0

STEAD, Jon (F) **140** **31**
H: 6 3 W: 13 03 b.Huddersfield 7-4-83
Source: Scholar. *Honours:* England Under-21.
2001–02 Huddersfield T 0 0
2002–03 Huddersfield T 42 6
2003–04 Huddersfield T 26 16 **68** **22**
2003–04 Blackburn R 13 6
2004–05 Blackburn R 29 2 **42** **8**
2005–06 Sunderland 30 1 **30** **1**

TAYLOR, Sean (D) **4** **0**
H: 5 8 W: 11 01 b.Amble 9-12-85
Source: Trainee.
2002–03 Sunderland 0 0
2003–04 Sunderland 0 0
2004–05 Sunderland 0 0
2005–06 Sunderland 0 0
2005–06 *Blackpool* 4 0 **4** **0**

WELSH, Andy (M) **112** **7**
H: 5 8 W: 10 03 b.Manchester 24-11-83
Source: Scholar.
2001–02 Stockport Co 15 0
2002–03 Stockport Co 13 2
2002–03 *Macclesfield T* 6 2 **6** **2**
2003–04 Stockport Co 34 1
2004–05 Stockport Co 13 0 **75** **3**
2004–05 Sunderland 7 1
2005–06 Sunderland 14 0 **21** **1**
2005–06 *Leicester C* 10 1 **10** **1**

WHITEHEAD, Dean (M) **201** **17**
H: 5 11 W: 12 06 b.Oxford 12-1-82
Source: Trainee.
1999–2000 Oxford U 0 0
2000–01 Oxford U 20 0
2001–02 Oxford U 40 1
2002–03 Oxford U 18 1
2003–04 Oxford U 44 7 **122** **9**
2004–05 Sunderland 42 5
2005–06 Sunderland 37 3 **79** **8**

WOODS, Martin (M) **14** **0**
H: 5 11 W: 11 13 b.Airdrie 1-1-86
Source: Trainee. *Honours:* Scotland Youth, Under-21.
2002–03 Leeds U 0 0
2003–04 Leeds U 0 0
2004–05 Leeds U 1 0 **1** **0**
2004–05 *Hartlepool U* 6 0 **6** **0**
2005–06 Sunderland 7 0 **7** **0**

WRIGHT, Stephen (D) **126** **2**
H: 6 0 W: 12 06 b.Liverpool 8-2-80
Source: Trainee. *Honours:* England Youth, Under-21.
1997–98 Liverpool 0 0
1998–99 Liverpool 0 0
1999–2000 Liverpool 0 0
1999–2000 *Crewe Alex* 23 0 **23** **0**
2000–01 Liverpool 2 0
2001–02 Liverpool 12 0 **14** **0**
2002–03 Sunderland 26 0
2003–04 Sunderland 22 1
2004–05 Sunderland 39 1
2005–06 Sunderland 2 0 **89** **2**

Scholars
Backhouse, Christopher David; Carson, Trevor; Chandler, Jamie; Chapman, Lee; Connolly, Liam David; Donoghue, Gavin; Dowson, David; Hartley, Peter; Smith, Richard; Weir, Robert James.

SWANSEA C (79)

AKINFENWA, Adebayo (F) **107** **32**
H: 5 11 W: 13 07 b.Nigeria 10-5-82
2001 Atlantas 19 4
2002 Atlantas 4 1 **23** **5**
From Barry T
2003–04 Boston U 3 0 **3** **0**
2003–04 Leyton Orient 1 0 **1** **0**
2003–04 Rushden & D 0 0
2003–04 Doncaster R 9 4 **9** **4**
2004–05 Torquay U 37 14 **37** **14**
2005–06 Swansea C 34 9 **34** **9**

ANDERSON, Ijah (D) **278** **4**
H: 5 9 W: 11 04 b.Hackney 30-12-75
Source: Tottenham H Trainee.
1994–95 Southend U 0 0
1995–96 Brentford 25 2
1996–97 Brentford 46 1
1997–98 Brentford 17 0
1998–99 Brentford 38 1
1999–2000 Brentford 31 0
2000–01 Brentford 1 0
2001–02 Brentford 35 0
2002–03 Brentford 9 0 **202** **4**
2002–03 *Wycombe W* 5 0 **5** **0**
2002–03 Bristol R 14 0
2003–04 Bristol R 39 0
2004–05 Bristol R 0 0 **53** **0**
2004–05 Swansea C 13 0
2005–06 Swansea C 5 0 **18** **0**

AUSTIN, Kevin (D) **374** **5**
H: 6 1 W: 14 08 b.Hackney 12-2-73
Source: Saffron Walden. *Honours:* Trinidad & Tobago 1 full cap.
1993–94 Leyton Orient 30 0
1994–95 Leyton Orient 39 2
1995–96 Leyton Orient 40 1 **109** **3**
1996–97 Lincoln C 44 1
1997–98 Lincoln C 46 0
1998–99 Lincoln C 39 1 **129** **2**
1999–2000 Barnsley 3 0
2000–01 Barnsley 0 0 **3** **0**
2000–01 *Brentford* 3 0 **3** **0**
2001–02 Cambridge U 6 0 **6** **0**
2002–03 Bristol R 33 0
2003–04 Bristol R 23 0 **56** **0**
2004–05 Swansea C 42 0
2005–06 Swansea C 26 0 **68** **0**

BOND, Chad (F) **0** **0**
H: 6 0 W: 11 00 b.Neath 20-4-87
Source: Scholar. *Honours:* Wales Youth.
2005–06 Swansea C 0 0

BRITTON, Leon (M) **135** **8**
H: 5 6 W: 10 00 b.Merton 16-9-82
Source: Trainee. *Honours:* England Youth.
1999–2000 West Ham U 0 0
2000–01 West Ham U 0 0
2001–02 West Ham U 0 0
2002–03 West Ham U 0 0
2002–03 *Swansea C* 25 0
2003–04 Swansea C 42 3
2004–05 Swansea C 30 1
2005–06 Swansea C 38 4 **135** **8**

FALLON, Rory (F) **161** **37**
H: 6 2 W: 11 09 b.Gisbourne 20-3-82
Source: North Shore U. *Honours:* England Youth.
1998–99 Barnsley 0 0
1999–2000 Barnsley 0 0
2000–01 Barnsley 1 0
2001–02 Barnsley 9 0
2001–02 *Shrewsbury T* 11 0 **11** **0**
2002–03 Barnsley 26 7
2003–04 Barnsley 16 4 **52** **11**
2003–04 Swindon T 19 6
2004–05 Swindon T 31 3
2004–05 *Yeovil T* 6 1 **6** **1**
2005–06 Swindon T 25 12 **75** **21**
2005–06 Swansea C 17 4 **17** **4**

FORBES, Adrian (F) **253** **33**
H: 5 8 W: 11 10 b.Greenford 23-1-79
Source: Trainee. *Honours:* England Youth.
1996–97 Norwich C 10 0
1997–98 Norwich C 33 4
1998–99 Norwich C 15 0
1999–2000 Norwich C 25 1
2000–01 Norwich C 29 3 **112** **8**
2001–02 Luton T 40 4
2002–03 Luton T 5 1
2003–04 Luton T 27 9 **72** **14**
2004–05 Swansea C 40 7
2005–06 Swansea C 29 4 **69** **11**

GUERET, Willy (G) **104** **0**
H: 6 1 W: 13 02 b.Saint Claude 3-8-73
Source: Le Mans.
2000–01 Millwall 11 0
2001–02 Millwall 1 0
2002–03 Millwall 0 0
2003–04 Millwall 2 0 **14** **0**
2004–05 Swansea C 44 0
2005–06 Swansea C 46 0 **90** **0**

IRIEKPEN, Ezomo (D) **109** **5**
H: 6 1 W: 12 02 b.East London 14-5-82
Source: Trainee. *Honours:* England Youth.
1998–99 West Ham U 0 0
1999–2000 West Ham U 0 0
2000–01 West Ham U 0 0
2001–02 West Ham U 0 0
2002–03 West Ham U 0 0
2002–03 *Leyton Orient* 5 1 **5** **1**
2002–03 *Cambridge U* 13 1 **13** **1**
2003–04 Swansea C 34 1
2004–05 Swansea C 29 2
2005–06 Swansea C 28 0 **91** **3**

KNIGHT, Leon (F) **191** **61**
H: 5 5 W: 9 06 b.Hackney 16-9-82
Source: Trainee. *Honours:* England Youth, Under-20.
1999–2000 Chelsea 0 0
2000–01 Chelsea 0 0
2000–01 *QPR* 11 0 **11** **0**
2001–02 Chelsea 0 0
2001–02 *Huddersfield T* 31 16 **31** **16**
2002–03 Chelsea 0 0
2002–03 *Sheffield W* 24 3 **24** **3**
2003–04 Chelsea 0 0

2003–04 Brighton & HA 44 25
2004–05 Brighton & HA 39 4
2005–06 Brighton & HA 25 5 **108 34**
2005–06 Swansea C 17 8 **17 8**

MACDONALD, Shaun (M) 7 0
H: 6 1 W: 11 04 b.Swansea 17-6-88
Source: Scholar. *Honours:* Wales Under-21.
2005–06 Swansea C 7 0 **7 0**

MARTINEZ, Roberto (M) 332 21
H: 5 9 W: 12 02 b.Balaguer 13-7-73
Source: Balaguer.
1995–96 Wigan Ath 42 9
1996–97 Wigan Ath 43 4
1997–98 Wigan Ath 33 1
1998–99 Wigan Ath 10 0
1999–2000 Wigan Ath 25 3
2000–01 Wigan Ath 34 0 **187 17**
2001–02 Motherwell 17 0 **17 0**
2002–03 Walsall 6 0 **6 0**
2002–03 Swansea C 19 2
2003–04 Swansea C 27 0
2004–05 Swansea C 37 0
2005–06 Swansea C 39 2 **122 4**

McLEOD, Kevin (M) 112 13
H: 5 11 W: 11 00 b.Liverpool 12-9-80
Source: Trainee.
1998–99 Everton 0 0
1999–2000 Everton 0 0
2000–01 Everton 5 0
2001–02 Everton 0 0
2002–03 Everton 0 0
2002–03 *QPR* 8 2
2003–04 Everton 0 0 **5 0**
2003–04 QPR 35 3
2004–05 QPR 24 1 **67 6**
2004–05 Swansea C 11 0
2005–06 Swansea C 29 7 **40 7**

MONK, Garry (D) 128 1
H: 6 0 W: 12 10 b.Bedford 6-3-79
Source: Trainee.
1995–96 Torquay U 5 0
1996–97 Southampton 0 0
1997–98 Southampton 0 0
1998–99 Southampton 4 0
1998–99 *Torquay U* 6 0 **11 0**
1999–2000 Southampton 2 0
1999–2000 *Stockport Co* 2 0 **2 0**
2000–01 Southampton 2 0
2000–01 *Oxford U* 5 0 **5 0**
2001–02 Southampton 2 0
2002–03 Southampton 1 0
2002–03 *Sheffield W* 15 0 **15 0**
2003–04 Southampton 0 0 **11 0**
2003–04 Barnsley 17 0 **17 0**
2004–05 Swansea C 34 0
2005–06 Swansea C 33 1 **67 1**

MURPHY, Brian (G) 14 0
H: 6 0 W: 13 00 b.Waterford 7-5-83
Honours: Eire Under-21.
2000–01 Manchester C 0 0
2001–02 Manchester C 0 0
2002–03 Manchester C 0 0
2002–03 *Oldham Ath* 0 0
2002–03 *Peterborough U* 1 0 **1 0**
From Waterford
2003–04 Swansea C 11 0
2004–05 Swansea C 2 0
2005–06 Swansea C 0 0 **13 0**

NUGENT, Kevin (F) 496 115
H: 6 1 W: 13 03 b.Edmonton 10-4-69
Source: Trainee. *Honours:* Eire Youth.
1987–88 Leyton Orient 11 3
1988–89 Leyton Orient 3 0
1989–90 Leyton Orient 11 0
1990–91 Leyton Orient 33 5
1991–92 Leyton Orient 36 12
1991–92 Plymouth Arg 4 0
1992–93 Plymouth Arg 45 11
1993–94 Plymouth Arg 39 14
1994–95 Plymouth Arg 37 7
1995–96 Plymouth Arg 6 0 **131 32**
1995–96 Bristol C 34 8
1996–97 Bristol C 36 6 **70 14**
1997–98 Cardiff C 4 0
1998–99 Cardiff C 41 15
1999–2000 Cardiff C 39 10
2000–01 Cardiff C 14 4
2001–02 Cardiff C 1 0 **99 29**
2001–02 Leyton Orient 9 1
2002–03 Leyton Orient 19 3 **122 24**
2002–03 Swansea C 15 5
2003–04 Swansea C 39 8
2004–05 Swansea C 19 3
2005–06 Swansea C 1 0 **74 16**

O'LEARY, Kristian (M) 250 9
H: 5 11 W: 12 09 b.Port Talbot 30-8-77
Source: Trainee. *Honours:* Wales Youth.
1995–96 Swansea C 1 0
1996–97 Swansea C 12 1
1997–98 Swansea C 29 0
1998–99 Swansea C 19 2
1999–2000 Swansea C 20 0
2000–01 Swansea C 24 2
2001–02 Swansea C 31 2
2002–03 Swansea C 33 0
2003–04 Swansea C 34 0
2004–05 Swansea C 32 1
2005–06 Swansea C 15 1 **250 9**

PRITCHARD, Mark (F) 4 0
H: 5 10 W: 12 04 b.Tredegar 23-11-85
Source: Scholar. *Honours:* Wales Under-21.
2003–04 Swansea C 4 0
2004–05 Swansea C 0 0
2005–06 Swansea C 0 0 **4 0**

RICKETTS, Sam (D) 131 2
H: 6 1 W: 12 01 b.Aylesbury 11-10-81
Source: Trainee. *Honours:* Wales 10 full caps.
1999–2000 Oxford U 0 0
2000–01 Oxford U 14 0
2001–02 Oxford U 29 1
2002–03 Oxford U 2 0 **45 1**
From Telford U
2004–05 Swansea C 42 0
2005–06 Swansea C 44 1 **86 1**

ROBINSON, Andy (M) 113 28
H: 5 8 W: 11 04 b.Birkenhead 3-11-79
Source: Cammell Laird.
2002–03 Tranmere R 0 0
2003–04 Swansea C 37 8
2004–05 Swansea C 37 8
2005–06 Swansea C 39 12 **113 28**

TATE, Alan (D) 119 1
H: 6 1 W: 13 05 b.Easington 2-9-82
Source: Scholar.
2000–01 Manchester U 0 0
2001–02 Manchester U 0 0
2002–03 Manchester U 0 0
2002–03 *Swansea C* 27 0
2003–04 Manchester U 0 0
2003–04 Swansea C 26 1
2004–05 Swansea C 23 0
2005–06 Swansea C 43 0 **119 1**

THORPE, Lee (F) 334 80
H: 6 0 W: 11 06 b.Wolverhampton 14-12-75
Source: Trainee.
1993–94 Blackpool 1 0
1994–95 Blackpool 1 0
1995–96 Blackpool 1 0
1996–97 Blackpool 9 0 **12 0**
1997–98 Lincoln C 44 14
1998–99 Lincoln C 38 8
1999–2000 Lincoln C 42 16
2000–01 Lincoln C 31 7
2001–02 Lincoln C 37 13 **192 58**
2001–02 Leyton Orient 0 0
2002–03 Leyton Orient 38 8
2003–04 Leyton Orient 17 4 **55 12**
2003–04 *Grimsby T* 6 0 **6 0**
2003–04 Bristol R 10 1
2004–05 Bristol R 25 3 **35 4**
2004–05 Swansea C 15 3
2005–06 Swansea C 3 0 **18 3**
2005–06 *Peterborough U* 6 0 **6 0**
2005–06 *Torquay U* 10 3 **10 3**

TRUNDLE, Lee (F) 203 85
H: 6 0 W: 11 06 b.Liverpool 10-10-76
Source: Rhyl.
2000–01 Wrexham 14 8
2001–02 Wrexham 36 8
2002–03 Wrexham 44 11 **94 27**
2003–04 Swansea C 31 16
2004–05 Swansea C 42 22
2005–06 Swansea C 36 20 **109 58**

TUDUR JONES, Owain (M) 21 3
H: 6 2 W: 12 00 b.Bangor 15-10-84
Source: Bangor C. *Honours:* Wales Under-21.
2005–06 Swansea C 21 3 **21 3**

WATT, Steven (D) 6 1
H: 6 2 W: 12 09 b.Aberdeen 1-5-85
Source: Trainee. *Honours:* Scotland Under-21, B.
2002–03 Chelsea 0 0
2003–04 Chelsea 0 0
2004–05 Chelsea 1 0
2005–06 Chelsea 0 0 **1 0**
2005–06 *Barnsley* 3 1 **3 1**
2005–06 Swansea C 2 0 **2 0**

WAY, Darren (M) 104 13
H: 5 7 W: 11 00 b.Plymouth 21-11-79
Source: Norwich C Trainee.
2003–04 Yeovil T 39 5
2004–05 Yeovil T 45 7
2005–06 Yeovil T 15 1 **99 13**
2005–06 Swansea C 5 0 **5 0**

WILLIAMS, Tom (M) 161 4
H: 5 11 W: 12 06 b.Carshalton 8-7-80
Source: Walton & Hersham.
1999–2000 West Ham U 0 0
2000–01 West Ham U 0 0
2000–01 *Peterborough U* 2 0
2001–02 Peterborough U 34 2
2001–02 Birmingham C 4 0
2002–03 Birmingham C 0 0
2002–03 *QPR* 26 1
2003–04 Birmingham C 0 0 **4 0**
2003–04 *QPR* 5 0 **31 1**
2003–04 *Peterborough U* 21 1 **57 3**
2004–05 Barnsley 39 0 **39 0**
2005–06 Gillingham 13 0 **13 0**
2005–06 Swansea C 17 0 **17 0**

SWINDON T (80)

BROWN, Aaron (M) 203 15
H: 5 10 W: 11 11 b.Bristol 14-3-80
Source: Trainee. *Honours:* England Schools.
1997–98 Bristol C 0 0
1998–99 Bristol C 14 0
1999–2000 Bristol C 13 2
1999–2000 *Exeter C* 5 1 **5 1**
2000–01 Bristol C 35 2
2001–02 Bristol C 36 1
2002–03 Bristol C 32 2
2003–04 Bristol C 30 5 **160 12**
2004–05 QPR 1 0
2004–05 *Torquay U* 5 0 **5 0**
2005–06 QPR 2 0 **3 0**
2005–06 *Cheltenham T* 3 0 **3 0**
2005–06 Swindon T 27 2 **27 2**

BULMAN, Matty (G) 0 0
H: 6 0 W: 11 05 b.Bristol 14-10-86
Source: Scholar.
2005–06 Swindon T 0 0

CATON, Andy (M) 8 1
H: 6 0 W: 12 03 b.Oxford 3-12-87
Source: Scholar.
2004–05 Swindon T 8 1
2005–06 Swindon T 0 0 **8 1**

COMYN-PLATT, Charlie (D) 26 1
H: 6 2 W: 12 00 b.Salford 2-10-85
Source: Scholar.
2003–04 Bolton W 0 0
2004–05 Bolton W 0 0
2004–05 *Wycombe W* 4 0 **4 0**
2005–06 Swindon T 22 1 **22 1**

CURETON, Jamie (F) 397 145
H: 5 8 W: 10 07 b.Bristol 28-8-75
Source: Trainee. *Honours:* England Youth.
1992–93 Norwich C 0 0
1993–94 Norwich C 0 0
1994–95 Norwich C 17 4
1995–96 Norwich C 12 2

1995–96	*Bournemouth*	5	0	**5**	**0**
1996–97	Norwich C	0	0	**29**	**6**
1996–97	Bristol R	38	11		
1997–98	Bristol R	43	13		
1998–99	Bristol R	46	25		
1999–2000	Bristol R	46	22		
2000–01	Bristol R	1	1	**174**	**72**
2000–01	Reading	43	26		
2001–02	Reading	38	15		
2002–03	Reading	27	9	**108**	**50**
From Busan Icons.					
2003–04	QPR	13	2		
2004–05	QPR	30	4	**43**	**6**
2005–06	Swindon T	30	7	**30**	**7**
2005–06	*Colchester U*	8	4	**8**	**4**

EVANS, Rhys (G) **140** **0**
H: 6 1 W: 13 12 b.Swindon 27-1-82
Source: Trainee. *Honours:* England Schools, Youth, Under-20, Under-21.

1998–99	Chelsea	0	0		
1999–2000	Chelsea	0	0		
1999–2000	*Bristol R*	4	0	**4**	**0**
2000–01	Chelsea	0	0		
2001–02	Chelsea	0	0		
2001–02	*QPR*	11	0	**11**	**0**
2002–03	Chelsea	0	0		
2002–03	*Leyton Orient*	7	0	**7**	**0**
2003–04	Swindon T	41	0		
2004–05	Swindon T	45	0		
2005–06	Swindon T	32	0	**118**	**0**

GURNEY, Andy (D) **427** **44**
H: 5 7 W: 10 08 b.Bristol 25-1-74
Source: Trainee.

1992–93	Bristol R	0	0		
1993–94	Bristol R	3	0		
1994–95	Bristol R	38	1		
1995–96	Bristol R	43	6		
1996–97	Bristol R	24	2	**108**	**9**
1997–98	Torquay U	44	9		
1998–99	Torquay U	20	1	**64**	**10**
1998–99	Reading	8	0		
1999–2000	Reading	38	2		
2000–01	Reading	21	1	**67**	**3**
2001–02	Swindon T	43	6		
2002–03	Swindon T	41	8		
2003–04	Swindon T	42	6		
2004–05	Swindon T	6	0		
2004–05	Swansea C	28	1		
2005–06	Swansea C	0	0	**28**	**1**
2005–06	Swindon T	28	1	**160**	**21**

HENRY, Leigh (D) **0** **0**
b.Swindon
Source: Scholar.

2005–06	Swindon T	0	0		

HOLGATE, Ashan (F) **8** **0**
H: 6 2 W: 12 00 b.Swindon 9-11-86
Source: Scholar.

2004–05	Swindon T	2	0		
2005–06	Swindon T	6	0	**8**	**0**

IFIL, Jerel (D) **109** **0**
H: 6 1 W: 12 10 b.Wembley 27-6-82
Source: Academy.

1999–2000	Watford	0	0		
2000–01	Watford	0	0		
2001–02	Watford	0	0		
2001–02	*Huddersfield T*	2	0	**2**	**0**
2002–03	Watford	1	0		
2002–03	*Swindon T*	9	0		
2003–04	Watford	10	0	**11**	**0**
2003–04	*Swindon T*	16	0		
2004–05	Swindon T	35	0		
2005–06	Swindon T	36	0	**96**	**0**

JENKINS, Steve (D) **509** **7**
H: 5 10 W: 10 09 b.Merthyr 16-7-72
Source: Trainee. *Honours:* Wales Youth, Under-21, 16 full caps.

1990–91	Swansea C	1	0		
1991–92	Swansea C	34	0		
1992–93	Swansea C	33	0		
1993–94	Swansea C	40	1		
1994–95	Swansea C	42	0		
1995–96	Swansea C	15	0	**165**	**1**
1995–96	Huddersfield T	31	1		
1996–97	Huddersfield T	33	0		
1997–98	Huddersfield T	29	1		
1998–99	Huddersfield T	36	1		
1999–2000	Huddersfield T	33	0		
2000–01	Huddersfield T	30	0		
2000–01	*Birmingham C*	3	0	**3**	**0**
2001–02	Huddersfield T	40	1		
2002–03	Huddersfield T	26	0	**258**	**4**
2002–03	Cardiff C	4	0	**4**	**0**
2003–04	Notts Co	17	0	**17**	**0**
2003–04	Peterborough U	8	0		
2004–05	Peterborough U	6	1	**14**	**1**
2004–05	Swindon T	24	0		
2005–06	Swindon T	24	1	**48**	**1**

JUTKIEWICZ, Lucas (F) **5** **0**
H: 6 1 W: 12 11 b.Southampton 20-3-89
Source: Scholar.

2005–06	Swindon T	5	0	**5**	**0**

LAPHAM, Kyle (D) **2** **0**
H: 5 11 W: 11 00 b.Swindon 5-1-86
Source: Scholar.

2004–05	Swindon T	2	0		
2005–06	Swindon T	0	0	**2**	**0**

MIGLIORANZI, Stefani (M) **159** **10**
H: 6 1 W: 12 07 b.Pacos de Caldas 20-9-77
Source: St Johns Univ.

1998–99	Portsmouth	7	0		
1999–2000	Portsmouth	13	2		
2000–01	Portsmouth	12	0		
2001–02	Portsmouth	3	0	**35**	**2**
2002–03	Swindon T	41	3		
2003–04	Swindon T	35	4		
2004–05	Swindon T	21	0		
2005–06	Swindon T	27	1	**124**	**8**

NICHOLAS, Andrew (D) **85** **1**
H: 6 2 W: 12 08 b.Liverpool 10-10-83
Honours: Liverpool Trainee.

2003–04	Swindon T	31	1		
2004–05	Swindon T	16	0		
2004–05	*Chester C*	5	0	**5**	**0**
2005–06	Swindon T	33	0	**80**	**1**

NICOLAU, Nicky (D) **36** **1**
H: 5 8 W: 10 03 b.Camden 12-10-83
Source: Trainee.

2002–03	Arsenal	0	0		
2003–04	Arsenal	0	0		
2003–04	*Southend U*	9	0		
2004–05	Southend U	22	1	**31**	**1**
2005–06	Swindon T	5	0	**5**	**0**

O'HANLON, Sean (D) **99** **9**
H: 6 1 W: 12 05 b.Southport 2-1-83
Honours: England Schools, Youth, Under-20.

1999–2000	Everton	0	0		
2000–01	Everton	0	0		
2001–02	Everton	0	0		
2002–03	Everton	0	0		
2003–04	Everton	0	0		
2003–04	Swindon T	19	2		
2004–05	Swindon T	40	3		
2005–06	Swindon T	40	4	**99**	**9**

PEACOCK, Lee (F) **383** **102**
H: 6 0 W: 12 08 b.Paisley 9-10-76
Source: Trainee. *Honours:* Scotland Youth, Under-21.

1993–94	Carlisle U	1	0		
1994–95	Carlisle U	7	0		
1995–96	Carlisle U	22	2		
1996–97	Carlisle U	44	9		
1997–98	Carlisle U	2	0	**76**	**11**
1997–98	Mansfield T	32	5		
1998–99	Mansfield T	45	17		
1999–2000	Mansfield T	12	7	**89**	**29**
1999–2000	Manchester C	8	0	**8**	**0**
2000–01	Bristol C	35	13		
2001–02	Bristol C	31	15		
2002–03	Bristol C	37	12		
2003–04	Bristol C	41	14	**144**	**54**
2004–05	Sheffield W	29	4		
2005–06	Sheffield W	22	2	**51**	**6**
2005–06	Swindon T	15	2	**15**	**2**

POOK, Michael (M) **35** **0**
H: 5 11 W: 11 10 b.Swindon 22-10-85
Source: Scholar.

2003–04	Swindon T	0	0		
2004–05	Swindon T	5	0		
2005–06	Swindon T	30	0	**35**	**0**

REEVES, Alan (D) **444** **27**
H: 6 0 W: 12 00 b.Birkenhead 19-11-67
Source: Heswall.

1988–89	Norwich C	0	0		
1988–89	*Gillingham*	18	0	**18**	**0**
1989–90	Chester C	30	2		
1990–91	Chester C	10	0	**40**	**2**
1991–92	Rochdale	34	3		
1992–93	Rochdale	41	3		
1993–94	Rochdale	41	3		
1994–95	Rochdale	5	0	**121**	**9**
1994–95	Wimbledon	31	3		
1995–96	Wimbledon	24	1		
1996–97	Wimbledon	2	0		
1997–98	Wimbledon	0	0	**57**	**4**
1998–99	Swindon T	24	2		
1999–2000	Swindon T	43	1		
2000–01	Swindon T	44	3		
2001–02	Swindon T	25	2		
2002–03	Swindon T	36	3		
2003–04	Swindon T	27	0		
2004–05	Swindon T	8	1		
2005–06	Swindon T	1	0	**208**	**12**

ROBERTS, Chris (F) **238** **48**
H: 5 11 W: 12 08 b.Cardiff 22-10-79
Source: Trainee. *Honours:* Wales Youth, Under-21.

1997–98	Cardiff C	11	3		
1998–99	Cardiff C	4	0		
1999–2000	Cardiff C	8	0	**23**	**3**
2000–01	Exeter C	42	8		
2001–02	Exeter C	37	11	**79**	**19**
2001–02	Bristol C	4	0		
2002–03	Bristol C	44	13		
2003–04	Bristol C	38	6		
2004–05	Bristol C	8	1	**94**	**20**
2004–05	Swindon T	21	3		
2005–06	Swindon T	21	3	**42**	**6**

SHAKES, Ricky (M) **45** **5**
H: 5 10 W: 12 00 b.Brixton 26-1-85
Source: Scholar. *Honours:* Trinidad & Tobago 1 full cap.

2003–04	Bolton W	0	0		
2004–05	Bolton W	0	0		
2004–05	*Bristol R*	1	0	**1**	**0**
2004–05	*Bury*	7	2	**7**	**2**
2005–06	Swindon T	37	3	**37**	**3**

SMITH, Jack (D) **63** **2**
H: 5 11 W: 11 05 b.Hemel Hempstead 14-10-83
Source: Scholar.

2001–02	Watford	0	0		
2002–03	Watford	1	0		
2003–04	Watford	17	2		
2004–05	Watford	7	0	**25**	**2**
2005–06	Swindon T	38	0	**38**	**0**

SMITH, Paul (M) **541** **34**
H: 5 11 W: 14 00 b.East Ham 18-9-71
Source: Trainee.

1989–90	Southend U	10	1		
1990–91	Southend U	2	0		
1991–92	Southend U	0	0		
1992–93	Southend U	8	0	**20**	**1**
1993–94	Brentford	32	3		
1994–95	Brentford	35	3		
1995–96	Brentford	46	4		
1996–97	Brentford	46	1	**159**	**11**
1997–98	Gillingham	46	3		
1998–99	Gillingham	45	6		
1999–2000	Gillingham	44	1		
2000–01	Gillingham	42	3		
2001–02	Gillingham	46	2		
2002–03	Gillingham	45	3		
2003–04	Gillingham	33	0		
2004–05	Gillingham	41	3		
2005–06	Walsall	8	1	**8**	**1**
2005–06	*Gillingham*	3	0	**345**	**21**
2005–06	Swindon T	9	0	**9**	**0**

STROUD, David (M) **2** **0**
H: 5 10 W: 12 04 b.Swindon 10-11-87
Source: Scholar.

2005–06	Swindon T	2	0	**2**	**0**

TAYLOR, Chris (D) **4 0**
H: 5 8 W: 10 05 b.Swindon 30-10-85
Source: Scholar.

2002–03	Swindon T	4	0		
2003–04	Swindon T	0	0		
2004–05	Swindon T	0	0		
2005–06	Swindon T	0	0	**4**	**0**

WELLS, Ben (M) **5 0**
H: 5 9 W: 10 07 b.Basingstoke 26-3-88
Source: Scholar.

2004–05	Swindon T	1	0		
2005–06	Swindon T	4	0	**5**	**0**

WHALLEY, Gareth (M) **363 14**
H: 5 10 W: 11 06 b.Manchester 19-12-73
Source: Trainee.

1992–93	Crewe Alex	25	1		
1993–94	Crewe Alex	15	1		
1994–95	Crewe Alex	40	1		
1995–96	Crewe Alex	44	2		
1996–97	Crewe Alex	38	3		
1997–98	Crewe Alex	18	1		
1998–99	Bradford C	45	2		
1999–2000	Bradford C	16	1		
2000–01	Bradford C	19	0		
2001–02	Bradford C	23	0	**103**	**3**
2001–02	*Crewe Alex*	7	0	**187**	**9**
2002–03	Cardiff C	19	0		
2003–04	Cardiff C	22	2		
2004–05	Cardiff C	0	0	**41**	**2**
2004–05	Wigan Ath	8	0	**8**	**0**
2005–06	Swindon T	24	0	**24**	**0**

TORQUAY U (81)

AFFUL, Leslie (F) **7 0**
H: 5 6 W: 10 00 b.Liverpool 4-2-84
Source: Scholar.

2001–02	Exeter C	2	0		
2002–03	Exeter C	0	0		
2003–04	Exeter C	0	0		
2004–05	Exeter C	0	0		
2005–06	Exeter C	0	0	**2**	**0**
2005–06	Torquay U	5	0	**5**	**0**

BEDEAU, Anthony (F) **308 58**
H: 5 10 W: 10 06 b.Hammersmith 24-3-79
Source: Trainee. *Honours:* Grenada full caps.

1995–96	Torquay U	4	0		
1996–97	Torquay U	8	1		
1997–98	Torquay U	34	5		
1998–99	Torquay U	36	9		
1999–2000	Torquay U	38	16		
2000–01	Torquay U	34	5		
2001–02	Torquay U	21	4		
2001–02	*Barnsley*	3	0	**3**	**0**
2002–03	Torquay U	40	6		
2003–04	Torquay U	24	1		
2004–05	Torquay U	35	2		
2005–06	Torquay U	31	9	**305**	**58**

BITTNER, Jamie (G) **0 0**
H: 6 2 W: 13 01 b.Devizes 2-2-82
Source: Exeter C.

2005–06	Torquay U	0	0		

COLEMAN, Liam (M) **14 0**
H: 5 5 W: 10 08 b.Colchester 11-1-86
Source: Colchester U Scholar.

2005–06	Torquay U	14	0	**14**	**0**

CONNELL, Alan (F) **76 15**
H: 6 0 W: 12 00 b.Enfield 5-2-83
Source: Ipswich T Trainee.

2002–03	Bournemouth	13	6		
2003–04	Bournemouth	7	0		
2004–05	Bournemouth	34	2	**54**	**8**
2005–06	Torquay U	22	7	**22**	**7**

FLYNN, Patrick (M) **1 0**
H: 5 11 W: 11 04 b.Dublin 13-1-85
Source: Scholar. *Honours:* Eire Youth.

2002–03	Wolverhampton W	0	0		
2003–04	Wolverhampton W	0	0		
2004–05	Wolverhampton W	0	0		
2005–06	Wolverhampton W	0	0		
2005–06	Torquay U	1	0	**1**	**0**

GARNER, Darren (M) **343 26**
H: 5 10 W: 12 02 b.Plymouth 10-12-71
Source: Trainee.

1988–89	Plymouth Arg	1	0		
1989–90	Plymouth Arg	1	0		
1990–91	Plymouth Arg	5	1		
1991–92	Plymouth Arg	10	0		
1992–93	Plymouth Arg	10	0		
1993–94	Plymouth Arg	0	0	**27**	**1**
From Dorchester T.					
1995–96	Rotherham U	31	1		
1996–97	Rotherham U	30	2		
1997–98	Rotherham U	40	3		
1998–99	Rotherham U	40	4		
1999–2000	Rotherham U	35	9		
2000–01	Rotherham U	31	1		
2001–02	Rotherham U	0	0		
2002–03	Rotherham U	26	3		
2003–04	Rotherham U	13	0		
2004–05	Rotherham U	18	0	**264**	**23**
2004–05	*Torquay U*	9	0		
2005–06	Torquay U	43	2	**52**	**2**

HANCOX, Richard (F) **83 10**
H: 5 10 W: 12 06 b.Stourbridge 4-10-70
Source: Stourbridge S.

1992–93	Torquay U	7	0		
1993–94	Torquay U	3	0		
1994–95	Torquay U	36	9		
1995–96	Torquay U	25	1		
1996–97	Torquay U	11	0		
1997–98	Torquay U	0	0		
1998–99	Torquay U	0	0		
2005–06	Torquay U	1	0	**83**	**10**

HEWLETT, Matt (M) **332 16**
H: 6 1 W: 12 07 b.Bristol 25-2-76
Source: Trainee. *Honours:* England Youth.

1993–94	Bristol C	12	0		
1994–95	Bristol C	1	0		
1995–96	Bristol C	27	2		
1996–97	Bristol C	36	2		
1997–98	Bristol C	34	4		
1998–99	Bristol C	10	1		
1998–99	*Burnley*	2	0	**2**	**0**
1999–2000	Bristol C	7	0	**127**	**9**
2000–01	Swindon T	26	0		
2001–02	Swindon T	39	1		
2002–03	Swindon T	40	1		
2003–04	Swindon T	43	3		
2004–05	Swindon T	31	1	**179**	**6**
2005–06	Torquay U	24	1	**24**	**1**

HILL, Kevin (M) **368 48**
H: 5 8 W: 10 06 b.Exeter 6-3-76
Source: Torrington.

1997–98	Torquay U	37	7		
1998–99	Torquay U	35	5		
1999–2000	Torquay U	43	2		
2000–01	Torquay U	44	9		
2001–02	Torquay U	44	2		
2002–03	Torquay U	39	4		
2003–04	Torquay U	45	5		
2004–05	Torquay U	39	5		
2005–06	Torquay U	42	9	**368**	**48**

HOCKLEY, Matthew (D) **173 9**
H: 5 10 W: 12 04 b.Paignton 5-6-82
Source: Trainee.

2000–01	Torquay U	6	1		
2001–02	Torquay U	12	0		
2002–03	Torquay U	40	2		
2003–04	Torquay U	45	5		
2004–05	Torquay U	34	1		
2005–06	Torquay U	36	0	**173**	**9**

LAWLESS, Alex (M) **14 0**
H: 5 11 W: 12 00 b.Tonypandy 26-3-85
Honours: Wales Under-21.

2003–04	Fulham	0	0		
2004–05	Fulham	0	0		
2005–06	Torquay U	14	0	**14**	**0**

LLOYD, Anthony (D) **62 3**
H: 5 7 W: 11 00 b.Taunton 14-3-84
Source: Scholar.

2003–04	Huddersfield T	31	3		
2004–05	Huddersfield T	11	0		
2005–06	Huddersfield T	0	0	**42**	**3**
2005–06	Torquay U	20	0	**20**	**0**

MARRIOTT, Andy (G) **411 0**
H: 6 2 W: 13 07 b.Sutton-in-Ashfield 11-10-70
Source: Trainee. *Honours:* England Schools, FA Schools, Youth, Under-21, Wales 5 full caps.

1988–89	Arsenal	0	0		
1989–90	Nottingham F	0	0		
1989–90	*WBA*	3	0	**3**	**0**
1989–90	*Blackburn R*	2	0	**2**	**0**
1989–90	*Colchester U*	10	0	**10**	**0**
1990–91	Nottingham F	0	0		
1991–92	Nottingham F	6	0		
1991–92	*Burnley*	15	0	**15**	**0**
1992–93	Nottingham F	5	0		
1993–94	Nottingham F	0	0	**11**	**0**
1993–94	Wrexham	36	0		
1994–95	Wrexham	46	0		
1995–96	Wrexham	46	0		
1996–97	Wrexham	43	0		
1997–98	Wrexham	42	0		
1998–99	Wrexham	0	0	**213**	**0**
1998–99	Sunderland	1	0		
1999–2000	Sunderland	1	0		
2000–01	Sunderland	0	0	**2**	**0**
2000–01	*Wigan Ath*	0	0		
2000–01	Barnsley	0	0		
2001–02	Barnsley	18	0		
2002–03	Barnsley	36	0	**54**	**0**
2002–03	Birmingham C	1	0	**1**	**0**
2003–04	Beira Mar	24	0	**24**	**0**
2004–05	Bury	19	0	**19**	**0**
2004–05	Torquay U	11	0		
2005–06	Torquay U	46	0	**57**	**0**

McGLINCHEY, Brian (D) **169 4**
H: 5 9 W: 11 00 b.Derry 26-10-77
Source: Trainee. *Honours:* Northern Ireland Youth, Under-21, B.

1995–96	Manchester C	0	0		
1996–97	Manchester C	0	0		
1997–98	Manchester C	0	0		
1998–99	Port Vale	15	1	**15**	**1**
1999–2000	Gillingham	13	1		
2000–01	Gillingham	1	0	**14**	**1**
2000–01	Plymouth Arg	20	0		
2001–02	Plymouth Arg	29	1		
2002–03	Plymouth Arg	19	1		
2003–04	Plymouth Arg	0	0	**68**	**2**
2003–04	Torquay U	34	0		
2004–05	Torquay U	33	0		
2005–06	Torquay U	5	0	**72**	**0**

OSEI-KUFFOUR, Jo (F) **159 31**
H: 5 8 W: 11 11 b.Edmonton 17-11-81
Source: Scholar.

2000–01	Arsenal	0	0		
2001–02	Arsenal	0	0		
2001–02	*Swindon T*	11	2	**11**	**2**
2002–03	Torquay U	30	5		
2003–04	Torquay U	41	10		
2004–05	Torquay U	34	6		
2005–06	Torquay U	43	8	**148**	**29**

PHILLIPS, Martin (M) **274 21**
H: 5 10 W: 11 10 b.Exeter 13-3-76
Source: Trainee.

1992–93	Exeter C	6	0		
1993–94	Exeter C	9	0		
1994–95	Exeter C	24	2		
1995–96	Exeter C	13	3		
1995–96	Manchester C	11	0		
1996–97	Manchester C	4	0		
1997–98	Manchester C	0	0		
1997–98	*Scunthorpe U*	3	0	**3**	**0**
1997–98	*Exeter C*	8	0	**60**	**5**
1998–99	Manchester C	0	0	**15**	**0**
1998–99	Portsmouth	17	1		
1998–99	*Bristol R*	2	0	**2**	**0**
1999–2000	Portsmouth	7	0	**24**	**1**
2000–01	Plymouth Arg	42	1		
2001–02	Plymouth Arg	39	6		
2002–03	Plymouth Arg	24	2		
2003–04	Plymouth Arg	9	1	**114**	**10**
2004–05	Torquay U	30	2		
2005–06	Torquay U	26	3	**56**	**5**

PRISO, Carl (F) **3** **0**
H: 6 1 W: 12 00 b.Cameroon 10-7-79
Source: Chemnitzer.

2005–06	Torquay U	3	0	**3**	**0**

ROBINSON, Paul (F) **125** **16**
H: 5 11 W: 11 00 b.Sunderland 20-11-78
Source: Trainee.

1995–96	Darlington	4	0		
1996–97	Darlington	3	0		
1997–98	Darlington	19	3	**26**	**3**
1997–98	Newcastle U	0	0		
1998–99	Newcastle U	0	0		
1999–2000	Newcastle U	11	0	**11**	**0**
2000–01	Wimbledon	2	0		
2000–01	*Burnley*	4	0	**4**	**0**
2001–02	Wimbledon	1	0	**3**	**0**
2001–02	*Grimsby T*	5	0		
2002–03	Grimsby T	12	1	**17**	**1**
2002–03	*Carlisle U*	5	1	**5**	**1**
2002–03	Blackpool	7	1	**7**	**1**
2003–04	Hartlepool U	31	7		
2004–05	Hartlepool U	0	0	**31**	**7**

From York C, Whitley Bay

2005–06	Torquay U	21	3	**21**	**3**

SAKO, Morike (M) **25** **3**
H: 6 7 W: 12 00 b.Paris 17-11-81
Source: Delemont.

2005–06	Torquay U	25	3	**25**	**3**

SHARP, James (D) **115** **3**
H: 6 1 W: 13 00 b.Reading 2-1-76
Source: Reading, Florida Tech, Aldershot T, Wokingham, Andover T.

2000–01	Hartlepool U	34	2		
2001–02	Hartlepool U	15	0		
2002–03	Hartlepool U	0	0	**49**	**2**
2003–04	Falkirk	30	1		
2004–05	Falkirk	4	0	**34**	**1**
2005–06	Torquay U	32	0	**32**	**0**

SKINNER, Nicholas (M) **0** **0**
H: 5 9 W: 10 00 b.Torquay 6-9-85
Source: Scholar.

2004–05	Torquay U	0	0		
2005–06	Torquay U	0	0		

SOW, Mamadou (F) **11** **0**
H: 5 9 W: 10 11 b.Clamart 22-8-81
Source: Villemondble.

2005–06	Torquay U	11	0	**11**	**0**

TAYLOR, Craig (D) **258** **13**
H: 6 2 W: 13 00 b.Plymouth 24-1-74
Source: Dorchester T.

1996–97	Swindon T	0	0		
1997–98	Swindon T	32	2		
1998–99	Swindon T	21	0		
1998–99	*Plymouth Arg*	6	1		
1999–2000	Swindon T	2	0	**55**	**2**
1999–2000	Plymouth Arg	41	3		
2000–01	Plymouth Arg	39	3		
2001–02	Plymouth Arg	1	0		
2002–03	Plymouth Arg	1	0	**88**	**7**
2002–03	*Torquay U*	5	0		
2003–04	Torquay U	43	4		
2004–05	Torquay U	36	0		
2005–06	Torquay U	31	0	**115**	**4**

VILLIS, Matt (D) **34** **0**
H: 6 2 W: 12 00 b.Bridgwater 13-4-84
Source: Bridgwater T.

2002–03	Plymouth Arg	0	0		
2003–04	Plymouth Arg	0	0		
2004–05	Plymouth Arg	0	0		
2004–05	*Torquay U*	22	0		
2005–06	Torquay U	12	0	**34**	**0**

WOODS, Steve (D) **231** **10**
H: 6 1 W: 13 00 b.Northwich 15-12-76
Source: Trainee.

1995–96	Stoke C	0	0		
1996–97	Stoke C	0	0		
1997–98	Stoke C	1	0		
1997–98	*Plymouth Arg*	5	0	**5**	**0**
1998–99	Stoke C	33	0	**34**	**0**
1999–2000	Chesterfield	25	0		
2000–01	Chesterfield	0	0	**25**	**0**
2001–02	Torquay U	38	2		
2002–03	Torquay U	9	0		
2003–04	Torquay U	46	6		
2004–05	Torquay U	36	2		
2005–06	Torquay U	38	0	**167**	**10**

TOTTENHAM H (82)

BARCHAM, Andy (F) **0** **0**
H: 5 8 W: 11 10 b.Basildon 16-12-86
Source: Scholar.

2005–06	Tottenham H	0	0		

BARNARD, Lee (F) **19** **0**
H: 5 10 W: 10 10 b.Romford 18-7-84
Source: Trainee.

2002–03	Tottenham H	0	0		
2002–03	*Exeter C*	3	0	**3**	**0**
2003–04	Tottenham H	0	0		
2004–05	Tottenham H	0	0		
2004–05	*Leyton Orient*	8	0	**8**	**0**
2004–05	*Northampton T*	5	0	**5**	**0**
2005–06	Tottenham H	3	0	**3**	**0**

BUNJEVCEVIC, Goran (D) **236** **21**
H: 6 3 W: 12 02 b.Karlovac 17-2-73
Honours: Serbia-Montenegro 17 full caps.

1994–95	Rad	17	0		
1995–96	Rad	13	2		
1996–97	Rad	30	3	**60**	**5**
1997–98	Red Star Belgrade	30	5		
1998–99	Red Star Belgrade	22	4		
1999–2000	Red Star Belgrade	40	7		
2000–01	Red Star Belgrade	33	0	**125**	**16**
2001–02	Tottenham H	6	0		
2002–03	Tottenham H	35	0		
2003–04	Tottenham H	7	0		
2004–05	Tottenham H	3	0		
2005–06	Tottenham H	0	0	**51**	**0**

BURCH, Rob (G) **0** **0**
H: 6 2 W: 12 13 b.Yeovil 8-10-83
Source: Trainee. *Honours:* England Under-20.

2002–03	Tottenham H	0	0		
2003–04	Tottenham H	0	0		
2004–05	Tottenham H	0	0		
2004–05	*West Ham U*	0	0		
2005–06	Tottenham H	0	0		
2005–06	*Bristol C*	0	0		

BUTTON, David (G) **0** **0**
H: 6 3 W: 13 00 b.Stevenage 27-2-89
Source: Scholar. *Honours:* England Youth.

2005–06	Tottenham H	0	0		

CARRICK, Michael (M) **208** **10**
H: 6 1 W: 11 10 b.Wallsend 28-7-81
Source: Trainee. *Honours:* England Youth, Under-21, B, 7 full caps.

1998–99	West Ham U	0	0		
1999–2000	West Ham U	8	1		
1999–2000	*Swindon T*	6	2	**6**	**2**
1999–2000	*Birmingham C*	2	0	**2**	**0**
2000–01	West Ham U	33	1		
2001–02	West Ham U	30	2		
2002–03	West Ham U	30	1		
2003–04	West Ham U	35	1		
2004–05	West Ham U	0	0	**136**	**6**
2004–05	Tottenham H	29	0		
2005–06	Tottenham H	35	2	**64**	**2**

CERNY, Radek (G) **3** **0**
H: 6 1 W: 14 02 b.Prague 18-2-74
Source: Slavia Prague. *Honours:* Czech Republic 3 full caps.

2004–05	Tottenham H	3	0		
2005–06	Tottenham H	0	0	**3**	**0**

DANIELS, Charlie (M) **0** **0**
H: 6 1 W: 12 12 b.Harlow 7-9-86
Source: Scholar.

2005–06	Tottenham H	0	0		

DAVENPORT, Calum (D) **112** **4**
H: 6 4 W: 14 00 b.Bedford 1-1-83
Source: Trainee. *Honours:* England Youth, Under-20, Under-21.

1999–2000	Coventry C	0	0		
2000–01	Coventry C	1	0		
2001–02	Coventry C	3	0		
2002–03	Coventry C	32	3		
2003–04	Coventry C	33	0		
2004–05	Coventry C	6	0	**75**	**3**
2004–05	*Southampton*	7	0	**7**	**0**
2004–05	Tottenham H	1	0		
2004–05	*West Ham U*	10	0	**10**	**0**
2005–06	Tottenham H	4	0	**5**	**0**
2005–06	*Norwich C*	15	1	**15**	**1**

DAVIDS, Edgar (M) **346** **34**
H: 5 7 W: 10 10 b.Paramaribo 13-3-73
Honours: Holland 74 full caps, 6 goals.

1991–92	Ajax	13	9		
1992–93	Ajax	28	1		
1993–94	Ajax	15	2		
1994–95	Ajax	22	5		
1995–96	Ajax	28	7	**106**	**24**
1996–97	AC Milan	15	0		
1997–98	AC Milan	3	0	**18**	**0**
1997–98	Juventus	20	1		
1998–99	Juventus	27	2		
1999–2000	Juventus	27	1		
2000–01	Juventus	26	1		
2001–02	Juventus	28	2		
2002–03	Juventus	26	1		
2003–04	Juventus	5	0	**159**	**8**
2003–04	Barcelona	18	1	**18**	**1**
2004–05	Internazionale	14	0	**14**	**0**
2005–06	Tottenham H	31	1	**31**	**1**

DAVIS, Jamie (M) **0** **0**
H: 5 7 W: 10 10 b.Braintree 25-10-88
Source: Scholar. *Honours:* England Youth.

2005–06	Tottenham H	0	0		

DAWKINS, Simon (F) **0** **0**
H: 5 10 W: 11 01 b.Edgware 1-12-87
Source: Scholar.

2005–06	Tottenham H	0	0		

DAWSON, Michael (D) **120** **7**
H: 6 2 W: 12 02 b.Northallerton 18-11-83
Source: School. *Honours:* England Youth, Under-21, B.

2000–01	Nottingham F	0	0		
2001–02	Nottingham F	1	0		
2002–03	Nottingham F	38	5		
2003–04	Nottingham F	30	1		
2004–05	Nottingham F	14	1	**83**	**7**
2004–05	Tottenham H	5	0		
2005–06	Tottenham H	32	0	**37**	**0**

DEFENDI, Rodrigo (D) **0** **0**
H: 6 2 W: 13 01 b.Ribeirao Preto 16-6-86
Source: Cruzeiro.

2004–05	Tottenham H	0	0		
2005–06	Tottenham H	0	0		

DEFOE, Jermain (F) **208** **76**
H: 5 7 W: 10 04 b.Beckton 7-10-82
Source: Charlton Ath. *Honours:* England Youth, Under-21, B, 16full caps, 1 goal.

1999–2000	West Ham U	0	0		
2000–01	West Ham U	1	0		
2000–01	*Bournemouth*	29	18	**29**	**18**
2001–02	West Ham U	35	10		
2002–03	West Ham U	38	8		
2003–04	West Ham U	19	11	**93**	**29**
2003–04	Tottenham H	15	7		
2004–05	Tottenham H	35	13		
2005–06	Tottenham H	36	9	**86**	**29**

EL HAMDAOUI, Mounir (F) **83** **35**
H: 6 0 W: 13 05 b.Rotterdam 14-7-84
Honours: Holland Under-21.

2001–02	Excelsior	6	2		
2002–03	Excelsior	21	2		
2003–04	Excelsior	33	17		
2004–05	Excelsior	14	11	**74**	**32**
2004–05	Tottenham H	0	0		
2005–06	Tottenham H	0	0		
2005–06	*Derby Co*	9	3	**9**	**3**

FORECAST, Tommy (G) **0** **0**
H: 6 6 W: 11 10 b.Newham 15-10-86
Source: Scholar.

2005–06	Tottenham H	0	0		

FULOP, Marton (G) **38** **0**
H: 6 6 W: 14 07 b.Budapest 3-5-83
Honours: Hungary Under-21, 1 full cap.

2004–05	Tottenham H	0	0		
2004–05	*Chesterfield*	7	0	**7**	**0**
2005–06	Tottenham H	0	0		
2005–06	*Coventry C*	31	0	**31**	**0**

GARDNER, Anthony (D) **143 5**
H: 6 3 W: 14 00 b.Stone 19-9-80
Source: Trainee. *Honours:* England Under-21, 1 full cap.

1998–99	Port Vale	15	1		
1999–2000	Port Vale	26	3	**41**	**4**
1999–2000	Tottenham H	0	0		
2000–01	Tottenham H	8	0		
2001–02	Tottenham H	15	0		
2002–03	Tottenham H	12	1		
2003–04	Tottenham H	33	0		
2004–05	Tottenham H	17	0		
2005–06	Tottenham H	17	0	**102**	**1**

GHALI, Hossam (M) **43 3**
H: 5 11 W: 12 04 b.Cairo 15-12-81

2003–04	Feyenoord	13	0		
2004–05	Feyenoord	20	1		
2005–06	Feyenoord	10	2	**43**	**3**
2005–06	Tottenham H	0	0		

HALLFREDSSON, Emil (M) **16 4**
H: 6 1 W: 13 01 b.Iceland 29-6-84
Honours: Iceland Under-21.

2004	FH	16	4	**16**	**4**
2004–05	Tottenham H	0	0		
2005–06	Tottenham H	*0*	*0*		

To Malmo January 2006

HUDDLESTONE, Tom (M) **105 1**
H: 6 2 W: 11 02 b.Nottingham 28-12-86
Source: Scholar. *Honours:* England Youth, Under-20, Under-21.

2003–04	Derby Co	43	0		
2004–05	Derby Co	45	0	**88**	**0**
2005–06	Tottenham H	4	0	**4**	**0**
2005–06	*Wolverhampton W*	13	1	**13**	**1**

IFIL, Phil (D) **18 0**
H: 5 10 W: 12 02 b.Willesden 18-11-86
Honours: England Youth, Under-20.

2004–05	Tottenham H	2	0		
2005–06	Tottenham H	0	0	**2**	**0**
2005–06	*Millwall*	16	0	**16**	**0**

JACKSON, Johnnie (M) **67 4**
H: 6 1 W: 12 00 b.Camden 15-8-82
Source: Trainee. *Honours:* England Youth, Under-20.

1999–2000	Tottenham H	0	0		
2000–01	Tottenham H	0	0		
2001–02	Tottenham H	0	0		
2002–03	Tottenham H	0	0		
2002–03	*Swindon T*	13	1	**13**	**1**
2002–03	*Colchester U*	8	0	**8**	**0**
2003–04	Tottenham H	11	1		
2003–04	*Coventry C*	5	2	**5**	**2**
2004–05	Tottenham H	8	0		
2004–05	*Watford*	15	0	**15**	**0**
2005–06	Tottenham H	1	0	**20**	**1**
2005–06	*Derby Co*	6	0	**6**	**0**

JENAS, Jermaine (M) **169 19**
H: 5 11 W: 11 00 b.Nottingham 18-2-83
Source: Scholar. *Honours:* England Youth, Under-21, B, 15 full caps.

1999–2000	Nottingham F	0	0		
2000–01	Nottingham F	1	0		
2001–02	Nottingham F	28	4	**29**	**4**
2001–02	Newcastle U	12	0		
2002–03	Newcastle U	32	6		
2003–04	Newcastle U	31	2		
2004–05	Newcastle U	31	1		
2005–06	Newcastle U	4	0	**110**	**9**
2005–06	Tottenham H	30	6	**30**	**6**

KANOUTE, Frederic (F) **184 52**
H: 6 3 W: 13 08 b.Ste. Foy-Les-Lyon 2-9-77
Honours: France Under-21, Mali 5 full caps, 4 goals.

1997–98	Lyon	18	6		
1998–99	Lyon	9	2		
1999–2000	Lyon	13	1	**40**	**9**
1999–2000	West Ham U	8	2		
2000–01	West Ham U	32	11		
2001–02	West Ham U	27	11		
2002–03	West Ham U	17	5	**84**	**29**
2003–04	Tottenham H	27	7		
2004–05	Tottenham H	32	7		
2005–06	Tottenham H	1	0	**60**	**14**

To Sevilla August 2005

KEANE, Robbie (F) **290 103**
H: 5 9 W: 12 02 b.Dublin 8-7-80
Source: Trainee. *Honours:* Eire Youth, B, 66 full caps, 26 goals.

1997–98	Wolverhampton W	38	11		
1998–99	Wolverhampton W	33	11		
1999–2000	Wolverhampton W	2	2	**73**	**24**
1999–2000	Coventry C	31	12	**31**	**12**
2000–01	Internazionale	6	0	**6**	**0**
2000–01	Leeds U	18	9		
2001–02	Leeds U	25	3		
2002–03	Leeds U	3	1	**46**	**13**
2002–03	Tottenham H	29	13		
2003–04	Tottenham H	34	14		
2004–05	Tottenham H	35	11		
2005–06	Tottenham H	36	16	**134**	**54**

KELLY, Stephen (D) **67 2**
H: 6 0 W: 12 04 b.Dublin 6-9-83
Source: Juniors. *Honours:* Eire Youth, Under-21, 1 full cap.

2000–01	Tottenham H	0	0		
2001–02	Tottenham H	0	0		
2002–03	Tottenham H	0	0		
2002–03	*Southend U*	10	0	**10**	**0**
2002–03	*QPR*	7	0	**7**	**0**
2003–04	Tottenham H	11	0		
2003–04	*Watford*	13	0	**13**	**0**
2004–05	Tottenham H	17	2		
2005–06	Tottenham H	9	0	**37**	**2**

KING, Ledley (D) **172 7**
H: 6 2 W: 14 05 b.Bow 12-10-80
Source: Trainee. *Honours:* England Youth, Under-21, 16 full caps, 1 goal.

1998–99	Tottenham H	1	0		
1999–2000	Tottenham H	3	0		
2000–01	Tottenham H	18	1		
2001–02	Tottenham H	32	0		
2002–03	Tottenham H	25	0		
2003–04	Tottenham H	29	1		
2004–05	Tottenham H	38	2		
2005–06	Tottenham H	26	3	**172**	**7**

LEE, Charlie (M) **0 0**
H: 5 11 W: 11 07 b.Whitechapel 5-1-87
Source: Scholar.

2005–06	Tottenham H	0	0		

LEE, Young-Pyo (D) **109 1**
H: 5 8 W: 10 10 b.Hong Chung 23-4-77
Source: Anyang Cheetahs. *Honours:* South Korea 88 full caps, 5 goals.

2002–03	PSV Eindhoven	15	0		
2003–04	PSV Eindhoven	32	0		
2004–05	PSV Eindhoven	31	1	**78**	**1**
2005–06	Tottenham H	31	0	**31**	**0**

LENNON, Aaron (M) **65 3**
H: 5 6 W: 10 03 b.Leeds 16-4-87
Source: Trainee. *Honours:* England Youth, Under-21, B, 4 full caps.

2003–04	Leeds U	11	0		
2004–05	Leeds U	27	1	**38**	**1**
2005–06	Tottenham H	27	2	**27**	**2**

LEWIS, Stuart (M) **0 0**
H: 5 10 W: 11 06 b.Welwyn 15-10-87
Source: Scholar.

2005–06	Tottenham H	0	0		

MAGHOMA, Jacques (M) **0 0**
H: 5 9 W: 11 06 b.Lubumbashi 23-10-87
Source: Scholar.

2005–06	Tottenham H	0	0		

MARNEY, Dean (M) **35 2**
H: 5 10 W: 11 09 b.Barking 31-1-84
Source: Scholar. *Honours:* England Under-21.

2002–03	Tottenham H	0	0		
2002–03	*Swindon T*	9	0	**9**	**0**
2003–04	Tottenham H	3	0		
2003–04	*QPR*	2	0	**2**	**0**
2004–05	Tottenham H	5	2		
2004–05	*Gillingham*	3	0	**3**	**0**
2005–06	Tottenham H	0	0	**8**	**2**
2005–06	*Norwich C*	13	0	**13**	**0**

MARTIN, Joe (M) **0 0**
H: 6 0 W: 12 13 b.Dagenham 29-11-88
Source: Scholar. *Honours:* England Youth.

2005–06	Tottenham H	0	0		

McKENNA, Kieran (M) **0 0**
H: 5 10 W: 10 07 b.London 14-5-86
Source: Academy.

2003–04	Tottenham H	0	0		
2004–05	Tottenham H	0	0		
2005–06	Tottenham H	0	0		

McKIE, Marcel (D) **0 0**
H: 5 11 W: 11 09 b.Edmonton 22-9-84
Source: Scholar. *Honours:* England Youth.

2001–02	Tottenham H	0	0		
2002–03	Tottenham H	0	0		
2003–04	Tottenham H	0	0		
2004–05	Tottenham H	0	0		
2005–06	Tottenham H	0	0		

MIDO (F) **139 59**
H: 6 2 W: 14 09 b.Cairo 23-2-83
Honours: Egypt 36 full caps, 24 goals.

1999–2000	Zamalek	4	3	**4**	**3**
2000–01	Gent	21	11	**21**	**11**
2001–02	Ajax	24	12		
2002–03	Ajax	16	9	**40**	**21**
2002–03	Celta Vigo	8	4	**8**	**4**
2003–04	Marseille	22	7	**22**	**7**
2004–05	Roma	8	0	**8**	**0**
2004–05	Tottenham H	9	2		
2005–06	Tottenham H	27	11	**36**	**13**

MILLS, Leigh (D) **0 0**
H: 6 2 W: 13 00 b.Winchester 8-2-88
Source: Scholar. *Honours:* England Youth.

2005–06	Tottenham H	0	0		

MURPHY, Danny (M) **386 60**
H: 5 10 W: 11 09 b.Chester 18-3-77
Source: Trainee. *Honours:* England Schools, Youth, Under-21, 9 full caps, 1 goal.

1993–94	Crewe Alex	12	2		
1994–95	Crewe Alex	35	5		
1995–96	Crewe Alex	42	10		
1996–97	Crewe Alex	45	10		
1997–98	Liverpool	16	0		
1998–99	Liverpool	1	0		
1998–99	*Crewe Alex*	16	1	**150**	**28**
1999–2000	Liverpool	23	3		
2000–01	Liverpool	27	4		
2001–02	Liverpool	36	6		
2002–03	Liverpool	36	7		
2003–04	Liverpool	31	5	**170**	**25**
2004–05	Charlton Ath	38	3		
2005–06	Charlton Ath	18	4	**56**	**7**
2005–06	Tottenham H	10	0	**10**	**0**

NAYBET, Nourredine (D) **330 17**
H: 6 0 W: 11 11 b.Casablanca 10-2-70
Source: WAC. *Honours:* Morocco 115 full caps, 3 goals.

1993–94	Nantes	34	1	**34**	**1**
1994–95	Sporting Lisbon	26	2		
1995–96	Sporting Lisbon	28	3	**54**	**5**
1996–97	La Coruna	34	1		
1997–98	La Coruna	31	4		
1998–99	La Coruna	30	0		
1999–2000	La Coruna	25	0		
2000–01	La Coruna	26	1		
2001–02	La Coruna	24	2		
2002–03	La Coruna	25	1		
2003–04	La Coruna	17	1	**212**	**10**
2004–05	Tottenham H	27	1		
2005–06	Tottenham H	3	0	**30**	**1**

O'HARA, Jamie (M) **19 5**
H: 5 11 W: 12 04 b.South London 25-9-86
Source: Scholar. *Honours:* England Youth.

2004–05	Tottenham H	0	0		
2005–06	Tottenham H	0	0		
2005–06	*Chesterfield*	19	5	**19**	**5**

REID, Andy (M) **170 22**
H: 5 9 W: 12 08 b.Dublin 29-7-82
Source: Trainee. *Honours:* Eire Youth, Under-21, 22 full caps, 3 goals.

1999–2000	Nottingham F	0	0		
2000–01	Nottingham F	14	2		
2001–02	Nottingham F	29	0		
2002–03	Nottingham F	30	1		
2003–04	Nottingham F	46	13		
2004–05	Nottingham F	25	5	**144**	**21**
2004–05	Tottenham H	13	1		
2005–06	Tottenham H	13	0	**26**	**1**

ROBINSON, Paul (G) **169 0**

H: 6 1 W: 14 07 b.Beverley 15-10-79

Source: Trainee. *Honours:* England Under-21, 26 full caps.

1996–97	Leeds U	0	0		
1997–98	Leeds U	0	0		
1998–99	Leeds U	5	0		
1999–2000	Leeds U	0	0		
2000–01	Leeds U	16	0		
2001–02	Leeds U	0	0		
2002–03	Leeds U	38	0		
2003–04	Leeds U	36	0	**95**	**0**
2003–04	Tottenham H	0	0		
2004–05	Tottenham H	36	0		
2005–06	Tottenham H	38	0	**74**	**0**

ROUTLEDGE, Wayne (M) **126 10**

H: 5 6 W: 11 02 b.Sidcup 7-1-85

Source: Scholar. *Honours:* England Youth, Under-20, Under-21.

2001–02	Crystal Palace	2	0		
2002–03	Crystal Palace	26	4		
2003–04	Crystal Palace	44	6		
2004–05	Crystal Palace	38	0	**110**	**10**
2005–06	Tottenham H	3	0	**3**	**0**
2005–06	*Portsmouth*	13	0	**13**	**0**

STALTERI, Paul (D) **183 7**

H: 5 11 W: 11 13 b.Etobicoke 18-10-77

Source: Malton Bullets, Toronto Lynx. *Honours:* Canada 50 full caps, 6 goals.

1999–2000	Werder Bremen	0	0		
2000–01	Werder Bremen	31	1		
2001–02	Werder Bremen	22	3		
2002–03	Werder Bremen	33	0		
2003–04	Werder Bremen	33	2		
2004–05	Werder Bremen	31	0	**150**	**6**
2005–06	Tottenham H	33	1	**33**	**1**

TAINIO, Teemu (M) **168 17**

H: 5 9 W: 11 09 b.Tornio 27-11-79

Honours: Finland Youth, Under-21, 33 full caps, 5 goals.

1996	Haka	20	4	**20**	**4**
1997–98	Auxerre	1	0		
1998–99	Auxerre	13	1		
1999–2000	Auxerre	25	3		
2000–01	Auxerre	10	1		
2001–02	Auxerre	28	3		
2002–03	Auxerre	25	1		
2003–04	Auxerre	22	3		
2004–05	Auxerre	0	0	**124**	**12**
2005–06	Tottenham H	24	1	**24**	**1**

YEATES, Mark (F) **60 5**

H: 5 8 W: 13 03 b.Dublin 11-1-85

Source: Trainee. *Honours:* Eire Youth, Under-21.

2002–03	Tottenham H	0	0		
2003–04	Tottenham H	1	0		
2003–04	*Brighton & HA*	9	0	**9**	**0**
2004–05	Tottenham H	2	0		
2004–05	*Swindon T*	4	0	**4**	**0**
2005–06	Tottenham H	0	0	**3**	**0**
2005–06	*Colchester U*	44	5	**44**	**5**

ZIEGLER, Reto (M) **79 1**

H: 6 0 W: 12 06 b.Nyon 16-1-86

Source: FC Gland, Servette, Terre-Sainte, Lausanne. *Honours:* Switzerland Under-21, 3 full caps.

2002–03	Grasshoppers	10	0		
2003–04	Grasshoppers	28	0	**38**	**0**
2004–05	Tottenham H	23	1		
2005–06	Tottenham H	0	0	**23**	**1**
2005–06	*Hamburg*	8	0	**8**	**0**
2005–06	*Wigan Ath*	10	0	**10**	**0**

Scholars

Archibald-Henville, Troy; Hamed, Radwan; Hughton, Cian James; Lake, Gregory James Stuart; Riley, Christopher Daniel; Smith, Alexander; Wells, Matthew Elliott.

TRANMERE R (83)

ACHTERBERG, John (G) **282 0**

H: 6 1 W: 14 03 b.Utrecht 8-7-71

Source: VV RUC, Utrecht.

1993–94	NAC	1	0		
1994–95	NAC	2	0		
1995–96	NAC	6	0	**9**	**0**
1996–97	Eindhoven	32	0	**32**	**0**
From Utrecht.					
1998–99	Tranmere R	24	0		
1999–2000	Tranmere R	26	0		
2000–01	Tranmere R	25	0		
2001–02	Tranmere R	25	0		
2002–03	Tranmere R	38	0		
2003–04	Tranmere R	45	0		
2004–05	Tranmere R	39	0		
2005–06	Tranmere R	19	0	**241**	**0**

AISTON, Sam (M) **230 10**

H: 6 1 W: 14 00 b.Newcastle 21-11-76

Source: Newcastle U Trainee. *Honours:* England Schools.

1995–96	Sunderland	14	0		
1996–97	Sunderland	2	0		
1996–97	*Chester C*	14	0		
1997–98	Sunderland	3	0		
1998–99	Sunderland	1	0		
1998–99	*Chester C*	11	0	**25**	**0**
1999–2000	Sunderland	0	0	**20**	**0**
1999–2000	*Stoke C*	6	0	**6**	**0**
1999–2000	*Shrewsbury T*	10	0		
2000–01	Shrewsbury T	42	2		
2001–02	Shrewsbury T	35	2		
2002–03	Shrewsbury T	21	2		
2003–04	Shrewsbury T	0	0		
2004–05	Shrewsbury T	35	1	**143**	**7**
2005–06	Tranmere R	36	3	**36**	**3**

BROWN, Paul (M) **4 0**

H: 5 8 W: 11 13 b.Liverpool 10-9-84

Source: Scholar.

2004–05	Tranmere R	4	0		
2005–06	Tranmere R	0	0	**4**	**0**

DAVIES, Steve (F) **22 2**

H: 6 0 W: 12 00 b.Liverpool 29-12-87

Source: Scholar.

2005–06	Tranmere R	22	2	**22**	**2**

FACEY, Delroy (F) **185 34**

H: 6 0 W: 15 02 b.Huddersfield 22-4-80

Source: Trainee.

1996–97	Huddersfield T	3	0		
1997–98	Huddersfield T	3	0		
1998–99	Huddersfield T	20	3		
1999–2000	Huddersfield T	2	0		
2000–01	Huddersfield T	34	10		
2001–02	Huddersfield T	13	2		
2002–03	Huddersfield T	0	0		
2002–03	*Bradford C*	6	1	**6**	**1**
2002–03	Bolton W	9	1		
2003–04	Bolton W	1	0	**10**	**1**
2003–04	*Burnley*	14	5	**14**	**5**
2003–04	WBA	9	0	**9**	**0**
2004–05	Hull C	21	4	**21**	**4**
2004–05	*Huddersfield T*	4	0	**79**	**15**
2004–05	Oldham Ath	6	0		
2005–06	Oldham Ath	3	0	**9**	**0**
2005–06	Tranmere R	37	8	**37**	**8**

FOWLER, Joe (M) **0 0**

H: 5 8 W: 11 07 b.Liverpool 19-8-86

Source: Scholar.

2005–06	Tranmere R	0	0		

GOODISON, Ian (D) **164 3**

H: 6 1 W: 13 04 b.St James, Jamaica 21-11-72

Source: Olympic Gardens. *Honours:* Jamaica full caps.

1999–2000	Hull C	18	0		
2000–01	Hull C	36	1		
2001–02	Hull C	16	0		
2002–03	Hull C	0	0	**70**	**1**
From Seba U.					
2003–04	Tranmere R	12	0		
2004–05	Tranmere R	44	1		
2005–06	Tranmere R	38	1	**94**	**2**

GREENACRE, Chris (F) **276 77**

H: 5 9 W: 12 09 b.Halifax 23-12-77

Source: Trainee.

1995–96	Manchester C	0	0		
1996–97	Manchester C	4	0		
1997–98	Manchester C	3	1		
1997–98	*Cardiff C*	11	2	**11**	**2**
1997–98	*Blackpool*	4	0	**4**	**0**
1998–99	Manchester C	1	0		
1998–99	*Scarborough*	12	2	**12**	**2**
1999–2000	Manchester C	0	0	**8**	**1**
1999–2000	Mansfield T	31	9		
2000–01	Mansfield T	46	19		
2001–02	Mansfield T	44	21	**121**	**49**
2002–03	Stoke C	30	4		
2003–04	Stoke C	13	2		
2004–05	Stoke C	32	1	**75**	**7**
2005–06	Tranmere R	45	16	**45**	**16**

HARRISON, Danny (M) **112 4**

H: 5 11 W: 12 04 b.Liverpool 4-11-82

Source: Scholar.

2001–02	Tranmere R	1	0		
2002–03	Tranmere R	12	0		
2003–04	Tranmere R	32	2		
2004–05	Tranmere R	32	0		
2005–06	Tranmere R	35	2	**112**	**4**

HENRY, Paul (M) **0 0**

H: 5 8 W: 11 06 b.Liverpool 28-1-88

Source: Scholar.

2005–06	Tranmere R	0	0		

JACKSON, Mike (D) **465 34**

H: 6 0 W: 13 08 b.Runcorn 4-12-73

Source: Trainee.

1991–92	Crewe Alex	1	0		
1992–93	Crewe Alex	4	0	**5**	**0**
1993–94	Bury	39	0		
1994–95	Bury	24	2		
1995–96	Bury	31	4		
1996–97	Bury	31	3	**125**	**9**
1996–97	Preston NE	7	0		
1997–98	Preston NE	40	2		
1998–99	Preston NE	44	8		
1999–2000	Preston NE	46	5		
2000–01	Preston NE	30	1		
2001–02	Preston NE	13	0		
2002–03	Preston NE	22	1		
2002–03	*Tranmere R*	6	0		
2003–04	Preston NE	43	0	**245**	**17**
2004–05	Tranmere R	43	5		
2005–06	Tranmere R	41	3	**90**	**8**

JAMES, Oliver (D) **1 0**

H: 6 0 W: 11 10 b.Birkenhead 13-1-87

Source: Scholar.

2004–05	Tranmere R	0	0		
2005–06	Tranmere R	1	0	**1**	**0**

JENNINGS, Steven (M) **53 1**

H: 5 7 W: 11 11 b.Liverpool 28-10-84

Source: Scholar.

2002–03	Tranmere R	0	0		
2003–04	Tranmere R	4	0		
2004–05	Tranmere R	11	0		
2005–06	Tranmere R	38	1	**53**	**1**

JOHNSTON, Michael (D) **0 0**

b. 16-12-87

2005–06	Tranmere R	0	0		

JONES, Mike (M) **1 0**

b.Birkenhead 15-8-87

Source: Scholar.

2005–06	Tranmere R	1	0	**1**	**0**

LINWOOD, Paul (D) **53 0**

H: 6 2 W: 13 03 b.Birkenhead 24-10-83

Source: Scholar.

2001–02	Tranmere R	0	0		
2002–03	Tranmere R	0	0		
2003–04	Tranmere R	20	0		
2004–05	Tranmere R	10	0		
2005–06	Tranmere R	14	0	**44**	**0**
2005–06	*Wrexham*	9	0	**9**	**0**

MARTIN, Paul (D) **0 0**

H: 6 1 W: 13 05 b.Liverpool 29-10-85

2005–06	Tranmere R	0	0		

McATEER, Jason (M) **402 24**
H: 5 11 W: 13 01 b.Birkenhead 18-6-71
Source: Marine. *Honours:* Eire B, 52 full caps, 3 goals.
1991–92 Bolton W 0 0
1992–93 Bolton W 21 0
1993–94 Bolton W 46 3
1994–95 Bolton W 43 5
1995–96 Bolton W 4 0 **114 8**
1995–96 Liverpool 29 0
1996–97 Liverpool 37 1
1997–98 Liverpool 21 2
1998–99 Liverpool 13 0 **100 3**
1998–99 Blackburn R 13 1
1999–2000 Blackburn R 28 2
2000–01 Blackburn R 27 1
2001–02 Blackburn R 4 0 **72 4**
2001–02 Sunderland 26 2
2002–03 Sunderland 9 1
2003–04 Sunderland 18 2 **53 5**
2004–05 Tranmere R 34 4
2005–06 Tranmere R 29 0 **63 4**

PALETHORPE, Philip (G) **0 0**
H: 6 2 W: 11 08 b.Wallasey 17-9-86
Source: Scholar.
2003–04 Tranmere R 0 0
2004–05 Tranmere R 0 0
2005–06 Tranmere R 0 0

RANKINE, Mark (M) **613 33**
H: 5 7 W: 12 02 b.Doncaster 30-9-69
Source: Trainee.
1987–88 Doncaster R 18 2
1988–89 Doncaster R 46 11
1989–90 Doncaster R 36 2
1990–91 Doncaster R 40 2
1991–92 Doncaster R 24 3 **164 20**
1991–92 Wolverhampton W 15 1
1992–93 Wolverhampton W 27 0
1993–94 Wolverhampton W 31 0
1994–95 Wolverhampton W 27 0
1995–96 Wolverhampton W 32 0
1996–97 Wolverhampton W 0 0 **132 1**
1996–97 Preston NE 23 0
1997–98 Preston NE 35 1
1998–99 Preston NE 42 3
1999–2000 Preston NE 44 0
2000–01 Preston NE 44 4
2001–02 Preston NE 26 4
2002–03 Preston NE 19 0 **233 12**
2002–03 *Sheffield U* 6 0
2003–04 Sheffield U 13 0 **19 0**
2004–05 Tranmere R 41 0
2005–06 Tranmere R 24 0 **65 0**

ROBERTS, Gareth (D) **281 13**
H: 5 8 W: 11 12 b.Wrexham 6-2-78
Source: Trainee. *Honours:* Wales Under-21, B, 9 full caps.
1995–96 Liverpool 0 0
1996–97 Liverpool 0 0
1997–98 Liverpool 0 0
1998–99 Liverpool 0 0
1999–2000 Tranmere R 37 1
2000–01 Tranmere R 34 0
2001–02 Tranmere R 45 2
2002–03 Tranmere R 37 4
2003–04 Tranmere R 44 1
2004–05 Tranmere R 40 3
2005–06 Tranmere R 44 2 **281 13**

SHARPS, Ian (D) **170 6**
H: 6 3 W: 14 07 b.Warrington 23-10-80
Source: Trainee.
1998–99 Tranmere R 1 0
1999–2000 Tranmere R 0 0
2000–01 Tranmere R 0 0
2001–02 Tranmere R 29 0
2002–03 Tranmere R 30 3
2003–04 Tranmere R 27 1
2004–05 Tranmere R 44 1
2005–06 Tranmere R 39 1 **170 6**

SUMMERBEE, Nicky (M) **469 26**
H: 5 11 W: 12 08 b.Altrincham 26-8-71
Source: Trainee. *Honours:* England Under-21.
1989–90 Swindon T 1 0
1990–91 Swindon T 7 0
1991–92 Swindon T 27 0
1992–93 Swindon T 39 3
1993–94 Swindon T 38 3
1994–95 Manchester C 41 1
1995–96 Manchester C 37 1
1996–97 Manchester C 44 4
1997–98 Manchester C 9 0
1997–98 Sunderland 25 3
1998–99 Sunderland 36 3
1999–2000 Sunderland 32 1
2000–01 Sunderland 0 0 **93 7**
2000–01 Bolton W 12 1 **12 1**
2001–02 Manchester C 0 0 **131 6**
2001–02 Nottingham F 17 2 **17 2**
2002–03 Leicester C 29 0 **29 0**
2003–04 Bradford C 35 1
2004–05 Bradford C 33 3 **68 4**
2005–06 Swindon T 1 0 **113 6**
2005–06 Tranmere R 6 0 **6 0**

TREMARCO, Carl (D) **21 1**
H: 5 8 W: 11 11 b.Liverpool 11-10-85
Source: Scholar.
2003–04 Tranmere R 0 0
2004–05 Tranmere R 3 0
2005–06 Tranmere R 18 1 **21 1**

VAUGHAN, James (D) **0 0**
H: 5 10 W: 11 10 b.Liverpool 6-12-86
Source: Scholar.
2004–05 Tranmere R 0 0
2005–06 Tranmere R 0 0

WHITMORE, Theo (M) **117 14**
H: 5 11 W: 12 09 b.Montego Bay 5-8-72
Source: Seba U. *Honours:* Jamaica full caps.
1999–2000 Hull C 17 2
2000–01 Hull C 26 5
2001–02 Hull C 34 2 **77 9**
From Seba U
2003–04 Livingston 3 0 **3 0**
2004–05 Tranmere R 33 5
2005–06 Tranmere R 4 0 **37 5**

WILSON, Steve (G) **327 0**
H: 6 0 W: 11 02 b.Hull 24-4-74
Source: Trainee.
1990–91 Hull C 2 0
1991–92 Hull C 3 0
1992–93 Hull C 26 0
1993–94 Hull C 9 0
1994–95 Hull C 20 0
1995–96 Hull C 19 0
1996–97 Hull C 15 0
1997–98 Hull C 37 0
1998–99 Hull C 23 0
1999–2000 Hull C 27 0
2000–01 Hull C 0 0 **181 0**
2000–01 *Macclesfield T* 1 0
2001–02 Macclesfield T 38 0
2002–03 Macclesfield T 44 0
2003–04 Macclesfield T 32 0
2004–05 Macclesfield T 19 0 **134 0**
2005–06 Tranmere R 12 0 **12 0**

ZOLA, Calvin (F) **62 11**
H: 6 3 W: 14 06 b.Kinshasa 31-12-84
Source: Scholar.
2001–02 Newcastle U 0 0
2002–03 Newcastle U 0 0
2003–04 Newcastle U 0 0
2003–04 *Oldham Ath* 25 5 **25 5**
2004–05 Tranmere R 15 2
2005–06 Tranmere R 22 4 **37 6**

WALSALL (84)

ATIENO, Taiwo (F) **25 3**
H: 6 2 W: 12 13 b.Brixton 6-8-85
Source: Scholar.
2004–05 Walsall 3 0
2004–05 *Rochdale* 13 2 **13 2**
2004–05 *Chester C* 4 1 **4 1**
2005–06 Walsall 2 0 **5 0**
2005–06 *Darlington* 3 0 **3 0**

BARROWMAN, Andrew (F) **23 2**
H: 5 11 W: 11 06 b.Wishaw 27-11-84
Source: Scholar. *Honours:* Scotland Youth.
2001–02 Birmingham C 0 0
2002–03 Birmingham C 0 0
2003–04 Birmingham C 1 0
2003–04 *Crewe Alex* 4 1 **4 1**
2004–05 Birmingham C 0 0 **1 0**
2004–05 *Blackpool* 2 0 **2 0**
2004–05 Mansfield T 3 0
2005–06 Mansfield T 0 0 **3 0**
2005–06 Walsall 13 1 **13 1**

BRADLEY, Mark (D) **4 0**
H: 6 0 W: 11 05 b.Dudley 14-1-88
Source: Scholar.
2004–05 Walsall 1 0
2005–06 Walsall 3 0 **4 0**

BROAD, Joseph (M) **38 0**
H: 5 11 W: 12 07 b.Bristol 24-8-82
Source: Trainee.
2000–01 Plymouth Arg 0 0
2001–02 Plymouth Arg 7 0
2002–03 Plymouth Arg 5 0
2003–04 Plymouth Arg 0 0 **12 0**
2003–04 Torquay U 14 0 **14 0**
2004–05 Walsall 10 0
2005–06 Walsall 2 0 **12 0**

CLAYTON, Lee (D) **0 0**
H: 6 1 W: 11 08 b.Wolverhampton 24-3-88
Source: Scholar.
2005–06 Walsall 0 0

COLEMAN, Dean (G) **2 0**
H: 6 1 W: 12 10 b.Dudley 18-9-85
Source: Scholar.
2004–05 Walsall 2 0
2005–06 Walsall 0 0 **2 0**

CONSTABLE, James (F) **17 3**
H: 6 2 W: 12 12 b.Malmesbury 4-10-84
Source: Chippenham T.
2005–06 Walsall 17 3 **17 3**

DANN, Scott (D) **1 0**
H: 6 2 W: 12 00 b.Liverpool 14-2-87
Source: Scholar.
2004–05 Walsall 1 0
2005–06 Walsall 0 0 **1 0**

DEAKIN, Graham (M) **0 0**
H: 5 10 W: 11 05 b.Birmingham 24-4-87
Source: Scholar.
2005–06 Walsall 0 0

DEMONTAGNAC, Ishmel (F) **24 2**
H: 5 10 W: 11 05 b.London 15-6-88
Source: Charlton Ath Scholar. *Honours:* England Youth.
2005–06 Walsall 24 2 **24 2**

DEVLIN, Paul (M) **503 88**
H: 5 7 W: 11 13 b.Birmingham 14-4-72
Source: Stafford R. *Honours:* Scotland 10 full caps.
1991–92 Notts Co 2 0
1992–93 Notts Co 32 3
1993–94 Notts Co 41 7
1994–95 Notts Co 40 9
1995–96 Notts Co 26 6
1995–96 Birmingham C 16 7
1996–97 Birmingham C 38 16
1997–98 Birmingham C 22 5
1997–98 Sheffield U 10 1
1998–99 Sheffield U 33 5
1998–99 *Notts Co* 5 0 **146 25**
1999–2000 Sheffield U 44 11
2000–01 Sheffield U 41 5
2001–02 Sheffield U 19 2 **147 24**
2001–02 Birmingham C 13 1
2002–03 Birmingham C 32 3
2003–04 Birmingham C 2 0 **123 32**
2003–04 Watford 39 3
2004–05 Watford 17 1
2005–06 Watford 23 2 **79 6**
2005–06 Walsall 8 1 **8 1**

FOX, Daniel (D) **44 1**
H: 5 11 W: 12 06 b.Crewe 29-5-86
Source: Scholar.
2004–05 Everton 0 0
2004–05 *Stranraer* 11 1 **11 1**
2005–06 Walsall 33 0 **33 0**

GERRARD, Anthony (D) 42 0
H: 6 2 W: 13 07 b.Liverpool 6-2-86
Source: Scholar.
2004–05 Everton 0 0
2004–05 *Walsall* 8 0
2005–06 Walsall 34 0 **42 0**

GILMARTIN, Rene (G) 2 0
H: 6 5 W: 13 06 b.Dublin 31-5-87
Source: St Patrick's BC. *Honours:* Eire Youth, Under-21.
2005–06 Walsall 2 0 **2 0**

HARKNESS, Jonny (M) 2 0
H: 5 11 W: 11 12 b.Belfast 18-11-85
Source: Scholar. *Honours:* Northern Ireland Youth.
2004–05 Walsall 1 0
2005–06 Walsall 1 0 **2 0**

KEATES, Dean (M) 293 26
H: 5 6 W: 10 06 b.Walsall 30-6-78
Source: Trainee.
1996–97 Walsall 2 0
1997–98 Walsall 33 1
1998–99 Walsall 43 2
1999–2000 Walsall 35 1
2000–01 Walsall 33 4
2001–02 Walsall 13 1
2002–03 Hull C 36 4
2003–04 Hull C 14 0 **50 4**
2003–04 Kidderminster H 8 2
2004–05 Kidderminster H 41 5 **49 7**
2005–06 Lincoln C 21 4 **21 4**
2005–06 Walsall 14 2 **173 11**

KINSELLA, Mark (M) 458 47
H: 5 8 W: 11 04 b.Dublin 12-8-72
Source: Home Farm. *Honours:* Eire 48 full caps, 3 goals.
1989–90 Colchester U 6 0
1990–91 Colchester U 0 0
1991–92 Colchester U 0 0
1992–93 Colchester U 38 6
1993–94 Colchester U 42 8
1994–95 Colchester U 42 6
1995–96 Colchester U 45 5
1996–97 Colchester U 7 2 **180 27**
1996–97 Charlton Ath 37 6
1997–98 Charlton Ath 46 6
1998–99 Charlton Ath 38 2
1999–2000 Charlton Ath 38 3
2000–01 Charlton Ath 32 2
2001–02 Charlton Ath 17 0
2002–03 Charlton Ath 0 0 **208 19**
2002–03 Aston Villa 19 0
2003–04 Aston Villa 2 0 **21 0**
2003–04 WBA 18 1 **18 1**
2004–05 Walsall 22 0
2005–06 Walsall 9 0 **31 0**

LARROSA, Ruben Dario (F) 7 0
H: 6 2 W: 13 09 b.Buenos Aires 4-12-79
Source: Perlis FC.
2005–06 Walsall 7 0 **7 0**

LEITAO, Jorge (F) 230 57
H: 5 11 W: 13 04 b.Oporto 14-1-74
Source: Feirense.
2000–01 Walsall 44 18
2001–02 Walsall 38 8
2002–03 Walsall 44 11
2003–04 Walsall 39 7
2004–05 Walsall 42 8
2005–06 Walsall 23 5 **230 57**

McDERMOTT, David (M) 1 0
H: 5 5 W: 10 00 b.Stourbridge 6-2-88
Source: Scholar.
2004–05 Walsall 0 0
2005–06 Walsall 1 0 **1 0**

McKEOWN, James (G) 0 0
H: 6 1 W: 13 07 b.Birmingham 24-7-89
Source: Scholar.
2005–06 Walsall 0 0

MERSON, Paul (M) 621 125
H: 6 0 W: 13 02 b.Harlesden 20-3-68
Source: Apprentice. *Honours:* England Youth, Under-21, B, 21 full caps, 3 goals.
1985–86 Arsenal 0 0
1986–87 Arsenal 7 3
1986–87 *Brentford* 7 0 **7 0**
1987–88 Arsenal 15 5
1988–89 Arsenal 37 10
1989–90 Arsenal 29 7
1990–91 Arsenal 37 13
1991–92 Arsenal 42 12
1992–93 Arsenal 33 6
1993–94 Arsenal 33 7
1994–95 Arsenal 24 4
1995–96 Arsenal 38 5
1996–97 Arsenal 32 6 **327 78**
1997–98 Middlesbrough 45 11
1998–99 Middlesbrough 3 0 **48 11**
1998–99 Aston Villa 26 5
1999–2000 Aston Villa 32 5
2000–01 Aston Villa 38 6
2001–02 Aston Villa 21 2 **117 18**
2002–03 Portsmouth 45 12 **45 12**
2003–04 Walsall 34 4
2004–05 Walsall 36 2
2005–06 Walsall 7 0 **77 6**

NICHOLLS, Alex (F) 8 0
H: 5 10 W: 11 00 b.Stourbridge 9-12-87
Source: Scholar.
2005–06 Walsall 8 0 **8 0**

OAKES, Andy (G) 97 0
H: 6 3 W: 12 04 b.Northwich 11-1-77
Source: Burnley Trainee.
1995–96 Bury 0 0
1996–97 Bury 0 0
1997–98 Bury 0 0
From Winsford U.
1998–99 Hull C 19 0 **19 0**
1999–2000 Derby Co 0 0
1999–2000 *Port Vale* 0 0
2000–01 Derby Co 6 0
2001–02 Derby Co 20 0
2002–03 Derby Co 7 0
2003–04 Derby Co 10 0
2004–05 Derby Co 0 0 **43 0**
2004–05 *Bolton W* 1 0 **1 0**
2004–05 Walsall 9 0
2005–06 Walsall 25 0 **34 0**

OSBORN, Simon (M) 433 33
H: 5 9 W: 11 04 b.Croydon 19-1-72
Source: Apprentice.
1989–90 Crystal Palace 0 0
1990–91 Crystal Palace 4 0
1991–92 Crystal Palace 14 2
1992–93 Crystal Palace 31 2
1993–94 Crystal Palace 6 1 **55 5**
1994–95 Reading 32 5 **32 5**
1995–96 QPR 9 1 **9 1**
1995–96 Wolverhampton W 21 2
1996–97 Wolverhampton W 35 5
1997–98 Wolverhampton W 24 2
1998–99 Wolverhampton W 37 2
1999–2000 Wolverhampton W 25 0
2000–01 Wolverhampton W 20 0 **162 11**
2000–01 Tranmere R 9 1 **9 1**
2001–02 Port Vale 7 0 **7 0**
2001–02 Gillingham 28 4
2002–03 Gillingham 18 1 **46 5**
2003–04 Walsall 43 3
2004–05 Walsall 38 0
2005–06 Walsall 32 2 **113 5**

PEAD, Craig (M) 94 3
H: 5 9 W: 11 06 b.Bromsgrove 15-9-81
Source: Trainee. *Honours:* England Youth, Under-20.
1998–99 Coventry C 0 0
1999–2000 Coventry C 0 0
2000–01 Coventry C 0 0
2001–02 Coventry C 1 0
2002–03 Coventry C 24 2
2003–04 Coventry C 17 1
2004–05 Coventry C 0 0 **42 3**
2004–05 *Notts Co* 5 0 **5 0**
2004–05 *Walsall* 8 0
2005–06 Walsall 39 0 **47 0**

PLATT, Sean (M) 0 0
H: 5 9 W: 11 05 b.Bloxwich 21-10-85
Source: Scholar.
2005–06 Walsall 0 0

ROPER, Ian (D) 279 2
H: 6 3 W: 14 00 b.Nuneaton 20-6-77
Source: Trainee.
1994–95 Walsall 0 0
1995–96 Walsall 5 0
1996–97 Walsall 11 0
1997–98 Walsall 21 0
1998–99 Walsall 32 1
1999–2000 Walsall 34 1
2000–01 Walsall 25 0
2001–02 Walsall 27 0
2002–03 Walsall 40 0
2003–04 Walsall 33 0
2004–05 Walsall 26 0
2005–06 Walsall 25 0 **279 2**

SMITH, Emmanuel (D) 0 0
H: 6 2 W: 12 03 b.Birmingham 8-11-88
Source: Scholar.
2005–06 Walsall 0 0

STANDING, Michael (M) 82 6
H: 5 10 W: 10 07 b.Shoreham 20-3-81
Source: Trainee. *Honours:* England Schools.
1997–98 Aston Villa 0 0
1998–99 Aston Villa 0 0
1999–2000 Aston Villa 0 0
2000–01 Aston Villa 0 0
2001–02 Aston Villa 0 0
2001–02 Bradford C 0 0
2002–03 Bradford C 24 2
2003–04 Bradford C 6 0 **30 2**
2004–05 Walsall 32 4
2005–06 Walsall 20 0 **52 4**

STAUNTON, Steve (D) 481 21
H: 6 0 W: 12 12 b.Drogheda 19-1-69
Source: Dundalk. *Honours:* Eire Under-21, 102 full caps, 7 goals.
1986–87 Liverpool 0 0
1987–88 Liverpool 0 0
1987–88 *Bradford C* 8 0 **8 0**
1988–89 Liverpool 21 0
1989–90 Liverpool 20 0
1990–91 Liverpool 24 0
1991–92 Aston Villa 37 4
1992–93 Aston Villa 42 2
1993–94 Aston Villa 24 2
1994–95 Aston Villa 35 5
1995–96 Aston Villa 13 0
1996–97 Aston Villa 30 2
1997–98 Aston Villa 27 1
1998–99 Liverpool 31 0
1999–2000 Liverpool 12 0
2000–01 Liverpool 1 0 **109 0**
2000–01 *Crystal Palace* 6 1 **6 1**
2000–01 Aston Villa 14 0
2001–02 Aston Villa 33 0
2002–03 Aston Villa 26 0
2003–04 Aston Villa 0 0 **281 16**
2003–04 Coventry C 35 3
2004–05 Coventry C 35 1 **70 4**
2005–06 Walsall 7 0 **7 0**

SZTYBEL, Jay (M) 1 0
H: 5 9 W: 11 00 b.Redditch 11-10-87
Source: Scholar.
2005–06 Walsall 1 0 **1 0**

TAYLOR, Daryl (F) 30 3
H: 5 10 W: 11 03 b.Birmingham 14-11-84
Source: Scholar.
2004–05 Walsall 19 3
2005–06 Walsall 11 0 **30 3**

TAYLOR, Kris (M) 45 5
H: 5 9 W: 11 05 b.Stafford 12-1-84
Source: Scholar. *Honours:* England Schools, Youth.
2000–01 Manchester U 0 0
2001–02 Manchester U 0 0
2002–03 Manchester U 0 0
2002–03 Walsall 0 0
2003–04 Walsall 11 1
2004–05 Walsall 12 2
2005–06 Walsall 22 2 **45 5**

TILT, Luke (G) 1 0
H: 6 1 W: 12 00 b.Dudley 28-6-88
Source: Scholar.
2005–06 Walsall 1 0 **1 0**

VAUGHAN, Lee (D)				**0**	**0**
H: 5 7 W: 11 00 b.Birmingham 15-7-86					
Source: Scholar.					
2005–06	Walsall	0	0		

WESTWOOD, Chris (D)				**283**	**11**
H: 5 11 W: 12 10 b.Dudley 13-2-77					
Source: Trainee.					
1995–96	Wolverhampton W	0	0		
1996–97	Wolverhampton W	0	0		
1997–98	Wolverhampton W	4	1		
1998–99	Wolverhampton W	0	0	**4**	**1**
1998–99	Hartlepool U	4	0		
1999–2000	Hartlepool U	37	0		
2000–01	Hartlepool U	46	1		
2001–02	Hartlepool U	35	1		
2002–03	Hartlepool U	46	1		
2003–04	Hartlepool U	45	0		
2004–05	Hartlepool U	37	4	**250**	**7**
2005–06	Walsall	29	3	**29**	**3**

WRACK, Darren (M)				**324**	**46**
H: 5 9 W: 12 02 b.Cleethorpes 5-5-76					
Source: Trainee.					
1994–95	Derby Co	16	1		
1995–96	Derby Co	10	0	**26**	**1**
1996–97	Grimsby T	12	1		
1996–97	*Shrewsbury T*	4	0	**4**	**0**
1997–98	Grimsby T	1	0	**13**	**1**
1998–99	Walsall	46	13		
1999–2000	Walsall	44	4		
2000–01	Walsall	28	4		
2001–02	Walsall	43	4		
2002–03	Walsall	43	6		
2003–04	Walsall	27	6		
2004–05	Walsall	43	7		
2005–06	Walsall	7	0	**281**	**44**

WRIGHT, Mark (M)				**87**	**6**
H: 5 11 W: 11 00 b.Wolverhampton 24-2-82					
Source: Scholar.					
2000–01	Walsall	4	0		
2001–02	Walsall	0	0		
2002–03	Walsall	5	0		
2003–04	Walsall	11	2		
2004–05	Walsall	37	2		
2005–06	Walsall	30	2	**87**	**6**

WATFORD (85)

BANGURA, Alhassan (M)				**37**	**1**
H: 5 11 W: 10 07 b.Freetown 24-1-88					
Source: Scholar.					
2004–05	Watford	2	0		
2005–06	Watford	35	1	**37**	**1**

BLIZZARD, Dominic (M)				**29**	**2**
H: 6 2 W: 12 04 b.High Wycombe 2-9-83					
Source: Scholar.					
2001–02	Watford	0	0		
2002–03	Watford	0	0		
2003–04	Watford	2	1		
2004–05	Watford	17	1		
2005–06	Watford	10	0	**29**	**2**

BOUAZZA, Hameur (F)				**64**	**5**
H: 5 10 W: 12 01 b.Evry 22-2-85					
Source: Scholar.					
2003–04	Watford	9	1		
2004–05	Watford	28	1		
2005–06	Watford	14	1	**51**	**3**
2005–06	*Swindon T*	13	2	**13**	**2**

CAMPANA, Alex (M)				**0**	**0**
H: 5 11 W: 12 01 b.Harrow 11-10-88					
Source: Scholar.					
2005–06	Watford	0	0		

CARLISLE, Clarke (D)				**256**	**20**
H: 6 2 W: 14 11 b.Preston 14-10-79					
Source: Trainee. *Honours:* England Under-21.					
1997–98	Blackpool	11	2		
1998–99	Blackpool	39	1		
1999–2000	Blackpool	43	4	**93**	**7**
2000–01	QPR	27	3		
2001–02	QPR	0	0		
2002–03	QPR	36	2		
2003–04	QPR	33	1	**96**	**6**
2004–05	Leeds U	35	4	**35**	**4**
2005–06	Watford	32	3	**32**	**3**

CHAMBERLAIN, Alec (G)				**678**	**0**
H: 6 1 W: 14 01 b.March 20-6-64					
Source: Ramsey T.					
1981–82	Ipswich T	0	0		
1982–83	Colchester U	4	0		
1983–84	Colchester U	46	0		
1984–85	Colchester U	46	0		
1985–86	Colchester U	46	0		
1986–87	Colchester U	46	0	**188**	**0**
1987–88	Everton	0	0		
1987–88	*Tranmere R*	15	0	**15**	**0**
1988–89	Luton T	6	0		
1989–90	Luton T	38	0		
1990–91	Luton T	38	0		
1991–92	Luton T	24	0		
1992–93	Luton T	32	0	**138**	**0**
1992–93	*Chelsea*	0	0		
1993–94	Sunderland	43	0		
1994–95	Sunderland	18	0		
1994–95	*Liverpool*	0	0		
1995–96	Sunderland	29	0	**90**	**0**
1996–97	Watford	4	0		
1997–98	Watford	46	0		
1998–99	Watford	46	0		
1999–2000	Watford	27	0		
2000–01	Watford	21	0		
2001–02	Watford	32	0		
2002–03	Watford	42	0		
2003–04	Watford	21	0		
2004–05	Watford	5	0		
2005–06	Watford	3	0	**247**	**0**

CHAMBERS, James (D)				**151**	**0**
H: 5 10 W: 11 11 b.West Bromwich 20-11-80					
Source: Trainee. *Honours:* England Youth.					
1998–99	WBA	0	0		
1999–2000	WBA	12	0		
2000–01	WBA	31	0		
2001–02	WBA	5	0		
2002–03	WBA	8	0		
2003–04	WBA	17	0		
2004–05	WBA	0	0	**73**	**0**
2004–05	Watford	40	0		
2005–06	Watford	38	0	**78**	**0**

DEMERIT, Jay (D)				**56**	**5**
H: 6 2 W: 12 13 b.Green Bay 4-12-79					
Source: Chicago Fire, Univ of Illinois, Northwood.					
2004–05	Watford	24	3		
2005 06	Watford	32	2	**56**	**5**

DIAGOURAGA, Toumani (M)				**9**	**0**
H: 6 2 W: 11 05 b.Corbeil-Essones 10-6-87					
Source: Scholar.					
2004–05	Watford	0	0		
2005–06	Watford	1	0	**1**	**0**
2005–06	*Swindon T*	8	0	**8**	**0**

DOYLEY, Lloyd (D)				**124**	**0**
H: 5 10 W: 12 13 b.Whitechapel 1-12-82					
Source: Scholar.					
2000–01	Watford	0	0		
2001–02	Watford	20	0		
2002–03	Watford	22	0		
2003–04	Watford	9	0		
2004–05	Watford	29	0		
2005–06	Watford	44	0	**124**	**0**

FERDINAND, Les (F)				**443**	**184**
H: 5 11 W: 13 05 b.Acton 8-12-66					
Source: Hayes. *Honours:* England B, 17 full caps, 5 goals.					
1986–87	QPR	2	0		
1987–88	QPR	1	0		
1987–88	*Brentford*	3	0	**3**	**0**
1988–89	QPR	0	0		
1988–89	*Besiktas*	24	14	**24**	**14**
1989–90	QPR	9	2		
1990–91	QPR	18	8		
1991–92	QPR	23	10		
1992–93	QPR	37	20		
1993–94	QPR	36	16		
1994–95	QPR	37	24	**163**	**80**
1995–96	Newcastle U	37	25		
1996–97	Newcastle U	31	16	**68**	**41**
1997–98	Tottenham H	21	5		
1998–99	Tottenham H	24	5		
1999–2000	Tottenham H	9	2		
2000–01	Tottenham H	28	10		
2001–02	Tottenham H	25	9		
2002–03	Tottenham H	11	2	**118**	**33**
2002–03	West Ham U	14	2	**14**	**2**
2003–04	Leicester C	29	12	**29**	**12**
2004–05	Bolton W	12	1	**12**	**1**
2004–05	Reading	12	1	**12**	**1**
2005–06	Watford	0	0		

FRANCIS, Fran (M)				**1**	**0**
H: 6 2 W: 14 03 b.Jamaica 18-1-87					
Source: Stoke C Scholar.					
2005–06	Watford	1	0	**1**	**0**

GILL, Ben (M)				**0**	**0**
H: 5 9 W: 10 11 b.Harrow 9-10-87					
Source: Scholar.					
2005–06	Watford	0	0		

GRANT, Joel (F)				**7**	**0**
H: 6 0 W: 12 01 b.Hammersmith 26-8-87					
Source: Scholar.					
2005–06	Watford	7	0	**7**	**0**

HAND, Jamie (M)				**86**	**0**
H: 6 0 W: 11 08 b.Uxbridge 7-2-84					
Source: Scholar. *Honours:* England Youth.					
2001–02	Watford	10	0		
2002–03	Watford	23	0		
2003–04	Watford	22	0		
2004–05	Watford	0	0		
2004–05	*Oxford U*	11	0	**11**	**0**
2005–06	Watford	0	0	**55**	**0**
2005–06	*Peterborough U*	9	0	**9**	**0**
From Fisher Ath.					
2005–06	Northampton T			**11**	**0**

HENDERSON, Darius (F)				**153**	**41**
H: 6 3 W: 14 03 b.Sutton 7-9-81					
Source: Trainee.					
1999–2000	Reading	6	0		
2000–01	Reading	4	0		
2001–02	Reading	38	7		
2002–03	Reading	22	4		
2003–04	Reading	1	0	**71**	**11**
2003–04	*Brighton & HA*	10	2	**10**	**2**
2003–04	Gillingham	4	0		
2004–05	Gillingham	32	9	**36**	**9**
2004–05	*Swindon T*	6	5	**6**	**5**
2005–06	Watford	30	14	**30**	**14**

KING, Marlon (F)				**254**	**85**
H: 5 10 W: 12 10 b.Dulwich 26-4-80					
Source: Trainee. *Honours:* Jamaica 11 full caps.					
1998–99	Barnet	22	6		
1999–2000	Barnet	31	8	**53**	**14**
2000–01	Gillingham	38	15		
2001–02	Gillingham	42	17		
2002–03	Gillingham	10	4		
2003–04	Gillingham	11	4	**101**	**40**
2003–04	Nottingham F	24	5		
2004–05	Nottingham F	26	5		
2004–05	*Leeds U*	9	0	**9**	**0**
2005–06	Nottingham F	0	0	**50**	**10**
2005–06	Watford	41	21	**41**	**21**

LEE, Richard (G)				**37**	**0**
H: 6 0 W: 12 06 b.Oxford 5-10-82					
Source: Scholar. *Honours:* England Under-20.					
2000–01	Watford	0	0		
2001–02	Watford	0	0		
2002–03	Watford	4	0		
2003–04	Watford	0	0		
2004–05	Watford	33	0		
2005–06	Watford	0	0	**37**	**0**
2005–06	*Blackburn R*	0	0		

MACKAY, Malky (D)				**375**	**30**
H: 6 2 W: 14 07 b.Bellshill 19-2-72					
Source: Queen's Park Youth. *Honours:* Scotland 5 full caps.					
1990–91	Queen's Park	10	0		
1991–92	Queen's Park	27	3		
1992–93	Queen's Park	33	3	**70**	**6**
1993–94	Celtic	0	0		
1994–95	Celtic	1	0		
1995–96	Celtic	11	1		
1996–97	Celtic	20	1		
1997–98	Celtic	4	1		

1998–99 Celtic 1 1 **37 4**
1998–99 Norwich C 27 1
1999–2000 Norwich C 21 0
2000–01 Norwich C 38 1
2001–02 Norwich C 44 3
2002–03 Norwich C 37 6
2003–04 Norwich C 45 4
2004–05 Norwich C 0 0 **212 15**
2004–05 West Ham U 18 2
2005–06 West Ham U 0 0 **18 2**
2005–06 Watford 38 3 **38 3**

MAHON, Gavin (M) 288 14
H: 5 11 W: 13 07 b.Birmingham 2-1-77
Source: Trainee.
1995–96 Wolverhampton W 0 0
1996–97 Hereford U 11 1
1997–98 Hereford U 0 0
1998–99 Hereford U 0 0 **11 1**
1998–99 Brentford 29 4
1999–2000 Brentford 37 3
2000–01 Brentford 40 1
2001–02 Brentford 35 0 **141 8**
2001–02 Watford 6 0
2002–03 Watford 17 0
2003–04 Watford 32 2
2004–05 Watford 43 0
2005–06 Watford 38 3 **136 5**

MARIAPPA, Adrian (D) 3 0
H: 5 10 W: 11 12 b.Harrow 3-10-86
Source: Scholar.
2005–06 Watford 3 0 **3 0**

McNAMEE, Anthony (M) 84 2
H: 5 6 W: 10 03 b.Kensington 13-7-84
Source: Scholar. *Honours:* England Youth, Under-20.
2001–02 Watford 7 1
2002–03 Watford 23 0
2003–04 Watford 2 0
2004–05 Watford 14 0
2005–06 Watford 38 1 **84 2**

OSBORNE, Junior (D) 2 0
H: 5 11 W: 11 13 b.Watford 12-2-88
Source: Scholar.
2004–05 Watford 1 0
2005–06 Watford 1 0 **2 0**

ROBINSON, Theo (M) 1 0
b.Birmingham 22-1-89
Source: Scholar.
2005–06 Watford 1 0 **1 0**

SIETES, Jose Riva (D) 281 5
H: 5 10 W: 11 07 b.Sietes 18-2-74
1993–94 Oviedo B 26 1 **26 1**
1993–94 Oviedo 9 2
1994–95 Oviedo 31 0 **40 2**
1995–96 Valencia 20 1
1996–97 Valencia 9 0 **29 1**
1997–98 Racing 32 1
1998–99 Racing 34 0
1999–2000 Racing 32 0
2000–01 Racing 20 0
2001–02 Racing 39 0
2002–03 Racing 17 0 **174 1**
2003–04 Alaves 12 0 **12 0**
2004–05 Murcia 0 0
2005–06 Watford 0 0

SPRING, Matthew (M) 302 34
H: 5 11 W: 12 05 b.Harlow 17-11-79
Source: Trainee.
1997–98 Luton T 12 0
1998–99 Luton T 45 3
1999–2000 Luton T 45 6
2000–01 Luton T 41 4
2001–02 Luton T 42 6
2002–03 Luton T 41 5
2003–04 Luton T 24 1 **250 25**
2004–05 Leeds U 13 1
2005–06 Leeds U 0 0 **13 1**
2005–06 Watford 39 8 **39 8**

STEWART, Jordan (D) 149 6
H: 6 0 W: 12 09 b.Birmingham 3-3-82
Source: Trainee. *Honours:* England Youth, Under-21.
1999–2000 Leicester C 1 0
1999–2000 *Bristol R* 4 0 **4 0**
2000–01 Leicester C 0 0
2001–02 Leicester C 12 0
2002–03 Leicester C 37 4
2003–04 Leicester C 25 1
2004–05 Leicester C 35 1 **110 6**
2005–06 Watford 35 0 **35 0**

YOUNG, Ashley (M) 78 16
H: 5 10 W: 10 03 b.Stevenage 9-7-85
Source: Juniors.
2002–03 Watford 0 0
2003–04 Watford 5 3
2004–05 Watford 34 0
2005–06 Watford 39 13 **78 16**

WBA (86)

ALBRECHTSEN, Martin (D) 216 4
H: 6 1 W: 12 13 b.Copenhagen 31-3-80
Honours: Denmark Youth, Under-21, 3 full caps.
1998–99 Aalborg 9 1
1999–2000 Aalborg 31 1
2000–01 Aalborg 30 0
2001–02 Aalborg 19 1 **89 3**
2001–02 FC Copenhagen 14 0
2002–03 FC Copenhagen 27 0
2003–04 FC Copenhagen 31 0 **72 0**
2004–05 WBA 24 0
2005–06 WBA 31 1 **55 1**

CAMPBELL, Kevin (F) 480 148
H: 6 0 W: 13 08 b.Lambeth 4-2-70
Source: Trainee. *Honours:* England Under-21, B.
1987–88 Arsenal 1 0
1988–89 Arsenal 0 0
1988–89 *Leyton Orient* 16 9 **16 9**
1989–90 Arsenal 15 2
1989–90 *Leicester C* 11 5 **11 5**
1990–91 Arsenal 22 9
1991–92 Arsenal 31 13
1992–93 Arsenal 37 4
1993–94 Arsenal 37 14
1994–95 Arsenal 23 4 **166 46**
1995–96 Nottingham F 21 3
1996–97 Nottingham F 17 6
1997–98 Nottingham F 42 23 **80 32**
1998–99 Trabzonspor 17 5 **17 5**
1998–99 Everton 8 9
1999–2000 Everton 26 12
2000–01 Everton 29 9
2001–02 Everton 23 4
2002–03 Everton 36 10
2003–04 Everton 17 1
2004–05 Everton 6 0 **145 45**
2004–05 WBA 16 3
2005–06 WBA 29 3 **45 6**

CARTER, Darren (M) 75 5
H: 6 2 W: 12 11 b.Solihull 18-12-83
Source: Scholar. *Honours:* England Youth, Under-20.
2001–02 Birmingham C 13 1
2002–03 Birmingham C 12 0
2003–04 Birmingham C 5 0
2004–05 Birmingham C 15 2 **45 3**
2004–05 *Sunderland* 10 1 **10 1**
2005–06 WBA 20 1 **20 1**

CHAPLOW, Richard (M) 87 8
H: 5 9 W: 9 03 b.Accrington 2-2-85
Source: Scholar. *Honours:* England Youth, Under-20, Under-21.
2002–03 Burnley 5 0
2003–04 Burnley 39 5
2004–05 Burnley 21 2 **65 7**
2004–05 WBA 4 0
2005–06 WBA 7 0 **11 0**
2005–06 *Southampton* 11 1 **11 1**

CLEMENT, Neil (D) 259 21
H: 6 0 W: 12 03 b.Reading 3-10-78
Source: Trainee. *Honours:* England Schools, Youth.
1995–96 Chelsea 0 0
1996–97 Chelsea 1 0
1997–98 Chelsea 0 0
1998–99 Chelsea 0 0
1998–99 *Reading* 11 1 **11 1**
1998–99 *Preston NE* 4 0 **4 0**
1999–2000 Chelsea 0 0 **1 0**
1999–2000 *Brentford* 8 0 **8 0**
1999–2000 *WBA* 8 0
2000–01 WBA 45 5
2001–02 WBA 45 6
2002–03 WBA 36 3
2003–04 WBA 35 2
2004–05 WBA 35 3
2005–06 WBA 31 1 **235 20**

DAVIES, Curtis (D) 89 4
H: 6 2 W: 11 13 b.Waltham Forest 15-3-85
Source: Scholar. *Honours:* England Under-21.
2003–04 Luton T 6 0
2004–05 Luton T 44 1
2005–06 Luton T 6 1 **56 2**
2005–06 WBA 33 2 **33 2**

DAVIES, Rob (M) 0 0
H: 5 9 W: 11 02 b.Tywyn 24-3-87
Source: Scholar. *Honours:* Wales Under-21.
2005–06 WBA 0 0

ELLINGTON, Nathan (F) 281 99
H: 5 10 W: 13 01 b.Bradford 2-7-81
Source: Walton & Hersham.
1998–99 Bristol R 10 1
1999–2000 Bristol R 37 4
2000–01 Bristol R 42 15
2001–02 Bristol R 27 15 **116 35**
2001–02 Wigan Ath 3 2
2002–03 Wigan Ath 42 15
2003–04 Wigan Ath 44 18
2004–05 Wigan Ath 45 24 **134 59**
2005–06 WBA 31 5 **31 5**

ELVINS, Rob (F) 0 0
b.Alvechurch 17-9-86
Source: Scholar.
2005–06 WBA 0 0

FORSYTH, Jeff (D) 0 0
H: 5 10 W: 12 02 b.Hexham 14-10-87
Source: Scholar.
2005–06 WBA 0 0

GAARDSOE, Thomas (D) 184 14
H: 6 2 W: 12 08 b.Randers 23-11-79
Honours: Denmark Under-23, 2 full caps, 1 goal.
1996–97 Aalborg 1 0
1997–98 Aalborg 6 1
1998–99 Aalborg 17 2
1999–2000 Aalborg 18 2
2000–01 Aalborg 20 0 **62 5**
2001–02 Ipswich T 4 1
2002–03 Ipswich T 37 4 **41 5**
2003–04 WBA 45 4
2004–05 WBA 29 0
2005–06 WBA 7 0 **81 4**

GERA, Zoltan (M) 183 44
H: 6 0 W: 11 11 b.Pecs 22-4-79
Source: Hakarny. *Honours:* Hungary 35 full caps, 9 goals.
1999–2000 Pecsi 15 4 **15 4**
2000–01 Ferencvaros 32 7
2001–02 Ferencvaros 27 8
2002–03 Ferencvaros 26 6
2003–04 Ferencvaros 30 11 **115 32**
2004–05 WBA 38 6
2005–06 WBA 15 2 **53 8**

GREENING, Jonathan (M) 210 8
H: 5 11 W: 11 00 b.Scarborough 2-1-79
Source: Trainee. *Honours:* England Youth, Under-21.
1996–97 York C 5 0
1997–98 York C 20 2 **25 2**
1997–98 Manchester U 0 0
1998–99 Manchester U 3 0
1999–2000 Manchester U 4 0
2000–01 Manchester U 7 0 **14 0**
2001–02 Middlesbrough 36 1
2002–03 Middlesbrough 38 2
2003–04 Middlesbrough 25 1 **99 4**
2004–05 WBA 34 0
2005–06 WBA 38 2 **72 2**

HODGKISS, Jared (M) **1 0**
H: 5 6 W: 11 02 b.Stafford 15-11-86
Source: Scholar.

2005–06	WBA	1	0	**1**	**0**

HORSFIELD, Geoff (F) **275 74**
H: 6 0 W: 11 07 b.Barnsley 1-11-73

1992–93	Scarborough	6	1		
1993–94	Scarborough	6	0	**12**	**1**
From Witton Alb					
1998–99	Halifax T	10	7	**10**	**7**
1998–99	Fulham	28	15		
1999–2000	Fulham	31	7	**59**	**22**
2000–01	Birmingham C	34	7		
2001–02	Birmingham C	40	11		
2002–03	Birmingham C	31	5		
2003–04	Birmingham C	3	0	**108**	**23**
2003–04	Wigan Ath	16	7	**16**	**7**
2003–04	WBA	20	7		
2004–05	WBA	29	3		
2005–06	WBA	18	4	**67**	**14**
2005–06	*Sheffield U*	3	0	**3**	**0**

HOULT, Russell (G) **378 0**
H: 6 3 W: 14 09 b.Ashby 22-11-72
Source: Trainee.

1990–91	Leicester C	0	0		
1991–92	Leicester C	0	0		
1991–92	*Lincoln C*	2	0		
1991–92	*Blackpool*	0	0		
1992–93	Leicester C	10	0		
1993–94	Leicester C	0	0		
1993–94	*Bolton W*	4	0	**4**	**0**
1994–95	Leicester C	0	0	**10**	**0**
1994–95	*Lincoln C*	15	0	**17**	**0**
1994–95	*Derby Co*	15	0		
1995–96	Derby Co	41	0		
1996–97	Derby Co	32	0		
1997–98	Derby Co	2	0		
1998–99	Derby Co	23	0		
1999–2000	Derby Co	10	0	**123**	**0**
1999–2000	Portsmouth	18	0		
2000–01	Portsmouth	22	0	**40**	**0**
2000–01	WBA	13	0		
2001–02	WBA	45	0		
2002–03	WBA	37	0		
2003–04	WBA	44	0		
2004–05	WBA	36	0		
2005–06	WBA	1	0	**176**	**0**
2005–06	*Nottingham F*	8	0	**8**	**0**

INAMOTO, Junichi (M) **198 20**
H: 6 0 W: 11 11 b.Kagoshima 18-9-79
Honours: Japan 65 full caps, 4 goals.

1997	Gamba Osaka	27	3		
1998	Gamba Osaka	28	6		
1999	Gamba Osaka	22	1		
2000	Gamba Osaka	28	4		
2001	Gamba Osaka	13	2	**118**	**16**
2001–02	Arsenal	0	0		
2002–03	Fulham	19	2		
2003–04	Fulham	22	2	**41**	**4**
2004–05	WBA	3	0		
2004–05	*Cardiff C*	14	0	**14**	**0**
2005–06	WBA	22	0	**25**	**0**

JOHNSON, Andy (M) **317 29**
H: 6 0 W: 13 00 b.Bristol 2-5-74
Source: Trainee. *Honours:* England Youth, Wales 15 full caps.

1991–92	Norwich C	2	0		
1992–93	Norwich C	2	1		
1993–94	Norwich C	2	0		
1994–95	Norwich C	7	0		
1995–96	Norwich C	26	7		
1996–97	Norwich C	27	5	**66**	**13**
1997–98	Nottingham F	34	4		
1998–99	Nottingham F	28	0		
1999–2000	Nottingham F	25	2		
2000–01	Nottingham F	31	3		
2001–02	Nottingham F	1	0	**119**	**9**
2001–02	WBA	32	4		
2002–03	WBA	32	1		
2003–04	WBA	38	2		
2004–05	WBA	22	0		
2005–06	WBA	8	0	**132**	**7**

KAMARA, Diomansy (F) **138 23**
H: 6 0 W: 11 05 b.Paris 8-11-80
Honours: Senegal full caps.

1999–2000	Catanzaro	11	4		
2000–01	Catanzaro	23	5	**34**	**9**
2001–02	Chievo	0	0		
2001–02	Modena	24	4		
2002–03	Modena	29	5	**53**	**9**
2004–05	Portsmouth	25	4	**25**	**4**
2005–06	WBA	26	1	**26**	**1**

KANU, Nwankwo (F) **298 78**
H: 6 5 W: 12 08 b.Owerri 1-8-76
Honours: Nigeria 42 full caps, 7 goals.

1991–92	Federation Works	30	9	**30**	**9**
1992–93	Iwanyanwu	30	6	**30**	**6**
1993–94	Ajax	6	2		
1994–95	Ajax	18	10		
1995–96	Ajax	30	13	**54**	**25**
1996–97	Internazionale	0	0		
1997–98	Internazionale	11	1		
1998–99	Internazionale	1	0	**12**	**1**
1998–99	Arsenal	12	6		
1999–2000	Arsenal	31	12		
2000–01	Arsenal	27	3		
2001–02	Arsenal	23	3		
2002–03	Arsenal	16	5		
2003–04	Arsenal	10	1	**119**	**30**
2004–05	WBA	28	2		
2005–06	WBA	25	5	**53**	**7**

KOUMAS, Jason (M) **255 51**
H: 5 10 W: 11 02 b.Wrexham 25-9-79
Source: Trainee. *Honours:* Wales 17 full caps, 1 goal.

1997–98	Tranmere R	0	0		
1998–99	Tranmere R	23	3		
1999–2000	Tranmere R	23	2		
2000–01	Tranmere R	39	10		
2001–02	Tranmere R	38	8		
2002–03	Tranmere R	4	2	**127**	**25**
2002–03	WBA	32	4		
2003–04	WBA	42	10		
2004–05	WBA	10	0		
2005–06	WBA	0	0	**84**	**14**
2005–06	*Cardiff C*	44	12	**44**	**12**

KUSZCZAK, Tomasz (G) **31 0**
H: 6 3 W: 13 03 b.Krosno Odrzansia 20-3-82
Source: Uerdingen. *Honours:* Poland 4 full caps.

2001–02	Hertha Berlin	0	0		
2002–03	Hertha Berlin	0	0		
2003–04	Hertha Berlin	0	0		
2004–05	WBA	3	0		
2005–06	WBA	28	0	**31**	**0**

MARTINEZ, Williams (D) **2 1**
H: 6 0 W: 12 00 b.Montevideo 18-12-82
Source: Defensor. *Honours:* Uruguay full caps.

2005–06	WBA	2	1	**2**	**1**

McGOVERN, Jamie (M) **0 0**

2005–06	WBA	0	0		

NICHOLSON, Stuart (F) **4 0**
H: 5 10 W: 11 09 b.Newcastle 3-2-86
Source: Scholar. *Honours:* England Youth.

2005–06	WBA	4	0	**4**	**0**

QUASHIE, Nigel (M) **295 24**
H: 6 0 W: 13 10 b.Peckham 20-7-78
Source: Trainee. *Honours:* England Youth, Under-21, B, Scotland 12 full caps, 1 goal.

1995–96	QPR	11	0		
1996–97	QPR	13	0		
1997–98	QPR	33	3		
1998–99	QPR	0	0	**57**	**3**
1998–99	Nottingham F	16	0		
1999–2000	Nottingham F	28	2	**44**	**2**
2000–01	Portsmouth	31	5		
2001–02	Portsmouth	35	2		
2002–03	Portsmouth	42	5		
2003–04	Portsmouth	21	1		
2004–05	Portsmouth	19	0	**148**	**13**
2004–05	Southampton	13	1		
2005–06	Southampton	24	4	**37**	**5**
2005–06	WBA	9	1	**9**	**1**

ROBINSON, Paul (D) **313 9**
H: 5 9 W: 11 12 b.Watford 14-12-78
Source: Trainee. *Honours:* England Under-21.

1996–97	Watford	12	0		
1997–98	Watford	22	2		
1998–99	Watford	29	0		
1999–2000	Watford	32	0		
2000–01	Watford	39	0		
2001–02	Watford	38	3		
2002–03	Watford	37	3		
2003–04	Watford	10	0	**219**	**8**
2003–04	WBA	31	0		
2004–05	WBA	30	1		
2005–06	WBA	33	0	**94**	**1**

SMIKLE, Brian (M) **0 0**
b.Tipton 3-11-85
Source: Scholar.

2005–06	WBA	0	0		

WALLWORK, Ronnie (M) **126 6**
H: 5 10 W: 12 09 b.Manchester 10-9-77
Source: Trainee. *Honours:* England Youth.

1994–95	Manchester U	0	0		
1995–96	Manchester U	0	0		
1996–97	Manchester U	0	0		
1997–98	Manchester U	1	0		
1997–98	*Carlisle U*	10	1	**10**	**1**
1997–98	*Stockport Co*	7	0	**7**	**0**
1998–99	Manchester U	0	0		
1999–2000	Manchester U	5	0		
2000–01	Manchester U	12	0		
2001–02	Manchester U	1	0	**19**	**0**
2002–03	WBA	27	0		
2003–04	WBA	5	0		
2003–04	*Bradford C*	7	4	**7**	**4**
2004–05	WBA	20	1		
2005–06	WBA	31	0	**83**	**1**

WATSON, Steve (D) **405 27**
H: 6 0 W: 12 07 b.North Shields 1-4-74
Source: Trainee. *Honours:* England Youth, Under-21, B.

1990–91	Newcastle U	24	0		
1991–92	Newcastle U	28	1		
1992–93	Newcastle U	2	0		
1993–94	Newcastle U	32	2		
1994–95	Newcastle U	27	4		
1995–96	Newcastle U	23	3		
1996–97	Newcastle U	36	1		
1997–98	Newcastle U	29	1		
1998–99	Newcastle U	7	0	**208**	**12**
1998–99	Aston Villa	27	0		
1999–2000	Aston Villa	14	0	**41**	**0**
2000–01	Everton	34	0		
2001–02	Everton	25	4		
2002–03	Everton	18	5		
2003–04	Everton	24	5		
2004–05	Everton	25	0	**126**	**14**
2005–06	WBA	30	1	**30**	**1**

Scholars
Baker, Lee; Bateman, John; Daniels, Luke Matthew; Darg, Rhys; Downing, Leigh; Manchester, Adrian; Mcdonald, Garth Rodgers; McGovern, Jaimie Eugene; McQuilkin, James Robbie Leonard; Nicholson, Dean Michael; Sissoko, Ibrahim.

WEST HAM U (87)

ASHIKODI, Moses (M) **9 0**
H: 6 0 W: 11 09 b.Lagos 27-6-87
Honours: FA Schools, England Youth.

2002–03	Millwall	5	0		
2003–04	Millwall	0	0	**5**	**0**
2004–05	West Ham U	0	0		
2005–06	West Ham U	0	0		
2005–06	*Gillingham*	4	0	**4**	**0**

To Rangers January 2006

ASHTON, Dean (F) **214 80**
H: 6 2 W: 14 07 b.Crewe 24-11-83
Source: Schoolboy. *Honours:* England Youth, Under-20, Under-21.

2000–01	Crewe Alex	21	8		
2001–02	Crewe Alex	31	7		
2002–03	Crewe Alex	39	9		

2003–04	Crewe Alex	44	19		
2004–05	Crewe Alex	24	17	**159**	**60**
2004–05	Norwich C	16	7		
2005–06	Norwich C	28	10	**44**	**17**
2005–06	West Ham U	11	3	**11**	**3**

BARADJI, Sekou (M) **1** **0**

H: 6 1 W: 12 02 b.Paris 24-4-84

2004–05	Le Mans	0	0		
2005–06	West Ham U	0	0		
2005–06	*Reading*	1	0	**1**	**0**

BENAYOUN, Yossi (M) **255** **86**

H: 5 10 W: 11 00 b.Beer Sheva 6-6-80

Honours: Israel 49 full caps, 11 goals.

1997–98	Hapoel Beer Sheva	25	15	**25**	**15**
1998–99	Maccabi Haifa	29	16		
1999–2000	Maccabi Haifa	38	19		
2000–01	Maccabi Haifa	37	13		
2001–02	Maccabi Haifa	26	7	**130**	**55**
2002–03	Santander	31	4		
2003–04	Santander	35	7		
2004–05	Santander	0	0	**66**	**11**
2005–06	West Ham U	34	5	**34**	**5**

BLEWITT, Darren (M) **1** **0**

H: 6 2 W: 13 00 b.Newham 3-9-85

Source: Scholar.

2004–05	West Ham U	0	0		
2004–05	*Southend U*	1	0	**1**	**0**
2005–06	West Ham U	0	0		

BYWATER, Steve (G) **79** **0**

H: 6 2 W: 12 10 b.Manchester 7-6-81

Source: Trainee. *Honours:* England Youth, Under-20, Under-21.

1997–98	Rochdale	0	0		
1998–99	West Ham U	0	0		
1999–2000	West Ham U	4	0		
1999–2000	*Wycombe W*	2	0	**2**	**0**
1999–2000	*Hull C*	4	0	**4**	**0**
2000–01	West Ham U	1	0		
2001–02	West Ham U	0	0		
2001–02	*Wolverhampton W*	0	0		
2001–02	*Cardiff C*	0	0		
2002–03	West Ham U	0	0		
2003–04	West Ham U	17	0		
2004–05	West Ham U	36	0		
2005–06	West Ham U	1	0	**59**	**0**
2005–06	*Coventry C*	14	0	**14**	**0**

CARROLL, Roy (G) **249** **0**

H: 6 2 W: 13 12 b.Enniskillen 30-9-77

Source: Trainee. *Honours:* Northern Ireland Youth, Under-21, 17 full caps.

1995–96	Hull C	23	0		
1996–97	Hull C	23	0	**46**	**0**
1996–97	Wigan Ath	0	0		
1997–98	Wigan Ath	29	0		
1998–99	Wigan Ath	43	0		
1999–2000	Wigan Ath	34	0		
2000–01	Wigan Ath	29	0	**135**	**0**
2001–02	Manchester U	7	0		
2002–03	Manchester U	10	0		
2003–04	Manchester U	6	0		
2004–05	Manchester U	26	0	**49**	**0**
2005–06	West Ham U	19	0	**19**	**0**

CLARKE, Clive (D) **225** **9**

H: 5 11 W: 12 03 b.Dublin 14-1-80

Source: Trainee. *Honours:* Eire Under-21, 2 full caps.

1996–97	Stoke C	0	0		
1997–98	Stoke C	0	0		
1998–99	Stoke C	2	0		
1999–2000	Stoke C	42	1		
2000–01	Stoke C	21	0		
2001–02	Stoke C	43	1		
2002–03	Stoke C	31	3		
2003–04	Stoke C	42	3		
2004–05	Stoke C	42	1	**223**	**9**
2005–06	West Ham U	2	0	**2**	**0**

COHEN, Chris (M) **48** **1**

H: 5 11 W: 10 11 b.Norwich 5-3-87

Source: Scholar. *Honours:* England Youth.

2003–04	West Ham U	7	0		
2004–05	West Ham U	11	0		
2005–06	West Ham U	0	0	**18**	**0**
2005–06	*Yeovil T*	30	1	**30**	**1**

COLLINS, James (D) **80** **5**

H: 6 2 W: 14 05 b.Newport 23-8-83

Source: Scholar. *Honours:* Wales Youth, Under-21, 13 full caps.

2000–01	Cardiff C	3	0		
2001–02	Cardiff C	7	1		
2002–03	Cardiff C	2	0		
2003–04	Cardiff C	20	1		
2004–05	Cardiff C	34	1	**66**	**3**
2005–06	West Ham U	14	2	**14**	**2**

DAILLY, Christian (D) **422** **28**

H: 6 1 W: 12 10 b.Dundee 23-10-73

Source: 'S' Form. *Honours:* Scotland Schools, Youth, Under-21, B, 61 full caps, 5 goals.

1990–91	Dundee U	18	5		
1991–92	Dundee U	8	0		
1992–93	Dundee U	14	4		
1993–94	Dundee U	38	4		
1994–95	Dundee U	33	4		
1995–96	Dundee U	30	1	**141**	**18**
1996–97	Derby Co	36	3		
1997–98	Derby Co	30	1		
1998–99	Derby Co	1	0	**67**	**4**
1998–99	Blackburn R	17	0		
1999–2000	Blackburn R	43	4		
2000–01	Blackburn R	10	0	**70**	**4**
2000–01	West Ham U	12	0		
2001–02	West Ham U	38	0		
2002–03	West Ham U	26	0		
2003–04	West Ham U	43	2		
2004–05	West Ham U	3	0		
2005–06	West Ham U	22	0	**144**	**2**

EPHRAIM, Hogan (F) **0** **0**

H: 5 9 W: 10 06 b.Islington 31-3-88

Source: Scholar. *Honours:* England Youth.

2004–05	West Ham U	0	0		
2005–06	West Ham U	0	0		

ETHERINGTON, Matthew (M) **216** **19**

H: 5 10 W: 10 12 b.Truro 14-8-81

Source: School. *Honours:* England Youth, Under-21.

1996–97	Peterborough U	1	0		
1997–98	Peterborough U	2	0		
1998–99	Peterborough U	29	3		
1999–2000	Peterborough U	19	3	**51**	**6**
1999–2000	Tottenham H	5	0		
2000–01	Tottenham H	6	0		
2001–02	*Bradford C*	13	1	**13**	**1**
2001–02	Tottenham H	11	0		
2002–03	Tottenham H	23	1	**45**	**1**
2003–04	West Ham U	35	5		
2004–05	West Ham U	39	4		
2005–06	West Ham U	33	2	**107**	**11**

FERDINAND, Anton (D) **82** **3**

H: 6 2 W: 11 00 b.Peckham 18-2-85

Source: Trainee. *Honours:* England Youth, Under-20, Under-21.

2002–03	West Ham U	0	0		
2003–04	West Ham U	20	0		
2004–05	West Ham U	29	1		
2005–06	West Ham U	33	2	**82**	**3**

FITZGERALD, Lorcan (D) **0** **0**

H: 5 9 W: 10 09 b.Republic of Ireland 3-1-89

Source: Scholar.

2005–06	West Ham U	0	0		

FLETCHER, Carl (M) **240** **22**

H: 5 10 W: 11 07 b.Camberley 7-4-80

Source: Trainee. *Honours:* Wales 15 full caps.

1997–98	Bournemouth	1	0		
1998–99	Bournemouth	1	0		
1999–2000	Bournemouth	25	3		
2000–01	Bournemouth	43	6		
2001–02	Bournemouth	35	5		
2002–03	Bournemouth	42	1		
2003–04	Bournemouth	40	2		
2004–05	Bournemouth	6	2	**193**	**19**
2004–05	West Ham U	32	2		
2005–06	West Ham U	12	1	**44**	**3**
2005–06	*Watford*	3	0	**3**	**0**

GABBIDON, Daniel (D) **249** **10**

H: 6 0 W: 13 05 b.Cwmbran 8-8-79

Source: Trainee. *Honours:* Wales Youth, Under-21, 26 full caps.

1998–99	WBA	2	0		
1999–2000	WBA	18	0		
2000–01	WBA	0	0	**20**	**0**
2000–01	Cardiff C	43	3		
2001–02	Cardiff C	44	3		
2002–03	Cardiff C	24	0		
2003–04	Cardiff C	41	3		
2004–05	Cardiff C	45	1	**197**	**10**
2005–06	West Ham U	32	0	**32**	**0**

HALES, Lee (M) **0** **0**

H: 5 9 W: 11 00 b.Sidcup 15-2-89

Source: Scholar. *Honours:* England Schools, Youth.

2005–06	West Ham U	0	0		

HAREWOOD, Marlon (F) **298** **96**

H: 6 1 W: 13 07 b.Hampstead 25-8-79

Source: Trainee.

1996–97	Nottingham F	0	0		
1997–98	Nottingham F	1	0		
1998–99	Nottingham F	23	1		
1998–99	*Ipswich T*	6	1	**6**	**1**
1999–2000	Nottingham F	34	4		
2000–01	Nottingham F	33	3		
2001–02	Nottingham F	28	11		
2002–03	Nottingham F	44	20		
2003–04	Nottingham F	19	12	**182**	**51**
2003–04	West Ham U	28	13		
2004–05	West Ham U	45	17		
2005–06	West Ham U	37	14	**110**	**44**

HISLOP, Shaka (G) **371** **0**

H: 6 4 W: 14 04 b.Hackney 22-2-69

Source: Howard Univ, USA. *Honours:* England Under-21, Trinidad & Tobago 26 full caps.

1992–93	Reading	12	0		
1993–94	Reading	46	0		
1994–95	Reading	46	0	**104**	**0**
1995–96	Newcastle U	24	0		
1996–97	Newcastle U	16	0		
1997–98	Newcastle U	13	0	**53**	**0**
1998–99	West Ham U	37	0		
1999–2000	West Ham U	22	0		
2000–01	West Ham U	34	0		
2001–02	West Ham U	12	0		
2002–03	Portsmouth	46	0		
2003–04	Portsmouth	30	0		
2004–05	Portsmouth	17	0	**93**	**0**
2005–06	West Ham U	16	0	**121**	**0**

KATAN, Yaniv (F) **229** **40**

H: 6 1 W: 12 13 b.Kiryat Ata 27-1-81

Honours: Israel 24 full caps, 5 goals.

1998–99	Maccabi Haifa	26	1		
1999–2000	Maccabi Haifa	36	3		
2000–01	Maccabi Haifa	35	5		
2001–02	Maccabi Haifa	19	5		
2002–03	Maccabi Haifa	32	6		
2003–04	Maccabi Haifa	28	7		
2004–05	Maccabi Haifa	32	8		
2005–06	Maccabi Haifa	15	5	**223**	**40**
2005–06	West Ham U	6	0	**6**	**0**

KONCHESKY, Paul (D) **198** **6**

H: 5 10 W: 11 07 b.Barking 15-5-81

Source: Trainee. *Honours:* England Youth, Under-20, Under-21, 2 full caps.

1997–98	Charlton Ath	3	0		
1998–99	Charlton Ath	2	0		
1999–2000	Charlton Ath	8	0		
2000–01	Charlton Ath	23	0		
2001–02	Charlton Ath	34	1		
2002–03	Charlton Ath	30	3		
2003–04	Charlton Ath	21	0		
2003–04	*Tottenham H*	12	0	**12**	**0**
2004–05	Charlton Ath	28	1	**149**	**5**
2005–06	West Ham U	37	1	**37**	**1**

McCLENAHAN, Trent (D) **39** **0**

H: 5 11 W: 12 00 b.Sydney 4-2-85

Source: Scholar. *Honours:* Australia Under-20.

2004–05	West Ham U	2	0		
2004–05	*Milton Keynes D*	8	0		
2005–06	West Ham U	0	0	**2**	**0**
2005–06	*Milton Keynes D*	29	0	**37**	**0**

MIKOLANDA, Petr (F) **29** **1**
H: 6 3 W: 13 05 b.Prague 12-9-84
Honours: Czech Republic Under-21.

2002–03	Slavia Prague	0	0		
2003–04	Viktoria Zizkov	13	0		
2004–05	Viktoria Zizkov	0	0	**13**	**0**
2005–06	West Ham U	0	0		
2005–06	*Northampton T*	2	0	**2**	**0**
2005–06	*Swindon T*	5	0	**5**	**0**
2005–06	*Rushden & D*	9	1	**9**	**1**

MULLINS, Hayden (D) **321** **19**
H: 5 11 W: 11 12 b.Reading 27-3-79
Source: Trainee. *Honours:* England Under-21.

1996–97	Crystal Palace	0	0		
1997–98	Crystal Palace	0	0		
1998–99	Crystal Palace	40	5		
1999–2000	Crystal Palace	45	10		
2000–01	Crystal Palace	41	1		
2001–02	Crystal Palace	43	0		
2002–03	Crystal Palace	43	2		
2003–04	Crystal Palace	10	0	**222**	**18**
2003–04	West Ham U	27	0		
2004–05	West Ham U	37	1		
2005–06	West Ham U	35	0	**99**	**1**

NEWTON, Shaun (M) **407** **33**
H: 5 8 W: 11 00 b.Camberwell 20-8-75
Source: Trainee. *Honours:* England Under-21.

1992–93	Charlton Ath	2	0		
1993–94	Charlton Ath	19	2		
1994–95	Charlton Ath	26	0		
1995–96	Charlton Ath	41	5		
1996–97	Charlton Ath	43	3		
1997–98	Charlton Ath	41	5		
1998–99	Charlton Ath	16	0		
1999–2000	Charlton Ath	42	5		
2000–01	Charlton Ath	10	0	**240**	**20**
2001–02	Wolverhampton W	45	8		
2002–03	Wolverhampton W	33	3		
2003–04	Wolverhampton W	28	0		
2004–05	Wolverhampton W	24	1	**130**	**12**
2004–05	West Ham U	11	0		
2005–06	West Ham U	26	1	**37**	**1**

NOBLE, Mark (M) **23** **0**
H: 5 11 W: 12 00 b.West Ham 8-5-87
Source: Scholar. *Honours:* England Youth.

2004–05	West Ham U	13	0		
2005–06	West Ham U	5	0	**18**	**0**
2005–06	*Hull C*	5	0	**5**	**0**

REED, Matthew (G) **4** **0**
H: 6 0 W: 11 00 b.Dartford 24-12-86

2005–06	West Ham U	0	0		
2005–06	*Barnet*	4	0	**4**	**0**

REID, Kyel (M) **2** **0**
H: 5 10 W: 12 05 b.South London 26-11-87
Source: Scholar. *Honours:* England Youth.

2004–05	West Ham U	0	0		
2005–06	West Ham U	2	0	**2**	**0**

REO-COKER, Nigel (M) **143** **16**
H: 5 8 W: 12 03 b.Southwark 14-5-84
Source: Scholar. *Honours:* England Youth, Under-20, Under-21.

2001–02	Wimbledon	1	0		
2002–03	Wimbledon	32	2		
2003–04	Wimbledon	25	4	**58**	**6**
2003–04	West Ham U	15	2		
2004–05	West Ham U	39	3		
2005–06	West Ham U	31	5	**85**	**10**

REPKA, Tomas (D) **411** **9**
H: 6 0 W: 12 04 b.Slavicin Zlin 2-1-74
Honours: Czechoslovakia 1 full cap, Czech Republic 46 full caps, 1 goal.

1991–92	Banik Ostrava	16	1		
1992–93	Banik Ostrava	19	0		
1993–94	Banik Ostrava	26	2		
1994–95	Banik Ostrava	16	0	**77**	**3**
1995–96	Sparta Prague	29	3		
1996–97	Sparta Prague	25	1		
1997–98	Sparta Prague	28	2	**82**	**6**
1998–99	Fiorentina	31	0		
1999–2000	Fiorentina	29	0		
2000–01	Fiorentina	28	0	**88**	**0**
2001–02	West Ham U	31	0		
2002–03	West Ham U	32	0		
2003–04	West Ham U	40	0		
2004–05	West Ham U	42	0		
2005–06	West Ham U	19	0	**164**	**0**

To Sparta Prague January 2006

SCALONI, Lionel (D) **263** **21**
H: 5 10 W: 12 04 b.Santa Fe 16-5-78
Honours: Argentina 7 full caps.

1995–96	Newell's Old Boys	12	0	**12**	**0**
1996–97	Estudiantes	21	3		
1997–98	Estudiantes	16	4	**37**	**7**
1997–98	La Coruna	19	2		
1998–99	La Coruna	21	0		
1999–2000	La Coruna	14	0		
2000–01	La Coruna	25	3		
2001–02	La Coruna	25	2		
2002–03	La Coruna	32	3		
2003–04	La Coruna	23	2		
2004–05	La Coruna	27	2		
2005–06	La Coruna	15	0	**201**	**14**
2005–06	West Ham U	13	0	**13**	**0**

SHERINGHAM, Teddy (F) **698** **270**
H: 6 0 W: 12 05 b.Highams Park 2-4-66
Source: Apprentice. *Honours:* England Youth, 51 full caps, 11 goals.

1983–84	Millwall	7	1		
1984–85	Millwall	0	0		
1984–85	*Aldershot*	5	0	**5**	**0**
1985–86	Millwall	18	4		
1986–87	Millwall	42	13		
1987–88	Millwall	43	22		
1988–89	Millwall	33	11		
1989–90	Millwall	31	9		
1990–91	Millwall	46	33	**220**	**93**
1991–92	Nottingham F	39	13		
1992–93	Nottingham F	3	1	**42**	**14**
1992–93	Tottenham H	38	21		
1993–94	Tottenham H	19	13		
1994–95	Tottenham H	42	18		
1995–96	Tottenham H	38	16		
1996–97	Tottenham H	29	7		
1997–98	Manchester U	31	9		
1998–99	Manchester U	17	2		
1999–2000	Manchester U	27	5		
2000–01	Manchester U	29	15	**104**	**31**
2001–02	Tottenham H	34	10		
2002–03	Tottenham H	36	12	**236**	**97**
2003–04	Portsmouth	32	9	**32**	**9**
2004–05	West Ham U	33	20		
2005–06	West Ham U	26	6	**59**	**26**

STOKES, Tony (M) **19** **0**
H: 5 10 W: 11 10 b.East London 7-1-87
Source: Scholar.

2005–06	West Ham U	0	0		
2005–06	*Rushden & D*	19	0	**19**	**0**

TOMKINS, James (D) **0** **0**
H: 6 3 W: 11 10 b.Basildon 29-3-89
Source: Scholar. *Honours:* England Schools, Youth.

2005–06	West Ham U	0	0		

WALKER, Jim (G) **416** **0**
H: 5 11 W: 13 04 b.Sutton-in-Ashfield 9-7-73
Source: Trainee.

1991–92	Notts Co	0	0		
1992–93	Notts Co	0	0		
1993–94	Walsall	31	0		
1994–95	Walsall	4	0		
1995–96	Walsall	26	0		
1996–97	Walsall	36	0		
1997–98	Walsall	46	0		
1998–99	Walsall	46	0		
1999–2000	Walsall	43	0		
2000–01	Walsall	44	0		
2001–02	Walsall	43	0		
2002–03	Walsall	41	0		
2003–04	Walsall	43	0	**403**	**0**
2004–05	West Ham U	10	0		
2005–06	West Ham U	3	0	**13**	**0**

WARD, Elliot (D) **34** **1**
H: 6 2 W: 13 00 b.Harrow 19-1-85
Source: Scholar.

2001–02	West Ham U	0	0		
2002–03	West Ham U	0	0		
2003–04	West Ham U	0	0		
2004–05	West Ham U	11	0		
2004–05	*Bristol R*	3	0	**3**	**0**
2005–06	West Ham U	4	0	**15**	**0**
2005–06	*Plymouth Arg*	16	1	**16**	**1**

ZAMORA, Bobby (F) **230** **94**
H: 6 1 W: 11 11 b.Barking 16-1-81
Source: Trainee. *Honours:* England Under-21.

1999–2000	Bristol R	4	0	**4**	**0**
1999–2000	*Brighton & HA*	6	6		
2000–01	Brighton & HA	43	28		
2001–02	Brighton & HA	41	28		
2002–03	Brighton & HA	35	14	**125**	**76**
2003–04	Tottenham H	16	0	**16**	**0**
2003–04	West Ham U	17	5		
2004–05	West Ham U	34	7		
2005–06	West Ham U	34	6	**85**	**18**

Scholars
Blackmore, David; Collison, Jack David; Hales, Lee Adam; Hines, Zavon; Jeffery, Jack; Widdowson, Joseph.

WIGAN ATH (88)

BAINES, Leighton (D) **110** **1**
H: 5 8 W: 11 00 b.Liverpool 11-12-84
Source: Trainee. *Honours:* England Under-21.

2002–03	Wigan Ath	6	0		
2003–04	Wigan Ath	26	0		
2004–05	Wigan Ath	41	1		
2005–06	Wigan Ath	37	0	**110**	**1**

CAMARA, Henri (F) **192** **73**
H: 5 9 W: 10 08 b.Dakar 10-5-77
Honours: Senegal 39 full caps, 9 goals.

1999–2000	Neuchatel Xamax	20	12		
2000–01	Neuchatel Xamax	12	5	**32**	**17**
2000–01	Grasshoppers	11	3	**11**	**3**
2001–02	Sedan	25	8		
2002–03	Sedan	34	14	**59**	**22**
2003–04	Wolverhampton W	30	7		
2004–05	Wolverhampton W	0	0	**30**	**7**
2004–05	*Celtic*	18	8	**18**	**8**
2004–05	*Southampton*	13	4	**13**	**4**
2005–06	Wigan Ath	29	12	**29**	**12**

CHIMBONDA, Pascal (D) **189** **11**
H: 5 10 W: 11 05 b.Les Abymes 21-2-79
Honours: France 1 full cap.

1999–2000	Le Havre	2	0		
2000–01	Le Havre	32	1		
2001–02	Le Havre	27	2		
2002–03	Le Havre	24	2	**85**	**5**
2003–04	Bastia	31	1		
2004–05	Bastia	36	3	**67**	**4**
2005–06	Wigan Ath	37	2	**37**	**2**

CONNOLLY, David (F) **283** **122**
H: 5 9 W: 11 00 b.Willesden 6-6-77
Source: Trainee. *Honours:* Eire Under-21, 41 full caps, 9 goals.

1994–95	Watford	2	0		
1995–96	Watford	11	8		
1996–97	Watford	13	2	**26**	**10**
1997–98	Feyenoord	10	2		
1998–99	Wolverhampton W	32	6	**32**	**6**
1999–2000	Excelsior	32	29	**32**	**29**
2000–01	Feyenoord	15	5	**25**	**7**
2001–02	Wimbledon	35	18		
2002–03	Wimbledon	28	24	**63**	**42**
2003–04	West Ham U	39	10	**39**	**10**
2004–05	Leicester C	44	13		
2005–06	Leicester C	5	4	**49**	**17**
2005–06	Wigan Ath	17	1	**17**	**1**

DE ZEEUW, Arjan (D) **503** **23**
H: 6 0 W: 13 06 b.Castricum 16-4-70
Source: Vitesse 22.

1992–93	Telstar	30	1		
1993–94	Telstar	31	2		
1994–95	Telstar	29	1		
1995–96	Telstar	12	1	**102**	**5**
1995–96	Barnsley	31	1		
1996–97	Barnsley	43	2		
1997–98	Barnsley	26	0		
1998–99	Barnsley	38	4	**138**	**7**
1999–2000	Wigan Ath	39	3		

2000–01	Wigan Ath	45	1		
2001–02	Wigan Ath	42	2		
2002–03	Portsmouth	38	1		
2003–04	Portsmouth	36	1		
2004–05	Portsmouth	32	3	**106**	**5**
2005–06	Wigan Ath	31	0	**157**	**6**

EDWARDS, Phil (D) **0** **0**

H: 5 8 W: 11 03 b.Kirkby 8-11-85

Source: Scholar.

2005–06	Wigan Ath	0	0		

EMERSON (D) **171** **3**

H: 6 2 W: 13 07 b.Porto Alegre 30-3-72

Source: Benfica.

1997–98	Sheffield W	6	0		
1998–99	Sheffield W	38	1		
1999–2000	Sheffield W	17	0	**61**	**1**
1999–2000	Chelsea	20	0		
2000–01	Chelsea	1	0	**21**	**0**
2000–01	Sunderland	31	1		
2001–02	Sunderland	12	1		
2002–03	Sunderland	1	0		
2003–04	Sunderland	0	0	**44**	**2**
2003–04	Bolton W	26	0	**26**	**0**
2004–05	Wigan Ath	15	0		
2005–06	Wigan Ath	0	0	**15**	**0**
2005–06	*Derby Co*	4	0	**4**	**0**

FILAN, John (G) **404** **0**

H: 6 2 W: 14 07 b.Sydney 8-2-70

Honours: Australia Under-20, Under-23, 2 full caps.

1989–90	St George	26	0		
1990–91	St George	26	0	**52**	**0**
1991–92	Wollongong Wolves	23	0		
1992–93	Wollongong Wolves	6	0	**29**	**0**
1992–93	Cambridge U	6	0		
1993–94	Cambridge U	46	0		
1994–95	Cambridge U	16	0	**68**	**0**
1994–95	*Nottingham F*	0	0		
1994–95	Coventry C	2	0		
1995–96	Coventry C	13	0		
1996–97	Coventry C	1	0	**16**	**0**
1997–98	Blackburn R	7	0		
1998–99	Blackburn R	26	0		
1999–2000	Blackburn R	16	0		
2000–01	Blackburn R	13	0		
2001–02	Blackburn R	0	0	**62**	**0**
2001–02	Wigan Ath	25	0		
2002–03	Wigan Ath	46	0		
2003–04	Wigan Ath	45	0		
2004–05	Wigan Ath	46	0		
2005–06	Wigan Ath	15	0	**177**	**0**

FRANCIS, Damien (M) **190** **30**

H: 6 0 W: 11 10 b.Wandsworth 27-2-79

Source: Trainee. *Honours:* Jamaica 1 full cap.

1996–97	Wimbledon	0	0		
1997–98	Wimbledon	2	0		
1998–99	Wimbledon	0	0		
1999–2000	Wimbledon	9	0		
2000–01	Wimbledon	29	8		
2001–02	Wimbledon	23	1		
2002–03	Wimbledon	34	6	**97**	**15**
2003–04	Norwich C	41	7		
2004–05	Norwich C	32	7	**73**	**14**
2005–06	Wigan Ath	20	1	**20**	**1**

HENCHOZ, Stephane (D) **377** **3**

H: 6 1 W: 12 08 b.Billens 7-9-74

Source: Bulle. *Honours:* Switzerland 72 full caps.

1992–93	Neuchatel Xamax	35	0		
1993–94	Neuchatel Xamax	21	1		
1994–95	Neuchatel Xamax	35	0	**91**	**1**
1995–96	Hamburg	31	2		
1996–97	Hamburg	18	0	**49**	**2**
1997–98	Blackburn R	36	0		
1998–99	Blackburn R	34	0	**70**	**0**
1999–2000	Liverpool	29	0		
2000–01	Liverpool	32	0		
2001–02	Liverpool	37	0		
2002–03	Liverpool	19	0		
2003–04	Liverpool	18	0	**135**	**0**
2004–05	*Celtic*	6	0	**6**	**0**
2005–06	Wigan Ath	26	0	**26**	**0**

JACKSON, Matt (D) **484** **13**

H: 6 1 W: 14 00 b.Leeds 19-10-71

Source: School. *Honours:* England Schools, Under-21.

1990–91	Luton T	0	0		
1990–91	*Preston NE*	4	0	**4**	**0**
1991–92	Luton T	9	0	**9**	**0**
1991–92	Everton	30	1		
1992–93	Everton	27	3		
1993–94	Everton	38	0		
1994–95	Everton	29	0		
1995–96	Everton	14	0		
1995–96	*Charlton Ath*	8	0	**8**	**0**
1996–97	Everton	0	0	**138**	**4**
1996–97	*QPR*	7	0	**7**	**0**
1996–97	*Birmingham C*	10	0	**10**	**0**
1996–97	Norwich C	19	2		
1997–98	Norwich C	41	3		
1998–99	Norwich C	37	1		
1999–2000	Norwich C	38	0		
2000–01	Norwich C	26	0		
2001–02	Norwich C	0	0	**161**	**6**
2001–02	Wigan Ath	26	0		
2002–03	Wigan Ath	45	1		
2003–04	Wigan Ath	24	1		
2004–05	Wigan Ath	36	1		
2005–06	Wigan Ath	16	0	**147**	**3**

JOHANSSON, Andreas (M) **247** **71**

H: 5 11 W: 12 05 b.Vanersborg 5-7-78

Honours: Sweden 12 full caps.

1993	Melleruds	2	0		
1994	Melleruds	15	1		
1995	Melleruds	21	10	**38**	**11**
1996	Degerfors	10	1		
1997	Degerfors	23	4		
1998	Degerfors	23	5	**56**	**10**
1999	AIK	12	1	**12**	**1**
2000	Djurgaarden	24	7		
2001	Djurgaarden	25	5		
2002	Djurgaarden	26	10		
2003	Djurgaarden	26	12		
2004	Djurgaarden	23	11	**124**	**45**
2004–05	Wigan Ath	1	0		
2005–06	Wigan Ath	16	4	**17**	**4**

KAVANAGH, Graham (M) **434** **66**

H: 5 10 W: 13 03 b.Dublin 2-12-73

Source: Home Farm. *Honours:* Eire Schools, Youth, Under-21, B, 15 full caps, 1 goal.

1991–92	Middlesbrough	0	0		
1992–93	Middlesbrough	10	0		
1993–94	Middlesbrough	11	2		
1993–94	*Darlington*	5	0	**5**	**0**
1994–95	Middlesbrough	7	0		
1995–96	Middlesbrough	7	1		
1996–97	Middlesbrough	0	0	**35**	**3**
1996–97	Stoke C	38	4		
1997–98	Stoke C	44	5		
1998–99	Stoke C	36	11		
1999–2000	Stoke C	45	7		
2000–01	Stoke C	43	8	**206**	**35**
2001–02	Cardiff C	43	13		
2002–03	Cardiff C	44	5		
2003–04	Cardiff C	27	7		
2004–05	Cardiff C	28	3	**142**	**28**
2004–05	Wigan Ath	11	0		
2005–06	Wigan Ath	35	0	**46**	**0**

LEE, Kevin (D) **0** **0**

H: 6 0 W: 11 10 b.Knowsley 4-11-85

Source: Scholar.

2005–06	Wigan Ath	0	0		
2005–06	*Blackpool*	0	0		

McCULLOCH, Lee (F) **317** **62**

H: 6 1 W: 13 07 b.Bellshill 14-5-78

Source: Cumbernauld U. *Honours:* Scotland Youth, Under-21, B, 7 full caps.

1995–96	Motherwell	1	0		
1996–97	Motherwell	15	0		
1997–98	Motherwell	25	2		
1998–99	Motherwell	26	3		
1999–2000	Motherwell	29	9		
2000–01	Motherwell	26	8	**122**	**22**
2000–01	Wigan Ath	10	3		
2001–02	Wigan Ath	34	6		
2002–03	Wigan Ath	38	6		
2003–04	Wigan Ath	41	6		
2004–05	Wigan Ath	42	14		
2005–06	Wigan Ath	30	5	**195**	**40**

McMILLAN, Steve (D) **244** **6**

H: 5 9 W: 12 05 b.Edinburgh 19-1-76

Source: Troon Juniors. *Honours:* Scotland Under-21.

1993–94	Motherwell	1	0		
1994–95	Motherwell	3	0		
1995–96	Motherwell	12	0		
1996–97	Motherwell	16	0		
1997–98	Motherwell	34	1		
1998–99	Motherwell	30	2		
1999–2000	Motherwell	31	3		
2000–01	Motherwell	25	0	**152**	**6**
2000–01	Wigan Ath	6	0		
2001–02	Wigan Ath	29	0		
2002–03	Wigan Ath	32	0		
2003–04	Wigan Ath	15	0		
2004–05	Wigan Ath	8	0		
2005–06	Wigan Ath	2	0	**92**	**0**

MOORE, David (F) **3** **0**

H: 5 10 W: 12 13 b.Worsley 4-4-85

Source: Scholar.

2004–05	Wigan Ath	0	0		
2004–05	*Bury*	3	0	**3**	**0**
2005–06	Wigan Ath	0	0		

POLLITT, Mike (G) **486** **0**

H: 6 4 W: 15 03 b.Farnworth 29-2-72

Source: Trainee.

1990–91	Manchester U	0	0		
1990–91	*Oldham Ath*	0	0		
1991–92	Bury	0	0		
1992–93	Lincoln C	27	0		
1993–94	Lincoln C	30	0	**57**	**0**
1994–95	Darlington	40	0		
1995–96	Darlington	15	0	**55**	**0**
1995–96	Notts Co	0	0		
1996–97	Notts Co	8	0		
1997–98	Notts Co	2	0	**10**	**0**
1997–98	*Oldham Ath*	16	0	**16**	**0**
1997–98	*Gillingham*	6	0	**6**	**0**
1997–98	*Brentford*	5	0	**5**	**0**
1997–98	Sunderland	0	0		
1998–99	Rotherham U	46	0		
1999–2000	Rotherham U	46	0		
2000–01	Chesterfield	46	0	**46**	**0**
2001–02	Rotherham U	46	0		
2002–03	Rotherham U	41	0		
2003–04	Rotherham U	43	0		
2004–05	Rotherham U	45	0	**267**	**0**
2005–06	Wigan Ath	24	0	**24**	**0**

ROBERTS, Jason (F) **287** **107**

H: 6 0 W: 14 01 b.Park Royal 25-1-78

Source: Hayes. *Honours:* Grenada 6 full caps.

1997–98	Wolverhampton W	0	0		
1997–98	*Torquay U*	14	6	**14**	**6**
1997–98	*Bristol C*	3	1	**3**	**1**
1998–99	Bristol R	37	16		
1999–2000	Bristol R	41	22	**78**	**38**
2000–01	WBA	43	14		
2001–02	WBA	14	7		
2002–03	WBA	32	3		
2003–04	WBA	0	0	**89**	**24**
2003–04	*Portsmouth*	10	1	**10**	**1**
2003–04	Wigan Ath	14	8		
2004–05	Wigan Ath	45	21		
2005–06	Wigan Ath	34	8	**93**	**37**

SCHARNER, Paul (D) **150** **16**

H: 6 3 W: 12 09 b.Scheibbs 11-3-80

Source: St Polten. *Honours:* Austria 14 full caps.

1998–99	FK Austria	4	0		
1999–2000	FK Austria	12	0		
2000–01	FK Austria	14	0		
2001–02	FK Austria	16	1		
2002–03	FK Austria	29	1		
2003–04	FK Austria	9	1	**84**	**3**
2003–04	Salzburg	13	2		
2004–05	Salzburg	5	1	**18**	**3**
2004	Brann	7	1		
2005	Brann	25	6	**32**	**7**
2005–06	Wigan Ath	16	3	**16**	**3**

SKOKO, Josip (M) **276 32**

H: 5 9 W: 12 02 b.Mount Gambier 10-12-75

Honours: Australia Under-20, Under-23, 46 full caps, 8 goals.

1995–96	Hajduk Split	14	1		
1996–97	Hajduk Split	27	10		
1997–98	Hajduk Split	26	5		
1998–99	Hajduk Split	24	3		
1999–2000	Hajduk Split	15	0	**106**	**19**
1999–2000	Genk	9	1		
2000–01	Genk	28	3		
2001–02	Genk	32	2		
2002–03	Genk	29	1	**98**	**7**
2003–04	Genclerbirligi	28	2		
2004–05	Genclerbirligi	30	2	**58**	**4**
2005–06	Wigan Ath	5	0	**5**	**0**
2005–06	*Stoke C*	9	2	**9**	**2**

TAYLOR, Ryan (M) **109 14**

H: 5 8 W: 10 04 b.Liverpool 19-8-84

Source: Scholar. *Honours:* England Youth, Under-21.

2001–02	Tranmere R	0	0		
2002–03	Tranmere R	25	1		
2003–04	Tranmere R	30	5		
2004–05	Tranmere R	43	8	**98**	**14**
2005–06	Wigan Ath	11	0	**11**	**0**

TEALE, Gary (F) **320 35**

H: 5 11 W: 12 02 b.Glasgow 21-7-78

Honours: Scotland Under-21, B, 3 full caps.

1996–97	Clydebank	33	6		
1997–98	Clydebank	27	6		
1998–99	Clydebank	8	2	**68**	**14**
1998–99	Ayr U	23	4		
1999–2000	Ayr U	32	0		
2000–01	Ayr U	29	5		
2001–02	Ayr U	18	4	**102**	**13**
2001–02	Wigan Ath	23	1		
2002–03	Wigan Ath	38	2		
2003–04	Wigan Ath	28	2		
2004–05	Wigan Ath	37	3		
2005–06	Wigan Ath	24	0	**150**	**8**

THOMPSON, David (M) **198 27**

H: 5 7 W: 10 00 b.Birkenhead 12-9-77

Source: Trainee. *Honours:* England Youth, Under-21.

1994–95	Liverpool	0	0		
1995–96	Liverpool	0	0		
1996–97	Liverpool	2	0		
1997–98	Liverpool	5	1		
1997–98	*Swindon T*	10	0	**10**	**0**
1998–99	Liverpool	14	1		
1999–2000	Liverpool	27	3	**48**	**5**
2000–01	Coventry C	25	3		
2001–02	Coventry C	37	12		
2002–03	Coventry C	4	0	**66**	**15**
2002–03	Blackburn R	23	4		
2003–04	Blackburn R	11	1		
2004–05	Blackburn R	24	0		
2005–06	Blackburn R	6	0	**64**	**5**
2005–06	Wigan Ath	10	2	**10**	**2**

WALSH, Gary (G) **241 0**

H: 6 3 W: 14 06 b.Wigan 21-3-68

Source: Apprentice. *Honours:* England Under-21.

1984–85	Manchester U	0	0		
1985–86	Manchester U	0	0		
1986–87	Manchester U	14	0		
1987–88	Manchester U	16	0		
1988–89	Manchester U	0	0		
1988–89	*Airdrieonians*	3	0	**3**	**0**
1989–90	Manchester U	0	0		
1990–91	Manchester U	5	0		
1991–92	Manchester U	2	0		
1992–93	Manchester U	0	0		
1993–94	Manchester U	3	0		
1993–94	*Oldham Ath*	6	0	**6**	**0**
1994–95	Manchester U	10	0	**50**	**0**
1995–96	Middlesbrough	32	0		
1996–97	Middlesbrough	12	0		
1997–98	Middlesbrough	0	0		
1997–98	Bradford C	35	0		
1998–99	Bradford C	46	0		
1999–2000	Bradford C	11	0		
2000–01	Bradford C	19	0		
2000–01	*Middlesbrough*	3	0	**47**	**0**
2001–02	Bradford C	18	0		
2002–03	Bradford C	3	0	**132**	**0**
2003–04	Wigan Ath	3	0		
2004–05	Wigan Ath	0	0		
2005–06	Wigan Ath	0	0	**3**	**0**

WRIGHT, David (D) **249 3**

H: 5 11 W: 11 01 b.Warrington 1-5-80

Source: Trainee. *Honours:* England Youth.

1997–98	Crewe Alex	3	0		
1998–99	Crewe Alex	20	1		
1999–2000	Crewe Alex	45	0		
2000–01	Crewe Alex	42	0		
2001–02	Crewe Alex	30	0		
2002–03	Crewe Alex	31	1		
2003–04	Crewe Alex	40	1	**211**	**3**
2004–05	Wigan Ath	31	0		
2005–06	Wigan Ath	2	0	**33**	**0**
2005–06	*Norwich C*	5	0	**5**	**0**

Scholars

Blaney, Ryan Trevor Joseph; Maloney, Dean Paul; Montrose, Lewis Robert Egerton; Moore, Peter Francis; Owens, David Michael; Perry-Acton, Benjamin; Saunders, Russell; Smith, Jonathan Robert.

WOLVERHAMPTON W (89)

ANDERTON, Darren (M) **405 45**

H: 6 1 W: 12 05 b.Southampton 3-3-72

Source: Trainee. *Honours:* England Youth, Under-21, B, 30 full caps, 7 goals.

1989–90	Portsmouth	0	0		
1990–91	Portsmouth	20	0		
1991–92	Portsmouth	42	7	**62**	**7**
1992–93	Tottenham H	34	6		
1993–94	Tottenham H	37	6		
1994–95	Tottenham H	37	5		
1995–96	Tottenham H	8	2		
1996–97	Tottenham H	16	3		
1997–98	Tottenham H	15	0		
1998–99	Tottenham H	32	3		
1999–2000	Tottenham H	22	3		
2000–01	Tottenham H	23	2		
2001–02	Tottenham H	35	3		
2002–03	Tottenham H	20	0		
2003–04	Tottenham H	20	1	**299**	**34**
2004–05	Birmingham C	20	3		
2005–06	Birmingham C	0	0	**20**	**3**
2005–06	Wolverhampton W	24	1	**24**	**1**

CAMERON, Colin (M) **450 91**

H: 5 8 W: 11 00 b.Kirkcaldy 23-10-72

Source: Lochore Welfare. *Honours:* Scotland B, 29 full caps, 2 goals.

1990–91	Raith R	0	0		
1991–92	*Sligo R*	0	0		
1992–93	Raith R	16	1		
1993–94	Raith R	41	6		
1994–95	Raith R	35	7		
1995–96	Raith R	30	9	**122**	**23**
1995–96	Hearts	4	2		
1996–97	Hearts	36	7		
1997–98	Hearts	31	8		
1998–99	Hearts	11	6		
1999–2000	Hearts	32	8		
2000–01	Hearts	37	12		
2001–02	Hearts	4	3	**155**	**46**
2001–02	Wolverhampton W	41	4		
2002–03	Wolverhampton W	33	7		
2003–04	Wolverhampton W	30	4		
2004–05	Wolverhampton W	37	3		
2005–06	Wolverhampton W	27	4	**168**	**22**
2005–06	*Millwall*	5	0	**5**	**0**

CLARKE, Leon (F) **62 8**

H: 6 2 W: 14 02 b.Birmingham 10-2-85

Source: Scholar.

2003–04	Wolverhampton W	0	0		
2003–04	*Kidderminster H*	4	0	**4**	**0**
2004–05	Wolverhampton W	28	7		
2005–06	Wolverhampton W	24	1	**52**	**8**
2005–06	*QPR*	1	0	**1**	**0**
2005–06	*Plymouth Arg*	5	0	**5**	**0**

CLYDE, Mark (D) **48 0**

H: 6 1 W: 13 00 b.Limavady 27-12-82

Source: Scholar. *Honours:* Northern Ireland Under-21, 3 full caps.

2001–02	Wolverhampton W	0	0		
2002–03	Wolverhampton W	17	0		
2002–03	*Kidderminster H*	4	0	**4**	**0**
2003–04	Wolverhampton W	9	0		
2004–05	Wolverhampton W	18	0		
2005–06	Wolverhampton W	0	0	**44**	**0**

CORNES, Chris (M) **10 3**

H: 5 8 W: 14 02 b.Worcester 20-12-86

Source: Scholar.

2004–05	Wolverhampton W	0	0		
2005–06	*Port Vale*	10	3	**10**	**3**
2005–06	Wolverhampton W	0	0		

CORT, Carl (F) **185 55**

H: 6 4 W: 12 04 b.Southwark 1-11-77

Source: Trainee. *Honours:* England Under-21.

1996–97	Wimbledon	1	0		
1996–97	*Lincoln C*	6	1	**6**	**1**
1997–98	Wimbledon	22	4		
1998–99	Wimbledon	16	3		
1999–2000	Wimbledon	34	9	**73**	**16**
2000–01	Newcastle U	13	6		
2001–02	Newcastle U	8	1		
2002–03	Newcastle U	1	0		
2003–04	Newcastle U	0	0	**22**	**7**
2003–04	Wolverhampton W	16	5		
2004–05	Wolverhampton W	37	15		
2005–06	Wolverhampton W	31	11	**84**	**31**

CRADDOCK, Jody (D) **393 8**

H: 6 0 W: 12 04 b.Redditch 25-7-75

Source: Christchurch.

1993–94	Cambridge U	20	0		
1994–95	Cambridge U	38	0		
1995–96	Cambridge U	46	3		
1996–97	Cambridge U	41	1	**145**	**4**
1997–98	Sunderland	32	0		
1998–99	Sunderland	6	0		
1999–2000	Sunderland	19	0		
1999–2000	*Sheffield U*	10	0	**10**	**0**
2000–01	Sunderland	34	0		
2001–02	Sunderland	30	1		
2002–03	Sunderland	25	1	**146**	**2**
2003–04	Wolverhampton W	32	1		
2004–05	Wolverhampton W	42	1		
2005–06	Wolverhampton W	18	0	**92**	**2**

DAVIES, Mark (M) **20 1**

H: 5 11 W: 11 08 b.Wolverhampton 18-2-88

Source: Scholar. *Honours:* England Youth.

2004–05	Wolverhampton W	0	0		
2005–06	Wolverhampton W	20	1	**20**	**1**

EDWARDS, Rob (D) **85 2**

H: 6 1 W: 11 10 b.Telford 25-12-82

Source: Trainee. *Honours:* Wales Youth, 11 full caps.

1999–2000	Aston Villa	0	0		
2000–01	Aston Villa	0	0		
2001–02	Aston Villa	0	0		
2002–03	Aston Villa	8	0		
2003–04	Aston Villa	0	0	**8**	**0**
2003–04	*Crystal Palace*	7	1	**7**	**1**
2003–04	*Derby Co*	11	1	**11**	**1**
2004–05	Wolverhampton W	17	0		
2005–06	Wolverhampton W	42	0	**59**	**0**

FRANKOWSKI, Tomasz (F) **199 119**

H: 5 8 W: 10 01 b.Poland 16-8-74

Source: Bialystok, Strasbourg, Grampus Eight, Poitiers, Martigues. *Honours:* Poland 18 full caps, 10 goals.

1998–99	Wisla Krakow	29	21		
1999–2000	Wisla Krakow	26	17		
2000–01	Wisla Krakow	28	18		
2001–02	Wisla Krakow	26	9		
2002–03	Wisla Krakow	12	6		
2003–04	Wisla Krakow	22	15		
2004–05	Wisla Krakow	26	25	**169**	**111**
2005–06	Elche	14	8	**14**	**8**
2005–06	Wolverhampton W	16	0	**16**	**0**

GANEA, Viorel (F) 285 83
H: 5 9 W: 11 02 b.Fagaras 10-8-73
Honours: Romania 44 full caps, 19 goals.

1994–95	Brasov	30	0		
1995–96	Brasov	20	4	**50**	**4**
1995–96	Uni Craiova	17	5		
1996–97	Uni Craiova	19	6		
1997–98	Uni Craiova	26	11	**62**	**22**
1998–99	Rapid Bucharest	16	11	**16**	**11**
1999–2000	Stuttgart	29	7		
2000–01	Stuttgart	32	8		
2001–02	Stuttgart	23	10		
2002–03	Stuttgart	23	9	**107**	**34**
2003–04	Bursa	16	5	**16**	**5**
2003–04	Wolverhampton W	16	3		
2004–05	Wolverhampton W	0	0		
2005–06	Wolverhampton W	18	4	**34**	**7**

GOBERN, Lewis (M) 17 2
H: 5 10 W: 11 07 b.Birmingham 28-1-85
Source: Scholar.

2003–04	Wolverhampton W	0	0		
2004–05	Wolverhampton W	0	0		
2004–05	*Hartlepool U*	1	0	**1**	**0**
2005–06	Wolverhampton W	1	0	**1**	**0**
2005–06	*Blackpool*	8	1	**8**	**1**
2005–06	*Bury*	7	1	**7**	**1**

GYEPES, Gabor (D) 134 12
H: 6 3 W: 13 01 b.Hungary 26-6-81
Honours: Hungary 22 full caps, 1 goal.

1999–2000	Ferencvaros	2	0		
2000–01	Ferencvaros	29	2		
2001–02	Ferencvaros	33	3		
2002–03	Ferencvaros	17	2		
2003–04	Ferencvaros	7	0		
2004–05	Ferencvaros	26	5	**114**	**12**
2005–06	Wolverhampton W	20	0	**20**	**0**

HENNESSEY, Wayne (G) 0 0
b.Anglesey 24-1-87
Source: Scholar. *Honours:* Wales Schools, Youth, Under-21.

2004–05	Wolverhampton W	0	0		
2005–06	Wolverhampton W	0	0		

IKEME, Carl (G) 9 0
H: 6 2 W: 13 09 b.Sutton Coldfield 8-6-86
Source: Scholar.

2005–06	Wolverhampton W	0	0		
2005–06	*Stockport Co*	9	0	**9**	**0**

INCE, Paul (M) 605 71
H: 5 10 W: 12 02 b.Ilford 21-10-67
Source: Trainee. *Honours:* England Youth, Under-21, B, 53 full caps, 2 goals.

1985–86	West Ham U	0	0		
1986–87	West Ham U	10	1		
1987–88	West Ham U	28	3		
1988–89	West Ham U	33	3		
1989–90	West Ham U	1	0	**72**	**7**
1989–90	Manchester U	26	0		
1990–91	Manchester U	31	3		
1991–92	Manchester U	33	3		
1992–93	Manchester U	41	5		
1993–94	Manchester U	39	8		
1994–95	Manchester U	36	5	**206**	**24**
1995–96	Internazionale	30	3		
1996–97	Internazionale	24	6	**54**	**9**
1997–98	Liverpool	31	8		
1998–99	Liverpool	34	6	**65**	**14**
1999–2000	Middlesbrough	32	3		
2000–01	Middlesbrough	30	2		
2001–02	Middlesbrough	31	2	**93**	**7**
2002–03	Wolverhampton W	37	2		
2003–04	Wolverhampton W	32	2		
2004–05	Wolverhampton W	28	3		
2005–06	Wolverhampton W	18	3	**115**	**10**

JONES, Daniel (D) 1 0
H: 6 2 W: 13 00 b.Wordsley 14-7-86
Source: Scholar.

2005–06	Wolverhampton W	1	0	**1**	**0**

KENNEDY, Mark (M) 321 31
H: 5 11 W: 11 09 b.Dublin 15-5-76
Source: Belvedere, Trainee. *Honours:* Eire Under-21, 34 full caps, 3 goals.

1992–93	Millwall	1	0		
1993–94	Millwall	12	4		
1994–95	Millwall	30	5	**43**	**9**
1994–95	Liverpool	6	0		
1995–96	Liverpool	4	0		
1996–97	Liverpool	5	0		
1997–98	Liverpool	1	0	**16**	**0**
1997–98	*QPR*	8	2	**8**	**2**
1997–98	Wimbledon	4	0		
1998–99	Wimbledon	17	0	**21**	**0**
1999–2000	Manchester C	41	8		
2000–01	Manchester C	25	0	**66**	**8**
2001–02	Wolverhampton W	35	5		
2002–03	Wolverhampton W	31	3		
2003–04	Wolverhampton W	31	2		
2004–05	Wolverhampton W	30	0		
2005–06	Wolverhampton W	40	2	**167**	**12**

LESCOTT, Jolean (D) 212 13
H: 6 2 W: 13 00 b.Birmingham 16-8-82
Source: Trainee. *Honours:* England Youth, Under-20, Under-21.

1999–2000	Wolverhampton W	0	0		
2000–01	Wolverhampton W	37	2		
2001–02	Wolverhampton W	44	5		
2002–03	Wolverhampton W	44	1		
2003–04	Wolverhampton W	0	0		
2004–05	Wolverhampton W	41	4		
2005–06	Wolverhampton W	46	1	**212**	**13**

LITTLE, Mark (D) 0 0
b.Worcester 20-8-88
Source: Scholar. *Honours:* England Youth.

2005–06	Wolverhampton W	0	0		

LOWE, Keith (D) 35 0
H: 6 2 W: 13 03 b.Wolverhampton 13-9-85
Source: Scholar.

2004–05	Wolverhampton W	11	0		
2005–06	Wolverhampton W	3	0	**14**	**0**
2005–06	*Burnley*	16	0	**16**	**0**
2005–06	*QPR*	1	0	**1**	**0**
2005–06	*Swansea C*	4	0	**4**	**0**

McNAMARA, Jackie (D) 345 13
H: 5 9 W: 10 04 b.Glasgow 24-10-73
Source: Gairdoch U. *Honours:* Scotland B, Under-21, 9 full caps.

1991–92	Dunfermline Ath	0	0		
1992–93	Dunfermline Ath	3	0		
1993–94	Dunfermline Ath	39	0		
1994–95	Dunfermline Ath	30	2		
1995–96	Dunfermline Ath	7	1	**79**	**3**
1995–96	Celtic	26	1		
1996–97	Celtic	30	1		
1997–98	Celtic	31	2		
1998–99	Celtic	16	0		
1999–2000	Celtic	23	0		
2000–01	Celtic	30	3		
2001–02	Celtic	20	0		
2002–03	Celtic	19	1		
2003–04	Celtic	27	1		
2004–05	Celtic	34	1	**256**	**10**
2005–06	Wolverhampton W	10	0	**10**	**0**

MILLER, Kenny (F) 242 72
H: 5 10 W: 10 09 b.Edinburgh 23-12-79
Source: Hutchison Vale. *Honours:* Scotland Under-21, B, 26 full caps, 7 goals.

1996–97	Hibernian	0	0		
1997–98	Hibernian	7	0		
1998–99	Hibernian	7	1		
1999–2000	Hibernian	31	11	**45**	**12**
2000–01	Rangers	27	8		
2001–02	Rangers	3	0	**30**	**8**
2001–02	Wolverhampton W	20	2		
2002–03	Wolverhampton W	43	19		
2003–04	Wolverhampton W	25	2		
2004–05	Wolverhampton W	44	19		
2005–06	Wolverhampton W	35	10	**167**	**52**

MURRAY, Matt (G) 45 0
H: 6 4 W: 13 10 b.Solihull 2-5-81
Source: Trainee. *Honours:* England Youth, Under-21.

1997–98	Wolverhampton W	0	0		
1998–99	Wolverhampton W	0	0		
1999–2000	Wolverhampton W	0	0		
2000–01	Wolverhampton W	0	0		
2001–02	Wolverhampton W	0	0		
2002–03	Wolverhampton W	40	0		
2003–04	Wolverhampton W	1	0		
2004–05	Wolverhampton W	1	0		
2005–06	Wolverhampton W	1	0	**43**	**0**
2005–06	*Tranmere R*	2	0	**2**	**0**

NAYLOR, Lee (D) 290 7
H: 5 9 W: 11 03 b.Walsall 19-3-80
Source: Trainee. *Honours:* England Youth, Under-21.

1997–98	Wolverhampton W	16	0		
1998–99	Wolverhampton W	23	1		
1999–2000	Wolverhampton W	30	2		
2000–01	Wolverhampton W	46	1		
2001–02	Wolverhampton W	27	0		
2002–03	Wolverhampton W	32	1		
2003–04	Wolverhampton W	38	0		
2004–05	Wolverhampton W	38	1		
2005–06	Wolverhampton W	40	1	**290**	**7**

NDAH, George (F) 248 39
H: 6 1 W: 12 05 b.Dulwich 23-12-74
Source: Trainee.

1992–93	Crystal Palace	13	0		
1993–94	Crystal Palace	1	0		
1994–95	Crystal Palace	12	1		
1995–96	Crystal Palace	23	4		
1995–96	*Bournemouth*	12	2	**12**	**2**
1996–97	Crystal Palace	26	3		
1997–98	Crystal Palace	3	0	**78**	**8**
1997–98	*Gillingham*	4	0	**4**	**0**
1997–98	Swindon T	14	2		
1998–99	Swindon T	41	11		
1999–2000	Swindon T	12	1	**67**	**14**
1999–2000	Wolverhampton W	4	0		
2000–01	Wolverhampton W	29	6		
2001–02	Wolverhampton W	15	1		
2002–03	Wolverhampton W	25	7		
2003–04	Wolverhampton W	0	0		
2004–05	Wolverhampton W	0	0		
2005–06	Wolverhampton W	14	1	**87**	**15**

O'CONNOR, Kevin (M) 7 1
H: 5 11 W: 12 02 b.Dublin 19-10-85
Source: Scholar. *Honours:* Eire Under-21.

2003–04	Wolverhampton W	0	0		
2004–05	Wolverhampton W	0	0		
2005–06	Wolverhampton W	0	0		
2005–06	*Stockport Co*	7	1	**7**	**1**

OAKES, Michael (G) 251 0
H: 6 2 W: 14 06 b.Northwich 30-10-73
Source: Trainee. *Honours:* England Under-21.

1991–92	Aston Villa	0	0		
1992–93	Aston Villa	0	0		
1993–94	Aston Villa	0	0		
1993–94	*Scarborough*	1	0	**1**	**0**
1993–94	*Tranmere R*	0	0		
1994–95	Aston Villa	0	0		
1995–96	Aston Villa	0	0		
1996–97	Aston Villa	20	0		
1997–98	Aston Villa	8	0		
1998–99	Aston Villa	23	0		
1999–2000	Aston Villa	0	0	**51**	**0**
1999–2000	Wolverhampton W	28	0		
2000–01	Wolverhampton W	46	0		
2001–02	Wolverhampton W	46	0		
2002–03	Wolverhampton W	6	0		
2003–04	Wolverhampton W	21	0		
2004–05	Wolverhampton W	35	0		
2005–06	Wolverhampton W	17	0	**199**	**0**

OLOFINJANA, Seyi (M) 89 16
H: 6 4 W: 11 10 b.Lagos 30-6-80
Source: Kwara United Ilorin. *Honours:* Nigeria full caps.

2003	Brann	25	9		
2004	Brann	9	2	**34**	**11**
2004–05	Wolverhampton W	42	5		
2005–06	Wolverhampton W	13	0	**55**	**5**

POSTMA, Stefan (G) 140 0
H: 6 6 W: 15 00 b.Utrecht 6-10-76

1995–96	Utrecht	5	0		
1996–97	Utrecht	12	0		
1997–98	Utrecht	13	0		
1998–99	Utrecht	1	0		
1999–2000	Utrecht	2	0	**33**	**0**
2000–01	De Graafschap	34	0		
2001–02	De Graafschap	33	0	**67**	**0**
2002–03	Aston Villa	6	0		
2003–04	Aston Villa	2	0		
2004–05	Aston Villa	3	0		

2005–06 Aston Villa 0 0 **11 0**
2005–06 Wolverhampton W 29 0 **29 0**

RAFFERTY, Conor (D) 0 0
b.Dundalk 3-2-87
Source: Scholar. *Honours:* Eire Schools, Youth.
2004–05 Wolverhampton W 0 0
2005–06 Wolverhampton W 0 0

RICKETTS, Rohan (M) 68 2
H: 5 10 W: 11 07 b.Clapham 22-12-82
Source: Scholar. *Honours:* England Youth, Under-20.
2001–02 Arsenal 0 0
2002–03 Tottenham H 0 0
2003–04 Tottenham H 24 1
2004–05 Tottenham H 6 0 **30 1**
2004–05 *Coventry C* 6 0 **6 0**
2004–05 *Wolverhampton W* 7 1
2005–06 Wolverhampton W 25 0 **32 1**

RILEY, Martin (D) 0 0
b.Wolverhampton 5-12-86
Source: Scholar. *Honours:* England Under-20.
2004–05 Wolverhampton W 0 0
2005–06 Wolverhampton W 0 0

ROSA, Denes (M) 194 29
H: 5 8 W: 10 05 b.Hungary 7-4-77
Honours: Hungary 9 full caps.
1996–97 BVSC 12 0
1997–98 BVSC 26 5
1998–99 BVSC 13 4
1999–2000 BVSC 0 0
1999–2000 Gyor 8 1
2000–01 Gyor 25 1
2001–02 BVSC 0 0 **51 9**
2001–02 Gyor 12 1 **45 3**
2002–03 Dunaferr 14 0 **14 0**
2002–03 Ujpest 9 1 **9 1**
2003–04 Ferencvaros 25 2
2004–05 Ferencvaros 27 8
2005–06 Ferencvaros 14 4 **66 14**
2005–06 Wolverhampton W 9 2 **9 2**

ROSS, Maurice (D) 96 2
H: 5 11 W: 11 01 b.Dundee 3-2-81
Honours: Scotland 13 full caps.
1999–2000 Rangers 1 0
2000–01 Rangers 1 0
2001–02 Rangers 21 0
2002–03 Rangers 20 1
2003–04 Rangers 20 1
2004–05 Rangers 13 0
2005–06 Rangers 1 0 **77 2**
2005–06 Sheffield W 1 0 **1 0**
2005–06 Wolverhampton W 18 0 **18 0**

SEOL, Ki-Hyun (F) 165 36
H: 6 0 W: 11 07 b.South Korea 8-1-79
Honours: South Korea 69 full caps, 13 goals.
2000–01 Antwerp 25 10 **25 10**
2001–02 Anderlecht 20 3
2002–03 Anderlecht 32 12
2003–04 Anderlecht 19 3 **71 18**
2004–05 Wolverhampton W 37 4
2005–06 Wolverhampton W 32 4 **69 8**

STEWART, Thomas (F) 0 0
b.Craigavon 12-11-86
Source: Portadown. *Honours:* Northern Ireland Schools, Youth, Under-21.
2004–05 Wolverhampton W 0 0
2005–06 Wolverhampton W 0 0

WREXHAM (90)

BAYLISS, Dave (D) 258 9
H: 6 0 W: 12 11 b.Liverpool 8-6-76
Source: Trainee.
1994–95 Rochdale 1 0
1995–96 Rochdale 28 0
1996–97 Rochdale 24 0
1997–98 Rochdale 29 2
1998–99 Rochdale 25 1
1999–2000 Rochdale 29 3
2000–01 Rochdale 41 3
2001–02 Rochdale 9 0
2001–02 Luton T 18 0
2002–03 Luton T 13 0
2003–04 Luton T 6 0
2004–05 Luton T 0 0 **37 0**
2004–05 *Chester C* 9 0 **9 0**
2005–06 Wrexham 22 0 **22 0**
2005–06 *Rochdale* 4 0 **190 9**

BENNETT, Dean (M) 220 18
H: 5 11 W: 11 00 b.Wolverhampton 13-12-77
Source: Aston Villa Juniors.
1996–97 WBA 1 0
1997–98 WBA 0 0 **1 0**
2000–01 Kidderminster H 42 4
2001–02 Kidderminster H 42 8
2002–03 Kidderminster H 32 1
2003–04 Kidderminster H 38 3 **154 16**
2002–03 Wrexham 18 0
2003–04 Wrexham 0 0
2004–05 Wrexham 14 0
2005–06 Wrexham 33 2 **65 2**

CROWELL, Matt (M) 72 4
H: 5 11 W: 10 10 b.Bridgend 3-7-84
Source: Scholar. *Honours:* Wales Youth, Under-21.
2001–02 Southampton 0 0
2002–03 Southampton 0 0
2003–04 Wrexham 15 1
2004–05 Wrexham 28 0
2005–06 Wrexham 29 3 **72 4**

DONE, Matt (M) 6 0
H: 5 10 W: 10 04 b.Oswestry 22-6-88
Source: Scholar.
2005–06 Wrexham 6 0 **6 0**

EVANS, Gareth (D) 0 0
H: 6 1 W: 12 12 b.Wrexham 10-1-87
Source: Scholar.
2005–06 Wrexham 0 0

FERGUSON, Darren (M) 421 28
H: 6 0 W: 11 10 b.Glasgow 9-2-72
Source: Trainee. *Honours:* Scotland Youth, Under-21.
1990–91 Manchester U 5 0
1991–92 Manchester U 4 0
1992–93 Manchester U 15 0
1993–94 Manchester U 3 0 **27 0**
1993–94 Wolverhampton W 14 0
1994–95 Wolverhampton W 24 0
1995–96 Wolverhampton W 33 1
1996–97 Wolverhampton W 16 3
1997–98 Wolverhampton W 26 0
1998–99 Wolverhampton W 4 0
1999–2000 Wolverhampton W 0 0 **117 4**
1999–2000 Wrexham 37 4
2000–01 Wrexham 43 9
2001–02 Wrexham 38 3
2002–03 Wrexham 41 2
2003–04 Wrexham 39 1
2004–05 Wrexham 40 3
2005–06 Wrexham 39 2 **277 24**

HARRIS, Mark (D) 0 0
H: 5 11 W: 10 10 b.Liverpool 15-8-83
Source: Scholar.
2005–06 Wrexham 0 0

HOLT, Andy (M) 292 22
H: 6 1 W: 12 07 b.Stockport 21-5-78
Source: Trainee.
1996–97 Oldham Ath 1 0
1997–98 Oldham Ath 14 1
1998–99 Oldham Ath 43 5
1999–2000 Oldham Ath 46 3
2000–01 Oldham Ath 20 1 **124 10**
2000–01 *Hull C* 10 2
2001–02 Hull C 30 0
2002–03 Hull C 6 0
2002–03 *Barnsley* 7 0 **7 0**
2002–03 *Shrewsbury T* 9 0 **9 0**
2003–04 Hull C 25 1 **71 3**
2004–05 Wrexham 45 6
2005–06 Wrexham 36 3 **81 9**

INGHAM, Michael (G) 99 0
H: 6 4 W: 13 10 b.Preston 7-9-80
Source: Malachians. *Honours:* Northern Ireland Youth, Under-21, 2 full caps.
1998–99 Cliftonville 18 0 **18 0**
1999–2000 Sunderland 0 0
1999–2000 *Carlisle U* 7 0 **7 0**
2000–01 Sunderland 0 0
2001–02 Sunderland 0 0
2001–02 *Stoke C* 0 0
2002–03 Sunderland 0 0
2002–03 *Darlington* 3 0 **3 0**
2002–03 *York C* 17 0 **17 0**
2003–04 Sunderland 0 0
2003–04 *Wrexham* 11 0
2004–05 Sunderland 2 0 **2 0**
2004–05 *Doncaster R* 1 0 **1 0**
2005–06 Wrexham 40 0 **51 0**

JONES, Mark (M) 82 17
H: 5 11 W: 10 12 b.Wrexham 15-8-83
Source: Scholar. *Honours:* Wales Under-21.
2002–03 Wrexham 1 0
2003–04 Wrexham 13 1
2004–05 Wrexham 26 3
2005–06 Wrexham 42 13 **82 17**

JONES, Michael (G) 8 0
H: 6 4 W: 12 05 b.Liverpool 3-12-87
Source: Scholar.
2004–05 Wrexham 1 0
2005–06 Wrexham 7 0 **8 0**

LAWRENCE, Dennis (D) 195 14
H: 6 7 W: 11 13 b.Trinidad 1-8-74
Source: Defence Force. *Honours:* Trinidad & Tobago 66 full caps, 4 goals.
2000–01 Wrexham 3 0
2001–02 Wrexham 32 2
2002–03 Wrexham 32 1
2003–04 Wrexham 45 5
2004–05 Wrexham 44 4
2005–06 Wrexham 39 2 **195 14**

MACKIN, Levi (M) 28 0
H: 6 1 W: 11 04 b.Chester 4-4-86
Source: Scholar. *Honours:* Wales Under-21.
2003–04 Wrexham 1 0
2004–05 Wrexham 10 0
2005–06 Wrexham 17 0 **28 0**

McEVILLY, Lee (F) 108 32
H: 6 0 W: 13 00 b.Liverpool 15-4-82
Source: Burscough. *Honours:* Northern Ireland Under-21, 1 full cap.
2001–02 Rochdale 18 4
2002–03 Rochdale 37 15
2003–04 Rochdale 30 6 **85 25**
From Accrington S
2005–06 Wrexham 23 7 **23 7**

PEJIC, Shaun (D) 122 0
H: 6 0 W: 11 07 b.Hereford 16-11-82
Source: Trainee. *Honours:* Wales Under-21.
2000–01 Wrexham 1 0
2001–02 Wrexham 12 0
2002–03 Wrexham 27 0
2003–04 Wrexham 21 0
2004–05 Wrexham 35 0
2005–06 Wrexham 26 0 **122 0**

REED, Jamie (F) 3 0
H: 5 11 W: 11 07 b.Deeside 13-8-87
Source: Scholar.
2005–06 Wrexham 3 0 **3 0**
To Glentoran (loan) January 2006

ROCHE, Lee (D) 113 3
H: 5 10 W: 10 11 b.Bolton 28-10-80
Source: Trainee. *Honours:* England Youth, Under-21.
1998–99 Manchester U 0 0
1999–2000 Manchester U 0 0
2000–01 Manchester U 0 0
2000–01 *Wrexham* 41 0
2001–02 Manchester U 0 0
2002–03 Manchester U 1 0 **1 0**
2003–04 Burnley 25 1
2004–05 Burnley 29 1 **54 2**
2005–06 Wrexham 17 1 **58 1**

SMITH, Alex (M) 198 7
H: 5 8 W: 10 09 b.Liverpool 15-2-76
Source: Trainee.
1994–95 Everton 0 0
1995–96 Everton 0 0
1995–96 Swindon T 8 0
1996–97 Swindon T 18 1

1997–98	Swindon T	5	0	**31**	**1**
1997–98	Huddersfield T	6	0	**6**	**0**
1998–99	Chester C	32	2	**32**	**2**
1998–99	Port Vale	8	0		
1999–2000	Port Vale	13	0		
2000–01	Port Vale	37	2	**58**	**2**
2001–02	Reading	13	2		
2002–03	Reading	1	0		
2002–03	*Shrewsbury T*	13	0	**13**	**0**
2003–04	Reading	0	0	**14**	**2**
2004–05	Wrexham	24	0		
2005–06	Wrexham	20	0	**44**	**0**

SPENDER, Simon (D) **38** **2**

H: 5 11 W: 11 00 b.Mold 15-11-85

Source: Scholar. *Honours:* Wales Youth, Under-21.

2003–04	Wrexham	6	0		
2004–05	Wrexham	13	0		
2005–06	Wrexham	19	2	**38**	**2**

WALTERS, Jon (F) **101** **12**

H: 6 0 W: 12 06 b.Birkenhead 20-9-83

Source: Blackburn R Scholar. *Honours:* Eire Under-21.

2001–02	Bolton W	0	0		
2002–03	Bolton W	4	0		
2002–03	*Hull C*	11	5		
2003–04	Bolton W	0	0	**4**	**0**
2003–04	Crewe Alex	0	0		
2003–04	*Barnsley*	8	0	**8**	**0**
2003–04	Hull C	16	1		
2004–05	Hull C	21	1	**48**	**7**
2004–05	*Scunthorpe U*	3	0	**3**	**0**
2005–06	Wrexham	38	5	**38**	**5**

WHITLEY, Jim (M) **209** **2**

H: 5 9 W: 10 12 b.Zambia 14-4-75

Source: Trainee. *Honours:* Northern Ireland B, 3 full caps.

1993–94	Manchester C	0	0		
1994–95	Manchester C	0	0		
1995–96	Manchester C	0	0		
1996–97	Manchester C	0	0		
1997–98	Manchester C	19	0		
1998–99	Manchester C	18	0		
1999–2000	Manchester C	1	0		
1999–2000	*Blackpool*	8	0	**8**	**0**
2000–01	Manchester C	0	0	**38**	**0**
2000–01	*Norwich C*	8	1	**8**	**1**
2000–01	*Swindon T*	2	0	**2**	**0**
2000–01	*Northampton T*	13	0	**13**	**0**
2000–01	*Nottingham F*	0	0		
2001–02	Wrexham	34	0		
2002–03	Wrexham	44	1		
2003–04	Wrexham	36	0		
2004–05	Wrexham	16	0		
2005–06	Wrexham	10	0	**140**	**1**

WILLIAMS, Danny (M) **222** **16**

H: 6 1 W: 13 00 b.Wrexham 12-7-79

Source: Trainee. *Honours:* Wales Under-21.

1996–97	Liverpool	0	0		
1997–98	Liverpool	0	0		
1998–99	Liverpool	0	0		
1998–99	Wrexham	0	0		
1999–2000	Wrexham	24	1		
2000–01	Wrexham	15	2		
2001–02	Kidderminster H	38	1		
2002–03	Kidderminster H	45	2		
2003–04	Kidderminster H	28	5	**111**	**8**
2003–04	Bristol R	6	1	**6**	**1**
2004–05	Wrexham	21	0		
2005–06	Wrexham	45	4	**105**	**7**

WILLIAMS, Marc (F) **4** **0**

H: 5 10 W: 11 12 b.Colwyn Bay 27-7-88

Source: Scholar. *Honours:* Wales Under-21.

2005–06	Wrexham	4	0	**4**	**0**

WILLIAMS, Mike (D) **12** **0**

H: 5 11 W: 12 00 b.Colwyn Bay 27-10-86

Source: Scholar. *Honours:* Wales Under-21.

2005–06	Wrexham	12	0	**12**	**0**

WYCOMBE W (91)

ANTWI, Will (D) **9** **0**

H: 6 2 W: 12 08 b.Epsom 19-10-82

Source: Scholar.

2002–03	Crystal Palace	4	0		
2003–04	Crystal Palace	0	0	**4**	**0**
From Aldershot T					
2005–06	Wycombe W	5	0	**5**	**0**

ANYA, Ikechi (M) **5** **0**

H: 5 5 W: 11 04 b.Glasgow 3-1-88

Source: Scholar.

2004–05	Wycombe W	3	0		
2005–06	Wycombe W	2	0	**5**	**0**

BETSY, Kevin (M) **200** **30**

H: 6 1 W: 12 00 b.Seychelles 20-3-78

Source: Woking.

1998–99	Fulham	7	1		
1999–2000	Fulham	2	0		
1999–2000	*Bournemouth*	5	0	**5**	**0**
1999–2000	*Hull C*	2	0	**2**	**0**
2000–01	Fulham	5	0		
2001–02	Fulham	1	0	**15**	**1**
2001–02	Barnsley	10	0		
2002–03	Barnsley	39	5		
2003–04	Barnsley	45	10		
2004–05	Barnsley	0	0	**94**	**15**
2004–05	*Hartlepool U*	6	1	**6**	**1**
2004–05	Oldham Ath	36	5	**36**	**5**
2005–06	Wycombe W	42	8	**42**	**8**

BLOOMFIELD, Matt (M) **77** **8**

H: 5 9 W: 11 00 b.Ipswich 8-2-84

Source: Scholar. *Honours:* England Youth, Under-20.

2001–02	Ipswich T	0	0		
2002–03	Ipswich T	0	0		
2003–04	Ipswich T	0	0		
2003–04	Wycombe W	12	1		
2004–05	Wycombe W	26	2		
2005–06	Wycombe W	39	5	**77**	**8**

BURNELL, Joe (M) **188** **1**

H: 5 8 W: 12 00 b.Bristol 10-10-80

Source: Trainee.

1999–2000	Bristol C	17	0		
2000–01	Bristol C	23	0		
2001–02	Bristol C	30	0		
2002–03	Bristol C	44	0		
2003–04	Bristol C	17	1	**131**	**1**
2004–05	Wycombe W	24	0		
2005–06	Wycombe W	33	0	**57**	**0**

CADMORE, Tom (D) **0** **0**

b.Rickmansworth 26-1-88

Source: Scholar.

2005–06	Wycombe W	0	0		

CHRISTON, Lewis (M) **0** **0**

b.Milton Keynes 21-1-89

Source: Scholar.

2005–06	Wycombe W	0	0		

DIXON, Jonny (F) **63** **6**

H: 5 9 W: 11 01 b.Murcia 16-1-84

Source: Scholar.

2002–03	Wycombe W	22	5		
2003–04	Wycombe W	8	0		
2004–05	Wycombe W	16	1		
2005–06	Wycombe W	17	0	**63**	**6**

EASTER, Jermaine (F) **109** **23**

H: 5 9 W: 12 02 b.Cardiff 15-1-82

Source: Trainee. *Honours:* Wales Youth.

2000–01	Wolverhampton W	0	0		
2000–01	Hartlepool U	4	0		
2001–02	Hartlepool U	12	2		
2002–03	Hartlepool U	8	0		
2003–04	Hartlepool U	3	0	**27**	**2**
2003–04	*Cambridge U*	15	2		
2004–05	Cambridge U	24	6	**39**	**8**
2004–05	Boston U	9	3	**9**	**3**
2005–06	Stockport Co	19	8	**19**	**8**
2005–06	Wycombe W	15	2	**15**	**2**

EASTON, Clint (M) **191** **8**

H: 5 11 W: 11 00 b.Barking 1-10-77

Source: Trainee. *Honours:* England Youth.

1996–97	Watford	17	1		
1997–98	Watford	12	0		
1998–99	Watford	7	0		
1999–2000	Watford	17	0		
2000–01	Watford	11	0	**64**	**1**
2001–02	Norwich C	14	1		
2002–03	Norwich C	26	2		
2003–04	Norwich C	10	2	**50**	**5**
2004–05	Wycombe W	33	1		
2005–06	Wycombe W	44	1	**77**	**2**

FAULKNER, James (F) **0** **0**

b.Aylesbury 22-11-87

Source: Scholar.

2005–06	Wycombe W	0	0		

GREGORY, Steven (D) **1** **0**

b.Aylesbury 19-3-87

Source: Scholar.

2005–06	Wycombe W	1	0	**1**	**0**

GRIFFIN, Charlie (F) **50** **5**

H: 6 0 W: 12 07 b.Bath 25-6-79

Source: Bristol R Schoolboy.

1998–99	Swindon T	5	1		
1999–2000	Swindon T	21	1		
2000–01	Swindon T	2	0	**28**	**2**
From Forest Green R.					
2005–06	Wycombe W	22	3	**22**	**3**

JOHNSON, Roger (D) **157** **19**

H: 6 3 W: 11 00 b.Ashford 28-4-83

Source: Trainee.

1999–2000	Wycombe W	1	0		
2000–01	Wycombe W	1	0		
2001–02	Wycombe W	7	1		
2002–03	Wycombe W	33	3		
2003–04	Wycombe W	28	2		
2004–05	Wycombe W	42	6		
2005–06	Wycombe W	45	7	**157**	**19**

LEE, Robert (M) **703** **105**

H: 5 10 W: 11 10 b.West Ham 1-2-66

Source: Hornchurch. *Honours:* England Under-21, 21 full caps, 2 goals.

1983–84	Charlton Ath	11	4		
1984–85	Charlton Ath	39	10		
1985–86	Charlton Ath	35	8		
1986–87	Charlton Ath	33	3		
1987–88	Charlton Ath	23	2		
1988–89	Charlton Ath	31	5		
1989–90	Charlton Ath	37	1		
1990–91	Charlton Ath	43	13		
1991–92	Charlton Ath	39	12		
1992–93	Charlton Ath	7	1	**298**	**59**
1992–93	Newcastle U	36	10		
1993–94	Newcastle U	41	7		
1994–95	Newcastle U	35	9		
1995–96	Newcastle U	36	8		
1996–97	Newcastle U	33	5		
1997–98	Newcastle U	28	4		
1998–99	Newcastle U	26	0		
1999–2000	Newcastle U	30	0		
2000–01	Newcastle U	22	0		
2001–02	Newcastle U	16	1	**303**	**44**
2001–02	Derby Co	13	0		
2002–03	Derby Co	35	2	**48**	**2**
2003–04	West Ham U	16	0		
2004–05	West Ham U	0	0	**16**	**0**
2004–05	Oldham Ath	0	0		
2004–05	Wycombe W	7	0		
2005–06	Wycombe W	31	0	**38**	**0**

MARTIN, Russell (M) **30** **3**

H: 6 0 W: 11 08 b.Brighton 4-1-86

2004–05	Wycombe W	7	0		
2005–06	Wycombe W	23	3	**30**	**3**

MOONEY, Tommy (F) **560** **162**

H: 5 10 W: 13 05 b.Billingham 11-8-71

Source: Trainee.

1989–90	Aston Villa	0	0		
1990–91	Scarborough	27	13		
1991–92	Scarborough	40	8		
1992–93	Scarborough	40	9	**107**	**30**
1993–94	Southend U	14	5	**14**	**5**
1993–94	*Watford*	10	2		
1994–95	Watford	29	3		
1995–96	Watford	42	6		
1996–97	Watford	37	13		
1997–98	Watford	45	6		
1998–99	Watford	36	9		
1999–2000	Watford	12	2		
2000–01	Watford	39	19	**250**	**60**

2001–02	Birmingham C	33	13		
2002–03	Birmingham C	1	0	**34**	**13**
2002–03	*Stoke C*	12	3	**12**	**3**
2002–03	*Sheffield U*	3	0	**3**	**0**
2002–03	*Derby Co*	8	0	**8**	**0**
2003–04	Swindon T	45	19	**45**	**19**
2004–05	Oxford U	42	15	**42**	**15**
2005–06	Wycombe W	45	17	**45**	**17**

NETHERCOTT, Stuart (D) **336** **12**

H: 6 0 W: 13 01 b.Ilford 21-3-73

Source: Trainee. *Honours:* England Under-21.

1991–92	Tottenham H	0	0		
1991–92	*Maidstone U*	13	1	**13**	**1**
1991–92	*Barnet*	3	0	**3**	**0**
1992–93	Tottenham H	5	0		
1993–94	Tottenham H	10	0		
1994–95	Tottenham H	17	0		
1995–96	Tottenham H	13	0		
1996–97	Tottenham H	9	0		
1997–98	Tottenham H	0	0	**54**	**0**
1997–98	Millwall	10	0		
1998–99	Millwall	37	2		
1999–2000	Millwall	37	0		
2000–01	Millwall	35	2		
2001–02	Millwall	46	3		
2002–03	Millwall	36	2		
2003–04	Millwall	14	1	**215**	**10**
2003–04	Wycombe W	22	1		
2004–05	Wycombe W	29	0		
2005–06	Wycombe W	0	0	**51**	**1**

OAKES, Stefan (M) **158** **9**

H: 6 1 W: 13 07 b.Leicester 6-9-78

Source: Trainee.

1997–98	Leicester C	0	0		
1998–99	Leicester C	3	0		
1999–2000	Leicester C	22	1		
2000–01	Leicester C	13	0		
2001–02	Leicester C	21	1		
2002–03	Leicester C	5	0	**64**	**2**
2002–03	*Crewe Alex*	7	0	**7**	**0**
2003–04	Walsall	5	0	**5**	**0**
2003–04	Notts Co	14	0		
2004–05	Notts Co	31	5	**45**	**5**
2005–06	Wycombe W	37	2	**37**	**2**

RYAN, Keith (M) **351** **29**

H: 5 10 W: 12 06 b.Northampton 25-6-70

Source: Berkhamsted T.

1993–94	Wycombe W	42	1		
1994–95	Wycombe W	24	4		
1995–96	Wycombe W	23	4		
1996–97	Wycombe W	0	0		
1997–98	Wycombe W	40	3		
1998–99	Wycombe W	28	1		
1999–2000	Wycombe W	38	6		
2000–01	Wycombe W	30	4		
2001–02	Wycombe W	35	1		
2002–03	Wycombe W	36	2		
2003–04	Wycombe W	17	1		
2004–05	Wycombe W	38	2		
2005–06	Wycombe W	0	0	**351**	**29**

SENDA, Danny (M) **276** **9**

H: 5 10 W: 10 02 b.Harrow 17-4-81

Source: Southampton Trainee. *Honours:* England Youth.

1998–99	Wycombe W	6	0		
1999–2000	Wycombe W	27	1		
2000–01	Wycombe W	31	2		
2001–02	Wycombe W	43	0		
2002–03	Wycombe W	41	2		
2003–04	Wycombe W	40	0		
2004–05	Wycombe W	44	4		
2005–06	Wycombe W	44	0	**276**	**9**

STONEBRIDGE, Ian (F) **239** **44**

H: 6 0 W: 11 04 b.Lewisham 30-8-81

Source: Tottenham H Trainee. *Honours:* England Youth.

1999–2000	Plymouth Arg	31	9		
2000–01	Plymouth Arg	31	11		
2001–02	Plymouth Arg	42	8		
2002–03	Plymouth Arg	37	5		
2003–04	Plymouth Arg	30	5	**171**	**38**
2004–05	Wycombe W	38	4		
2005–06	Wycombe W	27	2	**65**	**6**
2005–06	*Torquay U*	3	0	**3**	**0**

TALIA, Frank (G) **273** **0**

H: 6 1 W: 13 06 b.Melbourne 20-7-72

Honours: Australia Schools, Under-20.

1990–91	Sunshine	11	0		
1991–92	Sunshine	0	0	**11**	**0**
1992–93	Blackburn R	0	0		
1992–93	*Hartlepool U*	14	0	**14**	**0**
1993–94	Blackburn R	0	0		
1994–95	Blackburn R	0	0		
1995–96	Blackburn R	0	0		
1995–96	Swindon T	16	0		
1996–97	Swindon T	15	0		
1997–98	Swindon T	2	0		
1998–99	Swindon T	43	0		
1999–2000	Swindon T	31	0	**107**	**0**
2000–01	Wolverhampton W	0	0		
2000–01	Sheffield U	6	0	**6**	**0**
2001–02	Antwerp	3	0	**3**	**0**
2001–02	Reading	0	0		
2002–03	Wycombe W	35	0		
2003–04	Wycombe W	17	0		
2004–05	Wycombe W	45	0		
2005–06	Wycombe W	35	0	**132**	**0**

TORRES, Sergio (M) **24** **1**

H: 6 2 W: 12 04 b.Mar del Plata 8-11-83

Source: Basingstoke T.

2005–06	Wycombe W	24	1	**24**	**1**

WILLIAMS, Steve (G) **21** **0**

H: 6 6 W: 13 10 b.Oxford 21-4-83

Source: Scholar.

2001–02	Wycombe W	0	0		
2002–03	Wycombe W	0	0		
2003–04	Wycombe W	19	0		
2004–05	Wycombe W	1	0		
2005–06	Wycombe W	1	0	**21**	**0**

WILLIAMSON, Mike (D) **90** **7**

H: 6 4 W: 13 03 b.Stoke 8-11-83

Source: Trainee.

2001–02	Torquay U	3	0		
2001–02	Southampton	0	0		
2002–03	Southampton	0	0		
2003–04	Southampton	0	0		
2003–04	*Torquay U*	11	0	**14**	**0**
2003–04	*Doncaster R*	0	0		
2004–05	Southampton	0	0		
2004–05	*Wycombe W*	37	2		
2005–06	Wycombe W	39	5	**76**	**7**

YEOVIL T (92)

ALVAREZ, Luciano (F) **63** **19**

H: 6 0 W: 12 02 b.Buenos Aires 30-11-78

2002	Inter Turku	18	2		
2003	Inter Turku	23	12		
2004	Inter Turku	18	4	**59**	**18**
2005–06	Yeovil T	4	1	**4**	**1**

AMANKWAAH, Kevin (D) **125** **2**

H: 6 1 W: 12 12 b.Harrow 19-5-82

Source: Scholar. *Honours:* England Youth.

1999–2000	Bristol C	5	0		
2000–01	Bristol C	14	0		
2001–02	Bristol C	24	1		
2002–03	Bristol C	1	0		
2002–03	*Torquay U*	6	0	**6**	**0**
2003–04	Bristol C	5	0		
2003–04	*Cheltenham T*	12	0	**12**	**0**
2004–05	Bristol C	5	0	**54**	**1**
2004–05	Yeovil T	15	0		
2005–06	Yeovil T	38	1	**53**	**1**

BARKER, Danny (G) **0** **0**

H: 6 1 W: 11 05 b.Oxford 30-1-87

2005–06	Yeovil T	0	0		

BARRY, Anthony (M) **4** **0**

H: 5 7 W: 10 00 b.Liverpool 29-5-86

Source: Everton.

2004–05	Coventry C	0	0		
From Accrington S.					
2005–06	Yeovil T	4	0	**4**	**0**

BASTIANINI, Pablo (F) **45** **4**

H: 6 2 W: 14 00 b.Zarate 9-11-82

2003–04	Quilmes	8	0		
2004–05	Quilmes	17	1	**25**	**1**
2005–06	Yeovil T	20	3	**20**	**3**

COLLIS, Steve (G) **43** **0**

H: 6 3 W: 12 05 b.Harrow 18-3-81

Source: Barnet Juniors.

1999–2000	Barnet	0	0		
2000–01	Nottingham F	0	0		
2001–02	Nottingham F	0	0		
2003–04	Yeovil T	11	0		
2004–05	Yeovil T	9	0		
2005–06	Yeovil T	23	0	**43**	**0**

CULLINGFORD, Richard (M) **0** **0**

H: 5 11 W: 11 09 b.Yeovil 17-1-87

2005–06	Yeovil T	0	0		

DAVIES, Arron (M) **66** **16**

H: 5 9 W: 11 00 b.Cardiff 22-6-84

Source: Trainee. *Honours:* Wales Under-21, 1 full cap.

2002–03	Southampton	0	0		
2003–04	Southampton	0	0		
2003–04	*Barnsley*	4	0	**4**	**0**
2004–05	Southampton	0	0		
2004–05	Yeovil T	23	8		
2005–06	Yeovil T	39	8	**62**	**16**

EDWARDS, Jake (F) **48** **9**

H: 6 1 W: 13 01 b.Prestwich 11-5-76

Source: James Maddison Uni.

1998–99	Wrexham	9	1		
1999–2000	Wrexham	2	1	**11**	**2**
From Telford U.					
2003–04	Yeovil T	27	6	**27**	**6**
From Exeter C.					
2005–06	*Chester C*	10	1	**10**	**1**

GALL, Kevin (F) **173** **18**

H: 5 9 W: 10 08 b.Merthyr 4-2-82

Source: Trainee. *Honours:* Wales Schools, Youth, Under-21.

1998–99	Newcastle U	0	0		
1999–2000	Newcastle U	0	0		
2000–01	Newcastle U	0	0		
2000–01	Bristol R	10	2		
2001–02	Bristol R	31	3		
2002–03	Bristol R	9	0	**50**	**5**
2003–04	Yeovil T	43	8		
2004–05	Yeovil T	43	3		
2005–06	Yeovil T	37	2	**123**	**13**

GUYETT, Scott (D) **61** **2**

H: 6 2 W: 13 06 b.Ascot 20-1-76

Source: Brisbane C, Gresley R, Southport.

2001–02	Oxford U	22	0	**22**	**0**
From Chester C.					
2004–05	Yeovil T	18	2		
2005–06	Yeovil T	21	0	**39**	**2**

HARROLD, Matt (F) **80** **13**

H: 6 1 W: 11 10 b.Leyton 25-7-84

Source: Harlow T.

2003–04	Brentford	13	2		
2004–05	Brentford	19	0	**32**	**2**
2004–05	*Grimsby T*	6	2	**6**	**2**
2005–06	Yeovil T	42	9	**42**	**9**

JEVONS, Phil (F) **179** **63**

H: 5 11 W: 12 00 b.Liverpool 1-8-79

Source: Trainee.

1996–97	Everton	0	0		
1997–98	Everton	0	0		
1998–99	Everton	1	0		
1999–2000	Everton	3	0		
2000–01	Everton	4	0	**8**	**0**
2001–02	Grimsby T	31	6		
2002–03	Grimsby T	3	0		
2002–03	*Hull C*	24	3	**24**	**3**
2003–04	Grimsby T	29	12	**63**	**18**
2004–05	Yeovil T	46	27		
2005–06	Yeovil T	38	15	**84**	**42**

JOHNSON, Lee (M) **115** **14**

H: 5 6 W: 10 07 b.Newmarket 7-6-81

Source: Trainee.

1998–99	Watford	0	0		
1999–2000	Watford	0	0		
2000–01	Brighton & HA	0	0		
2000–01	Brentford	0	0		
2001–02	Brentford	0	0		
2003–04	Yeovil T	45	5		
2004–05	Yeovil T	44	7		
2005–06	Yeovil T	26	2	**115**	**14**

To Hearts January 2006

JONES, Nathan (M) **310** **9**
H: 5 6 W: 10 06 b.Rhondda 28-5-73
Source: Cardiff C Trainee, Maesteg Park, Ton Pentre, Merthyr T.

1995–96	Luton T	0	0		
Badajoz, Numaicia					
1997–98	Southend U	39	0		
1998–99	Southend U	17	0		
1998–99	*Scarborough*	9	0	**9**	**0**
1999–2000	Southend U	43	2	**99**	**2**
2000–01	Brighton & HA	40	4		
2001–02	Brighton & HA	36	2		
2002–03	Brighton & HA	28	1		
2003–04	Brighton & HA	36	0		
2004–05	Brighton & HA	19	0	**159**	**7**
2005–06	Yeovil T	43	0	**43**	**0**

LINDEGAARD, Andy (M) **75** **3**
H: 5 8 W: 11 04 b.Taunton 10-9-80
Source: Westland Sp.

2003–04	Yeovil T	23	2		
2004–05	Yeovil T	29	1		
2005–06	Yeovil T	23	0	**75**	**3**

LOCKWOOD, Adam (D) **82** **7**
H: 6 0 W: 12 07 b.Wakefield 26-10-81
Source: Reading Trainee.

2003–04	Yeovil T	43	4		
2004–05	Yeovil T	10	0		
2005–06	Yeovil T	20	0	**73**	**4**
2005–06	*Torquay U*	9	3	**9**	**3**

McCALLUM, Gavin (M) **0** **0**
H: 5 9 W: 12 00 b.Mississauga 24-8-87
Honours: Canada Under-20.

2005–06	Yeovil T	0	0		

MELONO, Alejandro (D) **1** **0**
H: 6 3 W: 13 05 b.Montevideo 27-4-77
Source: Chacarita Juniors.

2005–06	Yeovil T	1	0	**1**	**0**
To Dep Quito October 2005					

MILES, Colin (D) **92** **4**
H: 6 0 W: 13 10 b.Edmonton 6-9-78
Source: Trainee.

1996–97	Watford	0	0		
1997–98	Watford	1	0		
1998–99	Watford	0	0	**1**	**0**
1999–2000	Morton	4	0	**4**	**0**
From Dover Ath					
2003–04	Yeovil T	36	4		
2004–05	Yeovil T	21	0		
2005–06	Yeovil T	30	0	**87**	**4**

OLIVER, Luke (D) **7** **0**
H: 6 6 W: 14 05 b.Hammersmith 1-5-84
Source: Brook House.

2002–03	Wycombe W	2	0		
2003–04	Wycombe W	2	0	**4**	**0**
From Woking					
2005–06	Yeovil T	3	0	**3**	**0**

POOLE, David (M) **25** **2**
H: 5 8 W: 12 00 b.Manchester 25-11-84
Source: Trainee.

2002–03	Manchester U	0	0		
2003–04	Manchester U	0	0		
2004–05	Manchester U	0	0		
2005–06	Yeovil T	25	2	**25**	**2**

RAMOS, Francisco (G) **0** **0**
H: 6 3 W: 12 08 b.Lisbon 9-10-83

2005–06	Yeovil T	0	0		

REED, Steve (D) **19** **0**
H: 5 8 W: 12 02 b.Barnstaple 18-6-85
Source: Juniors.

2003–04	Yeovil T	5	0		
2004–05	Yeovil T	3	0		
2005–06	Yeovil T	0	0	**8**	**0**
2005–06	*Torquay U*	11	0	**11**	**0**

ROSE, Michael (D) **59** **1**
H: 5 11 W: 12 04 b.Salford 28-7-82
Source: Trainee.

1999–2000	Manchester U	0	0		
2000–01	Manchester U	0	0		
2001–02	Manchester U	0	0		
From Hereford U					
2004–05	Yeovil T	40	1		
2005–06	Yeovil T	1	0	**41**	**1**
2005–06	*Cheltenham T*	3	0	**3**	**0**
2005–06	*Scunthorpe U*	15	0	**15**	**0**

SKIVERTON, Terry (D) **120** **13**
H: 6 1 W: 13 06 b.Mile End 26-6-75
Source: Trainee.

1993–94	Chelsea	0	0		
1994–95	Chelsea	0	0		
1994–95	*Wycombe W*	10	0		
1995–96	Chelsea	0	0		
1995–96	Wycombe W	4	1		
1996–97	Wycombe W	6	0	**20**	**1**
From Welling U					
2003–04	Yeovil T	26	2		
2004–05	Yeovil T	38	4		
2005–06	Yeovil T	36	6	**100**	**12**

TERRY, Paul (M) **115** **8**
H: 5 10 W: 12 06 b.Barking 3-4-79
Source: Dagenham & R.

2003–04	Yeovil T	34	1		
2004–05	Yeovil T	39	6		
2005–06	Yeovil T	42	1	**115**	**8**

THOMAS, Bradley (D) **0** **0**
H: 6 2 W: 13 02 b.Forest Green 29-3-84
Source: Scholar.

2003–04	Peterborough U	0	0		
2004–05	Peterborough U	0	0		
From Eastleigh.					
2005–06	Yeovil T	0	0		

VINCENT, Jamie (D) **298** **10**
H: 5 10 W: 11 08 b.Wimbledon 18-6-75
Source: Trainee.

1993–94	Crystal Palace	0	0		
1994–95	Crystal Palace	0	0		
1994–95	*Bournemouth*	8	0		
1995–96	Crystal Palace	25	0		
1996–97	Crystal Palace	0	0	**25**	**0**
1996–97	Bournemouth	29	0		
1997–98	Bournemouth	44	3		
1998–99	Bournemouth	32	2	**113**	**5**
1998–99	Huddersfield T	7	0		
1999–2000	Huddersfield T	36	2		
2000–01	Huddersfield T	16	0	**59**	**2**
2000–01	Portsmouth	14	0		
2001–02	Portsmouth	34	1		
2002–03	Portsmouth	0	0		
2003–04	Portsmouth	0	0	**48**	**1**
2003–04	*Walsall*	12	0	**12**	**0**
2003–04	Derby Co	7	1		
2004–05	Derby Co	15	1	**22**	**2**
2005–06	Millwall	19	0	**19**	**0**
2005–06	Yeovil T	0	0		

WEALE, Chris (G) **98** **0**
H: 6 2 W: 13 03 b.Yeovil 9-2-82
Source: Juniors.

2003–04	Yeovil T	35	0		
2004–05	Yeovil T	38	0		
2005–06	Yeovil T	25	0	**98**	**0**

WEBB, Daniel (F) **114** **9**
H: 6 1 W: 11 08 b.Poole 2-7-83

2000–01	Southend U	15	1		
2001–02	Southend U	16	2		
2001–02	*Brighton & HA*	12	1		
2002–03	Southend U	0	0	**31**	**3**
2002–03	*Brighton & HA*	3	0	**15**	**1**
2002–03	Hull C	12	0		
2002–03	*Lincoln C*	5	1	**5**	**1**
2003–04	Hull C	4	0	**16**	**0**
2003–04	Cambridge U	21	3		
2004–05	Cambridge U	22	1		
2005–06	Cambridge U	0	0	**43**	**4**
2005–06	Yeovil T	4	0	**4**	**0**

WILLIAMS, Dale (F) **1** **0**
H: 6 0 W: 11 04 b.Neath 26-3-87
Source: Scholar. *Honours:* Wales Youth, Under-21.

2004–05	Yeovil T	0	0		
2005–06	Yeovil T	1	0	**1**	**0**

ENGLISH LEAGUE PLAYERS – INDEX

TRANSFERS 2005–06

JUNE 2005	*From*	*To*	*Fee in £*
2 Bent, Darren	Ipswich Town	Charlton Athletic	3,000,000
7 Campbell, Dudley J.	Yeading	Brentford	undisclosed
29 Doherty, Thomas	Bristol City	Queens Park Rangers	undisclosed
6 Evatt, Ian R.	Chesterfield	Queens Park Rangers	undisclosed
8 Heffernan, Paul	Bristol City	Doncaster Rovers	100,000
16 Lynch, Mark J.	Sunderland	Hull City	undisclosed
3 Macken, Jonathan P.	Manchester City	Crystal Palace	1,100,000
14 Moore, Stefan	Aston Villa	Queens Park Rangers	undisclosed
15 Parker, Scott M.	Chelsea	Newcastle United	6,500,000
30 Pollitt, Michael F.	Rotherham United	Wigan Athletic	200,000
16 Stead, Jonathan	Blackburn Rovers	Sunderland	1,800,000
10 Van der Sar, Edwin	Fulham	Manchester United	undisclosed
11 Vernon, Scott M.	Oldham Athletic	Blackpool	undisclosed
29 Villis, Matthew	Plymouth Argyle	Torquay United	undisclosed
1 Webber, Daniel V.	Watford	Sheffield United	500,000
9 Wellens, Richard P.	Blackpool	Oldham Athletic	undisclosed
JULY 2005			
11 Ambrose, Darren	Newcastle United	Charlton Athletic	700,000
8 Artell, David J.	Mansfield Town	Chester City	undisclosed
7 Bellamy, Craig D.	Newcastle United	Blackburn Rovers	5,000,000
28 Blake, Robert J.	Birmingham City	Leeds United	800,000
15 Blundell, Gregg	Doncaster Rovers	Chester City	105,000
5 Breckin, Ian	Wigan Athletic	Nottingham Forest	350,000
26 Bridges, Michael	Sunderland	Bristol City	undisclosed
20 Carruthers, Christopher P.A.	Northampton Town	Bristol Rovers	undisclosed
5 Carter, Darren A.	Birmingham City	West Bromwich Albion	1,500,000
21 Cole, Andrew A.	Fulham	Manchester City	undisclosed
14 Cole, Mitchell J.	Grays Athletic	Southend United	undisclosed
26 Coles, Daniel R.	Bristol City	Hull City	200,000
12 Coughlan, Graham	Plymouth Argyle	Sheffield Wednesday	undisclosed
20 Crouch, Peter J.	Southampton	Liverpool	7,000,000
2 Davis, Kelvin G.	Ipswich Town	Sunderland	1,250,000
14 Dichio, Daniele S.E.	Millwall	Preston North End	160,000
1 Eaden, Nicholas J.	Wigan Athletic	Nottingham Forest	Free
4 Forssell, Mikael K.	Chelsea	Birmingham City	3,000,000
19 Foster, Benjamin	Stoke City	Manchester United	1,000,000
27 Gilbert, Peter	Plymouth Argyle	Leicester City	200,000
22 Gunnarsson, Brynjar B.	Watford	Reading	undisclosed
8 Hargreaves, Christian	Brentford	Oxford United	undisclosed
13 Harrold, Matthew	Brentford	Yeovil	undisclosed
11 Heath, Matthew P.	Leicester City	Coventry City	200,000
7 Helguson, Heidar	Watford	Fulham	1,300,000
30 Huddlestone, Thomas A.	Derby County	Tottenham Hotspur	2,500,000
21 Hughes, Andrew J.	Reading	Norwich City	undisclosed
21 Hulse, Robert W.	West Bromwich Albion	Leeds United	800,000
7 Johnson, Brett	Aldershot Town	Northampton Town	undisclosed
5 Konchesky, Paul M.	Charlton Athletic	West Ham United	1,500,000
20 Lennon, Aaron J.	Leeds United	Tottenham Hotspur	1,000,000
14 Lita, Leroy	Bristol City	Reading	1,000,000
4 Louis-Jean, Matthieu	Nottingham Forest	Norwich City	undisclosed
15 Martin, Daniel A.	Derby County	Notts County	undisclosed
20 Nade, Raphael	Woking	Carlisle United	25,000
7 O'Brien, Andrew J.	Newcastle United	Portsmouth	2,000,000
25 Parkin, Sam	Swindon Town	Ipswich Town	450,000
6 Phillips, Kevin	Southampton	Aston Villa	750,000
22 Prendergast, Rory	Accrington Stanley	Blackpool	undisclosed
6 Purser, Wayne M.	Peterborough United	Weymouth	undisclosed
22 Rodgers, Luke J.	Shrewsbury Town	Crewe Alexandra	undisclosed
20 Shipperley, Neil J.	Crystal Palace	Sheffield United	undisclosed
15 Stewart, Jordan B.	Leicester City	Watford	125,000
13 Talbot, Stewart D.	Brentford	Boston United	undisclosed
13 Taylor, Ryan A.	Tranmere Rovers	Wigan Athletic	750,000
19 Thornton, Sean	Sunderland	Doncaster Rovers	175,000
27 Vassell, Darius	Aston Villa	Manchester City	2,000,000
22 Vine, Rowan	Portsmouth	Luton Town	250,000
12 Williamson, Lee	Northampton Town	Rotherham United	undisclosed
19 Wright-Phillips, Shaun C.	Manchester City	Chelsea	21,000,000
13 Yakubu, Ayegbeni	Portsmouth	Middlesbrough	7,500,000

TEMPORARY TRANSFERS

14 Beckett, Luke J. – Sheffield United – Oldham Athletic
6 Davies, Andrew – Middlesbrough – Derby County
26 Denton, Samuel E. – Bradford City – Harrogate Town
15 Diouf, El Hadji O. – Liverpool – Bolton Wanderers
1 Duffy, Richard – Portsmouth – Coventry City
26 Eagles, Christopher M. – Manchester United – Sheffield Wednesday
30 Elebert, David – Preston North End – Scarborough
6 Johnson, Edward W. – Manchester United – Crewe Alexandra
12 King, Marlon F. – Nottingham Forest – Watford
18 Kirkland, Christopher E. – Liverpool – West Bromwich Albion
26 McArdle, Rory A. – Sheffield Wednesday – Rochdale
7 Robert, Laurent – Newcastle United – Portsmouth
6 Sawyer, Gary D. – Plymouth Argyle – Exeter City
15 Smertin, Alexei – Chelsea – Charlton Athletic
11 Spector, Jonathan M. – Manchester United – Charlton Athletic
18 Stack, Graham – Arsenal – Reading
1 Symes, Michael – Bradford City – Macclesfield Town
21 Young, Jamie – Reading – Rushden & Diamonds

AUGUST 2005

	Player	From	To	Fee
22	Anderton, Darren R.	Birmingham City	Wolverhampton Wanderers	undisclosed
25	Asaba, Carl	Stoke City	Millwall	undisclosed
23	Baros, Milan	Liverpool	Aston Villa	6,500,000
3	Broomes, Marlon C.	Preston North End	Stoke City	undisclosed
8	Camara, Henri	Wolverhampton Wanderers	Wigan Athletic	3,000,000
8	Carlisle, Clarke J.	Leeds United	Watford	100,000
31	Clare, Daryl A.	Boston United	Crawley Town	undisclosed
1	Clarke, Clive	Stoke City	West Ham United	275,000
31	Connolly, David J.	Leicester City	Wigan Athletic	2,000,000
31	Courtney, Duane	AFC Telford United	Burnley	25,000
24	Cresswell, Richard P.W.	Preston North End	Leeds United	1,150,000
5	Cullip, Daniel	Sheffield United	Nottingham Forest	undisclosed
25	Dadi, Eugene	Tranmere Rovers	Nottingham Forest	undisclosed
31	Davies, Curtis E.	Luton Town	West Bromwich Albion	undisclosed
11	De Zeeuw, Arjan	Portsmouth	Wigan Athletic	500,000
24	Devaney, Martin T.	Watford	Barnsley	undisclosed
15	Ellington, Nathan L.F.	Wigan Athletic	West Bromwich Albion	3,000,000
5	Francis, Damien J.	Norwich City	Wigan Athletic	1,500,000
5	Fuller, Ricardo	Portsmouth	Southampton	340,000
11	Graham, David	Wigan Athletic	Sheffield Wednesday	250,000
11	Gray, Andrew D.	Sheffield United	Sunderland	1,100,000
31	Hammond, Elvis Z.	Fulham	Leicester City	undisclosed
30	Harley, Jon	Sheffield United	Burnley	150,000
4	Henderson, Darius A.	Gillingham	Watford	450,000
6	Hughes, Aaron W.	Newcastle United	Aston Villa	1,500,000
31	Hume, Iain	Tranmere Rovers	Leicester City	500,000
31	Jenas, Jermaine A.	Newcastle United	Tottenham Hotspur	7,000,000
31	Johnson, Gavin	Boston United	Northampton Town	undisclosed
25	Morrison, Clinton	Birmingham City	Crystal Palace	2,000,000
11	Murphy, Joseph	West Bromwich Albion	Sunderland	undisclosed
3	Neal, Lewis	Stoke City	Preston North End	undisclosed
4	Neville, Philip	Manchester United	Everton	3,500,000
30	Nowland, Adam C.	Nottingham Forest	Preston North End	undisclosed
19	Pogliacomi, Leslie A.	Oldham Athletic	Blackpool	undisclosed
31	Sabin, Eric	Northampton Town	Oxford United	undisclosed
18	Sharp, William	Sheffield United	Scunthorpe United	100,000
31	Solano, Nolberto A.	Aston Villa	Newcastle United	1,500,000
25	Spicer, John W.	AFC Bournemouth	Burnley	undisclosed
19	Spring, Matthew	Leeds United	Watford	100,000
31	Thirlwell, Paul	Sheffield United	Derby County	undisclosed
26	Torres, Sergio P.	Basingstoke Town	Wycombe Wanderers	undisclosed
17	Unsworth, David G.	Portsmouth	Sheffield United	undisclosed
31	Williams, Thomas A.	Barnsley	Gillingham	undisclosed

TEMPORARY TRANSFERS

25 Aliadiere, Jeremie – Arsenal – West Ham United
4 Andrew, Calvin H. – Luton Town – Grimsby Town
12 Angel, Mark – Kings Lynn – Cambridge United
12 Anyon, Joseph – Port Vale – Stafford Rangers
15 Ashikodi, Moses – West Ham United – Gillingham
11 Atieno, Taiwo L. – Walsall – Kidderminster Harriers
31 Bakke, Eirik – Leeds United – Aston Villa
17 Bellion, David – Manchester United – West Ham United
31 Bentley, David M. – Arsenal – Blackburn Rovers
17 Bermingham, Karl – Manchester City – Burnley
4 Best, Leon J. – Southampton – Sheffield Wednesday
12 Blewitt, Darren L. – West Ham United – Hereford United
12 Bond, Andrew M. – Crewe Alexandra – Lancaster City
19 Bossu, Bertrand – Darlington – Accrington Stanley
22 Brooks, Jamie P. – Oxford United – Slough Town
31 Brown, Paul H. – Tranmere Rovers – Accrington Stanley
10 Brown, Wayne L. – Chester City – Hereford United
17 Bruce, Alex – Birmingham City – Tranmere Rovers
31 Burch, Robert K. – Tottenham Hotspur – Bristol City
4 Butt, Nicholas – Newcastle United – Birmingham City
3 Bywater, Stephen – West Ham United – Coventry City
5 Carlisle, Clarke J. – Leeds United – Watford
4 Chadwick, Luke H. – West Ham United – Stoke City
2 Clarke, Ryan J. – Bristol Rovers – Forest Green Rovers
31 Clingan, Samuel G. – Wolverhampton Wanderers – Chesterfield
26 Coleman, Dean S. – Walsall – Hailsowen Town
12 Collins, Neill – Sunderland – Hartlepool United
3 Collins, Patrick – Sheffield Wednesday – Swindon Town
28 Cornes, Christopher R. – Wolverhampton Wanderers – Port Vale
26 Denton, Samuel E. – Bradford City – Guiseley
31 Derbyshire, Matthew – Blackburn Rovers – Plymouth Argyle
31 Diao, Salif – Liverpool – Portsmouth
10 Dormand, James – Birmingham City – Tamworth
19 Douglas, Jonathan – Blackburn Rovers – Leeds United
5 Duke, Matthew – Hull City – Stockport County
8 Fish, Mark A. – Charlton Athletic – Ipswich Town
18 Flood, William – Manchester City – Coventry City
31 Foley-Sheridan, Steven – Aston Villa – AFC Bournemouth
31 Forte, Jonathan – Sheffield United – Doncaster Rovers
2 Foster, Benjamin – Manchester United – Watford
30 Fox, Michael J.S. – Chesterfield – Belper Town
29 Gallagher, Paul – Blackburn Rovers – Stoke City
12 Gordon, Christopher – Lincoln City – Gainsborough Trinity
9 Graham, Luke – Northampton Town – Forest Green Rovers
11 Guyett, Scott B. – Yeovil Town – Aldershot Town
12 Haldane, Lewis O. – Bristol Rovers – Forest Green Rovers
19 Hammond, Elvis Z. – Fulham – Leicester City
19 Harkness, Jonathan – Walsall – Cambridge United
26 Harley, Jon – Sheffield United – Burnley
19 Harper, Adrian – Sheffield United – Scarborough
27 Harris, Neil – Nottingham Forest – Gillingham
19 Heath, Colin – Manchester United – Swindon Town
19 Heaton, Thomas D. – Manchester United – Swindon Town
4 Henderson, Wayne – Aston Villa – Brighton & Hove Albion
5 Horwood, Evan D. – Sheffield United – Scunthorpe United
9 Howell, Simieon – Reading – Forest Green Rovers
31 Hoyte, Justin R. – Arsenal – Sunderland
18 Hurst, Kevan – Sheffield United – Chesterfield
31 Ikeme, Carl – Wolverhampton Wanderers – Stockport County
22 Jarosik, Jiri – Chelsea – Birmingham City
3 Jones, David F.L. – Manchester United – Preston North End
22 Jones, Paul S. – Wolverhampton Wanderers – Millwall
30 Jubb, Anthony P. – Chesterfield – Belper Town

8 Keenan, Joseph J. – Chelsea – Brentford
3 Le Tallec, Anthony – Liverpool – Sunderland
31 Leary, Michael – Luton Town – Bristol Rovers
25 Lee, Richard A. – Watford – Blackburn Rovers
26 Lowe, Keith S. – Wolverhampton Wanderers – Burnley
2 Marney, Dean E. – Tottenham Hotspur – Norwich City
18 McClenahan, Trent – West Ham United – Milton Keynes Dons
31 McDermott, Neale T. – Fulham – Swindon Town
30 McEveley, James – Blackburn Rovers – Ipswich Town
6 McGurk, David – Darlington – York City
12 McPhee, Christopher S. – Brighton & Hove Albion – Aldershot Town
19 McShane, Luke – Peterborough United – Gravesend & Northfleet
4 McShane, Paul D. – Manchester United – Brighton & Hove Albion
31 Mills, Pablo – Derby County – Milton Keynes Dons
31 Milner, James P. – Newcastle United – Aston Villa
5 Molango, Maheta – Brighton & Hove Albion – Lincoln City
31 Nethercott, Stuart – Wycombe Wanderers – Woking
26 Nowland, Adam C. – Nottingham Forest – Preston North End
12 O'Grady, Christopher – Leicester City – Rushden & Diamonds
31 Oliver, Luke – Yeovil Town – Woking
3 Palmer, Jermaine – Grimsby Town – Scarborough
18 Picken, Philip J. – Manchester United – Chesterfield
8 Platt, Sean – Walsall – Willenhall Town
20 Poke, Michael H. – Southampton – Oldham Athletic
31 Poom, Mart – Sunderland – Arsenal
19 Postma, Stefan – Aston Villa – Wolverhampton Wanderers
30 Pratley, Darren – Fulham – Brentford
26 Randolph, Darren E. – Charlton Athletic – Accrington Stanley
19 Rankine, Michael – Scunthorpe United – Barrow
31 Rasiak, Grzegorz – Derby County – Tottenham Hotspur
15 Reed, Stephen – Yeovil Town – Woking
25 Rose, Michael C. – Yeovil Town – Cheltenham Town
26 Ross, Ian – Sheffield United – Boston United
31 Scully, Anthony D.T. – Notts County – Exeter City
3 Surman, Andrew R. – Southampton – AFC Bournemouth
2 Taylor, Andrew D. – Middlesbrough – Bradford City
5 Thelwell, Paul – Sheffield United – Derby County
2 Turnbull, Ross – Middlesbrough – Crewe Alexandra
26 Vaughan, Anthony J. – Barnsley – Stockport County
9 Vaughan, Lee – Walsall – Willenhall Town
5 Vincent, Jamie R. – Derby County – Millwall
26 Welsh, John J. – Liverpool – Hull City
31 Williams, Ryan N. – Bristol Rovers – Aldershot Town
31 Wright, Jake M. – Bradford City – Halifax Town
31 Wright, Thomas – Leicester City – Blackpool
5 Yeates, Mark – Tottenham Hotspur – Colchester United

SEPTEMBER 2005

12 Rasiak, Grzegorz	Derby County	Tottenham Hotspur	£2,250,000

TEMPORARY TRANSFERS

22 Agbonlahor, Gabriel – Aston Villa – Watford
8 Bacon, Daniel S. – Lincoln City – Burton Albion
26 Bailey, Matthew – Crewe Alexandra – Hereford United
1 Baradji, Sekou – West Ham United – Reading
21 Benjamin, Trevor J. – Peterborough United – Watford
19 Bermingham, Karl – Manchester City – Burnley
23 Berry, Tyrone – Crystal Palace – Notts County
16 Blayney, Alan – Southampton – Brighton & Hove Albion
16 Boucaud, Andre – Peterborough United – Aldershot Town
2 Broad, Joseph R. – Walsall – Redditch United
20 Brooks, Jamie P. – Oxford United – Slough Town
23 Brown, Aaron – Queens Park Rangers – Cheltenham Town
8 Brown, Christopher – Sunderland – Hull City
30 Burch, Robert K. – Tottenham Hotspur – Bristol City
9 Campbell, Darren – Reading – Tamworth
27 Campbell-Ryce, Jamal – Rotherham United – Southend United
15 Castle, Peter – Reading – St Albans City
27 Clarke, Darrell J. – Hartlepool United – Port Vale
29 Cornes, Christopher R. – Wolverhampton Wanderers – Port Vale
12 Davenport, Calum R.P. – Tottenham Hotspur – Norwich City
27 Dyer, Lloyd – West Bromwich Albion – Queens Park Rangers
16 El Hamdaoui, Mounir – Tottenham Hotspur – Derby County
14 Fadiga, Khalilou – Bolton Wanderers – Derby County
15 Fletcher, Carl N. – West Ham United – Watford
21 Flood, William – Manchester City – Coventry City
2 Fontaine, Liam V.H. – Fulham – Yeovil Town
27 Forte, Jonathan – Sheffield United – Doncaster Rovers
26 Francis, Simon C. – Sheffield United – Grimsby Town
23 Frecklington, Lee – Lincoln City – Stamford
5 Friars, Emmett – Notts County – AFC Telford United
8 Gallagher, Paul – Blackburn Rovers – Stoke City
30 Gillett, Simon J. – Southampton – Walsall
14 Guyett, Scott B. – Yeovil Town – Aldershot Town
11 Haldane, Lewis O. – Bristol Rovers – Forest Green Rovers
23 Hand, Jamie – Watford – Peterborough United
1 Harris, Neil – Nottingham Forest – Gillingham
15 Hoult, Russell – West Bromwich Albion – Nottingham Forest
9 Husbands, Michael P. – Rushall Olympic – Walsall
12 Ifil, Phillip – Tottenham Hotspur – Millwall
16 Jackson, Johnnie – Tottenham Hotspur – Derby County
16 John, Stern – Coventry City – Derby County
26 Jones, Paul S. – Wolverhampton Wanderers – Millwall
13 Keene, James D. – Portsmouth – AFC Bournemouth
23 Leadbitter, Grant – Sunderland – Rotherham United
15 Lindegaard, Andrew – Yeovil Town – Crawley Town
9 Lisbie, Kevin – Charlton Athletic – Norwich City
30 McAliskey, John – Huddersfield Town – Torquay United
23 McGoldrick, David J. – Southampton – Notts County
14 McPhee, Christopher S. – Brighton & Hove Albion – Aldershot Town
16 Mikolanda, Petr – West Ham United – Northampton Town
22 Miller, Adam E. – Queens Park Rangers – Peterborough United
23 Morris, Ian – Leeds United – Blackpool
23 Mulligan, Gary – Sheffield United – Port Vale
30 O'Brien, Alan – Newcastle United – Carlisle United
16 Palmer, Jermaine – Grimsby Town – York City
14 Pericard, Vincent D.P. – Portsmouth – Sheffield United
12 Platt, Sean – Walsall – Willenhall Town
23 Quinn, Stephen – Sheffield United – Milton Keynes Dons
23 Randolph, Darren E. – Charlton Athletic – Accrington Stanley
20 Rankine, Michael – Scunthorpe United – Barrow
27 Ross, Ian – Sheffield United – Boston United
23 Ruddy, John T.G. – Everton – Walsall
27 Sankofa, Osey O.K. – Charlton Athletic – Bristol City
23 Sanna, Christopher – Stoke City – Watford
8 Saunders, Mark P. – Gillingham – Welling United
23 Scully, Anthony D.T. – Notts County – Exeter City
30 Smith, Ryan C.M. – Arsenal – Leicester City
13 Vaughan, Lee – Walsall – Willenhall Town
7 Wallis, Jonathan – Gillingham – Hastings United
15 Whittingham, Peter – Aston Villa – Derby County
12 Williams, Adrian – Coventry City – Millwall
2 Williams, Dale T. – Yeovil Town – Tiverton Town
29 Wright, Jake M. – Bradford City – Halifax Town
13 Wright, Jermaine M. – Leeds United – Millwall

OCTOBER 2005

TEMPORARY TRANSFERS

28 Agbonlahor, Gabriel – Aston Villa – Sheffield Wednesday
25 Andrew, Calvin H. – Luton Town – Grimsby Town
27 Anyon, Joseph – Port Vale – Harrogate Town

13 Armstrong, Christopher – Sheffield United – Blackpool
26 Bailey, Matthew – Crewe Alexandra – Hereford United
7 Bell, Lee – Crewe Alexandra – Burton Albion
28 Bevan, Scott – Milton Keynes Dons – Tamworth
27 Blackstock, Dexter A. – Southampton – Derby County
17 Blayney, Alan – Southampton – Brighton & Hove Albion
7 Bouazza, Hameur – Watford – Swindon Town
26 Brooks, Jamie P. – Oxford United – Slough
6 Butcher, Richard T. – Oldham Athletic – Lincoln City
7 Coleman, Omari – Lincoln City – Aldershot Town
14 Conlon, Barry J. – Barnsley – Rotherham United
21 Cureton, Jamie – Swindon Town – Colchester United
28 Dann, Scott – Walsall – Redditch United
20 D'Laryea, Jonathan A. – Manchester City – Mansfield Town
18 Dolan, Joseph – Leyton Orient – Stockport County
31 Dyer, Lloyd – West Bromwich Albion – Queens Park Rangers
28 Dyer, Nathan A.J. – Southampton – Burnley
10 Edwards, Philip – Wigan Athletic – Accrington Stanley
26 Frecklington, Lee – Lincoln City – Stamford
4 Friars, Emmett – Notts County – AFC Telford United
28 Fulop, Marton – Tottenham Hotspur – Coventry City
21 Hand, Jamie – Watford – Peterborough United
27 Hardiker, John – Bury – Morecambe
18 Harkness, Jonathan – Walsall – Halesowen Town
28 Harley, Ryan B. – Bristol City – Forest Green Rovers
17 Hoult, Russell – West Bromwich Albion – Nottingham Forest
25 Huddlestone, Thomas A. – Tottenham Hotspur – Wolverhampton Wanderers
13 Husbands, Michael P. – Rushall Olympic – Port Vale
10 Jackson, Mark – Preston North End – Shrewsbury Town
28 Johnson, Jemal J. – Blackburn Rovers – Preston North End
31 Jones, Paul S. – Wolverhampton Wanderers – Millwall
4 Kay, Jamie – Stockport County – Woodleigh Sports
17 Keene, James D. – Portsmouth – AFC Bournemouth
21 Leadbitter, Grant – Sunderland – Rotherham United
4 Leary, Michael – Luton Town – Bristol Rovers
10 Lee, Kevin – Wigan Athletic – Accrington Stanley
16 Lindegaard, Andrew – Yeovil Town – Crawley Town
8 Lonergan, Andrew – Preston North End – Wycombe Wanderers
14 Lowe, Keith S. – Wolverhampton Wanderers – Burnley
14 Mendes, Albert J.H.A. – Huddersfield Town – Northampton Town
24 Morris, Ian – Leeds United – Blackpool
25 Mulligan, Gary – Sheffield United – Port Vale
27 Mullins, John – Reading – Kidderminster Harriers
21 Murphy, Joseph – Sunderland – Walsall
14 Nalis, Lilian B.P. – Sheffield United – Coventry City
21 O'Leary, Stephen – Luton Town – Tranmere Rovers
4 Oliver, Luke – Yeovil Town – Woking
21 Palmer, Jermaine – Grimsby Town – Hinckley United
18 Poke, Michael H. – Southampton – Northampton Town
10 Proudlock, Adam D. – Sheffield Wednesday – Ipswich Town
21 Quinn, James S. – Peterborough United – Bristol City
30 Randolph, Darren E. – Charlton Athletic – Accrington Stanley
14 Rankine, Michael – Scunthorpe United – Barrow
14 Rix, Benjamin – Crewe Alexandra – Scarborough
20 Robinson, Trevor K. – Millwall – Tamworth
27 Rose, Jason – Millwall – Aldershot Town
27 Ross, Ian – Sheffield United – Boston United
28 Ross, Maurice – Sheffield Wednesday – Wolverhampton Wanderers
21 Sanna, Christopher – Stoke City – Watford
14 Saunders, Ben – Doncaster Rovers – Worksop Town
28 Smith, Paul W. – Walsall – Gillingham
6 Strachan, Gavin D. – Hartlepool United – Stockport County
28 Thome, Emerson A. – Wigan Athletic – Derby County
6 Till, Peter – Birmingham City – Scunthorpe United
21 Tomlinson, Ezekiel – Stockport County – AFC Telford United
21 Warrender, Daniel J. – Manchester City – Blackpool
28 Watt, Steven – Chelsea – Barnsley
14 Wijnhard, Clyde – Darlington – Macclesfield Town
21 Wilson, Kyle P. – Crewe Alexandra – Altrincham
13 Youga, Kelly A. – Charlton Athletic – Bristol City

NOVEMBER 2005

TEMPORARY TRANSFERS

24 Abbey, Nathanael – Boston United – Leyton Orient
25 Agbonlahor, Gabriel – Aston Villa – Sheffield Wednesday
18 Anaclet, Edward B. – Southampton – Tamworth
11 Andrews, Lee D. – Carlisle United – York City
10 Armstrong, Christopher – Sheffield United – Blackpool
23 Barwick, Terence P. – Grimsby Town – York City
6 Bell, Lee – Crewe Alexandra – Burton Albion
28 Bevan, Scott – Milton Keynes Dons – Tamworth
28 Blackstock, Dexter A. – Southampton – Derby County
7 Bouazza, Hameur – Watford – Swindon Town
4 Breach, Christopher B. – Brighton & Hove Albion – Bognor Regis Town
15 Bridges, Michael – Bristol City – Carlisle United
18 Broad, Joseph R. – Walsall – Redditch United
24 Brown, Aaron – Tamworth – Reading
24 Brown, Aaron – Queens Park Rangers – Swindon Town
9 Cohen, Christopher D. – West Ham United – Yeovil Town
24 Coleman, Omari – Lincoln City – Gravesend & Northfleet
2 Collins, Sam – Port Vale – Hull City
21 Constable, James A. – Chippenham Town – Walsall
4 Constantine, Leon – Torquay United – Port Vale
3 Cornes, Christopher R. – Wolverhampton Wanderers – Port Vale
18 Cureton, Jamie – Swindon Town – Colchester United
18 Dann, Scott – Walsall – Redditch United
24 De Bolla, Mark – Chesterfield – Notts County
22 D'Laryea, Jonathan A. – Manchester City – Mansfield Town
24 Dobson, Michael W. – Brentford – Reading
24 Dolan, Joseph – Leyton Orient – Fisher Athletic
24 Doyle, Colin – Birmingham City – Millwall
24 Drench, Steven M. – Blackburn Rovers – Morecambe
4 Dyer, Bruce A. – Stoke City – Millwall
28 Dyer, Lloyd – West Bromwich Albion – Queens Park Rangers
25 Dyer, Nathan A.J. – Southampton – Burnley
14 Edwards, Philip – Wigan Athletic – Accrington Stanley
23 Elliot, Robert – Charlton Athletic – Accrington Stanley
11 Etuhu, Dixon P. – Preston North End – Norwich City
18 Evans, Paul S. – Nottingham Forest – Rotherham United
23 Fitzgerald, Scott – Brentford – Oxford United
18 Forte, Jonathan – Sheffield United – Doncaster Rovers
10 Fortune, Clayton A. – Bristol City – Port Vale
10 Fowler, Lee A. – Huddersfield Town – Scarborough
18 Francis, Simon C. – Sheffield United – Tranmere Rovers
23 Frecklington, Lee – Lincoln City – Stamford
24 Gilbert, Peter – Leicester City – Sheffield Wednesday
10 Gillespie, Steven – Bristol City – Cheltenham Town
24 Gobern, Lewis T. – Wolverhampton Wanderers – Blackpool
24 Graham, Daniel A.W. – Middlesbrough – Derby County
15 Grant, Lee A. – Derby County – Burnley
22 Green, Francis – Lincoln City – Boston United
10 Griffin, Adam – Oldham Athletic – Oxford United
28 Hand, Jamie – Watford – Peterborough United
11 Harding, Benjamin S. – Milton Keynes Dons – Forest Green Rovers
15 Harkins, Gary – Blackburn Rovers – Blackpool
24 Horwood, Evan D. – Sheffield United – York City
23 Huddlestone, Thomas A. – Tottenham Hotspur – Wolverhampton Wanderers
21 Husbands, Michael P. – Rushall Olympic – Port Vale
24 Hutchison, Donald – Millwall – Coventry City
24 Jarrett, Jason L. – Norwich City – Plymouth Argyle
11 Johnson, Bradley – Northampton Town – Gravesend & Northfleet
24 Johnson, Brett – Northampton Town – Gravesend & Northfleet
24 Jones, Zachariah S. – Blackburn Rovers – Southampton
10 Joseph, Marc E. – Hull City – Bristol City

11 Kandol, Tresor O. – Dagenham & Redbridge – Darlington
8 Kay, Jamie – Stockport County – Woodleigh Sports
21 Keene, James D. – Portsmouth – AFC Bournemouth
9 Keogh, Richard J. – Bristol City – Wycombe Wanderers
22 Knowles, Daniel – Gillingham – East Thurrock United
24 Koo-Boothe, Nathan – Milton Keynes Dons – Grays Athletic
24 Kuipers, Michael – Brighton & Hove Albion – Boston United
7 Leary, Michael – Luton Town – Bristol Rovers
2 Lloyd, Anthony – Huddersfield Town – Torquay United
18 Lloyd, Callum – Mansfield Town – Alfreton Town
24 Lloyd, Robert F. – Crewe Alexandra – Witton Albion
18 Lockwood, Adam B. – Yeovil Town – Torquay United
18 Logan, Richard J. – Peterborough United – Lincoln City
24 MacKenzie, Neil – Macclesfield Town – Scunthorpe United
17 Madjo, Guy B. – Bristol City – Forest Green Rovers
11 Martin, Richard W. – Brighton & Hove Albion – Kingstonian
24 Maynard, Nicholas D. – Crewe Alexandra – Witton Albion
17 McDonald, Dean L. – Ipswich Town – Hartlepool United
24 Melton, Stephen – Boston United – Tamworth
17 Mendes, Albert J.H.A. – Huddersfield Town – Northampton Town
24 Mikolanda, Petr – West Ham United – Swindon Town
4 Miller, Liam W. – Manchester United – Leeds United
23 Morgan, Daniel F. – Oxford United – Basingstoke Town
23 Morris, Ian – Leeds United – Blackpool
24 Motteram, Carl – Birmingham City – Tamworth
28 Mulligan, Gary – Sheffield United – Port Vale
29 Mullins, John – Reading – Kidderminster Harriers
24 Murphy, Darryl – Sunderland – Sheffield Wednesday
21 Murphy, Joseph – Sunderland – Walsall
23 Noble, David J. – Boston United – Bristol City
23 Oji, Samuel U.U. – Birmingham City – Doncaster Rovers
8 Oliver, Luke – Yeovil Town – Woking
24 Parton, Andrew – Scunthorpe United – Scarborough
9 Paynter, William P. – Port Vale – Hull City
28 Pidgeley, Leonard J. – Chelsea – Millwall
17 Poke, Michael H. – Southampton – Northampton Town
24 Pope, Thomas J. – Crewe Alexandra – Lancaster City
24 Prendergast, Rory – Blackpool – Halifax Town
11 Quinn, Stephen – Sheffield United – Milton Keynes Dons
4 Reet, Daniel – Sheffield Wednesday – Bury
3 Ricketts, Mark J. – Charlton Athletic – Milton Keynes Dons
23 Rigoglioso, Adriano – Doncaster Rovers – Southport
23 Roach, Neville – Eastleigh – Oxford United
22 Roberts, Mark A. – Crewe Alexandra – Southport
24 Robinson, Carl P. – Sunderland – Norwich City
3 Robinson, Steven E. – Lincoln City – Worksop Town
10 Ruddy, John T.G. – Everton – Rushden & Diamonds
18 Russell, Allan – Macclesfield Town – Mansfield Town
4 Ryan, Oliver – Lincoln City – Ilkeston Town
1 Sankofa, Osey O.K. – Charlton Athletic – Bristol City
12 Saunders, Ben – Doncaster Rovers – Worksop Town
24 Savage, Basir M. – Coventry City – Bristol City
24 Scully, Anthony D.T. – Notts County – Crawley Town
4 Sedgemore, Jake O. – Bury – Burton Albion
23 Seremet, Dino – Luton Town – Doncaster Rovers
11 Skora, Eric – Preston North End – Walsall
24 Speight, Jake – Scarborough – Bury
4 Stonebridge, Ian R. – Wycombe Wanderers – Torquay United
24 Sutton, Ritchie A. – Crewe Alexandra – Leek Town
6 Till, Peter – Birmingham City – Scunthorpe United
10 Togwell, Samuel J. – Crystal Palace – Port Vale
9 Turner, Iain R. – Everton – Wycombe Wanderers
11 Tyson, Nathan – Wycombe Wanderers – Nottingham Forest
17 Vernazza, Paulo A.P. – Rotherham United – Barnet
18 Vincent, Ashley D. – Cheltenham Town – Aldershot Town
22 Ward, Elliott L. – West Ham United – Plymouth Argyle
15 Warrender, Daniel J. – Manchester City – Blackpool
4 Weaver, Nicholas – Manchester City – Sheffield Wednesday
24 Whitbread, Zak B. – Liverpool – Millwall
24 Wilcox, Jason M. – Leicester City – Blackpool
4 Wilkinson, Neil – Hartlepool United – Blyth Spartans
9 Williams, Gavin J. – West Ham United – Ipswich Town
18 Wilson, Kyle P. – Crewe Alexandra – Altrincham
4 Winter, James H. – Hartlepool United – Gateshead
3 Woodman, Craig A. – Bristol City – Torquay United
17 Wright, David – Wigan Athletic – Norwich City
1 Wright, Jake M. – Bradford City – Halifax Town
10 Youga, Kelly A. – Charlton Athletic – Bristol City

DECEMBER 2005

28 Diouf, El Hadji O. Liverpool Bolton Wanderers undisclosed

TEMPORARY TRANSFERS

19 Anaclet, Edward B. – Southampton – Tamworth
12 Andrews, Lee D. – Carlisle United – York City
16 Appleby, Andrew – Hartlepool United – Blyth Spartans
16 Breach, Christopher B. – Brighton & Hove Albion – Bognor Regis Town
23 Brooks, Jamie P. – Oxford United – Brackley Town
2 Chilaka, Chibuzor – Notts County – Hinckley United
8 Cohen, Christopher D. – West Ham United – Yeovil Town
23 Coleman, Omari – Lincoln City – Gravesend & Northfleet
2 Corneille, Mark – Gillingham – Eastbourne Borough
30 Crane, Anthony S. – Grimsby Town – Worksop Town
16 D'Laryea, Jonathan A. – Manchester City – Mansfield Town
30 Dolan, Joseph – Leyton Orient – Fisher Athletic
23 Doyle, Colin – Birmingham City – Millwall
22 Drench, Steven M. – Blackburn Rovers – Morecambe
12 Edwards, Philip – Wigan Athletic – Accrington Stanley
30 Elliot, Robert – Charlton Athletic – Accrington Stanley
29 Foley-Sheridan, Steven – Aston Villa – AFC Bournemouth
10 Fowler, Lee A. – Huddersfield Town – Scarborough
19 Francis, Simon C. – Sheffield United – Tranmere Rovers
16 Grant, Lee A. – Derby County – Burnley
23 Hardiker, John – Bury – Morecambe
11 Harding, Benjamin S. – Milton Keynes Dons – Forest Green Rovers
16 Hicks, David – Northampton Town – Hitchin Town
12 Johnson, Bradley – Northampton Town – Gravesend & Northfleet
23 Johnson, Brett – Northampton Town – Gravesend & Northfleet
30 Johnson, Edward W. – Manchester United – Crewe Alexandra
15 Joseph, Marc E. – Hull City – Bristol City
3 Kay, Jamie – Stockport County – Woodleigh Sports
30 Kennedy, Luke D. – Rushden & Diamonds – Cambridge City
30 Knight, David – Middlesbrough – Darlington
22 Knowles, Daniel – Gillingham – East Thurrock United
5 Lamb, Alan – Grimsby Town – Eastwood Town
19 Lloyd, Robert F. – Crewe Alexandra – Witton Albion
22 Lockwood, Adam B. – Yeovil Town – Torquay United
24 Logan, Conrad – Leicester City – Boston United
18 Logan, Richard J. – Peterborough United – Lincoln City
12 Martin, Richard W. – Brighton & Hove Albion – Kingstonian
19 Maynard, Nicholas D. – Crewe Alexandra – Witton Albion
30 McClenahan, Trent – West Ham United – Milton Keynes Dons
30 Melton, Stephen – Boston United – Tamworth
23 Morgan, Daniel F. – Oxford United – Basingstoke Town
28 Nethercott, Stuart – Wycombe Wanderers – Woking
2 Palmer, Jermaine – Grimsby Town – Hinckley United
29 Picken, Philip J. – Manchester United – Chesterfield
20 Platt, Sean – Walsall – Hednesford Town
20 Poom, Mart – Sunderland – Arsenal
23 Pope, Thomas J. – Crewe Alexandra – Lancaster City
29 Prendergast, Rory – Blackpool – Halifax Town

5 Reet, Daniel – Sheffield Wednesday – Bury
7 Ricketts, Mark J. – Charlton Athletic – Milton Keynes Dons
1 Robinson, Steven E. – Lincoln City – Worksop Town
16 Ruddy, John T.G. – Everton – Chester City
5 Ryan, Oliver – Lincoln City – Ilkeston Town
16 Saunders, Ben – Doncaster Rovers – Worksop Town
2 Sedgemore, Jake O. – Bury – Burton Albion
30 Smith, Ryan C.M. – Arsenal – Leicester City
5 Stonebridge, Ian R. – Wycombe Wanderers – Torquay United
21 Sutton, Ritchie A. – Crewe Alexandra – Leek Town
28 Turnbull, Ross – Middlesbrough – Crewe Alexandra
20 Ward, Elliot L. – West Ham United – Plymouth Argyle
19 Warrender, Daniel J. – Manchester City – Blackpool
18 Weaver, Nicholas – Manchester City – Sheffield Wednesday
23 Wilcox, Jason M. – Leicester City – Blackpool
2 Wilkinson, Neil – Hartlepool United – Blyth Spartans
7 Williams, Christopher – Stockport County – Leigh RMI
6 Williams, Gavin J. – West Ham United – Ipswich Town
22 Wilson, Kyle P. – Crewe Alexandra – Barrow
22 Winters, Thomas R. – Oxford United – Brackley Town

JANUARY 2006

27 Akinbiyi, Adeola P.	Burnley	Sheffield United	1,750,000
24 Ashton, Dean	Norwich City	West Ham United	7,000,000
31 Barrowman, Andrew	Birmingham City	Walsall	undisclosed
23 Bean, Marcus T.	Queens Park Rangers	Blackpool	Free
12 Bell, David A.	Rushden & Diamonds	Luton Town	100,000
10 Bennett, Julian L.	Walsall	Nottingham Forest	100,000
17 Bent, Marcus N.	Everton	Charlton Athletic	2,000,000
31 Bentley, David M.	Arsenal	Blackburn Rovers	undisclosed
31 Berry, Tyrone	Crystal Palace	Rushden & Diamonds	undisclosed
5 Blayney, Alan	Southampton	Doncaster Rovers	50,000
1 Brown, Aaron	Tamworth	Reading	undisclosed
13 Brown, Aaron	Queens Park Rangers	Swindon Town	undisclosed
31 Brown, Michael R.	Tottenham Hotspur	Fulham	1,500,000
13 Burgess, Andrew J.	Rushden & Diamonds	Oxford United	35,000
1 Burton, Deon J.	Rotherham United	Sheffield Wednesday	100,000
31 Campbell, Dudley J.	Brentford	Birmingham City	500,000
31 Castle, Peter	Reading	Rushden & Diamonds	undisclosed
5 Chadwick, Luke H.	West Ham United	Stoke City	100,000
31 Christie, Iyseden combined	Kidderminster Harriers	Rochdale	35,000
20 Clarke, Jamie W.	Rochdale	Boston United	Free
24 Clingan, Samuel G.	Wolverhampton Wanderers	Nottingham Forest	nominal
2 Collins, Sam	Port Vale	Hull City	65,000
1 Constable, James A.	Chippenham Town	Walsall	4000
3 Constantine, Leon	Torquay United	Port Vale	20,000
17 Crane, Anthony S.	Grimsby Town	Worksop Town	undisclosed
12 Da Silva Mendes, Pedro M. combined	Tottenham Hotspur	Portsmouth	7,000,000
16 Dagnall, Christopher	Tranmere Rovers	Rochdale	25,000
12 Davis, Sean combined	Tottenham Hotspur	Portsmouth	7,000,000
31 Delap, Rory J.	Southampton	Sunderland	Free
13 Dempster, John	Rushden & Diamonds	Oxford United	10,000
30 Dyer, Lloyd	West Bromwich Albion	Millwall	Free
31 Earnshaw, Robert	West Bromwich Albion	Norwich City	2,750,000
31 Easter, Jermaine	Stockport County	Wycombe Wanderers	80,000
11 Edwards, Philip	Wigan Athletic	Accrington Stanley	undisclosed
3 Etuhu, Dixon P.	Preston North End	Norwich City	450,000
28 Foley-Sheridan, Steven	Aston Villa	AFC Bournemouth	20,000
30 Fowler, Robert B.	Manchester City	Liverpool	Free
10 Fryatt, Matthew C.	Walsall	Leicester City	750,000
12 Futcher, Benjamin P.	Boston United	Grimsby Town	undisclosed
5 Gilbert, Peter	Leicester City	Sheffield Wednesday	undisclosed
31 Gillespie, Steven	Bristol City	Cheltenham Town	undisclosed
3 Golbourne, Scott J.	Bristol City	Reading	undisclosed
31 Gritton, Martin	Grimsby Town	Lincoln City	nominal
19 Halls, John	Stoke City	Reading	250,000
20 Hatswell, Wayne	Kidderminster Harriers	Rushden & Diamonds	undisclosed
18 Heckingbottom, Paul	Sheffield Wednesday	Barnsley	undisclosed
31 Jackson, Mark G. combined	Kidderminster Harriers	Rochdale	35,000
12 Joseph, Marc E.	Hull City	Blackpool	Free
30 Kandol, Tresor O.	Dagenham & Redbridge	Barnet	50,000
25 Kiely, Dean L.	Charlton Athletic	Portsmouth	500,000
3 King, Marlon F.	Nottingham Forest	Watford	500,000
13 Lee, Graeme B.	Sheffield Wednesday	Doncaster Rovers	50,000
9 Lee, Jason	Boston United	Northamptonn Town	Free
6 Lloyd, Anthony	Huddersfield Town	Torquay United	undisclosed
1 MacKenzie, Neil	Macclesfield Town	Scunthorpe United	Free
13 Martin, David E.	Milton Keynes Dons	Liverpool	undisclosed
18 McGregor, Mark D.T.	Blackpool	Port Vale	Free
31 Mills, Matthew C.	Southampton	Manchester City	750,000
26 Moore, Darren M.	West Bromwich Albion	Derby County	500,000
31 Murphy, Daniel B.	Charlton Athletic	Tottenham Hotspur	2,000,000
10 Niemi, Antti	Southampton	Fulham	1,000,000
10 Noble, David J.	Boston United	Bristol City	undisclosed
26 Odubade, Yemi	Eastbourne Borough	Oxford United	15,000
27 Oliver, Luke	Yeovil Town	Stevenage Borough	15,000
30 Ormerod, Brett R.	Southampton	Preston North End	Free
18 Otsemobor, John	Rotherham United	Crewe Alexandra	Free
12 Pamarot, Noe combined	Tottenham Hotspur	Portsmouth	7,000,000

12	Parkin, Jonathan	Macclesfield Town	Hull City	150,000
2	Paynter, William P.	Port Vale	Hull City	150,000
10	Postma, Stefan	Aston Villa	Wolverhampton Wanderers	undisclosed
24	Price, Jason	Hull City	Doncaster Rovers	undisclosed
1	Proudlock, Adam D.	Sheffield Wednesday	Ipswich Town	Free
31	Quashie, Nigel F.	Southampton	West Bromwich Albion	1,500,000
30	Ramsden, Simon	Grimsby Town	Rochdale	Free
13	Reet, Daniel	Sheffield Wednesday	Mansfield Town	25,000
17	Robinson, Carl P.	Sunderland	Norwich City	50,000
26	Ross, Maurice	Sheffield Wednesday	Wolverhampton Wanderers	Free
30	Sills, Timothy	Aldershot Town	Oxford United	undisclosed
25	Smith, Kevin	Leeds United	Sunderland	Free
11	Sodje, Efetobore	Yeovil Town	Southend United	undisclosed
3	Speight, Jake	Scarborough	Bury	nominal
1	Stack, Graham	Arsenal	Reading	undisclosed
16	Stock, Brian B.	AFC Bournemouth	Preston North End	125,000
20	Stubbs, Alan	Sunderland	Everton	undisclosed
17	Taylor, Scott J.	Plymouth Argyle	Milton Keynes Dons	100,000
30	Thomas, Bradley M.	Eastleigh	Yeovil Town	undisclosed
5	Tudgay, Marcus	Derby County	Sheffield Wednesday	undisclosed
31	Turner, John A.J.	Cambridge United	Rushden & Diamonds	Free
20	Tynan, Scott J.	Barnet	Rushden & Diamonds	10,000
3	Tyson, Nathan	Wycombe Wanderers	Nottingham Forest	675,000
23	Warrender, Daniel J.	Manchester City	Blackpool	undisclosed
2	Welsh, John J.	Liverpool	Hull City	undisclosed
9	Whaley, Simon	Bury	Preston North End	250,000
4	Williams, Gavin J.	West Ham United	Ipswich Town	300,000
31	Willock, Calum	Peterborough United	Brentford	undisclosed
31	Wood, Neil A.	Coventry City	Blackpool	undisclosed
27	Woodhouse, Curtis	Hull City	Grimsby Town	Free
1	Wright, Thomas	Leicester City	Barnsley	undisclosed

TEMPORARY TRANSFERS

6 Adaggio, Marco – Shrewsbury Town – AFC Telford United
27 Afful, Leslie S. – Exeter City – Torquay United
30 Andrew, Calvin H. – Luton Town – Bristol City
31 Angus, Stevland D. – Grays Athletic – Barnet
13 Asamoah, Derek – Lincoln City – Chester City
12 Bailey, Matthew – Crewe Alexandra – Southport
20 Bean, Marcus T. – Queens Park Rangers – Blackpool
31 Benjamin, Trevor J. – Peterborough United – Swindon Town
13 Berry, Tyrone – Crystal Palace – Rushden & Diamonds
31 Best, Leon J. – Southampton – Sheffield Wednesday
27 Black, Thomas R. – Crystal Palace – Gillingham
1 Bloomer, Matthew – Lincoln City – Grimsby Town
27 Bowditch, Dean – Ipswich Town – Wycombe Wanderers
20 Bridge, Wayne M. – Chelsea – Fulham
13 Castle, Peter – Reading – Rushden & Diamonds
13 Cecila Batista, Ricardo J. – Fulham – Milton Keynes Dons
31 Clarke, Leon M. – Wolverhampton Wanderers – Queens Park Rangers
10 Cohen, Christopher D. – West Ham United – Yeovil Town
13 Collins, Aiden – Ipswich Town – Wycombe Wanderers
13 Corden, Simon W. – Scunthorpe United – Chester City
4 Corneille, Mark – Gillingham – Easbourne Borough
19 Craddock, Darren – Hartlepool United – York City
9 Crooks, Lee R. – Bradford City – Notts County
20 Dadi, Eugene – Nottingham Forest – Notts County
13 Dagnall, Christopher – Tranmere Rovers – Rochdale
30 Dixon, Jonathan J. – Wycombe Wanderers – Aldershot Town
31 Dobson, Michael W. – Brentford – Reading
20 Doolan, John – Blackpool – Rochdale
20 Dootson, Craig R. – Bury – Hinckley United
12 Doyle, Colin – Birmingham City – Millwall
31 Drench, Steven M. – Blackburn Rovers – Morecambe
13 Duke, Matthew – Hull City – Wycombe Wanderers
6 Eagles, Christopher M. – Manchester United – Watford
30 Easter, Jermaine – Stockport County – Wycombe Wanderers
20 Edwards, Andrew D. – Southend United – Grays Athletic
31 El Hamdaoui, Mounir – Tottenham Hotspur – Derby County
23 Elphick, Gary – Brighton & Hove Albion – Aldershot Town
12 Flitcroft, Garry W. – Blackburn Rovers – Sheffield United
31 Folly, Yoann – Southampton – Sheffield Wednesday
16 Fontaine, Liam V.H. – Fulham – Bristol City
9 Forte, Jonathan – Sheffield United – Rotherham United
10 Fortune, Clayton A. – Bristol City – Port Vale
4 Fowler, Lee A. – Huddersfield Town – Scarborough
23 Francis, Simon C. – Sheffield United – Tranmere Rovers
12 Fuller, Barry M. – Charlton Athletic – Barnet
30 Fulop, Marton – Tottenham Hotspur – Coventry City
31 Gallagher, Paul – Blackburn Rovers – Stoke City
1 Gillespie, Steven – Bristol City – Cheltenham Town
4 Gobern, Lewis T. – Wolverhampton Wanderers – Blackpool
1 Graham, Daniel A.W. – Middlesbrough – Derby County
23 Graham, David – Sheffield Wednesday – Huddersfield Town
13 Grant, Anthony P.S. – Chelsea – Oldham Athletic
31 Grant, Lee A. – Derby County – Oldham Athletic
20 Green, Adam – Fulham – Bristol City
20 Griffin, Adam – Oldham Athletic – Stockport County
6 Hall, Asa – Birmingham City – Boston United
12 Hayes, Jonathan – Reading – Forest Green Rovers
13 Heckingbottom, Paul – Sheffield Wednesday – Barnsley
19 Hicks, David – Northampton Town – Hitchin Town
6 Hopkins, Paul D. – Everton – Darlington
31 Horwood, Evan D. – Sheffield United – Chester City
13 Howarth, Christopher – Bolton Wanderers – Stockport County
5 Huddlestone, Thomas A. – Tottenham Hotspur – Wolverhampton Wanderers
20 Hurst, Kevan – Sheffield United – Chesterfield
5 Hutchison, Donald – Millwall – Coventry City
20 Ifil, Phillip – Tottenham Hotspur – Millwall
12 Igoe, Samuel – Millwall – Bristol Rovers
4 James, Kevin E. – Nottingham Forest – Walsall
25 Jarman, Nathan G. – Barnsley – Bury
20 Jarrett, Albert O. – Brighton & Hove Albion – Swindon Town
26 Jaszczun, Antony J. – Rochdale – Cambridge United
31 Johansson, Jonatan L. – Charlton Athletic – Norwich City
18 Johnson, Bradley – Northampton Town – Gravesend & Northfleet
20 Johnson, Brett – Northampton Town – Grays Athletic
26 Jones, Zachariah S. – Blackburn Rovers – Southampton
10 Joseph, Marc E. – Hull City – Blackpool
13 Keene, James D. – Portsmouth – Boston United
31 Kell, Richard – Barnsley – Scarborough
6 Knight, David – Middlesbrough – Darlington
24 Knowles, Daniel – Gillingham – East Thurrock United
23 Kuqi, Njazi – Birmingham City – Blackpool
6 Lafferty, Kyle – Burnley – Darlington

5 Lamb, Alan – Grimsby Town – Eastwood Town
31 Lapham, Kyle J. – Swindon Town – Cirencester Town
6 Leary, Michael – Luton Town – Walsall
18 Lee, Thomas E. – Manchester United – Macclesfield Town
6 Logan, Conrad – Leicester City – Boston United
31 Lowe, Keith S. – Wolverhampton Wanderers – Queens Park Rangers
12 Marrison, Colin – Sheffield United – Bury
16 Martin, Richard W. – Brighton & Hove Albion – Kingstonian
2 McArdle, Rory A. – Sheffield Wednesday – Rochdale
26 McCombe, John – Huddersfield Town – Torquay United
24 McGurk, David – Darlington – York City
1 McShane, Paul D. – Manchester United – Brighton & Hove Albion
19 Mellor, Neil A. – Liverpool – Wigan Athletic
18 Mendes, Albert J.H.A. – Huddersfield Town – Grimsby Town
27 Mikolanda, Petr – West Ham United – Rushden & Diamonds
6 Miller, Liam W. – Manchester United – Leeds United
27 Morais, Filipe A. – Chelsea – Milton Keynes Dons
1 Morris, Ian – Leeds United – Blackpool
31 Mulligan, Gary – Sheffield United – Gillingham
10 Mullins, John – Reading – Kidderminster Harriers
26 Nade, Raphael – Carlisle United – Weymouth
12 Nash, Gerard – Ipswich Town – Hartlepool United
27 Nicolau, Nicky G. – Swindon Town – Hereford United
20 N'Toya, Zoa T. – Chesterfield – York City
13 O'Hara, Jamie – Tottenham Hotspur – Chesterfield
20 O'Leary, Stephen – Luton Town – Tranmere Rovers
31 Osborne, Junior – Watford – Kidderminster Harriers
20 Palmer, Jermaine – Grimsby Town – Kettering Town
19 Partridge, David W. – Bristol City – Milton Keynes Dons
13 Pittman, Jon P. – Nottingham Forest – Hartlepool United
18 Poke, Thomas J. – Crewe Alexandra – Lancaster City
26 Potter, Darren M. – Liverpool – Southampton
10 Pratley, Darren – Fulham – Brentford
19 Quinn, Stephen – Sheffield United – Rotherham United
31 Raven, David H. – Liverpool – Tranmere Rovers
20 Rayner, Simon – Lincoln City – Alfreton Town
31 Reed, Matthew – West Ham United – Barnet
31 Rehman, Zeshan – Fulham – Norwich City
9 Ricketts, Mark J. – Charlton Athletic – Milton Keynes Dons
31 Ricketts, Michael B. – Leeds United – Burnley
31 Rix, Benjamin – Crewe Alexandra – AFC Bournemouth
6 Roach, Neville – Eastleigh – Oxford United
20 Roache, Lee P. – Barnet – Yeading
31 Roberts, Mark A. – Crewe Alexandra – Chester City
3 Roberts, Mark A. – Crewe Alexandra – Southport
31 Robertson, Christopher – Sheffield United – Chester City
1 Robinson, Trevor K. – Millwall – Cambridge United
20 Rogers, Alan – Nottingham Forest – Hull City
1 Rose, Michael C. – Yeovil Town – Scunthorpe United
30 Routledge, Wayne N.A. – Tottenham Hotspur – Portsmouth
1 Saunders, Ben – Doncaster Rovers – Bury
6 Scarsella, David D.A. – Barnsley – Tooting & Mitcham United
13 Schmeichel, Kasper – Manchester City – Darlington
3 Sedgemore, Jacob O. – Bury – Burton Albion
1 Seremet, Dino – Luton Town – Tranmere Rovers
12 Silk, Gary L. – Portsmouth – Boston United
31 Sinama-Pongolle, Florent – Liverpool – Blackburn Rovers
12 Smith, Dan – Sunderland – Huddersfield Town
11 Smith, Grant G. – Bristol City – Walsall
6 Sodje, Efetobore – Yeovil Town – Southend United
14 Stock, Brian B. – AFC Bournemouth – Preston North End
6 Stokes, Tony – West Ham United – Rushden & Diamonds
31 Symes, Michael – Bradford City – Stockport County
13 Taylor, Andrew – Blackburn Rovers – Queens Park Rangers
6 Taylor, Daryl S. – Walsall – Hereford United
17 Taylor, Gareth K. – Nottingham Forest – Crewe Alexandra
12 Taylor, Kris – Walsall – Burton Albion
24 Taylor, Sean – Sunderland – Blackpool
12 Till, Peter – Birmingham City – Boston United
6 Timm, Mads – Manchester United – Walsall
5 Togwell, Samuel J. – Crystal Palace – Port Vale
1 Tudgay, Marcus – Derby County – Sheffield Wednesday
6 Turner, John A.J. – Cambridge United – Rushden & Diamonds
20 Varney, Alexander – Charlton Athletic – Barnet
6 Vaughan, Lee – Walsall – AFC Telford United
1 Walker, James L.N. – Charlton Athletic – Hartlepool United
26 Ward, Elliott L. – West Ham United – Plymouth Argyle
20 Watkins, Robert J. – Fulham – Gravesend & Northfleet
3 Weaver, Nicholas – Manchester City – Sheffield Wednesday
4 Whitbread, Zak B. – Liverpool – Millwall
31 White, Andrew – Notts County – Kidderminster Harriers
10 Williams, Anthony S. – Carlisle United – Bury
20 Williams, Matthew – Notts County – Tamworth
22 Wilson, Kyle P. – Crewe Alexandra – Barrow
20 Winters, Thomas R. – Oxford United – Brackley Town
19 Wood, Neil A. – Coventry City – Blackpool
23 Ziegler, Reto – Tottenham Hotspur – Wigan Athletic

FEBRUARY 2006

TEMPORARY TRANSFERS

24 Albrighton, Mark – Doncaster Rovers – Chester City
13 Aliadiere, Jeremie – Arsenal – Wolverhampton Wanderers
27 Andrew, Calvin H. – Luton Town – Bristol City
9 Anyinsah, Joseph G. – Preston North End – Bury
23 Anyon, Joseph – Port Vale – Harrogate Town
4 Barnes, Philip K. – Sheffield United – Queens Park Rangers
28 Black, Thomas R. – Crystal Palace – Gillingham
27 Bowditch, Dean – Ipswich Town – Wycombe Wanderers
27 Brevett, Rufus E. – Plymouth Argyle – Leicester City
17 Brown, Aaron – Reading – AFC Bournemouth
24 Cecila Baptista, Ricardo J. – Fulham – Milton Keynes Dons
8 Chaplow, Richard D. – West Bromwich Albion – Southampton
13 Chillingworth, Daniel T. – Rushden & Diamonds – Notts County
9 Cochrane, Justin v. – Crewe Alexandra – Gillingham
15 Collins, Aiden – Ipswich Town – Wycombe Wanderers
17 Collins, Neill – Sunderland – Sheffield United
14 Cooke, Andrew R. – Bradford City – Darlington
8 Corneille, Mark – Gillingham – Folkestone Invicta
24 Doyle, Nathan – Derby County – Notts County
24 Ehui, Ismael – Fulham – Scunthorpe United
24 Ellender, Paul – Boston United – Chester City
16 Fitzgerald, Scott – Brentford – Walsall
10 Fordyce, Daryl T. – Portsmouth – AFC Bournemouth
6 Forte, Jonathan – Sheffield United – Rotherham United
16 Fuller, Barry M. – Charlton Athletic – Barnet
24 Fuller, Ricardo – Southampton – Ipswich Town
10 Goodhind, Warren – Rochdale – Oxford United
14 Hand, Jamie – Fisher Athletic – Northampton Town
28 Harthill, Oliver – Birmingham City – Alvechurch
17 Healy, Joe B. – Millwall – Walton & Hersham
10 Horlock, Kevin – Ipswich Town – Doncaster Rovers
13 Horsfield, Geoffrey M. – West Bromwich Albion – Sheffield United
13 Hughes, Mark A. – Everton – Stockport County
13 Igoe, Samuel – Millwall – Bristol Rovers
21 Jarrett, Albert O. – Brighton & Hove Albion – Swindon Town
27 Johnson, Thomas – Scunthorpe United – Tamworth
16 Kuipers, Michael – Brighton & Hove Albion – Boston United
9 Lafferty, Kyle – Burnley – Darlington
8 Lamb, Alan – Grimsby Town – Eastwood Town
10 Lasley, Keith – Plymouth Argyle – Blackpool

14 Lee, Thomas E. – Manchester United – Macclesfield Town
22 Lisbie, Kevin – Charlton Athletic – Derby County
17 Makabu-Ma-Kalamby, Yves – Chelsea – Watford
13 Marrison, Colin – Sheffield United – Bury
17 McCammon, Mark J. – Brighton & Hove Albion – Bristol City
13 McDermott, Neale T. – Fulham – Darlington
24 McSporran, Jermaine – Doncaster Rovers – Boston United
10 Mills, Pablo – Derby County – Portsmouth
27 Nade, Raphael – Carlisle United – Weymouth
27 Nix, Kyle – Sheffield United – Barnsley
10 Noble, Mark – West Ham United – Hull City
10 Oyedele, Ade S. – Milton Keynes Dons – Woking
20 Pearson, Gregory – Rushden & Diamonds – Hucknall Town
10 Pericard, Vincent D.P. – Portsmouth – Plymouth Argyle
19 Quinn, Stephen – Sheffield United – Rotherham United
8 Rasiak, Grzegorz – Tottenham Hotspur – Southampton
22 Rayner, Simon – Lincoln City – Alfreton Town
24 Roache, Lee P. – Barnet – Yeading
16 Roma, Dominic – Sheffield United – Tamworth
23 Schmeichel, Kasper – Manchester City – Bury
8 Skoko, Josip – Wigan Athletic – Stoke City
17 Smikle, Brian J. – West Bromwich Albion – Halifax Town
15 Smith, Daniel – Sunderland – Huddersfield Town
18 Smylie, Daryl – Newcastle United – Stockport County
24 Stockdale, Robert K. – Hull City – Darlington
9 Talbot, Jason C. – Mansfield Town – Port Vale
15 Taylor, Andrew – Blackburn Rovers – Blackpool
24 Taylor, Sean – Sunderland – Blackpool
24 Timlin, Michael – Fulham – Scunthorpe United
17 Watkins, Robert J. – Fulham – Gravesend & Northfleet
23 Westerveld, Sander – Portsmouth – Everton
10 Wheater, David J. – Middlesbrough – Doncaster Rovers
15 Wilkinson, Neil – Hartlepool United – Blyth Spartans
16 Williams, Christopher – Stockport County – Northwich Victoria
27 Williams, Matthew – Notts County – Tamworth
24 Willis, Paul – Liverpool – Stockport County
20 Wilson, Kyle P. – Crewe Alexandra – Barrow
9 Wilson, Laurence T. – Everton – Mansfield Town
23 Wright, Alan – Sheffield United – Derby County
8 Wright, Jermaine M. – Leeds United – Southampton

MARCH 2006

20 Beckford, Jermaine P.	Wealdstone	Leeds United	undisclosed
31 Makofo, Serge	Milton Keynes Dons	Kettering Town	undisclosed

TEMPORARY TRANSFERS

24 Albrighton, Mark – Doncaster Rovers – Chester City
23 Aliadiere, Jeremie – Arsenal – Wolverhampton Wanderers
23 Alsop, Sam – Birmingham City – Yeovil Town
17 Andrews, Lee D. – Carlisle United – Torquay United
28 Anyon, Joseph – Port Vale – Harrogate Town
31 Appleby, Andrew – Hartlepool United – Blyth Spartans
22 Atieno, Taiwo L. – Walsall – Darlington
10 Bailey, Matthew – Crewe Alexandra – Lancaster City
16 Bardsley, Philip A. – Manchester United – Burnley
23 Beaumont, James – Nottingham Forest – Darlington
17 Beckwith, Robert – Luton Town – Chesterfield
10 Bischoff, Mikkel – Manchester City – Sheffield Wednesday
2 Bloomer, Matthew – Lincoln City – Cambridge United
17 Bond, Clay – Plymouth Argyle – Torquay United
23 Bowditch, Ben E. – Barnet – Yeading
10 Bradshaw, Gary – Cheltenham Town – North Ferriby United
24 Breach, Christopher B. – Brighton & Hove Albion – Bognor Regis Town
23 Brevett, Rufus E. – Plymouth Argyle – Leicester City
23 Burns, Jamie D. – Blackpool – Bury
3 Cameron, Colin – Wolverhampton Wanderers – Millwall
23 Campbell-Ryce, Jamal – Rotherham United – Colchester United
10 Carson, Scott P. – Liverpool – Sheffield Wednesday
17 Chillingworth, Daniel T. – Rushden & Diamonds – Notts County
23 Claridge, Stephen E. – Bradford City – Walsall
23 Clarke, Leon M. – Wolverhampton Wanderers – Plymouth Argyle
23 Clarke, William C. – Ipswich Town – Colchester United
14 Cochrane, Justin V. – Crewe Alexandra – Gillingham
23 Coleman, Liam – Torquay United – Forest Green Rovers
16 Collins, Aiden – Ipswich Town – Stockport County
14 Cooke, Andrew R. – Bradford City – Darlington
23 Corden, Wayne – Scunthorpe United – Leyton Orient
17 Daly, Jonathan M. – Hartlepool United – Bury
13 Dann, Scott – Walsall – Hednesford Town
23 Diagouraga, Toumani – Watford – Swindon Town
3 Doherty, Thomas – Queens Park Rangers – Yeovil Town
16 Dove, Craig – Chester City – Forest Green Rovers
24 Doyle, Nathan – Derby County – Notts County
21 Edwards, Jake – Exeter City – Chester City
24 Ehui, Ismael – Fulham – Scunthorpe United
23 Forrester, Jamie – Bristol Rovers – Lincoln City
13 Forte, Jonathan – Sheffield United – Rotherham United
30 Friars, Emmett – Notts County – Alfreton Town
23 Fuller, Barry M. – Charlton Athletic – Barnet
23 Gobern, Lewis T. – Wolverhampton Wanderers – Bury
13 Goodhind, Warren – Rochdale – Oxford United
23 Graham, Daniel A.W. – Middlesbrough – Leeds United
17 Gray, Andrew D. – Sunderland – Burnley
21 Griffiths, Anthony J. – Doncaster Rovers – Oxford United
23 Guatelli, Andrea – Portsmouth – Oxford United
4 Hall, Asa – Birmingham City – Boston United
20 Healy, Joe B. – Millwall – Walton & Hersham
23 Hegarty, Nick – Grimsby Town – Willenhall Town
20 Hollands, Daniel T. – Chelsea – Torquay United
10 Horlock, Kevin – Ipswich Town – Doncaster Rovers
23 Horsted, Liam A. – Portsmouth – Oxford United
23 Jackson, Mark – Preston North End – Southport
7 Jarrett, Jason L. – Norwich City – Preston North End
10 Johnson, Jemal J. – Blackburn Rovers – Darlington
9 Jordan, Michael W. – Arsenal – Yeovil Town
21 Kuipers, Michael – Brighton & Hove Albion – Boston United
17 Kuqi, Njazi – Birmingham City – Peterborough United
7 Lapham, Kyle J. – Swindon Town – Cirencester Town
23 Lee, Kevin – Wigan Athletic – Blackpool
16 Lee, Thomas E. – Manchester United – Macclesfield Town
22 Lisbie, Kevin – Charlton Athletic – Derby County
8 Lucketti, Christopher J. – Preston North End – Sheffield United
23 Mahon, Alan – Wigan Athletic – Burnley
23 Marques, Rui M. – Leeds United – Hull City
13 Marrison, Colin – Sheffield United – Bury
23 McCammon, Mark J. – Brighton & Hove Albion – Bristol City
8 McIndoe, Michael – Doncaster Rovers – Derby County
23 McLachlan, Fraser – Mansfield Town – Morecambe
2 McNeil, Mathew – Hyde United – Macclesfield Town
23 McPhee, Christopher S. – Brighton & Hove Albion – Swindon Town
10 Morais, Filipe A. – Chelsea – Milton Keynes Dons
17 Mulligan, Gary – Sheffield United – Gillingham
22 Murray, Matthew W. – Wolverhampton Wanderers – Tranmere Rovers
24 Nade, Raphael – Carlisle United – Weymouth
23 Nash, Gerard – Ipswich Town – Southend United
23 Newby, Jon P.R. – Bury – Kidderminster Harriers
13 Noble, Mark – West Ham United – Hull City
23 Noel-Williams, Gifton R. – Burnley – Brighton & Hove Albion
23 N'Toya, Zoa – Chesterfield – Oxford United
23 O'Connor, Kevin J.A. – Wolverhampton Wanderers – Stockport County
23 Opara, Lloyd – Cheshunt – Peterborough United
29 Pope, Thomas J. – Crewe Alexandra – Stafford Rangers
10 Pulis, Anthony J. – Stoke City – Plymouth Argyle
23 Rayner, Simon – Lincoln City – Alfreton Town

7 Reed, Matthew – West Ham United – Barnet
3 Reed, Stephen – Yeovil Town – Torquay United
23 Richardson, Marcus G. – Chester City – Macclesfield Town
8 Rix, Benjamin – Crewe Alexandra – AFC Bournemouth
9 Roberts, Mark A. – Crewe Alexandra – Southport
23 Rocastle, Craig A. – Sheffield Wednesday – Yeovil Town
21 Roma, Dominic – Sheffield United – Tamworth
23 Ross, Ian – Sheffield United – Bury
28 Schmeichel, Kasper – Manchester City – Bury
23 Sherlock, James – Gainsborough Trinity – Lincoln City
17 Smikle, Brian J. – West Bromwich Albion – Halifax Town
14 Smith, James A. – Bristol City – Brentford
23 Smith, Jay A. – Southend United – Oxford United
21 Stewart, Marcus P. – Bristol City – Preston North End
17 Stockley, Sam J. – Colchester United – Blackpool
30 Sutton, Ritchie A. – Crewe Alexandra – Stafford Rangers
17 Taylor, Andrew – Blackburn Rovers – Blackpool
6 Taylor, Daryl S. – Walsall – Hereford United
17 Taylor, Jason J.F. – Oldham Athletic – Stockport County
3 Taylor, Michael – Cheltenham Town – Forest Green Rovers
23 Timlin, Michael – Fulham – Doncaster Rovers
17 Vernon, Scott M. – Blackpool – Colchester United
15 Vincent, Jamie R. – Yeovil Town – Millwall
7 Ward, Jamie J. – Aston Villa – Stockport County
1 Welsh, Andrew P.D. – Sunderland – Leicester City
10 Wheater, David J. – Middlesbrough – Doncaster Rovers
3 Wilbraham, Aaron – Milton Keynes Dons – Bradford City
31 Wilkinson, Jack L. – Hartlepool United – Newcastle Benfield (Bay Plastics)
30 Wilkinson, Neil – Hartlepool United – Whitby Town
17 Williams, Gareth A. – Colchester United – Blackpool
10 Wilson, Kelvin J. – Notts County – Preston North End
9 Wilson, Lawrence T. – Everton – Mansfield Town
9 Wilson, Marc D. – Portsmouth – Yeovil Town
23 Wright, Alan – Sheffield United – Derby County
7 Wright, Jermaine M. – Leeds United – Southampton

APRIL 2006

TEMPORARY TRANSFERS

7 Bischoff, Mikkel – Manchester City – Sheffield Wednesday
5 Bloomer, Matthew – Lincoln City – Cambridge United
6 Bradshaw, Gary – Cheltenham Town – North Ferriby United
2 Cameron, Colin – Wolverhampton Wanderers – Millwall
7 Carson, Scott P. – Liverpool – Sheffield Wednesday
16 Cooke, Andrew R. – Bradford City – Darlington
27 Forrester, Jamie – Bristol Rovers – Lincoln City
11 Johnson, Jemal J. – Blackburn Rovers – Darlington
10 Jordan, Michael W. – Arsenal – Yeovil Town
20 Logan, Conrad – Leicester City – Boston United
11 Mapes, Charles E. – Yeading – Yeovil Town
20 Mulligan, Gary – Sheffield United – Gillingham
7 Reed, Matthew – West Ham United – Barnet
4 Reed, Stephen – Yeovil Town – Torquay United
7 Rix, Benjamin – Crewe Alexandra – AFC Bournemouth
23 Ross, Ian – Sheffield United – Bury
23 Schmeichel, Kasper – Manchester City – Bury
18 Smikle, Brian J. – West Bromwich Albion – Halifax Town
19 Smith, James A. – Bristol City – Brentford
25 Taylor, Jason J.F. – Oldham Athletic – Stockport County
7 Taylor, Michael – Cheltenham Town – Forest Green Rovers
10 Ward, Jamie J. – Aston Villa – Stockport County
11 Wilson, Marc D. – Portsmouth – Yeovil Town

MAY 2006

18 Bullard, James R.	Wigan Athletic	Fulham	£2,500,000
31 Hart, Charles (Joe) J.J.	Shrewsbury Town	Manchester City	£600,000
26 Jarrett, Jason L.	Norwich City	Preston North End	undisclosed
24 Mahon, Alan	Wigan Athletic	Burnley	£200,000
19 O'Connor, James F.E.	AFC Bournemouth	Doncaster Rovers	£130,000
2 Rasiak, Grzegorz	Tottenham Hotspur	Southampton	£2,000,000
16 Sandell, Andrew C.	Bath City	Bristol Rovers	undisclosed
16 Sherlock, James	Gainsborough Trinity	Lincoln City	undisclosed
26 Wilson, Kelvin J.	Notts County	Preston North End	undisclosed

TEMPORARY TRANSFERS

5 Logan, Conrad – Leicester City – Boston United
9 Pratley, Darren – Fulham – Brentford
9 Smith, James A. – Bristol City – Brentford

THE NEW FOREIGN LEGION 2005–06

JULY 2005		*From*	*To*	*Fee in £*
27	Barragan-Fernandez, Antoni	Sevilla	Liverpool	undisclosed
25	Belozoglu, Emre	Internazionale	Newcastle United	3,800,000
27	Benayoun, Yossi	Racing Santander	West Ham United	2,500,000
25	Borgetti, Jared	Pachucha	Bolton Wanderers	1,000,000
26	Chimbonda, Pascal	Bastia	Wigan Athletic	undisclosed
1	Del Horno, Asier	Athletic Bilbao	Chelsea	8,000,000
22	Diarra, Lassana	Le Havre	Chelsea	2,800,000
15	Drobny, Jaroslav	Panionios	Fulham	300,000
13	Elrich, Ahmed	Busan Icons	Fulham	400,000
25	Karadas, Azar	Benfica	Portsmouth	loan
22	Kroldrup, Per	Udinese	Everton	5,000,000
15	Mannone, Vito	Atalanta	Arsenal	350,000
1	Moore, Craig	Borrusia Munchengladbach	Newcastle United	Free
11	Park, Ji-Sung	PSV Eindhoven	Manchester United	4,000,000
6	Reina, Jose	Villarreal	Liverpool	6,000,000
19	Sissoko, Mohamed	Valencia	Liverpool	5,600,000
11	Stalteri, Paul	Werder Bremen	Tottenham Hotspur	undisclosed
12	Tainio, Teema	Auxerre	Tottenham Hotspur	undisclosed
21	Viafara, John	Once Caldas	Portsmouth	1,500,000
28	Westerveld, Sander	Real Sociedad	Portsmouth	undisclosed
AUGUST 2005				
8	Antwi, Godwin	Zaragoza	Liverpool	undisclosed
24	Bassila, Christian	Strasbourg	Sunderland	Free
30	Bouma, Wilfred	PSV Eindhoven	Aston Villa	3,500,000
22	Brandao, Goncalo	Belenenses	Charlton Athletic	loan
5	Davids, Edgar	Internazionale	Tottenham Hotspur	undisclosed
19	Essien, Michael	Lyon	Chelsea	24,400,000
26	Ferrari, Matteo	Roma	Everton	loan
31	Gislason, Rurik	HJK Helsinki	Charlton Athletic	180,000
5	Hleb, Alexandr	Stuttgart	Arsenal	8,000,000
18	Hussian, Yasser	Al Sadd	Manchester City	loan
30	Idrizaj, Besian	Linz	Liverpool	undisclosed
31	Khizanishvili, Zurab	Rangers	Blackburn Rovers	loan
11	Krul, Tim	Den Haag	Newcastle United	200,000
31	Lee, Yong-Pyo	PSV Eindhoven	Tottenham Hotspur	1,360,000
26	Luque, Alberto	La Coruna	Newcastle United	9,600,000
3	Mbesuma, Collins	Kaizer Chiefs	Portsmouth	undisclosed
30	Nuno Valente	Porto	Everton	1,500,000
23	Mikolanda, Petr	Viktoria Zizkov	West Ham United	undisclosed
23	Nakata, Hidetoshi	Fiorentina	Bolton Wanderers	loan
25	Pogatetz, Emanuel	Leverkusen	Middlesbrough	1,800,000
23	Priske, Brian	Genk	Portsmouth	undisclosed
31	Rochemback, Fabio	Sporting Lisbon	Middlesbrough	undisclosed
19	Roque, Miguel	Lleida	Liverpool	undisclosed
31	Dario Silva, Debray	Sevilla	Portsmouth	1,500,000
19	Skoko, Josip	Genclerbirligi	Wigan Athletic	undisclosed
16	Song, Alexandre	Bastia	Arsenal	loan
31	Van der Meyde, Andy	Internazionale	Everton	1,800,000
31	Vukic, Zvonimir	Shakhtar Donetsk	Portsmouth	600,000
JANUARY 2006				
13	Adebayor, Emmanuel	Monaco	Arsenal	undisclosed
12	Agger, Daniel	Brondby	Liverpool	5,800,000
10	Al-Habsi, Ali	Lyn	Bolton Wanderers	Free
31	D'Alessandro, Andreas	Wolfsburg	Portsmouth	loan
13	Diaby, Vassiriki	Auxerre	Arsenal	3,500,000
6	Elliott, Simon	Columbus Crew	Fulham	Free
10	Evra, Patrice	Monaco	Manchester United	5,500,000
31	Ghali, Hossan	Feyenoord	Tottenham Hotspur	2,000,000
1	Haapala, Tuomas	MyPa	Manchester City	undisclosed
10	Hojsted, Ingi	B36 Torshavn	Birmingham City	Free
3	Katan, Yaniv	Maccabi Haifa	West Ham United	100,000
30	Koroman, Ognjien	Terek Groznyi	Portsmouth	loan
25	Kozak, Jan	Artmedia	West Bromwich Albion	loan
4	Kromkamp, Jan	Villarreal	Liverpool	exch.
31	Latka, Martin	Slavia Prague	Birmingham City	loan
4	Maniche	Dynamo Moscow	Chelsea	loan
6	Mwaruwari, Benjamin	Auxerre	Portsmouth	4,100,000
4	Olisadebe, Emanuel	Panathinaikos	Portsmouth	undisclosed
31	Olsson, Martin	Hogaborgs	Blackburn Rovers	nominal
31	Perez, Oscar	Cordoba	Bolton Wanderers	Free
5	Riera, Alberto	Espanyol	Manchester City	loan
31	Samaras, Georgios	Heerenveen	Manchester City	6,000,000
6	Scharner, Paul	Brann	Wigan Athletic	1,500,000
4	Vidic, Nemanja	Spartak Moscow	Manchester United	7,000,000

REFEREEING AND THE LAWS OF THE GAME

Most people will be delighted to learn that there are no substantive changes to the Laws for Season 2006/2007. There are several tidying up exercises, some of them very minor such as confirming that the basic equipment and particularly wearing apparel comprises separate items, so that combined garments are not permissible. Thus a jersey/shirt and shorts may not be joined together in any way. Of more importance is the Law comprising fouls and misconduct, where the position of substitutes comes under the microscope. It has now been laid down that either a substitute or substituted player will be cautioned and shown a yellow card where he/she commits the offences of being (a) guilty of unsporting behaviour (b) shows dissent by word or action or (c) delays the restart of play. Where such a substitute or substituted player is sent off, he/she must be shown a red card and sent from the vicinity of the field of play and the technical area.

In the section on delaying the restart there is an extra tactical nuance being prohibited, which is provoking a confrontation by deliberately touching the ball after the Referee has stopped play particularly after a goal has been scored. Whether Referees will studiously enforce this is arguable because other delaying tactics which include deliberately taking the kick from the wrong position; appearing to take a throw-in but then leaving it to a team mate; moving the ball after the Referee has stopped play and deliberately delaying leaving the field when being substituted are often partially or even completely ignored. An interesting alteration comes as a result of the ball at a corner only needing to touch the corner arc. Now instead of needing it to be ten yards (9.15 metres) from the ball, an opponent must be ten yards from the corner arc.

Again a number of minor changes have been introduced for the purposes of continuity. Last season a two metre rule for opponents was introduced at throw-ins so now a defender will be cautioned at a throw-in for failure to respect the required distance. At the taking of a penalty kick, an infringement by the kicker or his team mate resulting in a free kick will mean it being taken from the place at which the infringement incurs. An infringement by a goalkeeper's team mate will see a goal allowed if scored and if not scored a retake will be ordered. This makes these Rules consistent with others of the same ilk.

For the recent World Cup additional Rules were introduced and particular emphasis was given to preventing simulation (diving), shirt pulling and dissent. In the Tournament Referees were instructed to detect and eradicate "lunging" tackles with one or two feet and the deliberate use of elbows. These were to be treated as serious foul play with the punishment of a red card and instant dismissal. A yellow card caution was to be administered for preventing an opponent from playing the ball by holding or pulling him back irrespective of the position on the field of play. Finally and perhaps the most controversial was that no jewellery was to be permitted on the field even if taped over and this included rings, earrings and plastic wrist bands. Any player infringing the Rule was to be cautioned and made to leave the field to remove the offending article. Even wedding rings were to be removed prior to the game or the player would not be allowed to play. In this regard FIFA were concerned about an incident in a match well before the Tournament where a player celebrating a goal caught his ring on fencing which ultimately resulted in the amputation of the finger.

The number of yellow and red cards meted out again suggested the introduction of a sin bin would be both helpful and productive; whilst the failure to legislate to a return to the old system of a drop ball led to several unsavoury incidents as players did not do what their opponents expected. Obviously it will be interesting to see if any of these new concepts spill over into the domestic game in the coming months.

Incidentally, the English Officials at the Germany World Cup were Referee Graham Poll and Assistant Referees Glen Turner, Mike Tingay and Phil Sharp, the last named of whom had already appeared as one of the Assistants in the 2002 World Cup Final and also the Final of the 2004 Olympic Games.

The International Board have given a further go-ahead for some more tests with goal-line technology, but only for determining whether or not a goal has been scored and provided it gives an immediate indication. FIFA President Sepp Blatter's statement in May 2005 that it would be used in the 2006 World Cup therefore came to nought. Currently experiments are being tried commercially with chip-in-the-ball technology whilst the Italian FA was working on a digital camera system. The World Cup did see all the Referees with their Assistants and Fourth Officials wired up for sound communication, although using the word in its other context it did not always lead to a particularly sound type of communication.

The FA also during last season launched the country's first scholarship in refereeing. Working for two years on the project with Gloucester University and Gloucester County FA, the first recipient was Roger Goodwin, 18 years of age from Hay-on-Wye, Herefordshire. The scholarship is linked to the level 2 vocational qualification for match Officials. It is hoped to link more educational establishments to existing courses countrywide.

One referee who had an extraordinarily successful season in 2005/06 was Alan Wiley from Staffordshire who became the first man to referee both senior domestic Cup Finals when he took charge of the Carling Cup Final (League Cup) in February and the FA Cup Final the following May. In the latter case he stepped in because Mike Dean who it was announced would be the Official had to stand down because he comes from the Wirral which was too close to Liverpool who played West Ham in the Final.

So far as the current National List of Referees is concerned they can all take heart from the introduction domestically as from 1 October 2006 of the principles set out in the anti-age discrimination legislation whereby the compulsory retirement age of 48 may well have to be abandoned. This certainly has reprieved Dermot Gallagher from Oxfordshire who will still be officiating next season. Two Referees who have left the list are Steve Dunn who has retired and Matt Messias who left last February by mutual consent.

KEN GOLDMAN

NATIONAL LIST OF REFEREES FOR SEASON 2006–07

Armstrong, P (Paul) – Berkshire
Atkinson, M (Martin) – Yorkshire
Bates, A (Tony) – Staffordshire
Beeby, RJ (Richard) – Northamptonshire
Bennett, SG (Steve) – Kent
Booth, RJ (Russell) – Nottinghamshire
Boyeson, C (Carl) – Yorkshire
Bratt, SJ (Steve) – West Midlands
Clattenburg, M (Mark) – Tyne & Wear
Cowburn, MG (Mark) – Lancashire
Crossley, PT (Phil) – Kent
Deadman, D (Darren) – Cambridgeshire
Dean, ML (Mike) – Wirral
Desmond, RP (Bob) – Wiltshire
Dorr, SJ (Steve) – Worcestershire
Dowd, P (Phil) – Staffordshire
Drysdale, D (Darren) – Lincolnshire
D'Urso, AP (Andy) – Essex
Foster, D (David) – Tyne & Wear
Foy, CJ (Chris) – Merseyside
Friend, KA (Kevin) – Leicestershire
Gallagher, DJ (Dermot) – Oxfordshire
Graham, F (Fred) – Essex
Hall, AR (Andy) – West Midlands
Halsey, MR (Mark) – Lancashire
Haywood, M (Mark) – Yorkshire
Hegley, GK (Grant) – Hertfordshire
Hill, KD (Keith) – Hertfordshire
Ilderton, EL (Eddie) – Tyne & Wear
Jones, MJ (Michael) – Cheshire
Joslin, PJ (Phil) – Nottinghamshire
Kettle, TM (Trevor) – Rutland
Knight, B (Barry) – Kent
Laws, G (Graham) – Tyne & Wear
Lee, R (Ray) – Essex
Lewis, RL (Rob) – Shropshire
McDermid, D (Danny) – London
Marriner, AM (Andre) – West Midlands
Mason, LS (Lee) – Lancashire
Mathieson, SW (Scott) – Cheshire
Melin, PW (Paul) – Surrey
Miller, NS (Nigel) – Co. Durham
Miller, P (Pat) – Bedfordshire
Moss, J (Jon) – Yorkshire
Oliver, CW (Clive) – Northumberland
Olivier, RJ (Ray) – West Midlands
Parkes, TA (Trevor) – West Midlands
Penn, AM (Andy) – West Midlands
Penton, C (Clive) – Sussex
Pike, MS (Mike) – Cumbria
Poll, G (Graham) – Hertfordshire
Probert, LW (Lee) – Gloucestershire
Prosser, PJ (Phil) – Yorkshire
Rennie, UD (Uriah) – Yorkshire
Riley, MA (Mike) – Yorkshire
Robinson, JP (Paul) – Yorkshire
Russell, MP (Mike) – Hertfordshire
Salisbury, G (Graham) – Lancashire
Shoebridge, RL (Rob) – Derbyshire
Singh, J (Jarnail) – Middlesex
Stroud, KP (Keith) – Hampshire
Styles, R (Rob) – Hampshire
Sutton, GJ (Gary) – Lincolnshire
Swarbrick, ND (Neil) – Lancashire
Tanner SJ, (Steve) – Somerset
Taylor, A (Anthony) – Cheshire
Taylor, P (Paul) – Hertfordshire
Thorpe, M (Mike) – Norfolk
Walton, P (Peter) – Northamptonshire
Webb, HM (Howard) – Yorkshire
Webster, CH (Colin) – Tyne & Wear
Whitestone, D (Dean) – Northamptonshire
Wiley, AG (Alan) – Staffordshire
Williamson IG, (Iain) – Berkshire
Woolmer, KA (Andy) – Northamptonshire
Wright, KK (Kevin) – Cambridgeshire

ASSISTANT REFEREES

Artis, SG (Stephen) – Norfolk; Astley, MA (Mark) – Gtr Manchester; Atkins, G (Graeme) – Yorkshire; Attwell, SB (Stuart) – Warwickshire; Babski, DS (Dave) – Lincolnshire; Bannister, N (Nigel) – Yorkshire; Barker, CA (Craig) – Yorkshire; Barnes, PW (Paul) – Northamptonshire; Barratt, W (Wayne) – Worcestershire; Barrow, SJ (Simon) – Staffordshire; Bassindale, C (Carl) – Yorkshire; Beale, GA (Guy) – Somerset; Beck, SP (Simon) – Essex; Beevor, R (Richard) – Suffolk; Bennett, A (Andrew) – Devon; Bentley, I F (Ian) – Kent; Benton, DK (David) – Yorkshire; Birkett, DJ (Dave) – Lincolnshire; Bramley, P (Philip) – Yorkshire; Brittain, GM (Gary) – Yorkshire; Brown, M (Mark) – Yorkshire; Brumwell, CA (Chris) – Cumbria; Bryan, DS (Dave) – Lincolnshire; Buck, D (David) – Kent; Bull, M (Michael) – Essex; Buller, KR (Keith) – Somerset; Burt, S (Stuart) – Hampshire; Burton, R (Roy) – Staffordshire; Bushell, DD (David) – London; Butler, AN (Andrew) – Lancashire; Cairns, MJ (Mike) – Northamptonshire; Canadine, P (Paul) – Yorkshire; Cann, DJ (Darren) – Norfolk; Carter, JE (John) – Tyne & Wear; Cassidy, MT (Martin) – Somerset; Castle, S (Steve) – West Midlands; Chittenden, S (Steve) – Hertfordshire; Collin, J (Jake) – Merseyside; Cook, SD (Steven) – Surrey; Cook, SJ (Steve) – Derbyshire; Cooke, SG (Stephen) – Nottinghamshire; Coote, DH (David) – Nottinghamshire; Cox, JL (James) – Worcestershire; Creighton, SW (Steve) – Berkshire; Cummins, SP (Steven) – Cheshire; Curry, PE (Paul) – Northumberland; Devine, JP (Jim) – Cleveland; Dexter, MC (Martin) – Leicestershire; Drew, S (Steve) – Tyne & Wear; Duncan, SAJ (Scott) – Tyne & Wear; Dunn, C (Carl) – Staffordshire; East, R (Roger) – Wiltshire; Evans, C (Craig) – Lincolnshire; Evans, EM (Eddie) – Gtr Manchester; Evans, IA (Ian) – West Midlands; Evans, KG (Karl) – Gtr Manchester; Evetts, GS (Gary) – Hertfordshire; Farries, J (John) – Oxfordshire; Fletcher, R (Russell) – Derbyshire; Flynn, J (John) – Wiltshire; Ford, D (Declan) – London; Francis, CJ (Chris) – Cambridgeshire; Ganfield, RS (Ron) – Somerset; Garratt, AM (Andy) – West Midlands; Gibbs, PN (Phil) – West Midlands; Gosling, IJ (Ian) – Kent; Graham, P (Paul) – Gtr Manchester; Green, AJ (Tony) – Leicestershire; Green, RC (Russell) – Lancashire; Greenwood, AH (Alf) – Yorkshire; Grove, PJ (Peter) – West Midlands; Grunnill, W (Wayne) – Yorkshire; Haines, A (Andy) – Tyne & Wear; Halliday, A (Andy) – Yorkshire; Hambling, GS (Glenn) – Norfolk; Handley, D (Darren) – Lancashire; Harris, MA (Martin) – Lincolnshire; Harwood, CN (Colin) – Gtr Manchester; Hay, J (John) – Lancashire; Haycock, KW (Ken) – Yorkshire; Hayto, JM (John) – Essex; Hendley, AR (Andy) – West Midlands; Hewitt, RT (Richard) – Yorkshire; Heywood, M (Mark) – Cheshire; Hilton, G (Gary) – Lancashire; Hodgson, L (Lee) – Warwickshire; Holbrook, JH (John) – West Midlands; Hooper, SA (Simon) – Wiltshire; Hopkins, JD (John) – Essex; Horton, AJ (Tony) – West Midlands; Horwood, GD (Graham) – Bedfordshire; Hutchinson, AD (Andrew) – Cheshire; Hutchinson, SM (Mark) – Nottinghamshire; Ives, GL (Gary) – Essex; James, RG (Ron) – Buckinghamshire; Keane, PJ (Patrick) – West Midlands; Kellett, DG (Gary) – West Yorkshire; Kettlewell, PT (Paul) – Lancashire; Kinseley, N (Nick) – Essex; Kirkup, PJ (Peter) – Northamptonshire; Knapp, SC (Simon) – Gloucestershire; Langford, O (Oliver) – West Midlands; Laver, AA (Andrew) – Hampshire; Law, GC (Geoff) – Leicestershire; Lawson, KD (Keith) – Lincolnshire; Lawson, MR (Mark) – Northumberland; Lewis, GJ (Gary) – Cambridgeshire; Linington, JJ (James) – Isle of Wight; McCallum, DA (Dave) – Tyne & Wear; McCoy, MT (Michael) – Kent; McDonough, M (Mick) – Tyne & Wear; McGee, A (Tony) – Merseyside; McIntosh, WA (Wayne) – Lincolnshire; McPherson, MW (Michael) – Cambridgeshire; Mackrell, EB (Eric) – Hampshire; Malone, B (Brendan) – Wiltshire; Margetts, DS (David) – Essex; Martin, PC (Paul) – Northamptonshire; Martin, RW (Rob) – Yorkshire; Mason, T (Tony) – Kent; Massey, T (Trevor) – Cheshire; Matadar, M (Mo) – Lancashire; Mattocks, KJ (Kevin) – Lancashire; Mellor, G (Glyn) – Derbyshire; Mellor, GS (Gary) – Yorkshire; Merchant, R (Rob) – Staffordshire; Mullarkey, M (Mike) – Devon; Murphy, ME (Michael) – West Midlands; Murphy, N (Nigel) – Nottinghamshire; Naylor, D (Dave) – Nottinghamshire; Naylor, MA (Michael) – Yorkshire; Newbold, AM (Andrew) – Leicestershire; Newell, AC (Andy) – Lancashire; Nolan, I (Ian) – Lancashire; Norman, PV (Paul) – Dorset; Oliver, M (Michael) – Northumberland; Palmer, R (Richard) – Somerset; Pardoe, SA (Steve) – Cheshire; Parker, AR (Alan) – Derbyshire; Parry, B (Brian) – Co. Durham; Pawson, CL (Craig) – Yorkshire; Pearce, JE (John) – Norfolk; Phillips, D (David) – Sussex; Pike, K (Kevin) – Dorset; Pollock, RM (Bob) – Merseyside; Porter, W (Wayne) – Lincolnshire; Procter-green, SRM (Shaun) – Lincolnshire; Quinn, P (Peter) – Cleveland; Radford, N (Neil) – Worcestershire; Ramsay, W (William) – West Midlands; Rawcliffe, A (Allan) – Gtr Manchester; Rayner, AE (Amy) – Leicestershire; Reeves, CL (Christopher) – Yorkshire; Richards, DC (Ceri) – Carmarthenshire; Richardson, D (David) – Yorkshire; Roberts, B (Bob) – Lancashire; Roberts, DJ (Danny) – Gtr Manchester; Rodda, A (Andrew) – Devon; Ross, JJ (Joe) – London; Rowbury, J (John) – Kent; Rubery, SP (Steve) – Essex; Rushton, SJ (Steven) – Staffordshire; Russell, GR (Geoff) – Northamptonshire; Sainsbury, A (Andrew) – Wiltshire; Salt, RA (Richard – Yorkshire; Sarginson, CD (Christopher) – Staffordshire; Scarr, IK (Ian) – West Midlands; Scholes, MS (Mark) – Buckinghamshire; Scott, GD (Graham) – Oxfordshire; Scregg, AJ (Andrew) – Merseyside; Searle, IR (Ian) – Hertfordshire; Sharp, PR (Phil) – Hertfordshire; Sheffield, JA (Alan) – West Midlands; Sheldrake, D (Darren) – Surrey; Siddall, I (Iain) – Lancashire; Simpson, GH (George) – Yorkshire; Simpson, J (Jeremy) – Lancashire; Simpson, P (Paul) – Co. Durham; Slaughter, A (Ashley) – Sussex; Smallwood, W (William) – Cheshire; Smedley, I (Ian) – Derbyshire; Smith, AN (Andrew) – Yorkshire; Smith, EI (Eamonn) – Surrey; Smith, J (Jeff) – Yorkshire; Smith, N (Nigel) – Derbyshire; Smith, RH (Richard) – West Midlands; Snartt, SP (Simon) – Gloucestershire; Steans, RJ (Rob) – Leicestershire; Stewart, M (Matt) – Essex; Stokes, JD (John) – Wirral; Storrie, D (David) – Yorkshire; Stott, GT (Gary) – Gtr Manchester; Stretton, GS (Guy) – Leicestershire; Sutton, MA (Mark) – Derbyshire; Swabey, L (Lee) – Devon; Sygmuta, BC (Barry) – Yorkshire; Tattan, BJ (Brian) – Merseyside; Thompson, MF (Marvin) – Middlesex; Thompson, PI (Paul) – Derbyshire; Tierney, P (Paul) – Lancashire; Tiffin, R (Russell) – Co. Durham; Tincknell, SW (Steve) – Hertfordshire; Tingey, M (Mike) – Buckinghamshire; Tomlinson, SD (Stephen) – Hampshire; Turner, A (Andrew) – Devon; Turner, GB (Glenn) – Derbyshire; Tyas, J (Jason) – Yorkshire; Unsworth, D (David) – Lancashire; Varley, PC (Paul) – Yorkshire; Vaughan, RG (Roger) – Somerset; Wallace, G (Garry) – Tyne & Wear; Ward, GL (Gavin) – Kent; Waring, J (Jim) – Lancashire; Warren, MR (Mark) – West Midlands; Watts, AS (Adam) – Worcestershire; Waugh, J (Jock) – Yorkshire; Weaver, M (Mark) – West Midlands; West, MG (Malcolm) – Cornwall; West, RJ (Richard) – Yorkshire; Wigglesworth, RJ (Richard) – Yorkshire; Wilkinson, K (Keith) – Northumberland; Williams, MA (Andy) – Herefordshire; Woodward, IJ (Irvine) – Sussex; Yates, NA (Neil) – Lancashire; Yeo, KG (Keith) – Essex; Yerby, MS (Martin) – Kent; Young, GR (Gary) – Bedfordshire.

THE THINGS THEY SAID . . .

Arsene Wenger despairing of the Premier League's negative tactics:
"When somebody spends £50, £60 or £70 on a ticket, it is not because he wants to be bored. It is because he wants to enjoy a football game."

Former England international Terry Butcher discussing prospects for the 2006 World Cup in September:
"Sven doesn't look like changing his side. We could all name his starting 11 for the World Cup without breaking sweat."

As reported in the *Daily Mirror*'s Mania as a Daft quote of the Week:
"Northern Ireland are ten minutes away from their finest victory. There's 15 minutes to go here."

Charlton Athletic manager Alan Curbishley commenting on TV overkill:
"How can anybody sit down on a Sunday and be entertained by a Premiership game at 12 o'clock, one at two o'clock, a Football League game at three, a top Spanish game at six – another at nine, then throw an Italian game in there as well."

Gazza on Wayne Rooney:
"People tend to forget how old Wayne is. It is not fair relying on a 19 year old kid to win games for England. He should be welcomed, cuddled and caressed and looked after a little bit more."

Headline in *The Daily Telegraph* after George Reynolds, former Darlington supremo was jailed for tax evasion:
"Reynolds' grandiose Quakers schemes turn to porridge."

Jose Mourinho before Chelsea had lost a League game:
"Everybody was crying when we kept on winning and winning. So we draw at Goodison and that made people more happy. One day when we lose there will be a national holiday."

Danish referee Kim Milton Nielsen who sent off David Beckham against Argentina in the 1998 World Cup in France and after he had sent off Wayne Rooney in a Champions League match:
"After the red card Beckham started to concentrate on playing football instead of being a playboy."

David Beckham after England's dramatic late win over Argentina in Geneva:
"This was the performance that England needed. It will give us the confidence to go on from here."

Fireworks from Jose Mourinho on 5 November ahead of the visit to Old Trafford with Manchester United on two defeats in a row. (Final score was United 1 Chelsea 0):
"If I'd lost three games, I'd expect to be fired."

Chelsea captain John Terry on crutches after suffering 10 stitches in a seventh minute gashed foot following a Wayne Rooney challenge in the same match:
"I think I'd have had to have my foot amputated before I came off this pitch."

Ian Wright, ex-Arsenal and England striker sitting on the fence (?) while commenting on Sven-Goran Eriksson during his pre-Christmas USA TV broadcast:
"The man's like a wet fish. He's got as much passion as a tadpole. He's useless."

Luton manager Mike Newell on the growing problem of bungs as it applies to dealings with agents:
"Have I been offered money? Yes, of course. And I wouldn't entertain the idea. Never."

Agent Jake Duncan on the same subject:
"Normally there are only three people who know about a bung: the manager, the agent and the player. And they all have too much to lose to speak out. There is far too much money in football for there not to be a thick seam of corruption in the game."

Ken Bates, Leeds United chairman and ex-Chelsea of course dismissive of Jose Mourinho's achievements:
"Here's £200m, now go run Chelsea. Your grandmother could do it."

Sven-Goran Eriksson after the dust settled on his agreement to leave the England job in the wake of the *News of the World* allegations:
"It's a scandal. It could only happen in this country that's for sure."

Glenn Hoddle on Wayne Rooney:
"He is strong mentally but I think there is some work to be done with sports psychologists that could help him further. I saw them when I was a player."

Jose Mourinho in the wake of Chelsea crashing 3-0 to Middlesbrough:
"I like it when small teams fight for their lives against teams with more quality. I congratulate Middlesbrough."

Alan Pardew hitting out at the overuse of foreign players:
"The foreign players and coaches have added massively to the game, but we are losing the soul of British football and English players should be integrated into the teams."

Arsene Wenger replying to Pardew's point of view:
"My pride in my career is not to choose somebody because of his passport."

Birmingham City manager Steve Bruce in the wake of the 7-0 FA Cup defeat suffered at the hands of Liverpool:
"I'm shell-shocked, disappointed and humiliated. It was men against boys."

Among reasons for turning down the England job, Big Phil Scolari:
"I don't like this pressure, so I will definitely not be coach of England. There were 20 reporters in front of my house – that was too much and I didn't like it."

Jose Mourinho in the aftermath of winning the title with Chelsea for the second time, revealing earlier threats to quit and mentioning never once manager of the month:
"In this club, in this country, where people only see coins, pounds and numbers and transfer fees, this is the worst club in the world to be a manager and being recognised for what you do."

Peter Crouch after scoring for Liverpool against Wigan Athletic to end a goal famine lasting 24 hours eight minutes:
"It's been difficult for me. I'm a happy sort of person but it was getting me down a bit."

Brian Barwick, FA chief executive on the day Steve McClaren was appointed England head coach:
"He (Scolari) was not my first choice and was not offered the job. Steve was my first choice."

Steve McClaren on his appointment to succeed Sven Goran Eriksson at the England helm:
"The FA had to pick the best man for the job and I believe they have. I have the knowledge, the experience. I have won big games, worked in big tournaments."

Neil Warnock, manager of Sheffield United on gaining promotion to the Premier League:
"My wife will be glad about Mourinho coming to Bramall Lane because he's a good-looking swine, isn't he?"

Eriksson commenting on his surprise selection of Theo Walcott for the England squad to play in Germany during the World Cup:
"I have seen Walcott on videos a lot but never in the flesh. I spoke to him a couple of weeks ago. I said 'hello' after a training session."

After winning promotion to the Premier League in March, John Madejski, chairman of Reading:
"We've achieved what we set out to do 16 years ago and it's come courtesy of a lot of hard work by a lot of people. It is absolutely exhilarating – a dream come true."

Liverpool goalkeeper Jose Reina on his rollercoaster FA Cup final experience of conceding two soft goals before redeeming himself with a last gasp save and the crucial one in the shoot-out.
"I was afraid, it was a bad situation and it was because of me. My performance was really bad but football can change in a minute and this is what's happened."

Thierry Henry following the defeat of Arsenal in the Champions League final against Barcelona complaining about referee Terje Hauge:
"I don't know if the referee had a Barcelona shirt on because they kicked me all over the place. Maybe next time I'll learn how to dive."

Ali Boumnijel, the Tunisian goalkeeper, the oldest player in the World Cup and at 40 the only one in the competition alive when England won in 1966:
"It's a boyhood dream. I always wanted to play in it. This is my third World Cup, but we have never qualified for the knock-out stages."

West Ham United and Trinidad & Tobago goalkeeper Shaka Hislop speaking about his unexpected inclusion in the team against Sweden:
"Kelvin Jack said he was not fit after the warm-up – a selfless decision on his part. The coach came to me ten minutes before kick-off to say I was playing."

Asamoah Gyan of Ghana who scored the fastest goal in the finals in Germany:
"I couldn't believe my eyes when I scored against a team like the Czech Republic and so early on. It's incredible."

Harry Kewell reflecting on his feelings after scoring against Croatia:
"That goal I scored wasn't only for myself, it was for the whole team and the nation. The fans were just superb and they are our 12th man."

Graham Poll who announced his retirement from international football refereeing following the farce in which he booked Croatia's Josip Simunic three times:
"What I did was a public mistake but it didn't affect qualification or the outcome of the match. Nobody got hurt and nobody died."

Argentine Football Federation president Julio Grondona after the dismissal of his team against Germany:
"No team played better than Argentina. We just lacked luck and ability in the final metres."

Germany coach Jurgen Klinsmann who had chosen shoot-out hero Jens Lehmann over Oliver Kahn as goalkeeper:
"As a former striker, I wouldn't want to face him and he proved that he has a sense about where the ball is going."

AC Milan and Brazilian midfield player Kaka after the defeat suffered against France:
"At a time like this it is impossible to say. It's difficult to know exactly what we did wrong. If we had known we wouldn't have done it."

Sir Geoff Hurst talking about the unusual fact that two World Cup finalists have come from the same small town of Ashton-under-Lyne, himself a World Cup winner in 1966 for England, Simone Perrotta, of Italy in 2006:
"I don't know too much about Perrotta, but understand he wants to finish his career in England. Perhaps my old club West Ham should put in an offer for him."

Jose Mourinho believed the crucial penalty save by Portuguese goalkeeper Ricardo against Frank Lampard destroyed England:
"When the opposing team chooses its best penalty-taker to take the first kick and the goalkeeper saves, it gives a huge injection of confidence."

Gobsmacked Wayne Rooney commenting on his dismissal against Portugal with views supported by the Football Association:
"If anything, I feel we should have had a free-kick for the fouls committed on me during the same incident."

Sepp Blatter with his individual view on the Rooney sending-off:
"I can only say that the referee's decision is final and I have not seen any protest from fans or even team mates on the field of play."

Departing Eriksson:
"The preparation was perfect, fitness levels were perfect, we handled the heat very well, we've been preparing and taking advice from specialists about the heat. I wouldn't do anything different. The sending-off and penalties cost us."

Best remark from the World Cup from a German source repeated in *The Daily Telegraph*:
"An English player has failed a dope test. Theo Walcott has been found with Calpol in his system."

Second best quote of the World Cup – (anomymous, but name and address supplied – Ed):
"Peter Crouch is 6ft.7in. Unfortunately he only jumps 6ft.2in!"

Marcello Lippi after guiding Italy to World Cup victory in the final:
"I have won the European Cup, I have won the Inter-Continental Cup and I have won five Italian titles but I have never felt as happy as I do now."

French coach Raymond Domenech with his views on the sending-off of Zinedine Zidane:
"The sending-off of Zidane changed the match. That was the key moment. We had been playing better than Italy in extra time and you could see they were just waiting for penalties."

ENGLISH LEAGUE HONOURS 1888 TO 2006

FA PREMIER LEAGUE

MAXIMUM POINTS: *a* 126; *b* 114.

**Won or placed on goal average (ratio), goal difference or most goals scored. ††Not promoted after play-offs.*

	First	*Pts*	*Second*	*Pts*	*Third*	*Pts*
1992–93*a*	Manchester U	84	Aston Villa	74	Norwich C	72
1993–94*a*	Manchester U	92	Blackburn R	84	Newcastle U	77
1994–95*a*	Blackburn R	89	Manchester U	88	Nottingham F	77
1995–96*a*	Manchester U	82	Newcastle U	78	Liverpool	71
1996–97*b*	Manchester U	75	Newcastle U*	68	Arsenal*	68
1997–98*b*	Arsenal	78	Manchester U	77	Liverpool	65
1998–99*b*	Manchester U	79	Arsenal	78	Chelsea	75
1999–2000*b*	Manchester U	91	Arsenal	73	Leeds U	69
2000–01	Manchester U	80	Arsenal	70	Liverpool	69
2001–02	Arsenal	87	Liverpool	80	Manchester U	77
2002–03	Manchester U	83	Arsenal	78	Newcastle U	69
2003–04	Arsenal	90	Chelsea	79	Manchester U	75
2004–05	Chelsea	95	Arsenal	83	Manchester U	77
2005–06	Chelsea	91	Manchester U	83	Liverpool	82

FOOTBALL LEAGUE CHAMPIONSHIP

MAXIMUM POINTS: 138

2004–05	Sunderland	94	Wigan Ath	87	Ipswich T††	85
2005–06	Reading	106	Sheffield U	90	Watford	81

FIRST DIVISION

MAXIMUM POINTS: 138

1992–93	Newcastle U	96	West Ham U*	88	Portsmouth††	88
1993–94	Crystal Palace	90	Nottingham F	83	Millwall††	74
1994–95	Middlesbrough	82	Reading††	79	Bolton W	77
1995–96	Sunderland	83	Derby Co	79	Crystal Palace††	75
1996–97	Bolton W	98	Barnsley	80	Wolverhampton W††	76
1997–98	Nottingham F	94	Middlesbrough	91	Sunderland††	90
1998–99	Sunderland	105	Bradford C	87	Ipswich T††	86
1999–2000	Charlton Ath	91	Manchester C	89	Ipswich T	87
2000–01	Fulham	101	Blackburn R	91	Bolton W	87
2001–02	Manchester C	99	WBA	89	Wolverhampton W††	86
2002–03	Portsmouth	98	Leicester C	92	Sheffield U††	80
2003–04	Norwich C	94	WBA	86	Sunderland††	79

FOOTBALL LEAGUE CHAMPIONSHIP 1

MAXIMUM POINTS: 138

2004–05	Luton T	98	Hull C	86	Tranmere R††	79
2005–06	Southend U	82	Colchester U	79	Brentford††	76

SECOND DIVISION

MAXIMUM POINTS: 138

1992–93	Stoke C	93	Bolton W	90	Port Vale††	89
1993–94	Reading	89	Port Vale	88	Plymouth Arg*††	85
1994–95	Birmingham C	89	Brentford††	85	Crewe Alex††	83
1995–96	Swindon T	92	Oxford U	83	Blackpool††	82
1996–97	Bury	84	Stockport Co	82	Luton T††	78
1997–98	Watford	88	Bristol C	85	Grimsby T	72
1998–99	Fulham	101	Walsall	87	Manchester C	82
1999–2000	Preston NE	95	Burnley	88	Gillingham	85
2000–01	Millwall	93	Rotherham U	91	Reading††	86
2001–02	Brighton & HA	90	Reading	84	Brentford*††	83
2002–03	Wigan Ath	100	Crewe Alex	86	Bristol C††	83
2003–04	Plymouth Arg	90	QPR	83	Bristol C††	82

FOOTBALL LEAGUE CHAMPIONSHIP 2

MAXIMUM POINTS: 138

2004–05	Yeovil T	83	Scunthorpe U*	80	Swansea C	80
2005–06	Carlisle U	86	Northampton T	83	Leyton Orient	81

THIRD DIVISION

MAXIMUM POINTS: *a* 126; *b* 138.

1992–93*a*	Cardiff C	83	Wrexham	80	Barnet	79
1993–94*a*	Shrewsbury T	79	Chester C	74	Crewe Alex	73
1994–95*a*	Carlisle U	91	Walsall	83	Chesterfield	81
1995–96*b*	Preston NE	86	Gillingham	83	Bury	79
1996–97*b*	Wigan Ath*	87	Fulham	87	Carlisle U	84
1997–98*b*	Notts Co	99	Macclesfield T	82	Lincoln C	72
1998–99*b*	Brentford	85	Cambridge U	81	Cardiff C	80
1999–2000*b*	Swansea C	85	Rotherham U	84	Northampton T	82
2000–01	Brighton & HA	92	Cardiff C	82	Chesterfield¶	80
2001–02	Plymouth Arg	102	Luton T	97	Mansfield T	79
2002–03	Rushden & D	87	Hartlepool U	85	Wrexham	84
2003–04	Doncaster R	92	Hull C	88	Torquay U*	81

¶9pts deducted for irregularities.

FOOTBALL LEAGUE

MAXIMUM POINTS: ***a*** **44;** ***b*** **60**

	First	*Pts*	*Second*	*Pts*	*Third*	*Pts*
1888–89*a*	Preston NE	40	Aston Villa	29	Wolverhampton W	28
1889–90*a*	Preston NE	33	Everton	31	Blackburn R	27
1890–91*a*	Everton	29	Preston NE	27	Notts Co	26
1891–92*b*	Sunderland	42	Preston NE	37	Bolton W	36

FIRST DIVISION to 1991–92

MAXIMUM POINTS: ***a*** **44;** ***b*** **52;** ***c*** **60;** ***d*** **68;** ***e*** **76;** ***f*** **84;** ***g*** **126;** ***h*** **120;** ***k*** **114.**

	First	*Pts*	*Second*	*Pts*	*Third*	*Pts*
1892–93*c*	Sunderland	48	Preston NE	37	Everton	36
1893–94*c*	Aston Villa	44	Sunderland	38	Derby Co	36
1894–95*c*	Sunderland	47	Everton	42	Aston Villa	39
1895–96*c*	Aston Villa	45	Derby Co	41	Everton	39
1896–97*c*	Aston Villa	47	Sheffield U*	36	Derby Co	36
1897–98*c*	Sheffield U	42	Sunderland	37	Wolverhampton W*	35
1898–99*d*	Aston Villa	45	Liverpool	43	Burnley	39
1899–1900*d*	Aston Villa	50	Sheffield U	48	Sunderland	41
1900–01*d*	Liverpool	45	Sunderland	43	Notts Co	40
1901–02*d*	Sunderland	44	Everton	41	Newcastle U	37
1902–03*d*	The Wednesday	42	Aston Villa*	41	Sunderland	41
1903–04*d*	The Wednesday	47	Manchester C	44	Everton	43
1904–05*d*	Newcastle U	48	Everton	47	Manchester C	46
1905–06*e*	Liverpool	51	Preston NE	47	The Wednesday	44
1906–07*e*	Newcastle U	51	Bristol C	48	Everton*	45
1907–08*e*	Manchester U	52	Aston Villa*	43	Manchester C	43
1908–09*e*	Newcastle U	53	Everton	46	Sunderland	44
1909–10*e*	Aston Villa	53	Liverpool	48	Blackburn R*	45
1910–11*e*	Manchester U	52	Aston Villa	51	Sunderland*	45
1911–12*e*	Blackburn R	49	Everton	46	Newcastle U	44
1912–13*e*	Sunderland	54	Aston Villa	50	Sheffield W	49
1913–14*e*	Blackburn R	51	Aston Villa	44	Middlesbrough*	43
1914–15*e*	Everton	46	Oldham Ath	45	Blackburn R*	43
1919–20*f*	WBA	60	Burnley	51	Chelsea	49
1920–21*f*	Burnley	59	Manchester C	54	Bolton W	52
1921–22*f*	Liverpool	57	Tottenham H	51	Burnley	49
1922–23*f*	Liverpool	60	Sunderland	54	Huddersfield T	53
1923–24*f*	Huddersfield T*	57	Cardiff C	57	Sunderland	53
1924–25*f*	Huddersfield T	58	WBA	56	Bolton W	55
1925–26*f*	Huddersfield T	57	Arsenal	52	Sunderland	48
1926–27*f*	Newcastle U	56	Huddersfield T	51	Sunderland	49
1927–28*f*	Everton	53	Huddersfield T	51	Leicester C	48
1928–29*f*	Sheffield W	52	Leicester C	51	Aston Villa	50
1929–30*f*	Sheffield W	60	Derby Co	50	Manchester C*	47
1930–31*f*	Arsenal	66	Aston Villa	59	Sheffield W	52
1931–32*f*	Everton	56	Arsenal	54	Sheffield W	50
1932–33*f*	Arsenal	58	Aston Villa	54	Sheffield W	51
1933–34*f*	Arsenal	59	Huddersfield T	56	Tottenham H	49
1934–35*f*	Arsenal	58	Sunderland	54	Sheffield W	49
1935–36*f*	Sunderland	56	Derby Co*	48	Huddersfield T	48
1936–37*f*	Manchester C	57	Charlton Ath	54	Arsenal	52
1937–38*f*	Arsenal	52	Wolverhampton W	51	Preston NE	49
1938–39*f*	Everton	59	Wolverhampton W	55	Charlton Ath	50
1946–47*f*	Liverpool	57	Manchester U*	56	Wolverhampton W	56
1947–48*f*	Arsenal	59	Manchester U*	52	Burnley	52
1948–49*f*	Portsmouth	58	Manchester U*	53	Derby Co	53
1949–50*f*	Portsmouth*	53	Wolverhampton W	53	Sunderland	52
1950–51*f*	Tottenham H	60	Manchester U	56	Blackpool	50
1951–52*f*	Manchester U	57	Tottenham H*	53	Arsenal	53
1952–53*f*	Arsenal*	54	Preston NE	54	Wolverhampton W	51
1953–54*f*	Wolverhampton W	57	WBA	53	Huddersfield T	51
1954–55*f*	Chelsea	52	Wolverhampton W*	48	Portsmouth*	48
1955–56*f*	Manchester U	60	Blackpool*	49	Wolverhampton W	49
1956–57*f*	Manchester U	64	Tottenham H*	56	Preston NE	56
1957–58*f*	Wolverhampton W	64	Preston NE	59	Tottenham H	51
1958–59*f*	Wolverhampton W	61	Manchester U	55	Arsenal*	50
1959–60*f*	Burnley	55	Wolverhampton W	54	Tottenham H	53
1960–61*f*	Tottenham H	66	Sheffield W	58	Wolverhampton W	57
1961–62*f*	Ipswich T	56	Burnley	53	Tottenham H	52
1962–63*f*	Everton	61	Tottenham H	55	Burnley	54
1963–64*f*	Liverpool	57	Manchester U	53	Everton	52
1964–65*f*	Manchester U*	61	Leeds U	61	Chelsea	56
1965–66*f*	Liverpool	61	Leeds U*	55	Burnley	55
1966–67*f*	Manchester U	60	Nottingham F*	56	Tottenham H	56
1967–68*f*	Manchester C	58	Manchester U	56	Liverpool	55
1968–69*f*	Leeds U	67	Liverpool	61	Everton	57
1969–70*f*	Everton	66	Leeds U	57	Chelsea	55
1970–71*f*	Arsenal	65	Leeds U	64	Tottenham H*	52
1971–72*f*	Derby Co	58	Leeds U*	57	Liverpool*	57
1972–73*f*	Liverpool	60	Arsenal	57	Leeds U	53
1973–74*f*	Leeds U	62	Liverpool	57	Derby Co	48
1974–75*f*	Derby Co	53	Liverpool*	51	Ipswich T	51
1975–76*f*	Liverpool	60	QPR	59	Manchester U	56
1976–77*f*	Liverpool	57	Manchester C	56	Ipswich T	52
1977–78*f*	Nottingham F	64	Liverpool	57	Everton	55

	First	Pts	Second	Pts	Third	Pts
1978–79f	Liverpool	68	Nottingham F	60	WBA	59
1979–80f	Liverpool	60	Manchester U	58	Ipswich T	52
1980–81f	Aston Villa	60	Ipswich T	56	Arsenal	53
1981–82g	Liverpool	87	Ipswich T	83	Manchester U	78
1982–83g	Liverpool	82	Watford	71	Manchester U	70
1983–84g	Liverpool	80	Southampton	77	Nottingham F*	74
1984–85g	Everton	90	Liverpool*	77	Tottenham H	77
1985–86g	Liverpool	88	Everton	86	West Ham U	84
1986–87g	Everton	86	Liverpool	77	Tottenham H	71
1987–88h	Liverpool	90	Manchester U	81	Nottingham F	73
1988–89k	Arsenal*	76	Liverpool	76	Nottingham F	64
1989–90k	Liverpool	79	Aston Villa	70	Tottenham H	63
1990–91k	Arsenal†	83	Liverpool	76	Crystal Palace	69
1991–92g	Leeds U	82	Manchester U	78	Sheffield W	75

No official competition during 1915–19 and 1939–46; Regional Leagues operated. †2 pts deducted.

SECOND DIVISION to 1991–92

MAXIMUM POINTS: ***a*** **44;** ***b*** **56;** ***c*** **60;** ***d*** **68;** ***e*** **76;** ***f*** **84;** ***g*** **126;** ***h*** **132;** ***k*** **138.**

	First	Pts	Second	Pts	Third	Pts
1892–93a	Small Heath	36	Sheffield U	35	Darwen	30
1893–94b	Liverpool	50	Small Heath	42	Notts Co	39
1894–95c	Bury	48	Notts Co	39	Newton Heath*	38
1895–96c	Liverpool*	46	Manchester C	46	Grimsby T*	42
1896–97c	Notts Co	42	Newton Heath	39	Grimsby T	38
1897–98c	Burnley	48	Newcastle U	45	Manchester C	39
1898–99d	Manchester C	52	Glossop NE	46	Leicester Fosse	45
1899–1900d	The Wednesday	54	Bolton W	52	Small Heath	46
1900–01d	Grimsby T	49	Small Heath	48	Burnley	44
1901–02d	WBA	55	Middlesbrough	51	Preston NE*	42
1902–03d	Manchester C	54	Small Heath	51	Woolwich A	48
1903–04d	Preston NE	50	Woolwich A	49	Manchester U	48
1904–05d	Liverpool	58	Bolton W	56	Manchester U	53
1905–06e	Bristol C	66	Manchester U	62	Chelsea	53
1906–07e	Nottingham F	60	Chelsea	57	Leicester Fosse	48
1907–08e	Bradford C	54	Leicester Fosse	52	Oldham Ath	50
1908–09e	Bolton W	52	Tottenham H*	51	WBA	51
1909–10e	Manchester C	54	Oldham Ath*	53	Hull C*	53
1910–11e	WBA	53	Bolton W	51	Chelsea	49
1911–12e	Derby Co*	54	Chelsea	54	Burnley	52
1912–13e	Preston NE	53	Burnley	50	Birmingham	46
1913–14e	Notts Co	53	Bradford PA*	49	Woolwich A	49
1914–15e	Derby Co	53	Preston NE	50	Barnsley	47
1919–20f	Tottenham H	70	Huddersfield T	64	Birmingham	56
1920–21f	Birmingham*	58	Cardiff C	58	Bristol C	51
1921–22f	Nottingham F	56	Stoke C*	52	Barnsley	52
1922–23f	Notts Co	53	West Ham U*	51	Leicester C	51
1923–24f	Leeds U	54	Bury*	51	Derby Co	51
1924–25f	Leicester C	59	Manchester U	57	Derby Co	55
1925–26f	Sheffield W	60	Derby Co	57	Chelsea	52
1926–27f	Middlesbrough	62	Portsmouth*	54	Manchester C	54
1927–28f	Manchester C	59	Leeds U	57	Chelsea	54
1928–29f	Middlesbrough	55	Grimsby T	53	Bradford PA*	48
1929–30f	Blackpool	58	Chelsea	55	Oldham Ath	53
1930–31f	Everton	61	WBA	54	Tottenham H	51
1931–32f	Wolverhampton W	56	Leeds U	54	Stoke C	52
1932–33f	Stoke C	56	Tottenham H	55	Fulham	50
1933–34f	Grimsby T	59	Preston NE	52	Bolton W*	51
1934–35f	Brentford	61	Bolton W*	56	West Ham U	56
1935–36f	Manchester U	56	Charlton Ath	55	Sheffield U*	52
1936–37f	Leicester C	56	Blackpool	55	Bury	52
1937–38f	Aston Villa	57	Manchester U*	53	Sheffield U	53
1938–39f	Blackburn R	55	Sheffield U	54	Sheffield W	53
1946–47f	Manchester C	62	Burnley	58	Birmingham C	55
1947–48f	Birmingham C	59	Newcastle U	56	Southampton	52
1948–49f	Fulham	57	WBA	56	Southampton	55
1949–50f	Tottenham H	61	Sheffield W*	52	Sheffield U*	52
1950–51f	Preston NE	57	Manchester C	52	Cardiff C	50
1951–52f	Sheffield W	53	Cardiff C*	51	Birmingham C	51
1952–53f	Sheffield U	60	Huddersfield T	58	Luton T	52
1953–54f	Leicester C*	56	Everton	56	Blackburn R	55
1954–55f	Birmingham C*	54	Luton T*	54	Rotherham U	54
1955–56f	Sheffield W	55	Leeds U	52	Liverpool*	48
1956–57f	Leicester C	61	Nottingham F	54	Liverpool	53
1957–58f	West Ham U	57	Blackburn R	56	Charlton Ath	55
1958–59f	Sheffield W	62	Fulham	60	Sheffield U*	53
1959–60f	Aston Villa	59	Cardiff C	58	Liverpool*	50
1960–61f	Ipswich T	59	Sheffield U	58	Liverpool	52
1961–62f	Liverpool	62	Leyton Orient	54	Sunderland	53
1962–63f	Stoke C	53	Chelsea*	52	Sunderland	52
1963–64f	Leeds U	63	Sunderland	61	Preston NE	56
1964–65f	Newcastle U	57	Northampton T	56	Bolton W	50
1965–66f	Manchester C	59	Southampton	54	Coventry C	53
1966–67f	Coventry C	59	Wolverhampton W	58	Carlisle U	52
1967–68f	Ipswich T	59	QPR*	58	Blackpool	58
1968–69f	Derby Co	63	Crystal Palace	56	Charlton Ath	50

	First	Pts	Second	Pts	Third	Pts
1969–70f	Huddersfield T	60	Blackpool	53	Leicester C	51
1970–71f	Leicester C	59	Sheffield U	56	Cardiff C*	53
1971–72f	Norwich C	57	Birmingham C	56	Millwall	55
1972–73f	Burnley	62	QPR	61	Aston Villa	50
1973–74f	Middlesbrough	65	Luton T	50	Carlisle U	49
1974–75f	Manchester U	61	Aston Villa	58	Norwich C	53
1975–76f	Sunderland	56	Bristol C*	53	WBA	53
1976–77f	Wolverhampton W	57	Chelsea	55	Nottingham F	52
1977–78f	Bolton W	58	Southampton	57	Tottenham H*	56
1978–79f	Crystal Palace	57	Brighton & HA*	56	Stoke C	56
1979–80f	Leicester C	55	Sunderland	54	Birmingham C*	53
1980–81f	West Ham U	66	Notts Co	53	Swansea C*	50
1981–82g	Luton T	88	Watford	80	Norwich C	71
1982–83g	QPR	85	Wolverhampton W	75	Leicester C	70
1983–84g	Chelsea*	88	Sheffield W	88	Newcastle U	80
1984–85g	Oxford U	84	Birmingham C	82	Manchester C	74
1985–86g	Norwich C	84	Charlton Ath	77	Wimbledon	76
1986–87g	Derby Co	84	Portsmouth	78	Oldham Ath††	75
1987–88h	Millwall	82	Aston Villa*	78	Middlesbrough	78
1988–89k	Chelsea	99	Manchester C	82	Crystal Palace	81
1989–90k	Leeds U*	85	Sheffield U	85	Newcastle U††	80
1990–91k	Oldham Ath	88	West Ham U	87	Sheffield W	82
1991–92k	Ipswich T	84	Middlesbrough	80	Derby Co	78

No official competition during 1915–19 and 1939–46; Regional Leagues operated.

THIRD DIVISION to 1991–92

MAXIMUM POINTS: 92; 138 FROM 1981–82.

	First	Pts	Second	Pts	Third	Pts
1958–59	Plymouth Arg	62	Hull C	61	Brentford*	57
1959–60	Southampton	61	Norwich C	59	Shrewsbury T*	52
1960–61	Bury	68	Walsall	62	QPR	60
1961–62	Portsmouth	65	Grimsby T	62	Bournemouth*	59
1962–63	Northampton T	62	Swindon T	58	Port Vale	54
1963–64	Coventry C*	60	Crystal Palace	60	Watford	58
1964–65	Carlisle U	60	Bristol C*	59	Mansfield T	59
1965–66	Hull C	69	Millwall	65	QPR	57
1966–67	QPR	67	Middlesbrough	55	Watford	54
1967–68	Oxford U	57	Bury	56	Shrewsbury T	55
1968–69	Watford*	64	Swindon T	64	Luton T	61
1969–70	Orient	62	Luton T	60	Bristol R	56
1970–71	Preston NE	61	Fulham	60	Halifax T	56
1971–72	Aston Villa	70	Brighton & HA	65	Bournemouth*	62
1972–73	Bolton W	61	Notts Co	57	Blackburn R	55
1973–74	Oldham Ath	62	Bristol R*	61	York C	61
1974–75	Blackburn R	60	Plymouth Arg	59	Charlton Ath	55
1975–76	Hereford U	63	Cardiff C	57	Millwall	56
1976–77	Mansfield T	64	Brighton & HA	61	Crystal Palace*	59
1977–78	Wrexham	61	Cambridge U	58	Preston NE*	56
1978–79	Shrewsbury T	61	Watford*	60	Swansea C	60
1979–80	Grimsby T	62	Blackburn R	59	Sheffield W	58
1980–81	Rotherham U	61	Barnsley*	59	Charlton Ath	59
1981–82	Burnley*	80	Carlisle U	80	Fulham	78
1982–83	Portsmouth	91	Cardiff C	86	Huddersfield T	82
1983–84	Oxford U	95	Wimbledon	87	Sheffield U*	83
1984–85	Bradford C	94	Millwall	90	Hull C	87
1985–86	Reading	94	Plymouth Arg	87	Derby Co	84
1986–87	Bournemouth	97	Middlesbrough	94	Swindon T	87
1987–88	Sunderland	93	Brighton & HA	84	Walsall	82
1988–89	Wolverhampton W	92	Sheffield U*	84	Port Vale	84
1989–90	Bristol R	93	Bristol C	91	Notts Co	87
1990–91	Cambridge U	86	Southend U	85	Grimsby T*	83
1991–92	Brentford	82	Birmingham C	81	Huddersfield T	78

FOURTH DIVISION (1958–1992)

MAXIMUM POINTS: 92; 138 FROM 1981–82.

	First	Pts	Second	Pts	Third	Pts	Fourth	Pts
1958–59	Port Vale	64	Coventry C*	60	York C	60	Shrewsbury T	58
1959–60	Walsall	65	Notts Co*	60	Torquay U	60	Watford	57
1960–61	Peterborough U	66	Crystal Palace	64	Northampton T*	60	Bradford PA	60
1961–62†	Millwall	56	Colchester U	55	Wrexham	53	Carlisle U	52
1962–63	Brentford	62	Oldham Ath*	59	Crewe Alex	59	Mansfield T*	57
1963–64	Gillingham*	60	Carlisle U	60	Workington	59	Exeter C	58
1964–65	Brighton & HA	63	Millwall*	62	York C	62	Oxford U	61
1965–66	Doncaster R*	59	Darlington	59	Torquay U	58	Colchester U*	56
1966–67	Stockport Co	64	Southport*	59	Barrow	59	Tranmere R	58
1967–68	Luton T	66	Barnsley	61	Hartlepools U	60	Crewe Alex	58
1968–69	Doncaster R	59	Halifax T	57	Rochdale*	56	Bradford C	56
1969–70	Chesterfield	64	Wrexham	61	Swansea C	60	Port Vale	59
1970–71	Notts Co	69	Bournemouth	60	Oldham Ath	59	York C	56
1971–72	Grimsby T	63	Southend U	60	Brentford	59	Scunthorpe U	57
1972–73	Southport	62	Hereford U	58	Cambridge U	57	Aldershot*	56
1973–74	Peterborough U	65	Gillingham	62	Colchester U	60	Bury	59
1974–75	Mansfield T	68	Shrewsbury T	62	Rotherham U	59	Chester*	57

	First	*Pts*	*Second*	*Pts*	*Third*	*Pts*	*Fourth*	*Pts*
1975–76	Lincoln C	74	Northampton T	68	Reading	60	Tranmere R	58
1976–77	Cambridge U	65	Exeter C	62	Colchester U*	59	Bradford C	59
1977–78	Watford	71	Southend U	60	Swansea C*	56	Brentford	56
1978–79	Reading	65	Grimsby T*	61	Wimbledon*	61	Barnsley	61
1979–80	Huddersfield T	66	Walsall	64	Newport Co	61	Portsmouth*	60
1980–81	Southend U	67	Lincoln C	65	Doncaster R	56	Wimbledon	55
1981–82	Sheffield U	96	Bradford C*	91	Wigan Ath	91	Bournemouth	88
1982–83	Wimbledon	98	Hull C	90	Port Vale	88	Scunthorpe U	83
1983–84	York C	101	Doncaster R	85	Reading*	82	Bristol C	82
1984–85	Chesterfield	91	Blackpool	86	Darlington	85	Bury	84
1985–86	Swindon T	102	Chester C	84	Mansfield T	81	Port Vale	79
1986–87	Northampton T	99	Preston NE	90	Southend U	80	Wolverhampton W††	79
1987–88	Wolverhampton W	90	Cardiff C	85	Bolton W	78	Scunthorpe U††	77
1988–89	Rotherham U	82	Tranmere R	80	Crewe Alex	78	Scunthorpe U††	77
1989–90	Exeter C	89	Grimsby T	79	Southend U	75	Stockport Co††	74
1990–91	Darlington	83	Stockport Co*	82	Hartlepool U	82	Peterborough U	80
1991–92†*	Burnley	83	Rotherham U*	77	Mansfield T	77	Blackpool	76

†*Maximum points:* 88 owing to Accrington Stanley's resignation.
†**Maximum points:* 126 owing to Aldershot being expelled (and only 23 teams started the competition).

THIRD DIVISION—SOUTH (1920–1958)

1920–21 SEASON AS THIRD DIVISION. MAXIMUM POINTS: *a* 84; *b* 92.

	First	*Pts*	*Second*	*Pts*	*Third*	*Pts*
1920–21*a*	Crystal Palace	59	Southampton	54	QPR	53
1921–22*a*	Southampton*	61	Plymouth Arg	61	Portsmouth	53
1922–23*a*	Bristol C	59	Plymouth Arg*	53	Swansea T	53
1923–24*a*	Portsmouth	59	Plymouth Arg	55	Millwall	54
1924–25*a*	Swansea T	57	Plymouth Arg	56	Bristol C	53
1925–26*a*	Reading	57	Plymouth Arg	56	Millwall	53
1926–27*a*	Bristol C	62	Plymouth Arg	60	Millwall	56
1927–28*a*	Millwall	65	Northampton T	55	Plymouth Arg	53
1928–29*a*	Charlton Ath*	54	Crystal Palace	54	Northampton T*	52
1929–30*a*	Plymouth Arg	68	Brentford	61	QPR	51
1930–31*a*	Notts Co	59	Crystal Palace	51	Brentford	50
1931–32*a*	Fulham	57	Reading	55	Southend U	53
1932–33*a*	Brentford	62	Exeter C	58	Norwich C	57
1933–34*a*	Norwich C	61	Coventry C*	54	Reading*	54
1934–35*a*	Charlton Ath	61	Reading	53	Coventry C	51
1935–36*a*	Coventry C	57	Luton T	56	Reading	54
1936–37*a*	Luton T	58	Notts Co	56	Brighton & HA	53
1937–38*a*	Millwall	56	Bristol C	55	QPR*	53
1938–39*a*	Newport Co	55	Crystal Palace	52	Brighton & HA	49
1939–46	Competition cancelled owing to war. Regional Leagues operated.					
1946–47*a*	Cardiff C	66	QPR	57	Bristol C	51
1947–48*a*	QPR	61	Bournemouth	57	Walsall	51
1948–49*a*	Swansea T	62	Reading	55	Bournemouth	52
1949–50*a*	Notts Co	58	Northampton T*	51	Southend U	51
1950–51*b*	Nottingham F	70	Norwich C	64	Reading*	57
1951–52*b*	Plymouth Arg	66	Reading*	61	Norwich C	61
1952–53*b*	Bristol R	64	Millwall*	62	Northampton T	62
1953–54*b*	Ipswich T	64	Brighton & HA	61	Bristol C	56
1954–55*b*	Bristol C	70	Leyton Orient	61	Southampton	59
1955–56*b*	Leyton Orient	66	Brighton & HA	65	Ipswich T	64
1956–57*b*	Ipswich T*	59	Torquay U	59	Colchester U	58
1957–58*b*	Brighton & HA	60	Brentford*	58	Plymouth Arg	58

THIRD DIVISION—NORTH (1921–1958)

MAXIMUM POINTS: *a* 76; *b* 84; *c* 80; *d* 92.

	First	*Pts*	*Second*	*Pts*	*Third*	*Pts*
1921–22*a*	Stockport Co	56	Darlington*	50	Grimsby T	50
1922–23*a*	Nelson	51	Bradford PA	47	Walsall	46
1923–24*b*	Wolverhampton W	63	Rochdale	62	Chesterfield	54
1924–25*b*	Darlington	58	Nelson*	53	New Brighton	53
1925–26*b*	Grimsby T	61	Bradford PA	60	Rochdale	59
1926–27*b*	Stoke C	63	Rochdale	58	Bradford PA	55
1927–28*b*	Bradford PA	63	Lincoln C	55	Stockport Co	54
1928–29*b*	Bradford C	63	Stockport Co	62	Wrexham	52
1929–30*b*	Port Vale	67	Stockport Co	63	Darlington*	50
1930–31*b*	Chesterfield	58	Lincoln C	57	Wrexham*	54
1931–32*c*	Lincoln C*	57	Gateshead	57	Chester	50
1932–33*b*	Hull C	59	Wrexham	57	Stockport Co	54
1933–34*b*	Barnsley	62	Chesterfield	61	Stockport Co	59
1934–35*b*	Doncaster R	57	Halifax T	55	Chester	54
1935–36*b*	Chesterfield	60	Chester*	55	Tranmere R	55
1936–37*b*	Stockport Co	60	Lincoln C	57	Chester	53
1937–38*b*	Tranmere R	56	Doncaster R	54	Hull C	53
1938–39*b*	Barnsley	67	Doncaster R	56	Bradford C	52
1939–46	Competition cancelled owing to war. Regional Leagues operated.					
1946–47*b*	Doncaster R	72	Rotherham U	60	Chester	56
1947–48*b*	Lincoln C	60	Rotherham U	59	Wrexham	50
1948–49*b*	Hull C	65	Rotherham U	62	Doncaster R	50
1949–50*b*	Doncaster R	55	Gateshead	53	Rochdale*	51
1950–51*d*	Rotherham U	71	Mansfield T	64	Carlisle U	62
1951–52*d*	Lincoln C	69	Grimsby T	66	Stockport Co	59

	First	*Pts*	*Second*	*Pts*	*Third*	*Pts*
1952–53*d*	Oldham Ath	59	Port Vale	58	Wrexham	56
1953–54*d*	Port Vale	69	Barnsley	58	Scunthorpe U	57
1954–55*d*	Barnsley	65	Accrington S	61	Scunthorpe U*	58
1955–56*d*	Grimsby T	68	Derby Co	63	Accrington S	59
1956–57*d*	Derby Co	63	Hartlepools U	59	Accrington S*	58
1957–58*d*	Scunthorpe U	66	Accrington S	59	Bradford C	57

PROMOTED AFTER PLAY-OFFS

(NOT ACCOUNTED FOR IN PREVIOUS SECTION)

1986–87 Aldershot to Division 3.
1987–88 Swansea C to Division 3.
1988–89 Leyton Orient to Division 3.
1989–90 Sunderland to Division 1; Notts Co to Division 2; Cambridge U to Division 3.
1990–91 Notts Co to Division 1; Tranmere R to Division 2; Torquay U to Division 3.
1991–92 Blackburn R to Premier League; Peterborough U to Division 1.
1992–93 Swindon T to Premier League; WBA to Division 1; York C to Division 2.
1993–94 Leicester C to Premier League; Burnley to Division 1; Wycombe W to Division 2.
1994–95 Huddersfield T to Division 1.
1995–96 Leicester C to Premier League; Bradford C to Division 1; Plymouth Arg to Division 2.
1996–97 Crystal Palace to Premier League; Crewe Alex to Division 1; Northampton T to Division 2.
1997–98 Charlton Ath to Premier League; Colchester U to Division 2.
1998–99 Watford to Premier League; Scunthorpe U to Division 2.
1999–2000 Peterborough U to Division 2
2000–01 Walsall to Division 1; Blackpool to Division 2
2001–02 Birmingham C to Premier League; Stoke C to Division 1; Cheltenham T to Division 2
2002–03 Wolverhampton W to Premier League; Cardiff C to Division 1; Bournemouth to Division 2
2003–04 Crystal Palace to Premier League; Brighton & HA to Division 1; Huddersfield T to Division 2
2004–05 West Ham U to Premier League; Sheffield W to Championship; Southend U to Championship 1
2005–06 Watford to Premier League; Barnsley to Championship; Cheltenham T to Championship 1

LEAGUE TITLE WINS

FA PREMIER LEAGUE – Manchester U 8, Arsenal 3, Chelsea 2, Blackburn R 1.

FOOTBALL LEAGUE CHAMPIONSHIP – Reading 1, Sunderland 1.

LEAGUE DIVISION 1 – Liverpool 18, Arsenal 10, Everton 9, Sunderland 8, Aston Villa 7, Manchester U 7, Newcastle U 5, Sheffield W 4, Huddersfield T 3, Leeds U 3, Manchester C 3, Portsmouth 3, Wolverhampton W 3, Blackburn R 2, Burnley 2, Derby Co 2, Nottingham F 2, Preston NE 2, Tottenham H 2; Bolton W, Charlton Ath, Chelsea, Crystal Palace, Fulham, Ipswich T, Middlesbrough, Norwich C, Sheffield U, WBA 1 each.

FOOTBALL LEAGUE CHAMPIONSHIP 1 – Luton T 1, Southend U 1.

LEAGUE DIVISION 2 – Leicester C 6, Manchester C 6, Birmingham C (one as Small Heath) 5, Sheffield W 5, Derby Co 4, Liverpool 4, Preston NE 4, Ipswich T 3, Leeds U 3, Middlesbrough 3, Notts Co 3, Stoke C 3, Aston Villa 2, Bolton W 2, Burnley 2, Bury 2, Chelsea 2, Fulham 2, Grimsby T 2, Manchester U 2, Millwall 2, Norwich C 2, Nottingham F 2, Tottenham H 2, WBA 2, West Ham U 2, Wolverhampton W 2; Blackburn R, Blackpool, Bradford C, Brentford, Brighton & HA, Bristol C, Coventry C, Crystal Palace, Everton, Huddersfield T, Luton T, Newcastle U, QPR, Oldham Ath, Oxford U, Plymouth Arg, Reading, Sheffield U, Sunderland, Swindon T, Watford, Wigan Ath 1 each.

FOOTBALL LEAGUE CHAMPIONSHIP 2 – Carlisle U 1, Yeovil T 1.

LEAGUE DIVISION 3 – Brentford 2, Carlisle U 2, Oxford U 2, Plymouth Arg 2, Portsmouth 2, Preston NE 2, Shrewsbury T 2; Aston Villa, Blackburn R, Bolton W, Bournemouth, Bradford C, Brighton & HA, Bristol R, Burnley, Bury, Cambridge U, Cardiff C, Coventry C, Doncaster R. Grimsby T, Hereford U, Hull C, Leyton Orient, Mansfield T, Northampton T, Notts Co, Oldham Ath, QPR, Reading, Rotherham U, Rushden & D Southampton, Sunderland, Swansea C, Watford, Wigan Ath, Wolverhampton W, Wrexham 1 each.

LEAGUE DIVISION 4 – Chesterfield 2, Doncaster R 2, Peterborough U 2; Brentford, Brighton & HA, Burnley, Cambridge U, Darlington, Exeter C, Gillingham, Grimsby T, Huddersfield T, Lincoln C, Luton T, Mansfield T, Millwall, Northampton T, Notts Co, Port Vale, Reading, Rotherham U, Sheffield U, Southend U, Southport, Stockport Co, Swindon T, Walsall, Watford, Wimbledon, Wolverhampton W, York C 1 each.

TO 1957–58

DIVISION 3 (South) – Bristol C 3, Charlton Ath 2, Ipswich T 2, Millwall 2, Notts Co 2, Plymouth Arg 2, Swansea T 2; Brentford, Brighton & HA, Bristol R, Cardiff C, Coventry C, Crystal Palace, Fulham, Leyton Orient, Luton T, Newport Co, Norwich C, Nottingham F, Portsmouth, QPR, Reading, Southampton 1 each.

DIVISION 3 (North) – Barnsley 3, Doncaster R 3, Lincoln C 3, Chesterfield 2, Grimsby T 2, Hull C 2, Port Vale 2, Stockport Co 2; Bradford C, Bradford PA, Darlington, Derby Co, Nelson, Oldham Ath, Rotherham U, Scunthorpe U, Stoke C, Tranmere R, Wolverhampton W 1 each.

RELEGATED CLUBS

1891–92 League extended. Newton Heath, Sheffield W and Nottingham F admitted. *Second Division formed* including Darwen.
1892–93 In Test matches, Sheffield U and Darwen won promotion in place of Notts Co and Accrington S.
1893–94 In Tests, Liverpool and Small Heath won promotion. Newton Heath and Darwen relegated.
1894–95 After Tests, Bury promoted, Liverpool relegated.
1895–96 After Tests, Liverpool promoted, Small Heath relegated.
1896–97 After Tests, Notts Co promoted, Burnley relegated.
1897–98 Test system abolished after success of Stoke C and Burnley. League extended. Blackburn R and Newcastle U elected to First Division. *Automatic promotion and relegation introduced.*

FA PREMIER LEAGUE TO DIVISION 1

1992–93 Crystal Palace, Middlesbrough, Nottingham F
1993–94 Sheffield U, Oldham Ath, Swindon T
1994–95 Crystal Palace, Norwich C, Leicester C, Ipswich T
1995–96 Manchester C, QPR, Bolton W
1996–97 Sunderland, Middlesbrough, Nottingham F
1997–98 Bolton W, Barnsley, Crystal Palace
1998–99 Charlton Ath, Blackburn R, Nottingham F
1999–2000 Wimbledon, Sheffield W, Watford
2000–01 Manchester C, Coventry C, Bradford C
2001–02 Ipswich T, Derby Co, Leicester C
2002–03 West Ham U, WBA, Sunderland
2003–04 Leicester C, Leeds U, Wolverhampton W.

FA PREMIER LEAGUE TO CHAMPIONSHIP

2004–05 Crystal Palace, Norwich C, Southampton
2005–06 Birmingham C, WBA, Sunderland

DIVISION 1 TO DIVISION 2

1898–99 Bolton W and Sheffield W
1899–1900 Burnley and Glossop
1900–01 Preston NE and WBA
1901–02 Small Heath and Manchester C
1902–03 Grimsby T and Bolton W
1903–04 Liverpool and WBA
1904–05 League extended. Bury and Notts Co, two bottom clubs in First Division, re-elected.
1905–06 Nottingham F and Wolverhampton W
1906–07 Derby Co and Stoke C
1907–08 Bolton W and Birmingham C
1908–09 Manchester C and Leicester Fosse
1909–10 Bolton W and Chelsea
1910–11 Bristol C and Nottingham F
1911–12 Preston NE and Bury
1912–13 Notts Co and Woolwich Arsenal
1913–14 Preston NE and Derby Co
1914–15 Tottenham H and Chelsea*
1919–20 Notts Co and Sheffield W
1920–21 Derby Co and Bradford PA
1921–22 Bradford C and Manchester U
1922–23 Stoke C and Oldham Ath
1923–24 Chelsea and Middlesbrough
1924–25 Preston NE and Nottingham F
1925–26 Manchester C and Notts Co
1926–27 Leeds U and WBA
1927–28 Tottenham H and Middlesbrough
1928–29 Bury and Cardiff C
1929–30 Burnley and Everton
1930–31 Leeds U and Manchester U
1931–32 Grimsby T and West Ham U
1932–33 Bolton W and Blackpool
1933–34 Newcastle U and Sheffield U
1934–35 Leicester C and Tottenham H
1935–36 Aston Villa and Blackburn R
1936–37 Manchester U and Sheffield W
1937–38 Manchester C and WBA
1938–39 Birmingham C and Leicester C
1946–47 Brentford and Leeds U
1947–48 Blackburn R and Grimsby T
1948–49 Preston NE and Sheffield U
1949–50 Manchester C and Birmingham C
1950–51 Sheffield W and Everton
1951–52 Huddersfield T and Fulham
1952–53 Stoke C and Derby Co
1953–54 Middlesbrough and Liverpool
1954–55 Leicester C and Sheffield W
1955–56 Huddersfield T and Sheffield U
1956–57 Charlton Ath and Cardiff C
1957–58 Sheffield W and Sunderland
1958–59 Portsmouth and Aston Villa
1959–60 Luton T and Leeds U
1960–61 Preston NE and Newcastle U
1961–62 Chelsea and Cardiff C
1962–63 Manchester C and Leyton Orient
1963–64 Bolton W and Ipswich T
1964–65 Wolverhampton W and Birmingham C
1965–66 Northampton T and Blackburn R
1966–67 Aston Villa and Blackpool
1967–68 Fulham and Sheffield U
1968–69 Leicester C and QPR
1969–70 Sunderland and Sheffield W
1970–71 Burnley and Blackpool
1971–72 Huddersfield T and Nottingham F
1972–73 Crystal Palace and WBA
1973–74 Southampton, Manchester U, Norwich C
1974–75 Luton T, Chelsea, Carlisle U
1975–76 Wolverhampton W, Burnley, Sheffield U
1976–77 Sunderland, Stoke C, Tottenham H
1977–78 West Ham U, Newcastle U, Leicester C
1978–79 QPR, Birmingham C, Chelsea
1979–80 Bristol C, Derby Co, Bolton W
1980–81 Norwich C, Leicester C, Crystal Palace
1981–82 Leeds U, Wolverhampton W, Middlesbrough
1982–83 Manchester C, Swansea C, Brighton & HA
1983–84 Birmingham C, Notts Co, Wolverhampton W
1984–85 Norwich C, Sunderland, Stoke C
1985–86 Ipswich T, Birmingham C, WBA
1986–87 Leicester C, Manchester C, Aston Villa
1987–88 Chelsea**, Portsmouth, Watford, Oxford U
1988–89 Middlesbrough, West Ham U, Newcastle U
1989–90 Sheffield W, Charlton Ath, Millwall
1990–91 Sunderland and Derby Co
1991–92 Luton T, Notts Co, West Ham U
1992–93 Brentford, Cambridge U, Bristol R
1993–94 Birmingham C, Oxford U, Peterborough U
1994–95 Swindon T, Burnley, Bristol C, Notts Co
1995–96 Millwall, Watford, Luton T
1996–97 Grimsby T, Oldham Ath, Southend U
1997–98 Manchester C, Stoke C, Reading
1998–99 Bury, Oxford U, Bristol C
1999–2000 Walsall, Port Vale, Swindon T
2000–01 Huddersfield T, QPR, Tranmere R
2001–02 Crewe Alex, Barnsley, Stockport Co
2002–03 Sheffield W, Brighton & HA, Grimsby T
2003–04 Walsall, Bradford C, Wimbledon

***Relegated after play-offs.*

**Subsequently re-elected to Division 1 when League was extended after the War.*

FOOTBALL LEAGUE CHAMPIONSHIP TO FOOTBALL LEAGUE CHAMPIONSHIP 1

2004–05 Gillingham, Nottingham F, Rotherham U
2005–06 Crewe Alex, Millwall, Brighton & HA

DIVISION 2 TO DIVISION 3

1920–21 Stockport Co
1921–22 Bradford PA and Bristol C
1922–23 Rotherham Co and Wolverhampton W
1923–24 Nelson and Bristol C
1924–25 Crystal Palace and Coventry C
1925–26 Stoke C and Stockport Co
1926–27 Darlington and Bradford C
1927–28 Fulham and South Shields
1928–29 Port Vale and Clapton Orient
1929–30 Hull C and Notts Co
1930–31 Reading and Cardiff C
1931–32 Barnsley and Bristol C
1932–33 Chesterfield and Charlton Ath
1933–34 Millwall and Lincoln C
1934–35 Oldham Ath and Notts Co
1935–36 Port Vale and Hull C
1936–37 Doncaster R and Bradford C
1937–38 Barnsley and Stockport Co
1938–39 Norwich C and Tranmere R
1946–47 Swansea T and Newport Co
1947–48 Doncaster R and Millwall
1948–49 Nottingham F and Lincoln C
1949–50 Plymouth Arg and Bradford PA
1950–51 Grimsby T and Chesterfield
1951–52 Coventry C and QPR
1952–53 Southampton and Barnsley
1953–54 Brentford and Oldham Ath
1954–55 Ipswich T and Derby Co
1955–56 Plymouth Arg and Hull C
1956–57 Port Vale and Bury
1957–58 Doncaster R and Notts Co
1958–59 Barnsley and Grimsby T
1959–60 Bristol C and Hull C
1960–61 Lincoln C and Portsmouth
1961–62 Brighton & HA and Bristol R
1962–63 Walsall and Luton T
1963–64 Grimsby T and Scunthorpe U
1964–65 Swindon T and Swansea T
1965–66 Middlesbrough and Leyton Orient
1966–67 Northampton T and Bury
1967–68 Plymouth Arg and Rotherham U
1968–69 Fulham and Bury
1969–70 Preston NE and Aston Villa
1970–71 Blackburn R and Bolton W
1971–72 Charlton Ath and Watford
1972–73 Huddersfield T and Brighton & HA
1973–74 Crystal Palace, Preston NE, Swindon T
1974–75 Millwall, Cardiff C, Sheffield W
1975–76 Oxford U, York C, Portsmouth
1976–77 Carlisle U, Plymouth Arg, Hereford U
1977–78 Blackpool, Mansfield T, Hull C
1978–79 Sheffield U, Millwall, Blackburn R

1979–80 Fulham, Burnley, Charlton Ath
1980–81 Preston NE, Bristol C, Bristol R
1981–82 Cardiff C, Wrexham, Orient
1982–83 Rotherham U, Burnley, Bolton W
1983–84 Derby Co, Swansea C, Cambridge U
1984–85 Notts Co, Cardiff C, Wolverhampton W
1985–86 Carlisle U, Middlesbrough, Fulham
1986–87 Sunderland**, Grimsby T, Brighton & HA
1987–88 Huddersfield T, Reading, Sheffield U**
1988–89 Shrewsbury T, Birmingham C, Walsall
1989–90 Bournemouth, Bradford C, Stoke C
1990–91 WBA and Hull C
1991–92 Plymouth Arg, Brighton & HA, Port Vale
1992–93 Preston NE, Mansfield T, Wigan Ath, Chester C
1993–94 Fulham, Exeter C, Hartlepool U, Barnet
1994–95 Cambridge U, Plymouth Arg, Cardiff C, Chester C, Leyton Orient
1995–96 Carlisle U, Swansea C, Brighton & HA, Hull C
1996–97 Peterborough U, Shrewsbury T, Rotherham U, Notts Co
1997–98 Brentford, Plymouth Arg, Carlisle U, Southend U
1998–99 York C, Northampton T, Lincoln C, Macclesfield T
1999–2000 Cardiff C, Blackpool, Scunthorpe U, Chesterfield
2000–01 Bristol R, Luton T, Swansea C, Oxford U
2001–02 Bournemouth, Bury, Wrexham, Cambridge U
2002–03 Cheltenham T, Huddersfield T, Mansfield T Northampton T
2003–04 Grimsby T, Rushden & D, Notts Co, Wycombe W

FOOTBALL LEAGUE CHAMPIONSHIP 1 TO FOOTBALL LEAGUE CHAMPIONSHIP 2

2004–05 Torquay U, Wrexham, Peterborough U, Stockport Co
2005–06 Hartlepool U, Milton Keynes D, Swindon T, Walsall

DIVISION 3 TO DIVISION 4

1958–59 Stockport Co, Doncaster R, Notts Co, Rochdale
1959–60 York C, Mansfield T, Wrexham, Accrington S
1960–61 Tranmere R, Bradford C, Colchester U, Chesterfield
1961–62 Torquay U, Lincoln C, Brentford, Newport Co
1962–63 Bradford PA, Brighton & HA, Carlisle U, Halifax T
1963–64 Millwall, Crewe Alex, Wrexham, Notts Co
1964–65 Luton T, Port Vale, Colchester U, Barnsley
1965–66 Southend U, Exeter C, Brentford, York C
1966–67 Swansea T, Darlington, Doncaster R, Workington
1967–68 Grimsby T, Colchester U, Scunthorpe U, Peterborough U (demoted)
1968–69 Northampton T, Hartlepool, Crewe Alex, Oldham Ath
1969–70 Bournemouth, Southport, Barrow, Stockport Co
1970–71 Reading, Bury, Doncaster R, Gillingham
1971–72 Mansfield T, Barnsley, Torquay U, Bradford C
1972–73 Rotherham U, Brentford, Swansea C, Scunthorpe U
1973–74 Cambridge U, Shrewsbury T, Southport, Rochdale
1974–75 Bournemouth, Tranmere R, Watford, Huddersfield T
1975–76 Aldershot, Colchester U, Southend U, Halifax T
1976–77 Reading, Northampton T, Grimsby T, York C
1977–78 Port Vale, Bradford C, Hereford U, Portsmouth
1978–79 Peterborough U, Walsall, Tranmere R, Lincoln C
1979–80 Bury, Southend U, Mansfield T, Wimbledon
1980–81 Sheffield U, Colchester U, Blackpool, Hull C
1981–82 Wimbledon, Swindon T, Bristol C, Chester
1982–83 Reading, Wrexham, Doncaster R, Chesterfield
1983–84 Scunthorpe U, Southend U, Port Vale, Exeter C
1984–85 Burnley, Orient, Preston NE, Cambridge U
1985–86 Lincoln C, Cardiff C, Wolverhampton W, Swansea C
1986–87 Bolton W**, Carlisle U, Darlington, Newport Co
1987–88 Rotherham U**, Grimsby T, York C, Doncaster R
1988–89 Southend U, Chesterfield, Gillingham, Aldershot
1989–90 Cardiff C, Northampton T, Blackpool, Walsall
1990–91 Crewe Alex, Rotherham U, Mansfield T
1991–92 Bury, Shrewsbury T, Torquay U, Darlington

*** Relegated after play-offs.*

APPLICATIONS FOR RE-ELECTION

FOURTH DIVISION

Eleven: Hartlepool U.
Seven: Crewe Alex.
Six: Barrow (lost League place to Hereford U 1972), Halifax T, Rochdale, Southport (lost League place to Wigan Ath 1978), York C.
Five: Chester C, Darlington, Lincoln C, Stockport Co, Workington (lost League place to Wimbledon 1977).
Four: Bradford PA (lost League place to Cambridge U 1970), Newport Co, Northampton T.
Three: Doncaster R, Hereford U.
Two: Bradford C, Exeter C, Oldham Ath, Scunthorpe U, Torquay U.
One: Aldershot, Colchester U, Gateshead (lost League place to Peterborough U 1960), Grimsby T, Swansea C, Tranmere R, Wrexham, Blackpool, Cambridge U, Preston NE.
Accrington S resigned and Oxford U were elected 1962.
Port Vale were forced to re-apply following expulsion in 1968.
Aldershot expelled March 1992. Maidstone U resigned August 1992.

THIRD DIVISIONS NORTH & SOUTH

Seven: Walsall.
Six: Exeter C, Halifax T, Newport Co.
Five: Accrington S, Barrow, Gillingham, New Brighton, Southport.
Four: Rochdale, Norwich C.
Three: Crystal Palace, Crewe Alex, Darlington, Hartlepool U, Merthyr T, Swindon T.
Two: Aberdare Ath, Aldershot, Ashington, Bournemouth, Brentford, Chester, Colchester U, Durham C, Millwall, Nelson, QPR, Rotherham U, Southend U, Tranmere R, Watford, Workington.
One: Bradford C, Bradford PA, Brighton & HA, Bristol R, Cardiff C, Carlisle U, Charlton Ath, Gateshead, Grimsby T, Mansfield T, Shrewsbury T, Torquay U, York C.

LEAGUE STATUS FROM 1986–87

RELEGATED FROM LEAGUE

1986–87 Lincoln C
1987–88 Newport Co;
1988–89 Darlington
1989–90 Colchester U
1990–91 —
1991–92 —
1992–93 Halifax T
1993–94 —
1994–95 —
1995–96 —
1996–97 Hereford U
1997–98 Doncaster R
1998–99 Scarborough
1999–2000 Chester C
2000–01 Barnet
2001–02 Halifax T
2002–03 Shrewsbury T, Exeter C
2003–04 Carlisle U, York C
2004–05 Kidderminster H, Cambridge U
2005–06 Oxford U, Rushden & D

PROMOTED TO LEAGUE

1986–87 Scarborough
1987–88 Lincoln C
1988–89 Maidstone U
1989–90 Darlington
1990–91 Barnet
1991–92 Colchester U
1992–93 Wycombe W
1993–94 —
1994–95 —
1995–96 —
1996–97 Macclesfield T
1997–98 Halifax T
1998–99 Cheltenham T
1999–2000 Kidderminster H
2000–01 Rushden & D
2001–02 Boston U
2002–03 Yeovil T, Doncaster R
2003–04 Chester C, Shrewsbury T
2004–05 Barnet, Carlisle U
2005–06 Accrington S, Hereford U

LEAGUE ATTENDANCES SINCE 1946–47

Season	*Matches*	*Total*	*Div. 1*	*Div. 2*	*Div. 3 (S)*	*Div. 3 (N)*
1946–47	1848	35,604,606	15,005,316	11,071,572	5,664,004	3,863,714
1947–48	1848	40,259,130	16,732,341	12,286,350	6,653,610	4,586,829
1948–49	1848	41,271,414	17,914,667	11,353,237	6,998,429	5,005,081
1949–50	1848	40,517,865	17,278,625	11,694,158	7,104,155	4,440,927
1950–51	2028	39,584,967	16,679,454	10,780,580	7,367,884	4,757,109
1951–52	2028	39,015,866	16,110,322	11,066,189	6,958,927	4,880,428
1952–53	2028	37,149,966	16,050,278	9,686,654	6,704,299	4,708,735
1953–54	2028	36,174,590	16,154,915	9,510,053	6,311,508	4,198,114
1954–55	2028	34,133,103	15,087,221	8,988,794	5,996,017	4,051,071
1955–56	2028	33,150,809	14,108,961	9,080,002	5,692,479	4,269,367
1956–57	2028	32,744,405	13,803,037	8,718,162	5,622,189	4,601,017
1957–58	2028	33,562,208	14,468,652	8,663,712	6,097,183	4,332,661
		Total	*Div. 1*	*Div. 2*	*Div. 3*	*Div. 4*
1958–59	2028	33,610,985	14,727,691	8,641,997	5,946,600	4,276,697
1959–60	2028	32,538,611	14,391,227	8,399,627	5,739,707	4,008,050
1960–61	2028	28,619,754	12,926,948	7,033,936	4,784,256	3,874,614
1961–62	2015	27,979,902	12,061,194	7,453,089	5,199,106	3,266,513
1962–63	2028	28,885,852	12,490,239	7,792,770	5,341,362	3,261,481
1963–64	2028	28,535,022	12,486,626	7,594,158	5,419,157	3,035,081
1964–65	2028	27,641,168	12,708,752	6,984,104	4,436,245	3,512,067
1965–66	2028	27,206,980	12,480,644	6,914,757	4,779,150	3,032,429
1966–67	2028	28,902,596	14,242,957	7,253,819	4,421,172	2,984,648
1967–68	2028	30,107,298	15,289,410	7,450,410	4,013,087	3,354,391
1968–69	2028	29,382,172	14,584,851	7,382,390	4,339,656	3,075,275
1969–70	2028	29,600,972	14,868,754	7,581,728	4,223,761	2,926,729
1970–71	2028	28,194,146	13,954,337	7,098,265	4,377,213	2,764,331
1971–72	2028	28,700,729	14,484,603	6,769,308	4,697,392	2,749,426
1972–73	2028	25,448,642	13,998,154	5,631,730	3,737,252	2,081,506
1973–74	2027	24,982,203	13,070,991	6,326,108	3,421,624	2,163,480
1974–75	2028	25,577,977	12,613,178	6,955,970	4,086,145	1,992,684
1975–76	2028	24,896,053	13,089,861	5,798,405	3,948,449	2,059,338
1976–77	2028	26,182,800	13,647,585	6,250,597	4,152,218	2,132,400
1977–78	2028	25,392,872	13,255,677	6,474,763	3,332,042	2,330,390
1978–79	2028	24,540,627	12,704,549	6,153,223	3,374,558	2,308,297
1979–80	2028	24,623,975	12,163,002	6,112,025	3,999,328	2,349,620
1980–81	2028	21,907,569	11,392,894	5,175,442	3,637,854	1,701,379
1981–82	2028	20,006,961	10,420,793	4,750,463	2,836,915	1,998,790
1982–83	2028	18,766,158	9,295,613	4,974,937	2,943,568	1,552,040
1983–84	2028	18,358,631	8,711,448	5,359,757	2,729,942	1,557,484
1984–85	2028	17,849,835	9,761,404	4,030,823	2,667,008	1,390,600
1985–86	2028	16,488,577	9,037,854	3,551,968	2,490,481	1,408,274
1986–87	2028	17,379,218	9,144,676	4,168,131	2,350,970	1,715,441
1987–88	2030	17,959,732	8,094,571	5,341,599	2,751,275	1,772,287
1988–89	2036	18,464,192	7,809,993	5,887,805	3,035,327	1,791,067
1989–90	2036	19,445,442	7,883,039	6,867,674	2,803,551	1,891,178
1990–91	2036	19,508,202	8,618,709	6,285,068	2,835,759	1,768,666
1991–92	2064*	20,487,273	9,989,160	5,809,787	2,993,352	1,694,974
		Total	*FA Premier*	*Div. 1*	*Div. 2*	*Div. 3*
1992–93	2028	20,657,327	9,759,809	5,874,017	3,483,073	1,540,428
1993–94	2028	21,683,381	10,644,551	6,487,104	2,972,702	1,579,024
1994–95	2028	21,856,020	11,213,168	6,044,293	3,037,752	1,560,807
1995–96	2036	21,844,416	10,469,107	6,566,349	2,843,652	1,965,308
1996–97	2036	22,783,163	10,804,762	6,931,539	3,195,223	1,851,639
1997–98	2036	24,692,608	11,092,106	8,330,018	3,503,264	1,767,220
1998–99	2036	25,435,542	11,620,326	7,543,369	4,169,697	2,102,150
1999-2000	2036	25,341,090	11,668,497	7,810,208	3,700,433	2,161,952
2000–01	2036	26,030,167	12,472,094	7,909,512	3,488,166	2,160,395
2001–02	2036	27,756,977	13,043,118	8,352,128	3,963,153	2,398,578
2002–03	2036	28,343,386	13,468,965	8,521,017	3,892,469	2,460,935
2003–04	2036	29,197,510	13,303,136	8,772,780	4,146,495	2,975,099
		Total	*FA Premier*	*Championship*	*Championship 1*	*Championship 2*
2004–05	2036	29,245,870	12,878,791	9,612,761	4,270,674	2,483,644
2005–06	2036	29,089,084	12,871,643	9,719,204	4,183,011	2,315,226

**Figures include matches played by Aldershot.*
Football League official total for their three divisions in 2001–02 was 14,716,162.
The official Premiership total was 12,876,993 for 2005–06.

ENGLISH LEAGUE ATTENDANCES 2005–06

FA FA BARCLAYCARD PREMIERSHIP ATTENDANCES

	Average Gate			*Season 2005–06*	
	2004–05	2005–06	+/–%	Highest	Lowest
Arsenal	37,978	38,186	+0.55	38,389	37,867
Aston Villa	37,354	34,059	–8.82	42,551	26,422
Birmingham City	28,760	27,392	–4.76	29,312	24,010
Blackburn Rovers	22,314	21,015	–5.82	29,142	16,953
Bolton Wanderers	26,006	25,265	–2.85	27,718	22,733
Charlton Athletic	26,403	26,196	–0.78	27,111	23,453
Chelsea	41,870	41,902	+0.08	42,321	40,652
Everton	36,834	36,860	+0.07	40,158	34,333
Fulham	19,838	20,654	+4.11	22,486	16,550
Liverpool	42,587	44,236	+3.87	44,983	42,293
Manchester City	45,192	42,856	–5.17	47,192	40,256
Manchester United	67,871	68,765	+1.32	73,006	67,684
Middlesbrough	31,965	28,463	–10.96	31,908	25,971
Newcastle United	51,844	52,032	+0.36	52,327	50,451
Portsmouth	20,072	19,840	–1.16	20,240	19,030
Sunderland	28,821	33,904	+17.64	44,003	28,226
Tottenham Hotspur	35,883	36,074	+0.53	36,247	35,427
West Bromwich Albion	25,987	25,404	–2.24	27,623	23,144
West Ham United	27,403	33,743	+23.14	34,970	29,582
Wigan Athletic	11,571	20,610	+78.12	25,023	16,641

TOTAL ATTENDANCES:	12,871,643 (380 games) Average 33,873 (–0.06%)
HIGHEST:	73,006 Manchester United v Charlton Athletic
LOWEST:	16,550 Fulham v Birmingham City
HIGHEST AVERAGE:	68,765 Manchester United
LOWEST AVERAGE:	19,840 Portsmouth

FOOTBALL LEAGUE: CHAMPIONSHIP ATTENDANCES

	Average Gate			*Season 2005–06*	
	2004–05	2005–06	+/–%	Highest	Lowest
Brighton & Hove Albion	6,434	6,802	+5.7	7,999	5,859
Burnley	12,466	12,462	0.0	17,912	10,431
Cardiff City	12,976	11,720	–9.7	16,403	8,724
Coventry City	16,048	21,302	+32.7	26,851	16,156
Crewe Alexandra	7,403	6,732	–9.1	8,942	5,686
Crystal Palace	24,108	19,457	–19.3	23,843	17,291
Derby County	25,219	24,166	–4.2	30,391	21,434
Hull City	18,027	19,841	+10.1	23,486	17,698
Ipswich Town	25,651	24,253	–5.5	29,184	22,551
Leeds United	29,207	22,355	–23.5	27,843	18,353
Leicester City	24,137	22,234	–7.9	25,578	18,856
Luton Town	7,940	9,139	+15.1	10,248	7,474
Millwall	11,699	9,529	–18.5	13,209	7,108
Norwich City	24,354	24,952	+2.5	27,470	23,838
Plymouth Argyle	16,428	13,776	–16.1	17,726	10,460
Preston North End	13,889	14,617	+5.2	19,350	12,453
Queens Park Rangers	16,056	13,441	–16.3	16,152	10,901
Reading	17,169	20,207	+17.7	23,845	14,027
Sheffield United	19,594	23,650	+20.7	30,558	17,739
Sheffield Wednesday	23,100	24,853	+7.6	33,439	20,244
Southampton	30,610	23,614	–22.9	30,173	19,086
Stoke City	16,456	14,432	–12.3	20,408	10,121
Watford	14,290	15,415	+7.9	19,842	11,358
Wolverhampton Wanderers	26,620	23,624	–11.3	27,980	21,683

TOTAL ATTENDANCES:	9,719,204 (552 games) Average 17,607 (+1.1%)
HIGHEST:	33,439 Sheffield Wednesday v Sheffield United
LOWEST:	5,686 Crewe Alexandra v Ipswich Town
HIGHEST AVERAGE:	24,952 Norwich City
LOWEST AVERAGE:	6,732 Crewe Alexandra

Premiership and Football League attendance averages and highest crowd figures for 2005–06 are unofficial. The official Premiership total was 12,876,993.

FOOTBALL LEAGUE: CHAMPIONSHIP 1 ATTENDANCES

	Average Gate			*Season 2005–06*	
	2004–05	2005–06	+/–%	Highest	Lowest
Barnsley	9,779	9,054	–7.4	13,263	6,996
Blackpool	6,032	5,820	–3.5	8,541	4,326
AFC Bournemouth	7,123	6,458	–9.3	9,359	5,191
Bradford City	8,839	8,265	–6.5	15,608	6,745
Brentford	6,082	6,775	+11.4	9,903	5,131
Bristol City	11,391	11,725	+2.9	15,889	9,103
Chesterfield	4,961	4,772	–3.8	7,073	3,445
Colchester United	3,534	3,969	+12.3	5,920	2,721
Doncaster Rovers	6,886	6,139	–10.8	8,299	4,262
Gillingham	8,528	6,671	–21.8	8,128	4,861
Hartlepool United	5,182	4,812	–7.1	6,895	3,375
Huddersfield Town	11,905	13,058	+9.7	19,052	10,304
Milton Keynes Dons FC	4,896	5,776	+18.0	8,426	4,423
Nottingham Forest	23,608	20,257	–14.2	28,193	16,237
Oldham Athletic	6,462	5,797	–10.3	7,772	3,878
Port Vale	4,973	4,657	–6.4	6,793	3,452
Rotherham United	6,272	5,306	–15.4	7,625	3,537
Scunthorpe United	5,178	5,171	–0.1	7,152	3,786
Southend United	6,077	8,053	+32.5	11,387	5,261
Swansea City	8,458	14,112	+66.8	19,288	11,028
Swindon Town	5,835	5,951	+2.0	8,985	4,139
Tranmere Rovers	9,044	7,211	–20.3	9,152	6,210
Walsall	6,085	5,392	–11.4	8,703	4,293
Yeovil Town	6,320	6,668	+5.5	9,579	5,048

TOTAL ATTENDANCES: 4,183,011 (552 games)
Average 7,578 (–2.1%)
HIGHEST: 28,193 Nottingham Forest v Yeovil Town
LOWEST: 2,721 Colchester United v Barnsley, Colchester United v Doncaster Rovers
HIGHEST AVERAGE: 20,257 Nottingham Forest
LOWEST AVERAGE: 3,969 Colchester United

FOOTBALL LEAGUE: CHAMPIONSHIP 2 ATTENDANCES

	Average Gate			*Season 2005–06*	
	2004–05	2005–06	+/–%	Highest	Lowest
Barnet	2,512	2,578	+2.6	3,873	1,366
Boston United	2,932	2,519	–14.1	4,476	1,651
Bristol Rovers	7,077	5,989	–15.4	7,551	4,836
Bury	3,032	2,594	–14.4	4,276	1,673
Carlisle United	5,513	7,218	+30.9	13,467	5,190
Cheltenham Town	3,648	3,453	–5.3	6,005	2,531
Chester City	2,812	2,964	+5.4	4,801	1,806
Darlington	4,245	4,199	–1.1	8,640	2,905
Grimsby Town	4,943	5,151	+4.2	8,458	3,658
Leyton Orient	3,712	4,699	+26.6	6,720	3,463
Lincoln City	4,927	4,739	–3.8	7,182	2,956
Macclesfield Town	2,272	2,275	+0.1	4,553	1,576
Mansfield Town	4,092	3,560	–13.0	6,444	2,357
Northampton Town	5,927	5,935	+0.1	7,114	5,012
Notts County	5,384	5,467	+1.5	9,817	3,710
Oxford United	5,347	5,443	+1.8	12,243	3,702
Peterborough United	4,341	4,364	+0.5	8,637	2,833
Rochdale	2,690	2,808	+4.4	4,439	1,769
Rushden & Diamonds	3,321	3,162	–4.8	5,211	2,216
Shrewsbury Town	4,251	3,997	–6.0	6,249	2,469
Stockport County	5,000	4,772	–4.6	10,006	3,460
Torquay United	3,511	2,851	–18.8	5,697	2,010
Wrexham	4,751	4,478	–5.7	7,240	3,195
Wycombe Wanderers	4,937	5,445	+10.3	7,134	4,166

TOTAL ATTENDANCES: 2,315,226 (552 games)
Average 4,194 (–6.8%)
HIGHEST: 13,467 Carlisle United v Torquay United
LOWEST: 1,366 Barnet v Cheltenham Town
HIGHEST AVERAGE: 7,218 Carlisle United
LOWEST AVERAGE: 2,275 Macclesfield Town

LEAGUE CUP FINALISTS 1961–2006

Played as a two-leg final until 1966. All subsequent finals at Wembley until 2000, then at Millennium Stadium, Cardiff.

Year	*Winners*	*Runners-up*	*Score*
1961	Aston Villa	Rotherham U	0-2, 3-0 (aet)
1962	Norwich C	Rochdale	3-0, 1-0
1963	Birmingham C	Aston Villa	3-1, 0-0
1964	Leicester C	Stoke C	1-1, 3-2
1965	Chelsea	Leicester C	3-2, 0-0
1966	WBA	West Ham U	1-2, 4-1
1967	QPR	WBA	3-2
1968	Leeds U	Arsenal	1-0
1969	Swindon T	Arsenal	3-1 (aet)
1970	Manchester C	WBA	2-1 (aet)
1971	Tottenham H	Aston Villa	2-0
1972	Stoke C	Chelsea	2-1
1973	Tottenham H	Norwich C	1-0
1974	Wolverhampton W	Manchester C	2-1
1975	Aston Villa	Norwich C	1-0
1976	Manchester C	Newcastle U	2-1
1977	Aston Villa	Everton	0-0, 1-1 (aet), 3-2 (aet)
1978	Nottingham F	Liverpool	0-0 (aet), 1-0
1979	Nottingham F	Southampton	3-2
1980	Wolverhampton W	Nottingham F	1-0
1981	Liverpool	West Ham U	1-1 (aet), 2-1

MILK CUP

1982	Liverpool	Tottenham H	3-1 (aet)
1983	Liverpool	Manchester U	2-1 (aet)
1984	Liverpool	Everton	0-0 (aet), 1-0
1985	Norwich C	Sunderland	1-0
1986	Oxford U	QPR	3-0

LITTLEWOODS CUP

1987	Arsenal	Liverpool	2-1
1988	Luton T	Arsenal	3-2
1989	Nottingham F	Luton T	3-1
1990	Nottingham F	Oldham Ath	1-0

RUMBELOWS LEAGUE CUP

1991	Sheffield W	Manchester U	1-0
1992	Manchester U	Nottingham F	1-0

COCA-COLA CUP

1993	Arsenal	Sheffield W	2-1
1994	Aston Villa	Manchester U	3-1
1995	Liverpool	Bolton W	2-1
1996	Aston Villa	Leeds U	3-0
1997	Leicester C	Middlesbrough	1-1 (aet), 1-0 (aet)
1998	Chelsea	Middlesbrough	2-0 (aet)

WORTHINGTON CUP

1999	Tottenham H	Leicester C	1-0
2000	Leicester C	Tranmere R	2-1
2001	Liverpool	Birmingham C	1-1 (aet)
Liverpool won 5-4 on penalties			
2002	Blackburn R	Tottenham H	2-1
2003	Liverpool	Manchester U	2-0

CARLING CUP

2004	Middlesbrough	Bolton W	2-1
2005	Chelsea	Liverpool	3-2 (aet)
2006	Manchester U	Wigan Ath	4-0

LEAGUE CUP WINS

Liverpool 7, Aston Villa 5, Nottingham F 4, Chelsea 3, Leicester C 3, Tottenham H 3, Arsenal 2, Manchester C 2, Manchester U 2, Norwich C 2, Wolverhampton W 2, Birmingham C 1, Blackburn R 1, Leeds U 1, Luton T 1, Middlesbrough 1, Oxford U 1, QPR 1, Sheffield W 1, Stoke C 1, Swindon T 1, WBA 1.

APPEARANCES IN FINALS

Liverpool 10, Aston Villa 7, Manchester U 6, Nottingham F 6, Arsenal 5, Leicester C 5, Tottenham H 5, Chelsea 4, Norwich C 4, Manchester C 3, Middlesbrough 3, WBA 3, Birmingham C 2, Bolton W 2, Everton 2, Leeds U 2, Luton T 2, QPR 2, Sheffield W 2, Stoke C 2, West Ham U 2, Wolverhampton W 2, Blackburn R 1, Newcastle U 1, Oldham Ath 1, Oxford U 1, Rochdale 1, Rotherham U 1, Southampton 1, Sunderland 1, Swindon T 1, Tranmere R 1, Wigan Ath 1.

APPEARANCES IN SEMI-FINALS

Liverpool 13, Aston Villa 12, Arsenal 11, Manchester U 10, Tottenham H 10, Chelsea 8, West Ham U 7, Nottingham F 6, Blackburn R 5, Leeds U 5, Leicester C 5, Manchester C 5, Middlesbrough 5, Norwich C 5, Birmingham C 4, Bolton W 4, Sheffield W 4, WBA 4, Burnley 3, Crystal Palace 3, Everton 3, Ipswich T 3, QPR 3, Sunderland 3, Swindon T 3, Wolverhampton W 3, Bristol C 2, Coventry C 2, Luton T 2, Oxford U 2, Plymouth Arg 2, Southampton 2, Stoke C 2, Tranmere R 2, Watford 2, Wimbledon 2, Blackpool 1, Bury 1, Cardiff C 1, Carlisle U 1, Chester C 1, Derby Co 1, Huddersfield T 1, Newcastle U 1, Oldham Ath 1, Peterborough U 1, Rochdale 1, Rotherham U 1, Sheffield U 1, Shrewsbury T 1, Stockport Co 1, Walsall 1, Wigan Ath 1.

CARLING CUP 2005–06

▪ *Denotes player sent off.*

FIRST ROUND

Monday, 22 August 2005

Southend U (0) 0

Southampton (2) 3 *(Blackstock 44, Dyer 45, Ormerod 89)* 6358

Southend U: Flahavan; Hunt, Wilson, Maher, Barrett, Prior, Pettefer, Smith (Eastwood), Gray, Goater, Cole (Bentley).
Southampton: Smith; Cranie, Higginbotham, Delap, Hajto, Mills, Prutton (Wise), Folly, Jones (Ormerod), Blackstock, Dyer.

Tuesday, 23 August 2005

Blackpool (2) 2 *(Clarke 29 (pen), Grayson 39)*

Hull C (1) 1 *(Price 4)* 3819

Blackpool: Pogliacomi; Coid, Edwards, Grayson (Southern), McGregor, Clarke, Donnelly, Doolan, Murphy, Parker, Prendergast.
Hull C: Leite; Wiseman, Edge, Woodhouse (Fagan), Delaney, Joseph, Green, Welsh, Price (France), Burgess, Ellison (Elliott).

Bristol C (1) 2 *(Golbourne 14, Bridges 64)*

Barnet (1) 4 *(Lee 17, 53, Bailey 58, Roache 81)* 3383

Bristol C: Phillips; Carey, Golbourne, Partridge (Bridges), Fortune, Skuse, Murray, Grant, Brooker, Stewart, Smith G.
Barnet: Flitney; Hendon, King, Lee, Gross, Charles, Bowditch (Norville), Bailey, Grazioli (Roache), Strevens, Graham.

Burnley (0) 2 *(Duff 52, Akinbiyi 90)*

Carlisle U (0) 1 *(Murray A 74)* 5114

Burnley: Coyne; Duff (Lafferty), Branch, McCann, Thomas, McGreal, O'Connor J, Hyde, Akinbiyi, Noel-Williams, O'Connor G.
Carlisle U: Westwood; Andrews, Aranalde, McClen, Grand, Livesey, Hackney (McGill), Murray G (Hawley), Nade, Murray A, Murphy.

Bury (0) 0

Leicester C (2) 3 *(Hamill 37, Stearman 40, Gudjonsson 61 (pen))* 2759

Bury: Edwards; Hardiker, Fitzgerald (Kennedy), Scott, Challinor, Whaley, Flitcroft, Mattis, Smart▪, Newby (Barlow), Barry-Murphy (Unsworth).
Leicester C: Henderson; Stearman, Maybury, Williams, Gerrbrand (McCarthy), Johansson, Hamill, Gudjonsson (Kisnorbo), De Vries, Hammond, Tiatto (Wilcox).

Cheltenham T (1) 5 *(Melligan 5, Caines 55, Victory 69, McCann 78, 81)*

Brentford (0) 0 2113

Cheltenham T: Higgs; Wilson, Victory, McCann, Caines, Taylor, Melligan, Bird, Odejayi (Spencer), Vincent (Finnigan), Armstrong (Gill).
Brentford: Nelson; O'Connor (Tabb), Tillen, Osborne, Gayle, Turner, Peters (Steele), Keenan, Fitzgerald, Campbell, Brooker (Watts).

Crystal Palace (0) 3 *(Popovic 51 (pen), Granville 83, Hughes 87)*

Walsall (0) 0 5508

Crystal Palace: Speroni; Fray (Togwell), Granville, Butterfield, Popovic, Hudson, Black (Grabban), Hughes, Andrews, Kolkka (Berry), Riihilahti.
Walsall: Oakes; Pead, Fox, Osborn, Westwood, Bennett, Standing, Smith P (Larrosa), Leitao, Merson, Wright.

Gillingham (0) 1 *(Jarvis 83)*

Oxford U (0) 0 4149

Gillingham: Brown; Rose, Jackman, Flynn, Cox, Hope, Crofts, Jarvis, Claridge (Sancho), Byfield, Pouton (Hessenthaler).
Oxford U: Tardif; Mansell, Robinson, Quinn, Roget, Stirling, Bradbury (Beechers), Gray, Morgan, Davies (Basham), Hughes (Hackett).

Hartlepool U (1) 3 *(Daly 26, Proctor 76, 88)*

Darlington (0) 1 *(Logan 81)* 6163

Hartlepool U: Konstantopoulos; Williams D, Robson, Nelson, Collins, Strachan, Butler, Sweeney, Daly (Bullock), Boyd (Proctor), Humphreys.
Darlington: Bossu; Martis (Duke), Valentine, Hutchinson, Clarke, Peacock, Wainwright, Dickman (Jameson), Johnson S, Wijnhard (Sodje), Logan.

Ipswich T (0) 0

Yeovil T (1) 2 *(Way 45, Gall 87)* 11,299

Ipswich T: Price; Sito, Richards, Horlock, Collins, Naylor, Peters (Wilnis), Juan (Garvan), Currie (Westlake), Bowditch, McDonald.
Yeovil T: Weale; Amankwaah, Jones, Sodje, Skiverton, Miles (Lockwood), Johnson, Way, Bastianini (Terry), Harrold (Gall), Davies.

Leeds U (2) 2 *(Ricketts 20, Richardson 24)*

Oldham Ath (0) 0 14,970

Leeds U: Sullivan; Rui Marques, Crainey, Douglas, Gregan, Kilgallon, Richardson, Einarsson, Ricketts, Healy (Blake), Pugh.
Oldham Ath: Day; Scott, Forbes, Hughes (Bonner), Branston, Owen, Wellens, Warne (Edwards), Facey, Liddell, Tierney.

Leyton Orient (0) 1 *(McMahon 90)*

Luton T (1) 3 *(Coyne 45, Feeney 71, Alexander 76 (og))* 2383

Leyton Orient: Garner; Miller, Palmer, McMahon, Mackie (Dolan), Zakuani, Easton, Simpson, Alexander, Echanomi (Steele), Tudor (Keith).
Luton T: Beresford; Keane, Davis, Leary, Davies, Coyne (Perrett), Edwards, Nicholls (Holmes), Showunmi, Feeney, Morgan (O'Leary).

Lincoln C (2) 5 *(Beevers 6, Molango 35, Birch 64, 67, Robinson M 83)*

Crewe Alex (1) 1 *(Walker 44)* 2782

Lincoln C: Marriott; Beevers, Cryan, Kerr, Bloomer, McCombe, Brown (Folkes), Birch, Asamoah (Bacon), Molango (Robinson M), Keates.
Crewe Alex: Williams (Tomlinson); Moss, Tonkin, Jones B, Walker, Moses, Vaughan, Lunt, Varney, Ugarte (Johnson), Jones S.

Mansfield T (1) 1 *(Jelleyman 16)*

Stoke C (1) 1 *(Brammer 11 (pen))* 2799

Mansfield T: White; Peers, Talbot (Birchall), Buxton, Day, John-Baptiste, Uhlenbeek, Coke (Dawson), Barker, Beardsley (Brown), Jelleyman.
Stoke C: Simonsen; Halls (Buxton), Broomes, Hoefkens, Duberry, Henry, Brammer, Dyer (Russell), Sidibe, Kolar (Gudjonsson), Harper.
aet; Mansfield T won 3-0 on penalties.

Millwall (0) 2 *(Hayles 55, Fangueiro 85)*

Bristol R (0) 0 3079

Millwall: Jones; Dunne, Vincent, Livermore, Robinson P, Phillips, Igoe, Morris (Hutchison), May (Elliott), Hayles (Fangueiro), Simpson.
Bristol R: Shearer; Lescott, Ryan, Anderson, Hinton, Elliott, Campbell (Williams), Hunt, Louis (Walker), Agogo, Disley (Carruthers).

Milton Keynes D (0) 0

Norwich C (0) 1 *(McKenzie 120)* 4777

Milton Keynes D: Baker; Edds, Lewington (Carrilho), Chorley, Morgan, McClenahan, McKoy, Small, Wilbraham (Platt), McLeod (Kamara), Puncheon.
Norwich C: Green; Colin, Charlton, Fleming, Shackell, Safri, Marney (Jarrett), Brennan, McKenzie, Thorne (Doherty), McVeigh (Henderson).
aet.

Northampton T (1) 3 *(Kirk 19, McGleish 62, Sabin 90 (pen))*
QPR (0) 0 4537
Northampton T: Bunn; Bojic, Crowe, Taylor, Dyche, Chambers, Low (Gilligan), Hunt, McGleish (Sabin), Kirk (Dudfield), Jess.
QPR: Royce; Ukah, Milanese, Bean, Evatt■, Shimmin, Miller, Bircham (Baidoo), Moore, Gallen, Brown (Bignot).

Nottingham F (1) 2 *(Breckin 9, 83)*
Macclesfield T (2) 3 *(Whitaker 21, Townson 45, MacKenzie 80)* 5050
Nottingham F: Pedersen; Eaden, Padula, Morgan, Breckin, Gary Holt (Thompson), Southall, Gardner, Harris (Weir-Daley), Taylor (Johnson), Commons.
Macclesfield T: Fettis; Briscoe, Sandwith, Morley, Swailes, MacKenzie, Whitaker, Smart, Townson (Russell), Miles (Barras), Harsley.

Plymouth Arg (2) 2 *(Wotton 35 (pen), Taylor 38)*
Peterborough U (1) 1 *(Plummer 22)* 5974
Plymouth Arg: McCormick; Connolly, Barness, Wotton, Doumbe, Mendes, Norris, Buzsaky (Lasley), Evans (Zebroski), Taylor, Djordjic.
Peterborough U: Tyler; St Ledger-Hall, Burton, Arber, Plummer, Carden, Day (Semple), Newton, Farrell (Logan), Quinn (Benjamin), Gain.

Preston NE (0) 2 *(Dichio 77, Alexander 119 (pen))*
Barnsley (0) 2 *(Burns 81, 108)* 3137
Preston NE: Nash; Mears, Hill (Alexander), Jones, Lucketti, Davis, Sedgwick, McKenna, Agyemang (O'Neil), Nugent, Neal L (Dichio).
Barnsley: Flinders (Colgan); Tonge (Vaughan), Williams, Reid, Carbon, Kay (Burns), Wroe, Shuker, Hayes, Conlon, McPhail.
aet; Barnsley won 5-4 on penalties.

Reading (1) 3 *(Kitson 14, 95, Lita 114)*
Swansea C (1) 1 *(Akinfenwa 80)* 7603
Reading: Stack; Makin, Shorey, Ingimarsson, Sonko, Harper, Hunt, Sidwell, Kitson, Doyle (Gunnarsson), Oster (Little) (Lita).
Swansea C: Gueret; Ricketts, Austin (Anderson■), Britton, Tate, Edwards, Tudur-Jones (MacDonald), Martinez, Akinfenwa, Connor, McLeod.
aet.

Rochdale (0) 0
Bradford C (2) 5 *(Windass 7, 67, 77, Cadamarteri 40, Bridge-Wilkinson 82)* 2820
Rochdale: Gilks; Clarke, Goodall, Jones■, Gallimore, Boardman, Cartwright, Cooksey, Lambert, Holt, Jazsczun (Sturrock).
Bradford C: Howarth; Edghill, Emanuel, Crooks, Wetherall (Stewart), Bower, Muirhead (Morrison), Bridge-Wilkinson, Windass (Cooke), Cadamarteri, Petta.

Rotherham U (1) 3 *(Rowland 41 (og), Burton 71, Otsemobor 90)*
Port Vale (1) 1 *(Cummins 45)* 2809
Rotherham U: Cutler; Otsemobor, Robertson, McLaren, Murdock, Barker, Mullin, Williamson, Butler, Burton (Worrell), Keane.
Port Vale: Goodlad; Abbey (Rowland), Bell (Birchall), Dinning (Sam), Pilkington, Collins, Cummins, Sonner, Lowndes, Paynter, James.

Scunthorpe U (0) 2 *(Ryan 56, Hinds 82)*
Tranmere R (0) 1 *(Sharps 61)* 2738
Scunthorpe U: Musselwhite; Stanton, Williams, Crosby, Butler (Corden), Hinds, Sparrow (Taylor), Ryan, Sharp, Torpey (Johnson), Beagrie.
Tranmere R: Achterberg; Jennings, Roberts, Goodison, Jackson, Sharps, Harrison, Rankine (Bruce), Greenacre, Davies (Hume), Aiston.

Sheffield U (0) 1 *(Ross 50)*
Boston U (0) 0 6014
Sheffield U: Barnes; Kozluk (Wright), Geary, Quinn A, Morgan, Bromby, Gillespie (Forte), Ifill, Ross, Shaw (Mulligan), Armstrong.
Boston U: Abbey; Canoville, McCann (Whelan), Talbot, White, Ellender, Rusk (Maylett), Noble (Holland), Joachim, Lee, Thomas.

Shrewsbury T (1) 3 *(Stallard 22, Denny 89, 91)*
Brighton & HA (1) 2 *(McCammon 17, Robinson 80)* 2141
Shrewsbury T: Hart; Herd, Sharp, Tolley (Denny), Hogg (Ashton), Hope, Walton, Sorvel, Stallard (Langmead), McMenamin, Smith.
Brighton & HA: Chaigneau; El-Abd, Reid, Hammond, Butters, McShane, Carole (Jarrett) (Carpenter), McCammon, Knight, Kazim-Richards (Robinson), Nicolas.
aet.

Stockport Co (1) 2 *(Boshell 8, Le Fondre 108)*
Sheffield W (1) 4 *(Peacock 15, Partridge 107, Proudlock 116, 120)* 3001
Stockport Co: Spencer; Greenwood (Briggs), Robinson, Wolski, Clare, Williams A, Hamshaw (Coward), Boshell, Easter, Le Fondre, Singh.
Sheffield W: Lucas; Simek, Hills, Diallo, Coughlan (Wood), Whelan, Partridge, O'Brien, Graham (Proudlock), Peacock, Brunt (Rocastle).
aet.

Swindon T (0) 1 *(Pook 58)*
Wycombe W (1) 3 *(Stonebridge 12, Tyson 62, Dixon 75)* 3976
Swindon T: Heaton; Smith J, Whalley (Nicolau), Ifil, Reeves, Comyn-Platt, Heath, Shakes, Roberts (Cureton), Thorpe (Fallon), Pook.
Wycombe W: Talia; Senda, Easton, Oakes, Johnson, Williamson, Betsy, Stonebridge (Anya), Mooney, Tyson (Dixon), Lee.

Watford (2) 3 *(Young 13, Bouazza 34 (pen), Blizzard 48)*
Notts Co (0) 1 *(Palmer 76)* 7011
Watford: Chamberlain; Doyley, Mariappa, Bangura, DeMerit (Chambers), Carlisle, Spring, Blizzard (Grant), Bouazza, Young (Campana), McNamee.
Notts Co: Pilkington; O'Callaghan, Palmer, Edwards, Wilson, Baudet, Pipe, Gill, White (Scoffham), Martin (Ullathorne), Long.

Wolverhampton W (1) 5 *(Miller 6, Cameron 62, 74, Anderton 72, Ganea 79)*
Chester C (0) 1 *(Davies 83)* 9518
Wolverhampton W: Ikeme; Kennedy, Edwards, Cameron, Gyepes, Lescott (McNamara), Davies, Seol (Ndah), Clarke (Ganea), Miller, Anderton.
Chester C: MacKenzie; Regan (Bertos), McNiven, Curtis, Bolland, Dimech, Hessey, Walker (Blundell), Davies, Branch (Vaughan), Drummond.

Wrexham (0) 0
Doncaster R (0) 1 *(Hughes 86)* 2177
Wrexham: Ingham; Smith, Holt, Bennett (Mackin), Bayliss, Pejic (Warhurst), Mark Jones, Ferguson, Walters, Foy (Done), Williams D.
Doncaster R: Warrington; McGuire, Ryan, Fenton, Foster, Ravenhill (Hughes), Mulligan, Coppinger (Offiong), Guy, Fortune-West, McIndoe.

Wednesday, 24 August 2005

Chesterfield (1) 2 *(Niven 41, Hurst 60)*
Huddersfield T (1) 4 *(Abbott 9, Taylor-Fletcher 56, 76, 90)* 2922
Chesterfield: Muggleton; Kovacs, Picken, Niven, Blatherwick, Nicholson, Hall (Smith), Allott, Larkin, Allison (N'Toya), Hurst.
Huddersfield T: Rachubka; Holdsworth (Mendes), Adams, Collins, Clarke N, McIntosh (Clarke T), Brandon, Schofield, Abbott, Taylor-Fletcher, Carss.

Colchester U (0) 0
Cardiff C (2) 2 *(Purse 31 (pen), Jerome 34)* 1904
Colchester U: Gerken; Stockley (Williams), Brown, Baldwin (Elokobi), Chilvers, Watson (Howell), Izzet, Danns, Iwelumo, Halford, Yeates.
Cardiff C: Alexander; Weston, Barker (Parry), Boland, Purse, Loovens, Whitley, Koumas, Lee, Jerome (Ferretti), Cooper.

Derby Co (0) 0

Grimsby T (1) 1 *(Jones G 11)* 11,756

Derby Co: Grant; Kenna (Edworthy), Jackson, Nyatanga, Konjic, Johnson S, Holmes (Rasiak), Bolder, Tudgay, Peschisolido (Barnes), Smith.
Grimsby T: Mildenhall; McDermott, Cohen (Barwick), Ramsden, Jones R (Downey), Whittle, Kamudimba Kalala, Bolland, Parkinson, Jones G, Reddy.

Rushden & D (0) 0

Coventry C (2) 3 *(McSheffrey 10, Heath 41, Morrell 81)* 3240

Rushden & D: Young; Gier (Nicholls), Hawkins, McCafferty, Dempster (Okuonghae), Gulliver, Bell, Savage, Pearson (Taylor), O'Grady, Kelly.
Coventry C: Ince; Whing, Hall, Doyle, Williams, Heath, Morrell, Osbourne, John, McSheffrey (Adebola), Jorgensen (Wood).

Torquay U (0) 0

Bournemouth (0) 0 1876

Torquay U: Marriott; Hockley, Sharp (Osei-Kuffour), Hewlett, Villis, Taylor, Hill, Coleman (Woods), Bedeau, Constantine, Sako (Connell).
Bournemouth: Stewart; Cooper (Hart), O'Connor, Browning, Young, Gowling (Coutts), Cooke (Pitman), Stock, Hayter, Fletcher, Surman.
aet; Bournemouth won 4-3 on penalties.

SECOND ROUND

Tuesday, 20 September 2005

Barnet (1) 2 *(King 12, Grazioli 46)*

Plymouth Arg (1) 1 *(Buzsaky 19)* 1941

Barnet: Tynan; Hendon, King, Lee, Batt, Charles, Bailey, Sinclair, Grazioli (Norville), Strevens, Soares (Bowditch).
Plymouth Arg: McCormick; Barness, Capaldi, Lasley (Summerfield), Doumbe, West, Gudjonsson, Derbyshire, Chadwick, Taylor (Djordjic), Buzsaky.

Burnley (1) 3 *(Lowe 28, Akinbiyi 52, Spicer 59)*

Barnsley (0) 0 4501

Burnley: Coyne; Duff, Harley, Hyde (McCann), Lowe (Sinclair), McGreal, Spicer, O'Connor G, Akinbiyi (Noel-Williams), Branch, O'Connor J.
Barnsley: Flinders; Tonge, Williams, Burns (McPhail), Austin, Kay, Wroe, Shuker, Nardiello (Conlon), Richards (Hayes), Devaney.

Cardiff C (0) 2 *(Ledley 50, Koumas 81)*

Macclesfield T (1) 1 *(Bullock 5)* 3849

Cardiff C: Margetson; Weston, Barker, Ledley, Purse, Cox, Ardley, Whitley, Fleetwood (Ferretti), Lee, Parry (Koumas).
Macclesfield T: Fettis; Morley, Sandwith, Briscoe, Swailes, Barras (Beresford), Whitaker, Harsley, Miles, Bullock, McIntyre.

Charlton Ath (1) 3 *(Johansson 43 (pen), Bent D 73, Bothroyd 80)*

Hartlepool U (1) 1 *(Daly 40)* 10,328

Charlton Ath: Myhre; Young, Hreidarsson, Holland, Spector, Sorondo, Sam, Smertin (Murphy), Bartlett (Bent D), Johansson (Bothroyd), Thomas.
Hartlepool U: Konstantopoulos; Williams D, Humphreys, Nelson, Collins, Tinkler (Turnbull), Istead (Llewellyn), Sweeney, Proctor, Daly (Foley), Butler.

Crystal Palace (0) 1 *(Reich 67)*

Coventry C (0) 0 5341

Crystal Palace: Speroni; Butterfield, Fray, Hudson, Hall, Riihilahti, McAnuff (Berry), Togwell, Andrews (Grabban), Black (Reich), Danze.
Coventry C: Ince; Impey, Watson, Osbourne (Thornton), Page, Whing, Hughes (Scowcroft), Doyle, Morrell (Adebola), McSheffrey, Jorgensen.

Gillingham (1) 3 *(Byfield 42, Ashdown 56 (og), Crofts 94)*

Portsmouth (1) 2 *(O'Neil 24, Taylor 48 (pen))* 4903

Gillingham: Brown; Sancho, Rose, Flynn, Johnson, Hope (Jackman), Crofts, Hessenthaler (Williams), Shields (Hislop), Byfield, Jarvis.
Portsmouth: Ashdown; Priske, Vignal, Hughes, O'Brien, Stefanovic, O'Neil, Diao (Songo'o), Dario Silva (Todorov), Karadas, Taylor (Viafara).
aet.

Grimsby T (0) 1 *(Kamudimba Kalala 89)*

Tottenham H (0) 0 8206

Grimsby T: Mildenhall; McDermott, Cohen (Barwick), Kamudimba Kalala, Whittle, Jones R, Croft, Bolland, Parkinson, Jones G (Gritton), Reddy.
Tottenham H: Robinson; Stalteri, Lee, Brown, Naybet, King, Jenas, Carrick (Davis), Keane, Defoe, Reid (Lennon).

Leicester C (1) 2 *(De Vries 17, 79)*

Blackpool (0) 1 *(Parker 68)* 7386

Leicester C: Henderson; Stearman, Sheehan, Gudjonsson, McCarthy, Johansson, Sylla (Chambers), Kisnorbo, De Vries, Hammond (Hughes), Hamill (Wilcox).
Blackpool: Pogliacomi; McGregor, Burns, Grayson (Anderson), Butler, Clarke, Wiles, Doolan, Vernon (Parker), Donnelly, Prendergast (Blinkhorn).

Mansfield T (0) 1 *(Coke 68)*

Southampton (0) 0 3739

Mansfield T: Pressman; Peers, Jelleyman, McLachlan, Day, John-Baptiste, Talbot, Coke, Barker, Brown, Birchall.
Southampton: Smith; Cranie, Baird, Delap, Kenton, Mills, McCann, Dyer, Jones, Blackstock (McGoldrick), Folly (Walcott).

Norwich C (1) 2 *(Huckerby 34 (pen), Ashton 78)*

Northampton T (0) 0 16,766

Norwich C: Ward; Hughes, Drury, Brennan, Shackell, Fleming, Henderson, Jarrett (Safri), Doherty, Ryan Jarvis (McVeigh), Huckerby (Ashton).
Northampton T: Bunn; Crowe, Johnson G (Brett Johnson), Chambers, Dyche, Doig, Low, Jess (Galbraith), McGleish (Gilligan), Mikolanda, Rowson.

Reading (0) 1 *(Oster 80)*

Luton T (0) 0 6941

Reading: Hahnemann; Murty, Makin, Ingimarsson, Sonko, Harper, Oster, Doyle (Lita), Baradji, Obinna (Cox), Hunt.
Luton T: Brill; Edwards, Barnett (Keane), Holmes, Coyne, Davis, Brkovic, Nicholls, Howard, Feeney, Morgan.

Rotherham U (0) 0

Leeds U (2) 2 *(Cresswell 19, 28)* 5445

Rotherham U: Cutler; Worrell (Otsemobor), Robertson, McLaren, Gilchrist (Murdock), Barker, Mullin, Williamson, Butler, Burton, Keane.
Leeds U: Sullivan; Richardson, Crainey, Pugh, Kilgallon, Gregan, Douglas, Einarsson, Cresswell, Hulse (Derry), Moore.

Scunthorpe U (0) 0

Birmingham C (1) 2 *(Forssell 15, 70 (pen))* 6109

Scunthorpe U: Musselwhite; Byrne (Parton), Williams, Crosby, Stanton (Ridley), Ryan, Taylor, Sparrow, Keogh, Sharp, Corden.
Birmingham C: Vaesen; Martin Taylor, Clapham, Johnson, Upson, Tebily, Pennant (Till), Izzet (Kilkenny), Forssell (Painter), Pandiani, Gray.

Sheffield W (0) 2 *(Coughlan 76, Graham 77)*

West Ham U (1) 4 *(Zamora 2, 63, Dailly 54, Bellion 84)* 14,976

Sheffield W: Lucas; Ross, Bullen, Whelan (O'Brien), Coughlan, Wood, McGovern (Hills), Rocastle, Graham, Corr (Peacock), Brunt.
West Ham U: Hislop; Repka (Stokes), Collins, Williams (Ephraim), Cohen, Ward, Newton, Dailly, Harewood (Bellion), Zamora, Noble.

Shrewsbury T (0) 0

Sheffield U (0) 0 4250

Shrewsbury T: Hart; Herd, Ashton, Tolley (Sharp), Whitehead, Hope, Denny, Sorvel, Darby (Stallard), McMenamin, Smith (Hogg).
Sheffield U: Barnes; Geary, Wright, Francis, Morgan, Quinn S, Gillespie (McFadzean), Nalis, Webber (Marrison), Mulligan (Nix), Tonge.
aet; Sheffield U won 4-3 on penalties.

Sunderland (0) 1 *(Le Tallec 92)*

Cheltenham T (0) 0 11,969

Sunderland: Alnwick; Nosworthy, Smith■, Bassila, Collins D, Caldwell, Piper (Welsh), Robinson (Whitehead), Stead (Elliott), Le Tallec, Lawrence.
Cheltenham T: Higgs; Wilson, Victory, McCann, Caines, Townsend, Melligan (Gill), Finnigan, Odejayi (Spencer), Vincent (Duff), Bird.
aet.

WBA (2) 4 *(Ellington 23, 72, Kamara 33, Earnshaw 77)*

Bradford C (1) 1 *(Schumacher 45)* 10,792

WBA: Kuszczak; Watson, Albrechtsen■, Chaplow, Moore, Clement, Greening (Kanu), Carter, Ellington, Earnshaw, Kamara (Scimeca).
Bradford C: Howarth; Holloway, Edghill, Schumacher, Wetherall, Bower, Muirhead, Crooks, Windass, Cooke, Petta.

Watford (1) 2 *(Carlisle 45, 104)*

Wolverhampton W (1) 1 *(Miller 12)* 9296

Watford: Chamberlain; Chambers, Stewart, Spring, Carlisle, Doyley, Bangura (Gill), Diagouraga (Osborne), Bouazza, Francis (Grant), McNamee.
Wolverhampton W: Postma; Edwards, Naylor, Olofinjana, Gyepes (Lescott), Craddock, Davies, Cameron (Ricketts), Ganea (Ndah), Miller, Seol.
aet.

Wigan Ath (0) 1 *(Roberts 86)*

Bournemouth (0) 0 3346

Wigan Ath: Filan; Wright, McMillan, Skoko, Jackson, Emerson, Teale (Connolly), Taylor, Camara, Johansson (Roberts), Mahon.
Bournemouth: Stewart; Cooper, Coutts (Pitman), Hart, Young, Stock, Foley-Sheridan, Keene (Hudson), Hayter, Rodrigues (Whisken), Surman.

Wycombe W (3) 3 *(Tyson 6, Johnson 18, Mooney 39)*

Aston Villa (1) 8 *(Davis 14, 90, Baros 48, Milner 64, 86, Easton 69 (og), Barry 73 (pen), 78)* 5365

Wycombe W: Talia; Senda, Easton, Oakes, Johnson, Williamson, Burnell (Anya), Bloomfield, Mooney (Stonebridge), Tyson (Torres), Dixon.
Aston Villa: Sorensen; Samuel, Cahill, Davis, Hughes (De la Cruz), Ridgewell, Milner, Berger (Hendrie), Angel (Moore), Baros, Barry.

Yeovil T (0) 1 *(Davies 87)*

Millwall (0) 2 *(Dunne 48, Asaba 53)* 5108

Yeovil T: Weale; Amankwaah, Melono, Way, Skiverton, Fontaine■, Gall (Harrold), Johnson, Bastianini (Davies), Jevons, Jones (Sodje).
Millwall: Marshall; Dunne, Vincent, Livermore, Robinson P, Phillips, Igoe (Hutchison), Morris (Craig), Asaba (Fangueiro), Hayles, Serioux.

Wednesday, 21 September 2005

Blackburn R (1) 3 *(Bellamy 11, 84, Khizanishvili 60)*

Huddersfield T (0) 1 *(Abbott 79)* 11,755

Blackburn R: Friedel; Neill, Gray (Mokoena), Tugay, Nelsen, Khizanishvili, Emerton (Pedersen), Savage, Dickov (Kuqi), Bellamy, Bentley.
Huddersfield T: Rachubka; Holdsworth, Adams, Schofield (Hudson), Clarke N, McCombe, Worthington, Mendes (Brandon), Abbott, Booth (Taylor-Fletcher), Carss.

Doncaster R (0) 1 *(McIndoe 118 (pen))*

Manchester C (0) 1 *(Vassell 95 (pen))* 8228

Doncaster R: Warrington (Budtz); McGuire, McDaid, Roberts S, Albrighton, Green, Coppinger, Predic (Ravenhill), Guy (Heffernan), Fortune-West, McIndoe.
Manchester C: James; Onuoha■, Thatcher, Dunne, Distin, Ireland, Jihai, Reyna (Jordan), Sibierski, Vassell, Hussein (Croft).
aet; Doncaster R won 3-0 on penalties.

Fulham (2) 5 *(Rehman 26, Helguson 31, Rosenior 93, Radzinski 95, McBride 120)*

Lincoln C (0) 4 *(Green 70, Volz 82 (og), Kerr 101, Robinson M 115)* 5365

Fulham: Batista; Rosenior, Green, Rehman (Volz), Goma, Christanval, Elrich, Leacock (Radzinski), Helguson, John (McBride), Timlin.
Lincoln C: Marriott; Beevers (Robinson M), Cryan, Kerr, Morgan, McAuley, Keates (Mayo), Birch, Molango (Asamoah), Green, Brown.
aet.

THIRD ROUND

Tuesday, 25 October 2005

Aston Villa (1) 1 *(Phillips 22)*

Burnley (0) 0 26,872

Aston Villa: Sorensen; Delaney, Samuel, Davis, Mellberg, Ridgewell, Milner, McCann, Angel (Moore), Phillips, Barry.
Burnley: Jensen; Duff, Harley, McCann (Courtney), Lowe, Sinclair, Elliott (Karbassiyoon), O'Connor J, Akinbiyi, O'Connor G, Spicer (Noel-Williams).

Blackburn R (0) 3 *(Emerton 60, Dickov 76, Neill 89)*

Leeds U (0) 0 15,631

Blackburn R: Friedel; Neill, Gray, Tugay, Todd, Khizanishvili (Mokoena), Emerton, Savage, Dickov (Jansen), Kuqi (Bellamy), Pedersen.
Leeds U: Sullivan; Richardson, Harding, Gregan (Douglas), Butler, Kilgallon, Moore, Einarsson■, Healy, Blake (Hulse), Pugh (Lewis).

Crystal Palace (1) 2 *(Freedman 37, Reich 66)*

Liverpool (1) 1 *(Gerrard 40)* 19,673

Crystal Palace: Speroni; Boyce, Borrowdale, Hudson, Hall, Watson, Reich (Togwell), Hughes, Morrison (Andrews), Freedman (Black), Soares.
Liverpool: Carson; Raven, Warnock (Traore), Hamann, Whitbread, Hyypia, Potter, Gerrard, Crouch, Morientes (Sinama-Pongolle), Kewell (Luis Garcia).

Doncaster R (0) 2 *(Heffernan 84, 89)*

Gillingham (0) 0 6874

Doncaster R: Budtz; Marples, McDaid, Albrighton, Roberts S, Green, Coppinger, Ravenhill (Thornton), Roberts N (Heffernan), Guy (Fortune-West), McIndoe.
Gillingham: Bullock; Wallis, Williams, Flynn, Cox, Hope, Crofts, Hessenthaler (Saunders), Hislop (Jarvis), Collin, Jackman (Corneille).

Fulham (0) 2 *(Boa Morte 63, Helguson 90)*

WBA (1) 3 *(Earnshaw 3, Kanu 88, Inamoto 99)* 7373

Fulham: Warner; Leacock, Rosenior, Legwinski (Diop), Knight, Rehman, Malbranque, Elrich (John), Helguson, Pearce (Bocanegra), Boa Morte.
WBA: Kuszczak; Scimeca, Robinson■, Wallwork, Moore, Clement, Inamoto, Carter (Chaplow), Kanu (Gaardsoe), Earnshaw, Kamara (Campbell).
aet.

Mansfield T (0) 2 *(Brown 67, Barker 68)*

Millwall (1) 3 *(May 25, Robinson 61, Livermore 90)* 4133

Mansfield T: Pressman; Buxton, Jelleyman, Coke, Hjelde, John-Baptiste, Uhlenbeek, D'Laryea, Barker, Brown, Rundle.
Millwall: Marshall; Dunne, Craig, Livermore, Robinson P, Lawrence, Elliott (Cogan), Hutchison (Morris), Asaba, May, Hayles (Braniff).

Reading (0) 2 *(Kitson 54, 75)*
Sheffield U (0) 0 11,607
Reading: Stack; Murty, Shorey, Ingimarsson, Sonko, Baradji, Oster, Sidwell, Kitson (Cox), Obinna, Hunt (Little).
Sheffield U: Barnes; Geary, Wright, Quinn S, Bromby, Francis (Horwood), Marrison (Law), Ross, Webber (Nix), Forte, Tonge.

Sunderland (0) 0
Arsenal (0) 3 *(Eboue 61, Van Persie 67 (pen), 87)* 47,366
Sunderland: Alnwick; Nosworthy, Hoyte, Robinson (Whitehead), Collins D (Smith), Caldwell, Lawrence, Woods, Stead, Le Tallec, Welsh (Murphy D).
Arsenal: Almunia; Eboue, Cygan, Song Billong, Campbell, Senderos, Larsson (Cregg), Muamba, Lupoli (Stokes), Van Persie, Owusu-Abeyie (Bendtner).

Wigan Ath (0) 3 *(Taylor 98 (pen), Johansson 117, 120)*
Watford (0) 0 4531
Wigan Ath: Pollitt; Wright, McMillan (Waterhouse), Skoko, Emerson, Jackson, Taylor, Bullard (Kavanagh), Teale, Johansson, Mahon.
Watford: Chamberlain; Chambers, Stewart, Mahon (Mariappa), Mackay, DeMerit, Diagouraga (Gill), Bangura, Henderson (Francis), Grant, McNamee.
aet.

Wednesday, 26 October 2005

Birmingham C (1) 2 *(Pennant 5, Jarosik 86)*
Norwich C (1) 1 *(Martin Taylor 41 (og))* 28,825
Birmingham C: Vaesen; Johnson, Clapham, Butt, Upson, Martin Taylor, Pennant, Kilkenny, Forssell (Birley), Heskey (Pandiani), Jarosik.
Norwich C: Green; Fleming, Brennan, Hughes, Doherty, Davenport, Marney (Rossi Jarvis), Jarrett (McVeigh), Huckerby, Ashton, Charlton (Henderson).

Bolton W (0) 1 *(Borgetti 64)*
West Ham U (0) 0 10,927
Bolton W: Walker; O'Brien, Gardner, Diagne-Faye (Djetou), Ben Haim, Jaidi, Fernandes (N'Gotty), Nolan, Borgetti, Fadiga, Giannakopoulos (Pedersen).
West Ham U: Hislop; Repka, Konchesky, Collins, Ward, Mullins, Bellion, Dailly, Harewood (Fletcher), Sheringham (Aliadiere), Clarke (Newton).

Cardiff C (0) 0
Leicester C (1) 1 *(Johansson 11)* 8727
Cardiff C: Margetson; Weston (Ardley), Barker, Ledley, Purse, Loovens, Koumas, Whitley, Jerome, Lee, Parry (Ferretti).
Leicester C: Henderson; Maybury, Johansson, Williams, McCarthy, Gerrbrand, Gudjonsson, Hamill, Dublin (De Vries), Hammond, Tiatto (Kisnorbo).

Chelsea (1) 1 *(Terry 41)*
Charlton Ath (1) 1 *(Bent D 45)* 42,198
Chelsea: Cudicini; Paulo Ferreira, Bridge (Lampard), Geremi, Terry, Huth, Wright-Phillips (Cole J), Essien, Crespo (Drogba), Gudjohnsen, Robben.
Charlton Ath: Andersen; Young, Powell, Holland, El Karkouri, Hreidarsson, Murphy (Kishishev), Ambrose (Bothroyd), Bent D, Hughes, Rommedahl (Thomas).
aet; Charlton Ath won 5-4 on penalties.

Everton (0) 0
Middlesbrough (1) 1 *(Hasselbaink 38)* 25,844
Everton: Martyn; Hibbert, Ferrari (Bent), Yobo, Weir, Arteta, Davies (Osman), Neville, Beattie, McFadden (Van der Meyde), Kilbane.
Middlesbrough: Schwarzer; Parnaby, Queudrue, Doriva, Ehiogu (Bates), Riggott, Morrison, Rochemback, Hasselbaink (Nemeth), Viduka (Yakubu), Pogatetz.

Grimsby T (0) 0
Newcastle U (0) 1 *(Shearer 80)* 9311
Grimsby T: Mildenhall; McDermott, Newey, Kamudimba Kalala, Whittle, Jones R, Andrew (Parkinson), Bolland, Reddy, Jones G (Gritton), Cohen.
Newcastle U: Given; Ramage, Babayaro, Faye (Brittain), Taylor, Bramble, Solano (Clark), Parker, Shearer, Chopra, N'Zogbia.

Manchester U (2) 4 *(Miller 4, Richardson 19, Rossi 51, Ebanks-Blake 89)*
Barnet (0) 1 *(Sinclair 74)* 43,673
Manchester U: Howard; Bardsley, Eckersley, Miller, Brown, Pique, Martin (Gibson), Jones, Rossi, Ebanks-Blake, Richardson.
Barnet: Flitney■; Hendon, King, Lee (Batt), Yakubu, Gross, Bailey, Sinclair, Grazioli (Hatch), Strevens, Soares (Tynan).

FOURTH ROUND

Tuesday, 29 November 2005

Arsenal (2) 3 *(Reyes 12, Van Persie 42, Lupoli 65)*
Reading (0) 0 36,167
Arsenal: Almunia; Eboue, Gilbert, Flamini, Larsson, Senderos, Muamba, Djourou, Owusu-Abeyie (Bendtner), Van Persie (Lupoli), Reyes (Cygan).
Reading: Stack (Hahnemann); Murty, Shorey (Makin), Ingimarsson, Sonko, Harper, Oster, Sidwell, Lita (Doyle), Kitson, Hunt.

Doncaster R (1) 3 *(McIndoe 20 (pen), Heffernan 53, Thornton 79)*
Aston Villa (0) 0 10,590
Doncaster R: Seremet; Fenton, Mulligan, Foster, Roberts S, Ravenhill, Coppinger, Thornton, Guy (Green), Heffernan, McIndoe.
Aston Villa: Sorensen; Hughes, Samuel (Phillips), Davis, Mellberg, Ridgewell, Milner, McCann, Baros, Angel, Barry.

Millwall (0) 2 *(Dunne 57, Elliott 116)*
Birmingham C (1) 2 *(Gray 10, Heskey 102)* 7732
Millwall: Pidgeley; Dunne, Craig, Elliott, Robinson P, Livermore, Ifil (Fangueiro), Morris (Simpson), Asaba (May), Hayles, Wright.
Birmingham C: Vaesen; Melchiot, Clapham, Clemence (Jarosik), Upson, Martin Taylor, Pennant, Butt, Pandiani (Dunn), Heskey, Gray (Lazaridis).
aet; Birmingham C won 4-3 on penalties.

Wednesday, 30 November 2005

Bolton W (0) 2 *(Borgetti 104, Vaz Te 106)*
Leicester C (0) 1 *(Williams 110)* 13,067
Bolton W: Jaaskelainen; Hunt, Gardner, Djetou, Ben Haim, Jaidi, Okocha (Fadiga), Nakata, Vaz Te, Davies (Borgetti), Speed (Campo).
Leicester C: Douglas; Stearman (Sheehan), Maybury, Hughes (Sylla), Dublin, Johansson, Williams, Hamill, De Vries, Gudjonsson, Tiatto (McCarthy).

Charlton Ath (1) 2 *(Ambrose 37, Murphy 50)*
Blackburn R (0) 3 *(Kuqi 75, Thompson 81, Bentley 88)* 14,093
Charlton Ath: Kiely; Young (Spector), Powell (Bothroyd), Smertin, El Karkouri, Hreidarsson, Kishishev, Murphy, Bent D, Ambrose, Johansson (Hughes).
Blackburn R: Friedel; Khizanishvili, Gray, Savage (Thompson), Todd, Nelsen, Emerton (Kuqi), Reid, Bellamy, Bentley (Mokoena), Pedersen.

Manchester U (2) 3 *(Ronaldo 12 (pen), Saha 16, O'Shea 56)*
WBA (0) 1 *(Ellington 77)* 48,924
Manchester U: Howard; Neville, O'Shea (Pique), Fletcher (Jones), Ferdinand, Silvestre, Ronaldo, Richardson, Rossi, Saha, Park (Bardsley).
WBA: Hoult; Albrechtsen, Robinson, Wallwork, Moore (Gaardsoe), Clement, Kamara (Earnshaw), Inamoto, Ellington, Horsfield (Chaplow), Carter.

Middlesbrough (0) 2 *(Viduka 52, Nemeth 55)*
Crystal Palace (1) 1 *(Queudrue 31 (og))* 10,791
Middlesbrough: Schwarzer; Parnaby, Queudrue, Southgate, Ehiogu, Doriva, Rochemback (Bates), Boateng, Hasselbaink (Maccarone), Viduka, Nemeth (Pogatetz).
Crystal Palace: Speroni; Boyce, Borrowdale, Hudson, Popovic, Watson, McAnuff (Black), Andrews, Johnson (Morrison), Macken (Freedman), Leigertwood.

Wigan Ath (0) 1 *(Connolly 88 (pen))*
Newcastle U (0) 0 11,574
Wigan Ath: Pollitt; Taylor, McMillan (Baines), Skoko, Emerson (Henchoz), Jackson, Teale, Mahon, Connolly, Johansson (Roberts), McCulloch.
Newcastle U: Given; Ramage, N'Zogbia, Parker, Elliott, Boumsong, Solano, Emre (Faye), Shearer, Luque (Chopra), Bowyer (Brittain).

QUARTER-FINALS

Tuesday, 20 December 2005

Birmingham C (0) 1 *(Jarosik 75)*
Manchester U (0) 3 *(Saha 46, 63, Park 50)* 20,454
Birmingham C: Maik Taylor; Johnson, Painter, Clemence, Upson, Martin Taylor, Pennant, Butt (Clapham), Heskey (Forssell), Jarosik, Dunn (Kilkenny).
Manchester U: Howard; Neville, Richardson, O'Shea (Jones), Brown, Silvestre (Ferdinand), Fletcher, Park, Saha, Rossi (Rooney), Ronaldo.

Wigan Ath (2) 2 *(Roberts 40, 45)*
Bolton W (0) 0 13,401
Wigan Ath: Pollitt; Taylor (Chimbonda), Baines, Kavanagh, Jackson, De Zeeuw, Francis, Mahon (Teale), Roberts, Johansson (Camara), McCulloch.
Bolton W: Jaaskelainen; O'Brien, Gardner, Diagne-Faye (Okocha), Ben Haim, Jaidi, Nolan, Nakata (Diouf), Davies, Speed, Giannakopoulos (Vaz Te).

Wednesday, 21 December 2005

Doncaster R (1) 2 *(McIndoe 4, Green 104)*
Arsenal (0) 2 *(Owusu-Abeyie 63, Silva 120)* 10,006
Doncaster R: Budtz; Fenton, McDaid, Foster, Roberts S, Ravenhill, Coppinger (Roberts N), Thornton (Green), Guy (Oji), Heffernan, McIndoe.
Arsenal: Almunia; Eboue, Cygan, Silva, Senderos, Djourou, Hleb, Song Billong, Van Persie (Bendtner), Lupoli (Gilbert), Owusu-Abeyie (Larsson).
aet; Arsenal won 3-1 on penalties.

Middlesbrough (0) 0
Blackburn R (0) 1 *(Dickov 90)* 14,710
Middlesbrough: Schwarzer; Bates (Parnaby), Pogatetz, Doriva, Riggott, Southgate, Rochemback, Boateng (Queudrue), Hasselbaink, Yakubu, Johnson (Maccarone).
Blackburn R: Friedel; Neill, Gray, Tugay, Todd, Nelsen, Bentley (Reid), Savage, Dickov, Kuqi, Pedersen (Emerton).

SEMI-FINALS FIRST LEG

Tuesday, 10 January 2006

Wigan Ath (0) 1 *(Sharner 78)*
Arsenal (0) 0 12,181
Wigan Ath: Pollitt; Chimbonda, McMillan, Kavanagh, Henchoz, De Zeeuw, Teale, Bullard, Roberts, Connolly (Johansson), McCulloch (Scharner).
Arsenal: Almunia; Gilbert (Larsson), Cygan, Silva, Djourou, Senderos, Ljungberg, Flamini, Reyes (Fabregas), Owusu-Abeyie (Lupoli), Hleb.

Wednesday, 11 January 2006

Blackburn R (1) 1 *(Pedersen 35)*
Manchester U (1) 1 *(Saha 30)* 24,348
Blackburn R: Friedel; Neill, Gray, Tugay (Reid), Todd, Nelsen, Bentley (Emerton), Savage, Bellamy, Kuqi (Dickov), Pedersen.
Manchester U: Van der Sar; Neville, Silvestre, Smith, Ferdinand, Brown, Ronaldo, Fletcher (O'Shea), Saha (Van Nistelrooy), Rooney, Giggs.

SEMI-FINALS SECOND LEG

Tuesday, 24 January 2006

Arsenal (0) 2 *(Henry 65, Van Persie 108)*
Wigan Ath (0) 1 *(Roberts 119)* 34,692
Arsenal: Almunia; Gilbert, Lauren, Silva, Campbell, Senderos, Hleb (Pires), Diaby (Flamini), Henry (Van Persie), Bergkamp, Reyes.
Wigan Ath: Pollitt; Chimbonda, Baines, Kavanagh, Henchoz, Scharner, Teale, Bullard, Mellor (Johansson), Roberts, Mahon (Ziegler).
aet.

Wednesday, 25 January 2006

Manchester U (1) 2 *(Van Nistelrooy 8, Saha 51)*
Blackburn R (1) 1 *(Reid 32)* 61,637
Manchester U: Van der Sar; Neville, Evra (Silvestre), Fletcher, Ferdinand, Brown, Richardson, Saha, Van Nistelrooy (Vidic), Rooney, Giggs (Smith).
Blackburn R: Friedel; Neill, Gray, Tugay (Peter), Khizanishvili, Nelsen, Reid, Savage, Bentley, Kuqi (Emerton), Pedersen.

FINAL (AT MILLENNIUM STADIUM)

Sunday, 26 February 2006

Manchester U (1) 4 *(Rooney 33, 61, Saha 55, Ronaldo 59)*
Wigan Ath (0) 0 66,866
Manchester U: Van der Sar; Neville, Silvestre (Evra), Park, Brown (Vidic), Ferdinand, Ronaldo (Richardson), O'Shea, Saha, Rooney, Giggs.
Wigan Ath: Pollitt (Filan); Chimbonda, Baines, Kavanagh (Ziegler), Henchoz (McCulloch), De Zeeuw, Teale, Bullard, Camara, Roberts, Scharner.
Referee: A. Wiley (Staffordshire).

FOOTBALL LEAGUE COMPETITION ATTENDANCES

LEAGUE CUP ATTENDANCES

Season	*Attendances*	*Games*	*Average*
1960–61	1,204,580	112	10,755
1961–62	1,030,534	104	9,909
1962–63	1,029,893	102	10,097
1963–64	945,265	104	9,089
1964–65	962,802	98	9,825
1965–66	1,205,876	106	11,376
1966–67	1,394,553	118	11,818
1967–68	1,671,326	110	15,194
1968–69	2,064,647	118	17,497
1969–70	2,299,819	122	18,851
1970–71	2,035,315	116	17,546
1971–72	2,397,154	123	19,489
1972–73	1,935,474	120	16,129
1973–74	1,722,629	132	13,050
1974–75	1,901,094	127	14,969
1975–76	1,841,735	140	13,155
1976–77	2,236,636	147	15,215
1977–78	2,038,295	148	13,772
1978–79	1,825,643	139	13,134
1979–80	2,322,866	169	13,745
1980–81	2,051,576	161	12,743
1981–82	1,880,682	161	11,681
1982–83	1,679,756	160	10,498
1983–84	1,900,491	168	11,312
1984–85	1,876,429	167	11,236
1985–86	1,579,916	163	9,693
1986–87	1,531,498	157	9,755
1987–88	1,539,253	158	9,742
1988–89	1,552,780	162	9,585
1989–90	1,836,916	168	10,934
1990–91	1,675,496	159	10,538
1991–92	1,622,337	164	9,892
1992–93	1,558,031	161	9,677
1993–94	1,744,120	163	10,700
1994–95	1,530,478	157	9,748
1995–96	1,776,060	162	10,963
1996–97	1,529,321	163	9,382
1997–98	1,484,297	153	9,701
1998–99	1,555,856	153	10,169
1999–2000	1,354,233	153	8,851
2000–01	1,501,304	154	9,749
2001–02	1,076,390	93	11,574
2002-03	1,242,478	92	13,505
2003-04	1,267,729	93	13,631
2004-05	1,313,693	93	14,216

CARLING CUP 2005–06

Round	*Aggregate*	*Games*	*Average*
One	171,659	36	4,768
Two	175,905	24	7,329
Three	313,565	16	19,598
Four	152,938	8	19,117
Quarter-finals	58,571	4	14,643
Semi-finals	132,858	4	33,215
Final	66,866	1	66,866
Total	1,072,362	93	11,531

FOOTBALL LEAGUE TROPHY 2005–06

Round	*Aggregate*	*Games*	*Average*
One	51,538	28	1,841
Two	29,730	16	1,858
Area Quarter-finals	19,161	8	2,395
Area Semi-finals	14,660	4	3,665
Area finals	19,825	4	4,956
Final	42,028	1	42,028
Total	176,942	61	2,901

FA CUP ATTENDANCES 1968–2006

	1st Round	*2nd Round*	*3rd Round*	*4th Round*	*5th Round*	*6th Round*	*Semi-finals & Final*	*Total*	*No. of matches*	*Average per match*
2005–06	188,876	107,456	654,570	388,339	286,225	163,449	177,723	1,966,638	160	12,291
2004–05	161,197	98,702	602,152	477,472	339,082	127,914	193,233	1,999,752	146	13,697
2003–04	162,738	117,967	624,732	347,964	292,521	156,780	167,401	1,870,103	149	12,551
2002–03	189,905	104,103	577,494	404,599	242,483	156,244	175,498	1,850,326	150	12,336
2001–02	198,369	119,781	566,284	330,434	249,190	173,757	171,278	1,809,093	148	12,224
2000–01	171,689	122,061	577,204	398,241	256,899	100,663	177,778	1,804,535	151	11,951
1999–2000	181,485	127,728	514,030	374,795	182,511	105,443	214,921	1,700,913	158	10,765
1998–99	191,954	132,341	609,486	431,613	359,398	181,005	202,150	2,107,947	155	13,599
1997–98	204,803	130,261	629,127	455,557	341,290	192,651	172,007	2,125,696	165	12,883
1996–97	209,521	122,324	651,139	402,293	199,873	67,035	191,813	1,843,998	151	12,211
1995–96	185,538	115,669	748,997	391,218	274,055	174,142	156,500	2,046,199	167	12,252
1994–95	219,511	125,629	640,017	438,596	257,650	159,787	174,059	2,015,249	161	12,517
1993–94	190,683	118,031	691,064	430,234	172,196	134,705	228,233	1,965,146	159	12,359
1992–93	241,968	174,702	612,494	377,211	198,379	149,675	293,241	2,047,670	161	12,718
1991–92	231,940	117,078	586,014	372,576	270,537	155,603	201,592	1,935,340	160	12,095
1990–91	194,195	121,450	594,592	530,279	276,112	124,826	196,434	2,038,518	162	12,583
1989–90	209,542	133,483	683,047	412,483	351,423	123,065	277,420	2,190,463	170	12,885
1988–89	212,775	121,326	690,199	421,255	206,781	176,629	167,353	1,966,318	164	12,173
1987–88	204,411	104,561	720,121	443,133	281,461	119,313	177,585	2,050,585	155	13,229
1986–87	209,290	146,761	593,520	349,342	263,550	119,396	195,533	1,877,400	165	11,378
1985–86	171,142	130,034	486,838	495,526	311,833	184,262	192,316	1,971,951	168	11,738
1984–85	174,604	137,078	616,229	320,772	269,232	148,690	242,754	1,909,359	157	12,162
1983–84	192,276	151,647	625,965	417,298	181,832	185,382	187,000	1,941,400	166	11,695
1982–83	191,312	150,046	670,503	452,688	260,069	193,845	291,162	2,209,625	154	14,348
1981–82	236,220	127,300	513,185	356,987	203,334	124,308	279,621	1,840,955	160	11,506
1980–81	246,824	194,502	832,578	534,402	320,530	288,714	339,250	2,756,800	169	16,312
1979–80	267,121	204,759	804,701	507,725	364,039	157,530	355,541	2,661,416	163	16,328
1978–79	243,773	185,343	880,345	537,748	243,683	263,213	249,897	2,604,002	166	15,687
1977–78	258,248	178,930	881,406	540,164	400,751	137,059	198,020	2,594,578	160	16,216
1976–77	379,230	192,159	942,523	631,265	373,330	205,379	258,216	2,982,102	174	17,139
1975–76	255,533	178,099	867,880	573,843	471,925	206,851	205,810	2,759,941	161	17,142
1974–75	283,956	170,466	914,994	646,434	393,323	268,361	291,369	2,968,903	172	17,261
1973–74	214,236	125,295	840,142	747,909	346,012	233,307	273,051	2,779,952	167	16,646
1972–73	259,432	169,114	938,741	735,825	357,386	241,934	226,543	2,928,975	160	18,306
1971–72	277,726	236,127	986,094	711,399	486,378	230,292	248,546	3,158,562	160	19,741
1970–71	329,687	230,942	956,683	757,852	360,687	304,937	279,644	3,220,432	162	19,879
1969–70	345,229	195,102	925,930	651,374	319,893	198,537	390,700	3,026,765	170	17,805
1968–69	331,858	252,710	1,094,043	883,675	464,915	188,121	216,232	3,431,554	157	21,857

FOOTBALL LEAGUE TROPHY 2005–06

▪ *Denotes player sent off.*

NORTHERN SECTION FIRST ROUND

Tuesday, 18 October 2005

Barnsley (1) 2 *(Foster 6 (og), Nardiello 90)*

Doncaster R (1) 5 *(Guy 39, 86, Kay 72 (og), Offiong 79, Austin 82 (og))* 4095

Barnsley: Flinders; Austin, Williams, Howard, Hassell, Kay, Burns (Nardiello), Shuker, Hayes, Richards, Devaney.
Doncaster R: Richardson; McGuire, Mulligan, Foster, Fenton, Hughes, Offiong (Roberts S), Predic (Thornton), Guy, Fortune-West, Forte (Heffernan).

Blackpool (1) 4 *(Blinkhorn 2, McGregor 84, Southern 99, Vernon 104)*

Wrexham (0) 3 *(Mark Jones 77, 78, Ferguson 96)* 3239

Blackpool: Pogliacomi; Coid (Grayson), Armstrong, Doolan, McGregor, Clarke, Wiles, Southern, Wright (Vernon), Blinkhorn, Burns (Prendergast).
Wrexham: Ingham; Smith, Holt, Lawrence (Mackin), Bayliss (Foy), Spender (McEvilly), Mark Jones, Ferguson, Walters, Bennett, Williams D.
aet.

Cambridge U (0) 3 *(Bridges 65, Smith 79, Onibuje 90)*

Chester C (0) 0 1224

Cambridge U: Howie; Morrison, Okai (Angel), Duncan, Peters, Smith, Bridges, Hanlon, Nolan (Onibuje), Westcarr (Atkins), Quinton.
Chester C: MacKenzie; Bertos, El Kholti, Vaughan, Bolland, Hessey, Rutherford (McNiven), Walker, Richardson, Curle (Davies), Dove.

Grimsby T (0) 1 *(Ashton 67)*

Morecambe (1) 1 *(Lloyd 45)* 1131

Grimsby T: Mildenhall; Hegarty (Chamberlain), Cohen, Ramsden, Whittle, Crane, Francis (Palmer), Toner, Gritton, Slade (Ashton), Barwick.
Morecambe: Robinson; Blackburn, Howard (Gray), Lloyd, Kempson, Bentley, Smith, Stringfellow, Dodgson (Perkins), O'Connor (Carlton), Hunter.
aet; Morecambe won 4-3 on penalties.

Halifax T (2) 6 *(Midgley 17 (pen), Mansaram 29, 47, Haslam 52, Killeen 56, Parrish 76 (og))*

Bury (0) 1 *(Sedgemore 50)* 1191

Halifax T: Butler; Haslam, Doughty, Leister, Young, Quinn, Foster (Thompson), Bowler (Forrest), Killeen, Mansaram, Midgley (Wright).
Bury: Dootson▪; Hardiker (Quigley), Kennedy (Adams), Scott, Fitzgerald, Parrish, Sedgemore, Whaley, Youngs (Grundy), Barlow, Buchanan.

Kidderminster H (1) 2 *(Hatwell 45, Sheldon 83 (pen))*

Darlington (1) 1 *(N'Dumbu Nsungu 16 (pen))* 696

Kidderminster H: Lewis; Evans, Hatswell, Fleming, Jackson, Burgess, Russell, O'Connor (Wilson), Christie, Heslop, Sheldon.
Darlington: Russell; Wainwright, Valentine, Martis, Clarke, Hutchinson, Peacock, Appleby (Thomas) (Jameson), Johnson S, N'Dumbu Nsungu, Webster (Sodje).

Macclesfield T (0) 2 *(Wijnhard 51, Beresford 82)*

Chesterfield (0) 0 796

Macclesfield T: Fettis; Bailey, McIntyre, Morley, Swailes, Navarro, Whitaker, Harsley, Beresford, Wijnhard, Bullock.
Chesterfield: Roche; Bailey, Nicholson, O'Hare, Blatherwick, Niven (Allott), Smith, Hurst, De Bolla (N'Toya), Allison (Larkin), Clingan.

Mansfield T (0) 0

Hereford U (1) 1 *(Day 12 (og))* 1393

Mansfield T: White; Jacobs, Arnold, Talbot (Jelleyman), Day, John-Baptiste, Lloyd, McLachlan (Coke), Littlejohn, Birchall, Dawson.
Hereford U: Mawson; Green, Jeannin, Mkandawire, James, Pitman, Ferrell, Brady, Bailey (Ipoua), Williams (Evans), Purdie.

Oldham Ath (0) 1 *(Liddell 78 (pen))*

Carlisle U (1) 1 *(Hawley 5)* 2226

Oldham Ath: Day; Scott, Forbes (Tierney), Hall D, Branston, Hughes, Wellens (Porter), Eyres, Warne, Beckett (Hall C), Liddell.
Carlisle U: Westwood; Beharall, Aranalde, Billy, Gray (Grand), Murphy, Hackney (McClen), Holmes (Murray G), Nade, Hawley, Lumsdon.
aet; Carlisle U won 6-5 on penalties.

Rochdale (2) 3 *(Raynes 7 (og), Holt 21 (pen), Griffin D 58 (og))*

Stockport Co (1) 1 *(Goodhind 15 (og))* 1683

Rochdale: Gilks; Goodhind, Gallimore, Clarke (Cooksey), Griffiths, Boardman, Cartwright, Jones, Lambert (Sturrock), Holt, Goodall (Kitchen).
Stockport Co: Spencer; Briggs, Griffin D, Greenwood, Raynes, Dolan (Clare), Hamshaw (Williams C), Boshell, Bramble, Robinson, Singh (Le Fondre).

Rotherham U (2) 3 *(Butler 10, Hoskins 24, Newsham 120)*

Accrington S (1) 3 *(Mangan 18, Williams 75, Brown D 104)* 1888

Rotherham U: Montgomery; Otsemobor, Hurst, Leadbitter (Brogan), Gilchrist, Minto, Mullin, Monkhouse (Newsham), Butler, Conlon (Vernazza), Hoskins.
Accrington S: Dibble; Ventre, Butler, Lee (Barry), Williams, Craney, Jagielka (Brown D), Boco, Mangan, Edwards (Flynn), Roberts.
aet; Rotherham U won 3-2 on penalties.

Scunthorpe U (0) 1 *(Crosby 85 (pen))*

Hartlepool U (0) 0 2028

Scunthorpe U: Evans; Byrne, Ridley, Crosby, Butler, Ryan (Baraclough), Sparrow, Till, Johnson, Parton (Taylor), Corden.
Hartlepool U: Konstantopoulos; Craddock, Brackstone, Jones (Maidens), Collins, Tinkler (Clark▪), Llewellyn (Istead), Sweeney, Williams E, Bullock, Butler.

Tranmere R (1) 2 *(Rankine 33, Jennings 75)*

Lincoln C (1) 1 *(Brown 45)* 3210

Tranmere R: Achterberg; Goodison, Roberts, Linwood, Jackson, Sharps, Jennings, Rankine, Facey, Greenacre (Davies), Aiston (Zola).
Lincoln C: Marriott; Beevers, Bloomer, McAuley, Morgan, Cryan, Foster, Birch (Molango), Asamoah, Robinson M, Brown (Green).

SOUTHERN SECTION FIRST ROUND

Tuesday, 18 October 2005

Barnet (1) 3 *(Bailey 42, Norville 59, Sinclair 70)*

Bristol C (1) 2 *(Murray 44, Madjo 81)* 1031

Barnet: Tynan; Hendon, Batt, Bailey, Yakubu, Gross, Bowditch, Sinclair, Norville (Graham), Strevens, Soares (Hatch).
Bristol C: Phillips; Carey, Woodman, Sankofa, Fortune (Bridges), Skuse, Murray, Wilkshire, Cotterill, Stewart, Brown (Madjo).

Bournemouth (1) 4 *(Pitman 33 (pen), Keene 76, 83, Cooke 80 (pen))*

Aldershot T (0) 1 *(Heald 65)* 2657

Bournemouth: Moss; Hart, Purches (O'Connor), Browning, Cooper, Gowling, Coutts, Stock, Pitman (Foley-Sheridan), Rodrigues (Keene), Cooke.
Aldershot T: Bull; Somner, Reed, Boucaud, Heald, Jinadu, Sulaimani, Scott, Coleman, Sills (Crittenden), Holloway (Deen).

Brentford (1) 1 *(Fitzgerald 9)*

Oxford U (1) 1 *(Roget 41)* 1785

Brentford: Bankole; Osborne, Charles, Hutchinson (Moleski) (Watts), Gayle, Mousinho, Dobson, Newman, Fitzgerald, Peters (Ide), Tillen.
Oxford U: Tardif; Stirling, Robinson, Quinn, Roget, Willmott, Hackett, Bradbury, Basham, Davies, Hughes (Beechers).
aet; Oxford U won 4-3 on penalties.

Gillingham (0) 2 *(Jackman 94, Collin 107)*
Crawley T (0) 0 1988
Gillingham: Bullock; Wallis, Williams, Saunders, Johnson■, Rose, Crofts, Hessenthaler (Jackman), Hislop (Collin), Jarvis, Spiller (Harris).
Crawley T: Smith; Judge, Jenkins, Lindegaard (Cade), Woozley, Giles, Armstrong, Wormull (Blackburn), Clare, Burton■, Opinel (Douglas).
aet.

Leyton Orient (1) 2 *(Hanson 37, Alexander 76)*
Yeovil T (0) 0 958
Leyton Orient: Morris; Palmer, Hanson, McMahon, Miller, Zakuani, Duncan (Saah), Easton, Alexander, Echanomi, Carlisle (Demetriou).
Yeovil T: Weale; Amankwaah, Miles (Jones), Johnson, Skiverton, Sodje, Terry, Harrold (Gall), Bastianini, Jevons, Davies (Alvarez).

Milton Keynes D (1) 3 *(Smith 23, 89 (pen), Wilbraham 62)*
Exeter C (0) 2 *(Phillips 73, Taylor 83)* 2745
Milton Keynes D: Martin; Edds (Kamara), Lewington, Crooks, Morgan, Mills, McKoy (Harding), Smith, Wilbraham, McLeod, Rizzo (Quinn).
Exeter C: Rice; Hiley, Vinnicombe■, Taylor, Gaia, Sawyer, Mackie, Clay, Watkins (McConnell), Phillips, Afful (Ghiglia).

Northampton T (3) 5 *(Mendes 15, Cross 16, 22, McGleish 87, 90)*
Notts Co (1) 2 *(Long 3, McMahon 57 (pen))* 2041
Northampton T: Poke; Bojic, Galbraith (Bonner), Dolman, Doig, Brad Johnson, Low, Rowson, Cross (McGleish), Mendes, Smith (Crowe).
Notts Co: Marshall; Chilaka, Ullathorne (Palmer), Edwards, Wilson, Baudet, Long, McMahon, Berry, White, Williams (McGoldrick).

Peterborough U (1) 2 *(Crow 35, Logan 90)*
Bristol R (1) 1 *(Walker 11)* 1477
Peterborough U: Harrison; St Ledger-Hall, Holden, Arber, Plummer (Burton), Carden, Farrell (Semple), Newton, Thorpe, Crow (Logan), Gain.
Bristol R: Shearer; Lescott, Ryan, Campbell (Carruthers), Hinton, Elliott, Leary (Haldane), Hunt, Walker, Agogo, Disley.

Rushden & D (1) 1 *(Pearson 32)*
Southend U (0) 0 1300
Rushden & D: Woodman; Gier, Hawkins, McCafferty, Dempster, Gulliver, Pearson (Bell), Nicholls, Broughton (Tomlin), O'Grady (Okuonghae), Kelly.
Southend U: Flahavan; Jupp, Wilson, Maher, Barrett, Prior, Campbell-Ryce, Smith (Bentley), Gray, Eastwood, Gower (Lawson).

Shrewsbury T (0) 0
Cheltenham T (1) 2 *(Spencer 8, Connolly 74)* 2146
Shrewsbury T: Thompson; Herd (Adaggio), Ashton, Hogg, Whitehead, Cowan, Denny, Tolley (Edwards), Stallard, Lyng (Langmead), Jackson.
Cheltenham T: Higgs; Duff (Townsend), Wilson, McCann, Caines, Connolly, Melligan (Gill), Bird, Odejayi (Guinan), Spencer, Armstrong.

Swindon T (1) 2 *(Fallon 4, Bouazza 53)*
Stevenage B (0) 0 1771
Swindon T: Heaton; Gurney, Jenkins (Cureton), Nicholas, O'Hanlon, McDermott, Pook, Whalley (Comyn-Platt), Fallon (Thorpe), Bouazza, Roberts.
Stevenage B: Gore; Weatherstone, Perpetuini, Bulman, Henry, Quinn, Brough (Nurse), Berquez, Elding (Schillaci), Stamp (Boyd), Sullivan.

Torquay U (1) 1 *(Osei-Kuffour 24)*
Swansea C (0) 3 *(Forbes 65, Akinfenwa 86, Robinson 88)* 1025
Torquay U: Marriott; Hockley, Hill, Hewlett, Taylor, Sharp, Coleman (Phillips), Garner, Connell (Constantine), Osei-Kuffour, Bedeau (Sow).
Swansea C: Murphy; Tate, Ricketts, O'Leary, Austin, MacDonald (Martinez), Forbes (Iriekpen), Goodfellow, Akinfenwa, Pritchard (Trundle), Robinson.

Woking (1) 3 *(Rawle 11, 53, Richards 65)*
Nottingham F (2) 2 *(Bopp 20, Weir-Daley 38)* 3127
Woking: Davies; Jackson, El-Salahi, Murray, Oliver, Aggrey, Ferguson (Cockerill S), Selley, Richards (Sharpling), Rawle (Cockerill L), Blackman.
Nottingham F: Gerrard; James, Vickerton, Thompson, Fernandez, Gary Holt, Bopp (Pitman), Gardner, Dadi, Weir-Daley, Bastians.

Wycombe W (0) 2 *(Easton 64, 112)*
Dagenham & R (1) 1 *(Benson 26)* 1094
Wycombe W: Talia; Senda, Martin, Lee, Johnson, Williamson, Betsy (Bloomfield), Torres, Mooney, Tyson (Griffin), Stonebridge (Easton).
Dagenham & R: Roberts; Goodwin, Griffiths (Ward), Blackett, Uddin, Saunders (Lettejallon), Marwa, Southam, Moore, Benson (Vickers), Kandol.
aet.

NORTHERN SECTION FIRST ROUND

Wednesday, 19 October 2005

Boston U (1) 2 *(White 28, Maylett 74)*
Huddersfield T (0) 1 *(Mirfin 68)* 1593
Boston U: Abbey; Canoville, White, Holland, Greaves, Futcher, Maylett (Thomas), Talbot, Joachim, Dudfield (Lee), Ross.
Huddersfield T: Rachubka; Hardy, Lloyd, Collins, McCombe, Clarke T, Worthington (Holdsworth), Hand, Abbott (Clarke N), Taylor-Fletcher (Mirfin), Young.

NORTHERN SECTION SECOND ROUND

Tuesday, 22 November 2005

Cambridge U (2) 3 *(Morrison 8, Onibuje 34, Hanlon 78)*
Doncaster R (1) 2 *(Fortune-West 40, 69)* 1435
Cambridge U: Howie; Bunce, Morrison, Duncan, Peters, Smith, Gleeson, Bridges, Onibuje, Westcarr, Hanlon.
Doncaster R: Richardson (Budtz); Mulligan, McDaid, Albrighton, Fenton, Green, Offiong (Guy), Hughes, Roberts N, Fortune-West, Forte (Nelthorpe).

Carlisle U (0) 2 *(Hawley 63, Holmes 67)*
Blackpool (0) 1 *(Harkins 62)* 2987
Carlisle U: Westwood; Arnison (Beharall), Murphy, Murray A, Gray, Livesey, Hackney (McClen), Holmes (McGill), Nade, Hawley, Lumsdon.
Blackpool: Pogliacomi; Warrender, Coid, Harkins (Wiles), Butler, Edwards, Donnelly (Doolan), Southern, Murphy, Wright (Parker), Morris.

Hereford U (1) 2 *(Carey-Bertram 14, Mkandawire 102)*
Port Vale (1) 1 *(Smith 45)* 1355
Hereford U: Mawson; Green (Travis), Jeannin, Pitman (Stansfield), Mkandawire, Beckwith, Brady, Stanley, Ipoua (Evans), Carey-Bertram, Purdie.
Port Vale: Brain; Togwell, James, Dinning, Pilkington, Sonner (Rowland), Cornes, Innes, Lowndes, Mulligan (Husbands), Smith (Cardle).
aet.

Morecambe (0) 0
Bradford C (0) 1 *(Brown 90)* 1649
Morecambe: Robinson (Davies); Walmsley, Howard, Brannan, Kempson, Bentley, Thompson, Perkins, Twiss, Carlton, Curtis (Dodgson).
Bradford C: Howarth; Holloway, Taylor, Kearney, Stewart, Bower, Morrison (Muirhead), Bridge-Wilkinson, Claridge (Brown), Cooke, Petta (Emanuel).

Rotherham U (1) 1 *(Evans 24)*
Macclesfield T (0) 2 *(Parkin 56, Sandwith 85)* 1646
Rotherham U: Cutler; Worrell, Hurst, McLaren, Gilchrist, Barker, Otsemobor (Hoskins), Monkhouse (Brogan), Newsham, Mullin, Evans.
Macclesfield T: Fettis; Teague (Beresford), Sandwith, Morley, Swailes, Navarro, Whitaker, Harsley, Townson, Parkin, McIntyre.

Tranmere R (1) 3 *(Facey 6, Harrison 67, Greenacre 74 (pen))*

Rochdale (2) 2 *(Tait 9, 40)* 2867

Tranmere R: Achterberg; Jennings (Dagnall), Roberts, Goodison, Jackson, Sharps, Harrison, Rankine, Facey, Greenacre, O'Leary.
Rochdale: Gilks; Brown, Goodall, Brisco, Griffiths, Boardman, Warner, Jones (Clarke), Lambert, Tait, Sturrock.

SOUTHERN SECTION SECOND ROUND

Tuesday, 22 November 2005

Barnet (0) 0

Milton Keynes D (2) 3 *(Wilbraham 9, Small 39, Smith 88)* 991

Barnet: Tynan; Batt (Devera), King, Lee, Yakubu, Charles, Bailey, Norville, Roache (Hatch), Bowditch, Strevens (Soares).
Milton Keynes D: Martin; Edds, Lewington, Crooks, Koo-Boothe, Mills, Kamara (McKoy), Smith, Wilbraham, Small (Quinn), Rizzo (Puncheon).

Gillingham (2) 2 *(Jarvis 23, 27)*

Wycombe W (2) 2 *(Griffin 39, 42 (pen))* 2111

Gillingham: Bullock; Clohessy (Corneille), Williams, Smith, Johnson, Cox, Crofts, Spiller (Jackman), Harris (Shields), Byfield, Jarvis.
Wycombe W: Turner; Senda, Martin (Easton), Burnell (Philo), Johnson, Williamson, Betsy, Torres (Anya), Dixon, Griffin, Bloomfield.
aet; Wycombe W won 3-1 on penalties.

Peterborough U (1) 2 *(Hand 11, Benjamin 55 (pen))*

Swindon T (0) 1 *(Roberts 68)* 959

Peterborough U: Harrison; St Ledger-Hall, Holden, Arber, Burton, Day, Semple (Newton), Carden, Willock, Benjamin, Hand.
Swindon T: Heaton; Jenkins, Nicholas, Ifil, O'Hanlon, Comyn-Platt, Heath (Holgate), Whalley (McDermott), Fallon, Bouazza, Roberts.

Swansea C (1) 4 *(Robinson 20, 65, Monk 76, Connor 89)*

Rushden & D (0) 0 5321

Swansea C: Murphy; Fisken, Austin, MacDonald, Monk, O'Leary (Tudur-Jones), Forbes, Martinez, Goodfellow, Connor, Robinson (Bond).
Rushden & D: Ruddy; Gier, Hawkins, McCafferty, Dempster, Gulliver, Burgess, Mills, Armstrong (Tomlin), O'Grady (Taylor), Kelly.

Walsall (0) 1 *(Fryatt 67)*

Bournemouth (0) 0 2031

Walsall: Murphy; Pead, Fox, Skora, Roper, Bennett, Westwood (Staunton), Demontagnac (Constable), Fryatt, Leitao, Larrosa (Taylor D).
Bournemouth: Moss; Hart, O'Connor, Purches (Stock), Young, Cooper, Foley-Sheridan, Rodrigues (Pitman), Hayter, Fletcher (Cooke), Surman.

Woking (1) 1

Cheltenham T (1) 2 1159

Abandoned due to fog.

NORTHERN SECTION SECOND ROUND

Wednesday, 23 November 2005

Boston U (0) 0

Kidderminster H (3) 3 *(Christie 26, 28, Blackwood 40)* 1131

Boston U: Abbey; Canoville, McCann, Holland (Rusk), Futcher, Ellender, Ross, Talbot, Whelan (Lee), Dudfield, Thomas (Maylett).
Kidderminster H: Lewis; Mullins, Burgess, Blackwood (Graves), Jackson, Hatswell, Penn, Pugh (Wilson), Christie (Thompson), Atieno, Heslop.

SOUTHERN SECTION SECOND ROUND

Wednesday, 23 November 2005

Colchester U (0) 3 *(Elokobi 57, Garcia 90, Danns 101)*

Northampton T (1) 2 *(Kirk 26, Bojic 67)* 1719

Colchester U: Gerken; Stockley, Elokobi (Yeates), Baldwin, Richards, Halford (Iwelumo), Izzet (Watson), Danns, Williams, Garcia, Duguid.
Northampton T: Poke; Bojic, Low (Crowe), Taylor, Doig, Chambers, Rowson, Hunt (Galbraith), McGleish, Kirk, Mendes (Jess).
aet.

Oxford U (1) 1 *(Sabin 27)*

Leyton Orient (0) 0 1521

Oxford U: Turley; Mansell, Robinson, Quinn, Roget, Willmott, Hackett (E'Beyer), Hargreaves, Sabin, Basham (Bradbury), Griffin.
Leyton Orient: Morris (Garner); Barnard (Demetriou), Palmer, Easton, Mackie, Carlisle, Hanson, McMahon, Steele, Ibehre (Alexander), Duncan.

Monday, 28 November 2005

Woking (1) 1 *(Blackman 18)*

Cheltenham T (0) 5 *(Gillespie 59, Victory 101, Wilson 112, 118, Armstrong 117)* 883

Woking: Davies; El-Salahi, Cockerill L (McAllister), Ruby, Watson (Murray), Aggrey, Evans, Selley, Rawle, Blackman (Richards), Cockerill S.
Cheltenham T: Higgs; Gill, Victory, McCann, Caines, Duff, Melligan (Wilson), Finnigan (Bird), Odejayi (Spencer), Gillespie, Armstrong.
aet.

NORTHERN QUARTER-FINAL

Tuesday, 13 December 2005

Macclesfield T (3) 4 *(Wijnhard 12, 45, Sandwith 34, Parkin 61)*

Cambridge U (1) 2 *(Bridges 17, Atkins 47)* 860

Macclesfield T: Fettis; Harsley, Sandwith, Morley, Teague, Navarro, Whitaker, Bullock, Parkin, Wijnhard, McIntyre (Swailes).
Cambridge U: Howie; Gleeson (Robbins), Morrison, Duncan (Onibuje), Peters, Quinton, Bridges (Porter), Hanlon, Atkins, Westcarr, Bunce.

NORTHERN SECTION SECOND ROUND

Tuesday, 13 December 2005

Halifax T (0) 1 *(Doughty 88)*

Scunthorpe U (1) 3 *(Sharp 9, Keogh 59, Johnson 77)* 1124

Halifax T: Butler; Ingram, Doughty, Foster, Atherton, Young, Midgley, Jacobs (Thompson), Forrest, Senior (Mansaram), Bowler (Killeen).
Scunthorpe U: Evans; Byrne, Ridley, Hinds, Butler (Goodwin), Baraclough, Taylor, MacKenzie, Keogh, Sharp (Johnson), Corden (Beagrie).

SOUTHERN QUARTER-FINAL

Tuesday, 13 December 2005

Swansea C (0) 3 *(Akinfenwa 94, 109, Robinson 99)*

Peterborough U (0) 1 *(Crow 93)* 5474

Swansea C: Murphy; Ricketts, Austin, O'Leary (Tudur-Jones), Monk, MacDonald (Martinez), Forbes, McLeod, Akinfenwa, Connor (Trundle), Robinson.
Peterborough U: Tyler; Holden, St Ledger-Hall, Arber, Burton, Huke (Plummer), Newton, Benjamin, Quinn (Semple), Willock (Crow), Carden■.
aet.

NORTHERN QUARTER-FINALS

Tuesday, 20 December 2005

Hereford U (2) 2 *(Stansfield 17, Mkandawire 44)*

Scunthorpe U (0) 0 1452

Hereford U: Mawson; Travis, Jeannin, Mkandawire, James (Beckwith), Pitman, Ferrell, Purdie, Stansfield (Evans), Ipoua (Brady), Williams.
Scunthorpe U: Evans; Goodwin, Ridley, Crosby (Ryan), Byrne, Baraclough, Taylor, MacKenzie, Keogh, Johnson (Torpey), Corden (Sharp).

Kidderminster H (1) 2 *(Christie 16, Penn 60)*

Bradford C (0) 1 *(Brown 70)* 1276

Kidderminster H: Lewis; Mullins, Hatswell, Flynn, Jackson, Fleming, Blackwood (Sheldon), Penn, Christie, Heslop, Thompson.
Bradford C: Ricketts; Edghill, Taylor, Kearney, Wetherall, Bower, Emanuel (Schumacher), Crooks■, Cadamarteri (Muirhead), Cooke, Petta (Brown).

Tranmere R (0) 0

Carlisle U (0) 0 3054

Tranmere R: Wilson; Linwood, Roberts, Tremarco (Whitmore), Jackson, Sharps, Jennings, Harrison, Facey, Davies, Aiston (Brown).
Carlisle U: Westwood; Arnison, Murphy, Billy, Gray (Hackney), Grand, McGill (Nade), Lumsdon, Holmes (Murray G), Hawley, Aranalde.
aet; Carlisle U won 11-10 on penalties.

SOUTHERN QUARTER-FINALS

Tuesday, 20 December 2005

Cheltenham T (1) 2 *(Gillespie 1, Duff 60)*

Oxford U (0) 1 *(Mansell 84)* 1825

Cheltenham T: Higgs; Gill, Armstrong, McCann, Caines, Duff, Melligan (Finnigan), Bird, Odejayi (Spencer), Gillespie (Guinan), Wilson.
Oxford U: Tardif; Stirling, Robinson, Quinn, Roget, Willmott, Mansell, E'Beyer (Davies), Roach (Basham), Sabin, Griffin (Hackett).

Milton Keynes D (0) 1 *(Mills 58)*

Colchester U (0) 2 *(Duguid 61, Danns 74)* 2649

Milton Keynes D: Martin; Edds, Lewington, Crooks (Baldock), Morgan, Mills, Rizzo, Small (Kamara), Wilbraham, McLeod, McKoy (Quinn).
Colchester U: Gerken; Stockley, Elokobi, Baldwin, Richards, King (Danns), Guy (Halford), Izzet, Williams, Garcia, Duguid.

Walsall (2) 3 *(Constable 17, Bennett 22, Leitao 88)*

Wycombe W (1) 2 *(Griffin 6, 83)* 2571

Walsall: Murphy; Pead, Bennett, Kinsella (Bradley), Roper, Gerrard, Taylor K, Standing, Fryatt, Leitao, Constable (Nicholls).
Wycombe W: Williams; Senda, Easton, Martin, Johnson, Williamson, Betsy, Philo (Torres), Mooney, Griffin, Bloomfield.

NORTHERN SEMI-FINALS

Tuesday, 24 January 2006

Carlisle U (0) 1 *(Murray G 87)*

Kidderminster H (0) 0 4432

Carlisle U: Westwood; Arnison, Murphy, Billy, Gray, Livesey, Rivers (Hackney), Lumsdon, Holmes (Murray G), Hawley, Aranalde.
Kidderminster H: Danby; Mullins, Harkness, Fleming, Jackson, Burgess, Russell (Francis), Penn (Howarth), Christie, Sheldon (Pugh), Blackwood.

Macclesfield T (2) 2 *(Whitaker 19, Harsley 45)*

Hereford U (0) 0 1315

Macclesfield T: Fettis; Harsley, Sandwith, Morley, Swailes, Navarro, Whitaker, Bullock, Townson (Miles), Wijnhard, McIntyre.
Hereford U: Mawson; Travis, Jeannin, Mkandawire, Beckwith, Pitman, Williams (Evans), Stanley, Ipoua, Carey-Bertram, Ferrell (Purdie).

SOUTHERN SEMI-FINALS

Tuesday, 24 January 2006

Cheltenham T (0) 0

Colchester U (1) 1 *(Garcia 21)* 2243

Cheltenham T: Higgs; Gill, Bell (Wylde), Bird, Caines, Townsend, Melligan (Armstrong), Finnigan, Spencer, Gillespie (Odejayi), Wilson.
Colchester U: Gerken; Stockley, Elokobi, King (White), Baldwin, Richards, Halford, Izzet, Williams, Garcia (Guy), Duguid.

Swansea C (1) 2 *(Knight 8, Robinson 83)*

Walsall (0) 2 *(Nicholls 69, Constable 85)* 6670

Swansea C: Gueret; Ricketts, Austin, Britton (Forbes), Monk, Tate, Robinson, Martinez, Knight, Trundle (Akinfenwa), McLeod (Way).
Walsall: Oakes; Pead, Fox, Smith G, Westwood, Gerrard, Wright, Standing, McDermott (Deakin), Demontagnac (Constable), Nicholls.
aet; Swansea C won 6-5 on penalties.

NORTHERN FINAL FIRST LEG

Tuesday, 21 February 2006

Carlisle U (1) 2 *(Hawley 20, Murphy 90)*

Macclesfield T (1) 1 *(Smart 9)* 5706

Carlisle U: Westwood; Arnison, Aranalde, Billy, Livesey, Murphy, Rivers (Hackney), Murray A, Holmes (Murray G), Hawley, Lumsdon.
Macclesfield T: Lee; Teague, Sandwith, Morley, Swailes, Smart, Whitaker, Harsley, Bullock, Wijnhard, McIntyre.

NORTHERN FINAL SECOND LEG

Tuesday, 7 March 2006

Macclesfield T (2) 3 *(Teague 4, McNeil 28, Townson 120)*

Carlisle U (1) 2 *(Hawley 42, Grand 109)* 3598

Macclesfield T: Fettis; Teague (Beresford), Sandwith, Morley, Swailes, Miles (Townson), Whitaker, Harsley, McNeil (Smart), Bullock, McIntyre.
Carlisle U: Westwood; Arnison, Aranalde, Billy, Livesey, Murphy (Grand), Hackney (McGill), Murray A, Holmes (Murray G), Hawley, Lumsdon.
aet.

SOUTHERN FINAL FIRST LEG

Tuesday, 7 March 2006

Swansea C (1) 1 *(Akinfenwa 40)*

Colchester U (0) 0 7285

Swansea C: Gueret; Ricketts (MacDonald), Tate, Britton, Monk, Way, Forbes, McLeod (Martinez), Akinfenwa, Trundle (Knight), Robinson.
Colchester U: Gerken; Stockley, Elokobi (Izzet), Brown, Chilvers, Watson, Duguid, Danns, Iwelumo, Williams (Guy), Garcia (Baldwin).

SOUTHERN FINAL SECOND LEG

Tuesday, 14 March 2006

Colchester U (0) 1 *(Danns 46)*

Swansea C (0) 2 *(Britton 52, Knight 56)* 3236

Colchester U: Gerken; Baldwin, White (Williams), Brown, Chilvers, Watson, Halford, Danns, Iwelumo, Yeates (Guy), Duguid.
Swansea C: Gueret; Ricketts, Tate, O'Leary, Monk, Lowe (Forbes), Britton, Martinez, Akinfenwa, Knight (Trundle), Robinson (Way).

FINAL (AT MILLENNIUM STADIUM)

Sunday, 2 April 2006

Carlisle U (1) 1 *(Murray A 40)*

Swansea C (1) 2 *(Trundle 3, Akinfenwa 81)* 42,028

Carlisle U: Westwood; Arnison (Grand), Aranalde, Billy, Gray, Livesey, Lumsdon, Murray A (Hackney), Holmes (Murray G), Hawley, Murphy.
Swansea C: Gueret; Ricketts, Tate, O'Leary (Knight), Monk, Lowe, Britton, Tudur-Jones, Akinfenwa, Trundle, Robinson (Martinez).
Referee: T. Leake (Lancashire).

FA CUP FINALS 1872–2006

1872 and 1874–92	Kennington Oval	1910	Replay at Everton
1873	Lillie Bridge	1911	Replay at Old Trafford
1886	Replay at Derby (Racecourse Ground)	1912	Replay at Bramall Lane
		1915	Old Trafford, Manchester
1893	Fallowfield, Manchester	1920–22	Stamford Bridge
1894	Everton	1923 to 2000	Wembley
1895–1914	Crystal Palace	1970	Replay at Old Trafford
1901	Replay at Bolton	2001 to date	Millennium Stadium, Cardiff

Year	*Winners*	*Runners-up*	*Score*
1872	Wanderers	Royal Engineers	1-0
1873	Wanderers	Oxford University	2-0
1874	Oxford University	Royal Engineers	2-0
1875	Royal Engineers	Old Etonians	2-0 (after 1-1 draw aet)
1876	Wanderers	Old Etonians	3-0 (after 1-1 draw aet)
1877	Wanderers	Oxford University	2-1 (aet)
1878	Wanderers*	Royal Engineers	3-1
1879	Old Etonians	Clapham R	1-0
1880	Clapham R	Oxford University	1-0
1881	Old Carthusians	Old Etonians	3-0
1882	Old Etonians	Blackburn R	1-0
1883	Blackburn Olympic	Old Etonians	2-1 (aet)
1884	Blackburn R	Queen's Park, Glasgow	2-1
1885	Blackburn R	Queen's Park, Glasgow	2-0
1886	Blackburn R†	WBA	2-0 (after 0-0 draw)
1887	Aston Villa	WBA	2-0
1888	WBA	Preston NE	2-1
1889	Preston NE	Wolverhampton W	3-0
1890	Blackburn R	The Wednesday	6-1
1891	Blackburn R	Notts Co	3-1
1892	WBA	Aston Villa	3-0
1893	Wolverhampton W	Everton	1-0
1894	Notts Co	Bolton W	4-1
1895	Aston Villa	WBA	1-0
1896	The Wednesday	Wolverhampton W	2-1
1897	Aston Villa	Everton	3-2
1898	Nottingham F	Derby Co	3-1
1899	Sheffield U	Derby Co	4-1
1900	Bury	Southampton	4-0
1901	Tottenham H	Sheffield U	3-1 (after 2-2 draw)
1902	Sheffield U	Southampton	2-1 (after 1-1 draw)
1903	Bury	Derby Co	6-0
1904	Manchester C	Bolton W	1-0
1905	Aston Villa	Newcastle U	2-0
1906	Everton	Newcastle U	1-0
1907	The Wednesday	Everton	2-1
1908	Wolverhampton W	Newcastle U	3-1
1909	Manchester U	Bristol C	1-0
1910	Newcastle U	Barnsley	2-0 (after 1-1 draw)
1911	Bradford C	Newcastle U	1-0 (after 0-0 draw)
1912	Barnsley	WBA	1-0 (aet, after 0-0 draw)
1913	Aston Villa	Sunderland	1-0
1914	Burnley	Liverpool	1-0
1915	Sheffield U	Chelsea	3-0
1920	Aston Villa	Huddersfield T	1-0 (aet)
1921	Tottenham H	Wolverhampton W	1-0
1922	Huddersfield T	Preston NE	1-0
1923	Bolton W	West Ham U	2-0
1924	Newcastle U	Aston Villa	2-0
1925	Sheffield U	Cardiff C	1-0
1926	Bolton W	Manchester C	1-0
1927	Cardiff C	Arsenal	1-0
1928	Blackburn R	Huddersfield T	3-1
1929	Bolton W	Portsmouth	2-0
1930	Arsenal	Huddersfield T	2-0
1931	WBA	Birmingham	2-1
1932	Newcastle U	Arsenal	2-1
1933	Everton	Manchester C	3-0
1934	Manchester C	Portsmouth	2-1
1935	Sheffield W	WBA	4-2
1936	Arsenal	Sheffield U	1-0
1937	Sunderland	Preston NE	3-1
1938	Preston NE	Huddersfield T	1-0 (aet)
1939	Portsmouth	Wolverhampton W	4-1
1946	Derby Co	Charlton Ath	4-1 (aet)
1947	Charlton Ath	Burnley	1-0 (aet)
1948	Manchester U	Blackpool	4-2
1949	Wolverhampton W	Leicester C	3-1
1950	Arsenal	Liverpool	2-0
1951	Newcastle U	Blackpool	2-0
1952	Newcastle U	Arsenal	1-0
1953	Blackpool	Bolton W	4-3
1954	WBA	Preston NE	3-2
1955	Newcastle U	Manchester C	3-1
1956	Manchester C	Birmingham C	3-1

Year	*Winners*	*Runners-up*	*Score*
1957	Aston Villa	Manchester U	2-1
1958	Bolton W	Manchester U	2-0
1959	Nottingham F	Luton T	2-1
1960	Wolverhampton W	Blackburn R	3-0
1961	Tottenham H	Leicester C	2-0
1962	Tottenham H	Burnley	3-1
1963	Manchester U	Leicester C	3-1
1964	West Ham U	Preston NE	3-2
1965	Liverpool	Leeds U	2-1 (aet)
1966	Everton	Sheffield W	3-2
1967	Tottenham H	Chelsea	2-1
1968	WBA	Everton	1-0 (aet)
1969	Manchester C	Leicester C	1-0
1970	Chelsea	Leeds U	2-1 (aet)
	(after 2-2 draw, after extra time)		
1971	Arsenal	Liverpool	2-1 (aet)
1972	Leeds U	Arsenal	1-0
1973	Sunderland	Leeds U	1-0
1974	Liverpool	Newcastle U	3-0
1975	West Ham U	Fulham	2-0
1976	Southampton	Manchester U	1-0
1977	Manchester U	Liverpool	2-1
1978	Ipswich T	Arsenal	1-0
1979	Arsenal	Manchester U	3-2
1980	West Ham U	Arsenal	1-0
1981	Tottenham H	Manchester C	3-2
	(after 1-1 draw, after extra time)		
1982	Tottenham H	QPR	1-0
	(after 1-1 draw, after extra time)		
1983	Manchester U	Brighton & HA	4-0
	(after 2-2 draw, after extra time)		
1984	Everton	Watford	2-0
1985	Manchester U	Everton	1-0 (aet)
1986	Liverpool	Everton	3-1
1987	Coventry C	Tottenham H	3-2 (aet)
1988	Wimbledon	Liverpool	1-0
1989	Liverpool	Everton	3-2 (aet)
1990	Manchester U	Crystal Palace	1-0
	(after 3-3 draw, after extra time)		
1991	Tottenham H	Nottingham F	2-1 (aet)
1992	Liverpool	Sunderland	2-0
1993	Arsenal	Sheffield W	2-1 (aet)
	(after 1-1 draw, after extra time)		
1994	Manchester U	Chelsea	4-0
1995	Everton	Manchester U	1-0
1996	Manchester U	Liverpool	1-0
1997	Chelsea	Middlesbrough	2-0
1998	Arsenal	Newcastle U	2-0
1999	Manchester U	Newcastle U	2-0
2000	Chelsea	Aston Villa	1-0
2001	Liverpool	Arsenal	2-1
2002	Arsenal	Chelsea	2-0
2003	Arsenal	Southampton	1-0
2004	Manchester U	Millwall	3-0
2005	Arsenal	Manchester U	0-0 (aet)
	(Arsenal won 5-4 on penalties)		
2006	Liverpool	West Ham U	3-3 (aet)
	(Liverpool won 3-1 on penalties)		

** Won outright, but restored to the Football Association. † A special trophy was awarded for third consecutive win.*

FA CUP WINS

Manchester U 11, Arsenal 10, Tottenham H 8, Aston Villa 7, Liverpool 7, Blackburn R 6, Newcastle U 6, Everton 5, The Wanderers 5, WBA 5, Bolton W 4, Manchester C 4, Sheffield U 4, Wolverhampton W 4, Chelsea 3, Sheffield W 3, West Ham U 3, Bury 2, Nottingham F 2, Old Etonians 2, Preston NE 2, Sunderland 2, Barnsley 1, Blackburn Olympic 1, Blackpool 1, Bradford C 1, Burnley 1, Cardiff C 1, Charlton Ath 1, Clapham R 1, Coventry C 1, Derby Co 1, Huddersfield T 1, Ipswich T 1, Leeds U 1, Notts Co 1, Old Carthusians 1, Oxford University 1, Portsmouth 1, Royal Engineers 1, Southampton 1, Wimbledon 1.

APPEARANCES IN FINALS

Arsenal 17, Manchester U 17, Liverpool 13, Newcastle U 13, Everton 12, Aston Villa 10, WBA 10, Tottenham H 9, Blackburn R 8, Manchester C 8, Wolverhampton W 8, Bolton W 7, Chelsea 7, Preston NE 7, Old Etonians 6, Sheffield U 6, Sheffield W 6, Huddersfield T 5, *The Wanderers 5, West Ham U 5, Derby Co 4, Leeds U 4, Leicester C 4, Oxford University 4, Royal Engineers 4, Southampton 4, Sunderland 4, Blackpool 3, Burnley 3, Nottingham F 3, Portsmouth 3, Barnsley 2, Birmingham C 2, *Bury 2, Cardiff C 2, Charlton Ath 2, Clapham R 2, Notts Co 2, Queen's Park (Glasgow) 2, *Blackburn Olympic 1, *Bradford C 1, Brighton & HA 1, Bristol C 1, *Coventry C 1, Crystal Palace 1, Fulham 1, *Ipswich T 1, Luton T 4, Middlesbrough 1, Millwall 1, *Old Carthusians 1, QPR 1, Watford 1, *Wimbledon 1.
** Denotes undefeated.*

APPEARANCES IN SEMI-FINALS

Arsenal 25, Manchester U 24, Everton 23, Liverpool 22, Aston Villa 19, WBA 19, Blackburn R 17, Newcastle U 17, Tottenham H 17, Chelsea 16, Sheffield W 16, Wolverhampton W 14, Bolton W 13, Derby Co 13, Sheffield U 13, Nottingham F 12, Sunderland 12, Southampton 11, Manchester C 10, Preston NE 10, Birmingham C 9, Burnley 8, Leeds U 8, Leicester C 8, Huddersfield T 7, West Ham U 7, Old Etonians 6, Fulham 6, Oxford University 6, Notts Co 5, Portsmouth 5, The Wanderers 5, Luton T 4, Millwall 4, Queen's Park (Glasgow) 4, Royal Engineers 4, Watford 4, Blackpool 3, Cardiff C 3, Clapham R 3, Crystal Palace (professional club) 3, Ipswich T 3, Middlesbrough 3, Norwich C 3, Old Carthusians 3, Oldham Ath 3, Stoke C 3, The Swifts 3, Barnsley 2, Blackburn Olympic 2, Bristol C 2, Bury 2, Charlton Ath 2, Grimsby T 2, Swansea T 2, Swindon T 2, Wimbledon 2, Bradford C 1, Brighton & HA 1, Cambridge University 1, Chesterfield 1, Coventry C 1, Crewe Alex 1, Crystal Palace (amateur club) 1, Darwen 1, Derby Junction 1, Glasgow R 1, Hull C 1, Marlow 1, Old Harrovians 1, Orient 1, Plymouth Arg 1, Port Vale 1, QPR 1, Reading 1, Shropshire W 1, Wycombe W 1, York C 1.

THE FA CUP 2005–06

PRELIMINARY AND QUALIFYING ROUNDS

EXTRA PRELIMINARY ROUND

Newcastle Benfield (Bay Plastics) v Bedlington Terriers	2-4
Bacup Borough v Pickering Town	0-5
Jarrow Roofing Boldon CA v Sheffield	0-4
Blackpool Mechanics v Newcastle Blue Star	1-2
Nelson v Retford United	2-4
Esh Winning v Ashington	4-4, 0-1
Prudhoe Town v Horden CW	1-3
Skelmersdale United v Liversedge	1-0
Curzon Ashton v Darwen	2-1
Oldham Town v Morpeth Town	1-0
Guisborough Town v Great Harwood Town	1-1, 3-3
Great Harwood Town won 4-2 on penalties.	
Cheadle Town v Abbey Hey	3-2
Brandon United v Billingham Synthonia	0-5
Tow Law Town v Squires Gate	2-0
Formby v Consett	1-1, 1-5
Winsford United v Alsager Town	1-1, 1-0
Flixton v Hebburn Town	1-2
Rossington Main v Garforth Town	1-1, 0-3
Cammell Laird v West Allotment Celtic	4-1
West Auckland Town v Shildon	2-1
Winterton Rangers v North Shields	1-0
Studley v Oadby Town	1-3
Sutton Town v Loughborough Dynamo	5-1
Stourbridge v Glossop North End	3-0
Borrowash Victoria v Ford Sports Daventry	1-1, 2-1
Long Eaton United v Quorn	2-1
Congleton Town v Romulus	2-0
Norton United v Alvechurch	1-0
Shirebrook Town v Teversal	2-3
Oldbury United v Racing Club Warwick	2-1
Witham Town v Hadleigh United	1-0
Hullbridge Sports v Wisbech Town	2-5
Chalfont St Peter v Buckingham Town	1-0
Brook House v Leiston	1-1, 3-1
Wembley v St Neots Town	0-2
Aylesbury Vale v Kirkley	2-2, 3-0
Ware v Sporting Bengal United	2-0
Concord Rangers v Kingsbury Town	0-1
Harpenden Town v Sawbridgeworth Town	2-1
Soham Town Rangers v Yaxley	2-1
Stanway Rovers v Norwich United	4-1
Fakenham Town v Long Buckby	2-0
Gorleston v North Greenford United	2-4
Haringey Borough v Felixstowe & Walton United	0-3
Bowers & Pitsea v Stotfold	2-2, 3-3
Stotfold won 4-2 on penalties.	
London APSA v Halstead Town	0-2
Broxbourne Borough V&E v Holmer Green	1-4
Eton Manor v Leverstock Green	0-1
St Margaretsbury v St Ives Town	2-1
Wootton Blue Cross v Desborough Town	2-0
Romford v Waltham Abbey	1-3
Biggleswade United v Haverhill Rovers	6-0
Harefield United v Langford	2-3
Southend Manor v Woodford United	0-1
Woodbridge Town v Lowestoft Town	3-3, 0-5
Saffron Walden Town v Flackwell Heath	1-1, 1-3
Erith Town v Hassocks	0-3
Thamesmead Town v Abingdon United	2-4
Saltdean United v Wantage Town	0-0, 2-0
AFC Totton v Milton United	5-0
Eastbourne United v Ash United	1-2
Hythe Town v Raynes Park Vale	4-1
Moneyfields v Abingdon Town	6-1
Fareham Town v Selsey	0-0, 2-3
Gosport Borough v Sandhurst Town	6-1
East Grinstead Town v VCD Athletic	0-7
AFC Newbury v Farnham Town	2-2, 3-2
Erith & Belvedere v Hamble ASSC	4-2
Lancing v Whitehawk	1-2
Westfield v Godalming Town	1-2
Chichester City United v East Preston	1-2
Sidley United v Pagham	3-1
Sevenoaks Town v Chertsey Town	4-2
Andover v Didcot Town	4-4, 0-2
Hungerford Town v North Leigh	0-4
Horsham YMCA v Hailsham Town	1-0
Three Bridges v Shoreham	2-0
Westbury United v Newquay	2-1
Willand Rovers v Hamworthy United	0-1
Tuffley Rovers v Elmore	0-0, 0-1
Bishop's Cleeve v Corsham Town	1-0
Hallen v Porthleven	3-0
Calne Town v Shortwood United	0-2
Minehead v Almondsbury Town	1-2
Slimbridge v Wimborne Town	0-1
Odd Down v Portland United	2-1

PRELIMINARY ROUND

Bridlington Town v Whitley Bay	2-2, 0-4
Tow Law Town v Padiham	1-3
Colne v Chadderton	1-2
Warrington Town v Penrith	2-2, 2-1
Ramsbottom United v Marske United	3-1
Thornaby v Peterlee Newtown	3-0
Hebburn Town v Winterton Rangers	1-1, 2-0
Cheadle Town v Bamber Bridge	2-1
Pontefract Collieries v Bishop Auckland	2-3
Eccleshill United v Chester-le-Street Town	1-2
Selby Town v Billingham Town	1-3
Skelmersdale United v Colwyn Bay	2-0
Crook Town v St Helens Town	0-3
Curzon Ashton v Garforth Town	1-0
Rossendale United v Sunderland Nissan	1-1, 4-1
Norton & Stockton Ancients v Great Harwood Town	0-4
Spennymoor Town v Consett	0-2
Durham City v Brodsworth MW	5-0
Seaham Red Star v Atherton Collieries	2-0
Cammell Laird v Alnwick Town	6-0
Brigg Town v Holker Old Boys	4-0
Retford United v Parkgate	4-3
Horden CW v Kendal Town	1-2
Tadcaster Albion v Chorley	2-2, 0-2
Oldham Town v Hall Road Rangers	2-0
Pickering Town v Ashington	2-2, 2-1
Washington v Stocksbridge Park Steels	0-0, 1-1
Stocksbridge Park Steels won 4-2 on penalties.	
Thackley v South Shields	2-0
Newcastle Blue Star v Hallam	2-0
Sheffield v Mossley	2-2, 0-1
Yorkshire Amateur v Bedlington Terriers	2-1
Glasshoughton Welfare v Woodley Sports	0-2
Maine Road v Armthorpe Welfare	0-2
Billingham Synthonia v Fleetwood Town	2-0
Ossett Albion v Dunston FB	0-3
Atherton LR v Goole	1-1, 0-2
Whickham v West Auckland Town	1-5
Harrogate Railway v Clitheroe	1-2
New Mills v Salford City	0-2
Trafford v Silsden	3-1
Northallerton Town v Winsford United	4-0
(Abandoned 80 minutes; Winsford United reduced to six players).	
Willenhall Town v Blackstones	1-0
Shepshed Dynamo v Carlton Town	4-1
Newcastle Town v Buxton	1-1, 2-1
Chasetown v Causeway United	2-0
Congleton Town v Corby Town	1-2
Solihull Borough v Eccleshall	2-0
Westfields v Sutton Coldfield Town	3-0
Rushall Olympic v Gedling Town	0-2
Bromsgrove Rovers v Bourne Town	4-1
Glapwell v Barwell	3-1
Spalding United v Staveley MW	0-1
Nantwich Town v Gresley Rovers	3-1
Long Eaton United v Boston Town	4-2
Coalville Town v Borrowash Victoria	3-0
Deeping Rangers v Norton United	0-0, 0-1
Stourport Swifts v Stratford Town	1-2
Oldbury United v Stone Dominoes	4-0
Bedworth United v Rocester	3-1
Oadby Town v Stamford	3-3, 1-0
Malvern Town v Mickelover Sports	4-3
Cradley Town v Biddulph Victoria	2-1
Holbeach United v Boldmere St Michaels	0-2
Teversal v Pegasus Juniors	1-1, 2-3
Leamington v Sutton Town	0-0, 2-2
Leamington won 9-8 on penalties.	
Lincoln Moorlands v Eastwood Town	0-0, 2-3
Belper Town v Leek CSOB	1-0
South Normanton Athletic v Arnold Town	1-0
Stourbridge v Kidsgrove Athletic	2-2, 2-5
Ilford v Brackley Town	0-2
Long Melford v AFC Sudbury	0-1
Wootton Blue Cross v Barton Rovers	1-1, 1-4
Ware v Northampton Spencer	2-4
AFC Hornchurch v Chalfont St Peter	0-0, 2-1
Barkingside v Leverstock Green	2-2, 4-3
Harlow Town v Newport Pagnell Town	4-2
Uxbridge v Great Wakering Rovers	2-3
Tiptree United v Potton United	2-3
Bury Town v Ely City	1-1, 8-0
Needham Market v Diss Town	2-5
Marlow v Arlesey Town	2-3
Welwyn Garden City v Aylesbury Vale	2-0
St Neots Town v Hemel Hempstead Town	1-4
Harwich & Parkeston v Holmer Green	2-2, 5-2
Aveley v Kingsbury Town	5-1
Thame United v Brentwood Town	0-1
Fakenham Town v Waltham Forest	1-4

Berkhamsted Town v Newmarket Town 2-0
Mildenhall Town v Potters Bar Town 3-1
Stotfold v Clapton 1-2
Barking & East Ham United v St Margaretsbury 1-1, 0-2
Leighton Town v Wroxham 1-1, 1-4
Soham Town Rangers v Enfield Town 1-2
Cogenhoe United v Hanwell Town 4-1
March Town United v Harpenden Town 4-1
Stowmarket Town v Ipswich Wanderers 2-2, 1-3
Oxhey Jets v Lowestoft Town 1-2
Royston Town v Clacton Town 1-2
Burnham Ramblers v Flackwell Heath 4-3
Southall v Enfield 5-0
Felixstowe & Walton United v Dunstable Town 1-2
Tilbury v Wivenhoe Town 0-3
London Colney v Rothwell Town 2-3
Raunds Town v Beaconsfield SYCOB 0-2
Woodford United v Wisbech Town 1-0
Boreham Wood v Dereham Town 3-0
Great Yarmouth Town v Stanway Rovers 2-3
Henley Town v Witham Town 2-4
Tring Athletic v Biggleswade United 1-2
North Greenford United v Brook House 1-6
Waltham Abbey v Wingate & Finchley 6-2
Stansted v Langford 2-1
Hertford Town v Ruislip Manor 1-2
Halstead Town v Cornard United 7-0
Lymington & New Milton v Dover Athletic 0-2
Mile Oak v Camberley Town 1-1
Tie awarded to Camberley Town; Mile Oak fielded an ineligible player.
Horsham YMCA v Corinthian Casuals 2-0
Moneyfields v Rye & Iden United 4-0
Lordswood v Saltdean United 3-2
Carterton v Didcot Town 0-3
Kingstonian v Ringmer 2-1
Tonbridge Angels v Horsham 3-1
Ashford Town v Slade Green 3-1
Cobham v Egham Town 0-2
Reading Town v Eastbourne Town 1-3
Molesey v Burgess Hill Town 2-4
Bashley v Hythe Town 4-0
Ash United v Leatherhead 1-1, 2-3
Herne Bay v Sevenoaks Town 3-2
Burnham v Selsey 2-0
Sittingbourne v Chessington & Hook United 2-4
Erith & Belvedere v Tooting & Mitcham United 1-2
Croydon Athletic v Redhill 4-2
Oxford City v Newport (IW) 3-2
East Preston v Cowes Sports 0-1
Chatham Town v North Leigh 2-0
Metropolitan Police v Bracknell Town 0-0, 2-0
VCD Athletic v Hastings United 0-2
Croydon v Frimley Green 1-1, 2-0
Mole Valley (Predators) v Gosport Borough 0-8
Winchester City v Maidstone United 0-3
Sidlesham v Bedfont 1-2
Thatcham Town v Cove 3-0
Chipstead v Brockenhurst 4-2
Whitstable Town v Fleet Town 3-3, 1-2
Godalming Town v Dulwich Hamlet 1-2
Ashford Town (Middlesex) v Whyteleafe 3-1
Merstham v Ramsgate 1-4
Steyning Town v Cray Wanderers 0-6
BAT Sports v Abingdon United 0-3
Dartford v Dorking 1-2
Epsom & Ewell v AFC Newbury 6-1
Hillingon Borough v Hassocks 0-0, 1-2
Banstead Athletic v Alton Town 1-0
Whitehawk v AFC Totton 0-2
Three Bridges v Walton Casuals 1-0
Wick v Arundel 1-1, 2-1
Littlehampton Town v Tunbridge Wells 1-1, 2-2
Tunbridge Wells won 16-15 on penalties.
Sidley United v Deal Town 1-1, 1-2
Elmore v Torrington 2-0
Shortwood United v Bodmin Town 2-3
Liskeard Athletic v Brislington 2-0
Melksham Town v Westbury United 2-2, 3-2
Hamworthy United v Backwell United 4-0
Frome Town v St Blazey 0-0
Tie awarded to St Blazey; Frome Town unable to fulfil the tie.
Hallen v Swindon Supermarine 1-3
Almondsbury Town v Cinderford Town 3-5
Penzance v Street 2-2, 0-0
Penzance won 4-2 on penalties.
Bemerton Heath Harlequins v Ilfracombe Town 1-0
Chard Town v Wimborne Town 0-0, 0-2
Shepton Mallet v Bournemouth 0-2
Taunton Town v Bristol Manor Farm 1-0
Highworth Town v Welton Rovers 1-0
Bridgwater Town v Paulton Rovers 0-1
Barnstaple Town v Clevedon United 4-1
Odd Down v Exmouth Town 3-2
Bitton v Dawlish Town 2-1
Witney United v Clevedon Town 0-0, 2-3
Fairford Town v Devizes Town 0-0, 3-0
Christchurch v Bishop Sutton 5-0
Bishop's Cleeve v Bideford 3-1
Bridport v Falmouth Town 0-3

FIRST QUALIFYING ROUND

Oldham Town v Great Harwood Town 1-2
Wakefield & Emley v Blyth Spartans 1-2
Armthorpe Welfare v Mossley 3-1
Goole v Clitheroe 5-3
Billingham Synthonia v Retford United 4-2
Trafford v Yorkshire Amateur 4-1
Kendal Town v Witton Albion 2-3
Durham City v Hebburn Town 0-2
Runcorn FC Halton v Skelmersdale United 2-3
Curzon Ashton v Chester-le-Street Town 0-2
Burscough v Ashton United 3-2
Pickering Town v Farsley Celtic 1-2
Cammell Laird v Radcliffe Borough 2-1
Stocksbridge Park Steels v Ossett Town 1-3
Chorley v Bishop Auckland 0-0, 1-2
Dunston FB v Thackley 4-1
Woodley Sports v Prescot Cables 2-4
Seaham Red Star v Consett 2-1
Bradford Park Avenue v Padiham 1-1, 4-1
Marine v Cheadle Town 4-0
St Helens Town v Northallerton Town 3-3, 3-2
Frickley Athletic v Chadderton 2-0
Gateshead v Warrington Town 4-0
Guiseley v Salford City 0-1
Rossendale United v Billingham Town 2-2, 3-2
Thornaby v West Auckland Town 4-3
Newcastle Blue Star v Whitby Town 1-2
North Ferriby United v Brigg Town 3-1
Whitley Bay v Ramsbottom United 1-2
Willenhall Town v Malvern Town 1-1, 0-1
Bedworth United v Solihull Borough 1-1, 2-3
Stratford Town v Glapwell 1-3
Bromsgrove Rovers v Newcastle Town 2-0
Ilkeston Town v Coalville Town 1-0
Kidsgrove Athletic v Leamington 0-1
Staveley MW v Norton United 2-1
Halesowen Town v South Normanton Athletic 5-3
Leek Town v Long Eaton United 7-0
Westfields v Belper Town 1-2
Oadby Town v Oldbury United 3-3, 3-0
Boldmere St Michaels v Nantwich Town 0-3
Matlock Town v Pegasus Juniors 4-0
Cradley Town v Eastwood Town 0-6
Grantham Town v Lincoln United 4-0
Chasetown v Gedling Town 2-1
AFC Telford United v Rugby Town 1-1, 3-2
Corby Town v Shepshed Dynamo 2-0
Chesham United v Brackley Town 0-1
St Margaretsbury v Billericay Town 0-0, 3-2
Northwood v March Town United 3-0
Rothwell Town v Wivenhoe Town 1-3
Welwyn Garden City v Beaconsfield SYCOB 3-2
Ruislip Manor v Redbridge 1-1, 1-2
Wroxham v Diss Town 2-0
Woodford United v Harwich & Parkeston 5-0
East Thurrock United v Harrow Borough 1-2
Hampton & Richmond Borough v Witham Town 3-0
Halstead Town v Lowestoft Town 1-3
Aveley v Burnham Ramblers 1-2
Brentwood Town v Great Wakering Rovers 3-1
Barkingside v Maldon Town 1-6
Brook House v Clacton Town 9-1
Bedford Town v AFC Sudbury 2-2, 1-2
AFC Hornchurch v Stansted 2-0
Cogenhoe United v Clapton 4-2
Heybridge Swifts v Arlesey Town 1-0
Stanway Rovers v Wealdstone 0-0, 0-3
Chelmsford City v Harlow Town 1-1, 1-0
Ipswich Wanderers v Hemel Hempstead Town 1-1, 1-4
Potton United v Leyton 0-1
Hitchin Town v Waltham Forest 4-1
Enfield Town v Waltham Abbey 3-0
Bury Town v Boreham Wood 2-2, 2-4
Northampton Spencer v Aylesbury United 1-2
Staines Town v Dunstable Town 1-1, 1-0
Hendon v Biggleswade United 6-0
Southall v Mildenhall Town 6-3
Banbury United v King's Lynn 2-1
Berkhamsted Town v Barton Rovers 3-0
Cheshunt v Braintree Town 1-2
Slough Town v Oxford City 4-1
Camberley Town v Epsom & Ewell 1-0
Cray Wanderers v Kingstonian 4-1
Fleet Town v Thatcham Town 3-2
Lordswood v AFC Totton 1-2
Didcot Town v Herne Bay 0-0, 6-2
Bashley v Dover Athletic 0-1
Burgess Hill Town v Walton & Hersham 0-4
Abingdon United v Dulwich Hamlet 1-1, 2-3
Banstead Athletic v Moneyfields 3-0
Three Bridges v Chipstead 1-3
Croydon Athletic v Ramsgate 1-3
Bedfont v Bromley 1-4
Horsham YMCA v Croydon 1-2

AFC Wimbledon v Ashford Town (Middlesex) 2-2, 2-0
Ashford Town v Windsor & Eton 0-3
Maidstone United v Burnham 1-2
Folkestone Invicta v Egham Town 3-1
Chessington & Hook United v Hassocks 0-3
Wick v Worthing 0-4
Eastbourne Town v Gosport Borough 1-2
Margate v Cowes Sports 4-0
Dorking v Deal Town 1-3
Fisher Athletic v Tooting & Mitcham United 6-2
Chatham Town v Leatherhead 3-4
Metropolitan Police v Tunbridge Wells 2-0
Hastings United v Tonbridge Angels 3-3, 1-2
Swindon Supermarine v Melksham Town 1-0
Fairford Town v Bishop's Cleeve 0-1
Liskeard Athletic v Bitton 1-1, 0-1
Cirencester Town v Wimborne Town 5-3
Bath City v Cinderford Town 1-0
Clevedon Town v Salisbury City 1-1, 2-4
Taunton Town v Odd Down 3-0
Paulton Rovers v Barnstaple Town 3-2
Chippenham Town v Falmouth Town 4-0
Penzance v Bemerton Heath Harlequins 0-1
Gloucester City v Christchurch 0-0, 0-3
Tiverton Town v Evesham United 1-1, 1-0
Yate Town v Bodmin Town 2-0
Merthyr Tydfil v St Blazey 3-2
Bournemouth v Mangotsfield United 1-1, 0-7
Hamworthy United v Team Bath 0-2
Highworth Town v Elmore 2-1

SECOND QUALIFYING ROUND

Consett v Ossett Town 1-5
Billingham Synthonia v North Ferriby United 0-3
Blyth Spartans v Prescot Cables 1-0
Armthorpe Welfare v Rossendale United 0-2
Dunston FB v Thornaby 1-1, 1-2
Trafford v Whitby Town 1-1, 0-6
Harrogate Town v Great Harwood Town 3-0
Chester-le-Street Town v Leigh RMI 1-3
Marine v Cammell Laird 1-1, 1-3
Worksop Town v Witton Albion 0-1
Skelmersdale United v Bishop Auckland 0-0, 2-1
Hyde United v Lancaster City 2-1
St Helens Town v Alfreton Town 0-2
Vauxhall Motors v Ramsbottom United 2-0
Barrow v Hebburn Town 5-1
Farsley Celtic v Bradford Park Avenue 2-0
Gainsborough Trinity v Goole 2-2, 2-1
Frickley Athletic v Northwich Victoria 1-4
Droylsden v Burscough 1-2
Salford City v Gateshead 1-0
Stalybridge Celtic v Workington 0-0, 1-2
Bromsgrove Rovers v Hinckley United 3-1
Leamington v Oadby Town 2-2, 1-1
Leamington won 4-2 on penalties.
Chasetown v Belper Town 3-3, 4-1
Brackley Town v Banbury United 1-1, 2-5
Eastwood Town v Cambridge City 1-1, 1-3
Nuneaton Borough v AFC Telford United 3-1
Matlock Town v Corby Town 2-0
Glapwell v Halesowen Town 0-1
Redditch United v Woodford United 1-1, 2-2
Woodford United won 10-9 on penalties.
Malvern Town v Histon 1-4
Hednesford Town v Moor Green 2-0
Leek Town v Grantham Town 1-0
Kettering Town v Stafford Rangers 1-0
Cogenhoe United v Staveley MW 3-2
Solihull Borough v Ilkeston Town 3-0
Nantwich Town v Hucknall Town 0-1
Thurrock v Hemel Hempstead Town 3-2
Boreham Wood v Welling United 0-2
Wivenhoe Town v Heybridge Swifts 1-4
Bognor Regis Town v Basingstoke Town 1-1, 1-2
Yeading v Maidenhead United 3-0
Hendon v Metropolitan Police 0-0, 0-1
AFC Hornchurch v Worthing 1-4
Burnham v Lowestoft Town 1-1, 1-1
Burnham won 4-2 on penalties.
Bromley v Chipstead 2-1
Staines Town v Croydon 1-1, 2-1
Redbridge v Eastbourne Borough 2-2, 1-5
Deal Town v Hitchin Town 1-3
Chelmsford City v Dover Athletic 1-0
AFC Wimbledon v Walton & Hersham 0-3
Cray Wanderers v Camberley Town 4-1
Leyton v Lewes 0-1
St Margaretsbury v Folkestone Invicta 0-1
Braintree Town v Didcot Town 2-0
Brentwood Town v Windsor & Eton 1-2
Wroxham v Slough Town 2-0
Fisher Athletic v Tonbridge Angels 2-3
Northwood v Aylesbury United 0-0, 0-2
Margate v Carshalton Athletic 1-0
Hayes v Brook House 1-1, 4-0
Welwyn Garden City v AFC Sudbury 4-2
Hassocks v Dulwich Hamlet 0-1
Ramsgate v Southall 1-0
Farnborough Town v Berkhamsted Town 3-0
Enfield Town v St Albans City 1-1, 0-3
Sutton United v Maldon Town 2-0
Banstead Athletic v Wealdstone 1-4
Harrow Borough v Burnham Ramblers 2-1
Hampton & Richmond Borough v Leatherhead 1-1, 1-2
Fleet Town v Bishop's Stortford 0-2
Highworth Town v Tiverton Town 1-7
Yate Town v Salisbury City 0-2
Christchurch v Cirencester Town 0-2
Worcester City v Bemerton Heath Harlequins 7-0
Taunton Town v Merthyr Tydfil 1-1, 1-2
Gosport Borough v Bath City 3-4
Mangotsfield United v Swindon Supermarine 4-2
Bishop's Cleeve v Bitton 3-0
Dorchester Town v Team Bath 4-2
Weston-Super-Mare v Weymouth 2-2, 0-1
Chippenham Town v Newport County 4-0
AFC Totton v Paulton Rovers 2-1
Eastleigh v Havant & Waterlooville 0-0, 1-4

THIRD QUALIFYING ROUND

Northwich Victoria v North Ferriby United 1-0
Vauxhall Motors v Skelmersdale United 4-3
Leigh RMI v Gainsborough Trinity 1-1, 1-2
Rossendale United v Blyth Spartans 0-1
Leek Town v Thornaby 2-1
Matlock Town v Ossett Town 3-6
Harrogate Town v Witton Albion 2-0
Hucknall Town v Cammell Laird 2-2, 1-0
Alfreton Town v Whitby Town 2-1
Burscough v Workington 2-0
Salford City v Farsley Celtic 0-1
Hyde United v Barrow 2-3
Thurrock v Solihull Borough 1-0
Banbury United v Hednesford Town 3-4
Leamington v Woodford United 2-0
Cogenhoe United v Chasetown 1-1, 3-4
Hayes v Bishop's Stortford 2-0
Wroxham v Aylesbury United 1-1, 2-4
Cambridge City v Hitchin Town 4-1
Heybridge Swifts v Braintree Town 1-1, 1-3
Harrow Borough v Welling United 0-1
Wealdstone v Burnham 2-4
Halesowen Town v Bromsgrove Rovers 0-2
Histon v Welwyn Garden City 2-1
St Albans City v Kettering Town 0-0, 0-4
Nuneaton Borough v Chelmsford City 1-1, 2-1
Bishop's Cleeve v AFC Totton 1-1, 4-0
Metropolitan Police v Eastbourne Borough 3-3, 2-3
Bromley v Mangotsfield United 0-0, 1-0
Worcester City v Tonbridge Angels 3-0
Cirencester Town v Havant & Waterlooville 2-1
Worthing v Basingstoke Town 2-4
Yeading v Dorchester Town 1-1, 2-3
Merthyr Tydfil v Salisbury City 2-1
Folkestone Invicta v Staines Town 2-0
Tiverton Town v Windsor & Eton 2-1
Leatherhead v Farnborough Town 0-2
Chippenham Town v Sutton United 1-0
Ramsgate v Walton & Hersham 1-0
Margate v Cray Wanderers 0-3
Lewes v Dulwich Hamlet 1-0
Weymouth v Bath City 1-0

FOURTH QUALIFYING ROUND

Harrogate Town v Scarborough 1-0
Tamworth v Altrincham 3-1
Southport v Kidderminster Harriers 1-0
Hucknall Town v Burscough 0-0, 2-6
Blyth Spartans v Chasetown 2-2, 0-1
Northwich Victoria v Barrow 4-1
Gainsborough Trinity v York City 0-4
Ossett Town v Leamington 2-4
Accrington Stanley v Worcester City 1-1, 2-3
Hednesford Town v Vauxhall Motors 3-0
Halifax Town v Farsley Celtic 2-0
Burton Albion v Leek Town 2-0
Hereford United v Alfreton Town 0-0, 1-1
Hereford United won 4-3 on penalties.
Bromsgrove Rovers v Morecambe 0-2
Crawley Town v Braintree Town 0-1
Canvey Island v Burnham 1-1, 1-2
Kettering Town v Gravesend & Northfleet 3-0
Dorchester Town v Welling United 1-2
Bromley v Aldershot Town 0-1
Histon v Hayes 3-1
Grays Athletic v Cray Wanderers 2-0
Nuneaton Borough v Tiverton Town 0-0, 1-0
Exeter City v Stevenage Borough 0-1
Woking v Thurrock 3-0
Basingstoke Town v Chippenham Town 0-1
Cambridge City v Lewes 2-1
Merthyr Tydfil v Farnborough Town 2-0
Aylesbury United v Folkestone Invicta 0-2
Forest Green Rovers v Dagenham & Redbridge 2-3
Ramsgate v Cirencester Town 3-0
Weymouth v Cambridge United 2-1
Bishop's Cleeve v Eastbourne Borough 0-1

THE FA CUP 2005–06

COMPETITION PROPER

▪ *Denotes player sent off.*

FIRST ROUND

Friday, 4 November 2005

Cambridge C (0) 0

Hereford U (0) 1 *(Brady 78)* 1116

Cambridge C: Naisbitt; Pope, Langston, Simpson J (Southon), Chaffey, Fuff, Dobson (Gash), Molesley, Simpson R, Booth, Binns.
Hereford U: Mawson; Green, Jeannin, Pitman, Mkandawire, James, Brady, Stanley, Williams (Evans), Ipoua, Purdie.

Merthyr T (1) 1 *(Williams S 29)*

Walsall (2) 2 *(Fryatt 17 (pen), Kinsella 25)* 3046

Merthyr T: Morris; Keddle (Williams D), Williams S, Fowler, Needs, Eckhardt, Griffiths (Shephard), Cochlin, Welsh (Somers), Steins, Dorrian.
Walsall: Gilmartin; Staunton, Fox, Kinsella, Roper, Bennett, Gerrard, Broad, Fryatt, Leitao, Taylor K.

Port Vale (1) 2 *(Husbands 20, Constantine 65)*

Wrexham (0) 1 *(McEvilly 63)* 5046

Port Vale: Goodlad; Rowland, Bell, James, Pilkington, Dinning, Birchall, Husbands (Smith), Lowndes, Constantine, Innes (Porter).
Wrexham: Ingham; Roche, Smith, Bayliss, Lawrence, Spender (Foy), Mark Jones, Ferguson, Walters (Bennett), McEvilly, Williams D.

Saturday, 5 November 2005

Barnet (0) 0

Southend U (1) 1 *(Eastwood 2)* 3545

Barnet: Flitney; Hendon, King, Soares (Batt), Yakubu, Gross, Bailey, Sinclair, Hatch (Grazioli), Norville, Strevens (Roache).
Southend U: Griemink; Hunt, Wilson, Maher, Barrett, Edwards, Campbell-Ryce, Guttridge, Eastwood, Goater, Cole (Lawson).

Barnsley (1) 1 *(Hayes 5)*

Darlington (0) 0 6059

Barnsley: Colgan; Tonge, Austin, Howard, Hassell, Kay (Williams), Devaney, Shuker (Jarman), Hayes (Nardiello), Richards, McPhail.
Darlington: Russell; Valentine, Kendrick, Martis, Clarke, Peacock (N'Dumbu-Nsungu), Wainwright, Appleby, Johnson S, Sodje, Dickman (Stamp).

Bournemouth (1) 1 *(Stock 45)*

Tamworth (1) 2 *(Ward 29, Storer 82)* 4550

Bournemouth: Stewart; Hart (Rodrigues), O'Connor, Browning (Coutts), Young, Cooper, Foley-Sheridan, Stock, Hayter, Keene (Cooke), Surman.
Tamworth: Bevan; Touhy, Stamps, Storer, Bampton, Brown, Robinson, Cooper, Heggs (Jackson), Edwards, Ward.

Bristol C (0) 0

Notts Co (1) 2 *(Tann 45, Baudet 68)* 4221

Bristol C: Phillips; Orr, Youga, Carey (Heywood), Partridge (Russell), Skuse▪, Murray, Wilkshire, Brooker, Quinn, Cotterill (Gillespie).
Notts Co: Pilkington; Pipe, Tann, McMahon (O'Callaghan), Edwards, Baudet, Ullathorne, Gill, Scoffham (White), Hurst, Long.

Burnham (0) 1 *(Miller 88)*

Aldershot T (0) 3 *(Brough 54, Heald 71, Deen 85)* 1623

Burnham: Jackson; Brown (Miller), Horstead, Jones S (Leacock), Brett, Smith, Logie (Williams), Saunders, Alleyne, Jones D, Romeo.
Aldershot T: Bull; Somner, Barnard, Boucaud, Brough, Heald, Crittenden, Scott, Coleman, Sills (Deen), Holloway.

Burscough (1) 3 *(Bell 10, Cox 89 (og), Rowan 90)*

Gillingham (0) 2 *(Jarvis 58, Saunders 77)* 1927

Burscough: Boswell; Barlow, Crowder (Bowen), Parry, Bell, Tong, Byrne (Rowan), Blakeman, Gray, Eaton, Hussey.
Gillingham: Bullock; Wallis, Williams, Flynn▪, Cox, Hope, Smith, Hessenthaler (Collin), Harris, Jarvis, Crofts (Saunders).

Bury (0) 2 *(Kennedy 52 (pen), Scott 70)*

Scunthorpe U (2) 2 *(Keogh 6, Baraclough 41)* 2940

Bury: Dootson; Scott, Kennedy, Whaley, Challinor, Woodthorpe, Flitcroft, Mattis (Quigley), Tipton (Reet), Adams, Buchanan.
Scunthorpe U: Musselwhite; Byrne, Williams, Crosby, Butler, Baraclough, Sparrow, Hinds, Keogh, Sharp, Beagrie (Corden) (Taylor).

Cheltenham T (0) 1 *(McCann 64)*

Carlisle U (0) 0 2405

Cheltenham T: Higgs; Gill, Victory, McCann, Caines, Duff, Melligan (Bird), Wilson (Vincent), Odejayi, Guinan (Spencer), Armstrong.
Carlisle U: Westwood; Arnison, Murphy, Billy, Gray, Livesey, Hackney (Murray G), Holmes (Grand), Nade (McGill), Hawley, Lumsdon.

Chester C (0) 2 *(Branch 55 (pen), Lowe 71)*

Folkestone I (1) 1 *(Flanagan 10)* 2503

Chester C: MacKenzie; McNiven, Regan, Curtis, Artell, Dimech, Drummond, Davies (Vaughan), Richardson (El Kholti), Branch, Lowe.
Folkestone I: Kessell; Everitt J (Sly), Norman, Everitt M, Flanagan, Guest, Lamb (Neilson), Chandler (Lindsey), Jones, Dryden, Myall.

Chippenham T (0) 1 *(Constable 47)*

Worcester C (1) 1 *(Webster 6)* 2815

Chippenham T: Vaughan; Adams, Thorne W, Thorne G, McEntegart, Allison, Harvey, Badman (Kirk), Constable (Charity), Gilroy, Herring.
Worcester C: McDonnell; Lyttle, Warner, Warmer, Thompson, Smith C, Wedgebury (Colley), Hodnett (Hyde), Webster, Kelly (Preece), McDonald.

Colchester U (2) 9 *(Halford 39, Brown 44, Iwelumo 48, Cureton 60, 70, Watson 63, Yeates 67, Danns 89, 90)*

Leamington (0) 1 *(Adams R 72)* 3513

Colchester U: Davison; Stockley (Garcia), Duguid, Brown, Chilvers, Watson, Halford, Izzet (Danns), Iwelumo (Williams), Cureton, Yeates.
Leamington: Morris; Parisi (Smith), Blake, Morgan, Tank, Gregory, Adams J, Adams R, Thompson (Eden), Howell, Rodman (Kelsall).

Eastbourne B (0) 1 *(Rowland O 90 (pen))*

Oxford U (0) 1 *(Basham 70)* 3770

Eastbourne B: Hook; Austin, Tuck, Atkin (Piper), Baker, Warner, Cox (Simmonds), Smart, Ramsay, Marney (Odubade), Rowland O.
Oxford U: Turley; Ashton, Robinson, Quinn, Roget, Willmott, Mansell, Hargreaves, Sabin, Basham, Bradbury.

Grimsby T (0) 1 *(Jones G 49)*

Bristol R (1) 2 *(Agogo 28, 87)* 2680

Grimsby T: Mildenhall; McDermott, Newey, Kamudimba Kalala, Whittle, Jones R (Ramsden), Cohen, Bolland, Parkinson, Jones G (Gritton), Reddy.
Bristol R: Shearer; Lescott, Ryan, Carruthers, Hinton, Elliott, Gibb (Campbell), Hunt, Walker, Agogo, Disley.

Hartlepool U (1) 2 *(Nelson 34, Butler 83)*
Dagenham & R (1) 1 *(Kandol 32)* 3655

Hartlepool U: Konstantopoulos; Craddock, Humphreys, Williams D, Nelson, Bullock (Clark), Maidens (Istead), Sweeney, Williams E, Daly (Proctor), Butler.
Dagenham & R: Roberts; Goodwin, Griffiths (Bruce), Marwa, Uddin, Blackett, Foster, Southam, Moore, Mackail-Smith (Benson), Kandol.

Histon (1) 4 *(Jackman 10, 58, Cambridge I 50, Nightingale 84)*
Hednesford T (0) 0 1080

Histon: Key; Okay, Haniver, Cambridge A, Hipperson, Jackman, Barker, Nightingale, Cambridge I (Knight-Percival), Gutzmore (Farrington), Andrews N.
Hednesford T: Brush; Brannan (Brindley), Branch, Williams, Adams, Teesdale, McMahon, Heath, Bell, Anthrobus (Marshall T), Hunter.

Kettering T (1) 1 *(Midgley 14)*
Stevenage B (2) 3 *(Stamp 8, Boyd 43, Elding 69)* 4548

Kettering T: Osborn; Diuk, Theobald, Gould (Burgess), Brown, McIllain, Hall, Patterson, Moore, Midgley (Difante), Nicell.
Stevenage B: Julian; Warner, Perpetuini, Bulman, Laker, Quinn, Brough (Gregory), Berquez, Nurse (Elding), Stamp, Boyd (Lewis).

Leyton Orient (0) 0
Chesterfield (0) 0 3554

Leyton Orient: Garner; Miller, Lockwood, Easton, Mackie, Zakuani, Tudor, Simpson (McMahon), Alexander, Ibehre (Echanomi), Keith (Carlisle).
Chesterfield: Roche; Bailey, Nicholson, Hazell, Blatherwick, Niven, Hall, Allott, Larkin (Hurst), Allison, Davies.

Lincoln C (1) 1 *(Robinson M 29)*
Milton Keynes D (1) 1 *(Edds 45)* 3508

Lincoln C: Marriott; Beevers, Cryan, McAuley, Morgan, Keates■, Kerr, Birch (Green), Asamoah, Robinson M, Brown.
Milton Keynes D: Baker; Edds (Rizzo), Ricketts, Mitchell, Morgan, McClenahan, Crooks, Small, Platt, McLeod (Kamara), McKoy (Smith).

Macclesfield T (0) 1 *(Wijnhard 48)*
Yeovil T (0) 1 *(Jevons 81)* 1943

Macclesfield T: Fettis; Bailey, McIntyre, Morley, Swailes■, Navarro, Whitaker, Bullock (Parkin), Beresford (Briscoe), Wijnhard, Harsley.
Yeovil T: Weale (Collis); Amankwaah, Jones, Davies, Skiverton, Miles (Fontaine), Terry, Johnson, Bastianini, Jevons, Harrold (Gall).

Morecambe (0) 1 *(Carlton 84)*
Northwich Vic (2) 3 *(Brayson 19, 41, 67)* 2166

Morecambe: Robinson; Blackburn (Thompson), Howard, Kelly (Stringfellow), Kempson, Bentley, Walmsley, Perkins, Twiss, Curtis, O'Connor (Carlton).
Northwich Vic: Rodgers; McCarthy, Chapman, Elliott, Charnock (Payne), Handyside, Mayman, Carr, Brayson, Allan, Roca (Battersby).

Nottingham F (1) 1 *(Gary Holt 39)*
Weymouth (0) 1 *(Harris 56)* 10,305

Nottingham F: Pedersen; Eaden, Thompson, Morgan, Breckin, Gary Holt, Southall (Cullip), Perch, Johnson, Lester, Bopp.
Weymouth: Matthews; Tully, Challis, Wilkinson, O'Brien, Bound, Clark, Harris, Eribenne, Jackson, Elam.

Nuneaton B (2) 2 *(Oddy 15, Staff 34)*
Ramsgate (0) 0 2153

Nuneaton B: Acton; Oddy, Love, Fitzpatrick, Wilkin (Rea), Angus, Collins, Noon, Quailey, Frew■, Staff.
Ramsgate: Twyman; Vahid E, Cassar, Laslett, Morris (Pettit), Schulz O, Ball, Munday (Yianni), Vahid S (Suter), Welford, Schulz W.

Peterborough U (0) 0
Burton A (0) 0 3856

Peterborough U: Tyler; St Ledger-Hall, Holden, Arber, Burton, Carden, Semple (Farrell), Newton, Crow, Benjamin (Willock), Gain.
Burton A: Deeney; Henshaw, Webster, Stride, Tinson, Austin, Hall, Sedgemore, Shaw, Harrad (Ducros), Todd.

Rochdale (0) 0
Brentford (1) 1 *(O'Connor 45 (pen))* 2928

Rochdale: Gilks; Goodhind (Tait), Goodall, Clarke, Gallimore, McArdle, Jaszczun, Cooksey (Warner), Lambert (Sturrock), Holt, Jones.
Brentford: Nelson; O'Connor, Frampton, Lewis (Newman), Sodje, Turner, Pratley, Brooker (Dobson), Owusu, Rankin (Tillen), Tabb.

Rotherham U (2) 3 *(McLaren 30, 38, Burton 54)*
Mansfield T (2) 4 *(Brown 28, Coke 37, Barker 75, 90)* 4089

Rotherham U: Montgomery; Worrell, Hurst, McLaren, Gilchrist, Barker, Mullin (Williamson), Leadbitter (Monkhouse), Butler, Burton, Keane■.
Mansfield T: Pressman; Buxton, Uhlenbeek■, Coke, Hjelde (Day), John-Baptiste, Dawson, Talbot (Birchall), Barker, Brown, Rundle.

Shrewsbury T (3) 4 *(McMenamin 2 (pen), Tolley 5, Hope 44, Edwards 55)*
Braintree T (0) 1 *(Quinton 78)* 2969

Shrewsbury T: Hart; Herd, Ashton, Edwards, Whitehead, Hope, Smith, Tolley, Darby, McMenamin (Hogg), Langmead (Jackson).
Braintree T: Morgan; Burgess, Joseph (Martin R), Revell, Adedeji, Lorraine, Porter, Quinton, Wild (Baker), Ofori (Toku), Jones.

Southport (0) 1 *(Leadbetter 64)*
Woking (1) 1 *(Evans 32)* 1417

Southport: Dickinson; Powell, Fitzgerald, Lynch (Booth), Davis, Fitzhenry, Baker, Morley, Leadbetter, Daly (Robinson), McGinn.
Woking: Jalal; Jackson, El-Salahi, Murray, Nethercott, Oliver, Smith, Ferguson, Richards, McAllister (Rawle), Evans.

Stockport Co (1) 2 *(Easter 41, Briggs 53)*
Swansea C (0) 0 2978

Stockport Co: Spencer; Greenwood, Robinson, Briggs, Raynes, Clare, Hamshaw, Boshell (Wolski), Easter (Lefondre), Dje (Malcolm), Singh.
Swansea C: Gueret; Tate, Ricketts, Britton, Austin, Iriekpen, Tudur-Jones, Martinez (Robinson), Connor (Akinfenwa), Trundle, McLeod (Forbes).

Swindon T (1) 2 *(Gurney 32, Comyn-Platt 87)*
Boston U (2) 2 *(Rusk 25, Talbot 42)* 3814

Swindon T: Heaton; Nicholas, Jenkins, Ifil, O'Hanlon, Shakes, Miglioranzi (Comyn-Platt), Stroud (Pook), Gurney, Thorpe (Holgate), Heath.
Boston U: Abbey; Canoville, White, Holland, Greaves, Futcher, Maylett (Thomas), Talbot, Joachim, Dudfield (Ellender), Rusk.

Torquay U (0) 1 *(Stonebridge 80)*
Harrogate T (1) 1 *(Holland 20)* 2079

Torquay U: Marriott; Villis (Lloyd), Woodman, Hockley (Sako), Taylor, Woods, Phillips, Garner (Coleman), Stonebridge, Osei-Kuffour, Hill.
Harrogate T: Price; Wood L, Ellerker (Ryan), Grant, Brass, Stoneman (Lennon), Mason, Hunter, Smith, Holland, Philpott.

Wycombe W (0) 1 *(Burnell 90)*
Northampton T (0) 3 *(Doig 56, Smith 61, McGleish 80)* 3974

Wycombe W: Talia; Senda, Easton, Oakes (Lee), Johnson, Martin, Betsy, Burnell, Mooney (Griffin), Tyson, Torres (Bloomfield).
Northampton T: Harper; Crowe, Bojic, Chambers, Doig, Taylor, Low, Mendes (Kirk), McGleish, Smith (Rowson), Jess (Hunt).

York C (0) 0
Grays Ath (1) 3 *(Bishop A 15 (og), Slabber 58, Poole 87)* 3586
York C: Porter; Price, Merris, Dunning (Webster), Dudgeon, McGurk, Convery, Yalcin (Mallon), Donaldson, Bishop A, O'Neill (Stewart).
Grays Ath: Eyre; Sambrook, Nutter, Thurgood, Stuart, Angus, McLean (Hooper), Martin, Slabber, Oli (Poole), Kightly.

Sunday, 6 November 2005

Bradford C (0) 2 *(Crooks 56, Windass 59 (pen))*
Tranmere R (1) 1 *(Greenacre 6)* 6116
Bradford C: Ricketts; Edghill (Stewart), Emanuel, Schumacher, Wetherall, Bower, Muirhead, Crooks, Windass, Cooke, Morrison (Cadamarteri).
Tranmere R: Achterberg; Linwood, Roberts, Harrison, Jackson, Sharps, Jennings, Rankine (Aiston), Facey, Greenacre, Davies (Dagnall).

Chasetown (1) 1 *(Day 23 (og))*
Oldham Ath (1) 1 *(Eyres 31)* 1997
Chasetown: Taylor; Thompson, Aulton, Harrison (Turner), Slater, Edwards S, Harris, Horler, Bullimore, Edwards K, Whitcombe D.
Oldham Ath: Day (Cronin); Scott, Tierney, Hughes, Hall D, Owen, Wellens, Eyres, Porter (Beckett), Warne (Hall C), Liddell.

Doncaster R (1) 4 *(Heffernan 18, 72, McIndoe 53 (pen), 56 (pen))*
Blackpool (0) 1 *(Clarke 90 (pen))* 4332
Doncaster R: Budtz; Mulligan, McDaid, Foster, Fenton, Ravenhill, Offiong, Thornton (Green), Guy (Roberts N), Heffernan, McIndoe.
Blackpool: Pogliacomi; Warrender (Prendergast), Edwards, Doolan (Vernon), McGregor, Clarke, Grayson, Southern, Murphy, Blinkhorn, Wiles.

Halifax T (1) 1 *(Senior 45)*
Rushden & D (1) 1 *(Armstrong 2)* 2303
Halifax T: Butler; Haslam, Wright, Foster, Ingram, Quinn, Forrest, Thompson, Grant, Senior (Midgley), Bowler (Killeen).
Rushden & D: Young; Gier, Burgess, McCafferty, Dempster, Gulliver, Bell, Savage, Pearson (Tomlin), Armstrong, Kelly.

Huddersfield T (1) 4 *(Booth 27, 69, Schofield 50 (pen), Holdsworth 81)*
Welling U (0) 1 *(Moore C 83)* 5518
Huddersfield T: Rachubka; Holdsworth, Adams, Hudson, Mirfin, Clarke N, Worthington (Collins), Brandon (Abbott), Booth (Carss), Taylor-Fletcher, Schofield.
Welling U: Turner; Lee, Shearer, Clarke (Bodkin), Solomon (Lawson), Moore C, Carruthers (Moore D), Owen, Stadhart, Kedwell, Day.

FIRST ROUND REPLAYS

Monday, 14 November 2005

Weymouth (0) 0
Nottingham F (0) 2 *(Taylor 67, 73)* 6500
Weymouth: Matthews; Tully, Challis, Bound, Harris, O'Brien, Clark (Wheeler), Wilkinson (Dutton), Elam, Jackson (Taggart), Eribenne.
Nottingham F: Gerrard; Curtis (Eaden), Morgan, Cullip, Breckin, Gary Holt (Thompson), Southall, Perch, Johnson (Lester), Taylor, Gardner.

Worcester C (0) 1 *(Webster 76)*
Chippenham T (0) 0 4006
Worcester C: McDonnell; Thompson, Lyttle, Smith, Warner, Colley, Hyde (Preece), Warmer (McDonald), Hines, Kelly, Webster (Clegg).
Chippenham T: Trego; Adams, Thorne G, McEntegart, Thorne W (Griffin), Allison, Herring, Badman, Harvey■, Gilroy (Kirk), Constable.

Tuesday, 15 November 2005

Harrogate T (0) 0
Torquay U (0) 0 3317
Harrogate T: Price; Wood, Heard, Hunter, Brass, Ellerker, Mason, Philpott (Lennon), Smith, Grant, Holland.
Torquay U: Marriott; Lloyd, Woodman, Sharp, Taylor, Woods, Hockley, Garner (Coleman), Bedeau, Stonebridge, Hill.
aet; Torquay U won 6-5 on penalties.

Milton Keynes D (2) 2 *(Platt 14, 42)*
Lincoln C (1) 1 *(Mayo 24 (pen))* 4029
Milton Keynes D: Baker; Edds (McKoy), Lewington, McClenahan, Morgan, Mitchell, Rizzo (Crooks), Ricketts, Platt, McLeod, Small.
Lincoln C: Marriott; Beevers, Mayo, Cryan, Morgan, McCombe, Kerr, Birch (Green), Asamoah, Robinson M (Molango), Brown.

Rushden & D (0) 0
Halifax T (0) 0 2133
Rushden & D: Young; Gier, Burgess, McCafferty (Hawkins), Dempster, Gulliver, Bell (Mills), Savage, Tomlin (Pearson), Armstrong, Kelly.
Halifax T: Butler; Haslam■, Wright, Thompson, Ingram, Quinn, Forrest, Foster, Killeen (Senior), Mansaram (Grant), Bowler (Midgley).
aet; Rushden & D won 5-4 on penalties.

Scunthorpe U (0) 1 *(Johnson 117)*
Bury (0) 0 4006
Scunthorpe U: Musselwhite; Byrne, Williams, Stanton, Butler, Baraclough, Sparrow (Johnson), Hinds, Keogh, Sharp, Corden (Taylor).
Bury: Edwards; Scott, Kennedy, Whaley, Challinor, Woodthorpe, Flitcroft■, Mattis, Reet (Tipton), Adams, Buchanan (Fitzgerald).
aet.

Woking (0) 1 *(McAllister 114)*
Southport (0) 0 2298
Woking: Jalal; Jackson, El-Salahi, Murray, Nethercott, Oliver, Ferguson, Selley, Richards, Rawle (McAllister), Smith (Blackman).
Southport: Dickinson; Pickford, Fitzhenry, Morley, Davis, Fitzgerald, Baker, Krief (Lynch), Leadbetter, Daly, McGinn (Robinson).
aet.

Yeovil T (1) 4 *(Way 23, Terry 73, Johnson 75, Davies 90)*
Macclesfield T (0) 0 4456
Yeovil T: Weale; Amankwaah, Jones, Way (Sodje), Skiverton, Miles, Terry, Johnson, Bastianini (Harrold), Jevons (Davies), Gall.
Macclesfield T: Fettis; Morley, McIntyre, Harsley, Swailes, Navarro, Whitaker, Bullock (Briscoe), Parkin, Wijnhard, Beresford.

Wednesday, 16 November 2005

Boston U (4) 4 *(Joachim 10, 23, Maylett 40, Lee 45)*
Swindon T (0) 1 *(Fallon 83 (pen))* 2467
Boston U: Abbey; White, McCann, Holland, Greaves, Futcher, Maylett, Talbot (Noble), Joachim (Thomas), Lee (Dudfield), Rusk.
Swindon T: Heaton■; Jenkins, Smith J, Ifil, O'Hanlon, McDermott (Bulman), Gurney (Shakes), Nicholas, Fallon, Roberts, Pook (Comyn-Platt).

Burton Alb (0) 1 *(Harrad 73)*
Peterborough U (0) 0 2511
Burton Alb: Deeney; Henshaw, Webster, Stride, Tinson, Austin, Hall, Sedgemore, Shaw, Harrad (Corbett), Gilroy (Todd).
Peterborough U: Tyler; St Ledger-Hall, Holden, Arber, Plummer, Day, Carden, Newton (Semple), Crow (Willock), Thorpe (Benjamin), Gain.

Chesterfield (1) 1 *(Hurst 37)*
Leyton Orient (2) 2 *(Mackie 18, Tudor 43)* 4895
Chesterfield: Roche; Bailey, Nicholson, Hazell, Blatherwick, Niven (Davies), Hall (Smith), Allott, Larkin, Allison (N'Toya), Hurst.
Leyton Orient: Garner; Miller, Lockwood, Easton, Mackie, Zakuani, Tudor, Simpson, Alexander, Ibehre, Keith.

Oldham Ath (1) 4 *(Warne 31, Porter 56, 75, Hall C 84)*
Chasetown (0) 0 7235
Oldham Ath: Day; Forbes, Edwards, Hughes, Hall D, Owen, Wellens (Eyres), Butcher, Porter, Warne, Liddell (Hall C).
Chasetown: Bryan; Slater, Aulton (Bytheway), Harrison, Thompson, Edwards S, Harris (Turner), Horler, Bullimore, Edwards K, Whitcombe (Huckfield).

Oxford U (2) 3 *(Basham 20, 45, 90 (pen))*
Eastbourne B (0) 0 4396
Oxford U: Turley; Mansell, Robinson, Quinn, Roget (Stirling), Willmott, Hackett, Hargreaves, Basham, Sabin, Davies (Bradbury).
Eastbourne B: Hook; Austin, Tuck (Hemsley), Atkin, Baker, Warner, Cox, Smart (Simmonds), Odubade, Ramsay (Marney), Rowland.

SECOND ROUND

Friday, 2 December 2005

Mansfield T (2) 3 *(Barker 13, 42 (pen), Birchall 76)*
Grays Ath (0) 0 2992
Mansfield T: Pressman; Buxton, Jelleyman, Coke, Hjelde, John-Baptiste, Dawson, Birchall, Barker, Russell, Rundle.
Grays Ath: Bayes; Sambrook■, Nutter (Poole), Thurgood, Matthews, Angus, McLean, Martin, Slabber, Oli, Kightly (Hooper).

Port Vale (0) 1 *(Constantine 86)*
Bristol R (0) 1 *(Gibb 55)* 4483
Port Vale: Goodlad; Rowland, James, Dinning (Innes), Pilkington, Fortune, Husbands, Sonner, Mulligan (Lowndes), Constantine, Smith.
Bristol R: Shearer; Lescott, Carruthers, Campbell, Hinton, Elliott, Gibb (Williams), Hunt, Walker, Agogo, Disley.

Saturday, 3 December 2005

Aldershot T (0) 0
Scunthorpe U (1) 1 *(Keogh 14)* 3548
Aldershot T: Bull; Somner, Barnard, Tinnion, Brough (Jinadu), Heald, Crittenden, Scott (Watson), Turner, Holloway, Deen (Gearing).
Scunthorpe U: Evans; Byrne, Williams, Crosby, Butler, Baraclough (Ridley), MacKenzie, Till, Keogh, Sharp (Taylor), Beagrie.

Barnsley (1) 1 *(Hayes 43)*
Bradford C (0) 1 *(Edghill 82)* 7051
Barnsley: Flinders; Tonge (Wroe), Austin, Hassell, Carbon, Kay, Burns, Shuker, Hayes (Jarman), Richards, Devaney.
Bradford C: Ricketts; Edghill, Emanuel, Schumacher, Wetherall, Bower, Morrison (Claridge), Bridge-Wilkinson, Windass, Cadamarteri, Muirhead.

Burton Alb (0) 0
Burscough (0) 0 *Postponed; waterlogged pitch.*

Cheltenham T (1) 1 *(Guinan 14)*
Oxford U (0) 1 *(Sabin 52)* 4592
Cheltenham T: Higgs; Gill, Victory (Finnigan), McCann, Caines, Duff, Melligan, Wilson, Odejayi, Guinan (Spencer), Armstrong.
Oxford U: Turley; Mansell, Robinson, Quinn, Roget, Willmott, Bradbury, Hargreaves, Basham (Davies), Sabin, Griffin.

Chester C (1) 3 *(Lowe 40 (pen), 50, Richardson 55)*
Nottingham F (0) 0 4732
Chester C: MacKenzie; McNiven, Regan, Curtis, Artell, Dimech, Drummond, Davies (Dove), Richardson (El Kholti), Walker (Vaughan), Lowe.
Nottingham F: Gerrard; Thompson, Curtis, Cullip (Pittman) (Gardner), Morgan, Gary Holt■, Southall, Perch, Johnson, Taylor, Bopp (Bastians).

Hartlepool U (0) 1 *(Llewellyn 52 (pen))*
Tamworth (1) 2 *(Edwards 33, Redmile 48)* 3786
Hartlepool U: Konstantopoulos; Williams D, Brackstone, Nelson (Istead), Craddock, Tinkler (Williams E), Butler, Sweeney, McDonald, Llewellyn, Humphreys.
Tamworth: Bevan; Smith, Anaclet, Ward, Redmile, Bampton, Melton, Motteram (Cooper), Edwards, Jackson (Heggs), Storer (Turner).

Hereford U (0) 0
Stockport Co (1) 2 *(Easter 3, Wolski 57)* 3620
Hereford U: Mawson; Green, Jeannin, Pitman, Mkandawire, James, Purdie, Stanley, Ipoua (Stansfield), Carey-Bertram (Brady), Williams.
Stockport Co: Spencer; Greenwood, Robinson, Wolski, Raynes, Clare, Hamshaw, Boshell (Allen), Easter, Bramble, Singh.

Nuneaton B (1) 2 *(Collins 35, Quailey 52 (pen))*
Histon (2) 2 *(Barker 36, Knight-Percival 44)* 3366
Nuneaton B: Acton; Oddy, Love, Noon, Moore, Angus, Collins, Reeves, Frew (Murphy), Quailey, Staff.
Histon: Key; Jackman, Haniver, Farrington (Hipperson), Bowden, Okay, Cambridge A, Andrews, Barker, Gutzmore (Goddard), Knight-Percival.

Oldham Ath (0) 1 *(Liddell 57 (pen))*
Brentford (0) 1 *(Sodje 65)* 4365
Oldham Ath: Day; Forbes, Haining (Scott), Hughes, Branston, Tierney, Wellens, Butcher, Porter (Beckett), Warne, Liddell.
Brentford: Nelson; O'Connor, Frampton, Newman, Sodje, Turner, Pratley, Brooker (Tillen), Owusu, Campbell (Hutchinson), Tabb.

Rushden & D (0) 0
Leyton Orient (0) 1 *(Steele 66)* 3245
Rushden & D: Young; Hawkins (Mills), Burgess, McCafferty, Dempster, Gulliver, Bell, Savage, Broughton (Pearson), Armstrong (Tomlin), Kelly.
Leyton Orient: Garner; Barnard, Lockwood, McMahon, Miller (Saah), Zakuani, Tudor (Carlisle), Simpson, Alexander, Ibehre (Steele), Keith.

Shrewsbury T (1) 1 *(Edwards 45)*
Colchester U (1) 2 *(Cureton 23, Iwelumo 52)* 3695
Shrewsbury T: Hart; Herd, Ashton, Tolley, Whitehead, Hope, Edwards, Sorvel, Stallard (Darby), McMenamin, Smith (Langmead).
Colchester U: Davison; Stockley, White, Brown, Chilvers, Watson, Halford, Danns (Izzet), Iwelumo, Cureton (Garcia), Yeates (Duguid).

Southend U (0) 1 *(Eastwood 58)*
Milton Keynes D (1) 2 *(McLeod 16 (pen), Smith 71)* 5267
Southend U: Flahavan; Hunt, Wilson, Maher, Barrett, Prior, Campbell-Ryce (Lawson), Smith, Eastwood, Goater (Gray), Gower (Cole).
Milton Keynes D: Baker; Edds (Smith), Lewington, McClenahan, Morgan, Chorley, Mitchell, Small (Kamara), Platt (Wilbraham), McLeod, Quinn.

Stevenage B (1) 2 *(Boyd 5, Elding 83)*
Northampton T (0) 2 *(Bojic 67, McGleish 82 (pen))* 3937
Stevenage B: Julian; Warner, Gregory (Elding), Bulman, Laker, Quinn, Brough, Boyd, Nurse, Berquez, Perpetuini.
Northampton T: Harper; Low, Chambers, Bojic, Doig, Hunt (Johnson G), Rowson, Smith, McGleish, Kirk, Jess (Mendes).

Torquay U (1) 2 *(Bedeau 45, 69)*
Notts Co (0) 1 *(McMahon 54)* 2407
Torquay U: Marriott; Lloyd, Sharp, Hockley, Lockwood, Woods, Phillips (Taylor), Garner, Bedeau, Stonebridge (Hill), Osei-Kuffour.
Notts Co: Pilkington; O'Callaghan, Ullathorne (Long), Edwards, Wilson, Baudet, Pipe, McMahon, De Bolla (Gordon), Hurst, Sheridan (Palmer).

Walsall (1) 2 *(Fryatt 18 (pen), Leitao 83)*
Yeovil T (0) 0 4580
Walsall: Gilmartin; Pead, Fox, Staunton (Gerrard), Roper, Bennett, Taylor D, Osborn, Fryatt, Leitao (Nicholls), Demontagnac (Taylor K).
Yeovil T: Weale; Amankwaah, Miles (Davies) (Harrold), Cohen, Skiverton, Sodje, Terry, Johnson, Gall (Bastianini), Jevons, Jones.

Woking (0) 0
Northwich Vic (0) 0 2462
Woking: Jalal; Jackson, El-Salahi, Murray, Nethercott, Watson, Smith, Ferguson, Richards, McAllister, Cockerill L (Blackman).
Northwich Vic: Rodgers; McCarthy, Chapman, Elliott, Handyside, Charnock, Mayman, Carr, Brayson, Allan, Byrne (Roca).

Sunday, 4 December 2005

Boston U (0) 1 *(Futcher 90)*
Doncaster R (1) 2 *(Mulligan 29, 58)* 3995
Boston U: Wright; Canoville, McCann (Dudfield), Holland, White, Futcher, Maylett, Talbot, Joachim, Lee, Galbraith (Thomas).
Doncaster R: Budtz; Fenton, Mulligan, Foster, Roberts S, Ravenhill (Green), Coppinger, Thornton, Guy (Roberts N), Heffernan (Fortune-West), McIndoe.

Worcester C (0) 0
Huddersfield T (0) 1 *(Brandon 61)* 4163
Worcester C: McDonnell; Smith, Warner, Thompson, Lyttle, Hyde (Clegg), Colley (Wedgebury), Hines, Webster, Kelly, Warmer (Preece).
Huddersfield T: Rachubka; Holdsworth, Adams, Hudson, Mirfin, Clarke N, Worthington, Brandon, Taylor-Fletcher (Abbott), Booth, Schofield■.

Tuesday, 6 December 2005

Burton Alb (3) 4 *(Gilroy 8, 37, Stride 16, Harrad 84)*
Burscough (0) 1 *(Eaton 60)* 4499
Burton Alb: Deeney; Henshaw (Rowett), Corbett, Stride, Tinson, Austin, Hall (Todd), Sedgemore, Shaw, Harrad, Gilroy (Ducros).
Burscough: Boswell; Barlow, Danes (Rowan), Crowder, Bell, Tong (Underwood), Parry, Blakeman, Gray (McKevitt), Eaton, Bowen.

SECOND ROUND REPLAYS

Tuesday, 13 December 2005

Bradford C (1) 3 *(Cooke 34, Bower 67, Wetherall 73)*
Barnsley (0) 5 *(Hayes 51, 78, Reid 59, Devaney 96, 109)* 4738
Bradford C: Howarth; Edghill, Emanuel, Schumacher, Wetherall, Bower, Bridge-Wilkinson, Cadamarteri, Windass (Morrison), Cooke, Muirhead (Claridge).
Barnsley: Flinders; Hassell, Austin, Howard (Wroe), Reid, Kay, Burns, Shuker (Tonge), Hayes, Richards (Carbon), Devaney.
aet.

Brentford (0) 1 *(Owusu 78)*
Oldham Ath (0) 0 3146
Brentford: Nelson; O'Connor, Tillen, Newman, Sodje, Turner, Pratley (Peters), Brooker, Owusu, Campbell (Rankin), Tabb.
Oldham Ath: Day; Forbes, Scott, Hughes, Branston, Edwards, Wellens, Butcher (Owen■), Beckett (Tierney), Warne, Liddell.

Bristol R (0) 0
Port Vale (1) 1 *(Birchall 22)* 5623
Bristol R: Shearer; Lescott, Carruthers, Campbell, Hinton, Elliott, Gibb (Williams), Hunt, Walker (Haldane), Agogo, Disley (Forrester).
Port Vale: Goodlad; Rowland, James, Birchall (Husbands), Pilkington, Fortune, Innes (Porter), Sonner, Lowndes, Constantine, Bell.

Northampton T (2) 2 *(McGleish 44, 45)*
Stevenage B (0) 0 4407
Northampton T: Harper; Bojic, Crowe (Hunt), Chambers, Doig, Taylor (Dyche), Low, Jess, McGleish, Mendes (Kirk), Smith.
Stevenage B: Julian; Warner, Perpetuini, Bulman, Laker (Gregory), Quinn, Brough (Williams), Boyd, Elding, Nurse, Berquez (Stamp).

Northwich Vic (1) 2 *(Elliott 13, Brayson 60)*
Woking (1) 1 *(Ferguson 45)* 2302
Northwich Vic: Rodgers; McCarthy, Chapman, Charnock, Handyside (Payne), Carr, Mayman, Elliott, Allan, Brayson, Roca.
Woking: Jalal; Jackson, El-Salahi, Murray, Nethercott, Watson, Smith (Selley), Ferguson (Rawle), Richards, McAllister, Cockerill L (Evans).

Oxford U (0) 1 *(Basham 61)*
Cheltenham T (0) 2 *(Odejayi 51, Wilson 79)* 3455
Oxford U: Turley; Mansell, Robinson, Quinn, Roget, Willmott, Hackett, Bradbury, Basham (E'Beyer), Sabin, Griffin (Davies).
Cheltenham T: Higgs; Gill, Armstrong, McCann, Caines, Duff, Melligan (Bird), Finnigan, Odejayi, Guinan (Spencer), Wilson.

Wednesday, 14 December 2005

Histon (0) 1 *(Bowden 61)*
Nuneaton B (1) 2 *(Oddy 34, Moore 90)* 3000
Histon: Key; Okay, Bowden, Haniver (Cambridge I), Jackman, Hipperson, Barker, Andrews, Knight-Percival, Gutzmore (Nightingale), Cambridge A.
Nuneaton B: Acton; Oddy, Love, Noon, Moore, Angus, Reeves (Fitzpatrick), Collins, Quailey, Murphy (Frew), Staff.

THIRD ROUND

Friday, 6 January 2006

Port Vale (0) 2 *(Togwell 55, 73)*
Doncaster R (1) 1 *(Heffernan 27)* 4923
Port Vale: Goodlad; Rowland, James, Dinning, Pilkington, Fortune, Togwell, Cummins, Husbands, Constantine, Innes.
Doncaster R: Blayney; Fenton (Marples), McDaid, Albrighton, Foster, Ravenhill, Mulligan (Coppinger), Thornton (Green), Guy, Heffernan, McIndoe.

Saturday, 7 January 2006

Arsenal (2) 2 *(Pires 6, 18)*
Cardiff C (0) 1 *(Jerome 87)* 36,552
Arsenal: Almunia; Lauren, Gilbert, Silva, Djourou, Senderos, Reyes (Owusu-Abeyie), Flamini, Van Persie (Larsson), Bergkamp, Pires.
Cardiff C: Alexander; Weston, Barker, Cox, Purse, Loovens (Koskela), Ardley, Whitley, Jerome, Ledley, Cooper (Lee).

Barnsley (0) 1 *(Hayes 77)*
Walsall (0) 1 *(James 74)* 6884
Barnsley: Colgan; Tonge, Williams (Nardiello), Burns, Reid, Austin, Devaney, Shuker, Hayes, Richards (Wright), McPhail (Kell).
Walsall: Oakes; Pead, Fox, Osborn, Roper, Gerrard, Wright, Bennett, James, Timm (Nicholls), Leary.

Blackburn R (2) 3 *(Todd 17, Bellamy 36, 86)*

QPR (0) 0 12,705

Blackburn R: Friedel; Neill, Matteo, Tugay, Todd, Khizanishvili, Thompson, Savage (Pedersen), Dickov (Kuqi), Bellamy, Peter.
QPR: Royce; Bignot, Milanese, Rose, Shittu, Santos (Ainsworth), Rowlands, Langley, Furlong (Moore), Baidoo, Cook (Donnelly).

Brighton & HA (0) 0

Coventry C (0) 1 *(McSheffrey 50)* 6734

Brighton & HA: Chaigneau; El Abd (Reid), Mayo, McShane, Butters, Carpenter, Carole, Hammond, Hart (Robinson), Kazim Richards (McCammon), Frutos.
Coventry C: Ince; Duffy, Hall, Hughes (Jorgensen), Williams, Shaw, McSheffrey (Morrell), Doyle, Adebola, John (Whing), Scowcroft.

Chelsea (1) 2 *(Cole C 12, Gudjohnsen 82)*

Huddersfield T (0) 1 *(Taylor-Fletcher 75)* 41,650

Chelsea: Cudicini; Johnson, Bridge (Del Horno), Diarra, Huth, Ricardo Carvalho, Wright-Phillips (Paulo Ferreira), Cole J, Cole C, Gudjohnsen, Duff (Robben).
Huddersfield T: Senior; Holdsworth, Adams, Hudson, McIntosh (Mirfin), Clarke N, Ahmed (Clarke T), Brandon, Abbott, Taylor-Fletcher, Schofield (Collins).

Cheltenham T (0) 2 *(Melligan 59 (pen), Finnigan 74 (pen))*

Chester C (0) 2 *(Richardson 80, Drummond 90)* 4741

Cheltenham T: Brown; Gill, Victory, Bird, Caines, Townsend, Melligan (Armstrong), Finnigan, Odejayi, Guinan (Spencer), Wilson.
Chester C: Gillet; McNiven (Bolland), Regan, Walker, Artell, Dimech, Drummond, Davies (El Kholti), Richardson, Blundell (Vaughan), Curtis.

Crystal Palace (2) 4 *(Hughes 4, McAnuff 37, Johnson 53 (pen), Freedman 88 (pen))*

Northampton T (1) 1 *(Low 12)* 10,391

Crystal Palace: Kiraly; Boyce, Borrowdale, Hudson, Ward, Watson, McAnuff (Black), Hughes (Riihilati), Johnson (Berry), Freedman, Andrews.
Northampton T: Harper; Bojic (Brett Johnson), Crowe, Chambers, Doig, Taylor, Low, Hunt, McGleish, Kirk, Jess (Mendes).

Derby Co (1) 2 *(Peschisolido 18, 67)*

Burnley (1) 1 *(O'Connor G 29)* 12,713

Derby Co: Poole; Edworthy, Kenna, Thirlwell, Johnson M, Nyatanga, Johnson S, Idiakez, Peschisolido (Bolder), Smith, Holmes.
Burnley: Jensen; Duff (Thomas), Harley, Hyde, Sinclair, McGreal, Elliott (Branch), O'Connor J, Akinbiyi, McCann, O'Connor G.

Hull C (0) 0

Aston Villa (0) 1 *(Barry 61)* 17,051

Hull C: Myhill; France, Dawson (Lynch), Collins, Cort, Delaney, Price, Andrews, Fagan, Paynter (Green), Ellison (Elliott).
Aston Villa: Sorensen; Delaney, Barry, Davis, Hughes, Mellberg, Milner, McCann, Angel, Moore, Hendrie.

Ipswich T (0) 0

Portsmouth (1) 1 *(Dario Silva 37)* 15,593

Ipswich T: Supple; Wilnis, Barron, Williams, De Vos, Naylor, Westlake (Juan), Magilton (Sito), Currie, Haynes, Richards (Garvan).
Portsmouth: Westerveld; Priske, Vignal, Hughes, O'Brien, Stefanovic, O'Neil, Diao, Dario Silva (Todorov), Lua-Lua (Karadas), Taylor.

Luton T (2) 3 *(Howard 31, Robinson 43, Nicholls 53 (pen))*

Liverpool (1) 5 *(Gerrard 16, Sinama-Pongolle 62, 74, Xabi Alonso 69, 90)* 10,170

Luton T: Beresford; Foley, Underwood, Robinson, Coyne, Heikkenen (Barnett), Brkovic (Showunmi), Nicholls, Howard, Vine, Edwards (Feeney).
Liverpool: Carson; Finnan, Riise, Xabi Alonso, Carragher, Hyypia, Sissoko (Sinama-Pongolle), Gerrard, Crouch (Kromkamp), Cisse (Warnock), Kewell.

Manchester C (0) 3 *(Fowler 48, 56, 64 (pen))*

Scunthorpe U (1) 1 *(Keogh 17)* 27,779

Manchester C: James; Onuoha (Croft), Jordan, Dunne, Distin, Barton, Sinclair, Ireland, Sibierski (Wright-Phillips), Fowler, Jihai.
Scunthorpe U: Evans; Byrne (Sparrow), Rose, Crosby, Hinds, Baraclough, Taylor (Goodwin), MacKenzie, Keogh, Sharp, Beagrie (Torpey).

Millwall (1) 1 *(Williams M 39)*

Everton (0) 1 *(Osman 79)* 16,440

Millwall: Marshall; Robinson P, Craig, Elliott, Whitbread, Lawrence, Williams M, Livermore, Braniff (Fangueiro), May, Cogan.
Everton: Wright; Hibbert, Nuno Valente, Ferrari, Weir, Arteta, Neville (Osman), Cahill, Bent (Ferguson), McFadden (Beattie), Kilbane.

Newcastle U (0) 1 *(Shearer 80)*

Mansfield T (0) 0 41,459

Newcastle U: Given; Carr (Ramage), Babayaro, Clark, Bramble, Boumsong, Solano, Brittain (Chopra), Shearer, Luque (O'Brien), N'Zogbia.
Mansfield T: Pressman; Buxton, Jelleyman, Coke, Day, John-Baptiste, Uhlenbeek (Arnold), Dawson, Barker, Russell (Birchall), Rundle.

Norwich C (0) 1 *(McVeigh 72 (pen))*

West Ham U (1) 2 *(Mullins 6, Zamora 57)* 23,968

Norwich C: Green (Ward); Jarrett (Spillane), Drury, Fleming, Doherty, Charlton, Henderson, Rossi Jarvis (Cave-Brown), McVeigh, Thorne, Etuhu.
West Ham U: Hislop; Repka, Konchesky, Collins, Gabbidon, Mullins (Fletcher), Newton, Reo-Coker, Harewood, Zamora (Katan), Etherington (Dailly).

Nuneaton B (0) 1 *(Murphy 90 (pen))*

Middlesbrough (1) 1 *(Mendieta 15)* 6000

Nuneaton B: Acton; Oddy, Love, Fitzpatrick (Reeves), Moore, Angus, Noon, Staff (Whittaker), Collins, Murphy, Quailey (Frew).
Middlesbrough: Jones; Parnaby, Pogatetz, Southgate, Bates, Doriva, Mendieta, Morrison, Yakubu, Viduka, Cattermole.

Preston NE (0) 2 *(Alexander 62, Sedgwick 86)*

Crewe Alex (1) 1 *(Jones B 35)* 8380

Preston NE: Nash; Alexander, Davidson, Mears, Lucketti, Mawene (Anyinsah), Sedgwick, Davis, Agyemang (Hibbert), Nugent, Neal (Dichio).
Crewe Alex: Tomlinson; Moss, Moses, Jones B (Varney), Walker, McCready, Vaughan (Bell), Lunt, Higdon, Rivers, Roberts.

Sheffield U (1) 1 *(Kabba 5)*

Colchester U (1) 2 *(Danns 33, Williams 72)* 11,820

Sheffield U: Barnes; Kozluk, Armstrong, Jagielka, Morgan, Quinn (Forte), Ifill (Haidong), Nalis, Kabba (Montgomery), Gillespie, Tonge.
Colchester U: Davison; Halford, White, Brown, Baldwin, Watson, Duguid, Danns, Iwelumo, Garcia (Williams), Yeates.

Sheffield W (1) 2 *(Heckingbottom 16, 60)*

Charlton Ath (3) 4 *(Rommedahl 13, 44, Holland 27, Bent D 87)* 14,851

Sheffield W: Lucas; Simek, Heckingbottom, Whelan, Coughlan, Wood, O'Brien, Corr, Tudgay, Partridge (Bullen), Brunt.
Charlton Ath: Myhre; Spector, Powell (Perry), Holland, Fortune, Hreidarsson, Kishishev, Hughes (Lisbie), Bent D, Bartlett, Rommedahl (Ambrose).

Southampton (1) 4 *(Prutton 40, Quashie 60, Walcott 66, Kenton 88)*

Milton Keynes D (0) 3 *(Lundekvam 59 (og), Rizzo 79, Edds 84)* 15,908

Southampton: Smith; Baird, Cranie, Prutton, Lundekvam, Kenton, Dyer (Walcott), Quashie, Ormerod (Fuller), Blackstock, Belmadi (Folly).
Milton Keynes D: Baker; Edds, Lewington, McClenahan (Rizzo), Morgan, Chorley, Mitchell, Small (Kamara), Platt (Wilbraham), McLeod, Crooks.

Stockport Co (1) 2 *(Easter 17, Briggs 48)*

Brentford (1) 3 *(Owusu 13, Campbell 65, Rankin 84)* 4078

Stockport Co: Spencer; Clare, Robinson, Allen, Raynes, Williams A, Briggs (Le Fondre), Boshell (Wolski), Hamshaw, Easter, Singh.
Brentford: Nelson; O'Connor, Tillen, Newman, Sodje, Turner, Brooker (Rankin), Hutchinson, Owusu, Campbell, Gayle (Frampton).

Stoke C (0) 0

Tamworth (0) 0 9366

Stoke C: Simonsen; Buxton, Broomes, Hoefkens, Henry, Russell, Chadwick (Harper), Brammer, Sidibe, Gallagher (Sigurdsson), Kopteff (Sweeney).
Tamworth: Bevan; Ward, Turner, Bampton (Cooper), Redmile, Smith, Melton, Touhy, Wright (Storer), Edwards, Anaclet.

Torquay U (0) 0

Birmingham C (0) 0 5974

Torquay U: Marriott; Lawless, Lloyd, Hewlett, Lockwood, Sharp, Phillips, Woods, Bedeau (Connell), Osei-Kuffour, Hill.
Birmingham C: Maik Taylor; Bruce (Kilkenny), Lazaridis, Butt, Martin Taylor, Cunningham, Pennant, Johnson, Heskey, Jarosik (Pandiani), Gray.

WBA (0) 1 *(Gera 82 (pen))*

Reading (0) 1 *(Doyle 84 (pen))* 19,197

WBA: Kirkland; Albrechtsen, Robinson, Wallwork, Davies C, Moore, Greening (Gera), Inamoto (Horsfield), Ellington (Campbell), Kanu, Carter.
Reading: Stack; Makin, Shorey, Ingimarsson, Gunnarsson, Harper, Oster, Sidwell, Kitson (Doyle), Long (Lita), Hunt (Little).

Watford (0) 0

Bolton W (2) 3 *(Borgetti 11, Giannakopoulos 34, Vaz Te 73)* 13,239

Watford: Foster; Doyley, Stewart, Mahon, Mackay, Carlisle, Eagles, Diagouraga, Henderson (Gill), King, McNamee.
Bolton W: Walker; O'Brien, Gardner, Fadiga (Fojut), Ben Haim, N'Gotty (Sissons), Okocha, Nakata, Borgetti (Ashton), Vaz Te, Giannakopoulos.

Wigan Ath (0) 1 *(Connolly 47)*

Leeds U (0) 1 *(Hulse 88)* 10,980

Wigan Ath: Filan; Taylor, McMillan, Skoko (Roberts), Henchoz, Jackson, Francis, Johansson (Kavanagh), Connolly, McCulloch, Mahon (Teale).
Leeds U: Sullivan; Kelly, Crainey, Derry, Butler, Kilgallon, Douglas (Cresswell), Miller, Hulse, Blake (Healy), Lewis.

Wolverhampton W (1) 1 *(Clarke 26)*

Plymouth Arg (0) 0 11,041

Wolverhampton W: Postma; Ross, Kennedy, Ince, Gyepes, Lescott, Cameron (Rosa), Seol (Cort), Clarke, Miller, Davies.
Plymouth Arg: Larrieu; Connolly, Barness, Wotton, Doumbe, Aljofree, Norris, Buzsaky (Taylor), Evans, Hodges (Djordjic), Capaldi.

Sunday, 8 January 2006

Burton Alb (0) 0

Manchester U (0) 0 6191

Burton Alb: Deeney; Sedgemore, Corbett, Stride, Tinson, Austin, Hall (Todd), Ducros, Shaw, Harrad (Anderson), Gilroy.
Manchester U: Howard; Brown, Bardsley, O'Shea, Pique, Silvestre, Jones R, Solskjaer (Ronaldo), Saha, Rossi (Rooney), Richardson.

Fulham (0) 1 *(John 50)*

Leyton Orient (2) 2 *(Easton 17, Keith 44)* 13,394

Fulham: Warner; Rosenior, Jensen N, Elliott, Knight, Pearce (Goma), Legwinski, Radzinski, Elrich (Timlin), John, Boa Morte.
Leyton Orient: Garner; Miller, Lockwood, Easton, Mackie, Zakuani, Tudor (McMahon), Simpson, Alexander (Barnard), Ibehre, Keith (Carlisle).

Leicester C (1) 3 *(Hammond 44, Hughes 57, De Vries 90)*

Tottenham H (2) 2 *(Jenas 20, Stalteri 41)* 19,844

Leicester C: Douglas; Stearman, Maybury, Williams, McCarthy, Johansson, Smith R (Kisnorbo), Gudjonsson, De Vries, Hamill (Hammond), Hughes.
Tottenham H: Robinson; Stalteri, Kelly, Gardner, Dawson, Lennon (Tainio), Jenas, Carrick, Rasiak, Keane, Brown (Defoe).

Sunderland (2) 3 *(Collins N 6, Whitehead 41, Le Tallec 70)*

Northwich Vic (0) 0 19,323

Sunderland: Davis; Hoyte, Collins D, Lawrence, Stubbs, Collins N, Whitehead (Welsh), Miller, Stead, Le Tallec (Murphy), Arca.
Northwich Vic: Rodgers; McCarthy, Chapman (Sale), Carr, Payne, Charnock, Mayman (Byrne), Elliott, Allan, Brayson, Roca (Devlin).

THIRD ROUND REPLAYS

Tuesday, 17 January 2006

Birmingham C (0) 2 *(Jarosik 61, Forssell 81)*

Torquay U (0) 0 24,650

Birmingham C: Maik Taylor; Melchiot (Bruce), Gray, Clemence, Upson, Martin Taylor (Painter), Pennant, Kilkenny, Forssell, Jarosik, Dunn.
Torquay U: Marriott; Lawless, Lloyd, Lockwood, Sharp, Woods (Hewlett), Phillips (Connell), Sako (Garner), Bedeau, Osei-Kuffour, Hill.

Chester C (0) 0

Cheltenham T (0) 1 *(Odejayi 52)* 5096

Chester C: Gillet; McNiven (El Kholti), Regan, Curtis, Artell, Dimech, Drummond, Davies, Branch, Blundell, Walker (Richardson).
Cheltenham T: Higgs; Gill, Armstrong, Bird, Caines, Townsend, Melligan, Finnigan, Odejayi (Spencer), Guinan, Wilson.

Leeds U (1) 3 *(Healy 41, 64 (pen), Kelly 116)*

Wigan Ath (1) 3 *(Johansson 24, Roberts 50, 103)* 15,243

Leeds U: Sullivan; Kelly, Crainey, Walton (Blake), Butler, Kilgallon, Douglas, Miller (Einarsson), Hulse, Healy, Lewis (Cresswell).
Wigan Ath: Filan; Chimbonda, Baines, Kavanagh, Jackson, De Zeeuw, Teale, Francis (Bullard), Roberts, Johansson, Skoko (Joyce).
aet; Wigan Ath won 4-2 on penalties.

Middlesbrough (2) 5 *(Riggott 34, Yakubu 42 (pen), 58, Parnaby 50, Viduka 63)*

Nuneaton B (0) 2 *(Murphy 71, 86 (pen))* 26,255

Middlesbrough: Jones; Bates, Taylor, Parnaby (Parlour), Riggott, Pogatetz, Mendieta, Cattermole, Yakubu, Viduka (Maccarone), Johnson.
Nuneaton B: Acton; Oddy, Love, Noon, Moore, Angus, Collins (Reeves), Fitzpatrick, Murphy, Quailey (Frew), Whittaker (Wilkin).

Reading (0) 3 *(Lita 50, 65, 93)*
WBA (2) 2 *(Chaplow 9, 32)* 16,737
Reading: Stack; Murty, Makin, Ingimarsson, Gunnarsson, Harper, Oster (Osano), Hunt, Lita (Cox), Sidwell, Long (Doyle).
WBA: Kirkland; Albrechtsen, Hodgkiss, Wallwork (Nicholson), Davies C, Chaplow, Greening (Dyer), Inamoto (Davies R), Ellington, Earnshaw, Carter.
aet.

Tamworth (1) 1 *(Jackson 42)*
Stoke C (0) 1 *(Gallagher 80)* 3812
Tamworth: Bevan; Touhy, Anaclet, Ward (Stamps), Redmile, Smith, Melton (Storer), Wright (Turner), Heggs, Jackson, Bampton.
Stoke C: Simonsen; Henry, Broomes (Rooney), Hoefkens, Duberry, Harper, Chadwick (Kopteff), Brammer (Junior), Sidibe, Gallagher, Buxton.
aet; Stoke C won 5-4 on penalties.

Walsall (0) 2 *(Leary 68, James 78)*
Barnsley (0) 0 4074
Walsall: Oakes; Pead, Fox, Osborn (Standing), Roper (Westwood), Gerrard, Wright, Leary, Demontagnac, Timm, James.
Barnsley: Colgan; Hassell, Austin (Nardiello), Howard, Carbon, Reid, Kell (Burns), Shuker, Hayes, Wright, Devaney (Richards).

Wednesday, 18 January 2006

Everton (0) 1 *(Cahill 72)*
Millwall (0) 0 25,800
Everton: Martyn; Hibbert, Nuno Valente, Weir (Kroldrup), Ferrari, Arteta, Osman, Neville, Beattie, Cahill, Kilbane (McFadden).
Millwall: Marshall; Dunne, Craig (Braniff), Lawrence, Robinson P, Whitbread, Elliott, Morris (Cogan), May, Williams M, Livermore.

Manchester U (2) 5 *(Saha 7, Rossi 23, 90, Richardson 52, Giggs 68)*
Burton Alb (0) 0 53,564
Manchester U: Howard; Bardsley, Silvestre, Brown (Neville), Pique, O'Shea (Ferdinand), Solskjaer, Fletcher (Giggs), Rossi, Saha, Richardson.
Burton Alb: Deeney; Sedgemore, Corbett, Stride, Tinson, Austin, Hall (Webster), Ducros, Shaw (Anderson), Harrad, Gilroy (Henshaw).

FOURTH ROUND

Saturday, 28 January 2006

Aston Villa (0) 3 *(Baros 70, 74, Davis 90)*
Port Vale (0) 1 *(Lowndes 85)* 30,434
Aston Villa: Sorensen; Hughes, Samuel, Davis, Mellberg, Delaney, Milner, McCann, Baros, Angel (Phillips), Hendrie.
Port Vale: Goodlad; Abbey, James, Dinning, Pilkington, Fortune (Birchall), Togwell, Cummins, Husbands, Constantine (Lowndes), Innes (Doherty).

Bolton W (0) 1 *(Giannakopoulos 84)*
Arsenal (0) 0 13,326
Bolton W: Jaaskelainen; O'Brien, Gardner, Campo (Vaz Te), Ben Haim, N'Gotty, Nolan, Nakata, Borgetti (Jansen), Davies, Giannakopoulos (Hunt).
Arsenal: Almunia; Gilbert, Djourou, Flamini, Campbell, Senderos, Hleb, Diaby, Reyes, Van Persie, Ljungberg.

Brentford (0) 2 *(Campbell 57, 89)*
Sunderland (0) 1 *(Arca 66)* 11,698
Brentford: Nelson; Frampton, Tillen (Brooker), Newman, Sodje, Turner, Mousinho, Rankin (Hutchinson), Owusu, Campbell, Tabb.
Sunderland: Davis; Hoyte, Collins D, Lawrence, Breen, Collins N, Whitehead, Miller, Stead (Le Tallec), Kyle (Gray), Arca.

Charlton Ath (1) 2 *(Fortune 7, Bothroyd 90)*
Leyton Orient (0) 1 *(Steele 53)* 22,029
Charlton Ath: Myhre; Young, Powell, Holland, Fortune, Hreidarsson, Kishishev (Thomas), Ambrose, Bent D, Bartlett (Bothroyd), Hughes (Smertin).
Leyton Orient: Garner; Miller, Lockwood, McMahon, Mackie, Zakuani, Tudor, Simpson, Alexander, Steele (Duncan), Keith.

Cheltenham T (0) 0
Newcastle U (2) 2 *(Chopra 41, Parker 43)* 7022
Cheltenham T: Higgs; Gill, Armstrong, Bird, Caines, Townsend, Melligan (Vincent), Finnigan, Odejayi, Guinan (Spencer), Wilson.
Newcastle U: Given; Ramage, Babayaro, Clark, Bramble, Boumsong, Solano (Emre), Parker (Luque), Shearer, Chopra (N'Zogbia), Ameobi.

Colchester U (1) 3 *(Danns 44, 52, Garcia 59)*
Derby Co (0) 1 *(Smith 79 (pen))* 5933
Colchester U: Gerken; Duguid, White, Izzet, Baldwin, Richards, Halford, Danns, Iwelumo, Garcia (Stockley), Yeates (Williams).
Derby Co: Camp; Hajto, Johnson M, Thirlwell, Davies, Nyatanga, Bisgaard, Idiakez, Peschisolido (Holdsworth), Smith, Bolder (Holmes).

Coventry C (0) 1 *(John 54)*
Middlesbrough (0) 1 *(Hasselbaink 46)* 28,120
Coventry C: Fulop; Duffy, Hall, Doyle, Williams, Shaw, Scowcroft, Hutchison (Jorgensen), Adebola, John (Morrell), McSheffrey (Impey).
Middlesbrough: Schwarzer; Parnaby, Pogatetz, Cattermole, Ehiogu (Bates), Southgate, Mendieta, Rochemback (Doriva), Yakubu (Viduka), Hasselbaink, Downing.

Everton (1) 1 *(McFadden 36)*
Chelsea (0) 1 *(Lampard 73)* 29,742
Everton: Martyn; Hibbert, Nuno Valente, Neville, Weir, Arteta, Osman, Davies (Anichebe), McFadden (Naysmith), Ferguson, Kilbane.
Chelsea: Cudicini; Johnson, Del Horno (Cole C), Makelele, Terry, Gallas, Robben, Lampard, Crespo, Maniche (Duff), Cole J (Huth).

Leicester C (0) 0
Southampton (0) 1 *(Jones 90)* 20,427
Leicester C: Douglas; Stearman, Maybury, Gerrbrand, McCarthy, Johansson, Hughes, Gudjonsson, Hume, Hammond (De Vries), Smith R.
Southampton: Bialkowski; Baird, Brennan, Potter, Lundekvam, Higginbotham, Dyer, Oakley, Pahars, Blackstock (Jones), Prutton (Gillett).

Manchester C (0) 1 *(Cole 84)*
Wigan Ath (0) 0 30,811
Manchester C: James; Jihai, Jordan, Dunne, Distin, Barton, Sinclair, Ireland (Sibierski), Cole, Vassell (Wright-Phillips), Riera (Musampa).
Wigan Ath: Filan; Chimbonda, Baines, Skoko (Henchoz), Jackson, Scharner, Francis, Mahon (Bullard), Mellor (Roberts), Johansson, Ziegler.

Preston NE (1) 1 *(O'Neil 27)*
Crystal Palace (1) 1 *(Johnson 8)* 9489
Preston NE: Nash; Mears, Davidson, O'Neil (Lucketti), Davis, Mawene, Sedgwick, Alexander, Agyemang, Hibbert, Neal (Dichio).
Crystal Palace: Kiraly; Hall, Boyce, Hudson, Popovic, Leigertwood, Andrews (Riihilahti), Morrison (Macken), Johnson, Freedman (Reich), Soares.

Reading (1) 1 *(Long 31)*
Birmingham C (0) 1 *(Dunn 67)* 23,762
Reading: Stack; Halls, Makin, Gunnarsson, Sonko, Harper, Oster, Sidwell, Lita, Long (Doyle), Hunt.
Birmingham C: Maik Taylor; Tebily, Lazaridis, Izzet (Kilkenny), Melchiot, Bruce, Pennant, Johnson, Sutton, Heskey (Dunn), Jarosik (Forssell).

Stoke C (1) 2 *(Sidibe 45, Chadwick 49)*
Walsall (0) 1 *(James 51)* 8834
Stoke C: Simonsen (De Goey); Buxton, Broomes, Hoefkens, Duberry, Henry, Chadwick (Kopteff), Brammer, Sidibe, Gallagher (Sigurdsson), Sweeney.
Walsall: Oakes; Pead, Fox, Leary, Westwood, Gerrard, Wright (Standing), Smith G, McDermott (Nicholls), Timm, James.

West Ham U (2) 4 *(Sheringham 33 (pen), Etherington 37, Khizanishvili 59 (og), Zamora 73)*
Blackburn R (1) 2 *(Bentley 1, Neill 65)* 23,700
West Ham U: Hislop; Dailly, Konchesky, Gabbidon, Ferdinand, Mullins, Benayoun (Fletcher), Reo-Coker, Zamora (Katan), Sheringham (Harewood), Etherington.
Blackburn R: Friedel; Neill, Gray, Mokoena (Tugay), Todd, Khizanishvili, Reid, Savage, Bentley (Johnson), Kuqi (Emerton), Pedersen.

Sunday, 29 January 2006

Portsmouth (0) 1 *(Davis 54)*
Liverpool (2) 2 *(Gerrard 37 (pen), Riise 41)* 17,247
Portsmouth: Kiely; Primus (Priske), Vignal (Todorov), Davis, O'Brien, Stefanovic, O'Neil, Pedro Mendes, Pericard (Karadas), Hughes, Taylor.
Liverpool: Reina; Kromkamp, Warnock, Xabi Alonso, Carragher, Hyypia, Sissoko, Gerrard (Finnan), Cisse (Kewell), Morientes (Crouch), Riise.

Wolverhampton W (0) 0
Manchester U (2) 3 *(Richardson 5, 52, Saha 45)* 28,333
Wolverhampton W: Postma; Edwards, Naylor, Ince, Gyepes, Lescott, Seol (Cameron), Anderton (Davies), Cort (Frankowski), Miller, Kennedy.
Manchester U: Van der Sar; Neville, Silvestre, Ferdinand, Brown (Smith), Vidic, Richardson (Evra), Saha (Fletcher), Van Nistelrooy, Rooney, Park.

FOURTH ROUND REPLAYS

Tuesday, 7 February 2006

Birmingham C (1) 2 *(Forssell 30, Gray 67)*
Reading (0) 1 *(Hunt 51)* 16,644
Birmingham C: Maik Taylor; Melchiot, Gray, Clemence (Oji), Bruce, Painter, Pennant, Clapham, Forssell, Jarosik, Birley (Sadler).
Reading: Stack; Halls, Makin, Ingimarsson, Sonko, Gunnarsson, Oster, Sidwell, Kitson, Long (Cox), Hunt.

Crystal Palace (1) 1 *(Ward 26)*
Preston NE (1) 2 *(Dichio 35, 88)* 7356
Crystal Palace: Kiraly; Ward, Borrowdale (Andrews), Hudson, Boyce, Riihilahti, McAnuff, Watson, Johnson, Freedman (Maken), Reich (Soares).
Preston NE: Nash; Mears, Hill, O'Neil (Hibbert), Lucketti, Mawene, Sedgwick, McKenna, Agyemang, Dichio, Neal (Nugent).

Wednesday, 8 February 2006

Chelsea (3) 4 *(Robben 22, Lampard 36 (pen), Crespo 39, Terry 74)*
Everton (0) 1 *(Arteta 72 (pen))* 39,301
Chelsea: Cudicini; Johnson, Gallas, Essien, Terry, Huth, Wright-Phillips, Lampard (Geremi), Crespo (Maniche), Gudjohnsen, Robben (Cole J).
Everton: Turner; Hibbert, Nuno Valente (Davies), Ferrari, Weir, Arteta, Osman (Carsley), Neville, Beattie (McFadden), Cahill, Kilbane.

Middlesbrough (1) 1 *(Hasselbaink 20)*
Coventry C (0) 0 14,131
Middlesbrough: Schwarzer; Parnaby, Pogatetz, Doriva, Riggott, Southgate, Mendieta (Bates), Rochemback, Hasselbaink, Yakubu (Maccarone), Taylor.
Coventry C: Fulop; Whing (Morrell), Hall, Doyle, Page, Williams, Scowcroft, Hutchison, Adebola, John, McSheffrey.

FIFTH ROUND

Saturday, 18 February 2006

Bolton W (0) 0
West Ham U (0) 0 17,120
Bolton W: Jaaskelainen; O'Brien, Gardner, Speed, Ben Haim, Jaidi, Okocha, Nakata, Nolan, Davies (Borgetti), Giannakopoulos (Vaz Te).
West Ham U: Hislop; Scaloni, Konchesky, Gabbidon, Ferdinand, Mullins, Benayoun (Dailly), Reo-Coker, Harewood (Zamora), Ashton (Sheringham), Etherington.

Charlton Ath (2) 3 *(Bent D 3, Bothroyd 45, Hughes 62)*
Brentford (0) 1 *(Rankin 83)* 22,098
Charlton Ath: Myhre; Young, Powell, Smertin, Perry, Hreidarsson, Kishishev (Ambrose), Hughes (Holland), Bent D, Bothroyd (Bartlett), Thomas.
Brentford: Nelson; O'Connor, Frampton, Newman (Rankin), Sodje, Turner, Pratley, Tillen (Brooker), Owusu, Gayle (Peters), Tabb.

Liverpool (1) 1 *(Crouch 19)*
Manchester U (0) 0 44,039
Liverpool: Reina; Finnan, Riise, Hamann, Carragher, Hyypia, Sissoko, Gerrard, Crouch (Cisse), Morientes (Luis Garcia), Kewell (Kromkamp).
Manchester U: Van der Sar; Neville, Silvestre (Saha), Fletcher (Smith) (Park), Brown, Vidic, Ronaldo, Richardson, Van Nistelrooy, Rooney, Giggs.

Newcastle U (0) 1 *(Dyer 68)*
Southampton (0) 0 40,975
Newcastle U: Given; Ramage, Elliott, Parker, Bramble, Boumsong, Solano, Emre, Dyer (Bowyer), Ameobi (Luque), N'Zogbia.
Southampton: Bialkowski; Ostlund, Brennan, Oakley, Lundekvam (Potter), Powell, Wright, Pahars (Dyer), Jones (Blackstock), Madsen, Cranie.

Sunday, 19 February 2006

Aston Villa (0) 1 *(Baros 72)*
Manchester C (0) 1 *(Richards 90)* 23,847
Aston Villa: Sorensen; Hughes, Samuel, Davis, Mellberg, Delaney (Ridgewell), Milner, McCann, Baros, Moore (Angel), Barry.
Manchester C: James; Richards, Jordan, Dunne, Distin, Barton, Musampa, Sibierski (Croft), Samaras, Vassell (Wright-Phillips), Riera.

Chelsea (1) 3 *(Paulo Ferreira 37, Cole J 79, 90)*
Colchester U (1) 1 *(Ricardo Carvalho 28 (og))* 41,810
Chelsea: Cudicini; Johnson, Paulo Ferreira, Diarra (Cole J), Huth, Ricardo Carvalho, Wright-Phillips, Maniche (Lampard), Drogba, Essien, Duff (Crespo).
Colchester U: Davison; Duguid, White, Baldwin, Brown, Watson, Halford, Danns, Iwelumo, Garcia (Williams), Yeates (Chilvers).

Preston NE (0) 0
Middlesbrough (0) 2 *(Yakubu 52, 77)* 19,877
Preston NE: Nash; Mears, Hill, O'Neil (Dichio), Davis, Mawene, Sedgwick (Neal), McKenna, Agyemang (Lucketti), Nugent, Davidson.
Middlesbrough: Schwarzer; Parnaby, Queudrue, McMahon (Hasselbaink), Riggott, Pogatetz, Mendieta, Boateng, Yakubu (Southgate), Rochemback (Cattermole), Downing.

Stoke C (0) 0
Birmingham C (0) 1 *(Forssell 47)* 18,768
Stoke C: Simonsen; Hill, Broomes (Rooney), Hoefkens, Duberry, Junior, Chadwick, Brammer, Sidibe, Bangoura, Sweeney (Sigurdsson).
Birmingham C: Maik Taylor; Melchiot, Gray, Clemence, Latka, Bruce, Pennant (Clapham), Butt, Forssell (Jarosik), Heskey, Johnson.

FIFTH ROUND REPLAYS

Tuesday, 14 March 2006

Manchester C (1) 2 *(Samaras 17, Vassell 49)*
Aston Villa (0) 1 *(Davis 85)* 33,006
Manchester C: James; Jihai, Jordan, Dunne, Richards, Barton, Sinclair, Musampa, Samaras (Sibierski), Vassell (Wright-Phillips), Riera.
Aston Villa: Sorensen; Hughes, Bouma, Davis, Mellberg, Ridgewell, McCann, Moore, Baros (Gardner), Phillips, Barry.

Wednesday, 15 March 2006

West Ham U (1) 2 *(Jaaskelainen 10 (og), Harewood 96)*
Bolton W (1) 1 *(Davies 31)* 24,685
West Ham U: Hislop; Scaloni, Konchesky, Gabbidon, Ferdinand, Mullins, Benayoun, Reo-Coker (Dailly), Harewood, Ashton (Sheringham), Etherington (Zamora).
Bolton W: Jaaskelainen; Hunt (Borgetti), Gardner, Diagne-Faye (Pedersen), Ben Haim, Jaidi, Okocha, Speed (Vaz Te), Nolan, Davies, Giannakopoulos.

SIXTH ROUND

Monday, 20 March 2006

Manchester C (0) 1 *(Musampa 85)*
West Ham U (1) 2 *(Ashton 41, 69)* 39,357
Manchester C: James; Richards, Jordan (Sommeil), Dunne, Distin, Barton (Ireland), Jihai■, Musampa, Wright-Phillips (Croft), Vassell, Riera.
West Ham U: Hislop; Dailly (Scaloni), Konchesky, Gabbidon, Collins, Mullins, Benayoun, Reo-Coker (Fletcher), Harewood, Ashton (Zamora), Etherington.

Tuesday, 21 March 2006

Birmingham C (0) 0
Liverpool (3) 7 *(Hyypia 1, Crouch 5, 38, Morientes 59, Riise 70, Cisse 89, Tebily 77 (og))* 27,378
Birmingham C: Maik Taylor; Melchiot, Clapham, Clemence, Martin Taylor (Tebily), Cunningham, Pennant, Johnson (Bruce), Forssell, Dunn (Kilkenny), Painter.
Liverpool: Reina; Finnan, Traore (Kewell), Xabi Alonso, Carragher, Hyypia, Sissoko, Gerrard (Cisse), Crouch (Morientes), Luis Garcia, Riise.

Wednesday, 22 March 2006

Chelsea (1) 1 *(Terry 4)*
Newcastle U (0) 0 42,279
Chelsea: Cudicini; Geremi, Del Horno, Makelele, Terry, Ricardo Carvalho, Cole J (Essien), Lampard, Drogba, Gudjohnsen (Crespo), Duff (Wright-Phillips).
Newcastle U: Given; Carr, Babayaro (Moore), Parker, Elliott■, Ramage, Solano (Emre), Bowyer, Shearer, Ameobi, Dyer.

Thursday, 23 March 2006

Charlton Ath (0) 0
Middlesbrough (0) 0 24,187
Charlton Ath: Myhre; Young, Powell, Holland, Perry, Hreidarsson, Kishishev (Rommedahl), Hughes, Bent D, Bartlett (Bothroyd), Thomas.
Middlesbrough: Schwarzer; Parnaby, Queudrue, Boateng, Ehiogu, Southgate, Mendieta (Morrison), Cattermole, Hasselbaink, Yakubu (Viduka), Downing.

SIXTH ROUND REPLAY

Wednesday, 12 April 2006

Middlesbrough (2) 4 *(Rochemback 11, Morrison 26, Hasselbaink 73, Viduka 77)*
Charlton Ath (1) 2 *(Hughes 13, Bothroyd 76)* 30,248
Middlesbrough: Schwarzer; Parnaby, Taylor, Boateng, Riggott, Southgate, Morrison, Rochemback, Hasselbaink (Ehiogu), Viduka, Downing.
Charlton Ath: Myhre; Spector, Powell, Holland (Thomas), Perry, Hreidarsson, Kishishev (Euell), Rommedahl, Bent D, Bartlett (Bothroyd), Hughes.

SEMI-FINALS

Saturday, 22 April 2006 (at Old Trafford)

Chelsea (0) 1 *(Drogba 70)*
Liverpool (1) 2 *(Riise 21, Luis Garcia 53)* 64,575
Chelsea: Cudicini; Paulo Ferreira, Del Horno (Robben), Makelele, Terry, Gallas, Geremi (Duff), Lampard, Drogba, Crespo (Cole J), Essien.
Liverpool: Reina; Finnan, Riise, Xabi Alonso, Carragher, Hyypia, Sissoko, Gerrard, Crouch (Cisse), Luis Garcia (Morientes), Kewell (Traore).

Sunday, 23 April 2006 (at Villa Park)

Middlesbrough (0) 0
West Ham U (0) 1 *(Harewood 78)* 39,148
Middlesbrough: Schwarzer (Jones); Parnaby, Queudrue, Boateng, Riggott, Southgate, Taylor (Maccarone), Rochemback (Parlour), Hasselbaink, Yakubu, Downing.
West Ham U: Hislop; Ferdinand, Konchesky, Gabbidon, Collins, Mullins, Benayoun, Reo-Coker, Harewood, Ashton (Zamora), Etherington (Newton).

THE FA CUP FINAL

Saturday, 13 May 2006
(at Millennium Stadium, Cardiff, attendance 74,000)

Liverpool (1) 3 West Ham U (2) 3

Liverpool: Reina; Finnan, Riise, Xabi Alonso (Kromkamp), Carragher, Hyypia, Sissoko, Gerrard, Crouch (Hamann), Cisse, Kewell (Morientes).

Scorers: (Cisse 32, Gerrard 54, 90)

West Ham U: Hislop; Scaloni, Konchesky, Gabbidon, Ferdinand, Fletcher (Dailly), Benayoun, Reo-Coker, Harewood, Ashton (Zamora), Etherington (Sheringham).

Scorers: (Carragher 21 (og), Ashton 28, Konchesky 64)

aet; Liverpool won 3-1 on penalties: Hamann scored; Zamora saved; Hyypia saved; Sheringham scored; Gerrard scored; Konchesky saved; Riise scored; Ferdinand saved.

Referee: A. Wiley (Staffordshire).

NATIONWIDE CONFERENCE 2005–06

Those who are unhappy that the play-offs discriminate against teams who finish one place short of automatic promotion, would at least be satisfied that the Conference in 2005–06 ended with the first two achieving Football League status. While Accrington Stanley were the champions, Hereford United managed to survive the play-offs this time.

Ironically the first table after just one round had put Hereford on top, but the complexion of affairs looked vastly different after ten matches had been completed.

Grays Athletic on the back of an outstanding season in the Ryman League previously and winning the FA Trophy, too, were the only undefeated team, though their lead was just on a better goal difference from Accrington.

York City were starting to make a more positive move and naturally Morecambe were in the frame as well, as indeed were Exeter City.

Grays were drawing a high proportion of their matches but were still keeping their unbeaten record. Significantly their first reverse came in mid-November at home to Accrington who beat them 2-1. Exeter, with one game more completed had taken over at the head of the table by a point.

A month on and Accrington were leading having played one more game than Grays, Exeter were third and Morecambe fourth. They were the second team to lower Grays' colours with an emphatic 3-0 victory.

By the turn of the year Accrington had games in hand of their nearest rivals and were two points ahead of Exeter. Stevenage were next to throw down the gauntlet but in early February Accrington's lead had shot up to ten points with Morecambe their nearest challengers.

In mid-February, Hereford had started to make more progress and Grays had fallen away to be even out of the play-off places. By March Accrington looked home and dry with a 16 point lead having played 31 matches.

Halifax Town were finding some consistency and put themselves in the frame and Grays started to revive, too. Even Accrington suffered the odd setback, but on 17 April at Woking a 1-0 win meant a return to the Football League they had resigned from in 1962.

At the time, Hereford were still second followed by Halifax, Grays and Morecambe. These proved to be the finishing positions in the League. From the play-offs, Halifax took a narrow 3-2 lead in their home leg with Grays and held on 2-2 in Essex. Hereford drew at Morecambe 1-1 but were forced into extra time in the return before emerging 4-3 winners on aggregate.

In the final Halifax pushed Hereford to overtime, too, but United prevailed 3-2, their return to the Football League being after nine years outside the competition.

However, at the foot of the table it was a different matter and one which precipitated a farce involving the futures of Altrincham and Scarborough.

Altrincham were docked 18 points for fielding an ineligible player. Scarborough who had come out of administration appeared to be saved as Canvey Island had resigned from the Conference. But Scarborough did not fulfil financial guidelines and were axed with Altrincham reprieved!

Stevenage again flattered to deceive and Exeter had another disappointing season by their ambitions. York also fell away when it seemed they had mounted a serious challenge and Burton Albion in a better financial position after their FA Cup meetings with Manchester United had to settle for ninth place which they occupied from March.

Dagenham & Redbridge were economical with their playing staff but were mid-table and Woking who threatened earlier in the season only finished as runners-up to Grays in the Trophy final.

Neither relegated teams Cambridge United and Kidderminster Harriers offered much of a challenge and Canvey's plight came about through their benefactor withdrawing his financial support.

Aldershot Town began poorly and despite a mid-season improvement endured their worst season since gaining Conference status. Gravesend & Northfleet were never in any danger and twice as high as ninth and Crawley Town's 17th position seemed unlikely for much of the season as they languished at the bottom, until a run of five successive wins.

Ironically their on-field revival came after financial problems off it. Southport hauled themselves away from trouble, too, losing just the final game of their last six, while those perennial survivors Forest Green Rovers achieved safety once more.

Tamworth had a fine FA Cup run but struggled in the Conference and at one stage were facing relegation had Altrincham's appeal succeeded.

NATIONWIDE CONFERENCE PLAY-OFFS 2005–06

CONFERENCE FIRST LEG

Saturday, 6 May 2006

Halifax T (3) 3 *(Bushell 17, Sugden 30, Killeen 32)*

Grays Ath (0) 2 *(Oli 65, 77)* 3848

Halifax T: Kennedy; Haslam, Doughty, Foster, Young, Quinn, Forrest, Bushell (Thompson), Killeen, Sugden, Grant (Atherton).

Grays Ath: Bayes; Mawer, Nutter, Thurgood, Stuart, Hanson (Sambrook), Kightly, Martin, McLean, Oli, Poole.

Sunday, 7 May 2006

Morecambe (1) 1 *(Bentley 22)*

Hereford U (0) 1 *(Purdie 54 (pen))* 5208

Morecambe: Drench; Brannan, Howard, McLachlan, Bentley (Kempson), Blackburn, Thompson, Hunter (Perkins), Twiss, Carlton, Curtis (Rigoglioso).

Hereford U: Brown; Green, Jeannin, Mkandawire, Purdie, Beckwith, Travis, Stanley, Stansfield (Fleetwood), Williams (Ipoua), Ferrell.

CONFERENCE SECOND LEG

Wednesday, 10 May 2006

Grays Ath (0) 2 *(Kightly 56, Nutter 57)*

Halifax T (1) 2 *(Foster 6, 63 (pen))* 2886

Grays Ath: Bayes; Sambrook, Nutter, Thurgood, Stuart, Mawer, Kightly (Hooper), Martin, McLean, Oli, Poole.

Halifax T: Kennedy; Haslam, Doughty, Atherton, Young, Quinn, Thompson, Foster, Killeen (Senior), Sugden (Grant), Forrest.

Thursday, 11 May 2006

Hereford U (2) 3 *(Mkandawire 6, Williams 13, Ipoua 107)*

Morecambe (1) 2 *(Curtis 8 (pen), Twiss 53)* 6278

Hereford U: Brown; Green, Jeannin (Pitman), Mkandawire, Purdie, Beckwith, Travis, Stanley, Stansfield (Fleetwood), Williams (Ipoua), Ferrell.

Morecambe: Drench; Brannan, Howard, McLachlan (Perkins), Bentley (Kempson), Blackburn, Thompson, Hunter, Twiss, Carlton, Curtis (Rigoglioso).

aet.

CONFERENCE FINAL (at Leicester)

Saturday, 20 May 2006

Halifax T (1) 2 *(Killeen 27, Grant 73)*

Hereford U (1) 3 *(Williams 34, Ipoua 80, Green 108)* 15,499

Halifax T: Kennedy; Haslam, Doughty (Senior), Atherton, Young (Bushell), Quinn, Thompson, Foster, Killeen, Sugden (Grant), Forrest.

Hereford U: Brown; Green, Jeannin, Mkandawire, Purdie, Beckwith, Travis, Stanley (Pitman), Stansfield (Fleetwood), Williams (Ipoua), Ferrell.

Referee: D. Whitestone (Northamptonshire).

aet.

NATIONWIDE CONFERENCE 2005–06 FINAL LEAGUE TABLE

			Home					*Away*					*Total*						
		P	*W*	*D*	*L*	*F*	*A*	*W*	*D*	*L*	*F*	*A*	*W*	*D*	*L*	*F*	*A*	*GD*	*Pts*
1	Accrington S	42	16	3	2	38	17	12	4	5	38	28	28	7	7	76	45	31	91
2	Hereford U	42	11	7	3	30	14	11	7	3	29	19	22	14	6	59	33	26	80
3	Grays Ath	42	7	9	5	46	32	14	4	3	48	23	21	13	8	94	55	39	76
4	Halifax T	42	14	6	1	31	11	7	6	8	24	29	21	12	9	55	40	15	75
5	Morecambe	42	15	4	2	44	17	7	4	10	24	24	22	8	12	68	41	27	74
6	Stevenage B	42	15	3	3	38	15	4	9	8	24	32	19	12	11	62	47	15	69
7	Exeter C	42	11	3	7	41	22	7	6	8	24	26	18	9	15	65	48	17	63
8	York C	42	10	5	6	36	26	7	7	7	27	22	17	12	13	63	48	15	63
9	Burton Alb	42	8	7	6	23	21	8	5	8	27	31	16	12	14	50	52	−2	60
10	Dagenham & R	42	8	4	9	31	32	8	6	7	32	27	16	10	16	63	59	4	58
11	Woking	42	8	7	6	30	20	6	7	8	28	27	14	14	14	58	47	11	56
12	Cambridge U	42	11	6	4	35	25	4	4	13	16	32	15	10	17	51	57	−6	55
13	Aldershot T	42	10	4	7	30	30	6	2	13	31	44	16	6	20	61	74	−13	54
14	Canvey Island*	42	6	8	7	23	27	7	4	10	24	31	13	12	17	47	58	−11	51
15	Kidderminster H	42	8	5	8	21	27	5	6	10	18	28	13	11	18	39	55	−16	50
16	Gravesend & N	42	8	4	9	25	25	5	6	10	20	32	13	10	19	45	57	−12	49
17	Crawley T	42	9	4	8	27	22	3	7	11	21	33	12	11	19	48	55	−7	47
18	Southport	42	7	3	11	24	38	3	7	11	12	30	10	10	22	36	68	−32	40
19	Forest Green R	42	7	7	7	30	27	1	7	13	19	35	8	14	20	49	62	−13	38
20	Tamworth	42	4	10	7	17	23	4	4	13	15	40	8	14	20	32	63	−31	38
21	Scarborough§	42	4	7	10	24	30	5	3	13	16	36	9	10	23	40	66	−26	37
22	Altrincham†	42	7	5	9	25	30	3	6	12	15	41	10	11	21	40	71	−31	23

**Canvey Island resigned from Football Conference and will play 2006-07 season in Ryman Premier League.*
†Altrincham deducted 18 points for breach of rule.
§Scarborough relegated for financial reasons.

NATIONWIDE CONFERENCE LEADING GOALSCORERS 2005–06

	League	*Play-offs*	*FA Cup*	*LDV*	*Trophy*	*Total*
Andy Bishop *(York C)*	23	0	2	0	1	26
Justin Richards *(Woking)*	21	0	0	1	0	22
Danny Carlton *(Morecambe)*	17	0	1	0	0	18
Colin Little *(Altrincham)*	17	0	0	0	0	17
Clayton Donaldson *(York C)*	16	0	1	0	0	17
Chris Moore *(Dagenham & R)*	15	0	2	0	3	20
Michael Kightly *(Grays Ath)*	14	1	1	0	2	18
Paul Mullin *(Accrington S)*	14	0	0	0	3	17
Glenn Poole *(Grays Ath)*	13	0	1	0	4	18
Lee Phillips *(Exeter C)*	13	0	0	1	3	17
Ian Craney *(Accrington S)*	13	0	0	0	3	16
Gary Roberts *(Accrington S)*	13	0	2	0	0	15
Daryl Clare *(Burton Albion)*	13	0	0	0	0	13

(Includes 11 League goals for Crawley T).

ATTENDANCES BY CLUB 2005–06

	Aggregate 2005–06	*Average 2005–06*	*Highest Attendance 2005–06*
Exeter City	79,590	3,790	6,682 v Grays Athletic
York City	60,281	2,871	4,921 v Scarborough
Hereford United	58,655	2,793	4,497 v Accrington Stanley
Cambridge United	54,739	2,607	3,697 v Stevenage Borough
Aldershot Town	48,172	2,294	3,136 v Exeter City
Stevenage Borough	45,746	2,178	3,463 v Cambridge United
Woking	40,943	1,950	3,244 v Aldershot Town
Accrington Stanley	39,791	1,895	3,320 v Scarborough
Morecambe	37,383	1,780	2,788 v Southport
Kidderminster Harriers	37,275	1,775	3,241 v Hereford United
Halifax Town	36,732	1,749	2,688 v Accrington Stanley
Burton Albion	36,212	1,724	2,680 v Tamworth
Scarborough	33,686	1,604	4,057 v York City
Crawley Town	32,192	1,533	2,454 v Exeter City
Grays Athletic	30,325	1,444	2,910 v Canvey Island
Tamworth	26,182	1,247	2,151 v Burton Albion
Southport	26,124	1,244	1,807 v Morecambe
Dagenham & Redbridge	26,110	1,243	2,017 v Grays Athletic
Gravesend & Northfleet	22,934	1,092	1,616 v Accrington Stanley
Altrincham	22,006	1,048	1,447 v Morecambe
Forest Green Rovers	20,517	977	1,957 v Hereford United
Canvey Island	16,938	807	1,458 v Dagenham & Redbridge

ACCRINGTON STANLEY ROLL CALL 2005–06

Player	Position	Height	Weight	Birthplace	Birthdate	Source
Alcock Danny	G	5 11	11 03	Staffordshire	15 2 84	Barnsley
Boco Romauld	M	5 10	10 12		8 7 85	
Brown David	F	5 10	12 07	Bolton	2 10 78	Hereford U
Cavanagh Peter	D			Liverpool	14 10 81	Liverpool
Craney Ian	M			Liverpool	21 7 82	Altrincham
Edwards Phil	D			Kirkby	8 11 85	Wigan Ath
Jagielka Steve	M	5 8	11 03	Manchester	10 3 78	Sheffield U
Mangan Andrew	F	5 9	10 03	Liverpool	30 8 86	Blackpool
Mullin Paul	F			Bury	16 3 74	Radcliffe Borough
Proctor Andy	M			Lancashire	13 3 83	
Richardson Leam	D	5 8	11 04	Blackpool	19 11 79	Leeds U
Roberts Gary	M			Wales	18 3 84	Welshpool T
Todd Andy	M	6 0	11 03	Nottingham	22 2 79	Burton Alb
Tretton Andy	D	6 0	11 07	Derby	9 10 76	Hereford U
Ventre Danny	D				23 1 86	
Welch Michael	D	6 3	11 12	Crewe	11 1 82	Macclesfield T
Williams Robbie	D			Liverpool	12 4 79	St Dominics

HEREFORD UNITED ROLL CALL 2005–06

Player	Position	Height	Weight	Birthplace	Birthdate	Source
Beckwith Dean	D	6 3	13 01	Southwark	18 9 83	Gillingham
Ferrell Andy	M	5 8	11 05	Newcastle	9 1 84	Watford
Fleetwood Stuart	F	5 9	12 02	Gloucester	23 4 86	Cardiff C
Green Ryan	D	5 7	10 10	Cardiff	20 10 80	Sheffield W
Ipoua Guy	F	6 1	13 10	Douala	14 1 76	Doncaster R
James Tony	D	6 3	14 02	Cardiff	27 6 76	WBA
Jeannin Alex	D	6 0	11 06	Troyes	30 12 77	Bristol R
Mawson Craig	G	6 2	13 04	Keighley	16 5 79	Oldham Ath
Mkandawire Tamika	D	6 0	12 03	Malawi	28 5 83	WBA
Pitman Jamie	M	5 9	10 09	Trowbridge	6 1 76	Woking
Purdie Rob	F	5 8	11 02	Leicester	28 9 82	Leicester C
Stanley Colin	M	5 8	10 08	Bedworth	3 3 83	Telford U
Stansfield Adam	F	5 11	11 02	Plymouth	10 9 78	Yeovil T
Travis Simon	D	5 10	11 00	Preston	22 3 77	Stevenage B
Williams Andy	F	5 11	11 02	Hereford	14 8 86	

ACCRINGTON STANLEY FL Championship 2

Ground: The Crown Ground, Livingstone Road, Accrington, Lancashire.
Tel: 01254 397 869.
Year Formed: 1968 (formerly 1893).
Record Gate: 2,270 (1992 v Gateshead FA Cup First Round) (in Football League 17,634).
Nickname: Stanley.
Manager: John Coleman.
Secretary: Philip Terry.
Colours: Red shirts, white shorts, red stockings.

ACCRINGTON STANLEY 2005–06 LEAGUE RECORD

Match No.	Date	Venue	Opponents	Result		H/T Score	Lg. Pos.	Goalscorers	Attendance
1	Aug 13	H	Canvey Is	W	1-0	0-0	—	Brown D [68]	1012
2	16	A	Altrincham	W	1-0	0-0	—	Welch [85]	1264
3	20	A	Cambridge U	L	1-3	0-3	4	Mangan [83]	2730
4	27	H	Exeter C	L	1-2	0-0	9	Mullin [58]	1312
5	29	A	Scarborough	D	2-2	2-1	—	Jagielka [1], Cavanagh (pen) [15]	1509
6	Sept 3	H	Woking	W	2-1	1-0	9	Brown D [32], Craney [62]	959
7	10	A	Burton Alb	W	2-0	1-0	6	Brown D [9], Mangan [73]	1374
8	17	H	Crawley T	W	4-2	1-1	4	Craney [4], Jagielka [57], Roberts [77], Mangan [90]	1365
9	20	H	Aldershot T	W	3-2	3-1	—	Jagielka [35], Brown D [41], Roberts [45]	1114
10	24	A	Dagenham & R	W	2-1	0-0	2	Brown D [49], Craney (pen) [59]	1331
11	27	A	Morecambe	L	2-3	1-1	—	Craney [45], Cavanagh (pen) [84]	2162
12	Oct 1	H	Gravesend & N	D	1-1	1-0	3	Craney [17]	1206
13	7	H	Hereford U	W	2-1	1-0	—	Craney [9], Brown D [55]	1603
14	15	A	Stevenage Bor	L	1-3	1-0	4	Jagielka [27]	2141
15	29	H	York C	W	2-1	1-0	3	Roberts [44], Mullin [68]	2193
16	Nov 12	A	Grays Ath	W	2-1	1-0	3	Mullin [37], Jagielka [63]	1985
17	18	H	Forest Green R	W	2-0	1-0	—	Roberts [33], Jagielka [47]	1506
18	26	H	Southport	W	4-0	2-0	2	Craney [32], Boco [36], Mullin [87], Mangan [90]	1630
19	Dec 3	H	Altrincham	W	1-0	0-0	1	Roberts [63]	1436
20	10	H	Kidderminster H	W	2-0	1-0	1	Roberts [13], Mullin [78]	1366
21	26	A	Halifax T	D	2-2	1-1	1	Boco [27], Roberts [90]	2688
22	Jan 2	H	Halifax T	D	1-1	0-0	1	Cavanagh (pen) [80]	3014
23	7	A	Canvey Is	W	2-0	1-0	1	Cavanagh [39], Mullin [66]	962
24	10	A	Tamworth	W	2-1	1-1	—	Mullin [3], Craney [56]	1094
25	21	H	Cambridge U	W	1-0	0-0	1	Craney [78]	1837
26	30	A	Exeter C	W	3-1	1-0	—	Roberts 2 [12, 68], Boco [53]	4624
27	Feb 11	H	Dagenham & R	W	1-0	0-0	1	Boco [53]	2156
28	17	A	Gravesend & N	W	3-1	1-0	—	Todd [35], Mullin 2 [66, 80]	1616
29	20	H	Morecambe	W	2-0	2-0	—	Todd [24], Mullin [27]	3041
30	25	H	Burton Alb	W	2-1	1-1	1	Mullin [9], Williams [90]	1946
31	Mar 4	A	Crawley T	W	1-0	1-0	1	Roberts [42]	1361
32	7	A	Aldershot T	W	4-1	0-0	—	Craney [48], Roberts 2 [61, 79], Mangan [67]	1645
33	11	A	Hereford U	D	2-2	1-0	1	Brown D [37], Mkandawire (og) [59]	4497
34	18	H	Stevenage Bor	D	1-1	0-1	1	Todd [79]	2119
35	21	A	Southport	L	0-2	0-1	—		1414
36	25	A	York C	W	4-2	1-2	1	Mullin 2 [35, 68], Brown D (pen) [49], Craney [71]	3912
37	Apr 1	H	Grays Ath	L	2-3	1-0	1	Roberts [18], Craney [65]	2642
38	7	A	Forest Green R	D	1-1	0-0	—	Todd [79]	1187
39	15	A	Woking	W	1-0	1-0	1	Mullin [38]	2665
40	17	H	Scarborough	W	1-0	0-0	1	Todd [90]	3320
41	22	H	Tamworth	W	2-1	0-0	1	Todd [63], Craney [68]	3014
42	29	A	Kidderminster H	L	0-2	0-0	1		1934

Final League Position: 1

GOALSCORERS

League (76): Mullin 14, Craney 13 (1 pen), Roberts 13, Brown D 8 (1 pen), Jagielka 6, Todd 6, Mangan 5, Boco 4, Cavanagh 4 (3 pens), Welch 1, Williams 1, own goal 1.
FA Cup (3): Roberts 2, Welch 1.
Football League Trophy (3): Brown D 1, Mangan 1, Williams 1.
FA Trophy (8): Craney 3, Mullin 3, Boko 1, Brown D 1.

Jones 2	Williams 35 + 1	Richardson 33	Barry 26	Welch 32 + 1	Flynn 12	Jagielka 22 + 8	Craney 38 + 1	Mangan 5 + 33	Mullin 40 + 1	Roberts 40 + 2	Cavanagh 19 + 5	Brown D 26 + 9	Proctor 3 + 3	O'Neill — + 3	Bossu 1	Randolph 14	Brown P 1 + 2	Boco 24 + 6	Navarro — + 3	Butler 3	Dibble 1	Ventre 10 + 2	Cook 1 + 3	Edwards 27	Elliott 23	Tretton 6 + 1	Todd 13 + 1	Boyd 4 + 2	Alcock 1	*Match No.*
1	2	3	4	5^1	6	7^2	8	9^3	10	11	12	13	14																	1
1	2	3^1	4	5	6	7^2	8	9	10	11^3	12	13		14																2
	2	3	4	5		12	8	13	10	11^3	6^1	9	7^2	14	1															3
	5	3^1	4		6	12	8^3	9	10	11	2	7^2	14	13		1														4
	13	3	4	5^2	6	7	8	14	10	12	2	9^3	11^1			1														5
	5	3	4		6	7^2	8	12	10	11	2	9^1				1	13													6
	5	3	4	12	6^1	7	8	13	10	11^2	2	9				1														7
	5	3	4		6	7^3	8	12	10	11^2	2	9^1				1	13	14												8
	5	3^1	4		6	7^2	8	14	10	11	2	9^3				1		13	12											9
	5		4		6	7	8	12	10	11		9				1	2^1			3										10
	5		4		6	7	8^1	14	10	11^2	2	9^3				1		13	12	3■										11
	5	3	4^2		6	7	8	14	10	11	2^1	9^3				1		12	13											12
		3	4	5	6	7	8	12	10	11		9^1				1				2										13
	5	3	4^2	6		7	8	14	10	11		9^3						12			1	2^1	13							14
		3	4	5		7	8	12	10	11		9^1				1						2		6						15
	5	3	4^1	6		7	8	13■	10	11		9^2				1							12	2						16
	5	3	4	6		7	8		10	11		9^1				1		12						2						17
	5	3	4	6		7	8	13	10	11	12					1		9^2						2^1						18
	5	3	4	6		7	8^1	12	10	11								9						2	1					19
	5	3	4	6		7		12	10	11		9^1						8						2	1					20
	5	3	4	6		7^3	8^2	13	10	11	14	12						9						2^1	1					21
	5	3	4^3	6		7^2	8	14	10	11	12	13						9						2^1	1					22
	5	3	4	6			8		10	11	2^1	12						9						7	1					23
	5	3	4	6			8	12	10	11^1	2^2	13						9						7	1					24
	5		4	6			8	12	10	11	2	9^1						7						3	1					25
	5	3^2	4	6			8	12	10	11	7^1							9						2	1	13				26
	5	3		6			8	13	10	11^2		12						9						2	1	4	7^1			27
	5	3		6			8^1		10	11								9					12	2	1	4	7			28
	5	3		6			8	13	10	11	2^1							9				12			1	4	7^2			29
	5	3		6			8		10	11		7						9						2	1	4				30
		3					8	12	10	11		7^1						9				5		2	1	4	6			31
		3■		6		12	8	13	10	11		7^2						9				5		2	1		4^1			32
	5			6		13	8	12	10	11^1		7^2						9				2■		3	1		4			33
	5	3■		6		4^1	8	13	10	11		7^2						9						2	1		12			34
	5■			6^1			8	13	10	11		12						9				2		3	1		7	4^2		35
				6		12	8	13	10	11	3	7^2						9				2		5	1		4^1			36
	5			6^1			8	14	10	11	3^2	7^3						9				13		2	1		4	12		37
	5			6		13	8	10^3		11^2	3	14						9				2^1		4	1		7	12		38
	5	3		6		12		13	10	11	2							9^2						4	1		7	8^1		39
	5	3				12		13	10^3	14		9^2	8^1					11				2		6	1		7	4		40
	5	3^1		6			8	12	10	11	2■							9						4	1		7			41
				6		7^1	14	9	13	11		10^3	12									2	8	3		5		4^2	1	42

FA Cup
Fourth Qual Worcester C (h) 1-1
(a) 2-3

Football League Trophy
First Round Rotherham U (a) 3-3

FA Trophy
First Round Altrincham (h) 2-0
Second Round Carshalton Ath (a) 2-2
(h) 2-0
Third Round Worksop T (h) 1-1
(a) 1-1

ALDERSHOT TOWN — Conference

Ground: Recreation Ground, High Street, Aldershot, Hampshire GU11 1TW.
Tel: (01252) 320 211.
Year Formed: 1992 (formerly 1926).
Record Gate: 7,500 (2000 v Brighton & Hove Albion FA Cup First Round) (in Football League 19,138).
Nickname: Shots.
Manager: Terry Brown.
Secretary: Andy Morgan.
Colours: Red shirts with blue trim, red shorts, red stockings with blue trim.

ALDERSHOT TOWN 2005–06 LEAGUE RECORD

Match No.	Date	Venue	Opponents	Result		H/T Score	Lg. Pos.	Goalscorers	Attendance
1	Aug 13	H	Tamworth	L	0-2	0-2	—		2641
2	16	A	Canvey Is	L	1-2	1-0	—	Guyett 20	1210
3	20	A	Halifax T	D	1-1	0-1	21	McPhee (pen) 51	1571
4	27	H	Altrincham	L	0-2	0-0	22		2235
5	29	A	Grays Ath	L	1-2	0-1	—	Crittenden N 54	1869
6	Sept 5	H	Crawley T	W	3-2	2-1	—	Williams 29, Sills 2 (1 pen) 43, 69 (p)	2371
7	10	A	Morecambe	L	2-5	2-2	22	Heald 32, McPhee 45	1429
8	17	H	Stevenage Bor	D	2-2	0-2	22	Williams 48, Sills 82	2563
9	20	A	Accrington S	L	2-3	1-3	—	Somner 24, Sills 71	1114
10	24	H	York C	W	2-1	1-0	19	Crittenden N 20, Barnard 88	2470
11	27	H	Hereford U	L	0-1	0-1	—		2656
12	Oct 2	A	Burton Alb	W	2-1	0-1	19	Sills 65, Crittenden N 66	1493
13	9	A	Dagenham & R	L	0-2	0-1	22		1512
14	15	H	Kidderminster H	W	1-0	0-0	18	Coleman 63	2315
15	29	A	Scarborough	D	2-2	1-0	16	Jinadu 45, Hughes (og) 50	1682
16	Nov 12	H	Gravesend & N	W	3-2	2-1	15	Sills 2 5, 90, Barnard (pen) 32	2415
17	19	A	Cambridge U	W	2-0	1-0	12	Tinnion 5, Sills 69	2905
18	26	H	Forest Green R	W	2-1	2-1	11	Heald 19, Jinadu 31	2290
19	Dec 10	H	Southport	W	2-0	2-0	11	Somner 27, Barnard (pen) 39	2066
20	26	A	Exeter C	L	0-4	0-2	13		4989
21	31	A	Forest Green R	L	2-4	1-2	15	Sills 45, Sulaiman 90	1051
22	Jan 2	H	Exeter C	W	1-0	1-0	14	Somner 16	3136
23	21	H	Halifax T	W	3-1	2-1	12	Holloway 22, Griffiths 2 45, 73	2417
24	24	H	Canvey Is	D	2-2	0-0	—	Sills 52, Griffiths 75	1800
25	28	A	Altrincham	L	1-5	1-3	13	Barnard (pen) 34	1115
26	Feb 4	A	Stevenage Bor	L	1-2	1-1	14	Crittenden N 18	2010
27	12	A	York C	L	2-3	1-1	15	Dixon 17, Williams 82	2401
28	18	H	Burton Alb	D	1-1	1-1	16	Dixon 45	2248
29	21	A	Hereford U	L	1-2	0-2	—	Holloway 60	2205
30	25	H	Morecambe	W	2-0	1-0	14	Dixon 3, Griffiths 47	1868
31	Mar 7	H	Accrington S	L	1-4	0-0	—	Griffiths 71	1645
32	11	H	Dagenham & R	W	3-1	2-0	13	Barnard 20, Williams 45, Holloway 84	2010
33	18	A	Kidderminster H	W	4-1	4-0	12	Barnard 6, Crittenden N 17, Williams 34, Hudson 45	1630
34	21	A	Woking	W	2-1	2-0	—	Crittenden N 28, Barnard (pen) 32	3244
35	25	H	Scarborough	L	0-1	0-1	10		2245
36	Apr 1	A	Gravesend & N	W	3-0	1-0	10	Williams 2 45, 46, Hudson 56	1131
37	4	A	Tamworth	L	1-2	0-1	—	Matthews 53	914
38	8	H	Cambridge U	L	1-3	1-0	11	Griffiths 34	2198
39	15	A	Crawley T	L	0-2	0-1	12		1764
40	17	H	Grays Ath	L	0-3	0-3	12		1879
41	22	H	Woking	D	1-1	0-1	12	Dixon 56	2704
42	29	A	Southport	W	1-0	0-0	13	Barnard (pen) 69	1709

Final League Position: 13

GOALSCORERS

League (61): Sills 10 (1 pen), Barnard 8 (5 pens), Williams 7, Crittenden N 6, Griffiths 6, Dixon 4, Holloway 3, Somner 3, Heald 2, Hudson 2, Jinadu 2, McPhee 2 (1 pen), Coleman 1, Guyett 1, Matthews 1, Sulaiman 1, Tinnion 1, own goal 1.
FA Cup (4): Brough 1, Deen 1, Heald 1, Sills 1.
Football League Trophy (1): Heald 1.
FA Trophy (1): Barnard 1 (pen).

Bull 42	Sulaiman 10+13	Hamilton 27+3	Lee 2	Brough 12+3	Matthews 2+5	Guyett 13	Crittenden N 38+3	Nurse 1	McPhee 12+2	Crockford 3+3	Brayley 2+3	Deen 9+3	Ahmad 2+5	Jinadu 10+3	Sills 20+1	Weait —+1	Gordon —+1	Winfield 6+6	Scott 16+11	Kitson —+1	Mustafa 5+3	Cozic 2	Somner 29+2	Watson 24+2	Heald 28	Gearing —+4	Williams 24+1	Boucaud 8+1	Reed 4+1	Holloway 25+4	Barnard 24+2	Coleman 3	Tinnion 7	Walker —+1	Vincent 3	Turner 3+1	Griffiths 15+2	Hudson 9+3	Elphick 2+1	Dixon 10	Simpemba 10	*Match No.*
1	2	3	4	5[1]		6	7[2]	8[3]	9		10	11		12	13		14																									1
1	2	3	4[1]			6	13		9		8[2]	11		5	10[3]			12	7	14																						2
1	2	3[1]				6	7		9		14	11[2]		5	10[3]				12		13	8	4																			3
1	12	3[1]				6	7		9		13			5	10[2]						2	11	4	8																		4
1	3[1]	12				6	7		9		13[3]	11		5[2]				14	10		2		4	8																		5
1		3				6	7		9[1]						10						2		4	8	5	12	11															6
1	12[2]	3		13[3]		6	7[1]		9						10						2		4	8	5	14	11															7
1	12	3				6	13		9						10						2[1]		4	8	5		7	11[2]														8
1	2[1]	12				6	7		9						10				13				4■		5		11[3]	8[2]	3	14												9
1		2				6	7		9			11[2]			10									8	5			4[1]	3	13	12											10
1		2				6	7		9			11[3]			10				12					8[1]	5			4[2]	3	13	14											11
1		2[1]					7		9[3]			14		6	10						12			8	5			4	3	13	11[2]											12
1						6	7		14						10				12				4	8[1]	5			11	13	2[2]	3	9[3]										13
1		2				6	7[2]		12			11[3]		13	10				14				5					4		8	3■	9[1]										14
1	2			13			10					11[1]		6					4		12				5			8		7	3	9[2]										15
1	12			4			7[3]					11[2]			10				8				2		5			13		9[1]	3		6	14								16
1	12			4			7								10				8				2		5					11	3		6		9[1]							17
1							7[1]							4	10■				8				2		5	13				11	3		6		9[2]	12						18
1				4			7					12							8				2	13	5	14				11[2]	3[1]		6		9[3]	10						19
1	2[1]			4			7					12			10			13	8				5	14						11[2]	3		6[3]			9						20
1	13			4[1]			7								10			12	8				2		5					11	3		6			9[2]						21
1				4[1]			7								10			12	13				2	8	5		11			9	3		6[2]									22
1	12	3		4			7								10				6				2		5		11[1]			8							9[2]	13				23
1		3					7								10								2	4	5		11			8							9		6			24
1	12	13		14			7												4[3]				2	8	5		11			10	3[2]						9		6[1]			25
1		2		4			7																12	6	5		11[1]			8	3■						9			10		26
1		3		5[1]			7												13				2	4[2]	6		11			8							9		12	10		27
1	12	3		5			7																2	4	6		11[1]			8							9			10		28
1	7[2]	2		5[1]										12									4		6		11			8	3						9	13		10		29
1							7							5					4				2	8	6		11				3						9			10		30
1		2					7							5					4					8	6		11[1]			9	3						12			10		31
1	12	2					7							5					13					4	6		11[2]			8	3[1]						9	14		10[3]		32
1		2[1]			13		7																12	4	6		11			8	3						9[2]	10			5	33
1	13	2			14		7												12					4[1]	6		11[2]			8	3						9	10[3]			5	34
1	12	2			13		7																	4	6		11[1]			8	3						9	10[2]			5	35
1	2				14		7[1]			13			12					6					3	4[2]			11			8							9[3]	10			5	36
1	2[1]	3			9		7			13			14					12	4[2]				6	8			11											10[3]			5	37
1[6]		3					7			4			12			15		6[1]	8				2				11										9	10			5	38
1		2			9[2]		7[1]			8			12					6	14				4				11				3						13	10[3]			5	39
1		2					7						12					6	4					8			11[1]				3						9			10	5	40
1		2[1]			14		7			12			11[3]					6					4				13			8	3							9[2]		10	5	41
1	12						13			4[3]			7[2]					6	14				2				11[1]			8	3							9		10	5	42

FA Cup

Fourth Qual	Bromley	(a)	1-0
First Round	Burnham	(a)	3-1
Second Round	Scunthorpe U	(h)	0-1

Football League Trophy

First Round	Bournemouth	(a)	1-4

FA Trophy

First Round	Grays Ath	(h)	1-1
		(a)	0-1

ALTRINCHAM Conference

Ground: Moss Lane, Altrincham WA15 8AP.
Tel: (0161) 928 1045.
Year Formed: 1903.
Record Gate: 10,275 (1991 Altrincham Boys v Sunderland Boys ESFA Shield).
Nickname: The Robins.
Manager: Graham Heathcote.
Secretary: Graham Heathcote.
Colours: Red and white striped shirts, black shorts, red stockings.

ALTRINCHAM 2005–06 LEAGUE RECORD

Match No.	*Date*	*Venue*	*Opponents*	*Result*	*H/T Score*	*Lg. Pos.*	*Goalscorers*	*Attendance*
1	Aug 13	A	Stevenage Bor	L 0-3	0-2	—		2008
2	16	H	Accrington S	L 0-1	0-0	—		1264
3	20	H	Forest Green R	W 2-1	1-0	16	Searle (og) [24], Potts [51]	804
4	27	A	Aldershot T	W 2-0	0-0	10	Olsen [71], Little [78]	2235
5	29	H	Morecambe	W 2-0	2-0	—	Little [30], Potts [34]	1447
6	Sept 3	A	Hereford U	D 0-0	0-0	7		2318
7	10	H	Dagenham & R	L 0-5	0-1	11		876
8	17	A	York C	L 0-5	0-2	13		2634
9	20	H	Scarborough	D 1-1	0-0	—	Little [59]	862
10	24	A	Cambridge U	L 0-4	0-2	15		2199
11	27	A	Halifax T	L 0-2	0-1	—		1453
12	Oct 1	H	Crawley T	D 1-1	0-1	18	Little (pen) [69]	819
13	8	A	Canvey Is	D 1-1	1-1	18	Little (pen) [45]	835
14	15	H	Southport	W 1-0	0-0	14	Potts [70]	1225
15	30	A	Burton Alb	L 0-1	0-1	15		1375
16	Nov 12	H	Exeter C	D 1-1	0-1	17	Little [70]	1366
17	19	A	Gravesend & N	L 0-2	0-1	19		1091
18	26	H	Tamworth	W 2-0	0-0	18	Little [89], Robinson [90]	824
19	Dec 3	A	Accrington S	L 0-1	0-0	18		1436
20	6	A	Grays Ath	D 1-1	0-1	—	Lugsden [90]	1028
21	10	H	Woking	L 0-4	0-2	17		825
22	26	A	Kidderminster H	D 1-1	0-1	17	Aspinall (pen) [80]	2206
23	31	A	Tamworth	D 1-1	1-1	17	Peyton [45]	1064
24	Jan 2	H	Kidderminster H	W 3-0	2-0	16	Little 2 [11, 77], Thornley [36]	1165
25	7	H	Stevenage Bor	D 1-1	0-1	17	Little [76]	914
26	21	A	Forest Green R	L 0-5	0-2	17		995
27	28	H	Aldershot T	W 5-1	3-1	17	Robinson 2 [8, 45], Thornley 2 [41, 78], Little [80]	1115
28	Feb 4	A	Scarborough	W 2-1	1-0	16	Little [26], Aspinall (pen) [69]	1405
29	11	H	Cambridge U	W 2-1	2-1	13	Robinson [4], Thornley [26]	1151
30	18	A	Crawley T	L 0-2	0-1	14		1085
31	21	H	Halifax T	L 1-2	0-1	—	Peyton [61]	1139
32	Mar 11	H	Canvey Is	L 0-1	0-0	17		903
33	18	A	Southport	D 1-1	0-1	17	Talbot [90]	1278
34	25	H	Burton Alb	L 1-2	1-1	17	Little [7]	1214
35	Apr 1	A	Exeter C	L 1-3	1-2	18	Little [19]	3134
36	4	H	York C	L 0-3	0-3	—		1237
37	8	H	Gravesend & N	D 2-2	2-1	18	Murphy [20], Little [21]	688
38	11	A	Dagenham & R	W 4-2	3-2	—	Potts [9], Murphy [33], Band [38], Little [70]	1058
39	15	H	Hereford U	L 0-1	0-0	18		1251
40	17	A	Morecambe	L 0-2	0-1	18		2118
41	22	H	Grays Ath	L 0-2	0-0	22		917
42	29	A	Woking	L 1-3	0-3	18	Little [72]	1650

Final League Position: 22

GOALSCORERS

League (40): Little 17 (2 pens), Potts 4, Robinson 4, Thornley 4, Aspinall 2 (2 pens), Murphy 2, Peyton 2, Band 1, Lugsden 1, Olsen 1, Talbot 1, own goal 1.
FA Cup (1): own goal 1.
FA Trophy (0).

Coburn 42	Band 39	Adams 31 + 1	Hawes 14	Maddox 27 + 2	Talbot 20 + 3	Munroe 13 + 8	Owen 32	Little 41 + 1	Williams G 6 + 6	Chalmers 13 + 16	Potts 19 + 16	Lugsden 1 + 26	Thornley 21 + 3	Rose 11 + 5	McKenzie 3 + 4	Olsen 5 + 4	Hendley — + 4	Aspinall 20 + 3	Melling 3 + 2	Hilton 3 + 1	Scott 27 + 1	James 2 + 1	McFadden 1 + 5	Wilson 4 + 1	Peyton 23 + 1	Butler 1	Robinson 8 + 6	Bushell 7	Murphy 22 + 1	Norton 3 + 3	*Match No.*
1	2	3	4	5	6	7[1]	8	9	10[2]	11[3]	12	13	14																		1
1	2	3	4	5[1]	6		8	9	10[3]	11[2]	7	14		12	13																2
1	2	3	4		6		8	9	10[3]	11[2]	7	14		5[1]	13	12															3
1	2	3	4		6		8	9	10[3]	11[2]	5			7[1]	12	13	14														4
1	2	3	4				8	9	13	14	10[3]			5[1]	11[2]	7		12	6												5
1	2	3	4	14	6[1]		8	9	10[3]	13	11[2]			5		7			12												6
1	2	3	4		6	12	8	9	10		7[2]		14	5[1]	13	11[3]															7
1	2	3	4	5		7	8	9	14					6[1]	11[2]		12		13	10[3]											8
1	2	3	4	5[1]		13	8	9			7[2]	12	10			11[3]			6	14											9
1	2		4	5		12	8	9	14			7[2]	10			11[3]	13		6[1]	3											10
1	2	3	4	5[1]		7	8	9	13	11[3]		14		6	10[2]	12															11
1	2	3	4	5[1]	6	7	8	9	13		11[2]		10[3]				14				12										12
1	2	3	4[2]	5[1]	6	7	8	9	13	14	11					12					10[3]										13
1	2	3	4	12	6	7	8[2]	9		13	5[1]		10[3]								11	14									14
1	2	3		5		7■	8	9		13	10[3]		12								4[1]	11	14	6[2]							15
1	2	3		5[1]	6[2]			9		11	12	14		13							8	10[3]		7	4						16
1	2			5			8	9		11[2]	12	14								7	4			10[3]	6	3[1]	13				17
1	2	3[1]		5			8	9		13	7[2]	14									4			10[3]	11		12	6			18
1	2■	3[1]		5			8	9		14	7[2]	12									4				10		13	6[3]	11		19
1		3		5		7	8	9			13	12									2			14	11[3]		10[2]	4[1]	6		20
1		3[2]				7[1]	8[3]	9		11	13	12		5				14			2				6		10		4		21
1	2	3		5				9		11[2]	13	14	10[3]	12				4[1]							7			8	6		22
1				5				9		11[2]		12	4[1]	6				2			3				10		13	7	8		23
1	2							9		11[2]	14	12	10[3]	5				3			4				7		13	6	8[1]		24
1	2			5			8	9			13	12	10[3]					4			3[1]				11		14	6	7[2]		25
1	2			5			8	9		12	13	14	10[3]					4			3				11■		7[2]		6[1]		26
1	2	3		5			8[2]	9[3]		13		14	10	12				4			6						11		7[1]		27
1	2	3		5			8	9[2]		12	14		10[3]	13				4			6						7[1]		11		28
1	2	3		5			8	9		12	13	14	10[3]					6[1]			4						11[2]		7		29
1	2	3		5	14		8	9				13	10[3]					4			6				12		11[2]		7[1]		30
1	2			5	14		8	9		12		13	10[3]	11[2]				4			3				7		6[1]				31
1	2	3[1]			6		8	9		14	13	12						5			4				11				7[2]	10[3]	32
1	2	3			6	12	8	9			13		10[3]					5					14		11				7[1]	4[2]	33
1	2	3			6		8	9		13	12	14	10[3]					5							11				7[1]	4[2]	34
1	2	3		5■	6	7	8[2]	9[3]			14							4			10[1]				11				13	12	35
1	2	3[2]			6[1]	7	8	9			14	12						5			4		13		11				10[3]		36
1	2	3[1]			6	12		9			8	13	10[2]					5			4				11				7		37
1	2				6	13		9		11[2]	7[1]		10[3]					5			4		14		3				8	12	38
1	2				6	13		9		11[2]	7[1]	14	10[3]					5			4				3				8	12	39
1	2	3[2]		5	6	13		14		12	8							4[1]			11		9[3]		10				7		40
1	2			5[1]	12	7		9[2]			6	13	10[3]					4			3		14		11				8		41
1	2	13		5[1]	6[2]	7		9		14	8		10					12			3				11				4[3]		42

FA Cup
Fourth Qual Tamworth (a) 1-3

FA Trophy
First Round Accrington S (a) 0-2

BURTON ALBION

Conference

Ground: Eton Park, Princess Way, Burton-on-Trent DE14 2RU.
Tel: (01283) 565 938.
Year Formed: 1950.
Record Gate: 5,806 (1964 v Weymouth Southern League Cup Final).
Nickname: Brewers.
Manager: Nigel Clough.
Secretary: Tony Kirkland.
Colours: All yellow with black trim.

BURTON ALBION 2005–06 LEAGUE RECORD

Match No.	Date	Venue	Opponents	Result		H/T Score	Lg. Pos.	Goalscorers	Attendance
1	Aug 13	H	Grays Ath	D	1-1	0-0	—	Webster (pen) [49]	1654
2	16	A	Halifax T	L	0-1	0-0	—		1681
3	20	A	Woking	D	2-2	2-0	19	Shaw [10], Harrad [32]	1692
4	27	H	Canvey Is	L	1-2	1-1	20	Todd [8]	1423
5	29	A	Southport	L	2-3	0-1	—	Krief (og) [70], Hall [73]	1253
6	Sept 3	H	Scarborough	W	2-1	1-0	18	Webster 2 (1 pen) [23 (p), 52]	1336
7	10	H	Accrington S	L	0-2	0-1	20		1374
8	17	A	Dagenham & R	L	1-3	0-1	20	Anderson [78]	1149
9	20	H	Morecambe	L	0-4	0-2	—		1352
10	24	A	Exeter C	W	2-1	0-1	21	Stride [81], Shaw [85]	4025
11	27	A	Cambridge U	D	2-2	1-0	—	Anderson [11], Gilroy [70]	2298
12	Oct 2	H	Aldershot T	L	1-2	1-0	22	Todd [30]	1493
13	8	H	Stevenage Bor	W	3-1	3-0	19	Webster [5], Shaw 2 [11, 30]	1319
14	15	A	Hereford U	L	0-2	0-1	21		2493
15	30	H	Altrincham	W	1-0	1-0	17	Anderson [20]	1375
16	Nov 12	A	York C	W	1-0	0-0	16	Hall [78]	2411
17	19	H	Crawley T	W	3-1	1-0	13	Harrad [13], Shaw 2 [76, 89]	1353
18	26	H	Kidderminster H	W	1-0	0-0	12	Bell [50]	1847
19	Dec 10	H	Gravesend & N	D	0-0	0-0	13		1733
20	13	A	Forest Green R	L	0-1	0-1	—		548
21	26	A	Tamworth	D	1-1	1-1	15	Shaw [34]	2151
22	30	A	Kidderminster H	W	1-0	0-0	—	Gilroy [66]	1749
23	Jan 2	H	Tamworth	D	1-1	0-1	13	Shaw [58]	2680
24	21	H	Woking	D	1-1	1-1	14	Hall [44]	2061
25	24	H	Halifax T	L	1-2	1-1	—	Taylor K [8]	1540
26	28	A	Canvey Is	W	2-0	2-0	12	Taylor K 2 [27, 44]	741
27	31	A	Grays Ath	W	3-2	2-1	—	Shaw [17], Hall [23], Webster [57]	858
28	Feb 4	A	Morecambe	L	1-3	0-1	10	Ducros [84]	1855
29	10	H	Exeter C	W	2-0	0-0	—	Gilroy [62], Harrad [64]	1924
30	18	A	Aldershot T	D	1-1	1-1	10	Webster [4]	2248
31	21	H	Cambridge U	W	2-0	0-0	—	Moore [46], Harrad [60]	1577
32	25	A	Accrington S	L	1-2	1-1	10	Shaw [45]	1946
33	Mar 11	A	Stevenage Bor	W	3-2	0-2	9	Shaw [63], Webster [78], Moore [90]	2081
34	18	H	Hereford U	L	0-1	0-1	9		2512
35	25	A	Altrincham	W	2-1	1-1	9	Webster [4], Harrad [48]	1214
36	Apr 1	H	York C	D	0-0	0-0	9		2605
37	8	A	Crawley T	D	1-1	0-0	9	Clare [59]	1341
38	15	A	Scarborough	L	0-3	0-1	9		1808
39	18	H	Southport	D	0-0	0-0	—		1488
40	22	H	Forest Green R	W	1-0	1-0	9	Harrad [45]	2331
41	25	H	Dagenham & R	D	2-2	2-1	—	Clare [14], Harrad [23]	1235
42	29	A	Gravesend & N	W	1-0	1-0	9	Taylor K [36]	912

Final League Position: 9

GOALSCORERS

League (50): Shaw 11, Webster 8 (2 pens), Harrad 7, Hall 4, Taylor K 4, Anderson 3, Gilroy 3, Clare 2, Moore 2, Todd 2, Bell 1, Ducros 1, Stride 1, own goal 1.
FA Cup (7): Gilroy 2, Harrad 2, Shaw 2, Stride 1.
FA Trophy (0).

Crane 12	Henshaw 16 + 12	Corbett 38 + 2	Stride 34 + 3	Tinson 41	Webster 33 + 1	Todd 10 + 11	Ducros 23 + 7	Shaw 35 + 6	Harrad 32 + 7	Gilroy 31 + 2	Hall 27 + 10	Clough 4 + 3	Anderson 8 + 12	Graves 1 + 3	Austin 28 + 2	Bacon 4 + 1	Deeney 30	Bell 6	Sedgemore 9	Rowett 15 + 2	Taylor K 16 + 2	Moore 2 + 13	Clare 7 + 1	Brayford — + 1	*Match No.*
1	2	3	4	5	6	7^1	8^2	9^3	10	11	12	13	14												1
1	2	3	4	5	6	7	8^2	9^3	10	11^1	12	13	14												2
1	2	3	4	5	6	7^1	8	9^3	10	11^2	13		12	14											3
1	2	3	4	5	6	7^1	8^2	9^3	10	11	12		13	14											4
1	2	3	4	5	6	14		12	10^1	11^2	13	8	9	7^3											5
1	2	3	4	5	6	12		9	10^1	11	13	8^2			7										6
1	2	3	4	5	6	7^1		9		11	12		13		8	10^2									7
1	2	3	4	5	6	14		9	12	11^3		8^1	13		7	10^2									8
1		3	4	5	6	7^1		9	10	11	12		13		2	8^2									9
1	2^1	3	4	5	6		13	9	10^2	12	7		14		11	8^3									10
1		3	4	5	6	12	8	9		11^1	7		10		2										11
1		3	4	5	6	7		9			8	11	10^1		2	12									12
	12	3	4	5	6	13		9	14	11^2	7		10^3		2		1	8^1							13
		3	4■	5	6	7^2	13	9	14		11^1		10^3	12	2		1	8							14
		3	4	5	6	12		9	13	11^1	7		10^2		2		1	8							15
	2	13	4	5^1	6	12		9	10^2		7				3		1	8	11						16
		14	4	5	6	12	13	9^2	10^3	11^1	7				3		1	8	2						17
	2	3		5^1				9	10	11	7				4		1	6	8	12					18
	2	3	4	5		13	12	9^2	10^3	11	7^1		14		6		1		8						19
		3	4	5		7^1	8	13	10^2		12		9		6		1		11	2					20
	12	3^1	4	5			8	9	10^2	11	7		13		6		1		2						21
	2	3	13	5		12	8^2	9	10^3	11	7^1		14		6		1		4						22
	12	3	4	5		7	8	9	13	11			10^2				1		2	6^1					23
		3	4	5	12		13	9	10^2	11	7				6		1		2^1		8				24
		3	4	5	2		8	9	13	11	7^2				6		1			12	10^1				25
	13			5	3	12	8^2	9	10^3	11	4^1		14		6		1			2	7				26
	13	3	4		6		8	9	10	11^2	7^1				5		1				2	12			27
	12	3	4^1	5	6		8	9	10^2	11					2		1				7	13			28
		2	13	5	3			9	10	11	7^1				12		1			6	8	4^2			29
	12	2		5	3		13	9	10^3	11^2	6				4		1			8^1	7	14			30
	12	2		5	3		8^1	13	10^2	11	14				6		1			4	7	9^3			31
	2	3	13	5	6		8	9	10		11^1				4		1				7^2	12			32
		3	4	5	6		8^1	9	10^2	12	7						1			2	11	13			33
		2	4	5	6		13	9^2	10	11	8^1						1			3	7	12			34
	12	2		5	6		8	9^2	10^3	11	4						1			3	7^1	14	13		35
		2	4	5	3		8	12	10	11^2	7^1						1			6	13		9		36
	12	2	4	5	3		8^1	13	10^2		7						1			6	11	14	9^3		37
	14	2■	4	5	3		8	13	10		7^2						1			6^1	11	12	9^3		38
		2	4	5	3		8	7^1	10^3	11^2					13		1			6	14	12	9		39
	12		4	5	3^1		8	10	14	11^3					6		1			2	7^2	13	9		40
	2	3	4	5			8		10^1		7				11		1			6		12	9		41
	2^1	3	4	5				10	8^2		7	13			6		1				11	14	9^3	12	42

FA Cup

Fourth Qual	Leek T	(h)	2-0
First Round	Peterborough U	(a)	0-0
		(h)	1-0
Second Round	Burscough	(h)	4-1
Third Round	Manchester U	(h)	0-0
		(a)	0-5

FA Trophy

First Round	Worksop T	(h)	0-1

CAMBRIDGE UNITED Conference

Ground: Abbey Stadium, Newmarket Road, Cambridge CB5 8LN.
Tel: (01223) 566 500.
Year Formed: 1912.
Record Gate: 14,000 (1970 v Chelsea, Friendly).
Nickname: The 'U's'.
Manager: Rob Newman.
Secretary: Andrew Pincher.
Colours: Navy and sky blue shirts, sky blue shorts, sky blue stockings.

CAMBRIDGE UNITED 2005–06 LEAGUE RECORD

Match No.	Date	Venue	Opponents	Result	H/T Score	Lg. Pos.	Goalscorers	Attendance
1	Aug 13	A	Forest Green R	L 0-1	0-0	—		1112
2	16	H	Hereford U	W 2-1	1-0	—	Smith [44], Bridges [70]	2924
3	20	H	Accrington S	W 3-1	3-0	3	Angel [17], Quinton [34], Bridges [45]	2730
4	27	A	Gravesend & N	D 0-0	0-0	5		1379
5	29	H	Kidderminster H	L 0-2	0-0	—		3161
6	Sept 2	A	York C	L 0-1	0-0	—		2666
7	10	A	Exeter C	L 0-4	0-2	16		3407
8	17	H	Woking	L 0-2	0-0	18		2345
9	20	A	Grays Ath	L 3-5	1-4	—	Hanlon 2 [13, 82], Peters [58]	1543
10	24	H	Altrincham	W 4-0	2-0	17	Pitt [15], Onibuje 2 [18, 79], Atkins [84]	2199
11	27	H	Burton Alb	D 2-2	0-1	—	Onibuje [46], Pitt [66]	2298
12	Oct 1	A	Southport	D 2-2	1-1	15	Onibuje [5], Westcarr [83]	1204
13	7	H	Tamworth	W 2-1	1-0	—	Onibuje [22], Duncan [71]	2606
14	15	A	Halifax T	L 0-1	0-0	15		1621
15	29	H	Crawley T	W 2-1	2-1	13	Chick [32], Hanlon [37]	2413
16	Nov 12	A	Morecambe	W 1-0	1-0	10	Bridges [17]	1648
17	19	H	Aldershot T	L 0-2	0-1	11		2905
18	26	A	Canvey Is	D 1-1	0-1	13	Duncan [52]	842
19	Dec 3	H	Scarborough	W 2-1	2-0	11	Westcarr [31], Morrison [35]	2809
20	10	A	Dagenham & R	L 0-1	0-1	12		1271
21	26	H	Stevenage Bor	W 1-0	1-0	11	Bridges [19]	3697
22	31	H	Canvey Is	W 3-1	0-0	10	Westcarr [47], Onibuje 2 [51, 78]	2594
23	Jan 2	A	Stevenage Bor	L 1-3	1-2	11	Pitt [7]	3463
24	7	H	Forest Green R	D 2-2	1-1	11	Duncan [18], Onibuje [67]	2344
25	21	A	Accrington S	L 0-1	0-0	13		1837
26	28	H	Gravesend & N	D 1-1	0-1	14	Pitt [77]	2459
27	31	A	Hereford U	L 0-3	0-2	—		2142
28	Feb 11	A	Altrincham	L 1-2	1-2	16	Bridges [35]	1151
29	18	H	Southport	W 2-1	1-0	13	Woolaston [15], Peters [85]	2310
30	21	A	Burton Alb	L 0-2	0-0	—		1577
31	Mar 4	A	Woking	W 1-0	0-0	14	Guy [72]	2066
32	7	H	Grays Ath	D 1-1	1-1	—	Westcarr [13]	1821
33	11	A	Tamworth	D 1-1	1-1	12	Westcarr [5]	1325
34	18	H	Halifax T	D 1-1	1-0	14	Westcarr [2]	2288
35	25	A	Crawley T	L 0-1	0-0	14		1472
36	Apr 1	H	Morecambe	D 2-2	1-1	14	Brady [21], Smith [71]	2129
37	4	H	Exeter C	W 2-1	1-0	—	Onibuje [14], Guy [90]	2358
38	8	A	Aldershot T	W 3-1	0-1	13	Morrison [48], Pitt [58], Westcarr [75]	2198
39	14	H	York C	W 2-0	0-0	—	Westcarr (pen) [61], Hotte (og) [79]	3188
40	17	A	Kidderminster H	L 0-1	0-1	10		1665
41	22	A	Scarborough	W 2-1	1-1	10	Woolaston 2 [45, 74]	1831
42	29	H	Dagenham & R	L 1-2	0-0	12	Peters [59]	3161

Final League Position: 12

GOALSCORERS

League (51): Onibuje 9, Westcarr 8 (1 pen), Bridges 5, Pitt 5, Duncan 3, Hanlon 3, Peters 3, Woolaston 3, Guy 2, Morrison 2, Smith 2, Angel 1, Atkins 1, Brady 1, Chick 1, Quinton 1, own goal 1.
FA Cup (1): Peters 1.
Football League Trophy (8): Bridges 2, Onibuje 2, Atkins 1, Hanlon 1, Morrison 1, Smith 1.
FA Trophy (2): Bridges 1, Morrison 1.

Behcet 7	Gleeson 23 + 1	Chick 6 + 1	Duncan 31 + 1	Peters 34 + 1	Smith 21 + 5	Bridges 33 + 2	Quinton 11 + 6	Onibuje 25 + 9	Turner 6 + 3	Angel 6 + 2	Duffy 5 + 4	Daniels 1 + 2	Okai 6 + 7	Harkness 7	Davies 8 + 4	Nolan 3 + 7	Hanlon 22 + 3	Pitt 29 + 1	Robbins 3 + 1	Howie 33	Westcarr 23 + 8	Atkins 1 + 8	Morrison 21 + 1	Fuller 1	Nicholls 3 + 1	Bunce 5 + 8	Heeroo 8 + 1	Porter 3 + 5	Robinson 3 + 1	Brady 19	Medine 2 + 3	Jaszczun 16	Woolaston 13	Coldicott 4	Guy 12	Bloomer 8	*Match No.*
1	2	3^{1}	4	5	6	7	8^{2}	9	10	11^{3}	12	13	14																								1
1	2	3	4	5	6	7	8	9^{2}	10	11^{1}	13		12																								2
1	2		4^{1}	5	6	7	8	9^{2}	10^{3}	11	13			3	12	14																					3
1	2		4	5	6	7^{1}	8	9	10^{3}	11^{2}	14		13	3	12																						4
1	2		4^{1}	5	6	7	8	9	14	11^{2}	10^{3}	13		3		12																					5
1	2		4	5	6^{1}	7		12	10	11^{2}	9^{3}		13	3		14	8																				6
1	2		4	5		7		9^{2}	14		10^{3}		12	3^{1}		13	8	11	6																		7
	2		4^{1}	5		7			10			6^{2}		3	12	9	8	11		1	13																8
	2			5	6	7		9^{3}					12	3^{1}	4	10^{2}	8	11		1	14	13															9
	2			5	6	7^{1}	12	9^{3}		13			3		4		8^{2}	11		1	10	14															10
	2			5	6	7	12	9^{2}					3		4		8	11^{1}		1	10	13															11
			12	5	6^{1}	7^{2}	13	9^{3}					3		4		8	11	2	1	10	14															12
	2		4	5	6	7		9^{1}					3			12	8	11		1	10																13
			4	5	6	7				14			3			13	8	11^{3}	2^{1}	1	10		12	9^{2}													14
		3	4	5	6	7		9	12				11				8			1	10^{1}		2														15
			4	5	6	7	8									9^{2}	13			1	12	10^{1}	2		11	3■											16
	2^{1}	3^{2}	4			7	8	9					13			12	6			1	10^{3}	14	5		11												17
	2		4	5	6	7		9									8			1	10		3			11											18
	2^{1}		4	5	6^{2}	7		9									8		12	1	10		3		13	11											19
		13	4	5		7^{1}	14	9							3		8			1	10	12	2		6^{2}	11^{3}											20
		11	4	5	6	7		9									8^{1}	13		1	10^{2}		3				2	12									21
		11^{1}	4	5	6^{2}	7	8	13										9^{3}		1	10		3			14	2	12									22
				5		7	12	9							6^{1}			11^{3}		1	10	14	3			13	2	4	8^{2}								23
			4	5	14		12^{2}	9^{3}									8^{1}	11		1	10		3			13		6	7	2							24
	2^{1}		4	5	12	7	8^{2}	13										9^{3}		1	10		3			14			11	6							25
	2^{2}		4	5^{1}	12	7		9										11		1	10		6							8	13	3					26
	11^{2}		4	5	6^{1}	7		13										9		1	10^{3}		2					14	12	8		3					27
			4	5^{1}		7									12			11		1	13		2							8		3^{2}	6	10	9		28
			4	5		7												11		1	13		2					12		6		3	8	10^{1}	9^{2}		29
			4	5		7		12										11		1			2							6		3	8	10^{1}	9		30
	2		4			7		9										11		1										6		3	8		10	5	31
	2		4					9^{2}										11		1	10							12		6	13	3	7	8^{1}		5	32
	2^{1}		4	12													13	11		1	10							8^{2}		6	9	3	7			5	33
			4				8											11		1	10	13				12	2			6	9^{2}	3^{1}	7			5	34
			4			7												11		1	10^{2}					12	2^{1}			6	13	3	8■		9	5	35
				5^{1}	6	7^{2}		9			1				2		12	11								13				8		3			10	4	36
	12			5^{1}	6			9^{3}			1				4^{2}		8	11			14					13				7		3			10	2	37
			4^{1}			13		9^{3}									8	11		1	14		5				12			6		3	7^{2}		10	2	38
				5				12									8	11		1	10		4				2			6		3	7		9^{1}		39
				5		13		12									8^{2}	11		1	10		4			3	2^{1}			6			7		9		40
	4				13	9^{2}		14									8	11^{1}		1	12		5				2			6		3	7		10^{3}		41
	2			5	12		8^{2}	13									6^{1}	11		1			4							7		3	9		10		42

FA Cup

Fourth Qual	Weymouth	(a)	1-2

FA Trophy

First Round	Dorchester T	(a)	2-3

Football League Trophy

First Round	Chester C	(h)	3-0
Second Round	Doncaster R	(h)	3-2
Quarter-Final	Macclesfield T	(a)	2-4

CANVEY ISLAND — Ryman Premier

Ground: Park Lane, Canvey Island, Essex SS8 7PX.
Tel: (01268) 511 888.
Year Formed: 1950.
Record Gate: 3,553 (2002 v Aldershot T Ryman Premier League).
Nickname: Gulls.
Manager: John Batch.
Secretary: Wayne Purser.
Colours: Yellow and blue.

CANVEY ISLAND 2005–06 LEAGUE RECORD

Match No.	Date	Venue	Opponents	Result		H/T Score	Lg. Pos.	Goalscorers	Attendance
1	Aug 13	A	Accrington S	L	0-1	0-0	—		1012
2	16	H	Aldershot T	W	2-1	0-1	—	Boylan 2 (1 pen) 86, 90 (p)	1210
3	20	H	Gravesend & N	L	1-2	1-1	15	Duffy 8	1070
4	27	A	Burton Alb	W	2-1	1-1	8	Boylan 2 45, 72	1423
5	29	H	Dagenham & R	L	1-2	0-1	—	Minton 50	1458
6	Sept 2	A	Kidderminster H	L	2-3	1-1	—	Ibe 5, Boylan (pen) 87	1842
7	10	A	Crawley T	L	1-3	0-1	18	Minton 46	1335
8	17	H	Scarborough	W	1-0	1-0	15	Kennedy 17	744
9	20	A	Woking	D	1-1	1-1	—	Ibe 42	1543
10	24	H	Southport	W	2-1	0-1	13	Ibe 48, Hallett 79	727
11	27	H	Stevenage Bor	D	1-1	0-0	—	Ibe 68	832
12	Oct 1	A	Hereford U	D	1-1	1-1	12	Green (og) 21	2500
13	8	H	Altrincham	D	1-1	1-1	13	Noto 34	835
14	15	A	York C	L	1-2	0-0	13	Hallett 83	3070
15	29	H	Morecambe	D	3-3	2-0	14	Tait 9, Boylan 25, Sedgemore 49	480
16	Nov 12	A	Forest Green R	W	2-1	1-1	12	Boylan 33, Minton 60	678
17	19	H	Tamworth	L	1-2	0-1	15	Tait 60	646
18	26	H	Cambridge U	D	1-1	1-0	14	Boylan 29	842
19	Dec 3	A	Exeter C	W	2-0	0-0	12	Sedgemore 55, Ibe 82	3465
20	10	H	Halifax T	L	0-1	0-0	14		664
21	27	A	Grays Ath	W	2-1	1-0	—	Hallett 40, Minton 81	2910
22	31	A	Cambridge U	L	1-3	0-0	14	Ibe 67	2594
23	Jan 2	H	Grays Ath	W	2-1	1-1	12	Hallett 15, Clarke 63	1445
24	7	H	Accrington S	L	0-2	0-1	13		962
25	20	A	Gravesend & N	L	0-2	0-1	—		1560
26	24	A	Aldershot T	D	2-2	0-0	—	Minton 87, Sedgemore 90	1800
27	28	H	Burton Alb	L	0-2	0-2	16		741
28	Feb 11	A	Southport	L	0-2	0-1	17		901
29	18	H	Hereford U	D	1-1	1-1	17	Gregory (pen) 18	784
30	21	A	Stevenage Bor	L	0-3	0-1	—		1403
31	25	H	Crawley T	W	1-0	0-0	17	Sterling 52	698
32	Mar 11	A	Altrincham	W	1-0	0-0	16	Boylan 90	903
33	18	H	York C	D	1-1	0-0	15	Boylan 76	754
34	21	A	Scarborough	W	2-1	0-0	—	Hallett 77, Minton 90	1153
35	25	A	Morecambe	L	0-1	0-1	16		1471
36	Apr 1	H	Forest Green R	D	1-1	0-0	15	Chenery 49	426
37	4	H	Woking	L	0-2	0-2	—		358
38	8	A	Tamworth	L	0-1	0-0	16		1156
39	14	H	Kidderminster H	W	2-1	2-0	—	Clarke 1, Hallett 45	621
40	17	A	Dagenham & R	D	2-2	2-1	15	Hallett 2 9, 16	1139
41	22	H	Exeter C	D	1-1	0-0	15	Boylan 90	641
42	29	A	Halifax T	W	2-0	1-0	14	Hallett 19, Boylan 88	2049

Final League Position: 14

GOALSCORERS

League (47): Boylan 12 (2 pens), Hallett 9, Ibe 6, Minton 6, Sedgemore 3, Clarke 2, Tait 2, Chenery 1, Duffy 1, Gregory 1 (pen), Kennedy 1, Noto 1, Sterling 1, own goal 1.
FA Cup (2): Ibe 2.
FA Trophy (4): Hallett 2, Boylan 1, Clarke 1.

McKinney 19	Clarke 32 + 4	Bimson 20 + 2	Duffy 29 + 1	Chenery 36 + 1	Theobald 3	Kennedy 38	Minton 38 + 2	Tait 10 + 16	Boylan 20 + 5	Sedgemore 34 + 1	Keeling 20 + 11	Gregory 5 + 10	Sterling 20 + 4	Ibe 21 + 14	Ward 30 + 2	Harrison — + 1	Potter 23	Bunce 2	Hallett 18 + 14	McGhee 17 + 3	Noto 15 + 12	Lowes — + 1	Dolan 4 + 1	Conroy 8 + 2	*Match No.*
1	2^{1}	3	4	5	6	7	8^{2}	9	10	11	12	13													1
1	2^{2}	3^{1}	4	5	6	7	8	9^{3}	10	11	12	14	13												2
1	2^{2}	3	4	5	6	7	8	9^{3}	10	11^{1}	13		12	14											3
1	2	3^{1}	4			7	8	13	10^{2}	11	12		6	9	5										4
1	2	3^{1}	4			7	8	14	10	11^{2}	13	12	6	9^{3}	5										5
1■	2^{1}	3	4			7	8	13	10^{G}	11	12		6	9^{2}	5	15									6
	14	3^{3}	4■			7	8	9		13	2^{1}	12	6	10^{2}	5		1	11							7
1	2	3		5		7	8			11		10^{1}	6	9	4				12						8
1	2^{2}	3		5		7	8	14		11	13	9^{1}	6	10^{3}	4				12						9
1	2	3^{1}		5		7	8	13		11		9^{3}	6^{2}	10	4				14	12					10
1	2	3^{2}	12	5		7	8	14		11			6	9	4^{1}				10^{3}	13					11
1	2		3	5		7	8■	13		11^{1}			6	9					10^{2}	4	12				12
1	2	12^{2}	3	5		7■		13	10	11			6	9^{3}	4^{1}				14		8				13
1	2	12	3	5			8^{2}	13	10^{3}	11			6	9	4^{1}				14		7				14
			3	5		7	8	9^{1}	10	11	2		6		4		1		12						15
			3	5		7	8	9^{2}	10^{3}	11	2		6^{1}	13	12		1		14	4					16
			3	5		7	8	9	10	11^{2}	2						1	4^{1}	13	6	12				17
			4	5		7	8	9^{3}	10	11	2^{2}			14	12		1		13	6	3^{1}				18
			2	5		7	8	9^{3}	10^{2}	11	3^{1}			14	4		1		13	6	12				19
	13		3	5		7	8		10	11	2^{2}			9^{3}	4		1		14	6^{1}	12				20
	2		4	5		7^{1}	8			11	3			13	10		1		9^{2}	6	12				21
	10		3	5		7■	8			11	2^{1}			13	4		1		9^{2}	6	12				22
	10^{1}		2	5			8			11	3	13	4	12			1		9^{2}	6	7				23
	10^{2}			5			8			11	7		3^{1}	13	4		1		9	6	2	12			24
1	10		3	2		7	8			6^{2}	11^{3}		12	14	4^{1}				9		13		5		25
1	11		3^{1}			7^{2}	8			4	13	14	6	9					10^{3}	2	12		5		26
1	11		3	13		7^{1}	8			4	2	14	6^{2}	9^{3}					10		12		5		27
1	10	3^{1}	4	2			8^{2}			11	12	13	6						9		7		5		28
1	13		3	2		7	12			11	6	10^{2}		9	4					5	8^{1}				29
1	14	3		2		7		13		11	6^{2}	10^{3}		9	5					4^{1}	8		12		30
	11		3	2		7	8	9^{1}		4	13		6	12	5		1		10^{2}						31
	11		3	2		7	8		13	4			6^{1}	9^{3}	5		1		10^{2}		12			14	32
	11		3	2		7^{1}	8		10	4		13		9^{2}	5		1			6	12				33
	11■	3		2		7	8		10^{2}	4				9^{1}	5		1		12	6				13	34
			3^{1}	2		7	8	13	10	11				9^{3}	5		1		14	6	12			4^{2}	35
	11	3		5		7	8^{2}	12	10					14	6		1		9^{3}	13	4^{1}			2	36
	11		3^{1}	5		7	8	13	10		12			9^{3}	6		1		14		4^{2}			2	37
	11	3		5		7	13	12	10		8^{2}			14			1		9^{3}	6	4^{1}			2	38
	11	3		5		7	8	13	12		2^{1}				4		1		9^{2}		10			6	39
	10	3		5		7	8	12	13		11^{1}				6		1		9^{2}		4			2	40
	10	3		5		7	8		13		11^{2}	12		14	6		1		9^{3}		4^{1}			2	41
	10^{3}	3^{1}		5		7	8		13		11		12	14	6		1		9^{2}		4			2	42

FA Cup

Fourth Qual	Burnham	(h)	1-1
		(a)	1-2

FA Trophy

First Round	Kingstonian	(h)	4-1
Second Round	Salisbury C	(h)	0-1

CRAWLEY TOWN Conference

Ground: Broadfield Ground, Broadfield Stadium, Brighton Road, West Sussex RH11 9RX.
Tel: (01293) 410 000.
Year Formed: 1896.
Record Gate: 4,522 (2004 v Weymouth Dr Martens League).
Nickname: The Reds.
Manager: John Hollins.
Secretary: Barry Munn.
Colours: All red.

CRAWLEY TOWN 2005–06 LEAGUE RECORD

Match No.	*Date*	*Venue*	*Opponents*	*Result*		*H/T Score*	*Lg. Pos.*	*Goalscorers*	*Attendance*
1	Aug 13	A	York C	D	0-0	0-0	—		2276
2	16	H	Dagenham & R	D	0-0	0-0	—		1734
3	20	H	Hereford U	L	0-2	0-0	20		1842
4	27	A	Morecambe	L	0-3	0-0	21		1473
5	29	H	Stevenage Bor	L	1-2	0-0	—	Douglas [59]	2019
6	Sept 5	A	Aldershot T	L	2-3	1-2	—	Clare [8], Wormull [83]	2371
7	10	H	Canvey Is	W	3-1	1-0	21	Armstrong [44], Opinel [50], Burton [72]	1335
8	17	A	Accrington S	L	2-4	1-1	21	Burton [23], Clare [67]	1365
9	20	A	Forest Green R	D	2-2	0-2	—	Clare (pen) [84], Judge [88]	916
10	24	H	Grays Ath	L	1-3	1-1	22	Wormull [12]	1471
11	27	H	Kidderminster H	W	2-0	1-0	—	Burgess (og) [3], Cade [82]	1012
12	Oct 1	A	Altrincham	D	1-1	1-0	21	Lindegaard [45]	819
13	8	A	Scarborough	W	2-1	1-1	17	Wormull [9], Giles [90]	1257
14	15	H	Exeter C	L	0-2	0-0	20		2454
15	29	A	Cambridge U	L	1-2	1-2	21	Cade [3]	2413
16	Nov 12	H	Southport	W	2-0	2-0	18	Cade [22], Clare [35]	2055
17	19	A	Burton Alb	L	1-3	0-1	20	Clare [78]	1353
18	26	H	Gravesend & N	L	1-2	0-2	20	Armstrong [71]	1426
19	Dec 3	A	Halifax T	D	2-2	1-0	19	Clare (pen) [13], Whitman [82]	1616
20	10	H	Tamworth	W	3-0	0-0	18	Woozley [79], Burton 2 [86, 90]	1448
21	26	A	Woking	D	0-0	0-0	18		2643
22	Jan 2	H	Woking	D	2-2	0-1	18	Clare 2 (1 pen) [60 (p), 64]	2073
23	7	H	York C	L	0-1	0-0	19		1514
24	21	A	Hereford U	L	1-2	0-1	20	Brown [63]	2782
25	28	H	Morecambe	L	1-3	0-0	21	Clare (pen) [76]	1253
26	Feb 11	A	Grays Ath	L	0-1	0-0	22		1038
27	18	H	Altrincham	W	2-0	1-0	21	Clare 2 [35, 60]	1085
28	21	A	Kidderminster H	L	0-1	0-1	—		1302
29	25	A	Canvey Is	L	0-1	0-0	21		698
30	28	A	Gravesend & N	D	1-1	0-0	—	Jenkins [90]	698
31	Mar 4	H	Accrington S	L	0-1	0-1	21		1361
32	11	H	Scarborough	W	2-0	1-0	19	Scully [42], Coleman [76]	1181
33	18	H	Forest Green R	W	1-0	1-0	18	Burton [38]	1067
34	25	H	Cambridge U	W	1-0	0-0	18	Giles [56]	1472
35	28	A	Dagenham & R	W	3-0	0-0	—	Coleman [57], Burton 2 [66, 72]	932
36	Apr 1	A	Southport	W	2-0	0-0	17	Clay [74], Coleman [90]	1308
37	8	H	Burton Alb	D	1-1	0-0	17	Scully [89]	1341
38	15	H	Aldershot T	W	2-0	1-0	16	Coleman [28], Bostwick [55]	1764
39	17	A	Stevenage Bor	L	1-2	1-1	17	Ekoku [20]	2410
40	22	H	Halifax T	D	2-2	2-0	17	Bostwick 2 [9, 16]	1285
41	25	A	Exeter C	L	0-4	0-3	—		1782
42	29	A	Tamworth	D	0-0	0-0	17		1545

Final League Position: 17

GOALSCORERS

League (48): Clare 11 (4 pens), Burton 7, Coleman 4, Bostwick 3, Cade 3, Wormull 3, Armstrong 2, Giles 2, Scully 2, Brown 1, Clay 1, Douglas 1, Ekoku 1, Jenkins 1, Judge 1, Lindegaard 1, Opinel 1, Whitman 1, Woozley 1, own goal 1.
FA Cup (0).
FA Trophy (5): Burton 2, Giles 1, Scully 1, Wormull 1.

Smith 38	Judge 39	Jenkins 14 + 9	Simpemba 26	Woozley 29 + 1	Brown 23	Elam 4 + 1	Wormull 21 + 2	Burton 29 + 7	Cade 15 + 4	Hodgson 4	Blackburn 24 + 11	Ekoku 8 + 19	Douglas 2 + 5	Davidson — + 2	Armstrong 29 + 1	Giles 22 + 6	Opinel 19 + 4	Donovan 1	Kember 4 + 1	Clare 25	Lindegaard 10	Ward 4	Keehan 1 + 1	Proffit — + 2	Whitman 3 + 2	Scully 20	El-Abd 1	Mendy 21	Coleman 6 + 3	Clay 8 + 3	Marshall 3 + 3	Gordon 3 + 2	Bostwick 5 + 3	Macleod 1	*Match No.*
1	2	3	4	5	6^1	7	8	9^2	10^3	11	12	13	14																						1
1	2	3	4	5		7	8	9	10^1	11	6	12																							2
1	2	3	4	5		7^1	8	9	10	11^2	6		12	13																					3
1	2		4	5	6	7^1	8	9	14	11^2	3■	10^3		13	12																				4
1	2		4	5	6		8	12	13			9^1	10^2		7	3	11																		5
1	2			5	6		8		13			14	10^3		7	3^1	11^2	4■	12	9															6
1	2		4	5			8	10	6						7	3	11			9															7
1	2		4	5			8	10^2	12		14	13			7^3	3	11			9	6^1														8
1	2		4	5			13	12	10		8^2				7	3^1	11			9	6														9
1			4	5		12	8^2	11	10		13				7	2^1	3			9	6														10
	2		4	5			8^2	10^3	11		13		14		7	12	3^1			9	6	1													11
	2		4	5			8^1	10	11		12		13		7		3			9^2	6	1													12
	2	13	4^1	5			8	10	11^2						7	12	3■			9	6	1													13
	2	3^1		5			8	10^2	11^3		12		13		7	4				9	6	1	14												14
1	2	11		5					10		8				7	3				9	4		6												15
1	2	3^1	4	5			8^2		10^3			13			7	12				9	6			14	11										16
1	2	3^1	4	5			8		10^2			13			7	14				9	6			12	11^3										17
1	2		4	5			8	14	10^3			13			6	12	3^1			9					11^2	7									18
1	2		4	5	6			10			13				8^1	3	11^2			9					12	7									19
1	2		4	5	6		8	10			13	12			7					9						11^2	3^1								20
1		3	4	5■	6		8^1	10			12						11			9						7		2							21
1	2	11	4				8	10			6						3			9						7		5							22
1	2	11^2	4		6		8^1	10^3			12					3	13			9					14	7		5							23
1	2		4		6			10			7	12			8^1	9	3									11		5							24
1		12	4	5	6		8^1	10^3			13	14			7^2	2	3			9						11									25
1	2	3^3	4^1	5			12				8^2	13			6		11			9						7		10	14						26
1	2		4	5				10^2			7^1	13			8		3			9^3						11		6		12	14				27
1	2		4	5^1				14			7^2	13			8		3			9						11		6		12		10^3			28
1	2^1		4	5				10^3			7^2	12			8		3			9						11		6		13		14			29
1	2^1	12			6			13			8^2	14			4	3				9						11		5		7		10^3			30
1	2	12			6			10^3			8	14			4^2	3				9						11^1		5	13	7					31
1	2	12			6			10			8				4	3										11^1		5	13	7		9^2			32
1	2	12			6			10			8^1				4	3										11^2		5	9	7			13		33
1	2				6			10			8	12			4	3										11		5	9^1	7					34
1	2	12			6			10^2			8	13			4	3										11^1		5	9	7					35
1	2				6						8	10^3			4^2	3	12									11		5	9	7^1	13		14		36
1	2				6			10			8	13				3										11		5^1	9	7	4^2		12		37
1	2	13		12	6			10^3			8	7				3^1												5	9^2		11	14	4		38
1	2	3^1		5	6			10			8	9					12		7									4					11		39
1	2	13		5^1	6			10			8	9				12			11									4			7^2		3		40
1	2	3^1		5	6			13			7	9^2				10^3	14		8									4			12		11		41
1	2	3^1			6			12	10		7	9							8									5					11	4	42

FA Cup

Fourth Qual	Braintree T	(h)	0-1

FA Trophy

First Round	Stevenage B	(a)	2-0
Second Round	Worcester C	(h)	3-1
Third Round	Boreham Wood	(h)	0-2

Football League Trophy

First Round	Gillingham	(a)	0-2

DAGENHAM & REDBRIDGE Conference

Ground: Victoria Road, Dagenham, Essex RM10 7XL.
Tel: (0208) 592 7194.
Year Formed: 1992.
Record Gate: 5,500 (1992 v Leyton Orient FA Cup First Round).
Nickname: Daggers.
Manager: John Still.
Secretary: Derek Almond.
Colours: Red shirts, white shorts, red stockings.

DAGENHAM & REDBRIDGE 2005–06 LEAGUE RECORD

Match No.	Date	Venue	Opponents	Result		H/T Score	Lg. Pos.	Goalscorers	Attendance
1	Aug 13	H	Southport	W	3-1	1-1	—	Mackail-Smith 2 31, 90, Leberl 51	1265
2	16	A	Crawley T	D	0-0	0-0	—		1734
3	20	A	Tamworth	D	2-2	2-0	8	Goodwin 21, Moore 45	1040
4	27	H	Scarborough	L	0-2	0-0	11		1074
5	29	A	Canvey Is	W	2-1	1-0	—	Goodwin 27, Mackail-Smith 79	1458
6	Sept 3	H	Exeter C	D	2-2	1-1	11	Southam 5, Moore 58	1372
7	10	A	Altrincham	W	5-0	1-0	7	Kandol 2 37, 57, Moore 51, Leberl 70, Mackail-Smith 81	876
8	17	H	Burton Alb	W	3-1	1-0	5	Goodwin 23, Moore 63, Kandol 82	1149
9	20	A	York C	D	1-1	0-1	—	Griffiths 90	2927
10	24	H	Accrington S	L	1-2	0-0	8	Kandol 64	1331
11	27	H	Grays Ath	L	1-2	0-1	—	Moore 48	2017
12	Oct 5	A	Stevenage Bor	L	1-2	0-1	—	Mackail-Smith 72	2447
13	9	H	Aldershot T	W	2-0	1-0	8	Kandol 2 26, 63	1512
14	15	A	Morecambe	L	0-2	0-1	10		1718
15	29	H	Forest Green R	D	1-1	1-1	10	Moore 6	1325
16	Nov 12	A	Halifax T	L	0-3	0-0	11		1532
17	19	H	Hereford U	L	0-1	0-1	14		1294
18	26	H	Woking	L	1-3	1-2	15	Bruce 12	1138
19	Dec 3	A	Kidderminster H	L	1-3	0-2	16	Southam 81	1559
20	10	H	Cambridge U	W	1-0	1-0	15	Akurang 45	1271
21	26	A	Gravesend & N	W	3-1	1-1	14	Goodwin 32, Moore 2 87, 90	1391
22	31	A	Woking	D	0-0	0-0	13		1806
23	Jan 2	H	Gravesend & N	L	1-2	0-0	15	Bruce 60	1405
24	7	A	Southport	W	2-1	2-0	12	Leberl 6, Mackail-Smith 17	1002
25	21	H	Tamworth	W	2-1	1-1	11	Moore 2 14, 63	1352
26	28	A	Scarborough	W	1-0	0-0	10	Griffiths 70	1505
27	Feb 11	A	Accrington S	L	0-1	0-0	12		2156
28	18	H	Stevenage Bor	D	2-2	2-2	12	Cole 11, Saunders 17	1427
29	21	A	Grays Ath	W	4-0	3-0	—	Bruce 11, Akurang 2 18, 66, Southam 44	1065
30	Mar 7	H	York C	L	0-2	0-0	—		973
31	11	A	Aldershot T	L	1-3	0-2	14	Mackail-Smith 69	2010
32	18	H	Morecambe	W	3-1	0-0	13	Mackail-Smith 46, Southam 63, Akurang 72	960
33	25	A	Forest Green R	W	3-0	0-0	11	Cole 62, Foster 70, Moore 90	625
34	28	H	Crawley T	L	0-3	0-0	—		932
35	Apr 1	H	Halifax T	W	1-0	1-0	11	Mackail-Smith 15	1078
36	8	A	Hereford U	D	1-1	0-0	10	Southam (pen) 83	2561
37	11	H	Altrincham	L	2-4	2-3	—	Bruce 41, Griffiths 45	1058
38	15	A	Exeter C	L	1-3	1-1	11	Cole 35	3186
39	17	H	Canvey Is	D	2-2	1-2	11	Moore 2 (1 pen) 19, 82 (p)	1139
40	22	H	Kidderminster H	W	3-0	3-0	11	Saunders 34, Mackail-Smith 2 44, 45	1038
41	25	A	Burton Alb	D	2-2	1-2	—	Moore 3, Akurang 72	1235
42	29	A	Cambridge U	W	2-1	0-0	10	Moore (pen) 55, Benson 79	3161

Final League Position: 10

GOALSCORERS

League (63): Moore 15 (2 pens), Mackail-Smith 11, Kandol 6, Akurang 5, Southam 5 (1 pen), Bruce 4, Goodwin 4, Cole 3, Griffiths 3, Leberl 3, Saunders 2, Benson 1, Foster 1.
FA Cup (4): Kandol 2, Moore 2.
Football League Trophy (1): Benson 1.
FA Trophy (10): Mackail-Smith 3, Moore 3, Southam 2, Saunders 1, own goal 1.

Roberts 42	Goodwin 22	Griffiths 42	Blackett 39	Uddin 38	Leberl 10 + 1	Foster 37	Southam 42	Moore 33 + 7	Mackail-Smith 36 + 3	Bruce 26	Vickers 9 + 13	Benson 13 + 13	Saunders 15 + 7	Kandol 10 + 2	Marwa 10 + 2	Cole 20 + 2	Akurang 12 + 6	Batt — + 2	Lettejallon 4 + 4	Clark 2	Match No.
1	2	3[1]	4	5	6	7	8	9[2]	10	11	12	13									1
1	2	3	4[1]	5	6	7	8	9[2]	10	11	12	13									2
1	2	3		5	6	7	8	9	10	11[1]	4		12								3
1	2[1]	3	4	5	6	7	8	9[3]	10	11[2]		12	13	14							4
1	2	3	4	5	6	7	8	9[1]	10			11[2]	12	13							5
1	2	3[1]	4	5	6	7	8	9[2]	10		12	11			13						6
1	2	3	4	5	6	7	8	9	10					11							7
1	2	3	4	5	6[1]	7	8	9	10[2]			13		11	12						8
1	2	3	4	5		7	8	9[1]	10			12		11	6						9
1	2	3	4	5		7[1]	8	9	10		13	12		11	6[2]						10
1	2	3	4	5		7	8	9	10		6			11							11
1	2	3	4	5			8	9	10		6[1]	12		11	7						12
1	2	3	4	5			8	9	10			6		11	7						13
1	2	3	4	5			8	9	10[1]		12	7		11	6						14
1	2	3[1]	4	5			8	9	12		6	10[2]	13	11	7						15
1	2	3	4	5		7	8		10	11[1]		9			6	12					16
1	2	3	4	5		7	8	9	10	11[1]		6				12					17
1	2	3	4	5		7[1]	8	9		11		12			6		10				18
1	2	3	4	5		7	8	9		11[1]		12			6		10				19
1		3	4	5		7	8	9		11					2	6	10				20
1	2	3	4	5		7	8	13	10[1]	11		9[2]				6		12			21
1	2	3	4	5		7	8	9	10	11						6					22
1		3	4	5	6	7[1]	8	9	12	11		10				2					23
1		3	4	5	6■	7	8	12	10	11		9[1]				2					24
1		3	4	5		7	8	9	10	11			6	2							25
1	2	3	4	5		7	8	9	10[2]	11[1]	13		12			6					26
1		3[1]	4	5			8	9	10	11	12		2			6	7				27
1		3	4	5		7	8	9	10[1]	11			2			6	12				28
1		3		5	12	7	8	14	10[3]	11[2]	6		2[1]			4	9		13		29
1		3	4	5		7	8	13	10		12		2			6	9[2]		11[1]		30
1		3	4	5		7[1]	8	9	10		13		2			6	12		11[2]		31
1		3[1]	4	5		7	8		10	11	12		2[2]			6	9		13		32
1		3[1]	4	5		7	8	13	10	11	12		2			6	9[2]				33
1		3	4	5[1]		7[2]	8	13	10	11	12		2			6	9				34
1		3	4	5		7	8	9	10[2]	11			2[1]			6	13		12		35
1		3	4	5		7	8	9[1]	10[2]	11		13	2			6	12				36
1		3	4■	5		7[1]	8	9[2]	10	11■		12	2			6	13				37
1		3		5		7	8	13	10		4	12	2[1]			6	9[2]		11		38
1		3	4			7	8	9	13		5	10[2]	12			2	11[1]		6		39
1		3	4[2]			7	8	9	10		13	11[3]	2			5[1]		14	12	6	40
1		3	4			7	8	9	10	11	5	13	12				6[2]			2[1]	41
1		3	4			7	8	9	10	11	5	6[1]	2				12				42

FA Cup

Fourth Qual	Forest Green R	(a)	3-2
First Round	Hartlepool U	(a)	1-2

Football League Trophy

First Round	Wycombe W	(a)	1-2

FA Trophy

First Round	Thurrock	(h)	2-0
Second Round	Kettering Town	(h)	2-1
Third Round	Tamworth	(a)	0-0
		(h)	3-0
Fourth Round	Grays Ath	(a)	1-1
		(h)	2-4

EXETER CITY Conference

Ground: St James Park, Exeter EX4 6PX.
Tel: (01392) 411 243.
Year Formed: 1904.
Record Gate: 20,984 v Sunderland, FA Cup 6th rd (replay), 4 March 1931.
Nickname: The Grecians.
Manager: Paul Tisdale.
Secretary: Sally Cooke.
Colours: Red and white shirts, white shorts, white stockings.

EXETER CITY 2005–06 LEAGUE RECORD

Match No.	Date	Venue	Opponents	Result		H/T Score	Lg. Pos.	Goalscorers	Attendance
1	Aug 13	A	Gravesend & N	W	2-0	1-0	—	Phillips 2 (1 pen) 44, 73 (p)	1578
2	16	H	Kidderminster H	W	1-0	0-0	—	Farrell 69	4914
3	20	H	Morecambe	W	2-0	2-0	1	Phillips 24, Todd 33	3978
4	27	A	Accrington S	W	2-1	0-0	1	Watkins 68, Todd 71	1312
5	29	H	Forest Green R	D	0-0	0-0	—		4696
6	Sept 3	A	Dagenham & R	D	2-2	1-1	2	Challinor 12, Todd 90	1372
7	10	H	Cambridge U	W	4-0	2-0	1	Scully 4, Phillips 14, Buckle 63, Challinor 67	3407
8	17	A	Southport	W	3-0	0-0	1	Farrell 2 46, 56, Phillips 48	1423
9	20	A	Stevenage Bor	L	0-2	0-0	—		2445
10	24	H	Burton Alb	L	1-2	1-0	3	Jones B 17	4025
11	27	H	Woking	D	1-1	1-0	—	Scully 27	3082
12	Oct 1	A	York C	L	2-4	1-2	5	Flack 23, Jones B (pen) 74	3503
13	8	H	Halifax T	W	4-2	2-2	4	Jones B (pen) 11, Flack 45, Afful 74, Farrell 75	3154
14	15	A	Crawley T	W	2-0	0-0	3	Challinor 2 89, 90	2454
15	29	H	Tamworth	W	3-0	1-0	2	Phillips 44, Farrell 2 67, 90	3369
16	Nov 5	A	Kidderminster H	W	2-1	0-0	—	Todd 59, Scully 77	1869
17	12	A	Altrincham	D	1-1	1-0	1	Challinor 32	1366
18	19	H	Grays Ath	L	1-2	0-0	3	Challinor 87	6682
19	26	A	Hereford U	W	2-0	0-0	3	Mackie 61, Challinor 67	3754
20	Dec 3	H	Canvey Is	L	0-2	0-0	3		3465
21	10	A	Scarborough	W	1-0	1-0	3	Farrell 45	1428
22	26	H	Aldershot T	W	4-0	2-0	2	Buckle 33, Jones B (pen) 38, Challinor 61, Phillips 70	4989
23	30	H	Hereford U	L	1-2	1-2	—	Phillips 5	4433
24	Jan 2	A	Aldershot T	L	0-1	0-1	2		3136
25	7	H	Gravesend & N	W	1-0	0-0	2	Phillips 80	3396
26	21	A	Morecambe	D	2-2	0-0	2	Jones B (pen) 55, Challinor 90	2073
27	30	H	Accrington S	L	1-3	0-1	—	Edwards 72	4624
28	Feb 10	A	Burton Alb	L	0-2	0-0	—		1924
29	18	H	York C	L	1-3	1-1	7	Carlisle 3	3381
30	21	A	Woking	L	0-1	0-0	—		1536
31	Mar 4	H	Southport	W	5-0	4-0	7	Flack 3 3, 5, 14, Phillips (pen) 33, Buckle 82	3485
32	11	A	Halifax T	L	0-2	0-2	8		2104
33	14	H	Stevenage Bor	L	0-2	0-1	—		3026
34	28	A	Tamworth	D	1-1	1-1	—	Challinor 1	823
35	Apr 1	H	Altrincham	W	3-1	2-1	8	Phillips 9, Mackie 29, Challinor 50	3134
36	4	A	Cambridge U	L	1-2	0-1	—	Phillips 82	2358
37	10	A	Grays Ath	L	0-3	0-1	—		1369
38	15	H	Dagenham & R	W	3-1	1-1	8	Jones B (pen) 45, Phillips 48, Gill 89	3186
39	17	A	Forest Green R	D	0-0	0-0	8		1334
40	22	A	Canvey Is	D	1-1	0-0	8	Jones B 84	641
41	25	H	Crawley T	W	4-0	3-0	—	Mackie 34, Seaborne 38, Farrell 41, Moxey 62	1782
42	29	H	Scarborough	D	1-1	0-0	7	Challinor 86	3382

Final League Position: 7

GOALSCORERS

League (65): Phillips 13 (2 pens), Challinor 12, Farrell 8, Jones B 7 (5 pens), Flack 5, Todd 4, Buckle 3, Mackie 3, Scully 3, Afful 1, Carlisle 1, Edwards 1, Gill 1, Moxey 1, Seaborne 1, Watkins 1.
FA Cup (0).
Football League Trophy (2): Phillips 1, Taylor 1.
FA Trophy (11): Phillips 3, Jones B 2, Challinor 1, Flack 1, Mackie 1, Robinson 1, Todd 1, own goal 1.

Jones P 37	Hiley 13 + 1	Vinnicombe 1 + 2	Taylor 29 + 6	Gaia 14 + 3	Todd 41	Challinor 40 + 2	Buckle 24 + 4	Flack 11 + 26	Phillips 34 + 3	Moxey 12 + 9	Cronin 28 + 2	Farrell 26 + 12	Afful 4 + 6	Jones B 36 + 1	Edwards 8 + 6	Sawyer 26 + 4	Watkins — + 5	Scully 10 + 3	Mackie 13 + 11	Woodards 27	Robinson — + 1	Gill 13 + 3	Carlisle 4 + 2	Rice 5	Seaborne 4	Clay 1 + 2	Friend 1	Bye — + 1	*Match No.*
1	2	3	4	5	6	7	8	9^{1}	10^{2}	11^{3}	12	13	14■																1
1	2		4^{1}	5	6	7	8	9^{2}	10		11	13		3	12														2
1	2	12	14	5^{1}	6	7^{2}	8	13	10		11	9		3	4^{3}														3
1	2		11^{2}	5^{1}	6	7	8	9^{3}	10		4			3	14	12	13												4
1	2		11		6	7^{1}	8^{2}	14	10		4		13	3	9^{3}	5	12												5
1	2		11^{1}		6	7^{2}	8	9^{3}	10		4	14		3		5	13	12											6
1	2		12		6	7	8^{1}	14	10^{3}		4	9	13	3		5		11^{2}											7
1	2		12		6	7^{1}	8	13	10^{2}		4	9^{3}		3		5	14	11											8
1	2		11^{2}		6	7	8	12	10		4	14		3	9^{3}	5^{1}		13											9
1	2		13		6	7^{1}	8^{2}	14	10		4	9^{3}	12	3		5		11											10
1	2		4	12	6^{1}	7			10^{3}			9	8	3	14	5		11^{2}	13										11
1	2		4		6	7		9^{3}	10^{2}			11	13	3		5	14	12	8^{1}										12
1	2^{1}		8	5	6	7^{2}		9^{3}	14		4	10	12	3		13		11											13
1	14		4	5^{1}	6	7		13	10^{2}		3	9	8^{3}	2		12		11											14
1			8	5		7	12		10^{2}		4	9		2		6		11	13	3^{1}									15
1			8^{1}	5	6	7		14	10^{3}	12	4	9^{2}		3				11	13	2									16
1			8	5	6	7		14	10^{3}	12	4^{1}	9^{2}		3				11	13	2									17
1			12^{2}		6	7		13	10■	11^{1}	4	9^{3}		3		5		8	14	2									18
1			8		6	7		12		13	4	9	11^{1}	3		5			10^{2}	2									19
1			8^{3}		6	7	12	13		14	4	9	11^{2}	3		5			10	2^{1}									20
1			13	5	6	7	8^{2}	10			4	9		3		12			11^{1}	2									21
1			11^{2}		6	7	8	14	10	13	4^{1}	9^{3}		3		5			12	2									22
1			7^{1}	12	6	11	8^{2}	14	10	13	4	9^{3}		3		5				2									23
1			11^{1}		6	7	8^{3}	14	10		4^{2}	9		3		5			12	2	13								24
1			4^{1}		6	7	8	14	10	11^{2}	13	9^{3}		3		5			12	2									25
1					6	11	8^{3}	12	10		4^{2}	14		3	9	5				2		13	7^{1}						26
1				12	6^{1}	11	13	14	10			8^{3}		3	9	5				2		4^{2}	7						27
1				5	6	11	8^{2}	12	10^{3}		4	14		3	9				7^{1}	2		13							28
1				5	6	11	8^{2}		10	3	4	9		13	12					2			7^{1}						29
1			8	5	6	11		12	14	3	4	10^{2}			9^{3}				13	2		7^{1}							30
1			2		6	11^{1}	8	9^{2}	10^{3}	3	4				14	5			13			7	12						31
1			11		6	12	8	14		3	4	13			9^{3}	5			10^{2}	2		7^{1}							32
1			7^{1}		6	11	8	9^{2}			4	10^{3}		3	14	5				2		13	12						33
1			4^{3}		6	11	13	12	10	14		9		3		5				2^{1}		8	7^{2}						34
1			4		6	7	8^{1}		10	12		13		3		5			9^{2}	2		11							35
1			4^{1}		6	11	8	9^{3}	10	13		12		3		5			14	2		7^{2}							36
1				5	6	11^{1}	8	12	10	3						4			9	2		7							37
			4		6	7^{1}		13	10^{2}	11		14		3					9^{3}	2		8		1	5	12			38
			8		6	13		9^{3}	14			12		3		5			10	2^{2}		11		1		7	4^{1}		39
			4		6	7		13	10	11^{1}		12		3					9^{2}	2		8		1	5				40
		12			6	7^{2}			10	11		9		3^{1}					4	2		8		1	5	13			41
					6	7		13	10	11		9^{2}		3^{1}					4	2		8		1	5			12	42

FA Cup

Fourth Qual	Stevenage B	(h)	0-1

Football League Trophy

First Round	Milton Keynes D	(a)	2-3

FA Trophy

First Round	Bishop's Stortford	(h)	2-1
Second Round	Histon	(h)	3-2
Third Round	Cambridge C	(h)	1-0
Fourth Round	Salisbury C	(h)	3-1
Semi-Final	Grays Ath	(h)	2-1
		(a)	0-2

FOREST GREEN ROVERS Conference

Ground: The Lawn, Nympsfield Road, Forest Green, Nailsworth GL6 0ET.
Tel: (01453) 834 860.
Year Formed: 1890.
Record Gate: 3,002 (1999 v St Albans City FA Umbro Trophy).
Nickname: Rovers.
Manager: Gary Owers.
Secretary: David Honeybill.
Colours: Black and white striped shirts, black shorts, red stockings.

FOREST GREEN ROVERS 2005–06 LEAGUE RECORD

Match No.	*Date*	*Venue*	*Opponents*	*Result*		*H/T Score*	*Lg. Pos.*	*Goalscorers*	*Attendance*
1	Aug 13	H	Cambridge U	W	1-0	0-0	—	Rendell [49]	1112
2	16	A	Tamworth	D	0-0	0-0	—		1258
3	20	A	Altrincham	L	1-2	0-1	12	Wanless (pen) [71]	804
4	27	H	Halifax T	D	2-2	1-0	13	Wanless 2 [2, 82]	905
5	29	A	Exeter C	D	0-0	0-0	—		4696
6	Sept 2	H	Grays Ath	L	1-2	1-1	—	Wanless (pen) [23]	1152
7	10	H	York C	L	1-2	0-1	17	Teixeira [89]	889
8	17	A	Kidderminster H	W	3-1	2-0	14	Wanless [19], Abbey 2 [34, 74]	1818
9	20	H	Crawley T	D	2-2	2-0	—	Wanless [2], Meechan [5]	916
10	24	A	Scarborough	L	0-1	0-0	16		1341
11	27	A	Gravesend & N	L	0-2	0-1	—		706
12	Oct 1	H	Morecambe	W	1-0	0-0	14	Teixeira [67]	802
13	7	A	Southport	L	1-3	1-3	—	Richardson [16]	1087
14	15	H	Woking	L	0-3	0-3	19		875
15	29	A	Dagenham & R	D	1-1	1-1	19	Wanless (pen) [34]	1325
16	Nov 12	H	Canvey Is	L	1-2	1-1	21	Meechan [23]	678
17	18	A	Accrington S	L	0-2	0-1	—		1506
18	26	A	Aldershot T	L	1-2	1-2	22	Madjo [7]	2290
19	Dec 10	A	Stevenage Bor	L	1-2	1-0	22	Harding [5]	1771
20	13	H	Burton Alb	W	1-0	1-0	—	Alsop [45]	548
21	26	H	Hereford U	D	2-2	1-0	20	Meechan [34], Madjo [80]	1957
22	31	H	Aldershot T	W	4-2	2-1	19	Alsop [7], Wanless [10], Madjo 2 [48, 71]	1051
23	Jan 2	A	Hereford U	D	1-1	0-1	19	Madjo [58]	3507
24	7	A	Cambridge U	D	2-2	1-1	18	Richardson [3], Teixeira [90]	2344
25	21	H	Altrincham	W	5-0	2-0	18	Madjo 2 [12, 73], Alsop [18], Meechan [66], Rendell [88]	995
26	24	H	Tamworth	L	1-3	0-1	—	Wanless [75]	788
27	28	A	Halifax T	L	0-1	0-1	19		1284
28	Feb 11	H	Scarborough	W	5-1	3-0	18	Alsop [2], Sall [5], Wanless (pen) [44], Hayes [80], Teixeira [89]	732
29	18	A	Morecambe	L	2-3	1-2	18	Madjo [16], Sall [88]	1486
30	21	H	Gravesend & N	D	0-0	0-0	—		582
31	25	A	York C	L	1-5	1-4	18	Sall [34]	2314
32	Mar 4	H	Kidderminster H	D	0-0	0-0	18		1033
33	11	H	Southport	L	1-2	1-1	18	Sall [3]	846
34	18	A	Crawley T	L	0-1	0-1	19		1067
35	25	H	Dagenham & R	L	0-3	0-0	20		625
36	Apr 1	A	Canvey Is	D	1-1	0-0	19	Brough (pen) [71]	426
37	7	H	Accrington S	D	1-1	0-0	—	Meechan [74]	1187
38	15	A	Grays Ath	D	2-2	1-1	22	Brough (pen) [38], Madjo [90]	1205
39	17	H	Exeter C	D	0-0	0-0	22		1334
40	22	A	Burton Alb	L	0-1	0-1	21		2331
41	25	A	Woking	L	1-2	1-1	—	Brough (pen) [38]	890
42	29	H	Stevenage Bor	W	2-0	1-0	20	Teixeira [43], Alsop [61]	1510

Final League Position: 19

GOALSCORERS

League (49): Wanless 10 (4 pens), Madjo 9, Alsop 5, Meechan 5, Teixeira 5, Sall 4, Brough 3 (3 pens), Abbey 2, Rendell 2, Richardson 2, Harding 1, Hayes 1.
FA Cup (2): Beswetherick 1, Meechan 1.
FA Trophy (5): Gadsby 1, Harding 1, Hayes 1, Madjo 1, Wanless 1.

Clarke 42	Simpson 31 + 2	Searle 37	Graham 24 + 3	Sall 24 + 2	Richardson 25	Gadsby 20 + 8	Wanless 30	Rendell 8 + 10	Teixeira 12 + 15	Meechan 41	Haldane 3 + 4	Beswetherick 11 + 4	Garner 16 + 4	Gosling 3 + 6	Abbey 18 + 8	Rogers 5 + 5	Howell 6 + 1	Harrison — + 1	Whittington — + 1	Harley 3	Alsop 20 + 3	Harding 9	Madjo 18 + 6	Hayes 4	Beesley 11 + 5	Brough 13 + 1	Byron 3	McConnell 2 + 2	Taylor 10	Anthony 1	Jones 9 + 1	Dove 1 + 4	Coleman 2	Stonehouse — + 2	*Match No.*
1	2	3	4	5▮	6	7	8	9^{1}	10^{2}	11	12	13																							1
1	2	3	4		6	7^{1}	8	9^{3}	10^{2}	11	14	12▮	5	13																					2
1	2	3	4		6		8	9	10^{2}	11	12		5	7^{1}	13																				3
1	2	3	4^{1}		6	7^{2}	8		14	11	10^{3}	12	5		9	13																			4
1	2	3			6	12	8	14	13	11^{3}	10^{2}	5	7		9	4^{1}																			5
1	2	3			6		8	10		11		5	4		9	7^{1}	12																		6
1	2		4	12	6		8		14	11	10^{3}	3^{2}	5	13	9	7^{1}																			7
1				5	6		8	10		11^{2}	13	3	2	4^{1}	9	12	7																		8
1			4	5	6		8^{1}	10		11		3	2		9	12	7																		9
1		3		5	6		8	10^{2}	13	11		7	2	12	9		4^{1}																		10
1		3		5^{1}	6		8	12	10	11		2	4	13	9		7^{2}																		11
1	12	3		5^{1}	6	13	8	14	10^{3}	11		2	4		9		7^{2}																		12
1	2	3^{1}			6	13	8	12	10	11		7^{3}	5	14	9		4^{2}																		13
1▮	2	3^{1}			6	7	8		10^{2}	11		12	5	4		9^{6}		15	13																14
1	2		4		6	7	8			11		10	5	12						3^{1}	9														15
1	2		4		6	12	8		13	11		7^{1}	5		14					10^{2}	9^{3}	3													16
1	2	3		5	6	7	8			11					10^{1}						9	4	12												17
1	2	3		5^{1}	6	7		13	14	11^{3}					12					4^{2}	9	8	10▮												18
1	2	3	5		6	7	8	12		11					10^{1}						9	4													19
1	2	3	4		6	7	8	12		11^{2}			13		10^{1}						9	5													20
1	2	3	4		6	7	8		10^{2}	11			12								9	5^{1}	13												21
1	2	3	4		6	7	8	13	12	11^{1}											9^{2}	5	10												22
1	2	3	4		6	7^{1}	8	12		11^{2}			13								9	5	10												23
1	2	3	4		6		8	7^{1}	12	11											9	5	10												24
1	2	3	4		6^{1}	7	8	13		11			12								9^{3}		10	5^{2}	14										25
1	2	3	4^{1}	12		7	8		14	11^{2}			5								9		10	6^{3}	13										26
1	2	3	4	5		12	8		13	11^{2}											9		10^{3}	7	14	6^{1}									27
1		3	12	5		2	8		14	11					13						9^{2}		10^{3}	6	7^{1}	4									28
1	2	3		5		7^{1}			8	11^{2}					14	12							10		9^{3}	4	6	13							29
1		3	12	5		14	8^{1}		7^{2}	11					9								10		4^{3}	6	2	13							30
1	12	3	4	5^{1}		7			14	11					9	13							10^{3}			6^{2}	2▮	8							31
1		3	4	5			8		13	11					9^{1}						12		10^{2}			6		7	2						32
1		3		5		7				11					9^{3}	8^{2}					14		10		13	6^{1}			4	2	12				33
1	2	3		5					13	11					14						9^{3}		10		8^{1}	7^{2}			4		6	12			34
1	2	3		5		13	8^{2}			11					9^{3}								12		14				7		6	4^{1}	10		35
1	2	3	4	5						11													10		9	12			6		8		7^{1}		36
1	2	3	4	5						11											12		10^{1}		9	8			7		6				37
1	2	3	4^{1}	5						11											9		13		10^{2}	6			7		8	12			38
1	2	3	4	5		14				11											9^{3}		13		10^{2}	7^{1}			6		8	12			39
1	2	3	4^{1}	5					13	11											9^{3}		14		10^{2}	7			6		8	12			40
1		3		5		7			8	11					13						9^{2}		10		4	2^{1}					6			12	41
1	2	3	13	5		7^{2}			8^{1}						14						9^{3}		10		4				11		6▮			12	42

FA Cup

Fourth Qual	Dagenham & R	(h)	2-3

FA Trophy

First Round	Weymouth	(a)	1-0
Second Round	Dorchester T	(h)	3-1
Third Round	Stafford R	(a)	1-2

GRAVESEND & NORTHFLEET Conference

Ground: Stonebridge Road, Northfleet, Kent DA11 9BA.
Tel: (01474) 533 796.
Year Formed: 1946.
Record Gate: 12,036 (1963 v Sunderland FA Cup Fourth Round).
Nickname: The Fleet.
Manager: Liam Daish.
Secretary: Roly Edwards.
Colours: Red shirts, white shorts, red stockings.

GRAVESEND & NORTHFLEET 2005–06 LEAGUE RECORD

Match No.	Date	Venue	Opponents	Result		H/T Score	Lg. Pos.	Goalscorers	Attendance
1	Aug 13	H	Exeter C	L	0-2	0-1	—		1578
2	16	A	Grays Ath	L	1-6	0-2	—	MacDonald 59	1562
3	20	A	Canvey Is	W	2-1	1-1	18	MacDonald 2 (1 pen) 36 (p), 90	1070
4	27	H	Cambridge U	D	0-0	0-0	19		1379
5	29	A	Woking	W	3-1	2-0	—	Jackson 8, Saunders 2 14, 50	1770
6	Sept 3	H	Southport	W	2-1	1-1	10	McCarthy 15, Slatter 67	813
7	10	A	Scarborough	L	1-3	0-3	12	Drury 72	1207
8	17	H	Halifax T	W	4-0	1-0	9	Graham-Smith 36, MacDonald 47, Slatter 49, Drury (pen) 90	918
9	20	A	Hereford U	D	1-1	0-0	—	Bowry 89	2396
10	24	H	Kidderminster H	L	1-2	0-1	12	MacDonald 62	1054
11	27	H	Forest Green R	W	2-0	1-0	—	MacDonald 35, Jackson 66	706
12	Oct 1	A	Accrington S	D	1-1	0-1	10	Sodje 66	1206
13	8	H	York C	D	2-2	1-1	11	Grant 30, Sodje 89	1133
14	15	A	Tamworth	L	0-1	0-0	11		1003
15	29	H	Stevenage Bor	L	0-2	0-1	12		1372
16	Nov 12	A	Aldershot T	L	2-3	1-2	13	MacDonald 2 (1 pen) 21 (p), 86	2415
17	19	H	Altrincham	W	2-0	1-0	10	Drury 43, MacDonald 53	1091
18	26	A	Crawley T	W	2-1	2-0	10	Johnson Bradley 25, Coleman 27	1426
19	Dec 3	H	Morecambe	W	1-0	1-0	9	MacDonald 31	1172
20	10	A	Burton Alb	D	0-0	0-0	10		1733
21	26	H	Dagenham & R	L	1-3	1-1	10	MacDonald 41	1391
22	Jan 2	A	Dagenham & R	W	2-1	0-0	10	Graham-Smith 86, Johnson Bradley 90	1405
23	7	A	Exeter C	L	0-1	0-0	10		3396
24	20	H	Canvey Is	W	2-0	1-0	—	McCarthy 38, MacDonald 90	1560
25	28	A	Cambridge U	D	1-1	1-0	11	Jackson 33	2459
26	Feb 11	A	Kidderminster H	W	2-0	1-0	11	Sodje 18, Drury 74	1575
27	17	H	Accrington S	L	1-3	0-1	—	Graham-Smith 90	1616
28	21	A	Forest Green R	D	0-0	0-0	—		582
29	25	H	Scarborough	D	0-0	0-0	11		930
30	28	H	Crawley T	D	1-1	0-0	—	Rawle 60	698
31	Mar 7	H	Hereford U	L	1-2	1-0	—	Jackson 33	618
32	11	A	York C	L	0-1	0-1	11		2902
33	18	H	Tamworth	W	2-0	1-0	11	Smith 43, Jackson 60	841
34	25	A	Stevenage Bor	L	0-2	0-2	13		1873
35	Apr 1	H	Aldershot T	L	0-3	0-1	13		1131
36	4	H	Grays Ath	L	1-3	0-0	—	Johnson Bradley 51	1245
37	8	A	Altrincham	D	2-2	1-2	14	Smith 34, Johnson Bradley (pen) 90	688
38	15	A	Southport	L	0-1	0-1	14		1301
39	17	H	Woking	W	2-0	1-0	14	Johnson Bradley 45, Moore 76	776
40	22	A	Morecambe	L	0-3	0-2	14		1991
41	25	A	Halifax T	L	0-2	0-0	—		1680
42	29	H	Burton Alb	L	0-1	0-1	16		912

Final League Position: 16

GOALSCORERS

League (45): MacDonald 12 (2 pens), Jackson 5, Johnson Bradley 5 (1 pen), Drury 4 (1 pen), Graham-Smith 3, Sodje 3, McCarthy 2, Saunders 2, Slatter 2, Smith 2, Bowry 1, Coleman 1, Grant 1, Moore 1, Rawle 1.
FA Cup (0).
FA Trophy (3): MacDonald 2, Smith 1.

Holloway 32 + 1	Gooding 24 + 4	Skinner 19 + 3	Saunders 24 + 2	Graham-Smith 39	McCarthy 30	Slatter 37 + 2	Bowry 35	Grant 5 + 2	MacDonald 20	Jackson 26 + 3	Kerr 5 + 1	Omoyinmi 5 + 7	Glozier 6 + 4	Mott — + 1	McShane 5	Protheroe 15 + 1	Surey 1 + 9	Drury 30 + 2	Moore 10 + 18	Sodje 8 + 6	Guy — + 1	Tann 1	Johnson Bradley 21 + 4	Smith 18 + 4	Johnson Brett 4	Coleman 6	Hodgson 1 + 4	Fuller 4 + 9	Watkins 12 + 1	Rawle 9 + 2	McKimm 6 + 4	Hawkins 4 + 1	Darvill — + 2	*Match No.*
1[6]	2	3	4[1]	5■	6	7	8	9	10	11	15	12																						1
	2	3[6]	4	5	6	7	8[1]	9[2]	10	11	1■	12	15	13																				2
		3		5	6	4[1]	8		10	11		9			1	2	12	7																3
		3	4	5	6	7	8		10	11		9[1]			1	2			12															4
	12	3	4	5	6	7[2]	8		10[3]	11		9			1	2[1]	13		14															5
		3	4	5	6	7	8		10[2]	11		9[1]			1	2	12	13																6
	12	3[2]	4	5	6	7	8[3]			11			13		1	2[1]		9	14	10														7
1		3	4	5	6	7[1]	8[2]		10[3]	11		14				2	13	9		12■														8
1			4	5	6	7	8[1]		10	11[2]		13	3			2	12	9																9
1		3	4	5	6	7[1]	8		10	11		12				2		9																10
1		3	4	5	6	7	8[1]	13	10[3]	11		14				2	12	9[2]																11
1		3	4	5	6	7	8	10		11[1]						2	13	9[2]		12														12
1	12	3	4	5	6	7	8[2]	9[3]		11						2[1]	13			10	14													13
1		3[1]	8	5	6	7[2]		9[3]		11		14	12			2	4	13		10														14
1				5	6	4[2]	8	12	10	11		9	3[1]				13	7[3]		14		2												15
1	12		4	5	6		8		10	11						2■		9[1]	13	7[2]			3											16
1	2	12	4	5			8		10	3								7	9[2]	13			11[1]	6										17
1	2[1]		4	5			8[2]		10[3]	13						12		7	14				11	6	3	9								18
1	2		4	5		13	8[1]		10									7					11[2]	6	3	9	12							19
1	2	3	4			13	8		10[2]									7					11[1]	6	5	9	12							20
1	2				6	4	8		10									7[1]	13				11[2]	5	3	9	12							21
1		3		5	6[1]	4	8									2		7	13				11	12		9	10[2]							22
1		3		5[1]	6	4[2]	8		10							2		7	14				11	12		9[3]	13							23
1	2			5	6	4	8		10	3								7	9[1]				11■					12						24
1	2			5	6■	4	8		10[2]	11								7	9[1]					12					3	13				25
1	2			5		4	8			11[2]								7[1]	14	9[3]				6				13	3	10	12			26
1	2[1]			5		4	8[2]											7	12	9			11[3]	6				14	3	10	13			27
1	2			5	6	4[1]	8[2]											7	14	9[3]			13					12	3	10	11			28
1	2			5	6	4[1]	8			12								7	14	9[3]			13						3	10	11[2]			29
1	2			5	6	4[1]				11								9[2]	10				7					13	3	12	8			30
1	2			5[1]	6[2]	4				11[3]									9	14			7	12				13	3	10	8			31
1	2		13		6	4[1]				11								9	12	14			7	5					3	10[3]	8[2]			32
1	2		4	5	6	7				11[2]								9[1]	14				12	8				13	3	10[3]				33
1	2		4	5	6[1]	7[2]	8												13				11	9				14	3	10[3]		12		34
1	2		4[1]	5		7	8												9				12	6				11	13	10[2]		3		35
	2			5		7	8[1]			11	1								12				9	10					3		4■	6		36
	2	12		5		7	8			11[2]	1							9[3]	13				10	6				14	3[1]			4		37
15	2	3[1]		5	6	4	8				1[6]		12					9	13				7	10				11[2]						38
1	2		12	5	6■	4	8[1]						3					7	9				11	10										39
1	2[1]	12	4	5		7							3					9	10				11	6				8[2]			13			40
1		3	4	5		7	8						2					9[1]	10				11	6									12	41
		3	4[2]	5		7				12	1		2[1]						9				11	10				8[3]			13	6	14	42

FA Cup

Fourth Qual	Kettering T	(a)	0-3

FA Trophy

First Round	East Thurrock U	(a)	2-0
Second Round	Boreham Wood	(a)	1-3

GRAYS ATHLETIC Conference

Ground: Recreation Ground, Bridge Road, Grays RM17 6BZ.
Tel: (01375) 391 649.
Year Formed: 1890.
Record Gate: 9500 (1959 v Chelmsford City, FA Cup).
Nickname: The Blues.
Manager: Frank Gray.
Secretary: Phil O'Reilly.
Colours: All sky blue.

GRAYS ATHLETIC 2005–06 LEAGUE RECORD

Match No.	Date	Venue	Opponents	Result		H/T Score	Lg. Pos.	Goalscorers	Attendance
1	Aug 13	A	Burton Alb	D	1-1	0-0	—	Battersby [74]	1654
2	16	H	Gravesend & N	W	6-1	2-0	—	Martin 3 (1 pen) [33, 63, 72 (p)], Oli [42], Poole [88], Slabber [90]	1562
3	20	H	York C	D	1-1	0-0	6	Thirgood (pen) [90]	1272
4	27	A	Hereford U	W	2-0	1-0	3	Battersby [14], Hooper [90]	2997
5	29	H	Aldershot T	W	2-1	1-0	—	Poole [35], Battersby [48]	1869
6	Sept 2	A	Forest Green R	W	2-1	1-1	—	Oli [18], Stuart [90]	1152
7	10	H	Kidderminster H	D	2-2	0-0	2	Hooper [53], Danby (og) [90]	1316
8	17	A	Tamworth	D	2-2	1-1	3	Oli [38], Poole [69]	1078
9	20	H	Cambridge U	W	5-3	4-1	—	Slabber 3 (1 pen) [7, 39, 48 (p)], Howie (og) [25], Hooper [35]	1543
10	24	A	Crawley T	W	3-1	1-1	1	Slabber [42], Oli 2 [76, 90]	1471
11	27	A	Dagenham & R	W	2-1	1-0	—	Thirgood [37], Angus [87]	2017
12	Oct 1	H	Halifax T	D	1-1	1-0	1	Matthews [42]	1807
13	8	A	Woking	D	1-1	1-1	1	Thirgood (pen) [25]	1995
14	15	H	Scarborough	W	5-0	1-0	1	Slabber [27], Poole [53], Hooper [69], Kightly [82], Thirgood (pen) [90]	1515
15	29	A	Southport	W	4-1	2-0	1	Kightly [7], Slabber [22], Stuart [67], Hooper [87]	1148
16	Nov 12	H	Accrington S	L	1-2	0-1	2	Kightly [52]	1985
17	19	A	Exeter C	W	2-1	0-0	1	Martin [56], Hooper [90]	6682
18	26	A	Stevenage Bor	W	1-0	0-0	1	Hooper [84]	2753
19	Dec 6	H	Altrincham	D	1-1	1-0	—	McLean [4]	1028
20	10	A	Morecambe	L	0-3	0-2	2		1785
21	27	H	Canvey Is	L	1-2	0-1	—	Martin [64]	2910
22	31	H	Stevenage Bor	D	2-2	1-0	3	Kightly 2 [16, 73]	1214
23	Jan 2	A	Canvey Is	L	1-2	1-1	3	Kightly [4]	1445
24	21	A	York C	W	2-1	1-1	3	McLean 2 [30, 89]	2461
25	28	H	Hereford U	D	2-2	2-0	4	McLean [28], Thirgood [43]	1528
26	31	H	Burton Alb	L	2-3	1-2	—	Martin [20], Thirgood (pen) [51]	858
27	Feb 11	H	Crawley T	W	1-0	0-0	4	Oli [70]	1038
28	18	A	Halifax T	L	1-2	1-1	6	Stuart [11]	1666
29	21	H	Dagenham & R	L	0-4	0-3	—		1065
30	Mar 4	H	Tamworth	W	5-0	3-0	5	McLean [12], Thirgood [28], Slabber 2 [45, 55], Kightly [87]	1117
31	7	A	Cambridge U	D	1-1	1-1	—	Slabber [38]	1821
32	11	H	Woking	D	2-2	2-1	6	Slabber [20], McLean [22]	1256
33	28	A	Kidderminster H	W	5-0	2-0	—	Oli [6], Kightly [32], Poole [47], Thirgood (pen) [72], Hooper [89]	1220
34	Apr 1	A	Accrington S	W	3-2	0-1	5	Poole 2 [58, 63], McLean [80]	2642
35	4	A	Gravesend & N	W	3-1	0-0	—	Poole [68], Kightly 2 [70, 72]	1245
36	10	H	Exeter C	W	3-0	1-0	—	Poole [34], Oli [64], Martin [70]	1369
37	15	H	Forest Green R	D	2-2	1-1	4	Oli [13], Poole [72]	1205
38	17	A	Aldershot T	W	3-0	3-0	4	Kightly [10], Poole [19], McLean [27]	1879
39	19	A	Scarborough	W	7-2	3-0	—	McLean 2 [6, 56], Kightly 3 [17, 80, 90], Poole 2 [43, 71]	1560
40	22	A	Altrincham	W	2-0	0-0	3	Maddox (og) [55], Thirgood (pen) [64]	917
41	25	H	Southport	D	1-1	0-0	—	De Bolla [49]	918
42	29	H	Morecambe	L	1-2	1-1	3	De Bolla [8]	1950

Final League Position: 3

GOALSCORERS

League (94): Kightly 14, Poole 13, Slabber 11 (1 pen), McLean 10, Oli 9, Thirgood 9 (6 pens), Hooper 8, Martin 7 (1 pen), Battersby 3, Stuart 3, De Bolla 2, Angus 1, Matthews 1, own goals 3.
FA Cup (5): Kightly 1, McLean 1, Poole 1, Slabber 1, own goal 1.
FA Trophy (12): Poole 4, Kightly 2, McLean 2, Nutter 1, Oli 1, Slabber 1, Stuart 1.
Play-Offs (4): Oli 2, Knightly 1, Nutter 1.

Bayes 25	Sambrook 23 + 2	Nutter 40	Thirgood 40	Stuart 34	Matthews 8 + 3	Kightly 27 + 8	Martin 31 + 3	Slabber 18 + 10	Oli 26 + 8	Poole 31 + 6	Hooper 16 + 22	Battersby 13 + 1	Brennan 6 + 2	Bruce 9 + 3	Mawer 16 + 2	Angus 11	McLean 28 + 2	Brayley — + 4	Eyre 17	Olayinka 6 + 9	Koo-Boothe 2	Williamson 4 + 9	Johnson 4 + 1	Hanson 18 + 1	Edwards 4 + 1	Williams — + 1	De Bolla 5 + 3	Match No.
1	2	3	4	5	6	7[1]	8	9[2]	10	11	12	13																1
1	2	3	4	5	6	12	8[3]	13	10[2]	11	7	9[1]	14															2
1	2	3	4	5	6	13	8	12	10	11	7[2]	9[1]																3
1		3	4	5			8	13	10[1]	11	7	9[2]	12	2	6													4
1		3	4	5			8	12[2]		11		9	7	13	2	6	10[1]											5
1		3	4	5			8		10	11	7[1]	9		6	2		12											6
1		3	4	5			8		10	11[2]	7	9[1]		6	2		12	13										7
1		3	4	5				13	10	11	7[1]		8	6	2		9[2]	12										8
		3	4	5		13		9	10	11	7[2]		8[1]		2	6			1	12								9
		3	4	5		12		9[3]	10	11[2]	7[1]		8		2	6		13	1	14								10
		3	4	5[1]	12			9	10	11[3]	13		8		2	6	7[2]	14	1									11
		3	4		5	12	14	9	10	11[3]	13		8[2]		2	6	7[1]		1									12
		3	4	5			8	9	10	11[1]	12				2	6	7		1									13
	2	3	4	5		12	8	9	10[2]	11[3]	13					6	7[1]		1	14								14
	2	3	4	5		7[2]	8	9[3]	10	13	14					6	11[1]		1	12								15
	2	3	4	5		11	8	9	10		12					6	7[1]		1									16
1	2	3	4	5	6	11[2]	8	9	10[3]	14	12						7[1]			13								17
1	2	3	4		6	11[1]	8	9	10	13	12						7[2]				5							18
		3	4		6	11	8	9	12	13	7[1]				2	5	10[2]		1									19
		3	4[3]	5	12	11	8	9		13	7[2]				2[1]		10		1		6	14						20
		3	4	5	6	7[1]	8	9	10	11	12			2					1									21
	2	3	4	5		7	8			11	12	9[1]		6			10		1									22
	2	3	4	5		7[1]	8		14		13	9[3]		12		6	10		1	11[2]								23
1	2		4			11[1]	8	13			7	9[2]					10					12	3	6	5			24
1	2		4			11	8	13	12		7	9[1]					10[2]						3	6	5			25
1	2	11	4			13	8	12	14		7[3]	9[2]					10						3[1]	6	5			26
1	2	3	4			7	8[2]	9[3]	14	13					12		10					11	5[1]	6				27
1	2	3		5		7	8	12		11	10	9[1]			13							4[2]		6[3]	14			28
1	2[1]	3	4	5		7	8[2]		14	11	10	9[3]										13		12	6			29
	12	3	4	5		7		14	10	11					2[1]		9[3]		1	8[2]				6		13		30
		3	4	5		7[1]	8	9	10[2]	11	12				2				1			13		6				31
	12	3	4	5		7	8	9		11					2[1]		10		1					6				32
1	2	3	4	5		7[1]			10[2]	11	13						9[3]			8		14		6			12	33
1	2	3	4	5		7	12			11	13						9			8[1]				6			10[2]	34
1	2	3	4	5		7	12			11[2]	14						9			8[1]		13		6			10[3]	35
1	2	3	4	5		7[2]	8		12	11[3]	13						9			14				6			10[1]	36
1	2	3	4	5		7[1]	8		10[3]	11[2]	12						9			13				6			14	37
1	2	3	4	5		7[2]		9[1]	12	11	13						10[3]			14		8		6				38
1	2[1]	3	4[2]	5		7	8		10	11	14			12			9[3]					13		6				39
1		3	4	5		7	8[1]		10[2]	11	13			2			9[3]					14		6			12	40
1		3[1]	4	5		7[2]	8		10	11[3]	13			2						12		14		6			9	41
		3			12	14			10[3]	11	7			5	2				1	8[2]		4	13	6[1]			9	42

FA Cup

Fourth Qual	Cray W	(h)	2-0
First Round	York C	(a)	3-0
Second Round	Mansfield T	(a)	0-3

Play-Offs

Semi-Final	Halifax T	(a)	2-3
		(h)	2-2

FA Trophy

Second Round	Kidderminster H	(a)	1-0
Third Round	Hereford U	(a)	1-0
Fourth Round	Dagenham & R	(h)	1-1
		(a)	4-2
Semi-Final	Exeter C	(a)	1-2
		(h)	2-0
Final *(at Upton Park)*	Woking		2-0

HALIFAX TOWN Conference

Ground: The Shay Stadium, Shay Syke, Halifax, West Yorkshire HX1 2YS.
Tel: (01422) 341 222.
Year Formed: 1911.
Record Gate: 36,885 (1953 v Tottenham Hotspur FA Cup Fifth Round).
Nickname: The Shaymen.
Manager: Chris Wilder
Secretary: Jenna Helliwell.
Colours: All blue.

HALIFAX TOWN 2005–06 LEAGUE RECORD

Match No.	Date	Venue	Opponents	Result		H/T Score	Lg. Pos.	Goalscorers	Attendance
1	Aug 13	A	Morecambe	L	0-1	0-1	—		2150
2	16	H	Burton Alb	W	1-0	0-0	—	Brabin 71	1681
3	20	H	Aldershot T	D	1-1	1-0	13	Grant 4	1571
4	27	A	Forest Green R	D	2-2	0-1	14	Midgley (pen) 54, Senior 65	905
5	29	H	York C	W	1-0	0-0	—	Midgley (pen) 62	2078
6	Sept 3	A	Stevenage Bor	L	0-1	0-1	12		1682
7	10	H	Tamworth	W	4-0	0-0	9	Midgley 46, Forrest 64, Grant 69, Senior 72	1453
8	17	A	Gravesend & N	L	0-4	0-1	11		918
9	20	A	Kidderminster H	W	1-0	1-0	—	Killeen 27	1566
10	24	H	Hereford U	W	2-1	0-1	7	Grant 48, Senior 86	1559
11	27	H	Altrincham	W	2-0	1-0	—	Midgley (pen) 21, Grant 83	1453
12	Oct 1	A	Grays Ath	D	1-1	0-1	6	Grant 58	1807
13	8	A	Exeter C	L	2-4	2-2	5	Grant 2, Killeen 27	3154
14	15	H	Cambridge U	W	1-0	0-0	7	Senior 77	1621
15	29	A	Woking	D	2-2	0-1	7	Killeen 51, Quinn 80	2054
16	Nov 12	H	Dagenham & R	W	3-0	0-0	6	Mansaram 2 71, 90, Killeen 86	1532
17	19	A	Southport	W	2-0	2-0	5	Foster 21, Forrest 22	1402
18	26	A	Scarborough	L	0-2	0-0	6		1843
19	Dec 3	H	Crawley T	D	2-2	0-1	5	Forrest 57, Grant 62	1616
20	10	A	Canvey Is	W	1-0	0-0	5	Quinn 90	664
21	26	H	Accrington S	D	2-2	1-1	5	Killeen 45, Grant 68	2688
22	30	H	Scarborough	W	1-0	0-0	—	Foster 84	1682
23	Jan 2	A	Accrington S	D	1-1	0-0	5	Forrest 58	3014
24	9	H	Morecambe	D	0-0	0-0	—		1962
25	21	A	Aldershot T	L	1-3	1-2	7	Killeen 16	2417
26	24	A	Burton Alb	W	2-1	1-1	—	Grant 45, Foster (pen) 76	1540
27	28	H	Forest Green R	W	1-0	1-0	3	Quinn 19	1284
28	Feb 4	H	Kidderminster H	D	0-0	0-0	3		1544
29	11	A	Hereford U	L	0-1	0-0	6		2555
30	18	H	Grays Ath	W	2-1	1-1	4	Thompson 22, Grant 89	1666
31	21	A	Altrincham	W	2-1	1-0	—	Killeen 5, Sugden 88	1139
32	25	A	Tamworth	W	2-1	1-0	2	Killeen 2, Senior 70	1672
33	Mar 11	H	Exeter C	W	2-0	2-0	3	Sugden 2 5, 38	2104
34	18	A	Cambridge U	D	1-1	0-1	3	Grant 84	2288
35	28	H	Woking	W	1-0	1-0	—	Bushell 38	1465
36	Apr 1	A	Dagenham & R	L	0-1	0-1	3		1078
37	8	H	Southport	W	2-1	1-0	3	Forrest 45, Sugden 90	1791
38	14	H	Stevenage Bor	D	1-1	1-0	—	Young 35	2253
39	17	A	York C	W	2-0	0-0	3	Grant 48, Bushell 83	4084
40	22	A	Crawley T	D	2-2	0-2	4	Senior 57, Killeen 69	1285
41	25	H	Gravesend & N	W	2-0	0-0	—	Sugden 2 52, 54	1680
42	29	H	Canvey Is	L	0-2	0-1	4		2049

Final League Position: 4

GOALSCORERS

League (55): Grant 12, Killeen 9, Senior 6, Sugden 6, Forrest 5, Midgley 4 (3 pens), Foster 3 (1 pen), Quinn 3, Bushell 2, Mansaram 2, Brabin 1, Thompson 1, Young 1.
FA Cup (3): Senior 3.
Football League Trophy (7): Mansaram 2, Doughty 1, Haslam 1, Killeen 1, Midgley 1 (pen), own goal 1.
FA Trophy (1): Forrest 1.
Play-Offs (7): Foster 2 (1 pen), Killeen 2, Bushell 1, Grant 1, Sugden 1.

Dunbavin 14	Haslam 40	Young 24 + 6	Brabin 4	Ingram 18 + 2	Atherton 12 + 2	Midgley 14 + 10	Foster 35 + 1	Grant 30 + 10	Sugden 12 + 10	Killeen 32 + 4	Bowler 5 + 14	Senior 10 + 20	Thompson 37 + 4	Leister 2 + 7	Doughty 31 + 1	Toulson 1 + 1	Quinn 37	Jacobs 8 + 3	Forrest 32 + 4	Wright 10 + 1	Butler 3	Mansaram 1 + 2	Legzdins 10	Prendergast 6	Bushell 7 + 7	Kennedy 15	Yates — + 3	Smickle 11 + 1	Howell 1	Match No.
1	2	3^1	4	5	6	7^2	8	9	10^3	11	12	13	14																	1
1	2	3	4	5	6	7^1	8	9	10^3	11^2	14	12	13																	2
1	2	3	4	5	6	7^2	8^1	9	10^3	11	13	12	14																	3
1	2	3^2	4	5	6^1	7	8	9	14			10^3	11	13	12															4
1				5		7^1	8	9	10^2	11			4	12	3	2	6	13												5
1	2			5		7^1	8	9		10^3	13	12	4		3		6	11^2	14											6
1	2	12		5		7	8	9^2	13			10^1	4		3■		6		11^3	14										7
1	2^1	3		5		7^2	8	9^3	14	12	13	10	4				6		11											8
1	2	12		5		14	8	13	10^3	11^2			7				6	9^1	4	3										9
1	2	14		5		12	8	9^3	10^2			13	7				6	11^1	4	3										10
1	2	12		5		7^2	8■	9			13	10^3	11	14			6		4^1	3										11
1	2			5				14	10^3	11^2		13	8	12	3		6	4^1	7	9										12
1	2	14		5■				9		10^3		12	7	13	11		6	8^2	4^1	3										13
1	2	3				13		9		10^3		14	7	12	11^2		6	4	8^1	5										14
	2			5			8	9^3		10^2	12	13	7		11^1		6		4	3	1	14								15
	2			5		12	8	9^2		14	11^1	10^3	4				6		7	3		13	1							16
				5	2	11^1	8	14		9^2	13		7	12			6		4	3		10^3	1							17
	2			5^1	12		8	10		9^2		13	4				6		7	3			1	11						18
	2	14			5	13	8	10		9				7^1	3		6	12	4^3				1	11^2						19
	2				5	13	8	10^3		9^2	14	12	7		3		6	11^1	4				1							20
	2			12	5	7^2	8	13		9			4		3		6		10				1	11^1						21
	2			12	5	7^2	8	13		9^3		14	4		3		6		10				1	11^1						22
	2			9^1	5		8	10		12		13	4		3		6		7				1	11^2						23
	2				5	12	8	10		9^2		13	7		3		6		4				1	11^1						24
	2	5					8			9	12	10	7^1		3		6	11^2	4				1		13					25
	2	5					8	13		9^1		10^2	7		3		6	12	11		1				4					26
	2	5				7^1	8	10^2		9	13		4		3		6		11		1				12					27
	2	5				12	8	9	13		7^1		4^2		3		6		10						11	1				28
	2	5^1				14	8^3	10	13	9			7	4^2	3		6		11							1	12			29
	2	5^3					8	9		12	13		7		3		6		10							1	14	11^1	4^2	30
	2	5						10^2	13	9	14	12	7		3		6		11^3						4	1		8^1		31
	2	5					8		10^3	9	4^1	12	7		3		6		14						13	1		11^2		32
	2	5^1			12			14	10^3	9	7^2		11		3		6		13						8	1		4		33
	2	5						14	10^3	9	11^2	13	7		3		6		12						8	1		4^1		34
	2^1	5					13	9^3		10		11	7		3^2		6		4						8	1	12	14		35
	2	5					8	9		10	12	13	7		3^1		6		4							1		11^2		36
	2	5				12	8	9^2	13	10		11^1	7		3		6		4							1				37
	2	5					8	13	10^2	9			7		3		6		4						12	1		11^1		38
	2	5					8	10^2	13	9			7		3		6		4						12	1		11^1		39
	2	5					8	10^3	14	9^2		12	7		3		6		4						13	1		11^1		40
	2	5					8	12	10^1	9		13	7		3		6		4^3						14	1		11^2		41
	2	5			6	7	8	9^3	14			10	13		3	12									4^2	1		11^1		42

FA Cup

Fourth Qual	Farsley C	(h)	2-0
First Round	Rushden & D	(h)	1-1
		(a)	0-0

FA Trophy

First Round	Southport	(h)	0-0
		(a)	1-0
Second Round	Hereford U	(h)	0-1

Football League Trophy

First Round	Bury	(h)	6-1
Second Round	Scunthorpe U	(h)	1-3

Play-Offs

Semi-Final	Grays Ath	(h)	3-2
		(a)	2-2
Final *(at Leicester)*	Hereford U		2-3

HEREFORD UNITED FL Championship 2

Ground: Edgar Street, Hereford, Herefordshire HR4 9JU.
Tel: (01432) 276 666.
Year Formed: 1924.
Record Gate: 18,114 (1958 v Sheffield Wednesday FA Cup Third Round).
Nickname: The Bulls.
Manager: Graham Turner.
Secretary: Joan Fennessy.
Colours: White and black shirts, black shorts, white stockings.

HEREFORD UNITED 2005–06 LEAGUE RECORD

Match No.	Date	Venue	Opponents	Result	H/T Score	Lg. Pos.	Goalscorers	Attendance
1	Aug 13	H	Scarborough	W 4-0	0-0	—	Beckwith [64], Ipoua [69], Green [85], Carey-Bertram [90]	3105
2	16	A	Cambridge U	L 1-2	0-1	—	Ipoua [62]	2924
3	20	A	Crawley T	W 2-0	0-0	2	Ipoua [58], Mkandawire [83]	1842
4	27	H	Grays Ath	L 0-2	0-1	7		2997
5	29	A	Tamworth	W 1-0	1-0	—	Jeannin [20]	1744
6	Sept 3	H	Altrincham	D 0-0	0-0	6		2318
7	10	A	Stevenage Bor	D 0-0	0-0	10		2404
8	17	H	Morecambe	W 1-0	1-0	7	Ferrell [41]	2422
9	20	H	Gravesend & N	D 1-1	0-0	—	Stanley [53]	2396
10	24	A	Halifax T	L 1-2	1-0	9	Carey-Bertram [8]	1559
11	27	A	Aldershot T	W 1-0	1-0	—	Carey-Bertram [2]	2656
12	Oct 1	H	Canvey Is	D 1-1	1-1	7	Bailey [15]	2500
13	7	A	Accrington S	L 1-2	0-1	—	Carey-Bertram [46]	1603
14	15	H	Burton Alb	W 2-0	1-0	9	Carey-Bertram [23], James (pen) [84]	2493
15	29	A	Kidderminster H	D 1-1	1-1	9	Pitman [7]	3241
16	Nov 12	H	Woking	W 4-0	1-0	8	Williams [29], Purdie 2 [56, 70], Ipoua [72]	2498
17	19	A	Dagenham & R	W 1-0	1-0	8	Williams [12]	1294
18	26	H	Exeter C	L 0-2	0-0	8		3754
19	Dec 10	H	York C	W 1-0	0-0	7	Stansfield [69]	1950
20	26	A	Forest Green R	D 2-2	0-1	7	Mkandawire [58], Jeannin [79]	1957
21	30	A	Exeter C	W 2-1	2-1	—	Ipoua [30], Jeannin [43]	4433
22	Jan 2	H	Forest Green R	D 1-1	1-0	7	Stansfield [29]	3507
23	7	A	Scarborough	W 1-0	1-0	5	Stansfield [11]	1582
24	21	H	Crawley T	W 2-1	1-0	4	Williams [7], Ipoua [88]	2782
25	28	A	Grays Ath	D 2-2	0-2	6	Mkandawire [71], Beckwith [82]	1528
26	31	H	Cambridge U	W 3-0	2-0	—	Stansfield [34], Williams 2 [42, 50]	2142
27	Feb 11	H	Halifax T	W 1-0	0-0	2	Stansfield [78]	2555
28	18	A	Canvey Is	D 1-1	1-1	3	Fleetwood [15]	784
29	21	H	Aldershot T	W 2-1	2-0	—	Williams [3], Fleetwood [29]	2205
30	27	H	Stevenage Bor	W 2-0	1-0	—	Williams [45], Fleetwood [51]	2394
31	Mar 7	A	Gravesend & N	W 2-1	0-1	—	King [74], Williams [80]	618
32	11	H	Accrington S	D 2-2	0-1	2	Fleetwood [73], Nicolau [90]	4497
33	14	A	Southport	W 2-1	2-0	—	Mkandawire [10], Ferrell [43]	1057
34	18	A	Burton Alb	W 1-0	1-0	2	Williams [40]	2512
35	25	H	Kidderminster H	L 0-1	0-0	2		4223
36	Apr 1	A	Woking	D 1-1	0-1	2	Mkandawire [90]	1929
37	4	A	Morecambe	D 2-2	0-1	—	Carey-Bertram 2 [49, 78]	1699
38	8	H	Dagenham & R	D 1-1	0-0	2	Purdie (pen) [77]	2561
39	15	A	Altrincham	W 1-0	0-0	2	Fleetwood [64]	1251
40	17	H	Tamworth	W 1-0	0-0	2	Carey-Bertram [58]	2809
41	22	H	Southport	D 1-1	0-0	2	Stansfield [76]	2547
42	29	A	York C	W 3-1	2-0	2	Williams [13], Purdie [35], Ipoua [90]	2755

Final League Position: 2

GOALSCORERS

League (59): Williams 10, Carey-Bertram 8, Ipoua 7, Stansfield 6, Fleetwood 5, Mkandawire 5, Purdie 4 (1 pen), Jeannin 3, Beckwith 2, Ferrell 2, Bailey 1, Green 1, James 1 (pen), King 1, Nicolau 1, Pitman 1, Stanley 1.
FA Cup (2): Barry 1, Stanley 1.
Football League Trophy (5): Mkandawire 2, Carey-Bertram 1, Stansfield 1, own goal 1.
FA Trophy (8): Purdie 2 (1 pen), Stansfield 2, Ipoua 1, Pitman 1, Stanley 1, Williams 1.
Play-Offs (7): Ipoua 2, Williams 2, Green 1, Mkandawire 1, Purdie 1 (pen).

Mawson 9	Green 25 + 2	Jeannin 37	Mkandawire 36 + 3	James 20 + 3	Beckwith 29 + 3	Brady 18 + 2	Coldicott 4 + 1	Stansfield 17 + 6	Ipoua 13 + 6	Ferrell 30 + 1	Purdie 33 + 7	Carey-Bertram 18 + 14	Stanley 35 + 3	Brown 33	Blewitt 10 + 1	Evans 2 + 5	Pitman 14 + 8	Williams 23 + 8	Bailey 5	Travis 15 + 3	Taylor 8 + 2	Nicolau 10	Fleetwood 13 + 4	Gwynne — + 1	King 5	*Match No.*
1	2	3	4	5	6	7^1	8	9^2	10^3	11	12	13	14													1
1	2	3	4	5	6	7	8^1	9	10	11^2	13	12														2
1	2	3	4	5	6	7	8^1	9	10^2		11	13	12													3
1	2	3	4	5^1	6	7	8	9	10		11^2	12	13													4
	2■	3		5	6	7^1		9		11	12	10^2	8	1	4	13										5
		3^2		5	6	7^1	13	9		11	2	10	8	1	4	12										6
		3		5	6	7				11	2	10	8	1	4	9^1	12									7
		3	12	5	6	9^2				11	2	10^1	7	1	4		8	13								8
	2^1	3	13	5	6	12				11	9	10^2	7	1	4		8									9
	2	3	12	5	6^1	7^2			9^3	11	14	10	8	1	4		13									10
	2	3	4	12		7				11	6	10	8	1	5				9^1							11
	2	3	4	12		7^2				11	6	10	8	1	5^1	13			9							12
	2	3	4	5		7				11	6	10^1	8	1				12	9							13
	2	3	4	5		7				11	6	10^2	8^1	1			12	13	9							14
			4	5	12	7			13	11	2	10^2	8	1	6^1		3	14	9^3							15
1	2	3	4	5		7^1			10^3	13	11	12	8			14	6	9^2								16
1	2	3	4	5	12	7^1			10		11	13	8				6	9^2								17
1		3	4	5		7^1			10		11	12	8				6	9		2						18
	2	3	4		6	7		12	10^2	11	5		8	1		9^1		13								19
1		3	4					9	10		6		8		5		7	11		2						20
		3	4		6^2			9^1	10■		7	12	8	1	13		5	11		2						21
	13	3	4		5	14		9^3	10		11	12	8	1			6^2	7^1		2						22
	12	3	4		5			9			11	10^3	8	1		13	6	14		2^1	7^2					23
		3	4	14	6			9^2	13	11	7^1	12	8	1			5	10^3		2						24
		3	4		6			9	10^1	7	5	12		1				8		2		11				25
		3	4		6			9^1		7	5	10		1				8		2		11	12			26
	2	3	4		6			9		11			8	1				10		12	13	5^2	7^1			27
	2	3■	4		6			9^2		7	13		8	1				5		12	14	11^1	10^3			28
	2		4		6					7	12		8	1				10		3	5^1	11	9			29
	2		4		6					7	13	12	8	1				9		3	5^1	11^2	10^3	14		30
	2		4		6					11	5		8	1				9			3■		10		7	31
	2		4		6					3	5		8	1				9				11	10		7	32
	2	3	4	5						7		13	8	1			12	9^2				11^1	10		6	33
		3	4	5						7	2	13	8	1			12	9				11^1	10^2		6	34
	2	3	4	5				13		11■	6		8	1			12	9			7^1		10^2			35
	2	3	4	5^1	12			14			11		8	1			13	9			7		10^3		6^2	36
	2^1	3	4		6			9^3			11	10	8	1			5	13		12	7^2		14			37
		3	4		6			12			11	10	8	1			5^2	9		2	7^1		13			38
		3	4		6				12	11	5	10	8	1				7^1		2			9			39
1		3	4		6			13	14	7	5	10^2					8	12		2		11^1	9^2			40
		3	4		6			14	12	11	5	10^3	8	1			13	7^1		2			9^2			41
	2	3	4		6			9^1	12	11	5		8	1				10^2		7			13			42

FA Cup

Fourth Qual	Alfreton T	(h)	0-0
		(a)	1-1
First Round	Cambridge C	(a)	1-0
Second Round	Stockport Co	(h)	0-2

Play-Offs

Semi-Final	Morecambe	(a)	1-1
		(h)	3-2
Final *(at Leicester)*	Halifax T		3-2

Football League Trophy

First Round	Mansfield T	(a)	1-0
Second Round	Port Vale	(h)	2-1
Quarter-Final	Scunthorpe U	(h)	2-0
Semi-Final	Macclesfield T	(a)	0-2

FA Trophy

First Round	Bognor Regis T	(a)	7-1
Second Round	Halifax T	(a)	1-0
Third Round	Grays Ath	(h)	0-1

KIDDERMINSTER HARRIERS Conference

Ground: Aggborough Stadium, Hoo Road, Kidderminster DY10 1NB.
Tel: (01562) 823 951.
Year Formed: 1886.
Record Gate: 9155 (1948 v Hereford U).
Nickname: Harriers.
Manager: Mark Yates.
Secretary: Roger Barlow.
Colours: Red shirts, white shorts, red stockings.

KIDDERMINSTER HARRIERS 2005–06 LEAGUE RECORD

Match No.	*Date*	*Venue*	*Opponents*	*Result*		*H/T Score*	*Lg. Pos.*	*Goalscorers*	*Attendance*
1	Aug 13	H	Woking	W	2-1	0-0	—	Atieno 2 (1 pen) [82 (p), 90]	1926
2	16	A	Exeter C	L	0-1	0-0	—		4914
3	20	A	Scarborough	D	1-1	1-0	11	Jackson [31]	1401
4	27	H	Southport	D	1-1	0-1	15	Hatswell [84]	1753
5	29	A	Cambridge U	W	2-0	0-0	—	Atieno [74], Sheldon [86]	3161
6	Sept 2	H	Canvey Is	W	3-2	1-1	—	Fleming [42], Atieno (pen) [89], Christie [90]	1842
7	10	A	Grays Ath	D	2-2	0-0	8	Christie 2 [48, 63]	1316
8	17	H	Forest Green R	L	1-3	0-2	10	Christie [73]	1818
9	20	H	Halifax T	L	0-1	0-1	—		1566
10	24	A	Gravesend & N	W	2-1	1-0	10	Christie [25], Hatswell [57]	1054
11	27	A	Crawley T	L	0-2	0-1	—		1012
12	Oct 1	H	Tamworth	L	0-1	0-1	13		1961
13	8	H	Morecambe	W	1-0	1-0	12	Sheldon [45]	1461
14	15	A	Aldershot T	L	0-1	0-0	12		2315
15	29	H	Hereford U	D	1-1	1-1	11	Atieno [28]	3241
16	Nov 5	H	Exeter C	L	1-2	0-0	—	Heslop [49]	1869
17	12	A	Stevenage Bor	L	1-3	0-2	14	Christie [67]	2207
18	19	H	York C	D	0-0	0-0	16		1768
19	26	A	Burton Alb	L	0-1	0-0	16		1847
20	Dec 3	H	Dagenham & R	W	3-1	2-0	15	Christie 2 [41, 66], Pugh [45]	1559
21	10	A	Accrington S	L	0-2	0-1	16		1366
22	26	H	Altrincham	D	1-1	1-0	16	Christie (pen) [23]	2206
23	30	H	Burton Alb	L	0-1	0-0	—		1749
24	Jan 2	A	Altrincham	L	0-3	0-2	17		1165
25	7	A	Woking	W	1-0	0-0	16	Mullins [69]	1514
26	21	H	Scarborough	W	2-1	1-0	16	Jackson [45], Mullins [50]	1740
27	28	A	Southport	W	4-1	3-1	15	Jackson [15], Harkness [25], Christie [34], Russell [58]	1076
28	Feb 4	A	Halifax T	D	0-0	0-0	13		1544
29	11	H	Gravesend & N	L	0-2	0-1	14		1575
30	18	A	Tamworth	D	1-1	0-1	15	White [48]	1278
31	21	H	Crawley T	W	1-0	1-0	—	Russell [24]	1302
32	Mar 4	A	Forest Green R	D	0-0	0-0	13		1033
33	11	A	Morecambe	L	0-2	0-1	15		1662
34	18	H	Aldershot T	L	1-4	0-4	16	Reynolds [53]	1630
35	25	A	Hereford U	W	1-0	0-0	15	Blackwood [73]	4223
36	28	H	Grays Ath	L	0-5	0-2	—		1220
37	Apr 1	H	Stevenage Bor	D	0-0	0-0	16		1490
38	9	A	York C	D	2-2	0-0	15	Fleming [72], Reynolds [77]	3376
39	14	A	Canvey Is	L	1-2	0-2	—	Reynolds [72]	621
40	17	H	Cambridge U	W	1-0	1-0	16	Peters (og) [14]	1665
41	22	A	Dagenham & R	L	0-3	0-3	16		1038
42	29	H	Accrington S	W	2-0	0-0	15	Thompson [48], Reynolds [56]	1934

Final League Position: 15

GOALSCORERS

League (39): Christie 10 (1 pen), Atieno 5 (2 pens), Reynolds 4, Jackson 3, Fleming 2, Hatswell 2, Mullins 2, Russell 2, Sheldon 2, Blackwood 1, Harkness 1, Heslop 1, Pugh 1, Thompson 1, White 1, own goal 1.
FA Cup (0).
Football League Trophy (7): Christie 3, Blackwood 1, Hatswell 1, Penn 1, Sheldon 1 (pen).
FA Trophy (4): Blackwood 1, Christie 1, Heslop 1, Thompson 1.

Danby 27	Evans 13	Burgess 34	Fleming 37 + 1	Jackson 26	Hatswell 24	O'Connor 12	Thompson 16 + 16	Blackwood 24 + 6	Russell 23 + 8	Christie 23 + 1	Atieno 13 + 9	Sheldon 24 + 10	Wilson 8 + 14	Burton 1 + 3	Graves 3 + 2	Hurren 10 + 3	Heslop 15 + 7	Lewis 15	Mullins 25	Pugh 5 + 2	Penn 22	Flynn 5	Harkness 13 + 1	Francis 3 + 3	Howarth — + 1	Sedgemore 11	Smith — + 3	White 5	Osborne 3	Hanley — + 1	Reynolds 8	McGrath 1 + 3	Rea 7	Newby 5 + 2	Walker 1 + 1	Byrne — + 2	*Match No.*
1	2	3	4	5	6	7	8^{1}	9	10^{2}	11	12	13																									1
1	2	3	4	5	6	7^{1}	8^{2}	9	10^{3}	11	14	13	12																								2
1	2	3^{1}		5	6	7^{3}	8		10		9	11^{2}	4	12	13	14																					3
1	2	3	4	5	6	7			10	9	13	11^{2}	8^{1}				12																				4
1	2	3	4	5	6	7^{1}	14		8	9^{2}	10^{3}	13	12				11																				5
1	2	3	4	5	6	7	13	12^{2}	8^{1}	9	10		14				11^{3}																				6
1	2	3	4	5	6	7^{2}			14	9	10	11^{1}	13	12	8^{3}																						7
1	2^{1}	3	4	5	6		12	14		9	10	11^{3}	8^{2}		7		13																				8
1	2^{1}	3	4	5	6	7^{2}	8	13	14	9	10^{3}				11		12																				9
1	2	3	4	5	6			8^{1}	10^{2}	9^{3}	14	12	7	13			11																				10
1	2	3	4■	5	6		12	8^{2}	10^{3}	9	13	14	7^{1}				11																				11
1		3		5	6		8^{2}	13	12	9	10	7^{1}	11	2			4																				12
1	2	3	4	5	6	7^{1}		10^{3}	8	9	13	11^{2}	12				14																				13
1	2^{1}	3	4	5	6	7^{3}	12		8^{2}	9	13	11	14				10																				14
		3	4	5	6	7	12		8		10	11^{1}					9	1	2																		15
		3	4	5	6	7^{1}	14		8^{2}	13	10	11^{3}	12				9	1	2																		16
		3	4^{1}	5	6		13	8		9^{2}	10		11				7	1	2	12																	17
		3	4	5				7		9	10						8	1	2	6	11																18
		3■	12	5	6			7		9	10						11	1	2	4^{1}	8																19
			4		6		8			9						7	11	1	2	10	3	5															20
			4	5	6		8	12			10		13				11^{2}	1	2	7^{1}	9	3															21
			4	5	6		8^{2}	10^{1}		9	13	12					11	1	2		7	3															22
			4	5	6		8^{2}	10		9	13	11					12	1	2		7^{1}	3															23
1		3	4	5	6		8	10	12	9		11^{1}					7					2															24
1		3	4	5	6			10	12	9		11^{1}					13		2	7^{2}	8																25
1		3	4	5				7^{2}	6^{1}	9		10^{3}			13				2	12	8		11	14													26
1		3	4	5			14	11^{2}	7	9^{3}			13				12		2		8^{1}		6	10													27
1		3	4					7^{2}	8			14							2		6		5^{1}	10^{3}	12	11	13	9									28
1		3	4				13	7^{1}	8			11	12						2				5	10^{2}		6		9									29
1			4				8	10^{2}	6			11	12						2		7^{1}					5	13	9	3								30
1			4				8		7^{1}			11^{2}	12			10			2				3			6	13	9	5								31
1		3					10^{3}	14	8			7^{1}	13			5			2		11^{2}		4	12		6		9									32
1		3	4^{1}				8^{2}	9	7			10^{3}	12			5			2		11		6	14						13							33
1		3					12	10^{3}	8			11	6			13			2		7		4^{2}						5^{1}		9	14					34
1		3	4				12	7	13			11							2		8		6								9^{2}		5	10^{1}			35
1		3^{1}	4				13	8	7			11				12			2		6		5^{2}										9	10			36
		3	4					8^{1}	14			13				6		1	2		7		12			11					9^{2}		5	10^{3}			37
			4				13	8■				12				6		1	2		7		3			11					9^{2}		5	10^{1}			38
			4				14					12				6		1			7		3			2					9	11^{2}	5	10^{3}	8^{1}	13	39
		3	4				10^{2}					11				6		1			7		2			8					9^{1}	12	5	13			40
		3	4				12	10	14			11				6		1	2		7					8^{2}					9^{3}		5^{1}	13			41
		3	4				10		8^{2}			11				5		1	2		7					6^{1}					9	13^{3}			12	14	42

FA Cup

Fourth Qual	Southport	(a)	0-1

Football League Trophy

First Round	Darlington	(h)	2-1
Second Round	Boston U	(a)	3-0
Quarter-Final	Bradford C	(h)	2-1
Semi-Final	Carlisle U	(a)	0-1

FA Trophy

First Round	Scarborough	(h)	4-0
Second Round	Grays Ath	(h)	0-1

MORECAMBE Conference

Ground: Christie Park, Lancaster Road, Morecambe, Lancashire LA4 5TJ.
Tel: (01524) 411 797.
Year Formed: 1920.
Record Gate: 9,326 (1962 v Weymouth FA Cup Third Round).
Nickname: The Shrimps.
Manager: Sammy McIlroy.
Secretary: Neil Marsdin.
Colours: Red shirts, white shorts, black stockings.

MORECAMBE 2005–06 LEAGUE RECORD

Match No.	Date	Venue	Opponents	Result		H/T Score	Lg. Pos.	Goalscorers	Attendance
1	Aug 13	H	Halifax T	W	1-0	1-0	—	Curtis [21]	2150
2	16	A	Scarborough	W	1-0	0-0	—	Carlton [81]	1759
3	20	A	Exeter C	L	0-2	0-2	5		3978
4	27	H	Crawley T	W	3-0	0-0	2	Twiss [54], Thompson 2 [65, 76]	1473
5	29	A	Altrincham	L	0-2	0-2	—		1447
6	Sept 3	H	Tamworth	D	0-0	0-0	8		1413
7	10	H	Aldershot T	W	5-2	2-2	5	Curtis [26], O'Connor [45], Twiss 2 [48, 84], Carlton [80]	1429
8	17	A	Hereford U	L	0-1	0-1	8		2422
9	20	A	Burton Alb	W	4-0	2-0	—	Carlton [14], Curtis [40], O'Connor [60], Twiss [75]	1352
10	24	H	Stevenage Bor	W	4-1	3-0	4	Twiss [12], Hunter [25], Thompson [40], Curtis [90]	1738
11	27	H	Accrington S	W	3-2	1-1	—	Twiss 2 [33, 51], Carlton [73]	2162
12	Oct 1	A	Forest Green R	L	0-1	0-0	4		802
13	8	A	Kidderminster H	L	0-1	0-1	5		1461
14	15	H	Dagenham & R	W	2-0	1-0	5	Moore (og) [7], Curtis [75]	1718
15	29	A	Canvey Is	D	3-3	0-2	6	Bentley [59], Twiss 2 [74, 82]	480
16	Nov 12	H	Cambridge U	L	0-1	0-1	7		1648
17	19	A	Woking	W	1-0	1-0	7	Carlton [19]	2069
18	26	H	York C	W	2-0	1-0	4	Thompson [29], O'Connor [81]	1778
19	Dec 3	A	Gravesend & N	L	0-1	0-1	4		1172
20	10	H	Grays Ath	W	3-0	2-0	4	Thompson [22], Carlton [38], Bentley [58]	1785
21	26	A	Southport	W	3-0	1-0	4	Carlton [32], Thompson [59], Roberts (og) [88]	1807
22	31	A	York C	D	1-1	0-1	4	Curtis [54]	2712
23	Jan 2	H	Southport	D	0-0	0-0	4		2788
24	9	A	Halifax T	D	0-0	0-0	—		1962
25	21	H	Exeter C	D	2-2	0-0	5	Barlow [68], Brannan [75]	2073
26	24	H	Scarborough	L	0-3	0-2	—		1478
27	28	A	Crawley T	W	3-1	0-0	5	Barlow 2 [49, 56], Perkins [78]	1253
28	Feb 4	H	Burton Alb	W	3-1	1-0	2	Blackburn [40], Barlow [88], Thompson [90]	1855
29	11	A	Stevenage Bor	L	0-1	0-1	5		2068
30	18	H	Forest Green R	W	3-2	2-1	2	Kelly [30], Barlow [45], Curtis [71]	1486
31	20	A	Accrington S	L	0-2	0-2	—		3041
32	25	A	Aldershot T	L	0-2	0-1	5		1868
33	Mar 11	H	Kidderminster H	W	2-0	1-0	5	Twiss [32], Curtis [86]	1662
34	18	A	Dagenham & R	L	1-3	0-0	6	Thompson [49]	960
35	25	H	Canvey Is	W	1-0	1-0	6	Carlton [44]	1471
36	Apr 1	A	Cambridge U	D	2-2	1-1	7	Carlton 2 [23, 54]	2129
37	4	H	Hereford U	D	2-2	1-0	—	Twiss [3], Carlton [51]	1699
38	8	H	Woking	W	3-1	3-0	7	Curtis [32], Carlton [37], Hunter [45]	1468
39	15	A	Tamworth	W	3-0	2-0	5	Curtis [2], Thompson [12], Carlton [77]	1176
40	17	H	Altrincham	W	2-0	1-0	5	Bentley [44], Carlton [63]	2118
41	22	H	Gravesend & N	W	3-0	2-0	5	Curtis [15], Carlton 2 [39, 46]	1991
42	29	A	Grays Ath	W	2-1	1-1	5	Carlton [33], Bentley [54]	1950

Final League Position: 5

GOALSCORERS

League (68): Carlton 17, Curtis 11, Twiss 11, Thompson 9, Barlow 5, Bentley 4, O'Connor 3, Hunter 2, Blackburn 1, Brannan 1, Kelly 1, Perkins 1, own goals 2.
FA Cup (3): Carlton 1, O'Connor 1, Walmsley 1.
Football League Trophy (1): Lloyd 1.
FA Trophy (4): Twiss 2, Bentley 1, Curtis 1.
Play-Offs (3): Bentley 1, Curtis 1 (pen), Twiss 1.

Robinson 18	Heard 4 + 2	Howard 28	Bentley 40	Kempson 30 + 2	Blackburn 35 + 3	Thompson 39 + 1	Perkins 34 + 2	Twiss 40 + 2	Curtis 37 + 3	Hunter 21 + 2	Carlton 27 + 13	O'Connor 4 + 10	Kelly 16 + 7	Ruffer — + 3	Stringfellow — + 6	Walmsley 10 + 7	Dodgson — + 4	Lloyd — + 5	Hardiker 15 + 2	Brannan 23 + 2	Drench 24 + 1	Barlow 10 + 6	Rigoglioso — + 7	McLachlan 7 + 1	*Match No.*
1	2^1	3	4	5	6	7^2	8	9	10	11^3	12	13	14												1
1	2^1	3	4	5	6	7	8^2	9	10^3	11	12		13■	14											2
1	2^1	3^2	4	5	6	7^3	8	9	10	11	12				13	14									3
1	12	3	4	5	6	7	8^2	9	10^3	11					13	2^1	14■								4
1	14	3	4	5	6^1	7^2	8	9	10	11	12				13	2^3									5
1	2^1		4	5	6	7	8	9	10^2	11	12	13	3												6
1		3^1	4	5	6	7	8	9	10^2	11	14	2^3			12		13								7
1		3	4	5	6■	7	8	9	10	11^1	12	2^2				13									8
1			4	5		7^1	8	9^2	11	6	10^3	14	3	12		2		13							9
1			4	5	13	7^2	8	9	11	6	10^3	14	3	12		2^1									10
1			4	5	12	7	8	9	11	6	10^2	13	3			2^1									11
1			4	5	3^1	7^2	8	9	11	6	10	12	2			13									12
1			4	5	13	7^1	8	9	11	6	10^3	14	3^2		12	2									13
1		3^1	4	5	6		8	9^2	10	14	13	11^3	7		12	2									14
1		3	4	5^1	6	14	8	9	10		13	11^3	7^2			2			12						15
1		3^1	4	5		7	8	9	11		10	12							2	6					16
1		3	4	5		7	8	9	11		10^1	12^2				13			2	6					17
		3	4	5		7	8	9	11		10^2	13	12						2	6^1	1				18
		3	4	5	6^1	7	8	9	11		10^2		13			12				2	1				19
		3	4		5	7	8	9^2	11		10		12					13	2	6^1	1				20
			4	5	6	7	8	9	11		10								2	3	1				21
		3	4		6	7	8^1	9	11		10		12						2	5	1				22
		3	4		6	7		9^1	11		10		8					12	2	5	1				23
		3	4		6	7	8	9	11		10								2	5	1				24
			4	5	6	7	8	9	13		10^2		11^1			12		14		2	1	3^3			25
			4	5	6	7^1	8	9	11		10		13			2^3		12	14	3^2	1				26
			4	5	6		8	9	11				7			2			3		1	10			27
			4	5	6	7	8	9^2	11		13		2						3	12	1	10^1			28
			4	5	6	7	8^1	9			12		3						2	11	1	10			29
			4	5^2	6	7	8	12	11		10		2^3			13			3	14	1	9^1			30
			4	5	6	7	8	13	10^2		12		11^1						3	2	1	9			31
1■		3	4	5	6	7	8	9	11^G		12		2								15	10^1			32
		3		5	6	7	8^1	9	13	12	11^3								2	4	1	10^2	14		33
		3	4	12	6	7	8	9^3	11^2		10								2^1	5	1	14	13		34
		3	4		6	7	8	9	12	2	10^1									5	1	11^2		13	35
		3	4^1	12	6	7		9		11	10									2	1	8^2	13	5	36
		3		5	6	7		9	11^1	8	10^2						12			2	1	13		4	37
		3	4		6	7^1		9	11	8	10									2	1		12	5	38
		3	4		6	7		9^2	11^1	8	10^3						12			5	1	14	13	2	39
		3^1	4		6	7	12	9^2	11	8	10^3									5	1	14	13	2	40
		3^1	4		6	7	12	9	11^2	8	10^3									5	1	14	13	2	41
		3	4		6	7		9	11	8	10^1									5	1	12		2	42

FA Cup

Fourth Qual	Bromsgrove R	(a)	2-0
First Round	Northwich Vic	(h)	1-3

Football League Trophy

First Round	Grimsby T	(a)	1-1
Second Round	Bradford C	(h)	0-1

FA Trophy

First Round	Vauxhall M	(a)	4-0
Second Round	Stafford R	(a)	0-1

Play-Offs

Semi-Final	Hereford U	(h)	1-1
		(a)	2-3

SCARBOROUGH Conference North

Ground: McCain Stadium, Seamer Road, Scarborough, Yorkshire YO12 4HF.
Tel: (01723) 375 094.
Year Formed: 1879.
Record Gate: 11,130 (1987 v Luton Town FA Cup Third Round).
Nickname: The Boro.
Manager: Mark Patterson.
Secretary: Kevin Philliskirk.
Colours: All red.

SCARBOROUGH 2005–06 LEAGUE RECORD

Match No.	*Date*	*Venue*	*Opponents*	*Result*	*H/T Score*	*Lg. Pos.*	*Goalscorers*	*Attendance*
1	Aug 13	A	Hereford U	L 0-4	0-0	—		3105
2	16	H	Morecambe	L 0-1	0-0	—		1759
3	20	H	Kidderminster H	D 1-1	0-1	22	Foot ^{90}	1401
4	27	A	Dagenham & R	W 2-0	0-0	17	Speight ^{85}, Wake ^{90}	1074
5	29	H	Accrington S	D 2-2	1-2	—	Quayle ^{45}, Speight ^{76}	1509
6	Sept 3	A	Burton Alb	L 1-2	0-1	19	Wake ^{50}	1336
7	10	H	Gravesend & N	W 3-1	3-0	13	Wake ^{31}, McCarthy (og) ^{38}, Nicholson ^{43}	1207
8	17	A	Canvey Is	L 0-1	0-1	16		744
9	20	A	Altrincham	D 1-1	0-0	—	Coulson ^{87}	862
10	24	H	Forest Green R	W 1-0	0-0	14	Redfearn (pen) ^{61}	1341
11	27	H	Southport	L 0-1	0-1	—		1280
12	Oct 1	A	Woking	L 0-4	0-2	16		1840
13	8	H	Crawley T	L 1-2	1-1	20	Coulson ^{45}	1257
14	15	A	Grays Ath	L 0-5	0-1	22		1515
15	29	H	Aldershot T	D 2-2	0-1	22	Quayle ^{56}, Coulson ^{57}	1682
16	Nov 12	A	Tamworth	W 1-0	1-0	19	Quayle ^{43}	1165
17	19	H	Stevenage Bor	D 1-1	1-0	18	Nicholson ^{44}	1152
18	26	H	Halifax T	W 2-0	0-0	17	Fowler ^{47}, Clark (pen) ^{73}	1843
19	Dec 3	A	Cambridge U	L 1-2	0-2	17	Hackworth ^{64}	2809
20	10	H	Exeter C	L 0-1	0-1	19		1428
21	26	A	York C	L 1-3	1-1	19	Wake ^{21}	4921
22	30	A	Halifax T	L 0-1	0-0	—		1682
23	Jan 2	H	York C	D 2-2	1-1	20	Wake ^{42}, Hughes ^{90}	4057
24	7	H	Hereford U	L 0-1	0-1	20		1582
25	14	A	Southport	W 2-0	2-0	—	McNiven ^{2}, Fowler ^{18}	1035
26	21	A	Kidderminster H	L 1-2	0-1	19	McNiven ^{73}	1740
27	24	A	Morecambe	W 3-0	2-0	—	McNiven ^{19}, Hughes ^{27}, Fowler ^{87}	1478
28	28	H	Dagenham & R	L 0-1	0-0	18		1505
29	Feb 4	H	Altrincham	L 1-2	0-1	18	McNiven ^{75}	1405
30	11	A	Forest Green R	L 1-5	0-3	19	McNiven ^{86}	732
31	18	H	Woking	D 1-1	1-0	19	Coulson ^{9}	1278
32	25	A	Gravesend & N	D 0-0	0-0	19		930
33	Mar 11	A	Crawley T	L 0-2	0-1	20		1181
34	21	H	Canvey Is	L 1-2	0-0	—	Coulson ^{84}	1153
35	25	A	Aldershot T	W 1-0	1-0	19	Coulson ^{24}	2245
36	Apr 8	A	Stevenage Bor	L 0-2	0-2	21		1861
37	11	H	Tamworth	D 0-0	0-0	—		1648
38	15	H	Burton Alb	W 3-0	1-0	21	Redfearn (pen) ^{35}, Hackworth ^{72}, Coulson ^{81}	1808
39	17	A	Accrington S	L 0-1	0-0	21		3320
40	19	H	Grays Ath	L 2-7	0-3	—	McNiven ^{55}, Weaver ^{61}	1560
41	22	H	Cambridge U	L 1-2	1-1	20	Redfearn ^{36}	1831
42	29	A	Exeter C	D 1-1	0-0	22	Hackworth ^{90}	3382

Final League Position: 21

GOALSCORERS

League (40): Coulson 7, McNiven 6, Wake 5, Fowler 3, Hackworth 3, Quayle 3, Redfearn 3 (2 pens), Hughes 2, Nicholson 2, Speight 2, Clark 1 (pen), Foot 1, Weaver 1, own goal 1.
FA Cup (0).
FA Trophy (0).

Walker 28	Lyth 21 + 9	Nicholson 38 + 1	Weaver 22	Elebert 11 + 1	Baker S 34 + 1	Bishop 23 + 1	Clark 20	Wake 7 + 6	Quayle 15 + 4	Hackworth 36 + 3	Redfearn 17 + 4	Palmer 2 + 2	Eccles 4 + 4	Coulson 11 + 22	Foot 14 + 6	Harper 4	Speight 5 + 3	Blott — + 3	Beadle 5 + 3	Carl 1 + 1	Cook 11	Rix 1	Hughes 22 + 2	Fowler 24 + 1	McClare 6 + 9	Parton 1 + 3	Atkinson 20 + 2	Dunbavin 14	Jarvis — + 1	Ingram 14 + 1	Yates — + 1	McNiven 16 + 2	Pounder 7 + 2	Baker T 1	Kell 2	Bertos 1	Blunt 4 + 1	*Match No.*
1	2[1]	3	4	5	6	7	8	9[2]	10	11[3]	12	13	14																									1
1	2[1]	3	4	5	6	7■	8[3]	13	10		11[2]	9	14	12																								2
1	2[1]	3	4	5	6		8[2]		10	11		9[3]	13	14	12	7																						3
1	12	3		5	6		8[3]	14	10	11			2[2]	7[1]	4	9	13																					4
1	12	3		5	6[1]		8		10	9		13	11[3]	7[2]	2	4	14																					5
1	14	3		5	6	7	8[3]	9	10	11[1]	12				2	4[2]	13																					6
1	14	3		5	6	7	8	9[3]	10[2]	11	12			13	4		2[1]																					7
1	12	3	4[1]	5	6	7	8		10[3]	11	2[2]			13			9	14																				8
1	13	3		5[1]	6	7	8			11[2]	4		9[3]	14	2		10	12																				9
1	12	3		5	6	7	8			11	4[1]		9[2]	13	2		10																					10
1	12	3		5[1]	6	7	9			11	8		13	4	2		10[2]																					11
1	2	3		12	6	7	8			9[2]	4[1]			11	5				10	13																		12
1	2	3			6	7	8		10					11	5				9	4																		13
1	2	13	4			7	8[2]	14	10[3]	12				11	5				6		3	9[1]																14
1	2	3	4		6	7	8[1]	13	9[2]	10				12							11		5															15
1	2	3	4		6		8		9[1]	10				12							5		11	7														16
1	2	3	4		6	12	8		9[2]	10				13							7		5[1]	11														17
1	2	3	4			7	8		9[2]	10											11		5	6[1]	12	13												18
1	2	3			6	7	8		9[3]	10				12							4[2]		5[1]	11		13	14											19
	2[1]	3	4		6	7	8[2]		13	10											11[3]		12	5		9		1	14									20
	2	3[1]			6	7		9[3]		10	14			13							11		4	8	5[2]		12	1										21
1	2		4		6	7		9[3]		10				13							11[2]		12	3[1]	8	14	5											22
1	2[2]		4		6[1]	7		9	14	10[3]				13	12						11■		8	3			5											23
1	2[1]	3			6	7		9[2]	12	10				13									11		8		5			4								24
1	2	3			6	7				10					5								8	4[1]							12	9	11					25
1		3			2[1]	7		12		10													4	8			5			6		9	11					26
1		3			2	7		12		10													8	4			5			6		9[1]	11					27
1	12	3			2[1]	7			14	10					13								8[2]	4[3]			5			6		9	11					28
1	2	3								10[3]				12	14								11[2]	4			5			6		9	13	7[1]	8			29
1		3[1]								10	8			13	2									11	14		5			4		9	12		6[3]	7[2]		30
	2	3	4[1]		12									10									11	7	8		5	1		6		9						31
	2	3								12	8			10[1]									7		6		5	1		4		9	11					32
	2	3								14	4			10[3]	13								8[2]	12	7[1]		5	1		6		9	11					33
		3	4		6					10				12									7	8			5	1		2		9[1]					11	34
		3	4		6[1]					10	8[2]			9[3]					12				7	2	13		5	1				14					11	35
		3	4		6					10	7			9									8[2]	2			5	1		12		13					11[1]	36
		3	4		6					10	11[2]			12									7[1]	8	13		5	1		2		9						37
		3	4		6					10	11[1]			12									7	8	13		5	1		2[2]		9						38
		3[1]	4		6					10	8[2]								14				11■	7	13		5	1		2		9[3]					12	39
			4							10	7[2]			12	2				13					8	14		5	1		6[3]		9	11				3[1]	40
		3	4		6					10	7[1]			12	2[2]			14	11					8	13		5	1				9[3]						41
		3[1]	4		6[2]					10	8			14	12				2		11			7	13		5	1				9[3]						42

FA Cup
Fourth Qual Harrogate T (a) 0-1

FA Trophy
First Round Kidderminster H (a) 0-4

SOUTHPORT Conference

Ground: Haig Avenue, Southport PR8 6JZ.
Tel: (01704) 533 422.
Year Formed: 1881.
Record Gate: 20,010 (1932 v Newcastle U, FA Cup).
Nickname: Sandgrounders.
Manager: Paul Cook.
Secretary: Ken Hilton.
Colours: Yellow shirts, black shorts, black stockings.

SOUTHPORT 2005–06 LEAGUE RECORD

Match No.	Date	Venue	Opponents	Result		H/T Score	Lg. Pos.	Goalscorers	Attendance
1	Aug 13	A	Dagenham & R	L	1-3	1-1	—	Daly 32	1265
2	16	H	York C	L	1-4	1-3	—	Daly 6	1646
3	20	H	Stevenage Bor	W	3-2	2-0	17	Baker (pen) 24, Robinson 2 35, 48	1007
4	27	A	Kidderminster H	D	1-1	1-0	18	Daly 45	1753
5	29	H	Burton Alb	W	3-2	1-0	—	Robinson 2 16, 66, Leadbetter 59	1253
6	Sept 3	A	Gravesend & N	L	1-2	1-1	14	Leadbetter 34	813
7	10	A	Woking	L	0-1	0-0	15		1477
8	17	H	Exeter C	L	0-3	0-0	19		1423
9	20	H	Tamworth	D	1-1	0-0	—	Baker 53	1012
10	24	A	Canvey Is	L	1-2	1-0	20	Ward (og) 35	727
11	27	A	Scarborough	W	1-0	1-0	—	Leadbetter 27	1280
12	Oct 1	H	Cambridge U	D	2-2	1-1	17	Baker 2 1, 50	1204
13	7	H	Forest Green R	W	3-1	3-1	—	Baker 2 9, 10, Daly 24	1087
14	15	A	Altrincham	L	0-1	0-0	16		1225
15	29	H	Grays Ath	L	1-4	0-2	18	Rogan 60	1148
16	Nov 12	A	Crawley T	L	0-2	0-2	20		2055
17	19	H	Halifax T	L	0-2	0-2	21		1402
18	26	A	Accrington S	L	0-4	0-2	21		1630
19	Dec 10	A	Aldershot T	L	0-2	0-2	21		2066
20	26	H	Morecambe	L	0-3	0-1	22		1807
21	Jan 2	A	Morecambe	D	0-0	0-0	22		2788
22	7	H	Dagenham & R	L	1-2	0-2	22	Baker 49	1002
23	14	H	Scarborough	L	0-2	0-2	—		1035
24	21	A	Stevenage Bor	W	1-0	0-0	22	Robinson (pen) 62	2231
25	24	A	York C	D	0-0	0-0	—		2176
26	28	H	Kidderminster H	L	1-4	1-3	22	Robinson 4	1076
27	Feb 11	H	Canvey Is	W	2-0	1-0	21	Daly 2 17, 69	901
28	18	A	Cambridge U	L	1-2	0-1	22	Daly 84	2310
29	Mar 4	A	Exeter C	L	0-5	0-4	22		3485
30	11	A	Forest Green R	W	2-1	1-1	22	Daly 18, Blakeman 73	846
31	14	H	Hereford U	L	1-2	0-2	—	Robinson (pen) 60	1057
32	18	H	Altrincham	D	1-1	1-0	22	Daly 4	1278
33	21	H	Accrington S	W	2-0	1-0	—	Daly 2 14, 61	1414
34	25	A	Tamworth	D	0-0	0-0	21		1442
35	Apr 1	H	Crawley T	L	0-2	0-0	21		1308
36	8	A	Halifax T	L	1-2	0-1	22	Pickford 73	1791
37	10	H	Woking	W	1-0	1-0	—	Blakeman 22	1054
38	15	H	Gravesend & N	W	1-0	1-0	20	Daly 15	1301
39	18	A	Burton Alb	D	0-0	0-0	—		1488
40	22	A	Hereford U	D	1-1	0-0	18	Blakeman 89	2547
41	25	A	Grays Ath	D	1-1	0-0	—	Pickford 67	918
42	29	H	Aldershot T	L	0-1	0-0	19		1709

Final League Position: 18

GOALSCORERS

League (36): Daly 12, Baker 7 (1 pen), Robinson 7 (2 pens), Blakeman 3, Leadbetter 3, Pickford 2, Rogan 1, own goal 1.
FA Cup (2): Lane 1, Leadbitter 1.
FA Trophy (0).

Dickinson 40	Lane 37	Fitzgerald 31 + 5	Morley 31 + 1	Kilbane 12 + 2	Davis 32 + 2	Pickford 34	Krief 11	Fearns 5 + 4	Daly 34 + 2	Robinson 26 + 6	Lynch 6 + 9	Baker 33 + 3	Booth 5 + 18	Leadbetter 20 + 7	McGinn 13 + 14	Fitzhenry 14 + 2	Speare 2	Powell 13 + 10	Field — + 2	Evans — + 1	Rogan 3 + 8	Brooks — + 1	Brass 5	Roberts 18	Rigoglioso 1	Stringfellow — + 1	Bailey 1 + 1	Blakeman 15 + 1	Aggrey 3	Brabin 12 + 2	Price 3 + 3	Jackson 2 + 6	*Match No.*
1	2	3	4	5	6	7	8^{1}	9^{2}	10	11^{3}	12	13	14																				1
1	2	3		5	6	7	8^{2}	9	10		13	4^{1}	12	11^{3}	14																		2
1	2	3		5	6	7	8		10^{3}	11	12	4^{1}	14	9^{2}	13																		3
1	2	3		5	6	7	8	12	10^{1}	11^{2}	13	4		9^{3}	14																		4
1	2	3		5	6	7^{2}	8	14	10^{3}	11	13	4^{1}	12	9																			5
1	2	3		5	6	7^{2}	8^{1}		10^{3}	11	13	9	12	4	14																		6
1	2	3		12	6	7	8	14	10	11^{3}		4		9^{2}	13	5^{1}																	7
1	2	3	4^{3}		6	7^{2}	8	9	10		14	11^{1}	12		13	5																	8
	2	3	4	14	6	7	8^{1}	9^{3}	10^{2}			11		13	12	5■	1																9
	2	3	4	5	6	7		9	10			11^{2}	13	12	8^{1}		1																10
1	2	3	4	5		7^{1}		14	10^{3}		12	8^{2}	13	9	11			6															11
1	2	3	4	5					10		7^{1}	8	12	9	11^{2}			6	13														12
1	2		4	5					10^{2}		7^{1}	11	14	9^{3}	8	6		3	12	13													13
1	2	3	4	5					10^{3}	12	7^{2}	8	14	9	11^{1}	6		13															14
1	2		4		6				10	11^{3}	7^{1}	8	13	9^{2}	12	5		3			14												15
1	2■	14	4	5							8	7^{1}	12	9^{3}	11^{2}	3		6			10	13											16
1		3	4		6	7	8		10^{2}	13		5■		9^{3}	11^{1}	2		12			14												17
1			4		6		8^{2}				12		13	9	14	2		7^{1}			11^{3}		3	5	10								18
1	2	3	4^{1}		6	7^{2}			10	9^{3}	8				13			12			14		11■	5									19
1	2^{1}	3	4		6	8			14	9		7^{2}			13			12			10		11^{3}	5									20
1	2	13			6	7			10^{2}	9^{1}		11		12	3			8					5	4									21
1	2		13		6^{1}	7			10■	9^{3}		4			11	12		8^{2}			14		5	3									22
1	2	13	4			7^{2}				11		8		10	3^{1}	5					14			6		12	9^{3}						23
1	2	3	4		6	7				9^{2}		11		10^{1}	12	5					13							8					24
1	2	3	4		6	7				11^{2}		8^{1}		10		5		12			13							9					25
1	2		4		6	7^{2}			13	11^{3}		8		10	3	5^{1}		12			14							9					26
1	2	3	4		6	7			10^{3}	9^{2}		11^{1}		13													14	8	5	12			27
1	2	3	4		6	7			10	11				9														8	5				28
1		3■	4			2^{1}			10	11		8		9^{3}	12	5		14										7	6^{2}	13			29
1	2		4			7			10^{1}	11		6				12		3						8■				9		5			30
1	2	12	4^{3}		6	7			10	11		8^{2}	13	14				3										9		5^{1}			31
1	2	13	4		6				10	11		7^{1}		12	9^{2}			3						8						5			32
1	2	3	4		6				10^{3}	9^{2}			14	13	7^{1}			11						8						5	12		33
1	2	3	4		6	7			10	11^{1}														8				9		5		12	34
1	2	3^{3}	4		6^{1}	7^{2}			10	11		13			14									8				9■		5		12	35
1	2	3			6	7			10	13		11^{2}	14					4^{1}						8						5	12	9^{3}	36
1	2	3	4		14	7			10			9^{3}	6^{1}											8				11^{2}		5	13	12	37
1	2	3	4		12	7			10^{2}	13		11^{1}	9^{3}											8				6		5		14	38
1	2	3	4		6	7			10	9^{2}			13											8				12		5	11^{1}		39
1		3			6	7			10^{3}	14		8	4^{1}					12						2				9		5	11^{2}	13	40
1		3			6	2				11^{2}		7	4^{1}					12						8				10		5	9	13	41
1	2	3	4^{1}		6	7^{2}			10^{3}	14		13	5					12						8				11				9	42

FA Cup

Fourth Qual	Kidderminster H	(h)	1-0
First Round	Woking	(h)	1-1
		(a)	0-1

FA Trophy

First Round	Halifax T	(a)	0-0
		(h)	0-1

STEVENAGE BOROUGH Conference

Ground: Broadhall Way Stadium, Broadhall Way, Stevenage, Hertfordshire SG2 8RH.
Tel: (01438) 223 223.
Year Formed: 1976.
Record Gate: 6,489 (1997 v Kidderminster Harriers Conference).
Nickname: The Boro.
Secretary: Mark Stimson.
Colours: Red and white shirts, black shorts, white stockings.

STEVENAGE BOROUGH 2005–06 LEAGUE RECORD

Match No.	*Date*	*Venue*	*Opponents*	*Result*		*H/T Score*	*Lg. Pos.*	*Goalscorers*	*Atten-dance*
1	Aug 13	H	Altrincham	W	3-0	2-0	—	Elding [15], Stamp [37], Maamria (pen) [73]	2008
2	16	A	Woking	L	2-3	2-1	—	Boyd 2 [37, 45]	2592
3	20	A	Southport	L	2-3	0-2	14	Elding [54], Stamp (pen) [56]	1007
4	27	H	Tamworth	W	3-1	1-0	6	Boyd [41], Elding [64], Goodliffe [79]	1635
5	29	A	Crawley T	W	2-1	0-0	—	Stamp (pen) [73], Williams D [83]	2019
6	Sept 3	H	Halifax T	W	1-0	1-0	3	Elding [23]	1682
7	10	H	Hereford U	D	0-0	0-0	4		2404
8	17	A	Aldershot T	D	2-2	2-0	6	Elding [29], Gregory [40]	2563
9	20	H	Exeter C	W	2-0	0-0	—	Boyd [70], Bulman [88]	2445
10	24	A	Morecambe	L	1-4	0-3	6	Nurse [60]	1738
11	27	A	Canvey Is	D	1-1	0-0	—	Berquez [63]	832
12	Oct 5	H	Dagenham & R	W	2-1	1-0	—	Vickers (og) [34], Boyd [90]	2447
13	8	A	Burton Alb	L	1-3	0-3	6	Elding [51]	1319
14	15	H	Accrington S	W	3-1	0-1	6	Nurse [53], Maamria (pen) [61], Williams (og) [81]	2141
15	29	A	Gravesend & N	W	2-0	1-0	5	Nurse [3], Boyd [71]	1372
16	Nov 12	H	Kidderminster H	W	3-1	2-0	4	Stamp 2 (2 pens) [25, 70], Laker [27]	2207
17	19	A	Scarborough	D	1-1	0-1	4	Elding [74]	1152
18	26	H	Grays Ath	L	0-1	0-0	5		2753
19	Dec 10	H	Forest Green R	W	2-1	0-1	6	Nurse [56], Laker [75]	1771
20	26	A	Cambridge U	L	0-1	0-1	6		3697
21	31	A	Grays Ath	D	2-2	0-1	7	Maamria [77], Louis [88]	1214
22	Jan 2	H	Cambridge U	W	3-1	2-1	6	Nurse [43], Louis [45], Boyd [55]	3463
23	7	A	Altrincham	D	1-1	1-0	7	Stamp [40]	914
24	10	A	York C	W	1-0	1-0	—	Louis [21]	2325
25	21	H	Southport	L	0-1	0-0	6		2231
26	24	H	Woking	D	1-1	0-0	—	Stamp [62]	2152
27	28	A	Tamworth	L	0-2	0-0	7		1228
28	Feb 4	H	Aldershot T	W	2-1	1-1	6	Boyd [16], Maamria [77]	2010
29	11	H	Morecambe	W	1-0	1-0	3	Nurse [35]	2068
30	18	A	Dagenham & R	D	2-2	2-2	5	Nurse [1], Maamria (pen) [6]	1427
31	21	H	Canvey Is	W	3-0	1-0	—	Maamria [16], Louis [54], Boyd [88]	1403
32	27	A	Hereford U	L	0-2	0-1	—		2394
33	Mar 11	H	Burton Alb	L	2-3	2-0	7	Maamria [7], Stamp [45]	2081
34	14	A	Exeter C	W	2-0	1-0	—	Stamp [38], Nurse [77]	3026
35	18	A	Accrington S	D	1-1	1-0	5	Stamp [2]	2119
36	25	H	Gravesend & N	W	2-0	2-0	4	Nurse [36], Stamp [45]	1873
37	Apr 1	A	Kidderminster H	D	0-0	0-0	4		1490
38	8	H	Scarborough	W	2-0	2-0	4	Miller [10], Boyd [21]	1861
39	14	A	Halifax T	D	1-1	0-1	—	Stamp [85]	2253
40	17	H	Crawley T	W	2-1	1-1	6	Louis 2 [3, 80]	2410
41	22	H	York C	D	1-1	1-1	6	Goodliffe [43]	2701
42	29	A	Forest Green R	L	0-2	0-1	6		1510

Final League Position: 6

GOALSCORERS

League (62): Stamp 12 (4 pens), Boyd 10, Nurse 9, Elding 7, Maamria 7 (3 pens), Louis 6, Goodliffe 2, Laker 2, Berquez 1, Bulman 1, Gregory 1, Miller 1, Williams D 1, own goals 2.
FA Cup (6): Boyd 2, Elding 2, Laker 1, Stamp 1.
Football League Trophy (0).
FA Trophy (0).

Julian 41	Warner 28 + 6	Gregory 20 + 9	Bulman 39	Goodliffe 14 + 2	Henry 32	Weatherstone 6 + 13	Boyd 42	Elding 16 + 1	Maamria 25 + 5	Stamp 29 + 5	Williams D 3 + 14	Berquez 17 + 13	Nurse 33 + 6	Gore 1	Hocking 15 + 2	Quinn 24 + 2	Perpetuini 12 + 7	Laker 21 + 2	Brough 5 + 1	Sullivan — + 1	Louis 12 + 10	Lewis — + 1	Miller 14 + 1	Obinna 1 + 8	Oliver 12	Duffy — + 1	*Match No.*
1	2	3	4	5	6	7^{1}	8	9	10^{2}	11^{3}	12	13	14														1
	2	3	4	5^{1}	6		8	9	10■	11^{2}	12	7	13	1													2
1	2	3	4	5^{1}	6^{2}	7	8	9		10		11^{3}	12		13	14											3
1	2	3	4	5		13	8^{1}	9		10^{3}		14	11^{2}		6	7	12										4
1	2	3	4	5		13	8	9^{1}		11	14	12	10^{3}		7^{2}	6											5
1	2	3	4		6	13	8^{3}	9		11	12		10^{1}		5	7^{2}		14									6
1	2	3^{1}	4		6■	14	8	9		10	13		7		5^{2}	11^{3}		12									7
1	2	3	4^{2}			12	8	9		10	14	13	7^{1}		5	11^{3}		6									8
1	2	3^{1}	4	12	6	7	8^{2}	9^{3}	14		13		10		11			5									9
1	2	3■	4		6	7	8	9	12			13	10		11^{2}			5^{1}									10
1	2		4	5^{1}	6	7	8	9^{2}	13			12	10		11			3									11
1		3	4		6	13	8	9	10^{3}		14	7^{2}	11^{1}		2	12		5									12
1	2^{1}	3	4		6	12	8	9	10		14	13	11^{3}		7			5^{2}									13
1	2■		4		6	13	8		10	9^{2}		7	11			3	12	5^{1}									14
1	2		4		6^{1}		8^{2}		10■	11			9^{3}			5	12	3	7	13	14						15
1	2	14	4			12	8^{2}	9^{3}		10		7				6	3	5	11^{1}		13						16
1	2	12	4				8	14	13	10		7	9			6	3^{2}	5^{1}	11^{3}								17
1	2	3^{1}	4				8	9^{3}	13■	10		7^{2}	11			6	12	5	14								18
1	2^{1}		4	13			8	9^{3}			12	11	10			6	3	5	7^{2}		14						19
1	2	12			6		8			10	13	11■	9			4	3^{2}	5^{1}	7^{3}		14						20
1	2	3^{1}	4		6		8		10	11^{2}	13		7			5	12				9						21
1	2	3^{1}	4		6		8		10	13	7	14	11^{2}			5	12				9^{3}						22
1	2		4				8		10	11	7	12			6^{1}		3	5			9						23
1	12		4		6		8		10	14		13	11^{2}		2	7	3^{1}	5			9^{3}						24
1	2	13	4		6		8			14	11^{3}		10		5^{1}	7	3^{2}				9	12					25
1		3	4				8			11	12		10		2	6^{1}	13	5^{2}			9^{3}		7	14			26
1	2^{2}	3	4				8			12	14		10			11		5^{1}			9^{3}		7	13	6		27
1			4		6		8		10	11			9^{1}			2	3						7	12	5		28
1	2	12	4		6		8		10	11			9^{2}			5	3				13		7^{1}				29
1	2	12	4		6		8		10			14	11^{2}			5	3^{1}				9^{3}		7	13			30
1	2^{1}		4		6		8		10^{2}	9^{3}		12			13	5	3				14		7	11			31
1		3■	4		6		8		10	12		11^{2}	14		2	5^{1}					9^{3}		7	13			32
1			4		6	13	8		10	9		11^{3}	14			2	3^{2}				12		7^{1}		5		33
1			4	5	6	12	8		10	11		7	9^{1}					3							2		34
1	12		4^{1}	5	6		8		10	11^{2}		7	9					3						13	2		35
1	12		4	5	6		8		10	11			9^{2}					2					7^{1}	13	3		36
1	2	3		5	6		8		10	11^{1}			9								12		7		4		37
1		12	4^{1}	5	6	14	8		10	11^{3}		3	9^{2}								13		7		2		38
1			4^{3}	5^{1}	6	14	8		10	11		7	9					2^{2}			12		13		3		39
1	13	14		5	6	7^{1}	8		10^{2}	11		4^{3}	12								9		2		3		40
1	12	13	4^{1}	5■	6		8		10	11■		14	9^{3}								7^{2}		2		3		41
1	12	3^{1}	4		6		8		10			5^{2}	11^{3}								9■		7	13	2	14	42

FA Cup

Fourth Qual	Exeter C	(a)	1-0
First Round	Kettering T	(a)	3-1
Second Round	Northampton T	(h)	2-2
		(a)	0-2

Football League Trophy

First Round	Swindon T	(a)	0-2

FA Trophy

First Round	Crawley T	(h)	0-2

TAMWORTH Conference

Ground: The Lamb Ground, Kettlebrook, Tamworth, Staffordshire B77 1AA.
Tel: (01827) 65798.
Year Formed: 1933.
Record Gate: 4,920 (1948 v Atherstone Town Birmingham Combination).
Nickname: Lambs.
Manager: Mark Cooper.
Secretary: Russell Moore.
Colours: Red shirts with white sleeves, black shorts, red stockings.

TAMWORTH 2005–06 LEAGUE RECORD

Match No.	Date	Venue	Opponents	Result		H/T Score	Lg. Pos.	Goalscorers	Attendance
1	Aug 13	A	Aldershot T	W	2-0	2-0	—	Brown 16, Hollis 22	2641
2	16	H	Forest Green R	D	0-0	0-0	—		1258
3	20	H	Dagenham & R	D	2-2	0-2	9	Whitman 48, Alsop 85	1040
4	27	A	Stevenage Bor	L	1-3	0-1	12	Redmile 75	1635
5	29	H	Hereford U	L	0-1	0-1	—		1744
6	Sept 3	A	Morecambe	D	0-0	0-0	16		1413
7	10	A	Halifax T	L	0-4	0-0	19		1453
8	17	H	Grays Ath	D	2-2	1-1	18	Stuart (og) 14, Mansaram 49	1078
9	20	A	Southport	D	1-1	0-0	—	Heggs 90	1012
10	24	H	Woking	L	0-1	0-0	18		1021
11	27	H	York C	L	0-3	0-1	—		1005
12	Oct 1	A	Kidderminster H	W	1-0	1-0	20	Heggs 40	1961
13	7	A	Cambridge U	L	1-2	0-1	—	Ward 53	2606
14	15	H	Gravesend & N	W	1-0	0-0	17	Bampton 59	1003
15	29	A	Exeter C	L	0-3	0-1	20		3369
16	Nov 12	H	Scarborough	L	0-1	0-1	22		1165
17	19	A	Canvey Is	W	2-1	1-0	17	Edwards 18, Jackson 65	646
18	26	A	Altrincham	L	0-2	0-0	19		824
19	Dec 10	A	Crawley T	L	0-3	0-0	20		1448
20	26	H	Burton Alb	D	1-1	1-1	21	Melton 35	2151
21	31	H	Altrincham	D	1-1	1-1	21	Edwards 24	1064
22	Jan 2	A	Burton Alb	D	1-1	1-0	21	Edwards 3	2680
23	10	H	Accrington S	L	1-2	1-1	—	Edwards (pen) 39	1094
24	21	A	Dagenham & R	L	1-2	1-1	21	Williams 42	1352
25	24	A	Forest Green R	W	3-1	1-0	—	Folkes 33, Davidson 78, Williams 90	788
26	28	H	Stevenage Bor	W	2-0	0-0	20	Heggs 62, Williams 73	1228
27	Feb 11	A	Woking	L	0-5	0-2	20		2030
28	18	H	Kidderminster H	D	1-1	1-0	20	Williams 4	1278
29	21	A	York C	L	1-2	0-1	—	Williams (pen) 90	2153
30	25	H	Halifax T	L	1-2	0-1	20	Heggs 89	1672
31	Mar 4	A	Grays Ath	L	0-5	0-3	20		1117
32	11	H	Cambridge U	D	1-1	1-1	21	Neilson 12	1325
33	18	A	Gravesend & N	L	0-2	0-1	21		841
34	25	H	Southport	D	0-0	0-0	22		1442
35	28	H	Exeter C	D	1-1	1-1	—	Cooper 18	823
36	Apr 4	H	Aldershot T	W	2-1	1-0	—	Heggs 10, Johnson 50	914
37	8	H	Canvey Is	W	1-0	0-0	19	Cooper 66	1156
38	11	A	Scarborough	D	0-0	0-0	—		1648
39	15	H	Morecambe	L	0-3	0-2	19		1176
40	17	A	Hereford U	L	0-1	0-0	19		2809
41	22	A	Accrington S	L	1-2	0-0	19	Storer (pen) 90	3014
42	29	H	Crawley T	D	0-0	0-0	21		1545

Final League Position: 20

GOALSCORERS

League (32): Heggs 5, Williams 5 (1 pen), Edwards 4 (1 pen), Cooper 2, Alsop 1, Bampton 1, Brown 1, Davidson 1, Folkes 1, Hollis 1, Jackson 1, Johnson 1, Mansaram 1, Melton 1, Neilson 1, Redmile 1, Storer 1 (pen), Ward 1, Whitman 1, own goal 1.
FA Cup (8): Edwards 3, Jackson 1, Redmile 1, Robinson 1, Storer 1, Wood 1.
FA Trophy (3): Anaclet 1, Davidson 1, Ward 1.

Bowles 15 / Dormand 14	Stamps 26 + 3	Bampton 24	Ward 34 + 1	Redmile 37	Brown 15	Whitman 14 + 5	Smith 36 + 1	Roma 15 / Alsop 7 + 2	McAuley 7 + 1	Starosta 3 + 1 / Hollis 5 + 2	Taylor 11 + 14	Storer 20 + 7	Turner 16 + 7	Summerbee 4 / Douglas — + 1	Heggs 18 + 9	Jackson 11 + 13	Cooper 9 + 6	Merson 1 / Campbell 2 + 1	Francis 3 + 8	Johnson 6 + 1 / Mansaram 4 + 2	Edwards 8	Dryden — + 1 / Bevan 10	Robinson 2 + 1	Touhy 12 + 3	Gayle 2 + 1	Reid 2 / Anaclet 8	Melton 7	Motteram 1 + 1	McConnell 2	Rickards 4 + 3	Wright 1	Williams 8	Davidson 14 + 4	Folkes 11 + 4	Neilson 12 + 1	Breedon 1	Lake — + 1	*Match No.*
1	2	3	4	5	6	7	8	9^{1}	10^{2}	11^{3}	12	13	14																									1
1		3^{1}	4	5	6	7^{2}	8	9	10^{3}	11	14		2	12	13																							2
1	2		4	5	6	7^{1}	8	9	11	12	10		3																									3
1	2	3^{2}	4	5		7^{3}	8	9	10	11^{1}	13		6		14	12																						4
1	2		4▮	5	6	13	3^{1}	9	8	14	10	11^{3}	12			7^{2}																						5
1	2	3		5	6	10		14	8^{2}	11^{1}	9^{3}	13	4			12	7																					6
1	2^{1}	3		5		10^{3}	4	13	7^{2}	11	9	12	6				8	14																				7
1	2	3		5	6	7	8	9			13		4					11^{1}	12	10^{2}																		8
1	2	3		5	6	7	8	9^{3}			14		4		13			11^{1}	12	10^{2}																		9
1	2	3	4	5	6	7					9^{2}		11^{1}		13		12		8	10																		10
1	2		4^{1}	5	6	10	8^{2}				14	13	3		7		12		11	9^{3}																		11
1	2	3^{1}	4	5	6	13	8				9	7	12		10^{3}				11^{2}	14																		12
1	2	3	4	5	6	12	8				10	7^{2}	11^{1}		9^{3}		13			14																		13
1	2	3	4	5^{1}	6^{2}	7^{3}	8				14	11	13		9				12		10																	14
	2	3	4		6	10	5▮					7	8^{1}		9^{2}	13			12			1	11															15
	2	3	4		6		13					7^{2}			9^{3}	14	8		12		10	1	11^{1}	5														16
		3^{1}	4	5	6▮		2				13^{3}	7			9	8^{2}					10		14	12	1	11												17
			4	5			8		12			7^{1}	13		9^{2}	10^{3}					11	1		2		3	6	14										18
		4	6	5			2^{1}						12		9	10	11		13			1				3	7	8^{2}										19
		5^{1}	4									8	6		9^{2}	13			12		10	1		2		11	7		3									20
			4	5			6					12	8				13				10	1		3		11	7^{2}		2^{1}	9								21
		3^{2}	4^{1}	5			2					13	6		12						10	1		8		11	7			9								22
	12	3		5			4						6^{1}			13					10	1		2		11	7			9^{2}	8							23
	3^{2}	4▮	6	5			8					13	14		12							1		2^{1}		11				9^{3}		7	10					24
			4	5			6								9	11	12					1^{6}		2	15		7^{1}			13		8	10^{2}	3				25
		3	4	5			6								9^{1}	11								2	1							8	10	7	12			26
	2		4^{2}	5		7^{1}	3						8			10			12											13		11^{3}	9	6		1	14	27
1	3^{1}		4				6	2		8				7^{2}	13	11														12		10	9	5				28
1		3	4	5			2	11		8^{1}				7	13	12																10	9^{2}	6				29
1		3	12	5			2	11						7^{1}	13			8														10^{2}	9	4	6			30
1	12	3▮	4	5			6	2						7^{2}	11^{1}	10				9^{3}													13	14	8			31
1	3		4	5^{1}				2		12		7			11					10													9	6	8			32
1	3^{1}		8^{2}					2		7	14	4			11	13						12				10^{3}							9	6	5			33
1	3			5			7	2			14	4^{1}			11	9^{2}	12									10^{3}							13	6	8			34
1	3	6^{1}		5			11	2			10^{3}	7^{2}			9	13	8▮																14	12▮	4			35
1	3		8	5			6	2			10^{2}	7			9	11^{1}				12													13		4			36
1	3		8	5			6	2			12	7					11			10^{1}													9		4			37
1	3		4^{1}	5			6	2			13	8					7			10^{2}				12									9		11			38
1	3^{1}		8	5			6	2			10^{3}	7^{2}				14				11				12									9	13	4			39
1			4	5		14	11	2			13	7				12				10^{3}				3									9^{2}	6	8^{1}			40
1			4	5		13	11	2^{1}			12	7				14	8							3								10^{2}	9^{3}	6				41
1	14		4	5		10	3^{1}	2^{2}			9	7				13	8							11^{3}										12	6			42

FA Cup

Fourth Qual	Altrincham	(h)	3-1
First Round	Bournemouth	(a)	2-1
Second Round	Hartlepool U	(a)	2-1
Third Round	Stoke C	(a)	0-0
		(h)	1-1

FA Trophy

First Round	Halesowen T	(a)	2-1
Second Round	St Albans C	(h)	1-0
Third Round	Dagenham & R	(h)	0-0
		(a)	0-3

WOKING Conference

Ground: Kingfield Sports Ground, Kingfield, Woking, Surrey GU22 9AA.
Tel: (01483) 772 470.
Year Formed: 1889.
Record Gate: 6,084 (1997 v Coventry City, FA Cup Third Round).
Nickname: The Cards.
Manager: Glenn Cockerill.
Secretary: Phil Ledger.
Colours: Red and white shirts, black shorts, red stockings.

WOKING 2005–06 LEAGUE RECORD

Match No.	Date	Venue	Opponents	Result		H/T Score	Lg. Pos.	Goalscorers	Attendance
1	Aug 13	A	Kidderminster H	L	1-2	0-0	—	Richards [54]	1926
2	16	H	Stevenage Bor	W	3-2	1-2	—	Selley (pen) [10], MacDonald [51], Ferguson [88]	2592
3	20	H	Burton Alb	D	2-2	0-2	10	McAllister [86], Selley (pen) [90]	1692
4	26	A	York C	L	1-2	0-0	—	Richards [58]	2302
5	29	H	Gravesend & N	L	1-3	0-2	—	Selley [71]	1770
6	Sept 3	A	Accrington S	L	1-2	0-1	20	Rawle [89]	959
7	10	H	Southport	W	1-0	0-0	14	Richards [90]	1477
8	17	A	Cambridge U	W	2-0	0-0	12	McAllister [54], Murray [78]	2345
9	20	H	Canvey Is	D	1-1	1-1	—	Chenery (og) [45]	1543
10	24	A	Tamworth	W	1-0	0-0	11	Richards [62]	1021
11	27	A	Exeter C	D	1-1	0-1	—	Murray [76]	3082
12	Oct 1	H	Scarborough	W	4-0	2-0	9	Richards 3 (1 pen) [5, 18 (p), 62], McAllister [46]	1840
13	8	H	Grays Ath	D	1-1	1-1	9	Richards [21]	1995
14	15	A	Forest Green R	W	3-0	3-0	8	McAllister [2], Murray [13], Richards [29]	875
15	29	H	Halifax T	D	2-2	1-0	8	Murray [22], Ferguson [63]	2054
16	Nov 12	A	Hereford U	L	0-4	0-1	9		2498
17	19	H	Morecambe	L	0-1	0-1	9		2069
18	26	A	Dagenham & R	W	3-1	2-1	9	Richards [4], Cockerill L [7], McAllister [85]	1138
19	Dec 10	A	Altrincham	W	4-0	2-0	9	Richards 2 [3, 54], Evans [42], Watson [62]	825
20	26	H	Crawley T	D	0-0	0-0	9		2643
21	31	H	Dagenham & R	D	0-0	0-0	9		1806
22	Jan 2	A	Crawley T	D	2-2	1-0	9	Richards [32], Selley [79]	2073
23	7	H	Kidderminster H	L	0-1	0-0	9		1514
24	21	A	Burton Alb	D	1-1	1-1	10	Murray [21]	2061
25	24	A	Stevenage Bor	D	1-1	0-0	—	McAllister [87]	2152
26	28	H	York C	W	2-0	1-0	9	Richards [24], Ferguson [52]	1938
27	Feb 11	H	Tamworth	W	5-0	2-0	9	Evans [28], Sharpling [31], Richards (pen) [61], Watson [81], Ferguson [90]	2030
28	18	A	Scarborough	D	1-1	0-1	9	Ferguson [90]	1278
29	21	H	Exeter C	W	1-0	0-0	—	Richards (pen) [81]	1536
30	Mar 4	H	Cambridge U	L	0-1	0-0	9		2066
31	11	A	Grays Ath	D	2-2	1-2	10	Richards 2 [17, 83]	1256
32	21	H	Aldershot T	L	1-2	0-2	—	MacDonald [84]	3244
33	28	A	Halifax T	L	0-1	0-1	—		1465
34	Apr 1	H	Hereford U	D	1-1	1-0	12	McAllister [45]	1929
35	4	A	Canvey Is	W	2-0	2-0	—	Murray [8], Ferguson [37]	358
36	8	A	Morecambe	L	1-3	0-3	12	Ferguson [63]	1468
37	10	A	Southport	L	0-1	0-1	—		1054
38	15	H	Accrington S	L	0-1	0-1	13		2665
39	17	A	Gravesend & N	L	0-2	0-1	13		776
40	22	A	Aldershot T	D	1-1	1-0	13	Richards [7]	2704
41	25	H	Forest Green R	W	2-1	1-1	—	Evans [15], Richards (pen) [55]	890
42	29	H	Altrincham	W	3-1	3-0	11	McAllister [17], Richards (pen) [32], Watson [40]	1650

Final League Position: 11

GOALSCORERS

League (58): Richards 21 (5 pens), McAllister 8, Ferguson 7, Murray 6, Selley 4 (2 pens), Evans 3, Watson 3, MacDonald 2, Cockerill L 1, Rawle 1, Sharpling 1, own goal 1.
FA Cup (6): Ferguson 2, Evans 1, Jackson 1, McAllister 1, Oliver 1.
Football League Trophy (4): Rawle 2, Blackman 1, Richards 1.
FA Trophy (16): McAllister 4, Ferguson 3, Evans 2, Hutchinson 2, Murray 1, Rawle 1, Selley 1 (pen), Sharpling 1, Smith 1.

Jalal 41	Jackson 33 + 2	Cockerill L 10 + 6	Murray 39	MacDonald 27 + 3	Aggrey 5	Blackman 11 + 16	Selley 18 + 5	Richards 35 + 3	McAllister 33 + 6	Evans 31 + 3	El-Salahi 17 + 5	Sharpling 5 + 3	Reed 4 + 2	Ferguson 35 + 2	Smith 27 + 5	Rawle 4 + 13	Nethercott 32 + 1	Oliver 13	Watson 14 + 1	Cockerill S — + 3	Hutchinson 19 + 1	Oyedele 6 + 5	Buari 2 + 4	Davies 1 + 1	*Match No.*
1	2	3	4	5	6^{1}	7	8	9	10^{2}	11	12	13													1
1	2		4■	5		12	8	9		11	6	7^{1}	3	10^{2}	13										2
1	2			5		7	8	9	12	11	6		3	10^{2}	4^{1}	13									3
1	2	12	4	5		7^{1}	8	9	13	11^{2}	6		3	10											4
1		3	4	5		7^{1}	8	9	14	12	6		11^{2}	13	2	10^{3}									5
1	12		4	3^{1}		7■	8	9^{2}	10^{3}	11	2			14		13	5	6							6
1	2		4	3				14	10	11	12		13	7^{1}	8^{2}	9^{3}	5	6							7
1	2		4	3		13		14	10^{2}	11^{1}			12	7	8	9^{3}	5	6							8
1	2		4	3				9	10	11				8	7		5	6							9
1	2		4	3		12		9^{2}	10	11				7^{1}	8	13	5	6							10
1	2		4	3		12		9^{2}	10	11				7	8^{1}	13	5	6							11
1	2		4	3		14	12	9^{3}	10^{2}	11				7	8^{1}	13	5	6							12
1	2		4	3^{1}			13	9	10^{3}	11	12			7	8^{2}	14	5	6							13
1	2	14	4			7^{1}	12	9	10^{3}		3			8^{2}	11	13	5	6							14
1	2		4			12		9	10^{2}	11	3			7^{1}	8	13	5	6							15
1	2		4			12	13	9	10^{3}	11^{2}	3			7	8^{1}	14	5	6							16
1	2	13	4			7^{2}	8	9	10		3^{1}			11		12	5	6							17
1	2	11	4			12	13	9	10^{2}					7^{1}	8		5	6	3						18
1	2	3				13		9^{3}	10	11	4			7^{1}	8^{2}	14	5		6	12					19
1	2		4		6		8	9	10	11	3			7					5						20
1	2		4		6		8	9	10	11				7^{1}		12	5		3						21
1	2		4		6	13	8	9		11				7		10^{2}	5^{1}		3		12				22
1	2		4		6		8	9	10^{2}	11^{1}		12		7		13			5		3				23
1	2		4				8	9		11				10	7		5		3		6				24
1	2^{1}		4				8	9	13	11^{3}	12	14		10	7^{2}		5		6		3				25
1			4	12			8	9	10	13	3	7^{1}		11^{2}	2		5				6				26
1		14	4	12				9	10^{3}	11	2	7^{2}		8			5^{1}		3		6	13			27
1			4	5				9	10^{1}	11	2	7		8					3		6	12			28
1			4	12				9■	10	11	2^{1}	7^{2}		8	13				3		6	5			29
1	2	13	4	5		9^{2}	8		10	11					7^{1}		12		3		6				30
1	13		4	5		12	8	9	10					7	11^{1}		6^{2}		3		2				31
1	2^{1}	13	4	5		10^{3}		9	14	11				8	12		6				3		7^{2}		32
1	2	3^{2}		5		14	8	9^{3}	10	12				7	11^{1}		6				4		13		33
1	2	3	4	5		12			10	11^{1}				9	7		6				8				34
1	2	3^{2}	4	5		12			10	11^{1}				9	7		6				8	13			35
1		3	4	5		8^{2}			10		2			9^{3}	7^{1}		6			14	11	12	13		36
1		11^{1}	4	5		7^{2}		14	13		2			9	12		6				3	8	10^{3}		37
1	2		4	5				9	10					8	11^{1}		6				3	7	12		38
1	2		4	5			8	9	10^{2}					7■	12		6				3	11^{1}	13		39
1	2	11^{2}	4	5		13		9	10	7^{1}					8		6				3	12			40
1^{G}	2		4	5				9	10	11					7^{1}		6		12		3■	8		15	41
	2		4	5		14		9	10^{3}	11	12				7		6^{1}		3	13		8^{2}		1	42

FA Cup

Fourth Qual	Thurrock	(h)	3-0
First Round	Southport	(a)	1-1
		(h)	1-0
Second Round	Northwich Vic	(h)	0-0
		(a)	1-2

Football League Trophy

First Round	Nottingham F	(h)	3-2
Second Round	Cheltenham T	(h)	1-5

FA Trophy

First Round	Uxbridge	(a)	2-1
Second Round	Northwich Vic	(h)	1-1
		(a)	2-1
Third Round	Welling U	(h)	3-2
Fourth Round	Stafford R	(h)	1-1
		(a)	4-2
Semi-Final	Boreham Wood	(a)	1-0
		(h)	2-0
Final *(at Upton Park)*	Grays Ath		0-2

YORK CITY

Conference

Ground: KitKat Crescent, York YO30 7AQ.
Tel: (01904) 624 447.
Year Formed: 1922.
Record Gate: 28,123 (1938 v Huddersfield T, FA Cup Sixth Round).
Nickname: Minster Men.
Manager: Billy McEwan.
Colours: Red shirts, navy shorts, navy stockings.

YORK CITY 2005–06 LEAGUE RECORD

Match No.	*Date*	*Venue*	*Opponents*	*Result*		*H/T Score*	*Lg. Pos.*	*Goalscorers*	*Attendance*
1	Aug 13	H	Crawley T	D	0-0	0-0	—		2276
2	16	A	Southport	W	4-1	3-1	—	O'Neill 3 [3, 37, 81], Convery [19]	1646
3	20	A	Grays Ath	D	1-1	0-0	7	Bishop [69]	1272
4	26	H	Woking	W	2-1	0-0	—	Bishop (pen) [75], Dudgeon [78]	2302
5	29	A	Halifax T	L	0-1	0-0	—		2078
6	Sept 2	H	Cambridge U	W	1-0	0-0	—	Donaldson [53]	2666
7	10	A	Forest Green R	W	2-1	1-0	3	Dudgeon [17], Convery [68]	889
8	17	H	Altrincham	W	5-0	2-0	2	O'Neill [25], Donaldson [38], Dudgeon [52], Bishop [62], Stewart [82]	2634
9	20	H	Dagenham & R	D	1-1	1-0	—	Bishop [36]	2927
10	24	A	Aldershot T	L	1-2	0-1	5	Donaldson [64]	2470
11	27	A	Tamworth	W	3-0	1-0	—	Donaldson 2 [27, 57], Convery [63]	1005
12	Oct 1	H	Exeter C	W	4-2	2-1	2	Bishop 2 (1 pen) [21 (p), 90], Stewart [38], Donaldson [70]	3503
13	8	A	Gravesend & N	D	2-2	1-1	3	Donaldson [10], Bishop [86]	1133
14	15	H	Canvey Is	W	2-1	0-0	2	Convery [78], Bishop [89]	3070
15	29	A	Accrington S	L	1-2	0-1	4	Bishop [63]	2193
16	Nov 12	H	Burton Alb	L	0-1	0-0	5		2411
17	19	A	Kidderminster H	D	0-0	0-0	6		1768
18	26	A	Morecambe	L	0-2	0-1	7		1778
19	Dec 10	A	Hereford U	L	0-1	0-0	8		1950
20	26	H	Scarborough	W	3-1	1-1	8	Bishop [45], Donaldson [57], McGurk [85]	4921
21	31	H	Morecambe	D	1-1	1-0	8	Convery [41]	2712
22	Jan 2	A	Scarborough	D	2-2	1-1	8	Bishop 2 [38, 72]	4057
23	7	A	Crawley T	W	1-0	0-0	8	Dudgeon [61]	1514
24	10	H	Stevenage Bor	L	0-1	0-1	—		2325
25	21	H	Grays Ath	L	1-2	1-1	8	O'Neill [5]	2461
26	24	H	Southport	D	0-0	0-0	—		2176
27	28	A	Woking	L	0-2	0-1	8		1938
28	Feb 12	H	Aldershot T	W	3-2	1-1	8	Convery [34], Bishop A [49], Donaldson [52]	2401
29	18	A	Exeter C	W	3-1	1-1	8	Dudgeon [33], Bishop N [48], Bishop A [72]	3381
30	21	H	Tamworth	W	2-1	1-0	—	Bishop A [2], Donaldson [63]	2153
31	25	H	Forest Green R	W	5-1	4-1	6	Bishop A 3 (1 pen) [15 (p), 39, 41], McGurk [24], Thomas [61]	2314
32	Mar 7	A	Dagenham & R	W	2-0	0-0	—	Donaldson [86], Bishop A [90]	973
33	11	H	Gravesend & N	W	1-0	1-0	4	Dudgeon [9]	2902
34	18	A	Canvey Is	D	1-1	0-0	4	Dunning [57]	754
35	25	H	Accrington S	L	2-4	2-1	5	Donaldson [22], Bishop A [41]	3912
36	Apr 1	A	Burton Alb	D	0-0	0-0	6		2605
37	4	A	Altrincham	W	3-0	3-0	—	Donaldson 2 [24, 40], Bishop A [33]	1237
38	9	H	Kidderminster H	D	2-2	0-0	6	Bishop A (pen) [52], Donaldson [89]	3376
39	14	A	Cambridge U	L	0-2	0-0	—		3188
40	17	H	Halifax T	L	0-2	0-0	7		4084
41	22	A	Stevenage Bor	D	1-1	1-1	7	Donaldson [37]	2701
42	29	H	Hereford U	L	1-3	0-2	8	Bishop A [57]	2755

Final League Position: 8

GOALSCORERS

League (63): Bishop A 23 (4 pens), Donaldson 16, Convery 6, Dudgeon 6, O'Neill 5, McGurk 2, Stewart 2, Bishop N 1, Dunning 1, Thomas 1.
FA Cup (4): Bishop A 2 (1 pen), Convery 1, Donaldson 1.
FA Trophy (1): Bishop A 1.

Porter 41	Price 21 + 1	Peat 20 + 3	Mallon 1 + 4	Hotte 16 + 4	McGurk 36	Convery 38 + 4	Panther 36 + 1	Donaldson 42	Mansaram 4 + 1	Dunning 41	Bishop A 35 + 5	Stewart 2 + 19	O'Neill 25 + 12	Merris 18 + 7	Dudgeon 30 + 1	Yalcin 4 + 7	Webster — + 3	Palmer — + 3	Andrews 9	Bertos 3 + 3	Stockdale 1 + 1	Horwood 4	Barwick 3	Craddock 4	N'Toya 2 + 1	Bishop N 14	Thomas 12 + 2	Kamara — + 2	Rhodes — + 1	Match No.
1	2	3	4[1]	5	6	7	8	9	10[2]	11	12	13																		1
1	2	3		5	6	7[3]	8	9	10[1]	11	12	13	4[2]	14																2
1	2	3		5■	6	7	8	9	10[1]	11	12		4[2]	13																3
1	2	3			6	7	8	9	10[2]	11[1]	13		4		5	12														4
1	2	3		5	6	7[1]	8	9		11[2]	10	12	4			13														5
1	2	3		5	6	7[1]	8	9	13	11	10		4[2]			12														6
1	2		12		6	7[2]	8	9		11[3]	10[1]		4	3	5	14	13													7
1	2				6	7[1]	8	9		11	10[3]	14	4[2]	3	5	12		13												8
1	2				6	7	8	9		11	10		4	3	5															9
1	2				6	7[2]	8	9		11	10	13	4	3	5[1]			12												10
1	2				6	7	8	9		4	10[2]	11[1]	12	3	5			13												11
1	2				6	7	8	9		4	10	11[1]	12	3	5															12
1	2			12	6	7	8	9		4	10	13	11[2]	3	5[1]															13
1	2	13		5[1]	6	7	8[3]	9		4	10	14	11	3[2]	12															14
1	2		12		6	7[1]		9		4	10	13	11[2]	3	5	8														15
1	2		12		6	7[1]		9		4	10	13	11[2]	3		8			5											16
1	2		13		6	7		9		4	10[2]		12	3		8			5	11[1]										17
1[G]	2				6	7[1]		9		4	10		12						8	11	15	3	5							18
					6	12		9		4		13	10		5	7[1]			2	3	1	11	8[2]							19
1				2	6	7	13	9		4	10	14	11[3]	12					5			3[1]	8[2]							20
1				5	6	7	8	9		4	10		11	12					2			3[1]								21
1				5		7[1]	8	9		4	10		11[2]	3	6	12			2	13										22
1				5		7	8	9[2]		4	10	13	11[1]	3	6				2	12										23
1				5		7[1]	8	9		4	10	12	11[2]	3	6				2	13										24
1				5		7[1]	8	9		4			11	3	6	12								2	10					25
1	12			5		7	8	9		4	13		11	3[1]	6									2	10[2]					26
1	12			5		7[2]	8	9		4	10		11	3[1]	6									2	13					27
1		3			6	7	8	9		4	10	12			5									2		11[1]				28
1		3			6	7	8[1]	9		4	10[2]		13		5		12									11	2			29
1		3			6	7	8	9		4[1]	10[2]	12	13		5											11	2			30
1		3		12	6	7	8	9		4[2]	10[3]	13	14		5[1]											11	2			31
1		3		5	6	7	8	9		4	10															11	2			32
1		3			6	7[1]	8	9		4[2]	10		13	12	5											11	2			33
1	12	3			6	7	8	9		4[2]	10			13	5											11	2[1]			34
1	2	3		12	6	7	8	9		4[3]	10		14		5[1]											11[2]	13			35
1	2[1]	3			6	7	8	9		4	10				5											11	12			36
1		3			6	7[1]	8	9		4[3]	10		13		5											11[2]	2	14	12	37
1		3			6	7	8	9		4[2]	10	12	13		5											11	2[1]			38
1		3■		12	6	7[2]	8	9		4[3]	10	14	13		5											11	2[1]			39
1				5	6	13	8	9		4[2]	10	12	11	3[1]	2												7			40
1	2	3			6	12	8	9			10		11[2]		5		13									7	4[1]			41
1		3[2]			6	14	8	9		4[3]	10		7	13	5											11	2[1]	12		42

FA Cup

Fourth Qual	Gainsborough T	(a)	4-0
First Round	Grays Ath	(h)	0-3

FA Trophy

First Round	Northwich Vic	(h)	1-2

NATIONWIDE CONFERENCE SECOND DIVISION 2005–06

NATIONWIDE CONFERENCE NORTH FINAL LEAGUE TABLE

			Home					Away					Total						
		P	W	D	L	F	A	W	D	L	F	A	W	D	L	F	A	GD	Pts
1	Northwich Victoria	42	16	3	2	53	16	13	2	6	44	33	29	5	8	97	49	48	92
2	Stafford Rangers	42	12	5	4	36	17	13	5	3	32	17	25	10	7	68	34	34	85
3	Nuneaton Borough	42	13	7	1	43	21	9	4	8	25	22	22	11	9	68	43	25	77
4	Droylsden	42	15	3	3	52	24	5	9	7	28	32	20	12	10	80	56	24	72
5	Harrogate Town	42	14	4	3	35	16	8	1	12	31	40	22	5	15	66	56	10	71
6	Kettering Town	42	14	2	5	38	18	5	8	8	25	31	19	10	13	63	49	14	67
7	Stalybridge Celtic	42	15	3	3	51	23	4	6	11	23	31	19	9	14	74	54	20	66
8	Worcester City	42	7	8	6	27	20	9	6	6	31	26	16	14	12	58	46	12	62
9	Moor Green	42	5	10	7	28	33	10	6	4	39	31	15	16	11	67	64	3	61
10	Hinckley United	42	7	7	7	31	28	7	9	5	29	27	14	16	12	60	55	5	58
11	Hyde United	42	7	6	8	39	37	8	5	8	29	24	15	11	16	68	61	7	56
12	Hucknall Town	42	9	6	6	33	25	5	7	9	23	29	14	13	15	56	54	2	55
13	Workington	42	7	6	8	29	29	7	7	7	31	33	14	13	15	60	62	−2	55
14	Barrow	42	9	6	6	39	33	3	5	13	23	34	12	11	19	62	67	−5	47
15	Lancaster City	42	7	8	6	29	26	5	3	13	23	40	12	11	19	52	66	−14	47
16	Gainsborough Trinity	42	6	8	7	26	30	5	5	11	19	35	11	13	18	45	65	−20	46
17	Alfreton Town	42	9	5	6	29	27	1	10	11	17	31	10	15	17	46	58	−12	45
18	Vauxhall Motors	42	6	3	12	28	37	6	4	11	22	34	12	7	23	50	71	−21	43
19	Worksop Town	42	7	8	6	27	31	3	3	15	19	40	10	11	21	46	71	−25	41
20	Leigh RMI	42	7	6	8	20	25	2	7	12	25	54	9	14	20	45	79	−34	40
21	Redditch United	42	6	5	10	29	34	3	7	11	23	44	9	12	21	52	78	−26	39
22	Hednesford	42	3	7	11	16	37	4	7	10	26	50	7	14	21	42	87	−45	35

NATIONWIDE CONFERENCE NORTH LEADING GOALSCORER

	League	*FA Cup*	*Trophy*	*Total*
Jon Allan (Northwich Victoria)	24	1	6	31

NATIONWIDE CONFERENCE SOUTH FINAL LEAGUE TABLE

			Home					Away					Total						
		P	W	D	L	F	A	W	D	L	F	A	W	D	L	F	A	GD	Pts
1	Weymouth	42	17	3	1	47	13	13	1	7	33	21	30	4	8	80	34	46	94
2	St Albans City	42	17	1	3	54	19	10	4	7	40	28	27	5	10	94	47	47	86
3	Farnborough	42	12	4	5	33	17	11	5	5	32	24	23	9	10	65	41	24	78
4	Lewes	42	12	4	5	38	27	9	6	6	40	30	21	10	11	78	57	21	73
5	Histon	42	12	4	5	41	30	9	4	8	29	26	21	8	13	70	56	14	71
6	Havant & Waterlooville	42	12	5	4	29	17	9	5	7	35	31	21	10	11	64	48	16	70
7	Cambridge City	42	10	4	7	35	23	10	6	5	43	23	20	10	12	78	46	32	67
8	Eastleigh	42	12	1	8	33	28	9	2	10	32	30	21	3	18	65	58	7	66
9	Welling United	42	11	8	2	32	20	5	9	7	27	24	16	17	9	59	44	15	65
10	Thurrock	42	9	2	10	33	31	7	8	6	27	29	16	10	16	60	60	0	58
11	Dorchester Town	42	7	5	9	32	41	9	2	10	28	32	16	7	19	60	73	−13	55
12	Bognor Regis Town	42	7	8	6	31	23	5	5	11	23	32	12	13	17	54	55	−1	49
13	Sutton United	42	9	7	5	28	25	4	3	14	20	36	13	10	19	48	61	−13	49
14	Weston-Super-Mare	42	5	4	12	25	46	9	3	9	31	42	14	7	21	56	88	−32	49
15	Bishop's Stortford	42	8	5	8	35	33	3	10	8	20	30	11	15	16	55	63	−8	48
16	Yeading	42	3	5	13	18	38	10	3	8	29	24	13	8	21	47	62	−15	47
17	Eastbourne Borough	42	4	12	5	24	24	6	4	11	27	36	10	16	16	51	60	−9	46
18	Newport County	42	7	3	11	28	34	5	5	11	22	33	12	8	22	50	67	−17	44
19	Basingstoke Town	42	6	5	10	21	37	6	3	12	26	35	12	8	22	47	72	−25	44
20	Hayes	42	8	1	12	26	28	3	8	10	21	32	11	9	22	47	60	−13	42
21	Carshalton Athletic	42	4	10	7	21	27	4	6	11	21	41	8	16	18	42	68	−26	40
22	Maidenhead United	42	3	5	13	25	49	5	4	12	24	50	8	9	25	49	99	−50	33

NATIONWIDE CONFERENCE SOUTH LEADING GOALSCORER

	League	*FA Cup*	*Trophy*	*Total*
Paul Booth (Cambridge City)	24	6	2	32

CONFERENCE SECOND DIVISION PLAY-OFFS

NORTH PLAY-OFF SEMI-FINALS
Nuneaton Borough 0, Droylsden 1
Stafford Rangers 1, Harrogate Town 0

FINAL
Droylsden 1, Stafford Rangers 1
Stafford Rangers won 5-3 on penalties.

SOUTH PLAY-OFF SEMI-FINAL
Farnborough Town 0, Histon 3
(Lewes declined to play in the play-offs).

FINAL
St Albans City 2, Histon 0

Stafford Rangers and St Albans City qualified for the Conference National.

NATIONWIDE CONFERENCE SECOND DIVISION NORTH RESULTS 2005–06

	Alfreton T	Barrow	Droylsden	Gainsborough T	Harrogate T	Hednesford T	Hinckley U	Hucknall T	Hyde U	Kettering T	Lancaster C	Leigh RMI	Moor Green	Northwich Vic	Nuneaton B	Redditch U	Stafford R	Stalybridge C	Vauxhall M	Worcester C	Workington	Worksop T
Alfreton T	—	2-1	1-3	1-2	4-1	3-2	1-1	1-1	2-0	1-1	0-2	1-1	1-1	2-4	1-0	2-1	2-1	0-0	1-2	1-0	1-3	2-1
Barrow	2-2	—	2-0	3-1	3-1	3-1	2-5	2-0	2-2	0-1	1-4	3-1	2-2	1-1	0-3	1-1	1-1	4-2	0-2	0-2	6-1	1-0
Droylsden	1-0	2-2	—	1-2	2-1	1-1	3-1	2-3	1-0	3-1	6-1	4-1	3-0	4-3	2-2	2-1	2-1	1-0	4-0	3-0	2-3	3-1
Gainsborough T	2-2	3-2	2-2	—	0-2	1-1	1-2	3-2	0-3	0-2	1-0	2-1	2-2	1-2	1-2	2-2	1-1	1-0	1-1	0-1	0-0	2-0
Harrogate T	1-0	2-1	1-1	2-0	—	2-3	2-1	1-0	1-0	1-1	3-1	3-0	3-0	0-2	2-0	1-1	0-2	1-0	2-1	4-1	1-1	2-0
Hednesford T	1-0	0-3	0-1	1-1	0-4	—	3-4	1-1	0-2	2-1	1-0	1-3	1-2	1-4	0-0	1-1	0-2	1-1	0-1	0-4	0-0	2-1
Hinckley U	2-2	1-0	1-1	1-0	1-3	1-2	—	3-1	2-1	1-1	3-3	5-1	1-2	1-3	0-1	1-1	0-1	1-1	2-1	1-3	0-0	3-0
Hucknall T	1-0	2-1	2-0	4-1	4-1	2-2	0-2	—	1-3	1-1	0-0	2-2	2-2	3-2	0-1	4-0	0-2	2-1	1-2	1-2	1-0	0-0
Hyde U	2-3	2-2	2-2	2-0	3-1	4-2	0-1	0-0	—	3-0	2-4	3-3	3-2	1-3	1-0	1-3	1-3	1-3	2-3	4-0	1-1	1-1
Kettering T	1-0	1-3	1-0	1-2	0-2	4-0	2-2	0-0	3-2	—	2-0	4-0	0-3	2-0	3-0	4-0	0-1	4-1	1-0	2-1	2-1	1-0
Lancaster C	2-2	3-0	2-2	2-3	2-1	1-0	2-2	0-1	1-3	0-1	—	2-0	3-3	1-2	1-1	1-0	1-1	2-2	1-0	0-0	0-1	2-1
Leigh RMI	0-0	1-1	0-1	0-0	3-1	0-0	1-0	2-1	1-1	0-2	1-2	—	1-3	2-1	1-0	2-1	1-3	2-1	1-1	1-4	0-1	0-1
Moor Green	0-0	1-1	1-1	1-1	2-2	1-2	1-1	2-4	1-2	1-1	3-1	4-1	—	1-2	0-4	2-1	0-1	1-1	2-1	1-1	1-4	1-0
Northwich Vic	1-1	2-0	2-1	2-0	3-0	8-0	2-0	2-0	1-2	4-1	3-2	1-0	1-1	—	2-2	5-1	3-1	1-0	3-1	0-1	4-1	4-1
Nuneaton B	1-0	2-1	2-2	3-1	4-0	3-2	2-0	2-2	1-0	2-2	3-0	3-1	2-2	1-2	—	2-1	1-1	0-0	3-2	0-0	3-1	3-1
Redditch U	1-0	2-1	4-1	1-1	1-3	1-2	1-1	1-1	1-1	2-1	0-1	1-2	0-1	1-2	3-0	—	0-1	1-4	3-0	2-2	3-6	0-3
Stafford R	1-0	3-1	0-0	3-0	0-1	1-1	2-3	2-0	1-0	1-3	3-0	0-0	1-3	2-0	2-0	3-0	—	1-0	3-0	1-1	2-2	4-2
Stalybridge C	3-0	2-1	1-1	1-0	3-1	3-0	1-1	2-1	1-2	2-0	2-1	6-1	4-1	3-3	2-0	5-1	2-3	—	2-1	2-3	2-1	2-1
Vauxhall M	3-1	0-1	2-4	1-2	0-2	0-0	0-1	0-2	0-2	1-1	1-0	4-4	1-2	0-3	1-2	1-2	1-3	4-2	—	1-0	2-1	5-2
Worcester C	2-2	1-0	1-2	2-1	2-0	6-2	0-0	0-1	2-2	2-0	2-0	2-0	0-2	0-1	0-1	2-2	1-1	0-1	0-0	—	1-1	1-1
Workington	2-0	0-0	2-1	2-0	2-4	2-0	1-1	1-1	1-0	3-2	1-1	0-0	1-4	5-2	0-2	1-2	0-1	1-2	1-2	2-2	—	1-2
Worksop T	1-1	2-1	3-2	1-1	1-0	3-3	0-0	2-1	1-1	2-1	2-0	3-3	0-2	1-2	0-4	1-1	0-1	2-1	1-1	0-3	1-2	—

NATIONWIDE CONFERENCE SECOND DIVISION SOUTH RESULTS 2005–06

	Basingstoke T	Bishop's Stortford	Bognor Regis T	Cambridge C	Carshalton Ath	Dorchester T	Eastbourne B	Eastleigh	Farnborough T	Havant & W	Hayes	Histon	Lewes	Maidenhead U	Newport Co	St Albans C	Sutton U	Thurrock	Welling U	Weston-S-Mare	Weymouth	Yeading
Basingstoke T	—	1-1	2-3	0-5	2-1	2-0	2-2	0-1	0-1	2-1	1-1	0-1	1-5	0-1	1-0	1-1	2-0	0-3	2-2	2-1	0-3	0-4
Bishop's Stortford	1-1	—	2-1	1-3	3-3	5-2	0-1	4-1	1-1	1-3	1-0	5-0	0-3	1-0	0-1	1-3	2-1	2-2	1-1	2-3	0-2	2-1
Bognor Regis T	2-1	2-2	—	4-2	1-1	1-1	2-1	2-0	0-1	0-1	1-1	3-1	2-2	8-1	1-1	2-1	0-0	0-1	0-0	0-1	0-2	0-2
Cambridge C	1-0	1-1	2-0	—	0-0	1-2	2-3	2-1	0-2	0-0	3-1	3-1	0-2	3-0	0-2	4-3	3-0	6-0	0-0	3-0	1-3	0-2
Carshalton Ath	1-2	0-0	1-1	0-2	—	3-1	2-2	1-3	2-2	1-3	1-2	0-0	2-2	0-1	1-0	0-2	0-0	0-0	1-0	1-1	2-1	2-2
Dorchester T	2-1	1-3	3-5	1-0	2-0	—	3-0	1-3	1-1	1-1	2-2	0-3	2-2	1-3	2-2	1-4	0-5	2-0	0-3	1-2	2-0	4-0
Eastbourne B	2-3	1-1	0-0	1-1	1-1	1-1	—	0-1	0-1	2-2	0-0	1-1	3-1	3-3	2-0	1-1	2-1	0-0	1-1	1-2	0-2	2-1
Eastleigh	0-3	0-1	1-0	1-1	3-1	1-2	2-1	—	2-0	2-6	2-1	1-2	2-0	2-1	2-0	0-2	2-0	3-0	1-3	4-1	2-0	0-3
Farnborough T	1-0	3-0	2-1	0-3	4-0	0-1	2-3	1-0	—	4-1	0-0	0-2	2-2	3-1	2-1	0-0	2-1	0-0	1-0	5-0	0-1	1-0
Havant & W	2-0	2-2	1-0	1-1	1-1	1-0	1-0	2-1	1-0	—	1-1	3-1	1-0	2-1	1-2	0-1	0-1	1-2	0-0	3-2	2-1	3-0
Hayes	1-2	2-0	1-2	2-0	1-2	0-1	0-2	1-0	0-1	1-2	—	2-1	2-2	2-1	3-2	0-1	2-1	0-1	1-3	4-1	1-2	0-1
Histon	2-0	3-2	2-2	1-0	0-1	4-1	3-1	1-0	3-6	3-1	2-3	—	1-1	3-0	2-3	0-5	3-0	3-1	1-1	1-1	2-1	1-0
Lewes	3-0	2-1	1-1	2-2	2-1	3-2	1-0	1-2	6-2	0-2	2-1	0-3	—	2-2	1-0	0-2	2-0	0-0	2-1	5-2	2-3	1-0
Maidenhead U	0-0	2-2	1-2	0-5	0-2	2-3	2-6	2-2	1-2	3-1	2-1	1-4	0-1	—	1-1	0-4	2-0	1-3	2-4	2-4	0-0	1-2
Newport Co	2-0	1-0	1-0	0-2	4-1	0-2	1-1	0-2	1-2	2-3	1-0	0-1	2-3	3-0	—	1-3	1-0	3-4	2-2	2-2	0-3	1-3
St Albans C	3-1	3-0	2-0	2-4	3-0	2-0	5-0	2-4	2-2	2-0	1-0	1-0	2-0	4-0	1-0	—	3-1	3-2	3-1	1-2	4-0	5-2
Sutton U	0-1	1-1	1-0	3-2	1-1	1-0	2-0	0-3	1-0	1-1	2-1	1-1	1-5	4-1	1-1	4-0	—	1-1	2-1	1-2	0-3	0-0
Thurrock	4-1	2-1	3-0	0-3	2-1	0-1	1-0	3-1	0-2	0-2	1-1	1-2	2-3	1-2	4-2	2-1	5-3	—	1-1	0-1	1-2	0-1
Welling U	3-2	0-0	2-0	1-1	2-0	4-3	1-2	2-1	1-0	2-2	1-0	1-1	2-1	3-3	1-1	3-1	0-0	1-1	—	1-0	1-0	0-1
Weston-S-Mare	4-3	0-1	2-2	1-3	2-0	0-4	1-0	1-4	1-1	1-3	1-1	1-4	1-2	1-1	2-1	3-1	2-3	0-5	0-1	—	1-3	0-3
Weymouth	1-1	3-1	2-0	1-1	4-0	1-0	2-1	2-0	1-2	1-0	5-1	1-0	2-0	4-0	4-0	3-2	3-1	2-0	2-1	2-1	—	1-1
Yeading	0-4	0-0	0-3	1-2	3-4	0-1	1-1	2-2	0-3	2-0	2-3	1-0	0-3	0-2	1-2	2-2	0-2	1-1	1-0	1-2	0-1	—

REVIEW OF THE SCOTTISH SEASON 2005–06

Gretna. Heart of Midlothian. In that order, I think. On to Celtic, St Mirren, Cowdenbeath. That about covers the season.

And the first two met in the Cup Final. Everyone seems to need a penalty shoot-out these days!

To business: In the SPL there was a surprising start to the season with a string of confident wins for Hearts, under George Burley, which put them firmly on top. When he departed, the magic was not easy to replace; there were a few stutters, which allowed Celtic to slide through into the first place, and they never lost it. Hearts continued to do well enough and took second place, brushing aside a late challenge from Rangers. All was not well at Ibrox, and their season was – for them – a mess. They could not settle down to steadiness in the league, although, as we shall see, they did well enough in Europe. Hibs often looked good, but had blind spots. Then came Kilmarnock, tipped by many of the 'pundits' for relegation. They had not reckoned with Jim Jefferies, and he led his team to a good final position. Aberdeen and Inverness slogged it out for the sixth place. Aberdeen won. Caley Thistle then, in the lower half, won their last five matches without conceding a goal. Dunfermline and Livingston were destined for the bottom place, but Jim Leishman once again produced the needed results. Storms over relegation, a regular feature for the last few seasons, seemed to be brewing, but they dispersed, and St Mirren are welcomed back to the SPL.

The First Division soon divided itself into three groups: going up (this group led for a while by Ross County, but taken over successfully by St Mirren); a middle group who were not too concerned with either promotion or relegation; and a group of three, two of whom might go down. In this third group, Brechin City once again could not hold on, and they were soon destined for the drop. Queen of the South had a poor season, until Ian McCall arrived, and managed to start finding some good results. It was touch-and-go for a while whether they or Stranraer would be involved in the play-offs, but the latter lost some vital points.

In the Second Division, Gretna were in the front all season. They were set on a further move upwards, and they succeeded in no uncertain manner. Although they lost a few games, it is a remarkable fact that for two complete seasons, they have finished no league game without scoring. They went their merry way, and were pursued, at a polite distance, by Morton, who finished second, and very comfortably clear of Peterhead and Partick Thistle, third and fourth. Stirling Albion started the season very badly, but suddenly found what was wrong, and started to move rapidly up the table, finally nearly challenging for the second play-off place. At the foot, Alloa were adrift. Again, a late charge took them out of bottom spot, leaving that to Dumbarton, and leaving a possible life-line with a play-off.

There was much activity at the top end of the Third Division. Berwick Rangers led the way for a while; then Stenhousemuir; and, at the finish, Cowdenbeath. I am tempted to say, at the Finnish.

Cowdenbeath duly celebrated with an enormous crowd on the last afternoon, and the trophy – brought post haste by David Thomson of the SFL (for any of the three teams could have been champions) – was presented by an enthusiastic supporter, local MP, Chancellor Gordon Brown. It was quite an occasion.

The play-offs followed. They are not at all popular with tired managers at the end of a long haul, but, my Goodness! they do draw the crowds and add piquancy to a dying season. Well, someone is happy; someone not so happy. Partick and Peterhead, having disposed of Stranraer and Morton, went into the final in the north with Peterhead having a one-goal advantage; they still had it with moments to go: there followed extra time and penalties, and Partick are happy to be returning to the First Division. The final in the other group saw Alloa triumphantly maintaining their place in the Second Division.

Then to the Cups: the League Challenge Cup was won by St Mirren, with most of the main teams reaching the later stages. Hamilton Accies, always there or thereabouts during the season, were the losing finalists. In the CIS Cup, Celtic disposed of Rangers, and went on to win the final against Dunfermline 2-1. As shortly before this Celtic had scored eight goals against them, the Pars did well to get as near as they did. Livingston reached a semi-final, having removed Hearts on the way. Then the Scottish Cup: Spartans did very well to reach the Fourth Round, where, in a replay, they lost to St Mirren. Incidentally, in that round, six of the eight matches went to replays, and one to penalties. Alloa took nine off luckless Selkirk, and also reached the Fourth, defeating Livingston in a replay in the Third, and at last going out to Accies (in a replay). Gretna scored a round dozen against lower opposition in the first rounds, losing three goals in the process. These were the only goals Gretna *did* lose till the final. The final, Gretna v Hearts, was greeted with tremendous enthusiasm throughout the country, and was wildly exciting. Hearts just made it in the end, fulfilling a promise made by their owner. It was a hard game, played in the best of spirits – and the Hearts crowd generously applauded their junior opponents at the end. Most of the Gretna inhabitants came to the final, together with a large number of others, to cheer on this extraordinary side. They are aiming to go higher. It takes a bold person to bet against it.

Celtic did not last long in Europe: Gordon Strachan's stock did not rise when they lost 5-0 on their first Champions League outing. It was a crushing blow, but Strachan soon took command of the situation, and achieved a solid championship season, meantime bringing on some of Scotland's own young players. Dundee United failed to progress in the UEFA Cup after seeming well set, and Hibs did not last. It was left to Rangers to salvage some pride, and they did this by reaching the knock-out stage of the Champions League. And they very nearly moved forward there, losing only in the last minutes to Villarreal.

Internationals? Walter Smith has had much to encourage him, and perhaps we may now have reached 'the end of the beginning' with him. There is an air of expectancy about, and there have been some spirited performances, culminating with victory in the Kirin Cup in Japan. Still there are not enough young Scots playing first team football in Scotland; but there are some coming through; and they are scoring goals. Isn't that what the game is all about?

ALAN ELLIOTT

Rangers' Alan Hutton (left) and Neil Lennon of Celtic dispute possession in an Auld Firm Game. (ASP)

SCOTTISH LEAGUE PLAY-OFFS 2005–06

SCOTTISH DIVISION 1 SEMI-FINAL FIRST LEG

Wednesday, 3 May 2006

Morton (0) 0

Peterhead (0) 0 3995

Morton: McGurn; Weatherson, Harding, Greacen, Macgregor, Millar, Walker A (Keenan), McLaughlin (Finlayson), McAlistair, McLaren (McLean), Lilley.
Peterhead: Mathers; Shand (Hegarty), Tully, Perry, Cameron, Gibson, Sharp, Buchan, Nicol, Linn (Bavidge), Wood.

Stranraer (1) 1 *(Swift 19)*

Partick T (0) 3 *(McCulloch 61, Roberts 68, 75 (pen))* 1100

Stranraer: Corr; Swift, Keddie■, Wingate, Henderson, Gilfillan■, Hamilton, Aitken (Higgins), Moore (Harty), Hinds, Sharp (Martin).
Partick T: Arthur; Murray, McCulloch, Brady, Smyth, Craig (Hodge), Gibson J (Snowdon), Gibson B, McConalogue (Nicholas), Roberts, Strachan.

SCOTTISH DIVISION 1 SEMI-FINAL SECOND LEG

Saturday, 6 May 2006

Partick T (0) 1 *(Roberts 87)*

Stranraer (0) 2 *(Ross 79, Hamilton 90)* 3596

Partick T: Arthur; Murray, Smyth, Hodge, McCulloch, Gibson J, Gibson B (Snowdon), Brady, Strachan (Nicholas), McConalogue (Ritchie), Roberts.
Stranraer: Morrison; Swift, Wingate, Henderson, Higgins (Hinds), Payne (Aitken), Ross, Hamilton, Sharp, Moore, Harty (Martin).

Peterhead (1) 1 *(Cameron 24 (pen))*

Morton (0) 0 3717

Peterhead: Mathers; Shand (Hegarty), Cameron, Tully, Perry, Gibson, Sharp (Youngson), Buchan, Linn (Bavidge), Wood, Nicol.
Morton: McGurn; Weatherson, Macgregor, Harding, Greacen, Finlayson (Walker J), Millar, McClean (McLaren), Lilley, McLaughlin, McAlistair.

SCOTTISH DIVISION 1 FINAL FIRST LEG

Wednesday, 10 May 2006

Partick T (1) 1 *(Gibson B 34)*

Peterhead (0) 2 *(Sharp 59, Bavidge 85)* 3400

Partick T: Arthur; Murray, Smyth, Hodge, McCulloch, Gibson J, Boyd, Gibson B, Strachan, McConalogue (Ritchie), Roberts.
Peterhead: Mathers; Shand, Tully, Perry, Cameron, Sharp, Buchan, Youngson (Hegarty), Linn (Bavidge), Wood, Nicol.

SCOTTISH DIVISION 1 FINAL SECOND LEG

Sunday, 14 May 2006

Peterhead (1) 1 *(Bavidge 5)*

Partick T (1) 2 *(Roberts 8, Gibson B 90)* 3700

Peterhead: Mathers; Shand (Gibson), Cameron, Tully, Perry, Hegarty (Youngson), Sharp, Buchan, Bavidge, Wood (Linn), Nicol.
Partick T: Arthur; Murray, McCulloch (Nicholas), Snowdon, Smyth, Boyd (Ritchie), Gibson J, McConalogue (Kilgannon), Gibson B, Roberts, Strachan.
aet; Partick T won 4-2 on penalties.

SCOTTISH DIVISION 2 SEMI-FINAL FIRST LEG

Wednesday, 3 May 2006

Arbroath (1) 1 *(Reilly 23)*

Alloa Ath (0) 1 *(Sloan 53)* 1163

Arbroath: Inglis; Rennie, McCulloch, Raeside, Dobbins, Bishop, Black■, McMullen, Reilly, Swankie (Taylor), Stein (Smith) (Miller).
Alloa Ath: Creer; Stevenson A, Ovenstone, Townsley, Bolochoweckjy (Forrest), McColligan, Hamilton, Grant, Brown, Stevenson J (McLeod), Sloan.

Stenhousemuir (0) 0

Berwick R (0) 1 *(Hutchison 75)* 593

Stenhousemuir: Fahey; Menzies, McAlpine, Henderson, McKeown, McBride, Cassidy, Murphy, Diack, Renwick, McGrillen (Templeton).
Berwick R: O'Connor; Murie, McGroaty, McNicoll, Horn, Manson, McLeish, Paliczka (McGarty), Hutchison, Haynes (Lucas), Swanson (Kane).

SCOTTISH DIVISION 2 SEMI-FINAL SECOND LEG

Saturday, 6 May 2006

Alloa Ath (0) 1 *(Stevenson J 69)*

Arbroath (0) 0 1318

Alloa Ath: Creer; Stevenson A, Ovenstone, Townsley, Bolochoweckjy, McColligan, Stevenson J, Grant (McGeown), Brown (Hamilton), McLeod, Sloan.
Arbroath: Inglis; Rennie, McCulloch, Raeside, Dobbins, Bishop, Miller (Watson), McMullen, Reilly (Taylor), Swankie, Stein.

Berwick R (0) 0

Stenhousemuir (0) 0 913

Berwick R: O'Connor; Ramsay (Kane), Horn, McNicoll, Cowan, Manson (Lucas), McLeish, Paliczka (Johnstone), Hutchison, Haynes, Swanson.
Stenhousemuir: McCulloch; Menzies, McAlpine (Fallon), Henderson, McKeown, McBride, Mercer, Murphy, Diack, Sinclair, McGrillen (Templeton).

SCOTTISH DIVISION 2 FINAL FIRST LEG

Wednesday, 10 May 2006

Alloa Ath (2) 4 *(Stevenson A 42 (pen), McLeod 45, Ovenstone 79, 89)*

Berwick R (0) 0 975

Alloa Ath: Creer; Stevenson A, Ovenstone, Townsley, Bolochoweckjy, McColligan, Stevenson J (Nicolson), McGeown, McLeod, Hamilton (Grant), Sloan.
Berwick R: O'Connor; Murie, Horn, Manson (Paliczka), Cowan, Connelly, McLeish, Swanson, Hutchison, Haynes, Little (Ramsay).

SCOTTISH DIVISION 2 FINAL SECOND LEG

Sunday, 14 May 2006

Berwick R (0) 2 *(Horn 55, 80)*

Alloa Ath (1) 1 *(Hamilton 18)* 866

Berwick R: O'Connor; Murie, McGarty, Horn, Cowan, Connelly, McLeish, Paliczka (Johnstone), Hutchison, Swanson (Lucas), Ramsay (Manson).
Alloa Ath: Creer; Stevenson A, Ovenstone, Townsley, Bolochoweckjy, McColligan (Learmonth), Stevenson J, McGeown, McLeod (Brown), Hamilton, Sloan.

ABERDEEN Premier League

Year Formed: 1903. *Ground & Address:* Pittodrie Stadium, Pittodrie St, Aberdeen AB24 5QH. *Telephone:* 01224 650400. *Fax:* 01224 644173. *E-mail:* david@afc.co.uk. *Website:* www.afc.co.uk
Ground Capacity: all seated: 21,421. *Size of Pitch:* 115yd × 72yd.
Executive Director: Duncan Fraser. *Director of Football:* Willie Miller. *Secretary:* David Johnston. *Operations Manager:* John Morgan.
Manager: Jimmy Calderwood. *Assistant Manager:* Jimmy Nichol. *U-19 Manager:* Neil Cooper. *Physios:* David Wylie, John Sharp. *Reserve Team Coach:* Sandy Clark.
Managers since 1975: Ally MacLeod, Billy McNeill, Alex Ferguson, Ian Porterfield, Alex Smith and Jocky Scott, Willie Miller, Roy Aitken, Alex Miller, Paul Hegarty, Ebbe Skovdahl, Steve Paterson. *Club Nicknames(s):* The Dons. *Previous Grounds:* None.
Record Attendance: 45,061 v Hearts, Scottish Cup 4th rd, 13 Mar 1954.
Record Transfer Fee received: £1.75 million for Eoin Jess to Coventry City (February 1996).
Record Transfer Fee paid: £1m+ for Paul Bernard from Oldham Athletic (September 1995).
Record Victory: 13-0 v Peterhead, Scottish Cup, 9 Feb 1923.
Record Defeat: 0-8 v Celtic, Division 1, 30 Jan 1965.
Most Capped Players: Jim Leighton, 91 (Scotland); Alex McLeish, 77 (Scotland); Willie Miller, 65 (Scotland); Gordon Strachan, 50 (Scotland).
Most League Appearances: 556: Willie Miller, 1973-90.
Most League Goals in Season (Individual): 38: Benny Yorston, Division I, 1929-30.
Most Goals Overall (Individual): 199: Joe Harper.

ABERDEEN 2005–06 LEAGUE RECORD

Match No.	Date	Venue	Opponents	Result		H/T Score	Lg. Pos.	Goalscorers	Attendance
1	Jul 30	A	Dundee U	D	1-1	0-1	—	Nicholson 47	12,404
2	Aug 6	H	Kilmarnock	L	1-2	1-1	8	Anderson 33	13,661
3	14	H	Rangers	W	3-2	2-1	6	Anderson 29, Lovell 37, Smith 87	18,182
4	20	A	Hearts	L	0-2	0-1	7		16,139
5	27	H	Falkirk	W	3-0	3-0	7	Smith 2 3, 21, Clark 32	12,249
6	Sept 10	A	Celtic	L	0-2	0-1	7		58,798
7	17	A	Dunfermline Ath	W	2-0	2-0	7	Crawford 32, Severin 44	6387
8	24	H	Livingston	D	0-0	0-0	6		12,402
9	Oct 1	H	Motherwell	D	2-2	0-0	6	Mackie 2 (1 pen) 78 (p), 83	11,448
10	15	A	Inverness CT	D	1-1	0-0	7	Smith 55	6809
11	22	H	Hibernian	L	0-1	0-0	7		13,375
12	25	H	Dundee U	W	2-0	2-0	—	Smith 36, Crawford 42	10,270
13	29	A	Kilmarnock	L	2-4	1-2	7	Anderson 11, Crawford 71	5798
14	Nov 5	A	Rangers	D	0-0	0-0	7		49,717
15	20	H	Hearts	D	1-1	1-0	7	Smith 13	14,901
16	26	A	Falkirk	W	2-1	1-0	6	Clark 43, Anderson 51	5826
17	Dec 4	H	Celtic	L	1-3	0-0	7	Winter 32	17,031
18	10	H	Dunfermline Ath	D	0-0	0-0	8		9881
19	17	A	Livingston	D	0-0	0-0	7		3223
20	26	A	Motherwell	L	1-3	0-2	8	Stewart 90	6555
21	31	H	Inverness CT	D	0-0	0-0	8		12,266
22	Jan 14	A	Hibernian	W	2-1	2-0	8	Crawford 4, Mackie 13	14,572
23	21	A	Dundee U	D	1-1	0-0	8	Mackie 48	9936
24	28	H	Kilmarnock	D	2-2	1-1	8	Nicholson 9, Anderson 73	10,540
25	Feb 8	H	Rangers	W	2-0	2-0	—	Smith 33, Lovell 42	17,087
26	11	A	Hearts	W	2-1	0-1	7	Pressley (og) 68, Clark 88	16,895
27	18	H	Falkirk	W	1-0	1-0	7	Smith 33	11,538
28	Mar 4	A	Celtic	L	0-3	0-0	7		59,657
29	11	A	Dunfermline Ath	L	0-1	0-0	8		5308
30	18	H	Livingston	W	3-0	1-0	6	Anderson 16, Lovell 62, Snoyl 81	9229
31	25	H	Motherwell	D	2-2	2-1	7	Lovell 2 13, 22	10,212
32	Apr 1	A	Inverness CT	W	1-0	0-0	6	Lovell 82	7368
33	8	H	Hibernian	W	1-0	1-0	6	Severin 20	14,110
34	15	A	Rangers	D	1-1	0-0	6	Severin 67	48,987
35	22	H	Kilmarnock	D	0-0	0-0	6		10,634
36	29	H	Hibernian	W	4-0	2-0	6	Crawford 14, Lovell 2 29, 53, Foster 63	10,490
37	May 3	A	Hearts	L	0-1	0-0	—		17,327
38	7	H	Celtic	D	2-2	0-1	6	Stewart 2 69, 72	14,597

Final League Position: 6

Honours
League Champions: Division I 1954-55. Premier Division 1979-80, 1983-84, 1984-85; *Runners-up:* Division I 1910-11, 1936-37, 1955-56, 1970-71, 1971-72. Premier Division 1977-78, 1980-81, 1981-82, 1988-89, 1989-90, 1990-91, 1992-93, 1993-94.
Scottish Cup Winners: 1947, 1970, 1982, 1983, 1984, 1986, 1990; *Runners-up:* 1937, 1953, 1954, 1959, 1967, 1978, 1993, 2000.
League Cup Winners: 1955-56, 1976-77, 1985-86, 1989-90, (Coca-Cola cup) 1995-96; *Runners-up:* 1946-47, 1978-79, 1979-80, 1987-88, 1988-89, 1992-93, 1999-2000.
Drybrough Cup Winners: 1971, 1980.

European: *European Cup:* 12 matches (1980-81, 1984-85, 1985-86); *Cup Winners' Cup:* 39 matches (1967-68, 1970-71, 1978-79, 1982-83 winners, 1983-84 semi-finals, 1986-87, 1990-91, 1993-94); *UEFA Cup:* 48 matches (*Fairs Cup:* 1968-69. *UEFA Cup:* 1971-72, 1972-73, 1973-74, 1977-78, 1979-80, 1981-82, 1987-88, 1988-89, 1989-90, 1991-92, 1994-95, 1996-97, 2000-01, 2002-03).

Club colours: Shirt, Shorts, Stockings: Red.

Goalscorers: *League* (46): Lovell 8, Smith 8, Anderson 6, Crawford 5, Mackie 4 (1 pen), Clark 3, Severin 3, Stewart 3, Nicholson 2, Foster 1, Snoyl 1, Winter 1, own goal 1.
Scottish Cup (3): Crawford 2, Nicholson 1.
CIS Cup (5): Lovell 1, Nicholson 1, Smith 1, Winter 1, own goal 1.

Esson R 18	Considine A 8 + 4	McNaughton K 34	Anderson R 36	Diamond A 31 + 2	Severin S 28	Nicholson B 32 + 1	Dempsey G 17 + 7	Stewart J 2 + 15	Smith J 35	Clark C 30 + 1	Maguire C — + 2	Winter J 4 + 3	Lovell S 22 + 5	Craig S — + 2	Muirhead S 10 + 8	Foster R 8 + 17	Byrne R 18 + 1	Crawford S 27 + 3	Mackie D 11 + 17	Hart M 4	Langfield J 20	Griffin D 9 + 1	Macfarlane N 2 + 4	Snoyl F 9 + 3	MacAulay K 3 + 2	Donald D — + 1	*Match No.*
1	2	3^{2}	4	5	6	7	8	9^{1}	10	11	12	13															1
1		3	4	5	6	7	8^{3}	14	10	11		2^{2}	9^{1}	12	13												2
1		3	4	5	6	7	8^{3}	14	10	11			9^{1}	12	2^{2}	13											3
1	2^{3}	3	4^{1}	5	6	7	8^{2}	13	10	11			9		12	14											4
1		3	4	5	6^{2}	7	12		10	11		13	9^{1}		8		2										5
1	12	3^{1}	4	5	6	7		14	10	8			9^{3}		13		2^{2}	11									6
1		3	4	5	6	7	13		10	8			9^{1}		2	12		11^{2}									7
1		3	4	5	6	7	2^{1}		10	8^{2}			9		12		13	11									8
1		3	4^{2}	5	6	7		14	10			8^{1}	9^{3}		13		2■	11	12								9
1		3	4	5	6	7	8^{2}	14	10			13	12		2			11^{3}	9^{1}								10
1		3^{1}	4	5^{3}	6	7	12	14	10				13				2	11	9^{2}	8							11
1	3		4	5	6	7	13		10				9^{1}				2	11^{2}	12	8							12
1	3^{1}		4	5	6	7		14	10	12					13		2^{2}	11	9^{3}	8							13
1			4	5	6	7	8^{2}		10^{1}	9					3	13	2	11	12								14
1	14		4	5^{3}		7	12		10	6					3	13	2	11	9^{2}	8^{1}							15
1	13	3^{2}	4	5		7			10	8					6	12	2	11	9^{1}								16
1	4	3		5		7			10	8		9			6^{1}		2	11	12								17
	6	3	4	5^{1}		7			10	8		9^{2}				13	2	11	12		1						18
	5^{1}	3	4	12		7		13	10	8					14	6	2	11^{3}	9^{2}		1						19
		3	4	5		7	6	13	9	8			10^{2}		2^{1}			11	12		1						20
		3	4			7	6^{3}	9	11	8			10^{2}		5^{1}	14	2	13	12		1						21
		3	4			7			10^{2}	8			12		13■	6	2	11^{1}	9		1	5					22
	13	3	4			7			10	8			12			6^{2}	2	11	9^{1}		1	5					23
		3^{1}	4		6	7			10	8			13			14	2^{3}	11	9^{2}		1	5	12				24
		3	4	14	6	7			10	5			11^{2}			12			13		1	2	9^{3}	8^{1}			25
		3	4	5	6	7			10^{3}	9			11^{2}						13		1	2	14	12	8^{1}		26
		3	4	5	6	7			10^{3}	9			11^{2}			13			12		1	2	14	8^{1}			27
		3	4	5	6	7^{1}				9			11			12		14	13		1	2^{3}	10	8^{2}			28
		3^{1}	4	5	6		14	13		9						7		11	10		1	2^{2}		12	8^{3}		29
		3	4	5	6		8	13	9^{2}	2			10^{3}			14		11^{1}	12		1			7			30
		3	4	5	6		8		9	2			10			12		11^{1}	13		1			7^{2}			31
		3	4	5^{3}	6		8	14	9	2			10			12		11^{2}			1		13	7^{1}			32
		3	4	5	6		8^{2}		9	2			10			14		11^{1}	12		1	13		7^{3}			33
		3	4	5	6	14	8		11^{1}	2			10^{2}			9		13	12		1			7^{3}			34
		3	4	5	6	7^{2}	8		10	2^{3}						12		11	13		1			9^{1}	14		35
		3	4	5	6	7	2^{2}	12	9^{3}				10^{1}			8		11			1			13	14		36
		3	4	5^{2}	6■	7	13		9				10^{1}			8	2	11	12		1						37
1	5	3				7	6^{3}	12			13					8	2	11^{2}	10			4^{1}			9	14	38

AIRDRIE UNITED — First Division

Year Formed: 2002. *Ground & Address:* Shyberry Excelsior Stadium, Broomfield Park, Craigneuk Avenue, Airdrie ML6 8QZ. *E-mail:* enquiries@airdrieunitedfc.com. *Website:* www.airdrieunited.com
Ground Capacity: all seated: 10,000. *Size of Pitch:* 112yd × 76yd.
Chairman: James Ballantyne. *Secretary:* Ann Marie Ballantyne. *Commercial Manager:* Les Jones.
Manager: Sandy Stewart.
Record Attendance: 5704 v Morton, Second Division, 15 May 2004.
Record Victory: 6-0 v Berwick R, Second Division, 3 Apr 2004.
Record Defeat: 1-6 v Morton, Second Division, 1 Nov 2003.
Most League Appearances: 101, Mark McGeown, 2002-05.
Most League Goals in Season (Individual): 18, Jerome Vareille, 2002-03.
Most Goals Overall (Individual): 28, Jerome Vareille, 2002-04.

AIRDRIE UNITED 2005–06 LEAGUE RECORD

Match No.	Date	Venue	Opponents	Result		H/T Score	Lg. Pos.	Goalscorers	Attendance
1	Aug 6	A	Stranraer	L	0-1	0-1	—		996
2	13	H	Ross Co	L	0-1	0-0	10		1164
3	20	A	Brechin C	D	1-1	0-1	9	McKeown [79]	668
4	27	H	St Johnstone	W	3-1	1-1	7	McKeown (pen) [27], Prunty [61], Twigg [82]	1522
5	Sept 10	A	Dundee	W	2-0	1-0	7	McDougall [5], Prunty [75]	4198
6	17	A	Hamilton A	D	1-1	1-0	6	McLaren [31]	2229
7	24	H	St Mirren	L	0-1	0-1	6		2073
8	Oct 1	H	Clyde	L	1-3	0-1	8	McKeown (pen) [75]	1603
9	7	A	Ross Co	D	2-2	1-2	x	Twigg [9], McLaren [73]	2004
10	15	A	Queen of the S	L	0-1	0-0	8		1638
11	22	H	Stranraer	W	1-0	0-0	7	Prunty [59]	1100
12	29	H	Dundee	W	4-0	2-0	7	McPhee 2 [1, 26], McKeown (pen) [78], Hardie [82]	1656
13	Nov 5	A	St Johnstone	L	0-1	0-1	7		2412
14	12	H	Hamilton A	D	2-2	1-0	7	McPhee [28], McLaren [89]	1375
15	26	A	Clyde	L	0-1	0-1	7		1263
16	29	A	St Mirren	D	1-1	1-1	—	McKeown [11]	2941
17	Dec 3	H	Queen of the S	W	4-0	2-0	7	Prunty [11], McLaren [27], McPhee 2 [79, 87]	1242
18	10	A	Stranraer	D	1-1	1-0	7	McKeown (pen) [30]	581
19	17	H	Brechin C	W	6-0	1-0	7	Prunty 2 [57, 46], Hardie 3 [59, 73, 86], McLaren [78]	1106
20	26	A	Dundee	W	3-2	0-2	—	Prunty 3 [58, 88, 89]	4378
21	31	H	St Johnstone	W	2-1	2-1	6	McKeown (pen) [22], McLaren [35]	1616
22	Jan 2	A	Hamilton A	L	0-1	0-1	—		2498
23	14	H	St Mirren	L	1-4	0-1	6	McPhee [87]	2661
24	21	H	Clyde	D	1-1	1-1	7	Prunty [11]	1623
25	28	A	Queen of the S	L	0-2	0-1	7		1650
26	Feb 11	A	Brechin C	D	0-0	0-0	7		602
27	18	H	Ross Co	L	2-3	1-2	7	McPhee [32], Prunty [69]	1119
28	Mar 4	A	St Johnstone	D	2-2	1-0	7	Twigg [2], Lovering [50]	2216
29	11	H	Dundee	W	7-0	5-0	7	McLaren 3 [15, 46, 78], Twigg 2 (1 pen) [17 (p), 43], McPhee [19], Coyle [84]	1127
30	18	H	Hamilton A	D	0-0	0-0	7		1326
31	25	A	St Mirren	L	1-2	1-1	7	Prunty [42]	3785
32	Apr 1	A	Clyde	L	1-3	0-2	7	Prunty [85]	1264
33	8	H	Queen of the S	D	1-1	1-0	7	Twigg [6]	1262
34	15	H	Stranraer	W	3-0	1-0	6	McLaren [17], Prunty [72], Barkey [87]	919
35	22	A	Ross Co	W	1-0	0-0	6	Twigg [52]	2066
36	29	H	Brechin C	D	3-3	1-1	6	Prunty [44], McPhee [51], McGowan [78]	1212

Final League Position: 6

Honours
League Champions: Second Division 2003-04.
Bell's League Challenge Cup runners-up: 2003-04.

Club colours: Shirt: White with red diamond. Shorts: White with two red horizontal stripes. Stockings: White with red hoops.

Goalscorers: *League* (57): Prunty 15, McLaren 10, McPhee 9, McKeown 7 (5 pens), Twigg 7 (1 pen), Hardie 4, Barkey 1, Coyle 1, Lovering 1, McDougall 1, McGowan 1.
Scottish Cup (5): Doherty 2, Hardie 1, McKeown 1, McLaren 1.
CIS Cup (0).
Challenge Cup (1): McPhee 1.

Hollis L 10	Coyle F 10 + 10	Lovering P 26 + 2	McGowan N 34 + 1	McManus A 30	Dunn D 16 + 11	Marshall C 1 + 2	Docherty S 18 + 7	Roberts M 2	McPhee B 25 + 7	McLaren W 30 + 3	McDougall S 19 + 12	Twigg G 15 + 9	McKeown S 30 + 1	Prunty B 31 + 1	McKenna S 31 + 1	Barkey K 17 + 6	McCluskey S — + 1	Hardie M 14 + 7	Robertson S 26	Holmes G 8 + 8	Taylor S 3 + 4	*Match No.*
1	2	3	4	5	6[1]	7	8	9[2]	10■	11	12	13										1
1	2	3	6	5	11	13	8	9[1]	10[2]		7	12	4									2
1	2[1]	3	4	5	11[2]		8		10	13	7	14	6	9[3]	12							3
1		3	4	5	14	13	8		10[1]	11[3]	7[2]	12	6	9	2							4
1			4[1]	5	3				10	11	7[3]	14	8[2]	9	2	6	12	13				5
1			4	5	3				7[1]	11	13	10[2]	8	9	2	6		12				6
1			4	5	3■		14		7	11	12	10	8[2]	9[1]	2	6[3]		13				7
1		3[2]	4	5			8		7[1]	11	12	10	13	9	2	14		6[3]				8
			4	5	3		8		12	11	14	10[3]	6[2]	9[1]	2	7		13	1			9
	12		4	5■	3[1]				13	11		10[2]	8	9	2	7		6	1			10
		13	4		3[2]		2		12	11		10[1]	8	9	5	7		6	1			11
	13	3	4	5	14		12		10		11[3]		8	9[1]	2	7[2]		6	1			12
		3	4	5	13		12		10[1]		11		8	9	2	7[2]		6	1			13
	14	3	4	5			12		10	13	11[3]		8	9	2	7[2]		6[1]	1			14
		3	4	5			8		10	12	11[1]		7	9[2]	2	6		13	1			15
	7	3	4	5			6■		10[1]	11			8	9	2			12	1			16
	7	3	4[1]	5	12				10	11	14		8[2]	9[3]	2			6	1	13		17
	7	3	4	5	13		12		10[2]	11			8[1]	9	2			6	1			18
	13	3	4	5	10[1]					11	7		8[3]	9	2[2]	14		6	1	12		19
		3	4	5	6[1]				13	11[3]	7		8	9	2	14		10[2]	1	12		20
	13	3	4	5			12		10	11	7[2]		8[3]	9	2			6[1]	1	14		21
		3	4	5			6[2]		10	11	7[1]		8	9	2			12	1	13		22
		3	4[1]	5■			7		10	11	12		8[2]	9	2			6	1	13		23
	7[1]	5			3				10[2]	11	12	13	8■	9	2			4	1	6		24
	7[1]	5	13		3[2]		2		10	11[3]	12	14		9	4			6	1	8		25
	2	3	4		12				10[2]	11[1]	7	13	8	9[3]	5	14			1	6		26
	3[1]	12	4				2		10[2]	11	7[3]	13	8	9	5	14			1	6		27
		3	4		12		2		10[1]	11	13	9[2]	8		5	7			1	6		28
	14	3	4	5	13				10	11	7[2]	9[1]			2	8			1	6[3]	12	29
		3	4	5	14		6[3]		10[1]	11	13	9[2]	8	12	2	7			1			30
		3	4	5	14				12■	11	7[1]	10	8[3]	9[2]	2	6			1		13	31
1	13	3	4	5	14		2[2]			11		10[3]	8[1]	9		7■				12	6	32
1	14	3[1]	4	5	6		13			11	7	10[2]		9	2					8[3]	12	33
	14		4	5	3		2			11	7	10[3]	8[2]	9		13			1	6[1]	12	34
			4	5	3				12	11[1]	13	10	8[2]	9	2	7			1		6	35
	14		4	5			2[3]		12	11	7[2]	10[1]		9	3	8			1	13	6	36

ALBION ROVERS Third Division

Year Formed: 1882. *Ground & Address:* Cliftonhill Stadium, Main St, Coatbridge ML5 3RB. *Telephone/Fax:* 01236 606334.
Ground capacity: 1249 (seated 489). *Size of Pitch:* 110yd × 72yd.
Chairman: Frank Meade ACMA, *Company Secretary:* David Shanks BSc. *General Manager:* John Reynolds. *Commercial Manager:* Patrick Rollink.
Manager: Jim Chapman. *Assistant Manager:* Graham Diamond. *Youth Development:* Jimmy Lindsay. *Physio:* Derek Kelly.
Managers since 1975: G. Caldwell, S. Goodwin, H. Hood, J. Baker, D. Whiteford, M. Ferguson, W. Wilson, B. Rooney, A. Ritchie, T. Gemmell, D. Provan, M. Oliver, B. McLaren, T. Gemmell, T Spence, J. Crease, V. Moore, B. McLaren, J. McVeigh, P. Hetherston, K. McAllister.
Club Nickname(s): The Wee Rovers. *Previous Grounds:* Cowheath Park, Meadow Park, Whifflet.
Record Attendance: 27,381 v Rangers, Scottish Cup 2nd rd, 8 Feb 1936.
Record Transfer Fee received: £40,000 from Motherwell for Bruce Cleland.
Record Transfer Fee paid: £7000 for Gerry McTeague to Stirling Albion, September 1989.
Record Victory: 12-0 v Airdriehill, Scottish Cup, 3 Sept 1887.
Record Defeat: 1-11 v Partick Th, League Cup, 11 Aug 1993.
Most Capped Player: Jock White, 1 (2), Scotland.
Most League Appearances: 399, Murdy Walls, 1921-36.
Most League Goals in Season (Individual): 41: Jim Renwick, Division II, 1932-33.
Most Goals Overall (Individual): 105: Bunty Weir, 1928-31.

ALBION ROVERS 2005–06 LEAGUE RECORD

Match No.	Date	Venue	Opponents	Result		H/T Score	Lg. Pos.	Goalscorers	Attendance
1	Aug 6	H	Arbroath	D	2-2	1-0	—	Young 21, Houston 88	394
2	13	A	Montrose	W	2-0	0-0	3	Chisholm 2 71, 78	307
3	20	H	Stenhousemuir	L	0-2	0-2	4		268
4	27	A	Queen's Park	L	1-3	1-0	6	Bonnar 16	503
5	Sept 10	H	East Fife	L	2-4	1-1	8	Wallace G 3, Donachy 70	317
6	17	A	Elgin C	D	2-2	0-0	6	Donachy 54, Wallace G 88	305
7	24	H	Berwick R	L	0-2	0-1	7		314
8	Oct 1	A	East Stirling	L	1-3	0-2	10	Mackay (og) 74	245
9	15	H	Cowdenbeath	L	0-3	0-1	10		322
10	22	A	Arbroath	W	2-1	1-1	8	Friel (pen) 35, Wallace G 68	503
11	25	H	Montrose	D	1-1	1-1	—	Wallace G 18	181
12	29	A	East Fife	D	1-1	1-0	8	Chaplain 11	505
13	Nov 5	H	Queen's Park	D	1-1	0-1	8	Bonnar 85	447
14	12	H	Elgin C	L	0-2	0-0	8		273
15	Dec 3	A	Cowdenbeath	L	1-2	0-1	9	Donachy 51	255
16	10	A	Berwick R	W	1-0	0-0	9	Chaplain 70	306
17	Jan 2	A	Queen's Park	D	1-1	1-0	—	Chaplain 12	576
18	7	H	East Stirling	W	4-2	2-1	9	Wallace G 18, Noble 45, Sim 68, Reid D 75	244
19	14	H	East Fife	W	3-1	2-0	7	Reid D 2 7, 67, Sim 40	303
20	21	A	Elgin C	L	1-2	1-0	8	Young 39	360
21	28	H	Berwick R	L	0-1	0-1	8		299
22	Feb 4	A	East Stirling	L	0-1	0-1	8		199
23	11	H	Cowdenbeath	L	1-3	1-0	9	Chaplain 7	313
24	18	A	Montrose	D	2-2	2-1	9	Chisholm 2, Donachy 4	280
25	25	H	Stenhousemuir	L	1-2	0-1	9	Chaplain 56	428
26	28	A	Stenhousemuir	L	0-1	0-1	—		278
27	Mar 7	H	Arbroath	L	0-2	0-1	—		217
28	11	A	East Fife	L	0-1	0-1	9		257
29	18	H	Elgin C	L	1-2	1-1	9	Reid D 10	319
30	21	H	Queen's Park	W	1-0	0-0	—	Young 82	331
31	25	A	Berwick R	L	1-2	0-1	9	Donnelly (pen) 90	402
32	Apr 1	H	East Stirling	W	2-0	2-0	8	Chaplain 2 3, 24	803
33	8	A	Cowdenbeath	L	1-2	1-0	8	Chaplain 40	350
34	15	A	Arbroath	L	0-1	0-1	8		563
35	22	H	Montrose	D	1-1	1-1	8	Donnelly (pen) 35	825
36	29	A	Stenhousemuir	L	2-4	1-2	8	McGhee 35, Young 77	391

Final League Position: 8

Honours
League Champions: Division II 1933-34, Second Division 1988-89; *Runners-up:* Division II 1913-14, 1937-38, 1947-48.
Scottish Cup Runners-up: 1920.

Club colours: Shirt: Primrose yellow. Shorts: Red. Stockings: Red.

Goalscorers: *League* (39): Chaplain 8, Wallace G 5, Donachy 4, Reid S 4, Young 4, Chisholm 3, Bonnar 2, Donnelly 2 (pens), Sim 2, Friel 1 (pen), Houston 1, McGhee 1, Noble 1, own goal 1.
Scottish Cup (2): Chisholm 1, Roberts 1.
CIS Cup (1): Chisholm 1.
Challenge Cup (0).

Ewings J 18+1	Lennox T 16+2	Bonnar M 25+1	O'Neil K 4	Lennon G 36	McGhee G 30	Chisholm I 18+10	Friel S 35	Sichi L 9+7	Young C 10+11	Franch T 1+4	Houston S 1+1	Selkirk A 4+7	Noble S 16+4	Donnelly C 32	Wilson L 3+5	Donachy S 25+2	Reid D 14+18	Wallace G 21+1	Mathie G 1+3	Chaplain S 28+1	Black D 11	Doyle J 10+5	Creer A 4	Love R —+1	Sim A 5+8	Aboubeaker M —+3	McGlynn G 13	Quitongo J 1	Oné A 2	Quinn M 1+1	Reid A 1	Stewart P 1	Match No.
1	2	3	4	5	6	7	8	9[2]	10[1]	11	12	13																					1
1	2	12	4	5	6	9	8	7[3]	10[2]			14	3[1]	11	13																		2
1	2[3]	11[2]		4	5	9	8	7	10	14	3			6[1]	12	13																	3
1	2	6[3]		4	5	10	8	7[1]	14	12			3		9[2]	11	13																4
1	2	10		5	6	13	4		14				3[1]	8[3]		11	7[2]	9	12														5
1	2[1]	8		4	5	7	6		10[2]				3[3]		12	9	13	11	14														6
1		6	4[3]	5	3	7	2			12		13	14	8		11[2]	9[1]	10															7
1		6	4	5	3	7	2[3]			13					8[1]	10	14	9	11[2]	12													8
1		11		6[1]	3	7	2							5	10[2]	13	12	9		8	4												9
1		10		4	3	7[2]	6							5		11	13	9[1]	12	8	2■												10
1	2	10		4	3	7	6							5		11[1]	12	9		8													11
1	3	10[1]		4		7	6					12		5			11	9		8	2												12
1		10		4	3	7[2]	6		12					5		11	13	9[1]		8	2												13
1	12	10■		4	3		6	13	9[1]					5		11	7			8	2[2]												14
1	12			4	3[3]	8[1]	6	13						5	14	11	7[2]	9		10	2												15
1	2			4	3		6		13				10[3]	5	14	11	7[1]	9[2]		8		12											16
	2			4		8[1]	6		14				3	5		11■	7[2]	9[3]		10		12	1	13									17
	2			4	3	12	6						11	5			10[2]	9		8		13	1		7[1]								18
	2[2]			4	3	13	6		12				10	5			11	9[1]		8[3]		14	1		7								19
				4	3	13	6		9				10	5		11[2]	7[1]			8	2[3]	12	1			14							20
				4	3[3]	12		13	9				10	5		11	7[2]			8	2[1]	6				14	1						21
				4	3	12	2[1]	14	11[2]				10[3]	5		7	13	9		8		6					1						22
		10[1]		4	3[2]	12	2							5		11	13	9		8		6					1	7					23
		10		4	3	7[1]	2					9[2]	13	5		11				8		6			12		1						24
		10[1]		4	3[2]	7[3]	2					14		5		11	13			8		6			12		1		9				25
		10[3]		4	3	12	2					14		5		11	13			8		6			7[1]		1		9[2]				26
		10[3]		4	3[1]	7	2						12	5		11[2]	13	9		8		6			14		1						27
1		10[2]		4	3[1]	7	2					14		5[3]		11	12	9		8		6			13								28
1	2			4		12	6	14	13			9[1]	3	5			11[3]			8		10			7[2]								29
	2			4		12	6	14	13			9[2]	3	5		11	7[3]			8		10[1]					1						30
	2	10[3]		4			6	12	14			9[1]	3	5		11	7[2]			8					13		1						31
	2	10		4			6	7[1]	13				3	5		11[3]	14	9[2]		8					12		1						32
		10		4	3		6	7[3]	12					5		11	13	9[2]		8	2[1]				14		1						33
		10		4	3		6	7[2]					11[1]	5			12	9		8	2				13		1[G]			15			34
		10		4	3		6	11[1]	9[2]				14	5			12	13		8	2				7[3]		1						35
12		10		4	3		6	7[2]	9[3]					5			13			8						14				1	2[1]	11	36

ALLOA ATHLETIC Second Division

Year Formed: 1878. *Ground & Address:* Recreation Park, Clackmannan Rd, Alloa FK10 1RY. *Telephone:* 01259 722695. *Fax:* 01259 210886. *E-mail:* fcadmin@alloaathletic.co.uk. *Website:* www.alloaathletic.co.uk
Ground Capacity: total: 3100, seated: 400. *Size of Pitch:* 110yd × 75yd.
Chairman: Ian Henderson. *Secretary:* Ewen G. Cameron.
Manager: Allan Maitland. *Physios:* Vanessa Smith & Stuart Murphy.
Managers since 1975: H. Wilson, A. Totten, W. Garner, J. Thomson, D. Sullivan, G. Abel, B. Little, H. McCann, W. Lamont, P. McAuley, T. Hendrie, T. Christie, T. Hendrie.
Club Nickname(s): The Wasps. *Previous Grounds:* West End Public Park, Gabberston Park, Belleview Park.
Record Attendance: 13,000 v Dunfermline Athletic, Scottish Cup 3rd rd replay, 26 Feb 1939.
Record Transfer Fee received: £100,000 for Martin Cameron to Bristol Rovers.
Record Transfer Fee paid: £26,000 for Ross Hamilton from Stenhousemuir.
Record Victory: 9-2 v Forfar Ath, Division II, 18 Mar 1933.
Record Defeat: 0-10 v Dundee, Division II, 8 Mar 1947 v Third Lanark, League Cup, 8 Aug 1953.
Most Capped Player: Jock Hepburn, 1, Scotland.
Most League Goals in Season (Individual): 49: 'Wee' Willie Crilley, Division II, 1921-22.

ALLOA ATHLETIC 2005–06 LEAGUE RECORD

Match No.	*Date*	*Venue*	*Opponents*	*Result*		*H/T Score*	*Lg. Pos.*	*Goalscorers*	*Attendance*
1	Aug 6	H	Peterhead	W	4-1	3-0	—	Thomson 15, Bolochoweckyj 23, Tully (og) 33, Ovenstone 52	507
2	13	A	Dumbarton	D	1-1	0-0	4	Sloan 60	879
3	20	H	Raith R	L	1-2	1-2	5	Stevenson J 30	931
4	27	A	Stirling A	W	2-1	1-0	4	Sloan (pen) 25, Greenhill 58	962
5	Sept 10	H	Forfar Ath	D	1-1	0-1	5	Sloan (pen) 87	505
6	17	A	Morton	L	2-5	0-2	5	Brown A 57, Stevenson J (pen) 90	2515
7	24	H	Gretna	L	0-3	0-1	7		663
8	Oct 1	H	Partick Th	L	1-6	0-2	8	Sloan 47	1347
9	7	A	Stirling A	D	0-0	0-0	8		874
10	15	A	Ayr U	D	1-1	1-0	7	Brown A 13	1046
11	22	A	Peterhead	L	1-3	1-0	8	Stevenson J (pen) 38	422
12	25	H	Dumbarton	L	1-4	0-2	—	Brown G 86	469
13	29	A	Forfar Ath	L	1-3	1-2	9	Brown G 8	486
14	Nov 5	H	Stirling A	L	2-4	0-3	10	Brown A 2 61, 81	870
15	12	H	Morton	L	0-3	0-2	10		920
16	26	A	Gretna	L	0-4	0-2	10		759
17	Dec 3	H	Ayr U	L	0-4	0-1	10		488
18	17	A	Partick Th	L	3-4	2-1	10	Stevenson J 30, Sloan 40, Brown A 69	1868
19	24	H	Peterhead	L	0-2	0-0	—		644
20	31	A	Raith R	L	2-4	2-2	10	Ovenstone 29, Stevenson J 32	1637
21	Jan 14	H	Forfar Ath	L	0-1	0-0	10		575
22	21	A	Morton	L	1-4	0-2	10	Brown G 84	2814
23	28	H	Gretna	L	0-3	0-1	10		625
24	Feb 11	A	Ayr U	W	1-0	0-0	9	Sloan 66	913
25	25	H	Raith R	D	1-1	0-1	10	Forrest 68	749
26	28	H	Partick Th	W	2-1	2-1	—	Hamilton R 8, Brown G 30	675
27	Mar 11	A	Forfar Ath	L	0-3	0-2	10		399
28	18	H	Morton	D	0-0	0-0	10		671
29	21	A	Dumbarton	W	1-0	0-0	—	Stevenson J 76	534
30	25	A	Gretna	L	1-2	1-1	10	Stevenson J 3	948
31	28	H	Stirling A	D	0-0	0-0	—		656
32	Apr 1	A	Partick Th	W	3-2	1-1	10	McLeod 24, Hamilton R 60, Brown G 71	1920
33	8	H	Ayr U	D	1-1	1-1	10	Stevenson J 24	601
34	15	A	Peterhead	L	0-3	0-1	10		752
35	22	H	Dumbarton	W	1-0	0-0	9	Stevenson J 64	784
36	29	A	Raith R	W	1-0	0-0	9	Brown G 65	1560

Final League Position: 9

Honours
League Champions: Division II 1921-22; Third Division 1997-98. *Runners-up:* Division II 1938-39. Second Division 1976-77, 1981-82, 1984-85, 1988-89, 1999-2000, 2001-02.
Bell's League Challenge Winners: 1999-2000; *Runners-up:* 2001-02.

Club colours: Shirt: Gold with black trim. Shorts: Black with gold stripe. Stockings: Gold with black hoop on top.

Goalscorers: *League* (36): Stevenson J 9 (2 pens), Brown G 6, Sloan 6 (2 pens), Brown A 5, Hamilton R 2, Ovenstone 2, Bolochoweckyj 1, Forrest 1, Greenhill 1, McLeod 1, Thomson 1, own goal 1.
Scottish Cup (13): Hamilton R 3, Nicolson 3, Sloan 3, Bolochoweckyj 1, Brown A 1, Quitongo 1, Stevenson J 1.
CIS Cup (3): Stevenson J 2, Brown A 1.
Challenge Cup (0).
Play-Offs (7): Overstone 2, Hamilton 1, McLeod 1, Sloan 1, Stevenson A 1, Stevenson J 1.

McGlynn G 14	Walker R 20	Thomson D 2 + 4	Bolochoweckyj M 27 + 1	Townsley C 33	Ovenstone J 32 + 1	Quitongo J 12 + 6	Nicolson I 16 + 5	Brown G 14 + 14	Hamilton R 27 + 5	Stevenson J 35	Sloan R 24 + 11	Mortimer P 9 + 2	Greenhill D 13 + 5	Brown A 16 + 1	Evans J 8 + 2	Learmonth S 11 + 9	McGeown D 7 + 5	Forrest F 12 + 2	Swaney S 1	McColligan B 16	Greer A 13	Hamilton S 5	Grant J 8 + 1	Stevenson A 11 + 1	McLeod P 9 + 3	Ferguson P 1 + 1	Stuart M — + 1	Match No.
1	2	3	4	5	6	7^{2}	8	9^{1}	10	11	12	13																1
1	2	13	4	5	6		3^{2}	12	9	8^{1}	7	10	11															2
1■	2	13	4	5^{3}	6		3		9	8	7^{2}	10^{1}	11	12	14													3
1	2		4	5	6		3	12	9		7	8	10	11^{1}														4
1	2		4	5	6	13	3	12	9^{2}	8	7		10	11^{1}														5
1	2		4	5	6	12	3		7^{1}	8	13		10	9		11^{2}												6
1	3	14	4	5	6	7^{3}	2	12		8	13	10	11^{1}	9^{2}														7
1	2		4	5	6	7	3	13	12	8	10		11^{1}	9^{2}														8
	2		4	5	6	7	3^{1}	13	10^{2}	8			11	9	1	12												9
	2	14	4	5	6	7		12	10^{2}	8^{3}	13		11	9^{1}	1	3												10
	2		4^{1}	5	6	7^{3}		9	10^{2}	8	13	12	14		1	3■	11											11
1	2	3^{3}		5^{1}	6	7^{2}		14	10	8	13	4	12	9			11											12
	2			5	6	12		7^{1}	14	8	13	4	11^{2}	9^{3}	1	3	10											13
	2		4	5	6	12		9^{3}	14	7	13		11^{1}	10	1	3	8^{2}											14
1	2		4	5	6	7^{3}	14	12	10	8	11^{2}		13	9^{1}		3												15
1	2		4	5	6	12	8		10^{2}	7	13		11^{1}	9		3												16
	2		4	5	6	7^{1}	11^{2}	12	10	8	13			9	1	3												17
1	2		4	5	6	7^{2}		13		10^{1}	11	8	12	9		3												18
1	2		4	5■	6	7		12		10	11	8		9^{1}		3												19
1^{6}	2				6■	7	13		12	10^{2}	11	8	4	9^{1}	15	3		5										20
				2		12	3	10^{1}	9	7	11				1		8	4	5	6								21
			4	2	6		3	9	7	10	11^{1}				1		12	5		8								22
				4	12		3^{1}	9	7	11	14					13	10^{3}	5		6	1	2^{2}	8■					23
				4	3				12	10^{2}	11					13		5		6	1	2	7	8	9^{1}			24
				4	3			12	10	8	11							5		6	1^{6}	2	13	7^{1}	9^{2}	15		25
				4	3			9^{1}	10	7	11							5		6	1	2		8	12			26
			12	4	3				10	7	11					13		5		6		2^{1}		8	9^{2}	1		27
			2	4	3			9^{1}	10	7	11						12	5		6	1		8					28
			2	4	3		14		10^{3}	7	11		13					5^{1}		6	1		8	12	9^{2}			29
			2	4	3				10	7	11					12				6	1		8	5	9^{1}			30
			2	4	3			12	10^{2}	7	11					14		13		6	1		8^{1}	5	9^{3}			31
			5	4^{1}	3		14	10^{3}	8	7^{2}	11						13	12		6	1			2	9			32
			5	4			3	10	8	7	11^{1}					12	13			6	1			2	9^{2}			33
			4				3	10^{2}		7	11					13	8^{1}	5		6	1			2	9		12	34
			4		3			9	10	7	11^{1}					12		5		6	1		8	2^{2}	13			35
			5	4	3		14	9^{2}	7^{1}	10	11						12			6	1		8^{3}	2	13			36

ARBROATH — Third Division

Year Formed: 1878. *Ground & Address:* Gayfield Park, Arbroath DD11 1QB. *Telephone:* 01241 872157. *Fax:* 01241 431125. *E-mail:* AFCwebmaster@arbroathfc.co.uk. *Website:* www.arbroathfc.co.uk
Ground Capacity: 4020, seated: 715. *Size of Pitch:* 115yd × 71yd.
President: John D. Christison. *Secretary:* Dr Gary Callon. *Administrator:* Mike Cargill.
Manager: John McGlashan. *Assistant Manager:* Robbie Raeside. *Physio:* Jim Crosby.
Managers since 1975: A. Henderson, I. J. Stewart, G. Fleming, J. Bone, J. Young, W. Borthwick, M. Lawson, D. McGrain MBE, J. Scott, J. Brogan, T. Campbell, G. Mackie, D. Baikie, J. Brownlie, S. Kirk, H. Cairney.
Club Nickname(s): The Red Lichties. *Previous Grounds:* None.
Record Attendance: 13,510 v Rangers, Scottish Cup 3rd rd, 23 Feb 1952.
Record Transfer Fee received: £120,000 for Paul Tosh to Dundee (Aug 1993).
Record Transfer Fee paid: £20,000 for Douglas Robb from Montrose (1981).
Record Victory: 36-0 v Bon Accord, Scottish Cup 1st rd, 12 Sept 1885.
Record Defeat: 1-9 v Celtic, League Cup 3rd rd, 25 Aug 1993.
Most Capped Player: Ned Doig, 2 (5), Scotland.
Most League Appearances: 445: Tom Cargill, 1966-81.
Most League Goals in Season (Individual): 45: Dave Easson, Division II, 1958-59.
Most Goals Overall (Individual): 120: Jimmy Jack, 1966-71.

ARBROATH 2005–06 LEAGUE RECORD

Match No.	Date	Venue	Opponents	Result	H/T Score	Lg. Pos.	Goalscorers	Attendance
1	Aug 6	A	Albion R	D 2-2	0-1	—	Miller 71, McCulloch 83	394
2	13	H	East Fife	W 1-0	0-0	4	Davidson 65	507
3	20	A	East Stirling	L 1-3	0-0	5	Black 87	225
4	27	A	Montrose	L 0-1	0-1	7		888
5	Sept 10	H	Stenhousemuir	D 1-1	0-0	6	Stein 47	429
6	17	A	Berwick R	L 0-3	0-1	8		367
7	24	H	Cowdenbeath	L 0-3	0-2	9		423
8	Oct 1	A	Queen's Park	D 2-2	0-0	9	Cook 50, Dobbins 78	446
9	7	A	East Fife	D 1-1	0-1	9	McCulloch 48	747
10	15	H	Elgin C	W 2-0	1-0	6	Bishop 18, Brazil (pen) 82	502
11	22	H	Albion R	L 1-2	1-1	6	Stein 28	503
12	29	A	Stenhousemuir	L 0-2	0-1	7		332
13	Nov 5	H	Montrose	W 2-1	0-1	7	Dobbins 71, Clarke 84	830
14	12	H	Berwick R	W 4-0	2-0	6	Rennie 19, Stein 2 44, 69, Brazil 51	460
15	26	H	East Stirling	W 7-2	3-1	6	Brazil 3 15, 25, 39, Clarke 3 66, 81, 89, Black 84	409
16	Dec 3	A	Elgin C	L 0-2	0-1	6		357
17	6	A	Cowdenbeath	L 2-3	1-1	—	Clarke 31, Cook 56	236
18	Jan 2	A	Montrose	W 1-0	0-0	—	Stein 63	455
19	14	H	Stenhousemuir	W 3-2	2-2	6	Brazil 2 (1 pen) 8, 16 (p), Swankie 49	560
20	21	A	Berwick R	L 1-2	0-2	6	Stein 77	416
21	28	H	Cowdenbeath	W 4-1	1-0	6	Swankie 30, Stein 76, Watson 87, Cook 89	583
22	Feb 4	A	Queen's Park	D 0-0	0-0	6		572
23	11	H	Elgin C	L 0-1	0-0	6		536
24	18	H	East Fife	W 2-1	1-1	6	Rennie 13, Voigt 75	570
25	25	A	East Stirling	W 4-0	1-0	6	McMullan 18, Swankie 70, Raeside 72, Taylor 85	252
26	Mar 7	A	Albion R	W 2-0	1-0	—	Watson 37, McMullan 76	217
27	11	A	Stenhousemuir	D 0-0	0-0	5		383
28	14	H	Queen's Park	D 1-1	1-0	—	Raeside 7	520
29	18	H	Berwick R	L 0-2	0-2	5		558
30	21	H	Montrose	W 3-0	3-0	—	Swankie 3 7, 32, 36	732
31	25	A	Cowdenbeath	L 2-4	1-1	5	Swankie 25, McMullan 47	351
32	Apr 1	H	Queen's Park	W 1-0	0-0	4	Reilly 62	724
33	8	A	Elgin C	L 1-4	1-3	6	Raeside 1	607
34	15	H	Albion R	W 1-0	1-0	6	Taylor 40	563
35	22	A	East Fife	W 3-0	1-0	4	Stein 18, Bishop 50, Smith N 86	547
36	29	H	East Stirling	W 2-1	2-0	4	Stein 8, Raeside 30	1050

Final League Position: 4

Honours
League Runners-up: Division II 1934-35, 1958-59, 1967-68, 1971-72; Second Division 2000-01; Third Division 1997-98.
Scottish Cup: Quarter-finals 1993.

Club colours: Shirt: Maroon with white trim. Shorts: White. Stockings: Maroon.

Goalscorers: *League* (57): Stein 9, Brazil 7 (2 pens), Swankie 7, Clarke 5, Raeside 4, Cook 3, McMullan 3, Bishop 2, Black 2, Dobbins 2, McCulloch 2, Rennie 2, Taylor 2, Watson 2, Davidson 1, Miller 1, Reilly 1, Smith N 1, Voigt 1.
Scottish Cup (1): Brazil 1.
CIS Cup (1): Brazil 1.
Challenge Cup (1): Brazil 1.
Play-Offs (1): Reilly 1.

Inglis N 8	McMullan K 31	Black R 24 + 7	Bishop J 17 + 7	Cormack P 3	McCulloch M 30 + 2	Miller G 21 + 5	Davidson H 12 + 2	Collier J 1	Reilly A 10 + 12	Stein J 34	Jackson C 12 + 6	Warren G — + 4	Brazil A 17	Smith J — + 1	Cairns M 3	Watson P 19 + 6	Dobbins I 31	Clarke P 13	Peat M 25 + 1	Smith N 6 + 6	Rennie S 20 + 2	Cook S 14 + 4	King M 2 + 2	Swankie G 18	Raeside R 17	Taylor S 4 + 5	McGlashan J 1	Voigt J 3 + 8	Henderson R — + 3	*Match No.*
1	2	3	4	5	6	7	8	9^{1}	10^{2}	11	12	13																		1
1	2	3	4	5^{1}	6	7	8			11	10		9	12																2
1	2	3	4	5	6	7	8^{1}		12	11^{2}	10	13	9																	3
	2	3	4		6	7	8		12	11	10		9		1	5^{1}														4
	2	3	4		6^{1}	7	8			11	12				1	10	5	9												5
	2		4		6	7	8^{2}			11^{1}	10	12			1^{G}	3	5	9	15	13										6
	2	6	4^{1}		13		7^{2}			11			9			3	5	10	1	8■	12									7
	2	4			6					11	8		9			3	5	10^{1}	1	12		7								8
	2	12	4		6		8			11	13		9			3^{2}	5	10	1			7^{1}								9
	2	3	4		6		8		12	11^{1}			9				5	10	1			7								10
	2	3^{1}	4		6		8^{2}			11		13	9			12	5	10	1			7								11
	2		12		6	13	14			11	8^{3}		9			3	5	10	1		4^{1}	7^{2}								12
	2	13			6	12				11^{2}	8^{1}		9			3	5	10	1		4	7								13
	2^{2}		12		6	13				11	8		9			3	5	10	1		4^{1}	7								14
		12	4^{1}		6	2	8		14	11			9^{3}			3	5	10	1	13		7^{2}								15
		14	4		6	2^{1}	8^{2}			11	13		9			3^{3}	5	10	1			7	12							16
	2	6	13			12				11	8^{1}		9			3■	5	10	1		4^{2}	7								17
	2	12	5		6	8	13		14	11	3^{1}		10■						1		4	7^{2}	9^{3}							18
	2^{2}	6	5			8			14	11	3		9				7		1		4^{1}	12	13	10^{3}						19
	2	6	5^{3}			8				11	3^{2}					14	7		1			13	9^{1}	10	4	12				20
	2	3				8			12	11						13	5		1			7		10	4	9^{1}	6^{2}			21
	2	3			14	8			12	11^{3}			9^{1}			6	5		1		13	7		10	4^{2}					22
	2^{2}	3			6	8			9^{1}	11						13	5		1		7			10	4			12		23
	2				6	8^{2}			9	11^{1}						3	5		1	13	7			10	4			12		24
	2		14		6	8			9^{1}	11						3	5		1		7			10^{2}	4^{3}	12		13		25
	2	11			6	8			9^{1}		13					3^{2}	5		1		7			10	4	12				26
	2	3			6	8			9^{1}	11^{2}						13	5		1		7			10	4			12		27
1	6^{3}	11^{2}			3	8			13		14					9	5				2			10^{1}	4	7		12		28
	6^{3}	7			3^{1}	8				11							5		1	12	2	14		10	4	9^{2}		13		29
	6	14	12		3				13	11						7	5^{1}		1	8^{3}	2			10^{2}	4			9		30
	6	13	14		3^{2}				12	11^{3}						7■	5		1	8	2			10	4			9^{1}		31
		7			3	8			12	11^{2}							5		1	6	2	13		10	4			9^{1}		32
1		7	13		3				9	11^{3}							5			6	2	8■		10^{1}	4^{2}			12	14	33
1		7	6		3	13			8^{2}	11							5				2			10^{3}	4	9^{1}		12	14	34
1	8	7	6		3				9	11							5^{2}			13	2^{3}			10^{1}	4	12			14	35
1	8	7^{1}			3				9^{2}	11						12	5			6	2			10	4	13				36

AYR UNITED Second Division

Year Formed: 1910. *Ground & Address:* Somerset Park, Tryfield Place, Ayr KA8 9NB. *Telephone:* 01292 263435. *E-mail:* info@ayrunitedfc.co.uk. *Website:* ayrunitedfc.co.uk
Ground Capacity: 10,185, seated: 1549. *Size of Pitch:* 110yd × 72yd.
Chairman: Donald Cameron. *Managing Director:* Hugh Cameron. *Administrator:* Lachlan Cameron. *Lottery Manager:* Andrew Downie.
Manager: Robert Connor. *Assistant Manager:* Robert Reilly. *Physio:* John Kerr.
Managers since 1975: Alex Stuart, Ally MacLeod, Willie McLean, George Caldwell, Ally MacLeod, George Burley, Simon Stainrod, Gordon Dalziel, Mark Shanks, Campbell Money. *Club Nickname(s):* The Honest Men. *Previous Grounds:* None.
Record Attendance: 25,225 v Rangers, Division I, 13 Sept 1969.
Record Transfer Fee received: £300,000 for Steven Nicol to Liverpool (Oct 1981).
Record Transfer Fee paid: £90,000 for Mark Campbell from Stranraer (March 1999).
Record Victory: 11-1 v Dumbarton, League Cup, 13 Aug 1952.
Record Defeat: 0-9 in Division I v Rangers (1929); v Hearts (1931); B Division v Third Lanark (1954).
Most Capped Player: Jim Nisbet, 3, Scotland.
Most League Appearances: 459, John Murphy, 1963-78.
Most League League and Cup Goals in Season (Individual): 66, Jimmy Smith, 1927-28.
Most League and Cup Goals Overall (Individual): 213, Peter Price, 1955-61.

AYR UNITED 2005–06 LEAGUE RECORD

Match No.	Date	Venue	Opponents	Result		H/T Score	Lg. Pos.	Goalscorers	Attendance
1	Aug 6	H	Dumbarton	W	2-0	1-0	—	Boyd 17, Wardlaw 74	1274
2	13	A	Forfar Ath	W	2-1	1-1	3	Robertson 2 45, 64	470
3	20	H	Peterhead	D	1-1	0-1	3	Hyslop 51	1283
4	27	A	Gretna	D	2-2	2-0	3	Wardlaw 25, Robertson 26	1195
5	Sept 10	H	Partick Th	D	2-2	2-1	3	Vareille 6, Hyslop 37	2282
6	17	A	Raith R	D	3-3	2-0	3	Logan 2 28, 90, Wardlaw 43	1846
7	24	H	Morton	L	0-1	0-0	4		2102
8	Oct 1	A	Stirling A	D	3-3	2-2	5	Vareille 3 2, 9, 50	709
9	8	A	Peterhead	D	3-3	0-1	5	Vareille 2 48, 70, Logan 79	490
10	15	H	Alloa Ath	D	1-1	0-1	5	Maisano 74	1046
11	22	A	Dumbarton	L	0-6	0-2	6		919
12	29	A	Partick Th	L	0-1	0-1	8		2478
13	Nov 5	H	Gretna	L	1-3	0-2	8	Logan 74	1375
14	22	H	Raith R	W	2-1	1-1	—	Robertson 33, Conway 53	930
15	Dec 3	A	Alloa Ath	W	4-0	1-0	6	Logan 28, Vareille 2 48, 50, Wardlaw 85	488
16	6	A	Morton	L	1-2	0-1	—	Wardlaw 80	1677
17	13	H	Forfar Ath	W	2-1	0-0	—	Wardlaw 53, Robertson 72	815
18	17	H	Stirling A	L	2-5	1-3	6	Strain 19, Robertson 86	1029
19	26	H	Dumbarton	W	2-0	2-0	—	Conway 26, Ramsay 31	1266
20	Jan 2	A	Gretna	L	0-3	0-1	—		1268
21	14	H	Partick Th	L	1-2	1-0	6	Wardlaw 32	1886
22	21	A	Raith R	D	1-1	0-1	6	Vareille 60	1467
23	28	H	Morton	D	1-1	1-0	6	Wardlaw 19	1792
24	Feb 4	A	Stirling A	L	0-1	0-0	7		795
25	11	H	Alloa Ath	L	0-1	0-0	7		913
26	18	A	Forfar Ath	L	0-1	0-1	7		477
27	25	H	Peterhead	L	1-2	1-1	7	Robertson 5	849
28	Mar 11	A	Partick Th	D	2-2	0-1	8	Robertson 55, Conway 77	2347
29	18	H	Raith R	D	0-0	0-0	8		1010
30	21	H	Gretna	L	2-4	1-2	—	Vareille 25, Conway 86	909
31	25	A	Morton	W	4-0	1-0	7	Weaver 44, McAnespie 65, Wardlaw 2 86, 88	2437
32	Apr 1	H	Stirling A	W	3-0	2-0	7	Vareille 6, Ramsay 25, O'Brien (og) 90	1035
33	8	A	Alloa Ath	D	1-1	1-1	7	Weaver 3	601
34	15	A	Dumbarton	W	5-4	3-0	7	Logan 6, Strain 11, Vareille 13, McAnespie 54, Robertson 79	937
35	22	H	Forfar Ath	L	0-1	0-0	8		956
36	29	A	Peterhead	W	2-1	0-0	6	Vareille 68, Wardlaw 90	703

Final League Position: 6

Honours
League Champions: Division II 1911-12, 1912-13, 1927-28, 1936-37, 1958-59, 1965-66. Second Division 1987-88, 1996-97;
Runners-up: Division II 1910-11, 1955-56, 1968-69.
Scottish Cup: Semi-finals 2002.
League Cup: Runners-up: 2001-02.
B&Q Cup Runners-up: 1990-91, 1991-92.

Club colours: Shirt: White with black trim. Shorts: Black. Stockings: White with black.

Goalscorers: *League* (56): Vareille 13, Wardlaw 11, Robertson 9, Logan 6, Conway 4, Hyslop 2, McAnespie 2, Ramsay 2, Strain 2, Weaver 2, Boyd 1, Maisano 1, own goal 1.
Scottish Cup (4): Robertson 2, Wardlaw 2.
CIS Cup (5): Strain 2, Boyd 1, Vareille 1, Wardlaw 1.
Challenge Cup (0).

McGeown M 36	McKinstry J 27	Reid A 15 + 14	McLaughlin B 21	Campbell M 16 + 3	Logan R 33	Hyslop P 13 + 6	Boyd S 3 + 2	Vareille J 27 + 1	Ramsay D 26 + 3	Robertson C 34 + 2	Casey M 16 + 7	Wardlaw G 19 + 14	Cashmore I 3 + 13	Strain C 18 + 8	Conway C 26 + 5	Essler A 3 + 3	Weaver P 21 + 5	Joyce G 1 + 2	Tait T 3	Maisano J 1 + 2	Anis J 4 + 1	Stirling J 1	Bailey J 2	McAnespie K 15	Lowing D 11 + 1	Templeton P 1	Pettigrew C — + 1	Match No.
1	2	3	4	5	6	7[1]	8[2]	9[3]	10	11	12	13	14															1
1	2	3[1]	4	5	6			9	8	11[3]	7	13	14	10[2]	12													2
1	2	3	4	5	6	7[3]		9[2]	8	11	14	13		10[1]	12													3
1	2	14	4	5[1]	6	7[2]			8	11	12	9[3]		13		3	10											4
1	2	3	4	5[3]	6	7		9[1]	8[2]	11	13		12				10■	14										5
1	2	3	5[1]		6	7	10		8	11[2]	4	9			13			12										6
1	2				6	7[2]	12		8	11		9			3[1]	13	10	5	4									7
1	2	3			6	7[1]		9	8	11	4	10[2]	13		12				5									8
1	2	3[3]			6	7[2]		9	8	10[1]	4	12			11	14			5	13								9
1	4	14			6	7[1]		9	8[2]	5		10			11	3[3]	13			12	2							10
1	4				6■	12	13	9[2]	8■	5		10[3]			7	3[1]	14			11	2							11
1		3	5			7[1]	8	9[2]		10	4		13	14	11	12	6[3]				2							12
1	2[3]		4	5	6	7			8[1]	9	12	10		14	13		11					3[2]						13
1		12	4	5	6[3]	7			13	9	2	10	14	3[1]	11		8[2]											14
1		12	4	5	6	7[1]		9[2]		10[3]	2	14	13	3	11		8											15
1		7	4	5	6			9[3]	13	10	2	12	14	3[1]	11		8[2]											16
1	2[2]		4	5	6	13		14	3	11		10[3]	9[1]	12	7		8											17
1	2		4		6	12		9[1]	3	5	13	10	14	7[3]	11		8[2]											18
1		3	4		6	12		9[3]	8	5	2	10	14	11[2]	7[1]		13											19
1		3[2]			6■			9	8	4	2	10[3]	14	11[1]	7		12				13		5					20
1		13	4	2[1]	6				8[2]	9	7	10			11		12						5	3				21
1	2	13	4	5				9		7	6	10[2]		12	11		8[1]							3				22
1	2	12	4	5	6			9[2]		11	8	10[1]	13		7									3				23
1	2[1]	14	4	5	6			9		11[3]	8	10[2]		13	7									3	12			24
1		13	4	5	6			9[1]	2	12		10		8[2]	7									11	3			25
1	2[3]	14	4	5	6				8	12		10	9[1]	13	7									11[2]	3			26
1	2	8[1]	5		6			9[2]		10		12		13	7		4							11	3			27
1	2	12			6			9	8	5				7[1]	11		10							3	4			28
1	2				6			9[1]	8	5		12	13	7[2]	11		10							3	4			29
1	2			12	6			9	8	5		13		7[1]	11		10[2]							3	4			30
1	2	14		12	6			9[2]	8[1]	5		13		7[3]	11		10							3	4			31
1	2	14		13	6			9[1]	8	5[3]		12		7[2]	11		10							3	4■			32
1	2	3			6			9[1]	8	5	4	12		7	11		10											33
1	2	11[1]			6			9	8[2]	5	13	12		7			10							3	4			34
1	2	12			6[3]	13			14	5		9	8	7[2]	11[1]		10							3	4			35
1		11[1]				13		9		5	6[3]	14		7			10				2[2]			3	4	8	12	36

BERWICK RANGERS — Third Division

Year Formed: 1881. *Ground & Address:* Shielfield Park, Tweedmouth, Berwick-upon-Tweed TD15 2EF. *Telephone:* 01289 307424. *Fax:* 01289 309424. *E-mail:* dennismccleary133.fsnet.co.uk. *Website:* berwickrangers.co.uk
Ground Capacity: 4131, seated: 1366. *Size of Pitch:* 110yd × 70yd.
Chairman: Robert L. Wilson. *Vice-chairman:* Moray McLaren. *Company Secretary:* Ross Hood. *Football Secretary:* Dennis McCleary. *Treasurer:* J. N. Simpson.
Manager: John Coughlin. *Coach:* Ian Smith. *Physios:* Ian Smith, Ian Oliver. *Ground/Kit:* Ian Oliver.
Managers since 1975: H. Melrose, G. Haig, W. Galbraith, D. Smith, F. Connor, J. McSherry, E. Tait, J. Thomson, J. Jefferies, R. Callachan, J. Anderson, J. Crease, T. Hendrie, I. Ross, J. Thomson, P. Smith, S. Clark.
Club Nickname(s): The Borderers. *Previous Grounds:* Bull Stob Close, Pier Field, Meadow Field, Union Park, Old Shielfield.
Record Attendance: 13,365 v Rangers, Scottish Cup 1st rd, 28 Jan 1967.
Record Victory: 8-1 v Forfar Ath, Division II, 25 Dec 1965; v Vale of Leithen, Scottish Cup, Dec 1966.
Record Defeat: 1-9 v Hamilton A, First Division, 9 Aug 1980.
Most League Appearances: 435: Eric Tait, 1970-87.
Most League Goals in Season (Individual): 33: Ken Bowron, Division II, 1963-64.
Most Goals Overall (Individual): 115: Eric Tait, 1970-87.

BERWICK RANGERS 2005–06 LEAGUE RECORD

Match No.	*Date*	*Venue*	*Opponents*	*Result*	*H/T Score*	*Lg. Pos.*	*Goalscorers*	*Attendance*
1	Aug 6	A	East Fife	W 4-0	3-0	—	Little [8], McLeish (pen) [11], Hutchison [33], Connelly [66]	498
2	13	H	East Stirling	W 3-2	2-1	1	McLeish 2 (1 pen) [13 (p), 16], Hutchison [64]	406
3	20	A	Queen's Park	W 3-1	2-0	1	McLeish [3], Hutchison [28], Little [74]	431
4	27	H	Elgin C	W 3-1	1-1	2	Arthur [39], Gordon [75], Haynes [89]	390
5	Sept 10	A	Cowdenbeath	W 1-0	1-0	1	Haynes [4]	265
6	17	H	Arbroath	W 3-0	1-0	1	Haynes 2 [10, 59], Little [77]	367
7	24	A	Albion R	W 2-0	1-0	1	McNicoll [42], Hutchison [85]	314
8	Oct 1	H	Montrose	D 1-1	0-0	1	Little [54]	465
9	8	H	Elgin C	D 1-1	1-0	1	McLeish [12]	294
10	15	A	Stenhousemuir	W 1-0	1-0	1	McLeish (pen) [25]	558
11	22	H	East Fife	W 3-0	1-0	1	Gordon 2 [2, 55], Hutchison [49]	555
12	25	A	East Stirling	W 2-1	0-1	—	McGroarty [57], Little [59]	197
13	29	H	Cowdenbeath	W 1-0	0-0	1	McGroarty [65]	715
14	Nov 5	A	Elgin C	D 2-2	0-0	1	Haynes 2 (1 pen) [47, 90 (p)]	384
15	12	A	Arbroath	L 0-4	0-2	1		460
16	Dec 3	H	Stenhousemuir	L 0-2	0-1	2		507
17	10	H	Albion R	L 0-1	0-0	3		306
18	26	A	East Fife	L 0-1	0-0	—		575
19	Jan 7	A	Montrose	D 0-0	0-0	2		276
20	14	A	Cowdenbeath	D 1-1	1-0	2	Little [11]	432
21	21	H	Arbroath	W 2-1	2-0	2	McGroarty [2], Haynes [6]	416
22	28	A	Albion R	W 1-0	1-0	2	Hutchison [12]	299
23	Feb 4	H	Montrose	D 1-1	0-0	2	Haynes [54]	343
24	11	A	Stenhousemuir	L 0-1	0-1	2		548
25	18	H	East Stirling	W 1-0	1-0	2-	McLeish (pen) [43]	357
26	25	A	Queen's Park	W 1-0	1-0	2	McGroarty [7]	537
27	Mar 7	H	Queen's Park	L 1-2	0-0	—	Cowan [49]	249
28	11	H	Cowdenbeath	W 1-0	1-0	2	Hutchison [31]	403
29	14	A	Elgin C	W 3-1	2-1	—	Hutchison [34], Haynes 2 [43, 57]	298
30	18	A	Arbroath	W 2-0	2-0	2	Haynes [9], Horn [25]	558
31	25	H	Albion R	W 2-1	1-0	2	McNicoll [14], Haynes [89]	402
32	Apr 1	A	Montrose	W 2-1	1-0	2	Haynes 2 [6, 63]	301
33	8	H	Stenhousemuir	W 3-0	1-0	2	Paliczka [29], Haynes [60], Swanson [75]	710
34	15	H	East Fife	D 1-1	0-1	2	McLeish (pen) [74]	629
35	22	A	East Stirling	W 1-0	0-0	2	Manson [86]	246
36	29	H	Queen's Park	W 1-0	0-0	2	Hutchison [60]	1015

Final League Position: 2

Honours
League Champions: Second Division 1978-79; *Runners-up:* Second Division 1993-94. Third Division 1999-2000.
Scottish Cup: Quarter-finals 1953-54, 1979-80.
League Cup: Semi-finals 1963-64.
Bell's League Challenge: Quarter-finals 2004-05

Club colours: Shirt: Black with broad gold vertical stripes. Shorts: Black with white trim. Stockings: Gold with black and white trim.

Goalscorers: *League* (54): Haynes 15 (1 pen), Hutchison 9, McLeish 8 (4 pens), Little 6, McGroarty 4, Gordon 3, McNicoll 2, Arthur 1, Connelly 1, Cowan 1, Horn 1, Manson 1, Paliczka 1, Swanson 1.
Scottish Cup (0).
CIS Cup (4): Hutchison 2, McLeish 1, McNicoll 1.
Challenge Cup (3): Connelly 1, Hutchison 1, McLeish 1.
Play-Offs (3): Horn 2, Hutchison 1.

Coyle C 13	Murie D 36	McGroarty C 33	McNicoll G 31	Cowan M 30	Greenhill G 14 + 11	Arthur R 12 + 2	McLeish K 34 + 2	Hutchison G 35	Haynes K 30 + 3	Little I 31	Connelly G 12 + 2	McGarty M 7 + 8	Gordon K 11 + 7	Swanson D 11 + 16	Da Silva B 1 + 8	Shields J 12	O'Connor G 23	Gibson J — + 1	Horn R 10 + 4	Ramsay M — + 11	Manson S 1 + 10	Paliczka S 9 + 5	Lucas S — + 1	*Match No.*
1	2	3	4	5^{2}	6	7^{1}	8	9	10^{3}	11	12	13	14											1
1	2	3	4	5	6^{2}	7^{3}	8	9	10	11^{1}		13	12	14										2
1	2^{2}	3	4	5		7	8	10	9^{1}	11^{3}		6	12	13	14									3
1	2	3	4	5	6^{1}	7^{2}	8^{3}	9	12	11		14	10	13										4
1	2	3	4	5		7	8	9^{3}	10^{1}	11			12	13	14	6^{2}								5
1	2	3	4	5	13	7^{3}	8	9	10^{1}	11			12	14		6^{2}								6
1	2	3	4	5	12	7	8^{3}	9	10^{2}	11		14	13			6^{1}								7
1	2	3	4	5	12		7	9	10^{2}	11			13	8^{1}		6								8
1	2	3	4	5		7^{1}	8	9		11			10^{2}	12	13	6								9
1	2	3	4	5	12	7^{2}	8	9^{3}	13	11			10		14	6^{1}								10
	2	3	4	5^{1}	12	7^{2}	8	9		11			10^{3}	13	14	6	1							11
	2	3			7		4	9	10^{1}	11		5	8		12	6	1							12
	2	3	4		8^{1}		7	5	9^{2}	11		13	10	12		6	1							13
	2	3	4		6^{1}	7^{2}	8^{3}	5	9	11		12	10	14	13■		1							14
1	2	3	4		8^{1}	12	7^{2}	9	10			5	11	13		6^{3}		14						15
1	2	3	4			7^{1}	8	5	9	11			10		12	6								16
1	2^{1}	3	4			13	7	8	9^{2}	11		12	10	14		6^{3}			5					17
	2	3	4	5	13		8	9	12	10		7^{2}	11^{1}				1		6					18
	2	3	6	5			7		9			8		10	11		1		4					19
	2	3	4	5	6		7^{3}	10	9^{2}	11	12			8^{1}			1			13	14			20
	2	3	4	5	6		8	9	10^{2}	11	7^{1}			12			1			13				21
	2	3^{1}	4	5	6		8^{2}	9	10	11	7^{3}			14			1		12		13			22
	2	3	4	5	6^{1}		8	9^{2}	10					7^{3}			1		14	12	11	13		23
	2	3	4	5	8^{2}		12	9	10		7^{1}			13			1		6	14		11^{3}		24
	2	3		5	8^{1}		7	6	10^{3}			12		9			1		4	13	14	11^{2}		25
	2	3		5			7^{2}	6		11	8			10			1		4	13	12	9^{1}		26
	2	3		5			7	9	10^{2}	11	6			8^{1}			1		4	13		12		27
	2	3	4	5	6^{1}		12	9	10^{3}	11	7						1			14	13	8^{2}		28
	2	3^{1}	4	5	13		7	9	10^{2}	11	6						1		12		14	8^{3}		29
	2		4	5^{1}			7	9	10^{3}	11	6						1		3	14	13	8^{2}	12	30
	2	3	4	5			7	9	10	11^{1}	8^{3}			13			1		6^{2}	14		12		31
	2	3	4	5	13		7	9	10	11				6^{2}			1			12		8^{1}		32
	2	3	4	5	12		7	9	10^{3}	11	6^{1}			13			1				14	8^{2}		33
	2	3	4^{2}	5	12		7	9	10	11				6			1		13			8^{1}		34
	2			5	13		7^{3}	9	10^{1}	11	6^{2}	3		8			1		4		14	12		35
	2		4	5■			7	9	10^{1}	11	6	3		8^{2}			1				12	13		36

BRECHIN CITY — Second Division

Year Formed: 1906. *Ground & Address:* Glebe Park, Trinity Rd, Brechin, Angus DD9 6BJ. *Telephone:* 01356 622856.
Fax (to Secretary): 01356 625524. *Website:* www.brechincity.com
Ground Capacity: total: 3060, seated: 1518. *Size of Pitch:* 110yd × 67yd.
Chairman: David Birse. *Vice-Chairman:* Hugh Campbell Adamson. *Secretary:* Ken Ferguson.
Manager: Michael O'Neill. *Assistant Manager:* Gareth Evans. *Physio:* Tom Gilmartin.
Managers since 1975: C. Dunn, I. Stewart, D. Houston, I. Fleming, J. Ritchie, I. Redford, J. Young, R. Campbell, I. Campbell.
Club Nickname(s): The City. *Previous Grounds:* Nursery Park.
Record Attendance: 8122 v Aberdeen, Scottish Cup 3rd rd, 3 Feb 1973.
Record Transfer Fee received: £100,000 for Scott Thomson to Aberdeen (1991).
Record Transfer Fee paid: £16,000 for Sandy Ross from Berwick Rangers (1991).
Record Victory: 12-1 v Thornhill, Scottish Cup 1st rd, 28 Jan 1926.
Record Defeat: 0-10 v Airdrieonians, Albion R and Cowdenbeath, all in Division II, 1937-38.
Most League Appearances: 459: David Watt, 1975-89.
Most League Goals in Season (Individual): 26: W. McIntosh, Division II, 1959-60.
Most Goals Overall (Individual): 131: Ian Campbell.

BRECHIN CITY 2005–06 LEAGUE RECORD

Match No.	Date	Venue	Opponents	Result		H/T Score	Lg. Pos.	Goalscorers	Attendance
1	Aug 6	H	Hamilton A	L	1-2	0-1	—	Johnson 63	736
2	13	A	Queen of the S	D	0-0	0-0	7		1480
3	20	H	Airdrie U	D	1-1	1-0	8	Johnson 24	668
4	27	A	St Mirren	L	0-1	0-1	9		2713
5	Sept 10	H	Clyde	D	1-1	1-0	9	Hampshire 4	680
6	17	A	Ross Co	L	0-1	0-1	9		2124
7	24	H	Stranraer	L	2-3	1-3	9	Byers 2 2, 56	502
8	Oct 1	H	Dundee	L	1-3	1-3	9	Callaghan 45	2037
9	15	A	St Johnstone	L	1-3	1-1	10	Hampshire 15	2031
10	22	A	Hamilton A	L	0-3	0-1	10		1226
11	25	H	Queen of the S	D	1-1	1-0	—	Byers 28	503
12	29	A	Clyde	L	1-2	0-1	10	Byers 49	829
13	Nov 12	H	Ross Co	L	1-4	1-2	10	Britton 25	502
14	15	H	St Mirren	L	2-3	1-1	—	Byers 30, Ritchie 82	713
15	19	A	Stranraer	D	1-1	1-0	10	Britton 35	448
16	26	A	Dundee	L	0-1	0-0	10		3278
17	Dec 3	H	St Johnstone	L	1-4	0-1	10	Britton 58	811
18	10	H	Hamilton A	L	0-1	0-1	10		480
19	17	A	Airdrie U	L	0-6	0-1	10		1106
20	26	H	Clyde	W	3-1	1-0	—	Hampshire 2 20, 55, Geddes 87	711
21	31	A	St Mirren	L	2-3	1-1	10	White 25, Smith 63	2913
22	Jan 2	A	Ross Co	L	0-2	0-2	—		2227
23	14	H	Stranraer	D	0-0	0-0	10		507
24	21	H	Dundee	L	0-3	0-1	10		1421
25	28	A	St Johnstone	L	0-3	0-2	10		2069
26	Feb 11	H	Airdrie U	D	0-0	0-0	10		602
27	18	A	Queen of the S	D	0-0	0-0	10		1844
28	Mar 11	A	Clyde	L	1-5	1-1	10	Callaghan 35	738
29	18	H	Ross Co	D	3-3	1-0	10	Walker 15, Hannah (pen) 55, Johnson 71	503
30	21	H	St Mirren	L	0-3	0-1	—		791
31	25	A	Stranraer	L	0-2	0-2	10		427
32	Apr 8	H	St Johnstone	L	0-2	0-2	10		876
33	11	A	Dundee	W	1-0	1-0	10	Burns 10	1841
34	15	A	Hamilton A	L	0-2	0-1	10		1117
35	22	H	Queen of the S	D	1-1	0-1	10	Callaghan 79	809
36	29	A	Airdrie U	D	3-3	1-1	10	Devlin 2 32, 48, Byers 69	1212

Final League Position: 10

Honours
League Champions: C Division 1953-54. Second Division 1982-83, 1989-90. Third Division 2001-02. *Runners-up:* Second Division 1992-93, 2002-03. Third Division 1995-96. Second Division 2004-05.
Bell's League Challenge: Runners-up 2002-03. Semi-finals 2001-02.

Club colours: Shirt, Shorts, Stockings: Red with white trimmings.

Goalscorers: *League* (28): Byers 6, Hampshire 4, Britton 3, Callaghan 3, Johnson 3, Devlin 2, Burns 1, Geddes 1, Hannah 1 (pen), Ritchie 1, Smith 1, Walker 1, White 1.
Scottish Cup (1): King 1.
CIS Cup (0).
Challenge Cup (3): Gibson 1, Hampshire 1, Ritchie 1.

Nelson C 33	McEwan C 16 + 2	Bollan G 17 + 1	Walker S 35	Deas P 15 + 1	Johnson G 19 + 4	King C 16 + 15	Mitchell A 26	Ritchie P 9 + 9	Hampshire S 28 + 3	Gibson G 5 + 3	Burns A 14 + 6	Callaghan S 19 + 10	White D 27 + 4	Byers K 23 + 4	Smith D 18 + 14	Hamilton S 6 + 1	Ferguson S 6	Winter C 14 + 4	Britton G 19 + 4	Hillcoat J 3 + 1	Geddes C 3 + 5	Devlin S 1 + 3	Grainger D 10	Wilson S 3 + 1	Nicol K 1	Strachan R — + 1	Templeman C 3 + 7	Hannah D 7	Match No.
1	2^{3}	3	4	5	6	7^{2}	8	9^{1}	10	11	12	13	14																1
1	2	3^{1}	4	5	8		6	9	7^{3}	11^{2}	10		12	13	14														2
1	2		5	3	8	13	7	9^{2}	10		11^{3}	6^{1}	4	14	12														3
1	2	3^{1}	6	5	8■		4	14	9		10	13	12	7^{2}	11^{3}														4
1		3	5	6		12	4	13	10^{2}		14				11^{1}	2	7	8^{3}	9■										5
1	2^{2}		6	3		7	4	9	10^{3}		14	12	5	8	13			11^{1}											6
1			6	3		7	4^{1}	13	11^{2}		14	10	5	2	12			8^{3}	9										7
1	2^{1}		6	3		7^{3}		9^{2}	13		14	11■	5	8	12		4		10										8
1		3	6		8^{3}	12	4	13	11^{1}		10		5	7		2		14	9^{2}										9
1		3	6		8			9^{1}	11			14	5	7	12	2^{2}	4^{3}	13	10										10
1		3	6		8^{3}	13		12	7			14	5	10	11^{2}	2		4	9^{1}										11
1		3	6	2	8	12		13	7^{2}			14	5^{3}	10	11			4^{1}	9										12
1		6	5	3^{1}		13	4		10				12	7	11		2	8^{2}	9										13
1		3	6			12	8	14				11^{1}	5	2	13	10^{3}	4^{2}	7	9										14
1■		6	5		8^{2}	13	11	12	7^{1}			3	4	10				2	9^{3}	14									15
	13	3	5		11^{2}	10	8	9				6	4	7	12			2^{1}		1									16
	11^{1}	3	5		13	7	10^{3}	14				6	4	8	12			2^{2}	9	1									17
1	14	3■	5		7^{2}	12	11	9				6	4	8^{1}	13			2^{3}	10										18
1	2^{2}		5		11	7	6	9^{1}	12			3	4	8^{3}	14			13	10										19
1		3	5			7^{2}	10		9^{3}		12	6	4	8	11^{1}			2■	14		13								20
1			5		2■	7	3^{3}		9		10	6	4	8^{1}	11^{2}				12		13	14							21
1			5			7^{2}			8		10	3	4		11^{1}	12	6	2^{3}	9		13	14							22
1			5			7^{2}	10		9		8	6	4		11^{1}			2	12		13		3						23
1			5^{3}	14		7	11		10		8	6	4		12	2^{2}		13	9^{1}				3						24
1		13	5	3		7			9^{1}		2	6									10^{2}	12	11	4^{3}	8	14			25
1		3	5		13	14	4^{2}				8			7	11^{3}				9^{1}		12		6	2			10		26
1		3	5		12	13	4^{1}		10		8	14		7^{2}	11^{3}								6	2			9		27
1			5		8^{3}	14	11		7^{1}	2	10^{2}	6			13				12				3■				9	4	28
1	2		5	3	8		7		9			12	4		11^{1}				10^{2}								13	6	29
1	2^{3}		5		8	14	7		9			12	4	6	11^{1}				10^{2}				3				13		30
1	2^{3}		5^{1}		8	12	7		9				4	14	11				10^{2}				3				13	6	31
1	2		5	3	6	10^{2}			9^{3}	12		14	4	8	11^{1}												13	7	32
1	2		5		12		8		10^{2}	13	11	7	4		9^{1}								3					6	33
1	2		5		6	8^{1}			10^{3}	14	11^{2}		4	7	9								3■	12			13		34
1	2		5	3		7^{3}			14	10^{1}		8	4	13	9^{2}						11						12	6	35
	2			3		13			9	8^{3}		10	4	6	14					1	11^{1}	7^{2}					12	5	36

CELTIC — Premier League

Year Formed: 1888. *Ground & Address:* Celtic Park, Glasgow G40 3RE. *Telephone:* 0845 671 1888. *Fax:* 0141 551 8106.
E-mail: customerservices@celticfc.co.uk. *Website:* www.celticfc.net
Ground Capacity: all seated: 60,355. *Size of Pitch:* 105m × 68m.
Chairman: Brian Quinn. *Chief Executive:* Peter Lawwell. *Secretary:* Robert Howat.
Manager: Gordon Strachan. *Assistant Manager:* Gary Pendry. *Youth Development Manager:* Tommy Burns. *Head Youth Coach:* Willie McStay. *Physio:* Tim Williamson. *Club Doctor:* Dr Roddy Macdonald. *Kit Manager:* John Clark.
Managers since 1975: Jock Stein, Billy McNeill, David Hay, Billy McNeill, Liam Brady, Lou Macari, Tommy Burns, Wim Jansen, Dr Jozef Venglos, John Barnes, Martin O'Neill. *Club Nickname(s):* The Bhoys. *Previous Grounds:* None.
Record Attendance: 92,000 v Rangers, Division I, 1 Jan 1938.
Record Transfer Fee received: £4,700,000 for Paolo Di Canio to Sheffield W (August 1997).
Record Transfer Fee paid: £6,000,000 for Chris Sutton from Chelsea (July 2000).
Record Victory: 11-0 Dundee, Division I, 26 Oct 1895.
Record Defeat: 0-8 v Motherwell, Division I, 30 Apr 1937.
Most Capped Player: Pat Bonner 80, Republic of Ireland.
Most League Appearances: 486: Billy McNeill, 1957-75.
Most League Goals in Season (Individual): 50: James McGrory, Division I, 1935-36.
Most Goals Overall (Individual): 397: James McGrory, 1922-39.

Honours
League Champions: (40 times) Division I 1892-93, 1893-94, 1895-96, 1897-98, 1904-05, 1905-06, 1906-07, 1907-08, 1908-09, 1909-10, 1913-14, 1914-15, 1915-16, 1916-17, 1918-19, 1921-22, 1925-26, 1935-36, 1937-38, 1953-54, 1965-66, 1966-67, 1967-68, 1968-69, 1969-70, 1970-71, 1971-72, 1972-73, 1973-74. Premier Division 1976-77, 1978-79, 1980-81, 1981-82, 1985-86, 1987-88, 1997-98, 2000-01, 2001-02, 2003–04, 2005–06. *Runners-up:* 27 times.

CELTIC 2005–06 LEAGUE RECORD

Match No.	Date		Venue	Opponents	Result		H/T Score	Lg. Pos.	Goalscorers	Attendance
1	Jul	30	A	Motherwell	D	4-4	3-1	—	Hartson 3 [14, 31, 43], Beattie [90]	9903
2	Aug	6	H	Dundee U	W	2-0	1-0	3	Hartson [37], Beattie [88]	55,456
3		13	H	Falkirk	W	3-1	0-1	2	Hartson [48], Thompson 2 [74, 89]	57,151
4		20	A	Rangers	L	1-3	0-1	3	Maloney (pen) [86]	49,699
5		28	A	Dunfermline Ath	W	4-0	2-0	2	Zurawski 2 [5, 73], Hartson [10], Nakamura [57]	8998
6	Sept	10	H	Aberdeen	W	2-0	1-0	2	Zurawski [13], Petrov [60]	58,798
7		18	A	Hibernian	W	1-0	1-0	2	Petrov [5]	15,649
8		24	H	Inverness CT	W	2-1	0-0	2	Beattie 2 [57, 67]	56,823
9	Oct	1	A	Livingston	W	5-0	2-0	2	McManus [35], Maloney [44], Zurawski [50], Sutton [61], Beattie [71]	8862
10		15	H	Hearts	D	1-1	1-1	2	Beattie [12]	59,463
11		23	A	Kilmarnock	W	1-0	1-0	2	Petrov [24]	10,544
12		26	H	Motherwell	W	5-0	3-0	—	Petrov 3 [13, 22, 79], Maloney [17], Nakamura [67]	56,575
13		30	A	Dundee U	W	4-2	3-2	1	Hartson [17], Sutton [28], Balde [32], Pearson [88]	11,942
14	Nov	6	A	Falkirk	W	3-0	2-0	1	Maloney [40], McGeady [42], Hartson [68]	6498
15		19	H	Rangers	W	3-0	1-0	1	Hartson [11], Balde [56], McGeady [60]	58,997
16		26	H	Dunfermline Ath	L	0-1	0-1	1		56,575
17	Dec	4	A	Aberdeen	W	3-1	0-0	1	McGeady [55], Petrov [57], Telfer [64]	17,031
18		10	H	Hibernian	W	3-2	1-0	1	Hartson 2 [40, 64], Maloney [57]	59,808
19		18	A	Inverness CT	D	1-1	1-1	1	Hartson [21]	7500
20		26	H	Livingston	W	2-1	1-0	1	Maloney [38], Nakamura [87]	58,953
21	Jan	1	A	Hearts	W	3-2	0-2	1	Pearson [55], McManus 2 [88, 90]	16,532
22		14	H	Kilmarnock	W	4-2	2-1	1	Nakamura [2], Maloney (pen) [15], McManus [52], Zurawski [66]	58,883
23		22	A	Motherwell	W	3-1	1-1	1	Zurawski [17], McGeady [71], Hartson [85]	11,503
24		28	H	Dundee U	D	3-3	1-1	1	Hartson [8], Zurawski [48], Petrov [66]	59,458
25	Feb	8	H	Falkirk	W	2-1	2-0	—	Keane [34], McManus [44]	56,713
26		12	A	Rangers	W	1-0	1-0	1	Zurawski [11]	49,788
27		19	A	Dunfermline Ath	W	8-1	4-1	1	Petrov [3], Hartson [23], Zurawski 4 [31, 40, 55, 87], Maloney [73], Lennon [81]	9017
28	Mar	4	H	Aberdeen	W	3-0	0-0	1	Petrov [66], Maloney [75], Zurawski [88]	59,657
29		12	A	Hibernian	W	2-1	1-1	1	Maloney [35], McManus [59]	14,719
30		22	H	Inverness CT	W	2-1	1-0	—	McManus [34], Maloney [78]	57,105
31		26	A	Livingston	W	2-0	0-0	1	Zurawski [47], Maloney [51]	6504
32	Apr	5	H	Hearts	W	1-0	1-0	—	Hartson [4]	59,694
33		9	A	Kilmarnock	W	4-1	1-0	1	Nakamura 2 [7, 82], Hartson [63], Dublin [83]	10,978
34		16	H	Hibernian	D	1-1	0-1	1	Zurawski [75]	59,359
35		23	H	Rangers	D	0-0	0-0	1		58,928
36		30	A	Hearts	L	0-3	0-2	1		16,795
37	May	3	H	Kilmarnock	W	2-0	0-0	—	Zurawski [54], Varga [64]	56,538
38		7	A	Aberdeen	D	2-2	1-0	1	Hartson [5], Maloney [61]	14,597

Final League Position: 1

Scottish Cup Winners: (33 times) 1892, 1899, 1900, 1904, 1907, 1908, 1911, 1912, 1914, 1923, 1925, 1927, 1931, 1933, 1937, 1951, 1954, 1965, 1967, 1969, 1971, 1972, 1974, 1975, 1977, 1980, 1985, 1988, 1989, 1995, 2001, 2004, 2005. *Runners-up:* 18 times.
League Cup Winners: (13 times) 1956-57, 1957-58, 1965-66, 1966-67, 1967-68, 1968-69, 1969-70, 1974-75, 1982-83, 1997-98, 1999-2000, 2000-01, 2005-06. *Runners-up:* 13 times.

European: *European Cup:* 104 matches (1966-67 winners, 1967-68, 1968-69, 1969-70 runners-up, 1970-71, 1971-72 semi-finals, 1972-73, 1973-74 semi-finals, 1974-75, 1977-78, 1979-80, 1981-82, 1982-83, 1986-87, 1988-89, 1998-99, 2001-02, 2002-03, 2003-04, 2005-06). *Cup Winners' Cup:* 39 matches (1963-64 semi-finals, 1965-66 semi-finals, 1975-76, 1980-81, 1984-85, 1985-86, 1989-90, 1995-96). *UEFA Cup:* 73 matches (*Fairs Cup:* 1962-63, 1964-65. *UEFA Cup:* 1976-77, 1983-84, 1987-88, 1991-92, 1992-93, 1993-94, 1996-97, 1997-98, 1998-99, 1999-2000, 2000-01, 2001-02, 2002-03 runners-up, 2003-04 quarter-finals).

Club colours: Shirt: Emerald green and white hoops. Shorts: White with emerald trim. Stockings: White.

Goalscorers: *League* (93): Hartson 18, Zurawski 16, Maloney 13 (2 pens), Petrov 10, McManus 7, Beattie 6, Nakamura 6, McGeady 4, Balde 2, Pearson 2, Sutton 2, Thompson 2, Dublin 1, Keane 1, Lennon 1, Telfer 1, Varga 1.
Scottish Cup (1): Zurawski 1.
CIS Cup (9): Maloney 3, Zurawski 3, Balde 1, Dublin 1, Hartson 1.

Marshall D 4	Telfer P 36	Camara M 18	Varga S 9 + 1	McManus S 36	Petrov S 36 + 1	Lennon N 32	Thompson A 11 + 6	McGeady A 11 + 9	Hartson J 29 + 6	Maloney S 27 + 9	Beattie C 7 + 6	Boruc A 34	Balde D 28	Nakamura S 30 + 3	Zurawski M 22 + 2	Virgo A 3 + 7	Lawson P 1 + 2	Pearson S 2 + 16	Sutton C 7 + 1	Agathe D — + 4	Wallace R 8 + 3	McGlinchey M — + 1	Keane R 10	Wilson M 14 + 1	Dublin D 3 + 8	*Match No.*
1	2	3	4	5	6	7	8	9^{1}	10	11	12															1
	2	3		5	6	7	8		10	12	13	1	4	9^{2}	11^{1}											2
	2	3		5	6	7	8		10	12	13	1	4	9^{2}	11^{1}											3
	2	3^{3}		5	6	7■	8■		10^{2}	12	11	1	4	9^{1}	13	14										4
	2	3		5	6			13	10		8	1	4	9	11^{2}	7^{1}	12									5
	2	3		5	6	7	8^{3}		10^{2}	12	13	1	4	9^{1}	11			14								6
	2	3		5	6	7	8^{1}		10^{2}	14	13	1	4	9^{3}	11			12								7
	2	3		5^{1}	6				10	11	8	1	4	9^{2}		12			7	13						8
	2	3		5	6				12	11	8^{2}	1	4	9	10^{1}				7	13						9
	2	3		5	6	7^{2}	8^{1}		13	12	11	1	4	9^{3}					10	14						10
	2	3		5	6	7	13	14	12	11^{2}	10^{1}	1	4	9^{3}					8							11
	2	3^{1}		5	6	7		14	13	11	10^{2}	1	4	9					8^{3}		12					12
	2	3		5	6	7		14	10^{1}	11^{3}	12^{2}	1	4	9				13	8							13
	2	3		5	6^{1}	7		8	10^{3}	11^{2}		1	4	9		14		12			13					14
	2	3		5	6	7	12	8	10	11^{1}		1	4	9^{2}						13						15
	2	3^{2}		5	6	7	8^{1}	11	10			1	4		12			13	9							16
	2			5	6	7		8	10^{2}	12		1	4	9	11^{1}	13					3					17
	2			5	6	7		8	10	11		1	4	9^{1}				12			3					18
	2			5	6	7		8^{1}	10	11		1	4	9					12		3					19
	2			5	6	7		8^{1}	10	11		1	4	9		13					3^{2}	12				20
	2			5	6^{1}	7^{2}	8	13	10	11		1	4	9				12			3					21
	2			4	6	7		12	10	11		1		8	9^{1}						3		5			22
	2	3	4		6	7		12	10	11		1		8^{1}	9^{2}	5		13								23
			4		6	7			10	11		1		8^{1}	9	5		12			3			2		24
	3			5	6		12			11		1	4	8^{1}	10								7	2	9	25
	3			5	6	7			10^{1}	11^{2}		1	4		9			13					8	2	12	26
	3			5	6^{3}	7	13		10^{1}	11		1	4	14	9								8^{2}	2	12	27
	3			5	6	7	13		10^{1}	11		1	4	12	9								8^{2}	2		28
	3			5	6	7				11		1	4	9^{1}	10			12					8	2		29
	3			5	6^{1}	7	14		10^{2}	11		1	4	8	9^{3}			12						2	13	30
	3^{1}		13	5	6	7			14	11		1	4	8	10						12			2^{2}	9^{3}	31
	3			5	6	7		14	10^{2}	11^{3}		1	4	8^{1}	9			12						2	13	32
1	3		4	5	6^{1}	7^{3}		9	10^{2}	11				8			14	12						2	13	33
	3		4	5	6^{1}	7			10^{2}	12		1		9	11			14					8^{3}	2	13	34
	3		4	5	6	7		13	10^{3}	11^{2}		1		12	9								8^{1}	2	14	35
	3		4	5	12	7^{1}			14	11		1		8	10^{2}			13					6	2	9^{3}	36
1			4	5	6		7	11^{1}		12					10^{2}	14		9			3^{3}		8	2	13	37
1	3	2	4	5			7	9^{1}	10^{2}	11						13	6	8						12		38

CLYDE First Division

Year Formed: 1877. *Ground & Address:* Broadwood Stadium, Cumbernauld, G68 9NE. *Telephone:* 01236 451511.
Website: www.clydefc.co.uk
Ground Capacity: all seated: 8200. *Size of Pitch:* 112yd × 76yd.
Chairman: Len McGuire. *Secretary:* John D. Taylor.
Manager: Graham Roberts. *Assistant Manager:* Joe Miller. *Physio:* Ian McKinlay.
Managers since 1975: S. Anderson, C. Brown, J. Clark, A. Smith, G. Speirs, A. Maitland, A. Kernaghan, B. Reid.
Club Nickname(s): The Bully Wee. *Previous Grounds:* Barrowfield Park 1877-97, Shawfield Stadium 1897-1986.
Record Attendance: 52,000 v Rangers, Division I, 21 Nov 1908.
Record Transfer Fee received: £175,000 for Scott Howie to Norwich City (Aug 1993).
Record Transfer Fee paid: £14,000 for Harry Hood from Sunderland (1966).
Record Victory: 11-1 v Cowdenbeath, Division II, 6 Oct 1951.
Record Defeat: 0-11 v Dumbarton, Scottish Cup 4th rd, 22 Nov, 1879; v Rangers, Scottish Cup 4th rd, 13 Nov 1880.
Most Capped Player: Tommy Ring, 12, Scotland.
Most League Appearances: 428: Brian Ahern.
Most League Goals in Season (Individual): 32: Bill Boyd, 1932-33.

CLYDE 2005–06 LEAGUE RECORD

Match No.	Date	Venue	Opponents	Result	H/T Score	Lg. Pos.	Goalscorers	Attendance
1	Aug 6	A	Ross Co	L 1-3	1-2	—	Bryson 31	2208
2	13	H	Dundee	D 1-1	0-0	8	Miller 76	1825
3	20	A	Stranraer	W 2-1	0-0	7	O'Donnell 2 59, 87	692
4	27	H	Queen of the S	W 1-0	1-0	4	Williams 15	1152
5	Sept 10	A	Brechin C	D 1-1	0-1	5	McHale 46	680
6	17	A	St Mirren	L 0-2	0-1	8		3068
7	24	H	St Johnstone	L 0-1	0-1	8		1220
8	Oct 1	A	Airdrie U	W 3-1	1-0	6	Williams 2 3, 66, Brighton 62	1603
9	15	H	Hamilton A	D 1-1	1-1	6	Williams 24	1392
10	22	H	Ross Co	W 1-0	1-0	6	Williams 25	922
11	26	A	Dundee	D 3-3	1-2	—	Brighton 35, O'Donnell 2 (1 pen) 78, 83 (p)	3360
12	29	H	Brechin C	W 2-1	1-0	5	Williams 31, McGowan 59	829
13	Nov 5	A	Queen of the S	W 2-1	0-0	5	McGregor N 57, Williams 75	1436
14	12	H	St Mirren	L 1-2	0-0	5	Williams 61	1904
15	19	A	St Johnstone	D 0-0	0-0	5		2195
16	26	H	Airdrie U	W 1-0	1-0	5	McGowan 23	1263
17	Dec 3	A	Hamilton A	D 1-1	0-0	5	Miller 85	1787
18	10	A	Ross Co	W 1-0	1-0	5	O'Donnell 7	2149
19	17	H	Stranraer	W 1-0	0-0	4	Masterton 90	901
20	26	A	Brechin C	L 1-3	0-1	—	Bryson 90	711
21	31	H	Queen of the S	W 3-0	2-0	2	Williams 2 7, 62, O'Donnell 40	1101
22	Jan 2	A	St Mirren	L 1-2	0-2	—	Brighton 47	4338
23	14	H	St Johnstone	L 2-3	0-2	5	Brighton 2 55, 61	1296
24	21	A	Airdrie U	D 1-1	1-1	5	Brighton 22	1623
25	28	H	Hamilton A	D 2-2	1-0	5	O'Donnell 2 28, 53	1423
26	Feb 11	A	Stranraer	W 5-0	4-0	5	Hunter 4 3, 5, 32, 83, Bouadji 29	552
27	18	H	Dundee	D 3-3	2-2	4	Brighton 15, McDonald K (og) 23, McHale 70	1062
28	Mar 4	A	Queen of the S	L 1-2	0-0	5	Imrie 78	1750
29	11	H	Brechin C	W 5-1	1-1	4	Malone 18, Williams 3 50, 53, 58, O'Donnell 78	738
30	18	H	St Mirren	L 0-1	0-0	4		2324
31	25	A	St Johnstone	L 0-1	0-1	4		1997
32	Apr 1	H	Airdrie U	W 3-1	2-0	5	McHale (pen) 29, Bouadji 42, Brighton 79	1264
33	8	A	Hamilton A	L 0-2	0-1	5		1360
34	15	H	Ross Co	W 2-0	1-0	5	O'Donnell 2 (1 pen) 22, 73 (p)	813
35	22	A	Dundee	W 1-0	0-0	5	Imrie 64	3199
36	29	H	Stranraer	D 1-1	0-1	5	McKeown 90	1254

Final League Position: 5

Honours
League Champions: Division II 1904-05, 1951-52, 1956-57, 1961-62, 1972-73. Second Division 1977-78, 1981-82, 1992-93, 1999-2000.
Runners-up: Division II 1903-04, 1905-06, 1925-26, 1963-64. Second Division 2003-04.
Scottish Cup Winners: 1939, 1955, 1958; *Runners-up:* 1910, 1912, 1949.
Bell's League Challenge: Quarter-finals 2004-05.

Club colours: Shirt: White with red and black trim. Shorts: Black. Stockings: white.

Goalscorers: *League* (54): Williams 13, O'Donnell 11 (2 pens), Brighton 8, Hunter 4, McHale 3 (1 pen), Bouadji 2, Bryson 2, Imrie 2, McGowan M 2, Miller 2, McGregor N 1, McKeown 1, Malone 1, Masterton 1, own goal 1.
Scottish Cup (2): Bryson 1, Malone 1.
CIS Cup (6): Brighton 2, Arbuckle 1, Bryson 1, McGregor N 1, O'Donnell 1.
Challenge Cup (2): McGregor N 1, Williams 1.

Jarvie P 18	McGregor N 22	Malone E 31	Higgins C 34	McKeown C 34	McHale P 16 + 1	Bryson C 30 + 3	O'Donnell S 32 + 1	Williams A 29 + 3	Brighton T 34 + 2	Harris R 15 + 5	McGowan M 34 + 1	Miller J 2 + 13	Hunter R 3 + 11	Brawley W — + 3	Dick A 2 + 6	Cherrie P 18 + 2	Arbuckle G 2 + 17	Masterton S 18 + 4	Bouadji R 9 + 4	Bradley K 1 + 7	McDonald K 4 + 7	Imrie D 8 + 3	McKenna S — + 1	*Match No.*
1	2^{1}	3^{2}	4	5	6	7	8	9^{3}	10	11	12	13	14											1
1	2	3	4^{1}	5	6^{3}	7	8	9^{2}	10		11	12	13	14										2
1	2	3^{1}	4	5	6	7	8	9^{2}	10^{3}		11	13		12	14									3
1^{G}	2	3	4	5	6	7^{1}	8	9^{2}	10		11			13		15	12							4
1	2■	3	4	5^{1}	6	7	8	9	10		11		13				12^{2}							5
1^{G}		3	4	5		7^{1}	8	9^{2}	10	2	11	12			6	15	13							6
1	2^{3}	3	4	5	6^{1}	7	8	9	10^{2}		11		13				12	14						7
1	2	3	4	5		7	8	9^{1}	10^{2}	6	11		12				13							8
1	2■	3	4	5		7	8	9^{1}	10	6^{2}	11				13				12					9
1		3	4	5		7^{2}	8	9	10^{3}	6^{1}	11		14		13			2	12					10
1	2	3	4^{1}	5		7	8	9^{2}	10	12	11							6		13				11
1	2	3^{1}	4	5		7	8	9^{3}	10	12	11						14	6^{2}		13				12
1	2	3	4	5		7^{2}	8	9^{1}	10^{3}		11				13		14	6		12				13
1	2	3	4	5		7	8^{2}	9^{1}	10		11		13				12	6						14
	2	3	4	5			8	9^{2}	10	7^{1}	11	13			12	1		6						15
	2		4	5			8	9^{2}	10	7	11	14			3^{1}	1	13	6^{3}		12				16
			4	5		7^{2}	8	9^{3}	10		11	13	12			1	14	6	3	2^{1}				17
	2		4	5		7	8	9^{1}	10^{2}		11	12				1	13	6	3					18
	2	3	4^{1}	5		12	8	9^{2}	10		11	13				1		6	7					19
	2	3	4	5		12	8	13	10		11^{2}	9^{3}	14			1		6	7^{1}					20
	2	3	4	5		7^{3}	8^{1}	9^{2}	10		11		13			1	12	6	14					21
	2	3	4	5		7	8■	9	10		11					1	12	6^{1}						22
	2	3		5		7		9^{1}	10	4^{3}	11	12	8^{2}			1	13	6		14				23
	2	3	4	5■		7	8	9^{2}	10	6^{3}	11^{1}	12	14			1	13							24
	2	3	4			7	8		10		11	9^{2}				1	13	6^{1}	5		12			25
1			4		6	13			14	3	11^{3}		8		12		10	7^{1}	2		5^{2}	9		26
1		3	4	5	13	7^{2}	8		10	12	11		9^{3}						2^{1}		6	14		27
1		3	4^{2}	5	6	7	8^{3}	12	10	2	11						9^{1}				14	13		28
		3	4	5	6	7	12	9^{1}	13	2	11					1					8^{2}	10^{3}	14	29
		3	4	5	6	7	8	9	10	2						1						11		30
1		3	4	5^{3}	6^{2}	7	8		10	2^{1}	11							12	13		14	9		31
		3	4^{3}	5	6	7		12	10		11					1	14	8^{2}	2		13	9^{1}		32
		3		5	6^{3}	7	8	9	10	12	11					1		4^{2}	2^{1}		14	13		33
		3	4	5	6^{3}	7	8^{2}	9^{1}	10		11	12				1		13			14	2		34
		3	4	5	6	7^{1}	8	9^{2}	10^{3}	14	11					1				13	12	2		35
			4^{2}	5	6^{1}		8	9	10	3	11	13				1		12		14	7	2^{3}		36

COWDENBEATH Second Division

Year Formed: 1881. *Ground & Address:* Central Park, Cowdenbeath KY4 9EY. *Telephone:* 01383 610166. *Fax:* 01383 512132. *E-mail:* bluebrazil@cowdenbeathfc.com. *Website:* www.cowdenbeathfc.com
Ground Capacity: total: 5268, seated: 1622. *Size of Pitch:* 107yd × 66yd.
Chairman: Gordon McDougall. *Secretary:* Tom Ogilvie. *Commercial Manager:* Joe MacNamara.
Manager: Mixu Paatelainen. *First Team Coaches:* S. McLeish, M. Renwick. *Physio:* Neil Bryson.
Managers since 1975: D. McLindon, F. Connor, P. Wilson, A. Rolland, H. Wilson, W. McCulloch, J. Clark, J. Craig, R. Campbell, J. Blackley, J. Brownlie, A. Harrow, J. Reilly, P. Dolan, T. Steven, S. Conn, C. Levein, G. Kirk, K. Wright, D. Baikie. *Previous Grounds:* North End Park, Cowdenbeath.
Record Attendance: 25,586 v Rangers, League Cup quarter-final, 21 Sept 1949.
Record Transfer Fee received: £30,000 for Nicky Henderson to Falkirk (March 1994).
Record Victory: 12-0 v Johnstone, Scottish Cup 1st rd, 21 Jan 1928.
Record Defeat: 1-11 v Clyde, Division II, 6 Oct 1951.
Most Capped Player: Jim Paterson, 3, Scotland.
Most League and Cup Appearances: 491 Ray Allan 1972-75, 1979-89.
Most League Goals in Season (Individual): 54, Rab Walls, Division II, 1938-39.
Most Goals Overall (Individual): 127, Willie Devlin, 1922-26, 1929-30.

COWDENBEATH 2005–06 LEAGUE RECORD

Match No.	Date	Venue	Opponents	Result	H/T Score	Lg. Pos.	Goalscorers	Attendance
1	Aug 6	A	East Stirling	W 1-0	0-0	—	Ward 63	263
2	13	H	Queen's Park	L 0-2	0-1	6		280
3	20	A	Elgin C	W 3-0	1-0	3	Mauchlen (pen) 15, McCallum 74, Buchanan 89	402
4	27	A	East Fife	L 0-1	0-1	4		729
5	Sept 10	H	Berwick R	L 0-1	0-1	5		265
6	17	H	Montrose	W 2-0	0-0	4	McCallum 53, Guy 57	216
7	24	A	Arbroath	W 3-0	2-0	3	Buchanan 28, Ritchie 39, McCallum 79	423
8	Oct 1	H	Stenhousemuir	W 4-1	3-0	3	Buchanan 27, Ward 31, McCallum 40, Jackson 74	338
9	15	A	Albion R	W 3-0	1-0	4	Downs 6, Paatelainen Markus 46, McCallum 52	322
10	22	H	East Stirling	W 5-1	4-1	3	Downs 2 1, 10, Ward 31, Paatelainen Markus 44, Jackson 62	267
11	25	A	Queen's Park	W 2-0	1-0	—	Jackson 17, Paatelainen Markus 80	391
12	29	A	Berwick R	L 0-1	0-0	3		715
13	Nov 5	H	East Fife	W 3-1	0-1	3	Ritchie 46, McCallum 66, Guy 84	587
14	12	A	Montrose	W 1-0	1-0	3	Paatelainen Markus 3	295
15	Dec 3	H	Albion R	W 2-1	1-0	3	Paatelainen Markus 33, Buchanan 67	255
16	6	H	Arbroath	W 3-2	1-1	—	Buchanan 2 3, 66, Jackson 68	236
17	17	A	Stenhousemuir	L 0-2	0-2	2		503
18	Jan 2	A	East Fife	L 1-2	0-2	—	Ward 55	867
19	14	H	Berwick R	D 1-1	0-1	3	Paatelainen Markus 52	432
20	21	H	Montrose	W 2-0	1-0	3	McKenna 4, Buchanan 83	295
21	28	A	Arbroath	L 1-4	0-1	3	Paatelainen Mikko 90	583
22	Feb 4	H	Stenhousemuir	D 1-1	1-1	3	Buchanan 42	462
23	11	A	Albion R	W 3-1	0-1	3	Buchanan 55, Paatelainen Mikko 60, Guy 80	313
24	18	H	Queen's Park	W 6-0	2-0	3	Paatelainen Mikko 3 23, 30, 85, Ritchie 47, Buchanan 79, McKenna (pen) 88	315
25	25	A	Elgin C	W 4-0	1-0	3	Paatelainen Mikko 2 35, 64, Ritchie 58, McKenna 68	677
26	Mar 11	A	Berwick R	L 0-1	0-1	3		403
27	18	A	Montrose	W 3-0	2-0	3	Ritchie 2 40, 45, Buchanan 69	306
28	21	H	East Fife	W 4-1	3-1	—	Oné 9, Buchanan 2 41, 45, Mauchlen 72	412
29	25	H	Arbroath	W 4-2	1-1	3	Oné 11, Buchanan 48, McKenna 2 73, 88	351
30	28	H	Elgin C	W 5-2	5-2	—	Oné 29, McKenna 2 44, 45, Ward 55, Mauchlen 82	259
31	Apr 1	A	Stenhousemuir	W 2-1	1-1	3	Hill 42, Buchanan 46	816
32	4	A	East Stirling	D 1-1	0-1	—	McBride P 71	403
33	8	H	Albion R	W 2-1	0-1	1	McKenna 2 73, 76	350
34	15	H	East Stirling	W 5-0	1-0	1	McKenna 2 17, 79, Oné 3 47, 70, 77	592
35	22	A	Queen's Park	D 2-2	1-2	1	Buchanan 26, Oné 46	1247
36	29	H	Elgin C	W 2-1	1-0	1	Buchanan 15, Oné 51	2596

Final League Position: 1

Honours
League Champions: Division II 1913-14, 1914-15, 1938-39; *Champions:* Third Division 2005-06. *Runners-up:* Division II 1921-22, 1923-24, 1969-70. Second Division 1991-92. *Runners-up:* Third Division 2000-01.
Scottish Cup: Quarter-finals 1931.
League Cup: Semi-finals 1959-60, 1970-71.

Club colours: Shirt: Royal blue with white cuffs and collar. Shorts: White. Stockings: White.

Goalscorers: *League* (81): Buchanan 17, McKenna 11 (1 pen), Oné 8, Mikko Paatelainen 7, McCallum 6, Markus Paatelainen 6, Ritchie 6, Ward 5, Jackson 4, Downs 3, Guy 3, Mauchlen 3 (1 pen), Hill 1, McBride P 1.
Scottish Cup (0).
CIS Cup (2): Gribben 1, Ward 1.
Challenge Cup (0).

Hay D 35	Wilson D 2 + 3	McBride K 33	Ward J 35	McGregor D 7 + 8	Millar M 22 + 3	Guy G 24 + 3	Fusco G 22 + 8	Downs R 7 + 2	Gribben D 2 + 1	Mauchlen I 13 + 5	Hill D 15 + 10	Allison J — + 2	Buchanan L 27 + 4	Baird S 1	Grant M 1	Ritchie I 24	Paatelainen Markus 24 + 1	McCallum R 13 + 3	Baxter M 25 + 2	Jackson A 13	Krobot L — + 9	Scullion P 7 + 4	Paatelainen Mikko 9	McKenna D 17	McBride P — + 6	Boyd S 1 + 1	Thomson D 6 + 4	Oné A 10 + 1	Carlin A 1	Hughes C — + 1	*Match No.*
1	2^{1}	3	4	5	6^{2}	7	8	9^{3}	10	11	12	13	14																		1
1		3	4	5■	14	2	8^{2}	9^{1}	10^{3}	7	13		12	6	11																2
1		3	4		10^{2}	2		9^{1}		7	5	13	11			6	8	12													3
1		3	4	13	10^{3}	2		9^{1}	12	7	5^{2}		11			6	8	14													4
1		3	4		10	6^{2}	12			7^{1}			11			5	8	13	2	9											5
1		3	4		7	6							11			5	8	9	2	10											6
1		3	4		7	6	13	12					11			5	8	9^{2}	2	10^{1}											7
1		3^{2}	4			6	7	12			13		11^{1}			5	8	9	2	10											8
1		3	4		12	6^{1}	7	11								5	8	9	2	10											9
1	13	3^{1}	4	14	7		6^{2}	11			12					5	8	9	2^{3}	10											10
1	12	3	4	14	7		6	11^{1}			13					5	8	9^{3}	2^{2}	10											11
1	11^{1}	3	4		7		6				12					5	8	9	2	10											12
1	14	3^{3}	4	13	7	12	6^{1}						11			5	8	9	2^{2}	10											13
1		3^{3}	4		7^{1}	6^{2}	12				14		11			5	8	9	2	10	13										14
1		3	4		7^{1}	6	12			14	13		11^{3}			5	8^{2}	9	2	10											15
1		3	4		7	6^{1}	12						11			5	8	9	2	10											16
1		3	4		7^{2}	6^{1}	13			12			11			5	8	9	2	10											17
1			4		7					11	3					5	8	9	2			6	10								18
1			4	6	7		12				3		13			5	8		2^{1}			11^{2}	9	10							19
1		3	4	6■	7		12			13	5		14				8		2			11^{1}	9^{3}	10^{2}							20
1		3	4		7					12■	5		11				8		2■			6^{1}	9	10^{2}	13						21
1^{1}		3	4	2■			6				5		10				8				13	7^{2}	9			11	12				22
1		3	4		7^{1}	2	6				5		11^{2}				8				12		9	10			13				23
1		3	4		7	2^{2}	6						11			5	8^{1}		13				9^{3}	10		14	12				24
1		3	4		7	14	6^{2}						11^{1}			5	8^{3}		2			13	9	10			12				25
1		3	4		7^{2}	12	6						11^{3}			5			2^{1}		13		9	10			8	14			26
1		3	4		13	2	6			7^{1}			11			5					14	12		10			8^{2}	9^{3}			27
1		3	4			2	6			7^{3}	13		11			5^{2}					14			10	12		8	9^{1}			28
1		3	4			2	6			7^{3}	12		11			5^{1}					14	13		10			8^{2}	9			29
1		3	4			2	6			7^{3}	5		11						12			14		10	13		8^{1}	9^{2}			30
1		3	4	12		2^{1}	6			7	5		11						8					10				9			31
1			4	5			6■			7^{2}	3		11						2		12			10	13		8^{1}	9			32
		3	4	6		2				7^{1}	5		11						8					10	12			9^{2}	1	13	33
1		3	4^{2}	13		2	6				5		11						7			8		10	12			9^{1}			34
1		3	4■	12		2	6				5		11				13		7		14	8^{3}		10^{1}				9^{2}			35
1		3		12		2	6			13	5		11			4^{1}	8		7					10				9^{2}			36

DUMBARTON — Third Division

Year Formed: 1872. *Ground:* Strathclyde Homes Stadium, Dumbarton G82 1JJ. *Telephone:* 01389 762569. *Fax:* 01389 762629. *E-mail:* dumbarton.footballclub@btopenworld.com
Ground Capacity: total: 2050. *Size of Pitch:* 110yd × 75yd.
Chairman: Neil Rankine. *Club Secretary:* David Prophet. *Company Secretary:* Gilbert Lawrie.
Manager: Gerry McCabe. *Assistant Manager:* Jim Clark. *Physio:* Lindsay Smart.
Managers since 1975: A. Wright, D. Wilson, S. Fallon, W. Lamont, D. Wilson, D. Whiteford, A. Totten, M. Clougherty, R. Auld, J. George, W. Lamont, M. MacLeod, J. Fallon, I. Wallace, J. Brown, T. Carson, D. Winnie, B. Fairley, P. Martin.
Club Nickname(s): The Sons. *Previous Grounds:* Broadmeadow, Ropework Lane, Townend Ground, Boghead Park.
Record Attendance: 18,000 v Raith Rovers, Scottish Cup, 2 Mar 1957.
Record Transfer Fee received: £125,000 for Graeme Sharp to Everton (March 1982).
Record Transfer Fee paid: £50,000 for Charlie Gibson from Stirling Albion (1989).
Record Victory: 13-1 v Kirkintilloch Central. 1st rd, 1 Sept 1888.
Record Defeat: 1-11 v Albion Rovers, Division II; 30 Jan, 1926: v Ayr United, League Cup, 13 Aug 1952.
Most Capped Player: James McAulay, 9, Scotland.
Most League Appearances: 297: Andy Jardine, 1957-67.
Most Goals in Season (Individual): 38: Kenny Wilson, Division II, 1971-72. *(League and Cup):* 46 Hughie Gallacher, 1955-56.
Most Goals Overall (Individual): 169: Hughie Gallacher, 1954-62 (including C Division 1954-55). *(League and Cup):* 202

DUMBARTON 2005–06 LEAGUE RECORD

Match No.	Date	Venue	Opponents	Result		H/T Score	Lg. Pos.	Goalscorers	Attendance
1	Aug 6	A	Ayr U	L	0-2	0-1	—		1274
2	13	H	Alloa Ath	D	1-1	0-0	6	Walker [90]	879
3	20	A	Partick Th	L	2-3	2-1	8	Smith [8], McQuilken [12]	2485
4	27	H	Morton	D	1-1	0-0	9	Russell (pen) [89]	1574
5	Sept 10	A	Peterhead	L	0-1	0-0	9		494
6	17	A	Forfar Ath	L	0-2	0-1	9		429
7	24	H	Stirling A	W	2-0	1-0	9	Rodgers 2 [14, 83]	877
8	Oct 1	A	Gretna	L	0-1	0-1	9		954
9	15	H	Raith R	L	1-2	0-1	9	Gemmell [81]	852
10	22	H	Ayr U	W	6-0	2-0	9	Gaughan [4], Rodgers 2 (1 pen) [34 (p), 76], Dillon [63], Smith [86], Russell [87]	919
11	25	A	Alloa Ath	W	4-1	2-0	—	Gentile [1], Dillon [33], Russell [53], Connell [82]	469
12	29	H	Peterhead	W	1-0	0-0	7	Boyle [87]	771
13	Nov 5	A	Morton	L	0-4	0-2	7		2818
14	12	H	Forfar Ath	W	2-0	2-0	5	Rodgers [7], McQuilken [27]	737
15	Dec 3	A	Raith R	L	2-3	2-2	8	Rodgers 2 [39, 45]	1060
16	7	A	Stirling A	D	0-0	0-0	—		530
17	17	H	Gretna	L	0-1	0-1	8		839
18	26	A	Ayr U	L	0-2	0-2	—		1266
19	31	H	Partick Th	L	1-2	1-2	9	Borris [4]	1581
20	Jan 2	H	Morton	L	0-2	0-1	—		1594
21	14	A	Peterhead	L	1-3	0-1	9	Gemmell [70]	705
22	21	A	Forfar Ath	W	3-2	0-1	9	Russell (pen) [59], Gemmell [86], Dubourdeau (og) [90]	446
23	28	H	Stirling A	W	3-2	2-1	8	Russell 2 [17, 75], Gemmell [26]	891
24	Feb 11	H	Raith R	L	0-1	0-0	8		822
25	Mar 7	A	Gretna	L	0-3	0-1	—		598
26	11	H	Peterhead	L	2-3	2-1	9	Russell [10], Rodgers [13]	626
27	14	A	Partick Th	L	1-2	0-1	—	Boyle [90]	1537
28	18	H	Forfar Ath	D	0-0	0-0	9		616
29	21	H	Alloa Ath	L	0-1	0-0	—		534
30	25	A	Stirling A	L	1-3	0-0	9	Russell [87]	604
31	28	A	Morton	L	0-4	0-1	—		1418
32	Apr 8	A	Raith R	D	0-0	0-0	9		1055
33	15	H	Ayr U	L	4-5	0-3	9	Rodgers 2 [47, 60], Gemmell [64], McQuilken [70]	937
34	18	H	Gretna	L	0-2	0-2	—		685
35	22	A	Alloa Ath	L	0-1	0-0	10		784
36	29	H	Partick Th	L	2-3	2-0	10	Rodgers 2 [40, 41]	1257

Final League Position: 10

Hughie Gallacher, 1954-62

Honours
League Champions: Division I 1890-91 (shared with Rangers), 1891-92. Division II 1910-11, 1971-72. Second Division 1991-92; *Runners-up:* First Division 1983-84. Division II 1907-08. Third Division 2001-02.
Scottish Cup Winners: 1883; *Runners-up:* 1881, 1882, 1887, 1891, 1897.

Club colours: Shirt: Gold with black sleeves and black panel down sides. Shorts: Black with three gold panels. Stockings: Black.

Goalscorers: *League* (40): Rodgers 12 (1 pen), Russell 8 (2 pens), Gemmell 5, McQuilken 3, Boyle 2, Dillon 2, Smith 2, Borris 1, Connell 1, Gaughan 1, Gentile 1, Walker 1, own goal 1.
Scottish Cup (4): Rodgers 2, McQuilken 1, Russell 1.
CIS Cup (1): Rodgers 1.
Challenge Cup (1): Rodgers 1.

Grindlay S 36	Ferry D 10 + 7	Brittain C 7 + 3	Walker R 22	Smith J 33	Dempsie M 25	Bannerman S 16 + 7	Connell G 16 + 11	Russell I 20 + 10	Gemmell J 14 + 12	Borris R 30	McQuilken P 24 + 10	Ronald P 2 + 3	Dillon J 11 + 12	McDonald K 7 + 5	Rodgers A 27 + 6	Gentile C 19 + 3	Gaughan K 25 + 1	Boyle C 26	Allan J 3 + 1	Ferguson S 11	Winter C 12	McNaught D — + 3	McDevitt G — + 1	Match No.
1	2	3	4	5	6	7^{3}	8^{2}	9	10^{1}	11	12	13	14											1
1	13	3^{1}	4	5	6	12	14			7	9	8^{3}	11■	2	10^{2}									2
1	12		4	5	6	11^{3}	8	13	14	7■	9^{2}			2	10^{1}	3								3
1		3	8	5	4	2	6	12			9^{2}	13		11	7^{1}	10								4
1	12		4	5	6	14	8^{3}	13		7	9		11^{1}	2	10^{2}	3								5
1	2		4	5	6^{1}	13		10^{3}		7	9	8^{2}	11		14	3	12							6
1	14		4	5		8^{3}	13	10^{1}		7^{2}	12		11	2	9	3	6							7
1		3	4	5	6	2		14		7	12		11^{2}	13	9^{3}	10^{1}	8							8
1			4		6		8	10	13	7	12		11^{1}	2	9^{2}		5	3						9
1				4	6	12	8^{1}	14		7^{2}	11		13	2^{3}	9	3	5	10						10
1		3^{3}		5	6	14	13	12		7	11		8		9^{1}	2	4	10^{2}						11
1				5	6	2	14	7^{1}	12		11		8^{2}	13	9^{3}	3	4	10						12
1				5	6^{2}	11	12	13	14	7	10^{3}		8^{1}		9	3	4	2						13
1	13		6	5		7	8	14	12	2^{2}	10^{1}				9^{3}	3	4	11						14
1		3^{3}	6	5		13		11^{1}		2^{2}	7			12	9	10■	4	8	14					15
1		12	6	5^{1}		8		10^{3}	14	7	2^{2}			13	9		4	3	11					16
1			6	5		2		11^{1}	12	7	10				9	8	4	3						17
1		12	6^{1}	5		8■	11	10^{2}	14	2	3		13		9	7^{3}	4							18
1				5	6		8	13	12	2	10^{2}		14		9^{1}	11^{3}	4	3	7					19
1				5	6	11^{2}	8	10	9^{3}	2			12	13	14		4	7	3^{1}					20
1		12		5	6^{2}			10	11	2	14		13		9^{3}	3	4	7^{1}		8				21
1				5	6	13	12	9^{1}	10	2■	11^{2}					3	4	7		8■				22
1				5	6	2	8	9	10^{1}		11^{2}	13	12				4	7			3			23
1				5		10		9	11^{1}		7				12	3	4	2		8	6			24
1	2	3	4	5	6		8	7	9^{2}				12		13	14		10^{1}		11^{3}				25
1			4	5	6		13	10	14	7	3^{1}		12		9^{3}	2^{2}		11		8				26
1	2^{2}		4	5	6		12	14	9	11	7^{3}				13			3		8	10^{1}			27
1			4	5	6			10	7	11	12		13		9^{1}			3^{2}		8	2			28
1	3		4	5		7	12	9^{2}	10	2	14		11		13					6^{1}	8^{3}			29
1	2			5		8^{3}	6^{2}	7	11^{1}		12		14		9	13	4	3			10			30
1	2		5		6			10^{1}	14	7	12				9^{3}	13	4	3		8^{2}	11			31
1	2^{1}			5	6		12			7	11^{2}				9		4	3		8	10	13		32
1	2^{1}			5^{3}	6		13		12	7	11				9		4	3		8^{2}	10	14		33
1	2		4				6		10	7	13		11^{2}		9		5^{1}	3			8		12	34
1	13			4	6■		8^{2}		11	3	2^{1}				9		5	7			10	12		35
1	12		6^{1}	5			8		10	7	3^{2}		13		9		4	11			2			36

DUNDEE First Division

Year Formed: 1893. *Ground & Address:* Dens Park Stadium, Sandeman St, Dundee DD3 7JY. *Telephone:* 01382 889966. *Fax:* 01382 832284.
Ground Capacity: all seated: 11,760. *Size of Pitch:* 101m × 66m.
Chairman: Bob Brannan. *Chief Executive:* David MacKinnon.
Manager: Alex Rae. *Assistant Manager:* Davie Farrell. *Youth Development Coach:* Gordon Wallace. *Community Coach:* Gavin Timley. *Physio:* Karen Gibson.
Managers since 1975: David White, Tommy Gemmell, Donald Mackay, Archie Knox, Jocky Scott, Dave Smith, Gordon Wallace, Iain Munro, Simon Stainrod, Jim Duffy, John McCormack, John Scott, Ivano Bonetti, Jim Duffy, Alan Kernaghan.
Club Nickname(s): The Dark Blues or The Dee. *Previous Grounds:* Carolina Port 1893-98.
Record Attendance: 43,024 v Rangers, Scottish Cup, 1953.
Record Transfer Fee received: £500,000 for Tommy Coyne to Celtic (March 1989).
Record Transfer Fee paid: £200,000 for Jim Leighton (Feb 1992).
Record Victory: 10-0 Division II v Alloa, 9 Mar 1947 and v Dunfermline Ath, 22 Mar 1947.
Record Defeat: 0-11 v Celtic, Division I, 26 Oct 1895.
Most Capped Player: Alex Hamilton, 24, Scotland. *Most League Appearances:* 341: Doug Cowie, 1945-61.
Most League Goals in Season (Individual): 52: Alan Gilzean, 1963-64.
Most Goals Overall (Individual): 113: Alan Gilzean.

DUNDEE 2005–06 LEAGUE RECORD

Match No.	Date	Venue	Opponents	Result		H/T Score	Lg. Pos.	Goalscorers	Attendance
1	Aug 6	H	St Mirren	W	3-2	1-1	—	Mann 10, Lynch 77, McManus 83	5003
2	13	A	Clyde	D	1-1	0-0	3	Lynch 61	1825
3	20	H	Queen of the S	W	3-1	2-1	1	Mann 2 25, 35, Anderson 62	3915
4	27	A	Hamilton A	D	1-1	1-0	2	Lynch 36	2091
5	Sept 10	H	Airdrie U	L	0-2	0-1	3		4198
6	17	A	St Johnstone	D	1-1	1-1	3	Craig 10	5172
7	24	H	Ross Co	D	0-0	0-0	5		4025
8	Oct 1	A	Brechin C	W	3-1	3-1	4	Lynch 2 14, 34, Craig 30	2037
9	15	H	Stranraer	D	1-1	0-0	5	Ferguson 82	3417
10	22	A	St Mirren	D	0-0	0-0	5		4027
11	26	H	Clyde	D	3-3	2-1	—	Lynch 22, McManus 2 42, 51	3360
12	29	A	Airdrie U	L	0-4	0-2	6		1656
13	Nov 12	H	St Johnstone	W	2-1	1-1	6	Lynch (pen) 18, McManus 73	5383
14	15	H	Hamilton A	D	1-1	0-0	—	Craig 87	3890
15	19	A	Ross Co	L	0-3	0-2	6		2862
16	26	H	Brechin C	W	1-0	0-0	6	Lynch (pen) 73	3278
17	Dec 3	A	Stranraer	D	0-0	0-0	6		550
18	10	H	St Mirren	W	4-0	1-0	6	McDonald K 3, O'Reilly 2 72, 76, Ferguson 82	4204
19	26	H	Airdrie U	L	2-3	2-0	—	O'Reilly 22, Mann 45	4378
20	31	A	Hamilton A	D	0-0	0-0	7		1533
21	Jan 2	A	St Johnstone	D	0-0	0-0	—		5170
22	14	H	Ross Co	D	0-0	0-0	7		3671
23	21	A	Brechin C	W	3-0	1-0	7	McDonald K 19, Dixon 53, Lynch (pen) 62	1421
24	28	H	Stranraer	W	2-1	1-1	6	Deasley 7, Lynch 65	3134
25	Feb 11	H	Queen of the S	L	2-3	1-1	6	Lynch 2 37, 58	3365
26	18	A	Clyde	D	3-3	2-2	6	McManus 2 4, 48, Marshall 26	1062
27	28	A	Queen of the S	D	0-0	0-0	—		1566
28	Mar 4	H	Hamilton A	L	2-4	0-2	6	Wilkie 85, Robertson 88	3540
29	11	A	Airdrie U	L	0-7	0-5	6		1127
30	18	H	St Johnstone	L	0-1	0-0	6		4193
31	Apr 4	A	Ross Co	D	0-0	0-0	—		1754
32	8	A	Stranraer	D	1-1	1-1	6	McDonald K 42	480
33	11	H	Brechin C	L	0-1	0-1	—		1841
34	15	A	St Mirren	L	1-2	0-1	7	Craig 46	7629
35	22	H	Clyde	L	0-1	0-0	7		3199
36	29	A	Queen of the S	W	3-1	3-0	7	Craig 2 25, 29, Dixon 26	2624

Final League Position: 7

Honours
League Champions: Division I 1961-62. First Division 1978-79, 1991-92, 1997-98. Division II 1946-47; *Runners-up:* Division I 1902-03, 1906-07, 1908-09, 1948-49, 1980-81.
Scottish Cup Winners: 1910; *Runners-up:* 1925, 1952, 1964, 2003.
League Cup Winners: 1951-52, 1952-53, 1973-74; *Runners-up:* 1967-68, 1980-81. *(Coca-Cola Cup):* 1995-96.
B&Q (Centenary) Cup Winners: 1990-91; *Runners-up:* 1994-95.

European: *European Cup:* 8 matches (1962-63 semi-finals). *Cup Winners' Cup:* 2 matches: (1964-65).
UEFA Cup: 22 matches: (*Fairs Cup:* 1967-68 semi-finals. *UEFA Cup:* 1971-72, 1973-74, 1974-75, 2003-04).

Club colours: Shirt: Navy with white and red shoulder and sleeve flashes. Shorts: White with navy/red piping. Stockings: Navy, top with two white hoops.

Goalscorers: *League* (43): Lynch 12 (3 pens), Craig 6, McManus 6, Mann 4, McDonald K 3, O'Reilly 3, Dixon 2, Ferguson 2, Anderson 1, Deasley 1, Marshall 1, Robertson 1, Wilkie 1.
Scottish Cup (8): Lynch 3, Deasley 2, Craig 1, Mann 1, O'Reilly 1.
CIS Cup (1): Lynch 1.
Challenge Cup (3): Anderson 1, Lynch 1, Robertson 1.

Jack K 14	Smith B 36	Dixon P 25 + 4	Brady G 22 + 7	Mann R 35	Madaschi A 9	Anderson I 12 + 1	Robertson S 31 + 4	Lynch S 28 + 5	McManus T 18 + 5	Robb S 23 + 2	Hutchinson T 6 + 1	Britton G 1 + 1	Ferguson A 2 + 13	Ela Eyene J — + 2	Fyfe G 1	Kitamarike J — + 1	McCluskey S 12 + 2	Craig S 17 + 3	McDonald K 24 + 2	Macdonald C 25 + 2	Keane K — + 1	Gates S 3 + 4	O'Reilly C 4 + 11	Soutar D 6	McNally S 5	Swankie G — + 2	Murray S 16 + 2	Deasley B 7 + 6	Marshall C 9 + 4	Law G 1 + 2	Wilkie L 1 + 1	Hendry R 1	Allison M 1	Black D 1	*Match No.*
1	2	3^{1}	4	5	6	7	8	9^{2}	10^{3}	11	12	13	14																						1
1	2		4	5	6	7	8	9	10	11	3																								2
1	2	14	4	5	6	7	8^{1}	9	10^{2}	11	3^{3}		13	12																					3
1	2		8	4	3	7	6^{2}	9		11	5	10^{1}	12	13																					4
1	6	3	7	4	5	10	8^{3}	9	12		2^{2}		14		11^{1}	13																			5
1	6	12		4	3	11^{1}	8	9	7^{3}		5		14				2	10^{2}	13																6
1	6			4	3	11^{2}	8	9^{3}	7^{1}		5		14				2	10		12	13														7
1	6	13		4	5		7	9^{3}					12				2	10^{1}	8	3		11^{2}	14												8
	6		14	4	5^{3}		7	9^{2}	10	12			13				2		8	3		11^{1}		1											9
	6		7	4			11	9	10^{1}	3							2		8	5			12	1											10
	6		7	4			11^{1}	9	10^{2}	3									8	5			13	1	2	12									11
	6	12	11	4			7^{1}	9	10	3									8^{2}	5			13	1	2										12
	6	3	8	4			12	9^{2}	10	11			13					7^{1}		5				1	2										13
	6	3	8	4			13	9	10^{1}	11^{2}								7		5				1^{0}	2	12	15								14
	6	3^{1}	8	4		12	13	9	10	11			14					7^{3}		5					2^{2}		1								15
1	6	3	13	4		8^{1}	2	9^{3}	10^{2}	11			12						7	5		14													16
1	6	3	14	4		8^{1}	2	9^{2}	10^{3}	11			13						7	5		12													17
1	6	3	13	4		8^{2}	2	10^{1}		11			14					9^{3}	7	5			12												18
1	6	3	8	4			2		13	11^{2}								9	7	5			10^{1}					12							19
	6	3	13	4		8^{2}	2	12		11								9^{1}	7	5			10				1								20
	6	3	12	4		8^{1}	2	9		11									7	5			10^{2}				1	13							21
	6	3	8^{2}	4			2	9		11									7	5			10^{1}				1	12	13						22
	6^{1}	3	8^{3}	4			2	9		11							12	13	7	5							1	10^{2}	14						23
	6	3	8	4			2	9		11^{1}								13	7	5							1	10^{2}	12						24
	6	3	8^{2}	4			2	9									13		7	5			12				1	10	11^{1}						25
1^{6}	6	3	8	4			2	9	10^{2}								11		7^{1}	5			13				15		12						26
	6	3		4					10				9^{3}				11	2^{2}	7	5^{1}		12					1	14	8	13					27
	6	3	8	4^{2}			2	9	14								11^{3}		7^{1}	5		12					1	10			13				28
	6						13						9					10		5		11^{1}	12				1		8	2		3	4	7^{2}	29
1	6	3	8	4			2	9^{3}	10								11	13	7^{2}	12								14			5^{1}				30
	6	3		4			2	13		11^{1}								9^{2}	7	5			14				1	10^{3}	8	12					31
	6	3		4			2	12		11^{2}							5	9	7				13				1	10^{1}	8						32
	6	3	12	4			2	13		11							5^{1}	9^{2}	7				14				1	10	8^{3}						33
	6	3	11	4			2	9	12								5	10^{1}	7								1		8						34
	6	3	11	4			2	9^{3}	14	12								10^{2}	7	5							1	13	8^{1}						35
	6	3	7	4			2	13	10^{2}	11								9	12	5							1		8^{1}						36

DUNDEE UNITED Premier League

Year Formed: 1909 (1923). *Ground & Address:* Tannadice Park, Tannadice St, Dundee DD3 7JW. *Telephone:* 01382 833166. *Fax:* 01382 889398. *E-mail:* enquiries@dundeeunited.co.uk. *Website:* www.dundeeunitedfc.co.uk
Ground Capacity: total: 14,223 all seated: stands: east 2868, west 2096, south 2201, Fair Play 1601, George Fox 5151, executive boxes 292.
Size of Pitch: 110yd × 72yd.
Chairman: Eddie Thompson, OBE. *Secretary:* Spence Anderson. *Commercial Manager:* Bill Campbell.
Manager: Craig Brewster. *Assistant Manager:* Malcolm Thomson. *First Team Coach:* Tony Docherty. *Coach:* Graeme Liveston. *Physio:* Jeff Clarke. *Stadium Manager:* Ron West.
Managers since 1975: J. McLean, I. Golac, W. Kirkwood, T. McLean, P. Sturrock, A. Smith, I. McCall, G. Chisholm.
Club Nickname(s): The Terrors. *Previous Grounds:* None.
Record Attendance: 28,000 v Barcelona, Fairs Cup, 16 Nov 1966.
Record Transfer Fee received: £4,000,000 for Duncan Ferguson from Rangers (July 1993).
Record Transfer Fee paid: £750,000 for Steven Pressley from Coventry C (July 1995).
Record Victory: 14-0 v Nithsdale Wanderers, Scottish Cup 1st rd, 17 Jan 1931.
Record Defeat: 1-12 v Motherwell, Division II, 23 Jan 1954.
Most Capped Player: Maurice Malpas, 55, Scotland.
Most League Appearances: 612, Dave Narey, 1973-94.
Most Appearances in European Matches: 76, Dave Narey (record for Scottish player).
Most League Goals in Season (Individual): 41: John Coyle, Division II, 1955-56.
Most Goals Overall (Individual): 158: Peter McKay.

DUNDEE UNITED 2005–06 LEAGUE RECORD

Match No.	Date	Venue	Opponents	Result		H/T Score	Lg. Pos.	Goalscorers	Attendance
1	Jul 30	H	Aberdeen	D	1-1	1-0	—	Miller [6]	12,404
2	Aug 6	A	Celtic	L	0-2	0-1	10		55,456
3	14	H	Hearts	L	0-3	0-2	10		11,654
4	20	A	Motherwell	W	5-4	1-2	9	Miller 2 [42, 66], Fernandez [52], Brebner 2 [70, 73]	4706
5	28	H	Inverness CT	D	1-1	0-0	8	Miller [65]	6178
6	Sept 10	A	Hibernian	L	1-2	1-1	9	Brebner [14]	12,026
7	17	H	Livingston	W	2-0	1-0	9	Fernandez [33], Canero [76]	6302
8	24	A	Dunfermline Ath	L	1-2	1-0	9	McCracken [40]	5229
9	Oct 1	H	Kilmarnock	D	0-0	0-0	9		6095
10	16	H	Rangers	D	0-0	0-0	9		11,696
11	22	A	Falkirk	W	3-1	0-1	9	Robson [48], Canero [72], Samuel [81]	5316
12	25	A	Aberdeen	L	0-2	0-2	—		10,270
13	30	H	Celtic	L	2-4	2-3	9	Sutton (og) [4], Samuel [30]	11,942
14	Nov 5	A	Hearts	L	0-3	0-2	9		16,617
15	19	H	Motherwell	D	1-1	0-0	10	McIntyre [68]	6305
16	26	A	Inverness CT	D	1-1	1-1	10	Miller [7]	3700
17	Dec 3	H	Hibernian	W	1-0	0-0	9	Samuel [60]	7976
18	10	A	Livingston	L	0-1	0-1	9		3345
19	20	H	Dunfermline Ath	W	2-1	2-1	—	Samuel [25], Robson [40]	5889
20	26	A	Kilmarnock	L	1-2	0-1	9	Samuel [50]	5749
21	31	A	Rangers	L	0-3	0-0	9		49,141
22	Jan 15	H	Falkirk	W	2-1	1-0	9	Fernandez [36], McInnes [89]	7948
23	21	H	Aberdeen	D	1-1	0-0	9	Archibald [52]	9936
24	28	A	Celtic	D	3-3	1-1	9	Fernandez 2 [39, 85], Miller [81]	59,458
25	Feb 7	H	Hearts	D	1-1	1-0	—	Brebner [34]	10,584
26	11	A	Motherwell	L	0-2	0-1	9		5257
27	18	H	Inverness CT	L	2-4	2-2	9	Mulgrew 2 [17, 40]	6419
28	25	A	Dunfermline Ath	D	1-1	1-1	—	Kenneth [7]	4697
29	Mar 4	A	Hibernian	L	1-3	0-3	9	Goodwillie [88]	16,266
30	11	H	Livingston	W	3-1	0-1	9	Miller 2 [68, 79], Kerr [76]	5730
31	25	H	Kilmarnock	D	2-2	0-2	9	McCracken [47], McInnes [50]	5830
32	Apr 2	H	Rangers	L	1-4	0-2	9	Samuel [66]	11,213
33	8	A	Falkirk	L	0-1	0-1	9		4435
34	15	A	Livingston	L	1-3	1-1	9	Robertson [18]	2298
35	22	A	Inverness CT	L	0-1	0-0	9		3609
36	29	H	Falkirk	L	0-2	0-2	9		5798
37	May 2	H	Dunfermline Ath	L	0-1	0-0	—		5034
38	6	A	Motherwell	D	1-1	0-0	9	Samuel [86]	5269

Final League Position: 9

Honours
League Champions: Premier Division 1982-83. Division II 1924-25, 1928-29; *Runners-up:* Division II 1930-31, 1959-60. First Division Runners-up 1995-96.
Scottish Cup Winners: 1994; *Runners-up:* 1974, 1981, 1985, 1987, 1988, 1991, 2005.
League Cup Winners: 1979-80, 1980-81; *Runners-up:* 1981-82, 1984-85, 1997-98.
Summer Cup Runners-up: 1964-65. *Scottish War Cup Runners-up:* 1939-40.

European: *European Cup:* 8 matches (1983-84, semi-finals). *Cup Winners' Cup:* 10 matches (1974-75, 1988-89, 1994-95). *UEFA Cup:* 86 matches (*Fairs Cup:* 1966-67, 1969-70, 1970-71. *UEFA Cup:* 1975-76, 1977-78, 1978-79, 1979-80, 1980-81, 1981-82, 1982-83, 1984-85, 1985-86, 1986-87 runners-up, 1987-88, 1989-90, 1990-91, 1993-94, 1997-98, 2005-06).

Club colours: Shirts: Tangerine. Shorts: Tangerine. Stockings: Tangerine.

Goalscorers: *League* (41): Miller 8, Samuel 7, Fernandez 5, Brebner 4, Canero 2, McCracken 2, McInnes 2, Mulgrew 2, Robson 2, Archibald 1, Goodwillie 1, Kenneth 1, Kerr 1, McIntyre 1, Robertson 1, own goal 1.
Scottish Cup (2): Fernandez 2.
CIS Cup (0).

Stillie D 30	Wilson M 20 + 1	McCracken D 34	Ritchie P 20 + 1	Archibald A 33	Kerr M 35	Brebner G 26	Duff S 24 + 5	Crawford S 4	McIntyre J 18 + 7	Miller L 22 + 12	Kenneth G 12 + 4	Samuel C 23 + 12	Robson B 30 + 1	Fernandez D 29 + 1	Canero P 9 + 2	McInnes D 9 + 3	Cameron G 2 + 2	Goodwillie D — + 10	Samson C 8	Mulgrew C 13	Brewster C — + 1	Robertson D 6 + 5	Mair L 5 + 1	Gardiner R 4	Abbott S 2 + 1	Easton W — + 1	Match No.
1	2	3	4^1	5	6	7	8	9	10	11^2	12	13															1
1	2	3		5	4	7	8	9	10	11		12	6^1														2
1	2	3		5	4	7	8	9^1	10	11			6	12													3
1	2	3		5	4	7	8	9^2	13	11		12	6^1	10													4
1	2		4	5	6	7			12	11	3	9^1	8	10													5
1	2		4	5	8	7	9^2		12	11	3		13	10	6^1												6
1	2	3	4	5	8	7	12		13	11^1			9^2	10	6												7
1	2^2	3	4	5	8	7				11		13	9	10	12	6^1											8
1	2	3	4	5	8	7			11^1	13		12	9	10	6^2												9
1	2	3	4	5	8	7			11^1	12		13	9	10^2	6												10
1	2	3	4	5	8	7			11^2	13		12	9	10^1	6												11
1	2	3	4^1	5	8^2	7			11	14	12	13	9	10^3	6												12
1	2		4	5	8	7			11^1	12	3	10	9		6												13
1	13	3	4	5	6	7^1				11		9	8	10^2	2	12											14
1	2	3	4■	5	6		12		10	11		8	7	9^1													15
1	2	3		5	4		6		10	11		8	7	9													16
1	2	3	4	5	6		8		12	11		9	7	10^1													17
1	2	3	4	5	6		8^2		12	11		9	7	10^1	13												18
1	2	3	4	5	8	7^2	12		10	13		11	9^3		6^1	14											19
1	2	3	4	5	6		8		10	11		9	7														20
1	2	3	4	5^2	6		8		10^3	13		9^1	7	11			12	14									21
		3	4^1	5	6	7^2	8		10^3	14	12	11		9		13			1	2							22
1		3		5	4	7	8		10	11^1		12		9^2		6				2	13^3	14					23
1		3		5	4	7	2		10	12		11	8	9^2		6^1		13									24
1		3		5	4	7	8			12		11^1	9■	10		6				2							25
1		3		5	4^2	7	8			12		11	9	10		6^1		13		2							26
1		3		5	4	7	8			9^3		11		10		6^2		14		2^1		13	12				27
1				5	4	7	8			11	3	12	9	10^1								6	2				28
		2		5	6	7	8^1			10^3	3	13	9	11^2				14	1			12	4				29
1		2			5					10	3	9^1	8	11		6		12				7	4				30
1		2					12			10	3	9	8	11		6				5		7^1	4				31
1		2			7		12			10	3	9	8^2	11^3		6^1	14			5		13	4				32
		2		4	7	6	9				3	10	8	11^1				12	1	5							33
		2	12	4	7	6	9				3^1	11	10						1	5		8					34
		2	3	4	7	6^2	9					11						12	1	5		8^1		10	13		35
		2	3^1	4	7		9		13		12	11						14	1	5		8^2		10^3	6		36
		2					7		8	13	4	9		11^2			6		1	5		12		10	3^1		37
		2					6		9^2	8	3	12	7	11^1			5	13	1	4^3				10		14	38

DUNFERMLINE ATHLETIC Premier League

Year Formed: 1885. *Ground & Address:* East End Park, Halbeath Rd, Dunfermline KY12 7RB. *Telephone:* 01383 724295. *Fax:* 01383 723468. *Ticket office telephone:* 0870 300 1201. *E-mail:* enquiries@dafc.co.uk. *Website:* www.dafc.co.uk
Ground Capacity: all seated: 12,500. *Size of Pitch:* 115yd × 71yd.
Chairman: John Yorkston. *Company Secretary:* William Hodgins. *Executive Secretary:* Susan McDade. *Sales & Marketing:* Tracy Martin. *Commercial Manager:* Karen Brown.
Director of Football: Jim Leishman. *Coach:* Craig Robertson. *Physio:* Paul Atkinson.
Assistant Coaches: Hamish French & Scott Y Thomson.
Managers since 1975: G. Miller, H. Melrose, P. Stanton, T. Forsyth, J. Leishman, I. Munro, J. Scott, B. Paton, R. Campbell, J. Calderwood, D. Hay.
Club Nickname(s): The Pars. *Previous Grounds:* None.
Record Attendance: 27,816 v Celtic, Division I, 30 Apr 1968.
Record Transfer Fee received: £650,000 for Jackie McNamara to Celtic (Oct 1995).
Record Transfer Fee paid: £540,000 for Istvan Kozma from Bordeaux (Sept 1989).
Record Victory: 11-2 v Stenhousemuir, Division II, 27 Sept 1930.
Record Defeat: 1-11 v Hibernian, Scottish Cup, 3rd rd replay, 26 Oct 1889.
Most Capped Player: Colin Miller 16 (61), Canada.
Most League Appearances: 497: Norrie McCathie, 1981-96.
Most League Goals in Season (Individual): 53: Bobby Skinner, Division II, 1925-26.
Most Goals Overall (Individual): 154: Charles Dickson.

DUNFERMLINE ATHLETIC 2005–06 LEAGUE RECORD

Match No.	Date	Venue	Opponents	Result	H/T Score	Lg. Pos.	Goalscorers	Attendance
1	Jul 30	A	Hibernian	D 1-1	1-0	—	Shields 12	13,004
2	Aug 6	A	Motherwell	L 0-1	0-0	9		4649
3	13	H	Inverness CT	L 0-1	0-1	11		5002
4	20	A	Livingston	D 1-1	1-0	11	Makel 43	3528
5	28	H	Celtic	L 0-4	0-2	11		8998
6	Sept 10	A	Kilmarnock	L 2-3	1-2	11	Burchill 3, Young Derek 66	4737
7	17	H	Aberdeen	L 0-2	0-2	11		6387
8	24	H	Dundee U	W 2-1	0-1	10	Tod 50, Ross 75	5229
9	Oct 1	A	Rangers	L 1-5	0-2	11	Hunt 54	48,374
10	15	H	Falkirk	L 0-1	0-1	11		7068
11	22	A	Hearts	L 0-2	0-2	11		16,500
12	26	H	Hibernian	L 1-2	0-0	—	Mason 87	6853
13	29	H	Motherwell	L 0-3	0-0	11		4421
14	Nov 5	A	Inverness CT	L 1-2	0-2	11	Makel 72	3770
15	19	H	Livingston	L 0-1	0-0	12		6016
16	26	A	Celtic	W 1-0	1-0	11	Ross 17	56,575
17	Dec 3	H	Kilmarnock	L 0-1	0-1	11		4319
18	10	A	Aberdeen	D 0-0	0-0	12		9881
19	20	A	Dundee U	L 1-2	1-2	—	Wilson S 30	5889
20	26	H	Rangers	D 3-3	2-1	12	Hunt 18, Burchill 23, Young Darren 90	9505
21	31	A	Falkirk	W 2-1	1-0	11	Burchill 44, Hunt 56	6253
22	Jan 14	H	Hearts	L 1-4	0-1	11	Burchill 57	8277
23	21	A	Hibernian	L 1-3	1-1	11	Donnelly 34	13,318
24	28	H	Motherwell	D 1-1	1-0	11	Young Darren 11	4847
25	Feb 8	H	Inverness CT	D 2-2	2-0	—	Hunt 8, Burchill 10	3355
26	11	A	Livingston	W 1-0	1-0	11	Roy (og) 11	3976
27	19	H	Celtic	L 1-8	1-4	11	Tod 13	9017
28	25	H	Dundee U	D 1-1	1-1	—	Burchill 13	4697
29	Mar 4	A	Kilmarnock	L 0-1	0-1	11		5507
30	11	H	Aberdeen	W 1-0	0-0	10	Burchill 48	5308
31	25	A	Rangers	L 0-1	0-0	10		49,017
32	Apr 1	H	Falkirk	D 1-1	0-1	10	Burchill 50	6836
33	8	A	Hearts	L 0-4	0-3	11		16,873
34	15	A	Falkirk	D 0-0	0-0	11		5329
35	22	H	Livingston	W 3-2	1-1	11	Burchill 3 (1 pen) 38 (p), 79, 84	5963
36	29	A	Motherwell	W 3-2	2-1	11	Campbell I 20, Burchill (pen) 29, Mason 50	3621
37	May 2	A	Dundee U	W 1-0	0-0	—	Daquin 77	5034
38	6	H	Inverness CT	L 0-1	0-0	11		5354

Final League Position: 11

Honours
League Champions: First Division 1988-89, 1995-96. Division II 1925-26. Second Division 1985-86; *Runners-up:* First Division 1986-87, 1993-94, 1994-95, 1999-2000. Division II 1912-13, 1933-34, 1954-55, 1957-58, 1972-73. Second Division 1978-79.
Scottish Cup Winners: 1961, 1968; *Runners-up:* 1965, 2004.
League Cup Runners-up: 1949-50, 1991-92, 2005-06.

European: *Cup Winners' Cup:* 14 matches (1961-62, 1968-69 semi-finals). *UEFA Cup:* 30 matches (*Fairs Cup:* 1962-63, 1964-65, 1965-66, 1966-67, 1969-70. *UEFA Cup:* 2004-05).

Club colours: Shirt: Black and white vertical stripes. Shorts: White. Stockings: White.

Goalscorers: *League* (33): Burchill 12 (2 pens), Hunt 4, Makel 2, Mason 2, Ross 2, Tod 2, Darren Young 2, Campbell I 1, Daquin 1, Donnelly 1, Shields 1, Wilson S 1, Derek Young 1, own goal 1.
Scottish Cup (3): Hunt 1, Mason 1, Derek Young 1.
CIS Cup (9): Burchill 3, Derek Young 3, McCunnie 1, Mason 1, Darren Young 1.

Halliwell B 12	Shields G 33	Wilson S 31	Thomson S 23 + 2	Morrison S 3	Young Darren 20 + 1	Mason G 29	Makel L 20	Donnelly S 8 + 5	Young Derek 13 + 5	Tod A 26 + 4	Skerla A 1 + 1	Burchill M 24 + 7	Hunt N 22 + 10	Tarachulski B 12 + 15	Labonte A 19 + 3	Campbell I 14 + 3	Ross G 21 + 2	Horsted L 6 + 5	McGregor A 26	McCunnie J 18 + 4	Zambernardi Y 14 + 2	Wilson C 5 + 9	Dunn J —	Gunnlaursen G — + 1	Muirhead S 11 + 1	Campbell A 1 + 4	Simmons S 3 + 3	Daquin F 2 + 7	Phinn N 1 + 2	*Match No.*
1	2	3	4^{1}	5	6	7	8	9^{3}	10^{2}	11	12	13	14																	1
1	2	3■	4	5	6	7	8	9^{2}	10^{1}	11		12		13																2
1	2		4	5	6	7	8	9^{1}	13	11	3^{3}	10^{2}	14	12																3
1	2^{1}	3			6	7	8		13	4		10^{3}	14	11^{2}	5	9	12													4
1		3	4^{3}		6	7^{1}	8		12	2		10^{2}	13	11		9	5	14												5
		3	4		6		8		9	2		10^{2}	13	11^{1}		7^{3}	5	14	1	12										6
	2	3	4		6		8		9			10^{1}	13	12				11^{2}	1	7	5									7
		3					8		10^{1}	4			12	11	5		6	9^{2}	1	7	2	13								8
1		3	4				8		10			13	12	11^{1}	5		6	9^{2}		7	2									9
	2	3	4		6	7^{3}		14	10^{2}	12			13	11^{1}				9	1	8	5									10
	2	3^{1}	4		6	7	8	14	10^{3}	12		11						9^{2}	1	13	5									11
	2		4		6	7	8	12		3			10^{2}	11^{1}	14			9^{3}	1		5■	13								12
	2		4^{1}		6	7	8	10		3			11^{2}		12	5			1		9	13								13
	2				6^{2}	7	8	10^{3}		3		13	11		4	5		12	1	14		9^{1}								14
	2	3				7			10	4		13	11			6	8	12	1^{1}		5^{2}	9								15
	2	3				7			10	9			11^{2}	13	4	12	8		1	6	5^{1}									16
	2	3				7			10	9		12	11^{2}		4	6	8	13	1	5^{1}										17
	2				13	7	9^{2}		10^{3}	3^{1}		12	11		4	6	8		1	5		14								18
	2	3	4^{1}			7	9		12	10		11^{2}	13		5	6	8^{3}		1			14								19
1	2	3	4^{1}		6	7	9■		14	5		10^{2}	11^{3}	13		12	8													20
	2	3	4		6	7				9		10^{1}	11^{2}	12	13		8		1	5										21
	2	3				7	9^{1}			5		10	11	12		6	8		1	4										22
	2	3			6		9	12		10^{1}				11^{2}		7	8^{3}		1	4	5	14		13						23
	2	3	13		6	8		10^{1}				11	9						1	4^{2}	5				7^{3}	12	14			24
1	2	3	14		6	8		10^{2}				11^{3}	9							4	5				7^{1}	12	13			25
1	2	3	4^{2}		6	8		14		10		11^{3}	9^{1}							5	13					12	7			26
1		3			6	7				10		11		12						4	2	8^{2}				5^{1}	9	13		27
	2				6					4		11^{2}	10	13	5		12		1		3	8^{3}			7		9^{1}	14		28
	2		4^{3}				8			10		11	9^{1}	13	5				1	3	14	6^{2}			7			12		29
	2	3	4			8			10^{1}	14		11^{2}	9^{3}	13	5		6		1						7			12		30
1	2	3	4			9	8^{1}	10		11				14	5		6^{3}			12					7^{2}			13		31
	2	3	4			9						11	10^{1}	12	5		6		1	8					7					32
	2	3	4							9		11^{2}	10^{1}	12	5		6■		1	8					7				13	33
	2	3	4							9		11	10	13	5	12			1	6^{1}					7^{2}				8	34
	2	3	4			8				13		11	10^{2}	9	5		6		1						7^{1}			12		35
	2	3	4^{2}			8						11^{1}		10^{3}	5	9	6		1			13				12	14	7		36
	2	3				8						11	10	9^{1}	5	7	4		1			13			12			6^{2}		37
1	2	3^{1}				8						11	10	9^{2}	5	7	4					14			6^{3}			13	12	38

EAST FIFE Third Division

Year Formed: 1903. *Ground & Address:* Bayview Stadium, Harbour View, Methil, Fife KY8 3RW. *Telephone:* 01333 426323. *Fax:* 01333 426376. *E-mail:* secretary@eastfife.org. *Website:* www.eastfife.org
Ground Capacity: all seated: 2000. *Size of Pitch:* 115yd × 75yd.
Chairman and Secretary: Derrick Brown.
Manager: David Baikie. *Assistant Manager:* Graeme Irons. *Physio:* Ian Barrett.
Managers since 1975: Frank Christie, Roy Barry, David Clarke, Gavin Murray, Alex Totten, Steve Archibald, James Bone, Steve Kirk, Rab Shannon, David Clarke, Jim Moffat.
Club Nickname(s): The Fifers. *Previous Ground:* Bayview Park.
Record Attendance: 22,515 v Raith Rovers, Division I, 2 Jan 1950.
Record Transfer Fee received: £150,000 for Paul Hunter from Hull C (March 1990).
Record Transfer Fee paid: £70,000 for John Sludden from Kilmarnock (July 1991).
Record Victory: 13-2 v Edinburgh City, Division II, 11 Dec 1937.
Record Defeat: 0-9 v Hearts, Division I, 5 Oct 1957.
Most Capped Player: George Aitken, 5 (8), Scotland.
Most League Appearances: 517: David Clarke, 1968-86.
Most League Goals in Season (Individual): 41: Jock Wood, Division II; 1926-27 and Henry Morris, Division II, 1947-48.
Most Goals Overall (Individual): 225: Phil Weir (215 in League).

EAST FIFE 2005–06 LEAGUE RECORD

Match No.	Date	Venue	Opponents	Result		H/T Score	Lg. Pos.	Goalscorers	Attendance
1	Aug 6	H	Berwick R	L	0-4	0-3	—		498
2	13	A	Arbroath	L	0-1	0-0	10		507
3	20	H	Montrose	W	3-2	0-0	8	Smart 68, McDonald 87, Martin 90	468
4	27	H	Cowdenbeath	W	1-0	1-0	5	Hampshire 10	729
5	Sept 10	A	Albion R	W	4-2	1-1	3	McDonald 2 42, 80, Smart 57, Bradford 62	317
6	17	A	Stenhousemuir	L	1-2	0-1	5	Noble 57	494
7	24	H	Queen's Park	W	1-0	1-0	4	Clark (og) 8	567
8	Oct 1	A	Elgin C	W	2-1	1-0	4	Smart 6, Bradford 48	380
9	7	H	Arbroath	D	1-1	1-0	4	Martin 23	747
10	15	H	East Stirling	W	3-1	1-0	3	Bradford 18, Paliczka 71, Mitchell 82	545
11	22	A	Berwick R	L	0-3	0-1	4		555
12	29	H	Albion R	D	1-1	0-1	4	McDonald 77	505
13	Nov 5	A	Cowdenbeath	L	1-3	1-0	4	Smart 27	587
14	12	H	Stenhousemuir	L	2-3	1-0	4	Fortune 31, Smart 50	567
15	26	A	Queen's Park	L	0-2	0-0	5		399
16	Dec 3	A	East Stirling	W	2-1	1-1	4	Noble 37, Hampshire 82	244
17	26	H	Berwick R	W	1-0	0-0	—	Paliczka 89	575
18	31	A	Montrose	L	1-3	0-0	—	Kelly (pen) 52	401
19	Jan 2	H	Cowdenbeath	W	2-1	2-0	—	Paliczka 16, Kelly 19	867
20	7	H	Elgin C	L	1-2	0-0	4	Martin 89	409
21	14	A	Albion R	L	1-3	0-2	5	Bradford 71	303
22	21	A	Stenhousemuir	L	2-4	1-1	5	Bradford 2 39, 87	420
23	28	H	Queen's Park	L	0-1	0-0	5		479
24	Feb 4	A	Elgin C	L	3-5	2-2	7	Lumsden 23, Gordon 29, Smart 46	386
25	11	H	East Stirling	L	1-2	0-0	7	Pelosi (pen) 73	309
26	18	A	Arbroath	L	1-2	1-1	7	Hampshire 42	570
27	25	H	Montrose	W	4-0	1-0	7	Hampshire 8, Gordon 2 54, 58, Savage 87	332
28	Mar 11	H	Albion R	W	1-0	1-0	7	McDonald 21	257
29	18	H	Stenhousemuir	W	2-1	0-0	7	McDonald 2 46, 56	375
30	21	A	Cowdenbeath	L	1-4	1-3	—	Kelly 37	412
31	25	A	Queen's Park	D	1-1	0-0	7	Beith 76	403
32	Apr 1	H	Elgin C	L	0-2	0-1	7		357
33	8	A	East Stirling	L	1-2	1-1	7	Smart 29	270
34	15	A	Berwick R	D	1-1	1-0	7	Hampshire 14	629
35	22	H	Arbroath	L	0-3	0-1	7		547
36	29	A	Montrose	W	2-0	1-0	7	Dodds K 3, Bradford 59	431

Final League Position: 7

Honours
League Champions: Division II 1947-48; *Runners-up:* Division II 1929-30, 1970-71. Second Division 1983-84, 1995-96. Third Division 2002-03.
Scottish Cup Winners: 1938; *Runners-up:* 1927, 1950.
League Cup Winners: 1947-48, 1949-50, 1953-54.

Club colours: Shirt: Gold and black. Shorts: White. Stockings: Black.

Goalscorers: *League* (48): Bradford 7, McDonald 7, Smart 7, Hampshire 5, Gordon 3, Kelly 3 (1 pen), Martin 3, Paliczka 3, Noble 2, Beith 1, Dodds K 1, Fortune 1, Lumsden 1, Mitchell 1, Pelosi 1 (pen), Savage 1, own goal 1.
Scottish Cup (0).
CIS Cup (0).
Challenge Cup (0).

Dodds J 30	Lumsden C 25 + 4	Donaldson E 3 + 7	McDonald G 29	Mathie G 1	Kelly G 27 + 3	Fortune S 24 + 7	Hampshire P 31 + 2	Paliczka S 8 + 12	Port G 2 + 2	Mitchell J 3 + 4	Graham R 1 + 3	Beith G 20 + 3	Crawford R — + 1	Pelosi M 21 + 1	Smart C 26 + 2	Martin J 17 + 7	Bain K 19 + 5	Bradford J 22 + 9	Noble S 9 + 2	Morrison S 6	Campbell A 17	Brash K 3	Taylor S — + 1	Condie C 1 + 2	Savage J 10 + 3	Smith E 12	Gordon K 14	Doyle P 11	Dodds K 4 + 1	Johnston C — + 1	Samson C — + 1	Match No.
1	2	3^{2}	4	5	6^{3}	7	8	9	10	11^{1}	12	13	14																			1
1	4	3	5		2	6	8					11		7^{1}	9	10	12															2
1	4		5		2	6	11			7^{1}		8		3	9	10		12														3
1		14	4		2	6^{1}	11^{3}		13	12		8		3	9	7	5	10^{2}														4
1			4		2	13	8^{2}	12				6		3	9	7	5	10	11^{1}													5
1			4		2		8	12				6		3	9	7^{1}	5	10	11													6
1			4		2	13	8	12				6^{2}		3	9	7	5	10	11^{1}													7
1		14	4		2	12	8^{3}	7^{2}				6		3	9	13	5	10	11^{1}													8
1			4		2	6	10	13				8		3	9^{1}	7	5	11^{2}	12													9
1	14		4^{3}		2	6	10	12		13		8		3		7	5	9^{2}	11^{1}													10
1			4		2	8	11	13		10^{2}		6^{1}		3	9	7	5	12														11
	4	14	5			8	6^{3}	13			12			3	10	7^{2}		9^{1}	11	1	2											12
	4	11	5		6	10^{1}		14						3	7	12	8^{3}	9^{2}	13	1	2											13
	4	13	5		6	8	11	7^{2}		12				3	9				10^{1}	1	2											14
1	4	13	5		6	8	11^{2}	7^{3}							9			12	10		2	3^{1}	14									15
1	4		5		2	6	8	13						10^{2}	9	7^{3}	12	14	11			3^{1}										16
1	4	13	6		2	12	10	14	11^{1}			8				7▪	5	9^{3}				3^{2}										17
1	2		5		8	6	11	7		12		3					4	9						10^{1}								18
1	5	14	8		2^{1}	10	11^{2}	9^{3}			12	3				7	6				4			13								19
1	4				6	8	11^{2}	7^{1}				3				10	5	13			2			12	9							20
	2		5			6	14	13			9^{1}	11^{2}			8	7	4	12		1	3				10^{3}							21
1	12		4			8	14	7^{2}	13			3			10		5^{1}	9			6				11^{3}	2						22
1	4					8	11^{2}	12				13		3	6		5	9							10^{1}	2	7					23
1	5				12	8^{1}	11^{2}							3	9		6	10								2	7	4	13			24
1	12		5^{3}		2^{2}	13	8							3▪	9	11	14	10^{1}			6					4	7					25
1	6				2^{2}	8	3								10	12		9^{1}			5				13	4	7	11				26
1	2		6^{2}		13	8	3								10^{1}	12		9^{3}			5				14	4	7	11				27
1	2		6		12		3^{2}					13		8^{1}				9			5				10	4	7	11				28
1	2		6		8		3^{2}							13	12			9			5				10^{1}	4	7	11				29
1	2		6		8		3								13	12		9^{1}			5				10^{2}	4	7	11				30
1	2		6			14	3^{2}					8		4	9	12	13				5▪				10^{1}		7^{3}	11				31
1	2		6			5	3					8		4^{1}	9	10^{2}		13							12		7	11				32
1	4				8		11					6			10	12	5	9^{1}								3	7		2			33
	13		6^{2}		8	12	11^{1}					10						14		1	5				9^{3}	3	7	4	2			34
	5				8	11^{1}								3	10		6	12		1					9▪		7	4	2			35
1	2^{1}				6	8									10^{2}		13	9			5▪					3	7	4	11^{3}	12	14	36

EAST STIRLINGSHIRE Third Division

Year Formed: 1880. *Ground & Address:* Firs Park, Firs St, Falkirk FK2 7AY. *Telephone:* 01324 623583. *Fax:* 01324 637 862. *E-mail:* lestshire@aol.com. *Website:* www.eaststirlingshire.com
Ground Capacity: total: 1880, seated: 200. *Size of Pitch:* 112yd × 72yd.
Chairman: A. Mackin. *Vice Chairman:* Douglas Morrison. *Chief Executive/Secretary:* Leslie G. Thomson.
Head Coach: Dennis Newall. *Assistant Coach:* Gordon Wylde. *Physio:* David Jenkins.
Managers since 1975: I. Ure, D. McLinden, W. P. Lamont, A. Ferguson, W. Little, D. Whiteford, D. Lawson, J. D. Connell, A. Mackin, D. Sullivan, B. McCulley, B. Little, J. Brownlie, H. McCann, G. Fairley, B. Ross, D. Diver.
Club Nickname(s): The Shire. *Previous Grounds:* Burnhouse, Randyford Park, Merchiston Park, New Kilbowie Park.
Record Attendance: 12,000 v Partick Th, Scottish Cup 3rd rd, 21 Feb 1921.
Record Transfer Fee received: £35,000 for Jim Docherty to Chelsea (1978).
Record Transfer Fee paid: £6,000 for Colin McKinnon from Falkirk (March 1991).
Record Victory: 11-2 v Vale of Bannock, Scottish Cup 2nd rd, 22 Sept 1888.
Record Defeat: 1-12 v Dundee United, Division II, 13 Apr 1936.
Most Capped Player: Humphrey Jones, 5 (14), Wales.
Most League Appearances: 415: Gordon Russell, 1983-2001.
Most League Goals in Season (Individual): 36: Malcolm Morrison, Division II, 1938-39.

EAST STIRLINGSHIRE 2005–06 LEAGUE RECORD

Match No.	Date	Venue	Opponents	Result		H/T Score	Lg. Pos.	Goalscorers	Attendance
1	Aug 6	H	Cowdenbeath	L	0-1	0-0	—		263
2	13	A	Berwick R	L	2-3	1-2	9	Thywissen [1], Diack [80]	406
3	20	H	Arbroath	W	3-1	0-0	6	Diack 2 [48, 73], Graham [89]	225
4	27	A	Stenhousemuir	L	1-6	1-2	9	Diack [31]	403
5	Sept 10	H	Montrose	D	1-1	0-0	9	Dymock [88]	195
6	17	A	Queen's Park	L	0-3	0-2	9		454
7	24	H	Elgin C	L	0-2	0-1	10		201
8	Oct 1	H	Albion R	W	3-1	2-0	6	Diack 2 (1 pen) [13 (p), 19], Brand [69]	245
9	15	A	East Fife	L	1-3	0-1	8	Dymock [88]	545
10	22	A	Cowdenbeath	L	1-5	1-4	10	Dymock [39]	267
11	25	H	Berwick R	L	1-2	1-0	—	Dymock [28]	197
12	29	A	Montrose	L	0-3	0-2	10		326
13	Nov 5	H	Stenhousemuir	D	0-0	0-0	10		388
14	26	A	Arbroath	L	2-7	1-3	10	Diack 2 [36, 88]	409
15	Dec 3	H	East Fife	L	1-2	1-1	10	Ure [26]	244
16	10	A	Elgin C	D	1-1	1-1	10	Livingstone [14]	311
17	13	H	Queen's Park	L	0-4	0-2	—		266
18	Jan 2	A	Stenhousemuir	L	0-5	0-1	—		482
19	7	A	Albion R	L	2-4	1-2	10	Brand (pen) [20], Patrick [64]	244
20	14	H	Montrose	W	1-0	1-0	10	Dymock [20]	199
21	21	A	Queen's Park	L	1-3	0-1	10	Ure [81]	514
22	28	H	Elgin C	L	0-2	0-0	10		184
23	Feb 4	H	Albion R	W	1-0	1-0	10	Ure [5]	199
24	11	A	East Fife	W	2-1	0-0	10	Dymock [55], Tyrrell P [82]	309
25	18	A	Berwick R	L	0-1	0-1	10		357
26	25	H	Arbroath	L	0-4	0-1	10		252
27	Mar 11	A	Montrose	L	0-2	0-2	10		241
28	18	H	Queen's Park	D	0-0	0-0	10		330
29	21	H	Stenhousemuir	L	0-7	0-3	—		271
30	25	A	Elgin C	L	0-3	0-3	10		355
31	Apr 1	A	Albion R	L	0-2	0-2	10		803
32	4	H	Cowdenbeath	D	1-1	1-0	—	Tweedie [34]	403
33	8	H	East Fife	W	2-1	1-1	10	Ure [4], Thywissen [85]	270
34	15	A	Cowdenbeath	L	0-5	0-1	10		592
35	22	H	Berwick R	L	0-1	0-0	10		246
36	29	A	Arbroath	L	1-2	0-2	10	Smith [66]	1050

Final League Position: 10

Honours
League Champions: Division II 1931-32; C Division 1947-48. *Runners-up:* Division II 1962-63. Second Division 1979-80. Division Three 1923-24.

Club colours: Shirt: Black with white. Shorts: Black with white. Stockings: Black with white hoops.

Goalscorers: *League* (28): Diack 8 (1 pen), Dymock 6, Ure 4, Brand 2 (1 pen), Thywissen 2, Graham 1, Livingstone 1, Patrick 1, Smith 1, Tweedie 1, Tyrrell P 1.
Scottish Cup (2): Dymock 1, Owen 1.
CIS Cup (1): Diack 1.
Challenge Cup (0).

Jackson D 33	McKay J 8 + 3	Livingstone S 22 + 5	Tyrrell M 27 + 2	Gaughan P 17 + 4	Tyrrell P 24 + 1	Brand A 16 + 4	Thywissen C 27 + 3	Diack I 14	Graham A 14	Ure D 31 + 3	Blair S 13 + 7	Oates S 21 + 8	Dymock S 21 + 11	Gordon B 3	Gillespie A 1 + 1	Smith J 23 + 2	Walker J 5	Lojman K 1 + 3	Owen A 12 + 1	Ross P — + 1	Sobolewski H 7 + 6	McWilliam G 5 + 1	Molloy M 11 + 1	Patrick A 9 + 4	McKenzie M 11	Thomson A 1	Walsh G 9	Tweedie P 8 + 1	Wilson E 1	Carr M 1	*Match No.*
1	2	3	4	5^{2}	6	7^{1}	8^{3}	9	10	11	12	13	14																		1
1		3		5	6		7	9^{1}	10	11	8	4	12	2																	2
1		3		5	6		7	9^{1}	10	11	8	4	12	2^{2}	13																3
1		3	12	5	6		7^{2}	9	10	11	8	4	13	2^{1}																	4
1	5	2	3		8		7	9	10	11	6^{1}	4	12																		5
1	5	2	3		8	14	7^{2}	9	10	11^{3}	6^{1}	4	12			13															6
	2^{2}	3	5		8^{1}	12	13	9	10	11		4	7		1		6														7
1	2	11	3			7	8^{2}	9^{1}	10	13		4	12			5	6														8
1	2	11^{2}	3		12	7	8^{1}	9	10	13		4	14			5^{3}	6														9
1	13	3	4			8^{1}	10	9^{2}		11		2	7			5	6	12													10
1	2^{2}	7	4			8	6^{3}	9	10	12		13	11^{1}			5			3	14											11
1		7^{2}	4	13	6	8^{1}	12	9	10			2	11			5			3												12
1			2	4	6	7^{2}	8	9	10	11^{1}	13		12			5[illegible]			3												13
1		13	2	5	6	7	8^{1}	9	10^{3}	11^{2}		12	14				4		3												14
1		12	2^{1}		8	7	6		10[illegible]	11		5	9			4			3												15
1		2^{1}	7	6		8	10			11		5	9			4		12	3												16
1		2^{1}	7	6		8	10			11		5^{2}	9			4		12	3		13										17
1		12	7^{1}	6^{3}	10	8	14			11		13	9			4		2			3^{2}	5									18
1		14	2	5	6	7				11^{2}	13	12	10			4					3^{1}		8	9^{3}							19
1		5	6			2^{1}	4				13	11	9						3		12		8	10^{2}	7						20
1		2	4		10		6			11	12	5	9^{1}						3				8	7							21
1		2	4		6		10			11	12	5^{2}	9								3	13	8	7^{1}							22
1		11^{2}	4	14	6		5			10	2		9						12				8^{3}	13		3^{1}	7				23
1		11	4	14	6		5			10^{3}	2	13	9			12			3				8^{1}	7^{2}							24
1			12		6		10			11	2^{1}	4	9			5			3				8	13			7^{2}				25
1			4		6		5			10	7	12	9			2			3^{2}		11^{1}		8	13							26
1			4	13	6	7	11			3^{3}	2	12				5					14		8^{2}		9		10^{1}				27
1				2^{2}	6	13				10	4		11			5					12			8^{1}	9		7	3			28
					6	12				10	2^{1}		8			4						5		3	9		7	11	1		29
1				4	6	2				3			9			5					13		8	11^{1}	7		10^{2}	12			30
1			4		6					3		2	7^{1}			5					12		8		10		11	9			31
1			4	8						11		2				5					3	6			9		7	10			32
1		13		6			2			8		3				4					11^{1}	5	12		9		7^{2}	10			33
1	13	10	2	6			8			11		3^{1}				5^{2}						4		12	7			9			34
1	12	2		6			4			10	13		8^{2}			5					3^{1}			11	7			9			35
	8^{1}	3	2	6			5			11	10		12			4									7			9		1	36

ELGIN CITY

Third Division

Year Formed: 1893. *Ground and Address:* Borough Briggs, Borough Briggs Road, Elgin IV30 1AP.
Telephone: 01343 551114. *Fax:* 01343 547921. *E-mail:* elgincityfc@ukonline.co.uk. *Website:* www.elgincity.com
Ground Capacity: 3927, seated 478, standing 3449. *Size of pitch:* 111yd × 72yd.
Chairman: Derek W. Shewan. *Secretary:* Ian A. Allan. *Administrator:* Audrey Fanning. *Commercial Manager:* Michael Teasdale.
Manager: Brian Irvine. *Director of Football:* Graham Tatters. *Physio:* Billy Belcher.
Managers since 1975: McHardy, Wilson, McHardy, Dickson, Shewan, Tedcastle, Grant, Cochran, Cumming, Cowie, Paterson, Winton, Black, Teasdale, Fleming, McHardy, Tatters, Caldwell, Robertson.
Previous names: 1893-1900 Elgin City, 1900-03 Elgin City United, 1903- Elgin City.
Club Nickname(s): City or Black & Whites. *Previous Grounds:* Association Park 1893-95; Milnfield Park 1895-1909; Station Park 1909-19; Cooper Park 1919-21.
Record Attendance: 12,608 v Arbroath, Scottish Cup, 17 Feb 1968.
Record Transfer Fee received: £32,000 for Michael Teasdale to Dundee (Jan 1994).
Record Transfer Fee paid: £10,000 to Fraserburgh for Russell McBride (July 2001).
Record Victory: 18-1 v Brora Rangers, North of Scotland Cup, 6 Feb 1960.
Record Defeat: 1-14 v Hearts, Scottish Cup, 4 Feb 1939.
Most League Appearances: 126: David Hind, 2001-06.
Most League Goals in Season (Individual): Martin Johnston, 20, 2005-06.
Most Goals Overall (Individual): Martin Johnston, 20, 2005-06.

ELGIN CITY 2005–06 LEAGUE RECORD

Match No.	Date	Venue	Opponents	Result		H/T Score	Lg. Pos.	Goalscorers	Attendance
1	Aug 6	H	Montrose	D	0-0	0-0	—		460
2	13	A	Stenhousemuir	L	1-3	0-2	7	Scullion [68]	278
3	20	H	Cowdenbeath	L	0-3	0-1	10		402
4	27	A	Berwick R	L	1-3	1-1	10	Muir [14]	390
5	Sept 10	H	Queen's Park	D	2-2	2-0	10	Johnston [24], Booth [26]	371
6	17	H	Albion R	D	2-2	0-0	10	Wood [75], Dickson [89]	305
7	24	A	East Stirling	W	2-0	1-0	6	Booth (pen) [43], Johnston [85]	201
8	Oct 1	H	East Fife	L	1-2	0-1	7	Johnston [56]	380
9	8	A	Berwick R	D	1-1	0-1	6	Johnston [79]	294
10	15	A	Arbroath	L	0-2	0-1	7		502
11	22	A	Montrose	L	0-2	0-1	9		288
12	25	H	Stenhousemuir	L	1-2	0-0	—	Johnston [53]	274
13	29	A	Queen's Park	L	0-3	0-2	9		424
14	Nov 5	H	Berwick R	D	2-2	0-0	9	Johnston [58], Scullion [78]	384
15	12	A	Albion R	W	2-0	0-0	9	Vigurs I [70], Napier [80]	273
16	Dec 3	H	Arbroath	W	2-0	1-0	8	Muir [25], McKenzie [53]	357
17	10	H	East Stirling	D	1-1	1-1	8	Johnston [10]	311
18	26	H	Montrose	W	1-0	0-0	—	Johnston [56]	437
19	Jan 7	A	East Fife	W	2-1	0-0	7	Nelson [64], Bremner [82]	409
20	14	H	Queen's Park	L	1-2	1-0	8	Booth (pen) [34]	442
21	21	H	Albion R	W	2-1	0-1	7	McKenzie [77], Booth [87]	360
22	28	A	East Stirling	W	2-0	0-0	7	Cumming [51], Nelson [68]	184
23	Feb 4	H	East Fife	W	5-3	2-2	5	Gardiner [21], Booth 3 [44, 53, 78], Tweedie [68]	386
24	11	A	Arbroath	W	1-0	0-0	5	Dickson [89]	536
25	18	A	Stenhousemuir	W	2-1	1-1	5	Gardiner [8], Johnston [64]	388
26	25	H	Cowdenbeath	L	0-4	0-1	5		677
27	Mar 11	A	Queen's Park	D	3-3	1-1	6	Kaczan [31], Johnston 2 [50, 56]	465
28	14	H	Berwick R	L	1-3	1-2	—	Nelson [25]	298
29	18	A	Albion R	W	2-1	1-1	6	Johnston [42], Gardiner [78]	319
30	25	H	East Stirling	W	3-0	3-0	6	Johnston 2 [2, 8], Kaczan [10]	355
31	28	A	Cowdenbeath	L	2-5	2-5	—	Johnston [25], Booth [37]	259
32	Apr 1	A	East Fife	W	2-0	1-0	6	Johnston 2 [14, 73]	357
33	8	H	Arbroath	W	4-1	3-1	4	Johnston 3 (1 pen) [3, 10 (p), 44], Kaczan [56]	607
34	15	A	Montrose	W	3-1	1-1	4	Booth (pen) [8], Kaczan 2 [72, 85]	406
35	22	H	Stenhousemuir	L	0-2	0-0	5		880
36	29	A	Cowdenbeath	L	1-2	0-1	5	Nelson [68]	2596

Final League Position: 5

Honours
Scottish Cup: Quarter-finals 1968.
Highland League Champions: winners 15 times.
Scottish Qualifying Cup (North): winners 7 times.
North of Scotland Cup: winners 17 times.
Highland League Cup: winners 5 times.
Inverness Cup: winners twice.

Club colours: Shirt: Black and white vertical stripes. Shorts: Black. Stockings: Red.

Goalscorers: *League* (55): Johnston 20 (1 pen), Booth 9 (3 pens), Kaczan 5, Nelson 4, Gardiner 3, Dickson 2, McKenzie 2, Muir 2, Scullion 2, Bremner 1, Cumming 1, Napier 1, Tweedie 1, Vigurs I 1, Wood 1.
Scottish Cup (1): Gardiner 1.
CIS Cup (2): Dickson 1, Muir 1.
Challenge Cup (1) Booth 1.

Renton K 36	Cumming S 35	Dempsie A 27	McKenzie J 25 + 5	Dickson H 27	Scullion P 13	Bremner F 12 + 22	Easton S 22 + 4	Johnston M 31 + 1	Booth M 23 + 2	Gardiner C 23 + 8	Vigurs I 6 + 2	Wood G 5 + 7	Reid P 2 + 2	Muir A 15 + 6	Kaczan P 31 + 1	Napier P 6 + 3	Melrose G — + 5	Hind D 25 + 2	Jack M 1 + 4	Nelson A 21	Ralph J 1 + 1	Lauchlan M 5 + 4	Shewan G 1 + 4	Tweedie G 2 + 4	Stirling J 1	McIntosh S — + 2	*Match No.*
1	2	3	4	5	6^{3}	7^{2}	8^{1}	9	10	11	12	13	14														1
1	2	3^{1}	4	5■	6	13	7^{2}	9	10	11		14		8^{3}	12												2
1	2^{3}		6		5	7^{1}	14	9	10	11^{2}	3	12		8	4	13											3
1	2		4	3	6	12		9	8^{2}	7		10	13	11^{1}	5												4
1	2	3	6	5	8^{1}	12		9	10	7^{3}		13		11^{2}	4		14										5
1	2	3	6	5	8	12		9	10^{1}	7^{2}		13		11^{3}	4		14										6
1	2	3	4		6^{3}	7^{1}	14	9	8	10^{2}		12		11	5		13										7
1	2	3	6	8	4^{1}	13	14	9	7^{3}	12		10		11^{2}	5												8
1	2	3	6^{2}	5	8^{1}	14		9			11	10		12	4	7^{3}		13									9
1	2	3	12	5		14		9		13	11^{3}	10		8	4	7^{2}		6^{1}									10
1	2	3	13	5^{3}	6^{2}	14		9			11	10^{1}			4	7		8	12								11
1	2	3	6■	5		7		9	10	13				11^{1}	4	12		8^{2}									12
1	2	3		5		7		9	10	13	14			11^{1}	4	12		8^{2}		6^{3}							13
1	2			5	4	7		9			3	13	8^{1}			11^{2}	12	6^{3}		10	14						14
1	2			5	4	7		9			3		8^{1}			11^{2}	12	6	13	10							15
1	2	3	10			13	5	9	11	12				7^{2}	4^{1}			6		8							16
1	2	3	10	5^{2}		13	6	9						7^{1}	4^{3}			8		11		12	14				17
1	7	3	10^{1}		5		14	4	9^{3}	12						2		13	6		8		11^{2}				18
1	7^{3}	3	8^{2}	5		14	4	9	13	12					2			6		10		11^{1}					19
1	7	3	10^{2}	5		14	4	9^{1}	6	12					2^{3}			8	13	11							20
1	7^{2}	3	13	5		12	4		6	9^{3}				11^{1}	2			8		10				14			21
1	7^{3}	3		5		14	4		6	9^{2}				12	2			8	13	10		11^{1}					22
1	7^{3}	3		5		13	4		10^{2}	9				11^{1}	2			6		8			14	12			23
1	7	3		5		12	4		10	9					2			6		8				11^{1}			24
1	7	3	14	5		11^{2}	4	12	10^{3}	9^{1}					2			6		8		13					25
1	7	3^{1}	10	5		12	4	9		11					2			6		8^{2}		13					26
1	8^{2}		3	5		13	4	9		7^{1}				12	2			6		10		11					27
1	2		3	5^{3}		13	4^{1}	9		7				12	8			6		10		11^{2}	14				28
1	2		8^{1}			14	4	9	13	10^{3}				12■	3			6		11		7^{2}			5		29
1	2		7			3	4	9		10					5			6^{1}		8			12	11^{2}		13	30
1	2		11			3	4	9	7	10					5			6		8							31
1	2	3	12			7^{2}	4	9	11	10^{1}				13	5			6		8							32
1	2	3	11			7^{1}	4	9^{3}		10				6■	5					8^{2}		12		13		14	33
1	7	3	8	5		12	4	9^{2}	11^{1}	10					2			6						13			34
1	7^{1}	3	8	5		12	4	9	11	10					2			6									35
1		3	7	5			4	9	11	10■					2			6		8							36

FALKIRK Premier League

Year Formed: 1876. *Ground & Address:* The Falkirk Stadium, Westfield, Falkirk FK2 9DX. *Telephone:* 01324 624121. *Fax:* 01324 612418. *Website:* www.falkirkfc.co.uk
Ground Capacity: seated: 6123. *Size of Pitch:* 110yd × 72yd.
Chairman: Campbell Christie. *Managing Director:* George Craig. *Head of Development:* Eddie May. *Secretary:* Alex Blackwood. *General Manager:* Crawford Baptie.
Head Coach: John Hughes. *Assistant Coach:* Brian Rice. *Director of Football:* Alex Totten. *Youth Co-ordinator:* Ian McIntyre.
Managers since 1975: J. Prentice, G. Miller, W. Little, J. Hagart, A. Totten, G. Abel, W. Lamont, D. Clarke, J. Duffy, W. Lamont, J. Jefferies, J. Lambie E. Bannon, A. Totten, I. McCall. *Club Nickname(s):* The Bairns. *Previous Grounds:* Randyford 1876-81; Blinkbonny Grounds 1881-83; Brockville Park 1883-2003.
Record Attendance: 23,100 v Celtic, Scottish Cup 3rd rd, 21 Feb 1953.
Record Transfer Fee received: £380,000 for John Hughes to Celtic (Aug 1995).
Record Transfer Fee paid: £225,000 to Chelsea for Kevin McAllister (Aug 1991).
Record Victory: 12-1 v Laurieston, Scottish Cup 2nd rd, 23 Sept 1893.
Record Defeat: 1-11 v Airdrieonians, Division I, 28 Apr 1951.
Most Capped Player: Alex Parker, 14 (15), Scotland.
Most League Appearances: (post-war): 353, George Watson, 1975-87.
Most League Goals in Season (Individual): 43: Evelyn Morrison, Division I, 1928-29.
Most Goals Overall (Individual): Dougie Moran, 86, 1957-61 and 1964-67.

FALKIRK 2005–06 LEAGUE RECORD

Match No.	Date	Venue	Opponents	Result	H/T Score	Lg. Pos.	Goalscorers	Attendance
1	Jul 30	H	Inverness CT	L 0-2	0-0	—		4561
2	Aug 6	A	Livingston	W 2-0	1-0	6	Latapy 28, Duffy 72	3911
3	13	A	Celtic	L 1-3	1-0	9	Duffy (pen) 39	57,151
4	20	H	Hibernian	L 0-2	0-1	10		6268
5	27	A	Aberdeen	L 0-3	0-3	10		12,249
6	Sept 10	H	Rangers	D 1-1	0-1	10	McBreen 77	6500
7	17	A	Motherwell	L 0-5	0-2	10		5625
8	24	A	Kilmarnock	D 1-1	1-1	11	Gow 10	5507
9	Oct 2	H	Hearts	D 2-2	1-0	10	Duffy 26, Pressley (og) 68	6342
10	15	A	Dunfermline Ath	W 1-0	1-0	10	Duffy 39	7068
11	22	H	Dundee U	L 1-3	1-0	10	Duffy 3	5316
12	25	A	Inverness CT	W 3-0	1-0	—	Thomson S 21, Duffy 70, Moutinho 78	3660
13	29	H	Livingston	D 1-1	1-0	10	Pinxten (og) 15	4786
14	Nov 6	H	Celtic	L 0-3	0-2	10		6498
15	19	A	Hibernian	W 3-2	0-2	9	Duffy 2 48, 72, Gow 54	13,092
16	26	H	Aberdeen	L 1-2	0-1	9	McBreen 83	5826
17	Dec 3	A	Rangers	D 2-2	0-1	10	Gow 69, Moutinho 71	48,042
18	10	H	Motherwell	L 0-1	0-0	10		4972
19	17	H	Kilmarnock	L 1-2	0-0	10	Milne 73	4708
20	26	A	Hearts	L 0-5	0-3	10		16,532
21	31	H	Dunfermline Ath	L 1-2	0-1	10	Duffy 67	6253
22	Jan 15	A	Dundee U	L 1-2	0-1	10	McBreen 68	7948
23	21	H	Inverness CT	L 1-4	1-3	10	Ireland 11	4548
24	28	A	Livingston	W 1-0	1-0	10	O'Donnell 35	4729
25	Feb 8	A	Celtic	L 1-2	0-2	—	Milne 82	56,713
26	11	H	Hibernian	D 0-0	0-0	10		5937
27	18	A	Aberdeen	L 0-1	0-1	10		11,538
28	Mar 4	H	Rangers	L 1-2	0-0	10	Latapy 65	6303
29	11	A	Motherwell	L 1-3	0-1	11	Cregg 54	8179
30	18	A	Kilmarnock	L 1-2	1-1	11	McBreen 18	5443
31	25	H	Hearts	L 1-2	1-1	11	Gow 45	5918
32	Apr 1	A	Dunfermline Ath	D 1-1	1-0	11	Ross 22	6836
33	8	H	Dundee U	W 1-0	1-0	10	Ross 22	4435
34	15	H	Dunfermline Ath	D 0-0	0-0	10		5329
35	22	H	Motherwell	D 1-1	1-0	10	Gow 15	4437
36	29	A	Dundee U	W 2-0	2-0	10	Gow 14, McBreen 38	5798
37	May 3	A	Inverness CT	L 0-2	0-2	—		3121
38	6	H	Livingston	W 1-0	0-0	10	McBreen 73	5315

Final League Position: 10

Honours

League Champions: Division II 1935-36, 1969-70, 1974-75. First Division 1990-91, 1993-94, 2002-03, 2004-05. Second Division 1979-80; *Runners-up:* Division I 1907-08, 1909-10. First Division 1985-86, 1988-89. Division II 1904-05, 1951-52, 1960-61.

Scottish Cup Winners: 1913, 1957; *Runners-up:* 1997. *League Cup Runners-up:* 1947-48. *B&Q Cup Winners:* 1993-94. *League Challenge Cup Winners:* 1997-98, 2004-05.

Club colours: Shirt: Navy blue with white seams. Shorts: Navy. Stockings: Navy with two white hoops.

Goalscorers: *League* (35): Duffy 9 (1 pen), Gow 6, McBreen 6, Latapy 2, Milne 2, Moutinho 2, Ross 2, Cregg 1, Ireland 1, O'Donnell 1, Thomson S 1, own goals 2.
Scottish Cup (5): Gow 3, McBreen 2.
CIS Cup (3): O'Donnell 2, Gow 1.

Glennon M 21	Lawrie A 27 + 2	Ireland C 23	McPherson C 12 + 6	Rodrigues T 31 + 1	O'Neil J 3 + 4	Thomson S 30 + 2	Lima V 21 + 7	Latapy R 24 + 6	Duffy D 19 + 2	Gow A 30 + 4	McBreen D 21 + 12	O'Donnell S 21 + 6	Scally N 13 + 5	MacSween I — + 1	Thomson A — + 4	Ross J 16 + 1	Milne K 32 + 1	McStay R 1 + 4	Moutinho P 8 + 20	Hughes J 1	Ferguson A 9	Cregg P 14 + 2	Craig L 10 + 6	Lecsinel J 8	Barr D — + 1	Twaddie M 5 + 1	Dodd K 8 + 1	Howard M 8	Scobbie T 2 + 1	Churchill G — + 1	*Match No.*
1	2	3	4^3	5	6^2	7	8	9	10	11^1	12	13	14																		1
1	2	3	4	5	6^2	7	8	9	10		11^1	13		12																	2
1	2	3	4^3	5	6^2	7	8	9	10	12	11^1	13			14																3
1	2	3	4^2	5		7	8	9	10	13	11^3	6^1			14	12															4
1	2	3	4^3	5		7	8	9^2	10		11^1	6	12		13		14														5
1	2	3	12	5		7	8		13	11	14	10^3	9			4^1	6^2														6
1	2	3		5^1		7	8	13	12	11^3	14	10	9^2			4	6														7
1	2	3		5		7	8	9^3	10	11^2	14	6^1			13		4	12													8
1	2	3		5	12	7	8	9	10^2	11^3	13	6^1					4		14												9
1	2	3■	12	5		7	8	9^2	10	11^1		6					4		13												10
1	2		12	5		7	8	9	10	11^3			13				4^2	6^1	14	3											11
1	2	3	6	5		7	13	9^1	10^3		12	11^2	8				4		14												12
1	2	3	6^3	5		7	12	9	10^2	14		11^1	8				4		13												13
1	2	3			13	7	12	9^3	10	11	14	6^2	5				4		8^1												14
1	2	3		5		7		12	10^2	9	11^1	6	8				4		13												15
1	2	3	6^1	5		7		13	10	11^3	12	9	8				4^2		14												16
1	2	3^1	12	5	13		6	9	10	11			8				4		7^2												17
1	2		3	5	14		6^3	9	10	11	12		8^2				4	13	7^1												18
1	2	3	5				6	9^2	10	11^1	12		8				4	13	7												19
1	2	3	5			12	6	9^1	10^3	11^2	14	7■	8				4		13												20
1	2	3	6^2	5^3		7^1	9	11	10	14	13		8				4	12													21
	2	3		5		13	7^2	9^3		11	10	6	8^1				4		12		1	14									22
	2	3^2		5		7	8^3	9		11	10	6^1					4		13		1	14	12								23
	12	3		5		7^3	13	10			11	8				2^1	4		9^2		1	6	14								24
		3		5		7^3	14			11	10	8^2				2	4		12		1	6	13	9^1							25
				5		7^2	14	9		11	10^3	8^1				2	4		13		1	3	12	6							26
	2			5^1		7				11	10						4		9		1	3	8	6^2	12	13					27
	2					7		9		11	10					3	4		12		1	5	8^1			6					28
	2			12		7		9		11	10					3^1	4		13		1	5^2	8			6					29
	2					7		9		11	10^2	12				3^3	4		13		1	5	8^1			6	14				30
			14	5		7		12		11		13				3			10^1			8	9^2	2		6^3	4	1			31
				5		7^1		12		11^2	10					3	4		13			8	9	2			6	1			32
	13			5		7				11^1	10					3^2	4		12			8	9	2			6	1			33
				5		7		12		11	10					3	4					8	9^1	2			6	1			34
				5		7^1	12			11	10^2	14				3	4		13			8	9^3			6	2	1			35
				5			9			11^1	10^3	7^2	13			3	4		14			8■	12				6	1	2		36
			12	5^2			8			11	10	7	13			3	4^1		14				9^3				6	1	2		37
							8			11	10^3	7^1				3	4		9			6	12	2^2			5	1	14	13	38

FORFAR ATHLETIC Second Division

Year Formed: 1885. *Ground & Address:* Station Park, Carseview Road, Forfar. *Telephone:* 01307 463576/462259. *Fax:* 01307 466956. *E-mail:* pat@ramsayladders.co.uk. *Website:* www.forfarathletic.co.uk
Ground Capacity: total: 5177, seated: 739. *Size of Pitch:* 115yd × 69yd.
Chairman and Secretary: David McGregor.
Manager: George Shaw. *Player/Assistant Manager:* Paul Tosh. *Physio:* Brian McNeil.
Managers since 1975: Jerry Kerr, Archie Knox, Alex Rae, Doug Houston, Henry Hall, Bobby Glennie, Paul Hegarty, Tommy Campbell, Ian McPhee, Neil Cooper, R. Stewart, Ray Farningham, Brian Fairley.
Club Nickname(s): Loons. *Previous Grounds:* None.
Record Attendance: 10,780 v Rangers, Scottish Cup 2nd rd, 2 Feb 1970.
Record Transfer Fee received: £65,000 for David Bingham to Dunfermline Ath (September 1995).
Record Transfer Fee paid: £50,000 for Ian McPhee from Airdrieonians (1991).
Record Victory: 14-1 v Lindertis, Scottish Cup 1st rd, 1 Sept 1988.
Record Defeat: 2-12 v King's Park, Division II, 2 Jan 1930.
Most League Appearances: 484: Ian McPhee, 1978-88 and 1991-98.
Most League Goals in Season (Individual): 45: Dave Kilgour, Division II, 1929-30.
Most Goals Overall (Individual): 124, John Clark.

FORFAR ATHLETIC 2005–06 LEAGUE RECORD

Match No.	Date	Venue	Opponents	Result		H/T Score	Lg. Pos.	Goalscorers	Attendance
1	Aug 6	A	Gretna	L	1-5	1-3	—	Sellars 15	936
2	13	H	Ayr U	L	1-2	1-1	10	Lunan 44	470
3	20	A	Morton	L	0-1	0-0	10		2778
4	27	H	Peterhead	W	3-2	3-1	7	Sellars 16, Forrest 35, Cameron 44	504
5	Sept 10	A	Alloa Ath	D	1-1	1-0	8	Sellars 44	505
6	17	H	Dumbarton	W	2-0	1-0	8	Gribben 4, Dunn 64	429
7	24	A	Partick Th	L	0-1	0-0	8		2003
8	Oct 1	A	Raith R	W	2-0	1-0	6	Waddell 7, Gribben 58	1809
9	15	H	Stirling A	W	3-0	2-0	6	Waddell 17, Gribben 36, Lunan 52	508
10	22	H	Gretna	L	1-3	0-1	5	Gribben 47	664
11	29	H	Alloa Ath	W	3-1	2-1	4	Gribben 5, Lunan 42, Voigt 76	486
12	Nov 5	A	Peterhead	L	2-4	1-3	6	Lunan 2, Forrest 49	549
13	12	A	Dumbarton	L	0-2	0-2	7		737
14	26	H	Partick Th	L	2-3	0-3	7	Cameron 53, Bonar 72	726
15	Dec 3	A	Stirling A	L	2-4	2-1	9	Cameron 1, Devine (og) 16	528
16	13	A	Ayr U	L	1-2	0-0	—	Bonar 79	815
17	24	A	Gretna	W	2-1	1-1	—	Gribben 2 29, 69	1213
18	31	H	Morton	L	0-1	0-0	8		778
19	Jan 2	H	Peterhead	L	0-1	0-1	—		685
20	14	A	Alloa Ath	W	1-0	0-0	8	Connelly 87	575
21	21	H	Dumbarton	L	2-3	1-0	8	Cameron 8, Forrest 81	446
22	28	A	Partick Th	L	0-1	0-0	9		2048
23	Feb 4	A	Raith R	L	0-1	0-0	9		1409
24	18	H	Ayr U	W	1-0	1-0	8	Lombardi 39	477
25	25	A	Morton	L	0-3	0-1	8		2211
26	Mar 11	H	Alloa Ath	W	3-0	2-0	7	Lunan 2 5, 24, McClune 81	399
27	18	A	Dumbarton	D	0-0	0-0	7		616
28	21	A	Peterhead	D	1-1	1-0	—	Jackson 23	463
29	25	H	Partick Th	D	0-0	0-0	8		631
30	28	H	Raith R	W	5-2	4-1	—	Jackson 2 1, 35, Sellars 26, Lombardi 32, Gribben 65	737
31	Apr 1	H	Raith R	L	0-2	0-1	8		581
32	4	H	Stirling A	L	1-2	1-1	—	Gribben 12	394
33	8	A	Stirling A	L	1-3	0-2	8	Lunan 58	496
34	15	H	Gretna	W	2-1	2-0	8	Jackson 2 8, 32	591
35	22	A	Ayr U	W	1-0	0-0	7	Gribben 80	956
36	29	H	Morton	L	0-2	0-0	8		567

Final League Position: 8

Honours
League Champions: Second Division 1983-84. Third Division 1994-95; *Runners-up:* 1996-97. C Division 1948-49.
Scottish Cup: Semi-finals 1982.
League Cup: Semi-finals 1977-78.
Bell's League Challenge: Semi-finals 2004-05.

Club colours: Shirt: Sky blue with navy side panels, shoulder/sleeve bands. Shorts: Navy with sky blue side trim. Stockings: Sky blue with navy band on top.

Goalscorers: *League* (44): Gribben 10, Lunan 7, Jackson 5, Cameron 4, Sellars 4, Forrest 3, Bonar 2, Lombardi 2, Waddell 2, Connelly 1, Dunn 1, McClune 1, Voigt 1, own goal 1.
Scottish Cup (4): Gribben 2, Bonar 1, Cameron 1.
CIS Cup (1): Conway 1.
Challenge Cup (0).

Meldrum C 1	Rattray A 26 + 1	Florence S 2 + 1	Forrest E 26 + 2	Dunn D 19 + 4	Bonar S 15 + 3	Lunan P 30	McClune D 24 + 6	Conway A 3 + 7	Sellars B 31 + 1	Waddell R 16 + 2	Voigt J 1 + 12	Ferrie N 1 + 1	Donald B 22 + 3	Lowing D 16 + 1	Cameron M 19 + 4	Gethins C 1	Peat M 1	Connelly C 4 + 6	Dubourdeau F 18	Barr D 14 + 1	Gribben D 24 + 5	King D 21 + 1	Cumming K — + 4	Murdoch S 13	Montgomery R 10 + 1	Keogh D 13 + 1	Lombardi M 10 + 3	Tosh P — + 8	Jackson A 13	Brown M 2	Match No.
1[6]	2	3	4	5	6	7[1]	8	9	10[2]	11	12	15	13																		1
			4	5	8	2	12	13	7	11		1	6[1]	3	9	10[2]															2
			4	5	8	2		10[1]	7	11	12		6[2]	3	9		1	13													3
			4	5	8	2	10[2]	13	7	11			6	3	9[1]				1	12											4
			4	5[2]	7	2	8	14	10	11			6[3]	13	9[1]				1	3	12										5
			4	5	7	2	8	12	6	11					9[1]				1	3	10										6
	14		4	5	8[2]	7	13	12	6	11				3[3]	9[1]				1	2	10										7
	4[2]		5	13	6	7			8	11	12			3	9[1]				1	2	10										8
			5	4		7	8	14	6[2]	11	12		13	3	9[1]				1	2	10[3]										9
			5	4		7[2]	8		6	11	12		13	3	9[1]				1	2	10										10
	4[1]	12	5		14	7	8[3]		6	11	13			3	9				1	2	10[2]										11
		3[1]	5		13	7[2]	8		6	11	14			4	9[3]				1	2	10	12									12
			5	12	6		8	7[2]	10	11	13			3[1]	9				1	2		4									13
	4[2]		5■	13	6		7		8	11	9[1]			3	12				1	2	10										14
	4			5	6[1]		7		8	11				3	9				1	2	10		12								15
	4		5		6		7	12		11[1]	13		8	3	9				1	2	10[2]										16
	4		5				11		7				8	3	9				1	2	10	6									17
	4		5		12		7		11	13			8[1]	3[2]	9					2	10	6		1							18
	4		5		11[3]	2	7		8[1]	12	13			3	9[2]			14			10	6		1							19
	4		5		6	7[1]			10		13		8[2]					2	1		9	3	12		11						20
	4		5		6	7	12				13		8[1]		9			2	1		10[2]	3			11						21
	4		5			7	6						8		9[1]				1			3	13		11[2]	2	10	12			22
	4		5	13		7	12		8				6[1]						1		11	3			14	2[2]	10[3]		9		23
	4		5			7	12		8				6								11[1]	3		1		2	10		9		24
	4		5			7	11		8				6								13	3		1		2[2]	10[1]	12	9		25
	4			5		7	6						8		13						10[1]	3	14	1	11[3]	2		12	9[2]		26
	4			5		7	6		12				8								10[1]	3		1	11	2			9		27
	4			5		7	6		10				8[2]								13	3		1	11[1]	2	12		9		28
	4			5		7	6		10				8[3]					13			12	3		1		2[2]	11[1]	14	9		29
	4[1]		12	5		7	6		10				8[2]					14			11	3		1		2[3]	13		9		30
	4			5		7	6		10						12			13			11[3]	3		1		2[2]	8[1]	14	9		31
	4[1]		5	2		7	6[3]		8						13			14			10	3		1	11		9[2]	12			32
	4		5■	2		7			6				8								10[2]	3		1	11[1]	12	13		9		33
	4			5		7			6				8									3		1	11	2	10		9		34
	4					7			6				8					2			12	5			11[1]	3	10[2]	13	9	1	35
	4		14			7	13		6				8[2]					2[3]			11	5				3	10[1]	12	9	1	36

GRETNA

First Division

Year Formed: 1946. *Ground & Address:* Raydale Park, Dominion Rd, Gretna DG16 5AP. *Telephone:* 01461 337602. *Fax:* 01461 338047. *E-mail:* info@gretnafootballclub.co.uk. *Website:* www.gretnafootballclub.co.uk
Ground Capacity: 2200.
Club Shop: Alan Watson, 01387 251550.
President: Brian Fulton. *Chairman:* Ron MacGregor. *Secretary:* Helen MacGregor. *Managing Director:* Brookes Mileson. *Chief Executive:* Graeme Muir.
Manager: Rowan Alexander. *Assistant Manager:* David Irons. *Senior Coach:* Derek Collins. *Physio:* William Bentley.
Record Attendance: 3000 v Dundee U, Scottish Cup, 17 Jan 2005.
Record Victory: 20-0 v Silloth, 1962.
Record Defeat: 0-6 v Worksop Town, 1994-95 and 0-6 v Bradford (Park Avenue) 1999-2000.
Most League Appearances: 88, David Irons, 2002-05.
Most League Goals in Season (Individual): 38, Kenny Deuchar, 2004-05.
Most Goals Overall (Individual): 56, Kenny Deuchar, 2004-06.

GRETNA 2005–06 LEAGUE RECORD

Match No.	*Date*	*Venue*	*Opponents*	*Result*		*H/T Score*	*Lg. Pos.*	*Goalscorers*	*Attendance*
1	Aug 6	H	Forfar Ath	W	5-1	3-1	—	McGuffie (pen) [23], Bingham [25], Deuchar [35], Grady [73], Nicholls [75]	936
2	13	A	Raith R	W	3-1	2-0	1	Deuchar 2 [4, 41], Grady [58]	2124
3	20	H	Stirling A	W	1-0	1-0	1	Grady [35]	1010
4	27	H	Ayr U	D	2-2	0-2	1	Townsley [66], Skelton [79]	1195
5	Sept 10	A	Morton	W	2-0	1-0	1	Deuchar [10], McGuffie [80]	3783
6	17	H	Partick Th	D	2-2	1-0	1	Bingham [31], Grady [49]	1920
7	24	A	Alloa Ath	W	3-0	1-0	1	Townsley [9], Innes [81], McGuffie [88]	663
8	Oct 1	H	Dumbarton	W	1-0	1-0	1	Tosh [4]	954
9	15	A	Peterhead	W	2-0	1-0	1	Grady [8], Innes [60]	742
10	22	A	Forfar Ath	W	3-1	1-0	1	Deuchar 2 [17, 82], Innes [74]	664
11	25	H	Raith R	W	5-1	3-1	—	Townsley [10], Grady 2 [21, 71], Deuchar [42], Tosh [66]	1074
12	29	H	Morton	W	3-1	0-0	1	Innes [58], McGuffie [87], Baldacchino [90]	2006
13	Nov 5	A	Ayr U	W	3-1	2-0	1	Deuchar [9], Tosh [27], Innes [58]	1375
14	12	A	Partick Th	D	3-3	1-0	1	McGuffie [22], Innes [50], Deuchar [72]	3158
15	26	H	Alloa Ath	W	4-0	2-0	1	Grady [18], Deuchar [39], McGuffie [70], Birch [81]	759
16	Dec 3	H	Peterhead	W	3-0	2-0	1	Bingham [16], Deuchar [28], Grady [70]	1060
17	17	A	Dumbarton	W	1-0	1-0	1	Grady [28]	839
18	24	H	Forfar Ath	L	1-2	1-1	—	Rattray (og) [44]	1213
19	Jan 2	H	Ayr U	W	3-0	1-0	—	Grady [41], Shields [82], Graham (pen) [89]	1268
20	14	A	Morton	D	2-2	2-1	1	Deuchar [11], Innes [36]	5202
21	21	H	Partick Th	W	6-1	2-0	1	Tosh 2 [25, 55], Graham 2 [37, 90], Skelton [75], Grady [85]	2109
22	28	A	Alloa Ath	W	3-0	1-0	1	Townsley [28], McGuffie (pen) [56], Skelton [81]	625
23	Feb 11	A	Peterhead	W	3-1	1-1	1	O'Neil [15], McGuffie [74], Skelton [85]	749
24	18	A	Raith R	W	1-0	1-0	1	Tosh [16]	1745
25	28	A	Stirling A	W	5-0	1-0	—	Grady [33], Skelton [52], Townsley [55], Jenkins [73], McGuffie [78]	786
26	Mar 7	H	Dumbarton	W	3-0	1-0	—	Grady [22], McGuffie [50], Deuchar [62]	598
27	11	H	Morton	L	1-2	0-0	1	Deuchar [89]	2150
28	18	A	Partick Th	W	2-0	1-0	1	Deuchar 2 [42, 73]	2447
29	21	A	Ayr U	W	4-2	2-1	—	O'Neil [20], McKinstry (og) [38], McGuffie 2 (1 pen) [89 (p), 90]	909
30	25	H	Alloa Ath	W	2-1	1-1	1	Tosh 2 [44, 67]	948
31	Apr 8	H	Peterhead	W	3-1	1-1	1	McQuilken [1], Shields [69], Berkeley [89]	1049
32	11	H	Stirling A	W	6-0	4-0	—	Tosh 3 [28, 37, 45], Grady [38], McQuilken [49], Shields [86]	804
33	15	A	Forfar Ath	L	1-2	0-2	1	Grady (pen) [73]	591
34	18	A	Dumbarton	W	2-0	2-0	—	McGuffie [11], Innes [17]	685
35	22	H	Raith R	W	2-1	1-0	1	Deuchar [9], Skelton [74]	2201
36	29	A	Stirling A	L	1-2	0-2	1	Deuchar [73]	668

Final League Position: 1

Honours
League Champions: Second Division 2005-06. Third Division 2004–05.
Bell's League Challenge: Quarter-finals 2004-05.
Scottish Cup Runners-up: 2006.

Club colours: Shirt: White with black detail. Shorts: White. Stockings: White topped with black hoops.

Goalscorers: *League* (97): Deuchar 18, Grady 16 (1 pen), McGuffie 13 (3 pens), Tosh 11, Innes 8, Skelton 6, Townsley 5, Bingham 3, Graham 3 (1 pen), Shields 3, McQuilken 2, O'Neil 2, Baldacchino 1, Berkeley 1, Birch 1, Jenkins 1, Nicholls 1, own goals 2.
Scottish Cup (21): Grady 8, Deuchar 5, McGuffie 2 (1 pen), Townsley 2, Bingham 1, Nicholls 1, Tosh 1, own goal 1.
CIS Cup (2): Deuchar 1, Grady 1.
Challenge Cup (2): Deuchar 1, Nicholls 1.

Main A 31	Collins D 7 + 3	McQuilken J 10 + 15	Nicholls D 24 + 4	Townsley D 33	Innes C 29 + 2	Baldacchino R 19 + 2	McGuffie R 33 + 1	Deuchar K 33 + 1	Bingham D 17 + 1	Skelton G 32 + 4	Grady J 29 + 3	Aitken A 5 + 2	Boyd M — + 1	Tosh S 32 + 1	Graham D 5 + 11	Birch M 25 + 2	Shields D 1 + 8	Jenkins A 9 + 3	O'Neil J 11 + 4	Canning M 2 + 4	Mathieson D 5	Paterson S 3 + 1	Berkeley M 1 + 2	*Match No.*
1	2	3^2	4	5	6	7	8	9^1	10^3	11	12	13	14											1
1	2	3		5	6	7	8	9	10	12	11			4^1										2
1	2	3	13	5	6	7	8	9^2	10^1	12	11			4										3
1	2^2	3^1		5	6	7	8	9	10	12	11^3	13		4	14									4
1		13		5	6	7	8	9	10^2	3^1	11	2		4		12								5
1			12	5	6	7	8	9	10	3	11^1	2		4										6
1		12	11^1	5	6	7	8	9^3	10^2	3		2		4	13	14								7
1	13	12		5	6	7^2	8	9	10^1	3	11	2		4										8
1	12	3		5	6	7	8	9^2		11	10	2^1		4	13									9
1	2	3		5	6	7	8	9	12	11	10^1			4										10
1		14	12	5	6	7	8^1	9^2	10^3	3	11			4	13	2								11
1				5	6	7	8	9	10	3	11			4		2								12
1	7^2	13	12	5	6		8	9	10^1	3	11			4		2								13
1	12		5		6	7	8	9	10	3	11			4		2^1								14
1		12	3	5		7	8	9^2	10	6	11			4^1	13	2								15
1		12	3	5		7^1	8	9^2	10	6	11			4	13	2								16
1			3	5		7^1	8	9	10	6	11			4	12	2								17
1		14	3	5	13	7^1	8	9	10^2	6^3	11			4	12	2								18
1			3	5	6		8■	9^2	10^1	12	11			4	7	2	13							19
1	2	3	8		6			9		11					10	5	12	4^1	7					20
1		13	3	5	6		8	9^1		11	12			4	10	2^2			7					21
1		14	3	5	6^2		8	9^1		11	12			4^3	10	2			7	13				22
1			3	5			8			11	9			4		2		7	10	6				23
1		12	3	5			8^1	9^2		11	10			4		2	13	7		6				24
1		12	3	5^2	6	14	8^3	9		11	10			4^1		2		7		13				25
1			3	5	6	12	8	9^3		11	10			4^1		2^2		7	14	13				26
1			3	5	6	7	8	9		11	10					2^1		4	12					27
1			3	5	6	7^1	8	9		11	10			4^2		2		13	12					28
1			3	5	6		8	9		11	10^2			4^1		2	13	12	7					29
		14	3	5	6^1		8	9		11				4		2	10^3	13	7	12^2	1			30
		3			6		8	9^2		11	10^3			4		2	13	7^1	12		1	5	14	31
		9	3	5	6		13	14		11^1	10^3			4^2			12	8	7		1	2		32
		3^1	8	5	13			9		11	10			12	14	2		7^3	4		1	6^2		33
		12	3	5	6		8			11				4	10	2^3	13		7^1		1	14	9^2	34
1			3	5	6		8	9^2		11	10			4	12	2^1	13		7					35
1		14	3^3	5	6		8	9		11	10^1			4	12	2^2			7■				13	36

HAMILTON ACADEMICAL First Division

Year Formed: 1874. *Ground:* New Douglas Park, Cadzow Avenue, Hamilton ML3 0FT. *Telephone:* 01698 368650. *Fax:* 01698 285422. *Ground Capacity:* 5396. *Size of Pitch:* 115yd × 75yd.
Chairman: Ronnie MacDonald. *Chief Executive:* George W. Fairley. *Secretary:* Scott A. Struthers BA. *Commercial Manager:* Derek McQuade.
Manager: Billy Reid. *Director of Football:* Stuart Balmer. *Physio/Sports Therapist:* Avril Downs.
Managers since 1975: J. Eric Smith, Dave McParland, John Blackley, Bertie Auld, John Lambie, Jim Dempsey, John Lambie, Billy McLaren, Iain Munro, Sandy Clark, Colin Miller, Ally Dawson, Chris Hillcoat, Alan Maitland.
Club Nickname(s): The Accies. *Previous Grounds:* Bent Farm, South Avenue, South Haugh, Douglas Park, Cliftonhill Stadium, Firhill Stadium.
Record Attendance: 28,690 v Hearts, Scottish Cup 3rd rd, 3 Mar 1937.
Record Transfer Fee received: £380,000 for Paul Hartley to Millwall (July 1996).
Record Transfer Fee paid: £60,000 for Paul Martin from Kilmarnock (Oct 1988) and for John McQuade from Dumbarton (Aug 1993).
Record Victory: 11-1 v Chryston, Lanarkshire Cup, 28 Nov 1885.
Record Defeat: 1-11 v Hibernian, Division I, 6 Nov 1965.
Most Capped Player: Colin Miller, 29, Canada, 1988-94.
Most League Appearances: 452: Rikki Ferguson, 1974-88.

HAMILTON ACADEMICAL 2005–06 LEAGUE RECORD

Match No.	Date	Venue	Opponents	Result		H/T Score	Lg. Pos.	Goalscorers	Attendance
1	Aug 6	A	Brechin C	W	2-1	1-0	—	Robertson [18], Hardy [90]	736
2	13	H	St Johnstone	L	0-1	0-1	5		1877
3	20	A	Ross Co	D	0-0	0-0	5		2005
4	27	H	Dundee	D	1-1	0-1	6	Carrigan [66]	2091
5	Sept 10	A	Stranraer	W	2-1	2-1	4	Tunbridge [1], Carrigan (pen) [23]	584
6	17	H	Airdrie U	D	1-1	0-1	4	Mackenzie [63]	2229
7	24	A	Queen of the S	W	2-1	1-0	3	Jones [6], Tunbridge [76]	1380
8	Oct 1	H	St Mirren	W	3-1	2-0	3	Ferguson [6], Carrigan 2 (1 pen) [44 (p), 47]	2683
9	15	A	Clyde	D	1-1	1-1	3	Keogh [76]	1392
10	22	H	Brechin C	W	3-0	1-0	2	Fleming [15], Neil [46], Keogh [62]	1226
11	25	A	St Johnstone	L	1-5	0-4	—	Keogh [57]	2233
12	29	H	Stranraer	W	2-0	1-0	2	Jones [42], Gilhaney [85]	1334
13	Nov 12	A	Airdrie U	D	2-2	0-1	4	Robertson [47], Ferguson [59]	1375
14	15	A	Dundee	D	1-1	0-0	—	Keogh [72]	3890
15	19	H	Queen of the S	W	5-2	3-1	3	McLeod 2 [5, 35], Fleming (pen) [32], McMullan [52], Ferguson [76]	1475
16	26	A	St Mirren	L	1-2	0-1	3	Gilhaney [80]	3197
17	Dec 3	H	Clyde	D	1-1	0-0	4	Carrigan [72]	1787
18	10	A	Brechin C	W	1-0	1-0	4	Neil [4]	480
19	17	H	Ross Co	W	2-1	1-0	2	Thomson [27], McLaughlin [51]	1250
20	26	A	Stranraer	L	4-5	1-0	—	Carrigan [38], Ferguson 2 [50, 61], Jones [70]	628
21	31	H	Dundee	D	0-0	0-0	3		1533
22	Jan 2	H	Airdrie U	W	1-0	1-0	—	McLaughlin [25]	2498
23	14	A	Queen of the S	D	1-1	1-1	2	McLeod [2]	1813
24	21	H	St Mirren	D	0-0	0-0	2		3320
25	28	A	Clyde	D	2-2	0-1	4	Balmer [58], Torres [59]	1423
26	Feb 11	A	Ross Co	L	1-2	1-1	4	Ferguson [34]	2151
27	18	H	St Johnstone	L	1-2	0-1	5	Tunbridge [74]	1576
28	Mar 4	A	Dundee	W	4-2	2-0	4	Ferguson [1], Keogh [20], Wake 2 [82, 87]	3540
29	18	A	Airdrie U	D	0-0	0-0	5		1326
30	25	H	Queen of the S	L	0-2	0-1	5		1409
31	28	H	Stranraer	W	1-0	0-0	—	Wake [68]	1135
32	Apr 1	A	St Mirren	W	2-0	0-0	4	Elebert [83], Wake [90]	4431
33	8	H	Clyde	W	2-0	1-0	4	Wake [1], Gilhaney [90]	1360
34	15	H	Brechin C	W	2-0	1-0	3	Juanjo [36], Gilhaney [52]	1117
35	22	A	St Johnstone	D	1-1	1-0	3	McArthur [1]	2235
36	29	H	Ross Co	D	0-0	0-0	3		1297

Final League Position: 3

Most League Goals in Season (Individual): 35: David Wilson, Division I; 1936-37.
Most Goals Overall (Individual): 246: David Wilson, 1928-39.

Honours
League Champions: First Division 1985-86, 1987-88; Third Division 2000-01. *Runners-up:* Division II 1903-04, 1952-53, 1964-65; Second Division 1996-97, 2003-04.
Scottish Cup Runners-up: 1911, 1935. *League Cup:* Semi-finalists three times.
B&Q Cup Winners: 1991-92, 1992-93.

Club colours: Shirt: Red and white hoops. Shorts: White. Stockings: White.

Goalscorers: *League* (53): Ferguson 7, Carrigan 6 (2 pens). Keogh 5, Wake 5, Gilhaney 4, Jones 3, McLeod 3, Tunbridge 3, Fleming 2 (1 pen), McLaughlin 2, Neil 2, Robertson 2, Balmer 1, Elebert 1, Hardy 1, Juanjo 1, McArthur 1, Mackenzie 1, McMullan 1, Thomson 1, Torres 1.
Scottish Cup (7): McLaughlin 2, Ferguson 1, McDonald 1, McManus 1, Neil 1, Torres 1.
CIS Cup (3): Tunbridge 2, Jones 1.
Challenge Cup (9): Ferguson 2, Keogh 2, Corrigan 1, Hardy 1, Neil 1, Thomson 1, Tunbridge 1.

McEwan D 32	Robertson J 24+1	Hodge A 9+5	Thomson S 29+3	McLaughlin M 21+1	Balmer S 15	Ferguson B 24+5	Wilson M 21	Keogh P 8+12	Bennett T 1	Carrigan B 20+5	Hardy L 2+1	Tunbridge S 18+6	McLeod P 6+4	Neil A 32+1	Anderson D 1+1	Jones G 8+5	McArthur J 12+8	Sim A —+1	Mackenzie S 20	Fleming D 21+1	Gilhaney M 14+12	McMullan P 12+2	Torres R 5+7	Coult L —+1	McJimpsey M 1+1	Jellema R 4	Juanjo J 10+1	Elebert D 11+1	Wake B 7+3	Agnew C 4+1	Galloway C 4+1	McCabe R —+2	Anson S —+1	McAlpine M —+1	*Match No.*
1	2^3	3^2	4	5	6	7	8	9	10^1	11	12	13	14																						1
1	2	13	4	5	3^2	12	8			11^1	10	7	14	6	9^3																				2
1	2	3	4	5		7	8			11^1	10	9^2	13	6^3		12	14																		3
1	2	3	4	5		7^3	8			11		9	10^1	6	12^2		14	13																	4
1	2	3	13		5	12	8			11^1		7		6		9^2			4	10															5
1	2		4	5			8	12		11		7^1		6		9			10	3															6
1		12	4	5	2	14	8	11^1		13		7		6		9^3			10	3^2															7
1		14	4	5	2	7	8^3			11^2		9^1		6		13			10	3	12														8
1	14		4	5^3	2	7^1	8	12		11^2		9		6		13			10	3															9
1	2	14	4		5	7^3	8	13				11		6^1		9^2			10	3	12														10
1	2	4			5	7^2	8^1	9^3		13		11		6		14			10	3	12														11
1	2		4		5		8	12		7^2		11		6		9^1			10	3	13														12
1	2	5				4	8	9^1		11^2		7		6					10	3	12	13													13
1	2	5				7	8	13		11		9^1		6^2			14		10	3	12	4^3													14
1	2	5				7	8			11^1			9^2	6			13		10	3	12	4													15
1	2	5^1	12			7	8			11^3			9	6			13		10	3^2	14	4													16
1	9		2	5		7	8			13			11^1	12			3		10		6	4^2													17
1	2		4	5		13	8	9^1					11^2	6		12			10		7	3^1													18
1	2		4	5			8	13		11^2		12		6		9^1			10	3	7														19
1	2	13	4	5^2		7		12		11^3		8^1		6		9			10	3	14														20
1	2		4	5		7				11				6		9^1	13		10	3	12	8^2													21
1	2		13	5	4					11^1				6			7		10	3		8^3	9^2	12	14										22
1	2		3	5	4	7						12	11^2	6^1			8		10		14	13	9^3												23
	2		4	5	8	13				11^1		9		6^3			14			3	7	10^2	12			1									24
	2		4	5^3	8					11		10	13	6							7	3^1	12			1	9^2	14							25
1	2		4		5	7	8	13									6^2				11		9				10^1	3	12						26
1	2		4		5	7^2		13				8		6							11		9^1				10	3	12						27
			4			7		9^3				13					6		5^1			11	10			1		2	14	3	8^2	12			28
1			4	5		7	8^1	10^2		14				6			12				11	3^3					13	2	9						29
1			4	5				13		12		14		6			8				7	11^1					10	2	9^2	3^3					30
1			4^1					11^2						6			8				14				5		7	2	9	3^3	10	12	13		31
1			4	5^1		2								6			8			12	11		14				7^3	3	9	13	10^2				32
1			4	5		10								6			8^2			3	11		12				7^1	2	9^1		13				33
1			4			2^2		14		9^1				6^3			8			3	11		12				7	5		10				13	34
1			4			2^1		12				10		6			8			3	11		13				7^2	5	9						35
			4	12		2^1						13		6			8			3	11		14			1	7^3	5	9		10^2				36

HEART OF MIDLOTHIAN Premier League

Year Formed: 1874. *Ground & Address:* Tynecastle Stadium, Gorgie Rd, Edinburgh EH11 2NL. *Telephone:* 0131 200 7200. *Fax:* 0131 200 7222. *E-mail:* hearts@homplc.co.uk. *Website:* www.heartsfc.co.uk
Ground Capacity: 17,402. *Size of Pitch:* 100m × 64m.
Chairman and Interim Chief Executive: Roman Romanov.
Head Coach: Valdes Ivanauskas. *Assistant Head Coach:* John McGlynn. *Physio:* Alan Rae.
Managers since 1975: J. Hagart, W. Ormond, R. Moncur, T. Ford, A. MacDonald, A. MacDonald & W. Jardine, A. MacDonald, J. Jordan, S. Clark, T. McLean, J. Jefferies, C. Levein, J. Robertson, G. Burley, G. Rix.
Club Nickname(s): Hearts, Jambo's. *Previous Grounds:* The Meadows 1874, Powderhall 1878, Old Tynecastle 1881, (Tynecastle Park, 1886).
Record Attendance: 53,396 v Rangers, Scottish Cup 3rd rd, 13 Feb 1932.
Record Transfer Fee received: £2,100,000 for Alan McLaren from Rangers (October 1994).
Record of Transfer paid: £750,000 for Derek Ferguson to Rangers (July 1990).
Record Victory: 21-0 v Anchor, EFA Cup, 30 Oct 1880.
Record Defeat: 1-8 v Vale of Leven, Scottish Cup, 1888.
Most Capped Player: Bobby Walker, 29, Scotland.
Most League Appearances: 515: Gary Mackay, 1980-97.
Most League Goals in Season (Individual): 44: Barney Battles.
Most Goals Overall (Individual): 214: John Robertson, 1983-98.

HEART OF MIDLOTHIAN 2005–06 LEAGUE RECORD

Match No.	Date	Venue	Opponents	Result	H/T Score	Lg. Pos.	Goalscorers	Attendance
1	Jul 30	A	Kilmarnock	W 4-2	1-1	—	Skacel ^{13}, Bednar ^{46}, Mikoliunas ^{61}, Hartley ^{89}	7487
2	Aug 7	H	Hibernian	W 4-0	1-0	—	Skacel ^{13}, Hartley ^{58}, Simmons ^{71}, Mikoliunas ^{83}	16,459
3	14	A	Dundee U	W 3-0	2-0	1	Pressley ^{7}, Bednar ^{13}, Skacel ^{90}	11,654
4	20	H	Aberdeen	W 2-0	1-0	1	Skacel ^{20}, Pospisil ^{85}	16,139
5	27	H	Motherwell	W 2-1	1-0	1	Skacel ^{40}, Jankauskas ^{69}	16,213
6	Sept 11	A	Livingston	W 4-1	3-1	1	Skacel ^{10}, Webster ^{26}, Hartley 2 $^{33, 66}$	7900
7	17	A	Inverness CT	W 1-0	1-0	1	Skacel ^{28}	6454
8	24	H	Rangers	W 1-0	1-0	1	Bednar ^{14}	17,379
9	Oct 2	A	Falkirk	D 2-2	0-1	1	Pressley 2 $^{71, 88}$	6342
10	15	A	Celtic	D 1-1	1-1	1	Skacel ^{15}	59,463
11	22	H	Dunfermline Ath	W 2-0	2-0	1	Skacel ^{21}, Pospisil ^{23}	16,500
12	25	H	Kilmarnock	W 1-0	1-0	—	Jankauskas ^{34}	16,536
13	29	A	Hibernian	L 0-2	0-0	2		17,180
14	Nov 5	H	Dundee U	W 3-0	2-0	2	Hartley ^{10}, Skacel ^{25}, Pospisil ^{57}	16,617
15	20	A	Aberdeen	D 1-1	0-1	2	Skacel ^{64}	14,901
16	26	A	Motherwell	D 1-1	0-1	2	Hartley ^{89}	8131
17	Dec 3	H	Livingston	W 2-1	2-0	2	Skacel 2 $^{8, 15}$	16,583
18	10	H	Inverness CT	D 0-0	0-0	2		16,373
19	17	A	Rangers	L 0-1	0-1	2		49,723
20	26	H	Falkirk	W 5-0	3-0	2	Hartley ^{20}, Skacel ^{25}, Elliot 2 $^{40, 89}$, Pospisil ^{72}	16,532
21	Jan 1	H	Celtic	L 2-3	2-0	—	Jankauskas ^{6}, Pressley ^{8}	16,532
22	14	A	Dunfermline Ath	W 4-1	1-0	2	Pressley ^{27}, Pospisil 2 $^{53, 66}$, Skacel ^{80}	8277
23	21	A	Kilmarnock	L 0-1	0-0	2		8811
24	28	H	Hibernian	W 4-1	3-0	2	Hartley 2 (1 pen) $^{26, 43 (p)}$, Skacel ^{40}, Elliot ^{50}	17,371
25	Feb 7	A	Dundee U	D 1-1	0-1	—	Hartley ^{82}	10,584
26	11	H	Aberdeen	L 1-2	1-0	2	Elliot ^{9}	16,895
27	18	H	Motherwell	W 3-0	2-0	2	Jankauskas 2 $^{3, 13}$, Elliot ^{78}	16,976
28	Mar 5	A	Livingston	W 3-2	1-0	2	Aguiar ^{17}, Jankauskas ^{71}, Bednar ^{87}	4458
29	11	A	Inverness CT	D 0-0	0-0	2		5027
30	19	H	Rangers	D 1-1	1-0	2	Jankauskas ^{9}	17,040
31	25	A	Falkirk	W 2-1	1-1	2	Hartley ^{22}, Jankauskas ^{81}	5918
32	Apr 5	A	Celtic	L 0-1	0-1	—		59,694
33	8	H	Dunfermline Ath	W 4-0	3-0	2	Pospisil ^{6}, Bednar ^{14}, Mikoliunas ^{25}, Makela ^{82}	16,873
34	15	H	Kilmarnock	W 2-0	0-0	2	Hartley ^{70}, Berra ^{87}	16,497
35	22	A	Hibernian	L 1-2	1-1	2	Bednar ^{44}	16,654
36	30	H	Celtic	W 3-0	2-0	2	McManus (og) ^{7}, Hartley ^{9}, Bednar ^{63}	16,795
37	May 3	H	Aberdeen	W 1-0	0-0	—	Hartley (pen) ^{53}	17,327
38	7	A	Rangers	L 0-2	0-1	2		49,792

Final League Position: 2

Honours
League Champions: Division I 1894-95, 1896-97, 1957-58, 1959-60. First Division 1979-80; *Runners-up:* Division I 1893-94, 1898-99, 1903-04, 1905-06, 1914-15, 1937-38, 1953-54, 1956-57, 1958-59, 1964-65. Premier Division 1985-86, 1987-88, 1991-92; *Runners-up:* 2005-06. First Division 1977-78, 1982-83.
Scottish Cup Winners: 1891, 1896, 1901, 1906, 1956, 1998;, 2006; *Runners-up:* 1903, 1907, 1968, 1976, 1986, 1996.
League Cup Winners: 1954-55, 1958-59, 1959-60, 1962-63; *Runners-up:* 1961-62, 1996-97.

European: *European Cup:* 4 matches (1958-59, 1960-61). *Cup Winners' Cup:* 10 matches (1976-77, 1996-97, 1998-99). *UEFA Cup:* 45 matches (*Fairs Cup:* 1961-62, 1963-64, 1965-66. *UEFA Cup:* 1984-85, 1986-87, 1988-89, 1990-91, 1992-93, 1993-94, 2000-01, 2003-04, 2004-05).

Club colours: Shirt: Maroon. Shorts: White. Stockings: Maroon.

Goalscorers: *League* (71): Skacel 16, Hartley 14 (2 pens), Jankauskas 8, Bednar 7, Pospisil 7, Elliot 5, Pressley 5, Mikoliunas 3, Aguiar 1, Berra 1, Makela 1, Simmons 1, Webster 1, own goal 1.
Scottish Cup (12): Hartley 3 (1 pen), Jankauskas 2, Pressley 2, Cesnauskis 1, Elliot 1, McAllister 1, Pospisil 1, Skacel 1.
CIS Cup (2): Jankauskas 2.

Gordon C 36	Neilson R 36 + 1	Webster A 30	Pressley S 29	MacFarlane N 1 + 2	McAllister J 8 + 9	Mikoliunas S 16 + 7	Skacel R 33 + 2	Hartley P 34	Jankauskas E 24 + 1	Bednar R 19 + 3	Elliot C 17 + 11	Simmons S 1 + 10	Brellier J 28 + 2	Wallace L 2 + 10	Fyssas P 32	Pospisil M 13 + 10	Cesnauskis D 15 + 10	Camazzola S 5 + 3	Banks S 2 + 1	Berra C 10 + 2	Barasa N 1 + 3	Hjalmar — + 1	Johnson L 1 + 3	McCann N 1	Petras M 4 + 1	Straceny L 1	Aguiar B 10	Beslija M 2 + 1	Hackett M 1 + 1	Gonçalves J 3 + 2	Makela J — + 2	Tall I 3 + 1	*Match No.*
1	2	3	4	5	6	7^2	8	9	10	11^1	12	13																					1
1	2	3	4	14	6	7	8	9		11^3	10^1	12	5^2	13																			2
1	2	3	4		12	7^1	8	9	10^3	11			6^2	13	5	14																	3
1	2	3	4		12	7^1	8^3	9	10	11^2		14	6		5	13																	4
1	2	3	4			7^1	8	9	10	11		12	6		5																		5
1	2	3	4		7^2		8^3	9	10^1	11		12	6	13	5		14																6
1	2	3	4		7^1		8	9	10^3	11		14	6	13	5^2			12															7
1	2	3	4		13		8	9	10	11^1		12	7	14	5^2			6^3															8
1■	2	3	4		6		8	9	10				7^2	13		11^1	14	5^3	12														9
	2	3	4				8	9	10		12		7		5	11^1		6	1														10
1	2	3	4■		14		8	9^3	10		13		7		5	11^2	12	6^1															11
1	2	3			6		8^3		10^2		13		7	14	5	11	9^1	12		4													12
1	2	3	4				8	9	10■		13		7^1	12	5	11^2		6															13
1	2	3	4		13	6	8^2	9^1			10	14	7	12	5	11^3																	14
1	2	3	4			6	8	9	10^2		12		7		5	11^1	13																15
1	2	3	4		6	10^2	8	9		13	11^3	12	7^1		5		14																16
1	2	3	4			6	8	9		11^2	10^3	12	7^1		5	13	14																17
1	2	3	4			14	8	9	13		10^2	7^1			5	11^3	6	12															18
1	2	3	4		5	13■	8	9	10^1	11	12		7				6^2																19
1	2	3	4	12	14		8	9^3	10^2		11		7^1		5	13	6																20
1	2	3	4				8	9	10^2		11		7	12	5	13	6^1																21
1	2	3	4			6^1	8	9			10^2		7^3		5	11					12	13	14										22
1	2	3			12	6^2		9			10		7		5^3	11	14			4	13			8^1									23
1	2	3			14	6^1	8	9			11^2		7		5	13	12			4			10^3										24
1	12		4			14	8	9			11		7■		5	10^2	13			3					2^1	6^3							25
1	2	3	4				8	9			11				5										6		7	10					26
1	2	3	4			14	8		10^1	12	11		7^3		5		6^2						13				9						27
1	2	3					8^2		10^1	12	11				5		7^3			4					6		9		13	14			28
1	2	3			12^2			9		11	10				5		6			4							8		7^1	13			29
1	2	3	4			13	8^2	9	10	11^1	12		7		5		6																30
1	2^3		4^1				8^2	9	10	11	13		7		5		6			12					14					3			31
1	2	3				8^2	13	9	10^1	11	14		7^3		5	12	6			4													32
1	2		4			8^2		9^3		11			14		5	10^1	6										7	13		3	12		33
1	2					6^2	8	9	10^3	11	14				5		13			4							7			3^1		12	34
1	2					8	12	9		11^2	10			3		13	6^1			4							7					5	35
1	2		4				8	9	10	11^1					5	12	6^3			13	14						7					3^2	36
1	2		4			12	8^1	9	10	11^2			14		5	13	6										7^3					3	37
						14	8				10		7^1	2		9^2			1	4	3		12		5		6	11^3			13		38

HIBERNIAN Premier League

Year Formed: 1875. *Ground & Address:* Easter Road Stadium, Albion Rd, Edinburgh EH7 5QG. *Telephone:* 0131 661 2159. *Fax:* 0131 659 6488. *E-mail:* club@hibernianfc.co.uk. *Website:* www.hibernianfc.co.uk
Ground Capacity: total: 17,400. *Size of Pitch:* 112yd × 74yd.
Chairman: Rod Petrie. *Club Secretary:* Garry O'Hagan. *Marketing & Communications Manager:* Colin McNeill.
Manager: Tony Mowbray. *Assistant Manager:* Mark Venus.
Managers since 1975: Eddie Turnbull, Willie Ormond, Bertie Auld, Pat Stanton, John Blackley, Alex Miller, Jim Duffy, Alex McLeish, Frank Sauzee, B. Williamson.
Club Nickname(s): Hibees. *Previous Grounds:* Meadows 1875-78, Powderhall 1878-79, Mayfield 1879-80, First Easter Road 1880-92, Second Easter Road 1892-.
Record Attendance: 65,860 v Hearts, Division I, 2 Jan 1950.
Record Victory: 22-1 v 42nd Highlanders, 3 Sept 1881.
Record Defeat: 0-10 v Rangers, 24 Dec 1898.
Most Capped Player: Lawrie Reilly, 38, Scotland.
Most League Appearances: 446: Arthur Duncan.
Most League Goals in Season (Individual): 42: Joe Baker.
Most Goals Overall (Individual): 364: Gordon Smith.

HIBERNIAN 2005–06 LEAGUE RECORD

Match No.	Date	Venue	Opponents	Result	H/T Score	Lg. Pos.	Goalscorers	Attendance
1	Jul 30	H	Dunfermline Ath	D 1-1	0-1	—	O'Connor 73	13,004
2	Aug 7	A	Hearts	L 0-4	0-1	11		16,459
3	13	H	Livingston	W 3-0	2-0	7	Murphy 40, Shiels 41, O'Connor 52	11,009
4	20	A	Falkirk	W 2-0	1-0	6	Brown Scott 35, Riordan (pen) 62	6268
5	27	A	Rangers	W 3-0	0-0	4	Sproule 3 66, 86, 89	49,754
6	Sept 10	H	Dundee U	W 2-1	1-1	4	O'Connor (pen) 17, Sproule 71	12,026
7	18	H	Celtic	L 0-1	0-1	4		15,649
8	24	A	Motherwell	W 3-1	1-0	3	Beuzelin 18, Stewart 67, Riordan 76	6461
9	Oct 2	H	Inverness CT	L 1-2	0-0	4	Fletcher 81	11,683
10	15	H	Kilmarnock	W 4-2	0-2	3	Caldwell 53, Beuzelin 2 60, 79, Riordan 81	11,731
11	22	A	Aberdeen	W 1-0	0-0	3	Riordan 54	13,375
12	26	A	Dunfermline Ath	W 2-1	0-0	—	O'Connor 2 48, 83	6853
13	29	H	Hearts	W 2-0	0-0	3	Beuzelin 78, O'Connor 80	17,180
14	Nov 5	A	Livingston	W 2-1	0-1	3	Shiels 82, O'Connor 86	8390
15	19	H	Falkirk	L 2-3	2-0	3	Riordan 2 1, 32	13,092
16	27	H	Rangers	W 2-1	2-0	3	Riordan 17, O'Connor 24	16,958
17	Dec 3	A	Dundee U	L 0-1	0-0	3		7976
18	10	A	Celtic	L 2-3	0-1	3	Beuzelin 47, Fletcher 52	59,808
19	17	H	Motherwell	W 2-1	1-1	3	Fletcher 3, Riordan 90	11,926
20	26	A	Inverness CT	L 0-2	0-2	3		7017
21	Jan 2	A	Kilmarnock	D 2-2	0-1	3	Hogg 59, O'Connor 84	9224
22	14	H	Aberdeen	L 1-2	0-2	3	Whittaker 90	14,572
23	21	H	Dunfermline Ath	W 3-1	1-1	3	Riordan 2 16, 70, Fletcher 89	13,318
24	28	A	Hearts	L 1-4	0-3	4	O'Connor 58	17,371
25	Feb 8	H	Livingston	W 7-0	2-0	—	Killen 19, Riordan 2 32, 64, O'Connor 48, Dair (og) 69, Fletcher 2 88, 90	12,170
26	11	A	Falkirk	D 0-0	0-0	3		5937
27	18	A	Rangers	L 0-2	0-1	4		49,720
28	Mar 4	H	Dundee U	W 3-1	3-0	4	Riordan 6, Killen 32, Samson (og) 40	16,266
29	12	H	Celtic	L 1-2	1-1	4	Riordan 23	14,719
30	18	A	Motherwell	D 2-2	0-1	5	Killen 46, Glass 77	6724
31	25	H	Inverness CT	L 0-2	0-0	5		12,805
32	Apr 5	H	Kilmarnock	W 2-1	0-1	—	Riordan 80, Dalglish 87	10,427
33	8	A	Aberdeen	L 0-1	0-1	4		14,110
34	16	A	Celtic	D 1-1	1-0	4	Fletcher 34	59,359
35	22	H	Hearts	W 2-1	1-1	4	Riordan 15, Benjelloun 78	16,654
36	29	A	Aberdeen	L 0-4	0-2	4		10,490
37	May 2	H	Rangers	L 1-2	0-1	—	Riordan 72	14,773
38	7	A	Kilmarnock	L 1-3	1-0	4	Fletcher 4	5732

Final League Position: 4

Honours
League Champions: Division I 1902-03, 1947-48, 1950-51, 1951-52. First Division 1980-81, 1998-99. Division II 1893-94, 1894-95, 1932-33; *Runners-up:* Division I 1896-97, 1946-47, 1949-50, 1952-53, 1973-74, 1974-75.
Scottish Cup Winners: 1887, 1902; *Runners-up:* 1896, 1914, 1923, 1924, 1947, 1958, 1972, 1979, 2001.
League Cup Winners: 1972-73, 1991-92; *Runners-up:* 1950-51, 1968-69, 1974-75, 1993-94, 2003-04.

European: *European Cup:* 6 matches (1955-56 semi-finals). *Cup Winners' Cup:* 6 matches (1972-73). *UEFA Cup:* 63 matches (*Fairs Cup:* 1960-61 semi-finals, 1961-62, 1962-63, 1965-66, 1967-68, 1968-69, 1970-71. *UEFA Cup:* 1973-74, 1974-75, 1975-76, 1976-77, 1978-79, 1989-90, 1992-93, 2001-02, 2005-06).

Club colours: Shirt: Green with white sleeves and collar. Shorts: White with green stripe. Stockings: White with green trim.

Goalscorers: *League* (61): Riordan 17 (1 pen), O'Connor 11 (1 pen), Fletcher 8, Beuzelin 5, Sproule 4, Killen 3, Shiels 2, Benjelloun 1, Scott Brown 1, Caldwell 1, Dalglish 1, Glass 1, Hogg 1, Murphy 1, Stewart 1, Whittaker 1, own goals 2.
Scottish Cup (14): O'Connor 3, Sproule 3, Scott Brown 2, Fletcher 2, Glass 1, Killen 1, Riordan 1, Stewart 1.
CIS Cup (2): Riordan 2.

Malkowski Z 31 + 1	Caldwell G 34	Smith G 19 + 1	Murphy D 30	Whittaker S 34	Stewart M 24 + 1	Beuzelin G 21	Fletcher S 16 + 18	Brown Scott 16 + 3	Riordan D 32 + 4	O'Connor G 24 + 2	Sproule I 18 + 14	Glass S 23 + 5	Thomson K 28 + 3	Konte A 1 + 12	Hogg C 21 + 2	Shiels D 8 + 8	Morrow S — + 8	Rudge H 4 + 2	McCluskey J — + 3	McDonald K — + 2	Brown Simon 7 + 1	Kondé O 7 + 4	Killen C 6 + 1	Dalglish P 4 + 7	Shields J 7	Benjelloun A 2 + 3	Lynch S — + 2	Murray A 1	Campbell R — + 1	Match No.
1	2	3	4	5	6	7²	8¹	9■	10³	11	12	13	14																	1
1	2¹	3	4	5	6	7			13	11	14	8²	9	10³	12															2
1		3	4	5	6	7	14	9	10³	11¹			13		2	8²	12													3
1		3	4	5	6³	7	12	9	10¹	11²			14		2	8	13													4
1		3	4	5	6	7	13	9		11¹	12	14	8³		2	10²														5
1		3	4	5	6	7		9²	12	11	13	14	8³		2	10¹														6
1	2		4	5	6³	7	14		13	11¹	9		8	12	3	10²														7
1	2		4	5	6	7	13		10²	11³	9	12	8¹		3		14													8
1	2		4	5	6	7¹	12		10³	11²	9		8		3	14	13													9
1	2			5²	6¹	7	8		10	11³	12	4	9		3		14	13												10
1	2		4		6	7	8	13	10²	11³	12		9¹	14	3			5												11
1	2		4³		6	7	8¹	12	10²	11	9	14			3		13	5												12
1	2	12	4		6²	7		9	10³	11	13		8		3¹	14		5												13
1	2		4		6	7¹	14	9	10³	11	13		8²		3	12		5												14
1	2			5	6¹	7²		9	10	11³	12	4	8		3	13	14													15
1	2	3		5		7	12	9	10²	11¹	8	4	6³			14	13													16
1	2	3		5		7¹	12	9³	10	11		4	6			8²			13	14										17
1	2	3		5		7²	8	9	10¹	11	12	4	6						13											18
1	2	3		5		7	8¹	9	10		11	4	6	12																19
1	2	3		5	13	7	8¹	9³	10	12	11	4	6²	14																20
1	2	3²		5		7¹	8³		10	11	9	4	6		12			13		14										21
1	2		4	5	8		13	9	10³	11	12	7¹	6		3²	14														22
	2	3	4²	5	8		13	9	10	11¹	12	7	6								1									23
	2	3■	4	5	8		13	9¹	10²	11³	7		6								1	12	14							24
	2³	3	4	5	8		12		10	11¹	9²	7		13							1	14	6							25
	2		4	5	8³		9		10	13	11²	7		12	3						1	14	6¹							26
	2		4	5	8		12		13	11³	9	7	6²	14	3						1			10¹						27
	2	3	4	5	8¹		14		10		13	7	6								1	12	9³	11²						28
12	2	3	4	5	8		13		10¹		11	7²	6								1■		9³	14						29
1	2	3	4	5			12		10³		9²	7	6	13					14				8	11¹						30
1	2	3	4	5	8²		12		10		11	7	6										9¹	13						31
1	2		4	5			9¹		10				6	12	3							8		13	7²	11³	14			32
1	2		4	5			9		10¹				6	12	3							8		13	7²	11				33
1	2		4	5			11		10²		12	7	6³		3	14						9¹			8	13				34
1	2		4	5			9²	12	10		11¹	7			3							8³		14	6	13				35
1	2		4	5			9		10		11³	7			3¹	14						8		13	6	12²				36
1	2		4	5			9¹		10³		11	7		13		8²						6		12	3		14			37
1■	2		4■	5			11¹					7		13		9³					14	8		10²	3			6	12	38

INVERNESS CALEDONIAN THISTLE

Premier League

Year Formed: 1994. *Ground & Address:* Tulloch Caledonian Stadium, East Longman, Inverness IV1 1FF. *Telephone:* 01463 222880. *Fax:* 01463 227479. *E-mail:* jimfalconer@caleythistleonline.com. *Website:* caleythistleonline.co.uk
Ground Capacity: seated: 7400. *Size of Pitch:* 115yd × 75yd.
Chairman: Confirmed at AGM end of August 2006. *President:* John MacDonald. *Secretary:* Jim Falconer. *Commercial Manager:* Laura Murray. *Football and Community Development Manager:* Danny MacDonald.
Manager: Charlie Christie. *Assistant Manager:* Donald Park. *First Team Coach:* John Docherty. *Physio:* David Brandie.
Managers since 1994: S. Baltacha, S. Paterson, J. Robertson, C. Brewster.
Record Attendance: 7100 v Celtic, SPL, 16 March 2005.
Record Victory: 8-1, v Annan Ath, Scottish Cup 3rd rd, 24 January 1998.
Record Defeat: 1-5, v Morton, First Division, 12 November 1999 and v Airdrieonians, First Division, 15 April 2000.
Most League Appearances: 362, Ross Tokely, 1995-2006.
Most League Goals in Season: 27, Iain Stewart, 1996-97; Denis Wyness, 2002-03.
Most Goals Overall (Individual): 91, Denis Wyness, 2000-03, 2005-06.

INVERNESS CALEDONIAN TH 2005–06 LEAGUE RECORD

Match No.	Date	Venue	Opponents	Result	H/T Score	Lg. Pos.	Goalscorers	Attendance
1	Jul 30	A	Falkirk	W 2-0	0-0	—	Brewster 2 [57, 82]	4561
2	Aug 6	H	Rangers	L 0-1	0-0	5		7512
3	13	A	Dunfermline Ath	W 1-0	1-0	5	Fox [42]	5002
4	20	H	Kilmarnock	D 2-2	1-0	5	Brewster 2 [39, 71]	4119
5	28	A	Dundee U	D 1-1	0-0	6	Brewster [84]	6178
6	Sept 10	H	Motherwell	L 1-2	1-0	6	Brewster [24]	4018
7	17	H	Hearts	L 0-1	0-1	8		6454
8	24	A	Celtic	L 1-2	0-0	8	Wyness [50]	56,823
9	Oct 2	A	Hibernian	W 2-1	0-0	8	Proctor [47], Wyness [64]	11,683
10	15	H	Aberdeen	D 1-1	0-0	8	Bayne [73]	6809
11	22	A	Livingston	D 1-1	0-1	8	Morgan [71]	3070
12	25	H	Falkirk	L 0-3	0-1	—		3660
13	29	A	Rangers	D 1-1	1-0	8	Dargo [25]	47,867
14	Nov 5	H	Dunfermline Ath	W 2-1	2-0	8	Black [5], Proctor [8]	3770
15	19	A	Kilmarnock	D 2-2	1-0	8	Bayne [30], Dargo [77]	4708
16	26	H	Dundee U	D 1-1	1-1	8	Tokely [20]	3700
17	Dec 3	A	Motherwell	W 2-0	0-0	6	Dargo 2 [64, 88]	4103
18	10	A	Hearts	D 0-0	0-0	6		16,373
19	18	H	Celtic	D 1-1	1-1	6	Dargo [1]	7500
20	26	H	Hibernian	W 2-0	2-0	6	Dargo 2 [7, 10]	7017
21	31	A	Aberdeen	D 0-0	0-0	7		12,266
22	Jan 14	H	Livingston	W 3-0	1-0	6	Dargo 2 (1 pen) [26, 56 (p)], Wyness [60]	3605
23	21	A	Falkirk	W 4-1	3-1	6	Wilson [2], Wyness [18], Dargo [38], Tokely [55]	4548
24	29	H	Rangers	L 2-3	1-2	6	Dargo [12], Wyness [72]	7380
25	Feb 8	A	Dunfermline Ath	D 2-2	0-2	—	Dargo [81], Wyness [87]	3355
26	11	H	Kilmarnock	D 3-3	1-1	6	Wyness [34], Dargo [68], Proctor [86]	3618
27	18	A	Dundee U	W 4-2	2-2	6	Dods [29], Wyness [44], Dargo [48], Morgan [84]	6419
28	Mar 4	H	Motherwell	L 0-1	0-0	6		3183
29	11	H	Hearts	D 0-0	0-0	6		5027
30	22	A	Celtic	L 1-2	0-1	—	Hart [89]	57,105
31	25	A	Hibernian	W 2-0	0-0	6	Dods [59], Wilson (pen) [79]	12,805
32	Apr 1	H	Aberdeen	L 0-1	0-0	8		7368
33	8	A	Livingston	L 1-2	1-1	8	Tokely [15]	2688
34	15	A	Motherwell	W 1-0	1-0	7	Dargo [27]	3438
35	22	H	Dundee U	W 1-0	0-0	7	Dargo [89]	3609
36	29	A	Livingston	W 1-0	0-0	7	Wilson [55]	2076
37	May 3	H	Falkirk	W 2-0	2-0	—	Duncan [17], Dargo [31]	3121
38	6	A	Dunfermline Ath	W 1-0	0-0	7	Morgan [52]	5354

Final League Position: 7

Honours
Scottish Cup: Semi-finals 2003, 2004; Quarter-finals 1996.
League Champions: First Division 2003-04. Third Division 1996-97; *Runners-up:* Second Division 1998-99.
Bell's League Challenge Cup Winners: 2003-04. *Runners-up:* 1999-2000.

Club colours: Shirts: Royal blue with red and black stripes. Shorts: Royal blue. Stockings: Royal blue.

Goalscorers: *League* (51): Dargo 17 (1 pen), Wyness 8, Brewster 6, Morgan 3, Proctor 3, Tokely 3, Wilson 3 (1 pen), Bayne 2, Dods 2, Black 1, Duncan 1, Fox 1, Hart 1.
Scottish Cup (6): Dargo 2 (1 pen), Wyness 2, McAllister 1, McBain 1.
CIS Cup (9): Wilson 2, Dargo 1, Duncan 1, Fox 1, Hart 1, McBain 1, Munro 1, Wyness 1.

Brown M 37	Hastings R 26 + 1	Golabek S 14 + 3	Munro G 32	Dods D 37	Proctor D 12 + 5	Black I 24 + 2	McBain R 17 + 1	Wilson B 33 + 1	Brewster C 16 + 1	Dargo C 31 + 2	Hislop S — + 3	Tokely R 34	Hart R 11 + 20	Fox L 9 + 8	Wyness D 18 + 9	Duncan R 28 + 2	Morgan A 15 + 7	McAllister R 2 + 12	Bayne G 8 + 9	Juanjo — + 2	McCaffrey S 7 + 1	Keogh L 5 + 3	Fraser M 1	Sutherland A 1	Soane S — + 1	*Match No.*
1	2	3	4	5	6	7	8	9	10	11^{1}	12															1
1	3	6	4	5		7	8^{2}	9^{3}	10	11^{1}	12	2	13	14												2
1	3^{1}	6	4	5		7	8	9^{3}	10	11^{2}	13	2	14	12												3
1		3	4	5		7^{2}	8	9	10^{3}	11^{1}		2	14	6	12	13										4
1		3	4	5		7	8	9	10	11^{2}		2	12	6^{1}	13											5
1		3	4	5		7	8^{3}	9	10	11^{2}		2	13	6^{1}	12		14									6
1		3	4	5	6	7	8^{1}	9^{2}	10	11^{3}		2	14	12			13									7
1			4	5	7			9^{3}	10^{1}	12		2	13	6^{2}	11	8	3	14								8
1			4	5	7	12		9^{2}	10▮	14		2	13	6^{1}	11^{3}	8	3									9
1	4			5	7	13		9^{3}	11^{1}			2	14	6^{2}	10	8	3		12							10
1			4	5	12			9		10		2	7^{1}	6	11	8	3									11
1	12		4	5	14			9		10		2	7^{3}	6^{2}	11	8	3^{1}		13							12
1	3		4	5	9	7				11^{1}		2			12	8	6		10▮							13
1	3		4	5	6	7		9^{3}	10^{2}	11^{1}		2	14		12	8		13								14
1	3		4	5	6	7^{1}		9	13	11^{3}		2		12		8			10^{2}	14						15
1	3		4	5	6^{1}	7		9^{3}		11^{2}		2	14			8	12		10	13						16
1	3		4	5		7		9^{2}	10	11		2	12	13		8	6^{1}									17
1	3		4		6^{1}	7		9	10	11		2	12			8					5					18
1	3		4	5		7	8	9^{2}	10	11^{1}		2	13		12	6										19
1	3		4	5		7	8	9^{3}	10^{1}	11^{2}		2	14			6		13	12							20
1	3		4	5		7	8	9	10			2			12	6		11^{1}								21
1	3		4	5	14	7^{2}	8	9^{3}		11		2	13		10^{1}	6		12								22
1	3	12	4	5	13	7^{1}	8	9^{3}		11		2^{2}	14		10	6										23
1	3^{3}	12	4	5			8	9		11		2	13	7^{2}	10	6^{1}			14							24
1	4^{2}	3		5			8^{1}	9		11		2	13	12	14	7			10^{3}		6					25
1	4	3^{1}		5	6			9		11			8^{2}		10	7	12				2	13				26
1	3		4	5	12	7		9^{1}		11		2	8^{2}		10^{3}		6	13			14					27
1	3^{3}		4	5	9^{1}	7				11		2	8		10	6^{2}	12		14			13				28
1	3		4	5		7				11		2	8			6	9		10							29
1	3		4	5		7^{1}		12					8		11	6	9	13	10^{2}		2					30
1	3	12	4^{1}	5		7		10					8		11^{3}	6	9^{2}		13		2	14				31
1	3^{2}		4	5		7^{3}		9		11^{1}		2	8		10	6	14	13	12							32
1	3		4	5				9		11		2	8^{1}		10	6	7	12								33
1		3	4	5			12	9^{2}		11		2	13			6	7^{1}	14	10^{3}			8				34
1	4	3		5			8^{1}	9		11		2	7		10^{2}		12	13				6				35
1		3	4	5			8	9^{2}		11^{1}		2		13	10^{3}	6		14	12			7				36
		3		5						11^{1}		2			10^{2}	6	7^{3}	12	13		4	8	1	9	14	37
1		3		5			8	9^{3}				2		13	12	14	6^{2}	10^{1}	11		4	7				38

KILMARNOCK Premier League

Year Formed: 1869. *Ground & Address:* Rugby Park, Kilmarnock KA1 2DP. *Telephone:* 01563 545300. *Fax:* 01563 522181. *Website:* www.kilmarnockfc.co.uk
Ground Capacity: all seated: 18,128. *Size of Pitch:* 115yd × 74yd.
Chairman: Michael Johnston. *Secretary:* Angela Burnett.
Manager: Jim Jefferies. *Assistant Manager:* Billy Brown. *Physio:* A. MacQueen.
Managers since 1975: W. Fernie, D. Sneddon, J. Clunie, E. Morrison, J. Fleeting, T. Burns, A. Totten, B. Brown, B. Williamson.
Club Nickname(s): Killie. *Previous Grounds:* Rugby Park (Dundonald Road); The Grange; Holm Quarry; Present ground since 1899.
Record Attendance: 35,995 v Rangers, Scottish Cup, 10 Mar 1962.
Record Transfer Fee received: £400,000 for Kris Boyd to Rangers (2006).
Record Transfer Fee paid: £300,000 for Paul Wright from St Johnstone (1995).
Record Victory: 11-1 v Paisley Academical, Scottish Cup, 18 Jan 1930 (15-0 v Lanemark, Ayrshire Cup, 15 Nov 1890).
Record Defeat: 1-9 v Celtic, Division I, 13 Aug 1938.
Most Capped Player: Joe Nibloe, 11, Scotland.
Most League Appearances: 481: Alan Robertson, 1972-88.
Most League Goals in Season (Individual): 34: Harry 'Peerie' Cunningham 1927-28 and Andy Kerr 1960-61.
Most Goals Overall (Individual): 148: W. Culley, 1912-23.

KILMARNOCK 2005–06 LEAGUE RECORD

Match No.	Date	Venue	Opponents	Result	H/T Score	Lg. Pos.	Goalscorers	Attendance
1	Jul 30	H	Hearts	L 2-4	1-1	—	Naismith 12, Greer 74	7487
2	Aug 6	A	Aberdeen	W 2-1	1-1	7	Johnston 1 Naismith 72	13,661
3	13	H	Motherwell	W 4-1	2-1	4	Johnston 12, Boyd 2 19, 73, McDonald 62	5035
4	20	A	Inverness CT	D 2-2	0-1	3	Nish 70, Boyd 72	4119
5	27	H	Livingston	W 3-0	3-0	3	Nish 3 28, 34, 42	4644
6	Sept 10	H	Dunfermline Ath	W 3-2	2-1	3	Dodds 8, Boyd 33, Invincibile 89	4737
7	17	A	Rangers	L 0-3	0-1	5		49,076
8	24	H	Falkirk	D 1-1	1-1	4	Boyd (pen) 23	5507
9	Oct 1	A	Dundee U	D 0-0	0-0	5		6095
10	15	A	Hibernian	L 2-4	2-0	5	Ford 6, Fowler 40	11,731
11	23	H	Celtic	L 0-1	0-1	5		10,544
12	25	A	Hearts	L 0-1	0-1	—		16,536
13	29	H	Aberdeen	W 4-2	2-1	5	Ford 17, Invincibile 18, Boyd 2 47, 56	5798
14	Nov 5	A	Motherwell	D 2-2	1-1	5	Boyd 2 8, 90	5107
15	19	H	Inverness CT	D 2-2	0-1	5	Boyd 53, Naismith 55	4708
16	26	A	Livingston	W 3-0	2-0	5	Boyd 2 25, 81, Naismith 28	2946
17	Dec 3	A	Dunfermline Ath	W 1-0	1-0	4	Boyd 41	4319
18	11	H	Rangers	L 2-3	0-1	5	McDonald 60, Boyd 81	12,426
19	17	A	Falkirk	W 2-1	0-0	5	Fowler 49, Boyd 89	4708
20	26	H	Dundee U	W 2-1	1-0	4	McDonald 36, Wales 89	5749
21	Jan 2	H	Hibernian	D 2-2	1-0	5	Naismith 29, Wales 89	9224
22	14	A	Celtic	L 2-4	1-2	5	Naismith (pen) 23, Invincibile 50	58,883
23	21	H	Hearts	W 1-0	0-0	5	Invincibile 46	8811
24	28	A	Aberdeen	D 2-2	1-1	5	Naismith (pen) 30, Lilley 85	10,540
25	Feb 8	H	Motherwell	W 2-0	1-0	—	Wales 2 33, 50	5169
26	11	A	Inverness CT	D 3-3	1-1	5	Naismith 27, Wales 2 69, 85	3618
27	18	H	Livingston	W 3-1	2-1	5	Wales 22, Naismith 26, Invincibile 58	5266
28	Mar 4	H	Dunfermline Ath	W 1-0	1-0	5	Invincibile 10	5507
29	11	A	Rangers	L 0-4	0-1	5		49,442
30	18	H	Falkirk	W 2-1	1-1	4	Invincibile 2, Naismith 73	5443
31	25	A	Dundee U	D 2-2	2-0	4	Naismith 2 13, 17	5830
32	Apr 5	A	Hibernian	L 1-2	1-0	—	Wales 19	10,427
33	9	H	Celtic	L 1-4	0-1	5	Nish 88	10,978
34	15	A	Hearts	L 0-2	0-0	5		16,497
35	22	A	Aberdeen	D 0-0	0-0	5		10,634
36	29	H	Rangers	L 1-3	1-0	5	Nish 27	11,752
37	May 3	A	Celtic	L 0-2	0-0	—		56,538
38	7	H	Hibernian	W 3-1	0-1	5	Naismith 50, Greer 71, Nish 74	5732

Final League Position: 5

Honours
League Champions: Division I 1964-65. Division II 1897-98, 1898-99; *Runners-up:* Division I 1959-60, 1960-61, 1962-63, 1963-64. First Division 1975-76, 1978-79, 1981-82, 1992-93. Division II 1953-54, 1973-74. Second Division 1989-90.
Scottish Cup Winners: 1920, 1929, 1997; *Runners-up:* 1898, 1932, 1938, 1957, 1960.
League Cup Runners-up: 1952-53, 1960-61, 1962-63, 2000-01.

European: *European Cup:* 4 matches (1965-66). *Cup Winners' Cup:* 4 matches (1997-98). *UEFA Cup:* 24 matches (*Fairs Cup:* 1964-65, 1966-67, 1969-70, 1970-71. *UEFA Cup:* 1998-99, 1999-2000, 2001-02).

Club colours: Shirt: Blue and white vertical stripes. Shorts: White. Stockings: White.

Goalscorers: *League* (63): Boyd 15 (1 pen), Naismith 13 (2 pens), Wales 8, Invincibile 7, Nish 7, McDonald 3, Ford 2, Fowler 2, Greer 2, Johnston 2, Dodds 1, Lilley 1.
Scottish Cup (1): Nish 1.
CIS Cup (7): Boyd 2, DiGiacomo 1, Dodds 1, Invincibile 1, Wales 1, own goal 1.

Combe A 32	Fowler J 38	Ford S 32	Greer G 27	Hay G 35	Leven P 4 + 2	Invincibile D 34 + 3	Locke G 10 + 5	McDonald G 16 + 11	Boyd K 18 + 1	Naismith S 32 + 4	Nish C 25 + 9	Johnston A 36 + 1	Lilley D 8 + 3	Di Giacomo P 2 + 10	Dodds R 6 + 5	Murray S 1 + 14	Wales G 18 + 12	Campbell R — + 2	Smith G 6 + 1	Wright F 27	Wilson L 11 + 2	*Match No.*
1	2	3	4	5	6^{2}	7^{1}	8	9	10	11	12	13										1
1	6	3	4	5			8	9	10^{1}	11^{2}	12	7	2^{3}	13	14							2
1	6	3	4	5		14	8	9^{2}	10^{3}	11^{1}	12	7	2		13							3
1	6	3	4	5		13	8	9^{3}	10	11^{1}	12	7	2^{2}			14						4
1	2	3	4	5		6	8	9^{1}	10^{2}		11^{3}	7			12		13	14				5
1	2	3	4	5		6		9	10	12	11^{1}	7^{3}	14		8^{2}		13					6
1	2	3	4	5	14	6		9	10^{2}	12	11^{1}	7^{3}			8		13					7
1	2	3	4	5	6^{1}	8		9^{2}	10^{3}	11		7			12	14	13					8
1	2	3	4	5		6^{1}	8	9	10	12	13	7					11^{2}					9
1	2	3	4	5		6	8	9	12	13	11^{2}	7					10^{1}					10
	3		4	5		6	8	9^{1}	10	11^{2}	12^{3}	7	2		14		13		1			11
	3		4	5		8		9	10^{2}	11		7			6^{1}	13	12		1	2		12
	2	3	4	5		9		14	10^{1}	11^{2}	12	7^{3}			8		13		1	6		13
1	2	3	4^{1}	5		9			10	11^{2}	13	7			8^{3}	12	14			6		14
1	2	3	4	5		9^{2}			10	11^{3}	12	7			8^{1}	13	14			6		15
1	2	3	4	5		8^{1}		12	10	11^{2}	9^{3}	7				14	13			6		16
1	2	3	4	5		8		12	10	11	9^{1}	7								6		17
1	2	3	4	5		8^{1}		9	10	11		7				12				6		18
1	2	3	4	5		8		9	10	11^{1}		7					12			6		19
1	2	3	4	5		8		9		11	10^{2}			13		7^{1}	12			6		20
1	3		4	5		8^{1}		12		11	10^{2}	7	2	13			9			6		21
1	4	3		5		12		8		11	10^{3}	7	2^{1}	14		13	9^{2}			6		22
1	4	3		5		8		12		11	10^{1}	7	2				9			6		23
1	4	3		5		8^{3}	14			11^{1}	10^{2}	7	2	12		13	9			6		24
1^{6}	4	3		5		8	12	13		11	10	7					9^{2}		15	2	6^{1}	25
	4	3		5		8	12			11^{1}	10	7	13				9		1	2	6^{2}	26
	4	3		5		8	12			11^{3}	10^{1}	7		14		13	9^{2}		1	2	6	27
1	4	3		5		9	8	12			10	7^{1}		11^{2}		13				2	6	28
1[illegible]	6	3		5		8^{3}		14		11	10^{2}	7	12	9				13		2	4^{1}	29
	6	3		5		8		13		11	10^{1}	7				12	9^{2}		1	2	4	30
1	6	3	5			8				11	10	7					9			2	4	31
1	6	3		5	13	8		12		11	10	7^{1}					9^{2}			2	4	32
1	6	3		5		8				11	10	7		12			9^{1}			2	4	33
1	6	3	4	5		8				11	10	7					9			2		34
1	6	3^{1}	4	5		8				11	10	7					9			2	12	35
1	6		4	5^{1}		8^{2}		12		11	10	7		13		14	9^{3}			2	3	36
1	5		4		6	8	13			11	10	7		12			9^{1}			2	3^{2}	37
1	3		4		6	8^{3}	5^{2}			11	10	7		14		12	9^{1}			2	13	38

LIVINGSTON First Division

Year Formed: 1974. *Ground:* Almondvale Stadium, Alderton Road, Livingston EH54 7DN. *Telephone:* 01506 417000. *Fax:* 01506 418888. *Email:* info@livingstonfc.co.uk. *Website:* www.livingstonfc.co.uk
Ground Capacity: 10,024 (all seated). *Size of Pitch:* 105yd × 72yd.
Chairman: Pearse Flynn. *Chief Executive:* Vivien Kyles. *General Manager:* David Hay. *Secretary:* M. Kaplan.
Team Manager: John Robertson. *Physios:* Arthur Duncan, Marie McPhail.
Managers since 1975: M. Lawson, T. Christie, W. MacFarlane, A. Ness, J. Bain, J. Leishman, R. Stewart, J. Leishman, M. Barcellos, D. Hay, A. Preston, R. Gough, P. Lambert.
Club Nickname: Livi Lions. *Previous Grounds:* None.
Record Attendance: 10,024 v Celtic, Premier League, 18 Aug 2001.
Record Transfer Fee received: £1,000,000 for D. Fernandez to Celtic (June 2002).
Record Transfer Fee paid: £60,000 for Barry Wilson from Inverness CT (May 2000).
Record Victory: 7-0 v Queen of the South, Scottish Cup, 29 Jan 2000.
Record Defeat: 0-8 v Hamilton A. Division II, 14 Dec 1974.
Most Capped Player (under 18): I. Little.
Most League Appearances: 446: Walter Boyd, 1979-89.
Most League Goals in Season (Individual): 21: John McGachie, 1986-87. *(Team):* 69; Second Division, 1986-87.
Most Goals Overall (Individual): 64: David Roseburgh, 1986-93.

LIVINGSTON 2005–06 LEAGUE RECORD

Match No.	*Date*	*Venue*	*Opponents*	*Result*		*H/T Score*	*Lg. Pos.*	*Goalscorers*	*Attendance*
1	Jul 31	A	Rangers	L	0-3	0-1	—		49,613
2	Aug 6	H	Falkirk	L	0-2	0-1	12		3911
3	13	A	Hibernian	L	0-3	0-2	12		11,009
4	20	H	Dunfermline Ath	D	1-1	0-1	12	Pereira 64	3528
5	27	A	Kilmarnock	L	0-3	0-3	12		4644
6	Sept 11	H	Hearts	L	1-4	1-3	12	Dalglish 44	7900
7	17	A	Dundee U	L	0-2	0-1	12		6302
8	24	A	Aberdeen	D	0-0	0-0	12		12,402
9	Oct 1	H	Celtic	L	0-5	0-2	12		8862
10	15	A	Motherwell	L	0-1	0-1	12		4507
11	22	H	Inverness CT	D	1-1	1-0	12	Pinxten 12	3070
12	26	H	Rangers	D	2-2	0-1	—	Snodgrass 2 55, 65	8081
13	29	A	Falkirk	D	1-1	0-1	12	Snodgrass 87	4786
14	Nov 5	H	Hibernian	L	1-2	1-0	12	Strong 42	8390
15	19	A	Dunfermline Ath	W	1-0	0-0	11	Dalglish 60	6016
16	26	H	Kilmarnock	L	0-3	0-2	12		2946
17	Dec 3	A	Hearts	L	1-2	0-2	12	Walker 62	16,583
18	10	H	Dundee U	W	1-0	1-0	11	Snodgrass 41	3345
19	17	H	Aberdeen	D	0-0	0-0	11		3223
20	26	A	Celtic	L	1-2	0-1	11	Dalglish 57	58,953
21	31	H	Motherwell	L	1-2	1-1	12	Pinxten 37	3931
22	Jan 14	A	Inverness CT	L	0-3	0-1	12		3605
23	21	A	Rangers	L	1-4	0-1	12	Vincze 51	49,211
24	28	H	Falkirk	L	0-1	0-1	12		4729
25	Feb 8	A	Hibernian	L	0-7	0-2	—		12,170
26	11	H	Dunfermline Ath	L	0-1	0-1	12		3976
27	18	A	Kilmarnock	L	1-3	1-2	12	Hislop 13	5266
28	Mar 5	H	Hearts	L	2-3	0-1	12	Brittain 59, Mackay 76	4458
29	11	A	Dundee U	L	1-3	1-0	12	Morrow 18	5730
30	18	A	Aberdeen	L	0-3	0-1	12		9229
31	26	H	Celtic	L	0-2	0-0	12		6504
32	Apr 1	A	Motherwell	L	1-2	0-1	12	Whelan 75	4458
33	8	H	Inverness CT	W	2-1	1-1	12	Brittain 36, Healy 81	2688
34	15	H	Dundee U	W	3-1	1-1	12	Morrow 9, Pinxten 48, Brittain (pen) 90	2298
35	22	A	Dunfermline Ath	L	2-3	1-1	12	Brittain (pen) 9, Healy 63	5963
36	29	H	Inverness CT	L	0-1	0-0	12		2076
37	May 3	H	Motherwell	L	0-1	0-0	—		2081
38	6	A	Falkirk	L	0-1	0-0	12		5315

Final League Position: 12

Honours
League Champions: First Division: Champions: 2000-01. Second Division 1986-87, 1998-99. Third Division 1995-96;
Runners-up: Second Division 1982-83. First Division 1987-88.
Scottish Cup: Semi-finals 2004.
League Cup Winners: 2003-04. Semi-finals 1984-85. *B&Q Cup:* Semi-finals 1992-93, 1993-94, 2001.
Bell's League Challenge Runners-up: 2000-01.

European: *UEFA Cup:* 4 matches (2002-03).

Club colours: Shirt: Gold with black sleeves and side panels. Shorts: Black. Stockings: Gold with black trim.

Goalscorers: *League* (25): Brittain 4 (2 pens), Snodgrass 4, Dalglish 3, Pinxten 3, Healy 2, Morrow 2, Hislop 1, Mackay 1, Pereira 1, Strong 1, Vincze 1, Walker 1, Whelan 1.
Scottish Cup (2): Brittain 1, Dalglish 1.
CIS Cup (5): Dalglish 2, Dair 1, Mackay 1, Pereira 1.

McKenzie R 32	Mackay D 38	Dorado E 17 + 4	Pinxten H 26	Tierney P 25 + 6	Brittain R 33 + 2	Tesovic D 2 + 2	Walker A 28 + 5	Adams D 21 + 4	Scott M 8 + 11	McPake J 5 + 10	Snodgrass R 12 + 15	Pereira R 5 + 5	McLaughlin S 2 + 2	Strong G 28 + 2	Vincze G 11 + 6	Dorrans G 4 + 4	Lambert P 8	Dair J 21 + 1	Boyd S 2 + 2	Dalglish P 15 + 2	Barrett N 6 + 3	Barrett G 5	Adam S — + 2	Miller G 2 + 2	Roy L 6	McNamee D 13 + 1	Houlahan W 14 + 2	Hislop S 7 + 7	Morrow S 11	Whelan N 5 + 2	Healy C 6 + 4	Weir S — + 1	*Match No.*
1	2	3	4	5	6■	7	8^{3}	9	10^{1}	11^{2}	12	13	14																				1
1	2	3	4^{3}	5		13	8	9	7	11	12	10^{1}	6^{2}	14																			2
1	2	3		5	4	7^{2}	8	9	10	11^{1}	12		14		6^{3}	13																	3
1	2	3^{3}		5	4		8	9	10		13	12			6		7^{1}	11^{2}	14														4
1	2	3		5	4	12	8	9^{1}	7	13		14			6^{2}			11^{3}		10													5
1	2	3			4			9	13	12	14				6			8^{3}	5	10^{1}	7^{2}	11											6
1	2	3			12			9^{3}	13		14		4	6			8^{2}	5	10	7^{1}	11												7
1	2	3^{2}			6		5	9		12		8^{3}		4	14			7	13	10^{1}		11											8
1	2	3		12	6		5^{3}	9			13	8^{1}		4	14			7		10^{2}		11											9
1	2		3	5	14		12	9			13	7^{3}		4			8^{1}	6		10^{2}		11											10
1	2		3	5	6		7^{2}	9	14		10^{3}			4				8^{1}			13	11	12										11
1	2		3	5	6		7	9^{2}	11	13	10^{3}	14		4			8^{1}				12												12
1	2		3	5	6		7	9^{3}	11^{2}	12	10			4							8^{1}		13	14									13
1	2	14	3	5	6		7		13	11^{2}	10^{1}			4				9^{3}		12	8												14
	2	14	3^{3}	5	6		7			12	13	11^{1}		4				9		10^{2}	8				1								15
	2		3	5	6		7^{3}			14	11^{1}	12		4	13			9^{2}		10	8				1								16
	2		3	5	6		7^{2}		13	11	12			4	8			9		10^{1}					1								17
	2		3	5	6		7		12	13	11			4	8			9^{1}		10^{2}					1								18
1	2		3	5	6				13	14	11			4	7		8^{1}	9^{2}		10^{3}	12												19
1	2	14	3	5	6		7^{1}		13	12	11^{2}			4	8			9		10^{3}													20
1	2		3	5	6		7^{2}		12		11			4	8			9^{1}		10						13							21
1	2	14	3		6		13							4	12		8^{1}	9		10						5^{2}	7	11^{3}					22
1	2		3	6	7		12				13			4	8			14		10^{2}						5^{1}	9^{3}	11					23
1	2		3		7		6		13		10^{1}			4			8			12■						5	9	11^{2}					24
1	2		3	6			7	14	12		13			4			8^{3}	9								5^{2}	10	11^{1}					25
	2	4	3	6			12	8			11					14		7^{3}							1	5^{1}	10^{2}	13	9				26
	2	4	3	5^{3}	6^{1}		13	9			12				7			8							1		14	10^{2}	11				27
1	2	4			6		7	9			13			3		8^{1}		10								5^{2}	12		11				28
1	2	4		12	6		7^{1}	9						3	14	8^{3}										5	10^{2}		11		13		29
1	2	4			6^{2}		7	9^{3}						3		8^{1}										5	10	13	11	12	14		30
1	2	4		5	8		7	9^{2}						3		13										6^{1}	10		11		12		31
1	2		4^{2}	5	6		7	9^{1}						3										13			8^{3}	10	11	14	12		32
1	2		4	5	6		7^{1}	14						3	12												9	13	11	10^{2}	8^{3}		33
1	2		4	14	6		7^{3}	12						3												5	9^{1}	13	11	10^{2}	8		34
1	2		4	13	6		7							3												5^{2}	9	12	11^{1}	10	8		35
1	2	3	4	14	6			7^{2}								13										5^{3}	9	12	11^{1}	10	8		36
1	2	3^{2}	4^{1}	5	6			13	7		10^{3}			12										9				11			8	14	37
1	2			13	6		7				14			3		8								11		4^{2}	9^{3}	12		10^{1}	5		38

MONTROSE Third Division

Year Formed: 1879. *Ground & Address:* Links Park, Wellington St, Montrose DD10 8QD. *Telephone:* 01674 673200.
Fax: 01674 677311. *E-mail:* montrosefootballclub@tesco.net. *Website:* www.montrosefc.co.uk
Ground Capacity: total: 3292, seated: 1338. *Size of Pitch:* 113yd × 70yd.
Chairman: John F. Paton. *Secretary:* Malcolm J. Watters. *Assistant Secretary:* Andrew Stephen.
Co-Managers: Ed Wolecki and David Robertson. *Physio:* Scott Shephard.
Managers since 1975: A. Stuart, K. Cameron, R. Livingstone, S. Murray, D. D'Arcy, I. Stewart, C. McLelland, D. Rougvie, J. Leishman, J Holt, A. Dornan, D. Smith, T. Campbell, K. Drinkell, H. Hall.
Club Nickname(s): The Gable Endies. *Previous Grounds:* None.
Record Attendance: 8983 v Dundee, Scottish Cup 3rd rd, 17 Mar 1973.
Record Transfer Fee received: £50,000 for Gary Murray to Hibernian (Dec 1980).
Record Transfer Fee paid: £17,500 for Jim Smith from Airdrieonians (Feb 1992).
Record Victory: 12-0 v Vale of Leithen, Scottish Cup 2nd rd, 4 Jan 1975.
Record Defeat: 0-13 v Aberdeen, 17 Mar 1951.
Most Capped Player: Alexander Keillor, 2 (6), Scotland.
Most League Appearances: 432: David Larter, 1987-98.
Most League Goals in Season (Individual): 28: Brian Third, Division II, 1972-73.

MONTROSE 2005–06 LEAGUE RECORD

Match No.	Date	Venue	Opponents	Result		H/T Score	Lg. Pos.	Goalscorers	Attendance
1	Aug 6	A	Elgin C	D	0-0	0-0	—		460
2	13	H	Albion R	L	0-2	0-0	8		307
3	20	A	East Fife	L	2-3	0-0	9	Fotheringham 2 [65, 72]	468
4	27	H	Arbroath	W	1-0	1-0	8	Martin [19]	888
5	Sept 10	A	East Stirling	D	1-1	0-0	7	Henslee [82]	195
6	17	A	Cowdenbeath	L	0-2	0-0	7		216
7	24	H	Stenhousemuir	L	0-3	0-1	8		301
8	Oct 1	A	Berwick R	D	1-1	0-0	8	Webster [65]	465
9	15	H	Queen's Park	L	0-1	0-0	9		310
10	22	H	Elgin C	W	2-0	1-0	7	Henslee [13], Kerrigan [61]	288
11	25	A	Albion R	D	1-1	1-1	—	Henslee [10]	181
12	29	H	East Stirling	W	3-0	2-0	6	Henslee 3 [11, 35, 67]	326
13	Nov 5	A	Arbroath	L	1-2	1-0	6	Fotheringham [4]	830
14	12	H	Cowdenbeath	L	0-1	0-1	7		295
15	26	A	Stenhousemuir	L	2-6	1-3	7	Henslee [16], Webster [75]	253
16	Dec 3	A	Queen's Park	W	3-0	0-0	7	Kerrigan [52], Fotheringham 2 [72, 76]	351
17	26	A	Elgin C	L	0-1	0-0	—		437
18	31	H	East Fife	W	3-1	0-0	—	Henslee [65], Fotheringham (pen) [74], Russell [90]	401
19	Jan 2	H	Arbroath	L	0-1	0-0	—		455
20	7	H	Berwick R	D	0-0	0-0	8		276
21	14	A	East Stirling	L	0-1	0-1	9		199
22	21	A	Cowdenbeath	L	0-2	0-1	9		295
23	28	H	Stenhousemuir	L	0-2	0-1	9		326
24	Feb 4	A	Berwick R	D	1-1	0-0	9	Middleton [60]	343
25	11	H	Queen's Park	D	0-0	0-0	8		385
26	18	H	Albion R	D	2-2	1-2	8	McLeod [38], Davidson [85]	280
27	25	A	East Fife	L	0-4	0-1	8		332
28	Mar 11	H	East Stirling	W	2-0	2-0	8	Henslee [13], Middleton [19]	241
29	18	H	Cowdenbeath	L	0-3	0-2	8		306
30	21	A	Arbroath	L	0-3	0-3	—		732
31	25	A	Stenhousemuir	L	1-5	1-1	8	Fotheringham [10]	424
32	Apr 1	H	Berwick R	L	1-2	0-1	9	Fotheringham [56]	301
33	8	A	Queen's Park	D	2-2	0-1	9	Henslee [54], Fraser [79]	369
34	15	H	Elgin C	L	1-3	1-1	9	Watson [41]	406
35	22	A	Albion R	D	1-1	1-1	9	Russell [12]	825
36	29	H	East Fife	L	0-2	0-1	9		431

Final League Position: 9

Honours
League Champions: Second Division 1984-85; *Runners-up:* 1990-91. Third Division, *Runners-up:* 1994-95.
Scottish Cup: Quarter-finals 1973, 1976.
League Cup: Semi-finals 1975-76.
B&Q Cup: Semi-finals 1992-93.
League Challenge Cup: Semi-finals 1996-97.

Club colours: Shirt: Royal blue. Shorts: Royal blue. Stockings: White.

Goalscorers: *League* (31): Henslee 10, Fotheringham 8 (1 pen), Kerrigan 2, Middleton 2, Russell 2, Webster 2, Davidson 1, Fraser 1, McLeod 1, Martin 1, Watson 1.
Scottish Cup (0).
CIS Cup (0).
Challenge Cup (1): Martin 1.

Reid A 16	Donachie B 23+3	Smith E 20	McKenzie J 15+1	Stephen N 15	Kerrigan S 19+3	Webster K 19+3	Fotheringham M 24+4	Watson C 16+10	Hall E 22+2	Henslee G 33	Dodds K 12+7	McLean D 3+2	Doyle P 16+6	Fraser S 25+5	Cargill A 3+4	Martin W 6+4	Butter J 4+1	Russell J 10+7	Don K —+3	Wood A 15	Hay G 14	Hanknson M 1	Smith R 1	Lombardi M —+1	Brash K 8+3	Davidson H 15	Middleton G 12+2	McManus S 4+2	McLeod I 6+3	Ferguson S 9+1	Rae C —+1	Reid P 1+4	Kelly D 8	Corre G —+4	Ralph J 1	*Match No.*
1	2	3	4	5	6	7^3	8	9^2	10^1	11	12	13	14																							1
1	2	3	4	5	6	7	8	13	10^2	11				9^1	12																					2
1	2	3	4	5	6	7^1	8			11	12		10			9																				3
1		3		5	6	7	8			11	2		4	10^1	12	9																				4
1		3	4		6		8	12	7	11	2		5		10^1	9																				5
1		3	4		6	13	8	12	7^2	11	2		5	10^1		9																				6
1		3	4	5^2	6	7^3	8	12	10	11	2		13	14		9^1																				7
1		3	4	5	6	7	8	9^1	11	10	2		12																							8
1	13	3	4		6	7	8	9^1	11	10	2^2		5	12																						9
1	13	3	4	5	9^3	7	8		11^1	10	2		6^2	12		14																				10
1^6		3	4^1	5	9	7	8		11^2	10	2		6	13		12	15																			11
1	3		4	5	6	7	8^3		11^2	9	2		12	10^1	14	13																				12
1	2	3	4	5		7	8■		11^2	9	13		6	10^1		12																				13
1	2	3	4^2	5■		7			11	9	6	12	13	14	8^3	10^1																				14
1	2	3	4		13	7^3		12	11^2	9	8	10^1	5	6				14																		15
	2	3		5	6	7	10	13	11	9^2	12		4	8^1			1																			16
	2^2	3	14	5	8		10	9	11^3	6	13	7^1	4		12		1																			17
	12	3		5^1			13	9^3	8	6	2	10^2	4	11			1	7	14																	18
	2	3	5				10	9	12	8	14		4	11^1	6^3		1	7^2	13																	19
	2	3			8		10^2	9	6		12		4	11				7^1	13	1	5															20
	2	3		4	10		13	9	8^3	6			12					7			5^1	1	11^2	14												21
1	2				6^1		8	10					4	11				12			5				3	7	9									22
	2							13	12				4	11^1				7		1	5				3^2	8	9	6^3	10	14						23
	2■								11	8^2				3				7^1		1	4					6	9	10		5	12	13				24
							7^3	14	2	8				3				13		1	4				12	6	9	10^1	11	5^2						25
					14		10^2	13	2	8				3				7		1	4				12	6			11			9^1	5^3			26
							7^1	10^2	2	8				3						1	4					6	11	13	9	5				12		27
	2							10^1		8				3				7^2		1					11^3	6	9		12	5		13	4	14		28
	2					13				8				3				7^2		1	4				11^1	6	9		10	5				12		29
	2■					13	7	12		8				3				14		1	4				11	6^2	9^3		10^1	5						30
						7^1	10	11^3		8				3						1	4					6	9^2		14	5		12	2	13		31
	2					7^1	9■	10		8				5						1						6	11			3		12	4			32
	6				13	7^3		9		8				5				14		1	4				12	10	11^1			3			2^2			33
	4				10■	7^1		9		8				3				12		1	5				11^2	6	13						2			34
	4					7^2	12			8				3				9		1	5				11	6^1	10^3	14	13				2			35
	6				10		14	9		11				5				12		1					3^2	7^3	13	8^1					2		4	36

MORTON **Second Division**

Year Formed: 1874. *Ground & Address:* Cappielow Park, Sinclair St, Greenock. *Telephone:* 01475 723571. *Fax:* 01475 781084. *E-mail:* info@gmfc.net. *Website:* www.gmfc.net
Ground Capacity: total: 11,612, seated: 6062. *Size of Pitch:* 110yd × 71yd.
Chairman: Douglas Rae. *Chief Executive:* Gillian Donaldson. *Company Secretary:* Mary Davidson. *Commercial Manager:* Susan Gregory.
Manager: Jim McInally. *Assistant Manager:* Martin Clark. *Physios:* Paul Kelly, Bruce Coyle. *Managers since 1975:* Joe Gilroy, Benny Rooney, Alex Miller, Tommy McLean, Willie McLean, Allan McGraw, Billy Stark, Ian McCall, Allan Evans, Peter Cormack, Dave McPherson, J. McCormack.
Club Nickname(s): The Ton. *Previous Grounds:* Grant Street 1874, Garvel Park 1875, Cappielow Park 1879, Ladyburn Park 1882, (Cappielow Park 1883).
Record Attendance: 23,500 v Celtic, 29 April 1922.
Record Transfer Fee received: £350,000 for Neil Orr to West Ham U.
Record Transfer Fee paid: £150,000 for Alan Mahood from Nottingham Forest (August 1998).
Record Victory: 11-0 v Carfin Shamrock, Scottish Cup 1st rd, 13 Nov 1886.
Record Defeat: 1-10 v Port Glasgow Ath, Division II, 5 May, 1894 and v St Bernards, Division II, 14 Oct 1933.
Most Capped Player: Jimmy Cowan, 25, Scotland.
Most League Appearances: 358: David Hayes, 1969-84.
Most League Goals in Season (Individual): 58: Allan McGraw, Division II, 1963-64.

MORTON 2005–06 LEAGUE RECORD

Match No.	*Date*	*Venue*	*Opponents*	*Result*		*H/T Score*	*Lg. Pos.*	*Goalscorers*	*Atten-dance*
1	Aug 6	H	Raith R	W	2-0	1-0	—	Weatherson ^{37}, McLaren ^{84}	3322
2	13	A	Stirling A	W	2-0	1-0	2	McLaren ^{43}, Lilley ^{68}	1453
3	20	H	Forfar Ath	W	1-0	0-0	2	Forrest (og) ^{74}	2778
4	27	A	Dumbarton	D	1-1	0-0	2	Weatherson ^{88}	1574
5	Sept 10	H	Gretna	L	0-2	0-1	2		3783
6	17	H	Alloa Ath	W	5-2	2-0	2	Weatherson ^{19}, Walker A ^{35}, Templeman ^{66}, Finlayson ^{68}, Millar ^{83}	2515
7	24	A	Ayr U	W	1-0	0-0	2	Walker J ^{88}	2102
8	Oct 1	H	Peterhead	W	2-1	1-1	2	Templeman ^{25}, McGregor ^{73}	2719
9	15	A	Partick Th	L	0-2	0-2	2		4354
10	22	A	Raith R	W	2-1	1-0	2	Walker A ^{34}, Greacen ^{49}	2446
11	25	H	Stirling A	L	1-2	0-1	—	Weatherson ^{67}	2052
12	29	A	Gretna	L	1-3	0-0	3	McLaughlin ^{89}	2006
13	Nov 5	H	Dumbarton	W	4-0	2-0	2	McLaren ^{1}, Lilley 2 $^{7, 83}$, Weatherson ^{86}	2818
14	12	A	Alloa Ath	W	3-0	2-0	2	McAlister ^{15}, Lilley ^{40}, Walker J ^{90}	920
15	Dec 3	H	Partick Th	W	2-1	1-1	2	McLaren ^{17}, Lilley ^{79}	4214
16	6	H	Ayr U	W	2-1	1-0	—	Lilley ^{39}, McAlister ^{74}	1677
17	17	A	Peterhead	L	0-1	0-0	2		880
18	26	H	Raith R	W	2-0	0-0	—	Millar ^{71}, McLaren ^{87}	2818
19	31	A	Forfar Ath	W	1-0	0-0	2	Lilley ^{71}	778
20	Jan 2	A	Dumbarton	W	2-0	1-0	—	Lilley ^{23}, Weatherson ^{49}	1594
21	14	H	Gretna	D	2-2	1-2	2	Lilley ^{41}, Weatherson ^{84}	5202
22	21	H	Alloa Ath	W	4-1	2-0	2	Weatherson ^{10}, McAlister ^{38}, McPake 2 $^{55, 78}$	2814
23	28	A	Ayr U	D	1-1	0-1	2	Weatherson ^{90}	1792
24	Feb 4	H	Peterhead	D	0-0	0-0	2		2693
25	11	A	Partick Th	D	1-1	0-1	2	Lilley ^{82}	3999
26	18	A	Stirling A	L	1-3	1-1	2	Walker A ^{45}	1337
27	25	H	Forfar Ath	W	3-0	1-0	2	McLaren ^{17}, Harding ^{75}, Millar ^{78}	2211
28	Mar 11	A	Gretna	W	2-1	0-0	2	Millar 2 $^{78, 80}$	2150
29	18	A	Alloa Ath	D	0-0	0-0	2		671
30	25	H	Ayr U	L	0-4	0-1	2		2437
31	28	H	Dumbarton	W	4-0	1-0	—	McAlister ^{19}, Weatherson ^{53}, Walker J 2 $^{78, 79}$	1418
32	Apr 1	A	Peterhead	L	1-2	1-0	2	Walker A ^{30}	815
33	8	H	Partick Th	W	1-0	0-0	2	Walker J ^{74}	3025
34	15	A	Raith R	D	1-1	0-1	2	McLaren ^{88}	1395
35	22	H	Stirling A	W	1-0	0-0	2	Greacen ^{82}	2111
36	29	A	Forfar Ath	W	2-0	0-0	2	Lilley 2 $^{54, 59}$	567

Final League Position: 2

Honours
League Champions: First Division 1977-78, 1983-84, 1986-87. Division II 1949-50, 1963-64, 1966-67. Second Division 1994-95. Third Division 2002-03. *Runners-up:* Division 1 1916-17, Division II 1899-1900, 1928-29, 1936-37.
Scottish Cup Winners: 1922; *Runners-up:* 1948. *League Cup Runners-up:* 1963-64.
B&Q Cup Runners-up: 1992-93.

European: *UEFA Cup:* 2 matches (*Fairs Cup:* 1968-69).

Club colours: Shirt: Royal blue with $3\frac{1}{2}$ inch white hoops. Shorts: White with royal blue panel down side. Stockings: Royal blue with white tops.

Goalscorers: *League* (58): Lilley 12, Weatherson 10, McLaren 7, Millar 5, Walker J 5, McAlister 4, Walker A 4, Greacen 2, McPake 2, Templeman 2, Finlayson 1, Harding 1, Macgregor 1, McLaughlin 1, own goal 1.
Scottish Cup (5): Lilley 2, Templeman 1,Walker J 1, Weatherson 1.
CIS Cup (1): Lilley 1.
Challenge Cup (7): Lilley 3, Walker J 2, McLaughlin 1, Templeman 1.
Play-Offs (0).

McGurn D 29	Weatherson P 35	Walker A 23 + 4	Harding R 33 + 2	Greacen S 26 + 1	McLaren A 26 + 8	Millar C 35	Finlayson K 30 + 5	Templeman C 9 + 10	Lilley D 30 + 3	McAlister J 35	Walker J 9 + 26	Keenan D 4 + 7	Macgregor D 26 + 5	Adam J 6 + 11	McLaughlin S 25 + 5	Gonet S 7	McPake J 3 + 8	Black C 1	McLeod D 1	Gilbride A 1	Fulton M 1	McLean K 1	Graham B — + 1	*Match No.*
1	2	3	4	5	6^{3}	7	8	9^{1}	10	11^{2}	12	13	14											1
1	2	3	4	5	6	7	8		10	11	9^{1}	12												2
1	2	3^{1}	4	5	6^{3}	7	8	13	10	11	9^{2}	12		14										3
1	2		4	5	6■	7	8	12^{2}	10	11	9^{1}	3■	13											4
1	2	3^{1}	4	5		7	8	9^{2}	10	11	12			6	13									5
1	2	3	4	5	6^{2}	7	8	9	10^{1}	11^{3}	13		14		12									6
1	2	3	4	5■	6^{3}	7	8	9^{2}	10^{1}	11	13		14		12									7
1	2	3^{3}	4		6^{2}	7	8	9	10^{1}	11	12	14	5		13									8
1	2	3	4	5	6	7	8^{3}	9^{2}	10^{1}	11	12		14		13									9
1	2	3	4^{1}	5	9^{2}	7	8		12	11	13		6		10									10
1	2	12	14	5	6	7	8	9^{1}	10^{3}	11	13		3^{2}		4									11
1	2	3^{1}	4	5	13	7	8^{3}		12	11	9^{2}		6	14	10									12
1	2	3	4		10^{1}	7	8^{2}	14	9	11^{3}	12		5	13	6									13
1	2	3	4		10^{1}	7	8	13	9^{2}	11	12		5		6									14
1	2	3	4		10^{2}	7	8^{1}	14	9^{3}	11	13		5	12	6									15
1	2	3	4		10^{2}	7^{3}	8^{1}	13	9	11	12		5	14	6									16
	2	3	4	5	12	7		9^{1}		11	13		6	8^{2}	10	1								17
	2^{3}	3^{2}	4	5	8	7	13	9^{1}		11	12		6	14	10	1								18
	2	3^{1}	4	5	8^{2}	7	13	14	9^{3}	11	12		6		10	1								19
	2	13	4	5	8^{1}	7	3	14	9^{3}	11^{2}	12		6		10	1								20
	2		4	5^{3}	8	7	12	14	9	11	13		3		6^{2}	1	10^{1}							21
	2	6	4	5	8^{3}	7	13		9^{2}	11	14		3		10^{1}	1	12							22
1	2	6^{1}	4^{2}	5		7	8	14	9^{3}	11	13		3	12			10							23
1	2		4	5	8^{3}	7	6		9	11^{2}	14		3	13	10^{1}		12							24
1	2		4^{2}	5	8^{1}	7	6		9	11	14		3	13	10^{3}		12							25
1	2	4^{1}	13	5	14	7	8		9^{2}	11	12			3	6		10^{3}							26
1	2		4	5■	8^{1}	7^{3}	6		9^{2}	11	13	14	3		10		12							27
1	2		4		8^{1}	7	6		9	11	12	13	3	5^{2}	10									28
1	2	12	4		8^{2}	7	6		9	11	13		3	5^{1}	10									29
1	2	13	4	5	8^{2}	7^{3}	6		9	11	12		3	14	10^{1}									30
1	2		4	5	13	7	6		9^{1}	11^{2}	8^{3}	14	3		10		12							31
1		2^{2}	4	5	13	7	6^{1}		9	11	8		3		10		12							32
1	2		4		9^{1}	7	6			11	8^{2}	5	3	13	10		12							33
1	2	8	4	14	13	7	6^{1}		12	11^{2}	9	5^{3}	3		10									34
1	2	8	4	5	12	7	13		9^{1}	11	10^{2}		3		6									35
	4				13		6		9^{1}			8		10		1	12	2	3	5	7^{2}	11^{3}	14	36

MOTHERWELL Premier League

Year Formed: 1886. *Ground & Address:* Fir Park Stadium, Motherwell ML1 2QN. *Telephone:* 01698 333333. *Fax:* 01698 338001. *Website:* www.motherwellfc.co.uk
Ground Capacity: all seated: 13,742. *Size of Pitch:* 110yd × 75yd.
Chairman: Willian H. Dickie. *Secretary:* Stewart Robertson.
Manager: Maurice Malpas. *Assistant Manager:* Paul Hegarty. *Physios:* John Porteous, Peter Salila.
Managers since 1975: Ian St. John, Willie McLean, Rodger Hynd, Ally MacLeod, David Hay, Jock Wallace, Bobby Watson, Tommy McLean, Alex McLeish, Harri Kampman, Billy Davies, Eric Black, Terry Butcher.
Club Nickname(s): The Well. *Previous Grounds:* Roman Road, Dalziel Park.
Record Attendance: 35,632 v Rangers, Scottish Cup 4th rd replay, 12 Mar 1952.
Record Transfer Fee received: £1,750,000 for Phil O'Donnell to Celtic (September 1994).
Record Transfer Fee paid: £500,000 for John Spencer from Everton (Jan 1999).
Record Victory: 12-1 v Dundee U, Division II, 23 Jan 1954.
Record Defeat: 0-8 v Aberdeen, Premier Division, 26 Mar 1979.
Most Capped Player: Tommy Coyne, 13, Republic of Ireland.
Most League Appearances: 626: Bobby Ferrier, 1918-37.
Most League Goals in Season (Individual): 52: Willie McFadyen, Division I, 1931-32.
Most Goals Overall (Individual): 283: Hugh Ferguson, 1916-25.

MOTHERWELL 2005–06 LEAGUE RECORD

Match No.	Date	Venue	Opponents	Result	H/T Score	Lg. Pos.	Goalscorers	Attendance
1	Jul 30	H	Celtic	D 4-4	1-3	—	Kerr 20, Hamilton 57, McDonald Scott 59, Kinniburgh 84	9903
2	Aug 6	H	Dunfermline Ath	W 1-0	0-0	x	Hamilton 89	4649
3	13	A	Kilmarnock	L 1-4	1-2	8	Clarkson 41	5035
4	20	H	Dundee U	L 4-5	2-1	8	McCormack 5, McDonald Scott 11, Fitzpatrick 50, Hamilton 56	4706
5	27	A	Hearts	L 1-2	0-1	9	Foran (pen) 75	16,213
6	Sept 10	A	Inverness CT	W 2-1	0-1	8	McDonald Scott 63, Kinniburgh 69	4018
7	17	H	Falkirk	W 5-0	2-0	6	Hamilton 31, Foran 2 41, 46, Fagan 57, McDonald Scott 63	5625
8	24	H	Hibernian	L 1-3	0-1	7	Foran (pen) 81	6461
9	Oct 1	A	Aberdeen	D 2-2	0-0	7	Clarkson 2 62, 67	11,448
10	15	H	Livingston	W 1-0	1-0	6	Foran 20	4507
11	22	A	Rangers	L 0-2	0-1	6		49,215
12	26	A	Celtic	L 0-5	0-3	—		56,575
13	29	A	Dunfermline Ath	W 3-0	0-0	6	Kerr 57, Corrigan 62, Hamilton 79	4421
14	Nov 5	H	Kilmarnock	D 2-2	1-1	6	McDonald Scott 23, Kerr 53	5107
15	19	A	Dundee U	D 1-1	0-0	6	McDonald Scott 71	6305
16	26	H	Hearts	D 1-1	1-0	7	McLean 40	8131
17	Dec 3	H	Inverness CT	L 0-2	0-0	8		4103
18	10	A	Falkirk	W 1-0	0-0	7	Hamilton 58	4972
19	17	A	Hibernian	L 1-2	1-1	8	McDonald Scott 17	11,926
20	26	H	Aberdeen	W 3-1	2-0	7	McDonald Scott 2 8, 26, McCormack 53	6555
21	31	A	Livingston	W 2-1	1-1	6	Foran 30, McBride 89	3931
22	Jan 14	H	Rangers	L 0-1	0-0	7		10,689
23	22	H	Celtic	L 1-3	1-1	7	Hamilton 41	11,503
24	28	A	Dunfermline Ath	D 1-1	0-1	7	Hamilton 52	4847
25	Feb 8	A	Kilmarnock	L 0-2	0-1	—		5169
26	11	H	Dundee U	W 2-0	1-0	8	Foran 2 26, 56	5257
27	18	A	Hearts	L 0-3	0-2	8		16,976
28	Mar 4	A	Inverness CT	W 1-0	0-0	8	Foran (pen) 51	3183
29	11	H	Falkirk	W 3-1	1-0	7	McDonald Scott 2 30, 47, Foran 52	8179
30	18	H	Hibernian	D 2-2	1-0	8	O'Donnell 40, Craigan 90	6724
31	25	A	Aberdeen	D 2-2	1-2	8	McLean 45, Foran (pen) 47	10,212
32	Apr 1	H	Livingston	W 2-1	1-0	7	Hamilton 40, McLean 89	4458
33	8	A	Rangers	L 0-1	0-1	7		49,481
34	15	H	Inverness CT	L 0-1	0-1	8		3438
35	22	A	Falkirk	D 1-1	0-1	8	O'Donnell 58	4437
36	29	H	Dunfermline Ath	L 2-3	1-2	8	Paterson 11, Craigan 65	3621
37	May 3	A	Livingston	W 1-0	0-0	—	Clarkson 74	2081
38	6	H	Dundee U	D 1-1	0-0	8	Hamilton 59	5269

Final League Position: 8

Honours
League Champions: Division I 1931-32. First Division 1981-82, 1984-85. Division II 1953-54, 1968-69; *Runners-up:* Premier Division 1994-95. Division I 1926-27, 1929-30, 1932-33, 1933-34. Division II 1894-95, 1902-03. *Scottish Cup:* 1952, 1991; *Runners-up:* 1931, 1933, 1939, 1951.
League Cup Winners: 1950-51. *Runners-up:* 1954-55, 2004-05. *Scottish Summer Cup:* 1944, 1965.

Club colours: Shirt: Amber with claret hoop and trimmings. Shorts: Amber. Stockings: Amber with claret trim.

European: *Cup Winners' Cup:* 2 matches (1991-92). *UEFA Cup:* 6 matches (1994-95, 1995-96).

Goalscorers: *League* (55): Foran 11 (4 pens), McDonald Scott 11, Hamilton 10, Clarkson 4, Kerr 3, McLean 3, Craigan 2, Kinniburgh 2, McCormack 2, O'Donnell 2, Corrigan 1, Fagan 1, Fitzpatrick 1, McBride 1, Paterson 1.
Scottish Cup (0).
CIS Cup (6): Clarkson 1, Foran 1, Hamilton 1, Kerr 1, McDonald Scott 1 (pen), Smith D 1.

Marshall G 1	Quinn P 15 + 3	Kinniburgh W 17 + 4	Hammell S 32 + 1	Craigan S 36	Paterson J 10 + 9	O'Donnell P 23 + 6	Leitch S 1	McCormack A 24	Hamilton J 30 + 4	McDonald Scott 31 + 4	Kerr B 32 + 4	Fagan S 11 + 5	Wright K — + 1	Smith G 30	Clarkson D 12 + 18	Smith A 3 + 4	Foran R 29 + 3	Meldrum C 7 + 1	Keogh D — + 1	Fitzpatrick M 1 + 8	McLean B 27 + 2	Smith D — + 1	McDonald Steven — + 1	Corrigan M 27 + 2	McBride K 15 + 6	Coakley A — + 1	McGarry S 2 + 7	Thermeus A — + 1	Reynolds M 1	Donnelly R 1 + 1	*Match No.*
1	2	3	4	5	6	7	8^{1}	9^{2}	10	11^{3}	12	13	14																		1
	2	3	4	5	6^{2}	7		9	10		8^{3}	14		1	11^{1}	12	13														2
	2	3	4	5	6	7		9^{1}	10^{2}	13	8			1	11^{3}	14	12														3
	2	3^{2}	4	5	6^{1}	7		9	10	11	8					14		1	12	13^{3}											4
	2	3	4	5		7^{1}			10	11^{2}	8	6^{3}		1	13	9	12			14											5
	2^{1}	3	4	5	13	7			10	11	6			1	14	9^{3}	8^{2}				12										6
	2	3	4	5					10^{1}	11	6	7		1	12	9^{2}	8^{3}				13	14									7
		3	4	5		7				10	8	6^{1}		1	11^{2}	12	9				2		13								8
	12	3^{1}	4	5	13	7				10	8	6		1	11		9^{2}				2										9
		3	4	5	14	7			13	10^{2}	8	6^{1}		1	11^{3}		9				2			12							10
		3	4	5	7^{1}				13	10	8	6		1	11^{2}		9			12				2							11
	12	3	4^{1}	5					10	11	8	7		1	13		9^{2}			14	6^{3}			2							12
	4	3^{1}		5		7^{2}			10^{3}	11	8	12		1	14		9			13	6			2							13
	4			5		7^{1}			10	11^{2}	8	6		1	13		9			12	3			2							14
	4			5				7	10	11^{1}	8	6		1	12		9				3			2							15
	4	14		5				7^{3}	10	11^{1}	8	6		1	12		9^{2}			13	3			2							16
		13	4	5^{2}				7	10^{1}	11	8	6^{3}		1	12		9				3			2	14						17
	6		4	5		13		7^{2}	10	12	8	14		1	11^{1}						3			2	9^{3}						18
	6		4	5		12		7	10	11^{2}	8			1	13						3			2	9^{1}						19
			4	5		7		6^{1}	10^{3}	11^{2}	8			1	13		9				3			2	12	14					20
			4	5		7			10^{1}	11	8			1	12		9				3			2	6						21
		3	4	5		7		6^{2}	10^{1}	11	8			1			9			13				2	12						22
		3	4	5				6	10	11	8			1			9							2	7						23
			4	5				6	10	11^{1}	8						9	1			3			2	7		12				24
			4	5		13		6	10^{1}	11^{2}	8			1			9				3			2	7^{3}		14	12■			25
			4	5		12		6^{2}	10	11^{3}	8	13		1			9				3			2	7^{1}		14				26
			4	5		13		6	10^{3}	11^{1}	8				14		9	1			3			2	7^{2}		12				27
			4	5	14	12		6		10^{2}	8				11		9^{3}	1			3			2	7^{1}		13				28
			4	5	14	8^{3}		6	10	11^{2}	12				13		9	1			3			2	7^{1}						29
	12		4	5	14	9^{2}		6	13	11	8						10	1			3			2^{1}	7^{3}						30
		13	4	5	14	9		6		11^{1}	8				12		10	1			3^{2}			2	7^{3}						31
			4	5	12	8		6	10^{2}	11				1	13		9				3			2	7^{1}						32
		3^{2}		5	9	8		6^{3}	12	11	14			1	13		10							2	7^{1}		4				33
		14	4	5	7^{2}	8		6■	10^{1}	11	12			1	13		9^{3}				3			2							34
			4	5	12	8			10^{2}	13	7			1	11^{3}		9				3			2	6^{1}		14				35
			4	5	6	8			10	13^{3}	7			1	11^{2}		9^{1}				3			2	12		14				36
	2^{2}		12		6				10^{1}		8			1	11					4	3			13	14		9		5^{3}	7	37
	5	9^{2}	4		7	8		6	10					1^{6}	11			15			3			2^{1}	12					13	38

PARTICK THISTLE First Division

Year Formed: 1876. *Ground & Address:* Firhill Stadium, 80 Firhill Rd, Glasgow G20 7AL. *Telephone:* 0141 579 1971. *Fax:* 0141 945 1525. *E-mail:* mail@ptfc.co.uk. *Website:* www.ptfc.co.uk
Ground Capacity: total: 13,141, seated: 10,921. *Size of Pitch:* 105yd × 68yd.
Chairman: Brown McMaster. *Secretary:* Antonia Kerr. *Commercial Manager:* Michael Max.
Manager: Dick Campbell. *Coach:* Jimmy Bone. *Physio:* George Hannah.
Managers since 1975: R. Auld, P. Cormack, B. Rooney, R. Auld, D. Johnstone, W. Lamont, S. Clark, J. Lambie, M. MacLeod, J. McVeigh, T. Bryce, J. Lambie, G. Collins, G. Britton & D. Whyte.
Club Nickname(s): The Jags. *Previous Grounds:* Jordanvale Park; Muirpark; Inchview; Meadowside Park.
Record Attendance: 49,838 v Rangers, Division I, 18 Feb 1922. *Ground Record:* 54,728, Scotland v Ireland, 25 Feb 1928.
Record Transfer Fee received: £200,000 for Mo Johnston to Watford.
Record Transfer Fee paid: £85,000 for Andy Murdoch from Celtic (Feb 1991).
Record Victory: 16-0 v Royal Albert, Scottish Cup 1st rd, 17 Jan 1931.
Record Defeat: 0-10 v Queen's Park, Scottish Cup, 3 Dec 1881.
Most Capped Player: Alan Rough, 51 (53), Scotland.
Most League Appearances: 410: Alan Rough, 1969-82.
Most League Goals in Season (Individual): 41: Alex Hair, Division I, 1926-27.

PARTICK THISTLE 2005–06 LEAGUE RECORD

Match No.	Date	Venue	Opponents	Result		H/T Score	Lg. Pos.	Goalscorers	Attendance
1	Aug 6	H	Stirling A	D	0-0	0-0	—		2830
2	13	A	Peterhead	D	1-1	1-0	5	Snowdon 29	1010
3	20	H	Dumbarton	W	3-2	1-2	4	Roberts 2 26, 62, Santala 69	2485
4	27	H	Raith R	L	1-3	1-1	6	Brady 26	2376
5	Sept 10	A	Ayr U	D	2-2	1-2	6	Santala 2 24, 75	2282
6	17	A	Gretna	D	2-2	0-1	7	Santala 50, Kilgannon (pen) 89	1920
7	24	H	Forfar Ath	W	1-0	0-0	5	Roberts 55	2003
8	Oct 1	A	Alloa Ath	W	6-1	2-0	3	Dorrans 23, McCulloch 31, Gibson J 58, Santala 2 76, 77, Gibson W 79	1347
9	15	H	Morton	W	2-0	2-0	3	Santala 29, McCulloch 45	4354
10	22	A	Stirling A	W	2-1	0-0	3	McCulloch 59, Brady 72	1634
11	25	H	Peterhead	L	1-3	0-2	—	Dorrans 85	1689
12	29	H	Ayr U	W	1-0	1-0	2	Santala 45	2478
13	Nov 5	A	Raith R	D	1-1	1-0	3	Brown (og) 5	2039
14	12	H	Gretna	D	3-3	0-1	3	McConalogue 81, Gibson W 85, Dorrans 86	3158
15	26	A	Forfar Ath	W	3-2	3-0	3	Roberts 2 (1 pen) 24 (p), 38, Dorrans 44	726
16	Dec 3	A	Morton	L	1-2	1-1	3	McConalogue 16	4214
17	17	H	Alloa Ath	W	4-3	1-2	3	McConalogue 45, Gibson W 61, McCulloch 81, Dorrans 85	1868
18	26	H	Stirling A	L	0-3	0-1	—		2472
19	31	A	Dumbarton	W	2-1	2-1	3	Santala 27, McCulloch (pen) 39	1581
20	Jan 2	H	Raith R	W	1-0	1-0	—	McConalogue 34	2118
21	14	A	Ayr U	W	2-1	0-1	3	McCulloch 54, Roberts 65	1886
22	21	A	Gretna	L	1-6	0-2	3	McCulloch 81	2109
23	28	H	Forfar Ath	W	1-0	0-0	3	Strachan 66	2048
24	Feb 11	H	Morton	D	1-1	1-0	3	Gibson W 34	3999
25	18	A	Peterhead	L	1-2	0-1	3	Ritchie 57	810
26	28	A	Alloa Ath	L	1-2	1-2	—	McConalogue 37	675
27	Mar 11	H	Ayr U	D	2-2	1-0	4	Roberts 18, Gibson W 47	2347
28	14	H	Dumbarton	W	2-1	1-0	—	Roberts 25, McConalogue 63	1537
29	18	H	Gretna	L	0-2	0-1	4		2447
30	21	A	Raith R	W	2-1	0-0	—	Hodge 48, Gibson J 90	1112
31	25	A	Forfar Ath	D	0-0	0-0	3		631
32	Apr 1	H	Alloa Ath	L	2-3	1-1	4	McCulloch 28, Roberts (pen) 68	1920
33	8	A	Morton	L	0-1	0-0	4		3025
34	15	A	Stirling A	W	2-1	0-1	4	Smyth 46, Craig 80	1729
35	22	H	Peterhead	L	0-1	0-0	4		2382
36	29	A	Dumbarton	W	3-2	0-2	4	McConalogue 2 55, 87, Roberts 69	1257

Final League Position: 4

Honours
League Champions: First Division 1975-76, 2001-02. Division II 1896-97, 1899-1900, 1970-71; Second Division 2000-01;
Runners-up: First Division 1991-92. Division II 1901-02.
Scottish Cup Winners: 1921; *Runners-up:* 1930; *Semi-finals:* 2002.
League Cup Winners: 1971-72; *Runners-up:* 1953-54, 1956-57, 1958-59.
Bell's League Challenge: Quarter-finals 2004-05.

European: *Fairs Cup:* 4 matches (1963-64). *UEFA Cup:* 2 matches (1972-73). *Intertoto Cup:* 4 matches 1995-96.

Club colours: Shirt: Red and yellow halves with black sleeves. Shorts: Black. Stockings: Black.

Goalscorers: *League* (57): Roberts 10 (2 pens), Santala 9, McConologue 8, McCulloch 8 (1 pen), Dorrans 5, Gibson W 5, Brady 2, Gibson J 2, Craig 1, Hodge 1, Kilgannon 1 (pen), Ritchie 1, Smyth 1, Snowdon 1, Strachan 1, own goal 1.
Scottish Cup (13): Roberts 7, Gillies 1, McConologue 1, McCulloch 1, Ritchie 1, Santala 1, Smyth 1.
CIS Cup (1): Gillies 1.
Challenge Cup (6): McConologue 2, Gibson A 1, Kilgannon 1, Roberts 1, Santala 1.
Play-Offs (7): Roberts 4, Gibson B 2, McCulloch 1.

Arthur K 24	Murray G 36	Snowdon W 11 + 9	Brady D 30 + 1	Smyth M 26	McCulloch S 27 + 2	Nicholas S 6 + 16	Gillies R 27 + 4	McConalogue S 23 + 8	Gibson J 25 + 1	Kilgannon S 19 + 8	Gibson A 1 + 3	Santala J 14 + 2	Fleming D 2	Noble S —	Roberts M 28 + 1	Gibson W 21 + 8	McGoldrick J — + 2	Strachan A 9 + 17	Dorrans G 13 + 2	Craig D 14 + 4	Stewart C 12	Ritchie P 9 + 2	Dodds W 2	Hodge A 9 + 2	Boyd S 7	Pronevych D 1 + 2	Quitongo J — + 2	*Match No.*
1	2	3	4	5	6	7	8	9^{2}	10^{1}	11	12	13																1
1	2	3	10	5		7	8^{1}	9^{2}	13	11	12	4	6															2
1	2	3	4^{2}			12	8	9^{3}	7	11		5	6^{1}		10	13	14											3
1	2	3	7	5	6	9^{3}	8^{2}	14		11^{1}	12	4			10			13										4
1	2		6	5	3■	13	8	9^{1}		11	7^{2}	4			10				12									5
1	2	3^{2}	4	5		13	8^{1}		7	11		9			10				12	6								6
	2			5	12	14	8	13	4	11^{1}		9^{2}			10	3^{3}			7	6	1							7
	2		6^{1}	5	3	14	8	13	7	11		4^{3}			10	12			9^{2}		1							8
	2		6	5	3	14	8	13	7	11^{3}		4^{2}			10^{1}	12			9		1							9
	2		6	5	3	14	8^{1}	9^{2}	4	11					10	12		13	7^{3}		1							10
	2		6	5^{2}	3		8	12	7^{3}	11		4^{1}			10	14			9	13	1							11
	2		6	5	3	14	8	12	7	11^{1}		4^{2}			10	13			9^{3}		1							12
	2		6	5	3		8	12	7	11^{2}		4^{1}			10			13	9		1							13
	2		6	5	3		8	12	7	11^{3}		4^{1}			10^{2}	13		14	9		1							14
	2	13	6	5			8^{1}	11^{2}	7■	12					10	4		14	9^{3}	3	1							15
	2	12	4	5	6^{2}		8	9		11		13				7		14	10^{3}	3^{1}	1							16
	2		4	5	3	13	8^{2}	10		11		9^{1}				6		12	7^{3}	14	1							17
	2	6	4	5	3		8	10		11^{1}						7		12	9		1							18
1	2	13	4	5	3^{2}		12	10^{3}	7			9				8		14	11^{1}	6								19
1	2	14	4^{1}	5	3		11^{3}	10	7	12						8		13		6		9^{2}						20
1	2	5	4		3^{2}	14	8	10^{3}		13					12	7		11^{1}		6		9						21
1	2	13		5	3		8^{2}		7						10	4		14		6^{1}		9	11^{3}	12				22
1	2		4^{1}		3		13		7						10	8		12		6		9	11^{2}	5				23
1	2			6			14	8^{1}	7	12					10	4		11^{3}		13		9		5^{2}	3			24
1	2	12	6^{3}	5^{1}			14	8	7	13					10^{2}	4		11				9			3			25
1	2		14					8	7						10^{3}	4		11^{2}		6		12		3	5	9^{1}	13	26
1	2	13	4		3			9^{3}	7	12					10	8		11^{1}				14		5^{2}	6			27
1	2		4		3	13	8^{2}	11	7						10^{1}	6		12				9^{3}			5	14		28
1	2		4^{1}		13	14	8	11^{2}	7						10	6		12				9^{3}		3	5			29
1	2	12			3	11	8		7	14					10	4^{3}		13				9^{2}		6	5^{1}			30
1	2	5			3	11^{2}	8^{1}		7■	12					10	4		9		13				6				31
1	2	5	7		3	11^{2}	8^{1}	9							10	4		12						6			13	32
1	2	14	4	5^{3}	3	13	8^{2}	9							10	7		12		6				11^{1}				33
1	2	4	8	5^{2}	3	14		9^{1}		11					10		12	7^{3}		6						13		34
1	2	4^{1}	8	5^{3}	3	13		9^{2}		11					10	12		7		6				14				35
1	2		4	5	3	12		9	7						10	8		11^{1}		6								36

PETERHEAD — Second Division

Year Formed: 1891. *Ground and Address:* Balmoor Stadium, Lord Catto Park, Peterhead AB42 1EU.
Telephone: 01779 478256. *Fax:* 01779 490682. *E-mail:* shona@peterheadfc.org.uk. *Website:* www.peterheadfc.org.uk.
Ground Capacity: 3250, seated 1000.
Chairman: Rodger Morrison. *General Manager:* Dave Watson. *Secretary:* George Moore.
Manager: Iain Stewart. *Assistant Manager:* Paul Mathers. *Coach:* Shaun McSkimming. *Physio:* Sandy Rennie.
Managers since 1975: C. Grant, D. Darcy, I. Taylor, J. Harper, D. Smith, J. Hamilton, G. Adams, J. Guyan, I. Wilson, D. Watson, R. Brown, D. Watson, I. Wilson.
Club Nickname(s): Blue Toon. *Previous Ground:* Recreation Park.
Record Attendance: 6310 friendly v Celtic, 1948.
Record Victory: 17-0 v Fort William, 1998-99 (in Highland League).
Record Defeat: 0-13 v Aberdeen, Scottish Cup, 1923-24.
Most League Appearances: 135, Martin Johnston, 2000-05.
Most League Goals in Season (Individual): 21, Iain Stewart, 2002-03; 21, S. Michie, 2004-05.
Most Goals Overall (Individual): 58, Iain Stewart, 2000-05.

PETERHEAD 2005–06 LEAGUE RECORD

Match No.	Date	Venue	Opponents	Result		H/T Score	Lg. Pos.	Goalscorers	Attendance
1	Aug 6	A	Alloa Ath	L	1-4	0-3	—	Bavidge [79]	507
2	13	H	Partick Th	D	1-1	0-1	8	Youngson [90]	1010
3	20	A	Ayr U	D	1-1	1-0	7	Cameron [44]	1283
4	27	A	Forfar Ath	L	2-3	1-3	9	Wood [43], Michie [88]	504
5	Sept 10	H	Dumbarton	W	1-0	0-0	7	Shand [63]	494
6	17	A	Stirling A	W	3-1	1-1	6	Shand [20], Cameron [56], Good [63]	509
7	24	H	Raith R	L	0-1	0-1	6		740
8	Oct 1	A	Morton	L	1-2	1-1	7	Linn (pen) [11]	2719
9	8	H	Ayr U	D	3-3	1-0	7	Buchan [20], Linn 2 [55, 85]	490
10	15	H	Gretna	L	0-2	0-1	8		742
11	22	H	Alloa Ath	W	3-1	0-1	7	Linn 2 [48, 51], Gibson [62]	422
12	25	A	Partick Th	W	3-1	2-0	—	Linn [15], Perry [30], Buchan [89]	1689
13	29	A	Dumbarton	L	0-1	0-0	6		771
14	Nov 5	H	Forfar Ath	W	4-2	3-1	4	Hegarty [3], Linn (pen) [23], Wood [41], Buchan [86]	549
15	12	H	Stirling A	L	1-3	0-3	4	Sharp [86]	547
16	26	A	Raith R	W	2-0	1-0	4	Linn [26], Wood [85]	1202
17	Dec 3	A	Gretna	L	0-3	0-2	4		1060
18	17	H	Morton	W	1-0	0-0	4	Michie [77]	880
19	24	A	Alloa Ath	W	2-0	0-0	—	Michie 2 (1 pen) [62 (p), 89]	644
20	Jan 2	A	Forfar Ath	W	1-0	1-0	—	Gibson [27]	685
21	14	H	Dumbarton	W	3-1	1-0	4	Gibson [35], Wood [55], Sharp [68]	705
22	21	A	Stirling A	L	1-2	0-1	4	Buchan [85]	735
23	28	H	Raith R	D	0-0	0-0	4		702
24	Feb 4	A	Morton	D	0-0	0-0	4		2693
25	11	H	Gretna	L	1-3	1-1	4	Nicol [35]	749
26	18	H	Partick Th	W	2-1	1-0	4	Nicol [12], Wood [68]	810
27	25	A	Ayr U	W	2-1	1-1	4	Linn [16], Sharp [61]	849
28	Mar 11	A	Dumbarton	W	3-2	1-2	3	Gibson [40], Linn 2 [70, 86]	626
29	18	H	Stirling A	W	2-0	1-0	3	Nicol [16], Sharp [70]	661
30	21	H	Forfar Ath	D	1-1	0-1	—	Bavidge [67]	463
31	25	A	Raith R	L	0-1	0-1	4		1098
32	Apr 1	H	Morton	W	2-1	0-1	3	Sharp [60], Bavidge [65]	815
33	8	A	Gretna	L	1-3	1-1	3	Cameron [29]	1049
34	15	H	Alloa Ath	W	3-0	1-0	3	Cameron (pen) [6], Wood [52], Bavidge [65]	752
35	22	A	Partick Th	W	1-0	0-0	3	Buchan [50]	2382
36	29	H	Ayr U	L	1-2	0-0	3	Gibson [89]	703

Final League Position: 3

Honours
Third Division Runners up: 2004-05.
Scottish Cup: Quarter-finals 2001.
Highland League Champions: winners 5 times.
Scottish Qualifying Cup (North): winners 6 times.
North of Scotland Cup: winners 5 times.
Aberdeenshire Cup: winners: 20 times.

Club colours: Shirt: Royal blue with white; Shorts: Royal blue; Stockings: Royal blue tops with white hoops.

Goalscorers: *League* (53): Linn 11 (2 pens), Wood 6, Buchan 5, Gibson 5, Sharp 5, Bavidge 4, Cameron 4 (1 pen), Michie 4 (1 pen), Nicol 3, Shand 2, Good 1, Hegarty 1, Perry 1, Youngson 1.
Scottish Cup (3): Linn 1, Sharp 1, Wood 1.
CIS Cup (3): Linn 1, Michie 1 (pen), Youngson 1.
Challenge Cup (1): Bavidge 1.
Play-Offs (4): Bavidge 1, Bridges 1, Cameron 1, Sharp 1.

Mathers P 34	Tully C 28 + 3	Good I 17 + 1	Raeside R 6 + 1	Perry M 36	Gibson K 29 + 1	Sharp G 24 + 11	Buchan J 35 + 1	Bavidge M 8 + 10	Linn R 29 + 7	Hagen D 13 + 2	Stewart G 1	Cameron D 28 + 6	Youngson A 17 + 13	Wood M 30 + 4	Shand C 20 + 2	Hegarty C 17 + 2	Duncan R — + 2	Michie S 8 + 18	McCafferty J 2	Robertson C — + 2	Nicol K 12	Stephen N 2 + 1	*Match No.*
1	2	3	4	5	6	7	8	9	10	11													1
1	2	3	4^{3}	5		12	8	9	10	7^{2}	6^{1}	11	13	14									2
1	2		4	5	6	7^{2}	8	9	10^{1}			11	13	12	3^{3}	14							3
1	2		4^{2}	5	6	12	8		9			11	3^{1}	10		7^{3}	13	14					4
1		3		5	6^{1}	10^{3}	8		14	4^{2}		11	13	7	2	12		9					5
1		3		5	6	12	8		13	4^{1}		11		10	2	7		9^{2}					6
1	12	3		5	6^{1}	7	8		13	4		11		10	2			9^{2}					7
1		3	4^{3}	5		13	8		10	11^{1}		6	12	9	2	7^{2}		14					8
1	14	3	4^{3}	5			8		9	11^{1}		6	12	10	2^{2}	7		13					9
	4	3		5		12	8	13	9	11^{1}		6^{3}	14	10^{2}	2	7			1				10
1	4	3		5	6^{3}	14	8	10^{1}	9			13	11^{2}	12	2	7							11
1	4	3		5	6	12	8		9^{3}			13	11^{1}	10	2	7^{2}		14					12
1	4	3		5	6	12	8		9				11	10	2^{1}	7^{2}		13					13
1	4	3		5	6	13	8		9^{2}			12	11^{1}	10^{3}		2	14	7					14
1	4	3		5	6	13	8		9			12	11^{1}	10		2		7^{2}					15
1	4	3		5	6	7	8		9^{2}			12	11^{1}	10		2		13					16
1	4	3	14	5	6^{1}	7	8		9^{2}			12	11	10^{3}		2[illegible]		13					17
1	4			5	6	7^{2}	8		9	11		3	2^{1}	10				12		13			18
1	4			5	6	7	8		9^{1}	11		3	2^{2}	10				12		13			19
1	4			5	6	7	8		9^{1}	11		3	12	10		2							20
1	4			5	6	7^{1}	8		9	11		3^{2}	13	10		2		12					21
1	4			5	6	7^{3}	8		9	11^{1}		3	14	10	12	2^{2}		13					22
1	4			5	6	7	8	13	9			3	12	10^{2}	2			11^{1}					23
1	4			5	6	7	8	12	9			3		10^{2}	2^{1}			13			11		24
1	4^{3}			5	6	7	8	10^{1}	12			3	14	13	2			9^{2}			11		25
1	4			5	6	7	8	12	9^{2}			3		10	2^{1}			13			11		26
1	4			5	6	7	8	12	9^{2}			3	2^{1}	10				13			11		27
1	4			5	6	7	8		9			3	2	10^{1}				12			11		28
1	4			5	6	7^{2}	8	13	9			3	2^{1}	10^{3}	12			14			11		29
1	4			5	6	7	8	12	9			3	2^{1}	10^{2}				13			11		30
1	4			5	6^{2}	7	8	12	9			3	13	10^{1}	2^{3}			14			11		31
1		13		5	6^{2}	7	8	12	9^{1}			3	4	10	2^{3}						11	14	32
1		3		5		7	8	9^{1}	12	13		6		10^{2}	2						11	4	33
1	4	3^{1}		5		7	8	9^{2}	13	12		6^{3}	14	10	2						11		34
1	4			5	13	14	8	9	12			6	3^{3}	10	2	7^{1}					11^{2}		35
	12			5^{1}	6	11	13	14	9			3^{2}	8		2	7^{3}		10	1			4	36

QUEEN OF THE SOUTH First Division

Year Formed: 1919. *Ground & Address:* Palmerston Park, Dumfries DG2 9BA. *Telephone and Fax:* 01387 254853. *E-mail:* admin@qosfc.com. *Website:* www.qosfc.co.uk
Ground Capacity: total: 7412, seated: 3509. *Size of Pitch:* 112yd × 73yd.
Chairman: David Rae. *Vice-Chairman:* Thomas Harkness. *Commercial Manager:* Margaret Heuchan. *Physio/Business Development Manager:* Kenny Crichton.
Manager: Ian McCall. *First Team Coach:* Stevie Morrison.
Managers since 1975: M. Jackson, W. Hunter, B. Little, G. Herd, H. Hood, A. Busby, R. Clark, M. Jackson, D. Wilson, W. McLaren, F. McGarvey, A. MacLeod, D. Frye, W. McLaren, M. Shanks, R. Alexander, J. Connolly, Ian Scott.
Club Nickname(s): The Doonhamers. *Previous Grounds:* None.
Record Attendance: 26,552 v Hearts, Scottish Cup 3rd rd, 23 Feb 1952.
Record Transfer Fee received: £250,000 for Andy Thomson to Southend U (1994).
Record Transfer Fee paid: £30,000 for Jim Butter from Alloa Athletic (1995).
Record Victory: 11-1 v Stranraer, Scottish Cup 1st rd, 16 Jan 1932.
Record Defeat: 2-10 v Dundee, Division I, 1 Dec 1962.
Most Capped Player: Billy Houliston, 3, Scotland.
Most League Appearances: 731: Allan Ball, 1963-82.
Most League Goals in Season (Individual): 37: Jimmy Gray, Division II, 1927-28.

QUEEN OF THE SOUTH 2005–06 LEAGUE RECORD

Match No.	Date	Venue	Opponents	Result		H/T Score	Lg. Pos.	Goalscorers	Attendance
1	Aug 6	A	St Johnstone	L	0-4	0-2	—		2401
2	13	H	Brechin C	D	0-0	0-0	9		1480
3	20	A	Dundee	L	1-3	1-2	10	Lyle 39	3915
4	27	A	Clyde	L	0-1	0-1	10		1152
5	Sept 10	H	St Mirren	L	0-1	0-1	10		1688
6	17	A	Stranraer	D	0-0	0-0	10		1032
7	24	H	Hamilton A	L	1-2	0-1	10	O'Neill (pen) 63	1380
8	Oct 1	A	Ross Co	D	1-1	1-0	10	O'Neill 32	2203
9	15	H	Airdrie U	W	1-0	0-0	9	Burns 90	1638
10	22	H	St Johnstone	L	1-3	1-2	9	McLaughlin 25	1370
11	25	A	Brechin C	D	1-1	0-1	—	Hamilton (og) 60	503
12	29	A	St Mirren	L	0-2	0-1	9		3361
13	Nov 5	H	Clyde	L	1-2	0-0	9	McNiven 88	1436
14	12	H	Stranraer	D	1-1	1-1	9	O'Neill 28	2086
15	19	A	Hamilton A	L	2-5	1-3	9	O'Neill 2 (1 pen) 45 (p), 58	1475
16	26	H	Ross Co	L	2-3	1-1	9	O'Neill 9, Lyle 49	1276
17	Dec 3	A	Airdrie U	L	0-4	0-2	9		1242
18	10	A	St Johnstone	L	1-2	0-1	9	Wood 90	2091
19	26	H	St Mirren	D	0-0	0-0	—		2421
20	31	A	Clyde	L	0-3	0-2	9		1101
21	Jan 2	A	Stranraer	L	0-1	0-0	—		1548
22	14	H	Hamilton A	D	1-1	1-1	9	Lovell 37	1813
23	21	A	Ross Co	L	1-3	0-1	9	Thomson A 75	2152
24	28	H	Airdrie U	W	2-0	1-0	9	O'Neill (pen) 9, Burns 75	1650
25	Feb 11	A	Dundee	W	3-2	1-1	9	Thomson A 34, Mullen 67, Wood 80	3365
26	18	H	Brechin C	D	0-0	0-0	9		1844
27	28	H	Dundee	D	0-0	0-0	—		1566
28	Mar 4	H	Clyde	W	2-1	0-0	9	O'Neill (pen) 53, Thomson A 87	1750
29	11	A	St Mirren	L	0-1	0-0	9		3436
30	18	H	Stranraer	W	1-0	0-0	8	Bowey 48	2790
31	25	A	Hamilton A	W	2-0	1-0	9	Burns 36, O'Neill 58	1409
32	Apr 1	H	Ross Co	D	0-0	0-0	8		1630
33	8	A	Airdrie U	D	1-1	0-1	8	Weir 58	1262
34	15	H	St Johnstone	W	3-2	2-2	8	O'Neill (pen) 18, Weir 29, James (og) 75	2036
35	22	A	Brechin C	D	1-1	1-0	8	O'Connor 22	809
36	29	H	Dundee	L	1-3	0-3	8	Burns 50	2624

Final League Position: 8

Most Goals in Season: 41: Jimmy Rutherford, 1931-32.
Most Goals Overall (Individual): 250: Jim Patterson, 1949-63.

Honours
League Champions: Division II 1950-51. Second Division 2001-02. *Runners-up:* Division II 1932-33, 1961-62, 1974-75. Second Division 1980-81, 1985-86.
Scottish Cup: semi-finals 1949-50.
League Cup: semi-finals 1950-51, 1960-61.
B&Q Cup: semi-finals 1991-92. *League Challenge Cup Winners:* 2002-03; *Runners-up:* 1997-98.

Club colours: Shirt: Royal blue with white sleeves. Shorts: White with blue piping. Stockings: Royal blue.

Goalscorers: *League* (31): O'Neill 10 (5 pens), Burns 4, Thompson A 3, Lyle 2, Weir 2, Wood 2, Bowey 1, Lovell 1, McLaughlin 1, McNiven 1, Mullen 1, O'Connor 1, own goals 2.
Scottish Cup (1): Lyle 1.
CIS Cup (1): McNiven 1.
Challenge Cup (5): Burns 1, Lovell 1, Lyle 1, McLaughlin 1, McNiven 1.

Barnard R 16 + 1	Wood G 20 + 7	English T 14 + 2	McColligan B 10 + 1	Reid B 11 + 1	Carr C 6 + 5	Lovell S 26	Paton E 32 + 3	McNiven D 8 + 8	McLaughlin B 9 + 4	Payne S 6 + 3	Thomson J 33 + 1	Lyle D 18 + 10	Burns P 28 + 3	Bowey S 24 + 5	Gibson W 25 + 6	Hill S 7 + 1	O'Neill J 25 + 2	Scott C 20	Ardjogon T — + 1	Robertson S 2 + 5	Pronevych D — + 2	Dillon S 4 + 3	Weir G 15	McStay R 14	Mullen M 1 + 9	Thomson A 8 + 5	Aitken A 12 + 1	O'Connor S 2 + 2	*Match No.*
1	2■	3	4^{3}	5^{1}	6	7	8	9	10^{2}	11	12	13	14																1
1		3	4	5		7	2	9	12	11^{2}	6	10^{1}		8	13														2
1	2	3	4^{2}	5	12	7	11^{3}	9^{1}			6	10■	14	8	13														3
1	10	3	4	5		7	2	9		11	6			8															4
1	3		4					12	9		6	10^{1}	2	8	11	5	7												5
	4		11			7^{1}	12		9		6		2	8	3	5	10	1											6
	12	14	10^{1}	5			13	9	11		6		2^{2}	8	3	4^{3}	7	1											7
	9■	3	14	5^{1}			2	13		4	6		7	8■	11^{3}		10	1	12^{2}										8
		3					2	12	9^{1}	7^{2}	6	13	4		11^{3}	5	10	1		8	14								9
		3					2	12	9	14	6		4	8	11^{2}	5	10^{1}	1		7^{3}	13								10
		3					2	9	11		6	10	4	8^{1}	12	5	7	1											11
	11				3		2^{1}	9	12		6	10	4	8^{2}	13	5	7	1											12
	5		4^{2}		3		2	12	8^{1}		6	10	7^{3}	13	11		9	1		14									13
	4		11		5		2^{1}	9		12	6		7	8	3		10	1											14
	4		5■		12		2	13		7^{2}	6	9^{3}	3	8	11^{1}		10	1		14									15
	5				7	4	2	12			6	9^{1}	11	8	3		10	1											16
	5				7^{2}	4	2^{3}	12		13	6	9^{1}	11	8	3	14	10	1											17
15	5	3			13	4^{1}	2				6	9^{2}	7	8	11		10	1^{0}		12									18
1	4■	3		5	12	9^{2}	2				6^{1}	13	7	8	11		10												19
1		3		5^{2}	13	9	2		12		6	4^{1}	7^{3}	8	11		10			14									20
1	3	13		5		4^{1}	2		12		6	9	7	8	11^{2}		10												21
1		11		5^{2}		4	2				6	8	7				13			14		3	9^{1}	10^{3}	12				22
1				5^{2}		4	2				6	8^{3}	7	13	12							3	11^{1}	10	14	9			23
						5	2				6		7	12	11		4	1				3	8^{2}	10^{1}	13	9^{3}	14		24
	14					4	2^{3}		3^{2}		6	12	7		11			1					8^{1}	10	13	9	5		25
	14					4	2				6	13	7		11		3^{2}	1					8^{1}	10	12	9^{3}	5		26
	12					4	2				6	13	7	3	11			1					8^{3}	10^{2}	14	9^{1}	5		27
						4	2				6	9^{3}	7	12	11		3	1					8^{2}	10^{1}	14	13	5		28
	9					4	2^{1}				6		13	3	11		7	1				12	8^{3}	10^{2}	14		5		29
	14	3^{1}				4	2				6	13	7	11				1				12	8^{2}	10		9^{3}	5		30
1	12					4	2				6^{1}	9	7	11			13					3	8^{3}	10^{2}		14	5		31
1	13					4	2				6	7^{2}		11	3		10						8^{3}		14	9^{1}	5	12	32
1	2					4	13				6	9^{1}		11^{2}	3		10						8^{3}	7		14	5	12	33
1	3^{1}					4	2				6	13		12	11		7						8	10^{3}		14	5	9^{2}	34
1	3					4	2^{1}					14	7		11		6					12	8^{2}	10		13	5	9^{3}	35
1	6^{2}	3		13		4	2					14	7		12								8	10	9^{3}	11^{1}	5		36

QUEEN'S PARK Third Division

Year Formed: 1867. *Ground & Address:* Hampden Park, Mount Florida, Glasgow G42 9BA. *Telephone:* 0141 632 1275. *Fax:* 0141 636 1612. *E-mail:* secretary@queensparkfc.co.uk. *Website:* queensparkfc.co.uk
Ground Capacity: all seated: 52,000. *Size of Pitch:* 115yd × 75yd.
President: Garry Templeman. *Secretary:* Alistair Mackay. *Treasurer:* David Gordon.
Coach: Billy Stark. *Physio:* R. C. Findlay.
Coaches since 1975: D. McParland, J. Gilroy, E. Hunter, H. McCann, J. McCormack, K. Brannigan.
Club Nickname(s): The Spiders. *Previous Grounds:* 1st Hampden (Recreation Ground); (Titwood Park was used as an interim measure between 1st & 2nd Hampdens); 2nd Hampden (Cathkin); 3rd Hampden.
Record Attendance: 95,772 v Rangers, Scottish Cup, 18 Jan 1930.
Record for Ground: 149,547 Scotland v England, 1937.
Record Transfer Fee received: Not applicable due to amateur status.
Record Transfer Fee paid: Not applicable due to amateur status.
Record Victory: 16-0 v St. Peters, Scottish Cup 1st rd, 29 Aug 1885.
Record Defeat: 0-9 v Motherwell, Division I, 26 Apr 1930.
Most Capped Player: Walter Arnott, 14, Scotland.
Most League Appearances: 532: Ross Caven.
Most League Goals in Season (Individual): 30: William Martin, Division I, 1937-38.
Most Goals Overall (Individual): 163: J. B. McAlpine.

QUEEN'S PARK 2005–06 LEAGUE RECORD

Match No.	Date	Venue	Opponents	Result		H/T Score	Lg. Pos.	Goalscorers	Attendance
1	Aug 6	H	Stenhousemuir	L	1-2	1-1	—	Kettlewell 33	487
2	13	A	Cowdenbeath	W	2-0	1-0	5	Weir 23, Reilly (pen) 66	280
3	20	H	Berwick R	L	1-3	0-2	7	Kettlewell 74	431
4	27	H	Albion R	W	3-1	0-1	3	Ferry 2 46, 49, Felvus 90	503
5	Sept 10	A	Elgin C	D	2-2	0-2	4	Weatherston 80, Reilly (pen) 85	371
6	17	H	East Stirling	W	3-0	2-0	3	Harvey 17, Ferry 18, Weir 82	454
7	24	A	East Fife	L	0-1	0-1	5		567
8	Oct 1	H	Arbroath	D	2-2	0-0	5	Proctor 61, Trouten (pen) 63	446
9	15	A	Montrose	W	1-0	0-0	5	Weatherston 55	310
10	22	A	Stenhousemuir	L	0-1	0-0	5		444
11	25	H	Cowdenbeath	L	0-2	0-1	—		391
12	29	H	Elgin C	W	3-0	2-0	5	Reilly (pen) 31, Trouten 35, Ferry 68	424
13	Nov 5	A	Albion R	D	1-1	1-0	5	Weatherston 26	447
14	26	H	East Fife	W	2-0	0-0	4	Murray 55, Trouten 65	399
15	Dec 3	H	Montrose	L	0-3	0-0	5		351
16	13	A	East Stirling	W	4-0	2-0	—	Mackay (og) 8, Reilly (pen) 37, Felvus 53, Ferry 78	266
17	26	H	Stenhousemuir	W	2-0	1-0	—	Weatherston 6, Reilly (pen) 64	543
18	Jan 2	H	Albion R	D	1-1	0-1	—	Ferry 76	576
19	14	A	Elgin C	W	2-1	0-1	4	Quinn 2 61, 78	442
20	21	H	East Stirling	W	3-1	1-0	4	Trouten 16, Dunlop 69, Proctor 89	514
21	28	A	East Fife	W	1-0	0-0	4	Reilly (pen) 89	479
22	Feb 4	H	Arbroath	D	0-0	0-0	4		572
23	11	A	Montrose	D	0-0	0-0	4		385
24	18	A	Cowdenbeath	L	0-6	0-2	4		315
25	25	H	Berwick R	L	0-1	0-1	4		537
26	Mar 7	A	Berwick R	W	2-1	0-0	—	Weatherston 46, Clark 83	249
27	11	H	Elgin C	D	3-3	1-1	4	Kettlewell 5, Ferry 48, Sinclair 90	465
28	14	A	Arbroath	D	1-1	0-1	—	Weatherston 56	520
29	18	A	East Stirling	D	0-0	0-0	4		330
30	21	A	Albion R	L	0-1	0-0	—		331
31	25	H	East Fife	D	1-1	0-0	4	Clark 50	403
32	Apr 1	A	Arbroath	L	0-1	0-0	5		724
33	8	H	Montrose	D	2-2	1-0	5	Harvey 26, Felvus 51	369
34	15	A	Stenhousemuir	W	2-1	0-0	5	Canning 2 71, 90	552
35	22	H	Cowdenbeath	D	2-2	2-1	6	Ferry 13, Weatherston 29	1247
36	29	A	Berwick R	L	0-1	0-0	6		1015

Final League Position: 6

Honours
League Champions: Division II 1922-23. B Division 1955-56. Second Division 1980-81. Third Division 1999-2000.
Scottish Cup Winners: 1874, 1875, 1876, 1880, 1881, 1882, 1884, 1886, 1890, 1893; *Runners-up:* 1892, 1900.
League Cup: —.
FA Cup runners-up: 1884, 1885.

Club colours: Shirt: White and black hoops. Shorts: White. Stockings: Black with white tops.

Goalscorers: *League* (47): Ferry 8, Weatherston 7, Reilly 6 (6 pens), Trouten 4 (1 pen), Felvus 3, Kettlewell 3, Canning 2, Clark 2, Harvey 2, Proctor 2, Quinn 2, Weir 2, Dunlop 1, Murray 1, Sinclair 1, own goal 1.
Scottish Cup (4): Weatherston 2, Felvus 1, Trouten 1.
CIS Cup (3): Ferry 1, Harvey 1, Weatherston 1.
Challenge Cup (0).

Crawford D 34	Clark R 28 + 6	Molloy S 10 + 7	Reilly S 31	Sinclair R 24	Harvey P 18 + 6	Kettlewell S 29 + 2	Quinn A 26 + 4	Bowers R 3 + 4	Weatherston D 29 + 4	Ferry M 35 + 1	Weir J 3 + 10	Whelan J 5 + 10	Felvus B 11 + 13	McGinty A 8 + 1	Trouten A 23 + 1	Dunlop M 28	Proctor K 7 + 5	Paton P 22	Murray T 9 + 7	Agostini D 7 + 1	Cairney P 1 + 1	Canning S 3 + 3	Cairns M 2 + 1	Match No.
1	2	3	4	5	6	7^{1}	8	9^{2}	10^{3}	11	12	13	14											1
1	2	3	4	5	6		8		10	11	7	9^{1}	12											2
1	2	3^{3}	4	5	6	13	8	12	10	11	7^{2}		9^{1}	14										3
1	2	13	4	5^{2}	6	7	8	9^{3}		11	10^{1}	14	12	3										4
1	2	3^{2}	4			7	8	9^{1}	12	11	13	10		5	6									5
1	2		4		6^{3}	7^{2}	8	12	10	11	14	9^{1}		5	13	3								6
1	2	14		4		7	8^{2}		10	11	13	9^{1}	12	5	6	3^{3}								7
1	2			4		7	8		10	11^{2}	13		12	5	6	3	9^{1}							8
1	2			4	6^{1}	7	8		9^{2}	11	13	14		5	10^{3}	3	12							9
1	2	6	4			7	8		9	11				5	10	3								10
1	2^{1}	13	4			7	8^{3}		9	11	12	14		5	6	3	10^{2}							11
1			4	5		7	8^{2}		9^{3}	11	13	14			6	3	12	2	10^{1}					12
1	2		4	5		7^{1}	8		9	11	12				6	3			10					13
1	2	14	4			7		12	9^{2}	11^{3}		13			6	3		8	10^{1}	5				14
1	2		4			7			9	11^{2}		13			6	3	12	8^{3}	10^{1}	5	14			15
1	2^{1}	14	4			7	12		9^{2}	11^{3}			10		6	3		8	13	5				16
1	2		4		13	7^{1}	12		9^{3}	11			10^{2}			6	3		8	14	5			17
1	2	14	4		13	7	12		9	11			10^{2}		6	3^{3}		8^{1}		5				18
1	13	12	4			7^{2}	8		9	11			10^{3}		6	3		2	14	5^{1}				19
1	8	5	4			7		13	9^{2}	11			10^{1}		6	3	12	2						20
1	14	6^{2}	4	5	13	7			9^{3}	11			10^{1}		2	3	12	8						21
1	13		4	5	12	7^{1}	8		9^{2}	11					6	3■	10	2						22
1	12	3	4	5	10^{1}	7^{2}	8			11					6		9	2	13					23
1	12	3		5	10	7	8			11^{2}					6^{1}		9	2	13	4				24
1		3			10	7^{1}	8		11	12^{3}		4	13		6		9^{2}	2	14	5				25
1	12		4	5	10	7	8^{1}		9^{2}	11			13		6	3		2						26
1	8^{2}		4	5	10	7			9	11			13		6^{1}	3		2	12					27
1	6		4	5	12	7	8		9^{2}	11			13			3		2	10^{1}					28
1	6		4	5	10^{3}	7	14		9^{2}	11			13		8^{1}	3		2	12					29
1	6^{2}		4	5	13	7	8		12	11			9			3		2	10^{1}					30
1	6		4	5	10^{3}	12	8^{1}		9^{2}	11		14	7			3		2				13		31
1	6		4	5	10^{2}	7^{1}	8		12	11			9			3		2				13		32
1^{6}	6		4	5	10^{2}		8		7	11^{1}	12		9			3		2				13	15	33
	6		4	5	10^{3}		8		12	11		14	13		7^{2}	3		2^{1}				9	1	34
	2		4	5	10^{1}		8		7	11			12			3			6			9	1	35
1	6		4■	5	10				7^{2}	11		12	13			3		2■	8^{1}			9		36

RAITH ROVERS — Second Division

Year Formed: 1883. *Ground & Address:* Stark's Park, Pratt St, Kirkcaldy KY1 1SA. *Telephone:* 01592 263514. *Fax:* 01592 642833. *E-mail:* office@raithroversfc.com. *Website:* www.raithroversfc.com
Ground Capacity: all seated: 10,104. *Size of Pitch:* 113yd × 70yd.
Chairman: David Sinton. *Office Manager/Club Secretary:* Bob Mullen.
Manager: Gordon Dalziel. *Coach:* Shaun Dennis.
Managers since 1975: R. Paton, A. Matthew, W. McLean, G. Wallace, R. Wilson, F. Connor, J. Nicholl, J. Thomson, T. McLean, I. Munro, J. Nicholl, J. McVeigh, P. Hetherston, J. Scott, A. Calderon, C. Anelka.
Club Nickname: Rovers. *Previous Grounds:* Robbie's Park.
Record Attendance: 31,306 v Hearts, Scottish Cup 2nd rd, 7 Feb 1953.
Record Transfer Fee received: £900,000 for S. McAnespie to Bolton Wanderers (Sept 1995).
Record Transfer Fee paid: £225,000 for Paul Harvey from Airdrieonians (1996).
Record Victory: 10-1 v Coldstream, Scottish Cup 2nd rd, 13 Feb 1954.
Record Defeat: 2-11 v Morton, Division II, 18 Mar 1936.
Most Capped Player: David Morris, 6, Scotland.
Most League Appearances: 430: Willie McNaught.
Most League Goals in Season (Individual): 38: Norman Haywood, Division II, 1937-38.
Most Goals Overall (Individual): 154: Gordon Dalziel (League), 1987-94.

RAITH ROVERS 2005–06 LEAGUE RECORD

Match No.	*Date*	*Venue*	*Opponents*	*Result*	*H/T Score*	*Lg. Pos.*	*Goalscorers*	*Attendance*
1	Aug 6	A	Morton	L 0-2	0-1	—		3322
2	13	H	Gretna	L 1-3	0-2	9	Crilly ^{50}	2124
3	20	A	Alloa Ath	W 2-1	2-1	6	Lumsden ^{14}, Annand (pen) ^{42}	931
4	27	A	Partick Th	W 3-1	1-1	5	McManus ^{8}, McLeod ^{75}, Fairbairn ^{76}	2376
5	Sept 10	H	Stirling A	W 5-2	1-1	4	McManus 2 $^{7, 81}$, Crilly ^{54}, Ellis ^{63}, Jablonski ^{71}	1997
6	17	H	Ayr U	D 3-3	0-2	4	Crabbe ^{49}, McManus ^{63}, Jablonski ^{73}	1846
7	24	A	Peterhead	W 1-0	1-0	3	McManus ^{8}	740
8	Oct 1	H	Forfar Ath	L 0-2	0-1	4		1809
9	15	A	Dumbarton	W 2-1	1-0	4	Ellis ^{4}, McLeod ^{65}	852
10	22	H	Morton	L 1-2	0-1	4	Harding (og) ^{47}	2446
11	25	A	Gretna	L 1-5	1-3	—	Ellis ^{33}	1074
12	29	A	Stirling A	L 0-1	0-1	5		868
13	Nov 5	H	Partick Th	D 1-1	0-1	5	Fairbairn ^{48}	2039
14	22	A	Ayr U	L 1-2	1-1	—	Annand ^{36}	930
15	26	H	Peterhead	L 0-2	0-1	6		1202
16	Dec 3	H	Dumbarton	W 3-2	2-2	5	Jablonski ^{25}, McManus ^{32}, Davidson ^{77}	1060
17	26	A	Morton	L 0-2	0-0	—		2818
18	31	H	Alloa Ath	W 4-2	2-2	7	McManus 3 (1 pen) $^{3, 55, 69 (p)}$, Jablonski ^{19}	1637
19	Jan 2	A	Partick Th	L 0-1	0-1	—		2118
20	14	H	Stirling A	L 2-3	1-1	7	McNally (og) ^{40}, McManus (pen) ^{54}	2236
21	21	H	Ayr U	D 1-1	1-0	7	Crilly ^{23}	1467
22	28	A	Peterhead	D 0-0	0-0	7		702
23	Feb 4	H	Forfar Ath	W 1-0	0-0	6	Sellars (og) ^{67}	1409
24	11	A	Dumbarton	W 1-0	0-0	6	McManus ^{48}	822
25	18	H	Gretna	L 0-1	0-1	6		1745
26	25	A	Alloa Ath	D 1-1	1-0	6	Davidson ^{39}	749
27	Mar 11	A	Stirling A	D 2-2	1-2	6	Crilly ^{24}, McManus ^{70}	1079
28	18	A	Ayr U	D 0-0	0-0	6		1010
29	21	H	Partick Th	L 1-2	0-0	—	Lumsden ^{85}	1112
30	25	H	Peterhead	W 1-0	1-0	6	Adam ^{16}	1098
31	28	A	Forfar Ath	L 2-5	1-4	—	Campbell ^{45}, McManus ^{62}	737
32	Apr 1	A	Forfar Ath	W 2-0	1-0	6	McManus ^{41}, Jablonski ^{79}	581
33	8	H	Dumbarton	D 0-0	0-0	6		1055
34	15	H	Morton	D 1-1	1-0	6	McManus ^{20}	1395
35	22	A	Gretna	L 1-2	0-1	6	Silvestro ^{53}	2201
36	29	H	Alloa Ath	L 0-1	0-0	7		1560

Final League Position: 7

Honours
League Champions: First Division: 1992-93, 1994-95. Division II 1907-08, 1909-10 (shared), 1937-38, 1948-49; *Runners-up:* Division II 1908-09, 1926-27, 1966-67. Second Division 1975-76, 1977-78, 1986-87.
Scottish Cup Runners-up: 1913. *League Cup Winners: (Coca-Cola Cup):* 1994-95. *Runners-up:* 1948-49.

European: *UEFA Cup:* 6 matches (1995-96).

Club colours: Shirt: Navy blue with white sleeves. Shorts: White with navy and red trim. Stockings: Navy blue with white turnover.

Goalscorers: *League* (44): McManus 15 (2 pens), Jablonski 5, Crilly 4, Ellis 3, Annand 2, Davidson 2, Fairbairn 2, Lumsden 2, McLeod 2, Adam 1, Campbell 1, Crabbe 1, Silvestro 1, own goals 3.
Scottish Cup (0).
CIS Cup (3): Annand 1, Jablonski 1, McManus 1.
Challenge Cup (6) : McManus 3, Crabbe 1, own goals 2.

Brown A 35	Lyle W 28 + 2	Ellis L 33 + 2	Silvestro C 31 + 2	Lumsden T 36	McLeod C 25 + 4	Jablonski N 18 + 11	Ferguson D 7 + 1	Crabbe S 17 + 6	McManus P 36	Crilly M 28	Annand E 7 + 8	Fairbairn B 24 + 12	Jaconelli E 1 + 11	Davidson I 25 + 4	Hilland P 5 + 2	Tulloch S 1 + 3	Wilson S 5 + 1	Leiper C — + 1	Bagan D 1 + 9	Stirling J 1 + 1	Clarke P 2 + 5	Hall S 1	Campbell M 14	Bonar S 10 + 2	Adam S 5 + 3	*Match No.*
1	2	3	4	5	6	7^{2}	8	9^{1}	10^{3}	11	12	13	14													1
1	2	3	4	5	6	11^{1}	8		10	7	9^{2}	12	13													2
1	2	3	4	5	6	11	8^{1}		10^{3}	7	9^{2}	12	14	13												3
1	2	11	4	5	6			9^{1}	10^{2}	7	13	12		8	3											4
1	2	11	4^{1}	5	6	8			10^{2}	7	13	9		12	3											5
1	2	11	8^{1}	5	6	12		9^{2}	10		14	7^{3}		4	3	13										6
1	2	3	8^{1}	5	6	12			10^{3}		9	7	13	11			4^{2}	14								7
1	2	3	8^{3}	5	6		14		10^{2}		9	7	13	11	12		4^{1}									8
1	2	3	12	5	6		8^{3}		10^{2}	7^{1}	13	9		11			4		14							9
1	2	3		5	6		8	9^{3}	10	7	14	13		11^{2}	12		4^{1}									10
1	2^{3}	11	4	5	6	14	8^{1}	9■	10	7		12			3^{2}		13									11
1	2	11	13	5	6	4^{3}			10	9	12	7		8^{3}	3^{2}				14							12
1	2	3	4^{3}	5	6	12	8	13	10^{2}	11^{1}	9	7							14							13
1	2^{1}	3	4	5	6	11		8	10		9	7							12							14
1	2^{1}	3	4	5	6	11^{3}		8	10		9^{2}	7	14	13					12							15
1	2	11	4	5	6^{2}	10		9^{3}	8		14	7		12		3^{1}			13							16
1	2■	3	4	5	12■	11		10^{1}	8	7^{2}		9	13	6												17
1		3	2	5		11^{1}		10^{2}	8	9		7	4^{3}	6		14			13	12						18
1	2^{3}	3	4	5	14			13	8	9		7		6					10^{2}	11^{1}	12					19
1		3	2	5	6	11		10^{2}	8	9^{1}		7	12	4^{3}					14		13					20
1		3	2	5		7^{2}		10^{1}	8	9		11		4			6		13		12					21
	2	3	4	5	6	7^{1}		13	8	11		12		10							9^{2}	1				22
1	13	3	4	6		14		9	8^{1}	11		12		2									5	7^{2}	10^{3}	23
1	2	3	4	6		9^{2}		14	8^{3}	7^{1}		13		10									5	12	11	24
1	2^{2}	3	4	6	12	14			8	7		9^{3}		10									5	13	11^{1}	25
1	2^{1}	11	4	6	3	9^{3}		14	8^{2}	10		12		7									5		13	26
1	2	11^{1}	4	6	3			9^{2}	8	7		12		10							13		5			27
1	2	13	4^{2}	6	3	12			8	9		11^{1}		10									5	7		28
1	2	11^{2}		6	3	12			8			7		10							9^{1}		5	4	13	29
1	2	13		6	3	12			8	9		7^{3}		10							14		5	4^{1}	11^{2}	30
1	2^{1}		4	6	3^{2}				8	9		12	14	10		13							5	7	11^{3}	31
1		3	4	6		9^{1}			8	11		7	12	10									5	2		32
1		3	4	6		9^{1}		12	8	11		7		10									5	2		33
1	2	3	4	6		12		9^{1}	8	11		7											5	10		34
1	13	11	4	6	3	10^{3}		9^{2}	8			7^{1}	12										5	2	14	35
1		3	4	6	13	12		9^{1}	8	11^{2}		7		10									5	2		36

RANGERS Premier League

Year Formed: 1873. *Ground & Address:* Ibrox Stadium, 150 Edmiston Drive, Glasgow G51 2XD.
Telephone: 0870 600 1972. *Fax:* 0870 600 1978. *Website:* www.rangers.co.uk
Ground Capacity: all seated: 50,444. *Size of Pitch:* 114.5m × 81.5m.
Executive Chairman: David Murray. *Chief Executive:* Martin Bain. *Head of Football Administration:* Andrew Dickson.
Manager: Paul Le Guen. *Assistant Manager:* Yves Colleu. *Physio:* David Henderson.
Managers since 1975: Jock Wallace, John Greig, Jock Wallace, Graeme Souness, Walter Smith, Dick Advocaat, Alex McLeish.
Club Nickname(s): The Gers. *Previous Grounds:* Flesher's Haugh, Burnbank, Kinning Park, Old Ibrox.
Record Attendance: 118,567 v Celtic, Division I, 2 Jan 1939.
Record Transfer Fee received: £8,500,000 for G. Van Bronckhorst to Arsenal (2001).
Record Transfer Fee paid: £12 million for Tore Andre Flo from Chelsea (November 2000).
Record Victory: 14-2 v Blairgowrie, Scottish Cup 1st rd, 20 Jan, 1934. *Record Defeat:* 2-10 v Airdrieonians; 1886.
Most Capped Player: Ally McCoist, 60, Scotland. *Most League Appearances:* 496: John Greig, 1962-78.
Most League Goals in Season (Individual): 44: Sam English, Division I, 1931-32.
Most Goals Overall (Individual): 355: Ally McCoist; 1985-98.

Honours
League Champions: (51 times) Division I 1890-91 (shared), 1898-99, 1899-1900, 1900-01, 1901-02, 1910-11, 1911-12, 1912-13, 1917-18, 1919-20, 1920-21, 1922-23, 1923-24, 1924-25, 1926-27, 1927-28, 1928-29, 1929-30, 1930-31, 1932-33, 1933-34, 1934-35, 1936-37, 1938-39, 1946-47, 1948-49, 1949-50, 1952-53, 1955-56, 1956-57, 1958-59, 1960-61, 1962-63, 1963-64, 1974-75. Premier Division: 1975-76, 1977-78, 1986-87, 1988-89, 1989-90, 1990-91, 1991-92, 1992-93, 1993-94, 1994-95, 1995-96, 1996-97, 1998-99, 1999-2000, 2002-03, 2004-05; *Runners-up:* 25 times.

RANGERS 2005–06 LEAGUE RECORD

Match No.	Date	Venue	Opponents	Result	H/T Score	Lg. Pos.	Goalscorers	Attendance
1	Jul 31	H	Livingston	W 3-0	1-0	—	Prso [22], Pierre-Fanfan [62], Lovenkrands [90]	49,613
2	Aug 6	A	Inverness CT	W 1-0	0-0	2	Ferguson [59]	7512
3	14	A	Aberdeen	L 2-3	1-2	3	Prso [38], Lovenkrands [48]	18,182
4	20	H	Celtic	W 3-1	1-0	2	Prso [33], Buffel [50], Novo (pen) [87]	49,699
5	27	H	Hibernian	L 0-3	0-0	5		49,754
6	Sept 10	A	Falkirk	D 1-1	1-0	5	Novo (pen) [38]	6500
7	17	H	Kilmarnock	W 3-0	1-0	3	Prso (pen) [8], Ferguson 2 [67, 80]	49,076
8	24	A	Hearts	L 0-1	0-1	5		17,379
9	Oct 1	H	Dunfermline Ath	W 5-1	2-0	3	Buffel [15], Prso [37], Lovenkrands [74], Nieto [75], McCormack [85]	48,374
10	16	A	Dundee U	D 0-0	0-0	4		11,696
11	22	H	Motherwell	W 2-0	1-0	4	Burke [1], Lovenkrands [71]	49,215
12	26	A	Livingston	D 2-2	1-0	—	Ferguson [14], Burke [54]	8081
13	29	H	Inverness CT	D 1-1	0-1	4	Thompson [53]	47,867
14	Nov 5	H	Aberdeen	D 0-0	0-0	4		49,717
15	19	A	Celtic	L 0-3	0-1	4		58,997
16	27	A	Hibernian	L 1-2	0-2	4	Ferguson [59]	16,958
17	Dec 3	H	Falkirk	D 2-2	1-0	5	Buffel [31], Lovenkrands [56]	48,042
18	11	A	Kilmarnock	W 3-2	1-0	4	Lovenkrands 3 [16, 62, 72]	12,426
19	17	H	Hearts	W 1-0	1-0	4	Lovenkrands [35]	49,723
20	26	A	Dunfermline Ath	D 3-3	1-2	5	Lovenkrands 2 [22, 64], Burke [70]	9505
21	31	H	Dundee U	W 3-0	0-0	4	Buffel [67], Thompson [82], Lovenkrands [85]	49,141
22	Jan 14	A	Motherwell	W 1-0	0-0	4	Lovenkrands [54]	10,689
23	21	H	Livingston	W 4-1	1-0	4	Boyd 2 [7, 55], Prso 2 [89, 90]	49,211
24	29	A	Inverness CT	W 3-2	2-1	3	Boyd 2 [6, 52], Andrews [26]	7380
25	Feb 8	A	Aberdeen	L 0-2	0-2	—		17,087
26	12	H	Celtic	L 0-1	0-1	4		49,788
27	18	H	Hibernian	W 2-0	1-0	3	Boyd [40], Ferguson [73]	49,720
28	Mar 4	A	Falkirk	W 2-1	0-0	3	Boyd [57], Twaddle (og) [70]	6303
29	11	H	Kilmarnock	W 4-0	1-0	3	Boyd [12], Rodriguez [70], Prso (pen) [84], Lovenkrands [87]	49,442
30	19	A	Hearts	D 1-1	0-1	3	Buffel [64]	17,040
31	25	H	Dunfermline Ath	W 1-0	0-0	3	Kyrgiakos [70]	49,017
32	Apr 2	A	Dundee U	W 4-1	2-0	3	Prso [28], Boyd 3 [30, 53, 82]	11,213
33	8	H	Motherwell	W 1-0	1-0	3	Boyd [26]	49,481
34	15	H	Aberdeen	D 1-1	0-0	3	Boyd [50]	48,987
35	23	A	Celtic	D 0-0	0-0	3		58,928
36	29	A	Kilmarnock	W 3-1	0-1	3	Andrews 2 [50, 79], Boyd [64]	11,752
37	May 2	A	Hibernian	W 2-1	1-0	—	Boyd 2 [23, 36]	14,773
38	7	H	Hearts	W 2-0	1-0	3	Boyd 2 [36, 72]	49,792

Final League Position: 3

Scottish Cup Winners: (31 times) 1894, 1897, 1898, 1903, 1928, 1930, 1932, 1934, 1935, 1936, 1948, 1949, 1950, 1953, 1960, 1962, 1963, 1964, 1966, 1973, 1976, 1978, 1979, 1981, 1992, 1993, 1996, 1999, 2000, 2002, 2003; *Runners-up:* 17 times.
League Cup Winners: (24 times) 1946-47, 1948-49, 1960-61, 1961-62, 1963-64, 1964-65, 1970-71, 1975-76, 1977-78, 1978-79, 1981-82, 1983-84, 1984-85, 1986-87, 1987-88, 1988-89, 1990-91, 1992-93, 1993-94, 1996-97, 1998-99, 2001-02, 2002-03, 2004-05; *Runners-up:* 6 times.

European: *European Cup:* 127 matches (1956-57, 1957-58, 1959-60 semi-finals, 1961-62, 1963-64, 1964-65, 1975-76, 1976-77, 1978-79, 1987-88, 1989-90, 1990-91, 1991-92, 1992-93 final pool, 1993-94, 1994-95, 1995-96; 1996-97, 1997-98, 1999-2000, 2000-01, 2003-04, 2005-06).
Cup Winners' Cup: 54 matches (1960-61 runners-up, 1962-63, 1966-67 runners-up, 1969-70, 1971-72 winners, 1973-74, 1977-78, 1979-80, 1981-82, 1983-84). *UEFA Cup:* 58 matches (*Fairs Cup:* 1967-68, 1968-69 semi-finals, 1970-71.
UEFA Cup: 1982-83, 1984-85, 1985-86, 1986-87, 1988-89, 1997-98, 1998-99, 1999-2000, 2000-01, 2002-03, 2004-05).

Club colours: Shirt: Royal blue with red and white trim. Shorts: White with red and blue trim. Stockings: Black with red tops.

Goalscorers: *League* (67): Boyd 17, Lovenkrands 14, Prso 9 (2 pens), Ferguson 6, Buffel 5, Andrews 3, Burke 3, Novo 2 (2 pens), Thompson 2, Kyrgiakos 1, McCormack 1, Nieto 1, Pierre-Fanfan 1, Rodriguez 1, own goal 1.
Scottish Cup (5): Boyd 3, Kyrgiakos 1, McCormack 1.
CIS Cup (5): Buffel 2, Nieto 2, Andrews 1.

Waterreus R 36	Ricksen F 20 + 1	Andrews M 21 + 2	Pierre-Fanfan J 7	Murray I 26 + 4	Rae A 5 + 4	Ferguson B 32	Buffel T 25 + 4	Prso D 29 + 3	Novo I 10 + 14	Lovenkrands P 23 + 10	Thompson S 4 + 10	McCormack R 2 + 6	Adam C — + 1	Malcolm R 11 + 3	Rodriguez J 20 + 1	Ball M 2	Ross M — + 1	Kyrgiakos S 28	Namouchi H 6 + 1	Jeffers F 4 + 4	Bernard O 9	Nieto F — + 3	Burke C 25 + 2	Lowing A 1 + 1	Hemdani B 18	Hutton A 17 + 2	Klos S 2	Smith S 16 + 2	Boyd K 15 + 2	Rae G 4 + 4	Ashikodi M — + 1	Match No.
1	2	3	4	5	6	7	8^{2}	9^{1}	10^{3}	11	12	13	14																			1
1	2	3	4	5	6^{2}	7	8	9^{1}	10	11	12			13																		2
1	2■		4	8	13	7		9	10^{2}	11^{3}	12			6^{1}	3	5	14															3
1		3	4^{2}	8	6^{1}	7	9	11	10	12				13	2	5																4
1	2		4	5	6	7	8^{1}	11	10	12	9^{2}	13			3																	5
1	2		4	6		7	9^{1}	11	10	13					3			5	8^{2}	12												6
1	2	14		6		7	13	9	12	11					3			4^{3}	8^{2}	10^{1}	5											7
1	6	3		8		7	13	11	10^{1}						5^{2}			4	9^{3}	12	2	14										8
1	2			6		7^{3}	9^{2}	10		11		12			5			4			3	13	8^{1}	14								9
1	2					7		9		11^{3}		14			5			4■	13	10^{1}	3	12	8^{2}		6							10
1	2	3		12		7		9^{3}		11	14	10^{1}			5						4		8		6^{2}	13						11
1	2	3	4	8^{1}		7		10		11	12										5		9		6							12
1	2	3				7		10		11	12			6							5		9^{1}		8	4						13
	6			12		7		10		11^{2}	9				2			5		14	3		13		8^{1}	4^{3}	1					14
1	2	3		8		7		11^{2}		12	13							5	9	10					6	4^{1}						15
1		3		2	6	7■				14	13	11		12				5^{1}	8	10^{2}			9^{3}			4						16
1	2	3		7			8^{1}			10^{2}	11	13		6				5		12			9			4						17
1	2^{1}	3		9		7	8		13	11^{2}				6				4					10			12		5				18
1		3		6		7	8			11^{2}	12	13		5				4	10^{1}				9					2				19
1		3		6		7	8		12	11^{1}	10			5				4■					9					2				20
1	2	3		6		7	8		10^{1}	11	12												9	5				4				21
1		3		6		7	8^{1}	12	13	11^{2}				5				4					9					2	10			22
1	2	3		6		7	8	13	14	11^{2}				5				4^{1}					9					12	10^{3}			23
1	2	3		7			8	12	13	11				6				4					9^{1}			5			10^{2}			24
1	2	3		6		7	13	9		11				5				4^{1}					8					12	10^{2}			25
1		3				7	8^{3}	11	10^{1}	12				6	13			4^{2}					9			5		2	14			26
1						7	8	11							3			4					9		6^{1}	5		2	10	12		27
1						7		9	11^{2}	13					3			4			6^{1}		12		8	5		2	10			28
1	14			5		7^{3}	9	11	13	12					3			4					8^{2}		6	2			10^{1}			29
1				5		7	9	11^{2}	13	10^{1}					3			4					8		6	2			12			30
						7	9^{1}	11	13	12					3			4					8^{2}		6	2	1	5	10			31
1						7^{1}	9	11	13	8					3			4							6	2		5	10^{2}	12		32
1				14		7	9^{2}	11	12	8^{3}					3			4							6	2		5	10^{1}	13		33
1				12		7	9^{2}	11	13						3			4					8		6^{3}	2^{1}		5	10	14		34
1							9	11	12						3			4					8^{2}		6	2		5	10^{1}	7	13	35
1		12		4	14		9	11^{2}	13						3								8		6	2^{1}		5	10	7^{3}		36
1		3		2^{2}	13		9^{1}	11		12								4					8		6			5	10	7		37
1		3		2	12		13	11		9^{2}								4					8		6			5^{1}	10	7		38

ROSS COUNTY First Division

Year Formed: 1929. *Ground & Address:* Victoria Park, Dingwall IV15 9QW. *Telephone:* 01349 860860. *Fax:* 01349 866277.
E-mail: donnie@rosscountyfootballclub.co.uk. *Website:* www.rosscountyfootballclub.co.uk
Ground Capacity: 6700. *Size of Ground:* 105×68m.
Chairman: Peter Swanson. *Secretary:* Donnie MacBean.
Manager: Scott Leitch. *Director of Football:* George Adams. *Physio:* Douglas Sim.
Managers since 1975: N. Cooper, A. Smith, J. Robertson.
Club Nickname(s): The Staggies.
Record Attendance: 6600, benefit match v Celtic, 31 August 1970.
Record Transfer Fee Received: £200,000 for Neil Tarrant to Aston Villa (April 1999).
Record Transfer Fee Paid: £25,000 for Barry Wilson from Southampton (Oct. 1992).
Record Victory: 11-0 v St Cuthbert Wanderers, Scottish Cup, 11 Dec 1993.
Record Defeat: 1-10 v Inverness Thistle, Highland League.
Most League Appearances: 157: David Mackay, 1995-2001.
Most League Goals in Season: 22: D. Adams, 1996-97.
Most League Goals (Overall): 44: Steven Ferguson, 1996-2002.

ROSS COUNTY 2005–06 LEAGUE RECORD

Match No.	*Date*	*Venue*	*Opponents*	*Result*		*H/T Score*	*Lg. Pos.*	*Goalscorers*	*Attendance*
1	Aug 6	H	Clyde	W	3-1	2-1	—	Rankin [3], Burke [10], Higgins [67]	2208
2	13	A	Airdrie U	W	1-0	0-0	2	McGarry [49]	1164
3	20	H	Hamilton A	D	0-0	0-0	2		2005
4	27	H	Stranraer	W	2-1	1-0	1	Burke [8], Taylor [70]	1962
5	Sept 10	A	St Johnstone	D	1-1	1-1	1	Nuckowski [2]	2172
6	17	H	Brechin C	W	1-0	1-0	1	Burke [22]	2124
7	24	A	Dundee	D	0-0	0-0	1		4025
8	Oct 1	H	Queen of the S	D	1-1	0-1	1	Webb [83]	2203
9	7	H	Airdrie U	D	2-2	2-1	x	Rankin [36], Winters [43]	2004
10	15	A	St Mirren	L	0-2	0-1	2		2314
11	22	A	Clyde	L	0-1	0-1	4		922
12	29	H	St Johnstone	W	2-1	1-0	4	Rankin [5], Rutkiewicz (og) [66]	2557
13	Nov 5	A	Stranraer	W	3-2	1-2	3	Cowie 2 [34, 54], Rankin [82]	434
14	12	A	Brechin C	W	4-1	2-1	2	Canning [35], Rankin [41], Winters [48], Cowie [57]	502
15	19	H	Dundee	W	3-0	2-0	2	Rankin 3 [8, 41, 63]	2862
16	26	A	Queen of the S	W	3-2	1-1	2	Winters [6], McSwegan [84], Rankin [87]	1276
17	Dec 3	H	St Mirren	L	0-4	0-1	2		3393
18	10	H	Clyde	L	0-1	0-1	3		2149
19	17	A	Hamilton A	L	1-2	0-1	5	Higgins [79]	1250
20	26	A	St Johnstone	D	1-1	1-0	—	Higgins [6]	2499
21	Jan 2	H	Brechin C	W	2-0	2-0	—	Rankin 2 [29, 45]	2227
22	14	A	Dundee	D	0-0	0-0	4		3671
23	21	H	Queen of the S	W	3-1	1-0	4	McKinlay [27], Rankin [49], Burke [71]	2152
24	28	A	St Mirren	W	1-0	0-0	3	Higgins [80]	3659
25	Feb 11	H	Hamilton A	W	2-1	1-1	2	Higgins [26], Winters [75]	2151
26	18	A	Airdrie U	W	3-2	2-1	2	Winters [4], Higgins [44], Cowie [59]	1119
27	25	H	Stranraer	D	1-1	1-0	2	Higgins [7]	1975
28	Mar 11	H	St Johnstone	D	2-2	0-1	2	Higgins [70], Winters (pen) [82]	2220
29	18	A	Brechin C	D	3-3	0-1	3	Djebi-Zadi [50], Webb [82], Winters [83]	503
30	21	A	Stranraer	D	2-2	0-1	—	Winters (pen) [50], Higgins [57]	436
31	Apr 1	A	Queen of the S	D	0-0	0-0	3		1630
32	4	H	Dundee	D	0-0	0-0	—		1754
33	8	H	St Mirren	L	0-2	0-1	3		3588
34	15	A	Clyde	L	0-2	0-1	4		813
35	22	H	Airdrie U	L	0-1	0-0	4		2066
36	29	A	Hamilton A	D	0-0	0-0	4		1297

Final League Position: 4

Honours
League Champions: Third Division: 1998-99. *Bell's League Challenge Cup: Runners up:* 2004-05.

Club colours: Shirt: Navy blue with white trim. Shorts: White with navy side panels. Stockings: Navy blue with two white hoops.

Goalscorers: *League* (47): Rankin 12, Higgins 9, Winters 8 (2 pens), Burke 4, Cowie 4, Webb 2, Canning 1, Djebi-Zadi 1, McGarry 1, McKinlay 1, McSwegan 1, Nuckowski 1, Taylor 1, own goal 1.
Scottish Cup (6): Cowie 3, Burke 1, Higgins 1, McKinlay 1.
CIS Cup (5): Higgins 1, McGarry 1, Webb 1, Winters 1, own goal 1.
Challenge Cup (2): Rankin 1, Winters 1.

McCaldon I 10	Macdonald N 8 + 2	Djebi-Zadi L 36	Webb S 27	Canning M 19	Taylor S 4 + 4	Rankin J 36	McCulloch M 31	Burke A 25 + 3	McGarry S 10 + 4	Winters D 18 + 15	Higgins S 19 + 6	Niven D 2 + 1	McKinlay K 14 + 13	Cowan D 21	Nuckowski M 7 + 5	Tiernan F 17 + 3	Garden S 23 + 1	Cowie D 29 + 3	McSwegan G 6 + 10	Lauchlan J 25 + 1	Gunn C — + 8	Malin J 3 + 2	Anderson S 5 + 1	Hooks N 1	Match No.
1	2^{2}	3	4	5	6	7	8	9^{3}	10	11^{1}	12	13	14												1
1		3	4	5	8	7	6	12	10	13	11^{2}			2	9^{1}										2
1		3	4	5		7	6	13	10^{2}	12	11^{1}			2	9	8									3
		3	4	5	8^{2}	7	6	9	10^{3}	11^{1}			12	2	14	13	1								4
		3	4	5		7	8	9^{2}	10^{3}	13				2	11^{1}	6	1	12	14						5
		3	4	5		7	2	9^{3}	10^{1}	14	12				11^{2}	6	1	8	13						6
		3	4	5		7	2	9	10		12				11^{1}	6	1	8							7
		3	4	5		7	2	9	10^{2}	12			13		11^{1}	6^{3}	1	8	14						8
		3	4	5	12	7	2	9^{3}	10^{1}	11			13		14	6	1	8^{2}							9
		3	4	5		7^{1}	8	9	10	11^{2}	13^{3}			2		6	1	14		12					10
1^{G}		3		5	$13^{■}$	7	8	9		11				2		6^{1}	15	12	10^{2}	4					11
		3		5		7	6	9^{3}	12	11^{1}			13	2^{2}		8	1	10	14	4					12
	2	3		5	13	7	8	9^{1}	12	11						6	1	10^{2}		4					13
	2	3		5		7^{3}	8	9^{1}	12	11^{2}			14			6	1	10	13	4					14
	2	3		5		7^{3}	8	9^{2}	13	11^{1}	12		14			6	1	10		4					15
	2	3		5		7	8^{3}	9^{1}		11			13		12	6^{2}	1	10	14	4					16
		3		5^{1}		7	8	9^{3}		11			12	2	13	6^{2}	1	10	14	4					17
		3	5		12	7^{3}	2	8		11			14		13	6^{1}	1	10	9^{2}	4					18
1		3	5		6	7	8	11^{3}		14	12		13	2	9^{1}			10^{2}		4					19
	13	3^{2}	5			7^{1}	6	8^{3}		12	9		11	2			1	10	14	4					20
		3	5			7	6	8		12	9^{1}		11^{2}	2			1	10		4	13				21
		3		5		7	6	8^{1}		13	9^{2}		11	2			1	10		4	12				22
		3		5		7	6	8^{1}		12	9		11	2			1	10		4					23
	12	3	5			7	6	8^{2}		13	9		11	2^{1}			1	10		4					24
	2	3	5			7	6	8^{2}		12	9		11^{1}				1	10	13	4					25
	2	3	5			7	6			8	9^{1}		11				1	10	12	4					26
	2	3	5			7	6			8	9		11^{1}				1	10		4	12				27
		3	5			7	6^{1}			12	9		11	2		13	1^{G}	10	8^{2}	4		15			28
1		3	5			7	6^{1}			11	9		12	2				10	8^{2}	4	13				29
1		3	5			7	6	12		11	9			2				10	8^{1}	4					30
1		3	5			7				11^{2}	9		12	2		13		10	8^{1}	4			6		31
1		3	5			7				12	9^{1}		11	2		8^{2}		10		4	13		6		32
1^{G}		3	5			7	6^{2}	8^{1}		12	9		11	2				10		4		15	13		33
		3	5			7		8^{1}			9		11	2				10		4	12	1	6		34
		3	5			7				8^{1}	9	2	11					10		4	12	1	6		35
		3	5			8					9	2	11			6^{1}		10			12	1	4	7	36

ST JOHNSTONE First Division

Year Formed: 1884. *Ground & Address:* McDiarmid Park, Crieff Road, Perth PH1 2SJ. *Telephone:* 01738 459090. *Fax:* 01738 625 771. *Clubcall:* 0898 121559. *E-mail:* angome@saints.sol.co.uk. *Website:* www.stjohnstonefc.co.uk
Ground Capacity: all seated: 10,673. *Size of Pitch:* 115yd × 75yd.
Chairman: G.S. Brown. *Secretary and Managing Director:* Stewart Duff. *Sales Executive:* Susan Weir.
Manager: Owen Coyle. *Coach:* Jim Weir. *Youth Coach:* Tommy Campbell.
Managers since 1975: J. Stewart, J. Storrie, A. Stuart, A. Rennie, I. Gibson, A. Totten, J. McClelland, P. Sturrock, S. Clark, B. Stark, J. Connolly.
Club Nickname(s): Saints. *Previous Grounds:* Recreation Grounds, Muirton Park.
Record Attendance: (McDiarmid Park): 10,545 v Dundee, Premier Division, 23 May 1999.
Record Transfer Fee received: £1,750,000 for Calum Davidson to Blackburn R (March 1998).
Record Transfer Fee paid: £400,000 for Billy Dodds from Dundee (1994).
Record Victory: 9-0 v Albion R, League Cup, 9 Mar 1946.
Record Defeat: 1-10 v Third Lanark, Scottish Cup, 24 Jan 1903.
Most Capped Player: Nick Dasovic, 26, Canada.
Most League Appearances: 298: Drew Rutherford.
Most League Goals in Season (Individual): 36: Jimmy Benson, Division II, 1931-32.
Most Goals Overall (Individual): 140: John Brogan, 1977-83.

ST JOHNSTONE 2005–06 LEAGUE RECORD

Match No.	*Date*	*Venue*	*Opponents*	*Result*		*H/T Score*	*Lg. Pos.*	*Goalscorers*	*Attendance*
1	Aug 6	H	Queen of the S	W	4-0	2-0	—	Milne 2 [31, 42], Stevenson [50], Campbell [55]	2401
2	13	A	Hamilton A	W	1-0	1-0	1	Dobbie [42]	1877
3	20	H	St Mirren	L	1-2	0-0	3	MacDonald (pen) [65]	3089
4	27	A	Airdrie U	L	1-3	1-1	5	Scotland [23]	1522
5	Sept 10	H	Ross Co	D	1-1	1-1	6	MacDonald [39]	2172
6	17	H	Dundee	D	1-1	1-1	5	Rutkiewicz [13]	5172
7	24	A	Clyde	W	1-0	1-0	5	Milne [33]	1220
8	Oct 1	A	Stranraer	D	1-1	0-0	5	Stevenson [72]	643
9	15	H	Brechin C	W	3-1	1-1	2	Stevenson [5], James [72], Milne [75]	2031
10	22	A	Queen of the S	W	3-1	2-1	4	Milne [5], Sheerin 2 (1 pen) [29, 65 (p)]	1370
11	25	H	Hamilton A	W	5-1	4-0	—	Scotland [27], Stevenson [36], Sheerin 2 (1 pen) [44 (p), 45], Stanik [72]	2233
12	29	A	Ross Co	L	1-2	0-1	3	Scotland [65]	2557
13	Nov 5	H	Airdrie U	W	1-0	1-0	2	Scotland [29]	2412
14	12	A	Dundee	L	1-2	1-1	3	Mann (og) [1]	5383
15	19	H	Clyde	D	0-0	0-0	4		2195
16	26	H	Stranraer	D	1-1	0-1	4	Sheerin [82]	1687
17	Dec 3	A	Brechin C	W	4-1	1-0	3	Scotland 2 [43, 77], Stevenson [53], Sheerin [56]	811
18	10	H	Queen of the S	W	2-1	1-0	2	Scotland [19], Milne [64]	2091
19	17	A	St Mirren	D	0-0	0-0	3		3729
20	26	H	Ross Co	D	1-1	0-1	—	Scotland [58]	2499
21	31	A	Airdrie U	L	1-2	1-2	4	Sheerin (pen) [20]	1616
22	Jan 2	H	Dundee	D	0-0	0-0	—		5170
23	14	A	Clyde	W	3-2	2-0	3	Sheerin (pen) [39], Scotland [42], James [51]	1296
24	21	A	Stranraer	W	2-0	1-0	2	Scotland [18], Mensing [79]	620
25	28	H	Brechin C	W	3-0	2-0	2	Rutkiewicz [23], James [36], Sheerin [66]	2069
26	Feb 11	H	St Mirren	D	0-0	0-0	3		4515
27	18	A	Hamilton A	W	2-1	1-0	3	James [45], Scotland [72]	1576
28	Mar 4	H	Airdrie U	D	2-2	0-1	3	Hardie [61], James [88]	2216
29	11	A	Ross Co	D	2-2	1-0	3	Lauchlan (og) [23], Glennan [89]	2220
30	18	A	Dundee	W	1-0	0-0	2	Jack (og) [53]	4193
31	25	H	Clyde	W	1-0	1-0	2	Mensing [31]	1997
32	Apr 1	H	Stranraer	W	3-2	2-1	2	Scotland 3 [3, 37, 74]	1676
33	8	A	Brechin C	W	2-0	2-0	2	Milne [17], Scotland [20]	876
34	15	A	Queen of the S	L	2-3	2-2	2	James [38], Sheerin [42]	2036
35	22	H	Hamilton A	D	1-1	0-1	2	Mensing [86]	2235
36	29	A	St Mirren	W	1-0	0-0	2	Milne [67]	6726

Final League Position: 2

Honours
League Champions: First Division 1982-83, 1989-90, 1996-97. Division II 1923-24, 1959-60, 1962-63; *Runners-up:* Division II 1931-32. Second Division 1987-88.
Scottish Cup: Semi-finals 1934, 1968, 1989, 1991.
League Cup: Runners-up: 1969-70, 1998-99.
League Challenge Cup: Runners-up: 1996-97.

European: *UEFA Cup:* 10 matches (1971-72, 1999-2000).

Club colours: Shirt: Royal blue with white trim. Shorts: White. Stockings: Royal blue with white hoops.

Goalscorers: *League* (59): Scotland 15, Sheerin 10 (4 pens), Milne 8, James 6, Stevenson 5, Mensing 3, MacDonald 2 (1 pen), Rutkiewicz 2, Campbell 1, Dobbie 1, Glennan 1, Hardie 1, Stanik 1, own goals 3.
Scottish Cup (0).
CIS Cup (3): Dobbie 2, Milne 1.
Challenge Cup (12): Milne 4, Dobbie 2, Rutkiewicz 2, Janczyk 1, MacDonald 1, Mensing 1, Scotland 1.

Cuthbert K 23	Stevenson R 29 + 6	Stanik G 35	Mensing S 28 + 1	Campbell M 3	James K 31	McCann R 7 + 9	Sheridan D 32	Milne S 25 + 4	Dobbie S 7 + 13	Janczyk N 4 + 8	Henry J 17 + 7	MacDonald P 2 + 7	Sheerin P 33 + 3	Anderson S 19 + 4	Paston M 1	Scotland J 31	Rutkiewicz K 31	Hannah D 1 + 2	Paterson S 3 + 1	Coyle O 5 + 10	Doris S — + 3	Dyer W 1 + 2	Fotheringham K 2 + 3	Jackson A — + 2	Glennan M 12	Winter J 5 + 3	Hardie M 9	McCallum N — + 3	Moon K — + 1	*Match No.*
1	2	3	4	5	6	7^{1}	8^{3}	9^{2}	10	11	12	13	14																	1
1	2	3	5		6	7	8	9^{3}	10^{1}	11^{2}	14	12	13	4																2
1	2	3	4	5	6	7^{2}	8	9	10^{1}	11^{3}	13	12	14																	3
	7	3	2^{3}	5■	6		8	9^{2}	14	13		12	11^{1}	4	1	10														4
1	13	3	5			7	8	9	12			10^{1}	11	2^{3}			4	6^{2}	14											5
1	12	3	6			7	8	9				13	11	2		10^{2}	5^{1}		4											6
1		3	2■		6	7^{1}	8	9^{3}				13	11	14		10^{2}	5	12	4■											7
1	4	3^{1}	2		6		8	9				10	11	12		7	5													8
1	4	3	2		6		8	9	10^{1}		12		11			7^{2}	5			13										9
1	4	3	2		6	12	8	9^{3}	13		7^{1}		11			10^{2}	5			14										10
1	4	3	2		6	12	8	9^{3}	13		7^{1}		11			10^{2}	5			14										11
1	4^{2}	3	2		6	13	8	9^{3}	12		7		11^{1}			10	5			14										12
1	4	3	2		6	12	8	9^{2}	13		7^{1}		11			10	5													13
1	4	3				13	8	9	10^{3}	14	7^{2}		11	2			5	12	6^{1}											14
1	4	3			6	7^{2}	8	9^{1}	12				11	2		10	5			13										15
1	4^{1}	3	13		6	12	8	9					7	2^{2}		10	5			11^{3}	14									16
1	4		2		6	12	8^{1}	9		13	7		11^{2}			10	5					3								17
1	4^{2}	3	2		6^{1}	13	8	9	14		7		11	12		10^{3}	5													18
1	4	3	2^{1}		6	13^{3}	8	9		14	7^{2}		11	12		10	5													19
1	4^{1}	3			6		8	9^{3}	12	13	7		11^{2}	2		10	5				14									20
1	4	3	8■		6			9^{3}	12		7^{2}		11	2		10^{1}	5				14		13							21
1	4	3			6			9^{2}		8^{1}	7		11	2		10	5						12	13						22
1	2^{3}	3^{2}	8		6					14	7		11	4		10	5			9^{1}		13		12						23
1	13	3	2		6		8		12	14	7^{2}		11	4		10^{3}	5			9^{1}										24
	2	3	4		6		8		12		13		11			10^{1}	5			9					1	7^{2}				25
	2	3	4		6		8					12	11			10^{1}	5								1	7	9			26
	2	3	4		6				9^{2}				11			10	5			13					1	8^{1}	7	12		27
	2^{2}	3			6		8		12				11	4		10	5			13					1	7^{1}	9			28
	14	3			6^{1}		8	13	9^{2}				11	4		10	5						12		1	2^{3}	7			29
	2	3					8	12			7^{1}		11	4		10	5						6		1		9			30
	12	3	2				8	13			7^{3}		11	4		10^{2}	5						6^{1}		1	14	9			31
	13	3^{2}	2		6		8	12			7^{3}		11	4^{1}		10	5			14					1		9			32
	2	3	4		6		8^{1}	9^{2}			14		11^{3}			10	5			13					1	12	7			33
	2^{2}	3	4		6		8^{1}	9			12		11			10	5			13					1		7■			34
	2^{1}	3	7		6		8^{2}			13			11	4^{3}		10	5			9					1	12		14		35
	2^{1}	3	4^{2}		6		8	9^{3}			7		11	5		10						12			1			14	13	36

ST MIRREN Premier League

Year Formed: 1877. *Ground & Address:* St Mirren Park, Love St, Paisley PA3 2EA. *Telephone:* 0141 889 2558/0141 840 1337. *Fax:* 0141 848 6444. *E-mail:* commercial@saintmirren,net. *Website:* saintmirren.net.
Ground Capacity: 10,866 (all seated). *Size of Pitch:* 112yd × 73yd.
Chairman: Stewart Gilmour. *Vice-Chairman:* George Campbell. *Secretary:* Allan Marshall.
Manager: Gus MacPherson. *Assistant Manager:* Andy Millen. *Commercial Manager:* Campbell Kennedy. *Youth Development Officer:* David Longwell.
Managers since 1975: Alex Ferguson, Jim Clunie, Rikki MacFarlane, Alex Miller, Alex Smith, Tony Fitzpatrick, David Hay, Jimmy Bone, Tony Fitzpatrick, Tom Hendrie, John Coughlin. *Club Nickname(s):* The Buddies. *Previous Grounds:* Short Roods 1877-79, Thistle Park Greenhill 1879-83, Westmarch 1883-94.
Record Attendance: 47,438 v Celtic, League Cup, 20 Aug 1949.
Record Transfer Fee received: £850,000 for Ian Ferguson to Rangers (1988).
Record Transfer Fee paid: £400,000 for Thomas Stickroth from Bayer Uerdingen (1990).
Record Victory: 15-0 v Glasgow University, Scottish Cup 1st rd, 30 Jan 1960.
Record Defeat: 0-9 v Rangers, Division I, 4 Dec 1897.
Most Capped Player: Godmundor Torfason, 29, Iceland.
Most League Appearances: 351: Tony Fitzpatrick, 1973-88.
Most League Goals in Season (Individual): 45: Dunky Walker, Division I, 1921-22.
Most Goals Overall (Individual): 221: David McCrae, 1923-34.

ST MIRREN 2005–06 LEAGUE RECORD

Match No.	*Date*	*Venue*	*Opponents*	*Result*		*H/T Score*	*Lg. Pos.*	*Goalscorers*	*Attendance*
1	Aug 6	A	Dundee	L	2-3	1-1	—	Kean [25], Baird [87]	5003
2	13	H	Stranraer	D	0-0	0-0	6		2614
3	20	A	St Johnstone	W	2-1	0-0	4	Kean [59], McGowne [85]	3089
4	27	H	Brechin C	W	1-0	1-0	3	Kean (pen) [39]	2713
5	Sept 10	A	Queen of the S	W	1-0	1-0	2	Lappin [21]	1688
6	17	H	Clyde	W	2-0	1-0	2	Kean (pen) [28], Sutton [71]	3068
7	24	A	Airdrie U	W	1-0	1-0	2	Adam [32]	2073
8	Oct 1	A	Hamilton A	L	1-3	0-2	2	Kean [65]	2683
9	15	H	Ross Co	W	2-0	1-0	1	Sutton 2 [9, 65]	2314
10	22	H	Dundee	D	0-0	0-0	1		4027
11	25	A	Stranraer	W	2-1	1-0	—	Van Zanten [22], Kean [90]	703
12	29	H	Queen of the S	W	2-0	1-0	1	Potter [28], Kean [49]	3361
13	Nov 12	A	Clyde	W	2-1	0-0	1	Adam [70], Sutton [80]	1904
14	15	A	Brechin C	W	3-2	1-1	—	Sutton 2 [36, 67], Kean [69]	713
15	26	H	Hamilton A	W	2-1	1-0	1	Broadfoot [23], Lappin [84]	3197
16	29	H	Airdrie U	D	1-1	1-1	—	Van Zanten [5]	2941
17	Dec 3	A	Ross Co	W	4-0	1-0	1	Kean [9], Van Zanten [61], Sutton (pen) [73], Murray [77]	3393
18	10	A	Dundee	L	0-4	0-1	1		4204
19	17	H	St Johnstone	D	0-0	0-0	1		3729
20	26	A	Queen of the S	D	0-0	0-0	—		2421
21	31	H	Brechin C	W	3-2	1-1	1	Adam [36], Kean (pen) [58], Corcoran [81]	2913
22	Jan 2	H	Clyde	W	2-1	2-0	—	Corcoran [27], Kean (pen) [40]	4338
23	14	A	Airdrie U	W	4-1	1-0	1	McKenna (og) [24], Anderson 2 [61, 78], Corcoran [72]	2661
24	21	A	Hamilton A	D	0-0	0-0	1		3320
25	28	H	Ross Co	L	0-1	0-0	1		3659
26	Feb 11	A	St Johnstone	D	0-0	0-0	1		4515
27	18	H	Stranraer	W	3-1	1-1	1	Anderson [28], Lappin [47], Sutton (pen) [89]	3375
28	Mar 11	H	Queen of the S	W	1-0	0-0	1	Adam [90]	3436
29	18	A	Clyde	W	1-0	0-0	1	Adam [72]	2324
30	21	A	Brechin C	W	3-0	1-0	—	Sutton 3 [24, 52, 88]	791
31	25	H	Airdrie U	W	2-1	1-1	1	Sutton 2 [8, 47]	3785
32	Apr 1	H	Hamilton A	L	0-2	0-0	1		4431
33	8	A	Ross Co	W	2-0	1-0	1	Kean [16], Sutton [63]	3588
34	15	H	Dundee	W	2-1	1-0	1	Broadfoot [18], Mehmet [86]	7629
35	22	A	Stranraer	W	1-0	1-0	1	Mehmet [77]	1109
36	29	H	St Johnstone	L	0-1	0-0	1		6726

Final League Position: 1

Honours
League Champions: First Division 1976-77, 1999-2000, 2005-06; *Runners-up:* 2004-05. Division II 1967-68; *Runners-up:* 1935-36.
Scottish Cup Winners: 1926, 1959, 1987. *Runners-up:* 1908, 1934, 1962.
League Cup Runners-up: 1955-56.
B&Q Cup Runners-up: 1993-94. *Anglo-Scottish Cup:* 1979-80.

European: *Cup Winners' Cup:* 4 matches (1987-88). *UEFA Cup:* 10 matches (1980-81, 1983-84, 1985-86).

Club colours: Shirt: Black and white vertical stripes. Shorts: White with black trim. Stockings: White with 2 black hoops. Change colours: Predominantly red.

Goalscorers: *League* (52): Sutton 14 (2 pens), Kean 12 (4 pens), Adam 5, Anderson 3, Corcoran 3, Lappin 3, Van Zanten 3, Broadfoot 2, Mehmet 2, Baird 1, McGowne 1, Murray 1, Potter 1, own goal 1.
Scottish Cup (6): Adam 3, Maxwell 1, Potter 1, Sutton 1.
CIS Cup (1): McGowne 1.
Challenge Cup (8): Lappin 2, Sutton 2, Adam 1, Corcoran 1, Murray 1, Reid 1.

Hinchcliffe C 3	Van Zanten D 31 + 1	Broadfoot K 25 + 2	Millen A 27 + 1	McGowne K 32	Reilly M 11 + 3	Murray H 27 + 2	Lappin S 33 + 2	Kean S 29 + 6	Reid A 15 + 9	Corcoran M 11 + 16	Baird J — + 2	Maxwell I 16 + 5	McKenna D — + 3	Potter J 35	Mehmet W 10 + 19	McGinty B — + 8	Smith C 21 + 2	Sutton J 28 + 3	Adam C 24 + 5	Anderson I 5 + 6	Bullock A 12	Molloy C 1 + 1	*Match No.*
1	2	3	4	5	6^{3}	7	8	9	10^{2}	11^{1}	12	13	14										1
1	14	3	4	5		7	8	9	2^{3}	12		11^{1}		6	10^{2}	13							2
1	2	3	4	5		7	8	9	11		13			6^{2}	10^{1}	12							3
	2	3	4	5		7	8	9	11^{2}	13				6	10^{1}	12	1						4
		3	4			7	8	9	2	11^{2}		6		5	12	13	1	10^{1}					5
		3	4			7	8^{2}	9^{1}	2	13		6		5	12		1	10	11				6
	2	3	4	5		7	12	13	11	14				6	10^{2}		1	9^{3}	8^{1}				7
	2	3^{2}	4^{1}	5		7	8	9	11	12		13		6	10^{3}		1	14					8
	2	3	4	5		7	11^{1}	9	12					6	13		1	10^{2}	8				9
	2	3	4	5^{1}		7	11	9		14		12		6	13		1	10^{2}	8^{3}				10
	2	3			4	7	11^{2}	9		13		5		6	12		1	10	8^{1}				11
	2		4	5		7^{3}	11	9	12	14		3^{1}		6	13		1	10^{2}	8				12
	2	3	4	5^{1}	8		11^{3}	9	12	13				6	7^{2}		1	10	14				13
	2	3	14	5	4	7	11^{1}	9^{2}		12				6	13		1	10	8^{3}				14
	2	3	4	5		7	11	9^{1}	13					6		12	1	10	8^{2}				15
	2	3		5^{2}	4	7	11	9^{3}		12				6	14	13	1	10	8^{1}				16
	2	3	4^{2}	5	13	7	8^{3}	9^{1}	11					6	12		1	10	14				17
	2	3	4^{2}	5		7	8	9^{3}	11^{1}	14				6	13		1	10	12				18
	2	3	4	5		7	11	9^{1}		13				6	12		1	10	8^{2}				19
	2		4	5		7	11	9^{2}		13		3		6	12		1	10	8^{1}				20
	2	3			4	7	11	9^{3}	12	13		5^{1}	14	6			1	10	8^{2}				21
	2	3^{2}	4	5		7^{1}	8	9^{3}	10	11		13	14	6			1		12				22
	2		4^{3}	5	14		7	9^{2}	8^{1}	11		3		6			1	13	10	12			23
	2		4	5			7	12		11^{1}		3		6			1	9	10	8			24
	2^{3}		4	5		13	7^{2}	9^{1}	14	11		3		6				8	10	12	1		25
	2		4	5		7	8	9^{2}	11^{3}	10^{1}		3		6	13			12	14		1		26
	2		4	5			11	9^{1}		12		3		6	13			10	8^{2}	7	1		27
	2	12		5^{1}	4	7	8^{3}	14		11		3		6	13			9^{2}	10		1		28
	2			5	4	7^{1}	8	14		11^{3}		3		6	13			9^{2}	10	12	1		29
	2	12		5	4	7	8			11^{2}		3^{1}		6	13			9	10^{3}	14	1		30
	2	3		5	4	12	8	13	14	11^{1}				6	10^{2}			9		7^{3}	1		31
	2	3		5	4		8^{1}	13	12					6	11^{2}	14		9	10	7^{3}	1		32
	2	3^{1}	4	5		7^{3}	11	10	12					6	13			9^{2}	8	14	1		33
	2	3	4	5		7	11	10^{2}						6	13		15	9	8^{1}	12	1^{G}		34
		3^{1}	4	5			14	10	2			12		6	11^{3}			9	8^{2}	7	1	13	35
			4^{1}	5	12			10	2			3		6	11	13	15	9	8		1^{G}	7^{2}	36

STENHOUSEMUIR — Third Division

Year Formed: 1884. *Ground & Address:* Ochilview Park, Gladstone Rd, Stenhousemuir FK5 4QL. *Telephone:* 01324 562992. *Fax:* 01324 562980. *E-mail:* stenhousemuirfc@talk21.com. *Website:* www.stenhousemuirfc.com
Ground Capacity: total: 2654, seated: 626. *Size of Pitch:* 110yd × 72yd.
Chairman: David O. Reid. *Secretary:* Margaret Kilpatrick. *Commercial Manager:* Brian McGinlay.
Manager: Des McKeown. *Assistant Manager:* Paul Smith. *Physio:* Alain Davidson.
Managers since 1975: H. Glasgow, J. Black, A. Rose, W. Henderson, A. Rennie, J. Meakin, D. Lawson, T. Christie, G. Armstrong, B. Fairley, J. Bone, J. McVeigh, T. Smith.
Club Nickname(s): The Warriors. *Previous Grounds:* Tryst Ground 1884-86, Goschen Park 1886-90.
Record Attendance: 12,500 v East Fife, Scottish Cup 4th rd, 11 Mar 1950.
Record Transfer Fee received: £70,000 for Euan Donaldson to St Johnstone (May 1995).
Record Transfer Fee paid: £20,000 to Livingston for Ian Little (June 1995).
Record Victory: 9-2 v Dundee U, Division II, 16 Apr 1937.
Record Defeat: 2-11 v Dunfermline Ath, Division II, 27 Sept 1930.
Most League Appearances: 360: Archie Rose.
Most League Goals in Season (Individual): 32: Robert Taylor, Division II, 1925-26.

STENHOUSEMUIR 2005–06 LEAGUE RECORD

Match No.	Date	Venue	Opponents	Result		H/T Score	Lg. Pos.	Goalscorers	Attendance
1	Aug 6	A	Queen's Park	W	2-1	1-1	—	McInally [18], McGrillen [85]	487
2	13	H	Elgin C	W	3-1	2-0	2	Cramb 2 [18, 44], Mercer [80]	278
3	20	A	Albion R	W	2-0	2-0	2	McAlpine [13], Mercer [34]	268
4	27	H	East Stirling	W	6-1	2-1	1	McGrillen 3 (1 pen) [1, 7 (p), 80], Mercer 2 [76, 83], Cramb [89]	403
5	Sept 10	A	Arbroath	D	1-1	0-0	2	McGrillen (pen) [89]	429
6	17	H	East Fife	W	2-1	1-0	2	Cramb 2 [22, 70]	494
7	24	A	Montrose	W	3-0	1-0	2	Mercer [6], McGrillen 2 (1 pen) [60 (p), 85]	301
8	Oct 1	A	Cowdenbeath	L	1-4	0-3	2	Carroll [88]	338
9	15	H	Berwick R	L	0-1	0-1	2		558
10	22	H	Queen's Park	W	1-0	0-0	2	Cramb [89]	444
11	25	A	Elgin C	W	2-1	0-0	—	Cramb [71], McGrillen [88]	274
12	29	H	Arbroath	W	2-0	1-0	2	Cramb [7], Mercer [75]	332
13	Nov 5	A	East Stirling	D	0-0	0-0	2		388
14	12	A	East Fife	W	3-2	0-1	2	Cramb [76], McGrillen [78], Templeton [89]	567
15	26	H	Montrose	W	6-2	3-1	2	McBride [9], Sinclair [23], Cramb [29], McAlpine [54], Templeton 2 [82, 88]	253
16	Dec 3	A	Berwick R	W	2-0	1-0	1	McBride [36], Cramb [52]	507
17	17	H	Cowdenbeath	W	2-0	2-0	1	Mercer [37], Cramb [69]	503
18	26	A	Queen's Park	L	0-2	0-1	—		543
19	Jan 2	H	East Stirling	W	5-0	1-0	—	Diack [28], McGrillen 3 [58, 62, 79], Templeton [87]	482
20	14	A	Arbroath	L	2-3	2-2	1	Gibson [25], McKeown [40]	560
21	21	H	East Fife	W	4-2	1-1	1	Diack [16], Sinclair [72], Templeton 2 [88, 90]	420
22	28	A	Montrose	W	2-0	1-0	1	Diack [15], McBride (pen) [85]	326
23	Feb 4	A	Cowdenbeath	D	1-1	1-1	1	McBride (pen) [34]	462
24	11	H	Berwick R	W	1-0	1-0	1	Murphy [44]	548
25	18	H	Elgin C	L	1-2	1-1	1	Murphy [14]	388
26	25	A	Albion R	W	2-1	1-0	1	Cramb [19], Sinclair [72]	428
27	28	H	Albion R	W	1-0	1-0	—	McGrillen [43]	278
28	Mar 11	H	Arbroath	D	0-0	0-0	1		383
29	18	A	East Fife	L	1-2	0-0	1	McBride (pen) [74]	375
30	21	A	East Stirling	W	7-0	3-0	—	Sinclair [10], Templeton 2 [17, 52], Cramb 2 [45, 69], Diack 2 [74, 90]	271
31	25	H	Montrose	W	5-1	1-1	1	Sinclair 2 [18, 63], Cramb (pen) [60], Diack [75], McGrillen [81]	424
32	Apr 1	H	Cowdenbeath	L	1-2	1-1	1	Mercer [37]	816
33	8	A	Berwick R	L	0-3	0-1	3		710
34	15	H	Queen's Park	L	1-2	0-0	3	Clark (og) [80]	552
35	22	A	Elgin C	W	2-0	0-0	3	Diack 2 [47, 51]	880
36	29	H	Albion R	W	4-2	2-1	3	Diack [21], McKeown [25], McGrillen (pen) [73], McBride [90]	391

Final League Position: 3

Honours
League Champions: Third Division runners-up: 1998-99.
Scottish Cup: Semi-finals 1902-03. Quarter-finals 1948-49, 1949-50, 1994-95.
League Cup: Quarter-finals 1947-48, 1960-61, 1975-76.
League Challenge Cup: Winners: 1995-96.

Club colours: Shirt: Maroon with dark blue trim. Shorts: White. Stockings: Maroon.

Goalscorers: *League* (78): Cramb 16 (1 pen), McGrillen 15 (4 pens), Diack 9, Mercer 8, Templeton 8, McBride 6 (3 pens), Sinclair 6, McAlpine 2, McKeown 2, Murphy 2, Carroll 1, Gibson 1, McInally 1, own goal 1.
Scottish Cup (4): Cramb 1, Mercer 1, Renwick 1, Sinclair 1.
CIS Cup (0).
Challenge Cup (8): Cramb 2, McGrillen 2, Carroll 1, Denham 1, Mercer 1, Savage 1.
Play-Offs (0).

McCulloch W 30	Renwick M 26 + 3	Henderson R 25 + 1	Denham G 31	McKeown J 19	McBride J 32 + 1	McKenzie M 1 + 5	Collins L 8	Carroll F 10 + 3	Cramb C 25 + 2	McInally D 2 + 3	Sinclair T 21 + 7	McGrillen P 26 + 5	Savage J 2 + 5	McAlpine J 28 + 3	Menzies C 18	Mercer J 24 + 6	McGregor S 2	Arbuckle A 2 + 1	Murphy P 23 + 3	Tait J — + 1	Templeton D 4 + 14	Fallon S 9 + 2	Diack I 11 + 4	Gibson A 9	Cassidy P 2 + 4	Fahey C 6	*Match No.*
1	2	3	4	5	6^1	7	8	9	10^3	11^2	12	13	14														1
1	2	3			6^1	12	8	9	10			11		4	5	7											2
1	2	3	4	5	6^2	13	8	9^3		12		11	14	10^1		7											3
1	2	3	4	5	6	14	8^3	9	12			11^2	13	10^1		7											4
1	2	3	4		6	13	8	9^1	10■			11	12			7	5^2										5
1	2	3	4	5	6		8	13	10		7^1	11		9^2				12									6
1	2	3	4	5	6		8	9			13	11		12		7^1		10^2									7
1	2	3	4	5			8^3	9	10		13	11		14		6^1		7^2	12								8
1	2	3^1	4	5	6			9^3	10	7^2		11	14	12		13			8								9
1	2		4	5	6				10			11	9	3	7	8											10
1	2		4	5	6				10			11	9^1	3	7	8			12								11
1	2		4	5	6				10		12	11		3	7	9			8^1								12
1	2		4	5■	6				10		8^1	11		3	7	9				12							13
1	2	12	4^1		6				10		8	11		3	7	9^3	5^2		13		14						14
1	2		4		6	13			10^3	14	8^2	11		3	7	9^1			5		12						15
1	2	11	4		6				10		8			3	7	9^1			5		12						16
1	2	11	4		6			12	10		8^1			3	7	9			5								17
1	2	11	4		6			10			8^1			3	7^2	9			5		12	13					18
1	2		4	5						13	8	11		3	7^2	9^1			6		14	12	10^3				19
1	2		4	5	6			12			10^1	11		3					8				9	7			20
1	2		4						10^2		8	11		3		13			6		12	5	9^1	7			21
1		5	4		14				10^1		8	11^3		3	2	12			6		13		9^2	7			22
1	13	5	4^2		11				10^1		8			3	2	12			6		14		9^3	7			23
1	13	5	4		6						10	12		3^2	2	11			8				9^1	7			24
1	4	5^3			6				13		11^1	12		3	2^2	10			8				9	7	14		25
1	2	5		4	6			9^2	10		12	11		3					8		13			7^1			26
1		5		4	6				10		9	11		3					8		12	2		7^1			27
1		3	4	5	6				10			11				9			8			2	12	7^1			28
1		3	4	5	6^3				10		12	11				7^1			8		13	2	9^2		14		29
		5	4		6				10^3		11	14		3		7^1			8^2		9	2	12		13	1	30
	12	5	4^1		6				10		11	14		3		7^2			8		9^3	2	13			1	31
		5	4		6				10^1		7	11^2		3		9			8		13	2	12			1	32
1		5	4		6				10^1		7			3■		11			8		9	2			12		33
	2	5	4		6						12	11^2			7^1	13			8		9	3	10			1	34
	2		4	5	6						10	11		3	7						12		9^1		8	1	35
	2			5	6						10^1	11		3	7	12			4		13		9		8^2	1	36

STIRLING ALBION — Second Division

Year Formed: 1945. *Ground & Address:* Forthbank Stadium, Springkerse Industrial Estate, Stirling FK7 7UJ. *Telephone:* 01786 450399. *Fax:* 01786 448400. *E-mail:* stirlingalbion.footballclub@virgin.net. *Website:* www.stirlingalbion.com
Ground Capacity: 3808, seated: 2508. *Size of Pitch:* 110yd × 74yd.
Chairman: Peter McKenzie. *Secretary:* Mrs Marlyn Hallam.
Manager: Allan Moore. *Assistant Managers:* Mark McNally, David Gemmell. *Physio:* Graeme Lister.
Managers since 1975: A. Smith, G. Peebles, J. Fleeting, J. Brogan, K. Drinkell, J. Philliben, R. Stewart.
Club Nickname(s): The Binos. *Previous Grounds:* Annfield 1945-92.
Record Attendance: 26,400 (at Annfield) v Celtic, Scottish Cup 4th rd, 14 Mar 1959; 3808 v Aberdeen, Scottish Cup 4th rd, 15 February 1996 (Forthbank).
Record Transfer Fee received: £90,000 for Stephen Nicholas to Motherwell (Mar 1999).
Record Transfer Fee paid: £25,000 for Craig Taggart from Falkirk (Aug 1994).
Record Victory: 20-0 v Selkirk, Scottish Cup 1st rd, 8 Dec 1984.
Record Defeat: 0-9 v Dundee U, Division I, 30 Dec 1967.
Most League Appearances: 504: Matt McPhee, 1967-81.
Most League Goals in Season (Individual): 27: Joe Hughes, Division II, 1969-70.
Most Goals Overall (Individual): 129: Billy Steele, 1971-83.

STIRLING ALBION 2005–06 LEAGUE RECORD

Match No.	Date	Venue	Opponents	Result	H/T Score	Lg. Pos.	Goalscorers	Attendance
1	Aug 6	A	Partick Th	D 0-0	0-0	—		2830
2	13	H	Morton	L 0-2	0-1	7		1453
3	20	A	Gretna	L 0-1	0-1	9		1010
4	27	H	Alloa Ath	L 1-2	0-1	10	Graham [90]	962
5	Sept 10	A	Raith R	L 2-5	1-1	10	O'Brien [24], Hay C [48]	1997
6	17	H	Peterhead	L 1-3	1-1	10	Connolly [42]	509
7	24	A	Dumbarton	L 0-2	0-1	10		877
8	Oct 1	H	Ayr U	D 3-3	2-2	10	Connolly [13], Hay P [42], Dunn [51]	709
9	7	H	Alloa Ath	D 0-0	0-0	10		874
10	15	A	Forfar Ath	L 0-3	0-2	10		508
11	22	H	Partick Th	L 1-2	0-0	10	Bell S [60]	1634
12	25	A	Morton	W 2-1	1-0	—	Connolly [45], Forsyth [54]	2052
13	29	H	Raith R	W 1-0	1-0	10	Nugent [44]	868
14	Nov 5	A	Alloa Ath	W 4-2	3-0	9	Aitken [11], Connolly 2 [15, 41], O'Brien [57]	870
15	12	A	Peterhead	W 3-1	3-0	8	Aitken [12], Wilson [26], O'Brien [35]	547
16	Dec 3	H	Forfar Ath	W 4-2	1-2	7	Hay C 3 (1 pen) [41, 60 (p), 80], Connolly [63]	528
17	7	H	Dumbarton	D 0-0	0-0	—		530
18	17	A	Ayr U	W 5-2	3-1	5	Graham [12], Fraser [26], Hay C [35], Connolly [66], Aitken [75]	1029
19	26	A	Partick Th	W 3-0	1-0	—	Connolly 2 [17, 52], Aitken [63]	2472
20	Jan 14	A	Raith R	W 3-2	1-1	5	Wilson [24], Aitken (pen) [65], O'Brien [78]	2236
21	21	H	Peterhead	W 2-1	1-0	5	Wilson [7], Devine [60]	735
22	28	A	Dumbarton	L 2-3	1-2	5	Aitken [45], Devine [63]	891
23	Feb 4	H	Ayr U	W 1-0	0-0	5	Aitken (pen) [49]	795
24	18	H	Morton	W 3-1	1-1	5	Bell S [35], Aitken [50], O'Brien [65]	1337
25	28	H	Gretna	L 0-5	0-1	—		786
26	Mar 11	H	Raith R	D 2-2	2-1	5	O'Brien [9], Connolly [37]	1079
27	18	A	Peterhead	L 0-2	0-1	5		661
28	25	H	Dumbarton	W 3-1	0-0	5	Connolly [68], Wilson [72], McVicar [86]	604
29	28	A	Alloa Ath	D 0-0	0-0	—		656
30	Apr 1	A	Ayr U	L 0-3	0-2	5		1035
31	4	A	Forfar Ath	W 2-1	1-1	—	Aitken 2 [35, 46]	394
32	8	H	Forfar Ath	W 3-1	2-0	5	Aitken 2 (1 pen) [9 (p), 51], Connolly [34]	496
33	11	A	Gretna	L 0-6	0-4	—		804
34	15	H	Partick Th	L 1-2	1-0	5	Aitken (pen) [6]	1729
35	22	A	Morton	L 0-1	0-0	5		2111
36	29	H	Gretna	W 2-1	2-0	5	Hay P [22], Connolly [44]	668

Final League Position: 5

Honours
League Champions: Division II 1952-53, 1957-58, 1960-61, 1964-65. Second Division 1976-77, 1990-91, 1995-96; *Runners-up:* Division II 1948-49, 1950-51. Third Division 2003-04.
League Cup: Semi-finals 1961-62.

Club colours: Shirt: Red with white side panels and trim. Shorts: Red with white side design. Stockings: White with red front stripe.

Goalscorers: *League* (54): Connolly 14, Aitken 13 (4 pens), Hay C 5 (1 pen), O'Brien 5, Wilson 4, Bell S 2, Devine 2, Graham 2, Hay P 2, Dunn 1, Forsyth 1, Fraser 1, McVicar 1, Nugent 1.
Scottish Cup (3): Connolly 1, Forsyth 1, Hay C 1.
CIS Cup (3): Connolly 2, Boyack 1.
Challenge Cup (4): Aitken 1, Boyack 1, Fraser 1, Hay P 1.

Hogarth M 31	Nugent P 23	Forsyth R 31 + 3	McNally M 29	Roycroft S 7 + 3	Boyack S 8 + 6	Hay P 26 + 2	Devine S 25 + 6	Turnbull D 4 + 4	Connolly P 35 + 1	O'Brien D 29 + 6	Dunn R 5 + 11	Wilson D 19 + 11	Graham A 30	Fraser J 28	Hutchison S 1 + 2	Aitken C 23 + 2	Hay C 8 + 17	Millar J 1 + 3	Christie S 1	Giacomi R 4	Scotland C 1	Bell S 25 + 1	McClare S 2 + 1	Taggart N — + 1	Bell A — + 1	McVicar N — + 5	*Match No.*
1	2	3	4	5	6	7	8	9^{1}	10^{2}	11	12	13															1
1	2			5	6	7	3^{2}	12	9	11	10^{1}	13	4	8^{3}	14												2
1	2	3^{2}	4	11	6	7		10	9^{1}	13	12	14	5			8^{3}											3
1	2	3		5	6	8^{1}	13	9^{3}	14	11	10	7^{2}	4			12											4
1	2	3	4		6^{2}	7	12		9	11^{1}		13	5			8	10^{3}	14									5
	5	3	4^{2}		14	2	11^{3}	12	9	13		7		6		8	10^{1}		1								6
	2	3^{1}	4				13	10	9^{3}	12			5	8^{2}		11	14			1	6	7■					7
	2	3	4^{1}		7^{3}	6	12		10^{2}	11	9	13	5	8						1			14				8
	2	3				4	13		10^{3}	11	9^{1}	14	5	6^{2}			12			1		7	8				9
	2	3				4^{1}	12		9	11		13	5	6			10^{2}			1		7	8				10
1	2	10	4				3		9	11		7^{1}	5	6								8		12			11
1	2	10	4			13	3		9^{1}	11		7^{2}	5	6			12					8					12
1	2	10	4				3		9	11		7	5	6								8					13
1	2	10	4			3			9^{1}	11		7	5			6	12					8					14
1	2	10	4			13	3		9^{1}	11		7	5			6^{2}	12					8					15
1			4		12	2	3^{2}	14	9	11			5	6	8		10^{3}					7^{1}			13		16
1	2	10^{1}	4			8	3		9	11			5	6			12					7					17
1	2	3	4			7		13	9^{2}		12		5	6^{3}	14	11	10^{1}					8					18
1	2	3	4^{2}			7			9^{3}	13	12	14	5	6		11	10^{1}					8					19
1	2	10	4			5	3		9	11	12	7^{1}		6		8											20
1	2	10	4				3		9^{2}	11	14	7^{1}	5	6		8^{3}	13					12					21
1	2	10	4				3		9	11	12	7^{2}	5			6	13					8^{1}					22
1	2	10	4				3		9^{2}	11		12	5	6		7^{1}	13					8					23
1	2^{1}	13	4				3		9^{3}	11	14	7	5	6		8^{2}	12					10					24
1		13	4			2^{3}	3^{2}		9^{1}	11	12	7	5	6		8	14					10					25
1		12	4	14		2	3^{3}		9^{2}	11		7	5	6		10^{1}	13					8					26
1		10	4■	12		2^{1}	3		9^{3}	11		7	5	6^{2}		13	14					8					27
1		4			14	2	3		9^{2}	11		7^{3}	5	6		8	13	10^{1}								12	28
1		4				2	3		9	11		7	5	6		10^{1}						8				12	29
1		3^{2}	4			2^{1}	11		9	12		13	5	6		7	10^{3}					8				14	30
1		10	4			2	3		9	11			5■	6		8						7					31
1		5	4	13	12	2^{2}	3		9^{3}	11		7		6		10						8^{1}				14	32
1		6	4	2	10		3		9^{1}	11		7^{3}	5^{2}			8	13	12								14	33
1		5	4		14	2	3^{1}		9^{2}	11	12	7		6^{3}		10	13					8					34
1		5		4	12	2	3		9^{2}	11	10^{1}	14		6		7^{3}	13					8					35
1		11	4^{3}	2	3	7			9^{2}	14	13		5	6			10^{1}	12				8					36

STRANRAER Second Division

Year Formed: 1870. *Ground & Address:* Stair Park, London Rd, Stranraer DG9 8BS. *Telephone:* 01776 703271. *E-mail:* grodgers_sfc@yahoo.co.uk. *Website:* www.stranraerfc.org
Ground Capacity: 5600, seated: 1830. *Size of Pitch:* 110yd × 70yd.
Chairman: James Robertson. *Secretary:* Graham Rodgers. *Commercial Manager:* Ian Alldred.
Manager: Gerry Britton. *Assistant Manager:* Derek Ferguson.
Managers since 1975: J. Hughes, N. Hood, G. Hamilton, D. Sneddon, J. Clark, R. Clark, A. McAnespie, C. Money, W. McLaren, N. Watt.
Club Nickname(s): The Blues. *Previous Grounds:* None.
Record Attendance: 6500 v Rangers, Scottish Cup 1st rd, 24 Jan 1948.
Record Transfer Fee received: £90,000 for Mark Campbell to Ayr U (1999).
Record Transfer Fee paid: £15,000 for Colin Harkness from Kilmarnock (Aug 1989).
Record Victory: 7-0 v Brechin C, Division II, 6 Feb 1965.
Record Defeat: 1-11 v Queen of the South, Scottish Cup 1st rd, 16 Jan 1932.
Most League Appearances: 301, Keith Knox, 1986-90; 1999-2001.
Most League Goals in Season (Individual): 59, Tommy Sloan.

STRANRAER 2005–06 LEAGUE RECORD

Match No.	*Date*	*Venue*	*Opponents*	*Result*		*H/T Score*	*Lg. Pos.*	*Goalscorers*	*Attendance*
1	Aug 6	H	Airdrie U	W	1-0	1-0	—	Hamilton [37]	996
2	13	A	St Mirren	D	0-0	0-0	4		2614
3	20	H	Clyde	L	1-2	0-0	6	Swift [75]	692
4	27	A	Ross Co	L	1-2	0-1	8	Hamilton [79]	1962
5	Sept 10	H	Hamilton A	L	1-2	1-2	8	Moore [30]	584
6	17	H	Queen of the S	D	0-0	0-0	8		1032
7	24	A	Brechin C	W	3-2	3-1	7	Henderson 2 [12, 13], Jenkins [19]	502
8	Oct 1	H	St Johnstone	D	1-1	0-0	7	Moore [87]	643
9	15	A	Dundee	D	1-1	0-0	7	Henderson [50]	3417
10	22	A	Airdrie U	L	0-1	0-0	8		1100
11	25	H	St Mirren	L	1-2	0-1	—	Hinds [64]	703
12	29	A	Hamilton A	L	0-2	0-1	8		1334
13	Nov 5	H	Ross Co	L	2-3	2-1	8	Hamilton 2 (1 pen) [44, 45 (p)]	434
14	12	A	Queen of the S	D	1-1	1-1	8	Jenkins [25]	2086
15	19	H	Brechin C	D	1-1	0-1	8	Hamilton [73]	448
16	26	A	St Johnstone	D	1-1	1-0	8	Hamilton [38]	1687
17	Dec 3	H	Dundee	D	0-0	0-0	8		550
18	10	H	Airdrie U	D	1-1	0-1	8	Sharp [75]	581
19	17	A	Clyde	L	0-1	0-0	8		901
20	26	H	Hamilton A	W	5-4	0-1	—	Ross [49], Moore 3 [57, 61, 67], Shields [81]	628
21	Jan 2	H	Queen of the S	W	1-0	0-0	—	Sharp [66]	1548
22	14	A	Brechin C	D	0-0	0-0	8		507
23	21	H	St Johnstone	L	0-2	0-1	8		620
24	28	A	Dundee	L	1-2	1-1	8	Walker [28]	3134
25	Feb 11	H	Clyde	L	0-5	0-4	8		552
26	18	A	St Mirren	L	1-3	1-1	8	Moore [21]	3375
27	25	A	Ross Co	D	1-1	0-1	8	Hamilton [70]	1975
28	Mar 18	A	Queen of the S	L	0-1	0-0	9		2790
29	21	H	Ross Co	D	2-2	1-0	—	Moore [2], Swift [87]	436
30	25	H	Brechin C	W	2-0	2-0	8	Swift [6], Hamilton (pen) [10]	427
31	28	A	Hamilton A	L	0-1	0-0	—		1135
32	Apr 1	A	St Johnstone	L	2-3	1-2	9	Martin [21], Hamilton [56]	1676
33	8	H	Dundee	D	1-1	1-1	9	Payne [10]	480
34	15	A	Airdrie U	L	0-3	0-1	9		919
35	22	H	St Mirren	L	0-1	0-1	9		1109
36	29	A	Clyde	D	1-1	1-0	9	Swift [27]	1254

Final League Position: 9

Honours
League Champions: Second Division 1993-94, 1997-98; *Runners-up:* 2004-05. Third Division 2003-04.
Qualifying Cup Winners: 1937.
Scottish Cup: Quarter-finals 2003
League Challenge Cup Winners: 1996-97.

Club colours: Shirt: Blue with white side panels. Shorts: Blue with white side panels. Stockings: Blue with two white hoops.

Goalscorers: *League* (33): Hamilton 9 (2 pens), Moore 7, Swift 4, Henderson 3, Jenkins 2, Sharp 2, Hinds 1, Martin 1, Payne 1, Ross 1, Shields 1, Walker 1.
Scottish Cup (0).
CIS Cup (4): Hinds 2, Hamilton 1, Jenkins 1.
Challenge Cup (4): Hamilton 2, Jenkins 1, own goal 1.
Play-Offs (3): Hamilton 1, Ross 1, Swift 1.

Corr B 36	Swift S 25 + 1	Keddie A 35	Higgins C 26 + 6	Henderson M 34	Jenkins A 21	Hamilton D 34 + 1	Walker P 11 + 12	Moore M 28 + 1	Hinds L 24 + 7	Ross I 9 + 5	Aitken S 16 + 7	McLean S 1 + 2	Dowie A 18 + 4	Sharp L 26 + 4	Wingate D 11 + 4	Gaughan K — + 1	Marshall C 1 + 7	Shields D 3 + 8	Martin W 5 + 9	Gilfillan B 14 + 1	Payne S 13 + 2	Maisano J 1 + 2	McPhee G 1	Harty I 3 + 2	*Match No.*
1	2	3	4^3	5	6^2	7	8	9■	10^1	11	12	13	14												1
1	2	3	4	5	6	7	9		10^1	11		12	8												2
1	2	3	4	5	6	7^2	8		10	11^3	14	9^1	13	12											3
1	2^3	3	4	5	6	7	12		10	13			9	11^2	8^1	14									4
1	2	3	4	5	6	7	14	9	10^2	11^3			8^1				12	13							5
1	2	3		5	6	7		9	12		8			11	4			10^1							6
1	2^2	3	12	5	6	7	14	9	10^3		8^1			11	4		13								7
1		3		5	6	7	13	9	10^2	12			2	11^3	4		8^1	14							8
1		3	2^2	5	6	7	10	9		12			8	11^1	4		13								9
1		3	2	5^3	6	7	10^2	9	13		14		8^1	11	4		12								10
1	2^1	3	5		6	7	12	9^3	10		8^2		13	11	4			14							11
1		3	2^2	5	6	7	13	9	10^3		8^1			11	4		12	14							12
1		3	12	5	6	7	13	9	10^2	2	8^1			11^3	4		14								13
1		3	4	5	6	7		9		2^2	8^1		13	11			12	10							14
1	2	3	4	5	6	7	12	9^3	13	8	14			11^1				10^2							15
1	2^3	3	8	5	6	7	10^2	9^1	14				4	11	13			12							16
1	2	3	8	5	6	7	10^1	9					4	11				12							17
1	2	3	8^1	5	6	7	12	9	10				4	11											18
1	2	3	8	5	6	7		9	10^1	13			4	11^2				12							19
1	2^1	3	12^3	5	6	7	13	9	10	8			4	11^2				14							20
1		3	2	5	6	7		9	10^1	8			4	11					12						21
1	2	3	12	5		7		9	10^2				4	11					13	6	8^1				22
1	2	3	13	5		7	9		10^3		14		4	11^2					12	6	8^1				23
1	2	3	11	5			9		10		14		4	13	12				7^2	6^3	8^1				24
1	2	3	11	5		7	9		10^3		13		4	12					8^2	6^1	14				25
1	2	3	12	5^1		7	10	9	14		8^2		4	11^3						6	13				26
1	13	3	2	5		7	12	9			8^1		4	11^2						6	10				27
1	2	3	4	5		7	12	9	10					11^2					13	6	8^1				28
1	2	3	4	5		7		9	10		8								12	6^1	11				29
1	2	3	4	5		7		9	10^1		8								12	6	11				30
1	2	3	4	5		7		9^1	10■		8^3			13	14				12	6^2	11				31
1	2	3		5		7					8				4				9^2	12	11	13	6^1	10	32
1		3	4	5		7		9	12		8^1			2					13	6	11			10^2	33
1			4	5		7		9^3	12	13	8^2			11	14				3^1	6	2			10	34
1		3	4	5		7		9	10^1		8^2			11					14	6	2^3	13		12	35
1	2^2	3				13^3		14	10		8			11	4				9	6	7	5^1		12	36

SCOTTISH LEAGUE TABLES 2005–06

SCOTTISH PREMIER LEAGUE

		Home						Away					Total						
		P	W	D	L	F	A	W	D	L	F	A	W	D	L	F	A	GD	Pts
1	Celtic	38	14	4	1	41	15	14	3	2	52	22	28	7	3	93	37	56	91
2	Hearts	38	15	2	2	43	9	7	6	6	28	22	22	8	8	71	31	40	74
3	Rangers	38	13	4	2	38	11	8	6	5	29	26	21	10	7	67	37	30	73
4	Hibernian	38	11	1	7	39	24	6	4	9	22	32	17	5	16	61	56	5	56
5	Kilmarnock	38	11	3	5	39	29	4	7	8	24	35	15	10	13	63	64	–1	55
6	Aberdeen	38	8	9	3	30	17	5	6	7	16	23	13	15	10	46	40	6	54
7	Inverness CT	38	5	6	7	21	21	10	7	3	30	17	15	13	10	51	38	13	58
8	Motherwell	38	7	5	7	35	31	6	5	8	20	30	13	10	15	55	61	–6	49
9	Dundee U	38	5	8	6	22	28	2	4	13	19	38	7	12	19	41	66	–25	33
10	Falkirk	38	2	6	11	14	30	6	3	10	21	34	8	9	21	35	64	–29	33
11	Dunfermline Ath	38	3	5	11	17	39	5	4	10	16	29	8	9	21	33	68	–35	33
12	Livingston	38	3	4	12	15	33	1	2	16	10	46	4	6	28	25	79	–54	18

After 33 matches, the first six clubs play once against each other; bottom six likewise. Thus the finishing position of Inverness CT moves them from fourth to seventh place.

SCOTTISH FOOTBALL LEAGUE FIRST DIVISION

		Home						Away					Total						
		P	W	D	L	F	A	W	D	L	F	A	W	D	L	F	A	GD	Pts
1	St Mirren	36	11	4	3	23	12	12	3	3	29	16	23	7	6	52	28	24	76
2	St Johnstone	36	8	9	1	30	14	10	3	5	29	20	18	12	6	59	34	25	66
3	Hamilton A	36	9	6	3	25	12	6	8	4	28	27	15	14	7	53	39	14	59
4	Ross Co	36	8	6	4	24	19	6	8	4	23	21	14	14	8	47	40	7	56
5	Clyde	36	9	5	4	30	18	6	5	7	24	24	15	10	11	54	42	12	55
6	Airdrie U	36	8	5	5	41	21	3	7	8	16	22	11	12	13	57	43	14	45
7	Dundee	36	6	5	7	26	25	3	11	4	17	25	9	16	11	43	50	–7	43
8	Queen of the S	36	5	7	6	17	19	2	5	11	14	35	7	12	17	31	54	–23	33
9	Stranraer	36	4	7	7	20	27	1	7	10	13	26	5	14	17	33	53	–20	29
10	Brechin C	36	1	7	10	18	36	1	4	13	10	38	2	11	23	28	74	–46	17

SCOTTISH FOOTBALL LEAGUE SECOND DIVISION

		Home						Away					Total						
		P	W	D	L	F	A	W	D	L	F	A	W	D	L	F	A	GD	Pts
1	Gretna	36	14	2	2	53	15	14	2	2	44	15	28	4	4	97	30	67	88
2	Morton	36	13	2	3	36	16	8	5	5	22	17	21	7	8	58	33	25	70
3	Peterhead	36	9	4	5	29	22	8	2	8	24	25	17	6	13	53	47	6	57
4	Partick Th	36	8	4	6	25	27	8	5	5	32	29	16	9	11	57	56	1	57
5	Stirling A	36	8	4	6	28	28	7	2	9	26	35	15	6	15	54	63	–9	51
6	Ayr U	36	5	5	8	23	26	5	7	6	33	35	10	12	14	56	61	–5	42
7	Raith R	36	5	5	8	25	28	6	4	8	19	26	11	9	16	44	54	–10	42
8	Forfar Ath	36	8	1	9	29	25	4	3	11	15	30	12	4	20	44	55	–11	40
9	Alloa Ath	36	3	5	10	15	37	5	3	10	21	40	8	8	20	36	77	–41	32
10	Dumbarton	36	5	3	10	26	26	2	2	14	14	37	7	5	24	40	63	–23	26

SCOTTISH FOOTBALL LEAGUE THIRD DIVISION

		Home						Away					Total						
		P	W	D	L	F	A	W	D	L	F	A	W	D	L	F	A	GD	Pts
1	Cowdenbeath	36	14	2	2	51	18	10	2	6	30	16	24	4	8	81	34	47	76
2	Berwick R	36	11	4	3	28	14	12	3	3	26	13	23	7	6	54	27	27	76
3	Stenhousemuir	36	13	1	4	45	17	10	3	5	33	21	23	4	9	78	38	40	73
4	Arbroath	36	12	2	4	35	18	4	5	9	22	29	16	7	13	57	47	10	55
5	Elgin C	36	6	5	7	28	30	9	2	7	27	28	15	7	14	55	58	–3	52
6	Queen's Park	36	6	7	5	29	24	7	5	6	18	18	13	12	11	47	42	5	51
7	East Fife	36	9	2	7	24	24	4	2	12	24	40	13	4	19	48	64	–16	43
8	Albion R	36	4	4	10	20	31	3	4	11	19	29	7	8	21	39	60	–21	29
9	Montrose	36	5	3	10	15	23	1	7	10	16	36	6	10	20	31	59	–28	28
10	East Stirling	36	5	4	9	14	30	1	1	16	14	59	6	5	25	28	89	–61	23

SCOTTISH LEAGUE HONOURS 1890 to 2006

*On goal average (ratio)/difference. †Held jointly after indecisive play-off. ‡Won on deciding match. ††Held jointly. ¶Two points deducted for fielding ineligible player. Competition suspended 1940–45 during war; Regional Leagues operating. ‡‡Two points deducted for registration irregularities. §Not promoted after play-offs,

PREMIER LEAGUE

	First	Pts	Second	Pts	Third	Pts
			Maximum points: 108			
1998–99	Rangers	77	Celtic	71	St Johnstone	57
1999–2000	Rangers	90	Celtic	69	Hearts	54
			Maximum points: 114			
2000–01	Celtic	97	Rangers	82	Hibernian	66
2001–02	Celtic	103	Rangers	85	Livingston	58
2002–03	Rangers*	97	Celtic	97	Hearts	63
2003–04	Celtic	98	Rangers	81	Hearts	68
2004–05	Rangers	93	Celtic	92	Hibernian*	61
2005–06	Celtic	91	Hearts	74	Rangers	73

PREMIER DIVISION

	First	Pts	Second	Pts	Third	Pts
			Maximum points: 72			
1975–76	Rangers	54	Celtic	48	Hibernian	43
1976–77	Celtic	55	Rangers	46	Aberdeen	43
1977–78	Rangers	55	Aberdeen	53	Dundee U	40
1978–79	Celtic	48	Rangers	45	Dundee U	44
1979–80	Aberdeen	48	Celtic	47	St Mirren	42
1980–81	Celtic	56	Aberdeen	49	Rangers*	44
1981–82	Celtic	55	Aberdeen	53	Rangers	43
1982–83	Dundee U	56	Celtic*	55	Aberdeen	55
1983–84	Aberdeen	57	Celtic	50	Dundee U	47
1984–85	Aberdeen	59	Celtic	52	Dundee U	47
1985–86	Celtic*	50	Hearts	50	Dundee U	47
			Maximum points: 88			
1986–87	Rangers	69	Celtic	63	Dundee U	60
1987–88	Celtic	72	Hearts	62	Rangers	60
			Maximum points: 72			
1988–89	Rangers	56	Aberdeen	50	Celtic	46
1989–90	Rangers	51	Aberdeen*	44	Hearts	44
1990–91	Rangers	55	Aberdeen	53	Celtic*	41
			Maximum points: 88			
1991–92	Rangers	72	Hearts	63	Celtic	62
1992–93	Rangers	73	Aberdeen	64	Celtic	60
1993–94	Rangers	58	Aberdeen	55	Motherwell	54
			Maximum points: 108			
1994–95	Rangers	69	Motherwell	54	Hibernian	53
1995–96	Rangers	87	Celtic	83	Aberdeen*	55
1996–97	Rangers	80	Celtic	75	Dundee U	60
1997–98	Celtic	74	Rangers	72	Hearts	67

FIRST DIVISION

	First	Pts	Second	Pts	Third	Pts
			Maximum points: 52			
1975–76	Partick Th	41	Kilmarnock	35	Montrose	30
			Maximum points: 78			
1976–77	St Mirren	62	Clydebank	58	Dundee	51
1977–78	Morton*	58	Hearts	58	Dundee	57
1978–79	Dundee	55	Kilmarnock*	54	Clydebank	54
1979–80	Hearts	53	Airdrieonians	51	Ayr U*	44
1980–81	Hibernian	57	Dundee	52	St Johnstone	51
1981–82	Motherwell	61	Kilmarnock	51	Hearts	50
1982–83	St Johnstone	55	Hearts	54	Clydebank	50
1983–84	Morton	54	Dumbarton	51	Partick Th	46
1984–85	Motherwell	50	Clydebank	48	Falkirk	45
1985–86	Hamilton A	56	Falkirk	45	Kilmarnock	44
			Maximum points: 88			
1986–87	Morton	57	Dunfermline Ath	56	Dumbarton	53
1987–88	Hamilton A	56	Meadowbank T	52	Clydebank	49
			Maximum points: 78			
1988–89	Dunfermline Ath	54	Falkirk	52	Clydebank	48
1989–90	St Johnstone	58	Airdrieonians	54	Clydebank	44
1990–91	Falkirk	54	Airdrieonians	53	Dundee	52
			Maximum points: 88			
1991–92	Dundee	58	Partick Th*	57	Hamilton A	57
1992–93	Raith R	65	Kilmarnock	54	Dunfermline Ath	52
1993–94	Falkirk	66	Dunfermline Ath	65	Airdrieonians	54
			Maximum points: 108			
1994–95	Raith R	69	Dunfermline Ath*	68	Dundee	68
1995–96	Dunfermline Ath	71	Dundee U*	67	Morton	67
1996–97	St Johnstone	80	Airdieonians	60	Dundee*	58
1997–98	Dundee	70	Falkirk	65	Raith R*	60
1998–99	Hibernian	89	Falkirk	66	Ayr U	62
1999–2000	St Mirren	76	Dunfermline Ath	71	Falkirk	68

	First	*Pts*	*Second*	*Pts*	*Third*	*Pts*
2000–01	Livingston	76	Ayr U	69	Falkirk	56
2001–02	Partick Th	66	Airdrieonians	56	Ayr U	52
2002–03	Falkirk	81	Clyde	72	St Johnstone	67
2003–04	Inverness CT	70	Clyde	69	St Johnstone	57
2004–05	Falkirk	75	St Mirren*	60	Clyde	60
2005–06	St Mirren	76	St Johnstone	66	Hamilton A	59

SECOND DIVISION

Maximum points: 52

	First	*Pts*	*Second*	*Pts*	*Third*	*Pts*
1975–76	Clydebank*	40	Raith R	40	Alloa Ath	35
			Maximum points: 78			
1976–77	Stirling A	55	Alloa Ath	51	Dunfermline Ath	50
1977–78	Clyde*	53	Raith R	53	Dunfermline Ath	48
1978–79	Berwick R	54	Dunfermline Ath	52	Falkirk	50
1979–80	Falkirk	50	East Stirling	49	Forfar Ath	46
1980–81	Queen's Park	50	Queen of the S	46	Cowdenbeath	45
1981–82	Clyde	59	Alloa Ath*	50	Arbroath	50
1982–83	Brechin C	55	Meadowbank Th	54	Arbroath	49
1983–84	Forfar Ath	63	East Fife	47	Berwick R	43
1984–85	Montrose	53	Alloa Ath	50	Dunfermline Ath	49
1985–86	Dunfermline Ath	57	Queen of the S	55	Meadowbank Th	49
1986–87	Meadowbank Th	55	Raith R*	52	Stirling A*	52
1987–88	Ayr U	61	St Johnstone	59	Queen's Park	51
1988–89	Albion R	50	Alloa Ath	45	Brechin C	43
1989–90	Brechin C	49	Kilmarnock	48	Stirling A	47
1990–91	Stirling A	54	Montrose	46	Cowdenbeath	45
1991–92	Dumbarton	52	Cowdenbeath	51	Alloa Ath	50
1992–93	Clyde	54	Brechin C*	53	Stranraer	53
1993–94	Stranraer	56	Berwick R	48	Stenhousemuir*	47
			Maximum points: 108			
1994–95	Morton	64	Dumbarton	60	Stirling A	58
1995–96	Stirling A	81	East Fife	67	Berwick R	60
1996–97	Ayr U	77	Hamilton A	74	Livingston	64
1997–98	Stranraer	61	Clydebank	60	Livingston	59
1998–99	Livingston	77	Inverness CT	72	Clyde	53
1999–2000	Clyde	65	Alloa Ath	64	Ross Co	62
2000–01	Partick Th	75	Arbroath	58	Berwick R*	54
2001–02	Queen of the S	67	Alloa Ath	59	Forfar Ath	53
2002–03	Raith R	59	Brechin C	55	Airdrie U	54
2003–04	Airdrie U	70	Hamilton A	62	Dumbarton	60
2004–05	Brechin C	72	Stranraer	63	Morton	62
2005–06	Gretna	88	Morton§	70	Peterhead*§	57

THIRD DIVISION

Maximum points: 108

	First	*Pts*	*Second*	*Pts*	*Third*	*Pts*
1994–95	Forfar Ath	80	Montrose	67	Ross Co	60
1995–96	Livingston	72	Brechin C	63	Inverness CT	57
1996–97	Inverness CT	76	Forfar Ath*	67	Ross Co	67
1997–98	Alloa Ath	76	Arbroath	68	Ross Co*	67
1998–99	Ross Co	77	Stenhousemuir	64	Brechin C	59
1999–2000	Queen's Park	69	Berwick R	66	Forfar Ath	61
2000–01	Hamilton A*	76	Cowdenbeath	76	Brechin C	72
2001–02	Brechin C	73	Dumbarton	61	Albion R	59
2002–03	Morton	72	East Fife	71	Albion R	70
2003–04	Stranraer	79	Stirling A	77	Gretna	68
2004–05	Gretna	98	Peterhead	78	Cowdenbeath	51
2005–06	Cowdenbeath*	76	Berwick R§	76	Stenhousemuir§	73

FIRST DIVISION to 1974–75

Maximum points: a 36; *b* 44; *c* 40; *d* 52; *e* 60; *f* 68; g 76; *h* 84.

	First	*Pts*	*Second*	*Pts*	*Third*	*Pts*
1890–91*a*	Dumbarton††	29	Rangers††	29	Celtic	21
1891–92*b*	Dumbarton	37	Celtic	35	Hearts	34
1892–93*a*	Celtic	29	Rangers	28	St Mirren	20
1893–94*a*	Celtic	29	Hearts	26	St Bernard's	23
1894–95*a*	Hearts	31	Celtic	26	Rangers	22
1895–96*a*	Celtic	30	Rangers	26	Hibernian	24
1896–97*a*	Hearts	28	Hibernian	26	Rangers	25
1897–98*a*	Celtic	33	Rangers	29	Hibernian	22
1898–99*a*	Rangers	36	Hearts	26	Celtic	24
1899–1900*a*	Rangers	32	Celtic	25	Hibernian	24
1900–01*c*	Rangers	35	Celtic	29	Hibernian	25
1901–02*a*	Rangers	28	Celtic	26	Hearts	22
1902–03*b*	Hibernian	37	Dundee	31	Rangers	29
1903–04*d*	Third Lanark	43	Hearts	39	Celtic*	38
1904–05*d*	Celtic‡	41	Rangers	41	Third Lanark	35
1905–06*e*	Celtic	49	Hearts	43	Airdrieonians	38
1906–07*f*	Celtic	55	Dundee	48	Rangers	45
1907–08*f*	Celtic	55	Falkirk	51	Rangers	50
1908–09*f*	Celtic	51	Dundee	50	Clyde	48
1909–10*f*	Celtic	54	Falkirk	52	Rangers	46
1910–11*f*	Rangers	52	Aberdeen	48	Falkirk	44
1911–12*f*	Rangers	51	Celtic	45	Clyde	42
1912–13*f*	Rangers	53	Celtic	49	Hearts*	41

	First	*Pts*	*Second*	*Pts*	*Third*	*Pts*
1913–14*g*	Celtic	65	Rangers	59	Hearts*	54
1914–15*g*	Celtic	65	Hearts	61	Rangers	50
1915–16*g*	Celtic	67	Rangers	56	Morton	51
1916–17*g*	Celtic	64	Morton	54	Rangers	53
1917–18*f*	Rangers	56	Celtic	55	Kilmarnock*	43
1918–19*f*	Celtic	58	Rangers	57	Morton	47
1919–20*h*	Rangers	71	Celtic	68	Motherwell	57
1920–21*h*	Rangers	76	Celtic	66	Hearts	50
1921–22*h*	Celtic	67	Rangers	66	Raith R	51
1922–23*g*	Rangers	55	Airdrieonians	50	Celtic	46
1923–24*g*	Rangers	59	Airdrieonians	50	Celtic	46
1924–25*g*	Rangers	60	Airdrieonians	57	Hibernian	52
1925–26*g*	Celtic	58	Airdrieonians*	50	Hearts	50
1926–27*g*	Rangers	56	Motherwell	51	Celtic	49
1927–28*g*	Rangers	60	Celtic*	55	Motherwell	55
1928–29*g*	Rangers	67	Celtic	51	Motherwell	50
1929–30*g*	Rangers	60	Motherwell	55	Aberdeen	53
1930–31*g*	Rangers	60	Celtic	58	Motherwell	56
1931–32*g*	Motherwell	66	Rangers	61	Celtic	48
1932–33*g*	Rangers	62	Motherwell	59	Hearts	50
1933–34*g*	Rangers	66	Motherwell	62	Celtic	47
1934–35*g*	Rangers	55	Celtic	52	Hearts	50
1935–36*g*	Celtic	66	Rangers*	61	Aberdeen	61
1936–37*g*	Rangers	61	Aberdeen	54	Celtic	52
1937–38*g*	Celtic	61	Hearts	58	Rangers	49
1938–39*g*	Rangers	59	Celtic	48	Aberdeen	46
1946–47*e*	Rangers	46	Hibernian	44	Aberdeen	39
1947–48*e*	Hibernian	48	Rangers	46	Partick Th	36
1948–49*e*	Rangers	46	Dundee	45	Hibernian	39
1949–50*e*	Rangers	50	Hibernian	49	Hearts	43
1950–51*e*	Hibernian	48	Rangers*	38	Dundee	38
1951–52*e*	Hibernian	45	Rangers	41	East Fife	37
1952–53*e*	Rangers*	43	Hibernian	43	East Fife	39
1953–54*e*	Celtic	43	Hearts	38	Partick Th	35
1954–55*e*	Aberdeen	49	Celtic	46	Rangers	41
1955–56*f*	Rangers	52	Aberdeen	46	Hearts*	45
1956–57*f*	Rangers	55	Hearts	53	Kilmarnock	42
1957–58*f*	Hearts	62	Rangers	49	Celtic	46
1958–59*f*	Rangers	50	Hearts	48	Motherwell	44
1959–60*f*	Hearts	54	Kilmarnock	50	Rangers*	42
1960–61*f*	Rangers	51	Kilmarnock	50	Third Lanark	42
1961–62*f*	Dundee	54	Rangers	51	Celtic	46
1962–63*f*	Rangers	57	Kilmarnock	48	Partick Th	46
1963–64*f*	Rangers	55	Kilmarnock	49	Celtic*	47
1964–65*f*	Kilmarnock*	50	Hearts	50	Dunfermline Ath	49
1965–66*f*	Celtic	57	Rangers	55	Kilmarnock	45
1966–67*f*	Celtic	58	Rangers	55	Clyde	46
1967–68*f*	Celtic	63	Rangers	61	Hibernian	45
1968–69*f*	Celtic	54	Rangers	49	Dunfermline Ath	45
1969–70*f*	Celtic	57	Rangers	45	Hibernian	44
1970–71*f*	Celtic	56	Aberdeen	54	St Johnstone	44
1971–72*f*	Celtic	60	Aberdeen	50	Rangers	44
1972–73*f*	Celtic	57	Rangers	56	Hibernian	45
1973–74*f*	Celtic	53	Hibernian	49	Rangers	48
1974–75*f*	Rangers	56	Hibernian	49	Celtic	45

SECOND DIVISION to 1974–75

Maximum points: a 76; *b* 72; *c* 68; *d* 52; *e* 60; *f* 36; *g* 44.

	First	Pts	Second	Pts	Third	Pts
1893–94*f*	Hibernian	29	Cowlairs	27	Clyde	24
1894–95*f*	Hibernian	30	Motherwell	22	Port Glasgow	20
1895–96*f*	Abercorn	27	Leith Ath	23	Renton	21
1896–97*f*	Partick Th	31	Leith Ath	27	Kilmarnock*	21
1897–98*f*	Kilmarnock	29	Port Glasgow	25	Morton	22
1898–99*f*	Kilmarnock	32	Leith Ath	27	Port Glasgow	25
1899–1900*f*	Partick Th	29	Morton	28	Port Glasgow	20
1900–01*f*	St Bernard's	25	Airdrieonians	23	Abercorn	21
1901–02*g*	Port Glasgow	32	Partick Th	31	Motherwell	26
1902–03*g*	Airdrieonians	35	Motherwell	28	Ayr U*	27
1903–04*g*	Hamilton A	37	Clyde	29	Ayr U	28
1904–05*g*	Clyde	32	Falkirk	28	Hamilton A	27
1905–06*g*	Leith Ath	34	Clyde	31	Albion R	27
1906–07*g*	St Bernard's	32	Vale of Leven*	27	Arthurlie	27
1907–08*g*	Raith R	30	Dumbarton*‡‡	27	Ayr U	27
1908–09*g*	Abercorn	31	Raith R*	28	Vale of Leven	28
1909–10*g*	Leith Ath‡	33	Raith R	33	St Bernard's	27
1910–11*g*	Dumbarton	31	Ayr U	27	Albion R	25
1911–12*g*	Ayr U	35	Abercorn	30	Dumbarton	27
1912–13*d*	Ayr U	34	Dunfermline Ath	33	East Stirling	32
1913–14*g*	Cowdenbeath	31	Albion R	27	Dunfermline Ath*	26
1914–15*d*	Cowdenbeath*	37	St Bernard's*	37	Leith Ath	37
1921–22*a*	Alloa Ath	60	Cowdenbeath	47	Armadale	45
1922–23*a*	Queen's Park	57	Clydebank¶	50	St Johnstone¶	45
1923–24*a*	St Johnstone	56	Cowdenbeath	55	Bathgate	44
1924–25*a*	Dundee U	50	Clydebank	48	Clyde	47

	First	*Pts*	*Second*	*Pts*	*Third*	*Pts*
1925–26*a*	Dunfermline Ath	59	Clyde	53	Ayr U	52
1926–27*a*	Bo'ness	56	Raith R	49	Clydebank	45
1927–28*a*	Ayr U	54	Third Lanark	45	King's Park	44
1928–29*b*	Dundee U	51	Morton	50	Arbroath	47
1929–30*a*	Leith Ath*	57	East Fife	57	Albion R	54
1930–31*a*	Third Lanark	61	Dundee U	50	Dunfermline Ath	47
1931–32*a*	East Stirling*	55	St Johnstone	55	Raith R*	46
1932–33*c*	Hibernian	54	Queen of the S	49	Dunfermline Ath	47
1933–34*c*	Albion R	45	Dunfermline Ath*	44	Arbroath	44
1934–35*c*	Third Lanark	52	Arbroath	50	St Bernard's	47
1935–36*c*	Falkirk	59	St Mirren	52	Morton	48
1936–37*c*	Ayr U	54	Morton	51	St Bernard's	48
1937–38*c*	Raith R	59	Albion R	48	Airdrieonians	47
1938–39*c*	Cowdenbeath	60	Alloa Ath*	48	East Fife	48
1946–47*d*	Dundee	45	Airdrieonians	42	East Fife	31
1947–48*e*	East Fife	53	Albion R	42	Hamilton A	40
1948–49*e*	Raith R*	42	Stirling A	42	Airdrieonians*	41
1949–50*e*	Morton	47	Airdrieonians	44	Dunfermline Ath*	36
1950–51*e*	Queen of the S*	45	Stirling A	45	Ayr U*	36
1951–52*e*	Clyde	44	Falkirk	43	Ayr U	39
1952–53*e*	Stirling A	44	Hamilton A	43	Queen's Park	37
1953–54*e*	Motherwell	45	Kilmarnock	42	Third Lanark*	36
1954–55*e*	Airdrieonians	46	Dunfermline Ath	42	Hamilton A	39
1955–56*b*	Queen's Park	54	Ayr U	51	St Johnstone	49
1956–57*b*	Clyde	64	Third Lanark	51	Cowdenbeath	45
1957–58*b*	Stirling A	55	Dunfermline Ath	53	Arbroath	47
1958–59*b*	Ayr U	60	Arbroath	51	Stenhousemuir	46
1959–60*b*	St Johnstone	53	Dundee U	50	Queen of the S	49
1960–61*b*	Stirling A	55	Falkirk	54	Stenhousemuir	50
1961–62*b*	Clyde	54	Queen of the S	53	Morton	44
1962–63*b*	St Johnstone	55	East Stirling	49	Morton	48
1963–64*b*	Morton	67	Clyde	53	Arbroath	46
1964–65*b*	Stirling A	59	Hamilton A	50	Queen of the S	45
1965–66*b*	Ayr U	53	Airdrieonians	50	Queen of the S	47
1966–67*a*	Morton	69	Raith R	58	Arbroath	57
1967–68*b*	St Mirren	62	Arbroath	53	East Fife	49
1968–69*b*	Motherwell	64	Ayr U	53	East Fife*	48
1969–70*b*	Falkirk	56	Cowdenbeath	55	Queen of the S	50
1970–71*b*	Partick Th	56	East Fife	51	Arbroath	46
1971–72*b*	Dumbarton*	52	Arbroath	52	Stirling A	50
1972–73*b*	Clyde	56	Dumfermline Ath	52	Raith R*	47
1973–74*b*	Airdrieonians	60	Kilmarnock	58	Hamilton A	55
1974–75*a*	Falkirk	54	Queen of the S*	53	Montrose	53

Elected to First Division: 1894 Clyde; 1895 Hibernian; 1896 Abercorn; 1897 Partick Th; 1899 Kilmarnock; 1900 Morton and Partick Th; 1902 Port Glasgow and Partick Th; 1903 Airdrieonians and Motherwell; 1905 Falkirk and Aberdeen; 1906 Clyde and Hamilton A; 1910 Raith R; 1913 Ayr U and Dumbarton.

RELEGATED FROM PREMIER LEAGUE

1998–99 Dunfermline Ath
1999–2000 *No relegation due to League reorganization*
2000–01 St Mirren
2001–02 St Johnstone
2002–03 *No relegated team*
2003–04 Partick Th
2004–05 Dundee
2005–06 Livingston

RELEGATED FROM PREMIER DIVISION

1974–75 *No relegation due to League reorganization*
1975–76 Dundee, St Johnstone
1976–77 Hearts, Kilmarnock
1977–78 Ayr U, Clydebank
1978–79 Hearts, Motherwell
1979–80 Dundee, Hibernian
1980–81 Kilmarnock, Hearts
1981–82 Partick Th, Airdrieonians
1982–83 Morton, Kilmarnock
1983–84 St Johnstone, Motherwell
1984–85 Dumbarton, Morton
1985–86 *No relegation due to League reorganization*
1986–87 Clydebank, Hamilton A
1987–88 Falkirk, Dunfermline Ath, Morton
1988–89 Hamilton A
1989–90 Dundee
1990–91 *None*
1991–92 St Mirren, Dunfermline Ath
1992–93 Falkirk, Airdrieonians
1993–94 *See footnote*
1994–95 Dundee U
1995–96 Partick Th, Falkirk
1996–97 Raith R
1997–98 Hibernian

RELEGATED FROM DIVISION 1

1974–75 *No relegation due to League reorganization*
1975–76 Dunfermline Ath, Clyde
1976–77 Raith R, Falkirk
1977–78 Alloa Ath, East Fife
1978–79 Montrose, Queen of the S
1979–80 Arbroath, Clyde
1980–81 Stirling A, Berwick R
1981–82 East Stirling, Queen of the S
1982–83 Dunfermline Ath, Queen's Park
1983–84 Raith R, Alloa Ath
1984–85 Meadowbank Th, St Johnstone
1985–86 Ayr U, Alloa Ath
1986–87 Brechin C, Montrose
1987–88 East Fife, Dumbarton
1988–89 Kilmarnock, Queen of the S
1989–90 Albion R, Alloa Ath
1990–91 Clyde, Brechin C
1991–92 Montrose, Forfar Ath
1992–93 Meadowbank Th, Cowdenbeath
1993–94 *See footnote*
1994–95 Ayr U, Stranraer
1995–96 Hamilton A, Dumbarton
1996–97 Clydebank, East Fife
1997–98 Partick Th, Stirling A
1998–99 Hamilton A, Stranraer
1999–2000 Clydebank
2000–01 Morton, Alloa Ath
2001–02 Raith R
2002–03 Alloa Ath, Arbroath
2003–04 Ayr U, Brechin C
2004–05 Partick Th, Raith R
2005–06 Stranraer, Brechin C

RELEGATED FROM DIVISION 2

1994–95 Meadowbank Th, Brechin C
1995–96 Forfar Ath, Montrose
1996–97 Dumbarton, Berwick R
1997–98 Stenhousemuir, Brechin C
1998–99 East Fife, Forfar Ath
1999–2000 Hamilton A**
2000–01 Queen's Park, Stirling A
2001–02 Morton
2002–03 Stranraer, Cowdenbeath
2003–04 East Fife, Stenhousemuir
2004–05 Arbroath, Berwick R
2005–06 Dumbarton

RELEGATED FROM DIVISION 1 (TO 1973–74)

1921–22 *Queen's Park, Dumbarton, Clydebank
1922–23 Albion R, Alloa Ath
1923–24 Clyde, Clydebank
1924–25 Third Lanark, Ayr U
1925–26 Raith R, Clydebank
1926–27 Morton, Dundee U
1927–28 Dunfermline Ath, Bo'ness
1928–29 Third Lanark, Raith R
1929–30 St Johnstone, Dundee U
1930–31 Hibernian, East Fife
1931–32 Dundee U, Leith Ath
1932–33 Morton, East Stirling
1933–34 Third Lanark, Cowdenbeath
1934–35 St Mirren, Falkirk
1935–36 Airdrieonians, Ayr U
1936–37 Dunfermline Ath, Albion R
1937–38 Dundee, Morton
1938–39 Queen's Park, Raith R
1946–47 Kilmarnock, Hamilton A
1947–48 Airdrieonians, Queen's Park
1948–49 Morton, Albion R
1949–50 Queen of the S, Stirling A
1950–51 Clyde, Falkirk
1951–52 Morton, Stirling A
1952–53 Motherwell, Third Lanark
1953–54 Airdrieonians, Hamilton A
1954–55 *No clubs relegated*
1955–56 Stirling A, Clyde
1956–57 Dunfermline Ath, Ayr U
1957–58 East Fife, Queen's Park
1958–59 Queen of the S, Falkirk
1959–60 Arbroath, Stirling A
1960–61 Ayr U, Clyde
1961–62 St Johnstone, Stirling A
1962–63 Clyde, Raith R
1963–64 Queen of the S, East Stirling
1964–65 Airdrieonians, Third Lanark
1965–66 Morton, Hamilton A
1966–67 St Mirren, Ayr U
1967–68 Motherwell, Stirling A
1968–69 Falkirk, Arbroath
1969–70 Raith R, Partick Th
1970–71 St Mirren, Cowdenbeath
1971–72 Clyde, Dunfermline Ath
1972–73 Kilmarnock, Airdrieonians
1973–74 East Fife, Falkirk

*Season 1921–22 – only 1 club promoted, 3 clubs relegated. ***15pts deducted for failing to field a team.*

Scottish League Championship wins: Rangers 51, Celtic 40, Aberdeen 4, Hearts 4, Hibernian 4, Dumbarton 2, Dundee 1, Dundee U 1, Kilmarnock 1, Motherwell 1, Third Lanark 1.

At the end of the 1993–94 season four divisions were created assisted by the admission of two new clubs Ross County and Caledonian Thistle. Only one club was promoted from Division 1 and Division 2. The three relegated from the Premier joined with teams finishing second to seventh in Division 1 to form the new Division 1. Five relegated from Division 1 combined with those who finished second to sixth to form a new Division 2 and the bottom eight in Division 2 linked with the two newcomers to form a new Division 3. At the end of the 1997–98 season the nine clubs remaining in the Premier Division plus the promoted team from Division 1 formed a breakaway Premier League. At the end of the 1999–2000 season two teams were added to the Scottish League. There was no relegation from the Premier League but two promoted from the First Division and three from each of the Second and Third Divisions. One team was relegated from the First Division and one from the Second Division, leaving 12 teams in each division. In season 2002–03, Falkirk were not promoted to the Premier League due to the failure of their ground to meet League rules. Inverness CT were promoted after a previous refusal in 2003–04 because of ground sharing. At the end of 2005–06 the Scottish League introduced play-offs for the team finishing second from the bottom of Division 1 against the winners of the second, third and fourth finishing teams in Division 2 and with a similar procedure for Division 2 and Division 3.

Celebrations by the Hearts players at their penalty shoot-out triumph over Gretna in the Tennent's Scottish Cup Final at Hampden Park. (Lee Smith Livepic/Actionimages)

SCOTTISH LEAGUE CUP FINALS 1946–2006

Season	*Winners*	*Runners-up*	*Score*
1946–47	Rangers	Aberdeen	4-0
1947–48	East Fife	Falkirk	4-1 after 0-0 draw
1948–49	Rangers	Raith R	2-0
1949–50	East Fife	Dunfermline Ath	3-0
1950–51	Motherwell	Hibernian	3-0
1951–52	Dundee	Rangers	3-2
1952–53	Dundee	Kilmarnock	2-0
1953–54	East Fife	Partick Th	3-2
1954–55	Hearts	Motherwell	4-2
1955–56	Aberdeen	St Mirren	2-1
1956–57	Celtic	Partick Th	3-0 after 0-0 draw
1957–58	Celtic	Rangers	7-1
1958–59	Hearts	Partick Th	5-1
1959–60	Hearts	Third Lanark	2-1
1960–61	Rangers	Kilmarnock	2-0
1961–62	Rangers	Hearts	3-1 after 1-1 draw
1962–63	Hearts	Kilmarnock	1-0
1963–64	Rangers	Morton	5-0
1964–65	Rangers	Celtic	2-1
1965–66	Celtic	Rangers	2-1
1966–67	Celtic	Rangers	1-0
1967–68	Celtic	Dundee	5-3
1968–69	Celtic	Hibernian	6-2
1969–70	Celtic	St Johnstone	1-0
1970–71	Rangers	Celtic	1-0
1971–72	Partick Th	Celtic	4-1
1972–73	Hibernian	Celtic	2-1
1973–74	Dundee	Celtic	1-0
1974–75	Celtic	Hibernian	6-3
1975–76	Rangers	Celtic	1-0
1976–77	Aberdeen	Celtic	2-1
1977–78	Rangers	Celtic	2-1
1978–79	Rangers	Aberdeen	2-1
1979–80	Dundee U	Aberdeen	3-0 after 0-0 draw
1980–81	Dundee U	Dundee	3-0
1981–82	Rangers	Dundee U	2-1
1982–83	Celtic	Rangers	2-1
1983–84	Rangers	Celtic	3-2
1984–85	Rangers	Dundee U	1-0
1985–86	Aberdeen	Hibernian	3-0
1986–87	Rangers	Celtic	2-1
1987–88	Rangers	Aberdeen	3-3
		(Rangers won 5-3 on penalties)	
1988–89	Rangers	Aberdeen	3-2
1989–90	Aberdeen	Rangers	2-1
1990–91	Rangers	Celtic	2-1
1991–92	Hibernian	Dunfermline Ath	2-0
1992–93	Rangers	Aberdeen	2-1
1993–94	Rangers	Hibernian	2-1
1994–95	Raith R	Celtic	2-2
		(Raith R won 6-5 on penalties)	
1995–96	Aberdeen	Dundee	2-0
1996–97	Rangers	Hearts	4-3
1997–98	Celtic	Dundee U	3-0
1998–99	Rangers	St Johnstone	2-1
1999–2000	Celtic	Aberdeen	2-0
2000–01	Celtic	Kilmarnock	3-0
2001–02	Rangers	Ayr U	4-0
2002–03	Rangers	Celtic	2-1
2003–04	Livingston	Hibernian	2-0
2004–05	Rangers	Motherwell	5-1
2005–06	Celtic	Dunfermline Ath	3-0

SCOTTISH LEAGUE CUP WINS

Rangers 24, Celtic 13, Aberdeen 5, Hearts 4, Dundee 3, East Fife 3, Dundee U 2, Hibernian 2, Livingston 1, Motherwell 1, Partick Th 1, Raith R 1.

APPEARANCES IN FINALS

Rangers 30, Celtic 26, Aberdeen 12, Hibernian 8, Dundee 6, Hearts 6, Dundee U 5, Kilmarnock 4, Partick Th 4, Dunfermline Ath 3, East Fife 3, Motherwell 3, Raith R 2, St Johnstone 2, Ayr U 1, Falkirk 1, Livingston 1, Morton 1, St Mirren 1, Third Lanark 1.

CIS SCOTTISH LEAGUE CUP 2005–06

■ *Denotes player sent off.*

FIRST ROUND

Tuesday, 9 August 2005

Alloa Ath (1) 2 *(Stevenson J 18, 119)*

Arbroath (1) 1 *(Brazil 44)* 303

Alloa Ath: McGlynn; Walker, Thomson (Sloan), Bolochoweckyj, Townsley, Ovenstone, Quitongo (Mortimer), Nicolson, Brown, Hamilton (Greenhill), Stevenson J.
Arbroath: Cairns; McMullan, Black, Bishop, Cormack, McCulloch, Miller, Davidson (Cook), Brazil, Jackson (Warren), Stein.
aet.

Berwick R (0) 4 *(Hutchison 53, 70, McNicoll 58, McLeish 90)*

Elgin C (2) 2 *(Muir 7, Dickson 30)* 269

Berwick R: Coyle; Murie, McGroarty, McNicoll, Cowan, Greenhill, Arthur (Swanson), McLeish, Hutchison, Haynes, Little.
Elgin C: Renton; Cumming, Dempsie, McKenzie J, Dickson, Scullion (Wood), Bremner (Reid), Muir (Easton), Johnston, Booth, Gardiner.

Brechin C (0) 0

Partick T (0) 0 603

Brechin C: Nelson; Hamilton (White), Deas, Walker, Craig, Callaghan, King (Ritchie), Ferguson■, Hampshire (Burns), Winter, Gibson.
Partick T: Arthur; Murray, Snowdon, Santala, Smyth, McCulloch (Fleming), Nicholas (McGoldrick), Gillies, McConalogue (Gibson A), Brady, Kilgannon.
aet; Partick T won 3-1 on penalties.

Cowdenbeath (1) 2 *(Ward 28, Gribben 69)*

St Johnstone (2) 3 *(Dobbie 12, 30, Milne 85)* 849

Cowdenbeath: Hay; Guy, McBride, Ward, McGregor, Ritchie, Mauchlen, Fusco■, Downs (Grant), Gribben, Hill.
St Johnstone: Cuthbert; Stevenson, Stanik, Mensing, Campbell■, James, McCann (Henry), Sheerin, Milne, Dobbie (MacDonald), Janczyk.

East Fife (0) 0

Stranraer (0) 1 *(Hinds 72)* 235

East Fife: Dodds; Kelly, Donaldson, Lumsden, McDonald G, Beith, Paliczka (Fortune), Hampshire, Smart, Martin, Pelosi (Port).
Stranraer: Morrison; Swift, Keddie, Higgins, Henderson, Jenkins, Hamilton, Dowie (Sharp), McLean (Hinds), Walker, Ross.

East Stirling (0) 1 *(Diack 57)*

Queen's Park (3) 3 *(Ferry 22, Weatherston 32, Harvey 45)* 200

East Stirling: Jackson; Oates, Gourlay, Mackay (Gordon), Livingstone, Tyrrell P, Dymock, Blair■, Diack, Graham, Ure.
Queen's Park: Crawford; Clark, Molloy, Reilly, Sinclair, Harvey, Weir, Quinn, Whelan (Felvus), Weatherston, Ferry.

Forfar Ath (0) 1 *(Conway 86)*

Ross Co (1) 4 *(Webb 18, Winters 91, Higgins 112, McGarry 114)* 296

Forfar Ath: Ferrie; Bonar, Lowing, Forrest, Dunn, Donald, Sellars, McClune (Florence), Voigt (Rattray), Conway, Waddell.
Ross Co: McCaldon; McCulloch, Djebi-Zadi, Webb, Canning, Taylor (Hooks), Rankin, Higgins, Burke (Nuckowski), McGarry, McKinlay (Winters).
aet.

Hamilton A (0) 2 *(Tunbridge 84, 86)*

Dumbarton (1) 1 *(Rodgers 10)* 627

Hamilton A: McEwan; Stevenson, Hodge, Thomson, Ferguson (McLaughlin), McArthur (Robertson), Sim (Keogh), Bennett, Tunbridge, Hardy, Carrigan.
Dumbarton: Wight; Smith, Walker, Dobbins, Ronald, MacDonald, Borris, Dillon, McQuilken (Gentile), Rodgers (Russell), Allan (Ferry).

Montrose (0) 0

Clyde (1) 1 *(Brighton 11)* 414

Montrose: Butter; Dodds, Smith E, Doyle (Mackenzie), Stephen, Kerrigan, Webster, Fotheringham, Martin (Donachie), Watson (McLean), Henslee.
Clyde: Jarvie; McGregor N, Malone, Higgins, McKeown, McHale, Bryson, O'Donnell, Williams (Miller), Brighton (Hunter), McGowan.

Morton (0) 1 *(Lilley 60)*

Ayr U (2) 2 *(Strain 8, 18)* 2397

Morton: McGurn; Weatherson, Walker A, Harding, Greacen, McLaren, Millar, Finlayson, Templeman (Walker J), Lilley, McAlister.
Ayr U: McGeown; McKinstry, Reid, McLaughlin, Campbell, Logan, Hyslop (Casey), Ramsay, Vareille (Wardlaw), Strain (Cashmore), Robertson.

Raith R (1) 2 *(Annand 6, Jablonski 57)*

Airdrie U (0) 0 1237

Raith R: Brown; Lyle, Ellis, Silvestro, Lumsden, McLeod, Crilly, Ferguson, Annand (Jaconelli), McManus (Fairbairn), Jablonski.
Airdrie U: Hollis; Coyle, Lovering (Dunn), McGowan, McManus, McKeown, Marshall (McDougall), Docherty, Roberts, Twigg, McLaren.

Stenhousemuir (0) 0

Peterhead (1) 1 *(Linn 37)* 182

Stenhousemuir: McCulloch; Renwick, Henderson, Denham (McInally), McKeown, Mercer, McKenzie (Morrison), Collins, Carroll, Cramb (Savage), McGrillen.
Peterhead: Mathers; Tully, Good, Raeside, Shand, Gibson, Sharp, Buchan (Stewart G), Bavidge, Linn (Hegarty), Cameron (Hagen).

Wednesday, 10 August 2005

Albion R (0) 1 *(Chisholm 89)*

Gretna (1) 2 *(Deuchar 6, Grady 75)* 273

Albion R: Ewings; Lennox, Black, O'Neil (Sichi), Lennon, McGhee, Bonnar (Franch), Friel, Chisholm, Young, Donnelly (Wilson).
Gretna: Main; Nicholls (McQuilken), Aitken, McGuffie, Townsley, Innes, Baldacchino, Grady, Deuchar, Bingham, Skelton (Tosh).

Stirling Albion (2) 2 *(Connolly 10, 12)*

Queen of the S (1) 1 *(McNiven 32)* 723

Stirling Albion: Hogarth; Nugent, Devine, Roycroft, Graham, Boyack, Hay P, Fraser, Dunn (Hay C), Connolly, O'Brien.
Queen of the S: Barnard; Paton (Burns), English, Gibson W, Wood, Carr (Thomson), Lovell, Bowey, McNiven, Lyle, Payne.

SECOND ROUND

Tuesday, 23 August 2005

Aberdeen (1) 3 *(Winter 38, McNicoll (og) 52, Lovell 71)*

Berwick R (0) 0 4398

Aberdeen: Langfield; Byrne, McNaughton, Dempsey (Muirhead), Diamond, Severin, Nicholson, Winter, Lovell (Craig), Smith (Stewart), Clark.
Berwick R: Coyle; Murie, McGroarty, McNicoll, Horn, McGarty (Greenhill), Gordon (Da Silva), Arthur, Hutchison, McLeish, Little (Swanson).

Falkirk (2) 2 *(O'Donnell 9, 26)*

Partick T (1) 1 *(Gillies 22)* 2575

Falkirk: Glennon; Lawrie, McPherson, Lima (Scally), Rodrigues, Ireland (Ross), Thomson S, O'Donnell, McBreen (Gow), Latapy, Duffy.
Partick T: Arthur; Murray, Snowdon, Santala, Smyth (Gibson A), McCulloch, Gibson J (Gibson W), Gillies, Nicholas (McConalogue), Brady, Kilgannon.

Gretna (0) 0

Dunfermline (1) 1 *(Burchill 17)* 1405

Gretna: Main; Collins (Nicholls), McQuilken (Skelton), Tosh, Townsley, Innes, Baldacchino, McGuffie, Deuchar, Bingham, Grady.
Dunfermline: Halliwell; Campbell, Wilson S, Thomson, Labonte, Darren Young, Makel, Mason, Tarachulski (Derek Young), Tod, Burchill (Hunt).

Inverness CT (4) 6 *(Wilson 19, Hart 20, McBain 37, Duncan 42, Munro 47, Wyness 86)*

Alloa Ath (1) 1 *(Brown A 45)* 917

Inverness CT: Brown; Tokely (Parratt), Golabek, Proctor, Munro, Duncan, Wilson (McAllister), Wyness, Dargo, Hart, McBain (Fox).
Alloa Ath: Evans J; Walker, Thomson (Sloan), Bolochoweckyj, Townsley, Ovenstone, Brown A (Brown G), Mortimer, Hamilton (Quitongo), Stevenson J, Nicolson.

Kilmarnock (1) 4 *(Dodds 42, Invincibile 56, Wales 75, Di Giacomo 81)*

Stirling Albion (1) 1 *(Boyack 11)* 3124

Kilmarnock: Combe; Fowler, Ford, Greer, Hay, Leven, Murray (Johnston), Dodds, Invincibile, Nish (Di Giacomo), Naismith (Wales).
Stirling Albion: Hogarth; Nugent, Forsyth, Graham, Roycroft, Hay P, Wilson (Dunn), Boyack, Turnbull, Devine (Hutchison), O'Brien.

Motherwell (1) 2 *(McDonald 40, Hamilton 84)*

Hamilton A (1) 1 *(Jones 33)* 4619

Motherwell: Meldrum; Quinn, Donnelly R, Hammell, Fagan (Foran), McCormack (Keogh), O'Donnell, Kerr, Smith A, Hamilton, McDonald.
Hamilton A: McEwan; Robertson, Hodge, Thomson, McLaughlin, Neil■, Ferguson, Wilson, Jones (Tunbridge), Hardy■, Carrigan (McArthur).

Peterhead (2) 2 *(Youngson 33, Michie 43 (pen))*

Clyde (1) 3 *(McGregor N 3, Arbuckle 55, Brighton 73)* 584

Peterhead: Mathers; Tully, Cameron, Raeside, Perry, Gibson, Hegarty, Buchan, Michie (Bavidge) (Linn), Wood, Youngson (Sharp).
Clyde: Cherrie; McGregor N, Malone, Higgins■, McKeown, McHale, Bryson, O'Donnell, Williams (Arbuckle), Brighton (Hunter), McGowan (Brawley).

Queen's Park (0) 0

Hearts (2) 2 *(Jankauskis 15, 44)* 2429

Queen's Park: Crawford; Clark, Molloy, McGinty, Sinclair, Harvey (Reilly), Kettlewell, Quinn, Bowers (Weatherston), Weir (Whelan), Ferry.
Hearts: Gordon; Tierney, Wallace, Berra, Webster, Simmons, Cesnauskis (Elliot), McAllister, Jankauskis (Mikoliunas), Pospisil, MacFarlane (Hartley).

Raith R (1) 1 *(McManus 44)*

Livingston (0) 2 *(Dair 54, Dalglish 69)* 2077

Raith R: Brown; Lyle, Tulloch (Davidson), Silvestro, Lumsden, McLeod, Fairbairn (Jaconelli), Crilly, Annand (Crabbe), McManus, Ellis.
Livingston: McKenzie; Brittain, Tierney, Boyd, Mackay, Lambert (Walker), Vincze, Adams, Scott (McLaughlin), Dair, Dalglish (Pereira).

Ross Co (1) 1 *(Campbell (og) 20)*

Ayr U (2) 2 *(Boyd 6, Vareille 31)* 869

Ross Co: Garden; Cowan, Djebi-Zadi, Webb, Canning, Tiernan (McKinlay), Rankin, McCulloch, Nuckowski (McGarry), Burke, Winters (Higgins).
Ayr U: McGeown; McKinstry, Essler (Casey), McLaughlin, Campbell, Logan, Boyd (Reid), Ramsay, Vareille (Cashmore), Weaver, Robertson.

St Johnstone (0) 0

St Mirren (1) 1 *(McGowne 4)* 2219

St Johnstone: Paston; Mensing, Stanik, Anderson, Campbell (MacDonald), James, McCann (Stevenson), Sheridan, Milne, Dobbie (Coyle), Janczyk.
St Mirren: Hinchcliffe; Van Zanten, Broadfoot, Millen, McGowne, Potter, Murray, Lappin, Kean (Baird), Mehmet (McGinty), Reid.

Stranraer (2) 3 *(Jenkins 17, Hamilton 28, Hinds 84)*

Dundee (0) 1 *(Lynch 66)* 569

Stranraer: Corr; Swift (Dowie), Keddie, Higgins, Henderson, Jenkins, Hamilton, Wingate, Moore (Ross), Hinds (Gaughan), Sharp.
Dundee: Jack; Smith, Hutchinson (Britton), Brady, Mann, Madaschi, Anderson, Dixon, Lynch, McManus, Robb (Eyene).

THIRD ROUND

Tuesday, 20 September 2005

Inverness CT (2) 2 *(Fox 2, Wilson 41)*

Dundee U (0) 0 1984

Inverness CT: Brown; Dods, Wilson, Hart, Duncan, Munro, Proctor, Wyness, Morgan, Fox, McAllister (Black).
Dundee U: Stillie; Wilson, McCracken, Ritchie, Archibald, Canero (McInnes), Duff (Samuel), Brebner, Miller (McIntyre), Fernandez, Robson.

Kilmarnock (0) 3 *(Boyd 55, 90, Wilson S (og) 70)*

Dunfermline Ath (3) 4 *(McCunnie 7, Derek Young 8, 16, 64)* 3191

Kilmarnock: Combe; Dodds (Murray), Ford, Greer, Johnston, Leven (Naismith), Invincibile, Locke (Lilley), McDonald, Boyd, Nish.
Dunfermline Ath: McGregor; Wilson S, McCunnie, Thomson, Zambernardi, Darren Young, Horsted, Labonte, Makel, Derek Young (Hunt), Tarachulski (Tod).

Rangers (1) 5 *(Buffel 5, 74, Nieto 98, 113, Andrews 111)*

Clyde (0) 2 *(Bryson 52, O'Donnell 73 (pen))* 30,104

Rangers: Waterreus; Lowing, Andrews, Bernard, Kyrgiakos, Malcolm (Ferguson), Murray, Buffel, Jeffers (Nieto), Novo (Namouchi), Lovenkrands.
Clyde: Jarvie; McGregor N, Malone, Harris (Brawley), McKeown, McHale, Bryson (Dick), O'Donnell, Williams, Brighton (Arbuckle), McGowan.
aet.

St Mirren (0) 0

Motherwell (0) 2 *(Clarkson 94, Smith D 104)* 4192

St Mirren: Smith; Van Zanten, Broadfoot, Millen (Corcoran), McGowne, Potter, Murray, Lappin (Adam), Sutton, Mehmet (Kean), Reid.
Motherwell: Smith G; Quinn (McLean), Hammell, Kerr, Craigan, Clarkson, McDonald, Fagan, Foran (Keogh), Smith A (Smith D), Kinniburgh.
aet

Stranraer (0) 0

Aberdeen (0) 2 *(Smith 57, Nicholson 67)* 1575

Stranraer: Corr; Swift, Keddie, Wingate, Henderson, Jenkins, Hamilton, Aitken (Ross), Moore, Hinds (Shields), Sharp (Higgins).
Aberdeen: Esson; Considine (Dempsey), McNaughton, Anderson, Diamond, Severin, Smith, Nicholson, Crawford, Muirhead, Clark.

Wednesday, 21 September 2005

Ayr U (0) 1 *(Wardlaw 86)*

Hibernian (2) 2 *(Riordan 37, 41)* 2539

Ayr U: McGeown; McKinstry, Essler, Weaver (Boyd), Joyce, Logan, Hyslop, Ramsay (Maisano), Wardlaw, Strain (Robertson), Conway.
Hibernian: Simon Brown; Caldwell, Stevenson, Hogg, Rudge, Glass, Sproule (McDonald), Beuzelin, Riordan, Morrow (Konte), Fletcher (Shiels).

Celtic (0) 2 *(Zurawski 61, Hartson 94)*

Falkirk (0) 1 *(Gow 54)* 19,422

Celtic: Boruc; Telfer, Camara, Balde, McManus, Petrov, Zurawski, Nakamura, Sutton (Lawson), Maloney (McGeady), Beattie (Hartson).
Falkirk: Glennon; Lawrie, Milne, Thomson, Rodrigues, Ireland, O'Donnell (McStay), Gow, Lima, Latapy (McPherson), Duffy (McBreen).

Livingston (0) 1 *(Pereira 54)*
Hearts (0) 0 3762
Livingston: McKenzie; Mackay, Dorado, Strong, Dair, Walker (Vincze), Barrett N (Brittain), Adams (Scott), Pereira, Barrett G, Dalglish.
Hearts: Gordon; Neilson, Wallace, Pressley, Camazzola (Skacel), Webster, Simmons, Cesnauskis (Berra), Mole (Elliot), Hartley, McAllister.

QUARTER-FINALS

Tuesday, 8 November 2005

Dunfermline Ath (0) 3 *(Burchill 15, 45, Mason 90)*
Hibernian (0) 0 6262
Dunfermline Ath: McGregor; Shields, Ross, Labonte, Zambernardi, Campbell (Horsted), Wilson C, Mason, Hunt (Tarachulski), Tod, Burchill (Derek Young).
Hibernian: Malkowski; Rudge (Sproule), Smith G, Hogg, Murphy, Thomson (Fletcher), Beuzelin, Shiels, Scott Brown, O'Connor, Riordan (Morrow).

Livingston (1) 2 *(Mackay 44, Dalglish 116)*
Inverness CT (1) 1 *(Dargo 1)* 1531
Livingston: Roy; Mackay, Pinxten, Strong, Tierney, Brittain, Walker, Barrett N (Dorado), Snodgrass (Dalglish), McPake (Pereira), Dair.
Inverness CT: Brown; Tokely, Duncan, Dods, Munro, Hastings, Proctor, Black, Wilson (Morgan), Dargo (Wyness), Bayne (McAllister).
aet.

Motherwell (1) 1 *(Kerr 5)*
Aberdeen (0) 0 3989
Motherwell: Smith G; Fagan, Hammell, Kerr, Craigan, McCormack (Corrigan), McDonald (Clarkson), Quinn (Fitzpatrick), Foran, McLean, Hamilton.
Aberdeen: Langfield; Byrne (Mackie), Dempsey (Stewart), Anderson, Diamond■, Severin (Foster), Nicholson, Muirhead, Clark, Smith, Crawford.

Wednesday, 9 November 2005

Celtic (1) 2 *(Maloney 25, Balde 82)*
Rangers (0) 0 57,813
Celtic: Boruc; Telfer, Camara, Balde, McManus, Petrov, Nakamura, Lennon, McGeady (Thompson), Hartson, Maloney.
Rangers: Klos; Ricksen, Bernard (Lovenkrands), Kyrgiakos■, Rodriguez (Pierre Fanfan), Hutton, Ferguson, Murray, Namouchi, Prso, Thompson (Jeffers).

SEMI-FINALS (at Easter Road)

Wednesday, 25 January 2006

Dunfermline Ath (1) 1 *(Darren Young 35)*
Livingston (0) 0 4360
Dunfermline Ath: McGregor; Shields, Wilson S, McCunnie, Zambernardi, Darren Young, Wilson C (Ross), Mason, Donnelly, Burchill (Labonte), Hunt (Tarachulski).
Livingston: McKenzie; McNamee (Walker), Mackay, Pinxten, Strong, Tierney, Brittain, Vincze (Dair), Dalglish, Hoolahan, Hislop (Snodgrass).

Wednesday, 1 February 2006

Motherwell (1) 1 *(Foran 11)*
Celtic (1) 2 *(Zurawski 28, Maloney 89)* 22,595
Motherwell: Smith; Corrigan, Hammell, Kerr, Craigan, McCormack, McDonald, Hamilton (Thermeus), Foran, McBride (O'Donnell), McLean.
Celtic: Boruc; Virgo (Keane), Camara (Pearson), Varga, McManus, Petrov, Nakamura (Thompson), Lennon, Zurawski, Hartson, Maloney.

FINAL (at Hampden Park)

Sunday, 19 March 2006

Celtic (1) 3 *(Zurawski 43, Maloney 76, Dublin 90)*
Dunfermline Ath (0) 0 50,090
Celtic: Boruc; Telfer, Wallace, Balde, McManus, Petrov, Lennon, Keane (Dublin), Nakamura, Zurawski, Maloney.
Dunfermline Ath: McGregor; Shields, Wilson S, Thomson, Labonte, Ross (Donnelly), Makel, Mason, Campbell (Derek Young), Daquin (Tarachulski), Burchill.
Referee: Stuart Dougal.

SCOTTISH LEAGUE ATTENDANCES 2005–06

PREMIER LEAGUE

	Average	Highest	Lowest
Aberdeen	12,705	18,182	9229
Celtic	58,154	59,808	55,456
Dundee U	8154	12,404	5034
Dunfermline Ath	6182	9505	3355
Falkirk	5487	6500	4435
Hearts	16,718	17,379	16,139
Hibernian	13,682	17,180	10,427
Inverness CT	5082	7512	3121
Kilmarnock	7080	12,426	4644
Livingston	4526	8862	2076
Motherwell	6257	11,503	3438
Rangers	49,245	49,792	47,867

FIRST DIVISION

	Average	Highest	Lowest
Airdrie U	1428	2661	919
Brechin C	770	2037	480
Clyde	1260	2324	738
Dundee	3777	5383	1841
Hamilton A	1733	3320	1117
Queen of the S	1804	2790	1276
Ross Co	2311	3588	1754
St Johnstone	2659	5172	1676
St Mirren	3792	7629	2314
Stranraer	692	1548	427

SECOND DIVISION

	Average	Highest	Lowest
Alloa Ath	704	1347	469
Ayr U	1264	2282	815
Dumbarton	944	1594	534
Forfar Ath	560	778	394
Gretna	1292	2201	598
Morton	2812	5202	1418
Partick Th	2473	4354	1537
Peterhead	680	1010	422
Raith R	1624	2446	1055
Stirling A	905	1729	496

THIRD DIVISION

	Average	Highest	Lowest
Albion R	367	825	181
Arbroath	581	1050	409
Berwick R	474	1015	249
Cowdenbeath	473	2596	216
East Fife	507	867	257
East Stirling	254	403	184
Elgin C	427	880	274
Montrose	362	888	241
Queen's Park	506	1247	351
Stenhousemuir	442	816	253

BELL'S LEAGUE CHALLENGE 2005–06

▪ *Denotes player sent off.*

FIRST ROUND

Saturday, 30 July 2005

Arbroath (0) 1 *(Brazil 90)*

Stranraer (0) 3 *(Hamilton 51, 87, Davidson (og) 69)* 319

Arbroath: Inglis; McMullan, Black, Bishop, Cormack, McCulloch, Miller, Davidson (Reilly), Brazil, King (Cook), Stein.
Stranraer: Corr; Hamilton, Keddie, Higgins, Henderson, Jenkins, Walker, McPhee (Swift), McLean (Dowie), Hinds, Ross (Sharp).

Ayr U (0) 0

Stirling Albion (0) 1 *(Boyack 116)* 895

Ayr U: McGeown; McKinstry, Essler (Reid), McLaughlin, Campbell, Logan, Hyslop (Strain), Ramsay, Vareille (Robertson), Wardlaw, Cashmore.
Stirling Albion: Hogarth; Nugent (Hay P), Forsyth, McNally, Graham, Roycroft, Boyack, Fraser▪, Connolly (O'Brien), Devine (Aitken), Turnbull.
aet.

Brechin C (1) 3 *(Ritchie 10, Gibson 79, Hampshire 103)*

Clyde (1) 2 *(Williams 3, McGregor 85)* 547

Brechin C: Nelson; McEwan, Bolan, Walker, Deas, Callaghan, Byers (Mitchell), Johnson, Ritchie (Gibson), Hampshire, King (Darren Smith).
Clyde: Jarvie; McGregor N, Malone, Higgins, McKeown, McHale, Bryson, O'Donnell (Masterton), Williams, Miller (Bradley), Bouadji (Harris).
aet.

East Fife (0) 0

Stenhousemuir (2) 4 *(Denham 15, Carroll 17, Cramb 46, Savage 86)* 310

East Fife: Dodds; Lumsden, Donaldson, McDonald G, Mathie, Kelly (Fortune), Martin, Hampshire, Bradford (Smart▪), Mitchell, Pelosi.
Stenhousemuir: McCulloch; Renwick, Henderson, Denham, McKeown, Mercer (McBride), McKenzie (Sinclair), Collins, Carroll, Cramb (Savage), McInally.

Morton (1) 3 *(Lilley 3, 112, Walker J 108)*

Gretna (0) 2 *(Nicholls 67, Deuchar 92)* 2857

Morton: McGurn; Weatherson, Walker A (Keenan), Harding, Greacen, McLaren (Adam), Millar, Finlayson, Lilley, Templeman (Walker J), McAlister.
Gretna: Main; Collins, McQuilken, Nicholls (Boyd), Townsley, Innes▪, Baldacchino (Aitken), McGuffie, Deuchar (Graham), Bingham, Skelton.
aet.

Partick T (1) 2 *(McConalogue 31, Gibson A 55)*

Cowdenbeath (0) 0 1527

Partick T: Arthur; Murray, Snowdon, Brady, Smyth, McCulloch, Gibson A (McGoldrick), Gillies, McConalogue (Stewart), Gibson J, Kilgannon (Gibson W).
Cowdenbeath: Hay; Wilson, McBride, Hill, Ward, Ritchie, Allison (Gribben), McGregor, Buchanan, Downs (McCallum), Fusco.

Peterhead (1) 1 *(Bavidge 3)*

Berwick R (0) 2 *(Hutchison 71, Connelly 113)* 578

Peterhead: Mathers; Tully, Good, Raeside (Linn), Perry, Gibson, Sharp (Cameron), Buchan, Wood (Michie), Bavidge, Hagen.
Berwick R: Coyle; Murie, McGroarty, McNicoll▪, Cowan, Greenhill (Connelly), Arthur, McLeish, Haynes (Gordon), Hutchison (Da Silva), Little.
aet.

Queen of the S (1) 4 *(Lovell 32, Lyle 51, McNiven 72, McLaughlin 78)*

Albion R (0) 0 1492

Queen of the S: Barnard; Wood (Paton), English, McLaughlin, Reid, Carr, Lovell, Bowey (McColligan), McNiven, O'Neill (Lyle), Payne.
Albion R: Ewings; Friel, Houston (Franch), O'Neil, Lennon, McGhee, Lennox (Young), Bonnar, Wallace, Donnelly, Noble (Sichi).

Queen's Park (0) 0

Hamilton A (0) 3 *(Thomson 58, Ferguson 79, Hardy 84)* 755

Queen's Park: Crawford; Clark, Molloy, Reilly, Sinclair, Harvey, Kettlewell (Weatherston), Quinn, Bowers (Whelan), Weir (Felvus), Ferry.
Hamilton A: Jellema; Ferguson, Hodge, Thomson, Balmer, Carrigan (Jones), Sim (McLaughlin), Bennett, Keogh, Hardy, Gilhaney (Wilson).

Raith R (1) 3 *(Crabbe 21, McManus 94, Cumming (og) 109)*

Elgin C (1) 1 *(Booth 28)* 1418

Raith R: Brown; Davidson, Leiper (Fairbairn), Crilly, Lumsden, McLeod, Jablonski, Ferguson (Silvestro), Crabbe (Annand), McManus, Ellis.
Elgin C: Renton; Cumming, Dempsie (Vigurs I), McKenzie J, Dickson, Scullion, Bremner (Reid), Easton (Muir), Johnston, Booth, Gardiner.
aet.

Ross Co (1) 2 *(Rankin 45, Winters 60)*

Montrose (1) 1 *(Martin 34)* 805

Ross Co: McCaldon; MacDonald (Taylor), Djebi-Zadi, Webb, Canning, Tiernan, Rankin, McCulloch, Higgins (McKinlay), McGarry (Burke), Winters.
Montrose: Reid; Donachie, Smith E, Doyle (Fraser), Mackenzie, Kerrigan, Webster, Fotheringham (Cargill), Martin, Watson (Hall), Henslee.

St Johnstone (0) 2 *(Milne 66, Dobbie 76)*

Alloa Ath (0) 0 1592

St Johnstone: Cuthbert; Stevenson, Stanik, Anderson, Campbell, James, McCann (Henry), Sheridan, Milne, Dobbie (Coyle), Janczyk (Sheerin).
Alloa Ath: McGlynn; Walker, Thomson, Mortimer (Bolochoweckyj), Townsley, Ovenstone, Quitongo, Nicolson, Brown, Stevenson J, Greenhill.

St Mirren (0) 1 *(Reid 101)*

Forfar Ath (0) 0 1732

St Mirren: Hinchcliffe; Van Zanten (Maxwell), Broadfoot, Millen, McGowne, Reilly (Baird), Murray (Potter), Lappin, Kean, Corcoran, Reid.
Forfar Ath: Meldrum; Lunan (Rattray), Lowing, Forrest, Dunn, Bonar (Donald), Sellars, McClune, Voigt (Conway), Shields, Waddell.
aet.

Sunday, 31 July 2005

Dundee (2) 2 *(Anderson 24, Lynch 29)*

East Stirling (0) 0 2554

Dundee: Jack; Smith, Dixon, Brady (Swankie), Mann, Madaschi, Anderson, Robertson, Lynch (Ferguson), McManus, Robb.
East Stirling: Jackson; Mackay, Livingstone, Tyrrell M, Gaughan, Tyrrell P (Blair), Brand (Dymock), Thywissen, Diack, Graham, Ure (Gordon).

SECOND ROUND

Tuesday, 30 August 2005

Brechin C (0) 0

Morton (2) 2 *(Templeman 25, Lilley 43)* 583

Brechin C: Nelson; McEwan, Deas, White, Walker, Callaghan (Burns), King, Johnson, Hampshire (Ritchie), Mitchell, Darren Smith (Winter).
Morton: McGurn; Weatherson, Adam (Macgregor), Harding, Greacen, McLaren, Millar, Finlayson, Templeman (Walker J), Lilley, McAlister.

Dundee (1) 1 *(Robertson 33)*

Airdrie U (0) 1 *(McPhee 52)* 1857

Dundee: Murray; Smith, Dixon, Mann, Hutchinson (Kitamirike), Madaschi, Anderson, Brady (Eyene), Lynch, McManus (Ferguson), Robertson.
Airdrie U: Hollis; McKenna, Dunn, McGowan, McManus, McKeown, McDougall (Barkey), Docherty (Coyle), Prunty, McPhee (Twigg), McLaren.
aet; Dundee won 3-2 on penalties.

Partick T (0) 4 *(Roberts 61, Santala 90, McConalogue 104, Kilgannon 117 (pen))*

St Johnstone (0) 4 *(MacDonald 63, Rutkiewicz 80, Dobbie 108, Janczyk 119)* 1315

Partick T: Arthur; Murray, Snowdon (Gibson A), Brady, Smyth, McCulloch, Nicholas (Santala), Gillies (McGoldrick), McConalogue, Roberts, Kilgannon.
St Johnstone: Cuthbert; Anderson, Stanik, McCann, Rutkiewicz, James (Hannah), Sheerin (Janczyk), Sheridan, Milne (Dobbie), Scotland, MacDonald.
aet; St Johnstone won 4-3 on penalties.

Raith R (0) 2 *(Dempsie (og) 112, McManus 118)*

Dumbarton (0) 1 *(Rodgers 98)* 1382

Raith R: Brown; Lyle, Hilland, Davidson (Jablonski), Lumsden, McLeod, Fairbairn (Silvestro), Crilly, Annand (Crabbe), McManus, Ellis.
Dumbarton: Grindlay; MacDonald, Gentile, Walker, Smith, Dempsie, Borris, Connell (Bannerman), McQuilken, Russell (Rodgers), Dillon.
aet.

Ross Co (0) 0

Hamilton A (1) 1 *(Neil 45)* 770

Ross Co: Garden; McCulloch, Djebi-Zadi, Webb, Canning, Tiernan (Higgins), Rankin, Taylor (Niven), Burke, McGarry (McKinlay), Nuckowski.
Hamilton A: McEwan; Robertson, Hodge, Thomson, McLaughlin, Neil, Nieto (Hardy), Wilson, Tunbridge (Buckley), Fleming (Ferguson), Carrigan.

Wednesday, 31 August 2005

Queen of the S (0) 1 *(Burns 57)*

St Mirren (1) 2 *(Corcoran 20, Murray 59)* 1415

Queen of the S: Barnard; Carr (McNiven), Gibson W, Burns, Reid, Thomson, Lovell (Paton), Bowey, Wood, Lyle, McLaughlin.
St Mirren: Smith; Van Zanten, Maxwell, Millen, Potter, Reid, Murray, Lappin (Adam), Kean, McGinty, Corcoran (Baird).

Stirling Albion (1) 2 *(Aitken 40, Hay P 70)*

Berwick R (0) 1 *(McLeish 48)* 467

Stirling Albion: Hogarth; Nugent, Graham (Wilson), McNally, Roycroft, Aitken, Hay P, Boyack, Dunn (Turnbull), Connolly, O'Brien.
Berwick R: O'Connor; Murie, McGroarty, McNicoll, Cowan, Horn, McLeish, Little, Hutchison, Haynes (Shields), Gordon (Da Silva).

Stranraer (1) 1 *(Jenkins 42)*

Stenhousemuir (1) 2 *(Cramb 45, McGrillen 51)* 366

Stranraer: Morrison; Walker, Keddie, Higgins, Henderson, Jenkins, Hamilton, Aitken (Wingate), Moore, Hinds (Shields), Ross (Sharp).
Stenhousemuir: McCulloch; Renwick, Henderson, Denham, McGregor, McBride (McKenzie), Mercer, Collins, Carroll, Cramb, McGrillen.

QUARTER-FINALS

Tuesday, 13 September 2005

Hamilton A (1) 2 *(Carrigan 30, Keogh 53)*

Dundee (0) 0 609

Hamilton A: McEwan; Ferguson, Fleming, Thomson, McLaughlin, Neil, Tunbridge (Hardy), Wilson, Keogh (Hodge), MacKenzie, Carrigan (Nieto).
Dundee: Jack; Robertson, Dixon, Mann, Hutchinson (Eyene), Madaschi, Smith (McDonald K), Brady, Lynch, McManus (Ferguson), Anderson.

St Johnstone (3) 5 *(Milne 31, 42, 69, Scotland 36, Mensing 48)*

Raith R (1) 1 *(McManus 20)* 1672

St Johnstone: Cuthbert; Mensing, Stanik (Moon), Paterson, Campbell, Rutkiewicz, McCann, Hannah, Milne (Dobbie), Scotland (Coyle), Sheerin.
Raith R: Brown; Lyle, Hilland (Crabbe), Davidson, Lumsden, McLeod, Crilly (Annand), Jablonski, Fairbairn, McManus, Ellis (Tulloch).

St Mirren (3) 3 *(Lappin 20, Adam 21, Sutton 23)*

Stenhousemuir (2) 2 *(Mercer 33, McGrillen 37)* 1121

St Mirren: Smith; Reid, Broadfoot, Millen, Potter, Maxwell, Murray, Lappin, Kean (Mehmet), Sutton, Adam (McGinty).
Stenhousemuir: McCulloch; Renwick, McAlpine, Henderson, McKeown, McBride, Mercer, Collins, Arbuckle (Sinclair), Murphy (Savage), McGrillen.

Wednesday, 14 September 2005

Stirling Albion (1) 1 *(Fraser 33)*

Morton (1) 2 *(Walker J 28, McLaughlin 84)* 1083

Stirling Albion: Hogarth (Christie); Nugent, Forsyth, McNally, Fraser, Aitken, Hay P, Boyack (Wilson), Hay C (Turnbull), Connolly, Devine.
Morton: McGurn; Weatherson, Adam (McLaughlin), Macgregor, Greacen, McLaren, Millar, Finlayson, Walker J (Keenan), Lilley, McAlister.

SEMI-FINALS

Tuesday, 27 September 2005

St Johnstone (1) 1 *(Rutkiewicz 38)*

Hamilton A (1) 2 *(Keogh 33, Ferguson 83)* 1880

St Johnstone: Cuthbert; Anderson (Dobbie), McAnespie, Paterson, Campbell, Rutkiewicz, Hannah (McCann), Sheridam, Milne, Scotland (MacDonald), Sheerin.
Hamilton A: McEwan; Balmer, Fleming, Thomson, McLaughlin, Neil, Ferguson, Wilson, Keogh (Tunbridge), MacKenzie, Carrigan (Gilhaney) (Hardy).

St Mirren (0) 0

Morton (0) 0 7007

St Mirren: Smith; Van Zanten, Broadfoot, Millen (Mehmet), McGowne, Potter, Murray, Maxwell (Reid), Kean, Sutton, Corcoran (Adam).
Morton: McGurn; Weatherson, Walker A (Keenan), Harding, Greacen, McLaren, Millar, Finlayson, Templeman (Walker J), Lilley (McLaughlin), McAlister.
aet; St Mirren won 4-2 on penalties.

FINAL (at Excelsior Stadium, Airdrie)

Sunday, 6 November 2005

St Mirren (1) 2 *(Lappin 23, Sutton 80)*

Hamilton A (0) 1 *(Tunbridge 46)* 9612

St Mirren: Smith; Van Zanten, Broadfoot, Millen (Reilly), McGowne, Potter, Murray, Adam (Mehmet), Kean, Sutton, Lappin.
Hamilton A: McEwan; Balmer (Robertson), Fleming, Thomson, McLaughlin, Neil, Tunbridge, Wilson, Jones (Carrigan), MacKenzie, Keogh (Gilhaney).
Referee: Stuart Dougal.

SCOTTISH CUP FINALS 1874–2006

Year	*Winners*	*Runners-up*	*Score*
1874	Queen's Park	Clydesdale	2-0
1875	Queen's Park	Renton	3-0
1876	Queen's Park	Third Lanark	2-0 after 1-1 draw
1877	Vale of Leven	Rangers	3-2 after 0-0 and 1-1 draws
1878	Vale of Leven	Third Lanark	1-0
1879	Vale of Leven*	Rangers	
1880	Queen's Park	Thornlibank	3-0
1881	Queen's Park†	Dumbarton	3-1
1882	Queen's Park	Dumbarton	4-1 after 2-2 draw
1883	Dumbarton	Vale of Leven	2-1 after 2-2 draw
1884	Queen's Park‡	Vale of Leven	
1885	Renton	Vale of Leven	3-1 after 0-0 draw
1886	Queen's Park	Renton	3-1
1887	Hibernian	Dumbarton	2-1
1888	Renton	Cambuslang	6-1
1889	Third Lanark§	Celtic	2-1
1890	Queen's Park	Vale of Leven	2-1 after 1-1 draw
1891	Hearts	Dumbarton	1-0
1892	Celtic¶	Queen's Park	5-1
1893	Queen's Park	Celtic	2-1
1894	Rangers	Celtic	3-1
1895	St Bernard's	Renton	2-1
1896	Hearts	Hibernian	3-1
1897	Rangers	Dumbarton	5-1
1898	Rangers	Kilmarnock	2-0
1899	Celtic	Rangers	2-0
1900	Celtic	Queen's Park	4-3
1901	Hearts	Celtic	4-3
1902	Hibernian	Celtic	1-0
1903	Rangers	Hearts	2-0 after 1-1 and 0-0 draws
1904	Celtic	Rangers	3-2
1905	Third Lanark	Rangers	3-1 after 0-0 draw
1906	Hearts	Third Lanark	1-0
1907	Celtic	Hearts	3-0
1908	Celtic	St Mirren	5-1
1909	••		
1910	Dundee	Clyde	2-1 after 2-2 and 0-0 draws
1911	Celtic	Hamilton A	2-0 after 0-0 draw
1912	Celtic	Clyde	2-0
1913	Falkirk	Raith R	2-0
1914	Celtic	Hibernian	4-1 after 0-0 draw
1920	Kilmarnock	Albion R	3-2
1921	Partick Th	Rangers	1-0
1922	Morton	Rangers	1-0
1923	Celtic	Hibernian	1-0
1924	Airdrieonians	Hibernian	2-0
1925	Celtic	Dundee	2-1
1926	St Mirren	Celtic	2-0
1927	Celtic	East Fife	3-1
1928	Rangers	Celtic	4-0
1929	Kilmarnock	Rangers	2-0
1930	Rangers	Partick Th	2-1 after 0-0 draw
1931	Celtic	Motherwell	4-2 after 2-2 draw
1932	Rangers	Kilmarnock	3-0 after 1-1 draw
1933	Celtic	Motherwell	1-0
1934	Rangers	St Mirren	5-0
1935	Rangers	Hamilton A	2-1
1936	Rangers	Third Lanark	1-0
1937	Celtic	Aberdeen	2-1
1938	East Fife	Kilmarnock	4-2 after 1-1 draw
1939	Clyde	Motherwell	4-0
1947	Aberdeen	Hibernian	2-1
1948	Rangers	Morton	1-0 after 1-1 draw
1949	Rangers	Clyde	4-1
1950	Rangers	East Fife	3-0
1951	Celtic	Motherwell	1-0
1952	Motherwell	Dundee	4-0
1953	Rangers	Aberdeen	1-0 after 1-1 draw
1954	Celtic	Aberdeen	2-1
1955	Clyde	Celtic	1-0 after 1-1 draw
1956	Hearts	Celtic	3-1
1957	Falkirk	Kilmarnock	2-1 after 1-1 draw
1958	Clyde	Hibernian	1-0
1959	St Mirren	Aberdeen	3-1
1960	Rangers	Kilmarnock	2-0
1961	Dunfermline Ath	Celtic	2-0 after 0-0 draw
1962	Rangers	St Mirren	2-0
1963	Rangers	Celtic	3-0 after 1-1 draw

Year	Winners	Runners-up	Score
1964	Rangers	Dundee	3-1
1965	Celtic	Dunfermline Ath	3-2
1966	Rangers	Celtic	1-0 after 0-0 draw
1967	Celtic	Aberdeen	2-0
1968	Dunfermline Ath	Hearts	3-1
1969	Celtic	Rangers	4-0
1970	Aberdeen	Celtic	3-1
1971	Celtic	Rangers	2-1 after 1-1 draw
1972	Celtic	Hibernian	6-1
1973	Rangers	Celtic	3-2
1974	Celtic	Dundee U	3-0
1975	Celtic	Airdrieonians	3-1
1976	Rangers	Hearts	3-1
1977	Celtic	Rangers	1-0
1978	Rangers	Aberdeen	2-1
1979	Rangers	Hibernian	3-2 after 0-0 and 0-0 draws
1980	Celtic	Rangers	1-0
1981	Rangers	Dundee U	4-1 after 0-0 draw
1982	Aberdeen	Rangers	4-1 (aet)
1983	Aberdeen	Rangers	1-0 (aet)
1984	Aberdeen	Celtic	2-1 (aet)
1985	Celtic	Dundee U	2-1
1986	Aberdeen	Hearts	3-0
1987	St Mirren	Dundee U	1-0 (aet)
1988	Celtic	Dundee U	2-1
1989	Celtic	Rangers	1-0
1990	Aberdeen	Celtic	0-0 (aet)
		(Aberdeen won 9-8 on penalties)	
1991	Motherwell	Dundee U	4-3 (aet)
1992	Rangers	Airdrieonians	2-1
1993	Rangers	Aberdeen	2-1
1994	Dundee U	Rangers	1-0
1995	Celtic	Airdrieonians	1-0
1996	Rangers	Hearts	5-1
1997	Kilmarnock	Falkirk	1-0
1998	Hearts	Rangers	2-1
1999	Rangers	Celtic	1-0
2000	Rangers	Aberdeen	4-0
2001	Celtic	Hibernian	3-0
2002	Rangers	Celtic	3-2
2003	Rangers	Dundee	1-0
2004	Celtic	Dunfermline Ath	3-1
2005	Celtic	Dundee U	1-0
2006	Hearts	Gretna	1-1 (aet)
		(Hearts won 4-2 on penalties)	

*Vale of Leven awarded cup, Rangers failing to appear for replay after 1-1 draw.
†After Dumbarton protested the first game, which Queen's Park won 2-1.
‡Queen's Park awarded cup, Vale of Leven failing to appear.
§Replay by order of Scottish FA because of playing conditions in first match, won 3-0 by Third Lanark.
¶After mutually protested game which Celtic won 1-0.
••Owing to riot, the cup was withheld after two drawn games – between Celtic and Rangers 2-2 and 1-1.

SCOTTISH CUP WINS

Celtic 33, Rangers 31, Queen's Park 10, Aberdeen 7, Hearts 7, Clyde 3, Kilmarnock 3, St Mirren 3, Vale of Leven 3, Dunfermline Ath 2, Falkirk 2, Hibernian 2, Motherwell 2, Renton 2, Third Lanark 2, Airdrieonians 1, Dumbarton 1, Dundee 1, Dundee U 1, East Fife 1, Morton 1, Partick Th 1, St Bernard's 1.

APPEARANCES IN FINAL

Celtic 52, Rangers 48, Aberdeen 15, Hearts 13, Queen's Park 12, Hibernian 11, Dundee U 8, Kilmarnock 8, Vale of Leven 7, Clyde 6, Dumbarton 6, Motherwell 6, St Mirren 6, Third Lanark 6, Dundee 5, Renton 5, Airdrieonians 4, Dunfermline Ath 4, East Fife 3, Falkirk 3, Hamilton A 2, Morton 2, Partick Th 2, Albion R 1, Cambuslang 1, Clydesdale 1, Gretna 1, Raith R 1, St Bernard's 1, Thornlibank 1.

LEAGUE CHALLENGE FINALS 1991–2006

Year	Winners	Runners-up	Score
1990–91	Dundee	Ayr U	3-2
1991–92	Hamilton A	Ayr U	1-0
1992–93	Hamilton A	Morton	3-2
1993–94	Falkirk	St Mirren	3-0
1994–95	Airdrieonians	Dundee	3-2
1995–96	Stenhousemuir	Dundee U	0-0
	(Stenhousemuir won 5-4 on penalties)		
1996–97	Stranraer	St Johnstone	1-0
1997–98	Falkirk	Queen of the South	1-0
1998–99	no competition		
1999–2000	Alloa Ath	Inverness CT	4-4
	(Alloa Ath won 5-4 on penalties)		
2000–01	Airdrieonians	Livingston	2-2
	(Airdrieonians won 3-2 on penalties)		
2001–02	Airdrieonians	Alloa Ath	2-1
2002–03	Queen of the S	Brechin C	2-0
2003–04	Inverness CT	Airdrie U	2-0
2004–05	Falkirk	Ross Co	2-1
2005–06	St Mirren	Hamilton A	2-1

TENNENT'S SCOTTISH CUP 2005–06

▪ *Denotes player sent off.*

FIRST ROUND

Saturday, 19 November 2005

Partick T (1) 1 *(Roberts 20)*
Albion R (0) 1 *(Donachy 56)* 1758

Partick T: Stewart; Murray, Craig, Gibson W, Smyth, Brady, Gibson J, Gillies, McConalogue, Roberts (Santala), Kilgannon (Strachan).
Albion R: Ewings; Black, McGhee, Lennon (Wilson), Donnelly, Friel▪, Reid (Lennox), Chaplain, Wallace, Bonnar, Donachy (Sichi).

Preston Ath (0) 2 *(Hobbins 87, McAuley 89)*
Gretna (3) 6 *(Grady 10, 17, 60, Townsley 19, Deuchar 61, Bingham 65)* 713

Preston Ath: Gilpin; Murray, Costello, McCann (McColl), Scott, McAuley, Houston, Lockart (Barton), Hobbins (Eadie), Rennie, Wilson.
Gretna: Main; Birch (Collins), Nicholls, Tosh, Townsley, Skelton (Grainger), Baldacchino, McGuffie, Deuchar (Graham), Bingham, Grady.

Saturday, 26 November 2005

Cowdenbeath (0) 0
Morton (1) 3 *(Lilley 22, 75, Walker J 79)* 634

Cowdenbeath: Hay; Baxter, McBride, Ward, Ritchie, McGregor (Hill), Millar, Guy, McCallum, Buchanan, Mauchlen.
Morton: McGurn; Weatherson, Walker A, Harding (Adam), Macgregor, McLaughlin, Millar, Finlayson (Walker J), Lilley, McLaren (Templeman), McAlister.

Dumbarton (3) 4 *(Russell 7, Rodgers 19, 60, McQuilken 39)*
Forres Mechanics (1) 1 *(Mackay 34)* 755

Dumbarton: Grindlay; McQuilken, Gentile, Gaughan (Young), Smith, Walker, Borris, Connell (Brittain), Rodgers, Russell (McDonald), Boyle.
Forres Mechanics: Rae; Grant, Mackay, McGinlay, Mackinnon, Campbell (Rogers), White, Brown (MacMillan), Sanderson, Munro (Matheson), Green.

Spartans (0) 1 *(Henretty 59)*
Berwick R (0) 0 343

Spartans: Brown; O'Donnell, Fowlis, Burns, Seeley J, Bennett, Smart (Manson), Thomson, Johnson (Seeley C), McLeod (Mitchell), Henretty.
Berwick R: Coyle; Murie, McGarty, McNicoll, Hutchison, Greenhill (Swanson), Arthur, McLeish, Haynes (Da Silva), Gordon, Little.

Stirling Albion (2) 2 *(Forsyth 14, Connolly 40)*
Elgin C (0) 1 *(Gardiner 62)* 478

Stirling Albion: Hogarth; Nugent, Devine, McNally, Graham, Aitken, Wilson (Hay P), Hutchison (Boyack), Connolly, Forsyth, O'Brien.
Elgin C: Renton; Cumming, Dempsie, Scullion, Dickson, McKenzie J, Bremner (Gardiner), Hind (Reid), Johnston, Nelson, Napier (Vigurs I).

Monday, 28 November 2005

Alloa Ath (3) 9 *(Hamilton 6, 23, Brown A 18, Sloan 50, 86, Nicolson 54, 78, 82, Quitongo 68)*
Selkirk (0) 0 327

Alloa Ath: McGlynn; Walker, Learmonth, Bolochoweckyj, Townsley, Ovenstone, Quitongo, Stevenson J (Greenhill), Brown A (Sloan), Hamilton (Brown G), Nicolson.
Selkirk: Watson; Tyson, Moffat, Lothian G, Cockburn, Potts, McShane, Lothian C, Darling (Kerr), Biggs (Hossack), Livingston (Hastie).

Stenhousemuir (2) 3 *(Mercer 7, Sinclair 10, Cramb 72)*
East Stirling (1) 2 *(Owen 39, Dymock 58)* 405

Stenhousemuir: McCulloch; Renwick, McAlpine, Denham▪, Murphy, McBride, Menzies, Sinclair (Henderson), Mercer, Cramb (Templeton), McGrillen▪.
East Stirling: Jackson; Oates (Dymock), Owen, Smith, Gaughan (Lezman), Tyrrell P, Livingston, Tyrrell M, Diack, Graham (Thywissen), Ure.

FIRST ROUND REPLAY

Tuesday, 22 November 2005

Albion R (0) 1 *(Chisholm 72)*
Partick T (1) 3 *(Roberts 42, 83, Smyth 78)* 598

Albion R: Ewings; Black, McGhee (Young), Lennon, Donnelly, Bonnar, Lennox (Chisholm), Chaplain, Wallace (Wilson), Reid, Donachy.
Partick T: Stewart; Murray, Craig, Gibson W, Smyth, Brady (Snowdon), Gibson J, Gillies, McConalogue, Roberts, Santala.

SECOND ROUND

Sunday, 11 December 2005

Alloa Ath (1) 1 *(Stevenson J 23)*
Montrose (0) 0 326

Alloa Ath: McGlynn; Walker, Learmonth, Bolochoweckyj, Townsley, Ovenstone, Quitongo (Sloan), Stevenson J, Brown A (Brown G), Hamilton, Greenhill.
Montrose: Butter; Donnachie, Smith, Doyle, Stephen, Kerrigan, Webster (Dodds), Fraser (McLean), Henslee, Fotheringham, Hall (Watson).

Arbroath (1) 1 *(Brazil 16)*
Dumbarton (0) 0 596

Arbroath: Peat; McMullan, Watson, Rennie, Dobbins, McCulloch, Cook (Smith), Miller, Brazil, Black, Stein (King).
Dumbarton: Grindlay; McQuilken (Gemmell), Boyle, Gaughan, Walker, Allan (Russell), Borris, Bannerman, Rodgers, Gentile (MacDonald), Brittain.

Ayr U (0) 3 *(Wardlaw 51, Robertson 61, 64)*
Morton (0) 2 *(Weatherson 67, Templeman 80)* 1672

Ayr U: McGeown; McKinstry (Hyslop), Ramsay, McLaughlin, Campbell, Logan, Conway, Weaver▪, Cashmore (Boyd), Wardlaw, Robertson (Reid).
Morton: McGurn (Gonet); Weatherson, Walker A (Greacen), Harding, Macgregor, McLaughlin, Millar, Walker J▪, Lilley▪, McLaren (Templeman), McAlister.

East Fife (0) 0
Peterhead (2) 3 *(Wood 38, Sharp 40, Linn 75)* 441

East Fife: Dodds; Lumsden, Pelosi, Bain, McDonald G, Fortune (Bradford), Martin (Palicska), Kelly, Smart, Hampshire (Beith), Noble.
Peterhead: Mathers; Hegarty, Good (Hagen), Tully (Youngson), Perry, Gibson, Sharp (Michie), Buchan, Linn, Wood, Cameron.

Gretna (3) 6 *(Grady 2, 77, Deuchar 13, Townsley 45, McGuffie 64, Nicholls 82)*
Cove R (1) 1 *(Clark 32)* 570

Gretna: Main; Birch, Nicholls, Tosh, Townsley, Skelton (McQuilken), Baldacchino (Graham), McGuffie, Deuchar, Bingham, Grady.
Cove R: Pirie; Cruickshank, Livingstone, Hendry, Fraser S, Morrison, Tindal, Clark (Brown), Milne (Gordon), Steele (Bain), Fraser G.

Lossiemouth (0) 0
Spartans (1) 5 *(McLeod 32, 71, 85, Smart 59, Manson 87)* 420

Lossiemouth: Dunn; Reid, Youngson (Moir), Adams (Smith), Dixon, Hendry, McMullan, Ellis, McIntosh (Main), Morrison, Kennedy.
Spartans: Brown; O'Donnell, Fowlie, Burns, Seeley J, Bennett, Smart (Kadir), Thomson, Johnson (Mitchell), McLeod, Henretty (Manson).

Queen's Park (1) 2 *(Weatherston 1, Felvus 76)*
Raith R (0) 0 781
Queen's Park: Crawford; Clark, Dunlop, Reilly, Agostini, Trouten, Kettlewell, Paton, Weatherston, Murray (Felvus), Ferry.
Raith R: Brown; Lyle, Stirling, Silvestro, Lumsden, Davidson (McLeod), Fairbairn, McManus, Crabbe, Jablonski (Annand), Ellis.

Stenhousemuir (1) 1 *(Renwick 1)*
Partick T (2) 4 *(McCulloch 26, Gillies 41, Santala 79, McConalogue 85)* 1064
Stenhousemuir: McCulloch; Renwick, McAlpine, Henderson, Murphy, McBride, Menzies (Carroll), Sinclair (Templeton), Mercer, Cramb, McGrillen.
Partick T: Stewart; Murray, McCulloch, Brady, Smyth, Gibson W, Gibson J, Gillies, Santala (Strachan), McConalogue (Gibson A), Kilgannon (Craig).

Stirling Albion (0) 1 *(Hay C 89)*
Inverurie (0) 0 691
Stirling Albion: Hogarth; Nugent, Devine, McNally, Graham, Fraser (Turnbull), Hay P (Hay C), Bell, Connolly, Forsyth, O'Brien.
Inverurie: Gray; Walker, Buchan, Wilson■, Simpson, Mess, Singer (Milne), Ross, McKay, Roddie (Graham), McLean.

Threave R (0) 0
Forfar Ath (3) 4 *(Gribben 10, 51, Bonar 12, Cameron 18)* 520
Threave R: Hair; McMinn, Fingland, Carlyle, Watson (Harrison), Green, Hogg, Donley, Adams (Kerr), Rudd (Struthers), Warren.
Forfar Ath: Dubourdeau; Barr, Lowing, Rattray (Dunn), Forrest, Bonar, McClune, Sellars■, Cameron (Voigt), Gribben, Waddell (Donald).

THIRD ROUND

Saturday, 7 January 2006

Alloa Ath (0) 1 *(Bolochoweckyj 66)*
Livingston (0) 1 *(Brittain 90)* 1341
Alloa Ath: Evans J; Bolochoweckyj, Nicolson, Townsley, Forrest, Mortimer, Walker, McGeown (Learmonth), Hamilton, Stevenson J (Brown G), Sloan.
Livingston: McKenzie; Tierney, Mackay, Pinxten, Strong, Brittain, Lambert, Vincze, Dair (Hoolahan), Dalglish (Dorrans), Snodgrass.

Dundee U (2) 2 *(Fernandez 26, 28)*
Aberdeen (0) 3 *(Crawford 62, 63, Nicholson 79)* 8218
Dundee U: Stillie; Wilson, McCracken, Archibald, Mulgrew, Kerr, McIntyre, Robson, Duff (Miller), Fernandez, Samuel.
Aberdeen: Langfield; Byrne, McNaughton, Anderson, Griffin, Dempsey (Foster), Nicholson, Clark, Lovell (Mackie), Smith, Crawford (Considine).

Dunfermline Ath (2) 3 *(Mason 16, Hunt 23, Derek Young 85)*
Airdrie U (1) 4 *(Docherty 31, 89, Hardie 52, McKeown 88)* 4090
Dunfermline Ath: McGregor; Shields, McCunnie, Thomson (Campbell), Tod, Darren Young, Labonte, Mason, Makel■, Derek Young, Hunt (Tarachulski).
Airdrie U: Robertson; McKenna, Lovering, McGowan (McDougall), McManus, Hardie, Docherty, McKeown, Prunty, McPhee, McLaren.

Falkirk (1) 2 *(Gow 32, 64)*
Brechin C (1) 1 *(King 38)* 2248
Falkirk: Ferguson; Lawrie, Ireland, Rodrigues, Milne (McPherson), Lima, Scally (Cregg), O'Donnell, Latapy, Gow, McBreen (Moutinho).
Brechin C: Nelson; Winter (Geddes), Callaghan, White, Walker, Burns, King, Johnson, Hampshire, Mitchell, Darren Smith (Britton).

Hearts (1) 2 *(Pressley 23, McAllister 75)*
Kilmarnock (0) 1 *(Nish 84)* 13,704
Hearts: Gordon; Neilson, Fyssas, Pressley, Webster, Skacel, Jankauskas (Pospisil), Hartley, Mikoliunas (McAllister), Elliot (Berra), Brellier.
Kilmarnock: Combe; Fowler, Hay, Lilley, Greer (Murray), Ford, Wales (DiGiacomo), Johnston, Naismith, Nish, Wright.

Hibernian (2) 6 *(Scott Brown 39, 77, Sproule 44, Stewart 62, O'Connor 73, Fletcher 84)*
Arbroath (0) 0 10,523
Hibernian: Simon Brown; Caldwell, Hogg, Murphy, Whittaker, Glass, Stewart (McCluskey), Morrow (O'Connor), Scott Brown, Riordan (Fletcher), Sproule.
Arbroath: Peat; McMullan, Jackson (Davidson), Rennie, Bishop, McCulloch, Cook, Miller, King (Reilly), Watson, Stein (Black).

Inverness CT (0) 1 *(McAllister 52)*
Ayr U (0) 1 *(Wardlaw 53)* 2153
Inverness CT: Brown; Tokely, Golabek, Dods, McCaffrey, Wilson, Duncan, Wyness (Dargo), Morgan, Fox (Hart), McAllister.
Ayr U: McKeown; McKinstry, Ramsay, McLaughlin, Baillie, Casey, Hyslop (Reid), Robertson, Vareille (Strain), Wardlaw (Cashmore), Conway.

Queen of the S (0) 1 *(Lyle 81)*
Hamilton A (0) 1 *(McLaughlin 46)* 1823
Queen of the S: Ballard; Paton, English, Lovell, Reid, Thomson, Burns, Bowey (McLaughlin), Wood (Gibson W), O'Neil (Robertson), Lyle.
Hamilton A: McEwan; Robertson, Fleming, Balmer, McLaughlin, Neil, Torres (McMullan), McArthur, Jones (Gilhaney), MacKenzie, Carrigan (Ferguson).

Rangers (1) 5 *(Kyrgiakos 34, Boyd 49, 54, 71, McCormack 74)*
Peterhead (0) 0 39,870
Rangers: Waterreus; Malcolm (Rae A), Andrewa, Murray (Lowing), Kyrgiakos, Smith S, Ferguson, Burke, Boyd, Novo, Lovenkrands (McCormack).
Peterhead: Mathers; Hegarty, Cameron, Tully, Perry, Gibson, Sharp (Robertson), Buchan, Linn (Youngson), Wood (Michie), Hagen.

Ross Co (2) 5 *(Burke 11, Higgins 35, Cowie 47, 48, McKinlay 77)*
Forfar Ath (0) 0 1151
Ross Co: Garden; Cowan, Djebi-Zadi, Lauchlan, Canning, McCulloch (Tiernan), Rankin (Gunn), Burke, Higgins (Winters), Cowie, McKinlay.
Forfar Ath: Dubourdeau; Lunan (Connolly), Lowing, Rattray, Forrest, King, McClune (Waddell), Sellars, Cameron, Gribben (Bonar), Donald.

Spartans (1) 3 *(Mitchell 44, Seeley J 50, Henretty 67)*
Queen's Park (1) 2 *(Trouten 6, Weatherston 70)* 763
Spartans: Brown; O'Donnell (Gerrard), Fowlie, Burns, Seeley J, Bennett, Manson (Kadir), Thomson, Mitchell (Johnson), Smart, Henretty.
Queen's Park: Crawford; Clark (Felvus), Dunlop, Reilly, Agostini, Trouten, Kettlewell, Quinn (Murray), Weatherston, Harvey, Ferry.

St Johnstone (0) 0
Gretna (1) 1 *(Tosh 11)* 2658
St Johnstone: Cuthbert; Anderson, Stanik, Stevenson, Rutkiewicz, James, Henry (Coyle), Fotheringham K, Jackson (Dobbie), Scotland, Sheerin (Janczyk).
Gretna: Main; Birch, McQuilken, Tosh, Townsley, Innes, McGuffie, Nicholls, Deuchar (Shields), Graham, Skelton.

St Mirren (1) 3 *(Adam 22, 89, Potter 74)*
Motherwell (0) 0 6757
St Mirren: Smith; Van Zanten, Maxwell, Millen, McGowne, Potter, Lappin, Reid, Kean (Sutton), Adam, Corcoran (Anderson).
Motherwell: Smith G; Corrigan, Hammell, Kerr (Clarkson), McCormack, McDonald, Foran (Kinniburgh), O'Donnell, Hamilton, McBride, McLean.

Stirling Albion (0) 0

Partick T (1) 1 *(Ritchie 11)* 2031

Stirling Albion: Hogarth; Nugent, Forsyth, McNally, Graham, Aitken, Hay P (Wilson), Fraser (Hay C), Connolly, Dunn (O'Brien), Bell.
Partick T: Arthur; Murray, McCulloch, Brady (Snowdon), Smyth (Gillies), Craig, Gibson J, Gibson W, Ritchie, McConalogue (Roberts), Strachan.

Sunday, 8 January 2006

Clyde (2) 2 *(Bryson 31, Malone 35)*

Celtic (0) 1 *(Zurawski 82)* 7589

Clyde: Cherrie; McGregor N, Malone, Higgins, McKeown, Masterton, Bryson (Bouadji), O'Donnell, Williams (Miller), Brighton (Arbuckle), McGowan.
Celtic: Boruc; Telfer, Wallace (McGeady), McManus, Wei (Virgo), Nakamura, Keane, Lennon, Pearson, Hartson (Zurawski), Maloney.

Dundee (0) 2 *(O'Reilly 47, Lynch 80)*

Stranraer (0) 0 2580

Dundee: Murray; Robertson, Dixon, Mann, Macdonald C, Smith, McDonald K, Brady, Lynch (Craig), O'Reilly (Deasley), Robb.
Stranraer: Corr; Walker (Higgins), Keddie, Dowie, Henderson, Jenkins, Hamilton (Aitken), Ross, Moore, Hinds, Sharp (Martin).

THIRD ROUND REPLAYS

Wednesday, 11 January 2006

Livingston (1) 1 *(Dalglish 37 (pen))*

Alloa Ath (0) 2 *(Hamilton 69, Sloan 81)* 1518

Livingston: McKenzie; Mackay, Pinxten, Strong, Dorado (Hoolahan), Brittain, Lambert (Dair), Walker, Tierney, Snodgrass, Dalglish (Dorrans).
Alloa Ath: Evans J; Townsley, Nicolson, Forrest, Bolochoweckyj, Sloan, Stevenson (Learmonth), McGeown, Hamilton, Brown (Mortimer), Ovenstone.

Monday, 16 January 2006

Ayr U (0) 0

Inverness CT (1) 2 *(Dargo 38 (pen), Wyness 76)* 2774

Ayr U: McGeown■; McKinstry, Ramsay (Robertson), McLaughlin, Baillie, Logan, Hyslop, Casey, Vareille (Phillips), Wardlaw (Cashmore), Conway.
Inverness CT: Brown; Tokely, Dods, Munro, Hastings, Black, McBain (Golabek), Duncan, Wilson (Proctor), Dargo (McAllister), Wyness.

Tuesday, 17 January 2006

Hamilton A (0) 1 *(Torres 91)*

Queen of the S (0) 0 1747

Hamilton A: Jellema; Robertson, Fleming, Thomson, McLaughlin, Neil, Ferguson, Tunbridge, McLeod (Torres), MacKenzie (McArthur), Carrigan (Gilhaney).
Queen of the S: Barnard; Paton, English, Lovell, Reid (McLaughlin), Thomson, Burns, Bowey, Lyle, O'Neil (Carr), Wood (Gibson W).
aet.

FOURTH ROUND

Saturday, 4 February 2006

Airdrie U (0) 1 *(McLaren 59)*

Dundee (1) 1 *(Deasley 21)* 3557

Airdrie U: Robertson; Docherty (McKenna), Lovering, McGowan, McManus, Holmes, McDougall, McKeown, Prunty, McPhee (Twigg), McLaren.
Dundee: Murray; Robertson, Dixon, Mann, Macdonald C, Smith, McDonald K (McCluskey), Brady, Lynch (McManus), Deasley (O'Reilly), Robb.

Clyde (0) 0

Gretna (0) 0 2540

Clyde: Cherrie; Bouadji, Malone, Higgins■, McKeown, McDonald (Masterton), Bryson, O'Donnell, Williams■, Brighton, McGowan (Miller).
Gretna: Main; Birch, Nicholls, Tosh, Townsley, Innes■, O'Neil, McGuffie, Grady, Graham (Deuchar), Skelton.

Falkirk (0) 1 *(McBreen 78)*

Ross Co (1) 1 *(Cowie 16)* 3640

Falkirk: Ferguson; Ross, Milne, Ireland (Gow), Rodrigues, Cregg, Thomson S, O'Donnell (Craig), Latapy, Moutinho, McBreen.
Ross Co: Garden; MacDonald, Djebi-Zadi, Lauchlan, Webb, McCulloch, Rankin, Burke (Winters), Higgins, Cowie, McKinlay.

Hamilton A (0) 0

Alloa Ath (0) 0 1866

Hamilton A: McEwan; Robertson, Balmer, Thomson, McLaughlin, Neil, Juanjo, Tunbridge, Wake (Keogh), Gilhaney, Carrigan (McArthur).
Alloa Ath: Evans J (Ferguson); Bolochoweckyj (Nicolson), Ovenstone, Townsley, Forrest, McColligan, Greenhill, Learmonth (Muir), Hamilton, Stevenson J, Sloan.

Hearts (3) 3 *(Pospisil 21, Elliot 34, Pressley 45)*

Aberdeen (0) 0 17,456

Hearts: Gordon; Neilson, Pressley, Webster, Beslija (Wallace), Cesnauskis, Pospisil, Elliot (Makela), Brellier (McAllister), Johnson, Goncalves.
Aberdeen: Langfield; McNaughton, Anderson, Diamond■, Severin, Smith (Snoyl), Nicholson, Clark, Foster (Stewart), Crawford, Griffin (MacAulay).

Inverness CT (0) 2 *(McBain 59, Dargo 77)*

Partick T (1) 2 *(Roberts 44, 90)* 3325

Inverness CT: Brown; Tokely, Dods, Munro (Fox), Hastings, Duncan, Black (Golabek), McBain, Wilson, Dargo, Wyness (Bayne).
Partick T: Arthur; Murray, McCulloch (Boyd), Smyth, Hodge, Gibson W, Gibson J, Gillies (Dodds), Ritchie, Roberts, Strachan.

Rangers (0) 0

Hibernian (0) 3 *(O'Connor 49, Sproule 58, Killen 77)* 40,142

Rangers: Waterreus; Ricksen, Andrews, Kyrgiakos, Malcolm (Prso), Murray, Ferguson, Burke, Buffell, Boyd, Lovenkrands (Novo).
Hibernian: Simon Brown; Caldwell, Hogg, Murphy, Whittaker, Thomson (Glass), Stewart, Fletcher (Riordan), Scott Brown (Killen), Sproule, O'Connor.

Sunday, 5 February 2006

Spartans (0) 0

St Mirren (0) 0 3360

Spartans: Brown; Gerrard, Fowlie, Burns, Seeley J, Bennett, Smart (Manson), Thomson, Johnson (Mitchell), McLeod, Henretty (Kadir).
St Mirren: Bullock; Van Zanten (Reid), Maxwell, Millen, McGowne, Potter, Murray (Anderson), Lappin, Sutton (Kean), Adam, Corcoran.

FOURTH ROUND REPLAYS

Tuesday, 7 February 2006

Alloa Ath (0) 0

Hamilton A (2) 3 *(McLaughlin 13, Neil 19, Ferguson 85)* 1210

Alloa Ath: Ferguson; Nicolson, Ovenstone, Townsley, Forrest, McColligan, Grant, McGeown (Learmonth), Muir (Mortimer), Stevenson J, Sloan.
Hamilton A: McEwan; Robertson, Juanjo (Wake), Thomson, McLaughlin (Elebert), Neil, Ferguson, Wilson, Keogh (Tunbridge), Torres, Gilhaney.

Tuesday, 14 February 2006

Dundee (1) 2 *(Deasley 8, Lynch 71)*

Airdrie U (0) 0 3824

Dundee: Jack; Robertson, Dixon, Mann, Macdonald C, Smith, McDonald K, Brady, Lynch, Deasley (O'Reilly), McCluskey.
Airdrie U: Robertson; McKenna, Lovering (Dunn), McGowan (Docherty), McManus, Holmes, McDougall, McKeown, Prunty, McPhee, McLaren.

Gretna (1) 4 *(Grady 25, 70, 82, Deuchar 69)*

Clyde (0) 0 2410

Gretna: Main; Birch, Nicholls, Tosh, Townsley, Innes, O'Neil (McQuilken) (Shields), McGuffie, Deuchar, Grady, Skelton.

Clyde: Cherrie; McGregor N (Bouadji), Malone, Imre (Arbuckle), McKeown■, Masterton (Miller), Bryson, O'Donnell, Williams, Brighton, McGowan.

Ross Co (0) 0

Falkirk (0) 1 *(Gow 62)* 2372

Ross Co: Garden; MacDonald, Djebi-Zadi, Lauchlan, Webb, McCulloch (McSwegan), Rankin, Burke (Winters), Higgins, Cowie, McKinlay (Gunn).
Falkirk: Ferguson; Ross (Lawrie), Rodrigues, Milne, Lecsinel (Twaddle), Cregg, Thomson S, Craig, Gow, Moutinho, McBreen.

St Mirren (2) 3 *(Sutton 11, Adam 26, Maxwell 67)*

Spartans (0) 0 4295

St Mirren: Bullock; Van Zanten, Maxwell, Millen (Murray), McGowne, Potter, Anderson, Adam (Lappin), Kean, Sutton (Mehmet), Corcoran.
Spartans: Brown; Gerrard, Fowlie, Burns, Seeley J, Bennett, Manson (Mitchell), Thomson, Johnson (Smart), McLeod, Henretty (Antoni).

Wednesday, 15 February 2006

Partick T (1) 1 *(Roberts 15)*

Inverness CT (1) 1 *(Wyness 24)* 3166

Partick T: Arthur; Murray, Boyd, Gibson W, Smyth, Brady (Snowdon), Gibson J, McConalogue (Kilgannon), Ritchie (Gillies), Roberts, Strachan.
Inverness CT: Brown; Tokely, Dods, Munro, Hastings, Duncan (Proctor), Black (Fox), Hart, Wilson, Dargo, Wyness.
aet; Partick T won 4-2 on penalties.

QUARTER-FINALS

Saturday, 25 February 2006

Falkirk (0) 1 *(McBreen 70)*

Hibernian (1) 5 *(Riordan 9, O'Connor 65, Sproule 73, Glass 76, Fletcher 88)* 6034

Falkirk: Ferguson; Lawrie, Milne, Ross, Twaddle (Lima), Thomson S, Cregg, Craig (Latapy), Moutinho, Gow, McBreen.
Hibernian: Simon Brown; Caldwell (McCluskey), Smith G, Murphy, Whittaker, Glass, Thomson, Stewart, Sproule (Konde), Riordan (Fletcher), O'Connor.

Gretna (0) 1 *(Deuchar 73)*

St Mirren (0) 0 2850

Gretna: Main; Birch, Nicholls, Tosh, Townsley, Innes, McQuilken, McGuffie, Deuchar, Grady, Skelton.
St Mirren: Bullock; Van Zanten, Maxwell (Mehmet), Millen, McGowne, Potter, Anderson (Murray), Lappin, Sutton, Adam, Kean (Corcoran).

Hamilton A (0) 0

Dundee (0) 0 4486

Hamilton A: McEwan; Robertson, Balmer, Thomson, McLaughlin, Neil (Ferguson), Tunbridge, McArthur (Keogh), Wake (Torres), Juanjo, Gilhaney.
Dundee: Murray; Robertson, Dixon, Mann, Macdonald C, Smith, McDonald K (Gates), Brady, Lynch, McManus (Deasley), McCluskey.

Hearts (1) 2 *(Jankauskas 6, Cesnauskis 52)*

Partick T (0) 1 *(Roberts 53)* 16,698

Hearts: Gordon; Neilson, Fyssas, Pressley, Webster, Skacel (Mikoliunas), Jankauskas, Hartley, Cesnauskis (Berra), Elliot (Bednar■), Brellier.
Partick T: Arthur; Murray, Hodge, Gibson W, Smyth, Boyd, Gibson J, McConalogue (Gillies), Ritchie (Brady), Roberts, Strachan.

QUARTER-FINAL REPLAY

Sunday, 5 March 2006

Dundee (0) 3 *(Mann 56, Lynch 68, Craig 91)*

Hamilton A (0) 2 *(Juanjo 75, Keogh 82)* 7460

Dundee: Jack; Robertson, Dixon, Mann, Wilkie, McCluskey, McDonald K, Brady, Lynch (Macdonald C), Deasley (Craig), McManus (Ferguson).
Hamilton A: McEwan; Robertson, Balmer, Thomson (Keogh), McLaughlin, Neil, Ferguson (Juanjo), McArthur, Wake, Tunbridge (Wilson), Gilhaney.
aet.

SEMI-FINALS (at Hampden Park)

Saturday, 1 April 2006

Gretna (1) 3 *(Deuchar 45, McGuffie 58 (pen), Smith (og) 82)*

Dundee (0) 0 14,179

Gretna: Main; Birch, Townsley, Innes, McGuffie, O'Neil, Nicholls (McQuilken), Tosh, Skelton, Deuchar, Grady (Shields).
Dundee: Jack; Robertson, Dixon, Mann, Macdonald C, Smith, Brady (Robb), McManus (Craig), Lynch, Deasley, McCluskey (McDonald K).

Sunday, 2 April 2006

Hibernian (0) 0

Hearts (1) 4 *(Hartley 27, 58, 87 (pen), Jankauskas 80)* 43,180

Hibernian: Malkowski; Caldwell, Smith G■, Murphy, Whittaker, Hogg, Glass (Konté), Thomson, Sproule■, Benjelloun (Konde), Fletcher (McCluskey).
Hearts: Gordon; Neilson, Pressley (Fyssas), Webster, Goncalves (Mikoliunas), Cesnauskis, Aguiar, Hartley, Skacel, Elliot (Pospisil), Jankauskas.

FINAL (at Hampden Park)

Saturday, 13 May 2006

Hearts (1) 1 *(Skacel 39)*

Gretna (0) 1 *(McGuffie 76)* 51,232

Hearts: Gordon; Neilson, Pressley, Tall, Fyssas, Cesnauskis (Mikoliunas), Aguiar (Brellier), Hartley■, Skacel, Bednar (Pospisil), Jankauskas.
Gretna: Main; Birch, Townsley, Innes, Nicholls (Graham), McGuffie, Tosh, O'Neil, Skelton, Grady, Deuchar (McQuilken).
aet; Hearts won 4-2 on penalties.
Referee: Douglas McDonald.

SCOTLAND B INTERNATIONALS (FUTURE)

Kilmarnock, 6 December 2005, 3092

Scotland (1) 2 *(McDonald 38, Miller L 48)*

Poland (0) 0

Scotland: Marshall (Combe 46), Neilson, Greer, Virgo (Berra 70), Hay (Wallace 63), Teale, Montgomery, McDonald (McAllister 46), Robson (Kerr 63), Duffy (Miller L 46), Boyd.

Inverness, 15 March 2006, 5481

Scotland (0) 2 *(Naismith 42, Miller L 71)*

Turkey (1) 3 *(Kabze 7, Kaloglu 25, Tatan 61)* Ak■

Scotland: Brown (Turner 46); Corrigan, Hammell, Virgo (McNamee 66), Berra, Robson (Rankin 75), Naismith (Black! 46), Kerr, Miller L, Dargo (Duffy 46), McIndoe.

FUTURE TOURNAMENT (over two years)

	P	*W*	*D*	*L*	*F*	*A*	*Pts*
Turkey	4	3	1	0	9	4	10
Germany	4	2	1	1	10	5	7
Poland	4	2	0	2	4	6	6
Scotland	4	1	0	3	5	8	3
Austria	4	1	0	3	6	11	3

Turkey won the tournament.

WELSH FOOTBALL 2005–06

"If you're good enough, you're old enough" . . . never has the old saying seemed more appropriate.

As Wales prepare to begin their first full qualification campaign under John Toshack, the manager has shown that he is more than willing to give youth its head by blooding youngsters as and when he sees fit.

Indeed, history was made twice within three months as first Lewin Nyatanga and then Gareth Bale were awarded their first caps. At the age of 17 years and 195 days, the Derby central defender produced an assured performance in a 0-0 draw against Paraguay on St David's Day – only for Southampton's left-back to break the record by coming on as a substitute and setting up the winning goal against Trinidad & Tobago in Austria in May.

Bale, one of four debutants against England's 2006 World Cup group opponents, made his bow when he was just 16 years and 315 days old – three days before his former room-mate at Southampton, Theo Walcott, first played for England at the age of 17 years and 75 days. Bale's debut completed a remarkable clean sweep because it meant he had represented Wales at Under-17, 19 and 21 levels as well as making his senior Southampton debut all in the same season.

After the Under-21s had finished their season with three successive wins against Estonia (5-1 and 2-0) and Cyprus (1-0), it was perhaps no surprise that seven of Brian Flynn's team were on the pitch at the final whistle in Graz.

To be honest, Toshack has no alternative but to look to the future. With so many experienced players having departed, he must develop new talent as Wales attempt to qualify for Euro 2008 from a group containing Germany, the Czech Republic, Slovakia, Republic of Ireland, Cyprus and San Marino.

Their World Cup qualifying campaign during the 2005–06 season began with a whimper and ended with a bang as defeats by England and Poland were followed by victories over Northern Ireland – an exhilarating 3-2 win in Belfast – and Azerbaijan. But Wales came down to earth with a bump after an appalling display in Cyprus before drawing with Paraguay and beating Trinidad & Tobago.

On the domestic front, Cardiff flirted with the Championship play-offs but had to settle for a highly commendable mid-table finish and as their new stadium project drags on, manager Dave Jones deserves huge credit for turning the proverbial sow's ear into a relative silk purse.

Swansea came agonisingly close to pulling off back-to-back promotions by reaching the League One play-off final but produced a performance which sadly turned into a microcosm of their whole season. They dominated the game without taking their chances and their defensive vulnerability allowed Barnsley back into a match which was eventually decided on penalties. The Tykes showed typical Yorkshire grit to convert four superbly-struck spot kicks as the Swans lost their nerve.

After manager Denis Smith had managed to steer the Red Dragons to 13th place in League Two, Wrexham's future off the pitch was finally secured. The Football League accepted a rescue plan by a consortium led by local car dealer Neville Dickens to take the club out of administration and plans for a multi-million pound redevelopment near the Racecourse were given the go-ahead.

All three Welsh clubs playing in England failed to make their mark in the non-league pyramid. Merthyr missed out on the Southern Premier Division play-offs, Newport narrowly avoided being relegated from the Conference South for the second successive season and Colwyn Bay, after finishing just under half way in the First Division of the Unibond League, have appointed former Bangor boss Peter Davenport as their new manager.

TNS – to be known in the future as the New Saints – were hit for six by Liverpool in the first qualifying round of the Champions League but Carmarthen overcame Longford Town 5-3 to reach the second qualifying round of the UEFA Cup where they lost 4-0 to FC Copenhagen. Rhyl won their first European tie when they beat FK Atlantas 2-1 and then reached the UEFA Cup's second qualifying round on away goals before losing 3-1 to Viking. Bangor's Intertoto Cup campaign ended at the first hurdle when they lost 4-1 to Dinaburg.

TNS went on easily to retain their Welsh Premier League title and also won the League Cup – now called the Challenge Cup – by beating Port Talbot, Llanelli and Rhyl – who lifted the Welsh Cup, too, by defeating Bangor – secured the two UEFA Cup places with Carmarthen qualifying for the Intertoto Cup. Grange Quins were forced to resign from the league after struggling for much of their inaugural season while Swansea retained the FAW Premier Cup by again beating Wrexham in the final.

The new international season kicks off with a friendly against Bulgaria amid genuine grounds for cautious optimism. But John Toshack knows that the true test lies ahead. He wants to be judged on the performances of his side in a full qualifying campaign and that moment has now arrived. It's time for the more experienced players – including captain Ryan Giggs, Craig Bellamy, Simon Davies and Danny Gabbidon – to deliver and the promising youngsters to step up to the plate.

Eight years ago, another Ryan G – Ryan Green – was in Gareth Bale's position. The then Wolves full-back took Giggs' place in the record books by becoming the youngest Welsh player when he made his debut against Malta at the age of 17 years and 226 days. After drifting into non-league football, Green's career is now firmly back on track and it was fitting that his perseverance should be rewarded by him scoring the goal which returned Hereford United to the Football League via the play-offs. Green may be considered something of a veteran in comparison with the current new kids on the block, but I wonder if the Bristol Rovers player could complete his comeback by winning an international recall at the ripe old age of 25? Funny old game . . .

GRAHAME LLOYD

VAUXHALL MASTERFIT RETAILERS WELSH PREMIER LEAGUE 2005–06

			Home					*Away*					*Total*						
		P	*W*	*D*	*L*	*F*	*A*	*W*	*D*	*L*	*F*	*A*	*W*	*D*	*L*	*F*	*A*	*GD*	*Pts*
1	Total Network Solutions	34	15	2	0	47	5	12	3	2	40	12	27	5	2	87	17	70	86
2	Llanelli	34	9	4	4	30	14	12	1	4	34	14	21	5	8	64	28	36	68
3	Rhyl	34	10	5	2	34	13	8	5	4	31	17	18	10	6	65	30	35	64
4	Carmarthen Town	34	8	5	4	35	17	9	1	7	27	25	17	6	11	62	42	20	57
5	Port Talbot Town	34	7	7	3	20	12	8	4	5	27	18	15	11	8	47	30	17	56
6	Welshpool Town	34	10	4	3	37	23	5	5	7	22	25	15	9	10	59	48	11	54
7	Aberystwyth Town	34	8	6	3	32	19	6	4	7	27	29	14	10	10	59	48	11	52
8	Haverfordwest County	34	4	9	4	25	18	8	5	4	24	18	12	14	8	49	36	13	50
9	Bangor City	34	6	0	11	26	30	8	3	6	25	24	14	3	17	51	54	–3	45
10	Caersws	34	6	4	7	21	30	5	8	4	23	26	11	12	11	44	56	–12	45
11	Porthmadog	34	7	5	5	38	25	5	3	9	19	34	12	8	14	57	59	–2	44
12	Connah's Quay Nomads	34	7	2	8	15	17	3	6	8	21	29	10	8	16	36	46	–10	38
13	Caernarfon Town	34	4	5	8	23	26	5	5	7	24	29	9	10	15	47	55	–8	37
14	Newtown	34	4	2	11	23	33	6	4	7	19	28	10	6	18	42	61	–19	36
15	Newi Cefn Druids	34	5	8	4	27	24	2	3	12	15	34	7	11	16	42	58	–16	32
16	Airbus UK	34	4	2	11	17	30	4	6	7	18	30	8	8	18	35	60	–25	32
17	Cwmbran Town*	34	4	3	10	23	38	4	5	8	19	35	8	8	18	42	73	–31	19
18	Cardiff Grange Quins	34	3	1	13	14	50	1	3	13	9	60	4	4	26	23	110	–87	15

*Cwmbran Town deducted 13 points for fielding two ineligible players.

VAUXHALL MASTERFIT WELSH PREMIER LEAGUE RESULTS 2005–06

	Aberystwyth Town	Airbus UK	Bangor City	Caernarfon Town	Caersws	Cardiff G H	Carmarthen Town	Connah's Quay Nomads	Cwmbran Town	Haverfordwest County	Llanelli	Newi Cefn Druids	Newtown	Porthmadog	Port Talbot Town	Rhyl	Total Network Solutions	Welshpool Town
Aberystwyth Town	—	2-2	1-0	1-1	0-0	0-0	1-1	1-2	3-1	1-1	4-1	2-1	3-1	4-1	0-3	1-2	2-0	6-2
Airbus UK	0-1	—	2-1	1-2	1-1	2-0	1-3	2-2	1-3	1-2	1-0	3-2	0-2	0-1	0-1	1-2	0-5	0-2
Bangor City	3-1	1-2	—	1-0	1-2	5-1	1-2	0-2	3-0	0-1	1-3	2-1	0-2	1-2	3-2	0-3	2-3	2-4
Caernarfon Town	4-2	0-1	1-1	—	6-0	2-1	0-2	4-2	2-2	0-2	0-3	1-1	0-0	1-2	0-1	0-2	1-3	1-1
Caersws	1-1	3-1	0-6	3-4	—	2-2	1-2	1-0	1-2	1-0	1-4	1-0	2-1	2-1	1-1	1-1	0-2	0-2
Cardiff Grange Quins	2-5	0-1	2-3	4-1	0-5	—	0-6	1-4	1-1	1-0	0-5	3-1	0-1	0-2	0-5	0-2	0-3	0-5
Carmarthen Town	1-0	2-1	0-2	1-1	1-3	8-0	—	1-1	1-1	2-3	0-1	3-0	6-0	3-1	1-1	1-1	2-1	2-0
Connah's Quay Nomads	1-0	3-0	0-1	2-1	1-3	1-0	0-1	—	2-2	1-1	1-0	1-0	0-2	0-2	0-1	0-1	0-2	2-0
Cwmbran Town	1-3	1-1	1-2	0-1	2-2	1-1	3-2	2-1	—	3-2	0-1	1-2	0-1	3-1	2-5	1-7	1-4	1-2
Haverfordwest County	1-1	1-1	0-1	2-2	0-0	7-0	1-2	2-0	3-0	—	0-2	0-0	1-1	1-1	0-3	2-2	0-1	2-1
Llanelli	2-1	3-0	5-0	3-1	5-0	1-0	0-2	2-0	0-1	0-1	—	1-0	2-2	2-2	3-1	1-1	0-2	0-0
Newi Cefn Druids	2-2	0-0	2-2	3-2	2-0	7-0	1-2	2-2	0-0	0-1	2-5	—	3-0	1-1	0-0	1-1	0-6	1-0
Newtown	1-3	0-3	0-1	1-2	0-2	5-0	2-1	1-1	4-1	2-3	0-3	2-3	—	3-1	0-1	1-4	0-3	1-1
Porthmadog	0-2	3-1	1-2	2-3	3-3	4-0	3-0	2-2	5-1	1-4	1-2	5-0	1-1	—	1-1	2-1	2-2	2-0
Port Talbot Town	0-0	4-0	0-2	1-1	0-0	0-1	3-0	0-0	2-1	1-1	0-1	1-0	3-2	2-1	—	1-0	1-1	1-1
Rhyl	4-1	1-1	4-1	2-1	0-0	5-2	1-0	2-1	1-2	1-1	0-1	1-1	3-1	3-0	3-0	—	0-0	3-0
Total Network Solutions	5-0	3-0	2-0	2-1	2-0	7-0	4-1	2-0	1-0	2-0	0-0	4-1	3-1	7-0	1-0	1-0	—	1-1
Welshpool Town	1-4	3-3	2-0	0-0	2-2	2-1	3-0	4-1	5-1	1-1	3-2	3-2	1-2	1-0	2-1	3-1	1-2	—

PREVIOUS WELSH LEAGUE WINNERS

1993	Cwmbran Town	1997	Barry Town	2001	Barry Town	2005	TNS
1994	Bangor City	1998	Barry Town	2002	Barry Town	2006	TNS
1995	Bangor City	1999	Barry Town	2003	Barry Town		
1996	Barry Town	2000	TNS	2004	Rhyl		

WELSH CUP 2005–06

SECOND ROUND

Aberystwyth Town v Bettws	2-0
Airbus UK v Conwy United	4-1
Bala Town v Penrhyncoch	3-2
Bangor City v Llanberis	4-0
Caersws v Cardiff Grange Harlequins	5-3
Caldicot Town v Cwmbran Town	1-3
Cardiff Corinthians v Carmarthen Town	0-11
Chirk AAA v Nefyn United	1-2
Croesyceiliog v West End	3-2
Ento Aberaman v Briton Ferry Athletic	0-1
Glantraeth v Guilsfield	6-1
Gresford Athletic v Porthmadog	1-2
Haverfordwest County v Goytre United	1-2
Holyhead Hotspur v Caernarfon Town	1-3
Lex XI v Connah's Quay Nomads	4-2
Llanelli v Risca United	8-2
Llanfyllin Town v Buckley Town	1-3
Llanrwst United v Llandudno	3-2
Mold Alexandra v Myndd Isa	4-3
Newtown v Llandymog United	5-1
Pontyclun v Maesteg Park Athletic	2-1
Pontypridd Town v Ton Pentre *(Including penalties).*	7-6
Port Talbot Town v Newport YMCA	3-2
Rhayader Town v Llangefni Town	2-4
Presteigne St Andrews v Prestatyn Town	2-4
Rhyl v Sealand Rovers	4-0
Summerhill Brymbo v Newi Cefn Druids	2-3
TNS v Welshpool Town	4-1
Treharris Athletic v Ely Rangers	1-3
Troedyrhiw v Taffs Well	3-2
UWIC v AFC Llwydcoed	2-1
Ystradgynlais v Bryntirion Athletic	2-3

THIRD ROUND

Bala Town v Buckley Town	4-3
Bangor City v Airbus UK	4-2
Caersws v Croesceiliog	3-1
Carmarthen Town v Briton Ferry Athletic	4-0
Ely Rangers v Cwmbran Town	1-4
Glantraeth v Rhyl	2-5
Goytre United v Troedyrhiw	6-3
Llangefni Town v Llanrwst	3-0
Mold Alexander v Prestatyn Town	0-5
Newi Cefn Druids v Nefyn United	3-1
Newtown v Pontyclun	6-0
Porthmadog v Caernarfon Town	0-3
Port Talbot Town v Bryntirion Athletic	4-0
Pontypridd Town v Aberystwyth Town	1-0
TNS v Lex XI	4-0
UWIC v Llanelli	1-3

FOURTH ROUND

Bangor City v Newtown	2-1
Caernarfon Town v Bala Town	4-0
Caersws v Llangefni Town	1-3
Cwmbran Town v Port Talbot Town	1-3
Llanelli v TNS	1-0
Newi Cefn Druids v Rhyl	3-5
Pontypridd Town v Goytre United	0-5
Prestatyn Town v Carmarthen Town	1-2

QUARTER-FINALS

Bangor City v Carmarthen Town	1-0
Llanelli v Caernarfon Town	3-0
Port Talbot Town v Llangefni Town	3-0
Rhyl v Goytre United	5-2

SEMI-FINALS

Rhyl v Port Talbot Town *(Rhyl won 5-4 on penalties).*	2-2
Llanelli v Bangor City	0-1

WELSH CUP FINAL

(at Wrexham)

6 May 2006

Rhyl (0) 2 Bangor City (0) 0

Rhyl: Gann; Connolly (Limbert 88), Graves (Adamson 80), Stones, Horan, Edwards, Wilson, Moran, Hunt (Sharp 84), Powell, Brewerton.

Scorers: Moran 48 (pen), Wilson 78.

Bangor City: Havard; Blackmore, O'Neill, Jones K, Beattie, Jones C, Killackey, Priest■, Linnecar, Roberts, Lamb.

Attendance: 1743.

■ *Denotes player sent off.*

PREVIOUS WELSH CUP WINNERS

1878	Wrexham Town	1908	Chester	1948	Lovell's Athletic	1978	Wrexham
1879	White Star Newtown	1909	Wrexham	1949	Merthyr Tydfil	1979	Shrewsbury Town
1880	Druids	1910	Wrexham	1950	Swansea Town	1980	Newport County
1881	Druids	1911	Wrexham	1951	Merthyr Tydfil	1981	Swansea City
1882	Druids	1912	Cardiff City	1952	Rhyl	1982	Swansea City
1883	Wrexham	1913	Swansea Town	1953	Rhyl	1983	Swansea City
1884	Oswestry United	1914	Wrexham	1954	Flint Town United	1984	Shrewsbury Town
1885	Druids	1915	Wrexham	1955	Barry Town	1985	Shrewsbury Town
1886	Druids	1920	Cardiff City	1956	Cardiff City	1986	Wrexham
1887	Chirk	1921	Wrexham	1957	Wrexham	1987	Merthyr Tydfil
1888	Chirk	1922	Cardiff City	1958	Wrexham	1988	Cardiff City
1889	Bangor	1923	Cardiff City	1959	Cardiff City	1989	Swansea City
1890	Druids	1924	Wrexham	1960	Wrexham	1990	Hereford United
1891	Shrewsbury Town	1925	Wrexham	1961	Swansea Town	1991	Swansea City
1892	Chirk	1926	Ebbw Vale	1962	Bangor City	1992	Cardiff City
1893	Wrexham	1927	Cardiff City	1963	Borough United	1993	Cardiff City
1894	Chirk	1928	Cardiff City	1964	Cardiff City	1994	Barry Town
1895	Newtown	1929	Connah's Quay	1965	Cardiff City	1995	Wrexham
1896	Bangor	1930	Cardiff City	1966	Swansea Town	1996	TNS
1897	Wrexham	1931	Wrexham	1967	Cardiff City	1997	Barry Town
1898	Druids	1932	Swansea Town	1968	Cardiff City	1998	Bangor City
1899	Druids	1933	Chester	1969	Cardiff City	1999	Inter Cable-Tel
1900	Aberystwyth	1934	Bristol City	1970	Cardiff City	2000	Bangor City
1901	Oswestry United	1935	Tranmere Rovers	1971	Cardiff City	2001	Barry Town
1902	Wellington Town	1936	Crewe Alexandra	1972	Wrexham	2002	Barry Town
1903	Wrexham	1937	Crewe Alexandra	1973	Cardiff City	2003	Barry Town
1904	Druids	1938	Shrewsbury Town	1974	Cardiff City	2004	Rhyl
1905	Wrexham	1939	South Liverpool	1975	Wrexham	2005	TNS
1906	Wellington Town	1940	Wellington Town	1976	Cardiff City	2006	Rhyl
1907	Oswestry United	1947	Chester	1977	Shrewsbury Town		

FAW PREMIER LEAGUE CUP

FIRST ROUND
Cwmbran Town 1, Merthyr Tydfil 0
Caersws 5, Aberystwyth Town 1
Welshpool Town 0, Newtown 2
Porthmadog 1, Carmarthen Town 2

SECOND ROUND
Rhyl 1, Cwmbran Town 0
Bangor City 1, Carmarthen Town 2
Newtown 2, Haverfordwest County 1
Newport County 1, Caersws 0

QUARTER-FINALS
Carmarthen Town 2, Cardiff City 1
Newtown 2, TNS 5
Newport County 0, Wrexham 2
Rhyl 0, Swansea City 1

SEMI-FINALS
Wrexham 3, TNS 3
(Wrexham won 5-4 on penalties.)
Carmarthen Town 2, Swansea City 3

FAW CUP FINAL

(at Wrexham)

29 March 2006

Swansea City (2) 2 Wrexham (0) 1

Swansea City: Gueret; Ricketts, Tate, O'Leary, Monk, Lowe, Britton, Tudur-Jones, Fallon, Trundle, Robinson (Martinez 82).
Scorers: Williams D (og) 36, Fallon 42.
Wrexham: Ingham (Michael Jones 70); Bennett (Spender 46), Holt, Crowell, Lawrence, Pejic, Mark Jones (Mackin 76), Ferguson, Williams S, Derbyshire, Williams D.
Scorer: Spender 71.
Referee: C. Richards (Llangennech).
Attendance: 3032.

THE LOOSEMORES OF CARDIFF CHALLENGE CUP 2005-06

PRELIMINARY ROUND
Cardiff Grange Harlequins 1, Caernarfon Town 0
Newi Cefn Druids 2, Airbus UK 5

FIRST ROUND
Connah's Quay Nomads 0, Newtown 3
Cwmbran Town 1, Haverfordwest County 0
Cardiff Grange Harlequins 3, Caersws 1
Llanelli 3, Aberystwyth Town 0
Porthmadog 2, Airbus UK 3
Port Talbot Town 1, Carmarthen Town 0
Welshpool Town 0, TNS 2
Bangor City 2, Rhyl 4

QUARTER-FINALS
Port Talbot Town 2, Cwmbran Town 1
Llanelli 5, Cardiff Grange Harlequins 2
TNS 6, Newtown 1
Airbus UK 3, Rhyl 2

SEMI-FINALS FIRST LEG
Llanelli 0, Port Talbot Town 1
Airbus UK 1, TNS 2

SEMI-FINALS SECOND LEG
Port Talbot Town 0, Llanelli 1
(aet; Port Talbot Town won 7-6 on penalties.)
TNS 2, Airbus UK 0

CHALLENGE CUP FINAL

30 April 2006

TNS 4 *(Ward 7, Wilde 16, 61, 84)*

Port Talbot Town 0 **358**

TNS: Doherty; Carter, King, Hogan (Baker 71), Evans (Jones 85), Holmes, Leah (Davies 81), Jackson, Wilde, Toner, Ward.
Port Talbot Town: Rogers; Cockings, De Vulgt, Hanford (Davies 61), Rees, Surman, Pridham, Phillips (Jones 57), Griffiths, Pearson (Parry 80), Hooper.
Referee: R. Ellingham.

MACRON WEST WALES PRINT WELSH FOOTBALL LEAGUE 2005–06

DIVISION ONE

	P	W	D	L	F	A	GD	Pts
Goytre United	34	22	9	3	82	42	40	75
Neath Athletic	34	22	7	5	76	32	44	73
Pontardawe Town	34	18	9	7	57	35	22	63
Maesteg Park	34	18	9	7	61	40	21	63
UWIC	34	16	6	12	61	52	9	54
Bridgend Town	34	16	6	12	55	47	8	54
Afan Lido	34	13	8	13	46	41	5	47
Dinas Powys	34	13	8	13	42	44	–2	47
Bryntirion Athletic	34	13	6	15	62	58	4	45
Newport YMCA	34	11	11	12	48	54	–6	44
Barry Town	34	11	10	13	39	50	–11	43
Ely Rangers	34	12	5	17	47	59	–12	41
Ton Pentre	34	11	5	18	51	60	–9	38
Caerleon	34	11	4	19	33	58	–25	37
Taffs Well	34	9	9	16	46	62	–16	36
Bettws	34	10	5	19	46	63	–17	35
Briton Ferry	34	9	6	19	43	64	–21	33
AFC Llwydcoed	34	8	3	23	35	69	–34	27

HUWS GRAY-FITLOCK CYMRU ALLIANCE LEAGUE 2005–06

	P	W	D	L	F	A	GD	Pts
Glantraeth	34	21	7	6	83	36	47	70
Buckley Town	34	20	7	7	85	52	33	67
Flint Town United*	34	19	12	3	77	40	37	66
Guilsfield	34	16	12	6	73	44	29	60
Llangefni Town	34	17	7	10	68	46	22	58
Llandudno*	34	17	8	9	64	42	22	56
Bala Town	34	14	9	11	63	52	11	51
Lex XI	34	13	9	12	72	75	–3	48
CPD Bodedern	34	13	6	15	40	58	–18	45
Penrhyncoch	34	13	4	17	62	78	–16	43
Queen's Park	34	11	8	15	36	59	–23	41
Llanfair PG	34	11	6	17	58	73	–15	39
Llandyrnog	34	10	8	16	51	64	–13	38
Gresford Athletic	34	9	9	16	45	64	–19	36
Ruthin Town	34	7	13	14	43	55	–12	34
Holyhead Hotspur	34	8	9	17	44	67	–23	33
Holywell Town*	34	5	12	17	49	72	–23	24
Halkyn United	34	5	8	21	47	83	–36	23

**3 points deducted.*

NORTHERN IRISH FOOTBALL 2005–06

Northern Ireland football in many ways has experienced a remarkably successful season, with the highlight a David Healy goal which brought a never-to-be-forgotten 1-0 victory over England last September at Windsor Park. Yes, it has been success all the way. What a catalogue.

Healy's goal lifted the morale of the entire country – a goal which is now a piece of Irish football history. Along with the victory over Azerbaijan, it pushed manager Lawrie Sanchez's team into a comparatively respectable FIFA ranking after years hovering in the doldrums among fellow stragglers. That date, 7 September 2005, is now a golden chapter in the history of the Northern Ireland game.

Linfield won all four domestic trophies: Carnegie Irish Premiership, Nationwide Irish Cup, Crest Wear County Antrim Shield and the CIS Insurance League Cup.

Linfield, inspired by the motivational qualities of Manager of the Year David Jeffrey, maintained an admirable consistency, losing only the Setanta All-Ireland Cup – eliminated in the semi-final by eventual winners and a quality side Drogheda United.

Not only did Jeffrey, labelled by the fans as "The Special One", collect the Manager award, but Glenn Ferguson, veteran ex-Northern Ireland striker, was named Player of the Year and Peter Thompson, with 49 goals, was leading marksman and a transfer target for several English clubs.

From an international perspective, Northern Ireland finished fourth in the World Cup Group Six qualifying series behind England, Poland and Austria. They could have, with a bit of luck which now traditionally seems to elude them, got third place, but overall it was a commendable achievement considering the limited supply of talent.

Now there should be a promising throughput as the Under-21 side, twelve matches without defeat, are making an impact. So, overall it has been success, too, in the international arena.

Sanchez now finds himself with a corps of around 30 players thanks to those Under-21 triumphs and the emergence of some excellent young prospects – Sammy Clingan (Nottingham Forest), Kyle Lafferty (Burnley) and Aston Villa's Steve Davis, to name but three. The talent cupboard, which once lay so bare, is now reasonably well stocked.

Administratively, the controversy still continues over the proposed, but far from confirmed, move by the Government to establish a multi-purpose national stadium at The Maze, sight of a former prison. Supporters would prefer it to be constructed in Belfast, the capital, and they also query why Windsor Park, a stadium with an incomparable heritage which simply cannot be transferred, could not be refurbished. This is a controversy which looks like running continuously.

Vast changes have taken place in the Irish FA's constitution, which has been completely re-written, including those sections on Sunday football, while there is a groundswell for a complete reorganisation in the Irish Premier League format, reducing it from 16 teams to 12 teams. How this can be achieved remains to be seen, but there will certainly be opposition from the smaller clubs, who see those matches against Linfield and Glentoran as the financial bonanza to keep them ticking over.

The promotion of Crusaders, relegated only a season ago, was not surprising for they are well organised, within budgetary control and under manager Stephen Baxter, set about their task with true professionalism, while Donegal Celtic triumphed over Institute in the promotion–relegation play-off and despite some ill-founded concerns, have had their stadium at Suffolk given the green light for home matches.

This will add colour and spectacle to the local scene with the Donegal Celtic management claiming they will be no flash in the pan. They intend to establish themselves as a senior side and one with considerable support from West Belfast.

DR MALCOLM BRODIE MBE

CARNEGIE IRISH PREMIER LEAGUE

	P	W	D	L	F	A	GD	Pts
Linfield	30	23	6	1	88	23	65	75
Glentoran	30	19	6	5	60	28	32	63
Portadown	30	16	6	8	56	36	20	54
Dungannon Swifts	30	13	10	7	61	41	20	49
Cliftonville	30	13	8	9	45	35	10	47
Newry City	30	12	9	9	45	35	10	45
Ballymena United	30	13	6	11	42	48	–6	45
Lisburn Distillery	30	12	8	10	44	38	6	44
Coleraine	30	11	4	15	40	57	–17	37
Limavady United	30	9	9	12	42	49	–7	36
Loughgall	30	9	7	14	33	38	–5	34
Larne	30	7	9	14	42	63	–21	30
Glenavon	30	7	9	14	35	59	–24	30
Armagh City	30	9	3	18	38	69	–31	30
Institute†	30	6	8	16	37	58	–21	26
Ards*	30	6	2	22	31	62	–31	20

Ards 0, Glenavon 3; result annulled and Ards awarded 1-0 victory, Glenavon fielded an ineligible player.

**relegated; **promoted; †play-off.*

CARNEGIE IRISH FIRST DIVISION

	P	W	D	L	F	A	GD	Pts
Crusaders**	22	20	1	1	51	13	38	61
Donegal Celtic†	22	13	5	4	41	25	16	44
Dundela	22	10	5	7	32	28	4	35
Bangor	22	10	3	9	42	32	10	33
Banbridge Town	22	8	6	8	29	29	0	30
Tobermore United	22	8	5	9	33	37	–4	29
Carrick Rangers	22	8	4	10	25	29	–4	28
Coagh United	22	8	3	11	25	26	–1	27
HW Welders	22	7	4	11	21	31	–10	25
Moyola Park	22	7	3	12	32	50	–18	24
Ballyclare Cmrds*	22	6	5	11	32	37	–5	23
Ballymoney Utd*	22	3	4	15	18	44	–26	13

Promotion Play-off
Donegal Celtic 3, 0, Institute 1, 0.

CARNEGIE IRISH SECOND DIVISION

	P	W	D	L	F	A	GD	Pts
Portstewart**	20	12	5	3	33	15	18	41
Ballinamallard Utd**	20	11	7	2	48	22	26	40
PSNI	20	10	5	5	34	26	8	35
Lurgan Celtic	20	9	6	5	36	30	6	33
Annagh United	20	8	5	7	28	23	5	29
Dergview	20	8	2	10	34	37	–3	26
Chimney Corner	20	7	5	8	25	32	–7	26
Wakehurst	20	6	7	7	25	24	1	25
Brantwood	20	4	8	8	23	31	–8	20
Oxford United Stars	20	6	0	14	22	43	–21	18
Queens University	20	2	4	14	24	49	–25	10

Second Division Play-off
Trojan S 2, 3, Glebe Rangers 5, 4.

IRISH LEAGUE CHAMPIONSHIP WINNERS

1891 Linfield
1892 Linfield
1893 Linfield
1894 Glentoran
1895 Linfield
1896 Distillery
1897 Glentoran
1898 Linfield
1899 Distillery
1900 Belfast Celtic
1901 Distillery
1902 Linfield
1903 Distillery
1904 Linfield
1905 Glentoran
1906 Cliftonville
Distillery
1907 Linfield
1908 Linfield
1909 Linfield
1910 Cliftonville
1911 Linfield
1912 Glentoran
1913 Glentoran
1914 Linfield
1915 Belfast Celtic
1920 Belfast Celtic
1921 Glentoran
1922 Linfield
1923 Linfield
1924 Queen's Island
1925 Glentoran
1926 Belfast Celtic
1927 Belfast Celtic
1928 Belfast Celtic
1929 Belfast Celtic
1930 Linfield
1931 Glentoran
1932 Linfield
1933 Belfast Celtic
1934 Linfield
1935 Linfield
1936 Belfast Celtic
1937 Belfast Celtic
1938 Belfast Celtic
1939 Belfast Celtic
1940 Belfast Celtic
1948 Belfast Celtic
1949 Linfield
1950 Linfield
1951 Glentoran
1952 Glenavon
1953 Glentoran
1954 Linfield
1955 Linfield
1956 Linfield
1957 Glentoran
1958 Ards
1959 Linfield
1960 Glenavon
1961 Linfield
1962 Linfield
1963 Distillery
1964 Glentoran
1965 Derry City
1966 Linfield
1967 Glentoran
1968 Glentoran
1969 Linfield
1970 Glentoran
1971 Linfield
1972 Glentoran
1973 Crusaders
1974 Coleraine
1975 Linfield
1976 Crusaders
1977 Glentoran
1978 Linfield
1979 Linfield
1980 Linfield
1981 Glentoran
1982 Linfield
1983 Linfield
1984 Linfield
1985 Linfield
1986 Linfield
1987 Linfield
1988 Glentoran
1989 Linfield
1990 Portadown
1991 Portadown
1992 Glentoran
1993 Linfield
1994 Linfield
1995 Crusaders
1996 Portadown
1997 Crusaders
1998 Cliftonville
1999 Glentoran
2000 Linfield
2001 Linfield
2002 Portadown
2003 Glentoran
2004 Linfield
2005 Glentoran
2006 Linfield

FIRST DIVISION

1996 Coleraine
1997 Ballymena United
1998 Newry Town
1999 Distillery
2000 Omagh Town
2001 Ards
2002 Lisburn Distillery
2003 Dungannon Swifts
2004 Loughgall
2005 Armagh City
2006 Crusaders

SETANTA CUP

GROUP 1

	P	W	D	L	F	A	Pts
Cork City	6	5	1	0	11	2	16
Drogheda United	6	3	1	2	7	5	10
Dungannon Swifts	6	1	1	4	4	8	4
Portadown	6	0	3	3	4	11	3

GROUP 2

	P	W	D	L	F	A	Pts
Linfield	6	2	4	0	12	4	10
Shelbourne	6	2	3	1	6	2	9
Derry City	6	1	4	1	5	4	7
Glentoran	6	1	1	4	5	18	4

SEMI-FINALS

Cork City 2, Shelbourne 0 *(at Cork).*
Linfield 0, Drogheda United 1 *(at Windsor Park).*

SETANTA CUP FINAL

(at Tolka Park, Dublin, 22 April 2006)

Drogheda United (0) 1 *(Leech 103)*
Cork City (0) 0

Drogheda U: Connor; Shelley, Webb, Gartland, Gavin, Keegan, Robinson (Fahey 82), Bradley, O'Brien, Fitzpatrick (Leech 72), Keddy.
Cork C: Devine; Horgan, Bennett, Murray, Murphy, O'Donovan, O'Brien (Softic 103), Gamble, O'Callaghan (Woods 57), Fenn, Behan (McCarthey 100).
aet.
Referee: D. McKeon (Dublin).

ULSTER CUP WINNERS

1949 Linfield
1950 Larne
1951 Glentoran
1952
1953 Glentoran
1954 Crusaders
1955 Glenavon
1956 Linfield
1957 Linfield
1958 Distillery
1959 Glenavon
1960 Linfield
1961 Ballymena U
1962 Linfield
1963 Crusaders
1964 Linfield
1965 Coleraine
1966 Glentoran
1967 Linfield
1968 Coleraine
1969 Coleraine
1970 Linfield
1971 Linfield
1972 Coleraine
1973 Ards
1974 Linfield
1975 Coleraine
1976 Glentoran
1977 Linfield
1978 Linfield
1979 Linfield
1980 Ballymena U
1981 Glentoran
1982 Glentoran
1983 Glentoran
1984 Linfield
1985 Coleraine
1986 Coleraine
1987 Larne
1988 Glentoran
1989 Glentoran
1990 Portadown
1991 Bangor
1992 Linfield
1993 Crusaders
1994 Bangor
1995 Portadown
1996 Portadown
1997 Coleraine
1998 Ballyclare Comrades
1999 Distillery
2000 *No competition*
2001 *No competition*
2002 *No competition*
2003 Dungannon Swifts *(Confined to First Division clubs)*
2004 *No competition*
2005 *No competition*
2006 *No competition*

THE IRISH FA YOUTH LEAGUE PLAY-OFF

Linfield Rangers 2, Ballymena United III 0

IRISH LEAGUE YOUTH CUP

Glenavon III 2, Donegal Celtic 1

NATIONWIDE IRISH CUP 2005–06

FIFTH ROUND

Ards v Glentoran	1-2
Ballymena United v Kilmore Rec	4-0
Ballymoney United v Carrick Rangers	1-2
Ballynure OB v Ballyclare Comrades	0-4
Banbridge Town v Loughgall	0-0, 2-3
Cliftonville v Dungannon Swifts	1-1, 0-1
Coleraine v Newry City	1-1, 0-0
(Coleraine won 3-1 on penalties).	
Crusaders v Portadown	2-2, 0-1
Glenavon v Dundela	1-1, 2-1
HW Welders v Bangor	1-1, 1-3
Institute v Lisburn Distillery	1-3
Larne v Donegal Celtic	1-1, 3-1
Linfield v Armagh City	5-0
Newington YC v Coagh United	1-1, 2-0
PSNI v Limavady United	0-5
Tobermore United v Portstewart	2-3

SIXTH ROUND

Dungannon Swifts v Portadown	1-1, 1-3
Glenavon v Coleraine	3-0
Glentoran v Ballyclare Comrades	1-0
Larne v Carrick Rangers	3-0
Limavady United v Bangor	1-3
Linfield v Loughgall	1-1, 3-1
Lisburn Distillery v Ballymena United	0-0, 2-1
Newington YC v Portstewart	1-0

QUARTER-FINALS

Glentoran v Portadown	2-0
Linfield v Glenavon	3-0
Lisburn Distillery v Bangor	0-1
Newington YC v Larne	1-2

SEMI-FINALS

Glentoran v Larne	2-0
(at Windsor Park, Belfast)	
Linfield v Bangor	3-0
(at Seaview, Belfast)	

NATIONWIDE IRISH CUP FINAL 2005–06

(Windsor Park, 6 May 2006)

Linfield (1) 2 *(Thompson 45, 65)*
Glentoran (1) 1 *(Halliday 44)* 12,500

Linfield: Mannus; Ervin, McShane, Gault, Murphy, McAreavey (Hunter 85), Thompson, Mouncey, Ferguson, Kearney (McCann 74), Bailie.

Glentoran: Morris; Melaugh, Nixon, Simpson, Glendinning, Lockhart, Berry (Tolan 77), McDonagh, Ward, Halliday, Browne (Morgan 69).

Referee: M. Ross (Carrickfergus).

(Linfield's first Irish Cup Final win over Glentoran since 1945 ensured a four trophy clean sweep having already won the Carnegie Irish Premier Division, CIS Insurance Cup and Crest Wear Antrim Shield. For the first time in an Irish Cup Final there was a woman assistant referee, Andi Regan.)

IRISH CUP FINALS (from 1946–47)

1946–47 Belfast Celtic 1, Glentoran 0
1947–48 Linfield 3, Coleraine 0
1948–49 Derry City 3, Glentoran 1
1949–50 Linfield 2, Distillery 1
1950–51 Glentoran 3, Ballymena U 1
1951–52 Ards 1, Glentoran 0
1952–53 Linfield 5, Coleraine 0
1953–54 Derry City 1, Glentoran 0
1954–55 Dundela 3, Glenavon 0
1955–56 Distillery 1, Glentoran 0
1956–57 Glenavon 2, Derry City 0
1957–58 Ballymena U 2, Linfield 0
1958–59 Glenavon 2, Ballymena U 0
1959–60 Linfield 5, Ards 1
1960–61 Glenavon 5, Linfield 1
1961–62 Linfield 4, Portadown 0
1962–63 Linfield 2, Distillery 1
1963–64 Derry City 2, Glentoran 0
1964–65 Coleraine 2, Glenavon 1
1965–66 Glentoran 2, Linfield 0
1966–67 Crusaders 3, Glentoran 1
1967–68 Crusaders 2, Linfield 0
1968–69 Ards 4, Distillery 2
1969–70 Linfield 2, Ballymena U 1
1970–71 Distillery 3, Derry City
1971–72 Coleraine 2, Portadown 1
1972–73 Glentoran 3, Linfield 2
1973–74 Ards 2, Ballymena U 1
1974–75 Coleraine 1:0:1, Linfield 1:0:0
1975–76 Carrick Rangers 2, Linfield 1
1976–77 Coleraine 4, Linfield 1
1977–78 Linfield 3, Ballymena U 1
1978–79 Cliftonville 3, Portadown 2
1979–80 Linfield 2, Crusaders 0
1980–81 Ballymena U 1, Glenavon 0
1981–82 Linfield 2, Coleraine 1
1982–83 Glentoran 1:2, Linfield 1:1
1983–84 Ballymena U 4, Carrick Rangers 1
1984–85 Glentoran 1:1, Linfield 1:0
1985–86 Glentoran 2, Coleraine 1
1986–87 Glentoran 1, Larne 0
1987–88 Glentoran 1, Glenavon 0
1988–89 Ballymena U 1, Larne 0
1989–90 Glentoran 3, Portadown 0
1990–91 Portadown 2, Glenavon 1
1991–92 Glenavon 2, Linfield 1
1992–93 Bangor 1:1:1, Ards 1:1:0
1993–94 Linfield 2, Bangor 0
1994–95 Linfield 3, Carrick Rangers 1
1995–96 Glentoran 1, Glenavon 0
1996–97 Glenavon 1, Cliftonville 0
1997–98 Glentoran 1, Glenavon 0
1998–99 *Portadown awarded trophy after Cliftonville were eliminated for using an ineligible player in semi-final.*
1999–2000 Glentoran 1, Portadown 0
2000–01 Glentoran 1, Linfield 0
2001–02 Linfield 2, Portadown 1
2002–03 Coleraine 1, Glentoran 0
2003–04 Glentoran 1, Coleraine 0
2004–05 Portadown 5, Larne 1
2005–06 Linfield 2, Glentoran 1

CREST TEAM WEAR COUNTY ANTRIM SHIELD

FIRST ROUND

Linfield v Carrick Rangers	1-1, 2-1
Larne v Kilmore Rec	5-1
Lisburn Distillery v Donegal Celtic	5-0
Crusaders v Dundela	1-0
Glentoran v Bangor	4-0
Cliftonville v HW Welders	4-0
Ards v Ards Rangers	3-0
Ballymena United v Wakehurst	3-1

SECOND ROUND

Ballymena United v Cliftonville	2-0
Crusaders v Larne	1-2
Glentoran v Lisburn Distillery	3-2
Ards v Linfield	2-7

SEMI-FINALS

Ballymena United v Larne	3-0
(at Inver Park).	
Linfield v Glentoran	1-0
(at Windsor Park).	

COUNTY ANTRIM SHIELD FINAL

(at Seaview)

Ballymena United 1 Linfield 2

Ballymena United: McFrederick; Donaghy, McClean, Haveron (Charnock 61), Albert Watson, Smyth, Scates (Rowe 73), Aidan Watson, Sweeney (Hamill 73), Kelbie, King.
Scorer: Kelbie 32.

Linfield: Mannus; McShane, Murphy, Gault, Kingsberry (Picking 72), McAreavey, Kearney, Ervin, Ferguson, Thompson, Bailie.
Scorers: Kearney 50, Ferguson 86.

Referee: M. Ross (Carrickfergus).
Attendance: 3608

CIS INSURANCE IRISH LEAGUE CUP

FINAL SECTION TABLES

Group 1	P	W	D	L	F	A	Pts
Glentoran	6	5	1	0	14	7	16
Armagh City	6	2	2	2	12	9	8
Institute	6	1	2	3	9	13	5
Coleraine	6	0	2	4	3	9	2

Group 2	P	W	D	L	F	A	Pts
Portadown	6	4	2	0	10	5	14
Newry City	6	3	2	1	9	7	11
Ballymena United	6	2	2	2	6	6	8
Glenavon	6	0	0	6	5	12	0

Group 3	P	W	D	L	F	A	Pts
Linfield	6	6	0	0	20	1	18
Limavady United	6	3	1	2	9	12	10
Ards	6	2	1	3	6	12	7
Loughgall	6	0	0	6	7	15	0

Group 4	P	W	D	L	F	A	Pts
Lisburn Distillery	6	3	2	1	11	5	11
Dungannon Swifts	6	3	1	2	18	5	10
Cliftonville	6	1	4	1	6	7	7
Larne	6	1	1	4	7	17	4

QUARTER-FINALS

Glentoran v Newry City	2-1
Linfield v Dungannon Swifts	4-0
Portadown v Armagh City	4-2
Lisburn Distillery v Limavady United	6-0

SEMI-FINALS

Glentoran 2 *(Nixon 75, Glendinning 104)*
Portadown 1 *(Quinn 41)*
(at The Oval, 8 November 2005).

Linfield 5 *(McAreavey 29, Ferguson 35, Kearney 54, McShane 63 (pen), Larmour 90)*
Lisburn Distillery 0
(aet; at Seaview, Belfast, 8 November 2005).

CIS INSURANCE IRISH LEAGUE CUP FINAL

(at Windsor Park, Belfast, 10 December 2005)

Linfield 3 Glentoran 0

Linfield: Mannus; McShane, Murphy, Gault, Kearney, Ferguson (Larmour 88), Bailie, Mouncey (Kingsberry 64), McAreavey (O'Kane 89), Thompson, Ervin.
Scorer: Ferguson 2, 49, 75.

Glentoran: Morris; Nixon, Glendinning, Simpson, McGibbon, Holmes, Browne, Melaugh, Morgan (Halliday 72), McCann (Ward 72), Lockhart.
Referee: M. Ross (Carrickfergus).
Attendance: 7000.

LEADING GOALSCORERS

Ferguson (Linfield) 10
Halliday (Glentoran) 5
Thompson (Linfield) 5

SUNDAY LIFE TROPHY FOR LEADING GOALSCORERS

Peter Thompson *(Linfield)*	49	Oran Kearney *(Linfield)*	16	Lee Patrick *(Limavady Utd)*	12
Glenn Ferguson *(Linfield)*	42	Michael Ward *(Dungannon S)*	16	Gary Hamilton *(Portadown)*	12
Michael Halliday *(Glentoran)*	30	Kevin Kelbie *(Ballymena Utd)*	16	Michael Halliday *(Glentoran)*	12
Chris Morgan *(Glentoran)*	28	Mark Dickson *(Larne)*	15	Paul McAreavey *(Linfield)*	11
David Scullion *(Dungannon S)*	22	Marty Verner *(Glenavon)*	15	Vincent Sweeney *(Ballymena Utd)*	11
Timmy Adamson *(Dungannon S)*	21	Damien Whitehead *(Newry City)*	14	Damien Curran *(Newry City)*	11
Gary McCutcheon *(Larne)*	19	Nathan McConnell *(Cliftonville)*	12	David Ward *(Armagh City)*	11
Gary Browne *(Glentoran)*	18	Jason Hill *(Ards)*	12	John Martin *(Lisburn Distillery)*	11
Chris Morgan *(Glentoran)*	17	Marc McCann *(Portadown)*	12	Colin Nixon *(Glentoran)*	11

ROLL OF HONOUR SEASON 2005–06

Competition	*Winner*	*Runner-up*
Setanta Cup (all Ireland)	Cork City	Drogheda United
Carnegie Irish Premier	Linfield	Glentoran
Carnegie First Division	Crusaders	Donegal Celtic
CIS Insurance League Cup	Linfield	Glentoran
Nationwide Irish Cup	Linfield	Glentoran
Crest Wear County Antrim Shield	Linfield	Ballymena United
Steel & Sons Cup	Crusaders	Dundela
County Antrim Junior Shield	Ardoyne WMC	Temple Rangers
Belfast Telegraph Intermediate Cup	Donegal Celtic	Coagh United
Irish Junior Cup	Derryhirk United	Lincoln Court
Rushmere Shopping Mid Ulster Cup	Dungannon Swifts	Glenavon
North West Senior Cup	Coleraine	Institute
Harry Cavan Youth Cup	Ballinamallard United Youth	St Oliver Plunket Boys
George Wilson Memorial Cup	Dungannon Swifts Res	Glentoran II

CHAMPIONS LEAGUE REVIEW 2005–06

Barcelona, the best supported team in the competition and Arsenal with its miserly defence faced each other in the Champions League final. Each had a superstar. There was Ronaldinho the Brazilian fresh from being voted European and FIFA World Player of the Year, for the Gunners there was Thierry Henry the Football Writers' Association choice for an unprecedented third occasion. A mouth-watering prospect.

Certainly it was an intriguing tie with twists and turns in the unravelling, but neither Ronaldinho nor Henry lived up to their justified reputations. Arsenal suffered the early dismissal of goalkeeper Jens Lehmann. No debate about the foul: Samuel Eto'o pulled down by his ankle. But the ball eventually finished up in the net. A yellow card and a penalty would have been more appropriate.

Now the Arsenal rearguard had to take the stage. They stuck remarkably well to the task and from a dubious free-kick, Henry floated the ball in for Sol Campbell to soar above everyone to head them into a 34th minute lead.

Barcelona were finding it difficult to penetrate the Arsenal defence. Their best opportunities came from free-kicks outside the penalty area. But it was not Ronaldinho's day and he was wide of the target three times. In breakaways Henry was a constant threat but failed with a one-on-one with the goalkeeper.

There was even a suspicion of offside when Eto'o was nudged through by substitute Henrik Larsson for the Barcelona equaliser after 76 minutes. But it had started to become one-way traffic by then, Larsson again made the opening and Brazilian full-back Juliano Belletti squeezed the ball in just four minutes later. Heroism was not enough for Arsenal.

Naturally the beginning of the Champions League was an entirely different affair. None more so than the experience of the holders Liverpool who had to start the defence of their crown at the first qualifying stage. Actually it was touch and go whether they would be allowed in at all!

As fate would have it, the Welsh club TNS who had offered to play a qualifying match against the champions, were paired and duly lost both legs 3-0. Liverpool then disposed of Kaunas at which point Celtic were rudely beaten 5-0 by Artmedia the Bratislava club. Bravely Celtic pulled four goals back in the home leg.

The third qualifying round included Manchester United, Everton and Rangers. Everton went out to Villarreal, but naturally had another chance in the UEFA Cup, meanwhile their neighbours Liverpool won in Sofia against CSKA, but had to hang on in the return.

Enter Arsenal and Chelsea, the latter finding themselves in the same section as Liverpool. Arsenal impressively topped Group B dropping just two points, but Manchester United were eliminated at the bottom of Group D won by Villarreal.

Liverpool and Chelsea played out two goalless draws, while Rangers in a group headed by Internazionale managed a creditable second place.

There were shocks in the opening knockout round, with Benfica taking a slender home leg over Liverpool, Arsenal winning 2-1 in Madrid against Real and Chelsea losing at Stamford Bridge to Barcelona by the same scoreline. Rangers were held by Villarreal.

Chelsea managed a late draw away, Rangers drew again and sneaked through on away goals while Arsenal's defence kept Real out at Highbury. However Benfica piled on the agony at Anfield and scored twice, leaving the Gunners to carry on alone.

In the quarter-finals, Arsenal took a more than useful 2-0 lead over Juventus while Benfica and Barcelona were goalless, Internazionale edging Villarreal 2-1 and AC Milan holding Lyon in France.

Villarreal on away goals, AC Milan and Barcelona rather more comfortably joined Arsenal in the last four after the Londoners had held Juventus 0-0 in Turin. Then semi-final time saw Barca taking a 1-0 lead over AC Milan, Arsenal leading Villarreal by the same slender margin. With both second legs scoreless the dream final awaited.

Thierry Henry (left) and Barcelona's Carles Puyol had a personal duel in the Champions League Final. (ASP)

EUROPEAN CUP

EUROPEAN CUP FINALS 1956–1992

Year	Winners	Runners-up	Venue	Attendance	Referee
1956	Real Madrid 4	Reims 3	Paris	38,000	Ellis (E)
1957	Real Madrid 2	Fiorentina 0	Madrid	124,000	Horn (Ho)
1958	Real Madrid 3	AC Milan 2 *(aet)*	Brussels	67,000	Alsteen (Bel)
1959	Real Madrid 2	Reims 0	Stuttgart	80,000	Dutsch (WG)
1960	Real Madrid 7	Eintracht Frankfurt 3	Glasgow	135,000	Mowat (S)
1961	Benfica 3	Barcelona 2	Berne	28,000	Dienst (Sw)
1962	Benfica 5	Real Madrid 3	Amsterdam	65,000	Horn (Ho)
1963	AC Milan 2	Benfica 1	Wembley	45,000	Holland (E)
1964	Internazionale 3	Real Madrid 1	Vienna	74,000	Stoll (A)
1965	Internazionale 1	Benfica 0	Milan	80,000	Dienst (Sw)
1966	Real Madrid 2	Partizan Belgrade 1	Brussels	55,000	Kreitlein (WG)
1967	Celtic 2	Internazionale 1	Lisbon	56,000	Tschenscher (WG)
1968	Manchester U 4	Benfica 1 *(aet)*	Wembley	100,000	Lo Bello (I)
1969	AC Milan 4	Ajax 1	Madrid	50,000	Ortiz (Sp)
1970	Feyenoord 2	Celtic 1 *(aet)*	Milan	50,000	Lo Bello (I)
1971	Ajax 2	Panathinaikos 0	Wembley	90,000	Taylor (E)
1972	Ajax 2	Internazionale 0	Rotterdam	67,000	Helies (F)
1973	Ajax 1	Juventus 0	Belgrade	93,500	Guglovic (Y)
1974	Bayern Munich 1	Atletico Madrid 1	Brussels	49,000	Loraux (Bel)
Replay	Bayern Munich 4	Atletico Madrid 0	Brussels	23,000	Delcourt (Bel)
1975	Bayern Munich 2	Leeds U 0	Paris	50,000	Kitabdjian (F)
1976	Bayern Munich 1	St Etienne 0	Glasgow	54,864	Palotai (H)
1977	Liverpool 3	Moenchengladbach 1	Rome	57,000	Wurtz (F)
1978	Liverpool 1	FC Brugge 0	Wembley	92,000	Corver (Ho)
1979	Nottingham F 1	Malmo 0	Munich	57,500	Linemayr (A)
1980	Nottingham F 1	Hamburg 0	Madrid	50,000	Garrido (P)
1981	Liverpool 1	Real Madrid 0	Paris	48,360	Palotai (H)
1982	Aston Villa 1	Bayern Munich 0	Rotterdam	46,000	Konrath (F)
1983	Hamburg 1	Juventus 0	Athens	80,000	Rainea (R)
1984	Liverpool 1	Roma 1	Rome	69,693	Fredriksson (Se)
	(aet; Liverpool won 4-2 on penalties)				
1985	Juventus 1	Liverpool 0	Brussels	58,000	Daina (Sw)
1986	Steaua Bucharest 0	Barcelona 0	Seville	70,000	Vautrot (F)
	(aet; Steaua won 2-0 on penalties)				
1987	Porto 2	Bayern Munich 1	Vienna	59,000	Ponnet (Bel)
1988	PSV Eindhoven 0	Benfica 0	Stuttgart	70,000	Agnolin (I)
	(aet; PSV won 6-5 on penalties)				
1989	AC Milan 4	Steaua Bucharest 0	Barcelona	97,000	Tritschler (WG)
1990	AC Milan 1	Benfica 0	Vienna	57,500	Kohl (A)
1991	Red Star Belgrade 0	Marseille 0	Bari	56,000	Lanese (I)
	(aet; Red Star won 5-3 on penalties)				
1992	Barcelona 1	Sampdoria 0 *(aet)*	Wembley	70,827	Schmidhuber (G)

UEFA CHAMPIONS LEAGUE FINALS 1993–2006

Year	Winners	Runners-up	Venue	Attendance	Referee
1993	Marseille* 1	AC Milan 0	Munich	64,400	Rothlisberger (Sw)
1994	AC Milan 4	Barcelona 0	Athens	70,000	Don (E)
1995	Ajax 1	AC Milan 0	Vienna	49,730	Craciunescu (R)
1996	Juventus 1	Ajax 1	Rome	67,000	Vega (Sp)
	(aet; Juventus won 4-2 on penalties)				
1997	Borussia Dortmund 3	Juventus 1	Munich	59,000	Puhl (H)
1998	Real Madrid 1	Juventus 0	Amsterdam	47,500	Krug (G)
1999	Manchester U 2	Bayern Munich 1	Barcelona	90,000	Collina (I)
2000	Real Madrid 3	Valencia 0	Paris	78,759	Braschi (I)
2001	Bayern Munich 1	Valencia 1	Milan	71,500	Jol (Ho)
	(aet; Bayern Munich won 5-4 on penalties)				
2002	Real Madrid 2	Leverkusen 1	Glasgow	52,000	Meier (Sw)
2003	AC Milan 0	Juventus 0	Manchester	63,215	Merk (G)
	(aet; AC Milan won 3-2 on penalties)				
2004	Porto 3	Monaco 0	Gelsenkirchen	52,000	Nielsen (D)
2005	Liverpool 3	AC Milan 3	Istanbul	65,000	González (Sp)
	(aet; Liverpool won 3-2 on penalties)				
2006	Barcelona 2	Arsenal 1	Paris	79,500	Hauge (N)

**Subsequently stripped of title.*

UEFA CHAMPIONS LEAGUE 2005–06

■ *Denotes player sent off.*

FIRST QUALIFYING ROUND FIRST LEG

Tuesday, 12 July 2005

Dinamo Minsk (0) 1 *(Lentsevich 58)*

Anorthosis (1) 1 *(Froussos 44)* 3803

Dinamo Minsk: Lesko; Tigorev, Lentsevich, Pavlyukovich, Zoubek (Kachuro 58), Chalei, Edu, Volodenkov, Kislyak (Rozhkov 86), Razin (Kovel 26), Kozyr.
Anorthosis: Georgallides; Xenidis, Nikolaou (Konstantinou 85), Katsavakis, Poursaitidis, Ketsbaia, Haber, Louka, Tsitaishvili, Kinkladze (Marangos 76), Froussos (Tsolakidis 46).

Kairat (1) 2 *(Fomenko 39, Artemov 70)*

Artmedia (0) 0 7000

Kairat: Naboychenko; Artemov, Sosnovschi, Smakov, Irismetov F, Lovtchev, Likhobabenko, Aksenov (Assanbayev 37), Diku (Bogomolov 52), Fomenko, Karpenko (Irismetov J 46).
Artmedia: Cobej; Debnar (Kotula 80), Stano, Durica, Obzera, Tchur (Hellebrand 72), Gajdos, Borbely, Burak, Mikulic, Kozak (Vascak 62).

Levadia (1) 1 *(Nahk 45 (pen))*

Dinamo Tbilisi (0) 0 1600

Levadia: Kotenko; Kalimullin, Cepauskas, Sisov, Hohlov-Simson, Nahk, Vassiljev, Dovydenas, Dmitrijev, Teniste (Kazimir 46), Leitan (Purje 60).
Dinamo Tbilisi: Sturua; Aladashvili, Orbeldaze, Gigauri, Kandelski, Odikadze, Nozadze, Babunashvili, Navalovski, Megreladze (Bobokhidze 63), Melkadze.

Neftchi (1) 2 *(Mammadov 20, Misura 90)*

Hafnarfjordur (0) 0 8100

Neftchi: Hasanzade; Abramidze, Sadygov RF, Abbasov, Chertoganov, Boret, Mammadov (Misura 59), Nabiyev, Adamia, Tagizade, Cordas (Musayev 82).
Hafnarfjordur: Larusson; Helgason, Vidarsson, Nielsen, Bjarnason, Asgeirsson (Gardarsson J 90), Borgvardt, Bett, Gudmundsson, Gudjonsson (Snorrason 46), Stefansson.

Rabotnicki (1) 6 *(Kralevski 30, Ignatov 56 (pen), Nuhiji 65, 84, Trajcev 69, Maznov 76)*

Skonto Riga (0) 0 3000

Rabotnicki: Madzovski; Igorce Stojanov, Karcev, Kralevski, Jovanoski, Trajcev, Stojanov P, Ignatov (Mihajlovic 89), Nuhiji, Maznov (Ilijoski 84), Pejcic (Toleski 82).
Skonto Riga: Piedels; Zakresevskis, Isakovs, Zemlinskis (Adjan 74), Nguimbat, Eliava, Korgalidze (Pereplyotkin 61), Visnjakovs (Kalnins 56), Blanks, Menteshashvili, Chaladze.

Sliema Wanderers (0) 1 *(Bogdanovic 72)*

Serif (2) 4 *(Epureanu 21, 62, Kuchuk 25, Florescu 51)* 443

Sliema Wanderers: Akanji; Brincat (Muscat 63), Di Lello, Said, Woods (Mifsud A 84), Anonam, Turner (Farrugia 84), Bogdanovic, Doncic, Chetcuti, Giglio.
Serif: Hutan; Tassembedo, Testimitanu (Dinu 58), Tarkhnishvili, Florescu, Derme, Ionescu (Goghinashvili 57), Epureanu (Gnanou 63), Kuchuk, Cocis, Lacusta.

Wednesday, 13 July 2005

F91 Dudelange (0) 0

Zrinjski (1) 1 *(Maric B 15)* 1308

F91 Dudelange: Joubert J; Borbiconi, Mouny, Baudry, Crapa, Kabongo, Mazurier (Bellini 61), Di Gregorio (El Aouad 68), Remy (Saboga 78), Gruszczynski, Martine.
Zrinjski: Mitrovic; Vidic, Dzidic, Avdic (Vasilj 46), Karadza, Papic, Zurzinov, Mulina, Djuric (Semren 80), Smajic, Maric B (Sizovic 62).

Glentoran (0) 1 *(Ward 78)*

Shelbourne (0) 2 *(Byrne J 55, 65 (pen))* 2810

Glentoran: Morris; Nixon, Holmes, Walker, Leeman, Keegan, Ward, Tolan (Halliday 68), Parkhouse (Morgan 68), McCallion, Lockhart.
Shelbourne: Delaney; Heary, Crawley (Moore 46), Hawkins, Rogers, Hoolahan, Cahill, Byrne S, Byrne J (Crawford 79), Crowe (Fitzpatrick 76), Baker.

HB Torshavn (1) 2 *(Lag 29, 62)*

Kaunas (3) 4 *(Velicka 2, 25, Klimek 35, Zelmikas 63)* 400

HB Torshavn: Johannesen; Joensen Jo, Nielsen M, Joensen Ja, Lag (Mortensen■ 74), Larsen, Nolsoe Ru, Nielsen K, Borg, Jespersen (Mortansson 46), Danielsen (Akselsen 61).
Kaunas: Kurskis; Klimek (Rimkevicius 74), Zelmikas, Velicka, Kancelskis, Manchkhava, Baguzis (Kunevicius 74), Barevicius, Poderis, Kvaratskhelia (Papeckys 46), Tamosauskas.

HIT Gorica (0) 2 *(Kovacevic M 66, Birsa 82)*

Dinamo Tirana (0) 0 1432

HIT Gorica: Pirih; Suler, Handanagic, Srebrnic, Krsic, Zivec, Kovacevic N, Ranic (Demirovic 80), Burgic (Birsa 65), Kovacevic M, Pus.
Dinamo Tirana: Hidi; Sina, Dabulla, Salihi, Pisha, Hajdari, Ahmataj, Rraklli, Bulku, Bakalli, Mukaj.

Haka (1) 1 *(Pasoja 26)*

Pyunik (0) 0 1325

Haka: Vilmunen; Kangaskorpi, Karjalainen, Popovich, Pasoja, Lehtinen (Fowler 63), Innanen (Eerola 79), Kauppila, Manninen, Salli, Nenonen (Okkonen 52).
Pyunik: Bete; Tigranyan (Aleksanyan 88), Tadevosyan Al, Hovsepian, Mkrtchyan Ag, Diawara (Pachajyan 71), Arzumanyan, Nazaryan, Voskanyan, Davityan, Lombe (Sahakyan 84).

Liverpool (2) 3 *(Gerrard 8, 21, 89)*

TNS (0) 0 44,760

Liverpool: Reina; Finnan, Warnock (Zenden 64), Gerrard, Carragher, Hyypia, Potter (Cisse 76), Xabi Alonso, Le Tallec, Morientes, Riise.
TNS: Doherty; Baker, King, Ruscoe, Jackson, Evans, Wood, Holmes (Lawless 72), Ward (Leah 82), Wilde (Beck 59), Naylor.

FIRST QUALIFYING ROUND SECOND LEG

Tuesday, 19 July 2005

Dinamo Tbilisi (0) 2 *(Melkadze 48, Orbeldaze 50)*

Levadia (0) 0 5000

Dinamo Tbilisi: Sturua; Aladashvili, Kemoklidze, Orbeldaze, Kandelaki, Odikadze■, Nozadze, Babunashvili (Makharadze 73), Chelidze (Gigauri 66), Bobokhidze (Akobia 80), Melkadze.
Levadia: Kotenko; Kalimullin, Cepauskas, Sisov, Hohlov-Simson, Vassiljev, Nahk, Dmitrijev (Sadrin 60), Kazimir, Dovydenas (Purje 64), Zelinski (Leitan 46).

Kaunas (1) 4 *(Velicka 44, Rimkevicius 63, 82, Zelmikas 90)*

HB Torshavn (0) 0 2180

Kaunas: Kurskis; Klimek (Rimkevicius 46), Zelmikas, Papeckys, Kancelskis, Manchkhava, Barevicius (Maciulis 66), Velicka, Baguzis, Poderis (Pacevicius 72), Tamosauskas.
HB Torshavn: Johannesen; Joensen Jo, Nielsen M (Danielsen 59), Joensen Ja, Lag (Mortansson 59), Nolsoe Ru, Larsen (Akselsen 59), Borg, Nielsen K, Nolsoe Ra, Jacobsen.

TNS (0) 0

Liverpool (1) 3 *(Cisse 26, Gerrard 85, 86)* 8009

TNS: Doherty; Naylor, King, Baker, Evans (Jackson 78), Holmes, Ruscoe, Beck (Ward 68), Toner, Hogan, Wood (Lloyd-Williams 58).

Liverpool: Reina; Finnan, Riise, Hamann, Carragher (Whitbread 53), Hyypia, Potter, Xabi Alonso (Gerrard 67), Le Tallec (Luis Garcia 58), Cisse, Zenden.

Wednesday, 20 July 2005

Anorthosis (0) 1 *(Samaras 71)*

Dinamo Minsk (0) 0 6687

Anorthosis: Georgallides; Louka, Marangos, Katsavakis, Nikolaou (Konstantinou 88), Haber, Poursaitidis (Tsolakidis 64), Ketsbaia, Tsitaishvili, Kinkladze (Kampantais 46), Samaras.
Dinamo Minsk: Lesko; Tigorev, Lentsevich, Pavlyukovich, Zoubek (Kachuro 64), Chalei, Edu (Rozhkov 77), Volodenkov, Kovel, Kislyak, Kozyr.

Artmedia (1) 4 *(Borbely 21, Tchur 52, Kozak 94 (pen), Stano 121)*

Kairat (0) 1 *(Bogomolov 91)* 3204

Artmedia: Cobej; Kotula, Debnar, Durica, Hellebrand (Mikulic 72), Vascak (Gajdos 76), Fodrek, Obzera, Tchur (Stano 83), Borbely, Kozak.
Kairat: Naboychenko; Artemov, Sosnovschi, Smakov, Abdulin, Lovtchev, Likhobabenko, Aksenov (Karpenko 60), Diku (Bogomolov 58), Fomenko, Assanbayev (Tlekhougov 86).
aet.

Dinamo Tirana (2) 3 *(Rraklli 38, Dabulla 42, Salihi 47)*

HIT Gorica (0) 0 5000

Dinamo Tirana: Hidi; Sina, Dabulla, Salihi, Pisha, Hajdari, Ahmataj (Tafaj A 65), Bulku, Rraklli (Merkoci 78), Mukaj, Patushi (Bakalli 75).
HIT Gorica: Pirih; Suler, Handanagic, Srebrnic, Pus, Krsic (Sabec 77), Kovacevic N, Zivec (Demirovic 62), Ranic, Kovacevic M, Birsa (Burgic 55).

Hafnarfjordur (0) 1 *(Borgvardt 60)*

Neftchi (0) 2 *(Misura 51, Nabayev 75)* 1873

Hafnarfjordur: Larusson; Helgason, Saevarsson, Nielsen, Bjarnason (Albertsson 80), Asgeirsson, Borgvardt, Bett (Bjornsson 70), Gudmundsson, Vidarsson, Stefansson (Snorrason 57).
Neftchi: Hasanzade; Abramidze, Sadygov RF, Abbasov, Chertoganov■, Boret, Adamia, Nabayev (Rahmanov 85), Tagizade, Mammadov (Gafitullin 90), Misura (Musayev 71).

Pyunik (2) 2 *(Pachajyan 3, Diawara 30)*

Haka (1) 2 *(Mattila 38, Fowler 63)* 3395

Pyunik: Gasparyan; Tigranyan, Tadevosyan Al, Hovsepian, Diawara, Arzumanyan, Mkrtchyan Ag, Voskanyan (Aleksanyan 75), Pachajyan, Nazaryan, Davityan (Petrosyan V 75).
Haka: Vilmunen; Kangaskorpi, Karjalainen (Fowler 46), Okkonen, Pasoja, Eerola, Innanen, Kauppila, Manninen (Juuti 84), Salli, Mattila (Rosenberg 69).

Serif (0) 2 *(Derme 78, Cocis 83)*

Sliema Wanderers (0) 0 8800

Serif: Pasenco; Tassembedo (Goghinashvili 73), Gumeniuc, Testimitanu, Tarkhnishvili, Florescu (Dinu 67), Derme, Ionescu (Kuchuk 59), Epureanu, Cocis, Lacusta.
Sliema Wanderers: Akanji; Brincat, Chetcuti, Di Lello, Said, Woods (Mifsud A 75), Anonam (Muscat 86), Turner, Bogdanovic, Doncic, Giglio (Lombardi 86).

Shelbourne (2) 4 *(Heary 14, Byrne J 32 (pen), 71, Crowe 58)*

Glentoran (1) 1 *(McCann 21)* 6400

Shelbourne: Delaney; Heary, Crawley, Rogers, Hawkins, Baker, Byrne S, Cahill, Hoolahan (Crawford 73), Byrne J (O'Neill 82), Crowe (Fitzpatrick 82).
Glentoran: Morris; Nixon, Holmes, Walker, Leeman■, Ward (Parkhouse 66), McCann (Keegan 46) (Melaugh 88), McCallion, Morgan, Halliday, Lockhart.

Skonto Riga (0) 1 *(Pereplyotkin 90)*

Rabotnicki (0) 0 1945

Skonto Riga: Piedels; Zakresevskis, Isakovs, Nguimbat (Zemlinskis 75), Ussanov, Eliava, Visnjakovs, Menteshashvili, Semjonovs (Kalnins 81), Pereplyotkin, Miholaps (Blanks 73).
Rabotnicki: Madzovski; Karcev (Ilievski 75), Kralevski, Jovanoski, Igorce Stojanov, Mihajlovic, Jankep, Stojanov P (Trajcev 73), Ignatov (Pejcic 61), Toleski, Ilijoski.

Zrinjski (0) 0

F91 Dudelange (0) 4 *(Gruszczynski 93, 105, Di Gregorio 96, Hug 112)* 3600

Zrinjski: Mitrovic; Vidic, Dzidic, Sizovic (Semren 77), Karadza, Papic, Zurzinov, Mulina, Djuric (Landeka 54), Smajic, Maric B (Avdic 54).
F91 Dudelange: Joubert J; Borbiconi, Mouny, Baudry, Crapa (Di Gregorio 77), El Aouad (Gruszczynski 49), Kabongo, Remy, Hug, Cleiton (Bellini 57), Martine.
aet.

SECOND QUALIFYING ROUND FIRST LEG

Tuesday, 26 July 2005

Anderlecht (4) 5 *(Tihinen 21, Jestrovic 24, Mpenza 32, Goor 35, Vanderhaeghe 77)*

Neftchi (0) 0 21,055

Anderlecht: Zitka; Goor, Deschacht, Vanderhaeghe, Kompany, Tihinen, Vanden Borre, Jestrovic (Akin 74), Mpenza (Zewlakow 65), Wilhelmsson, Zetterberg (Baseggio 81).
Neftchi: Hasanzade (Micovic 46); Abramidze, Sadygov RF, Abbasov, Boret, Adamia, Nabayev, Mammadov, Misura (Subasic 74), Gafitullin (Getman 10), Cordas.

Anorthosis (1) 3 *(Nikolaou 25, Froussos 83, Tsitaishvili 90)*

Trabzonspor (0) 1 *(Fatih 75)* 14,613

Anorthosis: Georgallides; Kampantais (Froussos 77), Poursaitidis, Marangos, Ketsbaia (Kinkladze 54), Nikolaou, Tsitaishvili, Xenidis, Samaras (Haxhi 20), Katsavakis, Haber.
Trabzonspor: Galvao; Emrah, Erdinc, Dos Santos (Tayfun 81), Celaleddin (Lee 88), Huseyin, Volkan, Szymkowiak, Ibrahima■, Gokdeniz, Mehmet (Fatih 65).

Dinamo Tbilisi (0) 0

Brondby (0) 2 *(Skoubo 59, Elmander 83)* 8000

Dinamo Tbilisi: Sturua; Aladashvili, Gigauri, Orbeldaze, Amisulashvili■, Kandelaki, Nozadze (Grigalashvili 81), Babunashvili, Makharadze, Bobokhidze (Akobia 46), Melkadze (Iashvili 63).
Brondby: Ankergren; Sennels, Agger, Nielsen, Johansen, Lantz (Absalonsen 55), Jorgensen (Lorentzen 78), Daugaard, Retov, Skoubo (Kamper 70), Elmander.

Dynamo Kiev (2) 2 *(Gusev 20, Shatskikh 40)*

Thun (1) 2 *(Rodolfo 41 (og), Aegerter 66)* 17,000

Dynamo Kiev: Shovkovskyi; Yussuf, Nesmachny, Rodolfo, Rebrov, Gusev, Leko (Aliyev 69), Belkevich (Diogo Rincon 58), Gavrancic, Rotan, Shatskikh (Verpakovskis 58).
Thun: Jakupovic; Vieira (Bernardi 29), Milicevic, Pimenta (Rodrigues 90), Gerber (Goncalves 40), Deumi, Aegerter, Lustrinelli, Ferreira, Pallas, Hodzic.

Kaunas (1) 1 *(Barevicius 21)*

Liverpool (2) 3 *(Cisse 27, Carragher 30, Gerrard 54 (pen))* 6747

Kaunas: Kurskis; Zelmikas, Pacevicius (Petrenka 46), Kancelskis, Manchkhava, Barevicius (Papeckys 71), Rimkevicius, Klimek, Baguzis, Poderis, Tamosauskas (Maciulis 87).
Liverpool: Reina; Josemi, Riise, Alonso, Carragher, Hyypia, Potter (Luis Garcia 63), Gerrard (Sissoko 60), Crouch (Morientes 74), Cisse, Zenden.

Valerenga (0) 1 *(Dos Santos 50 (pen))*

Haka (0) 0 6297

Valerenga: Arason; Waehler, Brocken, Holm T, Muri, Dos Santos, Holm D, Hoset (Gashi 56), Flo, Ishizaki (Berre 46), Mabizela (Grindheim 46).
Haka: Vilmunen; Kangaskorpi, Popovich, Okkonen, Pasoja, Mattila (Lehtinen 51), Innanen (Rosenberg 90), Kauppila, Manninen (Eerola 82), Salli, Fowler.

Wednesday, 27 July 2005

Artmedia (1) 5 *(Halenar 43, 75, 90, Vascak 57, Mikulic 78)*

Celtic (0) 0 17,632

Artmedia: Cobej; Debnar, Durica, Kotula, Vascak (Mikulic 72), Obzera, Tchur, Halenar, Borbely, Fodrek, Kozak.
Celtic: Marshall; Telfer, Camara, Lennon, Varga, Balde, Zurawski (Maloney 60), Petrov, Hartson, Sutton (McGeady 17), Thompson (Aliadiere 66).

Debrecen (2) 3 *(Bogdanovic 26, 40, Kerekes 58)*

Hajduk Split (0) 0 7065

Debrecen: Csernyanszki; Mate, Szatmari, Dombi, Sandor, Bogdanovic (Brnovic 79), Kerekes (Bernath 72), Habi (Kiss 64), Nikolov, Halmosi, Eger.
Hajduk Split: Kale; Dolonga, Blatnjak, Kranjcar, Bartulovic, Damjanovic, Pralija, Zilic, Granic, Grgurevic (Makarin 80), Busic.

Dinamo Tirana (0) 0

CSKA Sofia (0) 2 *(Gueye 89, Gargorov 90)* 6000

Dinamo Tirana: Hidi; Sina (Fagu 90), Dabulla, Pisha, Bulku, Rraklli (Merkoci 46), Mukaj, Salihi, Hajdari (Behari 70), Ahmataj, Patushi.
CSKA Sofia: Hmaruc; Zabavnik, Iliev, Gueye, Tiago Silva (Matic 90), Hdiouad, Yanev, Gargorov, Todorov, Sakaliev (Dah Zadi 61), Matko (Dimitrov P 70).

F91 Dudelange (1) 1 *(Martine 8)*

Rapid Vienna (4) 6 *(Lawaree 2, 65, Akagunduz 3, 15, Hofmann 5, Kienast 84)* 1562

F91 Dudelange: Joubert; Borbiconi, Mouny, Baudry, Di Gregorio (Gruszczynski 58), Martine (El Aouad 79), Crapa (Bellini 72), Kabongo, Remy, Hug, Cleiton.
Rapid Vienna: Payer; Adamski, Korsos, Hlinka, Ivanschitz, Lawaree, Akagunduz (Kienast 72), Hofmann (Dollinger 46), Bejbl, Dober (Martinez 38), Vlachovic.

Malmo (1) 3 *(Osmanovski 33, Andersson D 48 (pen), Mattisson 68)*

Maccabi Haifa (2) 2 *(Harazi 2, Colautti 44)* 10,960

Malmo: Asper; Andersson A (Abelsson 89), Persson, Hoiland, Mattisson, Elanga, Alves, Osmanovski, Andersson P, Bech (Olsson 86), Andersson D.
Maccabi Haifa: Davidovitch; Harazi, Benado, Keise, Boccoli, Colautti, Tal, Saban (Olarra 75), Xavir, Zandberg (Biruk 88), Katan (Arbaitman 86).

Partizan Belgrade (0) 1 *(Odita 63)*

Serif (0) 0 13,116

Partizan Belgrade: Kralj; Vukcevic, Mirkovic, Bajic, Brnovic, Radonjic (Boya 46), Lomic, Odita (Grubjesic 82), Radovic, Rnic, Nadj (Vukajilovic 73).
Serif: Hutan; Tassembedo, Gumeniuc (Bychkov 84), Tarkhnishvili, Florescu, Kuchuk (Dinu 55), Derme, Ionescu (Goghinashvili 58), Epureanu, Cocis, Lacusta.

Rabotnicki (1) 1 *(Nuhiji 12)*

Lokomotiv Moskow (0) 1 *(Sychev 90)* 7000

Rabotnicki: Madzovski; Igorce Stojanov, Karcev, Kralevski, Jovanoski, Trajcev, Stojanov P (Mihajlovic 72), Ignatov (Jankep 90), Nuhiji, Maznov (Ilijoski 75), Pejcic.
Lokomotiv Moskow: Ovchinnikov; Lima, Evseev, Sennikov, Khokhlov (Samedov 62), Asatiani, Gurenko, Bilyaletdinov, Kanyenda (Lebedenko 75), Sychev, Poliakov.

Shelbourne (0) 0

Steaua (0) 0 8500

Shelbourne: Delaney; Heary, Rogers, Crawley, Hawkins, Baker, Cahill, Byrne S (Crawford 36), Moore, Byrne J (Fleming 77), Crowe (Harris 75).
Steaua: Hamutovski; Radoi, Dica (Oprita 89), Bostina, Nesu, Nicolita (Dinita 84), Iacob (Cristea 81), Ogararu, Paraschiv, Ghionea, Lovin.

SECOND QUALIFYING ROUND SECOND LEG

Tuesday, 2 August 2005

Celtic (2) 4 *(Thompson 22 (pen), Hartson 45, McManus 54, Beattie 82)*

Artmedia (0) 0 50,063

Celtic: Boruc; Telfer, Camara, Lennon, McManus, Balde, Thompson (Aliadiere 87), Wallace (Maloney 53), Hartson, Zurawski (Beattie 63), Petrov.
Artmedia: Cobej; Obzera, Debnar, Durica, Vascak (Mikulic 74), Tchur, Halenar (Bukvic 87), Borbely, Fodrek, Burak (Stano 67), Kozak.

Liverpool (0) 2 *(Gerrard 77, Cisse 86)*

Kaunas (0) 0 43,717

Liverpool: Carson; Finnan, Warnock, Hamann (Gerrard 75), Whitbread, Hyypia, Luis Garcia, Sissoko, Crouch (Potter 55), Morientes (Cisse 46), Zenden.
Kaunas: Kilijonas; Kancelskis, Zelmikas, Baguzis, Manchkhava, Pehlic (Barevicius 66), Petrenka (Klimek 46), Kvaratskhelia, Kunevicius, Poderis (Maciulis 87), Rimkevicius.

Wednesday, 3 August 2005

Brondby (2) 3 *(Lorentzen 9, Aladashvili 42 (og), Kamper 86)*

Dinamo Tbilisi (0) 1 *(Iashvili 65)* 13,165

Brondby: Ankergren; Sennels, Agger, Nielsen, Johansen (Schmidt 75), Lantz, Lorentzen, Daugaard, Jorgensen (Absalonsen 65), Skoubo, Elmander (Kamper 57).
Dinamo Tbilisi: Sturua; Aladashvili, Gigauri (Kemoklidze 46), Orbeldaze, Kandelaki (Akobia 73), Nozadze, Odikadze, Babunashvili, Makharadze, Melkadze, Megreladze (Iashvili 46).

CSKA Sofia (1) 2 *(Dah Zadi 2, Todorov 90)*

Dinamo Tirana (0) 0 3100

CSKA Sofia: Hmaruc; Zabavnik, Iliev (Matic 57), Gueye, Tiago Silva, Todorov, Yanev, Hdiouad, Gargorov (Yurukov 77), Sakaliev (Dimitrov P 57), Dah Zadi.
Dinamo Tirana: Hidi; Dabulla, Pisha, Behari, Bulku, Rraklli, Salihi (Fagu 82), Sina, Ahmataj (Tafaj 63), Patushi, Merkoci (Bakalli 58).

Hajduk Split (0) 0

Debrecen (3) 5 *(Halmosi 1, 27, Kerekes 22, Sidibe 76, Kiss 90)* 15,300

Hajduk Split: Kale; Dolonga, Blatnjak (Munhoz 46), Kranjcar, Bartulovic, Damjanovic, Zilic, Granic, Biscevic (Makarin 85), Grgurevic, Busic.
Debrecen: Csernyanszki; Mate, Szatmari, Vukmir, Dombi, Sandor, Bogdanovic (Kiss 56), Kerekes (Sidibe 57), Nikolov, Halmosi (Boor 76), Eger.

Haka (1) 1 *(Lehtinen 9)*

Valerenga (2) 4 *(Waehler 26, Flo 28, 74, Iversen 59)* 2051

Haka: Vilmunen; Kangaskorpi, Okkonen (Rosenberg 75), Pasoja, Eerola, Innanen, Manninen (Nenonen 58), Popovich, Salli, Lehtinen (Mattila 68), Fowler.
Valerenga: Arason; Waehler, Brocken, Holm T (Ishizaki 70), Dos Santos, Grindheim (Mabizela 68), Holm D, Johnsen, Gashi, Iversen (Hulsker 62), Flo.

Lokomotiv Moscow (0) 2 *(Sychev 75, Asatiani 85)*

Rabotnicki (0) 0 19,648

Lokomotiv Moscow: Ovchinnikov; Bikey, Evseev, Samedov (Maminov 73), Lima (Sennikov 82), Pachinine, Asatiani, Gurenko, Bilyaletdinov (Lebedenko 89), Khokhlov, Sychev.
Rabotnicki: Madzovski; Karcev, Igorce Stojanov (Ilija Stojanov 14), Kralevski, Jovanoski, Stojanov P, Trajcev, Ignatov (Jankep 55), Nuhiji (Ilijoski 77), Maznov, Pejcic.

Maccabi Haifa (1) 2 *(Colautti 10, Arbaitman 60)*

Malmo (1) 2 *(Alves 21, Abelsson 89)* 14,450

Maccabi Haifa: Davidovitch; Harazi, Benado, Keise, Boccoli, Colautti, Tal, Xavir, Zandberg (Biruk 77), Olarra, Katan (Arbaitman■ 56).
Malmo: Asper; Andersson A (Litmanen 61), Persson (Abelsson 85), Osmanovski (Barlay 88), Olsson, Andersson P, Elanga, Alves, Hoiland, Bech, Andersson D.

Neftchi (1) 1 *(Boret 5 (pen))*

Anderlecht (0) 0 8000

Neftchi: Micovic; Getman, Abramidze, Boret, Sadygov RF, Abbasov, Mammadov, Nabyev (Cordas 90), Subasic (Misura 76), Tagizade, Sadygov RA (Musayev 69).
Anderlecht: Zitka; Hasi, Deschacht, Vanderhaeghe, Goor (Akin 62), Zewlakow, Kompany (Deman 83), Tihinen, Mpenza (Jestrovic 70), Wilhelmsson, Vanden Borre.

Rapid Vienna (0) 3 *(Lawaree 47, 81, Dollinger 86)*

F91 Dudelange (2) 2 *(Tosun 7 (og), Gruszczynski 37)* 8623

Rapid Vienna: Hedl; Adamski, Korsos, Hlinka, Lawaree, Garics, Martinez (Kavlak 70), Dollinger, Kienast (Kincl 63), Prenner, Tosun (Vlachovic 63).
F91 Dudelange: Joubert; Borbiconi, Mouny, Baudry, Bellini (Martine 75), Crapa, El Aouad, Kabongo (Franceschi 66), Remy, Gruszczynski (Di Gregorio 54), Zeghdane.

Serif (0) 0

Partizan Belgrade (0) 1 *(Odita 74)* 11,000

Serif: Hutan; Tassembedo, Gumeniuc, Testemitanu, Tarkhnishvili, Florescu (Kuchuk 84), Derme, Ionescu (Goginashvili 73), Epureanu, Cocis, Lacusta.
Partizan Belgrade: Kralj; Vukcevic, Mirkovic (Cirkovic 89), Bajic, Brnovic, Boya, Radovic (Babovic 82), Lomic, Odita, Djordjevic, Nadj (Marinkovic 90).

Steaua (2) 4 *(Nicolita 20, Iacob 26, Dinita 62, Oprita 90 (pen))*

Shelbourne (1) 1 *(Byrne J 39)* 8781

Steaua: Hamutovski; Radoi, Dica■, Bostina (Oprita 75), Nesu, Nicolita (Paraschiv 90), Baciu, Iacob (Dinita■ 46), Ogararu, Ghionea, Lovin.
Shelbourne: Delaney; Heary, Crawley, Rogers■, Harris, Cahill, Byrne S, Crowe, Byrne J, Baker, Moore (Hoolahan 66).

Thun (0) 1 *(Bernardi 90)*

Dynamo Kiev (0) 0 25,728

Thun: Jakupovic; Goncalves, Milicevic, Pimenta (Bernardi 86), Gerber, Deumi, Aegerter, Lustrinelli (Rodrigues 90), Ferreira (Vieira 75), Pallas, Hodzic.
Dynamo Kiev: Shovkovskyi; Yussuf, Nesmachny, Rodolfo, Da Costa■, Cesnauskis (Diogo Rincon 56), Gusev, Rotan (Belkevich 68), Shatskikh (Kleber 61), Gavrancic, Cernat.

Trabzonspor (1) 1 *(Fatih 40)*

Anorthosis (0) 0 18,500

Trabzonspor: Galvao; Emrah, Erdinc (Ozgur 69), Dos Santos, Celaleddin, Huseyin, Adem (Mehmet 46), Szymkowiak, Volkan (Lee 59), Gokdeniz, Fatih.
Anorthosis: Georgallides; Marangos (Kinkladze 57), Poursaitidis, Louka, Haxhi, Tsitaishvili, Nikolaou, Katsavakis■, Froussos (Xenidis 75), Haber, Ketsbaia (Konstantinou 66).

THIRD QUALIFYING ROUND FIRST LEG

Tuesday, 9 August 2005

Anorthosis (0) 1 *(Froussos 72)*

Rangers (0) 2 *(Novo 64, Ricksen 71)* 16,990

Anorthosis: Georgallides; Poursaitidis (Tsolakidis 74), Haxhi, Louka, Xenidis, Marangos (Konstantinou 83), Froussos, Kinkladze, Tsitaishvili (Kampantais 70), Nikolaou, Ketsbaia.
Rangers: Waterreus; Pierre-Fanfan, Andrews, Rodriguez, Ball, Ricksen, Ferguson, Murray, Buffel (Lovenkrands 58), Novo (Burke 82), Prso (Thompson 74).

Betis (0) 1 *(Edu 90)*

Monaco (0) 0 19,122

Betis: Doblas; Melli, Juanito, Rivas, Luis Fernandez, Assuncao (Arzu 77), Rivera, Joaquin, Edu, Fernando (Denilson 57), Dani (Xisco 65).
Monaco: Roma; Maicon, Squillaci, Modesto, Evra, Meriem, Zikos, Bernardi, Sorlin (Gigliotti 82), Chevanton (Maoulida 69), Adebayor.

Everton (1) 1 *(Beattie 42)*

Villarreal (2) 2 *(Figueroa 27, Josico 45)* 37,685

Everton: Martyn; Hibbert, Pistone (McFadden 80), Yobo, Weir, Arteta, Davies, Neville, Beattie (Bent 63), Cahill, Kilbane (Ferguson 63).
Villarreal: Barbosa; Gonzalo Rodriguez, Arruabarrena, Quique Alvarez, Javi Venta, Josico, Marcos Senna, Sorin (Pena 89), Forlan (Guayre 85), Figueroa (Tacchinardi 65), Sanchez.

Manchester United (1) 3 *(Rooney 7, Van Nistelrooy 49, Ronaldo 63)*

Debrecen (0) 0 51,701

Manchester United: Van der Sar; Neville, O'Shea, Keane (Park 67), Ferdinand, Silvestre, Fletcher, Scholes, Van Nistelrooy (Rossi 81), Rooney, Ronaldo (Smith 67).
Debrecen: Csernyanszki; Nikolov, Eger, Mate, Szatmari, Dombi (Boor 85), Sandor, Vukmir, Halmosi, Kerekes (Sidibe 52), Bogdanovic (Kiss 60).

Valarenga (0) 1 *(Iversen 57)*

FC Brugge (0) 0 13,778

Valarenga: Arason; Skiri, Brocken, Holm T, Waehler, Dos Santos, Grindheim, Johnsen, Gashi, Iversen, Flo (Hoset 74).
FC Brugge: Butina; De Cock, Valgaeren, Klukowski, Clement, Maertens (Ishiaku 77), Vermant, Englebert, Leko, Verheyen, Balaban (Blondel 82).

Wisla (1) 3 *(Brozek 13, Uche 52, Frankowski 70)*

Panathinaikos (1) 1 *(Olisadebe 4)* 7227

Wisla: Majdan; Glowacki, Uche, Zienczuk, Cantoro, Frankowski, Blaszczykowski (Stolarczyk 76), Klos, Sobolewski (Paulista 68), Brozek (Penksa 65), Dudka.
Panathinaikos: Galinovic; Morris, Kotsios, Seric, Vintra, Biscan (Tziolis 62), Conceicao, Wooter (Theodoridis 75), Papadopoulos (Charalambides 81), Olisadebe, Gekas.

Wednesday, 10 August 2005

Anderlecht (2) 2 *(Goor 7, Mpenza 38)*

Slavia Prague (1) 1 *(Jarolim 21)* 17,866

Anderlecht: Zitka; Tihinen, Deschacht, Vanderhaeghe, Goor, Akin, Kompany, Jestrovic (Wilhelmsson 62), Mpenza, Vanden Borre, Zetterberg (Baseggio 81).
Slavia Prague: Kozacik; Latka, Vlcek (Pesir 84), Holenak, Gedeon, Jarolim, Zboncak, Pitak (Zabojnik 90), Hrdlicka (Svento 46), Kovac, Suchy.

Artmedia (0) 0

Partizan Belgrade (0) 0 16,127

Artmedia: Cobej; Kotula, Stano, Durica, Petras (Obzera 59), Vascak (Gomez 89), Borbely, Kozak, Tchur, Halenar, Fodrek.
Partizan Belgrade: Kralj; Mirkovic, Djordjevic, Bajic (Emeghara 46), Lomic, Nadj, Tomic, Brnovic, Vukcevic, Boya, Odita.

Basle (1) 2 *(Degen D 28, Rossi 52)*

Werder Bremen (0) 1 *(Klose 73)* 28,101

Basle: Zuberbuhler; Quennoz, Sterjovski (Kulaksioglu 71), Petric, Chipperfield (Rossi 46), Ba, Kleber, Delgado (Ergic 65), Degen D, Smiljanic, Zanni.
Werder Bremen: Reinke; Pasanen, Van Damme (Schulz 46), Naldo, Umit D (Owomoyela 65), Vranjes, Micoud, Frings, Borowski, Klose, Klasnic.

Brondby (1) 2 *(Skoubo 33, Escude 90 (og))*

Ajax (1) 2 *(Rosenberg 31, Babel 73)* 24,917

Brondby: Ankergren; Nielsen, Rytter, Sennels, Agger, Lantz (Absalonsen 81), Jorgensen (Kamper 39), Retov, Elmander, Skoubo, Lorentzen (Daugaard 66).
Ajax: Vonk; Escude, Grygera, Trabelsi, Maduro, De Jong, Pienaar, Emanuelson, Boukhari (Sneijder 77), Rosenberg (Charisteas 88), Babel.

CSKA Sofia (1) 1 *(Dimitrov V 45)*

Liverpool (2) 3 *(Cisse 25, Morientes 31, 58)* 16,553

CSKA Sofia: Hmaruc; Zabavnik, Matic, Todorov, Gueye, Tiago Silva, Gargorov, Hdiouad, Yanev (Dimitrov P 35), Dimitrov V (Sakaliev 58), Dah Zadi (Yordanov 79).
Liverpool: Reina; Finnan, Riise, Alonso (Hamann 65), Carragher, Hyypia, Luis Garcia, Gerrard (Sissoko 70), Cisse, Morientes (Barragan 78), Warnock.

Malmo (0) 0

Thun (1) 1 *(Pimenta 33)* 12,237

Malmo: Asper; Andersson A, Osmanovski, Abelsson, Pode, Hoiland, Elanga, Alves, Andersson P (Holgersson 87), Litmanen (Lawan 88), Andersson D.
Thun: Jakupovic; Goncalves, Milicevic, Bernardi, Pimenta, Gerber (Rodrigues 85), Deumi (Vieira 15), Lustrinelli, Ferreira (Sen 78), Pallas, Hodzic.

Rapid Vienna (0) 1 *(Vlachovic 75 (pen))*

Lokomotiv Moscow (1) 1 *(Samedov 10)* 17,500

Rapid Vienna: Payer; Adamski (Dollinger 78), Korsos (Dober 86), Hlinka, Ivanschitz, Akagunduz, Hofmann, Martinez, Bejbl, Kincl, Vlachovic.
Lokomotiv Moscow: Ovchinnikov; Bikey■, Lebedenko (Ruopolo 79), Samedov (Pachinine 76), Lima, Gurenko, Khokhlov (Evseev 90), Maminov, Asatiani, Sennikov, Bilyaletdinov.

Shakhtar Donetsk (0) 0

Internazionale (0) 2 *(Martins 68, Adriano 79)* 25,000

Shakhtar Donetsk: Lastuvka; Barcauan, Srna, Hubschman, Rat, Tymoschuk, Duljaj (Fernandinho 69), Matuzalem, Elano (Rodriguez 57), Bielik (Marica 71), Brandao.
Internazionale: Julio Cesar; Cordoba, Zanetti J, Stankovic, Cambiasso, Materazzi, Favalli, Martins, Adriano, Veron (Pizarro 76), Solari (Ze Maria 65).

Sporting Lisbon (0) 0

Udinese (1) 1 *(Iaquinta 27 (pen))* 35,474

Sporting Lisbon: Ricardo; Miguel Garcia (Rogerio 57), Anderson Polga, Beto, Custodio (Almeida 70), Joao Moutinho, Sa Pinto, Douala, Tello, Delvid (Silva 79), Liedson.
Udinese: De Sanctis; Bertotto, Natali, Zenoni, Candela, Obodo, Iaquinta, Di Natale (Rossini 82), Muntari (Mauri 72), Barreto (Vidigal 41), Felipe.

Steaua (1) 1 *(Iacob 30)*

Rosenborg (0) 1 *(Helstad 85)* 11,514

Steaua: Hamutovski; Radoi, Bostina, Nesu (Marin 79), Nicolita, Iacob, Ogararu, Cristea (Oprita 54), Paraschiv, Ghionea, Lovin.
Rosenborg: Johnsen E; Lago, Helstad (Odegaard 87), Braaten (Storflor 63), Basma, Strand (Winsnes 79), Berg, Dorsin, Johnsen F, Riseth, Solli.

THIRD QUALIFYING ROUND SECOND LEG

Tuesday, 23 August 2005

Liverpool (0) 0

CSKA Sofia (1) 1 *(Iliev 16)* 42,175

Liverpool: Carson; Finnan, Warnock (Zenden 64), Hamann, Josemi, Hyypia, Potter (Luis Garcia 46), Sissoko, Cisse (Sinama-Pongolle 83), Morientes, Riise.
CSKA Sofia: Maksic; Zabavnik, Iliev, Gueye, Tiago Silva, Todorov, Gargorov, Hdiouad, Yurukov (Sakaliev 72), Dimitrov V, Dah Zadi (Dimitrov P 84).

Lokomotiv Moscow (0) 0

Rapid Vienna (0) 1 *(Vlachovic 84)* 27,823

Lokomotiv Moscow: Ovchinnikov; Gurenko (Ruopolo 86), Evseev, Sennikov, Pachinine, Asatiani, Khokhlov, Maminov, Samedov (Izmailov 59), Bilyaletdinov, Lebedenko.
Rapid Vienna: Payer; Bejbl, Dober, Hlinka, Vlachovic, Adamski, Korsos (Martinez 75), Hofmann, Kincl, Akagunduz (Lawaree 56), Ivanschitz.

Monaco (1) 2 *(Gerard 33, Maoulida 63)*

Betis (1) 2 *(Oliveira 17, 75)* 13,011

Monaco: Warmuz; Evra, Squillaci, Sorlin (Gigliotti 82), Modesto, Maicon, Bernardi, Meriem, Adebayor, Gerard, Kapo (Maoulida 61).
Betis: Doblas; Luis Fernandez, Melli, Juanito, Rivas, Assuncao, Edu, Xisco, Joaquin (Varela 57), Oliveira, Rivera.

Panathinaikos (0) 4 *(Morris 62, Olisadebe 65, Papadopoulos 87, Kotsios 114)*

Wisla (0) 1 *(Sobolewski 78)* 43,741

Panathinaikos: Galinovic; Kotsios, Conceicao, Seric, Biscan (Elantiou 74), Morris, Vintra, Wooter (Papadopoulos 52), Charalambides, Olisadebe (Andric 69), Gekas.
Wisla: Majdan; Glowacki, Klos, Baszczynski, Dudka, Sobolewski■, Zienczuk (Rodriguez 62), Uche (Kuzba 75), Kantoro, Frankowski, Brozek (Penksa 63).
aet.

Partizan Belgrade (0) 0

Artmedia (0) 0 26,345

Partizan Belgrade: Kralj; Mirkovic, Djordjevic, Emeghara, Lomic (Bajic 106), Nadj, Tomic (Grubjesic 77), Brnovic, Vukcevic, Boya, Odita (Radovic 68).
Artmedia: Cobej; Burak (Mikulic 111), Borbely, Debnar, Durica, Tchur (Stano 54), Kozak, Fodrek, Petras, Halenar, Vascak (Gomez 95).
aet; Artmedia won 4-3 on penalties.

Rosenborg (1) 3 *(Solli 38, Odegaard 57, Radoi 60 (og))*

Steaua (0) 2 *(Radoi 74, Iacob 76)* 13,051

Rosenborg: Johnsen E; Basma, Riseth, Helstad (Solli 15), Dorsin, Lago (Braaten 46), Berg, Strand, Winsnes, Storflor (Odegaard 46), Johnsen F.
Steaua: Hamutovski; Marin (Dinita 85), Radoi, Ghionea, Ogararu, Nesu (Oprita 55), Paraschiv, Bostina, Nicolita, Lovin, Iacob.

Thun (2) 3 *(Bernardi 26, Lustrinelli 40, 66)*

Malmo (0) 0 31,243

Thun: Jakupovic; Pallas, Hodzic, Milicevic, Goncalves, Gerber (Leandro 70), Ferreira, Aegerter, Bernardi, Pimenta (Gelson 79), Lustrinelli (Sen 85).
Malmo: Asper; Hoiland, Elanga, Abelsson, Olsson (Litmanen 66), Andersson D, Osmanovski (Andersson A 62), Mattisson, Pode (Barlay 80), Bech, Alves.

Udinese (2) 3 *(Iaquinta 23 (pen), Natali 35, Barreto 89)*

Sporting Lisbon (1) 2 *(Douala 38, Pinilla 90)* 23,526

Udinese: De Sanctis; Bertotto, Natali, Felipe, Zenoni, Vidigal, Obodo, Muntari (Mauri 70), Candela, Di Natale (Barreto 82), Iaquinta.
Sporting Lisbon: Ricardo; Beto, Rogerio (Pinilla 82), Anderson Polga, Tello (Edson 46), Rochemback, Joao Moutinho, Luis Loureira, Douala, Sa Pinto (Delvid 46), Liedson.

Wednesday, 24 August 2005

Ajax (0) 3 *(Babel 50, Sneijder 80, 89)*

Brondby (1) 1 *(Elmander 44)* 39,075

Ajax: Vonk; Trabelski, Grygera, Escude, Maduro, Pienaar (Galasek 82), Babel, De Jong, Emanuelson, Rosenberg (Heitinga 90), Boukhari (Sneijder 62).
Brondby: Ankergren; Rytter, Nielsen, Lantz (Daugaard 81), Lorentzen (Kamper 57), Retov, Skoubo, Elmander, Sennels, Agger, Jorgensen (Absalonsen 74).

Debrecen (0) 0

Manchester United (1) 3 *(Heinze 20, 61, Richardson 65)* 25,000

Debrecen: Csernyanszki; Eger, Mate, Vukmir, Sandor, Dombi (Szatmari 57), Kiss, Boor (Madar 78), Halmosi, Bogdanovic (Brnovic 46), Kerekes.
Manchester United: Van der Sar; Neville (Richardson 13), Heinze, Brown, Ferdinand, Scholes (Bardsley 46), Fletcher (Miller 61), Van Nistelrooy, Smith, Giggs, Ronaldo.

FC Brugge (0) 1 *(Balaban 79)*
Valerenga (0) 0 20,144
FC Brugge: Butina; Vanaudenaerde (Dufer 69), Valgaeren, Klukowski, Clement, Maertens, Vermant, Englebert, Leko (Van Tornhout 77), Verheyen (Blondel 110), Balaban.
Valerenga: Arason; Skiri, Muri, Dos Santos, Holm D (Hulsker 77), Gashi, Berre (Mathisen 61), Iversen (Brocken 87), Grindheim, Johnsen, Waehler■.
aet; FC Brugge won 4-3 on penalties.

Internazionale (1) 1 *(Recoba 13)*
Shakhtar Donetsk (1) 1 *(Blumer 26)*
Internazionale: Julio Cesar; Zanetti J, Cordoba, Wome, Materazzi, Stankovic (Pizarro 46), Veron (Ze Maria 73), Solari, Cambiasso, Adriano (Cruz 83), Recoba.
Shakhtar Donetsk: Lastuvka; Lewandowski, Hubschman, Tymoschuk, Duljaj (Fernandinho 89), Matuzalem, Brandao, Rat, Marica (Bielik 71), Srna, Blumer (Jadson 65).
Behind closed doors.

Rangers (1) 2 *(Buffel 39, Prso 58)*
Anorthosis (0) 0 48,500
Rangers: Waterreus; Ricksen, Ball, Murray (Rae 85), Pierre-Fanfan, Rodriguez, Ferguson, Lovenkrands, Novo, Prso (Thompson 66), Buffel (McCormack 74).
Anorthosis: Georgallides; Poursaitides, Katsavakis, Louka, Xenidis, Haber, Marangos (Konstantinou 52), Nikolaou, Ketsbaia (Samaras 64), Tsitaishvili (Tsolakidis 72), Froussos.

Slavia Prague (0) 0
Anderlecht (0) 2 *(Akin 72, Mpenza 84)* 17,216
Slavia Prague: Kozacik; Svec (Fort 46), Latka, Vlcek, Holenak, Gedeon (Zabojnik 65), Suchy, Jarolim, Zboncak, Pitak, Hrdlicka (Svento 60).
Anderlecht: Zitka; Deschacht, Vanderhaeghe, Mpenza, Goor, Wilhelmsson (Zetterberg 88), Akin (Delorge 84), Kompany, Tihinen, Deman, Vanden Borre.

Villarreal (1) 2 *(Sorin 21, Forlan 90)*
Everton (0) 1 *(Arteta 69)* 22,000
Villarreal: Barbosa; Gonzalo Rodriguez, Josico, Figueroa (Tacchinardi 81), Arruabarrena, Sorin, Quique Alvarez, Javi Venta (Kromkamp 14), Marcos Senna, Riquelme, Forlan.
Everton: Martyn; Hibbert, Neville, Yobo, Weir, Arteta, Davies (McFadden 79), Cahill, Bent, Ferguson, Kilbane (Osman 56).

Werder Bremen (0) 3 *(Klasnic 65, 73, Borowski 68 (pen))*
Basle (0) 0 30,339
Werder Bremen: Reinke; Pasanen, Baumann (Jensen D 46), Schulz, Naldo, Owomoyela, Micoud (Vranjes 88), Frings, Borowski, Klasnic (Valdez 73), Klose■.
Basle: Zuberbuhler; Smiljanic, Quennoz (Sterjovski 69), Zanni, Kleber, Chipperfield, Degen D, Delgado, Ba, Rossi (Ergic 82), Eduardo Da Silva.

GROUP STAGE

GROUP A

Wednesday, 14 September 2005

FC Brugge (0) 1 *(Yulu-Matondo 85)*
Juventus (0) 2 *(Nedved 66, Trezeguet 75)* 29,975
FC Brugge: Stijnen; Spilar, Maertens, Valgaeren (Victor 75), De Cock, Vermant (Leko 84), Englebert, Vanaudenaerde, Yulu-Matondo, Portillo (Blondel 52), Balaban.
Juventus: Abbiati; Blasi, Kovac, Cannavaro, Zambrotta, Camoranesi (Giannichedda 88), Emerson, Vieira■, Nedved, Trezeguet (Zalayeta 88), Ibrahimovic.

Rapid Vienna (0) 0
Bayern Munich (0) 1 *(Guerrero 60)* 49,000
Rapid Vienna: Payer; Dober, Vlachovic, Bejbl, Adamski, Hofmann, Korsos (Martinez 64), Hlinka, Ivanschitz (Dollinger 84), Kincl, Lawaree (Agagunduz 74).
Bayern Munich: Kahn; Sagnol, Lucio, Ismael, Lizarazu (Demichelis 52), Schweinsteiger (Deisler 83), Hargreaves, Ze Roberto, Scholl, Pizarro (Guerrero 52), Makaay.

Tuesday, 27 September 2005

Bayern Munich (1) 1 *(Demichelis 32)*
FC Brugge (0) 0 65,527
Bayern Munich: Kahn; Sagnol, Lucio, Ismael, Lizarazu (Scholl 52), Demichelis, Schweinsteiger, Ze Roberto, Ballack (Jeremies 83), Makaay, Guerrero (Santa Cruz 72).
FC Brugge: Butina; De Cock, Maertens, Vandelannoite, Dufer, Englebert (Roelandts 85), Vermant, Blondel, Verheyen (Yulu-Matondo 75), Balaban, Leko (Portillo 67).

Juventus (1) 3 *(Trezeguet 27, Mutu 82, Ibrahimovic 85)*
Rapid Vienna (0) 0 11,156
Juventus: Abbiati; Zambrotta, Cannavaro, Thuram, Pessotto, Nedved, Emerson, Giannichedda (Blasi 83), Camoranesi (Mutu 65), Ibrahimovic, Trezeguet (Del Piero 60).
Rapid Vienna: Payer; Adamski, Bejbl, Vlachovic, Dober (Martinez 76), Ivanschitz, Hlinka, Korsos, Hofmann, Akagunduz (Lawaree 53), Kincl.

Tuesday, 18 October 2005

Bayern Munich (2) 2 *(Deisler 32, Demichelis 39)*
Juventus (0) 1 *(Ibrahimovic 90)* 60,000
Bayern Munich: Kahn; Sagnol, Lizarazu (Schweinsteiger 30), Ismael, Lucio, Demichelis, Ze Roberto, Ballack, Deisler, Santa Cruz (Scholl 88), Makaay.
Juventus: Abbiati; Zambrotta, Cannavaro, Thuram, Blasi (Chiellini 50), Nedved, Giannichedda, Emerson, Camoranesi (Del Piero 48), Trezeguet (Mutu 65), Ibrahimovic.

Rapid Vienna (0) 0
FC Brugge (0) 1 *(Balaban 75)* 45,000
Rapid Vienna: Payer; Dober (Martin Hiden 54), Valachovic, Bejbl (Martinez 73), Adamski, Hofmann, Korsos, Hlinka, Ivanschitz, Kincl, Lawaree (Akagunduz 73).
FC Brugge: Butina; Vanaudenaerde, Spilar, Maertens (Englebert 70), Blondel, Vermant, Clement, Leko, Dufer (Roelandts 90), Portillo (Verheyen 70), Balaban.

Wednesday, 2 November 2005

FC Brugge (2) 3 *(Portillo 8, Balaban 25, Verheyen 63)*
Rapid Vienna (1) 2 *(Kincl 1, Adamski 81)* 27,541
FC Brugge: Butina; Vanaudenaerde, Maertens, Spilar, Blondel, Vermant, Clement, Leko (Roelandts 86), Verheyen, Portillo (Victor 90), Balaban (Englebert 82).
Rapid Vienna: Hedl; Dober (Garics 83), Martin Hiden, Bejbl, Adamski, Hofmann, Korsos, Hlinka, Dollinger (Martinez 70), Kincl, Lawaree (Akagunduz 70).

Juventus (0) 2 *(Trezeguet 61, 85)*
Bayern Munich (0) 1 *(Deisler 66)* 16,076
Juventus: Abbiati; Thuram, Kovac (Camoranesi 58) (Mutu 76), Cannavaro, Chiellini, Emerson, Vieira, Zambrotta, Del Piero (Nedved 46), Trezeguet, Ibrahimovic■.
Bayern Munich: Kahn; Sagnol, Lucio, Ismael, Schweinsteiger, Deisler, Demichelis (Scholl 87), Ze Roberto, Ballack, Pizarro, Makaay (Guerrero 88).

Tuesday, 22 November 2005

Bayern Munich (1) 4 *(Deisler 21, Karimi 54, Makaay 72, 76)*

Rapid Vienna (0) 0 66,000

Bayern Munich: Kahn; Sagnol, Lizarazu (Lahm 62), Demichelis, Lucio, Ismael, Deisler, Karimi (Guerrero 83), Makaay, Pizarro, Ze Roberto (Schweinsteiger 46).
Rapid Vienna: Payer; Korsos, Martin Hiden, Bejbl, Katzer, Hofmann, Valachovic (Martinez 67), Hlinka (Garics 80), Ivanschitz (Dollinger 85), Akagunduz, Kincl.

Juventus (0) 1 *(Del Piero 80)*

FC Brugge (0) 0 9623

Juventus: Abbiati; Chiellini, Cannavaro, Thuram, Zambrotta, Nedved, Vieira, Emerson, Camoranesi, Del Piero, Trezeguet (Zalayeta 84).
FC Brugge: Butina; Clement (Englebert 50), Spilar, Maertens, Gvozdenovic, Vanaudenaerde, Leko, Vermant, Verheyen, Dufer (Serebrennikov 80), Portillo.

Wednesday, 7 December 2005

FC Brugge (1) 1 *(Portillo 32)*

Bayern Munich (1) 1 *(Pizarro 21)* 27,860

FC Brugge: Butina; Clement, Maertens, Spilar, Vandelannoite, Vermant, Englebert (Vanaudenaerde 90), Roelandts, Yulu-Matondo (Dufer 89), Lange (Gvozdenovic 77), Portillo.
Bayern Munich: Kahn; Lahm, Demichelis, Ismael, Lizarazu, Deisler, Hargreaves (Schweinsteiger 67), Karimi (Ze Roberto 46), Ballack, Pizarro, Makaay (Guerrero 46).

Rapid Vienna (0) 1 *(Kincl 52)*

Juventus (3) 3 *(Del Piero 35, 45, Ibrahimovic 42)* 46,500

Rapid Vienna: Payer; Dober, Martin Hiden, Valachovic, Katzer, Korsos (Martinez 80), Hlinka, Ivanschitz, Hofmann, Kincl, Akagunduz (Kienast 86).
Juventus: Abbiati; Balzaretti, Kovac, Thuram, Chiellini, Camoranesi (Giannichedda 78), Blasi, Vieira, Mutu (Pessotto 61), Del Piero, Ibrahimovic (Zalayeta 46).

Group A Final Table	*P*	*W*	*D*	*L*	*F*	*A*	*Pts*
Juventus	6	5	0	1	12	5	15
Bayern Munich	6	4	1	1	10	4	13
FC Brugge	6	2	1	3	6	7	7
Rapid Vienna	6	0	0	6	3	15	0

GROUP B

Wednesday, 14 September 2005

Arsenal (0) 2 *(Silva 51, Bergkamp 90)*

Thun (0) 1 *(Ferreira 53)* 34,498

Arsenal: Almunia; Lauren, Cole, Silva, Toure, Campbell, Ljungberg (Hleb 80), Fabregas (Bergkamp 72), Reyes (Owusu-Abeyie 80), Van Persie■, Pires.
Thun: Jakupovic; Orman, Hodzic, Milicevic, Goncalves, Gerber (Leandro 72), Bernardi, Adriano (Gelson 57), Aegerter, Ferreira, Lustrinelli (Faye 87).

Sparta Prague (0) 1 *(Matusovic 66)*

Ajax (0) 1 *(Sneijder 90)* 19,500

Sparta Prague: Blazek; Kadlec, Lukas, Petras, Pospech, Polacek (Dosek 79), Sivok, Kisel, Zelenka, Poborsky, Slepicka (Matusovic 49).
Ajax: Vonk; Emanuelson, Maduro, Grygera, Trabelsi, Lindenbergh, Sneijder, Galasek (Heitinga 90), Babel, Pienaar (Rosales 80), Rosenberg (Charisteas 76).

Tuesday, 27 September 2005

Ajax (0) 1 *(Rosenberg 71)*

Arsenal (1) 2 *(Ljungberg 2, Pires 69 (pen))* 48,000

Ajax: Vonk; De Jong, Grygera, Vermaelen, Emanuelson (Juanfran 85), Pienaar, Galasek, Lindenbergh, Babel, Boukhari (Manucharyan 69), Charisteas (Rosenberg 57).
Arsenal: Almunia; Lauren, Cole, Flamini, Toure, Campbell, Hleb (Cygan 90), Fabregas, Reyes (Owusu-Abeyie 81), Ljungberg, Pires (Clichy 88).

Thun (0) 1 *(Hodzic 89)*

Sparta Prague (0) 0 10,300

Thun: Jakupovic; Orman (Gerber 46), Deumi, Milicevic, Goncalves, Leandro, Hodzic, Adriano (Gelson 82), Aegerter, Ferreira, Lustrinelli (Sen 79).
Sparta Prague: Blazek; Pospech, Petras, Petrous, Kadlec, Kisel, Hasek, Sivok, Polacek (Dosek 84), Zelenka, Slepicka (Herzan 59).

Tuesday, 18 October 2005

Ajax (1) 2 *(Anastasiou 36, 55)*

Thun (0) 0 50,000

Ajax: Stekelenburg; Trabelsi, Grygera, Maduro, Emanuelson, Rosales (Heitinga 90), De Jong, Galasek, Pienaar (Boukhari 84), Anastasiou (Babel 82), Sneijder.
Thun: Jakupovic; Orman, Deumi, Milicevic, Goncalves, Leandro, Adriano (Sen 74), Aegerter, Ferreira, Gelson (Duruz 84), Lustrinelli (Faye 84).

Sparta Prague (0) 0

Arsenal (1) 2 *(Henry 21, 74)* 12,528

Sparta Prague: Blazek; Pergl (Matusovic 70), Petrous, Lukas, Kadlec, Petras, Pospech, Zelenka, Kisel, Polacek, Slepicka (Dosek 77).
Arsenal: Lehmann; Lauren, Clichy, Silva, Toure, Cygan, Flamini, Fabregas (Owusu-Abeyie 89), Reyes (Henry 15), Van Persie (Eboue 73), Pires.

Wednesday, 2 November 2005

Arsenal (1) 3 *(Henry 23, Van Persie 81, 86)*

Sparta Prague (0) 0 35,155

Arsenal: Almunia; Lauren, Clichy, Silva, Toure, Campbell, Reyes (Eboue 82), Flamini, Henry (Van Persie 66), Bergkamp, Pires (Fabregas 73).
Sparta Prague: Blazek; Pergl, Lukas, Petrous (Jeslinek 80), Kadlec, Pospech, Petras, Zelenka, Hasek, Polacek (Slepicka 58), Matusovic.

Thun (0) 2 *(Lustrinelli 56, Spadoto 74)*

Ajax (1) 4 *(Sneijder 26, Anastasiou 63, De Jong 89, Boukhari 90)* 31,340

Thun: Jakupovic; Goncalves, Milicevic (Spadoto 42), Deumi, Orman (Gerber 67), Leandro (Sen 81), Bernardi, Hodzic, Aegerter, Ferreira, Lustrinelli.
Ajax: Stekelenburg; Heitinga, Grygera, Maduro, Emanuelson, Pienaar, De Jong, Galasek, Sneijder (Boukhari 88), Babel, Anastasiou.

Tuesday, 22 November 2005

Ajax (0) 2 *(De Jong 68, 89)*

Sparta Prague (0) 1 *(Petrous 90)* 46,158

Ajax: Stekelenburg; Trabelsi, Grygera, Vermaelen, Emanuelson, Maduro, Sneijder, Lindenbergh (De Jong 53), Pienaar, Anastasiou (Rosenberg 62), Boukhari.
Sparta Prague: Blazek; Petras, Lukas, Petrous, Kadlec, Herzan (Simak 85), Hasek, Pospech, Zelenka (Slepicka 69), Polacek, Dosek.

Thun (0) 0

Arsenal (0) 1 *(Pires 88 (pen))* 31,330

Thun: Jakupovic; Orman, Hodzic, Deumi■, Goncalves (Bernardi 90), Ferreira, Milicevic, Aegerter, Leandro, Adriano, Lustrinelli (Sen 84).
Arsenal: Almunia; Eboue, Cygan (Lauren 67), Song Billong (Fabregas 56), Campbell, Senderos, Ljungberg, Flamini, Van Persie, Henry (Pires 70), Reyes.

Wednesday, 7 December 2005

Arsenal (0) 0

Ajax (0) 0 35,376

Arsenal: Almunia; Eboue, Lauren (Gilbert 73), Flamini, Toure, Senderos, Hleb (Fabregas 62), Larsson, Owusu-Abeyie, Henry, Reyes (Van Persie 65).
Ajax: Stekelenburg; Heitinga, Grygera (Trabelsi 15), Vermaelen, Juanfran, Maduro (De Jong 29), Galasek, Sneijder, Pienaar, Rosenberg, Boukhari (Babel 80).

Sparta Prague (0) 0

Thun (0) 0 9233

Sparta Prague: Blazek; Pospech, Petras■, Petrous, Kadlec, Simak (Jeslinek 60), Hasek (Herzan 82), Zelenka, Polacek, Dosek, Slepicka (Matusovic 66).
Thun: Jakupovic; Orman, Hodzic, Goncalves■, Duruz, Aegerter, Bernardi (Savic 70), Spadoto (Sen 57), Adriano (Gelson 83), Leandro, Lustrinelli.

Group B Final Table	P	W	D	L	F	A	Pts
Arsenal	6	5	1	0	10	2	16
Ajax	6	3	2	1	10	6	11
Thun	6	1	1	4	4	9	4
Sparta Prague	6	0	2	4	2	9	2

GROUP C

Wednesday, 14 September 2005

Udinese (1) 3 *(Iaquinta 28, 73, 76)*

Panathinaikos (0) 0 41,652

Udinese: De Sanctis; Felipe, Natali, Juarez (Sensini 86), Obodo (Pinzi 68), Candela, Muntari, Vidigal, Zenoni, Di Natale (Di Michele 79), Iaquinta.
Panathinaikos: Galinovic; Kotsios, Morris, Goumas, Seric, Gonzalez, Biscan, Nilsson, Wooter (Leontiou 79), Torghelle, Charalambides (Gekas 70).

Werder Bremen (0) 0

Barcelona (1) 2 *(Deco 13, Ronaldinho 77 (pen))* 42,466

Werder Bremen: Reinke; Owomoyela, Naldo, Pasanen, Schulz, Frings, Baumann (Jensen D 63), Borowski, Klasnic, Micoud, Valdez (Hunt 83).
Barcelona: Victor Valdes; Belletti (Edmilson 46), Puyol, Oleguer, Van Bronckhorst, Xavi (Van Bommel 79), Marquez, Deco, Giuly (Leo Messi 66), Eto'o, Ronaldinho.

Tuesday, 27 September 2005

Barcelona (3) 4 *(Ronaldinho 13, 32, 90 (pen), Deco 41)*

Udinese (1) 1 *(Felipe 24)* 74,730

Barcelona: Victor Valdes; Belletti, Puyol, Oleguer, Van Bronckhorst, Leo Messi (Ezquerro 70), Xavi, Van Bommel (Iniesta 62), Deco, Ronaldinho, Eto'o (Larsson 81).
Udinese: De Sanctis; Bertotto, Natali (Juarez 33), Felipe, Obodo, Zenoni, Vidigal■, Muntari (Di Michele 73), Candela, Di Natale (Mauri 51), Barreto.

Panathinaikos (2) 2 *(Gonzalez 6 (pen), Mantzios 8)*

Werder Bremen (1) 1 *(Klose 41)* 50,000

Panathinaikos: Galinovic; Vintra, Goumas (Kotsios 42), Morris, Darlas, Nilsson, Conceicao, Gonzalez, Seric, Mantzios (Gekas 72), Torghelle (Tziolis 58).
Werder Bremen: Reinke; Owomoyela, Andreasen, Naldo, Schulz (Valdez 74), Frings, Baumann (Hunt 63), Borowski, Klose, Micoud, Klasnic■.

Tuesday, 18 October 2005

Panathinaikos (0) 0

Barcelona (0) 0 65,000

Panathinaikos: Galinovic; Vyntra, Biscan, Morris, Darlas, Conceicao, Nilsson, Gonzalez (Papadopoulos 76), Seric (Wooter 87), Mantzios, Torghelle (Leontiou 59).
Barcelona: Valdes; Belletti, Puyol, Marquez, Van Bronckhorst, Xavi (Iniesta 76), Larsson (Messi 67), Van Bommel (Motta 56), Deco, Ronaldinho, Eto'o.

Udinese (0) 1 *(Di Natale 86)*

Werder Bremen (0) 1 *(Felipe 64 (og))* 43,952

Udinese: De Sanctis; Bertotto, Sensini, Felipe, Zenoni (Di Natale 76), Pinzi (Mauri 76), Obodo, Muntari, Candela, Iaquinta, Di Michele (Barreto 58).
Werder Bremen: Reinke; Owomoyela, Andreasen, Naldo, Schulz, Frings, Baumann, Borowski, Micoud, Valdez (Hunt 84), Klose.

Wednesday, 2 November 2005

Barcelona (4) 5 *(Van Bommel 1, Eto'o 14, 40, 65, Messi 34)*

Panathinaikos (0) 0 64,321

Barcelona: Valdes; Oleguer, Puyol, Edmilson, Van Bronckhorst, Messi, Van Bommel (Gabri 61), Xavi (Ezquerro 70), Iniesta (Motta 51), Ronaldinho, Eto'o.
Panathinaikos: Galinovic; Vyntra, Biscan (Kotsios 46), Morris, Darlas (Tziolis 60), Nilsson, Conceicao, Leontiou, Seric (Wooter 79), Gonzalez, Papadopoulos.

Werder Bremen (2) 4 *(Klose 15, Baumann 24, Micoud 51, 67)*

Udinese (0) 3 *(Di Natale 54, 57, Schulz 60 (og))* 35,424

Werder Bremen: Reinke; Owomoyela (Fahrenhorst 68), Andreasen, Naldo, Schulz, Borowski, Baumann (Vranjes 86), Frings, Valdez (Hunt 80), Micoud, Klose.
Udinese: De Sanctis; Bertotto, Sensini, Felipe, Zenoni (Mauri 50), Pinzi■, Obodo, Muntari (Di Natale 30), Candela, Iaquinta, Di Michele (Motta 73).

Tuesday, 22 November 2005

Barcelona (2) 3 *(Gabri 14, Ronaldinho 26, Larsson 71)*

Werder Bremen (1) 1 *(Borowski 22 (pen))* 67,273

Barcelona: Valdes; Oleguer, Puyol, Marquez (Belletti 74), Van Bronckhorst, Motta, Gabri (Iniesta 77), Deco, Giuly (Ezquerro 65), Ronaldinho, Larsson.
Werder Bremen: Reinke; Owomoyela, Fahrenhorst, Naldo, Schulz, Baumann, Frings, Borowski, Micoud, Valdez, Klose (Hunt 59).

Panathinaikos (1) 1 *(Charalambidis 45)*

Udinese (0) 2 *(Iaquinta 80, Candela 83)* 30,150

Panathinaikos: Galinovic; Kotsios, Morris, Conceicao, Goumas, Gonzalez, Papadopoulos (Andric 64), Charalambidis, Mantzios, Leontiou (Torghelle 83), Darlas.
Udinese: De Sanctis; Bertotto, Obodo, Sensini, Zenoni, Iaquinta, Di Natale (Barreto 62), Di Michele, Muntari (Mauri 77), Felipe, Candela.

Wednesday, 7 December 2005

Udinese (0) 0

Barcelona (0) 2 *(Ezquerro 85, Iniesta 90)* 38,500

Udinese: De Sanctis; Bertotto, Sensini, Juarez, Zenoni (Tissone 38), Vidigal, Obodo, Muntari (Mauri 65), Candela, Di Natale, Iaquinta (Di Michele 75).
Barcelona: Jorquera; Belletti, Oleguer, Puyol, Van Bronckhorst, Gabri (Iniesta 75), Edmilson, Deco, Giuly, Larsson, Ezquerro.

Werder Bremen (3) 5 *(Micoud 2 (pen), Valdez 28, 31, Klose 51, Frings 90)*

Panathinaikos (0) 1 *(Morris 53)* 38,000

Werder Bremen: Reinke; Owomoyela, Fahrenhorst, Andreasen, Schulz (Pasanen 50), Frings, Baumann (Jensen D 75), Vranjes, Micoud, Valdez (Hunt 79), Klose.
Panathinaikos: Galinovic; Vyntra, Morris, Biscan, Darlas (Wooter 71), Conceicao, Tziolis, Nilsson (Kotsios 78), Gonzalez, Papadopoulos, Torghelle (Mantzios 73).

Group C Final Table	P	W	D	L	F	A	Pts
Barcelona	6	5	1	0	16	2	16
Werder Bremen	6	2	1	3	12	12	7
Udinese	6	2	1	3	10	12	7
Panathinaikos	6	1	1	4	4	16	4

GROUP D

Wednesday, 14 September 2005

Benfica (0) 1 *(Miccoli 90)*

Lille (0) 0 38,000

Benfica: Moreira; Nelson, Luizao, Ricardo Rocha (Anderson 46), Leo, Geovanni (Mantorras 79), Petit (Karagounis 67), Manuel Fernandes, Simao Sabrosa, Miccoli, Nuno Gomes.
Lille: Sylva; Chalme, Plestan, Schmitz, Tafforeau, Makoun, Cabaye, Gygax (Debuchy 46), Bodmer, Dernis (Lichtsteiner 83), Moussilou (Odemwingie 70).

Villarreal (0) 0

Manchester United (0) 0 22,000

Villarreal: Viera; Kromkamp, Gonzalo Rodriguez, Quique Alvarez, Arruabarrena, Hector Font (Roger 70), Josico (Tacchinardi 46), Marcos Senna, Sorin, Forlan, Guayre (Figueroa 66).
Manchester United: Van der Sar; O'Shea, Heinze (Richardson 33), Smith, Ferdinand, Silvestre, Fletcher, Scholes, Van Nistelrooy (Park 80), Rooney■, Ronaldo (Giggs 80).

Tuesday, 27 September 2005

Lille (0) 0

Villarreal (0) 0 35,000

Lille: Sylva; Lichtsteiner, Plestan, Schmitz, Tafforeau, Debuchy, Makoun, Bodmer (Dumont 46), Acimovic (Dernis 84), Odemwingie, Moussilou (Fauverge 73).
Villarreal: Viera; Kromkamp, Quique Alvarez (Gonzalo Rodriguez 56), Pena, Arruabarrena, Riquelme, Tacchinardi, Josico, Sorin (Marcos Senna 46), Forlan (Guayre 84), Figueroa.
Played in Paris.

Manchester United (1) 2 *(Giggs 39, Van Nistelrooy 85)*

Benfica (0) 1 *(Simao Sabrosa 59)* 66,112

Manchester United: Van der Sar; Bardsley, Richardson, Smith, Ferdinand, O'Shea, Fletcher, Scholes, Van Nistelrooy, Giggs, Ronaldo.
Benfica: Moreira; Nelson, Luizao, Ricardo Rocha, Leo, Beto (Mantorras 87), Manuel Fernandes (Geovanni 87), Petit, Simao Sabrosa, Miccoli (Joao Pereira 80), Nuno Gomes.

Tuesday, 18 October 2005

Manchester United (0) 0

Lille (0) 0 60,626

Manchester United: Van der Sar; Bardsley, O'Shea, Smith, Ferdinand, Silvestre, Fletcher, Scholes■, Van Nistelrooy, Giggs (Park 83), Ronaldo.
Lille: Sylva; Vitakic, Tavlaridis, Schmitz, Tafforeau, Debuchy (Keita 83), Makoun, Bodmer, Chalme, Odemwingie (Moussilou 73), Acimovic (Dernis 60).

Villarreal (0) 1 *(Riquelme 73 (pen))*

Benfica (0) 1 *(Manuel 77)* 24,500

Villarreal: Viera; Kromkamp, Gonzalo Rodriguez, Arruabarrena (Josico 46), Arzo, Santi Cazorla, Tacchinardi (Roger 84), Sorin, Riquelme, Forlan, Jose Mari (Figueroa 79).
Benfica: Quim (Rui Nereu 28); Nelson, Luisao, Anderson, Ricardo Rocha, Karagounis (Karyaka 61), Petit, Manuel, Geovanni (Beto 90), Nuno Gomes, Simao Sabrosa.

Wednesday, 2 November 2005

Benfica (0) 0

Villarreal (0) 1 *(Marcos Senna 82)* 50,250

Benfica: Rui Nereu; Nelson, Luisao, Anderson (Nuno Assis 84), Leo, Geovanni (Joao Pereira 70), Manuel, Petit, Simao Sabrosa, Karagounis (Mantorras 70), Nuno Gomes.
Villarreal: Barbosa; Javi Venta, Gonzalo Rodriguez, Quique Alvarez, Arruabarrena, Marcos Senna (Pena 90), Josico, Riquelme, Sorin, Jose Mari (Guayre 71), Forlan (Figueroa 52).

Lille (1) 1 *(Acimovic 38)*

Manchester United (0) 0 66,470

Lille: Sylva; Chalme, Tavlaridis, Schmitz, Tafforeau, Debuchy, Makoun, Bodmer, Dernis (Gygax 79), Moussilou (Odemwingie 84), Acimovic (Cabaye 76).
Manchester United: Van der Sar; O'Shea, Silvestre, Smith, Ferdinand, Brown, Fletcher, Richardson (Park 65), Van Nistelrooy, Rooney, Ronaldo (Rossi 89).
Played in Paris.

Tuesday, 22 November 2005

Lille (0) 0

Benfica (0) 0 76,184

Lille: Sylva; Lichtsteiner, Tavlaridis, Schmitz, Tafforeau, Chalme (Mirallas 69), Bodmer, Acimovic (Fauvergue 87), Makoun, Dernis, Moussilou (Aboucherouane 75).
Benfica: Quim; Alcides, Luisao, Anderson, Ricardo Rocha, Nelson, Beto, Petit, Leo, Miccoli (Mantorras 44), Nuno Gomes.
Played in Paris.

Manchester United (0) 0

Villarreal (0) 0 67,471

Manchester United: Van der Sar; Brown (Neville 73), O'Shea, Smith (Saha 81), Ferdinand, Silvestre, Fletcher (Park 53), Scholes, Van Nistelrooy, Rooney, Ronaldo.
Villarreal: Barbosa; Javi Venta, Gonzalo Rodriguez, Pena, Arruabarrena, Roger (Hector Font 65), Tacchinardi (Josico 77), Marcos Senna, Sorin, Figueroa (Xisco Nadal 86), Jose Mari.

Wednesday, 7 December 2005

Benfica (2) 2 *(Geovanni 16, Beto 34)*

Manchester United (1) 1 *(Scholes 6)* 53,000

Benfica: Quim; Alcides, Luisao, Anderson, Leo (Ricardo Rocha 90), Nuno Assis (Joao Pereira 73), Petit, Beto, Nelson, Nuno Gomes, Geovanni (Mantorras 80).
Manchester United: Van der Sar; Neville, O'Shea (Richardson 85), Smith, Ferdinand, Silvestre, Ronaldo (Park 67), Scholes, Van Nistelrooy, Rooney, Giggs (Saha 61).

Villarreal (0) 1 *(Guayre 67)*

Lille (0) 0 21,000

Villarreal: Viera; Kromkamp, Gonzalo Rodriguez, Pena, Arruabarrena, Marcos Senna, Josico, Sorin (Hector Font 36), Riquelme, Jose Mari (Guayre 59), Forlan (Roger 83).
Lille: Sylva; Chalme, Tavlaridis, Vitakic, Tafforeau, Dumont, Makoun, Lichtsteiner (Moussilou 70), Bodmer, Dernis (Acimovic 60), Odemwingie (Mirallas 74).

Group D Final Table	*P*	*W*	*D*	*L*	*F*	*A*	*Pts*
Villarreal	6	2	4	0	3	1	10
Benfica	6	2	2	2	5	5	8
Lille	6	1	3	2	1	2	6
Manchester United	6	1	3	2	3	4	6

GROUP E

Tuesday, 13 September 2005

AC Milan (1) 3 *(Kaka 18, 86, Shevchenko 89)*

Fenerbahce (0) 1 *(Alex 63 (pen))* 34,619

AC Milan: Dida; Cafu, Nesta, Maldini, Kaladze, Gattuso (Serginho 71), Pirlo (Vogel 71), Ambrosini, Kaka, Shevchenko, Vieri (Gilardino 77).
Fenerbahce: Volkan; Serkan, Luciano, Onder, Umit O, Marco Aurelio, Selcuk, Appiah (Kemal 53) (Marcio Nobre 90), Alex, Anelka, Tuncay.

PSV Eindhoven (1) 1 *(Vennegoor of Hesselink 33)*

Schalke (0) 0 33,500

PSV Eindhoven: Gomes; Reiziger, Addo, Ooijer, Lucius, Afellay, Simons, Cocu (Lamey 82), Beasley, Vennegoor of Hesselink (De Pinho 86), Farfan.
Schalke: Rost; Altintop (Bajramovic 87), Krstajic, Bordon, Rafinha, Kobiashvili, Poulsen, Ernst (Varela 79), Kuranyi, Lincoln, Sand (Larsen 72).

Wednesday, 28 September 2005

Fenerbahce (1) 3 *(Alex 41 (pen), 68, Appiah 90)*

PSV Eindhoven (0) 0 21,895

Fenerbahce: Volkan; Serkan, Onder, Luciano, Umit O, Marco Aurelio, Appiah, Selcuk, Marcio Nobre (Mehmet 90), Anelka, Alex (Kemal 90).
PSV Eindhoven: Gomes; Ooijer, Alex, Simons, Cocu, Beasley, Lucius (Ferreyra 56), Farfan, Addo, Vennegoor of Hesselink■, Afellay.

Schalke (1) 2 *(Larsen 3, Altintop 70)*

AC Milan (1) 2 *(Seedorf 1, Shevchenko 59)* 60,881

Schalke: Rost; Rafinha, Bordon, Rodriguez, Krstajic, Ernst (Altintop 67), Poulsen (Bajramovic 85), Lincoln, Kobiashvili, Kuranyi (Sand 73), Larsen.
AC Milan: Dida; Cafu (Stam 76), Nesta, Maldini, Kaladze, Gattuso, Pirlo, Seedorf, Kaka (Rui Costa 74), Gilardino (Vieri 71), Shevchenko.

Wednesday, 19 October 2005

AC Milan (0) 0

PSV Eindhoven (0) 0 69,763

AC Milan: Dida; Cafu, Stam, Maldini, Kaladze, Pirlo, Gattuso, Seedorf (Serginho 74), Kaka, Shevchenko (Inzaghi 49), Vieri.
PSV Eindhoven: Gomes; Reiziger, Alex, Ooijer, Lamey, Afellay, Simons, Cocu, Beasley, Robert (Aissati 63), Farfan.

Fenerbahce (1) 3 *(Fabio Luciano 14, Marcio Nobre 73, Appiah 79)*

Schalke (0) 3 *(Lincoln 59, 62, Kuranyi 77)* 50,000

Fenerbahce: Volkan; Serkan, Onder, Fabio Luciano, Umit O, Selcuk, Marco Aurelio (Tuncay 69), Appiah, Alex■, Marcio Nobre, Anelka.
Schalke: Rost; Poulsen, Kobiashvili, Bordon, Altintop, Larsen, Lincoln, Sand (Kuranyi 46), Rodriguez, Rafinha, Krstajic.

Tuesday, 1 November 2005

PSV Eindhoven (1) 1 *(Farfan 12)*

AC Milan (0) 0 35,100

PSV Eindhoven: Gomes; Ooijer, Alex, Lamey, Afellay (Reiziger 58), Simons, Aissati, Cocu, Beasley, Vennegoor of Hesselink, Farfan (Addo 85).
AC Milan: Dida; Stam■, Nesta, Maldini, Kaladze (Serginho 46), Seedorf, Pirlo, Gattuso (Jankulovski 46), Kaka, Vieri, Gilardino (Shevchenko 73).

Schalke (1) 2 *(Kuranyi 32, Sand 90)*

Fenerbahce (0) 0 53,993

Schalke: Rost; Rafinha, Bordon, Rodriguez, Krstajic, Ernst (Varela 81), Poulsen, Altintop (Sand 64), Lincoln, Kobiashvili, Kuranyi (Bajramovic 90).
Fenerbahce: Volkan; Serkan, Onder, Fabio Luciano■, Umit O, Marco Aurelio■, Appiah, Selcuk, Marcio Nobre (Mehmet 46), Anelka, Tuncay.

Wednesday, 23 November 2005

Fenerbahce (0) 0

AC Milan (1) 4 *(Shevchenko 16, 52, 70, 76)* 51,200

Fenerbahce: Volkan; Serkan, Servet, Onder, Deniz, Selcuk (Kemal 28), Umit O, Appiah, Mehmet (Marcio Nobre 57), Tuncay, Anelka.
AC Milan: Dida; Simic, Nesta, Maldini, Serginho, Gattuso (Vogel 80), Pirlo, Kaka (Rui Costa 20), Seedorf, Shevchenko, Gilardino (Vieri 75).

Schalke (1) 3 *(Kobiashvili 18 (pen), 73, 79 (pen))*

PSV Eindhoven (0) 0 53,994

Schalke: Rost; Altintop, Bordon, Rodriguez, Krstajic, Poulsen, Lincoln, Ernst, Varela (Asamoah 74), Kuranyi (Sand 85), Kobiashvili (Bajramovic 89).
PSV Eindhoven: Gomes; Reiziger (Sibon 77), Ooijer, Alex, Lamey, Afellay, Cocu, Simons (Lucius 49), Farfan, Robert, Aissati (Vennegoor of Hesselink 49).

Tuesday, 6 December 2005

AC Milan (1) 3 *(Pirlo 42, Kaka 52, 60)*

Schalke (1) 2 *(Poulsen 44, Lincoln 66)* 43,816

AC Milan: Dida; Stam, Nesta, Maldini (Simic 30) (Kaladze 77), Serginho, Pirlo, Gattuso, Seedorf, Kaka, Inzaghi (Gilardino 85), Shevchenko.
Schalke: Rost; Rafinha, Bordon, Rodriguez, Krstajic (Larsen 84), Poulsen, Ernst (Asamoah 46), Altintop, Lincoln, Kobiashvili, Kuranyi (Sand 84).

PSV Eindhoven (1) 2 *(Cocu 14, Farfan 85)*

Fenerbahce (0) 0 35,100

PSV Eindhoven: Gomes; Lucius, Ooijer, Alex, Lamey, Simons, Afellay (Aissati 24), Cocu, Farfan, Vennegoor of Hesselink, Robert (Reiziger 67).
Fenerbahce: Volkan; Serkan, Onder, Fabio Luciano, Umit O, Appiah, Alex, Marco Aurelio, Tuncay, Anelka (Mehmet 65), Marcio Nobre (Semih 79).

Group E Final Table	*P*	*W*	*D*	*L*	*F*	*A*	*Pts*
AC Milan	6	3	2	1	12	6	11
PSV Eindhoven	6	3	1	2	4	6	10
Schalke	6	2	2	2	12	9	8
Fenerbahce	6	1	1	4	7	14	4

GROUP F

Tuesday, 13 September 2005

Lyon (3) 3 *(Carew 21, Juninho Pernambucano 26, Wiltord 31)*

Real Madrid (0) 0 39,500

Lyon: Coupet; Reveillere, Cris, Cacapa, Berthold, Diarra, Tiago (Pedretti 86), Juninho Pernambucano, Wiltord (Govou 80), Malouda, Carew (Fred 72).
Real Madrid: Casillas; Michel Salgado, Sergio Ramos, Helguera, Roberto Carlos, Beckham, Pablo Garcia, Gravesen (Guti 61), Julio Baptista, Robinho, Raul.

Olympiakos (1) 1 *(Lago 19 (og))*

Rosenborg (1) 3 *(Skjelbred 43, Mavrogenidis 47 (og), Storflor 90)* 30,000

Olympiakos: Nikopolidis; Mavrogenidis, Anatolakis, Kostoulas, Georgatos, Rivaldo (Dani 87), Toure (Kafes 90), Stoltidis, Babangida (Okkas 79), Konstantinou, Djordjevic.
Rosenborg: Johnsen E; Strand, Kvarme, Lago, Dorsin, Skjelbred (Riseth 85), Berg, Winsnes (Braaten 66), Solli, Helstad (Johnsen F 80), Storflor.

Wednesday, 28 September 2005

Real Madrid (1) 2 *(Raul 9, Soldado 87)*

Olympiakos (0) 1 *(Kafes 47)* 53,425

Real Madrid: Casillas; Michel Salgado (Diogo 80), Roberto Carlos, Sergio Ramos, Helguera, Julio Baptista (Soldado 79), Pablo Garcia (Gravesen 85), Beckham, Guti, Robinho, Raul.
Olympiakos: Nikopolidis; Mavrogenidis (Kapsis 39), Anatolakis, Kostoulas, Georgatos, Kafes, Toure, Stoltidis (Babangida 89), Rivaldo, Konstantinou (Okkas 84), Djordjevic.

Rosenborg (0) 0

Lyon (1) 1 *(Cris 45)* 20,620

Rosenborg: Johnsen E; Strand (Basma 66), Kvarme, Riseth, Dorsin, Skjelbred, Berg, Solli, Braaten, Helstad (Johnsen F 68), Storflor (Odegaard 59).
Lyon: Coupet; Reveillere, Cris, Cacapa, Berthold, Tiago, Diarra, Juninho Pernambucano, Govou (Wiltord 85), Carew (Fred 90), Malouda.

Wednesday, 19 October 2005

Lyon (1) 2 *(Juninho Pernambucano 4, Govou 89)*

Olympiakos (0) 1 *(Kafes 84)* 40,000

Lyon: Coupet; Reveillere, Cris, Cacapa, Abidal, Diarra, Tiago, Juninho Pernambucano, Fred (Carew 70), Govou (Clement 90), Malouda (Wiltord 75).
Olympiakos: Nikopolidis; Kapsis, Anatolakis (Babangida 90), Kostoulas, Pantos, Kafes, Toure, Stoltidis (Konstantinou 85), Bulut, Okkas, Djordjevic.

Real Madrid (0) 4 *(Woodgate 48, Raul 52, Helguera 68, Beckham 82)*

Rosenborg (1) 1 *(Strand 40)* 69,053

Real Madrid: Casillas; Diogo, Roberto Carlos, Helguera, Woodgate (Mejia 84), Pablo Garcia, Beckham, Zidane (Gravesen 70), Raul, Robinho, Julio Baptista (Guti 46).
Rosenborg: Johnsen E; Dorsin, Riseth, Kvarme, Basma, Solli, Skjelbred (Winsnes 75), Strand (Tettey 46), Storflor, Helstad (Johnsen F 63), Braaten.

Tuesday, 1 November 2005

Olympiakos (1) 1 *(Babangida 3)*

Lyon (2) 4 *(Juninho Pernambucano 41, Carew 43, 57, Diarra 55)* 29,555

Olympiakos: Giannou; Pantos, Kostoulas (Bulut 65), Anatolakis, Georgatos, Kafes, Toure, Rivaldo, Babangida, Okkas (D'Acol 81), Djordjevic (Stoltidis 65).
Lyon: Coupet; Reveillere, Cris, Cacapa, Abidal, Tiago (Clement 74), Diarra, Juninho Pernambucano (Pedretti 78), Govou, Carew, Malouda (Wiltord 67).

Rosenborg (0) 0

Real Madrid (2) 2 *(Dorsin 26 (og), Guti 41)* 20,122

Rosenborg: Johnsen E; Dorsin (Stensaas 74), Riseth, Kvarme, Basma, Storflor (Helstad 66), Solli, Skjelbred, Strand (Odegaard 82), Braaten, Johnsen F.
Real Madrid: Casillas; Michel Salgado (Meija 46), Roberto Carlos, Pavon, Woodgate, Guti (Raul Bravo 84), Sergio Ramos, Diogo, Beckham (De la Red 90), Robinho, Raul.

Wednesday, 23 November 2005

Real Madrid (1) 1 *(Guti 41)*

Lyon (0) 1 *(Carew 72)* 67,302

Real Madrid: Casillas; Diogo, Roberto Carlos, Sergio Ramos, Helguera, Pablo Garcia, Beckham (Michel Salgado 79), Zidane (Julio Baptista 76), Guti, Robinho, Pavon.
Lyon: Coupet; Monsoreau (Fred 70), Cacapa, Cris, Reveillere, Juninho Pernambucano (Clement 90), Diarra, Tiago, Malouda, Carew, Govou (Wiltord 69).

Rosenborg (0) 1 *(Helstad 88)*

Olympiakos (1) 1 *(Rivaldo 25)* 17,450

Rosenborg: Johnsen E; Basma, Riseth, Kvarme, Dorsin, Strand (Helstad 27), Solli, Skjelbred (Winsnes 10), Braaten (Odegaard 63), Johnsen F, Storflor.
Olympiakos: Nikopolidis; Pantos■, Anatolakis, Schurrer, Bulut, Kafes, Toure, Stoltidis, Babangida (Okkas 71), Rivaldo (Maric 86), Dani.

Tuesday, 6 December 2005

Lyon (1) 2 *(Benzema 33, Fred 90)*

Rosenborg (0) 1 *(Braaten 68)* 40,425

Lyon: Vercoutre; Reveillere (Clerc 82), Cris, Diatta, Monsoreau, Pedretti, Clement, Wiltord, Benzema (Beynie 90), Ben Arfa, Carew (Fred 55).
Rosenborg: Johnsen E; Basma, Lago, Kvarme, Dorsin, Winsnes, Riseth (Tettey 81), Johnsen F, Braaten, Helstad (Odegaard 56), Storflor (Eguren 83).

Olympiakos (0) 2 *(Bulut 50, Rivaldo 87)*

Real Madrid (1) 1 *(Sergio Ramos 7)* 31,456

Olympiakos: Nikopolidis; Mavrogenidis, Kapsis (Kostoulas 65), Schurrer, Bulut, Toure, Stoltidis, Rivaldo, Kafes (Babangida 80), Dani (Okkas 58), Djordjevic.
Real Madrid: Diego Lopez; Diogo, Pavon, Sergio Ramos, Raul Bravo, Balboa (Cardona 58), De la Red (Javi Garcia 81), Gravesen, Robinho (Jurado 80), Soldado, Julio Baptista.

Group F Final Table	*P*	*W*	*D*	*L*	*F*	*A*	*Pts*
Lyon	6	5	1	0	13	4	16
Real Madrid	6	3	1	2	10	8	10
Rosenborg	6	1	1	4	6	11	4
Olympiakos	6	1	1	4	7	13	4

GROUP G

Tuesday, 13 September 2005

Betis (0) 1 *(Arzu 51)*

Liverpool (2) 2 *(Sinama-Pongolle 2, Luis Garcia 14)* 45,000

Betis: Doblas; Melli, Juanito (Xisco 46), Rivas, Oscar Lopez, Arzu (Capi 72), Fernando (Dani 35), Assuncao, Joaquin, Varela, Oliveira.
Liverpool: Reina; Josemi, Traore, Xabi Alonso, Carragher, Hyypia, Luis Garcia, Sissoko, Crouch (Cisse 58), Sinama-Pongolle (Gerrard 74), Zenden (Riise 66).

Chelsea (1) 1 *(Lampard 19)*

Anderlecht (0) 0 29,575

Chelsea: Cech; Paulo Ferreira, Gallas, Makelele, Terry, Ricardo Carvalho, Duff (Cole J 77), Lampard, Drogba, Essien (Huth 90), Robben (Wright-Phillips 67).
Anderlecht: Zitka; Zewlakow (Jestrovic 81), Juhasz, Tihinen, Deschacht, Vanden Borre, Vanderhaeghe (Delorge 89), Deman, Goor, Mpenza, Akin (Wilhelmsson 70).

Wednesday, 28 September 2005

Anderlecht (0) 0

Betis (0) 1 *(Oliveira 69)* 27,500

Anderlecht: Proto; Vanden Borre, Deman, Tihinen (Akin 80), Deschacht, Wilhelmsson, Vanderhaeghe (Baseggio 86), Zetterberg, Goor, Mpenza, Jestrovic.
Betis: Doblas; Melli, Juanito, Rivas (Nano 73), Oscar Lopez, Varela, Rivera, Miguel Angel, Xisco (Fernando 77), Joaquin (Assuncio 90), Oliveira.

Liverpool (0) 0

Chelsea (0) 0 42,743

Liverpool: Reina; Finnan, Traore, Hamann, Carragher, Hyypia, Xabi Alonso, Gerrard, Crouch, Cisse (Sinama-Pongolle 78), Luis Garcia.
Chelsea: Cech; Paulo Ferreira, Gallas, Makelele, Terry, Ricardo Carvalho, Duff (Crespo 75), Lampard, Drogba (Huth 90), Essien, Robben (Wright-Phillips 65).

Wednesday, 19 October 2005

Anderlecht (0) 0

Liverpool (1) 1 *(Cisse 20)* 25,000

Anderlecht: Proto; Deschacht (Akin 75), Tihinen (Traore 50), De Man, Vanden Borre, Goor, Vanderhaeghe (Baseggio 61), Wilhelmsson, Zetterberg, Mpenza, Jestrovic.
Liverpool: Reina; Josemi, Traore, Hamann, Carragher, Hyypia, Sissoko (Zenden 82), Xabi Alonso, Cisse (Kewell 74), Luis Garcia, Riise (Warnock 88).

Chelsea (2) 4 *(Drogba 24, Ricardo Carvalho 44, Cole J 59, Crespo 64)*

Betis (0) 0 36,457

Chelsea: Cudicini; Ricardo Carvalho, Del Horno, Makelele (Diarra 76), Terry, Gallas, Wright-Phillips (Gujohnsen 66), Lampard, Drogba (Crespo 46), Essien, Cole J.
Betis: Doblas; Melli, Juanito, Rivas, Oscar Lopez (Xisco 46), Varela, Miguel Angel (Assuncao 56), Rivera, Edu, Oliveira, Joaquin.

Tuesday, 1 November 2005

Betis (1) 1 *(Dani 28)*

Chelsea (0) 0 55,000

Betis: Contreras; Varela, Juanito, Nano (Castellini 20), Melli, Joaquin, Rivera, Arzu, Edu, Capi (Fernando 84), Oliveira (Dani 25).
Chelsea: Cech; Paulo Ferreira, Gallas, Makelele, Terry, Ricardo Carvalho, Cole J (Wright-Phillips 42), Lampard, Gudjohnsen (Drogba 46), Essien, Robben (Duff 65).

Liverpool (1) 3 *(Morientes 34, Luis Garcia 61, Cisse 89)*

Anderlecht (0) 0 42,607

Liverpool: Reina; Finnan, Riise, Xabi Alonso, Carragher, Hyypia, Sissoko, Gerrard (Kewell 78), Crouch (Cisse 72), Morientes (Zenden 52), Luis Garcia.
Anderlecht: Proto; Zewlakow, Juhasz, Tihinen, Wilhelmsson, Vanderhaeghe (Pujol 70), De Man, Goor, Akin (Jestrovic■ 70), Zetterberg, Mpenza (Baseggio 82).

Wednesday, 23 November 2005

Anderlecht (0) 0

Chelsea (2) 2 *(Crespo 8, Ricardo Carvalho 15)* 21,845

Anderlecht: Proto; Deschacht, Tihinen, Kompany, Zewlakow, Goor, Vanderhaeghe (Iachtchouk 46), Vanden Borre, Akin (Ehret 74), Mpenza (Zetterberg 60), Wilhelmsson.
Chelsea: Cech; Del Horno, Gallas, Essien, Terry, Ricardo Carvalho, Duff, Lampard, Crespo (Cole C 86), Gudjohnsen (Geremi 77), Cole J (Diarra 63).

Liverpool (0) 0

Betis (0) 0 42,077

Liverpool: Reina; Finnan, Riise, Hamann, Carragher, Hyypia, Sissoko, Gerrard (Potter 90), Crouch (Kewell 83), Morientes (Cisse 66), Zenden.
Betis: Doblas; Melli, Juanito, Rivas, Oscar Lopez, Joaquin, Assuncao (Capi 69), Rivera, Arzu, Xisco, Fernando (Israel 78).

Tuesday, 6 December 2005

Betis (0) 0

Anderlecht (1) 1 *(Kompany 44)* 55,259

Betis: Doblas; Lembo, Rivas, Castellini, Rivera, Juandi (Assuncao 71), Juanlu (Xisco 46), Capi, Israel (Joaquin 46), Oscar Lopez, Fernando.
Anderlecht: Zitka; Juhasz, Kompany, Tiote (Zetterberg 84), Deschacht, Lovre (Tihinen 69), Delorge, Goor, Baseggio (Zewlakow 69), Pujol, Iachtchouk.

Chelsea (0) 0

Liverpool (0) 0 41,598

Chelsea: Cech; Paulo Ferreira (Del Horno 46), Gallas, Essien, Terry, Ricardo Carvalho, Duff (Wright-Phillips 73), Lampard, Drogba, Gudjohnsen, Robben (Cole C 73).
Liverpool: Reina; Finnan, Traore, Hamann, Carragher, Hyypia, Sissoko, Gerrard, Crouch (Morientes 68), Luis Garcia (Sinama-Pongolle 80), Riise (Kewell 60).

Group G Final Table	P	W	D	L	F	A	Pts
Liverpool	6	3	3	0	6	1	12
Chelsea	6	3	2	1	7	1	11
Betis	6	2	1	3	3	7	7
Anderlecht	6	1	0	5	1	8	3

GROUP H

Tuesday, 13 September 2005

Artmedia (0) 0

Internazionale (1) 1 *(Cruz 17)* 27,000

Artmedia: Cobej; Urbanek (Konecny 73), Durica, Debnar, Petras, Fodrek, Stano (Gomez 62), Kozak, Vascak, Halenar, Hartig.
Internazionale: Julio Cesar; Wome, Materazzi, Samuel, Cordoba, Stankovic, Veron■, Zanetti C, Figo (Martins 80), Cruz (Pizarro 65), Adriano.

Rangers (1) 3 *(Lovenkrands 35, Prso 59, Kyrgiakos 85)*

Porto (0) 2 *(Pepe 47, 71)* 48,599

Rangers: Waterreus; Ricksen, Rodriguez, Kyrgiakos, Bernard, Namouchi (Novo 72), Ferguson, Murray, Lovenkrands (Buffel 56), Prso, Jeffers (Thompson 84).
Porto: Vitor Baia; Pepe, Ricardo Costa, Pedro Emanuel (Sonkaya 41), Cesar Peixoto, Lucho Gonzalez, Diego (Quaresma 64), Ibson, Alan (Hugo Almeida 64), Sokota, Jorginho.

Wednesday, 28 September 2005

Internazionale (0) 1 *(Pizarro 49)*

Rangers (0) 0

Internazionale: Julio Cesar; Cordoba, Samuel, Materazzi, Wome, Figo (Ze Maria 75), Pizarro, Cambiasso, Solari (Gonzalez 84), Martins (Recoba 60), Cruz.
Rangers: Waterreus; Ricksen, Bernard, Ferguson, Rodriguez, Kyrgiakos, Namouchi (Thompson 89), Murray (Nieto 84), Prso, Buffel (Jeffers 78), Lovenkrands.
Behind closed doors.

Porto (2) 2 *(Gonzalez 32, Diego 39)*

Artmedia (1) 3 *(Petras 45, Kozak 54, Borbely 74)* 35,000

Porto: Vitor Baia; Bosingwa, Ricardo Costa (Alan 76), Bruno Alves, Cesar Peixoto, Ibson, Diego (Hugo Almeida 76), Gonzalez, Quaresma, McCarthy, Jorginho.
Artmedia: Cobej; Burak (Halenar 46), Borbely, Durica, Urbanek, Vascak, Debnar, Kozak, Fodrek, Petras (Stano 79), Hartig (Obzera 84).

Wednesday, 19 October 2005

Porto (2) 2 *(Materazzi 22 (og), McCarthy 35)*

Internazionale (0) 0 25,500

Porto: Vitor Baia; Bosingwa, Pedro Emanuel, Pepe, Cech, Lucho Gonzalez, Jorginho (Ibson 90), Paulo Assuncao, Quaresma (Ivanildo 82), McCarthy (Alan 60), Hugo Almeida.
Internazionale: Julio Cesar; Cordoba, Samuel, Materazzi, Favalli, Figo (Ze Maria 82), Pizarro (Recoba 53), Veron, Cambiasso, Solari (Adriano 67), Cruz.

Rangers (0) 0

Artmedia (0) 0 49,018

Rangers: Waterreus; Ricksen, Rodriguez, Kyrgiakos (Andrews 58), Bernard, Namouchi (Burke 75), Ferguson, Hemdani, Lovenkrands, Nieto (Thompson 37), Prso.
Artmedia: Cobej; Petras, Debnar, Durica, Urbanek, Vascak (Obzera 68), Kozak, Borbely, Fodrek, Halenar (Tchur 73), Hartig (Stano 83).

Tuesday, 1 November 2005

Artmedia (1) 2 *(Borbely 8, Kozak 59)*

Rangers (2) 2 *(Prso 3, Thompson 44)* 6527

Artmedia: Cobej; Petras, Debnar, Durica, Urbanek, Vascak (Tchur 83), Kozak, Borbely, Fodrek, Obzera (Stano 87), Hartig (Halenar 73).
Rangers: Waterreus; Hutton, Bernard (Murray 90), Ferguson, Kyrgiakos, Rodriguez, Ricksen, Hemdani, Prso, Thompson (Jeffers 70), Lovenkrands.

Internazionale (0) 2 *(Cruz 75 (pen), 82)*

Porto (1) 1 *(Hugo Almeida 16)*

Internazionale: Julio Cesar; Burdisso, Materazzi, Samuel (Mihajlovic 66), Favalli, Figo, Pizarro, Veron, Wome (Cambiasso 54), Adriano (Cruz 61), Martins.
Porto: Vitor Baia; Bosingwa, Pedro Emanuel, Pepe, Cech, Lucho Gonzalez, Paulo Assuncao (Bruno Alves 61), Jorginho, Quaresma, Alan (Raul Meireles 46), Hugo Almeida (McCarthy 76).
Behind closed doors.

Wednesday, 23 November 2005

Internazionale (2) 4 *(Figo 28, Adriano 41, 59, 74)*

Artmedia (0) 0

Internazionale: Julio Cesar; Zanetti J, Cordoba (Zanetti C 67), Samuel, Wome, Figo (Burdisso 47), Cambiasso, Veron (Stankovic 60), Solari, Adriano, Recoba.
Artmedia: Cobej; Petras, Debnar, Durica, Urbanek (Stano 78), Vascak (Mikulic 68), Kozak (Tchur 68), Borbely, Fodrek, Obzera, Halenar.
Behind closed doors.

Porto (0) 1 *(Lisandro Lopez 60)*

Rangers (0) 1 *(McCormack 83)* 39,439

Porto: Vitor Baia; Cesar Peixoto, Pepe, Pedro Emanuel (Hugo Almeida 46), Bosingwa, Diego (Bruno Alves 64), Paulo Assuncao, Lucho Gonzalez, Quaresma, Lisandro Lopez, Jorginho.
Rangers: Waterreus; Murray, Ricksen, Ferguson, Andrews, Kyrgiakos, Lovenkrands (Burke 78), Hemdani, Jeffers (McCormack 76), Namouchi, Rae (Thompson 62).

Tuesday, 6 December 2005

Artmedia (0) 0

Porto (0) 0 9542

Artmedia: Cobej; Petras, Debnar, Durica, Urbanek, Stano, Obzera (Halenar 87), Kozak, Borbely, Fodrek, Hartig (Vascak 61).
Porto: Vitor Baia; Ricardo Costa, Pepe, Pedro Emanuel (Bosingwa 58), Cesar Peixoto, Paulo Assuncao, Lucho Gonzalez, Diego (Hugo Almeida 46), Quaresma (Jorginho 62), Lisandro Lopez, McCarthy.

Rangers (1) 1 *(Lovenkrands 38)*

Internazionale (1) 1 *(Adriano 30)* 49,170

Rangers: Waterreus; Ricksen, Andrews, Kyrgiakos, Murray, Burke, Ferguson, Malcolm, Namouchi, Buffel, Lovenkrands.
Internazionale: Toldo; Andreolli (Zanetti J 70), Mihajlovic, Materazzi (Momente 41), Burdisso, Solari, Zanetti C■, Pizarro, Wome, Adriano (Maa Boumsong 81), Martins.

Group H Final Table	P	W	D	L	F	A	Pts
Internazionale	6	4	1	1	9	4	13
Rangers	6	1	4	1	7	7	7
Artmedia	6	1	3	2	5	9	6
Porto	6	1	2	3	8	9	5

KNOCK-OUT STAGE

KNOCK-OUT ROUND FIRST LEG

Tuesday, 21 February 2006

Bayern Munich (1) 1 *(Ballack 23)*
AC Milan (0) 1 *(Shevchenko 57 (pen))* 66,000
Bayern Munich: Rensing; Sagnol, Lucio, Ismael, Lahm, Demichelis, Salihamidzic (Karimi 58), Ze Roberto (Scholl 77), Ballack, Pizarro, Makaay (Guerrero 79).
AC Milan: Dida (Kalac 69); Stam, Nesta, Kaladze, Serginho, Gattuso (Vogel 85), Pirlo, Seedorf (Jankulovski 90), Kaka, Shevchenko, Gilardino.

Benfica (0) 1 *(Luisao 84)*
Liverpool (0) 0 65,000
Benfica: Moretto; Alcides, Luisao, Anderson, Leo (Ricardo Rocha 87), Robert (Nelson 76), Petit, Beto (Karagounis 58), Manuel, Simao Sabrosa, Nuno Gomes.
Liverpool: Reina; Finnan, Riise, Xabi Alonso, Carragher, Hyypia, Sissoko (Hamann 35), Luis Garcia, Fowler (Cisse), Morientes (Gerrard 78), Kewell.

PSV Eindhoven (0) 0
Lyon (0) 1 *(Juninho Pernambucano 65)* 29,400
PSV Eindhoven: Gomes; Reiziger, Ooijer, Alex, Lamey, Simons, Cocu, Afellay (Kone 73), Farfan, Vennegoor of Hesselink, Culina (Aissati 54).
Lyon: Coupet; Clerc, Cris (Wiltord 46), Muller, Abidal, Tiago, Diarra, Juninho Pernambucano, Govou■, Carew (Fred 63), Malouda.

Real Madrid (0) 0
Arsenal (0) 1 *(Henry 47)* 80,354
Real Madrid: Casillas; Cicinho, Sergio Ramos, Woodgate (Mejia 9), Roberto Carlos, Gravesen (Julio Baptista 76), Beckham, Guti, Zidane, Robinho (Raul 63), Ronaldo.
Arsenal: Lehmann; Eboue, Flamini, Silva, Toure, Senderos, Ljungberg, Fabregas (Song Billong 90), Reyes (Diaby 80), Henry, Hleb (Pires 76).

Wednesday, 22 February 2006

Ajax (2) 2 *(Huntelaar 16, Rosales 20)*
Internazionale (0) 2 *(Stankovic 49, Cruz 86)* 46,663
Ajax: Stekelenburg; Trabelsi, Heitinga, Vermaelen, Emanuelson, Maduro, Lindenbergh, Boukhari, Rosales (Babel 89), Rosenberg, Huntelaar.
Internazionale: Toldo; Zanetti J, Cordoba, Samuel, Burdisso, Figo, Cambiasso, Stankovic, Cesar (Pizarro 46), Cruz, Adriano (Martins 65).

Chelsea (0) 1 *(Motta 59 (og))*
Barcelona (0) 2 *(Terry 71 (og), Eto'o 80)* 39,521
Chelsea: Cech; Paulo Ferreira, Del Horno■, Makelele, Terry, Ricardo Carvalho, Cole J (Geremi 40), Lampard, Crespo (Drogba 46), Gudjohnsen, Robben (Wright-Phillips 78).
Barcelona: Valdes; Oleguer, Marquez, Puyol, Van Bronckhorst (Sylvinho 69), Messi, Deco (Iniesta 84), Edmilson, Motta (Larsson 65), Eto'o, Ronaldinho.

Rangers (1) 2 *(Lovenkrands 22, Pena 82 (og))*
Villarreal (2) 2 *(Riquelme 8 (pen), Forlan 35)* 49,372
Rangers: Waterreus; Hutton, Rodriguez, Kyrgiakos, Smith, Burke, Hemdani, Ferguson, Namouchi (Buffel 69), Prso (Boyd 89), Lovenkrands (Novo 75).
Villarreal: Viera; Javi Venta, Pena, Gonzalo Rodriguez, Arruabarrena (Sorin 61), Marcos Senna, Josico, Riquelme (Arzo 90), Tacchinardi, Forlan, Jose Mari (Roger 84).

Werder Bremen (1) 3 *(Schulz 39, Borowski 87, Micoud 90)*
Juventus (0) 2 *(Nedved 74, Trezeguet 82)* 36,500
Werder Bremen: Wiese; Owomoyela, Fahrenhorst, Naldo, Schulz, Frings, Baumann, Borowski, Micoud, Klose (Valdez 68), Klasnic.
Juventus: Buffon; Blasi, Thuram, Cannavaro, Balzaretti, Camoranesi (Zalayeta 76), Emerson, Vieira, Nedved, Trezeguet, Ibrahimovic (Del Piero 59).

KNOCK-OUT ROUND SECOND LEG

Tuesday, 7 March 2006

Barcelona (0) 1 *(Ronaldinho 78)*
Chelsea (0) 1 *(Lampard 90 (pen))* 98,436
Barcelona: Valdes; Oleguer, Puyol, Marquez, Van Bronckhorst, Deco, Edmilson, Motta, Messi (Larsson 25), Ronaldinho, Eto'o.
Chelsea: Cech; Paulo Ferreira, Gallas, Makelele, Terry, Ricardo Carvalho, Duff (Gudjohnsen 58), Lampard, Drogba (Crespo 58), Cole J (Huth 83), Robben.

Juventus (0) 2 *(Trezeguet 65, Emerson 88)*
Werder Bremen (1) 1 *(Micoud 13)* 40,226
Juventus: Buffon; Zebina, Thuram, Cannavaro, Zambrotta (Balzaretti 70), Camoranesi (Mutu 57), Emerson, Vieira, Nedved, Ibrahimovic (Del Piero 57), Trezeguet.
Werder Bremen: Wiese; Owomoyela, Naldo, Fahrenhorst, Schulz, Frings, Baumann (Pasanen 73), Micoud, Borowski, Klose, Klasnic (Valdez 81).

Villarreal (0) 1 *(Arruabarrena 49)*
Rangers (1) 1 *(Lovenkrands 12)* 23,000
Villarreal: Viera; Javi Venta (Hector Font 46), Gonzalo Rodriguez, Pena, Arruabarrena, Marcos Senna, Tacchinardi, Josico, Riquelme (Calleja 85), Forlan, Jose Mari (Franco 46).
Rangers: Waterreus; Hutton, Murray, Ferguson, Rodriguez, Kyrgiakos, Burke (Novo 87), Hemdani, Namouchi, Buffel (Boyd 64), Lovenkrands.

Wednesday, 8 March 2006

AC Milan (2) 4 *(Inzaghi 8, 47, Shevchenko 25, Kaka 59)*
Bayern Munich (1) 1 *(Ismael 36)* 71,032
AC Milan: Dida; Stam, Kaladze, Nesta, Serginho, Pirlo, Vogel, Seedorf, Kaka (Rui Costa 86), Shevchenko (Ambrosini 76), Inzaghi (Gilardino 71).
Bayern Munich: Kahn; Sagnol, Ismael, Lucio, Lizarazu (Ze Roberto 52), Demichelis, Deisler (Scholl 63), Schweinsteiger, Ballack, Pizarro, Makaay (Guerrero 46).

Arsenal (0) 0
Real Madrid (0) 0 35,487
Arsenal: Lehmann; Eboue, Flamini, Silva, Toure, Senderos, Reyes (Pires 68), Fabregas, Ljungberg, Henry, Hleb (Bergkamp 86).
Real Madrid: Casillas; Michel Salgado (Robinho 84), Sergio Ramos, Raul Bravo, Roberto Carlos, Beckham, Guti, Gravesen (Julio Baptista 67), Zidane, Raul (Cassano 73), Ronaldo.

Liverpool (0) 0
Benfica (1) 2 *(Simao Sabrosa 36, Miccoli 89)* 42,745
Liverpool: Reina; Finnan, Warnock (Hamman 70), Xabi Alonso, Carragher, Traore, Luis Garcia, Gerrard, Crouch, Morientes (Fowler 70), Kewell (Cisse 63).
Benfica: Moretto; Alcides, Luisao, Anderson, Leo, Robert (Ricardo Rocha 70), Beto, Manuel, Geovanni (Karagounis 60), Simao Sabrosa, Nuno Gomes (Miccoli 76).

Lyon (2) 4 *(Tiago 26, 45, Wiltord 71, Fred 90)*
PSV Eindhoven (0) 0 37,901
Lyon: Coupet; Clerc, Cris, Muller, Abidal, Tiago (Clement 80), Diarra, Juninho Pernambucano (Pedretti 76), Wiltord, Carew (Fred 66), Malouda.
PSV Eindhoven: Gomes; Lucius, Addo, Alex (Aissati 76), Reiziger, Simons, Afellay, Cocu■, Culina (Vayrynen 57), Kone, Farfan (Beasley 57).

Tuesday, 14 March 2006

Internazionale (0) 1 *(Stankovic 57)*
Ajax (0) 0 48,845
Internazionale: Toldo; Zanetti J, Materazzi, Samuel, Wome, Figo, Veron (Zanetti C 74), Cambiasso, Stankovic, Adriano, Martins (Recoba 83).

Ajax: Stekelenburg; Trabelsi, Maduro, Vermaelen, Juanfran, Pienaar, Lindenbergh, Boukhari, Rosales (Babel 71), Huntelaar, Rosenberg (Charisteas 74).

QUARTER-FINALS FIRST LEG

Tuesday, 28 March 2006

Arsenal (1) 2 *(Fabregas 40, Henry 69)*
Juventus (0) 0 35,472
Arsenal: Lehmann; Eboue, Flamini, Silva, Toure, Senderos, Hleb, Fabregas, Reyes (Van Persie 82), Henry, Pires.
Juventus: Buffon; Zebina■, Thuram, Cannavaro, Zambrotta, Camoranesi■, Vieira, Emerson, Mutu (Chiellini 71), Ibrahimovic, Trezeguet (Zalayeta 79).

Benfica (0) 0
Barcelona (0) 0 63,000
Benfica: Moretto; Ricardo Rocha, Luisao, Anderson, Leo, Beto, Petit, Manuel, Simao Sabrosa, Robert (Miccoli 46), Geovanni (Karagounis 68).
Barcelona: Valdes; Belletti, Oleguer, Motta, Van Bronckhorst, Deco (Gabri 76), Van Bommel, Iniesta, Larsson (Giuly 76), Ronaldinho, Eto'o.

Wednesday, 29 March 2006

Internazionale (1) 2 *(Adriano 7, Martins 54)*
Villarreal (1) 1 *(Forlan 1)* 49,153
Internazionale: Toldo; Zanetti J, Cordoba, Samuel, Wome, Stankovic (Kily Gonzalez 82), Veron, Cambiasso, Cesar (Materazzi 69), Recoba (Martins 28), Adriano.
Villarreal: Viera; Javi Venta, Gonzalo Rodriguez, Pena, Sorin, Riquelme, Arzo (Quique Alvarez 60), Marcos Senna, Calleja (Santi Cazorla 87), Jose Mari (Franco 76), Forlan.

Lyon (0) 0
AC Milan (0) 0 39,016
Lyon: Coupet; Clerc, Cris, Cacapa, Abidal, Tiago, Diarra, Pedretti (Clement 68), Wiltord, Carew (Fred 63), Malouda.
AC Milan: Dida; Costacurta (Maldini 62), Nesta, Kaladze, Serginho, Gattuso, Pirlo (Vogel 85), Seedorf, Kaka, Gilardino (Inzaghi 62), Shevchenko.

QUARTER-FINALS SECOND LEG

Tuesday, 4 April 2006

AC Milan (1) 3 *(Inzaghi 25, 88, Shevchenko 90)*
Lyon (1) 1 *(Diarra 31)* 78,894
AC Milan: Dida; Stam (Costacurta 24), Nesta, Kaladze, Serginho, Pirlo (Ambrosini 71), Gattuso (Maldini 78), Seedorf, Kaka, Inzaghi, Shevchenko.
Lyon: Coupet; Clerc, Cris, Cacapa, Abidal, Juninho Pernambucano, Diarra, Malouda, Wiltord, Fred (Carew 71), Govou (Reveillere 83).

Villarreal (0) 1 *(Arruabarrena 58)*
Internazionale (0) 0 22,800
Villarreal: Viera; Javi Venta, Quique Alvarez, Pena, Arruabarrena, Marcos Senna, Tacchinardi, Sorin (Josico 78), Riquelme, Forlan (Calleja 90), Jose Mari (Franco 78).
Internazionale: Toldo; Cordoba, Materazzi, Samuel, Zanetti J, Figo (Mihajlovic 75), Cambiasso, Veron (Cruz 89), Stankovic, Recoba (Martins 56), Adriano.

Wednesday, 5 April 2006

Barcelona (1) 2 *(Ronaldinho 19, Eto'o 88)*
Benfica (0) 0 89,875
Barcelona: Valdes; Van Bronckhorst, Oleguer, Puyol, Belletti, Deco, Iniesta, Van Bommel (Edmilson 84), Ronaldinho, Eto'o, Larsson (Giuly 86).
Benfica: Moretto; Ricardo Rocha, Luisao, Anderson, Leo, Beto (Robert 72), Petit, Manuel (Marcel 82), Geovanni (Karagounis 55), Miccoli, Simao Sabrosa.

Juventus (0) 0
Arsenal (0) 0 46,031
Juventus: Buffon; Zambrotta, Kovac, Cannavaro, Chiellini (Balzaretti 66), Mutu (Zalayeta 61), Emerson, Giannichedda, Nedved■, Trezeguet, Ibrahimovic.
Arsenal: Lehmann; Eboue, Flamini, Silva, Toure, Senderos, Hleb (Diaby 87), Fabregas, Reyes (Pires 62), Henry, Ljungberg.

SEMI-FINALS FIRST LEG

Tuesday, 18 April 2006

AC Milan (0) 0
Barcelona (0) 1 *(Giuly 57)* 76,883
AC Milan: Dida; Stam (Cafu 77), Kaladze, Nesta, Serginho, Gattuso (Ambrosini 73), Pirlo (Maldini 67), Seedorf, Kaka, Shevchenko, Gilardino.
Barcelona: Valdes; Oleguer (Motta 75), Puyol, Marquez, Van Bronckhorst, Edmilson, Van Bommel, Iniesta, Giuly (Belletti 70), Ronaldinho, Eto'o (Maxi Lopez 89).

Wednesday, 19 April 2006

Arsenal (1) 1 *(Toure 41)*
Villarreal (0) 0 35,438
Arsenal: Lehmann; Eboue, Flamini, Silva, Toure, Senderos, Hleb (Bergkamp 80), Fabregas, Ljungberg (Van Persie 80), Henry, Pires.
Villarreal: Barbosa; Javi Venta, Quique Alvarez, Arzo, Arruabarrena, Marcos Senna, Tacchinardi, Sorin (Josico 72), Riquelme, Jose Mari (Franco 55), Forlan (Calleja 90).

SEMI-FINALS SECOND LEG

Tuesday, 25 April 2006

Villarreal (0) 0
Arsenal (0) 0 22,000
Villarreal: Barbosa; Javi Venta, Pena, Quique Alvarez, Arruabarrena (Roger 82), Riquelme, Josico (Jose Mari 63), Marcos Senna, Sorin, Forlan, Franco.
Arsenal: Lehmann; Eboue, Flamini (Clichy 9), Silva, Toure, Campbell, Hleb, Fabregas, Reyes (Pires 69), Henry, Ljungberg.

Wednesday, 26 April 2006

Barcelona (0) 0
AC Milan (0) 0 95,661
Barcelona: Valdes; Belletti, Marquez, Puyol, Van Bronckhorst, Iniesta, Edmilson, Deco, Giuly (Larsson 68), Eto'o (Van Bommel 89), Ronaldinho.
AC Milan: Dida; Stam, Costacurta (Cafu 64), Kaladze, Serginho, Gattuso (Rui Costa 68), Pirlo, Seedorf, Shevchenko, Kaka, Inzaghi (Gilardino 80).

UEFA CHAMPIONS LEAGUE FINAL 2006

Wednesday, 17 May 2006

Barcelona (0) 2 *(Eto'o 76, Belletti 81)* **Arsenal (1) 1** *(Campbell 37)*

(at Stade de France, Paris, 79,500)

Barcelona: Valdes; Oleguer (Belletti 71), Van Bronckhorst, Marquez, Puyol, Edmilson (Iniesta 46), Giuly, Deco, Eto'o, Ronaldinho, Van Bommel (Larsson 61).

Arsenal: Lehmann■; Eboue, Cole, Silva, Toure, Campbell, Hleb (Reyes 85), Fabregas (Flamini 74), Henry, Ljungberg, Pires (Almunia 18).

Referee: T. Hauge (Norway).

Juliano Belletti (right) scoring the winning goal past Manuel Alumnia for Barcelona against Arsenal in the Champions League Cup Final. (Christophe Ena/AP/EMPICS)

UEFA CHAMPIONS LEAGUE 2006–07

(Early results)

FIRST QUALIFYING ROUND, FIRST LEG

Sioni	2	Baku	0
Elbasan	1	Ekranas	0
Pyunik	0	Sheriff	0
Dudelange	0	Rabotnicki	1
Birkirkara	0	B36	3
Linfield	1	Gorica	3
TVMK	2	Hafnarfjördur	3
Metalurgs	1	Aktobe	0
Cork	1	Apollon	0
MyPa	1	TNS	0
Shakhtyor	0	Široki Brijeg	1

EUROPEAN CUP-WINNERS' CUP FINALS 1961–99

Year	Winners	Runners-up	Venue	Attendance	Referee
1961	Fiorentina 2	Rangers 0 *(1st Leg)*	Glasgow	80,000	Steiner (A)
	Fiorentina 2	Rangers 1 *(2nd Leg)*	Florence	50,000	Hernadi (H)
1962	Atletico Madrid 1	Fiorentina 1	Glasgow	27,389	Wharton (S)
Replay	Atletico Madrid 3	Fiorentina 0	Stuttgart	38,000	Tschenscher (WG)
1963	Tottenham Hotspur 5	Atletico Madrid 1	Rotterdam	49,000	Van Leuwen (Ho)
1964	Sporting Lisbon 3	MTK Budapest 3 *(aet)*	Brussels	3000	Van Nuffel (Bel)
Replay	Sporting Lisbon 1	MTK Budapest 0	Antwerp	19,000	Versyp (Bel)
1965	West Ham U 2	Munich 1860 0	Wembley	100,000	Szolt (H)
1966	Borussia Dortmund 2	Liverpool 1 *(aet)*	Glasgow	41,657	Schwinte (F)
1967	Bayern Munich 1	Rangers 0 *(aet)*	Nuremberg	69,480	Lo Bello (I)
1968	AC Milan 2	Hamburg 0	Rotterdam	53,000	Ortiz (Sp)
1969	Slovan Bratislava 3	Barcelona 2	Basle	19,000	Van Ravens (Ho)
1970	Manchester C 2	Gornik Zabrze 1	Vienna	8,000	Schiller (A)
1971	Chelsea 1	Real Madrid 1 *(aet)*	Athens	42,000	Scheurer (Sw)
Replay	Chelsea 2	Real Madrid 1 *(aet)*	Athens	35,000	Bucheli (Sw)
1972	Rangers 3	Moscow Dynamo 2	Barcelona	24,000	Ortiz (Sp)
1973	AC Milan 1	Leeds U 0	Salonika	45,000	Mihas (Gr)
1974	Magdeburg 2	AC Milan 0	Rotterdam	4000	Van Gemert (Ho)
1975	Dynamo Kiev 3	Ferencvaros 0	Basle	13,000	Davidson (S)
1976	Anderlecht 4	West Ham U 2	Brussels	58,000	Wurtz (F)
1977	Hamburg 2	Anderlecht 0	Amsterdam	65,000	Partridge (E)
1978	Anderlecht 4	Austria/WAC 0	Paris	48,679	Adlinger (WG)
1979	Barcelona 4	Fortuna Dusseldorf 3 *(aet)*	Basle	58,000	Palotai (H)
1980	Valencia 0	Arsenal 0	Brussels	36,000	Christov (Cz)
	(aet; Valencia won 5-4 on penalties)				
1981	Dynamo Tbilisi 2	Carl Zeiss Jena 1	Dusseldorf	9000	Lattanzi (I)
1982	Barcelona 2	Standard Liege 1	Barcelona	100,000	Eschweiler (WG)
1983	Aberdeen 2	Real Madrid 1 *(aet)*	Gothenburg	17,804	Menegali (I)
1984	Juventus 2	Porto 1	Basle	60,000	Prokop (EG)
1985	Everton 3	Rapid Vienna 1	Rotterdam	50,000	Casarin (I)
1986	Dynamo Kiev 3	Atletico Madrid 0	Lyon	39,300	Wohrer (A)
1987	Ajax 1	Lokomotiv Leipzig 0	Athens	35,000	Agnolin (I)
1988	Mechelen 1	Ajax 0	Strasbourg	39,446	Pauly (WG)
1989	Barcelona 2	Sampdoria 0	Berne	45,000	Courtney (E)
1990	Sampdoria 2	Anderlecht 0	Gothenburg	20,103	Galler (Sw)
1991	Manchester U 2	Barcelona 1	Rotterdam	42,000	Karlsson (Se)
1992	Werder Bremen 2	Monaco 0	Lisbon	16,000	D'Elia (I)
1993	Parma 3	Antwerp 1	Wembley	37,393	Assenmacher (G)
1994	Arsenal 1	Parma 0	Copenhagen	33,765	Krondl (CzR)
1995	Zaragoza 2	Arsenal 1	Paris	42,424	Ceccarini (I)
1996	Paris St Germain 1	Rapid Vienna 0	Brussels	37,500	Pairetto (I)
1997	Barcelona 1	Paris St Germain 0	Rotterdam	45,000	Merk (G)
1998	Chelsea 1	Stuttgart 0	Stockholm	30,216	Braschi (I)
1999	Lazio 2	Mallorca 1	Villa Park	33,021	Benko (A)

INTER-CITIES FAIRS CUP FINALS 1958–71

(Winners in italics)

Year	First Leg	Attendance	Second Leg	Attendance
1958	London 2 Barcelona 2	45,466	*Barcelona* 6 London 0	62,000
1960	Birmingham C 0 Barcelona 0	40,500	*Barcelona* 4 Birmingham C 1	70,000
1961	Birmingham C 2 Roma 2	21,005	*Roma* 2 Birmingham C 0	60,000
1962	Valencia 6 Barcelona 2	65,000	Barcelona 1 *Valencia* 1	60,000
1963	Dynamo Zagreb 1 Valencia 2	40,000	*Valencia* 2 Dynamo Zagreb 0	55,000
1964	*Zaragoza* 2 Valencia 1	50,000	(in Barcelona)	
1965	*Ferencvaros* 1 Juventus 0	25,000	(in Turin)	
1966	Barcelona 0 Zaragoza 1	70,000	Zaragoza 2 *Barcelona* 4	70,000
1967	Dynamo Zagreb 2 Leeds U 0	40,000	Leeds U 0 *Dynamo Zagreb* 0	35,604
1968	Leeds U 1 Ferencvaros 0	25,368	Ferencvaros 0 *Leeds U* 0	70,000
1969	Newcastle U 3 Ujpest Dozsa 0	60,000	Ujpest Dozsa 2 *Newcastle U* 3	37,000
1970	Anderlecht 3 Arsenal 1	37,000	*Arsenal* 3 Anderlecht 0	51,612
1971	Juventus 0 Leeds U 0 *(abandoned 51 minutes)*	42,000		
	Juventus 2 Leeds U 2	42,000	*Leeds U* 1* Juventus 1	42,483

UEFA CUP FINALS 1972–97

(Winners in italics)

Year	First Leg	Attendance	Second Leg	Attendance
1972	Wolverhampton W 1 Tottenham H 2	45,000	*Tottenham H* 1 Wolverhampton W 1	48,000
1973	Liverpool 0 Moenchengladbach 0 *(abandoned 27 minutes)*	44,967		
	Liverpool 3 Moenchengladbach 0	41,169	Moenchengladbach 2 *Liverpool* 0	35,000
1974	Tottenham H 2 Feyenoord 2	46,281	*Feyenoord* 2 Tottenham H 0	68,000
1975	Moenchengladbach 0 Twente 0	45,000	Twente 1 *Moenchengladbach* 5	24,500
1976	Liverpool 3 FC Brugge 2	56,000	FC Brugge 1 *Liverpool* 1	32,000
1977	Juventus 1 Athletic Bilbao 0	75,000	Athletic Bilbao 2 *Juventus* 1*	43,000
1978	Bastia 0 PSV Eindhoven 0	15,000	*PSV Eindhoven* 3 Bastia 0	27,000
1979	Red Star Belgrade 1 Moenchengladbach 1	87,500	*Moenchengladbach* 1 Red Star Belgrade 0	45,000
1980	Moenchengladbach 3 Eintracht Frankfurt 2	25,000	*Eintracht Frankfurt* 1* Moenchengladbach 0	60,000
1981	Ipswich T 3 AZ 67 Alkmaar 0	27,532	AZ 67 Alkmaar 4 *Ipswich T* 2	28,500
1982	Gothenburg 1 Hamburg 0	42,548	Hamburg 0 *Gothenburg* 3	60,000
1983	Anderlecht 1 Benfica 0	45,000	Benfica 1 *Anderlecht* 1	80,000
1984	Anderlecht 1 Tottenham H 1	40,000	*Tottenham H* 1[1] Anderlecht 1	46,258
1985	Videoton 0 Real Madrid 3	30,000	*Real Madrid* 0 Videoton 1	98,300
1986	Real Madrid 5 Cologne 1	80,000	Cologne 2 *Real Madrid* 0	15,000
1987	Gothenburg 1 Dundee U 0	50,023	Dundee U 1 *Gothenburg* 1	20,911
1988	Espanol 3 Bayer Leverkusen 0	42,000	*Bayer Leverkusen* 3[2] Espanol 0	22,000
1989	Napoli 2 Stuttgart 1	83,000	Stuttgart 3 *Napoli* 3	67,000
1990	Juventus 3 Fiorentina 1	45,000	Fiorentina 0 *Juventus* 0	32,000
1991	Internazionale 2 Roma 0	68,887	Roma 1 *Internazionale* 0	70,901
1992	Torino 2 Ajax 2	65,377	*Ajax* 0* Torino 0	40,000
1993	Borussia Dortmund 1 Juventus 3	37,000	*Juventus* 3 Borussia Dortmund 0	62,781
1994	Salzburg 0 Internazionale 1	47,500	*Internazionale* 1 Salzburg 0	80,326
1995	Parma 1 Juventus 0	23,000	Juventus 1 *Parma* 1	80,750
1996	Bayern Munich 2 Bordeaux 0	62,000	Bordeaux 1 *Bayern Munich* 3	36,000
1997	Schalke 1 Internazionale 0	56,824	Internazionale 1 *Schalke* 0[3]	81,670

**won on away goals* [1]*aet; Tottenham H won 4-3 on penalties* [2]*aet; Bayer Leverkusen won 3-2 on penalties*
[3]*aet; Schalke won 4-1 on penalties*

UEFA CUP FINALS 1998–2006

Year	Winners	Runners-up	Venue	Attendance	Referee
1998	Internazionale 3	Lazio 0	Paris	42,938	Nieto (Sp)
1999	Parma 3	Marseille 0	Moscow	61,000	Dallas (S)
2000	Galatasaray 0 *(aet; Galatasaray won 4-1 on penalties).*	Arsenal 0	Copenhagen	38,919	Nieto (Sp)
2001	Liverpool 5 *(aet; Liverpool won on sudden death).*	Alaves 4	Dortmund	65,000	Veissiere (F)
2002	Feyenoord 3	Borussia Dortmund 2	Rotterdam	45,000	Pereira (P)
2003	Porto 3 *(aet).*	Celtic 2	Seville	52,972	Michel (Slv)
2004	Valencia 2	Marseille 0	Gothenburg	40,000	Collina (I)
2005	CSKA Moscow 3	Sporting Lisbon 1	Lisbon	48,000	Poll (E)
2006	Sevilla 4	Middlesbrough 0	Eindhoven	36,500	Fandel (G)

UEFA CUP 2005–06

▪ *Denotes player sent off.*

FIRST QUALIFYING ROUND, FIRST LEG

Allianssi (2) 3 *(Vajanne 34, Cleaver 41, Poulsen 85)*, Petange (0) 0 1709
Torpedo Kutaisi (0) 0, BATE Borisov (1) 1 *(Baga 27 (pen))* 5500
Banants (0) 2 *(Hakobian 82, Kharabakhtsyan 88)*, Lokomotivi Tbilisi (1) 3 *(Alaverdashvili 40, Kebadze 49, Oniani G 53)* 2000
Baskimi (0) 0, Zepce (0) 0 1500
Birkirkara (0) 0, Apoel (0) 2 *(Georgiou 72, Jovanovic 80)* 1000
Domagnano (0) 0, Domzale (1) 5 *(Stevanovic 14, Zavri 55, Nikezic 63, 86, Kacicnik 84)* 500
Elbasan (1) 1 *(Asllani 38), Vardar (0) 1 (Memeli 61)* 2000
Esbjerg (0) 1 *(Berglund 90)*, Flora (0) 2 *(Sirevicius 57, Sidorenkov 59)* 4223
Etzella (0) 0, Keflavik (1) 4 *(Sveinsson 17, 59, 76, 80)* 1000
Otaci (1) 3 *(Pancovici 12, Matiura 68 (pen), Blajco 89)*, Khazar (1) 1 *(Ramazonov 25)* 3000
Vaduz (0) 2 *(Gohouri 53, De Souza 72)*, Dacia (0) 0 850
Ferencvaros (0) 0, MTZ-RIPO (1) 2 *(Mkhitaryan 37, Tarashchik 89)* 5000
Omonia (1) 3 *(Mguni 30, Kozlej 46, Vakouftsis 84 (pen))*, Hibernians (0) 0 7500
Vestmann (1) 1 *(Sigurdsson P 25)*, B36 (1) 1 *(Gunnarsson 7)* 1000
Teuta (2) 3 *(Mancaku 31, 60, Xhafa 45)*, Siroki (0) 1 *(Abramovic 81)* 2500
Karat (0) 1 *(Sultanov 79)*, Zilina (0) 0 7000
Mainz (2) 4 *(Ruman 8, Auer 36, 67, Noveski 58)*, Mika (0) 0 22,000
Runavik (0) 0, Metalurgs (1) 3 *(Petersen J 23 (og), Karlsong 67, Grebis 77)* 500
VMK (1) 1 *(Teever 32)*, MyPa (0) 1 *(Kuparinen 78)* 1000
Sant Julia (0) 0, Rapid Bucharest (2) 5 *(Niculae 10, 34, 66, Vasilache 59, 77)* 500

Thursday, 14 July 2005

Ekranas (0) 0

Cork City (1) 2 *(O'Donovan 25, O'Callaghan 89)* 4100

Ekranas: Skrupskis; Klimavicius, Paulauskas, Gardzuauskas, Savenas, Banevicius (Saulenas 46), Kavaliauskas, Luksys, Skroblas, Tomkevicius, Galkevicius (Mizigurskis 71).
Cork City: Devine (Harrington 15); Horgan, Murray D, Murphy, O'Halloran, O'Donovan, Bennett, Gamble, Kearney (Woods 90), O'Callaghan, O'Flynn (Behan 89).

Linfield (1) 1 *(Mouncey 5)*

Ventspils (0) 0 2000

Linfield: Mannus; Ervin, McShane, McAreavey (Picking 68), Hunter, O'Kane (Kingsberry 64), Thompson, Mouncey, Larmour, Kearney (Gault 57), Bailie.
Ventspils: Romanovs; Logins, Soleicuks, Nalivaiko (Lukasevics 41), Zavoronkovs, Krohmer, Rekhviashvili, Stukalinas, Bicka, Agofonov (Gruber 33), Slesarcuks (Butriks 87).

Longford Town (1) 2 *(Paisley 35, Ferguson 55)*

Carmarthen (0) 0 2000

Longford Town: O'Brien; Murphy A, Dillon, Martin, Ferguson, Paisley, Kirby, Fitzgerald (Prunty 77), Myler (Baker 86), Keegan, Byrne.
Carmarthen: Pennock; Carter, Lloyd, Giles, Cochlan, Jones (James 90), Aherne-Evans, Kennedy, Dodds, Thomas, Smothers (Hardy 63).

Portadown (0) 1 *(Arkins 90 (pen))*

Viking (0) 2 *(Ostenstad 52 (pen), Kopteff 78)* 675

Portadown: Miskelly; Craig, O'Hara, Clarke, Convery, Kelly, McCann, Boyle (Quinn 85), Hamilton, Arkins, Neill.
Viking: Basso; Dahl, Deila, Hansen, Pereira, Kopteff (Berland 80), Hangeland, Nygaard, Gaarde, Ostenstad (Nhleko 71), Sigurdsson.

Rhyl (1) 2 *(Horan 12, Hunt 79)*

Atlantas (0) 1 *(Zvingilas 77)* 1570

Rhyl: McGuigan; Adamson, Powell M, Horan, Stones, Brewerton, Wilson (Morgan 86), Hunt (Powell G 86), Graves, Limbert, Moran (Thompson 90).
Atlantas: Lekevicius; Deveika, Maciulevicius, Gnedojus▪, Zernys (Zvingilas 46), Bartkus, Laurisas, Ksanavicius (Lapeikis 73), Zukauskas, Trakys, Petreikis.

FIRST QUALIFYING ROUND, SECOND LEG

Apoel (1) 4 *(Kaklamonos 38, 58, Neophytou 52, Georgiou 90)*, Birkirkara (0) 0 2500
B36 (1) 2 *(Morkore 1, Midjord 59)*, Vestmann (1) 1 *(Jeffs▪ 41) Sigurdsson P▪* 500
BATE Borisov (5) 5 *(Molosh 10, Lebedev 21, 26, Rubnenko 38, 43)*, Torpedo Kutaisi (0) 0 5000
Dacia (0) 1 *(Japalav 63)*, Vaduz (0) 0 500
Domzale (1) 3 *(Wilson 20, Nikezic 50, Zeljkovic 80 (pen))*, Domagnano (0) 0 1500
Flora (0) 0, Esbjerg (4) 6 *(Poulsen 15, Christensen 16, Berglund 23, Andreasen 41, Murcy 55, 86)* 1500
Hibernians (0) 0, Omonia (1) 3 *(Grozdanovski 5, 63, Vakouftsis 43 (pen))* 2500
Keflavik (0) 2 *(Sveinsson 76, Kristjansson 84) Antoniusson▪*, Etzella (0) 0 500
Khazar (0) 1 *(Aliyev 72)*, Otaci (2) 2 *(Lichioiu 19, 40)* 2500
Lokomotivi Tbilisi (0) 0, Banants (1) 2 *(Hakobian 22, Khachatryan 81)* 5500
Metalurgs (2) 3 *(Dobrecovs 4, 35, Klava 81)*, Runavik (0) 0 2000
Mika (0) 0, Mainz (0) 0 3000
MTZ-RIPO (0) 1 *(Kontsevoi 48)*, Ferencvaros (1) 2 *(Lipcsei 45, Rosa 90)* 4500
MyPa (0) 1 *(Rimas 57 (og))*, VMK (0) 0 *Neemelo▪* 3500
Petange (0) 1 *(Kefert 55)*, Allianssi (0) 1 *(Poulsen 63)* 500
Rapid Bucharest (4) 5 *(Buga 1, 14, 20, 29, Maldarasanu 80)*, Sant Julia (0) 0 4000
Siroki (2) 3 *(Medvid 33, Erceg 43, Wagner 70)*, Teuta (0) 0 2500
Vardar (0) 0, Elbasan (0) 0 3500
Zepce (0) 1 *(Mesic 80)*, Baskimi (0) 1 *(Gjurcevski 49)* 1500
Zilina (2) 3 *(Straka 7, Cisovsky 37, Labant 87)*, Karat (0) 1 *(Stolcers 70 (pen))* 5128

Thursday, 28 July 2005

Atlantas (1) 3 *(Laurisas 14 (pen), 68, Petreikis 78)*

Rhyl (1) 2 *(Stones 33, Powell G 62)* 1200

Atlantas: Valius; Deveika (Maciulevicius 53), Navikas, Tolis, Ringys (Zvingilas 46), Bartkus, Laurisas, Zernys▪, Zukauskas (Sarunas 59), Ksanavicius, Petreikis.
Rhyl: McGuigan; Adamson, Powell M, Horan, Stones, Brewerton, Morgan (Mutton 46), Powell G, Graves (Connelly 89), Limbert, Moran.

Carmarthen (1) 5 *(Thomas 15, 75, Lloyd 49, 54 (pen), Cotterrall 80)*

Longford Town (1) 1 *(Myler 20 (pen))* 850

Carmarthen: Pennock; Carter, Hardy, Lloyd, Giles, Jones, Evans, Kennedy, Dodds, Thomas (Walters 83), Smothers (Cotterrall 59).
Longford Town: O'Brien; O'Connor, Dillon, Martin, Ferguson, Paisley (Cawley 79), Kirby, Fitzgerald (Murphy A 68), Keegan, Myler (Baker 69), Byrne.

Cork City (0) 0

Ekranes (0) 1 *(Klimavicius 60)* 6000

Cork City: McNulty; Horgan, Bennett, Murray, Murphy, O'Donovan (O'Brien 87), O'Halloran, Gamble, Kearney (Woods 90), O'Callaghan, O'Flynn.
Ekranes: Skrupskis; Klimavicius, Paulauskas, Skroblas, Savenas, Gardzuauskas, Saulenas (Mykolaitis 79), Mizigurskis (Galkevicius 59), Tomkevicius, Kavaliauskas, Luksys.

Viking (0) 1 *(Nhleko 56)*
Portadown (0) 0 4372

Viking: Basso; Dahl, Deila, Hansen (Mambo Mumba 66), Pereira, Kopteff (Sorli 77), Hangeland, Nygaard, Gaarde, Nhleko (Sigurdsson 70), Ostenstad.
Portadown: Miskelly; Convery, Craig (Alderdice 84), Kelly, O'Hara, Clarke, Collins, Arkins, Boyle (Quinn 79), Hamilton, Neill (McCann 74).

Ventspils (1) 2 *(Rekhviashvili 39, Rimkus 90)*
Linfield (1) 1 *(Thompson 8)* 800

Ventspils: Davidovs; Kacanovs, Lukasevics, Soleicuks, Zavoronkovs, Stukalinas, Bicka, Gruber (Rimkus 46), Krohmer, Rekhviashvili (Modebadze 77), Slesarcuks (Butriks 55).
Linfield: Mannus; Ervin, McShane, Kearney, Murphy, O'Kane, Thompson (Larmour 82), Mouncey (Picking 85), Ferguson, Gault, Bailie.

SECOND QUALIFYING ROUND, FIRST LEG

Apoel (0) 1 *(Neophytou 63),* Maccabi Tel Aviv (0) 0 5500
Ashdod (2) 2 *(Rajovic 17, Dika 34),* Domzale (2) 2 *(Stevanovic 2, De Souza 24)* 3000
Banants (2) 2 *(Hakobian 23, 43),* Dnepr (0) 4 *(Ezerski 49, Kornilenko 82, 83, Balabanov 85)* 2000
Baskimi (0) 0, Maccabi Petah Tikva (3) 5 *(Megamadov 6, Tuaama 14, Asaf 22 (pen), Udi 71, Robel 90)* 1750
OFK Belgrade (2) 2 *(Kirovski 32, Ivanovic 39),* Lokomotiv Plovdiv (0) 1 *(Kamburov M■ 55)* 1000
Brann (0) 0 *MacAllister*■, Allianssi (0) 0 2579
Dinamo Bucharest (3) 3 *(Munteanu 15 (pen), Zicu 25, 44),* Omonia (1) 1 *(Konnafis 4) Georgiou*■ 6000
Esbjerg (0) 0, Tromso (1) 1 *(Strand 10)* 3742
Grasshoppers (0) 1 *(Eduardo 68),* Wisla Plock (0) 0 3600
Groclin (0) 4 *(Rocki 46, Wozniak 57 (og), Porazik 68, Oelusarski 83),* Bystrica (0) 1 *(Bazik 73)* 5000
Inter Zapresic (1) 1 *(Pecelj 41),* Red Star Belgrade (1) 3 *(Zigic 21, 51, Pantelic 82)* 2500
Krylia (1) 2 *(Adamu 8, Gusin 75 (pen)),* BATE Borisov (0) 0 26,000
Legia (0) 0 *Surma*■, Zurich (0) 1 *(Rafael 90)* 8000
Litets (0) 1 *(Zhelev 83),* Rijeka (0) 0 3000
Mainz (1) 2 *(Auer 10, Babatz 71),* Keflavik (0) 0 18,000
Matav (0) 0, Metalurg Donetsk (0) 3 *(Shyschenko 52, Oleksiyenko 87, 90)* 2000
Metalurgs (1) 2 *(Kalonas 13, Dobrecovs 82 (pen)),* Genk (0) 3 *(Vandenbergh 48, Daerden 60, Stojanovic 81)* 2500
Midtjylland (1) 2 *(Kristensen 38, 71),* B36 (0) 1 *(Hojsted 77)* 1500
MTZ-RIPO (0) 1 *(Kontsevoy 71),* Teplice (1) 1 *(Rilke 34)* 4000
Otaci (0) 0, Graz (0) 2 *(Schrott 55, Ehmann 57)* 3500
Pasching (1) 2 *(Chaile 33, Wisio 87),* Zenit (1) 2 *(Kerzhakov 16, Arshavin 73)* 4200
Publikum (0) 1 *(Bersnjak 67),* Levski (0) 0 1500
Rapid Bucharest (1) 3 *(Niculae 43, 50, Maldarasanu 67),* Vardar (0) 0 5000
Vaduz (0) 0, Besiktas (1) 1 *(Okan 12)* 2650
Zeta (0) 0, Siroki (0) 1 *(Erceg 90)* 2000
Zilina (1) 1 *(Bartos 40),* FK Austria (0) 2 *(Sebo 89, Linz 90)* 5500

Thursday, 11 August 2005

FC Copenhagen (0) 2 *(Dos Santos 48, Gravgaard 54)*
Carmarthen (0) 0 11,314

FC Copenhagen: Christiansen; Jacobsen, Van Heerden, Svensson, Bergdolmo, Linderoth, Dos Santos (Moller 80), Silberbauer, Ijeh (Saarinen 89), Gravgaard, Allback.
Carmarthen: Pennock; Hardy, Lloyd, Giles, Carter, Jones, Evans, Kennedy (Walters 70), Dodds, Thomas (Cotterall 58), Smothers (Burke 77).

Djurgaarden (0) 1 *(Amoah 80)*
Cork City (1) 1 *(Fenn 8)* 4854

Djurgaarden: Tourray; Concha, Stenman, Quivasto, Arneng, Hysen, Kusi Asare, Sjolund (Amoah 67), Jonson (Ba 46), Johannesson, Barsom (Arnason 71).
Cork City: Devine; Murphy, Bennett, O'Halloran, Horgan, Murray, Gamble, Fenn (O'Brien 81), O'Flynn, O'Donovan (Woods 86), Kearney.

Halmstad (1) 1 *(Johansson A 31)*
Linfield (0) 1 *(Kearney 72)* 1197

Halmstad: Johansson C; Johansson P, Djuric (Sashcheka 86), Jonsson, Jensen (Ingelsten 76), Preko (Johansson J 63), Zvirgzdauskas, Johansson A, Svensson, Thorvaldsson, Larsson.
Linfield: Mannus; Ervin, McShane, Kearney, Murphy, O'Kane (Kingsberry 71), Thompson, Mouncey, Ferguson (Larmour 90), Gault, Bailie.

MyPa (0) 0
Dundee United (0) 0 1820

MyPa: Korhonen; Kononen, Taipale, Lindstrom, Haapala, Tauriainen (Muinonen 74), Karhu, Huttunen, Tarvajarvi (Kaijasilta 79), Miranda, Munoz.
Dundee United: Stillie; Wilson, McCracken, Duff, Archibald, Kerr, Brebner, Miller, McIntyre, Crawford, Robson.

Rhyl (0) 0
Viking (1) 1 *(Kopteff 19)* 1540
(at Belle Vue).

Rhyl: McGuigan; Powell M, Horan, Stones, Brewerton, Graves, Limbert, Adamson, Wilson, Hunt, Moran (Mutton 78).
Viking: Basso; Dahl (Sorli 74), Hangeland, Hansen, Pereira, Kopteff, Mambo Mumba, Nygaard, Gaarde, Ostenstad, Sigurdsson (Nhleko 64).

SECOND QUALIFYING ROUND, SECOND LEG

Allianssi (0) 0, Brann (0) 2 *(Ludvigsen 57, Miller 87)* 1372
FK Austria (0) 2 *(Linz 65, 70),* Zilina (2) 2 *(Cisovsky 26, Gottwald 32)* 5800
B36 (1) 2 *(Midjord 4, Morkore 85), Joensen*■ Midtjylland (2) 2 *(Pimpong 17, Sorensen 35)* 1600
BATE Borisov (0) 0, Krylia (1) 2 *(Bulyga 5, Vinogradov 50)* 5500
Besiktas (1) 5 *(Ailton 35, Hasan 61, Ahmet 83 (pen), Adem 89, Pancu 90),* Vaduz (1) 1 *(De Souza 28)* 15,200
Bystrica (0) 0, Groclin (0) 0 4150
Dnepr (3) 4 *(Shelayev 10 (pen), 45, Rykun 32, Balabanov 70),* Banants (0) 0 *Oseyan*■ 5000
Domzale (0) 1 *(Nikezic 90),* Ashdod (0) 1 *(Ebiede 70)* 1500
Genk (3) 3 *(Vandenbergh 5, Daerden 17, Stojanovic 27),* Metalurgs (0) 0 6300
Graz (1) 1 *(Junuzovic 33),* Otaci (0) 0 5500
Keflavik (0) 0, Mainz (1) 2 *(Thurk 25, Geissler 84)* 888
Levski (1) 3 *(Yovov 41, 65, Domovchiyski 69),* Publikum (0) 0 12,000
Lokomotiv Plovdiv (0) 1 *(Stoynev 75),* OFK Belgrade (0) 0 10,000
Maccabi Petah Tikva (3) 6 *(Golan 9, 39, 89, Ganon 41, Sarsor 64, 66),* Baskimi (0) 0 3500
Maccabi Tel Aviv (0) 2 *(Nimni 63, Mesika 117),* Apoel (0) 2 *(Makridis 93, Neophytou 95) (aet).* 5000
Metalurg Donetsk (0) 2 *(Zakarlyuka 54, Oleksiyenko 89 (pen)),* Matav (0) 1 *(Cotan 86)* 12,500
Omonia (2) 2 *(Kaiafas 29, Kittos 31),* Dinamo Bucharest (0) 1 *(Niculescu 56)* 8000
Red Star Belgrade (3) 4 *(Jankovic 5, Pantelic 41, 85, Zigic*■ *45),* Inter Zapresic (0) 0 *Pecelj*■ 28,901
Rijeka (0) 2 *(Krpan 64, Randulic 90),* Litets (1) 1 *(Caillet 44 (pen))* 6000
Siroki (3) 4 *(Lukacevic 16, Juricic 18, Robiel 26, Bubalo 65),* Zeta (2) 2 *(Vukovic 4, 44) Marijan*■ 4000
Teplice (0) 2 *(Rilke 56, Masek 90),* MTZ-RIPO (0) 1 *(Mkhitaryan 69)* 4850
Tromso (0) 0, Esbjerg (1) 1 *(Lucena 17)* 4386
(aet; Tromso won 3-2 on penalties).
Vardar (1) 1 *(Naumov 40),* Rapid Bucharest (0) 1 *(Vasilache 60)* 4500
Wisla Plock (3) 3 *(Gesior 35, 38, Zilic*■ *69),* Grasshoppers (1) 2 *(Antonio Dos Santos 30, Eduardo 83)* 3000
Zenit (1) 1 *(Spivak 12 (pen)),* Pasching (0) 1 *(Gilewicz 88)* 22,500
Zurich (2) 4 *(Keita 25, 65, Dzemaili 29, Cesar 79 (pen)),* Legia (1) 1 *(Szalachowski 17)* 9600

Thursday, 25 August 2005

Carmarthen (0) 0

FC Copenhagen (2) 2 *(Moller 37, 39)* 882

Carmarthen: Pennock; Carter, Lloyd, Jones, Hardy, Giles, Cotterall (Smothers 67), Kennedy, Dodds (James 84), Thomas (Hughes 46), Evans.
FC Copenhagen: Christiansen; Jacobsen, Svensson, Linderoth (Saarinen 63), Silberbauer, Allback (Ijeh 63), Roll Larsen, Gravgaard, Bergdolmo, Van Heerden, Moller (Dos Santos 75).
(at Ninian Park).

Cork City (0) 0

Djurgaarden (0) 0 7000

Cork City: Devine; Horgan, Murphy, O'Callaghan, Bennett (O'Donovan 56), Murray, Gamble, O'Halloran, Fenn (Coughlan 90), O'Flynn, Kearney.
Djurgaarden: Tourray; Concha, Kuivasto, Johannesson, Stenman, Arneng, Rasck (Arnason 60), Sjolund (Amoah 90), Jonson, Kusi Asare (Barsom 46), Hysen.

Dundee United (2) 2 *(Kerr 15, Samuel 29)*

MyPa (0) 2 *(Adriano 74 (pen), 81)* 9600

Dundee United: Stillie; Wilson, Duff, Kerr, Ritchie, Archibald, Samuel (Crawford), Brebner, Miller, McIntyre, Robson.
MyPa: Korhonen: Huttunen; Miranda, Lindstrom, Kononen, Taipale (Kaijasilta 74), Karhu, Haapala, Kuparinen, Tarvajarvi (Manso 58), Adriano.

Linfield (0) 2 *(Mouncey 54, Ferguson 82)*

Halmstad (3) 4 *(Thorvaldsson 10, Jonsson 33, Preko 45, Djuric 74)* 4000

Linfield: Mannus; Douglas (Kingsberry 53), Murphy, Thompson, McShane, Kearney, O'Kane (McAreavey 58), Mouncey (Mulgrew 75), Gault■, Ferguson, Bailie.
Halmstad: Johansson C; Johansson P, Jonsson, Preko, Svensson (Sashcheka 77), Thorvaldsson (Anklev 85), Zvirgzdauskas, Johansson A, Djuric, Larsson, Jensen (Ingelsten 66).

Viking (2) 2 *(Nhleko 7, 25)*

Rhyl (1) 1 *(Adamson 36)* 3857

Viking: Basso; Dahl, Deila, Pereira, Ostenstad, Kopteff, Grande (Mambo Mumba 67), Hangeland, Sorli (Lundkvist 79), Hansen, Nhleko.
Rhyl: McGuigan; Powell M, Brewerton (Taylor 83), Connolly (Mutton 77), Horan, Stones, Graves■, Adamson, Hunt (Powell G 83), Moran, Wilson.

FIRST ROUND, FIRST LEG

Apoel (0) 0, Hertha Berlin (0) 1 *(Marcelinho 90 (pen))* 6362
Auxerre (0) 2 *(Poyet 53, Pieroni 84)*, Levski (1) 1 *(Bardon 35)* 5500
Banik Ostrava (2) 2 *(Klimpl 28, Magera 45 (pen))*, Heerenveen (0) 0 10,330
Basle (1) 5 *(Delgado 10, 78, 88, Ergic 70, Eduardo Da Silva 85)*, Siroki (0) 0 *Rezic*■ 14,458
Beerschott (0) 0, Marseille (0) 0 12,146
Besiktas (0) 0, Malmo (0) 1 *(Alves 70)* 31,000
Brann (1) 1 *(Winters 44)*, Lokomotiv Moscow (0) 2 *(Ruopolo 72, Lebedenko 78)* 5111
Brondby (1) 2 *(Skoubo 45, Johansen 74)*, Zurich (0) 0 13,614
CSKA Moscow (1) 3 *(Gusev 21, Daniel Carvalho 76, 79)*, Midtjylland (1) 1 *(Pimpong 24)*
(Behind closed doors).
Feyenoord (1) 1 *(Kuijt 40)*, Rapid Bucharest (0) 1 *(Vasilache 76 (pen)* 150
Grasshoppers (1) 1 *(Rogerio 1)*, MyPa (1) 1 *(Manso 20)* 3400
Graz (0) 0, Strasbourg (2) 2 *(Pagis 1, Lacour 45)* 6274
Guimaraes (1) 3 *(Cleber 24 (pen), Mario Sergio 70, Benachour 72)*, Wisla (0) 0 15,000
Halmstad (1) 1 *(Thorvaldsson 43 (pen))*, Sporting Lisbon (1) 2 *(Wender 45, Deivid 47)* 3246
Hamburg (1) 1 *(Van der Vaart 37)*, FC Copenhagen (1) 1 *(Van Heerden 40)* 43,085
Krylia (2) 5 *(Leilton 11, Adamu 45, Kovba 49, Gusin 63, Bobior 90)*, AZ (1) 3 *(Vlaar 20, Perez 58, Van Galen 85)* 26,000
Lens (1) 1 *(Hilton 13)*, Groclin (1) 1 *(Rocki 13)* 20,194
Leverkusen (0) 0, CSKA Sofia (1) 1 *(Todorov 18)* 20,000
Litets (0) 2 *(Venkov 65, Novakovic 90)*, Genk (0) 2 *(Daerden 54, Stojanovic 85)* 3500
Maccabi Petah Tikva (0) 0, Partizan Belgrade (1) 2 *(Vukcevic 33, Radonjic 46)* 3700
Monaco (1) 2 *(Kapo 24, Adebayor 48)*, Willem II (0) 0 9118
PAOK Salonika (1) 1 *(Salpigidis 23)*, Metalurg Donetsk (0) 1 *(Shyschenko 67)* 12,000
Palermo (2) 2 *(Corini 5, Brienza 29 (pen))*, Anorthosis (0) 1 *(Ketsbaia 77)* 13,047
Red Star Belgrade (0) 0, Braga (0) 0 32,706
Rennes (1) 3 *(Frei 28, 74, Hadji 83), Jeunechamp*■ Osasuna (0) 1 *(Milosevic 50)* 20,529
Roma (4) 5 *(Aquilani 1, Panucci 21, 43, Montella 27, Totti 53)*, Aris Salonika (1) 1 *(Sanjurgo 38)* 11,620
Setubal (0) 1 *(Tchomogo 47)*, Sampdoria (1) 1 *(Flachi 30)* 4152
Sevilla (0) 0, Mainz (0) 0 44,000
Shakhtar Donetsk (3) 4 *(Blumer 2, Brandao 32, 45 (pen), Vorobei 73)*, Debrecen (0) 1 *(Sidibe 89)* 18,500
Stuttgart (1) 2 *(Tomasson 7, Gentner 89)*, Domzale (0) 0 12,000
Teplice (0) 1 *(Tomas 48)*, Espanyol (0) 1 *(Luis Garcia 82)* 14,620
Tromso (0) 1 *(Szekeres 78)*, Galatasaray (0) 0 4764
Valerenga (0) 0, Steaua (2) 3 *(Radoi 22, Iacob 34, Goian 73)* 4192
Viking (0) 1 *(Mambo Mumba 71)*, FK Austria (0) 0 4716
Zenit (0) 0, AEK Athens (0) 0 20,000

Thursday, 15 September 2005

Bolton Wanderers (0) 2 *(Diouf 72, Borgetti 90)*

Lokomotiv Plovdiv (1) 1 *(Janchevski 28)* 19,723

Boldon Wanderers: Jaaskelainen; Hunt, Gardner, Campo, N'Gotty, Jaidi, Okocha (Nolan 67), Nakata, Diouf, Pedersen (Borgetti 57), Giannakopoulos (Fernandes 67).
Lokomotiv Plovdiv: Kolev; Ivanov, Iliev G(Vandev 81), Halimi (Georgiev 46), Tunchev, Kotev, Dimitrov, Krizmanich, Petrov, Djordani, Janchevski (Stoynev 90).

Dinamo Bucharest (1) 5 *(Niculescu 27, Zicu 55, Petre 71, Bratu 75, 90)*

Everton (1) 1 *(Yobo 30)* 11,500

Dinamo Bucharest: Gaev; Goian, Tamas, Moti, Pulhac, Petre (Galamaz 83), Margaritescu, Plesan (Munteanu 78), Grigorie, Zicu, Niculescu (Bratu 61).
Everton: Martyn; Hibbert, Nuno Valente, Yobo, Weir, Neville, Osman, McFadden (Ferguson 78), Bent, Cahill, Davies (Kilbane 73).

Hibernian (0) 0

Dnepr (0) 0 16,861

Hibernian: Malkowski; Whittaker, Hogg, Smith G (Caldwell 46), Murphy, Brown S (Glass 69), Beuzelin, Stewart (Sproule 52), Thomson, Shiels, O'Connor.
Dnepr: Kuslyi; Gritsay, Rusol, Shershun, Shelaev, Radchenko, Semochko, Andrienko (Motuz 77), Kravchenko (Kostyshin 80), Kotenko, Kornilenko (Balabanov 70).

Middlesbrough (1) 2 *(Boateng 28, Viduka 83)*

Xanthi (0) 0 14,191

Middlesbrough: Schwarzer; Xavier, Pogatetz, Boateng, Ehiogu, Bates, Parlour (Morrison 74), Doriva, Maccarone (Yakubu 74), Viduka, Johnson (Queudrue 60).
Xanthi: Pizanowski; Torosidis (Quintana 67), Sikov, Pavio (Kazakis 87), Papadimitriou, Maghradze (Leonardo 77), Antzas, Emerson, Andrade, Luciano, Labriakos.

Slavia Prague (0) 2 *(Hrdlicka 61, Pitak 79)*

Cork City (0) 0 4694

Slavia Prague: Kozacik; Zabojnik, Latka, Hubacek, Krajcik, Suchy, Jarolim (Fort 69), Hrdlicka, Svento, Pesir (Kratochvil 79), Pitak.
Cork City: Devine; Murphy, Murray, Bennett, Horgan, Kearney, O'Donovan, O'Callaghan, Gamble, O'Flynn, Fenn (O'Halloran 73).

FIRST ROUND, SECOND LEG

AEK Athens (0) 0, Zenit (0) 1 *(Arshavin 89)* 23,121
AZ (1) 3 *(Van Galen 45, Koevermans 79, Landzaat 85 (pen)),* Krylia (1) 1 *(Adamu 16■)* 8350
Anorthosis (0) 0, Palermo (1) 4 *(Caracciolo 5, Makinwa 46, 68, Santana 53)* 10,000
Aris Salonika (0) 0, Roma (0) 0 8500
FK Austria (1) 2 *(Rushfeldt 21, Lasnik 47),* Viking (1) 1 *(Nygaard 12)* 5800
Braga (0) 1 *(Jaime 85),* Red Star Belgrade (1) 1 *(Purovic 10)* 17,000
FC Copenhagen (0) 0, Hamburg (0) 1 *(Van der Vaart 90 (pen)) Boulahrouz■* 34,446
CSKA Sofia (0) 1 *(Hdiouad 67),* Leverkusen (0) 0 22,500
Debrecen (0) 0, Shakhtar Donetsk (2) 2 *(Brandao 18, Blumer 24)* 6500
Domzale (1) 1 *(Stevanovic 16), Elsner■* Stuttgart (0) 0 2600
Espanyol (0) 2 *(Fredson 81, Jofre 90),* Teplice (0) 0 9435
Galatasaray (0) 1 *(Hakan Sukur 78),* Tromso (1) 1 *(Bernier 32)* 34,651
Genk (0) 0, Litets (0) 1 *(Corea Sandrinho 56)* 6343
Groclin (0) 2 *(Sedlacek 57 (pen), Sablik 79),* Lens (2) 4 *(Cousin 23, 54, Dindane 30, Lachor 90)* 6000
Heerenveen (2) 5 *(Huntelaar 2, 59, 67, Nilsson 44, Yildirim 66),* Banik Ostrava (0) 0 16,500
Hertha Berlin (2) 3 *(Marcelinho 15, Rafael 25, Cairo 58),* Apoel (0) 1 *(Makridis 76)* 22,612
Levski (1) 1 *(Koprivarov 28),* Auxerre (0) 0 15,000
Lokomotiv Moscow (0) 3 *(Loskov 63, Asatiani 78, Bilyaletdinov 90),* Brann (1) 2 *(MacAllister 45, 75)* 13,422
Mainz (0) 0, Sevilla (2) 2 *(Kanoute 9, 40)* 33,400
(Played in Frankfurt).
Malmo (0) 1 *(Alves 61),* Besiktas (2) 4 *(Youla 28, 34, 52, Tumer 90)* 8070
Marseille (0) 0, Beerschot (0) 0 22,063
(aet; Marseille won 4-1 on penalties).
Metalurg Donetsk (1) 2 *(Kosyrin 39, Shyschenko 57),* PAOK Salonika (2) 2 *(Salpigidis 42, Konstantinidis 45) Karypidis■, Yiasoumi■* 17,000
Midtjylland (1) 1 *(Nielsen 14),* CSKA Moscow (0) 3 *(Daniel Carvalho 61, 77, Samodin 76)* 7022
MyPa (0) 0, *Manso■* Grasshoppers (0) 3 *(Toure 74, Salatic 80, Rogerio 86)* 4012
Osasuna (0) 0, Rennes (0) 0 17,000
Partizan Belgrade (2) 2 *(Radonjic 12 (pen), 41),* Maccabi Petah Tikvah (3) 5 *(Mashach 3 (pen), Golan 20, 45, 48, Lomic 87 (og))* 10,000
Rapid Bucharest (1) 1 *(Buga 12),* Feyenoord (0) 0 12,000
Sampdoria (1) 1 *(Gasbarroni 8),* Setubal (0) 0 18,558
Siroki (0) 0, Basle (1) 1 *(Petric 8)* 4000
Sporting Lisbon (1) 2 *(Wender 34, Zvirgzdauskas 103 (og))),* Halmstad (1) 2 *(Thorvaldsson 15, Zvirgzdauskas 89, Ingelsten 113)* 14,333
Steaua (2) 3 *(Dica 31, Bostina 41, Iacob 48),* Valerenga (0) 1 *(Hulsker 56)* 12,000
Strasbourg (2) 5 *(Haggui 6, Farnerud A 40, Farnerud P 50, Le Pen 60, Hosni 68),* Graz (0) 0 4184
Willem II (0) 1 *(Hadouir 84),* Monaco (0) 3 *(Maicon 48, Adebayor 55, Chevanton 89)* 11,600
Wisla (0) 0, Guimaraes (0) 1 *(Saganowski 82)* 14,500
Zurich (1) 2 *(Rafael 15, 89),* Brondby (0) 1 *(Elmander 46)* 8600

Thursday, 29 September 2005

Cork City (0) 1 *(O'Callaghan 66 (pen))*

Slavia Prague (1) 2 *(Pitak 27, Vlcek 63)* 6000

Cork City: Devine; Murphy, Bennett, O'Halloran (Gamble 59), Murray, Fenn (Bruton 67), O'Flynn, O'Callaghan, O'Donovan, Horgan, Kearney (Coughlan 76).
Slavia Prague: Kozacik; Latka, Hrdlicka (Cernoch 90), Jarolim, Krajcik, Pitak, Suchy, Svento, Zabojnik, Vlcek (Kratochvil 90), Fort (Pesir 82).

Dnepr (3) 5 *(Nazarenko 1, Shershun 26, Shelaev 39 (pen), Melaschenko 87, 90)*

Hibernian (1) 1 *(Riordan 24)* 20,000

Dnepr: Kuslyi; Gritsay, Shelaev, Kornilenko (Melaschenko 68), Kotenko (Kravchenko 62), Radchenko, Rusol, Semochko, Andrienko (Lysytskyi 46), Shershun, Nazarenko.
Hibernian: Malkowski; Beuzelin (Fletcher 66), Caldwell, Murphy, O'Connor (Morrow 77), Riordan, Sproule, Stewart (Shiels 72), Hogg, Thomson, Whittaker.

Everton (1) 1 *(Cahill 28)*

Dinamo Bucharest (0) 0 21,843

Everton: Martyn; Hibbert (Weir 24), Nuno Valente (Bent 68), Yobo, Ferrari, Arteta, Neville, Cahill, McFadden, Ferguson, Kilbane (Beattie 68).
Dinamo Bucharest: Hayeu; Galamaz, Tamas, Moti, Pulhac, Petre, Margaritescu, Grigorie, Plesan, Bratu (Chihaia 84), Zicu (Baltoi 75).

Lokomotiv Plovdiv (0) 1 *(Iliev G 51)*

Bolton Wanderers (0) 2 *(Tunchev 79 (og), Nolan 86)* 14,000

Lokomotiv Plovdiv: Kolev; Ivanov, Tunchev, Iliev G, Kotev, Vandev (Stoynev 62), Dimitrov, Krizmanich (Halimi 80), Jancevski, Djordani, Petrov.
Bolton Wanderers: Walker; Ben Haim, Pedersen, Diagne-Faye, N'Gotty, Fernandes (Nolan 56), Okocha, O'Brien (Nakata 66), Diouf, Borgetti (Davies 56), Giannakopoulos.

Xanthi (0) 0

Middlesbrough (0) 0 5013

Xanthi: Pizanowski; Papadimitriou, Torosidis (Kazakis 47), Sikov, Pavio, Antzas, Maghradze (Garpozis 68), Luciano, Labriakos, Emerson, Gomes Andrade (Leo Mineiro 60).
Middlesbrough: Jones; Xavier, Pogatetz, Doriva, Riggott, Southgate, Morrison, Boateng, Hasselbaink (Yakubu 71), Maccarone (Nemeth 71), Queudrue (Parnaby 78).

GROUP STAGE

GROUP A

Thursday, 20 October 2005

CSKA Sofia (0) 0

Hamburg (0) 1 *(Van der Vaart 57)* 22,000

CSKA Sofia: Maksic; Zabavnik, Iliev, Tiago Silva, Gueye, Jakirovic (Dah Zadi 66), Gargorov, Todorov, Yanev (Sakaliev 66), Dimitrov V (Yurukov 82), Hdiouad.
Hamburg: Wachter; Atouba, Van Buyten, Wicky, Demel (Klingbeil 46), Jarolim, Trochowski (Mahdavikia 59), Beinlich, Van der Vaart, Barbarez, Mpenza (Ziegler 87).

Viking (1) 1 *(Nhleko 18)*

Monaco (0) 0 9684

Viking: Basso; Hangeland, Hansen, Pereira, Kopteff, Grande (Mambo Mumba 73), Nygaard, Gaarde, Ostenstad, Nhleko (Svenning 89), Tengesdal.
Monaco: Warmuz; Evra (Zikos 46), Modesto, Maicon, Squillaci, Givet, Plasil (Gigliotti 46), Bernardi, Kapo (Maoulida 84), Meriem, Adebayor.

Thursday, 3 November 2005

Hamburg (1) 2 *(Van der Vaart 21, Lauth 66)*

Viking (0) 0 37,521

Hamburg: Wachter; Atouba, Van Buyten, Boulahrouz, Wicky (Laas 41), Barbarez (Kucukovic 76), Trochowski, Beinlich (Takyi 76), Van der Vaart, Lauth, Mahdavikia.
Viking: Basso; Dahl, Hangeland, Hansen, Svenning, Kopteff, Grande (Mambo Mumba 66), Nygaard, Gaarde (Tengesdal 70), Ostenstad, Nhelko (Lunde 76).

Slavia Prague (2) 4 *(Fort 5, 75, Vlcek 36, Pitak 56)*

CSKA Sofia (1) 2 *(Gargorov 10, Sakaliev 58)* 7171

Slavia Prague: Kozacik; Krajcik, Suchy, Latka, Hubacek, Pitak, Jarolim (Kratochvil 90), Hrdlicka, Svento, Vlcek (Svec 90), Fort (Pesir 87).
CSKA Sofia: Maksic; Zabavnik, Gueye, Yurukov (Ivanov A 46), Tiago Silva, Jakirovic, Todorov, Gargorov, Yanev (Dah Zadi 71), Sakaliev, Dimitrov V (Matko 90).

Thursday, 24 November 2005

Monaco (1) 2 *(Adebayor 44, Veigneau 90)*

Hamburg (0) 0 8500

Monaco: Warmuz; Evra, Modesto, Cubilier, Givet, Plasil (Maurice-Belay 58), Bernardi, Sorlin, Zikos, Meriem (Veigneau 75), Adebayor.
Hamburg: Wachter; Van Buyten, Wicky, Barbarez, Jarolim, Trochowski (Lauth 71), Klingbeil, Demel (Mahdavikia 46), Boulahrouz■, Van der Vaart, Mpenza.

Viking (1) 2 *(Nhleko 26, Gaarde 55)*

Slavia Prague (0) 2 *(Vlcek 51, Pitak 83)* 7941

Viking: Austbo; Dahl, Hangeland, Hansen, Pereira, Tengesdal, Gaarde, Nygaard, Kopteff, Nhleko (Berland 77), Ostenstad.
Slavia Prague: Kozacik; Hubacek (Zabojnik 79), Suchy, Latka, Krajcik, Svento, Hrdlicka, Jarolim, Pitak, Vlcek (Gedeon 90), Fort (Pesir 68).

Wednesday, 30 November 2005

CSKA Sofia (1) 2 *(Yanev 35 (pen), Dah Zadi 47)*

Viking (0) 0 10,000

CSKA Sofia: Maksic; Zabavnik, Iliev V, Tiago Silva, Gueye, Jakirovic, Yanev (Branekov 90), Gargorov, Todorov (Yurukov 81), Dimitrov V, Sakaliev (Dah Zadi 46).
Viking: Basso; Dahl, Hangeland, Hansen (Gabrielsen 50), Pereira, Tengesdal (Mambo Mumba 61), Nygaard (Bjarnason 79), Gaarde, Kopteff, Ostenstad, Nhleko.

Slavia Prague (0) 0

Monaco (1) 2 *(Maoulida 11, 71)* 12,540

Slavia Prague: Kozacik; Krajcik, Latka (Zabojnik 46), Suchy, Hubacek, Pitak, Hrdlicka, Jarolim, Svento, Vlcek (Svec 78), Fort (Pesir 74).
Monaco: Warmuz; Modesto, Cubilier, Evra, Givet, Bernardi (Zikos 58), Plasil (Veigneau 77), Perez, Sorlin, Maurice-Belay (Gigliotti 83), Maoulida.

Thursday, 15 December 2005

Hamburg (1) 2 *(Barbarez 9, Mpenza 57)*

Slavia Prague (0) 0 46,253

Hamburg: Kirschstein; Atouba, Van Buyten, Wicky (Laas 60), Mahadavikia, Barbarez (Takahara 70), Jarolim, Trochowski, Demel, Beinlich, Mpenza (Lauth 63).
Slavia Prague: Kozacik■, Latka, Vlcek (Pesir 81), Holenak, Gedeon, Fort (Seliga 29), Svento, Krajcik, Jarolim, Suchy, Hrdlicka (Svec 86).

Monaco (0) 2 *(Kapo 50, Squillaci 75)*

CSKA Sofia (0) 1 *(Dimitrov V 84)* 9279

Monaco: Warmuz; Modesto, Cubilier, Squillaci, Veigneau, Perez (Maurice-Belay 46), Plasil (Givet 68), Zikos, Kapo, Maoulida (Bernardi 46), Adebayor.
CSKA Sofia: Maksic; Zabavnik, Jakimovic, Yanev (Dah Zadi 23), Dimitrov V, Iliev, Hidiouad, Gargorov, Tiago Silva, Gueye (Yurukov 64), Todorov.

Group A Final Table	P	W	D	L	F	A	Pts
Monaco	4	3	0	1	6	2	9
Hamburg	4	3	0	1	5	2	9
Slavia Prague	4	1	1	2	6	8	4
Viking	4	1	1	2	3	6	4
CSKA Sofia	4	1	0	3	5	7	3

GROUP B

Wednesday, 19 October 2005

Lokomotiv Moscow (0) 0

Espanyol (0) 1 *(Tamudo 53)* 13,718

Lokomotiv Moscow: Ovchinnikov; Bugaev (Ruopolo 68), Pashinin, Sennikov, Asatiani, Gurenko, Bikey, Lima, Bilyaletdinov, Izmailov, Lebedenko.
Espanyol: Iraizoz; David Garcia (Moises Hurtado 78), Lopo, Pochettino, Jarque, Zabaleta, Ito, Fredson (Costa 66), Luis Garcia (Corominas 71), De la Pena, Tamudo.

Thursday, 20 October 2005

Maccabi Petah Tikva (1) 1 *(Golan 45)*

Palermo (1) 2 *(Brienza 11, Terlizzi 77)* 3964

Maccabi Petah Tikva: Cohen; Ganon, Megamadov, Amar, Tzemah, Mashiach (Sarsour 81), Lokembo Locaso, Caldeira, Edri (Gian 78), Golan, Mbamba.
Palermo: Andujar; Ferri, Rinaudo, Terlizzi, Grosso, Gonzalez, Mutarelli, Codrea (Corini 73), Bonanni (Santana 61), Brienza (Pepe 46), Caracciolo.

Thursday, 3 November 2005

Brondby (0) 2 *(Lantz 67, Absalonsen 83)*

Maccabi Petah Tikva (0) 0 14,188

Brondby: Ankergren; Nielsen, Johansen, Sennels, Andersen, Lantz, Lorentzen, Daugaard, Rasmussen (Absalonsen 81), Jorgensen (Kamper 46), Elmander (Bagger 86).
Maccabi Petah Tikva: Cohen; Amar, Megamadov, Lokembo Locaso, Ganon, Mashiach (Dobrovin 72), Caldeira, Edri, Tzemah, Golan, Mbamba.

Palermo (0) 0

Lokomotiv Moscow (0) 0 15,823

Palermo: Andujar; Grosso, Terlizzi, Barzagli, Ferri, Masiello, Gonzalez (Santana 66), Codrea, Mutarelli (Barone 46), Pepe, Caracciolo (Makinwa 43).
Lokomotiv Moscow: Ovchinnikov; Bikey, Evseev, Sennikov, Asatiani, Lima (Gurenko 76), Izmailov, Maminov, Khokhlov■, Bilyaletdinov, Ruopolo (Lebedenko 90).

Wednesday, 23 November 2005

Lokomotiv Moscow (0) 4 *(Loskov 60, 65, 84, Lebedenko 63)*

Brondby (2) 2 *(Retov 11, Skoubo 28)* 8700

Lokomotiv Moscow: Ovchinnikov; Evseev, Pashinin, Asatiani, Sennikov, Bikey, Samedov (Ruopolo 32), Loskov, Bilyaletdinov, Gurenko, Lebedenko (Bugaev 90).
Brondby: Ankergren; Rytter, Johansen, Nielsen, Sennels, Lorentzen (Christensen 74), Lantz, Daugaard, Rasmussen (Absalonsen 80), Retov (Kamper 46), Skoubo.

Thursday, 24 November 2005

Espanyol (0) 1 *(Luis Garcia 90)*

Palermo (1) 1 *(Gonzalez 45)* 9114

Espanyol: Iraizoz; David Garcia, Jarque, Moises Hurtado, Armando Sa (Fredson 77), Jofre (Corominas 61), Eduardo Costa, De la Pena, Zabaleta, Jonathan Soriano (Tamudo 61), Luis Garcia.
Palermo: Guardalben; Accardi, Barzagli (Ferri 87), Rinaudo, Zaccardo, Bonanni (Grosso 62), Barone, Codrea■, Gonzalez, Brienza, Makinwa (Caracciolo 74).

Wednesday, 30 November 2005

Brondby (0) 1 *(Skoubo 66)*

Espanyol (1) 1 *(Tamudo 42)* 21,399

Brondby: Ankergren; Rytter (Daugaard 71), Nielsen, Sennels, Rasmussen, Johansen■, Lantz, Elmander, Retov (Jorgensen 78), Lorentzen, Skoubo (Christensen 75).
Espanyol: Kameni; Lopo, Jarque, Domi, De la Pena (Jofre 84), Riera (Corominas 63), Fredson■, Zabaleta, Moises Hurtado, Tamudo, Luis Garcia (Ito 71).

Maccabi Petah Tikva (0) 0

Lokomotiv Moscow (1) 4 *(Loskov 27, Lebedenko 47, 48, Ruopolo 52)* 4000

Maccabi Petah Tikva: Cohen; Amar, Banay, Megamadov (Hadiya 60), Ganon, Caldeira, Tzemah, Edri (Toama 46), Mbamba, Golan, Dobrovin (David 54).
Lokomotiv Moscow: Polyakov; Bikey, Pashinin, Evseev, Sennikov, Asatiani (Omelyanchuk 86), Gurenko (Bugaev 80), Bilyaletdinov (Kruglov 83), Loskov, Lebedenko, Ruopolo.

Thursday, 15 December 2005

Espanyol (0) 1 *(Pochettino 83)*

Maccabi Petah Tikva (0) 0 5150

Espanyol: Iraizoz, Jarque, Lopo, David Garcia, Armando Sa (De la Pena 68), Pochettino, Ito, Moises Hurtado, Riera (Tamudo 67), Jonathan Soriano, Luis Garcia (Corominas 58).
Maccabi Petah Tikva: Cohen (Mizrahi 46), Pesser, Amar, Banai, Tzemah, Ganon, Caldeira, Toama (Edri 70), David■, Dubrovin, Golan (Mbamba 46).

Palermo (2) 3 *(Makinwa 24, Rinaudo 44, 88)*

Brondby (0) 0 4521

Palermo: Andujar; Zaccardo, Rinaudo, Barzagli, Grosso (Accardi 73), Gonzalez (Bonanni 68), Barone, Corini, Santana, Brienza, Makinwa.
Brondby: Ankergren; Rytter, Andersen, Nielsen (Agger 55), Sennels (Jorgensen 60), Daugaard, Retov, Lantz, Rasmussen, Skoubo, Lorentzen (Christensen 72).

Group B Final Table	P	W	D	L	F	A	Pts
Palermo	4	2	2	0	6	2	8
Espanyol	4	2	2	0	4	2	8
Lokomotiv Moscow	4	2	1	1	8	3	7
Brondby	4	1	1	2	5	8	4
Maccabi Petah Tikva	4	0	0	4	1	9	0

GROUP C

Thursday, 20 October 2005

Halmstad (0) 0

Hertha Berlin (0) 1 *(Neuendorf 67)* 2136

Halmstad: Johansson C; Johansson P (Delani 86), Jonsson, Jensen, Zvirgzdauskas, Anklev (Johansson J 74), Svensson, Johansson A, Djuric, Thorvaldsson, Preko (Ingelsten 75).
Hertha Berlin: Fiedler; Friedrich, Van Burik, Schroder, Simunic, Fathi, Dardai, Neuendorf (Marx 90), Basturk, Marcelinho, Rafael (Okoronkwo 89).
Played in Gothenburg.

Steaua (3) 4 *(Iacob 13, Goian 16, Dica 43, 63)*

Lens (0) 0 23,000

Steaua: Hamutovski; Goian, Radoi (Lovin 80), Ghionea, Ogararu, Nesu, Bostina, Paraschiv, Nicolita (Oprita 78), Iacob (Cristea 84), Dica.
Lens: Itandje; Hilton, Coulibaly (Jussie 46), Gillet, Barul, Assou-Ekotto, Diarra (Carriere 74), Demont, Keita (Leroy 46), Thomert, Dindane■.

Thursday, 3 November 2005

Lens (2) 5 *(Cousin 16, 23, 47, Jemaa 73, Lachor 90)*

Halmstad (0) 0 16,189

Lens: Itandje; Demont (Lacourt 65), Hilton, Gillet, Lachor, Barul, Keita, Leroy (Jemaa 72), Carriere, Cousin (Jussie 76), Thomert.
Halmstad: Johansson C; Johansson P, Jonsson, Svensson, Thorvaldsson, Zvirgzdauskas, Johansson A (Johansson J 74), Djuric, Larsson (Preko 74), Ingelsten, Jensen.

Sampdoria (0) 0

Steaua (0) 0 17,194

Sampdoria: Castellazzi; Zenoni, Castellini, Sala, Pisano, Gasbarroni (Diana 66), Volpi, Dalla Bona, Tonetto (Kutuzov 59), Zauli (Flachi 46), Bonazzoli.
Steaua: Hamutovski; Ogararu, Goian, Ghionea, Nesu (Marin 79), Nicolita (Dinita 82), Paraschiv, Lovin, Bostina, Dica (Dumitru 90), Iacob.

Thursday, 24 November 2005

Halmstad (1) 1 *(Djuric 18)*

Sampdoria (1) 3 *(Volpi 31, Diana 67, Bonazzoli 86)* 3126

Halmstad: Johansson C; Jensen, Zvirgzdauskas, Jonsson, Johansson P (Johansson J 78), Ingelsten, Anklev, Djuric, Svensson, Preko (Fribrock 69), Delani (Larsson 85).
Sampdoria: Castellazzi; Diana, Sala, Falcone, Dalla Bona, Bonazzoli (Borriello 87), Flachi (Kutuzov 68), Gasbarroni (Tonetto 46), Pisano, Volpi, Zenoni.

Hertha Berlin (0) 0

Lens (0) 0 18,514

Hertha Berlin: Fiedler; Friedrich, Van Burik, Simunic, Fathi, Kovac, Basturk, Dardai (Neuendorf 72), Marcelinho, Cairo (Boateng 63), Rafael (Samba 86).
Lens: Itandje; Hilton, Gillet, Demont, Assou-Ekotto, Keita, Jussie, Diarra, Barul, Jemaa (Thomert 82), Dindane (Cousin 82).

Wednesday, 30 November 2005

Sampdoria (0) 0

Hertha Berlin (0) 0 16,507

Sampdoria: Castellazzi; Zenoni, Falcone, Sala, Diana (Gasbarroni 67), Volpi, Pisano, Dalla Bona (Kutuzov 82), Tonetto, Flachi, Bonazzoli (Zauli 90).
Hertha Berlin: Fiedler; Friedrich, Madlung, Simunic, Fathi, Marx, Kovac, Boateng, Basturk, Marcelinho (Neuendorf 87), Rafael (Samba 90).

Steaua (1) 3 *(Radoi 11, Goian 63, Iacob 71)*

Halmstad (0) 0 25,000

Steaua: Hamutovski; Goian, Radoi (Lovin 83), Dica, Bostina (Dumitru 81), Nesu, Nicolita, Iacob (Cristea 74), Ogararu, Paraschiv, Ghionea.
Halmstad: Sahlman; Johansson P, Jonsson, Fribrock (Larsson 46), Delani (Johansson J 82), Svensson, Zvirgzdauskas, Djuric, Ingelsten, Anklev, Jensen.

Thursday, 15 December 2005

Hertha Berlin (0) 0

Steaua (0) 0 15,603

Hertha Berlin: Fiedler; Friedrich, Madlung, Fathi, Gilberto, Boateng (Okoronkwo 75), Basturk (Neuendorf 79), Kovac, Marcelinho, Chahed, Dejagah (Samba 90).
Steaua: Hamutovski; Ogararu, Goian, Ghionea, Nesu (Marin 74), Nicolita (Balan 84), Paraschiv, Radoi, Bostina, Iacob (Cristea 78), Dica.

Lens (1) 2 *(Thomert 10, Jemaa 90)*

Sampdoria (1) 1 *(Flachi 23)* 31,473

Lens: Itandje; Demont, Assou-Ekotto, Coulibaly, Gillet, Keita, Jussie (Carriere 65), Diarra, Dindane (Jemaa 78), Cousin, Thomert.
Sampdoria: Castellazzi, Volpi, Flachi (Borriello 65), Sala, Palombo, Bonazzoli, Falcone, Tonetto, Pisano, Diana, Zenoni.

Group C Final Table	P	W	D	L	F	A	Pts
Steaua	4	2	2	0	7	0	8
Lens	4	2	1	1	7	5	7
Hertha Berlin	4	1	3	0	1	0	6
Sampdoria	4	1	2	1	4	3	5
Halmstad	4	0	0	4	1	12	0

GROUP D

Thursday, 20 October 2005

Dnepr (0) 1 *(Matyukhin 70)*

AZ (1) 2 *(Arveladze 14, Sektioui 52)* 12,300

Dnepr: Kusliy; Yezerskyi, Radchenko, Matyukhin, Shershun (Motuz 64), Rusol, Shelaev, Semochko (Kornilenko 60), Andrienko (Kravchenko 42), Nazarenko, Melaschenko.
AZ: Timmer; Jaliens, Opdam, De Cler, Steinsson, Landzaat, Schaars, Arveladze (Ramzi 90), Huysegems, Perez, Sektioui (Meerdink 83).

Grasshoppers (0) 0

Middlesbrough (1) 1 *(Hasselbaink 10)* 8500

Grasshoppers: Coltorti; Stepanovs, Jaggy, Chihab (Toure 82), Mitreski, Renggli (Salatic 87), Cabanas, Antonio, Sutter, Eduardo, Rogerio.
Middlesbrough: Schwarzer; Parnaby, Pogatetz, Doriva, Riggott, Southgate, Mendieta (Queudrue 79), Boateng, Hasselbaink, Viduka (Yakubu 85), Nemeth (Morrison 67).

Thursday, 3 November 2005

Litets (1) 2 *(Novakovic 13, Sandrinho 81)*

Grasshoppers (0) 1 *(Antonio 90)* 4500

Litets: Vutov; Popov, Cichero, Venkov, Kirilov, Genchev, Caillet, Jelenkovic, Zlatinov (Berberovic 80), Sandrinho (Palankov 85), Novakovic (Lyubenov 89).
Grasshoppers: Coltorti; Stepanovs, Chihab (Hurlimann 9) (Salatic 76), Jaggy, Mitreski, Renggli, Antonio, Sutter, Cabanas, Eduardo, Rogerio.

Middlesbrough (1) 3 *(Yakubu 36, Viduka 50, 56)*

Dnepr (0) 0 12,953

Middlesbrough: Schwarzer; Parnaby, Queudrue, Riggott, Bates, Doriva, Mendieta (Kennedy 60), Morrison, Yakubu (Maccarone 57), Viduka (Nemeth 64), Pogatetz.
Dnepr: Kusliy; Shershun, Radchenko, Shelayev, Yezerskyi, Rusol (Lysytskiy 58), Semochko, Rykun, Mikhalenko (Motuz 66), Nazarenko, Kostyshin (Melaschenko 52).

Thursday, 24 November 2005

AZ (0) 0

Middlesbrough (0) 0 8461

AZ: Timmer; Jaliens, Mathijsen, De Cler, Landzaat, Arveladze (Koevermans 77), Van Galen, Perez, Sektioui (Meerdink 61), Steinsson, Schaars.
Middlesbrough: Jones; Bates, Pogatetz, Riggott, Ehiogu, Doriva, Morrison (Parnaby 64), Boateng, Hasselbaink, Viduka (Yakubu 64), Nemeth (Queudrue 75).

Dnepr (0) 0

Litets (0) 2 *(Novakovic 72, Nazarenko 90 (og))* 3000

Dnepr: Kernozenko; Lysytskiy, Yezerskyi, Radchenko■, Rusol, Shelayev (Kornilenko 56), Rykun, Semochko, Kravchenko (Kostyshin 73), Nazarenko, Balabanov (Grytsay 65).
Litets: Vutov; Popov, Cichero, Venkov, Caillet, Genchev, Jelenkovic, Zlatinov (Lyubenov 85), Berberovic (Hazurov 90), Sandrinho (Palankov 90), Novakovic.

Wednesday, 30 November 2005

Grasshoppers (0) 2 *(Toure 85, Renggli 90)*

Dnepr (1) 3 *(Nazarenko 39, Kravchenko 62, Mikhaylenko 83)* 1808

Grasshoppers: Coltorti; Stepanovs, Jaggy, Mitreski, Sutter (Chihab 58), Renggli, Cabanas, Antonio, Salatic (Pavlovic 63), Toure, Rogerio.
Dnepr: Kernozenko; Lysytskiy (Mikhaylenko 46), Yezerskyi (Matyukhin 22), Shelayev, Rusol, Grytsay, Kostyshin, Semochko, Kravchenko (Kornilenko 75), Nazarenko, Balabanov.

Litets (0) 0

AZ (1) 2 *(Van Galen 10, Sektioui 82)* 4000

Litets: Vutov; Popov■, Cichero, Venkov, Caillet, Genchev (Lyubenov 58), Sandrinho (Manolev 82), Jelenkovic, Zlatinov, Berberovic (Palankov 46), Novakovic.
AZ: Timmer; Jaliens, Mathijsen, Steinsson (Meerdink 68), Ramzi, Landzaat, Buskermolen (Vlaar 83), Van Galen (Huysegems 78), Sektioui, Koevermans, Schaars.

Thursday, 15 December 2005

AZ (0) 1 *(Koevermans 70)*

Grasshoppers (0) 0 8153

AZ: Timmer; Jaliens, Mathijsen, De Cler, Steinsson (Opdam 64), Landzaat, De Zeeuw (Ramzi 73), Medunjanin, Sektioui, Van Galen (Huysegems 64), Koevermans.
Grasshoppers: Coltori; Schwegler (Salatic 17), Denicola, Jaggy, Renggli, Cabanas,Mitreski, Antonio, Toure, Rogerio (Chihab 88), Sutter.

Middlesbrough (0) 2 *(Maccarone 80, 86)*

Litets (0) 0 9436

Middlesbrough: Jones; Bates, Queudrue, Riggott, Ehiogu, Doriva, Morrison, Kennedy, Hasselbaink (Cattermole 83), Maccarone, Johnson.
Litets: Vutov; Berberovic, Cichero, Caillet, Venkov, Palankov (Kirilov 77), Jelenkovic, Genchev, Sandrinho (Hazurov 87), Zlatinov (Lyubenov 74), Novakovic.

Group D Final Table	P	W	D	L	F	A	Pts
Middlesbrough	4	3	1	0	6	0	10
AZ	4	3	1	0	5	1	10
Litets	4	2	0	2	4	5	6
Dnepr	4	1	0	3	4	9	3
Grasshoppers	4	0	0	4	3	7	0

GROUP E

Thursday, 20 October 2005

Basle (0) 0

Strasbourg (2) 2 *(Diane 15, Boka 25)* 16,623

Basle: Zuberbuhler; Smiljanic, Muller■, Chipperfield, Ba, Delgado, Degen, Zanni, Eduardo Da Silva, Petric (Kulaksizoglu 63), Rossi (Sterjovski 76).
Strasbourg: Cassard; Deroff, Devaux, Boka (Farnerud P 64), Kante, Farnerud A, Hosni, Johansen, Lacour, Pagis (Faty 86), Diane (Le Pen 74).

Tromso (1) 1 *(Aarst 42)*

Roma (1) 2 *(Kuffour 35, Cufre 84)* 5982

Tromso: Hirschfeld; Nilsen (Hafstad 80), Kibebe, Pedersen, Yndestad (Szekeres 73), Walltin, Johansen B, Bernier, Essediri, Strand (Ademolu 68), Aarst.
Roma: Doni; Panucci (Cufre 66), Bovo, Kuffour, Mexes, Alvarez Reyes, Kharja, Dacourt (De Rossi 53), Perrotta■, Mancini (Taddei 80), Nonda.

Thursday, 3 November 2005

Red Star Belgrade (1) 1 *(Purovic 25)*

Basle (1) 2 *(Delgado 30 (pen), Rossi 88)*

Red Star Belgrade: Stojkovic; Lukovic, Dudic, Basta, Bisevac, Jankovic (Trajkovic 87), Perovic (Krivokapic 67), Kovacevic, Mladenovic, Purovic (Raskovic 84), Zigic.
Basle: Zuberbuhler; Quennoz, Smiljanic, Chipperfield, Ba, Zanni, Delgado, Degen (Sterjovski 84), Ergic (Petric 58), Eduardo Da Silva, Rossi.
Behind closed doors.

Strasbourg (1) 2 *(Pagis 38, Arrache 66)*

Tromso (0) 0 8516

Strasbourg: Cassard; Deroff, Devaux, Kante, Bellaid, Farnerud P (Krebs 60), Arrache (Mouloungui 69), Lacour, Faty, Pagis (Carlier 74), Diane.
Tromso: Hirschfeld; Kibebe, Pedersen, Yndestad, Nilsen, Bernier, Johansen B (Szekeres 80), Walltin, Ademolu, Strand (Normann 46), Essediri.

Thursday, 24 November 2005

Roma (0) 1 *(Cassano 73)*

Strasbourg (0) 1 *(Bellaid 52)* 8109

Roma: Curci; Panucci, Bovo, Mexes, Cufre, Aquilani (Taddei 71), Kharja, Dacourt, Totti (Alvarez Reyes 59), Cassano (De Rossi 80), Nonda.
Strasbourg: Puydebois; Kante (Schneider 70), Boka, Bellaid, Farnerud A (Krebs 46), Farnerud P, Johansen, Lacour, Faty (Arrache 80), Diane, Gmamdia.

Tromso (2) 3 *(Kibebe 22, Aarst 37, 74 (pen))*

Red Star Belgrade (1) 1 *(Zigic 24)* 4289

Tromso: Hirschfeld; Nilsen, Pedersen, Kibebe, Yndestad (Szekeres 64), Christensen, Walltin (Johansen B 84), Essediri, Bernier, Strand (Ademolu 71), Aarst.
Red Star Belgrade: Stojkovic; Lukovic, Dudic, Basta, Joksimovic, Djokaj (Trajkovic 78), Bisevac, Kovacevic, Mudrinic (Krivokapic 67), Zigic, Purovic.

Thursday, 1 December 2005

Basle (1) 4 *(Petric 17, Delgado 61, Chipperfield 67, Degen 75)*

Tromso (3) 3 *(Strand 2, 29, Aarst 19)* 14,718

Basle: Zuberbuhler; Petric, Chipperfield, Ba (Ergic 60), Muller, Delgado (Kulaksizoglu 80), Degen, Eduardo Da Silva, Smiljanic, Zanni, Rossi.
Tromso: Hirschfeld; Nilsen, Kibebe, Pedersen (Normann 44), Szekeres, Christensen (Ademolu 76), Bernier, Essediri, Walltin (Johansen B 66), Aarst, Strand.

Red Star Belgrade (1) 3 *(Zigic 37, 86, Purovic 77)*

Roma (1) 1 *(Nonda 23)* 35,186

Red Star Belgrade: Stojkovic; Lukovic, Dudic, Bisevac, Basta, Djokaj (Mudrinic 75), Jankovic, Kovacevic, Milovanovic (Purovic 58) (Joksimovic 87), Mladenovic, Zigic.
Roma: Curci; Panucci, Kuffour, Mexes, Cufre (Taddei 82), Alvarez Reyes (Rosi 72), Aquilani, Kharja, De Rossi, Cassano, Nonda.

Wednesday, 14 December 2005

Roma (2) 3 *(Taddei 14, Totti 45, Nonda 49)*

Basle (0) 1 *(Petric 78)* 16,000

Roma: Curci; Panucci (Chivu 40), Bovo, Cufre, Aquilani, De Rossi, Perrotta (Rosi 74), Totti, Taddei, Nonda (Mancini 84), Mexes.
Basle: Zuberbuhler; Zanni, Muller, Smiljanic, Chipperfield (Sterjovski 65), Ba (Petric 46), Ergic (Kulaksizoglu 72), Degen, Delgado, Rossi, Eduardo Da Silva.

Strasbourg (0) 2 *(Gameiro 79, 90)*

Red Star Belgrade (1) 2 *(Basta 34, Djokaj 64)* 13,416

Strasbourg: Cassard; Deroff, Boka, Bellaid (Haggui 76), Schneider, Krebs, Le Pen, Johansen (Lacour 72), Faty, Diane, Gameiro.
Red Star Belgrade: Stojkovic; Lukovic, Dudic, Bisevac, Djokaj (Dramen 77), Jankovic, Kovacevic, Basta, Milovanovic, Mladenovic (Mudrinic 70), Zigic (Purovic 89).

Group E Final Table	*P*	*W*	*D*	*L*	*F*	*A*	*Pts*
Strasbourg	4	2	2	0	7	3	8
Roma	4	2	1	1	7	6	7
Basle	4	2	0	2	7	9	6
Red Star Belgrade	4	1	1	2	7	8	4
Tromso	4	1	0	3	7	9	3

GROUP F

Thursday, 20 October 2005

CSKA Moscow (0) 1 *(Vagner Love 80)*

Marseille (2) 2 *(Lamouchi 23, Niang 38)* 12,000

CSKA Moscow: Akinfeev; Semberas, Ignashevich, Berezutski A, Berezutski V (Zhirkov 46), Odiah, Rahimic, Aldonin, Krasic (Vagner Love 57), Gusev, Samodin (Salougin 79).
Marseille: Barthez; Ferreira, Andre Luis, Beye, Cesar, Taiwo, Cana, Oruma, Lamouchi, Ribery (Gimenez 73), Niang (Nasri 77).

Dinamo Bucharest (0) 0

Heerenveen (0) 0 10,000

Dinamo Bucharest: Gaev; Pulhac, Galamaz, Tamas, Moti, Margaritescu, Petre, Grigorie (Munteanu 72), Plesan (Cristea 78), Zicu (Baltoi 72), Bratu.
Heerenveen: Waterman; Hansson, Breuer, Drost J, Seip, Yildirim, Bosvelt, Pranjic, Kissi, Huntelaar, Nilsson.

Thursday, 3 November 2005

Heerenveen (0) 0

CSKA Moscow (0) 0 20,200

Heerenveen: Waterman; Breuer, Seip, Bosvelt, Yildirim (Bruggink 73), Huntelaar, Nilsson (Samaras 63), Drost J, Derveld, Kissi, Pranjic.
CSKA Moscow: Akinfeev; Semberas, Ignashevich, Berezutski A, Daniel Carvalho, Gusev, Vagner Love (Samodin 80), Odiah, Zhirkov (Krasic 85), Aldonin, Rahimic.

Levski (0) 1 *(Angelov E 90)*

Dinamo Bucharest (0) 0 15,000

Levski: Petkov; Milanov, Tomasic, Topuzakov (Angelov S 67), Wagner, Eromoigbe, Borimirov, Telkiyski, Domovchiyski (Angelov E 77), Bardon, Koprivarov (Yovov 66).
Dinamo Bucharest: Gaev; Pulhac, Tamas, Moti, Galamaz, Grigorie (Bratu 70), Cristea, Margaritescu, Petre, Baltoi■, Zicu.

Thursday, 24 November 2005

CSKA Moscow (0) 2 *(Vagner Love 49, 73)*

Levski (0) 1 *(Domovchiyski 90)* 6000

CSKA Moscow: Akinfeev; Semberas, Ignashevich, Berezutski A, Gusev (Krasic 87), Daniel Carvalho (Dudu 78), Odiah, Zhirkov (Berezutski V 90), Aldonin, Rahimic, Vagner Love.
Levski: Petkov; Milanov, Tomasic, Wagner, Topuzakov, Eromoigbe, Borimirov, Telkiyski (Bukarev 86), Angelov E (Yovov 64), Domovchiyski, Bardon (Koprivarov 74).

Marseille (0) 1 *(Taiwo 90 (pen))*

Heerenveen (0) 0 14,777

Marseille: Barthez; Andre Luis, Taiwo, Meite, Cesar, Delfin, Oruma, Lamouchi (Mendoza 82), Ribery, Koke (Nasri 61), Niang (Cana 90).
Heerenveen: Vandenbussche; Hansson, Breuer, Seip, Drost J, Derveld (Bruggink 90), Yildirim, Drost H, Pranjic, Huntelaar (Nilsson 31), Samaras.

Thursday, 1 December 2005

Dinamo Bucharest (0) 1 *(Munteanu 72)*

CSKA Moscow (0) 0 13,000

Dinamo Bucharest: Gaev; Galamaz, Tamas, Moti, Pulhac, Petre (Balan 70), Cristea, Grigorie, Munteanu (Bratu 77), Niculescu (Daouda 84), Zicu.
CSKA Moscow: Akinfeev; Semberas (Krasic 75), Berezutski V, Ignashevich, Berezutski A, Odiah (Gusev 78), Daniel Carvalho, Zhirkov, Aldonin, Rahimic, Vagner Love.

Levski (0) 1 *(Yovov 56)*

Marseille (0) 0 20,000

Levski: Petkov; Wagner, Milanov, Tomasic, Topuzakov, Borimirov, Bardon, Eromoigbe, Telkiyski (Bukarev 90), Yovov (Angelov S 71), Domovchiyski (Angelov E 61).
Marseille: Barthez; Andre Luis, Ferreira (Ribery 66), Beye, Nakata, Delfim, Cesar, Nasri (Oruma 79), Koke (Niang 66), Gimenez, Mendoza.

Wednesday, 14 December 2005

Heerenveen (0) 2 *(Samaras 54, Hanssen 90)*

Levski (0) 1 *(Ivanov 52)* 20,025

Heerenveen: Vandenbussche; Hansson, Breuer, Bosvelt (Hanssen 63), Yildirim, Huntelaar, Drost J. Bruggink (Derveld 83), Samaras, Drost H, Pranjic.
Levski: Petkov; Milanov, Eromoigbe, Yovov, Topuzakov, Bukarev, Ivanov (Domovchiyski 67), Angelov S, Telkiyski (Vergilov 88), Wagner, Angelov E (Koprivarov 80).

Marseille (2) 2 *(Cesar 39, Delfim 45)*

Dinamo Bucharest (0) 1 *(Niculescu 52)* 15,909

Marseille: Barthez; Andre Luis, Taiwo, Ferreira, Delfim, Ribery, Gimenez (Mendoza 67), Lamouchi (Oruma 72), Cana, Nasri (Begeorgi 77), Cesar.
Dinamo Bucharest: Gaev; Daouda, Pulhac, Tamas, Margaritescu, Petre, Niculescu, Grigorie (Baltoi 87), Galamaz, Bratu (Chihaia 84), Munteanu.

Group F Final Table	*P*	*W*	*D*	*L*	*F*	*A*	*Pts*
Marseille	4	3	0	1	5	3	9
Levski	4	2	0	2	4	4	6
Heerenveen	4	1	2	1	2	2	5
CSKA Moscow	4	1	1	2	3	4	4
Dinamo Bucharest	4	1	1	2	2	3	4

GROUP G

Thursday, 20 October 2005

Rennes (0) 0

Stuttgart (0) 2 *(Tomasson 87, Ljuboja 90 (pen))* 22,847

Rennes: Pouplin; Adailton, Bourillon, Faty, Edman (N'Guema 90), M'bia (Gourcuff 61), Didot, Monterubbio, Hadji (Briand 64), Utaka, Frei.
Stuttgart: Hildebrand; Delpierre, Magnin, Stranzl, Meira, Hitzlsperger, Tiffert, Soldo, Gronkjaer (Ljuboja 51), Tomasson, Cacau (Carevic 69).

Shakhtar Donetsk (0) 1 *(Brandao 68 (pen))*

PAOK Salonika (0) 0 24,650

Shakhtar Donetsk: Shutkov; Lewandowski, Rat, Seyhan, Tymoschuk, Duljaj, Matuzalem, Srna, Elano, Brandao, Marica (Aghahowa 59).
PAOK Salonika: Fernandes; Akyel (Christodoulopoulos 88), Chasiotis, Udeze, Charalambous, Zagorakis (Engomitis 86), Balafas (Sikabala 71), Iliadis, Konstantinidis, Salpigidis, Mieciel.

Thursday, 3 November 2005

Rapid Bucharest (1) 2 *(Niculae 42, Buga 67)*

Rennes (0) 0 18,926

Rapid Bucharest: Coman; Rada, Badoi, Karamian, Ilyes, Maldarasanu, Niculae (Burdujan 88), Constantin M, Maftei, Constantin N (Dica 53), Buga (Vasilache 71).
Rennes: Pouplin; Ouaddou, Adailton (Briand 69), Bourillon, Utaka, Edman, Gourcuff, M'bia, Monterubbio, Didot (Barbosa 76), Frei (Sow 83).

Stuttgart (0) 0

Shakhtar Donetsk (1) 2 *(Fernandinho 31, Marica 88)* 15,200

Stuttgart: Heinen; Stranzl, Meira, Delpierre, Magnin, Meissner (Gronkjaer 56), Tiffert, Soldo, Gentner (Cacau 46), Tomasson (Streller 71), Ljuboja.
Shakhtar Donetsk: Shutkov; Seyhan, Lewandowski, Rat, Tymoschuk, Duljaj, Fernandinho (Vorobei 75), Srna, Matuzalem (Marica 84), Elano, Brandao (Bielik 90).

Thursday, 24 November 2005

PAOK Salonika (0) 1 *(Karipidis 48)*

Stuttgart (0) 2 *(Ljuboja 85, 90 (pen))* 29,000

PAOK Salonika: Fernandes; Karipidis, Udeze■, Charalambous, Zagorakis, Feutchine (Christodoulopoulos 87), Azmy Megahed (Balafas 57), Konstantinidis, Salpigidis, Mieciel (Maladenis 77), Chasiotis.
Stuttgart: Hildebrand; Stranzl (Carevic 71), Meira, Delpierre, Magnin, Meissner■, Hitzlsperger, Soldo, Tiffert, Ljuboja, Tomasson (Gomez 61).

Shakhtar Donetsk (0) 0

Rapid Bucharest (0) 1 *(Maldarasanu 87)* 17,700

Shakhtar Donetsk: Lastuvka; Lewandowski, Hubschman, Rat, Tymoschuk, Matuzalem, Duljaj, Elano (Jadson 71), Bielik, Stoican (Srna 46), Aghahowa (Fernandinho 54).
Rapid Bucharest: Coman; Rada, Badoi, Karamian (Perja 81), Ilyes (Burdujan 76), Maldarasanu, Niculae, Constantin M, Maftei, Constantin N (Dica 51), Buga.

Thursday, 1 December 2005

Rapid Bucharest (1) 1 *(Maldarasanu 45)*

PAOK Salonika (0) 0 12,100

Rapid Bucharest: Coman; Rada, Constantin M, Maftei, Constantin N (Dica 61), Badoi, Karamian (Perja 86), Ilyes (Burdujan 75), Maldarasanu, Niculae, Buga.
PAOK Salonika: Fernandes; Karipidis, Chasiotis, Zagorakis (Vangelis 38), Feutchine (Azmy Megahed 46), Iliadis, Konstantinidis, Charalambous, Salpigidis (Sikabala 56), Mieciel, Christodoulopoulos.

Rennes (0) 0

Shakhtar Donetsk (1) 1 *(Elano 38 (pen))* 18,727

Rennes: Pouplin; Ouaddou, Faty (Adailton 46), Edman, M'bia, Didot, Gourcuff, Kallstrom (Mvuemba 46), Monterubbio, Utaka (Briand 66), Frei.
Shakhtar Donetsk: Shutkov; Lewandowski, Hubschman, Rat, Srna, Tymoschuk, Matuzalem, Duljaj, Fernandinho (Fomin 90), Elano (Brandao 69), Aghahowa (Marica 79).

Wednesday, 14 December 2005

PAOK Salonika (2) 5 *(Rochat 4 (og), Christodoulopoulos 38, Yiasoumis 79, 89, Salpigidis 83 (pen))*

Rennes (0) 1 *(Briand 70)* 3000

PAOK Salonika: Fernandes; Udeze, Karipidis, Engomitis (Andralas 75), Feutchine, Konstantinidis, Balafas, Maladenis (Iliadis 46), Sikabala, Yiasoumis, Christodoulopoulos (Salpigidis 73).
Rennes: Pouplin, Perrier-Doumbe, Adailton, Bourillon, Sepsi, Barbosa (Kallstrom 72), Briand, Rochat, N'Guema (Utaka 72), Mvuemba, Sow (Frei 72).

Stuttgart (2) 2 *(Gomez 20, 37)*

Rapid Bucharest (0) 1 *(Burdujan 80)* 14,000

Stuttgart: Heinen; Hinkel, Babbel, Gerber, Delpierre, Hitzlsperger, Gronkjaer (Stranzl 89), Gentner, Carevic, Cacau (Tiffert 76), Gomez (Streller 59).
Rapid Bucharest: Minca; Rada, Constantin M, Maftei, Constantin N (Vasilache 52), Badoi, Karamian, Ilyes (Burdujan 76), Maldarasanu, Niculae, Buga (Dica 63).

Group G Final Table	*P*	*W*	*D*	*L*	*F*	*A*	*Pts*
Rapid Bucharest	4	3	0	1	5	2	9
Shakhtar Donetsk	4	3	0	1	4	1	9
Stuttgart	4	3	0	1	6	4	9
PAOK Salonika	4	1	0	3	6	5	3
Rennes	4	0	0	4	1	10	0

GROUP H

Thursday, 20 October 2005

Besiktas (1) 1 *(Ailton 7)*

Bolton Wanderers (1) 1 *(Borgetti 29)* 17,027

Besiktas: Cordoba; Adem, Ibrahim T (Gokhan 46) (Mustafa 70), Cagdas, Koray, Ibrahim A, Tayfur, Kleberson, Tumer (Ibrahim U 36), Ailton, Ahmed.
Bolton Wanderers: Walker; Jaidi, Gardner, Diagne-Faye, Ben Haim, Fadiga, Fernandes (Nolan 59), Nakata, Diouf, Borgetti, O'Brien.

Zenit (1) 2 *(Spivak 39 (pen), Arshavin 54)*

Guimaraes (0) 1 *(Neca 59)* 20,500

Zenit: Contofalsky; Aniukov, Hagen, Skrtel, Mares (Flachbart 40), Denisov, Gorshkov (Sumulikoski 77), Radimov■, Spivak, Arshavin (Poskus 66), Kerzhakov A.
Guimaraes: Nilson; Mario Sergio, Dragoner, Medeiros■, Cleber, Svard, Neca, Flavio Meireles, Benachour, Targino (Paulo Sergio 79), Saganowski.

Thursday, 3 November 2005

Bolton Wanderers (1) 1 *(Nolan 24)*

Zenit (0) 0 15,905

Bolton Wanderers: Jaaskelainen; O'Brien, Gardner, Diagne-Faye, N'Gotty, Ben Haim, Giannakopoulos, Nakata (Okocha 66), Nolan (Diouf 85), Davies (Borgetti 74), Speed.
Zenit: Contofalsky; Aniukov, Hagen, Skrtel (Gorshkov 25), Flachbart, Vjestica, Sumulikoski, Vlasov (Kozlov 90), Denisov, Kerzhakov A, Arshavin.

Sevilla (0) 3 *(Saviola 64, Kanoute 65, 89)*

Besiktas (0) 0 38,500

Sevilla: Notario; Daniel Alves, Javi Navarro, Aitor Ocio, David, Fernando Sales (Jordi Lopez 71), Maresca, Marti, Adriano Correia (Puerta 77), Saviola, Luis Fabiano (Kanoute 58).
Besiktas: Cordoba; Ali, Ibrahim T, Kleberson (Pancu 75), Cagdas, Adem, Koray, Okan (Ahmed 68), Ibrahim A (Youla 65), Tumer, Ailton.

Thursday, 24 November 2005

Guimaraes (0) 1 *(Saganowski 86)*

Bolton Wanderers (0) 1 *(Vaz Te 88)* 20,000

Guimaraes: Paiva; Mario Sergio, Dragoner, Cleber, Rogerio Matias, Svard, Flavio Meireles, Benachour, Neca (Paulo Sergio 82), Dario Monteiro (Targino 60), Saganowski.
Bolton Wanderers: Jaaskelainen; O'Brien, Gardner, Diagne Faye, Ben Haim, N'Gotty, Okocha (Vaz Te 87), Nakata (Speed 59), Borgetti (Diouf 64), Nolan, Giannakopoulos.

Zenit (1) 2 *(Kerzhakov A 11, 89)*

Sevilla (0) 1 *(Puerta 90)* 17,000

Zenit: Contofalsky; Kerzhakov A, Flachbart, Hagen, Krizanac, Mares, Gorshkov, Aniukov, Radimov (Denisov 67), Spivak (Vlasov 88), Arshavin (Sumulikoski 90).
Sevilla: Notario; David (Jesus Navas 53), Daniel Alves, Dragutinovic, Aitor Ocio, Fernando Sales (Kanoute 63), Puerta, Renato (Jordi Lopez 15), Maresca, Saviola, Kepa.

Thursday, 1 December 2005

Besiktas (1) 1 *(Ibrahim A 25)*

Zenit (1) 1 *(Gorshkov 30)* 16,440

Besiktas: Cordoba; Ali, Ahmed, Adem (Ailton 65), Mustafa, Cagdas, Ibrahim T, Okan (Veysel 80), Sergen (Kleberson 59), Ibrahim U, Ibrahim A.
Zenit: Contofalsky; Flachbart, Hagen, Krizanac, Mares, Aniukov (Vlasov 90), Gorshkov, Radimov (Denisov 64), Spivak, Kerzhakov A, Arshavin (Sumulikoski 69).

Sevilla (3) 3 *(Saviola 10, 27, Adriano Correia 39)*

Guimaraes (1) 1 *(Benachour 44)* 35,000

Sevilla: Palop; Daniel Alves, Aitor Ocio, Dragutinovic, Puerta, Jesus Navas, Marti, Maresca, Adriano Correia (Diego Capel 72), Saviola (Jordi Lopez 76), Kanoute (Kepa 51).
Guimaraes: Paiva; Mario Sergio, Cleber, Dragoner, Rogerio Matias, Moreno, Svard, Benachour, Neca (Manoel 74), Targino (Paulo Sergio 62), Saganowski (Dario Monteiro 46).

Wednesday, 14 December 2005

Bolton Wanderers (0) 1 *(N'Gotty 65)*

Sevilla (0) 1 *(Adriano Correia 74)* 15,623

Bolton Wanderers: Walker; Hunt, Gardner (N'Gotty 46), Diagne-Faye (Speed 55), Ben Haim, Jaidi, Diouf, Nakata, Fadiga, Davies (Vaz Te 46), Okocha.
Sevilla: Notario; Crespo, David Prieto, Pablo Alfaro, Dragutinovic, Jordi Lopez (Adriano Correia 67), Pablo (Aitor Ocio 58), Marti, Puerta, Kepa (Saviola 73), Luis Fabiano.

Guimaraes (1) 1 *(Saganowski 12)*

Besiktas (2) 3 *(Ibrahim T 9, 60, Youla 18)* 5000

Guimaraes: Nilson; Svard, Mario Sergio, Medeiros, Geromel, Rogerio Matias (Helder Cabral 80), Neca, Moreno, Saganowski, Manoel (Targino 46), Clayton (Paulo Sergio 46).
Besiktas: Cordoba; Adem, Cagdas, Ibrahim T, Sergen (Tumer 62), Kleberson, Ahmed (Veysel 59), Ibrahim U, Ali, Koray, Youla (Pancu 83).

Group H Final Table	*P*	*W*	*D*	*L*	*F*	*A*	*Pts*
Sevilla	4	2	1	1	8	4	7
Zenit	4	2	1	1	5	4	7
Bolton Wanderers	4	1	3	0	4	3	6
Besiktas	4	1	2	1	5	6	5
Guimaraes	4	0	1	3	4	9	1

KNOCKOUT STAGE

THIRD ROUND, FIRST LEG

Wednesday, 15 February 2006

Artmedia (0) 0

Levski (1) 1 *(Angelov E 9)* 5720

Artmedia: Kamenar; Burak, Stano, Tchur, Hartig, Fodrek, Petras, Straka, Kubala (Reiter 53), Obzera (Konecny 86), Halenar (Mikulic 75).
Levski: Petkov; Tomasic, Topuzakov, Angelov S, Wagner, Eromoigbe, Borimirov, Telkiyski (Koprivarov 71), Yovov (Domovchiyski 86), Bardon, Angelov E (Hristov 90).

Basle (0) 1 *(Degen 78)*

Monaco (0) 0 14,143

Basle: Zuberbuhler; Majstorovic, Sterjovski (Kuzmanovic 89), Petric (Kulaksizoglu 69), Ba, Delgado (Ergic 77), Degen, Eduardo Da Silva, Berner, Smiljanic, Zanni.
Monaco: Warmuz; Maicon, Squillaci, Givet (Modesto 20), Dos Santos, Gakpe, Bernardi, Zikos, Plasil (Veigneau 65), Meriem (Gigliotti 89), Vieri.

Betis (0) 2 *(Diego Tardelli 70, Robert 79)*

AZ (0) 0 18,000

Betis: Contreras; Luis Fernandez, Juanito, Dani (Diego Tardelli 63), Arzu, Joaquin (Oscar Lopez 87), Rivera, Edu, Varela, Melli, Robert (Israel 80).
AZ: Timmer; Jaliens, Mathijsen, De Cler, Landzaat, Arveladze, Van Galen (Huysegems 64), Perez, Meerdink (Ikedia 80), Steinsson, Molhoek (De Zeeuw 32).

Bolton Wanderers (0) 0

Marseille (0) 0 19,288

Bolton Wanderers: Jaaseklainen; O'Brien, Gardner, Diagne-Faye, Ben Haim, N'Gotty, Okocha (Speed), Nolan, Borgetti (Vaz Te), Davies, Giannakopoulos.
Marseille: Barthez; Ferreira, Beye, Dehu, Cesar, Taiwo, Nasri (Gimenez 73), Cana, Oruma, Ribery, Niang (Cantareil 90).

FC Brugge (0) 1 *(Portillo 61)*

Roma (1) 2 *(Vanaudenaerde 44 (og), Perrotta 74)* 27,138

FC Brugge: Butina (Stijnen 16); Vanaudenaerde (Gvozdenovic 85), Maertens, De Cock, Klukowski, Dufer, Roelandts (Ishiaku 53), Vermant, Leko, Portillo, Balaban.
Roma: Curci; Panucci, Kuffour, Mexes, Cufre, Dacourt, De Rossi■, Tommasi, Mancini (Alvarez Reyes 89), Perrotta (Kharja 88), Montella (Taddei 66).

Heerenveen (1) 1 *(Bruggink 24)*

Steaua (1) 3 *(Dica 29, Goian 76, Paraschiv 78)* 20,500

Heerenveen: Vandenbussche; Hansson, Breuer, Seip, Bosvelt, Drost J (Derveld 80), Norregaard (Hanssen 74), Nilsson, Pranjic, Bruggink (De Vries 74), Yildirim.
Steaua: Carlos; Goian, Radoi, Ghionea, Ogararu, Nesu, Paraschiv (Oprita 83), Bostina (Lovin 90), Iacob, Nicolita, Dica (Cristocea 87).

Hertha Berlin (0) 0

Rapid Bucharest (0) 1 *(Negru 68 (pen))* 13,430

Hertha Berlin: Fiedler; Friedrich, Madlung■, Chahed, Fathi (Dejagah 77), Cairo, Boateng■, Gilberto, Basturk, Marcelinho (Samba 78), Sverkos (Okoronkwo 70).
Rapid Bucharest: Coman; Constantin M, Maftei, Rada, Badoi, Dica, Maldarasanu, Karamian (Perja 90), Buga (Vasilache 85), Burdujan (Negru 63), Niculae.

Lille (1) 3 *(Fauvergue 19, Dernis 57, Odemwingie 77)*

Shakhtar Donetsk (0) 2 *(Brandao 89, Marica 90)* 19,880

Lille: Malicki (Pichon 50); Debuchy, Tavlaridis, Schmitz, Dernis (Keita 71), Bodmer, Fauvergue (Cabaye 79), Odemwingie, Makoun, Vitakic, Lichtsteiner.
Shakhtar Donetsk: Shust; Hubschman, Chygrynskyi, Rat, Duljaj (Marica 68), Lewandowski (Tymoschuk 59), Matuzalem, Fernandinho, Elano (Jadson 74), Brandao, Srna.

Litets (0) 0

Strasbourg (1) 2 *(Le Pen 2, Diane 82)* 3000

Litets: Vutov; Kirilov, Cichero, Caillet, Zanev, Genchev (Lyubenov 62), Grujic, Jelenkovic, Zlatinov (Zhelev 80), Sandrinho (Hazurov 46), Novakovic.
Strasbourg: Puydebois; Lacour, Haggui, Kante, Abou Moslem, Gnoleba Loue, Diane, Abdessadki (Deroff 81), Farnerud P, Le Pen, Gameiro (Farnerud A 65).

Lokomotiv Moscow (0) 0

Sevilla (0) 1 *(Jordi Lopez 75)* 10,223

Lokomotiv Moscow: Polyakov; Bikey, Spahic, Gurenko, Pashinin, Kingston (Maminov 60), Asatiani, Loskov, Bilyaletdinov (Izmailov 81), Samedov, Parks (Lebedenko 46).
Sevilla: Notario; David, Javi Navarro, Dragutinovic, Daniel Alves, Adriano Correia (Escude 86), Jordi Lopez, Marti, Jesus Navas (Puerta 78), Luis Fabiano (Saviola 68), Kanoute.

Rosenborg (0) 0

Zenit (2) 2 *(Arshavin 22, Kerzhakov A 32)* 11,082

Rosenborg: Johnsen E; Dorsin, Kvarme, Riseth, Basma, Solli (Stensaas 82), Tettey (Berg 46), Strand, Storflor (Kone 66), Johnsen F, Braaten.
Zenit: Contofalsky; Skrtel, Hagen, Krizanac, Aniukov, Sirl, Radimov, Gorshkov (Sumulikoski 83), Spivak, Arshavin, Kerzhakov A (Denisov 90).

Schalke (0) 2 *(Bordon 67, Ernst 88)*

Espanyol (1) 1 *(Luis Garcia 34)* 53,642

Schalke: Rost; Poulsen, Bordon, Ernst, Larsen, Lincoln, Rafinha, Krstajic, Kuranyi (Sand 80), Bajramovic (Asamoah 46), Boenisch (Varela 67).
Espanyol: Iraizoz; Armando Sa, David Garcia (Sergio Sanchez 82), Lopo, Eduardo Costa, Luis Garcia (Corominas 71), Ito (De la Pena 78), Pandiani, Domi, Zabaleta, Jarque.

Udinese (1) 3 *(Di Natale 35, Barreto 61, 82)*

Lens (0) 0 6928

Udinese: De Sanctis; Zapata, Natali, Felipe, Candela, Obodo, Zenoni, Muntari (Tissone 68), Baronio, Di Natale (Barreto 55), Rossini (Iaquinta 84).
Lens: Itandje; Demont, Assou-Ekotto, Coulibaly, Hilton, Diarra (Khiter 74), Keita, Thomert, Cousin, Frau (Carriere 63), Jussie (Jemaa 63).

Thursday, 16 February 2006

Slavia Prague (1) 2 *(Jarolim 28, Barzagli 49 (og))*

Palermo (1) 1 *(Conteh 40)* 6706

Slavia Prague: Vorel; Hubacek, Dosoudil, Suchy, Svento, Krajcik (Svec 77), Jarolim, Hrdlicka (Holenak 46), Vlcek, Fort (Hercegfalvi 82), Pitak.
Palermo: Andujar; Grosso, Terlizzi, Conteh, Barzagli (Rinaudo 52), Tedesco, Corini, Santana, Mutarelli (Barone 69), Brienza (Gonzalez 60), Makinwa.

Stuttgart (0) 1 *(Ljuboja 86)*

Middlesbrough (1) 2 *(Hasselbaink 20, Parnaby 46)* 21,000

Stuttgart: Hildebrand; Stranzl (Beck 46), Meira, Delpierre, Gerber, Gronkjaer, Meissner (Gentner 80), Soldo, Hitzlsperger (Gomez 66), Tomasson, Ljuboja.
Middlesbrough: Schwarzer; Parnaby, Pogatetz, Doriva, Riggott, Southgate, Davies, Boateng (Kennedy 81), Hasselbaink (Yakubu 85), Rochemback, Downing (Johnson 73).

THIRD ROUND, SECOND LEG

Thursday, 23 February 2006

AZ (2) 2 *(Arveladze 26, Jaliens 35)*

Betis (0) 1 *(Melli 94)* 8500

AZ: Timmer; Jaliens, Mathijsen, Opdam, De Cler■, Landzaat, Sektioui (Meerdink 103), Schaars (Molhoek 86), Arveladze, Van Galen (Koevermans 90), Perez.
Betis: Contreras; Juanito, Rivas, Varela (Rivera 61), Arzu, Capi (Dani 86), Joaquin, Oscar Lopez (Luis Fernandez 51), Edu, Melli, Robert.
aet.

Espanyol (0) 0

Schalke (0) 3 *(Kuranyi 54, Sand 70, Lincoln 73)* 18,100

Espanyol: Kameni; Armando Sa (Corominas 57), Lopo, Pochettino, Jarque, Domi (Juanfran 68), De la Pena, Eduardo Costa, Zabaleta (Jofre 68), Luis Garcia, Pandiani.
Schalke: Rost; Kobiashvili, Krstajic, Bordon (Klasener 76), Rafinha, Poulsen, Bajramovic, Ernst, Lincoln, Kuranyi (Larsen 74), Asamoah (Sand 66).

Hamburg (2) 2 *(Van Buyten 2, 33)*

Thun (0) 0 40,254

Hamburg: Wachter; Atouba, Van Buyten, Boulahrouz, Trochowski (Van der Vaart 64), Wicky, Barbarez, Jarolim■, De Jong (Demel 86), Takahara (Lauth 71), Mahdavikia.
Thun: Jakupovic; Vieira (Sen 52), Milicevic, Hodzic, Duruz, Deumi, Adriano (Cengel 78), Friedli, Aegerter, Ferreira (Bernardi 84), Omar.

Lens (0) 1 *(Frau 55)*

Udinese (0) 0 26,292

Lens: Chabbert; Barul (Feindouno 82), Assou-Ekotto, Coulibaly, Gillet, Carriere, Lacourt, Frau, Jemaa (Cousin 61), Dindane (Demont 73), Khiter.
Udinese: De Sanctis; Zapata, Bertotto, Vidigal, Iaquinta (Tissone 67), Muntari (Baronio 90), Felipe, Rossini, Aguilar (Obodo 58), Candela, Defendi.

Levski (2) 2 *(Angelov E 14, 57)*

Artmedia (0) 0 23,441

Levski: Petkov; Angelov S, Tomasic, Topuzakov, Wagner, Eromoigbe, Borimirov, Telkiyski, Bardon (Ivanov 88), Yovov (Domovchiyski 85), Angelov E (Koprivarov 76).
Artmedia: Kamenar; Petras, Stano, Tchur (Gajdos 83), Hartig, Mikulic (Kubala 55), Fodrek, Urbanek, Burak, Reiter (Halenar 66), Straka.

Marseille (1) 2 *(Ribery 45, Ben Haim 68 (og))*

Bolton Wanderers (1) 1 *(Giannakopoulos 25)* 38,351

Marseille: Barthez; Taiwo, Ferreira (Deruda 66), Dehu, Meite, Beye, Oruma, Cana (Civelli 90), Nasri, Ribery (Cantareil 80), Niang.
Bolton Wanderers: Jaaskelainen; O'Brien, Gardner, Diagne-Faye (Pedersen 73) (Borgetti 87), Ben Haim, N'Gotty, Okocha, Speed (Vaz Te 84), Nolan, Davies, Giannakopoulos.

Middlesbrough (0) 0

Stuttgart (1) 1 *(Tiffert 13)* 24,018

Middlesbrough: Schwarzer; Parnaby, Queudrue, Boateng, Riggott, Southgate, Mendieta (Ehiogu 86), Cattermole, Hasselbaink (Yakubu 86), Davies, Downing (Taylor 90).
Stuttgart: Hildebrand; Hinkel, Babbel, Delpierre, Magnin (Hitzlsperger 80), Soldo, Tiffert, Meissner (Cacau 75), Gentner, Gronkjaer (Gomez 64), Ljuboja.

Monaco (1) 1 *(Vieri 21 (pen))*
Basle (0) 1 *(Majstorovic 56)* 11,955
Monaco: Roma; Dos Santos, Modesto, Plasil (Chevanton 61), Squillaci, Maicon, Bernardi, Meriem (Kapo 75), Zikos, Gakpe (Maurice-Belay 62), Vieri.
Basle: Zuberbuhler; Majstorovic, Sterjovski (Kulaksizoglu 85), Petric, Ba, Delgado (Ergic 82), Degen, Eduardo Da Silva, Berner, Smiljanic, Zanni.

Palermo (0) 1 *(Godeas 51)*
Slavia Prague (0) 0 8063
Palermo: Andujar; Conteh, Barzagli, Terlizzi, Grosso, Tedesco, Codrea, Santana (Gonzalez 80), Brienza (Barone 59), Makinwa (Godeas 46), Mutarelli.
Slavia Prague: Vorel; Hubacek, Svec (Kratochvil 56), Dosoudil, Suchy, Krajcik, Svento (Janda 77), Holenak, Pitak, Vicek, Fort (Hercegfalvi 77).

Rapid Bucharest (0) 2 *(Niculae 50, Buga 79)*
Hertha Berlin (0) 0 16,300
Rapid Bucharest: Coman; Rada, Constantin M, Maftei, Negru (Constantin N 49), Badoi, Karamian, Dica, Maldarasanu (Stancu C 86), Niculae (Vasilache 89), Buga.
Hertha Berlin: Fiedler; Friedrich, Van Burik (Samba 76), Chahed, Fathi, Gilberto, Marcelinho (Dejagah 78), Schmidt, Marx (Cairo 67), Okoronkwo, Sverkos.

Roma (0) 2 *(Mancini 55, Bovo 71)*
FC Brugge (0) 1 *(Verheyen 60)* 15,209
Roma: Curci; Bovo, Kuffour, Mexes, Cufre, Alvarez Reyes (Perrotta 70), Aquilani, Kharja, Mancini (Chivu 88), Montella (Taddei 73), Tommasi.
FC Brugge: Stijnen; De Cock, Klukowski (Roelandts 62), Clement, Verheyen (Portillo 62), Englebert, Vermant (Leko 62), Balaban, Gvozdenovic, Maertens, Matondo.

Sevilla (1) 2 *(Maresca 34, Puerta 90)*
Lokomotiv Moscow (0) 0 25,000
Sevilla: Notario; Daniel Alves, Javi Navarro (Aitor Ocio 83), Dragutinovic, David, Jesus Navas, Jordi Lopez, Maresca, Puerta, Luis Fabiano (Kepa 70), Saviola (Adriano Correia 46).
Lokomotiv Moscow: Polyakov; Pashinin (Parks 68), Asatiani, Lebedenko, Spahic, Bikey, Maminov, Gurenko, Loskov, Samedov, Bilyaletdinov (Izmailov 61).

Shakhtar Donetsk (0) 0
Lille (0) 0 23,250
Shakhtar Donetsk: Shust; Rat, Chygrynskyi, Seyhan, Duljaj, Fernandinho (Vorobei 63), Matuzalem, Srna, Elano (Jadson 71), Marica, Brandao (Aghahowa 81).
Lille: Sylva; Tavlaridis, Schmitz, Tafforeau, Lichtsteiner (Keita 58), Debuchy, Cabaye (Fauvergue 67), Dernis, Bodmer, Chalme, Odemwingie (Franquart 77).

Steaua (0) 0
Heerenveen (0) 1 *(Bruggink 85)* 50,000
Steaua: Carlos; Goian, Radoi, Ogararu, Baciu, Bostina (Cristocea 87), Nesu, Paraschiv, Nicolita (Oprita 72), Iacob (Cristea 80), Dica.
Heerenveen: Vandenbussche; Hansson, Breuer (Drost J 47), Seip, Derveld, Norregaard (Bruggink 48), Nilsson (Hanssen 70), Prager, Pranjic, De Vries, Yildirim.

Strasbourg (0) 0
Litets (0) 0 9610
Strasbourg: Puydebois; Deroff, Devaux, Boka, Haggui, Abdessadki, Krebs (Gameiro 60), Le Pen (Farnerud P 75), Lacour, Farnerud A, Diane (Gnoleba Loue 68).
Litets: Vutov; Cichero, Kirilov, Zanev, Berberovic, Grujic, Jelenkovic, Palankov (Hazurov 83), Popov (Lyubenov 62), Sandrinho (Zlatinov 62), Novakovic.

Zenit (0) 2 *(Kerzhakov A 55, Denisov 86)*
Rosenborg (1) 1 *(Riseth 45)* 21,500
Zenit: Contofalsky (Malafeev 24); Aniukov, Krizanac, Hagen, Skrtel, Spivak (Hyun 66), Gorshkov (Denisov 73), Radimov, Sirl, Kerzhakov A, Arshavin.
Rosenborg: Johnsen E; Basma (Koppinen 46), Riseth, Kvarme, Dorsin, Strand (Tettey 90), Berg, Solli, Braaten, Johnsen F, Storflor (Kone 78).

FOURTH ROUND, FIRST LEG

Thursday, 9 March 2006

Basle (1) 2 *(Delgado 8, Kuzmanovic 89)*
Strasbourg (0) 0 14,243
Basle: Zuberbuhler; Majstorovic, Berner, Smiljanic, Zanni, Sterjovski, Petric, Ba (Ergic 83), Degen (Kuzmanovic 77), Delgado, Eduardo Da Silva.
Strasbourg: Puydebois; Deroff, Kante, Abou Moslem, Haggui (Bellaid 87), Hosni, Farnerud A, Lacour (Boka 63), Gnoleba Loue (Abdessadki 39), Farnerud P, Diane.

Lille (1) 1 *(Dernis 24)*
Sevilla (0) 0 11,009
Lille: Sylva; Schmitz, Plestan, Vitakic, Chalme, Dernis, Dumont (Franquart 88), Bodmer, Makoun, Moussilou (Mirallas 59), Keita (Lichtsteiner 75).
Sevilla: Notario; Javi Navarro, David, Dragutinovic, Daniel Alves, Marti (Jordi Lopez 72), Renato, Jesus Navas, Adriano Correia (Puerta 75), Luis Fabiano (Saviola 55), Kanoute.

Marseille (0) 0
Zenit (0) 1 *(Arshavin 51)* 25,500
Marseille: Barthez; Taiwo, Ferreira (Gimenez 61), Dehu, Ribery■, Oruma, Niang, Meite, Lamouchi (Delfim 82), Nasri (Deruda 82), Beye.
Zenit: Malafeev; Aniukov, Skrtel, Hagen, Krizanac, Sirl, Denisov (Hyun 90), Radimov, Spivak (Trifonov 62), Kerzhakov A, Arshavin (Poskus 90).

Middlesbrough (1) 1 *(Yakubu 12 (pen))*
Roma (0) 0 25,354
Middlesbrough: Schwarzer; Davies, Pogatetz, Boateng, Riggott, Southgate, Mendieta, Cattermole, Hasselbaink, Yakubu (Viduka 81), Downing (Queudrue 90).
Roma: Curci; Panucci, Kuffour, Mexes, Cufre, Dacourt (Aquilani 84), Kharja, Taddei (Okaka Chuka 61), Mancini, Tommasi (Alvarez Reyes 73), Perrotta.

Palermo (1) 1 *(Brienza 15)*
Schalke (0) 0 10,581
Palermo: Andujar; Tedesco (Mutarelli 61), Barone, Brienza (Gonzalez 69), Santana, Codrea, Terlizzi, Conteh, Accardi, Barzagli, Godeas (Caracciolo 88).
Schalke: Rost; Poulsen, Kobiashvili (Rodriguez 78), Bordon, Ernst, Larsen, Sand, Asamoah (Varela 80), Rafinha, Krstajic, Bajramovic.

Rapid Bucharest (1) 2 *(Niculae 45, Buga 88)*
Hamburg (0) 0 16,300
Rapid Bucharest: Coman; Constantin M, Maftei■, Rada, Badoi, Stancu C, Dica (Negru 13), Karamian (Stancu I 20), Burdujan (Moldovan 71), Niculae, Buga.
Hamburg: Wachter; Mahdavikia, Boulahrouz, Van Buyten, Demel, Wicky, Trochowski (Klingbeil 46), De Jong■, Van der Vaart, Takahara (Laas 71), Barbarez (Kucukovic 46).

Steaua (0) 0
Betis (0) 0 45,023
Steaua: Carlos; Goian, Radoi, Dica, Bostina (Oprita 70), Nesu, Nicolita (Cristocea 89), Iacob, Ogararu, Paraschiv (Lovin 75), Ghionea.
Betis: Doblas; Luis Fernandez, Juanito, Rivas, Varela (Dani 85), Capi, Joaquin (Diego Tardelli 90), Rivera, Edu, Melli, Robert (Arzu 79).

Udinese (0) 0
Levski (0) 0 7650
Udinese: De Sanctis; Bertotto, Felipe (Defendi 52), Zapata, Zenoni, Obodo, Baronio, Tissone, Candela (Muntari 60), Rossini, Di Natale (Barreto 67).
Levski: Petkov; Milanov, Topuzakov, Angelov S, Wagner, Eromoigbe, Borimirov, Telkiyski, Bardon (Hristov 90), Yovov (Bukarev 82), Angelov E (Domovchiyski 64).

FOURTH ROUND, SECOND LEG

Wednesday, 15 March 2006

Hamburg (2) 3 *(Lauth 24, Barbarez 36, Van der Vaart 62)*
Rapid Bucharest (0) 1 *(Buga 51)* 37,866

Hamburg: Kirschstein; Atouba, Van Buyten, Wicky, Mahdavikia, Barbarez, Lauth (Reinhardt 83), Jarolim, Demel (Takahara 53), Boulahrouz, Van der Vaart.
Rapid Bucharest: Coman; Stancu I, Rada, Badoi, Dica (Negru 46), Perja, Niculae, Constantin M, Stancu C, Constantin N (Moldovan 46), Buga (Burdujan 70).

Roma (1) 2 *(Mancini 43, 66 (pen))*
Middlesbrough (1) 1 *(Hasselbaink 32)* 32,642

Roma: Curci; Kuffour, Bovo, Mexes■, Chivu (Panucci 86), Taddei, Alvarez Reyes (Aquilani 71), Mancini, Dacourt (Okaka Chuka 63), De Rossi, Perrotta.
Middlesbrough: Schwarzer; Davies (Queudrue 46), Pogatetz, Boateng, Riggott, Southgate, Mendieta, Cattermole, Hasselbaink, Yakubu (Parlour 58), Downing.

Sevilla (2) 2 *(Kanoute 29, Luis Fabiano 45)*
Lille (0) 0 37,000

Sevilla: Palop; Daniel Alves (Jordi Lopez 65), Javi Navarro, Dragutinovic, David, Jesus Navas■, Renato, Marti, Adriano Correia (Escude 90), Kanoute, Luis Fabiano (Aitor Ocio 74).
Lille: Sylva; Chalme, Tavlaridis, Schmitz, Tafforeau, Makoun, Lichtsteiner, Dumont (Keita 58), Bodmer■, Dernis (Fauvergue 77), Moussilou (Odemwingie 46).

Thursday, 16 March 2006

Betis (0) 0
Steaua (0) 3 *(Nicolita 4, 82, Iacob 78)* 15,851

Betis: Contrereas; Melli, Juanito, Nano, Luis Fernandez, Rivera, Arzu (Dani 57), Joaquin■, Edu, Diego Tardelli (Xisco 56), Robert.
Steaua: Carlos; Ogararu, Ghionea, Goian, Marin, Nicolita (Cristea 86), Paraschiv, Radoi (Lovin 81), Bostina (Oprita 72), Dica, Iacob.

Levski (0) 2 *(Borimirov 51, Tomasic 63)*
Udinese (1) 1 *(Tissone 22)* 37,136

Levski: Petkov; Angelov S, Tomasic, Topuzakov, Wagner, Telkiyski, Borimirov, Eromoigbe, Bardon (Bukarev 85), Yovov (Koprivarov 78), Angelov E (Domovchiyski 46).
Udinese: De Sanctis; Zapata, Bertotto, Juarez, Vidigal (Barreto 73), Tissone, Morosini, Pieri (Osso Armellino 90), Baronio (Obodo 58), Rossini, Lazzari.

Schalke (1) 3 *(Kobiashvili 44 (pen), Larsen 72, Azaouagh 80)*
Palermo (0) 0 52,151

Schalke: Rost; Poulsen, Kobiashvili, Azaouagh (Baumjohann 90), Ernst (Varela 68), Larsen, Asamoah, Rodriguez, Rafinha, Krstajic, Bajramovic (Sand 85).
Palermo: Andujar; Corini■, Barone, Santana (Makinwa 65), Gonzalez (Brienza 76), Mutarelli, Terlizzi, Conteh (Tedesco 50), Zaccardo, Barzagli, Godeas.

Strasbourg (1) 2 *(Carlier 11, Kante 78)*
Basle (2) 2 *(Eduardo Da Silva 3, 26)* 8115

Strasbourg: Puydebois; Deroff, Kante, Boka, Bellaid, Abou Moslem, Farnerud P, Johansen, Faty, Farnerud A, Carlier.
Basle: Zuberbuhler; Majstorovic, Berner (Chipperfield 80), Smiljanic, Zanni, Sterjovski, Ba, Delgado (Ergic 66), Degen, Petric, Eduardo Da Silva (Kulaksizoglu 86).

Zenit (0) 1 *(Kerzhakov A 69)*
Marseille (0) 1 *(Dehu 74)* 21,838

Zenit: Malafeev; Vjestica, Hagen, Krizanac, Aniukov, Denisov, Gorshkov (Sumulikoski 80), Radimov, Sirl (Mares 63), Arshavin, Kerzhakov A (Trifonov 90).
Marseille: Carrasso■; Meite, Dehu, Beye, Taiwo, Civelli (Deruda 76), Cana, Nasri, Lamouchi (Begeorgi 77), Gimenez (Delfim 84), Niang.

QUARTER-FINALS, FIRST LEG

Thursday, 30 March 2006

Basle (2) 2 *(Delgado 43, Degen 45)*
Middlesbrough (0) 0 23,639

Basle: Zuberbuhler; Majstorovic, Berner, Smiljanic, Sterjovski (Chipperfield 64), Ba, Delgado, Degen, Zanni, Eduardo Da Silva, Petric (Ergic 85).
Middlesbrough: Schwarzer; Parnaby, Queudrue, Doriva, Riggott, Pogatetz (Ehiogu 68), Mendieta (Rochemback 74), Parlour, Hasselbaink (Yakubu 74), Viduka, Downing.

Levski (1) 1 *(Borimirov 6)*
Schalke (0) 3 *(Varela 48, Lincoln 69, Asamoah 79)* 38,000

Levski: Petkov; Milanov, Topuzakov, Tomasic, Wagner, Borimirov, Angelov S, Telkiyski (Bukarev 75), Bardon■, Yovov(Koprivarov 70), Domovchiyski (Angelov E 58).
Schalke: Rost; Altintop, Bordon, Krstajic (Rodriguez 83), Kobiashvili, Poulsen, Ernst, Lincoln, Larsen (Varela 46), Asamoah, Kuranyi (Sand 74).

Rapid Bucharest (0) 1 *(Moldovan 50)*
Steaua (1) 1 *(Nicolita 5)* 19,000

Rapid Bucharest: Coman; Constantin M, Maftei, Rada, Badoi, Dica (Negru 79), Stancu C, Stancu I (Grigore 46), Niculae, Moldovan (Burdujan 65), Buga.
Steaua: Carlos; Ogararu, Goian, Ghionea, Marin, Nicolita (Nesu 90), Radoi, Paraschiv (Cristocea 67), Dica, Oprita, Cristea (Lovin 60).

Sevilla (1) 4 *(Saviola 15, 80, Marti 56 (pen), Adriano Correia 90)*
Zenit (1) 1 *(Kerzhakov A 45)* 28,663

Sevilla: Palop; Marti (Maresca 75), Javi Navarro, Escude, David, Fernando Sales (Puerta 63), Jordi Lopez (Blanco 81), Renato, Adriano Correia, Saviola, Kanoute.
Zenit: Malafeev; Aniukov, Krizanac, Hagen■, Skrtel, Sirl (Mares 76), Sumulikoski (Gorshkov 88), Radimov, Denisov (Spivak 29), Arshavin■, Kerzhakov A.

QUARTER-FINALS, SECOND LEG

Thursday, 6 April 2006

Middlesbrough (1) 4 *(Viduka 33, 57, Hasselbaink 79, Maccarone 90)*
Basle (1) 1 *(Eduardo Da Silva 23)* 24,521

Middlesbrough: Schwarzer; Parnaby, Queudrue (Maccarone 67), Boateng, Riggott, Southgate, Morrison (Hasselbaink 46), Rochemback (Taylor 90), Yakubu, Viduka, Downing.
Basle: Zuberbuhler; Zanni, Majstorovic■, Smiljanic, Berner, Degen (Chipperfield 61), Delgado (Ergic 70), Ba, Petric, Sterjovski (Quennoz 85), Eduardo Da Silva.

Schalke (0) 1 *(Lincoln 58)*
Levski (1) 1 *(Angelov E 24)* 52,973

Schalke: Rost; Rafinha, Bordon, Rodriguez, Poulsen, Kobiashvili, Lincoln (Azaouagh 85), Bajramovic, Kuranyi (Sand 78), Asamoah (Altintop 73), Larsen.
Levski: Petkov; Hristov (Bukarev 5), Milanov, Tomasic, Borimirov, Domovchiyski, Ivanov (Telkiyski 65), Angelov S, Koprivarov (Yovov 62), Wagner, Angelov E.

Steaua (0) 0
Rapid Bucharest (0) 0 45,000

Steaua: Carlos; Goian, Ghionea, Marin (Lovin 78), Ogararu, Paraschiv, Radoi, Dica, Oprita (Nesu 67), Nicolita, Cristea (Balan 90).
Rapid Bucharest: Coman; Stancu I, Rada, Maftei, Constantin M, Badoi, Grigore, Stancu C (Dica 64), Buga (Vasilache 76), Moldovan (Burdujan 70), Niculae.

Zenit (0) 1 *(Hyun 50)*
Sevilla (0) 1 *(Kepa 66)* 18,500

Zenit: Malafeev; Aniukov, Krizanac■, Skrtel, Mares, Hyun (Kozhanov 58), Radimov, Vlasov, Sirl (Trifonov 79), Poskus, Kerzhakov A.
Sevilla: Palop; David, Javi Navarro, Escude, Daniel Alves, Jesus Navas, Marti, Maresca (Renato 70), Aitor Ocio, Adriano Correia (Fernando Sales 56), Luis Fabiano (Kepa■ 65).

SEMI-FINALS, FIRST LEG

Thursday, 20 April 2006

Schalke (0) 0

Sevilla (0) 0 53,551

Schalke: Rost; Krstajic■, Bordon, Altintop (Lincoln 46), Rafinha, Poulsen, Kobiashvili, Ernst (Bajramovic 74), Varela (Kuranyi 65), Larsen, Asamoah.
Sevilla: Palop; Javi Navarro, David, Daniel Alves, Escude, Marti, Maresca, Puerta (Adriano Correia 82), Jesus Navas, Saviola (Luis Fabiano 61), Kanoute (Renato 32).

Steaua (1) 1 *(Dica 30)*

Middlesbrough (0) 0 22,000

Steaua: Carlos; Ogararu, Ghionea, Goian, Marin, Radoi, Bostina, Parashiv (Lovin 86), Dica, Nicolita, Oprita (Cristea 89).
Middlesbrough: Schwarzer; Parnaby, Queudrue, Boateng, Ehiogu, Bates, Morrison (Parlour 70), Rochemback, Hasselbaink, Yakubu (Maccarone 70), Downing.

SEMI-FINALS, SECOND LEG

Thursday, 27 April 2006

Middlesbrough (1) 4 *(Maccarone 33, 89, Viduka 64, Riggott 73)*

Steaua (2) 2 *(Dica 16, Goian 24)* 34,622

Middlesbrough: Jones; Parnaby, Queudrue, Boateng, Riggott, Southgate (Maccarone 26), Taylor (Yakubu 55), Rochemback, Hasselbaink (Ehiogu 90), Viduka, Downing.
Steaua: Carlos; Ogararu, Ghionea, Goian, Marin, Oprita (Baciu 81), Radoi, Lovin, Bostina (Nesu 86), Dica, Iacob (Balan 65).

Sevilla (0) 1 *(Puerta 101)*

Schalke (0) 0 45,000

Sevilla: Palop; Daniel Alves, Aitor Ocio, Escude, David, Jesus Navas, Marti, Maresca, Adriano Correia (Puerta 77), Luis Fabiano (Renato 99), Saviola (Makukula 107).
Schalke: Rost; Rafinha, Bordon, Rodriguez, Kobiashvili, Poulsen, Ernst, Asamoah, Lincoln, Bajramovic (Varela 62), Kuranyi.
aet.

UEFA CUP FINAL 2006

Wednesday, 10 May 2006
(in Eindhoven, 31,000)

Middlesbrough (0) 0 Sevilla (1) 4 *(Luis Fabiano 26, Maresca 78, 84, Kanoute 89)*

Middlesbrough: Schwarzer; Parnaby, Queudrue (Yakubu 70), Boateng, Riggott, Southgate, Morrison (Maccarone 46), Rochemback, Hasselbaink, Viduka (Cattermole 85), Downing.

Sevilla: Palop; Daniel Alves, Javi Navarro, Escude, David, Jesus Navas, Marti, Maresca, Adriano Correia (Puerta 85), Luis Fabiano (Renato 73), Saviola (Kanoute 46).

Referee: H. Fandel (Germany).

Frederic Kanoute (right) scores Sevilla's fourth goal in the 4-0 win against Middlesbrough in the UEFA Cup Final. (Michael Sohn/AP/EMPICS)

INTERTOTO CUP 2005

FIRST ROUND, FIRST LEG
Beitar Jerusalem 4, Sileks 3
Bohemians 1, Gent 0
Cluj-Napoca 3, Vetra 2
Tiligul 0, Pogon 3
Dinamo Tirana 2, Varteks 1
Slaven 1, Drava 0
Olympiakos (Cy) 0, Gloria 5,
Skala 0, Tampere U 2
Trans 0, Lokeren 2
Valletta 0, Buducnost 5
Vasas 0, Dubnica 0
Victoria 1, IFK Gothenburg 2
Ararat 1, Neuchatel Xamax 3
Smederevo 0, Pobeda 1
Karvan 1, Lech 2
Venecia 1, Sturm Graz 1
Neman 0, Zlin 1
FC Inter 0, IA Akranes 0
Bangor C 1, Dinaburg 2
Zalgiris 1, Lisburn 0
Lombard 2, WIT Georgia 1

FIRST ROUND, SECOND LEG
Buducnost 2, Valletta 2
Sileks 1, Beitar Jerusalem 2
Gent 3, Bohemians 1
IFK Gothenburg 3, Victoria 1
Lech 2, Karvan 0
Lisburn 0, Zalgiris 1
Lokeren 0, Trans 1
Neuchatel Xamax 6, Ararat 0
Drava 0, Slaven 1
Pogon 6, Tiligul 2
Sturm Graz 5, Venecia 0
Varteks 4, Dinamo Tirana 1
Dinaburg 2, Bangor C 0
Pobeda 2, Smederevo 0
Zlin 0, Neman 0
Vetra 1, Cluj-Napoca 4
Gloria 11, Olympiakos (Cy) 0
IA Akranes 0, FC Inter 4
Tampere U 1, Skala 0
WIT Georgia 0, Lombard 1
Dubnica 2, Vasas 0

SECOND ROUND, FIRST LEG
Ankara 0, Dubnica 4
Cluj-Napoca 1, Athletic Bilbao 0
La Coruna 3, Buducnost 0
Gent 1, Zlin 0
Hamburg 4, Pobeda 1
Slovan Liberec 5, Beitar Jerusalem 1
Lokeren 1, Young Boys 4
Slaven 3, Gloria 2
Sigma Olomouc 1, Pogon 0
St Etienne 1, Neuchatel Xamax 1
Varteks 4, FC Inter 3
Wolfsburg 2, Sturm Graz 2
Lens 2, Lech 1
Lombard 2, IFK Gothenburg 3
Tampere U 1, Charleroi 0
Zalgiris 2, Dinaburg 0

SECOND ROUND, SECOND LEG
Athletic Bilbao 0, Cluj-Napoca 1
Buducnost 2, La Coruna 1
Charleroi 0, Tampere U 0
Dinaburg 2, Zalgiris 1
IFK Gothenburg 1, Lombard 0
Pogon 0, Sigma Olomouc 0
Sturm Graz 1, Wolfsburg 3
Dubnica 0, Ankara 1
Beitar Jerusalem 1, Slovan Liberec 2
FC Inter 2, Varteks 2
Pobeda 1, Hamburg 4
Zlin 0, Gent 0
Gloria 0, Slaven 1
Lech 0, Lens 1
Neuchatel Xamax 1, St Etienne 2
Young Boys 2, Lokeren 1

THIRD ROUND, FIRST LEG
Aigaleo 1, Zalgiris 3
Borussia Dortmund 1, Sigma Olomouc 1
La Coruna 1, Slaven 0
Roda JC 0, Slovan Liberec 0
Uniao Leiria 0, Hamburg 1
Varteks 1, Lens 1
Young Boys 2, Marseille 3
Gent 0, Valencia 0
Cluj-Napoca 1, St Etienne 1
IFK Gothenburg 0, Wolfsburg 2
Lazio 3, Tampere U 0
Dubnica 1, Newcastle U 3

THIRD ROUND, SECOND LEG
Zalgiris 2, Aigaleo 3
Hamburg 2, Uniao Leiria 0
Lens 4, Varteks 1
Slovan Liberec 1, Roda JC 1
Marseille 2, Young Boys 1
Slaven 0, La Coruna 3
Newcastle U 2, Dubnica 0
Sigma Olomouc 0, Borussia Dortmund 0
Tampere U 1, Lazio 1
Valencia 2, Gent 0
Wolfsburg 2, IFK Gothenburg 0
St Etienne 2, Cluj-Napoca 2

SEMI-FINAL, FIRST LEG
La Coruna 2, Newcastle U 1
Lazio 1, Marseille 1
Sigma Olomouc 0, Hamburg 1
Wolfsburg 0, Lens 0
Zalgiris 1, Cluj-Napoca 2
Valencia 4, Roda JC 0

SEMI-FINAL, SECOND LEG
Cluj-Napoca 5, Zalgiris 1
Hamburg 3, Sigma Olomouc 0
Lens 4, Wolfsburg 0
Marseille 3, Lazio 0
Newcastle U 1, La Coruna 2
Roda JC 0, Valencia 0

FINAL FIRST LEG
Cluj-Napoca 1, Lens 1
Hamburg 1, Valencia 0
La Coruna 2, Marseille 0

FINAL SECOND LEG
Lens 3, Cluj-Napoca 1
Marseille 5, La Coruna 1
Valencia 0, Hamburg 0
Hamburg, Lens and Marseille qualify for the UEFA Cup.

Dubnica (1) 1 *(Tesak 42)*

Newcastle U (2) 3 *(Chopra 4, Shearer 6, Milner 70)*

Newcastle: Harper; Taylor, Babayaro, Faye, Elliott, Boumsong, Milner, Butt, Shearer, Chopra (Brittain 58), N'Zogbia.

Newcastle U (0) 2 *(Shearer 72, 90)*

Dubnica (0) 0 25,135

Newcastle U: Given; Carr, Babayaro, Faye, Taylor, Boumsong, Jenas, Bowyer, Shearer, Milner, N'Zogbia (Brittain 60).

La Coruna (1) 2 *(Ruben Castro 11, Andrade 58)*

Newcastle U (0) 1 *(Bowyer 47)*

Newcastle U: Given; Carr, Babayaro, Faye, Taylor, Boumsong, Milner (Chopra 71), Butt, Shearer, Bowyer, N'Zogbia.

Newcastle U (1) 1 *(Milner 39)*

La Coruna (1) 2 *(Andrade 45, Munitis 48)* 35,200

Newcastle U: Given; Carr, Elliott, Faye (Ameobi 53), Taylor, Boumsong, Milner (N'Zogbia 72), Bowyer, Shearer, Parker, Emre (Brittain 90).

UEFA CHAMPIONS LEAGUE 2006–07

Champions League 2006–07 participating clubs

IOC	*Stage*	*Club*
ESP	Grp	FC Barcelona (holders)
ESP	Grp	Real Madrid CF
ESP	Q3	Valencia CF
ESP	Q3	CA Osasuna
ENG	Grp	Chelsea FC
ENG	Grp	Manchester United FC
ENG	Q3	Liverpool FC
ENG	Q3	Arsenal FC
ITA	Grp	Juventus
ITA	Grp	AC Milan
ITA	Q3	FC Internazionale Milano
ITA	Q3	ACF Fiorentina
FRA	Grp	Olympique Lyonnais
FRA	Grp	FC Girondins de Bordeaux
FRA	Q3	LOSC Lille Métropole
GER	Grp	FC Bayern München
GER	Grp	Werder Bremen
GER	Q3	Hamburger SV
POR	Grp	FC Porto
POR	Grp	Sporting Clube de Portugal
POR	Q3	SL Benfica
NED	Grp	PSV Eindhoven
NED	Q3	AFC Ajax
GRE	Grp	Olympiacos CFP
GRE	Q3	AEK Athens FC
BEL	Grp	RSC Anderlecht
BEL	Q3	R. Standard de Liège
SCO	Grp	Celtic FC
SCO	Q2	Heart of Midlothian FC
TUR	Q3	Galatasaray SK
TUR	Q2	Fenerbahçe SK
CZE	Q3	FC Slovan Liberec
CZE	Q2	FK Mladá Boleslav
RUS	Q3	PFC CSKA Moskva
RUS	Q2	FC Spartak Moskva
AUT	Q3	FK Austria Wien
AUT	Q2	SV Austria Salzburg
UKR	Q3	FC Shakhtar Donetsk
UKR	Q2	FC Dynamo Kyiv
ISR	Q3	Maccabi Haifa FC
SCG	Q2	FK Crvena Zvezda
POL	Q2	Legia Warszawa
SUI	Q2	FC Zürich
NOR	Q2	Vålerenga IF
BUL	Q2	PFC Levski Sofia
CRO	Q2	NK Dinamo Zagreb
DEN	Q2	FC København
HUN	Q2	Debreceni VSC
ROU	Q2	FC Steaua Bucuresti
SWE	Q2	Djurgårdens IF
SVK	Q2	MFK Ružomberok
SLO	Q1	NK Gorica
CYP	Q1	Apollon Limassol FC
BIH	Q1	NK Široki Brijeg
LAT	Q1	FHK Liepajas Metalurgs
FIN	Q1	Myllykosken Pallo-47
MOL	Q1	FC Sheriff
GEO	Q1	FC Sioni Bolnisi
LIT	Q1	FK Ekranas
ISL	Q1	FH Hafnarfjördur
MKD	Q1	FK Rabotnicki
IRL	Q1	Cork City FC
BLS	Q1	FC Shakhtyor Soligorsk
ARM	Q1	FC Pyunik
MLT	Q1	Birkirkara FC
ALB	Q1	KS Elbasani
EST	Q1	FC TVMK Tallinn
NIR	Q1	Linfield FC
WAL	Q1	The New Saints FC
LUX	Q1	F91 Dudelange
AZE	Q1	FK Baku
FAR	Q1	B36 Tórshavn
KAZ	Q1	FK Aktobe

UEFA CUP 2006–07

UEFA Cup 2006–07 participating clubs

IOC	*Round*	*Club*
ESP	1st	Sevilla FC (holders)
ESP	1st	RCD Espanyol *
ESP	1st	RC Celta de Vigo
ENG	1st	Tottenham Hotspur FC
ENG	1st	Blackburn Rovers FC
ENG	1st	West Ham United FC **
ITA	1st	AS Roma
ITA	1st	S.S. Lazio
ITA	1st	AC Chievo Verona
FRA	1st	Paris Saint-Germain FC
FRA	1st	RC Lens
FRA	1st	AS Nancy-Lorraine ***
GER	1st	FC Schalke 04
GER	1st	Bayer 04 Leverkusen
GER	1st	Eintracht Frankfurt **
POR	1st	SC Braga
POR	1st	CD Nacional
POR	1st	Vitória FC **
NED	1st	FC Groningen
NED	1st	AZ Alkmaar
NED	1st	Feyenoord
NED	1st	SC Heerenveen
GRE	1st	Panathinaikos FC
GRE	1st	Iraklis FC
GRE	1st	Skoda Xanthi FC
GRE	1st	Atromitos FC
BEL	1st	SV Zulte-Waregem *
BEL	Q2	Club Brugge KV
BEL	Q1	KSV Roeselare *****
SCO	1st	Rangers FC
SCO	Q2	Gretna FC
TUR	1st	Beşiktaş JK
TUR	Q2	Trabzonspor
CZE	1st	AC Sparta Praha *
CZE	Q2	SK Slavia Praha
RUS	1st	FC Lokomotiv Moskva
RUS	Q2	FC Rubin Kazan
AUT	1st	SV Pasching
AUT	Q2	SV Mattersburg
UKR	Q2	FC Chornomorets Odesa
UKR	Q2	FC Metalurh Zaporizhya **
ISR	Q2	Hapoel Tel-Aviv FC *
ISR	Q2	Beitar Jerusalem FC
ISR	Q2	Bnei Yehuda Tel-Aviv FC
SCG	Q2	FK Partizan
SCG	Q2	FK Hajduk Kula
SCG	Q2	OFK Beograd **
POL	Q2	Wisła Plock *
POL	Q2	Wisła Kraków
POL	Q1	Zagębie Lubin
SUI	Q2	FC Sion *
SUI	Q1	FC Basel 1893
SUI	Q1	BSC Young Boys
NOR	Q2	Molde FK *
NOR	Q1	IK Start
NOR	Q1	SFK Lyn Oslo
NOR	Q1	SK Brann *****
BUL	Q1	PFC CSKA Sofia *
BUL	Q1	PFC Litex Lovech
BUL	Q1	PFC Lokomotiv Sofia
CRO	Q1	HNK Rijeka *
CRO	Q1	NK Varteks
DEN	Q1	Randers FC *
DEN	Q1	Brøndby IF
HUN	Q1	FC Fehérvár *
HUN	Q1	Újpesti TE
ROU	Q1	AFC Rapid Bucuresti *
ROU	Q1	FC Dinamo 1948 Bucuresti
SWE	Q1	IFK Göteborg
SWE	Q1	Åtvidabergs FF **
SWE	Q1	Gefle IF *****
SVK	Q1	FC Artmedia
SVK	Q1	FC Spartak Trnava
SLO	Q1	FC Koper *
SLO	Q1	NK Domžale
CYP	Q1	APOEL FC *
CYP	Q1	AC Omonia
BIH	Q1	NK Orašje *
BIH	Q1	FK Sarajevo
LAT	Q1	FK Ventspils *
LAT	Q1	Skonto FC
FIN	Q1	FC Haka *
FIN	Q1	HJK Helsinki
MOL	Q1	CSF Zimbru Chisinau
MOL	Q1	FC Nistru Otaci **
GEO	Q1	FC Ameri Tbilisi *
GEO	Q1	FC WIT Georgia
LIT	Q1	FBK Kaunas *
LIT	Q1	FK Suduva
ISL	Q1	Valur Reykjavík *
ISL	Q1	ÍA Akranes
MKD	Q1	FK Makedonija GP Skopje *
MKD	Q1	FK Vardar
IRL	Q1	Drogheda United FC *
IRL	Q1	Derry City FC
BLS	Q1	FC BATE Borisov *
BLS	Q1	FC Dinamo Minsk
LIE	Q1	FC Vaduz ****
ARM	Q1	FC MIKA *
ARM	Q1	FC Banants
MLT	Q1	Hibernians FC *
MLT	Q1	Sliema Wanderers FC
ALB	Q1	KF Tirana *
ALB	Q1	KS Dinamo Tirana
EST	Q1	FC Levadia Tallinn
EST	Q1	FC Flora **
NIR	Q1	Glentoran FC
NIR	Q1	Portadown FC
WAL	Q1	Rhyl FC *
WAL	Q1	Llanelli FC
LUX	Q1	AS Jeunesse Esch
LUX	Q1	FC Etzella Ettlebrück
AZE	Q1	FK Karabakh *
AZE	Q1	FK Karvan Evlakh
FAR	Q1	GÍ Gøta *
FAR	Q1	Skála Ítróttarfelag
KAZ	Q1	FC Tobol Kostanay
KAZ	Q1	FC Kairat Almaty
AND	Q1	FC Rànger's
SMR	Q1	S.S. Murata
TBC	Q2	11 Teams as winners of UEFA Intertoto Cup

* domestic cup winners, ** losing domestic cup finalists, *** domestic league cup winners, **** national domestic title winners, ***** Fair Play winners.

SUMMARY OF APPEARANCES

EUROPEAN CUP AND CHAMPIONS LEAGUE (1955–2006)

ENGLISH CLUBS
17 Manchester U
16 Liverpool
10 Arsenal
4 Chelsea, Everton, Leeds U
3 Derby Co, Wolverhampton W, Aston Villa, Newcastle U, Nottingham F
1 Burnley, Tottenham H, Ipswich T, Manchester C, Blackburn R

SCOTTISH CLUBS
25 Rangers
21 Celtic
3 Aberdeen
2 Hearts
1 Dundee, Dundee U, Kilmarnock, Hibernian

WELSH CLUBS
6 Barry T
2 TNS
1 Cwmbran T, Rhyl

NORTHERN IRELAND CLUBS
21 Linfield
11 Glentoran
3 Crusaders, Portadown
1 Glenavon, Ards, Distillery, Derry C, Coleraine, Cliftonville

EIRE CLUBS
7 Shamrock R, Dundalk
6 Shelbourne, Waterford
4 Bohemians
3 Drumcondra, St Patrick's Ath,
2 Sligo R, Limerick, Athlone T, Derry C*
1 Cork Hibs, Cork Celtic, Cork City

Winners: Celtic 1966–67; Manchester U 1967–68, 1998–99; Liverpool 1976–77, 1977–78, 1980–81, 1983–84, 2004–05; Nottingham F 1978–79, 1979–80; Aston Villa 1981–82

Finalists: Celtic 1969–70; Leeds U 1974–75; Liverpool 1984–85; Arsenal 2005–06

EUROPEAN CUP-WINNERS' CUP (1960–99)

ENGLISH CLUBS
6 Tottenham H
5 Manchester U, Liverpool, Chelsea
4 West Ham U
3 Arsenal, Everton
2 Manchester C
1 Wolverhampton W, Leicester C, WBA, Leeds U, Sunderland, Southampton, Ipswich T, Newcastle U

SCOTTISH CLUBS
10 Rangers
8 Aberdeen, Celtic
3 Hearts
2 Dunfermline Ath, Dundee U
1 Dundee, Hibernian, St Mirren, Motherwell, Airdrieonians, Kilmarnock

WELSH CLUBS
14 Cardiff C
8 Wrexham
7 Swansea C
3 Bangor C
1 Borough U, Newport Co, Merthyr Tydfil, Barry T, Llansantfraid, Cwmbran T

NORTHERN IRELAND CLUBS
9 Glentoran
5 Glenavon
4 Ballymena U, Coleraine
3 Crusaders, Linfield
2 Ards, Bangor
1 Derry C, Distillery, Portadown, Carrick Rangers, Cliftonville

EIRE CLUBS
6 Shamrock R
4 Shelbourne
3 Limerick, Waterford, Dundalk, Bohemians
2 Cork Hibs, Galway U, Derry C*, Cork City
1 Cork Celtic, St Patrick's Ath, Finn Harps, Home Farm, University College Dublin, Bray W, Sligo R

Winners: Tottenham H 1962–63; West Ham U 1964–65; Manchester C 1969–70; Chelsea 1970–71, 1997–98; Rangers 1971–72; Aberdeen 1982–83; Everton 1984–85; Manchester U 1990–91; Arsenal 1993–94

Finalists: Rangers 1960–61, 1966–67; Liverpool 1965–66; Leeds U 1972–73; West Ham U 1975–76; Arsenal 1979–80, 1994–95

EUROPEAN FAIRS CUP & UEFA CUP (1955–2006)

ENGLISH CLUBS
13 Leeds U
12 Liverpool
10 Aston Villa, Ipswich T
9 Arsenal, Newcastle U
7 Everton, Manchester U
6 Southampton, Tottenham H, Chelsea
5 Nottingham F, Manchester C
4 Birmingham C, Wolverhampton W, WBA, Blackburn R
3 Sheffield W
2 Stoke C, Derby Co, QPR, Leicester C, Middlesbrough
1 Burnley, Coventry C, Millwall, Norwich C, London Rep XI, Watford, West Ham U, Fulham, Bolton W

SCOTTISH CLUBS
19 Dundee U
16 Hibernian
15 Aberdeen, Celtic
14 Rangers
12 Hearts
7 Kilmarnock
6 Dunfermline Ath
5 Dundee
3 St Mirren
2 Partick T, Motherwell, St Johnstone
1 Morton, Raith R, Livingston

WELSH CLUBS
4 Bangor C, TNS
3 Inter Cardiff (formerly Inter Cable-Tel), Cwmbran T
2 Newtown, Barry T
1 Afan Lido, Haverfordwest, Rhyl, Carmarthen T

NORTHERN IRELAND CLUBS
15 Glentoran
9 Linfield
8 Coleraine
7 Glenavon, Portadown
3 Crusaders
1 Ards, Ballymena U, Bangor

EIRE CLUBS
12 Bohemians
7 Shelbourne
6 Dundalk
5 Shamrock R, Cork City
3 Finn Harps, St Patrick's Ath, Derry C*, Longford T
2 Drumcondra,
1 Cork Hibs, Athlone T, Limerick, Drogheda U, Galway U, Bray Wanderers

Winners: Leeds U 1967–68, 1970–71; Newcastle U 1968–69; Arsenal 1969–70; Tottenham H 1971–72, 1983–84; Liverpool 1972–73, 1975–76, 2000–01; Ipswich T 1980–81

Finalists: London 1955–58, Birmingham C 1958–60, 1960–61; Leeds U 1966–67; Wolverhampton W 1971–72; Tottenham H 1973–74; Dundee U 1986–87; Middlesbrough 2005–06

** Now play in League of Ireland*

WORLD CLUB CHAMPIONSHIP

Played annually up to 1974 and intermittently since then between the winners of the European Cup and the winners of the South American Champions Cup — known as the Copa Libertadores. In 1980 the winners were decided by one match arranged in Tokyo in February 1981 which remained the venue until 2004, when the match was superseded by the FIFA Club World Championship. AC Milan replaced Marseille who had been stripped of their European Cup title in 1993.

1960 Real Madrid beat Penarol 0-0, 5-1
1961 Penarol beat Benfica 0-1, 5-0, 2-1
1962 Santos beat Benfica 3-2, 5-2
1963 Santos beat AC Milan 2-4, 4-2, 1-0
1964 Inter-Milan beat Independiente 0-1, 2-0, 1-0
1965 Inter-Milan beat Independiente 3-0, 0-0
1966 Penarol beat Real Madrid 2-0, 2-0
1967 Racing Club beat Celtic 0-1, 2-1, 1-0
1968 Estudiantes beat Manchester United 1-0, 1-1
1969 AC Milan beat Estudiantes 3-0, 1-2
1970 Feyenoord beat Estudiantes 2-2, 1-0
1971 Nacional beat Panathinaikos* 1-1, 2-1
1972 Ajax beat Independiente 1-1, 3-0
1973 Independiente beat Juventus* 1-0
1974 Atlético Madrid* beat Independiente 0-1, 2-0
1975 Independiente and Bayern Munich could not agree dates; no matches.
1976 Bayern Munich beat Cruzeiro 2-0, 0-0
1977 Boca Juniors beat Borussia Moenchengladbach* 2-2, 3-0
1978 Not contested
1979 Olimpia beat Malmö* 1-0, 2-1
1980 Nacional beat Nottingham Forest 1-0
1981 Flamengo beat Liverpool 3-0
1982 Penarol beat Aston Villa 2-0
1983 Gremio Porto Alegre beat SV Hamburg 2-1
1984 Independiente beat Liverpool 1-0
1985 Juventus beat Argentinos Juniors 4-2 on penalties after a 2-2 draw
1986 River Plate beat Steaua Bucharest 1-0
1987 FC Porto beat Penarol 2-1 after extra time
1988 Nacional (Uru) beat PSV Eindhoven 7-6 on penalties after 1-1 draw
1989 AC Milan beat Atletico Nacional (Col) 1-0 after extra time
1990 AC Milan beat Olimpia 3-0
1991 Red Star Belgrade beat Colo Colo 3-0
1992 Sao Paulo beat Barcelona 2-1
1993 Sao Paulo beat AC Milan 3-2
1994 Velez Sarsfield beat AC Milan 2-0
1995 Ajax beat Gremio Porto Alegre 4-3 on penalties after 0-0 draw
1996 Juventus beat River Plate 1-0
1997 Borussia Dortmund beat Cruzeiro 2-0
1998 Real Madrid beat Vasco da Gama 2-1
1999 Manchester U beat Palmeiras 1-0
2000 Boca Juniors beat Real Madrid 2-1
2001 Bayern Munich beat Boca Juniors 1-0 after extra time
2002 Real Madrid beat Olimpia 2-0
2003 Boca Juniors beat AC Milan 3-1 on penalties after 1-1 draw
2004 Porto beat Once Caldas 8-7 on penalties after 0-0 draw

*European Cup runners-up; winners declined to take part.

FIFA CLUB WORLD CHAMPIONSHIP 2005

(In Japan)

QUARTER-FINALS

Al Ittihad (0) 1 *(Noor 78),* **Al Ahly (0) 0**
att: 28,281 in Tokyo.

Sydney FC (0) 0, Deportivo Saprissa (0) 1 *(Bolanos 47)*
att: 28,538 in Toyota.

SEMI-FINALS

Al Ittihad (1) 2 *(Noor 33, Al Montashari 68)*
Sao Paulo (1) 3 *(Amoroso 16, 47, Rogerio Ceni 57 (pen))*
att: 31,510 in Tokyo.

Deportivo Saprissa (0) 0, Liverpool (2) 3 *(Crouch 3, 58, Gerrard 32)*
Liverpool: Reina; Josemi, Traore, Xabi Alonso (Hamann 79), Carragher, Hyypia (Luis Garcia 72), Sissoko, Gerrard (Sinama-Pongolle 64), Crouch, Cisse, Riise.
att: 43,902 in Yokohama.

MATCH FOR 5TH PLACE

Al Ahly (1) 1 *(Motab 45),* **Sydney FC (1) 2** *(Yorke 35, Carney 66)*
att: 15,951 in Tokyo.

MATCH FOR 3RD PLACE

Al Ittihad (1) 2 *(Kallon 28, Job 53 (pen))*
Deportivo Saprissa (1) 3 *(Saborio 13, 85 (pen), Gomez 89)*
in Yokohama.

FINAL

Sao Paulo (1) 1 *(Mineiro 27)*
Liverpool (0) 0
Sao Paulo: Rogerio Ceni; Cicinho, Fabao, Edcarlos, Lugano, Junior, Mineiro, Josue, Danilo, Amoroso, Aloisio (Grafite 75).
Liverpool: Reina; Finnan, Warnock (Riise 79), Xabi Alonso, Carragher, Hyypia, Sissoko (Sinama Pongolle 79), Gerrard, Luis Garcia, Morientes (Crouch 85), Kewell.
att: 66,821 in Yokohama.

EUROPEAN SUPER CUP

Played annually between the winners of the European Champions' Cup and the European Cup-Winners' Cup (UEFA Cup from 2000). AC Milan replaced Marseille in 1993–94.

1972 Ajax beat Rangers 3-1, 3-2
1973 Ajax beat AC Milan 0-1, 6-0
1974 Not contested
1975 Dynamo Kiev beat Bayern Munich 1-0, 2-0
1976 Anderlecht beat Bayern Munich 4-1, 1-2
1977 Liverpool beat Hamburg 1-1, 6-0
1978 Anderlecht beat Liverpool 3-1, 1-2
1979 Nottingham F beat Barcelona 1-0, 1-1
1980 Valencia beat Nottingham F 1-0, 1-2
1981 Not contested
1982 Aston Villa beat Barcelona 0-1, 3-0
1983 Aberdeen beat Hamburg 0-0, 2-0
1984 Juventus beat Liverpool 2-0
1985 Juventus v Everton not contested due to UEFA ban on English clubs
1986 Steaua Bucharest beat Dynamo Kiev 1-0
1987 FC Porto beat Ajax 1-0, 1-0
1988 KV Mechelen beat PSV Eindhoven 3-0, 0-1
1989 AC Milan beat Barcelona 1-1, 1-0
1990 AC Milan beat Sampdoria 1-1, 2-0
1991 Manchester U beat Red Star Belgrade 1-0
1992 Barcelona beat Werder Bremen 1-1, 2-1
1993 Parma beat AC Milan 0-1, 2-0
1994 AC Milan beat Arsenal 0-0, 2-0
1995 Ajax beat Zaragoza 1-1, 4-0
1996 Juventus beat Paris St Germain 6-1, 3-1
1997 Barcelona beat Borussia Dortmund 2-0, 1-1
1998 Chelsea beat Real Madrid 1-0
1999 Lazio beat Manchester U 1-0
2000 Galatasaray beat Real Madrid 2-1
2001 Liverpool beat Bayern Munich 3-2
2002 Real Madrid beat Feyenoord 3-1
2003 AC Milan beat Porto 1-0
2004 Valencia beat Porto 2-1
2005 Liverpool beat CSKA Moscow 3-1

EUROPEAN SUPER CUP 2005–06

26 August 2005, in Monaco (attendance 16,000)

Liverpool (0) 3 *(Cisse 82, 102, Luis Garcia 109)* **CSKA Moscow (1) 1** *(Daniel Carvalho 28)*

Liverpool: Reina; Josemi, Riise (Cisse 79), Hamann, Carragher, Hyypia, Finnan (Sinama-Pongolle 54), Xabi Alonso (Sissoko 70), Luis Garcia, Morientes, Zenden.

CSKA Moscow: Akinfeev; Odiah Chidi, Zhirkov (Semberas 65), Berezoutski V, Ignashevich, Berezoutski A, Rahmic, Krasic (Dudu 84), Vagner Love, Daniel Carvalho, Aldonin.

Referee: R. Timmink (Holland).

INTERNATIONAL DIRECTORY

The latest available information has been given regarding numbers of clubs and players registered with FIFA, the world governing body. Where known, official colours are listed. With European countries, League tables show a number of signs. * indicates relegated teams, + play-offs, *+ relegated after play-offs, ++ promoted.

There are 207 member associations. The four home countries, England, Scotland, Northern Ireland and Wales, are dealt with elsewhere in the Yearbook; but basic details appear in this directory.

EUROPE

ALBANIA

The Football Association of Albania, Rruga Labinoti, Pallati Perballe Shkolles 'Gjuhet e Huaja'.
Founded: 1930; *Number of Clubs:* 49; *Number of Players:* 5,192; *National Colours:* Red shirts, black shorts, red stockings.
Telephone: 00-355-43/46 601; *Fax:* 00-355-43/46 609.

International matches 2005
Ukraine (h) 0-2, Turkey (a) 0-2, Greece (a) 0-2, Poland (a) 0-1, Georgia (h) 3-2, Denmark (a) 1-3, Azerbaijan (h) 2-1, Kazakhstan (h) 2-1, Ukraine (a) 2-2, Turkey (h) 0-1.

League Championship wins (1930–37; 1945–2006)
SK Tirana 22 (including 17 Nentori 8); Dinamo Tirana 16; Partizani Tirana 15; Vllaznia 9; Elbasan 2 (including Labinoti 1); Flamurtari 1; Skenderbeu 1; Teuta 1.

Cup wins (1948–2006)
Partizani Tirana 15; Dinamo Tirana 13; SK Tirana 12 (including 17 Nentori 8); Vllaznia 5; Teuta 3; Elbasan 2 (including Labinoti 1); Flamurtari 2; Apolonia 1.

Final League Table 2005–06

	P	*W*	*D*	*L*	*F*	*A*	*Pts*
Elbasan	36	21	10	5	50	22	73
SK Tirana	36	17	11	8	54	33	62
Dinamo Tirana	36	17	10	9	53	35	61
Partizani	36	18	6	12	51	35	60
Besa	36	13	7	16	49	42	46
Vllaznia	36	13	6	17	39	45	45
Shkumbini	36	12	7	17	31	49	43
Teuta+	36	11	9	16	32	45	42
Skenderbeu+	36	12	6	18	33	50	42
Lushnja*	36	5	10	21	22	58	25

Top scorer: Salihi (SK Tirana) 28.
Cup Final: SK Tirana 1, Vllaznia 0.

ANDORRA

Federacio Andorrana de Futbol, Avinguda Carlemany 67, 3er Pis, Apartado postal 65, Escaldes-Engordany, Principat D'Andorra.
Founded: 1994; *Number of Clubs:* 12; *Number of Players:* 300; *National Colours:* Yellow shirts, red shorts, blue stockings.
Telephone: 00376/805 830; *Fax:* 00376/862 006.

International matches 2005
Macedonia (a) 0-0, Armenia (a) 1-2, Czech Republic (h) 0-4, Czech Republic (a) 1-8, Romania (a) 0-2, Finland (h) 0-0, Holland (a) 0-4, Armenia (h) 0-3.

League Championship wins (1996–2006)
Principat 3; Encamp 2; Santa Coloma 2; Dicoansa 1; Constelacio 1; St Julia 1; Rangers 1.

Cup wins (1996–2006)
Santa Coloma 5; Principat 4; Constelacio 1; Lusitanos 1.

Qualifying League Table 2005–06

	P	*W*	*D*	*L*	*F*	*A*	*Pts*
Rangers	14	12	1	1	62	7	37
St Julia	14	10	2	2	53	12	32
Santa Coloma	14	9	1	4	41	12	28
Lusitanos	14	8	0	6	26	29	24
Inter	14	7	2	5	22	23	23
Atletic	14	3	3	8	10	24	12
Principat	14	1	2	11	12	45	5
Extremenya	14	0	1	13	9	83	1

Championship Play-Offs

	P	*W*	*D*	*L*	*F*	*A*	*Pts*
Rangers	20	16	3	1	73	12	51
St Julia	20	12	3	5	61	19	39
Santa Coloma	20	11	3	6	47	17	36
Lusitanos	20	9	1	10	30	41	28

Relegation Play-Offs

	P	W	D	L	F	A	Pts
Inter	20	11	3	6	36	28	36
Atletic	20	8	4	8	21	27	28
Principat	20	3	2	15	18	55	11
Extremenya*	20	0	1	19	11	98	1

Cup Final: Santa Coloma 1, Rangers 1
Santa Coloma won 5-3 on penalties.

ARMENIA

Football Federation of Armenia, Saryan 38, Yerevan, 375 010, Armenia.
Founded: 1992; *Number of Clubs:* 32; *Number of Players:* 15,000; *National Colours:* Red shirts, blue shorts, orange stockings.
Telephone: 00374-1/535 084; *Fax:* 00374-1/539517.

International matches 2005
Kuwait (a) 1-3, Andorra (h) 2-1, Holland (a) 0-2, Macedonia (h) 1-2, Romania (a) 0-3, Jordan (a) 0-0, Holland (h) 0-1, Czech Republic (a) 1-4, Andorra (a) 3-0.

League Championship wins (1992–2006)
Pyunik 8 (including Homenetmen 2); Shirak Gyumri 4*; Ararat Yerevan 2*; FC Yerevan 1; Tsement 1; Araks 1.
*Includes one unofficial title.

Cup wins (1992–2006)
Mika 5; Ararat Yerevan 4; Pyunik 3; Tsement 2; Banants 1.

Qualifying League Table 2005

	P	*W*	*D*	*L*	*F*	*A*	*Pts*
Pyunik	16	11	5	0	32	6	38
Mika	16	10	5	1	27	11	35
Banants	16	10	4	2	32	17	34
Esteghlal	16	7	7	2	28	15	28
Kilikia	16	6	3	7	29	25	21
Dinamo-Zenit	16	4	3	9	20	26	15
Shirak+	16	3	2	11	18	34	11
Ararat+	16	3	1	12	9	38	10
Lernayin+	16	3	0	13	14	37	9

Kotiak renamed Esteghlal; Lernayin withdrew after 11 matches, remaining games awarded 0-3 against them.

Championship League Table 2005

	P	*W*	*D*	*L*	*F*	*A*	*Pts*
Pyunik	20	11	6	3	35	15	39
Mika	20	9	8	3	30	16	35
Banants	20	9	6	5	31	27	33
Esteghlal	20	8	7	5	22	19	31
Kilikia	20	4	5	11	20	32	17
Dinamo-Zenit	20	2	2	16	12	41	8

Relegation Table 2005

	P	*W*	*D*	*L*	*F*	*A*	*Pts*
Ararat	18	4	2	12	11	39	14
Shirak	18	3	3	12	19	36	12
Lernayin	16	3	0	13	14	37	9

Play-Off: Shirak 5, Gandzasar 1.
Top scorer: Erzrumian (Kilikia) 18.
Cup Final: Mika 1, Pyunik 0.

AUSTRIA

Oesterreichischer Fussball-Bund, Ernst-Happel Stadion – Sektor A/F, Postfach 340, Meierestrasse 7, Wien 1021.
Founded: 1904; *Number of Clubs:* 2,081; *Number of Players:* 253,576; *National Colours:* White shirts, black shorts, white stockings.
Telephone: 0043-1/727 180; *Fax:* 0043-1/ 728 1632.

International matches 2005
Cyprus (a) 1-1, Latvia (a) 1-1, Wales (a) 2-0, Wales (h) 1-0, Scotland (h) 2-2, Poland (a) 2-3, Azerbaijan (a) 0-0, England (a) 0-1, Northern Ireland (h) 2-0.

League Championship wins (1912–2006)
Rapid Vienna 31; FK Austria 24; Tirol-Svarowski-Innsbruck 10; Admira-Energie-Wacker 9; First Vienna 6; Wiener Sportklub 3; Austria Salzburg 3; Sturm Graz 2; FAC 1; Hakoah 1; Linz ASK 1; WAF 1; Voest Linz 1; Graz 1.

Cup wins (1919–2006)
FK Austria 28; Rapid Vienna 14; TS Innsbruck (formerly Wacker Innsbruck) 7; Admira-Energie-Wacker (formerly Sportklub Admira & Admira-Energie) 5; Graz 4; First Vienna 3; Sturm Graz 3; Linz ASK 1; Wacker Vienna 1; WAF 1; Wiener Sportklub 1; Stockerau 1; Ried 1; Karnten 1.

Final League Table 2005–06

	P	*W*	*D*	*L*	*F*	*A*	*Pts*
FK Austria	36	19	10	7	51	33	67
Salzburg	36	20	3	13	62	42	63
Pasching	36	16	10	10	43	32	58
Ried	36	13	13	10	48	47	52
Rapid	36	13	10	13	51	41	49
Graz	36	13	6	17	47	48	45
Mattersburg	36	12	8	16	40	54	44
Sturm Graz	36	10	12	14	44	51	42
Tirol	36	10	12	14	44	55	42
Admira Modling*	36	9	6	21	42	69	33

Top scorers: Linz (FK Austria), Kuljic (Ried) 15.
Cup Final: FK Austria 3, Mattersburg 0.

AZERBAIJAN

Association of Football Federations of Azerbaijan, 42 Gussi Gadjiev Street, Baku 370 009.
Founded: 1992; *Number of Clubs:* 1,500;. *Number of Players:* 95,000; *National Colours:* White shirts, blue shorts, white stockings.
Telephone: 00994-12/944 916; *Fax:* 00994-12/ 989 393.

International matches 2005
Trinidad & Tobago (a) 0-1, Trinidad & Tobago (a) 0-2, Moldova (h) 0-0, Poland (a) 0-8, England (a) 0-2, Iran (a) 1-2, Poland (h) 0-3, Albania (a) 1-2, Northern Ireland (a) 0-2, Austria (h) 0-0, Wales (a) 0-2.

League Championship wins (1992–2006)
Neftchi 4; Kopaz 3; Shamkir 3; Karabakh 2; Turan 1; Baku 1.
Includes one unofficial title for Shamkir in 2002.

Cup wins (1992–2006)
Kopaz 4; Neftchi 4; Karabakh 2; Inshatchi 1; Shafa 1; Baku 1.

Final League Table 2005–06

	P	*W*	*D*	*L*	*F*	*A*	*Pts*
Baku	26	18	4	4	42	12	58
Karvan	26	17	6	3	50	9	57
Neftchi	26	15	9	2	51	16	54
Inter	26	14	8	4	35	14	50
Karabakh	26	12	4	10	32	32	40
Turan	26	11	5	10	27	21	38
Xazar	26	9	9	8	27	18	36
Shahdagh	26	10	5	11	26	36	35
MKT Araz	26	9	8	9	31	36	35
Ganca	26	7	7	12	35	44	28
Ganclarbirliyi	26	6	9	11	25	37	27
Olimpik	26	5	8	13	15	27	23
MOIK*	26	2	3	21	11	67	9
Geyazan*	26	0	9	17	14	52	9

Olimpik is the new name for AMMK Baku.
Shamkir, Karat and Energetik all withdrew for financial reasons. MOIK reinstated.
Top scorer: Bamba (Karvan) 16.
Cup Final: Karabakh 2, Karvan 1.

BELARUS

Belarus Football Federation, Kirova Street 8/2, Minsk 220 600, Belarus.
Founded: 1992; *Number of Clubs:* 455; *Number of Players:* 120,000; *National Colours:* Red shirts, green shorts, red stockings.
Telephone: 00375-17/227 2920; *Fax:* 00375-17/227 2920.

International matches 2005
Poland (a) 3-1, Slovenia (a) 1-1, Slovenia (h) 1-1, Scotland (h) 0-0, Lithuania (a) 0-1, Moldova (a) 0-2, Italy (h) 1-4, Scotland (a) 1-0, Norway (h) 0-1, Latvia (h) 3-1.

League Championship wins (1992–2005)
Dynamo Minsk 7; Slavia Mozyr (formerly MPKC Mozyr) 2; BATE Borisov 2; Dnepr Mogilev 1; Belshina 1; Gomel 1; Shakhtyor 1.

Cup wins (1992–2006)
Belshina 3; Dynamo Minsk 3; Slavia Mozyr (formerly MPKC Mozyr) 2; Neman 1; Dynamo 93 Minsk 1; Lokomotiv 96 1; Gomel 1; Shakhtyor 1; MTZ-RIPA 1; BATE Borisov 1.

Final League Table 2005

	P	*W*	*D*	*L*	*F*	*A*	*Pts*
Shakhtyor	26	19	6	1	59	14	63
Dynamo Minsk	26	15	5	6	50	26	50
MTZ-RIPA	26	16	1	9	43	30	49
Topedo Zhodino	26	14	5	7	40	25	47
BATE Borisov	26	12	11	3	42	27	47
Dnepr	26	12	7	7	48	36	43
Gomel	26	12	3	11	34	32	39
Dynamo Brest	26	11	3	12	39	33	36
Naftan	26	10	3	13	43	44	33
Daryda	26	7	8	11	30	36	29
Lakamatyu	26	7	5	14	30	43	26
Neman	26	7	3	16	20	50	24
Zvezda*	26	3	5	18	24	60	14
Slavia*	26	2	5	19	14	60	11

Promoted Vedrych 97 declined to take part; Torpedo Minsk ceased operating leaving 14 clubs to participate.
Top scorer: Stripeikis (Naftan) 15.
Cup Final: BATE Borisov 3, Shakhtyor 1.

BELGIUM

Union Royale Belge Des Societes De Football Association, 145 Avenue Houba de Strooper, B-1020 Bruxelles.
Founded: 1895; *Number of Clubs:* 2,120; *Number of Players:* 390,468; *National Colours:* All red.
Telephone: 0032-2/477 1211; *Fax:* 0032-2/ 478 2391.

International matches 2005
Egypt (a) 0-4, Bosnia (h) 4-1, San Marino (a) 2-1, Serbia & Montenegro (a) 0-0, Greece (h) 2-0, Bosnia (a) 0-1, San Marino (h) 8-0, Spain (h) 0-2, Ukraine (a) 1-1.

League Championship wins (1896–2006)
Anderlecht 28; FC Brugge 13; Union St Gilloise 11; Standard Liege 8; Beerschot 7; RC Brussels 6; FC Liege 5; Daring Brussels 5; Antwerp 4; Mechelen 4; Lierse SK 4; SV Brugge 3; Beveren 2; Genk 2; RWD Molenbeek 1.

Cup wins (1954–2006)
FC Brugge 9; Anderlecht 8; Standard Liege 5; Beerschot 3; Waterschei 2; Beveren 2; Gent 2; Antwerp 2; Lierse SK 2; Genk 2; Racing Doornik 1; Waregem 1; SV Brugge 1; Mechelen 1; FC Liege 1; Ekeren 1; Westerlo 1; La Louviere 1; Waregem 1.

Final League Table 2005–06

	P	*W*	*D*	*L*	*F*	*A*	*Pts*
Anderlecht	34	20	10	4	72	27	70
Standard Liege	34	19	8	7	51	28	65
FC Brugge	34	18	10	6	51	33	64
Gent	34	18	7	9	48	34	61
Genk	34	16	9	9	52	38	57
Beerschot	34	14	7	13	50	45	49
Waregem	34	14	7	13	51	49	49
Lokeren	34	12	11	11	48	49	47
Westerlo	34	13	7	14	42	48	46
FC Brussels	34	12	10	12	30	30	46
Charleroi	34	11	12	11	39	39	45

Roeselare	34	10	11	13	44	42	41
Mouscron	34	11	4	19	43	43	37
CS Brugge	34	10	7	17	38	61	37
St Truiden	34	8	10	16	36	49	34
Beveren	34	9	6	19	35	55	33
Lierse+	34	8	8	18	22	52	32
La Louviere*	34	4	14	16	26	56	26

Top scorer: Dosunmu (Beerschot) 17.
Cup Final: Waregem 2, Mouscron 1.

BOSNIA-HERZEGOVINA

Football Federation of Bosnia & Herzegovina, Ferhadija 30, Sarajevo 71000.
Founded: 1992; *National Colours:* White shirts, blue shorts, white stockings.
Telephone: 00387-33/276 660; *Fax:* 00387-33/444 332.

International matches 2005
Iran (a) 1-2, Belgium (a) 1-4, Lithuania (h) 1-1, San Marino (a) 3-1, Spain (a) 1-1, Estonia (a) 0-1, Belgium (h) 1-0, Lithuania (a) 1-0, San Marino (h) 3-0, Serbia & Montenegro (a) 0-1.

League Championship wins (1996–2006)
Zeljeznicar 3; Siroki 2; Brotnjo 1; Leotar 1; Zrinjski 1.

Cup wins (1996–2006)
Sarajevo 3; Zeljeznicar 3; Bosna 1; Celik 1; Modrica 1; Orasje 1.

Final League Table 2005–06

	P	*W*	*D*	*L*	*F*	*A*	*Pts*
Siroki	30	19	6	5	38	19	63
Sarajevo	30	18	6	6	57	26	60
Zrinjski	30	17	3	10	47	29	54
Modrica	30	17	2	11	53	30	53
Slavija	30	12	5	13	41	47	41
Zeljeznicar	30	11	7	12	38	33	40
Jedinstvo	30	13	1	16	38	40	40
Zepce	30	11	7	12	29	40	40
Leotar	30	12	3	15	43	48	39
Posusje	30	12	3	15	38	46	39
Sloboda	30	11	6	13	31	40	39
Orasje	30	12	2	16	50	51	38
Radnik	30	11	5	14	37	52	38
Celik	30	10	5	15	33	45	35
Travnik*	30	10	4	16	33	41	34
Buducnost*	30	10	3	17	29	48	33

Top scorer: Jelic (Modrica) 19.
Cup Final: Siroki 0, 0, Orasje 0, 3.

BULGARIA

Bulgarian Football Union, Karnigradska Street 19, BG-1000 Sofia.
Founded: 1923; *Number of Clubs:* 376; *Number of Players:* 48,240; *National Colours:* White shirts, green shorts, white stockings.
Telephone: 00359-2/987 7490; *Fax:* 00359-2/986 2538.

International matches 2005
Serbia & Montenegro (h) 0-0, Sweden (h) 0-3, Hungary (a) 1-1, Croatia (h) 1-3, Turkey (h) 3-1, Sweden (a) 0-3, Iceland (h) 3-2, Hungary (h) 2-0, Malta (a) 1-1, Georgia (h) 6-2, Mexico (a) 3-0.

League Championship wins (1925–2006)
CSKA Sofia 30; Levski Sofia 24; Slavia Sofia 7; Vladislav Varna 3; Lokomotiv Sofia 3; Liteks 2; Trakia Plovdiv 2; AC 23 Sofia 1; Botev Plovdiv 1; SC Sofia 1; Sokol Varna 1; Spartak Plovdiv 1; Tichka Varna 1; JSZ Sofia 1; Beroe Stara Zagora 1; Etur 1; Lokomotiv Plovdiv 1.

Cup wins (1946–2006)
Levski Sofia 23; CSKA Sofia 18; Slavia Sofia 7; Lokomotiv Sofia 4; Liteks 2; Botev Plovdiv 1; Spartak Plovdiv 1; Spartak Sofia 1; Marek Stanke 1; Trakia Plovdiv 1; Spartak Varna 1; Sliven 1.

Final League Table 2005-06

	P	*W*	*D*	*L*	*F*	*A*	*Pts*
Levski Sofia	28	21	5	2	71	23	68
CSKA Sofia	28	20	5	3	73	22	65
Liteks	28	18	6	4	51	22	60
Lokomotiv Sofia	28	18	0	10	49	29	54
Lokomotiv Plovdiv	28	11	7	10	43	42	40
Belasitsa	28	11	6	11	33	33	39
Slavia Sofia	28	12	3	13	33	34	39
ChernoVarna	28	10	7	11	29	27	37
Vihren	28	10	2	16	35	55	32
Beroe	28	8	8	12	36	53	32
Marek	28	8	7	13	23	37	31
Rodopa	28	7	4	17	23	52	25
Botev Plovdiv	28	4	12	12	20	38	24
Pirin 1922*	28	5	8	15	23	46	23
Naftex*	28	4	6	18	14	43	18

Pirin were excluded after two matches relegated to regional level for reasons of financial failure.
Top scorer: Furtado (Vihren/CSKA Sofia) 17.
Cup Final: CSKA Sofia 3, Cherno Varna 1.

CROATIA

Croatian Football Federation, Rusanova 13, Zagreb, 10 3000, Croatia.
Founded: 1912; *Number of Clubs:* 1,221; *Number of Players:* 78,127; *National Colours:* Red & white shirts, white shorts, blue stockings.
Telephone: 00385-1/236 1555; *Fax:* 00385-1/244 1501.

International matches 2005
Israel (a) 3-3, Iceland (h) 4-0, Malta (h) 3-0, Bulgaria (a) 3-1, Brazil (h) 1-1, Iceland (a) 3-1, Malta (a) 1-1, Sweden (h) 1-0, Hungary (a) 0-0, Portugal (a) 0-2.

League Championship wins (1941–44; 1992–2006)
Dynamo Zagreb (formerly Croatia Zagreb) 8; Hajduk Split 6; Gradanski 3; Concordia 1; Zagreb 1.

Cup wins (1993–2006)
Dynamo Zagreb (formerly Croatia Zagreb) 7; Hajduk Split 4; Rijeka 2, Osijek 1.

Qualifying Table 2005–06

	P	*W*	*D*	*L*	*F*	*A*	*Pts*
Dynamo Zagreb	22	18	2	2	61	11	56
Rijeka	22	14	3	5	42	28	45
Osijek	22	10	4	8	25	32	34
Varteks	22	10	1	11	34	35	31
Hajduk Split	22	7	8	7	28	21	29
Kamen	22	8	5	9	26	30	29
Pula	22	8	4	10	29	26	28
Zagreb	22	8	3	11	19	27	27
Cibalia	22	7	5	10	24	35	26
Slaven	22	5	7	10	29	38	22
Inter	22	6	4	12	17	34	22
Medimurje	22	5	6	11	26	43	21

Championship Play-Off Table 2005-06

	P	*W*	*D*	*L*	*F*	*A*	*Pts*
Dynamo Zagreb	32	24	4	4	78	21	76
Rijeka	32	20	5	7	61	36	65
Varteks	32	15	2	15	51	48	47
Osijek	32	13	5	14	31	48	44
Hajduk Split	32	10	10	12	40	35	40
Kamen	32	11	5	16	33	47	38

Relegation Table 2005-06

	P	*W*	*D*	*L*	*F*	*A*	*Pts*
Pula	32	13	6	13	44	36	45
Slaven	32	10	11	11	46	48	41
Cibalia	32	9	10	13	33	47	37
Zagreb	32	11	4	17	26	43	37
Medimurje+	32	9	9	14	40	51	36
Inter*	32	8	7	17	30	53	31

Top scorer: Bosnjak (Dynamo Zagreb) 22.
Cup Final: Rijeka 4, 1, Varteks 0, 5.

CYPRUS

Cyprus Football Association, 1 Stasinos Str., Engomi, P.O. Box 25071, Nicosia 2404.
Founded: 1934; *Number of Clubs:* 85; *Number of Players:* 6,000; *National Colours:* Blue shirts, white shorts, blue stockings.
Telephone: 00357-22/590 960; *Fax:* 00357-22/590 544.

International matches 2005
Austria (h) 1-1, Finland (h) 1-2, Jordan (h) 2-1, Switzerland (a) 0-1, Iraq (h) 2-1, Faeroes (a) 3-0, Switzerland (h) 1-3, Republic of Ireland (h) 0-1, France (a) 0-4, Wales (h) 1-0.

League Championship wins (1935–2006)
Omonia 19; Apoel 18; Anorthosis 12; AEL 5; EPA 3; Olympiakos 3; Apollon 3; Pezoporikos 2; Chetin Kayal 1; Trast 1.

Cup wins (1935–2006)
Apoel 18; Omonia 12; Anorthosis 7; AEL 6; EPA 5; Apollon 5; Trast 3; Chetin Kayal 2; Olympiakos 1; Pezoporikos 1; Salamina 1; AEK 1.

Final League Table 2005–06

	P	*W*	*D*	*L*	*F*	*A*	*Pts*
Apollon	26	19	7	0	68	24	64
Omonia	26	20	3	3	59	20	63
Apoel	26	19	5	2	63	22	62
Anorthosis	26	15	8	3	55	26	53
ENP	26	12	7	7	40	28	43
NEA Salamina	26	12	5	9	53	48	41
AEL	26	10	5	11	44	48	35
AEK	26	9	4	13	39	37	31
Ethnikos Achnas	26	8	4	14	42	43	28
Digenis	26	7	7	12	33	45	28
Olympiakos	26	6	9	11	40	50	27
APOP*	26	5	3	18	35	65	18
APEP*	26	1	5	20	17	72	8
ENTHOI*	26	1	4	21	15	75	7

Top scorer: Sosin (Apollon) 28.
Cup Final: Apoel 3, AEK 2.

CZECH REPUBLIC

Football Association of Czech Republic, Diskarska 100, Prague 6 16017 – Strahov, Czech Republic.
Founded: 1901; *Number of Clubs:* 3,836; *Number of Players:* 319,500; *National Colours:* Red shirts, white shorts, blue stockings.
Telephone: 00420-2/3302 9111; *Fax:* 00420-2/3335 3107.

International matches 2005
Slovenia (a) 3-0, Finland (h) 4-3, Andorra (a) 4-0, Andorra (h) 8-1, Macedonia (h) 6-1, Sweden (a) 1-2, Romania (a) 0-2, Armenia (h) 4-1, Holland (h) 0-2, Finland (a) 3-0, Norway (a) 1-0, Norway (h) 1-0.

League Championship wins (1926–93)
Sparta Prague 19; Slavia Prague 12; Dukla Prague (prev. UDA) 11; Slovan Bratislava 7; Spartak Trnava 5; Banik Ostrava 3; Inter-Bratislava 1; Spartak Hradec Kralove 1; Viktoria Zizkov 1; Zbrojovka Brno 1; Bohemians 1; Vitkovice 1.

Cup wins (1961–93)
Dukla Prague 8; Sparta Prague 8; Slovan Bratislava 5; Spartak Trnava 4; Banik Ostrava 3; Lokomotiv Kosice 3; TJ Gottwaldov 1; Dunajska Streda 1.
From 1993–94, there were two separate countries; the Czech Republic and Slovakia.

League Championship wins (1994–2006)
Sparta Prague 9; Slovan Liberec 2; Slavia Prague 1; Banik Ostrava 1.

Cup wins (1994–2006)
Slavia Prague 4; Sparta Prague 3; Viktoria Zizkov 2; Spartak Hradec Kralove 1; Jablonec 1; Slovan Liberec 1; Teplice 1; Banik Osrava 1.

Final League Table 2005–06

	P	*W*	*D*	*L*	*F*	*A*	*Pts*
Slovan Liberec	30	16	11	3	43	22	59
Mlada	30	16	6	8	50	36	54
Slavia Prague	30	15	9	6	56	34	54
Teplice	30	12	16	2	38	24	52
Sparta Prague	30	13	6	11	43	39	45
Banik Ostrava	30	10	10	10	35	32	40
Slovacko	30	9	11	10	29	28	38
Jablonec	30	10	7	13	35	39	37
Sigma Olomouc	30	10	7	13	34	44	37
Siad	30	10	6	14	34	41	36
Zlin	30	8	11	11	27	33	35
Brno	30	7	14	9	35	36	35
Marila Pribram	30	8	10	12	36	36	34
Viktoria Plzen	30	7	10	13	30	43	31
Vysocina*	30	6	11	13	20	36	29
Chmel Blsany*	30	5	11	14	22	44	26

Top scorers: Ivana (Slovacko), Kulic (Mlada), Vlcek (Slavia Prague) 11.
Cup Final: Sparta Prague 0, Banik Ostrava 0
Sparta Prague won 4-2 on penalties.

DENMARK

Danish Football Association, Idraettens Hus, Brondby Stadion 20, DK-2605, Brondby.
Founded: 1889; *Number of Clubs:* 1,555; *Number of Players:* 268,517; *National Colours:* Red shirts, white shorts, red stockings.
Telephone: 0045-43/262 222; *Fax:* 0045-43/262 245.

International matches 2005
Greece (a) 1-2, Kazakhstan (h) 3-0, Ukraine (a) 0-1, Finland (a) 1-0, Albania (h) 3-1, England (h) 4-1, Turkey (a) 2-2, Georgia (h) 6-1, Greece (h) 1-0, Kazakhstan (a) 2-1.

League Championship wins (1913–2006)
KB Copenhagen 15; B 93 Copenhagen 10; Brondby 10; AB (Akademisk) 9; B 1903 Copenhagen 7; Frem 6; Esbjerg BK 5; Vejle BK 5; AGF Aarhus 5; FC Copenhagen 5; Hvidovre 3; Odense BK 3; AaB Aalborg 2; B 1909 Odense 2; Koge BK 2; Lyngby 2; Silkeborg 1; Herfolge 1.

Cup wins (1955–2006)
Aarhus GF 9; Vejle BK 6; Brondby 5; OB Odense 4; Randers Freja 4; Lyngby 3; FC Copenhagen 3; B1909 Odense 2; Aalborg BK 2; Esbjerg BK 2; Frem 2; B 1903 Copenhagen 2; B 93 Copenhagen 1; KB Copenhagen 1; Vanlose 1; Hvidovre 1; B1913 Odense 1, AB Copenhagen 1, Viborg 1; Silkeborg 1.

Final League Table 2005–06

	P	*W*	*D*	*L*	*F*	*A*	*Pts*
FC Copenhagen	33	22	7	4	62	27	73
Brondby	33	21	4	8	60	34	67
Odense	33	17	7	9	49	28	58
Viborg	33	15	9	9	62	43	54
Aalborg	33	11	12	10	48	44	45
Esbjerg	33	12	6	15	43	45	42
Midtjylland	33	10	11	12	42	52	41
Silkeborg	33	11	6	16	33	50	39
Nordsjaelland	33	9	11	13	49	55	38
Horsens	33	8	13	12	29	41	37
SonderjyskE*	33	6	8	19	39	70	26
Aarhus*	33	4	10	19	36	63	22

Top scorers: Junker (Nordsjaelland), Santos (FC Copenhagen), Allback (FC Copenhagen), Hojer (Viborg) 15.
Cup Final: Randers 1, Esbjerg 0.

ENGLAND

The Football Association, 25 Soho Square, London W1D 4FA.
Founded: 1863; *Number of Clubs:* 42,000; *Number of Players:* 2,250,000; *National Colours:* White shirts with navy blue collar, navy shorts, white stockings.
Telephone: 020 7745 4545, 020 7402 7151; *Fax:* 020 7745 4546; *Website:* www.the-fa.org

ESTONIA

Estonian Football Association, Rapia 8/10, Tallinn 11312.
Founded: 1921; *Number of Clubs:* 40; *Number of Players:* 12,000; *National Colours:* Blue shirts, black shorts, white stockings.
Telephone: 00372-6/512 720; *Fax:* 00372-6/512 729.

International matches 2005
Venezuela (a) 0-3, Slovakia (h) 1-2, Russia (h) 1-1, Norway (h) 1-2, Liechtenstein (h) 2-0, Portugal (h) 0-1, Bosnia (h) 1-0, Latvia (h) 2-1, Slovakia (a) 0-1, Luxembourg (a) 2-0, Finland (a) 2-2, Poland (a) 1-3.

League Championship wins (1922–40; 1992–2005)
Flora Tallinn 7; Sport 8; Estonia 5; Levadia 3; Norma Tallinn 2; Tallinn JK 2; Kalev 2; LFLS 1; Olimpia 1; Lantana 1; VMK 1.

Cup wins (1992–2006)
Levadia (merged with Sadam) 4; Levadia Tallinn 3; VMV Tallinn 1; Nikol Tallinn 1; Norma Tallinn 1; Lantana 1; Flora Tallinn 1; Trans 1; VMK 1.

Final League Table 2005

	P	W	D	L	F	A	Pts
VMK	36	30	5	1	138	21	95
Levadia Tallinn	36	28	5	3	97	25	89
Trans	36	23	6	7	99	34	75
Flora	36	21	6	9	81	36	69
Viljandi	36	12	11	13	46	48	47
Merkuur	36	11	7	18	52	86	40
Tammeka	36	8	5	23	50	88	29
Valga	36	8	4	24	38	78	28
Kuressaare+	36	7	6	23	40	96	27
Dynamo*	36	3	3	30	28	157	12

Tervis declined promotion; Kuressaare promoted in their place.
Top scorer: Neemelo (VMK) 39.
Cup Final: VMK 1, Flora 0.

FAEROE ISLANDS

Fotboltssamband Foroya, The Faeroes' Football Assn., Gundalur, P.O. Box 3028, FR-110, Torshavn.
Founded: 1979; *Number of Clubs:* 16; *Number of Players:* 1,014; *National Colours:* White shirts, blue shorts, white stockings.
Telephone: 00298/316 707; *Fax:* 00298/319 079.

International matches 2005
Switzerland (h) 1-3, Republic of Ireland (h) 0-2, Cyprus (h) 0-3, France (a) 0-3, Israel (h) 0-2, Israel (a) 1-2.

League Championship wins (1942–2005)
HB Torshavn 18; KI Klaksvik 16; B36 Torshavn 8; TB Tvoroyri 7; GI Gotu 7; B68 Toftir 3; SI Sorvag 1; IF Fuglafjordur 1; B71 Sandur 1; VB 1.

Cup wins (1955–2005)
HB Torshavn 26; GI Gotu 6; KI Klaksvik 5; TB Tvoroyri 4; B36 Torshavn 3; NSI Runavik 2; VB Vagur 1; B71 Sandur 1.

Final League Table 2005

	P	W	D	L	F	A	Pts
B36	27	15	9	3	38	17	54
Skala	27	13	11	3	55	30	50
HB	27	15	5	7	66	35	50
NSI	27	14	8	5	58	44	50
EB/Streymur	27	11	10	6	48	35	43
IF	27	6	9	12	32	57	27
KI	27	7	4	16	40	52	25
VB	27	6	6	15	36	57	24
GI+	27	6	5	16	35	58	23
TB*	27	5	7	15	26	49	22

Top scorer: Jacobsen (NSI) 18.
Cup Final: GI 4, IF 1.

FINLAND

Suomen Palloliitto Finlands Bollfoerbund, Urheilukatu 5, P.O. Box 191, Helsinki 00251.
Founded: 1907; *Number of Clubs:* 1,135; *Number of Players:* 66,100; *National Colours:* White shirts, blue shorts, white stockings.
Telephone: 00358-9/7421 51; *Fax:* 00358-9/7421 4200.

International matches 2005
Latvia (a) 2-1, Cyprus (a) 2-1, Kuwait (a) 1-0, Saudi Arabia (a) 4-1, Czech Republic (a) 3-4, Denmark (h) 0-1, Holland (h) 0-4, Macedonia (a) 3-0, Andorra (a) 0-0, Macedonia (h) 5-1, Romania (h) 0-1, Czech Republic (h) 0-3, Estonia (h) 2-2.

League Championship wins (1949–2005)
HJK Helsinki 12; Valkeakosken Haka 9; Turun Palloseura 5; Kuopion Palloseura 5; Kuusysi 4; Lahden Reipas 3; IF Kamraterna 3; Ilves-Kissat 2; Jazz Pori 2; Kotkan TP 2; OPS Oulu 2; Torun Pyrkiva 1; IF Kronohagens 1; Helsinki PS 1; Kokkolan PV 1; Vasa 1; TPV Tampere 1; Tampere U 1; MyPa 1.

Cup wins (1955–2005)
Valkeakosken Haka 12; HJK Helsinki 8; Lahden Reipas 7; Kotkan TP 4; MyPa 3; Mikkeli 2; Kuusysi 2; Kuopion Palloseura 2; Ilves Tampere 2; TPS Turku 2; IFK Abo 1; Drott 1; Helsinki PS 1; Pallo-Peikot 1; Rovaniemi PS 1; Jokerit 1 (formerly PK-35); Atlantis 1.

Final League Table 2005

	P	W	D	L	F	A	Pts
MyPa	26	17	5	4	51	18	56
HJK Helsinki	26	15	7	4	43	26	52
Tampere U	26	15	6	5	38	21	51
Haka	26	13	11	2	47	19	50
Inter	26	12	8	6	38	20	44
Lahti	26	11	5	10	39	36	38
Allianssi	26	8	10	8	33	41	34
KooTeePee	26	9	6	11	35	42	33
TPS Turku	26	8	6	12	30	35	30
KuPS	26	8	5	13	32	45	29
Jaro	26	6	8	12	21	31	26
Mariehamn	26	6	5	15	27	43	23
RoPS+	26	3	8	15	18	50	17
TP 47*	26	4	4	18	22	47	16

Top scorer: Maleka (HJK Helsinki) 16.
Cup Final: Haka 4, TPS Turku 1.

FRANCE

Federation Francaise De Football, 60 Bis Avenue d'Iena, Paris 75116.
Founded: 1919; *Number of Clubs:* 21,629; *Number of Players:* 1,692,205; *National Colours:* Blue shirts, white shorts, red stockings.
Telephone: 0033-1/ 4431 7300; *Fax:* 0033-1/4720 8296.

International matches 2005
Sweden (h) 1-1, Switzerland (h) 0-0, Israel (a) 1-1, Hungary (h) 2-1, Ivory Coast (h) 3-0, Faeroes (h) 3-0, Republic of Ireland (a) 1-0, Switzerland (a) 1-1, Cyprus (h) 4-0, Costa Rica (h) 3-2, Germany (h) 0-0.

League Championship wins (1933–2006)
Saint Etienne 10; Olympique Marseille 8; Nantes 8; AS Monaco 7; Stade de Reims 6; Girondins Bordeaux 5; Lyon 5; OGC Nice 4; Lille OSC 3; Paris St Germain 2; FC Sete 2; Sochaux 2; Racing Club Paris 1; Roubaix-Tourcoing 1; Strasbourg 1; Auxerre 1; Lens 1.

Cup wins (1918–2006)
Olympique Marseille 10; Paris St Germain 7; Saint Etienne 6; AS Monaco 5; Lille OSC 5; Racing Club Paris 5; Red Star 5; Auxerre 4; Olympique Lyon 3; Girondins Bordeaux 3; OGC Nice 3; Nantes 3; Racing Club Strasbourg 3; CAS Genereaux 2; Nancy 2; Sedan 2; FC Sete 2; Stade de Reims 2; SO Montpellier 2; Stade Rennes 2; AS Cannes 1; Club Français 1; Excelsior Roubaix 1; Le Havre 1; Olympique de Pantin 1; CA Paris 1; Sochaux 1; Toulouse 1; Bastia 1; Metz 1; Lorient 1.

Final League Table 2005–06

	P	W	D	L	F	A	Pts
Lyon	38	25	9	4	73	31	84
Bordeaux	38	18	15	5	43	25	69
Lille	38	16	14	8	56	31	62
Lens	38	14	18	6	48	34	60
Marseille	38	16	12	10	44	35	60
Auxerre	38	17	8	13	50	39	59
Rennes	38	18	5	15	48	49	59
Nice	38	16	10	12	36	31	58
Paris St Germain	38	13	13	12	44	38	52
Monaco	38	13	13	12	42	36	52
Le Mans	38	13	13	12	33	36	52
Nancy	38	12	12	14	35	37	48
St Etienne	38	11	14	13	29	39	47
Nantes	38	11	12	15	37	41	45
Sochaux	38	11	11	16	34	47	44
Toulouse	38	10	11	17	36	47	41
Troyes	38	9	12	17	37	47	39
Ajaccio*	38	8	9	21	27	53	33
Strasbourg*	38	5	14	19	33	56	29
Metz*	38	6	11	21	26	59	29

Top scorer: Pauleta (Paris St Germain) 21.
Cup Final: Paris St Germain 2, Marseille 1.

GEORGIA

Georgian Football Federation, 76a Tchavtchavadze Avenue, Tbilisi 380062.
Founded: 1990; *Number of Clubs:* 4,050. *Number of Players:* 115,000; *National Colours:* All white.
Telephone: 00995-32/912 610; *Fax:* 00995-32/001 128.

International matches 2005
Lithuania (h) 1-0, Greece (h) 1-3, Turkey (h) 2-5, Albania (a) 2-3, Kazakhstan (a) 2-1, Ukraine (h) 1-1, Denmark (a) 1-6, Kazakhstan (h) 0-0, Greece (a) 0-1, Bulgaria (a) 2-6, Jordan (a) 3-2.

League Championship wins (1990–2006)
Dynamo Tbilisi 12; Torpedo Kutaisi 3; WIT 1; Sioni 1.

Cup wins (1990–2006)
Dynamo Tbilisi 8; Lokomotivi 3; Torpedo Kutaisi 2; Dynamo Batumi 1; Guria 1; Ameri 1.

Final League Table 2005–06

	P	*W*	*D*	*L*	*F*	*A*	*Pts*
Sioni	30	23	4	3	57	17	73
WIT	30	21	5	4	53	17	68
Dynamo Tbilisi	30	20	4	6	61	22	64
Zestafoni	30	18	7	5	44	22	61
Borjomi	30	19	2	9	50	26	59
Dynamo Batumi	30	17	7	6	42	21	58
Ameri	30	15	4	11	32	26	49
Lokomotivi	30	11	4	15	41	48	37
Kakheti	30	10	4	16	33	46	34
Kolkheti	30	9	5	16	26	36	32
Dila Gori	30	9	4	17	35	44	31
Torpedo Kutaisi	30	8	6	16	28	42	30
Tbilisi+	30	9	2	19	29	44	29
Tskhinvali+	30	8	3	19	30	61	27
Dynamo Sokhumi*	30	5	3	22	26	70	18
Spartak Tbilisi*	30	3	6	21	12	57	15

Top scorer: Dvali (Dynamo Tbilisi) 21.
Cup Final: Ameri 2, Zestafoni 2.
Ameri won 4-3 on penalties.

GERMANY

Deutscher Fussball-Bund, Otto-Fleck-Schneise 6, Postfach 710265, Frankfurt Am Main 60492.
Founded: 1900; *Number of Clubs:* 26,760; *Number of Players:* 5,260,320; *National Colours:* White shirts, black shorts, white stockings.
Telephone: 0049-69/678 80; *Fax:* 0049-69/678 8266.

International matches 2005
Argentina (h) 2-2, Slovenia (a) 1-0, Northern Ireland (a) 4-1, Russia (h) 2-2, Australia (h) 4-3, Tunisia (h) 3-0, Argentina (h) 2-2, Brazil (h) 2-3, Mexico (h) 3-3, Holland (a) 2-2, Slovakia (a) 0-2, South Africa (h) 4-2, Turkey (a) 1-2, China (h) 1-0, France (a) 0-0.

League Championship wins (1903–2006)
Bayern Munich 20; 1.FC Nuremberg 9; Schalke 04 7; Borussia Dortmund 6; SV Hamburg 6; Borussia Moenchengladbach 5; VfB Stuttgart 4; 1.FC Kaiserslautern 4; Werder Bremen 4; VfB Leipzig 3; SpVgg Furth 3; 1.FC Cologne 3; Viktoria Berlin 2; Hertha Berlin 2; Hannover 96 2; Dresden SC 2; Munich 1860 1; Union Berlin 1; FC Freiburg 1; Phoenix Karlsruhe 1; Karlsruher FV 1; Holstein Kiel 1; Fortuna Dusseldorf 1; Rapid Vienna 1; VfR Mannheim 1; Rot-Weiss Essen 1; Eintracht Frankfurt 1; Eintracht Brunswick 1.

Cup wins (1935–2006)
Bayern Munich 13; Werder Bremen 5; 1.FC Cologne 4; Eintracht Frankfurt 4; Schalke 04 4; 1.FC Nuremberg 3; SV Hamburg 3; Moenchengladbach 3; VfB Stuttgart 3; Dresden SC 2; Fortuna Dusseldorf 2; Karlsruhe SC 2; Munich 1860 2; Borussia Dortmund 2; 1.FC Kaiserslautern 2; First Vienna 1; VfB Leipzig 1; Kickers Offenbach 1; Rapid Vienna 1; Rot-Weiss Essen 1; SW Essen 1; Bayer Uerdingen 1; Hannover 96 1; Leverkusen 1.

Final League Table 2005–06

	P	*W*	*D*	*L*	*F*	*A*	*Pts*
Bayern Munich	34	22	9	3	67	32	75
Werder Bremen	34	21	7	6	79	37	70
Hamburg	34	21	5	8	53	30	68
Schalke	34	16	13	5	47	31	61
Leverkusen	34	14	10	10	64	49	52
Hertha	34	12	12	10	52	48	48
Borussia Dortmund	34	11	13	10	45	42	46
Nuremberg	34	12	8	14	49	51	44
Stuttgart	34	9	16	9	37	39	43
Moenchengladbach	34	10	12	12	42	50	42
Mainz	34	9	11	14	46	47	38
Hannover	34	7	17	10	43	47	38
Arminia	34	10	7	17	32	47	37
Eintracht Frankfurt	34	9	9	16	42	51	36
Wolfsburg	34	7	13	14	33	55	34
Kaiserslautern*	34	8	9	17	47	71	33
Cologne*	34	7	9	18	49	71	30
Duisburg*	34	5	12	17	34	63	27

Top scorer: Klose (Werder Bremen) 25.
Cup Final: Bayern Munich 1, Eintracht Frankfurt 0.

GREECE

Hellenic Football Federation, Singrou Avenue 137, Nea Smirni, 17121 Athens.
Founded: 1926; *Number of Clubs:* 4,050; *Number of Players:* 180,000; *National Colours:* Blue shirts, white shorts, blue stockings.
Telephone: 0030-210/930 6000; *Fax:* 0030-210/935 9666.

International matches 2005
Denmark (h) 2-1, Georgia (a) 3-1, Albania (h) 2-0, Turkey (a) 0-0, Ukraine (h) 0-1, Brazil (n) 0-3, Japan (n) 0-1, Mexico (n) 0-0, Kazakhstan (a) 2-1, Denmark (a) 0-1, Georgia (h) 1-0, Belgium (a) 0-2, Hungary (h) 2-1.

League Championship wins (1928–2006)
Olympiakos 34; Panathinaikos 19; AEK Athens 11; Aris Salonika 3; PAOK Salonika 2; Larisa 1.

Cup wins (1932–2006)
Olympiakos 23; Panathinaikos 17; AEK Athens 13; PAOK Salonika 4; Panionios 2; Aris Salonika 1; Ethnikos 1; Iraklis 1; Kastoria 1; Larisa 1; OFI Crete 1.

Final League Table 2005–06

	P	*W*	*D*	*L*	*F*	*A*	*Pts*
Olympiakos	30	23	1	6	63	23	70
AEK Athens	30	21	4	5	42	20	67
Panathinaikos	30	21	4	5	55	23	67
Iraklis	30	15	6	9	39	31	51
Xanthi	30	13	8	9	31	25	47
PAOK Salonika	30	13	7	10	44	31	46
Atromitos	30	12	6	12	36	37	42
Larisa	30	10	9	11	31	37	39
Apollon	30	10	8	12	32	36	38
Aigaleo	30	8	9	13	23	41	33
Panionios	30	9	5	16	33	45	32
Ionikos	30	6	14	10	36	41	32
OFI Crete	30	7	10	13	23	37	31
Levadiakos*	30	8	7	15	24	36	31
Kalithea*	30	4	8	18	28	49	20
Akratitos*	30	4	6	20	19	47	18

Top scorer: Salpigidis (PAOK Salonika) 17.
Cup Final: Olympiakos 3, AEK Athens 0.

HOLLAND

Koninklijke Nederlandsche Voetbalbond, Woudenbergseweg 56–58, Postbus 515, NL-3700 AM, Zeist.
Founded: 1889; *Number of Clubs:* 3,097; *Number of Players:* 962,397; *National Colours:* Orange shirts, black shorts, orange stockings.
Telephone: 0031-343/499 201; *Fax:* 0031-343/499 189.

International matches 2005
England (a) 0-0, Romania (a) 2-0, Armenia (h) 2-0, Romania (h) 2-0, Finland (a) 4-0, Germany (h) 2-2, Armenia (a) 1-0, Andorra (h) 4-0, Czech Republic (a) 2-0, Macedonia (h) 0-0, Italy (h) 1-3.

League Championship wins (1898–2006)
Ajax Amsterdam 29; PSV Eindhoven 19; Feyenoord 14; HVV The Hague 8; Sparta Rotterdam 6; Go Ahead Deventer 4; HBS The Hague 3; Willem II Tilburg 3; RAP 2; Heracles 2; ADO The Hague 2; Quick The Hague 1; BVV Den Bosch 2; NAC Breda 1; Eindhoven 1; Enschede 1; Volewijckers Amsterdam 1; Limburgia 1; Rapid JC Heerlen 3; DOS Utrecht 1; DWS Amsterdam 1; Haarlem 1; Be Quick Groningen 1; AZ 67 Alkmaar 1.

Cup wins (1899–2006)
Ajax Amsterdam 16; Feyenoord 10; PSV Eindhoven 8; Quick The Hague 4; AZ 67 Alkmaar 3; Rotterdam 3; Utrecht 3; DFC 2; Fortuna Geleen 2; Haarlem 2; HBS The Hague 2; RCH Haarlem 2; Roda 2; VOC 2; Wageningen 2; Willem II Tilburg 2; FC Den Haag 2;

Twente Enschede 2; Concordia Rotterdam 1; CVV 1; Eindhoven 1; HVV The Hague 1; Longa 1; Quick Nijmegen 1; RAP 1; Roermond 1; Schoten 1; Velocitas Breda 1; Velocitas Groningen 1; VSV 1; VUC 1; VVV Groningen 1; ZFC 1; NAC Breda 1.

Final League Table 2005–06

	P	*W*	*D*	*L*	*F*	*A*	*Pts*
PSV Eindhoven	34	26	6	2	71	23	84
AZ	34	23	5	6	78	32	74
Feyenoord	34	21	8	5	79	34	71
Ajax	34	18	6	10	66	41	60
Groningen	34	16	8	10	46	43	56
Utrecht	34	16	7	11	48	44	55
Heerenveen	34	14	8	12	63	58	50
Roda JC	34	15	5	14	57	54	50
Twente	34	13	8	13	44	36	47
NEC Nijmegen	34	13	8	13	43	43	47
Vitesse	34	13	5	16	52	54	44
RKC Waalwijk	34	11	6	17	48	58	39
Heracles	34	11	6	17	35	58	39
Sparta	34	10	7	17	34	50	37
Den Haag	34	10	5	19	36	62	35
NAC Breda+	34	8	9	17	45	66	33
Willem II+	34	7	7	20	45	66	28
Roosendaal*	34	1	6	27	22	90	9

Play-Offs: UEFA Competitions rules after series of matches Twente enter Inter-Toto, AZ and Feyenoord in UEFA Cup.
Top scorer: Huntelaar (Ajax) 33 (Heerenveen 17, Ajax 16).
Cup Final: Ajax 2, PSV Eindhoven 1.

HUNGARY

Hungarian Football Federation, Robert Karoly krt 61-65, Robert Haz Budapest 1134.
Founded: 1901; *Number of Clubs:* 1,944; *Number of Players:* 95,986; *National Colours:* Red shirts, white shorts, green stockings.
Telephone: 0036-1/412 3340; *Fax:* 0036-1/452 0360.

International matches 2005
Saudi Arabia (h) 0-0, Wales (a) 0-2, Bulgaria (h) 1-1, France (a) 1-2, Iceland (a) 3-2, Argentina (h) 1-2, Malta (h) 4-0, Sweden (h) 0-1, Bulgaria (a) 0-2, Croatia (h) 0-0, Greece (a) 1-2, Mexico (a) 0-2, Antigua (a) 3-0.

League Championship wins (1901–2006)
Ferencvaros 28; MTK-VM Budapest 21; Ujpest Dozsa 20; Kispest Honved 13; Vasas Budapest 6; Csepel 4; Raba Gyor 3; BTC 2; Debrecen 2; Nagyvarad 1; Vac 1; Dunaferr 1; Zalaegerszeg 1.

Cup wins (1910–2006)
Ferencvaros 19; MTK-VM Budapest 12; Ujpest Dozsa 9; Raba Gyor 4; Kispest Honved 5; Vasas Budapest 4; Diösgyör 2; Debrecen 2; Bocskai 1; III Ker 1; Kispesti AC 1; Soroksar 1; Szolnoki MAV 1; Siofok Banyasz 1; Bekescsaba 1; Pecsi 1; Matav 1; Fehervar 1.
Cup not regularly held until 1964.

Final League Table 2005–06

	P	*W*	*D*	*L*	*F*	*A*	*Pts*
Debrecen	30	20	8	2	69	34	68
Ujpest	30	20	5	5	74	37	65
Fehervar	30	19	7	4	52	24	64
MTK	30	18	6	6	65	33	60
Tatabanya	30	11	8	11	46	45	41
Ferencvaros	30	10	11	9	43	38	41
Kaposvar	30	10	7	13	35	41	37
Diosgyor	30	10	7	13	33	44	37
Gyor	30	9	9	12	47	50	36
Matav	30	9	8	13	39	39	35
Zalaegerszeg	30	9	8	13	42	47	35
Pecsi	30	8	9	13	37	41	33
Honved	30	8	9	13	33	52	33
Rakospalotai	30	7	5	18	30	59	26
Vasas*	30	5	10	15	32	47	25
Lombard*	30	5	7	18	30	76	22

Honved were excluded on 29 September for a financial irregularity, but the ruling was revoked by the Hungarian F.A. Matav renamed Sopron.
Top scorer: Rajczi (Ujpest) 22.
Cup Final: Fehervar 2, Vasas 2.
Fehervar won 6-5 on penalties.

ICELAND

Knattspyrnusamband Island, Laugardal, 104 Reykjavik.
Founded: 1929; *Number of Clubs:* 73; *Number of Players:* 23,673; *National Colours;* All blue.
Telephone: 00354/510 2900; *Fax:* 00354/568 9793.

International matches 2005
Croatia (a) 0-4, Italy (a) 0-0, Hungary (h) 2-3, Malta (h) 4-1, South Africa (h) 4-1, Croatia (h) 1-3, Bulgaria (a) 2-3, Poland (a) 2-3, Sweden (a) 1-3.

League Championship wins (1912–2005)
KR 24; Valur 19; Fram 18; IA Akranes 18; Vikingur 5; IBV Vestmann 4; IBK Keflavik 3; FH Hafnarfjordur 2; KA Akureyri 1.

Cup wins (1960–2005)
KR 10; Valur 9; Fram 7; IA Akranes 8; IBV Vestmann 4; IBK Keflavik 3; Fylkir 2; IBA Akureyri 1; Vikingur 1.

Final League Table 2005

	P	*W*	*D*	*L*	*F*	*A*	*Pts*
FH	18	16	0	2	53	11	48
Valur	18	10	2	6	29	16	32
IA	18	10	2	6	24	20	32
Keflavik	18	7	6	5	28	31	27
Fylkir	18	8	2	8	28	28	26
KR	18	8	1	9	22	24	25
Grindavik	18	5	3	10	23	41	18
IBV	18	5	2	11	18	30	17
Fram*	18	5	2	11	19	32	17
Throttur*	18	4	4	10	21	32	16

Top scorer: Gudmundsson (FH) 16.
Cup Final: Valur 1, Fram 0.

REPUBLIC OF IRELAND

The Football Association of Ireland (Cumann Peile Na H-Eireann), 80 Merrion Square, South Dublin 2.
Founded: 1921; *Number of Clubs:* 3,190; *Number of Players:* 124,615; *National Colours:* Green shirts, white shorts, green and white stockings.
Telephone: 00353-1/676 6864; *Fax:* 00353-1/661 0931.

League Championship wins (1922–2005)
Shamrock Rovers 15; Shelbourne 12; Dundalk 9; Bohemians 9; St Patrick's Athletic 8; Waterford 6; Cork United 5; Drumcondra 5; St James's Gate 2; Cork Athletic 2; Sligo Rovers 2; Limerick 2; Athlone Town 2; Derry City 2; Cork City 2; Dolphin 1; Cork Hibernians 1; Cork Celtic 1.

Cup wins (1922–2005)
Shamrock Rovers 24; Dundalk 9; Shelbourne 6; Bohemians 6; Drumcondra 5; Derry City 3; Cork Athletic 2; Cork United 2; St James's Gate 2; St Patrick's Athletic 2; Cork Hibernians 2; Limerick 2; Waterford 2; Athlone Town 2; Sligo 2; Bray Wanderers 2; Longford Town 2; Cork City 2; Alton United 1; Fordsons 1; Transport 1; Finn Harps 1; Home Farm 1; UCD 1; Galway United 1; Drogheda United 1.

Final League Table 2005

	P	*W*	*D*	*L*	*F*	*A*	*Pts*
Cork City	33	22	8	3	53	18	74
Derry City	33	22	6	5	56	25	72
Shelbourne	33	20	7	6	62	25	67
Drogheda United	33	12	12	9	40	33	48
Longford Town	33	12	9	12	29	32	45
Bohemians	33	13	6	14	42	47	45
Bray Wanderers	33	11	6	16	40	57	39
Waterford United	33	9	7	17	30	49	34
UCD	33	7	12	14	28	44	33
St Patrick's Ath	33	7	11	15	26	36	32
Shamrock Rovers+	33	9	8	16	33	52	27
Finn Harps*	33	5	6	22	30	51	21

Shamrock Rovers deducted 8 points for financial irregularities.
Top scorer: Byrne J (Shelbourne) 22.
Cup Final: Drogheda United 2, Cork City 0.

ISRAEL

Israel Football Association, Ramat-Gan Stadium, 299 Aba Hilell Street, Ramat-Gan 52134.
Founded: 1948; *Number of Clubs:* 544; *Number of Players:* 30,449; *National Colours:* Blue shirts, white shorts, blue stockings.
Telephone: 00972-3/617 1503; *Fax:* 00972-3/ 570 2044.

International matches 2005
Croatia (h) 3-3, Republic of Ireland (h) 1-1, France (h) 1-1, Republic of Ireland (a) 2-2, Ukraine (h) 0-0, Poland (h) 2-3, Switzerland (a) 1-1, Faeroes (a) 2-0, Faeroes (h) 2-1.

League Championship wins (1932–2006)
Maccabi Tel Aviv 19; Hapoel Tel Aviv 13; Maccabi Haifa 10; Hapoel Petach Tikva 6; Maccabi Netanya 5; Beitar Jerusalem 4; Hakoah Ramat Gan 2; Hapoel Beersheba 2; Bnei Yehouda 1; British Police 1; Hapoel Kfar Sava 1; Hapoel Ramat Gan 1; Hapoel Haifa 1.

Cup wins (1928–2006)
Maccabi Tel Aviv 22; Hapoel Tel Aviv 12; Beitar Jerusalem 5; Maccabi Haifa 5; Hapoel Haifa 3; Hapoel Kfar Sava 3; Beitar Tel Aviv 2; Bnei Yehouda 2; Hakoah Ramat Gan 2; Hapoel Petah Tikva 2; Maccabi Petach Tikva 2; British Police 1; Hapoel Jerusalem 1; Hapoel Lod 1; Maccabi Netanya 1; Hapoel Beersheba 1; Hapoel Ramat Gan 1; Hapoel Bnei Sakhnin 1.

Final League Table 2005-06

	P	*W*	*D*	*L*	*F*	*A*	*Pts*
Maccabi Haifa	33	23	6	4	65	25	75
Hapoel Tel Aviv	33	16	11	6	51	25	59
Beitar Jerusalem	33	17	7	9	51	33	58
Bnei Yehouda	33	14	7	12	37	41	49
Maccabi Petah Tikva	33	12	8	13	37	38	44
Maccabi Tel Aviv	33	11	11	11	35	37	44
Maccabi Netanya	33	11	8	14	40	45	41
Ashdod	33	9	12	12	46	47	39
Hapoel Petah Tikva	33	9	10	14	38	50	36
Hapoel Kfar Saba	33	8	10	15	30	41	34
Hapoel Nazareth*	33	8	10	15	25	47	34
Hapoel Bnei Sakhnin	*33	5	10	18	28	54	25

Top scorer: Holtzman (Ashdod) 18.
Cup Final: Hapoel Tel Aviv 1, Bnei Yehouda 0.

ITALY

Federazione Italiana Giuoco Calcio, Via Gregorio Allegri 14, Roma 00198.
Founded: 1898; *Number of Clubs:* 20,961; *Number of Players:* 1,420,160; *National Colours:* Blue shirts, white shorts, blue stockings.
Telephone: 0039-06/84 911; *Fax:* 0039-06/84 912 526.

International matches 2005
Russia (h) 2-0, Scotland (h) 2-0, Iceland (h) 0-0, Norway (a) 0-0, Serbia & Montenegro (h) 1-1, Ecuador (a) 1-1, Republic of Ireland (a) 2-1, Scotland (a) 1-1, Belarus (a) 4-1, Slovenia (h) 1-0, Moldova (h) 2-1, Holland (a) 3-1, Ivory Coast (a) 1-1.

League Championship wins (1898–2006)
Juventus 29; AC Milan 17; Inter-Milan 13; Genoa 9; Torino 8; Pro Vercelli 7; Bologna 7; AS Roma 3; Fiorentina 2; Lazio 2; Napoli 2; Casale 1; Novese 1; Cagliari 1; Verona 1; Sampdoria 1.

Cup wins (1922–2006)
Juventus 9; AS Roma 8; Fiorentina 6; AC Milan 5; Inter-Milan 5; Torino 4; Sampdoria 4; Lazio 4; Napoli 3; Parma 3; Bologna 2; Atalanta 1; Genoa 1; Vado 1; Venezia 1; Vicenza 1.

Final League Table 2005–06

	P	*W*	*D*	*L*	*F*	*A*	*Pts*
Juventus	38	27	10	1	71	24	91
AC Milan	38	28	4	6	85	31	88
Internazionale	38	23	7	8	68	30	76
Fiorentina	38	22	8	8	66	41	74
Roma	38	19	12	7	70	42	69
Lazio	38	16	14	8	57	47	62
Chievo	38	13	15	10	54	49	54
Palermo	38	13	13	12	50	52	52
Livorno	38	12	13	13	37	44	49
Empoli	38	13	6	19	47	61	45
Parma	38	12	9	17	46	60	45
Ascoli	38	9	16	13	43	53	43
Udinese	38	11	10	17	40	54	43
Sampdoria	38	10	11	17	47	51	41
Reggina	38	11	8	19	39	65	41
Cagliari	38	8	15	15	42	55	39
Siena	38	9	12	17	42	60	39
Messina*	38	6	13	19	33	59	31
Lecce*	38	7	8	23	30	57	29
Treviso*	38	3	12	23	24	56	21

Top scorer: Toni (Fiorentina) 31.
Cup Final: Roma 1, 1, Internazionale 1, 3.

KAZAKHSTAN

The Football Union of Kazakhstan, Satpayev Street, 29/3 Almaty 480 072, Kazakhstan.
Founded: 1914; *Number of Clubs:* 5,793; *Number of Players:* 260,000; *National Colours:* Blue shirts, blue shorts, yellow stockings.
Telephone: 007-3272/920 444; *Fax:* 007-3272/921 885.

International matches 2005
Japan (a) 0-4, Denmark (a) 0-3, Ukraine (a) 0-2, Turkey (h) 0-6, Georgia (h) 1-2, Albania (a) 1-2, Greece (h) 1-2, Georgia (a) 0-0, Denmark (h) 1-2.

League Championship wins (1992-2005)
Irtysh 5; Yelimai 3; Zhenis 2; Kairat 2; Taraz 1; Aqtobe 1.

Cup wins (1992–2005)
Kairat 5; Zhenis 3; Dostyk 1; Vostok 1; Yelimai 1; Irtysh 1; Kaisar 1; Taraz 1.

Final League Table 2005

	P	*W*	*D*	*L*	*F*	*A*	*Pts*
Aqtobe	30	22	4	4	50	27	70
Tobol	30	21	6	3	53	21	69
Qayrat	30	18	8	4	56	22	62
Shakhter	30	19	2	9	37	22	59
Irtysh	30	18	3	9	51	24	57
Ordabasy	30	14	7	9	30	27	49
Yesil Bogatyr	30	15	3	12	38	25	48
Jenis	30	11	10	9	35	23	43
Oqjetpes	30	11	4	15	26	32	37
Atyrau	30	10	7	13	32	36	37
Taraz	30	10	6	14	32	36	36
Yekibastuzets	30	8	10	12	30	32	34
Almaty	30	9	3	18	30	43	30
Vostok	30	9	1	20	24	49	28
Jetisu*	30	4	7	19	28	60	19
Bolat*	30	0	1	29	15	88	1

Top scorer: Tleshev (Irtysh) 20.
Cup Final: Zhenis 2, Kairat 1.

LATVIA

Latvian Football Federation, Augsiela 1, LV-1009, Riga.
Founded: 1921; *Number of Clubs:* 50; *Number of Players:* 12,000; *National Colours:* Carmine red shirts, white shorts, carmine red stockings.
Telephone: 00371/729 2988; *Fax:* 00371/ 731 5604.

International matches 2005
Finland (n) 1-2, Austria (n) 1-1, Luxembourg (h) 4-0, Lithuania (a) 0-2, Russia (a) 0-2, Liechtenstein (h) 1-0, Russia (h) 1-1, Estonia (a) 1-2, Slovakia (h) 1-1, Japan (h) 2-2, Portugal (a) 0-3, Belarus (a) 1-3, Thailand (n) 1-1, North Korea (n) 1-1, Oman (n) 2-1, North Korea (n) 2-1.

League Championship wins (1922–2005)
Skonto Riga 14; ASK Riga 9; RFK Riga 8; Olympia Liepaya 7; Sarkanais Metalurgs Liepaya 7; VEF Riga 6; Energija Riga 4; Elektrons Riga 3; Torpedo Riga 3; Daugava Liepaya 2; ODO Riga 2; Khimikis Daugavpils 2; RAF Yelgava 2; Keisermezhs Riga 2; Dinamo Riga 1; Zhmilyeva Team 1; Darba Rezervi 1; REZ Riga 1; Start Brotseni 1; Venta Ventspils 1; Yurnieks Riga 1; Alfa Riga 1; Gauya Valmiera 1; Metalurgs Liepaya 1.

Cup wins (1937–2005)
Elektrons Riga 7; Skonto Riga 7; Sarkanais Metalurgs Liepaya 5; ODO Riga 3; VEF Riga 3; ASK Riga 3;

Tseltnieks Riga 3; RAF Yelgava 3; FK Ventspils 3; RFK Riga 2; Daugava Liepaya 2; Start Brotseni 2; Selmash Liepaya 2; Yurnieks Riga 2; Khimikis Daugavpils 2; Rigas Vilki 1; Dinamo Liepaya 1; Dinamo Riga 1; REZ Riga 1; Voulkan Kouldiga 1; Baltija Liepaya 1; Venta Ventspils 1; Pilot Riga 1; Lielupe Yurmala 1; Energija Riga 1; Torpedo Riga 1; Daugava SKIF Riga 1; Tseltnieks Daugavpils 1; Olympia Riga 1; FK Riga 1.

Final League Table 2005

	P	*W*	*D*	*L*	*F*	*A*	*Pts*
Metalurgs Liepaya	28	22	5	1	85	19	71
Skonto Riga	28	17	7	4	59	25	58
FK Ventspils	28	16	7	5	56	30	55
Dinaburg	28	9	8	11	37	43	35
FK Riga	28	9	7	12	36	42	34
Jurmala	28	9	5	14	37	38	32
Olimps Riga+	28	5	4	19	24	68	19
Venta Kuldiga*	28	2	3	23	18	79	9

Zibens refused place in the league and were replaced by Olimps Riga.
Top scorers: Dobrecovs (Metalurgs Liepaya), Siesarcuks (FK Ventspils) 18.
Cup Final: Metalurgs Liepaya 1, FK Ventspils 2.

LIECHTENSTEIN

Liechtensteiner Fussball-Verband, Malbuner Huus Altenbach 11, Postfach 165, 9490 Vaduz.
Founded: 1934; *Number of Clubs:* 7; *Number of Players:* 1,247; *National Colours:* Blue shirts, red shorts, blue stockings.
Telephone: 00423/237 4747; *Fax:* 00423/237 4748.

International matches 2005
Russia (h) 1-2, Estonia (a) 0-2, Latvia (a) 0-1, Slovakia (h) 0-0, Russia (a) 0-2, Luxembourg (h) 3-0, Portugal (a) 1-2, Macedonia (h) 1-2.
Liechtenstein has no national league. Teams compete in Swiss regional leagues.

Cup wins (1946–2006)
Vaduz 35; Balzers 11; Triesen 8; Eschen/Mauren 4; Schaan 3.
Cup Final: Vaduz 4, Balzers 2 (aet).

LITHUANIA

Lithuanian Football Federation, Seimyniskiu str. 15, 2005 Vilnius.
Founded: 1922; *Number of Clubs:* 152; *Number of Players:* 16,600; *National Colours:* Yellow shirts, green shorts, yellow stockings.
Telephone: 00370/5263 8741; *Fax:* 00370/5263 8740.

International matches 2005
Georgia (a) 0-1, Bosnia (a) 1-1, Latvia (h) 2-0, Spain (a) 0-1, Belarus (h) 1-0, Serbia & Montenegro (a) 0-2, Bosnia (h) 0-1, Serbia & Montenegro (h) 0-2, Belgium (h) 1-1.

League Championship wins (1937–2005)
FBK Kaunas 6 (including Zalgiris Kaunas 1); Zalgiris Vilnius 3; Kareda 2; Inkaras Kaunas 2; Ekranas Panevezys 2; Sirijus Klaipeda 1; ROMAR Mazeikiai 1.

Cup wins (1992–2005)
Zalgiris Vilnius 4; FBK Kaunas 3; Kareda 2; Ekranas 2; Atlantas 2; Lietuvos 1; Inkaras 1.

Final League Table 2005

	P	*W*	*D*	*L*	*F*	*A*	*Pts*
Ekranas	36	29	5	2	87	23	92
FBK Kaunas	36	26	4	6	89	25	82
Suduva	36	16	11	9	67	43	59
Vetra	36	17	6	13	45	45	57
FK Vilnius	36	11	14	11	36	29	47
Silute	36	12	8	16	44	61	44
Atlantas	36	11	8	17	40	52	41
Zalgiris	36	11	8	17	40	52	41
Siauliai	36	8	9	19	40	61	33
Nevezis	36	0	5	31	18	115	5

Top scorer: Savenas (Ekranas) 27.
Cup Final: FBK Kaunas 2, Vetra 0

LUXEMBOURG

Federation Luxembourgeoise De Football (F.L.F.), 68 Rue De Gasperich, Luxembourg 1617.
Founded: 1908; *Number of Clubs:* 126; *Number of Players:* 21,684; *National Colours:* All red.
Telephone: 00352/488 665 1; *Fax:* 00352/488 665 82.

International matches 2005
Latvia (a) 0-4, Slovakia (h) 0-4, Portugal (a) 0-6, Liechtenstein (a) 0-3, Russia (a) 1-5, Estonia (h) 0-2, Canada (h) 0-1.

League Championship wins (1910–2006)
Jeunesse Esch 27; Spora Luxembourg 11; Stade Dudelange 10; Avenir Beggen 7; Red Boys Differdange 6; US Hollerich-Bonnevoie 5; Fola Esch 5; US Luxembourg 5; F91 Dudelange 5; Aris Bonnevoie 3; Progres Niedercorn 3; Grevenmacher 1.

Cup wins (1922–2006)
Red Boys Differdange 16; Jeunesse Esch 12; US Luxembourg 10; Spora Luxembourg 8; Avenir Beggen 7; Stade Dudelange 4; Progres Niedercorn 4; Fola Esch 3; Grevenmacher 3; Alliance Dudelange 2; US Rumelange 2; F91 Dudelange 2; Aris Bonnevoie 1; US Dudelange 1; Jeunesse Hautcharage 1; National Schiffige 1; Racing Luxembourg 1; SC Tetange 1; Hesperange 1; Etzella 1; Petange 1.

Qualifying Table 2005–06

	P	*W*	*D*	*L*	*F*	*A*	*Pts*
F91 Dudelange	22	16	3	3	63	15	51
Jeunesse Esch	22	14	2	6	49	19	44
Etzella	22	13	1	8	48	36	40
Grevenmacher	22	12	2	8	51	27	38
FC Wiltz 71	22	9	7	6	36	27	34
Kaerjeng	22	10	4	8	36	33	34
Union Luxembourg	22	10	4	8	31	30	34
Petange	22	10	2	10	29	33	32
Hesperange	22	6	8	8	31	37	26
Victoria Rosport	22	6	5	11	24	42	23
Rumelange	22	3	3	16	20	58	12
Avenir Beggen	22	0	5	17	10	71	5

Championship Table 2005–06

	P	*W*	*D*	*L*	*F*	*A*	*Pts*
F91 Dudelange	28	20	4	4	83	22	64
Jeunesse Esch	28	17	2	9	58	36	53
Etzella	28	16	1	11	59	47	49
Grevenmacher	28	13	3	12	58	39	42

Promotion/Relegation Table 2005–06

Group A	*P*	*W*	*D*	*L*	*F*	*A*	*Pts*
FC Wiltz 71	28	13	8	7	49	36	47
Union Luxembourg	28	12	5	11	40	39	41
Hesperange	28	9	9	10	41	44	36
Rumelange*	28	4	4	20	25	70	16

Group B	*P*	*W*	*D*	*L*	*F*	*A*	*Pts*
Petange	28	12	4	12	39	40	40
Kaerjeng	28	10	7	11	44	46	37
Victoria Rosport	28	8	8	12	34	50	32
Avenir Beggen*	28	4	5	19	18	79	17

Top scorers: Rosamilia (FC Wiltz 71), Di Gregorio (F91 Dudelange) 22.
Cup Final: F91 Dudelange 3, Jeunesse Esch 2.

MACEDONIA

Football Association of Macedonia, VIII-ma Udarna Brigada 31-A, Skopje 1000.
Founded: 1948; *Number of Clubs:* 598; *Number of Players:* 15,165; *National Colours:* All red.
Telephone: 00389-2/3129 291; *Fax:* 00389-2/3165 448.

International matches 2005
Andorra (h) 0-0, Romania (h) 1-2, Armenia (a) 2-1, Czech Republic (a) 1-6, Finland (h) 0-3, Finland (a) 1-5, Holland (a) 0-0, Liechtenstein (a) 2-1.

League Championship wins (1993–2006)
Vardar 5; Sileks 3; Sloga 3; Rabotnicki 2; Pobeda 1.

Cup wins (1993–2006)
Vardar 4; Sloga 2; Sileks 1; Pellister 1; Pobeda 1; Cement 1; Baskimi 1; Makedonija 1.

Final League Table 2005–06

	P	W	D	L	F	A	Pts
Rabotnicki	33	21	9	3	64	26	72
Makedonija	33	21	6	6	55	23	69
Vardar	33	19	7	7	42	19	64
Pobeda	33	16	6	11	58	46	54
Shkendija	33	15	4	14	48	47	49
Baskimi	33	13	6	14	50	49	45
Renova	33	13	5	15	45	49	44
Vlazrimi	33	13	4	16	44	57	43
Sileks+	33	10	11	12	54	58	41
Bregalnica+	33	10	6	17	44	55	36
Cement*	33	8	8	17	38	51	32
Belasica*	33	2	2	29	22	84	8

Top scorer: Ristic (Sileks) 27.
Cup Final: Makedonija 3, Shkendija 2.

MALTA

Malta Football Association, 280 St Paul Street, Valletta VLT07.
Founded: 1900; *Number of Clubs:* 252; *Number of Players:* 5,544; *National Colours:* Red shirts, white shorts, red stockings.
Telephone: 00356-21/232 581; *Fax:* 00356-21/245 136.

International matches 2005
Norway (h) 0-3, Croatia (a) 0-3, Sweden (a) 0-6, Iceland (a) 1-4, Northern Ireland (h) 1-1, Hungary (a) 0-4, Croatia (h) 1-1, Bulgaria (h) 1-1.

League Championship wins (1910–2006)
Sliema Wanderers 26; Floriana 25; Valletta 18; Hibernians 9; Hamrun Spartans 7; Rabat Ajax 2; Birkirkara 2; St George's 1; KOMR 1.

Cup wins (1935–2006)
Sliema Wanderers 19; Floriana 18; Valletta 10; Hibernians 7; Hamrun Spartans 6; Birkirkara 3; Gzira United 1; Melita 1; Zurrieq 1; Rabat Ajax 1.

Qualifying League Table 2005–06

	P	W	D	L	F	A	Pts
Birkirkara	18	13	2	3	48	21	41
Sliema Wanderers	18	12	3	3	37	12	39
Hibernians	18	12	1	5	37	19	37
Marsaxlokk	18	10	4	4	36	23	34
Valletta	18	7	2	9	22	31	23
St Joseph	18	6	3	9	28	33	21
Floriana	18	4	7	7	24	28	19
Hamrun Spartans	18	6	1	11	29	41	19
Pieta Hotspurs	18	4	3	11	22	39	15
Mosta	18	2	2	14	20	56	8

Championship Table 2005–06

	P	W	D	L	F	A	Pts
Birkirkara	28	19	5	4	68	27	42
Sliema Wanderers	28	17	5	6	58	27	37
Marsaxlokk	28	16	5	7	52	36	36
Hibernians	28	14	4	10	49	37	28
Valletta	28	10	5	13	37	49	24
St Joseph	28	6	7	15	40	59	15

Promotion/Relegation Table 2005–06

	P	W	D	L	F	A	Pts
Floriana	24	6	9	9	36	37	18
Pieta Hotspurs	24	6	6	12	31	47	17
Mosta*	24	5	5	14	32	63	16
Hamrun Spartans*	24	6	3	15	35	56	12

Top scorer: Galea (Birkirkara) 19.
Cup Final: Hibernians 1, Floriana 0.

MOLDOVA

Football Association of Moldova, 39 Tricolorului Str, 2012, Chisinau.
Founded: 1990; *Number of Clubs:* 143; *Number of Players:* 75,000; *National Colours:* Red shirts, blue shorts, red stockings.
Telephone: 00373-22/210 413; *Fax:* 00373-22/210 432.

International matches 2005
Azerbaijan (a) 0-0, Norway (h) 0-0, Scotland (a) 0-2, Belarus (h) 2-0, Slovenia (h) 1-2, Norway (a) 0-1, Italy (a) 1-2.

League Championship wins (1992–2006)
Zimbru Chisinau 8; Serif 5; Constructorul 1.

Cup wins (1992–2006)
Tiligul 4; Zimbru Chisinau 4; Serif 4; Combat 1; Constructorul 1; Otaci 1.

Final League Table 2005-06

	P	W	D	L	F	A	Pts
Serif	28	22	5	1	57	11	71
Zimbru Chisinau	28	15	8	5	47	20	53
Tiraspol	28	8	13	7	24	21	37
Tiligul	28	7	13	8	22	23	34
Otaci	28	6	13	9	24	27	31
Dacia	28	7	9	12	28	39	30
Politehnica+	28	5	10	13	18	37	25
Dinamo*	28	2	9	17	17	59	15

Top scorer: Kuciuk (Serif) 13.
Cup Final: Serif 2, Otaci 0.

NORTHERN IRELAND

Irish Football Association Ltd, 20 Windsor Avenue, Belfast BT9 6EE.
Founded: 1880; *Number of Clubs:* 1,555; *Number of Players:* 24,558; *National Colours:* Green shirts, white shorts, green stockings.
Telephone: 0044-28/9066 9458; *Fax:* 0044-28/9066 7620.

NORWAY

Norges Fotballforbund, Ullevaal Stadion, Sognsveien 75J, Serviceboks 1, Oslo 0855.
Founded: 1902; *Number of Clubs:* 1,810; *Number of Players:* 300,000; *National Colours:* Red shirts, white shorts, blue stockings.
Telephone: 0047/2102 9300; *Fax:* 0047/2102 9301.

International matches 2005
Kuwait (a) 1-1, Bahrain (a) 1-0, Jordan (a) 0-0, Malta (a) 3-0, Moldova (a) 0-0, Estonia (a) 2-1, Costa Rica (h) 1-0, Italy (h) 0-0, Sweden (a) 3-2, Switzerland (h) 0-2, Slovenia (a) 3-2, Scotland (h) 1-2, Moldova (h) 1-0, Belarus (a) 1-0, Czech Republic (h) 0-1, Czech Republic (a) 0-1.

League Championship wins (1938–2005)
Rosenborg Trondheim 18; Fredrikstad 9; Viking Stavanger 8; Lillestroem 6; Valerenga 5; Larvik Turn 3; Brann Bergen 2; Lyn Oslo 2; IK Start 2; Friedig 1; Skeid Oslo 1; Strömsgodset Drammen 1; Moss 1.

Cup wins (1902–2005)
Odds Bk Skien 11; Fredrikstad 10; Lyn Oslo 8; Skeid Oslo 8; Rosenborg Trondheim 8; Sarpsborg FK 6; Brann Bergen 6; Viking Stavanger 5; Orn F Horten 4; Lillestroem 4; Strömsgodset Drammen 4; Frigg 3; Mjondalens F 3; Valerenga 3; Bodo-Glimt 2; Mercantile 2; Tromso 2; Molde 2; Grane Nordstrand 1; Kvik Halden 1; Sparta 1; Gjovik 1; Moss 1; Byrne 1; Stabaek 1; Odd Grenland 1.
(Known as the Norwegian Championship for HM The King's Trophy).

Final League Table 2005

	P	W	D	L	F	A	Pts
Valerenga	26	13	7	6	40	27	46
Start	26	13	6	7	47	35	45
Lyn	26	12	8	6	37	21	44
Lillestrom	26	12	6	8	37	31	42
Viking	26	12	5	9	37	32	41
Brann	26	10	7	9	43	32	37
Rosenborg	26	10	4	12	50	42	34
Tromso	26	8	10	8	31	30	34
Odd	26	9	6	11	28	51	33
Hamark	26	8	7	11	31	37	31
Fredrikstad	26	8	7	11	35	44	31
Molde+	26	8	6	12	40	46	30
Aalesunds*	26	6	9	11	30	42	27
Bodo-Glimt*	26	6	6	14	29	45	24

Top scorer: Arst (Tromso) 16.
Cup Final: Molde 4, Lillestrom 2.

POLAND

Polish Football Association, Polski Zwiazek Pilki Noznej, Miodowa 1, Warsaw 00-080.
Founded: 1919; *Number of Clubs:* 5,881; *Number of Players:* 317,442; *National Colours:* White shirts, red shorts, white stockings.
Telephone: 0048-22/827 0914; *Fax:* 0048-22/827 0704.

International matches 2005
Belarus (h) 1-3, Azerbaijan (h) 8-0, Northern Ireland (h) 1-0, Mexico (a) 1-1, Albania (h) 1-0, Azerbaijan (a) 3-0, Serbia & Montenegro (h) 3-2, Israel (h) 3-2, Austria (h) 3-2, Wales (h) 1-0, Iceland (h) 3-2, England (a) 1-2, Ecuador (a) 3-0, Estonia (h) 3-1.

League Championship wins (1921–2006)
Gornik Zabrze 14; Ruch Chorzow 13; Wisla Krakow 11; Legia Warsaw 8; Widzew Lodz 6; Lech Poznan 5; Pogon Lwow 4; Cracovia 3; Warta Poznan 2; Polonia Bytom 2; Stal Mielec 2; LKS Lodz 2; Polonia Warsaw 2; Garbarnia Krakow 1; Slask Wroclaw 1; Szombierki Bytom 1; Zaglebie Lubin 1.

Cup wins (1951–2006)
Legia Warsaw 12; Gornik Zabrze 6; Zaglebie Sosnowiec 4; Lech Poznan 4; GKS Katowice 3; Ruch Chorzow 3; Amica Wronki 3; Wisla Krakow 3; Slask Wroclaw 2; Polonia Warsaw 2; Gwardia Warsaw 1; LKS Lodz 1; Stal Rzeszow 1; Arka Gdynia 1; Lechia Gdansk 1; Widzew Lodz 1; Miedz Legnica 1; Groclin 1; Wisla Plock 1.

Final League Table 2005–06

	P	*W*	*D*	*L*	*F*	*A*	*Pts*
Legia	30	20	6	4	47	17	66
Wisla	30	19	7	4	50	20	64
Zaglebie	30	14	7	9	45	32	49
Amica	30	14	7	9	50	28	49
Korona	30	12	11	7	46	33	47
Lech	30	11	9	10	45	45	42
Odra	30	10	10	10	23	27	40
GKS Belchatow	30	10	9	11	32	31	39
Groclin	30	10	7	13	37	45	37
Cracovia	30	10	7	13	32	44	37
Pogon	30	9	10	11	29	34	37
Wisla Plock	30	10	4	16	30	45	34
Leczna	30	7	11	12	22	33	32
Gornik Zabrze+	30	8	5	17	29	46	29
Arka*	30	4	15	11	21	33	27
Polonia*	30	6	7	17	20	45	25

Top scorer: Piechna (Korona) 21.
Cup Final: Zaglebie 2, 1, Wisla Plock 3, 3.

PORTUGAL

Federacao Portuguesa De Futebol, Praca De Alegria N.25, Apartado 21.100, P-1127, Lisboa 1250-004.
Founded: 1914; *Number of Clubs:* 204; *Number of Players:* 79,235; *National Colours:* Red shirts, green shorts, red stockings.
Telephone: 00351-21/325 2700; *Fax:* 00351-21/325 2780.

International matches 2005
Republic of Ireland (a) 0-1, Canada (h) 4-1, Slovakia (a) 1-1, Slovakia (h) 2-0, Estonia (a) 1-0, Egypt (h) 2-0, Luxembourg (h) 6-0, Russia (a) 0-0, Liechtenstein (h) 2-1, Latvia (h) 3-0, Croatia (h) 2-0, Northern Ireland (a) 1-1.

League Championship wins (1935–2006)
Benfica 31; FC Porto 21; Sporting Lisbon 18; Belenenses 1; Boavista 1.

Cup wins (1939–2006)
Benfica 24; Sporting Lisbon 13; FC Porto 13; Boavista 5; Belenenses 3; Vitoria Setubal 3; Academica Coimbra 1; Leixoes Porto 1; Sporting Braga 1; Amadora 1; Beira Mar 1.

Final League Table 2005–06

	P	*W*	*D*	*L*	*F*	*A*	*Pts*
Porto	34	24	7	3	54	16	79
Sporting Lisbon	34	22	6	6	50	24	72
Benfica	34	20	7	7	51	29	67
Braga	34	17	7	10	38	22	58
Nacional	34	14	10	10	40	32	52
Boavista	34	12	14	8	37	29	50
Uniao Leiria	34	13	8	13	44	42	47
Setubal	34	14	4	16	28	33	46
Amadora	34	12	9	13	31	33	45
Maritimo	34	10	14	10	38	37	44
Ferreira	34	11	9	14	38	49	42
Gil Vicente	34	11	7	16	37	42	40
Naval	34	11	6	17	35	48	39
Academica	34	10	9	15	37	48	39
Belenenses*	34	11	6	17	40	42	39
Rio Ave*	34	8	10	16	34	53	34
Guimaraes*	34	8	10	16	28	41	34
Penafiel*	34	2	9	23	21	61	15

Top scorer: Meyong (Belenenses) 17.
Cup Final: Porto 1, Setubal 0.

ROMANIA

Federatia Romana De Fotbal, House of Football, Str. Serg. Serbanica Vasile 12, Bucharest 73412.
Founded: 1909; *Number of Clubs:* 414; *Number of Players:* 22,920; *National Colours:* All yellow.
Telephone: 0040-21/325 0678; *Fax:* 0040-21/325 0679.

International matches 2005
Slovakia (h) 2-2, Holland (h) 0-2, Macedonia (a) 2-1, Holland (a) 0-2, Armenia (h) 3-0, Andorra (h) 2-0, Czech Republic (h) 2-0, Finland (a) 1-0, Ivory Coast (h) 1-2, Nigeria (h) 3-0.

League Championship wins (1910–2006)
Steaua Bucharest 23; Dinamo Bucharest 17; Venus Bucharest 8; Chinezul Timisoara 6; UT Arad 6; Ripensia Temesvar 4; Uni Craiova 4; Petrolul Ploesti 3; Rapid Bucharest 3; Olimpia Bucharest 2; Colentina Bucharest 2; Arges Pitesti 2; ICO Oradea 2; Soc RA Bucharest 1; Prahova Ploesti 1; Coltea Brasov 1; Juventus Bucharest 1; Metalochimia Resita 1; Ploesti United 1; Unirea Tricolor 1.

Cup wins (1934–2006)
Steaua Bucharest 21; Dinamo Bucharest 12; Rapid Bucharest 12; Uni Craiova 6; UT Arad 2; Ripensia Temesvar 2; Politehnica Timisoara 2; Petrolul Ploesti 2; ICO Oradeo 1; Metalochimia Resita 1; Stinta Cluj 1; CFR Turnu Severin 1; Chimia Ramnicu Vilcea 1; Jiul Petroseni 1; Progresul Bucharest 1; Progresul Oradea 1; Gloria Bistrita 1.

Final League Table 2005–06

	P	*W*	*D*	*L*	*F*	*A*	*Pts*
Steaua	30	19	7	4	49	16	64
Rapid	30	17	8	5	47	23	59
Dinamo Bucharest	30	17	5	8	56	32	56
Sportul	30	17	5	8	54	35	56
Ecomax Cluj	30	14	8	8	36	37	50
National	30	13	7	10	32	37	46
Farul	30	14	3	13	39	38	45
Timisoara	30	10	10	10	34	31	40
Otelul	30	10	9	11	35	37	39
Gloria	30	11	6	13	27	34	39
Poli	30	11	6	13	28	31	39
Arges	30	8	8	14	27	37	32
Jiul	30	7	9	14	28	39	30
Vaslui	30	6	11	13	23	37	29
Pandurii*	30	6	7	17	22	44	25
Bacau*	30	3	5	22	16	55	14

Top scorer: Mazilu (Sportul) 22.
Cup Final: Rapid 1, National 0.

RUSSIA

Football Union of Russia; Luzhnetskaya Naberezyhnaja 8, Moscow 119 992.
Founded: 1912; *Number of Clubs:* 43,700; *Number of Players:* 785,000; *National Colours:* All white.
Telephone: 007-095/201 1637; *Fax:* 007-502/220 2037.

International matches 2005
Italy (a) 0-2, Liechtenstein (a) 2-1, Estonia (a) 1-1, Latvia (h) 2-0, Germany (a) 2-2, Latvia (a) 1-1, Liechtenstein (h) 2-0, Portugal (h) 0-0, Luxembourg (h) 5-1, Slovakia (a) 0-0.

League Championship wins (1945–2005)
Spartak Moscow 20; Dynamo Kiev 13; Dynamo Moscow 11; CSKA Moscow 9; Torpedo Moscow 3; Dynamo Tbilisi 2; Dnepr Dnepropetrovsk 2; Lokomotiv Moscow 2; Saria Voroshilovgrad 1; Ararat Erevan 1; Dynamo

Minsk 1; Zenit Leningrad 1; Spartak Vladikavkaz 1.

Cup wins (1936–2006)
Spartak Moscow 13; Dynamo Kiev 10; CSKA Moscow 8; Torpedo Moscow 7; Dynamo Moscow 7; Lokomotiv Moscow 6; Shakhtjor Donetsk 4; Dynamo Tbilisi 2; Ararat Erevan 2; Zenit Leningrad 2; Karpaty Lvov 1; SKA Rostov 1; Metallist Kharkov 1; Dnepr 1; Terek 1.

Final League Table 2005

	P	*W*	*D*	*L*	*F*	*A*	*Pts*
CSKA Moscow	30	18	8	4	48	20	62
Spartak Moscow	30	16	8	6	47	26	56
Lokomotiv Moscow	30	14	14	2	41	18	56
Rubin	30	14	9	7	45	31	51
FK Moscow	30	14	8	8	36	26	50
Zenit	30	13	10	7	45	26	49
Torpedo Moscow	30	12	9	9	37	33	45
Dynamo Moscow	30	12	2	16	36	46	38
Shinnik	30	9	11	10	26	31	38
Tomsk	30	9	10	11	28	33	37
Saturn	30	8	9	13	23	25	33
Amkar	30	7	12	11	25	36	33
Rostov	30	8	7	15	26	41	31
Krylia Sovekov	30	7	8	15	29	44	29
Alania*	30	5	8	17	27	53	23
Terek*	30	5	5	20	20	50	14

Terek six points deducted for delayed transfer payment.
Top scorer: Kirichenko (FK Moscow) 14.
Cup Final: CSKA Moscow 3, Spartak Moscow 0.

SAN MARINO

Federazione Sammarinese Giuoco Calcio, Viale Campo dei Giudei, 14; Rep. San Marino 47890.
Founded: 1931; *Number of Clubs:* 17; *Number of Players:* 1,033; *National Colours:* All light blue.
Telephone: 00378-054/999 0515; *Fax:* 00378-054/999 2348.

International matches 2005
Spain (a) 0-5, Belgium (h) 1-2, Bosnia (h) 1-3, Belgium (a) 0-8, Bosnia (a) 0-3, Spain (h) 0-6.

League Championship wins (1986–2006)
Tre Fiori 4; Domagnano 4; Faetano 3; Folgore 3; Fiorita 2; Montevito 1; Libertas 1; Cosmos 1; Pennarossa 1; Murata 1.

Cup wins (1986–2005)
Domagnano 7; Libertas 3; Faetano 3; Cosmos 2; Pennarossa 2; Fiorita 1; Tre Penne 1; Murata 1.

Qualifying League Table 2005–06

Group A	*P*	*W*	*D*	*L*	*F*	*A*	*Pts*
Tre Fiore	21	14	5	2	37	12	47
Domagnano	21	12	6	3	52	23	42
Tre Penne	21	11	6	4	27	15	39
Folgore/Falciano	21	9	4	8	22	25	31
La Fiorita	21	7	7	7	31	35	28
Faetano	21	6	3	12	32	40	21
Cosmos	21	5	5	11	13	22	20
San Giovanni	21	1	2	18	13	60	5

Group B	*P*	*W*	*D*	*L*	*F*	*A*	*Pts*
Murata	20	15	4	1	49	20	49
Pennarossa	20	12	6	2	38	19	42
Libertas	20	10	3	7	42	22	33
Virtus	20	7	4	9	23	33	25
Juvenes/Dogana	20	3	8	9	27	44	17
Cailungo	20	4	4	12	11	25	16
Fiorentino	20	3	3	14	30	52	12

Fiorentino formerly Montevito.
Play-Offs: Domagnano 1, Libertas 4; Pennarrossa 1, Tre Penne 1 *(Tre Penne won 3-2 on penalties);* Tre Fiore 1, Tre Penne 0; Murata 3, Libertas 1; Tre Penne 1, Domagnano 1 *(Tre Penne won 5-3 on penalties);* Libertas 0, Pennarossa 2; Tre Fiore 0, Murata 1; Tre Penne 2, Pennarossa 3; Tre Fiore 1, Pennarossa 2.
Final: Murata 1, Pennarossa 0.
Top scorer: De Luigi (Murata) 19.
2005 Cup Final: Pennarossa 4, Tre Penne 1.

SCOTLAND

The Scottish Football Association Ltd, Hampden Park, Glasgow G42 9AY.
Founded: 1873; *Number of Clubs:* 6,148; *Number of Players:* 135,474; *National Colours:* Dark blue shirts, white shorts, dark blue stockings.
Telephone: 0044-141/616 6000; *Fax:* 0044-141/616 6001.

SERBIA-MONTENEGRO

Football Association of Serbia and Montenegro, Terazije 35, P.O. Box 263, 11000 Beograd.
Founded: 1919; *Number of Clubs:* 6,532; *Number of Players:* 229,024; *National Colours:* Blue shirts, white shorts, red stockings.
Telephone: 00381-11/ 323 4253; *Fax:* 00381-11/323 3433.

International matches 2005
Bulgaria (a) 0-0, Spain (h) 0-0, Belgium (h) 0-0, Italy (a) 1-1, Poland (n) 2-3, Ukraine (n) 1-2, Lithuania (h) 2-0, Spain (a) 1-1, Lithuania (a) 2-0, Bosnia (h) 1-0, China (a) 2-0, South Korea (a) 0-2.

League Championship wins (1923–2006)
Red Star Belgrade 24; Partizan Belgrade 19; Hajduk Split 9; Gradjanski Zagreb 5; BSK Belgrade 5; Dynamo Zagreb 4; Jugoslavija Belgrade 2; Concordia Zagreb 2; FC Sarajevo 2; Vojvodina Novi Sad 2; HASK Zagreb 1; Zeljeznicar 1; Obilic 1.

Cup wins (1947–2006)
Red Star Belgrade 21; Hajduk Split 9; Partizan Belgrade 9; Dynamo Zagreb 8; BSK Belgrade 2; OFK Belgrade 2; Rijeka 2; Velez Mostar 2; Vardar Skopje 1; Borac Banjaluka 1; Sartid 1; Zeleznik 1.

Final League Table 2005–06

	P	*W*	*D*	*L*	*F*	*A*	*Pts*
Red Star Belgrade	30	25	3	2	73	23	78
Partizan Belgrade	30	22	5	3	53	17	71
Vozdovac**	30	15	6	9	52	38	51
Hajduk Kula	30	13	11	6	41	26	50
Golubovci	30	14	5	11	42	36	47
OFK Belgrade	30	13	5	12	35	29	44
Borac	30	12	8	10	32	27	44
Buducnost Dvor	30	13	5	12	34	31	44
Vojvodina	30	11	10	9	28	27	43
Zemun	30	11	8	11	34	39	41
Smederevo	30	11	6	13	30	37	39
Habitfarm*	30	8	8	14	22	35	32
Rad*	30	9	4	17	27	35	31
Buducnost Podgorica*	30	6	10	14	24	43	25
Obilic*	30	3	6	21	23	53	15
Jedinstvo*	30	3	2	25	18	72	11

*** Zeleznik merged with Vozdovac.*
Buducnost Podgorica three points deducted for walking off in round 21.
Javor renamed Habitfarm.
With Montenegro voting for independence Golubovci move to Montenegro, but Zemun and Smederevo stay in the competition.
Top scorer: Radonjic (Partizan Belgrade) 20.
Cup Final: Red Star Belgrade 4, OFK Belgrade 2.

SLOVAKIA

Slovak Football Association, Junacka 6, 83280 Bratislava, Slovakia.
Founded: 1993; *Number of Clubs:* 2,140; *Number of Players:* 141,000; *National Colours:* All blue and white.
Telephone: 00421-2/4924 9151; *Fax:* 00421-2/4924 9595.

International matches 2005
Romania (a) 2-2, Estonia (a) 2-1, Portugal (h) 1-1, Portugal (a) 0-2, Luxembourg (a) 4-0, Liechtenstein (a) 0-0, Germany (h) 2-0, Latvia (a) 1-1, Estonia (h) 1-0, Russia (h) 0-0, Spain (a) 1-5, Spain (h) 1-1.

League Championship wins (1939–44; 1994–2006)
Slovan Bratislava 8; Zilina 3; Kosice 2; Inter 2; Bystrica 1; OAP Bratislava 1; Petrzalka 1; Ruzomberok 1.

Cup wins (1994–2006)
Inter 3; Slovan Bratislava 2; Tatran Presov 1; Humenne 1; Spartak Trnava 1; Koba 1; Matador 1; Petrzalka 1; Bystrica 1; Ruzomberok 1.

Final League Table 2005-06

	P	*W*	*D*	*L*	*F*	*A*	*Pts*
Ruzomberok	36	26	2	8	65	28	80
Artmedia	36	23	5	8	58	33	74
Spartak Trnava	36	21	5	10	57	31	68

Zilina	36	18	6	12	69	44	60
Nitra	36	12	9	15	42	48	45
Trencin	36	11	9	16	31	49	42
Bystrica	36	12	6	18	36	43	41
Dubnica	36	10	10	16	41	55	39
Inter	36	7	9	20	28	61	30
Matador*	36	7	5	24	29	64	26

Top scorers: Rak (Nitra), Jendrisek (Ruzomberok) 21.
Cup Final: Ruzomberok 0, Spartak Trnava 0.
Ruzomberok won 4-3 on penalties.

SLOVENIA

Football Association of Slovenia, Nogometna zveza Slovenije, Cerinova 4, P.P. 3986, 1001 Ljubljana, Slovenia.
Founded: 1920; *Number of Clubs:* 375; *Number of Players:* 20,117; *National Colours:* White shirts with green sleeves, white shorts, white stockings.
Telephone: 00386-1/530 0400; *Fax:* 00386-1/530 0410.

International matches 2005
Czech Republic (h) 0-3, Germany (h) 0-1, Belarus (h) 1-1, Belarus (a) 1-1, Wales (a) 0-0, Norway (h) 2-3, Moldova (a) 2-1, Italy (a) 0-1, Scotland (h) 0-3.

League Championship wins (1992–2006)
Maribor 7; SCT Olimpija 4; Gorica 4.

Cup wins (1992–2006)
Maribor 5; SCT Olimpija 4; Gorica 2; Mura 1; Rudar 1; Publikum 1; Koper 1.

Final League Table 2005–06

	P	*W*	*D*	*L*	*F*	*A*	*Pts*
Gorica	36	21	10	5	75	30	73
Domzale	36	20	11	5	69	28	71
Koper	36	16	9	11	49	39	57
Maribor	36	16	6	14	51	42	54
Drava	36	15	9	12	50	46	54
Publikum	36	15	4	17	48	59	49
Nafta	36	13	7	16	42	52	46
Primorje	36	11	10	15	43	50	43
Bela Krajina+	36	7	13	16	35	61	34
Rudar*	36	2	9	25	28	83	15

Top scorer: Burgic (Gorica) 24.
Cup Final: Koper 1, Publikum 1.
Koper won 5-3 on penalties.

SPAIN

Real Federacion Espanola De Futbol, Ramon y Cajal, s/n, Apartado Postale 385, Madrid 28230.
Founded: 1913; *Number of Clubs:* 10,240; *Number of Players:* 408,135; *National Colours:* Red shirts, blue shorts, blue stockings with red, blue and yellow border.
Telephone: 0034-91/495 9800; *Fax:* 0034-91/495 9801.

International matches 2005
San Marino (h) 5-0, China (h) 3-0, Serbia & Montenegro (a) 0-0, Lithuania (h) 1-0, Bosnia (h) 1-1, Uruguay (h) 2-0, Canada (h) 2-1, Serbia & Montenegro (h) 1-1, Belgium (a) 2-0, San Marino (a) 6-0, Slovakia (h) 5-1, Slovakia (a) 1-1.

League Championship wins (1929–36; 1940–2006)
Real Madrid 29; Barcelona 18; Atletico Madrid 9; Athletic Bilbao 8; Valencia 6; Real Sociedad 2; Real Betis 1; Seville 1; La Coruna 1.

Cup wins (1902–2006)
Barcelona 24; Athletic Bilbao 23; Real Madrid 17; Atletico Madrid 9; Valencia 6; Real Zaragoza 6; Espanyol 4; Real Union de Irun 3; Seville 3; La Coruna 2; Real Betis 2; Arenas 1; Ciclista Sebastian 1; Racing de Irun 1; Vizcaya Bilbao 1; Real Sociedad 1; Mallorca 1.

Final League Table 2005–06

	P	*W*	*D*	*L*	*F*	*A*	*Pts*
Barcelona	38	25	7	6	80	35	82
Real Madrid	38	20	10	8	70	40	70
Valencia	38	19	12	7	58	33	69
Osasuna	38	21	5	12	49	43	68
Sevilla	38	20	8	10	54	39	68
Celta Vigo	38	20	4	14	45	33	64
Villarreal	38	14	15	9	50	39	57
La Coruna	38	15	10	13	47	45	55
Getafe	38	15	9	14	54	49	54
Atletico Madrid	38	13	13	12	45	37	52
Zaragoza	38	10	16	12	46	51	46
Athletic Bilbao	38	11	12	15	40	46	45
Mallorca	38	10	13	15	37	51	43
Betis	38	10	12	16	34	51	42
Espanyol	38	10	11	17	36	56	41
Real Sociedad	38	11	7	20	48	65	40
Santander	38	9	13	16	36	49	40
Alaves*	38	9	12	17	35	54	39
Cadiz*	38	8	12	18	36	52	36
Malaga*	38	5	9	24	36	68	24

Top scorer: Eto'o (Barcelona) 26.
Cup Final: Espanyol 4, Zaragoza 1.

SWEDEN

Svenska Fotbollfoerbundet, Box 1216, S-17123 Solna.
Founded: 1904; *Number of Clubs:* 3,250; *Number of Players:* 485,000; *National Colours:* Yellow shirts, blue shorts, yellow stockings.
Telephone: 0046-8/735 0900; *Fax:* 0046-8/735 0901.

International matches 2005
South Korea (h) 1-1, Mexico (a) 0-0, France (a) 1-1, Bulgaria (a) 3-0, Malta (h) 6-0, Norway (h) 2-3, Czech Republic (h) 2-1, Bulgaria (h) 3-0, Hungary (a) 1-0, Croatia (a) 0-1, Iceland (h) 3-1, South Korea (a) 2-2.

League Championship wins (1896–2005)
IFK Gothenburg 18; Malmo FF 15; Oergryte IS Gothenburg 14; IFK Norrköping 11; Djurgaarden 11; AIK Stockholm 10; GAIS Gothenburg 6; IF Helsingborg 6; Boras IF Elfsborg 4; Oster Vaxjo 4; Halmstad 4; Atvidaberg 2; IFK Ekilstune 1; IF Gavic Brynas 1; IF Gothenburg 1; Fassbergs 1; Norrköping IK Sleipner 1; Hammarby 1.

Cup wins (1941–2005)
Malmo FF 13; AIK Stockholm 8; IFK Norrköping 6; IFK Gothenburg 4; Djurgaarden 4; Atvidaberg 2; Kalmar 2; Helsingborg 2; GAIS Gothenburg 1; IF Raa 1; Landskrona 1; Oster Vaxjo 1; Degerfors 1; Halmstad 1; Orgryte 1; Elfsborg 1.

Final League Table 2005

	P	*W*	*D*	*L*	*F*	*A*	*Pts*
Djurgaarden	26	16	5	5	60	26	53
IFK Gothenburg	26	14	7	5	38	22	49
Kalmar	26	11	10	5	36	21	43
Hammarby	26	12	7	7	43	30	43
Malmo	26	12	5	9	38	27	41
Helsingborg	26	12	3	11	32	38	39
Elfsborg	26	10	7	9	35	43	37
Hacken	26	11	3	12	29	29	36
Orgryte	26	10	5	11	37	38	35
Halmstad	26	9	5	12	38	38	32
Gefle	26	9	4	13	27	33	31
Landskrona+	26	8	6	12	26	44	30
Sundsvall*	26	6	7	13	31	46	25
Assyriska*	26	4	2	20	17	52	14

Top scorer: Thorvaldsson (Halmstad) 16.
Cup Final: Djurgaarden 2, Atvidaberg 0.

SWITZERLAND

Schweizerisher Fussballverband, Postfach 3000, Berne 15.
Founded: 1895; *Number of Clubs:* 1,473; *Number of Players:* 185,286; *National Colours:* Red shirts, white shorts, red stockings.
Telephone: 0041-31/950 8111; *Fax:* 0041-31/950 8181.

International matches 2005
UAE (a) 2-1, France (a) 0-0, Cyprus (h) 1-0, Faeroes (a) 3-1, Norway (a) 2-0, Israel (h) 1-1, Cyprus (a) 3-1, France (h) 1-1, Republic of Ireland (a) 0-0, Turkey (h) 2-0, Turkey (a) 2-4.

League Championship wins (1898–2006)
Grasshoppers 26; Servette 17; Young Boys Berne 11; FC Basle 11; FC Zurich 10; Lausanne 7; La Chaux-de-Fonds 3; FC Lugano 3; Winterthur 3; FX Aarau 3; Neuchatel Xamax 3; Sion 2; St Gallen 2; FC Anglo-American 1; FC Brühl 1; Cantonal-Neuchatel 1; Biel 1; Bellinzona 1; FC Etoile La Chaux-de-Fonds 1; Lucerne 1.

Cup wins (1926–2006)
Grasshoppers 18; FC Sion 10; Lausanne 9; Servette 7; FC Basle 7; FC Zurich 7; La Chaux-de-Fonds 6; Young Boys Berne 6; Lucerne 2; FC Lugano 2; FC Granges 1; St Gallen 1; Urania Geneva 1; Young Fellows Zurich 1; Aarau 1; Wil 1.

Final League Table 2005–06

	P	W	D	L	F	A	Pts
Zurich	36	23	9	4	86	36	78
Basle	36	23	9	4	87	42	78
Young Boys	36	17	11	8	60	46	62
Grasshoppers	36	14	13	9	44	33	55
Thun	36	14	7	15	50	53	49
St Gallen	36	11	7	18	51	56	40
Aarau	36	8	11	17	29	63	35
Schaffhausen	36	7	12	17	32	55	33
Neuchatel Xamax+	36	9	6	21	41	70	33
Yverdon*	36	9	5	22	38	64	32

Top scorer: Keita (Zurich) 19.
Cup Final: Sion 1, Young Boys 1.
Sion won 5-3 on penalties.

TURKEY

Turkiye Futbol Federasyonu, Konaklar Mah. Ihlamurlu Sok. 9, 4 Levent, Istanbul 80620.
Founded: 1923; *Number of Clubs:* 230; *Number of Players:* 64,521; *National Colours:* All white.
Telephone: 0090-212/282 7020; *Fax:* 0090-212/282 7015.

International matches 2005
Albania (h) 2-0, Georgia (a) 5-2, Greece (h) 0-0, Kazakhstan (a) 6-0, Bulgaria (a) 1-3, Denmark (h) 2-2, Ukraine (a) 1-0, Germany (h) 2-1, Albania (a) 1-0, Switzerland (a) 0-2, Switzerland (h) 4-2.

League Championship wins (1960–2006)
Fenerbahce 16; Galatasaray 16; Besiktas 11; Trabzonspor 6.

Cup wins (1963–2006)
Galatasaray 14; Trabzonspor 7; Besiktas 7; Fenerbahce 4; Goztepe Izmir 2; Altay Izmir 2; Ankaragucu 2; Genclerbirligi 2; Kocaeli 2; Eskisehirspor 1; Bursapor 1; Sakaryaspor 1.

Final League Table 2005–06

	P	W	D	L	F	A	Pts
Galatasaray	34	26	5	3	82	34	83
Fenerbahce	34	25	6	3	90	34	81
Besiktas	34	15	9	10	52	39	54
Trabzonspor	34	15	7	12	51	42	52
Kayseri Erciyes	34	15	6	13	59	42	51
Genclerbirligi	34	14	9	11	47	39	51
Konya	34	12	10	12	39	43	46
Sivas	34	10	13	11	34	44	43
Rize	34	10	11	13	35	44	41
Kayseri Erciy	34	9	13	12	36	47	40
Gaziantep	34	10	10	14	34	50	40
Vestel	34	11	7	16	52	61	40
Ankaragucu	34	10	9	15	43	48	39
Ankara	34	9	12	13	44	51	39
Denizli	34	9	10	15	41	50	37
Malatya*	34	9	9	16	34	50	36
Samsun*	34	9	9	16	45	62	36
Diyarbakir*	34	8	5	21	31	69	29

Top scorer: Gokhan (Kayseri Erciyes) 25.
Cup Final: Besiktas 3, Fenerbahce 2.

UKRAINE

Football Federation of Ukraine, Laboratorna Str. 1, P.O. Box 293, Kiev 03150.
Founded: 1991; *Number of Clubs:* 1,500; *Number of Players:* 759,500; *National Colours:* All yellow and blue.
Telephone: 00380-44/252 8498; *Fax:* 00380-44/252 8513.

International matches 2005
Albania (a) 2-0, Denmark (h) 1-0, Kazakhstan (h) 2-0, Greece (a) 1-0, Israel (n) 0-0, Serbia & Montenegro (n) 2-1, Georgia (a) 1-1, Turkey (h) 0-1, Albania (h) 2-2, Japan (h) 1-0.

League Championship wins (1992–2006)
Dynamo Kiev 10; Shakhtar Donetsk 3; Tavriya Simferopol 1.

Cup wins (1992–2006)
Dynamo Kiev 8; Shakhtar Donetsk 5; Chernomorets 2.

Final League Table 2005–06

	P	W	D	L	F	A	Pts
Shakhtar Donetsk	30	23	6	1	64	14	75
Dynamo Kiev	30	23	6	1	68	20	75
Chernomorets	30	13	6	11	36	31	45
Mariupol	30	12	7	11	30	34	43
Metalist	30	12	7	11	35	42	43
Dnepro	30	11	10	9	33	23	43
Tavriya	30	11	6	13	29	31	39
Metalurg Zapor	30	11	6	13	32	40	39
Metalurg Donetsk	30	10	9	11	35	35	39
Vorskla	30	9	10	11	28	34	37
Stal	30	9	9	12	26	39	36
Arsenal Kiev	30	9	8	13	31	39	35
Kharkiv	30	9	6	15	29	36	33
Krivbas	30	9	6	15	27	35	33
Volyn*	30	9	6	15	31	45	33
Zakarpattja*	30	3	6	21	17	53	15

Championship Play-Off: Shakhtar Donetsk 2, Dynamo Kiev 1.
Kharkiv formerly Arsenal Kharkiv.
Top scorers: Brandao (Shakhtar Donetsk), Okoduwa (Arsenal Kiev) 15.
Cup Final: Dynamo Kiev 1, Metalurg Zapor 0.

WALES

The Football Association of Wales Limited, Plymouth Chambers, 3 Westgate Street, Cardiff, CF10 1DP.
Founded: 1876; *Number of Clubs:* 2,326; *Number of Players:* 53,926; *National Colours:* All red.
Telephone: 0044-29/2037 2325; *Fax:* 0044-29/2034 3961.

SOUTH AMERICA

ARGENTINA

Asociacion Del Futbol Argentina, Viamonte 1366/76, 1053 Buenos Aires.
Founded: 1893; *Number of Clubs:* 3,035; *Number of Players:* 306,365; *National Colours:* Light blue and white vertical striped shirts, dark blue shorts, white stockings.
Telephone: 0054-11/4372 7900; *Fax:* 0054-11/4375 4410.
International matches 2005
Germany (a) 2-2, Mexico (h) 1-1, Bolivia (a) 2-1, Colombia (h) 1-0, Ecuador (a) 0-2, Brazil (h) 3-1, Tunisia (n) 2-1, Australia (n) 4-2, Germany (n) 2-2, Mexico (n) 1-1, Brazil (n) 1-4, Hungary (a) 2-1, Paraguay (a) 0-1, Peru (h) 2-0, Uruguay (a) 0-1, England (n) 2-3, Qatar (a) 3-0.

BOLIVIA

Federacion Boliviana De Futbol, Av. Libertador Bolivar No. 1168, Casilla de Correo 484, Cochabamba, Bolivia.
Founded: 1925; *Number of Clubs:* 305; *Number of Players:* 15,290; *National Colours:* Green shirts, white shorts, green stockings.
Telephone: 00591-4/424 4982; *Fax:* 00591-4/428 2132.
International matches 2005
Argentina (h) 1-2, Venezuela (h) 3-1, Chile (a) 1-3, Paraguay (a) 1-4, Ecuador (h) 1-2, Brazil (h) 1-1, Peru (a) 1-4.

BRAZIL

Confederacao Brasileira De Futebol, Rua Victor Civita 66, Bloco 1-Edificio 5-5 Andar, Barra da Tijuca, Rio De Janeiro 22775-040.
Founded: 1914; *Number of Clubs:* 12,987; *Number of Players:* 551,358; *National Colours:* Yellow shirts with green collar and cuffs, blue shorts, white stockings with green and yellow border.

Telephone: 0055-21/3870 3610; Fax: 0055-21/3870 3612.
International matches 2005
Hong Kong (a) 7-1, Peru (h) 1-0, Uruguay (a) 1-1, Guatemala (h) 3-0, Paraguay (h) 4-1, Argentina (a) 1-3, Greece (n) 3-0, Mexico (n) 0-1, Japan (n) 2-2, Germany (n) 3-2, Argentina (n) 4-1, Croatia (a) 1-1, Chile (h) 5-0, Bolivia (a) 1-1, Venezuela (h) 3-0, UAE (a) 8-0.

CHILE

Federacion De Futbol De Chile, Avda. Quillin No. 5635, Casilla postal 3733, Correo Central, Santiago de Chile.
Founded: 1895; *Number of Clubs:* 4,598; *Number of Players:* 609,724; *National Colours:* Red shirts with blue collar and cuffs, blue shorts, white stockings.
Telephone: 0056-2/284 9000; *Fax:* 0056-2/284 3510.
International matches 2005
Ecuador (h) 3-0, Uruguay (h) 1-1, Paraguay (a) 1-2, Bolivia (h) 3-1, Venezuela (h) 2-1, Peru (a) 1-3, Brazil (a) 0-5, Colombia (a) 1-1, Ecuador (h) 0-0.

COLOMBIA

Federacion Colombiana De Futbol, Avenida 32, No. 16–22 piso 4o. Apartado Aereo 17602, Santafe de Bogota.
Founded: 1924; *Number of Clubs:* 3,685; *Number of Players:* 188,050; *National Colours:* Yellow shirts, blue shorts, red stockings.
Telephone: 0057-1/288 9740; *Fax:* 0057-1/288 9559.
International matches 2005
South Korea (h) 2-1, Guatemala (h) 1-1, Mexico (a) 1-1, USA (a) 0-3, Venezuela (a) 0-0, Argentina (a) 0-1, England (h) 2-3, Peru (h) 5-0, Ecuador (h) 3-0, Panama (n) 0-1, Honduras (n) 1-2, Trinidad & Tobago (n) 2-0, Mexico (n) 2-1, Panama (n) 2-3, Uruguay (a) 2-3, Chile (h) 1-1, Paraguay (a) 1-0.

ECUADOR

Federacion Ecuatoriana del Futbol, km 4 1/2 via a la Costa (Avda. del Bombero), PO Box 09-01-7447 Guayaquil.
Founded: 1925; *Number of Clubs:* 170; *Number of Players:* 15,700; *National Colours:* Yellow shirts, blue shorts, red stockings.
Telephone: 00593-4/235 2372; *Fax:* 00593-4/235 2116.
International matches 2005
Panama (h) 2-0, Panama (h) 2-0, Chile (a) 0-3, Costa Rica (a) 2-1, Paraguay (h) 5-2, Peru (a) 2-2, Paraguay (h) 1-0, Argentina (h) 2-0, Colombia (a) 0-3, Italy (h) 1-1, Venezuela (h) 3-1, Bolivia (a) 2-1, Uruguay (h) 0-0, Chile (a) 0-0, Poland (a) 0-3, Senegal (n) 1-2, Uganda (n) 1-2.

PARAGUAY

Asociacion Paraguaya de Futbol, Estadio De Los Defensores del Chaco, Calles Mayor Martinez 1393, Asuncion.
Founded: 1906; *Number of Clubs:* 1,500; *Number of Players:* 140,000; *National Colours:* Red and white shirts, blue shorts, blue stockings.
Telephone: 00595-21/480 120; *Fax:* 00595-21/480 124.
International matches 2005
South Korea (h) 1-1, Guatemala (h) 2-1, Ecuador (a) 2-5, Chile (h) 2-1, Paraguay (a) 1-0, Brazil (a) 1-4, Bolivia (h) 4-1, El Salvador (h) 3-0, Argentina (h) 1-0, Venezuela (a) 1-0, Colombia (h) 0-1, Togo (h) 4-2, Macedonia (a) 1-0.

PERU

Federacion Peruana De Futbol, Av. Aviacion 2085, San Luis, Lima 30.
Founded: 1922; *Number of Clubs:* 10,000; *Number of Players:* 325,650; *National Colours:* White shirts with red stripe, white shorts with red lines, white stockings with red line.
Telephone: 0051-1/225 8236; *Fax:* 0051-1/225 8240.
International matches 2005
Brazil (a) 0-1, Ecuador (h) 2-2, Japan (a) 1-0, UAE (a) 0-0, Colombia (a) 0-5, Uruguay (h) 0-0, Chile (h) 3-1, Venezuela (a) 1-4, Argentina (a) 0-2, Bolivia (h) 4-1.

URUGUAY

Asociacion Uruguaya De Futbol, Guayabo 1531, 11200 Montevideo.
Founded: 1900; *Number of Clubs:* 1,091; *Number of Players:* 134,310; *National Colours:* Sky blue shirts with white collar/cuffs, black shorts and stockings with sky blue borders.
Telephone: 0059-82/400 4814; *Fax:* 0059-82/409 0550.
International matches 2005
Chile (a) 1-1, Brazil (h) 1-1, Venezuela (a) 1-1, Peru (a) 0-0, Spain (a) 0-2, Colombia (h) 3-2, Ecuador (a) 0-0, Argentina (h) 1-0, Mexico (a) 1-3, Australia (h) 1-0, Australia (a) 0-1.

VENEZUELA

Federacion Venezolana De Futbol, Avda. Santos Erminy Ira, Calle las Delicias Torre Mega II, P.H. Sabana Grande, Caracas 1050.
Founded: 1926; *Number of Clubs:* 1,753; *Number of Players:* 63,175; *National Colours:* Burgundy shirts, white shorts and stockings.
Telephone: 0058-212/762 4472; *Fax:* 0058-212/762 0596.
International matches 2005
Estonia (h) 3-0, Colombia (h) 0-0, Bolivia (a) 1-3, Panama (h) 1-1, Uruguay (h) 1-1, Chile (a) 1-2, Ecuador (a) 1-3, Peru (h) 4-1, Paraguay (h) 0-1, Brazil (a) 0-3.

ASIA

AFGHANISTAN

Afghanistan Football Federation, PO Box 5099, Kabul.
Founded: 1933; *Number of Clubs:* 30; *Number of Players:* 3,300; *National Colours:* All white with red lines.
Telephone: 0093-20/210 2417; *Fax:* 0093-20/210 2417

BAHRAIN

Bahrain Football Association, P.O. Box 5464, Manama.
Founded: 1957; *Number of Clubs:* 25; *Number of Players:* 2,030; *National Colours:* All red.
Telephone: 00973/689 569; *Fax:* 00973/781 188.

BANGLADESH

Bangladesh Football Federation, Bangabandhu National Stadium-1, Dhaka 1000.
Founded: 1972; *Number of Clubs:* 1,265; *Number of Players:* 30,385; *National Colours:* Orange shirts, white shorts, green stockings.
Telephone: 00880-2/955 6072; *Fax:* 00880-2/956 3419.

BHUTAN

Bhutan Football Federation, P.O. Box 365, Thimphu.
National Colours: All yellow and red.
Telephone: 00975-2/322 350; *Fax:* 00975-2/321 131.

BRUNEI DARUSSALAM

The Football Association of Brunei Darussalam, P.O. Box 2010, 1920 Bandar Seri Begawan BS 8674.
Founded: 1959; *Number of Clubs:* 22; *Number of Players:* 830; *National Colours:* Yellow shirts, black shorts, black and white stockings.
Telephone: 00673-2/382 761; *Fax:* 00673-2/382 760.

CAMBODIA

Cambodian Football Federation, Chaeng Maeng Village, Rd. Kab Srov, Sangkat Samrong Krom, Khan Dangkor, Phnom-Penh .
Founded: 1933; *Number of Clubs:* 30; *Number of Players:* 650; *National Colours:* All blue.
Telephone: 00855-23/364 889; *Fax:* 00855-23/220 780.

CHINA PR

Football Association of The People's Republic of China, 9 Tiyuguan Road, Beijing 100763.
Founded: 1924; *Number of Clubs:* 1,045; *Number of Players:* 2,250,000; *National Colours:* All white.
Telephone: 0086-10/6711 7019; *Fax:* 0086-10/6714 2533.

CHINESE TAIPEI

Chinese Taipei Football Association, 2F No. Yu Men St., Taipei, Taiwan 104.
Founded: 1936; *Number of Players:* 17,000; *National Colours:* Blue shirts and shorts, white stockings.
Telephone: 00886-2/2596 1185; *Fax:* 00886-2/2595 1594.

GUAM

Guam Football Association, P.O.Box 5093, Agana, Guam 96932.
Founded: 1975; *National Colours:* Blue shirts, white shorts, blue stockings.
Telephone: 001-671/477 5423; *Fax:* 001-671/477 5424.

HONG KONG

The Hong Kong Football Association Ltd, 55 Fat Kwong Street, Homantin, Kowloon, Hong Kong.
Founded: 1914; *Number of Clubs:* 69; *Number of Players:* 3,274; *National Colours:* All red.
Telephone: 00852/2712 9122; *Fax:* 00852/2760 4303.

INDIA

All India Football Federation, Nehru Stadium (West Stand), Fatorda Margao-Goa 403 602.
Founded: 1937; *Number of Clubs:* 2,000; *Number of Players:* 56,000; *National Colours:* Sky blue shirts, navy blue shorts, sky and navy blue stockings.
Telephone: 0091-832/2742 603; *Fax:* 0091-832/2741 172.

INDONESIA

Football Association of Indonesia, Gelora Bung Karno, Pintu X-XI, Jakarta 10270.
Founded: 1930; *Number of Clubs:* 2,880; *Number of Players:* 97,000; *National Colours:* Red shirts, white shorts, red stockings.
Telephone: 0062-21/570 4762; *Fax:* 0062-21/573 4386.

IRAN

IR Iran Football Federation, No. 16-4th deadend, Pakistan Street, PO Box 15316-6967 Shahid Beheshti Avenue, Tehran 15316.
Founded: 1920; *Number of Clubs:* 6,326; *Number of Players:* 306,000; *National Colours:* All white.
Telephone: 0098-21/873 2754; *Fax:* 0098-21/873 0305.

IRAQ

Iraqi Football Association, Olympic Committee Building, Palestine Street, PO Box 484, Baghdad.
Founded: 1948; *Number of Clubs:* 155; *Number of Players:* 4,400; *National Colours:* All black.
Telephone: 00964-1/772 9990; *Fax:* 00964-1/885 4321.

JAPAN

Japan Football Association, JFA House, 3-10-15, Hongo, Bunkyo-ku, Tokyo 113-0033.
Founded: 1921; *Number of Clubs:* 13,047; *Number of Players:* 358,989; *National Colours:* Blue shirts, white shorts, blue stockings.
Telephone: 0081-3/3830 2004; *Fax:* 0081-3/3830 2005.

JORDAN

Jordan Football Association, P.O. Box 962024 Al Hussein Sports City, 11196 Amman.
Founded: 1949; *Number of Clubs:* 98; *Number of Players:* 4,305; *National Colours:* All white and red.
Telephone: 00962-6/565 7662; *Fax:* 00962-6/565 7660.

KOREA, NORTH

Football Association of The Democratic People's Rep. of Korea, Kumsong-dong, Kwangbok Street, Mangyongdae Distr, PO Box 56, Pyongyang FNJ-PRK.
Founded: 1945; *Number of Clubs:* 90; *Number of Players:* 3,420; *National Colours:* All white.
Telephone: 00850-2/18 222; *Fax:* 00850-2/381 4403.

KOREA, SOUTH

Korea Football Association, 1-131 Sinmunno, 2-ga, Jongno-Gu, Seoul 110-062.
Founded: 1928; *Number of Clubs:* 476; *Number of Players:* 2,047; *National Colours:* Red shirts, blue shorts, red stockings.
Telephone: 0082-2/733 6764; *Fax:* 0082-2/735 2755.

KUWAIT

Kuwait Football Association, P.O. Box 2029, Udiliya, Block 4 Al-Ittihad Street, Safat 13021.
Founded: 1952; *Number of Clubs:* 14 (senior); *Number of Players:* 1,526; *National Colours:* All blue.
Telephone: 00965/255 5851; *Fax:* 00965/254 9955.

KYRGYZSTAN

Football Federation of Kyrgyz Republic, PO Box 1484, Kurenkeeva Street 195, Bishkek 720040, Kyrgyzstan.
Founded: 1992; *Number of Players:* 20,000; *National Colours:* Red shirts, white shorts, red stockings.
Telephone: 00996-312/670 573; *Fax:* 00996-312/670 573.

LAOS

Federation Lao de Football, National Stadium, Kounboulo Street, PO Box 3777, Vientiane 856-21, Laos.
Founded: 1951; *Number of Clubs:* 76; *Number of Players:* 2,060; *National Colours:* All red.
Telephone: 00856-21/251 593; *Fax:* 00856-21/213 460.

LEBANON

Federation Libanaise De Football-Association, P.O. Box 4732, Verdun Street, Bristol, Radwan Centre Building, Beirut.
Founded: 1933; *Number of Clubs:* 105; *Number of Players:* 8,125; *National Colours:* Red shirts, white shorts, red stockings.
Telephone: 00961-1/745 745; *Fax:* 00961-1/349 529.

MACAO

Associacao De Futebol De Macau (AFM), Ave. da Amizade 405, Seng Vo Kok, 13 Andar "A", Macau.
Founded: 1939; *Number of Clubs:* 52; *Number of Players:* 800; *National Colours:* All green.
Telephone: 00853/781 883; *Fax:* 00853/782 383.

MALAYSIA

Football Association of Malaysia, 3rd Floor, Wisma Fam, Jalan, SSA/9, Kelana Jaya Selangor Darul Ehsan 47301.
Founded: 1933; *Number of Clubs:* 450; *Number of Players:* 11,250; *National Colours:* All yellow and black.
Telephone: 0060-3/7876 3766; *Fax:* 0060-3/7875 7984.

MALDIVES REPUBLIC

Football Association of Maldives, National Stadium G. Banafsaa Magu 20-04, Male.
Founded: 1982; *Number of Clubs: Number of Players: National Colours:* Red shirts, Green shorts, white stockings.
Telephone: 00960/317 006; *Fax:* 00960/317 005.

MONGOLIA

Mongolia Football Federation, PO Box 259 Ulaan-Baatar 210646.
National Colours: White shirts, red shorts, white stockings.
Telephone: 00976-11/312 145; *Fax:* 00976-11/312 145.

MYANMAR

Myanmar Football Federation, Youth Training Centre, Thingankyun Township, Yangon.
Founded: 1947; *Number of Clubs:* 600; *Number of Players:* 21,000; *National Colours:* Red shirts, white shorts, red stockings.
Telephone: 00951/577 366; *Fax:* 00951/570 000.

NEPAL

All-Nepal Football Association, AMFA House, Ward No. 4, Bishalnagar, PO Box 12582, Kathmandu.
Founded: 1951; *Number of Clubs:* 85; *Number of Players:* 2,550; *National Colours:* All red.
Telephone: 00977-1/5539 059; *Fax:* 00977-1/442 4314.

OMAN

Oman Football Association, P.O. Box 3462, Ruwi Postal Code 112.
Founded: 1978; *Number of Clubs:* 47; *Number of Players:* 2,340; *National Colours:* All white.
Telephone: 00968/787 635; *Fax:* 00968/787 632.

PAKISTAN

Pakistan Football Federation, 6 National Hockey Stadium, Feroze Pure Road, Lahore, Pakistan.
Founded: 1948; *Number of Clubs:* 882; *Number of Players:* 21,000; *National Colours:* All green and white.
Telephone: 0092-42/923 0821; *Fax:* 0092-42/923 0823.

PALESTINE

Palestinian Football Federation, Al-Yarmouk, Gaza.
Founded: 1928; *Number of Clubs:* 377; *Number of Players:* 37,190; *National Colours:* White shirts, black shorts, white stockings.
Telephone: 00972-8/283 4339; *Fax:* 00972-8/282 5208.

PHILIPPINES

Philippine Football Federation, Room 405, Building V, Philsports Complex, Meralco Avenue, Pasig City, Metro Manila.
Founded: 1907; *Number of Clubs:* 650; *Number of Players:* 45,000; *National Colours:* All blue.
Telephone: 0063-2/687 1594; *Fax:* 0063-2/687 1598.

QATAR

Qatar Football Association, 7th Floor, QNOC Building, Cornich, P.O. Box 5333, Doha.
Founded: 1960; *Number of Clubs:* 8 (senior); *Number of Players:* 1,380; *National Colours:* All white.
Telephone: 00974/494 4411; *Fax:* 00974/494 4414.

SAUDI ARABIA

Saudi Arabian Football Federation, Al Mather Quarter (Olympic Complex), Prince Faisal Bin Fahad Street, P.O. Box 5844, Riyadh 11432.
Founded: 1959; *Number of Clubs:* 120; *Number of Players:* 9,600; *National Colours:* White shirts, green shorts, white stockings.
Telephone: 00966-1/482 2240; *Fax:* 00966-1/482 1215.

SINGAPORE

Football Association of Singapore, Jalan Besar Stadium, 100 Tyrwhitt Road, Singapore 207542.
Founded: 1892; *Number of Clubs:* 250; *Number of Players:* 8,000; *National Colours:* All red.
Telephone: 0065/6348 3477; *Fax:* 0065/6293 3728.

SRI LANKA

Football Federation of Sri Lanka, 100/9, Independence Avenue, Colombo 07.
Founded: 1939; *Number of Clubs:* 600; *Number of Players:* 18,825; *National Colours:* All white.
Telephone: 0094-11/268 6120; *Fax:* 0094-11/2682 471.

SYRIA

Syrian Football Federation, PO Box 421, Maysaloon Street, Damascus.
Founded: 1936; *Number of Clubs:* 102; *Number of Players:* 30,600; *National Colours:* All red.
Telephone: 00963-11/333 5866; *Fax:* 00963-11/333 1511.

TAJIKISTAN

Tajikistan Football Federation, 22 Shotemur Ave., Dushanbe 734 025.
Founded: 1991; *Number of Clubs:* 1,804; *Number of Players:* 71,400; *National Colours:* All white.
Telephone: 00992-372/210 265; *Fax:* 00992-372/510 157.

THAILAND

The Football Association of Thailand, Gate 3, Rama I Road, Patumwan, Bangkok 10330.
Founded: 1916; *Number of Clubs:* 168; *Number of Players:* 15,000; *National Colours:* All red.
Telephone: 0066-2/216 4691; *Fax:* 0066-2/215 4494.

TIMOR-LESTE

Federacao Futebol Timor-Leste, Rua 12 de Novembro Str., Cruz, Dili.
Founded: 2002; *National Colours:* Red shirts, black shorts, red stockings.
Telephone: 00669 8511878; *Fax:* 00669 9554509.

TURKMENISTAN

Football Association of Turkmenistan, 32 Belinskiy Street, Stadium Kopetdag, Ashgabat 744 001.
Founded: 1992; *Number of Players:* 75,000; *National Colours:* Green shirts, white shorts, green stockings.
Telephone: 00993-12/362 392; *Fax:* 00993-12/362 355.

UNITED ARAB EMIRATES

United Arab Emirates Football Association, P.O. Box 916, Abu Dhabi.
Founded: 1971; *Number of Clubs:* 23 (senior); *Number of Players:* 1,787; *National Colours:* All white.
Telephone: 00971-2/444 5600; *Fax:* 00971-2/444 8558.

UZBEKISTAN

Uzbekistan Football Federation, Massiv Almazar Furkat Street 15/1, 700003 Tashkent, Uzbekistan.
Founded: 1946; *Number of Clubs:* 15,000; *Number of Players:* 217,000; *National Colours:* All white.
Telephone: 00998-71/144 1684; *Fax:* 00998-71/144 1683.

VIETNAM

Vietnam Football Federation, 18 Ly van Phuc, Dong Da District, Hanoi 844.
Founded: 1962; *Number of Clubs:* 55 (senior); *Number of Players:* 16,000; *National Colours:* All red.
Telephone: 0084-4/845 2480; *Fax:* 0084-4/823 3119.

YEMEN

Yemen Football Association, Quarter of Sport – Al Jeraf, Behind the Stadium of Ali Mushsen, Al Moreissy in the Sport, Al-Thawra City.
Founded: 1962; *Number of Clubs:* 26; *Number of Players:* 1,750; *National Colours:* All green.
Telephone: 00967-1/310 927. *Fax:* 00967-1/310 921.

CONCACAF

ANGUILLA

Anguilla Football Association, P.O. Box 1318, The Valley, Anguilla, BWI.
National Colours: Turquoise, white, orange and blue shirts and shorts, turquoise and orange stockings.
Telephone: 001-264/497 7323; *Fax:* 001-264/497 7324.

ANTIGUA & BARBUDA

The Antigua/Barbuda Football Association, Newgate Street, P.O. Box 773, St John's.
Founded: 1928; *Number of Clubs:* 60; *Number of Players:* 1,008; *National Colours:* Red, black, yellow and blue shirts, black shorts and stockings.
Telephone: 001-268/727 8869; *Fax:* 001-268/562 1681.

ARUBA

Arubaanse Voetbal Bond, Ferguson Street, Z/N P.O. Box 376, Oranjestad, Aruba.
Founded: 1932; *Number of Clubs:* 50; *Number of Players:* 1,000; *National Colours:* Yellow shirts, blue shorts, yellow and blue stockings.
Telephone: 00297/829 550; *Fax:* 00297/829 550.

BAHAMAS

Bahamas Football Association, Plaza on the Way, West Bay Street, P.O. Box N 8434, Nassau, NP.
Founded: 1967; *Number of Clubs:* 14; *Number of Players:* 700; *National Colours:* Yellow shirts, black shorts, yellow stockings.
Telephone: 001-242/322 5897; *Fax:* 001-242/322 5898.

BARBADOS

Barbados Football Association, Hildor No. 4, 10th Avenue, P.O. Box 1362, Belleville-St. Michael, Barbados.
Founded: 1910; *Number of Clubs:* 92; *Number of Players:* 1,100; *National Colours:* Royal blue and gold shirts, gold shorts, white, gold and blue stockings.
Telephone: 001-246/228 1707; *Fax:* 001-246/228 6484.

BELIZE

Belize National Football Association, 26 Hummingbird Highway, Belmopan, P.O. Box 1742, Belize City.
Founded: 1980; *National Colours:* Red, white and black shirts, black shorts, red and black stockings.
Telephone: 00501-822/3410; *Fax:* 00501-822/3377.

BERMUDA

The Bermuda Football Association, 48 Cedar Avenue, Hamilton HM12.
Founded: 1928; *Number of Clubs:* 30; *Number of Players:* 1,947; *National Colours:* All blue.
Telephone: 001-441/295 2199; *Fax:* 001-441/295 0773.

BRITISH VIRGIN ISLANDS

British Virgin Islands Football Association, P.O. Box 29, Road Town, Tortola, BVI.
National Colours: Gold and green shirts, green shorts, and stockings.
Telephone: 001-284/494 5655; *Fax:* 001-284/494 8968.

US VIRGIN ISLANDS

USVI Soccer Federation Inc., 54, Castle Coakley, PO Box 2346, Kingshill, St Croix 00851.
National Colours: Royal blue and gold shirts, royal blue shorts and stockings.
Telephone: 001-340/711 9676; *Fax:* 00-340/711 9707.

CANADA

The Canadian Soccer Association, Place Soccer Canada, 237 Metcalfe Street, Ottawa, ONT K2P 1R2.
Founded: 1912; *Number of Clubs:* 1,600; *Number of Players:* 224,290; *National Colours:* All red.
Telephone: 001-613/237 7678; *Fax:* 001-613/237 1516.

CAYMAN ISLANDS

Cayman Islands Football Association, PO Box 178 GT, Truman Bodden Sports Complex, Olympic Way Off

Walkers Rd, George Town, Grand Cayman, Cayman Islands WI.
Founded: 1966; *Number of Clubs:* 25; *Number of Players:* 875; *National Colours:* Red and white shirts, blue and white shorts, white and red stockings.
Telephone: 001-345/949 5775. *Fax:* 001-345/945 7673.

COSTA RICA

Federacion Costarricense De Futbol, Costado Norte Estatua Leon Cortes, San Jose 670-1000.
Founded: 1921; *Number of Clubs:* 431; *Number of Players:* 12,429; *National Colours:* Red shirts, blue shorts, white stockings.
Telephone: 00506/222 1544; *Fax:* 00506/255 2674.

CUBA

Asociacion de Futbol de Cuba, Calle 13 No. 661, Esq. C. Vedado, ZP 4, La Habana.
Founded: 1924; *Number of Clubs:* 70; *Number of Players:* 12,900; *National Colours:* All red, white and blue.
Telephone: 0053-7/545 024; *Fax:* 0053-7/335 310.

DOMINICA

Dominica Football Association, 33 Great Marlborough Street, Roseau.
Founded: 1970; *Number of Clubs:* 30; *Number of Players:* 500; *National Colours:* Emerald green shirts, black shorts, green stockings.
Telephone: 001-767/448 7577; *Fax:* 001-767/448 7587.

DOMINICAN REPUBLIC

Federacion Dominicana De Futbol, Centro Olimpico Juan Pablo Duarte, Ensanche Miraflores, Apartado De Correos No. 1953, Santo Domingo.
Founded: 1953; *Number of Clubs:* 128; *Number of Players:* 10,706; *National Colours:* Navy blue shirts, white shorts, red stockings.
Telephone: 001-809/542 6923; *Fax:* 001-809/547 5363.

EL SALVADOR

Federacion Salvadorena De Futbol, Primera Calle Poniente No. 2025, San Salvador CA1029.
Founded: 1935; *Number of Clubs:* 944; *Number of Players:* 21,294; *National Colours:* All blue.
Telephone: 00503/263 7525; *Fax:* 00503/260 3129.

GRENADA

Grenada Football Association, P.O. Box 326, National Stadium, Queens Park, St George's, Grenada, W.I.
Founded: 1924; *Number of Clubs:* 15; *Number of Players:* 200; *National Colours:* Green and yellow striped shirts, red shorts, yellow stockings.
Telephone: 001-473/440 9903; *Fax:* 001-473/440 9973.

GUATEMALA

Federacion Nacional de Futbol de Guatemala, 2a Calle 15-57, Zona 15, Boulevard Vista Hermosa, Guatemala City 01009.
Founded: 1946; *Number of Clubs:* 1,611; *Number of Players:* 43,516; *National Colours:* Blue shirts, white shorts, blue stockings.
Telephone: 00502/279 1746; *Fax:* 00502/379 8345.

GUYANA

Guyana Football Federation, 159 Rupununi Street, Bel Air Park, P.O. Box 10727, Georgetown.
Founded: 1902; *Number of Clubs:* 103; *Number of Players:* 1,665; *National Colours:* Green shirts and shorts, yellow stockings.
Telephone: 00592-2/278 758; *Fax:* 00592-2/262 641.

HAITI

Federation Haitienne De Football, 128 Avenue Christiophe, P.O. Box 2258, Port-Au-Prince.
Founded: 1904; *Number of Clubs:* 40; *Number of Players:* 4,000; *National Colours:* Blue shirts, red shorts, blue stockings.
Telephone: 00509/244 0115; *Fax:* 00509/244 0117.

HONDURAS

Federacion Nacional Autonoma De Futbol De Honduras, Colonia Florencia Norte, Ave Roble, Edificio Plaza America, Ave. Roble 1 y 2 Nivel, Tegucigalpa, D.C.
Founded: 1951; *Number of Clubs:* 1,050; *Number of Players:* 15,300; *National Colours:* All white.
Telephone: 00504/232 0572; *Fax:* 00504/239 8826.

JAMAICA

Jamaica Football Federation Ltd, 20 St Lucia Crescent, Kingston 5.
Founded: 1910; *Number of Clubs:* 266; *Number of Players:* 45,200; *National Colours:* Gold shirts, black shorts, gold stockings.
Telephone: 001-876/929 8036; *Fax:* 001-876/929 0483.

MEXICO

Federacion Mexicana De Futbol Asociacion, A.C., Colima No. 373, Colonia Roma Mexico DF 06700.
Founded: 1927; *Number of Clubs:* 77 (senior); *Number of Players:* 1,402,270; *National Colours:* Green shirts with white collar, white shorts, red stockings.
Telephone: 0052-55/5241 0190; *Fax:* 0052-55/5241 0191.

MONSERRAT

Monserrat Football Association Inc., P.O. Box 505, Woodlands, Monserrat.
National Colours: Green shirts with black and white stripes, green shorts with white stripes, green stockings with black and white stripes.
Telephone: 001-664/491 8744; *Fax:* 001-664/491 8801.

NETHERLANDS ANTILLES

Nederlands Antiliaanse Voetbal Unie, Bonamweg 49, Curacao, NA.
Founded: 1921; *Number of Clubs:* 85; *Number of Players:* 4,500; *National Colours:* White shirts with red and blue stripes, red shorts with blue and white stripes, white stockings with red stripes.
Telephone: 00599-9736 5040; *Fax:* 00599/9736 5047.

NICARAGUA

Federacion Nicaraguense De Futbol, Hospital Pautista 1, Cuadra avajo, 1 cuada al Sur y 1/2, Cuadra Abajo, Managua 976.
Founded: 1931; *Number of Clubs:* 31; *Number of Players:* 160 (senior); *National Colours:* Blue shirts, white shorts, blue stockings.
Telephone: 00505/222 7035; *Fax:* 00505/222 7885.

PANAMA

Federacion Panamena De Futbol, Estadio Rommel Fernandez, Puerta 24, Ave. Jose Aeustin Araneo, Apartado Postal 8-391, Zona 8, Panama.
Founded: 1937; *Number of Clubs:* 65; *Number of Players:* 4,225; *National Colours:* All red.
Telephone: 00507/233 3896; *Fax:* 00507/233 0582.

PUERTO RICO

Federacion Puertorriquena De Futbol, P.O. Box 193590 San Juan 00919.
Founded: 1940; *Number of Clubs:* 175; *Number of Players:* 4,200; *National Colours:* Red, blue and white shirts and shorts, red and blue stockings.
Telephone: 001-787/759 7544; *Fax:* 001-787/759 7544.

SAINT KITTS & NEVIS

St Kitts & Nevis Football Association, P.O. Box 465, Warner Park, Basseterre, St Kitts, W.I.
Founded: 1932; *Number of Clubs:* 36; *Number of Players:* 600; *National Colours:* Green and yellow shirts, red shorts, yellow stockings.
Telephone: 001-869/466 8502; *Fax:* 001-869/465 9033.

SAINT LUCIA

St Lucia National Football Association, PO Box 255, Sans Souci, Castries, St Lucia.
Founded: 1979; *Number of Clubs:* 100; *Number of Players:* 4,000; *National Colours:* White shirts and shorts with yellow, blue and black stripes, white, blue and yellow stockings.
Telephone: 001-758/453 0687; *Fax:* 001-758/456 0510.

SAINT VINCENT & THE GRENADINES

St Vincent & The Grenadines Football Federation, Sharpe Street, PO Box 1278, Saint George.
Founded: 1979; *Number of Clubs:* 500; *Number of Players:* 5,000; *National Colours:* Green shirts with yellow border, blue shorts, yellow stockings.
Telephone: 001-784/456 1092; *Fax:* 001-784/457 2193.

SURINAM

Surinaamse Voetbal Bond, Letitia Vriesde Laan 7, P.O. Box 1223, Paramaribo.
Founded: 1920; *Number of Clubs:* 168; *Number of Players:* 4,430; *National Colours:* White, green and red shirts, green and white shirts and stockings.
Telephone: 00597/473 112; *Fax:* 00597/479 718.

TRINIDAD & TOBAGO

Trinidad & Tobago Football Federation, 24–26 Dundonald Street, PO Box 400, Port of Spain.
Founded: 1908; *Number of Clubs:* 124; *Number of Players:* 5,050; *National Colours:* Red shirts, black shorts, white stockings.
Telephone: 001-868/623 7312; *Fax:* 001-868/623 8109.

TURKS & CAICOS

Turks & Caicos Islands Football Association, P.O. Box 626, Tropicana Plaza, Leeward Highway, Providenciales.
National Colours: All white.
Telephone: 001-649/941 5532; *Fax:* 001-649/941 5554.

USA

US Soccer Federation, US Soccer House, 1801–1811 S. Prairie Avenue, Chicago, Illinois 60616.
Founded: 1913; *Number of Clubs:* 7,000; *Number of Players:* 1,411,500; *National Colours:* White shirts, blue shorts, white stockings.
Telephone: 001-312/808 1300; *Fax:* 001-312/808 1301.

OCEANIA

AMERICAN SAMOA

American Samoa Football Association, P.O. Box 282, Pago Pago AS 96799.
National Colours: Navy blue shirts, white shorts, red stockings.
Telephone: 00684/699 7380; *Fax:* 00684/699 7381.

AUSTRALIA

Soccer Australia Ltd, Level 3, East Stand, Stadium Australia, Edwin Flack Avenue, Homebush, NSW 2127.
Founded: 1961; *Number of Clubs:* 6,816; *Number of Players:* 433,957; *National Colours:* All green with gold trim.
Telephone: 0061-2/9739 5555; *Fax:* 0061-2/9739 5590.

COOK ISLANDS

Cook Islands Football Association, Victoria Road, Tupapa, P.O. Box 29, Avarua, Rarotonga, Cook Islands.
Founded: 1971; *Number of Clubs:* 9; *National Colours:* Green shirts with white sleeves, green shorts, white stockings.
Telephone: 00682/28 980; *Fax:* 00682/28 981.

FIJI

Fiji Football Association, PO Box 2514, Government Buildings, Suva.
Founded: 1938; *Number of Clubs:* 140; *Number of Players:* 21,300; *National Colours:* White shirts, blue shorts and stockings.
Telephone: 00679/330 0453; *Fax:* 00679/330 4642.

NEW CALEDONIA

Federation Caledonienne de Football, 7 bis, Rue Suffren Quartien latin, BP 560, 99845 Noumea, New Caledonia.
Founded: 1928; *National Colours:* Grey shirts, red shorts, grey stockings.
Telephone: 00687 272383; *Fax:* 00687 263249.

NEW ZEALAND

New Zealand Soccer Inc., PO Box 301 043, Albany, Auckland, New Zealand.
Founded: 1891; *Number of Clubs:* 312; *Number of Players:* 52,969; *National Colours:* All white.
Telephone: 0064-9/414 0175; *Fax:* 0064-9/414 0176.

PAPUA NEW GUINEA

Papua New Guinea Football Association, PO Box 957, Room II Level I, Haus Tisa, Lae.
Founded: 1962; *Number of Clubs:* 350; *Number of Players:* 8,250; *National Colours:* Red and yellow shirts, black shorts, yellow stockings.
Telephone: 00675/479 1998; *Fax:* 00675/479 1999.

SAMOA

The Samoa Football Soccer Federation, P.O. Box 960, Apia.
Founded: 1968; *National Colours:* Blue, white and red shirts, blue and white shorts, red and blue stockings.
Telephone: 00685/26 504; *Fax:* 00685/20 341.

SOLOMON ISLANDS

Solomon Islands Football Federation, PO Box 854, Honiara, Solomon Islands.
Founded: 1978; *Number of Players:* 4,000; *National Colours:* Gold and blue shirts, blue and white shorts, white and blue stockings.
Telephone: 00677/26 496; *Fax:* 00677/26 497.

TAHITI

Federation Tahitienne de Football, Rue Coppenrath Stade de Fautana, PO Box 50858 Pirae 98716.
Founded: 1989; *National Colours:* Red shirts, white shorts, red stockings.
Telephone: 00689/540 954; *Fax:* 00689/419 629.

TONGA

Tonga Football Association, Tungi Arcade, Taufa'Ahau Road, P.O. Box 852, Nuku'Alofa, Tonga.
Founded: 1965; *Number of Clubs:* 23; *Number of Players:* 350; *National Colours:* Red shirts, white shorts, red stockings.
Telephone: 00676/24 442; *Fax:* 00676/23 340.

VANUATU

Vanuatu Football Federation, P.O. Box 266, Port Vila, Vanuatu.
Founded: 1934; *National Colours:* Gold and black shirts, black shorts, gold and black stockings.
Telephone: 00678/25 236; *Fax:* 00678/25 236.

AFRICA

ALGERIA

Federation Algerienne De Foot-ball, Chemin Ahmed Ouaked, Boite Postale No. 39, Dely-Ibrahim-Alger.
Founded: 1962; *Number of Clubs:* 780; *Number of Players:* 58,567; *National Colours:* Green shirts, white shorts, green stockings.
Telephone: 00213-21/372 929; *Fax:* 00213-21/367 266.

ANGOLA

Federation Angolaise De Football, Compl. da Cidadela Desportiva, B.P. 3449, Luanda.
Founded: 1979; *Number of Clubs:* 276; *Number of Players:* 4,269; *National Colours:* Red shirts, black shorts, red stockings.
Telephone: 00244-2/264 948; *Fax:* 00244-2/260 566.

BENIN

Federation Beninoise De Football, Stade Rene Pleven d'Akpakpa, B.P. 965, Cotonou 01.
Founded: 1962; *Number of Clubs:* 117; *Number of Players:* 6,700; *National Colours:* Green shirts, Yellow shorts, red stockings.
Telephone: 00229/330 537; *Fax:* 00229/330 537

BOTSWANA

Botswana Football Association, P.O. Box 1396, Gabarone.
Founded: 1970; *National Colours:* Blue, white and black striped shirts, blue, white and black shorts and stockings.
Telephone: 00267/390 0279; *Fax:* 00267/ 390 0280.

BURKINA FASO

Federation Burkinabe De Foot-Ball, 01 B.P. 57, Ouagadougou 01.
Founded: 1960; *Number of Clubs:* 57; *Number of Players:* 4,672; *National Colours:* All green, red and white.
Telephone: 00226/318 815; *Fax:* 00226/318 843.

BURUNDI

Federation De Football Du Burundi, Bulding Nyogozi, Boulevard de l'Uprona, B.P. 3426, Bujumbura.
Founded: 1948; *Number of Clubs:* 132; *Number of Players:* 3,930; *National Colours:* Red and white shirts, white and red shorts, green stockings.
Telephone : 00257/921 105; *Fax:* 00257/242 892.

CAMEROON

Federation Camerounaise De Football, B.P. 1116, Yaounde.
Founded: 1959; *Number of Clubs:* 200; *Number of Players:* 9,328; *National Colours:* Green shirts, red shorts, yellow stockings.
Telephone: 00237/221 0012; *Fax:* 00237/221 6662.

CAPE VERDE ISLANDS

Federacao Cabo-Verdiana De Futebol, Praia Cabo Verde, FCF CX, P.O. Box 234, Praia.
Founded: 1982; *National Colours:* Blue and white shirts and shorts, blue and red stockings.
Telephone : 00238/611 362; *Fax:* 00238/611 362.

CENTRAL AFRICAN REPUBLIC

Federation Centrafricaine De Football, Immeuble Soca Constructa, B.P. 344, Bangui.
Founded: 1937; *Number of Clubs:* 256; *Number of Players:* 7,200; *National Colours:* Blue and white shirts, white shorts, blue stockings.
Telephone: 00236/619 545; *Fax:* 00236/615 660.

CHAD

Federation Tchadienne de Football, B.P. 886, N'Djamena.
Founded: 1962; *National Colours:* Blue shirts, yellow shorts, red stockings.
Telephone: 00235/515 982; *Fax:* 00235/525 538.

COMOROS

Comoros FA, BP 798, Moroni.
Founded: 1979.
Telephone: 00269 733179; *Fax:* 00269 733236.

CONGO

Federation Congolaise De Football, 80 Rue Eugene-Etienne, Centre Ville, PO Box 11, Brazzaville.
Founded: 1962; *Number of Clubs:* 250; *Number of Players:* 5,940; *National Colours:* Green shirts, yellow shorts, red stockings.
Telephone: 00242/811 563; *Fax:* 00242/812 524.

CONGO DR

Federation Congolaise De Football-Association, Av. de l'Enseignemt 210, C/Kasa-Vubu, Kinshasa 1.
Founded: 1919; *Number of Clubs:* 3,800; *Number of Players:* 64,627; *National Colours:* Blue and yellow shirts, yellow and blue shorts, white and blue stockings.
Telephone: 00243/993 9635; *Fax:* 00243/139 8426.

DJIBOUTI

Federation Djiboutienne de Football, Stade el Haoj Hassan Gouled, B.P. 2694, Djibouti.
Founded: 1977; *Number of Players:* 2,000; *National Colours:* Green shirts, white shorts, blue stockings.
Telephone: 00253/341 964; *Fax:* 00253/341 963.

EGYPT

Egyptian Football Association, 5 Gabalaya Street, Guezira, El Borg Post Office, Cairo.
Founded: 1921; *Number of Clubs:* 247; *Number of Players:* 19,735; *National Colours:* Red shirts, white shorts, black stockings.
Telephone: 0020-2/735 1793; *Fax:* 0020-2/736 7817.

ERITREA

The Eritrean National Football Federation, Sematat Avenue 29–31, P.O. Box 3665, Asmara.
National Colours: Blue shirts, red shorts, green stockings.
Telephone: 00291-1/120 335; *Fax:* 00291-1/126 821.

ETHIOPIA

Ethiopia Football Federation, Addis Ababa Stadium, P.O. Box 1080, Addis Ababa.
Founded: 1943; *Number of Clubs:* 767; *Number of Players:* 20,594; *National Colours:* Green shirts, yellow shorts, red stockings.
Telephone: 00251-1/514 453; *Fax:* 00251-1/515 899.

GABON

Federation Gabonaise De Football, B.P. 181, Libreville.
Founded: 1962; *Number of Clubs:* 320; *Number of Players:* 10,000; *National Colours:* Green, yellow and blue shirts, blue and yellow shorts, white stockings with tri-colour trims.
Telephone: 00241/730 460; *Fax:* 00241/730 460.

GAMBIA

Gambia Football Association, Independence Stadium, Bakau, P.O. Box 523, Banjul.
Founded: 1952; *Number of Clubs:* 30; *Number of Players:* 860; *National Colours:* All red, blue and white.
Telephone: 00220/494 509; *Fax:* 00220/494 509.

GHANA

Ghana Football Association, National Sports Council, P.O. Box 1272, Accra.
Founded: 1957; *Number of Clubs:* 347; *Number of Players:* 11,275; *National Colours:* All yellow.
Telephone: 00233-21/671 501; *Fax:* 00233-21/668 590.

GUINEA

Federation Guineenne De Football, P.O. Box 3645, Conakry.
Founded: 1959; *Number of Clubs:* 351; *Number of Players:* 10,000; *National Colours:* Red shirts, yellow shorts, green stockings.
Telephone: 00224/455 878; *Fax:* 00224/455 879.

GUINEA-BISSAU

Federacao De Football Da Guinea-Bissau, Alto Bandim (Nova Sede), PO Box 375 Bissau 1035.
Founded: 1974; *National Colours:* Red, green and yellow shirts, green and yellow shorts, red, green and yellow stockings.
Telephone: 00245/201 918; *Fax:* 00245/211 414.

GUINEA, EQUATORIAL

Federacion Ecuatoguineana De Futbol, c/P Patricio Lumumba (Estadio La Paz), Malabo 1071.
Founded: 1986; *National Colours:* All red.
Telephone: 00240-9/74 049; *Fax:* 00240-9/2257.

IVORY COAST

Federation Ivoirienne De Football, 01 PO Box 1202, Abidjan 01.
Founded: 1960; *Number of Clubs:* 84 (senior); *Number of Players:* 3,655; *National Colours:* Orange shirts, black shorts, green stockings.
Telephone: 00225/2124 0027; *Fax:* 00225/2125 9352.

KENYA

Kenya Football Federation, Nyayo National Stadium, P.O. Box 40234, Nairobi.
Founded: 1960; *Number of Clubs:* 351; *Number of Players:* 8,880; *National Colours:* All red.
Telephone: 00254-2/608 422; *Fax:* 00254-2/249 855.

LESOTHO

Lesotho Football Association, P.O. Box 1879, Maseru-100, Lesotho.
Founded: 1932; *Number of Clubs:* 88; *Number of Players:* 2,076; *National Colours:* Blue shirts, green shorts, white stockings.
Telephone: 00266/2231 1879; *Fax:* 00266/2231 0586.

LIBERIA

Liberia Football Association, Broad and Center Streets, PO Box 10-1066, Monrovia 1000.
Founded: 1936; *National Colours:* Blue shirts, white shorts, red stockings.
Telephone: 00231/226 385; *Fax:* 00231/226 092.

LIBYA

Libyan Football Federation, Asayadi Street, Near Janat Al-Areet, P.O. Box 5137, Tripoli.
Founded: 1963; *Number of Clubs:* 89; *Number of Players:* 2,941; *National Colours:* Green and black shirts, black shorts and stockings.
Telephone: 00218-21/334 3600; *Fax:* 00218-21/444 1274.

MADAGASCAR

Federation Malagasy de Football, Immeuble Preservatrice Vie-Lot IBF-9B, Rue Rabearivelo-Antsahavola, PO Box 4409, Antananarivo 101.
Founded: 1961; *Number of Clubs:* 775; *Number of Players:* 23,536; *National Colours:* Red and green shirts, white and green shorts, green and white stockings.
Telephone: 00261-20/226 8374; *Fax:* 00261-20/226 8373.

MALAWI

Football Association of Malawi, Mpira House, Old Chileka Road, P.O. Box 865, Blantyre.
Founded: 1966; *Number of Clubs:* 465; *Number of Players:* 12,500; *National Colours:* Red shirts, white shorts, red and black stockings.
Telephone: 00265-1/623 197; *Fax:* 00265-1/623 204.

MALI
Federation Malienne De Football, Avenue du Mali, Hamdallaye ACI 2000, PO Box 1020, Bamako 12582.
Founded: 1960; *Number of Clubs:* 128; *Number of Players:* 5,480; *National Colours:* Green shirts, yellow shorts, red stockings.
Telephone: 00223/223 8844; *Fax:* 00223/222 4254.

MAURITANIA
Federation De Foot-Ball De La Rep. Islamique. De Mauritanie, B.P. 566, Nouakchott.
Founded: 1961; *Number of Clubs:* 59; *Number of Players:* 1,930; *National Colours:* Green and yellow shirts, yellow shorts, green stockings.
Telephone: 00222-5/241 860; *Fax:* 00222-5/241 861.

MAURITIUS
Mauritius Football Association, Chancery House, 2nd Floor Nos. 303–305, 14 Lislet Geoffroy Street, Port Louis.
Founded: 1952; *Number of Clubs:* 397; *Number of Players:* 29,375; *National Colours:* All red.
Telephone: 00230/212 1418; *Fax:* 00230/208 4100.

MOROCCO
Federation Royale Marocaine De Football, 51 Bis Av. Ibn Sina, PO Box 51, Agdal, Rabat 10 000.
Founded: 1955; *Number of Clubs:* 350; *Number of Players:* 19,768; *National Colours:* All green white and red.
Telephone: 00212-37/672 706; *Fax:* 00212-37/671 070.

MOZAMBIQUE
Federacao Mocambicana De Futebol, Av. Samora Machel 11-2, Caixa Postal 1467, Maputo.
Founded: 1978; *Number of Clubs:* 144; *National Colours:* Red shirts, black shorts, red and black stockings.
Telephone: 00258-1/300 366; *Fax:* 00258-1/300 367.

NAMIBIA
Namibia Football Association, Abraham Mashego Street 8521, Katurua Council of Churches in Namibia, P.O. Box 1345, Windhoek 9000, Namibia.
Founded: 1990; *Number of Clubs:* 244; *Number of Players:* 7,320; *National Colours:* All red.
Telephone: 00264-61/265 691; Fax: 00264-61/265 693.

NIGER
Federation Nigerienne De Football, Rue de la Tapoa, PO Box 10299, Niamey.
Founded: 1967; *Number of Clubs:* 64; *Number of Players:* 1,525; *National Colours:* Orange shirts, white shorts, green stockings.
Telephone: 00227/725 127; *Fax:* 00227/725 127.

NIGERIA
Nigeria Football Association, Plot 2033, Olusegun, Obasanjo Way, Zone 7, Wuse Abuja, PO Box 5101 Garki, Abuja, Nigeria.
Founded: 1945; *Number of Clubs:* 326; *Number of Players:* 80,190; *National Colours:* All green and white.
Telephone: 00234-9/523 7326; *Fax:* 00234-9/523 7327.

RWANDA
Federation Rwandaise De Football Amateur, B.P. 2000, Kigali.
Founded: 1972; *Number of Clubs:* 167; *National Colours:* Red, green and yellow shirts, green shorts, red stockings.
Telephone: 00250/571 596; *Fax:* 00250/571 597.

SENEGAL
Federation Senegalaise De Football, Stade Leopold Sedar Senghor, Route De L'Aeroport De Yoff, B.P. 130 21, Dakar.
Founded: 1960; *Number of Clubs:* 75 (senior); *Number of Players:* 3,977; *National Colours:* All white and green.
Telephone: 00221/827 2935; *Fax:* 00221/827 3524.

SEYCHELLES
Seychelles Football Federation, P.O. Box 843, People's Stadium, Victoria-Mahe, Seychelles.
Founded: 1979; *National Colours:* Red and green shirts and shorts, red stockings.
Telephone: 00248/324 632; *Fax:* 00248/225 468.

ST THOMAS AND PRINCIPE
Federation Santomense De Futebol, Rua Ex-Joao de Deus No. QXXIII-426/26, PO Box 440, Sao Tome.
Founded: 1975; *National Colours:* Green and red shirts, yellow shorts, green stockings.
Telephone: 00239-2/22 4231; *Fax:* 00239-2/21 333.

SIERRA LEONE
Sierra Leone Football Association, 21 Battery Street, Kingtorn, P.O. Box 672, National Stadium, Brookfields, Freetown.
Founded: 1967; *Number of Clubs:* 104; *Number of Players:* 8,120; *National Colours:* Green and blue shirts, green, blue and white shorts and stockings.
Telephone: 00232-22/241 872; *Fax:* 00232-22/227 771.

SOMALIA
Somali Football Federation, PO Box 222, Mogadishu BN 03040.
Founded: 1951; *Number of Clubs:* 46 (senior); *Number of Players:* 1,150; *National Colours:* Sky blue and white shirts and shorts, white and sky blue stockings.
Telephone: 00252-1/229 843; *Fax:* 00252-1/215 513.

SOUTH AFRICA
South African Football Association, First National Bank Stadium, PO Box 910, Johannesburg 2000, South Africa.
Founded: 1991; *Number of Clubs:* 51,944; *Number of Players:* 1,039,880; *National Colours:* White shirts with yellow striped sleeves, white shorts with yellow stripes, white stockings.
Telephone: 0027-11/494 3522; *Fax:* 0027-11/494 3013.

SUDAN
Sudan Football Association, Bladia Street, Khartoum.
Founded: 1936; *Number of Clubs:* 750; *Number of Players:* 42,200; *National Colours:* Red shirts, white shorts, black stockings.
Telephone: 00249-11/773 495; *Fax:* 00249-11/776 633.

SWAZILAND
National Football Association of Swaziland, Sigwaca House, Plot 582, Sheffield Road, PO Box 641, Mbabane H100.
Founded: 1968; *Number of Clubs:* 136; *National Colours:* Blue shirts, gold shorts, red stockings.
Telephone: 00268/404 6852; *Fax:* 00268/404 6206.

TANZANIA
Football Association of Tanzania, Uhuru/Shaurimoyo Road, Karume Memorial Stadium, P.O. Box 1574, Ilala/Dar Es Salaam.
Founded: 1930; *Number of Clubs:* 51; *National Colours:* Green, yellow and blue shirts, black shorts, green stockings with horizontal stripe.
Telephone: 00255-22/286 1815; *Fax:* 00255-22/286 1815.

TOGO
Federation Togolaise De Football, C.P. 5, Lome.
Founded: 1960; *Number of Clubs:* 144; *Number of Players:* 4,346; *National Colours:* White shirts, green shorts, red stockings with yellow and green stripes.
Telephone: 00228/221 2698; *Fax:* 00228/222 1413.

TUNISIA
Federation Tunisienne De Football, Maison des Federations Sportives, Cite Olympique, Tunis 1003.
Founded: 1956; *Number of Clubs:* 215; *Number of Players:* 18,300; *National Colours:* Red shirts, white shorts, red stockings.
Telephone: 00216-71/233 303; *Fax:* 00216-71/767 929.

UGANDA
Federation of Uganda Football Associations, Plot No. 879, Kyadondo Block 8, Mengo Wakaliga Road, P.O. Box 22518, Kampala.
Founded: 1924; *Number of Clubs:* 400; *Number of Players:* 1,518; *National Colours:* All yellow, red and white.
Telephone: 00256-41/272 702; *Fax:* 00256-41/272 702.

ZAMBIA
Football Association of Zambia, Football House, Alick Nkhata Road, P.O. Box 34751, Lusaka.
Founded: 1929; *Number of Clubs:* 20 (senior); *Number of Players:* 4,100; *National Colours:* White and green shirts, green and white shorts, white and green stockings.
Telephone: 00260-1/250 946; *Fax:* 00260-1/250 946.

ZIMBABWE
Zimbabwe Football Association, P.O. Box CY 114, Causeway, Harare.
Founded: 1965; *National Colours:* All green and gold.
Telephone: 00263-4/721 026; *Fax:* 00263-4/721 045.

THE WORLD CUP 2006

QUALIFYING RESULTS – EUROPE

* *Qualify with best second-placed record.*
† *Qualify for play-offs.*
▪ *Denotes player sent off.*

GROUP 1

Skopje, 18 August 2004, 10,000

Macedonia (2) 3 *(Pandev 5, Sakiri 38, Sumolikoski 90)*

Armenia (0) 0

Macedonia: Milosevski; Stavrevski, Krstev M, Mitreski I, Mitreski A, Trajanov V (Vasoski 67), Sumulikoski, Pandev, Sakiri (Toleski G 85), Dimitrovski, Sedloski.
Armenia: Ambartsumian; Melikian, Hovsepian, Vardanian▪, Dokhoyan, Khachatrian (Aleksanian K 46), Petrossian, Nazarian, Sargsian A, Art Karamian, Movsesian.
Referee: Genov (Bulgaria).

Bucharest, 18 August 2004, 15,000

Romania (0) 2 *(Mutu 50, Petre 89)*

Finland (0) 1 *(Eremenko Jr 90 (pen))*

Romania: Lobont; Stoican (Iencsi 84), Rat, Barcauan▪, Ghioane, Radoi, Dica (Soava 75), Petre, Caramarin (Cernat 46), Mutu, Danciulescu.
Finland: Niemi; Pasanen (Koppinen 60), Saarinen, Hyypia, Vayrynen▪, Nurmela (Kopteff 84), Litmanen (Eremenko Jr 57), Kolkka, Quivasto, Riihilahti, Johansson.
Referee: Gilewski (Poland).

Tampere, 4 September 2004, 7437

Finland (1) 3 *(Eremenko Jr 41, 63, Riihilahti 57)*

Andorra (0) 0

Finland: Niemi; Pasanen, Hyypia, Nurmela, Litmanen (Johansson 70), Kolkka (Heikkinen 81), Quivasto, Pohja (Kopteff 58), Riihilahti, Forssell, Eremenko Jr.
Andorra: Koldo; Ayala, Txema, Juli, Lima A, Sonejee, Pujol, Juli Sanchez (Silva 74), Sivera, Moreno, Ruiz (Jimenez 70).
Referee: Siric (Croatia).

Craiova, 4 September 2004, 26,000

Romania (1) 2 *(Pancu 15, Mutu 87)*

Macedonia (0) 1 *(Vasovski 75)*

Romania: Lobont; Stoican, Rat, Iencsi, Moldovan, Soava, Dica (Neaga 80), Petre F, Pancu (Marica 62), Mutu, Danciulescu (Cernat 46).
Macedonia: Milosevski; Jancevski (Trajanov V 88), Krstev M (Bozinovski 46), Stojanovski, Mitreski I, Mitreski A, Vasoski, Sumulikoski▪, Popov, Sakiri (Toleski G 83), Pandev.
Referee: Plautz (Austria).

La Valle, 8 September 2004, 900

Andorra (1) 1 *(Pujol 30 (pen))*

Romania (3) 5 *(Cernat 2, Pancu 5, 85, Niculae 16, 72)*

Andorra: Koldo; Txema, Lima I▪, Fernandez (Sonejee 73), Lima A, Sivera, Ruiz, Bernaus, Juli Sanchez (Jimenez 13), Ayala, Pujol.
Romania: Lobont; Cernat, Pancu, Niculae (Dica 85), Barcauan, Rat, Stoican, Iencsi, Soava, Caramarin (Paraschiv 75), Neaga (Marica 60).
Referee: Kircher (Germany).

Erevan, 8 September 2004, 10,000

Armenia (0) 0

Finland (1) 2 *(Forssell 24, Eremenko Jr 67)*

Armenia: Ambartsumian; Melikian, Dokhoyan, Hovsepian, Mkrtchian, Khachatrian, Art Petrossian, Nazarian (Aleksanian K 73), Sarkissian (Manucharian 54), Arman Karamian (Gregorian 79), Movsesian.
Finland: Niemi; Nurmela, Quivasto, Hyypia, Pasanen, Riihilahti, Litmanen (Lagerblom 46), Eremenko Jr (Kopteff 73), Vayrynen, Kolkka (Pohja 85), Forssell.
Referee: Malzinskas (Lithuania).

Amsterdam, 8 September 2004, 48,000

Holland (1) 2 *(Van Hooijdonk 33, 84)*

Czech Republic (0) 0

Holland: Van der Sar; De Jong, Heitinga, Ooijer, Sneijder, Van der Vaart (Boulahrouz 64), Van Bommel, Davids, Castelen (Makaay 74), Van Hooijdonk (Van Bronckhorst 86), Kuijt.
Czech Republic: Cech; Ujfalusi, Bolf, Jiranek (Grygera 58), Jankulovski, Rosicky, Hubschman (Vachousek 62), Tyce (Lokvenc 76), Heinz, Baros, Koller.
Referee: Merk (Germany).

Prague, 9 October 2004, 16,028

Czech Republic (1) 1 *(Koller 36 (pen))*

Romania (0) 0

Czech Republic: Cech; Ujfalusi, Jankulovski, Galasek, Bolf, Jiranek, Rosicky (Kovak 90), Vachousek, Baros (Jarosik 84), Koller, Heinz (Sionko 69).
Romania: Lobont; Stoican, Rat, Petre F (Sernat 58), Iencsi, Barcauan (Moldovan 46), Soava, Codrea, Marica, Mutu, Pancu (Dica 75).
Referee: Rosetti (Italy).

Tampere, 9 October 2004, 16,000

Finland (2) 3 *(Kuqi 8, 87, Eremenko Jr 28)*

Armenia (1) 1 *(Shakhgeldian 32)*

Finland: Niemi; Nurmela, Pasanen, Saarinen (Kallio 68), Kuivasto (Tainio 46), Hyypia, Riihilahti, Eremenko Jr, Kolkka (Johansson 83), Kuqi, Vayrynen.
Armenia: Ambartsumian; Dokhoyan, Hovsepian, Vardanian, Khachatrian (Aleksanian K 37), Nazarian, Mkhitarian, Shahgeldian, Movsesian, Gregorian (Manucharian 61), Tadevosian.
Referee: Fandel (Germany).

Skopje, 9 October 2004, 20,000

Macedonia (1) 2 *(Pandev 45, Stoikov 70)*

Holland (1) 2 *(Bouma 43, Kuijt 65)*

Macedonia: Nikoloski; Bozinovski, Sedloski, Mitreski I, Vasoski, Krstev M, Mitreski A, Jancevski (Trajanov V 71), Sakiri, Pandev (Grozdanovski 87), Stoikov (Bajevski 75).
Holland: Van der Sar; Boulahrouz, De Jong, Cocu (Van der Vaart 60), Bouma (Landzaat 81), Van Bommel, Sneijder, Davids, Van Hooijdonk (Makaay 60), Kuijt, Castelen.
Referee: Frojdpeldt (Sweden).

La Valle, 13 October 2004, 200

Andorra (0) 1 *(Bernaus 60)*

Macedonia (0) 0

Andorra: Koldo; Escura, Lima A, Fernandez, Txema, Sonejee, Pujol (Garcia 78), Silva (Juli Sanchez 85), Bernaus, Ruiz (Jonas 90), Sivera.
Macedonia: Nikoloski; Mitreski I, Mitreski A (Bozinovski 78), Stavrevski, Trajanov V (Bajevski 46), Jancevski, Grozdanovski, Stojanovski, Sakiri, Pandev, Stoikov.
Referee: Podeschi (San Marino).

Erevan, 13 October 2004, 8000

Armenia (0) 0

Czech Republic (2) 3 *(Koller 3, 78, Rosicky 30)*

Armenia: Bete; Dokhoyan (Mkrtchian 46), Hovsepian, Vardanian, Melikian, Nazarian, Mkhitarian, Shahgeldian (Movsesian 83), Aleksanian K (Sarkissian 73), Petrossian, Manucharian.
Czech Republic: Cech; Grygera, Bolf, Ujfalusi, Jankulovski, Galasek (Kovac 60), Sionko, Rosicky, Vachousek, Koller (Lokvenc 82), Heinz.
Referee: Granat (Poland).

Amsterdam, 13 October 2004, 49,000

Holland (2) 3 *(Sneijder 39, Van Nistelrooy 41, 63)*

Finland (1) 1 *(Tainio 14)*

Holland: Van der Sar; De Jong, Landzaat, Van der Vaart (Van Bronkhorst 72), Heitinga, Cocu, Sneijder (Van Bommel 83), Castelen (Makaay 77), Van Nistelrooy, Kuijt, Davids.
Finland: Niemi; Pasanen, Nurmela, Riihilahti (Johansson 60), Quivasto, Hyypia, Vayrynen (Pohja 85), Tainio, Kolkka, Kuqi, Eremenko Jr (Saarinen 72).
Referee: Bennett (England).

Barcelona, 17 November 2004, 2000

Andorra (0) 0

Holland (2) 3 *(Cocu 21, Robben 31, Sneijder 78)*

Andorra: Koldo; Escura, Fernandez, Lima A, Lima I, Sivera (Garcia 86), Txema, Jimenez (Ayala 78), Ruiz, Sonejee, Silva (Juli Sanchez 71).
Holland: Van der Sar; Ooijer, Van Bronckhorst, Cocu (Mathijsen 82), Melchiot, Sneijder, Van Galen (Van Hooijdonk 67), Landzaat, Kuijt, Van Nistelrooy (Makaay 35), Robben.
Referee: Yefet (Israel).

Erevan, 17 November 2004, 2500

Armenia (0) 1 *(Dokhoyan 62)*

Romania (1) 1 *(Marica 29)*

Armenia: Bete; Dokhoyan, Tadevosian, Hovsepian, Vardanian, Nazarian, Shahgeldian (Aleksanian K 87), Mkhitarian, Gregorian (Mkrtchian A 73), Manucharian, Aram Voskanian (Arman Karamian 74).
Romania: Lobont; Stoican, Barcauan, Moldovan, Dancia, Paraschiv (Bratu 74), Caramarian (Dica 46), Tararache, Cernat, Marica, Neaga.
Referee: De Bleeckere (Belgium).

Skopje, 17 November 2004, 12,000

Macedonia (0) 0

Czech Republic (0) 2 *(Lokvenc 88, Koller 90)*

Macedonia: Milosevski; Noveski, Sedloski, Mitreski I, Mitreski A, Krstev M (Jancevski 46), Pandev, Sakiri (Ignatov 77), Cadikovski (Stoikov 64), Bozinovski, Vasoski.
Czech Republic: Cech; Grygera (Lokvenc 77), Galasek, Bolf, Jankulovski, Poborsky, Koller, Rosicky, Vachousek (Jun 59), Baros (Heinz 17), Ujfalusi.
Referee: Meier (Switzerland).

Skopje, 9 February 2005, 1000

Macedonia (0) 0

Andorra (0) 0

Macedonia: Milosevski; Sedloski, Novevski, Mitreski A, Vasoski (Stavrevski 46), Krstev, Stoikov (Rajevski 68), Bozinovski (Popov G 75), Pandev, Sakiri, Cadikovski.
Andorra: Koldo; Txema, Escura, Lima A, Lima I, Pujol (Jonas 90), Sonejee, Silva (Juli Sanchez 62), Ruiz (Garcia 85), Sivera, Bernaus.
Referee: Verlist (Belgium).

Erevan, 26 March 2005, 9566

Armenia (1) 2 *(Hakobian 32, Khachatrian 73)*

Andorra (0) 1 *(Silva 57)*

Armenia: Berezovski; Aleksanian K, Arzumanian, Dokhoyan, Melikian, Khachatrian, Ara Hakobian (Voskanian 90), Art Karamian (Mkrtchian 72), Nazarian (Jenebian 73), Shahgeldian, Mkhitarian.
Andorra: Koldo; Ayala, Escura, Fernandez, Txema, Sonejee, Pujol, Sivera (Juli Sanchez 89), Silva (Javi Sanchez 90), Jimenez (Genis Garcia 79), Ruiz.
Referee: Attard (Malta).

Teplice, 26 March 2005, 16,200

Czech Republic (2) 4 *(Baros 8, Rosicky 34, Polak 58, Lokvenc 87)*

Finland (0) 3 *(Litmanen 46, Riihilahti 73, Johansson 79)*

Czech Republic: Cech; Jirasek, Bolf, Ujfalusi, Jankulovski, Poborsky, Rosicky, Polak (Jun 82), Sionko (Jarosik 72), Lokvenc, Baros (Plasil 53).
Finland: Jaaskelainen; Pasanen, Kopteff, Nurmela, Tihinen, Hyypia, Litmanen (Johansson 78), Riihilahti, Kolkka (Eremenko Jr 60), Ilola, Kuqi.
Referee: Bo Larsen (Denmark).

Bucharest, 26 March 2005, 19,000

Romania (0) 0

Holland (1) 2 *(Cocu 1, Babel 85)*

Romania: Lobont; Ogararu, Radoi, Chiu, Marin, Petre F, Ghioane (Plesan 46), Pancu, Munteanu D, Moldovan (Cristea 69), Ilie (Bucur 86).
Holland: Van der Sar; Kromkamp, Boulahrouz, Mathijsen, Van Bronckhorst, Van Bommel (Maduro 73), Landzaat, Cocu, Kuijt (Kastelen 90), Van Nistelrooy, Robben (Babel 74).
Referee: Cantalejo (Spain).

La Valle, 30 March 2005, 1000

Andorra (0) 0

Czech Republic (2) 4 *(Jankulovski 31 (pen), Baros 40, Lokvenc 53, Rosicky 90 (pen))*

Andorra: Koldo; Escura, Txema (Ayala 59), Lima I, Sonejee, Pujol, Sivera, Silva (Juli Sanchez 65), Bernaus, Lima A, Ruiz (Fernandez 67).
Czech Republic: Cech; Jiranek (Plasil 75), Rozehnal, Ujfalusi, Jankulovski, Poborsky, Tyce (Polak 46), Rosicky, Vachousek, Lokvenc, Baros (Jun 60).
Referee: Messner (Austria).

Eindhoven, 30 March 2005, 34,000

Holland (2) 2 *(Castelen 3, Van Nistelrooy 34)*

Armenia (0) 0

Holland: Van der Sar; Kromkamp, Van Bronckhorst, Mathijsen, Bouma, Van Bommel, Landzaat (Van der Vaart 50), Cocu, Castelen (Babel 50), Van Nistelrooy, Kujit (Vennegoor of Hesselink 80).
Armenia: Berezovski; Hovsepian, Dokhoyan, Arzumanian (Tadevosian 85), Melikan, Mkhitarian, Shahgeldian, Khachatrian, Gregorian (Art Karamian 60), Aram Voskanian, Ara Hakobian (Nazarian 46).
Referee: Trefoloni (Italy).

Skopje, 30 March 2005, 12,000

Macedonia (1) 1 *(Maznov 31)*

Romania (1) 2 *(Mitea 18, 58)*

Macedonia: Milosevski; Popov R, Petrov (Bozinovski 46), Sedloski, Vasoski, Grozdanovski, Mitreski A, Krstev M, Sumulikoski (Ignatov 72), Jancevski (Bajevski 81), Maznov.
Romania: Lobont; Contra, Radoi, Chivu (Ghionea 46), Rat, Petre F, Dica, Pancu, Munteanu D, Moldovan (Cristea 78), Mitea (Ghioane 70).
Referee: Ovrebo (Norway).

Erevan, 4 June 2005, 8000

Armenia (0) 1 *(Manucharyan 55)*

Macedonia (1) 2 *(Pandev 29 (pen), 46)*

Armenia: Berezovski; Hovsepian, Dokhoyan, Tadevosian, Khachatrian, Sarkissian, Mkrtchian, Mkhitarian (Manucharyan 52), Aleksanian K (Dzenebian 78), Aram Voskanian (Ara Hakobian 67), Shahgeldian.
Macedonia: Madzovski; Petrov, Popov G (Krstev M 57), Sedloski, Vasoski, Grozdanovski, Mitreski A, Sumulikoski (Kralevski 83), Lazarevski, Pandev, Maznov (Ismaili 66).
Referee: Mikulski (Poland).

Liberec, 4 June 2005, 9520

Czech Republic (3) 8 *(Lokvenc 13, 90, Koller 29, Smicer 38, Galasek 52 (pen), Baros 80, Rosicky 85 (pen), Polak 87)*

Andorra (1) 1 *(Riera 35)*

Czech Republic: Cech; Ujfalusi, Grygera, Rozehnal (Polak 46), Galasek, Poborsky, Rosicky, Smicer (Plasil 46), Lokvenc, Koller (Jun 64), Baros.
Andorra: Koldo; Txema, Fernandez, Sonejee, Lima A, Escura, Ayala, Ruiz■, Jimenez (Moreno 88), Riera (Andorra 70), Sivera (Garcia 80).
Referee: Selcuk (Turkey).

Rotterdam, 4 June 2005, 50,000

Holland (1) 2 *(Robben 26, Kuijt 46)*

Romania (0) 0

Holland: Van der Sar; Lucius, Heitinga, Opdam, Van Bronkhorst, Landzaat, Van Bommel (De Jong 49), Van der Vaart (Maduro 80), Kuijt, Van Nistelrooy (Van Persie 62), Robben.
Romania: Lobont; Contra, Tamas, Chivu, Stoica, Petre F, Munteanu D, Mitea (Niculae 65), Mutu (Coman 83), Niculescu C, Pancu.
Referee: De Santis (Italy).

Teplice, 8 June 2005, 14,150

Czech Republic (2) 6 *(Koller 42, 45, 49, 53, Rosicky 74 (pen), Baros 88)*

Macedonia (1) 1 *(Pandev 14)*

Czech Republic: Cech; Grygera, Hubschman, Ujfalusi, Poborsky (Zelenka 78), Galasek, Rosicky, Smicer (Plasil 61), Baros, Koller, Lokvenc (Polak 46).
Macedonia: Madzovski; Lazarevski, Petrov, Popov G, Sedloski, Vasoski, Krstev M (Banduliev 74), Mitreski A, Sumulikoski (Kralevski 70), Maznov, Pandev (Grozdanovski 67).
Referee: Ibanez (Spain).

Helsinki, 8 June 2005, 37,000

Finland (0) 0

Holland (2) 4 *(Van Nistelrooy 36, Kuijt 77, Cocu 84, Van Persie 87)*

Finland: Jaaskelainen; Nurmela, Tihinen, Hyypia, Saarinen, Tainio (Forssell 74), Riihilahti, Vayrynen, Litmanen (Johansson 29), Eremenko Jr (Kopteff 81), Kuqi.
Holland: Van der Sar; Lucius (Melchiot 27), Heitinga, Opdam, Van Bronckhorst, De Jong (Maduro 67), Landzaat, Cocu, Kuijt, Van Nistelrooy (Van Persie 74), Robben.
Referee: Hamer (Luxembourg).

Constanta, 8 June 2005, 15,000

Romania (2) 3 *(Petre 29, Bucur 40, 80)*

Armenia (0) 0

Romania: Lobont; Contra (Stoican 68), Tamas, Chivu, Rat, Petre O, Piesan, Munteanu D (Mazilu 87), Coman (Mitea 79), Niculae, Bucur.
Armenia: Berezovski; Melikian, Dokhoyan, Hovsepian, Khachatrian, Mkhitarian (Grigorian 82), Ara Hakobian, Aram Voskanian (Arzumanian 46), Tadevosian, Manucharian (Arman Karamian 50), Shahgeldian.
Referee: Briakos (Greece).

Skopje, 17 August 2005, 7000

Macedonia (0) 0

Finland (2) 3 *(Eremenko Jr 8, 45, Roiha 87)*

Macedonia: Madzovski; Sedloski, Petrov, Sumulikoski, Popov G, Vasoski (Popov R 66), Noveski, Mitreski A, Maznov, Nuhiji (Grozdanovski 62), Pandev (Nalimi 31).
Finland: Jaaskelainen; Tihinen, Hyypia, Pasanen, Heikkinen, Tainio, Kallio, Lagerblom (Litmanen 79), Eremenko Jr (Saarinen 85), Forssell (Roiha 62), Kuqi.
Referee: Messias (England).

Constanta, 17 August 2005, 8200

Romania (2) 2 *(Mutu 29, 41)*

Andorra (0) 0

Romania: Lobont; Contra, Chivu, Tamas, Rat (Pascovici 79), Dica, Petre F (Balan 72), Munteanu D (Tararache 46), Mutu, Niculescu C, Cocis.
Andorra: Koldo; Lima, Sivera, Escura (Javi Sanchez 46), Sonejee, Pujol, Ayala, Bernaus, Silva, Riera (Moreno 79), Rodriguez (Garcia 90).
Referee: Jakov (Israel).

La Vella, 3 September 2005, 1000

Andorra (0) 0

Finland (0) 0

Andorra: Koldo; Escura, Sivera, Lima I, Lima A, Jimenez, Juli Sanchez, Javi Sanchez (Riera 73), Ruiz (Fernandez 88), Sonejee, Pujol (Garcia 84).
Finland: Kaven; Kallio, Hyypia, Tihinen, Kopteff (Lagerblom 46), Saarinen, Kuivasto, Eremenko Jr (Riihilahti 64), Tainio, Forssell (Sjolund 75), Kuqi.
Referee: Vereecke (Belgium).

Erevan, 3 September 2005, 6000

Armenia (0) 0

Holland (0) 1 *(Van Nistelrooy 63)*

Armenia: Berezovski; Hovsepian, Dokhoyan, Arzumanian, Tadevosian, Khachatrian, Aleksanian K, Mkhitarian, Melikian (Aleksanian V 84), Manucharian (Ara Hakobian 17), Aram Hakobian (Aram Voskanian 80).
Holland: Van der Sar; Kromkamp (Vennegoor of Hesselink 63), Boulahrouz, Opdam, Van Bronckhorst, Landzaat (Sneijder 51), Maduro, Cocu, Kuijt, Van Nistelrooy, Van Persie (Van der Vaart 75).
Referee: Dougal (Scotland).

Constanza, 3 September 2005, 7000

Romania (1) 2 *(Mutu 28, 56)*

Czech Republic (0) 0

Romania: Lobont; Contra, Tamas, Chivu, Rat, Petre F (Badoi 52), Petre O, Munteanu D (Codrea 70), Cocis, Mazilu, Mutu (Bucur 87).
Czech Republic: Cech; Grygera, Bolf (Sivok 58), Ujfalusi, Jankulovsi (Pospech 14), Šmicer, Poborsky, Polak, Heinz (Jun 72), Koller, Baros.
Referee: Hauge (Norway).

Olomouc, 7 September 2005, 12,015

Czech Republic (0) 4 *(Heinz 47, Polak 52, 76, Baros 58)*

Armenia (0) 1 *(Ara Hakobian 86)*

Czech Republic: Blazek; Grygera, Polak, Galasek, Poborsky, Koller, Skacel (Smicer 46), Baros (Jun 80), Heinz, Ujfalusi, Rozehnal (Sivok 70).
Armenia: Berezovski; Hovsepian, Dokhoyan, Arzumanian, Tadevosian (Melikian 64), Aleksanian V, Khachatrian (Tigranian 71), Aleksanian K, Mkrtchian, Ara Hakobian, Aram Hakobian (Petrosian 57).
Referee: Hansson (Sweden).

Tampere, 7 September 2005, 8000

Finland (3) 5 *(Forssell 11, 13, 62, Tihinen 42, Eremenko Jr 55)*

Macedonia (0) 1 *(Maznov 49)*

Finland: Kaven; Pasanen, Saarinen (Nyman 53), Hyypia, Tihinen, Heikkinen, Tainio (Johansson 82), Riihilahti (Kopteff 72), Kallio, Eremenko Jr, Forssell.
Macedonia: Jovcev; Bozinovski, Lazarevski, Mitreski A, Noveski, Mustafi, Popov R, Sumulikoski (Popov G 46), Grozdanovski (Ignatov 58), Pandev, Maznov.
Referee: Jakobsson (Iceland).

Eindhoven, 7 September 2005, 35,000

Holland (3) 4 *(Van der Vaart 23, Lima T 27 (og), Van Nistelrooy 42, 89)*

Andorra (0) 0

Holland: Van der Sar; Lucius (Vennegoor of Hesselink 67), De Cler, Cocu■, Boulahrouz, Opdam, Sneijder (Maduro 78), Van der Vaart, Van Nistelrooy, Robben, Van Persie.
Andorra: Koldo; Javi Sanchez, Fernandez, Lima T, Sivera, Sonejee, Jimenez (Juli Sanchez 76), Ayala, Bernaus, Ruiz (Escura 30), Silva (Riera 54).
Referee: Hanacsek (Hungary).

Prague, 8 October 2005, 17,478

Czech Republic (0) 0

Holland (2) 2 *(Van der Vaart 30, Opdam 37)*

Czech Republic: Cech; Grygera, Jiranek (Smicer 44), Ujfalusi, Rozehnal, Polak (Heinz 57), Rosicky, Poborsky, Galasek, Baros, Stajner (Jarolim 77).
Holland: Van der Sar; Kromkamp (De Jong 84), Boulahrouz (Vlaar 57), Opdam, Van Bronckhorst, Maduro, Landzaat, Van der Vaart, Van Nistelrooy, Kuijt, Robben (Van Persie 77).
Referee: Sars (France).

Helsinki, 8 October 2005, 10,117

Finland (0) 0

Romania (1) 1 *(Mutu 41 (pen))*

Finland: Jaaskelainen; Kallio, Hyypia, Kuivasto, Lagerblom, Saarinen (Kopteff 76), Heikkinen, Nyman (Johansson 63), Tainio, Forssell (Sjolund 74), Eremenko Jr.
Romania: Lobont; Contra (Badoi 54), Tamas, Iencsi, Rat, Petre F, Petre O, Cocis, Munteanu D, Mutu (Rosu 81), Mazilu (Niculae 90).
Referee: Guenov (Bulgaria).

La Valle, 12 October 2005, 250

Andorra (0) 0

Armenia (1) 3 *(Sonejee 39 (og), Aram Hakobian 52, Ara Hakobian 62)*

Andorra: Koldo; Ayala, Lima A, Lima I, Javi Sanchez, Riera (Jimenez 82), Ruiz, Sivera (Juli Sanchez 18), Sonejee, Bernaus, Vieira (Clemente 56).
Armenia: Kasparov; Aleksanian V (Melkonian 77), Aleksanian K, Arzumanian, Dokhoyan, Khachatrian, Tadevosian, Melikian, Mkhitarian (Art Voskanian 82), Ara Hakobian, Aram Hakobian (Aram Voskanian 80).
Referee: Stokes (Republic of Ireland).

Helsinki, 12 October 2005, 11,234

Finland (0) 0

Czech Republic (1) 3 *(Jun 6, Rosicky 51, Heinz 58)*

Finland: Jaaskelainen; Saarinen (Kopteff 12), Hyypia, Kuivasto, Kolkka, Kallio, Heikkinen, Lagerblom (Nyman 60), Tainio, Sjolund (Forssell 61), Johansson.
Czech Republic: Cech; Grygera, Rozehnal, Ujfalusi, Mares, Poborsky, Galasek, Rosicky (Stajner 86), Heinz, Smicer (Polak 60), Jun (Kovac 73).
Referee: Gonzalez (Spain).

Amsterdam, 12 October 2005, 50,000

Holland (0) 0

Macedonia (0) 0

Holland: Van der Sar; De Jong, Boulahrouz, Opdam, Van Bronckhorst, Landzaat (Sneijder 46), Maduro (Davids 64), Van der Vaart, Kuijt, Van Nistelrooy, Van Persie (Babel 85).
Macedonia: Milosevski; Noveski, Popov G (Sumulikoski 54), Mitreski I, Sedloski, Vasoski, Meglehski, Tasevski (Stojkov 71), Masev, Naumoski (Hristov 90), Pandev.
Referee: Farina (Italy).

Group 1 Final table

	P	W	D	L	F	A	Pts
Holland	12	10	2	0	27	3	32
†Czech Republic	12	9	0	3	35	12	27
Romania	12	8	1	3	20	10	25
Finland	12	5	1	6	21	19	16
Macedonia	12	2	3	7	11	24	9
Armenia	12	2	1	9	9	25	7
Andorra	12	1	2	9	4	34	5

GROUP 2

Tirana, 4 September 2004, 19,000

Albania (2) 2 *(Murati 2, Aliaj 11)*

Greece (1) 1 *(Giannakopoulos 38)*

Albania: Strakosha; Beqiri E, Hasi, Aliaj, Cana, Lala, Skela, Duro (Beqiri A 86), Murati, Myrtaj (Dragusha 76), Tare.
Greece: Nikopolidis; Seitaridis, Fyssas (Tsartas 32), Dabizas (Giannakopoulos 27), Kapsis, Basinas, Zagorakis, Katsouranis, Charisteas, Karagounis, Vryzas (Papadopoulos 66).
Referee: Gonzalez (Spain).

Copenhagen, 4 September 2004, 36,335

Denmark (1) 1 *(Jorgensen 9)*

Ukraine (0) 1 *(Gusin 56)*

Denmark: Sorensen; Bogelund (Priske 43), Poulsen (Jensen C 65), Kroldrup, Jensen N, Helveg, Gravesen, Gronkjaer, Tomasson, Jorgensen, Madsen (Pedersen 79).
Ukraine: Shovkovskyi; Nesmachni, Rusol, Tymoschuk, Yezerski, Shelayev, Shevchenko, Gusin (Matykhin 67), Gusev (Zakarliuka 75), Starostiak, Vorobei (Radchenko 83).
Referee: Meier (Switzerland).

Trabzon, 4 September 2004, 15,000

Turkey (0) 1 *(Fatih 49)*

Georgia (0) 1 *(Astiani M 85)*

Turkey: Rustu; Serkan, Umit O, Deniz, Ibrahim, Okan B, Emre B, Tuncay (Huseyin 72), Hasan Sas■, Hakan Sukur (Nihat 79), Fatih (Gokdeniz 72).
Georgia: Devadze; Mzhavanadze, Khizanishvili, Khizaneishvili, Kaladze, Tskitshvili, Kvirkevlia, Rekhviashvili (Asatiani M 80), Jamarauli, Arveladze S, Demetradze (Jakobia 75).
Referee: Medina (Spain).

Tbilisi, 8 September 2004, 22,000

Georgia (1) 2 *(Iashvili 15, Demetradze 90)*

Albania (0) 0

Georgia: Devadze; Mzhavanadze, Kaladze, Khizanieshvili, Salukvadze, Tskitishvili, Jamarauli (Kvirkvelia 78), Asatiani M (Kankava 60), Kobiashvili, Iashvili, Arveladze S (Demetradze 89).
Albania: Strakosha; Beqiri A■, Cana, Aliaj, Hasi, Duro (Dragusha 59), Lala, Skela, Murati (Shkembi 81), Tare, Myrtaj (Bushi 63).
Referee: Courtney (Northern Ireland).

Piraeus, 8 September 2004, 33,000

Greece (0) 0

Turkey (0) 0

Greece: Nikopolidis; Seitaridis, Katsouranis, Kapsis, Fyssas (Papadopoulos 80), Karagounis, Giannakopoulos (Tsartas 80), Zagorakis, Basinas, Vryzas, Charisteas.
Turkey: Rustu; Serkan, Deniz, Servet, Umit O, Ibrahim, Okan B (Huseyin 73), Emre B, Gokdeniz, Fatih (Hamit Altintop 89), Nihat (Serhat 90).
Referee: Frisk (Sweden).

Almaty, 8 September 2004, 24,500

Kazakhstan (1) 1 *(Karpovich 35)*

Ukraine (1) 2 *(Bielik 15, Rotan 90)*

Kazakhstan: Novikov; Familtsev, Avdeyev, Irismetov, Dubinsky, Smakov (Musin 72), Baltiev, Chichulin (Urazbakhtin 53), Nizovtsev, Tieshev (Radionov 63), Karpovich.
Ukraine: Shovkovskyi; Rusol, Yezersky, Tymoschuk, Nesmachni, Gusin (Rotan 67), Bielik (Chelayev 90), Gusev, Zakarliouka, Starostiak (Voronin 51), Vorobei.
Referee: Garcia (Portugal).

Tirana, 9 October 2004, 20,000

Albania (0) 0

Denmark (0) 2 *(Jorgensen 52, Tomasson 72)*

Albania: Strakosha; Beqiri A, Murati, Haxhi, Cana, Hasi, Skela, Lala, Muka (Bushaj 78), Duro, Tare.
Denmark: Skov-Jensen; Priske, Helveg, Kroldrup, Jensen N, Poulsen, Gravesen, Tomasson, Gronkjaer (Kahlenberg 77), Jorgensen (Kristiansen 82), Pedersen (Rommedahl 46).
Referee: Baskalov (Russia).

Istanbul, 9 October 2004, 45,000

Turkey (1) 4 *(Gokdeniz 17, Nihat 50, Fatih 89, 90)*

Kazakhstan (0) 0

Turkey: Rustu; Umit O, Tolga, Servet, Deniz, Huseyin, Serkan (Hasan Sas 64), Gokdeniz (Tuncay 69), Necati, Nihat (Hamit Altintop 84), Fatih.
Kazakhstan: Novikov (Morev 52); Avdeyev, Chichulin (Baltiev 33), Dubinski, Lyapkin, Smakov (Kozulin 59), Irismetov, Karpovich, Nizovtsev, Buleshev, Familtsev.
Referee: Hrinak (Slovakia).

Kiev, 9 October 2004, 62,000

Ukraine (0) 1 *(Shevchenko 48)*

Greece (0) 1 *(Tsartas 81)*

Ukraine: Shovkovskyi; Nesmachni, Fedorov, Tymoschuk, Yezerski, Rusol, Shevchenko, Shelayev (Zakarliuka 85), Gusev, Voronin (Belik 90), Vorobei (Gusin 65).

Greece: Nikopolidis; Dellas, Seitaridis, Kapsis, Fyssas, Basinas (Georgiadis 78), Karagounis, Zagorakis, Giannakopoulos (Charisteas 61), Katsouranis, Vryzas (Tsartas 69).
Referee: Gonzalez (Spain).

Copenhagen, 13 October 2004, 41,331

Denmark (1) 1 *(Tomasson 27 (pen))*

Turkey (0) 1 *(Nihat 70)*

Denmark: Skov-Jensen; Priske, Jensen N, Gravesen, Poulsen, Kroldrup, Helveg, Tomasson, Perez (Rommedahl 62), Jorgensen (Kristiansen 77), Gronkjaer■.
Turkey: Rustu; Umit O, Ibrahim (Tuncay 46), Okan B, Tolga, Servet (Necati 67), Huseyin, Gokdeniz (Serkan 83), Fatih, Nihat, Emre B.
Referee: De Santis (Italy).

Almaty, 13 October 2004, 26,000

Kazakhstan (0) 0

Albania (0) 1 *(Bushaj 60)*

Kazakhstan: Morev; Lyapkin, Avdeyev, Smakov (Kamelov 53), Dubinski, Familtsev, Baltiev, Karpovitch (Shevchenko 62), Irismetov, Nizovtsev, Ourazbakhtin (Boulechev 56).
Albania: Strakosha; Beqiri A, Dragusha (Shkembi 90), Cana, Hasi, Lala, Skela, Bushaj (Rraklli 85), Haxhi, Luka (Lici 53), Tare.
Referee: Stuchlik (Austria).

Lvov, 13 October 2004, 28,000

Ukraine (1) 2 *(Bielik 9, Shevchenko 80)*

Georgia (0) 0

Ukraine: Shovkovskyi; Yezerski (Checher 46), Fedorov, Rusol, Nesmachni, Gusev, Tymoschuk, Gusin, Bielik, Shevchenko, Vorinin (Shelayev 39) (Zakarliouka 64).
Georgia: Devadze; Saluquaze, Khizaneishvili, Khizanishvili, Mjavanadze (Burduli 46), Asatiani M, Jamarauli (Demetradze 85), Tskitishvili, Kobiashvili, Arveladze S, Iashvili.
Referee: Stark (Germany).

Tbilisi, 17 November 2004, 30,000

Georgia (1) 2 *(Demetradze 33, Asatiani 74)*

Denmark (1) 2 *(Tomasson 9, 64)*

Georgia: Devadze; Khizaneishvili, Khizanishvili, Kaladze, Mzhavanadze, Kobiashvili, Tskitishvili, Jikia (Kvirkvelia 72), Asatiani M, Iashvili (Arveladze S 73), Demetradze.
Denmark: Sorensen; Poulsen, Priske, Kroldrup, Jensen N, Lustu, Gravesen, Jensen D (Skoubo 84), Tomasson, Jorgensen (Lovenkrands 84), Perez (Rommedahl 46).
Referee: Ceferin (Slovenia).

Athens, 17 November 2004, 35,000

Greece (2) 3 *(Charisteas 24, 45, Katsouranis 86)*

Kazakhstan (0) 1 *(Baltiev 88 (pen))*

Greece: Nikopolidis; Dellas, Fyssas, Kapsis (Katsouranis 60), Zagorakis (Kaves 71), Seitaridis, Basinas, Karagounis, Tsartas (Georgiadis 72), Charisteas, Vryzas.
Kazakhstan: Novikov; Chichulin, Dubinsky, Lyapkin, Smakov, Irismetov, Karpovich, Urazbakhtin (Rodionov 53), Baltiev, Buleshev (Shevchenko 66), Zhalmagambetov (Kamelov 68).
Referee: Kostadinov (Bulgaria).

Istanbul, 17 November 2004, 52,000

Turkey (0) 0

Ukraine (2) 3 *(Gusev 9, Shevchenko 17, 90)*

Turkey: Rustu; Deniz, Servet (Tuncay 28), Umit O, Seyhan, Okan B, Huseyin (Necati 66), Emre B, Gokdeniz (Basturk 54), Nihat, Fatih.
Ukraine: Shovkovskyi; Gusev, Fedorov, Nesmachni, Rusol, Yezerski, Gusin, Shelayev, Vorobei (Dmitrulin 75), Shevchenko (Nazarenko 90), Voronin (Rykun 61).
Referee: Baptista (Portugal).

Tirana, 9 February 2005, 14,000

Albania (0) 0

Ukraine (1) 2 *(Rusol 39, Gusin 59)*

Albania: Strakosha; Duro, Cana, Haxhi, Cipi (Osmani 58), Lala, Aliaj, Skela, Tare (Bogdani 65), Bushi (Myrtaj 76), Dullku.
Ukraine: Shovkovskyi; Tymoschuk, Nesmachni, Yerzersky, Rusol, Shelayev, Gusev, Shevchenko, Voronin (Rykun 80), Rotan (Vorobei 66), Gusin.
Referee: Bennett (England).

Piraeus, 9 February 2005, 32,430

Greece (2) 2 *(Zakorakis 25, Basinas 31 (pen))*

Denmark (1) 1 *(Rommedahl 45)*

Greece: Nikopolidis; Seitaridis, Fyssas, Katsouranis, Dellas, Zakorakis (Kyrgiakos 46), Basinas, Giannakopoulos, Karagounis (Kafes 61), Charisteas, Vryzas (Amantidis 83).
Denmark: Sorensen; Poulsen, Kroldrup, Lustu (Nielsen P 64), Jensen N (Madsen 64), Priske, Gravesen, Rommedahl, Tomasson, Jensen D, Perez (Jorgensen 46).
Referee: Collina (Italy).

Copenhagen, 26 March 2005, 20,980

Denmark (2) 3 *(Moller 10, 48, Poulsen 33)*

Kazakhstan (0) 0

Denmark: Sorensen; Priske, Laursen, Helveg, Jensen N, Poulsen, Tomasson (Perez 46), Jensen D (Jensen C 46), Gronkjaer (Silberbauer 74), Moller, Jorgensen.
Kazakhstan: Novikov; Familtsev, Avdejev, Smakov, Lyapin, Chichulin (Larim 46), Travin (Baizhanov 56), Baltiev, Karpovich, Utabajev (Baizjanov 78), Rodionov.
Referee: Gilewski (Poland).

Tbilisi, 26 March 2005, 25,000

Georgia (1) 1 *(Asatiani 23)*

Greece (2) 3 *(Kapsis 44, Vryzas 45, Giannakopoulos 54)*

Georgia: Lomaia; Mzhavanadze, Khizanishvili, Khizaneishvili, Kaladze, Kvirkvelia, Gogua (Tskitishvili 46), Asatiani M, Kobiashvili, Demetradze, Arveladze S (Iashvili 62).
Greece: Nikopolidis; Seitaridis, Goumas, Kapsis, Katsouranis, Zagorakis, Basinas, Karagounis, Giannakopoulos, Charisteas, Vryzas.
Referee: Rosetti (Italy).

Istanbul, 26 March 2005, 30,000

Turkey (2) 2 *(Necati 3 (pen), Beqiri E 5 (og))*

Albania (0) 0

Turkey: Rustu; Avci, Seyhan, Balci, Umit O, Ibrahim, Emre B (Bulent K 84), Basturk, Altintop (Gokdeniz 76), Necati, Fatih (Ayhan 63).
Albania: Lika; Beqiri E, Dalku, Haxhi, Lala, Duro (Bushi 79), Cana, Bogdani, Aliaj, Skela, Tare.
Referee: Plautz (Austria).

Tbilisi, 30 March 2005, 20,000

Georgia (2) 2 *(Amisulashvili 13, Iashvili 41)*

Turkey (3) 5 *(Seyhan 12, Fatih 19, 35, Koray 74, Tuncay 85)*

Georgia: Asatiani M; Mzhavanadze, Khizaneishvili (Salukvadze 17), Kaladze, Devadze (Lomaia 20), Gogua■, Tskitishvili (Burduli 71), Iashvili, Kobiashvili, Amisulashvili, Ashvetia.
Turkey: Rustu; Seyhan, Ibrahim, Umit O, Koray, Basturk (Huseyin 46), Emre B, Gokdeniz, Hamit Altintop, Fatih, Necati (Tuncay 64).
Referee: Hauge (Norway).

Athens, 30 March 2005, 38,000

Greece (1) 2 *(Charisteas 35, Karagounis 85)*

Albania (0) 0

Greece: Nikopolidis; Seitaridis, Goumas, Kyrgiakos, Katsouranis, Zagorakis, Basinas, Karagounis, Giannakopoulos (Amanatidis 87), Charisteas, Vryzas (Gekas 89).
Albania: Lika; Beqiri E, Haxhi, Lici, Lala, Duro (Dalku 84), Cana, Osmani, Mukaj (Rraklli 46), Skela, Bogdani (Tare 65).
Referee: Layec (France).

Kiev, 30 March 2005, 55,000

Ukraine (0) 1 *(Voronin 67)*

Denmark (0) 0

Ukraine: Shovkoskyi; Sviderski, Yezersky, Rusol, Nesmachni, Gusev, Tymoschuk, Vorobei, Gusin, Voronin (Matyshin 90), Kosyrin (Bielik 59) (Radchenko 80).

Denmark: Sorensen; Priske, Helveg, Kroldrup, Jensen N (Moller 70), Gravesen, Jorgensen (Jensen C 84), Poulsen, Rommedahl (Silberbauer 75), Tomasson, Gronkjaer.
Referee: Michel (Slovakia).

Tirana, 4 June 2005

Albania (2) 3 *(Tare 6, 55, Skela 33)*

Georgia (0) 2 *(Burduli 85, Kobiashvili 90)*

Albania: Lika; Hasi, Beqiri E, Osmani (Cipi 27), Aliaj, Haxhi, Duro, Skela (Shkembi 85), Jupi, Tare, Bogdani (Myrtaj 64).
Georgia: Sturua; Khizanishvili, Kaladze, Salukvadze, Rekhviashvili, Kobiashvili, Asatiani M (Daraselia 58), Kvirkvelia, Magradze (Burduli 64), Demetradze (Bobokhidze 76), Jakobia.
Behind closed doors.
Referee: Tudor (Romania).

Istanbul, 4 June 2005, 32,000

Turkey (0) 0

Greece (0) 0

Turkey: Rustu; Tolga, Ibrahim, Umit O, Mustafa (Tuncay 46), Hamit Altintop, Emre B (Serkan 78), Basturk■, Huseyin, Gokdeniz (Necati 60), Fatih.
Greece: Nikopolidis; Seitaridis, Goumas, Kapsis, Fyssas, Karagounis, Basinas, Katsouranis, Giannakopoulos (Lakis 66), Charisteas, Vryzas.
Referee: Merk (Germany).

Kiev, 4 June 2005, 40,000

Ukraine (1) 2 *(Shevchenko 18, Avdeyev 83 (og))*

Kazakhstan (0) 0

Ukraine: Shovkovskyi; Yezersky, Nesmachni, Rusol, Radchenko (Fedorov 86), Tymoschuk, Rotan, Gusev (Gusin 46), Shevchenko, Vorobei, Voronin (Bielik 69).
Kazakhstan: Novikov; Lyapkin, Familtsev (Travin 78), Avdeyev, Dubinsky, Smakov (Nizovtsev 55), Karpovich, Baizhanov, Rodionov (Chichulin 30), Baltiev, Krokhmal.
Referee: Lehner (Austria).

Copenhagen, 8 June 2005, 26,366

Denmark (1) 3 *(Larsen S 4, 46, Jorgensen 54)*

Albania (0) 1 *(Bogdani 72)*

Denmark: Sorensen; Helveg, Nielsen P, Kroldrup, Jensen N, Poulsen, Gravesen (Jensen D 60), Tomasson (Perez 87), Rommedahl (Silberbauer 71), Larsen S, Jorgensen.
Albania: Lika; Beqiri E, Osmani, Hasi, Allaj, Cana, Lala, Jupi (Sina 90), Skela (Duro 67), Tare (Myrtaj 81), Bogdani.
Referee: Frojdfeldt (Sweden).

Piraeus, 8 June 2005, 33,000

Greece (0) 0

Ukraine (0) 1 *(Gusin 82)*

Greece: Nikopolidis; Seitaridis, Kapsis (Vyntra 58), Goumas (Papadopoulos 86), Fyssas, Basinas, Zagorakis, Karagounis (Tsartas 35), Giannakopoulos, Charisteas, Vryzas.
Ukraine: Shovkovskyi; Fedorov, Rusol, Yezersky, Nesmachni, Gusev, Gusin, Tymoshchuk, Vorobei (Rotan 55), Shevchenko (Bielik 80), Voronin (Shelayev 90).
Referee: Temmink (Holland).

Almaty, 8 June 2005, 20,000

Kazakhstan (0) 0

Turkey (3) 6 *(Fatih 13, 80, Ibrahim 15, Tuncay 38, 90, Hamit Altintop 88)*

Kazakhstan: Novikov; Lyapkin, Avdejev, Baizhanov (Chichulin 46), Baltiev, Karpovich, Familtsev (Smakov 62), Nizovtsev, Rodionov (Larin 73), Krokhmal, Dubinsky.
Turkey: Omer; Hamit Altintop, Tolga, Ibrahim, Umit O, Gokdeniz (Serhat 68), Huseyin, Emre B (Serkan 66), Necati (Halil Altintop 46), Tuncay, Fatih.
Referee: Kassai (Hungary).

Almaty, 17 August 2005, 9000

Kazakhstan (1) 1 *(Kenzhekhanov 20)*

Georgia (0) 2 *(Demetradze 51, 84)*

Kazakhstan: Lorya; Irismetov, Familtsev, Zhumaskaliyev, Kuchma, Azovsky M, Baizhanov, Travin, Kenzhekhanov (Nizovtsev 60), Larin (Chichulin 85), Khokhlov.
Georgia: Lomaia; Kaladze, Khizanishvili, Mentesheshvili (Mujiri 66), Tskitishvili, Gakhokidze, Kobiashvili, Kankava, Aladashvili (Ganugrava 90), Iashvili, Demetradze.
Referee: Stredak (Slovakia).

Tirana, 3 September 2005, 2000

Albania (0) 2 *(Myrtaj 54, Bogdani 56)*

Kazakhstan (0) 1 *(Nizovtsev 64)*

Albania: Lika; Hasi, Murati, Beqiri E, Cana, Lala, Skela, Haxhi (Agolli 46), Jupi, Myrtaj (Kapllani 90), Bogdani (Bushi 85).
Kazakhstan: Loriya; Irismetov, Smakov, Travin, Kuchma, Baltiev, Larin, Kenzhekhanov, Baizhanov (Nizovtsev 55), Zhumaskaliev (Karpovich 61), Khokhlov.
Referee: Slupik (Poland).

Tbilisi, 3 September 2005, 10,000

Georgia (0) 1 *(Gakhokidze 89)*

Ukraine (1) 1 *(Rotan 44)*

Georgia: Lomaia; Tskitishvili, Khizanishvili, Odikadze, Kaladze, Gakhokidze, Kankava, Kobiashvili (Gogua 75), Mentesheshvili (Mujiri 75), Asatiani M (Ashvetia 86), Demetradze.
Ukraine: Shovkovskyi; Fedorov, Nesmachni, Yezerski, Rusol, Shychenko (Rebrov 66), Gusin, Tymoschuk, Rotan, Shevchenko, Voronin (Nazarenko 73).
Referee: Ovrebo (Norway).

Istanbul, 3 September 2005, 30,000

Turkey (0) 2 *(Okan B 48, Tumer 81)*

Denmark (1) 2 *(Jensen C 41, Larsen 90)*

Turkey: Volkan; Hamit Altintop, Alpay, Ibrahim, Umit O, Hasan Sas (Okan B 46), Selcuk, Basturk (Huseyin 46), Tumer (Tolga 85), Hakan Sukur, Fatih.
Denmark: Sorensen; Priske (Gravgaard 46), Helveg, Agger, Jensen N (Larsen S 85), Poulsen, Jensen C, Gravesen, Rommedahl, Tomasson, Jorgensen (Gronkjaer 79).
Referee: Gonzalez (Spain).

Copenhagen, 7 September 2005, 27,177

Denmark (3) 6 *(Jensen C 9, Poulsen 30, Agger 42, Tomasson 54, Larsen 79, 83)*

Georgia (1) 1 *(Demetradze 36 (pen))*

Denmark: Sorensen; Helveg, Jensen N, Gravesen, Gravgaard, Agger, Poulsen (Kahlenberg 62), Jensen C (Larsen S 63), Tomasson (Perez 67), Jorgensen, Rommedahl.
Georgia: Lomaia; Kaladze, Khizanishvili■, Asatiani M, Gakhokidze, Odikadze (Ganugrava 62), Kobiashvili (Salukvadze 81), Demetradze (Mujiri 67), Mentesheshvili, Gogua, Tskitishvili.
Referee: Bozinovski (Macedonia).

Almaty, 7 September 2005, 15,000

Kazakhstan (0) 1 *(Zhumaskaliev 53)*

Greece (0) 2 *(Giannakopoulos 79, Liberopoulos 90)*

Kazakhstan: Loriya; Familtsev (Travin 74), Avdeyev, Smakov, Azovsky M (Larin 52), Kuchma, Karpovich■, Khokhlov, Zhumaskaliev (Baltiev 81), Litvinenko, Rodionov■.
Greece: Nikopolidis; Fyssas (Gekas 76), Kapsis, Seitaridis, Basinas, Giannakopoulos, Karagounis, Katsouranis (Kafes 60), Zagorakis, Charisteas, Vryzas (Liberopoulos 55).
Referee: Tudor (Romania).

Kiev, 7 September 2005, 60,000

Ukraine (0) 0

Turkey (0) 1 *(Tumer 55)*

Ukraine: Shovkovskyi; Fedorov, Vaschuk, Rusol, Nesmachni, Tymoschuk, Gusev, Rotan (Venhlinsky 68), Shelayev (Rebrov 79), Voronin (Gusin 84), Bielik.
Turkey: Volkan; Hamit Altintop, Alpay, Ibrahim, Umit D, Okan (Serhat 90), Selcuk, Gokdeniz (Huseyin 46), Tumer, Fatih (Hasan Sas 83), Hakan Sukur.
Referee: Sars (France).

Copenhagen, 8 October 2005, 42,099

Denmark (1) 1 *(Gravgaard 39)*

Greece (0) 0

Denmark: Sorensen; Poulsen, Gravgaard, Nielsen, Jensen N, Priske, Gravesen, Jensen C (Larsen S 85), Tomasson, Jorgensen, Rommedahl (Gronkjaer 71).
Greece: Nikopolidis; Seitaridis, Basinas (Salpingidis 46), Zagorakis, Giannakopoulos, Vryzas (Gekas 76), Kapsis, Karagounis, Katsouranis, Kyrgiakos, Liberopoulos (Kafes 51).
Referee: De Bleeckere (Belgium).

Tbilisi, 8 October 2005, 10,000

Georgia (0) 0

Kazakhstan (0) 0

Georgia: Revishvili; Mjavanadze, Asatiani M, Salukvadze, Kaladze, Ganugrava, Kankava, Kobiashvili, Mujiri, Ashvetia (Tsinamdzgvrishvili 86), Demetradze.
Kazakhstan: Loriya; Mukanov, Kuchma (Familtsev 50), Smakov, Irismetov, Larin (Khokhlov 51), Azovsky M, Travin, Nizovtsev, Zhumaskaliev, Litvinenko (Kenzhekhanov 64).
Referee: Hyytia (Finland).

Dnepr, 8 October 2005, 26,000

Ukraine (1) 2 *(Shevchenko 45, Rotan 86)*

Albania (0) 2 *(Bogdani 75, 82)*

Ukraine: Shovkovskyi; Fedorov, Tymoschuk, Shelayev, Rusol, Rotan, Gusev, Voronin, Nazarenko (Vorobei 70), Shevchenko (Bielik 58), Shevchuk.
Albania: Lika; Beqiri E, Dallku, Cana, Hasi (Murati 84), Aliaj, Skela, Lala, Tare (Kapllani 70), Bogdani, Haxhi.
Referee: Verbist (Belgium).

Tirana, 12 October 2005, 13,200

Albania (0) 0

Turkey (0) 1 *(Tumer 57)*

Albania: Lika; Hasi, Dallku (Jupi 63), Beqiri E, Cana, Lala, Skela, Haxhi (Murati 50), Aliaj, Tare (Kapllani 73), Bogdani.
Turkey: Volkan; Hamit Altintop, Alpay, Ibrahim, Umit D, Okan B (Nihat 46), Huseyin, Basturk, Selcuk (Emre B 46), Tumer, Halil Altintop (Necati 90).
Referee: Ibanez (Spain).

Athens, 12 October 2005, 25,000

Greece (1) 1 *(Papadopoulos 17)*

Georgia (0) 0

Greece: Nikopolidis; Seitaridis, Dellas (Anatolakis 64), Goumas, Kapsis, Katsouranis, Zagorakis (Kafes 54), Basinas, Mantzios (Vryzas 46), Salpingidis, Papadopoulos.
Georgia: Revishvili; Mjavanadze, Khizanishvili, Salukvadze (Tsinamdzghvrishvili 46), Kaladze, Ganugrava, Kankava, Mujiri, Kobiashvili, Gogua, Demetradze (Gakhokidze 86).
Referee: Trefoloni (Italy).

Almaty, 12 October 2005, 17,000

Kazakhstan (0) 1 *(Kuchma 86)*

Denmark (0) 2 *(Gravgaard 46, Tomasson 49)*

Kazakhstan: Novikov; Avdeyev■, Familtsev (Larin 56), Irismetov (Travin 66), Khokhlov, Kuchma, Litvinenko (Kenzhekhanov 51), Mukanov, Smakov, Zhumaskaliev, Karpovich.
Denmark: Sorensen (Christiansen 46); Priske, Gravgaard, Nielsen P, Jensen N (Helveg 88), Rommedahl (Kahlenberg 46), Poulsen, Jensen D, Jorgensen, Tomasson, Larsen S.
Referee: Trivkovic (Croatia).

Group 2 Final table

	P	W	D	L	F	A	Pts
Ukraine	12	7	4	1	18	7	25
†Turkey	12	6	5	1	23	9	23
Denmark	12	6	4	2	24	12	22
Greece	12	6	3	3	15	9	21
Albania	12	4	1	7	11	20	13
Georgia	12	2	4	6	14	25	10
Kazakhstan	12	0	1	11	6	29	1

GROUP 3

Vaduz, 18 August 2004, 1000

Liechtenstein (0) 1 *(D'Elia 48)*

Estonia (1) 2 *(Viikmae 31, Lindpere 80)*

Liechtenstein: Heeb; Hasler D, Ritter■, Michael Stocklasa, Telser, Gerster■, Martin Stocklasa, Beck R (Rohrer 65), Beck T (Vogt 80), Frick M, D'Elia.
Estonia: Kojenko; Allas, Jaager, Piiroja, Rooba U, Rahn, Smirnov (Haavistu 66), Reim, Viikmae, Zahhovaiko, Terehhov (Lindpere 60).
Referee: Bozinovski (Macedonia).

Bratislava, 18 August 2004, 4500

Slovakia (1) 3 *(Vittek 26, Gresko 48, Demo 89)*

Luxembourg (1) 1 *(Strasser 2)*

Slovakia: Konig; Kratochvil, Varga, Zabavnik, Gresko, Janocko (Demo 68), Karhan, Michalik (Sech 46), Mintal, Nemeth (Sestak 84), Vittek.
Luxembourg: Besic; Braun G (Molitor 61), Cardoni, Hoffmann, Huss (Leweck C 73), Leweck A (Mannon 61), Peters, Reiter, Remy, Schauls, Strasser.
Referee: Kassai (Hungary).

Tallinn, 4 September 2004, 4200

Estonia (2) 4 *(Teever 7, Schauls 41 (og), Oper 61, Viikmae 67)*

Luxembourg (0) 0

Estonia: Poom; Allas, Jaager, Piiroja, Rooba U, Rahn, Teever, Reim (Leetmae 75), Viikmae, Zahhovaiko (Oper 46), Lindpere (Klavan 64).
Luxembourg: Besic; Peters, Reiter (Hellenbrand 88), Hoffmann, Strasser, Remy, Schauls, Cardoni (Di Domenico 81), Huss■, Leweck A, Braun G (Leweck C 68).
Referee: Kelly (Republic of Ireland).

Riga, 4 September 2004, 9500

Latvia (0) 0

Portugal (0) 2 *(Ronaldo 58, Pauleta 59)*

Latvia: Kolinko; Isakov, Zemlinsky, Stepanovs, Laizans, Bleidelis, Lobanov, Astafjevs, Rubins, Prohorenkovs (Rimkus 77), Verpakovskis.
Portugal: Ricardo; Paulo Ferreira, Ricardo Carvalho, Jorge Andrade, Nuno Valente (Caneira 74), Costinha, Maniche, Simao Sabrosa (Boa Morte 68), Deco, Ronaldo (Petit 82), Pauleta.
Referee: Poll (England).

Moscow, 4 September 2004, 14,000

Russia (1) 1 *(Bulykin 14)*

Slovakia (0) 1 *(Vittek 87)*

Russia: Malafeev; Aniukov, Sharonov, Kolodin, Evseev (Sennikov 46), Smertin, Alenichev, Khokhlov (Boyarintsev 66), Bulykin, Karayaka, Kerzahkov.
Slovakia: Contofalsky; Zabavnik, Kratochvil, Varga, Gresko, Karhan, Hanek (Reiter 84), Mintal, Vittek, Michalik (Cech 76), Nemeth (Breska 76).
Referee: Mejuto (Spain).

Luxembourg, 8 September 2004, 2000

Luxembourg (1) 3 *(Braun G 11, Leweck A 55, Cardoni 62)*

Latvia (2) 4 *(Verpakovskis 4, Zemlinsky 40 (pen), Hoffmann 65 (og), Prohorenkovs 67)*

Luxembourg: Besic; Peters (Di Domenico 90), Hellenbrand, Hoffmann, Strasser, Remy, Schauls, Leweck A (Colette 87), Braun G (Leweck C 77), Cardoni, Molitor.
Latvia: Kolinko; Stepanovs, Astafjevs, Zemlinsky, Laizans, Lobanov, Isakov, Bleidelis (Prohorenkovs 32), Verpakovskis, Rubins, Rimkus (Semyonovs 64).
Referee: Kasnaferis (Greece).

Leiria, 8 September 2004, 27,214

Portugal (0) 4 *(Ronaldo 75, Helder Postiga 84, 90, Pauleta 87)*

Estonia (0) 0

Portugal: Ricardo; Paulo Ferreira, Ricardo Carvalho, Jorge Andrade, Rui Jorge (Miguel 56), Costinha, Maniche (Helder Postiga 46), Simao Sabrosa (Boa Morte 70), Deco, Ronaldo, Pauleta.
Estonia: Poom; Allas, Piroja, Rooba U (Klavan 46), Jaager, Leetma, Reim, Teever (Viikmae 62), Lindpere, Oper, Terehhov (Zahovaiko 70).
Referee: Demirlek (Turkey).

Bratislava, 8 September 2004, 5620

Slovakia (2) 7 *(Vitek 15, 59, 81 (pen), Karhan 41, Nemeth 84, Mintal 85, Zabavnik 90)*

Liechtenstein (0) 0

Slovakia: Contofalsky; Zabavnik, Kratochvil (Petrus 46), Gresko (Breska 67), Karhan, Demo (Janocko 46), Mintal, Vitek, Nemeth, Hanek, Cech.
Liechtenstein: Heeb; Telser, Vogt, D'Elia, Martin Stocklasa, Rohrer (Frick C 70), Buchel R (Alabor 76), Burgmeier, Frick M, Beck R, Beck T.
Referee: Delevic (Serbia-Montenegro).

Vaduz, 9 October 2004, 3518

Liechtenstein (0) 2 *(Burgmeier 48, Beck T 76)*

Portugal (2) 2 *(Pauleta 23, Hasler 39 (og))*

Liechtenstein: Jehle; Telser, Michael Stocklasa, Martin Stocklasa, Hasler, Ritter, Rohrer (Beck R 46), Frick M (Frick D 90), Gerster, Burgmeier, Beck T (Buchel 89).
Portugal: Ricardo; Paulo Ferreira, Jorge Ribeiro, Maniche, Ricardo Carvalho, Jorge Andrade, Costinha (Tiago 46), Simao Sabrosa (Petit 57), Pauleta, Deco, Ronaldo (Helder Postiga 61).
Referee: Panic (Bosnia).

Luxembourg, 9 October 2004, 4000

Luxembourg (0) 0

Russia (0) 4 *(Sychev 56, 69, 86, Arshavin 62)*

Luxembourg: Besic; Federspiel, Hoffmann, Schauls (Schnell 58), Strasser, Cardoni (Leweck C 77), Leweck A, Molitor (Mannon 77), Peters, Remy, Braun G.
Russia: Malafeev; Aniukov, Bugaev, Evseev, Ignachevitch, Gusev (Aldonin 75), Kantonistov (Boyarintsev 46), Smertin, Arshavin, Bulykin (Kirichenko 67), Sychev.
Referee: Braamhaar (Holland).

Bratislava, 9 October 2004, 13,025

Slovakia (0) 4 *(Nemeth 47, Reiter 50, Karhan 55, 87)*

Latvia (1) 1 *(Verpakovskis 3)*

Slovakia: Contofalsky; Zabavnik, Gresko, Hanek, Kratochvl (Reiter 46), Varga, Karhan, Mintal (Janocko 46), Michalik (Cech 75), Vittek, Nemeth.
Latvia: Kolinko; Isakov, Koravlovs, Smirnovs, Zirnis, Astafjevs (Kolesnicenko 90), Bleidelis (Semyonovs 87), Lobanov, Laizans, Rimkus (Mikholap 76), Verpakovskis.
Referee: Farina (Italy).

Riga, 13 October 2004, 8200

Latvia (0) 2 *(Astafjevs 65, Laizans 82)*

Estonia (0) 2 *(Oper 72, Teever 79)*

Latvia: Kolinko; Isakov, Zemlinksy, Zirinis, Laizans, Bleidelis (Rimkus 81), Lobanov, Astafjevs, Stepanovs (Rubins 46), Verpakovskis, Prohorenkovs.
Estonia: Poom; Allas, Jaager, Piroja, Rooba U, Rhan, Teever (Leetma 85), Oper, Lindpere, Viikmae, Terehhov (Kruglov 85).
Referee: Meier (Germany).

Luxembourg, 13 October 2004, 3500

Luxembourg (0) 0

Liechtenstein (2) 4 *(Martin Stocklasa 41, Burgmeier 44, 85, Frick M 57 (pen))*

Luxembourg: Besic; Federspiel, Hoffmann, Strasser, Hellenbrand, Leweck C, Molitor (Colette 46), Cardoni, Remy, Braun G, Leweck A (Di Domenico 74).
Liechtenstein: Jehle; Telser, Hasler D, Ritter, Michael Stocklasa, Beck R (D'Elia 57), Martin Stocklasa, Frick M (Rohrer 81), Gerster, Burgmeier, Beck T (Buchel 87).
Referee: Jara (Czech Republic).

Lisbon, 13 October 2004, 27,578

Portugal (3) 7 *(Ronaldo 39, 69, Pauleta 26, Deco 45, Simao Sabrosa 82, Petit 89, 90)*

Russia (0) 1 *(Arshavin 79)*

Portugal: Ricardo; Miguel, Paulo Ferreira, Maniche (Petit 73), Ricardo Carvalho, Jorge Andrade, Costinha, Simao Sabrosa, Pauleta (Nuno Gomes 67), Deco, Ronaldo (Boa Morte 84).
Russia: Malafeev; Aniukov, Bougayev, Ignachevitch, Sennikov (Gusev 46), Arshavin, Smertin, Aldonin (Boyarintsev 71), Evseev, Bulykin, Sychev (Kiritchenko 46).
Referee: Vassaras (Greece).

Vaduz, 17 November 2004, 1500

Liechtenstein (1) 1 *(Frick M 31)*

Latvia (1) 3 *(Verpakovsky 7, Zemlinsky 57 (pen), Prohorenkovs 89)*

Liechtenstein: Jehle; Hasler D, Ritter, Michael Stocklasa, Vogt (Buchel R 88), Burgmeier, Gerster (Frick D 82), Martin Stocklasa, Beck R (Rohrer 65), Beck T, Frick M.
Latvia: Kolinko; Isakovs, Stepanovs, Zemlinsky, Zirnis, Astafjevs, Bleidelis, Laizans (Lobanov 90), Rubins (Zakresevski 90), Rimkus (Prohorenkovs 59), Verpakovskis.
Referee: Szabo (Hungary).

Luxembourg, 17 November 2004, 8300

Luxembourg (0) 0

Portugal (2) 5 *(Federspiel 11 (og), Ronaldo 28, Maniche 51, Pauleta 67, 83 (pen))*

Luxembourg: Besic; Federspiel, Hoffmann, Peters, Reiter, Schauls, Leweck A, Mannon (Di Domenico 78), Remy, Huss (Colette 78), Leweck C.
Portugal: Ricardo; Jorge Andrade, Ribeiro, Paulo Ferreira, Ricardo Carvalho, Costinha (Petit 59), Deco (Tiago 73), Maniche, Boa Morte (Quaresma 46), Ronaldo, Pauleta.
Referee: Godulyan (Ukraine).

Krasnodar, 17 November 2004, 28,000

Russia (3) 4 *(Karayaka 25, Izmailov 27, Sychev 34, Lozkov 69 (pen))*

Estonia (0) 0

Russia: Malafeev; Evseev, Bugaev, Smertin, Berezutski A, Izmailov, Khokhlov (Gusev 87), Lozkov (Shemshov 82), Karayaka, Kerzhakov, Sychev.
Estonia: Kaalma; Allas, Jaager, Piroja, Rooba U, Rahn, Teever (Kruglov 90), Lindpere, Viikmae, Oper, Terehhov (Klavan 82).
Referee: Busacca (Switzerland).

Tallinn, 26 March 2005, 4000

Estonia (0) 1 *(Oper 58)*

Slovakia (0) 2 *(Mintal 59, Reiter 66)*

Estonia: Kotenka; Allas, Stepanov, Jaager, Rooba U (Klavan 79), Reim, Lindpere (Zahovaiko 86), Oper, Terehhov (Teever 79), Viikmae, Kruglov.
Slovakia: Contofalsky; Zabavnik, Valachovic, Varga, Petras, Kisel (Jakubko 54), Hlinka, Karhan, Mintal, Michalik (Reiter 46), Nemeth (Cech 90).
Referee: Frojdfeldt (Sweden).

Vaduz, 26 March 2005, 2500

Liechtenstein (1) 1 *(Beck T 40)*

Russia (2) 2 *(Kerzhakov 23, Karayaka 37)*

Liechtenstein: Jehle; Telser, Ritter, Hasler D, Michael Stocklasa, Beck R (Vogt 60), D'Elia (Buchel R 53), Gerster, Burgmeier, Frick M, Beck T.
Russia: Malafeev; Berezutski A, Berezutski V, Evseev, Ignachevitch, Arshavin (Sychev 55), Bystrov (Izmailov 67), Karayaka, Khokhlov (Aldonin 78), Lozkov, Kerzhakov.
Referee: Berntsen (Norway).

Tallinn, 30 March 2005, 9300

Estonia (0) 1 *(Terehhov 63)*

Russia (1) 1 *(Arshavin 18)*

Estonia: Kotenko; Allas, Stepanov, Jaager, Kruglov, Rahn, Reim, Oper, Terehhov (Smirnov 83), Lindpere (Klavan 24), Viikmae (Teever 90).
Russia: Akinfeev; Smertin, Ignachevitch, Berezutski V, Berezutski A, Bystrov, Khokhlov (Kolodin 63), Loskov, Zhirkov (Kariaka 72), Arshavin (Sychev 67), Kerzhakov.
Referee: Paparesta (Italy).

Riga, 30 March 2005, 3000

Latvia (2) 4 *(Bleidelis 33, Laizans 38 (pen), Verpakovskis 73, 90)*

Luxembourg (0) 0

Latvia: Kolinko; Zirnis, Smirnovs, Stepanovs, Bleidelis (Miholaps 68), Astafjevs, Laizans, Rubins (Zavoronkovs 39), Morozs, Verpakovskis, Prohorekovs (Rimkus 82).
Luxembourg: Oberweis; Schauls (Lang 82), Hoffmann, Strasser, Heinz, Capela, Pace (Mannon 89), Remy, Peters (Leweck C 50), Durrer, Collette.
Referee: Kovacic (Croatia).

Bratislava, 30 March 2005, 30,000

Slovakia (1) 1 *(Karhan 7 (pen))*

Portugal (0) 1 *(Helder Postiga 62)*

Slovakia: Contofalsky; Zabavnik, Varga, Hanek (Kisel 80), Petras, Hlinka, Karhan, Mintel, Michalik (Had 35), Jakubko (Reiter 64), Nemeth.
Portugal: Ricardo; Paulo Ferreira (Miguel 63), Ricardo Carvalho, Jorge Andrade, Nuno Valente, Costinha, Maniche, Ronaldo, Deco, Pauleta (Helder Postiga 56), Simao Sabrosa (Viana 90).
Referee: Sars (France).

Tallinn, 4 June 2005, 5000

Estonia (1) 2 *(Stepanov 27, Oper 57)*

Liechtenstein (0) 0

Estonia: Kotenko; Allas, Stepanov, Jaager, Kruglov, Reim, Lindpere, Oper, Terehhov (Smirnov 89), Viikmae (Teever 71), Klavan (Saharov 87).
Liechtenstein: Jehle; Telser, D'Elia (Alabor 84), Hasler D, Ritter, Martin Stocklasa, Beck R (Buchel R 56), Gerster, Beck T, Frick M, Burgmeier.
Referee: Whitby (Wales).

Lisbon, 4 June 2005, 60,000

Portugal (2) 2 *(Fernando Meira 21, Ronaldo 41)*

Slovakia (0) 0

Portugal: Ricardo; Alex, Fernando Meira, Jorge Andrade, Caneira, Petit, Maniche, Figo, Deco (Tiago 88), Ronaldo (Ricardo Quaresma 76), Pauleta (Helder Postiga 78).
Slovakia: Contofalsky; Zabavnik, Varga, Petras, Had, Hanek (Kisel 64), Karhan, Hlinka, Mintal, Jakubko (Vittek 59), Nemeth (Slovak 59).
Referee: Collina (Italy).

St Petersburg, 4 June 2005, 8400

Russia (0) 2 *(Arshavin 57, Loskov 78 (pen))*

Latvia (0) 0

Russia: Akinfeev; Berezutski A, Smertin, Berezutski V, Aldonin (Bistrov 56), Semchov (Sennikov 67), Anukov, Arshavin (Izmailov 82), Loskov, Jirkov, Kerzhakov.
Latvia: Piedels; Stepanovs, Astafjevs, Smirnovs, Laizans, Zirnis, Isakovs (Zavoronkovs 84), Bleidelis, Rubins, Prohorenkovs (Rimkus 78), Verpakovskis.
Referee: Poulat (France).

Tallinn, 8 June 2005, 7000

Estonia (0) 0

Portugal (1) 1 *(Ronaldo 33)*

Estonia: Kotenko; Allas, Stepanov, Jaager, Rooba U, Terehhov (Saharov 79), Reim, Rahn, Kruglov (Klavan 80), Oper, Viikmae (Zahovaiko 55).
Portugal: Ricardo; Alex, Fernando Meira, Jorge Andrade, Caneira, Costinha, Deco, Maniche (Petit 73), Figo, Pauleta (Helder Postiga 66), Ronaldo (Tiago 90).
Referee: Riley (England).

Riga, 8 June 2005, 8000

Latvia (1) 1 *(Bleidelis 16)*

Liechtenstein (0) 0

Latvia: Piedels; Astafjevs, Stepanovs, Laizans, Smirnovs, Bleidelis, Korablovs, Zavoronkovs, Rubins, Verpakovskis, Prohorenkovs (Rimkus 60).
Liechtenstein: Jehle; Telser, Hasler D, Ritter, D'Elia (Vogt 56), Beck R (Rohrer 77), Buchel R (Buchel M 90), Martin Stocklasa, Burgmeier, Frick M, Beck T.
Referee: Eriksson (Sweden).

Luxembourg, 8 June 2005, 4000

Luxembourg (0) 0

Slovakia (2) 4 *(Nemeth 5, Mintal 15, Kisel 54, Reiter 60)*

Luxembourg: Oberweis; Federspiel (Sabotic 62), Heinz, Hoffmann, Reiter, Lang (Durrer 90), Strasser, Leweck A, Collette, Leweck C, Remy.
Slovakia: Contofalsky; Had (Slovak 46), Varga, Petras (Reiter 59), Kisel, Hanek, Karhan, Hlinka (Sninsky 46), Nemeth, Mintal, Vittek.
Referee: Styles (England).

Riga, 17 August 2005, 9500

Latvia (1) 1 *(Astafjevs 6)*

Russia (1) 1 *(Arshavin 26)*

Latvia: Kolinko; Smirnovs, Stepanovs, Korablovs, Zirnis, Astafjevs, Bleidelis, Rubins, Laizans, Verpakovskis, Rimkus (Prohorenkovs 77).
Russia: Akinfeev; Evseev, Ignachevitch, Berezutski A, Sennikov, Arshavin, Karyaka (Bystrov 59), Khokhlov (Semshov 67), Kerzhakov, Aldonin, Bilyaletdinov (Kirichenko 83).
Referee: Poll (England).

Vaduz, 17 August 2005, 1150

Liechtenstein (0) 0

Slovakia (0) 0

Liechtenstein: Jehle; Michael Stocklasa (Ritzberger 89), Telser, Vogt (Frick D 80), Martin Stocklasa, Beck T, Wolfinger, Buchel R, Rohrer (Alabor 87), Buchel M, Beck R.
Slovakia: Contofalsky; Karhan, Kratochvil, Zabavnik, Had, Kisel, Mintal, Hlinka (Sninsky 46), Gresko (Slovak 56), Vittek, Jakubko (Reiter 46).
Referee: Layec (France).

Tallinn, 3 September 2005, 3000

Estonia (1) 2 *(Oper 11, Smirnov 70)*

Latvia (0) 1 *(Laizans 90)*

Estonia: Kotenko; Piiroja, Stepanov, Jaager, Kruglov, Leetma, Dmitrijev, Viikmae (Neemelo 57), Terehhov, Smirnov (Teever 78), Oper.
Latvia: Kolinko; Stepanovs, Smirnovs, Zirnis (Morozs 86), Korablovs, Laizans, Astafjevs, Bleidelis, Rubins, Verpakovskis (Solonicins 81), Rimkus (Prohorenkovs 75).
Referee: Mallenco (Spain).

Faro, 3 September 2005, 26,340

Portugal (3) 6 *(Jorge Andrade 22, Ricardo Carvalho 30, Pauleta 36, 56, Simao Sabrosa 78, 84)*

Luxembourg (0) 0

Portugal: Ricardo; Paulo Ferreira, Ricardo Carvalho, Jorge Andrade, Nuno Valente, Costinha, Deco (Helder Postiga 66), Maniche (Joao Moutinho 46), Figo, Pauleta, Ronaldo (Simao Sabrosa 60).

Luxembourg: Oberweis; Federspiel, Heinz, Strasser, Lang (Schnell 39), Reiter, Pace (Sagramola 61), Collette, Leweck A, Hoffmann, Remy (Sabotic 66).
Referee: Van Egmond (Holland).

Moscow, 3 September 2005, 18,123

Russia (1) 2 *(Kerzhakov 27, 66)*
Liechtenstein (0) 0

Russia: Akinfeev; Berezutski A, Ignachevitch, Berezutsky V, Anyukov, Smertin, Izmailov, Arshavin (Titov 74), Bilyaletdinov, Kerzhakov (Kirichenko 82), Pavluchenko (Aldonin 65).
Liechtenstein: Jehle; D'Elia, Buchel M (Fischer 68), Telser, Michael Stocklasa, Martin Stocklasa, Buchel R, Burgmeier, Vogt (Rohrer 46), Frick M, Beck T (Frick D 85).
Referee: Hyytia (Finland).

Riga, 7 September 2005, 8800

Latvia (0) 1 *(Laizans 74)*
Slovakia (1) 1 *(Vittek 35)*

Latvia: Kolinko; Korablovs (Zavoronkovs 24), Isakovs, Zakresevskis, Zirnis, Astafjevs, Bleidelis, Laizans, Rubins, Rimkus (Morozs 71), Verpakovskis.
Slovakia: Contofalsky; Had, Kratochvil, Skrtel, Valachovic (Varga 86), Zabavnik, Gresko, Karhan, Holosko (Kisel 77), Mintal (Hlinka 65), Vittek.
Referee: Plautz (Austria).

Vaduz, 7 September 2005, 1000

Liechtenstein (1) 3 *(Frick M 38, Fischer 77, Beck T 90)*
Luxembourg (0) 0

Liechtenstein: Jehle; Michael Stocklasa, Telser, Buchel M (Rohrer 76), Martin Stocklasa, Beck T, Buchel R (Beck R 83), Burgmeier, D'Elia, Fischer, Frick M (Frick D 89).
Luxembourg: Oberweis; Federspiel, Hoffmann, Strasser, Remy (Sabotic 63), Collette (Pace 80), Leweck C, Schnell, Reiter, Joachim■, Sagramola (Da Luz 69).
Referee: Skomina (Slovenia).

Moscow, 7 September 2005, 28,800

Russia (0) 0
Portugal (0) 0

Russia: Akinfeev; Berezutski A, Ignachevitch, Berezutski V, Sennikov, Bilyaletdinov, Aldonin, Izmailov (Semak 74), Smertin■, Arshavin (Anyukov 87), Kerzhakov.
Portugal: Ricardo; Paulo Ferreira, Jorge Andrade, Nuno Valente, Ricardo Carvalho, Costinha, Maniche (Joao Moutinho 83), Deco (Simao Sabrosa 76), Figo, Pauleta (Helder Postiga 68), Ronaldo.
Referee: Merk (Germany).

Aveiro, 8 October 2005, 30,000

Portugal (0) 2 *(Pauleta 49, Nuno Gomes 86)*
Liechtenstein (1) 1 *(Fischer 33)*

Portugal: Ricardo; Jorge Andrade, Nuno Valente, Paulo Ferreira, Ricardo Carvalho, Figo, Maniche (Tiago 72), Petit, Simao Sabrosa (Hugo Viana 75), Pauleta, Ronaldo (Nuno Gomes 84).
Liechtenstein: Jehle; Hasler, Martin Stocklasa, Telser, Michael Stocklasa, Beck T (Frick D 88), Buchel R, Burgmeier, D'Elia, Frick M (Rohrer 52), Fischer (Beck R 57).
Referee: Gilewski (Poland).

Moscow, 8 October 2005, 25,000

Russia (2) 5 *(Izmailov 7, Kerzhakov 18, Pavluchenko 65, Kirichenko 75, 90)*
Luxembourg (0) 1 *(Reiter 52 (pen))*

Russia: Akinfeev; Anyukov, Berezutski A, Sennikov, Berezutski V, Gusev, Izmailov (Semak 55), Loskov, Semshov, Arshavin (Pavluchenko 61), Kerzhakov (Kirichenko 68).
Luxembourg: Gillet; Hoffmann, Reiter, Schnell, Leweck A, Peters, Remy, Collette (Sabotic 77), Leweck C (Federspiel 76), Mannon (Da Luz 86), Mutsch.
Referee: Tudor (Romania).

Bratislava, 8 October 2005, 12,837

Slovakia (0) 1 *(Hlinka 76)*
Estonia (0) 0

Slovakia: Contofalsky; Had (Reiter 71), Kratochvil, Skrtel, Zabavnik, Hlinka, Hodur (Sapara 80), Kisel, Nemeth, Sestak (Holosko 46), Vittek.
Estonia: Kotenko; Jaager, Kruglov, Piiroja, Stepanov, Dmitrijev, Leetma (Rahn 86), Smirnov, Terehhov, Oper, Viikmae (Neemelo 37).
Referee: Allaerts (Belgium).

Luxembourg, 12 October 2005, 1000

Luxembourg (0) 0
Estonia (1) 2 *(Oper 7, 79 (pen))*

Luxembourg: Gillet; Kintziger, Leweck A, Hoffmann, Collette, Peters, Mutsch (Federspiel 73), Reiter, Remy, Leweck C (Da Luz 78), Mannon (Kitenge 57).
Estonia: Kotenko; Dmitrijev, Jaager, Piiroja, Klavan, Kruglov, Viikmae, Terehhov (Smirnov 63), Rahn (Reim 63), Oper, Neemelo.
Referee: Dereli (Turkey).

Oporto, 12 October 2005, 36,860

Portugal (2) 3 *(Pauleta 18, 20, Hugo Viana 85)*
Latvia (0) 0

Portugal: Quim; Miguel, Fernando Meira, Jorge Andrade, Caneira, Maniche, Tiago, Deco, Figo (Hugo Viana 80), Pauleta (Helder Postiga 56), Ronaldo (Nuno Gomes 46).
Latvia: Kolinko; Stepanovs, Astafjevs, Zakresevskis, Morozs, Isakovs, Zirnis, Solonicins (Visnakovs 52), Rimkus (Kalnins 56), Verpakovskis (Korablovs 73), Rubins.
Referee: Frofdfeldt (Sweden).

Bratislava, 12 October 2005, 30,000

Slovakia (0) 0
Russia (0) 0

Slovakia: Contofalsky; Kratochvil, Skrtel, Valachovic, Zabavnik, Hodur (Holosko 56), Karhan (Kisel 67), Hlinka, Had, Vittek, Nemeth (Durica 82).
Russia: Akinfeev; Berezutski A, Sennikov, Berezutski V, Bilyaletdinov (Semak 58), Arshavin, Anyukov (Pavluchenko 83), Smertin, Loskov, Kerzhakov (Kirichenko 67), Izmailov.
Referee: Rosetti (Italy).

Group 3 Final table

	P	*W*	*D*	*L*	*F*	*A*	*Pts*
Portugal	12	9	3	0	35	5	30
†Slovakia	12	6	5	1	24	8	23
Russia	12	6	5	1	23	12	23
Estonia	12	5	2	5	16	17	17
Latvia	12	4	3	5	18	21	15
Liechtenstein	12	2	2	8	13	23	8
Luxembourg	12	0	0	12	5	48	0

GROUP 4

Saint-Denis, 4 September 2004, 43,526

France (0) 0
Israel (0) 0

France: Coupet; Gallas, Squillaci, Givet, Mendy (Giuly 57), Makelele, Vieira, Rothen (Pires 66), Evra, Henry, Saha.
Israel: Davidovitch; Ben-Haim, Saban, Antebi (Keisi 12), Benado, Afek (Gazal 71), Badir, Katan, Benayoun (Nimni 80), Goian, Tal.
Referee: Temmink (Holland).

Dublin, 4 September 2004, 35,900

Republic of Ireland (2) 3 *(Morrison 33, Reid A 38, Robbie Keane 55 (pen))*
Cyprus (0) 0

Republic of Ireland: Given; Carr (Finnan 70), O'Shea (Maybury 83), Kavanagh, O'Brien, Cunningham, Reid A, Kilbane, Robbie Keane, Morrison (Lee 81), Duff.

Cyprus: Panayiotou N; Theodotou, Kakoyiannis, Okkarides, Lambrou, Charalambous (Ilia 65), Makirdis, Satsias, Okkas (Krassas 77), Charalambides (Michael 70), Konstantinou M.
Referee: Paniashvili (Georgia).

Basle, 4 September 2004, 13,013

Switzerland (4) 6 *(Vonlanthen 10, 14, 57, Rey 29, 44, 55)*

Faeroes (0) 0

Switzerland: Zuberbuhler; Haas, Yakin M, Muller, Spycher (Magnin 46), Cabanas (Huggel 63), Vogel, Wicky, Yakin H, Rey (Haberli 75), Vonlanthen.
Faeroes: Knudsen; Thorsteinsson, Johannesen O, Jacobsen JR, Olsen, Borg (Danielsen 64), Johnsson J, Benjaminsen, Jorgensen (Hansen 70), Frederiksberg, Petersen J (Jacobsen R 57).
Referee: Tudor (Romania).

Torshavn, 8 September 2004, 6000

Faeroes (0) 0

France (1) 2 *(Giuly 37, Cisse 73)*

Faeroes: Mikkelsen; Thorsteinsson, Olsen, Johannesen O, Jacobsen JR, Jacobsen R (Flotum 75), Borg, Benjaminsen, Johnsson J, Jorgensen (Danielsen A 83), Frederiksberg (Petersen J 68).
France: Coupet; Gallas, Evra, Vieira■, Squillaci, Givet, Giuly, Pedretti, Saha (Cisse 9), Henry (Dhorasoo 64), Pires.
Referee: Thompson (Scotland).

Tel Aviv, 8 September 2004, 17,000

Israel (0) 2 *(Benayoun 64, Badir 74)*

Cyprus (0) 1 *(Konstantinou M 58)*

Israel: Davidovich; Saban, Ben-Haim, Benado, Keissi, Nimny (Balili 57), Badir, Benayoun, Tal (Afek 71), Katan (Gazal 84), Goian.
Cyprus: Panayiotou N; Okkarides, Kakoyiannis, Nikolaou, Theodotou (Georgiou 30), Makirdis, Satsias, Ilia, Charalambides (Michail 72), Okkas (Yiasoumi 79), Konstantinou M.
Referee: Shmolik (Belarus).

Basle, 8 September 2004, 28,000

Switzerland (1) 1 *(Yakin H 17)*

Republic of Ireland (1) 1 *(Morrison 8)*

Switzerland: Zuberbuhler; Vogel, Barnetta, Yakin M, Muller, Magnin, Haas, Cabanas, Yakin H, Vonlanthen (Lonfat 73), Rey.
Republic of Ireland: Given; Carr, Finnan, Roy Keane, O'Brien, Cunningham, Reid A (Kavanagh 73), Kilbane, Robbie Keane, Morrison (Doherty 84), Duff.
Referee: Vassaras (Greece).

Nicosia, 9 October 2004, 3000

Cyprus (1) 2 *(Konstantinou 14 (pen), Okkas 82)*

Faeroes (2) 2 *(Jorgensen 22, Jacobsen R 43)*

Cyprus: Panayiotou N; Nikolaou, Okkarides (Kaiafas 51), Makridis, Okkas (Kakoyiannis 69), Charalambides, Konstantinou, Charalambous, Georgiou, Elia, Krassias (Satsias 46).
Faeroes: Mikkelsen; Thorsteinsson, Johannesen O, Jacobsen JR (Petersen J 76), Olsen, Johnsson J, Benjaminsen, Borg, Jorgensen (Danielsen A 46), Jacobsen R, Frederiksberg (Flotum 69).
Referee: Gadiev (Azerbaijan).

Saint-Denis, 9 October 2004, 78,863

France (0) 0

Republic of Ireland (0) 0

France: Barthez; Gallas, Silvestre, Mavuba, Squillaci, Givet, Wiltord, Dacourt (Diarra 64), Cisse (Gouvou 83), Henry, Pires.
Republic of Ireland: Given; Carr, O'Shea, Roy Keane, O'Brien, Cunningham, Finnan, Kilbane, Robbie Keane, Morrison (Reid A 41), Duff.
Referee: Ibanez (Spain).

Tel Aviv, 9 October 2004, 37,981

Israel (1) 2 *(Benayoun 9, 48)*

Switzerland (2) 2 *(Frei 26, Vonlanthen 34)*

Israel: Davidovich; Benado, Ben-Haim, Gershon (Saban 78), Gazal (Nimny 46), Badir, Tal, Keissi, Afek, Benayoun, Balili (Golan 58).
Switzerland: Zuberbuhler; Haas, Magnin, Vogel, Yakin M (Henchoz 63), Muller, Cabanas, Barnetta (Gygax 33), Frei, Vonlanthen, Yakin H (Lonfat 80).
Referee: Shield (Australia).

Nicosia, 13 October 2004, 4000

Cyprus (0) 0

France (1) 2 *(Wiltord 38, Henry 72)*

Cyprus: Panayiotou N; Ilia, Charalambous, Okkarides, Nikolaou (Lambrou 77), Kakoyiannis, Georgiou (Yiasoumi 83), Satsias, Charalambides (Makridis 56), Okkas, Konstantinou M.
France: Barthez; Gallas, Silvestre, Vieira, Squillaci, Givet, Wiltord, Dacourt (Diarra 90), Luyindula (Evra 66), Henry, Pires (Moreira 46).
Referee: Larsen (Denmark).

Dublin, 13 October 2004, 36,000

Republic of Ireland (2) 2 *(Robbie Keane 14 (pen), 32)*

Faeroes (0) 0

Republic of Ireland: Given; Carr, O'Shea (Miller 57), Roy Keane, O'Brien A, Cunningham, Finnan, Kilbane, Robbie Keane, Duff, Reid A.
Faeroes: Mikkelsen; Thorsteinsson, Olsen, Johnsson J, Johannesen O, Jacobsen JR, Borg (Danielsen 85), Benjaminsen, Petersen J, Frederiksberg (Flotum 82), Jacobsen R (Lakjuni 58).
Referee: Lajuks (Latvia).

Nicosia, 17 November 2004, 3500

Cyprus (1) 1 *(Okkas 45)*

Israel (1) 2 *(Keissi 17, Nimny 86)*

Cyprus: Panayiotou N; Kaiafas, Kakoyannis, Okkarides, Makrides, Okkas (Yiasoumi 55), Charalambides (Nikolaou 85), Konstantinou M, Charalambous, Georgiou (Goumenos 70), Ilia.
Israel: Davidovich; Benado, Ben-Haim, Keissi, Balili (Goian 53), Nimny, Badir, Benayoun, Afek (Revivo 79), Kafan, Saban.
Referee: Kaldma (Estonia).

Paris, 26 March 2005, 79,373

France (0) 0

Switzerland (0) 0

France: Barthez; Sagnol, Boumsong, Givet, Gallas, Giuly, Pedretti, Vieira, Dhorasoo (Meriem 59), Trezeguet, Wiltord (Govou 82).
Switzerland: Zuberbuhler; Degen P, Senderos, Muller, Spycher, Gygax (Henchoz 90), Lonfat (Huggel 29), Cabanas, Vogel, Ziegler (Magnin 69), Frei.
Referee: De Santis (Italy).

Tel Aviv, 26 March 2005, 44,000

Israel (0) 1 *(Swan 90)*

Republic of Ireland (1) 1 *(Morrison 4)*

Israel: Awat; Afek (Nimny 65), Ben-Haim, Gershon, Benado, Keissi, Badir, Benayoun, Tal (Balili 65), Katan, Golan (Swan 73).
Republic of Ireland: Given; Carr, O'Shea, Finnan, O'Brien A, Cunningham, Duff, Roy Keane, Robbie Keane, Morrison (Holland 85), Kilbane.
Referee: Ivanov (Russia).

Tel Aviv, 30 March 2005, 43,000

Israel (0) 1 *(Badir 83)*

France (0) 1 *(Trezeguet 50)*

Israel: Awat; Sabas, Gershon, Ben-Haim, Keissi, Badir, Nimny, Tal (Afek 67), Katan, Benayoun, Balili.
France: Barthez; Sagnol, Boumsong, Givet, Gallas, Vieira, Pedreti, Diarra, Wiltord (Dhorasoo 90), Trezeguet■, Malouda.
Referee: Merk (Germany).

Zurich, 30 March 2005, 16,066

Switzerland (0) 1 *(Frei 88)*

Cyprus (0) 0

Switzerland: Zuberbuhler; Degen P, Muller, Senderos, Spycher (Magnin 82), Gygax, Lonfat (Yakin H 62), Vogel, Cabanas, Ziegler (Vonlanthen 41), Frei.
Cyprus: Panayiotou N■; Elia, Louka, Lambrou, Garpozis (Aloneftis 90), Charalambides, Makridis (Michael 65), Satsias, Krassas (Yiasoumi 80), Okkas, Constantinou A.
Referee: Dougal (Scotland).

Toftir, 4 June 2005, 2043

Faeroes (0) 1 *(Jacobsen R 70)*

Switzerland (1) 3 *(Wicky 25, Frei 73, 86)*

Faeroes: Mikkelsen; Hansen, Johannesen Y, Jacobsen JR, Olsen, Danielsen A, Borg (Frederiksberg 66), Benjaminsen, Jacobsen R, Jorgensen (Lakjuni 75), Flotum (Jacobsen C 63).
Switzerland: Zuberbuhler; Degen P, Muller, Rochat, Magnin, Gygas, Vogel, Wicky (Lonfat 90), Barnetta (Margairaz 68), Frei, Vonlanthen (Ziegler 77).
Referee: Gumienny (Belgium).

Dublin, 4 June 2005, 36,000

Republic of Ireland (2) 2 *(Harte 6, Robbie Keane 11)*

Israel (2) 2 *(Yehiel 39, Nimni 45 (pen))*

Republic of Ireland: Given; O'Shea, O'Brien A■, Cunningham, Harte, Holland, Kilbane, Duff, Robbie Keane (Kavanagh 27), Morrison, Reid A (Doherty 64).
Israel: Awat; Yehiel, Gershon, Benado, Saban, Suan, Tal, Nimni (Goian 79), Keissi, Benayoun, Katan (Balili 66).
Referee: Vassaras (Greece).

Torshavn, 8 June 2005, 10,000

Faeroes (0) 0

Republic of Ireland (0) 2 *(Harte 51 (pen), Kilbane 58)*

Faeroes: Mikkelsen; Hansen, Johannesen O, Danielsen A, Olsen, Johnsson J, Benjaminsen (Borg 79), Jorgensen (Akselsen 79), Jacobsen R, Lakjuni, Flotum (Jacobsen C 59).
Republic of Ireland: Given; Carr, Harte, Roy Keane, O'Shea, Cunningham, Reid, Kilbane, Morrison (Doherty 79), Elliott, Duff.
Referee: Genov (Bulgaria).

Toftir, 17 August 2005, 1500

Faeroes (0) 0

Cyprus (1) 3 *(Konstantinou M 39, 86 (pen), Krassas 90)*

Faeroes: Knudsen; Hansen, Johannesen O, Jacobsen JR, Danielsen, Olsen (Horg 14), Borg, Jacobsen R, Jorgensen, Flotum, Jonsson (Jacobsen C 46).
Cyprus: Morfis; Louka, Michael, Garpozis (Okkarides 63), Krassas, Charalambides, Theodotou (Charalambous 80), Makridis, Lufteris■, Okkas, Konstantinou M (Yiasoumi 87).
Referee: Johannesson (Sweden).

Lens, 3 September 2005, 40,126

France (2) 3 *(Cisse 13, 76, Olsen 19 (og))*

Faeroes (0) 0

France: Coupet; Sagnol, Thuram (Squillaci 76), Boumsong, Gallas, Makelele, Vieira, Zidane (Dhorasoo 58), Malouda, Cisse, Henry (Wiltord 67).
Faeroes: Mikkelsen; Horg (Jacobsen C 56), Johannesen O, Jacobsen JR, Olsen, Borg, Jorgensen (Lakjuni 76), Hojsted, Benjaminsen, Flotum, Jonsson (Jacobsen R 67).
Referee: Jara (Czech Republic).

Basle, 3 September 2005, 30,000

Switzerland (1) 1 *(Frei 5)*

Israel (1) 1 *(Keisi 20)*

Switzerland: Zuberbuhler; Degen P, Senderos, Muller, Magnin (Spycher 89), Gygax, Vogel, Barnetta, Yakin H (Cabanas 65), Frei, Vonlanthen (Lustrinelli 82).
Israel: Davidovitch; Saban, Harazi, Benado, Ben Haim, Nimni (Zandberg 71), Badir, Keisi, Tal, Benayoun (Suan 90), Katan (Golan 65).
Referee: Rosetti (Italy).

Nicosia, 7 September 2005, 3500

Cyprus (1) 1 *(Aloneftis 35)*

Switzerland (1) 3 *(Frei 15, Senderos 70, Gygax 84)*

Cyprus: Morfis; Elia, Okkarides (Lambrou 46), Louka, Aloneftis, Krassias (Nikolaou 64), Okkas, Charalambides, Konstantinou M, Michael (Yiasoumi 82), Charalambous.
Switzerland: Zuberbuhler; Degen P, Muller, Senderos, Spycher, Gygax, Vogel, Barnetta (Huggel 89), Wicky, Frei (Yakin H 73), Vonlanthen (Lustrinelli 81).
Referee: Ivanov (Russia).

Torshavn, 7 September 2005, 2240

Faeroes (0) 0

Israel (0) 2 *(Nimni 55, Katan 80)*

Faeroes: Mikkelsen; Horg, Johannesen O, Jacobsen JR, Olsen, Benjaminsen, Hojsted (Flotum 61), Borg (Lakjuni 69), Jacobsen R, Jorgensen (Samuelsen 85), Jacobsen C.
Israel: Davidovitch; Benado, Harazi, Ben Haim, Benayoun, Keissi, Nimni, Suan, Badir, Balili (Tal 66), Katan (Biton 86).
Referee: Vink (Holland).

Dublin, 7 September 2005, 36,000

Republic of Ireland (0) 0

France (0) 1 *(Henry 67)*

Republic of Ireland: Given; Carr, O'Shea, Roy Keane, Cunningham, Dunne, Reid A, Kilbane (Doherty 79), Robbie Keane, Morrison (Harte 79), Duff.
France: Coupet; Sagnol (Givet 89), Thuram, Gallas, Boumsong, Makelele, Wiltord, Vieira, Dhorasoo, Henry (Cisse 75), Zidane (Malouda 69).
Referee: Fandel (Germany).

Nicosia, 8 October 2005, 13,546

Cyprus (0) 0

Republic of Ireland (1) 1 *(Elliott 6)*

Cyprus: Panayiotou N; Elia (Maragos 74), Lambrou, Louka, Makridis, Michael, Konstantinou M (Krassas 30), Charalambides, Aloneftis, Okkas (Yiasoumi 70), Garpozis.
Republic of Ireland: Given; Carr, O'Shea, Kavanagh, Dunne, Cunningham, Finnan (Holland 46), Kilbane, Robbie Keane (Connolly 88), Elliott, Duff (Reid S 61).
Referee: Kassai (Hungary).

Tel Aviv, 8 October 2005, 21,500

Israel (1) 2 *(Benayoun 1, Zandberg 89)*

Faeroes (0) 1 *(Samuelsen 90)*

Israel: Davidovitch; Harazi, Benado, Keisi, Ben Haim, Badir, Suan (Zandberg 46), Nimni, Benayoun, Katan (Balili 73), Golan (Arbeitman 66).
Faeroes: Mikkelsen; Horg, Johannesen O, Jacobsen JR, Hansen (Danielsen 15), Benjaminsen, Flotum (Frederiksberg 66), Jacobsen C (Samuelsen 80), Hojsted, Jacobsen R, Jorgensen.
Referee: Brugger (Austria).

Berne, 8 October 2005, 31,400

Switzerland (0) 1 *(Magnin 79)*

France (0) 1 *(Cisse 52)*

Switzerland: Zuberbuhler; Degen P, Magnin, Muller, Senderos, Barnetta (Behrami 90), Cabanas, Vogel, Wicky (Lustrinelli 83), Frei, Vonlanthen (Gygax 60).
France: Coupet; Thuram, Gallas, Makelele, Reveillere, Boumsong, Malouda (Govou 90), Vieira, Dhorasoo (Cisse 46), Wiltord, Zidane.
Referee: Hauge (Norway).

Saint-Denis, 12 October 2005, 80,000

France (3) 4 *(Zidane 29, Wiltord 31, Dhorasoo 43, Giuly 84)*

Cyprus (0) 0

France: Coupet; Sagnol, Thuram, Boumsong, Gallas, Dhorasoo, Zidane, Vieira (Diarra 25), Govou (Jurietti 90), Cisse, Wiltord (Giuly 59).

Cyprus: Morfis; Elia, Lambrou, Louka, Garpozis (Maragos 46), Charalambides, Charalambous, Makridis (Nicolaou 81), Krassas, Yiasoumi (Filaniotis 63), Aloneftis.
Referee: Stark (Germany).

Dublin, 12 October 2005, 36,000

Republic of Ireland (0) 0

Switzerland (0) 0

Republic of Ireland: Given; Carr, Harte, O'Shea, Dunne, Cunningham, Holland, Reid A (Reid S 80), Morrison (Doherty 87), Robbie Keane (Elliott 68), Kilbane.
Switzerland: Zuberbuhler; Degen P, Muller, Senderos, Magnin, Barnetta (Gygax 89), Vogel, Cabanas, Wicky, Vonlanthen (Streller 53), Frei.
Referee: Merk (Germany).

Group 4 Final table

	P	W	D	L	F	A	Pts
France	10	5	5	0	14	2	20
†Switzerland	10	4	6	0	18	7	18
Israel	10	4	6	0	15	10	18
Republic of Ireland	10	4	5	1	12	5	17
Cyprus	10	1	1	8	8	20	4
Faeroes	10	0	1	9	4	27	1

GROUP 5

Palermo, 4 September 2004, 21,463

Italy (1) 2 *(De Rossi 4, Toni 79)*

Norway (1) 1 *(Carew 1)*

Italy: Buffon; Bonera, Nesta, Materazzi, Favalli (Diana 67), Fiore, Gattuso, De Rossi, Zambrotta, Gilardino (Corradi 59), Miccoli (Toni 68).
Norway: Johnsen E; Basma, Riseth, Lundekvam, Riise, Hoseth (Solli 90), Andresen, Sorensen (Pedersen M 85), Johnsen F, Rudi, Carew (Rushfeldt 72).
Referee: Sars (France).

Celje, 4 September 2004, 4000

Slovenia (2) 3 *(Acimovic 6, 28, 49)*

Moldova (0) 0

Slovenia: Mavric B; Karic, Pokore (Sukalo 81), Mavric M, Knavs, Seslar, Komac (Tanjic 74), Ceh (Koren 89), Acimovic, Dedic, Siljak.
Moldova: Hmaruc; Covalenco (Ivanov 71), Lascencov, Olexici (Lungu 46), Catinsus, Priganiuc, Covalciuc, Savinov, Rogaciov (Dadu 82), Cebotari, Miterev.
Referee: Hyytia (Finland).

Chisinau, 8 September 2004, 8500

Moldova (0) 0

Italy (1) 1 *(Del Piero 33)*

Moldova: Hmaruc; Lungu, Olexici, Catinsus, Lascencov, Priganiuc, Covalciuc, Ivanov, Rogaciov (Cebotari 81), Bursuc, Mitere (Dadu 62).
Italy: Buffon; Bonera (Blasi 84), Nesta, Materazzi, Zambrotta, Gattuso, Pirlo, Ambrosini (Oddo 74), Diana, Del Piero, Gilardino (Toni 80).
Referee: Benes (Czech Republic).

Oslo, 8 September 2004, 25,272

Norway (1) 1 *(Riseth 39)*

Belarus (0) 1 *(Kutuzov 77)*

Norway: Myhre; Hoiland, Riseth, Lundekvam, Riise, Andresen, Hoseth, Johnsen F, Rudi (Sorensen 46), Pedersen M, Rushfeldt (Carew 81).
Belarus: Khomutovski; Kulchi, Omelyanchuk, Shtanyuk, Yaskovich, Lavrik, Gurenko, Bulyga (Sashcheka 63), Romashchenko, Hleb V (Blizuk 44) (Suchkov 90), Kutuzov.
Referee: Costa (Portugal).

Glasgow, 8 September 2004, 38,278

Scotland (0) 0

Slovenia (0) 0

Scotland: Gordon; Caldwell G, Naysmith (Holt 59), Ferguson B, Webster, Mackay, McNamara, Fletcher, Dickov (Crawford 79), Quashie, McFadden.

Slovenia: Mavric B; Pokorn, Mavric M, Knavs, Karic, Ceh, Seslar, Komac, Acimovic, Siljak (Lavric 64), Dedic (Sukalo 79).
Referee: Larsen (Denmark).

Minsk, 9 October 2004, 20,000

Belarus (1) 4 *(Omelianchuk 44, Kutuzov 65, Bulyga 76, Romashchenko 90)*

Moldova (0) 0

Belarus: Khomutovski; Kulchi (Kovba 79), Yaskovich, Omelyanchuk, Shtanyuk, Gurenko, Lavrik, Belkevich (Koval 83), Romashchenko, Korytko, Kutuzov (Bulyga 66).
Moldova: Hmaruc; Savinov, Lascencov, Olexici, Catinsus, Barisev (Pobreban 79), Covalciuc (Epureanu 84), Ivanov, Rogaciov, Bursuc, Miterev (Golban 77).
Referee: Selcuk (Turkey).

Glasgow, 9 October 2004, 48,882

Scotland (0) 0

Norway (0) 1 *(Iversen 55 (pen))*

Scotland: Gordon; Caldwell G, Naysmith, Ferguson B, Anderson, Webster, Fletcher, Holt (Thompson 80), Dickov (Miller 75), McFadden■, Hughes (Pearson 63).
Norway: Myhre; Bergdolmo, Hagen, Lundekvam, Riise, Sorensen (Andresen 74), Solli, Hoseth (Pedersen M 58), Carew, Iversen (Johnsen F 89), Larsen.
Referee: Allaerts (Belgium).

Celje, 9 October 2004, 9000

Slovenia (0) 1 *(Cesar 82)*

Italy (0) 0

Slovenia: Mavric B; Pokorn, Mavric M, Mitrakovic (Cesar 76), Karic (Dedic 65), Sukalo, Komac, Ceh (Lazic 88), Acimovic, Siljak, Seslar.
Italy: Buffon; Bonera, Zambrotta, De Rossi, Cannavaro, Nesta, Gattuso, Camoranesi (Di Vaio 83), Gilardino (Toni 69), Totti, Esposito (Fiore 69).
Referee: De Bleeckere (Belgium).

Parma, 13 October 2004, 16,510

Italy (2) 4 *(Totti 26 (pen), 73, De Rossi 33, Gilardino 86)*

Belarus (0) 3 *(Romashchenko 52, 90, Bulyga 77)*

Italy: Buffon; Oddo (Cannavaro 68), Pancaro, De Rossi (Blasi 75), Nesta, Materazzi, Diana (Perrotta 65), Gattuso, Gilardino, Totti, Zambrotta.
Belarus: Khomutovski; Kulchi (Koval 84), Shtanyuk, Yaskovich■, Gurenko, Lavrik (Kovba 76), Tarlovski, Korytko (Bulyga 35), Belkevich, Kutuzov, Romashchenko.
Referee: Davila (Spain).

Chisinau, 13 October 2004, 4500

Moldova (1) 1 *(Dadu 27)*

Scotland (1) 1 *(Thompson 30)*

Moldova: Hmaruc; Lascencov, Savinov, Ivanov, Catinsus, Priganiuc, Olexici (Cebotari 38), Bursuc, Dadu, Rogaciov, Covalciuc.
Scotland: Gordon; Caldwell G, Naysmith (Murray 46), Ferguson B, Caldwell S, Webster, Fletcher (Miller 66), Holt, Crawford, Thompson (McCulloch 86), Cameron.
Referee: Jacobsson (Iceland).

Oslo, 13 October 2004, 24,907

Norway (1) 3 *(Carew 7, Pedersen 60, Odegaard 90)*

Slovenia (0) 0

Norway: Myhre; Bergdolmo, Riise, Andresen, Hagen, Lundekvam, Solli, Larsen, Carew (Rushfeldt 77), Iversen (Johnsen F 88), Pedersen M (Odegaard 80).
Slovenia: Mavric B; Pokorn, Mitrakovic, Seslar (Komac 66), Mavric M, Cesar, Sukalo, Ceh, Lavric (Dedic 78), Siljak, Acimovic.
Referee: Ivanov (Russia).

Milan, 26 March 2005, 40,745

Italy (1) 2 *(Pirlo 35, 85)*

Scotland (0) 0

Italy: Buffon; Bonera, Cannavaro, Materazzi, Chiellini, Camoranesi, Pirlo, Totti (De Rossi 72), Gattuso, Gilardino, Cassano (Toni 83).

Scotland: Douglas (Gordon 38); McNamara, Naysmith, Caldwell G, Weir, Pressley, Hartley (Crawford 76), Ferguson, Miller (O'Connor 86), McCulloch, Quashie.
Referee: Vassaras (Greece).

Chisinau, 30 March 2005, 6000

Moldova (0) 0

Norway (0) 0

Moldova: Hmaruc; Savinov, Lascencov (Bursuc 85), Olexici, Epureanu (Barisev 80), Catinsus, Priganiuc, Boret, Ivanov, Dadu, Rogaciov (Frunza 89).
Norway: Myhre; Bergdolmo, Riise, Larsen F, Hagen, Lundekvam, Solli, Hoset (Carew 59), Pedersen M, Iversen, Rushfeldt (Karadas 81).
Referee: Meyer (Germany).

Celje, 30 March 2005, 6000

Slovenia (1) 1 *(Rodic 44)*

Belarus (0) 1 *(Kulchi 49)*

Slovenia: Handanovic; Ilic, Mavric M (Rodic 29), Knavs, Filekovic (Siljak 54), Komac, Cipot (Koren 71), Ceh, Seslar, Acimovic, Lazic.
Belarus: Zhevnov; Belkevich, Gurenko, Hleb, Katskevich (Ostrovski 85), Kovba, Kulchi, Kutuzov (Bulyga 64), Omelyanchuk, Romashchenko (Kalatzov 76), Lavrik.
Referee: Al Ghamdi (Saudi Arabia).

Minsk, 4 June 2005, 20,000

Belarus (1) 1 *(Belkevich 19)*

Slovenia (1) 1 *(Ceh 16)*

Belarus: Zhevnov; Gurenko, Yaskovich (Lavrik 76), Omelyanchuk (Tarlovsky 85), Shtanyuk, Kulchi, Kovba, Belkevich, Hleb A, Bulyga, Kutuzov (Kornilenko 72).
Slovenia: Handanovic; Cipot, Mavric M, Cesar, Ilic (Sukalo 68), Filekovic, Pokorn, Komac (Zlogar 90), Ceh, Lavric, Rodic Cimirotic 58).
Referee: Hansson (Sweden).

Oslo, 4 June 2005, 24,829

Norway (0) 0

Italy (0) 0

Norway: Myhre; Bergdolmo, Hagen, Lundekvam, Riise, Solli (Karadas 71), Andresen, Hestad, Pedersen M, Iversen (Johnsen F 84), Carew.
Italy: Buffon; Bonera (Diana 81), Cannavaro, Materazzi, Grosso, Camoranesi, Pirlo, De Rossi, Zambrotta, Vieri (Toni 57), Cassano (Iaquinta 68).
Referee: Gonzalez (Spain).

Glasgow, 4 June 2005, 45,317

Scotland (0) 2 *(Dailly 53, McFadden 89)*

Moldova (0) 0

Scotland: Gordon; Pressley, Webster (Dailly 26), Ferguson B, Weir, Alexander G, McNamara, Hartley, Fletcher, Miller, McCulloch (McFadden 74).
Moldova: Hmaruc; Olexici, Priganiuc, Lascencov (Covalenko 46), Catinsus, Epureanu, Boret, Ivanov, Dadu, Savinov (Covalciuc 60), Rogaciov (Frunza 82).
Referee: Braamhaar (Holland).

Minsk, 8 June 2005, 20,000

Belarus (0) 0

Scotland (0) 0

Belarus: Zhevnov; Omelyanchuk, Kalachev (Hleb V 61), Gurenko, Shtanyuk, Jaskovic, Kovba, Hleb A, Bulyga (Kulchi 86), Belkevich, Kornichenko.
Scotland: Gordon; Weir, Webster, Caldwell G, Pressley, Dailly, Fletcher, Ferguson B, Miller (McFadden 76), Alexander G, McCulloch.
Referee: Benquerenca (Portugal).

Chisinau, 3 September 2005, 5000

Moldova (1) 2 *(Rogaciov 15, 49)*

Belarus (0) 0

Moldova: Hmaruc; Rebeja, Olexici, Catinsus, Priganiuc, Covalciuc (Frunza 86), Ivanov, Savinov, Rogaciov (Popovici 55), Boret (Bordian 46), Dadu.
Belarus: Zhevnov; Shtanyuk, Kulchi, Yaskovic, Omelyanchuk, Belkevich, Gurenko, Hleb A, Kalachev (Bulyga 56), Korytko (Hleb V 69), Kutuzov.
Referee: Duhamel (France).

Glasgow, 3 September 2005, 50,185

Scotland (1) 1 *(Miller 13)*

Italy (0) 1 *(Grosso 76)*

Scotland: Gordon; Alexander G, McNamara, Dailly, Weir, Webster, Hartley, Ferguson B, Miller (Beattie 77), Quashie (McCann 67), Fletcher.
Italy: Peruzzi; Zaccardo (Grosso 46), Nesta, Cannavaro, Zambrotta, Gattuso, Pirlo, Totti, De Rossi (Camoranesi 60), Iaquinta (Toni 71), Vieri.
Referee: Lubos (Slovakia).

Celje, 3 September 2005, 9000

Slovenia (1) 2 *(Cimirotic 3, Zlogar 83)*

Norway (2) 3 *(Carew 1, Lundekvam 24, Pedersen M 90)*

Slovenia: Mavric B; Knavs, Mavric M, Cesar, Ceh, Zlogar, Komac, Acimovic (Lavric 56), Filekovic (Koren 60), Cimirotic, Rodic.
Norway: Myhre; Hoiland, Lundekvam, Hagen, Bergdolmo, Solli (Andresen 66), Hestad, Grindheim, Pedersen M, Iversen (Braaten 11) (Arst 82), Carew.
Referee: Cantalejo (Spain).

Minsk, 7 September 2005, 38,000

Belarus (1) 1 *(Kutuzov 4)*

Italy (3) 4 *(Toni 6, 14, 55, Camoranesi 45)*

Belarus: Zhevnov; Yaskovic (Tarlovsky 33), Omelyanchuk, Shtanyuk, Lavrik, Kulchi (Korytko 80), Kovba, Belkevich, Hleb A, Bulyga, Kutuzov (Hleb V 76).
Italy: Peruzzi; Zaccardo, Nesta, Cannavaro, Grosso, Camoranesi (Barzagli 83), Pirlo, Gattuso, Totti, Gilardino (Barone 57), Toni (Iaquinta 67).
Referee: Temmink (Holland).

Chisinau, 7 September 2005, 7000

Moldova (1) 1 *(Rogaciov 34)*

Slovenia (0) 2 *(Lavric 47, Mavric M 57)*

Moldova: Hmaruc; Olexici, Savinov, Rebeja, Catinsus, Priganiuc, Covalciuc (Epureanu 89), Ivanov, Rogaciov (Popovici 90), Bordian, Dadu (Frunza 83).
Slovenia: Handanovic; Filekovic (Lavric 46), Mavric M, Cesar, Knavs, Koren, Ceh, Zlogar, Cimirotic (Pecnik 46), Rodic (Sukalo 89), Seslar.
Referee: Baskakov (Russia).

Oslo, 7 September 2005, 24,904

Norway (0) 1 *(Arst 89)*

Scotland (2) 2 *(Miller 21, 31)*

Norway: Myhre; Bergdolmo, Riise, Grindheim, Lundekvam, Riseth, Solli (Hestad 46), Andresen, Carew, Ostenstad (Arst 46), Valencia (Braaten 46).
Scotland: Gordon; Alexander G, Webster, Ferguson B, Weir, Pressley, Fletcher, McNamara, Hartley, Miller (McCann 40), McFadden (Beattie 72).
Referee: Hamer (Luxembourg).

Palermo, 8 October 2005, 19,611

Italy (0) 1 *(Zaccardo 77)*

Slovenia (0) 0

Italy: Peruzzi; Zambrotta, Nesta, Cannavaro, Grosso, Camoranesi, Pirlo (De Rossi 81), Gattuso, Toni (Vieri 88), Gilardino (Zaccardo 59), Totti.
Slovenia: Mavric B; Mavric M, Knavs, Cesar, Filekovic, Komac, Zlogar, Koren, Acimovic, Rodic (Siljak 87), Pokorn (Cimirotic 46).
Referee: Poulat (France).

Oslo, 8 October 2005, 23,409

Norway (0) 1 *(Rushfeldt 49)*

Moldova (0) 0

Norway: Myhre; Bergdolmo, Hagen, Hangeland, Grindheim, Hestad, Pedersen M, Riise, Iversen (Helstad 90), Johnsen M (Solli 63), Rushfeldt (Braaten 82).

Moldova: Hmaruc; Bordian (Boret 68), Catinsus, Lascencov, Olexici, Priganiuc, Savinov, Covalciuc, Ivanov (Gatcan 82), Dadu (Popovici 73), Rogaciov.
Referee: Bennett (South Africa).

Glasgow, 8 October 2005, 51,105

Scotland (0) 0

Belarus (1) 1 *(Kutuzov 6)*

Scotland: Gordon; Alexander G, Murray (Maloney 46), Ferguson, Pressley, Weir, Fletcher, Dailly, McCulloch, Miller, Hartley.
Belarus: Khomutovsky; Kulchi, Korytko, Ostrovski, Tarlovsky, Kovba, Bulyga (Sascheka 89), Lavrik, Hleb A, Kalachev, Kutuzov.
Referee: Szabo (Hungary).

Minsk, 12 October 2005, 16,000

Belarus (0) 0

Norway (0) 1 *(Helstad 72)*

Belarus: Khomutovsky; Kulchi, Ostrovski, Shtanyuk, Kalachev, Tarlovsky, Kovba (Kirilchik 58), Omelyanchuk, Sashcheka (Loshankov 64), Bulyga, Kutuzov.
Norway: Myhre; Hoiland, Hagen (Borgersen 81), Hangeland, Riise, Stromstad, Grindheim, Solli (Gashi 73), Pedersen M, Rushfeldt (Helstad 46), Iversen.
Referee: Plautz (Austria).

Lecce, 12 October 2005, 28,167

Italy (0) 2 *(Vieri 71, Gilardino 85)*

Moldova (0) 1 *(Gatcan 76)*

Italy: De Sanctis; Zaccardo, Bonera (Blasi 46), Materazzi, Grosso (Zambrotta 62), Diana, De Rossi, Barone, Iaquinta (Gilardino 68), Vieri, Del Piero.
Moldova: Pascenco; Lascencov, Catinsus, Priganiuc, Savinov, Olexici, Gatcan, Boret, Covalciuc, Rogaciov (Miterev 87), Dadu.
Referee: Benquerenca (Portugal).

Celje, 12 October 2005, 10,000

Slovenia (0) 0

Scotland (1) 3 *(Fletcher 4, McFadden 47, Hartley 84)*

Slovenia: Handanovic; Mavric M (Pecnik 25) (Ilic 62), Knavs, Cesar, Komac, Koren, Zlogar, Ceh, Acimovic, Cimirotic, Rodic (Siljak 53).
Scotland: Gordon; Alexander G, Murray, Dailly, Pressley (O'Connor 46), Weir, Fletcher, Quashie (Caldwell S 72), McFadden, Miller (Caldwell G 46), Hartley.
Referee: Temmink (Holland).

Group 5 Final table

	P	*W*	*D*	*L*	*F*	*A*	*Pts*
Italy	10	7	2	1	17	8	23
†Norway	10	5	3	2	12	7	18
Scotland	10	3	4	3	9	7	13
Slovenia	10	3	3	4	10	13	12
Belarus	10	2	4	4	12	14	10
Moldova	10	1	2	7	5	16	5

GROUP 6

Vienna, 4 September 2004, 48,500

Austria (0) 2 *(Kollmann 71, Ivanschitz 73)*

England (1) 2 *(Lampard 24, Gerrard 64)*

Austria: Manninger; Standfest, Stranzl, Martin Hiden, Pogatetz, Sick, Kuhbauer, Aufhauser (Kiesenebner 74), Ivanschitz, Glieder (Kollmann 68), Haas (Hleblinger 89).
England: James; Neville G, Cole A, Gerrard (Carragher 82), Terry, King, Beckham, Lampard, Smith (Defoe 74), Owen, Bridge (Cole J 84).
Referee: Michel (Slovakia).

Baku, 4 September 2004, 15,000

Azerbaijan (0) 1 *(Sadykhov 56)*

Wales (0) 1 *(Speed 48)*

Azerbaijan: Kramarenko; Shukurov, Hajiev, Agayev, Sadykhov, Kurbanov M, Huseynov (Mamedov A 73), Ponomarev (Kurbanov I 84), Kurbanov G, Aliyev (Noybiyev 71), Kerimov.
Wales: Jones P; Delaney, Gabbidon, Savage, Melville, Page, Koumas (Earnshaw 87), Speed, Hartson, Bellamy, Pembridge (Oster 46).
Referee: Trivkovic (Croatia).

Belfast, 4 September 2004, 14,000

Northern Ireland (0) 0

Poland (2) 3 *(Zurawski 4, Wlodarczyk 37, Krzynowek 57)*

Northern Ireland: Taylor; Hughes A, Capaldi, Whitley, Williams, Craigan, Johnson, Hughes M (Jones S 53), Quinn (Smith 73), Healy, Elliott (McVeigh 62).
Poland: Dudek; Michal Zewlakow, Bak, Glowacki, Rzasa, Krzynowek (Gorawski 67), Lewandowski M, Mila (Radomski 75), Zienczuk, Wlodarczyk■, Zurawski (Kryszalowicz 84).
Referee: Wegereef (Holland).

Vienna, 8 September 2004, 26,400

Austria (2) 2 *(Stranzl 23, Kollmann 44)*

Azerbaijan (0) 0

Austria: Manninger; Standfest, Stranzl, Martin Hiden, Pogatetz, Schopp (Dollinger 57), Kuhbauer, Aufhauser, Ivanschitz, Haas (Glieder 72), Kollmann (Linz 79).
Azerbaijan: Kramarenko; Agayev, Hajiev, Sadykhov, Shukurov, Guseynov, Kurbanov M (Mamedov I 46), Kerimov, Ponomarev (Nabiyev 46), Kurbanov G, Aliyev (Kurbanov I 46).
Referee: Sammut (Malta).

Chorzow, 8 September 2004, 38,000

Poland (0) 1 *(Zurawski 48)*

England (1) 2 *(Defoe 37, Glowacki 58 (og))*

Poland: Dudek; Michal Zewlakow, Bak, Glowacki, Krzynowek, Rzasa, Lewandowski M, Mila (Kukielka 63), Kosowski (Gorawski 80), Zurawski, Rasiak (Niedzielan 69).
England: Robinson; Neville G (Carragher 32), Cole A, Gerrard, Terry, King, Beckham (Hargreaves 90), Lampard, Defoe (Dyer 87), Owen, Bridge.
Referee: Farina (Italy).

Cardiff, 8 September 2004, 63,500

Wales (1) 2 *(Hartson 32, Earnshaw 75)*

Northern Ireland (2) 2 *(Whitley 11, Healy 21)*

Wales: Jones P; Delaney (Earnshaw 28), Thatcher (Parry 63), Savage■, Collins J, Gabbidon, Oster, Speed, Hartson, Bellamy, Koumas.
Northern Ireland: Taylor; Clyde, Capaldi (McCartney 90), Murdock, Hughes A, Williams, Johnson, Whitley, Quinn (Smith 58) (McVeigh 89), Healy■, Hughes M■.
Referee: Messina (Italy).

Vienna, 9 October 2004, 46,100

Austria (1) 1 *(Schopp 30)*

Poland (1) 3 *(Kaluzny 9, Krzynowek 79, Frankowski 90)*

Austria: Manninger; Standfest, Pogatetz, Schopp, Stranzl, Martin Hiden, Kuhbauer, Aufhauser (Kiesenebner 46), Ivanschitz, Haas (Kollmann 38), Vastic (Mayrleb 80).
Poland: Dudek; Baszczynski, Rzasa, Hajto, Bak, Mila, Krzynowek, Zajac (Kosowski 46), Kaluzny (Radomski■ 72), Zurawski, Rasiak (Frankowski 67).
Referee: Batista (Portugal).

Baku, 9 October 2004, 20,000

Azerbaijan (0) 0

Northern Ireland (0) 0

Azerbaijan: Hasanzade; Amirbekov, Hajiev, Kuliyev E, Kuliyev K, Kurbanov M (Ponomarev 58), Nabiyev, Sadykhov, Mamedov I (Kurbanov I 55), Aliyev (Kurbanov G), Shukurov.
Northern Ireland: Taylor; Clyde, Hughes A, Doherty, Williams, Murdock, Johnson, Whitley, Quinn (Smith 76), Elliott, Baird (Gillespie 9).
Referee: Hanaczek (Hungary).

Old Trafford, 9 October 2004, 65,224

England (1) 2 *(Lampard 4, Beckham 76)*

Wales (0) 0

England: Robinson; Neville G, Cole A, Butt, Campbell, Ferdinand, Beckham (Hargreaves 85), Rooney (King 86), Owen, Defoe (Smith 70), Lampard.
Wales: Jones P; Delaney, Thatcher, Pembridge (Robinson 59), Gabbidon, Speed, Koumas (Earnshaw 73), Bellamy, Hartson, Giggs, Davies S.
Referee: Haughe (Norway).

Baku, 13 October 2004, 20,000

Azerbaijan (0) 0

England (1) 1 *(Owen 22)*

Azerbaijan: Hasanzade; Hajiev, Shukurov, Kuliyev E (Kurbanov I 75), Sadykhov, Amirbekov, Kerimov, Ponomarev, Kuliyev K, Nabiyev (Abdullayev 79), Aliyev (Kurbanov G 59).
England: Robinson; Neville G, Cole A, Butt, Campbell, Ferdinand, Jenas (Wright-Phillips 72), Rooney (Cole J 85), Owen, Defoe (Smith 55), Lampard.
Referee: Hamer (Luxembourg).

Belfast, 13 October 2004, 11,830

Northern Ireland (1) 3 *(Healy 36, Murdock 60, Elliott 90)*

Austria (1) 3 *(Schopp 14, 72, Mayrleb 61)*

Northern Ireland: Carroll; Hughes A, McCarthy, Doherty (Jones S 86), Williams, Murdock (Elliott 78), Gillespie, Whitley (McVeigh 89), Quinn, Healy, Johnson.
Austria: Manninger; Ibertsberger, Pogatetz, Kuhbauer, Martin Hiden, Feldhofer, Schopp (Sick 81), Kiesenebner, Kirchler (Ivanschitz 64), Vastic, Mayrleb (Kollmann 81).
Referee: Shield (Australia).

Cardiff, 13 October 2004, 74,000

Wales (0) 2 *(Earnshaw 56, Hartson 90)*

Poland (0) 3 *(Frankowski 72, Zurawski 81, Krzynowek 85)*

Wales: Jones P; Delaney, Thatcher, Savage, Gabbidon, Collins J, Davies S, Speed (Hartson 79), Earnshaw, Bellamy, Koumas (Parry 86).
Poland: Dudek; Baszczynski, Krzynowek, Szymkowiak, Hajto, Bak (Klos 46), Kosowski, Kaluzny (Mila 71), Zurawski, Wlodarczyk (Frankowski 60), Rzasa.
Referee: Sars (France).

Old Trafford, 26 March 2005, 65,239

England (0) 4 *(Cole J 47, Owen 52, Baird 54 (og), Lampard 67)*

Northern Ireland (0) 0

England: Robinson; Neville G, Cole A, Gerrard (Hargreaves 72), Ferdinand, Terry, Beckham (Dyer 72), Lampard, Owen, Rooney (Defoe 80), Cole J.
Northern Ireland: Taylor; Baird, Capaldi, Doherty (Davis 59), Hughes A, Murdock, Gillespie, Johnson, Healy (Kirk 88), Elliott, Whitley (Jones S 80).
Referee: Stark (Germany).

Warsaw, 26 March 2005, 12,500

Poland (3) 8 *(Frankowski 12, 62, 65, Hajiev 16 (og), Kosowski 40, Krzynowek 71, Saganowski 83, 90)*

Azerbaijan (0) 0

Poland: Dudek; Baszczynski, Bak, Klos, Rzasa, Kosowski (Smolarek 46), Szymkowiak, Sobolewski, Krzynowek, Frankowski (Niedzielan 66), Zurawski (Saganowski 73).
Azerbaijan: Kramarenko; Hajiev, Sadykhov, Amirbekov, Kuliyev E (Malikov 20), Sjoeboerov, Kerimov (Actianov 46), Kuliyev V, Nadyov (Kurbanov I 46), Kurbanov G, Nabiev.
Referee: Vollquartz (Denmark).

Cardiff, 26 March 2005, 47,760

Wales (0) 0

Austria (0) 2 *(Vastic 82, Stranzl 86)*

Wales: Coyne; Delaney, Ricketts, Robinson, Gabbidon, Page, Davies S (Earnshaw 75), Fletcher, Hartson, Bellamy, Giggs.
Austria: Payer; Dospel, Pogatetz, Ehmann, Katzer, Kirchler, Stranzl, Aufhauser, Ivanschitz (Hleblinger 90), Mayrleb (Mair 87), Haas (Vastic 78).
Referee: Allaerts (Belgium).

Vienna, 30 March 2005, 29,500

Austria (0) 1 *(Aufhauser 87)*

Wales (0) 0

Austria: Payer; Stranzl, Dospel (Kiesenebner 84), Ehmann, Katzer, Kirchler (Mair 77), Kuhbauer, Aufhauser, Ivanschitz, Mayrleb, Haas (Vastic 55).
Wales: Coyne; Delaney, Ricketts, Robinson, Gabbidon, Collins J (Page 58), Partridge, Fletcher, Davies S, Bellamy, Giggs.
Referee: Gonzalez (Spain).

Newcastle, 30 March 2005, 49,046

England (0) 2 *(Gerrard 51, Beckham 62)*

Azerbaijan (0) 0

England: Robinson; Neville G, Cole A, Ferdinand (King 77), Terry, Gerrard, Beckham (Defoe 84), Lampard, Owen, Rooney (Dyer 77), Cole J.
Azerbaijan: Kramarenko; Abdurahmanov, Amirbekov (Kuliyev V 46), Sadykhov, Hajiev, Hashimov, Bakhshiev, Malikov, Kerimov, Kurbanov G (Actiamov 74), Nabiev (Ponomarev 74).
Referee: Gomes Costa (Portugal).

Warsaw, 30 March 2005, 25,000

Poland (0) 1 *(Zurawski 86)*

Northern Ireland (0) 0

Poland: Dudek; Baszczynski, Bak, Klos, Rzasa (Kielbowicz 46), Karwan (Rasiak 74), Kaluzny (Mila 67), Symkowiak, Krzynowek, Frankowski, Zurawski.
Northern Ireland: Taylor; Baird, Capaldi, Williams (Elliott 88), Hughes A, Murdock, Gillespie, Davis, Quinn (Feeney 35), Healy (Smith 81), Whitley.
Referee: Frojdfeldt (Sweden).

Baku, 4 June 2005, 8000

Azerbaijan (0) 0

Poland (1) 3 *(Frankowski 27, Klos 56, Zurawski 77)*

Azerbaijan: Gasanzade; Kuliyev K, Sadykhov, Hajiev (Ismailov 75), Chukurov, Abdurahmanov (Kurbanov I 75), Kuliyev E, Abdullayev, Malikov (Ramazanov 59), Karimov, Kurbanov G.
Poland: Dudek; Baszczynski, Bak, Klos, Rzasa, Kosowski, Sobolewski, Szymkowiak (Radomski 89), Mila (Zienczuk 84), Frankowski (Niedzielan 55), Zurawski.
Referee: Mallenco (Spain).

Belfast, 3 September 2005, 11,909

Northern Ireland (0) 2 *(Elliott 60, Feeney 85 (pen))*

Azerbaijan (0) 0

Northern Ireland: Taylor; Baird, Capaldi, Davis, Hughes A, Craigan, Gillespie, Johnson, Quinn (Feeney 72), Healy (Jones S 79), Elliott (Robinson 89).
Azerbaijan: Kramarenko; Hajiyev, Sadygov, Amirbekov, Tagizade (Nabiyev 84), Kerimov, Kurbanov M (Ponomarev 65), Kuliyev E, Imamaliev, Muzika, Aliyev (Chukurov 74).
Referee: Stanisic (Serbia & Montenegro).

Chorzow, 3 September 2005, 45,000

Poland (2) 3 *(Smolarek 13, Kosowski 22, Michal Zewlakow 68)*

Austria (0) 2 *(Linz 61, 80)*

Poland: Boruc; Baszczynski (Michal Zewlakow 88), Bak, Klos, Rzasa, Sobolewski (Mila 73), Szymkowiak (Radomski 83), Kosowski, Zurawski, Rasiak, Smolarek.
Austria: Schranz; Hieblinger, Pogatetz, Standfest, Ehmann, Kuhbauer, Aufhauser, Stranzl, Ivanschitz, Schopp (Kiesenebner 81), Mayrleb (Linz 46) (Kuljic 84).
Referee: De Santis (Italy).

Cardiff, 3 September 2005, 70,715

Wales (0) 0

England (0) 1 *(Cole J 54)*

Wales: Coyne; Page (Collins J 65), Duffy, Robinson (Koumas 55), Gabbidon, Partridge, Davies S (Earnshaw 69), Fletcher, Hartson, Giggs, Ricketts.
England: Robinson; Young, Cole A, Gerrard (Richardson 84), Ferdinand, Carragher, Wright-Phillips (Defoe 68), Beckham, Rooney, Lampard, Cole J (Hargreaves 76).
Referee: Ivanov (Russia).

Baku, 7 September 2005, 5012

Azerbaijan (0) 0

Austria (0) 0

Azerbaijan: Kramarenko; Amirbekov, Hajiyev, Muzika (Bakhshiyev 78), Akhmedov, Kuliyev E, Kuliyev K, Tagizade (Nabiyev 88), Chukurov, Kerimov, Kurbanov G (Aliyev 90).
Austria: Schranz; Ibertsberger, Stranzl (Hieblinger 50), Pogatetz, Gercaliv (Kovacevic 83), Morz, Mayrleb (Kuljic 62), Kuhbauer, Linz, Ivanschitz, Amerhauser.
Referee: Verbist (Belgium).

Belfast, 7 September 2005, 14,000

Northern Ireland (0) 1 *(Healy 74)*

England (0) 0

Northern Ireland: Taylor; Baird, Capaldi, Davis, Hughes A, Craigan, Gillespie, Johnson, Quinn (Feeney 79), Healy (Sproule 88), Elliott (Duff 90).
England: Robinson; Young, Cole A, Beckham, Ferdinand, Carragher, Lampard (Hargreaves 80), Gerrard (Defoe 75), Owen, Rooney, Wright-Phillips (Cole J 54).
Referee: Busacca (Switzerland).

Warsaw, 7 September 2005, 13,500

Poland (0) 1 *(Zurawski 54 (pen))*

Wales (0) 0

Poland: Boruc; Baszczynski, Jop, Bak, Rzasa, Smolarek (Michal Zewlakow 86), Sobolewski, Szymkowiak, Kosowski (Radomski 79), Zurawski, Rasiak (Frankowski 65).
Wales: Coyne; Edwards (Duffy 45), Ricketts, Fletcher, Gabbidon, Collins J, Davies S, Koumas (Davies C 68), Earnshaw (Ledley 80), Giggs, Partridge.
Referee: Larsen (Denmark).

Old Trafford, 8 October 2005, 64,822

England (1) 1 *(Lampard 25 (pen))*

Austria (0) 0

England: Robinson; Young, Carragher, Gerrard, Terry, Campbell (Ferdinand 65), Beckham■, Lampard, Crouch, Owen (Richardson 81), Cole J (King 62).
Austria: Macho; Dober, Scharner, Stranzl, Ibertsberger (Lasnik 80), Schopp (Kuljic 64), Aufhauser, Kiesenebner, Weissenberger (Sariyar 46), Ivanschitz, Linz.
Referee: Cantalejo (Spain).

Belfast, 8 October 2005, 14,000

Northern Ireland (0) 2 *(Gillespie 46, Davis 50)*

Wales (2) 3 *(Davies S 27, Robinson 38, Giggs 61)*

Northern Ireland: Taylor; Duff (Jones S 82), Capaldi, Davis, Murdock, Craigan, Gillespie, Johnson, Quinn, Healy, Elliott (Brunt 65).
Wales: Jones P; Delaney, Ricketts (Collins D 87), Fletcher, Partridge, Collins J (Duffy 52), Davies S, Robinson, Hartson, Earnshaw (Vaughan 77), Giggs.
Referee: Bossen (Holland).

Vienna, 12 October 2005, 20,000

Austria (1) 2 *(Aufhauser 44, 90)*

Northern Ireland (0) 0

Austria: Macho; Dober (Ibertsberger 46), Scharner, Pogatetz■, Stranzl, Schopp (Standfest 55), Kiesenebner, Aufhauser, Ivanschitz, Wallner (Gercaliv 77), Linz.
Northern Ireland: Taylor; Duff, Baird, Davis, Murdock, Craigan, Gillespie, Johnson■, Healy, Quinn (Feeney 56), Brunt (Elliott 76).
Referee: Briakos (Greece).

Old Trafford, 12 October 2005, 65,467

England (1) 2 *(Owen 44, Lampard 80)*

Poland (1) 1 *(Frankowski 45)*

England: Robinson; Young, Carragher, King, Terry, Ferdinand, Wright-Phillips (Crouch 66), Lampard, Rooney, Owen (Jenas 83), Cole J (Smith 86).
Poland: Boruc; Baszczynski, Jop, Bak, Kosowski, Sobolewski (Radomski 78), Lewandowski M, Michal Zewlakow, Smolarek (Krzynowek 46), Zurawski (Frankowski 38), Rasiak.
Referee: Nielsen (Denmark).

Cardiff, 12 October 2005, 50,000

Wales (1) 2 *(Giggs 3, 51)*

Azerbaijan (0) 0

Wales: Jones P; Duffy, Collins D (Ricketts 54), Fletcher (Crofts 69), Gabbidon, Vaughan, Davies S, Robinson, Hartson, Giggs (Cotterill 73), Collins J.
Azerbaijan: Kramarenko; Chukurov (Poladov 69), Agayev, Sadygov, Amirbekov (Bakhshiyev 80), Kerimov, Kuliyev V, Muzika, Ismailov, Imamaliev, Tagizade.
Referee: Hansson (Sweden).

Group 6 Final table

	P	W	D	L	F	A	Pts
England	10	8	1	1	17	5	25
*Poland	10	8	0	2	27	9	24
Austria	10	4	3	3	15	12	15
Northern Ireland	10	2	3	5	10	18	9
Wales	10	2	2	6	10	15	8
Azerbaijan	10	0	3	7	1	21	3

GROUP 7

Charleroi, 4 September 2004, 20,000

Belgium (0) 1 *(Sonck 61)*

Lithuania (0) 1 *(Jankauskas 72)*

Belgium: Peersman; Deflandre (Kompany 46), Dheedene, Simons, Van Buyten, Clement, Goor, Mpenza M (Dufer 22), Vernant (Pieroni 73), Buffel, Sonck.
Lithuania: Karcemarskas; Dziaukstas, Skarbalius (Morinas 8), Skerla, Stankevicius, Barasa, Cesnauskis E, Vencevicius (Razanauskas 57), Danelevicius (Mikoliunas 66), Jankauskas, Poskus.
Referee: Loizou (Cyprus).

Serravalle, 4 September 2004, 500

San Marino (0) 0

Serbia-Montenegro (2) 3 *(Vukic 5, Jestrovic 15, 82)*

San Marino: Gasperoni F; Valentini C, Michele Marani, Bacciocchi, Della Valle, Crescentini (Moretti M 46), Domenicioni, Gasperoni A (Maiani 85), Ciacci, Vannucci, Ugolini (Montagna 23).
Serbia-Montenegro: Jevric; Dragutinovic, Mladenovic (Duljaj 82), Vidic, Gavrancic, Koroman, Milosevic (Kezman 68), Stankovic, Jestrovic, Vukic (Brnovic 86), Krstajic.
Referee: Kholmatov (Kazakhstan).

Zenica, 8 September 2004, 15,000

Bosnia (0) 1 *(Bolic 74)*

Spain (0) 1 *(Vicente 66)*

Bosnia: Hasagic; Salihamidzic, Bajic, Spahic, Music, Grujic, Barbarez, Beslija, Baljic (Blatnjak 63), Misimovic, Bolic (Hililovic 83).
Spain: Casillas; Michel Salgado, Romero, Albelda (Xabi Alonso 71), Puyol, Helguera, Victor (Morientes 50), Baraja (Valeron 58), Reyes, Raul, Vicente.
Referee: De Santis (Italy).

Kaunas, 8 September 2004, 5000

Lithuania (1) 4 *(Jankauskas 18, 50, Danilevicius 65, Gedgaudas 90)*

San Marino (0) 0

Lithuania: Karcemarskas; Stankevicius, Dziaukstas, Skerla, Barasa, Vencevicius, Mikoliunas (Gedgaudas 74), Cesnauskis E (Morinas 46), Danilevicius, Poskus, Jankauskas (Radzinevicius 68).
San Marino: Gasperoni F; Valentini C, Bacciocchi, Della Valle, Michele Marani, Albani (Maiani 87), Domeniconi, Gasperoni A, Giacci, Vannucci (Nanni 82), Montagna (Moretti M 65).
Referee: Jareci (Albania).

Sarajevo, 9 October 2004, 32,000

Bosnia (0) 0

Serbia-Montenegro (0) 0

Bosnia: Tolja; Blatnjak, Spahic, Bajic (Hrgovic 62), Papac (Crnogorac 79), Grlic, Misimovic, Bolic, Barbarez, Baljic (Baiano 80), Beslija.

Serbia-Montenegro: Jevric; Gavrancic, Krstajic, Djordjevic N (Markovic 57), Duljaj, Dragutinovic, Stankovic, Koroman (Brnovic 90), Vukic, Milosevic (Pantelic 77), Ljuboja.
Referee: Veissiere (France).

Santander, 9 October 2004, 20,000

Spain (0) 2 *(Luque 59, Raul 63)*

Belgium (0) 0

Spain: Casillas; Michel Salgado, Del Horno, Albelda (Xabi Alonso 58), Marchena, Puyol, Joachim, Xavi (Baraja 73), Raul, Fernando Torres (Luque 53), Reyes.
Belgium: Peersman; Deflandre■, Deschacht, Clement, Kompany, Van Buyten, Buffel (Dufer 79), Bisconti (Doll 60), Mpenza M (Huysegems 73), Sonck, Goor■.
Referee: Nielsen (Denmark).

Vilnius, 13 October 2004, 6000

Lithuania (0) 0

Spain (0) 0

Lithuania: Karcemarskas; Stankevicius, Dziaukstas, Skerla, Skarbalius, Gedgaudas (Mikoliunas 75), Vencevcius, Barasa, Cesnauskas N, Jankauskas, Danilevicius (Radzinevicius 82).
Spain: Casillas; Michel Salgado, Capdevila (Torres 79), Albelda, Puyol, Marchena, Victor (Tamudo 53), Baraja (Reyes 65), Xavi, Raul, Luque.
Referee: Poulat (France).

Belgrade, 13 October 2004, 3000

Serbia-Montenegro (2) 5 *(Milosevic 35, Stankovic 45, 50, Koroman 52, Vukic 69)*

San Marino (0) 0

Serbia-Montenegro: Jevric; Markovic, Gavrancic, Dragutinovic (Vitakic 62), Koroman, Krstajic, Duljaj, Vukic, Stankovic, Milosevic, Ljuboja (Pantelic 70).
San Marino: Gasperoni F; Valentini C, Michele Marani, Bacciocchi, Della Valle, Albani, Domeniconi (Moretti L 90), Vannucci, Ciacci (De Luigi 77), Gasperoni A, Moretti M (Gasperoni B 65).
Referee: Isaksen (Faeroes).

Brussels, 17 November 2004, 32,000

Belgium (0) 0

Serbia-Montenegro (1) 2 *(Vukic 7, Kezman 59)*

Belgium: Proto; De Cock, Kompany, Simons, Deschacht (Daerden 27), Van der Heyden, Bisconti (Pieroni 58), Baseggio, Clement, Buffel, Sonck (Huysegems 65).
Serbia-Montenegro: Jevric; Markovic, Mladenovic (Djordjevic N 77), Gavrancic, Dragutinovic, Stankovic, Djordjevic P, Koroman (Duljaj 55), Vukic, Milosevic (Kezman 29), Vidic.
Referee: Frojdfeldt (Sweden).

Serravalle, 17 November 2004, 1457

San Marino (0) 0

Lithuania (1) 1 *(Cesnauskis D 41)*

San Marino: Gasperoni F; Valentini C, Michele Marani, Bacciocchi, Della Valle, Albani, Muccioli (Domeniconi 67), Gasperoni A, De Luigi (Bonifazi 82), Selva A, Vannucci.
Lithuania: Karcemarkas; Semberas, Dziaukstas, Stankevicius, Gedgaudas (Vencevicius 85), Zvirgzdauskas, Skarbalius, Cesnauskis E, Danilevicius, Cesnauskis D (Mikoliunas 76), Radzinevicius (Morinas 46).
Referee: Nalbandyan (Armenia).

Almeria, 9 February 2005, 15,000

Spain (3) 5 *(Joaquin 14, Torres 32, Raul 42, Guti 65, Del Horno 79)*

San Marino (0) 0

Spain: Casillas; Marchena, Puyol, Michel Salgado, De la Pena (Guayre 76), Del Horno, Joaquin, Xavi, Luque (Guti 46), Raul (Villa 46), Torres.
San Marino: Gasperoni F; Albani, Andreini (Gasperoni B 58), Bacciocchi, Domeniconi (Moretti M 75), Vannucci, Della Valle, Gasperoni A, Michele Marani, Valentini C, Selva A.
Referee: Clark (Scotland).

Brussels, 26 March 2005, 35,000

Belgium (2) 4 *(Mpenza E 15, 54, Daerden 44, Buffel 76)*

Bosnia (1) 1 *(Bajramovic 1)*

Belgium: Proto; Doll, Kompany, Van Buyten, Vanderheyden, Buffel (Bisconti 90), Vanderheyghe, Simons, Daerden, Mpenza E (Clement 90), Pieroni (Vandenbergh 86).
Bosnia: Hasagic; Spahic, Bajic, Milenkovic, Papac (Misimovic 58), Beslija, Grlic (Grujic 72), Barbarez, Bolic, Baljic (Halimovic 58), Bajramovic.
Referee: Hrinak (Slovakia).

Sarajevo, 30 March 2005, 15,000

Bosnia (1) 1 *(Bolic 21)*

Lithuania (0) 1 *(Stankevicius 64)*

Bosnia: Hasagic; Spahic, Bajic (Halilovic 73), Milenkovic, Vidic, Bajramovic, Grlic, Beslija (Baljic 46), Misimovic (Grujic 64), Barbarez, Bolic.
Lithuania: Karcemarskas; Stankevicius■, Skerla, Zutartas, Dziaukstas, Cesnauskis D (Barasa 54), Semberas, Cesnauskis E, Poskus, Danilevicius (Vencevicius 90), Jankauskas.
Referee: Baskakov (Russia).

Serravalle, 30 March 2005, 3000

San Marino (1) 1 *(Selva A 40)*

Belgium (1) 2 *(Simons 19 (pen), Van Buyten 65)*

San Marino: Gasperoni F; Albani, Della Valle, Bacciocchi, Michele Marani, Valentini C, Vannucci, Domeniconi (Montagna 89), Gasperoni A, Ciacci (Gasperoni B 61), Selva A.
Belgium: Proto; Doll (Vandenbergh 58), Kompany, Van Buyten, Van der Heyden, Buffel (Chatelle 38), Simons, Vanderhaeghe, Daerden, Pieroni (Bisconti 83), Mpenza E.
Referee: Kasnaferis (Greece).

Belgrade, 30 March 2005, 56,000

Serbia-Montenegro (0) 0

Spain (0) 0

Serbia-Montenegro: Jevric; Vidic, Gavrancic, Krstajic, Dragutinovic, Koroman (Basta 77), Duljaj, Stankovic, Djordjevic P, Kezman (Jestrovic 80), Milosevic (Ilic 65).
Spain: Casillas; Sergio Ramos, Pablo, Puyol (Juanito 46), Del Horno, Xavi, Albelda, De La Pena (Raul 46), Joaquin, Fernando Torres, Reyes (Antonio Lopez 62).
Referee: Busacca (Switzerland).

Serravalle, 4 June 2005, 747

San Marino (1) 1 *(Selva A 40)*

Bosnia (2) 3 *(Salihamidzic 17, 39, Barbarez 75)*

San Marino: Ceccoli; Valentini C (Gasperoni B 65), Crescentini, Della Valle, Bacciocchi, Michele Marani, Gasperoni D, Domeniconi, Vannucci, De Luigi (Andreini 72), Selva A (Montagna 85).
Bosnia: Tolja; Berberovic, Vidic, Papac, Milenkovic, Beslija (Bartolovic 56), Grlic, Bajramovic (Kerkez 82), Misimovic (Halilovic 59), Barbarez, Salihamidzic.
Referee: Demirlek (Turkey).

Belgrade, 4 June 2005, 45,000

Serbia-Montenegro (0) 0

Belgium (0) 0

Serbia-Montenegro: Jevric; Dragutinovic, Krstajic, Gavrancic, Vidic, Vukic, Duljaj, Koroman (Vukcevic 81), Stankovic (Mladenovic 82), Ljuboja, Jestrovic (Vucinic 53).
Belgium: Proto; Clement, Van Buyten, Deschacht, Borre, Vanderhaeghe, Bisconti, Daerden (Leonard 79), Buffel (Pieroni 88), Mpenza E, Mpenza M (Vandenbergh 83).
Referee: Ivanov (Russia).

Valencia, 4 June 2005, 25,000

Spain (0) 1 *(Luque 68)*

Lithuania (0) 0

Spain: Casillas; Michel Salgado, Marchena, Puyol, Del Horno (Luis Garcia 61), Joaquim, Xavi, Albelda, Vicente, Fernando Torres (Luque 59), Raul (Sergio 79).
Lithuania: Karcemarskas; Skerla, Dziaukstas, Zvirgzdauskas, Paulauskas, Barasa, Kucys (Preksaitis 46), Cesnauskis D (Mikoliunas 73), Danilevicius, Poskus, Morinas (Cesnauskis E 77).
Referee: Farina (Italy).

Valencia, 8 June 2005, 36,400

Spain (0) 1 *(Marchena 90)*

Bosnia (1) 1 *(Misimovic 38)*

Spain: Casillas; Michel Salgado, Marchena, Puyol (Juanito 8), Antonio Lopez (Xabi Alonso 62), Joaquin, Xavi, Albelda, Vicente, Raul, Fernando Torres (Luque 35).
Bosnia: Tolja; Spahic, Bajic, Vidic (Milenkovic 76), Music, Grlic, Bajramovic, Grujic (Damjanovic 74), Barbarez, Misimovic (Halilovic■ 65), Beslija■.
Referee: Bennett (England).

Zenica, 3 September 2005, 15,000

Bosnia (0) 1 *(Barbarez 62)*

Belgium (0) 0

Bosnia: Hasagic; Spahic, Berberovic, Papac, Music, Bartolovic (Jakirovic 88), Grujic, Bajramovic, Milenkovic (Hrgovic 77), Barbarez, Bolic (Misimovic 72).
Belgium: Proto; Vanden Borre (Daerden 78), Kompany, Van Buyten, Deschacht, Mpenza M, Vanderhaeghe, Simons, Van Damme (Garaerts 78), Buffel (Vandenbergh 68), Pieroni.
Referee: Benquerenca (Portugal).

Belgrade, 3 September 2005, 25,000

Serbia-Montenegro (1) 2 *(Kezman 18, Ilic 75)*

Lithuania (0) 0

Serbia-Montenegro: Jevric; Gavrancic, Vidic, Krstajic, Dragutinovic, Duljaj, Stankovic, Djordjevic P, Ilic (Vukic 82), Kezman (Zigic 74), Milosevic (Koroman 59).
Lithuania: Karcemarskas; Semberas, Dziaukstas (Zutautas 80), Paulauskas, Skerla, Skarbalius, Cesnauskis E, Jankauskas, Savenas (Preiksaitis 70), Mikoliunas (Radzinevicius 66), Cesnauskis D.
Referee: Nielsen (Denmark).

Antwerp, 7 September 2005, 8000

Belgium (3) 8 *(Simons 34 (pen), Daerden 39, 67, Buffel 44, Mpenza M 52, 71, Vandenbergh 53, Van Buyten 83)*

San Marino (0) 0

Belgium: Proto; Deschacht, Kompany (Daerden 12), Simons, Van Buyten, Vanden Borre (Hoefkens 69), Goor, Vanderhaeghe (Bisconti 69), Buffel, Mpenza M, Vandenbergh.
San Marino: Ceccoli; Valentini C■, Andreini, Crescentini (Nanni L 76), Della Valle, Bacciocchi, Maiani (Selva R 61), Domeniconi, Gasperoni A, Selva A, Moretti M (Ciacci 70).
Referee: Stokes (Republic of Ireland).

Vilnius, 7 September 2005, 4000

Lithuania (0) 0

Bosnia (1) 1 *(Barbarez 28)*

Lithuania: Karcemarskas; Semberas, Dziaukstas, Stankevicius, Cesnauskis D (Mikoliunas 66), Zvirgzdauskas, Skarbalius (Savenas 46), Cesnauskis E■, Jankauskas, Danilevicius, Poskus.
Bosnia: Hasagic; Milenkovic, Bajic, Papac, Berberovic, Grlic, Bajramovic, Music (Jakirovic 64), Beslija (Bartolovic 59), Barbarez, Bolic (Misimovic 87).
Referee: Kassai (Hungary).

Madrid, 7 September 2005, 55,000

Spain (1) 1 *(Raul 18)*

Serbia-Montenegro (0) 1 *(Kezman 68)*

Spain: Casillas; Michel Salgado, Del Horno, Marchena, Xabi Alonso, Puyol, Vicente (Luque 74), Xavi, Raul, Fernando Torres (Tamudo 53), Joaquin (Luis Garcia 66).
Serbia-Montenegro: Jevric; Djordjevic P, Dragutinovic, Gavrancic, Krstajic, Vidic, Duljaj■, Koroman (Maric 84), Ilic (Zigic 46) (Kovacevic N 90), Stankovic, Kezman.
Referee: Farina (Italy).

Brussels, 8 October 2005, 40,000

Belgium (0) 0

Spain (0) 2 *(Fernando Torres 56, 59)*

Belgium: Proto; Deschacht, Hoefkens, Simons, Van Buyten, Vanden Borre (Deflandre 61), Goor, Vanderhaeghe, Buffel (Walasiak 61), Mpenza M (Pieroni 74), Mpenza E.
Spain: Casillas; Michel Salgado, Antonio Lopez, Marchena, Puyol, Albelda, Xavi, Joaquin (Villa 52), Vicente (Reyes 52), Fernando Torres (Baraja 68), Raul.
Referee: Michel (Slovakia).

Zenica, 8 October 2005, 7000

Bosnia (0) 3 *(Bolic 48, 75, 85)*

San Marino (0) 0

Bosnia: Hasagic; Spahic, Music, Bajic, Konjic, Grlic, Grujic, Barbarez, Salihamidzic, Bolic, Bartolovic.
San Marino: Ceccoli; Andreini, Vannucci, Crescentini (Palazzi 71), Della Valle, Nanni L, Domeniconi (Moretti M 90), Gasperoni A, Selva A, Manuel Marani (Montagna 80), Michele Marani.
Referee: Hamer (Luxembourg).

Vilnius, 8 October 2005, 3000

Lithuania (0) 0

Serbia-Montenegro (1) 2 *(Kezman 42, Vukic 88)*

Lithuania: Karcemarskas; Stankevicius, Dziaukstas, Paulauskas (Laurisas 77), Skerla, Preiksaitis, Savenas, Cesnauskis D, Jankauskas, Mikoliunas (Morinas 60), Danilevicius (Radzinevicius 88).
Serbia-Montenegro: Jevric; Vidic, Gavrancic, Nadj, Kezman, Stankovic (Mladenovic 10), Djordjevic P, Vukic, Lukovic, Zigic (Ljuboja 56), Krstajic.
Referee: Wegereef (Holland).

Vilnius, 12 October 2005, 2000

Lithuania (1) 1 *(Deschacht 38 (og))*

Belgium (1) 1 *(Garaerts 20)*

Lithuania: Karcemarskas; Zutautas, Skerla, Dziaukstas, Paulauskas, Preiksaitis, Semberas■, Stankevicius (Radzinevicius 90), Morinas (Mikoliunas 83), Danilevicius, Savenas.
Belgium: Proto; Deflandre, Hoefkens (Maertens 46), Simons, Deschacht, Walasiak, Vanderhaeghe, Garaerts (Vanden Borre 46), Goor, Mpenza M, Mpenza E.
Referee: Riley (England).

Serravalle, 12 October 2005, 3400

San Marino (0) 0

Spain (3) 6 *(Antonio Lopez 1, Fernando Torres 10, 76 (pen), 88, Sergio Ramos 30, 49)*

San Marino: Gasperoni F; Andreini (Palazzi 84), Bacciocchi, Nanni L, Della Valle, Vannucci, Gasperoni A, Domeniconi, Manuel Marani (Nanni F 87), Michele Marani, Montagna (Masi 71).
Spain: Casillas; Sergio Ramos, Juanito, Pablo, Antonio Lopez, De La Pena, Albelda, Raul (Mista 73), Reyes (Vicente 68), Fernando Torres, Villa (Baraja 58).
Referee: Meyer (Germany).

Belgrade, 12 October 2005, 55,000

Serbia-Montenegro (1) 1 *(Kezman 7)*

Bosnia (0) 0

Serbia-Montenegro: Jevric; Gavrancic, Vidic■, Krstajic, Koroman, Nadj (Ilic 72), Duljaj, Djordjevic P, Vukic (Mladenovic 66), Kezman (Lukovic 87), Zigic.
Bosnia: Hasagic; Berberovic, Music (Beslija 65), Spahic, Bajramovic, Milenkovic, Salihamidzic, Barbarez, Grlic (Bartolovic 46), Jakirovic, Bolic (Misimovic 70).
Referee: Vassaras (Greece).

Group 7 Final table

	P	*W*	*D*	*L*	*F*	*A*	*Pts*
Serbia-Montenegro	10	6	4	0	16	1	22
†Spain	10	5	5	0	19	3	20
Bosnia	10	4	4	2	12	9	16
Belgium	10	3	3	4	16	11	12
Lithuania	10	2	4	4	8	9	10
San Marino	10	0	0	10	2	40	0

GROUP 8

Zagreb, 4 September 2004, 25,000

Croatia (1) 3 *(Prso 32, Klasnic 57, Gyepes 80 (og))*

Hungary (0) 0

Croatia: Butina; Srna (Mornar 84), Simunic, Kovac R, Tudor, Vranjes, Kranjcar (Leko I 77), Babic, Prso (Olic 75), Kovac N, Klasnic.
Hungary: Kiraly; Bodnar, Huszti■, Stark (Gyepes 59), Toth A (Kovacs 81), Molnar, Rosa, Szabics, Gera, Simek (Low 18), Juhasz.
Referee: Riley (England).

Reykjavik, 4 September 2004, 5000

Iceland (0) 1 *(Gudjohnsen E 51 (pen))*

Bulgaria (1) 3 *(Berbatov 35, 49, Yanev 62)*

Iceland: Arason; Bjarnason, Sigurdsson K, Gunnarsson B■, Sigurdsson I (Helgason 65), Gretarsson (Gudjonsson J 57), Hreidarsson, Einarsson, Gudjohnsen E, Gudjonsson T, Helguson (Sigurdsson H 70).
Bulgaria: Ivankov; Kishishev, Kirilov, Petkov I, Yankov (Kamburov 80), Berbatov, Lazarov (Yanev 42), Hristov, Petrov S, Bojinov (Bukarev 72), Stoyanov.
Referee: Hamer (Luxembourg).

Ta'Qali, 4 September 2004, 4000

Malta (0) 0

Sweden (3) 7 *(Ibrahimovic 4, 11, 14, 71, Ljungberg 46, 74, Larsson 76)*

Malta: Muscat; Briffa, Pullicino, Said, Azzopardi, Dimech, Giglio, Woods (Mallia 79), Zahra (Agius G 57), Mifsud M, Galea.
Sweden: Isaksson; Lucic, Mellberg (Nilsson 61), Hansson (Ostlund 49), Edman, Linderoth, Wilhelmsson (Jonson M 76), Anders Svensson, Ljungberg, Ibrahimovic, Larsson.
Referee: Jakov (Israel).

Budapest, 8 September 2004, 8000

Hungary (0) 3 *(Gera 62, Torghelle 76, Szabics 80)*

Iceland (1) 2 *(Gudjohnsen E 40, Sigurdsson I 78)*

Hungary: Kiraly; Juhasz, Gyepes, Toth A, Szelesi (Szabics 46), Molnar, Rosa, Bodnar, Simek (Low 18), Gera, Kovacs (Torghelle 66).
Iceland: Arason; Sigurdsson K, Bjarnason, Hreidarsson, Gudjonsson T (Einarsson 75), Gretarsson (Gunnarsson V 85), Vidarsson, Gudjonsson J, Sigurdsson I, Helguson, Gudjohnsen E (Sigurdsson H 86).
Referee: Ovrebo (Norway).

Gothenburg, 8 September 2004, 40,023

Sweden (0) 0

Croatia (0) 1 *(Srna 64)*

Sweden: Isaksson; Ostlund, Mellberg, Lucic (Allback 80), Edman, Linderoth, Wilhelmsson, Anders Svensson (Jonson M 73), Ljungberg, Larsson, Ibrahimovic.
Croatia: Butina; Kovac R, Tudor, Simunic, Srna, Kovac N, Kranjcar (Leko J 63), Vranjes, Babic, Prso (Tokic 90), Klasnic (Olic 46).
Referee: Ibanez (Spain).

Zagreb, 9 October 2004, 30,000

Croatia (2) 2 *(Srna 15, 32 (pen))*

Bulgaria (0) 2 *(Petrov M 77, Berbatov 86)*

Croatia: Butina; Srna, Simunic, Kovac N, Kovac R (Banovic 77), Tokic, Babic, Vranjes, Kranjcar (Balaban 69), Prso, Klasnic (Leko J 57).
Bulgaria: Ivankov; Kishishev (Manchev 55), Markov, Petkov I, Stoyanov, Petrov S, Yankov, Berbatov, Bojinov (Yanev 55), Petrov M, Georgiev (Paskov 90).
Referee: Collina (Italy).

Valletta, 9 October 2004, 6000

Malta (0) 0

Iceland (0) 0

Malta: Haber; Azzopardi, Briffa, Ciantar, Dimech, Said, Agius G (Mallia 65), Giglio, Mattocks, Woods (Galea 78), Mifsud M.
Iceland: Arason; Bjarnason, Hreidarsson, Gunnarsson B (Gretarsson 78), Sigurdsson K, Einarsson, Gudjonsson T (Gunnarsson V 68), Sigurdsson I (Sigurdsson H 59), Helguson, Gudjohnsen E, Vidarsson.
Referee: Corpodean (Romania).

Stockholm, 9 October 2004, 32,228

Sweden (1) 3 *(Ljungberg 26, Larsson 50, Svensson 67)*

Hungary (0) 0

Sweden: Isaksson; Ostlund, Lucic, Linderoth, Mellberg, Mjallby (Nilsson 46), Wilhelmsson (Alexandersson N 74), Ljungberg, Allback, Larsson, Anders Svensson (Kallstrom 80).
Hungary: Kiraly; Gyepes, Bodnar (Feher C 80), Dardai, Stark, Toth A, Molnar (Hajnal 55), Gera, Szabics, Torghelle (Kovacs 70), Bodor.
Referee: Dougal (Scotland).

Sofia, 13 October 2004, 17,700

Bulgaria (1) 4 *(Berbatov 43, 66, Yanev 47, Yankov 87)*

Malta (1) 1 *(Mifsud M 12)*

Bulgaria: Ivankov; Stoyanov, Petkov I, Georgiev, Petrov S, Yankov, Yanev (Kirilov 71), Bojinov (Sakaliev 67), Manchev (Gargorov 64), Berbatov, Petrov M.
Malta: Haber; Briffa (Zahra 46), Said, Azzopardi, Ciantar, Dimech, Woods (Pulicino 75), Giglio, Agius G, Mattocks, Mifsud M.
Referee: Richards (Wales).

Reykjavik, 13 October 2004, 7035

Iceland (0) 1 *(Gudjohnsen E 66)*

Sweden (4) 4 *(Larsson 24, 39, Allback 27, Wilhelmsson 44)*

Iceland: Arason; Bjarnason (Gudjonsson T 57), Sigurdsson L (Jonsson 25), Gunnarsson B, Sigurdsson K, Einarsson, Marteinsson, Hreidarsson, Helguson (Sigurdsson H 81), Gudjohnsen E, Gudjonsson J.
Sweden: Isaksson (Hedman 31); Ostlund, Lucic, Linderoth, Mellberg, Nilsson, Wilhelmsson, Ljungberg (Alexandersson N 57), Allback, Larsson (Ibrahimovic 53), Anders Svensson.
Referee: Busacca (Switzerland).

Ta'Qali, 17 November 2004, 2000

Malta (0) 0

Hungary (1) 2 *(Gera 39, Kovacs 90)*

Malta: Haber; Ciantar, Azzopardi, Briffa, Said, Dimech, Agius G (Barbara 86), Giglio, Mifsud M, Woods (Cohen 73), Mattocks (Galea 60).
Hungary: Kiraly; Rosa (Gyepes 90), Huszti, Juhasz, Stark, Hajnal, Feher C, Dardai, Torghelle (Kovacs 66), Gera, Wallner (Lipcsei 79).
Referee: Asumaa (Finland).

Sofia, 26 March 2005, 42,563

Bulgaria (0) 0

Sweden (1) 3 *(Ljungberg 17, 90, Edman 74)*

Bulgaria: Ivankov; Markov■, Stoyanov, Petkov I, Kishishev (Kirilov 74), Borimirov (Janev 76), Yankov, Georgiev, Berbatov, Ivanov G, Lazarov (Topuzakov 60).
Sweden: Isaksson; Ostlund, Mellberg, Lucic, Edman, Alexandersson N (Wilhelmsson 61), Linderoth, Anders Svensson, Ljungberg, Ibrahimovic, Jonson M (Allback 80).
Referee: Fandel (Germany).

Zagreb, 26 March 2005, 25,000

Croatia (1) 4 *(Kovac N 39, 76, Simunic 71, Prso 90)*

Iceland (0) 0

Croatia: Butina; Tomas, Tudor, Simunic, Seric (Bosnjak 86), Srna, Kovac N, Leko I (Leko J 79), Kranjcar, Klasnic (Olic 73), Prso.
Iceland: Arason; Bjarnason, Sigurdsson K, Gunnarsson B, Sigurdsson I, Sigurdsson H (Steinsson 50), Vidarsson, Helguson (Gislason 73), Einarsson, Gudjonsson I (Gudjonsson B 60), Marteinsson.
Referee: Damon (South Africa).

Zagreb, 30 March 2005, 10,000

Croatia (2) 3 *(Prso 24, 35, Tudor 80)*

Malta (0) 0

Croatia: Butina; Tomas, Kovac R (Olic 46), Tudor, Bosnjak (Tokic 68), Kovac N (Vranjes 77), Leko I, Kranjcar, Babic, Prso, Klasnic.

Malta: Haber; Pollicino, Said (Mallia 59), Dimech, Azzopardi, Agius G, Sammut, Grima (Woods 46), Giglio, Mattocks, Mifsud M (Barbara 68).
Referee: Kapitanis (Cyprus).

Budapest, 30 March 2005, 12,000

Hungary (0) 1 *(Rajczi 90)*

Bulgaria (0) 1 *(Petrov S 52)*

Hungary: Kiraly; Juhasz, Stark, Komlosi, Bodnar, Boor, Vincze (Rajczi 79), Korsos G (Kerekes 74), Huszti, Szabics, Torghelle.
Bulgaria: Ivankov; Kirilov, Stojanov, Petkov I, Georgiev, Lazarov (Borimirov 75), Petrov S, Yankov (Manchev 64), Petrov M (Ivanov 79), Berbatov, Topuzakov.
Referee: Wegereef (Holland).

Sofia, 4 June 2005, 30,738

Bulgaria (0) 1 *(Petrov M 73)*

Croatia (1) 3 *(Babic 18, Tudor 58, Kranjcar 80)*

Bulgaria: Ivankov; Kirilov, Stoyanov, Iliev V, Kishishev (Lazarov 54), Yankov, Petrov S, Georgiev, Berbatov, Ivanov G (Bojinov 46), Petrov M.
Croatia: Butina; Tomas, Kovac R, Tudor, Simunic, Srna, Kovac N, Babic, Kranjcar (Leko J 82), Olic (Balaban 90), Prso.
Referee: Nielsen (Denmark).

Reykjavik, 4 June 2005, 4613

Iceland (1) 2 *(Gudjohnsen E 18, Sigurdsson K 69)*

Hungary (1) 3 *(Gera 45 (pen), 56 (pen), Huszti 73)*

Iceland: Arason; Sigurdsson K, Bjarnasson■, Gislason, Sigurdsson I, Gunnarsson B, Marteinsson (Gudmundsson H 25), Steinsson (Arnason 46), Einarsson (Thorvaldsson 57), Vidarsson, Gujohnsen E.
Hungary: Kiraly; Bodnar, Stark, Huszti, Vanczak (Balog Z 14), Takacs, Hajnal, Baranyos (Szabics 75), Toth N (Rajczi 90), Gera, Kerekes.
Referee: Batista (Portugal).

Gothenburg, 4 June 2005, 40,000

Sweden (4) 6 *(Jonson M 6, Anders Svensson 18, Wilhelmsson 30, Ibrahimovic 40, Ljungberg 57, Elmander 81)*

Malta (0) 0

Sweden: Isaksson; Alexandersson N (Elmander 77), Mellberg, Lucic, Edman, Linderoth, Wilhelmsson, Anders Svensson (Kallstrom 62), Ljungberg, Ibrahimovic, Jonson M (Allback 62).
Malta: Haber; Pullicino, Dimech, Said, Pulis, Sammut, Giglio, Agius (Mallia 73), Pace (Briffa 46), Woods, Mifsud M.
Referee: Ivanov (Russia).

Reykjavik, 8 June 2005, 4884

Iceland (2) 4 *(Thorvaldsson 28, Gudjohnsen E 34, Gudmundsson T 75, Gunnarsson V 86)*

Malta (0) 1 *(Said 59)*

Iceland: Arason; Vidarsson, Helgason, Gunnarsson B, Steinsson, Gislason, Gunnarsson V, Arnason (Hardarson 63), Thorvaldsson (Sigurdsson H 84), Gudmundsson T, Gudjohnsen E (Danielsson 81).
Malta: Gauci; Said, Dimech, Briffa, Pulis, Agius G, Sammut, Pullicino, Mattocks (Cohen 59), Mallia, Mifsud M.
Referee: Skomina (Slovenia).

Budapest, 3 September 2005, 10,000

Hungary (1) 4 *(Torghelle 35, Wellman 57 (og), Takacs 65, Rajczi 85)*

Malta (0) 0

Hungary: Kiraly; Bodnar, Juhasz, Vanczak, Halmosi, Boor (Huszti 58), Gera (Buzsaky 76), Takacs, Hajnal, Kenesei (Rajczi 69), Torghelle.
Malta: Haber; Pullicino, Wellman, Said, Scicluna (Zahra 54), Mattocks, Briffa, Woods, Grima (Sammut 68), Anonam, Cohen (Ciantar 85).
Referee: Godulyan (Ukraine).

Reykjavik, 3 September 2005, 5000

Iceland (1) 1 *(Gudjohnsen E 24)*

Croatia (1) 3 *(Balaban 56, 61, Srna 82)*

Iceland: Arason; Sigurdsson K, Helgason (Arnason 79), Hreidarsson, Sigurdsson I (Vidarsson 43), Steinsson, Gunnarsson B, Gislason, Einarsson, Gudjohnsen E, Helguson (Thorvaldsson 24).
Croatia: Pletikosa; Srna, Kovac R, Simunic, Simic, Tudor, Kovac N, Kranjcar, Babic (Bosnjak 82), Balaban, Prso.
Referee: Stark (Germany).

Stockholm, 3 September 2005, 33,883

Sweden (0) 3 *(Ljungberg 60, Mellberg 75, Ibrahimovic 90)*

Bulgaria (0) 0

Sweden: Isaksson; Ostlund, Mellberg, Lucic, Edman, Wilhelmsson (Jonson M 80), Linderoth, Kallstrom (Alexandersson N 72), Ljungberg (Andersson D 90), Ibrahimovic, Larsson.
Bulgaria: Ivankov; Kishishev, Iliev V, Topuzakov, Petkov I, Georgiev■, Yankov (Iliev G 77), Petrov S, Petrov M, Lazarov (Kamburov 77), Ivanov G (Gargorov 58).
Referee: De Bleeckere (Belgium).

Sofia, 7 September 2005, 4836

Bulgaria (1) 3 *(Berbatov 21, Iliev G 69, Petrov M 86)*

Iceland (2) 2 *(Steinsson 9, Hreidarsson 16)*

Bulgaria: Ivankov; Iliev V, Petkov I, Kishishev, Topuzakov, Gargorov (Karaslavov 90), Yankov (Iliev G 46), Berbatov, Lazarov (Genkov 77), Petrov M, Petrov S.
Iceland: Arason; Sigurdsson K, Hreidarsson, Sigurdsson I, Gunnarsson B, Gislason, Helgason, Arnason (Vidarsson 75), Steinsson, Helguson, Gudjohnsen E.
Referee: Demirlek (Turkey).

Budapest, 7 September 2005, 30,000

Hungary (0) 0

Sweden (0) 1 *(Ibrahimovic 90)*

Hungary: Kiraly; Bodnar, Juhasz (Gyepes 46), Eger, Vanczak, Boor (Halmosi 87), Takacs, Hajnal (Kerekez 90), Huszti, Gera, Torghelle.
Sweden: Isaksson; Andersson C, Lucic, Ostlund, Mellberg, Alexandersson N, Linderoth, Wilhelmsson, Ibrahimovic (Allback 90), Larsson (Jonson M 82), Ljungberg.
Referee: Poll (England).

Ta'Qali, 7 September 2005, 4000

Malta (0) 1 *(Wellman 74)*

Croatia (1) 1 *(Kranjcar 19)*

Malta: Haber; Wellman, Scicluna (Sammut 46), Said, Pullicino, Agius G, Briffa, Anonam, Woods, Mattocks (Ciantar 73), Cohen (Grima 89).
Croatia: Pletikosa; Simunic, Tokic, Simic (Klasnic 80), Seric (Leko J 67), Babic, Kovac N, Srna, Kranjcar, Prso, Balaban (Bosnjak 68).
Referee: Briakos (Greece).

Sofia, 8 October 2005, 4652

Bulgaria (1) 2 *(Berbatov 30, Lazarov 55)*

Hungary (0) 0

Bulgaria: Ivankov; Iliev V, Topuzakov, Venkov, Iliev G, Kishishev, Lazarov (Georgiev 61), Petrov S (Kamburov 73), Yankov (Gargorov 68), Berbatov, Petrov M.
Hungary: Kiraly; Bodnar, Gyepes, Stark, Vanczak, Buzsaky (Kovacs 75), Hajnal, Halmosi (Kerekes 46), Huszti, Balog Z, Torghelle■.
Referee: Delevic (Serbia-Montenegro).

Zagreb, 8 October 2005, 15,000

Croatia (0) 1 *(Srna 56 (pen))*

Sweden (0) 0

Croatia: Butina; Srna, Simunic, Kovac R, Tudor, Tomas, Kranjcar, Babic, Prso (Simic 90), Kovac N, Klasnic (Bosnjak 70).
Sweden: Isaksson; Ostlund, Mellberg, Lucic, Edman, Linderoth (Wilhelmsson 66), Alexandersson N, Anders Svensson (Kallstrom 71), Ljungberg, Jonson M (Elmander 66), Larsson.
Referee: De Santis (Italy).

Budapest, 12 October 2005, 11,000

Hungary (0) 0

Croatia (0) 0

Hungary: Kiraly; Bodnar, Stark, Gyepes, Vanczak, Korsos G, Boor, Huszti, Baranyos (Buzsaky 76), Hajnal, Kovacs.
Croatia: Butina; Srna, Kovac R, Tudor, Vranjes, Babic, Tokic, Tomas, Leko I (Leko J 63), Klasnic (Bosnjak 63) (Simic 90), Balaban.
Referee: Larsen (Denmark).

Valletta, 12 October 2005, 6000

Malta (0) 1 *(Barbara 78)*

Bulgaria (0) 1 *(Yankov 66)*

Malta: Haber; Ciantar, Azzopardi (Zahra 65), Said, Dimech, Briffa, Wellman, Pullicino, Woods (Barbara 70), Mallia, Cohen (Grima 88).
Bulgaria: Kolev; Iliev V, Tupyzakov, Venkov, Gargarov, Iliev G, Kishishev (Kamburov 87), Yankov, Petrov M (Lazarov 46), Berbatov, Bojinov (Georgiev 60).
Referee: Godulyan (Ukraine).

Stockholm, 12 October 2005, 33,716

Sweden (2) 3 *(Ibrahimovic 29, Larsson 42, Kallstrom 90)*

Iceland (1) 1 *(Arnason 25)*

Sweden: Isaksson; Ostlund, Mellberg, Lucic, Edman, Wilhelmsson (Alexandersson N 66), Linderoth, Anders Svensson (Kallstrom 74), Ljungberg, Ibrahimovic (Allback 74), Larsson.
Iceland: Arason; Sigurdsson K, Helgason, Jonsson, Sigurdsson I, Steinsson, Gunnarsson G (Vidarsson 84), Thorvaldsson (Sigurdsson H 74), Gislason, Arnason (Einarsson 70), Helguson.
Referee: Ivanov (Russia).

Group 8 Final table

	P	W	D	L	F	A	Pts
Croatia	10	7	3	0	21	5	24
*Sweden	10	8	0	2	30	4	24
Bulgaria	10	4	3	3	17	17	15
Hungary	10	4	2	4	13	14	14
Iceland	10	1	1	8	14	27	4
Malta	10	0	3	7	4	32	3

PLAY-OFFS – EUROPE

PLAY-OFFS FIRST LEG

Oslo, 12 November 2005, 24,264

Norway (0) 0

Czech Republic (1) 1 *(Smicer 31)*

Norway: Myhre; Bergdolmo, Hagen, Hangeland, Riise, Solli (Braaten 46), Hestad, Grindheim (Stromstad 85), Pedersen M, Carew, Iversen (Aarst 77).
Czech Republic: Cech; Grygera, Jankulovski, Rozehnal, Ujfalusi, Galasek, Nedved, Poborsky, Rosicky (Jarosik 86), Smicer (Heinz 77), Baros (Polak 60).
Referee: Bussacca (Switzerland).

Madrid, 12 November 2005, 54,851

Spain (2) 5 *(Luis Garcia 10, 18, 74, Fernando Torres 65 (pen), Morientes 79)*

Slovakia (0) 1 *(Nemeth 49)*

Spain: Casillas; Michel Salgado, Del Horno, Puyol, Pablo, Albelda (Xabi Alonso 66), Xavi, Luis Garcia (Morientes 76), Fernando Torres, Reyes (Vicente 56), Raul.
Slovakia: Contofalsky; Petras, Skrtel, Kratochvil, Had■, Zabavnik, Karhan (Janocko 73), Hlinka, Hodur (Gresko 67), Holosko (Nemeth 46), Vittek.
Referee: De Sanctis (Italy).

Berne, 12 November 2005, 31,130

Switzerland (1) 2 *(Senderos 41, Behrami 86)*

Turkey (0) 0

Switzerland: Zuberbuhler; Magnin, Muller, Senderos, Degen P, Vogel, Barnetta (Behrami 83), Cabanas, Gygax, Streller (Vonlanthen 77), Frei.
Turkey: Volkan; Serkan, Alpay, Ibrahim, Umit O (Halil Altintop 77), Huseyin, Tuncay (Ergun 83), Selcuk, Tumer, Nihat (Okan B 46), Hakan Sukur.
Referee: Michel (Slovakia).

Montevideo, 12 November 2005, 75,000

Uruguay (1) 1 *(Rodriguez D 35)*

Australia (0) 0

Uruguay: Carini; Diogo, Diego Lopez (Rodriguez G 62), Montero, Rodriguez D, Perez, Pablo Garcia, Recoba, Zalayeta (Estoyanoff 62), Morales, Forlan (Dario Silva 17).
Australia: Schwarzer; Neill, Vidmar, Popovic, Grella, Emerton, Culina, Chipperfield, Kewell, Thompson (Bresciano 52), Viduka (Aloisi 79).
Referee: Larsen (Denmark).

PLAY-OFFS SECOND LEG

Sydney, 16 November 2005, 82,698

Australia (1) 1 *(Bresciano 35)*

Uruguay (0) 0

Australia: Schwarzer; Neill, Chipperfield, Cahill, Vidmar, Emerton (Skoko 110), Viduka, Grella, Bresciano (Aloisi 96), Culina, Popovic (Kewell 31).
Uruguay: Carini; Lugano, Rodriguez G, Pablo Garcia, Rodriguez D, Montero (Sosa 81), Varela, Diogo, Morales, Recoba (Zalayeta 72), Regueiro (Estoyanoff 97).
aet; Australia won 4-2 on penalties.
Referee: Cantalejo (Spain).

Prague, 16 November 2005, 17,464

Czech Republic (1) 1 *(Rosicky 35)*

Norway (0) 0

Czech Republic: Cech; Grygera, Ujfalusi, Rozehnal, Poborsky, Smicer (Stajner 75), Rosicky (Kovac 67), Nedved, Polak, Baros (Plasil 90), Jankulovski.
Norway: Myhre; Hoiland, Hagen, Hangeland, Riise (Johnsen M 88), Helstad (Arst 57), Hestad, Stromstad, Pedersen M, Carew, Iversen (Solli 46).
Referee: Poll (England).

Bratislava, 16 November 2005, 23,567

Slovakia (0) 1 *(Holosko 50)*

Spain (0) 1 *(Villa 70)*

Slovakia: Contofalsky; Skrtel, Kratochvil, Gresko (Cech 78), Durica, Zabavnik, Hlinka, Krajcik, Vittek, Hodur (Holosko 46), Nemeth (Fodrek 83).
Spain: Casillas; Michel Salgado, Antonio Lopez, Puyol, Baraja, Xavi (Sergio Ramos 74), Vicente, Raul (Morientes 65), Fernando Torres (Villa 61), Xabi Alonso, Pablo.
Referee: Merk (Germany).

Istanbul, 16 November 2005, 40,000

Turkey (2) 4 *(Tuncay 22, 36, 89, Necati 52 (pen))*

Switzerland (1) 2 *(Frei 2 (pen), Streller 84)*

Turkey: Volkan; Tolga, Necati (Fatih 81), Alpay, Emre B (Basturk 82), Ergun, Selcuk, Serhat (Tumer 70), Hakan Sukur, Hamit Altintop, Tuncay.
Switzerland: Zuberbuhler; Senderos, Degen P (Behrami 46), Spycher, Muller, Barnetta, Wicky, Cabanas, Vogel, Gygax (Streller 33) (Huggel 86), Frei.
Referee: De Bleeckere (Belgium).

QUALIFYING RESULTS – SOUTH AMERICA

Buenos Aires, 6 September 2003, 35,372

Argentina (2) 2 *(Kily Gonzalez 32, Aimar 36)*

Chile (0) 2 *(Mirosevic 60, Navia 77)*

Argentina: Cavallero; Vivas, Ayala, Samuel■, Zanetti, Veron (Almeyda 65), Kily Gonzalez, Aimar, D'Alessandro, Delgado, Crespo (Saviola 71).
Chile: Tapia N; Alvarez■, Contreras, Olarra, Perez, Martel, Marcos Gonzalez, Melendez (Mirosevic 38), Mark Gonzalez (Acuna 57), Tapia H (Pinilla 57), Navia■.
Referee: Aquino (Paraguay).

Quito, 6 September 2003, 30,000

Ecuador (1) 2 *(Espinoza G 6, Tenorio C 67)*

Venezuela (0) 0

Ecuador: Cevallos; De la Cruz, Espinoza G, Hurtado I, Reasco, Ayovi M, Obregon, Mendez, Chala, Aguinaga (Tenorio O 43), Tenorio C.
Venezuela: Angelucci; Vallenilla, Rey, Alvarado, Rojas, Mea Vitali, Jimenez, Arango, Paez (Noriega 60), Urdaneta (Gonzalez H 60), Moran (Casseres 67).
Referee: Selman (Chile).

Lima, 6 September 2003, 43,000

Peru (2) 4 *(Solano 34, Mendoza 42, Jorge Soto 83, Farfan 90)*

Paraguay (1) 1 *(Gamarra 24)*

Peru: Delgado; Jorge Soto, Rebosio, Galliquio, Hidalgo, Jayo, Zegarra, Solano (Jose Soto 89), Palacios (Ciurlizza 76), Mendoza (Farfan 70), Pizarro.
Paraguay: Tavarelli; Arce, Gamarra, Da Silva, Caceres J, Toledo (Alvarenga 60), Enciso, Paredes, Bonet (Cuevas 81), Santa Cruz, Cardozo.
Referee: Baldassi (Argentina).

Barranquilla, 7 September 2003, 55,000

Colombia (1) 1 *(Angel 38)*

Brazil (1) 2 *(Ronaldo 25, Kaka 60)*

Colombia: Cordoba O; Martinez, Cordoba I, Yepes, Bedoya (Perea 35), Caballero, Restrepo (Becerra 63), Grisales, Patino (Molina 75), Hernandez, Angel.
Brazil: Dida; Cafu, Lucio, Roque Junior, Roberto Carlos, Emerson (Renato 59), Gilberto Silva, Ze Roberto, Alex (Kaka 59), Ronaldo, Rivaldo (Diego 87).
Referee: Elizondo (Argentina).

Montevideo, 7 September 2003, 42,000

Uruguay (2) 5 *(Forlan 17, Chevanton 38, 60, Abeijon 82, Bueno 87)*

Bolivia (0) 0

Uruguay: Munua; Gonzalez, Lopez, Lago, Sosa (Abeijon 69), Liguera (Oliveira 77), Nunez, Recoba, Bueno, Chevanton, Forlan (Sanchez 76).
Bolivia: Fernandez L; Hoyos, Sanchez O, Pena, Gatti Ribeiro (Baldivieso 46), Rojas, Cristaldo, Ricardi■, Morejon (Botero 46), Castillo, Mendez.
Referee: Hidalgo (Peru).

Santiago, 9 September 2003, 55,000

Chile (1) 2 *(Pinilla 35, Norambuena 70)*

Peru (0) 1 *(Mendoza 57)*

Chile: Tapia N; Rojas R, Contreras, Olarra, Martel (Mark Gonzalez 46), Acuna, Marcos Gonzalez (Pizarro 46), Mirosevic, Perez, Tapia H (Norambuena 67), Pinilla.
Peru: Delgado; Jorge Soto, Galliquio, Rebosio, Hidalgo, Jayo, Zegarra, Solano (Jose Soto 81), Palacios (Farfan 75), Mendoza, Pizarro.
Referee: Aquino (Paraguay).

Caracas, 9 September 2003, 25,000

Venezuela (0) 0

Argentina (3) 3 *(Aimar 7, Crespo 25, Delgado 32)*

Venezuela: Angelucci; Gonzalez H (Vallenilla 46), Rey, Alvaravo, Rojas, Vera, Jimenez, Arango (Moreno 61), Paez, Moran (Urdaneta 46), Noriega.
Argentina: Cavallero; Vivas, Ayala, Piacente, Zanetti, Veron, Kily Gonzalez, Aimar (Heinze 63), D'Alessandro (Gonzalez L 85), Delgado (Almeyda 81), Crespo.
Referee: Vazquez (Uruguay).

La Paz, 10 September 2003, 30,000

Bolivia (2) 4 *(Baldivieso 12, Botero 28, 49, 58)*

Colombia (0) 0

Bolivia: Fernandez L (Fernandez JC 46); Paz Garcia, Pena, Sanchez O, Gatti Ribeiro, Rojas (Garcia R 74), Cristaldo, Baldivieso, Mendez, Botero, Suarez (Justinano 62).
Colombia: Cordoba O; Martinez, Cordoba I■, Yepes, Cortes, Viafara, Vargas (Restrepo 46), Patino (Molina 46), Hernandez (Castillo 46), Angel, Aristizabal.
Referee: Oliveira (Brazil).

Manaus, 10 September 2003, 35,000

Brazil (1) 1 *(Ronaldinho 13)*

Ecuador (0) 0

Brazil: Dida; Cafu, Lucio, Roque Junior, Roberto Carlos, Emerson (Renato 62), Gilberto Silva, Ze Roberto, Ronaldinho (Kaka 68), Ronaldo, Rivaldo (Alex 90).
Ecuador: Cevallos; De la Cruz, Hurtado I, Espinoza G, Reasco, Obregon, Tenorio E, Ayovi M, Mendez, Chala, Tenorio C (Tenorio O 83).
Referee: Solozano (Venezuela).

Asuncion, 10 September 2003, 20,000

Paraguay (1) 4 *(Cardozo 27, 58, 73, Paredes 54)*

Uruguay (1) 1 *(Chevanton 24)*

Paraguay: Villar; Arce, Gamarra, Da Silva, Caceres JC, Bonet, Enciso (Ortiz 90), Paredes, Santa Cruz, Cardozo, Campos (Gavilan 81).
Uruguay: Munua; Gonzalez, Sorondo, Aguiai, Regueiro (Nunez 78), Abeijon, Oliveira, Giacomazzi (Liguera 46), Chevanton, Bueno (Recoba 61), Forlan.
Referee: Ruiz (Colombia).

Buenos Aires, 15 November 2003, 30,042

Argentina (0) 3 *(D'Alessandro 56, Crespo 61, Aimar 63)*

Bolivia (0) 0

Argentina: Cavallero; Quiroga, Ayala, Samuel, Zanetti, Almeyda (Cambiasso 89), Kily Gonzalez, Aimar, D'Alessandro (Sorin 84), Crespo (Saviola 80), Delgado.
Bolivia: Fernandez L; Raldes, Sanchez O, Paz Garcia, Ricaldi, Gatti Ribeiro, Justiniano, Reyes, Suarez (Etcheverry 69), Mercado (Castillo 64), Botero (Mendez 64).
Referee: Hidalgo (Peru).

Barranquilla, 15 November 2003, 20,000

Colombia (0) 0

Venezuela (1) 1 *(Arango 8)*

Colombia: Mondragon; Vallejo, Perez, Yepes, Viveros, Lozano, Bolano (Arriaga 54), Hernandez (Patino 46), Grisales, Becerra, Angel.
Venezuela: Angelucci; Vallenilla, Hernandez, Rey, Cichero, Jimenez, Mea Vitali (Vielna 6), Paez (Gonzalez H 57), Urdaneta (Rojas 57), Arango, Noriega.
Referee: Chandia (Chile).

Asuncion, 15 November 2003, 30,000

Paraguay (1) 2 *(Santa Cruz 30, Cardozo 70)*

Ecuador (0) 1 *(Mendez 59)*

Paraguay: Villar; Arce, Caceres JC, Gamarra, Caniza, Bonet (Gavilan 72), Ortiz, Paredes, Campos (Cuevas 61), Santa Cruz, Cardozo (Alvarenga 87).
Ecuador: Cevallos; De la Cruz, Hurtado I, Espinoza G, Corozo, Mendez, Tenorio E (Fernandez 63), Ambrossi (Salas 77), Gomez, Chala, Ordonez.
Referee: Paniagua (Bolivia).

Montevideo, 15 November 2003, 60,000

Uruguay (1) 2 *(Chevanton 31, Romero 48)*

Chile (1) 1 *(Melendez 20)*

Uruguay: Munua; Gonzalez, Lopez, Lago, Munoz (Romero 46), Sosa, Nunez, Liguera (Recoba 70), Chevanton, Bueno, Forlan (Hornos 46).
Chile: Tapia N; Rojas R, Olarra, Ramirez, Perez, Martel (Ormazabal 53), Nunoz, Melendez, Mark Gonzalez (Mirosevic 53), Navia (Norambuena 75), Pinilla.
Referee: Martin (Argentina).

Lima, 16 November 2003, 70,000

Peru (0) 1 *(Solano 58)*

Brazil (1) 1 *(Rivaldo 20 (pen))*

Peru: Ibanez; Jorge Soto, Galliquio, Rebosio, Hidalgo (Salas 52), Jayo, Ciurlizza, Solano, Palacios (Garcia 74), Mendoza, Pizarro.
Brazil: Dida; Cafu, Lucio, Roque Junior, Junior, Gilberto Silva, Ze Roberto, Emerson (Renato 61), Kaka (Alex 74), Rivaldo (Luis Fabiano 84), Ronaldo.
Referee: Ruiz (Colombia).

Santiago, 18 November 2003, 63,000

Chile (0) 0

Paraguay (1) 1 *(Paredes 30)*

Chile: Tapia N; Contreras, Ramirez, Olarra, Alvarez (Ormazabal 46), Marcos Gonzalez (Melendez 46), Perez, Mirosevic, Pizarro, Pinilla, Navia (Norambuena 62).
Paraguay: Villar; Arce, Caceres JC, Gamarra, Caniza, Bonet (Gavilan 79), Ortiz, Paredes (Da Silva 88), Enciso, Santa Cruz, Cardozo (Alvarenga 87).
Referee: Mendez (Uruguay).

Maracaibo, 18 November 2003, 25,000

Venezuela (0) 2 *(Rey 89, Arango 90)*

Bolivia (0) 1 *(Botero 60)*

Venezuela: Angelucci; Vallenilla, Cichero, Rey, Hernandez (Rojas 61), Jimenez, Arango, Urdaneta, Paez, Moran (Rondon 59), Noriega (Moreno 52).
Bolivia: Fernandez L; Raldes (Sandy 79), Sanchez O, Paz Garcia, Reyes, Alvarez, Gatti Ribeiro, Justiniano, Suarez (Mendez 69), Mercado (Vaca J 66), Botero.
Referee: Reinoso (Ecuador).

Barranquilla, 19 November 2003, 30,000

Colombia (0) 1 *(Angel 47)*

Argentina (1) 1 *(Crespo 26)*

Colombia: Cordoba O; Martinez, Cordoba I, Yepes, Viveros, Grisales, Viafara, Lozano (Bolano 20), Patino (Arriaga 46), Montoya (Becerra 71), Angel.
Argentina: Cavallero; Quiroga, Ayala, Samuel, Zanetti, Almeyda, Piacente, Kily Gonzalez, Aimar (D'Alessandro 70), Delgado (Veron 46), Crespo (Saviola 71).
Referee: Simon (Brazil).

Quito, 19 November 2003, 43,000

Ecuador (0) 0

Peru (0) 0

Ecuador: Cevallos; De la Cruz, Hurtado I, Reasco, Espinoza G, Ayovi M, Obregon (Fernandez 66), Chala (Aguinaga 79), Mendez, Tenorio C, Ordonez (Salas 46).
Peru: Ibanez; Jorge Soto, Rebosio, Galliquio, Salas, Jayo, Ciurlizza, Garcia, Palacios (Moran 53), Mendoza (Farfan 46), Pizarro.
Referee: Gonzalez (Paraguay).

Curitiba, 19 November 2003, 30,000

Brazil (2) 3 *(Kaka 19, Ronaldo 29, 87)*

Uruguay (0) 3 *(Forlan 57, 76, Gilberto Silva 79 (og))*

Brazil: Dida; Cafu, Lucio, Roque Junior, Junior, Renato (Juninho Pernambucano 79), Gilberto Silva, Ze Roberto, Kaka (Alex 72), Rivaldo (Luis Fabiano 80), Ronaldo.
Uruguay: Munua; Romero (Recoba 46), Bizera, Lopez, Lago, Sosa, Abeijon (Nunez 36), Liguera, Hornos (Chevanton 55), Zalayeta, Forlan.
Referee: Elizondo (Argentina).

Buenos Aires, 30 March 2004, 55,000

Argentina (0) 1 *(Crespo 60)*

Ecuador (0) 0

Argentina: Cavallero; Ayala, Sorin, Rodriguez C, Gonzalez L, Heinze, Gonzalez M (Tevez 46), D'Alessandro, Aimar (Riquelme 55), Delgado (Burdisso 66), Crespo.
Ecuador: Cevallos; Hurtado I, De la Cruz, Obregon, Tenorio C (Salas 73), Ayovi M, Chala (Delgado 63), Espinoza G, Reasco, Mendez, Tenorio E (Kaviedes 67).
Referee: Vazquez (Uruguay).

La Paz, 30 March 2004, 42,000

Bolivia (0) 0

Chile (1) 2 *(Villarroel 38, Mark Gonzalez 60)*

Bolivia: Fernandez L; Sanchez, Pena, Pizarro, Suarez (Gatti Ribeiro 46), Angulo, Reyes (Vaca J 61), Pachi, Da Rosa, Castillo, Botero (Mendez 46).
Chile: Tapia N; Rojas R, Vargas, Olarra, Perez, Villarroel (Maldonado 55), Melendez, Mark Gonzalez, Martel (Valenzuela 74), Salas, Galaz (Pinilla 55).
Referee: Martin (Argentina).

Asuncion, 31 March 2004, 40,000

Paraguay (0) 0

Brazil (0) 0

Paraguay: Tavarelli; Arce, Caceres JC (Da Silva 73), Gamarra, Bonet (Ortiz 30), Paredes, Toledo (Campos 56), Enciso, Caniza, Cardozo, Santa Cruz.
Brazil: Dida; Cafu, Lucio, Roque Junior, Roberto Carlos, Renato (Juninho Pernambucano 67), Gilberto Silva, Ze Roberto, Kaka, Ronaldinho, Ronaldo.
Referee: Ruiz (Colombia).

Lima, 31 March 2004, 29,325

Peru (0) 0

Colombia (2) 2 *(Grisales 30, Oviedo 42)*

Peru: Ibanez; Rebosio, Jorge Soto, Hidalgo (Farfan 46), Jayo, Palacios (Silva 58), Quinteros (Salas 46), Ciurlizza, Galliquio, Pizarro, Mendoza.
Colombia: Calero; Cordoba I, Yepes, Vargas, Oviedo, Murillo (Viveros 72), Perea L, Ramirez (Viafara 90), Grisales (Patino 78), Bedoya, Angel.
Referee: Rezende (Brazil).

Montevideo, 31 March 2004, 40,000

Uruguay (0) 0

Venezuela (1) 3 *(Urdaneta 18, Gonzalez H 65, Arango 80)*

Uruguay: Munua; Lopez■, Sorondo, Rodriguez D, Liguera, Sosa, Nunez, Recoba, Chevanton (Correa 59), Hornos (Pandiani 46), Forlan (Bueno 72).
Venezuela: Angelucci; Vallenilla, Rey, Cichero, Hernandez, Jimenez, Vera, Paez (Rojas 61), Arango (Gonzalez A 83), Urdaneta (Gonzalez H 61), Rondon.
Referee: Ortube (Bolivia).

La Paz, 1 June 2004, 20,000

Bolivia (1) 2 *(Cristaldo 9, Suarez 72)*

Paraguay (1) 1 *(Cardozo 33)*

Bolivia: Fernandez L; Jauregui, Raldes, Pena■, Gatti Ribeiro (Solis 90), Cristaldo, Sanchez O, Alvarez (Suarez 60), Baldivieso, Gutierrez (Angulo 86), Botero.
Paraguay: Villa; Espinola, Lugo (Cabanas 82), Gamarra, Da Silva, Edgar Gonzalez, Ortiz, Duarte (De Los Santos 74), Enciso, Cardozo, Santa Cruz (Ramirez 63).
Referee: Resende de Freitas (Brazil).

Montevideo, 1 June 2004, 30,000

Uruguay (0) 1 *(Forlan 73)*

Peru (2) 3 *(Solano 12, Pizarro 19, Farfan 62)*

Uruguay: Munua; De Souza, Sorondo■, Lembo, Guigou (Romero 46), Sosa, Garcia, Pacheco (Forlan 46), Nunez, Chevanton, Pandiani (Dario Silva 72).
Peru: Ibanez; Galliquio, Acasiete, Rebosio (Garcia 80), Vilchez, Zegarra, Solano, Jayo, Palacios (Jose Soto 59), Pizarro (Mendoza 46), Farfan.
Referee: Selma (Chile).

San Cristobal, 1 June 2004, 30,000

Venezuela (0) 0

Chile (0) 1 *(Pinilla 84)*

Venezuela: Angelucci; Vallenilla (Gonzalez H 65), Cichero, Rey, Hernandez, Jimenez, Vielma (Gonzalez A 75), Urdaneta (Margiotta 46), Paez, Arango, Rondon.
Chile: Tapia N; Rojas R, Vargas, Olarra, Perez, Maldonado, Melendez, Mark Gonzalez (Mirosevic 59), Pizarro (Valenzuela 79), Galaz (Pinilla 46), Navia.
Referee: Torres (Paraguay).

Belo Horizonte, 2 June 2004, 48,000

Brazil (1) 3 *(Ronaldo 16 (pen), 67 (pen), 90 (pen))*

Argentina (0) 1 *(Sorin 80)*

Brazil: Dida; Cafu, Juan, Roque Junior, Roberto Carlos, Edmilson, Juninho Pernambucano (Julio Baptista 75), Ze Roberto, Kaka (Alex 75), Luis Fabiano, Ronaldo.
Argentina: Cavallero; Quiroga, Samuel, Heinze, Zanetti, Mascherano, Gonzalez L (Aimar 61), Sorin, Delgado (Rosales 36) (Saviola 61), Crespo, Kily Gonzalez.
Referee: Ruiz (Colombia).

Quito, 2 June 2004, 40,000

Ecuador (1) 2 *(Delgado 3, Salas 66)*

Colombia (0) 1 *(Oviedo 56)*

Ecuador: Espinoza J; De la Cruz, Hurtado I, Espinoza G, Ambrossi, Ayovi M (Lastra 87), Tenorio E, Mendez (Aguinaga 65), Chala, Figueroa (Salas 50), Delgado.
Colombia: Calero; Perea L, Yepes, Cordoba I, Bedoya (Ferreira 78), Vargas, Ramirez, Viafara (Viveros 46), Oviedo, Valentierra (Murillo■ 70), Rey.
Referee: Baldassi (Argentina).

Quito, 5 June 2004, 40,000

Ecuador (3) 3 *(Solis 29 (og), Delgado 33, De la Cruz 40)*

Bolivia (0) 2 *(Gutierrez 58, Castillo 75)*

Ecuador: Espinoza J; De la Cruz, Hurtado I, Espinoza G, Reasco, Tenorio E, Obregon (Aguinaga 70), Ambrossi (Ayovi M 80), Chala (Mendez 66), Delgado, Salas.
Bolivia: Fernandez L; Solis (Gatti Ribeiro 46), Sanchez O, Raldes, Jauregui, Alvarez, Angulo (Galindo 46), Suarez (Castillo 67), Baldivieso, Botero, Gutierrez.
Referee: Brand (Venezuela).

Buenos Aires, 6 June 2004, 30,000

Argentina (0) 0

Paraguay (0) 0

Argentina: Abbondanzieri; Ayala, Samuel, Heinze, Gonzalez L (Rosales 69), Mascherano, Sorin, Tevez, Saviola, Crespo, Kily Gonzalez.
Paraguay: Villar; Caniza, Caceres JC, Gamarra, Da Silva, Gavilan (Sarabia 90), Ortiz■, Toledo (Edgar Gonzalez 64), Enciso, Santa Cruz, Cardozo (Ramirez 84).
Referee: Simon (Brazil).

Santiago, 6 June 2004, 65,000

Chile (0) 1 *(Navia 89 (pen))*

Brazil (1) 1 *(Luis Fabiano 16)*

Chile: Tapia N; Rojas R (Alvarez 46), Fuentes, Olarra, Perez, Helo (Galaz 46), Melendez, Maldonado, Mark Gonzalez (Mirosevic 56), Pizarro, Navia.
Brazil: Dida; Cafu, Roberto Carlos, Juninho Pernambucano, Juan, Roque Junior, Edmilson, Kaka (Julio Baptista 72), Ronaldo, Luis Fabiano, Edu.
Referee: Elizondo (Argentina).

Barranquilla, 6 June 2004, 20,000

Colombia (3) 5 *(Pacheco 18, 32, Moreno 20, Restrepo 81, Herrera 86)*

Uruguay (0) 0

Colombia: Calero; Palacios, Perea L, Yepes, Bedoya, Ramirez, Restrepo, Oviedo (Vargas 74), Pacheco (Ferreira 84), Moreno (Arriaga 74), Herrera.
Uruguay: Munua; Gonzalez, Lembo, De Souza (Lago 64), Romero (De Los Santos 46), Romero, Pablo Garcia, Delgado, Canobbio (Forlan 46), Recoba, Chevanton.
Referee: Carlos (Paraguay).

Lima, 6 June 2004, 45,000

Peru (0) 0

Venezuela (0) 0

Peru: Ibanez; Jorge Soto, Rebosio, Acasiete, Hidalgo (Vilchez 67), Jayo, Zegarra, Solano, Palacios (Orejuela 67), Farfan, Mendoza (Silva 79).
Venezuela: Angelucci; Vallenilla, Cichero, Rey, Hernandez, Mea Vitali, Jimenez, Urdaneta (Margiotta 79), Paez (Gonzalez H 66), Arango, Rondon (Moran 61).
Referee: Larrionda (Uruguay).

Lima, 4 September 2004, 60,000

Peru (0) 1 *(Jorge Soto 62)*

Argentina (1) 3 *(Rosales 14, Coloccini 66, Sorin 90)*

Peru: Ibanez; Salas, Acasiete, Galliquio, Vilchez, Jayo, Solano, Palacios (Olcese 76), Jorge Soto (Garcia 77), Mendoza, Farfan.
Argentina: Abbondanzieri; Coloccini, Heinze, Milito G, Zanetti, Mascherano, Kily Gonzalez■, D'Alessandro (Milito D 64), Delgado (Sorin 70), Tevez (Medina 83), Rosales.
Referee: Simon (Brazil).

Sao Paulo, 5 September 2004, 72,000

Brazil (3) 3 *(Ronaldo 1, Ronaldinho 13 (pen), Adriano 44)*

Bolivia (0) 1 *(Cristaldo 48)*

Brazil: Julio Cesar; Belletti, Edmilson, Roque Junior, Roberto Carlos, Juninho Pernambucano (Renato 60), Gilberto Silva, Edu (Robinho 72), Ronaldinho (Alex 60), Ronaldo, Adriano.
Bolivia: Fernandez L; Ribeiro (Arena 46), Alvarez, Pena, Raldes, Cristaldo, Sanchez O, Colque (Tufino 46), Gutierrez (Coimbra 76), Pizarro, Botero.
Referee: Baldassi (Argentina).

Santiago, 5 September 2004, 63,000

Chile (0) 0

Colombia (0) 0

Chile: Tapia N; Villaroel, Fuentes, Olarra, Perez■, Maldonado■, Acuna, Mirosevic (Tello 60), Pizarro (Valenzuela 60), Navia (Salas 46), Pinilla.
Colombia: Calero; Perea L, Cordoba I, Yepes, Bedoya, Vargas, Viafara■, Oviedo (Perea E 87), Hernandez (Patino■ 56), Castillo, Preciado (Murillo 65).
Referee: Mendonca (Brazil).

Asuncion, 5 September 2004, 45,000

Paraguay (0) 1 *(Gamarra 53)*

Venezuela (0) 0

Paraguay: Villar; Sarabia, Caceres JC, Gamarra (Mansur 84), Da Silva, Paredes, Enciso, Gavilan (Barreto 78), Quevas, Cardozo (Ramirez 58), Santa Cruz.
Venezuela: Angelucci; Vallenilla, Rey, Cichero, Rojas, Jimenez, Vera, Paez (Rondon 68), Urdaneta (Gonzalez H 71), Arango, Castellin (Moreno 77).
Referee: Mendez (Uruguay).

Montevideo, 5 September 2004, 40,000

Uruguay (0) 1 *(Bueno 58)*

Ecuador (0) 0

Uruguay: Viera; Bizera, Montero, Rodriguez D, Diogo, Sosa, Delgado, Recoba (Perez 78), Rodriguez C (Estoyanoff 57), Dario Silva (Sanchez 25), Bueno.
Ecuador: Villafuerte; De la Cruz, Hurtado I, Espinoza, Reasco, Ayovi M, Soledispa (Quinonez 70), Mendez, Ayovi W (Valencia 75), Baldeon (Delgado 60), Tenorio C.
Referee: Hidalgo (Peru).

Buenos Aires, 9 October 2004, 60,000

Argentina (3) 4 *(Gonzalez L 6, Figueroa 33, 54, Zanetti 45)*

Uruguay (0) 2 *(Rodriguez C 63, Chevanton 86 (pen))*

Argentina: Abbondanzieri; Coloccini, Gonzalez L (Rodriguez M 68), Samuel, Heinze, Zanetti, Cambiasso, Saviola, Figueroa (Insua 81), Riquelme, Sorin.
Uruguay: Viera; Bizera (Lago 57), Lembo, Rodriguez D, Diogo, Sosa, Diego Perez (Garcia 55), Delgado, Rodriguez C, Dario Silva (Forlan 55), Chevanton.
Referee: Mendonca (Brazil).

La Paz, 9 October 2004, 30,000

Bolivia (0) 1 *(Botero 56)*

Peru (0) 0

Bolivia: Fernandez L; Arana, Sanchez O, Raldes, Ribeiro■, Garcia R, Cristaldo, Sanchez E (Tufino 86), Colque, Botero, Gutierrez (Galindo 90).
Peru: Ibanez; Rodriguez, Galliquio (La Rosa 72), Acasiete, Salas, Jorge Soto, Jayo, Garcia (Palacios 56), Ciurlizza (Carty 64), Guerrero, Farfan.
Referee: Reynoso (Ecuador).

Baranquilla, 9 October 2004, 25,000

Colombia (1) 1 *(Grisales 17)*

Paraguay (0) 1 *(Torres 78)*

Colombia: Calero; Perea L, Cordoba I, Yepes, Bedoya, Diaz (Rodriguez 81), Restrepo, Oviedo, Grisales (Moreno 67), Pacheco, Angel.
Paraguay: Villar; Caniza, Caceres JC, Sarabia, Da Silva, Ortiz (Gavilan 46), Enciso, Paredes, Torres (Monges 81), Bareiro (Cuevas 60), Cardozo.
Referee: Elizondo (Argentina).

Maracaibo, 9 October 2004, 35,000

Venezuela (0) 2 *(Moran 80, 90)*

Brazil (2) 5 *(Kaka 6, 35, Ronaldo 49, 51, Adriano 75)*

Venezuela: Angelucci; Vallenilla, Rey, Cichero, Hernandez (Vielma 55), Vera (Gonzalez C 68), Jimenez, Arango, Vargas, Margiotta (Gonzalez H 46), Moran.
Brazil: Dida; Cafu, Roberto Carlos, Juninho Pernambucano (Edu 62), Roque Junior, Juan, Renato, Ze Roberto, Ronaldo (Alex 72), Ronaldinho, Kaka (Adriano 68).
Referee: Chandia (Chile).

Quito, 10 October 2004, 26,000

Ecuador (0) 2 *(Kaviedes 59, Mendez 64)*

Chile (0) 0

Ecuador: Villafuerte; De la Cruz, Hurtado I, Espinoza G, Guerron, Tenorio E, Ayovi M, Ayovi W (Salas 46), Mendez, Kaviedes (Fernandez 88), Ordonez (Ambrossi 61).
Chile: Tapia N; Rojas R, Fuentes, Olarra, Contreras, Martel (Beausejour 46), Gonzalez L, Melendez, Valenzuela (Mirosevic 58), Salas, Galaz (Quinteros 76).
Referee: Ortube (Bolivia).

La Paz, 12 October 2004, 28,000

Bolivia (0) 0

Uruguay (0) 0

Bolivia: Fernandez L; Carballo (Colque 65), Arana, Raldes, Sanchez O, Garcia (Cabrera 46), Cristaldo, Sanchez E, Alvarez (Galindo 80), Gutierrez, Botero.
Uruguay: Viera; Diogo, Rodriguez G, Pouso■, Lago, Rodriguez D, Varela, Pablo Garcia, Morales R (Chevanton 78), Sanchez (Sosa 76), Regueiro (Parodi 73).
Referee: De Freitas (Brazil).

Maceio, 13 October 2004, 30,000

Brazil (0) 0

Colombia (0) 0

Brazil: Dida; Cafu, Roberto Carlos, Magrao (Elano 59), Roque Junior, Juan, Renato, Ze Roberto (Edu 84), Ronaldo, Ronaldinho, Alex (Adriano 58).
Colombia: Calero; Perea L, Cordoba I, Yepes, Bedoya, Grisales (Leal 87), Restrepo, Diaz, Oviedo (Moreno 86), Pacheco (Viveros 77), Angel.
Referee: Larrionda (Uruguay).

Santiago, 13 October 2004, 45,000

Chile (0) 0

Argentina (0) 0

Chile: Tapia N; Rojas R (Olarra 46), Fuentes, Vargas, Contreras, Alvarez, Melendez (Mirosevic 60), Valenzuela, Valdivia (Quinteros 72), Salas, Navia.
Argentina: Abbondanzieri; Coloccini, Samuel, Heinze, Zanetti, Cambiasso, Riquelme, Sorin, Gonzalez L (Mascherano 46), Saviola (D'Alessandro 76), Figueroa (Tevez 63).
Referee: Amarilla (Paraguay).

Asuncion, 13 October 2004, 30,000

Paraguay (1) 1 *(Paredes 29)*

Peru (0) 1 *(Solano 74 (pen))*

Paraguay: Villar; Caniza, Caceres JC, Manzur, Da Silva, Enciso, Paredes, Gavilan (Bareiro 83), Torres (Cuevas 53), Haedo, Cardozo (Monges 73).
Peru: Ibanez; Galliquio (Ciurlizza 46), Rebosio, Acasiete, Vargas, Solano, Jayo, Palacios, Jorge Soto, Mendoza (Guerrero 67), Farfan.
Referee: Ruiz (Colombia).

San Cristobal, 14 October 2004, 20,000

Venezuela (1) 3 *(Urdaneta 21 (pen), Moran 73, 81)*

Ecuador (1) 1 *(Ayovi M 42 (pen))*

Venezuela: Dudamel; Vallenilla (Gonzalez H 66), Rey, Cichero, Rojas, Vera, Jimenez (Paez 64), Arango, Urdaneta, Rondon (Garcia 61), Moran.
Ecuador: Villafuerte; Reasco, Hurtado I, Espinoza, Guerron, Tenorio E, Ayovi M, Ambrossi, Mendez, Kaviedes, Salas (Baldeon 72).
Referee: Lecca (Peru).

Buenos Aires, 17 November 2004, 30,000

Argentina (2) 3 *(Rey 3 (og), Riquelme 46, Saviola 65)*

Venezuela (1) 2 *(Moran 31, Vielma 72)*

Argentina: Abbondanzieri; Rodriguez G, Sorin, Zanetti, Mascherano, Milito G, Riquelme, Figueroa, Solari (Gonzalez L 65), Cambiasso (Placente 79), Delgado (Saviola 58).
Venezuela: Dudamel; Vallenilla, Rey, Cichero, Vera, Paez (Vielma 70), Jimenez (Casseres 77), Moran, Rojas, Arango, Hernandez (Urdaneta 52).
Referee: Hidalgo (Peru).

Barranquilla, 17 November 2004, 25,000

Colombia (1) 1 *(Yepes 18)*

Bolivia (0) 0

Colombia: Calero; Cordoba I, Yepes, Viveros, Oviedo (Perez 62), Angel, Pacheco (Hernandez 76), Murillo (Ferreira 70), Perea L, Grisales, Restrepo.
Bolivia: Fernandez L; Pena (Arce 80), Jauregui, Alvarez, Cristaldo, Tufino (Vaca Diez 76), Coimbra (Galindo 46), Gutierrez, Raldes, Botero, Arana.
Referee: Torres (Paraguay).

Quito, 17 November 2004, 38,308

Ecuador (0) 1 *(Mendez 77)*

Brazil (0) 0

Ecuador: Villafuerte; Hurtado I, De La Cruz, Mendez, Kaviedes (Ayovi W 75), Delgado (Reasco 90), Ambrosi, Urrutia (Salas 46), Ayovi M, Espinoza G, Tenorio E.
Brazil: Dida; Cafu, Juan, Roque Junior, Renato, Roberto Carlos, Juninho Pernambucano (Dudu 74), Kaka (Adriano 81), Ronaldo, Ronaldinho, Kleberson (Ricardinho 64).
Referee: Ruiz (Colombia).

Lima, 17 November 2004, 39,752

Peru (0) 2 *(Farfan 56, Guerrero 85)*

Chile (0) 1 *(Gonzalez S 90)*

Peru: Ibanez; Acasiete■, Jorge Soto, Vargas, Solano, Jayo, Palacios, Pizarro (Guerrero 71), Farfan, Ciurlizza (Zegarra 37) (Villalta 62), Rodriguez.
Chile: Tapia N; Alvarez, Maldonado (Valdivia 75), Contreras, Valenzuela (Gonzalez L 46), Pizarro, Pinilla, Melendez■, Olarra (Gonzalez S 62), Mark Gonzalez, Fuentes.
Referee: Baldassi (Argentina).

Montevideo, 17 November 2004, 35,000

Uruguay (0) 1 *(Montero 78)*

Paraguay (0) 0

Uruguay: Viera; Lugano, Rodriguez G, Montero, Garcia, Lopez, Varela (Estoyanoff 67), Dario Silva (Morales 46), Recoba (Sanchez 70), Delgado, Chevanton.
Paraguay: Villar; Caceres JC, Gamarra, Monges (Gavilan 80), Barreto (Bareiro 80), Paredes, Da Silva, Ortiz, Cardozo, Caniza, Cuevas (Ramirez 68).
Referee: Simon (Brazil).

La Paz, 26 March 2005, 35,000

Bolivia (0) 1 *(Castillo 49)*

Argentina (0) 2 *(Figueroa 58, Galletti 63)*

Bolivia: Fernandez L; Colque (Pachi 46), Sanchez O, Raldes, Alvarez L, Angulo (Cabrera 68), Pizarro, Galindo (Garcia 86), Sanchez E, Castillo, Botero.
Argentina: Abbondanzieri; Cufre, Burdisso, Milito G, Rodriguez C, Scaloni, Cambiasso, Duscher, Rodriguez M (Porzini 64), Galletti (Palacio 84), Figueroa (Zarate 73).
Referee: Larrionda (Uruguay).

Santiago, 26 March 2005, 45,000

Chile (0) 1 *(Mirosevic 47)*

Uruguay (1) 1 *(Requeiro 4)*

Chile: Tapia N; Fuentes, Rojas R, Conteras (Valdivia 46), Alvarez, Maldonado, Pizarro, Mark Gonzalez (Valenzuela 82), Mirosevic (Gonzalez S 82), Salas, Pinilla.
Uruguay: Viera; Lopez, Lugano, Monero, Rodriguez D, Diogo, Olivera (Sosa 59), Pablo Garcia, Requeiro (Sanchez 81), Forlan, Zalayeta (Morales 69).
Referee: Ruiz (Colombia).

Maracaibo, 26 March 2005, 20,000

Venezuela (0) 0

Colombia (0) 0

Venezuela: Dudamel; Gonzalez H, Rey, Cichero, Hernandez, Vielma, Jimenez, Maldonado, Urdaneta (Gonzalez A 65), Castellin (Gonzalez C 56), Margiotta (Noriega 74).
Colombia: Calero; Orozco, Cordoba I, Yepes, Bedoya, Restrepo, Ramirez (Vargas 72), Ferreira, Hernandez (Pacheco 73), Castillo (Herrera 86), Perea E.
Referee: Simon (Brazil).

Goiania, 27 March 2005, 52,000

Brazil (0) 1 *(Kaka 74)*

Peru (0) 0

Brazil: Dida; Cafu, Roberto Carlos, Juninho Pernambucano (Robinho 46), Lucio, Juan, Emerson, Kaka (Renato 83), Ronaldo, Ronaldinho, Ze Roberto.
Peru: Ibanez; Jorge Soto, Rebosio, Rodriguez (Guadalupe 73), Vilchez, Jayo, Zegarra, Solano (Cominges 68), Palacios (Olcese 46), Farfan, Pizarro.
Referee: Amarilla (Paraguay).

Quito, 27 March 2005, 25,000

Ecuador (2) 5 *(Valencia 32, 49, Mendez 45, 47, Marlon Ayovi M 77 (pen))*

Paraguay (2) 2 *(Cardozo 9 (pen), Cabanas 14)*

Ecuador: Villafuerte; De la Cruz, Ambrossi, Espinoza, Hurtado I, Ayovi M, Tenorio E (Caicedo 78), Mendez, Valencia, Tenorio O (Salas 57), Delgado (Kaviedes 78).
Paraguay: Villar; Sarabia, Gamarra, Da Silva, Caniza, Gavilan (Cuevas 52), Ortiz, Bonet, Monges (Barreto 52), Cabanas, Cardozo.
Referee: Mendez (Uruguay).

La Paz, 29 March 2005, 15,000

Bolivia (2) 3 *(Cichero 2 (og), Castillo 25, Vaca J 83)*

Venezuela (0) 1 *(Maldonado 71)*

Bolivia: Fernandez L; Jauregui, Raldes, Sanchez O, Alvarez, Pizarro, Garcia R (Vaca J 19), Galindo, Sanchez E (Pachi 80), Botero, Castillo.
Venezuela: Dudamel; De Ornelas (Rondon 70), Rey, Cichero (Noriega 46), Hernandez, Fuenmayor, Gonzalez A, Gonzalez H, Vera, Urdaneta (Gonzalez C 57), Maldonado.
Referee: Lecca (Peru).

Buenos Aires, 30 March 2005, 44,000

Argentina (0) 1 *(Crespo 65)*

Colombia (0) 0

Argentina: Abbondanzieri; Zanetti, Ayala, Heinze, Sorin, Gonzalez L, Mascherano (Galletti 55), Cambiasso, Riquelme, Saviola (Palcente 79), Crespo.
Colombia: Calero; Orozco, Cordoba I, Yepes, Bedoya, Viafara, Restrepo (Pacheco 79), Vargas■, Oviedo, Hernandez (Viveros 46), Perea E (Castillo 68).
Referee: Amarilla (Paraguay).

Asuncion, 30 March 2005, 35,000

Paraguay (1) 2 *(Morinigo 37, Cardozo 59)*

Chile (0) 1 *(Fuentes 72)*

Paraguay: Villar; Bonet, Caceres JC, Gamarra, Da Silva, Nunez, Paredes (Gavilan 82), Ortiz, Morinigo (Barreto 60), Cabanas, Cardozo (Valdez 71).
Chile: Tapia N; Rojas R, Fuentes, Olarra, Perez (Alvarez 46), Melendez (Pizarro 53), Maldonado, Mirosevic (Gonzalez S 64), Mark Gonzalez, Salas, Pinilla.
Referee: Elizondo (Argentina).

Lima, 30 March 2005, 45,000

Peru (1) 2 *(Guerrero 1, Farfan 58)*

Ecuador (2) 2 *(De la Cruz 3, Valencia 43)*

Peru: Ibanez; Jorge Soto (Salas 60), Rebosio, Acasiete, Vargas, Jayo, Solano (Mendoza 84), Zegarra (Palacios 60), Farfan, Pizarro, Guerrero.
Ecuador: Villafuerte; De la Cruz, Espinoza G, Hurtado I, Ambrossi, Ayovi M (Caicado 71), Tenorio E, Valencia, Mendez (Ayovi W 85), Baldeon (Salas 46), Delgado.
Referee: Chandia (Chile).

Montevideo, 30 March 2005, 50,000

Uruguay (0) 1 *(Forlan 48)*

Brazil (0) 1 *(Emerson 68)*

Uruguay: Viera; Lopez, Lugano, Montero, Rodriguez D, Olivera (Chevanton 72), Pablo Garcia, Diogo (De Los Santos 86), Requeiro (Delgado 58), Forlan, Zalayeta.
Brazil: Dida; Cafu, Roberto Carlos, Ricardo Oliveira (Robinho 63), Lucio, Luisao, Emerson, Kaka, Ronaldo, Ronaldinho, Ze Roberto (Renato 69).
Referee: Baldassi (Argentina).

Santiago, 4 June 2005, 35,000

Chile (2) 3 *(Fuentes 7, 35, Salas 69)*

Bolivia (0) 1 *(Castillo 85 (pen))*

Chile: Tapia N; Gonzalez S■, Fuentes, Rojas R, Villarroel, Rojas F, Maldonado, Pizarro, Melendez (Acuna 13), Jimenez (Tello 76), Salas (Galaz 75).
Bolivia: Fernandez L; Alvarez, Raldes, Arana, Castillo, Justiniano, Gutierrez, Coimbra, Pachi (Arce 46), Jauregui (Parada 81), Garcia (Vaca J 35).
Referee: Rezende (Brazil).

Barranquilla, 4 June 2005, 25,000

Colombia (1) 5 *(Rey 29, Soto E 56, Angel 59, Restrepo 76, Perea E 78)*

Peru (0) 0

Colombia: Mondragon; Palacio, Perea L, Yepes (Mendoza 80), Bedoya, Viafara, Restrepo, Soto E, Moreno, Angel (Perea E 65), Rey (Arzuaga 72).
Peru: Flores; Solano, Acasiete, Rebosio, Vilches (Guerrero 46), Jayo■, Juan Vargas, La Rosa, Palacios (Cominges 64), Farfan (Mendoza 64), Pizarro.
Referee: Torres (Paraguay).

Quito, 4 June 2005, 37,500

Ecuador (0) 2 *(Lara 53, Delgado 88)*

Argentina (0) 0

Ecuador: Villafuerte; Ambrossi, Espinoza G, Hurtado I, De la Cruz, Ayovi M, Tenorio E, Delgado, Valencia (Tenorio C 83), Gomez (Lara 46), Reasco (Quiroz 76).
Argentina: Franco; Zanetti, Coloccini, Samuel, Milito G (Figueroa 68), Duscher (Tevez 31), Cambiasso■, Aimar (D'Alessandro 74), Kily Gonzalez, Galletti, Maxi Rodriguez.
Referee: Selman (Chile).

Maracaibo, 4 June 2005, 30,000

Venezuela (0) 1 *(Maldonado 73)*

Uruguay (1) 1 *(Forlan 2)*

Venezuela: Dudamel; Gonzalez H, Rojas J, Rey, Cichero, Vera, Arango, Vielma (Urdaneta 38), Paez (Casseres 63), Moran, Maldonado.
Uruguay: Viera; Diogo■, Lopez, Lugano, Montero, Rodriguez D (De Los Santos 62), Olivera, Sosa, Requeiro (Perez 41), Forlan (Chevanton 76), Zalayeta.
Referee: Brazenas (Argentina).

Porto Alegre, 5 June 2005, 55,000

Brazil (2) 4 *(Ronaldinho 33 (pen), 42 (pen), Ze Roberto 71, Robinho 83)*

Paraguay (0) 1 *(Santa Cruz 73)*

Brazil: Dida; Belletti, Lucio■, Roque Junior, Roberto Carlos, Emerson (Gilberto Silva 76), Ze Roberto, Kaka, Ronaldinho, Robinho (Juan 84), Adriano (Ricardo Oliveira 76).
Paraguay: Villa; Caniza, Gamarra, Manzur, Da Silva, Bonet (Barreto 46), Ortiz, Paredes, Torres, Santa Cruz, Cabanas (Cuevas 64).
Referee: Broquetas (Uruguay).

Lima, 7 June 2005, 28,000

Peru (0) 0

Uruguay (0) 0

Peru: Flores; Cominges (Palacios 62), Rebosio, Mendoza, Vilchez, La Rosa (Solano 86), Villalta, Guadelupe, Farfan, Guerrero, Pizarro.
Uruguay: Viera; Rodriguez G, Lopez (Perez 31), Lugano, Rodriguez D, Oliveira, Pablo Garcia, Delgado, Chevanton (Estoyanoff 71), Zalayeta (Morales 83), Forlan.
Referee: Baldassi (Argentina).

Buenos Aires, 8 June 2005, 60,000

Argentina (3) 3 *(Crespo 4, 40, Riquelme 18)*

Brazil (0) 1 *(Roberto Carlos 71)*

Argentina: Abbondanzieri; Coloccini, Ayala, Heinze, Gonzalez L (Zanetti 70), Mascherano, Riquelme, Sorin, Kily Gonzalez, Saviola (Tevez 82), Crespo.
Brazil: Dida; Cafu, Roberto Carlos, Emerson, Juan, Roque Junior, Ronaldinho, Kaka, Adriano, Robinho (Renato 61), Ze Roberto.
Referee: Mendez (Uruguay).

Santiago, 8 June 2005, 35,000

Chile (1) 2 *(Jimenez 30, 59)*

Venezuela (0) 1 *(Moran 82)*

Chile: Tapia N; Fuentes, Rojas R, Contreras, Villarroel, Acuna, Maldonado, Rojas F, Pizarro (Gonzalez J 89), Jimenez (Valdivia 81), Galaz (Villanueva 62).
Venezuela: Dudamel; De Ornela (Vallenilla 46), Rey, Cichero, Hernandez, Jimenez, Gonzalez A (Perez 71), Urdaneta, Arango, Casseres (Gonzalez C 57), Moran.
Referee: Torres (Paraguay).

Barranquilla, 8 June 2005, 35,000

Colombia (2) 3 *(Moreno 5, 8, Arzuaga 70)*

Ecuador (0) 0

Colombia: Mondragon; Palacio, Yepes, Perea L, Benitez, Viafara, Restrepo, Soto E (Vargas 36), Rey (Hurtado 66), Moreno (Arzuaga 68), Angel.
Ecuador: Villafuerte; De la Cruz, Hurtado I, Espinoza G, Reasco, Quiroz, Tenorio C, Ayovi M (Caicedo 46), Valencia (Ayovi W 54), Ambrossi (Lara 60), Delgado.
Referee: Simon (Brazil).

Asuncion, 8 June 2005, 45,000

Paraguay (2) 4 *(Gamarra 17, Santa Cruz 45, Caceres JC 54, Nunez 68)*

Bolivia (1) 1 *(Galindo 30)*

Paraguay: Villar; Caceres JD, Caceres JC, Gamarra, Nunez, Ortiz, Paredes, Barreto (Gavilan 75), Cardozo (Salcedo 64), Santa Cruz, Cabanas (Cuevas 77).
Bolivia: Galerza; Alvarez, Raldes, Flores, Galindo, Jauregui, Centeno, Gutierrez L, Mojica (Vaca 78), Castillo (Arce 65), Parada (Coimbra 46).
Referee: Brand (Venezuela).

La Paz, 3 September 2005, 25,000

Bolivia (1) 1 *(Vaca D 41)*

Ecuador (1) 2 *(Delgado 7, 49)*

Bolivia: Arias; Jauregui, Vaca D, Raldes, Gomez, Alvarez, Galindo, Mendez (Lider Paz 53), Pachi (Vaca J 53), Botero, Flores (Arce 68).
Ecuador: Mora; De la Cruz, Hurtado I, Espinoza, Reasco (Lara 77), Ayovi M (Castillo 89), Valencia (Salas 46), Tenorio E, Ambrossi, Mendez, Delgado.
Referee: Baldassi (Argentina).

Asuncion, 3 September 2005, 40,000

Paraguay (1) 1 *(Santa Cruz 15)*

Argentina (0) 0

Paraguay: Villar; Caniza, Caceres JC, Gamarra, Nunez, Barreto, Acuna, Paredes, Dos Santos (Cuevas 88), Haedo Valdez, Santa Cruz (Cabanas 46).
Argentina: Abbondanzieri; Coloccini, Ayala, Heinze■, Zabaleta, Gonzalez L, Riquelme (D'Alessandro 72), Cambiasso, Sorin, Delgado (Messi 81), Farias.
Referee: Simon (Brazil).

Maracaibo, 3 September 2005, 15,000

Venezuela (1) 4 *(Maldonado 17, Arango 60, Torrealba 73, 80)*

Peru (0) 1 *(Farfan 63)*

Venezuela: Angelucci; Gonzalez H, Vielma, Cichero, Rojas J, Vera, Urdaneta, Paez, Arango (Jimenez 81), Moran (Gonzalez A 56), Maldonado (Torrealba 71).
Peru: Delgado; Guadalupe, Villalta, La Rosa■, Vilchez (Alva Niezen 46), Vargas, Perez, Huaman, Cominges (Mostto 76), Guerrero, Farfan.
Referee: Rezende (Bolivia).

Brasilia, 4 September 2005, 40,000

Brazil (4) 5 *(Juan 11, Robinho 21, Adriano 26, 29, 90)*

Chile (0) 0

Brazil: Dida; Cafu, Roberto Carlos (Juninho Pernambucano 65), Ze Roberto, Juan, Lucio, Emerson (Gilberto Silva 58), Ronaldo (Ricardinho 46), Adriano, Kaka, Robinho.
Chile: Tapia N; Rojas R, Fuentes, Contreras (Acuna 58), Alvarez, Melendez, Maldonado, Tello (Perez 58), Pizarro, Rubio, Pinilla (Jimenez 58).
Referee: Amarilla (Paraguay).

Montevideo, 4 September 2005, 50,000

Uruguay (1) 3 *(Zalayeta 42, 50, 85)*

Colombia (0) 2 *(Soto E 78, Angel 81)*

Uruguay: Carini; Varela (Sanchez 82), Montero, Diego Lopez, Rodriguez G, Perez, Pablo Garcia, Recoba (Estoyanoff 78), Forlan, Morales (Sosa■ 69), Zalayeta.
Colombia: Calero; Orozco, Perea L, Cordoba I, Bedoya (Oviedo 89), Viafara (Vargas 59), Rey (Arzuaga 81), Restrepo, Soto E, Moreno, Angel.
Referee: Elizondo (Argentina).

Barranquilla, 8 October 2005, 15,000

Colombia (1) 1 *(Rey 24)*

Chile (0) 1 *(Rojas R 63)*

Colombia: Calero; Palacio, Cordoba I, Yepes, Bedoya, Restrepo, Soto E, Vargas (Ferreira 72), Pacheco (Patino 62), Rey (Arzuaga 67), Angel.
Chile: Bravo; Rojas R, Fuentes, Contreras (Navia 62), Villarroel (Mirosevic 62), Maldonado, Acuna, Perez, Pizarro, Jimenez, Pinilla (Valdivia 81).
Referee: Souza (Brazil).

Quito, 8 October 2005, 44,000

Ecuador (0) 0

Uruguay (0) 0

Ecuador: Mora; De la Cruz, Hurtado I, Espinoza, Ambrossi, Tenorio E, Ayovi M, Valencia (Lara 59), Mendez, Borja (Mina 76), Delgado.
Uruguay: Carini; Diego Lopez, Lugano, Rodriguez G, Rodriguez D, Pouso, Pablo Garcia, Varela, Regueiro (Nunez 69), Recoba (Forlan 82), Morales (Dario Silva 75).
Referee: Rezende (Brazil).

Maracaibo, 8 October 2005, 25,000

Venezuela (0) 0

Paraguay (0) 1 *(Haedo Valdez 65)*

Venezuela: Angelucci; Gonzalez H, Rey, Cichero, Rojas J, Vera, Arango, Paez, Urdaneta (Gonzalez A 69), Maldonado (Moreno 75), Moran (Torrealba 55).
Paraguay: Gomez; Caniza, Gamarra, Caceres JD, Nunez, Acuna, Gavilan (Da Silva 87), Fatecha, Dos Santos (Montiel 77), Santa Cruz, Haedo Valdez (Cuevas 88).
Referee: Elizondo (Argentina).

Buenos Aires, 9 October 2005, 35,000

Argentina (0) 2 *(Riquelme 81, Guadalupe 90 (og))*

Peru (0) 0

Argentina: Abbondanzieri; Coloccini, Ayala, Milito, Sorin, Gonzalez L, Battaglia, Kily Gonzalez (Tevez 58), Riquelme (Santana 84), Messi, Crespo.
Peru: Butron■; Gallquio (Ross 89), Rodriguez, Guadalupe, Hidalgo, Jorge Soto, Ciurliza, Torres, Garcia (Delgado 79), Farfan (Cominges 82), Guerrero.
Referee: Torres (Paraguay).

La Paz, 9 October 2005, 30,000

Bolivia (0) 1 *(Castillo 49)*

Brazil (1) 1 *(Juninho Pernambucano 25)*

Bolivia: Arias; Jauregui, Vaca D, Raldes, Hoyos (Pachi 46), Angulo, Cristaldo, Baldivieso, Galindo, Botero (Lider Paz 77), Gutierrez (Castillo 46).
Brazil: Julio Cesar; Cicinho, Luisao, Roque Junior, Gilberto (Gustavo Nery 58), Gilberto Silva, Renato (Alex 58), Juninho Pernambucano (Julio Baptista 80), Ricardinho, Adriano, Robinho.
Referee: Larrionda (Uruguay).

Belem, 12 October 2005, 45,000

Brazil (1) 3 *(Adriano 28, Ronaldo 51, Roberto Carlos 62)*

Venezuela (0) 0

Brazil: Dida; Cafu, Roberto Carlos, Emerson, Juan, Lucio, Ze Roberto (Juninho Pernambucano 68), Kaka, Adriano (Robinho 64), Ronaldo, Ronaldinho (Alex 69).
Venezuela: Dudamel; Vallenilla, Rey, Cichero, Hernandez, Jimenez, Vielma, Urdaneta (Rojas 60), Paez (Gonzalez H 50), Arango, Maldonado (Torrealba 70).
Referee: Baldassi (Argentina).

Santiago, 12 October 2005, 40,000

Chile (0) 0

Ecuador (0) 0

Chile: Bravo; Perez, Rojas R, Fuentes, Villarroel (Mirosevic 63), Jimenez (Fernandez 70), Maldonado, Pizarro, Valdivia (Suazo 55), Navia, Melendez.
Ecuador: Villafuerte; Cortez (De la Cruz 60), Reasco, Espinoza, Lara (Ambrossi 70), Borja (Mina 84), Saritama, Tenorio E, Caicedo, Guagua, Castillo.
Referee: Elizondo (Argentina).

Asuncion, 12 October 2005, 35,000

Paraguay (0) 0

Colombia (1) 1 *(Rey 7)*

Paraguay: Villa; Montiel, Manzur, Caceres JC, Caniza, Acuna, Fatecha, Cabanas (Lopez 63), Dos Santos (Cardozo 75), Cuevas, Nunez (Caceres JD 60).
Colombia: Mondragon; Perea L, Cordoba I, Yepes, Passo, Viafara, Restrepo, Rey (Renteria 79), Soto E, Angel (Vanegas 90), Moreno (Vargas 74).
Referee: Rezende (Brazil).

Tacna, 12 October 2005, 20,000

Peru (3) 4 *(Vassallo 10, Acasiete 38, Farfan 45, 82)*

Bolivia (0) 1 *(Gutierrez 66)*

Peru: Delgado; Hidalgo, Jorge Soto, Guadalupe, Acasiete, Torres, Galliquio (Mendoza 46), Ciurlizza■, Cominges (Garcia 83), Farfan, Vassallo (Ross 60).
Bolivia: Arias; Galindo (Vaca J 83), Jauregui, Vaca D, Raldes, Pachi, Angulo, Gomez (Lider Paz 60), Baldivieso (Gutierrez■ 46), Castillo, Botero.

Montevideo, 12 October 2005, 70,000

Uruguay (0) 1 *(Recoba 46)*

Argentina (0) 0

Uruguay: Carini; Diogo, Lugano, Montero, Rodriguez D, Varela, Pablo Garcia, Recoba (Estoyanoff 70), Forlan (Diego Lopez 89), Morales, Zalayeta (Pouso 61).
Argentina: Abbondanzieri; Ponzio, Ayala, Samuel, Sorin, Gonzalez L (Messi 79), Battaglia, Riquelme, Kily Gonzalez (Aimar 61), Tevez, Crespo (Delgado 61).
Referee: Souza (Brazil).

South America Final table

	P	*W*	*D*	*L*	*F*	*A*	*Pts*
Brazil	18	9	7	2	35	17	34
Argentina	18	10	4	4	29	17	34
Ecuador	18	8	4	6	23	19	28
Paraguay	18	8	4	6	23	23	28
Uruguay	18	6	7	5	23	28	25
Colombia	18	6	6	6	24	16	24
Chile	18	5	7	6	18	22	22
Peru	18	4	6	8	20	28	18
Venezuela	18	5	3	10	20	28	18
Bolivia	18	4	2	12	20	37	14

Top four qualify for finals; Uruguay played Australia (Oceania winner) for place in finals.

QUALIFYING RESULTS – ASIA

FIRST STAGE

Group 1
Jordan 1, Qatar 0; Laos 0, Iran 7; Iran 3, Qatar 1; Jordan 5, Laos 0; Iran 0, Jordan 1; Qatar 5, Laos 0; Jordan 0, Iran 2; Laos 1, Qatar 6; Laos 2, Jordan 3; Qatar 2, Iran 3.

Group 2
Palestine 1, Iraq 1; Taiwan 0, Uzbekistan 1; Palestine 8, Taiwan 0; Uzbekistan 1, Iraq 1; Uzbekistan 3, Palestine 0; Iraq 6, Taiwan 1; Palestine 0, Uzbekistan 3; Taiwan 1, Iraq 4; Iraq 1, Uzbekistan 2; Taiwan 0, Palestine 1.

Group 3
India 1, Singapore 0; Japan 1, Oman 0; India 1, Oman 5; Singapore 1, Japan 2; Japan 7, India 0; Oman 7, Singapore 0; India 0, Japan 4; Singapore 0, Oman 2; Oman 0, Japan 1; Singapore 2, India 0.

Group 4
China 1, Kuwait 0; Malaysia 1, Hong Kong 3; Hong Kong 0, China 1; Malaysia 0, Kuwait 2; China 4, Malaysia 0; Kuwait 4, Hong Kong 0; Hong Kong 0, Kuwait 2; Malaysia 0, China 1; Hong Kong 2, Malaysia 0; Kuwait 1, China 0.

Group 5
UAE 1, Thailand 0; Yemen 1, North Korea 1; North Korea 0, UAE 0; Yemen 0, Thailand 3; Thailand 1, North Korea 4; UAE 3, Yemen 0; North Korea 4, Thailand 1; Yemen 3, UAE 1; North Korea 2, Yemen 1; Thailand 3, UAE 0.

Group 6
Bahrain 2, Syria 1; Kyrgyzstan 1, Tajikistan 2; Kyrgyzstan 1, Syria 1; Tajikistan 0, Bahrain 0; Bahrain 5, Kyrgyzstan 0; Syria 3, Tajikistan 1; Kyrgyzstan 1, Bahrain 2; Tajikistan 0, Syria 1; Syria 2, Bahrain 2; Tajikistan 2, Kyrgyzstan 1.

Group 7
South Korea 2, Lebanon 0; Vietnam 4, Maldives 0; Maldives 0, South Korea 0; Vietnam 0, Lebanon 2; Lebanon 3, Maldives 0; South Korea 2, Vietnam 0; Maldives 2, Lebanon 5; Vietnam 1, South Korea 2; Lebanon 1, South Korea 1; Maldives 3, Vietnam 0.

Group 8
Saudi Arabia 3, Indonesia 0; Turkmenistan 2, Sri Lanka 0; Sri Lanka 0, Saudi Arabia 1; Turkmenistan 3, Indonesia 1; Indonesia 1, Sri Lanka 0; Saudi Arabia 3, Turkmenistan 0; Sri Lanka 2, Indonesia 2; Turkmenistan 0, Saudi Arabia 1; Indonesia 1, Saudi Arabia 3.

SECOND STAGE

Group A
South Korea 2, Kuwait 0; Uzbekistan 1, Saudi Arabia 1, Kuwait 2, Uzbekistan 1; Saudi Arabia 2, South Korea 0; Kuwait 0, Saudi Arabia 0; South Korea 2, Uzbekistan 1; Saudi Arabia 3, Kuwait 0; Uzbekistan 1, South Korea 1; Kuwait 0, South Korea 4; Saudi Arabia 3, Uzbekistan 0; Uzbekistan 3, Kuwait 2; South Korea 0, Saudi Arabia 1.

Group B
Bahrain 0, Iran 0; Japan 2, North Korea 1; Iran 2, Japan 1; North Korea 1, Bahrain 2; Japan 1, Bahrain 0; North Korea 0, Iran 2; Iran 1, North Korea 0; Bahrain 0, Japan 1; Iran 1, Bahrain 0; North Korea 0, Japan 2; Bahrain 2, North Korea 3; Japan 2, Iran 1.

Top two in each group qualify for finals: Saudi Arabia, South Korea, Iran, Japan.

Play-off for match with fourth place in Concacaf.

First Leg
Uzbekistan 1, Bahrain 0
(FIFA ruled match null and void; referee gave wrong disqualification for Uzbekistan penalty!)

Replay
Uzbekistan 1, Bahrain 1.

Second Leg
Bahrain 0, Uzbekistan 0.

Play-off for Concacaf/Asia

First Leg
Trinidad & Tobago 1, Bahrain 1.

Second Leg
Bahrain 0, Trinidad & Tobago 1.

QUALIFYING RESULTS – CONCACAF

FIRST STAGE

Group 1

Game 1 – Grenada 5, Guyana 0; Guyana 1, Grenada 3.
Game 2 – USA 3, Grenada 0; Grenada 2, USA 3.

Group 2

Game 1 – Bermuda 13, Montserrat 0; Montserrat 0, Bermuda 7.
Game 2 – El Salvador 2, Bermuda 1; Bermuda 2, El Salvador 2.

Group 3

Game 1 – Haiti 5, Turks & Caicos Islands 0; Turks & Caicos Islands 0, Haiti 2.
Game 2 – Haiti 1, Jamaica 1; Jamaica 3, Haiti 0.

Group 4

Game 1 – British Virgin Islands 0, St Lucia 1; St Lucia 9, British Virgin Islands 0.
Game 2 – Panama 4, St Lucia 0; St Lucia 0, Panama 3.

Group 5

Game 1 – Cayman Islands 1, Cuba 2; Cuba 3, Cayman Islands 0.
Game 2 – Cuba 2, Costa Rica 2; Costa Rica 1, Cuba 1.

Group 6

Game 1 – Aruba 1, Surinam 2; Surinam 8, Aruba 1.
Game 2 – Surinam 1, Guatemala 1; Guatemala 3, Surinam 1.

Group 7

Game 1 – Antigua & Barbuda 2, Netherlands Antilles 0; Netherlands Antilles 3, Antigua & Barbuda 0.
Game 2 – Netherlands Antilles 1, Honduras 2; Honduras 4, Netherlands Antilles 0.

Group 8
Canada 4, Belize 0; Belize 0, Canada 4.

Group 9

Game 1 – Dominica 1, Bahamas 1; Bahamas 1, Dominica 3.
Game 2 – Dominica 0, Mexico 10; Mexico 8, Dominica 0.

Group 10

Game 1 – US Virgin Islands 0, St Kitts & Nevis 4; St Kitts & Nevis 7, US Virgin Islands 0.
Game 2 – Barbados 0, St Kitts & Nevis 2; St Kitts & Nevis 3, Barbados 2.

Group 11

Game 1 – Dominican Republic 0, Anguilla 0; Anguilla 0, Dominican Republic 6.
Game 2 – Dominican Republic 0, Trinidad & Tobago 2; Trinidad & Tobago 4, Dominican Republic 0.

Group 12

Game 1 – Nicaragua 2, St Vincent & the Grenadines 2; St Vincent & the Grenadines 4, Nicaragua 1.

Game two group winners to second stage.

SECOND STAGE

Group 1
El Salvador 2, Panama 1; Jamaica 1, USA 1; Jamaica 1, Panama 2; USA 2, El Salvador 0; El Salvador 0, Jamaica 3; Panama 1, USA 1; El Salvador 0, USA 2; Panama 1, Jamaica 1; Jamaica 0, El Salvador 0; USA 6, Panama 0.

Group 2
Canada 0, Guatemala 2; Costa Rica 2, Honduras 5; Canada 1, Honduras 1; Guatemala 2, Costa Rica 1; Costa Rica 1, Canada 0; Honduras 2, Guatemala 2; Costa Rica 5, Guatemala 0; Honduras 1, Canada 1; Canada 1, Costa Rica 3; Guatemala 1, Honduras 0.

Group 3
St Vincent & the Grenadines 0, Trinidad & Tobago 2; St Kitts & Nevis 1, Trinidad & Tobago 2; Trinidad & Tobago 1, Mexico 3; Mexico 7, St Vicent & the Grenadines 0; St Vincent & the Grenadines 0, Mexico 1; Trinidad & Tobago 5, St Kitts & Nevis 1; Mexico 3, Trinidad & Tobago 0; St Kitts & Nevis 0, St Vincent & the Grenadines 3.

Top two from each group to third stage.

THIRD STAGE

Costa Rica 1, Mexico 2; Panama 0, Guatemala 0; Trinidad & Tobago 1, United States 2; Costa Rica 2, Panama 1; Guatemala 5, Trinidad & Tobago 1; Mexico 2, United States 1; Panama 1, Mexico 1; Trinidad & Tobago 0, Costa Rica 0; United States 2, Guatemala 0; Guatemala 0, Mexico 2; Trinidad & Tobago 2, Panama 0; United States 3, Costa Rica 0; Costa Rica 3, Guatemala 2; Mexico 2, Trinidad & Tobago 0; Panama 0, United States 3; Mexico 2, Costa Rica 0; Guatemala 2, Panama 1; United States 1, Trinidad & Tobago 0; United States 2, Mexico 0; Panama 1, Costa Rica 3; Trinidad & Tobago 3, Guatemala 2; Costa Rica 2, Trinidad & Tobago 0; Guatemala 0, USA 0; Mexico 5, Panama 0; Mexico 5, Guatemala 2; Costa Rica 3, USA 0; Panama 0, Trinidad & Tobago 1; USA 2, Panama 0; Trinidad & Tobago 2, Mexico 1; Guatemala 3, Costa Rica 1.

USA, Mexico and Costa Rica qualify for finals; Trinidad & Tobago played Bahrain (fifth-placed Asian team) for place in finals.

QUALIFYING RESULTS – OCEANIA

FIRST STAGE

Group 1
Solomon Islands 6, Tonga 0; Tahiti 2, Cook Islands 0; Solomon Islands 5, Cook Islands 0; Tahiti 0, New Caledonia, 0; Tonga 2, Cook Islands 1; Solomon Islands 2, New Caledonia 0; New Caledonia 8, Cook Islands 0; Tahiti 2, Tonga 0; New Caledonia 8, Tonga 0; Solomon Islands 1, Tahiti 1.

Group 2
Papua New Guinea 1, Vanuatu 1; Samoa 4, American Samoa 0; American Samoa 1, Vanuatu 9; Fiji 4, Papua New Guinea 2; Fiji 11, American Samoa 0; Samoa 0, Vanuatu 3; American Samoa 0, Papua New Guinea 10; Samoa 0, Fiji 4; Fiji 0, Vanuatu 3; Samoa 1, Papua New Guinea 4.
Top two from each group in the second stage joining Australia and New Zealand.

SECOND STAGE

Six qualifiers in final group; winners and runners-up advance to third stage.
Vanuatu 0, Solomon Islands 1; Tahiti 0, Fiji 0; Australia 1, New Zealand 0; New Zealand 3, Solomon Islands 0; Australia 9, Tahiti 0; Fiji 1, Vanuatu 0; Australia 6, Fiji 1; Tahiti 0, Solomon Islands 4; New Zealand 2, Vanuatu 4; New Zealand 10, Tahiti 0; Fiji 1, Solomon Islands 2; Vanuatu 0, Australia 3, Tahiti 2, Vanuatu 1; Fiji 0, New Zealand 2; Solomon Islands 2, Australia 2.

THIRD STAGE

Two qualifiers Australia and Solomon Islands play-off.
First Leg: Australia 7, Solomon Island 0; *Second Leg:* Solomon Islands 1, Australia 2.
Australia played Uruguay (fifth-placed South American team) for place in finals.

QUALIFYING RESULTS – AFRICA

Group 1
Senegal 2, Congo 0; Zambia 1, Togo 0; Liberia 1, Mali 0; Mali 1, Zambia 1; Congo 3, Liberia 0; Togo 3, Senegal 1; Senegal 1, Zambia 0; Congo 1, Mali 0; Liberia 0, Togo 0; Zambia 1, Liberia 0; Mali 2, Senegal 2; Togo 2, Congo 0; Congo 2, Zambia 3; Togo 1, Mali 0; Liberia 0, Senegal 3; Senegal 6, Liberia 1; Zambia 2, Congo 0; Mali 1, Togo 2; Congo 0, Senegal 0; Mali 4, Liberia 1; Togo 4, Zambia 1; Senegal 2, Togo 2; Zambia 2, Mali 1; Liberia 0, Congo 2; Zambia 0, Senegal 1; Mali 2, Congo 0; Togo 3, Liberia 0; Congo 2, Togo 3; Senegal 3, Mali 0; Liberia 0, Zambia 5.

Group 2
Burkina Faso 1, Ghana 0; South Africa 2, Cape Verde Islands 1; Uganda 1, DR Congo 0; Cape Verde Islands 1, Uganda 0; Ghana 3, South Africa 0; DR Congo 3, Burkina Faso 2; Cape Verde Islands 1, DR Congo 1; South Africa 2, Burkina Faso 0; Uganda 1, Ghana 1; Burkina Faso 2, Uganda 0; DR Congo 1, South Africa 0; Ghana 2, Cape Verde Islands 0; Cape Verde Islands 1, Burkina Faso 0; Uganda 0, South Africa 1; Ghana 0, DR Congo 0; Burkina Faso 1, Cape Verde Islands 2; South Africa 2, Uganda 1; DR Congo 1, Ghana 1; Cape Verde Islands 1, South Africa 2; DR Congo 4, Uganda 0; Ghana 2, Burkina Faso 1; Burkina Faso 2, DR Congo 0; South Africa 0, Ghana 2; Uganda 1, Cape Verde Islands 0; Burkina Faso 3, South Africa 1; DR Congo 2, Cape Verde Islands 1; Ghana 2, Uganda 0; Cape Verde Islands 0, Ghana 4; South Africa 2, DR Congo 2; Uganda 2, Burkina Faso 2.

Group 3
Cameroon 2, Benin 1; Ivory Coast 2, Libya 0; Sudan 0, Egypt 3; Liberia 0, Cameroon 0; Benin 1, Sudan 1; Egypt 1, Ivory Coast 2; Sudan 0, Libya 1; Benin 3, Egypt 3; Cameroon 2, Ivory Coast 0; Libya 4, Benin 1; Egypt 3, Cameroon 2; Ivory Coast 5, Sudan 0; Libya 2, Egypt 1; Sudan 1, Cameroon 1; Benin 0, Ivory Coast 1; Cameroon 2, Sudan 1; Egypt 4, Libya 1; Ivory Coast 3, Benin 0; Libya 0, Ivory Coast 0; Benin 1, Cameroon 4; Egypt 6, Sudan 1; Cameroon 1, Libya 0; Ivory Coast 2, Egypt 0; Sudan 1, Benin 0; Libya 0, Sudan 0; Egypt 4, Benin 1; Ivory Coast 2, Cameroon 3; Sudan 1, Ivory Coast 3; Cameroon 1, Egypt 1; Benin 1, Libya 0.

Group 4
Algeria 0, Angola 0; Gabon 1, Zimbabwe 1; Nigeria 2, Rwanda 0; Rwanda 3, Gabon 1; Angola 1, Nigeria 0; Zimbabwe 1, Algeria 1; Gabon 2, Angola 2; Nigeria 1, Algeria 0; Rwanda 0, Zimbabwe 2; Zimbabwe 0, Nigeria 3; Algeria 0, Gabon 3; Angola 1, Rwanda 0; Gabon 1, Nigeria 1; Rwanda 1, Algeria 1; Angola 1, Zimbabwe 0; Nigeria 2, Gabon 0; Algeria 1, Rwanda 0; Zimbabwe 2, Angola 0; Angola 2, Algeria 1; Rwanda 1, Nigeria 1; Zimbabwe 1, Gabon 0; Gabon 3, Rwanda 0; Nigeria 1, Angola 1; Algeria 2, Zimbabwe 2; Zimbabwe 3, Rwanda 1; Angola 3, Gabon 0; Algeria 2, Nigeria 5; Rwanda 0, Angola 1; Nigeria 5, Zimbabwe 1; Gabon 0, Algeria 0.

Group 5
Malawi 1, Morocco 1; Tunisia 4, Botswana 1; Botswana 2, Malawi 0; Guinea 2, Tunisia 1; Botswana 0, Morocco 1; Malawi 1, Guinea 1; Kenya 3, Malawi 2; Morocco 1, Tunisia 1; Guinea 4, Botswana 0; Malawi 2, Tunisia 2; Botswana 2, Kenya 1; Guinea 1, Morocco 1; Kenya 2, Guinea 1; Morocco 5, Kenya 1; Kenya 1, Botswana 0; Morocco 1, Guinea 0; Tunisia 7, Malawi 0; Botswana 1, Tunisia 3; Morocco 4, Malawi 1; Guinea 1, Kenya 0; Tunisia 2, Guinea 0; Kenya 0, Morocco 0; Malawi 1, Botswana 3; Tunisia 1, Kenya 0; Morocco 1, Botswana 0; Kenya 0, Tunisia 2; Guinea 3, Malawi 1; Tunisia 2, Morocco 2; Botswana 1, Guinea 2; Malawi 3, Kenya 0.

Group winners qualify for finals: Togo, Ghana, Ivory Coast, Angola, Tunisia.

THE WORLD CUP 1930–2006

Year	Winners		Runners-up		Venue	Attendance	Referee
1930	Uruguay	4	Argentina	2	Montevideo	90,000	Langenus (B)
1934	Italy*	2	Czechoslovakia	1	Rome	50,000	Eklind (Se)
1938	Italy	4	Hungary	2	Paris	45,000	Capdeville (F)
1950	Uruguay	2	Brazil	1	Rio de Janeiro	199,854	Reader (E)
1954	West Germany	3	Hungary	2	Berne	60,000	Ling (E)
1958	Brazil	5	Sweden	2	Stockholm	49,737	Guigue (F)
1962	Brazil	3	Czechoslovakia	1	Santiago	68,679	Latychev (USSR)
1966	England*	4	West Germany	2	Wembley	93,802	Dienst (Sw)
1970	Brazil	4	Italy	1	Mexico City	107,412	Glockner (EG)
1974	West Germany	2	Holland	1	Munich	77,833	Taylor (E)
1978	Argentina*	3	Holland	1	Buenos Aires	77,000	Gonella (I)
1982	Italy	3	West Germany	1	Madrid	90,080	Coelho (Br)
1986	Argentina	3	West Germany	2	Mexico City	114,580	Filho (Br)
1990	West Germany	1	Argentina	0	Rome	73,603	Mendez (Mex)
1994	Brazil*	0	Italy	0	Los Angeles	94,194	Puhl (H)
	(Brazil won 3-2 on penalties)						
1998	France	3	Brazil	0	St-Denis	75,000	Belqola (Mor)
2002	Brazil	2	Germany	0	Yokohama	69,029	Collina (I)
2006	Italy	1	France	1	Berlin	69,000	Elizondo (Arg)
	(Italy won 5-3 on penalties)						

*(*After extra time)*

GOALSCORING AND ATTENDANCES IN WORLD CUP FINAL ROUNDS

Venue	*Matches*	*Goals (av)*	*Attendance (av)*
1930, Uruguay	18	70 (3.9)	434,500 (24,138)
1934, Italy	17	70 (4.1)	395,000 (23,235)
1938, France	18	84 (4.6)	483,000 (26,833)
1950, Brazil	22	88 (4.0)	1,337,000 (60,772)
1954, Switzerland	26	140 (5.4)	943,000 (36,270)
1958, Sweden	35	126 (3.6)	868,000 (24,800)
1962, Chile	32	89 (2.8)	776,000 (24,250)
1966, England	32	89 (2.8)	1,614,677 (50,458)
1970, Mexico	32	95 (2.9)	1,673,975 (52,311)
1974, West Germany	38	97 (2.5)	1,774,022 (46,684)
1978, Argentina	38	102 (2.7)	1,610,215 (42,374)
1982, Spain	52	146 (2.8)	2,064,364 (38,816)
1986, Mexico	52	132 (2.5)	2,441,731 (46,956)
1990, Italy	52	115 (2.2)	2,515,168 (48,368)
1994, USA	52	141 (2.7)	3,567,415 (68,604)
1998, France	64	171 (2.6)	2,775,400 (43,366)
2002, Japan/S. Korea	64	161 (2.5)	2,705,566 (42,274)
2006, Germany	64	147 (2.3)	3,354,646 (52,416)

LEADING GOALSCORERS

Year	*Player*	*Goals*
1930	Guillermo Stabile (Argentina)	8
1934	Angelo Schiavio (Italy), Oldrich Nejedly (Czechoslovakia), Edmund Conen (Germany)	4
1938	Leonidas da Silva (Brazil)	8
1950	Ademir (Brazil)	9
1954	Sandor Kocsis (Hungary)	11
1958	Just Fontaine (France)	13
1962	Valentin Ivanov (USSR), Leonel Sanchez (Chile), Garrincha, Vava (both Brazil), Florian Albert (Hungary), Drazen Jerkovic (Yugoslavia)	4
1966	Eusebio (Portugal)	9
1970	Gerd Muller (West Germany)	10
1974	Grzegorz Lato (Poland)	7
1978	Mario Kempes (Argentina)	6
1982	Paolo Rossi (Italy)	6
1986	Gary Lineker (England)	6
1990	Salvatore Schillaci (Italy)	6
1994	Oleg Salenko (Russia) Hristo Stoichkov (Bulgaria)	6
1998	Davor Suker (Croatia)	6
2002	Ronaldo (Brazil)	8
2006	Miroslav Klose (Germany)	5

WORLD CUP FINALS 2006 REVIEW

Whatever passed before the incident, the unfortunate confrontation between Zinedine Zidane of France and Marco Materazzi of Italy in the World Cup final tended to obliterate the previous month's events. Perhaps it summed up the tournament's impact overall.

Zidane clearly provoked by the Italian defender's remarks, the Frenchman coolly and deliberately headbutted his opponent and was eventually sent off when one official or another was able to verify the misdemeanour. That said Zidane still received the Golden Ball as the outstanding player in the finals; not the kind of message FIFA should be sending to aspiring youngsters.

Zidane had given France the lead with a delicate chip from the penalty spot which clipped the bar before falling majestically behind Gianluigi Buffon in the Italian goal. Materazzi equalised with a powerful header to leave it 1-1 at the break.

While Italy had enjoyed the better of the first half exchanges, it changed in the second half when France took a grip in midfield and Thierry Henry was giving the Italian defence problems. Extra time merely led to the inevitable penalty shoot-out which Italy won 5-3, only David Trezeguet who hit the bar himself actually failing to score.

Germany, the highest scorers with 14, deserved third place after beating Portugal and Miroslav Klose was top scorer with just five. Goalscoring generally was a poor 2.30 on average, the second worst ever behind 1990. Ronaldo, a portly figure in a disappointing Brazilian team, managed to overhaul Gerd Muller's record of finals goals to finish with 15. Brazil also set another with their 11th successive win in finals and shared the Fair Play Award with Spain.

Germany were also involved in the best game when they lost 2-0 to Italy in the quarter-final. Argentina had fallen to the Germans in the first knock-out round, unaided by poor judgement by the bench in substituting key players. They had arguably produced the best football and fashioned the finest goal in the high-scoring 6-0 rout of the Serbs: nine players, 24 passes, one goal – all in 57 seconds.

FIFA's crackdown on reckless tackling, diving and other frowned upon activities produced 345 yellow and 28 red cards, both records, but it was a charter for the cheats. Referees had a mixed time of it; Graham Poll managed to show a Croatian three yellow cards, Valentin Ivanov the Russian flashed 16 yellow and four reds in the record nine-a-side finishing Holland v Portugal match.

Crowds totalled 3,354,646 for an average of 52,416, the third best in history, but there were plenty of complaints about ticketing with corporate sponsorship getting more than their fair share.

Television viewing was estimated at 30 billion worldwide with more than one billion watching the final itself.

Oddities abounded: Switzerland became the first team to be eliminated from the finals without conceding a goal; Italy conceded two – an own goal and a penalty as Buffon won the Lev Yashin award as the best goalkeeper; Fabio Cannavaro, the outstanding Italian captain and centre-back, led his team to victory in his 100th appearance.

The Africans did better than expected, Ghana and Ivory Coast in particular. The South Americans disappointed apart from Argentina. Underachievers Spain flattered as ever, Trinidad & Tobago played above their status. France improved after an undistinguished start until the fateful final. Portuguese penalties finished off England, of course.

Holland, the Czechs and Ukraine threatened to do better before tailing away, Sweden were just thankful for a weak group, the USA had their moments and the Australians surprised expectations and gave Italy their most difficult match.

Only six countries: Costa Rica, Croatia, Iran, Italy, Paraguay and Saudi Arabia did not have a player from an English club!

Arsenal supplied the most with 15, Chelsea next with 14, Manchester United fifth with 12. Who said England had no real interest in the competition?

Italian players race to congratulate their fifth successful penalty-taker Fabio Grosso as the World Cup success is achieved. (Empics)

WORLD CUP FINALS 2006

GROUP A

Munich, 9 June 2006, 59,416

Germany (2) 4 *(Lahm 6, Klose 17, 61, Frings 87)*

Costa Rica (1) 2 *(Wanchope 12, 73)*

Germany: Lehmann; Friedrich, Mertesacker, Metzelder, Lahm, Frings, Schneider (Odonkor 90), Borowski (Kehl 72), Klose (Neuville 79), Podolski, Schweinsteiger.

Costa Rica: Porras; Umana, Sequeira, Marin, Martinez (Drummond 66), Fonseca, Gonzalez L, Solis (Bolanos 78), Gomez (Azofeifa 90), Wanchope, Centeno.

Referee: Elizondo (Argentina).

Gelsenkirchen, 9 June 2006, 48,426

Poland (0) 0

Ecuador (1) 2 *(Tenorio C 24, Delgado 80)*

Poland: Boruc; Baszczynski, Michal Zewlakow, Radomski, Bak, Jop, Sobolewski (Jelen 68), Smolarek, Zurawski (Brozek 84), Szymkowiak, Krzynowek (Kosowski 78).

Ecuador: Mora; De la Cruz, Reasco, Tenorio E, Hurtado I (Guagua 69), Espinoza G, Castillo, Valencia, Delgado (Urrutia 83), Tenorio C (Kaviedes 65), Mendez.

Referee: Kamikawa (Japan).

Dortmund, 14 June 2006, 65,000

Germany (0) 1 *(Neuville 90)*

Poland (0) 0

Germany: Lehmann; Friedrich (Odonkor 63), Lahm, Frings, Mertesacker, Metzelder, Schneider, Ballack, Klose, Podolski (Neuville 70), Schweinsteiger (Borowski 77).

Poland: Boruc; Baszczynski, Michal Zewlakow (Dudka 83), Sobolewski■, Bosacki, Bak, Jelen (Brozek 90), Radomski, Zurawski, Smolarek, Krzynowek (Lewandowski M 77).

Referee: Cantalejo (Spain).

Hamburg, 15 June 2006, 50,000

Ecuador (1) 3 *(Tenorio C 8, Delgado 54, Kaviedes 90)*

Costa Rica (0) 0

Ecuador: Mora; De la Cruz, Reasco, Tenorio E, Hurtado I, Espinoza G (Guagua 69), Valencia (Urrutia 73), Castillo, Delgado, Tenorio C (Kaviedes 46), Mendez.

Costa Rica: Porras; Sequeira, Fonseca (Saborio 29), Marin, Umana, Gonzalez L (Hernandez 56), Wallace, Solis, Wanchope, Gomez, Centeno (Bernard 84).

Referee: Codjia (Benin).

Hanover, 20 June 2006, 43,000

Costa Rica (1) 1 *(Gomez 24)*

Poland (1) 2 *(Bosacki 33, 66)*

Costa Rica: Porras; Umana, Drummond (Wallace 70), Marin, Badilla, Solis, Gonzalez L, Bolanos (Saborio 78), Wanchope, Centeno, Gomez (Hernandez 82).

Poland: Boruc; Baszczynski, Michal Zewlakow, Radomski (Lewandowski M 64), Bak, Bosacki, Smolarek (Rasiak 85), Szymkowiak, Jelen, Zurawski (Brozek 46), Krzynowek.

Referee: Maidin (Singapore).

Berlin, 20 June 2006, 72,000

Ecuador (0) 0

Germany (2) 3 *(Klose 4, 44, Podolski 57)*

Ecuador: Mora; De la Cruz, Ambrosi, Tenorio E, Guagua, Espinoza G, Valencia (Lara 63), Ayovi M (Urrutia 68), Borja (Benitez 46), Kaviedes, Mendez.

Germany: Lehmann; Friedrich, Lahm, Frings (Borowski 66), Mertesacker, Huth, Schneider (Asamoah 73), Ballack, Podolski, Klose (Neuville 66), Schweinsteiger.

Referee: Ivanov (Russia).

GROUP A FINAL TABLE	*P*	*W*	*D*	*L*	*F*	*A*	*Pts*
Germany	3	3	0	0	8	2	9
Ecuador	3	2	0	1	5	3	6
Poland	3	1	0	2	2	4	3
Costa Rica	3	0	0	3	3	9	0

GROUP B

Frankfurt, 10 June 2006, 43,324

England (1) 1 *(Gamarra 3 (og))*

Paraguay (0) 0

England: Robinson; Neville G, Cole A, Gerrard, Ferdinand, Terry, Beckham, Lampard, Crouch, Owen (Downing 56), Cole J (Hargreaves 83).

Paraguay: Villar (Bobadilla 8); Caniza, Toledo (Nunez 82), Toro Acuna, Caceres JC, Gamarra, Bonet (Cuevas 68), Paredes, Santa Cruz, Valdez, Riveros.

Referee: Moreno (Mexico).

Dortmund, 10 June 2006, 60,285

Trinidad & Tobago (0) 0

Sweden (0) 0

Trinidad & Tobago: Hislop; Gray, John A■, Birchall, Lawrence, Sancho, Yorke, Theobald (Whitley 67), John S, Samuel (Glen 53), Edwards.

Sweden: Shaaban; Alexandersson N, Edman, Linderoth (Kallstrom 78), Mellberg, Lucic, Wilhelmsson (Jonson M 79), Ljungberg, Ibrahimovic, Larsson, Anders Svensson (Allback 62).

Referee: Maidin (Singapore).

Nuremberg, 15 June 2006, 41,000

England (0) 2 *(Crouch 83, Gerrard 90)*

Trinidad & Tobago (0) 0

England: Robinson; Carragher (Lennon 58), Cole A, Gerrard, Ferdinand, Terry, Beckham, Lampard, Crouch, Owen (Rooney 58), Cole J (Downing 75).

Trinidad & Tobago: Hislop; Edwards, Gray, Yorke, Lawrence, Sancho, Birchall, Whitley, John S, Jones (Glen 70), Theobald (Wise 85).

Referee: Kamikawa (Japan).

Berlin, 15 June 2006, 72,000

Sweden (0) 1 *(Ljungberg 89)*

Paraguay (0) 0

Sweden: Isaksson; Alexandersson N, Edman, Linderoth, Mellberg, Lucic, Wilhelmsson (Jonson M 68), Kallstrom (Elmander 86), Ibrahimovic (Allback 46), Larsson, Ljungberg.

Paraguay: Bobadilla; Caniza, Nunez, Toro Acuna, Caceres JC, Gamarra, Bonet (Barreto 81), Paredes, Santa Cruz (Lopez 63), Valdez, Riveros (Dos Santos 62).

Referee: Michel (Slovakia).

Kaiserslautern, 20 June 2006, 46,000

Paraguay (1) 2 *(Sancho 25 (og), Cuevas 86)*

Trinidad & Tobago (0) 0

Paraguay: Bobadilla; Caniza (Da Silva 89), Nunez, Toro Acuna, Caceres JC (Manzur 77), Gamarra, Barreto, Dos Santos, Valdez (Cuevas 66), Santa Cruz, Paredes.

Trinidad & Tobago: Jack; Edwards, John A (Jones 31), Yorke, Lawrence, Sancho, Birchall, Whitley (Latapy 67), John S, Glen (Wise 41), Theobald.

Referee: Rosetti (Italy).

Cologne, 20 June 2006, 45,000

Sweden (0) 2 *(Allback 50, Larsson 90)*

England (1) 2 *(Cole J 34, Gerrard 85)*

Sweden: Isaksson; Alexandersson N, Edman, Linderoth (Andersson D 90), Mellberg, Lucic, Jonson M (Wilhelmsson 54), Kallstrom, Allback (Elmander 75), Larsson, Ljungberg.

England: Robinson; Carragher, Cole A, Hargreaves, Ferdinand (Campbell 56), Terry, Beckham, Lampard, Owen (Crouch 4), Rooney (Gerrard 69), Cole J.

Referee: Busacca (Switzerland).

GROUP B FINAL TABLE	*P*	*W*	*D*	*L*	*F*	*A*	*Pts*
England	3	2	1	0	5	2	7
Sweden	3	1	2	0	3	2	5
Paraguay	3	1	0	2	2	2	3
Trinidad & Tobago	3	0	1	2	0	4	1

GROUP C

Hamburg, 10 June 2006, 45,442

Argentina (2) 2 *(Crespo 24, Saviola 38)*

Ivory Coast (0) 1 *(Drogba 82)*

Argentina: Abbondanzieri; Burdisso, Sorin, Maxi Rodriguez, Ayala, Heinze, Cambiasso, Mascherano, Saviola (Gonzalez L 76), Crespo (Palacio 64), Riquelme (Aimar 90).
Ivory Coast: Tizie; Eboue, Boka, Toure Y, Toure K, Meite, Zokora, Keita (Kone A 77), Kalou (Dindane 56), Drogba, Akale (Kone B 62).
Referee: De Bleeckere (Belgium).

Leipzig, 11 June 2006, 37,216

Serbia & Montenegro (0) 0

Holland (1) 1 *(Robben 18)*

Serbia & Montenegro: Jevric; Djordjevic N (Koroman 43), Dragutinovic, Duljaj, Gavrancic, Krstajic, Stankovic, Nadj, Milosevic (Zigic 46), Kezman (Ljuboja 67), Djordjevic P.
Holland: Van der Sar; Heitinga, Van Bronckhorst, Van Bommel (Landzaat 60), Ooijer, Mathijsen (Boulahrouz 86), Sneijder, Cocu, Van Nistelrooy (Kuijt 69), Van Persie, Robben.
Referee: Merk (Germany).

Gelsenkirchen, 16 June 2006, 52,000

Argentina (3) 6 *(Maxi Rodriguez 6, 41, Cambiasso 31, Crespo 79, Tevez 84, Messi 89)*

Serbia & Montenegro (0) 0

Argentina: Abbondanzieri; Burdisso, Sorin, Mascherano, Ayala, Heinze, Gonzalez L (Cambiasso 17), Maxi Rodriguez (Messi 75), Crespo, Saviola (Tevez 59), Riquelme.
Serbia & Montenegro: Jevric; Duljaj, Krstajic, Nadj (Ergic 46), Dudic, Gavrancic, Koroman (Ljuboja 50), Djordjevic P, Milosevic (Vukic 70), Kezman■, Stankovic.
Referee: Rosetti (Italy).

Stuttgart, 16 June 2006, 52,000

Holland (2) 2 *(Van Persie 23, Van Nistelrooy 26)*

Ivory Coast (1) 1 *(Kone B 38)*

Holland: Van der Sar; Heitinga (Boulahrouz 46), Van Bronckhorst, Sneijder (Van der Vaart 50), Ooijer, Mathijsen, Van Persie, Van Bommel, Van Nistelrooy (Landzaat 73), Cocu, Robben.
Ivory Coast: Tizie; Eboue, Boka, Zokora, Toure K, Meite, Toure Y, Kone B (Dindane 62), Drogba, Kone A (Akale 73), Romaric (Yapi Yapo 62).
Referee: Acosta (Colombia).

Frankfurt, 21 June 2006, 48,000

Holland (0) 0

Argentina (0) 0

Holland: Van der Sar; Jaliens, De Cler, Sneijder (Maduro 86), Boulahrouz, Ooijer, Van Persie (Landzaat 67), Van der Vaart, Cocu, Van Nistelrooy (Babel 56), Kuijt.
Argentina: Abbondanzieri; Burdisso (Coloccini 24), Cufre, Mascherano, Ayala, Milito, Messi (Cruz 70), Maxi Rodriguez, Riquelme (Aimar 80), Cambiasso, Tevez.
Referee: Cantalejo (Spain).

Munich, 21 June 2006, 66,000

Ivory Coast (1) 3 *(Dindane 37 (pen), 67, Kalou B 85 (pen))*

Serbia & Montenegro (2) 2 *(Zigic 10, Ilic 20)*

Ivory Coast: Barry; Eboue, Boka, Zokora, Kouassi, Domoraud■, Keita (Kalou B 73), Toure Y, Dindane, Kone A, Akale (Kone B 60).
Serbia & Montenegro: Jevric; Djordjevic N, Dudic, Duljaj, Gavrancic, Krstajic (Nadj■ 16), Stankovic, Ergic, Zigic (Milosevic 67), Ilic, Djordjevic P.
Referee: Moreno (Mexico).

GROUP C FINAL TABLE	*P*	*W*	*D*	*L*	*F*	*A*	*Pts*
Argentina	3	2	1	0	8	1	7
Holland	3	2	1	0	3	1	7
Ivory Coast	3	1	0	2	5	6	3
Serbia & Montenegro	3	0	0	3	2	10	0

GROUP D

Cologne, 11 June 2006, 45,000

Angola (0) 0

Portugal (1) 1 *(Pauleta 4)*

Angola: Joao Ricardo; Loco, Delgado, Figueiredo (Miloy 80), Jamba, Kali, Andre Makanga, Mateus, Akwa (Mantorras 60), Ze Kalanga (Edson 70), Mendonca.
Portugal: Ricardo; Miguel, Nuno Valente, Petit (Maniche 72), Fernando Meira, Ricardo Carvalho, Ronaldo (Costinha 60), Figo, Pauleta, Tiago (Hugo Viana 82), Simao Sabrosa.
Referee: Larrionda (Uruguay).

Nuremberg, 11 June 2006, 36,898

Mexico (1) 3 *(Bravo 28, 76, Zinha 79)*

Iran (1) 1 *(Golmohammadi 36)*

Mexico: Sanchez O; Marquez, Salcido, Pardo, Osorio, Torrado (Perez L 46), Mendez, Bravo, Borgetti (Fonseca 52), Franco (Zinha 46), Pineda.
Iran: Mirzapour; Kaabi, Nosrati (Borhani 81), Teymourian, Golmohammadi, Rezaei, Mahdavikia, Nekounam, Daei, Hashemian, Karimi (Madanchi 63).
Referee: Rosetti (Italy).

Hanover, 16 June 2006, 43,000

Mexico (0) 0

Angola (0) 0

Mexico: Sanchez O; Marquez, Mendez, Osorio, Salcido, Pardo, Torrado, Zinha (Arellano 52), Bravo, Franco (Fonseca 74), Pineda (Morales 78).
Angola: Joao Ricardo; Loco, Delgado, Figueiredo (Rui Marques 73), Jamba, Kali, Andre Makanga■, Ze Kalanga (Miloy 83), Mendonca, Akwa, Mateus (Mantorras 68).
Referee: Maidin (Singapore).

Frankfurt, 17 June 2006, 48,000

Portugal (0) 2 *(Deco 63, Ronaldo 80 (pen))*

Iran (0) 0

Portugal: Ricardo; Miguel, Nuno Valente, Maniche (Petit 67), Fernando Meira, Ricardo Carvalho, Figo (Simao Sabrosa 88), Deco (Tiago 80), Pauleta, Costinha, Ronaldo.
Iran: Mirzapour; Kaabi, Nosrati, Teymourian, Golmohammadi (Bakhtiarizadeh 88), Rezaei, Mahdavikia, Karimi (Zandi 65), Hashemian, Nekounam, Madanchi (Khatibi 66).
Referee: Poulet (France).

Liepzig, 21 June 2006, 38,000

Iran (0) 1 *(Bakhtiarizadeh 75)*

Angola (0) 1 *(Flavio 60)*

Iran: Mirzapour; Kaabi (Borhani 67), Nosrati (Shojaei 13), Teymourian, Rezaei, Bakhtiarizadeh, Mahdavikia, Zandi, Hashemian (Khatibi 39), Daei, Madanchi.
Angola: Joao Ricardo; Loco, Delgado, Figueiredo (Rui Marques 73), Jamba, Kali, Ze Kalanga, Miloy, Akwa (Flavio 51), Mendonca, Mateus (Love 23).
Referee: Shield (Australia).

Gelsenkirchen, 21 June 2006, 52,000

Portugal (2) 2 *(Maniche 6, Simao Sabrosa 24 (pen))*

Mexico (1) 1 *(Fonseca 29)*

Portugal: Ricardo; Miguel (Paulo Ferreira 61), Caneira, Petit, Fernando Meira, Ricardo Carvalho, Figo (Boa Morte 80), Tiago, Helder Postiga (Nuno Gomes 69), Simao Sabrosa, Maniche.
Mexico: Sanchez O; Mendez (Franco 80), Marquez, Rodriguez (Zinha 46), Osorio, Salcido, Pardo, Perez L■, Fonseca, Bravo, Pineda (Castro 69).
Referee: Michel (Slovakia).

GROUP D FINAL TABLE	*P*	*W*	*D*	*L*	*F*	*A*	*Pts*
Portugal	3	3	0	0	5	1	9
Mexico	3	1	1	1	4	3	4
Angola	3	0	2	1	1	2	2
Iran	3	0	1	2	2	6	1

GROUP E

Hanover, 12 June 2006, 43,000

Italy (1) 2 *(Pirlo 40, Iaquinta 83)*

Ghana (0) 0

Italy: Buffon; Zaccardo, Grosso, De Rossi, Nesta, Cannavaro, Perrotta, Pirlo, Toni (Del Piero 82), Totti (Camoranesi 56), Gilardino (Iaquinta 64).
Ghana: Kingston; Pantsil, Pappoe (Shilla Illiasu 46), Muntari, Mensah, Kuffour, Appiah, Essien, Amoah (Pimpong 68), Gyan (Tachie-Mensah 89), Addo E.
Referee: Simon (Brazil).

Gelsenkirchen, 12 June 2006, 48,426
USA (0) 0
Czech Republic (2) 3 *(Koller 5, Rosicky 36, 76)*
USA: Keller; Cherundolo (O'Brien 46), Lewis, Mastroeni (Johnson 46), Pope, Onyewu, Beasley, Reyna, McBride (Wolff 77), Donovan, Convey.
Czech Republic: Cech; Grygera, Jankulovski, Galasek, Rozehnal, Ujfalusi, Poborsky (Polak 83), Nedved, Koller (Lokvenc 45), Rosicky (Stajner 86), Plasil.
Referee: Demarqui (Paraguay).

Cologne, 17 June 2006, 45,000
Czech Republic (0) 0
Ghana (1) 2 *(Gyan 2, Muntari 82)*
Czech Republic: Cech; Grygera, Jankulovski, Galasek (Polak 46), Rozehnal, Ujfalusi■, Poborsky (Stajner 56), Nedved, Lokvenc, Rosicky, Plasil (Sionko 68).
Ghana: Kingston; Pantsil, Mohamed, Essien, Mensah, Shilla Illiasu, Addo O (Boateng 46), Appiah, Amoah (Addo E 80), Gyan (Pimpong 85), Muntari.
Referee: Elizondo (Argentina).

Kaiserslautern, 17 June 2006, 46,000
Italy (1) 1 *(Gilardino 22)*
USA (1) 1 *(Zaccardo 27 (og))*
Italy: Buffon; Zaccardo (Del Piero 54), Zambrotta, De Rossi■, Nesta, Cannavaro, Pirlo, Perrotta, Toni (Iaquinta 61), Totti (Gattuso 35), Gilardino.
USA: Keller; Cherundolo, Bocanegra, Mastroeni■, Pope■, Onyewu, Dempsey (Beasley 62), Reyna, McBride, Donovan, Convey (Conrad 52).
Referee: Larrionda (Uruguay).

Hamburg, 22 June 2006, 50,000
Czech Republic (0) 0
Italy (1) 2 *(Materazzi 26, Inzaghi 87)*
Czech Republic: Cech; Grygera, Jankulovski, Polak■, Kovac R (Heinz 78), Rozehnal, Poborsky (Stajner 46), Nedved, Baros (Jarolim 64), Rosicky, Plasil.
Italy: Buffon; Zambrotta, Grosso, Gattuso, Nesta (Materazzi 17), Cannavaro, Pirlo, Camoranesi (Barone 74), Gilardino (Inzaghi 61), Totti, Perrotta.
Referee: Telez (Mexico).

Nuremberg, 22 June 2006, 41,000
Ghana (2) 2 *(Draman 22, Appiah 45 (pen))*
USA (1) 1 *(Dempsey 43)*
Ghana: Kingston; Pantsil, Mohamed, Essien, Mensah, Shilla Illiasu, Boateng (Addo O 46), Appiah, Amoah (Addo E 59), Pimpong, Draman (Tachie-Mensah 80).
USA: Keller; Cherundolo (Johnson 61), Bocanegra, Reyna (Olsen 40), Onyewu, Conrad, Dempsey, Donovan, McBride, Beasley, Lewis (Convey 74).
Referee: Merk (Germany).

GROUP E FINAL TABLE	P	W	D	L	F	A	Pts
Italy	3	2	1	0	5	1	7
Ghana	3	2	0	1	4	3	6
Czech Republic	3	1	0	2	3	4	3
USA	3	0	1	2	2	6	1

GROUP F

Kaiserslautern, 12 June 2006, 46,000
Australia (0) 3 *(Cahill 84, 89, Aloisi 90)*
Japan (1) 1 *(Nakamura 26)*
Australia: Schwarzer; Moore (Kennedy 61), Neill, Chipperfield, Grella, Wilkshire (Aloisi 75), Culina, Emerton, Viduka, Kewell, Bresciano (Cahill 53).
Japan: Kawaguchi; Komano, Santos, Nakata, Miyamoto, Nakazawa, Fukunishi, Tsuboi (Moniwa 56) (Oguro 90), Yanagisawa (Ono 79), Takahara, Nakamura.
Referee: El Fatah (Egypt).

Berlin, 13 June 2006, 72,000
Brazil (1) 1 *(Kaka 44)*
Croatia (0) 0
Brazil: Dida; Cafu, Roberto Carlos, Emerson, Lucio, Juan, Ze Roberto, Kaka, Adriano, Ronaldo (Robinho 69), Ronaldinho.
Croatia: Pletikosa; Srna, Babic, Simic, Kovac R, Simunic, Tudor, Kranjcar, Klasnic (Olic 56), Prso, Kovac N (Leko J 41).
Referee: Tellez (Mexico).

Munich, 18 June 2006, 66,000
Brazil (0) 2 *(Adriano 49, Fred 89)*
Australia (0) 0
Brazil: Dida; Cafu, Roberto Carlos, Emerson (Gilberto Silva 72), Juan, Lucio, Ze Roberto, Kaka, Ronaldo (Robinho 72), Adriano (Fred 88), Ronaldinho.
Australia: Schwarzer; Emerton, Chipperfield, Moore (Aloisi 69), Neill, Popovic (Bresciano 41), Culina, Grella, Viduka, Cahill (Kewell 56), Sterjovski.
Referee: Merk (Germany).

Nuremberg, 18 June 2006, 41,000
Japan (0) 0
Croatia (0) 0
Japan: Kawaguchi; Kaji, Santos, Fukunishi (Inamoto 46), Miyamoto, Nakazawa, Nakamura, Nakata H, Yanagisawa (Tamada 62), Takahara (Oguro 85), Ogasawara.
Croatia: Pletikosa; Simic, Tudor (Olic 70), Kovac R, Simunic, Kovac N, Srna (Bosnjak 87), Kranjcar (Modric 78), Klasnic, Prso, Babic.
Referee: De Bleeckere (Belgium).

Stuttgart, 22 June 2006, 52,000
Croatia (1) 2 *(Srna 2, Kovac N 56)*
Australia (1) 2 *(Moore 38 (pen), Kewell 79)*
Croatia: Pletikosa; Simic■, Babic, Kovac N, Tomas, Simunic■, Srna, Tudor, Prso, Olic (Modric 74), Kranjcar (Leko J 65).
Australia: Kalac; Emerton■, Chipperfield (Kennedy 75), Grella (Aloisi 63), Neill, Moore, Sterjovski (Bresciano 71), Culina, Viduka, Cahill, Kewell.
Referee: Poll (England).

Dortmund, 22 June 2006, 65,000
Japan (1) 1 *(Tamada 34)*
Brazil (1) 4 *(Ronaldo 45, 81, Juninho Pernambucano 53, Gilberto 59)*
Japan: Kawaguchi; Kaji, Santos, Nakata H, Tsuboi, Nakazawa, Nakamura, Inamoto, Maki (Takahara 60) (Oguro 66), Tamada, Ogasawara (Nakata K 56).
Brazil: Dida (Rogerio Ceni 82); Cicinho, Gilberto, Gilberto Silva, Lucio, Juan, Kaka (Ze Roberto 71), Juninho Pernambucano, Ronaldo, Robinho, Ronaldinho (Ricardinho 71).
Referee: Poulat (France).

GROUP F FINAL TABLE	P	W	D	L	F	A	Pts
Brazil	3	3	0	0	7	1	9
Australia	3	1	1	1	5	5	4
Croatia	3	0	2	1	2	3	2
Japan	3	0	1	2	2	7	1

GROUP G

Stuttgart, 13 June 2006, 56,000
France (0) 0
Switzerland (0) 0
France: Barthez; Sagnol, Abidal, Makelele, Thuram, Gallas, Wiltord (Dhorasoo 84), Vieira, Henry, Zidane, Ribery (Saha 70).
Switzerland: Zuberbuhler; Degen P, Magnin, Vogel, Muller (Djourou 75), Senderos, Barnetta, Wicky (Margairaz 82), Frei, Streller (Gygax 56), Cabanas.
Referee: Ivanov (Russia).

Frankfurt, 13 June 2006, 48,000
South Korea (0) 2 *(Lee C-S 54, Ahn 72)*
Togo (1) 1 *(Kader 31)*
South Korea: Lee W-J; Song C-G, Lee Y-P, Choi J-C, Kim Y-C, Kim J-K (Ahn 46), Ho Lee, Park J-S, Lee C-S, Cho J-J (Kim S-S 83), Lee E-Y (Kim N-I 68).
Togo: Agassa; Tchangai, Assemoassa (Forson 62), Romao, Abalo■, Nibombe, Senaya (Toure 55), Mamam, Adebayor, Kader, Salifou M (Aziawonou 86).
Referee: Poll (England).

Leipzig, 18 June 2006, 43,000
France (1) 1 *(Henry 9)*
South Korea (0) 1 *(Park J-S 81)*
France: Barthez; Sagnol, Abidal, Makelele, Thuram, Gallas, Wiltord (Ribery 60), Vieira, Henry, Zidane (Trezeguet 90), Malouda (Dhorasoo 88).
South Korea: Lee W-J; Lee Y-P, Kim D-J, Kim N-I, Choi J-C, Kim Y-C, Lee C-S (Ahn 72), Ho Lee (Kim S-S 69), Cho J-J, Lee E-Y (Seol K-H 46), Park J-S.
Referee: Tellez (Mexico).

Dortmund, 19 June 2006, 65,000
Togo (0) 0
Switzerland (1) 2 *(Frei 16, Barnetta 88)*
Togo: Agassa; Toure, Forson, Agboh (Salifou M 25), Tchangai, Nibombe, Dossevi (Senaya 69), Romao, Adebayor, Kader, Mamam (Malm 87).
Switzerland: Zuberbuhler; Degen P, Magnin, Vogel, Muller, Senderos, Barnetta, Cabanas (Streller 77), Gygax (Yakin 46), Frei (Lustrinelli 87), Wicky.
Referee: Demarqui (Paraguay).

Hanover, 23 June 2006, 43,000
Switzerland (1) 2 *(Senderos 23, Frei 77)*
South Korea (0) 0
Switzerland: Zuberbuhler; Degen P, Spycher, Vogel, Muller, Senderos (Djourou 54), Barnetta, Cabanas, Yakin (Margairaz 72), Frei, Wicky (Behrami 88).
South Korea: Lee W-J; Lee Y-P (Ahn 64), Kim D-J, Kim N-I, Choi J-C, Kim J-K, Park J-S, Ho Lee, Lee C-S, Cho J-J, Park C-J (Seol K-H 67).
Referee: Elizondo (Argentina).

Cologne, 23 June 2006, 45,000
Togo (0) 0
France (0) 2 *(Vieira 55, Henry 61)*
Togo: Agassa; Tchangai, Forson, Aziawonou, Abalo, Nibombe, Senaya, Mamam (Olufade 59), Adebayor (Dossevi 75), Kader, Salifou M.
France: Barthez; Sagnol, Silvestre, Makelele, Thuram, Gallas, Ribery (Gouvou 77), Vieira (Diarra 81), Trezeguet, Henry, Malouda (Wiltord 74).
Referee: Larrionda (Uruguay).

GROUP G FINAL TABLE	*P*	*W*	*D*	*L*	*F*	*A*	*Pts*
Switzerland	3	2	1	0	4	0	7
France	3	1	2	0	3	1	5
South Korea	3	1	1	1	3	4	4
Togo	3	0	0	3	1	6	0

GROUP H

Leipzig, 14 June 2006, 43,000
Spain (2) 4 *(Xabi Alonso 13, Villa 17, 48 (pen), Fernando Torres 81)*
Ukraine (0) 0
Spain: Casillas; Sergio Ramos, Pernia, Xabi Alonso (Albelda 55), Pablo, Puyol, Marcos Senna, Luis Garcia (Fabregas 77), Fernando Torres, Villa (Raul 55), Xavi.
Ukraine: Shovkovskyi; Yezerskiy, Nesmachni, Tymoschuk, Rusol, Vashchuk■, Gusev (Vorobei 46), Gusin (Shelayev 46), Voronin, Shevchenko, Rotan (Rebrov 64).
Referee: Busacca (Switzerland).

Munich, 14 June 2006, 66,000
Tunisia (1) 2 *(Jaziri 23, Jaidi 90)*
Saudi Arabia (0) 2 *(Al-Kahtani 57, Al-Jaber 84)*
Tunisia: Boumnijel; Trabelsi, Jemmali, Mnari, Haggui, Jaidi, Bouazizi (Nafti 55), Namouchi, Jaziri, Chikhaoui (Essediri 82), Chedli (Ghodhbane 69).
Saudi Arabia: Zaid; Dokhy, Sulimani, Aziz, Fallatah, Al-Montashari, Al-Ghamdi, Noor (Ameen 75), Al-Temyat (Mouath 67), Al-Kahtani (Al-Jaber 82), Khariri.
Referee: Shield (Australia).

Hamburg, 19 June 2006, 50,000
Saudi Arabia (0) 0
Ukraine (2) 4 *(Rusol 4, Rebrov 36, Shevchenko 46, Kalinichenko 84)*
Saudi Arabia: Zaid; Dokhy (Al-Khathran 55), Sulimani, Aziz, Al-Montashari, Fallatah, Al-Ghamdi, Noor (Al-Jaber 77), Ameen (Mouath 55), Al-Kahtani, Khariri.
Ukraine: Shovkovskyi; Gusev, Nesmachni, Tymoschuk, Sviderskiy, Rusol, Rebrov (Rotan 71), Shelayev, Voronin (Gusin 79), Shevchenko (Milevski 86), Kalinichenko.
Referee: Poll (England).

Stuttgart, 19 June 2006, 52,000
Spain (0) 3 *(Raul 71, Fernando Torres 76, 90 (pen))*
Tunisia (1) 1 *(Mnari 8)*
Spain: Casillas; Sergio Ramos, Pernia, Xabi Alonso, Puyol, Pablo, Marcos Senna (Fabregas 46), Luis Garcia (Raul 46), Fernando Torres, Villa (Joaquin 46), Xavi.
Tunisia: Boumnijel; Trabelsi, Ayari (Yahia A 57), Nafti, Haggui, Jaidi, Bouazizi (Ghodhbane 57), Namouchi, Jaziri, Mnari, Chedli (Guemamdia 80).
Referee: Simon (Brazil).

Kaiserslautern, 23 June 2006, 46,000
Saudi Arabia (0) 0
Spain (1) 1 *(Juanito 36)*
Saudi Arabia: Zaid; Dokhy, Al-Khathran, Khariri, Fallatah, Al-Montashari, Noor, Aziz (Al-Temyat 13), Al-Harthi, Al-Jaber (Mouath 68), Sulimani (Massad 81).
Spain: Canizares; Michel Salgado, Antonio Lopez, Albelda, Juanito, Marchena, Joaquin, Fabregas (Xavi 66), Reyes (Fernando Torres 69), Raul (Villa 46), Iniesta.
Referee: Codjia (Benin).

Berlin, 23 June 2006, 72,000
Ukraine (0) 1 *(Shevchenko 70 (pen))*
Tunisia (0) 0
Ukraine: Shovkovskyi; Gusev, Nesmachni, Tymoschuk, Sviderskiy, Rusol, Rebrov (Vorobei 55), Shelayev, Voronin, Shevchenko (Milevski 88), Kalinichenko (Gusin 75).
Tunisia: Boumnijel; Trabelsi, Ayari, Nafti (Ghodhbane 90), Haggui, Jaidi, Bouazizi (Ben Saada 80), Namouchi, Jaziri■, Mnari, Chedli (Santos 79).
Referee: Demarqui (Paraguay).

GROUP H FINAL TABLE	*P*	*W*	*D*	*L*	*F*	*A*	*Pts*
Spain	3	3	0	0	8	1	9
Ukraine	3	2	0	1	5	4	6
Tunisia	3	0	1	2	3	6	1
Saudi Arabia	3	0	1	2	2	7	1

SECOND ROUND

Liepzig, 24 June 2006, 43,000
Argentina (1) 2 *(Borgetti 9 (og), Maxi Rodriguez 98)*
Mexico (1) 1 *(Marquez 5)*
Argentina: Abbondanzieri; Scaloni, Sorin, Mascherano, Ayala, Heinze, Maxi Rodriguez, Cambiasso (Aimar 76), Crespo (Tevez 75), Saviola (Messi 84), Riquelme.
Mexico: Sanchez O; Mendez, Guardado (Pineda 67), Marquez, Osorio, Salcido, Castro, Pardo (Torrado 38), Borgetti, Fonseca, Morales (Zinha 74).
Referee: Busacca (Switzerland).

Munich, 24 June 2006, 66,000
Germany (2) 2 *(Podolski 4, 12)*
Sweden (0) 0
Germany: Lehmann; Friedrich, Lahm, Frings (Kehl 85), Mertesacker, Metzelder, Schneider, Ballack, Podolski (Neuville 74), Klose, Schweinsteiger (Borowski 72).
Sweden: Isaksson; Alexandersson N, Edman, Linderoth, Mellberg, Lucic■, Jonson M (Wilhelmsson 53), Kallstrom (Hansson 39), Ibrahimovic (Allback 72), Larsson, Ljungberg.
Referee: Simon (Brazil).

Stuttgart, 25 June 2006, 52,000
England (0) 1 *(Beckham 60)*
Ecuador (0) 0
England: Robinson; Hargreaves, Cole A, Carrick, Ferdinand, Terry, Beckham (Lennon 87), Lampard, Rooney, Gerrard (Downing 90), Cole J (Carragher 77).
Ecuador: Mora; De la Cruz, Reasco, Castillo, Hurtado I, Espinoza G, Valencia, Tenorio E (Lara 69), Delgado, Tenorio C (Kaviedes 71), Mendez.
Referee: De Bleeckere (Belgium).

Nuremberg, 25 June 2006, 41,000
Portugal (1) 1 *(Maniche 23)*
Holland (0) 0
Portugal: Ricardo; Miguel, Nuno Valente, Costinha■, Fernando Meira, Ricardo Carvalho, Deco■, Figo (Tiago 84), Pauleta (Petit 46), Maniche, Ronaldo (Simao Sabrosa 34).
Holland: Van der Sar; Boulahrouz■, Van Bronckhorst■, Sneijder, Ooijer, Mathijsen (Van der Vaart 56), Van Persie, Van Bommel (Heitinga 67), Kuijt, Cocu (Vennegoor of Hesselink 84), Robben.
Referee: Ivanov (Russia).

Kaiserslautern, 26 June 2006, 46,000
Italy (0) 1 *(Totti 90 (pen))*
Australia (0) 0
Italy: Buffon; Zambrotta, Grosso, Gattuso, Cannavaro, Materazzi■, Perrotta, Pirlo, Toni (Barzagli 56), Del Piero (Totti 75), Gilardino (Iaquinta 46).
Australia: Schwarzer; Culina, Wilkshire, Moore, Neill, Chipperfield, Grella, Sterjovski (Aloisi 81), Bresciano, Viduka, Cahill.
Referee: Cantalejo (Spain).

Cologne, 26 June 2006, 45,000
Switzerland (0) 0
Ukraine (0) 0
Switzerland: Zuberbuhler; Degen P, Magnin, Vogel, Djourou (Grichting 34), Muller, Wicky, Cabanas, Yakin (Streller 64), Frei (Lustrinelli 117), Barnetta.
Ukraine: Shovkovskyi; Gusev, Nesmachni, Tymoschuk, Gusin, Vashchuk, Vorobei (Rebrov 94), Shelayev, Voronin (Milevski 111), Shevchenko, Kalinichenko (Rotan 75).
aet; Ukraine won 3-0 on penalties: Shevchenko saved; Streller saved; Milevski scored; Barnetta hit bar; Rebrov scored; Cabanas saved; Gusev scored.
Referee: Tellez (Mexico).

Dortmund, 27 June 2006, 65,000
Brazil (2) 3 *(Ronaldo 5, Adriano 45, Ze Roberto 84)*
Ghana (0) 0
Brazil: Dida; Cafu, Roberto Carlos, Ze Roberto, Lucio, Juan, Emerson (Gilberto Silva 46), Kaka (Ricardinho 83), Ronaldo, Adriano (Juninho Pernambucano 61), Ronaldinho.
Ghana: Kingston; Pantsil, Pappoe, Addo E (Boateng 60), Mensah, Shilla Illiasu, Draman, Appiah, Amoah (Tachie-Mensah 70), Gyan■, Muntari.
Referee: Michel (Slovakia).

Hanover, 27 June 2006, 43,000
Spain (1) 1 *(Villa 28 (pen))*
France (1) 3 *(Ribery 41, Vieira 83, Zidane 90)*
Spain: Casillas; Sergio Ramos, Pernia, Xabi Alonso, Pablo, Puyol, Xavi (Marcos Senna 72), Fabregas, Fernando Torres, Villa (Joaquin 54), Raul (Luis Garcia 54).
France: Barthez; Sagnol, Abidal, Makelele, Thuram, Gallas, Ribery, Vieira, Henry (Wiltord 88), Zidane, Malouda (Govou 74).
Referee: Rosetti (Italy).

QUARTER FINALS

Berlin, 30 June 2006, 72,000
Germany (0) 1 *(Klose 80)*
Argentina (0) 1 *(Ayala 49)*
Germany: Lehmann; Friedrich, Lahm, Frings, Mertesacker, Metzelder, Schneider (Odonkor 62), Ballack, Podolski, Klose (Neuville 86), Schweinsteiger (Borowski 74).
Argentina: Abbondanzieri (Leo Franco 71); Coloccini, Sorin, Mascherano, Ayala, Heinze, Maxi Rodriguez, Gonzalez L, Crespo (Cruz 79), Riquelme (Cambiasso 72), Tevez.
aet; Germany won 4-2 on penalties: Neuville scored; Cruz scored; Ballack scored; Ayala saved; Podolski scored; Maxi Rodriguez saved; Borowski scored; Cambiasso saved. Unused sub Cufre■.
Referee: Michel (Slovakia).

Hamburg, 30 June 2006, 50,000
Italy (1) 3 *(Zambrotta 6, Toni 59, 69)*
Ukraine (0) 0
Italy: Buffon; Zambrotta, Grosso, Gattuso (Zaccardo 77), Cannavaro, Barzagli, Camoranesi (Oddo 68), Pirlo (Barone 68), Toni, Totti, Perrotta.
Ukraine: Shovkovskyi; Gusev, Nesmachni, Rusol (Vashchuk 45), Gusin, Sviderskiy (Vorobei 20), Tymoschuk, Shelayev, Milevski (Byelik 72), Shevchenko, Kalinichenko.
Referee: De Bleeckere (Belgium).

Frankfurt, 1 July 2006, 48,000
Brazil (0) 0
France (0) 1 *(Henry 57)*
Brazil: Dida; Cafu (Cicinho 76), Roberto Carlos, Gilberto Silva, Lucio, Juan, Ze Roberto, Juninho Pernambucano (Adriano 63), Ronaldo, Kaka (Robinho 79), Ronaldinho.
France: Barthez; Sagnol, Abidal, Makelele, Thuram, Gallas, Ribery (Govou 77), Vieira, Henry (Saha 86), Zidane, Malouda (Wiltord 81).
Referee: Cantalejo (Spain).

Gelsenkirchen, 1 July 2006, 52,000
England (0) 0
Portugal (0) 0
England: Robinson; Neville G, Cole A, Hargreaves, Ferdinand, Terry, Beckham (Lennon 52) (Carragher 119), Lampard, Rooney■, Gerrard, Cole J (Crouch 65).
Portugal: Ricardo; Miguel, Nuno Valente, Petit, Fernando Meira, Ricardo Carvalho, Figo (Helder Postiga 86), Maniche, Pauleta (Simao Sabrosa 63), Tiago (Hugo Viana 75), Ronaldo.
aet; Portugal won 3-1 on penalties: Simao Sabrosa scored; Lampard saved; Hugo Viana hit post; Hargreaves scored; Petit missed; Gerrard saved; Helder Postiga scored; Carragher scored ordered retaken saved; Ronaldo scored.
Referee: Elizondo (Argentina).

SEMI FINALS

Dortmund, 4 July 2006, 65,000
Germany (0) 0
Italy (0) 2 *(Grosso 119, Del Piero 102)*
Germany: Lehmann; Friedrich, Lahm, Kehl, Mertesacker, Metzelder, Schneider (Odonkor 83), Ballack, Podolski, Klose (Neuville 111), Borowski (Schweinsteiger 73).
Italy: Buffon; Zambrotta, Grosso, Gattuso, Materazzi, Cannavaro, Camoranesi (Iaquinta 91), Pirlo, Toni (Gilardino 74), Totti, Perrotta (Del Piero 104).
Referee: Tellez (Mexico).

Munich, 5 July 2006, 66,000
Portugal (0) 0
France (1) 1 *(Zidane 33 (pen))*
Portugal: Ricardo; Miguel (Paulo Ferreira 62), Nuno Valente, Costinha (Helder Postiga 75), Fernando Meira, Ricardo Carvalho, Figo, Deco, Pauleta (Simao Sabrosa 68), Maniche, Ronaldo.
France: Barthez; Sagnol, Abidal, Makelele, Thuram, Gallas, Ribery (Govou 72), Vieira, Henry (Saha 85), Zidane, Malouda (Wiltord 69).
Referee: Larrionda (Uruguay).

MATCH FOR THIRD PLACE

Stuttgart, 8 July 2006, 52,000
Germany (0) 3 *(Schweinsteiger 56, 78, Petit 61 (og))*
Portugal (0) 1 *(Nuno Gomes 88)*
Germany: Kahn; Lahm, Jansen, Frings, Nowotny, Metzelder, Schneider, Kehl, Podolski (Hanke 71), Klose (Neuville 65), Schweinsteiger (Hitzlsperger 79).
Portugal: Ricardo; Paulo Ferreira, Nuno Valente (Nuno Gomes 69), Costinha (Petit 46), Fernando Meira, Ricardo Costa, Ronaldo, Deco, Pauleta (Figo 77), Maniche, Simao Sabrosa.
Referee: Kamikawa (Japan).

THE WORLD CUP FINAL 2006

Berlin, 9 July 2006, 69,000

Italy (1) 1 *(Materazzi 19)* **France (1) 1** *(Zidane 7 (pen))*

Italy: Buffon; Zambrotta, Grosso, Gattuso, Cannavaro, Materazzi, Pirlo, Camoranesi (Del Piero 86), Toni, Totti (De Rossi 61), Perrotta (Iaquinta 61).

France: Barthez; Sagnol, Abidal, Makelele, Thuram, Gallas, Ribery (Trezeguet 100), Vieira (Diarra 56), Henry (Wiltord 107), Zidane■, Malouda.

aet; Italy won 5-3 on penalties: Pirlo scored; Wiltord scored; Materazzi scored; Trezeguet hit bar; De Rossi scored; Abidal scored; Del Piero scored; Sagnol scored; Grosso scored.

Referee: Elizondo (Argentina).

EURO 2008 QUALIFYING COMPETITION
(Fixtures)

Top two from each group qualify for finals; Austria and Switzerland qualify as co-hosts.
Final Tournament 7 to 29 June 2008.

GROUP A
16.08.06 Belgium v Kazakhstan
02.09.06 Poland v Finland
02.09.06 Serbia & Montenegro v Azerbaijan
06.09.06 Armenia v Belgium
06.09.06 Azerbaijan v Kazakhstan
06.09.06 Finland v Portugal
06.09.06 Poland v Serbia & Montenegro
07.10.06 Armenia v Finland
07.10.06 Kazakhstan v Poland
07.10.06 Portugal v Azerbaijan
07.10.06 Serbia & Montenegro v Belgium
11.10.06 Belgium v Azerbaijan
11.10.06 Kazakhstan v Finland
11.10.06 Poland v Portugal
11.10.06 Serbia & Montenegro v Armenia
15.11.06 Belgium v Poland
15.11.06 Finland v Armenia
15.11.06 Portugal v Kazakhstan
24.03.07 Kazakhstan v Serbia & Montenegro
24.03.07 Poland v Azerbaijan
24.03.07 Portugal v Belgium
28.03.07 Azerbaijan v Finland
28.03.07 Poland v Armenia
28.03.07 Serbia & Montenegro v Portugal
02.06.07 Azerbaijan v Poland
02.06.07 Belgium v Portugal
02.06.07 Finland v Serbia & Montenegro
02.06.07 Kazakhstan v Armenia
06.06.07 Armenia v Poland
06.06.07 Finland v Belgium
06.06.07 Kazakhstan v Azerbaijan
22.08.07 Armenia v Portugal
22.08.07 Belgium v Serbia & Montenegro
22.08.07 Finland v Kazakhstan
08.09.07 Azerbaijan v Armenia
08.09.07 Portugal v Poland
08.09.07 Serbia & Montengro v Finland
12.09.07 Armenia v Azerbaijan
12.09.07 Finland v Poland
12.09.07 Kazakhstan v Belgium
21.09.07 Portugal v Serbia & Montenegro
13.10.07 Armenia v Serbia & Montenegro
13.10.07 Azerbaijan v Portugal
13.10.07 Belgium v Finland
13.10.07 Poland v Kazakhstan
17.10.07 Azerbaijan v Serbia & Montenegro
17.10.07 Belgium v Armenia
17.10.07 Kazakhstan v Poland
17.11.07 Finland v Azerbaijan
17.11.07 Poland v Belgium
17.11.07 Portugal v Armenia
17.11.07 Serbia & Montenegro v Kazakhstan
21.11.07 Armenia v Kazakhstan
21.11.07 Azerbaijan v Belgium
21.11.07 Portugal v Finland
21.11.07 Serbia & Montenegro v Poland

GROUP B
16.08.06 Faeroes v Georgia
02.09.06 Georgia v France
02.09.06 Italy v Lithuania
02.09.06 Scotland v Faeroes
06.09.06 France v Italy
06.09.06 Lithuania v Scotland
06.09.06 Ukraine v Georgia
07.10.06 Faeroes v Lithuania
07.10.06 Italy v Ukraine
07.10.06 Scotland v France
11.10.06 France v Faeroes
11.10.06 Georgia v Italy
11.10.06 Ukraine v Scotland
24.03.07 Lithuania v France
24.03.07 Scotland v Georgia
28.03.07 Georgia v Faeroes
28.03.07 Italy v Scotland
28.03.07 Ukraine v Lithuania
02.06.07 France v Ukraine
02.06.07 Lithuania v Georgia
02.06.07 Faeroes v Italy
06.06.07 Faeroes v Scotland
06.06.07 France v Georgia
06.06.07 Lithuania v Italy
22.08.07 Faeroes v Ukraine
08.09.07 Georgia v Ukraine
08.09.07 Italy v France
08.09.07 Scotland v Lithuania
12.09.07 France v Scotland
12.09.07 Lithuania v Faeroes
12.09.07 Ukraine v Italy
13.10.07 Faeroes v France
13.10.07 Italy v Georgia
13.10.07 Scotland v Ukraine
17.10.07 France v Lithuania
17.10.07 Scotland v Georgia
17.10.07 Ukraine v Faeroes
17.11.07 Lithuania v Ukraine
17.11.07 Scotland v Italy
21.11.07 Georgia v Lithuania
21.11.07 Italy v Faeroes
21.11.07 Ukraine v France

GROUP C
02.09.06 Hungary v Norway
02.09.06 Malta v Bosnia
02.09.06 Moldova v Greece
06.09.06 Bosnia v Hungary
06.09.06 Norway v Moldova
06.09.06 Turkey v Malta
07.10.06 Greece v Norway
07.10.06 Hungary v Turkey
07.10.06 Moldova v Bosnia
11.10.06 Bosnia v Greece
11.10.06 Malta v Hungary
11.10.06 Turkey v Moldova
24.03.07 Greece v Turkey
24.03.07 Moldova v Malta
24.03.07 Norway v Bosnia
28.03.07 Hungary v Moldova
28.03.07 Malta v Greece
28.03.07 Turkey v Norway
02.06.07 Bosnia v Turkey
02.06.07 Greece v Hungary
02.06.07 Norway v Malta
06.06.07 Greece v Moldova
06.06.07 Bosnia v Malta
06.06.07 Norway v Hungary
08.09.07 Hungary v Bosnia
08.09.07 Malta v Turkey
08.09.07 Moldova v Norway
12.09.07 Bosnia v Moldova
12.09.07 Norway v Greece
12.09.07 Turkey v Hungary
13.10.07 Greece v Bosnia
13.10.07 Hungary v Malta
13.10.07 Moldova v Turkey
17.10.07 Bosnia v Norway
17.10.07 Malta v Moldova
17.10.07 Turkey v Greece
17.11.07 Greece v Malta
17.11.07 Moldova v Hungary
17.11.07 Norway v Turkey
21.11.07 Hungary v Greece
21.11.07 Malta v Norway
21.11.07 Turkey v Bosnia

GROUP D
02.09.06 Czech Republic v Wales
02.09.06 Germany v Republic of Ireland
02.09.06 Slovakia v Cyprus
06.09.06 San Marino v Germany
06.09.06 Slovakia v Czech Republic
07.10.06 Cyprus v Republic of Ireland
07.10.06 Czech Republic v San Marino
07.10.06 Wales v Slovakia
11.10.06 Republic of Ireland v Czech Republic
11.10.06 Slovakia v Germany
11.10.06 Wales v Cyprus
15.11.06 Cyprus v Germany
15.11.06 Republic of Ireland v San Marino
07.02.07 San Marino v Republic of Ireland
24.03.07 Cyprus v Slovakia
24.03.07 Czech Republic v Germany
24.03.07 Republic of Ireland v Wales
28.03.07 Czech Republic v Cyprus
28.03.07 Republic of Ireland v Slovakia
28.03.07 Wales v San Marino
02.06.07 Germany v San Marino
02.06.07 Wales v Czech Republic
06.06.07 Germany v Slovakia
22.08.07 San Marino v Cyprus
08.09.07 San Marino v Czech Republic
08.09.07 Slovakia v Republic of Ireland
08.09.07 Wales v Germany
12.09.07 Cyprus v San Marino
12.09.07 Czech Republic v Republic of Ireland
12.09.07 Slovakia v Wales
13.10.07 Cyprus v Wales
13.10.07 Republic of Ireland v Germany
13.10.07 Slovakia v San Marino

17.10.07 Germany v Czech Republic
17.10.07 Republic of Ireland v Cyprus
17.10.07 San Marino v Wales
17.11.07 Czech Republic v Slovakia
17.11.07 Czech Republic v Slovakia
17.11.07 Germany v Cyprus
17.11.07 Wales v Republic of Ireland
21.11.07 Cyprus v Czech Republic
21.11.07 Germany v Wales
21.11.07 San Marino v Slovakia

GROUP E

16.08.06 Estonia v Macedonia
02.09.06 England v Andorra
02.09.06 Estonia v Israel
06.09.06 Israel v Andorra
06.09.06 Macedonia v England
06.09.06 Russia v Croatia
07.10.06 Croatia v Andorra
07.10.06 England v Macedonia
07.10.06 Russia v Israel
11.10.06 Andorra v Macedonia
11.10.06 Croatia v England
11.10.06 Russia v Estonia
15.11.06 Israel v Croatia
15.11.06 Macedonia v Russia
24.03.07 Croatia v Macedonia
24.03.07 Estonia v Russia
24.03.07 Israel v England
28.03.07 Andorra v England
28.03.07 Israel v Estonia
02.06.07 Estonia v Croatia
02.06.07 Macedonia v Israel
02.06.07 Russia v Andorra
06.06.07 Andorra v Israel
06.06.07 Croatia v Russia
06.06.07 Estonia v England
22.08.07 Estonia v Andorra
08.09.07 Croatia v Estonia
08.09.07 England v Israel
08.09.07 Russia v Macedonia
12.09.07 Andorra v Croatia
12.09.07 England v Russia
12.09.07 Macedonia v Estonia
13.10.07 England v Estonia
17.10.07 Croatia v Russia
17.10.07 Macedonia v Andorra
17.10.07 Russia v England
17.11.07 Andorra v Estonia
17.11.07 Israel v Russia
17.11.07 Macedonia v Croatia
21.11.07 Andorra v Russia
21.11.07 England v Croatia
21.11.07 Israel v Macedonia

GROUP F

02.09.06 Latvia v Sweden
02.09.06 Northern Ireland v Iceland
02.09.06 Spain v Liechtenstein
06.09.06 Iceland v Denmark
06.09.06 Northern Ireland v Spain
06.09.06 Sweden v Liechtenstein
07.10.06 Denmark v Northern Ireland
07.10.06 Latvia v Iceland
07.10.06 Sweden v Spain
11.10.06 Iceland v Sweden
11.10.06 Liechtenstein v Denmark
11.10.06 Northern Ireland v Latvia
24.03.07 Liechtenstein v Northern Ireland
24.03.07 Spain v Denmark
28.03.07 Liechtenstein v Latvia
28.03.07 Northern Ireland v Sweden
28.03.07 Spain v Iceland
02.06.07 Denmark v Sweden
02.06.07 Iceland v Liechtenstein
02.06.07 Latvia v Spain
06.06.07 Latvia v Denmark
06.06.07 Liechtenstein v Spain
06.06.07 Sweden v Iceland
22.08.07 Northern Ireland v Liechtenstein
08.09.07 Iceland v Spain
08.09.07 Latvia v Northern Ireland
08.09.07 Sweden v Denmark
12.09.07 Denmark v Liechtenstein
12.09.07 Iceland v Northern Ireland
12.09.07 Spain v Latvia
13.10.07 Denmark v Spain
13.10.07 Iceland v Latvia
13.10.07 Liechtenstein v Sweden
17.10.07 Denmark v Latvia
17.10.07 Liechtenstein v Iceland
17.10.07 Sweden v Northern Ireland
17.11.07 Latvia v Liechtenstein
17.11.07 Northern Ireland v Denmark
17.11.07 Spain v Sweden
21.11.07 Denmark v Iceland
21.11.07 Spain v Northern Ireland
21.11.07 Sweden v Latvia

GROUP G

02.09.06 Belarus v Albania
02.09.06 Luxembourg v Holland
02.09.06 Romania v Bulgaria
06.09.06 Albania v Romania
06.09.06 Bulgaria v Slovenia
06.09.06 Holland v Belarus
07.10.06 Bulgaria v Holland
07.10.06 Romania v Belarus
07.10.06 Slovenia v Luxembourg
11.10.06 Belarus v Slovenia
11.10.06 Luxembourg v Bulgaria
11.10.06 Holland v Albania
24.03.07 Albania v Slovenia
24.03.07 Luxembourg v Belarus
24.03.07 Holland v Romania
28.03.07 Bulgaria v Albania
28.03.07 Romania v Luxembourg
28.03.07 Slovenia v Holland
02.06.07 Albania v Luxembourg
02.06.07 Belarus v Bulgaria
02.06.07 Slovenia v Romania
06.06.07 Bulgaria v Belarus
06.06.07 Luxembourg v Albania
06.06.07 Romania v Slovenia
08.09.07 Belarus v Romania
08.09.07 Luxembourg v Slovenia
08.09.07 Holland v Bulgaria
12.09.07 Albania v Holland
12.09.07 Bulgaria v Luxembourg
12.09.07 Slovenia v Belarus
13.10.07 Belarus v Luxembourg
13.10.07 Romania v Holland
13.10.07 Slovenia v Albania
17.10.07 Albania v Bulgaria
17.10.07 Luxembourg v Romania
17.10.07 Holland v Slovenia
17.11.07 Albania v Belarus
17.11.07 Bulgaria v Romania
17.11.07 Holland v Luxembourg
21.11.07 Belarus v Holland
21.11.07 Romania v Albania
21.11.07 Slovenia v Bulgaria

EUROPEAN FOOTBALL CHAMPIONSHIP

(formerly EUROPEAN NATIONS' CUP)

Year	*Winners*		*Runners-up*		*Venue*	*Attendance*
1960	USSR	2	Yugoslavia	1	Paris	17,966
1964	Spain	2	USSR	1	Madrid	120,000
1968	Italy After 1-1 draw	2	Yugoslavia	0	Rome	60,000 75,000
1972	West Germany	3	USSR	0	Brussels	43,437
1976	Czechoslovakia *(Czechoslovakia won on penalties)*	2	West Germany	2	Belgrade	45,000
1980	West Germany	2	Belgium	1	Rome	47,864
1984	France	2	Spain	0	Paris	48,000
1988	Holland	2	USSR	0	Munich	72,308
1992	Denmark	2	Germany	0	Gothenburg	37,800
1996	Germany *(Germany won on sudden death)*	2	Czech Republic	1	Wembley	73,611
2000	France *(France won on sudden death)*	2	Italy	1	Rotterdam	50,000
2004	Greece	1	Portugal	0	Lisbon	62,865

BRITISH AND IRISH INTERNATIONAL RESULTS 1872–2006

Note: In the results that follow, WC=World Cup, EC=European Championship, UI=Umbro International Trophy. TF = Tournoi de France. For Ireland, read Northern Ireland from 1921. *After extra time.

ENGLAND v SCOTLAND

Played: 110; England won 45, Scotland won 41, Drawn 24. Goals: England 192, Scotland 169.

Year	Date	Venue	E	S
1872	30 Nov	Glasgow	0	0
1873	8 Mar	Kennington Oval	4	2
1874	7 Mar	Glasgow	1	2
1875	6 Mar	Kennington Oval	2	2
1876	4 Mar	Glasgow	0	3
1877	3 Mar	Kennington Oval	1	3
1878	2 Mar	Glasgow	2	7
1879	5 Apr	Kennington Oval	5	4
1880	13 Mar	Glasgow	4	5
1881	12 Mar	Kennington Oval	1	6
1882	11 Mar	Glasgow	1	5
1883	10 Mar	Sheffield	2	3
1884	15 Mar	Glasgow	0	1
1885	21 Mar	Kennington Oval	1	1
1886	31 Mar	Glasgow	1	1
1887	19 Mar	Blackburn	2	3
1888	17 Mar	Glasgow	5	0
1889	13 Apr	Kennington Oval	2	3
1890	5 Apr	Glasgow	1	1
1891	6 Apr	Blackburn	2	1
1892	2 Apr	Glasgow	4	1
1893	1 Apr	Richmond	5	2
1894	7 Apr	Glasgow	2	2
1895	6 Apr	Everton	3	0
1896	4 Apr	Glasgow	1	2
1897	3 Apr	Crystal Palace	1	2
1898	2 Apr	Glasgow	3	1
1899	8 Apr	Birmingham	2	1
1900	7 Apr	Glasgow	1	4
1901	30 Mar	Crystal Palace	2	2
1902	3 Mar	Birmingham	2	2
1903	4 Apr	Sheffield	1	2
1904	9 Apr	Glasgow	1	0
1905	1 Apr	Crystal Palace	1	0
1906	7 Apr	Glasgow	1	2
1907	6 Apr	Newcastle	1	1
1908	4 Apr	Glasgow	1	1
1909	3 Apr	Crystal Palace	2	0
1910	2 Apr	Glasgow	0	2
1911	1 Apr	Everton	1	1
1912	23 Mar	Glasgow	1	1
1913	5 Apr	Chelsea	1	0
1914	14 Apr	Glasgow	1	3
1920	10 Apr	Sheffield	5	4
1921	9 Apr	Glasgow	0	3
1922	8 Apr	Aston Villa	0	1
1923	14 Apr	Glasgow	2	2
1924	12 Apr	Wembley	1	1
1925	4 Apr	Glasgow	0	2
1926	17 Apr	Manchester	0	1
1927	2 Apr	Glasgow	2	1
1928	31 Mar	Wembley	1	5
1929	13 Apr	Glasgow	0	1
1930	5 Apr	Wembley	5	2
1931	28 Mar	Glasgow	0	2
1932	9 Apr	Wembley	3	0
1933	1 Apr	Glasgow	1	2
1934	14 Apr	Wembley	3	0
1935	6 Apr	Glasgow	0	2
1936	4 Apr	Wembley	1	1
1937	17 Apr	Glasgow	1	3
1938	9 Apr	Wembley	0	1
1939	15 Apr	Glasgow	2	1
1947	12 Apr	Wembley	1	1
1948	10 Apr	Glasgow	2	0
1949	9 Apr	Wembley	1	3
WC1950	15 Apr	Glasgow	1	0
1951	14 Apr	Wembley	2	3
1952	5 Apr	Glasgow	2	1
1953	18 Apr	Wembley	2	2
WC1954	3 Apr	Glasgow	4	2
1955	2 Apr	Wembley	7	2
1956	14 Apr	Glasgow	1	1
1957	6 Apr	Wembley	2	1
1958	19 Apr	Glasgow	4	0
1959	11 Apr	Wembley	1	0
1960	9 Apr	Glasgow	1	1
1961	15 Apr	Wembley	9	3
1962	14 Apr	Glasgow	0	2
1963	6 Apr	Wembley	1	2
1964	11 Apr	Glasgow	0	1
1965	10 Apr	Wembley	2	2
1966	2 Apr	Glasgow	4	3
EC1967	15 Apr	Wembley	2	3
EC1968	24 Jan	Glasgow	1	1
1969	10 May	Wembley	4	1
1970	25 Apr	Glasgow	0	0
1971	22 May	Wembley	3	1
1972	27 May	Glasgow	1	0
1973	14 Feb	Glasgow	5	0
1973	19 May	Wembley	1	0
1974	18 May	Glasgow	0	2
1975	24 May	Wembley	5	1
1976	15 May	Glasgow	1	2
1977	4 June	Wembley	1	2
1978	20 May	Glasgow	1	0
1979	26 May	Wembley	3	1
1980	24 May	Glasgow	2	0
1981	23 May	Wembley	0	1
1982	29 May	Glasgow	1	0
1983	1 June	Wembley	2	0
1984	26 May	Glasgow	1	1
1985	25 May	Glasgow	0	1
1986	23 Apr	Wembley	2	1
1987	23 May	Glasgow	0	0
1988	21 May	Wembley	1	0
1989	27 May	Glasgow	2	0
EC1996	15 June	Wembley	2	0
EC1999	13 Nov	Glasgow	2	0
EC1999	17 Nov	Wembley	0	1

ENGLAND v WALES

Played: 99; England won 64, Wales won 14, Drawn 21. Goals: England 242, Wales 90.

Year	Date	Venue	E	W
1879	18 Jan	Kennington Oval	2	1
1880	15 Mar	Wrexham	3	2
1881	26 Feb	Blackburn	0	1
1882	13 Mar	Wrexham	3	5
1883	3 Feb	Kennington Oval	5	0
1884	17 Mar	Wrexham	4	0

			E	*W*
1885	14 Mar	Blackburn	1	1
1886	29 Mar	Wrexham	3	1
1887	26 Feb	Kennington Oval	4	0
1888	4 Feb	Crewe	5	1
1889	23 Feb	Stoke	4	1
1890	15 Mar	Wrexham	3	1
1891	7 May	Sunderland	4	1
1892	5 Mar	Wrexham	2	0
1893	13 Mar	Stoke	6	0
1894	12 Mar	Wrexham	5	1
1895	18 Mar	Queen's Club, Kensington	1	1
1896	16 Mar	Cardiff	9	1
1897	29 Mar	Sheffield	4	0
1898	28 Mar	Wrexham	3	0
1899	20 Mar	Bristol	4	0
1900	26 Mar	Cardiff	1	1
1901	18 Mar	Newcastle	6	0
1902	3 Mar	Wrexham	0	0
1903	2 Mar	Portsmouth	2	1
1904	29 Feb	Wrexham	2	2
1905	27 Mar	Liverpool	3	1
1906	19 Mar	Cardiff	1	0
1907	18 Mar	Fulham	1	1
1908	16 Mar	Wrexham	7	1
1909	15 Mar	Nottingham	2	0
1910	14 Mar	Cardiff	1	0
1911	13 Mar	Millwall	3	0
1912	11 Mar	Wrexham	2	0
1913	17 Mar	Bristol	4	3
1914	16 Mar	Cardiff	2	0
1920	15 Mar	Highbury	1	2
1921	14 Mar	Cardiff	0	0
1922	13 Mar	Liverpool	1	0
1923	5 Mar	Cardiff	2	2
1924	3 Mar	Blackburn	1	2
1925	28 Feb	Swansea	2	1
1926	1 Mar	Crystal Palace	1	3
1927	12 Feb	Wrexham	3	3
1927	28 Nov	Burnley	1	2
1928	17 Nov	Swansea	3	2
1929	20 Nov	Chelsea	6	0
1930	22 Nov	Wrexham	4	0
1931	18 Nov	Liverpool	3	1
1932	16 Nov	Wrexham	0	0
1933	15 Nov	Newcastle	1	2
1934	29 Sept	Cardiff	4	0
1936	5 Feb	Wolverhampton	1	2
1936	17 Oct	Cardiff	1	2
1937	17 Nov	Middlesbrough	2	1
1938	22 Oct	Cardiff	2	4
1946	13 Nov	Manchester	3	0
1947	18 Oct	Cardiff	3	0
1948	10 Nov	Aston Villa	1	0
wc1949	15 Oct	Cardiff	4	1
1950	15 Nov	Sunderland	4	2
1951	20 Oct	Cardiff	1	1
1952	12 Nov	Wembley	5	2
wc1953	10 Oct	Cardiff	4	1
1954	10 Nov	Wembley	3	2
1955	27 Oct	Cardiff	1	2
1956	14 Nov	Wembley	3	1
1957	19 Oct	Cardiff	4	0
1958	26 Nov	Aston Villa	2	2
1959	17 Oct	Cardiff	1	1
1960	23 Nov	Wembley	5	1
1961	14 Oct	Cardiff	1	1
1962	21 Oct	Wembley	4	0
1963	12 Oct	Cardiff	4	0
1964	18 Nov	Wembley	2	1
1965	2 Oct	Cardiff	0	0
EC1966	16 Nov	Wembley	5	1
EC1967	21 Oct	Cardiff	3	0
1969	7 May	Wembley	2	1
1970	18 Apr	Cardiff	1	1
1971	19 May	Wembley	0	0
1972	20 May	Cardiff	3	0
wc1972	15 Nov	Cardiff	1	0
wc1973	24 Jan	Wembley	1	1
1973	15 May	Wembley	3	0
1974	11 May	Cardiff	2	0
1975	21 May	Wembley	2	2
1976	24 Mar	Wrexham	2	1
1976	8 May	Cardiff	1	0
1977	31 May	Wembley	0	1
1978	3 May	Cardiff	3	1
1979	23 May	Wembley	0	0
1980	17 May	Wrexham	1	4
1981	20 May	Wembley	0	0
1982	27 Apr	Cardiff	1	0
1983	23 Feb	Wembley	2	1
1984	2 May	Wrexham	0	1
wc2004	9 Oct	Old Trafford	2	0
wc2005	3 Sept	Cardiff	1	0

ENGLAND v IRELAND

Played: 98; England won 75, Ireland won 7, Drawn 16. Goals: England 323, Ireland 81.

			E	*I*
1882	18 Feb	Belfast	13	0
1883	24 Feb	Liverpool	7	0
1884	23 Feb	Belfast	8	1
1885	28 Feb	Manchester	4	0
1886	13 Mar	Belfast	6	1
1887	5 Feb	Sheffield	7	0
1888	31 Mar	Belfast	5	1
1889	2 Mar	Everton	6	1
1890	15 Mar	Belfast	9	1
1891	7 Mar	Wolverhampton	6	1
1892	5 Mar	Belfast	2	0
1893	25 Feb	Birmingham	6	1
1894	3 Mar	Belfast	2	2
1895	9 Mar	Derby	9	0
1896	7 Mar	Belfast	2	0
1897	20 Feb	Nottingham	6	0
1898	5 Mar	Belfast	3	2
1899	18 Feb	Sunderland	13	2
1900	17 Mar	Dublin	2	0
1901	9 Mar	Southampton	3	0
1902	22 Mar	Belfast	1	0
1903	14 Feb	Wolverhampton	4	0
1904	12 Mar	Belfast	3	1
1905	25 Feb	Middlesbrough	1	1
1906	17 Feb	Belfast	5	0
1907	16 Feb	Everton	1	0
1908	15 Feb	Belfast	3	1
1909	13 Feb	Bradford	4	0
1910	12 Feb	Belfast	1	1
1911	11 Feb	Derby	2	1
1912	10 Feb	Dublin	6	1
1913	15 Feb	Belfast	1	2
1914	14 Feb	Middlesbrough	0	3
1919	25 Oct	Belfast	1	1
1920	23 Oct	Sunderland	2	0
1921	22 Oct	Belfast	1	1
1922	21 Oct	West Bromwich	2	0
1923	20 Oct	Belfast	1	2
1924	22 Oct	Everton	3	1
1925	24 Oct	Belfast	0	0
1926	20 Oct	Liverpool	3	3
1927	22 Oct	Belfast	0	2

Year	Date	Venue	E	I
1928	22 Oct	Everton	2	1
1929	19 Oct	Belfast	3	0
1930	20 Oct	Sheffield	5	1
1931	17 Oct	Belfast	6	2
1932	17 Oct	Blackpool	1	0
1933	14 Oct	Belfast	3	0
1935	6 Feb	Everton	2	1
1935	19 Oct	Belfast	3	1
1936	18 Nov	Stoke	3	1
1937	23 Oct	Belfast	5	1
1938	16 Nov	Manchester	7	0
1946	28 Sept	Belfast	7	2
1947	5 Nov	Everton	2	2
1948	9 Oct	Belfast	6	2
wc1949	16 Nov	Manchester	9	2
1950	7 Oct	Belfast	4	1
1951	14 Nov	Aston Villa	2	0
1952	4 Oct	Belfast	2	2
wc1953	11 Nov	Everton	3	1
1954	2 Oct	Belfast	2	0
1955	2 Nov	Wembley	3	0
1956	10 Oct	Belfast	1	1
1957	6 Nov	Wembley	2	3
1958	4 Oct	Belfast	3	3
1959	18 Nov	Wembley	2	1
1960	8 Oct	Belfast	5	2
1961	22 Nov	Wembley	1	1

Year	Date	Venue	E	I
1962	20 Oct	Belfast	3	1
1963	20 Nov	Wembley	8	3
1964	3 Oct	Belfast	4	3
1965	10 Nov	Wembley	2	1
EC1966	20 Oct	Belfast	2	0
EC1967	22 Nov	Wembley	2	0
1969	3 May	Belfast	3	1
1970	21 Apr	Wembley	3	1
1971	15 May	Belfast	1	0
1972	23 May	Wembley	0	1
1973	12 May	Everton	2	1
1974	15 May	Wembley	1	0
1975	17 May	Belfast	0	0
1976	11 May	Wembley	4	0
1977	28 May	Belfast	2	1
1978	16 May	Wembley	1	0
EC1979	7 Feb	Wembley	4	0
1979	19 May	Belfast	2	0
EC1979	17 Oct	Belfast	5	1
1980	20 May	Wembley	1	1
1982	23 Feb	Wembley	4	0
1983	28 May	Belfast	0	0
1984	24 Apr	Wembley	1	0
wc1985	27 Feb	Belfast	1	0
wc1985	13 Nov	Wembley	0	0
EC1986	15 Oct	Wembley	3	0
EC1987	1 Apr	Belfast	2	0
wc2005	26 Mar	Old Trafford	4	0
wc2005	7 Sept	Belfast	0	1

SCOTLAND v WALES

Played: 103; Scotland won 60, Wales won 20, Drawn 23. Goals: Scotland 238, Wales 116.

Year	Date	Venue	S	W
1876	25 Mar	Glasgow	4	0
1877	5 Mar	Wrexham	2	0
1878	23 Mar	Glasgow	9	0
1879	7 Apr	Wrexham	3	0
1880	3 Apr	Glasgow	5	1
1881	14 Mar	Wrexham	5	1
1882	25 Mar	Glasgow	5	0
1883	12 Mar	Wrexham	3	0
1884	29 Mar	Glasgow	4	1
1885	23 Mar	Wrexham	8	1
1886	10 Apr	Glasgow	4	1
1887	21 Mar	Wrexham	2	0
1888	10 Mar	Edinburgh	5	1
1889	15 Apr	Wrexham	0	0
1890	22 Mar	Paisley	5	0
1891	21 Mar	Wrexham	4	3
1892	26 Mar	Edinburgh	6	1
1893	18 Mar	Wrexham	8	0
1894	24 Mar	Kilmarnock	5	2
1895	23 Mar	Wrexham	2	2
1896	21 Mar	Dundee	4	0
1897	20 Mar	Wrexham	2	2
1898	19 Mar	Motherwell	5	2
1899	18 Mar	Wrexham	6	0
1900	3 Feb	Aberdeen	5	2
1901	2 Mar	Wrexham	1	1
1902	15 Mar	Greenock	5	1
1903	9 Mar	Cardiff	1	0
1904	12 Mar	Dundee	1	1
1905	6 Mar	Wrexham	1	3
1906	3 Mar	Edinburgh	0	2
1907	4 Mar	Wrexham	0	1
1908	7 Mar	Dundee	2	1
1909	1 Mar	Wrexham	2	3
1910	5 Mar	Kilmarnock	1	0
1911	6 Mar	Cardiff	2	2
1912	2 Mar	Tynecastle	1	0
1913	3 Mar	Wrexham	0	0
1914	28 Feb	Glasgow	0	0
1920	26 Feb	Cardiff	1	1

Year	Date	Venue	S	W
1921	12 Feb	Aberdeen	2	1
1922	4 Feb	Wrexham	1	2
1923	17 Mar	Paisley	2	0
1924	16 Feb	Cardiff	0	2
1925	14 Feb	Tynecastle	3	1
1925	31 Oct	Cardiff	3	0
1926	30 Oct	Glasgow	3	0
1927	29 Oct	Wrexham	2	2
1928	27 Oct	Glasgow	4	2
1929	26 Oct	Cardiff	4	2
1930	25 Oct	Glasgow	1	1
1931	31 Oct	Wrexham	3	2
1932	26 Oct	Edinburgh	2	5
1933	4 Oct	Cardiff	2	3
1934	21 Nov	Aberdeen	3	2
1935	5 Oct	Cardiff	1	1
1936	2 Dec	Dundee	1	2
1937	30 Oct	Cardiff	1	2
1938	9 Nov	Edinburgh	3	2
1946	19 Oct	Wrexham	1	3
1947	12 Nov	Glasgow	1	2
wc1948	23 Oct	Cardiff	3	1
1949	9 Nov	Glasgow	2	0
1950	21 Oct	Cardiff	3	1
1951	14 Nov	Glasgow	0	1
wc1952	18 Oct	Cardiff	2	1
1953	4 Nov	Glasgow	3	3
1954	16 Oct	Cardiff	1	0
1955	9 Nov	Glasgow	2	0
1956	20 Oct	Cardiff	2	2
1957	13 Nov	Glasgow	1	1
1958	18 Oct	Cardiff	3	0
1959	4 Nov	Glasgow	1	1
1960	20 Oct	Cardiff	0	2
1961	8 Nov	Glasgow	2	0
1962	20 Oct	Cardiff	3	2
1963	20 Nov	Glasgow	2	1
1964	3 Oct	Cardiff	2	3
EC1965	24 Nov	Glasgow	4	1
EC1966	22 Oct	Cardiff	1	1

			S	W
1967	22 Nov	Glasgow	3	2
1969	3 May	Wrexham	5	3
1970	22 Apr	Glasgow	0	0
1971	15 May	Cardiff	0	0
1972	24 May	Glasgow	1	0
1973	12 May	Wrexham	2	0
1974	14 May	Glasgow	2	0
1975	17 May	Cardiff	2	2
1976	6 May	Glasgow	3	1
wc1976	17 Nov	Glasgow	1	0
1977	28 May	Wrexham	0	0
wc1977	12 Oct	Liverpool	2	0
1978	17 May	Glasgow	1	1
1979	19 May	Cardiff	0	3
1980	21 May	Glasgow	1	0
1981	16 May	Swansea	0	2
1982	24 May	Glasgow	1	0
1983	28 May	Cardiff	2	0
1984	28 Feb	Glasgow	2	1
wc1985	27 Mar	Glasgow	0	1
wc1985	10 Sept	Cardiff	1	1
1997	27 May	Kilmarnock	0	1
2004	18 Feb	Cardiff	0	4

SCOTLAND v IRELAND

Played: 93; Scotland won 62, Ireland won 15, Drawn 16. Goals: Scotland 257, Ireland 81.

			S	I
1884	26 Jan	Belfast	5	0
1885	14 Mar	Glasgow	8	2
1886	20 Mar	Belfast	7	2
1887	19 Feb	Glasgow	4	1
1888	24 Mar	Belfast	10	2
1889	9 Mar	Glasgow	7	0
1890	29 Mar	Belfast	4	1
1891	28 Mar	Glasgow	2	1
1892	19 Mar	Belfast	3	2
1893	25 Mar	Glasgow	6	1
1894	31 Mar	Belfast	2	1
1895	30 Mar	Glasgow	3	1
1896	28 Mar	Belfast	3	3
1897	27 Mar	Glasgow	5	1
1898	26 Mar	Belfast	3	0
1899	25 Mar	Glasgow	9	1
1900	3 Mar	Belfast	3	0
1901	23 Feb	Glasgow	11	0
1902	1 Mar	Belfast	5	1
1902	9 Aug	Belfast	3	0
1903	21 Mar	Glasgow	0	2
1904	26 Mar	Dublin	1	1
1905	18 Mar	Glasgow	4	0
1906	17 Mar	Dublin	1	0
1907	16 Mar	Glasgow	3	0
1908	14 Mar	Dublin	5	0
1909	15 Mar	Glasgow	5	0
1910	19 Mar	Belfast	0	1
1911	18 Mar	Glasgow	2	0
1912	16 Mar	Belfast	4	1
1913	15 Mar	Dublin	2	1
1914	14 Mar	Belfast	1	1
1920	13 Mar	Glasgow	3	0
1921	26 Feb	Belfast	2	0
1922	4 Mar	Glasgow	2	1
1923	3 Mar	Belfast	1	0
1924	1 Mar	Glasgow	2	0
1925	28 Feb	Belfast	3	0
1926	27 Feb	Glasgow	4	0
1927	26 Feb	Belfast	2	0
1928	25 Feb	Glasgow	0	1
1929	23 Feb	Belfast	7	3
1930	22 Feb	Glasgow	3	1
1931	21 Feb	Belfast	0	0
1931	19 Sept	Glasgow	3	1
1932	12 Sept	Belfast	4	0
1933	16 Sept	Glasgow	1	2
1934	20 Oct	Belfast	1	2
1935	13 Nov	Edinburgh	2	1
1936	31 Oct	Belfast	3	1
1937	10 Nov	Aberdeen	1	1
1938	8 Oct	Belfast	2	0
1946	27 Nov	Glasgow	0	0
1947	4 Oct	Belfast	0	2
1948	17 Nov	Glasgow	3	2
1949	1 Oct	Belfast	8	2
1950	1 Nov	Glasgow	6	1
1951	6 Oct	Belfast	3	0
1952	5 Nov	Glasgow	1	1
1953	3 Oct	Belfast	3	1
1954	3 Nov	Glasgow	2	2
1955	8 Oct	Belfast	1	2
1956	7 Nov	Glasgow	1	0
1957	5 Oct	Belfast	1	1
1958	5 Nov	Glasgow	2	2
1959	3 Oct	Belfast	4	0
1960	9 Nov	Glasgow	5	2
1961	7 Oct	Belfast	6	1
1962	7 Nov	Glasgow	5	1
1963	12 Oct	Belfast	1	2
1964	25 Nov	Glasgow	3	2
1965	2 Oct	Belfast	2	3
1966	16 Nov	Glasgow	2	1
1967	21 Oct	Belfast	0	1
1969	6 May	Glasgow	1	1
1970	18 Apr	Belfast	1	0
1971	18 May	Glasgow	0	1
1972	20 May	Glasgow	2	0
1973	16 May	Glasgow	1	2
1974	11 May	Glasgow	0	1
1975	20 May	Glasgow	3	0
1976	8 May	Glasgow	3	0
1977	1 June	Glasgow	3	0
1978	13 May	Glasgow	1	1
1979	22 May	Glasgow	1	0
1980	17 May	Belfast	0	1
wc1981	25 Mar	Glasgow	1	1
1981	19 May	Glasgow	2	0
wc1981	14 Oct	Belfast	0	0
1982	28 Apr	Belfast	1	1
1983	24 May	Glasgow	0	0
1983	13 Dec	Belfast	0	2
1992	19 Feb	Glasgow	1	0

WALES v IRELAND

Played: 92; Wales won 43, Ireland won 27, Drawn 22. Goals: Wales 187, Ireland 131.

			W	I
1882	25 Feb	Wrexham	7	1
1883	17 Mar	Belfast	1	1
1884	9 Feb	Wrexham	6	0
1885	11 Apr	Belfast	8	2
1886	27 Feb	Wrexham	5	0
1887	12 Mar	Belfast	1	4
1888	3 Mar	Wrexham	11	0
1889	27 Apr	Belfast	3	1

			W	*I*
1890	8 Feb	Shrewsbury	5	2
1891	7 Feb	Belfast	2	7
1892	27 Feb	Bangor	1	1
1893	8 Apr	Belfast	3	4
1894	24 Feb	Swansea	4	1
1895	16 Mar	Belfast	2	2
1896	29 Feb	Wrexham	6	1
1897	6 Mar	Belfast	3	4
1898	19 Feb	Llandudno	0	1
1899	4 Mar	Belfast	0	1
1900	24 Feb	Llandudno	2	0
1901	23 Mar	Belfast	1	0
1902	22 Mar	Cardiff	0	3
1903	28 Mar	Belfast	0	2
1904	21 Mar	Bangor	0	1
1905	18 Apr	Belfast	2	2
1906	2 Apr	Wrexham	4	4
1907	23 Feb	Belfast	3	2
1908	11 Apr	Aberdare	0	1
1909	20 Mar	Belfast	3	2
1910	11 Apr	Wrexham	4	1
1911	28 Jan	Belfast	2	1
1912	13 Apr	Cardiff	2	3
1913	18 Jan	Belfast	1	0
1914	19 Jan	Wrexham	1	2
1920	14 Feb	Belfast	2	2
1921	9 Apr	Swansea	2	1
1922	4 Apr	Belfast	1	1
1923	14 Apr	Wrexham	0	3
1924	15 Mar	Belfast	1	0
1925	18 Apr	Wrexham	0	0
1926	13 Feb	Belfast	0	3
1927	9 Apr	Cardiff	2	2
1928	4 Feb	Belfast	2	1
1929	2 Feb	Wrexham	2	2
1930	1 Feb	Belfast	0	7
1931	22 Apr	Wrexham	3	2
1931	5 Dec	Belfast	0	4
1932	7 Dec	Wrexham	4	1
1933	4 Nov	Belfast	1	1
1935	27 Mar	Wrexham	3	1
1936	11 Mar	Belfast	2	3

			W	*I*
1937	17 Mar	Wrexham	4	1
1938	16 Mar	Belfast	0	1
1939	15 Mar	Wrexham	3	1
1947	16 Apr	Belfast	1	2
1948	10 Mar	Wrexham	2	0
1949	9 Mar	Belfast	2	0
wc1950	8 Mar	Wrexham	0	0
1951	7 Mar	Belfast	2	1
1952	19 Mar	Swansea	3	0
1953	15 Apr	Belfast	3	2
wc1954	31 Mar	Wrexham	1	2
1955	20 Apr	Belfast	3	2
1956	11 Apr	Cardiff	1	1
1957	10 Apr	Belfast	0	0
1958	16 Apr	Cardiff	1	1
1959	22 Apr	Belfast	1	4
1960	6 Apr	Wrexham	3	2
1961	12 Apr	Belfast	5	1
1962	11 Apr	Cardiff	4	0
1963	3 Apr	Belfast	4	1
1964	15 Apr	Cardiff	2	3
1965	31 Mar	Belfast	5	0
1966	30 Mar	Cardiff	1	4
EC1967	12 Apr	Belfast	0	0
EC1968	28 Feb	Wrexham	2	0
1969	10 May	Belfast	0	0
1970	25 Apr	Swansea	1	0
1971	22 May	Belfast	0	1
1972	27 May	Wrexham	0	0
1973	19 May	Everton	0	1
1974	18 May	Wrexham	1	0
1975	23 May	Belfast	0	1
1976	14 May	Swansea	1	0
1977	3 June	Belfast	1	1
1978	19 May	Wrexham	1	0
1979	25 May	Belfast	1	1
1980	23 May	Cardiff	0	1
1982	27 May	Wrexham	3	0
1983	31 May	Belfast	1	0
1984	22 May	Swansea	1	1
wc2004	8 Sept	Cardiff	2	2
wc2005	8 Oct	Belfast	3	2

OTHER BRITISH INTERNATIONAL RESULTS 1908–2006

ENGLAND

		v ALBANIA	*E*	*A*
wc1989	8 Mar	Tirana	2	0
wc1989	26 Apr	Wembley	5	0
wc2001	28 Mar	Tirana	3	1
wc2001	5 Sept	Newcastle	2	0

		v ARGENTINA	*E*	*A*
1951	9 May	Wembley	2	1
1953	17 May	Buenos Aires	0	0
(*abandoned after 21 mins*)				
wc1962	2 June	Rancagua	3	1
1964	6 June	Rio de Janeiro	0	1
wc1966	23 July	Wembley	1	0
1974	22 May	Wembley	2	2
1977	12 June	Buenos Aires	1	1
1980	13 May	Wembley	3	1
wc1986	22 June	Mexico City	1	2
1991	25 May	Wembley	2	2
wc1998	30 June	St Etienne	2	2
2000	23 Feb	Wembley	0	0
wc2002	7 June	Sapporo	1	0
2005	12 Nov	Geneva	3	2

		v AUSTRALIA	*E*	*A*
1980	31 May	Sydney	2	1
1983	11 June	Sydney	0	0
1983	15 June	Brisbane	1	0
1983	18 June	Melbourne	1	1
1991	1 June	Sydney	1	0
2003	12 Feb	West Ham	1	3

		v AUSTRIA	*E*	*A*
1908	6 June	Vienna	6	1
1908	8 June	Vienna	11	1
1909	1 June	Vienna	8	1
1930	14 May	Vienna	0	0
1932	7 Dec	Chelsea	4	3
1936	6 May	Vienna	1	2
1951	28 Nov	Wembley	2	2
1952	25 May	Vienna	3	2
wc1958	15 June	Boras	2	2
1961	27 May	Vienna	1	3
1962	4 Apr	Wembley	3	1
1965	20 Oct	Wembley	2	3
1967	27 May	Vienna	1	0
1973	26 Sept	Wembley	7	0
1979	13 June	Vienna	3	4
wc2004	4 Sept	Vienna	2	2
wc2005	8 Oct	Old Trafford	1	0

		v AZERBAIJAN	*E*	*A*
wc2004	13 Oct	Baku	1	0
wc2005	30 Mar	St James' Park	2	0

		v BELGIUM	*E*	*B*
1921	21 May	Brussels	2	0
1923	19 Mar	Highbury	6	1
1923	1 Nov	Antwerp	2	2
1924	8 Dec	West Bromwich	4	0
1926	24 May	Antwerp	5	3
1927	11 May	Brussels	9	1
1928	19 May	Antwerp	3	1
1929	11 May	Brussels	5	1
1931	16 May	Brussels	4	1

			E	*B*
1936	9 May	Brussels	2	3
1947	21 Sept	Brussels	5	2
1950	18 May	Brussels	4	1
1952	26 Nov	Wembley	5	0
WC1954	17 June	Basle	4	4*
1964	21 Oct	Wembley	2	2
1970	25 Feb	Brussels	3	1
EC1980	12 June	Turin	1	1
WC1990	27 June	Bologna	1	0*
1998	29 May	Casablanca	0	0
1999	10 Oct	Sunderland	2	1

		v BOHEMIA	*E*	*B*
1908	13 June	Prague	4	0

		v BRAZIL	*E*	*B*
1956	9 May	Wembley	4	2
WC1958	11 June	Gothenburg	0	0
1959	13 May	Rio de Janeiro	0	2
WC1962	10 June	Vina del Mar	1	3
1963	8 May	Wembley	1	1
1964	30 May	Rio de Janeiro	1	5
1969	12 June	Rio de Janeiro	1	2
WC1970	7 June	Guadalajara	0	1
1976	23 May	Los Angeles	0	1
1977	8 June	Rio de Janeiro	0	0
1978	19 Apr	Wembley	1	1
1981	12 May	Wembley	0	1
1984	10 June	Rio de Janeiro	2	0
1987	19 May	Wembley	1	1
1990	28 Mar	Wembley	1	0
1992	17 May	Wembley	1	1
1993	13 June	Washington	1	1
UI1995	11 June	Wembley	1	3
TF1997	10 June	Paris	0	1
2000	27 May	Wembley	1	1
WC2002	21 June	Shizuoka	1	2

		v BULGARIA	*E*	*B*
WC1962	7 June	Rancagua	0	0
1968	11 Dec	Wembley	1	1
1974	1 June	Sofia	1	0
EC1979	6 June	Sofia	3	0
EC1979	22 Nov	Wembley	2	0
1996	27 Mar	Wembley	1	0
EC1998	10 Oct	Wembley	0	0
EC1999	9 June	Sofia	1	1

		v CAMEROON	*E*	*C*
WC1990	1 July	Naples	3	2*
1991	6 Feb	Wembley	2	0
1997	15 Nov	Wembley	2	0
2002	26 May	Kobe	2	2

		v CANADA	*E*	*C*
1986	24 May	Burnaby	1	0

		v CHILE	*E*	*C*
WC1950	25 June	Rio de Janeiro	2	0
1953	24 May	Santiago	2	1
1984	17 June	Santiago	0	0
1989	23 May	Wembley	0	0
1998	11 Feb	Wembley	0	2

		v CHINA	*E*	*C*
1996	23 May	Beijing	3	0

		v CIS	*E*	*C*
1992	29 Apr	Moscow	2	2

		v COLOMBIA	*E*	*C*
1970	20 May	Bogota	4	0
1988	24 May	Wembley	1	1
1995	6 Sept	Wembley	0	0
WC1998	26 June	Lens	2	0
2005	31 May	New Jersey	3	2

		v CROATIA	*E*	*C*
1996	24 Apr	Wembley	0	0
2003	20 Aug	Ipswich	3	1
EC2004	21 June	Lisbon	4	2

		v CYPRUS	*E*	*C*
EC1975	16 Apr	Wembley	5	0
EC1975	11 May	Limassol	1	0

		v CZECHOSLOVAKIA	*E*	*C*
1934	16 May	Prague	1	2
1937	1 Dec	Tottenham	5	4
1963	29 May	Bratislava	4	2
1966	2 Nov	Wembley	0	0
WC1970	11 June	Guadalajara	1	0
1973	27 May	Prague	1	1
EC1974	30 Oct	Wembley	3	0
EC1975	30 Oct	Bratislava	1	2
1978	29 Nov	Wembley	1	0
WC1982	20 June	Bilbao	2	0
1990	25 Apr	Wembley	4	2
1992	25 Mar	Prague	2	2

		v CZECH REPUBLIC	*E*	*C*
1998	18 Nov	Wembley	2	0

		v DENMARK	*E*	*D*
1948	26 Sept	Copenhagen	0	0
1955	2 Oct	Copenhagen	5	1
WC1956	5 Dec	Wolverhampton	5	2
WC1957	15 May	Copenhagen	4	1
1966	3 July	Copenhagen	2	0
EC1978	20 Sept	Copenhagen	4	3
EC1979	12 Sept	Wembley	1	0
EC1982	22 Sept	Copenhagen	2	2
EC1983	21 Sept	Wembley	0	1
1988	14 Sept	Wembley	1	0
1989	7 June	Copenhagen	1	1
1990	15 May	Wembley	1	0
EC1992	11 June	Malmo	0	0
1994	9 Mar	Wembley	1	0
WC2002	15 June	Niigata	3	0
2004	16 Nov	Old Trafford	2	3
2005	17 Aug	Copenhagen	1	4

		v ECUADOR	*E*	*Ec*
1970	24 May	Quito	2	0
WC2006	25 June	Stuttgart	1	0

		v EGYPT	*E*	*Eg*
1986	29 Jan	Cairo	4	0
WC1990	21 June	Cagliari	1	0

		v FIFA	*E*	*FIFA*
1938	26 Oct	Highbury	3	0
1953	21 Oct	Wembley	4	4
1963	23 Oct	Wembley	2	1

		v FINLAND	*E*	*F*
1937	20 May	Helsinki	8	0
1956	20 May	Helsinki	5	1
1966	26 June	Helsinki	3	0
WC1976	13 June	Helsinki	4	1
WC1976	13 Oct	Wembley	2	1
1982	3 June	Helsinki	4	1
WC1984	17 Oct	Wembley	5	0
WC1985	22 May	Helsinki	1	1
1992	3 June	Helsinki	2	1
WC2000	11 Oct	Helsinki	0	0
WC2001	24 Mar	Liverpool	2	1

		v FRANCE	*E*	*F*
1923	10 May	Paris	4	1
1924	17 May	Paris	3	1
1925	21 May	Paris	3	2
1927	26 May	Paris	6	0
1928	17 May	Paris	5	1
1929	9 May	Paris	4	1
1931	14 May	Paris	2	5
1933	6 Dec	Tottenham	4	1
1938	26 May	Paris	4	2
1947	3 May	Highbury	3	0
1949	22 May	Paris	3	1

			E	*F*
1951	3 Oct	Highbury	2	2
1955	15 May	Paris	0	1
1957	27 Nov	Wembley	4	0
EC1962	3 Oct	Sheffield	1	1
EC1963	27 Feb	Paris	2	5
WC1966	20 July	Wembley	2	0
1969	12 Mar	Wembley	5	0
WC1982	16 June	Bilbao	3	1
1984	29 Feb	Paris	0	2
1992	19 Feb	Wembley	2	0
EC1992	14 June	Malmo	0	0
TF1997	7 June	Montpellier	1	0
1999	10 Feb	Wembley	0	2
2000	2 Sept	Paris	1	1
EC2004	13 June	Lisbon	1	2

		v GEORGIA	*E*	*G*
WC1996	9 Nov	Tbilisi	2	0
WC1997	30 Apr	Wembley	2	0

		v GERMANY	*E*	*G*
1930	10 May	Berlin	3	3
1935	4 Dec	Tottenham	3	0
1938	14 May	Berlin	6	3
1991	11 Sept	Wembley	0	1
1993	19 June	Detroit	1	2
EC1996	26 June	Wembley	1	1*
EC2000	17 June	Charleroi	1	0
WC2000	7 Oct	Wembley	0	1
WC2001	1 Sept	Munich	5	1

		v EAST GERMANY	*E*	*EG*
1963	2 June	Leipzig	2	1
1970	25 Nov	Wembley	3	1
1974	29 May	Leipzig	1	1
1984	12 Sept	Wembley	1	0

		v WEST GERMANY	*E*	*WG*
1954	1 Dec	Wembley	3	1
1956	26 May	Berlin	3	1
1965	12 May	Nuremberg	1	0
1966	23 Feb	Wembley	1	0
WC1966	30 July	Wembley	4	2*
1968	1 June	Hanover	0	1
WC1970	14 June	Leon	2	3*
EC1972	29 Apr	Wembley	1	3
EC1972	13 May	Berlin	0	0
1975	12 Mar	Wembley	2	0
1978	22 Feb	Munich	1	2
WC1982	29 June	Madrid	0	0
1982	13 Oct	Wembley	1	2
1985	12 June	Mexico City	3	0
1987	9 Sept	Dusseldorf	1	3
WC1990	4 July	Turin	1	1*

		v GREECE	*E*	*G*
EC1971	21 Apr	Wembley	3	0
EC1971	1 Dec	Piraeus	2	0
EC1982	17 Nov	Salonika	3	0
EC1983	30 Mar	Wembley	0	0
1989	8 Feb	Athens	2	1
1994	17 May	Wembley	5	0
WC2001	6 June	Athens	2	0
WC2001	6 Oct	Old Trafford	2	2

		v HOLLAND	*E*	*H*
1935	18 May	Amsterdam	1	0
1946	27 Nov	Huddersfield	8	2
1964	9 Dec	Amsterdam	1	1
1969	5 Nov	Amsterdam	1	0
1970	14 Jun	Wembley	0	0
1977	9 Feb	Wembley	0	2
1982	25 May	Wembley	2	0
1988	23 Mar	Wembley	2	2
EC1988	15 June	Dusseldorf	1	3
WC1990	16 June	Cagliari	0	0
2005	9 Feb	Villa Park	0	0
WC1993	28 Apr	Wembley	2	2
WC1993	13 Oct	Rotterdam	0	2
EC1996	18 June	Wembley	4	1
2001	15 Aug	Tottenham	0	2
2002	13 Feb	Amsterdam	1	1

		v HUNGARY	*E*	*H*
1908	10 June	Budapest	7	0
1909	29 May	Budapest	4	2
1909	31 May	Budapest	8	2
1934	10 May	Budapest	1	2
1936	2 Dec	Highbury	6	2
1953	25 Nov	Wembley	3	6
1954	23 May	Budapest	1	7
1960	22 May	Budapest	0	2
WC1962	31 May	Rancagua	1	2
1965	5 May	Wembley	1	0
1978	24 May	Wembley	4	1
WC1981	6 June	Budapest	3	1
WC1982	18 Nov	Wembley	1	0
EC1983	27 Apr	Wembley	2	0
EC1983	12 Oct	Budapest	3	0
1988	27 Apr	Budapest	0	0
1990	12 Sept	Wembley	1	0
1992	12 May	Budapest	1	0
1996	18 May	Wembley	3	0
1999	28 Apr	Budapest	1	1
2006	30 May	Old Trafford	3	1

		v ICELAND	*E*	*I*
1982	2 June	Reykjavik	1	1
2004	5 June	City of Manchester	6	1

		v REPUBLIC OF IRELAND	*E*	*RI*
1946	30 Sept	Dublin	1	0
1949	21 Sept	Everton	0	2
WC1957	8 May	Wembley	5	1
WC1957	19 May	Dublin	1	1
1964	24 May	Dublin	3	1
1976	8 Sept	Wembley	1	1
EC1978	25 Oct	Dublin	1	1
EC1980	6 Feb	Wembley	2	0
1985	26 Mar	Wembley	2	1
EC1988	12 June	Stuttgart	0	1
WC1990	11 June	Cagliari	1	1
EC1990	14 Nov	Dublin	1	1
EC1991	27 Mar	Wembley	1	1
1995	15 Feb	Dublin	0	1
(abandoned after 27 mins)				

		v ISRAEL	*E*	*I*
1986	26 Feb	Ramat Gan	2	1
1988	17 Feb	Tel Aviv	0	0

		v ITALY	*E*	*I*
1933	13 May	Rome	1	1
1934	14 Nov	Highbury	3	2
1939	13 May	Milan	2	2
1948	16 May	Turin	4	0
1949	30 Nov	Tottenham	2	0
1952	18 May	Florence	1	1
1959	6 May	Wembley	2	2
1961	24 May	Rome	3	2
1973	14 June	Turin	0	2
1973	14 Nov	Wembley	0	1
1976	28 May	New York	3	2
WC1976	17 Nov	Rome	0	2
WC1977	16 Nov	Wembley	2	0
EC1980	15 June	Turin	0	1
1985	6 June	Mexico City	1	2
1989	15 Nov	Wembley	0	0
WC1990	7 July	Bari	1	2
WC1997	12 Feb	Wembley	0	1
TF1997	4 June	Nantes	2	0
WC1997	11 Oct	Rome	0	0
2000	15 Nov	Turin	0	1
2002	27 Mar	Leeds	1	2

		v JAMAICA	*E*	*J*
2006	3 June	Old Trafford	6	0

		v JAPAN	*E*	*J*
UI1995	3 June	Wembley	2	1
2004	1 June	City of Manchester	1	1
		v KUWAIT	*E*	*K*
WC1982	25 June	Bilbao	1	0
		v LIECHTENSTEIN	*E*	*L*
EC2003	29 Mar	Vaduz	2	0
EC2003	10 Sept	Old Trafford	2	0
		v LUXEMBOURG	*E*	*L*
1927	21 May	Esch-sur-Alzette	5	2
WC1960	19 Oct	Luxembourg	9	0
WC1961	28 Sept	Highbury	4	1
WC1977	30 Mar	Wembley	5	0
WC1977	12 Oct	Luxembourg	2	0
EC1982	15 Dec	Wembley	9	0
EC1983	16 Nov	Luxembourg	4	0
EC1998	14 Oct	Luxembourg	3	0
EC1999	4 Sept	Wembley	6	0
		v MACEDONIA	*E*	*M*
EC2002	16 Oct	Southampton	2	2
EC2003	6 Sept	Skopje	2	1
		v MALAYSIA	*E*	*M*
1991	12 June	Kuala Lumpur	4	2
		v MALTA	*E*	*M*
EC1971	3 Feb	Valletta	1	0
EC1971	12 May	Wembley	5	0
2000	3 June	Valletta	2	1
		v MEXICO	*E*	*M*
1959	24 May	Mexico City	1	2
1961	10 May	Wembley	8	0
WC1966	16 July	Wembley	2	0
1969	1 June	Mexico City	0	0
1985	9 June	Mexico City	0	1
1986	17 May	Los Angeles	3	0
1997	29 Mar	Wembley	2	0
2001	25 May	Derby	4	0
		v MOLDOVA	*E*	*M*
WC1996	1 Sept	Chisinau	3	0
WC1997	10 Sept	Wembley	4	0
		v MOROCCO	*E*	*M*
WC1986	6 June	Monterrey	0	0
1998	27 May	Casablanca	1	0
		v NEW ZEALAND	*E*	*NZ*
1991	3 June	Auckland	1	0
1991	8 June	Wellington	2	0
		v NIGERIA	*E*	*N*
1994	16 Nov	Wembley	1	0
WC2002	12 June	Osaka	0	0
		v NORWAY	*E*	*N*
1937	14 May	Oslo	6	0
1938	9 Nov	Newcastle	4	0
1949	18 May	Oslo	4	1
1966	29 June	Oslo	6	1
WC1980	10 Sept	Wembley	4	0
WC1981	9 Sept	Oslo	1	2
WC1992	14 Oct	Wembley	1	1
WC1993	2 June	Oslo	0	2
1994	22 May	Wembley	0	0
1995	11 Oct	Oslo	0	0
		v PARAGUAY	*E*	*P*
WC1986	18 June	Mexico City	3	0
2002	17 Apr	Liverpool	4	0
WC2006	10 June	Frankfurt	1	0
		v PERU	*E*	*P*
1959	17 May	Lima	1	4
1962	20 May	Lima	4	0
		v POLAND	*E*	*P*
1966	5 Jan	Everton	1	1
1966	5 July	Chorzow	1	0
WC1973	6 June	Chorzow	0	2
WC1973	17 Oct	Wembley	1	1
WC1986	11 June	Monterrey	3	0
WC1989	3 June	Wembley	3	0
WC1989	11 Oct	Katowice	0	0
EC1990	17 Oct	Wembley	2	0
EC1991	13 Nov	Poznan	1	1
WC1993	29 May	Katowice	1	1
WC1993	8 Sept	Wembley	3	0
WC1996	9 Oct	Wembley	2	1
WC1997	31 May	Katowice	2	0
EC1999	27 Mar	Wembley	3	1
EC1999	8 Sept	Warsaw	0	0
WC2004	8 Sept	Katowice	2	1
WC2005	12 Oct	Old Trafford	2	1
		v PORTUGAL	*E*	*P*
1947	25 May	Lisbon	10	0
1950	14 May	Lisbon	5	3
1951	19 May	Everton	5	2
1955	22 May	Oporto	1	3
1958	7 May	Wembley	2	1
WC1961	21 May	Lisbon	1	1
WC1961	25 Oct	Wembley	2	0
1964	17 May	Lisbon	4	3
1964	4 June	São Paulo	1	1
WC1966	26 July	Wembley	2	1
1969	10 Dec	Wembley	1	0
1974	3 Apr	Lisbon	0	0
EC1974	20 Nov	Wembley	0	0
EC1975	19 Nov	Lisbon	1	1
WC1986	3 June	Monterrey	0	1
1995	12 Dec	Wembley	1	1
1998	22 Apr	Wembley	3	0
EC2000	12 June	Eindhoven	2	3
2002	7 Sept	Villa Park	1	1
2004	18 Feb	Faro	1	1
EC2004	24 June	Lisbon	2	2*
WC2006	1 July	Gelsenkirchen	0	0
		v ROMANIA	*E*	*R*
1939	24 May	Bucharest	2	0
1968	6 Nov	Bucharest	0	0
1969	15 Jan	Wembley	1	1
WC1970	2 June	Guadalajara	1	0
WC1980	15 Oct	Bucharest	1	2
WC1981	29 April	Wembley	0	0
WC1985	1 May	Bucharest	0	0
WC1985	11 Sept	Wembley	1	1
1994	12 Oct	Wembley	1	1
WC1998	22 June	Toulouse	1	2
EC2000	20 June	Charleroi	2	3
		v SAN MARINO	*E*	*SM*
WC1992	17 Feb	Wembley	6	0
WC1993	17 Nov	Bologna	7	1
		v SAUDI ARABIA	*E*	*SA*
1988	16 Nov	Riyadh	1	1
1998	23 May	Wembley	0	0
		v SERBIA-MONTENEGRO	*E*	*S-M*
2003	3 June	Leicester	2	1
		v SLOVAKIA	*E*	*S*
EC2002	12 Oct	Bratislava	2	1
EC2003	11 June	Middlesbrough	2	1
		v SOUTH AFRICA	*E*	*SA*
1997	24 May	Old Trafford	2	1
2003	22 May	Durban	2	1
		v SOUTH KOREA	*E*	*SK*
2002	21 May	Seoguipo	1	1
		v SPAIN	*E*	*S*
1929	15 May	Madrid	3	4
1931	9 Dec	Highbury	7	1
WC1950	2 July	Rio de Janeiro	0	1
1955	18 May	Madrid	1	1
1955	30 Nov	Wembley	4	1
1960	15 May	Madrid	0	3
1960	26 Oct	Wembley	4	2
1965	8 Dec	Madrid	2	0
1967	24 May	Wembley	2	0
EC1968	3 Apr	Wembley	1	0
EC1968	8 May	Madrid	2	1
1980	26 Mar	Barcelona	2	0
EC1980	18 June	Naples	2	1
1981	25 Mar	Wembley	1	2
WC1982	5 July	Madrid	0	0

Year	Date	Venue	*E*	*S*
1987	18 Feb	Madrid	4	2
1992	9 Sept	Santander	0	1
EC 1996	22 June	Wembley	0	0
2001	28 Feb	Villa Park	3	0
2004	17 Nov	Madrid	0	1

v SWEDEN

Year	Date	Venue	*E*	*S*
1923	21 May	Stockholm	4	2
1923	24 May	Stockholm	3	1
1937	17 May	Stockholm	4	0
1947	19 Nov	Highbury	4	2
1949	13 May	Stockholm	1	3
1956	16 May	Stockholm	0	0
1959	28 Oct	Wembley	2	3
1965	16 May	Gothenburg	2	1
1968	22 May	Wembley	3	1
1979	10 June	Stockholm	0	0
1986	10 Sept	Stockholm	0	1
WC1988	19 Oct	Wembley	0	0
WC1989	6 Sept	Stockholm	0	0
EC1992	17 June	Stockholm	1	2
UI1995	8 June	Leeds	3	3
EC1998	5 Sept	Stockholm	1	2
EC1999	5 June	Wembley	0	0
2001	10 Nov	Old Trafford	1	1
WC2002	2 June	Saitama	1	1
2004	31 Mar	Gothenburg	0	1
WC2006	20 June	Cologne	2	2

v SWITZERLAND

Year	Date	Venue	*E*	*S*
1933	20 May	Berne	4	0
1938	21 May	Zurich	1	2
1947	18 May	Zurich	0	1
1948	2 Dec	Highbury	6	0
1952	28 May	Zurich	3	0
WC1954	20 June	Berne	2	0
1962	9 May	Wembley	3	1
1963	5 June	Basle	8	1
EC1971	13 Oct	Basle	3	2
EC1971	10 Nov	Wembley	1	1
1975	3 Sept	Basle	2	1
1977	7 Sept	Wembley	0	0
WC1980	19 Nov	Wembley	2	1
WC1981	30 May	Basle	1	2
1988	28 May	Lausanne	1	0
1995	15 Nov	Wembley	3	1
EC1996	8 June	Wembley	1	1
1998	25 Mar	Berne	1	1
EC2004	17 June	Coimbra	3	0

v TRINIDAD & TOBAGO

Year	Date	Venue	*E*	*Tr*
WC2006	15 June	Nuremberg	2	0

v TUNISIA

Year	Date	Venue	*E*	*T*
1990	2 June	Tunis	1	1
WC1998	15 June	Marseilles	2	0

v TURKEY

Year	Date	Venue	*E*	*T*
WC1984	14 Nov	Istanbul	8	0
WC1985	16 Oct	Wembley	5	0
EC1987	29 Apr	Izmir	0	0
EC1987	14 Oct	Wembley	8	0
EC1991	1 May	Izmir	1	0
EC1991	16 Oct	Wembley	1	0
WC1992	18 Nov	Wembley	4	0
WC1993	31 Mar	Izmir	2	0
EC2003	2 Apr	Sunderland	2	0
EC2003	11 Oct	Istanbul	0	0

v UKRAINE

Year	Date	Venue	*E*	*U*
2000	31 May	Wembley	2	0
2004	18 Aug	St James' Park	3	0

v URUGUAY

Year	Date	Venue	*E*	*U*
1953	31 May	Montevideo	1	2
WC1954	26 June	Basle	2	4
1964	6 May	Wembley	2	1
WC1966	11 July	Wembley	0	0
1969	8 June	Montevideo	2	1
1977	15 June	Montevideo	0	0
1984	13 June	Montevideo	0	2
1990	22 May	Wembley	1	2
1995	29 Mar	Wembley	0	0
2006	1 Mar	Liverpool	2	1

v USA

Year	Date	Venue	*E*	*USA*
WC1950	29 June	Belo Horizonte	0	1
1953	8 June	New York	6	3
1959	28 May	Los Angeles	8	1
1964	27 May	New York	10	0
1985	16 June	Los Angeles	5	0
1993	9 June	Foxboro	0	2
1994	7 Sept	Wembley	2	0
2005	28 May	Chicago	2	1

v USSR

Year	Date	Venue	*E*	*USSR*
1958	18 May	Moscow	1	1
WC1958	8 June	Gothenburg	2	2
WC1958	17 June	Gothenburg	0	1
1958	22 Oct	Wembley	5	0
1967	6 Dec	Wembley	2	2
EC1968	8 June	Rome	2	0
1973	10 June	Moscow	2	1
1984	2 June	Wembley	0	2
1986	26 Mar	Tbilisi	1	0
EC1988	18 June	Frankfurt	1	3
1991	21 May	Wembley	3	1

v YUGOSLAVIA

Year	Date	Venue	*E*	*Y*
1939	18 May	Belgrade	1	2
1950	22 Nov	Highbury	2	2
1954	16 May	Belgrade	0	1
1956	28 Nov	Wembley	3	0
1958	11 May	Belgrade	0	5
1960	11 May	Wembley	3	3
1965	9 May	Belgrade	1	1
1966	4 May	Wembley	2	0
EC1968	5 June	Florence	0	1
1972	11 Oct	Wembley	1	1
1974	5 June	Belgrade	2	2
EC1986	12 Nov	Wembley	2	0
EC1987	11 Nov	Belgrade	4	1
1989	13 Dec	Wembley	2	1

SCOTLAND

v ARGENTINA

Year	Date	Venue	*S*	*A*
1977	18 June	Buenos Aires	1	1
1979	2 June	Glasgow	1	3
1990	28 Mar	Glasgow	1	0

v AUSTRALIA

Year	Date	Venue	*S*	*A*
WC1985	20 Nov	Glasgow	2	0
WC1985	4 Dec	Melbourne	0	0
1996	27 Mar	Glasgow	1	0
2000	15 Nov	Glasgow	0	2

v AUSTRIA

Year	Date	Venue	*S*	*A*
1931	16 May	Vienna	0	5
1933	29 Nov	Glasgow	2	2
1937	9 May	Vienna	1	1
1950	13 Dec	Glasgow	0	1
1951	27 May	Vienna	0	4
WC1954	16 June	Zurich	0	1
1955	19 May	Vienna	4	1
1956	2 May	Glasgow	1	1
1960	29 May	Vienna	1	4
1963	8 May	Glasgow (*abandoned after 79 mins*)	4	1
WC1968	6 Nov	Glasgow	2	1
WC1969	5 Nov	Vienna	0	2
EC1978	20 Sept	Vienna	2	3
EC1979	17 Oct	Glasgow	1	1
1994	20 Apr	Vienna	2	1
WC1996	31 Aug	Vienna	0	0
WC1997	2 Apr	Celtic Park	2	0
2003	30 Apr	Glasgow	0	2
2005	17 Aug	Graz	2	2

		v BELARUS	S	B
wc1997	8 June	Minsk	1	0
wc1997	7 Sept	Aberdeen	4	1
wc2005	8 June	Minsk	0	0
wc2005	8 Oct	Glasgow	0	1

		v BELGIUM	S	B
1947	18 May	Brussels	1	2
1948	28 Apr	Glasgow	2	0
1951	20 May	Brussels	5	0
EC1971	3 Feb	Liège	0	3
EC1971	10 Nov	Aberdeen	1	0
1974	2 June	Brussels	1	2
EC1979	21 Nov	Brussels	0	2
EC1979	19 Dec	Glasgow	1	3
EC1982	15 Dec	Brussels	2	3
EC1983	12 Oct	Glasgow	1	1
EC1987	1 Apr	Brussels	1	4
EC1987	14 Oct	Glasgow	2	0
wc2001	24 Mar	Glasgow	2	2
wc2001	5 Sept	Brussels	0	2

		v BOSNIA	S	B
EC1999	4 Sept	Sarajevo	2	1
EC1999	5 Oct	Glasgow	1	0

		v BRAZIL	S	B
1966	25 June	Glasgow	1	1
1972	5 July	Rio de Janeiro	0	1
1973	30 June	Glasgow	0	1
wc1974	18 June	Frankfurt	0	0
1977	23 June	Rio de Janeiro	0	2
wc1982	18 June	Seville	1	4
1987	26 May	Glasgow	0	2
wc1990	20 June	Turin	0	1
wc1998	10 June	Saint-Denis	1	2

		v BULGARIA	S	B
1978	22 Feb	Glasgow	2	1
EC1986	10 Sept	Glasgow	0	0
EC1987	11 Nov	Sofia	1	0
EC1990	14 Nov	Sofia	1	1
EC1991	27 Mar	Glasgow	1	1
2006	11 May	Kobe	5	1

		v CANADA	S	C
1983	12 June	Vancouver	2	0
1983	16 June	Edmonton	3	0
1983	20 June	Toronto	2	0
1992	21 May	Toronto	3	1
2002	15 Oct	Easter Road	3	1

		v CHILE	S	C
1977	15 June	Santiago	4	2
1989	30 May	Glasgow	2	0

		v CIS	S	C
EC1992	18 June	Norrkoping	3	0

		v COLOMBIA	S	C
1988	17 May	Glasgow	0	0
1996	30 May	Miami	0	1
1998	23 May	New York	2	2

		v COSTA RICA	S	CR
wc1990	11 June	Genoa	0	1

		v CROATIA	S	C
wc2000	11 Oct	Zagreb	1	1
wc2001	1 Sept	Glasgow	0	0

		v CYPRUS	S	C
wc1968	17 Dec	Nicosia	5	0
wc1969	11 May	Glasgow	8	0
wc1989	8 Feb	Limassol	3	2
wc1989	26 Apr	Glasgow	2	1

		v CZECHOSLOVAKIA	S	C
1937	22 May	Prague	3	1
1937	8 Dec	Glasgow	5	0
wc1961	14 May	Bratislava	0	4
wc1961	26 Sept	Glasgow	3	2
wc1961	29 Nov	Brussels	2	4*
1972	2 July	Porto Alegre	0	0
wc1973	26 Sept	Glasgow	2	1
wc1973	17 Oct	Prague	0	1
wc1976	13 Oct	Prague	0	2
wc1977	21 Sept	Glasgow	3	1

		v CZECH REPUBLIC	S	C
EC1999	31 Mar	Glasgow	1	2
EC1999	9 June	Prague	2	3

		v DENMARK	S	D
1951	12 May	Glasgow	3	1
1952	25 May	Copenhagen	2	1
1968	16 Oct	Copenhagen	1	0
EC1970	11 Nov	Glasgow	1	0
EC1971	9 June	Copenhagen	0	1
wc1972	18 Oct	Copenhagen	4	1
wc1972	15 Nov	Glasgow	2	0
EC1975	3 Sept	Copenhagen	1	0
EC1975	29 Oct	Glasgow	3	1
wc1986	4 June	Nezahualcayotl	0	1
1996	24 Apr	Copenhagen	0	2
1998	25 Mar	Glasgow	0	1
2002	21 Aug	Glasgow	0	1
2004	28 Apr	Copenhagen	0	1

		v ECUADOR	S	E
1995	24 May	Toyama	2	1

		v EGYPT	S	E
1990	16 May	Aberdeen	1	3

		v ESTONIA	S	E
wc1993	19 May	Tallinn	3	0
wc1993	2 June	Aberdeen	3	1
wc1997	11 Feb	Monaco	0	0
wc1997	29 Mar	Kilmarnock	2	0
EC1998	10 Oct	Edinburgh	3	2
EC1999	8 Sept	Tallinn	0	0
2004	27 May	Tallinn	1	0

		v FAEROES	S	F
EC1994	12 Oct	Glasgow	5	1
EC1995	7 June	Toftir	2	0
EC1998	14 Oct	Aberdeen	2	1
EC1999	5 June	Toftir	1	1
EC2002	7 Sept	Toftir	2	2
EC2003	6 Sept	Glasgow	3	1

		v FINLAND	S	F
1954	25 May	Helsinki	2	1
wc1964	21 Oct	Glasgow	3	1
wc1965	27 May	Helsinki	2	1
1976	8 Sept	Glasgow	6	0
1992	25 Mar	Glasgow	1	1
EC1994	7 Sept	Helsinki	2	0
EC1995	6 Sept	Glasgow	1	0
1998	22 Apr	Edinburgh	1	1

		v FRANCE	S	F
1930	18 May	Paris	2	0
1932	8 May	Paris	3	1
1948	23 May	Paris	0	3
1949	27 Apr	Glasgow	2	0
1950	27 May	Paris	1	0
1951	16 May	Glasgow	1	0
wc1958	15 June	Orebro	1	2
1984	1 June	Marseilles	0	2
wc1989	8 Mar	Glasgow	2	0
wc1989	11 Oct	Paris	0	3
1997	12 Nov	St Etienne	1	2
2000	29 Mar	Glasgow	0	2
2002	27 Mar	Paris	0	5

		v GERMANY	S	G
1929	1 June	Berlin	1	1
1936	14 Oct	Glasgow	2	0
EC1992	15 June	Norrkoping	0	2
1993	24 Mar	Glasgow	0	1
1998	28 Apr	Bremen	1	0
EC2003	7 June	Glasgow	1	1
EC2003	10 Sept	Dortmund	1	2

		v EAST GERMANY	S	EG
1974	30 Oct	Glasgow	3	0
1977	7 Sept	East Berlin	0	1
EC1982	13 Oct	Glasgow	2	0
EC1983	16 Nov	Halle	1	2
1985	16 Oct	Glasgow	0	0
1990	25 Apr	Glasgow	0	1

		v WEST GERMANY	S	WG
1957	22 May	Stuttgart	3	1
1959	6 May	Glasgow	3	2
1964	12 May	Hanover	2	2
WC1969	16 Apr	Glasgow	1	1
WC1969	22 Oct	Hamburg	2	3
1973	14 Nov	Glasgow	1	1
1974	27 Mar	Frankfurt	1	2
WC1986	8 June	Queretaro	1	2

		v GREECE	S	G
EC1994	18 Dec	Athens	0	1
EC1995	16 Aug	Glasgow	1	0

		v HOLLAND	S	H
1929	4 June	Amsterdam	2	0
1938	21 May	Amsterdam	3	1
1959	27 May	Amsterdam	2	1
1966	11 May	Glasgow	0	3
1968	30 May	Amsterdam	0	0
1971	1 Dec	Rotterdam	1	2
WC1978	11 June	Mendoza	3	2
1982	23 Mar	Glasgow	2	1
1986	29 Apr	Eindhoven	0	0
EC1992	12 June	Gothenburg	0	1
1994	23 Mar	Glasgow	0	1
1994	27 May	Utrecht	1	3
EC1996	10 June	Birmingham	0	0
2000	26 Apr	Arnhem	0	0
EC2003	15 Nov	Glasgow	1	0
EC2003	19 Nov	Amsterdam	0	6

		v HONG KONG XI	S	HK
†2002	23 May	Hong Kong	4	0

†*match not recognised by FIFA*

		v HUNGARY	S	H
1938	7 Dec	Glasgow	3	1
1954	8 Dec	Glasgow	2	4
1955	29 May	Budapest	1	3
1958	7 May	Glasgow	1	1
1960	5 June	Budapest	3	3
1980	31 May	Budapest	1	3
1987	9 Sept	Glasgow	2	0
2004	18 Aug	Glasgow	0	3

		v ICELAND	S	I
WC1984	17 Oct	Glasgow	3	0
WC1985	28 May	Reykjavik	1	0
EC2002	12 Oct	Reykjavik	2	0
EC2003	29 Mar	Glasgow	2	1

		v IRAN	S	I
WC1978	7 June	Cordoba	1	1

		v REPUBLIC OF IRELAND	S	RI
WC1961	3 May	Glasgow	4	1
WC1961	7 May	Dublin	3	0
1963	9 June	Dublin	0	1
1969	21 Sept	Dublin	1	1
EC1986	15 Oct	Dublin	0	0
EC1987	18 Feb	Glasgow	0	1
2000	30 May	Dublin	2	1
2003	12 Feb	Glasgow	0	2

		v ISRAEL	S	I
WC1981	25 Feb	Tel Aviv	1	0
WC1981	28 Apr	Glasgow	3	1
1986	28 Jan	Tel Aviv	1	0

		v ITALY	S	I
1931	20 May	Rome	0	3
WC1965	9 Nov	Glasgow	1	0
WC1965	7 Dec	Naples	0	3
1988	22 Dec	Perugia	0	2
WC1992	18 Nov	Glasgow	0	0
WC1993	13 Oct	Rome	1	3
WC2005	26 Mar	Milan	0	2
WC2005	3 Sept	Glasgow	1	1

		v JAPAN	S	J
1995	21 May	Hiroshima	0	0
2006	13 May	Saitama	0	0

		v LATVIA	S	L
WC1996	5 Oct	Riga	2	0
WC1997	11 Oct	Glasgow	2	0
WC2000	2 Sept	Riga	1	0
WC2001	6 Oct	Glasgow	2	1

		v LITHUANIA	S	L
EC1998	5 Sept	Vilnius	0	0
EC1999	9 Oct	Glasgow	3	0
EC2003	2 Apr	Kaunas	0	1
EC2003	11 Oct	Glasgow	1	0

		v LUXEMBOURG	S	L
1947	24 May	Luxembourg	6	0
EC1986	12 Nov	Glasgow	3	0
EC1987	2 Dec	Esch	0	0

		v MALTA	S	M
1988	22 Mar	Valletta	1	1
1990	28 May	Valletta	2	1
WC1993	17 Feb	Glasgow	3	0
WC1993	17 Nov	Valletta	2	0
1997	1 June	Valletta	3	2

		v MOLDOVA	S	M
EC2004	13 Oct	Chisinau	1	1
EC2005	4 June	Glasgow	2	0

		v MOROCCO	S	M
WC1998	23 June	St Etienne	0	3

		v NEW ZEALAND	S	NZ
WC1982	15 June	Malaga	5	2
2003	27 May	Tynecastle	1	1

		v NIGERIA	S	N
2002	17 Apr	Aberdeen	1	2

		v NORWAY	S	N
1929	28 May	Oslo	7	3
1954	5 May	Glasgow	1	0
1954	19 May	Oslo	1	1
1963	4 June	Bergen	3	4
1963	7 Nov	Glasgow	6	1
1974	6 June	Oslo	2	1
EC1978	25 Oct	Glasgow	3	2
EC1979	7 June	Oslo	4	0
WC1988	14 Sept	Oslo	2	1
WC1989	15 Nov	Glasgow	1	1
1992	3 June	Oslo	0	0
WC1998	16 June	Bordeaux	1	1
2003	20 Aug	Oslo	0	0
WC2004	9 Oct	Glasgow	0	1
WC2005	7 Sept	Oslo	2	1

		v PARAGUAY	S	P
WC1958	11 June	Norrkoping	2	3

		v PERU	S	P
1972	26 Apr	Glasgow	2	0
WC1978	3 June	Cordoba	1	3
1979	12 Sept	Glasgow	1	1

		v POLAND	S	P
1958	1 June	Warsaw	2	1
1960	4 June	Glasgow	2	3
WC1965	23 May	Chorzow	1	1
WC1965	13 Oct	Glasgow	1	2
1980	28 May	Poznan	0	1
1990	19 May	Glasgow	1	1
2001	25 Apr	Bydgoszcz	1	1

		v PORTUGAL	S	P
1950	21 May	Lisbon	2	2
1955	4 May	Glasgow	3	0
1959	3 June	Lisbon	0	1
1966	18 June	Glasgow	0	1
EC1971	21 Apr	Lisbon	0	2
EC1971	13 Oct	Glasgow	2	1
1975	13 May	Glasgow	1	0
EC1978	29 Nov	Lisbon	0	1

			S	*P*
EC1980	26 Mar	Glasgow	4	1
WC1980	15 Oct	Glasgow	0	0
WC1981	18 Nov	Lisbon	1	2
WC1992	14 Oct	Glasgow	0	0
WC1993	28 Apr	Lisbon	0	5
2002	20 Nov	Braga	0	2

		v ROMANIA	*S*	*R*
EC1975	1 June	Bucharest	1	1
EC1975	17 Dec	Glasgow	1	1
1986	26 Mar	Glasgow	3	0
EC1990	12 Sept	Glasgow	2	1
EC1991	16 Oct	Bucharest	0	1
2004	31 Mar	Glasgow	1	2

		v RUSSIA	*S*	*R*
EC1994	16 Nov	Glasgow	1	1
EC1995	29 Mar	Moscow	0	0

		v SAN MARINO	*S*	*SM*
EC1991	1 May	Serravalle	2	0
EC1991	13 Nov	Glasgow	4	0
EC1995	26 Apr	Serravalle	2	0
EC1995	15 Nov	Glasgow	5	0
WC2000	7 Oct	Serravalle	2	0
WC2001	28 Mar	Glasgow	4	0

		v SAUDI ARABIA	*S*	*SA*
1988	17 Feb	Riyadh	2	2

		v SLOVENIA	*S*	*SL*
WC2004	8 Sept	Glasgow	0	0
WC2005	12 Oct	Celje	3	0

		v SOUTH AFRICA	*S*	*SA*
2002	20 May	Hong Kong	0	2

		v SOUTH KOREA	*S*	*SK*
2002	16 May	Busan	1	4

		v SPAIN	*S*	*Sp*
WC1957	8 May	Glasgow	4	2
WC1957	26 May	Madrid	1	4
1963	13 June	Madrid	6	2
1965	8 May	Glasgow	0	0
EC1974	20 Nov	Glasgow	1	2
EC1975	5 Feb	Valencia	1	1
1982	24 Feb	Valencia	0	3
WC1984	14 Nov	Glasgow	3	1
WC1985	27 Feb	Seville	0	1
1988	27 Apr	Madrid	0	0
2004	3 Sept	Valencia	1	1

Match abandoned afer 60 minutes; floodlight failure.

		v SWEDEN	*S*	*Sw*
1952	30 May	Stockholm	1	3
1953	6 May	Glasgow	1	2
1975	16 Apr	Gothenburg	1	1
1977	27 Apr	Glasgow	3	1
WC1980	10 Sept	Stockholm	1	0
WC1981	9 Sept	Glasgow	2	0
WC1990	16 June	Genoa	2	1
1995	11 Oct	Stockholm	0	2
WC1996	10 Nov	Glasgow	1	0
WC1997	30 Apr	Gothenburg	1	2
2004	17 Nov	Edinburgh	1	4

		v SWITZERLAND	*S*	*Sw*
1931	24 May	Geneva	3	2
1948	17 May	Berne	1	2
1950	26 Apr	Glasgow	3	1
WC1957	19 May	Basle	2	1
WC1957	6 Nov	Glasgow	3	2
1973	22 June	Berne	0	1
1976	7 Apr	Glasgow	1	0
EC1982	17 Nov	Berne	0	2
EC1983	30 May	Glasgow	2	2
EC1990	17 Oct	Glasgow	2	1
EC1991	11 Sept	Berne	2	2
WC1992	9 Sept	Berne	1	3
WC1993	8 Sept	Aberdeen	1	1
WC1996	18 June	Birmingham	1	0
2006	1 Mar	Glasgow	1	3

		v TRINIDAD & TOBAGO	*S*	*TT*
2004	30 May	Edinburgh	4	1

		v TURKEY	*S*	*T*
1960	8 June	Ankara	2	4

		v URUGUAY	*S*	*U*
WC1954	19 June	Basle	0	7
1962	2 May	Glasgow	2	3
1983	21 Sept	Glasgow	2	0
WC1986	13 June	Nezahualcoyotl	0	0

		v USA	*S*	*USA*
1952	30 Apr	Glasgow	6	0
1992	17 May	Denver	1	0
1996	26 May	New Britain	1	2
1998	30 May	Washington	0	0
2005	11 Nov	Glasgow	1	1

		v USSR	*S*	*USSR*
1967	10 May	Glasgow	0	2
1971	14 June	Moscow	0	1
WC1982	22 June	Malaga	2	2
1991	6 Feb	Glasgow	0	1

		v YUGOSLAVIA	*S*	*Y*
1955	15 May	Belgrade	2	2
1956	21 Nov	Glasgow	2	0
WC1958	8 June	Vasteras	1	1
1972	29 June	Belo Horizonte	2	2
WC1974	22 June	Frankfurt	1	1
1984	12 Sept	Glasgow	6	1
WC1988	19 Oct	Glasgow	1	1
WC1989	6 Sept	Zagreb	1	3

		v ZAIRE	*S*	*Z*
WC1974	14 June	Dortmund	2	0

WALES

		v ALBANIA	*W*	*A*
EC1994	7 Sept	Cardiff	2	0
EC1995	15 Nov	Tirana	1	1

		v ARGENTINA	*W*	*A*
1992	3 June	Tokyo	0	1
2002	13 Feb	Cardiff	1	1

		v ARMENIA	*W*	*A*
WC2001	24 Mar	Erevan	2	2
WC2001	1 Sept	Cardiff	0	0

		v AUSTRIA	*W*	*A*
1954	9 May	Vienna	0	2
EC1955	23 Nov	Wrexham	1	2
EC1974	4 Sept	Vienna	1	2
1975	19 Nov	Wrexham	1	0
1992	29 Apr	Vienna	1	1
EC2005	26 Mar	Cardiff	0	2
EC2005	30 Mar	Vienna	0	1

		v AZERBAIJAN	*W*	*A*
EC2002	20 Nov	Baku	2	0
EC2003	29 Mar	Cardiff	4	0
WC2004	4 Sept	Baku	1	1
WC2005	12 Oct	Cardiff	2	0

		v BELARUS	*W*	*B*
EC1998	14 Oct	Cardiff	3	2
EC1999	4 Sept	Minsk	2	1
WC2000	2 Sept	Minsk	1	2
WC2001	6 Oct	Cardiff	1	0

		v BELGIUM	*W*	*B*
1949	22 May	Liège	1	3

			W	B
1949	23 Nov	Cardiff	5	1
EC1990	17 Oct	Cardiff	3	1
EC1991	27 Mar	Brussels	1	1
WC1992	18 Nov	Brussels	0	2
WC1993	31 Mar	Cardiff	2	0
WC1997	29 Mar	Cardiff	1	2
WC1997	11 Oct	Brussels	2	3

		v BOSNIA	W	B
2003	12 Feb	Cardiff	2	2

		v BRAZIL	W	B
WC1958	19 June	Gothenburg	0	1
1962	12 May	Rio de Janeiro	1	3
1962	16 May	São Paulo	1	3
1966	14 May	Rio de Janeiro	1	3
1966	18 May	Belo Horizonte	0	1
1983	12 June	Cardiff	1	1
1991	11 Sept	Cardiff	1	0
1997	12 Nov	Brasilia	0	3
2000	23 May	Cardiff	0	3

		v BULGARIA	W	B
EC1983	27 Apr	Wrexham	1	0
EC1983	16 Nov	Sofia	0	1
EC1994	14 Dec	Cardiff	0	3
EC1995	29 Mar	Sofia	1	3

		v CANADA	W	C
1986	10 May	Toronto	0	2
1986	20 May	Vancouver	3	0
2004	30 May	Wrexham	1	0

		v CHILE	W	C
1966	22 May	Santiago	0	2

		v COSTA RICA	W	CR
1990	20 May	Cardiff	1	0

		v CROATIA	W	C
2002	21 Aug	Varazdin	1	1

		v CYPRUS	W	C
WC1992	14 Oct	Limassol	1	0
WC1993	13 Oct	Cardiff	2	0
2005	16 Nov	Limassol	0	1

		v CZECHOSLOVAKIA	W	C
WC1957	1 May	Cardiff	1	0
WC1957	26 May	Prague	0	2
EC1971	21 Apr	Swansea	1	3
EC1971	27 Oct	Prague	0	1
WC1977	30 Mar	Wrexham	3	0
WC1977	16 Nov	Prague	0	1
WC1980	19 Nov	Cardiff	1	0
WC1981	9 Sept	Prague	0	2
EC1987	29 Apr	Wrexham	1	1
EC1987	11 Nov	Prague	0	2
WC1993	28 Apr	Ostrava†	1	1
WC1993	8 Sept	Cardiff†	2	2

†Czechoslovakia played as RCS (Republic of Czechs and Slovaks).

		v CZECH REPUBLIC	W	CR
2002	27 Mar	Cardiff	0	0

		v DENMARK	W	D
WC1964	21 Oct	Copenhagen	0	1
WC1965	1 Dec	Wrexham	4	2
EC1987	9 Sept	Cardiff	1	0
EC1987	14 Oct	Copenhagen	0	1
1990	11 Sept	Copenhagen	0	1
EC1998	10 Oct	Copenhagen	2	1
EC1999	9 June	Liverpool	0	2

		v ESTONIA	W	E
1994	23 May	Tallinn	2	1

		v FINLAND	W	F
EC1971	26 May	Helsinki	1	0
EC1971	13 Oct	Swansea	3	0
EC1987	10 Sept	Helsinki	1	1
EC1987	1 Apr	Wrexham	4	0
WC1988	19 Oct	Swansea	2	2
WC1989	6 Sept	Helsinki	0	1
2000	29 Mar	Cardiff	1	2
EC2002	7 Sept	Helsinki	2	0
EC2003	10 Sept	Cardiff	1	1

		v FAEROES	W	F
WC1992	9 Sept	Cardiff	6	0
WC1993	6 June	Toftir	3	0

		v FRANCE	W	F
1933	25 May	Paris	1	1
1939	20 May	Paris	1	2
1953	14 May	Paris	1	6
1982	2 June	Toulouse	1	0

		v GEORGIA	W	G
EC1994	16 Nov	Tbilisi	0	5
EC1995	7 June	Cardiff	0	1

		v GERMANY	W	G
EC1995	26 Apr	Dusseldorf	1	1
EC1995	11 Oct	Cardiff	1	2
2002	14 May	Cardiff	1	0

		v EAST GERMANY	W	EG
WC1957	19 May	Leipzig	1	2
WC1957	25 Sept	Cardiff	4	1
WC1969	16 Apr	Dresden	1	2
WC1969	22 Oct	Cardiff	1	3

		v WEST GERMANY	W	WG
1968	8 May	Cardiff	1	1
1969	26 Mar	Frankfurt	1	1
1976	6 Oct	Cardiff	0	2
1977	14 Dec	Dortmund	1	1
EC1979	2 May	Wrexham	0	2
EC1979	17 Oct	Cologne	1	5
WC1989	31 May	Cardiff	0	0
WC1989	15 Nov	Cologne	1	2
EC1991	5 June	Cardiff	1	0
EC1991	16 Oct	Nuremberg	1	4

		v GREECE	W	G
WC1964	9 Dec	Athens	0	2
WC1965	17 Mar	Cardiff	4	1

		v HOLLAND	W	H
WC1988	14 Sept	Amsterdam	0	1
WC1989	11 Oct	Wrexham	1	2
1992	30 May	Utrecht	0	4
WC1996	5 Oct	Cardiff	1	3
WC1996	9 Nov	Eindhoven	1	7

		v HUNGARY	W	H
WC1958	8 June	Sanviken	1	1
WC1958	17 June	Stockholm	2	1
1961	28 May	Budapest	2	3
EC1962	7 Nov	Budapest	1	3
EC1963	20 Mar	Cardiff	1	1
EC1974	30 Oct	Cardiff	2	0
EC1975	16 Apr	Budapest	2	1
1985	16 Oct	Cardiff	0	3
2004	31 Mar	Budapest	2	1
2005	9 Feb	Cardiff	2	0

		v ICELAND	W	I
WC1980	2 June	Reykjavik	4	0
WC1981	14 Oct	Swansea	2	2
WC1984	12 Sept	Reykjavik	0	1
WC1984	14 Nov	Cardiff	2	1
1991	1 May	Cardiff	1	0

		v IRAN	W	I
1978	18 Apr	Teheran	1	0

		v REPUBLIC OF IRELAND	W	RI
1960	28 Sept	Dublin	3	2
1979	11 Sept	Swansea	2	1

			W	RI
1981	24 Feb	Dublin	3	1
1986	26 Mar	Dublin	1	0
1990	28 Mar	Dublin	0	1
1991	6 Feb	Wrexham	0	3
1992	19 Feb	Dublin	1	0
1993	17 Feb	Dublin	1	2
1997	11 Feb	Cardiff	0	0

		v ISRAEL	*W*	*I*
WC1958	15 Jan	Tel Aviv	2	0
WC1958	5 Feb	Cardiff	2	0
1984	10 June	Tel Aviv	0	0
1989	8 Feb	Tel Aviv	3	3

		v ITALY	*W*	*I*
1965	1 May	Florence	1	4
WC1968	23 Oct	Cardiff	0	1
WC1969	4 Nov	Rome	1	4
1988	4 June	Brescia	1	0
1996	24 Jan	Terni	0	3
EC1998	5 Sept	Liverpool	0	2
EC1999	5 June	Bologna	0	4
EC2002	16 Oct	Cardiff	2	1
EC2003	6 Sept	Milan	0	4

		v JAMAICA	*W*	*J*
1998	25 Mar	Cardiff	0	0

		v JAPAN	*W*	*J*
1992	7 June	Matsuyama	1	0

		v LATVIA	*W*	*L*
2004	18 Aug	Riga	2	0

		v KUWAIT	*W*	*K*
1977	6 Sept	Wrexham	0	0
1977	20 Sept	Kuwait	0	0

		v LUXEMBOURG	*W*	*L*
EC1974	20 Nov	Swansea	5	0
EC1975	1 May	Luxembourg	3	1
EC1990	14 Nov	Luxembourg	1	0
EC1991	13 Nov	Cardiff	1	0

		v MALTA	*W*	*M*
EC1978	25 Oct	Wrexham	7	0
EC1979	2 June	Valletta	2	0
1988	1 June	Valletta	3	2
1998	3 June	Valletta	3	0

		v MEXICO	*W*	*M*
WC1958	11 June	Stockholm	1	1
1962	22 May	Mexico City	1	2

		v MOLDOVA	*W*	*M*
EC1994	12 Oct	Kishinev	2	3
EC1995	6 Sept	Cardiff	1	0

		v NORWAY	*W*	*N*
EC1982	22 Sept	Swansea	1	0
EC1983	21 Sept	Oslo	0	0
1984	6 June	Trondheim	0	1
1985	26 Feb	Wrexham	1	1
1985	5 June	Bergen	2	4
1994	9 Mar	Cardiff	1	3
WC2000	7 Oct	Cardiff	1	1
WC2001	5 Sept	Oslo	2	3
2004	27 May	Oslo	0	0

		v PARAGUAY	*W*	*P*
2006	1 Mar	Cardiff	0	0

		v POLAND	*W*	*P*
WC1973	28 Mar	Cardiff	2	0
WC1973	26 Sept	Katowice	0	3
1991	29 May	Radom	0	0
WC2000	11 Oct	Warsaw	0	0
WC2001	2 June	Cardiff	1	2
WC2004	13 Oct	Cardiff	2	3
WC2005	7 Sept	Warsaw	0	1

		v PORTUGAL	*W*	*P*
1949	15 May	Lisbon	2	3
1951	12 May	Cardiff	2	1
2000	2 June	Chaves	0	3

		v QATAR	*W*	*Q*
2000	23 Feb	Doha	1	0

		v ROMANIA	*W*	*R*
EC1970	11 Nov	Cardiff	0	0
EC1971	24 Nov	Bucharest	0	2
1983	12 Oct	Wrexham	5	0
WC1992	20 May	Bucharest	1	5
WC1993	17 Nov	Cardiff	1	2

		v RUSSIA	*W*	*R*
EC2003	15 Nov	Moscow	0	0
EC2003	19 Nov	Cardiff	0	1

		v SAN MARINO	*W*	*SM*
WC1996	2 June	Serravalle	5	0
WC1996	31 Aug	Cardiff	6	0

		v SAUDI ARABIA	*W*	*SA*
1986	25 Feb	Dahran	2	1

		v SERBIA-MONTENEGRO	*W*	*SM*
EC2003	20 Aug	Belgrade	0	1
EC2003	11 Oct	Cardiff	2	3

		v SLOVENIA	*W*	*S*
2005	17 Aug	Swansea	0	0

		v SPAIN	*W*	*S*
WC1961	19 Apr	Cardiff	1	2
WC1961	18 May	Madrid	1	1
1982	24 Mar	Valencia	1	1
WC1984	17 Oct	Seville	0	3
WC1985	30 Apr	Wrexham	3	0

		v SWEDEN	*W*	*S*
WC1958	15 June	Stockholm	0	0
1988	27 Apr	Stockholm	1	4
1989	26 Apr	Wrexham	0	2
1990	25 Apr	Stockholm	2	4
1994	20 Apr	Wrexham	0	2

		v SWITZERLAND	*W*	*S*
1949	26 May	Berne	0	4
1951	16 May	Wrexham	3	2
1996	24 Apr	Lugano	0	2
EC1999	31 Mar	Zurich	0	2
EC1999	9 Oct	Wrexham	0	2

		v TRINIDAD & TOBAGO	*W*	*TT*
2006	27 May	Graz	2	1

		v TUNISIA	*W*	*T*
1998	6 June	Tunis	0	4

		v TURKEY	*W*	*T*
EC1978	29 Nov	Wrexham	1	0
EC1979	21 Nov	Izmir	0	1
WC1980	15 Oct	Cardiff	4	0
WC1981	25 Mar	Ankara	1	0
WC1996	14 Dec	Cardiff	0	0
WC1997	20 Aug	Istanbul	4	6

		v REST OF UNITED KINGDOM	*W*	*UK*
1951	5 Dec	Cardiff	3	2
1969	28 July	Cardiff	0	1

		v UKRAINE	*W*	*U*
WC2001	28 Mar	Cardiff	1	1
WC2001	6 June	Kiev	1	1

		v USA	*W*	*USA*
2003	27 May	San Jose	0	2

		v URUGUAY	*W*	*U*
1986	21 Apr	Wrexham	0	0

		v USSR	W	USSR
wc1965	30 May	Moscow	1	2
wc1965	27 Oct	Cardiff	2	1
wc1981	30 May	Wrexham	0	0
wc1981	18 Nov	Tbilisi	0	3
1987	18 Feb	Swansea	0	0

		v YUGOSLAVIA	W	Y
1953	21 May	Belgrade	2	5
1954	22 Nov	Cardiff	1	3
EC1976	24 Apr	Zagreb	0	2
EC1976	22 May	Cardiff	1	1
EC1982	15 Dec	Titograd	4	4
EC1983	14 Dec	Cardiff	1	1
1988	23 Mar	Swansea	1	2

NORTHERN IRELAND

		v ALBANIA	NI	A
wc1965	7 May	Belfast	4	1
wc1965	24 Nov	Tirana	1	1
EC1982	15 Dec	Tirana	0	0
EC1983	27 Apr	Belfast	1	0
wc1992	9 Sept	Belfast	3	0
wc1993	17 Feb	Tirana	2	1
wc1996	14 Dec	Belfast	2	0
wc1997	10 Sept	Zurich	0	1

		v ALGERIA	NI	A
wc1986	3 June	Guadalajara	1	1

		v ARGENTINA	NI	A
wc1958	11 June	Halmstad	1	3

		v ARMENIA	NI	A
wc1996	5 Oct	Belfast	1	1
wc1997	30 Apr	Erevan	0	0
EC2003	29 Mar	Erevan	0	1
EC2003	10 Sept	Belfast	0	1

		v AUSTRALIA	NI	A
1980	11 June	Sydney	2	1
1980	15 June	Melbourne	1	1
1980	18 June	Adelaide	2	1

		v AUSTRIA	NI	A
wc1982	1 July	Madrid	2	2
EC1982	13 Oct	Vienna	0	2
EC1983	21 Sept	Belfast	3	1
EC1990	14 Nov	Vienna	0	0
EC1991	16 Oct	Belfast	2	1
EC1994	12 Oct	Vienna	2	1
EC1995	15 Nov	Belfast	5	3
wc2004	13 Oct	Belfast	3	3
wc2005	12 Oct	Vienna	0	2

		v AZERBAIJAN	NI	A
wc2004	9 Oct	Baku	0	0
wc2005	3 Sept	Belfast	2	0

		v BARBADOS	NI	B
2004	30 May	Waterford	1	1

		v BELGIUM	NI	B
wc1976	10 Nov	Liège	0	2
wc1977	16 Nov	Belfast	3	0
1997	11 Feb	Belfast	3	0

		v BRAZIL	NI	B
wc1986	12 June	Guadalajara	0	3

		v BULGARIA	NI	B
wc1972	18 Oct	Sofia	0	3
wc1973	26 Sept	Sheffield	0	0
EC1978	29 Nov	Sofia	2	0
EC1979	2 May	Belfast	2	0
wc2001	28 Mar	Sofia	3	4
wc2001	2 June	Belfast	0	1

		v CANADA	NI	C
1995	22 May	Edmonton	0	2
1999	27 Apr	Belfast	1	1
2005	9 Feb	Belfast	0	1

		v CHILE	NI	C
1989	26 May	Belfast	0	1
1995	25 May	Edmonton	1	2

		v COLOMBIA	NI	C
1994	4 June	Boston	0	2

		v CYPRUS	NI	C
EC1971	3 Feb	Nicosia	3	0
EC1971	21 Apr	Belfast	5	0
wc1973	14 Feb	Nicosia	0	1
wc1973	8 May	London	3	0
2002	21 Aug	Belfast	0	0

		v CZECHOSLOVAKIA	NI	C
wc1958	8 June	Halmstad	1	0
wc1958	17 June	Malmo	2	1*

**After extra time*

		v CZECH REPUBLIC	NI	C
wc2001	24 Mar	Belfast	0	1
wc2001	6 June	Teplice	1	3

		v DENMARK	NI	D
EC1978	25 Oct	Belfast	2	1
EC1979	6 June	Copenhagen	0	4
1986	26 Mar	Belfast	1	1
EC1990	17 Oct	Belfast	1	1
EC1991	13 Nov	Odense	1	2
wc1992	18 Nov	Belfast	0	1
wc1993	13 Oct	Copenhagen	0	1
wc2000	7 Oct	Belfast	1	1
wc2001	1 Sept	Copenhagen	1	1

		v ESTONIA	NI	E
2004	31 Mar	Tallinn	1	0
2006	1 Mar	Belfast	1	0

		v FAEROES	NI	F
EC1991	1 May	Belfast	1	1
EC1991	11 Sept	Landskrona	5	0

		v FINLAND	NI	F
wc1984	27 May	Pori	0	1
wc1984	14 Nov	Belfast	2	1
EC1998	10 Oct	Belfast	1	0
EC1998	9 Oct	Helsinki	1	4
2003	12 Feb	Belfast	0	1

		v FRANCE	NI	F
1928	21 Feb	Paris	0	4
1951	12 May	Belfast	2	2
1952	11 Nov	Paris	1	3
wc1958	19 June	Norrkoping	0	4
1982	24 Mar	Paris	0	4
wc1982	4 July	Madrid	1	4
1986	26 Feb	Paris	0	0
1988	27 Apr	Belfast	0	0
1999	18 Aug	Belfast	0	1

		v GERMANY	NI	G
1992	2 June	Bremen	1	1
1996	29 May	Belfast	1	1
wc1996	9 Nov	Nuremberg	1	1
wc1997	20 Aug	Belfast	1	3
EC1999	27 Mar	Belfast	0	3
EC1999	8 Sept	Dortmund	0	4
2005	4 June	Belfast	1	4

		v WEST GERMANY	NI	WG
WC1958	15 June	Malmo	2	2
WC1960	26 Oct	Belfast	3	4
WC1961	10 May	Hamburg	1	2
1966	7 May	Belfast	0	2
1977	27 Apr	Cologne	0	5
EC1982	17 Nov	Belfast	1	0
EC1983	16 Nov	Hamburg	1	0

		v GREECE	NI	G
WC1961	3 May	Athens	1	2
WC1961	17 Oct	Belfast	2	0
1988	17 Feb	Athens	2	3
EC2003	2 Apr	Belfast	0	2
EC2003	11 Oct	Athens	0	1

		v HOLLAND	NI	H
1962	9 May	Rotterdam	0	4
WC1965	17 Mar	Belfast	2	1
WC1965	7 Apr	Rotterdam	0	0
WC1976	13 Oct	Rotterdam	2	2
WC1977	12 Oct	Belfast	0	1

		v HONDURAS	NI	H
WC1982	21 June	Zaragoza	1	1

		v HUNGARY	NI	H
WC1988	19 Oct	Budapest	0	1
WC1989	6 Sept	Belfast	1	2
2000	26 Apr	Belfast	0	1

		v ICELAND	NI	I
WC1977	11 June	Reykjavik	0	1
WC1977	21 Sept	Belfast	2	0
WC2000	11 Oct	Reykjavik	0	1
WC2001	5 Sept	Belfast	3	0

		v REPUBLIC OF IRELAND	NI	RI
EC1978	20 Sept	Dublin	0	0
EC1979	21 Nov	Belfast	1	0
WC1988	14 Sept	Belfast	0	0
WC1989	11 Oct	Dublin	0	3
WC1993	31 Mar	Dublin	0	3
WC1993	17 Nov	Belfast	1	1
EC1994	16 Nov	Belfast	0	4
EC1995	29 Mar	Dublin	1	1
1999	29 May	Dublin	1	0

		v ISRAEL	NI	I
1968	10 Sept	Jaffa	3	2
1976	3 Mar	Tel Aviv	1	1
WC1980	26 Mar	Tel Aviv	0	0
WC1981	18 Nov	Belfast	1	0
1984	16 Oct	Belfast	3	0
1987	18 Feb	Tel Aviv	1	1

		v ITALY	NI	I
WC1957	25 Apr	Rome	0	1
1957	4 Dec	Belfast	2	2
WC1958	15 Jan	Belfast	2	1
1961	25 Apr	Bologna	2	3
1997	22 Jan	Palermo	0	2
2003	3 June	Campobasso	0	2

		v LATVIA	NI	L
WC1993	2 June	Riga	2	1
WC1993	8 Sept	Belfast	2	0
EC1995	26 Apr	Riga	1	0
EC1995	7 June	Belfast	1	2

		v LIECHTENSTEIN	NI	L
EC1994	20 Apr	Belfast	4	1
EC1995	11 Oct	Eschen	4	0
2002	27 Mar	Vaduz	0	0

		v LITHUANIA	NI	L
WC1992	28 Apr	Belfast	2	2
WC1993	25 May	Vilnius	1	0

		v LUXEMBOURG	NI	L
2000	23 Feb	Luxembourg	3	1

		v MALTA	NI	M
WC1988	21 May	Belfast	3	0
WC1989	26 Apr	Valletta	2	0
2000	28 Mar	Valletta	3	0
WC2000	2 Sept	Belfast	1	0
WC2001	6 Oct	Valletta	1	0
2005	17 Aug	Ta'Qali	1	1

		v MEXICO	NI	M
1966	22 June	Belfast	4	1
1994	11 June	Miami	0	3

		v MOLDOVA	NI	M
EC1998	18 Nov	Belfast	2	2
EC1999	31 Mar	Chisinau	0	0

		v MOROCCO	NI	M
1986	23 Apr	Belfast	2	1

		v NORWAY	NI	N
1922	25 May	Bergen	1	2
EC1974	4 Sept	Oslo	1	2
EC1975	29 Oct	Belfast	3	0
1990	27 Mar	Belfast	2	3
1996	27 Mar	Belfast	0	2
2001	28 Feb	Belfast	0	4
2004	18 Feb	Belfast	1	4

		v POLAND	NI	P
EC1962	10 Oct	Katowice	2	0
EC1962	28 Nov	Belfast	2	0
1988	23 Mar	Belfast	1	1
1991	5 Feb	Belfast	3	1
2002	13 Feb	Limassol	1	4
EC2004	4 Sept	Belfast	0	3
EC2005	30 Mar	Warsaw	0	1

		v PORTUGAL	NI	P
WC1957	16 Jan	Lisbon	1	1
WC1957	1 May	Belfast	3	0
WC1973	28 Mar	Coventry	1	1
WC1973	14 Nov	Lisbon	1	1
WC1980	19 Nov	Lisbon	0	1
WC1981	29 Apr	Belfast	1	0
EC1994	7 Sept	Belfast	1	2
EC1995	3 Sept	Lisbon	1	1
WC1997	29 Mar	Belfast	0	0
WC1997	11 Oct	Lisbon	0	1
2005	15 Nov	Belfast	1	1

		v ROMANIA	NI	R
WC1984	12 Sept	Belfast	3	2
WC1985	16 Oct	Bucharest	1	0
1994	23 Mar	Belfast	2	0
2006	27 May	Chicago	0	2

		v ST KITTS & NEVIS	NI	SK
2004	2 June	Basseterre	2	0

		v SERBIA-MONTENEGRO	NI	SM
2004	28 Apr	Belfast	1	1

		v SLOVAKIA	NI	S
1998	25 Mar	Belfast	1	0

		v SOUTH AFRICA	NI	SA
1924	24 Sept	Belfast	1	2

		v SPAIN	NI	S
1958	15 Oct	Madrid	2	6
1963	30 May	Bilbao	1	1
1963	30 Oct	Belfast	0	1
EC1970	11 Nov	Seville	0	3
EC1972	16 Feb	Hull	1	1
WC1982	25 June	Valencia	1	0
1985	27 Mar	Palma	0	0
WC1986	7 June	Guadalajara	1	2
WC1988	21 Dec	Seville	0	4
WC1989	8 Feb	Belfast	0	2
WC1992	14 Oct	Belfast	0	0
WC1993	28 Apr	Seville	1	3
1998	2 June	Santander	1	4

			NI	S
2002	17 Apr	Belfast	0	5
EC2002	12 Oct	Albacete	0	3
EC2003	11 June	Belfast	0	0

		v SWEDEN	NI	S
EC1974	30 Oct	Solna	2	0
EC1975	3 Sept	Belfast	1	2
WC1980	15 Oct	Belfast	3	0
WC1981	3 June	Solna	0	1
1996	24 Apr	Belfast	1	2

		v SWITZERLAND	NI	S
WC1964	14 Oct	Belfast	1	0
WC1964	14 Nov	Lausanne	1	2
1998	22 Apr	Belfast	1	0
2004	18 Aug	Zurich	0	0

		v THAILAND	NI	T
1997	21 May	Bangkok	0	0

		v TRINIDAD & TOBAGO	NI	TT
2004	6 June	Bacolet	3	0

		v TURKEY	NI	T
WC1968	23 Oct	Belfast	4	1
WC1968	11 Dec	Istanbul	3	0
EC1983	30 Mar	Belfast	2	1
EC1983	12 Oct	Ankara	0	1
WC1985	1 May	Belfast	2	0
WC1985	11 Sept	Izmir	0	0
EC1986	12 Nov	Izmir	0	0
EC1987	11 Nov	Belfast	1	0
EC1998	5 Sept	Istanbul	0	3
EC1999	4 Sept	Belfast	0	3

		v UKRAINE	NI	U
WC1996	31 Aug	Belfast	0	1
WC1997	2 Apr	Kiev	1	2
EC2002	16 Oct	Belfast	0	0
EC2003	6 Sept	Donetsk	0	0

		v URUGUAY	NI	U
1964	29 Apr	Belfast	3	0
1990	18 May	Belfast	1	0
2006	21 May	New Jersey	0	1

		v USSR	NI	USSR
WC1969	19 Sept	Belfast	0	0
WC1969	22 Oct	Moscow	0	2
EC1971	22 Sept	Moscow	0	1
EC1971	13 Oct	Belfast	1	1

		v YUGOSLAVIA	NI	Y
EC1975	16 Mar	Belfast	1	0
EC1975	19 Nov	Belgrade	0	1
WC1982	17 June	Zaragoza	0	0
EC1987	29 Apr	Belfast	1	2
EC1987	14 Oct	Sarajevo	0	3
EC1990	12 Sept	Belfast	0	2
EC1991	27 Mar	Belgrade	1	4
2000	16 Aug	Belfast	1	2

REPUBLIC OF IRELAND

		v ALBANIA	RI	A
WC1992	26 May	Dublin	2	0
WC1993	26 May	Tirana	2	1
EC2003	2 Apr	Tirana	0	0
EC2003	7 June	Dublin	2	1

		v ALGERIA	RI	A
1982	28 Apr	Algiers	0	2

		v ANDORRA	RI	A
WC2001	28 Mar	Barcelona	3	0
WC2001	25 Apr	Dublin	3	1

		v ARGENTINA	RI	A
1951	13 May	Dublin	0	1
†1979	29 May	Dublin	0	0
1980	16 May	Dublin	0	1
1998	22 Apr	Dublin	0	2

†*Not considered a full international.*

		v AUSTRALIA	RI	A
2003	19 Aug	Dublin	2	1

		v AUSTRIA	RI	A
1952	7 May	Vienna	0	6
1953	25 Mar	Dublin	4	0
1958	14 Mar	Vienna	1	3
1962	8 Apr	Dublin	2	3
EC1963	25 Sept	Vienna	0	0
EC1963	13 Oct	Dublin	3	2
1966	22 May	Vienna	0	1
1968	10 Nov	Dublin	2	2
EC1971	30 May	Dublin	1	4
EC1971	10 Oct	Linz	0	6
EC1995	11 June	Dublin	1	3
EC1995	6 Sept	Vienna	1	3

		v BELGIUM	RI	B
1928	12 Feb	Liège	4	2
1929	30 Apr	Dublin	4	0
1930	11 May	Brussels	3	1
WC1934	25 Feb	Dublin	4	4
1949	24 Apr	Dublin	0	2
1950	10 May	Brussels	1	5
1965	24 Mar	Dublin	0	2
1966	25 May	Liège	3	2
WC1980	15 Oct	Dublin	1	1
WC1981	25 Mar	Brussels	0	1
EC1986	10 Sept	Brussels	2	2
EC1987	29 Apr	Dublin	0	0
WC1997	29 Oct	Dublin	1	1
WC1997	16 Nov	Brussels	1	2

		v BOLIVIA	RI	B
1994	24 May	Dublin	1	0
1996	15 June	New Jersey	3	0

		v BRAZIL	RI	B
1974	5 May	Rio de Janeiro	1	2
1982	27 May	Uberlandia	0	7
1987	23 May	Dublin	1	0
2004	18 Feb	Dublin	0	0

		v BULGARIA	RI	B
WC1977	1 June	Sofia	1	2
WC1977	12 Oct	Dublin	0	0
EC1979	19 May	Sofia	0	1
EC1979	17 Oct	Dublin	3	0
WC1987	1 Apr	Sofia	1	2
WC1987	14 Oct	Dublin	2	0
2004	18 Aug	Dublin	1	1

		v CAMEROON	RI	C
WC2002	1 June	Niigata	1	1

		v CANADA	RI	C
2003	18 Nov	Dublin	3	0

		v CHILE	RI	C
1960	30 Mar	Dublin	2	0
1972	21 June	Recife	1	2
1974	12 May	Santiago	2	1
1982	22 May	Santiago	0	1
1991	22 May	Dublin	1	1
2006	24 May	Dublin	0	1

		v CHINA	RI	C
1984	3 June	Sapporo	1	0
2005	29 Mar	Dublin	1	0

		v CROATIA	RI	C
1996	2 June	Dublin	2	2
EC1998	5 Sept	Dublin	2	0

			RI	C
EC1999	4 Sept	Zagreb	0	1
2001	15 Aug	Dublin	2	2
2004	16 Nov	Dublin	1	0

		v CYPRUS	RI	C
wc1980	26 Mar	Nicosia	3	2
wc1980	19 Nov	Dublin	6	0
wc2001	24 Mar	Nicosia	4	0
wc2001	6 Oct	Dublin	4	0
wc2004	4 Sept	Dublin	3	0
wc2005	8 Oct	Nicosia	1	0

		v CZECHOSLOVAKIA	RI	C
1938	18 May	Prague	2	2
EC1959	5 Apr	Dublin	2	0
EC1959	10 May	Bratislava	0	4
wc1961	8 Oct	Dublin	1	3
wc1961	29 Oct	Prague	1	7
EC1967	21 May	Dublin	0	2
EC1967	22 Nov	Prague	2	1
wc1969	4 May	Dublin	1	2
wc1969	7 Oct	Prague	0	3
1979	26 Sept	Prague	1	4
1981	29 Apr	Dublin	3	1
1986	27 May	Reykjavik	1	0

		v CZECH REPUBLIC	RI	C
1994	5 June	Dublin	1	3
1996	24 Apr	Prague	0	2
1998	25 Mar	Olomouc	1	2
2000	23 Feb	Dublin	3	2
2004	31 Mar	Dublin	2	1

		v DENMARK	RI	D
wc1956	3 Oct	Dublin	2	1
wc1957	2 Oct	Copenhagen	2	0
wc1968	4 Dec	Dublin	1	1
(abandoned after 51 mins)				
wc1969	27 May	Copenhagen	0	2
wc1969	15 Oct	Dublin	1	1
EC1978	24 May	Copenhagen	3	3
EC1979	2 May	Dublin	2	0
wc1984	14 Nov	Copenhagen	0	3
wc1985	13 Nov	Dublin	1	4
wc1992	14 Oct	Copenhagen	0	0
wc1993	28 Apr	Dublin	1	1
2002	27 Mar	Dublin	3	0

		v ECUADOR	RI	E
1972	19 June	Natal	3	2

		v EGYPT	RI	E
wc1990	17 June	Palermo	0	0

		v ENGLAND	RI	E
1946	30 Sept	Dublin	0	1
1949	21 Sept	Everton	2	0
wc1957	8 May	Wembley	1	5
wc1957	19 May	Dublin	1	1
1964	24 May	Dublin	1	3
1976	8 Sept	Wembley	1	1
EC1978	25 Oct	Dublin	1	1
EC1980	6 Feb	Wembley	0	2
1985	26 Mar	Wembley	1	2
EC1988	12 June	Stuttgart	1	0
wc1990	11 June	Cagliari	1	1
EC1990	14 Nov	Dublin	1	1
EC1991	27 Mar	Wembley	1	1
1995	15 Feb	Dublin	1	0
(abandoned after 27 mins)				

		v ESTONIA	RI	E
wc2000	11 Oct	Dublin	2	0
wc2001	6 June	Tallinn	2	0

		v FAEROES	RI	F
EC2004	13 Oct	Dublin	2	0
EC2005	8 June	Toftir	2	0

		v FINLAND	RI	F
wc1949	8 Sept	Dublin	3	0
wc1949	9 Oct	Helsinki	1	1
1990	16 May	Dublin	1	1
2000	15 Nov	Dublin	3	0
2002	21 Aug	Helsinki	3	0

		v FRANCE	RI	F
1937	23 May	Paris	2	0
1952	16 Nov	Dublin	1	1
wc1953	4 Oct	Dublin	3	5
wc1953	25 Nov	Paris	0	1
wc1972	15 Nov	Dublin	2	1
wc1973	19 May	Paris	1	1
wc1976	17 Nov	Paris	0	2
wc1977	30 Mar	Dublin	1	0
wc1980	28 Oct	Paris	0	2
wc1981	14 Oct	Dublin	3	2
1989	7 Feb	Dublin	0	0
wc2004	9 Oct	Paris	0	0
wc2005	7 Sept	Dublin	0	1

		v GEORGIA	RI	G
EC2003	29 Mar	Tbilisi	2	1
EC2003	11 June	Dublin	2	0

		v GERMANY	RI	G
1935	8 May	Dortmund	1	3
1936	17 Oct	Dublin	5	2
1939	23 May	Bremen	1	1
1994	29 May	Hanover	2	0
wc2002	5 June	Ibaraki	1	1

		v WEST GERMANY	RI	WG
1951	17 Oct	Dublin	3	2
1952	4 May	Cologne	0	3
1955	28 May	Hamburg	1	2
1956	25 Nov	Dublin	3	0
1960	11 May	Dusseldorf	1	0
1966	4 May	Dublin	0	4
1970	9 May	Berlin	1	2
1975	1 Mar	Dublin	1	0†
1979	22 May	Dublin	1	3
1981	21 May	Bremen	0	3†
1989	6 Sept	Dublin	1	1

†*v West Germany 'B'*

		v GREECE	RI	G
2000	26 Apr	Dublin	0	1
2002	20 Nov	Athens	0	0

		v HOLLAND	RI	N
1932	8 May	Amsterdam	2	0
1934	8 Apr	Amsterdam	2	5
1935	8 Dec	Dublin	3	5
1955	1 May	Dublin	1	0
1956	10 May	Rotterdam	4	1
wc1980	10 Sept	Dublin	2	1
wc1981	9 Sept	Rotterdam	2	2
EC1982	22 Sept	Rotterdam	1	2
EC1983	12 Oct	Dublin	2	3
EC1988	18 June	Gelsenkirchen	0	1
wc1990	21 June	Palermo	1	1
1994	20 Apr	Tilburg	1	0
wc1994	4 July	Orlando	0	2
EC1995	13 Dec	Liverpool	0	2
1996	4 June	Rotterdam	1	3
wc2000	2 Sept	Amsterdam	2	2
wc2001	1 Sept	Dublin	1	0
2004	5 June	Amsterdam	1	0

		v HUNGARY	RI	H
1934	15 Dec	Dublin	2	4
1936	3 May	Budapest	3	3
1936	6 Dec	Dublin	2	3
1939	19 Mar	Cork	2	2
1939	18 May	Budapest	2	2
wc1969	8 June	Dublin	1	2
wc1969	5 Nov	Budapest	0	4
wc1989	8 Mar	Budapest	0	0
wc1989	4 June	Dublin	2	0
1991	11 Sept	Gyor	2	1

		v ICELAND	RI	I
EC1962	12 Aug	Dublin	4	2
EC1962	2 Sept	Reykjavik	1	1
EC1982	13 Oct	Dublin	2	0
EC1983	21 Sept	Reykjavik	3	0
1986	25 May	Reykjavik	2	1
wc1996	10 Nov	Dublin	0	0
wc1997	6 Sept	Reykjavik	4	2

		v IRAN	RI	I
1972	18 June	Recife	2	1
wc2001	10 Nov	Dublin	2	0
wc2001	15 Nov	Tehran	0	1

		v N. IRELAND	RI	NI
EC1978	20 Sept	Dublin	0	0
EC1979	21 Nov	Belfast	0	1
wc1988	14 Sept	Belfast	0	0
wc1989	11 Oct	Dublin	3	0
wc1993	31 Mar	Dublin	3	0
wc1993	17 Nov	Belfast	1	1
EC1994	16 Nov	Belfast	4	0
EC1995	29 Mar	Dublin	1	1
1999	29 May	Dublin	0	1

		v ISRAEL	RI	I
1984	4 Apr	Tel Aviv	0	3
1985	27 May	Tel Aviv	0	0
1987	10 Nov	Dublin	5	0
EC2005	26 Mar	Tel Aviv	1	1
EC2005	4 June	Dublin	2	2

		v ITALY	RI	I
1926	21 Mar	Turin	0	3
1927	23 Apr	Dublin	1	2
EC1970	8 Dec	Rome	0	3
EC1971	10 May	Dublin	1	2
1985	5 Feb	Dublin	1	2
wc1990	30 June	Rome	0	1
1992	4 June	Foxboro	0	2
wc1994	18 June	New York	1	0
2005	17 Aug	Dublin	1	2

		v JAMAICA	RI	J
2004	2 June	Charlton	1	0

		v LATVIA	RI	L
wc1992	9 Sept	Dublin	4	0
wc1993	2 June	Riga	2	1
EC1994	7 Sept	Riga	3	0
EC1995	11 Oct	Dublin	2	1

		v LIECHTENSTEIN	RI	L
EC1994	12 Oct	Dublin	4	0
EC1995	3 June	Eschen	0	0
wc1996	31 Aug	Eschen	5	0
wc1997	21 May	Dublin	5	0

		v LITHUANIA	RI	L
wc1993	16 June	Vilnius	1	0
wc1993	8 Sept	Dublin	2	0
wc1997	20 Aug	Dublin	0	0
wc1997	10 Sept	Vilnius	2	1

		v LUXEMBOURG	RI	I
1936	9 May	Luxembourg	5	1
wc1953	28 Oct	Dublin	4	0
wc1954	7 Mar	Luxembourg	1	0
EC1987	28 May	Luxembourg	2	0
EC1987	9 Sept	Dublin	2	1

		v MACEDONIA	RI	M
wc1996	9 Oct	Dublin	3	0
wc1997	2 Apr	Skopje	2	3
EC1999	9 June	Dublin	1	0
EC1999	9 Oct	Skopje	1	1

		v MALTA	RI	M
EC1983	30 Mar	Valletta	1	0
EC1983	16 Nov	Dublin	8	0
wc1989	28 May	Dublin	2	0
wc1989	15 Nov	Valletta	2	0

			RI	M
1990	2 June	Valletta	3	0
EC1998	14 Oct	Dublin	5	0
EC1999	8 Sept	Valletta	3	2

		v MEXICO	RI	M
1984	8 Aug	Dublin	0	0
wc1994	24 June	Orlando	1	2
1996	13 June	New Jersey	2	2
1998	23 May	Dublin	0	0
2000	4 June	Chicago	2	2

		v MOROCCO	RI	M
1990	12 Sept	Dublin	1	0

		v NIGERIA	RI	N
2002	16 May	Dublin	1	2
2004	29 May	Charlton	0	3

		v NORWAY	RI	N
wc1937	10 Oct	Oslo	2	3
wc1937	7 Nov	Dublin	3	3
1950	26 Nov	Dublin	2	2
1951	30 May	Oslo	3	2
1954	8 Nov	Dublin	2	1
1955	25 May	Oslo	3	1
1960	6 Nov	Dublin	3	1
1964	13 May	Oslo	4	1
1973	6 June	Oslo	1	1
1976	24 Mar	Dublin	3	0
1978	21 May	Oslo	0	0
wc1984	17 Oct	Oslo	0	1
wc1985	1 May	Dublin	0	0
1988	1 June	Oslo	0	0
wc1994	28 June	New York	0	0
2003	30 Apr	Dublin	1	0

		v PARAGUAY	RI	P
1999	10 Feb	Dublin	2	0

		v POLAND	RI	P
1938	22 May	Warsaw	0	6
1938	13 Nov	Dublin	3	2
1958	11 May	Katowice	2	2
1958	5 Oct	Dublin	2	2
1964	10 May	Kracow	1	3
1964	25 Oct	Dublin	3	2
1968	15 May	Dublin	2	2
1968	30 Oct	Katowice	0	1
1970	6 May	Dublin	1	2
1970	23 Sept	Dublin	0	2
1973	16 May	Wroclaw	0	2
1973	21 Oct	Dublin	1	0
1976	26 May	Poznan	2	0
1977	24 Apr	Dublin	0	0
1978	12 Apr	Lodz	0	3
1981	23 May	Bydgoszcz	0	3
1984	23 May	Dublin	0	0
1986	12 Nov	Warsaw	0	1
1988	22 May	Dublin	3	1
EC1991	1 May	Dublin	0	0
EC1991	16 Oct	Poznan	3	3
2004	28 Apr	Bydgoszcz	0	0

		v PORTUGAL	RI	P
1946	16 June	Lisbon	1	3
1947	4 May	Dublin	0	2
1948	23 May	Lisbon	0	2
1949	22 May	Dublin	1	0
1972	25 June	Recife	1	2
1992	7 June	Boston	2	0
EC1995	26 Apr	Dublin	1	0
EC1995	15 Nov	Lisbon	0	3
1996	29 May	Dublin	0	1
wc2000	7 Oct	Lisbon	1	1
wc2001	2 June	Dublin	1	1
2005	9 Feb	Dublin	1	0

		v ROMANIA	RI	R
1988	23 Mar	Dublin	2	0
wc1990	25 June	Genoa	0	0*
wc1997	30 Apr	Bucharest	0	1
wc1997	11 Oct	Dublin	1	1
2004	27 May	Dublin	1	0

		v RUSSIA	RI	R
1994	23 Mar	Dublin	0	0
1996	27 Mar	Dublin	0	2
2002	13 Feb	Dublin	2	0
EC2002	7 Sept	Moscow	2	4
EC2003	6 Sept	Dublin	1	1

		v SAUDI ARABIA	RI	SA
wc2002	11 June	Yokohama	3	0

		v SCOTLAND	RI	S
WC1961	3 May	Glasgow	1	4
WC1961	7 May	Dublin	0	3
1963	9 June	Dublin	1	0
1969	21 Sept	Dublin	1	1
EC1986	15 Oct	Dublin	0	0
EC1987	18 Feb	Glasgow	1	0
2000	30 May	Dublin	1	2
2003	12 Feb	Glasgow	2	0

		v SOUTH AFRICA	RI	SA
2000	11 June	New Jersey	2	1

		v SPAIN	RI	S
1931	26 Apr	Barcelona	1	1
1931	13 Dec	Dublin	0	5
1946	23 June	Madrid	1	0
1947	2 Mar	Dublin	3	2
1948	30 May	Barcelona	1	2
1949	12 June	Dublin	1	4
1952	1 June	Madrid	0	6
1955	27 Nov	Dublin	2	2
EC1964	11 Mar	Seville	1	5
EC1964	8 Apr	Dublin	0	2
WC1965	5 May	Dublin	1	0
WC1965	27 Oct	Seville	1	4
WC1965	10 Nov	Paris	0	1
EC1966	23 Oct	Dublin	0	0
EC1966	7 Dec	Valencia	0	2
1977	9 Feb	Dublin	0	1
EC1982	17 Nov	Dublin	3	3
EC1983	27 Apr	Zaragoza	0	2
1985	26 May	Cork	0	0
WC1988	16 Nov	Seville	0	2
WC1989	26 Apr	Dublin	1	0
WC1992	18 Nov	Seville	0	0
WC1993	13 Oct	Dublin	1	3
WC2002	16 June	Suwon	1	1

		v SWEDEN	RI	S
WC1949	2 June	Stockholm	1	3
WC1949	13 Nov	Dublin	1	3
1959	1 Nov	Dublin	3	2
1960	18 May	Malmo	1	4
EC1970	14 Oct	Dublin	1	1
EC1970	28 Oct	Malmo	0	1
1999	28 Apr	Dublin	2	0
2006	1 Mar	Dublin	3	0

		v SWITZERLAND	RI	S
1935	5 May	Basle	0	1
1936	17 Mar	Dublin	1	0
1937	17 May	Berne	1	0
1938	18 Sept	Dublin	4	0
1948	5 Dec	Dublin	0	1
EC1975	11 May	Dublin	2	1
EC1975	21 May	Berne	0	1
1980	30 Apr	Dublin	2	0
WC1985	2 June	Dublin	3	0
WC1985	11 Sept	Berne	0	0
1992	25 Mar	Dublin	2	1
EC2002	16 Oct	Dublin	1	2
EC2003	11 Oct	Basle	0	2
WC2004	8 Sept	Basle	1	1
WC2005	12 Oct	Dublin	0	0

		v TRINIDAD & TOBAGO	RI	TT
1982	30 May	Port of Spain	1	2

		v TUNISIA	RI	T
1988	19 Oct	Dublin	4	0

		v TURKEY	RI	T
EC1966	16 Nov	Dublin	2	1
EC1967	22 Feb	Ankara	1	2
EC1974	20 Nov	Izmir	1	1
EC1975	29 Oct	Dublin	4	0
1976	13 Oct	Ankara	3	3
1978	5 Apr	Dublin	4	2
1990	26 May	Izmir	0	0
EC1990	17 Oct	Dublin	5	0
EC1991	13 Nov	Istanbul	3	1
EC2000	13 Nov	Dublin	1	1
EC2000	17 Nov	Bursa	0	0
2003	9 Sept	Dublin	2	2

		v URUGUAY	RI	U
1974	8 May	Montevideo	0	2
1986	23 Apr	Dublin	1	1

		v USA	RI	USA
1979	29 Oct	Dublin	3	2
1991	1 June	Boston	1	1
1992	29 Apr	Dublin	4	1
1992	30 May	Washington	1	3
1996	9 June	Boston	1	2
2000	6 June	Boston	1	1
2002	17 Apr	Dublin	2	1

		v USSR	RI	USSR
WC1972	18 Oct	Dublin	1	2
WC1973	13 May	Moscow	0	1
EC1974	30 Oct	Dublin	3	0
EC1975	18 May	Kiev	1	2
WC1984	12 Sept	Dublin	1	0
WC1985	16 Oct	Moscow	0	2
EC1988	15 June	Hanover	1	1
1990	25 Apr	Dublin	1	0

		v WALES	RI	W
1960	28 Sept	Dublin	2	3
1979	11 Sept	Swansea	1	2
1981	24 Feb	Dublin	1	3
1986	26 Mar	Dublin	0	1
1990	28 Mar	Dublin	1	0
1991	6 Feb	Wrexham	3	0
1992	19 Feb	Dublin	0	1
1993	17 Feb	Dublin	2	1
1997	11 Feb	Cardiff	0	0

		v YUGOSLAVIA	RI	Y
1955	19 Sept	Dublin	1	4
1988	27 Apr	Dublin	2	0
EC1998	18 Nov	Belgrade	0	1
EC1999	1 Sept	Dublin	2	1

SIR BOBBY CHARLTON

Did Bobby Charlton play to more spectators than any other British player in history?

Manchester U (League)	26,189,139
Manchester U (FA Cup)	3,837,279
Manchester U (League Cup)	977,406
Manchester U (European Cup)	1,595,259
Manchester U (Cup-Winners' Cup)	273,719
Manchester U (Fairs Cup)	420,357
Preston NE (League)	411,609
Preston NE (FA Cup)	33,682
Preston NE (League Cup)	32,321
England	7,322,287
TOTAL	41,093,058

Figures do not include England schools, youth, six Under-23 matches, eight for the Football League and many other games.

Research conducted by Len Marsden.

OTHER BRITISH AND IRISH INTERNATIONAL MATCHES 2005–06

FRIENDLIES

Graz, 17 August 2005, 13,800

Austria (0) 2 *(Ibertsberger 83, Standfest 87)*

Scotland (2) 2 *(Miller 3, O'Connor 39)*

Austria: Payer (Schranz 46); Gercaliu, Dospel (Standfest 54), Pogatetz, Ehmann, Aufhauser, Schopp (Ibertsberger 68), Kuhbauer (Saumel 77), Mayrleb (Kuljic 66), Ivanschitz, Vastic (Akagunduz 66).
Scotland: Gordon; McNamara, Alexander G, Caldwell S, Pressley (Anderson 46), Webster, Dailly, O'Neil (Severin 46), O'Connor, Miller (Riordan 46), Quashie (Hughes R 73).
Referee: Selcuk (Turkey).

Glasgow, 12 November 2005, 26,708

Scotland (1) 1 *(Webster 37)*

USA (1) 1 *(Wolff 9 (pen))*

Scotland: Gordon; Alexander G, Webster, Dailly (Caldwell G 46), Weir, Pressley (Caldwell S 46), Fletcher, Quashie (Maloney 74), O'Connor (Brown 74), Hartley, McCann (McFadden 63).
USA: Keller; Spector, Bocanegra (Conrad 79), Cherundolo, Berhalter, Gaven (Quaranta 46), Carroll, Zavagnin (Olsen 46), Beasley (Pearce 76), Ching, Wolff (Rolfe 58).
Referee: A. Mallenco (Spain).

Glasgow, 1 March 2006, 20,952

Scotland (0) 1 *(Miller 55)*

Switzerland (2) 3 *(Barnetta 21, Gygax 41, Cabanas 69)*

Scotland: Gordon (Alexander N 49); Dailly, Alexander G, Ferguson (Teale 50), Weir (Caldwell S 56), Webster, Fletcher, Caldwell G, McFadden, Miller, Quashie.
Switzerland: Zuberbuhler (Coltorti 50); Degn, Senderos (Lustrinelli 73), Grichting, Behrami (Djourou 50), Barnetta, Vogel (Dzemaili 80), Cabanas, Wicky (Vonlanthen 50), Streller (Smiljanic 74), Gygax.
Referee: B. Coue (France).

Kobe, 11 May 2006, 5780

Bulgaria (1) 1 *(Todorov Y 26)*

Scotland (2) 5 *(Boyd 12, 43, McFadden 69, Burke 76, 88)*

Bulgaria: Kolev (Mihailov 71); Kirilov, Topuzakov, Karaslavov (Yanev 55), Wagner, Todorov Y, Telkiyski, Angelov, Domovchisky (Iliev 71), Petrov M, Todorov S (Genkov 71).
Scotland: Alexander N; Weir, Naysmith, Murty (McNamee 82), Anderson, Caldwell G, Fletcher, Severin (Rae 69), McCulloch (Murray 78), Teale (Burke 74), Boyd (McFadden 52).
Referee: T. Kamikawa (Japan).

Saitama, 13 May 2006, 58,648

Japan (0) 0

Scotland (0) 0

Japan: Kawaguchi; Miyamoto, Santos, Nakazawa (Tsuboi 50), Kaji, Fukunishi, Ogasawara, Ono, Endo (Sato 72), Kubo (Maki 62), Tamada.
Scotland: Alexander N; Weir, Naysmith (Murray 46), Murty (McNamee 79), Anderson, Caldwell G, Fletcher, Severin (Rae 46), McCulloch (Miller L 69), Teale (Burke 59), McFadden (Boyd 59).
Scotland won the Kirin Cup.
Referee: E. Gonzalez (Spain).

Copenhagen, 17 August 2005, 41,438

Denmark (0) 4 *(Rommedahl 60, Tomasson 63, Gravgaard 67, Larsen S 90)*

England (0) 1 *(Rooney 87)*

Denmark: Sorensen; Agger, Nielsen P (Gravgaard 46), Jensen N, Priske, Poulsen (Jensen D 87), Gravesen, Gronkjaer (Rommedahl 46), Jensen C (Perez 75), Tomasson (Larsen S 64), Jorgensen (Kahlenberg 46).
England: Robinson (James 46); Neville G (Johnson 46), Cole A, Gerrard (Jenas 84), Ferdinand, Terry (Carragher 46), Beckham, Lampard (Hargreaves 64), Rooney, Defoe (Owen 46), Cole J.
Referee: T. Ovrebo (Norway).

Geneva, 12 November 2005, 29,000

Argentina (1) 2 *(Crespo 34, Samuel 53)*

England (1) 3 *(Rooney 39, Owen 86, 90)*

Argentina: Abbondanzieri; Ayala (Coloccini 74), Sorin, Zanetti, Demichelis, Samuel, Riquelme (Gonzalez L 84), Rodriguez M, Cambiasso, Tevez (Cruz 80), Crespo (Saviola 70).
England: Robinson; Young (Crouch 80), Bridge (Konchesky 46), Ferdinand, Terry, King (Cole J 57), Beckham, Lampard, Rooney, Owen, Gerrard.
Referee: P. Lueuba (Switzerland).

Liverpool, 1 March 2006, 40,013

England (0) 2 *(Crouch 75, Cole J 90)*

Uruguay (1) 1 *(Pouso 26)*

England: Robinson; Neville, Bridge (Carragher 30), Gerrard (Jenas 46), Terry (King 46), Ferdinand, Beckham (Wright-Phillips 64), Carrick, Bent D (Defoe 82), Rooney (Crouch 64), Cole J.
Uruguay: Carini (Viera 46); Diogo, Lugano, Godin, Lima, Pouso, Perez (Gonzalez 88), Varela (Valdez 90), Vargas (Pereira 76), Regueiro (Martinez 83), Forlan (Medina 86).
Referee: S. Farina (Italy).

Reading, 25 May 2006, 22,032

England B (1) 1 *(Jenas 34)*

Belarus (0) 2 *(Kutuzov 50, Kornilenko 81)*

England: James (Green 46) (Carson 50); Hargreaves, Cole A, Carrick, Carragher, Campbell, Lennon, Jenas (Cole J 62), Crouch (Dawson 79), Owen (Walcott 62), Downing (Defoe 79).
Belarus: Zhevnov (Khomutovski 46); Kulchi, Lentsevich, Omelyanchuk■, Shtanyuk, Korytsko, Yurevich (Shagoiko 61), Bulyga (Kornilenko 46), Romaschenko (Kashevsky 74), Kalachev (Pankovets 80), Kutuzov (Kontsevoy 64).
Referee: D. McKeown (Ireland).

Old Trafford, 30 May 2006, 56,323

England (0) 3 *(Gerrard 47, Terry 51, Crouch 84)*

Hungary (0) 1 *(Dardai 55)*

England: Robinson; Neville G (Hargreaves 46), Cole A, Carragher, Ferdinand, Terry (Campbell 76), Beckham, Lampard, Gerrard (Crouch 65), Owen (Walcott 65), Cole J.
Hungary: Kiraly; Feher C, Komlosi (Vanczak 8), Halmosi, Eger, Molnar (Vadocz 82), Huszti, Dardai, Gera, Toth (Torghelle 62), Szabics (Polonkai 73).
Referee: P. Vink (Holland).

Old Trafford, 3 June 2006, 70,373

England (4) 6 *(Lampard 11, Taylor 17 (og), Crouch 29, 65, 89, Owen 32)*

Jamaica (0) 0

England: Robinson (James 46); Carragher, Cole A (Bridge 33), Gerrard, Ferdinand, Terry (Campbell 35), Beckham (Lennon 66), Lampard (Carrick 66), Crouch, Owen, Cole J.
Jamaica: Ricketts; Reid, Davis, Stewart, Daley, Hue (Johnson 85), Taylor (Crawford 46), Euell (Stephenson 78), Campbell-Ryce, Shelton (Burton 47), Fuller (Bennett 76).
Referee: K. Plautz (Austria).

Ta'Qali, 17 August 2005, 1850
Malta (1) 1 *(Woods 35)*
Northern Ireland (1) 1 *(Healy 9)*
Malta: Haber; Pullicino (Ciantar 62), Said, Dimech (Scicluna 62), Wellman, Woods■, Agius G (Mallia 74), Briffa, Mattocks, Anonam, Cohen (Sammut 86).
Northern Ireland: Taylor; Gillespie■, Hughes A, Davis (Mulryne 88), Murdock, Craigan, Johnson, Whitley (Jones S 59), Quinn (Feeney 69), Healy, Elliott (Brunt 59).
Referee: M. Riley (England).

Belfast, 15 November 2005, 20,000
Northern Ireland (0) 1 *(Feeney 54)*
Portugal (1) 1 *(Craigan 41 (og))*
Northern Ireland: Taylor; Gillespie (Shiels 86), Capaldi, Davis, Murdock, Craigan, Jones S (McAuley 46), Elliott (McCann 46), Quinn (Thompson 77), Feeney (Sproule 86), Brunt.
Portugal: Paulo Santos; Paulo Ferreira, Costinha (Alves 67), Petit, Ricardo Carvalho, Meira, Jorge Ribeiro, Ronaldo (Helder Postiga 69), Pauleta (Nuno Gomes 46), Boa Morte (Caneira 62), Tiago (Frechaut 76).
Referee: H. Webb (England).

Belfast, 1 March 2006, 14,000
Northern Ireland (1) 1 *(Sproule 2)*
Estonia (0) 0
Northern Ireland: Taylor; Duff, Capaldi, Davis (Elliott 68), Craigan (McLean 46), McAuley, Sproule (Jones 46), Baird, Quinn (Thompson 59), Healy (Feeney 59), Brunt (McCann 68).
Estonia: Poom; Jaager, Stepanov, Piiroja, Rooba U, Rahn (Reim 78), Teever (Kuresoo 73), Dmitrijev, Neemelo, Lindpere (Oper 54), Sidorenkov (Ahjupera 84).
Referee: P. Vink (Holland).

New Jersey, 21 May 2006, 4152
Northern Ireland (0) 0
Uruguay (1) 1 *(Estoyanoff 33)*
Northern Ireland: Ingham; Duff (Webb 82), Capaldi, Murdock (McAuley 82), Craigan, Davis, Jones S (Thompson 59), Clingan (Hughes M 82), Sproule, Quinn (Lafferty 75), Hughes J (Shiels 75).
Uruguay: Carini; Valdez, Godin, Scotti, Garcia, Lopez, Estoyanoff (Surraco 82), Perez, Abreu, Giacomazzi, Vargas.

Chicago, 27 May 2006, 15,000
Romania (2) 2 *(Balan 7, Niculae 13)*
Northern Ireland (0) 0
Romania: Coman; Goian (Iencsi 56), Maftei, Pulhac (Stoica 88), Radoi (Soava 46), Badoi, Balan (Vasile-Cocis 46), Bostina, Nicolita (Oprita 65), Niculae (Mutu 46), Buga.
Northern Ireland: Blayney; Duff, Capaldi (Hughes J 57), McAuley (Murdock 82), Craigan (Webb 71), Davis, Shiels (Jones S 66), Clingan, Sproule (Hughes M 57), Quinn■, Thompson (Lafferty 66).
Referee: M. Kennedy (USA).

Dublin, 17 August 2005, 44,000
Republic of Ireland (1) 1 *(Reid A 32)*
Italy (2) 2 *(Pirlo 10, Gilardino 31)*
Republic of Ireland: Given; Finnan (Carr 57), O'Shea (Miller 78), Holland (Harte 39), Cunningham, Dunne (O'Brien A 46), Reid A (Elliott 74), Reid S, Morrison, Kilbane, Duff.
Italy: Roma; Zaccardo, Zambrotta, Pirlo (Barone 76), Nesta (Materazzi 46), Cannavaro (Barzagli 63), Gattuso, De Rossi (Grosso 46), Del Piero (Iaquinta 46), Vieri, Gilardino (Diana 46).
Referee: Paulo Costa (Portugal).

Dublin, 1 March 2006, 34,000
Republic of Ireland (1) 3 *(Duff 35, Robbie Keane 47, Miller 70)*
Sweden (0) 0
Republic of Ireland: Given (Henderson 48); O'Brien J (Miller 61), Harte (Kilbane 61), O'Shea (Ireland 48), O'Brien A, Dunne, Elliott (Kavanagh 48), Reid S, Robbie Keane, Doyle (Morrison 68), Duff.
Sweden: Isaksson; Ostlund (Andersson C 74), Mellberg, Hansson, Edman, Linderoth (Andersson D 69), Elmander (Jonson 60), Kallstrom (Svensson A 60), Wilhelmsson, Ibrahimovic (Rosenberg 37), Larsson (Allback 78).
Referee: D. Ledentu (France).

Dublin, 24 May 2006, 41,200
Republic of Ireland (0) 0
Chile (0) 1 *(Iturra 49)*
Republic of Ireland: Given (Henderson 54); Kelly (Reid A 84), Dunne, Breen (Harte 53), Kilbane, Miller (Kavanagh 54), Reid S, O'Shea (McGeady 54), Doyle (Byrne 72), Robbie Keane, Duff.
Chile: Bravo; Jara, Vargas, Contreras, Olarra, Jimenez, Acuna, Iturra, Gonzalez M (Zenteno 90), Navia (Sanchez 76), Suazo (Galaz 81).
Referee: M. Ingvarsson (Sweden).

Swansea, 17 August 2005, 10,016
Wales (0) 0
Slovenia (0) 0
Wales: Coyne; Duffy (Edwards 73), Ricketts, Page, Gabbidon, Partridge (Roberts G 89), Robinson (Davies C 85), Vaughan (Parry 68), Hartson, Earnshaw (Williams G 62), Fletcher.
Slovenia: Mavric B (Handanovic 63); Cesar, Filekovic, Mavric M (Sukalo 46), Knavs, Acimovic (Cimirotic 46), Zlogar, Ceh, Pokorn (Ilic 56), Lavric (Rodic 46), Komac (Pecnik 87).
Referee: I. Stokes (Republic of Ireland).

Limassol, 16 November 2005, 1000
Cyprus (1) 1 *(Michael 42 (pen))*
Wales (0) 0
Cyprus: Morfis (Georgallides 71); Okkarides, Lambrou (Louka 79), Michael, Charalambidis, Elia (Theofilou 70), Garpozis, Krassas, Makrides, Okkas, Yiasoumi (Alecou 76).
Wales: Price; Duffy (Edwards 76), Collins D (Williams G 46), Gabbidon, Page, Fletcher, Ricketts, Robinson, Hartson, Bellamy, Vaughan (Earnshaw 66).
Referee: H. Jacov (Israel).

Cardiff, 1 March 2006, 12,324
Wales (0) 0
Paraguay (0) 0
Wales: Jones P (Price 66); Edwards, Ricketts, Gabbidon, Collins J, Nyatanga, Fletcher (Robinson 75), Bellamy (Earnshaw 78), Koumas (Ledley 70), Davies S (Crofts 76), Giggs (Cotterill 86).
Paraguay: Villar; Caceres J, Toledo, Caniza, Da Silva, Paredes, Ramirez (Cabanas 77), Barreto, Dos Santos (Riveros 67), Acuna, Haedo Valdez (Cardozo 71).
Referee: D. McDonald (Scotland).

Bilbao, 21 May 2006, 15,000
Basque Country (0) 0
Wales (0) 1 *(Giggs 76)*
Basque Country: Lafuente (Riesgo 46); Edu Alonso, Lopez Rekarte (Garrido 46), Campo (Sarriegi 46), Labaka, Punal, Preto, Guerrero (Munoz 46), Etxeberria, Alonso (Llorente 63), Gabilondo.
Wales: Jones P; Ledley, Nyatanga, Gabbidon, Collins J, Robinson (Cotterill 73), Fletcher, Bellamy (Crofts 56), Earnshaw, Davies S, Giggs.
Referee: E. Gonzalez (Spain).

Graz, 27 May 2006, 8000
Trinidad & Tobago (1) 1 *(John S 32)*
Wales (1) 2 *(Earnshaw 38, 87)*
Trinidad & Tobago: Jack; John A, Andrews, Lawrence (Samuell 35), Birchall, Gray, Edwards, John S, Jones (Latapy 62), Theobald (Whitley 77), Yorke.
Wales: Brown (Garner 46); Robinson, Ledley, Gabbidon, Collins J, Partridge (Nyatanga 46), Fletcher (Crofts 46), Earnshaw, Cotterill (Davies C 46), Davies S (Aaron Davies 78), Vaughan (Bale 55).
Referee: S. Messner (Austria).

INTERNATIONAL APPEARANCES 1872–2006

This is a list of full international appearances by Englishmen, Irishmen, Scotsmen and Welshmen in matches against the Home Countries and against foreign nations. It does not include unofficial matches against Commonwealth and Empire countries. The year indicated refers to the season; ie 2005 is the 2004–05 season. Actual match dates appear on pp. 883–902.

Explanatory code for matches played by all five countries: A represents Austria; Alb, Albania; Alg, Algeria; An, Angola; And, Andorra; Arg, Argentina; Arm, Armenia; Aus, Australia; Az, Azerbaijan; B, Bohemia; Bar, Barbados; Bel, Belgium; Bl, Belarus; Bol, Bolivia; Bos, Bosnia; Br, Brazil; Bul, Bulgaria; C,CIS; Ca, Canada; Cam, Cameroon; Ch, Chile; Chn, China; Co, Colombia; Cr, Costa Rica; Cro, Croatia; Cy, Cyprus; Cz, Czechoslovakia; CzR, Czech Republic; D, Denmark; E, England; Ec, Ecuador; Ei, Republic of Ireland; EG, East Germany; Eg, Egypt; Es, Estonia; F, France; Fa, Faeroes; Fi, Finland; G, Germany; Ge, Georgia; Gh, Ghana; Gr, Greece; H, Hungary; Hk, Hong Kong; Ho, Holland; Hon, Honduras; I, Italy; Ic, Iceland; Ir, Iran; Is, Israel; J, Japan; Jam, Jamaica; K, Kuwait; L, Luxembourg; La, Latvia; Li, Lithuania; Lie, Liechtenstein; M, Mexico; Ma, Malta; Mac, Macedonia; Mal, Malaysia; Mol, Moldova; Mor, Morocco; N, Norway; Ng, Nigeria; Ni, Northern Ireland; Nz, New Zealand; P, Portugal; Para, Paraguay; Pe, Peru; Pol, Poland; R, Romania; RCS, Republic of Czechs and Slovaks; R of E, Rest of Europe; R of UK, Rest of United Kingdom; R of W, Rest of World; Ru, Russia; S.Af, South Africa; S.Ar, Saudi Arabia; S, Scotland; Se, Sweden; Ser, Serbia-Montenegro; Sk, South Korea; Slo, Slovakia; Slv, Slovenia; Sm, San Marino; Sp, Spain; Stk, St Kitts & Nevis; Sw, Switzerland; T, Turkey; Th, Thailand; Tr, Trinidad & Tobago; Tun, Tunisia; U, Uruguay; Uk, Ukraine; US, United States of America; USSR, Soviet Union; W, Wales; WG, West Germany; Y, Yugoslavia; Z, Zaire.
As at July 2006.

ENGLAND

Abbott, W. (Everton), 1902 v W (1)
A'Court, A. (Liverpool), 1958 v Ni, Br, A, USSR; 1959 v W (5)
Adams, T. A. (Arsenal), 1987 v Sp, T, Br; 1988 v WG, T, Y, Ho, H, S, Co, Sw, Ei, Ho, USSR; 1989 v D, Se, S.Ar.; 1991 v Ei (2); 1993 v N, T, Sm, T, Ho, Pol, N; 1994 v Pol, Ho, D, Gr, N; 1995 v US, R, Ei, U; 1996 v Co, N, Sw, P, Chn, Sw, S, Ho, Sp, G; 1997 v Ge (2); 1998 v I, Ch, P, S.Ar, Tun, R, Co, Arg; 1999 v Se, F; 2000 v L, Pol, Bel, S (2), Uk, P; 2001 v F, G (66)
Adcock, H. (Leicester C), 1929 v F, Bel, Sp; 1930 v Ni, W (5)
Alcock, C. W. (Wanderers), 1875 v S (1)
Alderson, J. T. (C Palace), 1923 v F (1)
Aldridge, A. (WBA), 1888 v Ni; (with Walsall Town Swifts), 1889 v Ni (2)
Allen, A. (Stoke C) 1960 v Se, W, Ni (3)
Allen, A. (Aston Villa), 1888 v Ni (1)
Allen, C. (QPR), 1984 v Br (sub), U, Ch; (with Tottenham H), 1987 v T; 1988 v Is (5)
Allen, H. (Wolverhampton W), 1888 v S, W, Ni; 1889 v S; 1890 v S (5)
Allen, J. P. (Portsmouth), 1934 v Ni, W (2)
Allen, R. (WBA), 1952 v Sw; 1954 v Y, S; 1955 v WG, W (5)
Alsford, W. J. (Tottenham H), 1935 v S (1)
Amos, A. (Old Carthusians), 1885 v S; 1886 v W (2)
Anderson, R. D. (Old Etonians), 1879 v W (1)
Anderson, S. (Sunderland), 1962 v A, S (2)
Anderson, V. (Nottingham F), 1979 v Cz, Se; 1980 v Bul, Sp; 1981 v N, R, W, S; 1982 v Ni, Ic; 1984 v Ni; (with Arsenal), 1985 v T, Ni, Ei, R, Fi, S, M, US; 1986 v USSR, M; 1987 v Se, Ni (2), Y, Sp, T; (with Manchester U), 1988 v WG, H, Co (30)
Anderton, D. R. (Tottenham H), 1994 v D, Gr, N; 1995 v US, Ei, U, J, Se, Br; 1996 v H, Chn, Sw, S, Ho, Sp, G; 1998 v S.Ar, Mor, Tun, R, Co, Arg; 1999 v Se, Bul, L, CzR, F; 2001 v F, I (sub); 2002 v Se (sub) (30)
Angus, J. (Burnley), 1961 v A (1)
Armfield, J. C. (Blackpool), 1959 v Br, Pe, M, US; 1960 v Y, Sp, H, S; 1961 v L, P, Sp, M, I, A, W, Ni, S; 1962 v A, Sw, Pe, W, Ni, S, L, P, H, Arg, Bul, Br; 1963 v F (2), Br, EG, Sw, Ni, W, S; 1964 v R of W, W, Ni, S; 1966 v Y, Fi (43)
Armitage, G. H. (Charlton Ath), 1926 v Ni (1)
Armstrong, D. (Middlesbrough), 1980 v Aus; (with Southampton), 1983 v WG; 1984 v W (3)
Armstrong, K. (Chelsea), 1955 v S (1)
Arnold, J. (Fulham), 1933 v S (1)
Arthur, J. W. H. (Blackburn R), 1885 v S, W, Ni; 1886 v S, W; 1887 v W, Ni (7)
Ashcroft, J. (Woolwich Arsenal), 1906 v Ni, W, S (3)
Ashmore, G. S. (WBA), 1926 v Bel (1)
Ashton, C. T. (Corinthians), 1926 v Ni (1)
Ashurst, W. (Notts Co), 1923 v Se (2); 1925 v S, W, Bel (5)
Astall, G. (Birmingham C), 1956 v Fi, WG (2)
Astle, J. (WBA), 1969 v W; 1970 v S, P, Br (sub), Cz (5)
Aston, J. (Manchester U), 1949 v S, W, D, Sw, Se, N, F; 1950 v S, W, Ni, Ei, I, P, Bel, Ch, US; 1951 v Ni (17)
Athersmith, W. C. (Aston Villa), 1892 v Ni, 1897 v S, W, Ni; 1898 v S, W, Ni; 1899 v S, W, Ni; 1900 v S, W (12)
Atyeo, P. J. W. (Bristol C), 1956 v Br, Se, Sp; 1957 v D, Ei (2) (6)
Austin, S. W. (Manchester C), 1926 v Ni (1)
Bach, P. (Sunderland), 1899 v Ni (1)
Bache, J. W. (Aston Villa), 1903 v W; 1904 v W, Ni; 1905 v S; 1907 v Ni; 1910 v Ni; 1911 v S (7)
Baddeley, T. (Wolverhampton W), 1903 v S, Ni; 1904 v S, W, Ni (5)
Bagshaw, J. J. (Derby Co), 1920 v Ni (1)
Bailey, G. R. (Manchester U), 1985 v Ei, M (2)
Bailey, H. P. (Leicester Fosse), 1908 v W, A (2), H, B (5)
Bailey, M. A. (Charlton Ath), 1964 v US; 1965 v W (2)
Bailey, N. C. (Clapham Rovers), 1878 v S; 1879 v S, W; 1880 v S; 1881 v S; 1882 v S, W; 1883 v S, W; 1884 v S, W, Ni; 1885 v S, W, Ni; 1886 v S, W; 1887 v S, W (19)
Baily, E. F. (Tottenham H), 1950 v Sp; 1951 v Y, Ni, W; 1952 v A (2), Sw, W; 1953 v Ni (9)
Bain, J. (Oxford University), 1877 v S (1)
Baker, A. (Arsenal), 1928 v W (1)
Baker, B. H. (Everton), 1921 v Bel; (with Chelsea), 1926 v Ni (2)
Baker, J. H. (Hibernian), 1960 v Y, Sp, H, Ni, S; (with Arsenal) 1966 v Sp, Pol, Ni (8)
Ball, A. J. (Blackpool), 1965 v Y, WG, Se; 1966 v S, Sp, Fi, D, U, Arg, P, WG (2), Pol (2); (with Everton), 1967 v W, S, Ni, A, Cz, Sp; 1968 v W, S, USSR, Sp (2), Y, WG; 1969 v Ni, W, S, R (2), M, Br, U; 1970 v P, Co, Ec, R, Br, Cz (sub), WG, W, S, Bel; 1971 v Ma, EG, Gr, Ma (sub), Ni, S; 1972 v Sw, Gr; (with Arsenal) WG (2), S; 1973 v W (3), Y, S (2), Cz, Ni, Pol; 1974 v P (sub); 1975 v WG, Cy (2), Ni, W, S (72)
Ball, J. (Bury), 1928 v Ni (1)
Ball, M. J. (Everton), 2001 v Sp (sub) (1)
Balmer, W. (Everton), 1905 v Ni (1)
Bamber, J. (Liverpool), 1921 v W (1)
Bambridge, A. L. (Swifts), 1881 v W; 1883 v W; 1884 v Ni (3)
Bambridge, E. C. (Swifts), 1879 v S; 1880 v S; 1881 v S; 1882 v S, W, Ni; 1883 v W; 1884 v S, W, Ni; 1885 v S, W, Ni; 1886 v S, W; 1887 v S, W, Ni (18)
Bambridge, E. H. (Swifts), 1876 v S (1)
Banks, G. (Leicester C), 1963 v S, Br, Cz, EG; 1964 v W, Ni, S, R of W, U, P (2), US, Arg; 1965 v Ni, S, H, Y, WG, Se; 1966 v Ni, S, Sp, Pol (2), WG (2), Y, Fi, U, M, F, Arg, P; 1967 v Ni, W, S, Cz; (with Stoke C), 1968 v W, Ni, S, USSR (2), Sp, WG, Y; 1969 v Ni, S, R (2), F, U, Br; 1970 v W, Ni, S, Ho, Bel, Co, Ec, R, Br, Cz; 1971 v Gr, Ma (2), Ni, S; 1972 v Sw, Gr, WG (2), W, S (73)
Banks, H. E. (Millwall), 1901 v Ni (1)
Banks, T. (Bolton W), 1958 v USSR (3), Br, A; 1959 v Ni (6)
Bannister, W. (Burnley), 1901 v W; (with Bolton W), 1902 v Ni (2)
Barclay, R. (Sheffield U), 1932 v S; 1933 v Ni; 1936 v S (3)
Bardsley, D. J. (QPR), 1993 v Sp (sub), Pol (2)
Barham, M. (Norwich C), 1983 v Aus (2) (2)
Barkas, S. (Manchester C), 1936 v Bel; 1937 v S; 1938 v W, Ni, Cz (5)
Barker, J. (Derby Co), 1935 v I, Ho, S, W, Ni; 1936 v G, A, S, W, Ni; 1937 v W (11)
Barker, R. (Herts Rangers), 1872 v S (1)
Barker, R. R. (Casuals), 1895 v W (1)
Barlow, R. J. (WBA), 1955 v Ni (1)
Barmby, N. J. (Tottenham H), 1995 v U (sub), Se (sub); (with Middlesbrough), 1996 v Co, N, P, Chn, Sw (sub), Ho (sub), Sp (sub); 1997 v Mol; (with Everton), 2000 v Br

(sub), Uk (sub), Ma, G (sub), R (sub); (with Liverpool), 2001 v F, G, I, Sp; 2002 v Ho (sub), G, Alb, Gr (23)
Barnes, J. (Watford), 1983 v Ni (sub), Aus (sub), Aus (2); 1984 v D, L (sub), F (sub), S, USSR, Br, U, Ch; 1985 v EG, Fi, T, Ni, R, Fi, S, I (sub), M, WG (sub), US (sub); 1986 v R (sub), Is (sub), M (sub), Ca (sub), Arg (sub); 1987 v Se, T (sub), Br; (with Liverpool), 1988 v WG, T, Y, Is, Ho, S, Co, Sw, Ei, Ho, USSR; 1989 v Se, Gr, Alb, Pol, D; 1990 v Se, I, Br, D, U, Tun, Ei, Ho, Eg, Bel, Cam; 1991 v H, Pol, Cam, Ei, T, USSR, Arg; 1992 v Cz, Fi; 1993 v Sm, T, Ho, Pol, US, G; 1995 v US, R, Ng, U, Se; 1996 v Co (sub) (79)
Barnes, P. S. (Manchester C), 1978 v I, WG, Br, W, S, H; 1979 v D, Ei, Cz, Ni (2), S, Bul, A; (with WBA), 1980 v D, W; 1981 v Sp (sub), Br, W, Sw (sub); (with Leeds U), 1982 v N (sub), Ho (sub) (22)
Barnet, H. H. (Royal Engineers), 1882 v Ni (1)
Barrass, M. W. (Bolton W), 1952 v W, Ni; 1953 v S (3)
Barrett, A. F. (Fulham), 1930 v Ni (1)
Barrett, E. D. (Oldham Ath), 1991 v Nz; (with Aston Villa), 1993 v Br, G (3)
Barrett, J. W. (West Ham U), 1929 v Ni (1)
Barry, G. (Aston Villa), 2000 v Uk (sub), Ma (sub); 2001 v F, G (sub), Fi, I; 2003 v S.Af (sub), Ser (sub) (8)
Barry, L. (Leicester C), 1928 v F, Bel; 1929 v F, Bel, Sp (5)
Barson, F. (Aston Villa), 1920 v W (1)
Barton, J. (Blackburn R), 1890 v Ni (1)
Barton, P. H. (Birmingham), 1921 v Bel; 1922 v Ni; 1923 v F; 1924 v Bel, S, W; 1925 v Ni (7)
Barton, W. D. (Wimbledon), 1995 v Ei; (with Newcastle U), Se, Br (sub) (3)
Bassett, W. I. (WBA), 1888 v Ni, 1889 v S, W; 1890 v S, W; 1891 v S, Ni; 1892 v S; 1893 v S, W; 1894 v S; 1895 v S, Ni; 1896 v S, W, Ni (16)
Bastard, S. R. (Upton Park), 1880 v S (1)
Bastin, C. S. (Arsenal), 1932 v W; 1933 v I, Sw; 1934 v S, Ni, W, H, Cz; 1935 v S, Ni, I; 1936 v S, W, G, A; 1937 v W, Ni; 1938 v S, G, Sw, F (21)
Batty, D. (Leeds U), 1991 v USSR (sub), Arg, Aus, Nz, Mal; 1992 v G, T, H (sub), F, Se; 1993 v N, Sm, US, Br; (with Blackburn R), 1994 v D (sub); 1995 v J, Br; (with Newcastle U), 1997 v Mol (sub), Ge, I, M, Ge, S.Af (sub), Pol (sub), F; 1998 v Mol, I, Ch, Sw (sub), P, S.Ar, Tun, R, Co (sub), Arg (sub); 1999 v Bul (sub), L; (with Leeds U), H, Se, Bul; 2000 v L, Pol (42)
Baugh, R. (Stafford Road), 1886 v Ni; (with Wolverhampton W) 1890 v Ni (2)
Bayliss, A. E. J. M. (WBA), 1891 v Ni (1)
Baynham, R. L. (Luton T), 1956 v Ni, D, Sp (3)
Beardsley, P. A. (Newcastle U), 1986 v Eg (sub), Is, USSR, M, Ca (sub), P (sub), Pol, Para, Arg; 1987 v Ni (2), Y, Sp, Br, S; (with Liverpool), 1988 v WG, T, Y, Is, Ho, H, S, Co, Sw, Ei, Ho; 1989 v D, Se, S.Ar, Gr (sub), Alb (sub+1), Pol, D; 1990 v Se, Pol, I, Br, U (sub), Tun (sub), Ei, Eg (sub), Cam (sub), WG, I; 1991 v Pol (sub), Ei (2), USSR (sub); (with Newcastle U), 1994 v D, Gr, N; 1995 v Ng, Ei, U, J, Se; 1996 v P (sub), Chn (sub) (59)
Beasant, D. J. (Chelsea), 1990 v I (sub), Y (sub) (2)
Beasley, A. (Huddersfield T), 1939 v S (1)
Beats, W. E. (Wolverhampton W), 1901 v W; 1902 v S (2)
Beattie, J. S. (Southampton), 2003 v Aus, Ser (sub); 2004 v Cro (sub), Lie, D (sub) (5)
Beattie, T. K. (Ipswich T), 1975 v Cy (2), S; 1976 v Sw, P; 1977 v Fi, I (sub), Ho; 1978 v L (sub) (9)
Beckham, D. R. J. (Manchester U), 1997 v Mol, Pol, Ge, I, Ge, S.Af (sub), Pol, I, F; 1998 v Mol, I, Cam, P, S.Ar, Bel (sub), R (sub), Co, Arg; 1999 v L, CzR, F, Pol, Se; 2000 v L, Pol, S(2), Arg, Br, Uk, Ma, P, G, R; 2001 v F, G, I, Sp, Fi, Alb, M, Gr; 2002 v Ho, G, Alb, Gr, Se, Ho, I, Se, Arg, Ng, D, Br; 2003 v Slo, Mac, Aus, Lie, T, S.Af; (with Real Madrid), 2004 v Cro, Mac, Lie, T, D, P, J, Ic, F, Sw, Cro, P; 2005 v Uk, A, Pol, W, Sp, Ho, Ni, Az, Co; 2006 v D, W, Ni, A, Arg, U, H, Jam, Para, Tr, Se, Ec, P (94)
Becton, F. (Preston NE), 1895 v Ni; (with Liverpool), 1897 v W (2)
Bedford, H. (Blackpool), 1923 v Se; 1925 v Ni (2)
Bell, C. (Manchester C), 1968 v Se, WG; 1969 v W, Bul, F, U, Br; 1970 v Ni (sub), Ho (2), P, Br (sub), Cz, WG (sub); 1972 v Gr, WG (2), W, Ni, S; 1973 v W (3), Y, S (2), Ni, Cz, Pol; 1974 v A, Pol, I, W, Ni, S, Arg, EG, Bul, Y; 1975 v Cz, P, WG, Cy (2), Ni, S; 1976 v Sw, Cz (48)
Bennett, W. (Sheffield U), 1901 v S, W (2)
Benson, R. W. (Sheffield U), 1913 v Ni (1)
Bent, D. A. (Charlton Ath), 2006 v U (1)
Bentley, R. T. F. (Chelsea), 1949 v Se; 1950 v S, P, Bel, Ch, USA; 1953 v W, Bel; 1955 v W, WG, Sp, P (12)
Beresford, J. (Aston Villa), 1934 v Cz (1)
Berry, A. (Oxford University), 1909 v Ni (1)
Berry, J. J. (Manchester U), 1953 v Arg, Ch, U; 1956 v Se (4)
Bestall, J. G. (Grimsby T), 1935 v Ni (1)
Betmead, H. A. (Grimsby T), 1937 v Fi (1)
Betts, M. P. (Old Harrovians), 1877 v S (1)
Betts, W. (Sheffield W), 1889 v W (1)
Beverley, J. (Blackburn R), 1884 v S, W, Ni (3)
Birkett, R. H. (Clapham Rovers), 1879 v S (1)
Birkett, R. J. E. (Middlesbrough), 1936 v Ni (1)
Birley, F. H. (Oxford University), 1874 v S; (with Wanderers), 1875 v S (2)
Birtles, G. (Nottingham F), 1980 v Arg (sub), I; 1981 v R (3)
Bishop, S. M. (Leicester C), 1927 v S, Bel, L, F (4)
Blackburn, F. (Blackburn R), 1901 v S; 1902 v Ni; 1904 v S (3)
Blackburn, G. F. (Aston Villa), 1924 v F (1)
Blenkinsop, E. (Sheffield W), 1928 v F, Bel; 1929 v S, W, Ni, F, Bel, Sp; 1930 v S, W, Ni, G, A; 1931 v S, W, Ni, F, Bel; 1932 v S, W, Ni, Sp; 1933 v S, W, Ni, A (26)
Bliss, H. (Tottenham H), 1921 v S (1)
Blissett, L. (Watford), 1983 v WG (sub), L, W, Gr (sub), H, Ni, S (sub), Aus (1+1 sub); (with AC Milan), 1984 v D (sub), H, W (sub), S, USSR (14)
Blockley, J. P. (Arsenal), 1973 v Y (1)
Bloomer, S. (Derby Co), 1895 v S, Ni; 1896 v W, Ni; 1897 v S, W, Ni; 1898 v S; 1899 v S, W, Ni; 1900 v S; 1901 v S, W; 1902 v S, W, Ni; 1904 v S; 1905 v S, W, Ni; (with Middlesbrough), 1907 v S, W (23)
Blunstone, F. (Chelsea), 1955 v W, S, F, P; 1957 v Y (5)
Bond, R. (Preston NE), 1905 v Ni, W; 1906 v S, W, Ni; (with Bradford C), 1910 v S, W, Ni (8)
Bonetti, P. P. (Chelsea), 1966 v D; 1967 v Sp, A; 1968 v Sp; 1970 v Ho, P, WG (7)
Bonsor, A. G. (Wanderers), 1873 v S; 1875 v S (2)
Booth, F. (Manchester C), 1905 v Ni (1)
Booth, T. (Blackburn R), 1898 v W; (with Everton), 1903 v S (2)
Bould, S. A. (Arsenal), 1994 v Gr, N (2)
Bowden, E. R. (Arsenal), 1935 v W, I; 1936 v W, Ni, A; 1937 v H (6)
Bower, A. G. (Corinthians), 1924 v Ni, Bel; 1925 v W, Bel; 1927 v W (5)
Bowers, J. W. (Derby Co), 1934 v S, Ni, W (3)
Bowles, S. (QPR), 1974 v P, W, Ni; 1977 v I, Ho (5)
Bowser, S. (WBA), 1920 v Ni (1)
Bowyer, L. D. (Leeds U), 2003 v P (1)
Boyer, P. J. (Norwich C), 1976 v W (1)
Boyes, W. (WBA), 1935 v Ho; (with Everton), 1939 v W, R of E (3)
Boyle, T. W. (Burnley), 1913 v Ni (1)
Brabrook, P. (Chelsea), 1958 v USSR; 1959 v Ni; 1960 v Sp (3)
Bracewell, P. W. (Everton), 1985 v WG (sub), US; 1986 v Ni (3)
Bradford, G. R. W. (Bristol R), 1956 v D (1)
Bradford, J. (Birmingham), 1924 v Ni; 1925 v Bel; 1928 v S; 1929 v Ni, W, F, Sp; 1930 v S, Ni, G, A; 1931 v W (12)
Bradley, W. (Manchester U), 1959 v I, US, M (sub) (3)
Bradshaw, F. (Sheffield W), 1908 v A (1)
Bradshaw, T. H. (Liverpool), 1897 v Ni (1)
Bradshaw, W. (Blackburn R), 1910 v W, Ni; 1912 v Ni; 1913 v W (4)
Brann, G. (Swifts), 1886 v S, W; 1891 v W (3)
Brawn, W. F. (Aston Villa), 1904 v W, Ni (2)
Bray, J. (Manchester C), 1935 v W; 1936 v S, W, Ni, G; 1937 v S (6)
Brayshaw, E. (Sheffield W), 1887 v Ni (1)
Bridge W. M. (Southampton), 2002 v Ho, I, Para, Sk (sub), Cam, Arg (sub), Ng (sub); 2003 v P (sub), Mac, Lie, T, Ser (sub); (with Chelsea), 2004 v Cro (sub), Lie, D (sub), P (sub), Ic (sub); 2005 v A, Pol, Sp; 2006 v Arg, U, Jam (sub) (23)
Bridges, B. J. (Chelsea), 1965 v S, H, Y; 1966 v A (4)
Bridgett, A. (Sunderland), 1905 v S; 1908 v S, A (2), H, B; 1909 v Ni, W, H (2), A (11)
Brindle, T. (Darwen), 1880 v S, W (2)
Brittleton, J. T. (Sheffield W), 1912 v S, W, Ni; 1913 v S; 1914 v W (5)
Britton, C. S. (Everton), 1935 v S, W, Ni, I; 1937 v S, Ni, H, N, Se (9)
Broadbent, P. F. (Wolverhampton W), 1958 v USSR; 1959 v S, W, Ni, I, Br; 1960 v S (7)
Broadis, I. A. (Manchester C), 1952 v S, A, I; 1953 v S, Arg, Ch, U, US; (with Newcastle U), 1954 v S, H, Y, Bel, Sw, U (14)
Brockbank, J. (Cambridge University), 1872 v S (1)
Brodie, J. B. (Wolverhampton W), 1889 v S, Ni; 1891 v Ni (3)

Bromilow, T. G. (Liverpool), 1921 v W; 1922 v S, W; 1923 v Bel; 1926 v Ni (5)
Bromley-Davenport, W. E. (Oxford University), 1884 v S, W (2)
Brook, E. F. (Manchester C), 1930 v Ni; 1933 v Sw: 1934 v S, W, Ni, F, H, Cz; 1935 v S, W, Ni, I; 1936 v S, W, Ni; 1937 v H; 1938 v W, Ni (18)
Brooking, T. D. (West Ham U), 1974 v P, Arg, EG, Bul, Y; 1975 v Cz (sub), P; 1976 v P, W, Br, I, Fi; 1977 v Ei, Fi, I, Ho, Ni, W; 1978 v I, WG, W, S (sub), H; 1979 v D, Ei, Ni, W (sub), S, Bul, Se (sub), A; 1980 v D, Ni, Arg (sub), W, Ni, S, Bel, Sp; 1981 v Sw, Sp, R, H; 1982 v H, S, Fi, Sp (sub) (47)
Brooks, J. (Tottenham H), 1957 v W, Y, D (3)
Broome, F. H. (Aston Villa), 1938 v G, Sw, F; 1939 v N, I, R, Y (7)
Brown, A. (Aston Villa), 1882 v S, W, Ni (3)
Brown, A. S. (Sheffield U), 1904 v W; 1906 v Ni (2)
Brown, A. (WBA), 1971 v W (1)
Brown, G. (Huddersfield T), 1927 v S, W, Ni, Bel, L, F; 1928 v W; 1929 v S; (with Aston Villa), 1933 v W (9)
Brown, J. (Blackburn R), 1881 v W; 1882 v Ni; 1885 v S, W, Ni (5)
Brown, J. H. (Sheffield W), 1927 v S, W, Bel, L, F; 1930 v Ni (6)
Brown, K. (West Ham U), 1960 v Ni (1)
Brown, W. (West Ham U), 1924 v Bel (1)
Brown, W. M. (Manchester U), 1999 v H; 2001 v Fi (sub), Alb (sub); 2002 v Ho, Sk (sub), Cam; 2003 v Aus (sub); 2005 v Ho, US (9)
Bruton, J. (Burnley), 1928 v F, Bel; 1929 v S (3)
Bryant, W. I. (Clapton), 1925 v F (1)
Buchan, C. M. (Sunderland), 1913 v Ni; 1920 v W; 1921 v W, Bel; 1923 v F; 1924 v S (6)
Buchanan, W. S. (Clapham R), 1876 v S (1)
Buckley, F. C. (Derby Co), 1914 v Ni (1)
Bull, S. G. (Wolverhampton W), 1989 v S (sub), D (sub); 1990 v Y, Cz, D (sub), U (sub), Tun (sub), Ei (sub), Ho (sub), Eg, Bel (sub); 1991 v H, Pol (13)
Bullock, F. E. (Huddersfield T), 1921 v Ni (1)
Bullock, N. (Bury), 1923 v Bel; 1926 v W; 1927 v Ni (3)
Burgess, H. (Manchester C), 1904 v S, W, Ni; 1906 v S (4)
Burgess, H. (Sheffield W), 1931 v S, Ni, F, Bel (4)
Burnup, C. J. (Cambridge University), 1896 v S (1)
Burrows, H. (Sheffield W), 1934 v H, Cz; 1935 v Ho (3)
Burton, F. E. (Nottingham F), 1889 v Ni (1)
Bury, L. (Cambridge University), 1877 v S; (with Old Etonians), 1879 v W (2)
Butcher, T. (Ipswich T), 1980 v Aus; 1981 v Sp; 1982 v W, S, F, Cz, WG, Sp; 1983 v D, WG, L, W, Gr, H, Ni, S, Aus (3); 1984 v D, H, L, F, Ni; 1985 v EG, Fi, T, Ni, Ei, R, Fi, S, I, WG, US; 1986 v Is, USSR, S, M, Ca, P, Mor, Pol, Para, Arg; (with Rangers), 1987 v Se, Ni (2), Y, Sp, Br, S; 1988 v T, Y; 1989 v D, Se, Gr, Alb (2), Ch, S, Pol, D; 1990 v Se, Pol, I, Y, Br, Cz, D, U, Tun, Ei, Ho, Bel, Cam, WG (77)
Butler, J. D. (Arsenal), 1925 v Bel (1)
Butler, W. (Bolton W), 1924 v S (1)
Butt, N. (Manchester U), 1997 v M (sub), S.Af (sub); 1998 v Mol (sub), I (sub), Ch, Bel; 1999 v CzR, H; 2001 v I, Sp, Fi (sub), Alb, M (sub), Gr (sub); 2002 v Se, Ho (sub), I, Para, Arg, Ng, D, Br; 2003 v P, Slo, Mac (sub), Lie (sub), T; 2004 v Cro, Mac, T, D, P, Se, J (sub), Ic (sub); (with Newcastle U), 2005 v Uk, W, Az, Sp (39)
Byrne, G. (Liverpool), 1963 v S; 1966 v N (2)
Byrne, J. J. (C Palace), 1962 v Ni; (with West Ham U), 1963 v Sw; 1964 v S, U, P (2), Ei, Br, Arg; 1965 v W, S (11)
Byrne, R. W. (Manchester U), 1954 v S, H, Y, Bel, Sw, U; 1955 v S, W, Ni, WG, F, Sp, P; 1956 v S, W, Ni, Br, Se, Fi, WG, D, Sp; 1957 v S, W, Ni, Y, D (2), Ei (2); 1958 v W, Ni, F (33)

Callaghan, I. R. (Liverpool), 1966 v Fi, F; 1978 v Sw, L (4)
Calvey, J. (Nottingham F), 1902 v Ni (1)
Campbell, A. F. (Blackburn R), 1929 v W, Ni; (with Huddersfield T), 1931 v W, S, Ni; 1932 v W, Ni, Sp (8)
Campbell, S. (Tottenham H), 1996 v H (sub), S (sub); 1997 v Ge, I, Ge, S.Af (sub), Pol, F, Br; 1998 v Mol, I, Cam, Ch, P, Mor, Bel, Tun, R, Co, Arg; 1999 v Se, Bul, L, CzR, Pol, Se, Bul; 2000 v S (2), Arg, Br, Uk, Ma, P, G, R; 2001 v F, Sp, Fi, Alb; (with Arsenal), 2002 v G, Alb, Ho, I, Sk, Cam, Se, Arg, Ng, D, Br; 2003 v Mac, Aus, T; 2004 v Mac, T, J, Ic, F, Sw, Cro, P; 2005 v W, Az, US; 2006 v A, H (sub), Jam (sub), Se (sub) (69)
Camsell, G. H. (Middlesbrough), 1929 v F, Bel; 1930 v Ni, W; 1934 v F; 1936 v S, G, A, Bel (9)
Capes, A. J. (Stoke C), 1903 v S (1)
Carr, J. (Middlesbrough), 1920 v Ni; 1923 v W (2)
Carr, J. (Newcastle U), 1905 v Ni; 1907 v Ni (2)
Carr, W. H. (Owlerton, Sheffield), 1875 v S (1)
Carragher, J. L. (Liverpool), 1999 v H (sub); 2001 v I (sub), M (sub); 2002 v Ho, G (sub), Alb (sub), Se, Para (sub); 2003 v Ser (sub); 2004 v P (sub), Se, Ic; 2005 v Uk (sub), A (sub), Pol (sub), Sp (sub), Ho; 2006 v D (sub), W, Ni, A, Pol, U (sub), H, Jam, Tr, Se, Ec (sub), P (sub) (29)
Carrick, M. (West Ham U), 2001 v M (sub); 2002 v Ho (sub); (with Tottenham H), 2005 v US, Col; 2006 v U, Jam (sub), Ec (7)
Carter, H. S. (Sunderland), 1934 v S, H; 1936 v G; 1937 v S, Ni, H; (with Derby Co), 1947 v S, W, Ni, Ei, Ho, F, Sw (13)
Carter, J. H. (WBA), 1926 v Bel; 1929 v Bel, Sp (3)
Catlin, A. E. (Sheffield W), 1937 v W, Ni, H, N, Se (5)
Chadwick, A. (Southampton), 1900 v S, W (2)
Chadwick, E. (Everton), 1891 v S, W; 1892 v S; 1893 v S; 1894 v S; 1896 v Ni; 1897 v S (7)
Chamberlain, M (Stoke C), 1983 v L (sub); 1984 v D (sub), S, USSR, Br, U, Ch; 1985 v Fi (sub) (8)
Chambers, H. (Liverpool), 1921 v S, W, Bel; 1923 v S, W, Ni, Bel; 1924 v Ni (8)
Channon, M. R. (Southampton), 1973 v Y, S (2), Ni, W, Cz, USSR, I; 1974 v A, Pol, I, P, W, Ni, S, Arg, EG, Bul, Y; 1975 v Cz, P, WG, Cy (2), Ni (sub), W, S; 1976 v Sw, Cz, P, W, Ni, S, Br, I, Fi; 1977 v Fi, I, L, Ni, W, S, Br (sub), Arg, U; (with Manchester C), 1978 v Sw (46)
Charles, G. A. (Nottingham F), 1991 v Nz, Mal (2)
Charlton, J. (Leeds U), 1965 v S, H, Y, WG, Se; 1966 v W, Ni, S, A, Sp, Pol (2), WG (2), Y, Fi, D, U, M, F, Arg, P; 1967 v W, S, Ni, Cz; 1968 v W, Sp; 1969 v W, R, F; 1970 v Ho (2), P, Cz (35)
Charlton, R. (Manchester U), 1958 v S, P, Y; 1959 v S, W, Ni, USSR, I, Br, Pe, M, US; 1960 v W, S, Se, Y, Sp, H; 1961 v Ni, W, S, L, P, Sp, M, I, A; 1962 v W, Ni, S, A, Sw, Pe, L, P, H, Arg, Bul, Br; 1963 v S, F, Br, Cz, EG, Sw; 1964 v S, W, Ni, R of W, U, P, Ei, Br, Arg, US (sub); 1965 v Ni, S, Ho; 1966 v W, Ni, S, A, Sp, WG (2), Y, Fi, N, Pol, U, M, F, Arg, P; 1967 v Ni, W, S, Cz; 1968 v W, Ni, S, USSR (2), Sp (2), Se, Y; 1969 v S, W, Ni, R (2), Bul, M, Br; 1970 v W, Ni, Ho (2), P, Co, Ec, Cz, R, Br, WG (106)
Charnley, R. O. (Blackpool), 1963 v F (1)
Charsley, C. C. (Small Heath), 1893 v Ni (1)
Chedgzoy, S. (Everton), 1920 v W; 1921 v W, S, Ni; 1922 v Ni; 1923 v S; 1924 v W; 1925 v Ni (8)
Chenery, C. J. (C Palace), 1872 v S; 1873 v S; 1874 v S (3)
Cherry, T. J. (Leeds U), 1976 v W, S (sub), Br, Fi; 1977 v Ei, I, L, Ni, S (sub), Br, Arg, U; 1978 v Sw, L, I, Br, W; 1979 v Cz, W, Se; 1980 v Ei, Arg (sub), W, Ni, S, Aus, Sp (sub) (27)
Chilton, A. (Manchester U), 1951 v Ni; 1952 v F (2)
Chippendale, H. (Blackburn R), 1894 v Ni (1)
Chivers, M. (Tottenham H), 1971 v Ma (2), Gr, Ni, S; 1972 v Sw (1+1 sub), Gr, WG (2), Ni (sub), S; 1973 v W (3), S (2), Ni, Cz, Pol, USSR, I; 1974 v A, Pol (24)
Christian, E. (Old Etonians), 1879 v S (1)
Clamp, E. (Wolverhampton W), 1958 v USSR (2), Br, A (4)
Clapton, D. R. (Arsenal), 1959 v W (1)
Clare, T. (Stoke C), 1889 v Ni; 1892 v Ni; 1893 v W; 1894 v S (4)
Clarke, A. J. (Leeds U), 1970 v Cz; 1971 v EG, Ma, Ni, W (sub), S (sub); 1973 v S (2), W, Cz, Pol, USSR, I; 1974 v A, Pol, I; 1975 v P; 1976 v Cz, P (sub) (19)
Clarke, H. A. (Tottenham H), 1954 v S (1)
Clay, T. (Tottenham H), 1920 v W; 1922 v W, S, Ni (4)
Clayton, R. (Blackburn R), 1956 v Ni, Br, Se, Fi, WG, Sp; 1957 v S, W, Ni, Y, D (2), Ei (2); 1958 v S, W, Ni, F, P, Y, USSR; 1959 v S, W, Ni, USSR, I, Br, Pe, M, US; 1960 v W, Ni, S, Se, Y (35)
Clegg, J. C. (Sheffield W), 1872 v S (1)
Clegg, W. E. (Sheffield W), 1873 v S; (with Sheffield Albion), 1879 v W (2)
Clemence, R. N. (Liverpool), 1973 v W (2); 1974 v EG, Bul, Y; 1975 v Cz, P, WG, Cy, Ni, W, S; 1976 v Sw, Cz, P, W (2), Ni, S, Br, Fi; 1977 v Ei, Fi, I, Ho, L, S, Br, Arg, U; 1978 v Sw, L, I, WG, Ni, S; 1979 v D, Ei, Ni (2), S, Bul, A (sub); 1980 v D, Bul, Ei, Arg, W, S, Bel, Sp; 1981 v R, Sp, Br, Sw, H; (with Tottenham H), 1982 v N, Ni, Fi; 1983 v L; 1984 v L (61)
Clement, D. T. (QPR), 1976 v W (sub+1), I; 1977 v I, Ho (5)
Clough, B. H. (Middlesbrough), 1960 v W, Se (2)
Clough, N. H. (Nottingham F), 1989 v Ch; 1991 v Arg (sub), Aus, Mal; 1992 v F, Cz, C (sub); 1993 v Sp, T (sub), Pol (sub), N (sub), US, Br, G (14)
Coates, R. (Burnley), 1970 v Ni; 1971 v Gr (sub); (with Tottenham H), Ma, W (4)
Cobbold, W. N. (Cambridge University), 1883 v S, Ni; 1885 v S, Ni; 1886 v S, W; (with Old Carthusians), 1887 v S, W, Ni (9)

Cock, J. G. (Huddersfield T), 1920 v Ni; (with Chelsea), v S (2)
Cockburn, H. (Manchester U), 1947 v W, Ni, Ei; 1948 v S, I; 1949 v S, Ni, D, Sw, Se; 1951 v Arg, P; 1952 v F (13)
Cohen, G. R. (Fulham), 1964 v U, P, Ei, US, Br; 1965 v W, S, Ni, Bel, H, Ho, Y, WG, Se; 1966 v W, S, Ni, A, Sp, Pol (2), WG (2), N, D, U, M, F, Arg, P; 1967 v W, S, Ni, Cz, Sp; 1968 v W, Ni (37)
Cole, A. (Manchester U), 1995 v U (sub); 1997 v I (sub); 1999 v F (sub), Pol, Se; 2000 v S (sub), Arg (sub); 2001 v F, G, Fi, Sp, Fi, Alb; 2002 v Ho, Gr (sub) (15)
Cole, A. (Arsenal), 2001 v Alb, M, Gr; 2002 v Ho, G, Alb, Gr, Sk, Se, Arg, Ng, D, Br; 2003 v P, Slo, Mac, Aus, Ser, Slo; 2004 v Cro, Mac, T, D, P, J, Ic, F, Sw, Cro, P; 2005 v Uk, A, Pol, W, Az, Sp, Ho, Ni, Az, US, Col; 2006 v D, W, Ni, H, Jam, Para, Tr, Se, Ec, P (51)
Cole, J. J. (West Ham U), 2001 v M (sub); 2002 v Ho (sub), I (sub), Para (sub), Sk (sub), Cam, Se (sub); 2003 v P (sub), S.Af (sub), Ser (sub); (with Chelsea), 2004 v Cro (sub), Lie (sub), D, P (sub), Se (sub), J (sub), Ic (sub); 2005 v A (sub), Az (sub), Ni, Az, US, Col; 2006 v D, W, Ni (sub), A, Pol, Arg (sub), U, H, Jam, Para, Tr, Se, Ec, P (37)
Colclough, H. (C Palace), 1914 v W (1)
Coleman, E. H. (Dulwich Hamlet), 1921 v W (1)
Coleman, J. (Woolwich Arsenal), 1907 v Ni (1)
Collymore, S. V. (Nottingham F), 1995 v J, Br (sub); (with Aston Villa), 1998 v Mol (sub) (3)
Common, A. (Sheffield U), 1904 v W, Ni; (with Middlesbrough), 1906 v W (3)
Compton, L. H. (Arsenal), 1951 v W, Y (2)
Conlin, J. (Bradford C), 1906 v S (1)
Connelly, J. M. (Burnley), 1960 v W, Ni, S, Se; 1962 v W, A, Sw, P; 1963 v W, F; (with Manchester U), 1965 v H, Y, Se; 1966 v W, Ni, S, A, N, D, U (20)
Cook, T. E. R. (Brighton), 1925 v W (1)
Cooper, C. T. (Nottingham F), 1995 v Se, Br (2)
Cooper, N. C. (Cambridge University), 1893 v Ni (1)
Cooper, T. (Derby Co), 1928 v Ni; 1929 v W, Ni, S, F, Bel, Sp; 1931 v F; 1932 v W, Sp; 1933 v S; 1934 v S, H, Cz; 1935 v W (15)
Cooper, T. (Leeds U), 1969 v W, S, F, M; 1970 v Ho, Bel, Co, Ec, R, Cz, Br, WG; 1971 v EG, Ma, Ni, W, S; 1972 v Sw (2); 1975 v P (20)
Coppell, S. J. (Manchester U), 1978 v I, WG, Br, W, Ni, S, H; 1979 v D, Ei, Cz, Ni (2), W (sub), S, Bul, A; 1980 v D, Ni, Ei (sub), Sp, Arg, W, S, Bel, I; 1981 v R (sub), Sw, R, Br, W, S, Sw, H; 1982 v H, S, Fi, F, Cz, K, WG; 1983 v L, Gr (42)
Copping, W. (Leeds U), 1933 v I, Sw; 1934 v S, Ni, W, F; (with Arsenal), 1935 v Ni, I; 1936 v A, Bel; 1937 v N, Se, Fi; 1938 v S, W, Ni, Cz; 1939 v W, R of E; (with Leeds U), R (20)
Corbett, B. O. (Corinthians), 1901 v W (1)
Corbett, R. (Old Malvernians), 1903 v W (1)
Corbett, W. S. (Birmingham), 1908 v A, H, B (3)
Corrigan, J. T. (Manchester C), 1976 v I (sub), Br; 1979 v W; 1980 v Ni, Aus; 1981 v W, S; 1982 v W, Ic (9)
Cottee, A. R. (West Ham U), 1987 v Se (sub), Ni (sub); 1988 v H (sub); (with Everton) 1989 v D (sub), Se (sub), Ch (sub), S (7)
Cotterill, G. H. (Cambridge University), 1891 v Ni; (with Old Brightonians), 1892 v W; 1893 v S, Ni (4)
Cottle, J. R. (Bristol C), 1909 v Ni (1)
Cowan, S. (Manchester C), 1926 v Bel; 1930 v A; 1931 v Bel (3)
Cowans, G. (Aston Villa), 1983 v W, H, Ni, S, Aus (3); (with Bari), 1986 v Eg, USSR; (with Aston Villa), 1991 v Ei (10)
Cowell, A. (Blackburn R), 1910 v Ni (1)
Cox, J. (Liverpool), 1901 v Ni; 1902 v S; 1903 v S (3)
Cox, J. D. (Derby Co), 1892 v Ni (1)
Crabtree, J. W. (Burnley), 1894 v Ni; 1895 v Ni, S; (with Aston Villa), 1896 v W, S, Ni; 1899 v S, W, Ni; 1900 v S, W, Ni; 1901 v W; 1902 v W (14)
Crawford, J. F. (Chelsea), 1931 v S (1)
Crawford, R. (Ipswich T), 1962 v Ni, A (2)
Crawshaw, T. H. (Sheffield W), 1895 v Ni; 1896 v S, W, Ni; 1897 v S, W, Ni; 1901 v Ni; 1904 v W, Ni (10)
Crayston, W. J. (Arsenal), 1936 v S, W, G, A, Bel; 1938 v W, Ni, Cz (8)
Creek, F. N. S. (Corinthians), 1923 v F (1)
Cresswell, W. (South Shields), 1921 v W; (with Sunderland), 1923 v F; 1924 v Bel; 1925 v Ni; 1926 v W; 1927 v Ni; (with Everton), 1930 v Ni (7)
Crompton, R. (Blackburn R), 1902 v S, W, Ni; 1903 v S, W; 1904 v S, W, Ni; 1906 v S, W, Ni; 1907 v S, W, Ni; 1908 v S, W, Ni, A (2), H, B; 1909 v S, W, Ni, H (2), A; 1910 v S, W; 1911 v S, W, Ni; 1912 v S, W, Ni; 1913 v S, W, Ni; 1914 v S, W, Ni (41)
Crooks, S. D. (Derby Co), 1930 v S, G, A; 1931 v S, W, Ni, F, Bel; 1932 v S, W, Ni, Sp; 1933 v Ni, W, A; 1934 v S, Ni, W, F, H, Cz; 1935 v Ni; 1936 v S, W; 1937 v W, H (26)
Crouch, P. J. (Southampton), 2005 v Co; (with Liverpool), 2006 v A, Pol (sub), Arg (sub), U (sub), H (sub), Jam, Para, Tr, Se (sub), P (sub) (11)
Crowe, C. (Wolverhampton W), 1963 v F (1)
Cuggy, F. (Sunderland), 1913 v Ni; 1914 v Ni (2)
Cullis, S. (Wolverhampton W), 1938 v S, W, Ni, F, Cz; 1939 v S, Ni, R of E, N, I, R, Y (12)
Cunliffe, A. (Blackburn R), 1933 v Ni, W (2)
Cunliffe, D. (Portsmouth), 1900 v Ni (1)
Cunliffe, J. N. (Everton), 1936 v Bel (1)
Cunningham, L. (WBA), 1979 v W, Se, A (sub); (with Real Madrid), 1980 v Ei, Sp (sub); 1981 v R (sub) (6)
Curle, K. (Manchester C), 1992 v C (sub), H, D (3)
Currey, E. S. (Oxford University), 1890 v S, W (2)
Currie, A. W. (Sheffield U), 1972 v Ni; 1973 v USSR, I; 1974 v A, Pol, I; 1976 v Sw; (with Leeds U), 1978 v Br, W (sub), Ni, S, H (sub); 1979 v Cz, Ni (2), W, Se (17)
Cursham, A. W. (Notts Co), 1876 v S; 1877 v S; 1878 v S; 1879 v W; 1883 v S, W (6)
Cursham, H. A. (Notts Co), 1880 v W; 1882 v S, W, Ni; 1883 v S, W, Ni; 1884 v Ni (8)

Daft, H. B. (Notts Co), 1889 v Ni; 1890 v S, W; 1891 v Ni; 1892 v Ni (5)
Daley, A. M. (Aston Villa), 1992 v Pol (sub), C, H, Br, Fi (sub), D (sub), Se (7)
Danks, T. (Nottingham F), 1885 v S (1)
Davenport, P. (Nottingham F), 1985 v Ei (sub) (1)
Davenport, J. K. (Bolton W), 1885 v W; 1890 v Ni (2)
Davis, G. (Derby Co), 1904 v W, Ni (2)
Davis, H. (Sheffield W), 1903 v S, W, Ni (3)
Davison, J. E. (Sheffield W), 1922 v W (1)
Dawson, J. (Burnley), 1922 v S, Ni (2)
Day, S. H. (Old Malvernians), 1906 v Ni, W, S (3)
Dean, W. R. (Everton), 1927 v S, W, F, Bel, L; 1928 v S, W, Ni, F, Bel; 1929 v S, W, Ni; 1931 v S; 1932 v Sp; 1933 v Ni (16)
Deane, B. C. (Sheffield U), 1991 v Nz (sub + 1); 1993 v Sp (sub) (3)
Deeley, N. V. (Wolverhampton W), 1959 v Br, Pe (2)
Defoe, J. C. (Tottenham H), 2004 v Se (sub), Ic (sub); 2005 v Uk (sub), A (sub), Pol, W, Az, Sp (sub), Ni (sub), Az (sub), US (sub), Co (sub); 2006 v D, W (sub), Ni (sub), U (sub) (16)
Devey, J. H. G. (Aston Villa), 1892 v Ni; 1894 v Ni (2)
Devonshire, A. (West Ham U), 1980 v Aus (sub), Ni; 1982 v Ho, Ic; 1983 v WG, W, Gr; 1984 v L (8)
Dewhurst, F. (Preston NE), 1886 v W, Ni; 1887 v S, W, Ni; 1888 v S, W, Ni; 1889 v W (9)
Dewhurst, G. P. (Liverpool Ramblers), 1895 v W (1)
Dickinson, J. W. (Portsmouth), 1949 v N, F; 1950 v S, W, Ei, P, Bel, Ch, US, Sp; 1951 v Ni, W, Y; 1952 v W, Ni, S, A (2), I, Sw; 1953 v W, Ni, S, Bel, Arg, Ch, U, US; 1954 v W, Ni, S, R of E, H (2), Y, Bel, Sw, U; 1955 v Sp, P; 1956 v W, Ni, S, D, Sp; 1957 v W, Y, D (48)
Dimmock, J. H. (Tottenham H), 1921 v S; 1926 v W, Bel (3)
Ditchburn, E. G. (Tottenham H), 1949 v Sw, Se; 1953 v US; 1957 v W, Y, D (6)
Dix, R. W. (Derby Co), 1939 v N (1)
Dixon, J. A. (Notts Co), 1885 v W (1)
Dixon, K. M. (Chelsea), 1985 v M (sub), WG, US; 1986 v Ni, Is, M (sub), Pol (sub); 1987 v Se (8)
Dixon, L. M. (Arsenal), 1990 v Cz; 1991 v H, Pol, Ei (2), Cam, T, Arg; 1992 v G, T, Pol, Cz (sub); 1993 v Sp, N, T, Sm, T, Ho, N, US; 1994 v Sm; 1999 v F (22)
Dobson, A. T. C. (Notts Co), 1882 v Ni; 1884 v S, W, Ni (4)
Dobson, C. F. (Notts Co), 1886 v Ni (1)
Dobson, J. M. (Burnley), 1974 v P, EG, Bul, Y; (with Everton), 1975 v Cz (5)
Doggart, A. G. (Corinthians), 1924 v Bel (1)
Dorigo, A. R. (Chelsea), 1990 v Y (sub), Cz (sub), D (sub), I; 1991 v H (sub), USSR; (with Leeds U), 1992 v G, Cz (sub), H, Br; 1993 v Sm, Pol, US, Br; 1994 v Ho (15)
Dorrell, A. R. (Aston Villa), 1925 v W, Bel, F; 1926 v Ni (4)
Douglas, B. (Blackburn R), 1958 v S, W, Ni, F, P, Y, USSR (2), Br, A; 1959 v S, USSR; 1960 v Y, H; 1961 v Ni, W, S, L, P, Sp, M, I, A; 1962 v W, Ni, S, Pe, L, P, H, Arg, Bul, Br; 1963 v S, Br, Sw (36)
Downing, S. (Middlesbrough), 2005 v Ho (sub); 2006 v Para (sub), Tr (sub), Ec (sub) (4)
Downs, R. W. (Everton), 1921 v Ni (1)
Doyle, M. (Manchester C), 1976 v W, S (sub), Br, I; 1977 v Ho (5)
Drake, E. J. (Arsenal), 1935 v Ni, I; 1936 v W; 1937 v H; 1938 v F (5)
Dublin, D. (Coventry C), 1998 v Ch, Mor, Bel (sub); (with Aston Villa), 1999 v CzR (4)

Ducat, A. (Woolwich Arsenal), 1910 v S, W, Ni; (with Aston Villa), 1920 v S, W; 1921 v Ni (6)
Dunn, A. T. B. (Cambridge University), 1883 v Ni; 1884 v Ni; (with Old Etonians), 1892 v S, W (4)
Dunn, D. J. I. (Blackburn R), 2003 v P (sub) (1)
Duxbury, M. (Manchester U), 1984 v L, F, W, S, USSR, Br, U, Ch; 1985 v EG, Fi (10)
Dyer, K. C. (Newcastle U), 2000 v L, Pol (sub), Bel, Arg, Uk (sub); 2001 v F (sub), G (sub), I; 2002 v Para, Se (sub), D (sub), Br (sub); 2003 v Slo (sub), Aus, Lie, T (sub); 2004 v Cro (sub), Mac (sub), T (sub), P (sub), J (sub), Ic (sub), Sw (sub); 2005 v Uk (sub), Pol (sub), Ho (sub), Ni (sub), Az (sub) (28)

Earle, S. G. J. (Clapton), 1924 v F; (with West Ham U), 1928 v Ni (2)
Eastham, G. (Arsenal), 1963 v Br, Cz, EG; 1964 v W, Ni, S, R of W, U, P, Ei, US, Br, Arg; 1965 v H, WG, Se; 1966 v Sp, Pol, D (19)
Eastham, G. R. (Bolton W), 1935 v Ho (1)
Eckersley, W. (Blackburn R), 1950 v Sp; 1951 v S, Y, Arg, P; 1952 v A (2), Sw; 1953 v Ni, Arg, Ch, U, US; 1954 v W, Ni, R of E, H (17)
Edwards, D. (Manchester U), 1955 v S, F, Sp, P; 1956 v S, Br, Se, Fi, WG; 1957 v S, Ni, Ei (2), D (2); 1958 v W, Ni, F (18)
Edwards, J. H. (Shropshire Wanderers), 1874 v S (1)
Edwards, W. (Leeds U), 1926 v S, W; 1927 v W, Ni, S, F, Bel, L; 1928 v S, F, Bel; 1929 v S, W, Ni; 1930 v W, Ni (16)
Ehiogu, U. (Aston Villa), 1996 v Chn (sub); (with Middlesbrough), 2001 v Sp (sub); 2002 v Ho (sub), I (sub) (4)
Ellerington, W. (Southampton), 1949 v N, F (2)
Elliott, G. W. (Middlesbrough), 1913 v Ni; 1914 v Ni; 1920 v W (3)
Elliott, W. H. (Burnley), 1952 v I, A; 1953 v Ni, W, Bel (5)
Evans, R. E. (Sheffield U), 1911 v S, W, Ni; 1912 v W (4)
Ewer, F. H. (Casuals), 1924 v F; 1925 v Bel (2)

Fairclough, P. (Old Foresters), 1878 v S (1)
Fairhurst, D. (Newcastle U), 1934 v F (1)
Fantham, J. (Sheffield W), 1962 v L (1)
Fashanu, J. (Wimbledon), 1989 v Ch, S (2)
Felton, W. (Sheffield W), 1925 v F (1)
Fenton, M. (Middlesbrough), 1938 v S (1)
Fenwick, T. (QPR), 1984 v W (sub), S, USSR, Br, U, Ch; 1985 v Fi, S, M, US; 1986 v R, T, Ni, Eg, M, P, Mor, Pol, Arg; (with Tottenham H), 1988 v Is (sub) (20)
Ferdinand, L. (QPR), 1993 v Sm, Ho, N, US; 1994 v Pol, Sm; 1995 v US (sub); (with Newcastle U), 1996 v P, Bul, H; 1997 v Pol, Ge, I (sub); (with Tottenham H), 1998 v Mol, S.Ar (sub), Mor (sub), Bel (17)
Ferdinand, R. G. (West Ham U), 1998 v Cam (sub), Sw, Bel (sub); 1999 v L, CzR, F (sub), H, Se (sub); 2000 v Arg (sub); 2001 v I; (with Leeds U), Sp, Fi, Alb, M, Gr; 2002 v G, Alb, Gr, Se, Ho, Sk, Cam, Se, Arg, Ng, D, Br; (with Manchester U), 2003 v P, Aus, Lie, T, S.Af; 2004 v Cro; 2005 v W, Az, Sp, Ni, Az; 2006 v D, W, Ni, A (sub), Pol, Arg, U, H, Jam, Para, Tr, Se, Ec, P (52)
Field, E. (Clapham Rovers), 1876 v S; 1881 v S (2)
Finney, T. (Preston NE), 1947 v W, Ni, Ei, Ho, F, P; 1948 v S, W, Ni, Bel, Se, I; 1949 v S, W, Ni, Se, N, F; 1950 v S, W, Ni, Ei, I, P, Bel, Ch, US, Sp; 1951 v W, S, Arg, P; 1952 v W, Ni, S, F, I, Sw, A; 1953 v W, Ni, S, Bel, Arg, Ch, U, US; 1954 v W, S, Bel, Sw, U, H, Y; 1955 v WG; 1956 v S, W, Ni, D, Sp; 1957 v S, W, Y, D (2), Ei (2); 1958 v W, S, F, P, Y, USSR (2); 1959 v Ni, USSR (76)
Fleming, H. J. (Swindon T), 1909 v S, H (2); 1910 v W, Ni; 1911 v W, Ni; 1912 v Ni; 1913 v S, W; 1914 v S (11)
Fletcher, A. (Wolverhampton W), 1889 v W; 1890 v W (2)
Flowers, R. (Wolverhampton W), 1955 v F; 1959 v S, W, I, Br, Pe, US, M (sub); 1960 v W, Ni, S, Se, Y, Sp, H; 1961 v Ni, W, S, L, P, Sp, M, I, A; 1962 v W, Ni, S, A, Sw, Pe, L, P, H, Arg, Bul, Br; 1963 v Ni, W, S, F (2), Sw; 1964 v Ei, US, P; 1965 v W, Ho, WG; 1966 v N (49)
Flowers, T. D. (Southampton), 1993 v Br; (with Blackburn R), 1994 v Gr; 1995 v Ng, U, J, Se, Br; 1996 v Chn; 1997 v I; 1998 v Sw, Mor (11)
Forman, Frank (Nottingham F), 1898 v S, Ni; 1899 v S, W, Ni; 1901 v S; 1902 v S, Ni; 1903 v W (9)
Forman, F. R. (Nottingham F), 1899 v S, W, Ni (3)
Forrest, J. H. (Blackburn R), 1884 v W; 1885 v S, W, Ni; 1886 v S, W; 1887 v S, W, Ni; 1889 v S; 1890 v Ni (11)
Fort, J. (Millwall), 1921 v Bel (1)
Foster, R. E. (Oxford University), 1900 v W; (with Corinthians), 1901 v W, Ni, S; 1902 v W (5)
Foster, S. (Brighton & HA), 1982 v Ni, Ho, K (3)
Foulke, W. J. (Sheffield U), 1897 v W (1)
Foulkes, W. A. (Manchester U), 1955 v Ni (1)
Fowler, R. B. (Liverpool), 1996 v Bul (sub), Cro, Chn (sub), Ho (sub), Sp (sub); 1997 v M; 1998 v Cam; 1999 v CzR (sub), Bul; 2000 v L, Pol, Br (sub), Uk, Ma (sub); 2001 v I (sub), Fi (sub), M, Gr; 2002 v Ho, Alb (sub), Gr, Se (sub); (with Leeds U), I (sub), Para (sub), Cam (sub), D (sub) (26)
Fox, F. S. (Millwall), 1925 v F (1)
Francis, G. C. J. (QPR), 1975 v Cz, P, W, S; 1976 v Sw, Cz, P, W, Ni, S, Br, Fi (12)
Francis, T. (Birmingham C), 1977 v Ho, L, S, Br; 1978 v Sw, L, I (sub), WG (sub), Br, W, S, H; (with Nottingham F), 1979 v Bul (sub), Se, A (sub); 1980 v Ni, Bul, Sp; 1981 v Sp, R, S (sub), Sw; (with Manchester C), 1982 v N, Ni, W, S (sub), Fi (sub), F, Cz, K, WG, Sp; (with Sampdoria), 1983 v D, Gr, H, Ni, S, Aus (3); 1984 v D, Ni, USSR; 1985 v EG (sub), T (sub), Ni (sub), R, Fi, S, I, M; 1986 v S (52)
Franklin, C. F. (Stoke C), 1947 v S, W, Ni, Ei, Ho, F, Sw, P; 1948 v S, W, Ni, Bel, Se, I; 1949 v S, W, Ni, D, Sw, N, F, Se; 1950 v W, S, Ni, Ei, I (27)
Freeman, B. C. (Everton), 1909 v S, W; (with Burnley), 1912 v S, W, Ni (5)
Froggatt, J. (Portsmouth), 1950 v Ni, I; 1951 v S; 1952 v S, A (2), I, Sw; 1953 v Ni, W, S, Bel, US (13)
Froggatt, R. (Sheffield W), 1953 v W, S, Bel, US (4)
Fry, C. B. (Corinthians), 1901 v Ni (1)
Furness, W. I. (Leeds U), 1933 v I (1)

Galley, T. (Wolverhampton W), 1937 v N, Se (2)
Gardner, A. (Tottenham H), 2004 v Se (sub) (1)
Gardner, T. (Aston Villa), 1934 v Cz; 1935 v Ho (2)
Garfield, B. (WBA), 1898 v Ni (1)
Garraty, W. (Aston Villa), 1903 v W (1)
Garrett, T. (Blackpool), 1952 v S, I; 1954 v W (3)
Gascoigne, P. J. (Tottenham H), 1989 v D (sub), S.Ar (sub), Alb (sub), Ch, S (sub); 1990 v Se (sub), Br (sub), Cz, D, U, Tun, Ei, Ho, Eg, Bel, Cam, WG; 1991 v H, Pol, Cam; (with Lazio), 1993 v N, T, Sm, T, Ho, Pol, N; 1994 v Pol, D; 1995 v J (sub), Se (sub), Br (sub); (with Rangers), 1996 v Co, Sw, P, Bul, Cro, Chn, Sw, S, Ho, Sp, G; 1997 v Mol, Pol, Ge, S.Af, Pol, I (sub), F, Br; 1998 v Mol, I, Cam; (with Middlesbrough), S.Ar (sub), Mor, Bel (57)
Gates, E. (Ipswich T), 1981 v N, R (2)
Gay, L. H. (Cambridge University), 1893 v S; (with Old Brightonians), 1894 v S, W (3)
Geary, F. (Everton), 1890 v Ni; 1891 v S (2)
Geaves, R. L. (Clapham Rovers), 1875 v S (1)
Gee, C. W. (Everton), 1932 v W, Sp; 1937 v Ni (3)
Geldard, A. (Everton), 1933 v I, Sw; 1935 v S; 1938 v Ni (4)
George, C. (Derby Co), 1977 v Ei (1)
George, W. (Aston Villa), 1902 v S, W, Ni (3)
Gerrard, S. G. (Liverpool), 2000 v Uk, G (sub); 2001 v Fi, M, Gr; 2002 v G, Alb, Gr, Ho, Para; 2003 v P, Slo, Mac, Lie, T, S.Af, Ser, Slo; 2004 v Cro, Lie, T, Se, J, Ic, F, Sw, Cro, P; 2005 v Uk, A, Pol, Ho, Ni, Az; 2006 v D, W, Ni, A, Arg, U, H, Jam, Para, Tr, Se (sub), Ec, P (47)
Gibbins, W. V. T. (Clapton), 1924 v F; 1925 v F (2)
Gidman, J. (Aston Villa), 1977 v L (1)
Gillard, I. T. (QPR), 1975 v WG, W; 1976 v Cz (3)
Gilliat, W. E. (Old Carthusians), 1893 v Ni (1)
Goddard, P. (West Ham U), 1982 v Ic (sub) (1)
Goodall, F. R. (Huddersfield T), 1926 v S; 1927 v S, F, Bel, L; 1928 v S, W, F, Bel; 1930 v S, G, A; 1931 v S, W, Ni, Bel; 1932 v Ni; 1933 v W, Ni, A, I, Sw; 1934 v W, Ni, F (25)
Goodall, J. (Preston NE), 1888 v S, W; 1889 v S, W; (with Derby Co), 1891 v S, W; 1892 v S; 1893 v W; 1894 v S; 1895 v S, Ni; 1896 v S, W; 1898 v W (14)
Goodhart, H. C. (Old Etonians), 1883 v S, W, Ni (3)
Goodwyn, A. G. (Royal Engineers), 1873 v S (1)
Goodyer, A. C. (Nottingham F), 1879 v S (1)
Gosling, R. C. (Old Etonians), 1892 v W; 1893 v S; 1894 v W; 1895 v W, S (5)
Gosnell, A. A. (Newcastle U), 1906 v Ni (1)
Gough, H. C. (Sheffield U), 1921 v S (1)
Goulden, L. A. (West Ham U), 1937 v Se, N; 1938 v W, Ni, Cz, G, Sw, F; 1939 v S, W, R of E, I, R, Y (14)
Graham, L. (Millwall), 1925 v S, W (2)
Graham, T. (Nottingham F), 1931 v F; 1932 v Ni (2)
Grainger, C. (Sheffield U), 1956 v Br, Se, Fi, WG; 1957 v W, Ni; (with Sunderland), 1957 v S (7)
Gray, A. A. (C Palace), 1992 v Pol (1)
Gray, M. (Sunderland), 1999 v H (sub), Se (sub), Bul (3)
Greaves, J. (Chelsea), 1959 v Pe, M, US; 1960 v W, Se, Y, Sp; 1961 v Ni, W, S, L, P, Sp, I, A; (with Tottenham H), 1962 v S, Sw, Pe, H, Arg, Bul, Br; 1963 v Ni, W, S, F (2), Br, Cz, Sw; 1964 v W, Ni, R of W, P (2), Ei, Br, U, Arg; 1965 v Ni, S, Bel, Ho, H, Y; 1966 v W, A, Y, N, D, Pol, U, M, F; 1967 v S, Sp, A (57)
Green, F. T. (Wanderers), 1876 v S (1)

Green, G. H. (Sheffield U), 1925 v F; 1926 v S, Bel, W; 1927 v W, Ni; 1928 v F, Bel (8)
Green, R. P. (Norwich C), 2005 v Co (sub) (1)
Greenhalgh, E. H. (Notts Co), 1872 v S; 1873 v S (2)
Greenhoff, B. (Manchester U), 1976 v W, Ni; 1977 v Ei, Fi, I, Ho, Ni, W, S, Br, Arg, U; 1978 v Br, W, Ni, S (sub), H (sub); (with Leeds U), 1980 v Aus (sub) (18)
Greenwood, D. H. (Blackburn R), 1882 v S, Ni (2)
Gregory, J. (QPR), 1983 v Aus (3); 1984 v D, H, W (6)
Grimsdell, A. (Tottenham H), 1920 v S, W; 1921 v S, Ni; 1923 v W, Ni (6)
Grosvenor, A. T. (Birmingham), 1934 v Ni, W, F (3)
Gunn, W. (Notts Co), 1884 v S, W (2)
Guppy, S. (Leicester C), 2000 v Bel (1)
Gurney, R. (Sunderland), 1935 v S (1)

Hacking, J. (Oldham Ath), 1929 v S, W, Ni (3)
Hadley, H. (WBA), 1903 v Ni (1)
Hagan, J. (Sheffield U), 1949 v D (1)
Haines, J. T. W. (WBA), 1949 v Sw (1)
Hall, A. E. (Aston Villa), 1910 v Ni (1)
Hall, G. W. (Tottenham H), 1934 v F; 1938 v S, W, Ni, Cz; 1939 v S, Ni, R of E, I, Y (10)
Hall, J. (Birmingham C), 1956 v S, W, Ni, Br, Se, Fi, WG, D, Sp; 1957 v S, W, Ni, Y, D (2), Ei (2) (17)
Halse, H. J. (Manchester U), 1909 v A (1)
Hammond, H. E. D. (Oxford University), 1889 v S (1)
Hampson, J. (Blackpool), 1931 v Ni, W; 1933 v A (3)
Hampton, H. (Aston Villa), 1913 v S, W; 1914 v S, W (4)
Hancocks, J. (Wolverhampton W), 1949 v Sw; 1950 v W; 1951 v Y (3)
Hapgood, E. (Arsenal), 1933 v I, Sw; 1934 v S, Ni, W, H, Cz; 1935 v S, Ni, W, I, Ho; 1936 v S, Ni, W, G, A, Bel; 1937 v Fi; 1938 v S, G, Sw, F; 1939 v S, W, Ni, R of E, N, I, Y (30)
Hardinge, H. T. W. (Sheffield U), 1910 v S (1)
Hardman, H. P. (Everton), 1905 v W; 1907 v S, Ni; 1908 v W (4)
Hardwick, G. F. M. (Middlesbrough), 1947 v S, W, Ni, Ei, Ho, F, Sw, P; 1948 v S, W, Ni, Bel, Se (13)
Hardy, H. (Stockport Co), 1925 v Bel (1)
Hardy, S. (Liverpool), 1907 v S, W, Ni; 1908 v S; 1909 v S, W, Ni, H (2), A; 1910 v S, W, Ni; 1912 v Ni; (with Aston Villa), 1913 v S; 1914 v Ni, W, S; 1920 v S, W, Ni (21)
Harford, M. G. (Luton T), 1988 v Is (sub); 1989 v D (2)
Hargreaves, F. W. (Blackburn R), 1880 v W; 1881 v W; 1882 v Ni (3)
Hargreaves, J. (Blackburn R), 1881 v S, W (2)
Hargreaves, O. (Bayern Munich) 2002 v Ho, G (sub), I (sub), Para (sub), Sk, Cam, Se, Arg; 2003 v P (sub), Slo (sub), Aus (sub), Ser (sub), Slo (sub); 2004 v Mac, Lie (sub), P (sub), Se, J (sub), Ic (sub), F (sub), Sw (sub), P (sub); 2005 v Pol (sub), W (sub), Ho (sub), Ni (sub); 2006 v D (sub), W (sub), Ni (sub), H (sub), Para (sub), Se, Ec, P (34)
Harper, E. C. (Blackburn R), 1926 v S (1)
Harris, G. (Burnley), 1966 v Pol (1)
Harris, P. P. (Portsmouth), 1950 v Ei; 1954 v H (2)
Harris, S. S. (Cambridge University), 1904 v S; (with Old Westminsters), 1905 v Ni, W; 1906 v S, W, Ni (6)
Harrison, A. H. (Old Westminsters), 1893 v S, Ni (2)
Harrison, G. (Everton), 1921 v Bel; 1922 v Ni (2)
Harrow, J. H. (Chelsea), 1923 v Ni, Se (2)
Hart, E. (Leeds U), 1929 v W; 1930 v W, Ni; 1933 v S, A; 1934 v S, H, Cz (8)
Hartley, F. (Oxford C), 1923 v F (1)
Harvey, A. (Wednesbury Strollers), 1881 v W (1)
Harvey, J. C. (Everton), 1971 v Ma (1)
Hassall, H. W. (Huddersfield T), 1951 v S, Arg, P; 1952 v F; (with Bolton W), 1954 v Ni (5)
Hateley, M. (Portsmouth), 1984 v USSR (sub), Br, U, Ch; (with AC Milan), 1985 v EG (sub), Fi, Ni, Ei, Fi, S, I, M; 1986 v R, T, Eg, S, M, Ca, P, Mor, Para (sub); 1987 v T (sub), Br (sub), S; (with Monaco), 1988 v WG (sub), Ho (sub), H (sub), Co (sub), Ei (sub), Ho (sub), USSR (sub); (with Rangers), 1992 v Cz (32)
Hawkes, R. M. (Luton T), 1907 v Ni; 1908 v A (2), H, B (5)
Haworth, G. (Accrington), 1887 v Ni, W, S; 1888 v S; 1890 v S (5)
Hawtrey, J. P. (Old Etonians), 1881 v S, W (2)
Haygarth, E. B. (Swifts), 1875 v S (1)
Haynes, J. N. (Fulham), 1955 v Ni; 1956 v S, Ni, Br, Se, Fi, WG, Sp; 1957 v W, Y, D, Ei (2); 1958 v W, Ni, S, F, P, Y, USSR (3), Br, A; 1959 v S, Ni, USSR, I, Br, Pe, M, US; 1960 v Ni, Y, Sp, H; 1961 v Ni, W, S, L, P, Sp, M, I, A; 1962 v W, Ni, S, A, Sw, Pe, P, H, Arg, Bul, Br (56)
Healless, H. (Blackburn R), 1925 v Ni; 1928 v S (2)
Hector, K. J. (Derby Co), 1974 v Pol (sub), I (sub) (2)
Hedley, G. A. (Sheffield U), 1901 v Ni (1)
Hegan, K. E. (Corinthians), 1923 v Bel, F; 1924 v Ni, Bel (4)

Hellawell, M. S. (Birmingham C), 1963 v Ni, F (2)
Hendrie, L. A. (Aston Villa), 1999 v CzR (sub) (1)
Henfrey, A. G. (Cambridge University), 1891 v Ni; (with Corinthians), 1892 v W; 1895 v W; 1896 v S, W (5)
Henry, R. P. (Tottenham H), 1963 v F (1)
Heron, F. (Wanderers), 1876 v S (1)
Heron, G. H. H. (Uxbridge), 1873 v S; 1874 v S; (with Wanderers), 1875 v S; 1876 v S; 1878 v S (5)
Heskey, E. W. (Leicester C), 1999 v H (sub), Bul (sub); 2000 v Bel (sub), S (sub), Arg; (with Liverpool), Uk (sub), Ma (sub), P (sub), R (sub); 2001 v Fi, I, Sp (sub), Fi (sub), Alb (sub), M, Gr; 2002 v G, Alb, Gr, Se, Ho, I, Sk, Cam, Se, Arg, Ng, D, Br; 2003 v P, Slo, Lie, S.Af, Ser; 2004 v Cro, Mac (sub), T, D, P (sub), Se (sub); (with Birmingham C), J (sub), Ic (sub), F (sub) (43)
Hibbert, W. (Bury), 1910 v S (1)
Hibbs, H. E. (Birmingham), 1930 v S, W, A, G; 1931 v S, W, Ni; 1932 v W, Ni, Sp; 1933 v S, W, Ni, A, I, Sw; 1934 v Ni, W, F; 1935 v S, W, Ni, Ho; 1936 v G, W (25)
Hill, F. (Bolton W), 1963 v Ni, W (2)
Hill, G. A. (Manchester U), 1976 v I; 1977 v Ei (sub), Fi (sub), L; 1978 v Sw (sub), L (6)
Hill, J. H. (Burnley), 1925 v W; 1926 v S; 1927 v S, Ni, Bel, F; 1928 v Ni, W; (with Newcastle U), 1929 v F, Bel, Sp (11)
Hill, R. (Luton T), 1983 v D (sub), WG; 1986 v Eg (sub) (3)
Hill, R. H. (Millwall), 1926 v Bel (1)
Hillman, J. (Burnley), 1899 v Ni (1)
Hills, A. F. (Old Harrovians), 1879 v S (1)
Hilsdon, G. R. (Chelsea), 1907 v Ni; 1908 v S, W, Ni, A, H, B; 1909 v Ni (8)
Hinchcliffe, A. G. (Everton), 1997 v Mol, Pol, Ge; 1998 v Cam; (with Sheffield W), Sw, S.Ar; 1999 v Bul (7)
Hine, E. W. (Leicester C), 1929 v W, Ni; 1930 v W, Ni; 1932 v W, Ni (6)
Hinton, A. T. (Wolverhampton W), 1963 v F; (with Nottingham F), 1965 v W, Bel (3)
Hirst, D. E. (Sheffield W), 1991 v Aus, Nz (sub); 1992 v F (3)
Hitchens, G. A. (Aston Villa), 1961 v M, I, A; (with Inter-Milan), 1962 v Sw, Pe, H, Br (7)
Hobbis, H. H. F. (Charlton Ath), 1936 v A, Bel (2)
Hoddle, G. (Tottenham H), 1980 v Bul, W, Aus, Sp; 1981 v Sp, W, S; 1982 v N, Ni, W, Ic, Cz (sub), K; 1983 v L (sub), Ni, S; 1984 v H, L, F; 1985 v Ei (sub), S, I (sub), M, WG, US; 1986 v R, T, Ni, Is, USSR, S, M, Ca, P, Mor, Pol, Para, Arg; 1987 v Se, Ni, Y, Sp, T, S; (with Monaco), 1988 v WG, T (sub), Y (sub), Ho (sub), H (sub), Co (sub), Ei (sub), Ho, USSR (53)
Hodge, S. B. (Aston Villa), 1986 v USSR (sub), S, Ca, P (sub), Mor (sub), Pol, Para, Arg; 1987 v Se, Ni, Y; (with Tottenham H), Sp. Ni, T, S; (with Nottingham F), 1989 v D; 1990 v I (sub), Y (sub), Cz, D, U, Tun; 1991 v Cam (sub), T (sub) (24)
Hodgetts, D. (Aston Villa), 1888 v S, W, Ni; 1892 v S, Ni; 1894 v Ni (6)
Hodgkinson, A. (Sheffield U), 1957 v S, Ei (2), D; 1961 v W (5)
Hodgson, G. (Liverpool), 1931 v S, Ni, W (3)
Hodkinson, J. (Blackburn R), 1913 v W, S; 1920 v Ni (3)
Hogg, W. (Sunderland), 1902 v S, W, Ni (3)
Holdcroft, G. H. (Preston NE), 1937 v W, Ni (2)
Holden, A. D. (Bolton W), 1959 v S, I, Br, Pe, M (5)
Holden, G. H. (Wednesbury OA), 1881 v S; 1884 v S, W, Ni (4)
Holden-White, C. (Corinthians), 1888 v W, S (2)
Holford, T. (Stoke), 1903 v Ni (1)
Holley, G. H. (Sunderland), 1909 v S, W, H (2), A; 1910 v W; 1912 v S, W, Ni; 1913 v S (10)
Holliday, E. (Middlesbrough), 1960 v W, Ni, Se (3)
Hollins, J. W. (Chelsea), 1967 v Sp (1)
Holmes, R. (Preston NE), 1888 v Ni; 1891 v S; 1892 v S; 1893 v S, W; 1894 v Ni; 1895 v Ni (7)
Holt, J. (Everton), 1890 v W; 1891 v S, W; 1892 v S, Ni; 1893 v S; 1894 v S, Ni; 1895 v S; (with Reading), 1900 v Ni (10)
Hopkinson, E. (Bolton W), 1958 v W, Ni, S, F, P, Y; 1959 v S, I, Br, Pe, M, US; 1960 v W, Se (14)
Hossack, A. H. (Corinthians), 1892 v W; 1894 v W (2)
Houghton, W. E. (Aston Villa), 1931 v Ni, W, F, Bel; 1932 v S, Ni; 1933 v A (7)
Houlker, A. E. (Blackburn R), 1902 v S; (with Portsmouth), 1903 v S, W; (with Southampton), 1906 v W, Ni (5)
Howarth, R. H. (Preston NE), 1887 v Ni; 1888 v S, W; 1891 v S; (with Everton), 1894 v Ni (5)
Howe, D. (WBA), 1958 v S, W, Ni, F, P, Y, USSR (3), Br, A; 1959 v S, W, Ni, USSR, I, Br, Pe, M, US; 1960 v W, Ni, Se (23)
Howe, J. R. (Derby Co), 1948 v I; 1949 v S, Ni (3)
Howell, L. S. (Wanderers), 1873 v S (1)

Howell, R. (Sheffield U), 1895 v Ni; (with Liverpool) 1899 v S (2)
Howey, S. N. (Newcastle U), 1995 v Ng; 1996 v Co, P, Bul (4)
Hudson, A. A. (Stoke C), 1975 v WG, Cy (2)
Hudson, J. (Sheffield), 1883 v Ni (1)
Hudspeth, F. C. (Newcastle U), 1926 v Ni (1)
Hufton, A. E. (West Ham U), 1924 v Bel; 1928 v S, Ni; 1929 v F, Bel, Sp (6)
Hughes, E. W. (Liverpool), 1970 v W, Ni, S, Ho, P, Bel; 1971 v EG, Ma (2), Gr, W; 1972 v Sw, Gr, WG (2), W, Ni, S; 1973 v W (3), S (2), Pol, USSR, I; 1974 v A, Pol, I, W, Ni, S, Arg, EG, Bul, Y; 1975 v Cz, P, Cy (sub), Ni; 1977 v I, L, W, S, Br, Arg, U; 1978 v Sw, L, I, WG, Ni, S, H; 1979 v D, Ei, Ni, W, Se; (with Wolverhampton W), 1980 v Sp (sub), Ni, S (sub) (62)
Hughes, L. (Liverpool), 1950 v Ch, US, Sp (3)
Hulme, J. H. A. (Arsenal), 1927 v S, Bel, F; 1928 v S, Ni, W; 1929 v Ni, W; 1933 v S (9)
Humphreys, P. (Notts Co), 1903 v S (1)
Hunt, G. S. (Tottenham H), 1933 v I, Sw, S (3)
Hunt, Rev K. R. G. (Leyton), 1911 v S, W (2)
Hunt, R. (Liverpool), 1962 v A; 1963 v EG; 1964 v S, US, P; 1965 v W; 1966 v S, Sp, Pol (2), WG (2), Fi, N, U, M, F, Arg, P; 1967 v Ni, W, Cz, Sp, A; 1968 v W, Ni, USSR (2), Sp (2), Se, Y; 1969 v R (2) (34)
Hunt, S. (WBA), 1984 v S (sub), USSR (sub) (2)
Hunter, J. (Sheffield Heeley), 1878 v S; 1880 v S, W; 1881 v S, W; 1882 v S, W (7)
Hunter, N. (Leeds U), 1966 v WG, Y, Fi, Sp (sub); 1967 v A; 1968 v Sp, Se, Y, WG, USSR; 1969 v R, W; 1970 v Ho, WG (sub); 1971 v Ma; 1972 v WG (2), W, Ni, S; 1973 v W (2) USSR (sub); 1974 v A, Pol, Ni (sub), S; 1975 v Cz (28)
Hurst, G. C. (West Ham U), 1966 v S, WG (2), Y, Fi, D, Arg, P; 1967 v Ni, W, S, Cz, Sp, A; 1968 v W, Ni, S, Se (sub), WG, USSR (2); 1969 v Ni, S, R (2), Bul, F, M, U, Br; 1970 v W, Ni, S, Ho (1+1 sub), Bel, Co, Ec, R, Br, WG; 1971 v EG, Gr, W, S; 1972 v Sw (2), Gr, WG (49)

Ince, P. E. C. (Manchester U), 1993 v Sp, N, T (2), Ho, Pol, US, Br, G; 1994 v Pol, Ho, Sm, D, N; 1995 v R, Ei; (with Internazionale), 1996 v Bul, Cro, H, Sw, S, Ho, G; 1997 v Mol, Pol, Ge, I, M, Ge, Pol, I, F (sub), Br; (with Liverpool), 1998 v I, Cam, Ch (sub), Sw, P, Mor, Tun, R, Co, Arg; 1999 v Se, F; (with Middlesbrough), 2000 v Bel, S (2), Br, Ma (sub), P, G, R (53)
Iremonger, J. (Nottingham F), 1901 v S; 1902 v Ni (2)

Jack, D. N. B. (Bolton W), 1924 v S, W; 1928 v F, Bel; (with Arsenal), 1930 v S, G, A; 1933 v W, A (9)
Jackson, E. (Oxford University), 1891 v W (1)
James. D. B. (Liverpool), 1997 v M; (with Aston Villa), 2001 v I, Sp, M (sub); (with West Ham U), 2002 v Ho (sub + sub), I (sub), Sk (sub), Cam (sub); 2003 v P, Aus, Lie, T, S.Af, Ser, Slo; 2004 v Cro, Mac, Lie, T, D; (with Manchester C), P, Se, J, F, Sw, Cro, P; 2005 v Uk, A, US, Co; 2006 v D (sub), Jam (sub) (34)
Jarrett, B. G. (Cambridge University), 1876 v S; 1877 v S; 1878 v S (3)
Jefferis, F. (Everton), 1912 v S, W (2)
Jeffers, F. (Arsenal), 2003 v Aus (sub) (1)
Jenas, J. A. (Newcastle U), 2003 v Aus (sub), S.Af (sub), Ser (sub); 2004 v D (sub), P (sub), Se (sub); 2005 v Uk (sub), Az, Sp (sub), Ho (sub), US, Co; 2006 v D (sub); (with Tottenham H), Pol (sub), U (sub) (15)
Jezzard, B. A. G. (Fulham), 1954 v H; 1956 v Ni (2)
Johnson, A. (C Palace), 2005 v Ho (sub), US (2)
Johnson, D. E. (Ipswich T), 1975 v W, S; 1976 v Sw; (with Liverpool), 1980 v Ei, Arg, Ni, S, Bel (8)
Johnson, E. (Saltley College), 1880 v W; (with Stoke C), 1884 v Ni (2)
Johnson, G. M. C. (Chelsea), 2004 v D (sub); 2005 v Uk (sub), US, Co; 2006 v D (sub) (5)
Johnson, J. A. (Stoke C), 1937 v N, Se, Fi, S, Ni (5)
Johnson, S. A. M. (Derby Co), 2001 v I (sub) (1)
Johnson, T. C. F. (Manchester C), 1926 v Bel; 1930 v W; (with Everton), 1932 v S, Sp; 1933 v Ni (5)
Johnson, W. H. (Sheffield U), 1900 v S, W, Ni; 1903 v S, W, Ni (6)
Johnston, H. (Blackpool), 1947 v S, Ho; 1951 v S; 1953 v Arg, Ch, U, US; 1954 v W, Ni, H (10)
Jones, A. (Walsall Swifts), 1882 v S, W; (with Great Lever), 1883 v S (3)
Jones, H. (Blackburn R), 1927 v S, Bel, L, F; 1928 v S, Ni (6)
Jones, H. (Nottingham F), 1923 v F (1)
Jones, M. D. (Sheffield U), 1965 v WG, Se; (with Leeds U), 1970 v Ho (3)
Jones, R. (Liverpool), 1992 v F; 1994 v Pol, Gr, N; 1995 v US, R, Ng, U (8)
Jones, W. (Bristol C), 1901 v Ni (1)
Jones, W. H. (Liverpool), 1950 v P, Bel (2)
Joy, B. (Casuals), 1936 v Bel (1)

Kail, E. I. L. (Dulwich Hamlet), 1929 v F, Bel, Sp (3)
Kay, A. H. (Everton), 1963 v Sw (1)
Kean, F. W. (Sheffield W), 1923 v S, Bel; 1924 v W; 1925 v Ni; 1926 v Ni, Bel; 1927 v L; (with Bolton W), 1929 v F, Sp (9)
Keegan, J. K. (Liverpool), 1973 v W (2); 1974 v W, Ni, Arg, EG, Bul, Y; 1975 v Cz, WG, Cy (2), Ni, S; 1976 v Sw, Cz, P, W (2), Ni, S, Br, Fi; 1977 v Ei, Fi, I, Ho, L; (with SV Hamburg), W, Br, Arg, U; 1978 v Sw, I, WG, Br, H; 1979 v D, Ei, Cz, Ni, W, S, Bul, Se, A; 1980 v D, Ni, Ei, Sp (2), Arg, Bel, I; (with Southampton), 1981 v Sp, Sw, H; 1982 v N, H, Ni, S, Fi, Sp (sub) (63)
Keen, E. R. L. (Derby Co), 1933 v A; 1937 v W, Ni, H (4)
Kelly, R. (Burnley), 1920 v S; 1921 v S, W, Ni; 1922 v S, W; 1923 v S; 1924 v Ni; 1925 v W, Ni, S; (with Sunderland), 1926 v W; (with Huddersfield T), 1927 v L; 1928 v S (14)
Kennedy, A. (Liverpool), 1984 v Ni, W (2)
Kennedy, R. (Liverpool), 1976 v W (2), Ni, S; 1977 v L, W, S, Br (sub), Arg (sub); 1978 v Sw, L; 1980 v Bul, Sp, Arg, W, Bel (sub), I (17)
Kenyon-Slaney, W. S. (Wanderers), 1873 v S (1)
Keown, M. R. (Everton), 1992 v F, Cz, C, H, Br, Fi, D, F, Se; (with Arsenal), 1993 v Ho, G (sub); 1997 v M, S.Af, I, Br; 1998 v Sw, Mor, Bel; 1999 v CzR, F, Pol, H, Se; 2000 v L, Pol, Bel, S, Arg, Br, Ma, P (sub), G, R; 2001 v F, G, Fi, M, Gr; 2002 v Ho, Gr, Para, Sk (sub), Cam (sub) (43)
Kevan, D. T. (WBA), 1957 v S; 1958 v W, Ni, S, P. Y, USSR (3), Br, A; 1959 v M, US; 1961 v M (14)
Kidd, B. (Manchester U), 1970 v Ni, Ec (sub) (2)
King, L. B. (Tottenham H), 2002 v I (sub); 2003 v Aus (sub); 2004 v P, J (sub), Ic (sub), F, Cro (sub); 2005 v Uk, A, Pol, W (sub), Az (sub); 2006 v A (sub), Pol, Arg, U (sub) (16)
King, R. S. (Oxford University), 1882 v Ni (1)
Kingsford, R. K. (Wanderers), 1874 v S (1)
Kingsley, M. (Newcastle U), 1901 v W (1)
Kinsey, G. (Wolverhampton W), 1892 v W; 1893 v S; (with Derby Co), 1896 v W, Ni (4)
Kirchen, A. J. (Arsenal), 1937 v N, Se, Fi (3)
Kirton, W. J. (Aston Villa), 1922 v Ni (1)
Knight, A. E. (Portsmouth), 1920 v Ni (1)
Knight, Z. (Fulham), 2005 v US (sub), Co (2)
Knowles, C. (Tottenham H), 1968 v USSR, Sp, Se, WG (4)
Konchesky, P. M. (Charlton Ath), 2003 v Aus (sub); (with West Ham U), 2006 v Arg (sub) (2)

Labone, B. L. (Everton), 1963 v Ni, W, F; 1967 v Sp, A; 1968 v S, Sp, Se, Y, USSR, WG; 1969 v Ni, S, R, Bul, M, U, Br; 1970 v S, W, Bel, Co, Ec, R, Br, WG (26)
Lampard, F. J. (West Ham U), 2000 v Bel; 2001 v Sp (sub); (with Chelsea), 2002 v Ho (sub), Se (sub), Ho (sub), I, Para (sub); 2003 v Aus, S.Af (sub), Ser, Slo; 2004 v Cro (sub), Mac, Lie, T (sub), D, P, J, Ic, F, Sw, Cro, P; 2005 v Uk, A, Pol, W, Az, Sp, Ho, Ni, Az; 2006 v D, W, Ni, A, Pol, Arg, H, Jam, Para, Tr, Se, Ec, P (45)
Lampard, F. R. G. (West Ham U), 1973 v Y; 1980 v Aus (2)
Langley, E. J. (Fulham), 1958 v S, P, Y (3)
Langton, R. (Blackburn R), 1947 v W, Ni, Ei, Ho, F, Sw; 1948 v Se; (with Preston NE), 1949 v D, Se; (with Bolton W), 1950 v S; 1951 v Ni (11)
Latchford, R. D. (Everton), 1978 v I, Br, W; 1979 v D, Ei, Cz (sub), Ni (2), W, S, Bul, A (12)
Latheron, E. G. (Blackburn R), 1913 v W; 1914 v Ni (2)
Lawler, C. (Liverpool), 1971 v Ma, W, S; 1972 v Sw (4)
Lawton, T. (Everton), 1939 v S, W, Ni, R of E, N, I, R, Y; (with Chelsea), 1947 v S, W, Ni, Ei, Ho, F, Sw, P; 1948 v W, Ni, Bel; (with Notts Co), 1948 v S, Se, I; 1949 v D (23)
Leach, T. (Sheffield W), 1931 v W, Ni (2)
Leake, A. (Aston Villa), 1904 v S, Ni; 1905 v S, W, Ni (5)
Lee, E. A. (Southampton), 1904 v W (1)
Lee, F. H. (Manchester C), 1969 v Ni, W, S, Bul, F, M, U; 1970 v W, Ho (2), P, Bel, Co, Ec, R, Br, WG; 1971 v EG, Gr, Ma, Ni, W, S; 1972 v Sw (2), Gr, WG (27)
Lee, J. (Derby Co), 1951 v Ni (1)
Lee, R. M. (Newcastle U), 1995 v R, Ng; 1996 v Co (sub), N, Sw, Bul (sub), H; 1997 v M, Ge, S.Af, Pol, F (sub), Br (sub); 1998 v Cam (sub), Ch, Sw, Bel, Co (sub); 1999 v Se (sub), Bul, L (sub) (21)
Lee, S. (Liverpool), 1983 v Gr, L, W, Gr, H, S, Aus; 1984 v D, H, L, F, Ni, W, Ch (sub) (14)
Leighton, J. E. (Nottingham F), 1886 v Ni (1)
Lennon, A. J. (Tottenham H), 2006 v Jam (sub), Tr (sub), Ec (sub), P (sub) (4)

Le Saux, G. P. (Blackburn R), 1994 v D, Gr, N; 1995 v US, R, Ng, Ei, U, Se, Br; 1996 v Co, P (sub); 1997 v I, M, Ge, S.Af, Pol, I, F, Br; (with Chelsea), 1998 v I, Ch (sub), P, Mor, Bel, Tun, R, Co, Arg; 1999 v Se, Bul (sub), CzR, F, Pol, Se; 2001 v G (36)
Le Tissier, M. P. (Southampton), 1994 v D (sub), Gr (sub), N (sub); 1995 v R, Ng (sub), Ei; 1997 v Mol (sub), I (8)
Lilley, H. E. (Sheffield U), 1892 v W (1)
Linacre, H. J. (Nottingham F), 1905 v W, S (2)
Lindley, T. (Cambridge University), 1886 v S, W, Ni; 1887 v S, W, Ni; 1888 v S, W, Ni; (with Nottingham F), 1889 v S; 1890 v S, W; 1891 v Ni (13)
Lindsay, A. (Liverpool), 1974 v Arg, EG, Bul, Y (4)
Lindsay, W. (Wanderers), 1877 v S (1)
Lineker, G. (Leicester C), 1984 v S (sub); 1985 v Ei, R (sub), S (sub), I (sub), WG, US; (with Everton), 1986 v R, T, Ni, Eg, USSR, Ca, P, Mor, Pol, Para, Arg; (with Barcelona), 1987 v Ni (2), Y, Sp, T, Br; 1988 v WG, T, Y, Ho, H, S, Co, Sw, Ei, Ho, USSR; 1989 v Se, S.Ar, Gr, Alb (2), Pol, D; (with Tottenham H), 1990 v Se, Pol, I, Y, Br, Cz, D, U, Tun, Ei, Ho, Eg, Bel, Cam, WG, I; 1991 v H, Pol, Ei (2), Cam, T, Arg, Aus, Nz, Mal; 1992 v G, T, Pol, F (sub), Cz (sub), C, H, Br, Fi, D, F, Se (80)
Lintott, E. H. (QPR), 1908 v S, W, Ni; (with Bradford C), 1909 v S, Ni, H (2) (7)
Lipsham, H. B. (Sheffield U), 1902 v W (1)
Little, B. (Aston Villa), 1975 v W (sub) (1)
Lloyd, L. V. (Liverpool), 1971 v W; 1972 v Sw, Ni; (with Nottingham F), 1980 v W (4)
Lockett, A. (Stoke C), 1903 v Ni (1)
Lodge, L. V. (Cambridge University), 1894 v W; 1895 v S, W; (with Corinthians), 1896 v S, Ni (5)
Lofthouse, J. M. (Blackburn R), 1885 v S, W, Ni; 1887 v S, W; (with Accrington), 1889 v Ni; (with Blackburn R), 1890 v Ni (7)
Lofthouse, N. (Bolton W), 1951 v Y; 1952 v W, Ni, S, A (2), I, Sw; 1953 v W, Ni, S, Bel, Arg, Ch, U, US; 1954 v W, Ni, R of E, Bel, U; 1955 v Ni, S, F, Sp, P; 1956 v W, S, Sp, D, Fi (sub); 1959 v W, USSR (33)
Longworth, E. (Liverpool), 1920 v S; 1921 v Bel; 1923 v S, W, Bel (5)
Lowder, A. (Wolverhampton W), 1889 v W (1)
Lowe, E. (Aston Villa), 1947 v F, Sw, P (3)
Lucas, T. (Liverpool), 1922 v Ni; 1924 v F; 1926 v Bel (3)
Luntley, E. (Nottingham F), 1880 v S, W (2)
Lyttelton, Hon. A. (Cambridge University), 1877 v S (1)
Lyttelton, Hon. E. (Cambridge University), 1878 v S (1)

Mabbutt, G. (Tottenham H), 1983 v WG, Gr, L, W, Gr, H, Ni, S (sub); 1984 v H; 1987 v Y, Ni, T; 1988 v WG; 1992 v T, Pol, Cz (16)
Macaulay, R. H. (Cambridge University), 1881 v S (1)
McCall, J. (Preston NE), 1913 v S, W; 1914 v S; 1920 v S; 1921 v Ni (5)
McCann, G. P. (Sunderland), 2001 v Sp (sub) (1)
McDermott, T. (Liverpool), 1978 v Sw, L; 1979 v Ni, W, Se; 1980 v D, Ni (sub), Ei, Ni, S, Bel (sub), Sp; 1981 v N, R, Sw, R (sub), Br, Sw (sub), H; 1982 v N, H, W (sub), Ho, S (sub), Ic (25)
McDonald, C. A. (Burnley), 1958 v USSR (3), Br, A; 1959 v W, Ni, USSR (8)
Macdonald, M. (Newcastle U), 1972 v W, Ni, S (sub); 1973 v USSR (sub); 1974 v P, S (sub), Y (sub); 1975 v WG, Cy (2), Ni; 1976 v Sw (sub), Cz, P (14)
McFarland, R. L. (Derby Co), 1971 v Gr, Ma (2), Ni, S; 1972 v Sw, Gr, WG, W, S; 1973 v W (3), Ni, S, Cz, Pol, USSR, I; 1974 v A, Pol, I, W, Ni; 1976 v Cz, S; 1977 v Ei, I (28)
McGarry, W. H. (Huddersfield T), 1954 v Sw, U; 1956 v W, D (4)
McGuinness, W. (Manchester U), 1959 v Ni, M (2)
McInroy, A. (Sunderland), 1927 v Ni (1)
McMahon, S. (Liverpool), 1988 v Is, H, Co, USSR; 1989 v D (sub); 1990 v Se, Pol, I, Y (sub), Br, Cz (sub), D, Ei (sub), Eg, Bel, I; 1991 v Ei (17)
McManaman, S. (Liverpool), 1995 v Ng (sub), U (sub), J (sub); 1996 v Co, N, Sw, P (sub), Bul, Cro, Chn, Sw, S, Ho, Sp, G; 1997 v Pol, I, M; 1998 v Cam, Sw, Mor, Co (sub); 1999 v Pol, H; (with Real Madrid), 2000 v L, Pol, Uk, Ma (sub), P; 2001 v F (sub), Fi (sub+1), Alb, Gr (sub); 2002 v G (sub), Alb (sub), Gr (sub) (37)
McNab, R. (Arsenal), 1969 v Ni, Bul, R (1+1 sub) (4)
McNeal, R. (WBA), 1914 v S, W (2)
McNeil, M. (Middlesbrough), 1961 v W, Ni, S, L, P, Sp, M, I; 1962 v L (9)
Macrae, S. (Notts Co), 1883 v S, W, Ni; 1884 v S, Ni (5)
Maddison, F. B. (Oxford University), 1872 v S (1)
Madeley, P. E. (Leeds U), 1971 v Ni; 1972 v Sw (2), Gr, WG (2), W, S; 1973 v S, Cz, Pol, USSR, I; 1974 v A, Pol, I; 1975 v Cz, P, Cy; 1976 v Cz, P, Fi; 1977 v Ei, Ho (24)
Magee, T. P. (WBA), 1923 v W, Se; 1925 v S, Bel, F (5)
Makepeace, H. (Everton), 1906 v S; 1910 v S; 1912 v S, W (4)
Male, C. G. (Arsenal), 1935 v S, Ni, I, Ho; 1936 v S, W, Ni, G, A, Bel; 1937 v S, Ni, H, N, Se, Fi; 1939 v I, R, Y (19)
Mannion, W. J. (Middlesbrough), 1947 v S, W, Ni, Ei, Ho, F, Sw, P; 1948 v W, Ni, Bel, Se, I; 1949 v N, F; 1950 v S, Ei, P, Bel, Ch, US; 1951 v Ni, W, S, Y; 1952 v F (26)
Mariner, P. (Ipswich T), 1977 v L (sub), Ni; 1978 v L, W (sub), S; 1980 v W, Ni (sub), S, Aus, I (sub), Sp (sub); 1981 v N, Sw, Sp, Sw, H; 1982 v N, H, Ho, S, Fi, F, Cz, K, WG, Sp; 1983 v D, WG, Gr, W; 1984 v D, H, L; (with Arsenal), 1985 v EG, R (35)
Marsden, J. T. (Darwen), 1891 v Ni (1)
Marsden, W. (Sheffield W), 1930 v W, S, G (3)
Marsh, R. W. (QPR), 1972 v Sw (sub); (with Manchester C), WG (sub+1), W, Ni, S; 1973 v W (2), Y (9)
Marshall, T. (Darwen), 1880 v W; 1881 v W (2)
Martin, A. (West Ham U), 1981 v Br, S (sub); 1982 v H, Fi; 1983 v Gr, L, W, Gr, H; 1984 v H, L, W; 1985 v Ni; 1986 v Is, Ca, Para; 1987 v Se (17)
Martin, H. (Sunderland), 1914 v Ni (1)
Martyn, A. N. (C Palace), 1992 v C (sub), H; 1993 v G; (with Leeds U), 1997 v S.Af; 1998 v Cam, Ch, Bel; 1999 v CzR, F (sub); 2000 v L, Pol, Bel (sub), Uk, R; 2001 v Sp (sub), M; 2002 v Ho, Gr, Se, Ho, I, Sk, Cam (23)
Marwood, B. (Arsenal), 1989 v S.Ar (sub) (1)
Maskrey, H. M. (Derby Co), 1908 v Ni (1)
Mason, C. (Wolverhampton W), 1887 v Ni; 1888 v W; 1890 v Ni (3)
Matthews, R. D. (Coventry C), 1956 v S, Br, Se, WG; 1957 v Ni (5)
Matthews, S. (Stoke C), 1935 v W, I; 1936 v G; 1937 v S; 1938 v S, W, Cz, G, Sw, F; 1939 v S, W, Ni, R of E, N, I, Y; 1947 v S; (with Blackpool), 1947 v Sw, P; 1948 v S, W, Ni, Bel, I; 1949 v S, W, Ni, D, Sw; 1950 v Sp; 1951 v Ni, S; 1954 v Ni, R of E, H, Bel, U; 1955 v Ni, W, S, F, WG, Sp, P; 1956 v W, Br; 1957 v S, W, Ni, Y, D (2), Ei (54)
Matthews, V. (Sheffield U), 1928 v F, Bel (2)
Maynard, W. J. (1st Surrey Rifles), 1872 v S; 1876 v S (2)
Meadows, J. (Manchester C), 1955 v S (1)
Medley, L. D. (Tottenham H), 1951 v Y, W; 1952 v F, A, W, Ni (6)
Meehan, T. (Chelsea), 1924 v Ni (1)
Melia, J. (Liverpool), 1963 v S, Sw (2)
Mercer, D. W. (Sheffield U), 1923 v Ni, Bel (2)
Mercer, J. (Everton), 1939 v S, Ni, I, R, Y (5)
Merrick, G. H. (Birmingham C), 1952 v Ni, S, A (2), I, Sw; 1953 v Ni, W, S, Bel, Arg, Ch, U; 1954 v W, Ni, S, R of E, H (2), Y, Bel, Sw, U (23)
Merson, P. C. (Arsenal), 1992 v G (sub), Cz, H, Br (sub), Fi (sub), D, Se (sub); 1993 v Sp (sub), N (sub), Ho (sub), Br (sub), G; 1994 v Ho, Gr; 1997 v I (sub); (with Middlesbrough), 1998 v Sw, P (sub), Bel, Arg (sub); 1999 v Se (sub); (with Aston Villa), CzR (21)
Metcalfe, V. (Huddersfield T), 1951 v Arg, P (2)
Mew, J. W. (Manchester U), 1921 v Ni (1)
Middleditch, B. (Corinthians), 1897 v Ni (1)
Milburn, J. E. T. (Newcastle U), 1949 v S, W, Ni, Sw; 1950 v W, P, Bel, Sp; 1951 v W, Arg, P; 1952 v F; 1956 v D (13)
Miller, B. G. (Burnley), 1961 v A (1)
Miller, H. S. (Charlton Ath), 1923 v Se (1)
Mills, D. J. (Leeds U), 2001 v M (sub); 2002 v Ho (sub), Se (sub), I, Para (sub), Sk, Cam (sub), Se, Arg, Ng, D, Br; 2003 v P, Aus (sub), S.Af, Ser, Slo; 2004 v Cro (sub), P (sub) (19)
Mills, G. R. (Chelsea), 1938 v W, Ni, Cz (3)
Mills, M. D. (Ipswich T), 1973 v Y; 1976 v W (2), Ni, S, Br, I (sub), Fi; 1977 v Fi (sub), I, Ni, W, S; 1978 v WG, Br, W, Ni, S, H; 1979 v D, Ei, Ni (2), S, Bul, A; 1980 v D, Ni, Sp (2); 1981 v Sw (2), H; 1982 v N, H, S, Fi, F, Cz, K, WG, Sp (42)
Milne, G. (Liverpool), 1963 v Br, Cz, EG; 1964 v W, Ni, S, R of W, U, P, Ei, Br, Arg; 1965 v Ni, Bel (14)
Milton, C. A. (Arsenal), 1952 v A (1)
Milward, A. (Everton), 1891 v S, W; 1897 v S, W (4)
Mitchell, C. (Upton Park), 1880 v W; 1881 v S; 1883 v S, W; 1885 v W (5)
Mitchell, J. F. (Manchester C), 1925 v Ni (1)
Moffat, H. (Oldham Ath), 1913 v W (1)
Molyneux, G. (Southampton), 1902 v S; 1903 v S, W, Ni (4)
Moon, W. R. (Old Westminsters), 1888 v S, W; 1889 v S, W; 1890 v S, W; 1891 v S (7)
Moore, H. T. (Notts Co), 1883 v Ni; 1885 v W (2)
Moore, J. (Derby Co), 1923 v Se (1)

Moore, R. F. (West Ham U), 1962 v Pe, H, Arg, Bul, Br; 1963 v W, Ni, S, F (2), Br, Cz, EG, Sw; 1964 v W, Ni, S, R of W, U, P (2), Ei, Br, Arg; 1965 v Ni, S, Bel, H, Y, WG, Se; 1966 v W, Ni, S, A, Sp, Pol (2), WG (2), N, D, U, M, F, Arg, P; 1967 v W, Ni, S, Cz, Sp, A; 1968 v W, Ni, S, USSR (2), Sp (2), Se, Y, WG; 1969 v Ni, W, S, R, Bul, F, M, U, Br; 1970 v W, Ni, S, Ho, P, Bel, Co, Ec, R, Br, Cz, WG; 1971 v EG, Gr, Ma, Ni, S; 1972 v Sw (2), Gr, WG (2), W, S; 1973 v W (3), Y, S (2), Ni, Cz, Pol, USSR, I; 1974 v I (108)
Moore, W. G. B. (West Ham U), 1923 v Se (1)
Mordue, J. (Sunderland), 1912 v Ni; 1913 v Ni (2)
Morice, C. J. (Barnes), 1872 v S (1)
Morley, A. (Aston Villa), 1982 v H (sub), Ni, W, Ic; 1983 v D, Gr (6)
Morley, H. (Notts Co), 1910 v Ni (1)
Morren, T. (Sheffield U), 1898 v Ni (1)
Morris, F. (WBA), 1920 v S; 1921 v Ni (2)
Morris, J. (Derby Co), 1949 v N, F; 1950 v Ei (3)
Morris, W. W. (Wolverhampton W), 1939 v S, Ni, R (3)
Morse, H. (Notts Co), 1879 v S (1)
Mort, T. (Aston Villa), 1924 v W, F; 1926 v S (3)
Morten, A. (C Palace), 1873 v S (1)
Mortensen, S. H. (Blackpool), 1947 v P; 1948 v W, S, Ni, Bel, Se, I; 1949 v S, W, Ni, Se, N; 1950 v S, W, Ni, I, P, Bel, Ch, US, Sp; 1951 v S, Arg; 1954 v R of E, H (25)
Morton, J. R. (West Ham U), 1938 v Cz (1)
Mosforth, W. (Sheffield W), 1877 v S; (with Sheffield Albion), 1878 v S; 1879 v S, W; 1880 v S, W; (with Sheffield W), 1881 v W; 1882 v S, W (9)
Moss, F. (Arsenal), 1934 v S, H, Cz; 1935 v I (4)
Moss, F. (Aston Villa), 1922 v S, Ni; 1923 v Ni; 1924 v S, Bel (5)
Mosscrop, E. (Burnley), 1914 v S, W (2)
Mozley, B. (Derby Co), 1950 v W, Ni, Ei (3)
Mullen, J. (Wolverhampton W), 1947 v S; 1949 v N, F; 1950 v Bel (sub), Ch, US; 1954 v W, Ni, S, R of E, Y, Sw (12)
Mullery, A. P. (Tottenham H), 1965 v Ho; 1967 v Sp, A; 1968 v W, Ni, S, USSR, Sp (2), Se, Y; 1969 v Ni, S, R, Bul, F, M, U, Br; 1970 v W, Ni, S (sub), Ho (1 + 1 sub), P, Co, Ec, R, Cz, WG, Br; 1971 v Ma, EG, Gr; 1972 v Sw (35)
Murphy, D. B. (Liverpool), 2002 v Se (sub), I (sub), Para (sub), Sk; 2003 v P (sub), Aus (sub), Lie (sub); 2004 v Cro (sub), D (sub) (9)

Neal, P. G. (Liverpool), 1976 v W, I; 1977 v W, S, Br, Arg, U; 1978 v Sw, I, WG, Ni, S, H; 1979 v D, Ei, Ni (2), S, Bul, A; 1980 v D, Ni, Sp, Arg, W, Bel, I; 1981 v R, Sw, Sp, Br, H; 1982 v N, H, W, Ho, Ic, F (sub), K; 1983 v D, Gr, L, W, Gr, H, Ni, S, Aus (2); 1984 v D (50)
Needham, E. (Sheffield U), 1894 v S; 1895 v S; 1897 v S, W, Ni; 1898 v S, W; 1899 v S, W, Ni; 1900 v S, Ni; 1901 v S, W, Ni; 1902 v W (16)
Neville, G. A. (Manchester U), 1995 v J, Br; 1996 v Co, N, Sw, P, Bul, Cro, H, Chn, Sw, S, Ho, Sp; 1997 v Mol, Pol, I, Ge, Pol, I (sub), F, Br (sub); 1998 v Mol, Ch, P, S.Ar, Bel, R, Co, Arg; 1999 v Bul, Pol; 2000 v L (sub), Pol, Br, Ma, P, G, R; 2001 v G, I, Sp (sub), Fi, Alb; 2002 v Ho, G, Alb, Gr, Se, Ho, I (sub), Para; 2003 v Slo, Mac, Aus, Lie, T; 2004 v Mac, Lie, T, D, J, Ic, F, Sw, Cro, P; 2005 v Uk, A, Pol, W, Az, Sp, Ho, Ni, Az; 2006 v D, U, H, Para, P (81)
Neville, P. J. (Manchester U), 1996 v Chn; 1997 v S.Af, Pol (sub), I, F, Br; 1998 v Mol, Cam, Ch, P (sub), S.Ar (sub), Bel; 1999 v L, Pol (sub), H, Se, Bul; 2000 v L (sub), Pol (sub), Bel (sub), S (2), Arg (sub), Br, Uk, Ma, P, G, R; 2001 v Fi, Sp, M, Gr; 2002 v Se (sub), Ho (sub), I (sub), Para (sub); 2003 v S.Af, Ser, Slo; 2004 v Cro, Mac (sub), Lie (sub), D (sub), P, Se, J (sub), Ic (sub), Cro (sub), P (sub); 2005 v US (sub), Co (52)
Newton, K. R. (Blackburn R), 1966 v S, WG; 1967 v Sp, A; 1968 v W, S, Sp, Se, Y, WG; 1969 v Ni, W, S, R, Bul, M, U, Br, F; (with Everton), 1970 v Ni, S, Ho, Co, Ec, R, Cz, WG (27)
Nicholls, J. (WBA), 1954 v S, Y (2)
Nicholson, W. E. (Tottenham H), 1951 v P (1)
Nish, D. J. (Derby Co), 1973 v Ni; 1974 v P, W, Ni, S (5)
Norman, M. (Tottenham H), 1962 v Pe, H, Arg, Bul, Br; 1963 v S, F, Br, Cz, EG; 1964 v W, Ni, S, R of W, U, P (2), US, Br, Arg; 1965 v Ni, Bel, Ho (23)
Nuttall, H. (Bolton W), 1928 v W, Ni; 1929 v S (3)

Oakley, W. J. (Oxford University), 1895 v W; 1896 v S, W, Ni; (with Corinthians), 1897 v S, W, Ni; 1898 v S, W, Ni; 1900 v S, W, Ni; 1901 v S, W, Ni (16)
O'Dowd, J. P. (Chelsea), 1932 v S; 1933 v Ni, Sw (3)
O'Grady, M. (Huddersfield T), 1963 v Ni; (with Leeds U), 1969 v F (2)
Ogilvie, R. A. M. M. (Clapham R), 1874 v S (1)
Oliver, L. F. (Fulham), 1929 v Bel (1)
Olney, B. A. (Aston Villa), 1928 v F, Bel (2)
Osborne, F. R. (Fulham), 1923 v Ni, F; (with Tottenham H), 1925 v Bel; 1926 v Bel (4)
Osborne, R. (Leicester C), 1928 v W (1)
Osgood, P. L. (Chelsea), 1970 v Bel, R (sub), Cz (sub); 1974 v I (4)
Osman, R. (Ipswich T), 1980 v Aus; 1981 v Sp, R, Sw; 1982 v N, Ic; 1983 v D, Aus (3); 1984 v D (11)
Ottaway, C. J. (Oxford University), 1872 v S; 1874 v S (2)
Owen, J. R. B. (Sheffield), 1874 v S (1)
Owen, M. J. (Liverpool), 1998 v Ch, Sw, P (sub), Mor (sub), Bel (sub), Tun (sub), R (sub), Co, Arg; 1999 v Se, Bul, L, F; 2000 v L (sub), Pol (sub), Bel (sub), S (2), Br, P, G, R; 2001 v F (sub), G, Sp, Fi, Alb, M, Gr; 2002 v Ho (sub), G, Alb, I, Para, Sk, Cam, Se, Arg, Ng, D, Br; 2003 v P, Slo, Mac, Aus, Lie, T, S.Af, Ser, Slo; 2004 v Cro, Mac, Lie, P, J, Ic, F, Sw, Cro, P; (with Real Madrid), 2005 v Uk, A, Pol, W, Az, Sp, Ho, Ni, Az, Co; 2006 v D (sub); (with Newcastle U), Ni, A, Pol, Arg, H, Jam, Para, Tr, Se (80)
Owen, S. W. (Luton T), 1954 v H, Y, Bel (3)

Page, L. A. (Burnley), 1927 v S, W, Bel, L, F; 1928 v W, Ni (7)
Paine, T. L. (Southampton), 1963 v Cz, EG; 1964 v W, Ni, S, R of W, U, US, P; 1965 v Ni, H, Y, WG, Se; 1966 v W, A, Y, N, M (19)
Pallister, G. A. (Middlesbrough), 1988 v H; 1989 v S.Ar, (with Manchester U), 1991 v Cam (sub), T; 1992 v G; 1993 v N, US, Br, G; 1994 v Pol, Ho, Sm, D; 1995 v US, R, Ei, U, Se; 1996 v N, Sw; 1997 v Mol, Pol (sub) (22)
Palmer, C. L. (Sheffield W), 1992 v C, H, Br, Fi (sub), D, F, Se; 1993 v Sp (sub), N (sub), T, Sm, T, Ho, Pol, N, US, Br (sub); 1994 v Ho (18)
Pantling, H. H. (Sheffield U), 1924 v Ni (1)
Paravicini, P. J. de (Cambridge University), 1883 v S, W, Ni (3)
Parker, P. A. (QPR), 1989 v Alb (sub), Ch, D; 1990 v Y, U, Ho, Eg, Bel, Cam, WG, I; 1991 v H, Pol, USSR, Aus, Nz; (with Manchester U), 1992 v G; 1994 v Ho, D (19)
Parker, S. M. (Charlton Ath), 2004 v D (sub); (with Chelsea), v Se (sub) (2)
Parker, T. R. (Southampton), 1925 v F (1)
Parkes, P. B. (QPR), 1974 v P (1)
Parkinson, J. (Liverpool), 1910 v S, W (2)
Parlour, R. (Arsenal), 1999 v Pol (sub), Se (sub), Bul (sub); 2000 v L, S (sub), Arg (sub), Br (sub); 2001 v G (sub), Fi, I (10)
Parr, P. C. (Oxford University), 1882 v W (1)
Parry, E. H. (Old Carthusians), 1879 v W; 1882 v W, S (3)
Parry, R. A. (Bolton W), 1960 v Ni, S (2)
Patchitt, B. C. A. (Corinthians), 1923 v Se (2) (2)
Pawson, F. W. (Cambridge University), 1883 v Ni; (with Swifts), 1885 v Ni (2)
Payne, J. (Luton T), 1937 v Fi (1)
Peacock, A. (Middlesbrough), 1962 v Arg, Bul; 1963 v Ni, W; (with Leeds U), 1966 v W, Ni (6)
Peacock, J. (Middlesbrough), 1929 v F, Bel, Sp (3)
Pearce, S. (Nottingham F), 1987 v Br, S; 1988 v WG (sub), Is, H; 1989 v D, Se, S.Ar, Gr, Alb (2), Ch, S, Pol, D; 1990 v Se, Pol, I, Y, Br, Cz, D, U, Tun, Ei, Ho, Eg, Bel, Cam, WG; 1991 v H, Pol, Ei (2), Cam, T, Arg, Aus, Nz (2), Mal; 1992 v T, Pol, F, Cz, Br (sub), Fi, D, F, Se; 1993 v Sp, N, T; 1994 v Pol, Sm, Gr (sub); 1995 v R (sub), J, Br; 1996 v N, Sw, P, Bul, Cro, H, Sw, S, Ho, Sp, G; 1997 v Mol, Pol, I, M, S.Af, I; (with West Ham U), 2000 v L, Pol (78)
Pearson, H. F. (WBA), 1932 v S (1)
Pearson, J. H. (Crewe Alex), 1892 v Ni (1)
Pearson, J. S. (Manchester U), 1976 v W, Ni, S, Br, Fi; 1977 v Ei, Ho (sub), W, S, Br, Arg, U; 1978 v I (sub), WG, Ni (15)
Pearson, S. C. (Manchester U), 1948 v S; 1949 v S, Ni; 1950 v Ni, I; 1951 v P; 1952 v S, I (8)
Pease, W. H. (Middlesbrough), 1927 v W (1)
Pegg, D. (Manchester U), 1957 v Ei (1)
Pejic, M. (Stoke C), 1974 v P, W, Ni, S (4)
Pelly, F. R. (Old Foresters), 1893 v Ni; 1894 v S, W (3)
Pennington, J. (WBA), 1907 v S, W; 1908 v S, W, Ni, A; 1909 v S, W, H (2), A; 1910 v S, W; 1911 v S, W, Ni; 1912 v S, W, Ni; 1913 v S, W; 1914 v S, Ni; 1920 v S, W (25)
Pentland, F. B. (Middlesbrough), 1909 v S, W, H (2), A (5)
Perry, C. (WBA), 1890 v Ni; 1891 v Ni; 1893 v W (3)
Perry, T. (WBA), 1898 v W (1)
Perry, W. (Blackpool), 1956 v Ni, S, Sp (3)
Perryman, S. (Tottenham H), 1982 v Ic (sub) (1)
Peters, M. (West Ham U), 1966 v Y, Fi, Pol, M, F, Arg, P, WG; 1967 v Ni, W, S, Cz; 1968 v W, Ni, S, USSR (2), Sp (2), Se, Y; 1969 v Ni, S, R, Bul, F, M, U, Br; 1970 v Ho (2), P (sub), Bel; (with Tottenham H), W, Ni, S, Co, Ec, R, Br, Cz, WG; 1971 v EG, Gr, Ma (2), Ni, W, S; 1972 v

Sw, Gr, WG (1+1 sub), Ni (sub); 1973 v S (2), Ni, W, Cz, Pol, USSR, I; 1974 v A, Pol, I, P, S (67)
Phelan, M. C. (Manchester U), 1990 v I (sub) (1)
Phillips, K. (Sunderland), 1999 v H; 2000 v Bel, Arg (sub), Br (sub), Ma; 2001 v I (sub); 2002 v Se, Ho (sub) (8)
Phillips, L. H. (Portsmouth), 1952 v Ni; 1955 v W, WG (3)
Pickering, F. (Everton), 1964 v US; 1965 v Ni, Bel (3)
Pickering, J. (Sheffield U), 1933 v S (1)
Pickering, N. (Sunderland), 1983 v Aus (1)
Pike, T. M. (Cambridge University), 1886 v Ni (1)
Pilkington, B. (Burnley), 1955 v Ni (1)
Plant, J. (Bury), 1900 v S (1)
Platt, D. (Aston Villa), 1990 v I (sub), Y (sub), Br, D (sub), Tun (sub), Ho (sub), Eg (sub), Bel (sub), Cam, WG, I; 1991 v H, Pol, Ei (2), T, USSR, Arg, Aus, Nz (2), Mal; (with Bari), 1992 v G, T, Pol, Cz, C, Br, Fi, D, F, Se; (with Juventus), 1993 v Sp, N, T, Sm, T, Ho, Pol, N, Br (sub), G; (with Sampdoria), 1994 v Pol, Ho, Sm, D, Gr, N; 1995 v US, Ng, Ei, U, J, Se, Br; (with Arsenal), 1996 v Bul (sub), Cro, H, Sw (sub), Ho (sub), Sp, G (62)
Plum, S. L. (Charlton Ath), 1923 v F (1)
Pointer, R. (Burnley), 1962 v W, L, P (3)
Porteous, T. S. (Sunderland), 1891 v W (1)
Powell, C. G. (Charlton Ath), 2001 v Sp, Fi, M (sub); 2002 v Ho (sub+sub) (5)
Priest, A. E. (Sheffield U), 1900 v Ni (1)
Prinsep, J. F. M. (Clapham Rovers), 1879 v S (1)
Puddefoot, S. C. (Blackburn R), 1926 v S, Ni (2)
Pye, J. (Wolverhampton W), 1950 v Ei (1)
Pym, R. H. (Bolton W), 1925 v S, W; 1926 v W (3)

Quantrill, A. (Derby Co), 1920 v S, W; 1921 v W, Ni (4)
Quixall, A. (Sheffield W), 1954 v W, Ni, R of E; 1955 v Sp, P (sub) (5)

Radford, J. (Arsenal), 1969 v R; 1972 v Sw (sub) (2)
Raikes, G. B. (Oxford University), 1895 v W; 1896 v W, Ni, S (4)
Ramsey, A. E. (Southampton), 1949 v Sw; (with Tottenham H), 1950 v S, I, P, Bel, Ch, US, Sp; 1951 v S, Ni, W, Y, Arg, P; 1952 v S, W, Ni, F, A (2), I, Sw; 1953 v Ni, W, S, Bel, Arg, Ch, U, US; 1954 v R of E, H (32)
Rawlings, A. (Preston NE), 1921 v Bel (1)
Rawlings, W. E. (Southampton), 1922 v S, W (2)
Rawlinson, J. F. P. (Cambridge University), 1882 v Ni (1)
Rawson, H. E. (Royal Engineers), 1875 v S (1)
Rawson, W. S. (Oxford University), 1875 v S; 1877 v S (2)
Read, A. (Tufnell Park), 1921 v Bel (1)
Reader, J. (WBA), 1894 v Ni (1)
Reaney, P. (Leeds U), 1969 v Bul (sub); 1970 v P; 1971 v Ma (3)
Redknapp, J. F. (Liverpool), 1996 v Co, N, Sw, Chn, S (sub); 1997 v M (sub), Ge (sub), S.Af; 1999 v Se, Bul, F, Pol (sub), H (sub), Bul; 2000 v Bel, S (2) (17)
Reeves, K. (Norwich C), 1980 v Bul; (with Manchester C), Ni (2)
Regis, C. (WBA), 1982 v Ni (sub), W (sub), Ic; 1983 v WG; (with Coventry C), 1988 v T (sub) (5)
Reid, P. (Everton), 1985 v M (sub), WG, US (sub); 1986 v R, S (sub), Ca (sub), Pol, Para, Arg; 1987 v Br; 1988 v WG, Y (sub), Sw (sub) (13)
Revie, D. G. (Manchester C), 1955 v Ni, S, F; 1956 v W, D; 1957 v Ni (6)
Reynolds, J. (WBA), 1892 v S; 1893 v S, W; (with Aston Villa), 1894 v S, Ni; 1895 v S; 1897 v S, W (8)
Richards, C. H. (Nottingham F), 1898 v Ni (1)
Richards, G. H. (Derby Co), 1909 v A (1)
Richards, J. P. (Wolverhampton W), 1973 v Ni (1)
Richardson, J. R. (Newcastle U), 1933 v I, Sw (2)
Richardson, K. (Aston Villa), 1994 v Gr (1)
Richardson, K. E. (Manchester U), 2005 v US, Co (sub); 2006 v W (sub), A (sub) (4)
Richardson, W. G. (WBA), 1935 v Ho (1)
Rickaby, S. (WBA), 1954 v Ni (1)
Ricketts, M. B. (Bolton W), 2002 v Ho (1)
Rigby, A. (Blackburn R), 1927 v S, Bel, L, F; 1928 v W (5)
Rimmer, E. J. (Sheffield W), 1930 v S, G, A; 1932 v Sp (4)
Rimmer, J. J. (Arsenal), 1976 v I (1)
Ripley, S. E. (Blackburn R), 1994 v Sm; 1998 v Mol (sub) (2)
Rix, G. (Arsenal), 1981 v N, R, Sw (sub), Br, W, S; 1982 v Ho (sub), Fi (sub), F, Cz, K, WG, Sp; 1983 v D, WG (sub), Gr (sub); 1984 v Ni (17)
Robb, G. (Tottenham H), 1954 v H (1)
Roberts, C. (Manchester U), 1905 v Ni, W, S (3)
Roberts, F. (Manchester C), 1925 v S, W, Bel, F (4)
Roberts, G. (Tottenham H), 1983 v Ni, S; 1984 v F, Ni, S, USSR (6)
Roberts, H. (Arsenal), 1931 v S (1)
Roberts, H. (Millwall), 1931 v Bel (1)
Roberts, R. (WBA), 1887 v S; 1888 v Ni; 1890 v Ni (3)
Roberts, W. T. (Preston NE), 1924 v W, Bel (2)
Robinson, J. (Sheffield W), 1937 v Fi; 1938 v G, Sw; 1939 v W (4)
Robinson, J. W. (Derby Co), 1897 v S, Ni; (with New Brighton Tower), 1898 v S, W, Ni; (with Southampton), 1899 v W, S; 1900 v S, W, Ni; 1901 v Ni (11)
Robinson, P. W. (Leeds U), 2003 v Aus (sub), S.Af (sub); 2004 v Cro (sub), D (sub); (with Tottenham H), Ic; 2005 v Pol, W, Az, Sp, Ho, Ni, Az; 2006 v D, W, Ni, A, Pol, Arg, U, H, Jam, Para, Tr, Se, Ec, P (26)
Robson, B. (WBA), 1980 v Ei, Aus; 1981 v N, R, Sw, Sp, R, Br, W, S, Sw, H; 1982 v N; (with Manchester U), H, Ni, W, Ho, S, Fi, F, Cz, WG, Sp; 1983 v D, Gr, L, S; 1984 v H, L, F, Ni, S, USSR, Br, U, Ch; 1985 v EG, Fi, T, Ei, R, Fi, S, M, I, WG, US; 1986 v R, T, Is, M, P, Mor; 1987 v Ni (2), Sp, T, Br, S; 1988 v T, Y, Ho, H, S, Co, Sw, Ei, Ho, USSR; 1989 v D, Se, S.Ar, Gr, Alb (2), Ch, S, Pol, D; 1990 v Pol, I, Y, Cz, U, Tun, Ei, Ho; 1991 v Cam, Ei; 1992 v T (90)
Robson, R. (WBA), 1958 v F, USSR (2), Br, A; 1960 v Sp, H; 1961 v Ni, W, S, L, P, Sp, M, I; 1962 v W, Ni, Sw, L, P (20)
Rocastle, D. (Arsenal), 1989 v D, S.Ar, Gr, Alb (2), Pol (sub), D; 1990 v Se (sub), Pol, Y, D (sub); 1992 v Pol, Cz, Br (sub) (14)
Rooney, W. (Everton), 2003 v Aus (sub), Lie (sub), T, Ser (sub), Slo; 2004 v Mac, Lie, T, D, P, Se, J, Ic, F, Sw, Cro, P; (with Manchester U), 2005 v W, Az, Sp, Ho, Ni, Az; 2006 v D, W, Ni, Pol, Arg, U, Tr (sub), Se, Ec, P (33)
Rose, W. C. (Swifts), 1884 v S, W, Ni; (with Preston NE), 1886 v Ni; (with Wolverhampton W), 1891 v Ni (5)
Rostron, T. (Darwen), 1881 v S, W (2)
Rowe, A. (Tottenham H), 1934 v F (1)
Rowley, J. F. (Manchester U), 1949 v Sw, Se, F; 1950 v Ni, I; 1952 v S (6)
Rowley, W. (Stoke C), 1889 v Ni; 1892 v Ni (2)
Royle, J. (Everton), 1971 v Ma; 1973 v Y; (with Manchester C), 1976 v Ni (sub), I; 1977 v Fi, L (6)
Ruddlesdin, H. (Sheffield W), 1904 v W, Ni; 1905 v S (3)
Ruddock, N. (Liverpool), 1995 v Ng (1)
Ruffell, J. W. (West Ham U), 1926 v S; 1927 v Ni; 1929 v S, W, Ni; 1930 v W (6)
Russell, B. B. (Royal Engineers), 1883 v W (1)
Rutherford, J. (Newcastle U), 1904 v S; 1907 v S, Ni, W; 1908 v S, Ni, W, A (2), H, B (11)

Sadler, D. (Manchester U), 1968 v Ni, USSR; 1970 v Ec (sub); 1971 v EG (4)
Sagar, C. (Bury), 1900 v Ni; 1902 v W (2)
Sagar, E. (Everton), 1936 v S, Ni, A, Bel (4)
Salako, J. A. (C Palace), 1991 v Aus (sub), Nz (sub + 1), Mal; 1992 v G (5)
Sandford, E. A. (WBA), 1933 v W (1)
Sandilands, R. R. (Old Westminsters), 1892 v W; 1893 v Ni; 1894 v W; 1895 v W; 1896 v W (5)
Sands, J. (Nottingham F), 1880 v W (1)
Sansom, K. (C Palace), 1979 v W; 1980 v Bul, Ei, Arg, W (sub), Ni, S, Bel, I; (with Arsenal), 1981 v N, R, Sw, Sp, R, Br, W, S, Sw; 1982 v Ni, W, Ho, S, Fi, F, Cz, WG, Sp; 1983 v D, WG, Gr, L, Gr, H, Ni, S; 1984 v D, H, L, F, S, USSR, Br, U, Ch; 1985 v EG, Fi, T, Ni, Ei, R, Fi, S, I, M, WG, US; 1986 v R, T, Ni, Eg, Is, USSR, S, M, Ca, P, Mor, Pol, Para, Arg; 1987 v Se, Ni (2), Y, Sp, T; 1988 v WG, T, Y, Ho, S, Co, Sw, Ei, Ho, USSR (86)
Saunders, F. E. (Swifts), 1888 v W (1)
Savage, A. H. (C Palace), 1876 v S (1)
Sayer, J. (Stoke C), 1887 v Ni (1)
Scales, J. R. (Liverpool), 1995 v J, Se (sub), Br (3)
Scattergood, E. (Derby Co), 1913 v W (1)
Schofield, J. (Stoke C), 1892 v W; 1893 v W; 1895 v Ni (3)
Scholes, P. (Manchester U), 1997 v S.Af (sub), I, Br; 1998 v Mol, Cam, P, S.Ar, Tun, R, Co, Arg; 1999 v Se, Bul, L, F (sub), Pol, Se; 2000 v Pol, S (2), Arg, Br, Uk, Ma, P, G, R; 2001 v F, G, Fi, Sp, Fi, Alb, M, Gr; 2002 v Ho, G, Alb, Gr, Se, Ho, Para, Sk, Cam, Se, Arg, Ng, D, Br; 2003 v Slo, Mac, Aus, Lie, T, S.Af, Ser, Slo; 2004 v Cro, T, P, J, Ic, F, Sw, Cro, P (66)
Scott, L. (Arsenal), 1947 v S, W, Ni, Ei, Ho, F, Sw, P; 1948 v S, W, Ni, Bel, Se, I; 1949 v W, Ni, D (17)
Scott, W. R. (Brentford), 1937 v W (1)
Seaman, D. A. (QPR), 1989 v S.Ar, D (sub); 1990 v Cz (sub); (with Arsenal), 1991 v Cam, Ei, T, Arg; 1992 v Cz, H (sub); 1994 v Pol, Ho, Sm, D, N; 1995 v US, R, Ei; 1996 v Co, N, Sw, P, Bul, Cro, H, Sw, S, Ho, Sp, G; 1997 v Mol, Pol, Ge (2), Pol, F, Br; 1998 v Mol, I, P, S.Ar, Tun, R, Co, Arg; 1999 v Se, Bul, L, F, Pol, H, Se, Bul; 2000 v Bel, S (2), Arg, Br, P, G; 2001 v F, G, Fi (2), Alb, Gr; 2002 v G, Alb, Para, Se, Arg, Ng, D, Br; 2003 v Slo, Mac (75)

Seddon, J. (Bolton W), 1923 v F, Se (2); 1924 v Bel; 1927 v W; 1929 v S (6)
Seed, J. M. (Tottenham H), 1921 v Bel: 1923 v W, Ni, Bel; 1925 v S (5)
Settle, J. (Bury), 1899 v S, W, Ni; (with Everton), 1902 v S, Ni; 1903 v Ni (6)
Sewell, J. (Sheffield W), 1952 v Ni, A, Sw; 1953 v Ni; 1954 v H (2) (6)
Sewell, W. R. (Blackburn R), 1924 v W (1)
Shackleton, L. F. (Sunderland), 1949 v W, D; 1950 v W; 1955 v W, WG (5)
Sharp, J. (Everton), 1903 v Ni; 1905 v S (2)
Sharpe, L. S. (Manchester U), 1991 v Ei (sub); 1993 v T (sub), N, US, Br, G; 1994 v Pol, Ho (8)
Shaw, G. E. (WBA), 1932 v S (1)
Shaw, G. L. (Sheffield U), 1959 v S, W, USSR, I; 1963 v W (5)
Shea, D. (Blackburn R), 1914 v W, Ni (2)
Shearer, A. (Southampton), 1992 v F, C, F; (with Blackburn R), 1993 v Sp, N, T; 1994 v Ho, D, Gr, N; 1995 v US, R, Ng, Ei, J, Se, Br; 1996 v Co, N, Sw, P, H (sub), Chn, Sw, S, Ho, Sp, G; (with Newcastle U), 1997 v Mol, Pol, I, Ge, Pol, F, Br; 1998 v Ch (sub), Sw, P, S.Ar, Tun, R, Co, Arg; 1999 v Se, Bul, L, F, Pol, H, Se, Bul; 2000 v L, Pol, Bel, S (2), Arg, Br, Uk, Ma, P, G, R (63)
Shellito, K. J. (Chelsea), 1963 v Cz (1)
Shelton A. (Notts Co), 1889 v Ni; 1890 v S, W; 1891 v S, W; 1892 v S (6)
Shelton, C. (Notts Rangers), 1888 v Ni (1)
Shepherd, A. (Bolton W), 1906 v S; (with Newcastle U), 1911 v Ni (2)
Sheringham, E. P. (Tottenham H), 1993 v Pol, N; 1995 v US, R (sub), Ng (sub), U, J (sub), Se, Br; 1996 v Co (sub), N (sub), Sw, Bul, Cro, H, Sw, S, Ho, Sp, G; 1997 v Ge, M, Ge, S.Af, Pol, I, F (sub), Br; (with Manchester U), 1998 v I, Ch, Sw (sub), P, S.Ar, Tun, R; 1999 v Se (sub), Bul (sub), Bul; 2001 v Fi, Alb (sub), M (sub); (with Tottenham H), 2002 v Gr (sub), Se (sub), I (sub), Para (sub), Sk (sub), Cam (sub), Arg (sub), Ng (sub), D (sub), Br (sub) (51)
Sherwood, T. A. (Tottenham H), 1999 v Pol, H, Se (3)
Shilton, P. L. (Leicester C), 1971 v EG, W; 1972 v Sw, Ni; 1973 v Y, S (2), Ni, W, Cz, Pol, USSR, I; 1974 v A, Pol, I, W, Ni, S, Arg; (with Stoke C), 1975 v Cy; 1977 v Ni, W; (with Nottingham F), 1978 v W, H; 1979 v Cz, Se, A; 1980 v Ni, Sp, I; 1981 v N, Sw, R; 1982 v H, Ho, S, F, Cz, K, WG, Sp; (with Southampton), 1983 v D, WG, Gr, W, Gr, H, Ni, S, Aus (3); 1984 v D, H, F, Ni, W, S, USSR, Br, U, Ch; 1985 v EG, Fi, T, Ni, R, Fi, S, I, WG; 1986 v R, T, Ni, Eg, Is, USSR, S, M, Ca, P, Mor, Pol, Para, Arg; 1987 v Se, Ni (2), Sp, Br; (with Derby Co), 1988 v WG, T, Y, Ho, S, Co, Sw, Ei, Ho; 1989 v D, Se, Gr, Alb (2), Ch, S, Pol, D; 1990 v Se, Pol, I, Y, Br, Cz, D, U, Tun, Ei, Ho, Eg, Bel, Cam, WG, I (125)
Shimwell, E. (Blackpool), 1949 v Se (1)
Shutt, G. (Stoke C), 1886 v Ni (1)
Silcock, J. (Manchester U), 1921 v S, W; 1923 v Se (3)
Sillett, R. P. (Chelsea), 1955 v F, Sp, P (3)
Simms, E. (Luton T), 1922 v Ni (1)
Simpson, J. (Blackburn R), 1911 v S, W, Ni; 1912 v S, W, Ni; 1913 v S; 1914 v W (8)
Sinclair, T. (West Ham U), 2002 v Se, I, Para (sub), Sk (sub), Cam (sub), Arg (sub), Ng, D, Br; 2003 v P (sub), S.Af; (with Manchester C), 2004 v Cro (sub) (12)
Sinton, A. (QPR), 1992 v Pol, C, H (sub), Br, F, Se; 1993 v Sp, T, Br, G; (with Sheffield W), 1994 v Ho (sub), Sm (12)
Slater, W. J. (Wolverhampton W), 1955 v W, WG; 1958 v S, P, Y, USSR (3), Br, A; 1959 v USSR; 1960 v S (12)
Smalley, T. (Wolverhampton W), 1937 v W (1)
Smart, T. (Aston Villa), 1921 v S; 1924 v S, W; 1926 v Ni; 1930 v W (5)
Smith, A. (Nottingham F), 1891 v S, W; 1893 v Ni (3)
Smith, A. (Leeds U), 2001 v M (sub), Gr (sub); 2002 v Ho (sub); 2003 v P, Slo (sub), Mac; 2004 v P (sub), Se (sub); (with Manchester U), 2005 v Uk, A, W (sub), Az (sub), Sp (sub), US, Co (sub); 2006 v Pol (sub) (16)
Smith, A. K. (Oxford University), 1872 v S (1)
Smith, A. M. (Arsenal), 1989 v S.Ar (sub), Gr, Alb (sub), Pol (sub); 1991 v T, USSR, Arg; 1992 v G, T, Pol (sub), H (sub), D, Se (sub) (13)
Smith, B. (Tottenham H), 1921 v S; 1922 v W (2)
Smith, C. E. (C Palace), 1876 v S (1)
Smith, G. O. (Oxford University), 1893 v Ni; 1894 v W, S; 1895 v W; 1896 v Ni, W, S; (with Old Carthusians), 1897 v Ni, W, S; 1898 v Ni, W, S; (with Corinthians), 1899 v Ni, W, S; 1899 v Ni, W, S; 1901 v S (20)
Smith, H. (Reading), 1905 v W, S; 1906 v W, Ni (4)
Smith, J. (WBA), 1920 v Ni; 1923 v Ni (2)
Smith, Joe (Bolton W), 1913 v Ni; 1914 v S, W; 1920 v W, Ni (5)
Smith, J. C. R. (Millwall), 1939 v Ni, N (2)
Smith, J. W. (Portsmouth), 1932 v Ni, W, Sp (3)
Smith, Leslie (Brentford), 1939 v R (1)
Smith, Lionel (Arsenal), 1951 v W; 1952 v W, Ni; 1953 v W, S, Bel (6)
Smith, R. A. (Tottenham H), 1961 v Ni, W, S, L, P, Sp; 1962 v S; 1963 v S, F, Br, Cz, EG; 1964 v W, Ni, R of W (15)
Smith, S. (Aston Villa), 1895 v S (1)
Smith, S. C. (Leicester C), 1936 v Ni (1)
Smith, T. (Birmingham C), 1960 v W, Se (2)
Smith, T. (Liverpool), 1971 v W (1)
Smith, W. H. (Huddersfield T), 1922 v W, S; 1928 v S (3)
Sorby, T. H. (Thursday Wanderers, Sheffield), 1879 v W (1)
Southgate, G. (Aston Villa), 1996 v P (sub), Bul, H (sub), Chn, Sw, S, Ho, Sp, G; 1997 v Mol, Pol, Ge, M, Ge (sub), S.Af, Pol, I, F, Br; 1998 v Mol, I, Cam, Sw, S.Ar, Mor, Tun, Arg (sub); 1999 v Se, Bul, L, Bul; 2000 v Bel, S, Arg, Uk, Ma (sub), R (sub); 2001 v F (sub), G, Fi, I, M (sub); (with Middlesbrough), 2002 v Ho (sub), Se, Ho (sub), I, Para, Sk (sub), Cam (sub); 2003 v P, Slo, Lie, S.Af, Ser, Slo; 2004 v P, Se (sub) (57)
Southworth, J. (Blackburn R), 1889 v W; 1891 v W; 1892 v S (3)
Sparks, F. J. (Herts Rangers), 1879 v S; (with Clapham Rovers), 1880 v S, W (3)
Spence, J. W. (Manchester U), 1926 v Bel; 1927 v Ni (2)
Spence, R. (Chelsea), 1936 v A, Bel (2)
Spencer, C. W. (Newcastle U), 1924 v S; 1925 v W (2)
Spencer, H. (Aston Villa), 1897 v S, W; 1900 v W; 1903 v Ni; 1905 v W, S (6)
Spiksley, F. (Sheffield W), 1893 v S, W; 1894 v S, Ni; 1896 v Ni; 1898 v S, W (7)
Spilsbury, B. W. (Cambridge University), 1885 v Ni; 1886 v Ni, S (3)
Spink, N. (Aston Villa), 1983 v Aus (sub) (1)
Spouncer, W. A. (Nottingham F), 1900 v W (1)
Springett, R. D. G. (Sheffield W), 1960 v Ni, S, Y, Sp, H; 1961 v Ni, S, L, P, Sp, M, I, A; 1962 v W, Ni, S, A, Sw, Pe, L, P, H, Arg, Bul, Br; 1963 v Ni, W, F (2), Sw; 1966 v W, A, N (33)
Sproston, B. (Leeds U), 1937 v W; 1938 v S, W, Ni, Cz, G, Sw, F; (with Tottenham H), 1939 v W, R of E; (with Manchester C), N (11)
Squire, R. T. (Cambridge University), 1886 v S, W, Ni (3)
Stanbrough, M. H. (Old Carthusians), 1895 v W (1)
Staniforth, R. (Huddersfield T), 1954 v S, H, Y, Bel, Sw, U; 1955 v W, WG (8)
Starling, R. W. (Sheffield W), 1933 v S; (with Aston Villa), 1937 v S (2)
Statham, D. (WBA), 1983 v W, Aus (2) (3)
Steele, F. C. (Stoke C), 1937 v S, W, Ni, N, Se, Fi (6)
Stein, B. (Luton T), 1984 v F (1)
Stephenson, C. (Huddersfield T), 1924 v W (1)
Stephenson, G. T. (Derby Co), 1928 v F, Bel; (with Sheffield W), 1931 v F (3)
Stephenson, J. E. (Leeds U), 1938 v S; 1939 v Ni (2)
Stepney, A. C. (Manchester U), 1968 v Se (1)
Sterland, M. (Sheffield W), 1989 v S.Ar (1)
Steven, T. M. (Everton), 1985 v Ni, Ei, R, Fi, I, US (sub); 1986 v T (sub), Eg, USSR (sub), M (sub), Pol, Para, Arg; 1987 v Se, Y (sub), Sp (sub); 1988 v T, Y, Ho, H, S, Sw, Ho, USSR; 1989 v S; (with Rangers), 1990 v Cz, Cam (sub), WG (sub), I; 1991 v Cam; (with Marseille), 1992 v G, C, Br, Fi, D, F (36)
Stevens, G. A. (Tottenham H), 1985 v Fi (sub), T (sub), Ni; 1986 v S (sub), M (sub), Mor (sub), Para (sub) (7)
Stevens, M. G. (Everton), 1985 v I, WG; 1986 v R, T, Ni, Eg, Is, S, Ca, P, Mor, Pol, Para, Arg; 1987 v Br, S; 1988 v T, Y, Is, Ho, H (sub), S, Sw, Ei, Ho, USSR; (with Rangers), 1989 v D, Se, Gr, Alb (2), S, Pol; 1990 v Se, Pol, I, Br, D, Tun, Ei, I; 1991 v USSR; 1992 v C, H, Br, Fi (46)
Stewart, J. (Sheffield W), 1907 v S, W; (with Newcastle U), 1911 v S (3)
Stewart, P. A. (Tottenham H), 1992 v G (sub), Cz (sub), C (sub) (3)
Stiles, N. P. (Manchester U), 1965 v S, H, Y, Se; 1966 v W, Ni, S, A, Sp, Pol (2), WG (2), N, D, U, M, F, Arg, P; 1967 v Ni, W, S, Cz; 1968 v USSR; 1969 v R; 1970 v Ni, S (28)
Stoker, J. (Birmingham), 1933 v W; 1934 v S, H (3)
Stone, S. B. (Nottingham F), 1996 v N (sub), Sw (sub), P, Bul, Cro, Chn (sub), Sw (sub), S (sub), Sp (sub) (9)
Storer, H. (Derby Co), 1924 v F; 1928 v Ni (2)
Storey, P. E. (Arsenal), 1971 v Gr, Ni, S; 1972 v Sw, WG, W, Ni, S; 1973 v W (3), Y, S (2), Ni, Cz, Pol, USSR, I (19)
Storey-Moore, I. (Nottingham F), 1970 v Ho (1)

Strange, A. H. (Sheffield W), 1930 v S, A, G; 1931 v S, W, Ni, F, Bel; 1932 v S, W, Ni, Sp; 1933 v S, Ni, A, I, Sw; 1934 v Ni, W, F (20)
Stratford, A. H. (Wanderers), 1874 v S (1)
Streten, B. (Luton T), 1950 v Ni (1)
Sturgess, A. (Sheffield U), 1911 v Ni; 1914 v S (2)
Summerbee, M. G. (Manchester C), 1968 v S, Sp, WG; 1972 v Sw, WG (sub), W, Ni; 1973 v USSR (sub) (8)
Sunderland, A. (Arsenal), 1980 v Aus (1)
Sutcliffe, J. W. (Bolton W), 1893 v W; 1895 v S, Ni; 1901 v S; (with Millwall), 1903 v W (5)
Sutton, C. R. (Blackburn R), 1998 v Cam (sub) (1)
Swan, P. (Sheffield W), 1960 v Y, Sp, H; 1961 v Ni, W, S, L, P, Sp, M, I, A; 1962 v W, Ni, S, A, Sw, L, P (19)
Swepstone, H. A. (Pilgrims), 1880 v S; 1882 v S, W; 1883 v S, W, Ni (6)
Swift, F. V. (Manchester C), 1947 v S, W, Ni, Ei, Ho, F, Sw, P; 1948 v S, W, Ni, Bel, Se, I; 1949 v S, W, Ni, D, N (19)

Tait, G. (Birmingham Excelsior), 1881 v W (1)
Talbot, B. (Ipswich T), 1977 v Ni (sub), S, Br, Arg, U; (with Arsenal), 1980 v Aus (6)
Tambling, R. V. (Chelsea), 1963 v W, F; 1966 v Y (3)
Tate, J. T. (Aston Villa), 1931 v F, Bel; 1933 v W (3)
Taylor, E. (Blackpool), 1954 v H (1)
Taylor, E. H. (Huddersfield T), 1923 v S, W, Ni, Bel; 1924 v S, Ni, F; 1926 v S (8)
Taylor, J. G. (Fulham), 1951 v Arg, P (2)
Taylor, P. H. (Liverpool), 1948 v W, Ni, Se (3)
Taylor, P. J. (C Palace), 1976 v W (sub+1), Ni, S (4)
Taylor, T. (Manchester U), 1953 v Arg, Ch, U; 1954 v Bel, Sw; 1956 v S, Br, Se, Fi, WG; 1957 v Ni, Y (sub), D (2), Ei (2); 1958 v W, Ni, F (19)
Temple, D. W. (Everton), 1965 v WG (1)
Terry, J. G. (Chelsea), 2003 v Ser (sub); 2004 v Cro, Mac, Lie, T, D, Se, J, Sw, Cro, P; 2005 v Uk, A, Pol, Sp, Ni, Az; 2006 v D, A, Pol, Arg, U, H, Jam, Para, Tr, Se, Ec, P (29)
Thickett, H. (Sheffield U), 1899 v S, W (2)
Thomas, D. (Coventry C), 1983 v Aus (1+1 sub) (2)
Thomas, D. (QPR), 1975 v Cz (sub), P, Cy (sub+1), W, S (sub); 1976 v Cz (sub), P (sub) (8)
Thomas, G. R. (C Palace), 1991 v T, USSR, Arg, Aus, Nz (2), Mal; 1992 v Pol, F (9)
Thomas, M. L. (Arsenal), 1989 v S.Ar; 1990 v Y (2)
Thompson, A. (Celtic), 2004 v Se (1)
Thompson, P. (Liverpool), 1964 v P (2), Ei, US, Br, Arg; 1965 v Ni, W, S, Bel, Ho; 1966 v Ni; 1968 v Ni, WG; 1970 v S, Ho (sub) (16)
Thompson, P. B. (Liverpool), 1976 v W (2), Ni, S, Br, I, Fi; 1977 v Fi; 1979 v Ei (sub), Cz, Ni, S, Bul, Se (sub), A; 1980 v D, Ni, Bul, Ei, Sp (2), Arg, W, S, Bel, I; 1981 v N, R, H; 1982 v N, H, W, Ho, S, Fi, F, Cz, K, WG, Sp; 1983 v WG, Gr (42)
Thompson T. (Aston Villa), 1952 v W; (with Preston NE), 1957 v S (2)
Thomson, R. A. (Wolverhampton W), 1964 v Ni, US, P, Arg; 1965 v Bel, Ho, Ni, W (8)
Thornewell, G. (Derby Co), 1923 v Se (2); 1924 v F; 1925 v F (4)
Thornley, I. (Manchester C), 1907 v W (1)
Tilson, S. F. (Manchester C), 1934 v H, Cz; 1935 v W; 1936 v Ni (4)
Titmuss, F. (Southampton), 1922 v W; 1923 v W (2)
Todd, C. (Derby Co), 1972 v Ni; 1974 v P, W, Ni, S, Arg, EG, Bul, Y; 1975 v P (sub), WG, Cy (2), Ni, W, S; 1976 v Sw, Cz, P, Ni, S, Br, Fi; 1977 v Ei, Fi, Ho (sub), Ni (27)
Toone, G. (Notts Co), 1892 v S, W (2)
Topham, A. G. (Casuals), 1894 v W (1)
Topham, R. (Wolverhampton W), 1893 v Ni; (with Casuals), 1894 v W (2)
Towers, M. A. (Sunderland), 1976 v W, Ni (sub), I (3)
Townley, W. J. (Blackburn R), 1889 v W; 1890 v Ni (2)
Townrow, J. E. (Clapton Orient), 1925 v S; 1926 v W (2)
Tremelling, D. R. (Birmingham), 1928 v W (1)
Tresadern, J. (West Ham U), 1923 v S, Se (2)
Tueart, D. (Manchester C), 1975 v Cy (sub), Ni; 1977 v Fi, Ni, W (sub), S (sub) (6)
Tunstall, F. E. (Sheffield U), 1923 v S; 1924 v S, W, Ni, F; 1925 v Ni, S (7)
Turnbull, R. J. (Bradford), 1920 v Ni (1)
Turner, A. (Southampton), 1900 v Ni; 1901 v Ni (2)
Turner, H. (Huddersfield T), 1931 v F, Bel (2)
Turner, J. A. (Bolton W), 1893 v W; (with Stoke C), 1895 v Ni; (with Derby Co), 1898 v Ni (3)
Tweedy, G. J. (Grimsby T), 1937 v H (1)

Ufton, D. G. (Charlton Ath), 1954 v R of E (1)
Underwood, A. (Stoke C), 1891 v Ni; 1892 v Ni (2)
Unsworth, D. G. (Everton), 1995 v J (1)
Upson, M. J. (Birmingham C), 2003 v S.Af (sub), Ser, Slo; 2004 v Cro (sub), Lie, D; 2005 v Sp (sub) (7)
Urwin, T. (Middlesbrough), 1923 v Se (2); 1924 v Bel; (with Newcastle U), 1926 v W (4)
Utley, G. (Barnsley), 1913 v Ni (1)

Vassell, D. (Aston Villa), 2002 v Ho, I (sub), Para, Sk, Cam, Se, Ng (sub), Br (sub); 2003 v Mac (sub), Aus (sub), T (sub), S.Af (sub), Ser (sub), Slo (sub); 2004 v T (sub), Se, J (sub), Ic (sub), F (sub), Sw (sub), Cro (sub), P (sub) (22)
Vaughton, O. H. (Aston Villa), 1882 v S, W, Ni; 1884 v S, W (5)
Veitch, C. C. M. (Newcastle U), 1906 v S, W, Ni; 1907 v S, W; 1909 v W (6)
Veitch, J. G. (Old Westminsters), 1894 v W (1)
Venables, T. F. (Chelsea), 1965 v Bel, Ho (2)
Venison, B. (Newcastle U), 1995 v US, U (2)
Vidal, R. W. S. (Oxford University), 1873 v S (1)
Viljoen, C. (Ipswich T), 1975 v Ni, W (2)
Viollet, D. S. (Manchester U), 1960 v H; 1962 v L (2)
Von Donop (Royal Engineers), 1873 v S; 1875 v S (2)

Wace, H. (Wanderers), 1878 v S; 1879 v S, W (3)
Waddle, C. R. (Newcastle U), 1985 v Ei, R (sub), Fi (sub), S (sub), I, M (sub), WG, US; (with Tottenham H), 1986 v R, T, Ni, Is, USSR, S, M, Ca, P, Mor, Pol (sub), Arg (sub); 1987 v Se (sub), Ni (2), Y, Sp, T, Br, S; 1988 v WG, Is, H, S (sub), Co, Sw (sub), Ei, Ho (sub); 1989 v Se, S.Ar, Alb (2), Ch, S, Pol, D (sub); (with Marseille), 1990 v Se, Pol, I, Y, Br, D, U, Tun, Ei, Ho, Eg, Bel, Cam, WG, I (sub); 1991 v H (sub), Pol (sub); 1992 v T (62)
Wadsworth, S. J. (Huddersfield T), 1922 v S; 1923 v S, Bel; 1924 v S, Ni; 1925 v S, Ni; 1926 v W; 1927 v Ni (9)
Wainscoat, W. R. (Leeds U), 1929 v S (1)
Waiters, A. K. (Blackpool), 1964 v Ei, Br; 1965 v W, Bel, Ho (5)
Walcott, T. J. (Arsenal), 2006 v H (sub) (1)
Walden, F. I. (Tottenham H), 1914 v S; 1922 v W (2)
Walker, D. S. (Nottingham F), 1989 v D (sub), Se (sub), Gr, Alb (2), Ch, S, Pol, D; 1990 v Se, Pol, I, Y, Br, Cz, D, U, Tun, Ei, Ho, Eg, Bel, Cam, WG, I; 1991 v H, Pol, Ei (2), Cam, T, Arg, Aus, Nz (2), Mal; 1992 v T, Pol, F, Cz, C, H, Br, Fi, D, F, Se; (with Sampdoria), 1993 v Sp, N, T, Sm, T, Ho, Pol, N, US (sub), Br, G; (with Sheffield W), 1994 v Sm (59)
Walker, I. M. (Tottenham H), 1996 v H (sub), Chn (sub); 1997 v I; (with Leicester C), 2004 v Ic (sub) (4)
Walker, W. H. (Aston Villa), 1921 v Ni; 1922 v Ni, W, S; 1923 v Se (2); 1924 v S; 1925 v Ni, W, S, Bel, F; 1926 v Ni, W, S; 1927 v Ni, W; 1933 v A (18)
Wall, G. (Manchester U), 1907 v W; 1908 v Ni; 1909 v S; 1910 v W, S; 1912 v S; 1913 v Ni (7)
Wallace, C. W. (Aston Villa), 1913 v W; 1914 v Ni; 1920 v S (3)
Wallace, D. L. (Southampton), 1986 v Eg (1)
Walsh, P. (Luton T), 1983 v Aus (2 + 1 sub); 1984 v F, W (5)
Walters, A. M. (Cambridge University), 1885 v S, N; 1886 v S; 1887 v S, W; (with Old Carthusians), 1889 v S, W; 1890 v S, W (9)
Walters, K. M. (Rangers), 1991 v Nz (1)
Walters, P. M. (Oxford University), 1885 v S, Ni; (with Old Carthusians), 1886 v S, W, Ni; 1887 v S, W; 1888 v S, Ni; 1889 v S, W; 1890 v S, W (13)
Walton, N. (Blackburn R), 1890 v Ni (1)
Ward, J. T. (Blackburn Olympic), 1885 v W (1)
Ward, P. (Brighton & HA), 1980 v Aus (sub) (1)
Ward, T. V. (Derby Co), 1948 v Bel; 1949 v W (2)
Waring, T. (Aston Villa), 1931 v F, Bel; 1932 v S, W, Ni (5)
Warner, C. (Upton Park), 1878 v S (1)
Warren, B. (Derby Co), 1906 v S, W, Ni; 1907 v S, W, Ni; 1908 v S, W, Ni, A (2), H, B; (with Chelsea), 1909 v S, Ni, W, H (2), A; 1911 v S, Ni, W (22)
Waterfield, G. S. (Burnley), 1927 v W (1)
Watson, D. (Norwich C), 1984 v Br, U, Ch; 1985 v M, US (sub); 1986 v S; (with Everton), 1987 v Ni; 1988 v Is, Ho, S, Sw (sub), USSR (12)
Watson, D. V. (Sunderland), 1974 v P, S (sub), Arg, EG, Bul, Y; 1975 v Cz, P, WG, Cy (2), Ni, W, S; (with Manchester C), 1976 v Sw, Cz (sub), P; 1977 v Ho, L, Ni, W, S, Br, Arg, U; 1978 v Sw, L, I, WG, Br, W, Ni, S, H; 1979 v D, Ei, Cz, Ni (2), W, S, Bul, Se, A; (with Werder Bremen), 1980 v D; (with Southampton), Ni, Bul, Ei, Sp (2), Arg, Ni, S, Bel, I; 1981 v N, R, Sw, R, W, S, Sw, H; (with Stoke C), 1982 v Ni, Ic (65)
Watson, V. M. (West Ham U), 1923 v W, S; 1930 v S, G, A (5)
Watson, W. (Burnley), 1913 v S; 1914 v Ni; 1920 v Ni (3)
Watson, W. (Sunderland), 1950 v Ni, I; 1951 v W, Y (4)
Weaver, S. (Newcastle U), 1932 v S, 1933 v S, Ni (3)

Webb, G. W. (West Ham U), 1911 v S, W (2)
Webb, N. J. (Nottingham F), 1988 v WG (sub), T, Y, Is, Ho, S, Sw, Ei, USSR (sub); 1989 v D, Se, Gr, Alb (2), Ch, S, Pol, D; (with Manchester U), 1990 v Se, I (sub); 1992 v F, H, Br (sub), Fi, D (sub), Se (26)
Webster, M. (Middlesbrough), 1930 v S, A, G (3)
Wedlock, W. J. (Bristol C), 1907 v S, Ni, W; 1908 v S, Ni, W, A (2), H, B; 1909 v S, W, Ni, H (2), A; 1910 v S, W, Ni; 1911 v S, W, Ni; 1912 v S, W, Ni; 1914 v W (26)
Weir, D. (Bolton W), 1889 v S, Ni (2)
Welch, R. de C. (Wanderers), 1872 v S; (with Harrow Chequers), 1874 v S (2)
Weller, K. (Leicester C), 1974 v W, Ni, S, Arg (4)
Welsh, D. (Charlton Ath), 1938 v G, Sw; 1939 v R (3)
West, G. (Everton), 1969 v W, Bul, M (3)
Westwood, R. W. (Bolton W), 1935 v S, W, Ho; 1936 v Ni, G; 1937 v W (6)
Whateley, O. (Aston Villa), 1883 v S, Ni (2)
Wheeler, J. E. (Bolton W), 1955 v Ni (1)
Wheldon, G. F. (Aston Villa), 1897 v Ni; 1898 v S, W, Ni (4)
White, D. (Manchester C), 1993 v Sp (1)
White, T. A. (Everton), 1933 v I (1)
Whitehead, J. (Accrington), 1893 v W; (with Blackburn R), 1894 v Ni (2)
Whitfeld, H. (Old Etonians), 1879 v W (1)
Whitham, M. (Sheffield U), 1892 v Ni (1)
Whitworth, S. (Leicester C), 1975 v WG, Cy, Ni, W, S; 1976 v Sw, P (7)
Whymark, T. J. (Ipswich T), 1978 v L (sub) (1)
Widdowson, S. W. (Nottingham F), 1880 v S (1)
Wignall, F. (Nottingham F), 1965 v W, Ho (2)
Wilcox, J. M. (Blackburn R), 1996 v H; 1999 v F (sub); (with Leeds U), 2000 v Arg (3)
Wilkes, A. (Aston Villa), 1901 v S, W; 1902 v S, W, Ni (5)
Wilkins, R. G. (Chelsea), 1976 v I; 1977 v Ei, Fi, Ni, Br, Arg, U; 1978 v Sw (sub), L, I, WG, W, Ni, S, H; 1979 v D, Ei, Cz, Ni, W, S, Bul, Se (sub), A; (with Manchester U), 1980 v D, Ni, Bul, Sp (2), Arg, W (sub), Ni, S, Bel, I; 1981 v Sp (sub), R, Br, W, S, Sw, H (sub); 1982 v Ni, W, Ho, S, Fi, F, Cz, K, WG, Sp; 1983 v D, WG; 1984 v D, Ni, W, S, USSR, Br, U, Ch; (with AC Milan), 1985 v EG, Fi, T, Ni, Ei, R, Fi, S, I, M; 1986 v T, Ni, Is, Eg, USSR, S, M, Ca, P, Mor; 1987 v Se, Y (sub) (84)
Wilkinson, B. (Sheffield U), 1904 v S (1)
Wilkinson, L. R. (Oxford University), 1891 v W (1)
Williams, B. F. (Wolverhampton W), 1949 v F; 1950 v S, W, Ei, I, P, Bel, Ch, US, Sp; 1951 v Ni, W, S, Y, Arg, P; 1952 v W, F; 1955 v S, WG, F, Sp, P; 1956 v W (24)
Williams, O. (Clapton Orient), 1923 v W, Ni (2)
Williams, S. (Southampton), 1983 v Aus (1+1 sub); 1984 v F; 1985 v EG, Fi, T (6)
Williams, W. (WBA), 1897 v Ni; 1898 v W, Ni, S; 1899 v W, Ni (6)
Williamson, E. C. (Arsenal), 1923 v Se (2) (2)
Williamson, R. G. (Middlesbrough), 1905 v Ni; 1911 v Ni, S, W; 1912 v S, W; 1913 v Ni (7)
Willingham, C. K. (Huddersfield T), 1937 v Fi; 1938 v S, G, Sw, F; 1939 v S, W, Ni, R of E, N, I, Y (12)
Willis, A. (Tottenham H), 1952 v F (1)
Wilshaw, D. J. (Wolverhampton W), 1954 v W, Sw, U; 1955 v S, F, Sp, P; 1956 v W, Ni, Fi, WG; 1957 v Ni (12)
Wilson, C. P. (Hendon), 1884 v S, W (2)
Wilson, C. W. (Oxford University), 1879 v W; 1881 v S (2)
Wilson, G. (Sheffield W), 1921 v S, W, Bel; 1922 v S, Ni; 1923 v S, W, Ni, Bel; 1924 v W, Ni, F (12)
Wilson, G. P. (Corinthians), 1900 v S, W (2)
Wilson, R. (Huddersfield T), 1960 v S, Y, Sp, H; 1962 v W, Ni, S, A, Sw, Pe, P, H, Arg, Bul, Br; 1963 v Ni, F, Br, Cz, EG, Sw; 1964 v W, S, R of W, U, P (2), Ei, Br, Arg; (with Everton), 1965 v S, H, Y, WG, Se; 1966 v WG (sub), W, Ni, A, Sp, Pol (2), Y, Fi, D, U, M, F, Arg, P, WG; 1967 v Ni, W, S, Cz, A; 1968 v Ni, S, USSR (2), Sp (2), Y (63)
Wilson, T. (Huddersfield T), 1928 v S (1)
Winckworth, W. N. (Old Westminsters), 1892 v W; 1893 v Ni (2)
Windridge, J. E. (Chelsea), 1908 v S, W, Ni, A (2), H, B; 1909 v Ni (8)
Wingfield-Stratford, C. V. (Royal Engineers), 1877 v S (1)
Winterburn, N. (Arsenal), 1990 v I (sub); 1993 v G (sub) (2)
Wise, D. F. (Chelsea), 1991 v T, USSR, Aus (sub), Nz (2); 1994 v N; 1995 v R (sub), Ng; 1996 v Co, N, P, H (sub); 2000 v Bel (sub), Arg, Br, Ma, P (sub), G, R; 2001 v F, Fi (21)
Withe, P. (Aston Villa), 1981 v Br, W, S; 1982 v N (sub), W, Ic; 1983 v H, Ni, S; 1984 v H (sub); 1985 v T (11)
Wollaston, C. H. R. (Wanderers), 1874 v S; 1875 v S; 1877 v S; 1880 v S (4)
Wolstenholme, S. (Everton), 1904 v S; (with Blackburn R), 1905 v W, Ni (3)
Wood, H. (Wolverhampton W), 1890 v S, W; 1896 v S (3)
Wood, R. E. (Manchester U), 1955 v Ni, W; 1956 v Fi (3)
Woodcock, A. S. (Nottingham F), 1978 v Ni; 1979 v Ei (sub), Cz, Bul (sub), Se; 1980 v Ni; (with Cologne), Bul, Ei, Sp (2), Arg, Bel, I; 1981 v N, R, Sw, R, W (sub), S; 1982 v Ni (sub), Ho, Fi (sub), WG (sub), Sp; (with Arsenal), 1983 v WG (sub), Gr, L, Gr; 1984 v L, F (sub), Ni, W, S, Br, U (sub); 1985 v EG, Fi, T, Ni; 1986 v R (sub), T (sub), Is (sub) (42)
Woodgate, J. S. (Leeds U), 1999 v Bul; 2003 v P (sub), Slo, Mac; (with Newcastle U), 2004 v Se (5)
Woodger, G. (Oldham Ath), 1911 v Ni (1)
Woodhall, G. (WBA), 1888 v S, W (2)
Woodley, V. R. (Chelsea), 1937 v S, N, Se, Fi; 1938 v S, W, Ni, Cz, G, Sw, F; 1939 v S, W, Ni, R of E, N, I, R, Y (19)
Woods, C. C. E. (Norwich C), 1985 v US; 1986 v Eg (sub), Is (sub), Ca (sub); (with Rangers), 1987 v Y, Sp (sub), Ni (sub), T, S; 1988 v Is, H, Sw (sub), USSR; 1989 v D (sub); 1990 v Br (sub), D (sub); 1991 v H, Pol, Ei, USSR, Aus, Nz (2), Mal; (with Sheffield W), 1992 v G, T, Pol, F, C, Br, Fi, D, F, Se; 1993 v Sp, N, T, Sm, T, Ho, Pol, N, US (43)
Woodward, V. J. (Tottenham H), 1903 v S, W, Ni; 1904 v S, Ni; 1905 v S, W, Ni; 1907 v S; 1908 v S, W, Ni, A (2), H, B; 1909 v W, Ni, H (2), A; (with Chelsea), 1910 v Ni; 1911 v W (23)
Woosnam, M. (Manchester C), 1922 v W (1)
Worrall, F. (Portsmouth), 1935 v Ho; 1937 v Ni (2)
Worthington, F. S. (Leicester C), 1974 v Ni (sub), S, Arg, EG, Bul, Y; 1975 v Cz, P (sub) (8)
Wreford-Brown, C. (Oxford University), 1889 v Ni; (with Old Carthusians), 1894 v W; 1895 v W; 1898 v S (4)
Wright, E, G. D. (Cambridge University), 1906 v W (1)
Wright, I. E. (C Palace), 1991 v Cam, Ei (sub), USSR, Nz; (with Arsenal), 1992 v H (sub); 1993 v N, T (2), Pol (sub), N (sub), US (sub), Br, G (sub); 1994 v Pol, Ho (sub), Sm, Gr (sub), N (sub); 1995 v US (sub), R; 1997 v Ge (sub), I (sub), M (sub), S.Af, I, F, Br (sub); 1998 v Mol, I, S.Ar (sub), Mor; (with West Ham U), 1999 v L (sub), CzR (33)
Wright, J. D. (Newcastle U), 1939 v N (1)
Wright, M. (Southampton), 1984 v W; 1985 v EG, Fi, T, Ei, R, I, WG; 1986 v R, T, Ni, Eg, USSR; 1987 v Y, Ni, S; (with Derby Co), 1988 v Is, Ho (sub), Co, Sw, Ei, Ho; 1990 v Cz (sub), Tun (sub), Ho, Eg, Bel, Cam, WG, I; 1991 v H, Pol, Ei (2), Cam, USSR, Arg, Aus, Nz, Mal; (with Liverpool), 1992 v F, Fi; 1993 v Sp; 1996 v Cro, H (45)
Wright, R. I. (Ipswich T), 2000 v Ma; (with Arsenal), 2002 v Ho (sub) (2)
Wright, T. J. (Everton), 1968 v USSR; 1969 v R (2), M (sub), U, Br; 1970 v W, Ho, Bel, R (sub), Br (11)
Wright, W. A. (Wolverhampton W), 1947 v S, W, Ni, Ei, Ho, F, Sw, P; 1948 v S, W, Ni, Bel, Se, I; 1949 v S, W, Ni, D, Sw, Se, N, F; 1950 v S, W, Ni, Ei, I, P, Bel, Ch, US, Sp; 1951 v Ni, S, Arg; 1952 v W, Ni, S, F, A (2), I, Sw; 1953 v Ni, W, S, Bel, Arg, Ch, U, US; 1954 v W, Ni, S, R of E, H (2), Y, Bel, Sw, U; 1955 v W, Ni, S, WG, F, Sp, P; 1956 v Ni, W, S, Br, Se, Fi, WG, D, Sp; 1957 v S, W, Ni, Y, D (2), Ei (2); 1958 v W, Ni, S, P, Y, USSR (3), Br, A, F; 1959 v W, Ni, S, USSR, I, Br, Pe, M, US (105)
Wright-Phillips, S. C. (Manchester C), 2005 v Uk (sub), Az (sub), Sp (sub), Ho; (with Chelsea), 2006 v W, Ni, Pol, U (sub) (8)
Wylie, J. G. (Wanderers), 1878 v S (1)

Yates, J. (Burnley), 1889 v Ni (1)
York, R. E. (Aston Villa), 1922 v S; 1926 v S (2)
Young, A. (Huddersfield T), 1933 v W; 1937 v S, H, N, Se; 1938 v G, Sw, F; 1939 v W (9)
Young, G. M. (Sheffield W), 1965 v W (1)
Young, L. P. (Charlton Ath), 2005 v US (sub), Co (sub); 2006 v W, Ni, A, Pol, Arg (7)
R. E. Evans also played for Wales against E, Ni, S;
J. Reynolds also played for Ireland against E, W, S.
J. H. Edwards also played for W v S.

NORTHERN IRELAND

Addis, D. J. (Cliftonville), 1922 v N (1)
Aherne, T. (Belfast C), 1947 v E; 1948 v S; 1949 v W; (with Luton T), 1950 v W (4)
Alexander, T. E. (Cliftonville), 1895 v S (1)
Allan, C. (Cliftonville), 1936 v E (1)
Allen, J. (Limavady), 1887 v E (1)
Anderson, J. (Distillery), 1925 v S.Af (1)
Anderson, T. (Manchester U), 1973 v Cy, E, S, W; 1974 v Bul, P; (with Swindon T), 1975 v S (sub); 1976 v Is; 1977 v Ho, Bel, WG, E, S, W, Ic; 1978 v Ic, Ho, Bel; (with Peterborough U), S, E, W; 1979 v D (sub) (22)
Anderson, W. (Linfield), 1898 v W, E, S; (with Cliftonville), 1899 v S (4)
Andrews, W. (Glentoran), 1908 v S; (with Grimsby T), 1913 v E, S (3)
Armstrong, G. J. (Tottenham H), 1977 v WG, E, W (sub), Ic (sub); 1978 v Bel, S, E, W; 1979 v Ei, D, Bul, E, Bul, E, S, W, D; 1980 v E, Ei, Is, S, E, W, Aus (3); 1981 v Se; (with Watford), P, S, P, S, Se; 1982 v S, Is, E, F, W, Y, Hon, Sp, A, F; 1983 v A, T, Alb, S, E, W; (with Real Mallorca), 1984 v A, WG, E, W, Fi; 1985 v R, Fi, E, Sp; (with WBA), 1986 v T, R (sub), E (sub), F (sub); (with Chesterfield), D (sub), Br (sub) (63)

Baird, C. P. (Southampton), 2003 v I, Sp; 2004 v Uk, Arm, Gr, N, Es, Ser, Bar, Stk, Tr; 2005 v Az, Ca, E, Pol, G; 2006 v Az, E, A, Es (20)
Baird, G. (Distillery), 1896 v S, E, W (3)
Baird, H. C. (Huddersfield T), 1939 v E (1)
Balfe, J. (Shelbourne), 1909 v E; 1910 v W (2)
Bambrick, J. (Linfield), 1929 v W, S, E; 1930 v W, S, E; 1932 v W; (with Chelsea), 1935 v W; 1936 v E, S; 1938 v W (11)
Banks, S. J. (Cliftonville), 1937 v W (1)
Barr, H. H. (Linfield), 1962 v E; (with Coventry C), 1963 v E, Pol (3)
Barron, J. H. (Cliftonville), 1894 v E, W, S; 1895 v S; 1896 v S; 1897 v E, W (7)
Barry, J. (Cliftonville), 1888 v W, S; 1889 v E (3)
Barry, J. (Bohemians), 1900 v S (1)
Baxter, R. A. (Distillery), 1887 v S (1)
Baxter, S. N. (Cliftonville), 1887 v W (1)
Bennett, L. V. (Dublin University), 1889 v W (1)
Best, G. (Manchester U), 1964 v W, U; 1965 v E, Ho (2), S, Sw (2), Alb; 1966 v S, E, Alb; 1967 v E; 1968 v S; 1969 v E, S, W, T; 1970 v S, E, W, USSR; 1971 v Cy (2), Sp, E, S, W; 1972 v USSR, Sp; 1973 v Bul; 1974 v P; (with Fulham), 1977 v Ho, Bel, WG; 1978 v Ic, Ho (37)
Bingham, W. L. (Sunderland), 1951 v F; 1952 v E, S, W; 1953 v E, S, F, W; 1954 v E, S, W; 1955 v E, S, W; 1956 v E, S, W; 1957 v E, S, W, P (2), I; 1958 v S, E, W, I (2), Arg, Cz (2), WG, F; (with Luton T), 1959 v E, S, W, Sp; 1960 v S, E, W; (with Everton), 1961 v E, S, WG (2), Gr, I; 1962 v E, Gr; 1963 v E, S, Pol (2), Sp; (with Port Vale), 1964 v S, E, Sp (56)
Black, K. T. (Luton T), 1988 v Fr (sub), Ma (sub); 1989 v Ei, H, Sp (2), Ch (sub); 1990 v H, N, U; 1991 v Y (2), D, A, Pol, Fa; (with Nottingham F), 1992 v Fa, A, D, S, Li, G; 1993 v Sp, D (sub), Alb, Ei (sub), Sp; 1994 v D (sub), Ei (sub), R (sub) (30)
Black, T. (Glentoran), 1901 v E (1)
Blair, H. (Portadown), 1928 v F; 1931 v S; 1932 v S; (with Swansea), 1934 v S (4)
Blair, J. (Cliftonville), 1907 v W, E, S; 1908 v E, S (5)
Blair, R. V. (Oldham Ath), 1975 v Se (sub), S (sub), W; 1976 v Se, Is (5)
Blanchflower, J. (Manchester U), 1954 v W; 1955 v E, S; 1956 v S, W; 1957 v S, E, P; 1958 v S, E, I (2) (12)
Blanchflower, R. D. (Barnsley), 1950 v S, W; 1951 v E, S; (with Aston Villa), F; 1952 v W; 1953 v E, S, W, F; 1954 v E, S, W; 1955 v E, S; (with Tottenham H), W; 1956 v E, S, W; 1957 v E, S, W, I, P (2); 1958 v E, S, W, I (2), Cz (2), Arg, F, WG; 1959 v E, S, W, Sp; 1960 v E, S, W; 1961 v E, S, W, WG (2); 1962 v E, S, W, Gr, Ho; 1963 v E, S, Pol (2) (56)
Blayney, A. (Doncaster R), 2006 v R (1)
Bookman, L. J. O. (Bradford C), 1914 v W; (with Luton T), 1921 v S, W; 1922 v E (4)
Bothwell, A. W. (Ards), 1926 v S, E, W; 1927 v E, W (5)
Bowler, G. C. (Hull C), 1950 v E, S, W (3)
Boyle, P. (Sheffield U), 1901 v E; 1902 v E; 1903 v S, W; 1904 v E (5)
Braithwaite, R. M. (Linfield), 1962 v W; 1963 v Pol, Sp; (with Middlesbrough), 1964 v W, U; 1965 v E, S, Sw (2), Ho (10)
Breen, T. (Belfast C), 1935 v E, W; 1937 v E, S; (with Manchester U), 1937 v W; 1938 v E, S; 1939 v W, S (9)
Brennan, B. (Bohemians), 1912 v W (1)
Brennan, R. A. (Luton T), 1949 v W; (with Birmingham C), 1950 v E, S, W; (with Fulham), 1951 v E (5)
Briggs, W. R. (Manchester U), 1962 v W; (with Swansea T), 1965 v Ho (2)
Brisby, D. (Distillery), 1891 v S (1)
Brolly, T. H. (Millwall), 1937 v W; 1938 v W; 1939 v E, W (4)
Brookes, E. A. (Shelbourne), 1920 v S (1)
Brotherston, N. (Blackburn R), 1980 v S, E, W, Aus (3); 1981 v Se, P; 1982 v S, Is, E, F, S, W, Hon (sub), A (sub); 1983 v A (sub), WG, Alb, T, Alb, S (sub), E (sub), W; 1984 v T; 1985 v Is (sub), T (27)
Brown, J. (Glenavon), 1921 v W; (with Tranmere R), 1924 v E, W (3)
Brown, J. (Wolverhampton W), 1935 v E, W; 1936 v E; (with Coventry C), 1937 v E, W; 1938 v S, W; (with Birmingham C), 1939 v E, S, W (10)
Brown, N. M. (Limavady), 1887 v E (1)
Brown, W. G. (Glenavon), 1926 v W (1)
Browne, F. (Cliftonville), 1887 v E, S, W; 1888 v E, S (5)
Browne, R. J. (Leeds U), 1936 v E, W; 1938 v E, W; 1939 v E, S (6)
Bruce, A. (Belfast C), 1925 v S.Af (1)
Bruce, W. (Glentoran), 1961 v S; 1967 v W (2)
Brunt, C. (Sheffield W), 2005 v Sw (sub), G (sub); 2006 v Ma (sub), W (sub), A, P, Es (7)
Buckle, H. R. (Cliftonville), 1903 v S; (with Sunderland), 1904 v E; (with Bristol R), 1908 v W (3)
Buckle, J. (Cliftonville), 1882 v E (1)
Burnett, J. (Distillery), 1894 v E, W, S; (with Glentoran), 1895 v E, W (5)
Burnison, J. (Distillery), 1901 v E, W (2)
Burnison, S. (Distillery), 1908 v E; 1910 v E, S; (with Bradford), 1911 v E, S, W; (with Distillery), 1912 v E; 1913 v W (8)
Burns, J. (Glenavon), 1923 v E (1)
Burns, W. (Glentoran), 1925 v S.Af (1)
Butler, M. P. (Blackpool), 1939 v W (1)

Campbell, A. C. (Crusaders), 1963 v W; 1965 v Sw (2)
Campbell, D. A. (Nottingham F), 1986 v Mor (sub), Br; 1987 v E (2), T, Y; (with Charlton Ath), 1988 v Y, T (sub), Gr (sub), Pol (sub) (10)
Campbell, James (Cliftonville), 1897 v E, S, W; 1898 v E, S, W; 1899 v E; 1900 v E, S; 1901 v S, W; 1902 v S; 1903 v E; 1904 v S (14)
Campbell, John (Cliftonville), 1896 v W (1)
Campbell, J. P. (Fulham), 1951 v E, S (2)
Campbell, R. M. (Bradford C), 1982 v S, W (sub) (2)
Campbell, W. G. (Dundee), 1968 v S, E; 1969 v T; 1970 v S, W, USSR (6)
Capaldi, A. C. (Plymouth Arg), 2004 v Es, Ser, Bar, Stk, Tr; 2005 v Sw, Pol, W, Ca, E, Pol; 2006 v Az, E, W, P, Es, U, R (18)
Carey, J. J. (Manchester U), 1947 v E, S, W; 1948 v E; 1949 v E, S, W (7)
Carroll, E. (Glenavon), 1925 v S (1)
Carroll, R. E. (Wigan Ath), 1997 v Th (sub); 1999 v Ei (sub); 2000 v L, Ma; 2001 v Ma, D, Ic, CzR, Bul; (with Manchester U), 2002 v Lie (sub), Sp (sub); 2003 v Fi (sub), I (sub); 2004 v Ser (sub); 2005 v Sw, A, Ca (sub) (17)
Casey, T. (Newcastle U), 1955 v W; 1956 v W; 1957 v E, S, W, I, P (2); 1958 v WG, F; (with Portsmouth), 1959 v E, Sp (12)
Caskey, W. (Derby Co), 1979 v Bul, E, Bul, E, S (sub), D (sub); 1980 v E (sub); (with Tulsa R), 1982 v F (sub) (8)
Cassidy, T. (Newcastle U), 1971 v E (sub); 1972 v USSR (sub); 1974 v Bul (sub), S, E, W; 1975 v N; 1976 v S, E, W; 1977 v WG (sub); 1980 v E, Ei (sub), Is, S, E, W, Aus (3); (with Burnley), 1981 v Se, P; 1982 v Is, Sp (sub) (24)
Caughey, M. (Linfield), 1986 v F (sub), D (sub) (2)
Chambers, R. J. (Distillery), 1921 v W; (with Bury), 1928 v E, S, W; 1929 v E, S, W; 1930 v S, W; (with Nottingham F), 1932 v E, S, W (12)
Chatton, H. A. (Partick Th), 1925 v E, S; 1926 v E (3)
Christian, J. (Linfield), 1889 v S (1)
Clarke, C. J. (Bournemouth), 1986 v F, D, Mor, Alg (sub), Sp, Br; (with Southampton), 1987 v E, T, Y; 1988 v Y, T, Gr, Pol, F, Ma; 1989 v Ei, H, Sp (1+1 sub); (with QPR), Ma, Ch; 1990 v H, Ei, N; (with Portsmouth), 1991 v Y (sub), D, A, Pol, Y (sub), Fa; 1992 v Fa, A, D, S, G; 1993 v Alb, Sp, D (38)
Clarke, R. (Belfast C), 1901 v E, S (2)
Cleary, J. (Glentoran), 1982 v S, W; 1983 v W (sub); 1984 v T (sub); 1985 v Is (5)

Clements, D. (Coventry C), 1965 v W, Ho; 1966 v M; 1967 v S, W; 1968 v S, E; 1969 v T (2), S, W; 1970 v S, E, W, USSR (2); 1971 v Sp, E, S, W, Cy; (with Sheffield W), 1972 v USSR (2), Sp, E, S, W; 1973 v Bul, Cy (2), P, E, S, W; (with Everton), 1974 v Bul, P, S, E, W; 1975 v N, Y, E, S, W; 1976 v Se, Y; (with New York Cosmos), E, W (48)
Clingan, S. G. (Nottingham F), 2006 v U, R (2)
Clugston, J. (Cliftonville), 1888 v W; 1889 v W, S, E; 1890 v E, S; 1891 v E, W; 1892 v E, S, W; 1893 v E, S, W (14)
Clyde, M. G. (Wolverhampton W), 2005 v W, Az, G (3)
Cochrane, D. (Leeds U), 1939 v E, W; 1947 v E, S, W; 1948 v E, S, W; 1949 v S, W; 1950 v S, E (12)
Cochrane, G. (Cliftonville), 1903 v S (1)
Cochrane, G. T. (Coleraine), 1976 v N (sub); (with Burnley), 1978 v S (sub), E (sub), W (sub); 1979 v Ei (sub); (with Middlesbrough), D, Bul, E, Bul, E; 1980 v Is, E (sub), W (sub), Aus (1+2 sub); 1981 v Se (sub), P (sub), S, P, S, Se; 1982 v E (sub), F; (with Gillingham), 1984 v S, Fi (sub) (26)
Cochrane, M. (Distillery), 1898 v S, W, E; 1899 v E; 1900 v E, S, W; (with Leicester Fosse), 1901 v S (8)
Collins, F. (Celtic), 1922 v S (1)
Collins, R. (Cliftonville), 1922 v N (1)
Condy, J. (Distillery), 1882 v W; 1886 v E, S (3)
Connell, T. E. (Coleraine), 1978 v W (sub) (1)
Connor, J. (Glentoran), 1901 v S, E; (with Belfast C), 1905 v E, S, W; 1907 v E, S; 1908 v E, S; 1909 v W; 1911 v S, E, W (13)
Connor, M. J. (Brentford), 1903 v S, W; (with Fulham), 1904 v E (3)
Cook, W. (Celtic), 1933 v E, W, S; (with Everton), 1935 v E; 1936 v S, W; 1937 v E, S, W; 1938 v E, S, W; 1939 v E, S, W (15)
Cooke, S. (Belfast YMCA), 1889 v E; (with Cliftonville), 1890 v E, S (3)
Coote, A. (Norwich C), 1999 v Ca, Ei (sub); 2000 v Fi (sub), L (sub), Ma (sub), H (sub) (6)
Coulter, J. (Belfast C), 1934 v E, S, W; (with Everton), 1935 v E, S, W; 1937 v S, W; (with Grimsby T), 1938 v S, W; (with Chelmsford C), 1939 v S (11)
Cowan, J. (Newcastle U), 1970 v E (sub) (1)
Cowan, T. S. (Queen's Island), 1925 v W (1)
Coyle, F. (Coleraine), 1956 v E, S; 1957 v P; (with Nottingham F), 1958 v Arg (4)
Coyle, L. (Derry C), 1989 v Ch (sub) (1)
Coyle, R. I. (Sheffield W), 1973 v P, Cy (sub), W (sub); 1974 v Bul (sub), P (sub) (5)
Craig, A. B. (Rangers), 1908 v E, S, W; 1909 v S; (with Morton), 1912 v S, W; 1914 v E, S, W (9)
Craig, D. J. (Newcastle U), 1967 v W; 1968 v W; 1969 v T (2), E, S, W; 1970 v E, S, W, USSR; 1971 v Cy (2), Sp, S (sub); 1972 v USSR, S (sub); 1973 v Cy (2), E, S, W; 1974 v Bul, P; 1975 v N (25)
Craigan, S. J. (Partick Th), 2003 v Fi (sub), Arm, Gr; (with Motherwell), 2004 v Es, Ser, Bar, Stk, Tr; 2005 v Sw, Pol, Ca (sub), G; 2006 v Ma, Az, E, W, A, P, Es, U, R (21)
Crawford, A. (Distillery), 1889 v E, W; (with Cliftonville), 1891 v E, S, W; 1893 v E, W (7)
Croft, T. (Queen's Island), 1922 v N; 1924 v E; 1925 v S.Af (3)
Crone, R. (Distillery), 1889 v S; 1890 v E, S, W (4)
Crone, W. (Distillery), 1882 v W; 1884 v E, S, W; 1886 v E, S, W; 1887 v E; 1888 v E, W; 1889 v S; 1890 v W (12)
Crooks, W. J. (Manchester U), 1922 v W (1)
Crossan, E. (Blackburn R), 1950 v S; 1951 v E; 1955 v W (3)
Crossan, J. A. (Sparta-Rotterdam), 1960 v E; (with Sunderland), 1963 v W, P, Sp; 1964 v E, S, W, U, Sp; 1965 v E, S, Sw (2); (with Manchester C), W, Ho (2), Alb; 1966 v S, E, Alb, WG; 1967 v E, S; (with Middlesbrough), 1968 v S (24)
Crothers, C. (Distillery), 1907 v W (1)
Cumming, L. (Huddersfield T), 1929 v W, S; (with Oldham Ath), 1930 v E (3)
Cunningham, W. (Ulster), 1892 v S, E, W; 1893 v E (4)
Cunningham, W. E. (St Mirren), 1951 v W; 1953 v E; 1954 v S; 1955 v S; (with Leicester C), 1956 v E, S, W; 1957 v E, S, W, I, P (2); 1958 v S, W, I, Cz (2), Arg, WG, F; 1959 v E, S, W; 1960 v E, S, W; (with Dunfermline Ath), 1961 v W; 1962 v W, Ho (30)
Curran, S. (Belfast C), 1926 v S, W; 1928 v F, S (4)
Curran, J. J. (Glenavon), 1922 v W, N; (with Pontypridd), 1923 v E, S; (with Glenavon), 1924 v E (5)
Cush, W. W. (Glenavon), 1951 v E, S; 1954 v S, E; 1957 v W, I, P (2); (with Leeds U), 1958 v I (2), W, Cz (2), Arg, WG, F; 1959 v E, S, W, Sp; 1960 v E, S, W; (with Portadown), 1961 v WG, Gr; 1962 v Gr (26)

Dalrymple, J. (Distillery), 1922 v N (1)
Dalton, W. (YMCA), 1888 v S; (with Linfield), 1890 v S, W; 1891 v S, W; 1892 v E, S, W; 1894 v E, S, W (11)
D'Arcy, S. D. (Chelsea), 1952 v W; 1953 v E; (with Brentford), 1953 v S, W, F (5)
Darling, J. (Linfield), 1897 v E, S; 1900 v S; 1902 v E, S, W; 1903 v E, S (2), W; 1905 v E, S, W; 1906 v E, S, W; 1908 v W; 1909 v E; 1910 v E, S, W; 1912 v S (22)
Davey, H. H. (Reading), 1926 v E; 1927 v E, S; 1928 v E; (with Portsmouth), 1928 v W (5)
Davis, S. (Aston Villa), 2005 v Ca, E (sub), Pol, G; 2006 v Ma, Az, E, W, A, P, Es, U, R (13)
Davis, T. L. (Oldham Ath), 1937 v E (1)
Davison, A. J. (Bolton W), 1996 v Se; (with Bradford C), 1997 v Th; (with Grimsby T), 1998 v G (3)
Davison, J. R. (Cliftonville), 1882 v E, W; 1883 v E, W; 1884 v E, W, S; 1885 v E (8)
Dennison, R. (Wolverhampton W), 1988 v F, Ma; 1989 v H, Sp Ch (sub); 1990 v Ei, U; 1991 v Y (2), A. Pol, Fa (sub); 1992 v Fa, A, D (sub); 1993 v Sp (sub); 1994 v Co (sub); 1997 v I (sub) (18)
Devine, A. O. (Limavady), 1886 v E, W; 1887 v W; 1888 v W (4)
Devine, J. (Glentoran), 1990 v U (sub) (1)
Dickson, D. (Coleraine), 1970 v S (sub), W; 1973 v Cy, P (4)
Dickson, T. A. (Linfield), 1957 v S (1)
Dickson, W. (Chelsea), 1951 v W, F; 1952 v E, S, W; 1953 v E, S, W, F; (with Arsenal), 1954 v E, W; 1955 v E (12)
Diffin, W. J. (Belfast C), 1931 v W (1)
Dill, A. H. (Knock), 1882 v E, W; (with Down Ath), 1883 v W; (with Cliftonville), 1884 v E, S, W; 1885 v E, S, W (9)
Doherty, I. (Belfast C), 1901 v E (1)
Doherty, J. (Portadown), 1928 v F (1)
Doherty, J. (Cliftonville), 1933 v E, W (2)
Doherty, L. (Linfield), 1985 v Is; 1988 v T (sub) (2)
Doherty, M. (Derry C), 1938 v S (1)
Doherty, P. D. (Blackpool), 1935 v E, W; 1936 v E, S; (with Manchester C), 1937 v E, W; 1938 v E, S; 1939 v E, W; (with Derby Co), 1947 v E; (with Huddersfield T), W; 1948 v E, W; 1949 v S; (with Doncaster R), 1951 v S (16)
Doherty, T. E. (Bristol C), 2003 v I, Sp; 2004 v Uk, Arm, Ser; 2005 v Az, A, Ca, E (9)
Donaghey, B. (Belfast C), 1903 v S (1)
Donaghy, M. M. (Luton T), 1980 v S, E, W; 1981 v Se, P, S (sub); 1982 v S, Is, E, F, S, W, Y, Hon, Sp, F; 1983 v A, WG, Alb, T, Alb, S, E, W; 1984 v A, T, WG, S, E, W, Fi; 1985 v R, Fi, E, Sp, T; 1986 v T, R, E, F, D, Mor, Alg, Sp, Br; 1987 v E (2), T, Is, Y; 1988 v Y, T, Gr, Pol, F, Ma; 1989 v Ei, H; (with Manchester U), Sp (2), Ma, Ch; 1990 v Ei, N; 1991 v Y (2), D, A, Pol, Fa; 1992 v Fa, A, D, S, Li, G; (with Chelsea), 1993 v Alb, Sp, D, Alb, Ei, Sp, Li, La; 1994 v La, D, Ei, R, Lie, Co, M (91)
Donnelly, L. (Distillery), 1913 v W (1)
Doran, J. F. (Brighton), 1921 v E; 1922 v E, W (3)
Dougan, A. D. (Portsmouth), 1958 v Cz; (with Blackburn R), 1960 v S; 1961 v E, W, I, Gr; (with Aston Villa), 1963 v S, Pol (2); (with Leicester C), 1966 v S, E, Alb, W, WG, M; 1967 v E, S; (with Wolverhampton W), W; 1968 v S, W; 1969 v Is, T (2), E, S, W; 1970 v USSR (2), S, E; 1971 v Sp, Cy (2), E, S, W; 1972 v USSR (2), S, E, W; 1973 v Bul, Cy (43)
Douglas, J. P. (Belfast C), 1947 v E (1)
Dowd, H. O. (Glenavon), 1974 v W; (with Sheffield W), 1975 v N (sub), Se (3)
Dowie, I. (Luton T), 1990 v N (sub), U; 1991 v Y, D, A (sub), (with West Ham U), Y, Fa; (with Southampton) 1992 v Fa, A, D (sub), S (sub), Li; 1993 v Alb (2), Ei, Sp (sub), Li, La; 1994 v La, D, Ei (sub), R (sub), Lie, Co, M (sub); 1995 v A, Ei; (with C Palace), Ei, La, Ca, Ch, La; 1996 v P; (with West Ham U), A, N, G; 1997 v Uk, Arm, G, Alb, P, Uk, Arm, Th; 1998 v Alb, P; (with QPR), Slo, Sw, Sp; 1999 v T, Fi, Mol, G, Mol, Ca, Ei; 2000 v F, T, G (59)
Duff, M. J. (Cheltenham T), 2002 v Pol (sub); 2003 v Cy (sub); 2004 v Es (sub); (with Burnley), 2005 v Sw (sub); 2006 v E (sub), W, A, Es, U, R (10)
Duggan, H. A. (Leeds U), 1930 v E; 1931 v E, W; 1933 v E; 1934 v E; 1935 v S, W; 1936 v S (8)
Dunlop, G. (Linfield), 1985 v Is; 1987 v E, Y; 1990 v Ei (4)
Dunne, J. (Sheffield U), 1928 v W; 1931 v W, E; 1932 v E, S; 1933 v E, W (7)

Eames, W. L. E. (Dublin U), 1885 v E, S, W (3)
Eglington, T. J. (Everton), 1947 v S, W; 1948 v E, S, W; 1949 v E (6)
Elder, A. R. (Burnley), 1960 v W; 1961 v S, E, W, WG (2), Gr; 1962 v E, S, Gr; 1963 v E, S, W, Pol (2), Sp; 1964 v W, U; 1965 v E, S, W, Sw (2), Ho (2), Alb; 1966 v E, S, W, M, Alb; 1967 v E, S, W; (with Stoke C), 1968 v E, W; 1969 v E (sub), S, W; 1970 v USSR (40)

Elleman, A. R. (Cliftonville), 1889 v W; 1890 v E (2)
Elliott, S. (Motherwell), 2001 v Ma, D, Ic, N (sub), CzR, Bul (2), CzR; 2002 v D (sub), Ma, Pol (sub), Lie (sub), Sp; (with Hull C), 2003 v Fi (sub), Arm (sub), I (sub); 2004 v Gr, Bar (sub), Stk, Tr; 2005 v Sw, Pol, Az, A (sub), E, Pol (sub), G; 2006 v Ma, Az, E, W, A (sub), P, Es (sub) (34)
Elwood, J. H. (Bradford), 1929 v W; 1930 v E (2)
Emerson, W. (Glentoran), 1920 v E, S, W; 1921 v E; 1922 v E, S; (with Burnley), 1922 v W; 1923 v E, S, W; 1924 v E (11)
English, S. (Rangers), 1933 v W, S (2)
Enright, J. (Leeds C), 1912 v S (1)

Falloon, E. (Aberdeen), 1931 v S; 1933 v S (2)
Farquharson, T. G. (Cardiff C), 1923 v S, W; 1924 v E, S, W; 1925 v E, S (7)
Farrell, P. (Distillery), 1901 v S, W (2)
Farrell, P. (Hibernian), 1938 v W (1)
Farrell, P. D. (Everton), 1947 v S, W; 1948 v E, S, W; 1949 v E, W (7)
Feeney, J. M. (Linfield), 1947 v S; (with Swansea T), 1950 v E (2)
Feeney, W. (Glentoran), 1976 v Is (1)
Feeney, W. J. (Bournemouth), 2002 v Lie, Sp; 2003 v Cy (sub); (with Luton T), 2005 v Pol (sub), G (sub); 2006 v Ma (sub), Az (sub), E (sub), A (sub), P, Es (sub) (11)
Ferguson, G. (Linfield), 1999 v Ca (sub); 2001 v N, CzR (sub), Bul (sub), CzR (sub) (5)
Ferguson, W. (Linfield), 1966 v M; 1967 v E (2)
Ferris, J. (Belfast C), 1920 v E, W; (with Chelsea), 1921 v S, E; (with Belfast C), 1928 v F, S (6)
Ferris, R. O. (Birmingham C), 1950 v S; 1951 v F; 1952 v S (3)
Fettis, A. W. (Hull C), 1992 v D, Li; 1993 v D; 1994 v M; 1995 v P, Ei, La, Ca, Ch, La; 1996 v P, Lie, A; (with Nottingham F), v N, G; 1997 v Uk, Arm (2); (with Blackburn R), 1998 v P, Slo, Sw, Sp; 1999 v T, Fi, Mol (25)
Finney, T. (Sunderland), 1975 v N, E (sub), S, W; 1976 v N, Y, S; (with Cambridge U), 1980 v E, Is, S, E, W, Aus (2) (14)
Fitzpatrick, J. C. (Bohemians), 1896 v E, S (2)
Flack, H. (Burnley), 1929 v S (1)
Fleming, J. G. (Nottingham F), 1987 v E (2), Is, Y; 1988 v T, Gr, Pol; 1989 v Ma, Ch; (with Manchester C), 1990 v H, Ei; (with Barnsley), 1991 v Y; 1992 v Li (sub), G; 1993 v Alb, Sp, D, Alb, Sp, Li, La; 1994 v La, D, Ei, R, Lie, Co, M; 1995 v P, A, Ei (31)
Forbes, G. (Limavady), 1888 v W; (with Distillery), 1891 v E, S (3)
Forde, J. T. (Ards), 1959 v Sp; 1961 v E, S, WG (4)
Foreman, T. A. (Cliftonville), 1899 v S (1)
Forsythe, J. (YMCA), 1888 v E, S (2)
Fox, W. T. (Ulster), 1887 v E, S (2)
Frame, T. (Linfield), 1925 v S.Af (1)
Fulton, R. P. (Larne), 1928 v F; (Belfast C), 1930 v W; 1931 v E, S, W; 1932 v W, E; 1933 v E, S; 1934 v E, W, S; 1935 v E, W, S; 1936 v S, W; 1937 v E, S, W; 1938 v W (21)

Gaffikin, G. (Linfield Ath), 1890 v S, W; 1891 v S, W; 1892 v E, S, W; 1893 v E, S, W; 1894 v E, S, W; 1895 v E, W (15)
Galbraith, W. (Distillery), 1890 v W (1)
Gallagher, P. (Celtic), 1920 v E, S; 1922 v S; 1923 v S, W; 1924 v S, W; 1925 v S, W, E; (with Falkirk), 1927 v S (11)
Gallogly, C. (Huddersfield T), 1951 v E, S (2)
Gara, A. (Preston NE), 1902 v E, S, W (3)
Gardiner, A. (Cliftonville), 1930 v S, W; 1931 v S; 1932 v E, S (5)
Garrett, J. (Distillery), 1925 v W (1)
Gaston, R. (Oxford U), 1969 v Is (sub) (1)
Gaukrodger, G. (Linfield), 1895 v W (1)
Gaussen, A. D. (Moyola Park), 1884 v E, S; (with Magherafelt), 1888 v E, W; 1889 v E, W (6)
Geary, J. (Glentoran), 1931 v S; 1932 v S (2)
Gibb, J. T. (Wellington Park) 1884 v S, W; 1885 v S, E, W; 1886 v S; 1887 v S, E, W; (with Cliftonville), 1889 v S (10)
Gibb, T. J. (Cliftonville), 1936 v W (1)
Gibson W. K. (Cliftonville), 1894 v S, W, E; 1895 v S; 1897 v W; 1898 v S, W, E; 1901 v S, W, E; 1902 v S, W; 1903 v S (14)
Gillespie, K. R. (Manchester U), 1995 v P, A, Ei; (with Newcastle U), Ei, La, Ca, Ch (sub), La (sub); 1996 v P, A, N, G; 1997 v Uk, Arm, Bel, P, Uk; 1998 v G, Alb, Slo, Sw; 1999 v T, Fi, Mol; (with Blackburn R), G, Mol; 2000 v F (sub), T (sub), G (sub), L, Ma, H; 2001 v Y (sub), CzR, Bul (2); 2002 v D, Ic, Pol, Lie, Sp; 2003 v Cy, Sp, Uk, Fi, Arm, Gr; (with Leicester C), 2004 v Uk, Arm, Gr, N, Ser, Bar, Stk (sub), Tr (sub); 2005 v Sw, Az (sub), A, Ca, E, Pol, G; (with Sheffield U), 2006 v Ma, Az, E, W, A, P (68)
Gillespie, S. (Hertford), 1886 v E, S, W; 1887 v E, S, W (6)
Gillespie, W. (Sheffield U), 1913 v E, S; 1914 v E, W; 1920 v S, W; 1921 v E; 1922 v E, S, W; 1923 v E, S, W; 1924 v E, S, W; 1925 v E, S; 1926 v S, W; 1927 v E, W; 1928 v E; 1929 v E; 1931 v E (25)
Gillespie, W. (West Down), 1889 v W (1)
Goodall, A. L. (Derby Co), 1899 v S, W; 1900 v E, W; 1901 v E; 1902 v S; 1903 v E, W; (with Glossop), 1904 v E, W (10)
Goodbody, M. F. (Dublin University), 1889 v E; 1891 v W (2)
Gordon, H. (Linfield), 1895 v E; 1896 v E, S (3)
Gordon R. W. (Linfield), 1891 v S; 1892 v W, E, S; 1893 v E, S, W (7)
Gordon, T. (Linfield), 1894 v W; 1895 v E (2)
Gorman, W. C. (Brentford), 1947 v E, S, W; 1948 v W (4)
Gough, J. (Queen's Island), 1925 v S.Af (1)
Gowdy, J. (Glentoran), 1920 v E; (with Queen's Island), 1924 v W; (with Falkirk), 1926 v E, S; 1927 v E, S (6)
Gowdy, W. A. (Hull C), 1932 v S; (with Sheffield W), 1933 v S; (with Linfield), 1935 v E, S, W; (with Hibernian), 1936 v W (6)
Graham, W. G. L. (Doncaster R), 1951 v W, F; 1952 v E, S, W; 1953 v S, F; 1954 v E, W; 1955 v S, W; 1956 v E, S; 1959 v E (14)
Gray, P. (Luton T), 1993 v D (sub), Alb, Ei, Sp; (with Sunderland), 1994 v La, D, Ei, R, Lie (sub); 1995 v P, A, Ei, Ca, Ch (sub); 1996 v P (sub), Lie, A; (with Nancy), 1997 v Uk, Arm, G (sub); (with Luton T), 1999 v Mol (sub); (with Burnley), 2001 v Ma (sub), D (sub), Ic (sub); (with Oxford U), N (sub), CzR (sub) (26)
Greer, W. (QPR), 1909 v E, S, W (3)
Gregg, H. (Doncaster R), 1954 v W; 1957 v E, S, W, I, P (2); 1958 v E, I; (with Manchester U), 1958 v Cz, Arg, WG, F, W; 1959 v E, W; 1960 v S, E, W; 1961 v E, S; 1962 v S, Gr; 1964 v S, E (25)
Griffin, D. J. (St Johnstone), 1996 v G; 1997 v Uk, I, Bel (sub), Th; 1998 v G (sub), Alb; 1999 v Mol, Ei (sub); 2000 v L, Ma, H; (with Dundee U), 2001 v Y (sub), N (sub), CzR, Bul (2), CzR; 2002 v D, Ic, Ma, Pol; 2003 v Cy, I, Sp; 2004 v Uk, Arm, Gr; (with Stockport Co), N (29)

Hall, G. (Distillery), 1897 v E (1)
Halligan, W. (Derby Co), 1911 v W; (with Wolverhampton W), 1912 v E (2)
Hamill, M. (Manchester U), 1912 v E; 1914 v E, S; (with Belfast C), 1920 v E, S, W; (with Manchester C), 1921 v S (7)
Hamill, R. (Glentoran), 1999 v Ca (sub) (1)
Hamilton, B. (Linfield), 1969 v T; 1971 v Cy (2), E, S, W; (with Ipswich T), 1972 v USSR (1+1 sub), Sp; 1973 v Bul, Cy (2), P, E, S, W; 1974 v Bul, S, E, W; 1975 v N, Se, Y, E; 1976 v Se, N, Y; (with Everton), Is, S, E, W; 1977 v Ho, Bel, WG, E, S, W, Ic; (with Millwall), 1978 v S, E, W; 1979 v Ei (sub); (with Swindon T), Bul (2), E, S, W, D; 1980 v Aus (2 sub) (50)
Hamilton, G. (Portadown), 2003 v I (sub); 2004 v Ser (sub), Bar (sub), Stk; 2005 v Sw (sub) (5)
Hamilton, J. (Knock), 1882 v E, W (2)
Hamilton, R. (Rangers), 1928 v S; 1929 v E; 1930 v S, E; 1932 v S (5)
Hamilton, W. D. (Dublin Association), 1885 v W (1)
Hamilton, W. J. (Distillery), 1908 v W (1)
Hamilton, W. J. (Dublin Association), 1885 v W (1)
Hamilton, W. R. (QPR), 1978 v S (sub); (with Burnley), 1980 v S, E, W, Aus (2); 1981 v Se, P, S, P, S, Se; 1982 v S, Is, E, W, Y, Hon, Sp, A, F; 1983 v A, WG, Alb (2), S, E, W; 1984 v A, T, WG, S, E, W, Fi; (with Oxford U), 1985 v R, Sp; 1986 v Mor (sub), Alg, Sp (sub), Br (sub) (41)
Hampton, H. (Bradford C), 1911 v E, S, W; 1912 v E, W; 1913 v E, S, W; 1914 v E (9)
Hanna, J. (Nottingham F), 1912 v S, W (2)
Hanna, J. D. (Royal Artillery, Portsmouth), 1899 v W (1)
Hannon, D. J. (Bohemians), 1908 v E, S; 1911 v E, S; 1912 v W; 1913 v E (6)
Harkin, J. T. (Southport), 1968 v W; 1969 v T; (with Shrewsbury T), W (sub); 1970 v USSR; 1971 v Sp (5)
Harland, A. I. (Linfield), 1922 v N; 1923 v E (2)
Harris, J. (Cliftonville), 1921 v W; (with Glenavon), 1925 v S.Af (2)
Harris, V. (Shelbourne), 1906 v E; 1907 v E, W; 1908 v E, W, S; (with Everton), 1909 v E, W, S; 1910 v E, S, W; 1911 v E, S, W; 1912 v E; 1913 v E, S; 1914 v S, W (20)
Harvey, M. (Sunderland), 1961 v I; 1962 v Ho; 1963 v W, Sp; 1964 v S, E, W, U, Sp; 1965 v E, S, W, Sw (2), Ho (2), Alb; 1966 v S, E, W, M, Alb, WG; 1967 v E, S; 1968 v E, W; 1969 v Is, T (2), E; 1970 v USSR; 1971 v Cy, W (sub) (34)
Hastings, J. (Knock), 1882 v E, W; (with Ulster), 1883 v W; 1884 v E, S; 1886 v E, S (7)

Hatton, S. (Linfield), 1963 v S, Pol (2)
Hayes, W. E. (Huddersfield T), 1938 v E, S; 1939 v E, S (4)
Healy, D. J. (Manchester U), 2000 v L, Ma, H; 2001 v Y, Ma, D, Ic; (with Preston NE), N, CzR, Bul (2), CzR; 2002 v D, Ic, Ma, Pol, Lie, Sp; 2003 v Cy, Sp (sub), Uk, Fi, Arm, Gr, I, Sp; 2004 v Uk, Arm, Gr, N, Es, Ser, Bar, Stk (sub), Tr; 2005 v Sw, Pol, W, A; (with Leeds U), Ca, E, Pol, G; 2006 v Ma, Az, E, W, A, Es (49)
Healy, P. J. (Coleraine), 1982 v S, W, Hon (sub); (with Glentoran), 1983 v A (sub) (4)
Hegan, D. (WBA), 1970 v USSR; (with Wolverhampton W), 1972 v USSR, E, S, W; 1973 v Bul, Cy (7)
Henderson, J. (Ulster), 1885 v E, S, W (3)
Hewison, G. (Moyola Park), 1885 v E, S (2)
Hill, C. F. (Sheffield U), 1990 v N, U; 1991 v Pol, Y; 1992 v A, D; (with Leicester C), 1995 v Ei, La; 1996 v P, Lie, A, N, Se, G; 1997 v Uk, Arm, G, Alb, P, Uk, Arm, Th; (with Trelleborg), 1998 v G, Alb, P; (with Northampton T), Slo; 1999 v T (27)
Hill, M. J. (Norwich C), 1959 v W; 1960 v W; 1961 v WG; 1962 v S; (with Everton), 1964 v S, E, Sp (7)
Hinton, E. (Fulham), 1947 v S, W; 1948 v S, E, W; (with Millwall), 1951 v W, F (7)
Holmes, S. P. (Wrexham), 2002 v Lie (sub) (1)
Hopkins, J. (Brighton), 1926 v E (1)
Horlock, K. (Swindon T), 1995 v La, Ca; 1997 v G, Alb, I; (with Manchester C), v Bel, Uk, Arm, Th; 1998 v G, Alb, P; 1999 v T, Fi, G, Mol, Ca; 2000 v F, T, G, Ma (sub); 2001 v Y, Ma, D, Ic; 2002 v D, Ic, Ma, Sp; 2003 v Cy, Sp, Uk (32)
Houston, J. (Linfield), 1912 v S, W; 1913 v W; (with Everton), 1913 v E, S; 1914 v S (6)
Houston, W. (Linfield), 1933 v W (1)
Houston, W. J. (Moyola Park), 1885 v E, S (2)
Hughes, A. W. (Newcastle U), 1998 v Slo, Sw, Sp; 1999 v T, Fi, Mol (sub), Ca, Ei; 2000 v F, T, L, H; 2001 v Y, Ma, D, Ic, N, CzR, Bul, CzR; 2002 v D, Ic, Pol, Sp; 2003 v Sp, Uk, Fi, Arm, Gr, I, Sp; 2004 v Uk, Arm, Gr, N; 2005 v Sw, Pol, W, Az, A, Ca, E, Pol; (with Aston Villa), 2006 v Ma, Az, E (46)
Hughes, J. (Lincoln C), 2006 v U, R (sub) (2)
Hughes, M.A. (Oldham Ath), 2006 v U (sub), R (sub) (2)
Hughes, M. E. (Manchester C), 1992 v D, S, Li, G; (with Strasbourg), 1993 v Alb, Sp, D, Ei, Sp, Li, La; 1994 v La, D, Ei, R, Lie, Co, M; 1995 v P, A, Ei (2) La, Ca, Ch, La; 1996 v P, Lie, A, N, G; (with West Ham U), 1997 v Uk, Arm, G, Alb, I, Uk; 1998 v G; (with Wimbledon), P, Slo, Sw, Sp; 1999 v T, Fi, Mol, G, Mol; 2000 v F, T, G, Fi, L (sub), Ma, H; 2001 v CzR, Bul (2), CzR; 2002 v D, Ic, Ma, Pol, Lie (sub); 2003 v Sp (sub), Uk; (with C Palace), 2004 v Uk, Gr, N, Ser (sub); 2005 v Pol, W (71)
Hughes, P. A. (Bury), 1987 v E, T, Is (3)
Hughes, W. (Bolton W), 1951 v W (1)
Humphries, W. M. (Ards), 1962 v W; (with Coventry C), 1962 v Ho; 1963 v E, S, W, Pol, Sp; 1964 v S, E, Sp; 1965 v S, Ho; (with Swansea T), 1965 v W, Alb (14)
Hunter, A. (Distillery), 1905 v W; 1906 v W, E, S; (with Belfast C), 1908 v W; 1909 v W, E, S (8)
Hunter, A. (Blackburn R), 1970 v USSR; 1971 v Cy (2), E, S, W; (with Ipswich T), 1972 v USSR (2), Sp, E, S, W; 1973 v Bul, Cy (2), P, E, S, W; 1974 v Bul, S, E, W; 1975 v N, Se, Y, E, S, W; 1976 v Se, N, Y, Is, S, E, W; 1977 v Ho, Bel, WG, E, S, W, Ic; 1978 v Ic, Ho, Bel; 1979 v Ei, D, S, W, D; 1980 v E, Ei (53)
Hunter, B. V. (Wrexham), 1995 v La; 1996 v P, Lie, A, Se, G; (with Reading), 1997 v Arm, G, Alb, I, Bel; 1999 v Ca, Ei; 2000 v F, T (15)
Hunter, R. J. (Cliftonville), 1884 v E, S, W (3)
Hunter, V. (Coleraine), 1962 v E; 1964 v Sp (2)

Ingham, M. G. (Sunderland), 2005 v G (sub); (with Wrexham), 2006 v U (2)
Irvine, R. J. (Linfield), 1962 v Ho; 1963 v E, S, W, Pol (2), Sp; (with Stoke C), 1965 v W (8)
Irvine, R. W. (Everton), 1922 v S; 1923 v E, W; 1924 v E, S; 1925 v E; 1926 v E; 1927 v E, W; 1928 v E, S; (with Portsmouth), 1929 v E; 1930 v S; (with Connah's Quay), 1931 v E; (with Derry C), 1932 v W (15)
Irvine, W. J. (Burnley), 1963 v W, Sp; 1965 v S, W, Sw, Ho (2), Alb; 1966 v S, E, W, M, Alb; 1967 v E, S; 1968 v E, W; (with Preston NE), 1969 v Is, T, E; (with Brighton & HA), 1972 v E, S, W (23)
Irving, S. J. (Dundee), 1923 v S, W; 1924 v S, E, W; 1925 v S, E, W; 1926 v S, W; (with Cardiff C), 1927 v S, E, W; 1928 v S, E, W; (with Chelsea), 1929 v E; 1931 v W (18)

Jackson, T. A. (Everton), 1969 v Is, E, S, W; 1970 v USSR (1+1 sub); (with Nottingham F), 1971 v Sp; 1972 v E, S, W; 1973 v Cy, E, S, W; 1974 v Bul, P, S (sub), E (sub), W (sub); 1975 v N (sub), Se, Y, E, S, W; (with Manchester U); 1976 v Se, N, Y; 1977 v Ho, Bel, WG, E, S, W, Ic (35)
Jamison, J. (Glentoran), 1976 v N (1)
Jenkins, I. (Chester C), 1997 v Arm, Th; 1998 v Slo; (with Dundee U), Sw, Sp; 2000 v Fi (6)
Jennings, P. A. (Watford), 1964 v W, U; (with Tottenham H), 1965 v E, S, Sw (2), Ho, Alb; 1966 v S, E, W, Alb, WG; 1967 v E, S; 1968 v S, E, W; 1969 v Is, T (2), E, S, W; 1970 v S, E, USSR (2); 1971 v Cy (2), E, S, W; 1972 v USSR, Sp, S, E, W; 1973 v Bul, Cy, P, E, S, W; 1974 v P, S, E, W; 1975 v N, Se, Y, E, S, W; 1976 v Se, N, Y, Is, S, E, W; 1977 v Ho, Bel, WG, E, S, W, Ic; (with Arsenal), 1978 v Ic, Ho, Bel; 1979 v Ei, D, Bul, E, Bul, E, S, W, D; 1980 v E, Ei, Is; 1981 v S, P, S, Se; 1982 v S, Is, E, W, Y, Hon, Sp, F; 1983 v Alb, S, E, W; 1984 v A, T, WG, S, W, Fi; 1985 v R, Fi, E, Sp, T; (with Tottenham H), 1986 v T, R, E, F, D, Mor, Alg, Sp, Br (119)
Johnson, D. M. (Blackburn R), 1999 v Ei (sub); 2000 v Fi (sub), L, Ma (sub), H (sub); 2001 v Y, Ma, Ic, N (sub), Bul (sub+1), CzR; 2002 v Ma, Pol; (with Birmingham C), Lie, Sp; 2003 v Cy, Sp, Uk, Fi, Arm, Gr, I, Sp; 2004 v Uk, Arm, N, Bar, Stk (sub), Tr; 2005 v Sw, Pol, W, Az, A, E, G; 2006 v Ma, Az, E, W, A (42)
Johnston, H. (Portadown), 1927 v W (1)
Johnston, R. S. (Distillery), 1882 v E, W; 1884 v E; 1886 v E, S (5)
Johnston, R. S. (Distillery), 1905 v W (1)
Johnston, S. (Linfield), 1890 v W; 1893 v S, W; 1894 v E (4)
Johnston, W. (Oldpark), 1885 v S, W (2)
Johnston, W. C. (Glenavon), 1962 v W; (with Oldham Ath), 1966 v M (sub) (2)
Jones, J. (Linfield), 1930 v S, W; 1931 v S, W, E; 1932 v S, E; 1933 v S, E, W; 1934 v S, E, W; 1935 v S, E, W; 1936 v E, S; (with Hibernian), 1936 v W; 1937 v E, W, S; (with Glenavon), 1938 v E (23)
Jones, J. (Glenavon), 1956 v W; 1957 v E, W (3)
Jones, S. (Distillery), 1934 v E; (with Blackpool), 1934 v W (2)
Jones, S. G. (Crewe Alex), 2003 v I (sub), Sp; 2004 v Uk (sub), Arm (sub), Gr (sub), N (sub), Es, Ser (sub), Bar (sub), Stk (sub), Tr (sub); 2005 v Pol (sub), A (sub), Ca (sub), E (sub), G; 2006 v Ma (sub), Az (sub), W (sub), A (sub), P, Es (sub), U, R (sub) (24)
Jordan, T. (Linfield), 1895 v E, W (2)

Kavanagh, P. J. (Celtic), 1930 v E (1)
Keane, T. R. (Swansea T), 1949 v S (1)
Kearns, A. (Distillery), 1900 v E, S, W; 1902 v E, S, W (6)
Kee, P. V. (Oxford U), 1990 v N; 1991 v Y (2), D, A, Pol, Fa; (with Ards), 1995 v A, Ei (9)
Keith, R. M. (Newcastle U), 1958 v E, W, Cz (2), Arg, I, WG, F; 1959 v E, S, W, Sp; 1960 v S, E; 1961 v S, E, W, I, WG (2), Gr; 1962 v W, Ho (23)
Kelly, H. R. (Fulham), 1950 v E, W; (with Southampton), 1951 v E, S (4)
Kelly, J. (Glentoran), 1896 v E (1)
Kelly, J. (Derry C), 1932 v E, W; 1933 v E, W, S; 1934 v W; 1936 v E, S, W; 1937 v S, E (11)
Kelly, P. J. (Manchester C), 1921 v E (1)
Kelly, P. M. (Barnsley), 1950 v S (1)
Kennedy, A. L. (Arsenal), 1923 v W; 1925 v E (2)
Kennedy, P. H. (Watford), 1999 v Mol, G (sub); 2000 v F, T, G, Fi; 2001 v N, Bul (sub), CzR (sub); (with Wigan Ath), 2002 v D, Ic, Ma, Pol; 2003 v Cy, Fi, I, Sp; 2004 v Uk, Gr, N (20)
Kernaghan, N. (Belfast C), 1936 v W; 1937 v S; 1938 v E (3)
Kirk, A. R. (Hearts), 2000 v H; 2001 v N (sub); 2003 v Uk (sub), Fi (sub), Gr (sub); (with Boston U), 2005 v Ca (sub); (with Northampton T), E (sub), G (sub) (8)
Kirkwood, H. (Cliftonville), 1904 v W (1)
Kirwan, J. (Tottenham H), 1900 v W; 1902 v E, W; 1903 v E, S, W; 1904 v E, S, W; 1905 v E, S, W; (with Chelsea), 1906 v E, S, W; 1907 v W; (with Clyde), 1909 v S (17)

Lacey, W. (Everton), 1909 v E, S, W; 1910 v E, S, W; 1911 v E, S, W; 1912 v E; (with Liverpool), 1913 v W; 1914 v E, S, W; 1920 v E, S, W; 1921 v E, S, W; 1922 v E, S; (with New Brighton), 1925 v E (23)
Lafferty, K. (Burnley), 2006 v U (sub), R (sub) (2)
Lawther, R. (Glentoran), 1888 v E, S (2)
Lawther, W. I. (Sunderland), 1960 v W; 1961 v I; (with Blackburn R), 1962 v S, Ho (4)
Leatham, J. (Belfast C), 1939 v W (1)
Ledwidge, J. J. (Shelbourne), 1906 v S, W (2)
Lemon, J. (Glentoran), 1886 v W; (with Belfast YMCA), 1888 v S; 1889 v W (3)
Lennon, N. F. (Crewe Alex), 1994 v M (sub); 1995 v Ch; 1996 v P, Lie, A; (with Leicester C), v N; 1997 v Uk, Arm, G, Alb, Bel, P, Uk, Arm, Th; 1998 v G, Alb, P, Slo, Sw,

Sp; 1999 v T, Fi, Mol, G, Mol, Ei; 2000 v F, T, G, Fi, Ma, H; 2001 v D, Ic; (with Celtic), N, CzR, Bul (2); 2002 v Pol (sub) (40)
Leslie, W. (YMCA), 1887 v E (1)
Lewis, J. (Glentoran), 1899 v S, E, W; (with Distillery), 1900 v S (4)
Lockhart, H. (Russell School), 1884 v W (1)
Lockhart, N. H. (Linfield), 1947 v E; (with Coventry C), 1950 v W; 1951 v W; 1952 v W; (with Aston Villa), 1954 v S, E; 1955 v W; 1956 v W (8)
Lomas, S. M. (Manchester C), 1994 v R, Lie, Co (sub), M; 1995 v P, A; 1996 v P, Lie, A, N, Se, G; 1997 v Uk, Arm, G, Alb, I, Bel; (with West Ham U), P, Uk, Arm, Th; 1998 v Alb, P, Slo, Sw; 1999 v Mol, G, Mol, Ca; 2000 v F, T, G, L, Ma; 2001 v Ma, D, Ic; 2002 v Pol, Lie; 2003 v Sp, Uk, Fi, Arm, Gr (45)
Loyal, J. (Clarence), 1891 v S (1)
Lutton, R. J. (Wolverhampton W), 1970 v S, E; (with West Ham U), 1973 v Cy (sub), S (sub), W (sub); 1974 v P (6)
Lynas, R. (Cliftonville), 1925 v S.Af (1)
Lyner, D. R. (Glentoran), 1920 v E, W; 1922 v S, W; (with Manchester U), 1923 v E; (with Kilmarnock), 1923 v W (6)
Lytle, J. (Glentoran), 1898 W (1)

McAdams, W. J. (Manchester C), 1954 v W; 1955 v S; 1957 v E; 1958 v S, I; (with Bolton W), 1961 v E, S, W, I, WG (2), Gr; 1962 v E, Gr; (with Leeds U), Ho (15)
McAlery, J. M. (Cliftonville), 1882 v E, W (2)
McAlinden, J. (Belfast C), 1938 v S; 1939 v S; (with Portsmouth), 1947 v E; (with Southend U), 1949 v E (4)
McAllen, J. (Linfield), 1898 v E; 1899 v E, S, W; 1900 v E, S, W; 1901 v W; 1902 v S (9)
McAlpine, S. (Cliftonville), 1901 v S (1)
McArthur, A. (Distillery), 1886 v W (1)
McAuley, G. (Lincoln C), 2005 v G (sub); 2006 v P (sub), Es, U (sub), R (5)
McAuley, J. L. (Huddersfield T), 1911 v E, W; 1912 v E, S; 1913 v E, S (6)
McAuley, P. (Belfast C), 1900 v S (1)
McBride, S. D. (Glenavon), 1991 v D (sub), Pol (sub); 1992 v Fa (sub), D (4)
McCabe, J. J. (Leeds U), 1949 v S, W; 1950 v E; 1951 v W; 1953 v W; 1954 v S (6)
McCabe, W. (Ulster), 1891 v E (1)
McCambridge, J. (Ballymena), 1930 v S, W; (with Cardiff C), 1931 v W; 1932 v E (4)
McCandless, J. (Bradford), 1912 v W; 1913 v W; 1920 v W, S; 1921 v E (5)
McCandless, W. (Linfield), 1920 v E, W; 1921 v E; (with Rangers), 1921 v W; 1922 v S; 1924 v W, S; 1925 v S; 1929 v W (9)
McCann, G. S. (West Ham U), 2002 v Ma (sub), Pol (sub), Lie; 2003 v Sp (sub), Uk (sub); (with Cheltenham T), Arm, Gr; 2004 v Arm, Es (sub); 2006 v P (sub), Es (sub) (11)
McCann, P. (Belfast C), 1910 v E, S, W; 1911 v E; (with Glentoran), 1911 v S; 1912 v E; 1913 v W (7)
McCarthy, J. D. (Port Vale), 1996 v Se; 1997 v I, Arm, Th; (with Birmingham C), 1998 v P (sub), Slo (sub), Sp; 1999 v Fi (sub), Mol (sub), G (sub), Ca, Ei; 2000 v F, T, G, Fi; 2001 v N, Bul (sub) (18)
McCartney, A. (Ulster), 1903 v S, W; (with Linfield), 1904 v S, W; (with Everton), 1905 v E, S; (with Belfast C), 1907 v E, S, W; 1908 v E, S, W; (with Glentoran), 1909 v E, S, W (15)
McCartney, G. (Sunderland), 2002 v Ic, Ma, Pol (sub), Lie, Sp; 2003 v Cy, Sp, Uk, Fi, Gr, I, Sp; 2004 v Uk, Arm, Gr, N; 2005 v W (sub), A, Ca, G (20)
McCashin, J. W. (Cliftonville), 1896 v W; 1898 v S, W; 1899 v S; 1903 v S (5)
McCavana, W. T. (Coleraine), 1955 v S; 1956 v E, S (3)
McCaw, J. H. (Linfield), 1927 v W; 1928 v F; 1930 v S; 1931 v E, S, W (6)
McClatchey, J. (Distillery), 1886 v E, S, W (3)
McClatchey, T. (Distillery), 1895 v S (1)
McCleary, J. W. (Cliftonville), 1955 v W (1)
McCleery, W. (Cliftonville), 1922 v N; (Linfield), 1930 v E, W; 1931 v E, S, W; 1932 v S, W; 1933 v E, W (10)
McClelland, J. (Mansfield T), 1980 v S (sub), Aus (3); 1981 v Se, S; (with Rangers), S, Se (sub); 1982 v S, W, Y, Hon, Sp, A, F; 1983 v A, WG, Alb, T, Alb, S, E, W; 1984 v A, T, WG, S, E, W, Fi; 1985 v R, Is; (with Watford), Fi, E, Sp, T; 1986 v T, F (sub); 1987 v E (2), T, Is, Y; 1988 v T, Gr, F, Ma; 1989 v Ei, H, Sp (2), Ma; (with Leeds U), 1990 v N (53)
McClelland, J. T. (Arsenal), 1961 v W, I, WG (2), Gr; (with Fulham), 1966 v M (6)
McCluggage, A. (Cliftonville), 1922 v N; (Bradford), 1924 v E; (with Burnley), 1927 v S, W; 1928 v S, E, W; 1929 v S, E, W; 1930 v W; 1931 v E, W (13)
McClure, G. (Cliftonville), 1907 v S, W; 1908 v E; (with Distillery), 1909 v E (4)
McConnell, E. (Cliftonville), 1904 v S, W; (with Glentoran), 1905 v S; (with Sunderland), 1906 v E; 1907 v E; 1908 v S, W; (with Sheffield W), 1909 v S, W; 1910 v S, W, E (12)
McConnell, P. (Doncaster R), 1928 v W; (with Southport), 1932 v E (2)
McConnell, W. G. (Bohemians), 1912 v W; 1913 v E, S; 1914 v E, S, W (6)
McConnell, W. H. (Reading), 1925 v W; 1926 v E, W; 1927 v E, S, W; 1928 v E, W (8)
McCourt, F. J. (Manchester C), 1952 v E, W; 1953 v E, S, W, F (6)
McCourt, P. J. (Rochdale), 2002 v Sp (sub) (1)
McCoy, R. K. (Coleraine), 1987 v Y (sub) (1)
McCoy, S. (Distillery), 1896 v W (1)
McCracken, E. (Barking), 1928 v F (1)
McCracken, R. (C Palace), 1921 v E; 1922 v E, S, W (4)
McCracken, R. (Linfield), 1922 v N (1)
McCracken, W. R. (Distillery), 1902 v E, W; 1903 v S, E; 1904 v E, S, W; (with Newcastle U), 1905 v E, S, W; 1907 v E; 1920 v E; 1922 v E, S, W; (with Hull C), 1923 v S (16)
McCreery, D. (Manchester U), 1976 v S (sub), E, W; 1977 v Ho, Bel, WG, E, S, W, Ic; 1978 v Ic, Ho, Bel, S, E, W; 1979 v Ei, D, Bul, E, Bul, W, D; (with QPR), 1980 v E, Ei, S (sub), E (sub), W (sub), Aus (1+1 sub); 1981 v Se (sub), P (sub); (with Tulsa R), S, P, Se; 1982 v S, Is, E (sub), F, Y, Hon, Sp, A, F; (with Newcastle U), 1983 v A; 1984 v T (sub); 1985 v R, Sp (sub); 1986 v T (sub), R, E, F, D, Alg, Sp, Br; 1987 v T, E, Y; 1988 v Y; 1989 v Sp, Ma, Ch; (with Hearts), 1990 v H, Ei, N, U (sub) (67)
McCrory, S. (Southend U), 1958 v E (1)
McCullough, K. (Belfast C), 1935 v W; 1936 v E; (with Manchester C), 1936 v S; 1937 v E, S (5)
McCullough, W. J. (Arsenal), 1961 v I; 1963 v Sp; 1964 v S, E, W, U, Sp; 1965 v E, Sw; (with Millwall), 1967 v E (10)
McCurdy, C. (Linfield), 1980 v Aus (sub) (1)
McDonald, A. (QPR), 1986 v R, E, F, D, Mor, Alg, Sp, Br; 1987 v E (2), T, Is, Y; 1988 v Y, T, Pol, F, Ma; 1989 v Ei, H, Sp, Ch; 1990 v H, Ei, U; 1991 v Y, D, A, Fa; 1992 v Fa, S, Li, G; 1993 v Alb, Sp, D, Alb, Ei, Sp, Li, La; 1994 v D, Ei; 1995 v P, A, Ei, La, Ca, Ch, La; 1996 v A (sub), N (52)
McDonald, R. (Rangers), 1930 v S; 1932 v E (2)
McDonnell, J. (Bohemians), 1911 v E, S; 1912 v W; 1913 v W (4)
McElhinney, G. M. A. (Bolton W), 1984 v WG, S, E, W, Fi; 1985 v R (6)
McEvilly, L. R. (Rochdale), 2002 v Sp (sub) (1)
McFaul, W. S. (Linfield), 1967 v E (sub); (with Newcastle U), 1970 v W; 1971 v Sp; 1972 v USSR; 1973 v Cy; 1974 v Bul (6)
McGarry, J. K. (Cliftonville), 1951 v W, F, S (3)
McGaughey, M. (Linfield), 1985 v Is (sub) (1)
McGibbon, P. C. G. (Manchester U), 1995 v Ca (sub), Ch, La; 1996 v Lie (sub); 1997 v Th; (with Wigan Ath), 1998 v Alb; 2000 v L (sub) (7)
McGrath, R. C. (Tottenham H), 1974 v S, E, W; 1975 v N; 1976 v Is (sub); 1977; (with Manchester U), Ho, Bel, WG, E, S, W, Ic; 1978 v Ic, Ho, Bel, S, E, W; 1979 v Bul (sub), E (sub and sub) (21)
McGregor, S. (Glentoran), 1921 v S (1)
McGrillen, J. (Clyde), 1924 v S; (with Belfast C), 1927 v S (2)
McGuire, E. (Distillery), 1907 v S (1)
McGuire, J. (Linfield), 1928 v F (1)
McIlroy, H. (Cliftonville), 1906 v E (1)
McIlroy, J. (Burnley), 1952 v E, S, W; 1953 v E, S, W; 1954 v E, S, W; 1955 v E, S, W; 1956 v E, S, W; 1957 v E, S, W, I, P (2); 1958 v E, S, W, I (2), Cz (2), Arg, WG, F; 1959 v E, S, W, Sp; 1960 v E, S, W; 1961 v E, W, WG (2), Gr; 1962 v E, S, Gr, Ho; 1963 v E, S, Pol (2); (with Stoke C), 1963 v W; 1966 v S, E, Alb (55)
McIlroy, S. B. (Manchester U), 1972 v Sp, S (sub); 1974 v S, E, W; 1975 v N, Se, Y, E, S, W; 1976 v Se, N, Y, S, E, W; 1977 v Ho, Bel, E, S, W, Ic; 1978 v Ic, Ho, Bel, S, E, W; 1979 v Ei, D, Bul, E, Bul, E, S, W, D; 1980 v E, Ei, Is, S, E, W; 1981 v Se, P, S, P, S, Se; 1982 v S, Is; (with Stoke C), E, F, S, W, Y, Hon, Sp, A, F; 1983 v A, WG, Alb, T, Alb, S, E, W; 1984 v A, T, S, E, W, Fi; 1985 v Fi, E, T; (with Manchester C), 1986 v T, R, E, F, D, Mor, Alg, Sp, Br; 1987 v E (sub) (88)
McIlvenny, P. (Distillery), 1924 v W (1)
McIlvenny, R. (Distillery), 1890 v E; (with Ulster), 1891 v E (2)
McKeag, W. (Glentoran), 1968 v S, W (2)
McKeague, T. (Glentoran), 1925 v S.Af (1)

McKee, F. W. (Cliftonville), 1906 v S, W; (with Belfast C), 1914 v E, S, W (5)
McKelvey, H. (Glentoran), 1901 v W; 1903 v S (2)
McKenna, J. (Huddersfield), 1950 v E, S, W; 1951 v E, S, F; 1952 v E (7)
McKenzie, H. (Distillery), 1922 v N; 1923 v S (2)
McKenzie, R. (Airdrie), 1967 v W (1)
McKeown, N. (Linfield), 1892 v E, S, W; 1893 v S, W; 1894 v S, W (7)
McKie, H. (Cliftonville), 1895 v E, S, W (3)
Mackie, J. A. (Arsenal), 1923 v W; (with Portsmouth), 1935 v S, W (3)
McKinney, D. (Hull C), 1921 v S; (with Bradford C), 1924 v S (2)
McKinney, V. J. (Falkirk), 1966 v WG (1)
McKnight, A. D. (Celtic), 1988 v Y, T, Gr, Pol, F, Ma; (with West Ham U), 1989 v Ei, H, Sp (2) (10)
McKnight, J. (Preston NE), 1912 v S; (with Glentoran), 1913 v S (2)
McLaughlin, J. C. (Shrewsbury T), 1962 v E, S, W, Gr; 1963 v W; (with Swansea T), 1964 v W, U; 1965 v E, W, Sw (2); 1966 v W (12)
McLean, B. S. (Rangers), 2006 v Es (sub) (1)
McLean, T. (Limavady), 1885 v S (1)
McMahon, G. J. (Tottenham H), 1995 v Ca (sub), Ch, La; 1996 v Lie, N (sub), Se, G; (with Stoke C), 1997 v Arm (sub), Alb (sub), Bel, P (sub), Uk (sub), Arm (sub), Th (sub); 1998 v G (sub), Alb (sub), P (sub) (17)
McMahon, J. (Bohemians), 1934 v S (1)
McMaster, G. (Glentoran), 1897 v E, S, W (3)
McMichael, A. (Newcastle U), 1950 v E, S; 1951 v E, S, F; 1952 v E, S, W; 1953 v E, S, W, F; 1954 v E, S, W; 1955 v E, W; 1956 v W; 1957 v E, S, W, I, P (2); 1958 v E, S, W, I (2), Cz (2), Arg, WG, F; 1959 v S, W, Sp; 1960 v E, S, W (40)
McMillan, G. (Distillery), 1903 v E; 1905 v W (2)
McMillan, S. T. (Manchester U), 1963 v E, S (2)
McMillen, W. S. (Manchester U), 1934 v E; 1935 v S; 1937 v S; (with Chesterfield), 1938 v S, W; 1939 v E, S (7)
McMordie, A. S. (Middlesbrough), 1969 v Is, T (2), E, S, W; 1970 v E, S, W, USSR; 1971 v Cy (2), E, S, W; 1972 v USSR, Sp, E, S, W; 1973 v Bul (21)
McMorran, E. J. (Belfast C), 1947 v E; (with Barnsley), 1951 v E, S, W; 1952 v E, S, W; 1953 v E, S, F; (with Doncaster R), 1953 v W; 1954 v E; 1956 v W; 1957 v I, P (15)
McMullan, D. (Liverpool), 1926 v E, W; 1927 v S (3)
McNally, B. A. (Shrewsbury T), 1986 v Mor; 1987 v T (sub); 1988 v Y, Gr, Ma (sub) (5)
McNinch, J. (Ballymena), 1931 v S; 1932 v S, W (3)
McParland, P. J. (Aston Villa), 1954 v W; 1955 v E, S; 1956 v E, S; 1957 v E, S, W, P; 1958 v E, S, W, I (2), Cz (2), Arg, WG, F; 1959 v E, S, W, Sp; 1960 v E, S, W; 1961 v E, S, W, I, WG (2), Gr; (with Wolverhampton W), 1962 v Ho (34)
McShane, J. (Cliftonville), 1899 v S; 1900 v E, S, W (4)
McVeigh, P. (Tottenham H), 1999 v Ca (sub); (with Norwich C), 2002 v Ic (sub), Pol (sub); 2003 v Sp, Uk, Fi, Arm, Gr (sub), I, Sp (sub); 2004 v Arm (sub), N (sub), Ser (sub), Bar (sub), Stk, Tr (sub); 2005 v Sw (sub), Pol (sub), W (sub), A (sub) (20)
McVicker, J. (Linfield), 1888 v E; (with Glentoran), 1889 v S (2)
McWha, W. B. R. (Knock), 1882 v E, W; (with Cliftonville), 1883 v E, W; 1884 v E; 1885 v E, W (7)
Madden, O. (Norwich C), 1938 v E (1)
Magee, G. (Wellington Park), 1885 v E, S, W (3)
Magill, E. J. (Arsenal), 1962 v E, S, Gr; 1963 v E, S, W, Pol (2), Sp; 1964 v E, S, W, U, Sp; 1965 v E, S, Sw (2), Ho, Alb; 1966 v S; (with Brighton & HA), E, Alb, W, WG, M (26)
Magilton, J. (Oxford U), 1991 v Pol, Y, Fa; 1992 v Fa, A, D, S, Li, G; 1993 v Alb, D, Alb, Ei, Li, La; 1994 v La, D, Ei; (with Southampton), R, Lie, Co, M; 1995 v P, A, Ei (2), Ca, Ch, La; 1996 v P, N, G; 1997 v Uk (sub), Arm (sub), Bel, P; 1998 v G; (with Sheffield W), P, Sp; (with Ipswich T), 2000 v L; 2001 v Y, Ma, D, Ic, N, CzR, Bul; 2002 v D, Ic, Ma, Pol, Lie (52)
Maginnis, H. (Linfield), 1900 v E, S, W; 1903 v S, W; 1904 v E, S, W (8)
Mahood, J. (Belfast C), 1926 v S; 1928 v E, S, W; 1929 v E, S, W; 1930 v W; (with Ballymena), 1934 v S (9)
Mannus, A. (Linfield), 2004 v Tr (sub) (1)
Manderson, R. (Rangers), 1920 v W, S; 1925 v S, E; 1926 v S (5)
Mansfield, J. (Dublin Freebooters), 1901 v E (1)
Martin, C. (Cliftonville), 1882 v E, W; 1883 v E (3)
Martin, C. (Bo'ness), 1925 v S (1)
Martin, C. J. (Glentoran), 1947 v S; (with Leeds U), 1948 v E, S, W; (with Aston Villa), 1949 v E; 1950 v W (6)
Martin, D. K. (Belfast C), 1934 v E, S, W; 1935 v S; (with Wolverhampton W), 1935 v E; 1936 v W; (with Nottingham F), 1937 v S; 1938 v E, S; 1939 v S (10)
Mathieson, A. (Luton T), 1921 v W; 1922 v E (2)
Maxwell, J. (Linfield), 1902 v W; 1903 v W, E; (with Glentoran), 1905 v W, S; (with Belfast C), 1906 v W; 1907 v S (7)
Meek, H. L. (Glentoran), 1925 v W (1)
Mehaffy, J. A. C. (Queen's Island), 1922 v W (1)
Meldon, P. A. (Dublin Freebooters), 1899 v S, W (2)
Mercer, H. V. A. (Linfield), 1908 v E (1)
Mercer, J. T. (Distillery), 1898 v E, S, W; 1899 v E; (with Linfield), 1902 v E, W; (with Distillery), 1903 v S (2), W; (with Derby Co), 1904 v E, W; 1905 v S (12)
Millar, W. (Barrow), 1932 v W; 1933 v S (2)
Miller, J. (Middlesbrough), 1929 v W, S; 1930 v E (3)
Milligan, D. (Chesterfield), 1939 v W (1)
Milne, R. G. (Linfield), 1894 v E, S, W; 1895 v E, W; 1896 v E, S, W; 1897 v E, S; 1898 v E, S, W; 1899 v E, W; 1901 v W; 1902 v E, S, W; 1903 v E, S (2); 1904 v E, S, W; 1906 v E, S, W (28)
Mitchell, E. J. (Cliftonville), 1933 v S; (with Glentoran), 1934 v W (2)
Mitchell, W. (Distillery), 1932 v E, W; 1933 v E, W; (with Chelsea), 1934 v W, S; 1935 v S, E; 1936 v S, E; 1937 v E, S, W; 1938 v E, S (15)
Molyneux, T. B. (Ligoniel), 1883 v E, W; (with Cliftonville), 1884 v E, W, S; 1885 v E, W; 1886 v E, W, S; 1888 v S (11)
Montgomery, F. J. (Coleraine), 1955 v E (1)
Moore, C. (Glentoran), 1949 v W (1)
Moore, P. (Aberdeen), 1933 v E (1)
Moore, R. (Linfield Ath), 1891 v E, S, W (3)
Moore, R. L. (Ulster), 1887 v S, W (2)
Moore, W. (Falkirk), 1923 v S (1)
Moorhead, F. W. (Dublin University), 1885 v E (1)
Moorhead, G. (Linfield), 1923 v S; 1928 v F, S; 1929 v S (4)
Moran, J. (Leeds C), 1912 v S (1)
Moreland, V. (Derby Co), 1979 v Bul (2 sub), E, S; 1980 v E, Ei (6)
Morgan, G. F. (Linfield), 1922 v N; 1923 v E; (with Nottingham F), 1924 v S; 1927 v E; 1928 v E, S, W; 1929 v E (8)
Morgan, S. (Port Vale), 1972 v Sp; 1973 v Bul (sub), P, Cy, E, S, W; (with Aston Villa), 1974 v Bul, P, S, E; 1975 v Se; 1976 v Se (sub), N, Y; (with Brighton & HA), S, W (sub); (with Sparta Rotterdam), 1979 v D (18)
Morrison, R. (Linfield Ath), 1891 v E, W (2)
Morrison, T. (Glentoran), 1895 v E, S, W; (with Burnley), 1899 v W; 1900 v W; 1902 v E, S (7)
Morrogh, D. (Bohemians), 1896 v S (1)
Morrow, S. J. (Arsenal), 1990 v U (sub); 1991 v A (sub), Pol, Y; 1992 v Fa, S (sub), G (sub); 1993 v Sp (sub), Alb, Ei; 1994 v R, Co, M (sub); 1995 v P, Ei (2), La; 1996 v P, Se; 1997 v Uk, G, Alb, I, Bel; (with QPR), P, Uk, Arm; 1998 v G, P, Slo, Sw, Sp; 1999 v T, Fi, Mol, G, Mol; 2000 v G, Fi (39)
Morrow, W. J. (Moyola Park), 1883 v E, W; 1884 v S (3)
Muir, R. (Oldpark), 1885 v S, W (2)
Mulholland, T.S. (Belfast C), 1906 v S, E (2)
Mullan, G. (Glentoran), 1983 v S, E, W, Alb (sub) (4)
Mulligan, J. (Manchester C), 1921 v S (1)
Mulryne, P. P. (Manchester U), 1997 v Bel (sub), Arm (sub), Th; 1998 v Alb (sub), Sp (sub); 1999 v T, Fi; (with Norwich C), Ca; 2001 v Y, D (sub), Bul (sub), CzR; 2002 v D, Ic, Pol, Lie; 2003 v Sp, Uk; 2004 v Uk (sub), Arm (sub), Es, Ser, Bar, Stk (sub), Tr; 2005 v Ca (sub); (with Cardiff C), 2006 v Ma (sub) (27)
Murdock, C. J, (Preston NE), 2000 v L (sub), Ma, H (sub); 2001 v Y, Ma, D, Ic, N, CzR, Bul (2), CzR; 2002 v D, Ma; 2003 v Cy, Sp, Uk (sub); (with Hibernian), 2004 v Gr (sub), Bar (sub), Stk, Tr (sub); 2005 v Sw (sub), W, Az, A; (with Crewe Alex), Ca, E, Pol; (with Rotherham U), 2006 v Ma, W, A, P, U, R (sub) (34)
Murphy, J. (Bradford C), 1910 v E, S, W (3)
Murphy, N. (QPR), 1905 v E, S, W (3)
Murray, J. M. (Motherwell), 1910 v E, S; (with Sheffield W), W (3)

Napier, R. J. (Bolton W), 1966 v WG (1)
Neill, W. J. T. (Arsenal), 1961 v I, Gr, WG; 1962 v E, S, W, Gr; 1963 v E, W, Pol, Sp; 1964 v S, E, W, U, Sp; 1965 v E, S, W, Sw, Ho (2), Alb; 1966 v S, E, W, Alb, WG, M; 1967 v S, W; 1968 v S, E; 1969 v E, S, W, Is, T (2); 1970 v S, E, W, USSR (2); (with Hull C), 1971 v Cy, Sp; 1972 v USSR (2), Sp, S, E, W; 1973 v Bul, Cy (2), P, E, S, W (59)
Nelis, P. (Nottingham F), 1923 v E (1)

Nelson, S. (Arsenal), 1970 v W, E (sub); 1971 v Cy, Sp, E, S, W; 1972 v USSR (2), Sp, E, S, W; 1973 v Bul, Cy, P; 1974 v S, E; 1975 v Se, Y; 1976 v Se, N, Is, E; 1977 v Bel (sub), WG, W, Ic; 1978 v Ic, Ho, Bel; 1979 v Ei, D, Bul, E, Bul, E, S, W, D; 1980 v E, Ei, Is; 1981 v S, P, S, Se; (with Brighton & HA), 1982 v E, S, Sp (sub), A (51)
Nicholl, C. J. (Aston Villa), 1975 v Se, Y, E, S, W; 1976 v Se, N, Y, S, E, W; 1977 v W; (with Southampton), 1978 v Bel (sub), S, E, W; 1979 v Ei, Bul, E, Bul, E, W; 1980 v Ei, Is, S, E, W, Aus (3); 1981 v Se, P, S, P, S, Se; 1982 v S, Is, E, F, W, Y, Hon, Sp, A, F; 1983 v S (sub), E, W; (with Grimsby T), 1984 v A, T (51)
Nicholl, H. (Belfast C), 1902 v E, W; 1905 v E (3)
Nicholl, J. M. (Manchester U), 1976 v Is, W (sub); 1977 v Ho, Bel, E, S, W, Ic; 1978 v Ic, Ho, Bel, S, E, W; 1979 v Ei, D, Bul, E, Bul, E, S, W, D; 1980 v E, Ei, Is, S, E, W, Aus (3); 1981 v Se, P, S, P, S, Se; 1982 v S, Is, E; (with Toronto B), F, W, Y, Hon, Sp, A, F; (with Sunderland), 1983 v A, WG, Alb, T, Alb; (with Toronto B), S, E, W; 1984 v T; (with Rangers), WG, S, E; (with Toronto B), Fi; 1985 v R; (with WBA), Fi, E, Sp, T; 1986 v T, R, E, F, Alg, Sp, Br (73)
Nicholson, J. J. (Manchester U), 1961 v S, W; 1962 v E, W, Gr, Ho; 1963 v E, S, Pol (2); (with Huddersfield T), 1965 v W, Ho (2), Alb; 1966 v S, E, W, Alb, M; 1967 v S, W; 1968 v S, E, W; 1969 v S, E, W, T (2); 1970 v S, E, W, USSR (2); 1971 v Cy (2), E, S, W; 1972 v USSR (2) (41)
Nixon, R. (Linfield), 1914 v S (1)
Nolan, I. R. (Sheffield W), 1997 v Arm, G, Alb, P, Uk; 1998 v G, P; 2000 v G, Fi, L, Ma, H; (with Bradford C), 2001 v Y, Ma, Bul (2), CzR; (with Wigan Ath), 2002 v Sp (18)
Nolan-Whelan, J. V. (Dublin Freebooters), 1901 v E, W; 1902 v S, W; 1903 v S (5)

O'Boyle, G. (Dunfermline Ath), 1994 v Co (sub), M; (with St Johnstone), 1995 v P (sub), La (sub), Ca (sub), Ch (sub); 1996 v Se (sub), G (sub); 1997 v I (sub), Bel (sub); 1998 v Slo (sub), Sw (sub); 1999 v Fi (sub) (13)
O'Brien, M. T. (QPR), 1921 v S; (with Leicester C), 1922 v S, W; 1924 v S, W; (with Hull C), 1925 v S, E, W; 1926 v W; (with Derby Co), 1927 v W (10)
O'Connell, P. (Sheffield W), 1912 v E, S; (with Hull C), 1914 v E, S, W (5)
O'Doherty, A. (Coleraine), 1970 v E, W (sub) (2)
O'Driscoll, J. F. (Swansea T), 1949 v E, S, W (3)
O'Hagan, C. (Tottenham H), 1905 v S, W; 1906 v S, W, E; (with Aberdeen), 1907 v E, S, W; 1908 v S, W; 1909 v E (11)
O'Hagan, W. (St Mirren), 1920 v E, W (2)
O'Hehir, J. C. (Bohemians), 1910 v W (1)
O'Kane, W. J. (Nottingham F), 1970 v E, W, S (sub); 1971 v Sp, E, S, W; 1972 v USSR (2); 1973 v P, Cy; 1974 v Bul, P, S, E, W; 1975 v N, Se, E, S (20)
O'Mahoney, M. T. (Bristol R), 1939 v S (1)
O'Neill, C. (Motherwell), 1989 v Ch (sub); 1990 v Ei (sub); 1991 v D (3)
O'Neill, J. (Sunderland), 1962 v W (1)
O'Neill, J. P. (Leicester C), 1980 v Is, S, E, W, Aus (3); 1981 v P, S, P, S, Se; 1982 v S, Is, E, F, S, F (sub); 1983 v A, WG, Alb, T, Alb, S; 1984 v S (sub); 1985 v Is, Fi, E, Sp, T; 1986 v T, R, E, F, D, Mor, Alg, Sp, Br (39)
O'Neill, M. A. M. (Newcastle U), 1988 v Gr, Pol, F, Ma; 1989 v Ei, H, Sp (sub), Sp (sub), Ma (sub), Ch; (with Dundee U), 1990 v H (sub), Ei; 1991 v Pol; 1992 v Fa (sub), S (sub), G (sub); 1993 v Alb (sub + 1), Ei, Sp, Li, La; (with Hibernian), 1994 v Lie (sub); 1995 v A (sub), Ei; 1996 v Lie, A, N, Se; (with Coventry C), 1997 v Uk (sub), Arm (sub) (31)
O'Neill, M. H. M. (Distillery), 1972 v USSR (sub), (with Nottingham F), Sp (sub), W (sub); 1973 v P, Cy, E, S, W; 1974 v Bul, P, E (sub), W; 1975 v Se, Y, E, S; 1976 v Y (sub); 1977 v E (sub), S; 1978 v Ic, Ho, S, E, W; 1979 v Ei, D, Bul, E, Bul, D; 1980 v Ei, Is, Aus (3); 1981 v Se, P; (with Norwich C), P, S, Se; (with Manchester C), 1982 v S; (with Norwich C), E, F, S, Y, Hon, Sp, A, F; 1983 v A, WG, Alb, T, Alb, S, E; (with Notts Co), 1984 v A, T, WG, E, W, Fi; 1985 v R, Fi (64)
O'Reilly, H. (Dublin Freebooters), 1901 v S, W; 1904 v S (3)

Parke, J. (Linfield), 1964 v S; (with Hibernian), 1964 v E, Sp; (with Sunderland), 1965 v Sw, S, W, Ho (2), Alb; 1966 v WG; 1967 v E, S; 1968 v S, E (14)
Patterson, D. J. (C Palace), 1994 v Co (sub), M (sub); 1995 v Ei (sub+1), La, Ca, Ch (sub), La (sub); (with Luton T), 1996 v N (sub), Se; 1998 v Sw, Sp (sub); (with Dundee U), 1999 v Fi, Mol, G, Mol, Ei (17)
Peacock, R. (Celtic), 1952 v S; 1953 v F; 1954 v W; 1955 v E, S; 1956 v E, S; 1957 v W, I, P; 1958 v S, E, W, I (2), Arg, Cz (2), WG; 1959 v E, S, W; 1960 v S, E; 1961 v E, S, I, WG (2), Gr; (with Coleraine), 1962 v S (31)
Peden, J. (Linfield), 1887 v S, W; 1888 v W, E; 1889 v S, E; 1890 v W, S; 1891 v W, E; 1892 v W, E; 1893 v E, S, W; (with Distillery), 1896 v W, E, S; 1897 v W, S; 1898 v W, E, S; 1899 v W (24)
Penney, S. (Brighton & HA), 1985 v Is; 1986 v T, R, E, F, D, Mor, Alg, Sp; 1987 v E, T, Is; 1988 v Pol, F, Ma; 1989 v Ei, Sp (17)
Percy, J. C. (Belfast YMCA), 1889 v W (1)
Platt, J. A. (Middlesbrough), 1976 v Is (sub); 1978 v S, E, W; 1980 v S, E, W, Aus (3); 1981 v Se, P; 1982 v F, S, W (sub), A; 1983 v A, WG, Alb, T; (with Ballymena U), 1984 v E, W (sub); (with Coleraine), 1986 v Mor (sub) (23)
Pollock, W. (Belfast C), 1928 v F (1)
Ponsonby, J. (Distillery), 1895 v S, W; 1896 v E, S, W; 1897 v E, S, W; 1899 v E (9)
Potts, R. M. C. (Cliftonville), 1883 v E, W (2)
Priestley, T. J. M. (Coleraine), 1933 v S; (with Chelsea), 1934 v E (2)
Pyper, Jas. (Cliftonville), 1897 v S, W; 1898 v S, E, W; 1899 v S; 1900 v E (7)
Pyper, John (Cliftonville), 1897 v E, S, W; 1899 v E, W; 1900 v E, W, S; 1902 v S (9)
Pyper, M. (Linfield), 1932 v W (1)

Quinn, J. M. (Blackburn R), 1985 v Is, Fi, E, Sp, T; 1986 v T, R, E, F, D (sub), Mor (sub); 1987 v E (sub), T; (with Swindon T), 1988 v Y (sub), T, Gr, Pol, F (sub), Ma; (with Leicester C), 1989 v Ei, H (sub), Sp (sub+1); (with Bradford C), Ma, Ch; 1990 v H; (with West Ham U), N; 1991 v Y (sub); (with Bournemouth), 1992 v Li; (with Reading), 1993 v Sp, D, Alb (sub), Ei (sub), La (sub); 1994 v La, D (sub), Ei, R, Lie, Co, M; 1995 v P, A (sub), La (sub); 1996 v Lie, A (sub) (46)
Quinn, S. J. (Blackpool), 1996 v Se (sub); 1997 v Alb (sub), I, Bel, P, Uk (sub), Arm, Th (sub); 1998 v G, Alb; (with WBA), Slo, Sw; 1999 v T (sub), Fi (sub), Ei; 2000 v F (sub), T (sub), G (sub), Fi, L, Ma; 2001 v Y (sub), Bul (sub), CzR (sub); 2002 v Ma (sub); (with Willem II), 2003 v Cy, Fi, Arm, Gr; 2004 v Ser, Bar, Tr; 2005 v Pol, W, Az, A; (with Sheffield W), Pol; (with Peterborough U), 2006 v Ma, Az, E, W, A, P, Es, U, R (46)

Rafferty, P. (Linfield), 1980 v E (sub) (1)
Ramsey, P. C. (Leicester C), 1984 v A, WG, S; 1985 v Is, E, Sp, T; 1986 v T, Mor; 1987 v Is, E, Y (sub); 1988 v Y; 1989 v Sp (14)
Rankine, J. (Alexander), 1883 v E, W (2)
Rattray, D. (Avoniel), 1882 v E; 1883 v E, W (3)
Rea, R. (Glentoran), 1901 v E (1)
Redmond, R. (Cliftonville), 1884 v W (1)
Reid, G. H. (Cardiff C), 1923 v S (1)
Reid, J. (Ulster), 1883 v E; 1884 v W; 1887 v S; 1889 v W; 1890 v S, W (6)
Reid, S. E. (Derby Co), 1934 v E, W; 1936 v E (3)
Reid, W. (Hearts), 1931 v E (1)
Reilly, M. M. (Portsmouth), 1900 v E; 1902 v E (2)
Renneville, W. T. J. (Leyton), 1910 v S, E, W; (with Aston Villa), 1911 v W (4)
Reynolds, J. (Distillery), 1890 v E, W; (with Ulster), 1891 v E, S, W (5)
Reynolds, R. (Bohemians), 1905 v W (1)
Rice, P. J. (Arsenal), 1969 v Is; 1970 v USSR; 1971 v E, S, W; 1972 v USSR, Sp, E, S, W; 1973 v Bul, Cy, E, S, W; 1974 v Bul, P, S, E, W; 1975 v N, Y, E, S, W; 1976 v Se, N, Y, Is, S, E, W; 1977 v Ho, Bel, WG, E, S, Ic; 1978 v Ic, Ho, Bel; 1979 v Ei, D, E (2), S, W, D; 1980 v E (49)
Roberts, F. C. (Glentoran), 1931 v S (1)
Robinson, P. (Distillery), 1920 v S; (with Blackburn R), 1921 v W (2)
Robinson, S. (Bournemouth), 1997 v Th (sub); 1999 v Mol, Ei; 2000 v L (sub), H (sub); (with Luton T), 2006 v Az (sub) (6)
Rogan, A. (Celtic), 1988 v Y (sub), Gr, Pol (sub); 1989 v Ei (sub), H, Sp (2), Ma (sub), Ch; 1990 v H, N (sub), U; 1991 v Y (2), D, A; (with Sunderland), 1992 v Li (sub); (with Millwall), 1997 v G (sub) (18)
Rollo, D. (Linfield), 1912 v W; 1913 v W; 1914 v W, E; (with Blackburn R), 1920 v S, W; 1921 v E, S, W; 1922 v E; 1923 v E; 1924 v S, W; 1925 v W; 1926 v E; 1927 v E (16)
Roper, E. O. (Dublin University), 1886 v W (1)
Rosbotham, A. (Cliftonville), 1887 v E, S, W; 1888 v E, S, W; 1889 v E (7)
Ross, W. E. (Newcastle U), 1969 v Is (1)
Rowland, K. (West Ham U), 1994 v La (sub); 1995 v Ca, Ch, La; 1996 v P (sub), Lie (sub), N (sub), Se, G (sub); 1997 v Uk, Arm, I (sub); 1998 v Alb; (with QPR), 1999 v T, Fi, Mol, G, Ca, Ei (19)

Rowley, R. W. M. (Southampton), 1929 v S, W; 1930 v W, E; (with Tottenham H), 1931 v W; 1932 v S (6)
Rushe, F. (Distillery), 1925 v S.Af (1)
Russell, A. (Linfield), 1947 v E (1)
Russell, S. R. (Bradford C), 1930 v E, S; (with Derry C), 1932 v E (3)
Ryan, R. A. (WBA), 1950 v W (1)

Sanchez, L. P. (Wimbledon), 1987 v T (sub); 1989 v Sp, Ma (3)
Scott, E. (Liverpool), 1920 v S; 1921 v E, S, W; 1922 v E; 1925 v W; 1926 v E, S, W; 1927 v E, S, W; 1928 v E, S, W; 1929 v E, S, W; 1930 v E; 1931 v E; 1932 v W; 1933 v E, S, W; 1934 v E, S, W; (with Belfast C), 1935 v S; 1936 v E, S, W (31)
Scott, J. (Grimsby), 1958 v Cz, F (2)
Scott, J. E. (Cliftonville), 1901 v S (1)
Scott, L. J. (Dublin University), 1895 v S, W (2)
Scott, P. W. (Everton), 1975 v W; 1976 v Y; (with York C), Is, S, E (sub), W; 1978 v S, E, W; (with Aldershot), 1979 v S (sub) (10)
Scott, T. (Cliftonville), 1894 v E, S; 1895 v S, W; 1896 v S, E, W; 1897 v E, W; 1898 v E, S, W; 1900 v W (13)
Scott, W. (Linfield), 1903 v E, S, W; 1904 v E, S, W; (with Everton), 1905 v E, S; 1907 v E, S; 1908 v E, S, W; 1909 v E, S, W; 1910 v E, S; 1911 v E, S, W; 1912 v E; (with Leeds City), 1913 v E, S, W (25)
Scraggs, M. J. (Glentoran), 1921 v W; 1922 v E (2)
Seymour, H. C. (Bohemians), 1914 v W (1)
Seymour, J. (Cliftonville), 1907 v W; 1909 v W (2)
Shanks, T. (Woolwich Arsenal), 1903 v S; 1904 v W; (with Brentford), 1905 v E (3)
Sharkey, P. G. (Ipswich T), 1976 v S (1)
Sheehan, Dr G. (Bohemians), 1899 v S; 1900 v E, W (3)
Sheridan, J. (Everton), 1903 v W, E, S; 1904 v E, S; (with Stoke C), 1905 v E (6)
Sherrard, J. (Limavady), 1885 v S; 1887 v W; 1888 v W (3)
Sherrard, W. C. (Cliftonville), 1895 v E, W, S (3)
Sherry, J. J. (Bohemians), 1906 v E; 1907 v W (2)
Shields, R. J. (Southampton), 1957 v S (1)
Shiels, D. (Hibernian), 2006 v P (sub), U (sub), R (3)
Silo, M. (Belfast YMCA), 1888 v E (1)
Simpson, W. J. (Rangers), 1951 v W, F; 1954 v E, S; 1955 v E; 1957 v I, P; 1958 v S, E, W, I; 1959 v S (12)
Sinclair, J. (Knock), 1882 v E, W (2)
Slemin, J. C. (Bohemians), 1909 v W (1)
Sloan, A. S. (London Caledonians), 1925 v W (1)
Sloan, D. (Oxford U), 1969 v Is; 1971 v Sp (2)
Sloan, H. A. de B. (Bohemians), 1903 v E; 1904 v S; 1905 v E; 1906 v W; 1907 v E, W; 1908 v W; 1909 v S (8)
Sloan, J. W. (Arsenal), 1947 v W (1)
Sloan, T. (Manchester U), 1979 v S, W (sub), D (sub) (3)
Sloan, T. (Cardiff C), 1926 v S, W, E; 1927 v W, S; 1928 v E, W; 1929 v E; (with Linfield), 1930 v W, S; 1931 v S (11)
Small, J. M. (Clarence), 1887 v E; (with Cliftonville), 1893 v E, S, W (4)
Smith, A. W. (Glentoran), 2003 v I, Sp; 2004 v Uk (sub), Arm, Gr (sub), N, Es, Ser (sub), Bar (sub), Stk, Tr (sub); (with Preston NE), 2005 v Sw, Pol (sub), W (sub), Az (sub), Ca (sub), Pol (sub), G (sub) (18)
Smith, E. E. (Cardiff C), 1921 v S; 1923 v W, E; 1924 v E (4)
Smith, J. E. (Distillery), 1901 v S, W (2)
Smyth, R. H. (Dublin University), 1886 v W (1)
Smyth, S. (Wolverhampton W), 1948 v E, S, W; 1949 v S, W; 1950 v E, S, W; (with Stoke C), 1952 v E (9)
Smyth, W. (Distillery), 1949 v E, S; 1954 v S, E (4)
Snape, A. (Airdrie), 1920 v E (1)
Sonner, D. J. (Ipswich T), 1998 v Alb (sub); (with Sheffield W), 1999 v G (sub), Ca (sub); 2000 v L (sub), Ma (sub), H; (with Birmingham C), 2001 v N (sub); (with Nottingham F), 2004 v Es, Ser (sub), Bar, Stk, Tr (sub); (with Peterborough U), 2005 v Sw (13)
Spence, D. W. (Bury), 1975 v Y, E, S, W; 1976 v Se, Is, E, W, S (sub); (with Blackpool), 1977 v Ho (sub), WG (sub), E (sub), S (sub), W (sub), Ic (sub); 1979 v Ei, D (sub), E (sub), Bul (sub), E (sub), S, W, D; 1980 v Ei; (with Southend U), Is (sub), Aus (sub); 1981 v S (sub), Se (sub); 1982 v F (sub) (29)
Spencer, S. (Distillery), 1890 v E, S; 1892 v E, S, W; 1893 v E (6)
Spiller, E. A. (Cliftonville), 1883 v E, W; 1884 v E, W, S (5)
Sproule, I. (Hibernian), 2006 v E (sub), P (sub), Es, U, R (5)
Stanfield, O. M. (Distillery), 1887 v E, S, W; 1888 v E, S, W; 1889 v E, S, W; 1890 v E, S; 1891 v E, S, W; 1892 v E, S, W; 1893 v E, W; 1894 v E, S, W; 1895 v E, S; 1896 v E, S, W; 1897 v E, S, W (30)
Steele, A. (Charlton Ath), 1926 v W, S; (with Fulham), 1929 v W, S (4)
Stevenson, A. E. (Rangers), 1934 v E, S, W; (with Everton), 1935 v E, S; 1936 v S, W; 1937 v E, W; 1938 v E, W; 1939 v E, S, W; 1947 v S, W; 1948 v S (17)
Stewart, A. (Glentoran), 1967 v W; 1968 v S, E; (with Derby Co), 1968 v W; 1969 v Is, T (1+1 sub) (7)
Stewart, D. C. (Hull C), 1978 v Bel (1)
Stewart, I. (QPR), 1982 v F (sub); 1983 v A, WG, Alb, T, Alb, S, E, W; 1984 v A, T, WG, S, E, W, Fi; 1985 v R, Fi, Is, E, Sp, T; (with Newcastle U), 1986 v R, E, D, Mor, Alg (sub), Sp (sub), Br; 1987 v E, Is (sub) (31)
Stewart, R. K. (St Columb's Court), 1890 v E, S, W; (with Cliftonville), 1892 v E, S, W; 1893 v E, W; 1894 v E, S, W (11)
Stewart, T. C. (Linfield), 1961 v W (1)
Swan, S. (Linfield), 1899 v S (1)

Taggart, G. P. (Barnsley), 1990 v N, U; 1991 v Y, D, A, Pol, Fa; 1992 v Fa, A, D, S, Li, G; 1993 v Alb, Sp, D, Alb, Ei, Sp, Li, La; 1994 v La, D, Ei, R, Lie, Co, M; 1995 v P (sub), A, Ei (2), Ca, Ch, La; (with Bolton W), 1997 v G, Alb, I, Bel, P, Uk, Arm; 1998 v G, P, Sp; (with Leicester C), 2000 v H; 2001 v Ma, D, Ic, N; 2003 v Sp (51)
Taggart, J. (Walsall), 1899 v W (1)
Taylor, M. S. (Fulham), 1999 v G, Mol, Ca, Ei; 2000 v F, T, G, Fi, L (sub), Ma (sub), H; 2001 v Y, N, Bul, CzR; 2002 v D, Ic, Ma, Pol, Lie, Sp; 2003 v Cy, Sp, Uk, Fi, Arm, Gr, I, Sp; 2004 v Uk, Arm, Gr, N; (with Birmingham C), Es, Ser, Bar, Stk, Tr; 2005 v Pol, W, Az, Ca, E, Pol, G; 2006 v Ma, Az, E, W, A, P, Es (52)
Thompson, F. W. (Cliftonville), 1910 v E, S, W; (with Linfield), 1911 v W; (with Bradford C), 1911 v E; 1912 v E, W; 1913 v E, S, W; (with Clyde), 1914 v E, S (12)
Thompson, J. (Distillery), 1897 v S (1)
Thompson, P. (Linfield), 2006 v P (sub), Es (sub), U (sub), R (4)
Thompson, R. (Queen's Island), 1928 v F (1)
Thompson, W. (Belfast Ath), 1889 v S (1)
Thunder, P. J. (Bohemians), 1911 v W (1)
Todd, S. J. (Burnley), 1966 v M (sub); 1967 v E; 1968 v W; 1969 v E, S, W; 1970 v S, USSR; (with Sheffield W), 1971 v Cy (2), Sp (sub) (11)
Toner, C. (Leyton Orient), 2003 v I (sub), Sp (sub) (2)
Toner, J. (Arsenal), 1922 v W; 1923 v W; 1924 v W, E; 1925 v E, S; (with St Johnstone), 1927 v E, S (8)
Torrans, R. (Linfield), 1893 v S (1)
Torrans, S. (Linfield), 1889 v S; 1890 v S, W; 1891 v S, W; 1892 v E, S, W; 1893 v E, S; 1894 v E, S, W; 1895 v E; 1896 v E, S, W; 1897 v E, S, W; 1898 v E, S; 1899 v E, W; 1901 v S, W (26)
Trainor, D. (Crusaders), 1967 v W (1)
Tully, C. P. (Celtic), 1949 v E; 1950 v E; 1952 v S; 1953 v E, S, W, F; 1954 v S; 1956 v E; 1959 v Sp (10)
Turner, A. (Cliftonville), 1896 v W (1)
Turner, E. (Cliftonville), 1896 v E (1)
Turner, W. (Cliftonville), 1886 v E, S; 1888 v S (3)
Twomey, J. F. (Leeds U), 1938 v W; 1939 v E (2)

Uprichard, W. N. M. C. (Swindon T), 1952 v E, S, W; 1953 v E, S; (with Portsmouth), 1953 v W, F; 1955 v E, S, W; 1956 v E, S, W; 1958 v S, I, Cz; 1959 v S, Sp (18)

Vernon, J. (Belfast C), 1947 v E, S; (with WBA), 1947 v W; 1948 v E, S, W; 1949 v E, S, W; 1950 v E, S; 1951 v E, S, W, F; 1952 v S, E (17)

Waddell, T. M. R. (Cliftonville), 1906 v S (1)
Walker, J. (Doncaster R), 1955 v W (1)
Walker, T. (Bury), 1911 v S (1)
Walsh, D. J. (WBA), 1947 v S, W; 1948 v E, S, W; 1949 v E, S, W; 1950 v W (9)
Walsh, W. (Manchester C), 1948 v E, S, W; 1949 v E, S (5)
Waring, J. (Cliftonville), 1899 v E (1)
Warren, P. (Shelbourne), 1913 v E, S (2)
Watson, J. (Ulster), 1883 v E, W; 1886 v E, S, W; 1887 v S, W; 1889 v E, W (9)
Watson, P. (Distillery), 1971 v Cy (sub) (1)
Watson, T. (Cardiff C), 1926 v S (1)
Wattie, J. (Distillery), 1899 v E (1)
Webb, C. G. (Brighton), 1909 v S, W; 1911 v S (3)
Webb, S. M. (Ross Co), 2006 v U (sub), R (sub) (2)
Weir, E. (Clyde), 1939 v W (1)
Welsh, E. (Carlisle U), 1966 v W, WG, M; 1967 v W (4)
Whiteside, N. (Manchester U), 1982 v Y, Hon, Sp, A, F; 1983 v WG, Alb, T; 1984 v A, T, WG, S, E, W, Fi; 1985 v R, Fi, Is, E, Sp, T; 1986 v R, E, F, D, Mor, Alg, Sp, Br; 1987 v E (2), Is, Y; 1988 v T, Pol, F; (with Everton), 1990 v H, Ei (38)
Whiteside, T. (Distillery), 1891 v E (1)
Whitfield, E. R. (Dublin University), 1886 v W (1)

Whitley, Jeff (Manchester C), 1997 v Bel (sub), Th (sub); 1998 v Sp (sub); 2000 v Fi; 2001 v Y, D, N; (with Sunderland), 2004 v Gr, Es, Ser, Stk, Tr; 2005 v Pol, W, Az, A, Ca, E, Pol; (with Cardiff C), 2006 v Ma (20)
Whitley, Jim (Manchester C), 1998 v Sp; 1999 v T (sub); 2000 v Fi (sub) (3)
Williams, J. R. (Ulster), 1886 v E, S (2)
Williams, M. S. (Chesterfield), 1999 v G, Mol, Ca, Ei; (with Watford), 2000 v F, T, G, Fi, L, Ma, H (sub); (with Wimbledon), 2001 v Y, Ic (sub), N (sub), CzR, Bul, CzR; 2002 v Lie, Sp; 2003 v Cy, Fi; (with Stoke C), Arm, Gr, I (sub), Sp (sub); (with Wimbledon), 2004 v N (sub), Es, Ser, Bar, Tr; (with Milton Keynes D), 2005 v Sw, Pol, W, Az, A, Pol (36)
Williams, P. A. (WBA), 1991 v Fa (sub) (1)
Williamson, J. (Cliftonville), 1890 v E; 1892 v S; 1893 v S (3)
Willighan, T. (Burnley), 1933 v W; 1934 v S (2)
Willis, G. (Linfield), 1906 v S, W; 1907 v S; 1912 v S (4)
Wilson, D. J. (Brighton & HA), 1987 v T, Is, E (sub); (with Luton T), 1988 v Y, T, Gr, Pol, F, Ma; 1989 v Ei, H, Sp, Ma, Ch; 1990 v H, Ei, N, U; (with Sheffield W), 1991 v Y, D, A, Fa; 1992 v A (sub), S (24)
Wilson, H. (Linfield), 1925 v W, S.Af (2)
Wilson, K. J. (Ipswich T), 1987 v Is, E, Y; (with Chelsea), 1988 v Y, T, Gr (sub), Pol (sub), F (sub); 1989 v H (sub), Sp (2), Ma, Ch; 1990 v Ei (sub), N, U; 1991 v Y (2), A, Pol, Fa; 1992 v Fa, A, D, S; (with Notts Co), Li, G; 1993 v Alb, Sp, D, Sp, Li, La; 1994 v La, D, Ei, R, Lie, Co, M; (with Walsall), 1995 v Ei (sub), La (42)
Wilson, M. (Distillery), 1884 v E, S, W (3)
Wilson, R. (Cliftonville), 1888 v S (1)
Wilson, S. J. (Glenavon), 1962 v S; 1964 v S; (with Falkirk), 1964 v E, W, U, Sp; 1965 v E, Sw; (with Dundee), 1966 v W, WG; 1967 v S; 1968 v E (12)
Wilton, J. M. (St Columb's Court), 1888 v E, W; 1889 v S, E; (with Cliftonville), 1890 v E; (with St Columb's Court), 1893 v W, S (7)
Wood, T. J. (Walsall), 1996 v Lie (sub) (1)
Worthington, N. (Sheffield W), 1984 v W, Fi (sub); 1985 v Is, Sp (sub); 1986 v T, R (sub), E (sub), D, Alg, Sp; 1987 v E (2), T, Is, Y; 1988 v Y, T, Gr, Pol, F, Ma; 1989 v Ei, H, Sp, Ma; 1990 v H, Ei, U; 1991 v Y, D, A, Fa; 1992 v A, D, S, Li, G; 1993 v Alb, Sp, D, Ei, Sp, Li, La; 1994 v La, D, Ei, Lie, Co, M; (with Leeds U), 1995 v P, A, Ei (2), La, Ca (sub), Ch, La; 1996 v P, Lie, A, N, Se, G; (with Stoke C), 1997 v I, Bel (sub) (66)
Wright, J. (Cliftonville), 1906 v E, S, W; 1907 v E, S, W (6)
Wright, T. J. (Newcastle U), 1989 v Ma, Ch; 1990 v H, U; 1992 v Fa, A, S, G; 1993 v Alb, Sp, Alb, Ei, Sp, Li, La; 1994 v La; (with Nottingham F), D, Ei, R, Lie, Co, M (sub); 1997 v G, Alb, I, Bel; (with Manchester C), P, Uk; 1998 v Alb; 1999 v Ca (sub); 2000 v F (sub) (31)

Young, S. (Linfield), 1907 v E, S; 1908 v E, S; (with Airdrie), 1909 v E; 1912 v S; (with Linfield), 1914 v E, S, W (9)

SCOTLAND

Adams, J. (Hearts), 1889 v Ni; 1892 v W; 1893 v Ni (3)
Agnew, W. B. (Kilmarnock), 1907 v Ni; 1908 v W, Ni (3)
Aird, J. (Burnley), 1954 v N (2), A, U (4)
Aitken, A. (Newcastle U), 1901 v E; 1902 v E; 1903 v E, W; 1904 v E; 1905 v E, W; 1906 v E; (with Middlesbrough), 1907 v E, W; 1908 v E; (with Leicester Fosse), 1910 v E; 1911 v E, Ni (14)
Aitken, G. G. (East Fife), 1949 v E, F; 1950 v W, Ni, Sw; (with Sunderland), 1953 v W, Ni; 1954 v E (8)
Aitken, R. (Dumbarton), 1886 v E; 1888 v Ni (2)
Aitken, R. (Celtic), 1980 v Pe (sub), Bel, W (sub), E, Pol; 1983 v Bel, Ca (1+1 sub); 1984 v Bel (sub), Ni, W (sub); 1985 v E, Ic; 1986 v W, EG, Aus (2), Is, R, E, D, WG, U; 1987 v Bul, Ei (2), L, Bel, E, Br; 1988 v H, Bel, Bul, L, S.Ar, Ma, Sp, Co, E; 1989 v N, Y, I, Cy, F, Cy, E, Ch; 1990 v Y, F, N; (with Newcastle U), Arg (sub), Pol, Ma, Cr, Se, Br; (with St Mirren), 1992 v R (sub) (57)
Aitkenhead, W. A. C. (Blackburn R), 1912 v Ni (1)
Albiston, A. (Manchester U), 1982 v Ni; 1984 v U, Bel, EG, W, E; 1985 v Y, Ic, Sp (2), W; 1986 v EG, Ho, U (14)
Alexander, D. (East Stirlingshire), 1894 v W, Ni (2)
Alexander, G. (Preston NE), 2002 v Ng (sub), Sk, S.Af (sub), Hk (sub); 2003 v D (sub), Fa (sub), Ca, P, Ei, Ic, Li, Nz (sub); 2004 v Li (sub), R; 2005 v Mol, Bl; 2006 v A, I, N, Bl, Slv, US, Sw (23)
Alexander, N. (Cardiff C), 2006 v Sw (sub), Bul, J (3)
Allan, D. S. (Queen's Park), 1885 v E, W; 1886 v W (3)
Allan, G. (Liverpool), 1897 v E (1)
Allan, H. (Hearts), 1902 v W (1)
Allan, J. (Queen's Park), 1887 v E, W (2)
Allan, T. (Dundee), 1974 v WG, N (2)
Ancell, R. F. D. (Newcastle U), 1937 v W, Ni (2)
Anderson, A. (Hearts), 1933 v E; 1934 v A, E, W, Ni; 1935 v E, W, Ni; 1936 v E, W, Ni; 1937 v G, E, W, Ni, A; 1938 v E, W, Ni, Cz, Ho; 1939 v W, H (23)
Anderson, F. (Clydesdale), 1874 v E (1)
Anderson, G. (Kilmarnock), 1901 v Ni (1)
Anderson, H. A. (Raith R), 1914 v W (1)
Anderson, J. (Leicester C), 1954 v Fi (1)
Anderson, K. (Queen's Park), 1896 v Ni; 1898 v E, Ni (3)
Anderson, R. (Aberdeen), 2003 v Ic (sub), Ca, P, Ei; 2005 v N, Se; 2006 v A (sub), Bul, J (9)
Anderson, W. (Queen's Park), 1882 v E; 1883 v E, W; 1884 v E; 1885 v E, W (6)
Andrews, P. (Eastern), 1875 v E (1)
Archibald, A. (Rangers), 1921 v W; 1922 v W, E; 1923 v Ni; 1924 v E, W; 1931 v E; 1932 v E (8)
Archibald, S. (Aberdeen), 1980 v P (sub); (with Tottenham H), Ni, Pol, H; 1981 v Se (sub), Is, Ni, Is, Ni, E; 1982 v Ni, P, Sp (sub), Ho, Nz (sub), Br, USSR; 1983 v EG, Sw (sub), Bel; 1984 v EG, E, F; (with Barcelona), 1985 v Sp, E, Ic (sub); 1986 v WG (27)
Armstrong, M. W. (Aberdeen), 1936 v W, Ni; 1937 v G (3)
Arnott, W. (Queen's Park), 1883 v W; 1884 v E, Ni; 1885 v E, W; 1886 v E; 1887 v E, W; 1888 v E; 1889 v E; 1890 v E; 1891 v E; 1892 v E; 1893 v E (14)
Auld, J. R. (Third Lanark), 1887 v E, W; 1889 v W (3)
Auld, R. (Celtic), 1959 v H, P; 1960 v W (3)

Baird, A. (Queen's Park), 1892 v Ni; 1894 v W (2)
Baird, D. (Hearts), 1890 v Ni; 1891 v E; 1892 v W (3)
Baird, H. (Airdrieonians), 1956 v A (1)
Baird, J. C. (Vale of Leven), 1876 v E; 1878 v W; 1880 v E (3)
Baird, S. (Rangers), 1957 v Y, Sp (2), Sw, WG; 1958 v F, Ni (7)
Baird, W. U. (St Bernard), 1897 v Ni (1)
Bannon, E. (Dundee U), 1980 v Bel; 1983 v Ni, W, E, Ca; 1984 v EG; 1986 v Is, R, E, D (sub), WG (11)
Barbour, A. (Renton), 1885 v Ni (1)
Barker, J. B. (Rangers), 1893 v W; 1894 v W (2)
Barrett, F. (Dundee), 1894 v Ni; 1895 v W (2)
Battles, B. (Celtic), 1901 v E, W, Ni (3)
Battles, B. jun. (Hearts), 1931 v W (1)
Bauld, W. (Hearts), 1950 v E, Sw, P (3)
Baxter, J. C. (Rangers), 1961 v Ni, Ei (2), Cz; 1962 v Ni, W, E, Cz (2), U; 1963 v W, Ni, E, A, N, Ei, Sp; 1964 v W, E, N, WG; 1965 v W, Ni, Fi; (with Sunderland), 1966 v P, Br, Ni, W, E, I; 1967 v W, E, USSR; 1968 v W (34)
Baxter, R. D. (Middlesbrough), 1939 v E, W, H (3)
Beattie, A. (Preston NE), 1937 v E, A, Cz; 1938 v E; 1939 v W, Ni, H (7)
Beattie, C. (Celtic), 2006 v I (sub), N (sub) (2)
Beattie, R. (Preston NE), 1939 v W (1)
Begbie, I. (Hearts), 1890 v Ni; 1891 v E; 1892 v W; 1894 v E (4)
Bell, A. (Manchester U), 1912 v Ni (1)
Bell, J. (Dumbarton), 1890 v Ni; 1892 v E; (with Everton), 1896 v E; 1897 v E; 1898 v E; (with Celtic), 1899 v E, W, Ni; 1900 v E, W (10)
Bell, M. (Hearts), 1901 v W (1)
Bell, W. J. (Leeds U), 1966 v P, Br (2)
Bennett, A. (Celtic), 1904 v W; 1907 v Ni; 1908 v W; (with Rangers), 1909 v W, Ni, E; 1910 v E, W; 1911 v E, W; 1913 v Ni (11)
Bennie, R. (Airdrieonians), 1925 v W, Ni; 1926 v Ni (3)
Bernard, P. R. J. (Oldham Ath), 1995 v J (sub), Ec (2)
Berry, D. (Queen's Park), 1894 v W; 1899 v W, Ni (3)
Berry, W. H. (Queen's Park), 1888 v E; 1889 v E; 1890 v E; 1891 v E (4)
Bett, J. (Rangers), 1982 v Ho; 1983 v Bel; (with Lokeren), 1984 v Bel, W, E, F; 1985 v Y, Ic, Sp (2), W, E, Ic; (with Aberdeen), 1986 v W, Is, Ho; 1987 v Bel; 1988 v H (sub); 1989 v Y; 1990 v F (sub), N, Arg, Eg, Ma, Cr (25)
Beveridge, W. W. (Glasgow University), 1879 v E, W; 1880 v W (3)
Black, A. (Hearts), 1938 v Cz, Ho; 1939 v H (3)
Black, D. (Hurlford), 1889 v Ni (1)
Black, E. (Metz), 1988 v H (sub), L (sub) (2)
Black, I. H. (Southampton), 1948 v E (1)
Blackburn, J. E. (Royal Engineers), 1873 v E (1)
Blacklaw, A. S. (Burnley), 1963 v N, Sp; 1966 v I (3)
Blackley, J. (Hibernian), 1974 v Cz, E, Bel, Z; 1976 v Sw; 1977 v W, Se (7)

Blair, D. (Clyde), 1929 v W, Ni; 1931 v E, A, I; 1932 v W, Ni; (with Aston Villa), 1933 v W (8)
Blair, J. (Sheffield W), 1920 v E, Ni; (with Cardiff C), 1921 v E; 1922 v E; 1923 v E, W, Ni; 1924 v W (8)
Blair, J. (Motherwell), 1934 v W (1)
Blair, J. A. (Blackpool), 1947 v W (1)
Blair, W. (Third Lanark), 1896 v W (1)
Blessington, J. (Celtic), 1894 v E, Ni; 1896 v E, Ni (4)
Blyth, J. A. (Coventry C), 1978 v Bul, W (2)
Bone, J. (Norwich C), 1972 v Y (sub); 1973 v D (2)
Booth, S. (Aberdeen), 1993 v G (sub), Es (2 subs); 1994 v Sw, Ma (sub); 1995 v Fa, Ru; 1996 v Fi, Sm, Aus (sub), US, Ho, Sw (sub); (with Borussia Dortmund), 1998 v D, Fi, Co (sub), Mor (sub); (with Twente), 2001 v Pol; 2002 v Cro, Bel (sub), La (sub) (21)
Bowie, J. (Rangers), 1920 v E, Ni (2)
Bowie, W. (Linthouse), 1891 v Ni (1)
Bowman, D. (Dundee U), 1992 v Fi, US (sub); 1993 v G, Es; 1994 v Sw, I (6)
Bowman, G. A. (Montrose), 1892 v Ni (1)
Boyd, J. M. (Newcastle U), 1934 v Ni (1)
Boyd, K. (Rangers) 2006 v Bul, J (sub) (2)
Boyd, R. (Mossend Swifts), 1889 v Ni; 1891 v W (2)
Boyd, T. (Motherwell), 1991 v R (sub), Sw, Bul, USSR; (with Chelsea), 1992 v Sw, R; (with Celtic), Fi, Ca, N, C; 1993 v Sw, P, I, Ma, G, Es (2); 1994 v I, Ma (sub), Ho (sub), A; 1995 v Fi, Fa, Ru, Gr, Ru, Sm; 1996 v Gr, Fi, Se, Sm, Aus, D, US, Co, Ho, E, Sw; 1997 v A, La, Se, Es (2), A, Se, W, Ma, Bl; 1998 v Bl, La, F, D, Fi (sub), Co, US, Br, N, Mor; 1999 v Li, Es, Fa, CzR, G, Fa, CzR; 2001 v La, Cro, Aus, Bel, Sm (sub), Pol; 2002 v Bel (72)
Boyd, W. G. (Clyde), 1931 v I, Sw (2)
Bradshaw, T. (Bury), 1928 v E (1)
Brand, R. (Rangers), 1961 v Ni, Cz, Ei (2); 1962 v Ni, W, Cz, U (8)
Brandon, T. (Blackburn R), 1896 v E (1)
Brazil, A. (Ipswich T), 1980 v Pol (sub), H; 1982 v Sp, Ho (sub), Ni, W, E, Nz, USSR (sub); 1983 v EG, Sw; (with Tottenham H), W, E (sub) (13)
Breckenridge, T. (Hearts), 1888 v Ni (1)
Bremner, D. (Hibernian), 1976 v Sw (sub) (1)
Bremner, W. J. (Leeds U), 1965 v Sp; 1966 v E, Pol, P, Br, I (2); 1967 v W, Ni, E; 1968 v W, E; 1969 v W, E, Ni, D, A, WG, Cy (2); 1970 v Ei, WG, A; 1971 v W, E; 1972 v P, Bel, Ho, Ni, W, E, Y, Cz, Br; 1973 v D (2), E (2), Ni (sub), Sw, Br; 1974 v Cz, WG, Ni, W, E, Bel, N, Z, Br, Y; 1975 v Sp (2); 1976 v D (54)
Brennan, F. (Newcastle U), 1947 v W, Ni; 1953 v W, Ni, E; 1954 v Ni, E (7)
Breslin, B. (Hibernian), 1897 v W (1)
Brewster, G. (Everton), 1921 v E (1)
Brogan, J. (Celtic), 1971 v W, Ni, P, E (4)
Brown, A. (St Mirren), 1890 v W; 1891 v W (2)
Brown, A. (Middlesbrough), 1904 v E (1)
Brown, A. D. (East Fife), 1950 v Sw, P, F; (with Blackpool), 1952 v USA, D, Se; 1953 v W; 1954 v W, E, N (2), Fi, A, U (14)
Brown, G. C. P. (Rangers), 1931 v W; 1932 v E, W, Ni; 1933 v E; 1934 v A; 1935 v E, W; 1936 v E, W; 1937 v G, E, W, Ni, Cz; 1938 v E, W, Cz, Ho (19)
Brown, H. (Partick Th), 1947 v W, Bel, L (3)
Brown, J. B. (Clyde), 1939 v W (1)
Brown, J. G. (Sheffield U), 1975 v R (1)
Brown, R. (Cambuslang), 1890 v W (1)
Brown, R. (Dumbarton), 1884 v W, Ni (2)
Brown, R. (Rangers), 1947 v Ni; 1949 v Ni; 1952 v E (3)
Brown, R. jun. (Dumbarton), 1885 v W (1)
Brown, S. (Hibernian), 2006 v US (sub) (1)
Brown, W. D. F. (Dundee), 1958 v F; 1959 v E, W, Ni; (with Tottenham H), 1960 v W, Ni, Pol, A, H, T; 1962 v Ni, W, E, Cz; 1963 v W, Ni, E, A; 1964 v Ni, W, N; 1965 v E, Fi, Pol, Sp; 1966 v Ni, Pol, I (28)
Browning, J. (Celtic), 1914 v W (1)
Brownlie, J. (Third Lanark), 1909 v E, Ni; 1910 v E, W, Ni; 1911 v W, Ni; 1912 v W, Ni, E; 1913 v W, Ni, E; 1914 v W, Ni, E (16)
Brownlie, J. (Hibernian), 1971 v USSR; 1972 v Pe, Ni, E; 1973 v D (2); 1976 v R (7)
Bruce, D. (Vale of Leven), 1890 v W (1)
Bruce, R. F. (Middlesbrough), 1934 v A (1)
Buchan, M. M. (Aberdeen), 1972 v P (sub), Bel; (with Manchester U), W, Y, Cz, Br; 1973 v D (2), E; 1974 v WG, Ni, W, N, Br, Y; 1975 v EG, Sp, P; 1976 v D, R; 1977 v Fi, Cz, Ch, Arg, Br; 1978 v EG, W (sub), Ni, Pe, Ir, Ho; 1979 v A, N, P (34)
Buchanan, J. (Cambuslang), 1889 v Ni (1)
Buchanan, J. (Rangers), 1929 v E; 1930 v E (2)
Buchanan, P. S. (Chelsea), 1938 v Cz (1)
Buchanan, R. (Abercorn), 1891 v W (1)
Buckley, P. (Aberdeen), 1954 v N; 1955 v W, Ni (3)
Buick, A. (Hearts), 1902 v W, Ni (2)
Burchill, M. J. (Celtic), 2000 v Bos (sub), Li, E (sub + sub), F (sub), Ho (sub) (6)
Burke, C. (Rangers), 2006 v Bul (sub), J (sub) (2)
Burley, C. W. (Chelsea), 1995 v J, Ec, Fa; 1996 v Gr, Se, Aus, D, US, Co (sub), Ho (sub), E (sub), Sw; 1997 v A, La, Se, Es, A, Se, Ma, Bl; (with Celtic), 1998 v Bl, La, F, Co, US (sub), Br, N, Mor; 1999 v Fa, CzR; 2000 v Bos, Es, Bos, Li, E (2); (with Derby Co), Ho, Ei; 2001 v Cro, Aus, Bel, Sm; 2002 v Cro, Bel, La; 2003 v A (46)
Burley, G. (Ipswich T), 1979 v W, Ni, E, Arg, N; 1980 v P, Ni, E (sub), Pol; 1982 v W (sub), E (11)
Burns, F. (Manchester U), 1970 v A (1)
Burns, K. (Birmingham C), 1974 v WG; 1975 v EG (sub), Sp (2); 1977 v Cz (sub), W, Se, W (sub); (with Nottingham F), 1978 v Ni (sub), W, E, Pe, Ir; 1979 v N; 1980 v Pe, A, Bel; 1981 v Is, Ni, W (20)
Burns, T. (Celtic), 1981 v Ni; 1982 v Ho (sub), W; 1983 v Bel (sub), Ni, Ca (1 + 1 sub); 1988 v E (sub) (8)
Busby, M. W. (Manchester C), 1934 v W (1)

Cairns, T. (Rangers), 1920 v W; 1922 v E; 1923 v E, W; 1924 v Ni; 1925 v W, E, Ni (8)
Calderhead, D. (Q of S Wanderers), 1889 v Ni (1)
Calderwood, C. (Tottenham H), 1995 v Ru, Sm, J, Ec, Fa; 1996 v Gr, Fi, Se, Sm, US, Co, Ho, E, Sw; 1997 v A, La, Se, Es (2), A, Se; 1998 v Bl, La, F, D, Fi, Co, US, Br, N; 1999 v Li, Es; (with Aston Villa), Fa, CzR; 2000 v Bos (1 + sub) (36)
Calderwood, R. (Cartvale), 1885 v Ni, E, W (3)
Caldow, E. (Rangers), 1957 v Sp (2), Sw, WG, E; 1958 v Ni, W, Sw, Par, H, Pol, Y, F; 1959 v E, W, Ni, WG, Ho, P; 1960 v E, W, Ni, A, H, T; 1961 v E, W, Ni, Ei (2), Cz; 1962 v Ni, W, E, Cz (2), U; 1963 v W, Ni, E (40)
Caldwell, G. (Newcastle U), 2002 v F, Ng (sub), Sk, S.Af; (with Hibernian), 2004 v R, D, Es, Tr; 2005 v H, Bl, Sp, Slv, N, Mol, I; 2006 v Slv (sub), US (sub), Sw, Bul, J (20)
Caldwell, S. (Newcastle U), 2001 v Pol (sub); 2003 v Ei; 2004 v W, Tr (sub); (with Sunderland), 2005 v Mol; 2006 v A, Slv (sub), US (sub), Sw (sub) (9)
Callaghan, P. (Hibernian), 1900 v Ni (1)
Callaghan, W. (Dunfermline Ath), 1970 v Ei (sub), W (2)
Cameron, C. (Hearts), 1999 v G (sub), Fa (sub); 2000 v Li (sub), F, Ei (sub); 2001 v La (sub), Sm, Cro, Aus, Sm, Pol; (with Wolverhampton W), 2002 v Cro (sub), Bel (sub), La, F; 2003 v Ei (sub), Li (sub), A (sub), G; 2004 v N, Fa, G, Li, W, R, D; 2005 v Sp (sub), Mol (28)
Cameron, J. (Rangers), 1886 v Ni (1)
Cameron, J. (Queen's Park), 1896 v Ni (1)
Cameron, J. (St Mirren), 1904 v Ni; (with Chelsea), 1909 v E (2)
Campbell, C. (Queen's Park), 1874 v E; 1876 v W; 1877 v E, W; 1878 v E; 1879 v E; 1880 v E; 1881 v E; 1882 v E, W; 1884 v E; 1885 v E; 1886 v E (13)
Campbell, H. (Renton), 1889 v W (1)
Campbell, Jas (Sheffield W), 1913 v W (1)
Campbell, J. (South Western), 1880 v W (1)
Campbell, J. (Kilmarnock), 1891 v Ni; 1892 v W (2)
Campbell, John (Celtic), 1893 v E, Ni; 1898 v E, Ni; 1900 v E, Ni; 1901 v E, W, Ni; 1902 v W, Ni; 1903 v W (12)
Campbell, John (Rangers), 1899 v E, W, Ni; 1901 v Ni (4)
Campbell, K. (Liverpool), 1920 v E, W, Ni; (with Partick Th), 1921 v W, Ni; 1922 v W, Ni, E (8)
Campbell, P. (Rangers), 1878 v W; 1879 v W (2)
Campbell, P. (Morton), 1898 v W (1)
Campbell, R. (Falkirk), 1947 v Bel, L; (with Chelsea), 1950 v Sw, P, F (5)
Campbell, W. (Morton), 1947 v Ni; 1948 v E, Bel, Sw, F (5)
Canero, P. (Leicester C), 2004 v D (sub) (1)
Carabine, J. (Third Lanark), 1938 v Ho; 1939 v E, Ni (3)
Carr, W. M. (Coventry C), 1970 v Ni, W, E; 1971 v D; 1972 v Pe; 1973 v D (sub) (6)
Cassidy, J. (Celtic), 1921 v W, Ni; 1923 v Ni; 1924 v W (4)
Chalmers, S. (Celtic), 1965 v W, Fi; 1966 v P (sub), Br; 1967 v Ni (5)
Chalmers, W. (Rangers), 1885 v Ni (1)
Chalmers, W. S. (Queen's Park), 1929 v Ni (1)
Chambers, T. (Hearts), 1894 v W (1)
Chaplin, G. D. (Dundee), 1908 v W (1)
Cheyne, A. G. (Aberdeen), 1929 v E, N, G, Ho; 1930 v F (5)
Christie, A. J. (Queen's Park), 1898 v W; 1899 v E, Ni (3)
Christie, R. M. (Queen's Park), 1884 v E (1)
Clark, J. (Celtic), 1966 v Br; 1967 v W, Ni, USSR (4)
Clark, R. B. (Aberdeen), 1968 v W, Ho; 1970 v Ni; 1971 v W, Ni, E, D, P, USSR; 1972 v Bel, Ni, W, E, Cz, Br; 1973 v D, E (17)
Clarke, S. (Chelsea), 1988 v H, Bel, Bul, S.Ar, Ma; 1994 v Ho (6)

Cleland, J. (Royal Albert), 1891 v Ni (1)
Clements, R. (Leith Ath), 1891 v Ni (1)
Clunas, W. L. (Sunderland), 1924 v E; 1926 v W (2)
Collier, W. (Raith R), 1922 v W (1)
Collins, J. (Hibernian), 1988 v S.Ar; 1990 v EG, Pol (sub), Ma (sub); (with Celtic), 1991 v Sw (sub), Bul (sub); 1992 v Ni (sub), Fi; 1993 v P, Ma, G, P, Es (2); 1994 v Sw, Ho (sub), A, Ho; 1995 v Fi, Fa, Ru, Gr, Ru, Sm, Fa; 1996 v Gr, Fi, Se, Sm, Aus, D, US (sub), Co, Ho, E, Sw; (with Monaco), 1997 v A, La, Se, Es, A, Se, Ma; 1998 v Bl, La, F, Fi, Co, US, Br, N, Mor; (with Everton), 1999 v Li; 2000 v Bos, Es, Bos, E (2) (58)
Collins, R. Y. (Celtic), 1951 v W, Ni, A; 1955 v Y, A, H; 1956 v Ni, W; 1957 v E, W, Sp (2), Sw, WG; 1958 v Ni, W, Sw, H, Pol, Y, F, Par; (with Everton), 1959 v E, W, Ni, WG, Ho, P; (with Leeds U), 1965 v E, Pol, Sp (31)
Collins, T. (Hearts), 1909 v W (1)
Colman, D. (Aberdeen), 1911 v E, W, Ni; 1913 v Ni (4)
Colquhoun, E. P. (Sheffield U), 1972 v P, Ho, Pe, Y, Cz, Br; 1973 v D (2), E (9)
Colquhoun, J. (Hearts), 1988 v S.Ar (sub), Ma (sub) (2)
Combe, J. R. (Hibernian), 1948 v E, Bel, Sw (3)
Conn, A. (Hearts), 1956 v A (1)
Conn, A. (Tottenham H), 1975 v Ni (sub), E (2)
Connachan, E. D. (Dunfermline Ath), 1962 v Cz, U (2)
Connelly, G. (Celtic), 1974 v Cz, WG (2)
Connolly, J. (Everton), 1973 v Sw (1)
Connor, J. (Airdrieonians), 1886 v Ni (1)
Connor, J. (Sunderland), 1930 v F; 1932 v Ni; 1934 v E; 1935 v Ni (4)
Connor, R. (Dundee), 1986 v Ho; (with Aberdeen), 1988 v S.Ar (sub); 1989 v E; 1991 v R (4)
Cook, W. L. (Bolton W), 1934 v E; 1935 v W, Ni (3)
Cooke, C. (Dundee), 1966 v W, I; (with Chelsea), P, Br; 1968 v E, Ho; 1969 v W, Ni, A, WG (sub), Cy (2); 1970 v A; 1971 v Bel; 1975 v Sp, P (16)
Cooper, D. (Rangers), 1980 v Pe, A (sub); 1984 v W, E; 1985 v Y, Ic, Sp (2), W; 1986 v W (sub), EG, Aus (2), Ho, WG (sub), U (sub); 1987 v Bul, L, Ei, Br; (with Motherwell), 1990 v N, Eg (22)
Cormack, P. B. (Hibernian), 1966 v Br; 1969 v D (sub); 1970 v Ei, WG; (with Nottingham F), 1971 v D (sub), W, P, E; 1972 v Ho (sub) (9)
Cowan, J. (Aston Villa), 1896 v E; 1897 v E; 1898 v E (3)
Cowan, J. (Morton), 1948 v Bel, Sw; F; 1949 v E, W, F; 1950 v E, W, Ni, Sw, P, F; 1951 v E, W, Ni, A (2), D, F, Bel; 1952 v Ni, W, USA, D, Se (25)
Cowan, W, D. (Newcastle U), 1924 v E (1)
Cowie, D. (Dundee), 1953 v E, Se; 1954 v Ni, W, Fi, N, A, U; 1955 v W, Ni, A, H; 1956 v W, A; 1957 v Ni, W; 1958 v H, Pol, Y, Par (20)
Cox, C. J. (Hearts), 1948 v F (1)
Cox, S. (Rangers), 1949 v E, F; 1950 v E, F, W, Ni, Sw, P; 1951 v E, D, F, Bel, A; 1952 v Ni, W, USA, D, Se; 1953 v W, Ni, E; 1954 v W, Ni, E (24)
Craig, A. (Motherwell), 1929 v N, Ho; 1932 v E (3)
Craig, J. (Celtic), 1977 v Se (sub) (1)
Craig, J. P. (Celtic), 1968 v W (1)
Craig, T. (Rangers), 1927 v Ni; 1928 v Ni; 1929 v N, G, Ho; 1930 v Ni, E, W (8)
Craig, T. B. (Newcastle U), 1976 v Sw (1)
Crainey, S. (Celtic), 2002 v F, Ng; 2003 v D (sub), Fa; (with Southampton), 2004 v R (sub), D (6)
Crapnell, J. (Airdrieonians), 1929 v E, N, G; 1930 v F; 1931 v Ni, Sw; 1932 v E, F; 1933 v Ni (9)
Crawford, D. (St Mirren), 1894 v W, Ni; (with Rangers), 1900 v W (3)
Crawford, J. (Queen's Park), 1932 v F, Ni; 1933 v E, W, Ni (5)
Crawford, S. (Raith R), 1995 v Ec (sub); (with Dunfermline Ath), 2001 v Pol (sub); 2002 v F; 2003 v Fa (sub), Ic, Ca, P, Ei, Ic, Li, A (sub), Nz, G; 2004 v N, Fa, Li, Ho (sub), R (sub), Es (sub), Tr; (with Plymouth Arg), 2005 v H (sub), Sp, Slv (sub), Mol, Se (sub) (25)
Crerand, P. T. (Celtic), 1961 v Ei (2), Cz; 1962 v Ni, W, E, Cz (2), U; 1963 v W, Ni; (with Manchester U), 1964 v Ni; 1965 v E, Pol, Fi; 1966 v Pol (16)
Cringan, W. (Celtic), 1920 v W; 1922 v E, Ni; 1923 v W, E (5)
Crosbie, J. A. (Ayr U), 1920 v W; (with Birmingham), 1922 v E (2)
Croal, J. A. (Falkirk), 1913 v Ni; 1914 v E, W (3)
Cropley, A. J. (Hibernian), 1972 v P, Bel (2)
Cross, J. H. (Third Lanark), 1903 v Ni (1)
Cruickshank, J. (Hearts), 1964 v WG; 1970 v W, E; 1971 v D, Bel; 1976 v R (6)
Crum, J. (Celtic), 1936 v E; 1939 v Ni (2)
Cullen, M. J. (Luton T), 1956 v A (1)
Cumming, D. S. (Middlesbrough), 1938 v E (1)
Cumming, J. (Hearts), 1955 v E, H, P, Y; 1960 v E, Pol, A, H, T (9)
Cummings, G. (Partick Th), 1935 v E; 1936 v W, Ni; (with Aston Villa), E; 1937 v G; 1938 v W, Ni, Cz; 1939 v E (9)
Cummings, W. (Chelsea), 2002 v Hk (sub) (1)
Cunningham, A. N. (Rangers), 1920 v Ni; 1921 v W, E; 1922 v Ni; 1923 v E, W; 1924 v E, Ni; 1926 v E, Ni; 1927 v E, W (12)
Cunningham, W. C. (Preston NE), 1954 v N (2), U, Fi, A; 1955 v W, E, H (8)
Curran, H. P. (Wolverhampton W), 1970 v A; 1971 v Ni, E, D, USSR (sub) (5)

Dailly, C. (Derby Co), 1997 v W, Ma, Bl; 1998 v Bl, La, F, D, Fi, Co, US, Br, N, Mor; (with Blackburn R), 1999 v Li; 2000 v Bos (sub), Es, Bos, Li, E (2), F, Ho, Ei; 2001 v La, Sm, Aus; (with West Ham U), Pol; 2002 v Cro, Bel, La, F, Ng, Sk, S.Af, Hk; 2003 v D, Fa, Ic, Ca, P, Ei, Ic, Li, A, Nz, G; 2004 v N, G, Li, Ho, W, R, D; 2005 v Mol (sub), Bl; 2006 v A, I, Bl, Slv, US, Sw (61)
Dalglish, K. (Celtic), 1972 v Bel (sub), Ho; 1973 v D (1+1 sub), E (2), W, Ni, Sw, Br; 1974 v Cz (2), WG (2), Ni, W, E, Bel, N (sub), Z, Br, Y; 1975 v EG, Sp (sub+1), Se, P, W, Ni, E, R; 1976 v D (2), R, Sw, Ni, E; 1977 v Fi, Cz, W (2), Se, Ni, E, Ch, Arg, Br; (with Liverpool), 1978 v EG, Cz, W, Bul, Ni (sub), W, E, Pe, Ir, Ho; 1979 v A, N, P, W, Ni, E, Arg, N; 1980 v Pe, A, Bel (2), P, Ni, W, E, Pol, H; 1981 v Se, P, Is; 1982 v Se, Ni, P (sub), Sp, Ho, Ni, W, E, Nz, Br (sub); 1983 v Bel, Sw; 1984 v U, Bel, EG; 1985 v Y, Ic, Sp, W; 1986 v EG, Aus, R; 1987 v Bul (sub), L (102)
Davidson, C. I. (Blackburn R), 1999 v Li (sub), Es, Fa, CzR, G, Fa, CzR; 2000 v Es, Bos, Li, E, F; (with Leicester C), 2001 v La, Pol; 2002 v La; 2003 v Ic (sub), Ca (sub) (17)
Davidson, D. (Queen's Park), 1878 v W; 1879 v W; 1880 v W; 1881 v E, W (5)
Davidson, J. A. (Partick Th), 1954 v N (2), A, U; 1955 v W, Ni, E, H (8)
Davidson, S. (Middlesbrough), 1921 v E (1)
Dawson, A. (Rangers), 1980 v Pol (sub), H; 1983 v Ni, Ca (2) (5)
Dawson, J. (Rangers), 1935 v Ni; 1936 v E; 1937 v G, E, W, Ni, A, Cz; 1938 v W, Ho, Ni; 1939 v E, Ni, H (14)
Deans, J. (Celtic), 1975 v EG, Sp (2)
Delaney, J. (Celtic), 1936 v W, Ni; 1937 v G, E, A, Cz; 1938 v Ni; 1939 v W, Ni; (with Manchester U), 1947 v E; 1948 v E, W, Ni (13)
Devine, A. (Falkirk), 1910 v W (1)
Devlin, P. J. (Birmingham C), 2003 v Ca, P (sub), Ei (sub), Ic (sub), Li (sub), A, Nz, G; 2004 v N (sub), Fa (10)
Dewar, G. (Dumbarton), 1888 v Ni; 1889 v E (2)
Dewar, N. (Third Lanark), 1932 v E, F; 1933 v W (3)
Dick, J. (West Ham U), 1959 v E (1)
Dickie, M. (Rangers), 1897 v Ni; 1899 v Ni; 1900 v W (3)
Dickov, P. (Manchester C), 2001 v Sm (sub), Cro (sub), Aus (sub); (with Leicester C), 2003 v Fa; 2004 v Fa, Ho (2), W; (with Blackburn R), 2005 v Slv, N (10)
Dickson, W. (Dundee Strathmore), 1888 v Ni (1)
Dickson, W. (Kilmarnock), 1970 v Ni, W, E; 1971 v D, USSR (5)
Divers, J. (Celtic), 1895 v W (1)
Divers, J. (Celtic), 1939 v Ni (1)
Dobie, R. S. (WBA), 2002 v Sk, S.Af, Hk (sub); 2003 v D (sub), Fa, P (6)
Docherty, T. H, (Preston NE), 1952 v W; 1953 v E, Se; 1954 v N (2), A, U; 1955 v W, E, H (2), A; 1957 v E, Y, Sp (2), Sw, WG; 1958 v Ni, W, E, Sw; (with Arsenal), 1959 v W, E, Ni (25)
Dodds, D. (Dundee U), 1984 v U (sub), Ni (2)
Dodds, J. (Celtic), 1914 v E, W, Ni (3)
Dodds, W. (Aberdeen), 1997 v La (sub), W, Bl (sub); 1998 v Bl (sub); (with Dundee U), 1999 v Es (sub), Fa, G, Fa, CzR; 2000 v Bos, Es, Bos, Li (sub), E (2); (with Rangers), F, Ho, Ei; 2001 v La, Sm, Aus, Bel, Sm, Pol; 2002 v Cro (sub), Bel (26)
Doig, J. E. (Arbroath), 1887 v Ni; 1889 v Ni; (with Sunderland), 1896 v E; 1899 v E; 1903 v E (5)
Donachie, W. (Manchester C), 1972 v Pe, Ni, E, Y, Cz, Br; 1973 v D, E, W, Ni; 1974 v Ni; 1976 v R, Ni, W, E; 1977 v Fi, Cz, W (2), Se, Ni, E, Ch, Arg, Br; 1978 v EG, W, Bul, W, E, Ir, Ho; 1979 v A, N, P (sub) (35)
Donaldson, A. (Bolton W), 1914 v E, Ni, W; 1920 v E, Ni; 1922 v Ni (6)
Donnachie, J. (Oldham Ath), 1913 v E; 1914 v E, Ni (3)
Donnelly, S. (Celtic), 1997 v W (sub), Ma (sub); 1998 v La (sub), F (sub), D (sub), Fi (sub), Co (sub), US (sub); 1999 v Es (sub), Fa (10)
Dougall, C. (Birmingham C), 1947 v W (1)
Dougall, J. (Preston NE), 1939 v E (1)
Dougan, R. (Hearts), 1950 v Sw (1)

Douglas, A. (Chelsea), 1911 v Ni (1)
Douglas, J. (Renfrew), 1880 v W (1)
Douglas, R. (Celtic), 2002 v Ng, S.Af, Hk; 2003 v D, Fa, Ic, P, Ic, Nz, G; 2004 v N, Fa, G, Li, Ho (2), W; 2005 v I; (with Leicester C), 2006 v A (sub) (19)
Dowds, P. (Celtic), 1892 v Ni (1)
Downie, R. (Third Lanark), 1892 v W (1)
Doyle, D. (Celtic), 1892 v E; 1893 v W; 1894 v E; 1895 v E, Ni; 1897 v E; 1898 v E, Ni (8)
Doyle, J. (Ayr U), 1976 v R (1)
Drummond, J. (Falkirk), 1892 v Ni; (with Rangers), 1894 v Ni; 1895 v Ni, E; 1896 v E, Ni; 1897 v Ni; 1898 v E; 1900 v E; 1901 v E; 1902 v E, W, Ni; 1903 v Ni (14)
Dunbar, M. (Cartvale), 1886 v Ni (1)
Duncan, A. (Hibernian), 1975 v P (sub), W, Ni, E, R; 1976 v D (sub) (6)
Duncan, D. (Derby Co), 1933 v E, W; 1934 v A, W; 1935 v E, W; 1936 v E, W, Ni; 1937 v G, E, W, Ni; 1938 v W (14)
Duncan, D. M. (East Fife), 1948 v Bel, Sw, F (3)
Duncan, J. (Alexandra Ath), 1878 v W; 1882 v W (2)
Duncan, J. (Leicester C), 1926 v W (1)
Duncanson, J. (Rangers), 1947 v Ni (1)
Dunlop, J. (St Mirren), 1890 v W (1)
Dunlop, W. (Liverpool), 1906 v E (1)
Dunn, J. (Hibernian), 1925 v W, Ni; 1927 v Ni; 1928 v Ni, E; (with Everton), 1929 v W (6)
Durie, G. S. (Chelsea), 1988 v Bul (sub); 1989 v I (sub), Cy; 1990 v Y, EG, Eg, Se; 1991 v Sw (sub), Bul (2), USSR (sub), Sm; (with Tottenham H), 1992 v Sw, R, Sm, Ni (sub), Fi, Ca, N (sub), Ho, G; 1993 v Sw, I; 1994 v Sw, I; (with Rangers), Ho (2); 1996 v US, Ho, E, Sw; 1997 v A (sub), Se (sub), Ma (sub), Bl; 1998 v Bl, La, F, Fi (sub), Co, Br, N, Mor (43)
Durrant, I. (Rangers), 1988 v H, Bel, Ma, Sp; 1989 v N (sub); 1993 v Sw (sub), P (sub), I, P (sub); 1994 v I (sub), Ma; (with Kilmarnock), 1999 v Es, Fa (sub), G, Fa, CzR; 2000 v Bos (sub), Es, Ho (sub), Ei (sub) (20)
Dykes, J. (Hearts), 1938 v Ho; 1939 v Ni (2)

Easson, J. F. (Portsmouth), 1931 v A, Sw; 1934 v W (3)
Elliott, M. S. (Leicester C), 1998 v F (sub), D, Fi; 1999 v Li, Fa, CzR, Fa; 2000 v Ho, Ei; 2001 v La, Sm, Cro, Aus (sub), Bel, Sm; 2002 v Cro, Bel, La (18)
Ellis, J. (Mossend Swifts), 1892 v Ni (1)
Evans, A. (Aston Villa), 1982 v Ho, Ni, E, Nz (4)
Evans, R. (Celtic), 1949 v E, W, Ni, F; 1950 v W, Ni, Sw, P; 1951 v E, A; 1952 v Ni; 1953 v Se; 1954 v Ni, W, E, N, Fi; 1955 v Ni, P, Y, A, H; 1956 v E, Ni, W, A; 1957 v WG, Sp; 1958 v Ni, W, E, Sw, H, Pol, Y, Par, F; 1959 v E, WG, Ho, P; 1960 v E, Ni, W, Pol; (with Chelsea), 1960 v A, H, T (48)
Ewart, J. (Bradford C), 1921 v E (1)
Ewing, T. (Partick Th), 1958 v W, E (2)

Farm, G. N. (Blackpool), 1953 v W, Ni, E, Se; 1954 v Ni, W, E; 1959 v WG, Ho, P (10)
Ferguson, B. (Rangers), 1999 v Li (sub); 2000 v Bos, Es (sub), E (2), F, Ei; 2001 v La, Aus, Bel; 2003 v D, Fa, Ic, Ei, Ic; 2004 v N (with Blackburn R), Fa, G, Li, Ho (2); 2005 v H, Sp, Slv, N, Mol; (with Rangers), I, Mol, Bl; 2006 v I, N, Bl, Sw (33)
Ferguson, D. (Rangers), 1988 v Ma, Co (sub) (2)
Ferguson, D. (Dundee U), 1992 v US (sub), Ca, Ho (sub); 1993 v G; (with Everton), 1995 v Gr; 1997 v A, Es (7)
Ferguson, I. (Rangers), 1989 v I, Cy (sub), F; 1993 v Ma (sub), Es; 1994 v Ma, A (sub), Ho (sub); 1997 v Es (sub) (9)
Ferguson, J. (Vale of Leven), 1874 v E; 1876 v E, W; 1877 v E, W; 1878 v W (6)
Ferguson, R. (Kilmarnock), 1966 v W, E, Ho, P, Br; 1967 v W, Ni (7)
Fernie, W. (Celtic), 1954 v Fi, A, U; 1955 v W, Ni; 1957 v E, Ni, W, Y; 1958 v W, Sw, Par (12)
Findlay, R. (Kilmarnock), 1898 v W (1)
Fitchie, T. T. (Woolwich Arsenal), 1905 v W; 1906 v W, Ni; (with Queen's Park), 1907 v W (4)
Flavell, R. (Airdrieonians), 1947 v Bel, L (2)
Fleck, R. (Norwich C), 1990 v Arg, Se, Br (sub); 1991 v USSR (4)
Fleming, C. (East Fife), 1954 v Ni (1)
Fleming, J. W. (Rangers), 1929 v G, Ho; 1930 v E (3)
Fleming, R. (Morton), 1886 v Ni (1)
Fletcher, D. B. (Manchester U), 2004 v N (sub), Li (sub), Ho (2), W, D, Es, Tr; 2005 v H, Sp, Slv, N, Mol (2), Bl; 2006 v I, N, Bl, Slv, US, Sw, Bul, J (23)
Forbes, A. R. (Sheffield U), 1947 v Bel, L, E; 1948 v W, Ni; (with Arsenal), 1950 v E, P, F; 1951 v W, Ni, A; 1952 v W, D, Se (14)
Forbes, J. (Vale of Leven), 1884 v E, W, Ni; 1887 v W, E (5)
Ford, D. (Hearts), 1974 v Cz (sub), WG (sub), W (3)
Forrest, J. (Rangers), 1966 v W, I; (with Aberdeen), 1971 v Bel (sub), D, USSR (5)
Forrest, J. (Motherwell), 1958 v E (1)
Forsyth, A. (Partick Th), 1972 v Y, Cz, Br; 1973 v D; (with Manchester U), E; 1975 v Sp, Ni (sub), R, EG; 1976 v D (10)
Forsyth, C. (Kilmarnock), 1964 v E; 1965 v W, Ni, Fi (4)
Forsyth, T. (Motherwell), 1971 v D; (with Rangers), 1974 v Cz; 1976 v Sw, Ni, W, E; 1977 v Fi, Se, W, Ni, E, Ch, Arg, Br; 1978 v Cz, W, Ni, W (sub), E, Pe, Ir (sub), Ho (22)
Foyers, R. (St Bernards), 1893 v W; 1894 v W (2)
Fraser, D. M. (WBA), 1968 v Ho; 1969 v Cy (2)
Fraser, J. (Moffat), 1891 v Ni (1)
Fraser, M. J. E. (Queen's Park), 1880 v W; 1882 v W, E; 1883 v W, E (5)
Fraser, J. (Dundee), 1907 v Ni (1)
Fraser, W. (Sunderland), 1955 v W, Ni (2)
Freedman, D. A. (C Palace), 2002 v La, F (2)
Fulton, W. (Abercorn), 1884 v Ni (1)
Fyfe, J. H. (Third Lanark), 1895 v W (1)

Gabriel, J. (Everton), 1961 v W; 1964 v N (sub) (2)
Gallacher, H. K. (Airdrieonians), 1924 v Ni; 1925 v E, W, Ni; 1926 v W; (with Newcastle U), 1926 v E, Ni; 1927 v E, W, Ni; 1928 v E, W; 1929 v E, W, Ni; 1930 v W, Ni, F; (with Chelsea), 1934 v E; (with Derby Co), 1935 v E (20)
Gallacher, K. W. (Dundee U), 1988 v Co, E (sub); 1989 v N, I; (with Coventry C), 1991 v Sm; 1992 v R (sub), Sm (sub), Ni (sub), N (sub), Ho (sub), G (sub), C; 1993 v Sw (sub), P; (with Blackburn R), P, Es (2); 1994 v I, Ma; 1996 v Aus (sub), D, Co (sub), Ho; 1997 v Se (sub), Es (2), A, Se, W, Ma, Bl; 1998 v Bl, La, F, Fi (sub), US, Br, N, Mor; 1999 v Li, Es, Fa, CzR; 2000 v Bos (sub); (with Newcastle U), Bos, Li (sub), E, F, Ei (sub); 2001 v Sm, Cro, Bel (sub), Sm (sub) (53)
Gallacher, P. (Sunderland), 1935 v Ni (1)
Gallacher, P. (Dundee U), 2002 v Hk (sub); 2003 v Ca, Ei (sub), Li, A; 2004 v R, D, Es (8)
Gallagher, P. (Blackburn R), 2004 v W (sub) (1)
Galloway, M. (Celtic), 1992 v R (1)
Galt, J. H. (Rangers), 1908 v W, Ni (2)
Gardiner, I. (Motherwell), 1958 v W (1)
Gardner, D. R. (Third Lanark), 1897 v W (1)
Gardner, R. (Queen's Park), 1872 v E; 1873 v E; (with Clydesdale), 1874 v E; 1875 v E; 1878 v E (5)
Gemmell, T. (St Mirren), 1955 v P, Y (2)
Gemmell, T. (Celtic), 1966 v E; 1967 v W, Ni, E, USSR; 1968 v Ni, E; 1969 v W, Ni, E, D, A, WG, Cy; 1970 v E, Ei, WG; 1971 v Bel (18)
Gemmill, A. (Derby Co), 1971 v Bel; 1972 v P, Ho, Pe, Ni, W, E; 1976 v D, R, Ni, W, E; 1977 v Fi, Cz, W (2), Ni (sub), E (sub), Ch (sub), Arg, Br; 1978 v EG (sub); (with Nottingham F), Bul, Ni, W, E (sub), Pe (sub), Ir, Ho; 1979 v A, N, P, N; (with Birmingham C), 1980 v A, P, Ni, W, E, H; 1981 v Se, P, Is, Ni (43)
Gemmill, S. (Nottingham F), 1995 v J, Ec, Fa (sub); 1996 v Sm, D (sub), US; 1997 v Es, Se (sub), W, Ma (sub), Bl (sub); 1998 v D, Fi; (with Everton), 1999 v G, Fa (sub); 2001 v Sm (sub), Pol (sub); 2002 v Cro (sub), F (sub), Ng, Sk, S.Af, Hk; 2003 v Ca, Ei (sub), A (sub) (26)
Gibb, W. (Clydesdale), 1873 v E (1)
Gibson, D. W. (Leicester C), 1963 v A, N, Ei, Sp; 1964 v Ni; 1965 v W, Fi (7)
Gibson, J. D. (Partick Th), 1926 v E; 1927 v E, W, Ni; (with Aston Villa), 1928 v E, W; 1930 v W, Ni (8)
Gibson, N. (Rangers), 1895 v E, Ni; 1896 v E, Ni; 1897 v E, Ni; 1898 v E; 1899 v E, W, Ni; 1900 v E, Ni; 1901 v W; (with Partick Th), 1905 v Ni (14)
Gilchrist, J. E. (Celtic), 1922 v E (1)
Gilhooley, M. (Hull C), 1922 v W (1)
Gillespie, G. (Rangers), 1880 v W; 1881 v E, W; 1882 v E; (with Queen's Park), 1886 v W; 1890 v W; 1891 v Ni (7)
Gillespie, G. T. (Liverpool), 1988 v Bel, Bul, Sp; 1989 v N, F, Ch; 1990 v Y, EG, Eg, Pol, Ma, Br (sub); 1991 v Bul (13)
Gillespie, Jas (Third Lanark), 1898 v W (1)
Gillespie, John (Queen's Park), 1896 v W (1)
Gillespie, R. (Queen's Park), 1927 v W; 1931 v W; 1932 v F; 1933 v E (4)
Gillick, T. (Everton), 1937 v A, Cz; 1939 v W, Ni, H (5)
Gilmour, J. (Dundee), 1931 v W (1)
Gilzean, A. J. (Dundee), 1964 v W, E, N, WG; 1965 v Ni; (with Tottenham H), Sp; 1966 v Ni, W, Pol, I; 1968 v W; 1969 v W, E, WG, Cy (2), A (sub); 1970 v Ni, E (sub), WG, A; 1971 v P (22)
Glass, S. (Newcastle U), 1999 v Fa (sub) (1)
Glavin, R. (Celtic), 1977 v Se (1)
Glen, A. (Aberdeen), 1956 v E, Ni (2)

Glen, R. (Renton), 1895 v W; 1896 v W; (with Hibernian), 1900 v Ni (3)
Goram, A. L. (Oldham Ath), 1986 v EG (sub), R, Ho; 1987 v Br; (with Hibernian), 1989 v Y, I; 1990 v EG, Pol, Ma; 1991 v R, Sw, Bul (2), USSR, Sm; (with Rangers), 1992 v Sw, R, Sm, Fi, N, Ho, G, C; 1993 v Sw, P, I, Ma, P; 1994 v Ho; 1995 v Fi, Fa, Ru, Gr; 1996 v Se (sub), D (sub), Co, Ho, E, Sw; 1997 v A, La, Es; 1998 v D (sub) (43)
Gordon, C. S. (Hearts), 2004 v Tr; 2005 v Sp, Slv, N, Mol, I (sub), Mol, Bl; 2006 v A, I, N, Bl, Slv, US, Sw (15)
Gordon, J. E. (Rangers), 1912 v E, Ni; 1913 v E, Ni, W; 1914 v E, Ni; 1920 v W, E, Ni (10)
Gossland, J. (Rangers), 1884 v Ni (1)
Goudle, J. (Abercorn), 1884 v Ni (1)
Gough, C. R. (Dundee U), 1983 v Sw, Ni, W, E, Ca (3); 1984 v U, Bel, EG, Ni, W, E, F; 1985 v Sp, E, Ic; 1986 v W, EG, Aus, Is, R, E, D, WG, U; (with Tottenham H), 1987 v Bul, L, Ei (2), Bel, E, Br; 1988 v H; (with Rangers), S.Ar, Sp, Co, E; 1989 v Y, I, Cy, F, Cy; 1990 v F, Arg, EG, Eg, Pol, Ma, Cr; 1991 v USSR, Bul; 1992 v Sm, Ni, Ca, N, Ho, G, C; 1993 v Sw, P (61)
Gould, J. (Celtic), 2000 v Li; 2001 v Aus (2)
Gourlay, J. (Cambuslang), 1886 v Ni; 1888 v W (2)
Govan, J. (Hibernian), 1948 v E, W, Bel, Sw, F; 1949 v Ni (6)
Gow, D. R. (Rangers), 1888 v E (1)
Gow, J. J. (Queen's Park), 1885 v E (1)
Gow, J. R. (Rangers), 1888 v Ni (1)
Graham, A. (Leeds U), 1978 v EG (sub); 1979 v A (sub), N, W, Ni, E, Arg, N; 1980 v Pe (sub), A; 1981 v W (11)
Graham, G. (Arsenal), 1972 v P, Ho, Ni, Y, Cz, Br; 1973 v D (2); (with Manchester U), E, W, Ni, Br (sub) (12)
Graham, J. (Annbank), 1884 v Ni (1)
Graham, J. A. (Arsenal), 1921 v Ni (1)
Grant, J. (Hibernian), 1959 v W, Ni (2)
Grant, P. (Celtic), 1989 v E (sub), Ch (2)
Gray, A. (Hibernian), 1903 v Ni (1)
Gray, A. D. (Bradford C), 2003 v Li (sub), Nz (sub) (2)
Gray, A. M. (Aston Villa), 1976 v R, Sw; 1977 v Fi, Cz; 1979 v A, N; (with Wolverhampton W), 1980 v P, E (sub); 1981 v Se, P, Is (sub), Ni; 1982 v Se (sub), Ni (sub); 1983 v Ni, W, E, Ca (1+1 sub); (with Everton), 1985 v Ic (20)
Gray, D. (Rangers), 1929 v W, Ni, G, Ho; 1930 v W, E, Ni; 1931 v W; 1933 v W, Ni (10)
Gray, E. (Leeds U), 1969 v E, Cy; 1970 v WG, A; 1971 v W, Ni; 1972 v Bel, Ho; 1976 v W, E; 1977 v Fi, W (12)
Gray, F. T. (Leeds U), 1976 v Sw; 1979 v N, P, W, Ni, E, Arg (sub); (with Nottingham F), 1980 v Bel (sub); 1981 v Se, P, Is, Ni, Is, W; (with Leeds U), Ni, E; 1982 v Se, Ni, P, Sp, Ho, W, Nz, Br, USSR; 1983 v EG, Sw, Bel, Sw, W, E, Ca (32)
Gray, W. (Pollokshields Ath), 1886 v E (1)
Green, A. (Blackpool), 1971 v Bel (sub), P (sub), Ni, E; (with Newcastle U), 1972 v W, E (sub) (6)
Greig, J. (Rangers), 1964 v E, WG; 1965 v W, Ni, E, Fi (2), Sp, Pol; 1966 v Ni, W, E, Pol, I (2), P, Ho, Br; 1967 v W, Ni, E; 1968 v Ni, W, E, Ho; 1969 v W, Ni, E, D, A, WG, Cy (2); 1970 v W, E, Ei, WG, A; 1971 v D, Bel, W (sub), Ni, E; 1976 v D (44)
Groves, W. (Hibernian), 1888 v W; (with Celtic), 1889 v Ni; 1890 v E (3)
Gulliland, W. (Queen's Park), 1891 v W; 1892 v Ni; 1894 v E; 1895 v E (4)
Gunn, B. (Norwich C), 1990 v Eg; 1993 v Es (2); 1994 v Sw, I, Ho (sub) (6)

Haddock, H. (Clyde), 1955 v E, H (2), P, Y; 1958 v E (6)
Haddow, D. (Rangers), 1894 v E (1)
Haffey, F. (Celtic), 1960 v E; 1961 v E (2)
Hamilton, A. (Queen's Park), 1885 v E, W; 1886 v E; 1888 v E (4)
Hamilton, A. W. (Dundee), 1962 v Cz, U, W, E; 1963 v W, Ni, E, A, N, Ei; 1964 v Ni, W, E, N, WG; 1965 v Ni, W, E, Fi (2), Pol, Sp; 1966 v Pol, Ni (24)
Hamilton, G. (Aberdeen), 1947 v Ni; 1951 v Bel, A; 1954 v N (2) (5)
Hamilton, G. (Port Glasgow Ath), 1906 v Ni (1)
Hamilton, J. (Queen's Park), 1892 v W; 1893 v E, Ni (3)
Hamilton, J. (St Mirren), 1924 v Ni (1)
Hamilton, R. C. (Rangers), 1899 v E, W, Ni; 1900 v W; 1901 v E, Ni; 1902 v W, Ni; 1903 v E; 1904 v Ni; (with Dundee), 1911 v W (11)
Hamilton, T. (Hurlford), 1891 v Ni (1)
Hamilton, T. (Rangers), 1932 v E (1)
Hamilton, W. M. (Hibernian), 1965 v Fi (1)
Hammell, S. (Motherwell), 2005 v Se (sub) (1)
Hannah, A. B. (Renton), 1888 v W (1)
Hannah, J. (Third Lanark), 1889 v W (1)
Hansen, A. D. (Liverpool), 1979 v W, Arg; 1980 v Bel, P; 1981 v Se, P, Is; 1982 v Se, Ni, P, Sp, Ni (sub), W, E, Nz, Br, USSR; 1983 v EG, Sw, Bel, Sw; 1985 v W (sub); 1986 v R (sub); 1987 v Ei (2), L (26)
Hansen, J. (Partick Th), 1972 v Bel (sub), Y (sub) (2)
Harkness, J. D. (Queen's Park), 1927 v E, Ni; 1928 v E; (with Hearts), 1929 v W, E, Ni; 1930 v E, W; 1932 v W, F; 1934 v Ni, W (12)
Harper, J. M. (Aberdeen), 1973 v D (1+1 sub); (with Hibernian), 1976 v D; (with Aberdeen), 1978 v Ir (sub) (4)
Harper, W. (Hibernian), 1923 v E, Ni, W; 1924 v E, Ni, W; 1925 v E, Ni, W; (with Arsenal), 1926 v E, Ni (11)
Harris, J. (Partick Th), 1921 v W, Ni (2)
Harris, N. (Newcastle U), 1924 v E (1)
Harrower, W. (Queen's Park), 1882 v E; 1884 v Ni; 1886 v W (3)
Hartford, R. A. (WBA), 1972 v Pe, W (sub), E, Y, Cz, Br; (with Manchester C), 1976 v D, R, Ni (sub); 1977 v Cz (sub), W (sub), Se, W, Ni, E, Ch, Arg, Br; 1978 v EG, Cz, W, Bul, W, E, Pe, Ir, Ho; 1979 v A, N, P, W, Ni, E, Arg, N; (with Everton), 1980 v Pe, Bel; 1981 v Ni (sub), Is, W, Ni, E; 1982 v Se; (with Manchester C), Ni, P, Sp, Ni, W, E, Br (50)
Hartley, P. J. (Hearts), 2005 v I, Mol; 2006 v I, N, Bl, Slv, US (7)
Harvey, D. (Leeds U), 1973 v D; 1974 v Cz, WG, Ni, W, E, Bel, Z, Br, Y; 1975 v EG, Sp (2); 1976 v D (2); 1977 v Fi (sub) (16)
Hastings, A. C. (Sunderland), 1936 v Ni; 1938 v Ni (2)
Haughney, M. (Celtic), 1954 v E (1)
Hay, D. (Celtic), 1970 v Ni, W, E; 1971 v D, Bel, W, P, Ni; 1972 v P, Bel, Ho; 1973 v W, Ni, E, Sw, Br; 1974 v Cz (2), WG, Ni, W, E, Bel, N, Z, Br, Y (27)
Hay, J. (Celtic), 1905 v Ni; 1909 v Ni; 1910 v W, Ni, E; 1911 v Ni, E; (with Newcastle U), 1912 v E, W; 1914 v E, Ni (11)
Hegarty, P. (Dundee U), 1979 v W, Ni, E, Arg, N (sub); 1980 v W, E; 1983 v Ni (8)
Heggie, C. (Rangers), 1886 v Ni (1)
Henderson, G. H. (Rangers), 1904 v Ni (1)
Henderson, J. G. (Portsmouth), 1953 v Se; 1954 v Ni, E, N; 1956 v W; (with Arsenal), 1959 v W, Ni (7)
Henderson, W. (Rangers), 1963 v W, Ni, E, A, N, Ei, Sp; 1964 v W, Ni, E, N, WG; 1965 v Fi, Pol, E, Sp; 1966 v Ni, W, Pol, I, Ho; 1967 v W, Ni; 1968 v Ho; 1969 v Ni, E, Cy; 1970 v Ei; 1971 v P (29)
Hendry, E. C. J. (Blackburn R), 1993 v Es (2); 1994 v Ma, Ho, A, Ho; 1995 v Fi, Fa, Gr, Ru, Sm; 1996 v Fi, Se, Sm, Aus, D, US, Co, Ho, E, Sw; 1997 v A, Se, Es (2), A, Se; 1998 v La, D, Fi, Co, US, Br, N, Mor; (with Rangers), 1999 v Li, Es, Fa, G; 2000 v Bos, Es, Bos, E (2); (with Coventry C), F; 2001 v La, Sm, Cro, Aus (sub); (with Bolton W), Bel, Sm (51)
Hepburn, J. (Alloa Ath), 1891 v W (1)
Hepburn, R. (Ayr U), 1932 v Ni (1)
Herd, A. C. (Hearts), 1935 v Ni (1)
Herd, D. G. (Arsenal), 1959 v E, W, Ni; 1961 v Ei, Cz (5)
Herd, G. (Clyde), 1958 v E; 1960 v H, T; 1961 v W, Ni (5)
Herriot, J. (Birmingham C), 1969 v Ni, E, D, Cy (2), W (sub); 1970 v Ei (sub), WG (8)
Hewie, J. D. (Charlton Ath), 1956 v E, A; 1957 v E, Ni, W, Y, Sp (2), Sw, WG; 1958 v H, Pol, Y, F; 1959 v Ho, P; 1960 v Ni, W, Pol (19)
Higgins, A. (Kilmarnock), 1885 v Ni (1)
Higgins, A. (Newcastle U), 1910 v E, Ni; 1911 v E, Ni (4)
Highet, T. C. (Queen's Park), 1875 v E; 1876 v E, W; 1878 v E (4)
Hill, D. (Rangers), 1881 v E, W; 1882 v W (3)
Hill, D. A. (Third Lanark), 1906 v Ni (1)
Hill, F. R. (Aberdeen), 1930 v F; 1931 v W, Ni (3)
Hill, J. (Hearts), 1891 v E; 1892 v W (2)
Hogg, G (Hearts), 1896 v E, Ni (2)
Hogg, J. (Ayr U), 1922 v Ni (1)
Hogg, R. M. (Celtic), 1937 v Cz (1)
Holm, A. H. (Queen's Park), 1882 v W; 1883 v E, W (3)
Holt, D. D. (Hearts), 1963 v A, N, Ei, Sp; 1964 v WG (sub) (5)
Holt, G. J. (Kilmarnock), 2001 v La (sub), Cro (sub); (with Norwich C), 2002 v F (sub); 2004 v D, Es, Tr; 2005 v H, Slv (sub), N, Mol (10)
Holton, J. A. (Manchester U), 1973 v W, Ni, E, Sw, Br; 1974 v Cz, WG, Ni, W, E, N, Z, Br, Y; 1975 v EG (15)
Hope, R. (WBA), 1968 v Ho; 1969 v D (2)
Hopkin, D. (C Palace), 1997 v Ma, Bl; (with Leeds U), 1998 v Bl (sub), F (sub); 1999 v CzR; 2000 v Bos (2) (7)
Houliston, W. (Queen of the South), 1949 v E, Ni, F (3)
Houston, S. M. (Manchester U), 1976 v D (1)
Howden, W. (Partick Th), 1905 v Ni (1)

Howe, R. (Hamilton A), 1929 v N, Ho (2)
Howie, H. (Hibernian), 1949 v W (1)
Howie, J. (Newcastle U), 1905 v E; 1906 v E; 1908 v E (3)
Howieson, J. (St Mirren), 1927 v Ni (1)
Hughes, J. (Celtic), 1965 v Pol, Sp; 1966 v Ni, I (2); 1968 v E; 1969 v A; 1970 v Ei (8)
Hughes, R. D. (Portsmouth), 2004 v Es, Tr (sub); 2005 v N, Se (sub); 2006 v A (sub) (5)
Hughes, W. (Sunderland), 1975 v Se (sub) (1)
Humphries, W. (Motherwell), 1952 v Se (1)
Hunter, A. (Kilmarnock), 1972 v Pe, Y; (with Celtic), 1973 v E; 1974 v Cz (4)
Hunter, J. (Dundee), 1909 v W (1)
Hunter, J. (Third Lanark), 1874 v E; (with Eastern), 1875 v E; (with Third Lanark), 1876 v E; 1877 v W (4)
Hunter, R. (St Mirren), 1890 v Ni (1)
Hunter, W. (Motherwell), 1960 v H, T; 1961 v W (3)
Husband, J. (Partick Th), 1947 v W (1)
Hutchison, D. (Everton), 1999 v CzR (sub), G; 2000 v Bos, Es, Li, E (2), F, Ho, Ei; (with Sunderland), 2001 v La, Sm, Cro, Aus, Bel, Sm; (with West Ham U), 2002 v Cro, Bel, La; 2003 v Ei, Ic, Li, A; 2004 v N, Li (sub), Ho (sub) (26)
Hutchison, T. (Coventry C), 1974 v Cz (2), WG (2), Ni, W, Bel (sub), N, Z (sub), Y (sub); 1975 v EG, Sp (2), P, E (sub), R (sub); 1976 v D (17)
Hutton, J. (Aberdeen), 1923 v E, W, Ni; 1924 v Ni; 1926 v W, E, Ni; (with Blackburn R), 1927 v Ni; 1928 v W, Ni (10)
Hutton, J. (St Bernards), 1887 v Ni (1)
Hyslop, T. (Stoke C), 1896 v E; (with Rangers), 1897 v E (2)

Imlach, J. J. S. (Nottingham F), 1958 v H, Pol, Y, F (4)
Imrie, W. N. (St Johnstone), 1929 v N, G (2)
Inglis, J. (Rangers), 1883 v E, W (2)
Inglis, J. (Kilmarnock Ath), 1884 v Ni (1)
Irons, J. H. (Queen's Park), 1900 v W (1)
Irvine, B. (Aberdeen), 1991 v R; 1993 v G, Es (2); 1994 v Sw, I, Ma, A, Ho (9)

Jackson, A. (Cambuslang), 1886 v W; 1888 v Ni (2)
Jackson, A. (Aberdeen), 1925 v E, W, Ni; (with Huddersfield T), 1926 v E, W, Ni; 1927 v W, Ni; 1928 v E, W; 1929 v E, W, Ni; 1930 v E, W, Ni, F (17)
Jackson, C. (Rangers), 1975 v Se, P (sub), W; 1976 v D, R, Ni, W, E (8)
Jackson, D. (Hibernian), 1995 v Ru, Sm, J, Ec, Fa; 1996 v Gr, Fi (sub), Se (sub), Sm (sub), Aus (sub), D (sub), US; 1997 v La, Se, Es, A, Se, W, Ma, Bl; (with Celtic), 1998 v D, Fi, Co, US, Br, N; 1999 v Li, Es (sub) (28)
Jackson, J. (Partick Th), 1931 v A, I, Sw; 1933 v E; (with Chelsea), 1934 v E; 1935 v E; 1936 v W, Ni (8)
Jackson, T. A. (St Mirren), 1904 v W, E, Ni; 1905 v W; 1907 v W, Ni (6)
James, A. W. (Preston NE), 1926 v W; 1928 v E; 1929 v E, Ni; (with Arsenal), 1930 v E, W, Ni; 1933 v W (8)
Jardine, A. (Rangers), 1971 v D (sub); 1972 v P, Bel, Ho; 1973 v E, Sw, Br; 1974 v Cz (2), WG (2), Ni, W, E, Bel, N, Z, Br, Y; 1975 v EG, Sp (2), Se, P, W, Ni, E; 1977 v Se (sub), Ch (sub), Br (sub); 1978 v Cz, W, Ni, Ir; 1980 v Pe, A, Bel (2) (38)
Jarvie, A. (Airdrieonians), 1971 v P (sub), Ni (sub), E (sub) (3)
Jenkinson, T. (Hearts), 1887 v Ni (1)
Jess, E. (Aberdeen), 1993 v I (sub), Ma; 1994 v Sw (sub), I, Ho (sub), A, Ho (sub); 1995 v Fi (sub); 1996 v Se (sub), Sm; (with Coventry C), US, Co (sub), E (sub); (with Aberdeen), 1998 v D (sub); 1999 v CzR, G (sub), Fa (sub), CzR (sub) (18)
Johnston, A. (Sunderland), 1999 v Es, Fa, CzR (sub), G, Fa, CzR; 2000 v Es, F (sub), Ei (sub); (with Rangers), 2001 v Sm (sub), Cro, Sm; (with Middlesbrough), 2002 v Ng (sub), Sk, S.Af, Hk; 2003 v D (sub), Fa (18)
Johnston, L. H. (Clyde), 1948 v Bel, Sw (2)
Johnston, M. (Watford), 1984 v W (sub), E (sub), F; 1985 v Y; (with Celtic), Ic, Sp (2), W; 1986 v EG; 1987 v Bul, Ei (2), L; (with Nantes), 1988 v H, Bel, L, S.Ar, Sp, Co, E; 1989 v N, Y, I, Cy, F, Cy, E, Ch (sub); (with Rangers), 1990 v F, N, EG, Pol, Ma, Cr, Se, Br; 1992 v Sw, Sm (sub) (38)
Johnston, R. (Sunderland), 1938 v Cz (1)
Johnston, W. (Rangers), 1966 v W, E, Pol, Ho; 1968 v W, E; 1969 v Ni (sub); 1970 v Ni; 1971 v D; (with WBA), 1977 v Se, W (sub), Ni, E, Ch, Arg, Br; 1978 v EG, Cz, W (2), E, Pe (22)
Johnstone, D. (Rangers), 1973 v W, Ni, E, Sw, Br; 1975 v EG (sub), Se (sub); 1976 v Sw, Ni (sub), E (sub); 1978 v Bul (sub), Ni, W; 1980 v Bel (14)
Johnstone, J. (Abercorn), 1888 v W (1)
Johnstone, J. (Celtic), 1965 v W, Fi; 1966 v E; 1967 v W, USSR; 1968 v W; 1969 v A, WG; 1970 v E, WG; 1971 v D, E; 1972 v P, Bel, Ho, Ni, E (sub); 1974 v W, E, Bel, N; 1975 v EG, Sp (23)
Johnstone, Jas (Kilmarnock), 1894 v W (1)
Johnstone, J. A. (Hearts), 1930 v W; 1933 v W, Ni (3)
Johnstone, R. (Hibernian), 1951 v E, D, F; 1952 v Ni, E; 1953 v E, Se; 1954 v W, E, N, Fi; 1955 v Ni, H; (with Manchester C), 1955 v E; 1956 v E, Ni, W (17)
Johnstone, W. (Third Lanark), 1887 v Ni; 1889 v W; 1890 v E (3)
Jordan, J. (Leeds U), 1973 v E (sub), Sw (sub), Br; 1974 v Cz (sub+1), WG (sub), Ni (sub), W, E, Bel, N, Z, Br, Y; 1975 v EG, Sp (2); 1976 v Ni, W, E; 1977 v Cz, W, Ni, E; 1978 v EG, Cz, W; (with Manchester U), Bul, Ni, E, Pe, Ir, Ho; 1979 v A, P, W (sub), Ni, E, N; 1980 v Bel, Ni (sub), W, E, Pol; 1981 v Is, W, E; (with AC Milan), 1982 v Se, Ho, W, E, USSR (52)

Kay, J. L. (Queen's Park), 1880 v E; 1882 v E, W; 1883 v E, W; 1884 v W (6)
Keillor, A. (Montrose), 1891 v W; 1892 v Ni; (with Dundee), 1894 v Ni; 1895 v W; 1896 v W; 1897 v W (6)
Keir, L. (Dumbarton), 1885 v W; 1886 v Ni; 1887 v E, W; 1888 v E (5)
Kelly, H. T. (Blackpool), 1952 v USA (1)
Kelly, J. (Renton), 1888 v E; (with Celtic), 1889 v E; 1890 v E; 1892 v E; 1893 v E, Ni; 1894 v W; 1896 v Ni (8)
Kelly, J. C. (Barnsley), 1949 v W, Ni (2)
Kelso, R. (Renton), 1885 v W, Ni; 1886 v W; 1887 v E, W; 1888 v E; (with Dundee), 1898 v Ni (7)
Kelso, T. (Dundee), 1914 v W (1)
Kennaway, J. (Celtic), 1934 v A (1)
Kennedy, A. (Eastern), 1875 v E; 1876 v E, W; (with Third Lanark), 1878 v E; 1882 v W; 1884 v W (6)
Kennedy, J. (Hibernian), 1897 v W (1)
Kennedy, J. (Celtic), 1964 v W, E, WG; 1965 v W, Ni, Fi (6)
Kennedy, J. (Celtic), 2004 v R (1)
Kennedy, S. (Aberdeen), 1978 v Bul, W, E, Pe, Ho; 1979 v A, P; 1982 v P (sub) (8)
Kennedy, S. (Partick Th), 1905 v W (1)
Kennedy, S. (Rangers), 1975 v Se, P, W, Ni, E (5)
Ker, G. (Queen's Park), 1880 v E; 1881 v E, W; 1882 v W, E (5)
Ker, W. (Queen's Park), 1872 v E; 1873 v E (2)
Kerr, A. (Partick Th), 1955 v A, H (2)
Kerr, B. (Newcastle U), 2003 v Nz (sub); 2004 v Es (sub); Tr (sub) (3)
Kerr, P. (Hibernian), 1924 v Ni (1)
Key, G. (Hearts), 1902 v Ni (1)
Key, W. (Queen's Park), 1907 v Ni (1)
King, A. (Hearts), 1896 v E, W; (with Celtic), 1897 v Ni; 1898 v Ni; 1899 v Ni, W (6)
King, J. (Hamilton A), 1933 v Ni; 1934 v Ni (2)
King, W. S. (Queen's Park), 1929 v W (1)
Kinloch, J. D. (Partick Th), 1922 v Ni (1)
Kinnaird, A. F. (Wanderers), 1873 v E (1)
Kinnear, D. (Rangers), 1938 v Cz (1)
Kyle, K. (Sunderland), 2002 v Sk (sub), S.Af, Hk; 2003 v D, Fa, Ca (sub), P (sub), Nz; 2004 v D (9)

Lambert, P. (Motherwell), 1995 v J, Ec (sub); (with Borussia Dortmund), 1997 v La (sub), Se (sub), A, Se, Bl; 1998 v Bl, La; (with Celtic), Fi (sub), Co, US, Br, N, Mor; 1999 v Li, CzR, G, Fa, CzR; 2000 v Bos, Li, Ho, Ei; 2001 v Bel, Sm; 2002 v Cro, Bel, F, Ng; 2003 v D, Fa, Ic, P, Ei, Ic, Li, G; 2004 v N, G (40)
Lambie, J. A. (Queen's Park), 1886 v Ni; 1887 v Ni; 1888 v E (3)
Lambie, W. A. (Queen's Park), 1892 v Ni; 1893 v W; 1894 v E; 1895 v E, Ni; 1896 v E, Ni; 1897 v E, Ni (9)
Lamont, W. (Pilgrims), 1885 v Ni (1)
Lang, A. (Dumbarton), 1880 v W (1)
Lang, J. J. (Clydesdale), 1876 v W; (with Third Lanark), 1878 v W (2)
Latta, A. (Dumbarton), 1888 v W; 1889 v E (2)
Law, D. (Huddersfield T), 1959 v W, Ni, Ho, P; 1960 v Ni, W; (with Manchester C), 1960 v E, Pol, A; 1961 v E, Ni; (with Torino), 1962 v Cz (2), E; (with Manchester U), 1963 v W, Ni, E, A, N, Ei, Sp; 1964 v W, E, N, WG; 1965 v W, Ni, E, Fi (2), Pol, Sp; 1966 v Ni, E, Pol; 1967 v W, E, USSR; 1968 v Ni; 1969 v Ni, A, WG; 1972 v Pe, Ni, W, E, Y, Cz, Br; (with Manchester C), 1974 v Cz (2), WG (2), Ni, Z (55)
Law, G. (Rangers), 1910 v E, Ni, W (3)
Law, T. (Chelsea), 1928 v E; 1930 v E (2)
Lawrence, J. (Newcastle U), 1911 v E (1)
Lawrence, T. (Liverpool), 1963 v Ei; 1969 v W, WG (3)
Lawson, D. (St Mirren), 1923 v E (1)

Leckie, R. (Queen's Park), 1872 v E (1)
Leggat, G. (Aberdeen), 1956 v E; 1957 v W; 1958 v Ni, H, Pol, Y, Par; (with Fulham), 1959 v E, W, Ni, WG, Ho; 1960 v E, Ni, W, Pol, A, H (18)
Leighton, J. (Aberdeen), 1983 v EG, Sw, Bel, Sw, W, E, Ca (2); 1984 v U, Bel, Ni, W, E, F; 1985 v Y, Ic, Sp (2), W, E, Ic; 1986 v W, EG, Aus (2), Is, D, WG, U; 1987 v Bul, Ei (2), L, Bel, E; 1988 v H, Bel, Bul, L, S.Ar, Ma, Sp; (with Manchester U), Co, E; 1989 v N, Cy, F, Cy, E, Ch; 1990 v Y, F, N, Arg, Ma (sub, Cr, Se, Br; (with Hibernian), 1994 v Ma, A, Ho; 1995 v Gr (sub), Ru, Sm, J, Ec, Fa; 1996 v Gr, Fi, Se, Sm, Aus, D, US; 1997 v Se, Es, A, Se, W (sub), Ma, Bl; (with Aberdeen), 1998 v Bl, La, D, Fi, US, Br, N, Mor; 1999 v Li, Es (91)
Lennie, W. (Aberdeen), 1908 v W, Ni (2)
Lennox, R. (Celtic), 1967 v Ni, E, USSR; 1968 v W, E; 1969 v D, A, WG, Cy (sub); 1970 v W (sub) (10)
Leslie, L. G. (Airdrieonians), 1961 v W, Ni, Ei (2), Cz (5)
Levein, C. (Hearts), 1990 v Arg, EG, Eg (sub), Pol, Ma (sub), Se; 1992 v R, Sm; 1993 v P, G, P; 1994 v Sw, Ho; 1995 v Fi, Fa, Ru (16)
Liddell, W. (Liverpool), 1947 v W, Ni; 1948 v E, W, Ni; 1950 v E, W, P, F; 1951 v W, Ni, E, A; 1952 v W, Ni, E, USA, D, Se; 1953 v W, Ni, E; 1954 v W; 1955 v P, Y, A, H; 1956 v Ni (28)
Liddle, D. (East Fife), 1931 v A, I, Sw (3)
Lindsay, D. (St Mirren), 1903 v Ni (1)
Lindsay, J. (Dumbarton), 1880 v W; 1881 v W, E; 1884 v W, E; 1885 v W, E; 1886 v E (8)
Lindsay, J. (Renton), 1888 v E; 1893 v E, Ni (3)
Linwood, A. B. (Clyde), 1950 v W (1)
Little, R. J. (Rangers), 1953 v Se (1)
Livingstone, G. T. (Manchester C), 1906 v E; (with Rangers), 1907 v W (2)
Lochhead, A. (Third Lanark), 1889 v W (1)
Logan, J. (Ayr), 1891 v W (1)
Logan, T. (Falkirk), 1913 v Ni (1)
Logie, J. T. (Arsenal), 1953 v Ni (1)
Loney, W. (Celtic), 1910 v W, Ni (2)
Long, H. (Clyde), 1947 v Ni (1)
Longair, W. (Dundee), 1894 v Ni (1)
Lorimer, P. (Leeds U), 1970 v A (sub); 1971 v W, Ni; 1972 v Ni (sub), W, E; 1973 v D (2), E (2); 1974 v WG (sub), E, Bel, N, Z, Br, Y; 1975 v Sp (sub); 1976 v D (2), R (sub) (21)
Love, A. (Aberdeen), 1931 v A, I, Sw (3)
Low, A. (Falkirk), 1934 v Ni (1)
Low, J. (Cambuslang), 1891 v Ni (1)
Low, T. P. (Rangers), 1897 v Ni (1)
Low, W. L. (Newcastle U), 1911 v E, W; 1912 v Ni; 1920 v E, Ni (5)
Lowe, J. (St Bernards), 1887 v Ni (1)
Lundie, J. (Hibernian), 1886 v W (1)
Lyall, J. (Sheffield W), 1905 v E (1)

McAdam, J. (Third Lanark), 1880 v W (1)
McAllister, B. (Wimbledon), 1997 v W, Ma, Bl (sub) (3)
McAllister, G. (Leicester C), 1990 v EG, Pol, Ma (sub); (with Leeds U), 1991 v R, Sw, Bul, USSR (sub), Sm; 1992 v Sw (sub), Sm, Ni, Fi (sub), US, Ca, N, Ho, G, C; 1993 v Sw, P, I, Ma; 1994 v Sw, I, Ma, Ho, A, Ho; 1995 v Fi, Ru, Gr, Ru, Sm; 1996 v Gr, Fi, Se, Sm, Aus, D, US (sub), Co, Ho, E, Sw; (with Coventry C), 1997 v A, La, Es (2), A, Se, W, Ma, Bl; 1998 v Bl, La, F; 1999 v CzR (57)
McAllister, J. R. (Livingston), 2004 v Tr (1)
Macari, L. (Celtic), 1972 v W (sub), E, Y, Cz, Br; 1973 v D; (with Manchester U), E (2), W (sub), Ni (sub); 1975 v Se, P (sub), W, E (sub), R; 1977 v Ni (sub), E (sub), Ch, Arg; 1978 v EG, W, Bul, Pe (sub), Ir (24)
McArthur, D. (Celtic), 1895 v E, Ni; 1899 v W (3)
McAtee, A. (Celtic), 1913 v W (1)
McAulay, J. (Arthurlie), 1884 v Ni (1)
McAulay, J. D. (Dumbarton), 1882 v W; 1883 v E, W; 1884 v E; 1885 v E, W; 1886 v E; 1887 v E, W (9)
Macauley, A. R. (Brentford), 1947 v E; (with Arsenal), 1948 v E, W, Ni, Bel, Sw, F (7)
McAuley, R. (Rangers), 1932 v Ni, W (2)
McAvennie, F. (West Ham U), 1986 v Aus (2), D (sub), WG (sub); (with Celtic), 1988 v S.Ar (5)
McBain, E. (St Mirren), 1894 v W (1)
McBain, N. (Manchester U), 1922 v E; (with Everton), 1923 v Ni; 1924 v W (3)
McBride, J. (Celtic), 1967 v W, Ni (2)
McBride, P. (Preston NE), 1904 v E; 1906 v E; 1907 v E, W; 1908 v E; 1909 v W (6)
McCall, A. (Renton), 1888 v Ni (1)
McCall, J. (Renton), 1886 v W; 1887 v E, W; 1888 v E; 1890 v E (5)
McCall, S. M. (Everton), 1990 v Arg, EG, Eg (sub), Pol, Ma, Cr, Se, Br; 1991 v Sw, USSR, Sm; (with Rangers), 1992 v Sw, R, Sm, US, Ca, N, Ho, G, C; 1993 v Sw, P (2); 1994 v I, Ho, A (sub), Ho; 1995 v Fi (sub), Ru, Gr; 1996 v Gr, D, US (sub), Co, Ho, E, Sw; 1997 v A, La; 1998 v D (sub) (40)
McCalliog, J. (Sheffield W), 1967 v E, USSR; 1968 v Ni; 1969 v D; (with Wolverhampton W), 1971 v P (5)
McCallum, N. (Renton), 1888 v Ni (1)
McCann, N. (Hearts), 1999 v Li (sub); (with Rangers), CzR; 2000 v Bos, Es (sub), E, F (sub), Ho, Ei; 2001 v La, Sm, Aus (sub); 2002 v Cro, La, F, Ng; 2003 v Ei; (with Southampton), 2004 v Fa, G, Ho (2), R, D (sub); 2005 v I (sub); 2006 v I (sub), N (sub), US (26)
McCann, R. J. (Motherwell), 1959 v WG; 1960 v E, Ni, W; 1961 v E (5)
McCartney, W. (Hibernian), 1902 v Ni (1)
McClair, B. (Celtic), 1987 v L, Ei, E, Br (sub); (with Manchester U), 1988 v Bul, Ma (sub), Sp (sub); 1989 v N, Y, I (sub), Cy, F (sub); 1990 v N (sub), Arg (sub); 1991 v Bul (2), Sm; 1992 v Sw (sub), R, Ni, US, Ca (sub), N, Ho, G, C; 1993 v Sw, P (sub), Es (2) (30)
McClory, A. (Motherwell), 1927 v W; 1928 v Ni; 1935 v W (3)
McCloy, P. (Ayr U), 1924 v E; 1925 v E (2)
McCloy, P. (Rangers), 1973 v W, Ni, Sw, Br (4)
McCoist, A. (Rangers), 1986 v Ho; 1987 v L (sub), Ei (sub), Bel, E, Br; 1988 v H, Bel, Ma, Sp, Co, E; 1989 v Y (sub), F, Cy, E; 1990 v Y, F, N, EG (sub), Eg, Pol, Ma (sub), Cr (sub), Se (sub), Br; 1991 v R, Sw, Bul (2), USSR; 1992 v Sw, Sm, Ni, Fi (sub), US, Ca, N, Ho, G, C; 1993 v Sw, P, I, Ma, P; 1996 v Gr (sub), Fi (sub), Sm (sub), Aus, D (sub), Co, E (sub), Sw; 1997 v A, Se (sub), Es (sub), A (sub); 1998 v Bl (sub); (with Kilmarnock), 1999 v Li, Es (61)
McColl, I. M. (Rangers), 1950 v E, F; 1951 v W, Ni, Bel; 1957 v E, Ni, W, Y, Sp, Sw, WG; 1958 v Ni, E (14)
McColl, R. S. (Queen's Park), 1896 v W, Ni; 1897 v Ni; 1898 v Ni; 1899 v Ni, E, W; 1900 v E, W; 1901 v E, W; (with Newcastle U), 1902 v E; (with Queen's Park), 1908 v Ni (13)
McColl, W. (Renton), 1895 v W (1)
McCombie, A. (Sunderland), 1903 v E, W; (with Newcastle U), 1905 v E, W (4)
McCorkindale, J. (Partick Th), 1891 v W (1)
McCormick, R. (Abercorn), 1886 v W (1)
McCrae, D. (St Mirren), 1929 v N, G (2)
McCreadie, A. (Rangers), 1893 v W; 1894 v E (2)
McCreadie, E. G. (Chelsea), 1965 v E, Sp, Fi, Pol; 1966 v P, Ni, W, Pol, I; 1967 v E, USSR; 1968 v Ni, W, E, Ho; 1969 v W, Ni, E, D, A, WG, Cy (2) (23)
McCulloch, D. (Hearts), 1935 v W; (with Brentford), 1936 v E; 1937 v W, Ni; 1938 v Cz; (with Derby Co), 1939 v H, W (7)
McCulloch, L. (Wigan Ath), 2005 v Mol (sub), I, Mol, Bl; 2006 v Bl, Bul, J (7)
MacDonald, A. (Rangers), 1976 v Sw (1)
McDonald, J. (Edinburgh University), 1886 v E (1)
McDonald, J. (Sunderland), 1956 v W, Ni (2)
MacDougall, E. J. (Norwich C) 1975 v Se, P, W, Ni, E; 1976 v D, R (sub) (7)
McDougall, J. (Vale of Leven), 1877 v E, W; 1878 v E; 1879 v E, W (5)
McDougall, J. (Airdrieonians), 1926 v Ni (1)
McDougall, J. (Liverpool), 1931 v I, A (2)
McFadden, J. (Motherwell), 2002 v S.Af (sub); 2003 v Ca (sub), A, Nz; (with Everton), 2004 v Fa (sub), G, Li, Ho (2), W (sub), R (sub), D, Es, Tr; 2005 v H, Sp, Slv, N, Se, Mol (sub), Bl (sub); 2006 v N, Slv, US (sub), Sw, Bul (sub), J (27)
McFadyen, W. (Motherwell), 1934 v A, W (2)
Macfarlane, A. (Dundee), 1904 v W; 1906 v W; 1908 v W; 1909 v Ni; 1911 v W (5)
Macfarlane, W. (Hearts), 1947 v L (1)
McFarlane, R. (Greenock Morton), 1896 v W (1)
McGarr, E. (Aberdeen), 1970 v Ei, A (2)
McGarvey, F. P. (Liverpool), 1979 v Ni (sub), Arg; (with Celtic), 1984 v U, Bel (sub), EG (sub), Ni, W (7)
McGeoch, A. (Dumbreck), 1876 v E, W; 1877 v E, W (4)
McGhee, J. (Hibernian), 1886 v W (1)
McGhee, M. (Aberdeen), 1983 v Ca (1+1 sub); 1984 v Ni (sub), E (4)
McGinlay, J. (Bolton W), 1994 v A, Ho; 1995 v Fa, Ru, Gr, Ru, Sm, Fa; 1996 v Se; 1997 v Se, Es (1 + sub), A (sub) (13)
McGonagle, W. (Celtic), 1933 v E; 1934 v A, E, Ni; 1935 v Ni, W (6)
McGrain, D. (Celtic), 1973 v W, Ni, E, Sw, Br; 1974 v Cz (2), WG, W (sub), E, Bel, N, Z, Br, Y; 1975 v Sp, Se, P, W, Ni, E, R; 1976 v D (2), Sw, Ni, W, E; 1977 v Fi, Cz, W

(2), Se, Ni, E, Ch, Arg, Br; 1978 v EG, Cz; 1980 v Bel, P, Ni, W, E, Pol, H; 1981 v Se, P, Is, Ni, Is, W (sub), Ni, E; 1982 v Se, Sp, Ho, Ni, E, Nz, USSR (sub) (62)
McGregor, J. C. (Vale of Leven), 1877 v E, W; 1878 v E; 1880 v E (4)
McGrory, J. (Celtic), 1928 v Ni; 1931 v E; 1932 v Ni, W; 1933 v E, Ni; 1934 v Ni (7)
McGrory, J. E. (Kilmarnock), 1965 v Ni, Fi; 1966 v P (3)
McGuire, W. (Beith), 1881 v E, W (2)
McGurk, F. (Birmingham), 1934 v W (1)
McHardy, H. (Rangers), 1885 v Ni (1)
McInally, A. (Aston Villa), 1989 v Cy (sub), Ch; (with Bayern Munich), 1990 v Y (sub), F (sub), Arg, Pol (sub), Ma, Cr (8)
McInally, J. (Dundee U), 1987 v Bel, Br; 1988 v Ma (sub); 1991 v Bul (2); 1992 v US (sub), N (sub), C (sub); 1993 v G, P (10)
McInally, T. B. (Celtic), 1926 v Ni; 1927 v W (2)
McInnes, D. (WBA), 2003 v D (sub), P (sub) (2)
McInnes, T. (Cowlairs), 1889 v Ni (1)
McIntosh, W. (Third Lanark), 1905 v Ni (1)
McIntyre, A. (Vale of Leven), 1878 v E; 1882 v E (2)
McIntyre, H. (Rangers), 1880 v W (1)
McIntyre, J. (Rangers), 1884 v W (1)
MacKay, D. (Celtic), 1959 v E, WG, Ho, P; 1960 v E, Pol, A, H, T; 1961 v W, Ni; 1962 v Ni, Cz, U (sub) (14)
Mackay, D. C. (Hearts), 1957 v Sp; 1958 v F; 1959 v W, Ni; (with Tottenham H), 1959 v WG, E; 1960 v W, Ni, A, Pol, H, T; 1961 v W, Ni, E; 1963 v E, A, N; 1964 v Ni, W, N; 1966 v Ni (22)
Mackay, G. (Hearts), 1988 v Bul (sub), L (sub), S.Ar (sub), Ma (4)
Mackay, M. (Norwich C), 2004 v D, Es, Tr; 2005 v Sp, Slv (5)
McKay, J. (Blackburn R), 1924 v W (1)
McKay, R. (Newcastle U), 1928 v W (1)
McKean, R. (Rangers), 1976 v Sw (sub) (1)
McKenzie, D. (Brentford), 1938 v Ni (1)
Mackenzie, J. A. (Partick Th), 1954 v W, E, N, Fi, A, U; 1955 v E, H; 1956 v A (9)
McKeown, M. (Celtic), 1889 v Ni; 1890 v E (2)
McKie, J. (East Stirling), 1898 v W (1)
McKillop, T. R. (Rangers), 1938 v Ho (1)
McKimmie, S. (Aberdeen), 1989 v E, Ch; 1990 v Arg, Eg, Cr (sub), Br; 1991 v R, Sw, Bul, Sm; 1992 v Sw, R, Ni, Fi, US, Ca (sub), N (sub), Ho, G, C; 1993 v P, Es (sub); 1994 v Sw, I, Ho, A, Ho; 1995 v Fi, Fa, Ru, Gr, Ru, Fa; 1996 v Gr, Fi, Se, D, Co, Ho, E (40)
McKinlay, D. (Liverpool), 1922 v W, Ni (2)
McKinlay, T. (Celtic), 1996 v Gr, Fi, D, Co, E, Sw; 1997 v A, La, Se, Es (sub + 1), A, Se, W, Ma, Bl; 1998 v Bl, La (sub), F (sub), US, Br (sub), Mor (sub) (22)
McKinlay, W. (Dundee U), 1994 v Ma, Ho (sub), A, Ho; 1995 v Fa (sub), Ru, Gr, Ru (sub), Sm (sub), J, Ec, Fa; 1996 v Fi (sub), Se (sub); (with Blackburn R), Sm (sub), Aus, D (sub), Ho (sub); 1997 v Se, Es (sub); 1998 v La (sub), F, D, Fi, Co (sub), US, Br (sub); 1999 v Es, Fa (29)
McKinnon, A. (Queen's Park), 1874 v E (1)
McKinnon, R. (Rangers), 1966 v W, E, I (2), Ho, Br; 1967 v W, Ni, E; 1968 v Ni, W, E, Ho; 1969 v D, A, WG, Cy; 1970 v Ni, W, E, Ei, WG, A; 1971 v D, Bel, P, USSR, D (28)
McKinnon, R. (Motherwell), 1994 v Ma; 1995 v J, Fa (3)
MacKinnon, W. (Dumbarton), 1883 v E, W; 1884 v E, W (4)
MacKinnon, W. W. (Queen's Park), 1872 v E; 1873 v E; 1874 v E; 1875 v E; 1876 v E, W; 1877 v E; 1878 v E; 1879 v E (9)
McLaren, A. (St Johnstone), 1929 v N, G, Ho; 1933 v W, Ni (5)
McLaren, A. (Preston NE), 1947 v E, Bel, L; 1948 v W (4)
McLaren, A. (Hearts), 1992 v US, Ca, N; 1993 v I, Ma, G, Es (sub + 1); 1994 v I, Ma, Ho, A; 1995 v Fi, Fa; (with Rangers), Ru, Gr, Ru, Sm, J, Ec, Fa; 1996 v Fi, Se, Sm (24)
McLaren, A. (Kilmarnock), 2001 v Pol (sub) (1)
McLaren, J. (Hibernian), 1888 v W; (with Celtic), 1889 v E; 1890 v E (3)
McLean, A. (Celtic), 1926 v W, Ni; 1927 v W, E (4)
McLean, D. (St Bernards), 1896 v W; 1897 v Ni (2)
McLean, D. (Sheffield W), 1912 v E (1)
McLean, G. (Dundee), 1968 v Ho (1)
McLean, T. (Kilmarnock), 1969 v D, Cy, W; 1970 v Ni, W; 1971 v D (6)
McLeish, A. (Aberdeen), 1980 v P, Ni, W, E, Pol, H; 1981 v Se, Is, Ni, Is, Ni, E; 1982 v Se, Sp, Ni, Br (sub); 1983 v Bel, Sw (sub), W, E, Ca (3); 1984 v U, Bel, EG, Ni, W, E, F; 1985 v Y, Ic, Sp (2), W, E, Ic; 1986 v W, EG, Aus (2), E, Ho, D; 1987 v Bel, E, Br; 1988 v Bel, Bul, L, S.Ar (sub), Ma, Sp, Co, E; 1989 v N, Y, I, Cy, F, Cy, E, Ch; 1990 v Y, F, N, Arg, EG, Eg, Cr, Se, Br; 1991 v R, Sw, USSR, Bul; 1993 v Ma (77)
McLeod, D. (Celtic), 1905 v Ni; 1906 v E, W, Ni (4)
McLeod, J. (Dumbarton), 1888 v Ni; 1889 v W; 1890 v Ni; 1892 v E; 1893 v W (5)
MacLeod, J. M. (Hibernian), 1961 v E, Ei (2), Cz (4)
MacLeod, M. (Celtic), 1985 v E (sub); 1987 v Ei, L, E, Br; (with Borussia Dortmund), 1988 v Co, E; 1989 v I, Ch; 1990 v Y, F, N (sub), Arg, EG, Pol, Se Br; (with Hibernian), 1991 v R, Sw, USSR (sub) (20)
McLeod, W. (Cowlairs), 1886 v Ni (1)
McLintock, A. (Vale of Leven), 1875 v E; 1876 v E; 1880 v E (3)
McLintock, F. (Leicester C), 1963 v N (sub), Ei, Sp; (with Arsenal), 1965 v Ni; 1967 v USSR; 1970 v Ni; 1971 v W, Ni, E (9)
McLuckie, J. S. (Manchester C), 1934 v W (1)
McMahon, A. (Celtic), 1892 v E; 1893 v E, Ni; 1894 v E; 1901 v Ni; 1902 v W (6)
McMenemy, J. (Celtic), 1905 v Ni; 1909 v Ni; 1910 v E, W; 1911 v Ni, W, E; 1912 v W; 1914 v W, Ni, E; 1920 v Ni (12)
McMenemy, J. (Motherwell), 1934 v W (1)
McMillan, I. L. (Airdrieonians), 1952 v E, USA, D; 1955 v E; 1956 v E; (with Rangers), 1961 v Cz (6)
McMillan, J. (St Bernards), 1897 v W (1)
McMillan, T. (Dumbarton), 1887 v Ni (1)
McMullan, J. (Partick Th), 1920 v W; 1921 v W, Ni, E; 1924 v E, Ni; 1925 v E; 1926 v W; (with Manchester C), 1926 v E; 1927 v E, W; 1928 v E, W; 1929 v W, E, Ni (16)
McNab, A. (Morton), 1921 v E, Ni (2)
McNab, A. (Sunderland), 1937 v A; (with WBA), 1939 v E (2)
McNab, C. D. (Dundee), 1931 v E, W, A, I, Sw; 1932 v E (6)
McNab, J. S. (Liverpool), 1923 v W (1)
McNair, A. (Celtic), 1906 v W; 1907 v Ni; 1908 v E, W; 1909 v E; 1910 v W; 1912 v E, W, Ni; 1913 v E; 1914 v E, Ni; 1920 v E, W, Ni (15)
McNamara, J. (Celtic), 1997 v La (sub), Se, Es, W (sub); 1998 v D, Co, US (sub), N (sub), Mor; 2000 v Ho; 2001 v Sm; 2002 v Bel (sub), F (sub); 2003 v Ic (1+sub), Li, Nz, G (sub); 2004 v Fa, G, Li, Ho (2), W, Tr; 2005 v Sp, Slv, Se, I, Mol; (with Wolverhampton W), 2006 v A, I, N (33)
McNamee, D. (Livingston), 2004 v Es, Tr (sub); 2006 v Bul (sub), J (sub) (4)
McNaught, W. (Raith R), 1951 v A, W, Ni; 1952 v E; 1955 v Ni (5)
McNaughton, K. (Aberdeen), 2002 v Ng; 2003 v D; 2005 v Se (3)
McNeill, W. (Celtic), 1961 v E, Ei (2), Cz; 1962 v Ni, E, Cz, U; 1963 v Ei, Sp; 1964 v W, E, WG; 1965 v E, Fi, Pol, Sp; 1966 v Ni, Pol; 1967 v USSR; 1968 v E; 1969 v Cy, W, E, Cy (sub); 1970 v WG; 1972 v Ni, W, E (29)
McNiel, H. (Queen's Park), 1874 v E; 1875 v E; 1876 v E, W; 1877 v W; 1878 v E; 1879 v E, W; 1881 v E, W (10)
McNiel, M. (Rangers), 1876 v W; 1880 v E (2)
McPhail, J. (Celtic), 1950 v W; 1951 v W, Ni, A; 1954 v Ni (5)
McPhail, R. (Airdrieonians), 1927 v E; (with Rangers), 1929 v W; 1931 v E, Ni; 1932 v W, Ni, F; 1933 v E, Ni; 1934 v A, Ni; 1935 v E; 1937 v G, E, Cz; 1938 v W, Ni (17)
McPherson, D. (Kilmarnock), 1892 v Ni (1)
McPherson, D. (Hearts), 1989 v Cy, E; 1990 v N, Ma, Cr, Se, Br; 1991 v Sw, Bul (2), USSR (sub), Sm; 1992 v Sw, R, Sm, Ni, Fi, US, Ca, N, Ho, G, C; (with Rangers), 1993 v Sw, I, Ma, P (27)
McPherson, J. (Clydesdale), 1875 v E (1)
McPherson, J. (Vale of Leven), 1879 v E, W; 1880 v E; 1881 v W; 1883 v E, W; 1884 v E; 1885 v Ni (8)
McPherson, J. (Kilmarnock), 1888 v W; (with Cowlairs), 1889 v E; 1890 v Ni, E; (with Rangers), 1892 v W; 1894 v E; 1895 v E, Ni; 1897 v Ni (9)
McPherson, J. (Hearts), 1891 v E (1)
McPherson, R. (Arthurlie), 1882 v E (1)
McQueen, G. (Leeds U), 1974 v Bel; 1975 v Sp (2), P, W, Ni, E, R; 1976 v D; 1977 v Cz, W (2), Ni, E; 1978 v EG, Cz, W; (with Manchester U), Bul, Ni, W; 1979 v A, N, P, Ni, E, N; 1980 v Pe, A, Bel; 1981 v W (30)
McQueen, M. (Leith Ath), 1890 v W; 1891 v W (2)
McRorie, D. M. (Morton), 1931 v W (1)
McSpadyen, A. (Partick Th), 1939 v E, H (2)
McStay, P. (Celtic), 1984 v U, Bel, EG, Ni, W, E (sub); 1985 v Y (sub), Ic, Sp (2), W; 1986 v EG (sub), Aus, Is, U; 1987 v Bul, Ei (1+1 sub), L (sub), Bel, E, Br; 1988 v H, Bel, Bul, L, S.Ar, Sp, Co, E; 1989 v N, Y, I, Cy, F, Cy, E, Ch; 1990 v Y, F, N, Arg, EG (sub), Eg, Pol (sub), Ma, Cr, Se (sub), Br; 1991 v R, USSR, Bul; 1992 v Sm, Fi, US, Ca, N, Ho, G, C; 1993 v Sw, P, I, Ma, P, Es (2); 1994 v I (sub), Ho; 1995 v Fi, Fa, Ru; 1996 v Aus; 1997 v Es (2), A (sub) (76)

McStay, W. (Celtic), 1921 v W, Ni; 1925 v E, Ni, W; 1926 v E, Ni, W; 1927 v E, Ni, W; 1928 v W, Ni (13)
McSwegan, G. (Hearts), 2000 v Bos (sub), Li (2)
McTavish, J. (Falkirk), 1910 v Ni (1)
McWattie, G. C. (Queen's Park), 1901 v W, Ni (2)
McWilliam, P. (Newcastle U), 1905 v E; 1906 v E; 1907 v E, W; 1909 v E, W; 1910 v E; 1911 v W (8)
Madden, J. (Celtic), 1893 v W; 1895 v W (2)
Main, F. R. (Rangers), 1938 v W (1)
Main, J. (Hibernian), 1909 v Ni (1)
Maley, W. (Celtic), 1893 v E, Ni (2)
Maloney, S. R. (Celtic), 2006 v Bl (sub), US (sub) (2)
Malpas, M. (Dundee U), 1984 v F; 1985 v E, Ic; 1986 v W, Aus (2), Is, R, E, Ho, D, WG; 1987 v Bul, Ei, Bel; 1988 v Bel, Bul, L, S.Ar, Ma; 1989 v N, Y, I, Cy, F, Cy, E, Ch; 1990 v Y, F, N, Eg, Pol, Ma, Cr, Se, Br; 1991 v R, Bul (2), USSR, Sm; 1992 v Sw, R, Sm, Ni, Fi, US, Ca (sub), N, Ho, G; 1993 v Sw, P, I (55)
Marshall, D. J. (Celtic), 2005 v H, Se (2)
Marshall, G. (Celtic), 1992 v US (1)
Marshall, H. (Celtic), 1899 v W; 1900 v Ni (2)
Marshall, J. (Third Lanark), 1885 v Ni; 1886 v W; 1887 v E, W (4)
Marshall, J. (Middlesbrough), 1921 v E, W, Ni; 1922 v E, W, Ni; (with Llanelly), 1924 v W (7)
Marshall, J. (Rangers), 1932 v E; 1933 v E; 1934 v E (3)
Marshall, R. W. (Rangers), 1892 v Ni; 1894 v Ni (2)
Martin, B. (Motherwell), 1995 v J, Ec (2)
Martin, F. (Aberdeen), 1954 v N (2), A, U; 1955 v E, H (6)
Martin, N. (Hibernian), 1965 v Fi, Pol; (with Sunderland), 1966 v I (3)
Martis, J. (Motherwell), 1961 v W (1)
Mason, J. (Third Lanark), 1949 v W, Ni, E; 1950 v Ni; 1951 v Ni, Bel, A (7)
Massie, A. (Hearts), 1932 v Ni, W, F; 1933 v Ni; 1934 v E, Ni; 1935 v E, Ni, W; 1936 v W, Ni; (with Aston Villa), 1936 v E; 1937 v G, E, W, Ni, A; 1938 v W (18)
Masson, D. S. (QPR), 1976 v Ni, W, E; 1977 v Fi, Cz, W, Ni, E, Ch, Arg, Br; 1978 v EG, Cz, W; (with Derby Co), Ni, E, Pe (17)
Mathers, D. (Partick Th), 1954 v Fi (1)
Matteo, D. (Leeds U), 2001 v Aus, Bel, Sm; 2002 v Cro, Bel, F (6)
Maxwell, W. S. (Stoke C), 1898 v E (1)
May, J. (Rangers), 1906 v W, Ni; 1908 v E, Ni; 1909 v W (5)
Meechan, P. (Celtic), 1896 v Ni (1)
Meiklejohn, D. D. (Rangers), 1922 v W; 1924 v W; 1925 v W, Ni, E; 1928 v W, Ni; 1929 v E, Ni; 1930 v E, Ni; 1931 v E; 1932 v W, Ni; 1934 v A (15)
Menzies, A. (Hearts), 1906 v E (1)
Mercer, R. (Hearts), 1912 v W; 1913 v Ni (2)
Middleton, R. (Cowdenbeath), 1930 v Ni (1)
Millar, A. (Hearts), 1939 v W (1)
Millar, J. (Rangers), 1897 v E; 1898 v E, W (3)
Millar, J. (Rangers), 1963 v A, Ei (2)
Miller, C. (Dundee U), 2001 v Pol (1)
Miller, J. (St Mirren), 1931 v E, I, Sw; 1932 v F; 1934 v E (5)
Miller, K. (Rangers), 2001 v Pol (sub); (with Wolverhampton W), 2003 v Ic, Li, A (sub), G; 2004 v Li, Ho (sub + sub), W, R, Es, Tr (sub); 2005 v H, Sp (sub), N (sub), Mol (sub), Se, I, Mol, Bl; 2006 v A, I, N, Bl, Slv, Sw (26)
Miller, L. (Dundee U), 2006 v J (sub) (1)
Miller, P. (Dumbarton), 1882 v E; 1883 v E, W (3)
Miller, T. (Liverpool), 1920 v E; (with Manchester U), 1921 v E, Ni (3)
Miller, W. (Third Lanark), 1876 v E (1)
Miller, W. (Celtic), 1947 v E, W, Bel, L; 1948 v W, Ni (6)
Miller, W. (Aberdeen), 1975 v R; 1978 v Bul; 1980 v Bel, W, E, Pol, H; 1981 v Se, P, Is (sub), Ni, W, Ni, E; 1982 v Ni, P, Ho, Br, USSR; 1983 v EG, Sw (2), W, E, Ca (3); 1984 v U, Bel, EG, W, E, F; 1985 v Y, Ic, Sp (2), W, E, Ic; 1986 v W, EG, Aus (2), Is, R, E, Ho, D, WG, U; 1987 v Bul, E, Br; 1988 v H, L, S.Ar, Ma, Sp, Co, E; 1989 v N, Y; 1990 v Y, N (65)
Mills, W. (Aberdeen), 1936 v W, Ni; 1937 v W (3)
Milne, J. V. (Middlesbrough), 1938 v E; 1939 v E (2)
Mitchell, D. (Rangers), 1890 v Ni; 1892 v E; 1893 v E, Ni; 1894 v E (5)
Mitchell, J. (Kilmarnock), 1908 v Ni; 1910 v Ni, W (3)
Mitchell, R. C. (Newcastle U), 1951 v D, F (2)
Mochan, N. (Celtic), 1954 v N, A, U (3)
Moir, W. (Bolton W), 1950 v E (1)
Moncur, R. (Newcastle U), 1968 v Ho; 1970 v Ni, W, E, Ei; 1971 v D, Bel, W, P, Ni, E, D; 1972 v Pe, Ni, W, E (16)
Morgan, H. (St Mirren), 1898 v W; (with Liverpool), 1899 v E (2)
Morgan, W. (Burnley), 1968 v Ni; (with Manchester U), 1972 v Pe, Y, Cz, Br; 1973 v D (2), E (2), W, Ni, Sw, Br; 1974 v Cz (2), WG (2), Ni, Bel (sub), Br, Y (21)
Morris, D. (Raith R), 1923 v Ni; 1924 v E, Ni; 1925 v E, W, Ni (6)
Morris, H. (East Fife), 1950 v Ni (1)
Morrison, T. (St Mirren), 1927 v E (1)
Morton, A. L. (Queen's Park), 1920 v W, Ni; (with Rangers), 1921 v E; 1922 v E, W; 1923 v E, W, Ni; 1924 v E, W, Ni; 1925 v E, W, Ni; 1927 v E, Ni; 1928 v E, W, Ni; 1929 v E, W, Ni; 1930 v E, W, Ni; 1931 v E, W, Ni; 1932 v E, W, F (31)
Morton, H. A. (Kilmarnock), 1929 v G, Ho (2)
Mudie, J. K. (Blackpool), 1957 v W, Ni, E, Y, Sw, Sp (2), WG; 1958 v Ni, E, W, Sw, H, Pol, Y, Par, F (17)
Muir, W. (Dundee), 1907 v Ni (1)
Muirhead, T. A. (Rangers), 1922 v Ni; 1923 v E; 1924 v W; 1927 v Ni; 1928 v Ni; 1929 v W, Ni; 1930 v W (8)
Mulhall, G. (Aberdeen), 1960 v Ni; (with Sunderland), 1963 v Ni; 1964 v Ni (3)
Munro, A. D. (Hearts), 1937 v W, Ni; (with Blackpool), 1938 v Ho (3)
Munro, F. M. (Wolverhampton W), 1971 v Ni (sub), E (sub), D, USSR; 1975 v Se, W (sub), Ni, E, R (9)
Munro, I. (St Mirren), 1979 v Arg, N; 1980 v Pe, A, Bel, W, E (7)
Munro, N. (Abercorn), 1888 v W; 1889 v E (2)
Murdoch, J. (Motherwell), 1931 v Ni (1)
Murdoch, R. (Celtic), 1966 v W, E, I (2); 1967 v Ni; 1968 v Ni; 1969 v W, Ni, E, WG, Cy; 1970 v A (12)
Murphy, F. (Celtic), 1938 v Ho (1)
Murray, I. (Hibernian), 2003 v Ca (sub); 2005 v Mol (sub), Se; (with Rangers), 2006 v Bl, Bul (sub), J (sub) (6)
Murray, J. (Renton), 1895 v W (1)
Murray, J. (Hearts), 1958 v E, H, Pol, Y, F (5)
Murray, J. W. (Vale of Leven), 1890 v W (1)
Murray, P. (Hibernian), 1896 v Ni; 1897 v W (2)
Murray, S. (Aberdeen), 1972 v Bel (1)
Murty, G. S. (Reading), 2004 v W (sub); 2006 v Bul, J (3)
Mutch, G. (Preston NE), 1938 v E (1)

Napier, C. E. (Celtic), 1932 v E; 1935 v E, W; (with Derby Co), 1937 v Ni, A (5)
Narey, D. (Dundee U), 1977 v Se (sub); 1979 v P, Ni (sub), Arg; 1980 v P, Ni, Pol, H; 1981 v W, E (sub); 1982 v Ho, W, E, Nz (sub), Br, USSR; 1983 v EG, Sw, Bel, Ni, W, E, Ca (3); 1986 v Is, R, Ho, WG, U; 1987 v Bul, Ei, Bel; 1989 v I, Cy (35)
Naysmith, G. A. (Hearts), 2000 v Ei; 2001 v La (sub), Sm, Cro; (with Everton), 2002 v Cro, Bel; 2003 v D, Ic, P, Ei, Ic, Li, A, Nz, G; 2004 v N, Fa, G, Li, Ho (2), W; 2005 v H, Sp, Slv, N, Mol, I; 2006 v Bul, J (30)
Neil, R. G. (Hibernian), 1896 v W; (with Rangers), 1900 v W (2)
Neill, R. W. (Queen's Park), 1876 v W; 1877 v E, W; 1878 v W; 1880 v E (5)
Nellies, P. (Hearts), 1913 v Ni; 1914 v W (2)
Nelson, J. (Cardiff C), 1925 v W, Ni; 1928 v E; 1930 v F (4)
Nevin, P. K. F. (Chelsea), 1986 v R (sub), E (sub); 1987 v L, Ei, Bel (sub); 1988 v L; (with Everton), 1989 v Cy, E; 1991 v R (sub), Bul (sub), Sm (sub); 1992 v US, G (sub), C (sub); (with Tranmere R), 1993 v Ma, P (sub), Es; 1994 v Sw, Ma, Ho, A (sub), Ho (sub); 1995 v Fa, Ru (sub), Sm; 1996 v Se (sub), Sm, Aus (sub) (28)
Niblo, T. D. (Aston Villa), 1904 v E (1)
Nibloe, J. (Kilmarnock), 1929 v E, N, Ho; 1930 v W; 1931 v E, Ni, A, I, Sw; 1932 v E, F (11)
Nicholas, C. (Celtic), 1983 v Sw, Ni, E, Ca (3); (with Arsenal), 1984 v Bel, F (sub); 1985 v Y (sub), Ic (sub), Sp (sub), W (sub); 1986 v Is, R (sub), E, D, U (sub); 1987 v Bul, E (sub); (with Aberdeen), 1989 v Cy (sub) (20)
Nicholson, B. (Dunfermline Ath), 2001 v Pol; 2002 v La; 2005 v Se (3)
Nicol, S. (Liverpool), 1985 v Y, Ic, Sp, W; 1986 v W, EG, Aus, E, D, WG, U; 1988 v H, Bul, S.Ar, Sp, Co, E; 1989 v N, Y, Cy, F; 1990 v Y, F; 1991 v Sw, USSR, Sm; 1992 v Sw (27)
Nisbet, J. (Ayr U), 1929 v N, G, Ho (3)
Niven, J. B. (Moffat), 1885 v Ni (1)

O'Connor, G. (Hibernian), 2002 v Ng (sub), Sk, Hk (sub); 2005 v I (sub); 2006 v A, Slv (sub), US (7)
O'Donnell, F. (Preston NE), 1937 v E, A, Cz; 1938 v W; (with Blackpool), E, Ho (6)
O'Donnell, P. (Motherwell), 1994 v Sw (sub) (1)
Ogilvie, D. H. (Motherwell), 1934 v A (1)
O'Hare, J. (Derby Co), 1970 v W, Ni, E; 1971 v D, Bel, W, Ni; 1972 v P, Bel, Ho (sub), Pe, Ni, W (13)

O'Neil, B. (Celtic), 1996 v Aus; (with Wolfsburg), 1999 v G (sub); 2000 v Li, Ho (sub), Ei; (with Derby Co), 2001 v Aus; (with Preston NE), 2006 v A (7)
O'Neil, J. (Hibernian), 2001 v Pol (1)
Ormond, W. E. (Hibernian), 1954 v E, N, Fi, A, U; 1959 v E (6)
O'Rourke, F. (Airdrieonians), 1907 v Ni (1)
Orr, J. (Kilmarnock), 1892 v W (1)
Orr, R. (Newcastle U), 1902 v E; 1904 v E (2)
Orr, T. (Morton), 1952 v Ni, W (2)
Orr, W. (Celtic), 1900 v Ni; 1903 v Ni; 1904 v W (3)
Orrock, R. (Falkirk), 1913 v W (1)
Oswald, J. (Third Lanark), 1889 v E; (with St Bernards), 1895 v E; (with Rangers), 1897 v W (3)

Parker, A. H. (Falkirk), 1955 v P, Y, A; 1956 v E, Ni, W, A; 1957 v Ni, W, Y; 1958 v Ni, W, E, Sw; (with Everton), Par (15)
Parlane, D. (Rangers), 1973 v W, Sw, Br; 1975 v Sp (sub), Se, P, W, Ni, E, R; 1976 v D (sub); 1977 v W (12)
Parlane, R. (Vale of Leven), 1878 v W; 1879 v E, W (3)
Paterson, G. D. (Celtic), 1939 v Ni (1)
Paterson, J. (Leicester C), 1920 v E (1)
Paterson, J. (Cowdenbeath), 1931 v A, I, Sw (3)
Paton, A. (Motherwell), 1952 v D, Se (2)
Paton, D. (St Bernards), 1896 v W (1)
Paton, M. (Dumbarton), 1883 v E; 1884 v W; 1885 v W, E; 1886 v E (5)
Paton, R. (Vale of Leven), 1879 v E, W (2)
Patrick, J. (St Mirren), 1897 v E, W (2)
Paul, H. McD. (Queen's Park), 1909 v E, W, Ni (3)
Paul, W. (Partick Th), 1888 v W; 1889 v W; 1890 v W (3)
Paul, W. (Dykebar), 1891 v Ni (1)
Pearson, S. P. (Motherwell), 2004 v Ho (sub); (with Celtic), W; 2005 v H (sub), Sp (sub), N (sub), Se (6)
Pearson, T. (Newcastle U), 1947 v E, Bel (2)
Penman, A. (Dundee), 1966 v Ho (1)
Pettigrew, W. (Motherwell), 1976 v Sw, Ni, W; 1977 v W (sub), Se (5)
Phillips, J. (Queen's Park), 1877 v E, W; 1878 v W (3)
Plenderleith, J. B. (Manchester C), 1961 v Ni (1)
Porteous, W. (Hearts), 1903 v Ni (1)
Pressley, S. J. (Hearts), 2000 v F (sub), Ei (sub); 2003 v Ic, Ca, P, Ic, Li, A, Nz, G; 2004 v N, G, Li, Ho (2), R, D, Es, Tr; 2005 v H, I, Mol, Bl; 2006 v A, N, Bl, Slv, US (28)
Pringle, C. (St Mirren), 1921 v W (1)
Provan, D. (Rangers), 1964 v Ni, N; 1966 v I (2), Ho (5)
Provan, D. (Celtic), 1980 v Bel (2 sub), P (sub), Ni (sub); 1981 v Is, W, E; 1982 v Se, P, Ni (10)
Pursell, P. (Queen's Park), 1914 v W (1)

Quashie, N. F. (Portsmouth), 2004 v Es, Tr; 2005 v H, Sp, Slv, Se; (with Southampton), I; 2006 v A, I, Slv, US; (with WBA), Sw (12)
Quinn, J. (Celtic), 1905 v Ni; 1906 v Ni, W; 1908 v Ni, E; 1909 v E; 1910 v E, Ni, W; 1912 v E, W (11)
Quinn, P. (Motherwell), 1961 v E, Ei (2); 1962 v U (4)

Rae, G. (Dundee), 2001 v Pol; 2002 v La (sub); 2003 v G (sub); 2004 v N (sub), Fa (sub), G (sub), Li, Ho; (with Rangers), R; 2006 v Bul (sub), J (sub) (11)
Rae, J. (Third Lanark), 1889 v W; 1890 v Ni (2)
Raeside, J. S. (Third Lanark), 1906 v W (1)
Raisbeck, A. G. (Liverpool), 1900 v E; 1901 v E; 1902 v E; 1903 v E, W; 1904 v E; 1906 v E; 1907 v E (8)
Rankin, G. (Vale of Leven), 1890 v Ni; 1891 v E (2)
Rankin, R. (St Mirren), 1929 v N, G, Ho (3)
Redpath, W. (Motherwell), 1949 v W, Ni; 1951 v E, D, F, Bel, A; 1952 v Ni, E (9)
Reid, J. G. (Airdrieonians), 1914 v W; 1920 v W; 1924 v Ni (3)
Reid, R. (Brentford), 1938 v E, Ni (2)
Reid, W. (Rangers), 1911 v E, W, Ni; 1912 v Ni; 1913 v E, W, Ni; 1914 v E, Ni (9)
Reilly, L. (Hibernian), 1949 v E, W, F; 1950 v W, Ni, Sw, F; 1951 v W, E, D, F, Bel, A; 1952 v Ni, W, E, USA, D, Se; 1953 v Ni, W, E, Se; 1954 v W; 1955 v H (2), P, Y, A, E; 1956 v E, W, Ni, A; 1957 v E, Ni, W, Y (38)
Rennie, H. G. (Hearts), 1900 v E, Ni; (with Hibernian), 1901 v E; 1902 v E, Ni, W; 1903 v Ni, W; 1904 v Ni; 1905 v W; 1906 v Ni; 1908 v Ni, W (13)
Renny-Tailyour, H. W. (Royal Engineers), 1873 v E (1)
Rhind, A. (Queen's Park), 1872 v E (1)
Richmond, A. (Queen's Park), 1906 v W (1)
Richmond, J. T. (Clydesdale), 1877 v E; (with Queen's Park), 1878 v E; 1882 v W (3)
Ring, T. (Clyde), 1953 v Se; 1955 v W, Ni, E, H; 1957 v E, Sp (2), Sw, WG; 1958 v Ni, Sw (12)

Rioch, B. D. (Derby Co), 1975 v P, W, Ni, E, R; 1976 v D (2), R, Ni, W, E; 1977 v Fi, Cz, W; (with Everton), W, Ni, E, Ch, Br; 1978 v Cz; (with Derby Co), Ni, E, Pe, Ho (24)
Riordan, D. G. (Hibernian), 2006 v A (sub) (1)
Ritchie, A. (East Stirlingshire), 1891 v W (1)
Ritchie, H. (Hibernian), 1923 v W; 1928 v Ni (2)
Ritchie, J. (Queen's Park), 1897 v W (1)
Ritchie, P. S. (Hearts), 1999 v G (sub), CzR; 2000 v Li, E; (with Bolton W), F, Ho; (with Walsall), 2004 v W (7)
Ritchie, W. (Rangers), 1962 v U (sub) (1)
Robb, D. T. (Aberdeen), 1971 v W, E, P, D (sub), USSR (5)
Robb, W. (Rangers), 1926 v W; (with Hibernian), 1928 v W (2)
Robertson, A. (Clyde), 1955 v P, A, H; 1958 v Sw, Par (5)
Robertson, D. (Rangers), 1992 v Ni; 1994 v Sw, Ho (3)
Robertson, G. (Motherwell), 1910 v W; (with Sheffield W), 1912 v W; 1913 v E, Ni (4)
Robertson, G. (Kilmarnock), 1938 v Cz (1)
Robertson, H. (Dundee), 1962 v Cz (1)
Robertson, J. (Dundee), 1931 v A, I (2)
Robertson, J. (Hearts), 1991 v R, Sw, Bul (sub), Sm (sub); 1992 v Sm, Ni (sub), Fi; 1993 v I (sub), Ma (sub), G, Es; 1995 v J (sub), Ec, Fa (sub); 1996 v Gr (sub), Se (16)
Robertson, J. N. (Nottingham F), 1978 v Ni, W (sub), Ir; 1979 v P, N; 1980 v Pe, A, Bel (2), P; 1981 v Se, P, Is, Ni, Is, Ni, E; 1982 v Se, Ni (2), E (sub), Nz, Br, USSR; 1983 v EG, Sw; (with Derby Co), 1984 v U, Bel (28)
Robertson, J. G. (Tottenham H), 1965 v W (1)
Robertson, J. T. (Everton), 1898 v E; (with Southampton), 1899 v E; (with Rangers), 1900 v E, W; 1901 v W, Ni, E; 1902 v W, Ni, E; 1903 v E, W; 1904 v E, W, Ni; 1905 v W (16)
Robertson, P. (Dundee), 1903 v Ni (1)
Robertson, T. (Queen's Park), 1889 v Ni; 1890 v E; 1891 v W; 1892 v Ni (4)
Robertson, T. (Hearts), 1898 v Ni (1)
Robertson, W. (Dumbarton), 1887 v E, W (2)
Robinson, R. (Dundee), 1974 v WG (sub); 1975 v Se, Ni, R (sub) (4)
Ross, M. (Rangers), 2002 v Sk, S.Af, Hk; 2003 v D, Fa, Ic, Ca, P, Nz, G; 2004 v N, G (sub), Ho (sub) (13)
Rough, A. (Partick Th), 1976 v Sw, Ni, W, E; 1977 v Fi, Cz, W (2), Se, Ni, E, Ch, Arg, Br; 1978 v Cz, W, Ni, E, Pe, Ir, Ho; 1979 v A, P, W, Arg, N; 1980 v Pe, A, Bel (2), P, W, E, Pol, H; 1981 v Se, P, Is, Ni, Is, W, E; 1982 v Se, Ni, Sp, Ho, W, E, Nz, Br, USSR; (with Hibernian), 1986 v W (sub), E (53)
Rougvie, D. (Aberdeen), 1984 v Ni (1)
Rowan, A. (Caledonian), 1880 v E; (with Queen's Park), 1882 v W (2)
Russell, D. (Hearts), 1895 v E, Ni; (with Celtic), 1897 v W; 1898 v Ni; 1901 v W, Ni (6)
Russell, J. (Cambuslang), 1890 v Ni (1)
Russell, W. F. (Airdrieonians), 1924 v W; 1925 v E (2)
Rutherford, E. (Rangers), 1948 v F (1)

St John, I. (Motherwell), 1959 v WG; 1960 v E, Ni, W, Pol, A; 1961 v E; (with Liverpool), 1962 v Ni, W, E, Cz (2), U; 1963 v W, Ni, E, N, Ei (sub), Sp; 1964 v Ni; 1965 v E (21)
Sawers, W. (Dundee), 1895 v W (1)
Scarff, P. (Celtic), 1931 v Ni (1)
Schaedler, E. (Hibernian), 1974 v WG (1)
Scott, A. S. (Rangers), 1957 v Ni, Y, WG; 1958 v W, Sw; 1959 v P; 1962 v Ni, W, E, Cz, U; (with Everton), 1964 v W, N; 1965 v Fi; 1966 v P, Br (16)
Scott, J. (Hibernian), 1966 v Ho (1)
Scott, J. (Dundee), 1971 v D (sub), USSR (2)
Scott, M. (Airdrieonians), 1898 v W (1)
Scott, R. (Airdrieonians), 1894 v Ni (1)
Scoular, J. (Portsmouth), 1951 v D, F, A; 1952 v E, USA, D, Se; 1953 v W, Ni (9)
Sellar, W. (Battlefield), 1885 v E; 1886 v E; 1887 v E, W; 1888 v E; (with Queen's Park), 1891 v E; 1892 v E; 1893 v E, Ni (9)
Semple, W. (Cambuslang), 1886 v W (1)
Severin, S. D. (Hearts), 2002 v La (sub), Sk (sub), S.Af (sub), Hk; 2003 v D (sub), Ic (sub), Ca (sub), P (sub); (with Aberdeen), 2005 v H (sub), Se (sub); 2006 v A (sub), Bul, J (13)
Shankly, W. (Preston NE), 1938 v E; 1939 v E, W, Ni, H (5)
Sharp, G. M. (Everton), 1985 v Ic; 1986 v W, Aus (2 sub), Is, R, U; 1987 v Ei; 1988 v Bel (sub), Bul, L, Ma (12)
Sharp, J. (Dundee), 1904 v W; (with Woolwich Arsenal), 1907 v W, E; 1908 v E; (with Fulham), 1909 v W (5)
Shaw, D. (Hibernian), 1947 v W, Ni; 1948 v E, Bel, Sw, F; 1949 v W, Ni (8)
Shaw, F. W. (Pollokshields Ath), 1884 v E, W (2)
Shaw, J. (Rangers), 1947 v E, Bel, L; 1948 v Ni (4)

Shearer, D. (Aberdeen), 1994 v A (sub), Ho (sub); 1995 v Fi, Ru (sub), Sm, Fa; 1996 v Gr (7)
Shearer, R. (Rangers), 1961 v E, Ei (2), Cz (4)
Sillars, D. C. (Queen's Park), 1891 v Ni; 1892 v E; 1893 v W; 1894 v E; 1895 v W (5)
Simpson, J. (Third Lanark), 1895 v E, W, Ni (3)
Simpson, J. (Rangers), 1935 v E, W, Ni; 1936 v E, W, Ni; 1937 v G, E, W, Ni, A, Cz; 1938 v W, Ni (14)
Simpson, N. (Aberdeen), 1983 v Ni; 1984 v U (sub), F (sub); 1987 v E; 1988 v E (5)
Simpson, R. C. (Celtic), 1967 v E, USSR; 1968 v Ni, E; 1969 v A (5)
Sinclair, G. L. (Hearts), 1910 v Ni; 1912 v W, Ni (3)
Sinclair, J. W. E. (Leicester C), 1966 v P (1)
Skene, L. H. (Queen's Park), 1904 v W (1)
Sloan, T. (Third Lanark), 1904 v W (1)
Smellie, R. (Queen's Park), 1887 v Ni; 1888 v W; 1889 v E; 1891 v E; 1893 v E, Ni (6)
Smith, A. (Rangers), 1898 v E; 1900 v E, Ni, W; 1901 v E, Ni, W; 1902 v E, Ni, W; 1903 v E, Ni, W; 1904 v Ni; 1905 v W; 1906 v E, Ni; 1907 v W; 1911 v E, Ni (20)
Smith, D. (Aberdeen), 1966 v Ho; (with Rangers), 1968 v Ho (2)
Smith, G. (Hibernian), 1947 v E, Ni; 1948 v W, Bel, Sw, F; 1952 v E, USA; 1955 v P, Y, A, H; 1956 v E, Ni, W; 1957 v Sp (2), Sw (18)
Smith, H. G. (Hearts), 1988 v S.Ar (sub); 1992 v Ni, Ca (3)
Smith, J. (Ayr U), 1924 v E (1)
Smith, J. (Rangers), 1935 v Ni; 1938 v Ni (2)
Smith, J. (Aberdeen), 1968 v Ho (sub); (with Newcastle U), 1974 v WG, Ni (sub), W (sub) (4)
Smith, J. (Celtic), 2003 v Ei (sub), A (sub) (2)
Smith, J. E. (Celtic), 1959 v H, P (2)
Smith, Jas (Queen's Park), 1872 v E (1)
Smith, John (Mauchline), 1877 v E, W; 1879 v E, W; (with Edinburgh University), 1880 v E; (with Queen's Park), 1881 v W, E; 1883 v E, W; 1884 v E (10)
Smith, N. (Rangers), 1897 v E; 1898 v W; 1899 v E, W, Ni; 1900 v E, W, Ni; 1901 v Ni, W; 1902 v E, Ni (12)
Smith, R. (Queen's Park), 1872 v E; 1873 v E (2)
Smith, T. M. (Kilmarnock), 1934 v E; (with Preston NE), 1938 v E (2)
Somers, P. (Celtic), 1905 v E, Ni; 1907 v Ni; 1909 v W (4)
Somers, W. S. (Third Lanark), 1879 v E, W; (with Queen's Park), 1880 v W (3)
Somerville, G. (Queen's Park), 1886 v E (1)
Souness, G. J. (Middlesbrough), 1975 v EG, Sp, Se; (with Liverpool), 1978 v Bul, W, E (sub), Ho; 1979 v A, N, W, Ni, E; 1980 v Pe, A, Bel, P, Ni; 1981 v P, Is (2); 1982 v Ni, P, Sp, W, E, Nz, Br, USSR; 1983 v EG, Sw, Bel, Sw, W, E, Ca (2 + 1 sub); 1984 v U, Ni, W; (with Sampdoria), 1985 v Y, Ic, Sp (2), W, E, Ic; 1986 v EG, Aus (2), R, E, D, WG (54)
Speedie, D. R. (Chelsea), 1985 v E; 1986 v W, EG (sub), Aus, E; (with Coventry C), 1989 v Y (sub), I (sub), Cy (1+1 sub), Ch (10)
Speedie, F. (Rangers), 1903 v E, W, Ni (3)
Speirs, J. H. (Rangers), 1908 v W (1)
Spencer, J. (Chelsea), 1995 v Ru (sub), Gr (sub), Sm (sub), J; 1996 v Fi, Aus, D, US (sub), Co, Ho (sub), E, Sw (sub); 1997 v La; (with QPR), W (sub) (14)
Stanton, P. (Hibernian), 1966 v Ho; 1969 v Ni; 1970 v Ei, A; 1971 v D, Bel, P, USSR, D; 1972 v P, Bel, Ho, W; 1973 v W, Ni; 1974 v WG (16)
Stark, J. (Rangers), 1909 v E, Ni (2)
Steel, W. (Morton), 1947 v E, Bel, L; (with Derby Co), 1948 v F, E, W, Ni; 1949 v E, W, Ni, F; 1950 v E, W, Ni, Sw, P, F; (with Dundee), 1951 v W, Ni, E, A (2), D, F, Bel; 1952 v W; 1953 v W, E, Ni, Se (30)
Steele, D. M. (Huddersfield), 1923 v E, W, Ni (3)
Stein, C. (Rangers), 1969 v W, Ni, D, E, Cy (2); 1970 v A (sub), Ni (sub), W, E, Ei, WG; 1971 v D, USSR, Bel, D; 1972 v Cz (sub); (with Coventry C), 1973 v E (2 sub), W (sub), Ni (21)
Stephen, J. F. (Bradford), 1947 v W; 1948 v W (2)
Stevenson, G. (Motherwell), 1928 v W, Ni; 1930 v Ni, E, F; 1931 v E, W; 1932 v W, Ni; 1933 v Ni; 1934 v E; 1935 v Ni (12)
Stewart, A. (Queen's Park), 1888 v Ni; 1889 v W (2)
Stewart, A. (Third Lanark), 1894 v W (1)
Stewart, D. (Dumbarton), 1888 v Ni (1)
Stewart, D. (Queen's Park), 1893 v W; 1894 v Ni; 1897 v Ni (3)
Stewart, D. S. (Leeds U), 1978 v EG (1)
Stewart, G. (Hibernian), 1906 v W, E; (with Manchester C), 1907 v E, W (4)
Stewart, J. (Kilmarnock), 1977 v Ch (sub); (with Middlesbrough), 1979 v N (2)
Stewart, M. J. (Manchester U), 2002 v Ng (sub), Sk, S.Af (sub) (3)
Stewart, R. (West Ham U), 1981 v W, Ni, E; 1982 v Ni, P, W; 1984 v F; 1987 v Ei (2), L (10)
Stewart, W. G. (Queen's Park), 1898 v Ni; 1900 v Ni (2)
Stockdale, R. K. (Middlesbrough), 2002 v Ng, Sk (sub), S.Af, Hk; 2003 v D (5)
Storrier, D. (Celtic), 1899 v E, W, Ni (3)
Strachan, G. (Aberdeen), 1980 v Ni, W, E, Pol, H (sub); 1981 v Se, P; 1982 v Ni, P, Sp, Ho (sub), Nz, Br, USSR; 1983 v EG, Sw, Bel, Sw, Ni (sub), W, E, Ca (2 + 1 sub); 1984 v EG, Ni, E, F; (with Manchester U), 1985 v Sp (sub), E, Ic; 1986 v W, Aus, R, D, WG, U; 1987 v Bul, Ei (2); 1988 v H; 1989 v F (sub); (with Leeds U), 1990 v F; 1991 v USSR, Bul, Sm; 1992 v Sw, R, Ni, Fi (50)
Sturrock, P. (Dundee U), 1981 v W (sub), Ni, E (sub); 1982 v P, Ni (sub), W (sub), E (sub); 1983 v EG (sub), Sw, Bel (sub), Ca (3); 1984 v W; 1985 v Y (sub); 1986 v Is (sub), Ho, D, U; 1987 v Bel (20)
Sullivan, N. (Wimbledon), 1997 v W; 1998 v F, Co; 1999 v Fa, CzR, G, Fa, CzR; 2000 v Bos, Es, Bos, E (2), F, Ho, Ei; (with Tottenham H), 2001 v La, Sm, Cro, Bel, Sm, Pol; 2002 v Cro, Bel, La, F, Sk; 2003 v Ei (28)
Summers, W. (St Mirren), 1926 v E (1)
Symon, J. S. (Rangers), 1939 v H (1)

Tait, T. S. (Sunderland), 1911 v W (1)
Taylor, J. (Queen's Park), 1872 v E; 1873 v E; 1874 v E; 1875 v E; 1876 v E, W (6)
Taylor, J. D. (Dumbarton), 1892 v W; 1893 v W; 1894 v Ni; (with St Mirren), 1895 v Ni (4)
Taylor, W. (Hearts), 1892 v E (1)
Teale, G. (Wigan Ath), 2006 v Sw (sub), Bul, J (3)
Telfer, P. N. (Coventry C), 2000 v F (1)
Telfer, W. (Motherwell), 1933 v Ni; 1934 v Ni (2)
Telfer, W. D. (St Mirren), 1954 v W (1)
Templeton, R. (Aston Villa), 1902 v E; (with Newcastle U), 1903 v E, W; 1904 v E; (with Woolwich Arsenal), 1905 v W; (with Kilmarnock), 1908 v Ni; 1910 v E, Ni; 1912 v E, Ni; 1913 v W (11)
Thompson, S. (Dundee U), 2002 v F (sub), Ng, Hk; 2003 v D, Fa (sub), Ic, Ca; (with Rangers), Ei (sub), A, G (sub); 2004 v Fa (sub), G, R; 2005 v H (sub), N (sub), Mol (16)
Thomson, A. (Arthurlie), 1886 v Ni (1)
Thomson, A. (Third Lanark), 1889 v W (1)
Thomson, A. (Airdrieonians), 1909 v Ni (1)
Thomson, A. (Celtic), 1926 v E; 1932 v F; 1933 v W (3)
Thomson, C. (Hearts), 1904 v Ni; 1905 v E, Ni, W; 1906 v W, Ni; 1907 v E, W, Ni; 1908 v E, W, Ni; (with Sunderland), 1909 v W; 1910 v E; 1911 v Ni; 1912 v E, W; 1913 v E, W; 1914 v E, Ni (21)
Thomson, C. (Sunderland), 1937 v Cz (1)
Thomson, D. (Dundee), 1920 v W (1)
Thomson, J. (Celtic), 1930 v F; 1931 v E, W, Ni (4)
Thomson, J. J. (Queen's Park), 1872 v E; 1873 v E; 1874 v E (3)
Thomson, J. R. (Everton), 1933 v W (1)
Thomson, R. (Celtic), 1932 v W (1)
Thomson, R. W. (Falkirk), 1927 v E (1)
Thomson, S. (Rangers), 1884 v W, Ni (2)
Thomson, W. (Dumbarton), 1892 v W; 1893 v W; 1898 v Ni, W (4)
Thomson, W. (Dundee), 1896 v W (1)
Thomson, W. (St Mirren), 1980 v Ni; 1981 v Ni (sub+1) 1982 v P; 1983 v Ni, Ca; 1984 v EG (7)
Thornton, W. (Rangers), 1947 v W, Ni; 1948 v E, Ni; 1949 v F; 1952 v D, Se (7)
Toner, W. (Kilmarnock), 1959 v W, Ni (2)
Townsley, T. (Falkirk), 1926 v W (1)
Troup, A. (Dundee), 1920 v E; 1921 v W, Ni; 1922 v Ni; (with Everton), 1926 v E (5)
Turnbull, E. (Hibernian), 1948 v Bel, Sw; 1951 v A; 1958 v H, Pol, Y, Par, F (8)
Turner, T. (Arthurlie), 1884 v W (1)
Turner, W. (Pollokshields Ath), 1885 v Ni; 1886 v Ni (2)

Ure, J. F. (Dundee), 1962 v W, Cz; 1963 v W, Ni, E, A, N, Sp; (with Arsenal), 1964 v Ni, N; 1968 v Ni (11)
Urquhart, D. (Hibernian), 1934 v W (1)

Vallance, T. (Rangers), 1877 v E, W; 1878 v E; 1879 v E, W; 1881 v E, W (7)
Venters, A. (Cowdenbeath), 1934 v Ni; (with Rangers), 1936 v E; 1939 v E (3)

Waddell, T. S. (Queen's Park), 1891 v Ni; 1892 v E; 1893 v E, Ni; 1895 v E, Ni (6)

Waddell, W. (Rangers), 1947 v W; 1949 v E, W, Ni, F; 1950 v E, Ni; 1951 v E, D, F, Bel, A; 1952 v Ni, W; 1954 v Ni; 1955 v W, Ni (17)
Wales, H. M. (Motherwell), 1933 v W (1)
Walker, A. (Celtic), 1988 v Co (sub); 1995 v Fi, Fa (sub) (3)
Walker, F. (Third Lanark), 1922 v W (1)
Walker, G. (St Mirren), 1930 v F; 1931 v Ni, A, Sw (4)
Walker, J. (Hearts), 1895 v Ni; 1897 v W; 1898 v Ni; (with Rangers), 1904 v W, Ni (5)
Walker, J. (Swindon T), 1911 v E, W, Ni; 1912 v E, W, Ni; 1913 v E, W, Ni (9)
Walker, J. N. (Hearts), 1993 v G; (with Partick Th), 1996 v US (sub) (2)
Walker, R. (Hearts), 1900 v E, Ni; 1901 v E, W; 1902 v E, W, Ni; 1903 v E, W, Ni; 1904 v E, W, Ni; 1905 v E, W, Ni; 1906 v Ni; 1907 v E, Ni; 1908 v E, W, Ni; 1909 v E, W; 1912 v E, W, Ni; 1913 v E, W (29)
Walker, T. (Hearts), 1935 v E, W; 1936 v E, W, Ni; 1937 v G, E, W, Ni, A, Cz; 1938 v E, W, Ni, Cz, Ho; 1939 v E, W, Ni, H (20)
Walker, W. (Clyde), 1909 v Ni; 1910 v Ni (2)
Wallace, I. A. (Coventry C), 1978 v Bul (sub); 1979 v P (sub), W (3)
Wallace, W. S. B. (Hearts), 1965 v Ni; 1966 v E, Ho; (with Celtic), 1967 v E, USSR (sub); 1968 v Ni; 1969 v E (sub) (7)
Wardhaugh, J. (Hearts), 1955 v H; 1957 v Ni (2)
Wark, J. (Ipswich T), 1979 v W, Ni, E, Arg, N (sub); 1980 v Pe, A, Bel (2); 1981 v Is, Ni; 1982 v Se, Sp, Ho, Ni, Nz, Br, USSR; 1983 v EG, Sw (2), Ni, E (sub); 1984 v U, Bel, EG; (with Liverpool), E, F; 1985 v Y (29)
Watson, A. (Queen's Park), 1881 v E, W; 1882 v E (3)
Watson, J. (Sunderland), 1903 v E, W; 1904 v E; 1905 v E; (with Middlesbrough), 1909 v E, Ni (6)
Watson, J. (Motherwell), 1948 v Ni; (with Huddersfield T), 1954 v Ni (2)
Watson, J. A. K. (Rangers), 1878 v W (1)
Watson, P. R. (Blackpool), 1934 v A (1)
Watson, R. (Motherwell), 1971 v USSR (1)
Watson, W. (Falkirk), 1898 v W (1)
Watt, F. (Kilbirnie), 1889 v W, Ni; 1890 v W; 1891 v E (4)
Watt, W. W. (Queen's Park), 1887 v Ni (1)
Waugh, W. (Hearts), 1938 v Cz (1)
Webster, A. (Hearts), 2003 v A, Nz, G; 2004 v N, Fa, W (sub), Es (sub), Tr (sub); 2005 v H, Sp, Slv, N, Mol, Se, Mol, Bl; 2006 v A, I, N, Slv, US, Sw (22)
Weir, A. (Motherwell), 1959 v WG; 1960 v E, Pol, A, H, T (6)
Weir, D. G. (Hearts), 1997 v W, Ma (sub); 1998 v F, D (sub), Fi (sub), N (sub), Mor; 1999 v Es, Fa; (with Everton), CzR, G, Fa, CzR; 2000 v Bos, Es, Bos, Li, E (2), Ho; 2001 v La, Sm (sub), Cro, Aus, Bel, Sm, Pol (sub); 2002 v Cro, Bel, La, F, Ng, Sk, S.Af, Hk; 2003 v D, Fa; 2005 v I, Mol, Bl; 2006 v I, N, Bl, Slv, US, Sw, Bul, J (48)
Weir, J. (Third Lanark), 1887 v Ni (1)
Weir, J. B. (Queen's Park), 1872 v E; 1874 v E; 1875 v E; 1878 v W (4)
Weir, P. (St Mirren), 1980 v Ni, W, Pol (sub), H; (with Aberdeen), 1983 v Sw; 1984 v Ni (6)
White, John (Albion R), 1922 v W; (with Hearts), 1923 v Ni (2)
White, J. A. (Falkirk), 1959 v WG, Ho, P; 1960 v Ni; (with Tottenham H), 1960 v W, Pol, A, T; 1961 v W; 1962 v Ni, W, E, Cz (2); 1963 v W, Ni, E; 1964 v Ni, W, E, N, WG (22)
White, W. (Bolton W), 1907 v E; 1908 v E (2)
Whitelaw, A. (Vale of Leven), 1887 v Ni; 1890 v W (2)
Whyte, D. (Celtic), 1988 v Bel (sub), L; 1989 v Ch (sub); 1992 v US (sub); (with Middlesbrough), 1993 v P, I; 1995 v J (sub), Ec; 1996 v US; 1997 v La; (with Aberdeen), 1998 v Fi; 1999 v G (sub) (12)
Wilkie, L. (Dundee), 2002 v S.Af (sub), Hk; 2003 v Ic, Ca, P, Ic, Li, A; 2004 v Fa, Ho (2) (11)
Williams, G. (Nottingham F), 2002 v Ng, Sk (sub), S.Af, Hk (sub); 2003 v P (sub) (5)
Wilson, A. (Sheffield W), 1907 v E; 1908 v E; 1912 v E; 1913 v E, W; 1914 v Ni (6)
Wilson, A. (Portsmouth), 1954 v Fi (1)
Wilson, A. N. (Dunfermline), 1920 v E, W, Ni; 1921 v E, W, Ni; (with Middlesbrough), 1922 v E, W, Ni; 1923 v E, W, Ni (12)
Wilson, D. (Queen's Park), 1900 v W (1)
Wilson, D. (Oldham Ath), 1913 v E (1)
Wilson, D. (Rangers), 1961 v E, W, Ni, Ei (2), Cz; 1962 v Ni, W, E, Cz, U; 1963 v W, E, A, N, Ei, Sp; 1964 v E, WG; 1965 v Ni, E, Fi (22)
Wilson, G. W. (Hearts), 1904 v W; 1905 v E, Ni; 1906 v W; (with Everton), 1907 v E; (with Newcastle U), 1909 v E (6)
Wilson, Hugh, (Newmilns), 1890 v W; (with Sunderland), 1897 v E; (with Third Lanark), 1902 v W; 1904 v Ni (4)
Wilson, I. A. (Leicester C), 1987 v E, Br; (with Everton), 1988 v Bel, Bul, L (5)
Wilson, J. (Vale of Leven), 1888 v W; 1889 v E; 1890 v E; 1891 v E (4)
Wilson, P. (Celtic), 1926 v Ni; 1930 v F; 1931 v Ni; 1933 v E (4)
Wilson, P. (Celtic), 1975 v Sp (sub) (1)
Wilson, R. P. (Arsenal), 1972 v P, Ho (2)
Winters, R. (Aberdeen), 1999 v G (sub) (1)
Wiseman, W. (Queen's Park), 1927 v W; 1930 v Ni (2)
Wood, G. (Everton), 1979 v Ni, E, Arg (sub); (with Arsenal), 1982 v Ni (4)
Woodburn, W. A. (Rangers), 1947 v E, Bel, L; 1948 v W, Ni; 1949 v E, F; 1950 v E, W, Ni, P, F; 1951 v E, W, Ni, A (2), D, F, Bel; 1952 v E, W, Ni, USA (24)
Wotherspoon, D. N. (Queen's Park), 1872 v E; 1873 v E (2)
Wright, K. (Hibernian), 1992 v Ni (1)
Wright, S. (Aberdeen), 1993 v G, Es (2)
Wright, T. (Sunderland), 1953 v W, Ni, E (3)
Wylie, T. G. (Rangers), 1890 v Ni (1)

Yeats, R. (Liverpool), 1965 v W; 1966 v I (2)
Yorston, B. C. (Aberdeen), 1931 v Ni (1)
Yorston, H. (Aberdeen), 1955 v W (1)
Young, A. (Everton), 1905 v E; 1907 v W (2)
Young, A. (Hearts), 1960 v E, A (sub), H, T; 1961 v W, Ni; (with Everton), Ei; 1966 v P (8)
Young, G. L. (Rangers), 1947 v E, Ni, Bel, L; 1948 v E, Ni, Bel, Sw, F; 1949 v E, W, Ni, F; 1950 v E, W, Ni, Sw, P, F; 1951 v E, W, Ni, A (2), D, F, Bel; 1952 v E, W, Ni, USA, D, Se; 1953 v W, E, Ni, Se; 1954 v Ni, W; 1955 v W, Ni, P, Y; 1956 v Ni, W, E, A; 1957 v E, Ni, W, Y, Sp, Sw (53)
Young, J. (Celtic), 1906 v Ni (1)
Younger, T. (Hibernian), 1955 v P, Y, A, H; 1956 v E, Ni, W, A; (with Liverpool), 1957 v E, Ni, W, Y, Sp (2), Sw, WG; 1958 v Ni, W, E, Sw, H, Pol, Y, Par (24)

WALES

Adams, H. (Berwyn R), 1882 v Ni, E; (with Druids), 1883 v Ni, E (4)
Aizlewood, M. (Charlton Ath), 1986 v S.Ar, Ca (2); 1987 v Fi; (with Leeds U), USSR, Fi (sub); 1988 v D (sub), Se, Ma, I; 1989 v Ho, Se (sub), WG; (with Bradford C), 1990 v Fi, WG, Ei, Cr; (with Bristol C), 1991 v D, Bel (2), L, Ei, Ic, Pol, G; 1992 v Br, L, Ei, A, R, Ho, Arg, J; 1993 v Ei, Bel, Fa; 1994 v RCS, Cy; (with Cardiff C), 1995v Bul (39)
Allchurch, I. J. (Swansea T), 1951 v E, Ni, P, Sw; 1952 v E, S, Ni, R of UK; 1953 v S, E, Ni, F, Y; 1954 v S, E, Ni, A; 1955 v S, E, Ni, Y; 1956 v E, S, Ni, A; 1957 v E, S; 1958 v Ni, Is (2), H (2), M, Se, Br; (with Newcastle U), 1959 v E, S, Ni; 1960 v E, S; 1961 v Ni, H, Sp (2); 1962 v E, S, Br (2), M; (with Cardiff C), 1963 v S, E, Ni, H (2); 1964 v E; 1965 v S, E, Ni, Gr, I, USSR; (with Swansea T), 1966 v USSR, E, S, D, Br (2), Ch (68)
Allchurch, L. (Swansea T), 1955 v Ni; 1956 v A; 1958 v S, Ni, EG, Is; 1959 v S; (with Sheffield U), 1962 v S, Ni, Br; 1964 v E (11)
Allen, B. W. (Coventry C), 1951 v S, E (2)
Allen, M. (Watford), 1986 v S.Ar (sub), Ca (1 + 1 sub); (with Norwich C), 1989 v Is (sub); 1990 v Ho, WG; (with Millwall), Ei, Se, Cr (sub); 1991 v L (sub), Ei (sub); 1992 v A; 1993 v Ei (sub); (with Newcastle U), 1994 v R (sub) (14)
Arridge, S. (Bootle), 1892 v S, Ni; (with Everton), 1894 v Ni; 1895 v Ni; 1896 v E; (with New Brighton Tower), 1898 v E, Ni; 1899 v E (8)
Astley, D. J. (Charlton Ath), 1931 v Ni; (with Aston Villa), 1932 v E; 1933 v E, S, Ni; 1934 v E, S; 1935 v S; 1936 v E, Ni; (with Derby Co), 1939 v E, S; (with Blackpool), F (13)
Atherton, R. W. (Hibernian), 1899 v E, Ni; 1903 v E, S, Ni; (with Middlesbrough), 1904 v E, S, Ni; 1905 v Ni (9)

Bailiff, W. E. (Llanelly), 1913 v E, S, Ni; 1920 v Ni (4)
Baker, C. W. (Cardiff C), 1958 v M; 1960 v S, Ni; 1961 v S, E, Ei; 1962 v S (7)
Baker, W. G. (Cardiff C), 1948 v Ni (1)
Bale, G. (Southampton), 2006 v Tr (sub) (1)
Bamford, T. (Wrexham), 1931 v E, S, Ni; 1932 v Ni; 1933 v F (5)

Barnard, D. S. (Barnsley), 1998 v Jam; 1999 v I, D, Bl, I, D; 2000 v Bl, Sw, Q, Fi, Br (sub), P; 2001 v Uk, Pol, Uk; 2002 v Arm (sub); (with Grimsby T), 2003 v Cro, Az; 2004 v Ser, Ru (2), N (sub) (22)
Barnes, W. (Arsenal), 1948 v E, S, Ni; 1949 v E, S, Ni; 1950 v E, S, Ni, Bel; 1951 v E, S, Ni, P; 1952 v E, S, Ni, R of UK; 1954 v E, S; 1955 v S, Y (22)
Bartley, T. (Glossop NE), 1898 v E (1)
Bastock, A. M. (Shrewsbury), 1892 v Ni (1)
Beadles, G. H. (Cardiff C), 1925 v E, S (2)
Bell, W. S. (Shrewsbury Engineers), 1881 v E, S; (with Crewe Alex), 1886 v E, S, Ni (5)
Bellamy, C. D. (Norwich C), 1998 v Jam (sub), Ma, Tun; 1999 v D (sub), Sw (sub), I, D (sub); 2000 v Br (sub), P; (with Coventry C), 2001 v Bl, Arm, Uk; (with Newcastle U), 2002 v Arm, N, Bl, Arg; 2003 v Fi (sub), I, Bos, Az; 2004 v Ser, I, Ser, N, Ca; 2005 v La, Az, Ni, E, Pol, H, A (2); (with Blackburn R), 2006 v Cy, Para (35)
Bennion, S. R. (Manchester U), 1926 v S; 1927 v S; 1928 v S, E, Ni; 1929 v S, E, Ni; 1930 v S; 1932 v Ni (10)
Berry, G. F. (Wolverhampton W), 1979 v WG; 1980 v Ei, WG (sub), T; (with Stoke C), 1983 v E (sub) (5)
Blackmore, C. G. (Manchester U), 1985 v N (sub); 1986 v S (sub), H (sub), S.Ar, Ei, U; 1987 v Fi (2), USSR, Cz; 1988 v D (2), Cz, Y, Se, Ma, I; 1989 v Ho, Fi, Is, WG; 1990 v F; Ho, WG, Cr; 1991 v Bel, L; 1992 v Ei (sub), A, R (sub), Ho, Arg, J; 1993 v Fa, Cy, Bel, RCS; 1994 v Se (sub); (with Middlesbrough), 1997 v Bel (39)
Blake, N. A. (Sheffield U), 1994 v N, Se (sub); 1995 v Alb, Mol; 1996 v G (with Bolton W), I (sub); 1998 v T; 1999 v I, D, Bl; (with Blackburn R) Sw; 2000 v Bl, Sw, Q, Fi; 2001 v Bl (sub), N, Pol (2), Uk; 2002 v N (sub); (with Wolverhampton W), CzR; 2003 v I (sub); 2004 v Ser, I (sub), Fi (sub), Ser (sub), Ru (sub + sub) (29)
Blew, H. (Wrexham), 1899 v E, S, Ni; 1902 v S, Ni; 1903 v E, S; 1904 v E, S, Ni; 1905 v S, Ni; 1906 v E, S, Ni; 1907 v S; 1908 v E, S, Ni; 1909 v E, S; 1910 v E (22)
Boden, T. (Wrexham), 1880 v E (1)
Bodin, P. J. (Swindon T), 1990 v Cr; 1991 v D, Bel, L, Ei; (with C Palace), Bel, Ic, Pol. G; 1992 v Br, G, L (sub); (with Swindon T), Ei (sub), Ho, Arg; 1993 v Ei, Bel, RCS, Fa; 1994 v R, Se, Es (sub); 1995 v Alb (23)
Boulter, L. M. (Brentford), 1939 v Ni (1)
Bowdler, H. E. (Shrewsbury), 1893 v S (1)
Bowdler, J. C. H. (Shrewsbury), 1890 v Ni; (with Wolverhampton W), 1891 v S; 1892 v Ni; (with Shrewsbury), 1894 v E (4)
Bowen, D. L. (Arsenal), 1955 v S, Y; 1957 v Ni, Cz, EG; 1958 v E, S, Ni, EG, Is (2), H (2), M, Se, Br; 1959 v E, S, Ni (19)
Bowen, E. (Druids), 1880 v S; 1883 v S (2)
Bowen, J. P. (Swansea C), 1994 v Es; (with Birmingham C), 1997 v Ho (2)
Bowen, M. R. (Tottenham H), 1986 v Ca (2 sub); (with Norwich C), 1988 v Y (sub); 1989 v Fi (sub), Is, Se, WG (sub); 1990 v Fi (sub), Ho, WG, Se; 1992 v Br (sub), G, L, Ei, A, R, Ho (sub), J; 1993 v Fa, Cy, Bel (1 + sub), RCS (sub); 1994 v RCS, Se; 1995 v Mol, Ge, Bul (2), G, Ge; 1996 v Mol, G, Alb, Sw, Sm; (with West Ham U), 1997 v Sm, Ho (2), Ei (sub) (41)
Bowsher, S. J. (Burnley), 1929 v Ni (1)
Boyle, T. (C Palace), 1981 v Ei, S (sub) (2)
Britten, T. J. (Parkgrove), 1878 v S; (with Presteigne), 1880 v S (2)
Brookes, S. J. (Llandudno), 1900 v E, Ni (2)
Brown, A. I. (Aberdare Ath), 1926 v Ni (1)
Brown, J. R. (Gillingham), 2006 v Tr (1)
Browning, M. T. (Bristol R), 1996 v I (sub), Sm; 1997 v Sm, Ho (with Huddersfield T), S (sub) (5)
Bryan, T. (Oswestry), 1886 v E, Ni (2)
Buckland, T. (Bangor), 1899 v E (1)
Burgess, W. A. R. (Tottenham H), 1947 v E, S, Ni; 1948 v E, S; 1949 v E, S, Ni, P, Bel, Sw; 1950 v E, S, Ni, Bel; 1951 v S, Ni, P, Sw; 1952 v E, S, Ni, R of UK; 1953 v S, E, Ni, F, Y; 1954 v S, E, Ni, A (32)
Burke, T. (Wrexham), 1883 v E; 1884 v S; 1885 v E, S, Ni; (with Newton Heath), 1887 v E, S; 1888 v S (8)
Burnett, T. B. (Ruabon), 1877 v S (1)
Burton, A. D. (Norwich C), 1963 v Ni, H; (with Newcastle U), 1964 v E; 1969 v S, E, Ni, I, EG; 1972 v Cz (9)
Butler, J. (Chirk), 1893 v E, S, Ni (3)
Butler, W. T. (Druids), 1900 v S, Ni (2)

Cartwright, L. (Coventry C), 1974 v E (sub), S, Ni; 1976 v S (sub); 1977 v WG (sub); (with Wrexham), 1978 v Ir (sub); 1979 v Ma (7)
Carty, T. See McCarthy (Wrexham).
Challen, J. B. (Corinthians), 1887 v E, S; 1888 v E; (with Wellingborough GS), 1890 v E (4)
Chapman, T. (Newtown), 1894 v E, S, Ni; 1895 v S, Ni; (with Manchester C), 1896 v E; (with Grimsby T), 1897 v E (7)
Charles, J. M. (Swansea C), 1981 v Cz, T (sub), S (sub), USSR (sub); 1982 v Ic; 1983 v N (sub), Y (sub), Bul (sub), S, Ni, Br; 1984 v Bul (sub); (with QPR), Y (sub), S; (with Oxford U), 1985 v Ic (sub), Sp, Ic; 1986 v Ei; 1987 v Fi (19)
Charles, M. (Swansea T), 1955 v Ni; 1956 v E, S, A; 1957 v E, Ni, Cz (2), EG; 1958 v E, S, EG, Is (2), H (2), M, Se, Br; 1959 v E, S; (with Arsenal), 1961 v Ni, H, Sp (2); 1962 v E, S; (with Cardiff C), 1962 v Br, Ni; 1963 v S, H (31)
Charles, W. J. (Leeds U), 1950 v Ni; 1951 v Sw; 1953 v Ni, F, Y; 1954 v E, S, Ni, A; 1955 v S, E, Ni, Y; 1956 v E, S, A, Ni; 1957 v E, S, Ni, Cz (2), EG; (with Juventus), 1958 v Is (2), H (2) M, Se; 1960 v S; 1962 v E, Br (2), M; (with Leeds U), 1963 v S; (with Cardiff C), 1964 v S; 1965 v S, USSR (38)
Clarke, R. J. (Manchester C), 1949 v E; 1950 v S, Ni, Bel; 1951 v E, S, Ni, P, Sw; 1952 v S, E, Ni, R of UK; 1953 v S, E; 1954 v E, S, Ni; 1955 v Y, S, E; 1956 v Ni (22)
Coleman, C. (C Palace), 1992 v A (sub); 1993 v Ei (sub); 1994 v N, Es; 1995 v Alb, Mol, Ge, Bul (2), G; 1996 v Mol; (with Blackburn R), I, Sw, Sm; 1997 v Sm; 1998 v Br; (with Fulham), Jam, Ma, Tun; 1999 v I, D, Bl, Sw, D; 2000 v Bl, Sw, Q, Fi; 2001 v Bl, N, Pol; 2002 v G (sub) (32)
Collier, D. J. (Grimsby T), 1921 v S (1)
Collins, D. L. (Sunderland), 2005 v H (sub); 2006 v Ni (sub), Az (3)
Collins, J. M. (Cardiff C), 2004 v N, Ca; 2005 v La (sub), Ni, Pol, A; (with West Ham U), 2006 v E (sub), Pol, Ni, Az, Cy, Para, Tr (13)
Collins, W. S. (Llanelly), 1931 v S (1)
Conde, C. (Chirk), 1884 v E, S, Ni (3)
Cook, F. C. (Newport Co), 1925 v E, S; (with Portsmouth), 1928 v E, S; 1930 v E, S, Ni; 1932 v E (8)
Cornforth, J. M. (Swansea C), 1995 v Bul (sub), Ge (2)
Cotterill, D. R. G. B. (Bristol C), 2006 v Az (sub), Para (sub), Tr (3)
Coyne, D. (Tranmere R), 1996 v Sw; (with Grimsby T), 2002 v CzR (sub); (with Leicester C), 2004 v H (sub), N, Ca; (with Burnley), 2005 v H, A (2); 2006 v Slv, E, Pol (11)
Crofts, A. L. (Gillingham), 2006 v Az (sub), Para (sub), Tr (sub) (3)
Crompton, W. (Wrexham), 1931 v E, S, Ni (3)
Cross, E. A. (Wrexham), 1876 v S; 1877 v S (2)
Crosse, K. (Druids), 1879 v S; 1881 v E, S (3)
Crossley, M. G. (Nottingham F), 1997 v Ei; 1999 v Sw (sub); 2000 v Fi; (with Middlesbrough), 2002 v Arg (sub), G; 2003 v Bos (sub); (with Fulham), 2004 v S; 2005 v La (sub) (8)
Crowe, V. H. (Aston Villa), 1959 v E, Ni; 1960 v E, Ni; 1961 v S, E, Ni, Ei, H, Sp (2); 1962 v E, S, Br, M; 1963 v H (16)
Cumner, R. H. (Arsenal), 1939 v E, S, Ni (3)
Curtis, A. (Swansea C), 1976 v E, Y (sub), S, Ni, Y (sub), E; 1977 v WG, S (sub), Ni (sub); 1978 v WG, E, S; 1979 v WG, S; (with Leeds U), E, Ni, Ma; 1980 v Ei, WG, T; (with Swansea C), 1982 v Cz, Ic, USSR, Sp, E, S, Ni; 1983 v N; 1984 v R (sub); (with Southampton), S; 1985 v Sp, N (1 + 1 sub); 1986 v H; (with Cardiff C), 1987 v USSR (35)
Curtis, E. R. (Cardiff C), 1928 v S; (with Birmingham), 1932 v S; 1934 v Ni (3)

Daniel, R. W. (Arsenal), 1951 v E, Ni, P; 1952 v E, S, Ni, R of UK; 1953 v S, E, Ni, F, Y; (with Sunderland), 1954 v E, S, Ni; 1955 v E, Ni; 1957 v S, E, Ni, Cz (21)
Darvell, S. (Oxford University), 1897 v S, Ni (2)
Davies, A. (Manchester U), 1983 v Ni, Br; 1984 v E, Ni; 1985 v Ic (2), N; (with Newcastle U), 1986 v H; (with Swansea C), 1988 v Ma, I; 1989 v Ho; (with Bradford C), 1990 v Fi, Ei (13)
Davies, A. (Wrexham), 1876 v S; 1877 v S (2)
Davies, A. (Druids), 1904 v S; (with Middlesbrough), 1905 v S (2)
Davies, A. O. (Barmouth), 1885 v Ni; 1886 v E, S; (with Swifts), 1887 v E, S; 1888 v E, Ni; (with Wrexham), 1889 v S; (with Crewe Alex), 1890 v E (9)
Davies, A. R. (Yeovil T), 2006 v Tr (sub) (1)
Davies, A. T. (Shrewsbury), 1891 v Ni (1)
Davies, C. (Charlton Ath), 1972 v R (sub) (1)
Davies, C. M. (Oxford U), 2006 v Slv (sub), Pol (sub); (with Verona), Tr (sub) (3)
Davies, D. (Bolton W), 1904 v S, Ni; 1908 v E (sub) (3)
Davies, D. C. (Brecon), 1899 v Ni; (with Hereford); 1900 v Ni (2)
Davies, D. W. (Treharris), 1912 v Ni; (with Oldham Ath), 1913 v Ni (2)

Davies, E. Lloyd (Stoke C), 1904 v E; 1907 v E, S, Ni; (with Northampton T), 1908 v S; 1909 v Ni; 1910 v Ni; 1911 v E, S; 1912 v E, S; 1913 v E, S; 1914 v Ni, E, S (16)
Davies, E. R. (Newcastle U), 1953 v S, E; 1954 v E, S; 1958 v E, EG (6)
Davies, G. (Fulham), 1980 v T, Ic; 1982 v Sp (sub), F (sub); 1983 v E, Bul, S, Ni, Br; 1984 v R (sub), S (sub), E, Ni; 1985 v Ic; (with Manchester C), 1986 v S.Ar, Ei (16)
Davies, Rev. H. (Wrexham), 1928 v Ni (1)
Davies, Idwal (Liverpool Marine), 1923 v S (1)
Davies, J. E. (Oswestry), 1885 v E (1)
Davies, Jas (Wrexham), 1878 v S (1)
Davies, John (Wrexham), 1879 v S (1)
Davies, Jos (Newton Heath), 1888 v E, S, Ni; 1889 v S; 1890 v E; (with Wolverhampton W), 1892 v E; 1893 v E (7)
Davies, Jos (Everton), 1889 v S, Ni; (with Chirk), 1891 v Ni; (with Ardwick), v E, S; (with Sheffield U), 1895 v E, S, Ni; (with Manchester C), 1896 v E; (with Millwall), 1897 v E; (with Reading), 1900 v E (11)
Davies, J. P. (Druids), 1883 v E, Ni (2)
Davies, Ll. (Wrexham), 1907 v Ni; 1910 v Ni, S, E; (with Everton), 1911 v S, Ni; (with Wrexham), 1912 v Ni, S, E; 1913 v Ni, S, E; 1914 v Ni (13)
Davies, L. S. (Cardiff C), 1922 v E, S, Ni; 1923 v E, S, Ni; 1924 v E, S, Ni; 1925 v S, Ni; 1926 v E, Ni; 1927 v E, Ni; 1928 v S, Ni, E; 1929 v S, Ni, E; 1930 v E, S (23)
Davies, O. (Wrexham), 1890 v S (1)
Davies, R. (Wrexham), 1883 v Ni; 1884 v Ni; 1885 v Ni (3)
Davies, R. (Druids), 1885 v E (1)
Davies, R. O. (Wrexham), 1892 v Ni, E (2)
Davies, R. T. (Norwich C), 1964 v Ni; 1965 v E; 1966 v Br (2), Ch; (with Southampton), 1967 v S, E, Ni; 1968 v S, Ni, WG; 1969 v S, E, Ni, I, WG; 1970 v R of UK, E, S, Ni; 1971 v Cz, S, E, Ni; 1972 v R, E, S, Ni; (with Portsmouth), 1974 v E (29)
Davies, R. W. (Bolton W), 1964 v E; 1965 v E, S, Ni, D, Gr, USSR; 1966 v E, S, Ni, USSR, D, Br (2), Ch (sub); 1967 v S; (with Newcastle U), E; 1968 v S, Ni, WG; 1969 v S, E, Ni, I; 1970 v EG; 1971 v R, Cz; (with Manchester C), 1972 v E, S, Ni; (with Manchester U), 1973 v E, S (sub), Ni; (with Blackpool), 1974 v Pol (34)
Davies, S. (Tottenham H), 2001 v Uk (sub+1); 2002 v Arm, N, Bl, Arg, CzR, G; 2003 v Cro, Fi, I, Az, Bos, Az, US; 2004 v Ser, I, Fi, S; 2005 v E, Pol, H, A (2); (with Everton), 2006 v E, Pol, Ni, Az, Para, Tr (30)
Davies, S. I. (Manchester U), 1996 v Sw (sub) (1)
Davies, Stanley (Preston NE), 1920 v E, S, Ni; (with Everton), 1921 v E, S, Ni; (with WBA), 1922 v E, S, Ni; 1923 v S; 1925 v S, Ni; 1926 v S, E, Ni; 1927 v S; 1928 v S; (with Rotherham U), 1930 v Ni (18)
Davies, T. (Oswestry), 1886 v E (1)
Davies, T. (Druids), 1903 v E, Ni, S; 1904 v S (4)
Davies, W. (Wrexham), 1884 v Ni (1)
Davies, W. (Swansea T), 1924 v E, S, Ni; (with Cardiff C), 1925 v E, S, Ni; 1926 v E, S, Ni; 1927 v S; 1928 v Ni; (with Notts Co), 1929 v E, S, Ni; 1930 v E, S, Ni (17)
Davies, William (Wrexham), 1903 v Ni; 1905 v Ni; (with Blackburn R), 1908 v E, S; 1909 v E, S, Ni; 1911 v E, S, Ni; 1912 v Ni (11)
Davies, W. C. (C Palace), 1908 v S; (with WBA), 1909 v E; 1910 v S; (with C Palace), 1914 v E (4)
Davies, W. D. (Everton), 1975 v H, L, S, E, Ni; 1976 v Y (2), E, Ni; 1977 v WG, S (2), Cz, E, Ni; 1978 v K; (with Wrexham), S, Cz, WG, Ir, E, S, Ni; 1979 v Ma, T, WG, S, E, Ni, Ma; 1980 v Ei, WG, T, E, S, Ni, Ic; 1981 v T, Cz, Ei, T, S, E, USSR; (with Swansea C), 1982 v Cz, Ic, USSR, Sp, E, S, F; 1983 v Y (52)
Davies, W. H. (Oswestry), 1876 v S; 1877 v S; 1879 v E; 1880 v E (4)
Davis, G. (Wrexham), 1978 v Ir, E (sub), Ni (3)
Davis, W. O. (Millwall Ath), 1913 v E, S, Ni; 1914 v S, Ni (5)
Day, A. (Tottenham H), 1934 v Ni (1)
Deacy, N. (PSV Eindhoven), 1977 v Cz, S, E, Ni; 1978 v K (sub), S (sub), Cz (sub), WG, Ir, S (sub), Ni; (with Beringen), 1979 v T (12)
Dearson, D. J. (Birmingham), 1939 v S, Ni, F (3)
Delaney, M. A. (Aston Villa), 2000 v Sw, Q, Br, P; 2001 v N, Pol, Arm, Uk (2); 2002 v Arm, N, Bl, Arg, CzR, G; 2003 v Cro, Fi, I, Az; 2004 v Ser, I, Ser, Ru (2), N, Ca; 2005 v La, Az, Ni, E, Pol, A (2); 2006 v Ni (34)
Derrett, S. C. (Cardiff C), 1969 v S, WG; 1970 v I; 1971 v Fi (4)
Dewey, F. T. (Cardiff Corinthians), 1931 v E, S (2)
Dibble, A. (Luton T), 1986 v Ca (1+1 sub); (with Manchester C), 1989 v Is (3)
Doughty, J. (Druids), 1886 v S; (with Newton Heath), 1887 v S, Ni; 1888 v E, S, Ni; 1889 v S; 1890 v E (8)
Doughty, R. (Newton Heath), 1888 v S, Ni (2)
Duffy, R. M. (Portsmouth), 2006 v Slv, E, Pol (sub), Ni (sub), Az, Cy (6)
Durban, A. (Derby Co), 1966 v Br (sub); 1967 v Ni; 1968 v E, S, Ni, WG; 1969 v EG, S, E, Ni, WG; 1970 v E, S, Ni, EG, I; 1971 v R, S, E, Ni, Cz, Fi; 1972 v Fi, Cz, E, S, Ni (27)
Dwyer, P. (Cardiff C), 1978 v Ir, E, S, Ni; 1979 v T, S, E, Ni, Ma (sub); 1980 v WG (10)

Earnshaw, R. (Cardiff C), 2002 v G; 2003 v Cro, Az, Bos; 2004 v Ser (sub), I (sub), Fi, Ser, Ru (sub), S, H, N, Ca (sub); 2005 v Az (sub); (with WBA), Ni (sub), E (sub), Pol, H, A (sub); 2006 v Slv, E (sub), Pol, Ni, Cy (sub); (with Norwich C), Para (sub), Tr (26)
Edwards, C. (Wrexham), 1878 v S (1)
Edwards, C. N. H. (Swansea C), 1996 v Sw (sub) (1)
Edwards, G. (Birmingham C), 1947 v E, S, Ni; 1948 v E, S, Ni; (with Cardiff C), 1949 v Ni, P, Bel, Sw; 1950 v E, S (12)
Edwards, H. (Wrexham Civil Service), 1878 v S; (with Wrexham), 1880 v E, S; 1882 v E, S; 1883 v S; 1884 v Ni; 1887 v Ni (8)
Edwards, J. H. (Wanderers), 1876 v S (1)
Edwards, J. H. (Oswestry), 1895 v Ni; 1897 v E, Ni (3)
Edwards, J. H. (Aberystwyth), 1898 v Ni (1)
Edwards, L. T. (Charlton Ath), 1957 v Ni, EG (2)
Edwards, R. I. (Chester), 1978 v K (sub); 1979 v Ma, WG; (with Wrexham), 1980 v T (sub) (4)
Edwards, R. O. (Aston Villa), 2003 v Az (sub); 2004 v Ser (sub), S, H (sub), N (sub), Ca (sub); (with Wolverhampton W), 2005 v H; 2006 v Slv (sub), Pol, Cy (sub), Para (11)
Edwards, R. W. (Bristol C), 1998 v T (sub), Bel, Ma (sub), Tun (sub) (4)
Edwards, T. (Linfield), 1932 v S (1)
Egan, W. (Chirk), 1892 v S (1)
Ellis, B. (Motherwell), 1932 v E; 1933 v E, S; 1934 v S; 1936 v E; 1937 v S (6)
Ellis, E. (Nunhead), 1931 v S; (with Oswestry), E; 1932 v Ni (3)
Emanuel, W. J. (Bristol C), 1973 v E (sub), Ni (sub) (2)
England, H. M. (Blackburn R), 1962 v Ni, Br, M; 1963 v Ni, H; 1964 v E, S, Ni; 1965 v E, D, Gr (2), USSR, Ni, I; 1966 v E, S, Ni, USSR, D; (with Tottenham H), 1967 v S, E; 1968 v E, Ni, WG; 1969 v EG; 1970 v R of UK, EG, E, S, Ni, I; 1971 v R; 1972 v Fi, E, S, Ni; 1973 v E (3), S; 1974 v Pol; 1975 v H, L (44)
Evans, B. C. (Swansea C), 1972 v Fi, Cz; 1973 v E (2), Pol, S; (with Hereford U), 1974 v Pol (7)
Evans, D. G. (Reading), 1926 v Ni; 1927 v Ni, E; (with Huddersfield T), 1929 v S (4)
Evans, H. P. (Cardiff C), 1922 v E, S, Ni; 1924 v E, S, Ni (6)
Evans, I. (C Palace), 1976 v A, E, Y (2), E, Ni; 1977 v WG, S (2), Cz, E, Ni; 1978 v K (13)
Evans, J. (Oswestry), 1893 v Ni; 1894 v E, Ni (3)
Evans, J. (Cardiff C), 1912 v Ni; 1913 v Ni; 1914 v S; 1920 v S, Ni; 1922 v Ni; 1923 v E, Ni (8)
Evans, J. H. (Southend U), 1922 v E, S, Ni; 1923 v S (4)
Evans, Len (Aberdare Ath), 1927 v Ni; (with Cardiff C), 1931 v E, S; (with Birmingham), 1934 v Ni (4)
Evans, M. (Oswestry), 1884 v E (1)
Evans, P. S. (Brentford), 2002 v CzR (sub); (with Bradford C), Cro (sub) (2)
Evans, R. (Clapton), 1902 v Ni (1)
Evans, R. E. (Wrexham), 1906 v E, S; (with Aston Villa), Ni; 1907 v E; 1908 v E, S; (with Sheffield U), 1909 v S; 1910 v E, S, Ni (10)
Evans, R. O. (Wrexham), 1902 v Ni; 1903 v E, S, Ni; (with Blackburn R), 1908 v Ni; (with Coventry C), 1911 v E, Ni; 1912 v E, S, Ni (10)
Evans, R. S. (Swansea T), 1964 v Ni (1)
Evans, T. J. (Clapton Orient), 1927 v S; 1928 v E, S; (with Newcastle U), Ni (4)
Evans, W. (Tottenham H), 1933 v Ni; 1934 v E, S; 1935 v E; 1936 v E, Ni (6)
Evans, W. A. W. (Oxford University), 1876 v S; 1877 v S (2)
Evans, W. G. (Bootle), 1890 v E; (with Aston Villa), 1891 v E; 1892 v E (3)
Evelyn, E. C. (Crusaders), 1887 v E (1)
Eyton-Jones, J. A. (Wrexham), 1883 v Ni; 1884 v Ni, E, S (4)

Farmer, G. (Oswestry), 1885 v E, S (2)
Felgate, D. (Lincoln C), 1984 v R (sub) (1)
Finnigan, R. J. (Wrexham), 1930 v Ni (1)
Fletcher, C. N. (Bournemouth), 2004 v S (sub), H (sub), N, Ca; (with West Ham U), 2005 v H, A (2); 2006 v Slv, E, Pol, Ni, Az, Cy, Para, Tr (15)
Flynn, B. (Burnley), 1975 v L (2 sub), H (sub), S, E, Ni; 1976 v A, E, Y (2), E, Ni; 1977 v WG (sub), S (2), Cz, E,

Ni; 1978 v K (2), S; (with Leeds U), Cz, WG, Ir (sub), E, S, Ni; 1979 v Ma, T, S, E, Ni, Ma; 1980 v Ei, WG, E, S, Ni, Ic; 1981 v T, Cz, Ei, T, S, E, USSR; 1982 v Cz, USSR, E, S, Ni, F; 1983 v N; (with Burnley), Y, E, Bul, S, Ni, Br; 1984 v N, R, Bul, Y, S, N, Is (66)
Ford, T. (Swansea T), 1947 v S; (with Aston Villa), 1947 v Ni; 1948 v S, Ni; 1949 v E, S, Ni, P, Bel, Sw; 1950 v E, S, Ni, Bel; 1951 v S; (with Sunderland), 1951 v E, Ni, P, Sw; 1952 v E, S, Ni, R of UK; 1953 v S, E, Ni, F, Y; (with Cardiff C), 1954 v A; 1955 v S, E, Ni, Y; 1956 v S, Ni, E, A; 1957 v S (38)
Foulkes, H. E. (WBA), 1932 v Ni (1)
Foulkes, W. I. (Newcastle U), 1952 v E, S, Ni, R of UK; 1953 v E, S, F, Y; 1954 v E, S, Ni (11)
Foulkes, W. T. (Oswestry), 1884 v Ni; 1885 v S (2)
Fowler, J. (Swansea T), 1925 v E; 1926 v E, Ni; 1927 v S; 1928 v S; 1929 v E (6)
Freestone, R. (Swansea C), 2000 v Br (1)

Gabbidon, D. L. (Cardiff C), 2002 v CzR; 2003 v Cro, Fi, I; 2004 v Ser (2), Ru (2), S, H, N, Ca; 2005 v Az, Ni, E, Pol, H, A (2); (with West Ham U), 2006 v Slv, E, Pol, Az, Cy, Para, Tr (26)
Garner, G. (Leyton Orient), 2006 v Tr (sub) (1)
Garner, J. (Aberystwyth), 1896 v S (1)
Giggs, R. J. (Manchester U), 1992 v G (sub), L (sub), R (sub); 1993 v Fa (sub), Bel (sub + 1), RCS, Fa; 1994 v RCS, Cy, R; 1995 v Alb, Bul; 1996 v G, Alb, Sm; 1997 v Sm, T, Bel; 1998 v T, Bel; 1999 v I (2), D; 2000 v Bl, Fi; 2001 v Bl, N, Pol, Uk, Pol, Uk; 2002 v Arm, N, Arg, G; 2003 v Fi, I, Az (2); 2004 v Ser, I, Fi, Ser, Ru (2), S, Ca; 2005 v E, A (2); 2006 v E, Pol, Ni, Az, Para (56)
Giles, D. (Swansea C), 1980 v E, S, Ni, Ic; 1981 v T, Cz, T (sub), E (sub), USSR (sub); (with C Palace), 1982 v Sp (sub); 1983 v Ni (sub), Br (12)
Gillam, S. G. (Wrexham), 1889 v S (sub), Ni; (with Shrewsbury), 1890 v E, Ni; (with Clapton), 1894 v S (5)
Glascodine, G. (Wrexham), 1879 v E (1)
Glover, E. M. (Grimsby T), 1932 v S; 1934 v Ni; 1936 v S; 1937 v E, S, Ni; 1939 v Ni (7)
Godding, G. (Wrexham), 1923 v S, Ni (2)
Godfrey, B. C. (Preston NE), 1964 v Ni; 1965 v D, I (3)
Goodwin, U. (Ruthin), 1881 v E (1)
Goss, J. (Norwich C), 1991 v Ic, Pol (sub); 1992 v A; 1994 v Cy (sub), R (sub), Se; 1995 v Alb; 1996 v Sw (sub), Sm (sub) (9)
Gough, R. T. (Oswestry White Star), 1883 v S (1)
Gray, A. (Oldham Ath), 1924 v E, S, Ni; 1925 v E, S, Ni; 1926 v E, S; 1927 v S; (with Manchester C), 1928 v E, S; 1929 v E, S, Ni; (with Manchester Central), 1930 v S; (with Tranmere R), 1932 v E, S, Ni; (with Chester), 1937 v E, S, Ni; 1938 v E, S, Ni (24)
Green, A. W. (Aston Villa), 1901 v Ni; (with Notts Co), 1903 v E; 1904 v S, Ni; 1906 v Ni, E; (with Nottingham F), 1907 v E; 1908 v S (8)
Green, C. R. (Birmingham C), 1965 v USSR, I; 1966 v E, S, USSR, Br (2); 1967 v E; 1968 v E, S, Ni, WG; 1969 v S, I, Ni (sub) (15)
Green, G. H. (Charlton Ath), 1938 v Ni; 1939 v E, Ni, F (4)
Green, R. M. (Wolverhampton W), 1998 v Ma, Tun (2)
Grey, Dr W. (Druids), 1876 v S; 1878 v S (2)
Griffiths, A. T. (Wrexham), 1971 v Cz (sub); 1975 v A, H (2), L (2), E, Ni; 1976 v A, E, S, E (sub), Ni, Y (2); 1977 v WG, S (17)
Griffiths, F. J. (Blackpool), 1900 v E, S (2)
Griffiths, G. (Chirk), 1887 v Ni (1)
Griffiths, J. H. (Swansea T), 1953 v Ni (1)
Griffiths, L. (Wrexham), 1902 v S (1)
Griffiths, M. W. (Leicester C), 1947 v Ni; 1949 v P, Bel; 1950 v E, S, Bel; 1951 v E, Ni, P, Sw; 1954 v A (11)
Griffiths, P. (Chirk), 1884 v E, Ni; 1888 v E; 1890 v S, Ni; 1891 v Ni (6)
Griffiths, P. H. (Everton), 1932 v S (1)
Griffiths, T. P. (Everton), 1927 v E, Ni; 1929 v E; 1930 v E; 1931 v Ni; 1932 v Ni, S, E; (with Bolton W), 1933 v E, S, Ni; (with Middlesbrough), F; 1934 v E, S; 1935 v E, Ni; 1936 v S; (with Aston Villa), Ni; 1937 v E, S, Ni (21)

Hall, G. D. (Chelsea), 1988 v Y (sub), Ma, I; 1989 v Ho, Fi, Is; 1990 v Ei; 1991 v Ei; 1992 v A (sub) (9)
Hallam, J. (Oswestry), 1889 v E (1)
Hanford, H. (Swansea T), 1934 v Ni; 1935 v S; 1936 v E; (with Sheffield W), 1936 v Ni; 1938 v E, S; 1939 v F (7)
Harrington, A. C. (Cardiff C), 1956 v Ni; 1957 v E, S; 1958 v S, Ni, Is (2); 1961 v S, E; 1962 v E, S (11)
Harris, C. S. (Leeds U), 1976 v E, S; 1978 v WG, Ir, E, S, Ni; 1979 v Ma, T, WG, E (sub), Ma; 1980 v Ni (sub), Ic (sub); 1981 v T, Cz (sub), Ei, T, S, E, USSR; 1982 v Cz, Ic, E (sub) (24)
Harris, W. C. (Middlesbrough), 1954 v A; 1957 v EG, Cz; 1958 v E, S, EG (6)
Harrison, W. C. (Wrexham), 1899 v E; 1900 v E, S, Ni; 1901 v Ni (5)
Hartson, J. (Arsenal), 1995 v Bul, G (sub), Ge (sub); 1996 v Mol (sub), Sw; 1997 v Ho, T (sub), Ei; (with West Ham U), Bel (sub), S; 1998 v Bel, Jam, Ma, Tun; (with Wimbledon), 1999 v Sw (sub), I (sub), D; 2000 v Sw (sub); 2001 v N, Pol; (with Coventry C), Arm, Uk, Pol, Uk; (with Celtic), 2002 v N, Bl, Arg, CzR, G; 2003 v Cro, Fi, I, Az, Bos, Az; 2004 v I, Fi, Ser, Ru (2); 2005 v La, Az, Ni, E, Pol (sub), A; 2006 v Slv, E, Ni, Az, Cy (51)
Haworth, S. O. (Cardiff C), 1997 v S (sub); (with Coventry C), 1998 v Br, Jam (sub), Ma (sub), Tun (sub) (5)
Hayes, A. (Wrexham), 1890 v Ni; 1894 v Ni (2)
Hennessey, W. T. (Birmingham C), 1962 v Ni, Br (2); 1963 v S, E, H (2); 1964 v E, S; 1965 v S, E, D, Gr, USSR; 1966 v E, USSR; (with Nottingham F), 1966 v S, Ni, D, Br (2), Ch; 1967 v S, E; 1968 v E, S, Ni; 1969 v WG, EG; 1970 v R of UK, EG; (with Derby Co), E, S, Ni; 1972 v Fi, Cz, E, S; 1973 v E (39)
Hersee, A. M. (Bangor), 1886 v S, Ni (2)
Hersee, R. (Llandudno), 1886 v Ni (1)
Hewitt, R. (Cardiff C), 1958 v Ni, Is, Se, H, Br (5)
Hewitt, T. J. (Wrexham), 1911 v E, S, Ni; (with Chelsea), 1913 v E, S, Ni; (with South Liverpool), 1914 v E, S (8)
Heywood, D. (Druids), 1879 v E (1)
Hibbott, H. (Newtown Excelsior), 1880 v E, S; (with Newtown), 1885 v S (3)
Higham, G. G. (Oswestry), 1878 v S; 1879 v E (2)
Hill, M. R. (Ipswich T), 1972 v Cz, R (2)
Hockey, T. (Sheffield U), 1972 v Fi, R; 1973 v E (2); (with Norwich C), Pol, S, E, Ni; (with Aston Villa), 1974 v Pol (9)
Hoddinott, T. F. (Watford), 1921 v E, S (2)
Hodges, G. (Wimbledon), 1984 v N (sub), Is (sub); 1987 v USSR, Fi, Cz; (with Newcastle U), 1988 v D; (with Watford), D (sub), Cz (sub), Se, Ma (sub), I (sub); 1990 v Se, Cr; (with Sheffield U), 1992 v Br (sub), Ei (sub), A; 1996 v G (sub), I (18)
Hodgkinson, A. V. (Southampton), 1908 v Ni (1)
Holden, A. (Chester C), 1984 v Is (sub) (1)
Hole, B. G. (Cardiff C), 1963 v Ni; 1964 v Ni; 1965 v S, E, Ni, D, Gr (2), USSR, I; 1966 v E, S, Ni, USSR, D, Br (2), Ch; (with Blackburn R), 1967 v S, E, Ni; 1968 v E, S, Ni, WG; (with Aston Villa), 1969 v I, WG, EG; 1970 v I; (with Swansea C), 1971 v R (30)
Hole, W. J. (Swansea T), 1921 v Ni; 1922 v E; 1923 v E, Ni; 1928 v E, S, Ni; 1929 v E, S (9)
Hollins, D. M. (Newcastle U), 1962 v Br (sub), M; 1963 v Ni, H; 1964 v E; 1965 v Ni, Gr, I; 1966 v S, D, Br (11)
Hopkins, I. J. (Brentford), 1935 v S, Ni; 1936 v E, Ni; 1937 v E, S, Ni; 1938 v E, Ni; 1939 v E, S, Ni (12)
Hopkins, J. (Fulham), 1983 v Ni, Br; 1984 v N, R, Bul, Y, S, E, Ni, N, Is; 1985 v Ic (1 + 1 sub), N; (with C Palace), 1990 v Ho, Cr (16)
Hopkins, M. (Tottenham H), 1956 v Ni; 1957 v Ni, S, E, Cz (2), EG; 1958 v E, S, Ni, EG, Is (2), H (2), M, Se, Br; 1959 v E, S, Ni; 1960 v E, S; 1961 v Ni, H, Sp (2); 1962 v Ni, Br (2), M; 1963 v S, Ni, H (34)
Horne, B. (Portsmouth), 1988 v D (sub), Y, Se (sub), Ma, I; 1989 v Ho, Fi, Is; (with Southampton), Se, WG; 1990 v WG (sub), Ei, Se, Cr; 1991 v D, Bel (2), L, Ei, Ic, Pol, G; 1992 v Br, G, L, Ei, A, R, Ho, Arg, J; (with Everton), 1993 v Fa, Cy, Bel, Ei, Bel, RCS, Fa; 1994 v RCS, Cy, R, N, Se, Es; 1995 v Mol, Ge, Bul, G, Ge; 1996 v Mol, G, I, Sw, Sm; (with Birmingham C), 1997 v Sm, Ho, T, Ei, Bel (59)
Howell, E. G. (Builth), 1888 v Ni; 1890 v E; 1891 v E (3)
Howells, R. G. (Cardiff C), 1954 v E, S (2)
Hugh, A. R. (Newport Co), 1930 v Ni (1)
Hughes, A. (Rhos), 1894 v E, S (2)
Hughes, A. (Chirk), 1907 v Ni (1)
Hughes, C. M. (Luton T), 1992 v Ho (sub); 1994 v N (sub), Se (sub), Es; 1996 v Alb; 1997 v Ei (sub); (with Wimbledon), 1998 v T, Bel (8)
Hughes, E. (Everton), 1899 v S, Ni; (with Tottenham H), 1901 v E, S; 1902 v Ni; 1904 v E, Ni, S; 1905 v E, Ni, S; 1906 v E, Ni; 1907 v E (14)
Hughes, E. (Wrexham), 1906 v S; (with Nottingham F), 1906 v Ni; 1908 v S, E; 1910 v Ni, E, S; 1911 v Ni, E, S; (with Wrexham), 1912 v Ni, E, S; (with Manchester C), 1913 v E, S; 1914 v Ni (16)
Hughes, F. W. (Northwich Victoria), 1882 v E, Ni; 1883 v E, Ni, S; 1884 v S (6)
Hughes, I. (Luton T), 1951 v E, Ni, P, Sw (4)
Hughes, J. (Cambridge University), 1877 v S; (with Aberystwyth), 1879 v S (2)
Hughes, J. (Liverpool), 1905 v E, S, Ni (3)

Hughes, J. I. (Blackburn R), 1935 v Ni (1)
Hughes, L. M. (Manchester U), 1984 v E, Ni; 1985 v Ic, Sp, Ic, N, S, Sp, N; 1986 v S, H, U; (with Barcelona), 1987 v USSR, Cz; 1988 v D (2), Cz, Se, Ma, I; (with Manchester U), 1989 v Ho, Fi, Is, Se, WG; 1990 v Fi, WG, Cr; 1991 v D, Bel (2), L, Ic, Pol, G; 1992 v Br, G, L, Ei, R, Ho, Arg, J; 1993 v Fa, Cy, Bel, Ei, Bel, RCS, Fa; 1994 v RCS, Cy, N; 1995 v Ge, Bul, G, Ge; (with Chelsea), 1996 v Mol, I, Sm; 1997 v Sm, Ho, T, Ei, Bel; 1998 v T; (with Southampton), 1999 v I, D, Bl, Sw, I, D (72)
Hughes, P. W. (Bangor), 1887 v Ni; 1889 v Ni, E (3)
Hughes, W. (Bootle), 1891 v E; 1892 v S, Ni (3)
Hughes, W. A. (Blackburn R), 1949 v E, Ni, P, Bel, Sw (5)
Hughes, W. M. (Birmingham), 1938 v E, Ni, S; 1939 v E, Ni, S, F; 1947 v E, S, Ni (10)
Humphreys, J. V. (Everton), 1947 v Ni (1)
Humphreys, R. (Druids), 1888 v Ni (1)
Hunter, A. H. (FA of Wales Secretary), 1887 v Ni (1)

Jackett, K. (Watford), 1983 v N, Y, E, Bul, S; 1984 v N, R, Y, S, Ni, N, Is; 1985 v Ic, Sp, Ic, N, S, Sp, N; 1986 v S, H, S.Ar, Ei, Ca (2); 1987 v Fi (2); 1988 v D, Cz, Y, Se (31)
Jackson, W. (St Helens Rec), 1899 v Ni (1)
James, E. (Chirk), 1893 v E, Ni; 1894 v E, S, Ni; 1898 v S, E; 1899 v Ni (8)
James, E. G. (Blackpool), 1966 v Br (2), Ch; 1967 v Ni; 1968 v S; 1971 v Cz, S, E, Ni (9)
James, L. (Burnley), 1972 v Cz, R, S (sub); 1973 v E (3), Pol, S, Ni; 1974 v Pol, E, S, Ni; 1975 v A, H (2), L (2), S, E, Ni; 1976 v A; (with Derby Co), S, E, Y (2), Ni; 1977 v WG, S (2), Cz, E, Ni; 1978 v K (2); (with QPR), WG; (with Burnley), 1979 v T; (with Swansea C), 1980 v E, S, Ni, Ic; 1981 v T, Ei, T, S, E; 1982 v Cz, Ic, USSR, E (sub), S, Ni, F; (with Sunderland), 1983 v E (sub) (54)
James, R. M. (Swansea C), 1979 v Ma, WG (sub), S, E, Ni, Ma; 1980 v WG; 1982 v Cz (sub), Ic, Sp, E, S, Ni, F; 1983 v N, Y, E, Bul; (with Stoke C), 1984 v N, R, Bul, Y, S, E, Ni, N, Is; 1985 v Ic, Sp, Ic; (with QPR), N, S, Sp, N; 1986 v S, S.Ar, Ei, U, Ca (2); 1987 v Fi (2), USSR, Cz; (with Leicester C), 1988 v D (2); (with Swansea C), Y (47)
James, W. (West Ham U), 1931 v Ni; 1932 v Ni (2)
Jarrett, R. H. (Ruthin), 1889 v Ni; 1890 v S (2)
Jarvis, A. L. (Hull C), 1967 v S, E, Ni (3)
Jenkins, E. (Lovell's Ath), 1925 v E (1)
Jenkins, J. (Brighton), 1924 v Ni, E, S; 1925 v S, Ni; 1926 v E, S; 1927 v S (8)
Jenkins, R. W. (Rhyl), 1902 v Ni (1)
Jenkins, S. R. (Swansea C), 1996 v G; (with Huddersfield T), Alb, I; 1997 v Ho (sub), T, S; 1998 v T, Bel, Br, Jam; 1999 v I (sub), D; 2001 v Pol (sub), Uk (sub); 2002 v Arm, N (16)
Jenkyns, C. A. L. (Small Heath), 1892 v E, S, Ni; 1895 v E; (with Woolwich Arsenal), 1896 v S; (with Newton Heath), 1897 v Ni; (with Walsall), 1898 v S, E (8)
Jennings, W. (Bolton W), 1914 v E, S; 1920 v S; 1923 v Ni, E; 1924 v E, S, Ni; 1927 v S, Ni; 1929 v S (11)
John, R. F. (Arsenal), 1923 v S, Ni; 1925 v Ni; 1926 v E; 1927 v E; 1928 v E, Ni; 1930 v E, S; 1932 v E; 1933 v F, Ni; 1935 v Ni; 1936 v S; 1937 v E (15)
John, W. R. (Walsall), 1931 v Ni; (with Stoke C), 1933 v E, S, Ni, F; 1934 v E, S; (with Preston NE), 1935 v E, S; (with Sheffield U), 1936 v E, S, Ni; (with Swansea T), 1939 v E, S (14)
Johnson, A. J. (Nottingham F), 1999 v I, D, Bl, Sw; 2000 v Fi (sub), Br (sub), P (sub); (with WBA), 2003 v Cro, Fi, US; 2004 v I (sub), Fi (sub), Ru (2); 2005 v La (sub) (15)
Johnson, M. G. (Swansea T), 1964 v Ni (1)
Jones, A. (Port Vale), 1987 v Fi, Cz (sub); 1988 v D, (with Charlton Ath), D (sub), Cz (sub); 1990 v Hol (sub) (6)
Jones, A. F. (Oxford University), 1877 v S (1)
Jones, A. T. (Nottingham F), 1905 v E; (with Notts Co), 1906 v E (2)
Jones, Bryn (Wolverhampton W), 1935 v Ni; 1936 v E, S, Ni; 1937 v E, S, Ni; 1938 v E, S, Ni; (with Arsenal), 1939 v E, S, Ni; 1947 v S, Ni; 1948 v E; 1949 v S (17)
Jones, B. S. (Swansea T), 1963 v S, E, Ni, H (2); 1964 v S, Ni; (with Plymouth Arg), 1965 v D; (with Cardiff C), 1969 v S, E, Ni, I (sub), WG, EG; 1970 v R of UK (15)
Jones, Charlie (Nottingham F), 1926 v E; 1927 v S, Ni; 1928 v E; (with Arsenal), 1930 v E, S; 1932 v E; 1933 v F (8)
Jones, Cliff (Swansea T), 1954 v A; 1956 v E, Ni, S, A; 1957 v E, S, Ni, Cz (2), EG; 1958 v EG, E, S, Is (2); (with Tottenham H), Ni, H (2), M, Se, Br; 1959 v Ni; 1960 v E, S, Ni; 1961 v S, E, Ni, Sp, H, Ei; 1962 v E, Ni, S, Br (2), M; 1963 v S, Ni, H; 1964 v E, S, Ni; 1965 v E, S, Ni, D, Gr (2), USSR, I; 1967 v S, E; 1968 v E, S, WG; (with Fulham), 1969 v I; 1970 v R of UK (59)
Jones, C. W. (Birmingham), 1935 v Ni; 1939 v F (2)
Jones, D. (Chirk), 1888 v S, Ni; (with Bolton W), 1889 v E, S, Ni; 1890 v E; 1891 v S; 1892 v Ni; 1893 v E; 1894 v E; 1895 v E; 1898 v S; (with Manchester C), 1900 v E, Ni (14)
Jones, D. E. (Norwich C), 1976 v S, E (sub); 1978 v S, Cz, WG, Ir, E; 1980 v E (8)
Jones, D. O. (Leicester C), 1934 v E, Ni; 1935 v E, S; 1936 v E, Ni; 1937 v Ni (7)
Jones, Evan (Chelsea), 1910 v S, Ni; (with Oldham Ath), 1911 v E, S; 1912 v E, S; (with Bolton W), 1914 v Ni (7)
Jones, F. R. (Bangor), 1885 v E, Ni; 1886 v S (3)
Jones, F. W. (Small Heath), 1893 v S (1)
Jones, G. P. (Wrexham), 1907 v S, Ni (2)
Jones, H. (Aberaman), 1902 v Ni (1)
Jones, Humphrey (Bangor), 1885 v E, Ni, S; 1886 v E, Ni, S; (with Queen's Park), 1887 v E; (with East Stirlingshire), 1889 v E, S; 1890 v E, S, Ni; (with Queen's Park), 1891 v E, S (14)
Jones, Ivor (Swansea T), 1920 v S, Ni; 1921 v Ni, E; 1922 v S, Ni; (with WBA), 1923 v E, Ni; 1924 v S; 1926 v Ni (10)
Jones, Jeffrey (Llandrindod Wells), 1908 v Ni; 1909 v Ni; 1910 v S (3)
Jones, J. (Druids), 1876 v S (1)
Jones, J. (Berwyn Rangers), 1883 v S, Ni; 1884 v S (3)
Jones, J. (Wrexham), 1925 v Ni (1)
Jones, J. L. (Sheffield U), 1895 v E, S, Ni; 1896 v Ni, S, E; 1897 v Ni, S, E; (with Tottenham H), 1898 v Ni, E, S; 1899 v S, Ni; 1900 v S; 1902 v E, S, Ni; 1904 v E, S, Ni (21)
Jones, J. Love (Stoke C), 1906 v S; (with Middlesbrough), 1910 v Ni (2)
Jones, J. O. (Bangor), 1901 v S, Ni (2)
Jones, J. P. (Liverpool), 1976 v A, E, S; 1977 v WG, S (2), Cz, E, Ni; 1978 v K (2), S, Cz, WG, Ir, E, S, Ni; (with Wrexham), 1979 v Ma, T, WG, S, E, Ni, Ma; 1980 v Ei, WG, T, E, S, Ni, Ic; 1981 v T, Ei, T, S, E, USSR; 1982 v Cz, Ic, USSR, Sp, E, S, Ni, F; 1983 v N; (with Chelsea), Y, E, Bul, S, Ni, Br; 1984 v N, R, Bul, Y, S, E, Ni, N, Is; 1985 v Ic, N, S, N; (with Huddersfield T), 1986 v S, H, Ei, U, Ca (2) (72)
Jones, J. T. (Stoke C), 1912 v E, S, Ni; 1913 v E, Ni; 1914 v S, Ni; 1920 v E, S, Ni; (with C Palace), 1921 v E, S; 1922 v E, S, Ni (15)
Jones, K. (Aston Villa), 1950 v S (1)
Jones, Leslie J. (Cardiff C), 1933 v F; (with Coventry C), 1935 v Ni; 1936 v S; 1937 v E, S, Ni; (with Arsenal), 1938 v E, S, Ni; 1939 v E, S (11)
Jones, M. G. (Leeds U), 2000 v Sw (sub), Q, Br, P; 2001 v Pol (sub); (with Leicester C), Arm (sub), Uk, Pol (sub); 2002 v Arm (sub), N (sub), Bl; 2003 v Bos (sub), US (13)
Jones, P. L. (Liverpool), 1997 v S (sub); (with Tranmere R), 1998 v T (sub) (2)
Jones, P. S. (Stockport Co), 1997 v S (sub); (with Southampton), 1998 v T (sub), Br, Jam, Ma; 1999 v I, D, Bl, Sw, I, D; 2000 v Bl, Sw, Q; 2001 v Bl, N, Pol, Arm, Uk, Pol, Uk; 2002 v Arm, N, Bl, Arg; 2003 v Cro, Fi, I, Az (2), US; 2004 v Ser, I, Fi, Ser, Ru (2); (with Wolverhampton W), H; 2005 v La, Az, Ni, E, Pol; 2006 v Ni, Az; (with QPR), Para (46)
Jones, P. W. (Bristol R), 1971 v Fi (1)
Jones, R. (Bangor), 1887 v S; 1889 v E; (with Crewe Alex), 1890 v E (3)
Jones, R. (Leicester Fosse), 1898 v S (1)
Jones, R. (Druids), 1899 v S (1)
Jones, R. (Bangor), 1900 v S, Ni (2)
Jones, R. (Millwall), 1906 v S, Ni (2)
Jones, R. A. (Druids), 1884 v E, Ni, S; 1885 v S (4)
Jones, R. A. (Sheffield W), 1994 v Es (1)
Jones, R. S. (Everton), 1894 v Ni (1)
Jones, S. (Wrexham), 1887 v Ni; (with Chester), 1890 v S (2)
Jones, S. (Wrexham), 1893 v S, Ni; (with Burton Swifts), 1895 v S; 1896 v E, Ni; (with Druids), 1899 v E (6)
Jones, T. (Manchester U), 1926 v Ni; 1927 v E, Ni; 1930 v Ni (4)
Jones, T. D. (Aberdare), 1908 v Ni (1)
Jones, T. G. (Everton), 1938 v Ni; 1939 v E, S, Ni; 1947 v E, S; 1948 v E, S, Ni; 1949 v E, Ni, P, Bel, Sw; 1950 v E, S, Bel (17)
Jones, T. J. (Sheffield W), 1932 v Ni; 1933 v F (2)
Jones, V. P. (Wimbledon), 1995 v Bul (2), G, Ge; 1996 v Sw; 1997 v Ho, T, Ei, Bel (9)
Jones, W. E. A. (Swansea T), 1947 v E, S; (with Tottenham H), 1949 v E, S (4)
Jones, W. J. (Aberdare), 1901 v E, S; (with West Ham U), 1902 v E, S (4)
Jones, W. Lot (Manchester C), 1905 v E, Ni; 1906 v E, S, Ni; 1907 v E, S, Ni; 1908 v S; 1909 v E, S, Ni; 1910 v E; 1911 v E; 1913 v E, S; 1914 v S, Ni; (with Southend U), 1920 v E, Ni (20)
Jones, W. P. (Druids), 1889 v E, Ni; (with Wynnstay), 1890 v S, Ni (4)

Jones, W. R. (Aberystwyth), 1897 v S (1)

Keenor, F. C. (Cardiff C), 1920 v E, Ni; 1921 v E, Ni, S; 1922 v Ni; 1923 v E, Ni, S; 1924 v E, Ni, S; 1925 v E, Ni, S; 1926 v S; 1927 v E, Ni, S; 1928 v E, Ni, S; 1929 v E, Ni, S; 1930 v E, Ni, S; 1931 v E, Ni, S; (with Crewe Alex), 1933 v S (32)
Kelly, F. C. (Wrexham), 1899 v S, Ni; (with Druids), 1902 v Ni (3)
Kelsey, A. J. (Arsenal), 1954 v Ni, A; 1955 v S, Ni, Y; 1956 v E, Ni, S, A; 1957 v E, Ni, S, Cz (2), EG; 1958 v E, S, Ni, Is (2), H (2), M, Se, Br; 1959 v E, S; 1960 v E, Ni, S; 1961 v E, Ni, S, H, Sp (2); 1962 v E, S, Ni, Br (2) (41)
Kenrick, S. L. (Druids), 1876 v S; 1877 v S; (with Oswestry), 1879 v E, S; (with Shropshire Wanderers), 1881 v E (5)
Ketley, C. F. (Druids), 1882 v Ni (1)
King, J. (Swansea T), 1955 v E (1)
Kinsey, N. (Norwich C), 1951 v Ni, P, Sw; 1952 v E; (with Birmingham C), 1954 v Ni; 1956 v E, S (7)
Knill, A. R. (Swansea C), 1989 v Ho (1)
Koumas, J. (Tranmere R), 2001 v Uk (sub); 2002 v CzR; (with WBA), 2003 v Bos (sub), US; 2004 v I, Fi, Ru (2), H; 2005 v La, Az, Ni, E, Pol; 2006 v E (sub), Pol, Para (17)
Krzywicki, R. L. (WBA), 1970 v EG, I; (with Huddersfield T), Ni, E, S; 1971 v R, Fi; 1972 v Cz (sub) (8)

Lambert, R. (Liverpool), 1947 v S; 1948 v E; 1949 v P, Bel, Sw (5)
Latham, G. (Liverpool), 1905 v E, S; 1906 v S; 1907 v E, S, Ni; 1908 v E; 1909 v Ni; (with Southport Central), 1910 v E; (with Cardiff C), 1913 v Ni (10)
Law, B. J. (QPR), 1990 v Se (1)
Lawrence, E. (Clapton Orient), 1930 v Ni; (with Notts Co), 1932 v S (2)
Lawrence, S. (Swansea T), 1932 v Ni; 1933 v F; 1934 v S, E, Ni; 1935 v E, S; 1936 v S (8)
Lea, A. (Wrexham), 1889 v E; 1891 v S, Ni; 1893 v Ni (4)
Lea, C. (Ipswich T), 1965 v Ni, I (2)
Leary, P. (Bangor), 1889 v Ni (1)
Ledley, J. C. (Cardiff C), 2006 v Pol (sub), Para (sub), Tr (3)
Leek, K. (Leicester C), 1961 v S, E, Ni, H, Sp (2); (with Newcastle U), 1962 v S; (with Birmingham C), v Br (sub), M; 1963 v E; 1965 v S, Gr; (with Northampton T), 1965 v Gr (13)
Legg, A. (Birmingham C), 1996 v Sw, Sm (sub); 1997 v Ho (sub), Ei; (with Cardiff C), 1999 v D (sub); 2001 v Arm (6)
Lever, A. R. (Leicester C), 1953 v S (1)
Lewis, B. (Chester), 1891 v Ni; (with Wrexham), 1892 v S, E, Ni; (with Middlesbrough), 1893 v S, E; (with Wrexham), 1894 v S, E, Ni; 1895 v S (10)
Lewis, D. (Arsenal), 1927 v E; 1928 v Ni; 1930 v E (3)
Lewis, D. (Swansea C), 1983 v Br (sub) (1)
Lewis, D. J. (Swansea T), 1933 v E, S (2)
Lewis, D. M. (Bangor), 1890 v Ni, S (2)
Lewis, J. (Bristol R), 1906 v E (1)
Lewis, J. (Cardiff C), 1926 v S (1)
Lewis, T. (Wrexham), 1881 v E, S (2)
Lewis, W. (Bangor), 1885 v E; 1886 v E, S; 1887 v E, S; 1888 v E; 1889 v E, Ni, S; (with Crewe Alex), 1890 v E; 1891 v E, S; (with Chester), 1892 v E, S, Ni; 1894 v E, S, Ni; 1895 v S, Ni, E; 1896 v E, S, Ni; (with Manchester C), 1897 v E, S; (with Chester), 1898 v Ni (27)
Lewis, W. L. (Swansea T), 1927 v E, Ni; 1928 v E, Ni; 1929 v S; (with Huddersfield T), 1930 v E (6)
Llewellyn, C. M. (Norwich C), 1998 v Ma (sub), Tun (sub); (with Wrexham), 2004 v N (sub), Ca (sub) (4)
Lloyd, B. W. (Wrexham), 1976 v A, E, S (3)
Lloyd, J. W. (Wrexham), 1879 v S; (with Newtown), 1885 v S (2)
Lloyd, R. A. (Ruthin), 1891 v Ni; 1895 v S (2)
Lockley, A. (Chirk), 1898 v Ni (1)
Lovell, S. (C Palace), 1982 v USSR (sub); (with Millwall), 1985 v N; 1986 v S (sub), H (sub), Ca (1+1 sub) (6)
Lowndes, S. (Newport Co), 1983 v S (sub), Br (sub); (with Millwall), 1985 v N (sub); 1986 v S.Ar (sub), Ei, U, Ca (2); (with Barnsley), 1987 v Fi (sub); 1988 v Se (sub) (10)
Lowrie, G. (Coventry C), 1948 v E, S, Ni; (with Newcastle U), 1949 v P (4)
Lucas, P. M. (Leyton Orient), 1962 v Ni, M; 1963 v S, E (4)
Lucas, W. H. (Swansea T), 1949 v S, Ni, P, Bel, Sw; 1950 v E; 1951 v E (7)
Lumberg, A. (Wrexham), 1929 v Ni; 1930 v E, S; (with Wolverhampton W), 1932 v S (4)

McCarthy, T. P. (Wrexham), 1889 v Ni (1)
McMillan, R. (Shrewsbury Engineers), 1881 v E, S (2)
Maguire, G. T. (Portsmouth), 1990 v Fi (sub), Ho, WG, Ei, Se; 1992 v Br (sub), G (7)
Mahoney, J. F. (Stoke C), 1968 v E; 1969 v EG; 1971 v Cz; 1973 v E (3), Pol, S, Ni; 1974 v Pol, E, S, Ni; 1975 v A, H (2), L (2), S, E, Ni; 1976 v A, Y (2), E, Ni; 1977 v WG, Cz, S, E, Ni; (with Middlesbrough), 1978 v K (2), S, Cz, Ir, E (sub), S, Ni; 1979 v WG, S, E, Ni, Ma; (with Swansea C), 1980 v Ei, WG, T (sub); 1982 v Ic, USSR; 1983 v Y, E (51)
Mardon, P. J. (WBA), 1996 v G (sub) (1)
Margetson, M. W. (Cardiff C), 2004 v Ca (sub) (1)
Marriott, A. (Wrexham), 1996 v Sw (sub); 1997 v S; 1998 v Bel, Br (sub), Tun (5)
Martin, T. J. (Newport Co), 1930 v Ni (1)
Marustik, C. (Swansea C), 1982 v Sp, E, S, Ni, F; 1983 v N (6)
Mates, J. (Chirk), 1891 v Ni; 1897 v E, S (3)
Matthews, R. W. (Liverpool), 1921 v Ni; (with Bristol C), 1923 v E; (with Bradford), 1926 v Ni (3)
Matthews, W. (Chester), 1905 v Ni; 1908 v E (2)
Matthias, J. S. (Brymbo), 1896 v S, Ni; (with Shrewsbury), 1897 v E, S; (with Wolverhampton W), 1899 v S (5)
Matthias, T. J. (Wrexham), 1914 v S, E; 1920 v Ni, S, E; 1921 v S, E, Ni; 1922 v S, E, Ni; 1923 v S (12)
Mays, A. W. (Wrexham), 1929 v Ni (1)
Medwin, T. C. (Swansea T), 1953 v Ni, F, Y; (with Tottenham H), 1957 v E, S, Ni, Cz (2), EG; 1958 v E, S, Ni, Is (2), H (2), M, Br; 1959 v E, S, Ni; 1960 v E, S, Ni; 1961 v S, Ei, E, Sp; 1963 v E, H (30)
Melville, A. K. (Swansea C), 1990 v WG, Ei, Se, Cr (sub); (with Oxford U), 1991 v Ic, Pol, G; 1992 v Br, G, L, R, Ho, J (sub); 1993 v RCS, Fa (sub); (with Sunderland), 1994 v RCS (sub), R, N, Se, Es; 1995 v Alb, Mol (sub), Ge, Bul; 1996 v G, Alb, Sm; 1997 v Sm, Ho (2), T; 1998 v T; 1999 v I, D; (with Fulham), 2000 v Bl, Q, Fi, Br, P; 2001 v Bl, N, Pol, Arm, Uk, Pol, Uk; 2002 v Arm, Bl, Arg, CzR, G; 2003 v Cro, Fi, I, Az, Bos, Az, US; 2004 v Fi, Ru (2); (with West Ham U), S, H; 2005 v La, Az (65)
Meredith, S. (Chirk), 1900 v S; 1901 v S, E, Ni; (with Stoke C), 1902 v E; 1903 v Ni; 1904 v E; (with Leyton), 1907 v E (8)
Meredith, W. H. (Manchester C), 1895 v E, Ni; 1896 v E, Ni; 1897 v E, Ni, S; 1898 v E, Ni; 1899 v E; 1900 v E, Ni; 1901 v E, Ni; 1902 v E, S; 1903 v E, S, Ni; 1904 v E; 1905 v E, S; (with Manchester U), 1907 v E, S, Ni; 1908 v E, Ni; 1909 v E, S, Ni; 1910 v E, S, Ni; 1911 v E, S, Ni; 1912 v E, S, Ni; 1913 v E, S, Ni; 1914 v E, S, Ni; 1920 v E, S, Ni (48)
Mielczarek, R. (Rotherham U), 1971 v Fi (1)
Millership, H. (Rotherham Co), 1920 v E, S, Ni; 1921 v E, S, Ni (6)
Millington, A. H. (WBA), 1963 v S, E, H; (with C Palace), 1965 v E, USSR; (with Peterborough U), 1966 v Ch, Br; 1967 v E, Ni; 1968 v Ni, WG; 1969 v I, EG; (with Swansea C), 1970 v E, S, Ni; 1971 v Cz, Fi; 1972 v Fi (sub), Cz, R (21)
Mills, T. J. (Clapton Orient), 1934 v E, Ni; (with Leicester C), 1935 v E, S (4)
Mills-Roberts, R. H. (St Thomas' Hospital), 1885 v E, S, Ni; 1886 v E; 1887 v E; (with Preston NE), 1888 v E, Ni; (with Llanberis), 1892 v E (8)
Moore, G. (Cardiff C), 1960 v E, S, Ni; 1961 v Ei, Sp; (with Chelsea), 1962 v Br; 1963 v Ni, H; (with Manchester U), 1964 v S, Ni; (with Northampton T), 1966 v Ni, Ch; (with Charlton Ath), 1969 v S, E, Ni; 1970 v R of UK, E, S, Ni, I; 1971 v R (21)
Morgan, J. R. (Cambridge University), 1877 v S; (with Derby School Staff), 1879 v S; 1880 v E, S; 1881 v E, S; 1882 v E, S, Ni; 1883 v E (10)
Morgan, J. T. (Wrexham), 1905 v Ni (1)
Morgan-Owen, H. (Oxford University), 1902 v S; (with Corinthians), 1906 v E, Ni; 1907 v S (4)
Morgan-Owen, M. M. (Oxford University), 1897 v S, Ni; 1898 v E, S; 1899 v S; 1900 v E; (with Corinthians), 1901 v S, E; 1903 v S; 1906 v S, E, Ni; 1907 v E (13)
Morley, E. J. (Swansea T), 1925 v E; (with Clapton Orient), 1929 v E, S, Ni (4)
Morris, A. G. (Aberystwyth), 1896 v E, Ni, S; (with Swindon T), 1897 v E; 1898 v S; (with Nottingham F), 1899 v E, S; 1903 v E, S; 1905 v E, S; 1907 v E, S; 1908 v E; 1910 v E, S, Ni; 1911 v E, S, Ni; 1912 v E (21)
Morris, C. (Chirk), 1900 v E, S, Ni; (with Derby Co), 1901 v E, S, Ni; 1902 v E; 1903 v E, S, Ni; 1904 v Ni; 1905 v E, S, Ni; 1906 v S; 1907 v S; 1908 v E, S; 1909 v E, S, Ni; 1910 v E, S, Ni; (with Huddersfield T), 1911 v E, S, Ni (27)
Morris, E. (Chirk), 1893 v E, S, Ni (3)
Morris, H. (Sheffield U), 1894 v S; (with Manchester C), 1896 v E; (with Grimsby T), 1897 v E (3)
Morris, J. (Oswestry), 1887 v S (1)
Morris, J. (Chirk), 1898 v Ni (1)

Morris, R. (Chirk), 1900 v E, Ni; 1901 v Ni; 1902 v S; (with Shrewsbury T), 1903 v E, Ni (6)
Morris, R. (Druids), 1902 v E, S; (with Newtown), Ni; (with Liverpool), 1903 v S, Ni; 1904 v E, S, Ni; (with Leeds C), 1906 v S; (with Grimsby T), 1907 v Ni; (with Plymouth Arg), 1908 v Ni (11)
Morris, S. (Birmingham), 1937 v E, S; 1938 v E, S; 1939 v F (5)
Morris, W. (Burnley), 1947 v Ni; 1949 v E; 1952 v S, Ni, R of UK (5)
Moulsdale, J. R. B. (Corinthians), 1925 v Ni (1)
Murphy, J. P. (WBA), 1933 v F, E, Ni; 1934 v E, S; 1935 v E, S, Ni; 1936 v E, S, Ni; 1937 v S, Ni; 1938 v E, S (15)

Nardiello, D. (Coventry C), 1978 v Cz, WG (sub) (2)
Neal, J. E. (Colwyn Bay), 1931 v E, S (2)
Neilson, A. B. (Newcastle U), 1992 v Ei (sub); 1994 v Se, Es; 1995 v Ge; (with Southampton), 1997 v Ho (5)
Newnes, J. (Nelson), 1926 v Ni (1)
Newton, L. F. (Cardiff Corinthians), 1912 v Ni (1)
Nicholas, D. S. (Stoke C), 1923 v S; (with Swansea T), 1927 v E, Ni (3)
Nicholas, P. (C Palace), 1979 v S (sub), Ni (sub), Ma; 1980 v Ei, WG, T, E, S, Ni, Ic; 1981 v T, Cz, E; (with Arsenal), T, S, E, USSR; 1982 v Cz, Ic, USSR, Sp, E, S, Ni, F; 1983 v Y, Bul, S, Ni; 1984 v N (with C Palace), Bul, N, Is; 1985 v Sp; (with Luton T), N, S, Sp, N; 1986 v S, H, S.Ar, Ei, U, Ca (2); 1987 v Fi (2) USSR, Cz; (with Aberdeen), 1988 v D (2), Cz, Y, Se; (with Chelsea), 1989 v Ho, Fi, Is, Se, WG; 1990 v Fi, Ho, WG, Ei, Se, Cr; 1991 v D (sub), Bel, L, Ei; (with Watford), Bel, Pol, G; 1992 v L (73)
Nicholls, J. (Newport Co), 1924 v E, Ni; (with Cardiff C), 1925 v E, S (4)
Niedzwiecki, E. A. (Chelsea), 1985 v N (sub); 1988 v D (2)
Nock, W. (Newtown), 1897 v Ni (1)
Nogan, L. M. (Watford), 1992 v A (sub); (with Reading), 1996 v Mol (2)
Norman, A. J. (Hull C), 1986 v Ei (sub), U, Ca; 1988 v Ma, I (5)
Nurse, M. T. G. (Swansea T), 1960 v E, Ni; 1961 v S, E, H, Ni, Ei, Sp (2); (with Middlesbrough), 1963 v E, H; 1964 v S (12)
Nyatanga, L. J. (Derby Co), 2006 v Para, Tr (sub) (2)

O'Callaghan, E. (Tottenham H), 1929 v Ni; 1930 v S; 1932 v S, E; 1933 v Ni, S, E; 1934 v Ni, S, E; 1935 v E (11)
Oliver, A. (Blackburn R), 1905 v E; (with Bangor), S (2)
Oster, J. M. (Everton), 1998 v Bel (sub), Br, Jam; (with Sunderland), 2000 v Sw; 2003 v Bos (sub), Az, US; 2004 v Ser (sub), S, N, Ca; 2005 v Az (sub), Ni (13)
O'Sullivan, P. A. (Brighton), 1973 v S (sub); 1976 v S; 1979 v Ma (sub) (3)
Owen, D. (Oswestry), 1879 v E (1)
Owen, E. (Ruthin Grammar School), 1884 v E, Ni, S (3)
Owen, G. (Chirk), 1888 v S; (with Newton Heath), 1889 v S, Ni; (with Chirk), 1893 v Ni (4)
Owen, J. (Newton Heath), 1892 v E (1)
Owen, Trevor (Crewe Alex), 1899 v E, S (2)
Owen, T. (Oswestry), 1879 v E (1)
Owen, W. (Chirk), 1884 v E; 1885 v Ni; 1887 v E; 1888 v E; 1889 v E, Ni, S; 1890 v S, Ni; 1891 v E, S, Ni; 1892 v E, S; 1893 v S, Ni (16)
Owen, W. P. (Ruthin), 1880 v E, S; 1881 v E, S; 1882 v E, S, Ni; 1883 v E, S; 1884 v E, S, Ni (12)
Owens, J. (Wrexham), 1902 v S (1)

Page, M. E. (Birmingham C), 1971 v Fi; 1972 v S, Ni; 1973 v E (1+1 sub), Ni; 1974 v S, Ni; 1975 v H, L, S, E, Ni; 1976 v E, Y (2), E, Ni; 1977 v WG, S; 1978 v K (sub+1), WG, Ir, E, S; 1979 v Ma, WG (28)
Page, R. J. (Watford), 1997 v T, Bel, S; 1998 v T, Bel (sub), Br, I; 2000 v Bl, Sw, Q, Fi, Br, P; 2001 v Bl, N, Pol, Arm, Uk, Pol, Uk; (with Sheffield U), 2002 v N, Bl (sub), Arg, CzR, G; 2003 v Az, Bos, Az; 2004 v Ser, I, Fi, S, H; (with Cardiff C), 2005 v La, Az, H; (with Coventry C), A (1+sub); 2006 v Slv, E, Cy (41)
Palmer, D. (Swansea T), 1957 v Cz; 1958 v E, EG (3)
Parris, J. E. (Bradford), 1932 v Ni (1)
Parry, B. J. (Swansea T), 1951 v S (1)
Parry, C. (Everton), 1891 v E, S; 1893 v E; 1894 v E; 1895 v E, S; (with Newtown), 1896 v E, S, Ni; 1897 v Ni; 1898 v E, S, Ni (13)
Parry, E. (Liverpool), 1922 v S; 1923 v E, Ni; 1925 v Ni; 1926 v Ni (5)
Parry, M. (Liverpool), 1901 v E, S, Ni; 1902 v E, S, Ni; 1903 v E, S; 1904 v E, Ni; 1906 v E; 1908 v E, S, Ni; 1909 v E, S (16)
Parry, P. I. (Cardiff C), 2004 v S (sub), N, Ca; 2005 v Ni (sub), Pol (sub); 2006 v Slv (sub) (6)
Parry, T. D. (Oswestry), 1900 v E, S, Ni; 1901 v E, S, Ni; 1902 v E (7)
Parry, W. (Newtown), 1895 v Ni (1)
Partridge, D. W. (Motherwell), 2005 v H, A; (with Bristol C), 2006 v Slv, E, Pol, Ni, Tr (7)
Pascoe, C. (Swansea C), 1984 v N, Is; (with Sunderland), 1989 v Fi, Is, WG (sub); 1990 v Ho (sub), WG (sub); 1991 v Ei, Ic (sub); 1992 v Br (10)
Paul, R. (Swansea T), 1949 v E, S, Ni, P, Sw; 1950 v E, S, Ni, Bel; (with Manchester C), 1951 v S, E, Ni, P, Sw; 1952 v E, S, Ni, R of UK; 1953 v S, E, Ni, F, Y; 1954 v E, S, Ni; 1955 v S, E, Y; 1956 v E, Ni, S, A (33)
Peake, E. (Aberystwyth), 1908 v Ni; (with Liverpool), 1909 v Ni, S, E; 1910 v S, Ni; 1911 v Ni; 1912 v E; 1913 v E, Ni; 1914 v Ni (11)
Peers, E. J. (Wolverhampton W), 1914 v Ni, S, E; 1920 v E, S; 1921 v S, Ni, E; (with Port Vale), 1922 v E, S, Ni; 1923 v E (12)
Pembridge, M. A. (Luton T), 1992 v Br, Ei, R, Ho (with Derby Co), J (sub); 1993 v Bel (sub), Ei; 1994 v N (sub); 1995 v Alb (sub), Mol, Ge (sub); (with Sheffield W), 1996 v Mol, G, Alb, Sw, Sm; 1997 v Sm, Ho (2), T, Ei, Bel, S; 1998 v Bel, Br, Jam, Ma, Tun; (with Benfica), 1999 v D (sub), Bl, Sw, I (sub), D (sub); (with Everton), 2000 v Bl, Q, Fi; 2001 v Arm, Pol, Uk; 2002 v Bl, Arg, G; 2003 v Cro, Fi, I, Bos, Az, US; 2004 v Ser; (with Fulham), I, Fi; 2005 v La, Az, E (54)
Perry, E. (Doncaster R), 1938 v E, S, Ni (3)
Perry, J. (Cardiff C), 1994 v N (1)
Phennah, E. (Civil Service), 1878 v S (1)
Phillips, C. (Wolverhampton W), 1931 v Ni; 1932 v E; 1933 v S; 1934 v E, S, Ni; 1935 v E, S, Ni; 1936 v S; (with Aston Villa), 1936 v E, Ni; 1938 v S (13)
Phillips, D. (Plymouth Arg), 1984 v E, Ni, N; (with Manchester C), 1985 v Sp, Ic, S, Sp, N; 1986 v S, H, S.Ar, Ei, U; (with Coventry C), 1987 v Fi, Cz; 1988 v D (2), Cz, Y, Se; 1989 v Se, WG; (with Norwich C), 1990 v Fi, Ho, WG, Ei, Se; 1991 v D, Bel, Ic, Pol, G; 1992 v L, Ei, A, R, Ho (sub), Arg, J; 1993 v Fa, Cy, Bel, Ei, Bel (sub), RCS, Fa; (with Nottingham F), 1994 v RCS, Cy, R, N, Se, Es; 1995 v Alb, Mol, Ge, Bul (2), G, Ge; 1996 v Mol (sub), Alb, I (62)
Phillips, L. (Cardiff C), 1971 v Cz, S, E, Ni; 1972 v Cz, R, S, Ni; 1973 v E; 1974 v Pol (sub), Ni; 1975 v A; (with Aston Villa), H (2), L (2), S, E, Ni; 1976 v A, E, Y (2), E, Ni; 1977 v WG, S (2), Cz, E; 1978 v K (2), S, Cz, WG, E, S; 1979 v Ma; (with Swansea C), T, WG, S, E, Ni, Ma; 1980 v Ei, WG, T, S (sub), Ni, Ic; 1981 v T, Cz, T, S, E, USSR; (with Charlton Ath), 1982 v Cz, USSR (58)
Phillips, T. J. S. (Chelsea), 1973 v E; 1974 v E; 1975 v H (sub); 1978 v K (4)
Phoenix, H. (Wrexham), 1882 v S (1)
Pipe, D. R. (Coventry C), 2003 v US (sub) (1)
Poland, G. (Wrexham), 1939 v Ni, F (2)
Pontin, K. (Cardiff C), 1980 v E (sub), S (2)
Powell, A. (Leeds U), 1947 v E, S; 1948 v E, S, Ni; (with Everton), 1949 v E; 1950 v Bel; (with Birmingham C), 1951 v S (8)
Powell, D. (Wrexham), 1968 v WG; (with Sheffield U), 1969 v S, E, Ni, I, WG; 1970 v E, S, Ni, EG; 1971 v R (11)
Powell, I. V. (QPR), 1947 v E; 1948 v E, S, Ni; (with Aston Villa), 1949 v Bel; 1950 v S, Bel; 1951 v S (8)
Powell, J. (Druids), 1878 v S; 1880 v E, S; 1882 v E, S, Ni; 1883 v E, S, Ni; (with Bolton W), 1884 v E; (with Newton Heath), 1887 v E, S; 1888 v E, S, Ni (15)
Powell, Seth (Oswestry), 1885 v S; 1886 v E, Ni; (with WBA), 1891 v E, S; 1892 v E, S (7)
Price, H. (Aston Villa), 1907 v S; (with Burton U), 1908 v Ni; (with Wrexham), 1909 v S, E, Ni (5)
Price, J. (Wrexham), 1877 v S; 1878 v S; 1879 v E; 1880 v E, S; 1881 v E, S; 1882 v S, E, Ni; 1883 v S, Ni (12)
Price, L. P. (Ipswich T), 2006 v Cy, Para (sub) (2)
Price, P. (Luton T), 1980 v E, S, Ni, Ic; 1981 v T, Cz, Ei, T, S, E, USSR; (with Tottenham H), 1982 v USSR, Sp, F; 1983 v N, Y, E, Bul, S, Ni; 1984 v N, R, Bul, Y, S (sub) (25)
Pring, K. D. (Rotherham U), 1966 v Ch, D; 1967 v Ni (3)
Pritchard, H. K. (Bristol C), 1985 v N (sub) (1)
Pryce-Jones, A. W. (Newtown), 1895 v E (1)
Pryce-Jones, W. E. (Cambridge University), 1887 v S; 1888 v S, E, Ni; 1890 v Ni (5)
Pugh, A. (Rhostyllen), 1889 v S (1)
Pugh, D. H. (Wrexham), 1896 v S, Ni; 1897 v S, Ni; (with Lincoln C), 1900 v S; 1901 v S, E (7)
Pugsley, J. (Charlton Ath), 1930 v Ni (1)
Pullen, W. J. (Plymouth Arg), 1926 v E (1)

Rankmore, F. E. J. (Peterborough), 1966 v Ch (sub) (1)

Ratcliffe, K. (Everton), 1981 v Cz, Ei, T, S, E, USSR; 1982 v Cz, Ic, USSR, Sp, E; 1983 v Y, E, Bul, S, Ni, Br; 1984 v N, R, Bul, Y, S, E, Ni, N, Is; 1985 v Ic, Sp, Ic, N, S, Sp; 1986 v S, H, S.Ar, U; 1987 v Fi (2), USSR, Cz; 1988 v D (2), Cz; 1989 v Fi, Is, Se, WG; 1990 v Fi; 1991 v D, Bel (2), L, Ei, Ic, Pol, G; 1992 v Br, G; (with Cardiff C), 1993 v Bel (59)
Rea, J. C. (Aberystwyth), 1894 v Ni, S, E; 1895 v S; 1896 v S, Ni; 1897 v S, Ni; 1898 v Ni (9)
Ready, K. (QPR), 1997 v Ei; 1998 v Bel, Br, Ma, Tun (5)
Reece, G. I. (Sheffield U), 1966 v E, S, Ni, USSR; 1967 v S; 1970 v R of UK (sub), I (sub); 1971 v S, E, Ni, Fi; 1972 v Fi, R, E (sub), S, Ni; (with Cardiff C), 1973 v E (sub), Ni; 1974 v Pol (sub), E, S, Ni; 1975 v A, H (2), L (2), S, Ni (29)
Reed, W. G. (Ipswich T), 1955 v S, Y (2)
Rees, A. (Birmingham C), 1984 v N (sub) (1)
Rees, J. M. (Luton T), 1992 v A (sub) (1)
Rees, R. R. (Coventry C), 1965 v S, E, Ni, D, Gr (2), I, USSR; 1966 v E, S, Ni, USSR, D, Br (2), Ch; 1967 v E, Ni; 1968 v E, S, Ni; (with WBA), WG; 1969 v I; (with Nottingham F), 1969 v WG, EG, S (sub); 1970 v R of UK, E, S, Ni, EG, I; 1971 v Cz, R, E (sub), Ni (sub), Fi; 1972 v Cz (sub), R (39)
Rees, W. (Cardiff C), 1949 v Ni, Bel, Sw; (with Tottenham H), 1950 v Ni (4)
Richards, A. (Barnsley), 1932 v S (1)
Richards, D. (Wolverhampton W), 1931 v Ni; 1933 v E, S, Ni; 1934 v E, S, Ni; 1935 v E, S, Ni; 1936 v S; (with Brentford), 1936 v E, Ni; 1937 v S, E; (with Birmingham), Ni; 1938 v E, S, Ni; 1939 v E, S (21)
Richards, G. (Druids), 1899 v E, S, Ni; (with Oswestry), 1903 v Ni; (with Shrewsbury), 1904 v S; 1905 v Ni (6)
Richards, R. W. (Wolverhampton W), 1920 v E, S; 1921 v Ni; 1922 v E, S; (with West Ham U), 1924 v E, S, Ni; (with Mold), 1926 v S (9)
Richards, S. V. (Cardiff C), 1947 v E (1)
Richards, W. E. (Fulham), 1933 v Ni (1)
Ricketts, S. (Swansea C), 2005 v H, A (2); 2006 v Slv, E, Pol, Ni, Az (sub), Cy, Para (10)
Roach, J. (Oswestry), 1885 v Ni (1)
Robbins, W. W. (Cardiff C), 1931 v E, S; 1932 v Ni, E, S; (with WBA), 1933 v F, E, S, Ni; 1934 v S; 1936 v S (11)
Roberts, A. M. (QPR), 1993 v Ei (sub); 1997 v Sm (sub) (2)
Roberts, D. F. (Oxford U), 1973 v Pol, E (sub), Ni; 1974 v E, S; 1975 v A; (with Hull C), L, Ni; 1976 v S, Ni, Y; 1977 v E (sub), Ni; 1978 v K (1+1 sub), S, Ni (17)
Roberts, G. W. (Tranmere R), 2000 v Fi (sub), Br, P; 2001 v Bl; 2004 v H (sub), N (sub); 2005 v La (sub), H (sub); 2006 v Slv (sub) (9)
Roberts, I. W. (Watford), 1990 v Ho; (with Huddersfield T), 1992 v A, Arg, J; (with Leicester C), 1994 v Se; 1995 v Alb (sub), Mol; (with Norwich C), 2000 v Fi (sub), Br, P; 2001 v Bl, N (sub), Arm (sub); 2002 v Arm, Bl (sub) (15)
Roberts, Jas (Wrexham), 1913 v S, Ni (2)
Roberts, J. (Corwen), 1879 v S; 1880 v E, S; 1882 v E, S, Ni; (with Berwyn R), 1883 v E (7)
Roberts, J. (Ruthin), 1881 v S; 1882 v S (2)
Roberts, J. (Bradford C), 1906 v Ni; 1907 v Ni (2)
Roberts, J. G. (Arsenal), 1971 v S, E, Ni, Fi; 1972 v Fi, E, Ni; (with Birmingham C), 1973 v E (2), Pol, S, Ni; 1974 v Pol, E, S, Ni; 1975 v A, H, S, E; 1976 v E, S (22)
Roberts, J. H. (Bolton), 1949 v Bel (1)
Roberts, N. W. (Wrexham), 2000 v Sw (sub); (with Wigan Ath), 2003 v Az (sub), US (sub); 2004 v N (sub) (4)
Roberts, P. S. (Portsmouth), 1974 v E; 1975 v A, H, L (4)
Roberts, R. (Druids), 1884 v S; (with Bolton W), 1887 v S; 1888 v S, E; 1889 v S, E; 1890 v S; 1892 v Ni; (with Preston NE), S (9)
Roberts, R. (Wrexham), 1886 v Ni; 1887 v Ni; 1891 v Ni (3)
Roberts, R. (Rhos), 1891 v Ni; (with Crewe Alex), 1893 v E (2)
Roberts, R. L. (Chester), 1890 v Ni (1)
Roberts, S. W. (Wrexham), 2005 v H (sub) (1)
Roberts, W. (Llangollen), 1879 v E, S; 1880 v E, S; (with Berwyn R), 1881 v S; 1883 v S (6)
Roberts, W. (Rhyl), 1883 v E (1)
Roberts, W. (Wrexham), 1886 v E, S, Ni; 1887 v Ni (4)
Roberts, W. H. (Ruthin), 1882 v E, S; 1883 v E, S, Ni; (with Rhyl), 1884 v S (6)
Robinson, C. P. (Wolverhampton W), 2000 v Bl (sub), P (sub); 2001 v Arm (sub), Uk; 2002 v Arm, N, Bl (sub), Arg (sub); (with Portsmouth), 2003 v Cro, Az (1+sub), US (sub); 2004 v Ser, S (sub), H, N, Ca; (with Sunderland), 2005 v La (sub), E (sub), H, A (2); 2006 v Slv, E, Ni, Az, Cy; (with Norwich C), Para (sub), Tr (29)
Robinson, J. R. C. (Charlton Ath), 1996 v Alb (sub), Sw, Sm; 1997 v Sm, Ho (1 + sub), Ei, S; 1998 v Bel, Br; 1999 v I, D (sub), Bl, Sw, I, D; 2000 v Bl, Sw, Q, Fi, Br, P; 2001 v Bl, N, Pol, Arm; 2002 v N (sub), Bl, Arg (sub), CzR (30)
Rodrigues, P. J. (Cardiff C), 1965 v Ni, Gr (2); 1966 v USSR, E, S, D; (with Leicester C), Ni, Br (2), Ch; 1967 v S; 1968 v E, S, Ni; 1969 v E, Ni, EG; 1970 v R of UK, E, S, Ni, EG; (with Sheffield W), 1971 v R, E, S, Cz, Ni; 1972 v Fi, Cz, R, E, Ni (sub); 1973 v E (3), Pol, S, Ni; 1974 v Pol (40)
Rogers, J. P. (Wrexham), 1896 v E, S, Ni (3)
Rogers, W. (Wrexham), 1931 v E, S (2)
Roose, L. R. (Aberystwyth), 1900 v Ni; (with London Welsh), 1901 v E, S, Ni; (with Stoke C), 1902 v E, S; 1904 v E; (with Everton), 1905 v S, E; (with Stoke C), 1906 v E, S, Ni; 1907 v E, S, Ni; (with Sunderland), 1908 v E, S; 1909 v E, S, Ni; 1910 v E, S, Ni; 1911 v S (24)
Rouse, R. V. (C Palace), 1959 v Ni (1)
Rowlands, A. C. (Tranmere R), 1914 v E (1)
Rowley, T. (Tranmere R), 1959 v Ni (1)
Rush, I. (Liverpool), 1980 v S (sub), Ni; 1981 v E (sub); 1982 v Ic (sub), USSR, E, S, Ni, F; 1983 v N, Y, E, Bul; 1984 v N, R, Bul, Y, S, E, Ni; 1985 v Ic, N, S, Sp; 1986 v S, S.Ar, Ei, U; 1987 v Fi (2), USSR, Cz; (with Juventus), 1988 v D, Cz, Y, Se, Ma, I; (with Liverpool), 1989 v Ho, Fi, Se, WG; 1990 v Fi, Ei; 1991 v D, Bel (2), L, Ei, Pol, G; 1992 v G, L, R; 1993 v Fa, Cy, Bel (2), RCS, Fa; 1994 v RCS, Cy, R, N, Se, Es; 1995 v Alb, Ge, Bul, G, Ge; 1996 v Mol, I (73)
Russell, M. R. (Merthyr T), 1912 v S, Ni; 1914 v E; (with Plymouth Arg), 1920 v E, S, Ni; 1921 v E, S, Ni; 1922 v E, Ni; 1923 v E, S, Ni; 1924 v E, S, Ni; 1925 v E, S; 1926 v E, S; 1928 v S; 1929 v E (23)

Sabine, H. W. (Oswestry), 1887 v Ni (1)
Saunders, D. (Brighton & HA), 1986 v Ei (sub), Ca (2); 1987 v Fi, USSR (sub); (with Oxford U), 1988 v Y, Se, Ma, I (sub); 1989 v Ho (sub), Fi; (with Derby Co), Is, Se, WG; 1990 v Fi, Ho, WG, Se, Cr; 1991 v D, Bel (2), L, Ei, Ic, Pol, G; (with Liverpool), 1992 v Br, G, Ei, R, Ho, Arg, J; 1993 v Fa; (with Aston Villa), Cy, Bel (2), RCS, Fa; 1994 v RCS, Cy, R, N (sub); 1995 v Ge, Bul (2), G, Ge; (with Galatasaray), 1996 v G, Alb, Sm; (with Nottingham F), 1997 v Sm, Ho (2), T, Bel, S; 1998 v T, Bel, Br; (with Sheffield U), Ma, Tun; 1999 v I (sub), D, Bl; (with Benfica) Sw, I, D; (with Bradford C), 2000 v Bl, Sw, Fi (sub), Br; 2001 v Arm, Uk (sub) (75)
Savage, R. W. (Crewe Alex), 1996 v Alb (sub), Sw (sub), Sm (sub); 1997 v Ei (sub), S; (with Leicester C), 1998 v T, Bel, Jam, Tun; 1999 v I (sub), D, Bl, Sw; 2000 v Sw, Fi, Br; 2001 v Bl, N, Pol (2); 2002 v Arm, N, Arg, CzR, G; (with Birmingham C), 2003 v Fi, I, Bos, Az; 2004 v Ser, I, Ru (2), S, H; 2005 v La, Az, Ni, Pol (39)
Savin, G. (Oswestry), 1878 v S (1)
Sayer, P. (Cardiff C), 1977 v Cz, S, E, Ni; 1978 v K (2), S (7)
Scrine, F. H. (Swansea T), 1950 v E, Ni (2)
Sear, C. R. (Manchester C), 1963 v E (1)
Shaw, E. G. (Oswestry), 1882 v Ni; 1884 v S, Ni (3)
Sherwood, A. T. (Cardiff C), 1947 v E, Ni; 1948 v S, Ni; 1949 v E, S, Ni, P, Sw; 1950 v E, S, Ni, Bel; 1951 v E, S, Ni, P, Sw; 1952 v E, S, Ni, R of UK; 1953 v S, E, Ni, F, Y; 1954 v E, S, Ni, A; 1955 v S, E, Y, Ni; 1956 v E, S, Ni, A; (with Newport Co), 1957 v E, S (41)
Shone, W. W. (Oswestry), 1879 v E (1)
Shortt, W. W. (Plymouth Arg), 1947 v Ni; 1950 v Ni, Bel; 1952 v E, S, Ni, R of UK; 1953 v S, E, Ni, F, Y (12)
Showers, D. (Cardiff C), 1975 v E (sub), Ni (2)
Sidlow, C. (Liverpool), 1947 v E, S; 1948 v E, S, Ni; 1949 v S; 1950 v E (7)
Sisson, H. (Wrexham Olympic), 1885 v Ni; 1886 v S, Ni (3)
Slatter, N. (Bristol R), 1983 v S; 1984 v N (sub), Is; 1985 v Ic, Sp, Ic, N, S, Sp, N; (with Oxford U), 1986 v H (sub), S.Ar, Ca (2); 1987 v Fi (sub), Cz; 1988 v D (2), Cz, Ma, I; 1989 v Is (sub) (22)
Smallman, D. P. (Wrexham), 1974 v E (sub), S (sub), Ni; (with Everton), 1975 v H (sub), E, Ni (sub); 1976 v A (7)
Southall, N. (Everton), 1982 v Ni; 1983 v N, E, Bul, S, Ni, Br; 1984 v N, R, Bul, Y, S, E, Ni, N, Is; 1985 v Ic, Sp, Ic, N, S, Sp, N; 1986 v S, H, S.Ar, Ei; 1987 v USSR, Fi, Cz; 1988 v D, Cz, Y, Se; 1989 v Ho, Fi, Se, WG; 1990 v Fi, Ho, WG, Ei, Se, Cr; 1991 v D, Bel (2), L, Ei, Ic, Pol, G; 1992 v Br, G, L, Ei, A, R, Ho, Arg, J; 1993 v Fa, Cy, Bel, Ei, Bel, RCS, Fa; 1994 v RCS, Cy, R, N, Se, Es; 1995 v Alb, Mol, Ge, Bul (2), G, Ge; 1996 v Mol, G, Alb, I, Sm; 1997 v Sm, Ho (2), T, Bel; 1998 v T (92)
Speed, G. A. (Leeds U), 1990 v Cr (sub); 1991 v D, L (sub), Ei (sub), Ic, G (sub); 1992 v Br, G (sub), L, Ei, R, Ho,Arg,J; 1993 v Fa, Cy, Bel, Ei, Bel, Fa (sub); 1994 v RCS (sub), Cy, R, N, Se; 1995 v Alb, Mol, Ge, Bul (2), G; 1996 v Mol, G, I, Sw (sub); (with Everton), 1997 v Sm (sub), Ho (2), T, Ei, Bel, S; 1998 v T, Br; (with Newcastle U), Jam, Ma, Tun; 1999 v I, D, Sw, I, D; 2000 v Bl, Sw, Q, Fi, Br, P; 2001 v Bl, N, Pol, Arm, Uk, Pol, Uk; 2002 v Bl,

Arg, G; 2003 v Fi, I, Az, Bos, Az; 2004 v Ser, I, Fi, Ser, Ru (2), S; (with Bolton W), 2005 v La, Az, Ni, E, Pol (85)
Sprake, G. (Leeds U), 1964 v S, Ni; 1965 v S, D, Gr; 1966 v E, Ni, USSR; 1967 v S; 1968 v E, S; 1969 v S, E, Ni, WG; 1970 v R of UK, EG, I; 1971 v R, S, E, Ni; 1972 v Fi, E, S, Ni; 1973 v E (2), Pol, S, Ni; 1974 v Pol; (with Birmingham C), S, Ni; 1975 v A, H, L (37)
Stansfield, F. (Cardiff C), 1949 v S (1)
Stevenson, B. (Leeds U), 1978 v Ni; 1979 v Ma, T, S, E, Ni, Ma; 1980 v WG, T, Ic (sub); 1982 v Cz; (with Birmingham C), Sp, S, Ni, F (15)
Stevenson, N. (Swansea C), 1982 v E, S, Ni; 1983 v N (4)
Stitfall, R. F. (Cardiff C), 1953 v E; 1957 v Cz (2)
Sullivan, D. (Cardiff C), 1953 v Ni, F, Y; 1954 v Ni; 1955 v E, Ni; 1957 v E, S; 1958 v Ni, H (2), Se, Br; 1959 v S, Ni; 1960 v E, S (17)
Symons, C. J. (Portsmouth), 1992 v Ei, Ho, Arg, J; 1993 v Fa, Cy, Bel, Ei, RCS, Fa; 1994 v RCS, Cy, R; 1995 v Mol, Ge (sub), Bul, G, Ge; (with Manchester C), 1996 v Mol, G, I, Sw; 1997 v Ho (2), Ei, Bel, S; (with Fulham), 1999 v I, D, Bl, Sw; 2000 v Q (sub); 2001 v Pol; 2002 v Arm, N, Bl; (with C Palace), 2004 v S (sub) (37)

Tapscott, D. R. (Arsenal), 1954 v A; 1955 v S, E, Ni, Y; 1956 v E, Ni, S, A; 1957 v Ni, Cz, EG; (with Cardiff C), 1959 v E, Ni (14)
Taylor, G. K. (C Palace), 1996 v Alb, I (sub); (with Sheffield U), Sw; 1997 v Sm (sub), Ho (sub), Ei (sub); 1998 v Bel (sub), Jam; (with Burnley), 2002 v CzR (sub); 2003 v Cro (sub), Bos (sub), US; (with Nottingham F), 2004 v S (sub), H; 2005 v La (sub) (15)
Taylor, J. (Wrexham), 1898 v E (1)
Taylor, O. D. S. (Newtown), 1893 v S, Ni; 1894 v S, Ni (4)
Thatcher, B. D. (Leicester C), 2004 v H, N, Ca; (with Manchester C), 2005 v La, Ni, E, Pol (7)
Thomas, C. (Druids), 1899 v Ni; 1900 v S (2)
Thomas, D. A. (Swansea T), 1957 v Cz; 1958 v EG (2)
Thomas, D. S. (Fulham), 1948 v E, S, Ni; 1949 v S (4)
Thomas, E. (Cardiff Corinthians), 1925 v E (1)
Thomas, G. (Wrexham), 1885 v E, S (2)
Thomas, H. (Manchester U), 1927 v E (1)
Thomas, M. (Wrexham), 1977 v WG, S (1+1 sub), Ni (sub); 1978 v K (sub), S, Cz, Ir, E, Ni (sub); 1979 v Ma; (with Manchester U), T, WG, Ma (sub); 1980 v Ei, WG (sub), T, E, S, Ni; 1981 v Cz, S, E, USSR; (with Everton), 1982 v Cz; (with Brighton & HA), USSR (sub), Sp, E, S (sub), Ni (sub); 1983 (with Stoke C), v N, Y, E, Bul, S, Ni, Br; 1984 v R, Bul, Y; (with Chelsea), S, E; 1985 v Ic, Sp, Ic, S, Sp, N; 1986 v S; (with WBA), H, S.Ar (sub) (51)
Thomas, M. R. (Newcastle U), 1987 v Fi (1)
Thomas, R. J. (Swindon T), 1967 v Ni; 1968 v WG; 1969 v E, Ni, I, WG; 1970 v R of UK, E, S, Ni, EG, I; 1971 v S, E, Ni, R, Cz; 1972 v Fi, Cz, R, E, S, Ni; 1973 v E (3), Pol, S, Ni; 1974 v Pol; (with Derby Co), E, S, Ni; 1975 v H (2), L (2), S, E, Ni; 1976 v A, Y, E; 1977 v Cz, S, E, Ni; 1978 v K, S; (with Cardiff C), Cz (50)
Thomas, T. (Bangor), 1898 v S, Ni (2)
Thomas, W. R. (Newport Co), 1931 v E, S (2)
Thomson, D. (Druids), 1876 v S (1)
Thomson, G. F. (Druids), 1876 v S; 1877 v S (2)
Toshack, J. B. (Cardiff C), 1969 v S, E, Ni, WG, EG; 1970 v R of UK, EG, I; (with Liverpool), 1971 v S, E, Ni, Fi; 1972 v Fi, E; 1973 v E (3), Pol, S; 1975 v A, H (2), L (2), S, E; 1976 v Y (2), E; 1977 v S; 1978 v K (2), S, Cz; (with Swansea C), 1979 v WG (sub), S, E, Ni, Ma; 1980 v WG (40)
Townsend, W. (Newtown), 1887 v Ni; 1893 v Ni (2)
Trainer, H. (Wrexham), 1895 v E, S, Ni (3)
Trainer, J. (Bolton W), 1887 v S; (with Preston NE), 1888 v S; 1889 v E; 1890 v S; 1891 v S; 1892 v Ni, S; 1893 v E; 1894 v Ni, E; 1895 v Ni, E; 1896 v S; 1897 v Ni, S, E; 1898 v S, E; 1899 v Ni, S (20)
Trollope, P. J. (Derby Co), 1997 v S; 1998 v Br (sub); (with Fulham), Jam (sub), Ma, Tun; (with Coventry C), 2002 v CzR (sub); (with Northampton T), 2003 v Cro (sub), Az (sub+sub) (9)
Turner, H. G. (Charlton Ath), 1937 v E, S, Ni; 1938 v E, S, Ni; 1939 v Ni, F (8)
Turner, J. (Wrexham), 1892 v E (1)
Turner, R. E. (Wrexham), 1891 v E, Ni (2)
Turner, W. H. (Wrexham), 1887 v E, Ni; 1890 v S; 1891 v E, S (5)

Van Den Hauwe, P. W. R. (Everton), 1985 v Sp; 1986 v S, H; 1987 v USSR, Fi, Cz; 1988 v D (2), Cz, Y, I; 1989 v Fi, Se (13)
Vaughan, D. O. (Crewe Alex), 2003 v US; 2004 v H; 2006 v Slv, Ni (sub), Az, Cy, Tr (7)
Vaughan, Jas (Druids), 1893 v E, S, Ni; 1899 v E (4)
Vaughan, John (Oswestry), 1879 v S; (with Druids), 1880 v S; 1881 v E, S; 1882 v E, S, Ni; 1883 v E, S, Ni; (with Bolton W), 1884 v E (11)
Vaughan, J. O. (Rhyl), 1885 v Ni; 1886 v Ni, E, S (4)
Vaughan, N. (Newport Co), 1983 v Y (sub), Br; 1984 v N; (with Cardiff C), R, Bul, Y, Ni (sub), N, Is; 1985 v Sp (sub) (10)
Vaughan, T. (Rhyl), 1885 v E (1)
Vearncombe, G. (Cardiff C), 1958 v EG; 1961 v Ei (2)
Vernon, T. R. (Blackburn R), 1957 v Ni, Cz (2), EG; 1958 v E, S, EG, Se; 1959 v S; (with Everton), 1960 v Ni; 1961 v S, E, Ei; 1962 v Ni, Br (2), M; 1963 v S, E, H; 1964 v E, S; (with Stoke C), 1965 v Ni, Gr, I; 1966 v E, S, Ni, USSR, D; 1967 v Ni; 1968 v E (32)
Villars, A. K. (Cardiff C), 1974 v E, S, Ni (sub) (3)
Vizard, E. T. (Bolton W), 1911 v E, S, Ni; 1912 v E, S; 1913 v S; 1914 v E, Ni; 1920 v E; 1921 v E, S, Ni; 1922 v E, S; 1923 v E, Ni; 1924 v E, S, Ni; 1926 v E, S; 1927 v S (22)

Walley, J. T. (Watford), 1971 v Cz (1)
Walsh, I. (C Palace), 1980 v Ei, T, E, S, Ic; 1981 v T, Cz, Ei, T, S, E, USSR; 1982 v Cz (sub), Ic; (with Swansea C), Sp, S (sub), Ni (sub), F (18)
Ward, D. (Bristol R), 1959 v E; (with Cardiff C), 1962 v E (2)
Ward, D. (Notts Co), 2000 v P; (with Nottingham F), 2002 v CzR; 2003 v Bos, US (sub); 2004 v S (sub) (5)
Warner, J. (Swansea T), 1937 v E; (with Manchester U), 1939 v F (2)
Warren, F. W. (Cardiff C), 1929 v Ni; (with Middlesbrough), 1931 v Ni; 1933 v F, E; (with Hearts), 1937 v Ni; 1938 v Ni (6)
Watkins, A. E. (Leicester Fosse), 1898 v E, S; (with Aston Villa), 1900 v E, S; (with Millwall), 1904 v Ni (5)
Watkins, W. M. (Stoke C), 1902 v E; 1903 v E, S; (with Aston Villa); 1904 v E, S, Ni; (with Sunderland), 1905 v E, S, Ni; (with Stoke C), 1908 v Ni (10)
Webster, C. (Manchester U), 1957 v Cz; 1958 v H, M, Br (4)
Weston, R. D. (Arsenal), 2000 v P (sub); (with Cardiff C), 2003 v Cro (sub), Az (sub), Bos; 2004 v Fi, Ser; 2005 v H (sub) (7)
Whatley, W. J. (Tottenham H), 1939 v E, S (2)
White, P. F. (London Welsh), 1896 v Ni (1)
Wilcock, A. R. (Oswestry), 1890 v Ni (1)
Wilding, J. (Wrexham Olympians), 1885 v E, S, Ni; 1886 v E, Ni; (with Bootle), 1887 v E; 1888 v S, Ni; (with Wrexham), 1892 v S (9)
Williams, A. (Reading), 1994 v Es; 1995 v Alb, Mol, G (sub), Ge; 1996 v Mol, I; (with Wolverhampton W), 1998 v Br (sub), Jam; 1999 v I, D, I; (with Reading), 2003 v US (13)
Williams, A. L. (Wrexham), 1931 v E (1)
Williams, A. P. (Southampton), 1998 v Br (sub), Ma (2)
Williams, B. (Bristol C), 1930 v Ni (1)
Williams, B. D. (Swansea T), 1928 v Ni, E; 1930 v E, S; (with Everton), 1931 v Ni; 1932 v E; 1933 v E, S, Ni; 1935 v Ni (10)
Williams, D. G. (Derby Co), 1988 v Cz, Y, Se, Ma, I; 1989 v Ho, Is, Se, WG; 1990 v Fi, Ho; (with Ipswich T), 1993 v Ei; 1996 v G (sub) (13)
Williams, D. M. (Norwich C), 1986 v S.Ar (sub), U, Ca (2); 1987 v Fi (5)
Williams, D. R. (Merthyr T), 1921 v E, S; (with Sheffield W), 1923 v S; 1926 v S; 1927 v E, Ni; (with Manchester U), 1929 v E, S (8)
Williams, E. (Crewe Alex), 1893 v E, S (2)
Williams, E. (Druids), 1901 v E, Ni, S; 1902 v E, Ni (5)
Williams, G. (Chirk), 1893 v S; 1894 v S; 1895 v E, S, Ni; 1898 v Ni (6)
Williams, G. E. (WBA), 1960 v Ni; 1961 v S, E, Ei; 1963 v Ni, H; 1964 v E, S, Ni; 1965 v S, E, Ni, D, Gr (2), USSR, I; 1966 v Ni, Br (2), Ch; 1967 v S, E, Ni; 1968 v Ni; 1969 v I (26)
Williams, G. G. (Swansea T), 1961 v Ni, H, Sp (2); 1962 v E (5)
Williams, G. J. (Ipswich T), 2006 v Slv (sub), Cy (sub) (2)
Williams, G. J. J. (Cardiff C), 1951 v Sw (1)
Williams, G. O. (Wrexham), 1907 v Ni (1)
Williams, H. J. (Swansea), 1965 v Gr (2); 1972 v R (3)
Williams, H. T. (Newport Co), 1949 v Ni, Sw; (with Leeds U), 1950 v Ni; 1951 v S (4)
Williams, J. H. (Oswestry), 1884 v E (1)
Williams, J. J. (Wrexham), 1939 v F (1)
Williams, J. T. (Middlesbrough), 1925 v Ni (1)
Williams, J. W. (C Palace), 1912 v S, Ni (2)
Williams, R. (Newcastle U), 1935 v S, E (2)
Williams, R. P. (Caernarvon), 1886 v S (1)
Williams, S. G. (WBA), 1954 v A; 1955 v E, Ni; 1956 v E, S, A; 1958 v E, S, Ni, Is (2), H (2), M, Se, Br; 1959 v E, S, Ni;

1960 v E, S, Ni; 1961 v Ni, Ei, H, Sp (2); 1962 v E, S, Ni, Br (2), M; (with Southampton), 1963 v S, E, H (2); 1964 v E, S; 1965 v S, E, D; 1966 v D (43)
Williams, W. (Druids), 1876 v S; 1878 v S; (with Oswestry), 1879 v E, S; (with Druids), 1880 v E; 1881 v E, S; 1882 v E, S, Ni; 1883 v Ni (11)
Williams, W. (Northampton T), 1925 v S (1)
Witcomb, D. F. (WBA), 1947 v E, S; (with Sheffield W), 1947 v Ni (3)
Woosnam, A. P. (Leyton Orient), 1959 v S; (with West Ham U), E; 1960 v E, S, Ni; 1961 v S, E, Ni, Ei, Sp, H; 1962 v E, S, Ni, Br; (with Aston Villa), 1963 v Ni, H (17)
Woosnam, G. (Newtown Excelsior), 1879 v S (1)
Worthington, T. (Newtown), 1894 v S (1)
Wynn, G. A. (Wrexham), 1909 v E, S, Ni; (with Manchester C), 1910 v E; 1911 v Ni; 1912 v E, S; 1913 v E, S; 1914 v E, S (11)
Wynn, W. (Chirk), 1903 v Ni (1)

Yorath, T. C. (Leeds U), 1970 v I; 1971 v S, E, Ni; 1972 v Cz, E, S, Ni; 1973 v E, Pol, S; 1974 v Pol, E, S, Ni; 1975 v A, H (2), L (2), S; 1976 v A, E, S, Y (2), E, Ni; (with Coventry C), 1977 v WG, S (2), Cz, E, Ni; 1978 v K (2), S, Cz, WG, Ir, E, S, Ni; 1979 v T, WG, S, E, Ni; (with Tottenham H), 1980 v Ei, T, E, S, Ni, Ic; 1981 v T, Cz; (with Vancouver W), Ei, T, USSR (59)
Young, E. (Wimbledon), 1990 v Cr; (with C Palace), 1991 v D, Bel (2), L, Ei; 1992 v G, L, Ei, A; 1993 v Fa, Cy, Bel, Ei, Bel, Fa; 1994 v RCS, Cy, R, N; (with Wolverhampton W), 1996 v Alb (21)

REPUBLIC OF IRELAND

Aherne, T. (Belfast C), 1946 v P, Sp; (with Luton T), 1950 v Fi, E, Fi, Se, Bel; 1951 v N, Arg, N; 1952 v WG (2), A, Sp; 1953 v F; 1954 v F (16)
Aldridge, J. W. (Oxford U), 1986 v W, U, Ic, Cz; 1987 v Bel, S, Pol; (with Liverpool), S, Bul, Bel, Br, L; 1988 v Bul, Pol, N, E, USSR, Ho; 1989 v Ni, Tun, Sp, F (sub), H, Ma (sub), H; 1990 v WG; (with Real Sociedad), Ni, Ma, Fi (sub), T. E, Eg, Ho, R, I; 1991 v T, E (2), Pol; (with Tranmere R), 1992 v H (sub), T, W (sub), Sw (sub), US (sub), Alb, I, P (sub); 1993 v La, D, Sp, D, Alb, La, Li; 1994 v Li, Ni, CzR, I (sub), M (sub), N; 1995 v La, Ni, P, Lie; 1996 v La, P, Ho, Ru; 1997 v Mac (sub) (69)
Ambrose, P. (Shamrock R), 1955 v N, Ho; 1964 v Pol, N, E (5)
Anderson, J. (Preston NE), 1980 v Cz (sub), US (sub); 1982 v Ch, Br, Tr; (with Newcastle U), 1984 v Chn; 1986 v W, Ic, Cz; 1987 v Bul, Bel, Br, L; 1988 v R (sub), Y (sub); 1989 v Tun (16)
Andrews, P. (Bohemians), 1936 v Ho (1)
Arrigan, T. (Waterford), 1938 v N (1)

Babb, P. A. (Coventry C), 1994 v Ru, Ho, Bol, G, CzR (sub), I, M, N, Ho; (with Liverpool), 1995 v La, Lie, Ni (2), P, Lie, A; 1996 v La, P, Ho, CzR; 1997 v Ic; 1998 v Li (sub), R, Arg (sub), M; 1999 v Cro, Para (sub), Se (sub), Ni; 2000 v CzR (sub), S, M (sub), US, S.Af; (with Sunderland), 2003 v Ru (sub) (35)
Bailham, E. (Shamrock R), 1964 v E (1)
Barber, E. (Shelbourne), 1966 v Sp; (with Birmingham C), 1966 v Bel (2)
Barrett, G. (Arsenal), 2003 v Fi (sub); (with Coventry C), 2004 v Pol (sub), Ng (sub), Jam, Ho; 2005 v Cro (sub) (6)
Barry, P. (Fordsons), 1928 v Bel; 1929 v Bel (2)
Beglin, J. (Liverpool), 1984 v Chn; 1985 v M, D, I, Is, E, N, Sw; 1986 v Sw, USSR, D, W; 1987 v Bel (sub), S, Pol (15)
Bermingham, J. (Bohemians), 1929 v Bel (1)
Bermingham, P. (St James' Gate), 1935 v H (1)
Bonner, P. (Celtic), 1981 v Pol; 1982 v Alg; 1984 v Ma, Is, Chn; 1985 v I, Is, E, N; 1986 v U, Ic; 1987 v Bel (2), S (2), Pol, Bul, Br, L; 1988 v Bul, R, Y, N, E, USSR, Ho; 1989 v Sp, F, H, Sp, Ma, H; 1990 v WG, Ni, Ma, W, Fi, T, E, Eg, Ho, R, I; 1991 v Mor, T, E (2), W, Pol, US; 1992 v H, Pol, T, W, Sw, Alb, I; 1993 v La, D, Sp, W, Ni, D, Alb, La, Li; 1994 v Li, Sp, Ni, Ru, Ho, Bol, CzR, I, M, N, Ho; 1995 v Lie; 1996 v M, Bol (sub) (80)
Braddish, S. (Dundalk), 1978 v T (sub), Pol (2)
Bradshaw, P. (St James' Gate), 1939 v Sw, Pol, H (2), G (5)
Brady, F. (Fordsons), 1926 v I; 1927 v I (2)
Brady, T. R. (QPR), 1964 v A (2), Sp (2), Pol, N (6)
Brady, W. L. (Arsenal), 1975 v USSR, T, Sw, USSR, Sw, WG; 1976 v T, N, Pol; 1977 v E, T, F (2), Sp, Bul; 1978 v Bul, N; 1979 v Ni, E, D, Bul, WG; 1980 v W, Bul, E, Cy; (with Juventus), 1981 v Ho, Bel, F, Cy, Bel; 1982 v Ho, F, Ch, Br, Tr; (with Sampdoria), 1983 v Ho, Sp, Ic, Ma; 1984 v Ic, Ho, Ma, Pol, Is; (with Internazionale), 1985 v USSR, N, D, I, E, N, Sp, Sw; 1986 v Sw, USSR, D, W; (with Ascoli), 1987 v Bel, S (2), Pol; (with West Ham U), Bul, Bel, Br, L; 1988 v L, Bul; 1989 v F, H (sub), H (sub); 1990 v WG, Fi (72)
Branagan, K. G. (Bolton W), 1997 v W (1)
Breen, G. (Birmingham C), 1996 v P (sub), Cro, Ho, US, M, Bol (sub); 1997 v Lie, Mac, Ic; (with Coventry C), v Mac; 1998 v Li (sub), R, CzR, Arg, M; 1999 v Ma, Y, Para, Se, Mac; 2000 v Y, Cro, Ma, Mac, T (2), Gr, S, M, US, S.Af; 2001 v Ho, P, Es, Fi, Cy, And (2); 2002 v Cy, Ir (2), Ru (sub), US, Cam, G, S.Ar, Sp; (with West Ham U), 2003 v Fi, Ru, Sw, S, Ge, Alb, N, Alb, Ge; (with Sunderland), 2004 v Aus, Ru, T, Sw; 2005 v Bul (sub), Cro; 2006 v Ch (63)
Breen, T. (Manchester U), 1937 v Sw, F; (with Shamrock R), 1947 v E, Sp, P (5)
Brennan, F. (Drumcondra), 1965 v Bel (1)
Brennan, S. A. (Manchester U), 1965 v Sp; 1966 v Sp, A, Bel; 1967 v Sp, T, Sp; 1969 v Cz, D, H; 1970 v S, Cz, D, H, Pol (sub), WG; (with Waterford), 1971 v Pol, Se, I (19)
Brown, J. (Coventry C), 1937 v Sw, F (2)
Browne, W. (Bohemians), 1964 v A, Sp, E (3)
Buckley, L. (Shamrock R), 1984 v Pol (sub); (with Waregem), 1985 v M (2)
Burke, F. (Cork Ath), 1952 v WG (1)
Burke, J. (Shamrock R), 1929 v Bel (1)
Burke, J. (Cork), 1934 v Bel (1)
Butler, P. J. (Sunderland), 2000 v CzR (1)
Butler, T. (Sunderland), 2003 v Fi, Sw (sub) (2)
Byrne, A. B. (Southampton), 1970 v D, Pol, WG; 1971 v Pol, Se (2), I (2), A; 1973 v F, USSR (sub), F, N; 1974 v Pol (14)
Byrne, D. (Shelbourne), 1929 v Bel; (with Shamrock R), 1932 v Sp; (with Coleraine), 1934 v Bel (3)
Byrne, J. (Bray Unknowns), 1928 v Bel (1)
Byrne, J. (QPR), 1985 v I, Is (sub), E (sub), Sp (sub); 1987 v S (sub), Bel (sub), Br, L (sub); 1988 v L, Bul (sub), Is, R, Y (sub), Pol (sub); (with Le Havre), 1990 v WG (sub), W, Fi, T (sub), Ma; (with Brighton & HA), 1991 v W; (with Sunderland), 1992 v T, W; (with Millwall), 1993 v W (23)
Byrne, J. (Shelbourne), 2004 v Pol (sub); 2006 v Ch (sub) (2)
Byrne, P. (Dolphin), 1931 v Sp; (with Shelbourne), 1932 v Ho; (with Drumcondra), 1934 v Ho (3)
Byrne, P. (Shamrock R), 1984 v Pol, Chn; 1985 v M; 1986 v D (sub), W (sub), U (sub), Ic (sub), Cz (8)
Byrne, S. (Bohemians), 1931 v Sp (1)

Campbell, A. (Santander), 1985 v I (sub), Is, Sp (3)
Campbell, N. (St Patrick's Ath), 1971 v A (sub); (with Fortuna Cologne), 1972 v Ir, Ec, Ch, P; 1973 v USSR, F (sub); 1975 v WG; 1976 v N; 1977 v Sp, Bul (sub) (11)
Cannon, H. (Bohemians), 1926 v I; 1928 v Bel (2)
Cantwell, N. (West Ham U), 1954 v L; 1956 v Sp, Ho; 1957 v D, WG, E (2); 1958 v D, Pol, A; 1959 v Pol, Cz (2); 1960 v Se, Ch, Se; 1961 v N; (with Manchester U), S (2); 1962 v Cz (2), A; 1963 v Ic (2), S; 1964 v A, Sp, E; 1965 v Pol, Sp; 1966 v Sp (2), A, Bel; 1967 v Sp, T (36)
Carey, B. P. (Manchester U), 1992 v US (sub); 1993 v W; (with Leicester C), 1994 v Ru (3)
Carey, J. J. (Manchester U), 1938 v N, Cz, Pol; 1939 v Sw, Pol, H (2), G; 1946 v P, Sp; 1947 v E, Sp, P; 1948 v P, Sp; 1949 v Sw, Bel, P, Se, Sp; 1950 v Fi, E, Fi, Se; 1951 v N, Arg, N; 1953 v F, A (29)
Carolan, J. (Manchester U), 1960 v Se, Ch (2)
Carr, S. (Tottenham H), 1999 v Se, Ni, Mac; 2000 v Y (sub), Cro, Ma, T (2), S, M, US, S.Af; 2001 v Ho, P, Es, And (sub), P, Es; 2003 v S, Ge, Alb, N, Alb, Ge; 2004 v Aus, Ru, T (sub), Sw, Ca, Br; (with Newcastle U), 2005 v Bul (sub), Cy, Sw, F, Fa, Is, Fa; 2006 v I (sub), F, Cy, Sw (41)
Carroll, B. (Shelbourne), 1949 v Bel; 1950 v Fi (2)
Carroll, T. R. (Ipswich T), 1968 v Pol; 1969 v Pol, A, D; 1970 v Cz, Pol, WG; 1971 v Se; (with Birmingham C), 1972 v Ir, Ec, Ch, P; 1973 v USSR (2), Pol, F, N (17)
Carsley, L. K. (Derby Co), 1998 v R, Bel (1 + sub), CzR, Arg, M; 1999 v Cro (sub), Ma (sub), Para (sub); (with Blackburn R) Ni, Mac; 2000 v Y (sub), Cro, Ma, T; 2001 v Fi (sub); (with Coventry C), 2002 v Cro, Cy (sub), Ru (sub); (with Everton), S.Ar (sub); 2003 v Fi, Gr, S (sub), Ge, Alb, N (sub), Alb (sub), Ge; 2004 v Ru (29)
Cascarino, A. G. (Gillingham), 1986 v Sw, USSR, D; (with Millwall), 1988 v Pol, N (sub), USSR (sub), Ho (sub); 1989 v Ni, Tun, Sp, F, H, Sp, Ma, H; 1990 v WG (sub), Ni,

Ma; (with Aston Villa), W, Fi, T, E, Eg, Ho (sub), R (sub), I (sub); 1991 v Mor (sub),T(sub), E (2 sub), Pol (sub), Ch (sub), US; (with Celtic), 1992 v Pol, T; (with Chelsea), W, Sw, US (sub); 1993 v W, Ni (sub), D (sub), Alb (sub), La (sub); 1994 v Li (sub), Sp (sub), Ni (sub), Ru, Bol (sub), G, CzR, Ho (sub); (with Marseille), 1995 v La (sub), Ni (sub), P (sub), Lie (sub), A (sub); 1996 v A (sub), P (sub), Ho, Ru (sub), P, Cro (sub), Ho; 1997 v Lie (sub), Mac, Ic; (with Nancy), v W, Mac, R (sub), Lie (sub); 1998 v Li (sub), Ic (sub), Li, R, Bel (2); 1999 v Cro (sub), Ma (sub), Y (sub), Para (sub), Se (sub), Ni (sub), Mac (sub); 2000 v Y (sub), Cro, Mac (sub), T (1 + sub) (88)

Chandler, J. (Leeds U), 1980 v Cz (sub), US (2)

Chatton, H. A. (Shelbourne), 1931 v Sp; (with Dumbarton), 1932 v Sp; (with Cork), 1934 v Ho (3)

Clarke, C. R. (Stoke C), 2004 v Ng (sub), Jam (sub) (2)

Clarke, J. (Drogheda U), 1978 v Pol (sub) (1)

Clarke, K. (Drumcondra), 1948 v P, Sp (2)

Clarke, M. (Shamrock R), 1950 v Bel (1)

Clinton, T. J. (Everton), 1951 v N; 1954 v F, L (3)

Coad, P. (Shamrock R), 1947 v E, Sp, P; 1948 v P, Sp; 1949 v Sw, Bel, P, Se; 1951 v N (sub); 1952 v Sp (11)

Coffey, T. (Drumcondra), 1950 v Fi (1)

Colfer, M. D. (Shelbourne), 1950 v Bel; 1951 v N (2)

Colgan, N. (Hibernian), 2002 v D (sub); 2003 v S (sub), N (sub); 2004 v Aus, T, Ca (sub), Pol (sub), Ng (8)

Collins, F. (Jacobs), 1927 v I (1)

Conmy, O. M. (Peterborough U), 1965 v Bel; 1967 v Cz; 1968 v Cz, Pol; 1970 v Cz (5)

Connolly, D. J. (Watford), 1996 v P, Ho, US, M; 1997 v R, Lie; (with Feyenoord), 1998 v Li, Ic, Li, Bel (1 + sub), CzR, M; (with Wolverhampton W), 1999 v Y (sub), Para (sub), Se, Ni (sub), Mac (sub); (with Excelsior), 2000 v T (1 + sub), CzR (sub), Gr; 2001 v Ho (sub), Fi (sub), Cy, And; (with Feyenoord), And; (with Wimbledon), 2002 v Cro (sub), Cy, Ir, D (sub), US (sub), Ng (sub), Sp (sub); 2003 v S (sub), N, Alb; (with West Ham U), 2004 v Aus (sub), T, Sw; (with Wigan Ath), 2006 v Cy (sub) (41)

Connolly, H. (Cork), 1937 v G (1)

Connolly, J. (Fordsons), 1926 v I (1)

Conroy, G. A. (Stoke C), 1970 v Cz, D, H, Pol, WG; 1971 v Pol, Se (2), I; 1973 v USSR, F, USSR, N; 1974 v Pol, Br, U, Ch; 1975 v T, Sw, USSR, Sw, WG (sub); 1976 v T (sub), Pol; 1977 v E, T, Pol (27)

Conway, J. P. (Fulham), 1967 v Sp, T, Sp; 1968 v Cz; 1969 v A (sub), H; 1970 v S, Cz, D, H, Pol, WG; 1971 v I, A; 1974 v U, Ch; 1975 v WG (sub); 1976 v N, Pol; (with Manchester C), 1977 v Pol (20)

Corr, P. J. (Everton), 1949 v P, Sp; 1950 v E, Se (4)

Courtney, E. (Cork U), 1946 v P (1)

Coyle, O. C. (Bolton W), 1994 v Ho (sub) (1)

Coyne, T. (Celtic), 1992 v Sw, US, Alb (sub), US (sub), I (sub), P (sub); 1993 v W (sub), La (sub); (with Tranmere R), Ni; (with Motherwell), 1994 v Ru (sub), Ho, Bol, G (sub), CzR (sub), I, M, Ho; 1995 v Lie, Ni (sub), A; 1996 v Ru (sub); 1998 v Bel (sub) (22)

Crowe, G. (Bohemians), 2003 v Gr, N (sub) (2)

Cummins, G. P. (Luton T), 1954 v L (2); 1955 v N (2), WG; 1956 v Y, Sp; 1958 v D, Pol, A; 1959 v Pol, Cz (2); 1960 v Se, Ch, WG, Se; 1961 v S (2) (19)

Cuneen, T. (Limerick), 1951 v N (1)

Cunningham, K. (Wimbledon), 1996 v CzR, P, Cro, Ho (sub), US, Bol; 1997 v Ic (sub), W, R, Lie; 1998 v Li, Ic, Li, Bel (2), CzR; 1999 v Cro, Ma, Y, Para, Se, Ni, Mac; 2000 v Y, Cro, Ma, Mac, T (2), CzR, Gr; 2001 v Cy, And; 2002 v Ir (sub), Ru, D, US (sub), Ng, G (sub), Sp (sub); (with Birmingham C), 2003 v Fi, Ru, Sw, Gr, Ge, Alb (2), Ge; 2004 v Aus, Ru, Ca, Br, CzR, Pol, R, Ng, Ho; 2005 v Bul, Cy, Sw, F, Fa, Cro (sub), P, Is, Chn, Is, Fa; 2006 v I, F, Cy, Sw (72)

Curtis, D. P. (Shelbourne), 1957 v D, WG; (with Bristol C), 1957 v E (2); 1958 v D, Pol, A; (with Ipswich T), 1959 v Pol; 1960 v Se, Ch, WG, Se; 1961 v N, S; 1962 v A; 1963 v Ic; (with Exeter C), 1964 v A (17)

Cusack, S. (Limerick), 1953 v F (1)

Daish, L. S. (Cambridge U), 1992 v W, Sw (sub); (with Coventry C), 1996 v CzR (sub), Cro, M (5)

Daly, G. A. (Manchester U), 1973 v Pol (sub), N; 1974 v Br (sub), U (sub); 1975 v Sw (sub), WG; 1977 v E, T, F; (with Derby Co), F, Bul; 1978 v Bul, T, D; 1979 v Ni, E, D, Bul; 1980 v Ni, E, Cy, Sw, Arg; (with Coventry C), 1981 v WG 'B', Ho, Bel, Cy, W, Bel, Cz, Pol (sub); 1982 v Alg, Ch, Br, Tr; 1983 v Ho, Sp (sub); 1984 v Is (sub), Ma; (with Birmingham C), 1985 v M (sub), N, Sp, Sw; 1986 v Sw; (with Shrewsbury T), U, Ic (sub), Cz (sub); 1987 v S (sub) (48)

Daly, J. (Shamrock R), 1932 v Ho; 1935 v Sw (2)

Daly, M. (Wolverhampton W), 1978 v T, Pol (2)

Daly, P. (Shamrock R), 1950 v Fi (sub) (1)

Davis, T. L. (Oldham Ath), 1937 v G, H; (with Tranmere R), 1938 v Cz, Pol (4)

Deacy, E. (Aston Villa), 1982 v Alg (sub), Ch, Br, Tr (4)

Delap, R. J. (Derby Co), 1998 v CzR (sub), Arg (sub), M (sub); 2000 v T (2), Gr (sub); (with Southampton), 2002 v US; 2003 v Fi (sub), Gr (sub); 2004 v Ca (sub), CzR (sub) (11)

De Mange, K. J. P. P. (Liverpool), 1987 v Br (sub); (with Hull C), 1989 v Tun (sub) (2)

Dempsey, J. T. (Fulham), 1967 v Sp, Cz; 1968 v Cz, Pol; 1969 v Pol, A, D; (with Chelsea), 1969 v Cz, D; 1970 v H, WG; 1971 v Pol, Se (2), I; 1972 v Ir, Ec, Ch, P (19)

Dennehy, J. (Cork Hibernians), 1972 v Ec (sub), Ch; (with Nottingham F), 1973 v USSR (sub), Pol, F, N; 1974 v Pol (sub); 1975 v T (sub), WG (sub); (with Walsall), 1976 v Pol (sub); 1977 v Pol (sub) (11)

Desmond, P. (Middlesbrough), 1950 v Fi, E, Fi, Se (4)

Devine, J. (Arsenal), 1980 v Cz, Ni; 1981 v WG 'B', Cz; 1982 v Ho, Alg; 1983 v Sp, Ma; (with Norwich C), 1984 v Ic, Ho, Is; 1985 v USSR, N (13)

Doherty, G. M. T. (Luton T), 2000 v Gr (sub); (with Tottenham H), US, S.Af (sub); 2001 v Cy (sub), And (sub+1), P (sub), Es (sub); 2002 v US (sub); 2003 v Fi (sub), Ru (sub), Sw (sub), Gr, S, Ge, Alb (sub+sub), Ge; 2004 v Aus, Ru (sub), T, Ca, CzR, Pol, Ng, Jam; 2005 v Bul; (with Norwich C), Sw (sub), Fa (sub), Chn (sub), Is (sub), Fa (sub); 2006 v F (sub), Sw (sub) (34)

Donnelly, J. (Dundalk), 1935 v H, Sw, G; 1936 v Ho, Sw, H, L; 1937 v G, H; 1938 v N (10)

Donnelly, T. (Drumcondra), 1938 v N; (Shamrock R), 1939 v Sw (2)

Donovan, D. C. (Everton), 1955 v N, Ho, N, WG; 1957 v E (5)

Donovan, T. (Aston Villa), 1980 v Cz; 1981 v WG 'B'(sub) (2)

Douglas, J. (Blackburn R), 2004 v Pol (sub), Ng (sub) (2)

Dowdall, C. (Fordsons), 1928 v Bel; (with Barnsley), 1929 v Bel; (with Cork), 1931 v Sp (3)

Doyle, C. (Shelbourne), 1959 v Cz (1)

Doyle, D. (Shamrock R), 1926 v I (1)

Doyle, K. E. (Reading), 2006 v Se, Ch (2)

Doyle, L. (Dolphin), 1932 v Sp (1)

Doyle, M. P. (Coventry C), 2004 v Ho (sub) (1)

Duff, D. A. (Blackburn R), 1998 v CzR, M; 1999 v Cro, Ma, Y, Para, Se (sub), Ni, Mac; 2000 v Cro, Ma (sub), T (sub + sub), S (sub); 2001 v P (sub), Es (sub), Cy (sub), And, P (sub), Es; 2002 v Cro, Ho, Ru, D, US, Ng, Cam, G, S.Ar, Sp; 2003 v Fi, Ru, Sw, Ge, Alb, N, Alb; (with Chelsea), 2004 v Aus, Ru, T, Sw, Ca, CzR; 2005 v Bul, Cy, Sw, F, Fa, Cro, P, Is, Chn, Is, Fa; 2006 v I, F, Cy, Se, Ch (59)

Duffy, B. (Shamrock R), 1950 v Bel (1)

Duggan, H. A. (Leeds U), 1927 v I; 1930 v Bel; 1936 v H, L; (with Newport Co), 1938 v N (5)

Dunne, A. P. (Manchester U), 1962 v A; 1963 v Ic, S; 1964 v A, Sp, Pol, N, E; 1965 v Pol, Sp; 1966 v Sp (2), A, Bel; 1967 v Sp, T, Sp; 1969 v Pol, D, H; 1970 v H; 1971 v Se, I, A; (with Bolton W), 1974 v Br (sub), U, Ch; 1975 v T, Sw, USSR, Sw, WG; 1976 v T (33)

Dunne, J. (Sheffield U), 1930 v Bel; (with Arsenal), 1936 v Sw, H, L; (with Southampton), 1937 v Sw, F; (with Shamrock R), 1938 v N (2), Cz, Pol; 1939 v Sw, Pol, H (2), G (15)

Dunne, J. C. (Fulham), 1971 v A (1)

Dunne, L. (Manchester C), 1935 v Sw, G (2)

Dunne, P. A. J. (Manchester U), 1965 v Sp; 1966 v Sp (2), WG; 1967 v T (5)

Dunne, R. P. (Everton), 2000 v Gr, S (sub), M; 2001 v Ho, P, Es; (with Manchester C), Fi, And, P, Es; 2002 v Cro, Ho, Ru (sub), D (sub); 2003 v Gr, S (sub), N; 2004 v Aus (sub), T (sub), Ca; 2005 v Cro, P (sub), Chn; 2006 v I, F, Cy, Sw, Se, Ch (29)

Dunne, S. (Luton T), 1953 v F, A; 1954 v F, L; 1956 v Sp, Ho; 1957 v D, WG, E; 1958 v D, Pol, A; 1959 v Pol; 1960 v WG, Se (15)

Dunne, T. (St Patrick's Ath), 1956 v Ho; 1957 v D, WG (3)

Dunning, P. (Shelbourne), 1971 v Se, I (2)

Dunphy, E. M. (York C), 1966 v Sp; (with Millwall), 1966 v WG; 1967 v T, Sp, T, Cz; 1968 v Cz, Pol; 1969 v Pol, A, D (2), H; 1970 v D, H, Pol, WG (sub); 1971 v Pol, Se (2), I (2), A (23)

Dwyer, N. M. (West Ham U), 1960 v Se, Ch, WG, Se; (with Swansea T), 1961 v W, N, S (2); 1962 v Cz (2); 1964 v Pol (sub), N, E; 1965 v Pol (14)

Eccles, P. (Shamrock R), 1986 v U (sub) (1)

Egan, R. (Dundalk), 1929 v Bel (1)

Eglington, T. J. (Shamrock R), 1946 v P, Sp; (with Everton), 1947 v E, Sp, P; 1948 v P; 1949 v Sw, P, Se; 1951 v N, Arg; 1952 v WG (2), A, Sp; 1953 v F, A; 1954 v F, L, F; 1955 v N, Ho, WG; 1956 v Sp (24)
Elliott, S. W. (Sunderland), 2005 v Cro, Chn, Fa; 2006 v I (sub), Cy, Sw (sub), Se (7)
Ellis, P. (Bohemians), 1935 v Sw, G; 1936 v Ho, Sw, L; 1937 v G, H (7)
Evans, M. J. (Southampton), 1998 v R (sub) (1)

Fagan, E. (Shamrock R), 1973 v N (sub) (1)
Fagan, F. (Manchester C), 1955 v N; 1960 v Se; (with Derby Co), 1960 v Ch, WG, Se; 1961 v W, N, S (8)
Fagan, J. (Shamrock R), 1926 v I (1)
Fairclough, M. (Dundalk), 1982 v Ch (sub), Tr (sub) (2)
Fallon, S. (Celtic), 1951 v N; 1952 v WG (2), A, Sp; 1953 v F; 1955 v N, WG (8)
Fallon, W. J. (Notts Co), 1935 v H; 1936 v H; 1937 v H, Sw, F; 1939 v Sw, Pol; (with Sheffield W), 1939 v H, G (9)
Farquharson, T. G. (Cardiff C), 1929 v Bel; 1930 v Bel; 1931 v Sp; 1932 v Sp (4)
Farrell, P. (Hibernian), 1937 v Sw, F (2)
Farrell, P. D. (Shamrock R), 1946 v P, Sp; (with Everton), 1947 v Sp, P; 1948 v P, Sp; 1949 v Sw, P (sub), Sp; 1950 v E, Fi, Se; 1951 v Arg, N; 1952 v WG (2), A, Sp; 1953 v F, A; 1954 v F (2); 1955 v N, Ho, WG; 1956 v Y, Sp; 1957 v E (28)
Farrelly, G. (Aston Villa), 1996 v P, US, Bol; (with Everton), 1998 v CzR, M; (with Bolton W), 2000 v US (6)
Feenan, J. J. (Sunderland), 1937 v Sw, F (2)
Finnan, S. (Fulham), 2000 v Gr, S; 2001 v P (sub), Es (sub), Fi, And (sub+sub); 2002 v Cro (sub), Ho (sub), Cy, Ir (2), Ru, US, Ng, Cam (sub), G, S.Ar, Sp; 2003 v Ru, Gr, N (sub); (with Liverpool), 2004 v Aus, T, Sw (sub), R, Ng, Ho; 2005 v Bul, Cy (sub), Sw, F, Fa, Cro, P, Is; 2006 v I, Cy (38)
Finucane, A. (Limerick), 1967 v T, Cz; 1969 v Cz, D, H; 1970 v S, Cz; 1971 v Se, I (1+sub); 1972 v A (11)
Fitzgerald, F. J. (Waterford), 1955 v Ho; 1956 v Ho (2)
Fitzgerald, P. J. (Leeds U), 1961 v W, N, S; (with Chester), 1962 v Cz (2) (5)
Fitzpatrick, K. (Limerick), 1970 v Cz (1)
Fitzsimons, A. G. (Middlesbrough), 1950 v Fi, Bel; 1952 v WG (2), A, Sp; 1953 v F, A; 1954 v F, L, F; 1955 v Ho, N, WG; 1956 v Y, Sp, Ho; 1957 v D, WG, E (2); 1958 v D, Pol, A; 1959 v Pol; (with Lincoln C), 1959 v Cz (26)
Fleming, C. (Middlesbrough), 1996 v CzR (sub), P, Cro (sub), Ho (sub), US (sub), M, Bol; 1997 v Lie (sub); 1998 v R (sub), M (10)
Flood, J. J. (Shamrock R), 1926 v I; 1929 v Bel; 1930 v Bel; 1931 v Sp; 1932 v Sp (5)
Fogarty, A. (Sunderland), 1960 v WG, Se; 1961 v S; 1962 v Cz (2); 1963 v Ic (2), S (sub); 1964 v A (2); (with Hartlepools U), Sp (11)
Foley, D. J. (Watford), 2000 v S (sub), M (sub), US, S.Af; 2001 v Es (sub), Fi (6)
Foley, J. (Cork), 1934 v Bel, Ho; (with Celtic), 1935 v H, Sw, G; 1937 v G, H (7)
Foley, M. (Shelbourne), 1926 v I (1)
Foley, T. C. (Northampton T), 1964 v Sp, Pol, N; 1965 v Pol, Bel; 1966 v Sp (2), WG; 1967 v Cz (9)
Foy, T. (Shamrock R), 1938 v N; 1939 v H (2)
Fullam, J. (Preston NE), 1961 v N; (with Shamrock R), 1964 v Sp, Pol, N; 1966 v A, Bel; 1968 v Pol; 1969 v Pol, A, D; 1970 v Cz (sub) (11)
Fullam, R. (Shamrock R), 1926 v I; 1927 v I (2)

Gallagher, C. (Celtic), 1967 v T, Cz (2)
Gallagher, M. (Hibernian), 1954 v L (1)
Gallagher, P. (Falkirk), 1932 v Sp (1)
Galvin, A. (Tottenham H), 1983 v Ho, Ma; 1984 v Ho (sub), Is (sub); 1985 v M, USSR, N, D, I, N, Sp; 1986 v U, Ic, Cz; 1987 v Bel (2), S, Bul, L; (with Sheffield W), 1988 v L, Bul, R, Pol, N, E, USSR, Ho; 1989 v Sp; (with Swindon T), 1990 v WG (29)
Gannon, E. (Notts Co), 1949 v Sw; (with Sheffield W), 1949 v Bel, P, Se, Sp; 1950 v Fi; 1951 v N; 1952 v WG, A; 1954 v L, F; 1955 v N; (with Shelbourne), 1955 v N, WG (14)
Gannon, M. (Shelbourne), 1972 v A (1)
Gaskins, P. (Shamrock R), 1934 v Bel, Ho; 1935 v H, Sw, G; (with St James' Gate), 1938 v Cz, Pol (7)
Gavin, J. T. (Norwich C), 1950 v Fi (2); 1953 v F; 1954 v L; (with Tottenham H), 1955 v Ho, WG; (with Norwich C), 1957 v D (7)
Geoghegan, M. (St James' Gate), 1937 v G; 1938 v N (2)
Gibbons, A. (St Patrick's Ath), 1952 v WG; 1954 v L; 1956 v Y, Sp (4)
Gilbert, R. (Shamrock R), 1966 v WG (1)
Giles, C. (Doncaster R), 1951 v N (1)
Giles, M. J. (Manchester U), 1960 v Se, Ch; 1961 v W, N, S (2); 1962 v Cz (2), A; 1963 v Ic, S; (with Leeds U), 1964 v A (2), Sp (2), Pol, N, E; 1965 v Sp; 1966 v Sp (2), A, Bel; 1967 v Sp, T (2); 1969 v A, D, Cz; 1970 v S, Pol, WG; 1971 v I; 1973 v F, USSR; 1974 v Br, U, Ch; 1975 v USSR, T, Sw, USSR, Sw; (with WBA), 1976 v T; 1977 v E, T, F (2), Pol, Bul; (with Shamrock R), 1978 v Bul, T, Pol, N, D; 1979 v Ni, D, Bul, WG (59)
Given, S. J. J. (Blackburn R), 1996 v Ru, CzR, P, Cro, Ho, US, Bol; 1997 v Lie (2); (with Newcastle U), 1998 v Li, Ic, Li, Bel (2), CzR, Arg, M; 1999 v Cro, Ma, Y, Para, Se, Ni; 2000 v Gr, S.Af; 2001 v Fi, Cy, And (2), P, Es; 2002 v Cro, Ho, Cy, Ir (2), Ru, US, Ng, Cam, G, S.Ar, Sp; 2003 v Fi (sub), Ru, Sw, Gr, Ge, Alb, N, Alb, Ge; 2004 v Ru, Sw, Ca, Br, CzR, Pol, R, Ho; 2005 v Bul, Cy, Sw, F, Fa, Cro (sub), P, Is (2), Fa; 2006 v I, F, Cy, Sw, Se, Ch (76)
Givens, D. J. (Manchester U), 1969 v D, H; 1970 v S, Cz, D, H; (with Luton T), 1970 v Pol, WG; 1971 v Se, I (2), A; 1972 v Ir, Ec, P; (with QPR), 1973 v F, USSR, Pol, F, N; 1974 v Pol, Br, U, Ch; 1975 v USSR, T, Sw, USSR, Sw, WG; 1976 v T, N, Pol; 1977 v E, T, F (2), Sp, Bul; 1978 v Bul, N, D; (with Birmingham C), 1979 v Ni (sub), E, D, Bul, WG; 1980 v US (sub), Ni (sub), Sw, Arg; 1981 v Ho, Bel, Cy (sub), W; (with Neuchatel X), 1982 v F (sub) (56)
Glen, W. (Shamrock R), 1927 v I; 1929 v Bel; 1930 v Bel; 1932 v Sp; 1936 v Ho, Sw, H, L (8)
Glynn, D. (Drumcondra), 1952 v WG; 1955 v N (2)
Godwin, T. F. (Shamrock R), 1949 v P, Se, Sp; 1950 v Fi, E; (with Leicester C), 1950 v Fi, Se, Bel; 1951 v N; (with Bournemouth), 1956 v Ho; 1957 v E; 1958 v D, Pol (13)
Golding, J. (Shamrock R), 1928 v Bel; 1930 v Bel (2)
Goodman, J. (Wimbledon), 1997 v W, Mac, R (sub), Lie (sub) (4)
Goodwin, J. (Stockport Co), 2003 v Fi (sub) (1)
Gorman, W. C. (Bury), 1936 v Sw, H, L; 1937 v G, H; 1938 v N, Cz, Pol; 1939 v Sw, Pol; (with Brentford), H; 1947 v E, P (13)
Grace, J. (Drumcondra), 1926 v I (1)
Grealish, A. (Orient), 1976 v N, Pol; 1978 v N, D; 1979 v Ni, E, WG; (with Luton T), 1980 v W, Cz, Bul, US, Ni, E, Cy, Sw, Arg; 1981 v WG 'B', Ho, Bel, F, Cy, W, Bel, Pol; (with Brighton & HA), 1982 v Ho, Alg, Ch, Br, Tr; 1983 v Ho, Sp, Ic, Sp; 1984 v Ic, Ho; (with WBA), Pol, Chn; 1985 v M, USSR, N, D, Sp (sub), Sw; 1986 v USSR, D (45)
Gregg, E. (Bohemians), 1978 v Pol, D (sub); 1979 v E (sub), D, Bul, WG; 1980 v W, Cz (8)
Griffith, R. (Walsall), 1935 v H (1)
Grimes, A. A. (Manchester U), 1978 v T, Pol, N (sub); 1980 v Bul, US, Ni, E, Cy; 1981 v WG 'B' (sub), Cz, Pol; 1982 v Alg; 1983 v Sp (2); (with Coventry C), 1984 v Pol, Is; (with Luton T), 1988 v L, R (18)

Hale, A. (Aston Villa), 1962 v A; (with Doncaster R), 1963 v Ic; 1964 v Sp (2); (with Waterford), 1967 v Sp; 1968 v Pol (sub); 1969 v Pol, A, D; 1970 v S, Cz; 1971 v Pol (sub); 1972 v A (sub); 1974 v Pol (sub) (14)
Hamilton, T. (Shamrock R), 1959 v Cz (2) (2)
Hand, E. K. (Portsmouth), 1969 v Cz (sub); 1970 v Pol, WG; 1971 v Pol, A; 1973 v USSR, F, USSR, Pol, F; 1974 v Pol, Br, U, Ch; 1975 v T, Sw, USSR, Sw, WG; 1976 v T (20)
Harrington, W. (Cork), 1936 v Ho, Sw, H, L; 1938 v Pol (sub) (5)
Harte, I. P. (Leeds U), 1996 v Cro (sub), Ho, M, Bol; 1997 v Lie, Mac, Ic (sub), W, Mac (sub), R, Lie; 1998 v Li, Ic, Li, Bel (2), Arg, M; 1999 v Para; 2000 v Cro (sub), Ma (sub), CzR; 2001 v Ho, P, Es, Fi, Cy, And (2), P, Es; 2002 v Cro, Ho, Cy, Ir (2), Ru, D, US, Ng, Cam, G, S.Ar, Sp; 2003 v Fi, Ru, Sw, S, N; 2004 v Aus (sub), Ru (sub), T, Sw, Ca (sub), CzR, Pol; (with Levante), 2005 v Is, Fa; 2006 v I (sub), F (sub), Sw, Se, Ch (sub) (63)
Hartnett, J. B. (Middlesbrough), 1949 v Sp; 1954 v L (2)
Haverty, J. (Arsenal), 1956 v Ho; 1957 v D, WG, E (2); 1958 v D, Pol, A; 1959 v Pol; 1960 v Se, Ch; 1961 v W, N, S (2); (with Blackburn R), 1962 v Cz (2); (with Millwall), 1963 v S; 1964 v A, Sp, Pol, N, E; (with Celtic), 1965 v Pol; (with Bristol R), 1965 v Sp; (with Shelbourne), 1966 v Sp (2), WG, A, Bel; 1967 v T, Sp (32)
Hayes, A. W. P. (Southampton), 1979 v D (1)
Hayes, W. E. (Huddersfield T), 1947 v E, P (2)
Hayes, W. J. (Limerick), 1949 v Bel (1)
Healey, R. (Cardiff C), 1977 v Pol; 1980 v E (sub) (2)
Healy, C. (Celtic), 2002 v Ru, D (sub), US; 2003 v Fi (sub), Sw, Gr, S (sub), N (sub), Ge; (with Sunderland), 2004 v Aus (sub), Ru, T, Sw (13)
Heighway, S. D. (Liverpool), 1971 v Pol, Se (2), I, A; 1973 v USSR; 1975 v USSR, T, USSR, WG; 1976 v T, N; 1977 v E, F (2), Sp, Bul; 1978 v Bul, N, D; 1979 v Ni, Bul; 1980 v Bul, US, Ni, E, Cy, Arg; 1981 v Bel, F, Cy, W, Bel; (with Minnesota K), 1982 v Ho (34)

Henderson, B. (Drumcondra), 1948 v P, Sp (2)
Henderson, W. C. P. (Brighton & HA), 2006 v Se (sub), Ch (sub) (2)
Hennessy, J. (Shelbourne), 1965 v Pol, Bel, Sp; 1966 v WG; (with St Patrick's Ath), 1969 v A (5)
Herrick, J. (Cork Hibernians), 1972 v A, Ch (sub); (with Shamrock R), 1973 v F (sub) (3)
Higgins, J. (Birmingham C), 1951 v Arg (1)
Holland, M. R. (Ipswich T), 2000 v Mac (sub), M, US, S.Af; 2001 v P (sub), Fi, Cy (sub), And (2), P (sub), Es; 2002 v Ho, Cy, Ir (2), Ru (sub), D, US (sub), Ng, Cam, G, S.Ar, Sp; 2003 v Fi (sub), Ru, Sw, Gr, S, Ge, Alb, N, Alb, Ge; (with Charlton Ath), 2004 v Aus, Ru, Sw, Ca (sub), Br, CzR, R, Ng, Jam (sub), Ho; 2005 v P, Is (sub+1); 2006 v I, Cy (sub), Sw (49)
Holmes, J. (Coventry C), 1971 v A (sub); 1973 v F, USSR, Pol, F, N; 1974 v Pol, Br; 1975 v USSR, Sw; 1976 v T, N, Pol; 1977 v E, T, F, Sp; (with Tottenham H), F, Pol, Bul; 1978 v Bul, T, Pol, N, D; 1979 v Ni, E, D, Bul; (with Vancouver W), 1981 v W (30)
Horlacher, A. F. (Bohemians), 1930 v Bel; 1932 v Sp, Ho; 1934 v Ho (sub); 1935 v H;1936 v Ho, Sw (7)
Houghton, R. J. (Oxford U), 1986 v W, U, Ic, Cz; 1987 v Bel (2), S (2), Pol, L; 1988 v L, Bul; (with Liverpool), Is, Y, N, E, USSR, Ho; 1989 v Ni, Tun, Sp, F, H, Sp, Ma, H; 1990 v Ni, Ma, Fi, E, Eg, Ho, R, I; 1991 v Mor, T, E (2), Pol, Ch, US; 1992 v H, Alb, US, I, P; (with Aston Villa), 1993 v D, Sp, Ni, D, Alb, La, Li; 1994 v Li, Sp, Ni, Bol, G (sub), I, M, N, Ho; (with C Palace), 1995 v P, A; 1996 v A, CzR; 1997 v Lie, R, Lie; (with Reading), 1998 v Li, R, Bel (1 + sub) (73)
Howlett, G. (Brighton & HA), 1984 v Chn (sub) (1)
Hoy, M. (Dundalk), 1938 v N; 1939 v Sw, Pol, H (2), G (6)
Hughton, C. (Tottenham H), 1980 v US, E, Sw, Arg; 1981 v Ho, Bel, F, Cy, W, Bel, Pol; 1982 v F; 1983 v Ho, Sp, Ma, Sp; 1984 v Ic, Ho, Ma; 1985 v M (sub), USSR, N, I, Is, E, Sp; 1986 v Sw, USSR, U, Ic; 1987 v Bel, Bul; 1988 v Is, Y, Pol, N, E, USSR, Ho; 1989 v Ni, F, H, Sp, Ma, H; 1990 v W (sub), USSR (sub), Fi, T (sub), Ma; 1991 v T; (with West Ham U), Ch; 1992 v T (53)
Hurley, C. J. (Millwall), 1957 v E; (with Sunderland), 1958 v D, Pol, A; 1959 v Cz (2); 1960 v Se, Ch, WG, Se; 1961 v W, N, S (2); 1962 v Cz (2), A; 1963 v Ic (2), S; 1964 v A (2), Sp (2), Pol, N; 1965 v Sp; 1966 v WG, A, Bel; 1967 v T, Sp, T, Cz; 1968 v Cz, Pol; 1969 v Pol, D, Cz, (with Bolton W), H (40)
Hutchinson, F. (Drumcondra), 1935 v Sw, G (2)

Ireland S .J. (Manchester C), 2006 v Se (sub) (1)
Irwin, D. J. (Manchester U), 1991 v Mor, T, W, E, Pol, US; 1992 v H, Pol, W, US, Alb, US (sub), I; 1993 v La, D, Sp, Ni, D, Alb, La, Li; 1994 v Li, Sp, Ni, Bol, G, I, M; 1995 v La, Lie, Ni, E, Ni, P, Lie, A; 1996 v A, P, Ho, CzR; 1997 v Lie, Mac, Ic, Mac, R; 1998 v Li, Bel, Arg (sub); 1999 v Cro, Y, Para, Mac; 2000 v Y, Mac, T (2) (56)

Jordan, D. (Wolverhampton W), 1937 v Sw, F (2)
Jordan, W. (Bohemians), 1934 v Ho; 1938 v N (2)

Kavanagh, G. A. (Stoke C), 1998 v CzR (sub); 1999 v Se (sub), Ni (sub); (with Cardiff C), 2004 v Ca, Br; 2005 v Bul (sub), Cy, Sw (sub), Cro, P (sub); (with Wigan Ath), Chn, Is (sub); 2006 v Cy, Se (sub), Ch (sub) (15)
Kavanagh, P. J. (Celtic), 1931 v Sp; 1932 v Sp (2)
Keane, R. D. (Wolverhampton W), 1998 v CzR (sub), Arg, M; 1999 v Cro, Ma, Para, Se (sub), Ni, Mac; (with Coventry C), 2000 v Y, Ma, Mac, T, CzR, Gr, S, M, S.Af (sub); (with Internazionale), 2001 v Ho, P, Es, Fi, Cy, And, P; (with Leeds U), 2002 v Cro, Ho, Ir (2), Ru, D, US, Ng, Cam, G, S.Ar, Sp; 2003 v Fi; (with Tottenham H), Ru, Sw, Alb, N, Alb, Ge; 2004 v Aus, Sw, Ca, Br, CzR, R, Ng, Ho; 2005 v Cy, Sw, F, Fa, Cro, P, Is, Chn, Is; 2006 v F, Cy, Sw, Se, Ch (66)
Keane, R. M. (Nottingham F), 1991 v Ch; 1992 v H, Pol, W, Sw, Alb, US; 1993 v La, D, Sp, W, Ni, D, Alb, La, Li; (with Manchester U), 1994 v Li, Sp, Ni, Bol, G, CzR (sub), I, M, N, Ho; 1995 v Ni (2); 1996 v A, Ru; 1997 v Ic, W, Mac, R, Lie; 1998 v Li, Ic, Li; 1999 v Cro, Ma, Y, Para; 2000 v Y, T (2), CzR; 2001 v Ho, P, Es, Cy, And, P; 2002 v Cro, Ho, Cy, Ir, Ru, Ng; 2004 v R; 2005 v Bul, Sw, F, Fa, Is, Chn (sub), Fa; 2006 v F (67)
Keane, T. R. (Swansea T), 1949 v Sw, P, Se, Sp (4)
Kearin, M. (Shamrock R), 1972 v A (1)
Kearns, F. T. (West Ham U), 1954 v L (1)
Kearns, M. (Oxford U), 1971 v Pol (sub); (with Walsall), 1974 v Pol (sub), U, Ch; 1976 v N, Pol; 1977 v E, T, F (2), Sp, Bul; 1978 v N, D; 1979 v Ni, E; (with Wolverhampton W), 1980 v US, Ni (18)

Kelly, A. T. (Sheffield U), 1993 v W (sub); 1994 v Ru (sub), G; 1995 v La, Ni, E, Ni, P, Lie, A; 1996 v A, La, P, Ho; 1997 v Mac, Ic, Mac, R; 1998 v R, Arg (sub); 1999 v Para (sub), Mac; (with Blackburn R), 2000 v Y, Cro, Ma, Mac, T, CzR, S, US; 2001 v Ho, P, Es; 2002 v Cro (sub) (34)
Kelly, D. T. (Walsall), 1988 v Is, R, Y; (with West Ham U), 1989 v Tun (sub); (with Leicester C), 1990 v USSR, Ma; 1991 v Mor, W (sub), Ch, US; 1992 v H; (with Newcastle U), I (sub), P; 1993 v D (sub), W; (with Wolverhampton W), 1994 v Ru, N (sub); 1995 v E, Ni; (with Sunderland), 1996 v La (sub); 1997 v Ic, W (sub), Mac (sub); (with Tranmere R), 1998 v Li (sub), R (sub), Bel (sub) (26)
Kelly, G. (Leeds U), 1994 v Ru, Ho, Bol (sub), G (sub), CzR, N, Ho; 1995 v La, Lie, Ni (2), P, Lie, A; 1996 v A, La, P, Ho; 1997 v W (sub), R, Lie; 1998 v Ic, Li, Bel (2), CzR, Arg, M; 2000 v Cro, Mac, CzR; 2001 v Ho (sub), Fi, Cy, And (2), P, Es; 2002 v Cro, Ho, Ir (sub+sub), Ru (sub), D, US (sub), Ng (sub), Cam, G, S.Ar, Sp; 2003 v Fi, Sw (52)
Kelly, J. (Derry C), 1932 v Ho; 1934 v Bel; 1936 v Sw, L (4)
Kelly, J. A. (Drumcondra), 1957 v WG, E; (with Preston NE), 1962 v A; 1963 v Ic (2), S; 1964 v A (2), Sp (2), Pol; 1965 v Bel; 1966 v A, Bel; 1967 v Sp (2), T, Cz; 1968 v Pol, Cz; 1969 v Pol, A, D, Cz, D, H; 1970 v S, D, H, Pol, WG; 1971 v Pol, Se (2), I (2), A; 1972 v Ir, Ec, Ch, P; 1973 v USSR, F, USSR, Pol, F, N (47)
Kelly, J. P. V. (Wolverhampton W), 1961 v W, N, S; 1962 v Cz (2) (5)
Kelly, M. J. (Portsmouth), 1988 v Y, Pol (sub); 1989 v Tun; 1991 v Mor (4)
Kelly, N. (Nottingham F), 1954 v L (1)
Kelly, S. M. (Tottenham H), 2006 v Ch (1)
Kendrick, J. (Everton), 1927 v I; (with Dolphin) 1934 v Bel, Ho; 1936 v Ho (4)
Kenna, J. J. (Blackburn R), 1995 v P (sub), Lie (sub), A (sub); 1996 v La, P, Ho, Ru (sub), CzR, P, Cro, Ho, US; 1997 v Lie, Mac, Ic, R (sub), Lie; 1998 v Li, Ic, R, Bel (1 + sub), CzR, Arg; 1999 v Cro (sub), Ma; 2000 v T (sub) (27)
Kennedy, M. F. (Portsmouth), 1986 v Ic, Cz (sub) (2)
Kennedy, M. J. (Liverpool), 1996 v A, La (sub), P, Ru, CzR, Cro, Ho (sub), US (sub), M, Bol (sub); 1997 v R, Lie; 1998 v Li, Ic (sub), R, Bel (2), (with Wimbledon), M (sub); 1999 v Ma (sub), Se, Ni, Mac; (with Manchester C), 2000 v Y, Ma, Mac, CzR, S, M, US (sub), S.Af (sub); 2001 v And; (with Wolverhampton W), 2002 v Cro, Cy, Ru (sub) (34)
Kennedy, W. (St James' Gate), 1932 v Ho; 1934 v Bel, Ho (3)
Kenny, P. (Sheffield U), 2004 v CzR (sub), Jam; 2005 v Bul (sub), Cro, Chn (5)
Keogh, J. (Shamrock R), 1966 v WG (sub) (1)
Keogh, S. (Shamrock R), 1959 v Pol (1)
Kernaghan, A. N. (Middlesbrough), 1993 v La, D (2), Alb, La, Li; 1994 v Li; (with Manchester C), Sp, Ni, Bol (sub), CzR; 1995 v Lie, E; 1996 v A, P (sub), Ho (sub), Ru, P, Cro (sub), Ho, US, Bol (22)
Kiely, D. L. (Charlton Ath), 2000 v T (sub + 1), Gr (sub), M; 2002 v Ru (sub), D; 2003 v Fi, S (8)
Kiernan, F. W. (Shamrock R), 1951 v Arg, N; (with Southampton), 1952 v WG (2), A (5)
Kilbane, K. D. (WBA), 1998 v Ic, CzR (sub), Arg; 1999 v Se (sub), Mac (sub); 2000 v Y, Cro (sub), Ma, T (2); (with Sunderland), CzR, Gr, S, M (sub), US, S.Af (sub); 2001 v Ho, P, Es, Fi, Cy, And (2), P, Es; 2002 v Cro (sub), Ho, Cy, Ir (2), Ru, US, Ng, Cam, G, S.Ar, Sp; 2003 v Fi (sub), Ru, Sw, S, Ge, Alb, N, Alb, Ge; 2004 v Aus (sub); (with Everton), Ru, T, Sw, Ca (sub), Br, CzR; 2005 v Bul, Cy, Sw, F, Fa, Cro, P, Is, Chn, Is, Fa; 2006 v I, F, Cy, Sw, Se (sub), Ch (70)
Kinnear, J. P. (Tottenham H), 1967 v T; 1968 v Cz, Pol; 1969 v A; 1970 v Cz, D, H, Pol; 1971 v Se (sub), I; 1972 v Ir, Ec, Ch, P; 1973 v USSR, F; 1974 v Pol, Br, U, Ch; 1975 v USSR, T, Sw, USSR, WG; (with Brighton & HA), 1976 v T (sub) (26)
Kinsella, J. (Shelbourne), 1928 v Bel (1)
Kinsella, M. A. (Charlton Ath), 1998 v CzR, Arg; 1999 v Cro, Ma, Y, Para, Se, Ni, Mac; 2000 v Y, Cro, Ma, Mac, T, CzR, Gr; 2001 v Ho, P, Es, Fi, Cy, And, P, Es; 2002 v Ir, D, US, Ng (sub), Cam, G, S.Ar, Sp; 2003 v Fi; (with Aston Villa), Ru, Sw, S, Ge, Alb, N, Alb, Ge (sub); 2004 v Aus, T, Sw (sub); (with WBA), CzR (sub), Pol, Ng, Jam (48)
Kinsella, O. (Shamrock R), 1932 v Ho; 1938 v N (2)
Kirkland, A. (Shamrock R), 1927 v I (1)

Lacey, W. (Shelbourne), 1927 v I; 1928 v Bel; 1930 v Bel (3)
Langan, D. (Derby Co), 1978 v T, N; 1980 v Sw, Arg; (with Birmingham C), 1981 v WG 'B', Ho, Bel, F, Cy, W, Bel, Cz, Pol; 1982 v Ho, F; (with Oxford U), 1985 v N, Sp, Sw;

1986 v W, U; 1987 v Bel, S, Pol, Br (sub), L (sub); 1988 v L (26)
Lawler, J. F. (Fulham), 1953 v A; 1954 v L, F; 1955 v N, Ho, N, WG; 1956 v Y (8)
Lawlor, J. C. (Drumcondra), 1949 v Bel; (with Doncaster R), 1951 v N, Arg (3)
Lawlor, M. (Shamrock R), 1971 v Pol, Se (2), I (sub); 1973 v Pol (5)
Lawrenson, M. (Preston NE), 1977 v Pol; (with Brighton & HA), 1978 v Bul, Pol, N (sub), D; 1979 v Ni, E; 1980 v E, Cy, Sw; 1981 v Ho, Bel, F, Cy, Pol; (with Liverpool), 1982 v Ho, F; 1983 v Ho, Sp, Ic, Ma, Sp; 1984 v Ic, Ho, Ma, Is; 1985 v USSR, N, D, I, E, N; 1986 v Sw, USSR, D; 1987 v Bel, S; 1988 v Bul, Is (39)
Lee, A. D. (Rotherham U), 2003 v N (sub), Ge (sub); (with Cardiff C), 2004 v CzR (sub), Pol, Ng, Jam, Ho (sub); 2005 v Cy (sub) (8)
Leech, M. (Shamrock R), 1969 v Cz, D, H; 1972 v A, Ir, Ec, P; 1973 v USSR (sub) (8)
Lennon, C. (St James' Gate), 1935 v H, Sw, G (3)
Lennox, G. (Dolphin), 1931 v Sp; 1932 v Sp (2)
Lowry, D. (St Patrick's Ath), 1962 v A (sub) (1)
Lunn, R. (Dundalk), 1939 v Sw, Pol (2)
Lynch, J. (Cork Bohemians), 1934 v Bel (1)

McAlinden, J. (Portsmouth), 1946 v P, Sp (2)
McAteer, J. W. (Bolton W), 1994 v Ru, Ho (sub), Bol (sub), G, CzR (sub), I (sub), M (sub), N, Ho (sub); 1995 v La, Lie, Ni (2 sub), Lie; (with Liverpool), 1996 v La, P, Ho (sub), Ru; 1997 v Mac, Ic, W, Mac; 1998 v Ic (sub), Li, R; 1999 v Cro, Ma, Y; (with Blackburn R), Para, Se; 2000 v CzR (sub), S, M, US (sub), S.Af; 2001 v Ho, P, Es, Fi (sub), Cy; 2002 v Cro (sub), Ho; (with Sunderland), Ir (2), Ru (sub), D, Ng, Cam, S.Ar (sub); 2003 v Fi, Ru; 2004 v Br (sub) (52)
McCann, J. (Shamrock R), 1957 v WG (1)
McCarthy, J. (Bohemians), 1926 v I; 1928 v Bel; 1930 v Bel (3)
McCarthy, M. (Shamrock R), 1932 v Ho (1)
McCarthy, M. (Manchester C), 1984 v Pol, Chn; 1985 v M, D, I, Is, E, Sp, Sw; 1986 v Sw, USSR, W (sub), U, Ic, Cz; 1987 v S (2), Pol, Bul, Bel (with Celtic), Br, L; 1988 v Bul, Is, R, Y, N, E, USSR, Ho; 1989 v Ni, Tun, Sp, F, H, Sp; (with Lyon), 1990 v WG, Ni (with Millwall), W, USSR, Fi, T, E, Eg, Ho, R, I; 1991 v Mor, T, E, US; 1992 v H, T, Alb (sub), US, I, P (57)
McConville, T. (Dundalk), 1972 v A; (with Waterford), 1973 v USSR, F, USSR, Pol, F (6)
McDonagh, Jacko (Shamrock R), 1984 v Pol (sub), Ma (sub); 1985 v M (sub) (3)
McDonagh, J. (Everton), 1981 v WG 'B', W, Bel, Cz; (with Bolton W), 1982 v Ho, F, Ch, Br; 1983 v Ho, Sp, Ic, Ma, Sp; (with Notts Co), 1984 v Ic, Ho, Pol; 1985 v M, USSR, N, D, Sp, Sw; 1986 v Sw, USSR; (with Wichita Wings) D (25)
McEvoy, M. A. (Blackburn R), 1961 v S (2); 1963 v S; 1964 v A, Sp (2), Pol, N, E; 1965 v Pol, Bel, Sp; 1966 v Sp (2); 1967 v Sp, T, Cz (17)
McGeady, A. (Celtic), 2004 v Jam (sub); 2005 v Cro (sub), P (sub); 2006 v Ch (sub) (4)
McGee, P. (QPR), 1978 v T, N (sub), D (sub); 1979 v Ni, E, D (sub), Bul (sub); 1980 v Cz, Bul; (with Preston NE), US, Ni, Cy, Sw, Arg; 1981 v Bel (sub) (15)
McGoldrick, E. J. (C Palace), 1992 v Sw, US, I, P (sub); 1993 v D, W, Ni (sub), D; (with Arsenal), 1994 v Ni, Ru, Ho, CzR; 1995 v La (sub), Lie, E (15)
McGowan, D. (West Ham U), 1949 v P, Se, Sp (3)
McGowan, J. (Cork U), 1947 v Sp (1)
McGrath, M. (Blackburn R), 1958 v A; 1959 v Pol, Cz (2); 1960 v Se, WG, Se; 1961 v W; 1962 v Cz (2); 1963 v S; 1964 v A (2), E; 1965 v Pol, Bel, Sp; 1966 v Sp; (with Bradford), 1966 v WG, A, Bel; 1967 v T (22)
McGrath, P. (Manchester U), 1985 v I (sub), Is, E, N (sub), Sw (sub); 1986 v Sw (sub), D, W, Ic, Cz; 1987 v Bel (2), S (2), Pol, Bul, Br, L; 1988 v L, Bul, Y, Pol, N, E, Ho; 1989 v Ni, F, H, Sp, Ma, H; (with Aston Villa), 1990 v WG, Ma, USSR, Fi, T, E, Eg, Ho, R, I; 1991 v E (2), W, Pol, Ch (sub), US; 1992 v Pol, T, Sw, US, Alb, US, I, P; 1993 v La, Sp, Ni, D, La, Li; 1994 v Sp, Ni, G, CzR, I, M, N, Ho; 1995 v La, Ni, E, Ni, P, Lie, A; 1996 v A, La, P, Ho, Ru, CzR; (with Derby Co), 1997 v W (83)
McGuire, W. (Bohemians), 1936 v Ho (1)
Macken, A. (Derby Co), 1977 v Sp (1)
Macken J. P. (Manchester C), 2005 v Bul (sub) (1)
McKenzie, G. (Southend U), 1938 v N (2), Cz, Pol; 1939 v Sw, Pol, H (2), G (9)
Mackey, G. (Shamrock R), 1957 v D, WG, E (3)
McLoughlin, A. F. (Swindon T), 1990 v Ma, E (sub), Eg (sub); 1991 v Mor (sub), E (sub); (with Southampton), W, Ch (sub); 1992 v H (sub), W (sub); (with Portsmouth), US (1 + sub), I (sub), P; 1993 v W; 1994 v Ni (sub), Ru, Ho (sub); 1995 v Lie (sub); 1996 v P, Cro, Ho, US, M, Bol (sub); 1997 v Lie, Mac, Ic, W, Mac; 1998 v Li (sub), Ic, Li, R, Bel, CzR (sub); 1999 v Y, Para (sub), Se, Ni (sub); 2000 v Cro, Ma (sub), Mac (42)
McLoughlin, F. (Fordsons), 1930 v Bel; (with Cork), 1932 v Sp (2)
McMillan, W. (Belfast Celtic), 1946 v P, Sp (2)
McNally, J. B. (Luton T), 1959 v Cz; 1961 v S; 1963 v Ic (3)
McPhail, S. (Leeds U), 2000 v S, US, S.Af; 2002 v Cro (sub), Cy (sub); 2003 v Fi (sub), Gr; 2004 v T (sub), Ca (sub), Ng (10)
Madden, O. (Cork), 1936 v H (1)
Maguire, J. (Shamrock R), 1929 v Bel (1)
Mahon, A. J. (Tranmere R), 2000 v Gr (sub), S.Af (2)
Malone, G. (Shelbourne), 1949 v Bel (1)
Mancini, T. J. (QPR), 1974 v Pol, Br, U, Ch; (with Arsenal), 1975 v USSR (5)
Martin, C. (Bo'ness), 1927 v I (1)
Martin, C. J. (Glentoran), 1946 v P (sub), Sp; 1947 v E; (with Leeds U), 1947 v Sp; 1948 v P, Sp; (with Aston Villa), 1949 v Sw, Bel, P, Se, Sp; 1950 v Fi, E, Fi, Se, Bel; 1951 v Arg; 1952 v WG, A, Sp; 1954 v F (2), L; 1955 v N, Ho, N, WG; 1956 v Y, Sp, Ho (30)
Martin, M. P. (Bohemians), 1972 v A, Ir, Ec, Ch, P; 1973 v USSR; (with Manchester U), 1973 v USSR, Pol, F, N; 1974 v Pol, Br, U, Ch; 1975 v USSR, T, Sw, USSR, Sw, WG; (with WBA), 1976 v T, N, Pol; 1977 v E, T, F (2), Sp, Pol, Bul; (with Newcastle U), 1979 v D, Bul, WG; 1980 v W, Cz, Bul, US, Ni; 1981 v WG 'B', F, Bel, Cz; 1982 v Ho, F, Alg, Ch, Br, Tr; 1983 v Ho, Sp, Ma, Sp (52)
Maybury, A. (Leeds U), 1998 v CzR; 1999 v Ni; (with Hearts), 2004 v CzR, Pol (sub), R, Ng, Jam, Ho; 2005 v Cy (sub); (with Leicester C), Chn (10)
Meagan, M. K. (Everton), 1961 v S; 1962 v A; 1963 v Ic; 1964 v Sp; (with Huddersfield T), 1965 v Bel; 1966 v Sp (2), A, Bel; 1967 v Sp, T, Sp, T, Cz; 1968 v Cz, Pol; (with Drogheda), 1970 v S (17)
Meehan, P. (Drumcondra), 1934 v Ho (1)
Miller, L. W. P. (Celtic), 2004 v CzR (sub), Pol, R, Ng; (with Manchester U), 2005 v Bul, Fa (sub), Cro, P (sub), Chn (sub); 2006 v I (sub), Se (sub), Ch (12)
Milligan, M. J. (Oldham Ath), 1992 v US (sub) (1)
Monahan, P. (Sligo R), 1935 v Sw, G (2)
Mooney, J. (Shamrock R), 1965 v Pol, Bel (2)
Moore, A. (Middlesbrough), 1996 v CzR, Cro (sub), Ho, M, Bol; 1997 v Lie (sub), Mac (sub), Ic (sub) (8)
Moore, P. (Shamrock R), 1931 v Sp; 1932 v Ho; (with Aberdeen), 1934 v Bel, Ho; 1935 v H, G; (with Shamrock R), 1936 v Ho; 1937 v G, H (9)
Moran, K. (Manchester U), 1980 v Sw, Arg; 1981 v WG 'B', Bel, F, Cy, W (sub), Bel, Cz, Pol; 1982 v F, Alg; 1983 v Ic; 1984 v Ic, Ho, Ma, Is; 1985 v M; 1986 v D, Ic, Cz; 1987 v Bel (2), S (2), Pol, Bul, Br, L; 1988 v L, Bul, Is, R, Y, Pol, N, E, USSR, Ho; (with Sporting Gijon), 1989 v Ni, Sp, H, Sp, Ma, H; 1990 v Ni, Ma; (with Blackburn R), W, USSR (sub), Ma, E, Eg, Ho, R, I; 1991 v T (sub), W, E, Pol, Ch, US; 1992 v Pol, US; 1993 v D, Sp, Ni, Alb; 1994 v Li, Sp, Ho, Bol (71)
Moroney, T. (West Ham U), 1948 v Sp; 1949 v P, Se, Sp; 1950 v Fi, E, Fi, Bel; 1951 v N (2); 1952 v WG; (with Evergreen U), 1954 v F (12)
Morris, C. B. (Celtic), 1988 v Is, R, Y, Pol, N, E, USSR, Ho; 1989 v Ni, Tun, Sp, F, H (1+sub); 1990 v WG, Ni, Ma (sub), W, USSR, Fi (sub), T, E, Eg, Ho, R, I; 1991 v E; 1992 v H (sub), Pol, W, Sw, US (2), P; (with Middlesbrough), 1993 v W (35)
Morrison, C. H. (C Palace), 2002 v Cro (sub), Cy (sub), Ir (sub), Ru (sub), D, US (sub), Ng (sub); (with Birmingham C), 2003 v Ru (sub), Sw (sub), S; 2004 v Aus (sub), Ru, T (sub), Sw (sub), Ca (sub), Br, CzR, Pol, R, Jam, Ho; 2005 v Bul, Cy, Sw, F, P, Is, Chn (sub), Is, Fa; 2006 v I; (with C Palace), F, Sw, Se (sub) (34)
Moulson, C. (Lincoln C), 1936 v H, L; (with Notts Co), 1937 v H, Sw, F (5)
Moulson, G. B. (Lincoln C), 1948 v P, Sp; 1949 v Sw (3)
Muckian, C. (Drogheda U), 1978 v Pol (1)
Muldoon, T. (Aston Villa), 1927 v I (1)
Mulligan, P. M. (Shamrock R), 1969 v Cz, D, H; 1970 v S, Cz, D; (with Chelsea), 1970 v H, Pol, WG; 1971 v Pol, Se, I; 1972 v A, Ir, Ec, Ch, P; (with C Palace), 1973 v F, USSR, Pol, F, N; 1974 v Pol, Br, U, Ch; 1975 v USSR, T, Sw, USSR, Sw; (with WBA), 1976 v T, Pol; 1977 v E, T, F (2), Pol, Bul; 1978 v Bul, N, D; 1979 v E, D, Bul (sub), WG; (with Shamrock R), 1980 v W, Cz, Bul, US (sub) (50)
Munroe, L. (Shamrock R), 1954 v L (1)
Murphy, A. (Clyde), 1956 v Y (1)

Murphy, B. (Bohemians), 1986 v U (1)
Murphy, J. (C Palace), 1980 v W, US, Cy (3)
Murphy, J. (WBA), 2004 v T (sub) (1)
Murray, T. (Dundalk), 1950 v Bel (1)

Newman, W. (Shelbourne), 1969 v D (1)
Nolan, R. (Shamrock R), 1957 v D, WG, E; 1958 v Pol; 1960 v Ch, WG, Se; 1962 v Cz (2); 1963 v Ic (10)

O'Brien, A. J. (Newcastle U), 2001 v Es (sub); 2002 v Cro (sub), Ho (sub), Ru, US; 2003 v S (sub); 2004 v Aus (sub), T, Br, Pol (sub), R, Jam, Ho; 2005 v Cy, Sw, F, Fa, P, Is, Chn (sub), Is; (with Portsmouth), 2006 v I (sub), Se (23)
O'Brien, F. (Philadelphia F), 1980 v Cz, E, Cy (sub) (3)
O'Brien J. M. (Bolton W), 2006 v Se (1)
O'Brien, L. (Shamrock R), 1986 v U; (with Manchester U), 1987 v Br; 1988 v Is (sub), R (sub), Y (sub), Pol (sub); 1989 v Tun; (with Newcastle U), Sp (sub); 1992 v Sw (sub); 1993 v W; (with Tranmere R), 1994 v Ru; 1996 v Cro, Ho, US, Bol; 1997 v Mac (sub) (16)
O'Brien, M. T. (Derby Co), 1927 v I; (with Walsall), 1929 v Bel; (with Norwich C), 1930 v Bel; (with Watford), 1932 v Ho (4)
O'Brien, R. (Notts Co), 1976 v N, Pol; 1977 v Sp, Pol; 1980 v Arg (sub) (5)
O'Byrne, L. B. (Shamrock R), 1949 v Bel (1)
O'Callaghan, B. R. (Stoke C), 1979 v WG (sub); 1980 v W, US; 1981 v W; 1982 v Br, Tr (6)
O'Callaghan, K. (Ipswich T), 1981 v WG 'B', Cz, Pol; 1982 v Alg, Ch, Br, Tr (sub); 1983 v Sp, Ic (sub), Ma (sub), Sp (sub); 1984 v Ic, Ho, Ma; 1985 v M (sub), N (sub), D (sub); (with Portsmouth), E (sub); 1986 v Sw (sub), USSR (sub); 1987 v Br (21)
O'Connell, A. (Dundalk), 1967 v Sp; (with Bohemians), 1971 v Pol (sub) (2)
O'Connor, T. (Shamrock R), 1950 v Fi, E, Fi, Se (4)
O'Connor, T. (Fulham), 1968 v Cz; (with Dundalk), 1972 v A, Ir (sub), Ec (sub), Ch; (with Bohemians), 1973 v F (sub), Pol (sub) (7)
O'Driscoll, J. F. (Swansea T), 1949 v Sw, Bel, Se (3)
O'Driscoll, S. (Fulham), 1982 v Ch, Br, Tr (sub) (3)
O'Farrell, F. (West Ham U), 1952 v A; 1953 v A; 1954 v F; 1955 v Ho, N; 1956 v Y, Ho; (with Preston NE), 1958 v D; 1959 v Cz (9)
O'Flanagan, K. P. (Bohemians), 1938 v N, Cz, Pol; 1939 v Pol, H (2), G; (with Arsenal), 1947 v E, Sp, P (10)
O'Flanagan, M. (Bohemians), 1947 v E (1)
O'Hanlon, K. G. (Rotherham U), 1988 v Is (1)
O'Kane, P. (Bohemians), 1935 v H, Sw, G (3)
O'Keefe, E. (Everton), 1981 v W; (with Port Vale), 1984 v Chn; 1985 v M, USSR (sub), E (5)
O'Keefe, T. (Cork), 1934 v Bel; (with Waterford), 1938 v Cz, Pol (3)
O'Leary, D. (Arsenal), 1977 v E, F (2), Sp, Bul; 1978 v Bul, N, D; 1979 v E, Bul, WG; 1980 v W, Bul, Ni, E, Cy; 1981 v WG 'B',Ho, Cz, Pol; 1982 v Ho, F; 1983 v Ho, Ic, Sp; 1984 v Pol, Is, Chn; 1985 v USSR, N, D, Is, E (sub), N, Sp, Sw; 1986 v Sw, USSR, D, W; 1989 v Sp, Ma, H; 1990 v WG, Ni (sub), Ma, W (sub), USSR, Fi, T, Ma, R (sub); 1991 v Mor, T, E (2), Pol, Ch; 1992 v H, Pol, T, W, Sw, US, Alb, I, P; 1993 v W (68)
O'Leary, P. (Shamrock R), 1980 v Bul, US, Ni, E (sub), Cz, Arg; 1981 v Ho (7)
O'Mahoney, M. T. (Bristol R), 1938 v Cz, Pol; 1939 v Sw, Pol, H, G (6)
O'Neill, F. S. (Shamrock R), 1962 v Cz (2); 1965 v Pol, Bel, Sp; 1966 v Sp (2), WG, A; 1967 v Sp, T, Sp, T; 1969 v Pol, A, D, Cz, D (sub), H (sub); 1972 v A (20)
O'Neill, J. (Everton), 1952 v Sp; 1953 v F, A; 1954 v F, L, F; 1955 v N, Ho, N, WG; 1956 v Y, Sp; 1957 v D; 1958 v A; 1959 v Pol, Cz (2) (17)
O'Neill, J. (Preston NE), 1961 v W (1)
O'Neill, K. P. (Norwich C), 1996 v P (sub), Cro, Ho (sub), US (sub), M, Bol; 1997 v Lie, Mac (1 + sub); 1999 v Cro, Y (sub); (with Middlesbrough), Ni (sub); 2000 v Mac (sub) (13)
O'Neill, W. (Dundalk), 1936 v Ho, Sw, H, L; 1937 v G, H, Sw, F; 1938 v N; 1939 v H, G (11)
O'Regan, K. (Brighton & HA), 1984 v Ma, Pol; 1985 v M, Sp (sub) (4)
O'Reilly, J. (Brideville), 1932 v Ho; (with Aberdeen), 1934 v Bel, Ho; (with Brideville), 1936 v Ho; Sw, H, L; (with St James' Gate), 1937 v G, H, Sw, F; 1938 v N (2), Cz, Pol; 1939 v Sw, Pol, H (2), G (20)
O'Reilly, J. (Cork U), 1946 v P, Sp (2)
O'Shea, J. F. (Manchester U), 2002 v Cro (sub); 2003 v Gr, S, Ge, Alb (2), Ge; 2004 v Aus, Ru, Sw, Ca, Br, Pol, Jam; 2005 v Bul, Cy, F, Fa, Cro, P, Is, Chn, Is, Fa; 2006 v I, F, Cy, Sw, Se, Ch (30)

Peyton, G. (Fulham), 1977 v Sp (sub); 1978 v Bul, T, Pol; 1979 v D, Bul, WG; 1980 v W, Cz, Bul, E, Cy, Sw, Arg; 1981 v Ho, Bel, F, Cy; 1982 v Tr; 1985 v M (sub); 1986 v W, Cz; (with Bournemouth), 1988 v L, Pol; 1989 v Ni, Tun; 1990 v USSR, Ma; 1991 v Ch; (with Everton) 1992 v US (2), I (sub), P (33)
Peyton, N. (Shamrock R), 1957 v WG; (with Leeds U), 1960 v WG, Se (sub); 1961 v W; 1963 v Ic, S (6)
Phelan, T. (Wimbledon), 1992 v H, Pol (sub), T, W, Sw, US, I (sub), P; (with Manchester C), 1993 v La (sub), D, Sp, Ni, Alb, La, Li; 1994 v Li, Sp, Ni, Ho, Bol, G, CzR, I, M, Ho; 1995 v E; 1996 v La; (with Chelsea), Ho, Ru, P, Cro, Ho, US, M (sub), Bol; (with Everton), 1997 v W, Mac; 1998 v R; (with Fulham), 2000 v S (sub), M, US, S.Af (42)

Quinn, A. (Sheffield W), 2003 v N (sub); 2004 v Aus (sub), Jam, Ho; (with Sheffield U), 2005 v Bul (sub), Cro (sub) (6)
Quinn, B. S. (Coventry C), 2000 v Gr, M, US (sub), S.Af (sub) (4)
Quinn, N. J. (Arsenal), 1986 v Ic (sub), Cz; 1987 v Bul (sub), Br (sub); 1988 v L (sub), Bul (sub), Is, R (sub), Pol (sub), E (sub); 1989 v Tun (sub), Sp (sub), H (sub); (with Manchester C), 1990 v USSR, Ma, Eg (sub), Ho, R, I; 1991 v Mor, T, E(2) W, Pol; 1992 v H, W (sub), US, Alb, US, I, P; 1993 v La, D, Sp, Ni, D, Alb, La, Li; 1994 v Li, Sp, Ni; 1995 v La, Lie, Nl, E, Ni, P, Lie, A; 1996 v A, La, P, Ru, CzR, P (sub), Cro, Ho (sub), US; (with Sunderland), 1997 v Lie; 1998 v Li, Arg; 1999 v Ma, Y, Para, Se, Ni, Mac; 2000 v Y, Cro (sub), Ma, Mac, T, CzR, S, M, US (sub), S.Af; 2001 v Ho, P, Es, P, Es; 2002 v Ho (sub), Cy, Ir, Ru (sub), G (sub), S.Ar (sub), Sp (sub) (91)

Reid, A. M. (Nottingham F), 2004 v Ca, Br, CzR, Pol, R, Jam, Ho; 2005 v Bul, Cy, Sw, F (sub), Fa; (with Tottenham H), P, Chn, Is, Fa; 2006 v I, F, Cy (sub), Sw, Se, Ch (sub) (22)
Reid, C. (Brideville), 1931 v Sp (1)
Reid, S. J. (Millwall), 2002 v Cro, Ru, D (sub), US (sub), Ng (sub), Cam (sub), G (sub); 2003 v S, Alb (sub); (with Blackburn R), 2004 v Ru (sub), T (sub), Ca, Pol; 2006 v I, Sw (sub), Ch (16)
Richardson, D. J. (Shamrock R), 1972 v A (sub); (with Gillingham), 1973 v N (sub); 1980 v Cz (3)
Rigby, A. (St James' Gate), 1935 v H, Sw, G (3)
Ringstead, A. (Sheffield U), 1951 v Arg, N; 1952 v WG (2), A, Sp; 1953 v A; 1954 v F; 1955 v N; 1956 v Y, Sp, Ho; 1957 v E (2); 1958 v D, Pol, A; 1959 v Pol, Cz (2) (20)
Robinson, J. (Bohemians), 1928 v Bel; (with Dolphin), 1931 v Sp (2)
Robinson, M. (Brighton & HA), 1981 v WG 'B', F, Cy, Bel, Pol; 1982 v Ho, F, Alg, Ch; 1983 v Ho, Sp, Ic, Ma; (with Liverpool), 1984 v Ic, Ho, Is; 1985 v USSR, N; (with QPR), N, Sp, Sw; 1986 v D (sub), W, Cz (24)
Roche, P. J. (Shelbourne), 1972 v A; (with Manchester U), 1975 v USSR, T, Sw, USSR, Sw, WG; 1976 v T (8)
Rogers, E. (Blackburn R), 1968 v Cz, Pol; 1969 v Pol, A, D, Cz, D, H; 1970 v S, D, H; 1971 v I (2), A; (with Charlton Ath), 1972 v Ir, Ec, Ch, P; 1973 v USSR (19)
Rowlands, M. C. (QPR), 2004 v R (sub), Ng (sub), Jam (sub) (3)
Ryan, G. (Derby Co), 1978 v T; (with Brighton & HA), 1979 v E, WG; 1980 v W, Cy (sub), Sw, Arg (sub); 1981 v WG 'B' (sub), F (sub), Pol (sub); 1982 v Br (sub), Ho (sub), Alg (sub), Ch (sub), Tr; 1984 v Pol, Chn; 1985 v M (18)
Ryan, R. A. (WBA), 1950 v Se, Bel; 1951 v N, Arg, N; 1952 v WG (2), A, Sp; 1953 v F, A; 1954 v F, L, F; 1955 v N; (with Derby Co), 1956 v Sp (16)

Sadlier, R. T. (Millwall), 2002 v Ru (sub) (1)
Savage, D. P. T. (Millwall), 1996 v P (sub), Cro (sub), US (sub), M, Bol (5)
Saward, P. (Millwall), 1954 v L; (with Aston Villa), 1957 v E (2); 1958 v D, Pol, A; 1959 v Pol, Cz; 1960 v Se, Ch, WG, Se; 1961 v W, N; (with Huddersfield T), 1961 v S; 1962 v A; 1963 v Ic (2) (18)
Scannell, T. (Southend U), 1954 v L (1)
Scully, P. J. (Arsenal), 1989 v Tun (sub) (1)
Sheedy, K. (Everton), 1984 v Ho (sub), Ma; 1985 v D, I, Is, Sw; 1986 v Sw, D; 1987 v S, Pol; 1988 v Is, R, Pol, E (sub), USSR, Ho (sub); 1989 v Ni, Tun, H, Sp, Ma, H; 1990 v Ni, Ma, W (sub), USSR, Fi (sub), T, E, Eg, Ho, R, I; 1991 v W, E, Pol, Ch, US; 1992 v H, Pol, T, W; (with Newcastle U), Sw (sub), Alb; 1993 v La, W (sub) (46)
Sheridan, J. J. (Leeds U), 1988 v R, Y, Pol, N (sub); 1989 v Sp; (with Sheffield W), 1990 v W, T (sub), Ma, I (sub); 1991 v Mor (sub), T, Ch, US (sub); 1992 v H; 1993 v La

(sub); 1994 v Sp (sub), Ho, Bol, G, CzR, I, M, N, Ho; 1995 v La, Lie, Ni, E, Ni, P, Lie, A; 1996 v A, Ho (34)

Slaven, B. (Middlesbrough), 1990 v W, Fi, T (sub), Ma; 1991 v W, Pol (sub); 1993 v W (7)

Sloan, J. W. (Arsenal), 1946 v P, Sp (2)

Smyth, M. (Shamrock R), 1969 v Pol (sub) (1)

Squires, J. (Shelbourne), 1934 v Ho (1)

Stapleton, F. (Arsenal), 1977 v T, F, Sp, Bul; 1978 v Bul, N, D; 1979 v Ni, E (sub), D, WG; 1980 v W, Bul, Ni, E, Cy; 1981 v WG 'B', Ho, Bel, F, Cy, Bel, Cz, Pol; (with Manchester U), 1982 v Ho, F, Alg; 1983 v Ho, Sp, Ic, Ma, Sp; 1984 v Ic, Ho, Ma, Pol, Is, Chn; 1985 v N, D, I, Is, E, N, Sw; 1986 v Sw, USSR, D, U, Ic, Cz (sub); 1987 v Bel (2), S (2), Pol, Bul, L; (with Ajax), 1988 v L, Bul, R, Y, N, E, USSR, Ho; (with Le Havre), 1989 v F, Sp, Ma; (with Blackburn R), 1990 v WG, Ma (sub) (71)

Staunton, S. (Liverpool), 1989 v Tun, Sp (2), Ma, H; 1990 v WG, Ni, Ma, W, USSR, Fi, T, Ma, E, Eg, Ho, R, I; 1991 v Mor, T, E (2), W, Pol, Ch, US; (with Aston Villa), 1992 v Pol, T, Sw, US, Alb, US, I, P; 1993 v La, Sp, Ni, D, Alb, La, Li; 1994 v Li, Sp, Ho, Bol, G, CzR, I, M, N, Ho; 1995 v La, Lie, Ni, E, Ni, P, Lie, A; 1996 v La, P, Ru; 1997 v Lie, Mac (2), W, R, Lie; 1998 v Li, Ic, Li, Bel (2), Arg; (with Liverpool), 1999 v Cro, Ma, Y, Se; 2000 v Y, Cro, Ma, Mac, CzR (sub), Gr; 2001 v Ho (sub), Fi (sub); (with Aston Villa), And (sub), P, Es; 2002 v Cro, Ho, Cy, Ir (2), Ru (sub), D, US (sub), Ng, Cam, G, S.Ar, Sp (102)

Stevenson, A. E. (Dolphin), 1932 v Ho; (with Everton), 1947 v E, Sp, P; 1948 v P, Sp; 1949 v Sw (7)

Strahan, F. (Shelbourne), 1964 v Pol, N, E; 1965 v Pol; 1966 v WG (5)

Sullivan, J. (Fordsons), 1928 v Bel (1)

Swan, M. M. G. (Drumcondra), 1960 v Se (sub) (1)

Synnott, N. (Shamrock R), 1978 v T, Pol; 1979 v Ni (3)

Taylor, T. (Waterford), 1959 v Pol (sub) (1)

Thomas, P. (Waterford), 1974 v Pol, Br (2)

Thompson, J. (Nottingham F), 2004 v Ca (sub) (1)

Townsend, A. D. (Norwich C), 1989 v F, Sp (sub), Ma (sub), H; 1990 v WG (sub), Ni, Ma, W, USSR, Fi (sub), T, Ma (sub), E, Eg, Ho, R, I; (with Chelsea), 1991 v Mor, T, E (2), W, Pol, Ch, US; 1992 v Pol, W, US, Alb, US, I; 1993 v La, D, Sp, Ni, D, Alb, La, Li; (with Aston Villa), 1994 v Li, Ni, Ho, Bol, G, CzR, I, M, N, Ho; 1995 v La, Ni, E, Ni, P; 1996 v A, La, Ho, Ru, CzR, P; 1997 v Lie, Mac (2), Ic, R, Lie; 1998 v Li; (with Middlesbrough), Ic, Bel (2) (70)

Traynor, T. J. (Southampton), 1954 v L; 1962 v A; 1963 v Ic (2), S; 1964 v A (2), Sp (8)

Treacy, R. C. P. (WBA), 1966 v WG; 1967 v Sp, Cz; 1968 v Cz; (with Charlton Ath), 1968 v Pol; 1969 v Pol, Cz, D; 1970 v S, D, H (sub), Pol (sub), WG (sub); 1971 v Pol, Se (sub+1), I, A; (with Swindon T), 1972 v Ir, Ec, Ch, P; 1973 v USSR, F, USSR, Pol, F, N; 1974 v Pol; (with Preston NE), Br; 1975 v USSR, Sw (2), WG; 1976 v T, N (sub), Pol (sub); (with WBA), 1977 v F, Pol; (with Shamrock R), 1978 v T, Pol; 1980 v Cz (sub) (42)

Tuohy, L. (Shamrock R), 1956 v Y; 1959 v Cz (2); (with Newcastle U), 1962 v A; 1963 v Ic (2); (with Shamrock R), 1964 v A; 1965 v Bel (8)

Turner, C. J. (Southend U), 1936 v Sw; 1937 v G, H, Sw, F; 1938 v N (2); (with West Ham U), Cz, Pol; 1939 v H (10)

Turner, P. (Celtic), 1963 v S; 1964 v Sp (2)

Vernon, J. (Belfast C), 1946 v P, Sp (2)

Waddock, G. (QPR), 1980 v Sw, Arg; 1981 v W, Pol (sub); 1982 v Alg; 1983 v Ic, Ma, Sp, Ho (sub); 1984 v Ma (sub), Ic, Ho, Is; 1985 v I, Is, E, N, Sp; 1986 v USSR; (with Millwall), 1990 v USSR, T (21)

Walsh, D. J. (Linfield), 1946 v P, Sp; (with WBA), 1947 v Sp, P; 1948 v P, Sp; 1949 v Sw, P, Se, Sp; 1950 v E, Fi, Se; 1951 v N; (with Aston Villa), Arg, N; 1952 v Sp; 1953 v A; 1954 v F (2) (20)

Walsh, J. (Limerick), 1982 v Tr (1)

Walsh, M. (Blackpool), 1976 v N, Pol; 1977 v F (sub), Pol; (with Everton), 1979 v Ni (sub); (with QPR), D (sub), Bul, WG (sub); (with Porto), 1981 v Bel (sub), Cz; 1982 v Alg (sub); 1983 v Sp, Ho (sub), Sp (sub); 1984 v Ic (sub), Ma, Pol, Chn; 1985 v USSR, N (sub), D (21)

Walsh, M. (Everton), 1982 v Ch, Br, Tr; 1983 v Ic (4)

Walsh, W. (Manchester C), 1947 v E, Sp, P; 1948 v P, Sp; 1949 v Bel; 1950 v E, Se, Bel (9)

Waters, J. (Grimsby T), 1977 v T; 1980 v Ni (sub) (2)

Watters, F. (Shelbourne), 1926 v I (1)

Weir, E. (Clyde), 1939 v H (2), G (3)

Whelan, R. (St Patrick's Ath), 1964 v A, E (sub) (2)

Whelan, R. (Liverpool), 1981 v Cz (sub); 1982 v Ho (sub), F; 1983 v Ic, Ma, Sp; 1984 v Is; 1985 v USSR, N, I (sub), Is, E, N (sub), Sw (sub); 1986 v USSR (sub), W; 1987 v Bel (sub), S, Bul, Bel, Br, L; 1988 v L, Bul, Pol, N, E, USSR, Ho; 1989 v Ni, F, H, Sp, Ma; 1990 v WG, Ni, Ma, W, Ho (sub); 1991 v Mor, E; 1992 v Sw; 1993 v La, W (sub), Li (sub); 1994 v Li (sub), Sp, Ru, Ho, G (sub), N (sub); (with Southend U), 1995 v Lie, A (53)

Whelan, W. (Manchester U), 1956 v Ho; 1957 v D, E (2) (4)

White, J. J. (Bohemians), 1928 v Bel (1)

Whittaker, R. (Chelsea), 1959 v Cz (1)

Williams, J. (Shamrock R), 1938 v N (1)

England's youngest Theo Walcott in action during the friendly match against Hungary at Old Trafford in May 2006. (John Sibley Livepic/Actionimages)

BRITISH AND IRISH INTERNATIONAL GOALSCORERS SINCE 1872

Where two players with the same surname and initials have appeared for the same country, and one or both have scored, they have been distinguished by reference to the club which appears *first* against their name in the international appearances section.

ENGLAND	
A'Court, A.	1
Adams, T. A.	5
Adcock, H.	1
Alcock, C. W.	1
Allen, A.	3
Allen, R.	2
Amos, A.	1
Anderson, V.	2
Anderton, D. R.	7
Astall, G.	1
Athersmith, W. C.	3
Atyeo, P. J. W.	5
Bache, J. W.	4
Bailey, N. C.	2
Baily, E. F.	5
Baker, J. H.	3
Ball, A. J.	8
Bambridge, A. L.	1
Bambridge, E. C.	11
Barclay, R.	2
Barmby, N. J.	4
Barnes, J.	11
Barnes, P. S.	4
Barton, J.	1
Bassett, W. I.	8
Bastin, C. S.	12
Beardsley, P. A.	9
Beasley, A.	1
Beattie, T. K.	1
Beckham, D. R. J.	17
Becton, F.	2
Bedford, H.	1
Bell, C.	9
Bentley, R. T. F.	9
Bishop, S. M.	1
Blackburn, F.	1
Blissett, L.	3
Bloomer, S.	28
Bond, R.	2
Bonsor, A. G.	1
Bowden, E. R.	1
Bowers, J. W.	2
Bowles, S.	1
Bradford, G. R. W.	1
Bradford, J.	7
Bradley, W.	2
Bradshaw, F.	3
Brann, G.	1
Bridge, W. M.	1
Bridges, B. J.	1
Bridgett, A.	3
Brindle, T.	1
Britton, C. S.	1
Broadbent, P. F.	2
Broadis, I. A.	8
Brodie, J. B.	1
Bromley-Davenport, W.	2
Brook, E. F.	10
Brooking, T. D.	5
Brooks, J.	2
Broome, F. H.	3
Brown, A.	4
Brown, A. S.	1
Brown, G.	5
Brown, J.	3
Brown, W.	1
Buchan, C. M.	4
Bull, S. G.	4
Bullock, N.	2
Burgess, H.	4
Butcher, T.	3
Byrne, J. J.	8
Campbell, S. J.	1
Camsell, G. H.	18
Carter, H. S.	7
Carter, J. H.	4
Chadwick, E.	3
Chamberlain, M.	1
Chambers, H.	5
Channon, M. R.	21
Charlton, J.	6
Charlton, R.	49
Chenery, C. J.	1
Chivers, M.	13
Clarke, A. J.	10
Cobbold, W. N.	6
Cock, J. G.	2
Cole, A.	1
Cole, J. J.	6
Common, A.	2
Connelly, J. M.	7
Coppell, S. J.	7
Cotterill, G. H.	2
Cowans, G.	2
Crawford, R.	1
Crawshaw, T. H.	1
Crayston, W. J.	1
Creek, F. N. S.	1
Crooks, S. D.	7
Crouch, P. J.	6
Currey, E. S.	2
Currie, A. W.	3
Cursham, A. W.	2
Cursham, H. A.	5
Daft, H. B.	3
Davenport, J. K.	2
Davis, G.	1
Davis, H.	1
Day, S. H.	2
Dean, W. R.	18
Defoe, J. C.	1
Devey, J. H. G.	1
Dewhurst, F.	11
Dix, W. R.	1
Dixon, K. M.	4
Dixon, L. M.	1
Dorrell, A. R.	1
Douglas, B.	11
Drake, E. J.	6
Ducat, A.	1
Dunn, A. T. B.	2
Eastham, G.	2
Edwards, D.	5
Ehiogu, U.	1
Elliott, W. H.	3
Evans, R. E.	1
Ferdinand, L.	5
Ferdinand, R. G.	1
Finney, T.	30
Fleming, H. J.	9
Flowers, R.	10
Forman, Frank	1
Forman, Fred	3
Foster, R. E.	3
Fowler, R. B.	7
Francis, G. C. J.	3
Francis, T.	12
Freeman, B. C.	3
Froggatt, J.	2
Froggatt, R.	2
Galley, T.	1
Gascoigne, P. J.	10
Geary, F.	3
Gerrard, S. G.	9
Gibbins, W. V. T.	3
Gilliatt, W. E.	3
Goddard, P.	1
Goodall, J.	12
Goodyer, A. C.	1
Gosling, R. C.	2
Goulden, L. A.	4
Grainger, C.	3
Greaves, J.	44
Grovesnor, A. T.	2
Gunn, W.	1
Haines, J. T. W.	2
Hall, G. W.	9
Halse, H. J.	2
Hampson, J.	5
Hampton, H.	2
Hancocks, J.	2
Hardman, H. P.	1
Harris, S. S.	2
Hassall, H. W.	4
Hateley, M.	9
Haynes, J. N.	18
Hegan, K. E.	4
Henfrey, A. G.	2
Heskey, E. W.	5
Hilsdon, G. R.	14
Hine, E. W.	4
Hinton, A. T.	1
Hirst, D. E.	1
Hitchens, G. A.	5
Hobbis, H. H. F.	1
Hoddle, G.	8
Hodgetts, D.	1
Hodgson, G.	1
Holley, G. H.	8
Houghton, W. E.	5
Howell, R.	1
Hughes, E. W.	1
Hulme, J. H. A.	4
Hunt, G. S.	1
Hunt, R.	18
Hunter, N.	2
Hurst, G. C.	24
Ince, P. E. C.	2
Jack, D. N. B.	3
Jeffers, F.	1
Johnson, D. E.	6
Johnson, E.	2
Johnson, J. A.	2
Johnson, T. C. F.	5
Johnson, W. H.	1
Kail, E. I. L.	2
Kay, A. H.	1
Keegan, J. K.	21
Kelly, R.	8
Kennedy, R.	3
Kenyon-Slaney, W. S.	2
Keown, M. R.	2
Kevan, D. T.	8
Kidd, B.	1
King, L. B.	1
Kingsford, R. K.	1
Kirchen, A. J.	2
Kirton, W. J.	1
Lampard, F. J.	11
Langton, R.	1
Latchford, R. D.	5
Latheron, E. G.	1
Lawler, C.	1
Lawton, T.	22
Lee, F.	10
Lee, J.	1
Lee, R. M.	2
Lee, S.	2
Le Saux, G. P.	1
Lindley, T.	14
Lineker, G.	48
Lofthouse, J. M.	3
Lofthouse, N.	30
Hon. A. Lyttelton	1
Mabbutt, G.	1
Macdonald, M.	6
Mannion, W. J.	11
Mariner, P.	13
Marsh, R. W.	1
Matthews, S.	11
Matthews, V.	1
McCall, J.	1
McDermott, T.	3
McManaman, S.	3
Medley, L. D.	1
Melia, J.	1
Mercer, D. W.	1
Merson, P. C.	3
Milburn, J. E. T.	10
Miller, H. S.	1
Mills, G. R.	3
Milward, A.	3
Mitchell, C.	5
Moore, J.	1
Moore, R. F.	2
Moore, W. G. B.	2
Morren, T.	1
Morris, F.	1
Morris, J.	3
Mortensen, S. H.	23
Morton, J. R.	1
Mosforth, W.	3
Mullen, J.	6
Mullery, A. P.	1
Murphy, D. B	1
Neal, P. G.	5
Needham, E.	3
Nicholls, J.	1
Nicholson, W. E.	1
O'Grady, M.	3
Osborne, F. R.	3
Owen, M. J.	36
Own goals	26
Page, L. A.	1
Paine, T. L.	7
Palmer, C. L.	1
Parry, E. H.	1
Parry, R. A.	1

Pawson, F. W. 1
Payne, J. 2
Peacock, A. 3
Pearce, S. 5
Pearson, J. S. 5
Pearson, S. C. 5
Perry, W. 2
Peters, M. 20
Pickering, F. 5
Platt, D. 27
Pointer, R. 2

Quantrill, A. 1

Ramsay, A. E. 3
Revie, D. G. 4
Redknapp, J. F. 1
Reynolds, J. 3
Richardson, K. E. 2
Richardson, J. R. 2
Rigby, A. 3
Rimmer, E. J. 2
Roberts, F. 2
Roberts, H. 1
Roberts, W. T. 2
Robinson, J. 3
Robson, B. 26
Robson, R. 4
Rooney, W. 11
Rowley, J. F. 6
Royle, J. 2
Rutherford, J. 3

Sagar, C. 1
Sandilands, R. R. 3
Sansom, K. 1
Schofield, J. 1
Scholes, P. 14
Seed, J. M. 1
Settle, J. 6
Sewell, J. 3
Shackleton, L. F. 1
Sharp, J. 1
Shearer, A. 30
Shelton, A. 1
Shepherd, A. 2
Sheringham, E. P. 11
Simpson, J. 1
Smith, A. 1
Smith, A. M. 2
Smith, G. O. 11
Smith, Joe 1
Smith, J. R. 2
Smith, J. W. 4
Smith, R. 13
Smith, S. 1
Sorby, T. H. 1
Southgate, G. 2
Southworth, J. 3
Sparks, F. J. 3
Spence, J. W. 1
Spiksley, F. 5
Spilsbury, B. W. 5
Steele, F. C. 8
Stephenson, G. T. 2
Steven, T. M. 4
Stewart, J. 2
Stiles, N. P. 1
Storer, H. 1
Stone, S. B. 2
Summerbee, M. G. 1

Tambling, R. V. 1
Taylor, P. J. 2
Taylor, T. 16
Terry, J. G. 1
Thompson, P. B. 1
Thornewell, G. 1
Tilson, S. F. 6
Townley, W. J. 2
Tueart, D. 2

Vassell, D. 6
Vaughton, O. H. 6
Veitch, J. G. 3
Viollet, D. S. 1

Waddle, C. R. 6
Walker, W. H. 9
Wall, G. 2
Wallace, D. 1
Walsh, P. 1
Waring, T. 4
Warren, B. 2
Watson, D. V. 4
Watson, V. M. 4
Webb, G. W. 1
Webb, N. 4
Wedlock, W. J. 2
Weller, K. 1
Welsh, D. 1
Whateley, O. 2
Wheldon, G. F. 6
Whitfield, H. 1
Wignall, F. 2
Wilkes, A. 1
Wilkins, R. G. 3
Willingham, C. K. 1
Wilshaw, D. J. 10
Wilson, G. P. 1
Winckworth, W. N. 1
Windridge, J. E. 7
Wise, D. F. 1
Withe, P. 1
Wollaston, C. H. R. 1
Wood, H. 1
Woodcock, T. 16
Woodhall, G. 1
Woodward, V. J. 29
Worrall, F. 2
Worthington, F. S. 2
Wright, I. E. 9
Wright, M. 1
Wright, W. A. 3
Wright-Phillips, S. C. 1
Wylie, J. G. 1

Yates, J. 3

NORTHERN IRELAND

Anderson, T. 4
Armstrong, G. 12

Bambrick, J. 12
Barr, H. H. 1
Barron, H. 3
Best, G. 9
Bingham, W. L. 10
Black, K. 1
Blanchflower, D. 2
Blanchflower, J. 1
Brennan, B. 1
Brennan, R. A. 1
Brotherston, N. 3
Brown, J. 1
Browne, F. 2

Campbell, J. 1
Campbell, W. G. 1
Casey, T. 2
Caskey, W. 1
Cassidy, T. 1
Chambers, J. 3
Clarke, C. J. 13
Clements, D. 2
Cochrane, T. 1
Condy, J. 1
Connor, M. J. 1
Coulter, J. 1
Croft, T. 1
Crone, W. 1
Crossan, E. 1
Crossan, J. A. 10
Curran, S. 2
Cush, W. W. 5

Dalton, W. 4
D'Arcy, S. D. 1
Darling, J. 1
Davey, H. H. 1
Davis, S. 1
Davis, T. L. 1
Dill, A. H. 1
Doherty, L. 1
Doherty, P. D. 3
Dougan, A. D. 8
Dowie, I. 12
Dunne, J. 4

Elder, A. R. 1
Elliott, S. 4
Emerson, W. 1
English, S. 1

Feeney, W. J. 2
Ferguson, W. 1
Ferris, J. 1
Ferris, R. O. 1
Finney, T. 2

Gaffkin, J. 4
Gara, A. 3
Gaukrodger, G. 1
Gibb, J. T. 2
Gibb, T. J. 1
Gillespie, K. R. 2
Gillespie, W. 13
Goodall, A. L. 2
Griffin, D. J. 1
Gray, P. 6

Halligan, W. 1
Hamill, M. 1
Hamilton, B. 4
Hamilton, W. R. 5
Hannon, D. J. 1
Harkin, J. T. 2
Harvey, M. 3
Healy, D. J. 19
Hill, C. F. 1
Hughes, M. E. 5
Humphries, W. 1
Hunter, A. (*Distillery*) 1
Hunter, A. (*Blackburn R*) 1
Hunter, B. V. 1

Irvine, R. W. 3
Irvine, W. J. 8

Johnston, H. 2
Johnston, S. 2
Johnston, W. C. 1
Jones, S. 1
Jones, S. (*Crewe Alex*) 1
Jones, J. 1

Kelly, J. 4
Kernaghan, N. 2
Kirwan, J. 2

Lacey, W. 3
Lemon, J. 2
Lennon, N. F. 2
Lockhart, N. 3
Lomas, S. M. 3

Magilton, J. 5
Mahood, J. 2
Martin, D. K. 3
Maxwell, J. 2
McAdams, W. J. 7
McAllen, J. 1
Mcauley, J. L. 1
McCartney, G. 1
McCandless, J. 2
McCandless, W. 1
McCaw, J. H. 1
McClelland, J. 1
McCluggage, A. 2
McCracken, W. 1
McCrory, S. 1
McCurdy, C. 1
McDonald, A. 3
McGarry, J. K. 1
McGrath, R. C. 4
McIlroy, J. 10
McIlroy, S. B. 5
McKenzie, H 1
McKnight, J. 2
McLaughlin, J. C. 6
McMahon, G. J. 2
McMordie, A. S. 3
McMorran, E. J. 4
McParland, P. J. 10
McWha, W. B. R. 1
Meldon, P. A 1
Mercer, J. T. 1
Millar, W. 1
Milligan, D. 1
Milne, R. G. 2
Molyneux, T. B. 1
Moreland, V. 1
Morgan, S. 3
Morrow, S. J. 1
Morrow, W. J. 1
Mulryne, P. P. 3
Murdock, C. J. 1
Murphy, N. 1

Neill, W. J. T. 2
Nelson, S. 1
Nicholl, C. J. 3
Nicholl, J. M. 1
Nicholson, J. J. 6

O'Boyle, G. 1
O'Hagan, C. 2
O'Kane, W. J. 1
O'Neill, J. 2
O'Neill, M. A. 4
O'Neill, M. H. 8
Own goals 6

Patterson, D. J. 1
Peacock, R. 2
Peden, J. 7
Penney, S. 2
Pyper, James 2
Pyper, John 1

Quinn, J. M. 12
Quinn, S. J. 4

Reynolds, J. 1
Rowland, K. 1
Rowley, R. W. M. 2
Rushe, F. 1

Sheridan, J. 2
Sherrard, J. 1
Sherrard, W. C. 2
Simpson, W. J. 5
Sloan, H. A. de B. 4
Smyth, S. 5
Spence, D. W. 3
Sproule, I. 1
Stanfield, O. M. 11
Stevenson, A. E. 5
Stewart, I. 2

Taggart, G. P. 7
Thompson, F. W. 2
Torrans, S. 1
Tully, C. P. 3
Turner, A. 1

Walker, J. 1
Walsh, D. J. 5
Welsh, E. 1
Whiteside, N. 9
Whiteside, T. 1
Whitley, Jeff 2
Williams, J. R. 1
Williams, M. S. 1
Williamson, J. 1

Wilson, D. J. 1
Wilson, K. J. 6
Wilson, S. J. 7
Wilton, J. M. 2

Young, S. 1
N.B. In 1914 Young goal should be credited to Gillespie W v Wales

SCOTLAND
Aitken, R. (*Celtic*) 1
Aitken, R. (*Dumbarton*) 1
Aitkenhead, W. A. C. 2
Alexander, D. 1
Allan, D. S. 4
Allan, J. 2
Anderson, F. 1
Anderson, W. 4
Andrews, P. 1
Archibald, A. 1
Archibald, S. 4

Baird, D. 2
Baird, J. C. 2
Baird, S. 2
Bannon, E. 1
Barbour, A. 1
Barker, J. B. 4
Battles, B. Jr 1
Bauld, W. 2
Baxter, J. C. 3
Bell, J. 5
Bennett, A. 2
Berry, D. 1
Bett, J. 1
Beveridge, W. W. 1
Black, A. 3
Black, D. 1
Bone, J. 1
Booth, S. 6
Boyd, K 2
Boyd, R. 2
Boyd, T. 1
Boyd, W. G. 1
Brackenridge, T. 1
Brand, R. 8
Brazil, A. 1
Bremner, W. J. 3
Brown, A. D. 6
Buchanan, P. S. 1
Buchanan, R. 1
Buckley, P. 1
Buick, A. 2
Burke, C. 2
Burley, C. W. 3
Burns, K. 1

Cairns, T. 1
Caldwell, G. 1
Calderwood, C. 1
Calderwood, R. 2
Caldow, E. 4
Cameron, C. 2
Campbell, C. 1
Campbell, John (*Celtic*) 5
Campbell, John (*Rangers*) 4
Campbell, J. (*South Western*) 1
Campbell, P. 2
Campbell, R. 1
Cassidy, J. 1
Chalmers, S. 3
Chambers, T. 1
Cheyne, A. G. 4
Christie, A. J. 1
Clunas, W. L. 1
Collins, J. 12
Collins, R. Y. 10
Combe, J. R. 1
Conn, A. 1
Cooper, D. 6

Craig, J. 1
Craig, T. 1
Crawford, S. 4
Cunningham, A. N. 5
Curran, H. P. 1

Dailly, C. 5
Dalglish, K. 30
Davidson, D. 1
Davidson, J. A. 1
Delaney, J. 3
Devine, A. 1
Dewar, G. 1
Dewar, N. 4
Dickov, P. 1
Dickson, W. 4
Divers, J. 1
Dobie, R. S. 1
Docherty, T. H. 1
Dodds, D. 1
Dodds, W. 7
Donaldson, A. 1
Donnachie, J. 1
Dougall, J. 1
Drummond, J. 2
Dunbar, M. 1
Duncan, D. 7
Duncan, D. M. 1
Duncan, J. 1
Dunn, J. 2
Durie, G. S. 7

Easson, J. F. 1
Elliott, M. S. 1
Ellis, J. 1

Ferguson, B. 2
Ferguson, J. 6
Fernie, W. 1
Fitchie, T. T. 1
Flavell, R. 2
Fleming, C. 2
Fleming, J. W. 3
Fletcher, D. 3
Fraser, M. J. E. 3
Freedman, D. A. 1

Gallacher, H. K. 23
Gallacher, K. W. 9
Gallacher, P. 1
Galt, J. H. 1
Gemmell, T. (*St Mirren*) 1
Gemmell, T. (*Celtic*) 1
Gemmill, A. 8
Gemmill, S. 1
Gibb, W. 1
Gibson, D. W. 3
Gibson, J. D. 1
Gibson, N. 1
Gillespie, Jas. 3
Gillick, T. 3
Gilzean, A. J. 12
Gossland, J. 2
Goudie, J. 1
Gough, C. R. 6
Gourlay, J. 1
Graham, A. 2
Graham, G. 3
Gray, A. 7
Gray, E. 3
Gray, F. 1
Greig, J. 3
Groves, W. 4

Hamilton, G. 4
Hamilton, J. (*Queen's Park*) 3
Hamilton, R. C. 15
Harper, J. M. 2
Hartley, P. J. 1
Harrower, W. 5
Hartford, R. A. 4
Heggie, C. W 4
Henderson, J. G. 1

Henderson, W. 5
Hendry, E. C. J. 3
Herd, D. G. 3
Herd, G. 1
Hewie, J. D. 2
Higgins, A. (*Newcastle U*) 1
Higgins, A. (*Kilmarnock*) 4
Highet, T. C. 1
Holt, G.J. 1
Holton, J. A. 2
Hopkin, D. 2
Houliston, W. 2
Howie, H. 1
Howie, J. 2
Hughes, J. 1
Hunter, W. 1
Hutchison, D. 6
Hutchison, T. 1
Hutton, J. 1
Hyslop, T. 1

Imrie, W. N. 1

Jackson, A. 8
Jackson, C. 1
Jackson, D. 4
James, A. W. 4
Jardine, A. 1
Jenkinson, T. 1
Jess, E. 2
Johnston, A. 2
Johnston, L. H. 1
Johnston, M. 14
Johnstone, D. 2
Johnstone, J. 4
Johnstone, Jas. 1
Johnstone, R. 10
Johnstone, W. 1
Jordan, J. 11

Kay, J. L. 5
Keillor, A. 3
Kelly, J. 1
Kelso, R. 1
Ker, G. 10
King, A. 1
King, J. 1
Kinnear, D. 1
Kyle, K. 1

Lambert, P. 1
Lambie, J. 1
Lambie, W. A. 5
Lang, J. J. 2
Latta, A. 2
Law, D. 30
Leggat, G. 8
Lennie, W. 1
Lennox, R. 3
Liddell, W. 6
Lindsay, J. 6
Linwood, A. B. 1
Logan, J. 1
Lorimer, P. 4
Love, A. 1
Low, J. (*Cambuslang*) 1
Lowe, J. (*St Bernards*) 1

Macari, L. 5
MacDougall, E. J. 3
MacLeod, M. 1
Mackay, D. C. 4
Mackay, G. 1
MacKenzie, J. A. 1
MacKinnon, W. W. 5
Madden, J. 5
Marshall, H. 1
Marshall, J. 1
Mason, J. 4
Massie, A. 1
Masson, D. S. 5
McAdam, J. 1

McAllister, G. 5
McAulay, J. D. 1
McAvennie, F. 1
McCall, J. 1
McCall, S. M. 1
McCalliog, J. 1
McCallum, N. 1
McCann, N. 3
McClair, B. J. 2
McCoist, A. 19
McColl, R. S. 13
McCulloch, D. 3
McDougall, J. 4
McFarlane, A. 1
McFadden, J. 8
McFadyen, W. 2
McGhee, M. 2
McGinlay, J. 4
McGregor, J. 1
McGrory, J. 6
McGuire, W. 1
McInally, A. 3
McInnes, T. 2
McKie, J. 2
McKimmie, S. 1
McKinlay, W. 4
McKinnon, A. 1
McKinnon, R. 1
McLaren, A. 4
McLaren, J. 1
McLean, A. 1
McLean, T. 1
McLintock, F. 1
McMahon, A. 6
McMenemy, J. 5
McMillan, I. L. 2
McNeill, W. 3
McNiel, H. 5
McPhail, J. 3
McPhail, R. 7
McPherson, J. 5
McPherson, J. (*Vale of Leven*) 1
McPherson, R. 1
McQueen, G. 5
McStay, P. 9
McSwegan, G. 1
Meiklejohn, D. D. 3
Millar, J. 2
Miller, K. 7
Miller, T. 2
Miller, W. 1
Mitchell, R. C. 1
Morgan, W. 1
Morris, D. 1
Morris, H. 3
Morton, A. L. 5
Mudie, J. K. 9
Mulhall, G. 1
Munro, A. D. 1
Munro, N. 2
Murdoch, R. 5
Murphy, F. 1
Murray, J. 1

Napier, C. E. 3
Narey, D. 1
Naysmith, G. A. 1
Neil, R. G. 2
Nevin, P. K. F. 5
Nicholas, C. 5
Nisbet, J. 2

O'Connor, G. 1
O'Donnell, F. 2
O'Hare, J. 5
Ormond, W. E. 2
O'Rourke, F. 1
Orr, R. 1
Orr, T. 1
Oswald, J. 1
Own goals 17

Parlane, D.	1
Paul, H. McD.	2
Paul, W.	5
Pettigrew, W.	2
Provan, D.	1
Quashie, N. F.	1
Quinn, J.	7
Quinn, P.	1
Rankin, G.	2
Rankin, R.	2
Reid, W.	4
Reilly, L.	22
Renny-Tailyour, H. W.	1
Richmond, J. T.	1
Ring, T.	2
Rioch, B. D.	6
Ritchie, J.	1
Ritchie, P. S.	1
Robertson, A.	2
Robertson, J.	3
Robertson, J. N.	8
Robertson, J. T.	2
Robertson, T.	1
Robertson, W.	1
Russell, D.	1
Scott, A. S.	5
Sellar, W.	4
Sharp, G.	1
Shaw, F. W.	1
Shearer, D.	2
Simpson, J.	1
Smith, A.	5
Smith, G.	4
Smith, J.	1
Smith, John	13
Somerville, G.	1
Souness, G. J.	4
Speedie, F.	2
St John, I.	9
Steel, W.	12
Stein, C.	10
Stevenson, G.	4
Stewart, A.	1
Stewart, R.	1
Stewart, W. E.	1
Strachan, G.	5
Sturrock, P.	3
Taylor, J. D.	1
Templeton, R.	1
Thompson, S.	3
Thomson, A.	1
Thomson, C.	4
Thomson, R.	1
Thomson, W.	1
Thornton, W.	1
Waddell, T. S.	1
Waddell, W.	6
Walker, J.	2
Walker, R.	7
Walker, T.	9
Wallace, I. A.	1
Wark, J.	7
Watson, J. A. K.	1
Watt, F.	2
Watt, W. W.	1
Webster, A.	1
Weir, A.	1
Weir, D.	1
Weir, J. B.	2
White, J. A.	3
Wilkie, L.	1
Wilson, A.	2
Wilson, A. N.	13
Wilson, D. (*Queen's Park*)	2
Wilson, D. (*Rangers*)	9
Wilson, H.	1
Wylie, T. G.	1
Young, A.	5

WALES

Allchurch, I. J.	23
Allen, M.	3
Astley, D. J.	12
Atherton, R. W.	2
Bamford, T.	1
Barnes, W.	1
Bellamy, C. D.	9
Blackmore, C. G.	1
Blake, N. A.	4
Bodin, P. J.	3
Boulter, L. M.	1
Bowdler, J. C. H.	3
Bowen, D. L.	1
Bowen, M.	3
Boyle, T.	1
Bryan, T.	1
Burgess, W. A. R.	1
Burke, T.	1
Butler, W. T.	1
Chapman, T.	2
Charles, J.	1
Charles, M.	6
Charles, W. J.	15
Clarke, R. J.	5
Coleman, C.	4
Collier, D. J.	1
Crosse, K.	1
Cumner, R. H.	1
Curtis, A.	6
Curtis, E. R.	3
Davies, D. W.	1
Davies, E. Lloyd	1
Davies, G.	2
Davies, L. S.	6
Davies, R. T.	9
Davies, R. W.	6
Davies, Simon	5
Davies, Stanley	5
Davies, W.	6
Davies, W. H.	1
Davies, William	5
Davis, W. O.	1
Deacy, N.	4
Doughty, J.	6
Doughty, R.	2
Durban, A.	2
Dwyer, P.	2
Earnshaw, R.	11
Edwards, G.	2
Edwards, R. I.	4
England, H. M.	4
Evans, I.	1
Evans, J.	1
Evans, R. E.	2
Evans, W.	1
Eyton-Jones, J. A.	1
Flynn, B.	7
Ford, T.	23
Foulkes, W. I.	1
Fowler, J.	3
Giles, D.	2
Giggs, R. J.	11
Glover, E. M.	7
Godfrey, B. C.	2
Green, A. W.	3
Griffiths, A. T.	6
Griffiths, M. W.	2
Griffiths, T. P.	3
Harris, C. S.	1
Hartson, J.	14
Hersee, R.	1
Hewitt, R.	1
Hockey, T.	1
Hodges, G.	2
Hole, W. J.	1
Hopkins, I. J.	2
Horne, B.	2
Howell, E. G.	3
Hughes, L. M.	16
James, E.	2
James, L.	10
James, R.	7
Jarrett, R. H.	3
Jenkyns, C. A.	1
Jones, A.	1
Jones, Bryn	6
Jones, B. S.	2
Jones, Cliff	16
Jones, C. W.	1
Jones, D. E.	1
Jones, Evan	1
Jones, H.	1
Jones, I.	1
Jones, J. L.	1
Jones, J. O.	1
Jones, J. P.	1
Jones, Leslie J.	1
Jones, R. A.	2
Jones, W. L.	6
Keenor, F. C.	2
Koumas, J.	1
Krzywicki, R. L.	1
Leek, K.	5
Lewis, B.	4
Lewis, D. M.	2
Lewis, W.	8
Lewis, W. L.	3
Lovell, S.	1
Lowrie, G.	2
Mahoney, J. F.	1
Mays, A. W.	1
Medwin, T. C.	6
Melville, A. K	3
Meredith, W. H.	11
Mills, T. J.	1
Moore, G.	1
Morgan, J. R.	2
Morgan-Owen, H.	1
Morgan-Owen, M. M.	2
Morris, A. G.	9
Morris, H.	2
Morris, R.	1
Morris, S.	2
Nicholas, P.	2
O'Callaghan, E.	3
O'Sullivan, P. A.	1
Owen, G.	2
Owen, W.	4
Owen, W. P.	6
Own goals	12
Palmer, D.	3
Parry, P. I.	1
Parry, T. D.	3
Paul, R.	1
Peake, E.	1
Pembridge, M.	6
Perry, E.	1
Phillips, C.	5
Phillips, D.	2
Powell, A.	1
Powell, D.	1
Price, J.	4
Price, P.	1
Pryce-Jones, W. E.	3
Pugh, D. H.	2
Reece, G. I.	2
Rees, R. R.	3
Richards, R. W.	1
Roach, J.	2
Robbins, W. W.	4
Roberts, J. (*Corwen*)	1
Roberts, Jas.	1
Roberts, P. S.	1
Roberts, R. (*Druids*)	1
Roberts, W. (*Llangollen*)	2
Roberts, W. (*Wrexham*)	1
Roberts, W. H.	1
Robinson, C. P.	1
Robinson, J. R. C.	3
Rush, I.	28
Russell, M. R.	1
Sabine, H. W.	1
Saunders, D.	22
Savage, R. W.	2
Shaw, E. G.	2
Sisson, H.	4
Slatter, N.	2
Smallman, D. P.	1
Speed, G. A.	7
Symons, C. J.	2
Tapscott, D. R.	4
Taylor, G. K.	1
Thomas, M.	4
Thomas, T.	1
Toshack, J. B.	12
Trainer, H.	2
Vaughan, John	2
Vernon, T. R.	8
Vizard, E. T.	1
Walsh, I.	7
Warren, F. W.	3
Watkins, W. M.	4
Wilding, J.	4
Williams, A.	1
Williams, D. R.	2
Williams, G. E.	1
Williams, G. G.	1
Williams, W.	1
Woosnam, A. P.	3
Wynn, G. A.	1
Yorath, T. C.	2
Young, E.	1

REPUBLIC OF IRELAND

Aldridge, J.	19
Ambrose, P.	1
Anderson, J.	1
Barrett, G.	2
Bermingham, P.	1
Bradshaw, P.	4
Brady, L.	9
Breen, G.	6
Brown, J.	1
Byrne, D. (*Bray*)	1
Byrne, J.	4
Cantwell, J.	14
Carey, J.	3
Carroll, T.	1
Cascarino, A.	19
Coad, P.	3
Connolly, D. J.	9
Conroy, T.	2
Conway, J.	3
Coyne, T.	6
Cummins, G.	5
Curtis, D.	8

Name	Goals
Daly, G.	13
Davis, T.	4
Dempsey, J.	1
Dennehy, M.	2
Doherty, G. M. T.	4
Donnelly, J.	4
Donnelly, T.	1
Duff, D. A.	7
Duffy, B.	1
Duggan, H.	1
Dunne, J.	13
Dunne, L.	1
Dunne, R. P.	4
Eglington, T.	2
Elliott, S. W.	1
Ellis, P.	1
Fagan, F.	5
Fallon, S.	2
Fallon, W.	2
Farrell, P.	3
Finnan, S.	1
Fitzgerald, P.	2
Fitzgerald, J.	1
Fitzsimons, A.	7
Flood, J. J.	4
Fogarty, A.	3
Foley, D.	2
Fullam, J.	1
Fullam, R.	1
Galvin, A.	1
Gavin, J.	2
Geoghegan, M.	2
Giles, J.	5
Givens, D.	19
Glynn, D.	1
Grealish, T.	8
Grimes, A. A.	1
Hale, A.	2
Hand, E.	2
Harte, I. P.	11
Haverty, J.	3
Healy, C.	1
Holland, M. R.	5
Holmes, J.	1
Horlacher, A.	2
Houghton, R.	6
Hughton, C.	1
Hurley, C.	2
Irwin, D.	4
Jordan, D.	1
Kavanagh, G. A.	1
Keane, R. D.	26
Keane, R. M.	9
Kelly, D.	9
Kelly, G.	2
Kelly, J.	2
Kennedy, M.	4
Kernaghan, A. N.	1
Kilbane, K. D.	5
Kinsella, M. A.	3
Lacey, W.	1
Lawrenson, M.	5
Leech, M.	2
McAteer, J. W.	3
McCann, J.	1
McCarthy, M.	2
McEvoy, A.	6
McGee, P.	4
McGrath, P.	8
McLoughlin, A. F.	2
McPhail, S. J. P.	1
Mancini, T.	1
Martin, C.	6
Martin, M.	4
Miller, L. W. P.	1
Mooney, J.	1
Moore, P.	7
Moran, K.	6
Morrison, C. H.	9
Moroney, T.	1
Mulligan, P.	1
O'Brien, A. J.	1
O'Callaghan, K.	1
O'Connor, T.	2
O'Farrell, F.	2
O'Flanagan, K.	3
O'Keefe, E.	1
O'Leary, D. A.	1
O'Neill, F.	1
O'Neill, K. P.	4
O'Reilly, J. (*Brideville*)	2
O'Reilly, J. (*Cork*)	1
O'Shea, J. F.	1
Own goals	10
Quinn, N.	21
Reid, A. M.	3
Reid, S. J.	2
Ringstead, A.	7
Robinson, M.	4
Rogers, E.	5
Ryan, G.	1
Ryan, R.	3
Sheedy, K.	9
Sheridan, J.	5
Slaven, B.	1
Sloan, J.	1
Squires, J.	1
Stapleton, F.	20
Staunton, S.	7
Strahan, J.	1
Sullivan, J.	1
Townsend, A. D.	7
Treacy, R.	5
Touhy, L.	4
Waddock, G.	3
Walsh, D.	5
Walsh, M.	3
Waters, J.	1
White, J. J.	2
Whelan, R.	3

Peter Crouch climbs to head home England's opening goal in the 2-0 win over Trinidad and Tobago during the Group B World Cup match in Nuremberg. (Michael Regan Livepic/Actionimages)

SOUTH AMERICA

COPA LIBERTADORES 2005

FINAL FIRST LEG
Paranaense 1, Sao Paulo 1

FINAL SECOND LEG
Sao Paulo 4, Paranaense 0

TOURNAMENT LEADING GOALSCORER
Salcedo (Cerro Porteno) 9.

COPA LIBERTADORES 2006

PRELIMINARY ROUND FIRST LEG
Nacional (Par) 2, Universitario 2
Colo Colo 1, Guadalajara 3
Palmeiras 2, Dep Tachira 0
Dep Cuenca 1, Goias 1
River Plate 6, Oriente 0
Defensor 2, Indep Santa Fe 2

PRELIMINARY ROUND SECOND LEG
Universitario 0, Nacional (Par) 0
Guadalajara 5, Colo Colo 3
Dep Tachira 2, Palmeiras 4
Goias 3, Dep Cuenca 0
Oriente 0, River Plate 2
Indep Santa Fe 0, Defensor 0

GROUP 1	P	W	D	L	F	A	Pts
Sao Paulo	6	4	0	2	12	6	12
Guadalajara	6	3	3	0	6	3	12
Caracas	6	1	2	3	7	7	5
Cienciano	6	1	1	4	3	12	4

GROUP 2	P	W	D	L	F	A	Pts
Indep Santa Fe	6	3	1	2	9	7	10
Estudiantes	6	3	1	2	10	10	10
Sporting Cristal	6	2	1	3	11	12	7
Bolivar	6	2	1	3	7	8	7

GROUP 3	P	W	D	L	F	A	Pts
Goias	6	3	2	1	7	1	11
Newell's Old Boys	6	2	2	2	7	7	8
Union Espanola	6	2	2	2	3	5	8
The Strongest	6	2	0	4	4	8	6

GROUP 4	P	W	D	L	F	A	Pts
Corinthians	6	4	1	1	10	6	13
Tigres	6	3	1	2	12	10	10
Univ Catolica	6	3	1	2	12	11	10
Dep Cali	6	0	1	5	9	16	1

GROUP 5	P	W	D	L	F	A	Pts
Velez Sarsfield	6	5	1	0	18	6	16
LDU Quito	6	3	1	2	16	9	10
Rocha	6	1	2	3	4	16	5
Universitario	6	0	2	4	5	12	2

GROUP 6	P	W	D	L	F	A	Pts
Internacional	6	4	2	0	13	4	14
Nacional	6	2	3	1	6	6	9
Union At Maracaibo	6	2	2	2	7	8	8
Pumas	6	0	1	5	4	12	1

GROUP 7	P	W	D	L	F	A	Pts
At Nacional	6	3	1	2	13	9	10
Palmeiras	6	2	3	1	9	8	9
Cerro Porteno	6	2	2	2	9	12	8
Rosario Central	6	1	2	3	6	8	5

GROUP 8	P	W	D	L	F	A	Pts
Libertad	6	3	2	1	8	3	11
River Plate	6	3	0	3	10	10	9
El Nacional	6	1	3	2	8	10	6
Paulista	6	1	3	2	4	7	6

SECOND ROUND FIRST LEG
Estudiantes 2, Goias 0
LDU Quito 4, At Nacional 0
River Plate 3, Corinthians 2
Palmeiras 1, Sao Paulo 1
Guadalajara 3, Indep Santa Fe 0
Newell's Old Boys 2, Velez Sarsfield 4
Nacional 1, Internacional 2
Tigres 0, Libertad 0

SECOND ROUND SECOND LEG
Goias 3, Estudiantes 1
At Nacional 0, LDU Quito 1
Corinthians 1, River Plate 3
Sao Paulo 2, Palmeiras 1
Indep Santa Fe 3, Guadalajara 1
Velez Sarsfield 2, Newell's Old Boys 2
Internacional 0, Nacional 0
Libertad 0, Tigres 0
Tigres 0, Libertad 0
Libertad won 5-3 on penalties.

QUARTER-FINALS
Guadalajara 0, Velez Sarsfield 0
LDU Quito 2, Internacional 1
River Plate 2, Libertad 2
Estudiantes 1, Sao Paulo 0
Competition still being played.

COPA SUDAMERICANA 2005

FIRST PHASE
Byes to second phase:
Boca Juniors (holders), River Plate, Velez Sarsfield, Pumas UNAM, America, DC United.

SECTION 1 (Argentina)
Banfield 2, Estudiantes 0
Estudiantes 2, Banfield 1
Newell's Old Boys 0, Rosario Central 0
Rosario Central 1, Newell's Old Boys 0

SECTION 2 (Brazil)
Fluminense 2, Santos 1
Santos 2, Fluminense 1
Fluminense won 4-2 on penalties.
Goias 0, Corinthians 2
Corinthians 1, Goias 1
Internacional 2, Sao Paulo 1
Sao Paulo 1, Internacional 1
Juventude 1, Cruzeiro 3
Cruzeiro 0, Juventude 1

SECTION 3 (Chile, Peru)
First Stage
Univ de Chile 1, Univ Catolica 2
Univ Catolica 0, Univ de Chile 1
Universitario 1, Alianza Atletico 1
Alianza Atletico 1, Universitario 1
Alianza Atletico won 4-1 on penalties.

Second Stage
Univ Catolica 5, Alianza Atletico 0
Alianza Atletico 2, Univ Catolica 0

SECTION 4 (Bolivia, Ecuador)
First Stage
The Strongest 2, Bolivar 1
Bolivar 1, The Strongest 2
El Nacional 3, LDU Quito 4
LDU Quito 1, El Nacional 2
LDU Quito won on away goals.

Second Stage
The Strongest 2, LDU Quito 1
LDU Quito 0, The Strongest 3

SECTION 5 (Paraguay, Uruguay)
First Stage
Defensor 2, Danubio 3
Danubio 1, Defensor 3
Guarani 1, Cerro Porteno 2
Cerro Porteno 1, Guarani 2
Cerro Porteno won 4-3 on penalties.

Second Stage
Cerro Porteno 2, Defensor 0
Defensor 1, Cerro Porteno 1

SECTION 6 (Colombia, Venezuela)
First Stage
Dep Cali 2, At Nacional 0
At Nacional 2, Dep Cali 0
At Nacional won 7-6 on penalties.
Trujillanos 3, Mineros 1
Mineros 1, Trujillanos 2

Second Stage
Trujillanos 1, At Nacional 5
At Nacional 2, Trujillanos 0

SECOND PHASE
DC United 1, Univ Catolica 1
Univ Catolica 3, DC United 2
Corinthians 0, River Plate 0
River Plate 1, Corinthians 1
Corinthians won on away goals.
Velez Sarsfield 2, Cruzeiro 0
Cruzeiro 2, Velez Sarsfield 1
Fluminense 3, Banfield 1
Banfield 0, Fluminense 0
Rosario Central 0, Internacional 1
Internacional 1, Rosario Central 1
Cerro Porteno 2, Boca Juniors 2
Boca Juniors 5, Cerro Porteno 1
Pumas UNAM 3, The Strongest 1
The Strongest 2, Pumas UNAM 1
America 3, At Nacional 3
At Nacional 1, America 4

QUARTER-FINALS
Fluminense 2, Univ Catolica 1
Univ Catolica 2, Fluminense 0
Corinthians 2, Pumas UNAM 1
Pumas UNAM 3, Corinthians 0
Internacional 1, Boca Juniors 0
Boca Juniors 4, Internacional 1
America 0, Velez Sarsfield 2
Velez Sarsfield 2, America 0

SEMI-FINALS FIRST LEG
Velez Sarsfield 0, Pumas UNAM 0
Boca Juniors 2, Univ Catolica 2

SEMI-FINALS SECOND LEG
Pumas UNAM 4, Velez Sarsfield 0
Univ Catolica 0, Boca Juniors 1

FINAL
Pumas UNAM 1, Boca Juniors 1
Boca Juniors 1, Pumas UNAM 1
Boca Juniors won 4-3 on penalties.

AFRICA

AFRICAN NATIONS CUP 2006
Final Tournament in Egypt

GROUP A
Morocco 0, Ivory Coast 1
Egypt 3, Libya 0
Egypt 0, Morocco 0
Libya 1, Ivory Coast 2
Egypt 3, Ivory Coast 1
Libya 0, Morocco 0

GROUP B
Cameroon 3, Angola 1
Togo 0, DR Congo 2
Angola 0, DR Congo 0
Cameroon 2, Togo 0
Angola 3, Togo 2
Cameroon 2, DR Congo 0

GROUP C
South Africa 0, Guinea 2
Tunisia 4, Zambia 1
Tunisia 2, South Africa 0
Zambia 1, Guinea 2
Tunisia 0, Guinea 3
Zambia 1, South Africa 0

GROUP D
Nigeria 1, Ghana 0
Zimbabwe 0, Senegal 2
Ghana 1, Senegal 0
Nigeria 2, Zimbabwe 0
Ghana 1, Zimbabwe 2
Nigeria 2, Senegal 1

QUARTER-FINALS
Guinea 2, Senegal 3
Egypt 4, DR Congo 1
Cameroon 1, Ivory Coast 1
aet; Ivory Coast won 12-11 on penalties.
Nigeria 1, Tunisia 1
aet; Nigeria won 7-6 on penalties.

SEMI-FINALS
Egypt 2, Senegal 1
Nigeria 0, Ivory Coast 1

MATCH FOR THIRD PLACE
Nigeria 1, Senegal 0

FINAL
Egypt 0, Ivory Coast 0
aet; Egypt won 4-2 on penalties.

ASIA

ARAB CHAMPIONS LEAGUE FINAL

ENPPI (Cairo) 1, Raja Casablanca 2;
Raja Casablanca 1, ENPPI 0.

AFC CHALLENGE CUP

Sri Lanka 0, Tajikistan 4

UEFA UNDER-21 CHAMPIONSHIP 2004–06

GROUP 1
Romania 1, Finland 0
Macedonia 4, Armenia 0
Romania 5, Macedonia 1
Holland 0, Czech Republic 0
Armenia 0, Finland 1
Czech Republic 4, Romania 1
Finland 0, Armenia 1
Macedonia 0, Holland 2
Holland 4, Finland 1
Armenia 0, Czech Republic 4
Armenia 0, Romania 5
Macedonia 2, Czech Republic 2
Romania 2, Holland 0
Czech Republic 3, Finland 0
Holland 0, Armenia 0
Macedonia 1, Romania 0
Holland 2, Romania 0
Armenia 0, Macedonia 0
Czech Republic 2, Macedonia 0
Finland 1, Holland 2
Romania 2, Armenia 0

GROUP 2
Albania 1, Greece 1
Denmark 3, Ukraine 2
Turkey 0, Georgia 0
Kazakhstan 0, Ukraine 1
Georgia 2, Albania 1
Greece 2, Turkey 1
Albania 1, Denmark 2
Ukraine 1, Greece 0
Turkey 1, Kazakhstan 0
Kazakhstan 0, Albania 1
Ukraine 6, Georgia 0
Denmark 1, Turkey 1
Greece 5, Kazakhstan 0
Georgia 2, Denmark 4
Turkey 1, Ukraine 0
Albania 1, Ukraine 1
Greece 0, Denmark 1
Denmark 5, Kazakhstan 1
Georgia 1, Greece 1
Turkey 4, Albania 0
Georgia 0, Turkey 2
Greece 2, Albania 0
Ukraine 0, Denmark 1
Albania 0, Georgia 1
Ukraine 2, Kazakhstan 1
Turkey 0, Greece 2
Kazakhstan 2, Turkey 1
Denmark 7, Albania 0
Greece 0, Ukraine 1

GROUP 3
Slovakia 1, Luxembourg 0
Estonia 0, Luxembourg 0
Latvia 1, Portugal 2
Russia 4, Slovakia 0
Luxembourg 1, Latvia 2
Portugal 3, Estonia 0
Luxembourg 0, Russia 4
Slovakia 3, Latvia 1
Latvia 0, Estonia 0
Portugal 2, Russia 0
Russia 3, Estonia 0
Luxembourg 1, Portugal 6
Estonia 0, Slovakia 2
Latvia 2, Luxembourg 1
Slovakia 0, Portugal 1
Estonia 1, Russia 5
Portugal 2, Slovakia 1
Russia 1, Latvia 1
Luxembourg 0, Slovakia 2
Estonia 0, Portugal 5

GROUP 4
France 1, Israel 0
Republic of Ireland 3, Cyprus 0
Israel 1, Cyprus 0
Switzerland 4, Republic of Ireland 2
Israel 1, Switzerland 1
France 1, Republic of Ireland 0
Cyprus 0, France 1
Cyprus 0, Israel 1
Israel 3, Republic of Ireland 1
France 1, Switzerland 1
Israel 3, France 2
Switzerland 3, Cyprus 0
Republic of Ireland 2, Israel 2

GROUP 5
Italy 2, Norway 0
Slovenia 1, Moldova 0
Norway 2, Belarus 3
Scotland 1, Slovenia 1
Moldova 0, Italy 1
Belarus 2, Moldova 3
Scotland 0, Norway 2
Slovenia 0, Italy 3
Moldova 0, Scotland 0
Norway 0, Slovenia 0
Italy 2, Belarus 1
Italy 2, Scotland 0
Moldova 1, Norway 3
Slovenia 1, Belarus 4
Belarus 1, Slovenia 2
Scotland 0, Moldova 0
Norway 1, Italy 0
Belarus 3, Scotland 2

GROUP 6
Azerbaijan 0, Wales 1
Austria 0, England 2
Austria 3, Azerbaijan 0
Poland 1, England 3
Austria 0, Poland 3
England 2, Wales 0
Azerbaijan 0, Germany 2
Wales 2, Poland 2
Germany 2, Austria 0
Azerbaijan 0, England 0
Germany 1, Poland 1
Wales 0, Germany 4
Wales 1, Austria 0
Poland 3, Azerbaijan 0
England 2, Germany 2
Austria 2, Wales 0
England 2, Azerbaijan 0
Azerbaijan 1, Poland 1

GROUP 7
Belgium 3, Lithuania 0
San Marino 0, Serbia & Montenegro 5
Bosnia 0, Spain 2
Lithuania 2, San Marino 0
Bosnia 1, Serbia & Montenegro 3
Spain 2, Belgium 2
Serbia & Montenegro 9, San Marino 0
Lithuania 1, Spain 1
Belgium 4, Serbia & Montenegro 0
San Marino 1, Lithuania 2
Spain 14, San Marino 0
Belgium 2, Bosnia 1
Serbia & Montenegro 1, Spain 0
Bosnia 2, Lithuania 0
San Marino 0, Belgium 4
Serbia & Montenegro 1, Belgium 1
San Marino 1, Bosnia 4
Spain 2, Lithuania 0
Spain 4, Bosnia 2

GROUP 8
Iceland 3, Bulgaria 1
Croatia 1, Hungary 0
Malta 0, Sweden 1
Hungary 1, Iceland 0
Sweden 0, Croatia 2
Croatia 1, Bulgaria 0
Malta 1, Iceland 0
Sweden 2, Hungary 1
Iceland 3, Sweden 1
Bulgaria 2, Malta 1
Malta 0, Hungary 2
Bulgaria 1, Sweden 2
Croatia 2, Iceland 1
Hungary 1, Bulgaria 0
Croatia 1, Malta 0
Bulgaria 2, Croatia 1
Iceland 0, Hungary 1
Sweden 6, Malta 0
Iceland 0, Malta 0

PLAY-OFFS, FIRST LEG
Czech Republic 0, Germany 2
England 1, France 1
Hungary 1, Italy 1
Russia 0, Denmark 1
Serbia & Montenegro 3, Croatia 1
Slovenia 0, Holland 0
Switzerland 1, Portugal 1
Ukraine 2, Belgium 3

PLAY-OFFS, SECOND LEG
Belgium 1, Ukraine 3
Croatia 1, Serbia & Montenegro 2
Denmark 3, Russia 1
France 2, England 1
Germany 1, Czech Republic 0
Holland 2, Slovenia 0
Italy 1, Hungary 0
Portugal 2, Switzerland 1

Final Tournament (in Portugal)

GROUP A
Germany 0, Portugal 1
France 2, Serbia & Montenegro 0
France 3, Germany 0
Portugal 0, Serbia & Montenegro 2
Serbia & Montenegro 0, Germany 1
Portugal 0, France 1

GROUP B
Holland 1, Italy 0
Denmark 1, Ukraine 2
Denmark 1, Holland 1
Italy 1, Ukraine 0
Ukraine 2, Holland 1
Italy 3, Denmark 3

SEMI-FINALS
France 2, Holland 3
Ukraine 0, Serbia & Montenegro 0
Ukraine won 5-4 on penalties.

FINAL

Holland (2) 3 *(Huntelaar 11, 43 (pen), Hofs 90)* **Ukraine 0 (0)**

Holland: Vermeer; Tiendalli, Vlaar, Luirink, Emanuelson, Aissati (Zomer 78), De Zeeuw, Schaars, Hofs, Huntelaar, Castelen (De Ridder 69).
Ukraine: Pyatov; Yarmash, Chygrynskiy, Yatsenko, Romanchuk■, Mikhalik, Godin (Feschuk 46), Cheberyachko, Maksymov, Milevskiy, Fomin (Aliyev 46).

■ *Denotes player sent off.*

UEFA UNDER-17 CHAMPIONSHIP 2006

(Finals in Luxembourg)

GROUP A
Hungary 0, Russia 1
Luxembourg 1, Spain 7
Spain 3, Russia 0
Luxembourg 0, Hungary 4
Russia 2, Luxembourg 0
Spain 2, Hungary 0

GROUP B
Belgium 0, Germany 4
Serbia & Montenegro 1, Czech Republic 2
Belgium 1, Serbia & Montenegro 1
Germany 0, Czech Republic 0
Germany 4, Serbia & Montenegro 0
Czech Republic 3, Belgium 1

SEMI-FINALS
Germany 0, Russia 1
Spain 0, Czech Republic 2

MATCH FOR THIRD PLACE
Spain 1, Germany 1
Spain won 3-2 on penalties.

FINAL
Czech Republic 2, Russia 2
Russia won 5-3 on penalties.

UEFA UNDER-19 CHAMPIONSHIP 2006

(Finals in Northern Ireland)

GROUP A
Serbia & Montenegro 4, Germany 2
Northern Ireland 0, Greece 1
Greece 0, Germany 3
Northern Ireland 0, Serbia & Montenegro 1
Germany 2, Northern Ireland 1
Greece 0, Serbia & Montenegro 3

GROUP B
France 1, England 1
Norway 2, Armenia 0
Armenia 1, England 1
Norway 1, France 3
Armenia 0, France 1
England 3, Norway 2

SEMI-FINAL
Serbia & Montenegro 1, England 3
France 3, Germany 2

FINAL
England 1, France 3

WORLD YOUTH CUP UNDER-17 2006

(Finals in Peru)

GROUP A	P	W	D	L	F	A	Pts
Costa Rica	3	1	2	0	4	2	5
China	3	1	2	0	3	2	5
Ghana	3	0	3	0	3	3	3
Peru	3	0	1	2	1	4	1

GROUP B	P	W	D	L	F	A	Pts
Turkey	3	3	0	0	6	3	9
Mexico	3	2	0	1	6	2	6
Australia	3	1	0	2	2	5	3
Uruguay	3	0	0	3	3	7	0

GROUP C	P	W	D	L	F	A	Pts
USA	3	2	1	0	7	4	7
North Korea	3	1	1	1	6	4	4
Italy	3	1	1	1	6	7	4
Ivory Coast	3	0	1	2	4	8	1

GROUP D	P	W	D	L	F	A	Pts
Brazil	3	2	0	1	9	4	6
Holland	3	2	0	1	8	5	6
Gambia	3	2	0	1	6	4	6
Qatar	3	0	0	3	4	14	0

QUARTER-FINALS
Costa Rica 1, Mexico 3
Turkey 5, China 1
USA 0, Holland 2
Brazil 3, North Korea 1

SEMI-FINALS
Mexico 4, Holland 0
Turkey 3, Brazil 4

MATCH FOR THIRD PLACE
Holland 2, Turkey 1

FINAL
Mexico 3, Brazil 0

ENGLAND UNDER-21 RESULTS 1976–2006

EC UEFA Competition for Under-21 Teams

v ALBANIA

Year	Date		Venue	Eng	Alb
EC1989	Mar	7	Shkroda	2	1
EC1989	April	25	Ipswich	2	0
EC2001	Mar	27	Tirana	1	0
EC2001	Sept	4	Middlesbrough	5	0

v ANGOLA

Year	Date		Venue	Eng	Ang
1995	June	10	Toulon	1	0
1996	May	28	Toulon	0	2

v ARGENTINA

Year	Date		Venue	Eng	Arg
1998	May	18	Toulon	0	2
2000	Feb	22	Fulham	1	0

v AUSTRIA

Year	Date		Venue	Eng	Aus
1994	Oct	11	Kapfenberg	3	1
1995	Nov	14	Middlesbrough	2	1
EC2004	Sept	3	Krems	2	0
EC2005	Oct	7	Leeds	1	2

v AZERBAIJAN

Year	Date		Venue	Eng	Az
EC2004	Oct	12	Baku	0	0
EC2005	Mar	29	Middlesbrough	2	0

v BELGIUM

Year	Date		Venue	Eng	Bel
1994	June	5	Marseille	2	1
1996	May	24	Toulon	1	0

v BRAZIL

Year	Date		Venue	Eng	B
1993	June	11	Toulon	0	0
1995	June	6	Toulon	0	2
1996	June	1	Toulon	1	2

v BULGARIA

Year	Date		Venue	Eng	Bul
EC1979	June	5	Pernik	3	1
EC1979	Nov	20	Leicester	5	0
1989	June	5	Toulon	2	3
EC1998	Oct	9	West Ham	1	0
EC1999	June	8	Vratsa	1	0

v CROATIA

Year	Date		Venue	Eng	Cro
1996	Apr	23	Sunderland	0	1
2003	Aug	19	West Ham	0	3

v CZECHOSLOVAKIA

Year	Date		Venue	Eng	Cz
1990	May	28	Toulon	2	1
1992	May	26	Toulon	1	2
1993	June	9	Toulon	1	1

v CZECH REPUBLIC

Year	Date		Venue	Eng	CzR
1998	Nov	17	Ipswich	0	1

v DENMARK

Year	Date		Venue	Eng	Den
EC1978	Sept	19	Hvidovre	2	1
EC1979	Sept	11	Watford	1	0
EC1982	Sept	21	Hvidovre	4	1
EC1983	Sept	20	Norwich	4	1
EC1986	Mar	12	Copenhagen	1	0
EC1986	Mar	26	Manchester	1	1
1988	Sept	13	Watford	0	0
1994	Mar	8	Brentford	1	0
1999	Oct	8	Bradford	4	1
2005	Aug	16	Herning	1	0

v EAST GERMANY

Year	Date		Venue	Eng	EG
EC1980	April	16	Sheffield	1	2
EC1980	April	23	Jena	0	1

v FINLAND

Year	Date		Venue	Eng	Fin
EC1977	May	26	Helsinki	1	0
EC1977	Oct	12	Hull	8	1
EC1984	Oct	16	Southampton	2	0
EC1985	May	21	Mikkeli	1	3
EC2000	Oct	10	Valkeakoski	2	2
EC2001	Mar	23	Barnsley	4	0

v FRANCE

Year	Date		Venue	Eng	Fra
EC1984	Feb	28	Sheffield	6	1
EC1984	Mar	28	Rouen	1	0
1987	June	11	Toulon	0	2
EC1988	April	13	Besancon	2	4
EC1988	April	27	Highbury	2	2
1988	June	12	Toulon	2	4
1990	May	23	Toulon	7	3
1991	June	3	Toulon	1	0
1992	May	28	Toulon	0	0
1993	June	15	Toulon	1	0
1994	May	31	Aubagne	0	3
1995	June	10	Toulon	0	2
1998	May	14	Toulon	1	1
1999	Feb	9	Derby	2	1
EC2005	Nov	11	Tottenham	1	1
EC2005	Nov	15	Nancy	1	2

v GEORGIA

Year	Date		Venue	Eng	Geo
EC1996	Nov	8	Batumi	1	0
EC1997	April	29	Charlton	0	0
2000	Aug	31	Middlesbrough	6	1

v GERMANY

Year	Date		Venue	Eng	Ger
1991	Sept	10	Scunthorpe	2	1
EC2000	Oct	6	Derby	1	1
EC2001	Aug	31	Frieburg	2	1
2005	Mar	25	Hull	2	2
2005	Sept	6	Mainz	1	1

v GREECE

Year	Date		Venue	Eng	Gre
EC1982	Nov	16	Piraeus	0	1
EC1983	Mar	29	Portsmouth	2	1
1989	Feb	7	Patras	0	1
EC1997	Nov	13	Heraklion	0	2
EC1997	Dec	17	Norwich	4	2
EC2001	June	5	Athens	1	3
EC2001	Oct	5	Ewood Park	2	1

v HOLLAND

Year	Date		Venue	Eng	H
EC1993	April	27	Portsmouth	3	0
EC1993	Oct	12	Utrecht	1	1
2001	Aug	14	Reading	4	0
EC2001	Nov	9	Utrecht	2	2
EC2001	Nov	13	Derby	1	0
2004	Feb	17	Hull	3	2
2005	Feb	8	Derby	1	2

v HUNGARY

Year	Date		Venue	Eng	Hun
EC1981	June	5	Keszthely	2	1
EC1981	Nov	17	Nottingham	2	0
EC1983	April	26	Newcastle	1	0
EC1983	Oct	11	Nyiregyhaza	2	0
1990	Sept	11	Southampton	3	1
1992	May	12	Budapest	2	2
1999	April	27	Budapest	2	2

v ITALY

Year	Date		Venue	Eng	Italy
EC1978	Mar	8	Manchester	2	1
EC1978	April	5	Rome	0	0
EC1984	April	18	Manchester	3	1
EC1984	May	2	Florence	0	1
EC1986	April	9	Pisa	0	2
EC1986	April	23	Swindon	1	1
EC1997	Feb	12	Bristol	1	0
EC1997	Oct	10	Rieti	1	0
EC2000	May	27	Bratislava	0	2
2000	Nov	14	Monza*	0	0
2002	Mar	26	Valley Parade	1	1
EC2002	May	20	Basle	1	2
2003	Feb	11	Pisa	0	1

**Abandoned 11 mins; fog.*

v ISRAEL

Year	Date		Venue	Eng	Isr
1985	Feb	27	Tel Aviv	2	1

v LATVIA

Year	Date		Venue	Eng	Lat
1995	April	25	Riga	1	0
1995	June	7	Burnley	4	0

v LUXEMBOURG

Year	Date		Venue	Eng	Lux
EC1998	Oct	13	Greven Macher	5	0
EC1999	Sept	3	Reading	5	0

v MACEDONIA

Year	Date		Venue	Eng	M
EC2002	Oct	15	Reading	3	1
EC2003	Sept	5	Skopje	1	1

v MALAYSIA

Year	Date		Venue	Eng	Mal
1995	June	8	Toulon	2	0

v MEXICO

Year	Date		Venue	Eng	Mex
1988	June	5	Toulon	2	1
1991	May	29	Toulon	6	0
1992	May	25	Toulon	1	1
2001	May	24	Leicester	3	0

			v MOLDOVA	Eng	Mol
EC1996	Aug	31	Chisinau	2	0
EC1997	Sept	9	Wycombe	1	0

			v MOROCCO	Eng	Mor
1987	June	7	Toulon	2	0
1988	June	9	Toulon	1	0

			v NORWAY	Eng	Nor
EC1977	June	1	Bergen	2	1
EC1977	Sept	6	Brighton	6	0
1980	Sept	9	Southampton	3	0
1981	Sept	8	Drammen	0	0
EC1992	Oct	13	Peterborough	0	2
EC1993	June	1	Stavanger	1	1
1995	Oct	10	Stavanger	2	2
2006	Feb	28	Reading	3	1

			v POLAND	Eng	Pol
EC1982	Mar	17	Warsaw	2	1
EC1982	April	7	West Ham	2	2
EC1989	June	2	Plymouth	2	1
EC1989	Oct	10	Jastrzebie	3	1
EC1990	Oct	16	Tottenham	0	1
EC1991	Nov	12	Pila	1	2
EC1993	May	28	Zdroj	4	1
EC1993	Sept	7	Millwall	1	2
EC1996	Oct	8	Wolverhampton	0	0
EC1997	May	30	Katowice	1	1
EC1999	Mar	26	Southampton	5	0
EC1999	Sept	7	Plock	1	3
EC2004	Sept	7	Rybnik	3	1
EC2005	Oct	11	Hillsborough	4	1

			v PORTUGAL	Eng	Por
1987	June	13	Toulon	0	0
1990	May	21	Toulon	0	1
1993	June	7	Toulon	2	0
1994	June	7	Toulon	2	0
EC1994	Sept	6	Leicester	0	0
1995	Sept	2	Lisbon	0	2
1996	May	30	Toulon	1	3
2000	Apr	16	Stoke	0	1
EC2002	May	22	Zurich	1	3
EC2003	Mar	28	Rio Major	2	4
EC2003	Sept	9	Everton	1	2

			v REPUBLIC OF IRELAND	Eng	RoI
1981	Feb	25	Liverpool	1	0
1985	Mar	25	Portsmouth	3	2
1989	June	9	Toulon	0	0
EC1990	Nov	13	Cork	3	0
EC1991	Mar	26	Brentford	3	0
1994	Nov	15	Newcastle	1	0
1995	Mar	27	Dublin	2	0

			v ROMANIA	Eng	Rom
EC1980	Oct	14	Ploesti	0	4
EC1981	April	28	Swindon	3	0
EC1985	April	30	Brasov	0	0
EC1985	Sept	10	Ipswich	3	0

			v RUSSIA	Eng	Rus
1994	May	30	Bandol	2	0

			v SAN MARINO	Eng	SM
EC1993	Feb	16	Luton	6	0
EC1993	Nov	17	San Marino	4	0

			v SENEGAL	Eng	Sen
1989	June	7	Toulon	6	1
1991	May	27	Toulon	2	1

			v SERBIA-MONTENEGRO	Eng	S-M
2003	June	2	Hull	3	2

			v SCOTLAND	Eng	Sco
1977	April	27	Sheffield	1	0
EC1980	Feb	12	Coventry	2	1
EC1980	Mar	4	Aberdeen	0	0
EC1982	April	19	Glasgow	1	0
EC1982	April	28	Manchester	1	1
EC1988	Feb	16	Aberdeen	1	0
EC1988	Mar	22	Nottingham	1	0
1993	June	13	Toulon	1	0

			v SLOVAKIA	Eng	Slo
EC2002	June	1	Bratislava	0	2
EC2002	Oct	11	Trnava	4	0
EC2003	June	10	Sunderland	2	0

			v SLOVENIA	Eng	Slo
2000	Feb	12	Nova Gorica	1	0

			v SOUTH AFRICA	Eng	SA
1998	May	16	Toulon	3	1

			v SPAIN	Eng	Spa
EC1984	May	17	Seville	1	0
EC1984	May	24	Sheffield	2	0
1987	Feb	18	Burgos	2	1
1992	Sept	8	Burgos	1	0
2001	Feb	27	Birmingham	0	4
2004	Nov	16	Alcala	0	1

			v SWEDEN	Eng	Swe
1979	June	9	Vasteras	2	1
1986	Sept	9	Ostersund	1	1
EC1988	Oct	18	Coventry	1	1
EC1989	Sept	5	Uppsala	0	1
EC1998	Sept	4	Sundvall	2	0
EC1999	June	4	Huddersfield	3	0
2004	Mar	30	Kristiansund	2	2

			v SWITZERLAND	Eng	Swit
EC1980	Nov	18	Ipswich	5	0
EC1981	May	31	Neuenburg	0	0
1988	May	28	Lausanne	1	1
1996	April	1	Swindon	0	0
1998	Mar	24	Brugglifeld	0	2
EC2002	May	17	Zurich	2	1

			v TURKEY	Eng	Tur
EC1984	Nov	13	Bursa	0	0
EC1985	Oct	15	Bristol	3	0
EC1987	April	28	Izmir	0	0
EC1987	Oct	13	Sheffield	1	1
EC1991	April	30	Izmir	2	2
1991	Oct	15	Reading	2	0
EC1992	Nov	17	Orient	0	1
EC1993	Mar	30	Izmir	0	0
EC2000	May	29	Bratislava	6	0
EC2003	April	1	Newcastle	1	1
EC2003	Oct	10	Istanbul	0	1

			v UKRAINE	Eng	Uk
2004	Aug	17	Middlesbrough	3	1

			v USA	Eng	USA
1989	June	11	Toulon	0	2
1994	June	2	Toulon	3	0

			v USSR	Eng	USSR
1987	June	9	Toulon	0	0
1988	June	7	Toulon	1	0
1990	May	25	Toulon	2	1
1991	May	31	Toulon	2	1

			v WALES	Eng	Wales
1976	Dec	15	Wolverhampton	0	0
1979	Feb	6	Swansea	1	0
1990	Dec	5	Tranmere	0	0
EC2004	Oct	8	Blackburn	2	0
EC2005	Sept	2	Wrexham	4	0

			v WEST GERMANY	Eng	WG
EC1982	Sept	21	Sheffield	3	1
EC1982	Oct	12	Bremen	2	3
1987	Sept	8	Ludenscheid	0	2

			v YUGOSLAVIA	Eng	Yugo
EC1978	April	19	Novi Sad	1	2
EC1978	May	2	Manchester	1	1
EC1986	Nov	11	Peterborough	1	1
EC1987	Nov	10	Zemun	5	1
EC2000	Mar	29	Barcelona	3	0
2002	Sept	6	Bolton	1	1

BRITISH AND IRISH UNDER-21 TEAMS 2005–06

▪ *Denotes player sent off.*

ENGLAND UNDER-21 TEAMS 2005–06

Herning, 16 August 2005, 4012
Denmark (0) 0 *Rasmussen M*▪
England (0) 1 *(Ambrose 90)*
England: Carson (Camp 46); Hunt, Ridgewell (Whittingham 46), Reo-Coker (Soares 46), Dawson (Ferdinand 46), Davenport, Milner, Richardson, Cole C, Ashton (Stead 46), Downing (Ambrose 46).

Wrexham, 2 September 2005, 4109
Wales (0) 0
England (2) 4 *(Stead 5, Whittingham 27, 89, Dawson 68)*
Wales: Hennessey; Beevers, Gilbert, Birchall, Anthony, Nyatanga (Adam Davies 56), Crofts, Davies C (Fleetwood 72), Aaron Davies, Cotterill, Tudur-Jones.
England: Carson; Johnson, Dawson, Reo-Coker, Ferdinand, Ridgewell (Hunt 57), Milner, Ambrose, Cole C (Welsh 60), Stead (Nugent 60), Whittingham.

Mainz, 6 September 2005, 7000
Germany (1) 1 *(Kiessling 17)*
England (1) 1 *(Taylor S 42)*
England: Carson; Hunt (Baines 46), Taylor S, Dawson, Ferdinand, O'Neil, Welsh (Nugent 78), Reo-Coker, Cole C, Milner, Whittingham (Soares 46).

Leeds, 7 October 2005, 28,030
England (1) 1 *(Cole C 18)*
Austria (0) 2 *(Janko 56, 76)*
England: Carson; Taylor S, Baines, Dawson, Ferdinand (Taylor R 71), Huddlestone, Milner, Soares (Moore 61), Cole C (Jerome 87), Thomas, Lennon.

Hillsborough, 11 October 2005, 23,110
England (3) 4 *(Cole C 18, Thomas 21, Taylor S 37, 88)*
Poland (1) 1 *(Kukut 39)*
England: Carson; Taylor R (Onuoha 85), Whittingham, Taylor S, Ferdinand, Huddlestone, Reo-Coker, O'Neil, Cole C (Stead 87), Lennon, Thomas (Milner 65).

Tottenham, 11 November 2005, 34,494
England (0) 1 *(Ambrose 88)*
France (0) 1 *(Le Tallec 47)*
England: Carson; Taylor R, Whittingham, Dawson, Ferdinand, Huddlestone, Milner (Ashton 79), Ambrose, Cole C, Bent, Richardson.

Nancy, 15 November 2005, 13,045
France (0) 2 *(Ribery 58, Briand 85 (pen))*
England (0) 1 *(Bent 55)*
England: Carson; Taylor R, Onuoha (Whittingham 79), Huddlestone, Dawson, Ferdinand, Ambrose (Ashton 66), O'Neil, Bent, Cole C (Jerome 89), Richardson.

Reading, 28 February 2006, 15,022
England (1) 3 *(Whittingham 24, Bentley 54, 60)*
Norway (0) 1 *(Steenslid 52)*
England: Carson (Camp 46); Johnson (Hoyte 65), Whittingham (Taylor 65), Ridgewell (Davies 46), Ferdinand, Huddlestone, Reo-Coker (Soares 46), Bentley (Welsh 73), Nugent (Lita 46), Milner (Jerome 46), Routledge (McLeod 73).

SCOTLAND UNDER-21 TEAMS 2005–06

Koflach, 16 August 2005, 1200
Austria (0) 1 *(Thonhofer 51)*
Scotland (2) 3 *(Robertson 24, Beattie 32, 65)*
Scotland: Marshall; Berra, Whittaker, Brown, Diamond (Collins 46), Robertson, Thomson (Lawson 81), Morrison (Kinniburgh 31), Gallagher (Duffy 70), Maloney, Beattie.

Motherwell, 2 September 2005, 5913
Scotland (1) 2 *(Diamond 45, Gallagher 74)*
Italy (0) 2 *(Lazzari 53, Pepe*▪ *76) Motta*▪
Scotland: Marshall▪; Berra, Robertson, Diamond, Collins, Brown, Whittaker, Thomson (Lawson 64), Duffy (Turner 78), Wilson, Gallagher.
UEFA declared the match a 3-0 win for Italy; Scotland fielded Whittaker, a suspended player.

Drammen, 6 September 2005, 2207
Norway (0) 0
Scotland (1) 1 *(Gallagher 7)*
Scotland: Turner; Berra, Robertson, Watt, Collins, Brown, Wilson, Thomson, Clarkson (Brighton 85), Lawson, Gallagher.

Cumbernauld, 7 October 2005, 3192
Scotland (2) 2 *(Duffy 2, Robertson 45)*
Belarus (0) 3 *(McCunnie 58 (og), Kovel 66, Afanasyev 78) Kornilenko*▪
Scotland: Turner; Berra▪, Robertson, Watt, Collins, Wilson, Whittaker, McCunnie (Diamond 67), Duffy (Brighton 80), Lawson, Gallagher▪.

Velenje, 11 October 2005, 800
Slovenia (1) 3 *(Collins 35 (og), Stevanovic 60, 90)*
Scotland (0) 0
England: Smith; Diamond, Robertson, Watt (Mulgrew 46), Collins, McCormack, Whittaker, McCunnie, Duffy (Naismith 68), Lawson (Lappin 46), Clarkson.

Firhill, 28 February 2006, 1024
Scotland (3) 4 *(Naismith 1, Scott 19, Elliot 29, 57)*
Iceland (0) 0
Scotland: Marshall (Turner 46); Irvine, Diamond (Clarkson 67), Kinniburgh, Berra, Lawson, Scott (Foster 43), Naismith (Bryson 81), Elliot (Brighton 67), Woods (Quinn R 35), Adam.

Drumahoe, 16 May 2006, 350
Northern Ireland (0) 1 *(Stewart 62)*
Scotland (0) 0
Scotland: Marshall; Whittaker, Wilson, Lawson, Quinn P, Broadfoot, Foster, Naismith, Duffy (McCormack 77), Adam, Woods (Mulgrew 65).
Northern Ireland: McGovern; Ward S, Friars (McCaffrey 58), McVey (Callaghan 53), McChrystal, Evans, McGowan, Gilfillan, Stewart, Ramsey (Ward M 46), Scullion (Buchanan 71).

Kilmarnock, 19 May 2006, 2238
Scotland (0) 1 *(Naismith 46)*
Turkey (0) 1 *(Gulec 55 (pen))*
Scotland: Marshall; Irvine, Quinn P, Broadfoot, Mulgrew, Wilson, Whittaker, Quinn R (McCormack 74), Clarkson (Duffy 68), Adam▪, Naismith.

WALES UNDER-21 TEAMS 2005–06

Llanelli, 16 August 2005, 1157
Wales (1) 3 *(Crofts 12, Pritchard 52, Aaron Davies 74)*
Malta (0) 1 *(Bajada R 81)*
Wales: Hennessey (Worgan 46); Beevers (Martin 46), Gilbert (Adam Davies 46), Anthony (Jacobson 70), Pulis, Nyatanga, Crofts, Aaron Davies, Cotterill, Pritchard (Fleetwood 56), Birchall (Tudur-Jones 66).

Mosir, 6 September 2005, 2175
Poland (1) 3 *(Brozek P 18, 53, Gregorek 83)*
Wales (2) 2 *(Cotterill 13, Vaughan 38)*
Wales: Hennessey; Beevers, Gilbert, Tudur-Jones (Pulis 60), Anthony (Adam Davies 57), Nyatanga, Aaron Davies, Crofts, Calliste, Cotterill, Vaughan.

Braunschweig, 7 October 2005, 4500
Germany (1) 4 *(Rafael 3, 51, Fathi 54, Masmanidis 79)*
Wales (0) 0
Wales: Worgan; Spender, Nyatanga (Wiggins 86), Anthony, Adam Davies, Gilbert, Mark Jones (Birchall 68), Pulis, Calliste, Aaron Davies, Ledley.

Newport, 11 October 2005, 812
Wales (0) 3 *(Pritchard 65, Birchall 70, Gilbert 87)*
Azerbaijan (0) 0
Wales: Worgan; Beevers, Gilbert, Pulis (McDonald S 85), Morgan, Nyatanga, Birchall, Mark Jones, Calliste, Aaron Davies, McDonald C (Pritchard 59).

Paphos, 15 November 2005, 400
Cyprus (2) 3 *(Pavlou 16, 36, Eleftheriou 89)*
Wales (2) 3 *(Jones 31, Cotterill 40, Efthimiou 90 (og))*
Wales: Pearce (Letheren 75); Powell (Crowell■ 52), Spender, Jacobson (James 75), Nyatanga, Adam Davies (Anthony 52), Pulis (Wiggins 52), Crofts, Mark Jones, Calliste (Pritchard 60), Cotterill.

Llanelli, 28 February 2006
Wales (0) 0
Northern Ireland (1) 1 *(Morrow 25)*
Wales: Pearce; Lawless (Marc Williams 84), Wiggins (Jacobson 87), Mackin (Davies R 56), Adam Davies, Mike Williams, Aaron Davies, Hughes (Easter 46), MacDonald (James 56), Davies C (Pritchard 74), Calliste.
Northern Ireland: McGovern; Ward S, Hughes J, Clarke (McVey 66), McChrystal, McArdle, Gilfillan (Ervin 46), Clingan, Scullion (Friars 71), Lafferty (Smylie 84), Morrow (Stewart 87).

10 May 2006
Estonia (0) 0
Wales (1) 2 *(Cotterill 23, Calliste 89)*
Wales: Price; Duffy, Wiggins, Ledley (James 65), Morgan, Nyatanga, Aaron Davies, Crofts, Davies C (Calliste 86), Cotterill, McDonald.

16 May 2006
Wales (1) 1 *(Morgan 44)*
Cyprus (0) 0
Wales: Pearce; Gunter (Critchell 50), Wiggins (Calliste 46), Crowell (James 55), Morgan, Mike Williams, Spender (McDonald 51), Edwards (Davies R 64), Davies C, Aaron Davies, Bale.

24 May 2006
Wales (4) 5 *(Davies C 2, 27, 45, Aaron Davies 44, 73)*
Estonia (0) 1 *(Gussev 60)*
Wales: Price; Spender, Wiggins (Bale 68), Crofts (Davies R 75), Morgan, Mike Williams, MacDonald, Edwards, Davies C (Williams D 52), Calliste, Aaron Davies.

REPUBLIC OF IRELAND UNDER-21 TEAMS 2005–06

Belfast, 16 August 2005
Northern Ireland (1) 2 *(Sheehan 36 (og), Webb 51)*
Republic of Ireland (0) 2 *(Doyle 64, 72 (pen))*
Northern Ireland: McGovern; Hughes M, Webb, Gilfillan (Ward S 54), McCrystal, McLean, Gault (Smylie 73), Higgins, Morrow (Thompson 76), McCourt (Friars 70), Braniff (Shiels 76).
Republic of Ireland: Henderson; Foley, Whelan (Dawson 46), O'Brien, Sheehan, Kelly, Fitzgerald, Cregg (O'Donovan 59), Doyle, Murphy, Tabb.

Cork, 6 September 2005, 6100
Republic of Ireland (1) 1 *(Murphy 33)*
France (1) 2 *(Le Tallec 41 (pen), Bergougnoux 71)*
Republic of Ireland: Henderson; Kelly, Sheehan (Kearney 84), Dawson (O'Donovan 46), Fitzgerald, Paisley, Flood, O'Brien, Murphy, Doyle, McGeady.

Larnaca, 7 October 2005, 1200
Cyprus (1) 1 *(Panayi A 30)*
Republic of Ireland (0) 1 *(Flood 76)*
Republic of Ireland: Henderson; Keane (McStay 43), Ward (Bermingham 74), Painter, Potter, O'Brien (Whelan 46), Fitzgerald, McShane, Flood, Tabb, McGeady.

Dublin, 11 October 2005
Republic of Ireland (0) 0
Switzerland (1) 1 *(Degen D 13)*
Republic of Ireland: Henderson; Deery, Painter, O'Brien (O'Donovan 80), Fitzgerald, McShane, Flood, Whelan, Ward, Tabb, McGeady.

Madeira, 14 February 2006
Madeira (0) 1 *(Patricio 60)*
Republic of Ireland (0) 1 *(Hayes 80)*
Republic of Ireland: Quigley; Keane, Keogh R, Deans (Tyrrell 61), Hand, O'Donovan (Hayes 46), Dicker (O'Connor 61), Timlin■, O'Brien (Stokes 74), Ward (O'Carroll 46), Keogh A.

Madeira, 16 February 2006
Finland (0) 1 *(Hatemaj 67)*
Republic of Ireland (0) 2 *(Ward 49, Dicker 88)*
Republic of Ireland: Randolph; Keane, Keogh R, Deans, Hand, O'Donovan (O'Carroll 72), Dicker, Grant (O'Connor 72), Stokes, Ward (Tyrrell 90), Keogh A (O'Brien 46).

Madeira, 17 February 2006
Portugal (0) 1 *(Veloso 89)*
Republic of Ireland (2) 2 *(Grant 3, Ward 43)*
Republic of Ireland: Quigley; Keane, Keogh R, O'Dea, Hand, Grant (Deans 84), Dicker, Timlin, O'Brien (O'Donovan 90), Stokes, Ward.

Drogheda, 28 February 2006
Republic of Ireland (0) 1 *(Ward 77)*
Sweden (0) 0
Republic of Ireland: Quigley (Doyle 46); Foley, Painter (Hand 90), Whelan (Dicker 68), McShane, Bruce, Flood, Potter, Ward (Leech 79), Timlin, Yeates (Behan 90).

Baku, 11 May 2006, 1500
Azerbaijan (1) 1 *(Aghakishiyev 20)*
Republic of Ireland (0) 2 *(Keogh A 58, 88)*
Republic of Ireland: Quigley■; Foley, Keogh R, Bruce, Painter, Keegan, Flood, Timlin, O'Donovan (Long 62), Keogh A, McGeady.

Kilkenny, 18 May 2006, 1600
Republic of Ireland (1) 3 *(O'Donovan 37, Foley 69, Keogh A 65)*
Azerbaijan (0) 0
Republic of Ireland: Gilmartin; Foley, Keogh R, Bruce, Painter, Keegan (Dicker 85), Flood (Tabb 74), Timlin, O'Donovan, Keogh A (Behan 84), McGeady.

NORTHERN IRELAND UNDER-21 TEAMS 2005–06

Tel Aviv, 6 February 2006
Israel (0) 0
Northern Ireland (1) 1 *(Clingan 1)*
Northern Ireland: McGovern; Ward S, Friars (Hughes J), McArdle, McChrystal, Clingan, Gilfillan (Callaghan), Clarke, Smylie (McVey), Stewart, Scullion.

Tel Aviv, 8 February 2006, 350
Israel (0) 0
Northern Ireland (1) 1 *(Clarke 38)*
Northern Ireland: McGovern (Willis 46); Callaghan (Ward S 85), McCaffrey, Lindsay, Hughes J, McVey, Clingan, Ward J, McGowan, Clarke (Stewart 46), Smylie (Scullion 46).

Vaduz, 12 April 2006, 600
Liechtenstein (1) 1 *(Hughes J 7 (og))*
Northern Ireland (1) 4 *(Morrow 33, 61 Gilfillan 58, Scullion 84)*
Northern Ireland: McGovern; Ward S, Hughes J, Clingan, McChrystal, McArdle, Gilfillan (Ward J), Clarke (McVey), Morrow, Stewart (Smylie), Scullion.

Belfast, 16 May 2006
Northern Ireland (3) 4 *(Thompson 9, Clarke 41, Shiels 42, McArdle 78)*
Liechtenstein (0) 0
Northern Ireland: McGovern; Ward S, Hughes J (Friars 46), McArdle, McChrystal, Clarke (Lafferty 60), Gilfillan (Ward J 67), Clingan, Thompson, Shiels, Scullion.

BRITISH UNDER-21 APPEARANCES 1976–2006

ENGLAND

Ablett, G. (Liverpool), 1988 v F (1)
Adams, A. (Arsenal). 1985 v Ei, Fi; 1986 v D; 1987 v Se, Y (5)
Adams, N. (Everton), 1987 v Se (1)
Allen, B. (QPR), 1992 v H, M, Cz, F; 1993 v N (sub), T, P, Cz (sub) (8)
Allen, C. A. (Oxford U), 1995 v Br (sub), F (sub) (2)
Allen, C. (QPR), 1980 v EG (sub); (with C Palace), 1981 v N, R (3)
Allen, M. (QPR), 1987 v Se (sub); 1988 v Y (sub) (2)
Allen, P. (West Ham U), 1985 v Ei, R; (with Tottenham H), 1986 v R (3)
Allen, R. W. (Tottenham H), 1998 v F (sub), S.Af, Arg (sub) (3)
Ambrose, D. P. F. (Ipswich T), 2003 v I (sub); (with Newcastle U), Ser (sub); 2004 v Se (sub); 2005 v Sp, Az (sub); (with Charlton Ath), 2006 v D (sub), W, F (2) (9)
Ameobi, F. (Newcastle U), 2001 v Sp (sub), Fi (sub), Alb (sub), M, Gr (sub); 2002 v Ho (sub+1), Slv (sub), Sw (sub), I (sub), P (sub); 2003 v Y (sub), Slo, Mac, I, P, Ser, Slo; 2004 v Mac, P, T (19)
Anderson, V. A. (Nottingham F), 1978 v I (1)
Anderton, D. R. (Tottenham H), 1993 v Sp, Sm, Ho, Pol, N, P, Cz, Br, S, F; 1994 v Pol, Sm (12)
Andrews, I. (Leicester C), 1987 v Se (1)
Ardley, N. C. (Wimbledon), 1993 v Pol, N, P, Cz, Br, S, F, 1994 v Pol (sub), Ho, Sm (10)
Ashcroft, L. (Preston NE), 1992 v H (sub) (1)
Ashton, D. (Crewe Alex), 2004 v Ho, Se; 2005 v Uk (sub); (with Norwich C), Ho, G, Az ; 2006 v D, F (sub+sub) (9)
Atherton, P. (Coventry C), 1992 v T (1)
Atkinson, B. (Sunderland), 1991 v W (sub), Sen, M, USSR (sub), F; 1992 v Pol (sub) (6)
Awford, A. T. (Portsmouth), 1993 v Sp, N, T, P, Cz, Br, S, F; 1994 v Ho (9)

Bailey, G. R. (Manchester U), 1979 v W, Bul; 1980 v D, S (2), EG; 1982 v N; 1983 v D, Gr; 1984 v H, F (2), I, Sp (14)
Baines, L.J. (Wigan Ath), 2005 v A, Pol, Ho; 2006 v G (sub), A (5)
Baker, G. E. (Southampton), 1981 v N, R (2)
Ball, M. J. (Everton), 1999 v Se, Bul, L, CzR, Pol; 2000 v L, D (sub) (7)
Barker, S. (Blackburn R), 1985 v Is (sub), Ei, R; 1986 v I (4)
Barmby, N. J. (Tottenham H), 1994 v D; 1995 v P, A (sub); (with Everton), 1998 v Sw (4)
Bannister, G. (Sheffield W), 1982 v Pol (1)
Barnes, J. (Watford), 1983 v D, Gr (2)
Barnes, P. S. (Manchester C), 1977 v W (sub), S, Fi, N; 1978 v N, Fi, I (2), Y (9)
Barrett, E. D. (Oldham Ath), 1990 v P, F, USSR, Cz (4)
Barry, G. (Aston Villa), 1999 v CzR, F, H; 2000 v Y; 2001 v Sp, Fi, Alb; 2002 v Ho, G, Alb, Gr, Ho (sub), Slv, I, P, Sw, I, P; 2003 v Y, Slo, Mac, I, P, T, Slo; 2004 v Cro, P (27)
Barton, J. (Manchester C), 2004 v Mac, P (2)
Bart-Williams, C. G. (Sheffield W), 1993 v Sp, N, T; 1994 v D, Ru, F, Bel, P; 1995 v P, A, Ei (2), La (2); (with Nottingham F), 1996 v P (sub), A (16)
Batty, D. (Leeds U), 1988 v Sw (sub); 1989 v Gr (sub), Bul, Sen, Ei, US; 1990 v Pol (7)
Bazeley, D. S. (Watford), 1992 v H (sub) (1)
Beagrie, P. (Sheffield U), 1988 v WG, T (2)
Beardsmore, R. (Manchester U), 1989 v Gr, Alb (sub), Pol, Bul, USA (5)
Beattie, J. S. (Southampton), 1999 v CzR (sub), F (sub), Pol, H; 2000 v Pol (5)
Beckham, D. R. J. (Manchester U), 1995 v Br, Mal, An, F; 1996 v P, A (sub), Bel, An, P (9)
Bent, D. A. (Ipswich T), 2003 v I (sub), Ser (sub); 2004 v T (sub), Ho (sub), Se (sub); 2005 v Uk (sub), A (sub), Pol (sub), W (sub), Sp, G, Az; (with Charlton Ath), 2006 v F (2) (14)
Bent, M. N. (C Palace), 1998 v S.Af (sub), Arg (2)
Bentley, D. M. (Arsenal), 2004 v Ho, Se; 2005 v Pol; (with Blackburn R), 2006 v N (4)
Beeston, C (Stoke C), 1988 v USSR (1)
Benjamin, T. J. (Leicester C), 2001 v M (sub) (1)
Bertschin, K. E. (Birmingham C), 1977 v S; 1978 v Y (2) (3)
Birtles, G. (Nottingham F), 1980 v Bul, EG (sub) (2)
Blackwell, D. R. (Wimbledon), 1991 v W, T, Sen (sub), M, USSR, F (6)
Blake, M. A. (Aston Villa), 1990 v F (sub), Cz (sub); 1991 v H, Pol, Ei (2), W; 1992 v Pol (8)
Blissett, L. L. (Watford), 1979 v W, Bul (sub), Se; 1980 v D (4)
Booth, A. D. (Huddersfield T), 1995 v La (2 subs); 1996 v N (3)
Bothroyd, J. (Coventry C), 2001 v M (sub) (1)
Bowyer, L. D. (Charlton Ath), 1996 v N (sub), Bel, P, Br; (with Leeds U), 1997 v Mol, I, Sw, Ge; 1998 v Mol; 1999 v F, Pol; 2000 v D, Arg (13)
Bracewell, P. (Stoke C), 1983 v D, Gr (1 + 1 sub), H; 1984 v D, H, F (2), I (2), Sp (2); 1985 v T (13)
Bradbury, L. M. (Portsmouth), 1997 v Pol; (with Manchester C), 1998 v Mol (sub), I (sub) (3)
Bramble, T. M. (Ipswich T), 2001 v Ge, G, Fi, Alb (sub), M; 2002 v Ho (sub); (with Newcastle U), 2003 v Y, Slo, Mac, P (10)
Branch, P. M. (Everton), 1997 v Pol (sub) (1)
Bradshaw, P. W. (Wolverhampton W), 1977 v W, S; 1978 v Fi, Y (4)
Breacker, T. (Luton T), 1986 v I (2) (2)
Brennan, M. (Ipswich T), 1987 v Y, Sp, T, Mor, F (5)
Bridge, W. M. (Southampton), 1999 v H (sub); 2001 v Sp; 2002 v Ho, G, Alb, Gr, Ho (2) (8)
Bridges, M. (Sunderland), 1997 v Sw (sub); 1999 v F; (with Leeds U), 2000 v D (3)
Brightwell, I. (Manchester C), 1989 v D, Alb; 1990 v Se (sub), Pol (4)
Briscoe, L. S. (Sheffield W), 1996 v Cro, Bel (sub), An, Br; 1997 v Sw (sub) (5)
Brock, K. (Oxford U), 1984 v I, Sp (2); 1986 v I (4)
Broomes, M. C. (Blackburn R), 1997 v Sw, Ge (2)
Brown, M. R. (Manchester C), 1996 v Cro, Bel, An, P (4)
Brown, W. M. (Manchester U), 1999 v Se, Bul, L, CzR, Pol, Se, Bul; 2001 v G (8)
Bull, S. G. (Wolverhampton W), 1989 v Alb (2) Pol; 1990 v Se, Pol (5)
Bullock, M. J. (Barnsley), 1998 v Gr (sub) (1)
Burrows, D. (WBA), 1989 v Se (sub); (with Liverpool), Gr, Alb (2), Pol; 1990 v Se, Pol (7)
Butcher, T. I. (Ipswich T), 1979 v Se; 1980 v D, Bul, S (2), EG (2) (7)
Butt, N. (Manchester U), 1995 v Ei (2), La; 1996 v P, A; 1997 v Ge, Pol (7)
Butters, G. (Tottenham H), 1989 v Bul, Sen (sub), Ei (sub) (3)
Butterworth, I. (Coventry C), 1985 v T, R; (with Nottingham F), 1986 v R, T, D (2), I (2) (8)
Bywater, S. (West Ham U), 2001 v M (sub), Gr; 2002 v Ho (sub), I (sub); 2003 v P, Ser (sub) (6)

Cadamarteri, D. L. (Everton), 1999 v CzR (sub); 2000 v Y (sub); 2001 v M (sub) (3)
Caesar, G. (Arsenal), 1987 v Mor, USSR (sub), F (3)
Callaghan, N. (Watford), 1983 v D, Gr (sub), H (sub); 1984 v D, H, F (2), I, Sp (9)
Camp, L. M. J. (Derby Co), 2005 v Sp (sub), Ho (sub); 2006 v D (sub), N (sub) (4)
Campbell, A. P. (Middlesbrough), 2000 v Y, T (sub), Slo (sub); 2001 v Ge (sub) (4)
Campbell, K. J. (Arsenal), 1991 v H, T (sub); 1992 v G, T (4)
Campbell, S. (Tottenham), 1994 v D, Ru, F, US, Bel, P; 1995 v P, A, Ei; 1996 v N, A (11)
Carbon, M. P. (Derby Co), 1996 v Cro (sub); 1997 v Ge, I, Sw (4)
Carr, C. (Fulham), 1985 v Ei (sub) (1)
Carr, F. (Nottingham F), 1987 v Se, Y, Sp (sub), Mor, USSR; 1988 v WG (sub), T, Y, F (9)
Carragher, J. L. (Liverpool), 1997 v I (sub), Sw, Ge, Pol; 1998 v Mol (sub), I, Gr, Sw (sub), F, S.Af, Arg; 1999 v Se, Bul, L, CzR, F, Pol, Se, Bul; 2000 v L, Pol, D, Arg, Y, I, T, Slo (27)
Carlisle, C. J. (QPR), 2001 v Ge (sub), G (sub), Fi (sub) (3)
Carrick, M. (West Ham U), 2001 v Ge, G, Fi, I, Gr; 2002 v Gr, Ho (2), P; 2003 v Y, Slo, Mac, I, P (14)
Carson, S. P. (Leeds U), 2004 v Ho, Se; 2005 v Uk, A, Pol, W, Az, Sp; (with Liverpool), Ho, G, Az; 2006 v D, W, G, A, Pol, F (2), N (19)
Casper, C. M. (Manchester U), 1995 v Mal (1)
Caton, T. (Manchester C), 1982 v N, H (sub), Pol (2), S; 1983 v WG (2), Gr; 1984 v D, H, F (2), I (2) (14)

Chadwick, L. H. (Manchester U), 2000 v L, D, Arg, I (sub), Slo (sub); 2001 v Ge (sub), I, Sp, Fi, Alb; 2002 v Ho, G, Alb (13)
Challis, T. M. (QPR), 1996 v An, P (2)
Chamberlain, M. (Stoke C), 1983 v Gr; 1984 v F (sub), I, Sp (4)
Chaplow, R. D. (Burnley), 2004 v Ho (sub) (1)
Chapman, L. (Stoke C), 1981 v Ei (1)
Charles, G. A. (Nottingham F), 1991 v H, W (sub), Ei; 1992 v T (4)
Chettle, S. (Nottingham F), 1988 v M, USSR, Mor, F; 1989 v D, Se, Gr, Alb (2), Bul; 1990 v Se, Pol (12)
Chopra, R, M. (Newcastle U), 2004 v Se (sub) (1)
Clark, L. R. (Newcastle U), 1992 v Cz, F; 1993 v Sp, N, T, Ho (sub), Pol (sub), Cz, Br, S; 1994 v Ho (11)
Clarke, P. M. (Everton), 2003 v Slo (sub), I, T, Ser, Slo; 2004 v Cro, Mac, P (8)
Christie, M. N. (Derby Co), 2001 v Fi (sub), Sp, Fi, Alb, M, Gr; 2002 v Ho (sub), Gr (sub), Ho, Slv, P (11)
Clegg, M. J. (Manchester U), 1998 v Fr (sub), S.Af (sub) (2)
Clemence, S. N. (Tottenham H), 1999 v Se (sub) (1)
Clough, N. (Nottingham F), 1986 v D (sub); 1987 v Se, Y, T, USSR, F (sub), P; 1988 v WG, T, Y, S (2), M, Mor, F (15)
Cole, A. A. (Arsenal), 1992 v H, Cz (sub), F (sub); (with Bristol C), 1993 v Sm; (with Newcastle U), Pol, N; 1994 v Pol, Ho (8)
Cole, A. (Arsenal), 2001 v Ge, G, Fi, I (4)
Cole, C. (Chelsea), 2003 v T (sub), Ser (sub), Slo (sub); 2004 v Cro (sub), Ho, Se; 2005 v Uk, A, Pol, W, Sp, Ho; 2006 v D, W, G, A, Pol, F (2) (19)
Cole, J. J. (West Ham U), 2000 v Arg (sub); 2001 v Ge, Gr; 2002 v G; 2003 v Slo, Mac, P, T (8)
Coney, D. (Fulham), 1985 v T (sub); 1986 v R; 1988 v T, WG (4)
Connor, T. (Brighton & HA), 1987 v Y (1)
Cooke, R. (Tottenham H), 1986 v D (sub) (1)
Cooke, T. J. (Manchester U), 1996 v Cro, Bel, An (sub), P (4)
Cooper, C. (Middlesbrough), 1988 v F (2), M, USSR, Mor; 1989 v D, Se, Gr (8)
Corrigan, J. T. (Manchester C), 1978 v I (2), Y (3)
Cort, C. E. R. (Wimbledon), 1999 v L (sub), CzR, H (sub), Se, Bul; 2000 v L (sub), Pol, D (sub), Arg, I, T, Slo (12)
Cottee, A. (West Ham U), 1985 v Fi (sub), Is (sub), Ei, R, Fi; 1987 v Sp, P; 1988 v WG (8)
Couzens, A. J. (Leeds U), 1995 v Mal (sub), An, F (sub) (3)
Cowans, G. S. (Aston Villa), 1979 v W, Se; 1980 v Bul, EG; 1981 v R (5)
Cox, N. J. (Aston Villa), 1993 v T, Ho, Pol, N; 1994 v Pol, Sm (6)
Cranson, I. (Ipswich T), 1985 v Fi, Is, R; 1986 v R, I (5)
Cresswell, R. P. W. (York C), 1999 v F (sub); (with Sheffield W) H (sub), Se, Bul (4)
Croft, G. (Grimsby T), 1995 v Br, Mal, An, F (4)
Crooks, G. (Stoke C), 1980 v Bul, S (2), EG (sub) (4)
Crossley, M. G. (Nottingham F), 1990 v P, USSR, Cz (3)
Crouch, P. J. (Portsmouth), 2002 v I (sub), P (sub), Sw; (with Aston Villa), 2003 v Mac (sub), P (sub) (5)
Cundy, J. V. (Chelsea), 1991 v Ei (2); 1992 v Pol (3)
Cunningham, L. (WBA), 1977 v S, Fi, N (sub); 1978 v N, Fi, I (6)
Curbishley, L. C. (Birmingham C), 1981 v Sw (1)
Curtis, J. C. K. (Manchester U), 1998 v I (sub), Gr, Sw, F, S.Af, Arg; 1999 v Se (sub), Bul, L, CzR, F, Pol (sub), H, Se (sub), Bul; 2000 v Pol (16)

Daniel, P. W. (Hull C), 1977 v S, Fi, N; 1978 v Fi, I, Y (2) (7)
Davenport, C. R. P. (Tottenham H), 2005 v A, Pol, W, Az, Sp (sub), G, Az; 2006 v D (8)
Davies, A. J. (Middlesbrough), 2004 v T (1)
Davies, C. E. (WBA), 2006 v N (sub) (1)
Davies, K. C. (Southampton), 1998 v Gr (sub); (with Blackburn R), 1999 v CzR; (with Southampton), 2000 v Y (sub) (3)
Davis, K. G. (Luton T), 1995 v An; 1996 v Cro (sub), P (3)
Davis, P. (Arsenal), 1982 v Pol, S; 1983 v D, Gr (1 + 1 sub), H (sub); 1987 v T; 1988 v WG, T, Y, Fr (11)
Davis, S. (Fulham), 2001 v Fi, Alb, M, Gr; 2002 v Ho, G, Al, Ho (2), P, Sw (11)
Dawson, M. R. (Nottingham F), 2003 v Slo (sub), I, P, T; 2004 v P, Se; 2005 v Sp; (with Tottenham H), 2006 v D, W, G, A, F (2) (13)
Day, C. N. (Tottenham H), 1996 v Cro, Bel, Br; (with C Palace), 1997 v Mol, Ge, Sw (6)
D'Avray, M. (Ipswich T), 1984 v I, Sp (sub) (2)
Deehan, J. M. (Aston Villa), 1977 v N; 1978 v N, Fi, I; 1979 v Bul, Se (sub); 1980 v D (7)
Defoe, J. C. (West Ham U), 2001 v M, Gr; 2002 v Ho (sub), G (sub), Alb, Gr, Ho (2), Slv, I, P (sub), Sw, I, P; 2003 v Y, P, T, Ser, Slo; 2004 v Cro, Mac (sub), P (sub), T (23)
Dennis, M. E. (Birmingham C), 1980 v Bul; 1981 v N, R (3)
Dichio, D. S. E. (QPR), 1996 v N (sub) (1)
Dickens, A. (West Ham U), 1985 v Fi (sub) (1)
Dicks, J. (West Ham U), 1988 v Sw (sub), M, Mor, F (4)
Digby, F. (Swindon T), 1987 v Sp (sub), USSR, P; 1988 v T; 1990 v Pol (5)
Dillon, K. P. (Birmingham C), 1981 v R (1)
Dixon, K. (Chelsea), 1985 v Fi (1)
Dobson, A. (Coventry C), 1989 v Bul, Sen, Ei, US (4)
Dodd, J. R. (Southampton), 1991 v Pol, Ei, T, Sen, M, F; 1992 v G, Pol (8)
Donowa, L. (Norwich C), 1985 v Is, R (sub), Fi (sub) (3)
Dorigo, A. (Aston Villa), 1987 v Se, Sp, T, Mor, USSR, F, P; 1988 v WG, Y, S (2) (11)
Downing, S. (Middlesbrough), 2004 v Ho, Se; 2005 v Uk, A, W, Az (sub), Sp (sub); 2006 v D (8)
Dozzell, J. (Ipswich T), 1987 v Se, Y (sub), Sp, USSR, F, P; 1989 v Se, Gr (sub); 1990 v Se (sub) (9)
Draper, M. A. (Notts Co), 1991 v Ei (sub); 1992 v G, Pol (3)
Duberry, M. W. (Chelsea), 1997 v Mol, Pol, Ge; 1998 v Mol, Gr (5)
Dunn, D. J. I. (Blackburn R), 1999 v CzR (sub); 2000 v I (sub), T, Slo; 2001 v Ge, G, Fi, I, Sp, M, Gr; 2002 v Ho, Gr, Ho (2), Slv, P, Sw, I, P (20)
Duxbury, M. (Manchester U), 1981 v Sw (sub), Ei (sub), R (sub), Sw; 1982 v N; 1983 v WG (2) (7)
Dyer, B. A. (C Palace), 1994 v Ru, F, US, Bel, P; 1995 v P (sub); 1996 v Cro; 1997 v Mol, Ge; 1998 v Mol, Gr (10)
Dyer, K. C. (Ipswich T), 1998 v Mol, I, Gr, Sw, S.Af, Arg; 1999 v Se, Bul, CzR, Se; (with Newcastle U), 2000 v Y (11)
Dyson, P. I. (Coventry C), 1981 v N, R, Sw, Ei (4)

Eadie, D. M. (Norwich C), 1994 v F (sub), US; 1997 v Mol, Ge (2), I; 1998 v I (7)
Ebbrell, J. (Everton), 1989 v Sen, Ei, US (sub); 1990 v P, F, USSR, Cz; 1991 v H, Pol, Ei, W, T; 1992 v G, T (14)
Edghill, R. A. (Manchester C), 1994 v D, Ru; 1995 v A (3)
Ehiogu, U. (Aston Villa), 1992 v H, M, Cz, F; 1993 v Sp, N, T, Sm, T, Ho, Pol, N; 1994 v Pol, Ho, Sm (15)
Elliott, P. (Luton T), 1985 v Fi; 1986 v T, D (3)
Elliott, R. J. (Newcastle U), 1996 v P, A (2)
Elliott, S. W. (Derby Co), 1998 v F, Arg (sub) (2)
Etherington, N, (Tottenham H), 2002 v Slv (sub), I; 2003 v Y (sub) (3)
Euell, J. J. (Wimbledon), 1998 v F, Arg (sub); 1999 v Se (sub), Bul (se), Pol (sub), H (6)
Evans, R. (Chelsea), 2003 v Ser, Slo (2)

Fairclough, C. (Nottingham F), 1985 v T, Is, Ei; 1987 v Sp, T; (with Tottenham H), 1988 v Y, F (7)
Fairclough, D. (Liverpool), 1977 v W (1)
Fashanu, J. (Norwich C), 1980 v EG; 1981 v N (sub), R, Sw, Ei (sub), H; (with Nottingham F), 1982 v N, H, Pol, S; 1983 v WG (sub) (11)
Fear, P. (Wimbledon), 1994 v Ru, F, US (sub) (3)
Fenton, G. A. (Aston Villa), 1995 v Ei (1)
Fenwick, T. W. (C Palace), 1981 v N, R, Sw, Ei; (with QPR), R; 1982 v N, H, S (2); 1983 v WG (2) (11)
Ferdinand, A. J. (West Ham U), 2005 v Uk, A, Pol; 2006 v D (sub), W, G, A, Pol, F (2), N (11)
Ferdinand, R. G. (West Ham U), 1997 v Sw, Ge; 1998 v I, Gr; 2000 v Y (5)
Fereday, W. (QPR), 1985 v T, Ei (sub). Fi; 1986 v T (sub), I (5)
Flitcroft, G. W. (Manchester C), 1993 v Sm, Hol, N, P, Cz, Br, S, F; 1994 v Pol, Ho (10)
Flowers, T. (Southampton), 1987 v Mor, F; 1988 v WG (sub) (3)
Ford, M. (Leeds U), 1996 v Cro; 1997 v Mol (2)
Forster, N. M. (Brentford), 1995 v Br, Mal, An, F (4)
Forsyth, M. (Derby Co), 1988 v Sw (1)
Foster, S. (Brighton & HA), 1980 v EG (sub) (1)
Fowler, R. B. (Liverpool), 1994 v Sm, Ru (sub), F, US; 1995 v P, A; 1996 v P, A (8)
Froggatt, S. J. (Aston Villa), 1993 v Sp, Sm (sub) (2)
Futcher, P. (Luton T), 1977 v W, S, Fi, N; (with Manchester C), 1978 v N, Fi, I (2), Y (2); 1979 v D (11)

Gabbiadini, M. (Sunderland), 1989 v Bul, USA (2)
Gale, A. (Fulham), 1982 v Pol (1)
Gallen, K. A. (QPR), 1995 v Ei, La (2); 1996 v Cro (4)
Gardner, A. (Tottenham H), 2002 v I (sub) (1)
Gascoigne, P. (Newcastle U), 1987 v Mo, USSR, P; 1988 v WG, Y, S (2), F (2), Sw, M, USSR (sub), Mor (13)
Gayle, H. (Birmingham C), 1984 v I, Sp (2) (3)

Gernon, T. (Ipswich T), 1983 v Gr (1)
Gerrard, P. W. (Oldham Ath), 1993 v T, Ho, Pol, N, P, Cz, Br, S, F; 1994 v D, Ru; 1995 v P, A, Ei (2), La (2); 1996 v P (18)
Gerrard, S. G. (Liverpool), 2000 v L, Pol, D, Y (4)
Gibbs, N. (Watford), 1987 v Mor, USSR, F, P; 1988 v T (5)
Gibson, C. (Aston Villa), 1982 v N (1)
Gilbert, W. A. (C Palace), 1979 v W, Bul; 1980 v Bul; 1981 v N, R, Sw, R, Sw, H; 1982 v N (sub), H (11)
Goddard, P. (West Ham U), 1981 v N, Sw, Ei (sub); 1982 v N (sub), Pol, S; 1983 v WG (2) (8)
Gordon, D. (Norwich C), 1987 v T (sub), Mor (sub), F, P (4)
Gordon, D. D. (C Palace), 1994 v Ru, F, US, Bel, P; 1995 v P, A, Ei (2), La (2); 1996 v P, N (13)
Grant, A. J. (Everton), 1996 v An (sub) (1)
Grant, L. A. (Derby Co), 2003 v I (sub); 2004 v P, T, Se (sub) (4)
Granville, D. P. (Chelsea), 1997 v Ge (sub), Pol; 1998 v Mol (3)
Gray, A. (Aston Villa), 1988 v S, F (2)
Greening, J. (Manchester U), 1999 v H, Se (sub), Bul; 2000 v Pol; 2001 v Ge, G, Fi, I, Sp (sub), Fi, Alb; (with Middlesbrough), 2002 v Ho, G, Alb, Gr, Ho (sub), I, P (18)
Griffin, A. (Newcastle U), 1999 v H; 2001 v I, Sp (3)
Guppy, S. A. (Leicester C), 1998 v Sw (1)

Haigh, P. (Hull C), 1977 v N (sub) (1)
Hall, M. T. J. (Coventry C), 1997 v Pol (2), I, Sw, Ge; 1998 v Mol, Gr (2) (8)
Hall, R. A. (Southampton), 1992 v H (sub), F; 1993 v Sm, T, Ho, Pol, P, Cz, Br, S, F (11)
Hamilton, D. V. (Newcastle U), 1997 v Pol (1)
Harding, D. A. (Brighton & HA), 2005 v Uk (sub), W, Az, Sp (4)
Hardyman, P. (Portsmouth), 1985 v Ei; 1986 v D (2)
Hargreaves, O. (Bayern Munich), 2001 v Ge (sub), I, Sp (3)
Harley, J. (Chelsea), 2000 v Arg (sub), T (sub), Slo (3)
Hateley, M. (Coventry C), 1982 v Pol, S; 1983 v Gr (2), H; (with Portsmouth), 1984 v F (2), I, Sp (2) (10)
Hayes, M. (Arsenal), 1987 v Sp, T; 1988 v F (sub) (3)
Hazell, R. J. (Wolverhampton W), 1979 v D (1)
Heaney, N. A. (Arsenal), 1992 v H, M, Cz, F; 1993 v N, T (6)
Heath, A. (Stoke C), 1981 v R, Sw, H; 1982 v N, H; (with Everton), Pol, S; 1983 v WG (8)
Hendon, I. M. (Tottenham H), 1992 v H, M, Cz, F; 1993 v Sp, N, T (7)
Hendrie, L. A. (Aston Villa), 1996 v Cro (sub); 1998 v Sw (sub); 1999 v Se, Bul, L, F, Pol; 2000 v L, D, Arg, Y, I, Slo (sub) (13)
Hesford, I. (Blackpool), 1981 v Ei (sub), Pol (2), S (2); 1983 v WG (2) (7)
Heskey, E. W. I. (Leicester C), 1997 v I, Ge, Pol (2); 1998 v I, Gr (2), Sw, F, S.Af, Arg; 1999 v Se, Bul, L; 2000 v L; (with Liverpool), Y (16)
Hilaire, V. (C Palace), 1980 v Bul, S (1+1 sub), EG (2); 1981 v N, R, Sw (sub); 1982 v Pol (sub) (9)
Hill, D. R. L. (Tottenham H), 1995 v Br, Mal, An, F (4)
Hillier, D. (Arsenal), 1991 v T (1)
Hinchcliffe, A. (Manchester C), 1989 v D (1)
Hinshelwood, P. A. (C Palace), 1978 v N; 1980 v EG (2)
Hirst, D. (Sheffield W), 1988 v USSR, F; 1989 v D, Bul (sub), Sen, Ei, US (7)
Hislop, N. S. (Newcastle U), 1998 v Sw (1)
Hoddle, G. (Tottenham H), 1977 v W (sub); 1978 v Fi (sub), I (2), Y; 1979 v D, W, Bul; 1980 v S (2), EG (2) (12)
Hodge, S. (Nottingham F), 1983 v Gr (sub); 1984 v D, F, I, Sp (2); (with Aston Villa), 1986 v R, T (8)
Hodgson, D. J. (Middlesbrough), 1981 v N, R (sub), Sw, Ei; 1982 v Pol; 1983 v WG (6)
Holdsworth, D. (Watford), 1989 v Gr (sub) (1)
Holland, C. J. (Newcastle U), 1995 v La; 1996 v N (sub), A (sub), Cro, Bel, An, Br; 1997 v Mol, Pol, Sw (10)
Holland, P. (Mansfield T), 1995 v Br, Mal, An, F (4)
Holloway, D. (Sunderland), 1998 v Sw (sub) (1)
Horne, B. (Millwall), 1989 v Gr (sub), Pol, Bul, Ei, US (5)
Howe, E. J. F. (Bournemouth), 1998 v S.Af (sub), Arg (2)
Hoyte, J. R. (Arsenal), 2004 v Ho (sub), Se; 2005 v Uk (sub), A (sub), Pol (sub), Sp, Ho; 2006 v N (sub) (8)
Hucker, P. (QPR), 1984 v I, Sp (2)
Huckerby, D. (Coventry C), 1997 v I (sub), Sw, Ge (sub), Pol (sub) (4)
Huddlestone, T. A. (Derby Co), 2005 v Ho, G, Az ; (with Tottenham H), 2006 v A, Pol, F (2), N (8)
Hughes, S. J. (Arsenal), 1997 v I, Sw, Ge, Pol; 1998 v Mol, I, Gr, Sw (sub) (8)
Humphreys, R. J. (Sheffield W), 1997 v Pol, Ge (sub), Sw (3)
Hunt, N. B. (Bolton W), 2004 v Ho; 2005 v Uk, A, W, Az, Sp, G; 2006 v D, W (sub), G (10)

Impey, A. R. (QPR), 1993 v T (1)
Ince, P. (West Ham U), 1989 v Alb; 1990 v Se (2)

Jackson, M. A. (Everton), 1992 v H, M, Cz, F; 1993 v Sm (sub), T, Ho, Pol, N; 1994 v Pol (10)
Jagielka, P. N. (Sheffield U), 2003 v Ser, Slo; 2004 v Cro (sub), Mac, P, T (6)
James, D. (Watford), 1991 v Ei (2), T, Sen, M, USSR, F; 1992 v G, T, Pol (10)
James, J. C. (Luton T), 1990 v F, USSR (2)
Jansen, M. B (C Palace), 1999 v Se, Bul, L; (with Blackburn R), F (sub), Pol; 2000 v I (sub) (6)
Jeffers, F. (Everton), 2000 v L, Arg, I, T, Slo; 2001 v Ge; (with Arsenal), 2002 v Ho, G (sub), Alb; 2003 v Y, Slo, Mac, T; 2004 v Cro, Mac, P (16)
Jemson, N. B. (Nottingham F), 1991 v W (1)
Jenas, J. A. (Newcastle U), 2002 v Slo, I, P (sub); 2003 v Y, Slo, Mac, T; 2004 v Cro, T (9)
Jerome, C. (Cardiff C), 2006 v A (sub), F (sub), N (sub) (3)
Joachim, J. K. (Leicester C), 1994 v D (sub); 1995 v P, A, Ei, Br, Mal, An, F; 1996 v N (9)
Johnson, G. M. C. (West Ham U), 2003 v T (sub), Ser (sub); (with Chelsea), 2004 v Cro, Mac, P, T, Ho; 2005 v Pol, W, Az, Sp, G; 2006 v W, N (14)
Johnson, S. A. M. (Crewe Alex), 1999 v L (sub), CzR (sub), F (sub), Pol; (with Derby Co), Se, Bul; 2000 v D, Arg (sub), Y, I, T; 2001 v Fi; 2002 v Ho (sub), Alb (sub); (with Leeds U), P (15)
Johnson, T. (Notts Co), 1991 v H (sub), Ei (sub); 1992 v G, T, Pol; (with Derby Co), M, Cz (sub) (7)
Johnston, C. P. (Middlesbrough), 1981 v N, Ei (2)
Jones, D. R. (Everton), 1977 v W (1)
Jones, C. H. (Tottenham H), 1978 v Y (sub) (1)
Jones, D. F. L. (Manchester U), 2004 v Se (sub) (1)
Jones, R. (Liverpool), 1993 v Sm, Ho (2)

Keegan, G. A. (Manchester C), 1977 v W (1)
Kenny, W. (Everton), 1993 v T (1)
Keown, M. (Aston Villa), 1987 v Sp, Mor, USSR, P; 1988 v T, S, F (2) (8)
Kerslake, D. (QPR), 1986 v T (1)
Kilcline, B. (Notts C), 1983 v D, Gr (2)
Kilgallon, M. (Leeds U), 2004 v Se (sub); 2005 v Uk, Pol (sub), Az (sub) (4)
King, A. E. (Everton), 1977 v W; 1978 v Y (2)
King, L. B. (Tottenham H), 2000 v L (sub), I, T, Slo; 2001 v I, Sp (sub), Fi; 2002 v G, Alb, Gr, Ho (2) (12)
Kirkland, C. E. (Coventry C), 2001 v M; (with Liverpool), 2002 v Gr, Ho (2), P (sub); 2003 v Y, Mac; 2004 v Mac (8)
Kitson, P. (Leicester C), 1991 v Sen (sub), M, F; 1992 v Pol; (with Derby Co), M, Cz, F (7)
Knight, A. (Portsmouth), 1983 v Gr, H (2)
Knight, I. (Sheffield W), 1987 v Se (sub), Y (2)
Knight, Z. (Fulham), 2002 v Slo (sub), I (2), P (4)
Konchesky, P. M. (Charlton Ath), 2002 v Slo, P, Sw, I, P; 2003 Y, Slo, Mac, P, T, Ser, Slo; 2004 v Cro, Mac, P (15)
Kozluk, R. (Derby Co), 1998 v F, Arg (sub) (2)

Lake, P. (Manchester C), 1989 v D, Alb (2), Pol; 1990 v Pol (5)
Lampard, F. J. (West Ham U), 1998 v Gr (2), Sw, F, S.Af, Arg; 1999 v Se, Bul, L, CzR, F, Pol, Se; 2000 v L, Arg, Y, I, T, Slo (19)
Langley, T. W. (Chelsea), 1978 v I (sub) (1)
Lee, D. J. (Chelsea), 1990 v F; 1991 v H, Pol, Ei (2), T, Sen, USSR, F; 1992 v Pol (10)
Lee, R. (Charlton Ath), 1986 v I (sub); 1987 v Se (sub) (2)
Lee, S. (Liverpool), 1981 v R, Sw, H; 1982 v S; 1983 v WG (2) (6)
Lennon, A. J. (Tottenham H), 2006 v A, Pol (2)
Le Saux, G. (Chelsea), 1990 v P, F, USSR, Cz (4)
Lescott, J. P. (Wolverhampton W), 2003 v Y (sub), I (sub) (2)
Lita, L. H. (Bristol C), 2005 v Ho (sub); 2006 v N (sub) (2)
Lowe, D. (Ipswich T), 1988 v F, Sw (sub) (2)
Lukic, J. (Leeds U), 1981 v N, R, Ei, R, Sw, H; 1982 v H (7)
Lund, G. (Grimsby T), 1985 v T; 1986 v R, T (3)

McCall, S. H. (Ipswich T), 1981 v Sw, H; 1982 v H, S; 1983 v WG (2) (6)
McDonald, N. (Newcastle U), 1987 v Se (sub), Sp, T; 1988 v WG, Y (sub) (5)
McEveley, J. (Blackburn R), 2003 v I (sub) (1)
McGrath, L. (Coventry C), 1986 v D (1)

MacKenzie, S. (WBA), 1982 v N, S (2) (3)
McLeary, A. (Millwall), 1988 v Sw (1)
McLeod, I. M. (Milton Keynes D), 2006 v N (sub) (1)
McMahon, S. (Everton), 1981 v Ei; 1982 v Pol; 1983 v D, Gr (2); (with Aston Villa), 1984 v H (6)
McManaman, S. (Liverpool), 1991 v W, M (sub); 1993 v N, T, Sm, T; 1994 v Pol (7)
Mabbutt, G. (Bristol R), 1982 v Pol (2), S; (with Tottenham H), 1983 v D; 1984 v F; 1986 v D, I (7)
Makin, C. (Oldham Ath), 1994 v Ru (sub), F, US, Bel, P (5)
Marney, D. E. (Tottenham H), 2005 v Ho (sub) (1)
Marriott, A. (Nottingham F), 1992 v M (1)
Marsh, S. T. (Oxford U), 1998 v F (1)
Marshall, A. J. (Norwich C), 1995 v Mal, An; 1997 v Pol, I (4)
Marshall, L. K. (Norwich C), 1999 v F (sub) (1)
Martin, L. (Manchester U), 1989 v Gr (sub), Alb (sub) (2)
Martyn, N. (Bristol R), 1988 v S (sub), M, USSR, Mor, F; 1989 v D, Se, Gr, Alb (2); 1990 v Se (11)
Matteo, D. (Liverpool), 1994 v F (sub), Bel, P; 1998 v Sw (4)
Matthew, D. (Chelsea), 1990 v P, USSR (sub), Cz; 1991 v Ei, M, USSR, F; 1992 v G (sub), T (9)
May, A. (Manchester C), 1986 v I (sub) (1)
Merson, P. (Arsenal), 1989 v D, Gr, Pol (sub); 1990 v Pol (4)
Middleton, J. (Nottingham F), 1977 v Fi, N; (with Derby Co), 1978 v N (3)
Miller, A. (Arsenal), 1988 v Mor (sub); 1989 v Sen; 1991 v H, Pol (4)
Mills, D. J. (Charlton Ath), 1999 v Se, Bul (sub), L, Pol, H, Se; (with Leeds U), 2000 v L, Pol, D, Arg, Y (sub), I, T, Slo (14)
Mills, G. R. (Nottingham F), 1981 v R; 1982 v N (2)
Milner, J. P. (Leeds U), 2004 v Se (sub); (with Newcastle U), 2005 v Uk, A (sub), Pol, W, Az, Sp, Ho, G, Az; 2006 v D, W, G, A, Pol (sub), F, N (17)
Mimms, R. (Rotherham U), 1985 v Is (sub), Ei (sub); (with Everton), 1986 v I (3)
Minto, S. C. (Charlton Ath), 1991 v W; 1992 v H, M, Cz; 1993 v T; 1994 v Ho (6)
Moore, I. (Tranmere R), 1996 v Cro (sub), Bel (sub), An, P, Br; 1997 v Mol (sub); (with Nottingham F), Sw (sub) (7)
Moore, L. I. (Aston Villa), 2006 v A (sub) (1)
Moran, S. (Southampton), 1982 v N (sub); 1984 v F (2)
Morgan, S. (Leicester C), 1987 v Se, Y (2)
Morris, J. (Chelsea), 1997 v Pol (sub), Sw (sub), Ge (sub); 1999 v Bul (sub), L (sub), CzR; 2000 v Pol (7)
Mortimer, P. (Charlton Ath), 1989 v Sen, Ei (2)
Moses, A. P. (Barnsley), 1997 v Pol; 1998 v Gr (sub) (2)
Moses, R. M. (WBA), 1981 v N (sub), Sw, Ei, R, Sw, H; 1982 v N (sub); (with Manchester U), H (8)
Mountfield, D. (Everton), 1984 v Sp (1)
Muggleton, C. D. (Leicester C), 1990 v F (1)
Mullins, H. I. (C Palace), 1999 v Pol (sub), H, Bul (3)
Murphy, D. B. (Liverpool), 1998 v Mol, Gr (sub); 2000 v T, Slo (4)
Murray, P. (QPR), 1997 v I, Pol; 1998 v I, Gr (4)
Murray, M. W. (Wolverhampton W), 2003 v Slo, Mac (sub), I, T; 2004 v Cro (5)
Mutch, A. (Wolverhampton W), 1989 v Pol (1)
Myers. A. (Chelsea), 1995 v Br, Mal, An (sub), F (4)

Naylor, L. M. (Wolverhampton W), 2000 v Arg; 2001 v M, Gr (3)
Nethercott, S. (Tottenham), 1994 v D, Ru, F, US, Bel, P; 1995 v La (2) (8)
Neville, P. J. (Manchester U), 1995 v Br, Mal, An, F; 1996 v P, N (sub); 1997 v Ge (7)
Newell, M. (Luton T), 1986 v D (1 + 1 sub), I (1 + 1 sub) (4)
Newton, A. L. (West Ham U), 2001 v Ge (1)
Newton, E. J. I. (Chelsea), 1993 v T (sub); 1994 v Sm (2)
Newton, S. O. (Charlton Ath), 1997 v Mol, Pol, Ge (3)
Nicholls, A. (Plymouth Arg), 1994 v F (1)
Nolan, K. A. J. (Bolton W), 2003 v I (sub) (1)
Nugent, D. J. (Preston NE), 2006 v W (sub), G (sub), N (3)

Oakes, M. C. (Aston Villa), 1994 v D (sub), F (sub), US, Bel, P; 1996 v A (6)
Oakes, S. J. (Luton T), 1993 v Br (sub) (1)
Oakley, M. (Southampton), 1997 v Ge; 1998 v F, S.Af, Arg (4)
O'Brien, A. J. (Bradford C), 1999 v F (1)
O'Connor, J. (Everton), 1996 v Cro, An, Br (3)
O'Neil, G. P. (Portsmouth) 2005 v Uk, A, Pol, W, Az, G; 2006 v G, Pol, F (9)
Oldfield, D. (Luton T), 1989 v Se (1)
Olney, I. A. (Aston Villa), 1990 v P, F, USSR, Cz; 1991 v H, Pol, Ei (2), T; 1992 v Pol (sub) (10)
Onuoha C. (Manchester C), 2006 v Pol (sub), F (2)
Ord, R. J. (Sunderland), 1991 v W, M, USSR (3)
Osman, R. C. (Ipswich T), 1979 v W (sub), Se; 1980 v D, S (2), EG (2) (7)
Owen, G. A. (Manchester C), 1977 v S, Fi, N; 1978 v N, Fi, I (2), Y; 1979 v D, W; (with WBA), Bul, Se (sub); 1980 v D, S (2), EG; 1981 v Sw, R; 1982 v N (sub), H; 1983 v WG (2) (22)
Owen, M. J. (Liverpool), 1998 v Gr (1)

Painter, I. (Stoke C), 1986 v I (1)
Palmer, C. (Sheffield W), 1989 v Bul, Sen, Ei, US (4)
Parker, G. (Hull C), 1986 v I (2); (with Nottingham F), F; 1987 v Se, Y (sub), Sp (6)
Parker, P. (Fulham), 1985 v Fi, T, Is (sub), Ei, R, Fi; 1986 v T, D (8)
Parker, S. M. (Charlton Ath), 2001 v Ge (sub), G, Fi (sub), Alb (sub); 2002 v Ho (sub), G (sub), Alb, Slo, I (sub), Sw (sub), I (sub), P (sub) (12)
Parkes, P. B. F. (QPR), 1979 v D (1)
Parkin, S. (Stoke C), 1987 v Sp (sub); 1988 v WG (sub), T, S (sub), F (5)
Parlour, R. (Arsenal), 1992 v H, M, Cz, F; 1993 v Sp, N, T; 1994 v D, Ru, Bel, P; 1995 v A (12)
Parnaby, S. (Middlesbrough), 2003 v Y (sub), Ser, Slo; 2004 v Cro (4)
Peach, D. S. (Southampton), 1977 v S, Fi, N; 1978 v N, I (2) (6)
Peake, A. (Leicester C), 1982 v Pol (1)
Pearce, I. A. (Blackburn R), 1995 v Ei, La; 1996 v N (3)
Pearce, S. (Nottingham F), 1987 v Y (1)
Pennant, J. (Arsenal), 2001 v M (sub), Gr (sub); 2002 v Ho (sub), Alb (sub), Gr, Ho (2), Slv, I (sub), P (sub), Sw, I, P; 2003 v Y, P (sub), Ser, Slo; 2004 v Cro, Mac; 2005 v Uk, A, Pol, W, Az (24)
Pickering N. (Sunderland), 1983 v D (sub), Gr, H; 1984 v F (sub + 1), I (2), Sp; 1985 v Is, R, Fi; 1986 v R, T; (with Coventry C), D, I (15)
Platt, D. (Aston Villa), 1988 v M, Mor, F (3)
Plummer, C. S. (QPR), 1996 v Cro (sub), Bel, An, P (sub), Br (5)
Pollock, J. (Middlesbrough), 1995 v Ei (sub); 1996 v N, A (3)
Porter, G. (Watford), 1987 v Sp (sub), T, Mor, USSR, F, P (sub); 1988 v T (sub), Y, S (2), F, Sw (12)
Potter, G. S. (Southampton), 1997 v Mol (1)
Pressman, K. (Sheffield W), 1989 v D (sub) (1)
Proctor, M. (Middlesbrough), 1981 v Ei (sub), Sw; (with Nottingham F) 1982 v N, Pol (4)
Prutton, D. T. (Nottingham F), 2001 v Ge (sub), G (sub), Fi, Sp (sub), M, Gr (sub); 2002 v Ho (sub), G, Gr (sub), Slv (sub), I, Sw (sub), I, P; 2003 v Y, Slo, Mac; (with Southampton), I, P, T, Ser, Slo; 2004 v Cro, P, T (25)
Purse, D. J. (Birmingham C), 1998 v F. S.Af (2)

Quashie, N. F. (QPR), 1997 v Pol; 1998 v Mol, Gr, Sw (4)
Quinn, W. R. (Sheffield U), 1998 v Mol (sub), I (2)

Ramage, C. D. (Derby Co), 1991 v Pol (sub), W; 1992 v Fr (sub) (3)
Ranson, R. (Manchester C), 1980 v Bul, EG; 1981 v R (sub), R, Sw (1 + 1 sub), H, Pol (2), S (10)
Redknapp, J. F. (Liverpool), 1993 v Sm, Pol, N, P, Cz, Br, S, F; 1994 v Pol, Ho (sub), D, Ru, F, US, Bel, P; 1995 v P, A; 1998 v Sw (19)
Redmond, S. (Manchester C), 1988 v F (2), M, USSR, Mor, F; 1989 v D, Se, Gr, Alb (2), Pol; 1990 v Se, Pol (14)
Reeves, K. P. (Norwich C), 1978 v I, Y (2); 1979 v N, W, Bul, Sw; 1980 v D, S; (with Manchester C), EG (10)
Regis, C. (WBA), 1979 v D, Bul, Se; 1980 v S, EG; 1983 v D (6)
Reid, N. S. (Manchester C), 1981 v H (sub); 1982 v H, Pol (2), S (2) (6)
Reid, P. (Bolton W), 1977 v S, Fi, N; 1978 v Fi, I, Y (6)
Reo-Coker, N. S. A. (Wimbledon), 2004 v T (sub); (with West Ham U), Ho, Se; 2005 v Uk (sub), A, Pol, Az; 2006 v D, W, G, Pol, N (12)
Richards, D. I. (Wolverhampton W), 1995 v Br, Mal, An, F (4)
Richards, J. P. (Wolverhampton W), 1977 v Fi, N (2)
Richards, M. L. (Ipswich T), 2005 v Uk (1)
Richardson, K. E. (Manchester U), 2005 v Ho (sub), G, Az; 2006 v D, F (2) (6)
Rideout, P. (Aston Villa), 1985 v Fi, Is, Ei (sub), R; (with Bari), 1986 v D (5)
Ridgewell, L. M. (Aston Villa), 2004 v Ho, Se; 2005 v Sp (sub), Ho, G; 2006 v D, W, N (8)
Riggott, C. M. (Derby Co), 2001 v Sp (sub), Fi (sub), Alb, M (sub); 2002 v Ho (sub), Slv, P, Sw (8)

Ripley, S. (Middlesbrough), 1988 v USSR, F (sub); 1989 v D (sub), Se, Gr, Alb (2); 1990 v Se (8)
Ritchie, A. (Brighton & HA), 1982 v Pol (1)
Rix, G. (Arsenal), 1978 v Fi (sub), Y; 1979 v D, Se; 1980 v D (sub), Bul, S (7)
Roberts, A. J. (Millwall), 1995 v Ei, La (2); (with C Palace), 1996 v N, A (5)
Roberts, B. J. (Middlesbrough), 1997 v Sw (sub) (1)
Robins, M. G. (Manchester U), 1990 v P, F, USSR, Cz; 1991 v H (sub), Pol (6)
Robinson, P. P. (Watford), 1999 v Se, Bul; 2000 v Pol (3)
Robinson, P. W. (Leeds U), 2000 v D; 2001 v Ge, G, Fi, Sp; 2002 v Slv, I, P, Sw, I, P (11)
Robson, B. (WBA), 1979 v W, Bul (sub), Se; 1980 v D, Bul, S (2) (7)
Robson, S. (Arsenal), 1984 v I; 1985 v Fi, Is, Fi; 1986 v R, I; (with West Ham U), 1988 v S, Sw (8)
Rocastle, D. (Arsenal), 1987 v Se, Y, Sp, T; 1988 v WG, T, Y, S (2), F (2 subs), M, USSR, Mor (14)
Roche, L. P. (Manchester U), 2001 v Fi (1)
Rodger, G. (Coventry C), 1987 v USSR, F, P; 1988 v WG (4)
Rogers, A. (Nottingham F), 1998 v F, S.Af, Arg (3)
Rosario, R. (Norwich C), 1987 v T (sub), Mor, F, P (sub) (4)
Rose, M. (Arsenal), 1997 v Ge (sub), I (2)
Rosenior, L. J. (Fulham), 2005 v G (sub), Az (2)
Routledge, W. (C Palace), 2005 v Sp (sub), Ho, Az (sub); (with Tottenham H), 2006 v N (4)
Rowell, G. (Sunderland), 1977 v Fi (1)
Ruddock, N. (Southampton), 1989 v Bul (sub), Sen, Ei, US (4)
Rufus, R. R. (Charlton Ath), 1996 v Cro, Bel, An, P, Br; 1997 v I (6)
Ryan, J. (Oldham Ath), 1983 v H (1)
Ryder, S.H. (Walsall), 1995 v Br, An, F (3)

Samuel, J. (Aston Villa), 2002 v I; 2003 v Y, Slo, Mac, I, P, T (7)
Samways, V. (Tottenham H), 1988 v Sw (sub), USSR, F; 1989 v D, Se (5)
Sansom, K. G. (C Palace), 1979 v D, W, Bul, Se; 1980 v S (2), EG (2) (8)
Scimeca, R. (Aston Villa), 1996 v P; 1997 v Mol, Pol, Ge, I; 1998 v Mol, I, Gr (2) (9)
Scowcroft, J. B. (Ipswich T), 1997 v Pol, Ge (2), I (sub); 1998 v Gr (sub) (5)
Seaman, D. (Birmingham C), 1985 v Fi, T, Is, Ei, R, Fi; 1986 v R, F, D, I (10)
Sedgley, S. (Coventry C), 1987 v USSR, F (sub), P; 1988 v F; 1989 v D (sub), Se, Gr, Alb (2), Pol; (with Tottenham H), 1990 v Se (11)
Sellars, S. (Blackburn R), 1988 v S (sub), F, Sw (3)
Selley, I. (Arsenal), 1994 v Ru (sub), F (sub), US (3)
Serrant, C. (Oldham Ath), 1998 v Gr (2) (2)
Sharpe, L. (Manchester U), 1989 v Gr; 1990 v P (sub), F, USSR, Cz; 1991 v H, Pol (sub), Ei (8)
Shaw, G. R. (Aston Villa), 1981 v Ei, Sw, H; 1982 v H, S; 1983 v WG (2) (7)
Shearer, A. (Southampton), 1991 v Ei (2), W, T, Sen, M, USSR, F; 1992 v G, T, Pol (11)
Shelton, G. (Sheffield W), 1985 v Fi (1)
Sheringham, T. (Millwall), 1988 v Sw (1)
Sheron, M. N. (Manchester C), 1992 v H, F; 1993 v N (sub), T (sub), Sm, Ho, Pol, N, P, Cz, Br, S, F; 1994 v Pol (sub), Ho, Sm (16)
Sherwood, T. A. (Norwich C), 1990 v P, F, USSR, Cz (4)
Shipperley, N. J. (Chelsea), 1994 v Sm (sub); (with Southampton), 1995 v Ei, La (2); 1996 v P, N, A (7)
Sidwell, S. J. (Reading), 2003 v Ser, Slo; 2004 v Cro (sub), Mac, T (5)
Simonsen, S. P. A. (Tranmere R), 1998 v F; (with Everton), 1999 v CzR, F, Bul (4)
Simpson, P. (Manchester C), 1986 v D (sub); 1987 v Y, Mor, F, P (5)
Sims, S. (Leicester C), 1977 v W, S, Fi, N; 1978 v N, Fi, I (2), Y (2) (10)
Sinclair, T. (QPR), 1994 v Ho, Sm, D, Ru, F, US, Bel, P; 1995 v P, Ei (2), La; 1996 v P; (with West Ham U), 1998 v Sw (5)
Sinnott, L. (Watford), 1985 v Is (sub) (1)
Slade, S. A. (Tottenham H), 1996 v Bel, An, P, Br (4)
Slater, S. I. (West Ham U), 1990 v P, USSR (sub), Cz (sub) (3)
Small, B. (Aston Villa), 1993 v Sm, T, Ho, Pol, N, P, Cz, Br, S, F; 1994 v Pol, Sm (12)
Smith, A. (Leeds U), 2000 v D, Arg (sub); 2001 v G, Fi, Sp; 2002 v I, P, Sw, I, P (10)
Smith, D. (Coventry C), 1988 v M, USSR (sub), Mor; 1989 v D, Se, Alb (2), Pol; 1990 v Se, Pol (10)
Smith, M. (Sheffield W), 1981 v Ei, R, Sw, H; 1982 v Pol (sub) (5)
Smith, M. (Sunderland), 1995 v Ei (sub) (1)
Smith, T. W. (Watford), 2001 v Ge (sub) (1)
Snodin, I. (Doncaster R), 1985 v T, Is, R, Fi (4)
Soares T. J. (C Palace), 2006 v D (sub), G (sub), A, N (sub) (4)
Statham, B. (Tottenham H), 1988 v Sw; 1989 v D (sub), Se (3)
Statham, D. J. (WBA), 1978 v Fi, 1979 v W, Bul, Se; 1980 v D; 1983 v D (6)
Stead, J. G. (Blackburn R), 2004 v Ho (sub), Se (sub); 2005 v Uk, A, W, Az, Ho (sub), Az (sub); (with Sunderland), 2006 v D (sub), W, Pol (sub) (11)
Stein, B. (Luton T), 1984 v D, H, I (3)
Sterland, M. (Sheffield W), 1984 v D, H, F (2), I, Sp (2) (7)
Steven, T. (Everton), 1985 v Fi, T (2)
Stevens, G. (Brighton & HA), 1983 v H; (with Tottenham H), 1984 v H, F (1+1 sub), I (sub), Sp (1+1 sub); 1986 v I (8)
Stewart, J. (Leicester C), 2003 v P (sub) (1)
Stewart, P. (Manchester C), 1988 v F (1)
Stockdale, R. K. (Middlesbrough), 2001 v Ge (sub) (1)
Stuart, G. C. (Chelsea), 1990 v P (sub), F, USSR, Cz; 1991 v T (sub) (5)
Stuart, J. C. (Charlton Ath), 1996 v Bel, An, P, Br (4)
Suckling, P. (Coventry C), 1986 v D; (with Manchester C), 1987 v Se (sub), Y, Sp, T; (with C Palace), 1988 v S (2), F (2), Sw (10)
Summerbee, N. J. (Swindon T), 1993 v P (sub), S (sub), F (3)
Sunderland, A. (Wolverhampton W), 1977 v W (1)
Sutton, C. R. (Norwich), 1993 v Sp (sub), T (sub + 1), Ho, P (sub), Cz, Br, S, F; 1994 v Pol, Ho, Sm, D (13)
Swindlehurst, D. (C Palace), 1977 v W (1)
Sutch, D. (Norwich C), 1992 v H, M, Cz; 1993 v T (4)

Talbot, B. (Ipswich T), 1977 v W (1)
Taylor, A. (Blackburn R), 2006 v N (sub) (1)
Taylor, M. (Blackburn R), 2001 v M (sub) (1)
Taylor, M. S. (Portsmouth), 2003 v Slo (sub), I; 2004 v T (3)
Taylor, R. A. (Wigan Ath), 2006 v A (sub), Pol, F (2) (4)
Taylor, S. J. (Arsenal), 2002 v Ho, G, Alb (3)
Taylor, S. V. (Newcastle U), 2004 v Ho, Se; 2005 v W (sub), Ho, G (sub), Az; 2006 v G, A, Pol (9)
Terry, J. G. (Chelsea), 2001 v Fi, Sp, Fi, Alb, M, Gr; 2002 v Ho (3) (9)
Thatcher, B. D. (Millwall), 1996 v Cro; (with Wimbledon), 1997 v Mol, Pol; 1998 v I (4)
Thelwell, A. A. (Tottenham H), 2001 v Sp (sub) (1)
Thirlwell, P. (Sunderland), 2001 v Ge (sub) (1)
Thomas, D. (Coventry C), 1981 v Ei; 1983 v WG (2), Gr, H; (with Tottenham H), I, Sp (7)
Thomas, J. W. (Charlton Ath), 2006 v A, Pol (2)
Thomas, M. (Luton T), 1986 v T, D, I (3)
Thomas, M. (Arsenal), 1988 v Y, S, F (2), M, USSR, Mor; 1989 v Gr, Alb (2), Pol; 1990 v Se (12)
Thomas, R. E. (Watford), 1990 v P (1)
Thompson, A. (Bolton W), 1995 v La; 1996 v P (2)
Thompson, D. A. (Liverpool), 1997 v Pol (sub), Ge; 2000 v L (sub), Pol (sub), D (sub), I, T (sub) (7)
Thompson, G. L. (Coventry C), 1981 v R, Sw, H; 1982 v N, H, S (6)
Thorn, A. (Wimbledon), 1988 v WG (sub). Y, S, F, Sw (5)
Thornley, B. L. (Manchester U), 1996 v Bel, P, Br (3)
Tiler, C. (Barnsley), 1990 v P, USSR, Cz; 1991 v H, Pol, Ei (2), T, Sen, USSR, F; (with Nottingham F), 1992 v G, T (13)
Tonge, M. W. E. (Sheffield U), 2004 v Mac, Se (2)

Unsworth, D. G. (Everton), 1995 v A, Ei (2), La; 1996 v N, A (6)
Upson, M. J. (Arsenal), 1999 v Se, Bul, L, F; 2000 v L, Pol, D; 2001 v I, Sp (sub), M (sub), Gr (11)

Vassell, D. (Aston Villa), 1999 v H (sub); 2000 v Pol (sub); 2001 v Ge, G, Fi, I, Fi, Alb; 2002 v Ho, G, Gr (11)
Venison, B. (Sunderland), 1983 v D, Gr; 1985 v Fi, T, Is, Fi; 1986 v R, T, D (2) (10)
Vernazza, P. A. P. (Arsenal), 2001 v G (sub); (with Watford), M (sub) (2)
Vinnicombe, C. (Rangers), 1991 v H (sub), Pol, Ei (2), T, Sen, M, USSR (sub), F; 1992 v G, T, Pol (12)

Waddle, C. (Newcastle U), 1985 v Fi (1)
Wallace, D. (Southampton), 1983 v Gr, H; 1984 v D, H, F (2), I, Sp (sub); 1985 v Fi, T, Is; 1986 v R, D, I (14)
Wallace, Ray (Southampton), 1989 v Bul, Sen (sub), Ei; 1990 v Se (4)

Wallace, Rod (Southampton), 1989 v Bul, Ei (sub), US; 1991 v H, Pol, Ei, T, Sen, M, USSR, F (11)
Walker, D. (Nottingham F), 1985 v Fi; 1987 v Se, T; 1988 v WG, T, S (2) (7)
Walker, I. M. (Tottenham H), 1991 v W; 1992 v H, Cz, F; 1993 v Sp, N, T, Sm; 1994 v Pol (9)
Walsh, G. (Manchester U), 1988 v WG, Y (2)
Walsh, P. M. (Luton T), 1983 v D (sub), Gr (2), H (4)
Walters, K. (Aston Villa), 1984 v D (sub), H (sub); 1985 v Is, Ei, R; 1986 v R, T, D, I (sub) (9)
Ward, P. D. (Brighton & HA), 1978 v N; 1980 v EG (2)
Warhurst, P. (Oldham Ath), 1991 v H, Pol, W, Sen, M (sub), USSR, F (sub); (with Sheffield W), 1992 v G (8)
Watson, D. (Norwich C), 1984 v D, F (2), I (2), Sp (2) (7)
Watson, D. N. (Barnsley), 1994 v Ho, Sm; 1995 v Br, F; 1996 v N (5)
Watson, G. (Sheffield W), 1991 v Sen, USSR (2)
Watson, S. C. (Newcastle U), 1993 v Sp (sub), N; 1994 v Sm (sub), D; 1995 v P, A, Ei (2), La (2); 1996 v N, A (12)
Weaver, N. J. (Manchester C), 2000 v L, Pol, Arg, I, T, Slo; 2001 v I, Fi, Alb; 2002 v Slv (sub) (10)
Webb, N. (Portsmouth), 1985 v Ei; (with Nottingham F), 1986 v D (2) (3)
Welsh, J. J. (Liverpool), 2004 v Ho; 2005 v Ho (sub), G (sub), Az; 2006 v W (sub), G; (with Hull C), N (sub) (7)
Whelan, P. J. (Ipswich T), 1993 v Sp, T (sub), P (3)
Whelan, N. (Leeds U), 1995 v A (sub), Ei (2)
Whittingham, P. (Aston Villa), 2004 v Ho (sub); 2005 v Uk (sub), W (sub), Az, Sp, Ho, Az; 2006 v D (sub), W, G, Pol, F (1+sub), N (14)
Wilson, M. A. (Manchester U), 2001 v Sp, Fi (sub), Alb, M (sub); (with Middlesbrough), 2002 v Ho (sub), Alb (sub) (6)
White, D. (Manchester C), 1988 v S (2), F, USSR; 1989 v Se; 1990 v Pol (6)
Whyte, C. (Arsenal), 1982 v S (1+1 sub); 1983 v D, Gr (4)
Wicks, S. (QPR), 1982 v S (1)
Wilkins, R. C. (Chelsea), 1977 v W (1)
Wilkinson, P. (Grimsby T), 1985 v Ei, R (sub); (with Everton), 1986 v R (sub), I (4)
Williams, D. (Sunderland), 1998 v Sw (sub); 1999 v F (2)
Williams, P. (Charlton Ath), 1989 v Bul, Sen, Ei, US (sub) (4)
Williams, P. D. (Derby Co), 1991 v Sen, M, USSR; 1992 v G, T, Pol (6)
Williams, S. C. (Southampton), 1977 v S, Fi, N; 1978 v N, I (1 + 1 sub), Y (2); 1979 v D, Bul, Se (sub); 1980 v D, EG (2) (14)
Winterburn, N. (Wimbledon), 1986 v I (1)
Wise, D. (Wimbledon), 1988 v Sw (1)
Woodcook, A. S. (Nottingham F), 1978 v Fi, I (2)
Woodgate, J. S. (Leeds U), 2000 v Arg (1)
Woodhouse, C. (Sheffield U), 1999 v H, Se, Bul; 2000 v Pol (sub) (4)
Woods, C. C. E. (Nottingham F), 1979 v W (sub), Se; (with QPR), 1980 v Bul, EG; 1981 v Sw; (with Norwich C), 1984 v D (6)
Wright, A. G. (Blackburn), 1993 v Sp, N (2)
Wright, M. (Southampton), 1983 v Gr, H; 1984 v D, H (4)
Wright, R. I. (Ipswich T), 1997 v Ge, Pol; 1998 v Mol, I, Gr (2), S.Af, Arg; 1999 v Se, Bul, L, Pol, H, Se; 2000 v Y (15)
Wright, S. J. (Liverpool), 2001 v Ge (sub), G, M (sub); 2002 v Ho (sub), G, Alb, Ho, Slv, I, P (10)
Wright, W. (Everton), 1979 v D, W, Bul; 1980 v D, S (2) (6)
Wright-Phillips, S. C. (Manchester C), 2002 v I; 2003 v Y (sub), Mac (sub), I; 2004 v Mac (sub), T (6)

Yates, D. (Notts Co), 1989 v D (sub), Bul, Sen, Ei, US (5)
Young, L. P. (Tottenham H), 1999 v H; 2000 v D (sub), Arg (sub), T, Slo; (with Charlton Ath), 2002 v Ho, Gr, Ho, P (sub), Sw, I, P (12)

Zamora, R. L. (Brighton & HA), 2002 v P (sub), I (sub), P (sub); 2003 v I, Ser, Slo (sub) (6)

SCOTLAND

Adam, C. (Rangers), 2006 v Ic, Ni, T (3)
Aitken, R. (Celtic), 1977 v Cz, W, Sw; 1978 v Cz, W; 1979 v P, N (2); 1980 v Bel, E; 1984 v EG, Y (2); 1985 v WG, Ic, Sp (16)
Albiston, A. (Manchester U), 1977 v Cz, W, Sw; 1978 v Sw, Cz (5)
Alexander, N. (Stenhousemuir), 1997 v P; 1998 v Bl, Ei, I; (with Livingston), 1999 v Li, Es, Bel (2), CzR, G (10)
Anderson, I. (Dundee), 1997 v Co (sub), US, CzR, P; 1998 v Bl, La, Fi, D (sub), Ei (sub), Ni; 1999 v G (sub), Ei, Ni, CzR; (with Toulouse), 2000 v Bos (15)
Anderson, R. (Aberdeen), 1997 v Es, A, Se; 1998 v La (sub), Fi, Ei, I; 1999 v Es, Bel, G, Ei, Ni, CzR; 2000 v Bos, Es (15)
Anthony, M. (Celtic), 1997 v La (sub), Es (sub), Col (3)
Archdeacon, O. (Celtic), 1987 v WG (sub) (1)
Archibald, A. (Partick Th), 1998 v Fi, Ei, Ni, I; 1999 v Li (5)
Archibald, S. (Aberdeen), 1980 v B, E (2), WG; (with Tottenham H), 1981 v D (5)

Bagen, D. (Kilmarnock), 1997 v Es, A (sub), Se (sub), Bl (4)
Bain, K. (Dundee), 1993 v P, I, Ma, P (4)
Baker, M. (St Mirren), 1993 v F, M, E; 1994 v Ma, A; 1995 v Gr, M, F (sub), Sk (sub); 1996 v H (sub) (10)
Baltacha, S. S. (St Mirren), 2000 v Bos, Li (sub), F (sub) (3)
Bannon, E. J. P. (Hearts), 1979 v US; (with Chelsea), P, N (2); (with Dundee U), 1980 v Bel, WG, E (7)
Beattie, C. (Celtic), 2004 v H (sub), R, D (sub), Ei; 2006 v A (5)
Beattie, J. (St Mirren), 1992 v D, US, P, Y (4)
Beaumont, D. (Dundee U), 1985 v Ic (1)
Bell, D. (Aberdeen), 1981 v D; 1984 v Y (2)
Bernard, P. R. J. (Oldham Ath), 1992 v R (sub), D, Se (sub), US; 1993 v Sw, P, I, Ma, P, F, Bul, M, E; 1994 v I, Ma (15)
Berra, C. (Hearts), 2005 v I; 2006 v A, I, N, Bl, Ic (6)
Bett, J. (Rangers), 1981 v Se, D; 1982 v Se, D, I, E (2) (7)
Black, E. (Aberdeen), 1983 v EG, Sw (2), Bel; 1985 v Ic, Sp (2), Ic (8)
Blair, A. (Coventry C), 1980 v E; 1981 v Se; (with Aston Villa), 1982 v Se, D, I (5)
Bollan, G. (Dundee U), 1992 v D, G (sub), US, P, Y; 1993 v Sw, P, I, P, F, Bul, M, E; 1994 v Sw; 1995 v Gr; (with Rangers) v Ru, Sm (17)
Bonar, P. (Raith R), 1997 v A, La, Es (sub), Se (4)
Booth, S. (Aberdeen), 1991 v R (sub), Bul (sub + 1), Pol, F (sub); 1992 v Sw, R, D, Se, US, P, Y; 1993 v Ma, P (14)
Bowes, M. J. (Dunfermline Ath), 1992 v D (sub) (1)
Bowman, D. (Hearts), 1985 v WG (sub) (1)
Boyack, S. (Rangers), 1997 v Se (1)
Boyd, K. (Kilmarnock), 2003 v Bel (sub); 2004 v R (sub), D, Ei; 2005 v H, N, Mol (sub), I (sub) (8)
Boyd, T. (Motherwell), 1987 v WG, Ei (2), Bel; 1988 v Bel (5)
Brazil, A. (Hibernian), 1978 v W (1)
Brazil, A. (Ipswich T), 1979 v N; 1980 v Bel (2), E (2), WG; 1981 v Se; 1982 v Se (8)
Brebner, G. I. (Manchester U), 1997 v Col, CzR (sub), US (sub), P; 1998 v Bl, La, Fi, D; (with Reading), 1999 v Li, Es, Bel (2), CzR, G, Ei, Ni, CzR; (with Hibernian), 2000 v Bos (18)
Brighton, T. (Rangers), 2005 v Ni, I (sub), Mol (sub), Bl; (with Clyde), 2006 v N (sub), Bl (sub), Ic (sub) (7)
Broadfoot, K. (St Mirren), 2005 v Bl; 2006 v Ni, T (3)
Brough, J. (Hearts), 1981 v D (1)
Brown, A. H. (Hibernian), 2004 v D (1)
Brown, S. (Hibernian), 2005 v H, Sp, Slv, I, Mol; 2006 v A, I, N (8)
Browne, P. (Raith R), 1997 v A (1)
Bryson, C. (Clyde), 2006 v Ic (sub) (1)
Buchan, J. (Aberdeen), 1997 v Se, Col, CzR, P; 1998 v Bl, La, Fi; 1999 v Li, Es, Bel, CzR, G, Ei (13)
Burchill, M. (Celtic), 1998 v Fi, D (sub); 1999 v Li, Es (sub), Bel (2), CzR, Ei, Ni, CzR; 2000 v Bos, Es; 2001 v La, Bel, Pol (15)
Burke, A. (Kilmarnock), 1997 v Es, A, Bl (sub); 1998 v Ei (sub) (4)
Burke, C. (Rangers), 2004 v R (sub), D (sub); 2005 v Ni (sub) (3)
Burley, G. E. (Ipswich T), 1977 v Cz, W, Sw; 1978 v Sw, Cz (5)
Burley, C. (Chelsea), 1992 v D; 1993 v Sw, P, I, P; 1994 v Sw, I (sub) (7)
Burns, H. (Rangers), 1985 v Sp, Ic (sub) (2)
Burns, T. (Celtic), 1977 v Cz, W, E; 1978 v Sw; 1982 v E (5)

Caldwell, G. (Newcastle U), 2000 v F, Ni, W; 2002 v Cro, Bel, La; 2003 v Is (sub), Ic, Gh, Bel, Ei, Ic, Li, A, G; 2004 v N, G, Li, Cro (19)
Caldwell, S. (Newcastle U), 2001 v La, Cro, Bel; 2002 v Cro (4)
Campbell, S. (Dundee), 1989 v N (sub), Y, F (3)

Campbell, S. P. (Leicester C), 1998 v Fi (sub), D, Ei, Ni (sub), I; 1999 v Li, Es, Bel (2), CzR, G, Ei, Ni, CzR (sub); 2000 v Bos (sub) (15)
Canero, P. (Kilmarnock), 2000 v F; 2001 v La (sub), Cro (sub), Bel, Pol; 2002 v La (sub); 2003 v D, Ni, Bel (sub), Ei, ic, Li, A, G; 2004 v Li, Cro (2) (17)
Carey, L. A. (Bristol C), 1998 v D (1)
Casey, J. (Celtic), 1978 v W (1)
Christie, M. (Dundee), 1992 v D, P (sub), Y (3)
Clark, R. (Aberdeen), 1977 v Cz, W, Sw (3)
Clarke, S. (St Mirren), 1984 v Bel, EG, Y; 1985 v WG, Ic, Sp (2), Ic (8)
Clarkson, D. (Motherwell), 2004 v D (sub); 2005 v Sp, Slv, N (sub), Mol, Ni (sub), Mol (sub), Bl (sub); 2006 v A (sub), N, Slv, Ic (sub), T (13)
Cleland, A. (Dundee U), 1990 v F, N (2); 1991 v R, Sw, Bul; 1992 v Sw, R, G, Se (2) (11)
Collins, J. (Hibernian), 1988 v Bel, E; 1989 v N, Y, F; 1990 v Y, F, N (8)
Collins, N. (Sunderland), 2005 v Mol, Bl; 2006 v A (sub), I, N, Bl, Slv (7)
Connolly, P. (Dundee U), 1991 v R (sub), Sw, Bul (3)
Connor, R. (Ayr U), 1981 v Se; 1982 v Se (2)
Cooper, D. (Clydebank), 1977 v Cz, W, Sw, E; (with Rangers), 1978 v Sw, Cz (6)
Cooper, N. (Aberdeen), 1982 v D, E (2); 1983 v Bel, EG, Sw (2); 1984 v Bel, EG, Y; 1985 v Ic, Sp, Ic (13)
Crabbe, S. (Hearts), 1990 v Y (sub), F (2)
Craig, M. (Aberdeen), 1998 v Bl, La (2)
Craig, T. (Newcastle U), 1977 v E (1)
Crainey, S. D. (Celtic), 2000 v F (sub); 2003 v Bel, Ei (sub), A, G; 2004 v N, G (7)
Crainie, D. (Celtic), 1983 v Sw (sub) (1)
Crawford, S. (Raith R), 1994 v A, Eg, P, Bel; 1995 v Fi, Ru,Gr, Ru, Sm, M, F (sub), Sk (sub), Br (sub); 1996 v Gr, Fi (sub), H (1 + sub), Sp (sub), F (sub) (19)
Creaney, G. (Celtic), 1991 v Sw, Bul (2), Pol, F; 1992 v Sw, R, G (2), Se (2) (11)
Cummings, W. (Chelsea), 2000 v F, Ni; 2001 v La, Cro, Bel, Pol; 2002 v Cro, Bel (8)

Dailly, C. (Dundee U), 1991 v R; 1992 v US, R; 1993 v Sw, P, I, Ic, P, F, Bul, M, E; 1994 v Sw, I, Ma, A, Eg, P, Bel; 1995 v Fi, Ru, Gr, Ru, Sm, M, F, Sk, Br; 1996 v Fi, Sm, H (2), Sp, F (34)
Dalglish, P. (Newcastle U), 1999 v Es, Bel, CzR; (with Norwich C), 2000 v Es (sub), Bos, Li (sub) (6)
Dargo, C. (Raith R), 1998 v Fi, Ei, Ni (sub), I; 1999 v Es, Bel (1+sub), CzR (sub), G, Ni (sub) (10)
Davidson, C. (St Johnstone), 1997 v Se, Bl (2)
Davidson, H. N. (Dundee U), 2000 v Es (sub), Li, F (3)
Dawson, A. (Rangers), 1979 v P, N (2); 1980 v B (2), E (2), WG (8)
Deas, P. A. (St Johnstone), 1992 v D (sub); 1993 v Ma (2)
Dempster, J. (Rushden & D), 2004 v H (sub) (1)
Dennis, S. (Raith R), 1992 v Sw (1)
Diamond, A. (Aberdeen), 2004 v H (sub); 2005 v H, Sp, Slv, I; 2006 v A, I, Bl (sub), Slv, Ic (10)
Dickov, P. (Arsenal), 1992 v Y; 1993 v F, M, E (4)
Dodds, D. (Dundee U), 1978 v W (1)
Dods, D. (Hibernian), 1997 v La, Es, Se (2), Bl (5)
Doig, C. R. (Nottingham F), 2000 v Ni, W; 2001 v La, Cro, Pol; 2003 v D, Is, Ni, Ic, Gh, Bel, Ei; 2004 v N (sub) (13)
Donald, G. S. (Hibernian), 1992 v US (sub), P, Y (sub) (3)
Donnelly, S. (Celtic), 1994 v Eg, P, Bel; 1995 v Fi, Gr (sub); 1996 v Gr (sub), Sm, H (2), Sp, F (11)
Dow, A. (Dundee), 1993 v Ma (sub), Ic; (with Chelsea) 1994 v I (3)
Dowie, A. J. (Rangers), 2003 v D, Is; 2004 v N (sub), H, R, D. Ei; (with Partick Th), 2005 v Sp, Slv, N, Mol, Se, Ni, I (14)
Duffy, D. A. (Falkirk), 2005 v Se, Ni; 2006 v A (sub), I, Bl, Slv; (with Hull C), Ni, T (sub) (8)
Duffy, J. (Dundee), 1987 v Ei (1)
Duff, S. (Dundee U), 2003 v Is, Ni (sub), Ic, Gh, Bel, Ei (sub); 2004 v N, G, Cro (9)
Durie, G. S. (Chelsea), 1987 v WG, Ei, Bel; 1988 v Bel (4)
Durrant, I. (Rangers), 1987 v WG, Ei, Bel; 1988 v E (4)
Doyle, J. (Partick Th), 1981 v D, I (sub) (2)

Easton, C. (Dundee U), 1997 v Col, US, CzR, P; 1998 v Bl, Fi, D, Ei, Ni, I; 1999 v Li, Es, Bel (1+sub); 2000 v Li, F; 2001 v La (sub), Cro, Bel; 2002 v Cro, Bel (21)
Elliot, B. (Celtic), 1998 v Ni; 1999 v Li (sub) (2)
Elliot, C. (Hearts), 2006 v Ic (1)
Esson, R. (Aberdeen), 2000 v Li, Ni; 2001 v La, Cro, Bel, Pol; 2002 v Bel (7)

Fagan, S. M. (Motherwell), 2005 v N (1)
Ferguson, B. (Rangers), 1997 v Col (sub), US, CzR, P; 1998 v Bl, La, Fi, D (sub), Ei, Ni, I; 1999 v Bel (12)
Ferguson, D. (Rangers), 1987 v WG, Ei, Bel; 1988 v E; 1990 v Y (5)
Ferguson, D. (Dundee U), 1992 v D, G, Se (2); 1993 v Sw, I, Ma (7)
Ferguson, D. (Manchester U), 1992 v US, P (sub), Y; 1993 v Sw, Ma (5)
Ferguson, I. (Dundee), 1983 v EG (sub), Sw (sub); 1984 v Bel (sub), EG (4)
Ferguson, I. (Clyde), 1987 v WG (sub), Ei; (with St Mirren), Ei, Bel; 1988 v Bel; (with Rangers), E (sub) (6)
Ferguson, R. (Hamilton A), 1977 v E (1)
Findlay, W. (Hibernian), 1991 v R, Pol, Bul (2), Pol (5)
Fitzpatrick, A. (St Mirren), 1977 v W (sub), Sw (sub), E; 1978 v Sw, Cz (5)
Flannigan, C. (Clydebank), 1993 v Ic (sub) (1)
Fleck, R. (Rangers), 1987 v WG (sub), Ei, Bel; (with Norwich C), 1988 v E (2); 1989 v Y (6)
Fletcher, D. B. (Manchester U), 2003 v Ic (sub); 2004 v G (sub) (2)
Foster, R. M. (Aberdeen), 2005 v Mol, Se (sub); 2006 v Ic (sub), Ni (4)
Fotheringham, M. M. (Dundee), 2004 v R, D (sub), Ei (sub) (3)
Fowler, J. (Kilmarnock), 2002 v Cro (sub), Bel, La (3)
Foy, R. A. (Liverpool), 2004 v H, R (sub), D; 2005 v H, N (5)
Fraser, S. T. (Luton T), 2000 v Ni (sub), W; 2001 v La, Cro (4)
Freedman, D. A. (Barnet), 1995 v Ru (sub + 1), Sm, M, F, Sk, Br; (with C Palace), 1996 v Sm (sub) (8)
Fridge, L. (St Mirren), 1989 v F; 1990 v Y (2)
Fullarton, J. (St Mirren), 1993 v F, Bul; 1994 v Ma, A, Eg, P, Bel; 1995 v M, F, Sk, Br; 1996 v Gr, Fi, H (sub + 1), Sp (sub), F (17)
Fulton, M. (St Mirren), 1980 v Bel, WG, E; 1981 v Se, D (sub) (5)
Fulton, S. (Celtic), 1991 v R, Sw, Bul, Pol, F; 1992 v G (2) (7)

Gallacher, K. (Dundee U), 1987 v WG, Ei (2), Bel (sub); 1988 v E (2); 1990 v Y (7)
Gallacher, P. (Dundee U), 1999 v Ei, Ni, CzR; 2000 v Bos, Es, Bos, F (7)
Gallagher, P. (Blackburn R), 2003 v G (sub); 2004 v N (sub), Li (sub), D; 2005 v H, Se, Mol; 2006 v A, I, N, Bl (11)
Galloway, M. (Hearts), 1989 v F; (with Celtic), 1990 v N (2)
Gardiner, J. (Hibernian), 1993 v F (1)
Geddes, R. (Dundee), 1982 v Se, D, E (2); 1988 v E (5)
Gemmill, S. (Nottingham F), 1992 v Sw, R (sub), G (sub), Se (sub) (4)
Germaine, G. (WBA), 1997 v Se (1)
Gilles, R. (St Mirren), 1997 v A (1 + sub), La, Es (2), Se, Bl (7)
Gillespie, G. (Coventry C), 1979 v US; 1980 v E; 1981 v D; 1982 v Se, D, I (2), E (8)
Glass, S. (Aberdeen), 1995 v M, F, Sk, Br; 1996 v Gr, Fi, H, Sp; 1997 v A (2), Es (11)
Glover, L. (Nottingham F), 1988 v Bel (sub); 1989 v N; 1990 v Y (3)
Goram, A. (Oldham Ath), 1987 v Ei (1)
Gordon, C. (Hearts), 2003 v Is (sub), Gh; 2004 v N (sub), Cro (2) (5)
Gough, C. R. (Dundee U), 1983 v EG, Sw, Bel; 1984 v Y (2) (5)
Graham, D. (Rangers), 1998 v Bl (sub), La (sub), Fi (sub), D, Ei (sub), Ni, I; 1999 v Li (8)
Grant, P. (Celtic), 1985 v WG, Ic, Sp; 1987 v WG, Ei (2), Bel; 1988 v Bel, E (2) (10)
Gray S. (Celtic), 1995 v F, Sk, Br; 1996 v Gr, H, Sp, F (7)
Gray, S. (Aberdeen), 1987 v WG (1)
Gunn, B. (Aberdeen), 1984 v EG, Y (2); 1985 v WG, Ic, Sp (2), Ic; 1990 v F (9)

Hagen, D. (Rangers), 1992 v D (sub), US (sub), P, Y; 1993 v Sw (sub), P, Ic, P (8)
Hammell, S. (Motherwell), 2001 v Pol (sub); 2002 v La; 2003 v Is, Ni, Gh, Bel (sub), Ei; 2004 v N, Li, Cro (2) (11)
Hamilton, B. (St Mirren), 1989 v Y, F (sub); 1990 v F, N (4)
Hamilton, J. (Dundee) 1995 v Sm (sub), Br; 1996 v Fi (sub), Sm, H (sub), Sp (sub), F; 1997 v A, La, Es, Se; (with Hearts), Es, A, Se (14)
Handyside, P. (Grimsby T), 1993 v Ic (sub), Bul, M, E; 1995 v Ru; 1996 v Fi, Sm (7)
Hannah, D. (Dundee U), 1993 v F (sub), Bul, M; 1994 v A, Eg, P, Bel; 1995 v Fi, Ru (sub), Gr, Ru, M, F, Sk, Br; 1996 v Gr (16)

Harper, K. (Hibernian), 1995 v Ru (sub); 1996 v Fi; 1997 v A (2), La, Es, Se (7)
Hartford, R. A. (Manchester C), 1977 v Sw (1)
Hartley, P. (Millwall), 1997 v A (sub) (1)
Hegarty, P. (Dundee U), 1987 v WG, Bel; 1988 v E (2); 1990 v F, N (6)
Hendry, J. (Tottenham H), 1992 v D (sub) (1)
Hetherston, B. (St Mirren), 1997 v Es (sub) (1)
Hewitt, J. (Aberdeen), 1982 v I; 1983 v EG, Sw (2); 1984 v Bel, Y (sub) (6)
Hogg, G. (Manchester U), 1984 v Y; 1985 v WG, Ic, Sp (4)
Hood, G. (Ayr U), 1993 v F, E (sub); 1994 v A (3)
Horn, R. (Hearts), 1997 v US, CzR, P; 1998 v Bl, La, D (sub) (6)
Howie, S. (Cowdenbeath), 1993 v Ma, Ic, P; 1994 v Sw, I (5)
Hughes, R. D. (Bournemouth), 1999 v CzR, Ei, Ni, CzR; 2000 v Bos, Es; 2001 v La, Cro, Bel (9)
Hughes, S. (Rangers), 2002 v La; 2003 v D, Ic, Gh, Be, Ei (sub), Ic (sub), A; 2004 v N (sub), Li (sub), Cro (sub+sub) (12)
Hunter, G. (Hibernian), 1987 v Ei (sub); 1988 v Bel, E (3)
Hunter, P. (East Fife), 1989 v N (sub), F (sub); 1990 v F (sub) (3)
Hutton, A. (Rangers), 2004 v R, D; 2005 v H, Slv, Se, Ni (sub) (6)

Irvine, G. (Celtic), 2006 v Ic, T (2)

James, K. F. (Falkirk), 1997 v Bl (1)
Jardine, I. (Kilmarnock), 1979 v US (1)
Jess, E. (Aberdeen), 1990 v F (sub), N (sub); 1991 v R, Sw, Bul (2), Pol, F; 1992 v Sw, R, G (2), Se (1 + 1 sub) (14)
Johnson, G. I. (Dundee U), 1992 v US, P, Y; 1993 v Sw, P, Ma (6)
Johnston, A. (Hearts), 1994 v Bel; 1995 v Ru, 1996 v Sp (3)
Johnston, F. (Falkirk), 1993 v Ic (1)
Johnston, M. (Partick Th), 1984 v EG (sub); (with Watford), Y (2) (3)
Jordan, A. J. (Bristol C), 2000 v Bos (sub), Li, F (3)
Jupp, D. A. (Fulham), 1995 v Fi, Ru (2), Sm, M, F, Sk, Br; 1997 v Se (9)

Kirkwood, D. (Hearts), 1990 v Y (1)
Kennedy, J. (Celtic), 2003 v Is (sub), Ni, Ic, Gh, Bel, Ei, Ic, Li, A, G; 2004 v N (sub), Li, Cro (2), H (15)
Kerr, B. (Newcastle U), 2003 v D, Is, Ni, Ic, Gh, Bel, Ei, Ic, Li, A, G; 2004 v Li, Cro (2) (14)
Kerr, M. (Kilmarnock), 2001 v Pol (sub) (1)
Kerr, S. (Celtic), 1993 v Bul, M, E; 1994 v Ma, A, Eg, P, Bel; 1995 v Fi, Gr (10)
Kinniburgh, W. D. (Motherwell), 2004 v R (sub); 2006 v A (sub), Ic (3)
Kyle, K. (Sunderland), 2001 v La (sub), Cro (sub), Pol (sub); 2003 v Ic, Ei, Ic, Li, G; 2004 v N. G, Cro (2) (12)

Lambert, P. (St Mirren), 1991 v R, Sw, Bul (2), Pol, F; 1992 v Sw, R, G (2), Se (11)
Langfield, J. (Dundee), 2000 v W; 2002 v Cro (2)
Lappin, S. (St Mirren), 2004 v H, R, D, Ei; 2005 v H (sub), Slv, N, Mol, Se; 2006 v Slv (sub) (10)
Lauchlan, J. (Kilmarnock), 1998 v Ei, Ni, I; 1999 v CzR, G, Ni, CzR; 2000 v Bos, Es, Bos, Li (11)
Lavety, B. (St Mirren), 1993 v Ic, Bul (sub), M (sub), E; 1994 v Ma, A (sub), Eg (sub), Bel (sub); 1995 v Fi (sub) (9)
Lavin, G. (Watford), 1993 v F, Bul, M; 1994 v Ma, Eg, P, Bel (7)
Lawson, P. (Celtic), 2004 v H, R, Ei; 2006 v A (sub), I (sub), N, Bl, Slv, Ic, Ni (10)
Leighton, J. (Aberdeen), 1982 v I (1)
Levein, C. (Hearts), 1985 v Sp, Ic (2)
Leven, P. (Kilmarnock), 2005 v Se (sub), Ni (2)
Liddell, A. M. (Barnsley), 1994 v Ma (sub); 1995 v Sm (sub), M (sub), F, Sk; 1996 v Gr, Fi, Sm, H (2), Sp, F (sub) (12)
Lindsey, J. (Motherwell), 1979 v US (1)
Locke, G. (Hearts), 1994 v Ma, A, Eg, P; 1995 v Fi; 1996 v Fi, H; 1997 v Es, A, Bl (10)
Love, G. (Hibernian), 1995 v Ru (1)
Lynch, S. (Celtic), 2003 v Is (sub), Ni (sub), Ic (sub), Gh (sub), Bel; (with Preston NE), Ei (sub), Li (sub), A (sub), G; 2004 v N, G, Li, Cro (sub) (13)

McAllister, G. (Leicester C), 1990 v N (1)
McAlpine, H. (Dundee U), 1983 v EG, Sw (2), Bel; 1984 v Bel (5)
McAnespie, K. (St Johnstone), 1998 v Fi (sub); 1999 v G (sub); 2000 v Ni, W (4)
McAuley, S. (St Johnstone), 1993 v P (sub) (1)
McAvennie, F. (St Mirren), 1982 v I, E; 1985 v Is, Ei, R (5)
McBride, J. (Everton), 1981 v D (1)
McBride, J. P. (Celtic), 1998 v Ni (sub), I (sub) (2)
McCall, S. (Bradford C), 1988 v E; (with Everton), 1990 v F (2)
McCann, N. (Dundee), 1994 v A, Eg, P, Bel; 1995 v Fi, Gr (sub), Sm; 1996 v Fi, Sm (9)
McClair, B. (Celtic), 1984 v Bel (sub), EG, Y (1 + 1 sub); 1985 v WG, Ic, Sp, Ic (8)
McCluskey, G. (Celtic), 1979 v US, P; 1980 v Bel (2); 1982 v D, I (6)
McCluskey, S. (St Johnstone), 1997 v Es (2), A, Se, Col, US, CzR; 1998 v Bl, La, D, Ei (sub), Ni, I; 1999 v Li (14)
McCoist, A. (Rangers), 1984 v Bel (1)
McConnell, I. (Clyde), 1997 v A (sub) (1)
McCormack, R. (Rangers), 2006 v Slv, Ni (sub), T (sub) (3)
McCracken, D. (Dundee U), 2002 v La; 2004 v N, G, Li, Cro (5)
McCulloch, A. (Kilmarnock); 1981 v Se (1)
McCulloch, I. (Notts Co), 1982 v E (2)
McCulloch, L. (Motherwell), 1997 v La (sub), Es (1 + sub), Se (sub + 1), A (sub), Col (sub); 1998 v Bl (sub), Fi (sub), D, Ei, Ni; 1999 v CzR, G (14)
McCunnie, J. (Dundee U), 2001 v Pol; 2002 v Cro; 2003 v D. Is, Ni; (with Ross Co), 2004 v H, R, Ei; 2005 v H (sub), Sp, Slv, N (sub), Mol, Se, Ni, I, Mol, Bl; (with Dunfermline Ath), 2006 v Bl, Slv (20)
MacDonald, J. (Rangers), 1980 v WG (sub); 1981 v Se; 1982 v Se (sub), L, I (2), E (2 sub) (8)
McDonald, C. (Falkirk), 1995 v Fi (sub), Ru, M (sub), F (sub), Br (sub) (5)
McEwan, C. (Clyde), 1997 v Col, US (sub), CzR (sub), P; (with Raith R), 1998 v Bl, La, Fi, D, Ei, Ni, I; 1999 v Li, Es (sub), Bel (2), CzR, G (sub) (17)
McEwan, D. (Livingston), 2003 v Ni (sub), Gh (sub) (2)
McFadden, J. (Motherwell), 2003 v D (sub), Is, Ni, Gh, Ei (sub), Ic, Li (7)
McFarlane, D. (Hamilton A), 1997 v Col, US (sub), P (sub) (3)
McGarry, S. (St Mirren), 1997 v US, CzR, P (sub) (3)
McGarvey, F. (St Mirren), 1977 v E; 1978 v Cz; (with Celtic), 1982 v D (3)
McGarvey, S. (Manchester U), 1982 v E (sub); 1983 v Bel, Sw; 1984 v Bel (4)
McGhee, M. (Aberdeen), 1981 v D (1)
McGinnis, G. (Dundee U), 1985 v Sp (1)
McGregor, A. (Rangers), 2003 v D (sub), Is, Bel (sub), Ei (sub), A (sub); 2004 v N (6)
McGrillen, P. (Motherwell), 1994 v Sw (sub), I (2)
McGuire, D. (Aberdeen), 2002 v Bel, La (2)
McInally, J. (Dundee U), 1989 v F (1)
McKenzie, R. (Hearts), 1997 v Es, Bl (2)
McKimmie, S. (Aberdeen), 1985 v WG, Ic (2) (3)
McKinlay, T. (Dundee), 1984 v EG (sub); 1985 v WG, Ic, Sp (2), Ic (6)
McKinlay, W. (Dundee U), 1989 v N, Y (sub), F; 1990 v Y, F, N (6)
McKinnon, R. (Dundee U), 1991 v R, Pol (sub); 1992 v G (2), Se (2) (6)
McLaren, A, (Hearts), 1989 v F; 1990 v Y, N; 1991 v Sw, Bul, Pol, F; 1992 v R, G, Se (2) (11)
McLaren, A. (Dundee U), 1993 v I, Ma (sub); 1994 v Sw, I (sub) (4)
McLaughlin, B. (Celtic), 1995 v Ru, Sm, M, Sk (sub), Br (sub); 1996 v Gr (sub), Sm (sub), H (8)
McLaughlin, J. (Morton), 1981 v D; 1982 v Se, D, I, E (2); 1983 v EG, Sw (2), Bel (10)
McLean, S. (Rangers), 2003 v D (sub), Ni (sub), Gh (sub), Bel (sub) (4)
McLeish, A. (Aberdeen), 1978 v W; 1979 v US; 1980 v Bel, E (2); 1987 v Ei (6)
MacLeod, A. (Hibernian), 1979 v P, N (2) (3)
McLeod, J. (Dundee U), 1989 v N; 1990 v F (2)
MacLeod, M. (Dumbarton), 1979 v US; (with Celtic), P (sub), N (2); 1980 v Bel (5)
McManus, T. (Hibernian), 2001 v Bel (sub), Pol (sub); 2002 v Cro, Bel, La; 2003 v D (sub), Ni (sub), Ic, Gh, A, G (sub); 2004 v N (sub), Li (sub), Cro (14)
McMillan, S. (Motherwell), 1997 v A (sub + sub), Se, Bl (4)
McNab, N. (Tottenham H), 1978 v W (1)
McNally, M. (Celtic), 1991 v Bul; 1993 v Ic (2)
McNamara, J. (Dunfermline Ath), 1994 v A, Bel; 1995 v Gr, Ru, Sm; 1996 v Gr, Fi; (with Celtic), Sm, H (2), Sp, F (12)
McNaughton, K. (Aberdeen), 2002 v La (sub) (1)
McNichol, J. (Brentford), 1979 v P, N (2); 1980 v Bel (2), WG, E (7)
McNiven, D. (Leeds U), 1977 v Cz, W (sub), Sw (sub) (3)
McNiven, S. A. (Oldham Ath), 1996 v Sm (sub) (1)
McParland, A. (Celtic), 2003 v Gh (sub) (1)

McPhee, S. (Port Vale), 2002 v La (sub) (1)
McPherson, D. (Rangers), 1984 v Bel; 1985 v Sp; (with Hearts), 1989 v N, Y (4)
McQuilken, J. (Celtic), 1993 v Bul, E (2)
McStay, P. (Celtic), 1983 v EG, Sw (2); 1984 v Y (2) (5)
McWhirter, N. (St Mirren), 1991 v Bul (sub) (1)
Main, A. (Dundee U), 1988 v E; 1989 v Y; 1990 v N (3)
Malcolm, R. (Rangers), 2001 v Pol (1)
Maloney, S. (Celtic), 2002 v Cro (sub), Bel (sub), La; 2003 v D, Is, Ni, Bel, Ei, Ic (sub), Li (sub), A; 2004 v G (sub), Li, Cro (1+sub), H; 2005 v Ni, I, Mol, Bl; 2006 v A (21)
Malpas, M. (Dundee U), 1983 v Bel, Sw (1+1 sub); 1984 v Bel, EG, Y (2); 1985 v Sp (8)
Marshall, D. J. (Celtic), 2004 v H (sub), D; 2005 v I; 2006 v A, I, Ic, Ni, T (8)
Marshall, S. R. (Arsenal), 1995 v Ru, Gr; 1996 v H, Sp, F (5)
Mason, G. R. (Manchester C), 1999 v Li (sub); (with Dunfermline Ath), 2002 v Bel (2)
Mathieson, D. (Queen of the South), 1997 v Col; 1998 v La; 1999 v G (sub) (3)
May, E. (Hibernian), 1989 v Y (sub), F (2)
Meldrum, C. (Kilmarnock), 1996 v F (sub); 1997 v A (2), La, Es, Se (6)
Melrose, J. (Partick Th), 1977 v Sw; 1979 v US, P, N (2); 1980 v Bel (sub), WG, E (8)
Miller, C. (Rangers), 1995 v Gr, Ru; 1996 v Gr, Sp, F; 1997 v A, La, Es (8)
Miller, J. (Aberdeen), 1987 v Ei (sub); 1988 v Bel; (with Celtic), E; 1989 v N, Y; 1990 v F, N (7)
Miller, K. (Hibernian), 2000 v F, Ni, W; (with Rangers), 2001 v Cro, Bel; 2002 v Cro, Bel (7)
Miller, W. (Aberdeen), 1978 v Sw, Cz (2)
Miller, W. (Hibernian), 1991 v R, Sw, Bul, Pol, F; 1992 v R, G (sub) (7)
Milne, K. (Hearts), 2000 v F (1)
Milne, R. (Dundee U), 1982 v Se (sub); 1984 v Bel, EG (3)
Money, I. C. (St Mirren), 1987 v Ei; 1988 v Bel; 1989 v N (3)
Montgomery, N. A. (Sheffield U), 2003 v A (sub); 2004 v Cro (sub) (2)
Morrison, S. A. (Aberdeen), 2004 v H (sub), D (sub), Ei; 2005 v H, Sp, Mol, Se, Ni, I, Mol, Bl; (with Dunfermline Ath), 2006 v A (12)
Muir, L. (Hibernian), 1977 v Cz (sub) (1)
Mulgrew, C. (Celtic), 2006 v Slv (sub), Ni (sub), T (3)
Murray, H. (St Mirren), 2000 v F (sub), Ni (sub), W (sub) (3)
Murray, I. (Hibernian), 2001 v Bel (sub), Pol; 2002 v Cro, Bel, La; 2003 v D, Ic, Gh, Bel, Ic, Li, G; 2004 v G, Cro (2) (15)
Murray, N. (Rangers), 1993 v P (sub), Ma, Ic, P; 1994 v Sw, I; 1995 v Fi, Ru, Gr, Sm; 1996 v Gr (sub), Fi, Sm, H (2), F (16)
Murray, R. (Bournemouth), 1993 v Ic (sub) (1)
Murray, S. (Kilmarnock), 2004 v D (sub), Ei (sub) (2)

Narey, D. (Dundee U), 1977 v Cz, Sw; 1978 v Sw, Cz (4)
Naismith, S. (Kilmarnock), 2006 v Slv (sub), Ic, Ni, T (4)
Naysmith, G. (Hearts), 1997 v La, Es (1 + sub), Se, A, Col, US, CzR, P; 1998 v La, D; 1999 v Es, Bel (2), CzR, G, Ei, CzR; 2000 v Bos, Es, Bos, Li (22)
Neilson, R. (Hearts), 2000 v Ni (1)
Nevin, P. (Chelsea), 1985 v WG, Ic, Sp (2), Ic (5)
Nicholas, C. (Celtic), 1981 v Se; 1982 v Se; 1983 v EG, Sw, Bel; (with Arsenal), 1984 v Y (6)
Nicholson, B. (Rangers), 1999 v G, Ni, CzR (sub); 2000 v Bos (sub), Es, Bos, Li (7)
Nicol, S. (Ayr U), 1981 v Se; 1982 v Se, D; (with Liverpool), I (2), E (2); 1983 v EG, Sw (2), Bel; 1984 v Bel, EG, Y (14)
Nisbet, S. (Rangers), 1989 v N, Y, F; 1990 v Y, F (5)
Noble, D. J. (West Ham U), 2003 v A (sub); 2004 v N (sub) (2)
Notman, A. M. (Manchester U), 1999 v Li (sub), Es, Bel (sub+sub); 2000 v Li, F (sub), Ni, W; 2001 v La, Cro (10)

O'Brien, B. (Blackburn R), 1999 v Ei (sub), Ni (sub), CzR (sub); 2000 v Bos (sub); (with Livingston), 2003 v Is (sub), Gh (sub) (6)
O'Connor, G. (Hibernian), 2003 v D; 2004 v Cro, H, R; 2005 v Sp, Slv, N, Mol (8)
O'Donnell, P. (Motherwell), 1992 v Sw (sub), R, D, G (2), Se (1 + 1 sub); 1993 v P (8)
O'Neil, B. (Celtic), 1992 v D, G, Se (2); 1993 v Sw, P, I (7)
O'Neil, J. (Dundee U), 1991 v Bul (sub) (1)
O'Neill, M. (Clyde), 1995 v Ru (sub), F, Sk, Br; 1997 v Se (sub), Bl (sub) (6)
Orr, N. (Morton), 1978 v W (sub); 1979 v US, P, N (2); 1980 v Bel, E (7)

Parker, K. (St Johnstone), 2001 v Pol (sub) (1)
Parlane, D. (Rangers), 1977 v W (1)
Paterson, C. (Hibernian), 1981 v Se; 1982 v I (2)
Paterson, J. (Dundee U), 1997 v Col, US, CzR; 1999 v Bel (sub+sub); 2000 v Es, Bos, Li; 2002 v Cro (sub) (9)
Payne, G. (Dundee U), 1978 v Sw, Cz, W (3)
Peacock, L. A. (Carlisle U), 1997 v Bl (1)
Pearson, S. (Motherwell), 2003 v Is, Ni, Bel (sub), Ei, A, G; 2004 v N, G (8)
Pressley, S. (Rangers), 1993 v Ic, F, Bul, M, E; 1994 v Sw, I, M, A, Eg, P, Bel; 1995 v Fi; (with Coventry C), Ru (2), Sm, M, F, Sk, Br; (with Dundee U), 1996 v Gr, Sm, H (2), Sp, F (26)
Provan, D. (Kilmarnock), 1977 v Cz (sub) (1)
Prunty, B. (Aberdeen), 2004 v H, R (sub), Ei; 2005 v H (sub), Sp (sub), Slv (sub) (6)

Quinn, P. C. (Motherwell), 2004 v D; 2006 v Ni, T (3)
Quinn, R. (Celtic), 2006 v Ic (sub), T (2)

Rae, A. (Millwall), 1991 v Bul (sub + 1), F (sub); 1992 v Sw, R, G (sub), Se (2) (8)
Rae, G. (Dundee), 1999 v Ei (sub), Ni, CzR; 2000 v Bos, Es, Bos (6)
Redford, I. (Rangers), 1981 v Se (sub); 1982 v Se, D, I (2), E (6)
Reid, B. (Rangers), 1991 v F; 1992 v D, US, P (4)
Reid, C. (Hibernian), 1993 v Sw, P, I (3)
Reid, M. (Celtic), 1982 v E; 1984 v Y (2)
Reid, R. (St Mirren), 1977 v W, Sw, E (3)
Reilly, A. (Wycombe W), 2004 v H (sub) (1)
Renicks, S. (Hamilton A), 1997 v Bl (1)
Rice, B. (Hibernian), 1985 v WG (1)
Richardson, L. (St Mirren), 1980 v WG, E (sub) (2)
Riordan, D. G. (Hibernian), 2004 v R; 2005 v H (sub), Sp (sub), Slv (sub), I (5)
Ritchie, A. (Morton), 1980 v Bel (1)
Ritchie, P. R. (Hearts), 1996 v H; 1997 v A (2), La, Es (2), Se (7)
Robertson, A. (Rangers) 1991 v F (1)
Robertson, C. (Rangers), 1977 v E (sub) (1)
Robertson, D. (Aberdeen), 1987 v Ei (sub); 1988 v E (2); 1989 v N, Y; 1990 v Y, N (7)
Robertson, G. A. (Nottingham F), 2004 v Ei; 2005 v H, Sp, Slv, N, Mol, Se, Ni, Mol, Bl; (with Rotherham U), 2006 v A, I, N, Bl, Slv (15)
Robertson, H. (Aberdeen), 1994 v Eg; 1995 v Fi (2)
Robertson, J. (Hearts), 1985 v WG, Ic (sub) (2)
Robertson, L. (Rangers), 1993 v F, M (sub), E (sub) (3)
Robertson, S. (St Johnstone), 1998 v Fi, Ni (2)
Roddie, A. (Aberdeen), 1992 v US, P; 1993 v Sw (sub), P, Ic (5)
Ross, T. W. (Arsenal), 1977 v W (1)
Rowson, D. (Aberdeen), 1997 v La, Es, Se (2), Bl (5)
Russell, R. (Rangers), 1978 v W; 1980 v Bel; 1984 v Y (3)

Salton, D. B. (Luton T), 1992 v D, US, P, Y; 1993 v Sw, I (6)
Samson, C. I. (Kilmarnock), 2004 v R, Ei; 2005 v H, Ni, Mol, Bl (6)
Scott, M. (Livingston), 2006 v Ic (1)
Scott, P. (St Johnstone), 1994 v A (sub), Eg (sub), P, Bel (4)
Scrimgour, D. (St Mirren), 1997 v US, CzR; 1998 v D (3)
Seaton, A. (Falkirk), 1998 v Bl (sub) (1)
Severin, S. D. (Hearts), 2000 v Es, Bos, Li (sub), F, Ni, W; 2001 v La, Bel; 2002 v Cro, Bel (10)
Shannon, R. (Dundee), 1987 v WG, Ei (2), Bel; 1988 v Bel, E (2) (7)
Sharp, G. (Everton), 1982 v E (1)
Sharp, R. (Dunfermline Ath), 1990 v N (sub); 1991 v R, Sw, Bul (4)
Sheerin, P. (Southampton), 1996 v Sm (1)
Shields, G. (Rangers), 1997 v A, La (2)
Simmons, S. (Hearts), 2003 v Gh (sub) (1)
Simpson, N. (Aberdeen), 1982 v I (2), E; 1983 v EG, Sw (2), Bel; 1984 v Bel, EG, Y; 1985 v Sp (11)
Sinclair, G. (Dumbarton), 1977 v E (1)
Skilling, M. (Kilmarnock), 1993 v Ic (sub); 1994 v I (2)
Smith, B. M. (Celtic), 1992 v G (2), US, P, Y (5)
Smith, D. L. (Motherwell), 2006 v Slv (1)
Smith, G. (Rangers), 1978 v W (1)
Smith, G. (Rangers), 2004 v H, D (sub), Ei (sub); 2005 v H (sub), Sp, Slv, N, Mol (8)
Smith, H. G. (Hearts), 1987 v WG, Bel (2)
Sneddon, A. (Celtic), 1979 v US (1)
Soutar, D. (Dundee), 2003 v D, Ni, Ic, Bel, Ei, Ic, Li, A, G; 2004 v G, Li (11)
Speedie, D. (Chelsea), 1985 v Sp (1)
Spencer, J. (Rangers), 1991 v Sw (sub), F; 1992 v Sw (3)
Stanton, P. (Hibernian), 1977 v Cz (1)

Stark, W. (Aberdeen), 1985 v Ic (1)
Stephen, R. (Dundee), 1983 v Bel (sub) (1)
Stevens, G. (Motherwell), 1977 v E (1)
Stewart, C. (Kilmarnock), 2002 v La (1)
Stewart, J. (Kilmarnock), 1978 v Sw, Cz; (with Middlesbrough), 1979 v P (3)
Stewart, M. J. (Manchester U), 2000 v Ni; 2001 v La, Cro, Bel, Pol; 2002 v La; 2003 v D, Is, Ni, Ei (sub), Ic, Li, A; 2004 v N, G, Li, Cro (17)
Stewart, R. (Dundee U), 1979 v P, N (2); (with West Ham U), 1980 v Bel (2), E (2), WG; 1981 v D; 1982 v I (2), E (12)
Stillie, D. (Aberdeen), 1995 v Ru (2), Sm, M, F, Sk, Br; 1996 v Gr, Fi, Sm, H (2), Sp, F (14)
Strachan, G. D. (Aberdeen), 1980 v Bel (1)
Strachan, G. D. (Coventry C), 1998 v D, Ei; 1999 v Li, Es, Bel (2); 2000 v Li (7)
Sturrock, P. (Dundee U), 1977 v Cz, W, Sw, E; 1978 v Sw, Cz; 1982 v Se, I, E (9)
Sweeney, P. H. (Millwall), 2004 v H (sub), D, Ei (sub); 2005 v H, Sp, Slv, Se (sub), Mol (sub) (8)
Sweeney, S. (Clydebank), 1991 v R, Sw (sub), Bul (2), Pol; 1992 v Sw, R (7)

Tarrant, N. K. (Aston Villa), 1999 v Ni (sub); 2000 v Es (sub), Bos (sub), Li, Ni (sub) (5)
Teale, G. (Clydebank), 1997 v La (sub), Es, Bl; (with Ayr U), 1999 v CzR (sub), G (sub), Ei (sub) (6)
Telfer, P. (Luton T), 1993 v Ma, P; 1994 v Sw (3)
Thomas, K. (Hearts), 1993 v F (sub), Bul, M, E; 1994 v Sw, Ma; 1995 v Gr; 1997 v A (8)
Thompson, S. (Dundee U), 1997 v US, CzR, P; 1998 v Bl, La; 1999 v G (sub), Ei, Ni, CzR; 2000 v Bos, Es, Bos (12)
Thomson, K. (Hibernian), 2005 v Bl (sub); 2006 v A, I, N (4)
Thomson, W. (Partick Th), 1977 v E (sub); 1978 v W; (with St Mirren), 1979 v US, N (2); 1980 v Bel (2), E (2), WG (10)
Tolmie, J. (Morton), 1980 v Bel (sub) (1)
Tortolano, J. (Hibernian), 1987 v WG, Ei (2)
Turner, I. (Everton), 2005 v Sp (sub), Se; 2006 v I (sub), N, Bl, Ic (sub) (6)
Tweed, S. (Hibernian), 1993 v Ic; 1994 v Sw, I (3)

Wales, G. (Hearts), 2000 v F (1)
Walker, A. (Celtic), 1988 v Bel (1)
Wallace, I. (Coventry C), 1978 v Sw (1)
Wallace, R. (Celtic), 2004 v H (sub); 2005 v N (2)
Walsh, C. (Nottingham F), 1984 v EG, Sw (2), Bel; 1984 v EG (5)
Wark, J. (Ipswich T), 1977 v Cz, W, Sw; 1978 v W; 1979 v P; 1980 v E (2), WG (8)
Watson, A. (Aberdeen), 1981 v Se, D; 1982 v D, I (sub) (4)
Watson, K. (Rangers), 1977 v E; 1978 v Sw (sub) (2)
Watt, M. (Aberdeen), 1991 v R, Sw, Bul (2), Pol, F; 1992 v Sw, R, G (2), Se (2) (12)
Watt. S. M. (Chelsea), 2005 v Mol, Bl; 2006 v N, Bl, Slv (5)
Webster, A. (Hearts), 2003 v Ic, Li (2)
Whiteford, A. (St Johnstone), 1997 v US (1)
Whittaker, S. G. (Hibernian), 2005 v H (sub), Sp, Slv (sub), N, Mol, Se, Ni, I, Mol, Bl; 2006 v A, I, Bl, Slv, Ni, T (16)
Whyte, D. (Celtic), 1987 v Ei (2), Bel; 1988 v E (2); 1989 v N, Y; 1990 v Y, N (9)
Wilkie, L. (Dundee), 2000 v Bos, F, Ni, W; 2001 v La, Cro (6)
Will, J. A. (Arsenal), 1992 v D (sub), Y; 1993 v Ic (sub) (3)
Williams, G. (Nottingham F), 2002 v Bel (sub); 2003 v Ic, Ei, Ic, Li; 2004 v N, G, Li, Cro (9)
Wilson, M. (Dundee U), 2004 v H, R, D, Ei; 2005 v H, N, Mol, Se, Ni, I, Mol, Bl; 2006 v I, N, Bl, Ni, T (17)
Wilson, S. (Rangers), 1999 v Es, Bel (2), G, Ei, CzR; 2000 v Bos (7)
Wilson, T. (St Mirren), 1983 v Sw (sub) (1)
Wilson, T. (Nottingham F), 1988 v E; 1989 v N, Y; 1990 v F (4)
Winnie, D. (St Mirren), 1988 v Bel (1)
Woods, M. (Sunderland), 2006 v Ic, Ni (2)
Wright, P. (Aberdeen), 1989 v Y, F; (with QPR), 1990 v Y (sub) (3)
Wright, S. (Aberdeen), 1991 v Bul, Pol, F; 1992 v Sw, G (2), Se (2); 1993 v Sw, P, I, Ma; 1994 v I, Ma (14)
Wright, T. (Oldham Ath), 1987 v Bel (sub) (1)

Young, Darren (Aberdeen), 1997 v Es (sub), Se, Col, CzR (sub), P; 1998 v La (sub); 1999 v CzR (sub), G (sub) (8)
Young, Derek (Aberdeen), 2000 v W; 2001 v Cro (sub), Bel (sub), Pol; 2002 v Cro (5)

WALES

Aizlewood, M. (Luton T), 1979 v E; 1981 v Ho (2)
Anthony, B. (Cardiff C), 2005 v La (sub), E, Pol; 2006 v Ma, E, Pol, G, Cy (sub) (8)

Baddeley, L. M. (Cardiff C), 1996 v Mol (sub), G (sub) (2)
Balcombe, S. (Leeds U), 1982 v F (sub) (1)
Bale, G. (Southampton), 2006 v Cy, Es (sub) (2)
Barnhouse, D. J. (Swansea), 1995 v Mol; 1996 v Mol, Sm (3)
Bater, P. T. (Bristol R), 1977 v E, S (2)
Beevers, L. J. (Boston U), 2005 v G (sub); (with Lincoln C), A (2); 2006 v Ma, E, Pol, Az (7)
Bellamy, C. D. (Norwich C), 1996 v Sm (sub); 1997 v Sm, T, Bel; 1998 v T, Bel, I; 1999 v I (8)
Birchall, A. S. (Arsenal), 2003 v Fi, I, Az; 2005 v La, Az, E, Pol, A (sub +1); (with Mansfield T), 2006 v Ma, E, Az (12)
Bird, A. (Cardiff C), 1993 v Cy (sub); 1994 v Cy (sub); 1995 v Mol, Ge (sub), Bul; 1996 v G (sub) (6)
Blackmore, C. (Manchester U), 1984 v N, Bul, Y (3)
Blake, N. (Cardiff C), 1991 v Pol (sub); 1993 v Cy, Bel, RCS; 1994 v RCS (5)
Blaney, S. D. (West Ham U), 1997 v Sm, Ho, T (3)
Bodin, P. (Cardiff C), 1983 v Y (1)
Bowen, J. P. (Swansea C), 1993 v Cy, Bel (2); 1994 v RCS, R (sub) (5)
Bowen, M. (Tottenham H), 1983 v N; 1984 v Bul, Y (3)
Boyle, T. (C Palace), 1982 v F (1)
Brace, D. P. (Wrexham), 1995 v Ge, Bul (2); 1997 v Sm Ho; 1998 v T (6)
Brough, M. (Notts Co), 2003 v As (sub); 2004 v I, Fi (3)
Brown, J. R. (Gillingham), 2003 v Fi, I, Az; 2004 v Ser, I, Fi, Ser (7)
Byrne, M. T. (Bolton W), 2003 v Az (sub) (1)

Calliste, R. T. (Manchester U), 2005 v La (sub), Az, E, Pol, G, A (2); (with Liverpool), 2006 v Pol, G, Az, Cy, Ni, Es (sub), Cy (sub), Es (15)
Carpenter, R. E. (Burnley), 2005 v E (sub) (1)
Cegielski, W. (Wrexham), 1977 v E (sub), S (2)

Chapple, S. R. (Swansea C), 1992 v R; 1993 v Cy, Bel (2), RCS; 1994 v RCS; Bul (2) (8)
Charles, J. M. (Swansea C), 1979 v E; 1981 v Ho (2)
Clark, J. (Manchester U), 1978 v S; (with Derby Co), 1979 v E (2)
Coates, J. S. (Swansea C), 1996 v Mol, G; 1997 v Ho, T (sub); 1998 v T (sub) (5)
Coleman, C. (Swansea C), 1990 v Pol; 1991 v E, Pol (3)
Collins, J. M. (Cardiff C), 2003 v I (sub), Az (sub+1); 2004 v Ser, I, Fi (sub), Ser (7)
Cotterill D. (Bristol C), 2005 v A (sub+sub); 2006 v Ma, E, Pol, Cy, Es (7)
Coyne, D. (Tranmere R), 1992 v R; 1994 v Cy (sub), R; 1995 v Mol, Ge, Bul (2) (7)
Critchell, K. A. R. (Southampton), 2005 v A (sub); 2006 v Cy (sub) (2)
Crofts, A. L. (Gillingham), 2005 v G, A (2); 2006 v Ma, E, Pol, Cy, Es (2) (9)
Crowell, M. T. (Wrexham), 2004 v Ser (sub); 2005 v Az (sub), E (sub), Pol (sub), A (sub); 2006 v Cy (sub+1) (7)
Curtis, A. T. (Swansea C), 1977 v E (1)

Davies, A. (Manchester U), 1982 v F (2), Ho; 1983 v N, Y, Bul (6)
Davies, A. G. (Cambridge U), 2006 v Ma (sub), E (sub), Pol (sub), G, Cy, Ni (6)
Davies, A. R. (Southampton), 2005 v La (sub); (with Yeovil T), A (2); 2006 v Ma, E, Pol, G, Az, Ni, Es, Cy, Es (12)
Davies, C. M. (Oxford U), 2005 v A (2); 2006 v E; (with Verona), Ni (sub), Es, Cy, Es (7)
Davies, D. (Barry T), 1999 v D (sub) (1)
Davies, G. M. (Hereford U), 1993 v Bel, RCS; 1995 v Mol (sub), Ge, Bul (2); (with C Palace), 1996 v Mol (7)
Davies, I. C. (Norwich C), 1978 v S (sub) (1)
Davies, L. (Bangor C), 2005 v La (sub) (1)
Davies, R. J. (WBA), 2006 v Ni (sub), Cy (sub), Es (sub) (3)
Davies, S. (Peterborough U), 1999 v D, Bl, Sw, I, D; (with Tottenham H), 2000 v S; 2001 v Bl, N, Pol, Arm (10)

Day, R. (Manchester C), 2000 v S (sub), Ni; 2001 v Uk, Pol, Uk; 2002 v Arm, N, Bl; 2003 v Fi, I, Az; (with Mansfield T), Az; 2004 v Ser (11)
Deacy, N. (PSV Eindhoven), 1977 v S (1)
De-Vulgt, L. S. (Swansea C), 2002 v Arm (sub), Bl (2)
Dibble, A. (Cardiff C), 1983 v Bul; 1984 v N, Bul (3)
Doyle, S. C. (Preston NE), 1979 v E (sub); (with Huddersfield T), 1984 v N (2)
Duffy, R. M. (Portsmouth), 2005 v La, E, Pol, G, A (2); 2006 v Es (7)
Dwyer, P. J. (Cardiff C), 1979 v E (1)

Earnshaw, R. (Cardiff C), 1999 v P (sub), I, D; 2000 v S, Ni; 2001 v Bl (sub), N, Pol (2), Uk (10)
Easter, D. J. (Cardiff C), 2006 v Ni (1)
Ebdon, M. (Everton), 1990 v Pol; 1991 v E (2)
Edwards, C. N. H. (Swansea C), 1996 v G; 1997 v Sm, Ho (2), T, Bel; 1998 v T (7)
Edwards, D. A. (Shrewsbury T), 2006 v Cy, Es (2)
Edwards, R. I. (Chester), 1977 v S; 1978 v W (2)
Edwards, R. W. (Bristol C), 1991 v Pol; 1992 v R; 1993 v Cy, Bel (2), RCS; 1994 v RCS, Cy, R; 1995 v Ge, Bul; 1996 v Mol, G (13)
Evans, A. (Bristol R), 1977 v E (1)
Evans, K. (Leeds U), 1999 v I (sub), D; (with Cardiff C), 2001 v N (sub), Pol (sub) (4)
Evans, P. S. (Shrewsbury T), 1996 v G (1)
Evans, S. J. (C Palace), 2001 v Bl, Arm (2)
Evans, T. (Cardiff C), 1995 v Bul (sub); 1996 v Mol, G (3)

Fish, N. (Cardiff C), 2005 v La, Az (sub) (2)
Fleetwood, S. (Cardiff C), 2005 v La, Az; 2006 v Ma (sub), E (sub) (4)
Folland, R. W. (Oxford U), 2000 v Ni (sub) (1)
Foster, M. G. (Tranmere R), 1993 v RCS (1)
Fowler, L. A. (Coventry C), 2003 v I; (with Huddersfield T), 2004 v Ser, I, Fi; 2005 v La, Az, E, Pol, G (9)
Freestone, R. (Chelsea), 1990 v Pol (1)

Gabbidon, D. L. (WBA), 1999 v D, P, Sw, I (sub), D; 2000 v Bl, Sw, S, Ni; (with Cardiff C), 2001 v N, Pol, Arm, Uk, Pol, Uk; 2002 v Arm, N (17)
Gale, D. (Swansea C), 1983 v Bul; 1984 v N (sub) (2)
Gall, K. A. (Bristol R), 2002 v N (sub), Bl (sub); 2003 v Fi (sub), Az; (with Yeovil T), 2004 v Ser, I, Fi, Ser (8)
Gibson, N. D. (Tranmere R), 1999 v D (sub), Bl (sub), P; 2000 v S (sub), Ni; (with Sheffield W), 2001 v Uk, Pol, Uk; 2002 v Arm, N, Bl (11)
Giggs, R. (Manchester U), 1991 v Pol (1)
Gilbert, P. (Plymouth Arg), 2005 v La, Az, E, Pol, G, A (2); 2006 v Ma, E, Pol, G, Az (12)
Giles, D. C. (Cardiff C), 1977 v S; 1978 v S; (with Swansea C), 1981 v Ho; (with C Palace), 1983 v Y (4)
Giles, P. (Cardiff C), 1982 v F (2), Ho (3)
Graham, D. (Manchester U), 1991 v E (1)
Green, R. M. (Wolverhampton W), 1998 v I; 1999 v I, D, Bl, Sw, I, D; 2000 v Bl, S, Ni; 2001 v Bl, N, Pol, Arm, Uk, Pol (16)
Griffith, C. (Cardiff C), 1990 v Pol (1)
Griffiths, C. (Shrewsbury T), 1991 v Pol (sub) (1)
Gunter, C. (Cardiff C), 2006 v Cy (1)

Hall, G. D. (Chelsea), 1990 v Pol (1)
Hartson, J. (Luton T), 1994 v Cy, R; 1995 v Mol, Ge, Bul; (with Arsenal), 1996 v G, Sm; 1997 v Sm, Ho (9)
Haworth, S. O. (Cardiff C), 1997 v Ho, T, Bel; (with Coventry C), 1998 v T, Bel; I; 1999 v I, D; (with Wigan Ath), Bl, Sw; 2000 v Bl, Sw (12)
Hennessey, W. R. (Wolverhampton W), 2006 v Ma, E, Pol (3)
Hillier, I. M. (Tottenham H), 2001 v Uk (sub), Pol (sub), Uk; (with Luton T), 2002 v Arm, N (5)
Hodges, G. (Wimbledon), 1983 v Y (sub), Bul (sub); 1984 v N, Bul, Y (5)
Holden, A. (Chester C), 1984 v Y (sub) (1)
Holloway, C. D. (Exeter C), 1999 v P, D (2)
Hopkins, J. (Fulham), 1982 v F (sub), Ho; 1983 v N, Y, Bul (5)
Hopkins, S. A. (Wrexham), 1999 v P (sub) (1)
Huggins, D. S. (Bristol C), 1996 v Sm (1)
Hughes, D. (Kaiserslautern), 2005 v La; (with Regensburg), 2006 v Ni (2)
Hughes, D. R. (Southampton), 1994 v R (1)
Hughes, R. D. (Aston Villa), 1996 v Sm; 1997 v Sm (sub), Ho (2), T, Bel; 1998 v T, Bel, I; 1999 v I, Sw, I; (with Shrewsbury T), 2000 v Sw (13)
Hughes, I. (Bury), 1992 v R; 1993 v Cy, Bel (sub), RCS; 1994 v Cy, R; 1995 v Mol, Ge, Bul; 1996 v Mol (sub), G (11)
Hughes, L. M. (Manchester U), 1983 v N, Y; 1984 v N, Bul, Y (5)
Hughes, W. (WBA), 1977 v E, S; 1978 v S (3)

Jackett, K. (Watford), 1981 v Ho; 1982 v F (2)
Jacobson, J. M. (Cardiff C), 2006 v Ma (sub), Cy, Ni (sub) (3)
James, L. R. S. (Southampton), 2006 v Cy (sub), Ni (sub), Es (sub), Cy (sub) (4)
James, R. M. (Swansea C), 1977 v E, S; 1978 v S (3)
Jarman, L. (Cardiff C), 1996 v Sm; 1997 v Sm, Ho (2), Bel; 1998 v T, Bel; 1999 v I, P; 2000 v Bl (10)
Jeanne, L. C. (QPR), 1999 v P (sub), Sw, I; 2000 v Bl, Sw, S, Ni; 2001 v Bl (8)
Jelleyman, G. A. (Peterborough U), 1999 v D (sub) (1)
Jenkins, L. D. (Swansea C), 1998 v T (sub); 2000 v Bl, Sw, S, Ni; 2001 v N, Pol, Arm, Uk (9)
Jenkins, S. R. (Swansea C), 1993 v Cy (sub), Bel (2)
Jones, E. P. (Blackpool), 2000 v Ni (sub) (1)
Jones, F. (Wrexham), 1981 v Ho (1)
Jones, J. A. (Swansea C); 2001 v Pol, Uk; 2002 v N (sub) (3)
Jones, L. (Cardiff C), 1982 v F (2), Ho (3)
Jones, M. A. (Wrexham), 2004 v Ser; 2006 v G, Az, Cy (4)
Jones, M. G. (Leeds U), 1998 v Bel; 1999 v I, D, Bl, Sw, I; 2000 v Sw (7)
Jones, P. L. (Liverpool), 1992 v R; 1993 v Cy, Bel (2), RCS; 1994 v RCS (sub), Cy, R; 1995 v Mol, Ge; 1996 v Mol, G (12)
Jones, R. (Sheffield W), 1994 v R; 1995 v Bul (2) (3)
Jones, S. J. (Swansea C), 2005 v Az (1)
Jones, V. (Bristol R), 1979 v E; 1981 v Ho (2)

Kendall, L. M. (C Palace), 2001 v N, Pol (2)
Kendall, M. (Tottenham H), 1978 v S (1)
Kenworthy, J. R. (Tranmere R), 1994 v Cy; 1995 v Mol, Bul (3)
Knott, G. R. (Tottenham H), 1996 v Sm (1)

Law, B. J. (QPR), 1990 v Pol; 1991 v E (2)
Lawless, A. (Torquay U), 2006 v Ni (1)
Ledley, J. C. (Cardiff C), 2005 v G, A (2); 2006 v G, Es (5)
Letheran, G. (Leeds U), 1977 v E, S (2)
Letheran, K. C. (Swansea C), 2006 v Cy (sub) (1)
Lewis, D. (Swansea C), 1982 v F (2), Ho; 1983 v N, Y, Bul; 1984 v N, Bul, Y (9)
Lewis, J. (Cardiff C), 1983 v N (1)
Llewellyn, C. M. (Norwich C), 1998 v T (sub), Bel (sub), I; 1999 v I, D, Bl, I; 2000 v Bl, Sw, S; 2001 v N, Pol, Arm, Uk (14)
Loveridge, J. (Swansea C), 1982 v Ho; 1983 v N, Bul (3)
Low, J. D. (Bristol R), 1999 v P; (with Cardiff C), 2002 v Arm (sub), N (sub), Bl (1)
Lowndes, S. R. (Newport Co), 1979 v E; 1981 v Ho; (with Millwall), 1984 v Bul, Y (4)

MacDonald, S. B. (Swansea C), 2006 v Az (sub), Ni, Es (3)
McCarthy, A. J. (QPR), 1994 v RCS, Cy, R (3)
McDonald, C. (Cardiff C), 2006 v Az, Es, Cy (sub) (3)
Mackin, L. (Wrexham), 2006 v Ni (1)
Maddy, P. (Cardiff C), 1982 v Ho; 1983 v N (sub) (2)
Margetson, M. W. (Manchester C), 1992 v R; 1993 v Cy, Bel (2), RCS; 1994 v RCS, Cy (7)
Martin, A. P. (C Palace), 1999 v D (1)
Martin, D. A. (Notts Co), 2006 v Ma (sub) (1)
Marustik, C. (Swansea C), 1982 v F (2); 1983 v Y, Bul; 1984 v N, Bul, Y (7)
Maxwell, L. J. (Liverpool), 1999 v Sw (sub), I; 2000 v Sw (sub), S, Ni; 2001 v Bl, Pol, Arm, Uk, Pol, Uk; (with Cardiff C), 2002 v Arm, N, Bl (sub) (14)
Meaker, M. J. (QPR), 1994 v RCS (sub), R (sub) (2)
Melville, A. K. (Swansea C), 1990 v Pol; (with Oxford U), 1991 v E (2)
Micallef, C. (Cardiff C), 1982 v F, Ho; 1983 v N (3)
Morgan, A. M. (Tranmere R), 1995 v Mol, Bul; 1996 v Mol, G (4)
Morgan, C. (Wrexham), 2004 v Fi, Ser (sub); 2005 v La, G, A (2); (with Milton Keynes D), 2006 v Az, Es, Cy, Es (10)
Moss, D. M. (Shrewsbury T), 2003 v Fi, I, Az (2); 2004 v Ser (2) (6)
Mountain, P. D. (Cardiff C), 1997 v Ho, T (2)
Mumford, A. O. (Swansea C), 2003 v Fi, I, Az (2) (4)

Nardiello, D. (Coventry C), 1978 v S (1)
Neilson, A. B. (Newcastle U), 1993 v Cy, Bel (2), RCS; 1994 v RCS, Cy, R (7)
Nicholas, P. (C Palace), 1978 v S; 1979 v E; (with Arsenal), 1982 v F (3)
Nogan, K. (Luton T), 1990 v Pol; 1991 v E (2)
Nogan, L. (Oxford U) 1991 v E (1)

Nyatanga, L. J. (Derby Co), 2005 v G (sub); 2006 v Ma, E, Pol, G, Az, Cy, Es (8)

Oster, J. M. (Grimsby T), 1997 v Sm (sub), Ho (sub), T, Bel; (with Everton), 1998 v T, Bel, I; 1999 v I, Sw (9)
Owen, G. (Wrexham), 1991 v E (sub), Pol; 1992 v R; 1993 v Cy, Bel (2); 1994 v Cy, R (8)

Page, R. J. (Watford), 1995 v Mol, Ge, Bul; 1996 v Mol (4)
Parslow, D. (Cardiff C), 2005 v La, Az, E, Pol (4)
Partridge, D. W. (West Ham U), 1997 v T (1)
Pascoe, C. (Swansea C), 1983 v Bul (sub); 1984 v N (sub), Bul, Y (4)
Pearce, S. (Bristol C), 2006 v Cy, Ni, Cy (3)
Pejic, S. M. (Wrexham), 2003 v Fi, I, Az; 2004 v Ser, I, Fi (6)
Pembridge, M. (Luton T), 1991 v Pol (1)
Perry, J. (Cardiff C), 1990 v Pol; 1991 v E, Pol (3)
Peters, M. (Manchester C), 1992 v R; (with Norwich C), 1993 v Cy, RCS (3)
Phillips, D. (Plymouth Arg), 1984 v N, Bul, Y (3)
Phillips, G. R. (Swansea C), 2001 v Uk (sub); 2002 v Arm (sub), Bl (3)
Phillips, L. (Swansea C), 1979 v E; (with Charlton Ath), 1983 v N (2)
Pipe, D. R. (Coventry C), 2003 v As (2); 2004 v Ser, I, Fi, Ser;(with Notts Co), 2005 v La, Az, E, Pol, G, A (12)
Pontin, K. (Cardiff C), 1978 v S (1)
Powell, L. (Southampton), 1991 v Pol (sub); 1992 v R (sub); 1993 v Bel (sub); 1994 v RCS (4)
Powell, L. (Leicester C), 2004 v Ser (sub), I (sub) Fi (3)
Powell, R. (Bolton W), 2006 v Cy (1)
Price, J. J. (Swansea C), 1998 v I (sub); 1999 v I (sub), D, Bl, P; 2000 v Bl, Sw (7)
Price, L. P. (Ipswich T), 2005 v La, Az, E, Pol, G, A; 2006 v Es (2) (8)
Price, M. D. (Everton), 2001 v Uk. Pol (sub), Uk; (with Hull C), 2002 v Arm, N, Bl; 2003 v Fi, I; (with Scarborough), Az (2); 2004 v Ser, Fi, Ser (13)
Price, P. (Luton T), 1981 v Ho (1)
Pritchard, M. O. (Swansea C), 2006 v Ma, Az (sub), Cy (sub), Ni (sub) (4)
Pugh, D. (Doncaster R), 1982 v F (2) (2)
Pugh, S. (Wrexham), 1993 v Bel (sub + sub) (2)
Pulis, A. J. (Stoke C), 2006 v Ma, Pol (sub), G, Az, Cy (5)

Ramasut, M. W. T. (Bristol R), 1997 v Ho, Bel; 1998 v T, I (4)
Ratcliffe, K. (Everton), 1981 v Ho; 1982 v F (2)
Ready, K. (QPR), 1992 v R; 1993 v Bel (2); 1994 v RCS, Cy (5)
Rees, A. (Birmingham C), 1984 v N (1)
Rees, J. (Luton T), 1990 v Pol; 1991 v E, Pol (3)
Rees, M. R. (Millwall), 2003 v Fi (sub), Az; 2004 v Ser, I (4)
Roberts, A. (QPR), 1991 v E, Pol (2)
Roberts, C. J. (Cardiff C), 1999 v D (sub) (1)
Roberts, G. (Hull C), 1983 v Bul (1)
Roberts, G. W. (Liverpool), 1997 v Ho, T, Bel; 1998 v T, I; 1999 v I, D, Bl, P; (with Panionios), D; (with Tranmere R), 2000 v Sw (11)
Roberts, J. G. (Wrexham), 1977 v E (1)
Roberts, N. W. (Wrexham), 1999 v I (sub), P; 2000 v Sw (sub) (3)
Roberts, P. (Porthmadog), 1997 v Ho (sub) (1)
Roberts, S. I. (Swansea C), 1999 v Sw, I (sub), D; 2000 v Bl (sub), Ni; 2001 v Bl (sub), N, Pol, Arm, Uk; 2002 v Arm, N, Bl (13)
Roberts, S. W. (Wrexham), 2000 v S; 2001 v Bl, N (sub) (3)
Robinson, C. P. (Wolverhampton W), 1996 v Sm; 1997 v Sm, Ho (2), T, Bel (6)
Robinson, J. (Brighton & HA), 1992 v R; (with Charlton Ath), 1993 v Bel; 1994 v RCS, Cy, R (5)
Rowlands, A. J. R. (Manchester C), 1996 v Sm; 1997 v Sm, Ho (1 + sub), T (sub) (5)
Rush, I. (Liverpool), 1981 v Ho; 1982 v F (2)

Savage, R. W. (Crewe Alex), 1995 v Bul; 1996 v Mol, G (3)
Sayer, P. A. (Cardiff C), 1977 v E, S (2)
Searle, D. (Cardiff C), 1991 v Pol (sub); 1992 v R; 1993 v Cy, Bel (2), RCS; 1994 v RCS (6)
Slatter, D. (Chelsea), 2000 v Sw (sub), S; 2001 v Bl, N (sub), Pol (sub), Uk (sub) (6)
Slatter, N. (Bristol R), 1983 v N, Y, Bul; 1984 v N, Bul, Y (6)
Somner, M. J. (Brentford), 2004 v Ser (sub), I (2)
Speed, G. A. (Leeds U), 1990 v Pol; 1991 v E, Pol (3)
Spender, S. (Wrexham), 2005 v La (sub), Az (sub); 2006 v G, Cy (2), Es (6)
Stevenson, N. (Swansea C), 1982 v F, Ho (2)
Stevenson, W. B. (Leeds U), 1977 v E, S; 1978 v S (3)
Stock, B. B. (Bournemouth), 2003 v Fi (sub), I (sub); 2004 v Fi, Ser (4)
Symons, K. (Portsmouth), 1991 v E, Pol (2)

Taylor, G. K. (Bristol R), 1995 v Ge, Bul (2); 1996 v Mol (4)
Thomas, D. J. (Watford), 1998 v T, Bel (2)
Thomas, J. A. (Blackburn R), 1996 v Sm; 1997 v Sm, Ho (2), T, Bel; 1998 v Bel; 1999 v D, Bl, P; 2000 v Bl (sub); 2001 v Bl, N, Pol, Arm, Uk, Pol, Uk; 2002 v Arm, N, Bl (21)
Thomas, Martin R. (Bristol R), 1979 v E; 1981 v Ho (2)
Thomas, Mickey R. (Wrexham), 1977 v E; 1978 v S (2)
Thomas, S. (Wrexham), 2001 v Pol, Uk; 2002 v Arm, N, Bl (5)
Thomas, D. G. (Leeds U), 1977 v E; 1979 v E; 1984 v N (3)
Tibbott, L. (Ipswich T), 1977 v E, S (2)
Tipton, M. J. (Oldham Ath), 1998 v I (sub); 1999 v P, Sw (sub); 2000 v Ni; 2001 v Arm (sub), Uk (sub) (6)
Tolley, J. C. (Shrewsbury T), 2001 v Pol, Uk (sub); 2003 v Fi, I, Az (2); 2004 v Ser (2); 2005 v Az, E, Pol, G (sub) (12)
Tudur-Jones, O. (Swansea C), 2006 v Ma (sub), E, Pol (3)
Twiddy, C. (Plymouth Arg), 1995 v Mol, Ge; 1996 v G (sub) (3)

Vaughan, D. O. (Crewe Alex), 2003 v Fi, Az; 2004 v I; 2005 v Az, E, Pol, G; 2006 v Pol (8)
Vaughan, N. (Newport Co), 1982 v F, Ho (2)
Valentine, R. D. (Everton), 2001 v Pol, Uk; 2002 v Arm, N, Bl; (with Darlington), 2003 v Fi, I, Az (8)

Walsh, D. (Wrexham), 2000 v S, Ni; 2001 v Bl, Arm, Uk; 2002 v Arm, N, Bl (8)
Walsh, I. P. (C Palace), 1979 v E; (with Swansea C), 1983 v Bul (2)
Walton, M. (Norwich C.), 1991 v Pol (sub) (1)
Ward, D. (Notts Co), 1996 v Mol, G (2)
Weston, R. D. (Arsenal), 2001 v Bl, N, Pol; (with Cardiff C), Arm (4)
Whitfield, P. M. (Wrexham), 2003 v Az (1)
Wiggins, R. (Crystal Palace), 2006 v Cy (sub), Ni, Es, Cy, Es (5)
Williams, A. P. (Southampton), 1998 v Bel, I; 1999 v I, D (sub), Bl, Sw, I; 2000 v Bl, Sw (9)
Williams, A. S. (Blackburn R), 1996 v Sm; 1997 v Sm, Ho, Bel; 1998 v T, Bel, I; 1999 v I, D, Bl, P, Sw, I, D; 2000 v Bl, Sw (16)
Williams, D. (Bristol R), 1983 v Y (1)
Williams, D. I. L. (Liverpool), 1998 v I; 1999 v D, Bl; (with Wrexham) I, D; 2000 v Bl, S, Ni; 2001 v Bl (9)
Williams, D. T. (Yeovil T), 2006 v Es (sub) (1)
Williams, E. (Caernarfon T), 1997 v Ho (sub), T (sub) (2)
Williams, G. (Bristol R), 1983 v Y, Bul (2)
Williams, G. A. (C Palace), 2003 v I (sub), Az; 2004 v Ser, I, Ser (sub) (5)
Williams, M. (Manchester U), 2001 v Pol (sub), Uk (sub); 2002 v Bl (sub); 2003 v Fi, I, Az (sub); 2004 v Ser (sub), I (sub), Fi, Ser (10)
Williams, M. P. (Wrexham), 2006 v Ni, Cy, Es (3)
Williams, M. R. (Wrexham), 2006 v Ni (sub) (1)
Williams, S. J. (Wrexham), 1995 v Mol, Ge, Bul (2) (4)
Wilmot, R. (Arsenal), 1982 v F (2), Ho; 1983 v N, Y; 1984 v Y (6)
Worgan, L. J. (Milton Keynes D), 2005 v La (sub), A; (with Rushden & D), 2006 v Ma (sub), G, Az (5)
Wright, A. A. (Oxford U), 1998 v Bel, I (sub); 1999 v D (sub) (3)

Young, S. (Cardiff C), 1996 v Sm; 1997 v Sm, Ho (2), Bel (sub) (5)

NORTHERN IRELAND

Bailie, N. (Linfield), 1990 v Is; 1994 v R (sub) (2)
Baird, C. P. (Southampton), 2002 v G; 2003 v S, Sp, Uk, Fi, Gr (6)
Beatty, S. (Chelsea), 1990 v Is; (with Linfield), 1994 v R (2)
Black, J. (Tottenham H), 2003 v Uk (sub) (1)
Black, K. T. (Luton T), 1990 v Is (1)
Black, R. Z. (Morecambe), 2002 v G (1)
Blackledge, G. (Portadown), 1978 v Ei (1)
Blayney, A. (Southampton), 2003 v Fi (sub); 2004 v Uk, Arm, Gr (4)
Boyle, W. S. (Leeds U), 1998 v Sw (sub), S (sub); 2001 v CzR (sub), Bul (1+sub), CzR; 2002 v Ma (7)
Braniff, K. R. (Millwall), 2002 v G; 2003 v S (sub), Sp (sub), Fi, Arm (sub), Gr, Sp; 2004 v Gr (sub); 2005 v Sw, S; 2006 v Ei (11)
Brotherston, N. (Blackburn R), 1978 v Ei (sub) (1)
Browne, G. (Manchester C), 2003 v S, Sp, Uk, Fi (sub), Sp (5)
Brunt, C. (Sheffield W), 2005 v S (1)
Buchanan, D. T. H. (Bury), 2006 v S (sub) (1)
Buchanan, W. B. (Bolton W), 2002 v G (sub); 2003 v Uk (sub); (with Lisburn Distillery), 2004 v Uk, Arm, Gr (5)
Burns, L. (Port Vale), 1998 v Sw, S, Ei; 1999 v T, Fi, Mol, G, Mol, Ei; 2000 v F, T, G, Fi (13)

Callaghan, A. (Limavady U), 2006 v Is (sub+1), S (3)
Campbell, S. (Ballymena U), 2003 v Sp (sub) (1)
Capaldi, A. C. (Birmingham C), 2002 v D (sub), Ic, Ma, G; 2003 v S, Sp, Uk, Fi, Arm, Gr; (with Plymouth Arg), Sp; 2004 v Uk, Arm, Gr (14)
Carlisle, W. T. (C Palace), 2000 v Fi (sub); 2001 v Ma, Ic, Bul (1+sub), CzR; 2002 v D, Ic, Ma (9)
Carroll, R. E. (Wigan Ath), 1998 v S, Ei; 1999 v T, Fi, Mol, G, Mol, Ei; 2000 v T, G, Fi (11)
Carson, S. (Rangers), 2000 v Ma; (wirh Dundee U), 2002 v D (sub) (2)
Clarke, L. (Peterborough U), 2003 v Sp (sub); 2004 v Uk (sub), Arm (sub); 2005 v Sw (4)
Clarke, R. (Newry C), 2006 v Is (2), W, Lie (2) (5)
Clarke, R. D. J. (Portadown), 1999 v Ei (sub), S; 2000 v F (sub), S, W (sub) (5)
Clingan, S. G. (Wolverhampton W), 2003 v Arm (sub); 2004 v Uk, Arm, Gr; 2005 v Sw, S; (with Nottingham F), 2006 v Is (2), W, Lie (2) (11)
Close, B. (Middlesbrough), 2002 v Ic, Ma (sub), G; 2003 v S, Sp, Uk, Arm, Sp; 2004 v Arm, Gr (10)
Clyde, M. G. (Wolverhampton W), 2002 v G; 2003 v S, Sp, Uk, Fi (5)
Connell, T. E. (Coleraine), 1978 v Ei (sub) (1)
Coote, A. (Norwich C), 1998 v Sw (sub), S, Ei; 1999 v T, Fi,Mol, G, Mol, Ei; 2000 v F, T, G (12)
Convery, J. (Celtic), 2000 v S, W; 2001 v D, Ic (4)

Davey, H. (UCD), 2004 v Uk, Arm, Gr (3)
Davis, S. (Aston Villa), 2004 v Uk (sub), Arm (sub); 2005 v Sw (3)
Devine, D. (Omagh T), 1994 v R (1)
Devine, J. (Glentoran), 1990 v Is (1)
Dickson, H. (Wigan Ath). 2002 v Ma (1)
Dolan, J. (Millwall), 2000 v Fi, Ma, S; 2001 v Ma, D, Ic (6)
Donaghy, M. M. (Larne), 1978 v Ei (1)
Dowie, I. (Luton T), 1990 v Is (1)
Duff, S. (Cheltenham T), 2003 v Sp (1)

Elliott, S. (Glentoran), 1999 v Fi (sub), Ei, S (sub) (3)
Ervin, J. (Linfield), 2005 v Sw; 2006 v W (sub) (2)
Evans, J. (Manchester U), 2006 v S (1)

Feeney, L. (Linfield), 1998 v Ei (sub); 1999 v T, Fi, Mol; (with Rangers), G (sub), Ei, S; 2000 v Fi (8)
Feeney, W. (Bournemouth), 2002 v D, Ic (sub); 2003 v Fi, Arm, Gr; 2004 v Uk, Arm, Gr (8)
Ferguson, M. (Glentoran), 2000 v T (sub), Ma (sub) (2)
Fitzgerald, D. (Rangers), 1998 v Sw, S; 1999 v T (sub), Fi (4)
Friars, E. C. (Notts Co), 2005 v Sw, S; 2006 v Ei (sub), Is, W (sub), Lie (sub), S (7)
Friars, S. M. (Liverpool), 1998 v Sw, S, Ei; (with Ipswich T), 1999 v T, Fi, Mol, G, Mol; 2000 v F, T, G, Ma, S, W; 2001 v Ma, D, Ic, CzR, Bul (2), CzR (21)

Gault, M. (Linfield), 2005 v S (sub); 2006 v Ei (2)
Gilfillan, B. J. (Gretna), 2005 v S; 2006 v Ei, Is, W, Lie (2), S (7)
Gillespie, K. R. (Manchester U), 1994 v R (1)
Glendinning, M. (Bangor), 1994 v R (1)
Graham, G. L. (C Palace), 1999 v S; 2000 v F, T, G, Fi (5)
Graham, R. S. (QPR), 1999 v Fi (sub), Mol, Ei (sub); 2000 v F (sub), T (sub), G (sub), Fi (sub), Ma, S, W; 2001 v Ma, D, CzR (sub), Bul (sub), CzR (sub) (15)
Gray, P. (Luton T), 1990 v Is (sub) (1)
Griffin, D. J. (St Johnstone), 1998 v S (sub), Ei; 1999 v T, Fi, G, Mol, Ei, S; 2000 v F, T (10)

Hamilton, G. (Blackburn R), 2000 v Ma (sub), S, W (sub); 2001 v Ma, D, Ic, CzR, Bul (2), CzR; (with Portadown), 2002 v Ic, Ma (12)
Hamilton, W. R. (Linfield), 1978 v Ei (1)
Harkin, M. P. (Wycombe W), Ma (sub), S (sub), W; 2001 v Ma (sub), D (sub), Ic, CzR, Bul (sub+1) (9)
Harvey, J. (Arsenal), 1978 v Ei (1)
Hawe, S. (Blackburn R), 2001 v Cz (1+sub) (2)
Hayes, T. (Luton T), 1978 v Ei (1)
Healy, D. J. (Manchester U), 1999 v Mol (sub), G (sub), Ei (sub), S; 2000 v F (sub), T, G, Fi (8)
Herron, C. J. (QPR), 2003 v Arm, Gr (2)
Higgins, R. (Derry C), 2006 v Ei (1)
Holmes, S. (Manchester C), Ma, S, W; 2001 v Ma, D, Ic, CzR, Bul (2), CzR; (with Wrexham), 2002 v D, Ic, Ma (13)
Hughes, J. (Lincoln C), 2006 v Is (sub+1), W, Lie (2) (5)
Hughes, M. A. (Tottenham H), 2003 v Sp (sub), Uk (sub), Fi, Arm, Gr, Sp; 2004 v Uk, Arm, Gr (sub); 2005 v Sw, S; (with Oldham Ath), 2006 v Ei (12)
Hughes, M. E. (Manchester C), 1990 v Is (sub)
Hunter, M. (Glentoran), 2002 v G (sub) (1)

Ingham, M. (Sunderland), 2001 v CzR, Bul (2), CzR (4)

Johnson, D. M. (Blackburn R), 1998 v Sw, S, Ei; 1999 v T, Fi, G, Mol, Ei; 2000 v F, T, G (11)
Johnston, B. (Cliftonville), 1978 v Ei (1)
Julian, A. A. (Brentford), 2005 v Sw (1)

Kee, P. V. (Oxford U), 1990 v Is (1)
Kelly, D. (Derry C), 2000 v Ma, W; 2001 v Ma, Ic (sub), CzR, Bul (2), CzR; 2002 v D, Ic, Ma (11)
Kelly, N. (Oldham Ath), 1990 v Is (sub) (1)
Kirk, A. (Hearts), 1999 v S; 2000 v Ma, S, W; 2001 v Ma, D, Ic (sub); 2002 v D, Ic (9)

Lafferty, K. (Burnley), 2006 v W, Lie (sub) (2)
Lennon, N. F. (Manchester C), 1990 v Is; (with Crewe Alex), 1994 v R (2)
Lindsay, K. (Larne), 2006 v Is (1)
Lyttle, G. (Celtic), 1998 v Sw, S; (with Peterborough U), 1999 v T (sub), Mol (2), S; 2000 v G, Fi (8)

Magee, J. (Bangor), 1994 v R (sub) (1)
Magilton, J. (Liverpool), 1990 v Is (1)
Matthews, N. P. (Blackpool), 1990 v Is (1)
McArdle, R. (Sheffield W), 2006 v Is, W, Lie (2) (4)
McAreavey, P. (Swindon T), 2000 v Ma, S; 2001 v Ma, D; 2002 v D, Ic (sub), Ma (sub) (7)
McBride, J. (Glentoran), 1994 v R (sub) (1)
McCaffrey, D. (Hibernian), 2006 v Is, S (sub) (2)
McCallion, E. (Coleraine), 1998 v Sw (sub) (1)
McCann, G. S. (West Ham U), 2000 v S (sub), W; 2001 v D (sub), Ic, CzR, Bul (2), CzR; 2002 v D, Ic, Ma (11)
McCann, P. (Portadown), 2003 v Sp (1)
McCann, R. (Rangers), 2002 v G (sub); (with Linfield), 2003 v S (sub) (2)
McCartney, G. (Sunderland), 2001 v D, CzR, Bul (2); 2002 v D (5)
McChrystal, M. (Derry C), 2005 v Sw, S; 2006 v Ei, Is, W, Lie (2), S (8)
McCourt, P. J. (Rochdale), 2002 v G; 2003 v S (sub), Sp, Uk, Fi (sub), Arm (sub), Gr (sub); 2005 v Sw; (with Derry C), 2006 v Ei (8)
McCoy, R. K. (Coleraine), 1990 v Is (1)
McCreery, D. (Manchester U), 1978 v Ei (1)
McEvilly, L. (Rochdale), 2003 v S, Sp, Uk, Fi (sub), Arm, Gr (sub); 2004 v Uk, Arm, Gr (9)
McFlynn, T. M. (QPR), 2000 v Ma (sub), W (sub); 2001 v Ma (sub), CzR (sub), Bul (sub+sub), CzR; (with Woking), 2002 v D (sub), Ic (sub); (with Margate), G; 2003 v S (sub), Sp (sub), Fi (sub), Arm, Gr (sub), Sp (sub); 2004 v Uk, Arm (sub), Gr (19)
McGibbon, P. C. G. (Manchester U), 1994 v R (1)
McGlinchey, B. (Manchester C), 1998 v Sw, S, Ei; (with Port Vale), 1999 v T, Fi, Mol, G, Mol, Ei, S; (with Gillingham), 2000 v F, G, T, Fi (14)
McGovern, M. (Celtic), 2005 v S; 2006 v Ei, Is (2), W, Lie (2), S (8)

McGowan, M. V. (Clyde), 2006 v Is, S (2)
McIlroy, T. (Linfield), 1994 v R (sub) (1)
McKnight, P. (Rangers), 1998 v Sw; 1999 v T (sub), Mol (sub) (3)
McLean, B. S. (Rangers), 2006 v Ei (1)
McMahon, G. J. (Tottenham H),1994 v R (sub) (1)
McVeigh, A. (Ayr U), 2002 v G (sub) (1)
McVeigh, P. F. (Tottenham H), 1998 v S (sub), Ei; 1999 v T, Mol, G, Mol, Ei; 2000 v F, T (sub), G (sub), Fi (11)
McVey, K. (Coleraine), 2006 v Is (sub+1), W (sub), Lie (sub), S (5)
Melaugh, G. M. (Aston Villa), 2002 v G; 2003 v S, Sp, Uk, Fi, Arm, Gr, Sp; (with Glentoran), 2004 v Uk, Arm, Gr (11)
Millar, W. P. (Port Vale), 1990 v Is (1)
Miskelly, D. T. (Oldham Ath), 2000 v F, Ma, S, W; 2001 v Ma, D, Ic; 2002 v D, Ic, Ma (10)
Moreland, V. (Glentoran), 1978 v Ei (sub) (1)
Morgan, M, P. T. (Preston NE), 1999 v S (1)
Morris, E. J. (WBA), 2002 v G; (with Glentoran), 2003 v S, Sp, Uk, Fi, Arm, Gr, Sp (8)
Morrison, O. (Sheffield W), 2001 v Bul (sub); 2002 v Ma (sub); 2003 v S, Fi; (with Sheffield U), Arm, Gr, Sp (7)
Morrow, A. (Northampton T), 2001 v D (sub) (1)
Morrow, S. (Hibernian), 2005 v S (sub); 2006 v Ei, W, Lie (4)
Mulryne, P. P. (Manchester U), Sw, S, Ei; (with Norwich C), 1999 v G, Mol (5)
Murray, W. (Linfield), 1978 v Ei (sub) (1)
Murtagh, C. (Hearts), 2005 v S (sub) (1)

Nicholl, J. M. (Manchester U), 1978 v Ei (1)
Nixon, C. (Glentoran), 2000 v Fi (sub) (1)

O'Hara, G. (Leeds U), 1994 v R (1)
O'Neill, M. A. M. (Hibernian), 1994 v R (1)
O'Neill, J. P. (Leicester C), 1978 v Ei (1)

Patterson, D. J. (C Palace), 1994 v R (1)

Quinn, S. J. (Blackpool), 1994 v R (1)

Ramsey, K. (Institute), 2006 v S (1)
Robinson, S. (Tottenham H), 1994 v R (1)

Scullion, D. (Dungannon Swifts), 2006 v Is (1+sub), W, Lie (2), S (6)
Shiels, D. (Hibernian), 2005 v Sw (sub), S; 2006 v Ei (sub), Lie (4)
Simms, G. (Hartlepool U), 2001 v Bul (2), CzR; 2002 v D, Ic, Ma, G; 2003 v S, Sp, Uk, Fi, Arm, Gr, Sp (14)
Skates, G. (Blackburn R), 2000 v Ma; 2001 v Ic (sub), CzR (2) (4)
Sloan, T. (Ballymena U), 1978 v Ei (1)
Smylie, D. (Newcastle U), 2006 v Ei (sub), Is (2), W, Lie (sub) (5)
Stewart T. (Wolverhampton W), 2006 v Is (1+sub), W (sub), Lie, S (sub) (5)

Taylor, M. S. (Fulham), 1998 v Sw (1)
Thompson, P. (Linfield), 2006 v Ei (sub), Lie (2)
Toner, C. (Tottenham H), 2000 v Ma (sub), S (sub), W; 2001 v D, Ic, CzR, Bul (2), CzR; 2002 v D, Ic, Ma; (with Leyton Orient), 2003 v S, Sp, Uk, Fi, Gr (17)
Teggart, N. (Sunderland), 2005 v Sw (sub), S (sub) (2)

Ward, J. (Aston Villa), 2006 v Is, Lie (sub+sub) (3)
Ward, M. (Dungannon Swifts), 2006 v S (sub) (1)
Ward, S. (Glentoran), 2005 v S; 2006 v Ei (sub), Is (1+sub), W, Lie (2), S (8)
Waterman, D. G. (Portsmouth), 1998 v Sw, S, Ei; 1999 v T, Fi, Mol, G, Mol, Ei, S (sub); 2000 v F, T, G, Fi (14)
Webb, S. M. (Ross Co), 2004 v Uk, Arm, Gr; (with St Johnstone), 2005 v Sw, S; (with Ross Co), 2006 v Ei (6)
Wells, D. P. (Barry T), 1999 v S (1)
Whitley, Jeff (Manchester C), 1998 v Sw, S, Ei; 1999 v T, Fi, Mol, G, Ei, S; 2000 v F, G, T, Ma, S, W; 2001 v Ma, Ic (17)
Willis, P. (Liverpool), 2006 v Is (sub) (1)

OLYMPIC FOOTBALL

Previous medallists

Games	Medallists	Games	Medallists	Games	Medallists
1896 Athens*	1 Denmark 2 Greece	1948 London	1 Sweden 2 Yugoslavia 3 Denmark	1980 Moscow	1 Czechoslovakia 2 East Germany 3 USSR
1900 Paris*	1 Great Britain 2 France	1952 Helsinki	1 Hungary 2 Yugoslavia 3 Sweden	1984 Los Angeles	1 France 2 Brazil 3 Yugoslavia
1904 St Louis**	1 Canada 2 USA	1956 Melbourne	1 USSR 2 Yugoslavia 3 Bulgaria	1988 Seoul	1 USSR 2 Brazil 3 West Germany
1908 London	1 Great Britain 2 Denmark 3 Holland	1960 Rome	1 Yugoslavia 2 Denmark 3 Hungary	1992 Barcelona	1 Spain 2 Poland 3 Ghana
1912 Stockholm	1 England 2 Denmark 3 Holland	1964 Tokyo	1 Hungary 2 Czechoslovakia 3 East Germany	1996 Atlanta	1 Nigeria 2 Argentina 3 Brazil
1920 Antwerp	1 Belgium 2 Spain 3 Holland	1968 Mexico City	1 Hungary 2 Bulgaria 3 Japan	2000 Sydney	1. Cameroon 2. Spain 3. Chile
1924 Paris	1 Uruguay 2 Switzerland 3 Sweden	1972 Munich	1 Poland 2 Hungary 3 E Germany/ USSR	2004 Athens	1. Argentina 2. Paraguay 3. Italy
1928 Amsterdam	1 Uruguay 2 Argentina 3 Italy	1976 Montreal	1 East Germany 2 Poland 3 USSR		
1932 Los Angeles	no tournament				
1936 Berlin	1 Italy 2 Austria 3 Norway				

* No official tournament
** No official tournament but gold medal later awarded by IOC

FOUR NATIONS TOURNAMENT 2006

(in England)

23 May

England 2 *(Carr 74, Oli 82)*

Republic of Ireland 0 824

(in Eastbourne).
England: Jalal; Travis, Kempson, Charnock, Nutter (Blackett 89), Oli, Thurgood, Craney (Carr 70), Boyd, McLean (Mackail-Smith 85), Richards (Roberts 70).

25 May

England 1 *(Richards 29)*

Wales 1 *(Moore 79)* 1024

(in Eastbourne).
England: Jalal; Travis, Kempson, Charnock, Nutter, Oli, Thurgood, Craney (Carr 83), Boyd, McLean (Roberts 75), Richards (Mackail-Smith 60).

27 May

England 2 *(Richards 75, Mackail-Smith 90)*

Scotland 0 2036

(in Eastbourne).
England: Jalal; Travis, Charnock, Nutter, Henry, Carr, Thurgood, McLean, Southam, Boyd, Oli.
Subs: Richards, Blackett, Mackail-Smith, Roberts.
Scotland: Shearer; Chisholm, McNamara, Brown, Fowlie, McLean, Thomson, Smith, Low, McMillan, McKay.
Subs: Gunn, McKinnan, McAuley, Nicol, Seeley.

23 May

Wales 2 *(Evans 14, Moore 25)*

Scotland 1 *(Thomson 71)* 532

(in Bognor Regis).
Wales: Roberts T; Coupe (Thomas 68), Keddie, Jones D, Jones G, Fowler (Harris 77), Bale (Davies N 80), Holloway, Evans (Davies L 53), Moore (Roberts P 73), Searle.
Scotland: Ridgers; Smith, Thomson, Seeley (McAuley 68), Brown, Low (Mackay 78), Gunn, McKay, McLean, Chisholm, MacKinnan (McMillan 57).

25 May

Republic of Ireland 1 *(Nolan 87)*

Scotland 2 *(McMillan 5, McKay 46)* 383

(in Worthing).
Republic of Ireland: Masterson; McGee (Nolan 62), Lally, O'Donnell, Guthrie, Finn, Harte, Deegan, McEniff, Bracken (McGowan 87), Tyrell.
Scotland: Shearer; Smith (Nicol 86), Thomson, Brown, Low, McKay, McMillan (Gunn 73), McLean, Chisholm, Fowlie, McNamara.

27 May

Republic of Ireland 0

Wales 3 *(Davies L 43, 87, Moore 58)* 600

(in Worthing).
Republic of Ireland: Ferry; McGee, Lally, O'Donnell (Mulvenna 72), McGowan, Finn, Harte, Deegan, McEniff (Bracken 72), Nolan, Kileen.
Wales: Kendall; Keddie, Jones D, Jones G, Thomas (Moore 46), Bale, Davies N, Fowler, Davies L, Harris, Roberts P (Evans 68).

ENGLAND NATIONAL GAME XI 2005–06

16 Nov

Belgium 0

England 2 *(Bishop 18, Carey-Bertram 66)*

(in Wavre).
England: Robinson (Jones P 85); Mkandawire, Charnock, Perkins (Brown 90), Oli (Mackail-Smith 72), Craney, Wales, Carr, Boyd (Jones B 89), Bishop, Slabber (Carey-Bertram 60).

16 Feb

England 3 *(Bishop 4, Blackburn 78, Mackail-Smith 85)*

Italy 1 *(Ferrario 33)* 3025

(at Cambridge United).
England: Jalal (Jones P 86); Blackburn, Mkandawire, Charnock, Perkins, Baker (Mackail-Smith 46), Carr (Bridges 62), Craney, Boyd, Shaw (Roberts 55), Bishop (Austin 86).

FA SCHOOLS & YOUTH GAMES 2005–06

ENGLAND UNDER-20

Howard, Smith (Arsenal); Agbonlahor, Cahill (Aston Villa); Flinders (Barnsley); Hall, Kilkenny (Birmingham C); Barker, Taylor A (Blackburn R); Ashton (Charlton Ath); Jones B (Crewe Alex); Borrowdale (Crystal Palace); Doyle (Derby Co); Hopkins (Everton); Fontaine (Fulham); Fry (Hull C); Raven (Liverpool); Croft (Manchester C); Graham, Morrison (Middlesbrough); Martin (Milton Keynes D); Henderson (Norwich C); Nugent (Preston NE); Hoskins (Rotherham U); Nix, Ross (Sheffield U); Blackstock, Cranie (Southampton); Leadbitter (Sunderland); Ifil (Tottenham H); Chaplow (WBA); Riley (Wolverhampton W).

16 Aug

Russia 4 *(Logkin 26, Semen 36, Valeryi 70, Luchenko 82)*

England 0

(in Moscow).
England: Flinders (Howard 46); Jones B, Taylor A (Doyle 46), Hall, Fontaine (Ashton 46), Riley, Hoskins, Ross (Fry 46), Nugent, Nix (Hopkins 73), Barker (Agbonlahor 46).

9 Oct

England 2 *(Leadbitter 61, Blackstock 73)*

Holland 2 *(Schilder 51, Zoontjes 86)* 6851

(at Burnley).
England: Flinders (Martin 46); Ifil (Raven 75), Borrowdale, Cahill, Cranie, Morrison (Hoskins 62), Chaplow, Leadbitter, Smith R (Croft 82), Kilkenny (Henderson 46), Graham (Blackstock 46).

ENGLAND UNDER-19

Connolly, Gilbert, Smith, Walcott (Arsenal); Garner, (Blackburn R); Ashton, Walker, Weston (Charlton Ath); Grant, Mancienne, Smith J (Chelsea); Jones B, Roberts G (Crewe Alex); Ainsworth, Doyle, Holmes (Derby Co); Clarke T (Huddersfield T); Parker, Rothery, Walton (Leeds U); Porter, Stearman (Leicester C); Guthrie (Liverpool); Richards (Manchester C); Campbell, Jones R (Manchester U); Johnson, Knight, McMahon, Morrison, Taylor AD, Wheater (Middlesbrough); Martin (Milton Keynes D); Ryan Jarvis, Lewis (Norwich C); Ashikodi (Rangers); Golbourne (Reading); Hart (Shrewsbury T); Blackstock, Cranie, Dyer, Mills (Southampton); Alnwick, Leadbitter (Sunderland); Ifil (Tottenham H); Fryatt (Walsall); Nicholson (WBA); Ephraim, Noble, Reid (West Ham U); Davies (Wolverhampton W).

18 July

France 1 *(Balde 19)*

England 1 *(Fryatt 9)*

(in Belfast).
England: Martin; McMahon, Mills, Cranie, Taylor AD, Leadbitter, Noble, Jarvis (Blackstock 69), Morrison (Smith 72), Fryatt (Jones R 89), Holmes.

20 July

England 1 *(Petrosyan 72 (og))*

Armenia 1 *(Lombe 89)*

(in Ballymena).
England: Martin; Taylor AD, Mills, Cranie, Ifil, Leadbitter, Jones R (Jarvis 71), Noble, Holmes, Blackstock (Fryatt 61), Smith.

23 July

England 3 *(Mills 4, Blackstock 80, Wheater 84)*

Norway 2 *(Aoudia 23, Hanssen 79)*

(in Newry).
England: Martin; Ifil (Wheater 73), Mills, Cranie, Taylor AD, Leadbitter, Noble (Jones R 56), Jarvis (Blackstock 46), Morrison, Fryatt, Holmes.

26 July

Serbia & Montenegro 1 *(Marinkovic 87)*

England 3 *(Fryatt 18, 81, 90)*

(in Lurgan).
England: Martin; McMahon, Mills, Cranie, Taylor AD, Jones R, Leadbitter, Noble (Jarvis 46), Morrison, Fryatt, Holmes.

29 July

England 1 *(Holmes 43)*

France 3 *(Chakouri 56, Balde 75, Gouffran 88)* 4723

(in Belfast).
England: Martin; McMahon, Mills, Cranie, Taylor AD, Jones R (Jarvis 79), Leadbitter, Noble, Morrison (Smith 66), Fryatt (Blackstock 78), Holmes.

6 Sept

England 3 *(Clarke 5, Walker 39, Smith J 52)*

Belgium 2 *(Derijck 27, 76 (pen))* 3123

(at Darlington).
England: Alnwick (Hart 46); Gilbert, Stearman, Clarke (Mancienne 46), Golbourne (Parker 76), Reid (Dyer 66), Smith J, Roberts G, Johnson, Ephraim (Guthrie 58), Walker (Campbell 46).

7 Oct

England 1 *(Smith J 30)*

Czech Republic 2 *(Blazek 53, 82)*

(in Poznan).
England: Lewis; Jones B, Parker, Roberts G, Walton, Wheater, Holmes, Davies (Grant 16), Walker (Garner 57), Smith J (Mancienne 87), Johnson (Weston 80).

9 Oct

Poland A 0

England 2 *(Holmes 10, Rothery 50)*

(in Poznan).
England: Knight; Ashton, Jones B, Parker, Roberts G (Johnson 90), Holmes, Rothery, Weston, Garner, Smith J.

11 Oct

Poland B 2 *(Trytko 44, Napierata 75)*

England 1 *(Roberts G 39)*

England: Lewis; Parker, Walton, Wheater, Ashton, Smith J (Roberts G 20), Weston, Rothery, Johnson, Walker, Garner.

16 Nov

England 2 *(Ashikodi 68, 83)*

Switzerland 0

(at Wycombe).
England: Alnwick (Hart); Jones B (Doyle), Parker, Roberts G (Rothery), Richards, Wheater, Dyer (Porter), Grant, Garner (Ashikodi), Noble (Stearman), Johnson.

28 Feb

England 3 *(Holmes 43, Ashikodi 75, Walcott 80 (pen))*

Slovakia 0 6679

(at Northampton).
England: Hart (Lewis 46); Doyle, Golbourne (Ashton 46), Smith J (Rothery 65), Wheater, Clarke (Walton 46), Dyer (Ainsworth 60), Grant, Walcott, Holmes (Ashikodi 65), Johnson.

18 May

Belgium 2 *(Vermeulen 6, Legear 68)*

England 1 *(Garner 71)*

(in Tournai).
England: Hart; Jones B, Parker, Wheater (Connolly), Richards, Roberts, Davies, Johnson, Holmes, Dyer, Garner (Nicholson).

20 May

England (2) *(Holmes 40, Roberts 88)*

Northern Ireland 1 *(Catney R 78)*

(in Tubize).
England: Hart; Jones B, Parker, Connolly, Richards (Ashton 30), Roberts, Davies, Johnson, Smith J, Holmes (Dyer 90), Ashikodi (Garner 70).

22 May

England (0)

Serbia & Montenegro 1 *(Durisic 55)*

(in Tournai).
England: Hart; Jones B, Parker, Connolly, Wheater, Roberts, Davies, Johnson, Smith J, Holmes, Garner.

ENGLAND UNDER-18

Muamba, Simpson (Arsenal); Jones Z (Blackburn R); Sissons (Bolton W); Sullivan (Brighton & HA); Williams (Bristol C); Weston (Charlton Ath); Mancienne (Chelsea); Gooding (Coventry C); Straker (Crystal Palace); Barnes, Hanson (Derby Co); Phelan (Everton); Omozusi, Sankoh, Watts (Fulham); Mullan (Manchester U); Cattermole (Middlesbrough); Ryan Jarvis (Norwich C); Lallana (Southampton); Dowson (Sunderland); Davis, Mills, Riley (Tottenham H); Demontagnac (Walsall); Daniels (WBA); Ephraim (West Ham U); Little (Wolverhampton W).

15 Nov

Turkey 1 *(Yilmaz 31)*

England 0

(in Mersin).
England: Sullivan (Jones Z 85); Little (Omozusi 70), Straker (Riley 77), Cattermole, Mills, Mancienne, Barnes (Phelan 62), Muamba (Gooding 81), Demontagnac (Sankoh 56), Ephraim (Mullan 81), Weston.

17 Apr

England 2 *(Lallana 42, Phelan 56)*

Slovenia 1 *(Matavz 64)* 9594

(at Bournemouth).
England: Daniels (Jones Z 46); Omozusi, Straker (Watts 46), Mancienne, Rossi Jarvis, Muamba, Simpson (Davis 46) (Hanson 72), Ephraim, Weston (Sissons 67), Lallana (Dowson 67), Williams (Phelan 46).

ENGLAND UNDER-17

Rodgers, Randall (Arsenal); Clark (Aston Villa); Aluko (Birmingham C); Arestidou (Blackburn R); Wright, Yussuff (Charlton Ath); Bertrand, Cork, Sinclair, (Chelsea); Obadeyi (Coventry C); Ashton, Richards (Derby Co); Connor, Kissock, Molyneux (Everton); Smithies (Huddersfield T); Robinson, Upson (Ipswich T); Chambers, Magunda (Leicester C); Nardiello (Liverpool); Sturridge (Manchester C); Amos, Brandy (Manchester U); Porritt, Walker (Middlesbrough); Mills, Thomson, Walcott (Southampton); Chandler, Kay (Sunderland); Button (Tottenham H); Hales, Spence, Tomkins (West Ham U).

2 Aug

England 3 *(Ashton 42, Chandler 45, Mills 52)*

Finland 2 *(Pelvas 28, Minkenen 58)*

(in Reykjavik).
England: Arestidou; Robinson, Magunda, Spence, Rodgers, Chandler, Wright, Thompson (Richards 58), Porritt (Chambers 62), Ashton, Connor (Mills 51).

3 Aug

Faeroes 0

England 7 *(Chambers 14, 52, 54, Thompson 17 (pen), Spence 47, Ashton 72, Porritt 76)*

(in Kopavogur).
England: Smithies; Robinson (Rodgers 41), Spence (Magunda 67), Kay, Thompson, Chandler (Porritt 41), Richards, Randall, Connor (Wright 55), Chambers (Ashton 61), Mills (Hales 41).

5 Aug

England 2 *(Ashton 63, Magunda 74)*

Sweden 0

(in Akranes).
England: Arestidou; Robinson (Kay 78), Chandler, Magunda, Rodgers, Wright (Thompson 74), Spence, Hales (Randall 78), Porritt (Mills 68), Ashton (Richards 79), Connor (Chambers 63).

7 Aug

Republic of Ireland 2 *(Lyons 8, Sheridan 80)*

England 0

(in Reykjavik).
England: Smithies; Kay (Thompson 77), Chandler, Magunda, Rodgers (Robinson 72), Randall, Spence, Richards (Connor 72), Porritt, Ashton, Mills (Chambers 54).

31 Aug

England 3 *(Porritt 13, Sturridge 47, 62)*

Portugal 1 *(Matias 73)* 3370

(at Bristol City).
England: Button; Rodgers, Tomkins, Walker, Molyneux, Walcott, Wright (Thompson 62), Kissock (Randall 67), Chandler, Porritt (Nardiello 72), Sturridge.

2 Sept

England 0

USA 1 *(Williams 30)*

(at Swindon Town).
England: Amos; Tomkins, Walker, Brandy (Wright 15), Randall (Kissock 55), Sturridge, Nardiello (Porritt 60), Walcott, Cork, Magunda, Thompson.

4 Sept

England 1 *(Chandler 67)*

Italy 2 *(Palumbo 22, Tagliani 65)* 2534

(at Cheltenham).
England: Button; Rodgers, Cork, Tomkins, Molyneux, Kissock (Thomson 64), Randall (Walcott 53), Walker, Chandler, Porritt, Nardiello (Sturridge 46).

2 Nov

France 2 *(Pied 13, Obertan 51)*

England 2 *(Sturridge 18, 33)* 900

(in Mondorf-les-Bains).
England: Button; Molyneux, Tomkins, Walker, Yussuff (Richards 61), Chandler, Magunda, Cork, Aluko (Thomson 70), Sturridge, Sinclair.

13 Dec

England 1 *(Sturridge 80)*

Turkey 0

(at Notts County).
England: Button (Amos 40); Thomson, Clark, Chandler, Tomkins, Walker, Hales (Magunda 52), Upson (Richards 40), Sturridge, Ashton (Nardiello 70), Aluko (Obadeyi 65).

28 Mar

England 2 *(Thomson 25, 27)*

Italy 2 *(Mustacchio 24, Marconi 74)* 5165

(at Huddersfield).
England: Button; Cork, Tomkins, Clark, Bertrand, Thomson (Molyneux 74), Walker, Chandler (Wright 78), Sinclair, Brandy, Sturridge.

30 Mar

England 0

Bulgaria 0 4225

(at Barnsley).
England: Button; Cork, Clark, Tomkins, Bertrand, Thomson, Wright (Chandler 55), Walker, Porritt (Brandy 55), Sinclair (Nardiello 67), Sturridge.

1 Apr

England 1 *(Nardiello 5)*

Russia 2 *(Gorbatenko 13, Fomine 21)*

(at Scunthorpe).
England: Button; Cork, Molyneux, Clark, Rodgers (Thomson 40), Richards (Wright 53), Chandler, Walker, Sinclair, Nardiello, Sturridge.

ENGLAND UNDER-16

SKY SPORTS VICTORY SHIELD

Barnett, Lansbury, Murphy (Arsenal); Clancy, Parish (Aston Villa); Etheridge, Ofori, Taiwo, Woods (Chelsea); Moses (Crystal Palace); Broadbent, Smithies (Huddersfield T); Darville, Elliott, Rose (Leeds U); Chambers, Mattock (Leicester C); Norwood, Welbeck, Woods (Manchester U); Franks, Porritt, Steele (Middlesbrough); Reid (Nottingham F); Askham (Sheffield U); Asayile, Fraser-Allen (Tottenham H); Brookes, Harvey, Spence (West Ham U).

14 Oct

England 4 *(Franks 22, 46, Chambers 59, Rose 80)*

Wales 0

(at Telford).
England: Smithies; Ofori, Mattock (Brooks 65), Woods, Spence, Clancy, Franks, Lansbury (Harvey 46), Chambers, Asayile (Rose 46), Porritt (Welbeck 70).

3 Nov

England 0

Northern Ireland 1 *(Evans 80)* 1109

(at Chester).
England: Etheridge; Ofori, Reid, Brooks, Spence, Woods, Askham (Chambers 46), Harvey, Porritt, Mattock, Broadbent (Moses 67), Taiwo (Lansbury 46).

25 Nov

Scotland 1 *(Glen 1)*

England 2 *(Perry 27 (og), Porritt 58)*

(at Kilmarnock).
England: Woods; Barnett (Mattock 40), Brookes (Ofori 79), Moses (Asajile 80), Murphy, Porritt, Rose, Spence, Taiwo, Darville, Franks.

FRIENDLIES

22 Feb

Belgium 1 *(Dyck 33)*

England 2 *(Chambers 46 (pen), Harvey 54)*

(in Heist).
England: Woods (Parrish 41); Darville (Reid 41), Barnett, Norwood (Ofori 41), Spence (Harvey 46), Mattock, Fraser-Allen (Clancy 41), Lansbury, Chambers, Rose, Franks.

12 Apr*

England 2 *(Rose 2, 16)*

China 0

(in Mouilleron Le Captif).
England: Steele; Ofori, Reid, Spence, Franks, Murphy (Chambers 74), Woods (Taiwo 61), Rose (Elliott 68), Barnett (Mattock 44), Clancy, Lansbury (Harvey 27).

13 Apr*

England 0

France 1 *(Sakho 69)*

(in Mouilleron Le Captif).
England: Smithies; Ofori, Reid, Taiwo (Harvey 65), Spence, Mattock, Franks, Murphy, Woods, Rose, Chambers.

15 Apr*

England 1 *(Chambers 45)*

Tunisia 2

(in Montaigu).
England: Smithies; Spence (Mattock 54), Franks (Murphy 68), Harvey (Taiwo 40), Woods, Rose, Elliott (Chambers 40), Barnett, Clancy, Lansbury, Brookes (Ofori 72).

17 Apr*

England 1 *(Murphy 74)*

Japan 1

England won 4-3 on penalties.
(in Bouffere).
England: Smithies; Ofori, Reid (Brookes 74), Taiwo (Harvey 69), Mattock, Franks, Murphy, Chambers, Barnett (Woods 78), Clancy, Lansbury.

* Montaigu Tournament.

WOMEN'S FOOTBALL 2005-06

The domestic story of last term as it has been over the past few years is one of Arsenal triumphs. Like a hydrofoil powerfully gliding through the choppy waters of cups and league they were again the dominant force in women's football and had another tremendous season.

They started off on 5 August 2005 with a 4-0 victory over close rivals Charlton Athletic to lift the FA Women's Community Shield with a brace from Jayne Ludlow. When on 13 April 2006 they again defeated Charlton this time by 2-0 they became Premier League Champions for the third successive season. Not content with that, on the following 1 May they trounced a plucky Leeds United 5-0 to win the FA Women's Cup and to achieve the second highest scoreline in the Final. However, it failed to match the 8-2 margin by which Southampton Ladies beat QPR in 1978 but was still an awesome display. The goals came firstly through an unfortunate own goal by Lucy Ward in only the third minute from which the side never recovered and further strikes by Julie Fleeting, Rachel Yankey with a free kick, Kelly Smith with a penalty and Lianne Sanderson completed the scoring.

Charlton did prove that the Gunners were not invincible when on 5 March they defeated them 2-1 to win the FA Nationwide Women's Premier League Cup. Their young star in the making, Eni Aluko, netted twice in the 28th and 45th minutes, whilst Julie Fleeting pulled one back in the 76th minute. Aluko deservedly won the player of the match award in what was Charlton's second ever trophy, they having won the FA Cup last season. The above results determine that Arsenal completed their eighth League Championship in 14 seasons coupled with seven FA Cup victories.

For the remainder of the League scene, Sunderland and Chelsea just hung on to their Premier League status having to take part in the play-off system which is utilised to determine promotion and relegation. In a two-leg series Chelsea defeated Liverpool 4-1 on aggregate whilst Sunderland and Bristol City finished on a 5-5 aggregate but the Black Cats survived on the away goals rule. Sadly Fulham Ladies have dropped a little off the pace since again becoming part-time, having once been the only full-time outfit. They finished third from bottom in the League.

However it was all smiles for one club, in that Cardiff Ladies won the National League Southern Division which means they are now going to play in the top level next term. They became only the second Welsh Club to achieve this level. Barry Town actually played two seasons there between 2001 and 2003 but unfortunately were subsequently relegated and had the further misfortune through lack of players to have to fold. Cardiff topped the table only on goal difference, albeit by 15 goals, from runners-up Bristol City. The club were also good enough to annexe the Welsh Cup and that for the fourth successive season, beating Pwllheli Ladies 11-0 thus ensuring themselves a place alongside Arsenal in next season's Women's UEFA Cup.

Internationally England's teams go from strength to strength and there is now a very real possibility that in the next few years they could win something major in the women's game. The senior side under their coach Hope Powell played nine games and at the end of the season topped the World Cup qualifying group defeating Hungary on the way, in their own backyard, a record 13-0. England used 22 players and Rachel Unitt, the Everton left-back, was voted the England Women's Player of the Year.

In nine games from September 2005 England was unbeaten and Unitt scored one in a friendly with Sweden. The Under-21 side coached by Brent Hills also did well, whilst the Under-19's after a bright start lost to Denmark and were eliminated from the UEFA European Championship. However their coach Mo Marley, who has had so much to do with the rise of Everton Ladies, indicated that there were many positives to be taken from the last 12 months, not the least of which is the chance to upgrade the best girls to the Under-21 and full senior side next season. By the same token the best of the Under-17 squad will also gain promotion to more senior teams and they had the satisfaction of winning the Nationwide Tournament in April by beating Scotland 2-0.

Overall football remains the top female sport in the country with five teams out of ten in the National Division actually paying their players, but this by no means is intended to suggest those are full time professionals. However, the English FA is working towards the goal of professionalising the game which it believes will become inevitable. Currently 34 teams participate in the FA Nationwide Women's Premier League's three divisions, i.e. National, Northern and Southern divisions.

From observation there is no doubt that with improved coaching the enthusiasm and the willingness to learn, some girls, certainly at under-15 level could easily compete for capability with boys of the same age. Furthermore this is being recognised in the number of additional Leagues and Cups being set-up each year at junior level, whilst the number of spectators watching senior matches also continues to rise.

Apart from Rachel Unitt's Nationwide International Player of the Year honour, there were as usual a number of annual awards for the women's game. The full list is as follows:

THE UMBRO TOP GOALSCORER, NORTHERN DIVISION
Vicky Abbott – Tranmere Rovers

THE UMBRO TOP GOALSCORER, SOUTHERN DIVISION
Helen Lander – Watford

THE UMBRO TOP GOALSCORER, NATIONAL DIVISION
Kelly Smith – Arsenal

THE FA YOUNG PLAYER OF THE YEAR
Karen Carney – Birmingham City

BBC CLUB MEDIA AWARD
Nottingham Forest

THE FA CLUB MARKETING AWARD
Leeds United

NATIONWIDE MANAGER OF THE YEAR
Andrew McNally – Blackburn Rovers

NATIONWIDE CLUB OF THE YEAR
Newcastle United

SKY SPORTS NEWS BEST PROGRAMME AWARD
Nottingham Forest

THE FA FAIR PLAY AWARD
West Ham United

THE FA NATIONAL MEDIA AWARD
Women's Soccer Scene

THE FA REGIONAL MEDIA AWARD
Birmingham Evening Mail

NATIONWIDE INTERNATIONAL PLAYER OF THE YEAR
(voted by visitors to TheFA.com) – Rachel Unitt

THE FA SPECIAL ACHIEVEMENT AWARD
Sue Hector – Birmingham City Ladies

NATIONWIDE PLAYERS' PLAYER OF THE YEAR
(voted for by the players) Kelly Smith – Arsenal

KEN GOLDMAN

WOMEN'S PREMIER LEAGUE 2005–06

NATIONAL DIVISION

	P	W	D	L	F	A	GD	Pts
Arsenal	18	16	2	0	83	20	63	50
Everton	18	14	2	2	46	20	26	44
Charlton Athletic	18	12	3	3	41	13	28	39
Doncaster Rovers B	18	7	2	9	32	34	–2	23
Bristol Academy	18	4	8	6	19	29	–10	20
Birmingham City	18	6	2	10	24	40	–16	20
Leeds United	18	4	6	8	27	36	–9	18
Fulham	18	4	2	12	24	45	–21	14
Sunderland	18	3	4	11	22	57	–35	13
Chelsea	18	3	3	12	22	46	–24	12

NORTHERN DIVISION

	P	W	D	L	F	A	GD	Pts
Blackburn Rovers	22	20	2	0	55	12	43	62
Liverpool	22	15	3	4	39	17	22	48
Tranmere Rovers	22	13	4	5	41	29	12	43
Lincoln City	22	11	3	8	40	31	9	36
Nottingham Forest	22	8	6	8	33	30	3	30
Wolverhampton W	22	6	10	6	29	33	–4	28
Aston Villa	22	8	2	12	33	38	–5	26
Newcastle United	22	6	7	9	32	33	–1	25
Stockport County	22	5	7	10	24	31	–7	22
Curzon Ashton	22	4	6	12	27	64	–37	18
Manchester City	22	3	7	12	19	31	–12	16
Middlesbrough	22	3	3	16	18	41	–23	12

SOUTHERN DIVISION

	P	W	D	L	F	A	GD	Pts
Cardiff City	22	14	7	1	53	17	36	49
Bristol City	22	16	1	5	51	30	21	49
Watford	22	14	5	3	59	28	31	47
Portsmouth	22	12	4	6	58	39	19	40
Millwall Lionesses	22	11	5	6	51	31	20	38
West Ham United	22	8	4	10	31	33	–2	28
AFC Wimbledon	22	8	3	11	39	52	–13	27
Reading Royals	22	7	2	13	34	42	–8	23
Crystal Palace	22	7	1	14	38	52	–14	22
Southampton Saints	22	6	0	16	30	70	–40	18
Brighton & Hove A	22	4	5	13	33	53	–20	17
Langford	22	4	5	13	30	60	–30	17

NATIONAL DIVISION LEAGUE – PREVIOUS WINNERS

1992–93	Arsenal
1993–94	Doncaster Belles
1994–95	Arsenal
1995–96	Croydon
1996–97	Arsenal
1997–98	Everton
1998–99	Croydon
1999–00	Croydon
2000–01	Arsenal
2001–02	Arsenal
2002–03	Fulham
2003–04	Arsenal
2004–05	Arsenal
2005–06	Arsenal

THE FA WOMEN'S CUP 2005–06
IN PARTNERSHIP WITH NATIONWIDE

PRELIMINARY ROUND

Braintree Town v Eastbourne Borough 3-2
Basildon Town v Crowborough Athletic 0-2

FIRST QUALIFYING ROUND

Bradford City v Buxton 7-1
Barnsley v Darlington RA 5-0
Liverpool Manweb Feds v Warrington Town 4-0
Darwen v Macclesfield Town 10-0
Bury Girls & Ladies v Wigan 4-0
Durham City v Teesside Athletic 0-6
Blyth Town v Wakefield Hall Green 3-2
Lumley Ladies v Killingworth YPC 11-1
Ossett Albion v Morley Spurs 0-4
Penrith United v Windscale 2-4
Denton Town v Gateshead Cleveland Hall 3-1
York City v Kirklees 11-0
Bolton Ambassadors v Blyth Spartans 2-6
Huddersfield Town v Bolton Wanderers 6-2
Walsall v Notts County 4-4
Walsall won 4-3 on penalties.
Rushcliff Eagles v Creswell Wanderers 5-0
Cambridge Rangers v Dudley United 1-5
Loughborough Dynamo v Cambridge University 3-1
Corby S&L v AFC Telford United Ladies 2-4
Kettering Town v Birstall FL&E Ladies 5-4
Stoke City v University of Birmingham 0-1
South Notts v Colchester Town 5-0
Tamworth Lionesses v Copsewood (Coventry) 0-2
Southam United v Kirkley 7-0
Kettering United v Solihull Ladies 1-9
Broughton Rangers v Sandiacre Town 6-4
Leicester City Women's v Cambridge United 5-0
Florence v Peterborough 1-0
Wyrley v Stratford Town 5-1
Peterborough Azure v Lichfield Diamonds 2-5
Clapton Orient v Lewes 1-2
Upper Beeding v Barking 1-4
Thatcham Town v Braintree Town 3-1
Chelmsford City v Abbey Rangers 3-2
London Women v Woodbridge Town 0-3
Wycombe Wanderers v Harlow Athletic 3-1
AFC Kempston Rovers v Littlehampton Town 3-2
Hastings United w.o. v Leighton Linslade *withdrew*
Sawbridgeworth Town v Tottenham Hotspur 1-0
Lordswood v Aylesbury United 7-0
MK Wanderers v Gravesend & Northfleet 2-3
Concord Rangers v Hendon 0-2
Aylesbury Vale v Haywards Heath Town 2-3
Hoddesdon Owls v Crowborough Athletic 0-1
Tring Athletic v Acton Sports Club 1-3
Thurrock & Tilbury v Swale Magpies 0-4
Dynamo North London v Croydon Athletic 4-3
Banbury United v Brentwood Town 3-2
Eastbourne Town v Whitehawk 0-9
Henley Town v UKP 6-5

Billericay v Saffron Walden Town 2-1
Met Ladies v Newport Pagnell Town 1-3
Haringey Borough v Kent Magpies 7-3
Launton v Staines Town 0-10
Slough v Brentford 3-2
AFC Newbury Ladies v Kings Sports 4-1
Carterton v Corinthian Casuals 2-2
Carterton won 3-1 on penalties.
Battersea v Woking 1-2
Aldershot Town v Stevenage Borough 3-1
Dover Athletic v Arlesey Town 5-3
Launceston v Penzance 2-4
Worcester City v Yeovil Town 0-5
Hereford Pegasus v Brize Norton 9-0
Mansfield Road v Ross Town 2-3
Ilminster Town v Saltash United 1-6
Exeter City v Frome Town 1-2
Reading v Chinnor Youth Ladies 4-2
Gloucester City v Alphington 12-0
Team Bath v Central 3-2
Bath City v Holway United 5-2
Shanklin v St Peter's 2-0
AFC Bournemouth Ladies v Poole Town 5-1

SECOND QUALIFYING ROUND
Windscale v Barnsley 1-3
Liverpool Manweb Feds v Bury Girls & Ladies 3-5
York City v Denton Town 2-2
York City won 5-4 on penalties.
Teesside Athletic v Morley Spurs 1-7
Huddersfield Town v Darwen 4-0
Lumley Ladies v Blyth Spartans 1-3
Blyth Town v Bradford City 4-3
Florence v Broughton Rangers 2-1
Dudley United v Lichfield Diamonds 2-3
Rushcliffe Eagles v Kettering Town 1-2
Copsewood (Coventry) v Solihull Ladies 1-2
Wyrley v Walsall 4-2
Southam United v AFC Telford United Ladies 2-3
South Notts v University of Birmingham 1-3
Loughborough Dynamo v Leicester City Women's 0-6
Swale Magpies v Wycombe Wanderers 5-1
Henley Town v Dynamo North London 0-1
Hendon v Woodbridge Town 2-4
AFC Newbury Ladies v Lewes 2-6
Chelmsford City v Newport Pagnell Town 9-0
Sawbridgeworth Town v Whitehawk 2-4
Crowborough Athletic v Barking 2-0
Billericay v Lordswood 2-1
Staines Town v Acton Sports Club 4-2
Aldershot Town v Thatcham Town 2-3
Gravesend & Northfleet v Carterton 6-1
Slough v Haywards Heath Town 5-0
Haringey Borough v Banbury United 10-1
AFC Kempston Rovers v Woking 1-2
Hastings United v Dover Athletic 9-2
Gloucester City v Team Bath 2-3
Bath City v Frome Town 2-4
Penzance v Saltash United 11-0
Ross Town v Hereford Pegasus 3-4
Reading v Yeovil Town 0-7
Shanklin v AFC Bournemouth Ladies 1-1
Shanklin won 4-2 on penalties.

FIRST ROUND
Blyth Town v Leeds City Vixens 4-6
Florence v Morley Spurs 2-3
Bury Girls & Ladies v Huddersfield Town 2-4
Crewe v York City 1-2
Scunthorpe United v Garswood Saints 0-0
Garswood Saints won 4-2 on penalties.
Rotherham United v Chester City 6-1
Barnsley v Blyth Spartans 1-2
Blackpool Wren Rovers v Sheffield Wednesday 1-7
Doncaster Parkland Rovers v Chester-le-Street Town 0-2
Preston North End v South Durham Royals 8-0
University of Birmingham v Long Eaton Villa 1-5
Leicester City Women's v Solihull Ladies 12-1
Lichfield Diamonds v Wyrley 4-2
Ipswich Town v Kettering Town 7-0
Norwich City Ladies v Leicester City Ladies 0-0
Leicester City Ladies won 6-5 on penalties.
Northampton Town v Coventry City 2-1
TNS Ladies v AFC Telford United Ladies 8-0
Chesterfield v Shrewsbury Town 2-1
Leafield Athletic Triplex v Derby County 5-4
Loughborough Students v Stafford Rangers 7-0
Dagenham & Redbridge v Chelmsford City 5-2
Enfield Town v Luton Town Belles 3-1
Colchester United v Dynamo North London 7-0
Woodbridge Town v Slough 2-3
Crowborough Athletic v Queens Park Rangers 0-4
Lewes v Thatcham Town 7-0
Chesham United v Barnet FC Ladies 3-4
Sophtlogic v Bedford Town Belles 4-2
Haringey Borough v Staines Town 2-5
Billericay v Hastings United 1-6
Whitehawk v Swale Magpies 3-1
Gillingham v Leyton Orient 1-2
Gravesend & Northfleet v Woking 4-0
Keynsham Town v Shanklin 4-1
Oxford City v Frome Town 2-4
Forest Green Rovers v Newton Abbot 1-0
Plymouth Argyle v Hereford Pegasus 0-4
Penzance v Clevedon Town 2-1
Swindon Town v Yeovil Town 1-0
Newquay AFC Ladies v Team Bath 5-3

SECOND ROUND
Sheffield Wednesday v Rotherham United 1-2
Leeds City Vixens v York City 6-1
Morley Spurs v Huddersfield Town 0-0
Huddersfield Town won 4-2 on penalties.
Blyth Spartans v Chester-le-Street Town 3-2
Preston North End v Garswood Saints 8-1
Chesterfield v Northampton Town 0-2
Long Eaton Villa v Ipswich Town 3-3
Ipswich Town won 5-4 on penalties.
Leicester City Women's v Lichfield Diamonds 3-2
TNS Ladies v Leafield Athletic Triplex 1-1
TNS Ladies won 3-1 on penalties.
Loughborough Students v Leicester City Ladies 1-2
Whitehawk v Enfield Town 3-0
Sophtlogic v Staines Town 1-4
Gravesend & Northfleet v Colchester United 0-1
Queens Park Rangers v Lewes 6-0
Leyton Orient v Hastings United 5-3
Barnet FC Ladies v Dagenham & Redbridge 1-0
Hereford Pegasus v Penzance 3-0
Newquay AFC Ladies v Keynsham Town 1-5
Slough v Forest Green Rovers 1-0
Frome Town v Swindon Town 6-1

THIRD ROUND
Leeds City Vixens v Rotherham United 5-1
Blackburn Rovers v Lincoln City 3-1
Newcastle United v Huddersfield Town 7-2
Middlesbrough v Manchester City 1-2
Liverpool v Tranmere Rovers 2-1
Preston North End v Stockport County 1-2
Curzon Ashton v Blyth Spartans 6-0
Nottingham Forest v Leicester City Women's 3-1
Aston Villa v Wolverhampton Wanderers 1-0
Northampton Town v TNS Ladies 2-1
Ipswich Town v Leicester City Ladies 2-0
Colchester United v Staines Town 3-2
AFC Wimbledon v Crystal Palace 3-1
Watford v Queens Park Rangers 3-0
Portsmouth v Millwall Lionesses 2-1
Langford v Whitehawk 2-1
Barnet FC Ladies v West Ham United 4-1
Brighton & Hove Albion v Leyton Orient 3-0
Cardiff City v Keynsham Town 2-0
Reading Royals v Bristol City 0-1
After abandoned game due to fog, 2-4
Southampton Saints v Slough 3-1
Hereford Pegasus v Frome Town 3-3
Frome Town won 3-1 on penalties.

FOURTH ROUND
Leeds City Vixens v Aston Villa 4-5
Bristol City v Charlton Athletic 1-4
Leeds United v Doncaster Rovers Belles 2-1
Cardiff City v Arsenal 1-4
Fulham v Southampton Saints 6-0
Everton v Nottingham Forest 2-0
Liverpool v Colchester United 1-0
Sunderland AFC Ladies v Curzon Ashton 2-2
Curzon Ashton won 4-3 on penalties.
Manchester City v Barnet FC Ladies 0-2
AFC Wimbledon v Watford 1-3
Portsmouth v Bristol Academy 5-5
Bristol Academy won 6-5 on penalties.
Blackburn Rovers v Chelsea 1-2
Newcastle United v Northampton Town 3-1
Langford v Brighton & Hove Albion 0-1
Ipswich Town v Birmingham City 0-7
Stockport County v Frome Town 7-1

FIFTH ROUND

Fulham v Charlton Athletic	0-3
Brighton & Hove Albion v Bristol Academy	1-2
Barnet FC Ladies v Liverpool	2-3
Leeds United v Everton	3-1
Watford v Chelsea	0-1
Stockport County v Birmingham City	0-2
Newcastle United v Curzon Ashton	2-0
Aston Villa v Arsenal	0-3

SIXTH ROUND

Birmingham City v Leeds United	1-3
Chelsea v Arsenal	1-6
Bristol Academy v Charlton Athletic	0-5
Newcastle United v Liverpool	2-2
Liverpool won 9-8 on penalties.	

SEMI-FINALS

Leeds United v Liverpool	2-0
Arsenal v Charlton Athletic	2-1

THE FA WOMEN'S CUP FINAL (at Upton Park)

Monday, 1 May 2006

Arsenal 5 *(Ward 3 (og), Fleeting 34, Yankey 35, Smith 73 (pen), Sanderson 77)*

Leeds United 0 13,452

Arsenal: Byrne; Scott (Daniels 84), Champ, Ludlow (Grant 73), White, Phillip (McArthur 78), Asante, Smith, Fleeting, Yankey, Sanderson.

Leeds United: Fay; Cook (Walton 52), Culvin, Emmanuel, Haigh, Ward, Clarke, Burke, Walker (Panesar 85), Preston (Owen 85), Smith.

Referee: P. Crossley (Kent).

THE FA NATIONWIDE PREMIER LEAGUE CUP 2005–06

FIRST ROUND

AFC Wimbledon v West Ham	5-2
Arsenal v Wolverhampton Wanderers	5-0
Aston Villa v Everton	4-6
Blackburn Rovers v Curzon Ashton	5-0
Cardiff v Sunderland	1-5
Chelsea v Bristol City	3-5
Doncaster Rovers Belles v Liverpool	2-2
Doncaster Rovers Belles won 4-3 on penalties.	
Fulham v Manchester City	1-1
Manchester City won 6-5 on penalties.	
Leeds United v Bristol Academy	1-2
Millwall Lionesses v Nottingham Forest	1-0
Newcastle United v Middlesbrough	3-4
Portsmouth v Crystal Palace	1-0
Stockport County v Birmingham City	0-4
Tranmere Rovers v Brighton & Hove Albion	2-0
Watford v Southampton Saints	3-0
Reading Royals v Charlton Athletic	0-6

SECOND ROUND

Tranmere Rovers v Middlesbrough	7-0
Doncaster Rovers Belles v Birmingham City	3-0
Manchester City v Arsenal	0-4
Charlton Athletic v Portsmouth	13-0
AFC Wimbledon v Sunderland	0-3
Watford v Bristol Academy	2-5
Bristol City v Millwall Lionesses	3-2
Everton v Blackburn Rovers	2-0

THIRD ROUND

Arsenal v Bristol City	5-0
Doncaster Rovers Belles v Tranmere Rovers	3-2
Sunderland v Everton	1-3
Charlton Athletic v Bristol Academy	1-0

SEMI-FINALS

Everton v Arsenal	0-2
Doncaster Rovers Belles v Charlton Athletic	0-2

THE FA NATIONWIDE PREMIER LEAGUE CUP FINAL

Arsenal (1) *(Fleeting 76)*

Charlton Athletic (2) *(Aluko 28, 45)* 3506

(at Wycombe).

Arsenal: Byrne; Yankey (Grant 77), Tracy, Ludlow, Phillip, White, Asante, Smith, Sanderson, Fleeting, Scott.

Charlton Athletic: Cope; Stoney, Hickmott, Bertelli, Hills, Chapman, Snare, Pond, Aluko (Hincks 83), Barr, Potter.

Referee: P. Forrester.

UEFA WOMEN'S CUP 2005–06

FIRST QUALIFYING ROUND

GROUP 1
1. Dezembro 0, Montpellier 1
Cardiff 3, Glentoran 0
Montpellier 2, Cardiff 0
Glentoran 0, 1. Decembro 7
Montpellier 8, Glentoran 0
1. Decembro 3, Cardiff 0

GROUP 2
Bardolino 0, Neulengbach 0
Maksimir 0, UCD 2
Neulengbach 5, Maksimir 1
UCD 0, Bardolino 2
Neulengbach 5, UCD 1
Bardolino 3, Maksimir 0

GROUP 3
Saestum 1, Athletic 1
Wezemaal 5, Glasgow City 1
Athletic 3, Wezemaal 0
Glasgow City 0, Saestum 7
Athletic 6, Glasgow City 2
Saestum 2, Wezemaal 1

GROUP 4
United 2, Idrettslag 3
Parnu 1, Valur 8
Idrettslag 9, Parnu 1
Valur 2, United 1
Idrettslag 1, Valur 4
United 2, Parnu 0

GROUP 5
Codru 0, LUwin.ch 4
Shkiponjat 1, KI 1
LUwin.ch 7, Shkiponjat 0
KI 1, Codru 4
LUwin.ch 5, KI 1
Codru 4, Shkiponjat 1

GROUP 6
Vitebsk 0, Sparta 3
Gintra 2, Clujana 2
Sparta 8, Gintra 0
Clujana 2, Vitebsk 2
Sparta 1, Clujana 1
Vitebsk 2, Gintra 0

GROUP 7
M. Holon 0, Wroclaw 1
Kokkinochovion 0, Arsenal Kharkiv 20
Wroclaw 11, Kokkinochovion 0
Arsenal Kharkiv 8, M. Holon 1
Wroclaw 5, Arsenal Kharkiv 0
M. Holon 6, Kokkinochovion 0

GROUP 8
Novo Mesto 0, Toliatti 5
Bratislava 0, Sarajevo 1
Toliatti 6, Bratislava 0
Sarajevo 1, Novo Mesto 0
Toliatti 3, Sarajevo 0
Novo Mesto 1, Bratislava 4

GROUP 9
Alma 2, Aegina 3
Sofia 1, MTK 1
Aegina 1, Sofia 3
MTK 0, Alma 3
Aegina 2, MTK 2
Alma 5, Sofia 0

SECOND QUALIFYING ROUND

GROUP 1
Neulengbach 3, Saestum 4
Potsdam 0, Montpellier 0
Potsdam 2, Saestum 0
Montpellier 4, Neulengbach 0
Neulengbach 1, Potsdam 12
Saestum 1, Montpellier 2

GROUP 2
Nis 0, Djurgaarden/Alvsjo 7
Alma 0, Valur 8
Valur 3, Nis 0
Djurgaarden/Alvsjo 3, Alma 0
Djurgaarden/Alvsjo 2, Valur 1
Nis 3, Alma 5

GROUP 3
Gomrukcu Baku 1, Frankfurt 11
Sparta 1, LUwin.ch 0
Frankfurt 1, Sparta 1
LUwin.ch 5, Gomrukcu Baku 0
Frankfurt 4, LUwin.ch 0
Gomrukcu Baku 0, Sparta 3

GROUP 4
Brondby 1, Arsenal 0
Toliatti 3, Wroclaw 3
Arsenal 1, Toliatti 0
Wroclaw 1, Brondby 3
Arsenal 3, Wroclaw 1
Brondby 2, Toliatti 0

QUARTER-FINALS, FIRST LEG
Sparta 0, Djurgaarden/Alvsjo 2
Valur 1, Potsdam 8
Arsenal 1, Frankfurt 1
Montpellier 3, Brondby 0

QUARTER-FINALS, SECOND LEG
Djurgaarden/Alvsjo 0, Sparta 0
Brondby 1, Montpellier 3
Potsdam 11, Valur 1
Frankfurt 3, Arsenal 1

SEMI-FINALS, FIRST LEG
Frankfurt 0, Montpellier 1
Potsdam 2, Djurgaarden/Alvsjo 3

SEMI-FINALS, SECOND LEG
Montpellier 2, Frankfurt 3
Djurgaarden/Alvsjo 2, Potsdam 5

FINAL
Potsdam 0, Frankfurt 4
Frankfurt 3, Potsdam 2

ENGLAND WOMEN'S INTERNATIONAL MATCHES 2005–06

1 September 2005 (in Amsterdam)
Austria 1 *(Celouch 20)*
England 4 *(Williams 23 (pen), Smith K 35, Barr 55, Smith S 90)* 1700
England: Brown; Scott (Stoney 61), White, Phillip, Unitt, Carny, Chapman, Williams, Potter (Smith S 46), Smith K (Westwood 67), Barr.

27 October 2005 (in Tapolca)
Hungary 0
England 13 *(Smith K 3, Aluko 2, Scott 2, Williams 2, Yankey, Chapman, Handley, Potter).*
England: Brown (Chamberlain 72); Stoney, Phillip, Johnson, Unitt, Scott, Chapman, Williams, Yankey (Potter 40), Smith K, Aluko (Handley 63).

17 November 2005 (in Zwollen)
Holland 0
England 1 *(Williams 55 (pen))* 2319
England: Brown; Stoney, White, Phillip, Unitt, Carney (Potter 59), Exley (Asante 81), Williams, Yankey, Smith K, Aluko (Barr 46).

7 February 2006 (in Larnaca)
Sweden 0
England 0
England: Brown; Phillip, Stoney, Unitt, Asante (Potter 86), Chapman, Exley, Williams, Aluko (Barr 74), Carney (Handley 66), Yankey (Smith S 66).

9 February 2006 (in Achna)
Sweden 1 *(Aronsson 5)*
England 1 *(Unitt 64)*
England: Brown; Johnson, Unitt, Asante, Chapman, Phillip, Carney, Williams, Barr (Stoney 63), Smith K (Aluko 82), Potter.

9 March 2006 (in Norwich)
England 1 *(Carney 79)*
Iceland 0 9616
England: Brown (Chamberlain 46); Stoney (Johnson 46), Unitt, Asante, Chapman, Phillip, Carney, Williams, Aluko (Scott 60), Smith K, Yankey (Potter 67).

26 March 2006 (at Blackburn)
England 0
France 0 12,164
England: Brown; Stoney, Unitt, Asante (Exley 88), Chapman, Phillip, Carney, Williams, Aluko (Scott 75), Smith K, Yankey.

20 April 2006 (at Gillingham)
England 4 *(Spieler 36 (og), Williams 85, Smith S 87, Handley 90)*
Austria 0 8068
England: Brown; Johnson, Unitt, Chapman, White, Phillip, Carney, Williams, Barr (Handley 59), Smith K, Yankey (Smith S 84).

11 May 2006 (at Southampton)
England 2 *(Exley 41, Scott 90)*
Hungary 0 8817
England: Brown; Johnson (Stoney 69), Unitt, Asante, White, Phillip, Carney (Scott 57), Potter, Handley (Sanderson 54), Exley, Smith S.

Arsenal's Julie Fleeting gets ahead of Leeds United's Karen Burke in the Women's FA Cup Final at The New Den (Tony Marshall/EMPICS)

UNIBOND LEAGUE 2005–06

PREMIER DIVISION

		P	*W*	*D*	*L*	*F*	*A*	*W*	*D*	*L*	*F*	*A*	*W*	*D*	*L*	*F*	*A*	*GD*	*Pts*
1	Blyth Spartans	42	13	6	2	37	16	13	5	3	42	16	26	11	5	79	32	47	89
2	Frickley Athletic	42	13	5	3	35	17	13	3	5	37	19	26	8	8	72	36	36	86
3	Marine	42	12	6	3	33	12	11	6	4	28	13	23	12	7	61	25	36	81
4	Farsley Celtic	42	12	4	5	47	22	11	6	4	37	12	23	10	9	84	34	50	79
5	North Ferriby United	42	12	4	5	39	24	9	6	6	38	30	21	10	11	77	54	23	73
6	Whitby Town	42	13	4	4	39	23	5	6	10	21	36	18	10	14	60	59	1	64
7	Burscough	42	8	5	8	33	31	11	1	9	31	33	19	6	17	64	64	0	63
8	Witton Albion	42	7	5	9	30	22	10	4	7	37	31	17	9	16	68	55	14	60
9	Matlock Town	42	8	5	8	24	26	8	6	7	34	28	16	11	15	60	55	4	59
10	AFC Telford United	42	10	7	4	33	27	4	10	7	21	25	14	17	11	54	52	2	59
11	Ossett Town	42	11	3	7	36	30	6	4	11	21	31	17	7	18	57	61	–4	58
12	Leek Town	42	5	10	6	21	24	9	4	8	29	29	14	14	14	50	53	–3	56
13	Prescot Cables	42	7	6	8	23	26	8	2	11	26	34	15	8	19	49	60	–11	53
14	Guiseley	42	8	3	10	23	33	6	6	9	22	25	14	9	19	45	58	–13	51
15	Ashton United	42	8	5	8	42	31	5	5	11	20	32	13	10	19	62	63	–1	49
16	Ilkeston Town	42	10	5	6	26	16	2	8	11	22	35	12	13	17	48	51	–3	49
17	Gateshead	42	8	4	9	31	41	4	6	11	21	36	12	10	20	52	77	–25	46
18	Radcliffe Borough	42	8	2	11	36	30	4	6	11	18	32	12	8	22	54	62	–8	44
19	Lincoln United	42	3	8	10	21	31	7	6	8	23	33	10	14	18	44	64	–20	44
20	Wakefield & Emley	42	6	5	10	17	26	5	4	12	21	43	11	9	22	38	69	–31	42
21	Bradford Park Avenue	42	6	5	10	33	36	4	4	13	31	50	10	9	23	64	86	–22	39
22	Runcorn AFC Halton	42	4	6	11	21	51	2	5	14	15	57	6	11	25	36	108	–72	29

Farsley Celtic promoted to Conference North as Play-Off winners.
Lincoln United not relegated as they had a superior record to the club in the Isthmian League.

FIRST DIVISION

		P	*W*	*D*	*L*	*F*	*A*	*W*	*D*	*L*	*F*	*A*	*W*	*D*	*L*	*F*	*A*	*GD*	*Pts*
1	Mossley	42	15	3	3	54	21	8	6	7	29	34	23	9	10	83	55	28	78
2	Fleetwood Town	42	11	6	4	37	23	11	4	6	35	25	22	10	10	72	48	24	76
3	Kendal Town	42	9	6	6	37	29	13	4	4	44	29	22	10	10	81	58	23	76
4	Woodley Sports	42	13	5	3	48	22	9	3	9	37	31	22	8	12	85	53	32	74
5	Gresley Rovers	42	13	4	4	43	25	7	6	8	36	39	20	10	12	79	64	15	70
6	Stocksbridge Park Steels	42	11	4	6	38	23	6	12	3	28	20	17	16	9	66	43	23	67
7	Eastwood Town	42	9	8	4	42	30	7	6	8	24	28	16	14	12	66	58	8	62
8	Brigg Town	42	10	5	6	36	29	6	9	6	34	35	16	14	12	70	64	6	62
9	Belper Town	42	10	4	7	32	27	7	4	10	21	29	17	8	17	53	56	–3	59
10	Shepshed Dynamo	42	6	7	8	22	27	9	6	6	35	29	15	13	14	57	56	1	58
11	Bridlington Town	42	11	6	4	32	21	5	4	12	29	47	16	10	16	61	68	–7	58
12	Colwyn Bay	42	11	5	5	37	18	4	6	11	19	35	15	11	16	56	53	3	56
13	Bamber Bridge	42	9	6	6	38	31	4	9	8	27	28	13	15	14	65	59	6	54
14	Ossett Albion	42	8	4	9	26	27	7	5	9	28	37	15	9	18	54	64	–10	54
15	Rossendale United	42	6	9	6	33	30	6	8	7	25	31	12	17	13	58	61	–3	53
16	Clitheroe	42	11	4	6	34	29	4	4	13	20	44	15	8	19	54	73	–19	53
17	Kidsgrove Athletic	42	9	3	9	38	34	5	6	10	28	35	14	9	19	66	69	–3	51
18	Chorley	42	4	7	10	26	30	10	1	10	32	29	14	8	20	58	59	–1	50
19	Warrington Town	42	7	7	7	29	29	4	8	9	33	45	11	15	16	62	74	–12	48
20	Spalding United	42	6	9	6	27	31	4	6	11	22	39	10	15	17	49	70	–21	45
21	Goole Town*	42	4	8	9	29	50	7	3	11	26	35	11	11	20	55	85	–30	43
22	Bishop Auckland	42	2	3	16	18	47	1	3	17	21	52	3	6	33	39	99	–60	15

**Goole Town deducted 1 point for fielding an ineligible player.*
Kendal Town promoted to the Unibond Premier Division as Play-Off winners.
Goole Town not relegated as they had a superior record to the club in the Isthmian League.

LEADING GOALSCORERS (in order of League goals)

Premier Division	*Lge*	*Cup*	*Total*
Dale (Blyth Spartans)	32	5	37
Gray (Burscough)	20	13	33
Brunskill (Whitby Town)	17	2	19
Walshaw (Ossett Town)	16	16	32
Reeves (Farsley Celtic)	16	7	23
(Includes 7 League and 5 Cup goals for Wakefield & Emley).			
Callery (Frickley Athletic)	16	5	21
Foster (Radcliffe Borough)	16	5	21
Nagington (Leek Town)	16	5	21
Moseley (Witton Albion)	16	3	19
Johnstone (Gateshead)	16	2	18
Bell (Blyth Spartans)	16	1	17

First Division	*Lge*	*Cup*	*Total*
O'Connor (Gresley Rovers)	28	7	35
Zoll (Stocksbridge Park Steels)	23	5	28
Mitchell (Warrington Town)	19	3	22
Ashcroft (Kendal Town)	18	6	24
Wright (Chorley)	18	4	22
Downey (Mossley)	18	3	21
Edwards (Gresley Rovers)	18	2	20
Knox (Eastwood Town)	17	7	24
Kerley (Eastwood Town)	16	5	21
(Includes 1 League goal for Spalding United).			
Palmer (Bridlington Town)	15	4	19
Daniel (Woodley Sports)	15	3	18
Salmon (Woodley Sports)	15	3	18

ATTENDANCES

Premier Division
Highest Attendances:
2323 AFC Telford United v North Ferriby United
1835 AFC Telford United v Whitby Town
1782 AFC Telford United v Witton Albion
1720 AFC Telford United v Ashton United

First Division
Highest Attendances:
839 Colwyn Bay v Chorley
602 Fleetwood Town v Bamber Bridge
584 Fleetwood Town v Kendal Town
583 Fleetwood Town v Bridlington Town

UNIBOND LEAGUE CHALLENGE CUP 2005–06

FIRST ROUND
Blyth Spartans 1, Goole Town 2
Bridlington Town 2, Ossett Albion 1
Clitheroe 4, Woodley Sports 2
Colwyn Bay 2, Warrington Town 0
Kidsgrove Athletic 4, Chorley 2
Lincoln United 1, Frickley Athletic 1
Lincoln United won 2-0 on penalties.
Marine 3, Bamber Bridge 1
Ossett Town 0, Gateshead 1
Rossendale United 2, Fleetwood Town 4
Shepshed Dynamo 0, Stocksbridge Park Steels 3
Spalding United 1, Belper Town 0
Wakefield & Emley 4, Bishop Auckland 2

SECOND ROUND
AFC Telford United 3, Gresley Rovers 2
Bridlington Town 1, Lincoln United 0
Brigg Town 0, Stocksbridge Park Steels 0
Stocksbridge Park Steels won 8-7 on penalties.
Clitheroe 3, Kendal Town 4
Farsley Celtic 2, Bradford Park Avenue 2
Farsley Celtic won 4-1 on penalties.
Fleetwood Town 2, Burscough 1
Gateshead 2, Guiseley 4
Kidsgrove Athletic 1, Eastwood Town 1
Eastwood Town won 5-4 on penalties.
Leek Town 3, Ilkeston Town 1
Marine 3, Prescot Cables 2
Mossley 0, Witton Albion 2
North Ferriby United 3, Matlock Town 2
Radcliffe Borough 3, Colwyn Bay 1
Runcorn FC Halton 1, Ashton United 0
Wakefield & Emley 3, Spalding United 0
Whitby Town 4, Goole Town 3

THIRD ROUND
AFC Telford United 0, Witton Albion 1
Farsley Celtic 4, North Ferriby United 0
Fleetwood Town 0, Radcliffe Borough 1
Guiseley 1, Whitby Town 3
Kendal Town 0, Runcorn FC Halton 1
Marine 3, Leek Town 0
Stocksbridge Park Steels 3, Bridlington Town 1
Wakefield & Emley 0, Eastwood Town 1

FOURTH ROUND
Farsley Celtic 2, Whitby Town 1
Marine 3, Eastwood Town 0
Radcliffe Borough 3, Stocksbridge Park Steels 4
Witton Albion 1, Runcorn FC Halton 3

SEMI-FINALS
Farsley Celtic 5, Runcorn FC Halton 2
Stocksbridge Park Steels 2, Marine 1

FINAL
Farsley Celtic 1, Stocksbridge Park Steels 0

PRESIDENT'S CUP 2005–06

FIRST ROUND
Ashton United 0, Bradford Park Avenue 1
Brigg Town 2, Gateshead 0
Colwyn Bay 4, Clitheroe 2
Goole Town 2, Ilkeston Town 4
Kidsgrove Athletic 0, Mossley 1
Lincoln United 2, Spalding United 1
Matlock Town 4, Gresley Rovers 0
Prescot Cables 0, Burscough 1

SECOND ROUND
Burscough 1, Bradford Park Avenue 2
Ilkeston Town 1, Mossley 0
Lincoln United 1, Brigg Town 1
Brigg Town won 5-4 on penalties.
Matlock Town 2, Colwyn Bay 0

SEMI-FINALS
Brigg Town 1, Bradford Park Avenue 1
Bradford Park Avenue won 4-3 on penalties.
Matlock Town 3, Ilkeston Town 4

FINAL
Ilkeston Town 0, Bradford Park Avenue 1

CHAIRMAN'S CUP 2005–06

FIRST ROUND
Bamber Bridge 2, Belper Town 1
Ossett Albion 4, Shepshed Dynamo 1
Rossendale United 1, Frickley Athletic 3
Warrington Town 0, Woodley Sports 1

SECOND ROUND
Bamber Bridge 0, Ossett Town 2
Blyth Spartans 1, Ossett Albion 0
Frickley Athletic 4, Chorley 2
Woodley Sports 2, Bishop Auckland 0

SEMI-FINALS
Frickley Athletic 2, Blyth Spartans 2
Blyth Spartans won 5-3 on penalties.
Woodley Sports 2, Ossett Town 4

FINAL
Blyth Spartans 2, Ossett Town 0

UNIBOND PREMIER DIVISION PLAY-OFFS 2005–06

SEMI-FINALS
Frickley Athletic 0, North Ferriby United 0
North Ferriby United won 4-2 on penalties.
Marine 0, Farsley Celtic 1

FINAL
Farsley Celtic 2, North Ferriby United 1

UNIBOND LEAGUE FIRST DIVISION PROMOTION PLAY-OFFS 2005–06

SEMI-FINALS
Kendal Town 1, Stocksbridge Park Steels 1
Kendal Town won 4-2 on penalties.
Woodley Sports 0, Gresley Rovers 4

FINAL
Kendal Town 2, Gresley Rovers 1

SOUTHERN LEAGUE 2005–06

SOUTHERN LEAGUE PREMIER DIVISION 2005–06

			Home			*Away*			*Total*						
		P	*W*	*D*	*L*	*W*	*D*	*L*	*W*	*D*	*L*	*F*	*A*	*GD*	*Pts*
1	Salisbury City	42	16	2	3	14	3	4	30	5	7	83	27	56	95
2	Bath City	42	12	4	5	13	4	4	25	8	9	66	33	33	83
3	King's Lynn	42	14	3	4	11	4	6	25	7	10	73	41	32	82
4	Chippenham Town	42	14	5	2	8	6	7	22	11	9	69	45	24	77
5	Bedford Town	42	12	6	3	10	4	7	22	10	10	69	53	16	76
6	Yate Town	42	15	3	3	6	2	13	21	5	16	78	74	4	68
7	Banbury United	42	11	5	5	6	6	9	17	11	14	66	61	5	62
8	Halesowen Town	42	9	7	5	6	8	7	15	15	12	54	45	9	60
9	Merthyr Tydfil	42	9	4	8	8	5	8	17	9	16	62	58	4	60
10	Mangotsfield United	42	6	6	9	9	7	5	15	13	14	67	67	0	58
11	Grantham Town	42	6	8	7	9	3	9	15	11	16	49	49	0	56
12	Tiverton Town	42	9	5	7	5	5	11	14	10	18	69	65	4	52
13	Gloucester City	42	9	5	7	5	5	11	14	10	18	57	60	–3	52
14	Hitchin Town	42	9	6	6	4	6	11	13	12	17	59	76	–17	51
15	Rugby Town	42	8	4	9	5	7	9	13	11	18	58	66	–8	50
16	Cheshunt	42	8	4	9	5	5	11	13	9	20	57	70	–13	48
17	Team Bath	42	7	2	12	7	4	10	14	6	22	55	68	–13	48
18	Cirencester Town	42	6	3	12	8	1	12	14	4	24	49	68	–19	46
19	Northwood	42	7	5	9	5	1	15	12	6	24	53	88	–35	42
20	Evesham United	42	5	7	9	4	7	10	9	14	19	46	58	–12	41
21	Aylesbury United	42	7	4	10	2	8	11	9	12	21	43	69	–26	39
22	Chesham United	42	4	6	11	5	3	13	9	9	24	43	84	–41	36

SOUTHERN LEAGUE DIVISION ONE EAST 2005–06

			Home			*Away*			*Total*						
		P	*W*	*D*	*L*	*W*	*D*	*L*	*W*	*D*	*L*	*F*	*A*	*GD*	*Pts*
1	Boreham Wood	42	13	6	2	11	6	4	24	12	6	84	41	43	84
2	Corby Town	42	16	3	2	9	6	6	25	9	8	63	33	30	84
3	Enfield Town	42	10	5	6	14	4	3	24	9	9	75	43	32	81
4	Stamford	42	14	7	0	6	3	12	20	10	12	73	53	20	70
5	Barking & East Ham United	42	12	4	5	8	6	7	20	10	12	63	47	16	70
6	Wivenhoe Town	42	12	4	5	5	7	9	17	11	14	56	54	2	62
7	Dartford	42	9	8	4	7	5	9	16	13	13	65	57	8	61
8	Waltham Forest	42	10	4	7	7	4	10	17	8	17	64	66	–2	59
9	Harlow Town	42	9	8	4	5	8	8	14	16	12	57	56	1	58
10	Arlesey Town	42	8	4	9	7	7	7	15	11	16	58	65	–7	56
11	Rothwell Town	42	8	9	4	5	5	11	13	14	15	48	53	–5	53
12	Wingate & Finchley	42	8	6	7	5	8	8	13	14	15	57	64	–7	53
13	Great Wakering Rovers	42	11	3	7	2	9	10	13	12	17	65	67	–2	51
14	Uxbridge	42	6	4	11	7	7	7	13	11	18	62	64	–2	50
15	Potters Bar Town	42	7	8	6	6	3	12	13	11	18	60	66	–6	50
16	Enfield	42	7	6	8	6	5	10	13	11	18	52	64	–12	50
17	Chatham Town	42	10	4	7	3	6	12	13	10	19	51	57	–6	49
18	Sittingbourne	42	7	8	6	5	4	12	12	12	18	53	69	–16	48
19	Barton Rovers	42	8	4	9	5	4	12	13	8	21	59	73	–14	47
20	Aveley	42	8	6	7	3	7	11	11	13	18	51	70	–19	46
21	Ilford	42	6	9	6	2	8	11	8	17	17	35	59	–24	41
22	Berkhamsted Town	42	5	7	9	3	5	13	8	12	22	51	81	–30	36

SOUTHERN LEAGUE DIVISION ONE WEST 2005–06

			Home			*Away*			*Total*						
		P	*W*	*D*	*L*	*W*	*D*	*L*	*W*	*D*	*L*	*F*	*A*	*GD*	*Pts*
1	Clevedon Town	42	15	2	4	13	4	4	28	6	8	86	45	41	90
2	Ashford Town (Middlesex)	42	13	4	4	11	4	6	24	8	10	84	50	34	80
3	Brackley Town	42	12	4	5	11	5	5	23	9	10	71	34	37	78
4	Hemel Hempstead Town	42	10	5	6	12	4	5	22	9	11	86	47	39	75
5	Swindon Supermarine	42	10	7	4	12	2	7	22	9	11	70	47	23	75
6	Marlow	42	10	2	9	12	4	5	22	6	14	62	59	3	72
7	Sutton Coldfield Town	42	11	4	6	10	2	9	21	6	15	91	62	29	69
8	Leighton Town	42	10	2	9	9	6	6	19	8	15	55	48	7	65
9	Willenhall Town	42	11	4	6	6	8	7	17	12	13	78	61	17	63
10	Rushall Olympic	42	10	6	5	7	5	9	17	11	14	73	57	16	62
11	Bromsgrove Rovers	42	9	3	9	8	8	5	17	11	14	65	50	15	62
12	Solihull Borough	42	8	7	6	7	6	8	15	13	14	50	51	–1	58
13	Beaconsfield SYCOB	42	8	7	6	6	6	9	14	13	15	60	66	–6	55
14	Burnham	42	8	3	10	8	2	11	16	5	21	58	71	–13	53
15	Cinderford Town	42	8	2	11	6	7	8	14	9	19	71	79	–8	51
16	Bedworth United	42	7	4	10	7	5	9	14	9	19	46	57	–11	51
17	Paulton Rovers	42	7	6	8	5	4	12	12	10	20	55	76	–21	46
18	Taunton Town	42	8	3	10	4	6	11	12	9	21	67	81	–14	45
19	Bracknell Town	42	7	3	11	5	3	13	12	6	24	53	77	–24	42
20	Stourport Swifts	42	3	10	8	6	4	11	9	14	19	55	80	–25	41
21	Dunstable Town	42	6	7	8	2	5	14	8	12	22	45	91	–46	36
22	Thame United	42	2	5	14	2	0	19	4	5	33	30	122	–92	17

SOUTHERN LEAGUE PLAY-OFFS 2005–06

PREMIER DIVISION PLAY-OFF FINAL
Chippenham Town 2, Bedford Town 3 2029

DIVISION ONE EAST PLAY-OFF FINAL
Stamford 2, Wivenhoe Town 1 561

DIVISION ONE WEST PLAY-OFF FINAL
Brackley Town 2, Hemel Hempstead Town 3 655

SOUTHERN LEAGUE ATTENDANCES 2005–06

Premier Division Highest	2268	Bath City 0 Chippenham Town 2 (17 April 2006)
Division One East Highest	1340	Corby Town 1 Waltham Forest 0 (29 April 2006)
Division One West Highest	572	Brackley Town 0 Ashford Town (Middlesex) 1 (29 April 2006)

SOUTHERN LEAGUE LEADING GOALSCORERS 2005–06

PREMIER DIVISION

Joshua Sozzo (Hitchin Town)	30
David Gilroy (Chippenham Town)	26
Rene Howe (Bedford Town)	25
Paul Sales (Salisbury City)	22
Darren Edwards (Yate Town)	21
Scott Partridge (Bath City)	21
Matthew Tubbs (Salisbury City)	21
Richard Ball (Evesham United)	19
Sean Canham (Team Bath)	19
James Mudge (Tiverton Town)	19
Lloyd Opara (Cheshunt)	19
Jody Bevan (Gloucester City)	18
Robert Claridge (Mangotsfield United)	17

DIVISION ONE EAST

Richard Howard (Potters Bar Town)	26
Paul Barnes (Barton Rovers)	25
Brendan Cass (Dartford)	23
Rudi Hall (Enfield Town)	23
Neil Richmond (Great Wakering Rovers)	23
Leon Archer (Boreham Wood)	22
Garath Pritchard (Stamford)	22
Martin Wormall (Stamford)	22
Kevin Byrne (Corby Town)	21
Wayne Vaughan (Barking & East Ham United)	20
Simon Thomas (Wivenhoe Town)	17
Wesley Thomas (Waltham Forest)	17

DIVISION ONE WEST

Anthony Thomas (Hemel Hempstead Town)	31
Matthew Murphy (Brackley Town)	28
Jack Pitcher (Clevedon Town)	24
Justin Rowe (Sutton Coldfield Town)	24
Dean Perrow (Willenhall Town)	22
Scott Todd (Ashford Town (Middlesex))	22
Matthew Pratley (Swindon Supermarine)	20
Grant Carney (Hemel Hempstead Town)	19
Jonathon Douglas (Bedworth United)	18
Damien Markman (Sutton Coldfield Town)	18
Daniel Cleverley (Paulton Rovers)	17
Aaron Blakemore (Taunton Town)	16
Thomas Jacobs (Clevedon Town)	16

Up to and including 1 May 2006 – includes League and League Cup goals only

ERREA SOUTHERN LEAGUE CUP 2005–06

FIRST ROUND
Aveley 0, Potters Bar Town 0
Potters Bar Town won 5-3 on penalties.
Barking & East Ham United 2, Sittingbourne 1
Boreham Wood 1, Ashford Town (Middlesex) 4
Bracknell Town 1, Marlow 2
Bromsgrove Rovers 2, Stourport Swifts 1
Burnham 2, Beaconsfield SYCOB 0
Corby Town 4, Brackley Town 1
Dartford 0, Chatham Town 1
Dunstable Town 6, Stamford 5
Enfield Town 0, Wivenhoe Town 0
Wivenhoe Town won 5-4 on penalties.
Great Wakering Rovers 3, Enfield 4
Harlow Town 2, Ilford 1
Leighton Town 1, Barton Rovers 0
Rothwell Town 4, Arlesey Town 0
Solihull Borough 4, Bedworth United 0
Sutton Coldfield Town 2, Cinderford Town 1
Swindon Supermarine 2, Paulton Rovers 0
Taunton Town 0, Cleveland Town 2
Thame United 0, Berkhamsted Town 4
Uxbridge 0, Hemel Hempstead Town 5
Willenhall Town 0, Rushall Olympic 1
Wingate & Finchley 2, Waltham Forest 3

SECOND ROUND
Ashford Town (Middlesex) 5, Burnham 0
Barking & East Ham United 2, Chatham Town 3
Berkhamsted Town 1, Marlow 2
Dunstable Town 0, Hitchin Town 1
Enfield 0, Potters Bar Town 3
Hemel Hempstead Town 6, Leighton Town 0
Rothwell Town 1, Corby Town 2
Rushall Olympic 1, Sutton Coldfield Town 0
Solihull Borough 0, Bromsgrove Rovers 2
Swindon Supermarine 1, Clevedon Town 0
Waltham Forest 1, Cheshunt 5
Wivenhoe Town 1, Harlow Town 2
Tie awarded to Wivenhoe Town; Harlow Town fielded an illegible player.

THIRD ROUND
Banbury United 2, Halesowen Town 1
Bedford Town 1, Grantham Town 0
Chesham United 0, Cheshunt 1
Chippenham Town 1, Swindon Supermarine 0
Evesham United 0, Bromsgrove Rovers 5
Gloucester City 2, Cirencester Town 4
Hemel Hempsted Town 1, Potters Bar Town 4
Hitchin Town 2, Marlow 1
King's Lynn 5, Corby Town 0
Mangotsfield United 4, Merthyr Tydfil 1
Northwood 1, Ashford Town (Middlesex) 2
Rushall Olympic 2, Rugby Town 0
Salisbury City 3, Aylesbury United 0
Team Bath 4, Yate Town 1
Tiverton Town 1, Bath City 2
Wivenhoe Town 1, Chatham Town 4

FOURTH ROUND
Ashford Town (Middlesex) 1, Hitchin Town 4
Banbury United 1, Rushall Olympic 1
abandoned, frozen pitch; 1-0
Bedford Town 1, Cheshunt 0
Bromsgrove Rovers 1, King's Lynn 0
Chatham Town 2, Potters Bar Town 0
Chippenham Town 2, Team Bath 0
Mangotsfield United 2, Bath City 1
Salisbury City 3, Cirencester Town 2
abandoned, frozen pitch; 3-4

FIFTH ROUND
Banbury United 0, Bromsgrove Rovers 4
Chatham Town 0, Bedford Town 2
Chippenham Town 2, Mangotsfield United 0
Cirencester Town 0, Hitchin Town 7

SEMI-FINALS
Chippenham Town 1, Bromsgrove Rovers 2
Hitchin Town 2, Bedford Town 0

FINAL FIRST LEG
Hitchin Town 1, Bromsgrove Rovers 0

FINAL SECOND LEG
Bromsgrove Rovers 1, Hitchin Town 2

RYMAN LEAGUE 2005–06

RYMAN LEAGUE PREMIER DIVISION 2005–06

			Home					*Away*					*Total*						
		P	*W*	*D*	*L*	*F*	*A*	*W*	*D*	*L*	*F*	*A*	*W*	*D*	*L*	*F*	*A*	*GD*	*Pts*
1	Braintree Town	42	18	3	0	45	12	10	7	4	29	20	28	10	4	74	32	+42	94
2	Heybridge Swifts	42	14	3	4	32	16	14	0	7	38	30	28	3	11	70	46	+24	87
3	Fisher Athletic	42	10	6	5	36	24	16	1	4	48	22	26	7	9	84	46	+38	85
4	AFC Wimbledon	42	9	8	4	33	23	13	3	5	34	13	22	11	9	67	36	+31	77
5	Hampton & Richmond Borough	42	12	1	8	36	27	12	2	7	37	27	24	3	15	73	54	+19	75
6	Staines Town	42	9	4	8	31	26	11	6	4	43	30	20	10	12	74	56	+18	70
7	Billericay Town	42	10	5	6	38	28	9	7	5	31	17	19	12	11	69	45	+24	69
8	Worthing	42	12	4	5	41	26	7	6	8	30	34	19	10	13	71	60	+11	67
9	Walton & Hersham	42	11	3	7	28	23	8	4	9	27	27	19	7	16	55	50	+5	64
10	Chelmsford City	42	10	5	6	32	27	8	5	8	25	35	18	10	14	57	62	–5	64
11	Bromley	42	9	8	4	34	24	7	6	8	23	25	16	14	12	57	49	+8	62
12	East Thurrock United	42	10	2	9	33	34	8	3	10	27	26	18	5	19	60	60	0	59
13	Folkestone Invicta	42	11	4	6	28	19	5	6	10	19	32	16	10	16	47	51	–4	58
14	Margate	42	5	10	6	24	27	6	7	8	25	28	11	17	14	49	55	–6	50
15	Leyton	42	6	2	13	28	30	7	7	7	30	31	13	9	20	58	61	–3	48
16	Harrow Borough	42	7	7	7	32	31	6	2	13	24	42	13	9	20	56	73	–17	48
17	Slough Town	42	6	4	11	29	38	7	4	10	34	37	13	8	21	63	75	–12	47
18	Wealdstone	42	5	2	14	37	48	8	3	10	31	34	13	5	24	68	82	–14	44
19	Hendon	42	4	8	9	22	26	5	4	12	22	38	9	12	21	44	64	–20	39
20	Maldon Town	42	4	3	14	21	40	4	8	9	20	33	8	11	23	41	73	–32	35
21	Windsor & Eton	42	5	4	12	16	32	3	4	14	21	43	8	8	26	37	75	–38	32
22	Redbridge	42	3	2	16	17	48	0	3	18	11	49	3	5	34	28	97	–69	14

RYMAN LEAGUE DIVISION ONE 2005–06

			Home					*Away*					*Total*						
		P	*W*	*D*	*L*	*F*	*A*	*W*	*D*	*L*	*F*	*A*	*W*	*D*	*L*	*F*	*A*	*GD*	*Pts*
1	Ramsgate	44	13	6	3	53	22	11	8	3	31	16	24	14	6	84	38	+46	86
2	Horsham	44	14	5	3	53	29	11	6	5	41	26	25	11	8	94	55	+39	86
3	Tonbridge Angels	44	13	3	6	36	21	11	5	6	35	27	24	8	12	71	48	+23	80
4	Metropolitan Police	44	15	3	4	41	18	9	4	9	31	28	24	7	13	72	46	+26	79
5	Dover Athletic	44	13	7	2	39	19	8	7	7	30	27	21	14	9	69	46	+23	77
6	Tooting & Mitcham United	44	10	6	6	47	31	12	3	7	46	31	22	9	13	93	62	+31	75
7	Kingstonian	44	10	6	6	41	28	10	8	4	41	28	20	14	10	82	56	+26	74
8	Croydon Athletic	44	11	8	3	30	16	9	5	8	26	25	20	13	11	56	41	+15	73
9	Bashley	44	11	4	7	36	32	9	6	7	27	29	20	10	14	63	61	+2	70
10	Leatherhead	44	11	5	6	36	25	7	9	6	28	25	18	14	12	64	50	+14	68
11	Cray Wanderers	44	11	5	6	41	37	9	3	10	39	37	20	8	16	80	74	+6	68
12	Hastings United	44	10	4	8	41	33	9	6	7	24	25	19	10	15	65	58	+7	67
13	Dulwich Hamlet	44	10	4	8	26	18	9	4	9	29	25	19	8	17	55	43	+12	65
14	Fleet Town	44	8	9	5	23	24	5	10	7	27	32	13	19	12	50	56	–6	58
15	Walton Casuals	44	9	6	7	31	25	7	4	11	37	50	16	10	18	68	75	–7	58
16	Lymington & New Milton	44	6	5	11	27	33	6	6	10	34	47	12	11	21	61	80	–19	47
17	Molesey	44	7	6	9	30	32	5	4	13	26	47	12	10	22	56	79	–23	46
18	Whyteleafe	44	6	8	8	31	30	4	6	12	19	36	10	14	20	50	66	–16	44
19	Burgess Hill Town	44	8	4	10	38	36	2	6	14	19	47	10	10	24	57	83	–26	40
20	Banstead Athletic	44	6	6	10	22	33	2	7	13	21	38	8	13	23	43	71	–28	37
21	Ashford Town	44	5	4	13	21	44	3	7	12	20	37	8	11	25	41	81	–40	35
22	Newport IoW	44	0	10	12	21	43	6	1	15	17	54	6	11	27	38	97	–59	29
23	Corinthian Casuals	44	4	5	13	21	37	2	4	16	18	48	6	9	29	39	85	–46	27

RYMAN LEAGUE DIVISION TWO 2005–06

			Home					*Away*					*Total*						
		P	*W*	*D*	*L*	*F*	*A*	*W*	*D*	*L*	*F*	*A*	*W*	*D*	*L*	*F*	*A*	*GD*	*Pts*
1	Ware	30	10	2	3	42	18	9	2	4	35	18	19	4	7	77	36	+41	61
2	Witham Town	30	10	4	1	34	13	7	3	5	27	17	17	7	6	61	30	+31	58
3	Brook House	30	11	1	3	38	17	6	6	3	25	16	17	7	6	63	33	+30	58
4	Flackwell Heath	30	9	2	4	31	21	6	5	4	23	28	15	7	8	54	49	+5	52
5	Egham Town	30	9	2	4	23	15	6	3	6	16	21	15	5	10	39	36	+3	50
6	Chertsey Town	30	9	3	3	30	17	5	4	6	17	20	14	7	9	47	37	+10	49
7	Edgware Town	30	7	3	5	25	20	6	2	7	21	21	13	5	12	46	41	+5	44
8	Chalfont St Peter	30	8	1	6	25	21	5	1	9	25	32	13	2	15	50	53	–3	41
9	Dorking	30	5	5	5	27	30	6	3	6	21	21	11	8	11	48	51	–3	41
10	Croydon	30	5	5	5	25	23	6	2	7	18	20	11	7	12	43	43	0	40
11	Wembley	30	5	5	5	16	15	6	1	8	28	28	11	6	13	44	43	+1	39
12	Kingsbury Town	30	5	4	6	16	19	4	6	5	16	18	9	10	11	32	37	–5	37
13	Hertford Town	30	5	4	6	15	21	2	6	7	20	33	7	10	13	35	54	–19	31
14	Camberley Town	30	3	5	7	17	27	2	3	10	14	30	5	8	17	31	57	–26	23
15	Epsom & Ewell	30	2	4	9	16	30	3	2	10	16	34	5	6	19	32	64	–32	21
16	Clapton*	30	3	4	8	14	34	1	5	9	19	37	4	9	17	33	71	–38	16

**5 points deducted – breach of rule.*

RYMAN LEAGUE PLAY-OFFS 2005–06

PREMIER DIVISION PLAY-OFF FINAL
Fisher Athletic 3, Hampton & Richmond Borough 0

DIVISION ONE PLAY-OFF FINAL
Tonbridge Angels 3, Dover Athletic 2

RYMAN LEAGUE ATTENDANCES 2005–06

Premier Division Highest Average	2706	AFC Wimbledon
Division One Highest Average	816	Dover Athletic
Division One Highest Average	152	Ware

RYMAN LEAGUE LEADING GOALSCORERS 2005–06

PREMIER LEAGUE

		Games played	*Goals scored*
Beckford, J	Wealdstone	31	26
Hodges, I	Slough Town	33	19
Jolly, R	Heybridge Swifts	35	19
Watts, S	Fisher Athletic	33	17
Hockton, D	Margate	33	16
Revell, A	Braintree Town	35	16
Browne, S	Worthing	32	15
Yaku, L	Hampton & Richmond Borough	30	15
Akurang, C	Heybridge Swifts	18	14
Bajada, L	Leyton	30	14
Boot, A	Chelmsford City	30	13
Butler, R	AFC Wimbledon	27	13
Smeltz, S	AFC Wimbledon	32	13
Griffiths, L	Fisher Athletic	22	12
Nwokeji, M	Staines Town	28	12
Dryden, J	Folkestone Invicta	19	11
Godfrey, E	Hampton & Richmond Borough	34	11
Hunter, L	Billericay Town	30	11
McDonnell, N	Bromley	24	11
Ofori, E	Braintree Town	29	11

DIVISION ONE

Ruggles, P	Molesey	37	24
Cooper, K	Fleet Town	36	20
Gillespie, R	Bashley	36	20
Rose, J	Kingstonian	32	17
Taylor, J	Horsham	37	17
Welford, S	Ramsgate	35	17
Ball, G	Walton Casuals	29	16
Hastings, J	Tooting & Mitcham United	23	15
Allen, E	Croydon Athletic	30	14
Abbott, G	Cray Wanderers	33	13
Bremner, L	Cray Wanderers	32	13
Main, J	Tonbridge Angels	33	13
Moore, S	Corinthian Casuals	33	13
Smith, E	Fleet Town	32	13
Wilkens, C	Dover Athletic	36	13
Ojukwa, K	Kingstonian	29	12
Adams, S	Hastings United	32	11
Carpenter, M	Walton Casuals	32	10
Gedling, L	Burgess Hill Town	34	10
Mitchell, S	Banstead Athletic	26	10

DIVISION TWO

Blackburne, S	Edgware Town	23	17
Papali, D	Brook House	18	17
Frendo, J	Ware	9	16
Pomroy, J	Chertsey Town	23	13
Haastrup, H	Kingsbury Town	15	11
Budge, K	Witham Town	22	10
Bunce, A	Chalfont St Peter	20	10
Brosnan, B	Chalfont St Peter	18	9
Coleman, L	Egham Town	20	9
Da, Costa, J	Chertsey Town	22	9
Duffell, C	Dorking	16	9
Hill, G	Flackwell Heath	22	9
Stevens, J	Ware	18	9
Burnell, D	Flackwell Heath	19	8
Channell, L	Flackwell Heath	20	8
Shelton, P	Wembley	15	8
Bennett, G	Witham Town	19	7
Ellerbeck, C	Ware	21	7
Humphrey, A	Croydon	18	6
Jones, I	Brook House	16	6

WESTVIEW LEAGUE CUP 2005–06

FIRST ROUND

Banstead Athletic v Corinthian Casuals	2-1
Camberley Town v Edgware Town	0-1
Chertsey Town v Leatherhead	1-2
Dover Athletic v Ware	1-0
Dulwich Hamlet v Bashley	3-1
Egham Town v Fleet Town	2-3
Epsom & Ewell v Hastings United	0-3
Flackwell Heath v Witham Town	1-3
Horsham v Chalfont St Peter	6-1
Lymington & New Milton v Kingstonian	2-0
Metropolitan Police v Hertford Town	4-2
Ramsgate v Newport (IW)	1-2
Tonbridge Angels v Clapton	3-1
Walton Casuals v Tooting & Mitcham United	0-4
Wembley v Ashford Town	5-2
Whyteleafe v Dorking	1-3
Burgess Hill Town v Brook House	2-4
Croydon v Croydon Athletic	1-3
Kingsbury Town v Molesey	3-1

SECOND ROUND

Newport (IW) v Brook House	1-2
Cray Wanderers v Kingsbury Town	6-0
Dorking v Edgware Town	0-3
Dover Athletic v Wembley	5-0
Dulwich Hamlet v Banstead Athletic	3-2
Fleet Town v Hastings United	1-3
Tonbridge Angels v Tooting & Mitcham United	0-1
Witham Town v Croydon Athletic	0-2
Lymington & New Milton v Horsham	1-4
Leatherhead v Metropolitan Police	4-1

THIRD ROUND

Billericay Town v Maldon Town	2-1
Brook House v Hendon	1-2
Chelmsford City v Horsham	3-1
Dover Athletic v Leyton	2-0
East Thurrock United v Heybridge Swifts	0-3
Fisher Athletic v Folkestone Invicta	4-2
Hampton & Richmond Borough v Dulwich Hamlet	1-0
Harrow Borough v Windsor & Eton	1-0
Hastings United v Braintree Town	2-3
Leatherhead v Cray Wanderers	5-3
Margate v Bromley	2-3
Slough Town v Redbridge	3-2
Staines Town v AFC Wimbledon	0-2
Tooting & Mitcham United v Edgware Town	3-0
Wealdstone v Croydon Athletic	1-0
Worthing v Walton & Hersham	2-2

aet; Worthing won 5-4 on penalties.

FOURTH ROUND

Billericay Town v Tooting & Mitcham United	3-1
Braintree Town v Wealdstone	1-2
Dover Athletic v Bromley	0-2
Fisher Athletic v Hampton & Richmond Borough	2-1
Harrow Borough v Worthing	1-2
Heybridge Swifts v Chelmsford City	2-0
Leatherhead v Slough Town	0-2
AFC Wimbledon v Hendon	0-1

QUARTER-FINALS

Slough Town v Heybridge Swifts	3-0
Bromley v Wealdstone	3-2
Hendon v Fisher Athletic	0-1
Worthing v Billericay Town	1-3

SEMI-FINALS, FIRST LEG

Bromley v Billericay Town	2-2
Fisher Athletic v Slough Town	5-2

SEMI-FINALS, SECOND LEG

Billericay Town v Bromley	2-1
Slough Town v Fisher Athletic	3-1

FINAL

Billericay Town v Fisher Athletic	0-4

ASSOCIATE MEMBERS TROPHY

FIRST ROUND (IN FOUR GROUPS)

Ware 0, Clapton 1
Camberley Town 0, Epsom & Ewell 3
Edgware Town 4, Kingsbury Town 1
Wembley 0, Egham Town 2
Croydon 3, Dorking 0
Ware 2, Hertford Town 3
Kingsbury Town 1, Edgware Town 2
Wembley 1, Edgware Town 1
Chertsey Town 2, Flackwell Heath 2
Chertsey Town 2, Brook House 5
Flackwell Heath 3, Chalfont St Peter 1
Camberley Town 0, Croydon 1
Hertford Town 3, Witham Town 1
Witham Town 5, Ware 2
Chertsey Town 1, Chalfont St Peter 3
Flackwell Heath 1, Brook House 2
Kingsbury Town 1, Wembley 0
Clapton 1, Ware 0
Witham Town 2, Hertford Town 0
Chalfont St Peter 2, Flackwell Heath 1
Egham Town 2, Wembley 1
Epsom & Ewell 2, Camberley Town 1
Kingsbury Town 1, Edgware Town 0
Wembley 2, Kingsbury Town 0
Edgware Town 2, Egham Town 2
Chalfont St Peter 2, Chertsey Town 1
Brook House 4, Flackwell Heath 1
Camberley Town 0, Dorking 3
Hertford Town 1, Clapton 2
Croydon 1, Epsom & Ewell 1
Ware 6, Witham Town 3
Clapton 2, Witham Town 0
Dorking 2, Epsom & Ewell 3
Chalfont St Peter 3, Brook House 2
Dorking 1, Croydon 3
Egham Town 0, Kingsbury Town 3
Brook House 5, Chertsey Town 1
Egham Town 2, Edgware Town 1
Brook House 3, Chalfont St Peter 3
Flackwell Heath 0, Chertsey Town 0
Egham Town 5, Wembley 0
Hertford Town 4, Ware 1
Witham Town 5, Clapton 3
Croydon 3, Camberley Town 0
Epsom & Ewell 0, Dorking 1
Clapton 0, Hertford Town 1
Dorking 4, Camberley Town 0
Epsom & Ewell 1, Croydon 0

QUARTER-FINALS

Brook House 3, Epsom & Ewell 2
Croydon 2, Clapton 1
Egham Town 1, Chalfont St Peter 2
Hertford Town 3, Edgware Town 0

SEMI-FINALS

Chalfont St Peter 1, Brook House 2
Croydon 0, Hertford Town 1

FINAL

Brook House 3, Hertford Town 1

THE FA TROPHY 2005–06

IN PARTNERSHIP WITH CARLSBERG

FIRST QUALIFYING ROUND

Warrington Town v Frickley Athletic	1-1, 1-1
Warrington Town won 5-4 on penalties.	
North Ferriby United v Prescot Cables	1-1, 2-2
Prescot Cables won 4-3 on penalties.	
Rossendale United v Woodley Sports	0-1
Guiseley v Chorley	3-1
Farsley Celtic v Runcorn FC Halton	2-0
Wakefield & Emley v Fleetwood Town	0-5
Mossley v Shepshed Dynamo	3-2
Witton Albion v AFC Telford United	1-1, 1-2
Bradford Park Avenue v Gateshead	1-1, 3-4
Blyth Spartans v Belper Town	2-0
Bamber Bridge v Grantham Town	2-2, 0-3
Burscough v Leek Town	3-3, 3-1
Kidsgrove Athletic v Ashton United	3-1
Brigg Town v Matlock Town	0-1
Radcliffe Borough v Marine	1-2
Clitheroe v Spalding United	3-1
Ossett Albion v Kendal Town	0-4
Ossett Town v Stocksbridge Park Steels	1-1, 2-2
Ossett Town won 4-1 on penalties.	
Lincoln United v Colwyn Bay	2-1
Whitby Town v Eastwood Town	4-2
Gresley Rovers v Ilkeston Town	2-2, 3-2
Bashley v Margate	0-3
Enfield Town v Berkhamsted Town	3-0
Metropolitan Police v Maldon Town	4-1
Dover Athletic v Dartford	1-1, 2-3
Barton Rovers v Potters Bar Town	3-2
AFC Wimbledon v King's Lynn	1-0
Leyton v Arlesey Town	1-0
Enfield v Fleet Town	1-2
Folkestone Invicta v Whyteleafe	1-1, 2-1
Walton Casuals v Harlow Town	0-1
Slough Town v Croydon Athletic	1-3
Chelmsford City v Horsham	6-0
Waltham Forest v Burgess Hill Town	0-1
Kingstonian v Aveley	2-2, 1-0
Northwood v Ramsgate	2-4
Sittingbourne v Chatham Town	3-0
Staines Town v Wivenhoe Town	2-0
Tonbridge Angels v Cheshunt	1-0
Leatherhead v East Thurrock United	0-1
Braintree Town v Great Wakering Rovers	4-2
Rothwell Town v Molesey	3-1
Heybridge Swifts v Walton & Hersham	3-0
Billericay Town v Wingate & Finchley	1-0
Corinthian Casuals v Stamford	1-4
Lymington & New Milton v Worthing	0-4
Hastings United v Corby Town	0-0, 0-2
Hampton & Richmond Borough v Newport (IW)	0-2
Banstead Athletic v Redbridge	1-2
Boreham Wood v Ilford	1-0
Dulwich Hamlet v Barking & East Ham United	1-1, 0-2
Windsor & Eton v Uxbridge	1-2
Tooting & Mitcham United v Wealdstone	1-2
Fisher Athletic v Hendon	4-2
Ashford Town v Bromley	0-2
Team Bath v Hitchin Town	0-1
Thame United v Aylesbury United	0-5
Halesowen Town v Willenhall Town	0-0, 3-2
Tiverton Town v Mangotsfield United	0-0, 2-1
Cinderford Town v Chippenham Town	1-1, 1-3
Dunstable Town v Bath City	2-2, 0-5
Cirencester Town v Gloucester City	2-0
Evesham United v Solihull Borough	0-2
Brackley Town v Banbury United	1-1, 0-3
Stourport Swifts v Bedworth United	0-1
Paulton Rovers v Salisbury City	1-1, 1-3
Clevedon Town v Taunton Town	2-1
Hemel Hempstead Town v Swindon Supermarine	1-1, 1-0
Merthyr Tydfil v Rushall Olympic	0-3
Leighton Town v Rugby Town	2-1
Bromsgrove Rovers v Beaconsfield SYCOB	3-2
Sutton Coldfield Town v Chesham United	2-1
Marlow v Ashford Town (Middlesex)	1-2
Burnham v Yate Town	2-0
Bedford Town v Bracknell Town	3-0

SECOND QUALIFYING ROUND

Blyth Spartans v Whitby Town	2-0
Gresley Rovers v Mossley	1-4
Bishop Auckland v Woodley Sports	1-3
Ossett Town v Clitheroe	2-2, 1-1
Clitheroe won 4-2 on penalties.	
Burscough v Fleetwood Town	1-2
Grantham Town v Lincoln United	2-1
Guiseley v Kendal Town	2-2, 0-4
Gateshead v Kidsgrove Athletic	1-0
Gateshead removed from the competition for fielding an ineligible player.	
Marine v Matlock Town	2-1
AFC Telford United v Goole	1-1, 1-0
Prescot Cables v Farsley Celtic	1-2
Bridlington Town v Warrington Town	2-2, 0-1
Harlow Town v Barton Rovers	2-1
Boreham Wood v Bromley	4-1
Fleet Town v Kingstonian	0-1
Barking & East Ham United v Burgess Hill Town	4-1
Cray Wanderers v Staines Town	4-3
Folkestone Invicta v Wealdstone	5-3
Enfield Town v Redbridge	1-1, 1-2
Sittingbourne v Corby Town	1-0
Harrow Borough v Metropolitan Police	4-2
Margate v Dartford	0-1
Tonbridge Angels v Newport (IW)	2-1
East Thurrock United v Leyton	2-1
Croydon Athletic v Rothwell Town	2-2, 1-0
Heybridge Swifts v Billericay Town	2-1
Chelmsford City v Braintree Town	0-2
Fisher Athletic v Uxbridge	1-2
Worthing v Stamford	1-1, 0-2
Ramsgate v AFC Wimbledon	1-1, 1-2
Salisbury City v Clevedon Town	2-1
Hemel Hempstead Town v Chippenham Town	2-3
Burnham v Leighton Town	4-5
Rushall Olympic v Ashford Town (Middlesex)	3-4
Hitchin Town v Bedford Town	1-2
Solihull Borough v Tiverton Town	3-1
Halesowen Town v Aylesbury United	2-0
Banbury United v Cirencester Town	2-2, 4-3
Bedworth United v Sutton Coldfield Town	2-5
Bath City v Bromsgrove Rovers	2-0

THIRD QUALIFYING ROUND

Leigh RMI v Stafford Rangers	1-4
Vauxhall Motors v Mossley	2-1
Droylsden v Grantham Town	4-0
Worksop Town v AFC Telford United	1-1, 2-1
Fleetwood Town v Alfreton Town	1-3
Hucknall Town v Northwich Victoria	0-0, 1-2
Redditch United v Barrow	1-1, 0-2
Lancaster City v Workington	0-0, 2-1
Kettering Town v Gainsborough Trinity	1-0
Hinckley United v Histon	2-2, 1-2
Farsley Celtic v Nuneaton Borough	3-1
Marine v Blyth Spartans	0-1
Solihull Borough v Harrogate Town	1-0
Warrington Town v Kidsgrove Athletic	4-0
Clitheroe v Woodley Sports	2-1
Worcester City v Kendal Town	1-0
Sutton Coldfield Town v Halesowen Town	1-1, 0-3
Hednesford Town v Moor Green	1-1, 4-2
Hyde United v Stalybridge Celtic	1-5
Weston-Super-Mare v Bedford Town	4-0
Dartford v AFC Wimbledon	0-0, 0-2
Lewes v Dorchester Town	2-2, 1-3
Basingstoke Town v Welling United	0-2
Eastbourne Borough v Thurrock	0-3
Harlow Town v Folkestone Invicta	2-1
Ashford Town (Middlesex) v Bognor Regis Town	2-3
Maidenhead United v Bishop's Stortford	2-2, 1-2
Braintree Town v Hayes	0-1
Tonbridge Angels v East Thurrock United	0-0, 0-3
Farnborough Town v Banbury United	2-0
Barking & East Ham United v Croydon Athletic	2-1
Sittingbourne v Cambridge City	1-3
Weymouth v Havant & Waterlooville	2-1

Uxbridge v Sutton United	2-2, 1-0
Bath City v Yeading	1-2
Eastleigh v Leighton Town	1-2
Boreham Wood v Stamford	3-1
Salisbury City v Newport County	3-0
Redbridge v Harrow Borough	1-1, 3-2
Chippenham Town v Carshalton Athletic	0-2
Cray Wanderers v Kingstonian	1-1, 1-3
Heybridge Swifts v St Albans City	0-1

FIRST ROUND

Halesowen Town v Tamworth	1-2
York City v Northwich Victoria	1-2
Solihull Borough v Hednesford Town	2-1
Vauxhall Motors v Morecambe	0-4
Halifax Town v Southport	0-0, 1-0
Warrington Town v Blyth Spartans	1-2
Burton Albion v Worksop Town	0-1
Alfreton Town v Histon	1-1, 1-2
Barrow v Clitheroe	2-1
Accrington Stanley v Altrincham	2-0
Kidderminster Harriers v Scarborough	4-0
Stafford Rangers v Lancaster City	4-2
Stalybridge Celtic v Droylsden	1-0
Kettering Town v Farsley Celtic	2-1
Yeading v Carshalton Athletic	1-2
Salisbury City v Harlow Town	1-0
Aldershot Town v Grays Athletic	1-1, 0-1
Weston-Super-Mare v Barking & East Ham United	3-2
AFC Wimbledon v St Albans City	2-3
Stevenage Borough v Crawley Town	0-2
Exeter City v Bishop's Stortford	2-1
Bognor Regis Town v Hereford United	1-7
Dagenham & Redbridge v Thurrock	2-0
Uxbridge v Woking	1-2
Canvey Island v Kingstonian	4-1
Boreham Wood v Leighton Town	1-0
Worcester City v Hayes	1-0
Dorchester Town v Cambridge United	3-2
Weymouth v Forest Green Rovers	0-1
Farnborough Town v Cambridge City	0-2
East Thurrock United v Gravesend & Northfleet	0-2
Welling United v Redbridge	4-1

SECOND ROUND

Canvey Island v Salisbury City	0-1
Stalybridge Celtic v Solihull Borough	1-0
Halifax Town v Hereford United	0-1
Carshalton Athletic v Accrington Stanley	2-2, 0-2
Boreham Wood v Gravesend & Northfleet	3-1
Tamworth v St Albans City	1-0
Forest Green Rovers v Dorchester Town	3-1
Weston-Super-Mare v Worksop Town	1-1, 1-2
Woking v Northwich Victoria	1-1, 2-1
Barrow v Cambridge City	1-2
Exeter City v Histon	3-2
Dagenham & Redbridge v Kettering Town	2-1
Blyth Spartans v Welling United	1-3
Stafford Rangers v Morecambe	1-0
Crawley Town v Worcester City	3-1
Kidderminster Harriers v Grays Athletic	0-1

THIRD ROUND

Hereford United v Grays Athletic	0-1
Stafford Rangers v Forest Green Rovers	2-1
Crawley Town v Boreham Wood	0-2
Woking v Welling United	3-2
Tamworth v Dagenham & Redbridge	0-0, 0-3
Exeter City v Cambridge City	1-0
Accrington Stanley v Worksop Town	1-1, 1-1
Worksop Town won 4-2 on penalties.	
Salisbury City v Stalybridge Celtic	0-0, 1-0

FOURTH ROUND

Exeter City v Salisbury City	3-1
Worksop Town v Boreham Wood	0-1
Woking v Stafford Rangers	1-1, 4-2
Grays Athletic v Dagenham & Redbridge	1-1, 4-2

SEMI-FINALS (TWO LEGS)

Boreham Wood v Woking	0-1, 0-2
Exeter City v Grays Athletic	2-1, 0-2

THE FA TROPHY FINAL

Sunday, 14 May 2006
(at Upton Park)

Grays Athletic (2) 2 *(Oli 41, Poole 45)*
Woking (0) 0 13,800

Grays Athletic: Bayes; Sambrook, Nutter, Thurgood, Stuart, Hanson, Kightly (Williamson 90), Martin, McLean, Oli, Poole.

Woking: Jalal; Jackson, Hutchinson, Murray, Nethercott (Cockerill L 60), MacDonald, Smith (Watson 60), Ferguson, Richards, McAllister, Evans (Blackman 83).

Referee: H. Webb (Sheffield & Hallamshire).

Grays Athletic lift the FA Trophy after their 2-0 win over Woking at Upton Park.
(Henry Browne/Actionimages)

THE FA VASE 2005–06

IN PARTNERSHIP WITH CARLSBERG

FIRST QUALIFYING ROUND

Horden CW v Bacup Borough 2-3
Hall Road Rangers v Morpeth Town 3-5
Brandon United v Bottesford Town 4-3
Penrith v Clipstone Welfare 3-0
Tow Law Town v Trafford 1-2
Hallam v Padiham 1-2
North Shields v Cammell Laird 1-4
Ryton v Crook Town 1-2
Esh Winning v Flixton 0-1
Pontefract Collieries v Garforth Town 3-2
Winterton Rangers v Guisborough Town 3-1
Seaham Red Star w.o. v Shotton Comrades withdrew
Peterlee Newtown v Retford United 2-6
Easington Colliery v Armthorpe Welfare 0-6
Durham City v Eccleshill United 1-0
Ramsbottom United v Squires Gate 1-3
Yorkshire Amateur v Newcastle Blue Star 0-3
Glasshoughton Welfare v Chester-le-Street Town 2-0
Curzon Ashton v Newcastle Benfield (Bay Plastics) 0-1
Parkgate v Tadcaster Albion 2-0
Northallerton Town v Sunderland Nissan 0-1
Boston Town v Nuneaton Griff 0-2
Teversal v Norton United 1-1, 0-1
Malvern Town v Long Eaton United 4-2
Pilkington XXX v Pegasus Juniors 3-6
Causeway United v Graham St Prims 2-0
Gedling MW v Alvechurch 1-2
Deeping Rangers v Stapenhill 2-1
Tividale v Highgate United 4-1
Racing Club Warwick v Eccleshall 1-0
Leek CSOB v Gornal Athletic 2-0
Studley v Leamington 0-1
Shifnal Town v Coventry Copsewood 4-0
Westfields v Stratford Town 2-1
Bourne Town v Shirebrook Town 1-2
Blackstones v Dunkirk 1-0
Blaby & Whetstone Athletic v Loughborough Dynamo 3-1
St Andrews v Rolls Royce Leisure 3-1
Mickleover Sports v Pershore Town 1-2
Ellistown v Castle Vale 1-4
Kirby Muxloe v Sandiacre Town 2-2, 2-1
Atherstone Town v Ludlow Town 4-2
Friar Lane & Epworth v Holwell Sports 5-1
Bolehall Swifts v Buxton 1-5
Lincoln Moorlands v Nettleham 4-1
Biddulph Victoria v Brierley & Hagley 3-0
Stowmarket Town v Needham Market 0-5
Royston Town v Whitton United 0-0, 2-0
Southall v Wroxham 2-3
Ipswich Wanderers v Bowers & Pitsea 2-0
Tring Athletic v Stotfold 1-1, 0-2
Leiston v Ruislip Manor 3-1
Haverhill Rovers v Welwyn Garden City 2-4
Sawbridgeworth Town v Long Buckby 2-0
Tiptree United v London APSA 2-1
Buckingham Town v Barkingside 3-1
Woodbridge Town v Harwich & Parkeston 4-2
Harpenden Town v AFC Wallingford 1-2
Northampton Spencer v Cranfield United 3-0
Huntingdon Town v St Margaretsbury 1-3
Brimsdown Rovers v Biggleswade Town 1-2
London Colney v Eynesbury Rovers 4-1
Bedford United & Valerio v Basildon United 0-4
Hullbridge Sports v Cornard United 3-1
Hoddesdon Town v Yaxley 0-1
Flackwell Heath v Gorleston 1-2
Ware v Newport Pagnell Town 1-3
Biggleswade United v Walsham Le Willows 1-2
Godmanchester Rovers v St Neots Town 1-2
Harefield United v Witham Town 2-3
Wootton Blue Cross v Stansted 2-0
Kingsbury Town v Saffron Walden Town 3-1
Hertford Town v Dereham Town 1-2
Camberley Town v Godalming Town 2-4
Tunbridge Wells v Moneyfields 0-0, 0-5
Lymington Town v Sidlesham 3-0
Pagham v Hythe Town 2-6
Oakwood v VCD Athletic 1-4
Epsom & Ewell v Petersfield Town 3-1
Hartley Wintney v Alton Town 1-0
Bedfont v Littlehampton Town 1-2
Greenwich Borough v Chertsey Town 2-0
Farnham Town v Wantage Town 1-2
VT v Wick 4-3
Bedfont Green v Ash United 1-1, 0-4
Cobham v Sevenoaks Town 0-2
Fareham Town v Ringmer 0-1
AFC Totton v Mole Valley (Predators) 3-1
Westfield v Hungerford Town 0-2
Maidstone United v Cowes Sports 4-2
East Preston v Redhill 4-1
Chichester City United v Colliers Wood United 2-2, 1-2
Eastbourne United v Mile Oak 1-3
Slimbridge v Chipping Norton Town 3-0
Hamworthy United w.o. v Tuffley Rovers withdrew
Amesbury Town v Bishop Sutton 0-1
Harrow Hill v Penryn Athletic 2-3
Radstock Town v Barnstaple Town 3-1
Odd Down v Wadebridge Town 2-1
Westbury United v Shaftsbury 4-0
Fairford Town v Portland United 5-0
Wellington Town v Calne Town 3-1
Budleigh Salterton v Falmouth Town 1-1, 1-0
Downton v Street 1-2
Truro City v Launceston 3-1
Exmouth Town v St Blazey 1-4

SECOND QUALIFYING ROUND

Liversedge v Bacup Borough 1-0
Glasshoughton Welfare v Rossington Main 7-1
Abbey Hey v Formby 6-1
Newcastle Blue Star v Seaham Red Star 1-2
Cammell Laird v Atherton Collieries 4-0
Winsford United v Padiham 2-1
Silsden v Ashville 1-3
Hebburn Town v Prudhoe Town 0-2
Whickham v Chadderton 5-1
Atherton LR v Marske United 1-1, 2-4
Sunderland Nissan v Whitley Bay 4-2
Washington v West Auckland Town 1-2
Alsager Town v Newcastle Benfield (Bay Plastics) 2-4
Nelson v Flixton 3-2
Spennymoor Town v Crook Town 1-4
Oldham Town v Winterton Rangers 3-1
Willington v Darwen 2-4
Norton & Stockton Ancients v Sheffield 2-0
Maine Road v Daisy Hill 2-3
New Mills v Penrith 1-2
Morpeth Town v Salford City 1-1, 0-5
Great Harwood Town v Thornaby 0-3
Paulton Victoria v Parkgate 1-3
Durham City v Trafford 2-4
Shildon v Alnwick Town 1-1, 2-5
South Shields v Ashington 1-3
Pontefract Collieries v Darlington Railway Athletic 2-3
Consett v Worsborough Bridge MW 5-0
Brodsworth MW v Blackpool Mechanics 2-0
Retford United v Holker Old Boys 4-2
Cheadle Town v Armthorpe Welfare 2-4
Squires Gate v Brandon United 2-1
Buxton v Lincoln Moorlands 2-1
Sutton Town v Nuneaton Griff 0-0, 0-0
Sutton Town won 4-1 on penalties.
Ibstock United v Arnold Town
Tie abandoned at half time. *0-1*
Shawbury United v Glapwell 0-4
Blackstones v Racing Club Warwick 1-2
Cradley Town v Lye Town 2-1
Highfield Rangers v Downes Sports 2-1
Causeway United v Kirby Muxloe 2-3
Romulus v Birstall United 5-0
Pershore Town v Bridgnorth Town 0-2
Barrow Town v Congleton Town 3-2
Leamington w.o. v Radcliffe Olympic withdrew
Glossop North End v Staveley MW 3-2
Stone Dominoes withdrew v Biddulph Victoria w.o.
Carlton Town v Holbrook MW 2-1
South Normanton Athletic v Wolverhampton Casuals 2-1
Barwell v Leek CSOB 3-2
Radford v Pelsall Villa 1-2
St Andrews v Blidworth Welfare 5-1
Oadby Town v Friar Lane & Epworth 1-3
Ford Sports Daventry v Atherstone Town 1-0
Rainworth MW v Deeping Rangers 0-1
Tividale v Borrowash Victoria 1-1, 0-4
Kimberley Town v Alvechurch 1-4
Blackwell MW v Shirebrook Town 0-3
Norton United v Oldbury United 1-1, 0-2
Boldmere St Michaels v Meir KA 4-2
Malvern Town v Castle Vale 1-3
Bromyard Town v Heath Hayes 2-1
Barnt Green Spartak v Coleshill Town 2-4

Dudley Town v Anstey Nomads 1-0
Westfields v Pegasus Juniors 3-0
Daventry Town v Wellington 0-0
Wellington won 4-2 on penalties.
Blaby & Whetstone Athletic v Heanor Town 2-5
Shifnal Town v Nantwich Town 0-1
Newark Town v Coventry Sphinx 4-2
St Neots Town v Witham Town 0-0, 2-4
Wembley v Needham Market 0-4
Kirkley v Dereham Town 0-2
Sporting Bengal United v Felixstowe & Walton United 1-4
Biggleswade Town v Tiptree United 1-3
Downham Town v Leverstock Green 1-1, 1-5
Henley Town v Ely City 3-2
Stotfold v Gorleston 1-4
Southend Manor v Brentwood Town 3-0
Hullbridge Sports v Clacton Town 4-0
Arlesey Athletic v Concord Rangers 3-5
Woodbridge Town v Raunds Town 1-4
Great Yarmouth Town v Stanway Rovers 0-1
Thetford Town v Wootton Blue Cross 1-4
Cockfosters v Holmer Green 4-1
St Ives Town v Woodford United 0-2
Bicester Town v Buckingham Town 2-0
Romford v Oxhey Jets 2-0
Basildon United v Buckingham Athletic 2-1
Newmarket Town v Walsham Le Willows 2-1
Fakenham Town v Newport Pagnell Town 0-4
Rothwell Corinthians v Welwyn Garden City 1-3
Sawbridgeworth Town v Chalfont St Peter 1-3
Langford v Leiston 0-3
Broxbourne Borough V&E v St Margaretsbury 2-1
Royston Town v Norwich United 1-0
Bugbrooke St Michaels v Long Melford 0-4
Wroxham v Yaxley 0-2
Clapton v Haringey Borough 1-2
AFC Kempston Rovers v Colney Heath 0-3
Eton Manor v Kingsbury Town 1-4
Northampton Spencer v Ipswich Wanderers 1-3
Dunstable Town 98 v Wisbech Town 1-7
London Colney v Hadleigh United 2-1
AFC Wallingford v March Town United 1-0
Mildenhall Town v Diss Town 4-0
Sevenoaks Town v VT 2-3
Selsey v Lordswood 2-2, 2-0
Blackfield & Langley v Abingdon Town 4-5
Hailsham Town v Cove 2-5
Slade Green v East Preston 2-1
United Services Portsmouth v Sidley United 0-2
Worthing United v Three Bridges 0-5
Epsom & Ewell v Milton United 3-0
Lymington Town v Thamesmead Town 2-4
Colliers Wood United v Raynes Park Vale 3-0
Hamble ASSC v Steyning Town 4-0
Eastbourne Town v Maidstone United 0-3
Merstham v Reading Town 4-0
Peacehaven & Telscombe v Godalming Town 1-4
North Leigh v Hawley Town 2-0
Littlehampton Town v Hillingdon Borough 1-1, 1-3
Ardley United v Carterton 1-3
Mile Oak v BAT Sports 2-0
Shoreham v AFC Totton 6-2
Hassocks v Ash United 3-1
Guildford United v Andover 1-5
Wantage Town v Ringmer 3-2
Abingdon United v Sandhurst Town 4-1
Gosport Borough v Greenwich Borough 0-1
Arundel v Frimley Green 5-1
Chipstead v Brockenhurst 1-2
Hartley Wintney v Hungerford Town 1-1, 1-2
Hythe Town v Moneyfields 2-1
East Grinstead Town v Lancing 3-1
Saltdean United v VCD Athletic 0-3
Erith Town v Andover New Street 3-2
Ilfracombe Town v Bournemouth 2-4
Pewsey Vale v Westbury United 1-0
Welton Rovers v Sherborne Town 5-0
Porthleven v St Blazey 0-3
Chard Town v Melksham Town 4-1
Saltash United v Clevedon United 1-2
Devizes Town v Penzance 1-0
Budleigh Salterton v Witney United 0-6
Willand Rovers v Elmore 4-1
Wimborne Town v Shepton Mallet 3-0
Shortwood United v Cullompton Rangers 5-0
Odd Down v Bridport 3-0
Torrington v Truro City 0-4
Larkhall Athletic v Poole Town 1-4
Liskeard Athletic v Bemerton Heath Harlequins 1-4
Bristol Manor Farm v Minehead 2-1
Fairford Town v Radstock Town 1-2
Wootton Bassett Town v Christchurch 1-1, 0-1
Millbrook v Newton Abbot 2-3
Ottery St Mary v Tavistock 2-5
Wellington Town v Ringwood Town 1-0
Penryn Athletic v Hamworthy United 2-1
Newquay v Street 1-2
Malmsbury Victoria v Slimbridge 0-2
Almondsbury Town v Dawlish Town 0-1
Bishop Sutton v Hallen 0-2

FIRST ROUND

Trafford v Prudhoe Town 1-0
Darlington Railway Athletic v Dunston FB 2-2, 0-3
Armthorpe Welfare v Norton & Stockton Ancients 0-1
Sunderland Nissan v Abbey Hey 1-0
Daisy Hill v Nelson 0-1
Newcastle Benfield (Bay Plastics) v Whickham 3-1
Ashington v Thornaby 3-3, 3-4
Consett v Cammell Laird 0-1
Alnwick Town v Glasshoughton Welfare 1-3
Ashville v Penrith 3-1
Crook Town v Winsford United 2-0
Squires Gate v Salford City 3-0
Marske United v St Helens Town 2-3
Retford United v Brodsworth MW 4-0
Darwen v Harrogate Railway 2-4
Oldham Town v Seaham Red Star 3-1
West Auckland Town v Billingham Synthonia 0-2
Parkgate v Liversedge 3-3, 0-3
Wellington v Alvechurch 0-1
Holbeach United v Leamington 0-2
Biddulph Victoria v Castle Vale 2-1
Oldbury United v Coleshill Town 0-4
Barrow Town v Borrowash Victoria 4-3
Ford Sports Daventry v Sutton Town 2-1
Selby Town v South Normanton Athletic 3-1
Deeping Rangers v Buxton 0-4
Coalville Town v Dudley Town 7-0
Westfields v Bridgnorth Town 1-0
Nantwich Town v Boldmere St Michaels 1-0
Heanor Town v Arnold Town 0-2
Cradley Town v Newark Town 4-2
Rocester v Carlton Town 0-2
Racing Club Warwick v Barwell 1-0
Glossop North End v Romulus 6-4
Friar Lane & Epworth v Shirebrook Town 5-1
Newcastle Town v Glapwell 3-2
Highfield Rangers v St Andrews 2-0
Bromyard Town v Chasetown 0-1
Kirby Muxloe v Pelsall Villa 0-2
Cockfosters v Ipswich Wanderers 0-3
Tilbury v Burnham Ramblers 2-1
Felixstowe & Walton United v Chalfont St Peter 3-3, 1-2
Wootton Blue Cross v Royston Town 2-1
Leiston v Henley Town 3-2
Long Melford v Newmarket Town 1-2
Stanway Rovers v Basildon United 4-3
Newport Pagnell Town v Romford 0-1
London Colney v Tiptree United 5-3
Hullbridge Sports v Mildenhall Town 0-8
Yaxley v Southend Manor 8-1
AFC Wallingford v Wisbech Town 1-4
Hanwell Town v Colney Heath 4-1
Kingsbury Town v Haringey Borough 2-0
Woodford United v Broxbourne Borough V&E 3-4
Oxford City v Welwyn Garden City 1-3
Witham Town v Waltham Abbey 5-3
Aylesbury Vale v Bicester Town 1-2
Cogenhoe United v AFC Hornchurch 0-1
Gorleston v Raunds Town 1-0
Concord Rangers v Halsted Town 2-0
Leverstock Green v North Greenford United 3-1
Needham Market v Dereham Town 1-0
VT v Hythe Town 1-2
Thatcham Town v Selsey 4-2
Mile Oak v Slade Green 0-0, 4-1
Greenwich Borough v Colliers Wood United 1-3
Sidley United v Shoreham 3-0
Arundel v Croydon 4-2
Abingdon Town v Egham Town 0-2
Carterton v Hungerford Town 1-0
Merstham v Three Bridges 1-2
Erith Town v Whitehawk 2-0
Godalming Town v Hassocks 1-4
Brockenhurst v Abingdon United 2-1
Chessington & Hook United v Horsham YMCA 1-0
Herne Bay v Epsom & Ewell 4-2
East Grinstead Town v Rye Iden United 3-5
Erith & Belvedere v Hillingdon Borough 1-5
Wantage Town v Thamesmead Town 1-3
Dorking v Hamble ASSC 4-1
North Leigh v Maidstone United 0-4
Cove v VCD Athletic 0-2
Whitstable Town v Andover 1-3

Chard Town v Dawlish Town 1-1, 2-3
Poole Town v Bideford 1-2
Devizes Town v Pewsey Vale 0-0, 1-1
Devizes Town won 3-0 on penalties.
Shortwood United v Bishop's Cleeve 0-3
Bristol Manor Farm v Highworth Town 2-3
Newton Abbot v Corsham Town 1-0
Street v Christchurch 0-2
Truro City v Witney United 3-1
Tavistock v Penryn Athletic 3-0
Bournemouth v Odd Down 4-1
Clevedon United v St Blazey 2-4
Wimborne Town v Radstock Town 3-1
Hallen v Slimbridge 0-1
Wellington Town v Bemerton Heath Harlequins 1-2
Welton Rovers v Willand Rovers 2-3

SECOND ROUND
Glasshoughton Welfare v Squires Gate 1-2
Pickering Town v Oldham Town 1-0
Nelson v Ashville 0-1
Sunderland Nissan v Bedlington Terriers 3-3, 1-2
Thackley v Jarrow Roofing Boldon CA 3-0
Liversedge v Billingham Synthonia 5-4
Colne v Norton & Stockton Ancients 4-0
Crook Town v Billingham Town 4-0
Harrogate Railway v Cammell Laird 0-1
Newcastle Benfield (Bay Plastics) v Thornaby 5-1
St Helens Town v Dunston FB 1-3
Skelmersdale United v West Allotment Celtic 4-3
Retford United v Trafford 2-1
Selby Town v Westfields 3-3, 3-2
Barrow Town v Quorn 1-3
Arnold Town v Pelsall Villa 2-0
Newcastle Town v Cradley Town 1-0
Tipton Town v Racing Club Warwick 0-2
Biddulph Victoria v Leamington 1-2
Highfield Rangers v Gedling Town 2-3
Ford Sports Daventry v Coleshill Town 4-2
Friar Lane & Epworth v Stourbridge 1-5
Glossop North End v Carlton Town 3-4
Desborough Town v Coalville Town 0-1
Buxton v Alvechurch 4-0
Chasetown v Nantwich Town 0-1
Stanway Rovers v Broxbourne Borough V&E 5-5, 0-3
London Colney v Ipswich Wanderers 6-3
AFC Hornchurch v Soham Town Rangers 1-3
Lowestoft Town v Wootton Blue Cross 2-0
Gorleston v Mildenhall Town 0-0, 0-1
Abandoned 85 minutes; fog. 0-2
Leverstock Green v Chalfont St Peter 0-2
Needham Market v Potton United 3-1
Newmarket Town v Tilbury 2-1
Concord Rangers v Welwyn Garden City 1-2
Wisbech Town v Leiston 8-1
Yaxley v Witham Town 3-0
AFC Sudbury v Romford 4-0
Bury Town v Hanwell Town 3-0
Colliers Wood United v VCD Athletic 2-3
Sidley United v Erith Town 4-2
Chessington & Hook United v Carterton 2-0
Mile Oak v Deal Town 1-3
Bicester Town v Dorking 0-1
Maidstone United v Andover 4-0
Thamesmead Town v Brook House 0-4
Rye & Iden United v Hillingdon Borough 2-2, 0-1
Three Bridges v Arundel 0-1
Winchester City v AFC Newbury 5-0
Hythe Town v Thatcham Town 3-2
Didcot Town v Herne Bay 7-0
Brockenhurst v Egham Town 2-2, 1-0
Kingsbury Town v Hassocks 1-0
Bishop's Cleeve v Newton Abbot 1-0
Abandoned 48 minutes; fog. 3-0
Highworth Town v Wimborne Town 0-1
Bournemouth v Frome Town 1-0
Bridgwater Town v Slimbridge 0-1
Devizes Town v Brislington 2-1
Bodmin Town v Bitton 3-0
Christchurch v Truro City 3-2
Dawlish Town v Bideford 1-2
Ledbury Town v Willand Rovers 2-1
Abandoned 86 minutes; fog. 0-4
Bemerton Heath Harlequins v St Blazey 2-3
Tavistock v Backwell United 4-2

THIRD ROUND
Ashville v Racing Club Warwick 3-3, 2-2
Ashville won 4-3 on penalties.
Squires Gate v Skelmersdale United 2-1
Coalville Town v Arnold Town 3-3, 0-3
Thackley v Colne 2-1
Gedling Town v Carlton Town 4-3
Pickering Town v Dunston FB 1-0
Crook Town v Ford Sports Daventry 8-2
Quorn v Nantwich Town 0-1
Cammell Laird v Retford United 3-0
Newcastle Benfield (Bay Plastics) v Stourbridge 2-1
Newcastle Town v Bedlington Terriers 1-3
Leamington v Liversedge 2-1
Selby Town v Buxton 0-1
Hythe Town v Chalfont St Peter 2-1
Needham Market v Devizes Town 3-0
Maidstone United v Broxbourne Borough V&E 2-2, 3-3
Broxbourne Borough V&E won 5-4 on penalties.
Hillingdon Borough v Bideford 2-1
Yaxley v Winchester City 2-4
Arundel v VCD Athletic 1-2
Soham Town Rangers v Bury Town 1-2
AFC Sudbury v Bodmin Town 3-1
Lowestoft Town v Kingsbury Town 2-0
Sidley United v St Blazey 1-2
Wisbech Town v Brook House 4-4, 0-2
London Colney v Chessington & Hook United 1-2
Deal Town v Tavistock 2-4
Wimborne Town v Bishop's Cleeve 4-1
Dorking v Christchurch 5-2
Welwyn Garden City v Slimbridge 3-1
Bournemouth v Brockenhurst 1-2
Newmarket Town v Willand Rovers 1-0
Didcot Town v Mildenhall Town 4-4, 1-2

FOURTH ROUND
Crook Town v St Blazey 3-0
Pickering Town v Tavistock 3-0
Leamington v Wimborne Town 2-3
Needham Market v Nantwich Town 3-6
Thackley v Arnold Town 0-2
Dorking v Mildenhall Town 1-3
Newcastle Benfield (Bay Plastics) v Lowestoft Town 3-1
VCD Athletic v Broxbourne Borough V & E 1-0
Chessington & Hook United v Cammell Laird 1-2
Buxton v Ashville 1-0
Brockenhurst v Bury Town 0-2
Newmarket Town v Welwyn Garden City 2-2, 1-2
Tie awarded to Newmarket Town; Welwyn Garden City fielded an ineligible player.
Hillingdon Borough v Brook House 2-0
Squires Gate v Gedling Town 2-1
Hythe Town v Winchester City 1-3
AFC Sudbury v Bedlington Terriers 1-1, 3-1

FIFTH ROUND
AFC Sudbury v Bury Town 0-2
Wimborne Town v Pickering Town 1-2
Nantwich Town v Buxton 1-0
Cammell Laird v VCD Athletic 1-0
Hillingdon Borough v Mildenhall Town 4-0
Arnold Town v Crook Town 0-1
Winchester City v Newmarket Town 3-4
Squires Gate v Newcastle Benfield (Bay Plastics) 2-1

SIXTH ROUND
Hillingdon Borough v Squires Gate 2-0
Crook Town v Bury Town 0-1
Nantwich Town v Pickering Town 2-0
Newmarket Town v Cammell Laird 1-2

SEMI-FINAL (TWO LEGS)
Bury Town v Hillingdon Borough 1-1, 1-2
Cammell Laird v Nantwich Town 0-1, 0-4

THE FA VASE FINAL

Saturday, 6 May 2006

(at St Andrews, Birmingham City FC)

Hillingdon Borough (0) 1 *(Nelson 90)*

Nantwich Town (2) 3 *(Kinsey 14, 68, Scheuber 30)* 3286

Hillingdon Borough: Harris; Brown, Rundell (Fenton 80), Tilbury, Phillips, Kidson, Hibbs, Duncan (Nelson 47), Lawrence, Wharton (Lyons 37), Craft.
Nantwich Town: Hackney; Taylor A, Taylor P, Donnelly, Smith, Davis, Beasley, Scheuber (Parkinson 72), Blake (Scarlett 85), Kinsey (Marrow 72), Griggs.
Referee: P. Armstrong (Berkshire).

THE FA YOUTH CUP 2005–06

IN PARTNERSHIP WITH PEPSI

PRELIMINARY ROUND

Woodley Sports v Lancaster City 1-2
Chadderton v Marine 2-2
Marine won 8-7 on penalties.
Leigh RMI v Frickley Athletic 5-0
Belper Town v Eccleshall 1-0
Teversal v Eastwood Town 1-1
Teversal won 6-5 on penalties.
Burton Albion v Redditch United 4-0
Matlock Town v Ford Sports Daventry 3-3
Ford Sports Daventry won 7-6 on penalties.
Chasetown v Tamworth 3-2
AFC Telford United w.o. v Mickleover Sports withdrew
Nuneaton Borough v Sutton Coldfield Town 4-0
Blackstones v Corby Town 6-2
Stotfold v St Albans City 3-2
Aylesbury United v Chesham United 1-3
King's Lynn v Raunds Town 2-1
Harwich & Parkeston v Dereham Town 6-1
North Greenford United v Boreham Wood 3-1
Harlow Town v Brentwood Town 2-3
Hampton & Richmond Borough v Hayes 0-7
Long Buckby w.o. v Thame United withdrew
Harrow Borough v Enfield Town 2-1
Bury Town v Diss Town 12-0
Bugbrooke St Michaels v Histon 0-6
Harefield United v Royston Town 3-2
Concord Rangers v Grays Athletic 3-0
Redbridge v Berkhamsted Town 2-0
Whitton United v Great Yarmouth Town 1-1
Great Yarmouth Town won 4-2 on penalties.
Tring Athletic v Buckingham Town 5-0
Newport Pagnell Town v Barton Rovers 1-3
Colney Heath v Bedford Town 1-2
Sawbridgeworth Town v Wealdstone 0-4
AFC Kempston Rovers v St Margaretsbury 3-1
Long Melford v Southend Manor 4-0
East Thurrock United v Woodbridge Town 2-5
Halstead Town w.o. v Stansted withdrew
Ruislip Manor v Leighton Town 0-1
Burnham Ramblers v Hitchin Town 1-3
AFC Newbury v Westfield 0-5
Herne Bay w.o. v Ashford Town withdrew
Godalming Town v Fleet Town 2-0
Thamesmead Town v Bedfont 3-2
Camberley Town v AFC Wimbledon 0-4
Carshalton Athletic v Erith Town 4-1
Cobham v Ash United 2-2
Ash United won 5-3 on penalties.
Three Bridges w.o. v Havant & Waterlooville withdrew
Carterton v Oxford City 3-5
Reading Town v Ashford Town (Middlesex) 1-3

FIRST QUALIFYING ROUND

Atherton LR v Vauxhall Motors 0-3
Ossett Albion v Retford United 1-2
Dunston FB v Gateshead 2-1
Selby Town v Altrincham 2-1
Witton Albion v Yorkshire Amateur 0-1
Whitley Bay v Kendal Town 3-0
Trafford v Eccleshill United 4-3
Skelmersdale United v Alsager Town 11-1
Stocksbridge Park Steels v Leigh RMI 2-3
Winsford United v Warrington Town 1-4
Ryton v Scarborough 4-3
Northwich Victoria v Burscough 0-3
Stalybridge Celtic v Pontefract Collieries 1-2
AFC Emley v Morecambe 1-6
Bradford Park Avenue v Thackley 1-0
Goole v Guiseley 3-2
Prescot Cables v Daisy Hill 0-2
Halifax Town v North Ferriby United 0-3
Penrith withdrew v Workington w.o.
Formby v Lancaster City 1-2
Worksop Town v Garforth Town 0-3
Radcliffe Borough v Southport 1-2
York City v Marine 4-1
Chester-le-Street Town v Farsley Celtic 1-1
Farsley Celtic won 5-4 on penalties.
Nuneaton Borough v Oadby Town 3-1
Gresley Rovers v Kidderminster Harriers 0-3
Bedworth United v Nuneaton Griff 4-2
Long Eaton United v AFC Telford United 3-4
Rushall Olympic v Wellington 3-2
Racing Club Warwick v Cradley Town 4-2
Castle Vale v Boldmere St Michaels 1-3
Lye Town v Chasetown 2-4
Nantwich Town v Burton Albion 1-9
Rugby Town v Pershore Town 14-0
Kimberley Town v Alfreton Town 1-6
Gornal Athletic v Leek Town 0-3
Moor Green v Hinckley United 4-3
Ford Sports Daventry v Deeping Rangers 0-3
Blackstones v Stafford Rangers 1-3
Coleshill Town v Congleton Town 3-1
Hucknall Town v Arnold Town 1-6
Coventry Sphinx v Glossop North End 1-0
Hednesford Town v Newcastle Town 14-0
Bromsgrove Rovers v Belper Town 6-1
Stourbridge v Carlton Town 2-0
Kettering Town v Malvern Town 1-0
Stratford Town v Teversall 2-2
Stratford Town won 3-0 on penalties.
Alvechurch v Bourne Town 1-0
Heybridge Swifts v Chesham United 0-1
Hitchin Town v Uxbridge 1-1
Uxbridge won 4-3 on penalties.
Canvey Island v Leighton Town 1-2
Wealdstone v Banbury United 6-1
Barking & East Ham United v Leyton 5-3
Wingate & Finchley v Cambridge United 0-10
Staines Town v Stotfold 4-1
London Colney v Barton Rovers 0-2
Stevenage Borough v Redbridge 4-0
Haringey Borough v AFC Kempston Rovers 7-3
Fakenham Town v Ware 6-5
Lowestoft Town v Long Buckby 1-0
Potters Bar Town v Cogenhoe United 1-7
Clacton Town v Great Wakering Rovers 2-1
Clapton v Marlow 0-0
Marlow won 4-2 on penalties.
King's Lynn v Ely City 1-2
Hemel Hempstead Town v Thurrock 1-3
Ilford v Rothwell Corinthians 0-1
Wivenhoe Town v Broxbourne Borough V&E 5-6
Hendon v Kingsbury Town 3-0
AFC Hornchurch v Harefield United 1-2
Newmarket Town v Histon 0-3
Great Yarmouth Town v Witham Town 3-1
Northwood v Romford 3-2
Chalfont St Peter v Brook House 0-2
Bishop's Stortford v Woodbridge Town 2-1
Hayes v Cheshunt 1-1
Cheshunt won 4-3 on penalties.
Tring Athletic v Harwich & Parkeston 1-0
Bury Town v Long Melford 3-0
AFC Wallingford v Henley Town 1-2
Walsham Le Willows v Hullbridge Sports 2-3
Northampton Spencer v March Town United 5-1
Dagenham & Redbridge v Waltham Forest 0-1
Waltham Abbey v Billericay Town 0-3
Concord Rangers v Harrow Borough 0-1
North Greenford United v Cambridge City 0-3
Chelmsford City v Braintree Town 1-0
Bedford Town v Brentwood Town 5-2
Halstead Town v Buntingford Town 0-3
Beaconsfield SYCOB v Aveley 1-0
Wick v Eastbourne Borough 2-3
Burnham v Milton United 6-1
Farnborough Town v Steyning Town 4-1
Aldershot Town v Bromley 6-0
Dulwich Hamlet v Epsom & Ewell 6-1
Oxford City v Burgess Hill Town 9-1
Worthing v Lewes 5-2
Folkestone Invicta v Croydon Athletic 3-3
Folkestone Invicta won 5-4 on penalties.
Sevenoaks Town v Three Bridges 3-4
Basingstoke Town v Molesey 6-1
Saltdean United v Horsham 2-1

Ramsgate v Tonbridge Angels 2-1
Horsham YMCA v Ash United 2-1
Dover Athletic v Chatham Town 2-1
Bracknell Town v Eastleigh 4-2
Woking v Ashford Town (Middlesex) 4-0
Mile Oak v Alton Town 5-1
AFC Wimbledon v Erith & Belvedere 3-0
Moneyfields v Godalming Town 3-1
Mole Valley (Predators) v Corinthian Casuals 1-3
Whyteleafe v Carshalton Athletic 3-4
Hillingdon Borough v Crawley Town 2-0
Dartford v Gravesend & Northfleet 1-6
Sandhurst Town v Thatcham Town 1-0
Chipstead v Lewisham Borough 6-0
Herne Bay v Peacehaven & Telscombe 7-1
Fisher Athletic v Maidenhead United 2-3
Sutton United v Chertsey Town 4-1
South Park v Thamesmead Town 2-4
Pagham v Walton & Hersham 1-1
Pagham won 4-2 on penalties.
East Grinstead Town v Maidstone United 0-3
Westfield v Andover 2-1
Radstock Town v Forest Green Rovers 0-1
Weymouth v Westbury United 1-1
Weymouth won 3-1 on penalties.
Mangotsfield United v Gloucester City 0-2
Bath City v Bishop's Cleeve 2-0
Cinderford Town v Bristol Manor Farm 2-4
Wootton Bassett Town v Witney United 3-0
Bitton v Bridgwater Town 3-1
Tiverton Town v Exeter City 2-2
Tiverton Town won 9-8 on penalties.
Evesham United v Worcester City 1-5
Yate Town v Bournemouth 1-0
Cirencester Town v Merthyr Tydfil 1-2
Weston-Super-Mare v Newport County 2-5
Hereford United v Malmsbury Victoria 4-0
Poulton Rovers v Brislington 3-2
Taunton Town v Salisbury City 3-1
Chippenham Town v Poole Town 0-4

SECOND QUALIFYING ROUND

Pontefract Collieries v Workington 1-2
Skelmersdale United v Yorkshire Amateur 6-0
Whitley Bay v Dunston FB 0-3
Bradford Park Avenue v Southport 1-4
Trafford v York City 2-2
York City won 4-1 on penalties.
North Ferriby United v Garforth Town 3-0
Morecambe v Leigh RMI 2-1
Lancaster City v Selby Town 1-1
Lancaster City won 4-1 on penalties.
Ryton v Burscough 0-2
Farsley Celtic v Warrington Town 2-1
Daisy Hill v Retford United 3-1
Vauxhall Motors v Goole 2-1
Moor Green v Hednesford Town 0-1
Chasetown v Rushall Olympic 3-3
Chasetown won 4-2 on penalties.
Racing Club Warwick v Bedworth United 1-2
Stafford Rangers v Kettering Town 1-3
Boldmere St Michaels v Stratford Town 1-4
Coventry Sphinx v Stourbridge 2-1
Deeping Rangers v Burton Albion 1-4
Bromsgrove Rovers v AFC Telford United 2-3
Alfreton Town v Leek Town 2-5
Alvechurch v Rugby Town 3-2
Arnold Town v Kidderminster Harriers 4-0
Nuneaton Borough v Coleshill Town 0-1
Hendon v Wealdstone 1-2
Billericay Town v Tring Athletic 9-0
Hullbridge Sports v Rothwell Corinthians 0-2
Buntingford Town v Henley Town 1-0
Fakenham Town v Barton Rovers 1-7
Beaconsfield SYCOB v Cheshunt 1-0
Leighton Town v Ely City 2-3
Haringey Borough v Harefield United 1-1
Haringey Borough won 6-5 on penalties.
Great Yarmouth Town v Chesham United 1-2
Stevenage Borough v Uxbridge 6-1
Clacton Town v Waltham Forest 0-3
Thurrock v Northampton Spencer 1-3
Brook House v Bury Town 0-3
Broxbourne Borough V&E v Histon 1-2
Northwood v Lowestoft Town 7-1
Harrow Borough v Chelmsford City 1-4
Staines Town v Bishop's Stortford 10-0
Bedford Town v Cogenhoe United 1-2
Cambridge City v Cambridge United 1-0
Barking & East Ham United v Marlow 2-0
Hillingdon Borough v Horsham YMCA 3-3
Hillingdon Borough won 3-1 on penalties.
Sutton United v Herne Bay 4-0
Mile Oak v Dover Athletic 2-1
Eastbourne Borough v Burnham 0-1
Three Bridges v Worthing 2-4
Pagham v Farnborough Town 1-3
Thamesmead Town v Dulwich Hamlet 2-0
Chipstead v Moneyfields 2-0
Saltdean United v Gravesend & Northfleet 1-8
Westfield v Aldershot Town 0-2
Basingstoke Town v Maidstone United 5-3
Maidenhead United v Ramsgate 0-4
Bracknell Town v Woking 0-4
Corinthian Casuals v Burgess Hill Town 6-0
Sandhurst Town v AFC Wimbledon 1-1
Sandhurst Town won 12-11 on penalties.
Folkestone Invicta v Carshalton Athletic 2-2
Folkestone Invicta won 6-5 on penalties.
Bitton v Tiverton Town 1-4
Hereford United v Paulton Rovers 5-0
Bath City v Bristol Manor Farm 4-2
Poole Town v Merthyr Tydfil 3-2
Weymouth v Gloucester City 0-1
Newport County v Yate Town 2-1
Wootton Bassett Town v Taunton Town 1-2
Forest Green Rovers v Worcester City 1-3

THIRD QUALIFYING ROUND

Skelmersdale United v Vauxhall Motors 5-4
Workington v Burscough 0-11
Dunston FB v York City 3-2
Daisy Hill v Farsley Celtic 4-3
Southport v North Ferriby United 4-4
Southport won 4-2 on penalties.
Morecambe v Lancaster City 1-1
Morecambe won 4-1 on penalties.
Chasetown v Coleshill Town 1-2
Hednesford Town v Leek Town 4-3
Bedworth United v Stratford Town 0-2
Arnold Town v Alvechurch 2-1
Kettering Town v Coventry Sphinx 3-1
Burton Albion v AFC Telford United 7-0
Stevenage Borough v Haringey Borough 8-0
Northwood v Barton Rovers 1-5
Barking & East Ham United v Bury Town 4-3
Wealdstone v Ely City 3-2
Northampton Spencer v Cambridge City 1-2
Billericay Town v Waltham Forest 2-3
Histon v Cogenhoe United 2-3
Buntingford Town v Rothwell Corinthians 1-0
Beaconsfield SYCOB v Chelmsford City 3-2
Chesham United v Staines Town 3-2
Thamesmead Town v Chipstead 2-4
Woking v Corinthian Casuals 9-3
Burnham v Worthing 1-1
Worthing won 4-2 on penalties.
Folkestone Invicta v Basingstoke Town 3-2
Sutton United v Mile Oak 5-1
Ramsgate v Aldershot Town 0-4
Farnborough Town v Sandhurst Town 2-0
Hillingdon Borough v Gravesend & Northfleet 0-5
Newport County v Worcester City 2-0
Taunton Town v Tiverton Town 2-3
Hereford United v Bath City 1-5
Poole Town v Gloucester City 0-3

FIRST ROUND

Blackpool v Rotherham United 3-2
Bury v Grimsby Town 0-1
Daisy Hill v Doncaster Rovers 2-4
Stockport County v Scunthorpe United 1-1
Stockport County won 7-6 on penalties.
Huddersfield Town v Burscough 3-0
Morecambe v Darlington 1-3
Chesterfield v Tranmere Rovers 0-3
Rochdale v Southport 0-1
Wrexham v Skelmersdale United 3-0

Carlisle United v Macclesfield Town 3-1
Bradford City v Dunston FB 1-2
Hartlepool United v Chester City 1-2
Oldham Athletic v Barnsley 3-0
Mansfield Town v Notts County 1-0
Coleshill Town v Arnold Town 0-2
Cogenhoe United v Boston United 2-1
Rushden & Diamonds v Lincoln City 3-0
Kettering Town v Nottingham Forest 0-3
Burton Albion v Port Vale 3-4
Hednesford Town v Cambridge City 2-3
Stratford Town v Northampton Town 1-2
Walsall v Shrewsbury Town 2-1
Wycombe Wanderers v Gravesend & Northfleet 1-0
Brentford v Worthing 4-1
Barking & East Ham United v Sutton United 2-0
Wealdstone v Folkestone Invicta 1-1
Folkestone Invicta won 7-6 on penalties.
Southend United v Barton Rovers 3-1
Aldershot Town v Buntingford Town 3-3
Buntingford Town won 7-6 on penalties.
Waltham Forest v Leyton Orient 4-2
Milton Keynes Dons v Farnborough Town 4-0
Stevenage Borough v Woking 2-1
Gillingham v Barnet 3-3
Gillingham won 6-5 on penalties.
Chipstead v Chesham United 3-2
Beaconsfield SYCOB v Colchester United 1-5
Oxford United v Yeovil 3-5
AFC Bournemouth v Tiverton Town 2-0
Newport County v Swindon Town 3-4
Gloucester City v Bath City 1-2
Match abandoned 20 minutes; waterlogged pitch; 0-0.
Swansea City v Cheltenham Town 0-1
Bristol Rovers v Bristol City 3-5

SECOND ROUND
Cambridge City v Nottingham Forest 0-5
Rushden & Diamonds v Walsall 0-1
Oldham Athletic v Wrexham 1-1
Wrexham won 4-2 on penalties.
Northampton Town v Mansfield Town 5-0
Cogenhoe United v Southport 3-0
Stockport County v Chester City 0-1
Carlisle United v Doncaster Rovers 1-1
Carlisle United won 5-4 on penalties.
Darlington v Huddersfield Town 0-1
Blackpool v Tranmere Rovers 0-3
Dunston FB v Arnold Town 1-7
Port Vale v Grimsby Town 3-2
Southend United v Swindon Town 3-2
Folkestone Invicta v Chipstead 1-2
Wycombe Wanderers v AFC Bournemouth 4-3
Waltham Forest v Yeovil Town 2-0
Bath City v Cheltenham Town 0-1
Colchester United v Barking & East Ham United 3-2
Milton Keynes Dons v Stevenage Borough 1-0
Gillingham v Bristol City 1-2
Brentford v Buntingford Town 3-1

THIRD ROUND
Arnold Town v Sheffield United 0-4
Cheltenham Town v Wolverhampton Wanderers 2-3
Reading v Everton 3-2
Wycombe Wanderers v Tranmere Rovers 0-5
Plymouth Argyle v Sunderland 3-4
Newcastle United v Stoke City 0-0
Newcastle United won 8-7 on penalties.
Milton Keynes Dons v Watford 0-4
Cogenhoe United v Derby County 1-3
Norwich City v Chelsea 1-2
Walsall v Charlton Athletic 1-2
Leicester City v Huddersfield Town 1-1
Huddersfield Town won 5-4 on penalties.
Sheffield Wednesday v Southend United 2-0
Arsenal v Brentford 2-2
Brentford won 5-4 on penalties.
Middlesbrough v Fulham 1-3
Brighton & Hove Albion v Port Vale 2-1
Northampton Town v Nottingham Forest 2-3
West Ham United v Luton Town 2-1
Leeds United v Ipswich Town 0-1
Queens Park Rangers v Aston Villa 1-2
Crewe Alexandra v Preston North End 2-0
Crystal Palace v Colchester United 3-2
Waltham Forest v West Bromwich Albion 1-0
Carlisle United v Chipstead 5-1
Bristol City v Bolton Wanderers 0-1
Hull City v Burnley 2-3
Portsmouth v Millwall 0-2
Wrexham v Southampton 2-5
Blackburn Rovers v Tottenham Hotspur 2-0
Birmingham City v Manchester United 0-2
Chester City v Wigan Athletic 0-2
Liverpool v Cardiff City 2-0
Manchester City v Coventry City 3-2

FOURTH ROUND
Wolverhampton Wanderers v Charlton Athletic 1-2
Brentford v Waltham Forest 2-0
Brighton & Hove Albion v Chelsea 2-1
Nottingham Forest v Reading 2-2
Nottingham Forest won 5-4 on penalties.
Crystal Palace v Tranmere Rovers 3-1
Burnley v Fulham 2-1
West Ham United v Manchester City 2-4
Sunderland v Manchester United 1-2
Bolton Wanderers v Crewe Alexandra 1-0
Carlisle United v Huddersfield Town 2-1
Southampton v Aston Villa 1-0
Liverpool v Ipswich Town 2-1
Sheffield United v Wigan Athletic 5-0
Sheffield Wednesday v Newcastle United 1-2
Blackburn Rovers v Derby County 2-1
Millwall v Watford 1-3

FIFTH ROUND
Brentford v Newcastle United 1-2
Burnley v Liverpool 0-3
Carlisle United v Sheffield United 2-0
Crystal Palace v Watford 3-2
Blackburn Rovers v Brighton & Hove Albion 2-3
Nottingham Forest v Manchester City 0-3
Bolton Wanderers v Southampton 0-1
Manchester United v Charlton Athletic 2-1

SIXTH ROUND
Crystal Palace v Southampton 0-4
Manchester City v Manchester United 1-0
Newcastle United v Brighton & Hove Albion 0-0
Newcastle United won 3-2 on penalties.
Liverpool v Carlisle United 6-0

SEMI-FINALS (TWO LEGS)
Liverpool v Southampton 2-1, 2-3
Liverpool won 5-4 on penalties.
Newcastle United v Manchester City 2-3, 1-1

FINAL (First Leg)
Thursday, 13 April 2006

Liverpool (2) 3 *(Threlfall 18, Flynn 32, Roque 84)*
Manchester City (0) 0 12,744

Liverpool: Roberts; Darby, Hobbs, Antwii, Threlfall, Barnett, Flynn (Spearing 88), Barratt, Hamill (Roque 77), Anderson, Lindfield.
Manchester City: Matthewson; Obeng, Logan, Williamson, Breen, Marshall, Williams, Johnson, Etuhu, Sturridge, Moore (Evans 81).

FINAL (Second Leg)
Friday, 21 April 2006

Manchester City (1) 2 *(Sturridge 32, 56)*
Liverpool (0) 0 10,601

Manchester City: Matthewson; Obeng, Logan, Richards, Breen, Evans, Marshall, Johnson, Moore, Etuhu, Sturridge.
Liverpool: Roberts; Darby, Threlfall, Hobbs, Antwii, Barnett (Roque 46), Barratt, Flynn, Lindfield, Anderson, Hamill (Spearing 59).

THE FA SUNDAY CUP 2005–06

IN PARTNERSHIP WITH CARLSBERG

PRELIMINARY ROUND

Allerton v Blessed Sacrament	5-2
The Warby v Whetley Lane WMC	1-2
Bartley Green Sunday v AC Sportsman	2-1
Wainscott Arrows v Howbridge Swifts	2-0
Treble Chance v Grange Athletic	0-2
Broad Plain House v Holt	2-1

FIRST ROUND

Allerton v AFC Pudsey	6-0
James Cropper v Harrington Portland	1-2
Bolton Woods v Carrs Hotel	1-2
BRNESC v Britannia	1-7
Buttershaw Whitestar v Brow	0-1
Home & Bargain v Canada Edinburgh Park	2-1
Elland v Nicosia	0-3
Clifton v Fairweather Green WMC	6-6
Fairweather Green WMC won 4-1 on penalties.	
Oakenshaw v Queens Park	1-3
Elmhouse Canon v Rawdon	3-0
Queensbury v Hartlepool Athletic Rugby	2-1
Dock v Lobster	3-5
Redoubt v Orchard Park	1-2
Seaburn v Pablo Derby Arms	1-0
Halton Arms Sports v Ring o' Bells (Shipley)	1-2
Hartlepool Rovers Quoit v Paddock	0-1
Seymour KFCA v Shipley Town	5-2
Smith & Nephew v Thornaby Town	2-0
Whetley Lane WMC v Hartlepool Supporters Athletic	2-0
Bruce Ennis Square v St Aloysius E	1-6
Western Approaches v Shankhouse United	1-3
Hetton Lyons Cricket Club v Seaton Sluice SC	4-1
Maryport v Sunderland JWS Construction	2-3
Taxi Club withdrew v Hessle Rangers w.o.	
Melling Victoria v Irlam MS	1-1
Irlam MS won 4-2 on penalties.	
Sandon Dock v Norcoast	3-4
Hartlepool Lion Hillcarter v North Mersey Lions	1-2
61 FC (Sunday) v George & Dragon	4-1
Austin ex Apprentices v Birstall Stamford	1-2
Scots Grey v Tally Ho	5-3
Bartley Green Sunday v Loft Style St Andrews	0-2
AFC Hornets (Studham) v Pioneer	1-6
Brache Green Man v Dun Cow	3-1
Ashlyn's United v Grosvenor Park	1-4
Crawley Green (Sunday) v Belstone	2-3
Belt Road v Lodge Cottrell	0-1
Casino v St Margarets	2-0
Hammer v Lewsey Social	2-1
Wainscott Arrows v Nicholas Wybacks	2-0
The Clifton v Lashings	7-1
Diffusion v Lebeq Tavern Courage	1-2
Travellers v Moggerhanger Sunday	3-1
Rettendon Athletic v Snodland WMC	3-5
Rainham Sports v Toby	2-1
UK Flooring v Moat	5-2
FC Fellowship v Venceremos	3-1
Grange Athletic v Wernley	2-3
Green Baize v CB Hounslow United	4-2
Broad Plain House v Woolston T&L	2-1
Bowood v Sandford	0-3
Risden Wood v Skew Bridge	3-1
London Maccabi Lions v The Well	5-3
VS Villa v Hanham Sunday	3-2
Dees v Greyhound	0-2
Reading Irish w.o. v Shireway Sports withdrew	
St Joseph's (Luton) v Trooper	2-0
Bournemouth Electric v Bedfont Sunday	3-2
Richfield Rovers v Team Bristol	0-4
The Cutters Friday v Mackadown Lane S&S	0-4
Queensmen v Celtic SC (Luton)	2-3
FC Houghton Centre v Nirankari Sports Sabha	2-8
Red Star ICL v Enfield Rangers	0-3

SECOND ROUND

Harrington Portland v Allerton	1-2
Carrs Hotel v Home & Bargain	3-2
Fairweather Green WMC v Britannia	1-9
Brow v Nicosia	1-4
Queens Park v Lobster	2-4
Elmhouse Canon v Queensbury	0-0
Queensbury won 4-2 on penalties.	
Orchard Park v Paddock	5-4
Seaburn v Ring o' Bells (Shipley)	5-0
Smith & Nephew v St Aloysius E	1-2
Seymour KFCA v Whetley Lane WMC	5-1
Shankhouse United v Hetton Lyons Cricket Club	1-8
Sunderland JWS Construction v Albion Sports	3-2
Hessle Rangers v North Mersey Lions	2-2
Hessle Rangers won 4-2 on penalties.	
Irlam MS v Norcoast	2-1
Birstall Stamford v Gossoms End	1-0
61 FC (Sunday) v Scots Grey	1-2
Pioneer v FC Fellowship	6-2
Loft Style St Andrews v Grosvenor Park	3-6
Lodge Cottrell v Belstone	1-2
Casino v UK Flooring	1-2
The Clifton v London Maccabi Lions	0-2
Wainscott Arrows v VS Villa	2-1
Risden Wood v Travellers	2-1
Greyhound v Lebeq Tavern Courage	0-2
Snodland WMC v Brache Green Man	0-2
Rainham Sports v Hammer	3-1
Wernley v Green Baize	3-0
Sandford v Broad Plain House	3-3
Broad Plain House won 8-7 on penalties.	
Reading Irish v St Joseph's (Luton)	1-1
St Joseph's (Luton) won 5-4 on penalties.	
Bournemouth Electric v Team Bristol	2-0
Mackadown Lane S&S v Enfield Rangers	2-2
Mackadown Lane S&S won 6-5 on penalties.	
Celtic SC (Luton) v Nirankari Sports Sabha	6-3

THIRD ROUND

Queensbury v Hetton Lyons Cricket Club	0-5
Allerton v Nicosia	0-2
Sunderland JWS Construction v Orchard Park	0-1
Britannia v Lobster	2-5
Hessle Rangers v Carss Hotel	2-0
Seymour KFCA v Irlam MS	2-1
Seaburn v St Aloyius E	2-2
St Aloyius E won 4-2 on penalties.	
Birstall Stamford v Grosvenor Park	3-1
Scots Grey v Mackadown Lane S&S	5-4
Brache Green Man v Wernley	0-2
Belstone v Wainscott Arrows	0-5
Pioneer v Celtic SC (Luton)	3-3
Celtic SC (Luton) won 4-3 on penalties.	
Rainham Sports v St Joseph's (Luton)	2-6
London Maccabi Lions v Risden Wood	3-1
UK Flooring v Bournemouth Electric	0-1
Lebeq Tavern Courage v Broad Plain House	5-0

FOURTH ROUND

Nicosia v Hetton Lyons Cricket Club	2-5
Hessle Rangers v Seymour KFCA	0-1
Orchard Park v Scots Grey	3-2
St Aloyius E v Lobster	3-5
Wernley v Birstall Stamford	0-1
St Joseph's (Luton) v London Maccabi Lions	2-1
Wainscott Arrows v Lebeq Tavern Courage	1-0
Bournemouth Electric v Celtic SC (Luton)	0-2

FIFTH ROUND

Seymour KFCA v Hetton Lyons Cricket Club	0-2
Orchard Park v Lobster	0-2
Wainscott Arrows v Birstall Stamford	1-3
Celtic SC Luton v St Joseph's (Luton)	0-1

SEMI-FINALS

Hetton Lyons Cricket Club v Birstall Stamford	2-1
Lobster v St Joseph's (Luton)	0-2

FINAL

Hetton Lyons Cricket Club 5 *(Brightwell 3, Pearson, Johnston)*
St Joseph's (Luton) 3 *(Hayes 2, Fontanelle)*
(at Liverpool FC)

THE FA COUNTY YOUTH CUP 2005–06

IN PARTNERSHIP WITH PEPSI

FIRST ROUND

Durham v Leicestershire & Rutland	4-1
Cheshire v Isle of Man	6-0
West Riding v Birmingham	0-3
Lincolnshire v Westmoreland	4-1
Manchester v Nottinghamshire	3-1
Sheffield & Hallamshire v Cumberland	2-1
Essex v Hertfordshire	2-0
Gloucestershire v Huntingdonshire	0-1
Middlesex v Army	4-2
London v Berks & Bucks	0-3
Worcestershire v Dorset	2-3
Cambridgeshire v Wiltshire	0-3
Guernsey v Herefordshire	4-2
Devon v Surrey	2-3
Kent v Bedfordshire	0-3

Byes: Cornwall, Derbyshire, East Riding, Hampshire, Jersey, Lancashire, Liverpool, Norfolk, North Riding, Northamptonshire, Northumberland, Oxfordshire, Shropshire, Somerset, Staffordshire, Suffolk, Sussex.

SECOND ROUND

Sheffield & Hallamshire v Birmingham	1-4
Shropshire v Lancashire	1-5
Manchester v Northumberland	3-2
Lincolnshire v East Riding	2-1
Liverpool v Durham	1-7
Cheshire v North Riding	2-1
Derbyshire v Staffordshire	4-0
Jersey v Surrey	0-1
Suffolk v Guernsey	2-1
Cornwall v Bedfordshire	2-3
Sussex v Norfolk	3-1
Middlesex v Hampshire	1-5
Berks & Bucks v Somerset	1-0
Huntingdonshire v Wiltshire	1-2
Dorset v Northamptonshire	0-1
Oxfordshire v Essex	4-3

THIRD ROUND

Lincolnshire v Derbyshire	2-0
Berks & Bucks v Cheshire	0-3
Bedfordshire v Lancashire	2-1
Hampshire v Wiltshire	1-5
Northamptonshire v Manchester	2-0
Oxfordshire v Sussex	1-2
Surrey v Durham	2-3
Birmingham v Suffolk	4-2

FOURTH ROUND

Durham v Sussex	3-1
Wiltshire v Northamptonshire	3-2
Cheshire v Lincolnshire	1-2
Bedfordshire v Birmingham	1-0

SEMI-FINALS

Durham v Wiltshire	0-0
Durham won 5-4 on penalties.	
Lincolnshire v Bedfordshire	0-0
Bedfordshire won 3-1 on penalties.	

FINAL

(at Darlington FC)

Durham (0) 2 *(Forrest 60, Brown 73)*

Bedfordshire (1) 3 *(Cunnington 11 (pen), Grieve 84, Lewis 85)*

Durham: Lawson; Burns, Davidson, Basham▪, Brown, Hall▪, Forrest, Magnay, Pennock (Hunter 77), Thackray (McRow 46), Coe.
Bedfordshire: Tompkins; Lewis, Moulds, Grieve, Lynch, Walsh (Thrower 46), Hall, Darvall, Cunnington, Howson (Funge 74), Douglas (Woodley 86).

▪ *Denotes player sent off.*

SCHOOLS FOOTBALL 2005–06

BOODLE & DUNTHORNE INDEPENDENT SCHOOLS FA CUP 2005–06

FIRST ROUND

Alleyn's 1, Brentwood 0
Chigwell 3, Dover College 0
Dulwich 4, Aldenham 2
Forest 1, St Bede's College 2
Hulme GS 3, Winchester 1
John Lyon 4, Kimbolton 2
King's, Chester 3, Haileybury 1
Lancing 6, Malvern 0
Leeds GS 1, Manchester GS 3
St Bede's School 3, Grange 0
St Mary's, Crosby 1, Charterhouse 10

SECOND ROUND

Alleyn's 2, Bolton 2
(Bolton won 5-4 on penalties).
Ardingly 5, Birkdale 0
Bradfield 3, St Bede's College 2
Bury GS 1, QEGS, Blackburn 0
Charterhouse 3, St Bede's School 0
Chigwell 2, John Lyon 0
City of London 0, Shrewsbury 1
Dulwich 2, Eton 5
Hulme GS 0, Highgate 2
King's, Chester 3, Wolverhampton GS 1
Lancing 5, Oswestry 0
Latymer Upper 3, Norwich 1
Manchester GS 2, Hampton 4
Millfield 4, KES, Witley 0
Repton 3, Westminster 0
RGS, Newcastle 4, St Edmund's, Canterbury 2

THIRD ROUND

Ardingly 0, Hampton 1
Bolton 2, RGS, Newcastle 0
Chigwell 2, Bradfield 2
(Chigwell won 9-8 on penalties).
Highgate 4, Repton 1
Latymer Upper 0, Bury GS 2
Lancing 2, Charterhouse 1
Millfield 2, Eton 0
Shrewsbury 0, King's, Chester 1

FOURTH ROUND

Chigwell 1, Bolton 2
Highgate 2, Millfield 3
King's, Chester 2, Bury GS 1
Lancing 2, Hampton 2
(Hampton won 3-0 on penalties).

SEMI-FINALS

King's, Chester 2, Bolton 0
Millfield 3, Hampton 0

FINAL

(at Leicester City FC)

King's, Chester 2 *(Minshaw 2)*

Millfield 1 *(Rolli)*

King's, Chester: T. Mying; T. Bellis, L. West (A. O'Brien), M. Davies, M. Evered, A. Dyne, C. Martland, M. Pipe, J. Minshaw, R. Wildman (A. Fennell), J. Bedford (P. Boweyer).
Millfield: S. Cooper; S. Jenkinson, B. Middleton, O. Irish, R. Topp, M. Stephenson, A. Turner, F. Rolli, C. Ashling (J. Williams), L. Irish, J. Bisgrove (J. Dukes).
Referee: S. Bennett (Kent).

FA PREMIER RESERVE LEAGUES 2005–06

FA PREMIER RESERVE LEAGUE – NORTH SECTION

	P	W	D	L	F	A	GD	Pts
Manchester U	28	19	2	7	68	32	36	59
Aston Villa	28	16	8	4	59	26	33	56
Manchester C	28	15	8	5	47	37	10	53
Middlesbrough	28	15	7	6	50	27	23	52
Newcastle U	28	12	8	8	45	40	5	44
Liverpool	28	13	5	10	31	31	0	44
Sunderland	28	11	7	10	40	41	–1	40
Everton	28	10	8	10	31	35	–4	38
Leeds U	28	9	11	8	27	31	–4	38
Blackburn R	28	8	7	13	38	46	–8	31
Birmingham C	28	7	9	12	32	36	–4	30
Wolverhampton W	28	6	8	14	28	37	–9	26
Bolton W	28	6	6	16	25	46	–21	24
WBA	28	6	6	16	26	55	–29	24
Wigan Ath	28	5	4	19	24	51	–27	19

Leading Goalscorers		
Rossi G	Manchester U	26
Chopra M	Newcastle U	14
Miller I	Manchester C	13
Agbonlahor G	Aston Villa	11
Wright-Phillips B	Manchester C	11
Graham D	Middlesbrough	11
Williams S	Aston Villa	10
Craddock T	Middlesbrough	10
Anichebe V	Everton	9
Campbell F	Manchester U	9
Ebanks-Blake S	Manchester U	9
Finnigan C	Newcastle U	9
Nicholson S	WBA	8
Johnson J	Blackburn R	7
Peter S	Blackburn R	7
Calliste R	Liverpool	7
Murphy D	Sunderland	7
Johansson A	Wigan Ath	7
Whittingham P	Aston Villa	6
De Vita R	Blackburn R	6
Smith J	Bolton W	6
Johnson A	Middlesbrough	6

LEAGUE APPEARANCES AND GOALSCORERS

Manchester United: Neumayr 25, Rossi 25, Pique 21, Jones 20+1, Steele 15, Gibson 14+5, Bardsley 13, Martin 13, Evans J 12+4, Marsh 11+5, Campbell 11+3, Lee K 10+2, Simpson 10+2, Fox 10+1, Eckersley 8, Solskjaer 8, Cooper 7+8, Ebanks-Blake 7+2, Howard T 7, Rose 6+3, Howard M 6+1, Shawcross 5+5, Lee T 5, Mullan 4+3, Fortune 4, Moran 3+3, Barnes 3+2, Hewson 3+2, Richardson 3, Brown 2, Evra 2, Neville 2, Vidic 2, Gray 1+5, Cathcart 1+3, Brandy 1+2, Fletcher 1, Heath 1, Heaton 1, Heinze 1, O'Shea 1, Picken 1, Saha 1, Smith 1, Burns +2, Evans S +2, Fagan +1.

Goalscorers: Rossi 26 (5 pens), Campbell 9, Ebanks-Blake 9 (1 pen), Cooper 3, Evans J 3, Gibson 2, Heath 2, Neumayr 2, Solskjaer 2, Fagan 1, Fox 1, Howard M 1, Jones 1, Martin 1, Moran 1, Mullan 1, Smith 1, own goals 2.

FA PREMIER RESERVE LEAGUE – SOUTH SECTION

	P	W	D	L	F	A	GD	Pts
Tottenham H	26	20	3	3	57	13	44	63
Southampton	26	17	3	7	50	26	24	51
Arsenal	26	14	7	5	60	34	26	49
Charlton Ath	26	13	4	9	37	30	7	43
Coventry C	26	13	1	12	30	36	–6	40
Chelsea	26	10	9	7	34	24	10	39
Crystal Palace	26	11	5	10	44	41	3	38
Fulham	26	11	3	12	26	32	–6	36
Ipswich T	26	10	1	15	44	54	–10	31
West Ham U	26	7	8	11	37	38	–1	29
Leicester C	26	7	7	12	38	57	–19	28
Watford	26	8	3	15	25	51	–26	27
Portsmouth	26	6	4	16	35	54	–19	22
Norwich C	26	4	6	16	19	46	–27	18

Leading Goalscorers		
Barnard L	Tottenham H	20
Bendtner N	Arsenal	19
Lupoli A	Arsenal	17
McGoldrick D	Southampton	12
Reid C	Coventry C	10
Lisbie K	Charlton Ath	8
Andrews W	Crystal Palace	7
Grabban L	Crystal Palace	7
Bowditch D	Ipswich T	7
Dodds L	Leicester C	7
O'Grady C	Leicester C	7
Simpson J	Arsenal	6
Hollands D	Chelsea	6
Smith J	Chelsea	6
Hall R	Crystal Palace	6
Grant J	Watford	6

LEAGUE APPEARANCES AND GOALSCORERS

Tottenham Hotspur: Barnard 19+1, Bunjevcevic 18, Lee 16+1, Jackson 16, McKenna 15+3, Barcham 14+4, Daniels 13+3, Davis 12+2, Burch 12, O'Hara 11+2, Kelly 11, Lewis 10+3, Huddlestone 10, Cerny 9, Davenport 8, Reid 8, McKie 7+3, Hallfredsson 7, Marney 6+1, Ghaly 5, Pamarot 5, Rasiak 5, Martin 4+6, Brown 4, El Hamadoui 4, Gardner 4, Lennon 4, Riley 4, Maghoma 3+6, Mills 3+1, Forecast 3, Ifil 3, Routledge 3, Dawkins 2+6, Hamed 2+1, Fulop 2, Smith A 1+3, Kanoute 1, Murphy 1, Ziegler 1, Hughton +1, Seanla +1.

Goalscorers: Barnard 19 (1 pen), Jackson 5, Rasiak 4, Reid 4, Davenport 3, Barcham 2, Daniels 2, Dawkins 2, El Hamadoui 2, Kelly 2, McKenna 2, Marney 2, Bunjevcevic 1, Davis 1, Hallfredsson 1, Ifil 1, Kanoute 1, Lennon 1, Maghoma 1, Murphy 1.

PREMIER RESERVE LEAGUE PLAY-OFF

Manchester U (2) 2 *(Pique 24, Solskjaer 28)*

Tottenham H (0) 0 2416

at Old Trafford.

Manchester U: Howard; Gray, Lee, Pique, Evans, Gibson, Neumayr, Fletcher (Jones), Campbell, Solskjaer (Rossi), Rose (Mullan).

Tottenham H: Burch; McKenna, McKie (Martin), Marney, Lee, Bunjevcevic, Lewis (Riley), Jackson, Barcham (Hamad), Dawkins, Maghoma.

PONTIN'S RESERVE LEAGUES 2005–06

PONTIN'S HOLIDAYS LEAGUE

DIV ONE CENTRAL	P	W	D	L	F	A	GD	Pts
Sheffield W	18	10	5	3	26	13	13	35
Huddersfield T	18	10	4	4	24	16	8	34
Oldham Ath	18	9	5	4	29	17	12	32
Sheffield U A	18	9	3	6	42	28	14	30
Nottingham F	18	6	5	7	34	27	7	23
Stoke C	18	7	2	9	22	30	–8	23
Barnsley	18	6	4	8	26	33	–7	22
Walsall	18	6	3	9	29	41	–12	21
Rotherham U	18	3	8	7	26	30	–4	17
Bradford C	18	3	3	12	19	42	–23	12

DIV ONE WEST	P	W	D	L	F	A	GD	Pts
Carlisle U	18	11	4	3	39	16	23	37
Bury	18	9	4	5	31	25	6	31
Preston NE	18	7	8	3	32	22	10	29
Tranmere R	18	7	7	4	30	26	4	28
Blackpool	18	8	1	9	31	31	0	25
Shrewsbury T	18	6	6	6	23	25	–2	24
Rochdale	18	7	1	10	23	35	–12	22
Chester C	18	4	6	8	21	30	–9	18
Burnley*	18	5	5	8	26	31	–5	17
Wrexham	18	3	4	11	22	37	–15	13

**Burnley deducted three points.*

DIV ONE EAST	P	W	D	L	F	A	GD	Pts
Doncaster R	18	11	3	4	34	16	18	36
Sheffield U B	18	10	1	7	39	27	12	31
Hull C	18	8	7	3	28	24	4	31
Lincoln C	18	7	6	5	29	28	1	27
Darlington	18	8	3	7	24	38	–14	27
Scarborough	18	7	5	6	31	26	5	26
York C	18	8	2	8	26	23	3	26
Hartlepool U	18	7	4	7	33	24	9	25
Scunthorpe U	18	4	4	10	16	26	–10	16
Grimsby T	18	0	5	13	17	45	–28	5

PONTIN'S HOLIDAYS COMBINATION

CENTRAL DIVISION	P	W	D	L	F	A	GD	Pts
Reading	16	12	2	2	48	10	38	38
Millwall	16	10	2	4	37	21	16	32
Brighton & HA	16	9	2	5	40	21	19	29
Gillingham	16	8	3	5	25	25	0	27
QPR	16	5	6	5	30	26	4	21
Wycombe W	16	6	1	9	27	26	1	19
Aldershot T	16	5	1	10	24	42	–18	16
Crawley T	16	4	0	12	23	39	–16	12
Woking	16	3	3	10	12	56	–44	12

WALES AND WEST DIVISION	P	W	D	L	F	A	GD	Pts
Cheltenham T	16	13	2	1	36	17	16	41
Cardiff C	16	9	4	3	28	14	14	31
Swindon T	16	7	4	5	36	25	11	25
Bristol C	16	7	4	5	27	20	7	25
Yeovil T	16	5	4	7	33	26	7	19
Bristol R	16	5	3	8	29	26	3	18
Plymouth Arg	16	4	6	6	23	24	–1	18
AFC Bournemouth	16	5	2	9	30	37	–7	17
Swansea C	16	2	1	13	20	70	–50	7

EAST DIVISION	P	W	D	L	F	A	GD	Pts
Luton T	16	12	2	2	44	19	25	38
Northampton T	16	10	3	3	34	13	21	33
Colchester U	16	10	3	3	33	21	12	32
Milton Keynes D	16	7	5	4	27	18	9	26
Southend U	16	6	2	8	20	25	–5	20
Leyton Orient	16	5	1	10	20	31	–11	16
Barnet	16	5	1	10	25	40	–15	16
Stevenage B	16	5	1	10	15	30	–15	16
Oxford U	16	1	5	10	13	33	–20	8

FOOTBALL LEAGUE YOUTH TABLES 2005–06

NORTH AND MIDLANDS WEST CONFERENCE	P	W	D	L	F	A	GD	Pts
Oldham Ath	30	26	1	3	102	32	70	79
Preston NE	27	18	3	6	62	28	34	57
Tranmere R	28	15	5	8	59	40	19	50
Port Vale	29	14	7	8	56	45	11	49
Rochdale	29	15	3	11	58	46	12	48
Stockport Co	30	14	4	12	53	45	8	46
Burnley	27	15	1	11	55	65	–10	46
Chester C	30	10	7	13	52	53	–1	37
Carlisle U	28	10	7	11	35	51	–16	37
Walsall	29	10	6	13	42	46	–4	36
Wigan Ath	28	11	3	14	39	47	–8	36
Blackpool	28	11	2	15	25	41	–16	35
Bury	30	8	7	15	43	48	–5	31
Shrewsbury T	29	7	5	17	34	58	–24	26
Macclesfield T	30	6	7	17	31	69	–38	25
Wrexham	30	7	0	23	31	63	–32	21

NORTH AND MIDLANDS EAST CONFERENCE	P	W	D	L	F	A	GD	Pts
Chesterfield	26	18	5	3	67	30	37	59
Rotherham U	26	16	6	4	68	34	34	54
Hull C	26	15	5	6	49	30	19	50
Doncaster R	26	14	6	6	49	25	24	48
Bradford C	26	14	4	8	52	42	10	46
Darlington	26	14	4	8	50	40	10	46
Scunthorpe U	26	13	1	12	44	41	3	40
Grimsby T	26	11	3	12	55	46	9	36
Hartlepool U	26	10	4	12	58	61	–3	34
Notts Co	26	6	6	14	30	45	–15	24
Boston U	26	7	3	16	28	58	–30	24
Lincoln C	26	5	7	14	29	51	–22	22
Mansfield T	26	2	9	15	26	67	–41	15
York C	26	3	5	18	23	58	–35	14

SOUTH WEST CONFERENCE	P	W	D	L	F	A	GD	Pts
Yeovil T	22	16	1	5	62	30	32	49
Plymouth Arg	22	14	3	5	53	25	28	45
Bristol R	22	13	4	5	53	31	22	43
Swindon T	22	12	5	5	43	26	17	41
Exeter C	22	12	0	10	51	45	6	36
Cheltenham T	22	10	4	8	44	33	11	34
AFC Bournemouth	22	11	0	11	55	43	12	33
Newport Co	22	9	4	9	39	30	9	31
Oxford U	22	7	5	10	35	34	1	26
Cirencester	22	6	4	12	27	76	–49	22
Swansea C	22	3	7	12	46	53	–7	16
Hereford U	22	0	1	21	15	97	–82	1

SOUTH EAST CONFERENCE	P	W	D	L	F	A	GD	Pts
Brighton & HA	22	14	5	3	51	19	32	47
Rushden & D	22	12	5	5	43	25	18	41
QPR	22	12	4	6	44	34	10	40
Southend U	22	9	6	7	26	33	–7	33
Wycombe W	22	9	5	8	33	30	3	32
Gillingham	22	8	7	7	40	33	7	31
Brentford	22	9	3	10	40	52	–12	30
Leyton Orient	22	7	6	9	32	35	–3	27
Northampton T	22	8	3	11	30	36	–6	27
Colchester U	22	7	4	11	28	32	–4	25
Luton T	22	6	1	15	24	38	–14	19
Portsmouth	22	4	5	13	23	47	–24	17

THE YOUTH ALLIANCE CUP 2005–06

SOUTHERN SECTION

GROUP 1	P	W	D	L	F	A	GD	Pts
Plymouth Arg	5	5	0	0	14	2	12	15
Brighton & HA	6	4	0	2	12	4	8	12
Luton T	4	2	1	1	6	5	1	7
Wycombe W	4	2	0	2	7	10	–3	6
Exeter C	4	1	1	2	8	8	0	4
Swansea C	4	0	0	4	2	10	–8	0
Newport Co	3	0	0	3	1	11	–10	0

GROUP 2	P	W	D	L	F	A	GD	Pts
Leyton Orient	4	3	1	0	7	3	4	10
Portsmouth	5	3	0	2	13	8	5	9
Bristol R	5	3	0	2	7	7	0	9
Brentford	5	2	1	2	8	11	–3	7
QPR	5	2	0	3	9	8	1	6
Yeovil T	4	0	0	4	2	9	–7	0

GROUP 3	P	W	D	L	F	A	GD	Pts
Gillingham	5	4	1	0	15	2	13	13
Northampton T	5	3	1	1	13	7	6	10
Swindon T	5	2	2	1	16	5	11	8
AFC Bournemouth	5	2	1	2	5	4	1	7
Southend U	5	1	1	3	11	12	–1	4
Hereford U	5	0	0	5	1	31	–30	0

GROUP 4	P	W	D	L	F	A	GD	Pts
Colchester U	5	3	2	0	11	4	7	11
Oxford U	5	3	0	2	8	7	1	9
Cheltenham T	5	3	0	2	9	11	–2	9
Rushden & D	5	1	2	2	5	4	1	5
Cirencester	5	0	3	2	4	7	–3	3
Cambridge U	5	0	3	2	5	9	–4	3

NORTHERN SECTION

FIRST ROUND
Blackpool 2, Bradford C 3
Bury 2, Shrewsbury T 4
Doncaster R 3, Scunthorpe U 2
Grimsby T 1, Chester C 2
Mansfield T 3, Hartlepool U 4
Oldham Ath 2, Lincoln C 1
Port Vale 0, Preston NE 0
Preston NE won 4-1 on penalties.
Rochdale 0, Notts Co
Rochdale won 5-3 on penalties.
Rotherham U 1, Burnley 3
Stockport Co 2, Carlisle U 0
Tranmere R 2, Macclesfield T 0
Walsall 1, Hull C 2
Wigan Ath 1, Chesterfield 0
Wrexham 4, York C 0

Byes: Boston U and Darlington.

SECOND ROUND
Boston U 1, Burnley 2
Doncaster R 0, Preston NE 1
Oldham Ath 7, Hartlepool U 1
Rochdale 4, Darlington 1
Shrewsbury T 2, Chester C 3
Tranmere R 1, Hull C 0
Wigan Ath 1, Bradford C 3
Wrexham 1, Stockport Co 4

THIRD ROUND
Chester C 0, Burnley 1
Preston NE 2, Bradford C 1
Stockport Co 1, Rochdale 0
Tranmere R 2, Oldham Ath 1

THE YOUTH ALLIANCE CUP

QUARTER-FINALS

Southern Section
Colchester U 2, Leyton Orient 0
Gillingham 2, Plymouth Arg 1

Northern Section
Burnley 0, Tranmere R 3
Stockport Co 0, Preston NE 6

SEMI-FINALS

Southern Section
Colchester U 2, Gillingham 1

Northern Section
Tranmere R 1, Preston NE 2

FINAL
Colchester U v Preston NE

FA ACADEMY UNDER 18 LEAGUE 2005–06

GROUP A	P	W	D	L	F	A	GD	Pts
Southampton	28	17	5	6	72	35	37	56
Chelsea	28	17	5	6	45	21	24	56
West Ham U	28	13	6	9	51	41	10	45
Arsenal	28	11	5	12	47	47	0	38
Norwich C	28	10	6	12	31	34	–3	36
Fulham	28	9	5	14	30	46	–16	32
Ipswich T	28	8	7	13	53	64	–11	31
Crystal Palace	28	8	6	14	54	59	–5	30
Charlton Ath	28	8	4	16	36	52	–16	28
Millwall	28	6	8	14	30	52	–22	26

GROUP B	P	W	D	L	F	A	GD	Pts
Aston Villa	28	17	5	6	63	33	30	56
Leicester C	28	17	3	8	54	41	13	54
Bristol C	28	12	8	8	47	37	10	44
Coventry C	28	12	8	8	40	40	0	44
Watford	28	11	9	8	41	41	0	42
Tottenham H	28	11	5	12	45	49	–4	38
Cardiff C	28	10	5	13	36	41	–5	35
Milton Keynes D	28	10	5	13	37	48	–11	35
Reading	28	9	6	13	43	41	2	33
Birmingham C	28	8	8	12	33	45	–12	32

GROUP C	P	W	D	L	F	A	GD	Pts
Blackburn R	28	17	3	8	51	36	15	54
Manchester U	28	16	4	8	56	30	26	52
Manchester C	28	14	7	7	50	37	13	49
Everton	28	14	7	7	33	24	9	49
Liverpool	28	13	5	10	47	35	12	44
Stoke C	28	10	8	10	42	37	5	38
Bolton W	28	9	11	8	31	35	–4	38
Crewe Alex	28	9	8	11	38	42	–4	35
WBA	28	6	9	13	39	52	–13	27
Wolverhampton W	28	6	8	14	25	39	–14	26

GROUP D	P	W	D	L	F	A	GD	Pts
Derby Co	28	16	7	5	49	26	23	55
Leeds U	28	16	5	7	51	26	25	53
Newcastle U	28	12	5	11	37	37	0	41
Nottingham F	28	9	7	12	32	34	–2	34
Sunderland	28	10	4	14	31	37	–6	34
Sheffield U	28	8	8	12	32	40	–8	32
Middlesbrough	28	8	6	14	30	48	–18	30
Barnsley	28	7	7	14	22	42	–20	28
Sheffield W	28	7	4	17	29	55	–26	25
Huddersfield T	28	5	6	17	26	60	–34	21

NON-LEAGUE TABLES 2005–06

NATIONAL LEAGUE SYSTEM – STEP 5

ARNGROVE NORTHERN LEAGUE DIVISION ONE

	P	W	D	L	F	A	GD	Pts
Newcastle Blue Star	40	28	6	6	87	34	53	90
Bedlington Terriers	40	22	8	10	86	61	25	74
Dunston Fed Brewery	40	20	11	9	82	45	37	71
Billingham Town	40	18	13	9	81	54	27	67
West Auckland Town	40	20	7	13	76	53	23	67
Morpeth Town	40	19	10	11	68	50	18	67
Billingham Synthonia	40	17	12	11	65	58	7	63
Chester Le Street Town	40	18	9	13	64	64	0	63
Newcastle Benfield (BP)	40	18	8	14	81	62	19	62
Whitley Bay	40	17	9	14	68	51	17	60
Durham City	40	15	13	12	58	44	14	58
Tow Law Town	40	15	9	16	63	65	–2	54
West Allotment Celtic	40	14	8	18	77	83	–6	50
Sunderland Nissan	40	14	8	18	64	73	–9	50
Jarrow Roofing Boldon CA	40	14	7	19	65	76	–11	49
Ashington	40	13	9	18	64	60	4	48
Thornaby	40	14	6	20	72	85	–13	48
Horden CW	40	12	11	17	55	65	–10	47
Shildon	40	11	14	15	55	65	–10	47
Esh Winning	40	3	7	30	32	103	–71	16
Brandon United	40	4	3	33	35	147	–112	15

BADGER ALES SUSSEX COUNTY LEAGUE DIVISION ONE

	P	W	D	L	F	A	GD	Pts
Horsham YMCA	38	27	7	4	83	31	52	88
Ringmer	38	24	7	7	68	34	34	79
Whitehawk	38	20	7	11	66	36	30	67
Littlehampton Town	38	20	7	11	63	44	19	67
Eastbourne Town	38	19	8	11	69	44	25	65
Crowborough Athletic	38	19	8	11	68	45	23	65
Arundel	38	16	15	7	61	43	18	63
Chichester City United	38	17	9	12	61	55	6	60
Hassocks	38	15	12	11	63	48	15	57
Hailsham Town	38	13	13	12	43	46	–3	52
Sidley United	38	16	4	18	65	80	–15	52
Wick	38	14	9	15	56	49	7	51
Shoreham	38	15	6	17	58	59	–1	51
Eastbourne United Assoc	38	12	8	18	48	62	–14	44
Three Bridges	38	10	12	16	46	50	–4	42
East Preston	38	8	15	15	41	60	–19	39
Worthing United	38	9	12	17	41	60	–19	39
Redhill	38	10	4	24	39	78	–39	34
Rye & Iden United	38	4	8	26	38	83	–45	20
Southwick	38	2	9	27	28	98	–70	15

CHERRY RED COMBINED COUNTIES PREMIER DIVISION

	P	W	D	L	F	A	GD	Pts
Godalming Town	40	30	7	3	99	33	66	97
Merstham	40	24	9	7	64	26	38	81
Ash United	40	21	8	11	73	43	30	71
Colliers Wood United	40	22	4	14	93	63	30	70
Horley Town	40	20	9	11	54	41	13	69
Bedfont	40	19	10	11	69	45	24	67
Sandhurst Town	40	18	12	10	77	50	27	66
Chessington & Hook (–4)	40	17	12	11	82	46	36	59
Raynes Park Vale	40	18	3	19	71	82	–11	57
Reading Town	40	15	9	16	65	59	6	54
Westfield	40	15	9	16	60	58	2	54
Mole Valley Predators	40	16	5	19	65	90	–25	53
North Greenford United	40	15	7	18	72	70	2	52
Chipstead	40	13	10	17	56	65	–9	49
Cobham	40	12	8	20	55	60	–5	44
Cove	40	11	11	18	55	83	–28	44
Guildford United	40	11	9	20	53	83	–30	42
Frimley Green	40	11	8	21	45	78	–33	41
Bedfont Green	40	12	5	23	60	95	–35	41
Feltham	40	9	6	25	49	90	–41	33
Farnham Town	40	5	11	24	38	95	–57	26

EAGLE BITTER UNITED COUNTIES LEAGUE PREMIER DIVISION

	P	W	D	L	F	A	GD	Pts
Woodford United	42	28	8	6	102	32	70	92
Potton United	42	28	8	6	92	51	41	92
Northampton Spencer	42	28	5	9	92	36	56	89
St Neots Town	42	25	5	12	81	52	29	80
Cogenhoe United	42	23	8	11	86	64	22	77
Boston Town	42	22	9	11	88	60	28	75
Yaxley (–3)	42	21	6	15	71	49	22	66
Raunds Town	42	18	11	13	66	54	12	65
St Ives Town	42	18	4	20	64	76	–12	58
Blackstones	42	15	12	15	79	68	11	57
Stotfold	42	15	10	17	84	74	10	55
Wootton Blue Cross	42	15	9	18	65	59	6	54
Bourne Town	42	15	9	18	68	73	–5	54
Buckingham Town (–1)	42	15	7	20	77	84	–7	51
Newport Pagnell Town	42	14	8	20	48	66	–18	50
Stewarts & Lloyds	42	14	8	20	55	77	–22	50
Holbeach United	42	12	10	20	63	70	–7	46
Desborough Town (–1)	42	13	8	21	64	83	–19	46
Ford Sports Daventry	42	13	6	23	59	84	–25	45
Deeping Rangers	42	11	9	22	56	73	–17	42
Long Buckby	42	11	7	24	65	87	–22	40
Harrowby United	42	2	5	35	37	190	–153	11

GLS FOOTBALL HELLENIC LEAGUE PREMIER DIVISION

	P	W	D	L	F	A	GD	Pts
Didcot Town	40	34	3	3	124	31	93	105
Bishops Cleeve	40	29	5	6	108	45	63	92
Abingdon United	40	27	3	10	88	40	48	84
North Leigh	40	25	6	9	78	40	38	81
Slimbridge	40	24	6	10	90	45	45	78
Witney United	40	23	4	13	88	51	37	73
Carterton	40	23	3	14	73	51	22	72
Shrivenham	40	22	5	13	82	58	24	71
Wantage Town	40	19	7	14	73	70	3	64
Ardley United	40	18	6	16	70	63	7	60
Milton United	40	14	9	17	62	69	–7	51
Highworth Town	40	13	10	17	62	72	–10	49
Pegasus Juniors	40	12	11	17	53	74	–21	47
Almondsbury Town	40	13	6	21	50	64	–14	45
Shortwood United	40	12	6	22	55	79	–24	42
Hungerford Town	40	11	8	21	31	65	–34	41
Fairford Town	40	11	6	23	42	73	–31	39
Abingdon Town	40	9	10	21	45	88	–43	37
Chipping Norton Town	40	6	7	27	43	99	–56	25
Kidlington	40	7	1	32	42	108	–66	22
Henley Town	40	5	4	31	28	102	–74	19

HARVEY WORLD TRAVEL MIDLAND ALLIANCE

	P	W	D	L	F	A	GD	Pts
Chasetown	42	29	7	6	74	32	42	94
Stourbridge	42	29	5	8	110	55	55	92
Malvern Town	42	27	4	11	95	56	39	85
Romulus	42	23	11	8	84	49	35	80
Leamington	42	21	11	10	79	44	35	74
Racing Club Warwick	42	22	7	13	72	55	17	73
Quorn	42	21	6	15	71	51	20	69
Coalville Town	42	21	6	15	63	60	3	69
Barwell	42	20	8	14	83	66	17	68
Boldmere St Michaels	42	17	12	13	60	48	12	63
Tipton Town	42	15	13	14	74	69	5	58
Oldbury United	42	16	10	16	58	58	0	58
Loughborough Dynamo	42	16	8	18	53	53	0	56
Alvechurch	42	16	7	19	59	64	–5	55
Stratford Town	42	15	6	21	49	55	–6	51
Studley	42	14	7	21	54	81	–27	49
Biddulph Victoria	42	12	9	21	55	83	–28	45
Oadby Town	42	10	14	18	50	64	–14	44
Causeway United	42	9	7	26	49	89	–40	34
Westfields	42	8	9	25	48	88	–40	33
Cradley Town	42	5	9	28	38	94	–56	24
Rocester	42	4	8	30	36	100	–64	20

MOORE & CO NORTH WEST COUNTIES LEAGUE DIVISION ONE

	P	W	D	L	F	A	GD	Pts
Cammell Laird (–6)	42	35	3	4	126	36	90	102
Skelmersdale United	42	28	7	7	119	48	71	91
Alsager Town	42	27	7	8	87	43	44	88
Nantwich Town	42	26	6	10	91	37	54	84
Salford City	42	23	10	9	79	46	33	79
Newcastle Town	42	21	9	12	97	52	45	72
Curzon Ashton	42	20	8	14	72	66	6	68
St Helens Town	42	20	7	15	70	68	2	67
Colne (–6)	42	22	3	17	84	70	14	63
Maine Road	42	17	10	15	65	56	9	61
Silsden	42	16	8	18	76	75	1	56
Abbey Hey	42	14	12	16	61	70	–9	54
Congleton Town	42	15	8	19	50	63	–13	53
Squires Gate	42	12	15	15	43	62	–19	51
Trafford (–3)	42	13	13	16	71	56	15	49
Glossop North End	42	12	11	19	62	78	–16	47
Ramsbottom United	41	9	18	14	45	58	–13	45
Bacup Borough	41	12	8	21	42	62	–20	44
Atherton Collieries	42	7	9	26	43	93	–50	30
Atherton LR	42	7	8	27	40	115	–75	29
Stone Dominoes	42	5	5	32	39	146	–107	20
Formby	42	4	7	31	43	105	–62	19

NORTHERN COUNTIES EAST PREMIER

	P	W	D	L	F	A	GD	Pts
Buxton	38	30	5	3	102	27	75	95
Liversedge	38	25	5	8	106	49	57	80
Harrogate Railway	38	22	7	9	92	49	43	73
Sheffield	38	20	10	8	63	43	20	70
Arnold Town (–3)	38	21	7	10	72	45	27	67
Pickering Town	38	19	9	10	63	42	21	66
Sutton Town	38	17	9	12	78	57	21	60
Selby Town	38	17	5	16	58	60	–2	56
Thackley (–3)	38	18	3	17	59	62	–3	54
Garforth Town	38	12	11	15	61	68	–7	47
Armthorpe Welfare	38	13	8	17	65	77	–12	47
Glapwell	38	12	11	15	46	71	–25	47
Mickleover Sports	38	12	8	18	51	73	–22	44
Eccleshill United	38	12	7	19	66	70	–4	43
Shirebrook Town	38	13	4	21	59	85	–26	43
Glasshoughton Welfare	38	11	5	22	52	70	–18	38
Hallam	38	10	8	20	44	73	–29	38
Maltby Main (–1)	38	9	11	18	52	70	–18	37
Long Eaton United (–3)	38	8	8	22	47	86	–39	29
Brodsworth MW	38	6	5	27	47	106	–59	23

RIDGEONS EASTERN COUNTIES LEAGUE PREMIER DIVISION

	P	W	D	L	F	A	GD	Pts
Lowestoft Town	42	30	4	8	121	43	78	94
Bury Town	42	29	5	8	100	32	68	92
AFC Sudbury	42	28	5	9	114	56	58	89
Wisbech Town	42	25	7	10	98	55	43	82
Mildenhall Town	42	23	9	10	100	68	32	78
Needham Market	42	22	9	11	79	41	38	75
Ipswich Wanderers	42	23	6	13	69	38	31	75
Wroxham	42	21	6	15	77	62	15	69
Leiston	42	21	5	16	89	69	20	68
Soham Town Rangers	42	18	11	13	75	51	24	65
Diss Town	42	20	5	17	89	78	11	65
Dereham Town	42	18	10	14	99	64	35	64
Histon Reserves	42	15	11	16	71	84	–13	56
Kirkley	42	15	6	21	60	76	–16	51
King's Lynn Reserves	42	12	13	17	68	78	–10	49
Woodbridge Town	42	14	6	22	64	83	–19	48
Newmarket Town	42	13	6	23	53	91	–38	45
Halstead Town	42	11	7	24	67	124	–57	40
Cambridge City Reserves	42	10	8	24	60	107	–47	38
Norwich United	42	10	6	26	47	82	–35	36
Harwich & Parkeston	42	10	2	30	41	100	–59	32
Clacton Town	42	0	1	41	20	179	–159	1

RYMAN ISTHMIAN LEAGUE DIVISION TWO

	P	W	D	L	F	A	GD	Pts
Ware	30	19	4	7	77	36	41	61
Witham Town	30	17	7	6	61	30	31	58
Brook House	30	17	7	6	63	33	30	58
Flackwell Heath	30	15	7	8	54	49	5	52
Egham Town	30	15	5	10	39	36	3	50
Chertsey Town	30	14	7	9	47	37	10	49
Edgware Town	30	13	5	12	46	41	5	44
Chalfont St Peter	30	13	2	15	50	53	–3	41
Dorking	30	11	8	11	48	51	–3	41
Croydon	30	11	7	12	43	43	0	40
Wembley	30	11	6	13	44	43	1	39
Kingsbury Town	30	9	10	11	32	37	–5	37
Hertford Town	30	7	10	13	35	54	–19	31
Camberley Town	30	5	8	17	31	57	–26	23
Epsom & Ewell	30	5	6	19	32	64	–32	21
Clapton (–5)	30	4	9	17	33	71	–38	16

SPARTAN SOUTH MIDLANDS PREMIER DIVISION

	P	W	D	L	F	A	GD	Pts
Oxford City	38	27	7	4	91	41	50	88
Hillingdon Borough	38	28	4	6	80	41	39	88
Hanwell Town	38	24	6	8	95	45	50	78
Harefield United	38	23	9	6	81	38	43	78
Aylesbury Vale	38	23	5	10	79	52	27	74
Leverstock Green	38	18	9	11	64	51	13	63
Holmer Green	38	18	7	13	69	59	10	61
Welwyn Garden City	38	16	10	12	59	45	14	58
Biggleswade United	38	16	7	15	60	54	6	55
Tring Athletic	38	12	12	14	40	39	1	48
Broxbourne Borough V&E	38	14	5	19	66	63	3	47
St Margaretsbury	38	13	7	18	61	57	4	46
Oxhey Jets	38	12	8	18	54	60	–6	44
London Colney	38	11	8	19	49	68	–19	41
Biggleswade Town	38	11	8	19	52	74	–22	41
Ruislip Manor	38	10	8	20	44	56	–12	38
Langford	38	11	3	24	51	102	–51	36
Royston Town	38	10	5	23	39	86	–47	35
Haringey Borough	38	8	4	26	34	86	–52	28
Harpenden Town	38	6	6	26	33	84	–51	24

SYDENHAMS WESSEX LEAGUE DIVISION ONE

	P	W	D	L	F	A	GD	Pts
Winchester City	42	34	5	3	112	31	81	107
Thatcham Town	42	29	7	6	92	37	55	94
Andover	42	27	5	10	120	64	56	86
AFC Totton	42	25	9	8	101	40	61	84
Gosport Borough	42	23	10	9	85	44	41	79
Hamworthy United	42	21	12	9	65	40	25	75
Bournemouth	42	21	10	11	72	45	27	73
Poole Town	42	21	8	13	79	60	19	71
Fareham Town	42	19	10	13	74	61	13	67
Christchurch	42	17	9	16	72	62	10	60
Moneyfields	42	14	16	12	48	49	–1	58
Wimborne Town	42	15	10	17	60	61	–1	55
VT FC	42	13	15	14	65	66	–1	54
Bemerton Heath H	42	14	8	20	70	86	–16	50
Hamble ASSC	42	14	7	21	50	56	–6	49
Cowes Sports	42	12	10	20	48	67	–19	46
Lymington Town	42	10	14	18	42	71	–29	44
BAT Sports	42	10	6	26	61	109	–48	36
AFC Newbury	42	9	8	25	35	96	–61	35
Alton Town	42	8	9	25	51	99	–48	33
Brockenhurst	42	4	6	32	42	93	–51	18
Portland United	42	2	6	34	32	139	–107	12

TOOLSTATION WESTERN LEAGUE PREMIER DIVISION

	P	W	D	L	F	A	GD	Pts
Bideford	38	29	7	2	93	25	68	94
Corsham Town	38	24	10	4	78	30	48	82
Bristol Manor Farm	38	24	4	10	86	43	43	76
Welton Rovers	38	19	12	7	61	39	22	69
Calne Town	38	19	10	9	70	41	29	67
Willand Rovers	38	18	11	9	63	42	21	65
Frome Town	38	18	10	10	61	45	16	64
Bitton	38	18	9	11	63	41	22	63
Hallen	38	15	12	11	71	54	17	57
Brislington	38	15	8	15	55	53	2	53
Bridgwater Town	38	15	7	16	66	54	12	52
Radstock Town	38	14	5	19	62	73	–11	47
Barnstaple Town	38	12	9	17	54	62	–8	45
Melksham Town	38	12	8	18	43	68	–25	44
Odd Down	38	11	10	17	34	44	–10	43
Bishop Sutton	38	7	13	18	36	52	–16	34
Keynsham Town	38	5	11	22	34	78	–44	26
Devizes Town	38	7	5	26	27	94	–67	26
Torrington	38	6	7	25	33	89	–56	25
Backwell United	38	3	10	25	30	93	–63	19

WESTVIEW ESSEX SENIOR LEAGUE PREMIER DIVISION

	P	W	D	L	F	A	GD	Pts
AFC Hornchurch	30	25	3	2	71	21	50	78
Waltham Abbey	30	18	6	6	64	28	36	60
Tilbury	30	16	7	7	63	37	26	55
Barkingside	30	15	10	5	44	31	13	55
Burnham Ramblers	30	15	9	6	72	44	28	54
Sawbridgeworth Town	30	12	11	7	47	28	19	47
Concord Rangers	30	14	5	11	33	32	1	47
Brentwood Town	30	11	7	12	46	41	5	40
London APSA	30	7	11	12	36	52	–16	32
Southend Manor	30	9	5	16	38	57	–19	32
Basildon United (–1)	30	8	8	14	47	76	–29	31
Romford	30	6	11	13	38	54	–16	29
Eton Manor	30	6	8	16	35	54	–19	26
Hullbridge Sports	30	6	7	17	38	60	–22	25
Bowers & Pitsea	30	7	4	19	36	65	–29	25
Stansted	30	5	8	17	31	59	–28	23

NATIONAL LEAGUE SYSTEM – STEP 6

ARNGROVE NORTHERN LEAGUE DIVISION TWO

	P	W	D	L	F	A	GD	Pts
Consett	38	33	3	2	134	31	103	102
Northallerton Town	38	25	8	5	86	30	56	83
Darlington RA	38	23	5	10	83	46	37	74
Penrith	38	20	10	8	73	46	27	70
Crook Town	38	19	11	8	95	43	52	68
Washington	38	17	10	11	68	54	14	61
Norton & Stockton Ancients	38	17	9	12	83	73	10	60
Spennymoor Town	38	16	11	11	70	66	4	59
Whickham	38	16	10	12	84	64	20	58
Marske United	38	12	13	13	62	69	–7	49
Ryton	38	13	9	16	51	65	–14	48
North Shields	38	13	8	17	57	67	–10	47
Prudhoe Town	38	12	10	16	45	49	–4	46
Seaham Red Star	38	11	12	15	60	59	1	45
Hebburn Town	38	12	9	17	46	67	–21	45
Alnwick Town (–3)	38	12	1	25	62	93	–31	34
Kennek Ryhope CA	38	5	13	20	41	76	–35	28
South Shields (–6)	38	10	4	24	51	95	–44	28
Guisborough Town	38	7	7	24	35	86	–51	28
Peterlee Newtown	38	5	1	32	48	155	–107	16

BADGER ALES SUSSEX COUNTY LEAGUE DIVISION TWO

	P	W	D	L	F	A	GD	Pts
Oakwood	34	25	5	4	87	25	62	80
Selsey	34	23	6	5	80	28	52	75
St Francis Rangers (+3)	34	20	8	6	85	42	43	71
Westfield	34	18	4	12	67	52	15	58
Crawley Down	34	15	10	9	61	43	18	55
Wealden	34	16	7	11	64	62	2	55
East Grinstead Town	34	17	3	14	70	61	9	54
Mile Oak (–3)	34	15	7	12	61	53	8	49
Seaford	34	12	6	16	57	64	–7	42
Sidlesham	34	10	11	13	53	56	–3	41
Broadbridge Heath	34	12	5	17	53	69	–16	41
Lancing	34	11	7	16	42	53	–11	40
Pagham	34	9	12	13	65	63	2	39
Storrington	34	11	6	17	47	63	–16	39
Steyning Town	34	10	8	16	50	69	–19	38
Saltdean United	34	11	3	20	45	75	–30	36
Midhurst & Easebourne	34	8	7	19	42	70	–28	31
Bexhill United	34	3	5	26	28	109	–81	14

CHERRY RED COMBINED COUNTIES DIVISION ONE

	P	W	D	L	F	A	GD	Pts
Warlingham	32	25	4	3	102	37	65	79
AFC Wallingford	32	24	2	6	90	38	52	74
Bookham	32	22	7	3	113	33	80	73
Worcester Park	32	19	6	7	86	43	43	63
Hartley Wintney (–3)	32	21	3	8	74	44	30	63
Tongham	32	19	3	10	118	58	60	60
Hanworth Villa	32	18	5	9	94	53	41	59
Coney Hall	32	15	7	10	95	56	39	52
Farleigh Rovers	32	13	5	14	55	57	–2	44
Crescent Rovers	32	13	5	14	56	65	–9	44
Staines Lammas	32	11	4	17	58	70	–12	37
Sheerwater	32	9	4	19	44	90	–46	31
Monotype	32	8	6	18	45	89	–44	30
Merrow	32	6	2	24	47	114	–67	20
Chobham & Ottershaw	32	5	4	23	34	108	–74	19
Shottermill & Haslemere	32	5	3	24	36	98	–62	18
Netherne	32	3	2	27	38	132	–94	11

EAGLE BITTER UNITED COUNTIES LEAGUE DIVISION ONE

	P	W	D	L	F	A	GD	Pts
Sleaford Town	34	26	3	5	106	36	70	81
Wellingborough Town	34	22	11	1	74	19	55	77
Wellingborough Whitworths	34	21	5	8	77	38	39	68
AFC Kempston Rovers	34	19	7	8	61	38	23	64
Northampton ON Cheneks	34	19	5	10	66	43	23	62
Daventry Town	34	14	9	11	67	58	9	51
Eynesbury Rovers	34	15	5	14	63	68	–5	50
Olney Town	34	14	6	14	69	59	10	48
Peterborough Northern Star	34	13	9	12	71	63	8	48
Rothwell Corinthians	34	13	7	14	59	57	2	46
Bugbrooke St Michaels	34	12	7	15	45	65	–20	43
Huntingdon Town	34	12	5	17	45	53	–8	41
Northampton Sileby Rangers	34	12	4	18	59	81	–22	40
Blisworth (–1)	34	10	10	14	63	71	–8	39
Irchester United	34	11	4	19	48	65	–17	37
Thrapston Town	34	7	7	20	52	79	–27	28
Higham Town	34	6	4	24	35	105	–70	22
Burton Park Wanderers	34	3	6	25	26	88	–62	15

GLS FOOTBALL HELLENIC LEAGUE DIVISION ONE EAST

	P	W	D	L	F	A	GD	Pts
Hounslow Borough	34	23	4	7	99	45	54	73
Bicester Town	34	21	8	5	78	36	42	71
Wokingham & Emmbrook	34	21	5	8	86	47	39	68
Chalfont Wasps	34	20	4	10	80	49	31	64
Englefield Green Rovers	34	20	4	10	73	46	27	64
Penn & Tylers Green	34	20	4	10	69	46	23	64
Bisley Sports	34	19	5	10	81	51	30	62
Binfield	34	19	2	13	70	44	26	59
Kintbury Rangers	34	18	4	12	81	48	33	58
Eton Wick	34	17	5	12	73	64	9	56
Badshot Lea	34	13	6	15	81	74	7	45
Oxford Quarry Nomads (–3)	34	14	4	16	67	81	–14	43
Finchampstead	34	10	7	17	58	60	–2	37
Holyport	34	10	4	20	58	90	–32	34
Rayners Lane	34	11	1	22	57	90	–33	34
Chinnor	34	5	5	24	34	82	–48	20
Banbury United Reserves	34	4	4	26	29	108	–79	16
Prestwood	34	1	4	29	24	137	–113	7

GLS FOOTBALL HELLENIC LEAGUE DIVISION ONE WEST

	P	W	D	L	F	A	GD	Pts
Winterbourne United	34	24	5	5	98	36	62	77
Harrow Hill	34	18	9	7	61	40	21	63
Tytherington Rocks	34	19	5	10	79	54	25	62
Headington Amateurs	34	18	8	8	59	39	20	62
Wootton Bassett Town	34	17	10	7	58	30	28	61
Trowbridge Town	34	17	9	8	65	44	21	60
Old Woodstock Town	34	16	8	10	55	46	9	56
Cheltenham Saracens	34	14	12	8	54	40	14	54
Letcombe	34	14	6	14	51	45	6	48
Pewsey Vale	34	13	7	14	54	51	3	46
Hook Norton	34	13	7	14	57	58	–1	46
Cricklade Town	34	13	5	16	55	67	–12	44
Malmesbury Victoria	34	11	9	14	50	56	–6	42
Cirencester United	34	11	5	18	50	64	–14	38
Purton (–3)	34	7	9	18	33	64	–31	27
Easington Sports	34	6	9	19	37	71	–34	27
Clanfield	34	5	4	25	30	74	–44	19
Ross Town	34	5	3	26	36	103	–67	18

MIDLAND COMBINATION PREMIER DIVISION

	P	W	D	L	F	A	GD	Pts
Atherstone Town	42	32	7	3	131	27	104	103
Coventry Sphinx	42	33	4	5	148	60	88	103
Barnt Green Spartak	42	28	3	11	82	51	31	87
Feckenham	42	25	6	11	107	64	43	81
Bridgnorth Town	42	24	7	11	75	48	27	79
Bolehall Swifts	42	24	6	12	90	59	31	78
Shifnal Town	42	23	8	11	86	44	42	77
Nuneaton Griff	42	19	6	17	73	70	3	63
Castle Vale	42	18	8	16	73	76	–3	62
Alveston	42	18	4	20	65	61	4	58
Coleshill Town	42	14	9	19	79	93	–14	51
Brocton	42	13	10	19	56	70	–14	49
Coventry Copsewood	42	14	7	21	56	79	–23	49
Southam United	42	13	9	20	56	65	–9	48
Highgate United	42	13	8	21	51	86	–35	47
Pershore Town	42	14	3	25	63	88	–25	45
Meir KA	42	12	9	21	55	92	–37	45
Dudley Sports	42	11	11	20	51	71	–20	44
Pilkington XXX	42	11	8	23	61	109	–48	41
Massey Ferguson	42	11	5	26	46	90	–44	38
Cadbury Athletic (–4)	42	11	8	23	68	92	–24	37
Continental Star	42	5	6	31	51	128	–77	21

MOORE & CO NORTH WEST COUNTIES LEAGUE DIVISION TWO

	P	W	D	L	F	A	GD	Pts
FC United of Manchester	36	27	6	3	111	35	76	87
Flixton	36	24	7	5	93	37	56	79
Nelson	36	23	5	8	82	53	29	74
Winsford United	36	19	8	9	65	41	24	65
Padiham	36	19	5	12	76	52	24	62
Great Harwood Town	36	18	8	10	51	33	18	62
Ashton Town	36	17	7	12	59	57	2	58
Norton United	36	13	12	11	45	47	–2	51
Blackpool Mechanics	36	13	10	13	48	51	–3	49
Oldham Town	36	14	6	16	46	49	–3	48
Eccleshall	36	13	7	16	50	64	–14	46
New Mills	36	13	7	16	46	62	–16	46
Chadderton (–3)	36	13	8	15	51	62	–11	44
Cheadle Town (–6)	36	14	6	16	55	53	2	42
Holker Old Boys	36	11	8	17	58	74	–16	41
Darwen	36	11	2	23	47	61	–14	35
Leek CSOB	36	7	7	22	51	82	–31	28
Daisy Hill	36	7	6	23	38	75	–37	27
Castleton Gabriels (–8)	36	2	3	31	38	122	–84	1

NORTHERN COUNTIES EAST LEAGUE DIVISION ONE

	P	W	D	L	F	A	GD	Pts
Carlton Town	30	23	4	3	68	27	41	73
Retford United	30	20	5	5	74	28	46	65
Tadcaster Albion	30	21	1	8	55	35	20	64
Gedling Town	30	19	5	6	75	34	41	62
Winterton Rangers	30	18	7	5	71	27	44	61
Parkgate	30	18	5	7	87	40	47	59
Lincoln Moorlands	30	16	1	13	56	40	16	49
Borrowash Victoria	30	15	4	11	50	45	5	49
Worsborough Bridge	30	11	5	14	57	67	–10	38
Staveley MW	30	9	4	17	44	57	–13	31
Pontefract Collieries	30	6	7	17	43	64	–21	25
South Normanton Ath	30	7	4	19	45	86	–41	25
Rossington Main	30	6	5	19	37	67	–30	23
Hall Road Rangers	30	6	5	19	38	82	–44	23
Teversal	30	5	6	19	28	78	–50	21
Yorkshire Amateur	30	4	4	22	29	80	–51	16

RIDGEONS EASTERN COUNTIES LEAGUE DIVISION ONE

	P	W	D	L	F	A	GD	Pts
Stanway Rovers	42	33	4	5	106	29	77	103
Felixstowe & Walton	42	30	5	7	107	48	59	95
Fulbourn Institute	42	30	4	8	109	60	49	94
Tiptree United	42	29	3	10	125	56	69	90
Walsham le Willows	42	23	10	9	91	46	45	79
Whitton United	42	22	7	13	83	63	20	73
Ely City	42	20	10	12	88	68	20	70
Haverhill Rovers	42	21	7	14	77	60	17	70
Swaffham Town	42	19	12	11	90	71	19	69
Debenham LC	42	17	10	15	60	70	–10	61
Fakenham Town	42	15	11	16	64	69	–5	56
Saffron Walden Town	42	14	12	16	56	62	–6	54
Great Yarmouth Town	42	14	10	18	54	60	–6	52
Godmanchester Rovers	42	12	10	20	53	73	–20	46
Long Melford	42	9	11	22	59	84	–25	38
Stowmarket Town	42	10	8	24	63	95	–32	38
Cornard United	42	11	4	27	59	96	–37	37
Gorleston (–4)	42	9	12	21	50	74	–24	35
March Town United	42	9	6	27	46	91	–45	33
Downham Town	42	8	9	25	41	99	–58	33
Hadleigh United	42	6	13	23	38	78	–40	31
Thetford Town	42	7	10	25	47	114	–67	31

SPARTAN SOUTH MIDLANDS DIVISION ONE

	P	W	D	L	F	A	GD	Pts
Colney Heath	32	26	3	3	106	27	79	81
Brache Sparta	32	23	3	6	76	38	38	72
Stony Stratford Town	32	20	6	6	90	42	48	66
New Bradwell St Peter	32	16	4	12	60	54	6	52
Brimsdown Rovers	32	15	6	11	52	50	2	51
Arlesey Athletic	32	15	5	12	71	57	14	50
Hoddesdon Town	32	14	6	12	64	50	14	48
Cockfosters	32	14	6	12	63	61	2	48
Sun Postal Sports	32	13	5	14	58	61	–3	44
Bedford Utd & Valerio (–3)	32	15	2	15	52	86	–34	44
Kentish Town	32	11	8	13	65	68	–3	41
Dunstable Town 98	32	12	5	15	58	62	–4	41
Buckingham Athletic	32	12	4	16	46	54	–8	40
Winslow United	32	9	6	17	48	73	–25	33
Cranfield United	32	7	4	21	36	68	–32	25
Ampthill Town	32	6	3	23	43	90	–47	21
Amersham Town	32	4	4	24	30	77	–47	16

SYDENHAMS WESSEX LEAGUE DIVISION TWO

	P	W	D	L	F	A	GD	Pts
Locks Heath	42	31	5	6	96	28	68	98
Hayling United	42	27	8	7	99	39	60	89
Brading Town	42	27	7	8	96	50	46	88
Downton	42	27	6	9	108	64	44	87
Liss Athletic	42	26	5	11	99	57	42	83
Horndean	42	22	6	14	95	67	28	72
Fawley	42	20	9	13	76	53	23	69
Stockbridge	42	18	13	11	82	52	30	67
Ringwood Town	42	20	6	16	81	71	10	66
United Services Portsmouth	42	18	11	13	86	72	14	65
Farnborough North End	42	19	6	17	93	76	17	63
East Cowes Vics	42	16	10	16	76	70	6	58
Romsey Town	42	15	11	16	59	61	–2	56
Blackfield & Langley	42	14	13	15	81	69	12	55
Petersfield Town	42	12	8	22	58	91	–33	44
Shaftesbury	42	10	10	22	53	96	–43	40
Hythe & Dibden	42	11	7	24	50	98	–48	40
Andover New Street	42	10	9	23	61	96	–35	39
Amesbury Town	42	10	4	28	55	109	–54	34
Alresford Town	42	8	9	25	49	86	–37	33
Bishops Waltham Town	42	7	7	28	57	112	–55	28
Whitchurch United	42	5	8	29	44	137	–93	23

TOOLSTATION WESTERN LEAGUE DIVISION ONE

	P	W	D	L	F	A	GD	Pts
Dawlish Town	42	33	6	3	115	33	82	105
Chard Town	42	29	10	3	87	27	60	97
Street	42	24	11	7	80	39	41	83
Ilfracombe Town	42	23	9	10	82	50	32	78
Westbury United	42	22	10	10	95	50	45	76
Bridport	42	22	6	14	81	60	21	72
Larkhall Athletic	42	19	11	12	93	56	37	68
Portishead	42	18	12	12	59	49	10	66
Shrewton United	42	18	7	17	88	79	9	61
Bradford Town	42	15	13	14	71	81	–10	58
Clevedon United	42	15	12	15	62	67	–5	57
Longwell Green Sports	42	15	9	18	47	53	–6	54
Weston St Johns (–3)	42	18	3	21	63	81	–18	54
Cadbury Heath	42	15	8	19	70	62	8	53
Saltash United	42	15	7	20	71	84	–13	52
Biddestone	42	13	11	18	54	59	–5	50
Wellington	42	14	8	20	69	81	–12	50
Almondsbury	42	10	11	21	46	70	–24	41
Minehead	42	9	9	24	48	98	–50	36
Shepton Mallet	42	10	4	28	34	85	–51	34
Clyst Rovers	42	7	7	28	47	92	–45	28
Elmore	42	4	4	34	42	148	–106	16

WEST MIDLANDS LEAGUE PREMIER DIVISION

	P	W	D	L	F	A	GD	Pts
Market Drayton Town	42	32	8	2	102	33	69	104
Gornal Athletic	42	25	11	6	74	32	42	86
Great Wyrley (–1)	42	24	14	4	94	36	58	85
Bewdley Town	42	23	8	11	101	52	49	77
Wyrley Rangers	42	22	10	10	81	40	41	76
Lye Town	42	20	11	11	64	44	20	71
Goodrich	42	18	16	8	86	66	20	70
Tividale	42	20	8	14	73	50	23	68
Wellington	42	19	8	15	64	62	2	65
Dudley Town	42	18	8	16	74	71	3	62
Wednesfield	42	18	5	19	56	66	–10	59
Bustleholme	42	15	9	18	66	73	–7	54
Heath Hayes	42	14	12	16	53	64	–11	54
Pelsall Villa	42	16	5	21	61	69	–8	53
Shawbury United	42	15	6	21	74	87	–13	51
Ludlow Town (–2)	42	12	11	19	62	90	–28	45
Brierley & Hagley	42	11	6	25	50	83	–33	39
Bromyard Town	42	10	8	24	53	79	–26	38
Wolverhampton Casuals	42	11	5	26	60	99	–39	38
Smethwick Rangers (–1)	42	11	3	28	57	98	–41	35
Kington Town	42	8	7	27	41	103	–62	31
Ledbury Town	42	7	7	28	52	101	–49	28

SCOTTISH

SCOTS-ADS HIGHLAND FOOTBALL LEAGUE

Deveronvale	28	20	4	4	77	29	48	64
Inverurie Loco Works	28	19	3	6	72	26	46	60
Buckie Thistle	28	16	8	4	48	23	25	56
Forres Mechanics	28	17	3	8	76	37	39	54
Keith	28	16	4	8	63	41	22	52
Huntly	28	15	6	7	66	41	25	51
Fraserburgh	28	13	6	9	68	45	23	45
Cove Rangers	28	12	6	10	55	46	9	42
Clachnacuddin	28	12	5	11	56	57	–1	41
Nairn County	28	12	4	12	57	46	11	40
Rothes	28	9	1	18	48	75	–27	28
Wick Academy	28	7	4	17	41	67	–26	25
Lossiemouth	28	7	4	17	40	97	–57	25
Brora Rangers	28	4	1	23	31	82	–51	13
Fort William	28	1	1	26	18	104	–86	4

AMATEUR FOOTBALL ALLIANCE 2005–06

AFA SENIOR CUP

Sponsored by Alan Day Volkswagen

1st ROUND PROPER
Wood Green Old Boys 4 Old Finchleians 5
West Wickham 3 Hon Artillery Company 2
Old Reptonians 2 Old Wilsonians 4
Chislehurst Sports 1 William Fitt 3
Old Esthameians 7 Old Sedcopians 1
BB Eagles 1 Southgate Olympic 2
Bradfield Old Boys 0 Civil Service 5
Old Camdenians 1 Bromleians Sports 3
Alleyn Old Boys 4 Glyn Old Boys 0
Lloyds TSB Bank 2 Broomfield 8
Southgate County 6 Old Tiffinians 3
Enfield Old Grammarians w/o Old Chigwellians w/d
Weirside Rangers 3 Old Salvatorians 2
Bank of England 2 Brent 0
Centymca 1 Old Actonians Association 0
Old Suttonians 1 Carshalton 0
Old Woodhousians 0 Wake Green 4
Old Meadonians 2 Alexandra Park 0
Old Foresters 2 Old Brentwoods 8
Old Aloysians 3 Old Latymerians 2
Old Hamptonians 5 Old Wokingians 1
Old Challoners 0 Polytechnic 1
Winchmore Hill 4 Parkfield 1
Old Danes 0 South Bank Cuaco 3
Norsemen 7 Old Manorians 2
Old Parmiterians 0 Albanian 3
UCL Academicals 2 HSBC 0
Old Guildfordians 4 Cardinal Manning Old Boys 2
Sinjuns Gramm'ns 3 E Barnet Old Grammarians 4
Nottsborough 4 Old Bealonians 1
Old Isleworthians 3 Old Stationers 2
Old Salesians 0 Old Owens 1

2nd ROUND PROPER
Bank of England 1 Wake Green 2
Old Hamptonians 2 Old Guildfordians 0
Bromleians Sports 2 Nottsborough 1
Old Finchleians 0 Old Owens 4
Southgate County 2 Old Suttonians 0
Albanian 3 Polytechnic 5
Norsemen 1*:4p Civil Service 1*:2p
Centymca 0 West Wickham 4
Old Isleworthians 1 William Fitt 2
South Bank Cuaco 1*:5p Southgate Olympic 1*:4p
Enfield Old Grammarians 1 Winchmore Hill 2
Bromleians Sports 2 Nottsborough 1
Broomfield 2 UCL Academicals 1
Alleyn Old Boys 5 E Barnet Old Grammarians 6
Old Meadonians 2 Old Aloysians 1
Old Esthameians 2 Old Brentwoods 1
Old Wilsonians 2*:10p Weirside Rangers 2*:9p

3rd ROUND PROPER
Polytechnic 3 Old Hamptonians 2
William Fitt 1 Old Owens 3
Norsemen 0 West Wickham 4
South Bank Cuaco 4 Old Wilsonians 1
Broomfield 2*:2p E Barnet Old Grammarians 2*:4p
Wake Green 5 Southgate County 0
Winchmore Hill 4 Old Esthameians 1
Old Meadonians 3 Bromleians Sports 1

4th ROUND PROPER
South Bank Cuaco 0 Old Owens 2
West Wickham 0 Winchmore Hill 1
Old Meadonians 4 E Barnet Old Grammarians 1
Polytechnic 2 Wake Green 3

SEMI-FINALS
Old Meadonians 1*:2p Old Owens 1*:4p
Wake Green 0 Winchmore Hill 4

FINAL
Old Owens 0 Winchmore Hill 1

** after extra time*

OTHER CUP FINALS

MIDDLESEX / ESSEX SENIOR
Broomfield 0 Old Meadonians 5

SURREY / KENT SENIOR
Clapham Old Xaverians 2* Old Salesians 0*

INTERMEDIATE
Civil Service Res 0 Mill Hill Village 1st 4

JUNIOR
Civil Service 3rd 1*:4p Winchmore Hill 3rd 1*:3p

MINOR
Old Actonians 4th 5 Old Haileyburians 1st 4

VETERANS
William Fitt "A" 1 Sinjuns Grammarians 2

OPEN VETERANS
Port of London Authority 2 Chelsea Diamonds 1

MIDDLESEX / ESSEX INTERMEDIATE
Old Actonians Ass'n Res 1 Old Meadonians Res 3

SURREY / KENT INTERMEDIATE
Dresdner Kleinwort Wasserstein 3 Marsh 1

GREENLAND
Old Owens 3 UCL Academicals 0

SENIOR NOVETS
Civil Service 5th 1 Nat'l Westminster Bank 2

INTERMEDIATE NOVETS
Old Actonians 6th 3 Old Meadonians 6th 1

JUNIOR NOVETS
Old Actonians 7th 3 Old Meadonians 8th 0

WOMEN'S CUP†
East Barnet Old Grammarians 4 Alexandra Park 0

† New Competitions

SATURDAY YOUTH
U-18
Provident House 4 Hale End Athletic 0
U-17
Field Crusaders 2 Norsemen 1
U-16
Forty Hill 1 Norsemen 1
U-15
Bethwin SE 2* Old Bealonians 4*
U-14
Prydun 3 Norsemen "B" 2
U-13
Providence House 1*:5p Mill Hill Village 1*:3p
U-12
Cheshunt 2 Whitewebbs Eagles 1
U-11
Old Bealonians 0*:2p West Essex Colts 0*:4p
U-12 GIRLS†
Potters Bar United 5 Flamingoes 1

SUNDAY YOUTH
U-18
Chase Side 2*:3p Barnet 2*:5p
U-17
Cheshunt 3 Field Crusaders 4
U-16
Cheshunt 3 Forty Hill 1
U-15
Cheshunt 1 Whitewebbs Eagles 6
U-14
Prydun 2 Potters Bar United 0
U-13 (Tesco)
Chase Side 1 Broomfield PL 2
U-12
Whitewebbs Eagles 2 Southgate Adelaide 0
U-11
Trent Park 1 Potters Bar United 3
U-14 GIRLS†
William Fitt 2 Flamingoes 1

ARTHUR DUNN CUP FINAL

Old Carthusians 2 Old Westminsters 0

ARTHURIAN LEAGUE

PREMIER DIVISION	P	W	D	L	F	A	Pts
Old Carthusians	18	15	1	2	68	22	46
Old Harrovians	18	13	1	4	70	26	40
Old Etonians	18	11	4	3	52	24	37
Old Brentwoods	18	9	4	5	36	26	31
Lancing Old Boys	18	7	5	6	36	33	26
Old Foresters	18	7	3	8	40	43	24
Old Salopians	18	5	8	5	42	33	23
Old Reptonians*	18	2	5	11	25	65	8
Old Bradfieldian*	18	3	1	14	23	65	7
Old Chigwellians	18	1	2	15	14	69	5

DIVISION 1	P	W	D	L	F	A	Pts
Old Westminsters	14	9	3	2	40	24	30
Old Cholmeleians	14	9	0	5	29	23	27
Old Aldenhamians	14	7	4	3	40	27	25
Old Wykehamists	14	5	5	4	23	19	20
Old Malvernians	14	4	3	7	23	29	15
Old Haileyburians	14	2	7	5	23	27	13
Old Tonbridgians*	14	4	1	9	29	41	10
Old Haberdashers*	14	4	1	9	24	41	–5

DIVISION 2	P	W	D	L	F	A	Pts
Old Salopians Res	16	10	2	4	49	29	32
Old Foresters Res	16	10	2	4	46	29	32
Old Etonians 3rd	16	9	2	5	31	26	29
Old Chigwellians Res	16	7	3	6	38	28	24
Old Carthusians Res	16	7	3	6	35	29	24
Old Etonians Res	16	5	5	6	25	39	20
Old Westminsters Res	16	5	2	9	30	41	17
Old Carthusians 3rd	16	5	1	10	20	40	16
Old Cholmeleians Res*	16	3	2	11	21	34	8

DIVISION 3	P	W	D	L	F	A	Pts
Old Brentwoods Res	12	9	1	2	43	18	28
Old Radleians	12	8	2	2	33	16	26
Old Bradfieldians Res	12	6	1	5	29	30	19
Old Wellingtonians	12	4	2	6	25	33	14
Old Aldenhamians Res	12	4	2	6	26	36	14
Lancing Old Boys Res	12	2	4	6	23	33	10
Old Brentwoods 3rd	12	1	4	7	16	29	7

DIVISION 4	P	W	D	L	F	A	Pts
Old Chigwellians 3rd	14	10	2	2	33	16	32
Old Oundelians	14	8	1	5	32	17	25
Old Foresters 3rd	14	8	1	5	32	22	25
Old Malvernians Res*	14	7	2	5	30	29	20
Old Eastbournians	14	6	1	7	29	23	19
Old Brentwoods 4th	14	5	2	7	25	21	17
Old Berkhamstedians	14	5	1	8	29	36	16
Old Cholmeleians 3rd	14	1	2	11	11	57	5

DIVISION 5	P	W	D	L	F	A	Pts
Old Westminsters 3rd	15	9	2	4	31	21	29
Old Harrovians Res	15	7	4	4	30	32	25
Old Chigwellians 4th	15	6	5	4	24	14	23
Old Wykehamists Res*	15	8	1	6	32	25	22
Old Foresters 4th	15	5	2	8	25	25	17
Old Cholmeleians 4th*	15	2	2	11	20	45	–1

** Points deducted – breach of rules*

JUNIOR LEAGUE CUP
Old Harrovians Res 5 Old Chigwellians Res 2 aet

DERRIK MOORE VETERANS' CUP
Old Cholmeleians 3 Old Carthusians1

JIM DIXSON SIX-A-SIDE CUP
Won by Lancing Old Boys

LONDON FINANCIAL FOOTBALL ASSOCIATION

DIVISION 1	P	W	D	L	F	A	Pts
Marsh	16	11	4	1	41	15	37
NatWest Bank Res	16	8	5	3	38	31	29
Dresdner Kleinwort Wasserstein	16	5	4	7	29	33	19
Chislehurst Sports	16	4	5	7	26	36	17
NatWest Bank	16	0	6	10	16	35	6

DIVISION 2	P	W	D	L	F	A	Pts
Credit Suisse First Boston	14	11	2	1	54	17	35
Royal Bank of Scotland	14	10	3	1	38	23	33
Chislehurst Sports Res	14	6	5	3	39	25	23
Coutts & Co.	14	5	2	7	39	41	17
Zurich Eagle Star	14	5	2	7	39	41	17
Marsh Res	14	4	3	7	31	39	15
NatWest Bank 3rd	14	4	2	8	41	55	14
JP Morgan Chase	14	1	1	12	24	64	4

DIVISION 3	P	W	D	L	F	A	Pts
NatWest Bank 4th	16	13	3	0	47	12	42
Royal Bank of Scotland Res	16	10	3	3	36	16	33
Chislehurst Sports 3rd	16	7	6	3	31	25	27
British Council	16	7	2	7	25	30	23
Citigroup CIB	16	6	2	8	29	30	20
Royal Sun Alliance	16	6	2	8	24	32	20
Temple Bar	16	5	3	8	34	38	18
Foreign & Commonwealth Office	16	4	1	11	26	53	13
Royal Sun Alliance Res	16	2	2	12	25	41	8

CHALLENGE CUP
HSBC 0*:4p Weirside Rangers 0*:3p

SENIOR CUP
Marsh 2 Dresdner Kleinwort Wasserstein 1

JUNIOR CUP
Chislehurst Sports 0 Credit Suisse 1

JUNIOR CUP
National Westminster Bank 3 Zurich Eagle Star 1

LONDON LEGAL LEAGUE

DIVISION I	P	W	D	L	F	A	Pts
Linklaters	18	13	2	3	39	26	41
Slaughter & May	18	11	4	3	39	22	37
Stephenson Harwood	18	11	1	6	50	33	34
Macfarlanes	18	10	2	6	48	32	32
Watson Farley & Williams	18	8	4	6	24	23	28
Simmons & Simmons	18	8	1	9	37	37	25
Dechert*	18	5	5	8	34	36	19
Richards Butler	18	4	5	9	35	44	17
Clifford Chance	18	4	3	11	23	46	15
KPMG London*	18	2	1	15	26	56	6

DIVISION II	P	W	D	L	F	A	Pts
Financial Service A	18	14	2	2	57	17	44
Nabarro Nathanson	18	14	2	2	58	20	44
Gray's Inn	18	9	2	7	30	34	29
Allen & Overy	18	8	3	7	44	37	27
Barlow Lyde & Gilbert	18	7	1	10	48	46	22
Baker & McKenzie	18	7	0	11	31	45	21
Herbert Smith	18	6	3	9	31	47	21
Ashurst Morris Crisp*	18	6	4	8	30	31	20
Norton Rose	18	6	0	12	24	58	18
CMS Cameron McKenna*	18	3	3	12	24	42	8

DIVISION III	P	W	D	L	F	A	Pts
Lovells	16	11	1	4	48	29	34
Pegasus	16	9	3	4	47	32	30
Kirkpatrick & Lockhart N G	16	9	3	4	39	27	30
Withers	16	8	4	4	30	24	28
Freshfields Bruckhaus Deringer	16	7	1	8	39	34	22
Field Fisher Waterhouse*	16	5	3	8	45	37	17
BBC Post Production	16	4	4	8	30	34	16
Denton Wilde Sapte	16	5	1	10	24	45	16
Taylor Wessing	16	3	2	11	12	52	11

Farrer & Co withdrawn and record expunged
** Points deducted – breach of rules*

LEAGUE CHALLENGE CUP
Stephenson Harwood 4 Watson Farley & Williams 1

WEAVERS ARMS CUP
Macfarlanes 2 Lovells 4

INVITATION CUP
Field Fisher Waterhouse 3 Taylor Wessing 1

LONDON FOOTBALL LEAGUE

PREMIER DIVISION	P	W	D	L	F	A	Pts
Abbey	21	14	4	3	84	22	46
Alba	21	13	4	4	62	37	43
BNP Paribas	22	12	4	6	59	45	40
Invisible	21	12	3	6	69	36	39
Audit Commission	22	11	6	5	60	40	39
Warner Brothers	21	11	5	5	57	40	38
Warrington	22	10	6	6	50	44	36
Eastern Promise	22	10	5	7	56	42	35
Athletico Chips	22	5	1	16	37	73	16
Philosophy Football	22	4	4	14	28	75	16
Viacom Outdoor	22	3	2	17	26	73	11
Mother	22	2	2	18	22	83	8

DIVISION 1	P	W	D	L	F	A	Pts
MTV	21	17	3	1	68	17	54
Accenture	21	17	2	2	54	28	53
UBS	21	12	3	6	56	29	39
Davis Langdon	22	12	2	8	51	38	38
TNT Magazine	21	11	4	6	48	31	37
Sotheby's	22	10	2	10	42	49	32
BBC Post Production	21	9	3	9	47	43	30
London Reaction	22	8	1	13	34	52	25
Thorp Design	21	7	3	11	43	48	24
Hudson	22	6	2	14	51	74	20
Visa	22	3	3	16	31	65	12
Boodle Hatfield	22	2	2	18	29	80	8

LONDON OLD BOYS' CUPS

SENIOR
Old Meadonians 3 Southgate County 2
CHALLENGE
Old Kolsassions 0*:5p Fulham Compton Old Boys 0*:4p
INTERMEDIATE
Albanian Res 3 King's Old Boys Res 1
JUNIOR
Old Vaughanians 3rd 1 UCL Academicals 3rd 2
MINOR
Old Aloysians 4th 2 Parkfield 4th 3
DRUMMOND
Southgate County 4th 0 Albanian 5th 3
NEMEAN
Old Meadonians 8th 1*:2p Cardinal Manning Res 2*:4p
OLYMPIAN
Old Guildfordians Res 2 Old Bromleians 3rd 3
JACK PERRY VETERANS
Old Meadonians "A" 2 Old Woodhousians 3

OLD BOYS' INVITATION CUPS

SENIOR
Old Owens 2 Old Salesians 1
JUNIOR
Old Owens Res 1 Old Finchleians Res 0
MINOR
Old Tenisonians 3rd 3 Old Owens 3rd 1
4TH XIs
Old Finchleians 4th 1 Old Owens 4th 2
5TH XIs
Old Parmiterians 5th 1*:2p E Barnet Old Grammarians 5th 1*:3p
6TH XIs
Glyn Old Boys 6th 2 Old Parmiterians 6th 1
7TH XIs
Old Bealonians 7th 2 Old Suttonians 7th 5
VETERANS'
Old Aloysians 3 Old Woodhousians 0

MIDLAND AMATEUR ALLIANCE

PREMIER DIVISION	P	W	D	L	F	A	Pts
Underwood Villa	24	21	0	3	119	47	63
Racing Athletic	24	15	4	5	58	30	49
Ashland Rovers	24	15	4	5	58	40	49
Woodborough United	24	14	2	8	87	48	44
Beaufort United	24	13	5	6	68	39	44
Steelers	24	13	3	8	61	39	42
Old Elizabethans	24	11	6	7	49	46	39
Wollaton 3rd	24	10	4	10	66	59	34
Beeston Old Boys Assn	24	9	4	11	48	53	31
Lady Bay	24	6	2	16	47	80	20
Bassingfield	24	5	2	17	29	99	17
Derbyshire Amateurs Res	24	2	4	18	32	78	10
Sherwood Forest	24	1	2	21	25	89	5

DIVISION 1	P	W	D	L	F	A	Pts
Monty Hind Old Boys	26	19	7	0	73	27	64
County NALGO	26	17	5	4	64	34	56
Brunts Old Boys	26	14	3	9	66	64	45
Clinphone	26	11	7	8	61	50	40
Radcliffe Olympic 3rd	26	11	4	11	47	45	37
PASE	26	10	7	9	59	63	37
Old Bemrosians	26	11	3	12	46	40	36
Nottinghamshire Res	26	11	3	12	50	53	36
Old Elizabethans Res	26	11	1	14	57	62	34
Keyworth United 3rd	26	8	7	11	56	58	31
Southwell Amateurs	26	7	6	13	47	58	27
Wollaton 4th	26	7	6	13	44	59	27
Broadmeadows	26	6	5	15	57	60	23
West Bridgford United	26	5	4	17	40	94	19

DIVISION 2	P	W	D	L	F	A	Pts
FC 05	26	26	0	0	178	20	78
Acorn Athletic	26	20	2	4	128	62	62
Top Club	26	19	3	4	105	54	60
Calverton Miners Welfare 3rd	26	15	1	10	80	62	46
Ashland Rovers Res	26	14	3	9	75	80	45
Hickling	26	14	1	11	88	69	43
EMTEC	26	12	3	11	86	67	39
Nottinghamshire 3rd	26	10	4	12	60	70	34
Cambridge Knights	26	9	1	16	93	80	28
Derbyshire Amateurs 3rd	26	8	3	15	50	98	27
Ashfield Athletic	26	5	6	15	68	105	21
Old Bemrosians Res	26	6	2	18	34	92	20
Tibshelf Old Boys	26	5	3	18	47	110	18
Hare and Hounds	26	2	2	22	41	164	8

LEAGUE SENIOR CUP
Underwood Villa 3 Racing Athletic 1

LEAGUE INTERMEDIATE CUP
PASE 2 Clinphone 1

LEAGUE MINOR CUP
FC05 6 Hickling 1

SOUTHERN AMATEUR LEAGUE

SENIOR SECTION

DIVISION 1	P	W	D	L	F	A	Pts
Old Owens	20	14	1	5	51	19	43
West Wickham	20	12	6	2	41	15	42
Nottsborough	20	12	5	3	43	20	41
Winchmore Hill	20	13	2	5	31	15	41
Broomfield	20	7	6	7	26	35	27
Old Salesians	20	6	6	8	28	33	24
East Barnet Old Grammarians	20	6	5	9	27	34	23
Civil Service	20	4	5	11	31	40	17
Old Lyonians	20	5	2	13	22	47	17
Old Esthameians	20	2	10	8	23	42	16
Old Actonians Association	20	2	6	12	18	41	12

DIVISION 2	P	W	D	L	F	A	Pts
Alleyn Old Boys	20	12	2	6	48	26	38
Old Wilsonians	20	11	5	4	38	26	38
Norsemen	20	11	3	6	44	24	36
Ibis	20	11	2	7	51	42	35
Carshalton	20	8	6	6	46	41	30
Bank of England	20	7	5	8	31	33	26
Weirside Rangers	20	7	5	8	37	41	26
Polytechnic	20	7	4	9	36	39	25
HSBC	20	7	4	9	24	31	25
South Bank Cuaco	20	4	3	13	33	53	15
Old Finchleians	20	4	3	13	28	60	15

DIVISION 3	P	W	D	L	F	A	Pts
Merton	20	13	3	4	58	26	42
BB Eagles	20	11	7	2	55	27	40
Alexandra Park	20	12	3	5	59	35	39
Old Westminster Citizens	20	10	6	4	44	37	36
Old Parkonians	20	9	5	6	50	38	32
Crouch End Vampires	20	8	3	9	38	45	27
Old Stationers	20	7	4	5	46	52	25
Old Latymerians	20	7	2	13	27	43	23
Lloyds TSB Bank	20	6	3	16	39	62	21
Kew Association	20	3	3	10	28	59	12
Southgate Olympic	20	2	5	12	25	45	11

INTERMEDIATE SECTION
Division 1 – 11 teams – Won by Old Actonians Association Res
Division 2 – 11 teams – Won by Old Wilsonians Res
Division 3 – 11 teams – Won by Old Westminster Citizens Res

THIRD TEAM SECTION
Division 1 – 11 teams – Won by Winchmore Hill 3rd
Division 2 – 11 teams – Won by Old Stationers 3rd
Division 3 – 11 teams – Won by Southgate Olympic 3rd

MINOR SECTION
Division 3 North – 11 teams – Won by Old Owens 6th
Division 3 South – 10 teams – Won by BB Eagles 4th
Division 4 North – 11 teams – Won by Winchmore Hill 7th
Division 4 South – 10 teams – Won by Old Actonians Association 7th
Division 5 North – 10 teams – Won by Winchmore Hill 9th

Division 5 South – 11 teams – Won by Wearside Rangers 5th
Division 6 South – 11 teams – Won by Merton 5th
Division 7 South – 11 teams – Won by Lloyds TSB Bank 8th

CHALLENGE CUPS

Junior
Southgate Olympic 3rd 0 O Actonians Ass'n 3rd 1
Minor
Old Owens 4th 2*:6p Kew Association 4th 2*:7p
Senior Novets
Civil Service 5th 9 Old Stationers 5th 4
Intermediate Novets
Old Actonians Ass'n 6th 4 Crouch End Vamps 6th 1
Junior Novets
Winchmore Hill 7th 2*:3 Crouch End Vamps 7th 2*:2

U-16 GIRLS CENTRE OF EXCELLENCE LEAGUE

	P	W	D	L	F	A	Pts
Southampton	20	14	3	3	67	32	45
Arsenal	20	13	5	2	39	15	44
Millwall	20	14	1	5	50	25	43
Chelsea	20	13	3	4	50	19	42
Charlton Athletic	20	10	4	6	39	31	34
Reading	20	8	4	8	38	43	28
Watford	20	8	2	10	35	44	26
Colchester United	20	6	3	11	28	47	21
Fulham	20	6	2	12	37	43	20
Leyton Orient	20	2	2	16	16	44	8
Brighton	20	1	1	18	13	69	4

AMATEUR FOOTBALL COMBINATION

PREMIER DIVISION	P	W	D	L	F	A	Pts
Old Meadonians	18	12	6	0	53	15	42
Old Hamptonians	18	12	3	3	42	17	39
Honourable Artillery Company	18	11	4	3	62	19	37
Albanian	18	10	3	5	35	33	33
Old Bealonians	18	8	5	5	26	22	29
Parkfield	18	5	3	10	24	38	18
UCL Academicals	18	5	2	11	26	31	17
Old Aloysians	18	5	2	11	28	41	17
Hale End Athletic	18	5	1	12	21	42	16
Latymer Old Boys*	18	1	3	14	19	78	3

SENIOR DIVISION 1	P	W	D	L	F	A	Pts
Southgate County	18	12	3	3	51	26	39
Old Parmiterians	18	11	5	2	41	18	38
Enfield Old Grammarians	18	11	4	3	44	23	37
Glyn Old Boys	18	9	2	7	46	30	29
Old Salvatorians	18	8	5	5	43	36	29
Old Danes	18	6	6	6	24	34	24
Wood Green Old Boys	18	5	2	11	26	40	17
Old Tiffinians	18	4	3	11	22	38	15
Old Wokingians	18	4	2	12	27	45	14
Old Ignatians	18	3	2	13	16	50	11

SENIOR DIVISION 2	P	W	D	L	F	A	Pts
Sinjuns Grammarians	20	15	3	2	71	32	48
Old Challoners	20	14	3	3	50	26	45
Economicals	20	13	2	5	56	30	41
Old Suttonians	20	12	4	4	54	36	40
Clapham Old Xaverians	20	11	2	7	45	32	35
Shene Old Grammarians	20	9	4	7	50	47	31
Old Vaughanians	20	6	2	12	31	44	20
Old Aloysians Res	20	4	4	12	35	49	16
Old Dorkinians	20	3	4	13	38	57	13
Old Tenisonians	20	2	6	12	39	58	12
Old Isleworthians	20	2	4	14	22	80	10

SENIOR DIVISION 3 NORTH

	P	W	D	L	F	A	Pts
Old Meadonians Res	18	12	3	3	46	21	39
Old Salvatorians Res	18	12	3	3	50	27	39
Albanians Res	18	12	1	5	50	32	37
UCL Academicals Res	18	11	2	5	40	20	35
Hale End Athletic Res	18	9	3	6	50	36	30
Old Minchendenians	18	6	5	7	48	49	23
Old Manorians	18	6	3	9	32	42	21
Parkfield Res	18	4	3	11	37	42	15
Old Buckwellians	18	4	2	12	29	54	14
Pegasus	18	1	1	16	16	75	3

** Points deducted – breach of rules*

SENIOR DIVISION 3 SOUTH

	P	W	D	L	F	A	Pts
King's Old Boys	20	14	4	2	65	26	46
Old Paulines	20	11	4	5	54	34	37
Wandsworth Borough	20	11	4	5	52	38	37
Old Hamptonians Res	20	9	4	7	35	35	31
Hampstead Heathens	20	7	7	6	40	39	28
Fitzwilliam Old Boys	20	8	4	8	40	41	28
Old Guildfordians	20	8	3	9	34	37	27
John Fisher Old Boys	20	8	2	10	41	48	26
Old Reigatians	20	5	4	11	35	42	19
Queen Mary College Old Boys	20	5	2	13	29	42	17
Old Sedcopians	20	4	2	14	27	70	14

INTERMEDIATE DIVISION NORTH

	P	W	D	L	F	A	Pts
Mill Hill Village	20	17	2	1	77	25	53
Southgate County Res	20	13	3	4	52	39	42
Enfield Old Grammarians Res	20	12	2	6	57	37	38
Old Bealonians Res	20	8	5	7	33	28	29
Old Woodhouseians	20	7	4	9	43	43	25
Egbertian	20	6	6	8	39	44	24
UCL Academicals 3rd	20	7	3	10	42	50	24
Old Camdenians	20	7	2	11	33	48	23
Old Edmontonians	20	6	4	10	39	48	22
Old Buckwellians Res	20	4	4	12	34	59	16
Old Parmiterians Res	20	2	7	11	36	64	13

INTERMEDIATE DIVISION SOUTH

	P	W	D	L	F	A	Pts
H A C Res	20	13	6	1	65	23	45
Old Belgravians	20	12	2	6	78	44	38
Centymca	20	9	5	6	43	44	32
Witan	20	8	6	6	52	50	30
Kings Old Boys Res	20	8	5	7	50	41	29
Old Thorntonians	20	7	6	7	37	39	27
Old Suttonians Res	20	7	5	8	35	39	26
Old Josephians	20	7	3	10	60	63	24
Mickleham Old Boxhillians	20	6	6	8	46	53	24
Old Tenisonians Res	20	5	5	10	41	73	20
Old St Mary's	20	1	5	14	31	69	8

INTERMEDIATE DIVISION WEST

	P	W	D	L	F	A	Pts
Old Meadonians 3rd	20	14	1	5	64	37	43
Old Manorians Res	20	13	3	4	63	36	42
Brent	20	13	2	5	66	33	41
London Welsh	20	10	6	4	52	40	36
Cardinal Manning Old Boys	20	11	1	8	48	39	34
Old Challoners Res	20	10	2	8	40	32	32
Old Vaughanians Res	20	6	3	11	47	51	21
Parkfield 3rd	20	5	4	11	29	46	19
Old Danes Res	20	5	5	10	42	86	20
Old Salvatorians 3rd	20	3	4	13	34	58	13
Phoenix Old Boys	20	3	3	14	25	52	12

Intermediate Division North – 11 teams – Won by Mill Hill Village
Intermediate Division South – 11 teams – Won by Honourable Artillery Company Res
Intermediate Division West – 11 teams – Won by Old Meadonians 3rd

NORTHERN REGIONAL

Division 1 – 11 teams – Won by Old Parmiterians 3rd
Division 2 – 10 teams – Won by Old Aloysians 4th
Division 3 – 10 teams – Won by Ravenscroft Old Boys
Division 4 – 10 teams – Won by Mill Hill County Old Boys
Division 5 – 10 teams – Won by Old Parmiterians 5th
Division 6 – 10 teams – Won by Old Buckwellians 4th
Division 7 – 10 teams – Won by Old Tollingtonians Res
Division 8 – 9 teams – Won by Wood Green Old Boys 5th
Division 9 – 8 teams – Won by Old Parmiterians 7th

SOUTHERN REGIONAL

Division 1 – 10 teams – Won by Economicals Res
Division 2 – 11 teams – Won by Chertsey Old Salesians
Division 3 – 10 teams – Won by Old Tenisonians 3rd
Division 4 – 10 teams – Won by Witan Res
Division 5 – 10 teams – Won by Old Josephians 3rd
Division 6 – 10 teams – Won by Shene Old Grammarians 3rd
Division 7 – 10 teams – Won by Old Paulines 3rd
Division 8 – 10 teams – Won by Old Guildfordians 4th
Division 9 – 10 teams – Won by Economicals 4th

Division 10 – 10 teams – Won by John Fisher Old Boys 5th
Division 11 – 8 teams – Won by Kings Old Boys 3rd

WESTERN REGIONAL
Division 1 – 10 teams – Won by Old Vaughanians 3rd
Division 2 – 10 teams – Won by Old Uffingtonians Res
Division 3 – 11 teams – Won by Old Challoners 3rd
Division 4 – 9 teams – Won by Phoenix Old Boys 3rd
Division 5 – 10 teams – Won by Ealing Association Res

SPRING CUP FINALS
SENIOR
Old Aloysians 4 Old Manorians 2

INTERMEDIATE
Leyton County Old Boys 5 Old Uxonians Res 1

JUNIOR NORTH
Enfield Old Grammarians 4th 2 Leyton County OB 3rd 3

JUNIOR SOUTH
Clapham Old Xaverians 4th 2 Old Sedcopians Res 0

MINOR NORTH
Davenant Wanderers Res 9 Old Edmontonians 5th 2

MINOR SOUTH
Old Wokingians 6th 3 Economicals 4th 5

MINOR WEST
Phoenix Old Boys 4 Shene Old Grammarians 3rd 0

UNIVERSITY OF LONDON MEN'S INTER-COLLEGIATE LEAGUE

In all Leagues some games were not played and points awarded

WEEKEND ONE DIVISION	P	W	D	L	F	A	Pts
London School of Economics	11	9	2	0	44	6	29
Queen Mary College	11	6	4	1	27	11	22
Royal Holloway College	11	5	4	2	24	14	19
University College	11	5	3	3	21	22	18
Imperial College	11	4	3	4	20	14	15
King's College	11	4	4	3	27	22	16
R Free, Mx & Univ Coll Hosp MS	11	5	2	4	16	17	17
St Bart's & R London Hosps MS	11	3	3	5	11	17	12
School of Oriental & African Studies	11	4	0	7	15	31	12
London School Economics Res	11	2	3	6	12	19	9
Imperial College Res	11	2	1	8	6	34	7
University College Res	11	2	1	8	20	36	4

WEEKEND TWO DIVISION	P	W	D	L	F	A	Pts
Royal Holloway College Res	10	8	2	0	30	7	26
Imperial College Medicals	10	6	3	1	31	14	21
Guy's, King's, St Thomas's MS	10	6	2	2	30	12	20
Royal Holloway College 3rd	10	5	3	2	32	13	18
University College 3rd	10	5	1	4	17	21	16
St Georges Hospital MS	10	4	3	3	33	23	15
Queen Mary College Res	10	3	1	6	19	35	10
Imperial College 3rd	10	3	0	7	12	26	9
King's College Res	10	2	2	6	18	23	8
Imperial Medicals Res	10	2	2	6	9	31	8
St Georges Hospital Res	10	1	1	8	8	34	4

DIVISION ONE	P	W	D	L	F	A	Pts
Goldsmiths' College	22	18	3	1	73	27	57
London School of Economics 3rd	22	14	6	2	68	29	48
University College 5th	22	12	3	7	44	30	39
Royal Holloway College 4th	22	9	3	10	45	54	30
King's College 3rd	22	9	4	9	39	40	31
Royal Veterinary College	22	8	4	10	38	44	28
R Free, Mx & Univ Coll Hosp MS Res	22	8	3	11	53	54	27
Imperial College 5th	22	9	3	10	29	61	30
Guy's, King's, St Thomas's MS Res	22	12	2	8	52	25	38
University College 4th	22	6	5	11	43	42	23
Imperial College 4th	22	5	5	12	34	55	20
R Free, Mx & Univ Coll Hosp MS 3rd	22	1	1	20	17	74	4

DIVISION TWO	P	W	D	L	F	A	Pts
University College 6th	22	20	1	1	82	21	61
Queen Mary College 3rd	22	15	1	6	61	31	46
London School of Economics 4th	22	12	2	8	43	37	38
London School of Economics 5th	22	11	4	7	62	39	37
St Bart's & R London Hosps MS Res	22	10	5	7	40	26	35
Royal Holloway College 5th	22	9	2	11	45	49	29
Guy's, King's, St Thomas's MS 3rd	22	8	2	12	36	32	26
University College 7th	22	8	1	13	43	64	25
King's College 4th	22	7	4	11	39	63	25
Imperial Medicals 3rd	22	6	5	11	40	54	23
Royal School of Mines (IC)	22	6	4	12	39	63	22
King's College 5th	22	3	3	16	24	75	12

DIVISION THREE	P	W	D	L	F	A	Pts
Royal Holloway College 6th	20	13	2	5	61	33	41
King's College 6th	20	10	6	4	49	28	36
St Bart's & R London Hosps MS 3rd	20	10	4	6	52	38	34
Guy's, King's, St Thomas's MS 4th	20	8	8	4	51	43	32
Imperial College 6th	20	9	2	9	31	29	29
Guy's, King's, St Thomas's Hosp MS 5th	20	9	2	9	25	34	29
London School of Economics 7th	20	7	4	9	37	33	25
London School of Economics 6th	20	7	4	9	24	37	25
Goldsmiths' College Res	20	7	2	11	50	61	23
R Free, Mx & Univ Coll Hosp 4th	20	5	5	10	22	33	20
Queen Mary College 4th	20	4	3	13	31	64	15

DIVISION FOUR	P	W	D	L	F	A	Pts
University of the Arts	18	14	1	3	85	25	43
School of Pharmacy	18	13	1	4	81	40	40
Imperial College 7th	18	13	0	5	48	29	39
School of Oriental & African Studies Res	18	12	2	4	77	38	38
School of Slavonic & E European Studies	18	7	3	8	34	53	24
Goldsmiths' College 3rd	16	6	2	8	47	61	20
Queen Mary College 5th	18	6	1	11	37	51	19
Royal Veterinary College Res	18	5	3	10	37	72	18
Imperial Medicals 4th	18	4	1	13	40	87	13
St Georges Hospital MS 3rd	18	1	2	15	16	46	5

CHALLENGE CUP
University College 1 Royal Free, Mx & UCH Med School 3

RESERVES CHALLENGE CUP
Royal Holloway 3rd 2 University College 4th 1

RESERVES PLATE
University College 6th 3 Queen Mary College 3rd 2

VASE
St Barts & R London Med School 3rd 6* King's College 3rd 3*
* *After Extra Time*

UNIVERSITY OF LONDON WOMEN'S INTER-COLLEGIATE LEAGUE

PREMIER DIVISION	P	W	D	L	F	A	Pts
Guy's, King's, St Thomas's Hosp MS	10	8	1	1	77	21	25
Royal Holloway College	10	7	1	2	35	15	22
London School of Economics	10	6	2	2	43	13	20
Queen Mary College	10	3	0	7	35	59	9
University College	10	3	1	6	27	29	10
King's College	10	0	1	9	6	86	1

DIVISION ONE	P	W	D	L	F	A	Pts
Goldsmiths' College	8	6	1	1	34	10	19
Imperial College Medicals	8	4	3	1	29	9	15
R Free, Mx & Univ Coll Hosp MS	8	3	1	4	16	16	10
Royal Veterinary College	8	3	1	4	20	21	10
University College Res	8	1	0	7	7	50	3

DIVISION TWO	P	W	D	L	F	A	Pts
Guy's, King's, St Thomas's MS Res	8	6	1	1	28	16	19
Imperial Medicals Womens 1st	8	5	2	1	54	11	17
School of Oriental & African Studies	8	4	1	3	12	21	13
St George's Hospital MS	8	1	2	5	21	24	5
R Free, Mx & Univ Coll Hosp MS Res	8	0	2	6	6	49	2

WOMEN'S CHALLENGE CUP
Guy's King's St Thomas's 9 LSE 1

UNIVERSITY FOOTBALL 2005–06

122nd UNIVERSITY MATCH

(at Craven Cottage, 2 April 2006)

Oxford (0) 0 Cambridge (0) 1

Oxford: D. Robinson; *M. Elliot, *A. Barkhouse, *J. Hazzard, O. Price, J. Huxley, J. Butterfield, *M. Rigby, *V. Vitale, P. Kaliszewski, L. Burns.
Subs: P. Rainford, M. Hall, *L. Sullivan, J. Doree, *N. Baker.

Cambridge: *T. Savill; W. Stevenson, A. Murphy, *N. Pantelides, *C. Turnbull, J. Lockwood, *A. Coleman, M. Dankis, B. Threlfall, *M. Adams, *A. Mugan.
Subs: R. Payne, J. Brown, M. Ellis, D. Mills, J. Dean.
Scorer: R. Payne.

Referee: S. Bennett (Kent).

**denotes Old Blue.*

Cambridge drew level with Oxford after their 47th win, 28 matches have been drawn.

IMPORTANT ADDRESSES

The Football Association: The Secretary, 25 Soho Square, London W1D 4FA. *020 7745 4545*

Scotland: David Taylor, Hampden Park, Glasgow G42 9AY. *0141 616 6000*

Northern Ireland (Irish FA): Chief Executive: Howard J. C. Wells, 20 Windsor Avenue, Belfast BT9 6EG. *028 9066 9458*

Wales: D. Collins, 3 Westgate Street, Cardiff, South Glamorgan CF10 1DP. *029 2037 2325*

Republic of Ireland B. Menton (FA of Ireland): 80 Merrion Square South, Dublin 2. *00353 16766864*

International Federation (FIFA): P. O. Box 85 8030 Zurich, Switzerland. *00 411 384 9595. Fax: 00 411 384 9696*

Union of European Football Associations: Secretary, Route de Geneve 46, Case Postale CH-1260 Nyon, Switzerland. *0041 22 994 44 44. Fax: 0041 22 994 44 88*

THE LEAGUES

The Premier League: M. Foster, 11 Connaught Place, London W2 2ET. *020 7298 1600*

The Football League: Secretary, The Football League, Unit 5, Edward VII Quay, Navigation Way, Preston, Lancashire PR2 2YF. *0870 442 0 1888. Fax 0870 442 0 1188*

Scottish Premier League: R. Mitchell, Hampden Park, Somerville Drive, Glasgow G42 9BA. *0141 646 6962*

The Scottish League: P. Donald, Hampden Park, Glasgow G42 9AY. *0141 616 6000*

The Irish League: Secretary, 96 University Street, Belfast BT7 1HE. *028 9024 2888*

Football League of Ireland: D. Crowther, 80 Merrion Square, Dublin 2. *00353 16765120*

Conference National: Riverside House, 14b High Street, Crayford DA1 4HG. *01322 411021*

Eastern Counties League: B. A. Badcock, 18 Calford Drive, Hanchett Drive, Haverhill, Suffolk CB9 7WQ. *01440 708064*

Hellenic League: B. King, 83 Queens Road, Carterton, Oxon OX18 3YF. *01993 212738*

Kent League: R. Vinter, Bakery House, The Street, Chilham, Canterbury, Kent CT4 8BX. *01227 730457*

Leicestershire Senior League: R. J. Holmes, 9 Copse Close, Hugglescote, Coalville, Leicestershire LE67 2GL. *01530 831818*

Midland Combination: N. Harvey, 115 Millfield Road, Handsworth Wood, Birmingham B20 1ED. *0121 357 4172*

Northern Premier: R. D. Bayley, 22 Woburn Drive, Hale, Altrincham, Cheshire WA15 8LZ. *0161 980 7007*

Northern League: T. Golightly, 85 Park Road North, Chester-le-Street, Co Durham DH3 3SA. *0191 3882056*

Isthmian League: N. Robinson, Triumph House, Station Approach, Sanderstead Road, South Croydon, Surrey CR2 0PL. *020 8409 1978*

Southern League: D. J. Strudwick, 8 College Yard, Worcester WR1 2LA. *01905 330444*

Spartan South Midlands League: M. Mitchell, 26 Leighton Court, Dunstable, Beds LU6 1EW. *01582 667291*

United Counties League: R. Gamble, 8 Bostock Avenue, Northampton NN1 4LW. *01604 637766*

Western League: K. A. Clarke, 32 Westmead Lane, Chippenham, Wilts SN15 3HZ. *01249 464467*

West Midlands League: N. R. Juggins, 14 Badger Way, Blackwell, Bromsgrove, Worcs B60 1EX. *0121 445 2953*

Northern Counties (East): B. Wood, 6 Restmore Avenue, Guiseley, Leeds LS20 9DG. *01943 874558*

Central Midlands Football League: J. Worrall, 36 Spilsby Close, Cantley, Doncaster DN4 6TJ. *01302 370188*

Combined Counties League: L. Pharo, 17 Nigel Fisher Way, Chessington, Surrey KT9 2SN. *020 8391 0297*

Essex Senior League: D. Walls, 2 Hillsfield Cottage, Layer, Breton, Essex CO2 0PS. *01206 330146*

Midland Football Alliance: P. Dagger, 11 The Oval, Bicton, Nr Shrewsbury, Shropshire SY3 8ER. *01742 850859*

North West Counties Football League: G. J. Wilkinson, 46 Oaklands Drive, Penwortham, Preston, Lancs PR1 0XY. *01772 746312*

Wessex League: I. Craig, 7 Old River, Denmead, Hampshire PO7 6UX. *02392 230973*

South Western League: P. Lowe, 14 Anderton Court, Whitchurch, Tavistock, Devon PL19 9EX. *01822 613715*

Devon League: P. Hiscox, 19 Ivy Close, Wonford, Exeter, Devon EX2 5LX. *01392 493995*

Northern Alliance: J. McLackland, 92 Appletree Gardens, Walkerville, Newcastle-upon-Tyne NE6 4SX. *0191 262 6665*

Sussex County League: P. Beard, 2 Van Gogh Place, Bersted, Bognor Regis, West Sussex PO22 9BG. *01243 822063.*

Wearside League: T. Clark, 55 Vicarage Close, Silksworth, Sunderland, Tyne & Wear SR3 1UF. *0191 521 1242*

West Cheshire League: A. Green, 46 Bertram Drive, Meols, Wirral, Cheshire CH47 0LH. *0151 632 4946*

COUNTY FOOTBALL ASSOCIATIONS

Bedfordshire: P. D. Brown, Century House, Skimpot Road, Dunstable, Beds LU5 4JU. *01582 565111*

Berks and Bucks: B. G. Moore, 15a London Street, Faringdon, Oxon SN7 7HD. *01367 242099*

Birmingham County: D. Shelton, County FA Offices, Rayhall Lane, Great Barr, Birmingham B43 6JF. *0121 357 4278*

Cambridgeshire: R. K. Pawley, City Ground, Milton Road, Cambridge CB4 1FA. *01223 576770*

Cheshire: Ms M. Dunford, Hartford House, Hartford Moss Rec Centre, Northwich, Cheshire CW8 4BG. *01606 871166*

Cornwall: B. Cudmore, 1 High Cross Street, St. Austell, Cornwall PL25 4AB. *01726 74080*

Cumberland: G. Turrell, 17 Oxford Street, Workington, Cumbria CA14 2AL. *01900 872310*

Derbyshire: K. Compton, No 8–9 Stadium Business Court, Millenium Way, Pride Park, Derby DE24 8HZ *01332 361422*

Devon County: D. Richardson, County HQ, Coach Road, Newton Abbot, Devon TQ12 1EJ. *01626 332077*

Dorset County: P. Hough, County Ground, Blandford Close, Hamworthy, Poole, Dorset BH15 4BF. *01202 682375*

Durham: J. Topping, 'Codeslaw', Ferens Park, Durham DH1 1JZ. *0191 3848653*

East Riding County: D. R. Johnson, 50 Boulevard, Hull HU3 2TB. *01482 221158*

Essex County: P. Sammons, 31 Mildmay Road, Chelmsford, Essex CM2 0DN. *01245 357727*

Gloucestershire: P. Britton, Oaklands Park, Almondsbury, Bristol BS32 4AG. *01454 615888*

Guernsey: Matt Fallaize, Corbet Field, Grand Fort Road, St Sampson's, Guernsey GY2 4FG. *01481 200443*

Hampshire: Laurence Jones, William Pickford House, 8 Ashwood Gardens, off Winchester Road, Southampton SO16 7PW. *023 8079 1110*

Herefordshire: J. S. Lambert, County Ground Offices, Widemarsh Common, Hereford HR4 9NA. *01432 342179*

Hertfordshire: E. King, County Ground, Baldock Road, Letchworth, Herts SG6 2EN. *01462 677622*

Huntingdonshire: M. Frost, Cromwell Chambers, 8 St Johns Street, Huntingdon, Cambs PE29 3DD. *01480 414422*

Isle of Man: Mrs A. Garrett, P.O. Box 53, The Bowl, Douglas IOM IM99 1GY. *01624 615576*

Jersey: Gill Morgan, Springfield Stadium, St Helier, Jersey JE2 4LF. *01534 500165*
Kent County: K. T. Masters, 69 Maidstone Road, Chatham, Kent ME4 6DT. *01634 843824*
Lancashire: J. Kenyon, The County Ground, Thurston Road, Leyland, Preston, Lancs PR25 1LF. *01772 624000*
Leicestershire and Rutland: P. Morrison, Holmes Park, Dog and Gun Lane, Whetstone, Leicester LE8 6FA. *0116 2867828*
Lincolnshire: J. Griffin, PO Box 26, 12 Dean Road, Lincoln LN2 4DP. *01522 524917*
Liverpool County: S. Catterall, Walton Hall Avenue, Liverpool L4 9XP. *0151 523 4488*
London: D. Fowkes, 11 Hurlingham Business Park, Sullivan Road, Fulham SW6 3DU. *08707 743010*
Manchester County: John Dutton, Brantingham Road, Chorlton, Manchester M21 0TT. *0161 881 0299*
Middlesex County: P. J. Clayton, 39 Roxborough Road, Harrow, Middx HA1 1NS. *020 8424 8524*
Norfolk County: R. J. Howlett, Plantation Park, Blofield, Norwich, Norfolk, NR13 4PL. *01603 717177*
Northamptonshire: D. Payne, 9 Duncan Close, Red House Square, Moulton Park, Northampton NN3 6WL. *01604 670741*
North Riding County: M. Jarvis, Broughton Road, Stokesley, Middlesbrough TS9 5NY. *01642 717770*
Northumberland: R. E. Maughan, Whitley Park, Whitley Road, Newcastle-upon-Tyne NE12 9FA. *0191 270 0700*
Nottinghamshire: M. Kilbee, 7 Clarendon Street, Nottingham NG1 5HS. *0115 941 8954*
Oxfordshire: I. Mason, P.O. Box 62, Witney, Oxon OX28 1HA. *01993 778586*
Sheffield and Hallamshire: J. Hope-Gill, Clegg House, 69 Cornish Place, Cornish Street, Shalesmoor, Sheffield S6 3AF. *0114 241 4999*
Shropshire: D. Rowe, Gay Meadow, Abbey Foregate, Shrewsbury SY2 6AB. *01743 362769*
Somerset & Avon (South): Mrs H. Marchment, 30 North Road, Midsomer Norton, Radstock BA3 2QD. *01761 410280*
Staffordshire: B. J. Adshead, County Showground, Weston Road, Stafford ST18 0BD. *01785 256994*
Suffolk County: M. Head, The Buntings, Cedars Park, Stowmarket, Suffolk IP14 5GZ. *01449 616606*
Surrey County: R. Ward, 321 Kingston Road, Leatherhead, Surrey KT22 7TU. *01372 373543*
Sussex County: Ken Benham, County Office, Culver Road, Lancing, West Sussex BN15 9AX. *01903 753547*
Westmoreland: P. G. Ducksbury, Unit 1, Angel Court, 21 Highgate, Kendal, Cumbria LA9 4DA. *01539 730946*
West Riding County: R. Carter, Fleet Lane, Woodlesford, Leeds LS26 8NX. *0113 2821222*
Wiltshire: M. G. Benson, 18 Covingham Square, Covingham, Swindon SN3 5AY. *01793 486047*
Worcestershire: M. R. Leggett, Craftsman House, De Salis Drive, Hampton Lovett Industrial Estate, Droitwich WR9 0QE. *01905 827137*

OTHER USEFUL ADDRESSES

Amateur Football Alliance: M. L. Brown, 55 Islington Park Street, London N1 1QB. *020 7359 3493*
English Schools FA: Mike Spinks, 1/2 Eastgate Street, Stafford ST16 2NQ. *01785 251142*
Oxford University: Richard Tur, Oriel College, Oriel Square, Oxford OX1 4EW. *01865 276648*
Cambridge University: Dr J. A. Little, St Catherine's College, Cambridge CB2 1RL. *01223 334376*
Army: Major W. T. E. Thomson ASCB (MOD), Clayton Barracks, Thornhill Road, Aldershot, Hants GU11 2BG. *01252 348571/4*
Royal Air Force: Sqn Ldr N. Hope, SATCO, RAF Shawbury, Shropshire S74 4DZ. *01939 250351*
Royal Navy: Lt-Cdr S. Vasey, RN Sports Office, HMS Temeraire, Portsmouth, Hants PO1 2HB. *023 9272 2671*
British Universities Sports Association: G. Gregory-Jones, Chief Executive: BUSA, 8 Union Street, London SE1 1SZ. *020 7357 8555*
British Olympic Association: Church Row, Wandsworth Plain, London SW18 1EH. *0208 871 2677*
The Footbal Supporters Federation: Chairman: Ian D. Todd MBE, 8 Wyke Close, Wyke Gardens, Isleworth, Middlesex TW7 5PE. *020 8847 2905 (and fax). Mobile: 0961 558908*. National Secretary: Mike Williamson, 2 Repton Avenue, Torrishome, Morecambe, Lancs LA4 6RZ. *01524 425242, 07729 906329 (mobile)*. National Administrator: Mark Agate, 'The Stadium', 14 Coombe Close, Lordswood, Chatham, Kent ME5 8NU. *01634 319461 (and fax) 07931 635637 (mobile)*
National Playing Fields Association: Col. R. Satterthwaite, O.B.E., 578b Catherine Place, London, SW1
Professional Footballers' Association: G. Taylor, 2 Oxford Court, Bishopsgate, Off Lower Mosley Street, Manchester M2 3WQ. *0161 236 0575*
Referees' Association: A. Smith, 1 Westhill Road, Coundon, Coventry CV6 2AD. *024 7660 1701*
Women's Football Alliance: Miss K. Doyle, The Football Association, 25 Soho Square, London W1D 4FA. *020 7745 4545*
Institute of Football Management and Administration: Camkin House, 8 Charles Court, Budbrooke Road, Warwick CV34 5LZ. *01926 411884. Fax: 01926 411041*
Football Administrators Association: as above
Commercial and Marketing Managers Association: as above
Management Stats Association: as above
League Managers Association: as above
The Football Programme Directory: David Stacey, 'The Beeches', 66 Southend Road, Wickford, Essex SS11 8EN. *01268 732041 (and fax)*
England Football Supporters Association: Publicity Officer, David Stacey, 'The Beeches', 66 Southend Road, Wickford, Essex SS11 8EN. *01268 732041 (and fax)*
World Cup (1966) Association: Hon. Secretary, David Duncan, 96 Glenlea Road, Eltham, London SE9 1DZ
The Ninety-Two Club: 104 Gilda Crescent, Whitchurch, Bristol BS14 9LD
Scottish 38 Club: Mark Byatt, 6 Greenfields Close, Loughton, Essex IG10 3HG. *0208 508 6088*
The Football Trust: Second Floor, Walkden House, 10 Melton Street, London NW1 2EJ. *020 7388 4504*
Association of Provincial Football Supporters Clubs in London: Stephen Moon, 32 Westminster Gardens, Barking, Essex IG11 0BJ. *020 8594 2367*
World Association of Friends of English Football: Carlisle Hill, Gluck, Habichthof 2, D24939 Flensburg, Germany. *0049 461 4700222*
Football Postcard Collectors Club: PRO: Bryan Horsnell, 275 Overdown Road, Tilehurst, Reading RG31 6NX. *0118 942 4448 (and fax)*
UK Programme Collectors Club: Secretary, John Litster, 46 Milton Road, Kirkcaldy, Fife KY1 1TL. *01592 268718. Fax: 01592 595069*
Programme Monthly: as above
Scottish Football Historians Association: as above
Phil Gould (Licensed Football Agent), c/o Whoppit Management Ltd, P. O. Box 27204, London N11 2WS. *07071 732 468. Fax: 07070 732 469*
The Scandinavian Union of Supporters of British Football: Postboks, 15 Stovner, N-0913 Oslo, Norway
Football Writers' Association: Executive Secretary, Ken Montgomery, 6 Chase Lane, Barkingside, Essex IG6 1BH. *0208 554 2455 (and fax)*
Programme Promotions: 47 The Beeches, Lampton Road, Hounslow, Middlesex TW3 4DF.
Web: www.footballprogrammes.com

FOOTBALL CLUB CHAPLAINCY

The chairman's brow appeared even more furrowed than usual, so that his friend, the chaplain, felt constrained to invite the club's owner and inspiration to explain the reasons, should he wish to do so.

'I can cope with irksome newsmen, egotistical directors, know-it-all supporters and even players' agents, but sometimes situations arise which require something deeper – and I can't always find it, or even what it is.'

The chaplain smiled. 'Care to elaborate?' he asked.

'It isn't one thing in particular', mused his friend. 'The fact that several matters have arisen, all in the last forty-eight hours, and I'm finding them, in addition to my responsibilities here, quite overwhelming. Listen. The vice-chairman's wife is in hospital and has been diagnosed with cancer; the club captain's wife has lost the baby they were expecting next year; our star midfielder has learnt that he must spend time at Lilleshall and even then his full recovery from his injury isn't certain by any means; and my daughter's fiancé has upped and left her.'

'Things *are* tough for you,' agreed the chaplain. 'But listen. I can get to the hospital this afternoon and, should Beryl wish, I could also ask my friend the hospital chaplain to meet with her. Later, I'll ring the skipper: I could take a suitable little service for the baby – she could be buried in my churchyard if they wished. The football chaplains' conference is at Lilleshall in ten days time. I'll tell Gary I'm going to invite him for a chat about his future while I'm there. And please give your daughter my love and tell her one day that I prayed for 'The Unknown Girl' who became my wife for ten years before I met her!'

That conversation took place some eighteen months ago. Beryl is battling brilliantly – with *two* parsons to help, that isn't surprising! The captain and his wife have never forgotten the baby they lost, but visit her sometimes and are fully occupied with the one they have. The star midfielder is busy taking his coaching courses and has become a chaplains' devotee. The chairman's daughter is enjoying her single status, while quietly praying for her 'TUB', to whom the club chaplain has promised to marry her one day.

THE REV

OFFICIAL CHAPLAINS TO FA PREMIERSHIP AND FOOTBALL LEAGUE CLUBS

Rev Ken Baker – Aston Villa; Rev Ken Howles – Blackburn R; Rev Philip Mason – Bolton W; Revs Jeffrey Heskins and Matt Baker (Co-Chaplains) – Charlton Ath; Revs Henry Corbett and Harry Ross (Co-Chaplains) – Everton; Rev Gary Piper – Fulham; Rev Bill Bygroves – Liverpool; Rev Tony Porter – Manchester C; Rev John Boyers – Manchester U; Rev David Tully – Newcastle U; Mr Mick Mellows – Portsmouth; Rev Ken Hipkiss – WBA; Rev Elwin Cockett – West Ham U; Rev Peter Amos – Barnsley; Rev David Tidswell – Blackpool; Rev John Moore – Boston U; Rev Alan Fisher – Bournemouth; Rev Martin Short – Bradford C; Rev Derek Cleave – Bristol C; Rev Steven Hawkins – Bristol R; Rev Mark Hirst – Burnley; Mr Paul Bennett and Rev Malcolm Allen (Co-Chaplains) – Cheltenham T; Rev Jim McGlade – Chesterfield; Rev Simon Lawton – Crewe Alexandra; Rev Nigel Sands – Crystal Palace; Rev Phil Clarke – Darlington; Rev Tony Luke – Derby Co; Rev Brian Quar – Doncaster R; Rev Richard Hayton – Gillingham; Revs Vaughan Pollard and David Male (Co-Chaplains) – Huddersfield T; Rev Allen Bagshawe – Hull C; Rev Kevan McCormack – Ipswich T; Rev Paul C. Welch and Fr Steven Billington (Co-Chaplains) – Leeds U; Rev Bruce Nayden – Leicester C; Rev Alan Comfort – Leyton Orient; Rev Andrew Vaughan – Lincoln C; Rev Chandy Perera – Luton T; Revs Dean Shaw and Jeremy Tear (Co-Chaplains) – Macclesfield T; Fr Owen Beament – Millwall; Rev Ron Smith – Milton Keynes D; Rev Ken Baker – Northampton T; Revs Bert Cadmore and Arthur W. Bowles (Co-Chaplains) – Norwich C; Rev Richard Longfoot – Peterborough U; Rev Jeff Howden – Plymouth Arg; Rev John M. Hibberts – Port Vale; Rev Chris Nelson – Preston NE; Revs Bob Mayo and Cameron Collington – QPR; Rev Steve Prince – Reading; Canon Roger Knight – Rushden & D; Rev Alan Wright – Scunthorpe U; Rev David Jeans – Sheffield W; Rev Chris Sims – Shrewsbury T; Fr Andrew McMahon – Southampton; Rev Billy Montgomery – Stockport Co; Rev Simon Stevenette – Swindon T; Mr Reg Walton – Torquay U; Fr Gerald Courell – Tranmere R; Rev Martin Butt – Walsall; Rev Ray Dupere – Watford; Rev John Hall-Matthews – Wolverhampton W; Rev Paul Brown – Wrexham; Revs Tim O'Brien and John Roberts (Co-Chaplains) – Wycombe W; Rev Jim Pearce – Yeovil T.

The chaplains hope that those who read this page will see the value and benefit of chaplaincy work in football and will take appropriate steps to spread the word where this is possible. They would also like to thank the editors of the Football Yearbook *for their continued support for this specialist and growing area of work.*

The following addresses may be helpful: SCORE (Sports Chaplaincy Offering Resources and Encouragement), PO Box 123, Sale, Manchester M33 4ZA and Christians in Sport, Frampton House, Victoria Road, Bicester, OX26 6PB.

OBITUARIES

Percy Anderson (Born Cambridge, 22 September 1930. Died 4 March 2006.) Percy Anderson made just one appearance in senior football, featuring at left half for Stockport County at Southport in April 1954. In the 1970s he won fame in the fishing world, being capped by England and winning the National title in 1974.

Arthur Bailey (Born Beswick, Manchester, 11 January 1914. Died 2006.) Arthur Bailey spent three years on the books of Oldham Athletic in the 1930s, making over 50 first-team appearances. He also played for non-League clubs Manchester North End and Stalybridge Celtic.

Hugh Baird (Born Bellshill, Lanarkshire, 14 March 1930. Died 19 June 2006.) Hugh Baird was a prolific centre forward for Airdrieonians in the 1950s, scoring 156 goals in just 180 appearances. After finishing as the leading scorer in the top flight in 1956–57 with 33 goals he was sold to Leeds United. He did well at Elland Road too, averaging a goal every other game over two seasons before returning north to play for Aberdeen. Hugh spent four years at Pittodrie and featured in the side that lost out to St Mirren in the 1959 Scottish Cup final. He made one appearance for Scotland against Austria in 1956.

Matt Balunas (Born circa 1918. Died February 2006.) Matt Balunas was a solid and reliable defender who made over 300 appearances for Third Lanark in the period from 1946 to 1955, although he failed to score a single goal. He wound down his career with a season at Stranraer and later became a referee in Glasgow junior football.

Tony Banks, Lord Stratford (Born Belfast, 8 April 1943. Died Sanibel Island, Florida, United States, 8 January 2006.) Tony Banks served as Sports Minister in the Labour Government from 1997 to 1999 and led England's unsuccessful bid to host the 2006 World Cup finals. A Member of Parliament from 1987 to 2005, he was a long-time supporter of Chelsea FC.

Gordon Barker (Born Bramley, Leeds, 6 July 1931. Died Chelmsford, Essex, 10 February 2006.) Gordon Barker played as an amateur with West Auckland and Bishop Auckland before joining Southend in 1954. A versatile forward, he spent five years at Roots Hall making over 60 appearances. Gordon also played cricket for Essex, for whom he scored over 22,000 runs as an opening batsman between 1954 and 1971.

Vic Barney (Born Stepney, London, 3 April 1922. Died Oxford, 26 May 2006.) Vic Barney began his senior career in Italy with Napoli, where he was based with the British Army during the latter stages of the Second World War. On his return to England he signed for Reading, making his debut in the club's record 10-2 win against Crystal Palace. An inside forward, Vic subsequently played for Bristol City and Grimsby Town before joining non-League Headington United.

Bob Barrie (Born Blairgowrie, Perthshire, 1934. Died Grimsby, 2 October 2005.) Bob Barrie was a goalkeeper who began his career with Dunfermline Athletic, but failed to make the first team at East End Park. He went on to play for Brechin City and Cowdenbeath in the mid-1950s before moving south to join Grimsby Borough Police.

Bill Barron (Born Herrington, Co Durham, 26 October 1917. Died Northampton, 2 January 2006.) Bill Barron scored on his senior debut for Charlton against Brentford in February 1938, but played only twice more for the Addicks before joining Northampton. He went on to make over 250 first-team appearances, including wartime games for the Cobblers before retiring in 1951. Bill also played cricket for Lancashire and Northamptonshire.

Don Bates (Born Brighton, 10 May 1933. Died 29 May 2005.) Don Bates was on Brighton's books as a wing half for several seasons, but all of his 21 first-team appearances came in the 1957–58 campaign when Albion won the Division Three South title. He was better known as a cricketer for Sussex, for whom he took over 800 wickets as a fast medium bowler.

Ferenc Bene (Born Balatonujlak, Hungary, 17 December 1944. Died Budapest, Hungary, 27 February 2006.) Ferenc Bene was one of the all-time greats of Hungarian football, winning 76 caps for his country between 1962 and 1979. A pacy forward with a powerful shot, he was a member of the team that won the Olympic Games title in 1964, when he finished as the tournament's leading scorer with 12 goals included all six against Morocco. At club level he played for Ujpest and later went into coaching.

Alan Bennett (Born Stoke-on-Trent, 5 November 1931. Died Stoke-on-Trent, 17 January 2006.) Alan Bennett was a talented outside left who was capped by England Youths. He went on to make over 100 first-team appearances for Port Vale, mostly in the early 1950s, but stayed on the club's books until 1957. Alan concluded his career with a season at Crewe Alexandra.

George Best (Born Belfast, 22 May 1946. Died London, 29 November 2005.) George Best was one of the most talented footballers in the history of the game – a player of breathtaking skills he is one of just a handful of British players to truly warrant inclusion in a list of all-time world greats. An icon of modern youth during the 1960s, he was the country's first superstar footballer and at the height of his fame his popularity was on a similar scale to that of pop groups such as the Beatles. Signed as a teenager by Manchester United, he progressed through the club's junior and reserve teams, stepping up to make his senior debut in September 1963, and within a matter of months he had won a regular place in the line-up. Over the next few seasons George established himself as perhaps the most exciting player of his generation and certainly the best dribbler in the Football League. After assisting the Reds to the Division One title in 1966–67 he was one of the key figures in the side which defeated Benfica in the following season's European Cup final, when he scored a fine solo goal. The year 1968 was the peak of George's career for along with his European Cup winners' medal he also won the Football Writers' Association Footballer of the Year and the European Footballer of the Year titles. Thereafter George slowly became disillusioned with the game and eventually left Old Trafford early in 1974. His playing career after this was somewhat intermittent. There were short spells in South Africa and with Stockport and Cork Celtic before a more prolonged period at Fulham. George also enjoyed several seasons of football in the USA, where he often seemed to be more relaxed, featuring for Los Angeles Aztecs, Ford Lauderdale Strikers and San Jose Earthquakes. He eventually returned to Britain where he had brief associations with Hibernian and Bournemouth before leaving the game altogether. George was also a regular for Northern Ireland throughout his career, winning a total of 37 caps. After leaving the game he remained a high profile society figure, but constantly struggled to fight off his addiction to alcohol, before eventually passing away after a lengthy illness.

Laurie Blyth (Born Dundee, 1929. Died Dundee, 29 December 2005.) Laurie Blyth was believed to be only the second Catholic player to sign for Rangers when he joined the club in 1951. Although he failed to make the first team at Ibrox, the inside forward or wing half later played a handful of games for Dunfermline Athletic in the 1952–53 season.

George Best

Jackie Boden (Born Grimsby, 4 October 1926. Died Grimsby, 22 April 2006.) Jackie Boden was a prolific scorer in Lincolnshire League football and signed for Lincoln City in April 1948. At Sincil Bank he was principally a reserve, but scored two goals in his three Football League appearances for the Imps.

Gerry Bowler (Born Londonderry, 8 June 1919. Died Redhill, Surrey, 26 March 2006.) Gerry Bowler played Irish League football for Derry City and Distillery before signing for Portsmouth in August 1946. However, it was not until he joined Hull City some three years later that he saw regular first-team football. After a season at Boothferry Park the versatile defender was sold to Millwall where he made over 150 first-team appearances. Gerry was also capped three times by Northern Ireland.

George Bromilow (Born Southport, 4 December 1930. Died Southport, 19 November 2005.) George Bromilow was a centre forward who was capped by England Youths, but elected for a career as a schoolmaster, remaining an amateur throughout his career. He spent four years with Southport in the late 1950s, scoring 43 goals from 88 appearances, his tally including five in an FA Cup tie against Ashton United in November 1955. George won five caps for England Amateurs and also made three appearances for Great Britain in the Olympic Games matches.

Irvin Brown (Born Lewes, Sussex, 20 September 1935. Died Poole, Dorset, 20 December 2005.) Irvin Brown was a half back who made just three appearances for Brighton, although he was on the club's books for six years. In September 1958 he was transferred to Bournemouth, where he featured more regularly, playing over 70 games before departing in the summer of 1963.

Jock Brown (Born 21 February 1905. Died Prestwick, Ayrshire, 27 August 2005.) Jock Brown was a brave and reliable goalkeeper who spent his best years with Clyde in the seasons leading up to the outbreak of war. He was a member of the team that defeated Motherwell to win the Scottish Cup final in 1939 and also won a solitary cap for Scotland. Jock also played for Hibernian, Dundee and Kilmarnock and in later years served as the physio for Scotland's rugby union team.

Ken Burns (Born Ramsey, Isle of Man, 24 September 1923. Died Ramsey, Isle of Man, 5 May 2006.) Ken Burns was one of the few Manxmen to have played in the Football League. An inside forward, he had spells with Tranmere Rovers and Southport in the years immediately after the war before returning to the Isle of Man, where he continued playing until he was 60 years old.

Frank Butler, OBE (Born 16 September 1916. Died 2 January 2006.) After beginning his professional career with the Daily Express, Frank Butler rose to become Sports Editor of the Sunday Express in 1941. He subsequently switched to the News of the World in 1949 and served as Sports Editor from 1960 until his retirement in 1982. For many years he edited the News of the World Football Annual.

Eric Campbell (Born circa 1945. Died Manchester, 25 January 2006.) Eric Campbell was the assistant physio at Macclesfield Town for more than 20 years following his appointment in 1985, seeing the club on their path from the Northern Premier League through to becoming an established member of the Football League.

Noel Cantwell (Born Cork, Republic of Ireland, 28 December 1932. Died Peterborough, 7 September 2005.) Noel Cantwell was a cultured and reliable defender who made his name with West Ham before joining Manchester United in November 1960. He captained the United team that defeated Leicester City in the 1963 FA Cup final and in total made over 400 senior appearances. Noel was also a regular for the Republic of Ireland, winning 36 caps. After retiring as a player he went on to manager Coventry City (1967–1972) and Peterborough United (1972–1977 and 1986–1988). Noel was a dual international, also representing Ireland at cricket on five occasions.

Fred Chandler (Born Hythe, nr. Southampton, 2 August 1912. Died September 2005.) Fred Chandler began his career as an outside left with Reading in the 1930s and also played for Blackpool and Swindon before joining Crewe in the summer of 1937. He went on to play over 200 games for the Railwaymen, many in wartime, later switching to the full-back position.

Roy Clarke (Born Newport, South Wales, 1 June 1925. Died Sale, Cheshire, 13 March 2006.) Roy Clarke was an old-fashioned winger who began his career with Cardiff City, but it was only when he was transferred to Manchester City in April 1947 that he began to make a name for himself. He went on to make over 350 senior appearances in a decade at Maine Road, gaining an FA Cup winners' medal in 1956 when City defeated Birmingham. Roy also won 22 caps for Wales between 1949 and 1956. He finished off with a season at Stockport and later returned to Maine Road as the Social Club manager, a post he held for some 25 years.

Jimmy Clarkson (Born circa 1926. Died 24 January 2006.) Jimmy Clarkson was a tall stopper centre half who made almost 200 appearances for Dunfermline Athletic between 1948 and 1954, featuring in the side that lost out to East Fife in the 1949–50 Scottish League Cup final. He later played for Ayr United, St Johnstone and Forfar Athletic.

Alec Coxon (Born Huddersfield, 18 January 1916. Died Roker, Sunderland, 22 January 2006.) Alec Coxon made two appearances for Bradford Park Avenue in the emergency competitions during the Second World War, one at centre forward and one in defence. He was better known for his cricketing exploits with Yorkshire (1945–1950) and England (one cap against Australia in 1948).

John Craig (Born Glasgow, 10 April 1953. Died Tenerife, Spain, 19 November 2005.) A midfielder, John Craig began his career with Aberdeen, but although he was Scotland's Young Player of the Year in 1973 he failed to win a regular place at Pittodrie. He went on to assist Partick Thistle to the First Division title in 1975–76 and later played for Hearts and Morton. John was capped four times by Scotland U23s.

Johnny Crosland (Born Lytham St Anne's, Lancashire, 10 November 1922. Died Ely, Cambridgeshire, 5 May 2006.) Johnny Crosland was a full back who joined Blackpool from local football in the summer of 1946. He went on to play in the team that was defeated by Manchester United in the 1948 FA Cup final, and also won two caps for England B. In 1954 he moved on to Bournemouth, making over 100 appearances in a three-year stay at Dean Court.

Jack Cross (Born Bury, 5 February 1927. Died Bournemouth, 19 February 2006.) Jack Cross joined Blackpool in 1943 and played a number of wartime games for the Seasiders before Army service intervened, and he later signed for Guildford City prior to transfer to Bournemouth in the summer of 1947. Initially a right winger, he later converted to the centre-forward position and in a career that also saw him play for Northampton, Sheffield United and Reading, he scored 94 Football League goals from just over 200 appearances.

Eddie Crossan (Born Londonderry, 17 November 1925. Died Londonderry, 13 June 2006.) Eddie Crossan was a talented winger with excellent dribbling skills who joined Blackburn from Derry City in November 1947. He made over 300 appearances for Rovers, spending a decade on the books at Ewood Park, before winding down his career with a season at Tranmere. Eddie also won three caps for Northern Ireland.

Jim Davidson (Born circa 1944. Died November 2005) Goalkeeper Jim Davidson was capped three times by Scotland Schools and subsequently signed for Hearts. He stayed only briefly at Tynecastle before joining Alloa Athletic, for whom he made just one senior appearance in the 1960–61 season.

Ted Ditchburn (Born Gillingham, 24 October 1921. Died Ipswich, 26 December 2005.) Ted Ditchburn was one of the greatest goalkeepers in the history of Tottenham Hotspur FC. A product of the club's nursery team, Northfleet, he made over 450 appearances in the immediate post-war period, including a run of 247 consecutive Football League appearances. Ted was a member of the famous 'push-and-run' team that won back-to-back Second Division and Football League titles in 1949–50 and 1950–51. He was capped six times by England and featured in the squad for the 1950 World Cup finals in Brazil.

Arthur Dixon (Born Middleton, Lancs, 17 November 1921. Died 2006.) Arthur Dixon was a skilful inside forward who scored some 88 wartime goals for Queen's Park before joining Clyde in the summer of 1945. He later played for Hearts before moving south to join Northampton Town in November 1949. Arthur scored 21 goals in 68 Football League appearances for the Cobblers before concluding his career at Leicester. He later served Notts County as physio.

Jimmy Dudley (Born Gartcosh, Lanarkshire, 24 August 1928. Died West Bromwich, 25 April 2006.) Jimmy Dudley was an efficient right half who was a regular in the West Bromwich Albion line-up in the years immediately after the war. He played over 300 games for the Baggies and was a member of the side that defeated Preston North End to win the 1954 FA Cup final. Jimmy later spent five seasons at Walsall, helping the club win successive promotions in 1959–60 and 1960–61.

George Dunkley (Born Ipswich, 19 July 1924. Died Ipswich, 15 March 2006.) George Dunkley was a goalkeeper who joined Millwall in September 1942 after appearing for Leyton and Walthamstow Avenue. He made 40 wartime appearances for the club and was a regular in the 1945–46 season. He later played for Arsenal (without featuring at first-team level), Gravesend and Dover.

Malcolm Dunkley (Born Wolverhampton, 12 July 1961. Died 24 September 2005.) Malcolm Dunkley was a giant striker who moved from Stafford Rangers to Finland's Roivaniemen Palloseura in December 1987. He proved a great success, scoring 20 goals in 76 appearances and featuring for the club in UEFA Cup action. He subsequently had a brief spell with Lincoln City towards the end of the 1988–89 season, but quickly faded after scoring two on his debut against Cambridge United.

Tommy Dunlop (Born circa 1925. Died Dundee, 18 March 2006.) Tommy Dunlop was a centre half who made two appearances for Dundee United in the 1951–52 season. He was also prominent at Junior level, where his clubs included Dundee Osborne and Blair of Atholl.

Joe Dunn (Born Glasgow, 20 September 1925. Died December 2005.) Joe Dunn impressed sufficiently at Clyde to earn a transfer to Preston in August 1951. He went on to play almost 250 games for North End, where he established himself as a regular in the centre-half position. Joe later served Morecambe as player-manager.

Jimmy Dyet (Born Dailly, Ayrshire, 14 June 1908. Died Falkirk, 21 July 2005.) Jimmy Dyet created history when he scored eight goals on his debut for King's Park against Forfar Athletic in a Scottish League Division Two fixture in January 1930, this being a record for a player on his debut in senior British football. All told he scored 91 goals in just 106 appearances between 1930 and 1934, also featuring for Falkirk and Dundee United.

Tony Emery (Born Lincoln, 4 November 1927. Died Lincoln, 5 December 2005.) Tony Emery was a solid and reliable centre half who played over 400 games for Lincoln City between 1945 and 1959, his total of appearances standing as a club record for many years. He captained the side to the Third Division North title in 1951–52 and toured the Caribbean with an FA XI in the summer of 1955.

Ray Evans (Born Carlisle, 8 October 1929. Died December 2005.) Ray Evans was a goalkeeper who spent three seasons on the books of Crewe Alexandra between 1948 and 1951, making a total of 24 senior appearances.

Roy Farrington (Born Tonbridge, Kent, 6 June 1925. Died March 2006.) Roy Farrington joined Crystal Palace from Tonbridge junior football in November 1947, scoring on his debut in an FA Cup tie against Port Vale. However, he only made a handful more first-team appearances for the Eagles and left the club in 1949.

Vivien Felton (Born Southgate, Middlesex, 13 August 1929. Died 13 October 2005.) Vivien Felton joined Crystal Palace from Barnet in the summer of 1954, but made just two first-team appearances during his stay at Selhurst Park.

Ewan Fenton (Born Dundee, 17 November 1929. Died Limerick, Republic of Ireland, 3 April 2006.) Ewan Fenton joined Blackpool from Scottish Junior football in November 1946 and went on to make over 200 appearances for the Seasiders in a 13-year spell at the club. A regular in the line-up at right half from December 1952, he was a member of the team that won the FA Cup in 1953. He subsequently played for Wrexham, Limerick and Linfield, eventually settling in Limerick.

Bob Ferguson (Born Grangetown, nr. Middlesbrough, 27 July 1917. Died Marlow, Bucks, 17 June 2006) Bob Ferguson was a goalkeeper who signed for Middlesbrough in the summer of 1935 and made ten appearances in the pre-war period. In 1939 he moved on to York City and spent eight years on the books at Bootham Crescent, playing regularly during the wartime emergency competitions. Bob was a first choice in the 1946–47 season, but then left the club and later played in non-League for Peterborough United and Goole before a broken collarbone ended his career.

Ron Greenwood

Willie Finnigan (Born circa 1912. Died Oxford, April 1912.) Willie Finnigan joined Hibs as an outside left in 1939 and quickly established himself as a first-team regular but switched to the inside-right position early on. He made 225 wartime appearances for the club, when he was a member of the teams that won the Summer Cup in 1940–41 and the Southern League Cup in 1943–44. He went on to feature for Hibs when they won the Scottish League title in 1947–48 and later spent two seasons with Dunfermline before injury led to his retirement.

Ken Fish (Born Cape Town, South Africa, 20 February 1914. Died Stoke-on-Trent, 4 August 2005.) Ken Fish made a number of international appearances for South Africa in the late 1930s before moving to England where he signed for Aston Villa. He made no first-team appearances for Villa, but played a handful of games for Port Vale before moving on to Swiss club Young Boys of Berne. When he had retired from playing he became a respected trainer, serving Port Vale, Aston Villa, Birmingham City and Oxford United.

Bobby Foster (Born Sheffield, 19 July 1929. Died March 2006.) Bobby Foster spent most of his career at Preston for whom he made over 100 senior appearances and featured in the side that lost out to West Brom in the 1954 FA Cup final. An inside forward, he won representative honours for England B against France in May 1952 and also had spells on the books of Chesterfield and Rotherham United.

Les Gallantree (Born East Boldon, Co Durham, 25 December 1913. Died Durham, 2006.) Les Gallantree was a small, stocky winger who joined Newcastle United in the summer of 1931 and went on to make nine appearances for the Magpies. Later in the 1930s he had spells with Aldershot and Gateshead.

Tommy Garrett (Born South Shields, 28 February 1926. Died Wallsend, New South Wales, Australia, 16 April 2006.) Tommy Garrett was a full back who joined Blackpool from Horden Colliery in October 1944. He went on to make over 300 appearances for the Seasiders and was a member of the team for the famous 'Matthews Final' in 1953 when the Seasiders defeated Bolton Wanderers to win the FA Cup in dramatic fashion. He won three England caps in the early 1950s and also won representative honours for the Football League. Tommy later played for Millwall and Fleetwood before emigrating to Australia.

Shay Gibbons (Born Dublin, 19 May 1929. Died June 2006.) Shay Gibbons was a prolific scorer with League of Ireland club St Patrick's Athletic in the 1950s for whom he was a member of three Championship sides. He also played for Cork Hibs and Dundalk. Shay won four caps for the Republic of Ireland and won inter-league representative honours.

Ron Greenwood (Born Worsthorne, nr. Burnley, 11 November 1921. Died Suffolk, 9 February 2006.) As a player Ron Greenwood was a talented centre half who was on Chelsea's books during the war before being sold to Bradford Park Avenue in December 1945. He subsequently played for Brentford, Chelsea and Fulham, assisting the Blues to their first-ever Football League title in 1954–55. He also won representative honours for England B against Holland in March 1952. Ron subsequently embarked on an extremely successful career in coaching and management. After serving Arsenal as assistant-manager, he was appointed manager of West Ham in April 1961, leading the club to victory in both the FA Cup (1964) and European Cup Winners' Cup (1965). He stayed in the post until 1974, then becoming general manager at Upton Park. He was appointed manager of England in 1977, spending five years in the job and leading the team to qualification for the finals of the European Championship in 1980 and the World Cup two years later.

Wyn Griffiths (Born Blaengwynfi, nr. Maesteg, 17 October 1919. Died 28 May 2006.) Wyn Griffiths was an amateur goalkeeper who joined Cardiff City during the war, playing 72 games during the emergency competitions. He also guested for Arsenal and Derby, and was in goal for the Gunners in their famous encounter with Moscow Dynamo in November 1945. He made just four peacetime appearances, one for Cardiff and three for Newport County, preferring to concentrate on his career as a vet.

Harry Gunning (Born Leigh, Lancashire, 8 February 1932. Died July 2005.) Harry Gunning spent two years on the books of West Ham, but made just a single first-team appearance, at Lincoln in May 1953. A winger, he saw regular first-team football in three seasons with Crystal Palace before ending his career at Southend.

Phil Gwatkin (Born Harrow, Middlesex, 5 August 1929. Died Wallasey, 9 July 2006.) Phil Gwatkin joined Wrexham soon after completing a spell of National Service in the Army. He played 52 Football League games for the Racecourse club between 1952 and 1956 and then spent a season at Tranmere before dropping into non-League football.

Bernard Harrison (Born Worcester, 28 September 1934. Died March 2006.) Bernard Harrison was a winger who featured regularly for Crystal Palace in the 1950s, making almost 100 Football League appearances. He later had a season at Southampton, where he was understudy to Terry Paine, before concluding his career at Exeter. He also played cricket for Hampshire between 1957 and 1962.

Johnny Haynes

Bryan Harvey (Born Stepney, London, 26 August 1938. Died 2006.) After developing with Wisbech Town, goalkeeper Bryan Harvey joined Newcastle United in the summer of 1958. He took over from Ronnie Simpson as the Magpies' first-choice 'keeper, but in June 1961 he dropped back into non-League football, signing for Cambridge City. Bryan then had a brief spell at Blackpool, where he was principally a reserve, then moved to Northampton where he was a key figure in the club's rise through the divisions to the top flight in the mid-1960s.

Johnny Haynes (Born Edmonton, Middlesex, 17 October 1934. Died Edinburgh 18 October 2005.) Johnny Haynes was one of the most influential footballers of the late 1950s and arguably the greatest player in the history of Fulham Football Club. An inside left with sublime distribution skills, he had the ability to dictate the course of a game with his accurate passing allied with an excellent goal-scoring record. He was a fixture in the England line-up between 1955 and 1962, winning a total of 56 caps and captaining the side from May 1960 until his retirement from international football following the 1962 World Cup finals. Throughout his career, Johnny remained loyal to Fulham, despite the club's somewhat unfashionable status, leading them to the semi-final of the FA Cup in 1957–58 (as a Second Division side) and then promotion to the top flight the following season. When the maximum wage was lifted in 1961 it was widely reported that he had become the first player to earn £100 a week. He remained a potent force at club level through to the end of the 1969–70 season, by which time he had created new club records for both senior appearances (658) and goals (158). He subsequently moved to South Africa, where he played for Durban City.

Bobby Henderson (Died May 2006.) Bobby Henderson joined Partick Thistle from Glasgow Perthshire and made his first-team debut in September 1937. He remained at the club until the summer of 1951 and later played for Dundee, where he was a member of the team that defeated Kilmarnock to win the Scottish League Cup in 1952–53 before finishing his career with a brief spell at rivals Dundee United.

Ron Hepworth (Born Barnsley, 25 January 1919. Died 26 April 2006.) Ron Hepworth was a full back who signed for Bradford Park Avenue in the summer of 1939. He played 40 wartime games for the club and featured regularly in the late 1940s, accumulating over a century of appearances and featuring in the side that famously defeated Arsenal at Highbury in the FA Cup third round in January 1948.

Brian Hetherston (Born Bellshill, Lanarkshire, 27 November 1976. Died Coatbridge, Lanarkshire, 4 March 2006.) Brian Hetherston was a midfielder who played for St Mirren, Sligo Rovers and Raith in the early 1990s, winning one cap at Under 21 level. His sudden death came after suffering a suspected epileptic fit.

Oscar Hold (Born Carlton, Yorkshire, 19 October 1918. Died Sunderland, 11 October 2005.) Oscar Hold was a powerful forward who scored 40 goals in just over 100 senior appearances in the immediate post-war period. His travels took him to Aldershot, Norwich, Notts County, Chelmsford City, Everton and Queen's Park Rangers. On retiring as a player he became a respected manager and coach serving clubs throughout the globe.

Jimmy Holland (Born Burnley, 25 March 1928. Died Crete, Greece, 2006.) Jimmy Holland served Burnley as the club physio from 1965 to 1993, being awarded with a testimonial match against Oldham for his services.

Barry Hutchinson (Born Sheffield, 27 January 1936. Died Rotherham, 12 July 2005.) Barry Hutchinson began his senior career as a wing half, making over 150 appearances for Chesterfield in the 1950s. In July 1960 he joined Derby County where he made a successful switch to the centre-forward position, netting 57 goals in 116 games for the Rams. He later played for Weymouth, Lincoln City, Darlington, Halifax and Rochdale.

Jair (Born Quatis, Rio de Janeiro, Brazil, 21 March 1921. Died Rio de Janeiro, Brazil, 28 July 2005.) Jair was a talented inside forward with tremendous ball control who won 39 caps for Brazil. He featured in the squad for the 1950 World Cup finals when the team lost out to Uruguay for the title and played for a number of sides at club level including Flamengo, Vasco da Gama, Santos, Sao Paulo and Palmeiras.

Eddie Jenkins (Born Cardiff, 16 July 1909. Died Cardiff, 5 August 2005.) Eddie Jenkins represented Wales at Schoolboy international level and later signed for Cardiff City, featuring regularly in the line-up in the early 1930s, either at left back or left half. He also had spells on the books of Bristol City and Newport County.

William Johnston, MBE (Born Montrose, 25 October 1912. Died Dundee, 26 September 2005.) William Johnston was closely associated with Montrose FC for more than 60 years. A leading figure in the Supporters' Club before the war, he was elected to the club Board of Directors in 1949 and became Chairman in 1955. He held the position for over 30 years before taking on the role of President. He also served as chairman of the Forfarshire Football Association and as a member of the Scottish FA Council.

Jimmy Johnstone (Born Uddingston, Lanarkshire, 30 September 1944. Died 13 March 2006.) Jimmy Johnstone was one of the legendary figures in post-war Scottish football. A supremely talented winger he made over 500 appearances for Celtic after making his debut towards the end of the 1962–63 season. Although physically slight he possessed tremendous control and his ability to take the ball past man after man, mesmerising opponents, earned him the nickname 'Jinky'. Jimmy was a member of the great Celtic team of the late 1960s which won the Scottish league title nine times in a row and became the first British club to win the European Cup in 1967, defeating Inter Milan in Lisbon. He won 23 caps for Scotland and also had spells with San Jose Earthquakes, Sheffield United and Dundee. In 2002 he was diagnosed with Motor Neurone Disease and this eventually led to his untimely death.

Jimmy Johnstone

Dave Joyce (Born 1943. Died 16 December 2005.) Dave Joyce was secretary of Rushden & Diamonds from the club's formation in 1992 until his death. He played an important role in the club's progression from the Southern League through to winning Football League status.

Jason Kaminsky (Born Leicester, 5 December 1973. Died Leicester, 28 September 2005.) Jason Kaminsky made one senior appearance as a substitute for Nottingham Forest in the 1991–92 season. His tragically early death came from liver failure as a result of turning to alcohol.

Archie Kelly (Born Paisley, 9 December 1921. Died July 2005.) Archie Kelly was a strong and powerful centre forward who netted 170 goals in just under 300 senior games in Scottish football in the period after the war. His career took him to Hearts, Aberdeen, Motherwell, Stirling Albion, Ayr United and, briefly, Cowdenbeath. His greatest success came at Motherwell, where he won a Scottish League Cup winners' medal in 1950–51 and a Scottish Cup winners' medal the following season.

Fred Kelly (Born Wednesbury, Staffs, 11 February 1921. Died 15 June 2006.) Fred Kelly was a full back or centre forward for Walsall in the late 1940s. He scored seven goals in 20 peacetime appearances for the Saddlers, the highlight being when he netted against Liverpool in an FA Cup tie in January 1947.

Vince Kenny (Born Sheffield, 29 December 1924. Died 24 February 2006.) Vince Kenny was a solid full back who made over 250 appearances for Sheffield Wednesday and Carlisle in the 1940s and '50s. He was a member of the Owls' team that won the old Second Division title in 1951–52.

John Kerr (Born Birkenhead, 23 November 1959. Died Spain, 4 June 2006.) John Kerr was a centre forward who made over 250 appearances for Tranmere, Bristol City, Stockport and Bury between 1977 and 1986. He later went into coaching, enjoying spells with Chester, Shrewsbury and Walsall. At the time of his death he was Academy Manager at Cardiff City.

Billy Kiernan (Born Croydon, Surrey, 22 May 1925. Died Tunbridge Wells, Kent, 2 April 2006.) Billy Kiernan was a winger or inside forward who made over 400 appearances for Charlton between 1949 and 1961, scoring 93 goals. A player with good close control and an eye for goal, he won representative honours for England B against West Germany in 1955.

Brian Labone (Born Liverpool, 23 January 1940. Died Liverpool, 24 April 2006.) Brian Labone was a powerful, dominating centre half who made a total of 534 senior appearances for Everton, a club record for an outfield player. One of the key figures in the club's successful teams of the 1960s, he was a member of the team that won the FA Cup final in 1966 and the Football League title in 1969–70. He remained close to the club after leaving football and for a while worked in the commercial department. Brian also won 26 caps for England and was in the squad for the 1970 World Cup finals in Mexico.

Nobby Lawton (Born Manchester, 25 March 1940. Died Manchester, 22 April 2006.) An aggressive yet creative midfield player, Nobby began his career at Manchester United before moving on to Preston in March 1963. He went on to captain the North End team to a place in the FA Cup final in 1964, making over 150 appearances for the club. He later played for Brighton and Lincoln City.

Tommy Ledgerwood (Died 13 February 2006.) Tommy Ledgerwood was a sold, reliable goalkeeper who made almost 300 appearances for Partick Thistle in the immediate post-war period. He scored one goal, netting against Hearts in 1950 when he was injured during the game and switched to an outfield position. Tommy won representative honours for Scotland B and the Scottish League and ended his career with a brief spell at Morton.

Harry Leonard (Born Jarrow, 19 May 1924. Died Jarrow, 23 January 2006.) Harry Leonard was a full back or wing half who made a handful of wartime appearances for Darlington and later featured briefly for both Bradford Park Avenue and Hartlepools United.

Harry Lewis (Born Merthyr Tydfil, 25 October 1910. Died Southend, February 2006.) Capped by Wales as a schoolboy, Harry developed as a fine inside left with Rochdale in the early 1930s. In February 1931 he was sold to Arsenal, but he never managed to make the first team at Highbury. His career continued with spells at Southend, Notts County, West Ham, Swansea and Queen of the South before concluding at Watford during the war.

Jackie Lindsay (Born Cambuslang, Lanarkshire, 11 December 1921. Died Carlisle, 9 February 2006.) Jackie Lindsay was a regular scorer with Morton and Sheffield Wednesday in the later years of the war, but made only one peacetime appearance for the Owls. After a short spell with Bury he joined Carlisle United where he enjoyed the best years of his career, scoring 51 goals from just 109 appearances. Perhaps his best performance came against Scunthorpe in February 1952 when he scored four goals, including a hat-trick inside three minutes. He later had several seasons at Wigan in their non-League days, before returning to Carlisle, briefly, at the end of the 1954–55 campaign.

Aaron Lofting (Born Leicester, 15 April 1982. Died Leuchars, Fife, 14 May 2006.) Aaron Lofting made a total of 20 first-team appearances for East Fife, almost all as a substitute, between 2000 and 2002. He later switched to Junior football and was attached to St Andrew's United at the time of his tragic death.

John Lyall (Born Ilford, Essex, 24 February 1940. Died 18 April 2006.) John Lyall gave over 30 years service to West Ham United after joining the club groundstaff in 1955. He made his first-team debut in February 1960 but made just 31 Football league appearances before a knee injury ended his career. He subsequently joined the backroom staff at Upton Park and eventually rose to become manager in August 1974, staying in charge until 1989. He led the Hammers to success in the FA Cup in 1975 and 1980 and a place in the European Cup Winners' Cup final in 1976. John later had a spell as manager of Ipswich Town from 1990 to 1994, winning promotion to the Premiership in 1991–92.

Alex Macaulay (Born Clydebank, 23 September 1928. Died Stirling, 28 February 2006.) Alex Macaulay was a talented inside forward who appeared for Queen's Park, Dunfermline and East Fife in the immediate post-war period, making over 100 senior appearances. He also won two caps for Scotland at Amateur international level.

John McGarrity (Born 20 October 1925. Died Dundee, 23 March 2006.) Goalkeeper John McGarrity joined East Fife from Junior club Blairhall Colliery during the 1948–49 campaign and the following season he won a Scottish League Cup winners' medal after appearing in the final against Dunfermline. After leaving Bayview he later played for Arbroath and Cowdenbeath.

Gordon McKeag (Born Whickham, Northumberland, 1929. Died Northumberland, October 2005) Gordon McKeag was a solicitor who was appointed to the board of directors at Newcastle United in 1972 and remained until November 1992. He served as Chairman between 1988 and 1990.

Alf McMichael (Born Belfast, 1 October 1927. Died 7 January 2006.) Alf McMichael was a solid and consistent full back who developed with Cliftonville and Linfield, winning representative honours for the Irish League. In September 1949 he joined Newcastle United and went on to play over 400 games for the Magpies, featuring in the side that won the FA Cup in 1952. Alf was also a regular in the Northern Ireland international team in the 1950s, winning 40 caps and appearing in the quarter-finals of the World Cup in 1958. He later served South Shields and Irish league club Bangor City as manager.

Jimmy McNab (Born Denny, Stirlingshire, 13 April 1940. Died Sunderland, 29 June 2006.) Jimmy McNab was a tough-tackling left half who made over 300 appearances for Sunderland, featuring in the side that won promotion to the old First Division in 1963–64. In March 1967 he moved on to Preston, where he added another 200 games, later switching to the left-back position. He concluded his career with a spell at Stockport County.

Tom McNab (Born Glasgow, 15 July 1933. Died Otahuhu, Auckland, New Zealand, 5 April 2006.) Tom McNab was a wing half who joined Partick Thistle in December 1951 and went on to make over 200 senior appearances in a career that saw him play for Nottingham Forest, Wrexham, Barrow and East Stirling. In the 1960s he emigrated to New Zealand and won a number of caps for his adopted country. He spent the last 20 years of his life in a wheelchair after being paralysed in an accident at work.

Don McVicar (Born Perth, 6 November 1962. Died Dundee, 31 January 2006.) Don McVicar made over 200 first-team appearances for St Johnstone in two spells at the club (1981–85 and 1986–92), featuring in the sides that won the First Division title in 1982–83 and 1989–90. he also played for Tranmere Rovers, Montrose, Partick Thistle, Airdrieonians, Ayr, Forfar and Arbroath before leaving the game in 1997. His early death was a result of Motor Neurone Disease.

Jimmy Main (Born Motherwell, circa 1916. Died New Stevenston, Lanarkshire. 20 April 2006.) Jimmy Main was a half back who made a number of appearances for Motherwell in the late 1930s.

Davie Marshall (Born circa 1943. Died 2005.) Davie Marshall was a big, powerful centre forward who was a prolific goal-scorer with Airdrieonians, netting 79 goals from just over 200 senior appearances. He also had brief spells with Cowdenbeath and Forfar before leaving the senior game in the summer of 1972.

Stuart Mason (Born Whitchurch, Shropshire, 2 June 1948. Died 5 February 2006.) Stuart Mason was capped by England at Youth international and broke into the Wrexham first team as a teenager. In October 1966 he was sold to Liverpool, but failed to make the first team at Anfield, although he later saw plenty of first-team action for both Wrexham and Chester in the late 1960s and early '70s, making over 300 first-team appearances. He also had brief loan spells at Doncaster, Rochdale and Crewe.

Gerry Mays (Born Craigneuk, Lanarkshire, 18 July 1921. Died 21 March 2006.) Gerry Mays was an inside forward or winger who played for Hibernian and Hamilton Academical during the war before joining St Johnstone in the summer of 1947. He subsequently spent four seasons with Dunfermline Athletic, appearing in the side that reached the final of the Scottish League Cup in 1949–50. He later spent seven seasons at Kilmarnock where he helped the club win two promotions and was a prolific goal-scorer.

Jim Mechan (Died Worcester, May 2006.) Jim Mechan was an outside right who was on the books of Third Lanark without making a first-team appearance. He later joined Forfar Athletic where played 14 games in the 1951–52 season.

Wallace Mercer (Born Dunoon, Argyllshire, 1946. Died Edinburgh, 17 January 2006.) Wallace Mercer was a controversial Chairman of Heart of Midlothian for a 13-year period from 1981. He took over when the club faced the real possibility of extinction and revived their fortunes, although his proposal for a merger with city rivals Hibernian proved to be extremely unpopular with both sets of fans.

Jackie Milburn (Born Crook, circa 1921. Died 2006.) Jackie Milburn (no relation to the famous 'Wor Jackie') was a left winger who played for Crook Town, Willington and Stanley United before the war. He spent six years on Newcastle United's books during the hostilities, but mostly featured in the Northern Combination team, although he made one first-team appearance against Grimsby Town in December 1940.

Dick Neilson (Born Blackhall, Co Durham, 1916. Died Manchester, 14 December 2005.) Dick Neilson joined Manchester City from Dawdon Colliery in 1935 and made almost 50 appearances, including wartime games, during his stay at Maine Road.

Tony Nicholas (Born West Ham, 16 April 1938. Died London, 25 September 2005.) Tony Nicholas was capped by England at Youth international level and made over 60 appearances for Chelsea as an inside left in the late 1950s. He subsequently had spells with Brighton, Chelmsford City and Leyton Orient before leaving football to focus on his successful DIY business.

Albert Nightingale (Born Rotherham, 10 November 1923. Died Liverpool, 26 February 1926.) Albert Nightingale was a hard-working inside forward who made over 350 senior appearances in the 1940s and '50s. Immensely popular with the fans, he played for Sheffield United, Huddersfield, Blackburn and Leeds before injury brought his career to a close.

Alfie Noakes (Born Stratford, London, 14 August 1933. Died 24 October 2005.) Alfie Noakes joined Crystal Palace from Sittingbourne in June 1955, and went on to make over 200 senior appearances during his stay at Selhurst Park, helping the club win promotion from the old Fourth Division in 1960–61. He later spent two seasons at Portsmouth before moving on to Tunbridge Wells Rangers.

Peter Osgood

Shay Noonan (Died 14 September 2005.) Shay Noonan was a versatile defender with Drumcondra and Dundalk during the 1950s, winning FAI Cup winners' medals with both clubs. He also won seven caps for the League of Ireland representative side.

Kevin O'Flanagan (Born Dublin, 10 June 1919. Died 26 May 2006.) Kevin O'Flanagan was a talented all-round sportsman who was capped at both soccer and rugby union. As a youngster he played for Bohemians, but moved to London to train as a doctor. He featured as an amateur for both Arsenal and Brentford in the years immediately after the war and won ten full caps for the Republic of Ireland. In later years he was involved in the Olympic movement, serving on the International Olympic Committee.

Les Olive (Born Salford, Lancashire, 27 April 1928. Died 20 May 2006.) Les gave over 50 years loyal service to Manchester United after joining the staff at the age of 14. He made two first-team appearances as a goalkeeper in the 1952–53 season but was better known for his administrative role, serving as secretary for 30 years from 1958. He also had a spell as a director of the club from 1988.

Tommy O'Neil (Born St Helens, 25 October 1952. Died May 2006.) Tommy O'Neil was a full back who made over 50 appearances for Manchester United before moving on to Southport in the summer of 1973. He went on to clock up over 350 first-team appearances in a career which also saw him play for Tranmere and Halifax. He later joined the coaching staff at Old Trafford.

Peter Osgood (Born Windsor, 20 February 1947. Died Slough, 1 March 2006.) Peter Osgood was one of the most talented English centre forwards of the late 1960s and early '70s. Tall and robust, his strength on the ball made him an effective front man, but he was also very athletic and had the ability to control the ball and deliver a pass to a colleague in one seamless movement. He joined Chelsea as a 17-year-old and proved an immediate success, scoring two goals on his debut, and then quickly breaking through to gain regular first-team football. He led the Blues' scoring charts with 23 First Division goals in 1969–70, when he also helped the club win the FA Cup, and later had a successful spell at Southampton, where he was a member of the team that surprised the football world to defeat Manchester United and win the FA Cup in 1976. Peter also had a spell in the USA with Philadelphia Fury and concluded his playing career back at Stamford Bridge. He won four England caps and was a member of the squad for the 1970 World Cup finals.

John Page (Born Frimley Green, Surrey, 21 October 1934. Died July 2006.) John Page was a solid and reliable centre half who made over 200 appearances for Southampton between 1952 and 1961. He was also the club's penalty taker, and spot kicks accounted for the majority of his 25 first-team goals.

Albert Parker (Born Liverpool, 13 September 1927. Died Wrexham, 29 October 2005.) Albert Parker made over 300 senior appearances for Crewe and Wrexham between 1948 and 1959. A hard-tackling full back, his only senior goal came when he netted from some 60 yards against Workington. He later returned to the Racecourse as groundsman and also took up refereeing, reaching the UEFA linesman's list.

Willie Paton (Born circa 1925. Died 7 November 2005) Willie Paton was an inside forward who made over a century of appearances for both Rangers and Ayr United between 1947 and 1962. During his time at Ibrox he was a member of the team that won a domestic treble in 1948–49 and he also won a Scottish Cup winners' medal in 1953.

Matt Patrick (Born Slamannan, Stirlingshire, 13 June 1919. Died York, 14 July 2005.) Matt Patrick joined York City from Cowdenbeath in September 1940 and went on to make over 250 peacetime appearances, mostly as an inside forward or wing half. He finished joint-top scorer for the Minstermen in the 1950–51 season and stayed at Bootham Crescent until the summer of 1957.

Norman Pengelly (Born Looe, Cornwall, 6 October 1919. Died Plymouth, 10 October 2005.) Norman Pengelly had a brief spell on the books of Plymouth Argyle in the 1945–46 season and later played for Looe before rejoining the Pilgrims in June 1947. He made nine senior appearances for the club before his career was ended by a serious injury. He later became successful in dinghy sailing, winning the national Redwing championships on four occasions.

Mark Philo (Born Bracknell, Berks, 5 October 1984. Died Reading, 14 January 2006.) Mark Philo was a promising young midfielder who broke into the Wycombe Wanderers first-team squad in the closing stages of the 2003–04 season. Thereafter his career was affected by a string of injuries, although he featured in two Football League Trophy games for the Chairboys in 2005–06. His tragically early death came as a result of a car accident.

Ray Potter (Born Beckenham, Kent, 7 May 1936. Died 7 August 2005.) Ray Potter was a solid and dependable goalkeeper who made almost 250 appearances for West Bromwich Albion between 1958 and 1967, appearing in the side that won the Football League Cup in 1966. He began his career with Crystal palace and later played for Portsmouth.

Ted Powell (Born circa 1938. Died 22 September 2005.) Ted Powell was a wing half Sutton United, Wycombe Wanderers and Kingstonian in the 1960s winning 51 caps for England Amateurs and also featuring for the Great Britain Olympic side. Later he coached England U18s to victory in the 1993 UEFA Championships and more recently had coached at youth level with Tottenham.

John Prentice (Born Shotts, Lanarkshire, circa 1926. Died Australia, 9 February 2006.) John Prentice was a combative left half best known for his spells as a player with Rangers and Falkirk in the 1950s. He won a Scottish Cup winners' medal for Falkirk in 1957, when he captained the side, and also had spells with Dumbarton and Hearts. John later became a respected manager serving a string of clubs including Arbroath, Clyde, Falkirk and Dundee, and had a brief spell in charge of the Scotland national team during 1966.

Hugh Rainey (Born Dumbarton, 7 January 1935. Died 2005.) Hugh Rainey began his professional career at Portsmouth but made no appearances for Pompey. He had more success at his next club Aldershot, playing nine games as an inside forward or wing half in the 1957–58 season.

John Rawlingson (Born Wallsend, 7 April 1944. Died Newcastle upon Tyne, 14 March 2006.) John Rawlingson was a centre half who had spells with Bury and Barrow during the 1960s. He later won fame as a comedian on the Northern club circuit, adopting the stage name Spike Rawlings.

George Robertson (Born Kilmarnock, 7 September 1915. Died Irvine, Ayrshire, 2006.) George Robertson was a hard-working wing half who joined Kilmarnock in the summer of 1936 and was a regular in the line-up for the next two seasons. He featured in the team that lost out to East Fife in the 1938 Scottish Cup final and also won a single cap for Scotland against Czechoslovakia in December 1937. He spent much of the rest of his life in Southern Rhodesia.

Tommy Rowe (Born Poole, 1 January 1913. Died Dorchester, 9 May 2006.) Tommy Rowe was a centre half who joined Portsmouth from Poole Town in July 1934 and made his debut later the same year. He became a regular in the line-up in 1937–38 and the following season was a member of the Pompey team that defeated Wolves to win the FA Cup final at Wembley. He served in the RAF during the war, gaining the Distinguished Flying Cross for his exploits.

Tony Rowley (Born Porthcawl, 19 September 1929. Died Bromborough, Cheshire, 28 April 2006.) Tony Rowley was a winger who played for Liverpool and Tranmere Rovers in the 1950s. He had the distinction of scoring a hat-trick on his Football League debut for the Reds against Doncaster on the opening day of the 1954–55 season. Tony won a single cap for Wales, appearing against Northern Ireland in April 1959.

John Russell (Died Vancouver, British Colombia, Canada, 7 December 2005.) John Russell was a stocky wing half who joined Motherwell from Pollok Juniors in 1943, but he struggled to win regular first-team football with the club and in August 1950 he moved on to Kilmarnock. John spent six years at Rugby Park making over 150 appearances and featuring in the team that lost out in the final of the Scottish League Cup in 1952–53. He emigrated to Canada soon after leaving the senior game.

Drew Rutherford (Born Edinburgh, 4 October 1953. Died 14 December 2005.) Drew Rutherford was a committed defender who established a record total of 345 first-team appearances for St Johnstone between 1977 and 1985. A key figure in the team that won promotion in 1982–83, he began his career with East Fife and also had a spell on the books of Cowdenbeath.

Tele Santana (Born 31 July 1931. Died 21 April 2006.) Tele Santana had been a player with Fluminense during the 1950s, but went on to become one of the most successful coaches in the modern game. After winning South American and world club championships with the Sao Paulo club he was appointed coach to the Brazil national team, leading the side at both the 1982 and 1986 World Cup finals. His teams were known for their fair play and a cultured approach to the game.

Dennis Setterington (Born 1945. Died Stirling, 13 December 2005.) Dennis Setterington spent eight years as an inside forward on the books of Rangers, but was only ever on the fringes of the first-team squad. In June 1970 he moved on to Falkirk, where he experienced more regular first-team football, before concluding his career at Stirling Albion.

Tommy Singleton (Born Blackpool, 8 September 1940. Died Blackpool, 29 December 2005.) Tommy Singleton made a solitary appearance for Blackpool, but had more success in the lower divisions, featuring regularly for Peterborough, Chester and Bradford Park Avenue as a right back throughout the 1960s.

Ron Smillie (Born Grimethorpe, Yorkshire, 27 September 1933. Died Chelmsford, Essex, 17 August 2005.) Ron Smillie was a diminutive winger who also worked as a coal miner in the early years of his career. He joined Barnsley in December 1950, but it was only when he moved on to Lincoln City in the summer of 1956 that he gained regular first-team football. He played nearly 100 games for the Imps and returned to Oakwell for two seasons before switching to the Southern League with Chelmsford City.

John Sproates (Born Houghton-le-Spring, Co Durham, 11 April 1943. Died February 2006.) John Sproates made two first-team appearances at right half for Barnsley in the 1963–64 season. He also played for a string of non-League clubs in Yorkshire and the North East.

Joe Stapleton (Born Marylebone, London, 27 June 1928. Died July 2005.) Joe Stapleton was a wing half who made over 100 first-team appearances for Fulham in the 1950s, featuring in the side that reached the FA Cup semi-final in 1958. An ankle injury ended his senior career although he later played for Cambridge City and Bexleyheath & Welling.

Stan Steele (Born Fenton, Stoke-on-Trent, 5 January 1937. Died Fenton, Stoke-on-Trent, 15 July 2005.) Stan Steele was an industrious inside forward who spent most of his career with Port Vale, for whom he made over 300 first-team appearances in three separate spells. In between he spent time with West Brom and in South Africa with Port Elizabeth City.

Jimmy Stevenson (Born circa 1914. Died 2005.) Jimmy Stevenson was Sports Editor for the Daily Record for many years and served as President of the Scottish Football Writers' Association when it was formed in 1957.

Dennis Stokoe (Born Blyth, Northumberland, 6 June 1925. Died Chester-le-Street, Co Durham, 22 July 2005.) Dennis Stokoe began his professional career with Chesterfield, but did not experience first-team football until he moved on to Carlisle in 1948. He made a century of appearances for both the Brunton Park club and Workington before concluding his playing career at Gateshead.

George Swindin (Born Campsall, Yorkshire, 4 December 1914. Died Kettering, 26 October 2005.) George Swindin came to prominence as a goalkeeper with Bradford City in the mid-1930s and was snapped up by Arsenal in April 1936. A brave 'keeper who dominated his area, he featured in three Football League Championship teams for the Gunners (1937–38, 1947–48 and 1952–53) and also won an FA Cup winners' medal in 1950. He later had spells as manager of Peterborough United, Arsenal, Norwich and Cardiff.

Colin Taylor (Born Stourbridge, Worcs, 24 August 1940. Died Dudley, 29 June 2005.) Colin Taylor was a stocky left winger with a thunderbolt shot who was best known for his exploits with Walsall, for whom he made over 400 appearances and scored over 150 goals. He also had spells with Newcastle United and Crystal Palace before retiring from the game in the summer of 1973.

Wally Taylor (Born Kirton-in-Lindsey, Lincs, 30 October 1926. Died Scunthorpe, 18 August 2005.) Wally Taylor guested for both Notts County and Nottingham Forest during the war when he was also on the books of Grimsby Town. In July 1951 he moved on to Southport and became one of the greatest centre halves in the club's history making over 250 appearances and winning selection for the Division Three North representative team. He concluded his career at Oldham.

Roy Tickell (Born Liverpool, 25 April 1924. Died Southport, 8 February 2006.) An outside right, Roy Tickell served in the RAF during the war and made 11 appearances during the 1945–46 season for Exeter. However, when peacetime football resumed he was unable to break into the Grecians' first team again and his only further senior action came in a brief spell at Southport.

Maurice Tobin (Born Airdrie, 30 July 1920. Died Lakenham, Norwich, 19 August 2005.) Maurice Tobin joined Norwich City in the summer of 1938, but due to the intervention of the war he did not make his first-team debut until September 1946. He went on to make over 100 appearances for the Canaries, chiefly at left back and later worked on the club's backroom staff.

Eddie Wainwright (Born Southport, 22 June 1924. Died 30 September 2005.) Eddie Wainwright joined Everton after being spotted in Southport junior football. A talented inside forward, he went on to make almost 300 first-team appearances for the Toffees, including 66 during the war years. His form at Goodison brought him close to full international honours for he was selected for the Football League representative team that faced the Irish League in April 1950. He concluded his career at Rochdale, where his manager was Harry Catterick, a former colleague at Goodison.

Johnny Watts (Born Birmingham, 13 April 1931. Died March 2006.) Johnny Watts was a tireless half back who made over 200 appearances for Birmingham City between 1951 and 1953. Although slight in appearance he was a tremendous tackler and always showed 100 per cent commitment. One of the highlights of his career was appearing in the side that lost out to Barcelona over two legs in the Inter Cities Fairs Cup final in 1960.

Charlie Wayman (Born Chilton, Co Durham, 16 May 1921. Died Bishop Auckland, Co Durham, 26 February 2006.) Charlie Wayman was a prolific goal-scorer throughout his career, netting some 254 goals in just 382 appearances. Fast, brave and with an eye for the half-chance, perhaps his best years were at Preston, for whom he scored in every round of their FA Cup campaign in 1954, including their defeat by West Brom in the final. He had begun his career at Newcastle during the war and also played for Southampton, Middlesbrough and Darlington.

Tom Weir (Born Edinburgh. Died Kirkcaldy, Fife, 23 October 2005.) Tom Weir joined East Fife from Bayview Youth Club, but apart from an extended run in the side in the second half of the 1951–52 season he was mainly a reserve. Principally a centre half or right back, he later spent two years on the books of Raith Rovers before leaving the game.

Jimmy Whitehouse (Born West Bromwich, 19 September 1934. Died 20 September 2005.) Jimmy Whitehouse signed up for West Bromwich Albion, but he was unable to force his way in to the first team at the Hawthorns and in 1949 he moved on to join Walsall. However, it was not until he joined Rochdale in July 1950 that he became a regular first-teamer. He was later sold to Carlisle for a fee of £3,500 and proved to be an excellent signing for the Cumbrian club. His tally of a goal every other game included five in an 8-0 victory over Scunthorpe on Christmas Day 1950, while he remains the only player to net a century of Football League goals for the club in the post-war period.

Andy Whyte (Born Clacmannan. Date not known. Died 11 June 2006.) Andy Whyte was a tough-tackling right half who made over 100 appearances for Dunfermline Athletic between 1947 and 1951, later having several seasons on the books of East Fife. He was a part-time player throughout his career, also working as a coal miner in local pits.

Billy Williamson (Born Lenzie, Dunbartonshire, circa 1922. Died Kirkintilloch, Dunbartonshire, 30 January 2006.) Billy Williamson signed for Rangers from Junior club Petershill, but spent much of the war on active service as a PT Instructor with the Royal Navy. He occasionally turned out for the Ibrox club, also making over 50 appearances as a guest for Manchester City during the hostilities. Although never a regular for Rangers he made a significant impact as a goal-scoring forward in the immediate post-war years. In 1947 he scored one of the goals in the League Cup final victory over Aberdeen, whilst he also gained Scottish Cup winners' medals in 1948 and 1949, finding the net on both occasions. After spells with St Mirren and Stirling, Billy coached the Queen's Park club.

Glen Wilson (Born High Spen, Co Durham, 2 July 1929. Died Brighton, 8 November 2005.) Glen Wilson gave some 30 years service to Brighton & Hove Albion. As a player he made over 400 first-team appearances between 1949 and 1960, gaining representative honours for Division Three South against their northern counterparts. He later had two seasons as player-manager of Exeter City before returning to work behind the scenes at the Goldstone Ground.

Peter Wilson (Born circa 1943. Died Shrewsbury, 19 November 2005.) Peter Wilson was the Mansfield Town goalkeeping coach. He collapsed and died shortly before the match against Shrewsbury in November 2005, leading to the match being postponed.

Tom Wilson (Born Windygates, Fife, 25 July 1933. Died Bridgwater, Somerset, 4 April 2006.) A product of Scottish Junior football, Tom Wilson was an inside right who played for Reading and Exeter City in the late 1950s. He settled in the West Country, spending several years with Bridgwater Town before moving on to Street.

Telmo Zarra (Born Asua, Vizceya, Spain, 20 January 1921. Died Bilbao, Spain, 23 February 2006.) Telmo Zarra was the greatest goal-scorer in the history of Spanish club football, scoring over 250 goals, principally for Athletic Bilbao in the 1940s and '50s. He also won 20 caps for Spain, scoring at a rate of a goal a game.

Ian Nannestad, Soccer History Magazine

THE FA BARCLAYS PREMIERSHIP AND COCA-COLA FOOTBALL LEAGUE FIXTURES 2006–07

**Sky Sports; †PremPlus pay per view*

Saturday, 5 August 2006

Coca-Cola Football League Championship
Barnsley v Cardiff C
Birmingham C v Colchester U
Burnley v QPR
Ipswich T v Crystal Palace
Leeds U v Norwich C
Luton T v Leicester C* (12.30)
Plymouth Arg v Wolverhampton W
Preston NE v Sheffield W
Southend U v Stoke C
WBA v Hull C

Sunday, 6 August 2006

Coca-Cola Football League Championship
Coventry C v Sunderland* (1.30)
Derby Co v Southampton* (4.00)

Coca-Cola Football League One
Bournemouth v Chesterfield
Brentford v Blackpool
Bristol C v Scunthorpe U
Carlisle U v Doncaster R
Crewe Alex v Northampton T
Gillingham v Huddersfield T
Millwall v Yeovil T
Nottingham F v Bradford C
Port Vale v Leyton Orient
Rotherham U v Brighton & HA
Swansea C v Cheltenham T
Tranmere R v Oldham Ath

Coca-Cola Football League Two
Barnet v Torquay U
Chester C v Accrington S
Darlington v Macclesfield T
Grimsby T v Boston U
Hartlepool U v Swindon T
Lincoln C v Notts Co
Milton Keynes Dons v Bury
Peterborough U v Bristol R
Rochdale v Walsall
Shrewsbury T v Mansfield T
Stockport Co v Hereford U
Wycombe W v Wrexham

Tuesday, 8 August 2006

Coca-Cola Football League Championship
Cardiff C v WBA
Colchester U v Plymouth Arg
Crystal Palace v Southend U
Hull C v Barnsley
Leicester C v Burnley
Norwich C v Preston NE
QPR v Leeds U
Sheffield W v Luton T
Stoke C v Derby Co
Sunderland v Birmingham C
Wolverhampton W v Ipswich T

Coca-Cola Football League One
Blackpool v Nottingham F
Bradford C v Bristol C
Brighton & HA v Gillingham
Cheltenham T v Tranmere R
Doncaster R v Crewe Alex
Huddersfield T v Rotherham U
Leyton Orient v Millwall
Northampton T v Brentford
Oldham Ath v Port Vale
Scunthorpe U v Swansea C
Yeovil T v Bournemouth

Coca-Cola Football League Two
Accrington S v Darlington
Bristol R v Wycombe W
Bury v Chester C
Hereford U v Lincoln C
Macclesfield T v Hartlepool U
Mansfield T v Milton Keynes Dons
Notts Co v Shrewsbury T
Swindon T v Barnet
Torquay U v Rochdale
Walsall v Stockport Co
Wrexham v Grimsby T

Wednesday, 9 August 2006

Coca-Cola Football League Championship
Southampton v Coventry C

Coca-Cola Football League One
Chesterfield v Carlisle U

Coca-Cola Football League Two
Boston U v Peterborough U

Friday, 11 August 2006

Coca-Cola Football League Championship
Wolverhampton W v Preston NE* (7.45)

Saturday, 12 August 2006

Coca-Cola Football League Championship
Cardiff C v Coventry C
Colchester U v Barnsley
Hull C v Derby Co* (5.30)
Leicester C v Ipswich T
Norwich C v Luton T
QPR v Southend U
Sheffield W v Burnley
Southampton v WBA
Stoke C v Birmingham C* (12.30)
Sunderland v Plymouth Arg

Sunday, 13 August 2006

Coca-Cola Football League Championship
Crystal Palace v Leeds U* (12.00)

Coca-Cola Football League One
Blackpool v Rotherham U
Bradford C v Gillingham
Brighton & HA v Brentford
Cheltenham T v Port Vale
Chesterfield v Millwall
Doncaster R v Tranmere R
Huddersfield T v Bristol C
Leyton Orient v Bournemouth
Northampton T v Nottingham F
Oldham Ath v Swansea C
Scunthorpe U v Crewe Alex
Yeovil T v Carlisle U

Coca-Cola Football League Two
Accrington S v Barnet
Boston U v Darlington
Bristol R v Grimsby T
Bury v Shrewsbury T
Hereford U v Chester C
Macclesfield T v Milton Keynes Dons
Mansfield T v Stockport Co
Notts Co v Wycombe W
Swindon T v Rochdale
Torquay U v Lincoln C
Walsall v Hartlepool U
Wrexham v Peterborough U

Friday, 18 August 2006

Coca-Cola Football League Championship
Coventry C v Leicester C (7.45)

Saturday, 19 August 2006

Barclays Premiership
Arsenal v Aston Villa
Bolton W v Tottenham H† (5.15)
Everton v Watford
Newcastle U v Wigan Ath
Portsmouth v Blackburn R
Reading v Middlesbrough
Sheffield U v Liverpool* (12.45)
West Ham U v Charlton Ath

Coca-Cola Football League Championship
Barnsley v Southampton
Birmingham C v Crystal Palace
Burnley v Wolverhampton W
Derby Co v Norwich C
Ipswich T v Hull C
Leeds U v Cardiff C
Luton T v Stoke C
Plymouth Arg v Sheffield W
Preston NE v QPR

Southend U v Sunderland
WBA v Colchester U

Coca-Cola Football League One
Bournemouth v Cheltenham T
Brentford v Huddersfield T
Bristol C v Blackpool
Carlisle U v Leyton Orient
Crewe Alex v Bradford C
Gillingham v Northampton T
Millwall v Oldham Ath
Nottingham F v Brighton & HA
Port Vale v Chesterfield
Rotherham U v Scunthorpe U
Swansea C v Doncaster R
Tranmere R v Yeovil T

Coca-Cola Football League Two
Barnet v Hereford U
Chester C v Wrexham
Darlington v Swindon T
Grimsby T v Mansfield T
Hartlepool U v Torquay U
Lincoln C v Walsall
Milton Keynes Dons v Bristol R
Peterborough U v Macclesfield T
Rochdale v Notts Co
Shrewsbury T v Boston U
Stockport Co v Accrington S
Wycombe W v Bury

Sunday, 20 August 2006
Barclays Premiership
Chelsea v Manchester C* (4.00)
Manchester U v Fulham† (1.30)

Tuesday, 22 August 2006
Barclays Premiership
Charlton Ath v Manchester U
Middlesbrough v Chelsea
Tottenham H v Sheffield U
Watford v West Ham U
Wigan Ath v Arsenal

Wednesday, 23 August 2006
Barclays Premiership
Aston Villa v Reading
Blackburn R v Everton
Fulham v Bolton W
Manchester C v Portsmouth

Friday, 25 August 2006
Coca-Cola Football League Championship
QPR v Ipswich T* (7.45)

Saturday, 26 August 2006
Barclays Premiership
Aston Villa v Newcastle U
Charlton Ath v Bolton W
Fulham v Sheffield U
Liverpool v West Ham U† (12.45)
Manchester C v Arsenal† (5.15)
Tottenham H v Everton
Watford v Manchester U
Wigan Ath v Reading

Coca-Cola Football League Championship
Cardiff C v Birmingham C
Colchester U v Derby Co
Crystal Palace v Burnley
Hull C v Coventry C
Leicester C v Southend U
Norwich C v Barnsley
Southampton v Preston NE
Stoke C v Plymouth Arg
Wolverhampton W v Luton T

Coca-Cola Football League One
Blackpool v Gillingham
Bradford C v Rotherham U
Brighton & HA v Crewe Alex
Cheltenham T v Millwall
Chesterfield v Tranmere R
Doncaster R v Bournemouth
Huddersfield T v Nottingham F
Leyton Orient v Swansea C
Oldham Ath v Carlisle U
Scunthorpe U v Brentford
Yeovil T v Port Vale

Coca-Cola Football League Two
Accrington S v Rochdale
Boston U v Milton Keynes Dons
Bristol R v Shrewsbury T
Bury v Grimsby T
Hereford U v Hartlepool U
Macclesfield T v Wycombe W
Mansfield T v Lincoln C
Notts Co v Peterborough U
Swindon T v Stockport Co
Torquay U v Chester C
Walsall v Darlington
Wrexham v Barnet

Sunday, 27 August 2006
Barclays Premiership
Blackburn R v Chelsea* (4.00)

Coca-Cola Football League Championship
Sheffield W v Leeds U* (1.15)

Monday, 28 August 2006
Barclays Premiership
Middlesbrough v Portsmouth* (8.00)

Coca-Cola Football League Championship
Sunderland v WBA* (3.00)

Tuesday, 29 August 2006
Northampton T v Bristol C* (7.45)

Saturday, 2 September 2006
Coca-Cola Football League One
Bournemouth v Oldham Ath
Brentford v Bradford C
Bristol C v Brighton & HA
Carlisle U v Cheltenham T
Crewe Alex v Huddersfield T* (12.15)
Gillingham v Scunthorpe U
Millwall v Blackpool
Nottingham F v Chesterfield
Rotherham U v Northampton T
Swansea C v Yeovil T
Tranmere R v Leyton Orient

Coca-Cola Football League Two
Barnet v Walsall
Chester C v Swindon T
Darlington v Torquay U
Grimsby T v Macclesfield T
Hartlepool U v Boston U
Lincoln C v Accrington S
Milton Keynes Dons v Notts Co
Peterborough U v Bury
Rochdale v Hereford U
Shrewsbury T v Wrexham
Stockport Co v Bristol R
Wycombe W v Mansfield T

Sunday, 3 September 2006
Coca-Cola Football League One
Port Vale v Doncaster R* (4.00)

Saturday, 9 September 2006
Barclays Premiership
Arsenal v Middlesbrough
Bolton W v Watford
Chelsea v Charlton Ath
Everton v Liverpool† (12.45)
Manchester U v Tottenham H† (5.15)
Newcastle U v Fulham
Portsmouth v Wigan Ath
Sheffield U v Blackburn R

Coca-Cola Football League Championship
Barnsley v Stoke C
Birmingham C v Hull C
Burnley v Colchester U
Coventry C v Norwich C
Derby Co v Sunderland
Ipswich T v Southampton
Luton T v Crystal Palace
Plymouth Arg v QPR
Preston NE v Cardiff C
Southend U v Sheffield W
WBA v Leicester C

Coca-Cola Football League One
Bournemouth v Crewe Alex
Carlisle U v Northampton T
Cheltenham T v Huddersfield T
Chesterfield v Rotherham U
Doncaster R v Gillingham
Leyton Orient v Brentford
Millwall v Brighton & HA
Oldham Ath v Scunthorpe U
Port Vale v Blackpool
Swansea C v Bradford C
Tranmere R v Bristol C
Yeovil T v Nottingham F

Coca-Cola Football League Two
Boston U v Stockport Co
Bristol R v Rochdale
Bury v Torquay U
Grimsby T v Walsall
Macclesfield T v Barnet
Mansfield T v Hereford U
Milton Keynes Dons v Hartlepool U
Notts Co v Accrington S
Peterborough U v Darlington
Shrewsbury T v Lincoln C
Wrexham v Swindon T
Wycombe W v Chester C

Sunday, 10 September 2006
Barclays Premiership
West Ham U v Aston Villa* (4.00)

Coca-Cola Football League Championship
Leeds U v Wolverhampton W* (1.15)

Monday, 11 September 2006
Barclays Premiership
Reading v Manchester C* (8.00)

Tuesday, 12 September 2006
Coca-Cola Football League Championship
Burnley v Barnsley
Crystal Palace v Southampton
Ipswich T v Coventry C
Leeds U v Sunderland

Leicester C v Hull C
Luton T v Colchester U
Plymouth Arg v Cardiff C
Preston NE v WBA
QPR v Birmingham C
Sheffield W v Stoke C
Southend U v Norwich C
Wolverhampton W v Derby Co

Coca-Cola Football League One
Blackpool v Chesterfield
Bradford C v Carlisle U
Brentford v Swansea C
Brighton & HA v Bournemouth
Bristol C v Leyton Orient
Crewe Alex v Cheltenham T
Gillingham v Millwall
Huddersfield T v Doncaster R
Northampton T v Yeovil T
Nottingham F v Oldham Ath
Rotherham U v Tranmere R
Scunthorpe U v Port Vale

Coca-Cola Football League Two
Accrington S v Wrexham
Barnet v Boston U
Chester C v Notts Co
Darlington v Bury
Hartlepool U v Mansfield T
Hereford U v Wycombe W
Lincoln C v Macclesfield T
Rochdale v Grimsby T
Stockport Co v Shrewsbury T
Swindon T v Milton Keynes Dons
Torquay U v Bristol R
Walsall v Peterborough U

Friday, 15 September 2006
Coca-Cola Football League Championship
Hull C v Sheffield W* (7.45)

Saturday, 16 September 2006
Barclays Premiership
Blackburn R v Manchester C
Bolton W v Middlesbrough
Charlton Ath v Portsmouth† (12.45)
Everton v Wigan Ath
Sheffield U v Reading
Tottenham H v Fulham
Watford v Aston Villa† (5.15)

Coca-Cola Football League Championship
Barnsley v Wolverhampton W
Birmingham C v Ipswich T
Cardiff C v Luton T
Colchester U v QPR
Coventry C v Leeds U
Derby Co v Preston NE
Norwich C v Crystal Palace
Southampton v Plymouth Arg
Stoke C v Burnley
Sunderland v Leicester C
WBA v Southend U

Coca-Cola Football League One
Blackpool v Oldham Ath
Bradford C v Port Vale
Brentford v Bournemouth
Brighton & HA v Leyton Orient
Bristol C v Chesterfield
Crewe Alex v Millwall
Gillingham v Swansea C
Huddersfield T v Yeovil T
Northampton T v Tranmere R
Nottingham F v Carlisle U
Rotherham U v Doncaster R
Scunthorpe U v Cheltenham T

Coca-Cola Football League Two
Accrington S v Boston U
Barnet v Notts Co
Chester C v Grimsby T
Darlington v Bristol R
Hartlepool U v Shrewsbury T
Hereford U v Bury
Lincoln C v Milton Keynes Dons
Rochdale v Wycombe W
Stockport Co v Wrexham
Swindon T v Peterborough U
Torquay U v Mansfield T
Walsall v Macclesfield T

Sunday, 17 September 2006
Barclays Premiership
Chelsea v Liverpool* (1.30)
Manchester U v Arsenal* (4.00)
West Ham U v Newcastle U (3.00)

Wednesday, 20 September 2006
Barclays Premiership
Liverpool v Newcastle U (8.00)

Friday, 22 September 2006
Coca-Cola Football League Championship
Preston NE v Barnsley* (7.45)

Saturday, 23 September 2006
Barclays Premiership
Arsenal v Sheffield U
Aston Villa v Charlton Ath
Fulham v Chelsea
Liverpool v Tottenham H* (12.45)
Manchester C v West Ham U
Middlesbrough v Blackburn R
Reading v Manchester U† (5.15)
Wigan Ath v Watford

Coca-Cola Football League Championship
Burnley v Southampton
Crystal Palace v Coventry C
Ipswich T v Sunderland
Leeds U v Birmingham C
Leicester C v Colchester U
Luton T v WBA
Plymouth Arg v Norwich C
QPR v Hull C
Sheffield W v Derby Co
Wolverhampton W v Stoke C

Coca-Cola Football League One
Bournemouth v Scunthorpe U
Carlisle U v Brighton & HA
Cheltenham T v Bradford C
Chesterfield v Brentford
Doncaster R v Blackpool
Leyton Orient v Rotherham U
Millwall v Northampton T
Oldham Ath v Gillingham
Port Vale v Bristol C
Swansea C v Huddersfield T
Tranmere R v Nottingham F
Yeovil T v Crewe Alex

Coca-Cola Football League Two
Boston U v Rochdale
Bristol R v Walsall
Bury v Barnet
Grimsby T v Stockport Co
Macclesfield T v Torquay U
Mansfield T v Accrington S
Milton Keynes Dons v Chester C
Notts Co v Swindon T
Peterborough U v Hartlepool U
Shrewsbury T v Darlington
Wrexham v Hereford U
Wycombe W v Lincoln C

Sunday, 24 September 2006
Barclays Premiership
Newcastle U v Everton* (4.00)

Coca-Cola Football League Championship
Southend U v Cardiff C* (1.15)

Monday, 25 September 2006
Barclays Premiership
Portsmouth v Bolton W* (8.00)

Tuesday, 26 September 2006
Coca-Cola Football League One
Bournemouth v Bristol C
Carlisle U v Blackpool
Cheltenham T v Northampton T
Doncaster R v Bradford C
Leyton Orient v Gillingham
Millwall v Brentford
Oldham Ath v Rotherham U
Port Vale v Nottingham F
Swansea C v Crewe Alex
Tranmere R v Huddersfield T
Yeovil T v Brighton & HA

Coca-Cola Football League Two
Bristol R v Hereford U
Bury v Accrington S
Grimsby T v Hartlepool U
Macclesfield T v Chester C
Mansfield T v Darlington
Milton Keynes Dons v Torquay U
Notts Co v Stockport Co
Peterborough U v Barnet
Shrewsbury T v Walsall
Wrexham v Rochdale
Wycombe W v Swindon T

Wednesday, 27 September 2006
Coca-Cola Football League One
Chesterfield v Scunthorpe U

Coca-Cola Football League Two
Boston U v Lincoln C

Friday, 29 September 2006
Coca-Cola Football League Championship
Colchester U v Ipswich T* (7.45)

Saturday, 30 September 2006
Barclays Premiership
Blackburn R v Wigan Ath
Bolton W v Liverpool* (12.45)
Charlton Ath v Arsenal
Chelsea v Aston Villa
Everton v Manchester C
Manchester U v Newcastle U
Sheffield U v Middlesbrough† (5.15)
West Ham U v Reading

Coca-Cola Football League Championship
Barnsley v Luton T
Birmingham C v Leicester C
Cardiff C v Wolverhampton W
Coventry C v Plymouth Arg
Derby Co v Southend U
Hull C v Crystal Palace

Southampton v QPR
Stoke C v Preston NE
Sunderland v Sheffield W
WBA v Leeds U

Coca-Cola Football League One
Blackpool v Leyton Orient
Bradford C v Tranmere R
Brentford v Yeovil T
Brighton & HA v Chesterfield
Bristol C v Oldham Ath
Crewe Alex v Carlisle U
Gillingham v Cheltenham T
Huddersfield T v Bournemouth
Northampton T v Port Vale
Nottingham F v Swansea C
Rotherham U v Millwall
Scunthorpe U v Doncaster R

Coca-Cola Football League Two
Accrington S v Wycombe W
Barnet v Milton Keynes Dons
Chester C v Bristol R
Darlington v Grimsby T
Hartlepool U v Wrexham
Hereford U v Macclesfield T
Lincoln C v Bury
Rochdale v Shrewsbury T
Stockport Co v Peterborough U
Swindon T v Boston U
Torquay U v Notts Co
Walsall v Mansfield T

Sunday, 1 October 2006
Barclays Premiership
Tottenham H v Portsmouth* (4.00)

Coca-Cola Football League Championship
Norwich C v Burnley* (1.15)

Monday, 2 October 2006
Barclays Premiership
Watford v Fulham* (8.00)

Saturday, 7 October 2006
Coca-Cola Football League One
Bournemouth v Northampton T
Bradford C v Huddersfield T
Brentford v Bristol C
Carlisle U v Millwall
Crewe Alex v Gillingham
Doncaster R v Oldham Ath
Leyton Orient v Chesterfield
Nottingham F v Scunthorpe U* (12.15)
Port Vale v Rotherham U
Swansea C v Tranmere R
Yeovil T v Cheltenham T

Coca-Cola Football League Two
Accrington S v Swindon T
Bristol R v Boston U
Bury v Wrexham
Chester C v Walsall
Darlington v Rochdale
Lincoln C v Hartlepool U
Mansfield T v Notts Co
Milton Keynes Dons v Peterborough U
Shrewsbury T v Macclesfield T
Stockport Co v Barnet
Wycombe W v Torquay U

Sunday, 8 October 2006
Coca-Cola Football League One
Brighton & HA v Blackpool* (1.30)

Coca-Cola Football League Two
Grimsby T v Hereford U* (4.00)

Saturday, 14 October 2006
Barclays Premiership
Arsenal v Watford
Aston Villa v Tottenham H
Liverpool v Blackburn R
Manchester C v Sheffield U
Middlesbrough v Everton
Portsmouth v West Ham U
Reading v Chelsea† (5.15)
Wigan Ath v Manchester U* (12.45)

Coca-Cola Football League Championship
Burnley v Hull C
Crystal Palace v Cardiff C
Ipswich T v WBA
Leeds U v Stoke C
Leicester C v Southampton
Luton T v Birmingham C
Preston NE v Sunderland
QPR v Norwich C
Sheffield W v Barnsley
Southend U v Coventry C
Wolverhampton W v Colchester U

Coca-Cola Football League One
Blackpool v Yeovil T
Bristol C v Crewe Alex
Cheltenham T v Doncaster R
Chesterfield v Swansea C
Gillingham v Nottingham F
Huddersfield T v Carlisle U
Millwall v Bournemouth
Northampton T v Bradford C
Oldham Ath v Leyton Orient
Rotherham U v Brentford
Scunthorpe U v Brighton & HA
Tranmere R v Port Vale

Coca-Cola Football League Two
Barnet v Lincoln C
Boston U v Mansfield T
Hartlepool U v Stockport Co
Hereford U v Darlington
Macclesfield T v Bury
Notts Co v Bristol R
Peterborough U v Shrewsbury T
Rochdale v Chester C
Swindon T v Grimsby T
Torquay U v Accrington S
Walsall v Wycombe W
Wrexham v Milton Keynes Dons

Sunday, 15 October 2006
Barclays Premiership
Newcastle U v Bolton W* (4.00)

Coca-Cola Football League Championship
Plymouth Arg v Derby Co* (1.15)

Monday, 16 October 2006
Barclays Premiership
Fulham v Charlton Ath* (8.00)

Tuesday, 17 October 2006
Coca-Cola Football League Championship
Barnsley v Plymouth Arg
Birmingham C v Norwich C
Burnley v Southend U
Cardiff C v Southampton
Colchester U v Sheffield W
Crystal Palace v WBA
Hull C v Luton T
Ipswich T v Preston NE
Leeds U v Leicester C
QPR v Derby Co
Stoke C v Sunderland
Wolverhampton W v Coventry C

Saturday, 21 October 2006
Barclays Premiership
Aston Villa v Fulham† (5.15)
Blackburn R v Bolton W
Charlton Ath v Watford
Chelsea v Portsmouth
Everton v Sheffield U
Middlesbrough v Newcastle U
Tottenham H v West Ham U
Wigan Ath v Manchester C† (12.45)

Coca-Cola Football League Championship
Coventry C v Colchester U
Derby Co v Birmingham C
Leicester C v Crystal Palace
Luton T v Leeds U
Norwich C v Cardiff C
Plymouth Arg v Burnley
Preston NE v Hull C
Sheffield W v QPR
Southampton v Stoke C
Southend U v Ipswich T
Sunderland v Barnsley
WBA v Wolverhampton W

Coca-Cola Football League One
Bournemouth v Rotherham U
Bradford C v Scunthorpe U
Brentford v Gillingham
Brighton & HA v Northampton T
Carlisle U v Tranmere R
Crewe Alex v Blackpool
Doncaster R v Chesterfield
Leyton Orient v Cheltenham T
Nottingham F v Bristol C
Port Vale v Huddersfield T
Swansea C v Millwall
Yeovil T v Oldham Ath

Coca-Cola Football League Two
Accrington S v Walsall
Bristol R v Macclesfield T
Bury v Boston U
Chester C v Hartlepool U
Darlington v Barnet
Grimsby T v Notts Co
Lincoln C v Rochdale
Mansfield T v Wrexham
Milton Keynes Dons v Hereford U
Shrewsbury T v Swindon T
Stockport Co v Torquay U
Wycombe W v Peterborough U

Sunday, 22 October 2006
Barclays Premiership
Manchester U v Liverpool* (1.00)
Reading v Arsenal* (4.00)

Friday, 27 October 2006
Coca-Cola Football League Championship
Burnley v Preston NE* (7.45)

Saturday, 28 October 2006
Barclays Premiership
Arsenal v Everton
Bolton W v Manchester U

Fulham v Wigan Ath
Liverpool v Aston Villa
Newcastle U v Charlton Ath† (5.15)
Portsmouth v Reading
Sheffield U v Chelsea† (12.45)
Watford v Tottenham H

Coca-Cola Football League Championship
Barnsley v Coventry C
Birmingham C v WBA
Cardiff C v Derby Co
Colchester U v Southampton
Crystal Palace v Plymouth Arg
Hull C v Sunderland
Leeds U v Southend U
QPR v Leicester C
Stoke C v Norwich C
Wolverhampton W v Sheffield W

Coca-Cola Football League One
Blackpool v Bradford C
Bristol C v Doncaster R
Cheltenham T v Nottingham F
Chesterfield v Yeovil T
Gillingham v Carlisle U
Huddersfield T v Brighton & HA
Millwall v Port Vale
Northampton T v Swansea C
Oldham Ath v Brentford
Rotherham U v Crewe Alex
Scunthorpe U v Leyton Orient
Tranmere R v Bournemouth

Coca-Cola Football League Two
Barnet v Chester C
Boston U v Wycombe W
Hartlepool U v Darlington
Hereford U v Accrington S
Macclesfield T v Mansfield T
Notts Co v Bury
Peterborough U v Grimsby T
Rochdale v Stockport Co
Swindon T v Lincoln C
Torquay U v Shrewsbury T
Walsall v Milton Keynes Dons
Wrexham v Bristol R

Sunday, 29 October 2006
Barclays Premiership
West Ham U v Blackburn R* (4.00)

Coca-Cola Football League Championship
Ipswich T v Luton T* (1.15)

Monday, 30 October 2006
Barclays Premiership
Manchester C v Middlesbrough* (8.00)

Tuesday, 31 October 2006
Coca-Cola Football League Championship
Coventry C v Birmingham C
Leicester C v Stoke C
Luton T v Burnley
Norwich C v Colchester U
Plymouth Arg v Ipswich T
Preston NE v Leeds U
Sheffield W v Crystal Palace
Southend U v Hull C
Sunderland v Cardiff C
WBA v QPR

Wednesday, 1 November 2006
Coca-Cola Football League Championship
Derby Co v Barnsley
Southampton v Wolverhampton W

Saturday, 4 November 2006
Barclays Premiership
Aston Villa v Blackburn R
Bolton W v Wigan Ath
Charlton Ath v Manchester C
Fulham v Everton* (12.45)
Liverpool v Reading
Manchester U v Portsmouth
Newcastle U v Sheffield U† (5.15)
Watford v Middlesbrough

Coca-Cola Football League Championship
Barnsley v Leeds U
Burnley v Ipswich T
Colchester U v Cardiff C
Derby Co v WBA
Norwich C v Sunderland
Plymouth Arg v Birmingham C
Preston NE v Luton T
QPR v Crystal Palace
Sheffield W v Leicester C
Southampton v Hull C
Stoke C v Coventry C
Wolverhampton W v Southend U

Coca-Cola Football League One
Bradford C v Brighton & HA
Carlisle U v Rotherham U
Cheltenham T v Oldham Ath
Crewe Alex v Port Vale
Doncaster R v Leyton Orient
Gillingham v Chesterfield
Huddersfield T v Scunthorpe U
Northampton T v Blackpool
Nottingham F v Brentford
Swansea C v Bournemouth
Tranmere R v Millwall
Yeovil T v Bristol C

Coca-Cola Football League Two
Boston U v Notts Co
Bristol R v Mansfield T
Darlington v Chester C
Grimsby T v Milton Keynes Dons
Hartlepool U v Barnet
Peterborough U v Accrington S
Rochdale v Bury
Shrewsbury T v Wycombe W
Stockport Co v Lincoln C
Swindon T v Hereford U
Walsall v Torquay U
Wrexham v Macclesfield T

Sunday, 5 November 2006
Barclays Premiership
Tottenham H v Chelsea* (4.00)
West Ham U v Arsenal* (1.30)

Saturday, 11 November 2006
Barclays Premiership
Blackburn R v Manchester U† (5.15)
Chelsea v Watford
Everton v Aston Villa
Manchester C v Newcastle U* (12.45)
Middlesbrough v West Ham U
Portsmouth v Fulham
Sheffield U v Bolton W
Wigan Ath v Charlton Ath

Coca-Cola Football League Championship
Birmingham C v Barnsley
Cardiff C v Burnley
Coventry C v Derby Co
Crystal Palace v Stoke C
Hull C v Wolverhampton W
Ipswich T v Sheffield W
Leeds U v Colchester U
Leicester C v Plymouth Arg
Luton T v QPR
Southend U v Preston NE
Sunderland v Southampton
WBA v Norwich C

Sunday, 12 November 2006
Barclays Premiership
Arsenal v Liverpool* (4.00)
Reading v Tottenham H* (1.30)

Saturday, 18 November 2006
Barclays Premiership
Arsenal v Newcastle U
Chelsea v West Ham U
Everton v Bolton W
Manchester C v Fulham† (12.45)
Middlesbrough v Liverpool (5.15)
Portsmouth v Watford
Reading v Charlton Ath
Sheffield U v Manchester U

Coca-Cola Football League Championship
Birmingham C v Wolverhampton W
Cardiff C v QPR
Coventry C v Sheffield W
Crystal Palace v Barnsley
Hull C v Stoke C
Ipswich T v Norwich C
Leeds U v Southampton
Leicester C v Preston NE
Luton T v Derby Co
Southend U v Plymouth Arg
Sunderland v Colchester U
WBA v Burnley

Coca-Cola Football League One
Blackpool v Huddersfield T
Bournemouth v Carlisle U
Brentford v Crewe Alex
Brighton & HA v Tranmere R
Bristol C v Gillingham
Chesterfield v Cheltenham T
Leyton Orient v Yeovil T
Millwall v Doncaster R
Oldham Ath v Bradford C
Port Vale v Swansea C
Rotherham U v Nottingham F
Scunthorpe U v Northampton T

Coca-Cola Football League Two
Accrington S v Hartlepool U
Barnet v Rochdale
Bury v Bristol R
Chester C v Stockport Co
Hereford U v Walsall
Lincoln C v Darlington
Macclesfield T v Boston U
Mansfield T v Peterborough U
Milton Keynes Dons v Shrewsbury T
Notts Co v Wrexham
Torquay U v Swindon T
Wycombe W v Grimsby T

Sunday, 19 November 2006
Barclays Premiership
Blackburn R v Tottenham H* (4.00)
Wigan Ath v Aston Villa* (1.30)

Saturday, 25 November 2006
Barclays Premiership
Aston Villa v Middlesbrough
Bolton W v Arsenal† (5.15)
Charlton Ath v Everton† (12.45)
Fulham v Reading
Liverpool v Manchester C
Tottenham H v Wigan Ath
Watford v Blackburn R
West Ham U v Sheffield U

Coca-Cola Football League Championship
Barnsley v Ipswich T
Burnley v Birmingham C
Colchester U v Southend U
Derby Co v Leicester C
Norwich C v Hull C
Plymouth Arg v Leeds U
Preston NE v Crystal Palace
QPR v Coventry C
Sheffield W v Cardiff C
Southampton v Luton T
Stoke C v WBA
Wolverhampton W v Sunderland

Coca-Cola Football League One
Bradford C v Bournemouth
Carlisle U v Port Vale
Cheltenham T v Brentford
Crewe Alex v Chesterfield
Doncaster R v Brighton & HA
Gillingham v Rotherham U
Huddersfield T v Oldham Ath
Northampton T v Leyton Orient
Nottingham F v Millwall
Swansea C v Bristol C
Tranmere R v Blackpool
Yeovil T v Scunthorpe U

Coca-Cola Football League Two
Boston U v Hereford U
Bristol R v Barnet
Darlington v Milton Keynes Dons
Grimsby T v Accrington S
Hartlepool U v Wycombe W
Peterborough U v Torquay U
Rochdale v Mansfield T
Shrewsbury T v Chester C
Stockport Co v Macclesfield T
Swindon T v Bury
Walsall v Notts Co
Wrexham v Lincoln C

Sunday, 26 November 2006
Barclays Premiership
Manchester U v Chelsea* (4.00)
Newcastle U v Portsmouth* (1.30)

Tuesday, 28 November 2006
Barclays Premiership
Watford v Sheffield U* (8.00)

Coca-Cola Football League Championship
Barnsley v Southend U
Burnley v Leeds U
Colchester U v Hull C
Norwich C v Leicester C
Plymouth Arg v Luton T
Preston NE v Coventry C
QPR v Sunderland
Sheffield W v WBA
Stoke C v Cardiff C
Wolverhampton W v Crystal Palace

Wednesday, 29 November 2006
Barclays Premiership
Bolton W v Chelsea* (8.00)
Aston Villa v Manchester C
Fulham v Arsenal
Liverpool v Portsmouth
Manchester U v Everton

Coca-Cola Football League Championship
Derby Co v Ipswich T
Southampton v Birmingham C

Saturday, 2 December 2006
Barclays Premiership
Arsenal v Tottenham H† (12.45)
Blackburn R v Fulham
Chelsea v Newcastle U
Middlesbrough v Manchester U† (5.15)
Portsmouth v Aston Villa
Reading v Bolton W
Sheffield U v Charlton Ath
Wigan Ath v Liverpool

Coca-Cola Football League Championship
Birmingham C v Plymouth Arg
Cardiff C v Colchester U
Coventry C v Stoke C
Crystal Palace v QPR
Hull C v Southampton
Ipswich T v Burnley
Leeds U v Barnsley
Leicester C v Sheffield W
Luton T v Preston NE
Southend U v Wolverhampton W
Sunderland v Norwich C
WBA v Derby Co

Sunday, 3 December 2006
Barclays Premiership
Everton v West Ham U* (4.00)

Monday, 4 December 2006
Barclays Premiership
Manchester C v Watford* (8.00)

Tuesday, 5 December 2006
Barclays Premiership
Charlton Ath v Blackburn R
Tottenham H v Middlesbrough

Coca-Cola Football League One
Blackpool v Cheltenham T
Bournemouth v Nottingham F
Brentford v Doncaster R
Brighton & HA v Swansea C
Bristol C v Carlisle U
Leyton Orient v Bradford C
Millwall v Huddersfield T
Oldham Ath v Crewe Alex
Port Vale v Gillingham
Rotherham U v Yeovil T
Scunthorpe U v Tranmere R

Coca-Cola Football League Two
Accrington S v Shrewsbury T
Barnet v Grimsby T
Bury v Walsall
Chester C v Boston U
Hereford U v Peterborough U
Lincoln C v Bristol R
Macclesfield T v Rochdale
Mansfield T v Swindon T
Milton Keynes Dons v Stockport Co
Notts Co v Hartlepool U
Torquay U v Wrexham
Wycombe W v Darlington

Wednesday, 6 December 2006
Barclays Premiership
Newcastle U v Reading
West Ham U v Wigan Ath

Coca-Cola Football League One
Chesterfield v Northampton T

Saturday, 9 December 2006
Barclays Premiership
Blackburn R v Newcastle U
Bolton W v West Ham U† (5.15)
Liverpool v Fulham
Manchester U v Manchester C† (12.45)
Middlesbrough v Wigan Ath
Portsmouth v Everton
Tottenham H v Charlton Ath
Watford v Reading

Coca-Cola Football League Championship
Barnsley v WBA
Birmingham C v Preston NE
Cardiff C v Ipswich T
Coventry C v Burnley
Crystal Palace v Colchester U
Leeds U v Derby Co
Norwich C v Sheffield W
Plymouth Arg v Hull C
Southend U v Southampton
Stoke C v QPR
Sunderland v Luton T
Wolverhampton W v Leicester C

Coca-Cola Football League One
Blackpool v Swansea C
Bournemouth v Port Vale
Brentford v Tranmere R
Brighton & HA v Cheltenham T
Carlisle U v Scunthorpe U
Chesterfield v Oldham Ath
Crewe Alex v Nottingham F
Leyton Orient v Huddersfield T
Millwall v Bradford C
Northampton T v Doncaster R
Rotherham U v Bristol C
Yeovil T v Gillingham

Coca-Cola Football League Two
Accrington S v Milton Keynes Dons
Boston U v Wrexham
Bristol R v Hartlepool U
Chester C v Lincoln C
Grimsby T v Shrewsbury T
Hereford U v Torquay U
Mansfield T v Bury
Notts Co v Macclesfield T
Rochdale v Peterborough U
Stockport Co v Darlington
Walsall v Swindon T
Wycombe W v Barnet

Saturday, 10 December 2006
Barclays Premiership
Chelsea v Arsenal* (4.00)

Monday, 11 December 2006
Barclays Premiership
Sheffield U v Aston Villa* (8.00)

Saturday, 16 December 2006
Barclays Premiership
Arsenal v Portsmouth
Aston Villa v Bolton W
Charlton Ath v Liverpool† (12.45)
Fulham v Middlesbrough
Manchester C v Tottenham H† (5.15)
Newcastle U v Watford
Reading v Blackburn R
Wigan Ath v Sheffield U

Coca-Cola Football League Championship
Burnley v Sunderland
Colchester U v Stoke C
Derby Co v Crystal Palace
Hull C v Cardiff C
Ipswich T v Leeds U
Leicester C v Barnsley
Luton T v Southend U
Preston NE v Plymouth Arg
QPR v Wolverhampton W
Sheffield W v Birmingham C
Southampton v Norwich C
WBA v Coventry C

Coca-Cola Football League One
Bradford C v Chesterfield
Bristol C v Millwall
Cheltenham T v Rotherham U
Doncaster R v Yeovil T
Gillingham v Bournemouth
Huddersfield T v Northampton T
Nottingham F v Leyton Orient
Oldham Ath v Brighton & HA
Port Vale v Brentford
Scunthorpe U v Blackpool
Swansea C v Carlisle U
Tranmere R v Crewe Alex

Coca-Cola Football League Two
Barnet v Mansfield T
Bury v Stockport Co
Darlington v Notts Co
Hartlepool U v Rochdale
Lincoln C v Grimsby T
Macclesfield T v Accrington S
Milton Keynes Dons v Wycombe W
Peterborough U v Chester C
Shrewsbury T v Hereford U
Swindon T v Bristol R
Torquay U v Boston U
Wrexham v Walsall

Sunday, 17 December 2006
Barclays Premiership
Everton v Chelsea* (1.30)
West Ham U v Manchester U* (4.00)

Saturday, 23 December 2006
Barclays Premiership
Arsenal v Blackburn R
Aston Villa v Manchester U
Fulham v West Ham U* (12.45)
Liverpool v Watford
Manchester C v Bolton W
Middlesbrough v Charlton Ath
Newcastle U v Tottenham H
Portsmouth v Sheffield U
Reading v Everton
Wigan Ath v Chelsea† (5.15)

Coca-Cola Football League Championship
Burnley v Derby Co
Crystal Palace v Sunderland
Ipswich T v Stoke C
Leeds U v Hull C
Leicester C v Cardiff C
Luton T v Coventry C
Plymouth Arg v WBA
Preston NE v Colchester U
QPR v Barnsley
Sheffield W v Southampton
Southend U v Birmingham C
Wolverhampton W v Norwich C

Coca-Cola Football League One
Bournemouth v Blackpool
Carlisle U v Brentford
Cheltenham T v Bristol C
Chesterfield v Huddersfield T
Doncaster R v Nottingham F
Leyton Orient v Crewe Alex
Millwall v Scunthorpe U
Oldham Ath v Northampton T
Port Vale v Brighton & HA
Swansea C v Rotherham U
Tranmere R v Gillingham
Yeovil T v Bradford C

Coca-Cola Football League Two
Boston U v Walsall
Bristol R v Accrington S
Bury v Hartlepool U
Grimsby T v Torquay U
Macclesfield T v Swindon T
Mansfield T v Chester C
Milton Keynes Dons v Rochdale
Notts Co v Hereford U
Peterborough U v Lincoln C
Shrewsbury T v Barnet
Wrexham v Darlington
Wycombe W v Stockport Co

Tuesday, 26 December 2006
Barclays Premiership
Blackburn R v Liverpool† (3.00)
Bolton W v Newcastle U
Chelsea v Reading* (1.00)
Everton v Middlesbrough
Manchester U v Wigan Ath
Sheffield U v Manchester C
Tottenham H v Aston Villa
Watford v Arsenal* (5.30)
West Ham U v Portsmouth

Coca-Cola Football League Championship
Barnsley v Burnley
Birmingham C v QPR
Cardiff C v Plymouth Arg
Colchester U v Luton T
Coventry C v Ipswich T
Derby Co v Wolverhampton W
Hull C v Leicester C
Norwich C v Southend U
Southampton v Crystal Palace
Stoke C v Sheffield W
Sunderland v Leeds U
WBA v Preston NE

Coca-Cola Football League One
Blackpool v Carlisle U
Bradford C v Doncaster R
Brentford v Millwall
Brighton & HA v Yeovil T
Bristol C v Bournemouth
Crewe Alex v Swansea C
Gillingham v Leyton Orient
Huddersfield T v Tranmere R
Northampton T v Cheltenham T
Nottingham F v Port Vale
Rotherham U v Oldham Ath
Scunthorpe U v Chesterfield

Coca-Cola Football League Two
Accrington S v Bury
Barnet v Peterborough U
Chester C v Macclesfield T
Darlington v Mansfield T
Hartlepool U v Grimsby T
Hereford U v Bristol R
Lincoln C v Boston U
Rochdale v Wrexham
Stockport Co v Notts Co
Swindon T v Wycombe W
Torquay U v Milton Keynes Dons
Walsall v Shrewsbury T

Wednesday, 27 December 2006
Barclays Premiership
Charlton Ath v Fulham* (8.00)

Saturday, 30 December 2006
Barclays Premiership
Blackburn R v Middlesbrough
Bolton W v Portsmouth
Charlton Ath v Aston Villa
Chelsea v Fulham
Everton v Newcastle U
Manchester U v Reading
Sheffield U v Arsenal
Tottenham H v Liverpool
Watford v Wigan Ath
West Ham U v Manchester C

Coca-Cola Football League Championship
Barnsley v Sheffield W
Birmingham C v Luton T
Cardiff C v Crystal Palace
Colchester U v Wolverhampton W
Coventry C v Southend U
Derby Co v Plymouth Arg
Hull C v Burnley
Norwich C v QPR
Southampton v Leicester C
Stoke C v Leeds U
Sunderland v Preston NE
WBA v Ipswich T

Coca-Cola Football League One
Blackpool v Doncaster R
Bradford C v Cheltenham T
Brentford v Chesterfield
Brighton & HA v Carlisle U
Bristol C v Port Vale
Crewe Alex v Yeovil T
Gillingham v Oldham Ath
Huddersfield T v Swansea C
Northampton T v Millwall
Nottingham F v Tranmere R
Rotherham U v Leyton Orient
Scunthorpe U v Bournemouth

Coca-Cola Football League Two
Accrington S v Mansfield T
Barnet v Bury
Chester C v Milton Keynes Dons
Darlington v Shrewsbury T
Hartlepool U v Peterborough U
Hereford U v Wrexham
Lincoln C v Wycombe W
Rochdale v Boston U

Stockport Co v Grimsby T
Swindon T v Notts Co
Torquay U v Macclesfield T
Walsall v Bristol R

Monday, 1 January 2007

Barclays Premiership
Arsenal v Charlton Ath
Aston Villa v Chelsea
Fulham v Watford
Liverpool v Bolton W
Manchester C v Everton
Middlesbrough v Sheffield U
Newcastle U v Manchester U
Portsmouth v Tottenham H
Reading v West Ham U
Wigan Ath v Blackburn R

Coca-Cola Football League Championship
Burnley v Stoke C
Crystal Palace v Norwich C
Ipswich T v Birmingham C
Leeds U v Coventry C
Leicester C v Sunderland
Luton T v Cardiff C
Plymouth Arg v Southampton
Preston NE v Derby Co
QPR v Colchester U
Sheffield W v Hull C
Southend U v WBA
Wolverhampton W v Barnsley

Coca-Cola Football League One
Bournemouth v Brighton & HA
Carlisle U v Bradford C
Cheltenham T v Crewe Alex
Chesterfield v Blackpool
Doncaster R v Huddersfield T
Leyton Orient v Bristol C
Millwall v Gillingham
Oldham Ath v Nottingham F
Port Vale v Scunthorpe U
Swansea C v Brentford
Tranmere R v Rotherham U
Yeovil T v Northampton T

Coca-Cola Football League Two
Boston U v Barnet
Bristol R v Torquay U
Bury v Darlington
Grimsby T v Rochdale
Macclesfield T v Lincoln C
Mansfield T v Hartlepool U
Milton Keynes Dons v Swindon T
Notts Co v Chester C
Peterborough U v Walsall
Shrewsbury T v Stockport Co
Wrexham v Accrington S
Wycombe W v Hereford U

Saturday, 6 January 2007

Coca-Cola Football League One
Bournemouth v Brentford
Carlisle U v Nottingham F
Cheltenham T v Scunthorpe U
Chesterfield v Bristol C
Doncaster R v Rotherham U
Leyton Orient v Brighton & HA
Millwall v Crewe Alex
Oldham Ath v Blackpool
Port Vale v Bradford C
Swansea C v Gillingham
Tranmere R v Northampton T
Yeovil T v Huddersfield T

Coca-Cola Football League Two
Boston U v Accrington S
Bristol R v Darlington
Bury v Hereford U
Grimsby T v Chester C
Macclesfield T v Walsall
Mansfield T v Torquay U
Milton Keynes Dons v Lincoln C
Notts Co v Barnet
Peterborough U v Swindon T
Shrewsbury T v Hartlepool U
Wrexham v Stockport Co
Wycombe W v Rochdale

Saturday, 13 January 2007

Barclays Premiership
Blackburn R v Arsenal
Bolton W v Manchester C
Charlton Ath v Middlesbrough
Chelsea v Wigan Ath
Everton v Reading
Manchester U v Aston Villa
Sheffield U v Portsmouth
Tottenham H v Newcastle U
Watford v Liverpool
West Ham U v Fulham

Coca-Cola Football League Championship
Barnsley v Preston NE
Birmingham C v Leeds U
Cardiff C v Southend U
Colchester U v Leicester C
Coventry C v Crystal Palace
Derby Co v Sheffield W
Hull C v QPR
Norwich C v Plymouth Arg
Southampton v Burnley
Stoke C v Wolverhampton W
Sunderland v Ipswich T
WBA v Luton T

Coca-Cola Football League One
Blackpool v Port Vale
Bradford C v Swansea C
Brentford v Leyton Orient
Brighton & HA v Millwall
Bristol C v Tranmere R
Crewe Alex v Bournemouth
Gillingham v Doncaster R
Huddersfield T v Cheltenham T
Northampton T v Carlisle U
Nottingham F v Yeovil T
Rotherham U v Chesterfield
Scunthorpe U v Oldham Ath

Coca-Cola Football League Two
Accrington S v Notts Co
Barnet v Macclesfield T
Chester C v Wycombe W
Darlington v Peterborough U
Hartlepool U v Milton Keynes Dons
Hereford U v Mansfield T
Lincoln C v Shrewsbury T
Rochdale v Bristol R
Stockport Co v Boston U
Swindon T v Wrexham
Torquay U v Bury
Walsall v Grimsby T

Saturday, 20 January 2007

Barclays Premiership
Arsenal v Manchester U
Aston Villa v Watford
Fulham v Tottenham H
Liverpool v Chelsea
Manchester C v Blackburn R
Middlesbrough v Bolton W
Newcastle U v West Ham U
Portsmouth v Charlton Ath
Reading v Sheffield U
Wigan Ath v Everton

Coca-Cola Football League Championship
Burnley v Norwich C
Crystal Palace v Hull C
Ipswich T v Colchester U
Leeds U v WBA
Leicester C v Birmingham C
Luton T v Barnsley
Plymouth Arg v Coventry C
Preston NE v Stoke C
QPR v Southampton
Sheffield W v Sunderland
Southend U v Derby Co
Wolverhampton W v Cardiff C

Coca-Cola Football League One
Bournemouth v Huddersfield T
Carlisle U v Crewe Alex
Cheltenham T v Gillingham
Chesterfield v Brighton & HA
Doncaster R v Scunthorpe U
Leyton Orient v Blackpool
Millwall v Rotherham U
Oldham Ath v Bristol C
Port Vale v Northampton T
Swansea C v Nottingham F
Tranmere R v Bradford C
Yeovil T v Brentford

Coca-Cola Football League Two
Boston U v Swindon T
Bristol R v Chester C
Bury v Lincoln C
Grimsby T v Darlington
Macclesfield T v Hereford U
Mansfield T v Walsall
Milton Keynes Dons v Barnet
Notts Co v Torquay U
Peterborough U v Stockport Co
Shrewsbury T v Rochdale
Wrexham v Hartlepool U
Wycombe W v Accrington S

Saturday, 27 January 2007

Coca-Cola Football League One
Blackpool v Bournemouth
Bradford C v Yeovil T
Brentford v Carlisle U
Brighton & HA v Port Vale
Bristol C v Cheltenham T
Crewe Alex v Leyton Orient
Gillingham v Tranmere R
Huddersfield T v Chesterfield
Northampton T v Oldham Ath
Nottingham F v Doncaster R
Rotherham U v Swansea C
Scunthorpe U v Millwall

Coca-Cola Football League Two
Accrington S v Bristol R
Barnet v Shrewsbury T
Chester C v Mansfield T
Darlington v Wrexham
Hartlepool U v Bury
Hereford U v Notts Co
Lincoln C v Peterborough U
Rochdale v Milton Keynes Dons
Stockport Co v Wycombe W
Swindon T v Macclesfield T

Torquay U v Grimsby T
Walsall v Boston U

Tuesday, 30 January 2007
Barclays Premiership
Arsenal v Manchester C
Bolton W v Charlton Ath
Portsmouth v Middlesbrough
Reading v Wigan Ath
Sheffield U v Fulham

Coca-Cola Football League Championship
Barnsley v QPR
Birmingham C v Southend U
Cardiff C v Leicester C
Colchester U v Preston NE
Coventry C v Luton T
Hull C v Leeds U
Norwich C v Wolverhampton W
Stoke C v Ipswich T
Sunderland v Crystal Palace
WBA v Plymouth Arg

Wednesday, 31 January 2007
Barclays Premiership
Chelsea v Blackburn R
Everton v Tottenham H
Manchester U v Watford
Newcastle U v Aston Villa
West Ham U v Liverpool

Coca-Cola Football League Championship
Derby Co v Burnley
Southampton v Sheffield W

Saturday, 3 February 2007
Barclays Premiership
Aston Villa v West Ham U
Blackburn R v Sheffield U
Charlton Ath v Chelsea
Fulham v Newcastle U
Liverpool v Everton
Manchester C v Reading
Middlesbrough v Arsenal
Tottenham H v Manchester U
Watford v Bolton W
Wigan Ath v Portsmouth

Coca-Cola Football League Championship
Cardiff C v Barnsley
Colchester U v Birmingham C
Crystal Palace v Ipswich T
Hull C v WBA
Leicester C v Luton T
Norwich C v Leeds U
QPR v Burnley
Sheffield W v Preston NE
Southampton v Derby Co
Stoke C v Southend U
Sunderland v Coventry C
Wolverhampton W v Plymouth Arg

Coca-Cola Football League One
Blackpool v Brentford
Bradford C v Nottingham F
Brighton & HA v Rotherham U
Cheltenham T v Swansea C
Chesterfield v Bournemouth
Doncaster R v Carlisle U
Huddersfield T v Gillingham
Leyton Orient v Port Vale
Northampton T v Crewe Alex
Oldham Ath v Tranmere R
Scunthorpe U v Bristol C
Yeovil T v Millwall

Coca-Cola Football League Two
Accrington S v Chester C
Boston U v Grimsby T
Bristol R v Peterborough U
Bury v Milton Keynes Dons
Hereford U v Stockport Co
Macclesfield T v Darlington
Mansfield T v Shrewsbury T
Notts Co v Lincoln C
Swindon T v Hartlepool U
Torquay U v Barnet
Walsall v Rochdale
Wrexham v Wycombe W

Saturday, 10 February 2007
Barclays Premiership
Arsenal v Wigan Ath
Bolton W v Fulham
Chelsea v Middlesbrough
Everton v Blackburn R
Manchester U v Charlton Ath
Newcastle U v Liverpool
Portsmouth v Manchester C
Reading v Aston Villa
Sheffield U v Tottenham H
West Ham U v Watford

Coca-Cola Football League Championship
Barnsley v Colchester U
Birmingham C v Stoke C
Burnley v Sheffield W
Coventry C v Cardiff C
Derby Co v Hull C
Ipswich T v Leicester C
Leeds U v Crystal Palace
Luton T v Norwich C
Plymouth Arg v Sunderland
Preston NE v Wolverhampton W
Southend U v QPR
WBA v Southampton

Coca-Cola Football League One
Bournemouth v Leyton Orient
Brentford v Brighton & HA
Bristol C v Huddersfield T
Carlisle U v Yeovil T
Crewe Alex v Scunthorpe U
Gillingham v Bradford C
Millwall v Chesterfield
Nottingham F v Northampton T
Port Vale v Cheltenham T
Rotherham U v Blackpool
Swansea C v Oldham Ath
Tranmere R v Doncaster R

Coca-Cola Football League Two
Barnet v Accrington S
Chester C v Hereford U
Darlington v Boston U
Grimsby T v Bristol R
Hartlepool U v Walsall
Lincoln C v Torquay U
Milton Keynes Dons v Macclesfield T
Peterborough U v Wrexham
Rochdale v Swindon T
Shrewsbury T v Bury
Stockport Co v Mansfield T
Wycombe W v Notts Co

Saturday, 17 February 2007
Coca-Cola Football League Championship
Cardiff C v Leeds U
Colchester U v WBA
Crystal Palace v Birmingham C
Hull C v Ipswich T
Leicester C v Coventry C
Norwich C v Derby Co
QPR v Preston NE
Sheffield W v Plymouth Arg
Southampton v Barnsley
Stoke C v Luton T
Sunderland v Southend U
Wolverhampton W v Burnley

Coca-Cola Football League One
Blackpool v Bristol C
Bradford C v Crewe Alex
Brighton & HA v Nottingham F
Cheltenham T v Bournemouth
Chesterfield v Port Vale
Doncaster R v Swansea C
Huddersfield T v Brentford
Leyton Orient v Carlisle U
Northampton T v Gillingham
Oldham Ath v Millwall
Scunthorpe U v Rotherham U
Yeovil T v Tranmere R

Coca-Cola Football League Two
Accrington S v Stockport Co
Boston U v Shrewsbury T
Bristol R v Milton Keynes Dons
Bury v Wycombe W
Hereford U v Barnet
Macclesfield T v Peterborough U
Mansfield T v Grimsby T
Notts Co v Rochdale
Swindon T v Darlington
Torquay U v Hartlepool U
Walsall v Lincoln C
Wrexham v Chester C

Tuesday, 20 February 2007
Coca-Cola Football League Championship
Barnsley v Hull C
Birmingham C v Sunderland
Burnley v Leicester C
Coventry C v Southampton
Ipswich T v Wolverhampton W
Leeds U v QPR
Luton T v Sheffield W
Plymouth Arg v Colchester U
Preston NE v Norwich C
Southend U v Crystal Palace
WBA v Cardiff C

Coca-Cola Football League One
Bournemouth v Yeovil T
Brentford v Northampton T
Bristol C v Bradford C
Carlisle U v Chesterfield
Crewe Alex v Doncaster R
Gillingham v Brighton & HA
Millwall v Leyton Orient
Nottingham F v Blackpool
Port Vale v Oldham Ath
Rotherham U v Huddersfield T
Swansea C v Scunthorpe U
Tranmere R v Cheltenham T

Coca-Cola Football League Two
Barnet v Swindon T
Chester C v Bury

Darlington v Accrington S
Grimsby T v Wrexham
Hartlepool U v Macclesfield T
Lincoln C v Hereford U
Milton Keynes Dons v Mansfield T
Peterborough U v Boston U
Rochdale v Torquay U
Shrewsbury T v Notts Co
Stockport Co v Walsall
Wycombe W v Bristol R

Wednesday, 21 February 2007

Coca-Cola Football League Championship
Derby Co v Stoke C

Saturday, 24 February 2007

Barclays Premiership
Aston Villa v Arsenal
Blackburn R v Portsmouth
Charlton Ath v West Ham U
Fulham v Manchester U
Liverpool v Sheffield U
Manchester C v Chelsea
Middlesbrough v Reading
Tottenham H v Bolton W
Watford v Everton
Wigan Ath v Newcastle U

Coca-Cola Football League Championship
Cardiff C v Preston NE
Colchester U v Burnley
Crystal Palace v Luton T
Hull C v Birmingham C
Leicester C v WBA
Norwich C v Coventry C
QPR v Plymouth Arg
Sheffield W v Southend U
Southampton v Ipswich T
Stoke C v Barnsley
Sunderland v Derby Co
Wolverhampton W v Leeds U

Coca-Cola Football League One
Blackpool v Millwall
Bradford C v Brentford
Brighton & HA v Bristol C
Cheltenham T v Carlisle U
Chesterfield v Nottingham F
Doncaster R v Port Vale
Huddersfield T v Crewe Alex
Leyton Orient v Tranmere R
Northampton T v Rotherham U
Oldham Ath v Bournemouth
Scunthorpe U v Gillingham
Yeovil T v Swansea C

Coca-Cola Football League Two
Accrington S v Lincoln C
Boston U v Hartlepool U
Bristol R v Stockport Co
Bury v Peterborough U
Hereford U v Rochdale
Macclesfield T v Grimsby T
Mansfield T v Wycombe W
Notts Co v Milton Keynes Dons
Swindon T v Chester C
Torquay U v Darlington
Walsall v Barnet
Wrexham v Shrewsbury T

Saturday, 3 March 2007

Barclays Premiership
Arsenal v Reading
Bolton W v Blackburn R
Fulham v Aston Villa
Liverpool v Manchester U
Manchester C v Wigan Ath
Newcastle U v Middlesbrough
Portsmouth v Chelsea
Sheffield U v Everton
Watford v Charlton Ath
West Ham U v Tottenham H

Coca-Cola Football League Championship
Barnsley v Norwich C
Birmingham C v Cardiff C
Burnley v Crystal Palace
Coventry C v Hull C
Derby Co v Colchester U
Ipswich T v QPR
Leeds U v Sheffield W
Luton T v Wolverhampton W
Plymouth Arg v Stoke C
Preston NE v Southampton
Southend U v Leicester C
WBA v Sunderland

Coca-Cola Football League One
Bournemouth v Doncaster R
Brentford v Scunthorpe U
Bristol C v Northampton T
Carlisle U v Oldham Ath
Crewe Alex v Brighton & HA
Gillingham v Blackpool
Millwall v Cheltenham T
Nottingham F v Huddersfield T
Port Vale v Yeovil T
Rotherham U v Bradford C
Swansea C v Leyton Orient
Tranmere R v Chesterfield

Coca-Cola Football League Two
Barnet v Wrexham
Chester C v Torquay U
Darlington v Walsall
Grimsby T v Bury
Hartlepool U v Hereford U
Lincoln C v Mansfield T
Milton Keynes Dons v Boston U
Peterborough U v Notts Co
Rochdale v Accrington S
Shrewsbury T v Bristol R
Stockport Co v Swindon T
Wycombe W v Macclesfield T

Saturday, 10 March 2007

Coca-Cola Football League Championship
Barnsley v Sunderland
Birmingham C v Derby Co
Burnley v Plymouth Arg
Cardiff C v Norwich C
Colchester U v Coventry C
Crystal Palace v Leicester C
Hull C v Preston NE
Ipswich T v Southend U
Leeds U v Luton T
QPR v Sheffield W
Stoke C v Southampton
Wolverhampton W v WBA

Coca-Cola Football League One
Blackpool v Brighton & HA
Bristol C v Brentford
Cheltenham T v Yeovil T
Chesterfield v Leyton Orient
Gillingham v Crewe Alex
Huddersfield T v Bradford C
Millwall v Carlisle U
Northampton T v Bournemouth
Oldham Ath v Doncaster R
Rotherham U v Port Vale
Scunthorpe U v Nottingham F
Tranmere R v Swansea C

Coca-Cola Football League Two
Barnet v Stockport Co
Boston U v Bristol R
Hartlepool U v Lincoln C
Hereford U v Grimsby T
Macclesfield T v Shrewsbury T
Notts Co v Mansfield T
Peterborough U v Milton Keynes Dons
Rochdale v Darlington
Swindon T v Accrington S
Torquay U v Wycombe W
Walsall v Chester C
Wrexham v Bury

Tuesday, 13 March 2007

Coca-Cola Football League Championship
Coventry C v Wolverhampton W
Leicester C v Leeds U
Luton T v Hull C
Norwich C v Birmingham C
Plymouth Arg v Barnsley
Preston NE v Ipswich T
Sheffield W v Colchester U
Southend U v Burnley
Sunderland v Stoke C
WBA v Crystal Palace

Wednesday, 14 March 2007

Coca-Cola Football League Championship
Derby Co v QPR
Southampton v Cardiff C

Saturday, 17 March 2007

Barclays Premiership
Aston Villa v Liverpool
Blackburn R v West Ham U
Charlton Ath v Newcastle U
Chelsea v Sheffield U
Everton v Arsenal
Manchester U v Bolton W
Middlesbrough v Manchester C
Reading v Portsmouth
Tottenham H v Watford
Wigan Ath v Fulham

Coca-Cola Football League Championship
Coventry C v Barnsley
Derby Co v Cardiff C
Leicester C v QPR
Luton T v Ipswich T
Norwich C v Stoke C
Plymouth Arg v Crystal Palace
Preston NE v Burnley
Sheffield W v Wolverhampton W
Southampton v Colchester U
Southend U v Leeds U
Sunderland v Hull C
WBA v Birmingham C

Coca-Cola Football League One
Bournemouth v Millwall
Bradford C v Northampton T
Brentford v Rotherham U
Brighton & HA v Scunthorpe U
Carlisle U v Huddersfield T
Crewe Alex v Bristol C

Doncaster R v Cheltenham T
Leyton Orient v Oldham Ath
Nottingham F v Gillingham
Port Vale v Tranmere R
Swansea C v Chesterfield
Yeovil T v Blackpool

Coca-Cola Football League Two
Accrington S v Torquay U
Bristol R v Notts Co
Bury v Macclesfield T
Chester C v Rochdale
Darlington v Hereford U
Grimsby T v Swindon T
Lincoln C v Barnet
Mansfield T v Boston U
Milton Keynes Dons v Wrexham
Shrewsbury T v Peterborough U
Stockport Co v Hartlepool U
Wycombe W v Walsall

Saturday, 24 March 2007
Coca-Cola Football League One
Bournemouth v Tranmere R
Bradford C v Blackpool
Brentford v Oldham Ath
Brighton & HA v Huddersfield T
Carlisle U v Gillingham
Crewe Alex v Rotherham U
Doncaster R v Bristol C
Leyton Orient v Scunthorpe U
Nottingham F v Cheltenham T
Port Vale v Millwall
Swansea C v Northampton T
Yeovil T v Chesterfield

Coca-Cola Football League Two
Accrington S v Hereford U
Bristol R v Wrexham
Bury v Notts Co
Chester C v Barnet
Darlington v Hartlepool U
Grimsby T v Peterborough U
Lincoln C v Swindon T
Mansfield T v Macclesfield T
Milton Keynes Dons v Walsall
Shrewsbury T v Torquay U
Stockport Co v Rochdale
Wycombe W v Boston U

Saturday, 31 March 2007
Barclays Premiership
Aston Villa v Everton
Bolton W v Sheffield U
Charlton Ath v Wigan Ath
Fulham v Portsmouth
Liverpool v Arsenal
Manchester U v Blackburn R
Newcastle U v Manchester C
Tottenham H v Reading
Watford v Chelsea
West Ham U v Middlesbrough

Coca-Cola Football League Championship
Barnsley v Derby Co
Birmingham C v Coventry C
Burnley v Luton T
Cardiff C v Sunderland
Colchester U v Norwich C
Crystal Palace v Sheffield W
Hull C v Southend U
Ipswich T v Plymouth Arg
Leeds U v Preston NE
QPR v WBA
Stoke C v Leicester C
Wolverhampton W v Southampton

Coca-Cola Football League One
Blackpool v Crewe Alex
Bristol C v Nottingham F
Cheltenham T v Leyton Orient
Chesterfield v Doncaster R
Gillingham v Brentford
Huddersfield T v Port Vale
Millwall v Swansea C
Northampton T v Brighton & HA
Oldham Ath v Yeovil T
Rotherham U v Bournemouth
Scunthorpe U v Bradford C
Tranmere R v Carlisle U

Coca-Cola Football League Two
Barnet v Darlington
Boston U v Bury
Hartlepool U v Chester C
Hereford U v Milton Keynes Dons
Macclesfield T v Bristol R
Notts Co v Grimsby T
Peterborough U v Wycombe W
Rochdale v Lincoln C
Swindon T v Shrewsbury T
Torquay U v Stockport Co
Walsall v Accrington S
Wrexham v Mansfield T

Saturday, 7 April 2007
Barclays Premiership
Arsenal v West Ham U
Blackburn R v Aston Villa
Chelsea v Tottenham H
Everton v Fulham
Manchester C v Charlton Ath
Middlesbrough v Watford
Portsmouth v Manchester U
Reading v Liverpool
Sheffield U v Newcastle U
Wigan Ath v Bolton W

Coca-Cola Football League Championship
Birmingham C v Burnley
Cardiff C v Sheffield W
Coventry C v QPR
Crystal Palace v Preston NE
Hull C v Norwich C
Ipswich T v Barnsley
Leeds U v Plymouth Arg
Leicester C v Derby Co
Luton T v Southampton
Southend U v Colchester U
Sunderland v Wolverhampton W
WBA v Stoke C

Coca-Cola Football League One
Blackpool v Tranmere R
Bournemouth v Bradford C
Brentford v Cheltenham T
Brighton & HA v Doncaster R
Bristol C v Swansea C
Chesterfield v Crewe Alex
Leyton Orient v Northampton T
Millwall v Nottingham F
Oldham Ath v Huddersfield T
Port Vale v Carlisle U
Rotherham U v Gillingham
Scunthorpe U v Yeovil T

Coca-Cola Football League Two
Accrington S v Peterborough U
Barnet v Hartlepool U
Bury v Rochdale
Chester C v Darlington
Hereford U v Swindon T
Lincoln C v Stockport Co
Macclesfield T v Wrexham
Mansfield T v Bristol R
Milton Keynes Dons v Grimsby T
Notts Co v Boston U
Torquay U v Walsall
Wycombe W v Shrewsbury T

Monday, 9 April 2007
Barclays Premiership
Aston Villa v Wigan Ath
Bolton W v Everton
Charlton Ath v Reading
Fulham v Manchester C
Liverpool v Middlesbrough
Manchester U v Sheffield U
Newcastle U v Arsenal
Tottenham H v Blackburn R
Watford v Portsmouth
West Ham U v Chelsea

Coca-Cola Football League Championship
Barnsley v Birmingham C
Burnley v Cardiff C
Colchester U v Leeds U
Derby Co v Coventry C
Norwich C v WBA
Plymouth Arg v Leicester C
Preston NE v Southend U
QPR v Luton T
Sheffield W v Ipswich T
Southampton v Sunderland
Stoke C v Crystal Palace
Wolverhampton W v Hull C

Coca-Cola Football League One
Bradford C v Oldham Ath
Carlisle U v Bournemouth
Cheltenham T v Chesterfield
Crewe Alex v Brentford
Doncaster R v Millwall
Gillingham v Bristol C
Huddersfield T v Blackpool
Northampton T v Scunthorpe U
Nottingham F v Rotherham U
Swansea C v Port Vale
Tranmere R v Brighton & HA
Yeovil T v Leyton Orient

Coca-Cola Football League Two
Boston U v Macclesfield T
Bristol R v Bury
Darlington v Lincoln C
Grimsby T v Wycombe W
Hartlepool U v Accrington S
Peterborough U v Mansfield T
Rochdale v Barnet
Shrewsbury T v Milton Keynes Dons
Stockport Co v Chester C
Swindon T v Torquay U
Walsall v Hereford U
Wrexham v Notts Co

Saturday, 14 April 2007
Barclays Premiership
Arsenal v Bolton W
Blackburn R v Watford
Chelsea v Manchester U
Everton v Charlton Ath
Manchester C v Liverpool
Middlesbrough v Aston Villa
Portsmouth v Newcastle U

Reading v Fulham
Sheffield U v West Ham U
Wigan Ath v Tottenham H

Coca-Cola Football League Championship
Birmingham C v Southampton
Cardiff C v Stoke C
Coventry C v Preston NE
Crystal Palace v Wolverhampton W
Hull C v Colchester U
Ipswich T v Derby Co
Leeds U v Burnley
Leicester C v Norwich C
Luton T v Plymouth Arg
Southend U v Barnsley
Sunderland v QPR
WBA v Sheffield W

Coca-Cola Football League One
Blackpool v Northampton T
Bournemouth v Swansea C
Brentford v Nottingham F
Brighton & HA v Bradford C
Bristol C v Yeovil T
Chesterfield v Gillingham
Leyton Orient v Doncaster R
Millwall v Tranmere R
Oldham Ath v Cheltenham T
Port Vale v Crewe Alex
Rotherham U v Carlisle U
Scunthorpe U v Huddersfield T

Coca-Cola Football League Two
Accrington S v Grimsby T
Barnet v Bristol R
Bury v Swindon T
Chester C v Shrewsbury T
Hereford U v Boston U
Lincoln C v Wrexham
Macclesfield T v Stockport Co
Mansfield T v Rochdale
Milton Keynes Dons v Darlington
Notts Co v Walsall
Torquay U v Peterborough U
Wycombe W v Hartlepool U

Saturday, 21 April 2007
Barclays Premiership
Aston Villa v Portsmouth
Bolton W v Reading
Charlton Ath v Sheffield U
Fulham v Blackburn R
Liverpool v Wigan Ath
Manchester U v Middlesbrough
Newcastle U v Chelsea
Tottenham H v Arsenal
Watford v Manchester C
West Ham U v Everton

Coca-Cola Football League Championship
Barnsley v Crystal Palace
Burnley v WBA
Colchester U v Sunderland
Derby Co v Luton T
Norwich C v Ipswich T
Plymouth Arg v Southend U
Preston NE v Leicester C
QPR v Cardiff C
Sheffield W v Coventry C
Southampton v Leeds U
Stoke C v Hull C
Wolverhampton W v Birmingham C

Coca-Cola Football League One
Bradford C v Leyton Orient
Carlisle U v Bristol C
Cheltenham T v Blackpool
Crewe Alex v Oldham Ath
Doncaster R v Brentford
Gillingham v Port Vale
Huddersfield T v Millwall
Northampton T v Chesterfield
Nottingham F v Bournemouth
Swansea C v Brighton & HA
Tranmere R v Scunthorpe U
Yeovil T v Rotherham U

Coca-Cola Football League Two
Boston U v Chester C
Bristol R v Lincoln C
Darlington v Wycombe W
Grimsby T v Barnet
Hartlepool U v Notts Co
Peterborough U v Hereford U
Rochdale v Macclesfield T
Shrewsbury T v Accrington S
Stockport Co v Milton Keynes Dons
Swindon T v Mansfield T
Walsall v Bury
Wrexham v Torquay U

Saturday, 28 April 2007
Barclays Premiership
Arsenal v Fulham
Blackburn R v Charlton Ath
Chelsea v Bolton W
Everton v Manchester U
Manchester C v Aston Villa
Middlesbrough v Tottenham H
Portsmouth v Liverpool
Reading v Newcastle U
Sheffield U v Watford
Wigan Ath v West Ham U

Coca-Cola Football League Championship
Barnsley v Leicester C
Birmingham C v Sheffield W
Cardiff C v Hull C
Coventry C v WBA
Crystal Palace v Derby Co
Leeds U v Ipswich T
Norwich C v Southampton
Plymouth Arg v Preston NE
Southend U v Luton T
Stoke C v Colchester U
Sunderland v Burnley
Wolverhampton W v QPR

Coca-Cola Football League One
Blackpool v Scunthorpe U
Bournemouth v Gillingham
Brentford v Port Vale
Brighton & HA v Oldham Ath
Carlisle U v Swansea C
Chesterfield v Bradford C
Crewe Alex v Tranmere R
Leyton Orient v Nottingham F
Millwall v Bristol C
Northampton T v Huddersfield T
Rotherham U v Cheltenham T
Yeovil T v Doncaster R

Coca-Cola Football League Two
Accrington S v Macclesfield T
Boston U v Torquay U
Bristol R v Swindon T
Chester C v Peterborough U
Grimsby T v Lincoln C
Hereford U v Shrewsbury T
Mansfield T v Barnet
Notts Co v Darlington
Rochdale v Hartlepool U
Stockport Co v Bury
Walsall v Wrexham
Wycombe W v Milton Keynes Dons

Saturday, 5 May 2007
Barclays Premiership
Arsenal v Chelsea
Aston Villa v Sheffield U
Charlton Ath v Tottenham H
Everton v Portsmouth
Fulham v Liverpool
Manchester C v Manchester U
Newcastle U v Blackburn R
Reading v Watford
West Ham U v Bolton W
Wigan Ath v Middlesbrough

Coca-Cola Football League One
Bradford C v Millwall
Bristol C v Rotherham U
Cheltenham T v Brighton & HA
Doncaster R v Northampton T
Gillingham v Yeovil T
Huddersfield T v Leyton Orient
Nottingham F v Crewe Alex
Oldham Ath v Chesterfield
Port Vale v Bournemouth
Scunthorpe U v Carlisle U
Swansea C v Blackpool
Tranmere R v Brentford

Coca-Cola Football League Two
Barnet v Wycombe W
Bury v Mansfield T
Darlington v Stockport Co
Hartlepool U v Bristol R
Lincoln C v Chester C
Macclesfield T v Notts Co
Milton Keynes Dons v Accrington S
Peterborough U v Rochdale
Shrewsbury T v Grimsby T
Swindon T v Walsall
Torquay U v Hereford U
Wrexham v Boston U

Sunday, 6 May 2007
Coca-Cola Football League Championship
Burnley v Coventry C
Colchester U v Crystal Palace
Derby Co v Leeds U
Hull C v Plymouth Arg
Ipswich T v Cardiff C
Leicester C v Wolverhampton W
Luton T v Sunderland
Preston NE v Birmingham C
QPR v Stoke C
Sheffield W v Norwich C
Southampton v Southend U
WBA v Barnsley

Sunday, 13 May 2007
Barclays Premiership
Blackburn R v Reading
Bolton W v Aston Villa
Chelsea v Everton
Liverpool v Charlton Ath
Manchester U v West Ham U
Middlesbrough v Fulham
Portsmouth v Arsenal
Sheffield U v Wigan Ath
Tottenham H v Manchester C
Watford v Newcastle U

CONFERENCE NATIONAL FIXTURES 2006–07

Saturday, 12 August 2006
Aldershot T v Gravesend & N
Altrincham T v Stevenage B
Cambridge U v Northwich Vic
Crawley T v Rushden & D'monds
Forest Green R v Dagenham & Red
Grays Ath v Stafford R
Kidderminster H v St Albans
Morecambe v Burton Alb
Oxford U v Halifax T
Southport v Woking
Tamworth v Weymouth
York C v Exeter C

Tuesday, 15 August 2006
Burton Alb v Kidderminster H
Dagenham & Red v Oxford U
Exeter C v Forest Green R
Gravesend & N v Tamworth
Halifax T v Southport
Northwich Vic v Morecambe
Rushden & D'monds v Grays Ath
St Albans v Cambridge U
Stafford R v Altrincham T
Stevenage B v York C
Weymouth v Aldershot T
Woking v Crawley T

Saturday, 19 August 2006
Burton Alb v Oxford U
Dagenham & Red v Tamworth
Exeter C v Altrincham T
Gravesend & N v York C
Halifax T v Grays Ath
Northwich Vic v Kidderminster H
Rushden & D'monds v Forest Green R
St Albans v Aldershot T
Stafford R v Southport
Stevenage B v Crawley T
Weymouth v Cambridge U
Woking v Morecambe

Saturday, 26 August 2006
Aldershot T v Dagenham & Red
Altrincham T v St Albans
Cambridge U v Halifax T
Crawley T v Stafford R
Forest Green R v Gravesend & N
Grays Ath v Woking
Kidderminster H v Weymouth
Morecambe v Stevenage B
Oxford U v Northwich Vic
Southport v Rushden & D'monds
Tamworth v Exeter C
York C v Burton Alb

Monday, 28 August 2006
Burton Alb v Southport
Dagenham & Red v Cambridge U
Exeter C v Crawley T
Gravesend & N v Altrincham T
Halifax T v Morecambe
Northwich Vic v Grays Ath
Rushden & D'monds v York C
St Albans v Tamworth
Stafford R v Aldershot T
Stevenage B v Forest Green R
Weymouth v Oxford U
Woking v Kidderminster H

Saturday, 2 September 2006
Tamworth v Stevenage B

Sunday, 3 September 2006
Aldershot T v Halifax T
Altrincham T v Dagenham & Red
Cambridge U v Exeter C
Crawley T v Northwich Vic
Forest Green R v Woking
Grays Ath v Burton Alb
Kidderminster H v Rushden & D'monds
Morecambe v Weymouth
Oxford U v St Albans
Southport v Gravesend & N
York C v Stafford R

Saturday, 9 September 2006
Burton Alb v Weymouth
Crawley T v York C
Exeter C v Aldershot T
Forest Green R v Cambridge U
Grays Ath v Southport
Halifax T v Gravesend & N
Kidderminster H v Tamworth
Morecambe v Oxford U
Northwich Vic v St Albans
Rushden & D'monds v Altrincham T
Stevenage B v Stafford R
Woking v Dagenham & Red

Tuesday, 12 September 2006
Aldershot T v Stevenage B
Altrincham T v Halifax T
Cambridge U v Kidderminster H
Dagenham & Red v Crawley T
Gravesend & N v Grays Ath
Oxford U v Exeter C
Southport v Northwich Vic
St Albans v Woking
Stafford R v Burton Alb
Tamworth v Rushden & D'monds
Weymouth v Forest Green R
York C v Morecambe

Saturday, 16 September 2006
Aldershot T v Northwich Vic
Altrincham T v Woking
Cambridge U v Stevenage B
Dagenham & Red v Morecambe
Gravesend & N v Exeter C
Oxford U v Grays Ath
Southport v Crawley T
St Albans v Burton Alb
Stafford R v Rushden & D'monds
Tamworth v Forest Green R
Weymouth v Halifax T
York C v Kidderminster H

Tuesday, 19 September 2006
Burton Alb v Cambridge U
Crawley T v Oxford U
Exeter C v St Albans
Forest Green R v Altrincham T
Grays Ath v Aldershot T
Halifax T v Dagenham & Red
Kidderminster H v Southport
Morecambe v Tamworth
Northwich Vic v Stafford R
Rushden & D'monds v Gravesend & N
Stevenage B v Weymouth
Woking v York C

Saturday, 23 September 2006
Altrincham T v Tamworth
Burton Alb v Northwich Vic
Cambridge U v Aldershot T
Crawley T v Grays Ath
Dagenham & Red v Weymouth
Exeter C v Stevenage B
Halifax T v Forest Green R
Morecambe v Kidderminster H
St Albans v Gravesend & N
Stafford R v Oxford U
Woking v Rushden & D'monds
York C v Southport

Saturday, 30 September 2006
Aldershot T v Altrincham T
Forest Green R v Stafford R
Gravesend & N v Dagenham & Red
Grays Ath v Morecambe
Kidderminster H v Crawley T
Northwich Vic v Woking
Oxford U v York C
Rushden & D'monds v Burton Alb
Southport v Exeter C
Stevenage B v Halifax T
Tamworth v Cambridge U
Weymouth v St Albans

Tuesday, 3 October 2006
Aldershot T v Tamworth
Burton Alb v Crawley T
Cambridge U v Altrincham T
Grays Ath v Exeter C
Halifax T v Kidderminster H
Morecambe v Rushden & D'monds
Northwich Vic v York C
Oxford U v Southport
St Albans v Forest Green R
Stafford R v Dagenham & Red
Stevenage B v Woking
Weymouth v Gravesend & N

Saturday, 7 October 2006
Tamworth v Stafford R

Sunday, 8 October 2006
Altrincham T v Weymouth
Crawley T v Morecambe
Dagenham & Red v Northwich Vic
Exeter C v Halifax T
Forest Green R v Oxford U
Gravesend & N v Cambridge U
Kidderminster H v Grays Ath
Rushden & D'monds v Stevenage B
Southport v St Albans
Woking v Burton Alb
York C v Aldershot T

Tuesday, 10 October 2006
Altrincham T v Morecambe
Crawley T v Weymouth
Dagenham & Red v St Albans
Exeter C v Northwich Vic
Forest Green R v Burton Alb
Gravesend & N v Stafford R
Kidderminster H v Oxford U
Rushden & D'monds v Halifax T
Southport v Stevenage B
Tamworth v Grays Ath
Woking v Aldershot T
York C v Cambridge U

Saturday, 14 October 2006
Aldershot T v Kidderminster H
Burton Alb v Gravesend & N
Cambridge U v Crawley T
Grays Ath v Forest Green R

Halifax T v Tamworth
Morecambe v Exeter C
Northwich Vic v Rushden & D'monds
Oxford U v Altrincham T
St Albans v York C
Stafford R v Woking
Stevenage B v Dagenham & Red
Weymouth v Southport

Saturday, 21 October 2006
Aldershot T v Morecambe
Altrincham T v Southport
Cambridge U v Oxford U
Dagenham & Red v Kidderminster H
Exeter C v Stafford R
Forest Green R v Crawley T
Gravesend & N v Woking
Halifax T v Burton Alb
St Albans v Grays Ath
Stevenage B v Northwich Vic
Tamworth v York C
Weymouth v Rushden & D'monds

Friday, 3 November 2006
Burton Alb v Stevenage B

Saturday, 4 November 2006
Crawley T v St Albans
Grays Ath v Cambridge U
Kidderminster H v Forest Green R
Morecambe v Gravesend & N
Northwich Vic v Halifax T
Oxford U v Aldershot T
Rushden & D'monds v Dagenham & Red
Southport v Tamworth
Stafford R v Weymouth
Woking v Exeter C
York C v Altrincham T

Saturday, 18 November 2006
Aldershot T v Southport
Altrincham T v Crawley T
Cambridge U v Morecambe
Dagenham & Red v Burton Alb
Exeter C v Kidderminster H
Forest Green R v Northwich Vic
Gravesend & N v Oxford U
Halifax T v Stafford R
St Albans v Rushden & D'monds
Stevenage B v Grays Ath
Tamworth v Woking
Weymouth v York C

Saturday, 25 November 2006
Burton Alb v Exeter C
Crawley T v Halifax T
Grays Ath v Altrincham T
Kidderminster H v Stevenage B
Morecambe v Forest Green R
Northwich Vic v Gravesend & N
Oxford U v Tamworth
Rushden & D'monds v Aldershot T
Southport v Cambridge U
Stafford R v St Albans
Woking v Weymouth
York C v Dagenham & Red

Saturday, 2 December 2006
Aldershot T v Crawley T
Altrincham T v Burton Alb
Cambridge U v Stafford R
Dagenham & Red v Southport
Exeter C v Rushden & D'monds
Forest Green R v York C
Gravesend & N v Kidderminster H
Halifax T v Woking
St Albans v Morecambe
Stevenage B v Oxford U
Tamworth v Northwich Vic
Weymouth v Grays Ath

Saturday, 9 December 2006
Burton Alb v Aldershot T
Crawley T v Tamworth
Exeter C v Dagenham & Red
Forest Green R v Southport
Grays Ath v York C
Halifax T v St Albans
Kidderminster H v Altrincham T
Morecambe v Stafford R
Northwich Vic v Weymouth
Rushden & D'monds v Oxford U
Stevenage B v Gravesend & N
Woking v Cambridge U

Tuesday, 26 December 2006
Aldershot T v Forest Green R
Altrincham T v Northwich Vic
Cambridge U v Rushden & D'monds
Dagenham & Red v Grays Ath
Gravesend & N v Crawley T
Oxford U v Woking
Southport v Morecambe
St Albans v Stevenage B
Stafford R v Kidderminster H
Tamworth v Burton Alb
Weymouth v Exeter C
York C v Halifax T

Saturday, 30 December 2006
Aldershot T v Grays Ath
Altrincham T v Forest Green R
Cambridge U v Burton Alb
Dagenham & Red v Halifax T
Gravesend & N v Rushden & D'monds
Oxford U v Crawley T
Southport v Kidderminster H
St Albans v Exeter C
Stafford R v Northwich Vic
Tamworth v Morecambe
Weymouth v Stevenage B
York C v Woking

Monday, 1 January 2007
Burton Alb v Stafford R
Crawley T v Dagenham & Red
Exeter C v Oxford U
Forest Green R v Weymouth
Grays Ath v Gravesend & N
Halifax T v Altrincham T
Kidderminster H v Cambridge U
Morecambe v York C
Northwich Vic v Southport
Rushden & D'monds v Tamworth
Stevenage B v Aldershot T
Woking v St Albans

Saturday, 6 January 2007
Aldershot T v Exeter C
Altrincham T v Rushden & D'monds
Cambridge U v Forest Green R
Dagenham & Red v Woking
Gravesend & N v Halifax T
Oxford U v Morecambe
Southport v Grays Ath
St Albans v Northwich Vic
Stafford R v Stevenage B
Tamworth v Kidderminster H
Weymouth v Burton Alb
York C v Crawley T

Saturday, 20 January 2007
Burton Alb v St Albans
Crawley T v Southport
Exeter C v Gravesend & N
Forest Green R v Tamworth
Grays Ath v Oxford U
Halifax T v Weymouth
Kidderminster H v York C
Morecambe v Dagenham & Red
Northwich Vic v Aldershot T
Rushden & D'monds v Stafford R
Stevenage B v Cambridge U
Woking v Altrincham T

Tuesday, 23 January 2007
Burton Alb v Tamworth
Crawley T v Gravesend & N
Exeter C v Weymouth
Forest Green R v Aldershot T
Grays Ath v Dagenham & Red
Halifax T v York C
Kidderminster H v Stafford R
Morecambe v Southport
Northwich Vic v Altrincham T
Rushden & D'monds v Cambridge U
Stevenage B v St Albans
Woking v Oxford U

Saturday, 27 January 2007
Aldershot T v Burton Alb
Altrincham T v Kidderminster H
Cambridge U v Woking
Dagenham & Red v Exeter C
Gravesend & N v Stevenage B
Oxford U v Rushden & D'monds
Southport v Forest Green R
St Albans v Halifax T
Stafford R v Morecambe
Tamworth v Crawley T
Weymouth v Northwich Vic
York C v Grays Ath

Saturday, 3 February 2007
Burton Alb v Halifax T
Crawley T v Forest Green R
Grays Ath v St Albans
Kidderminster H v Dagenham & Red
Morecambe v Aldershot T
Northwich Vic v Stevenage B
Oxford U v Cambridge U
Rushden & D'monds v Weymouth
Southport v Altrincham T
Stafford R v Exeter C
Woking v Gravesend & N
York C v Tamworth

Saturday, 10 February 2007
Aldershot T v Oxford U
Altrincham T v York C
Cambridge U v Grays Ath
Dagenham & Red v Rushden & D'monds
Exeter C v Woking
Forest Green R v Kidderminster H
Gravesend & N v Morecambe
Halifax T v Northwich Vic
St Albans v Crawley T
Stevenage B v Burton Alb
Tamworth v Southport
Weymouth v Stafford R

Saturday, 17 February 2007
Burton Alb v Dagenham & Red
Crawley T v Altrincham T
Grays Ath v Stevenage B
Kidderminster H v Exeter C
Morecambe v Cambridge U

Northwich Vic v Forest Green R
Oxford U v Gravesend & N
Rushden & D'monds v St Albans
Southport v Aldershot T
Stafford R v Halifax T
Woking v Tamworth
York C v Weymouth

Saturday, 24 February 2007
Aldershot T v Rushden & D'monds
Altrincham T v Grays Ath
Cambridge U v Southport
Dagenham & Red v York C
Exeter C v Burton Alb
Forest Green R v Morecambe
Gravesend & N v Northwich Vic
Halifax T v Crawley T
St Albans v Stafford R
Stevenage B v Kidderminster H
Tamworth v Oxford U
Weymouth v Woking

Saturday, 3 March 2007
Burton Alb v Altrincham T
Crawley T v Aldershot T
Grays Ath v Weymouth
Kidderminster H v Gravesend & N
Morecambe v St Albans
Northwich Vic v Tamworth
Oxford U v Stevenage B
Rushden & D'monds v Exeter C
Southport v Dagenham & Red
Stafford R v Cambridge U
Woking v Halifax T
York C v Forest Green R

Tuesday, 6 March 2007
Altrincham T v Cambridge U
Crawley T v Burton Alb
Dagenham & Red v Stafford R
Exeter C v Grays Ath
Forest Green R v St Albans
Gravesend & N v Weymouth
Kidderminster H v Halifax T
Rushden & D'monds v Morecambe
Southport v Oxford U
Tamworth v Aldershot T
Woking v Stevenage B
York C v Northwich Vic

Saturday, 10 March 2007
Aldershot T v York C
Burton Alb v Woking
Cambridge U v Gravesend & N
Grays Ath v Kidderminster H
Halifax T v Exeter C
Morecambe v Crawley T
Northwich Vic v Dagenham & Red
Oxford U v Forest Green R
St Albans v Southport
Stafford R v Tamworth
Stevenage B v Rushden & D'monds
Weymouth v Altrincham T

Tuesday, 13 March 2007
Aldershot T v Woking
Burton Alb v Forest Green R
Cambridge U v York C
Grays Ath v Tamworth
Halifax T v Rushden & D'monds
Morecambe v Altrincham T
Northwich Vic v Exeter C
Oxford U v Kidderminster H
St Albans v Dagenham & Red
Stafford R v Gravesend & N
Stevenage B v Southport
Weymouth v Crawley T

Saturday, 17 March 2007
Altrincham T v Oxford U
Crawley T v Cambridge U
Dagenham & Red v Stevenage B
Exeter C v Morecambe
Forest Green R v Grays Ath
Gravesend & N v Burton Alb
Kidderminster H v Aldershot T
Rushden & D'monds v Northwich Vic
Southport v Weymouth
Tamworth v Halifax T
Woking v Stafford R
York C v St Albans

Sunday, 25 March 2007
Burton Alb v Morecambe
Dagenham & Red v Forest Green R
Exeter C v York C
Gravesend & N v Aldershot T
Halifax T v Oxford U
Northwich Vic v Cambridge U
Rushden & D'monds v Crawley T
St Albans v Kidderminster H
Stafford R v Grays Ath
Stevenage B v Altrincham T
Weymouth v Tamworth
Woking v Southport

Tuesday, 27 March 2007
Aldershot T v Weymouth
Altrincham T v Stafford R
Cambridge U v St Albans
Crawley T v Woking
Forest Green R v Exeter C
Grays Ath v Rushden & D'monds
Kidderminster H v Burton Alb
Morecambe v Northwich Vic
Oxford U v Dagenham & Red
Southport v Halifax T
Tamworth v Gravesend & N
York C v Stevenage B

Saturday, 31 March 2007
Aldershot T v St Albans
Altrincham T v Exeter C
Cambridge U v Weymouth
Crawley T v Stevenage B
Forest Green R v Rushden & D'monds
Grays Ath v Halifax T
Kidderminster H v Northwich Vic
Morecambe v Woking
Oxford U v Burton Alb
Southport v Stafford R
Tamworth v Dagenham & Red
York C v Gravesend & N

Saturday, 7 April 2007
Burton Alb v York C
Dagenham & Red v Aldershot T
Exeter C v Tamworth
Gravesend & N v Forest Green R
Halifax T v Cambridge U
Northwich Vic v Oxford U
Rushden & D'monds v Southport
St Albans v Altrincham T
Stafford R v Crawley T
Stevenage B v Morecambe
Weymouth v Kidderminster H
Woking v Grays Ath

Monday, 9 April 2007
Aldershot T v Stafford R
Altrincham T v Gravesend & N
Cambridge U v Dagenham & Red
Crawley T v Exeter C
Forest Green R v Stevenage B
Grays Ath v Northwich Vic
Kidderminster H v Woking
Morecambe v Halifax T
Oxford U v Weymouth
Southport v Burton Alb
Tamworth v St Albans
York C v Rushden & D'monds

Saturday, 14 April 2007
Burton Alb v Grays Ath
Dagenham & Red v Altrincham T
Exeter C v Cambridge U
Gravesend & N v Southport
Halifax T v Aldershot T
Northwich Vic v Crawley T
Rushden & D'monds v Kidderminster H
St Albans v Oxford U
Stafford R v York C
Stevenage B v Tamworth
Weymouth v Morecambe
Woking v Forest Green R

Saturday, 21 April 2007
Aldershot T v Cambridge U
Forest Green R v Halifax T
Gravesend & N v St Albans
Grays Ath v Crawley T
Kidderminster H v Morecambe
Northwich Vic v Burton Alb
Oxford U v Stafford R
Rushden & D'monds v Woking
Southport v York C
Stevenage B v Exeter C
Tamworth v Altrincham T
Weymouth v Dagenham & Red

Saturday, 28 April 2007
Altrincham T v Aldershot T
Burton Alb v Rushden & D'monds
Cambridge U v Tamworth
Crawley T v Kidderminster H
Dagenham & Red v Gravesend & N
Exeter C v Southport
Halifax T v Stevenage B
Morecambe v Grays Ath
St Albans v Weymouth
Stafford R v Forest Green R
Woking v Northwich Vic
York C v Oxford U

THE SCOTTISH PREMIER LEAGUE AND FOOTBALL LEAGUE FIXTURES 2006–07

Saturday, 29 July 2006

Bank of Scotland

Scottish Premier League
Celtic v Kilmarnock
Dundee U v Falkirk
Dunfermline Ath v Hearts
Hibernian v Aberdeen
Inverness CT v St Mirren

Sunday, 30 July 2006

Bank of Scotland

Scottish Premier League
Motherwell v Rangers

Saturday, 5 August 2006

Bank of Scotland

Scottish Premier League
Aberdeen v Inverness CT
Falkirk v Dunfermline Ath
Kilmarnock v Hibernian
Rangers v Dundee U
St Mirren v Motherwell

Bell's Scottish First Division
Airdrie U v Ross Co
Dundee v Partick T
Gretna v Hamilton A
Livingston v Queen of the S
St Johnstone v Clyde

Bell's Scottish Second Division
Cowdenbeath v Alloa Ath
Forfar Ath v Stranraer
Morton v Raith R
Peterhead v Brechin C
Stirling Alb v Ayr U

Bell's Scottish Third Division
Berwick R v Albion R
East Fife v Stenhousemuir
East Stirlingshire v Elgin C
Montrose v Dumbarton
Queen's Park v Arbroath

Sunday, 6 August 2006

Bank of Scotland

Scottish Premier League
Hearts v Celtic

Saturday, 12 August 2006

Bank of Scotland

Scottish Premier League
Celtic v St Mirren
Hearts v Falkirk
Inverness CT v Hibernian
Kilmarnock v Dundee U
Motherwell v Aberdeen

Bell's Scottish First Division
Clyde v Gretna
Hamilton A v Dundee
Partick T v Airdrie U
Queen of the S v St Johnstone
Ross Co v Livingston

Bell's Scottish Second Division
Alloa Ath v Peterhead
Ayr U v Cowdenbeath
Brechin C v Stirling Alb
Raith R v Forfar Ath
Stranraer v Morton

Bell's Scottish Third Division
Albion R v East Fife
Arbroath v Berwick R
Dumbarton v East Stirlingshire
Elgin C v Queen's Park
Stenhousemuir v Montrose

Sunday, 13 August 2006

Bank of Scotland

Scottish Premier League
Dunfermline Ath v Rangers

Saturday, 19 August 2006

Bank of Scotland

Scottish Premier League
Dundee U v Dunfermline Ath
Falkirk v Kilmarnock
Hibernian v Motherwell
Rangers v Hearts
St Mirren v Aberdeen

Bell's Scottish First Division
Airdrie U v Queen of the S
Dundee v Clyde
Gretna v Ross Co
Livingston v Partick T
St Johnstone v Hamilton A

Bell's Scottish Second Division
Cowdenbeath v Brechin C
Forfar Ath v Alloa Ath
Morton v Ayr U
Peterhead v Raith R
Stirling Alb v Stranraer

Bell's Scottish Third Division
Berwick R v Stenhousemuir
East Fife v Arbroath
East Stirlingshire v Albion R
Montrose v Elgin C
Queen's Park v Dumbarton

Sunday, 20 August 2006

Bank of Scotland

Scottish Premier League
Inverness CT v Celtic

Saturday, 26 August 2006

Bank of Scotland

Scottish Premier League
Aberdeen v Dunfermline Ath
Celtic v Hibernian
Falkirk v Motherwell
Hearts v Inverness CT
St Mirren v Dundee U

Bell's Scottish First Division
Airdrie U v Hamilton A
Clyde v Partick T
Dundee v Livingston
Queen of the S v Gretna
St Johnstone v Ross Co

Bell's Scottish Second Division
Alloa Ath v Stirling Alb
Ayr U v Stranraer
Brechin C v Forfar Ath
Peterhead v Morton
Raith R v Cowdenbeath

Bell's Scottish Third Division
Albion R v Queen's Park
Arbroath v Montrose
Berwick R v Dumbarton
East Stirlingshire v Stenhousemuir
Elgin C v East Fife

Sunday, 27 August 2006

Bank of Scotland

Scottish Premier League
Kilmarnock v Rangers

Sunday, 3 September 2006

Bell's Scottish Second Division
Cowdenbeath v Peterhead
Forfar Ath v Ayr U
Morton v Alloa Ath
Stirling Alb v Raith R
Stranraer v Brechin C

Bell's Scottish Third Division
Dumbarton v Arbroath
East Fife v East Stirlingshire
Montrose v Albion R
Queen's Park v Berwick R
Stenhousemuir v Elgin C

Saturday, 9 September 2006

Bank of Scotland

Scottish Premier League
Aberdeen v Celtic
Dundee U v Hibernian
Dunfermline Ath v Kilmarnock
Hearts v St Mirren
Motherwell v Inverness CT
Rangers v Falkirk

Bell's Scottish First Division
Gretna v Dundee
Hamilton A v Clyde
Livingston v Airdrie U
Partick T v St Johnstone
Ross Co v Queen of the S

Bell's Scottish Second Division
Ayr U v Peterhead
Brechin C v Alloa Ath
Cowdenbeath v Morton
Stirling Alb v Forfar Ath
Stranraer v Raith R

Bell's Scottish Third Division
Arbroath v Albion R
Berwick R v East Stirlingshire
Elgin C v Dumbarton
Montrose v East Fife
Stenhousemuir v Queen's Park

Saturday, 16 September 2006
Bank of Scotland
Scottish Premier League
Celtic v Dunfermline Ath
Falkirk v Aberdeen
Inverness CT v Dundee U
Motherwell v Hearts
St Mirren v Kilmarnock

Bell's Scottish First Division
Clyde v Ross Co
Dundee v Queen of the S
Gretna v Livingston
Hamilton A v Partick T
St Johnstone v Airdrie U

Bell's Scottish Second Division
Alloa Ath v Ayr U
Forfar Ath v Cowdenbeath
Morton v Stirling Alb
Peterhead v Stranraer
Raith R v Brechin C

Bell's Scottish Third Division
Albion R v Elgin C
Dumbarton v Stenhousemuir
East Fife v Berwick R
East Stirlingshire v Arbroath
Queen's Park v Montrose

Sunday, 17 September 2006
Bank of Scotland
Scottish Premier League
Hibernian v Rangers

Saturday, 23 September 2006
Bank of Scotland
Scottish Premier League
Aberdeen v Hearts
Celtic v Rangers
Dundee U v Motherwell
Dunfermline Ath v St Mirren
Hibernian v Falkirk
Kilmarnock v Inverness CT

Bell's Scottish First Division
Airdrie U v Dundee
Livingston v St Johnstone
Partick T v Gretna
Queen of the S v Clyde
Ross Co v Hamilton A

Bell's Scottish Second Division
Brechin C v Ayr U
Forfar Ath v Morton
Raith R v Alloa Ath
Stirling Alb v Peterhead
Stranraer v Cowdenbeath

Bell's Scottish Third Division
Dumbarton v Albion R
Elgin C v Berwick R
Montrose v East Stirlingshire
Queen's Park v East Fife
Stenhousemuir v Arbroath

Saturday, 30 September 2006
Bank of Scotland
Scottish Premier League
Hearts v Dundee U
Inverness CT v Dunfermline Ath
Motherwell v Kilmarnock
Rangers v Aberdeen
St Mirren v Hibernian

Bell's Scottish First Division
Clyde v Livingston
Dundee v St Johnstone
Gretna v Airdrie U
Hamilton A v Queen of the S
Partick T v Ross Co

Bell's Scottish Second Division
Alloa Ath v Stranraer
Ayr U v Raith R
Cowdenbeath v Stirling Alb
Morton v Brechin C
Peterhead v Forfar Ath

Bell's Scottish Third Division
Albion R v Stenhousemuir
Arbroath v Elgin C
Berwick R v Montrose
East Fife v Dumbarton
East Stirlingshire v Queen's Park

Sunday, 1 October 2006
Bank of Scotland
Scottish Premier League
Falkirk v Celtic

Saturday, 14 October 2006
Bank of Scotland
Scottish Premier League
Dundee U v Celtic
Falkirk v St Mirren
Hibernian v Hearts
Kilmarnock v Aberdeen
Motherwell v Dunfermline Ath
Rangers v Inverness CT

Bell's Scottish First Division
Airdrie U v Clyde
Livingston v Hamilton A
Queen of the S v Partick T
Ross Co v Dundee
St Johnstone v Gretna

Bell's Scottish Second Division
Alloa Ath v Cowdenbeath
Ayr U v Stirling Alb
Brechin C v Peterhead
Raith R v Morton
Stranraer v Forfar Ath

Bell's Scottish Third Division
Albion R v Berwick R
Arbroath v Queen's Park
Dumbarton v Montrose
Elgin C v East Stirlingshire
Stenhousemuir v East Fife

Saturday, 21 October 2006
Bank of Scotland
Scottish Premier League
Aberdeen v Dundee U
Celtic v Motherwell
Dunfermline Ath v Hibernian
Hearts v Kilmarnock
Inverness CT v Falkirk

Bell's Scottish First Division
Airdrie U v Partick T
Dundee v Hamilton A
Gretna v Clyde
Livingston v Ross Co
St Johnstone v Queen of the S

Bell's Scottish Second Division
Cowdenbeath v Ayr U
Forfar Ath v Raith R
Morton v Stranraer
Peterhead v Alloa Ath
Stirling Alb v Brechin C

Bell's Scottish Third Division
Berwick R v Arbroath
East Fife v Albion R
East Stirlingshire v Dumbarton
Montrose v Stenhousemuir
Queen's Park v Elgin C

Sunday, 22 October 2006
Bank of Scotland
Scottish Premier League
St Mirren v Rangers

Saturday, 28 October 2006
Bank of Scotland
Scottish Premier League
Aberdeen v Hibernian
Falkirk v Dundee U
Hearts v Dunfermline Ath
Kilmarnock v Celtic
Rangers v Motherwell
St Mirren v Inverness CT

Bell's Scottish First Division
Clyde v St Johnstone
Hamilton A v Gretna
Partick T v Dundee
Queen of the S v Livingston
Ross Co v Airdrie U

Bell's Scottish Second Division
Alloa Ath v Morton
Ayr U v Forfar Ath

Brechin C v Stranraer
Peterhead v Cowdenbeath
Raith R v Stirling Alb

Bell's Scottish Third Division
Albion R v Montrose
Arbroath v Dumbarton
Berwick R v Queen's Park
East Stirlingshire v East Fife
Elgin C v Stenhousemuir

Saturday, 4 November 2006

Bank of Scotland

Scottish Premier League
Celtic v Hearts
Dunfermline Ath v Falkirk
Hibernian v Kilmarnock
Inverness CT v Aberdeen
Motherwell v St Mirren

Bell's Scottish First Division
Airdrie U v Livingston
Clyde v Hamilton A
Dundee v Gretna
Queen of the S v Ross Co
St Johnstone v Partick T

Bell's Scottish Second Division
Cowdenbeath v Raith R
Forfar Ath v Brechin C
Morton v Peterhead
Stirling Alb v Alloa Ath
Stranraer v Ayr U

Bell's Scottish Third Division
Dumbarton v Berwick R
East Fife v Elgin C
Montrose v Arbroath
Queen's Park v Albion R
Stenhousemuir v East Stirlingshire

Sunday, 5 November 2006

Bank of Scotland

Scottish Premier League
Dundee U v Rangers

Saturday, 11 November 2006

Bank of Scotland

Scottish Premier League
Aberdeen v Motherwell
Dundee U v Kilmarnock
Falkirk v Hearts
Hibernian v Inverness CT
Rangers v Dunfermline Ath

Bell's Scottish First Division
Gretna v Queen of the S
Hamilton A v Airdrie U
Livingston v Dundee
Partick T v Clyde
Ross Co v St Johnstone

Bell's Scottish Second Division
Ayr U v Alloa Ath
Brechin C v Raith R
Cowdenbeath v Forfar Ath
Stirling Alb v Morton
Stranraer v Peterhead

Bell's Scottish Third Division
Arbroath v East Stirlingshire
Berwick R v East Fife
Elgin C v Albion R
Montrose v Queen's Park
Stenhousemuir v Dumbarton

Sunday, 12 November 2006

Bank of Scotland

Scottish Premier League
St Mirren v Celtic

Saturday, 18 November 2006

Bank of Scotland

Scottish Premier League
Aberdeen v St Mirren
Celtic v Inverness CT
Dunfermline Ath v Dundee U
Hearts v Rangers
Kilmarnock v Falkirk
Motherwell v Hibernian

Bell's Scottish First Division
Airdrie U v St Johnstone
Livingston v Gretna
Partick T v Hamilton A
Queen of the S v Dundee
Ross Co v Clyde

Saturday, 25 November 2006

Bank of Scotland

Scottish Premier League
Dundee U v St Mirren
Dunfermline Ath v Aberdeen
Inverness CT v Hearts
Motherwell v Falkirk
Rangers v Kilmarnock

Bell's Scottish First Division
Clyde v Queen of the S
Dundee v Airdrie U
Gretna v Partick T
Hamilton A v Ross Co
St Johnstone v Livingston

Bell's Scottish Second Division
Alloa Ath v Brechin C
Forfar Ath v Stirling Alb
Morton v Cowdenbeath
Peterhead v Ayr U
Raith R v Stranraer

Bell's Scottish Third Division
Albion R v Arbroath
Dumbarton v Elgin C
East Fife v Montrose
East Stirlingshire v Berwick R
Queen's Park v Stenhousemuir

Sunday, 26 November 2006

Bank of Scotland

Scottish Premier League
Hibernian v Celtic

Saturday, 2 December 2006

Bank of Scotland

Scottish Premier League
Celtic v Aberdeen
Hibernian v Dundee U
Inverness CT v Motherwell
Kilmarnock v Dunfermline Ath
St Mirren v Hearts

Bell's Scottish First Division
Clyde v Airdrie U
Dundee v Ross Co
Gretna v St Johnstone
Hamilton A v Livingston
Partick T v Queen of the S

Bell's Scottish Second Division
Alloa Ath v Raith R
Ayr U v Brechin C
Cowdenbeath v Stranraer
Morton v Forfar Ath
Peterhead v Stirling Alb

Bell's Scottish Third Division
Albion R v Dumbarton
Arbroath v Stenhousemuir
Berwick R v Elgin C
East Fife v Queen's Park
East Stirlingshire v Montrose

Sunday, 3 December 2006

Bank of Scotland

Scottish Premier League
Falkirk v Rangers

Saturday, 9 December 2006

Bank of Scotland

Scottish Premier League
Aberdeen v Falkirk
Dundee U v Inverness CT
Hearts v Motherwell
Kilmarnock v St Mirren
Rangers v Hibernian

Bell's Scottish First Division
Airdrie U v Gretna
Livingston v Clyde
Queen of the S v Hamilton A
Ross Co v Partick T
St Johnstone v Dundee

Sunday, 10 December 2006

Bank of Scotland

Scottish Premier League
Dunfermline Ath v Celtic

Saturday, 16 December 2006

Bank of Scotland

Scottish Premier League
Falkirk v Hibernian
Hearts v Aberdeen
Inverness CT v Kilmarnock
Motherwell v Dundee U
Rangers v Celtic
St Mirren v Dunfermline Ath

Bell's Scottish First Division
Clyde v Dundee
Hamilton A v St Johnstone
Partick T v Livingston
Queen of the S v Airdrie U
Ross Co v Gretna

Bell's Scottish Second Division
Brechin C v Morton
Forfar Ath v Peterhead
Raith R v Ayr U
Stirling Alb v Cowdenbeath
Stranraer v Alloa Ath

Bell's Scottish Third Division
Dumbarton v East Fife
Elgin C v Arbroath
Montrose v Berwick R
Queen's Park v East Stirlingshire
Stenhousemuir v Albion R

Saturday, 23 December 2006

Bank of Scotland

Scottish Premier League
Aberdeen v Rangers
Celtic v Falkirk
Dundee U v Hearts
Dunfermline Ath v Inverness CT
Hibernian v St Mirren
Kilmarnock v Motherwell

Tuesday, 26 December 2006

Bank of Scotland

Scottish Premier League
Aberdeen v Kilmarnock
Celtic v Dundee U
Dunfermline Ath v Motherwell
Hearts v Hibernian
St Mirren v Falkirk

Bell's Scottish First Division
Airdrie U v Ross Co
Dundee v Partick T
Gretna v Hamilton A
Livingston v Queen of the S
St Johnstone v Clyde

Bell's Scottish Second Division
Cowdenbeath v Alloa Ath
Forfar Ath v Stranraer
Morton v Raith R
Peterhead v Brechin C
Stirling Alb v Ayr U

Bell's Scottish Third Division
Berwick R v Albion R
East Fife v Stenhousemuir
East Stirlingshire v Elgin C
Montrose v Dumbarton
Queen's Park v Arbroath

Wednesday, 27 December 2006

Bank of Scotland

Scottish Premier League
Inverness CT v Rangers

Saturday, 30 December 2006

Bank of Scotland

Scottish Premier League
Dundee U v Aberdeen
Falkirk v Inverness CT
Hibernian v Dunfermline Ath
Kilmarnock v Hearts
Motherwell v Celtic
Rangers v St Mirren

Bell's Scottish First Division
Gretna v Dundee
Hamilton A v Clyde
Livingston v Airdrie U
Partick T v St Johnstone
Ross Co v Queen of the S

Bell's Scottish Second Division
Alloa Ath v Forfar Ath
Ayr U v Morton
Brechin C v Cowdenbeath
Raith R v Peterhead
Stranraer v Stirling Alb

Bell's Scottish Third Division
Albion R v East Stirlingshire
Arbroath v East Fife
Dumbarton v Queen's Park
Elgin C v Montrose
Stenhousemuir v Berwick R

Monday, 1 January 2007

Bank of Scotland

Scottish Premier League
Celtic v Kilmarnock
Dundee U v Falkirk
Dunfermline Ath v Hearts
Hibernian v Aberdeen
Inverness CT v St Mirren
Motherwell v Rangers

Tuesday, 2 January 2007

Bell's Scottish First Division
Airdrie U v Hamilton A
Clyde v Partick T
Dundee v Livingston
Queen of the S v Gretna
St Johnstone v Ross Co

Bell's Scottish Second Division
Alloa Ath v Stirling Alb
Ayr U v Stranraer
Brechin C v Forfar Ath
Peterhead v Morton
Raith R v Cowdenbeath

Bell's Scottish Third Division
Albion R v Queen's Park
Arbroath v Montrose
Berwick R v Dumbarton
East Stirlingshire v Stenhousemuir
Elgin C v East Fife

Saturday, 13 January 2007

Bank of Scotland

Scottish Premier League
Aberdeen v Inverness CT
Falkirk v Dunfermline Ath
Kilmarnock v Hibernian
Rangers v Dundee U
St Mirren v Motherwell

Bell's Scottish First Division
Airdrie U v Dundee
Livingston v St Johnstone
Partick T v Gretna
Queen of the S v Clyde
Ross Co v Hamilton A

Bell's Scottish Second Division
Cowdenbeath v Peterhead
Forfar Ath v Ayr U
Morton v Alloa Ath
Stirling Alb v Raith R
Stranraer v Brechin C

Bell's Scottish Third Division
Dumbarton v Arbroath
East Fife v East Stirlingshire
Montrose v Albion R
Queen's Park v Berwick R
Stenhousemuir v Elgin C

Sunday, 14 January 2007

Bank of Scotland

Scottish Premier League
Hearts v Celtic

Saturday, 20 January 2007

Bank of Scotland

Scottish Premier League
Celtic v St Mirren
Hearts v Falkirk
Inverness CT v Hibernian
Kilmarnock v Dundee U
Motherwell v Aberdeen

Bell's Scottish First Division
Clyde v Ross Co
Dundee v Queen of the S
Gretna v Livingston
Hamilton A v Partick T
St Johnstone v Airdrie U

Bell's Scottish Second Division
Alloa Ath v Ayr U
Forfar Ath v Cowdenbeath
Morton v Stirling Alb
Peterhead v Stranraer
Raith R v Brechin C

Bell's Scottish Third Division
Albion R v Elgin C
Dumbarton v Stenhousemuir
East Fife v Berwick R
East Stirlingshire v Arbroath
Queen's Park v Montrose

Sunday, 21 January 2007

Bank of Scotland

Scottish Premier League
Dunfermline Ath v Rangers

Saturday, 27 January 2007

Bank of Scotland

Scottish Premier League
Dundee U v Dunfermline Ath
Falkirk v Kilmarnock
Hibernian v Motherwell
Rangers v Hearts
St Mirren v Aberdeen

Bell's Scottish First Division
Airdrie U v Clyde
Livingston v Hamilton A
Queen of the S v Partick T
Ross Co v Dundee
St Johnstone v Gretna

Bell's Scottish Second Division
Ayr U v Peterhead
Brechin C v Alloa Ath
Cowdenbeath v Morton
Stirling Alb v Forfar Ath
Stranraer v Raith R

Bell's Scottish Third Division
Arbroath v Albion R
Berwick R v East Stirlingshire
Elgin C v Dumbarton
Montrose v East Fife
Stenhousemuir v Queen's Park

Sunday, 28 January 2007

Bank of Scotland

Scottish Premier League
Inverness CT v Celtic

Saturday, 3 February 2007

Bell's Scottish Second Division
Brechin C v Ayr U
Forfar Ath v Morton
Raith R v Alloa Ath
Stirling Alb v Peterhead
Stranraer v Cowdenbeath

Bell's Scottish Third Division
Dumbarton v Albion R
Elgin C v Berwick R
Montrose v East Stirlingshire
Queen's Park v East Fife
Stenhousemuir v Arbroath

Saturday, 10 February 2007

Bank of Scotland

Scottish Premier League
Aberdeen v Dunfermline Ath
Celtic v Hibernian
Falkirk v Motherwell
Hearts v Inverness CT
St Mirren v Dundee U

Bell's Scottish First Division
Clyde v Livingston
Dundee v St Johnstone
Gretna v Airdrie U
Hamilton A v Queen of the S
Partick T v Ross Co

Bell's Scottish Second Division
Alloa Ath v Stranraer
Ayr U v Raith R
Cowdenbeath v Stirling Alb
Morton v Brechin C
Peterhead v Forfar Ath

Bell's Scottish Third Division
Albion R v Stenhousemuir
Arbroath v Elgin C
Berwick R v Montrose
East Fife v Dumbarton
East Stirlingshire v Queen's Park

Sunday, 11 February 2007

Bank of Scotland

Scottish Premier League
Kilmarnock v Rangers

Saturday, 17 February 2007

Bank of Scotland

Scottish Premier League
Aberdeen v Celtic
Dundee U v Hibernian
Dunfermline Ath v Kilmarnock
Hearts v St Mirren
Motherwell v Inverness CT
Rangers v Falkirk

Bell's Scottish First Division
Airdrie U v Queen of the S
Dundee v Clyde
Gretna v Ross Co
Livingston v Partick T
St Johnstone v Hamilton A

Bell's Scottish Second Division
Cowdenbeath v Brechin C
Forfar Ath v Alloa Ath
Morton v Ayr U
Peterhead v Raith R
Stirling Alb v Stranraer

Bell's Scottish Third Division
Berwick R v Stenhousemuir
East Fife v Arbroath
East Stirlingshire v Albion R
Montrose v Elgin C
Queen's Park v Dumbarton

Saturday, 24 February 2007

Bell's Scottish First Division
Clyde v Gretna
Hamilton A v Dundee
Partick T v Airdrie U
Queen of the S v St Johnstone
Ross Co v Livingston

Bell's Scottish Second Division
Alloa Ath v Peterhead
Ayr U v Cowdenbeath
Brechin C v Stirling Alb
Raith R v Forfar Ath
Stranraer v Morton

Bell's Scottish Third Division
Albion R v East Fife
Arbroath v Berwick R
Dumbarton v East Stirlingshire
Elgin C v Queen's Park
Stenhousemuir v Montrose

Saturday, 3 March 2007

Bank of Scotland

Scottish Premier League
Celtic v Dunfermline Ath
Falkirk v Aberdeen
Inverness CT v Dundee U
Motherwell v Hearts
St Mirren v Kilmarnock

Bell's Scottish First Division
Gretna v Queen of the S
Hamilton A v Airdrie U
Livingston v Dundee
Partick T v Clyde
Ross Co v St Johnstone

Bell's Scottish Second Division
Cowdenbeath v Raith R
Forfar Ath v Brechin C
Morton v Peterhead
Stirling Alb v Alloa Ath
Stranraer v Ayr U

Bell's Scottish Third Division
Dumbarton v Berwick R
East Fife v Elgin C
Montrose v Arbroath
Queen's Park v Albion R
Stenhousemuir v East Stirlingshire

Sunday, 4 March 2007

Bank of Scotland

Scottish Premier League
Hibernian v Rangers

Saturday, 10 March 2007

Bank of Scotland

Scottish Premier League
Aberdeen v Hearts
Celtic v Rangers
Dundee U v Motherwell
Dunfermline Ath v St Mirren
Hibernian v Falkirk
Kilmarnock v Inverness CT

Bell's Scottish First Division
Airdrie U v Livingston
Clyde v Hamilton A
Dundee v Gretna
Queen of the S v Ross Co
St Johnstone v Partick T

Bell's Scottish Second Division
Alloa Ath v Morton
Ayr U v Forfar Ath
Brechin C v Stranraer
Peterhead v Cowdenbeath
Raith R v Stirling Alb

Bell's Scottish Third Division
Albion R v Montrose
Arbroath v Dumbarton
Berwick R v Queen's Park
East Stirlingshire v East Fife
Elgin C v Stenhousemuir

Saturday, 17 March 2007

Bank of Scotland

Scottish Premier League
Falkirk v Celtic
Hearts v Dundee U
Inverness CT v Dunfermline Ath
Motherwell v Kilmarnock
Rangers v Aberdeen
St Mirren v Hibernian

Bell's Scottish First Division
Airdrie U v St Johnstone
Livingston v Gretna
Partick T v Hamilton A
Queen of the S v Dundee
Ross Co v Clyde

Bell's Scottish Second Division
Ayr U v Alloa Ath
Brechin C v Raith R
Cowdenbeath v Forfar Ath

Stirling Alb v Morton
Stranraer v Peterhead

Bell's Scottish Third Division
Arbroath v East Stirlingshire
Berwick R v East Fife
Elgin C v Albion R
Montrose v Queen's Park
Stenhousemuir v Dumbarton

Saturday, 31 March 2007

Bank of Scotland

Scottish Premier League
Dundee U v Celtic
Falkirk v St Mirren
Hibernian v Hearts
Kilmarnock v Aberdeen
Motherwell v Dunfermline Ath
Rangers v Inverness CT

Bell's Scottish First Division
Clyde v Queen of the S
Dundee v Airdrie U
Gretna v Partick T
Hamilton A v Ross Co
St Johnstone v Livingston

Bell's Scottish Second Division
Alloa Ath v Brechin C
Forfar Ath v Stirling Alb
Morton v Cowdenbeath
Peterhead v Ayr U
Raith R v Stranraer

Bell's Scottish Third Division
Albion R v Arbroath
Dumbarton v Elgin C
East Fife v Montrose
East Stirlingshire v Berwick R
Queen's Park v Stenhousemuir

Tuesday, 3 April 2007

Bell's Scottish First Division
Airdrie U v Gretna
Queen of the S v Hamilton A
Ross Co v Partick T
St Johnstone v Dundee

Bell's Scottish Second Division
Brechin C v Morton
Forfar Ath v Peterhead
Raith R v Ayr U
Stranraer v Alloa Ath

Bell's Scottish Third Division
Dumbarton v East Fife
Elgin C v Arbroath
Queen's Park v East Stirlingshire
Stenhousemuir v Albion R

Wednesday, 4 April 2007

Bell's Scottish First Division
Livingston v Clyde

Bell's Scottish Second Division
Stirling Alb v Cowdenbeath

Bell's Scottish Third Division
Montrose v Berwick R

Saturday, 7 April 2007

Bank of Scotland

Scottish Premier League
Aberdeen v Dundee U
Celtic v Motherwell
Dunfermline Ath v Hibernian
Hearts v Kilmarnock
Inverness CT v Falkirk

Bell's Scottish First Division
Clyde v Airdrie U
Dundee v Ross Co
Gretna v St Johnstone
Hamilton A v Livingston
Partick T v Queen of the S

Bell's Scottish Second Division
Alloa Ath v Raith R
Ayr U v Brechin C
Cowdenbeath v Stranraer
Morton v Forfar Ath
Peterhead v Stirling Alb

Bell's Scottish Third Division
Albion R v Dumbarton
Arbroath v Stenhousemuir
Berwick R v Elgin C
East Fife v Queen's Park
East Stirlingshire v Montrose

Sunday, 8 April 2007

Bank of Scotland

Scottish Premier League
St Mirren v Rangers

Saturday, 14 April 2007

Bell's Scottish First Division
Clyde v St Johnstone
Hamilton A v Gretna
Partick T v Dundee
Queen of the S v Livingston
Ross Co v Airdrie U

Bell's Scottish Second Division
Alloa Ath v Cowdenbeath
Ayr U v Stirling Alb
Brechin C v Peterhead
Raith R v Morton
Stranraer v Forfar Ath

Bell's Scottish Third Division
Albion R v Berwick R
Arbroath v Queen's Park
Dumbarton v Montrose
Elgin C v East Stirlingshire
Stenhousemuir v East Fife

Saturday, 21 April 2007

Bell's Scottish First Division
Airdrie U v Partick T
Dundee v Hamilton A
Gretna v Clyde
Livingston v Ross Co
St Johnstone v Queen of the S

Bell's Scottish Second Division
Cowdenbeath v Ayr U
Forfar Ath v Raith R
Morton v Stranraer
Peterhead v Alloa Ath
Stirling Alb v Brechin C

Bell's Scottish Third Division
Berwick R v Arbroath
East Fife v Albion R
East Stirlingshire v Dumbarton
Montrose v Stenhousemuir
Queen's Park v Elgin C

Saturday, 28 April 2007

Bell's Scottish First Division
Clyde v Dundee
Hamilton A v St Johnstone
Partick T v Livingston
Queen of the S v Airdrie U
Ross Co v Gretna

Bell's Scottish Second Division
Alloa Ath v Forfar Ath
Ayr U v Morton
Brechin C v Cowdenbeath
Raith R v Peterhead
Stranraer v Stirling Alb

Bell's Scottish Third Division
Albion R v East Stirlingshire
Arbroath v East Fife
Dumbarton v Queen's Park
Elgin C v Montrose
Stenhousemuir v Berwick R

OTHER FIXTURES 2006–07

AUGUST 2006

Tue 1 UEFA Champions League 2Q (2)
Wed 2 UEFA Champions League 2Q (2)
Sat 5 FL Season Commences
Tue 8 UEFA Champions League 3Q (1)
Wed 9 UEFA Champions League 3Q (1)
Thu 10 UEFA Cup 2Q (1)
Sun 13 FA Community Shield
Wed 16 England v Greece (F)
Sat 19 FA Cup EP
PL Season Commences
Tue 22 UEFA Champions League 3Q (2)
Wed 23 FL Cup 1
UEFA Champions League 3Q (2)
Thu 24 UEFA Cup 2Q (2)
Fri 25 UEFA Super Cup

SEPTEMBER 2006

Sat 2 FA Cup P
England v Andorra – EURO 2008 Qualifier
Wed 6 Macedonia v England – EURO 2008 Qualifier
Sat 9 FA Vase 1Q
Mon 11 FA Youth Cup P**
Tue 12 UEFA Champions League MD 1
Wed 13 UEFA Champions League MD 1
Thu 14 UEFA Cup 1st Rd (1)
Sat 16 FA Cup 1Q
Wed 20 FL Cup 2
Sat 23 FA Vase 2Q
Sun 24 FA Sunday Cup P
Mon 25 FA Youth Cup 1Q**
Tue 26 UEFA Champions League MD 2
Wed 27 UEFA Champions League MD 2
Thu 28 UEFA Cup 1st Rd (2)
Sat 30 FA Cup 2Q

OCTOBER 2006

Sat 7 FA Trophy P
FA Vase 1P
England v Macedonia – EURO 2008 Qualifier
Sun 8 FA County Youth Cup 1*
Mon 9 FA Youth Cup 2Q**
Wed 11 Croatia v England – EURO 2008 Qualifier
Sat 14 FA Cup 3Q
Sun 15 FA Sunday Cup 1
Tue 17 UEFA Champions League MD 3
Wed 18 FL Trophy 1
UEFA Champions League MD 3
Thu 19 UEFA Cup MD 1
Sat 21 FA Trophy 1Q
Mon 23 FA Youth Cup 3Q**
Wed 25 FL Cup 3
Sat 28 FA Cup 4Q
Tue 31 UEFA Champions League MD 4

NOVEMBER 2006

Wed 1 FL Trophy 2
UEFA Champions League MD 4
Thu 2 UEFA Cup MD 2
Sat 4 FA Trophy 2Q
Sun 5 FA County Youth Cup 2*
FA Sunday Cup 2
Wed 8 FL Cup 4
Sat 11 FA Cup 1P
FA Youth Cup 1P*
Wed 15 Holland v England (F)
Sat 18 FA Vase 2P
Tue 21 UEFA Champions League MD 5
Wed 22 FA Cup 1P-R
UEFA Champions League MD 5
Thu 23 UEFA Cup MD 3
Sat 25 FA Trophy 3Q
FA Youth Cup 2P*
Sun 26 FA Sunday Cup 3
Wed 29 FL Trophy AQF
UEFA Cup MD 4
Thu 30 UEFA Cup MD 4

DECEMBER 2006

Sat 2 FA Cup 2P
Tue 5 UEFA Champions League MD 6
Wed 6 UEFA Champions League MD 6
Sat 9 FA Vase 3P
Sun 10 FA County Youth Cup 3*
Wed 13 FA Cup 2P-R
UEFA Cup MD 5
Thu 14 UEFA Cup MD 5
Sat 16 FA Trophy 1P
FA Youth Cup 3P*
Wed 20 FL Cup 5

JANUARY 2007

Sat 6 FA Cup 3P
Wed 10 FL Cup SF1
FL Trophy ASF
Sat 13 FA Trophy 2P
Sun 14 FA Sunday Cup 4
Wed 17 FA Cup 3P-R
Sat 20 FA Vase 4P
FA Youth Cup 4P*
Wed 24 FL Cup SF2
Sat 27 FA Cup 4P
Sun 28 FA County Youth Cup 4*
Wed 31 FL Trophy AF1

FEBRUARY 2007

Sat 3 FA Trophy 3P
FA Youth Cup 5P*
Wed 7 International Friendly
Sat 10 FA Cup 4P-R
(option 2 for clubs in UEFA Cup)
FA Vase 5P
Tue 13 FL Trophy AF2
Wed 14 FA Cup 4P-R
UEFA Cup Rd of 32 (1)
Thu 15 UEFA Cup Rd of 32 (1)
Sat 17 FA Cup 5P
FA Youth Cup 6P*
Tue 20 UEFA Champions League 1st KO Rd (1)
Wed 21 UEFA Champions League 1st KO Rd (1)
Thu 22 UEFA Cup Rd of 32 (2)
Sat 24 FA Trophy 4P
Sun 25 FA Sunday Cup 5
FL Cup Final
Wed 28 FA Cup 5P-R

MARCH 2007

Sat 3 FA Vase 6P
Sun 4 FA County Youth Cup SF*

Tue 6	UEFA Champions League 1st KO Rd (2)
Wed 7	UEFA Champions League 1st KO Rd (2)
Thu 8	UEFA Cup Rd of 16 (1)
Sat 10	FA Cup 6P FA Trophy SF1 FA Youth Cup SF1*
Wed 14	UEFA Cup Rd of 16 (2)
Thu 15	UEFA Cup Rd of 16 (2)
Sat 17	FA Trophy SF2
Sun 18	FL Trophy Final
Mon 19	FA Cup 6P-R
Sat 24	FA Vase SF1 FA Youth Cup SF2* Israel v England – EURO 2008 Qualifier
Sun 25	FA Sunday Cup SF
Wed 28	Andorra v England – EURO 2008 Qualifier
Sat 31	FA Vase SF2

APRIL 2007

Tue 3	UEFA Champions League QF (1)
Wed 4	UEFA Champions League QF (1)
Thu 5	UEFA Cup QF (1)
Fri 6	Good Friday
Sat 7	
Mon 9	Easter Monday
Tue 10	UEFA Champions League QF (2)
Wed 11	UEFA Champions League QF (2)
Thu 12	UEFA Cup QF (2)
Sat 14	FA Cup SF
Tue 24	UEFA Champions League SF (1)
Wed 25	UEFA Champions League SF (1)
Thu 26	UEFA Cup SF (1)
Sun 29	FA Sunday Cup Final (prov)

MAY 2007

Tue 1	UEFA Champions League SF (2)
Wed 2	UEFA Champions League SF (2)
Thu 3	UEFA Cup SF (2)
Sat 5	FL Season Ends
Mon 7	Bank Holiday
Sat 12	FA Vase Final PL Season Ends
Wed 16	UEFA Cup Final
Sat 19	FA Cup Final
Sun 20	FA Trophy Final
Wed 23	UEFA Champions League Final
Sat 26	FL2 Play-off
Sun 27	FL1 Play-off
Mon 28	FL Championship Play-off Bank Holiday

** closing date of round*
*** ties to be played in the week commencing*

DATES TO BE CONFIRMED

FA Women's Cup – all rounds
FA Youth Cup Final 1
FA Youth Cup Final 2
FA County Youth Cup Final

FURTHER INTERNATIONAL DATES – 2007

Wed 6 Jun	Estonia v England – EURO 2008 Qualifier
Sat 8 Sep	England v Israel – EURO 2008 Qualifier
Wed 12 Sep	England v Russia – EURO 2008 Qualifier
Sat 13 Oct	England v Estonia – EURO 2008 Qualifier
Wed 17 Oct	Russia v England – EURO 2008 Qualifier
Wed 21 Nov	England v Croatia – EURO 2008 Qualifier

BRITISH & IRISH INTERNATIONAL MANAGERS

England
Walter Winterbottom 1946–1962 (after period as coach); Alf Ramsey 1963–1974; Joe Mercer (caretaker) 1974; Don Revie 1974–1977; Ron Greenwood 1977–1982; Bobby Robson 1982–1990; Graham Taylor 1990–1993; Terry Venables (coach) 1994–1996; Glenn Hoddle 1996–1999; Kevin Keegan 1999–2000; Sven-Goran Eriksson 2001–06; Steve McClaren from August 2006.

Northern Ireland
Peter Doherty 1951–1952; Bertie Peacock 1962–1967; Billy Bingham 1967–1971; Terry Neill 1971–1975; Dave Clements (player-manager) 1975–1976; Danny Blanchflower 1976–1979; Billy Bingham 1980–1994; Bryan Hamilton 1994–1998; Lawrie McMenemy 1998–1999; Sammy McIlroy 2000–03; Lawrie Sanchez from January 2004.

Scotland (since 1967)
Bobby Brown 1967–1971; Tommy Docherty 1971–1972; Willie Ormond 1973–1977; Ally MacLeod 1977–1978; Jock Stein 1978–1985; Alex Ferguson (caretaker) 1985–1986 Andy Roxburgh (coach) 1986–1993; Craig Brown 1993–2001; Berti Vogts 2002–04; Walter Smith from December 2004.

Wales (since 1974)
Mike Smith 1974–1979; Mike England 1980–1988; David Williams (caretaker) 1988; Terry Yorath 1988–1993; John Toshack 1994 for one match; Mike Smith 1994–1995; Bobby Gould 1995–1999; Mark Hughes 1999–2004; John Toshack from November 2004.

Republic of Ireland
Liam Tuohy 1971–1972; Johnny Giles 1973–1980 (after period as player-manager); Eoin Hand 1980–1985; Jack Charlton 1986–1996; Mick McCarthy 1996–2002; Brian Kerr 2003–06; Steve Staunton from January 2006

STOP PRESS

Marcello Lippi (Italy) resigns, Jurgen Klinsmann (Germany) resigns . . . Juventus, Fiorentina and Lazio relegated in Italy over match-fixing, AC Milan deducted points . . . Rooney says stamping was an accident . . . Owen has to wait for his operation . . . O'Leary out at Villa . . . McCarthy in at Wolves . . . Community service for Zidane . . . Materazzi two match ban . . . Dunga is Brazil boss . . . Niall Quinn for Sunderland.

Summer transfers completed and pending: **Premier Division: Arsenal:** Tomas Rosicky (Borussia Dortmund) £7,000,000; Joe O'Cearuill (Watford); Vincent Van den Berg (Heerenveen). **Aston Villa:** Damian Bellon (St Gallen); Yago Bellon (St Gallen). **Blackburn R:** Francis Jeffers (Charlton Ath); Jason Roberts (Wigan Ath) £1,000,000; Jason Brown (Gillingham). **Bolton W:** Idan Tal (Maccabi Haifa); Dietmar Hamann (Liverpool); Abdoulaye Meite (Marseille). **Charlton Ath:** Simon Walton (Leeds U) £500,000; Gonzalo Sorondo (Internazionale) (after loan); Jimmy Floyd Hasselbaink (Middlesbrough); Cory Gibbs (Den Haag); Mark Staunton (Celtic). **Chelsea:** Andriy Shevchenko (AC Milan) £29,500,000; Jon Obi Mikel (Lyn) £16,000,000; Michael Ballack (Bayern Munich); Hilario (Nacional); Salomon Kalou (Feyenoord) £3,500,000. **Everton:** Tim Howard (Manchester U) Loan; Andy Johnson (Crystal Palace) £8,600,000; Joleon Lescott (Wolverhampton W) £5,000,000; Scott Spencer (Oldham Ath). **Fulham:** Jimmy Bullard (Wigan Ath) £2,500,000; Gabriel Zakuani (Leyton Orient) £1,000,000; Bjorn Runstrom (Hammarby) £700,000. **Liverpool:** Fabiano Aurelio (Valencia); Craig Bellamy (Blackburn R) £6,000,000; Mark Gonzalez (Banfield) £4,000,000 after year loaned out; Gabriel Paletta (Banfield) £2,000,000. **Manchester C:** Ousmane Dabo (Lazio); Paul Dickov (Blackburn R); Joe Hart (Shrewsbury T) £600,000; Dietmar Hamann (Bolton W); Bernardo Corradi (Valencia). **Middlesbrough:** Herold Goulon (Lyon). **Newcastle U:** Damien Duff (Chelsea) £5,000,000. **Portsmouth:** Glen Johnson (Chelsea) Loan. **Reading:** Sam Sodje (Brentford) £350,000; Ki-hyeon Seol (Wolverhampton W) £1,500,000. **Sheffield U:** Mikele Leigertwood (Crystal Palace) £600,000; Claude Davis (Preston NE); Chris Lucketti (Preston NE) £300,000; David Sommeil (Manchester C); Christian Nade (Troyes). **Tottenham H:** Benoit Assou-Ekotto (Lens); Dimitar Berbatov (Leverkusen) £10,900,000; Dorian Dervitte (Lille); Didier Zokora (St Etienne) £8,200,000. **Watford:** Chris Powell (Charlton Ath); Sheku Kamara (Charlton Ath); Claude Seanla (Tottenham H); Scott Loach (Lincoln C); Damien Francis (Wigan Ath) £1,500,000. **West Ham U:** Carlton Cole (Chelsea); Tyrone Mears (Preston NE) £1,000,000; Lee Bowyer (Newcastle U); Jonathan Spector (Manchester U) £500,000. **Wigan Ath:** Emile Heskey (Birmingham C) £5,500,000; Tomasz Cywka (Gwarek Zawrze); Fitz Hall (Crystal Palace) £3,000,000; Chris Kirkland (Liverpool) Loan; Denny Landzaat (AZ) £2,500,000.

Football League Championship: Barnsley: Michael Coulson (Scarborough); Michael McIndoe (Doncaster R); Sam Togwell (Crystal Palace). **Birmingham C:** Brno N'Gotty (Bolton W); Stephen Kelly (Tottenham H); Neil Danns (Colchester U) £850,000. **Burnley:** Alan Mahon (Wigan Ath); Steve Jones (Crewe Alex); Steve Foster (Crewe Alex); Andy Gray (Sunderland). **Cardiff C:** Roger Johnson (Wycombe W) £275,000; Nick McKoy (Milton Keynes D); Malvin Kamara (Milton Keynes D); Mark Howard (Arsenal); Kevin McNaughton (Aberdeen); Michael Chopra (Newcastle U); Stephen McPhail (Barnsley); Glenn Loovens (Feyenoord); Luigi Glombard (Nantes); Kerrea Gilbert (Arsenal) Loan. **Colchester U:** Johnnie Jackson (Tottenham H); Jamie Cureton (Swindon T). **Coventry C:** Jay Tabb (Brentford); Mikkel Bischoff (Manchester C); Colin Cameron (Wolverhampton W); Elliott Ward (West Ham U) £1,000,000; Wayne Andrews (Crystal Palace); David McNamee (Livingston); Andy Marshall (Millwall). **Crystal Palace:** Leon Cort (Hull C); Scott Flinders (Barnsley); Mark Kennedy (Wolverhampton W). **Derby Co:** Steve Howard (Luton T). **Hull C:** Michael Turner (Brentford) £350,000; Sam Ricketts (Swansea C); Dean Marney (Tottenham H). **Leeds U:** Sebastien Carole (Brighton & HA); David Livermore (Millwall). **Leicester C:** Darren Kenton (Southampton); Andy Johnson (WBA); Josh Low (Northampton T); Gareth McAuley (Lincoln C). **Luton T:** Richard Langley (QPR); Lewis Emanuel (Bradford C). **Plymouth Arg:** Sylvan Ebanks-Blake (Manchester U); Barry Hayles (Millwall). **Preston NE:** Sean St Ledger-Hall (Peterborough U) £225,000; Jason Jarrett (Norwich C); Kelvin Wilson (Notts Co); Danny Pugh (Leeds U); Liam Chilvers (Colchester U). **QPR:** Damion Stewart (Bradford C); Adam Czerkas (Korona Kielce); Egutu Oliseh (La Louviere); Nick Ward (Perth Glory). **Sheffield W:** Wade Small (Milton Keynes D); Kenny Lunt (Crewe Alex); Madjid Bougherra (Gueugnon); Yoann Folly (Southampton). **Southampton:** Bradley Wright-Phillips (Manchester C); Grzegorz Rasiak (Tottenham H) £2,000,000; Jermaine Wright (Leeds U); Peter Madsen (Cologne); Marcelo Sarmiento (Racing Cordoba); Kelvin Davis (Sunderland). **Southend U:** Jamal Campbell-Ryce (Rotherham U); Steven Hammell (Motherwell); Michael Ricketts (Leeds U); Simon Francis (Sheffield U); Steven Collis (Yeovil T). **Stoke C:** Vincent Pericard (Portsmouth). **Sunderland:** Kenny Cunningham (Birmingham C). **West Bromwich Albion:** Chris Perry (Charlton Ath); John Hartson (Celtic); Pascal Zuberbuhler (Basle). **Wolverhampton W:** Gary Breen (Sunderland).

Football League 1: Blackpool: Marcus Bean (QPR); Paul Tierney (Livingston); Rhys Evans (Swindon T); Wesley Hoolahan (Livingston); Adrian Forbes (Swansea C). **Bournemouth:** Danny Hollands (Chelsea); Daryl Taylor (Walsall). **Bradford C:** Matthew Clarke (Darlington); Jermaine Johnson (Tivoli Gardens); Eddie Johnson (Manchester U). **Brentford:** Chris Moore (Dagenham & R); Joe Osei-Kuffour (Torquay U); Adam Griffiths (Bournemouth); Thomas Pinault (Grimsby T). **Brighton & HA:** Alex Revell (Braintree T). **Bristol C:** Liam Fontaine (Fulham); Philip Jevons (Yeovil T); Chris Weale (Yeovil T); Enoch Showunmi (Luton T); Jamie McCombe (Lincoln C). **Carlisle U:** David Raven (Liverpool); Kevin Gall (Yeovil T). **Chesterfield:** Paul Shaw (Rotherham U); Phil Picken (Manchester U); Kevan Hurst (Sheffield U). **Crewe Alex:** Julian Baudet (Notts Co); Darran Kempson (Morecambe). **Doncaster R:** James O'Connor (AFC Bournemouth); Kevin Horlock (Ipswich T); Adam Lockwood (Yeovil T); Bruce Dyer (Sheffield U); Jonathan Forte (Sheffield U). **Gillingham:** Kelvin Jack (Dundee); Clint Easton (Wycombe W); Mark Bentley (Southend U); Duncan Jupp (Southend U); Dean McDonald (Ipswich T); Gary Mulligan (Sheffield U); Guylain Ndumbu-Nsungu (Cardiff C). **Huddersfield T:** Luke Beckett (Oldham Ath); Matthew Glennon (St Johnstone). **Leyton Orient:** Wayne Corden (Scunthorpe U). **Millwall:** Derek McInnes (Dundee U); Chris Day (Oldham Ath); Richard Shaw (Coventry C); Tom Brighton (Clyde); Filipe Morais (Chelsea); Zak Whitbread (Liverpool); Lenny Pidgeley (Chelsea); Gavin Grant (Gillingham); Adam Cottrell (Charlton Ath). **Northampton T:** Joe Burnell (Wycombe W); Sam Aiston (Shrewsbury T); Andy Holt (Wrexham). **Nottingham F:** Paul Smith (Southampton). **Oldham Ath:** Craig Rocastle (Sheffield W); John Mullin (Rotherham U); Leslie Pogliacomi (Blackpool); Gary McDonald (Kilmarnock); Moussa Dabo (Racing Paris). **Port Vale:** Colin Miles (Yeovil T); Danny Whitaker (Macclesfield T); Paul Harsley (Macclesfield T); Akpo Sodje (Darlington); Jason Talbot (Mansfield); Richard Walker (Crewe Alex). **Rotherham U:** Delroy Facey (Tranmere R); Justin Cochrane (Crewe Alex); Ian Sharps (Tranmere R); Ritchie Partridge (Sheffield W); Scott Wiseman (Hull C); Pablo Mills (Derby Co). **Scunthorpe U:** Ramon Calliste (Liverpool); David Mulligan (Doncaster R); Joe Murphy (Sunderland). **Swansea C:** Darren Pratley (Fulham). **Tranmere R:** Chris Shuker (Barnsley); Paul McLaren (Rotherham U); Gavin Ward (Preston NE); Kevin Ellison (Hull C); Robbie Stockdale (Hull C); Chris McCready (Crewe Alex). **Yeovil T:** Chris Cohen (West Ham U); Terrell Forbes (Oldham Ath); Jean-Paul Kamudimba Kala (Grimsby T); Wayne Gray (Southend U); Steve Mildenhall (Grimsby T); Darren Behcet (West Ham U); Stephen Maher (Dublin C).

Football League 2: Accrington S: Julien N'Da (Rouen); Andrew Todd (Burton Alb); Sean Doherty (Port Vale). **Barnet:** Lee Harrison (Peterborough U). **Boston U:** Paul Tait (Chester C); David Farrell (Peterborough U); Andy Marriott (Torquay U); Francis Green (Lincoln C); Mark Albrighton (Doncaster R); Tim Ryan (Peterborough U); Anthony Elding (Stevenage B); Richie Ryan (Scunthorpe U). **Bristol R:** Andrew Sandell (Bath C); Ryan Green (Hereford U); Oliver Barnes (Bristol C); Stephen Phillips (Bristol C). **Bury:** Marc Goodfellow (Grimsby T); Alan Fettis (Macclesfield T); Andy Bishop (York C); Richard Baker (Preston NE). **Chester C:** Ashley Westwood (Northampton T); Graham Allen (Rushden & D); Glenn Cronin (Exeter C); Kevin Sandwith (Macclesfield T); Jonathan Walters (Wrexham); Dean Bennett (Wrexham); Drewe Broughton (Rushden & D); Jermaine McSporran (Doncaster R); Jamie Hand (Northampton T); Laurence Wilson (Everton); John Danby (Kidderminster H); Phil Bolland (Peterborough U). **Darlington:** Patrick Collins (Sheffield W); Martin Smith (Northampton T); Barry Conlon (Barnsley); Michael Cummins (Port Vale); Gaetano Giallanza (Young Boys). **Grimsby T:** Phil Barnes (Sheffield U); Isaiah Rankin (Brentford); Gary Harkins (Blackburn R). **Hereford U:** Richard Rose (Gillingham); Tim Sills (Oxford U); John Wallis (Gillingham); Gareth Sheldon (Kidderminster H); Wayne Brown (Chester C); Dean Beckwith (Gillingham); Philip Gulliver (Rushden & D); Alan Connell (Torquay U). **Lincoln C:** James Sherlock (Gainsborough T); Adrian Moses (Crewe Alex); Jamie Forrester (Bristol R); Mark Stallard (Shrewsbury T). **Macclesfield T:** Colin Heath (Chesterfield); Carl Regan (Chester C); Marvin Robinson (Lincoln C); Matt McNeil (Hyde U); Tommy Lee (Manchester U). **Mansfield T:** Matthew Hamshaw (Stockport Co); Johnny Mullins (Reading); Carl Muggleton (Chesterfield). **Milton Keynes D:** Drissa Diallo (Sheffield W); Sean O'Hanlon (Swindon T); Jon-Paul McGovern (Sheffield W); Joe Tillen (Chelsea); Jamie Smith (Bristol C). **Notts Co:** Austin McCann (Boston U); Tommy Curtis (Chester C); Lawrie Dudfield (Boston U); Alan White (Boston U); Junior Mendes (Huddersfield T); Tcham N'Toya (Chesterfield); Andy Parkinson (Grimsby T); Stephen Hunt (Colchester U); Gary Silk (Portsmouth); Jason Lee (Northampton T); Matt Somner (Aldershot T); Ian Ross (Sheffield U); Daniel Gleeson (Cambridge U). **Peterborough U:** Jude Stirling (Lincoln C); Richard Butcher (Oldham Ath); Justin Richards (Woking); Guy Branston (Oldham Ath). **Rochdale:** Adam Rundle (Mansfield T). **Shrewsbury T:** Ryan Esson (Aberdeen); Ben Davies (Chester C); Chris MacKenzie (Chester C); Stuart Drummond (Chester C); Dale Williams (Yeovil T); Daniel Hall (Oldham Ath). **Stockport Co:** Gareth Owen (Oldham Ath); Michael Rose (Yeovil T); Tony Dinning (Port Vale). **Swindon T:** Folawiyo Onibuje (Cambridge U); Adrian Williams (Coventry C); Andy Monkhouse (Rotherham U); Gustavo Poyet (player-coach); Dennis Wise (Coventry C, player-manager). **Torquay U:** Lee Mansell (Oxford U); Jamie Ward (Aston Villa); Lee Andrews (Carlisle U); Mickey Evans (Plymouth Arg); Stephen Reed (Yeovil T). **Walsall:** Clayton Ince (Coventry C); Tony Bedeau (Torquay U); Michael Dobson (Brentford); Martin Butler (Rotherham U). **Wrexham:** Neil Roberts (Doncaster R); Chris Llewellyn (Hartlepool U); Steve Evans (TNS); Ryan Valentine (Darlington). **Wycombe W:** Chris Palmer (Notts Co); Sam Stockley (Colchester U); Anthony Grant (Chelsea).

Leaving the country: Robert Pires Arsenal to Villarreal; Asier Del Horno Chelsea to Valencia; Eidur Gudjohnsen Chelsea to Barcelona; Dean Furman Chelsea to Rangers; Djibril Cisse Liverpool to Marseille Loan; Fernando Morientes Liverpool to Valencia; Bruno Cheyrou Liverpool to Rennes; John Viafara Portsmouth to Real Sociedad; Mounir El Hamdaoui Tottenham H to Willem II; Shaka Hislop West Ham U to Dallas; Yaniv Katan West Ham U to Maccabi Haifa Loan; Nico Vaesen Birmingham C to Lierse.